Congressional Quarterly's

# Guide to U.S. Elections

## Third Edition

# Congressional Quarterly's

# Guide to U.S. Elections

## Third Edition

Congressional Quarterly Inc.
Washington, D.C.

*Editor*  John L. Moore
*Associate Editor*  Jon Preimesberger
*Major Contributors*  Rhodes Cook, Ronald D. Elving, Charles C. Euchner, Alice V. McGillivray, Robert H. Resnick
*Contributors*  Bob Benenson, Peter Bragdon, Phil Duncan, Thomas Galvin, Kenneth E. Jaques, Chris Karlsten, Kerry Kern, Ann O'Malley, Shirley Tutthill
*Graphic Artists*  Eloise Fuller, Joyce Kachergis
*General Indexers*  Foxon-Maddocks Associates
*Typesetter*  Jessica Forman
*Proofreader*  Jodean Marks

The cover designer was Anne Masters of Anne Masters Design, Washington, D.C. Congressional Quarterly wishes to thank the Smithsonian's National Museum of American History, especially political history museum specialist Harry Rubenstein, for use of the Smithsonian's political artifact collection. The photograph of the political buttons was taken by Fred Sons.

## Congressional Quarterly Inc.

Congressional Quarterly Inc., an editorial research service and publishing company, serves clients in the fields of news, education, business and government. It combines the specific coverage of Congress, government and politics contained in the *Congressional Quarterly Weekly Report* with the more general subject range of an affiliated service, the *CQ Researcher*.

Congressional Quarterly also publishes a variety of books, including college political science textbooks under the CQ Press imprint and public affairs paperbacks on developing issues and events. CQ Books researches, writes and publishes information directories and reference books on the federal government, national elections and politics, including the *Guide to the Presidency*, the *Guide to Congress*, the *Guide to the U.S. Supreme Court* and *Politics in America*. *CQ's Encyclopedia of American Government* is a three-volume reference work providing essential information about the U.S. government. The *CQ Almanac*, a compendium of legislation for one session of Congress, is published each year. *Congress and the Nation*, a record of government for a presidential term, is published every four years.

CQ publishes the *Congressional Monitor*, a daily report on current and future activities of congressional committees, and several newsletters including *Congressional Insight*, a weekly analysis of congressional action. The CQ FaxReport provides a daily update available every afternoon when Congress is in session. An electronic online information system, Washington Alert, provides immediate access to CQ's databases of legislative action, votes, schedules, profiles and analyses.

## Copyright © 1994 Congressional Quarterly Inc.

Printed in the United States of America

**Congressional Quarterly Inc.**
**1414 22nd St. N.W., Washington, D.C. 20037**

**Library of Congress Cataloging-in-Publication Data**

Congressional Quarterly's Guide to U.S. elections. — 3rd ed.
   p.    cm.
   Includes bibliographical references and indexes.
   ISBN: 0-87187-996-4
   1. Elections — United States — History — Statistics. 2. Political conventions — United States — History. 3. Political parties — United States — History.    I. Congressional Quarterly, inc. II. Title: Guide to U.S. elections.    III. Title: Guide to U.S. elections.
JK1967.C662 1994
324.973 — dc20                                                                94-19015
                                                                                    CIP

# Table of Contents

## Introduction

## Part I
## Political Parties

## Part II
## Presidential Elections

# Part III
# Gubernatorial and Congressional Elections

## Gubernatorial Elections

## Senate Elections

## House Elections

# Appendix

# Indexes

# List of Tables, Figures and Boxes

## Tables and Figures

### Political Parties

### Presidential Elections

### Gubernatorial and Congressional Elections

# Appendix

# Boxes

## Political Parties

## Presidential Elections

## Gubernatorial and Congressional Elections

# Editor's Note: How to Use the *Guide to U.S. Elections*

With its 1,500 pages of text and tabular material, the *Guide to U.S. Elections, Third Edition,* is almost twice the size of the original 1975 edition, which at the time was hailed as the most comprehensive collection of published data on presidential, gubernatorial and congressional elections.

The new 1994 edition is also considerably larger than the second edition, published in 1985, which was expanded to include new sections on gubernatorial and Senate primaries since 1956 and pre-1824 outcomes of the first contests for American state governorships.

More election returns — for president in 1988 and 1992, and for governor and Congress 1985-93 — of course account for some of the new guide's added bulk. But much of it is also due to new features and sections added to make the book even more complete and useful than its highly acclaimed predecessors.

Among the items new to this edition, besides the additional results, are:

● A narrative chronology of presidential elections, 1789-1992

● Listings of officers and keynote speakers at Democratic and Republican national nominating conventions

● Improved tables of popular vote returns for president, reformatted to show the total vote and winning party in each state

● A section on politics and issues 1945-92, to put in perspective the national and state elections held during that period

● An expanded summary table of House of Representative seats won by each party back to 1928

● Background boxes on the Democratic Party's long dominance in House elections

● New data and discussion of the 1990s efforts in several states to limit the terms of their House and Senate members

● More data on voter registration and turnout rates

● The status of House reapportionment and redistricting in the 1990s, including legal challenges to "racial gerrymandering"

This note explains the organization of the book and helps users to find the specific facts they want in the updated and expanded guide. There are four key aids to locating information in these pages. The Table of Contents offers an overall view of the book's scope and allows quick access to major sections. The List of Tables, Figures and Boxes allows quick identification of tabular, graphic and special information. Candidate Indexes pinpoint the returns for the more than 68,000 candidates listed. The General Index spans the broad range of subjects covered and contains references to all sections of the book except those covered by the Candidate Indexes.

## Structure of the Book

The Table of Contents *(pp. v-vi)* outlines the four major parts — Introduction, Elections: Key to Understanding America; Part I: Political Parties; Part II: Presidential Elections; Part III: Gubernatorial and Congressional Elections.

Part I contains primarily narrative material — Pre-Convention Politics, 1789-1828; Nominating Conventions; Convention Chronology, 1831-1992; and Historical Profiles of American Political Parties.

Readers of the convention chronology will find the results of important balloting from presidential nominating conventions broken down by state delegations in Key Convention Ballots *(pp. 191-256)*.

**Explanatory Introductions.** The subsections in Parts II and III have a basically parallel structure and contain common elements. Each subsection provides an introduction explaining the origins and development of election procedures for the office covered in that part of the guide. Thus, "The Electoral College" *(pp. 343-355)*, presents a comprehensive discussion of the constitutional origins and historical development of the Electoral College, details complex and little-known methods used in the various states through the first third of the 19th century to choose presidential electors, recounts historical anomalies in the functioning of the Electoral College and explains why a state's electoral votes frequently have been divided among several presidential candidates.

This subsection also covers the two occasions when a president was elected by the House of Representatives, the

# ICPSR Historical Election Returns File

The election returns obtained from the Inter-University Consortium for Political and Social Research for the *Guide to U.S. Elections* represent constituency-level totals for candidates appearing in elections for the offices of president from 1824 to 1916, for governor and U.S. representative from 1824 to 1973 and for U.S. senator from 1913 to 1973. Congressional Quarterly obtained returns for the more recent elections through 1993 from the Elections Research Center in Washington, D.C.

The 1824 starting point for the ICPSR Historical Election Returns File was based on consideration of factors such as the pronounced trend by that time toward popular election of presidential electors, as well as the availability, accessibility and quality of returns for presidential, gubernatorial and House elections.

## Collection of the Data

The original data collection effort, begun in 1962, was supported by the Social Science Research Council and the National Science Foundation. The continuing addition of contemporary election returns is supported by the annual membership fee of more than 300 colleges and universities affiliated with the consortium.

As in the case with any enterprise of the magnitude represented by this data collection, many individuals contributed to its development and growth. Those who provided the initial impetus for the project included Lee Benson, Allan G. Bogue, Dewey Grantham Jr., Samuel P. Hays, Morton P. Keller, V. O. Key, Richard P. McCormick, Phillip Mason, Warren E. Miller, Thomas J. Pressly, William H. Riker and Charles G. Sellers Jr. The ad hoc Committee to Collect the Basic Quantitative Data for American Political History of the American Historical Association obtained the assistance of more than 100 archivists, historians and political scientists in the collection of the data.

Through the efforts of Warren E. Miller, then executive director of the consortium, financial support was obtained for completion of the data collection, conversion to computer-readable form and the extensive data processing that followed. The data collection and processing effort was successively directed by Walter Dean Burnham, Howard W. Allen and Jerome M. Clubb at the Survey Research Center, and more recently the Center for Political Studies, in the Institute for Social Research, the University of Michigan.

The initial data collection was conducted by scholars in the various states who volunteered their time and effort in locating little-known publications, searching state and local archives for unpublished data, exploring newspaper files, and evaluating the accuracy and reliability of these sources. In as many cases as possible, multiple sources were consulted. While general preference was given to official sources, these scholars were charged with the task of evaluating all available sources in terms of their quality and completeness. While the complete source annotations for the collection are too extensive to publish here, information on the sources for returns from specific elections can be obtained from the ICPSR.

The result of this initial effort, and subsequent work by the ICPSR staff, was the recovery of returns for more than 90 percent of all the elections for president, governor, senator and representative in the period covering 1824 to 1973. This estimate was based on a review of the periodicity of elections by state and office, indicating where elections apparently occurred but no returns could be located. Such hypotheses were confirmed by reference to state manuals and histories or the *Biographical Directory of the United States Congress, 1774-1989*, U.S. Government Printing Office, Washington, D.C., 1989, which indicates the changes in the membership of state delegations.

## Format of the Election Returns File

In the computer-readable format in which these materials are stored and retrieved by the ICPSR, an election is defined as a set of returns by party or candidate for a specified office in a specified state at a specified time. As a result, the collection through 1973 included returns for more than 25,000 individual elections and records the names of almost 115,000 candidates.

A decision was reached early in the process of conversion of the data to machine-readable form to preserve the original party designations appearing on each original source. Consequently, almost 1,700 unique partisan labels appear in the collection, most of which, of course, represent short-lived or localized minor parties and the combinations and permutations of multi-party support received by individual candidates. In the ICPSR data collection, separate vote totals are recorded for candidates who appeared more than once on a ballot with different and distinct party designations. In short, the data appear in the collection virtually as they appeared in the original sources, with no combinations of either candidate or party totals. *(For details on presentation of these data in the* Guide to U.S. Elections, Third Edition, *see pages 428, 666, 814, 942.)*

A comprehensive series of manual and machine-aided error-checking procedures was carried out on these data, and errors discovered through them were corrected. The ICPSR maintains returns for these elections at the county level in separate and larger computer-readable files. Using these data, it was possible to ascertain that the individual candidate returns summed to the total number of votes cast in the county. Subsequently, county returns were summed as a check against the state or congressional district level returns, both by candidate and in terms of the total number of votes cast. All discrepancies encountered in this process were resolved where possible and appropriate corrections to the machine-readable files were made. No further systematic error checks are planned, although errors discovered through the use of the data are corrected as they are reported to the ICPSR.

**Requests for Computer-Readable Data.** Requests for data from the Historical Election Returns File in machine-readable form should be addressed to: Executive Director, Inter-University Consortium for Political and Social Research, Box 1248, Ann Arbor, Mich. 48106.

procedures for counting and challenging electoral votes in Congress and major points of the famous Hayes-Tilden contest for president in 1876. It concludes with a discussion of instances of presidential disability and ratification of the 25th Amendment.

In a similar fashion, the introductions to the subsections in Part III trace historical developments in election procedures for governors, senators and House representatives.

**Popular Election Returns.** The major sections of Parts II and III are listings of popular vote returns — since 1787 for gubernatorial elections; since 1824 for presidential and House elections; since 1913 for Senate elections; since 1919-20 for Southern primaries for governor and senator; and since 1956 for gubernatorial and Senate primaries outside the 11 states of the Old South.

Special research materials unique to Part II include maps displaying presidential Electoral College results since 1789, presidential primary returns from 1912 to 1992 and a Biographical Directory of Presidential and Vice Presidential Candidates. Part III contains a complete listing of all governors and senators since 1789. The lists are valuable complements to the gubernatorial and Senate election returns because they contain dates of service and footnotes explaining disputed elections and instances of succession to office by appointment or other non-elective procedures.

**Appendix.** The Appendix contains supplementary texts and tables relevant to U.S. elections, including state-by-state population growth 1790-1990, sessions and leaders of each Congress through the 103rd (1993-94), constitutional provisions on elections, an extensive list of political party abbreviations, summaries showing which party controlled the White House and Congress after each election, a chart showing changes in states' methods of choosing presidential electors 1789-1836, and suggestions for further reading.

## Candidate Indexes

Separate Candidate Indexes for the popular election returns appear on pages 1367 to 1501. The six indexes are: Presidential Candidates Index *(p. 1367)*, Gubernatorial Candidates Index *(p. 1368)*, Gubernatorial Primary Candidates Index *(p. 1381)*, Senate Candidates Index *(p. 1388)*, Senate Primary Candidates Index *(p. 1395)* and the House Candidates Index *(p. 1402)*. Each Candidate Index lists the *years* of candidacy for each candidate. Instructions for use of the candidate indexes appear on the first page of each index.

## General Index

The General Index, *(pp. 1503-1543)*, provides page references for all sections of the *Guide to U.S. Elections, Third Edition,* except the popular returns, which are indexed in the special Candidate Indexes described above. The General Index can be used independently as a source of information; for example, the index entry for Herbert C. Hoover *(p. 1521)* indicates that Hoover received votes in presidential primaries in 1920, 1928, 1932, 1936 and 1940; received votes at the 1920, 1928, 1932 and 1940 Republican nominating conventions; and was a presidential candidate in 1928 and 1932.

## ICPSR Election Data

Except where noted, the returns through 1972 for presidential, gubernatorial, Senate, House and Southern primary elections were obtained from the Inter-University Consortium for Political and Social Research. *(Description*

## Acknowledgments

Congressional Quarterly expresses appreciation to the following copyright owners for permission to use material from their books in the *Guide to U.S. Elections, Third Edition*:

● Brookings Institution, Washington, D.C.: *Convention Decisions and Voting Records*, by Richard C. Bain and Judith H. Parris. Copyright 1973.

● James W. Davis: *Presidential Primaries: Road to the White House*, Greenwood Press, Westport, Conn., and London, England, reprint. Copyright 1967, 1980.

● Joseph E. Kallenbach and Jessamine S. Kallenbach: *American State Governors, 1776-1976*, vol. 1, Oceana Publications, Dobbs Ferry, N.Y. Copyright 1977.

● Svend Petersen: *A Statistical History of the American Presidential Elections, With Supplementary Tables Covering 1968-1980*, Greenwood Press, Westport, Conn., and London, England, reprint. Copyright 1963, 1968, 1981.

Most of the photographs and engravings appearing in the *Guide to U.S. Elections, Third Edition,* were obtained from the collection of the Library of Congress. The National Portrait Gallery, Smithsonian Institution, Washington, D.C., provided the photographs of William Jennings Bryan on pages 70, 72, 76, the 1888 Republican convention on page 286 and the ballot-counting scene on page 572. Other photos and their sources were: Thomas E. Dewey, on pages 100, 103 — New York State Historical Society; Harry S. Truman on page 103 — Harry S. Truman Library.

of ICPSR Historical Election Returns File, p. x; details on the presentation of these returns in this book, pp. 428, 666, 814, 942)*

Congressional Quarterly is grateful to the ICPSR staff for its assistance and advice in supplementing this information since the first edition of the guide. We thank especially Richard C. Rockwell, executive director, and Erik W. Austin, director of archival development.

## Other Sources

Major sources used to update or supplement the ICPSR data are identified at the beginning of each section. Those cited most often are the biennial *America Votes* series compiled by Richard M. Scammon and Alice V. McGillivray (Washington, D.C.: Congressional Quarterly) and *American State Governors, 1776-1976*, vol. 1, by Joseph E. Kallenbach and Jessamine S. Kallenbach (Dobbs Ferry, N.Y.: Oceana Publishing, 1977).

Kenneth C. Martis, author and editor of *The Historical Atlas of United States Congressional Districts 1789-1983* (New York: The Free Press, 1982), provided information on several missing House elections that were verified for inclusion in the second and third editions.

Political scientist Nelson W. Polsby of the University of California-Berkeley wrote the introduction to the first edition of the guide; Alan Ehrenhalt, then political editor of the

## Editor's Note

*Congressional Quarterly Weekly Report,* wrote the second edition introduction; and Ronald D. Elving, the *Weekly Report*'s current political editor, wrote the introduction to this edition.

The help of these authors is gratefully acknowledged.

## The Writers

Introductions to major sections of the guide have been updated and revised for this edition. Original writers of that material were Rhodes Cook — political parties, convention functions and histories, party profiles (with Elizabeth Wehr); Charles C. Euchner — chronology of presidential elections; Warden Moxley (1939-84) — presidential, gubernatorial and House elections, reapportionment and redistricting, Southern primaries, Senate elections (with Matt Pinkus). Other contributors to this edition are listed on p. iv.

Associate Editor Jon Preimesberger contributed greatly to the expansion and improvement of this edition of the *Guide.* For months he masterfully oversaw the complex task of making and tracking the thousands of changes that were needed to keep pace with developments in the dynamic American electoral system.

Invariably in a project of this scope — particularly one involving the publication of a large computer data file — there will be some omissions or errors. We are grateful to the diligent readers who pointed out possible errors in the first and second editions. Where their information could be verified, the corrections have been made. Congressional Quarterly again invites comments and suggestions from scholars and other users of the *Guide to U.S. Elections.*

John L. Moore
June 1994

# Introduction

# Introduction

# Elections: Key to Understanding America

### By Ronald D. Elving
#### *Political Editor, Congressional Quarterly Weekly Report*

The *Guide to U.S. Elections, Third Edition,* offers such a wealth of information and research convenience that it scarcely needs further justification. Nevertheless, it has one: It illustrates how the political events of our own time are continuous with those of preceding generations. In politics, as in most things, people tend to notice what is new, whatever its relative importance. The eye is naturally drawn to the unfamiliar, the mind to the unknown. Yet what is old may be what matters most.

Richard M. Scammon, the political scientist for whom vote studies were a lifelong passion, liked to say that the two most important factors in an American national election were the Protestant Reformation of the 16th century and the American Civil War of the 19th century. Indeed, the meaning of any political development is largely determined by its relationship to previous trends and events. This guide is an unmatched compendium of such trends and events, presented partly in narrative text but primarily in straightforward, statistical detail.

## 'Grand and Vivid Landscape'

The guide provides an array of tools and instruments for researchers at different levels of interest and sophistication. It can be used as background or introductory reading, or it can be a microscope for inspecting the deep, elaborate roots of contemporary politics. It can also be viewed as a grand and vivid landscape, a historical canvas against which we can proportion each new political figure and judge each new movement and mood. It helps us to separate the truly notable from the merely novel.

The history of the presidency and the Congress can be glimpsed in outline in the guide, merely by reviewing the candidates and outcomes of the elections that filled these offices that matter most. The states are represented by their gubernatorial successions.

The Electoral College is explained and shown at work, with its occasional drama and frequent quirkiness, from the presidential election of George Washington in 1789 to the election of Bill Clinton in 1992. Also explored are such distinctly American phenomena as the Southern second primary, by which the one-party Democrats of Dixie assured a majoritarian winner, and the decennial processes of reapportioning the House of Representatives and recarving the districts within the several states.

## Trove of Information

The guide has long been acknowledged as a trove of verified and accessible information. The congressional scholar Kenneth C. Martis, in his *Historical Atlas of Political Parties in the United States Congress: 1789-1989,* paid tribute to the book as "undoubtedly one of the most remarkable compilations of American election statistics in print." The data at the heart of the guide, obtained from the Historical Archive of the Inter-University Consortium for Political and Social Research (ICPSR), had previously been available only on computer tape or printouts.

Added to this store of information from the beginning were portraits of the national parties, large and small, beginning with the earliest presidential politics. This section includes also the history of the major party conventions, documenting their roll-call votes and providing the highlights and flavor of each platform and the personality of every presidential ticket.

The second edition, published in 1985, brought in the results of all federal and gubernatorial elections from 1974 through 1984 and added previously unavailable data on gubernatorial elections back to 1787. Now, in this third edition, the guide is extended through two more presidential cycles and four more congressional cycles — updating the record through the special elections of 1993. In addition, discussions of salient and recurrent issues of public policy have been included in narrative form for the period since World War II.

Also new are examinations of several political phenomena specific to the decade between the second and third editions. The discussion of reapportionment and redistricting reflects the landmark 1990 census and the continuing progression of Supreme Court decisions requiring the creation of districts with African American or Hispanic American majorities. This edition also takes up the term-limitation movement, the re-emergence of an issue that had been debated at the Constitutional Convention of 1787. In its latest incarnation, the limitation concept began with state gubernatorial and legislative terms and quickly spread to congressional terms, raising constitutional as well as political issues.

Beyond all this fact gathering, the guide functions as something more, because the facts it contains, while old, are very much alive. The political landscape is constantly being made over. The action takes place over time, so gradually as to conjure a geologic analogy. But past elections are not like underlying layers of rock exposed by excavation, they are an organic component of current political reality. The elections held in each era and in every state represent a series of closely related moves and counter-moves, each shaped by the last and, in turn, shaping the next. Even minor political events leave some mark or coloration on what comes next.

That is why the guide can be a surprisingly entertaining read. The narratives are rich in historical perspective, and the tables can be remarkably absorbing as well. The maps of the Electoral College vote by state are endlessly diverting. Numbers may crowd these pages, but the events and people so carefully enumerated are, for those whose imaginations are stimulated by such facts, vibrant on every page.

## Three Eras of Politics

In the years since the first edition of the *Guide to U.S. Elections* appeared, three distinct eras have passed in the national politics of the United States. The first book appeared at the time of the Watergate scandal and the resignation of the President Richard Nixon. The Democrats in that era seized on Nixon's disgrace to solidify their majority status in the House and the Senate and in the nation's governorships. They rode the same momentum to the White House in 1976, when Jimmy Carter of Georgia became the first Democrat since Franklin D. Roosevelt to sweep the Old South (save only Virginia).

By the time the second edition appeared, a conservative resurgence led by President Ronald Reagan had not only returned the White House to Republican control but recaptured the Senate as well. Reagan had just carried 49 states in being re-elected and had seemingly restored the presidency to its postwar primacy. The Iran-contra scandal and the savings and loans debacle, which would tar the memory of the Reagan presidency, had yet to occur.

But the Republican Party found it difficult to sustain its march toward undisputed predominance. As any reader of the guide could have predicted, the outparty prospered in the second midterm elections in 1986. Since the popular election of senators began in 1914, presidents who have served two terms have seen their party lose an average of seven Senate seats in their second midterms. In 1986 the Democrats picked up a net of eight seats and took control. With the House having remained Democratic throughout the Reagan era, the Hill was once again a Democratic bastion.

The divided government produced a period of standoff between the legislative branch and the executive (which remained Republican with the election of President George Bush in 1988). The result of the electoral stasis was often an inability on the part of the federal government to pursue any consistent agenda or policy direction. The frustration of this political box came to be called gridlock, a term borrowed from traffic engineering. It suggested that, while the constitutional system of shared powers and checks and balances might still be a good thing, a government could get too much of it.

## Incumbency's Lost Magic

In the years since the 1985 edition of this book, Congress also has touched the heights and depths of its turnover range. The election of November 1988 produced just 34 new faces in the House: a turnover of less than 8 percent and one of the smallest freshman classes ever. The re-election rate among those seeking another term was higher than 98 percent. A scant nine House seats changed party, the smallest number ever.

Those numbers attracted enough notice to cause trouble for the institution. They inspired countless editorials regretting the long tenures of ossified congressmen. Few could draw a negative correlation between seniority and effectiveness, but incumbency nonetheless became a target for talk-show hosts and other professional critics of government. This atmosphere contributed to slightly higher turnover in 1990, when 45 seats got new occupants. But it was in 1992, after a round of redistricting and a scandal in the House bank, that incumbency seemed to be shorn of its magic. Its power was undermined from within: 65 members chose to leave the House on their own. The incoming class of 100 freshmen was the largest since 1948.

The new Congress sworn in on Jan. 3, 1993, was also the most diverse in the history of the institution. The House included 48 women, an increase of two-thirds over the previous record. It also included 58 African Americans and Hispanics, an increase of about one-half over the previous record. And the Senate the same day welcomed 13 freshmen and an unprecedented set of demographics. For the first time, there were six woman senators, including four newcomers, two of whom were from the same state (California). (A seventh woman senator, from Texas, was elected in a 1993 special election.) Carol Moseley-Braun of Illinois became the first African American woman in Senate history and the first black senator in more than a decade. Ben Nighthorse Campbell of Colorado became the first Native American senator since 1929.

And yet, no Congress is ever the product of a single election. Continuity was factory-installed by the Framers of the Constitution, who required just one-third of the Senate to stand for re-election in each biennium. In the House, the entire membership is theoretically vulnerable to voter recall every two years. But as a practical matter, those who seek to be re-elected nearly always win. So, even after a housecleaning year such as 1992 — or the "Watergate Baby" election of 1974 or the "Reagan Revolution" of 1980 — more than three out of four members are returnees from the last Congress. For that matter, even the freshmen can be viewed as the offspring of multiple elections — including elections held before they were born.

Previous elections have determined the form and focus of the government, modifying and preserving what is passed on to each succeeding generation. The results of all those elections live on in the structure of government, the laws it enforces (or allows to go unenforced) and the rules by which income is distributed and by which authority restrains itself.

The United States is the world's longest-running democracy, and the sheer longevity of the system matters. It provides some of the shared experience that European nations are more likely to derive from their common ethnicity and culture. That is why the results of U.S. elections are essential subtext for understanding not only the political system but the American nation itself.

# Political Parties

**"Interior of Tammany Hall, New York — The Democratic Convention in Session,"** *Harper's,* **July 1868.**

# Pre-Convention Politics, 1789-1828

For more than a century and a half the United States has had an established two-party system. The Framers of the Constitution, however, never envisioned such a system. They in fact viewed the existence of political parties with suspicion.

In his Farewell Address, written in 1796, President George Washington warned the American people of "the danger of parties." He went on to state:

> There is an opinion that parties in free countries are useful checks upon the administration of the government, and serve to keep alive the spirit of liberty. This within certain limits is probably true; and in governments of a monarchical cast patriotism may look with indulgence, if not with favor, upon the spirit of party. But in those of the popular character, in governments purely elective, it is a spirit not to be encouraged.... A fire not to be quenched, it demands a uniform vigilance to prevent its bursting into a flame, lest, instead of warming, it should consume.

Other early American leaders shared Washington's suspicion of parties. Alexander Hamilton remarked in 1787, "[N]othing could be more illjudged than that intolerant spirit which has at all times characterized political parties." Two years later Thomas Jefferson declared: "If I could not go to heaven but with a party, I would not go there at all." Even a generation later, after the establishment of a U.S. party system, two early 19th-century presidents continued to speak out against the existence of political parties. Andrew Jackson, 12 years before he was elected president, wrote in 1816: "Now is the time to exterminate the monster called party spirit." In 1822, after his unopposed 1820 election victory, President James Monroe characterized parties as "the curse of the country."

Early American leaders were heavily influenced in their attitude by a dominant anti-party theme in European political philosophy, which equated parties with factions and viewed both negatively. Thomas Hobbes (1588-1679), David Hume (1711-1776) and Jean Jacques Rousseau (1712-1778) — three European philosophers whose views strongly influenced the Founders — regarded parties as threats to state government. In England there was no formal party system until the 1820s, several decades after the formation of parties in the United States. In colonial America there were no parties, and there were none in the Continental Congress or under the Articles of Confederation.

The Constitution did not provide authority for political parties or prohibitions against them. Historians have pointed out that most of the Framers had only a dim understanding of the function of political parties and thus were ambivalent, if not hostile, toward parties when they laid down the foundation of the new government. Nevertheless, the delegates to the Constitutional Convention and their successors in Congress ensured a role for parties in the government when they gave protection to civil rights and the right to organize. The Founders set up what they regarded as safeguards against excesses of party activity by providing an elaborate governmental system of checks and balances. The prevailing attitude of the convention was summed up by James Madison, who wrote in *The Federalist* that the "great object" of the new government was "to secure the public good and private rights against the danger of such a faction [party], and at the same time to preserve the spirit and the form of popular government."

Madison's greatest fear was that a party would become a tyrannical majority. This could be avoided, he believed, through the republican form of government that the proponents of the Constitution advocated. In *The Federalist* Madison wrote, "Among the numerous advantages promised by a well-constructed Union, none deserved to be more

## Sources

Chambers, William N. *Political Parties in a New Nation: The American Experience, 1776-1809.* New York: Oxford University Press, 1963.

Key, V. O., Jr. *Politics, Parties and Pressure Groups.* 5th ed. New York: Thomas Y. Crowell, 1964.

Nichols, Roy F. *The Invention of the American Political Parties.* New York: Free Press, 1972.

Roseboom, Eugene H. *A History of Presidential Elections: From George Washington to Jimmy Carter.* 4th ed. New York: Macmillan, 1979.

Schlesinger, Arthur M., Jr. *History of U.S. Political Parties.* Vol. 1. 1973. Reprint. New York: Chelsea House, 1981.

Stanwood, Edward. *History of the Presidency.* Vol. 1. 1921. Reprint. New York: Kelley, 1975.

Stimpson, George W. *A Book about American Politics.* New York: Harper, 1952.

*"[N]othing could be more illjudged than that intolerant spirit which has at all times characterized political parties."*
—Alexander Hamilton, 1789

accurately developed than its tendency to break and control the violence of faction." A republic, as understood by Madison, was an elected body of wise, patriotic citizens, while a democracy was equated with mob rule. Madison dismissed the democratic form of government as a spectacle of "turbulence and contention."

Ironically, in this setting two competing parties grew up quickly. They developed as a result of public sentiment for and against adoption of the Constitution. The Federalist Party — a loose coalition of merchants, shippers, financiers and other business interests — favored the strong central government provided by the Constitution, while their opponents (at first called Anti-Federalists or Jeffersonians and later known as Democratic-Republicans) were intent upon preserving the sovereignty of the states. Underlying the controversy was the desire of the interests represented by the Federalists to create a government with power to guarantee the value of the currency (and thus protect the position of creditors) and the desire of the agrarians and frontiersmen who made up the Anti-Federalists to maintain easy credit conditions and the power of state legislatures to fend off encroachments by a remote federal government.

Unlike the Federalist Party, which was never more than a loose alliance of particular interests, the Anti-Federalists achieved a high degree of organization. The Federalists, in fact, never considered themselves a political party but rather a gentlemanly coalition of interests representing respectable society. What party management there was, they kept clandestine, a reflection of their own fundamental suspicion of parties.

There is no precise date for the beginning of parties, although both Thomas Jefferson and Alexander Hamilton (a Federalist) referred to the existence of a Jeffersonian republican "faction" in Congress as early as 1792.

While party organization became more formalized in the 1790s and early 1800s, particularly among the Jeffersonians, the parties never acquired nationally accepted names. The Jeffersonians most commonly referred to themselves as Republicans. Their opponents labeled them as Anti-Federalists, disorganizers, Jacobins (after the radical democrats in France) and Democrats — the latter an unflattering term in the early years of the Republic. To many Americans in the late 18th century, a democrat was considered a supporter of mob rule and revolution and often ideologically identified with the bloody French Revolution of 1789.

The designation Democrat-Republican was used by the Jeffersonians in several states but was never widely accepted as a party label. However, historians often refer to the Jeffersonians as the Democratic-Republicans, to avoid confusion with the later and unrelated Republican Party, founded in 1854.

Although the early American political leaders acknowledged the development of parties, they did not foresee the emergence of a two-party system. Rather, they often justified the existence of their own party as a reaction to an unacceptable opposition. Jefferson defended his party involvement as a struggle between good and evil: "[When] the principle of difference is as substantial and as strongly pronounced as between the republicans and the Monocrats of our country, I hold it as honorable to take a firm and decided part, and as immoral to pursue a middle line, as between the parties of Honest men, and Rogues, into which every country is divided."

# Presidential Politics

The rise of parties forced an alteration in the presidential selection method envisioned by the creators of the Constitution. Delegates to the Constitutional Convention of 1787 had sought a presidential selection method in which the "spirit of party" would play no part. The Electoral College system they finally settled on was a compromise born of a basic distrust in the political abilities of the populace, the complexities of the separation of powers system and the diversity in the states — slavery in the South and rivalries between the big and small states.

Rather than have the people vote directly for president, the choice was to be entrusted to presidential "electors," who the Founders hoped would be wise leaders in the separate states, able to choose the one person best qualified to be president. Under the Electoral College system, states were to choose electors as they saw fit; the electors would meet in their separate states some time after their selection to pick the next president. *(The Electoral College, p. 343)*

While it seems odd that the leaders of a new democracy would choose to bypass the general populace, the decision was not so far out of line with conditions of the day as it might appear. The electors would merely be a somewhat more sophisticated version of the 18th-century electorate, which was quite different from the voting population of today. The Constitution left it to the states to determine voting requirements. In all states only men could vote. Many states also limited voting rights to property owners. Indeed, property qualifications had existed in all the colonies and endured in several states, although the exact requirements differed among states.

Some states allowed personal property or the payment of taxes as a substitute for holding real estate. By 1800 four states had established universal manhood suffrage. But property requirements of one sort or another were not abandoned by all the states until 1856. While they lasted, such requirements were restrictive, but their effect can be overstated. Because the United States was predominantly a middle-class society with fairly widespread ownership of property, such qualifications were not so significant a limit as they at first might appear. And since women and many men already were excluded from voting, restricting presidential selection to an elite group did not have the effect that it would today under universal suffrage.

# Caucus System

While the Electoral College retained the power to *elect* the president, the state electors soon lost the authority to *nominate* the candidates and thus determine the field from which to choose a president. Strong political parties developed and removed the nomination process from the electors' hands. The parties created instead the first informal nominating device for choosing a president: a caucus of each party's members in Congress.

From 1796 until 1824, congressional caucuses — when a party had enough representatives to form one — chose almost all the candidates for president; the electors then chose from the party nominees. Only twice — in 1800 and 1824 — as a result of a failure of any candidate to receive a majority of electoral votes, were presidential elections decided by the House of Representatives, and even in those two cases political parties were instrumental in the election of the president.

### Election of 1789

In the first presidential election, held in 1789 shortly after the ratification of the Constitution, the nominating and electing process centered in the Electoral College. Electors chosen in the various states were, under the Constitution, entitled to cast two votes and required to cast each vote for a different person. The individual receiving votes of a majority of the electors was named president and the person receiving the second highest total was named vice president.

There were no formal nominations in 1789, but public opinion centered on George Washington of Virginia for president. He received 69 electoral votes, the maximum possible. John Adams of Massachusetts was the leading second choice, although he did not enjoy the degree of unanimity that surrounded Washington. Adams easily won the vice presidency, receiving 34 electoral votes.

### Election of 1792

The Federalists and Democratic-Republicans were emerging as competitive parties by the election of 1792. As a result, the Republic experienced the first modification in the presidential nominating process. No attempt was made to displace President Washington, but the Democratic-Republicans mounted a challenge to Vice President Adams. Meeting in Philadelphia in October 1792, a group of Democratic-Republican leaders from the Middle Atlantic states and South Carolina endorsed Gov. George Clinton of New York for the vice presidency, bypassing Sen. Aaron Burr of the same state. While Adams emerged victorious in the Electoral College, Clinton's endorsement by a meeting of party politicians was a milestone in the evolution of the presidential nominating process and a step away from the original Electoral College system.

### Election of 1796

The election of 1796 brought further modifications in the nominating method, evidenced by the appearance of the congressional caucus.

There was no opposition to Thomas Jefferson as the Democratic-Republican presidential candidate, and he was considered the party's standard-bearer by a consensus of party leaders. A caucus of Democratic-Republican senators, however, was unable to agree on a running mate, producing a tie vote between Burr and Sen. Pierce Butler of South Carolina that ended with a walk-out by Butler's supporters. As a result, there was no formal Democratic-Republican candidate to run with Jefferson.

The Federalists held what historian Roy F. Nichols described as a "quasi caucus" of the party's members of Congress in Philadelphia in May 1796. The gathering chose Vice President Adams and Minister to Great Britain Thomas Pinckney of South Carolina as the Federalist candidates.

## Presidents, 1789-1829

| Term | President | Vice President |
|---|---|---|
| 1789-93 | George Washington (FED) | John Adams (FED) |
| 1793-97 | George Washington (FED) | John Adams (FED) |
| 1797-1801 | John Adams (FED) | Thomas Jefferson (D-R) |
| 1801-05 | Thomas Jefferson (D-R) | Aaron Burr (D-R) |
| 1805-09 | Thomas Jefferson (D-R) | George Clinton (D-R) |
| 1809-13 | James Madison (D-R) | George Clinton (D-R) |
| 1813-17 | James Madison (D-R) | Elbridge Gerry (D-R) |
| 1817-21 | James Monroe (D-R) | Daniel D. Tompkins (D-R) |
| 1821-25 | James Monroe (D-R) | Daniel D. Tompkins (D-R) |
| 1825-29 | John Q. Adams (D-R) | John C. Calhoun (D-R) |

FED - Federalist;  D-R - Democratic-Republican

### Election of 1800

The election of 1800 was the first where both parties used the congressional caucus as the nominating body. Neither party, however, desired much publicity for the process, gathering in secret to deliberate. The proceedings were sketchily described by private correspondence and occasionally referred to in newspapers of the day. Unlike the public national conventions of later years, privacy was a hallmark of the early caucuses.

Although the actual dates of the 1800 caucuses are hazy, it is believed that both were held in May. The Democratic-Republican caucus was held in Marache's boardinghouse in Philadelphia, where 43 of the party's members of Congress selected Aaron Burr to run with Thomas Jefferson, the latter again the presidential candidate by consensus and not formally nominated by the caucus.

Federalist members of Congress met in the Senate chamber in Philadelphia and nominated President Adams and Gen. Charles Cotesworth Pinckney of South Carolina. Pinckney, the elder brother of the Federalist vice presidential candidate in 1796, was placed on the ticket at the insistence of Alexander Hamilton, who believed one of the South Carolina Pinckneys could win. Although the deliberations of the Federalist caucus were secret, the existence of the meeting was not. It was described by the local Democratic-Republican paper, the *Philadelphia Aurora*, as a "Jacobinical conclave." Further denunciations by the paper's author, Benjamin F. Bache, earned him a personal rebuke from the U.S. Senate.

### Election of 1804

The 1804 election was the first one held after the 12th Amendment to the Constitution went into effect, requiring electors to cast separate votes for president and vice presi-

*"If I could not go to heaven but with a party, I would not go there at all."*

—Thomas Jefferson, 1789

*"Among the numerous advantages promised by a well-constructed Union, none deserves to be more accurately developed than its tendency to break and control the violence of faction."*
—James Madison, 1787

dent. The amendment was designed to avoid the unwieldy situation that had developed in 1800, when the two leading Democratic-Republican candidates, Jefferson and Burr, both received the same number of electoral votes. The unexpected tie vote threw the presidential election into the House of Representatives, where 36 ballots were cast before Jefferson finally won. With ratification of the amendment, parties in 1804 and thereafter specifically designated their presidential and vice presidential candidates.

The Democratic-Republicans retained the caucus system of nomination in 1804, as they did for the next two decades, and for the first time they publicly reported their deliberations. The party caucus was held in February and attracted 108 of the party's senators and representatives. President Jefferson was renominated by acclamation, but Vice President Burr was not considered for a second term. On the first nominating roll call publicly reported in American political history, New York's Gov. Clinton was chosen to run for vice president. He received 67 votes to easily defeat Sen. John Breckinridge of Kentucky, who collected 20 votes. To "avoid unpleasant discussions" no names were placed in nomination, and the vote was taken by written ballot.

Before adjourning, the caucus appointed a 13-member committee to conduct the campaign. A forerunner of party national committees, the new campaign group included members of both the House and Senate, but with no two individuals from the same state.

The Federalists dropped the congressional caucus as their nominating method. Federalist leaders in 1804 informally chose Charles Cotesworth Pinckney for president and Rufus King of New York for vice president. But the details of how they formulated this ticket are not known. There is no record in 1804 of any Federalist meeting to nominate candidates.

## Election of 1808

The Democratic-Republican caucus was held in January 1808. For the first time a formal call was issued. Sen. Stephen R. Bradley of Vermont, the chairman of the 1804 caucus, issued the call to all 146 Democratic-Republicans in Congress and several Federalists sympathetic to the Democratic-Republican cause. His authority to call the caucus was questioned by several party leaders, but various reports indicate that 89 to 94 members of Congress attended.

As in 1804 the balloting was done without the formal placing of names in nomination. For president, Jefferson's handpicked successor, Secretary of State James Madison of Virginia, was an easy winner with 83 votes. Vice President Clinton and James Monroe of Virginia each received three votes. For vice president the caucus overwhelmingly renominated Clinton. He received 79 votes, while runner-up John Langdon of New Hampshire collected five. Even after the Democratic-Republicans renominated him for vice presi-

dent, Clinton's supporters continued to hope that the Federalists would nominate their man for president later in the year. But their hopes were dashed when the nomination ultimately went to Pinckney.

As in 1804 the Democratic-Republican caucus appointed a committee to conduct the campaign. Membership was expanded to 15 House and Senate members and it was formally called the "committee of correspondence and arrangement." The committee was authorized to fill any vacancies on the national ticket, should any occur.

Before adjournment a resolution was approved defending the caucus system as "the most practicable mode of consulting and respecting the interest and wishes of all." Later caucuses adopted similar resolutions throughout the history of the system.

The resolution was meant to stem the rumblings of opposition to the caucus system. Seventeen Democratic-Republican members of Congress signed a protest against Madison's selection and questioned the authority of the caucus as a nominating body. Vice President Clinton, himself selected by the caucus, wrote of his disapproval of the caucus system.

The Federalists in 1808 again altered their presidential selection process, holding a secret meeting of party leaders in August of that year to choose the ticket. The meeting, held in New York City, was initially called by the Federalist members of the Massachusetts legislature. Twenty-five to 30 party leaders from seven states, all north of the Potomac River except South Carolina, attended the national meeting. There was some discussion of choosing Vice President George Clinton, a dissident Democratic-Republican, for the presidency, but the meeting ultimately selected the Federalist candidates of 1804: Charles Cotesworth Pinckney and Rufus King.

## Election of 1812

The Democratic-Republicans held their quadrennial nominating caucus in May 1812. Eighty-three of the party's 138 members of Congress attended, with the New England and New York delegations poorly represented. The New York delegation was sympathetic to the candidacy of the state's lieutenant governor, De Witt Clinton, who was maneuvering for the Federalist nomination, while New England was noticeably upset with the Madison foreign policy that was leading to war with England. President Madison was renominated with a near-unanimous total, receiving 82 votes. John Langdon of New Hampshire was chosen for vice president by a wide margin, collecting 64 votes to 16 for Gov. Elbridge Gerry of Massachusetts. But Langdon declined the nomination, citing his age (70) as the reason. In a second caucus, held in June, Gerry was a runaway winner with 74 votes.

In 1812, as four years earlier, the Federalists held a secret meeting in New York City. It was more than twice the size of the 1808 gathering, with 70 representatives from 11 states attending the three-day meeting in September. Delegates were sent to the conference by Federalist general committees, with all but nine of the delegates coming from the New England and Middle Atlantic states.

Debate centered on whether to run a separate Federalist ticket or to endorse the candidacy of De Witt Clinton, the nephew of George Clinton. The younger Clinton already had been nominated for the presidency by the New York Democratic-Republican caucus, and the Federalists ultimately adopted a resolution approving his candidacy and that of

Jared Ingersoll. Ingersoll was a Pennsylvania Federalist who was initially nominated for vice president by a party legislative caucus in that state.

### Election of 1816

The Federalist Party was nearly extinct by 1816 and did not hold any type of meeting to nominate candidates for president and vice president. As a result, nomination by the Democratic-Republican caucus was tantamount to election. Only 58 members of Congress attended the first caucus in the House chamber. With the expectation of better attendance, a second caucus was held several days later in mid-March 1816 and drew 119 senators and representatives. By a vote of 65 to 54, Secretary of State James Monroe was nominated for president, defeating Secretary of War William H. Crawford of Georgia. Forty of Crawford's votes came from five states: Georgia, Kentucky, New Jersey, New York and North Carolina. The vice presidential nomination went to New York governor Daniel D. Tompkins, who easily outdistanced Pennsylvania governor Simon Snyder, 85 to 30. The nominations of Monroe and Tompkins revived a Virginia-New York alliance that extended back to the late 18th century. With the lone exception of 1812, every Democratic-Republican ticket from 1800 until 1824 was composed of a candidate from Virginia and a vice presidential candidate from New York.

While the collapse of the Federalists ensured Democratic-Republican rule, it also increased intraparty friction and spurred further attacks on the caucus system. Twenty-two Democratic-Republican members of Congress were absent from the second party caucus, and at least 15 were known to be opposed to the system. Historian Edward Stanwood wrote that there were mass meetings around the country to protest the caucus system. Opponents claimed that the writers of the Constitution did not envision the caucus, that presidential nominating should not be a function of Congress and that the caucus system encouraged candidates to curry the favor of Congress.

### Election of 1820

The 1820 election came during the "Era of Good Feelings," a phrase coined by a Boston publication, the *Columbian Centinel,* to describe a brief period of virtual one-party rule in the United States. With only one candidate, President James Monroe, there was no need for a caucus. One was called, but fewer than 50 of the Democratic-Republicans' 191 members of Congress attended. The caucus voted unanimously to make no nominations and passed a resolution explaining that it was inexpedient to do so. Despite the fact that Monroe and Tompkins were not formally renominated, electoral slates were filed on their behalf. They both received nearly unanimous Electoral College victories.

## Demise of the Caucus

In 1824 there was still only one party, but within this party there was an abundance of candidates for the presidency: Secretary of State John Quincy Adams of Massachusetts, Sen. Andrew Jackson of Tennessee, Secretary of War John C. Calhoun of South Carolina, House Speaker Henry Clay of Kentucky and Secretary of the Treasury William H. Crawford. It was generally assumed that Crawford was the strongest candidate among members of Congress and would

win a caucus if one were held; therefore, Crawford's opponents joined the growing list of caucus opponents.

In early February 1824, 11 Democratic-Republican members of Congress issued a call for a caucus to be held in the middle of the month. Their call was countered by 24 other members of Congress from 15 states who deemed it "inexpedient under existing circumstances" to hold a caucus. They claimed that 181 members of Congress were resolved not to attend if a caucus were held.

When the caucus convened in mid-February, only 66 members of Congress were present, with three-quarters of those attending from just four states — Georgia, New York, North Carolina and Virginia. As expected, Crawford won the presidential nomination, receiving 64 votes. Selected for vice president was Albert Gallatin of Pennsylvania, who received 57 votes. The caucus adopted a resolution defending its actions as "the best means of collecting and concentrating the feelings and wishes of the people of the Union upon this important subject." A committee was appointed to write an address to the people. As written, the text of the address viewed with alarm the "dismemberment" of the Democratic-Republican Party.

The caucus nomination proved to be an albatross for Crawford as his opponents denounced him as the candidate of "King Caucus." Reflecting the increasing democratization of American politics, other presidential candidates relied on nominations by state legislatures to legitimize their presidential ambitions. However, in an attempt to narrow the field, the candidates had to negotiate among themselves. Calhoun alone withdrew to become the vice presidential candidate of all the anti-caucus entries. Adams offered the vice presidency to Jackson as "an easy and dignified retirement to his old age." Jackson refused. Other maneuvers were equally unsuccessful, so that four presidential candidates remained in the field to collect electoral votes, subsequently throwing the election into the House of Representatives, where Adams won.

The election of 1828 proved to be a transitional one in the development of the presidential nominating process. The caucus was dead, but the national nominating convention was not yet born. Jackson was nominated by the legislature of his native Tennessee and in October 1825, three years before the election, accepted the nomination in a speech before the legislature. He accepted Vice President Calhoun as his running mate, after it was proposed in January 1827 by the *United States Telegraph,* a pro-Jackson paper in Washington. A Pennsylvania state convention paired President Adams with Secretary of the Treasury Richard Rush of Pennsylvania, a ticket that Adams' supporters in other states accepted. Both Jackson and Adams were endorsed by other legislatures, conventions and meetings.

*"We must always have party distinctions."*
—Martin Van Buren, 1827

# Trend Toward Conventions

The birth of the national convention system came in 1831, seven years after the death of the caucus. The caucus system collapsed when a field of candidates appeared who would not acquiesce to the choice of one caucus-approved candidate. But other factors were present to undermine the caucus system. These included changes in voting procedures and an expansion of suffrage. Between 1800 and 1824 the proportion of states in which the electors were chosen by popular vote rather than by the state legislature increased from 4 out of 16 to 18 out of 24. In 1828 the popular vote reached 1.1 million, compared with fewer than 400,000 in 1824. A broader base of support than the congressional caucus became essential for presidential aspirants.

State legislatures, state conventions and mass meetings all emerged in the 1820s to challenge the caucus. The trend to democratization of the presidential nominating process, as evidenced by the expansion of suffrage and increased importance of the popular vote for president, led shortly to creation of the national nominating convention. The convention system, initiated by the Anti-Masons in 1831, was adopted by all the major parties before the end of the decade. *(Anti-Masons, pp. 35, 261)*

The birth of the national nominating convention was a milestone in the evolution of the presidential nominating process. Political scientist V. O. Key Jr. summarized some of the major forces that brought about the rise of the convention system:

> The destruction of the caucus represented more than a mere change in the method of nomination. Its replacement by the convention was regarded as the removal from power of self-appointed oligarchies that had usurped the right to nominate. The new system, the convention, gave, or so it was supposed, the mass of party members an opportunity to participate in nominations. These events occurred as the domestic winds blew in from the growing West, as the suffrage was being broadened, and as the last vestiges of the early aristocratic leadership were disappearing. Sharp alterations in the distribution of power were taking place, and they were paralleled by the shifts in methods of nomination.

With the establishment of the national convention came the re-emergence of the two-party system. Unlike the Founders, who were suspicious of competitive parties, some political leaders in the late 1820s and 1830s viewed the existence of opposing parties favorably. One of the most prominent of these men, Martin Van Buren, a leading organizer of Jackson's 1828 election victory and himself president after Jackson, had written in 1827: "We must always have party distinctions."

# Nominating Conventions

Although the presidential nominating convention has been a target of criticism throughout its existence, it has survived to become a traditional fixture of American politics. The convention owes its longevity and general acceptance in large part to the multiplicity of functions that the convention uniquely combines.

The convention is a nominating body that the Democrats, Republicans and most of the principal third parties have used for 160 years to choose their candidates for president and vice president. The convention also produces a platform containing the party's positions on issues of the campaign. Convention delegates form the organization's supreme governing body and as such they make major decisions on party affairs. Between conventions such decisions are made by the national committee with the guidance of the party chair.

The convention provides a forum for compromise among the diverse elements within a party, allowing the discussion and often the satisfactory solution of differing points of view. As the ultimate campaign rally, the convention also gathers together thousands of party leaders and rank-and-file members from across the country in an atmosphere that varies widely, sometimes encouraging sober discussion but often resembling a carnival. But even though the process has drawn heavy criticism, the convention has endured because it successfully performs a variety of actions.

The convention is an outgrowth of the American political experience. Nowhere is it mentioned in the Constitution nor has the authority of the convention ever been a subject of congressional legislation. Rather, the convention has evolved along with the presidential selection process. The convention has been the accepted nominating method of the major political parties since the election of 1832, but internal changes within the convention system have been massive since the early, formative years.

## Convention Sites

Before the Civil War, conventions frequently were held in small buildings, even churches, and attracted only several hundred delegates and a minimum of spectators. Transportation and communications were slow, so most conventions were held in the late spring in a city with a central geographical location. Baltimore, Md., was the most popular convention city in this period, playing host to the first six Democratic conventions (1832 through 1852), two Whig conventions, one National Republican convention, and the 1831 Anti-Masonic gathering — America's first national nominating convention. With the nation's westward expansion, the heartland city of Chicago, Ill., emerged as the most frequent convention center. Since its first one in 1860, Chicago has been the site of 24 major party conventions (14 Republican, 10 Democratic).

### Location and Financing

Since 1976 presidential elections have been publicly funded and parties have depended on host cities to supplement the money the parties could legally spend on their conventions. In 1992 that amount was $11,048,000, which each major party received from the optional checkoff on federal income taxes for presidential campaigns. (Congress raised the original $1 checkoff to $3 per taxpayer beginning in 1993). The Federal Election Commission has ruled that host-city contributions are not prohibited contributions, and this has enabled the parties to far exceed the technical limit on convention spending. In 1992, for example, the Republicans spent $21.0 million on their Houston convention and the Democrats spent a record $38.6 on their New York City meeting, according to political scientist Herbert E. Alexander. In 1988 the comparable amounts were $18.0 million for the GOP at New Orleans and $22.5 million for the Democrats at Atlanta, each total including $9.2 million that the party received in public funds. To attract the Democratic convention, Atlanta levied a special tax on hotel guests, which enabled the host committee to offer a package of $5 million in borrowed money. For both 1988 conventions, General Motors (with FEC permission) provided fleets of cars at an estimated cost of $350,000.

No breakdown of the 1992 convention costs was available, but major outlays typically go for construction, administration, office space, convention committees and police and fire protection. Besides adequate hotel and convention hall facilities, safety of the delegates and other attendees is increasingly a major consideration in selection of a national party convention site. The island location of Miami Beach, for example, made it easier to contain protest demonstrators and reportedly was a factor in its selection by the Republicans in 1968 and by both parties in 1972. For the party that controls the White House, often the overriding factor in site selection is the president's personal preference — as in the GOP's decision to meet in 1992 at President George Bush's adopted home city of Houston.

# Sites of Major Party Conventions, 1832-1992

The following chart lists the 20 cities selected as the sites of major party conventions and the number of conventions they have hosted or were scheduled to host, from the first national gathering for the Democrats (1832) and the Republicans (1856) through the 1992 conventions.

| | Total Conventions | Democratic Conventions | | Republican Conventions | |
|---|---|---|---|---|---|
| | | Number | Last Hosted | Number | Last Hosted |
| Chicago, Ill. | 24 | 10 | 1968 | 14 | 1960 |
| Baltimore, Md. | 10 | 9 | 1912 | 1 | 1864 |
| Philadelphia, Pa. | 7 | 2 | 1948 | 5 | 1948 |
| St. Louis, Mo. | 5 | 4 | 1916 | 1 | 1896 |
| New York, N.Y. | 5 | 5 | 1992 | 0 | — |
| San Francisco, Calif. | 4 | 2 | 1984 | 2 | 1964 |
| Cincinnati, Ohio | 3 | 2 | 1880 | 1 | 1876 |
| Kansas City, Mo. | 3 | 1 | 1900 | 2 | 1976 |
| Miami Beach, Fla. | 3 | 1 | 1972 | 2 | 1972 |
| Cleveland, Ohio | 2 | 0 | — | 2 | 1936 |
| Houston, Texas | 2 | 1 | 1928 | 1 | 1992 |
| Atlanta, Ga. | 1 | 1 | 1988 | 0 | — |
| Atlantic City, N.J. | 1 | 1 | 1964 | 0 | — |
| Charleston, S.C. | 1 | 1 | 1860 | 0 | — |
| Dallas, Texas | 1 | 0 | — | 1 | 1984 |
| Denver, Colo. | 1 | 1 | 1908 | 0 | — |
| Detroit, Mich. | 1 | 0 | — | 1 | 1980 |
| Los Angeles, Calif. | 1 | 1 | 1960 | 0 | — |
| Minneapolis, Minn. | 1 | 0 | — | 1 | 1892 |
| New Orleans, La. | 1 | 0 | — | 1 | 1988 |

The national committees of the two parties select the sites about one year before the conventions are to take place.

## Call of the Convention

The second major step in the quadrennial convention process follows several months after the site selection with announcement of the convention call, the establishment of the three major convention committees — credentials, rules and platform (resolutions) — the appointment of convention officers and finally the holding of the convention itself. While these basic steps have undergone little change during the past 160 years, there have been major alterations within the nominating convention system.

The call to the convention sets the date and site of the meeting and is issued early in each election year, if not before. The call to the first Democratic convention, held in 1832, was issued by the New Hampshire legislature. Early Whig conventions were called by party members in Congress. With the establishment of national committees later in the 19th century, the function of issuing the convention call fell to these new party organizations. Each national committee currently has the responsibility for allocating delegates to each state.

## Delegate Selection

Both parties have modified the method of allocating delegates to the individual states and territories. From the beginning of the convention system in the 19th century, both the Democrats and Republicans distributed votes to the states based on their Electoral College strength. The first major deviation from this procedure was made by the Republicans after their divisive 1912 convention, in which President William Howard Taft won renomination over former president Theodore Roosevelt. Taft's nomination was due largely to almost solid support from the South — a region vastly over-represented in relation to its number of Republican voters. Before their 1916 convention the Republicans reduced the allocation of votes to the Southern states. At their 1924 convention the Republicans applied the first bonus system, by which states were awarded extra votes for supporting the Republican presidential candidate in the previous election. The concept of bonus votes, applied as a reward to the states for supporting the party ticket, has been used and expanded by both parties since that time.

The Democrats first used a bonus system in 1944, completing a compromise arrangement with Southern states for abolishing the party's controversial two-thirds nominating rule. Since then both parties have used various delegate-allocation formulas. At their 1972 convention the Republicans revised the formula and added more than 900 new delegate slots. The Ripon Society, an organization of liberal Republicans, sued to have the new rules overturned. They argued that, because of the extra delegates awarded to states that voted Republican in the previous presidential election, small Southern and Western states were favored at the expense of the more populous but less Republican Eastern states. The challenge failed when the Supreme Court in February 1976 refused to hear the case and thus let stand a U.S. Court of Appeals decision upholding the rules.

Only 116 delegates from 13 states attended the initial national nominating convention held by the Anti-Masons in 1831, but with the addition of more states and the adoption of increasingly complex voting-allocation formulas by the major parties, the size of conventions spiraled. The 1976 Republican convention had 2,259 delegates, while the Dem-

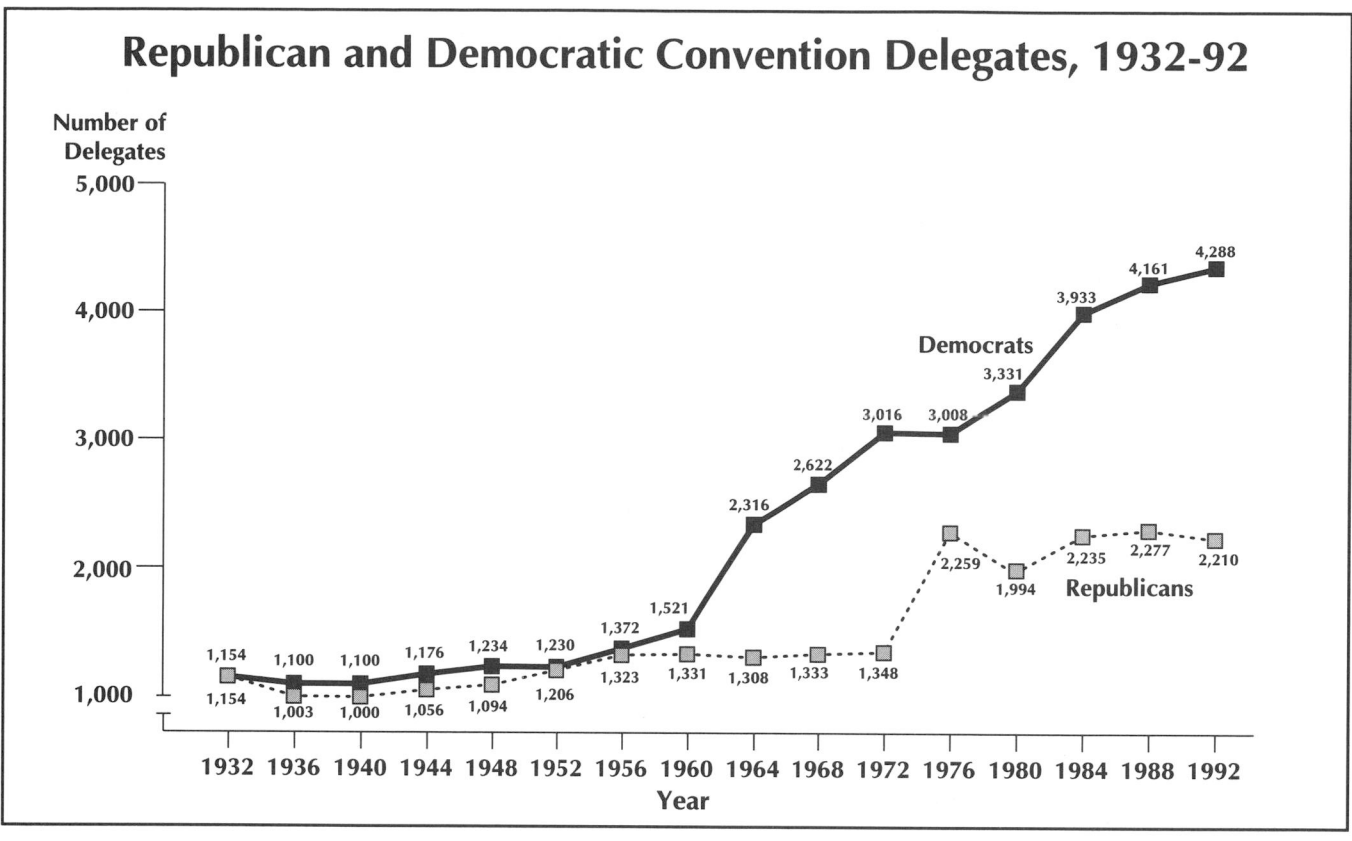

## Republican and Democratic Convention Delegates, 1932-92

Number of Delegates

ocrats in the same year had 3,075 delegates casting 3,008 votes. (The number of delegate votes was smaller than the number of delegates because the rules provided for fractional voting.)

The expanded size of modern conventions in part reflected their democratization, with less command by a few party leaders and dramatic growth among youth, women and minority delegations. Increased representation by such groups was one of the major reasons given by the Republicans for the 60 percent increase in delegate strength authorized by the 1972 convention (and effective for the 1976 gathering). The Democrats adopted new rules in June 1978, expanding the number of delegates by 10 percent to provide extra representation for state and local officials. The new rules also required that women account for at least 50 percent of the delegates beginning with the 1980 convention. The party's national convention continued to grow throughout the next decade — from 3,933 delegate votes in 1984 to 4,288 in 1992.

With the increased size of conventions has come a formalization in the method of delegate selection, which at first was often haphazard and informal. At the Democratic convention in 1835, for example, Maryland had 188 delegates to cast the state's 10 votes. In contrast, Tennessee's 15 votes were cast by a traveling businessman who happened to be in the convention city at the time. While the number of delegates and the number of votes allocated tended to be equal or nearly so later in the 19th century, a few party bosses frequently exercised domination of national conventions.

Two basic methods of delegate selection were employed in the 19th century and continued to be used into the 20th:

the caucus method, by which delegates were chosen by meetings at the local or state level, and the appointment method, by which delegates were appointed by the governor or a powerful state leader.

### Presidential Primaries

A revolutionary new mechanism for delegate selection emerged during the early 1900s: the presidential primary election in which the voters directly elected convention delegates.

Initiated in Florida in 1904, the presidential primary by 1912 was used by 13 states. In his first annual message to Congress the following year, President Woodrow Wilson advocated the establishment of a national primary to select presidential candidates: "I feel confident that I do not misinterpret the wishes or the expectations of the country when I urge the prompt enactment of legislation which will provide for primary elections throughout the country at which the voters of several parties may choose their nominees for the presidency without the intervention of nominating conventions." Wilson went on to suggest the retention of conventions for the purpose of declaring the results of the primaries and formulating the parties' platforms.

Before any action was taken on Wilson's proposal, the progressive spirit that spurred the growth of presidential primaries died out. Not until after World War II, when widespread pressures for change touched both parties but especially the Democratic, was there a rapid growth in presidential primaries. In the mid-1980s some states reverted to the caucus method of delegate selection, but the revival trend soon abated. A record 40 primaries were held

# Democratic Conventions, 1832-1992

| Year | City | Dates | Presidential Nominee | Vice Presidential Nominee | No. of Pres. Ballots |
|------|------|-------|----------------------|---------------------------|----------------------|
| 1832 | Baltimore | May 21-23 | Andrew Jackson | Martin Van Buren | 1 |
| 1835 | Baltimore | May 20-23 | Martin Van Buren | Richard M. Johnson | 1 |
| 1840 | Baltimore | May 5-6 | Martin Van Buren | —[1] | 1 |
| 1844 | Baltimore | May 27-29 | James K. Polk | George M. Dallas | 9 |
| 1848 | Baltimore | May 22-25 | Lewis Cass | William O. Butler | 4 |
| 1852 | Baltimore | June 1-5 | Franklin Pierce | William R. King | 49 |
| 1856 | Cincinnati | June 2-6 | James Buchanan | John C. Breckinridge | 17 |
| 1860 | Charleston | April 23-May 3 | Deadlocked | | 57 |
| | Baltimore | June 18-23 | Stephen A. Douglas | Benjamin Fitzpatrick Herschel V. Johnson[2] | 2 |
| 1864 | Chicago | Aug. 29-31 | George B. McClellan | George H. Pendleton | 1 |
| 1868 | New York | July 4-9 | Horatio Seymour | Francis P. Blair | 22 |
| 1872 | Baltimore | July 9-10 | Horace Greeley | Benjamin G. Brown | 1 |
| 1876 | St. Louis | June 27-29 | Samuel J. Tilden | Thomas A. Hendricks | 2 |
| 1880 | Cincinnati | June 22-24 | Winfield S. Hancock | William H. English | 2 |
| 1884 | Chicago | July 8-11 | Grover Cleveland | Thomas A. Hendricks | 2 |
| 1888 | St. Louis | June 5-7 | Grover Cleveland | Allen G. Thurman | 1 |
| 1892 | Chicago | June 21-23 | Grover Cleveland | Adlai E. Stevenson | 1 |
| 1896 | Chicago | July 7-11 | William J. Bryan | Arthur Sewall | 5 |
| 1900 | Kansas City | July 4-6 | William J. Bryan | Adlai E. Stevenson | 1 |
| 1904 | St. Louis | July 6-9 | Alton S. Parker | Henry G. Davis | 1 |
| 1908 | Denver | July 7-10 | William J. Bryan | John W. Kern | 1 |
| 1912 | Baltimore | June 25-July 2 | Woodrow Wilson | Thomas R. Marshall | 46 |
| 1916 | St. Louis | June 14-16 | Woodrow Wilson | Thomas R. Marshall | 1 |
| 1920 | San Francisco | June 28-July 6 | James M. Cox | Franklin D. Roosevelt | 44 |
| 1924 | New York | June 24-July 9 | John W. Davis | Charles W. Bryan | 103 |
| 1928 | Houston | June 26-29 | Alfred E. Smith | Joseph T. Robinson | 1 |
| 1932 | Chicago | June 27-July 2 | Franklin D. Roosevelt | John N. Garner | 4 |
| 1936 | Philadelphia | June 23-27 | Franklin D. Roosevelt | John N. Garner | Acclamation |
| 1940 | Chicago | July 15-18 | Franklin D. Roosevelt | Henry A. Wallace | 1 |
| 1944 | Chicago | July 19-21 | Franklin D. Roosevelt | Harry S. Truman | 1 |
| 1948 | Philadelphia | July 12-14 | Harry S. Truman | Alben W. Barkley | 1 |
| 1952 | Chicago | July 21-26 | Adlai E. Stevenson | John J. Sparkman | 3 |
| 1956 | Chicago | Aug. 13-17 | Adlai E. Stevenson | Estes Kefauver | 1 |
| 1960 | Los Angeles | July 11-15 | John F. Kennedy | Lyndon B. Johnson | 1 |
| 1964 | Atlantic City | Aug. 24-27 | Lyndon B. Johnson | Hubert H. Humphrey | Acclamation |
| 1968 | Chicago | Aug. 26-29 | Hubert H. Humphrey | Edmund S. Muskie | 1 |
| 1972 | Miami Beach | July 10-13 | George McGovern | Thomas F. Eagleton R. Sargent Shriver[3] | 1 |
| 1976 | New York | July 12-15 | Jimmy Carter | Walter F. Mondale | 1 |
| 1980 | New York | Aug. 11-14 | Jimmy Carter | Walter F. Mondale | 1 |
| 1984 | San Francisco | July 16-19 | Walter F. Mondale | Geraldine A. Ferraro | 1 |
| 1988 | Atlanta | July 18-21 | Michael S. Dukakis | Lloyd Bentsen | 1 |
| 1992 | New York | July 13-16 | Bill Clinton | Albert Gore Jr. | 1 |

1. *The 1840 Democratic convention did not nominate a candidate for vice president.*

2. *The 1860 Democratic convention nominated Benjamin Fitzpatrick, who declined the nomination shortly after the convention adjourned. On June 25 the Democratic National Committee selected Herschel V. Johnson as the party's candidate for vice president.*

3. *The 1972 Democratic convention nominated Thomas F. Eagleton, who withdrew from the ticket on July 31. On Aug. 8 the Democratic National Committee selected R. Sargent Shriver as the party's candidate for vice president.*

in 1992, including the District of Columbia and Puerto Rico. *(Selection by Caucus Method, box, p. 483)*

In most states participation in the presidential primary is restricted to voters belonging to the party holding the primary. In some states, however, participation by voters outside the party is allowed.

## Democratic Rules in the 1980s and 1990s

In June 1982 the Democratic National Committee (DNC) adopted several changes in the presidential nomi-

nating process recommended by the party's Commission on Presidential Nominations, chaired by Gov. James B. Hunt Jr. of North Carolina. The Hunt Commission, as it came to be known, suggested revisions to increase the power of party regulars and give the convention more freedom to act on its own. It was the fourth time in 12 years that the Democrats, struggling to repair their nominating process without repudiating earlier reforms, had rewritten their party rules. *(Changes in Democrats' Nominating Rules, box, p. 23)*

# Chief Officers and Keynote Speakers At Democratic National Conventions, 1832-1992

| Year | Chair National Committee | Temporary Chair | Permanent Chair | Keynote Speaker |
|------|--------------------------|-----------------|-----------------|-----------------|
| 1832 | | Robert Lucas, Ohio | Robert Lucas, Ohio | |
| 1836 | | Andrew Stevenson, Va. | Andrew Stevenson, Va. | |
| 1840 | | Isaac Hill, N.H. | William Carroll, Tenn. | |
| 1844 | | Hendrick B. Wright, Pa. | Hendrick B. Wright, Pa. | |
| 1848 | Benjamin Hallet, Mass. | J. S. Bryce, La. | Andrew Stevenson, Va. | |
| 1852 | Robert M. McLane, Md. | Gen. Romulus M. Saunders, N.C. | John W. Davis, Ind. | |
| 1856 | David A. Smalley, Vt. | Samuel Medary, Ohio | John E. Ward, Ga. | |
| 1860 | August Belmont, N.Y. | Francis B. Flournoy, Ark. | Caleb Cushing, Mass. | |
| 1864 | August Belmont, N.Y. | William Bigler, Pa. | Horatio Seymour, N.Y. | |
| 1868 | August Belmont, N.Y. | Henry L. Palmer, Wis. | Horatio Seymour, N.Y. | |
| 1872 | Augustus Schell, N.Y. | Thomas Jefferson Randolph, Va. | James R. Doolittle, Wis. | |
| 1876 | Abram Stevens Hewitt, N.Y. | Henry M. Watterson, Ky. | John A. McClernand, Ill. | |
| 1880 | William H. Barnum, Conn. | George Hoadly, Ohio | John W. Stevenson, Ky. | |
| 1884 | William H. Barnum, Conn. | Richard B. Hubbard, Texas | William F. Vilas, Wis. | |
| 1888 | William H. Barnum, Conn. | Stephen M. White, Calif. | Patrick A. Collins, Mass. | |
| 1892 | William F. Harrity, Penn. | William C. Owens, Ky. | William L. Wilson, W.Va. | |
| 1896 | James K. Jones, Ark. | John W. Daniel, Va. | Stephen M. White, Calif. | |
| 1900 | James K. Jones, Ark. | Charles S. Thomas, Colo. | James D. Richardson, Tenn. | |
| 1904 | Thomas Taggart, Ind. | John Sharp Williams, Miss. | Champ Clark, Mo. | |
| 1908 | Norman E. Mack, N.Y. | Theodore A. Bell, Calif. | Henry D. Clayton, Ala. | |
| 1912 | William F. McCombs, N.Y. | Alton B. Parker, N.Y. | Ollie M. James, Ky. | |
| 1916 | Vance C. McCormick, Pa. | Martin H. Glynn, N.Y. | Ollie M. James, Ky. | |
| 1920 | George H. White, Ohio | Homer S. Cummings, Conn. | Joseph T. Robinson, Ark. | |
| 1924 | Clem Shaver, W.Va. | Pat Harrison, Miss. | Thomas J. Walsh, Mont. | |
| 1928 | John J. Raskob, Md. | Claude G. Bowers, Ind. | Joseph T. Robinson, Ark. | |
| 1932 | James A. Farley, N.Y. | Alben W. Barkley, Ky. | Thomas J. Walsh, Mont. | |
| 1936 | James A. Farley, N.Y. | Alben W. Barkley, Ky. | Joseph T. Robinson, Ark. | Alben W. Barkley, Ky. |
| 1940 | Edward J. Flynn, N.Y. | William B. Bankhead, Ala. | Alben W. Barkley, Ky. | William B. Bankhead, Ala. |
| 1944 | Robert E. Hannegan, Mo. | Robert S. Kerr, Okla. | Samuel D. Jackson, Ind. | Robert S. Kerr, Okla. |
| 1948 | J. Howard McGrath, R.I. | Alben W. Barkley, Ky. | Sam Rayburn, Texas | Alben W. Barkley, Ky. |
| 1952 | Stephen A. Mitchell, Ill. | Paul A. Dever, Mass. | Sam Rayburn, Texas | Paul A. Dever, Mass. |
| 1956 | Paul M. Butler, Ind. | Frank G. Clement, Tenn. | Sam Rayburn, Texas | Frank Clement, Tenn. |
| 1960 | Henry Jackson, Wash. | Frank Church, Idaho | LeRoy Collins, Fla. | Frank Church, Idaho |
| 1964 | John M. Bailey, Conn. | John O. Pastore, R.I. | John W. McCormack, Mass. | John O. Pastore, R.I. |
| 1968 | Lawrence F. O'Brien, Mass. | Daniel K. Inouye, Hawaii | Carl B. Albert, Okla. | Daniel K. Inouye, Hawaii |
| 1972[1] | Lawrence F. O'Brien, Mass. | | Lawrence F. O'Brien, Mass. | Reubin Askew, Fla. |
| 1976 | Robert S. Strauss, Texas | | Lindy Boggs, La. | John Glenn, Ohio Barbara C. Jordan, Texas |
| 1980 | John C. White, Texas | | Thomas P. O'Neill Jr., Mass. | Morris K. Udall, Ariz. |
| 1984 | Charles T. Manatt, Calif. | | Martha Layne Collins, Ky. | Mario M. Cuomo, N.Y. |
| 1988 | Paul G. Kirk Jr., Mass. | | Jim Wright, Texas | Ann W. Richards, Texas |
| 1992 | Ronald H. Brown, D.C. | | Ann W. Richards, Texas | Bill Bradley, N.J. Zell Miller, Ga. Barbara C. Jordan, Texas |

1. A rule change eliminated the position of temporary chair.

One major change in the Democrats' rules was the creation of a new group of "superdelegates," party and elected officials who would go to the 1984 convention uncommitted and would cast about 14 percent of the ballots. The DNC also adopted a Hunt Commission proposal to weaken the rule binding delegates to vote for their original presidential preference on the first convention ballot. The new rule allowed a presidential candidate to replace any disloyal delegate with a more faithful one.

One of the most significant revisions was the Democrats' decision to relax proportional representation at the convention and end the ban on the "loophole" primary — winner take all by district. Proportional representation is the distribution of delegates among candidates to reflect their share of the primary or caucus vote. Mandated by party rules in 1980, it was blamed by some Democrats for the protracted primary fight between President Jimmy Carter and Sen. Edward M. Kennedy of Massachusetts. Because candidates needed only about 20 percent of the vote in most places to qualify for a share of the delegates,

# Republican Conventions, 1856-1992

| Year | City | Dates | Presidential Nominee | Vice Presidential Nominee | No. of Pres. Ballots |
|---|---|---|---|---|---|
| 1856 | Philadelphia | June 17-19 | John C. Fremont | William L. Dayton | 2 |
| 1860 | Chicago | May 16-18 | Abraham Lincoln | Hannibal Hamlin | 3 |
| 1864 | Baltimore | June 7-8 | Abraham Lincoln | Andrew Johnson | 1 |
| 1868 | Chicago | May 20-21 | Ulysses S. Grant | Schuyler Colfax | 1 |
| 1872 | Philadelphia | June 5-6 | Ulysses S. Grant | Henry Wilson | 1 |
| 1876 | Cincinnati | June 14-16 | Rutherford B. Hayes | William A. Wheeler | 7 |
| 1880 | Chicago | June 2-8 | James A. Garfield | Chester A. Arthur | 36 |
| 1884 | Chicago | June 3-6 | James G. Blaine | John A. Logan | 4 |
| 1888 | Chicago | June 19-25 | Benjamin Harrison | Levi P. Morton | 8 |
| 1892 | Minneapolis | June 7-10 | Benjamin Harrison | Whitelaw Reid | 1 |
| 1896 | St. Louis | June 16-18 | William McKinley | Garret A. Hobart | 1 |
| 1900 | Philadelphia | June 19-21 | William McKinley | Theodore Roosevelt | 1 |
| 1904 | Chicago | June 21-23 | Theodore Roosevelt | Charles W. Fairbanks | 1 |
| 1908 | Chicago | June 16-19 | William H. Taft | James S. Sherman | 1 |
| 1912 | Chicago | June 18-22 | William H. Taft | James S. Sherman Nicholas Murray Butler[1] | 1 |
| 1916 | Chicago | June 7-10 | Charles E. Hughes | Charles W. Fairbanks | 3 |
| 1920 | Chicago | June 8-12 | Warren G. Harding | Calvin Coolidge | 10 |
| 1924 | Cleveland | June 10-12 | Calvin Coolidge | Charles G. Dawes | 1 |
| 1928 | Kansas City | June 12-15 | Herbert Hoover | Charles Curtis | 1 |
| 1932 | Chicago | June 14-16 | Herbert Hoover | Charles Curtis | 1 |
| 1936 | Cleveland | June 9-12 | Alfred M. Landon | Frank Knox | 1 |
| 1940 | Philadelphia | June 24-28 | Wendell L. Willkie | Charles L. McNary | 6 |
| 1944 | Chicago | June 26-28 | Thomas E. Dewey | John W. Bricker | 1 |
| 1948 | Philadelphia | June 21-25 | Thomas E. Dewey | Earl Warren | 3 |
| 1952 | Chicago | July 7-11 | Dwight D. Eisenhower | Richard M. Nixon | 1 |
| 1956 | San Francisco | Aug. 20-23 | Dwight D. Eisenhower | Richard M. Nixon | 1 |
| 1960 | Chicago | July 25-28 | Richard M. Nixon | Henry Cabot Lodge | 1 |
| 1964 | San Francisco | July 13-16 | Barry Goldwater | William E. Miller | 1 |
| 1968 | Miami Beach | Aug. 5-8 | Richard M. Nixon | Spiro T. Agnew | 1 |
| 1972 | Miami Beach | Aug. 21-23 | Richard M. Nixon | Spiro T. Agnew | 1 |
| 1976 | Kansas City | Aug. 16-19 | Gerald R. Ford | Robert Dole | 1 |
| 1980 | Detroit | July 14-17 | Ronald Reagan | George Bush | 1 |
| 1984 | Dallas | Aug. 20-23 | Ronald Reagan | George Bush | 1 |
| 1988 | New Orleans | Aug. 15-18 | George Bush | Dan Quayle | 1 |
| 1992 | Houston | Aug. 17-20 | George Bush | Dan Quayle | 1 |

1. *The 1912 Republican convention nominated James S. Sherman, who died on Oct. 30. The Republican National Committee subsequently selected Nicholas Murray Butler to receive the Republican electoral votes for vice president.*

Kennedy was able to remain in contention. But while the system kept Kennedy going, it did nothing to help his chances of winning the nomination.

Although the Democrats' 1984 rules permitted states to retain proportional representation, they also allowed states to take advantage of two options that could help a front-running candidate build the momentum to wrap up the nomination early in the year.

One was a winner-take-more system. States could elect to keep proportional representation but adopt a winner bonus plan that would award the top vote-getter in each district one extra delegate.

The other option was a return to the loophole primary, which party rules outlawed in 1980 (with exemptions allowing Illinois and West Virginia to retain their loophole voting systems). In the loophole states, voters ballot directly for delegates, with each delegate candidate identified by presidential preference. Sometimes several presidential contenders win at least a fraction of the delegates in a given district,

but the most common result is a sweep by the presidential front-runner, even if he has less than an absolute majority. Loophole primaries aid the building of a consensus behind the front-runner, while still giving other candidates a chance to inject themselves back into the race by winning a major loophole state decisively.

The DNC retained the delegate-selection season adopted in 1978, a three-month period stretching from the second Tuesday in March to the second Tuesday in June. But, in an effort to reduce the growing influence of early states in the nominating process, the Democrats required Iowa and New Hampshire to move their highly publicized elections to late winter. Party rules maintained the privileged status of Iowa and New Hampshire before other states but mandated that their initial nominating rounds be held only eight days apart in 1984. Five weeks intervened between the Iowa caucuses and New Hampshire primary in 1980.

The DNC also retained rules requiring primary states to set candidate filing deadlines 30 to 90 days before the

# Chief Officers and Keynote Speakers
# At Republican National Conventions, 1856-1992

| Year | Chair National Committee | Temporary Chair | Permanent Chair | Keynote Speaker |
|---|---|---|---|---|
| 1856 | Edwin D. Morgan, N.Y. | Robert Emmet, N.Y. | Henry S. Lane, Ind. | |
| 1860 | Edwin D. Morgan, N.Y. | David Wilmot, Pa. | George Ashmun, Mass. | |
| 1864 | Edwin D. Morgan, N.Y. | Robert J. Breckinridge, Ky. | William Dennison, Ohio | |
| 1868 | Marcus L. Ward, N.J. | Carl Schurz, Mo. | Joseph R. Hawley, Conn. | |
| 1872 | William Claflin, Mass. | Morton McMichael, Pa. | Thomas Settle, N.C. | |
| 1876 | Edwin D. Morgan, N.Y. | Theodore M. Pomeroy, N.Y. | Edward McPherson, Pa. | |
| 1880 | J. Donald Cameron, Pa. | George F. Hoar, Mass. | George F. Hoar, Mass. | |
| 1884 | Dwight M. Sabin, Minn. | John R. Lynch, Miss. | John B. Henderson, Mo. | |
| 1888 | B. F. Jones, Pa. | John M. Thurston, Neb. | Morris M. Estee, Calif. | |
| 1892 | James S. Clarkson, Iowa | J. Sloat Fassett, N.Y. | William McKinley Jr., Ohio | |
| 1896 | Thomas H. Carter, Mont. | Charles W. Fairbanks, Ind. | John M. Thurston, Neb. | |
| 1900 | Marcus A. Hanna, Ohio | Edward O. Wolcott, Colo. | Henry Cabot Lodge, Mass. | |
| 1904 | Henry C. Payne, Wis. | Elihu Root, N.Y. | Joseph G. Cannon, Ill. | |
| 1908 | Harry S. New, Ind. | Julius C. Burrows, Mich. | Henry Cabot Lodge, Mass. | |
| 1912 | Victor Rosewater, Neb. | Elihu Root, N.Y. | Elihu Root, N.Y. | |
| 1916 | Charles D. Hilles, N.Y. | Warren G. Harding, Ohio | Warren G. Harding, Ohio | |
| 1920 | Will H. Hays, Ind. | Henry Cabot Lodge, Mass. | Henry Cabot Lodge, Mass. | Henry Cabot Lodge, Mass. |
| 1924 | John T. Adams, Iowa | Theodore E. Burton, Ohio | Frank W. Mortdell, Wyo. | |
| 1928 | William M. Butler, Mass. | Simeon D. Fess, Ohio | George H. Moses, N.H. | |
| 1932 | Simeon D. Fess, Ohio | L. J. Dickinson, Iowa | Bertrand H. Snell, N.Y. | |
| 1936 | Henry P. Fletcher, Pa. | Frederick Steiwer, Ore. | Bertrand H. Snell, N.Y. | Frederick Steiwer, Ore. |
| 1940 | John Hamilton, Kan. | Harold E. Stassen, Minn. | Joseph W. Martin Jr., Mass. | Harold E. Stassen, Minn. |
| 1944 | Harrison E. Spangler, Iowa | Earl Warren, Calif. | Joseph W. Martin Jr., Mass. | Earl Warren, Calif. |
| 1948 | Carroll Reece, Tenn. | Dwight H. Green, Ill. | Joseph W. Martin Jr., Mass. | Dwight H. Green, Ill. |
| 1952 | Guy George Gabrielson, N.J. | Walter S. Hallanan, W.Va. | Joseph W. Martin Jr., Mass. | Douglas MacArthur |
| 1956 | Leonard W. Hall, N.Y. | William F. Knowland, Calif. | Joseph W. Martin Jr., Mass. | Arthur B. Langlie, Wash. |
| 1960 | Thruston B. Morton. Ky. | Cecil H. Underwood, W. Va. | Charles A. Halleck, Ind. | Walter H. Judd, Minn. |
| 1964 | William E. Miller, N.Y. | Mark O. Hatfield, Ore. | Thruston B. Morton, Ky. | Mark O. Hatfield, Ore. |
| 1968 | Ray C. Bliss, Ohio | Edward W. Brooke, Mass. | Gerald R. Ford, Mich. | Daniel J. Evans, Wash. |
| 1972 | Robert Dole, Kan. | Ronald Reagan, Calif. | Gerald R. Ford, Mich. | Richard G. Lugar, Ind. Anne L. Armstrong, Texas |
| 1976 | Mary Louise Smith, Iowa | Robert Dole, Kan. | John J. Rhodes, Ariz. | Howard H. Baker Jr., Tenn. |
| 1980 | Bill Brock, Tenn. | Nancy Landon Kassebaum, Kan. | John J. Rhodes, Ariz. | Guy Vander Jagt, Mich. |
| 1984 | Frank J. Fahrenkopf Jr., Nev. | Howard H. Baker Jr., Tenn. | Robert H. Michel, Ill. | Katherine Ortega, N.M. |
| 1988 | Lee Atwater, S.C. | Elizabeth Hanford Dole, N.C. | Robert H. Michel, Ill. | Thomas H. Kean, N.J. |
| 1992 | Richard N. Bond, N.Y. | Kay Bailey Hutchison, Texas | Robert H. Michel, Ill. | Phil Gramm, Texas |

election and limiting participation in the delegate selection process to Democrats only. This last rule eliminated cross-over primaries where voters could participate in the Democratic primary without designating their party affiliation. Blacks and Hispanics won continued endorsement of affirmative action in the new party rules. Women gained renewed support for the equal division rule, which required state delegations at the national convention to be divided equally between men and women.

The Democratic Party's 1988 presidential nominating process remained basically the same as that used in 1984. The rules adopted by the national committee included only minor modifications suggested by the party's rules review panel, the Fairness Commission.

The bloc of uncommitted party and elected officials (superdelegates) was expanded slightly to 16 percent and rearranged to reserve more convention seats for members of Congress, governors and the DNC; the rules restricting participation in Democratic primaries and caucuses to Democrats only was relaxed so the open primaries in Wisconsin and Montana could be conducted with the approval of the national party; and the share of the vote a candidate must win in a primary or caucus to qualify for delegates was lowered from the 20 percent level used in most places in 1984 to 15 percent.

Only the rule regarding the 15 percent "threshold" spawned much debate during the rules-writing process, and though the discussion of the issue seldom was acrimonious, it did reveal a yawning chasm in the party on what the proper role of the national convention should be.

Most party leaders, including DNC Chairman Paul G. Kirk Jr., wanted a threshold of at least 15 percent because they thought it would help steadily shrink the field of presidential candidates during the primary and caucus season and ensure that the convention would be a "ratifying" body that confirmed the choice of the party's voters.

But civil rights leader and presidential candidate Jesse L. Jackson saw it differently, as did a cadre of liberal activists. They wanted a convention that was more "deliberative," and they complained that getting one was virtually

# Political Party Organization and Rules

Political parties in the United States are loosely organized. Anyone of voting age can become a party member simply by signing up. Millions of Americans do just that, while many others shun formal partisan affiliations but think of themselves as Democrats or Republicans nonetheless.

Cowboy humorist Will Rogers used to get laughs by saying, "I am not a member of any organized party. I am a Democrat." But the same line could also be applied to the Republicans, even if they sometimes seemed to be less disorganized than their major rivals.

Both parties have the same fluidity of membership, with the rolls open to independents as well as to supporters of the other party. Formally registering as a Democrat or Republican has the advantage of permitting the member to participate in the party's nominating primaries and caucuses. Most states bar crossover voting in the other party's elections, largely for fear that Democrats would try to nominate the weakest Republican candidates, and vice versa.

In 1992 almost 33 million Americans participated in presidential primaries — 20.2 million in Democratic and 12.7 million in Republican primaries. But many voters who passed up the partisan primaries went to the polls in the November general election — the first U.S. election with a turnout of more than 100 million voters. *(1992 presidential election results, p. 468; primaries results, p. 481)*

The larger Democratic showing reflects what the polls show — that a plurality of Americans think of themselves as Democrats. In a 1990 Gallup poll, 39 percent said they were Democrats; 31 percent, Republicans; and 30 percent, independents.

## Party Structure

Loose though it is, each major party has an organizational structure — a necessity for continuity as an institution, fund raising and conducting election campaigns. Congress has officially recognized the role of the parties and public funding is provided for their presidential nominating conventions. Some states also provide funding for election campaigns.

Beginning at the precinct or neighborhood level, a series of progressively larger units make up the national organization. Next up the line are city, county, legislative district, congressional district and, just below the national committee, the state organizations.

There is no "chain of command." Each unit is more or less independent. The national chair exerts influence mainly through prestige and force of personality, rather than through any specified powers. The national committee elects the chair, but the president actually designates the chair of the party controlling the White House.

With its 426 members, the DNC is more than twice the size of the 162-member Republican National Committee. Fifty-four members make up the DNC executive committee — the 9 officers, 20 regional representatives, 10 "at-large" members elected by the DNC and 15 others representing Democratic affiliates.

Since 1984 the Democrats have occupied their own $6.4 million national headquarters at 430 South Capitol Street, S.E., in Washington. Previous locations in New York and Washington (including the Watergate offices burglarized by the Republicans in 1972) were rented.

Besides the chair, eight other DNC officers are elected: five vice chairs, treasurer, secretary and national finance chair. Party organizations in the states and territories elect their DNC members for four-year terms, ending with the next convention. They are the state chair and the next highest-ranking member of the opposite sex. Another 200 votes are distributed on a population basis, with each state or territory guaranteed at least two, equally divided among men and women.

Other DNC members are two U.S. senators, two House members, two members of the College Democrats and three representatives each from among Democratic governors, mayors, state legislators, county officials, municipal officials, Young Democrats and the National Federation of Democratic Women.

The RNC elects four officers — the chair, co-chair, secretary and treasurer for two-year terms. The party owns its national headquarters at 310 First Street, S.E., in Washington. The Republicans maintain a large field staff and generally have more money than the Democrats to dispense to campaigns.

Because of their large sizes, the full national committees seldom meet more than a few times during the four years between the national conventions, which are the parties' supreme governing bodies. In both parties, the day-to-day work of the national organization is done by the chair and the headquarters staff, under direction of the executive committee.

## Operating Rules

The most important rules of both major parties deal largely with the selection of delegates to the quadrennial national nominating conventions. While the Democrats in recent years have experimented widely with these rules, mainly to give more representation to women, youth and minorities, Republicans have left their rules largely unchanged. *(GOP Primary Rules, box, p. 22)*

As they prepared for the 1992 convention, Democrats for the first time in two decades did not have a special commission intensively examining the nominating process. Nevertheless, the DNC again changed the rules somewhat. *(Democratic Rules in the 1980s and 1990s, p. 16)*

Beginning with reforms proposed by Sen. George S. McGovern of South Dakota, who won the nomination himself in 1972, the party attempted to "democratize" the process. A succession of commissions headed by Barbara A. Mikulski of Maryland (1972), Morley Winograd of Michigan (1976), Gov. James B. Hunt Jr. of North Carolina (1980) and Donald L. Fowler of South Carolina (1988), succeeded in gaining equal representation for women, requiring proportional representation of delegates among primary vote-getters and giving convention votes to "superdelegate" party and elected officials.

impossible under the system as it existed because it discriminated against long-shot candidates and produced an artificial consensus behind one candidate.

Most Democratic leaders were satisfied with the way the nominating process operated in 1984, and they felt it would be a disaster for the party to go through a free-wheeling, multi-ballot convention. Not since 1952 — at the beginning of the television age — has a national party taken more than one ballot to nominate its candidate.

At the DNC meeting, some black committee members joined with a few white liberal activists in proposing to eliminate the 15 percent threshold altogether. The proposal was rejected by voice vote. A second proposal to lower the threshold to 10 percent was defeated 92-178.

In 1990 the DNC made two basic changes that directly affected the delegate-selection process for the 1992 convention. One moved forward the officially sanctioned start of the presidential primary season by one week, from the second Tuesday in March to the first. This was an invitation to California to move its 1992 primary from June to March 3. (California declined; it held its primary June 2.) The second change banned winner-reward systems, which gave extra delegates to the winner of a primary or caucus. Fifteen states had used some form of winner-reward system in 1988.

The Democrats required all states in 1992 to divide their publicly elected delegates proportionally among candidates who drew at least 15 percent of the primary or caucus vote.

The Democratic Party also continued to use super-delegates, expanding their number to 772 for the 1992 convention, or 18 percent of the 4,288 delegate votes.

During the 1972-1992 period the Republican Party followed an entirely different approach and made few changes in its nominating rules. While the Democratic rules were revised somewhat for each presidential cycle, the GOP rules remained stable. *(GOP Primary Rules, box, p. 22)*

## Credentials Disputes

Before the opening of a convention the national committee compiles a temporary roll of delegates. The roll is referred to the convention's credentials committee, which holds hearings on the challenges and makes recommendations to the convention, the final arbiter of all disputes.

Some of the most bitter convention battles have concerned the seating of contested delegations. In the 20th century most of the heated credentials fights have concerned delegations from the South. In the Republican Party the challenges focused on the power of the Republican state organizations to dictate the selection of delegates. The issue was hottest in 1912 and 1952, when the party throughout most of the South was a skeletal structure whose power was restricted largely to selection of convention delegates. Within the Democratic Party the question of Southern credentials emerged after World War II on the volatile issues of civil rights and party loyalty. Important credentials challenges on these issues occurred at the 1948, 1952, 1964 and 1968 Democratic conventions.

There were numerous credentials challenges at the 1972 Democratic convention, but, unlike those at its immediate predecessors, the challenges involved delegations from across the nation and focused on violations of the party's newly adopted guidelines.

After their 1952 credentials battle, the Republicans established a contest committee within the national commit-

---

## Democrats' Two-Thirds Rule

At their first convention in 1832, the Democrats adopted a rule requiring a two-thirds majority for nomination. Two presidential candidates — Martin Van Buren in 1844 and Champ Clark in 1912 — received majorities but failed to attain the two-thirds requirement.

On the first ballot in 1844 Van Buren received 146 of the 266 convention votes, 54.9 percent of the total. His total fell under a simple majority on succeeding roll calls and on the ninth ballot the nomination went to a dark-horse candidate, former governor James K. Polk of Tennessee.

From the 10th through the 16th ballots in 1912 Clark recorded a simple majority. He reached his peak on the 10th ballot, receiving 556 of the 1,094 convention votes, 50.8 percent of the total. The nomination, however, ultimately went to New Jersey governor Woodrow Wilson, who was selected on the 46th ballot.

At their 1936 convention, the Democrats voted to end the requirement for a two-thirds majority for nomination.

---

tee to review credentials challenges before the convention. After their divisive 1968 convention the Democrats also created a formal credentials procedure to review all challenges before the opening of the convention.

Equally important to the settlement of credentials challenges are the rules under which the convention operates. The Republican Party adopts a completely new set of rules at every convention. Although large portions of the existing rules are enacted each time, general revision is always possible.

After its 1968 convention the Democratic Party set out to reform itself and the convention system. The Commission on Rules and the Commission on Party Structure and Delegate Selection, both created by the 1968 convention, proposed many changes that were accepted by the national committee. As a result, a formal set of rules was adopted for the first time at the party's 1972 convention.

## Controversial Rules

Although it did not have a formal set of rules before 1972, the Democratic Party operated with two controversial rules never used by the Republicans: the unit rule and the two-thirds nominating rule. The unit rule enabled the majority of a delegation, if authorized by its state party, to cast the entire vote of the delegation for one candidate or position. In use since the earliest Democratic conventions, the unit rule was abolished by the 1968 convention.

From their first convention in 1832 until the 1936 convention, the Democrats employed the two-thirds nominating rule, which required any candidate for president or vice president to win not just a simple majority but a two-thirds majority. Viewed as a boon to the South since it allowed that region a virtual veto power over any possible nominee, the rule was abolished with the stipulation that the South would receive an increased vote allocation at later conventions.

In its century of use the two-thirds rule frequently produced protracted, multi-ballot conventions, often giving

---

# GOP Primary Rules

The Republican Party, wrote political scientist Nelson W. Polsby, "in many respects remains unreformed." Virtually anything has been permitted in the nominating process so long as it was not baldly discriminatory. And that has been the way GOP leaders have wanted it.

While the Democratic Party has a tightly crafted, nationalized set of rules that govern its nominating process, Republicans historically have shunned control by a central authority. The individual GOP state parties are given wide latitude to determine how their delegates are selected, with guidelines from the national party kept to a minimum.

The result has been a nominating procedure with a simplicity and continuity that the Democrats lack. A more homogeneous party than the Democrats, the Republicans have not felt the pressure for rules reform that had engulfed the Democrats. No major rules changes were made by the Republicans between 1974 and 1992.

Republicans, however, have not been able to operate totally in their own world. Campaign finance laws and the rising influence of mass media affected Republicans as well as Democrats. And in states where legislatures accommodated the Democrats and created a presidential primary, the Republicans were dragged along.

Ironically, the GOP had been less hasty than the Democrats in abandoning primaries. There were a number of states where the GOP in 1984 elected delegates through primaries while the Democrats reverted to the caucus process. By 1992 both parties had returned almost equally to primaries — 40 for the Democrats and 39 for the Republicans.

---

the Democrats a degree of turbulence the Republicans, requiring only a simple majority, did not have. Between 1832 and 1932, seven Democratic conventions took more than 10 ballots to select a presidential candidate. In contrast, in their entire convention history, the Republicans have had just one convention that required more than 10 ballots to select a presidential candidate. *(Democrats' Two-Thirds Rule, box, p. 21)*

One controversy that surfaced during the 1980 Democratic Party convention concerned a rule that bound delegates to vote on the first ballot for the candidates under whose banner they had been elected. Supporters of Sen. Kennedy had devoted their initial energies to prying the nomination from incumbent President Carter by defeating that rule. The final tally on the rule showed 1,936.42 delegates favoring the binding rule and 1,390.58 opposing it. Passage of the binding rule ensured Carter's renomination, and shortly after the vote Kennedy announced that his name would not be placed in nomination.

## Convention Officers

Credentials, rules and platform are the three major convention committees, but each party has additional committees, including one in charge of convention arrangements.

Within the Republican Party the arrangements committee recommends a slate of convention officers to the national committee, which in turn refers the names to the committee on permanent organization for confirmation. The people the committee chooses are subject to the approval of the convention. In the Democratic Party, this function is performed by the rules committee.

In both the Democratic and Republican parties, the presiding officer during the bulk of the convention is the permanent chairman. Over the past quarter century the position usually has gone to the party's leader in the House of Representatives. *(National Party Chairs, box, p. 27)*

However, this loose precedent was broken in the Democratic Party by a rule adopted at the 1972 convention requiring that the presiding officer position alternate every four years between the sexes.

## Party Platforms

The adoption of a party platform is one of the principal functions of a convention. The platform committee is charged with the responsibility of writing a party platform to be presented to the convention for its approval.

The main challenge before the platform committee is to write a platform all party candidates can use in their campaigns. For this reason, platforms often fit the description given them by Wendell L. Willkie, Republican presidential candidate in 1940: "fusions of ambiguity."

Despite the best efforts of platform-builders to resolve their differences in the comparative privacy of the committee room, they sometimes encounter so controversial a subject that it cannot be compromised. Under these conditions dissident committee members often submit a minority report to the convention floor. Open floor fights are not unusual and, like credentials battles, often reflect the strength of the various candidates.

When the party has an incumbent president, the platform often is drafted in the White House or at least has the approval of the president. Rarely does a party adopt a platform that is critical of an incumbent president of the same party.

The first platform was adopted by the Democrats in 1840. It was a short document, fewer than 1,000 words. Since then the platforms with few exceptions have grown longer and longer, covering more issues and appealing to more and more interest groups. One of the exceptions to the growth trend was the 4,500-word Democratic platform of 1988 — about one-tenth the length of the 1984 platform. But by 1992 the Democrats' platform had grown again, to about 10,000 words, compared with about 40,000 words in its Republican counterpart.

The 1992 GOP platform was characterized by hard-line conservative stands on abortion and other social issues, leading to widespread journalistic speculation that it was the platform of the religious right rather than the George Bush White House. But in an analysis in *Political Science Quarterly* (Winter 1993-94) political scientist L. Sandy Maisel concluded that the platform was adopted largely as drafted by the president's advisers and that "it is clear the drafters had the most influence, not the vocal and visible representatives of the party's right wing."

### Third Parties: Radical Ideas

Throughout American history, many daring and controversial political platforms adopted by third parties have been rejected as too radical by the major parties. Yet

# Changes in Democrats' Nominating Rules

Between 1968 and 1992 Democrats tinkered with their nominating rules every four years, producing a system that, if not better than before, was always differ-ent. The following chart shows the ebb and flow of the Democratic Party's rules changes, with a "✔" indicating the years these major rules were in effect.

| | 1972 | 1976 | 1980 | 1984 | 1988 | 1992 |
|---|---|---|---|---|---|---|
| **Timing:** Restrict delegate-selection events to a three-month period (the "window"). | | | ✔ | ✔ | ✔ | ✔ |
| **Conditions of Participation:** Restrict participation in delegate-selection events to Democrats. | | ✔ | ✔ | ✔ | ✔ | ✔ |
| **Proportional Representation:** Ban all types of winner-take-all contests. | | | ✔ | | | ✔ |
| Ban all types of winner-reward contests (where winner receives extra delegates). | | | | | | ✔ |
| **Delegate Loyalty:** Give candidates the right to approve delegates identifying with their candidacy. | | ✔ | ✔ | ✔ | ✔ | ✔ |
| Bind delegates to vote for their original presidential preference at convention on first ballot. | | | ✔ | | | |
| **Party and Elected Officials:** Expand each delegation to include pledged party and elected officials. | | | ✔ | ✔ | ✔ | ✔ |
| Further expand each delegation to include uncommitted party and elected officials ("superdelegates"). | | | | ✔ | ✔ | ✔ |
| **Demographic Representation:** Encourage participation and representation of minorities and traditionally under-represented groups (affirmative action). | | | ✔ | ✔ | ✔ | ✔ |
| Require delegations to be equally divided between men and women. | | | ✔ | ✔ | ✔ | ✔ |

many of these proposals later have won popular acceptance and have made their way into the major party platforms — and into law.

Ideas such as the graduated income tax, popular election of senators, women's suffrage, minimum wages, Social Security and the 18-year-old vote were advocated by Populists, Progressives and other independents long before they were finally accepted by the nation as a whole.

The radical third parties and their platforms have been anathema to the established wisdom of the day, denounced as impractical, dangerous, destructive of moral virtues and even traitorous. They have been anti-establishment and more far-reaching in their proposed solutions to problems than the major parties have dared to be.

## Major Parties: Broader Appeal

In contrast with the third parties, Democrats and Republicans traditionally have been much more chary of adopting radical platform planks. Trying to appeal to a broad range of voters, the two major parties have tended to compromise differences or to reject controversial platform planks.

The Democratic Party has been more ready than the Republicans to adopt once-radical ideas, but there is usually a considerable time lag between their origin in third parties and their eventual adoption in Democratic plat-forms. For example, while the Democrats by 1912 had adopted many of the Populist planks of the 1890s, the Bull Moose Progressives of that year already were way ahead of them in proposals for social legislation. Not until 1932 were many of the 1912 Progressive planks adopted by the Democrats.

Similarly, it was not until the 1960s that Democratic platforms incorporated many of the more far-reaching pro-posals originally put forward by the Progressive Party in the late 1940s.

# Notable Credentials Fights

**1848, Democratic.** Two rival New York state factions, known as the Barnburners and the Hunkers, sent separate delegations. By a vote of 126 to 125, the convention decided to seat both delegations and split New York's vote between them. This compromise suited neither faction: the Barnburners bolted the convention; the Hunkers remained but refused to vote.

**1860, Democratic.** Dissatisfaction with the slavery plank in the party platform spurred a walkout by several dozen Southern delegates from the Charleston convention. When the tumultuous convention reconvened in Baltimore six weeks later, a credentials controversy developed on the status of the bolting delegates. The majority report of the credentials committee recommended that the delegates in question, except those from Alabama and Louisiana, be reseated. The minority report recommended that a larger majority of the withdrawing Charleston delegates be allowed to return. The minority report was defeated, 100-1/2 to 150, prompting a walkout by the majority of delegates from nine states.

**1880, Republican.** Factions for and against the candidacy of former president Ulysses S. Grant clashed on the credentials of the Illinois delegation. By a margin of 387 to 353, the convention rejected a minority report that proposed seating pro-Grant delegates elected at the state convention over other delegates elected at a congressional district caucus. Three other votes were taken on disputed credentials from different Illinois districts, but all were decided in favor of the anti-Grant forces by a similar margin. The votes indicated the weakness of the Grant candidacy. The nomination went to a dark-horse candidate, Rep. James A. Garfield of Ohio, on the 36th ballot.

**1912, Republican.** The furious struggle between President William Howard Taft and Theodore Roosevelt for the presidential nomination centered on credentials. The Roosevelt forces brought 72 delegate challenges to the floor of the convention, but the test of strength between the two candidates came on a procedural motion. By a vote of 567 to 507, the convention tabled a motion presented by the Roosevelt forces barring any of the delegates under challenge from voting on any of the credentials contests. This procedural vote clearly indicated Taft's control of the convention. All the credentials cases were settled in favor of the Taft delegates, and the presidential nomination ultimately went to the incumbent president.

**1932, Democratic.** Two delegations favorable to the front-runner for the presidential nomination, Franklin D. Roosevelt, came under challenge. However, in a show of strength, the Roosevelt forces won both contests: seating a Louisiana delegation headed by Sen. Huey P. Long by a vote of 638-3/4 to 514-1/4 and a Roosevelt delegation from Minnesota by an even wider margin, 658-1/4 to 492-3/4. Roosevelt won the nomination on the fourth ballot.

**1952, Democratic.** The refusal of three Southern states — Louisiana, South Carolina and Virginia — to agree to a party loyalty pledge brought their credentials into question. The Virginia delegation argued that the problem prompting the loyalty pledge was covered by state law. By a vote of 650-1/2 to 518, the convention approved the seating of the Virginia delegation. After Louisiana and South Carolina took positions similar to that of Virginia, they were seated by a voice vote.

**1952, Republican.** Sixty-eight delegates from three Southern states (Georgia, Louisiana and Texas) were the focal point of the fight for the presidential nomination between Gen. Dwight D. Eisenhower and Sen. Robert A. Taft of Ohio. The national committee, controlled by forces favorable to Taft, had voted to seat delegations friendly to the Ohio senator from these three states. But by a vote of 607 to 531 the convention seated the Georgia delegation favorable to Eisenhower. It seated the Eisenhower delegates from Louisiana and Texas without roll calls. The general went on to win the presidential nomination on the first ballot.

**1968, Democratic.** A struggle between the anti-Vietnam war forces, led by Sen. Eugene J. McCarthy of Minnesota, and the party regulars, headed by Vice President Hubert H. Humphrey, dominated the 17 cases considered by the credentials committee. Three of the cases, involving the Texas, Georgia and Alabama delegations, required roll calls on the convention floor. All were won by the Humphrey forces. By a vote of 1,368-1/4 to 956-3/4, the regular Texas delegation headed by Gov. John B. Connally was seated. A minority report to seat the entire Georgia delegation led by black leader Julian Bond was defeated, 1,043.55 to 1,415.45. And a minority report to seat a McCarthy-backed, largely black delegation from Alabama was also rejected, 880-3/4 to 1,607. Humphrey, having shown his strength during the credentials contests, went on to win an easy first ballot nomination.

**1972, Democratic.** The first test of strength at the convention between South Dakota senator George McGovern's delegates and party regulars came over credentials. Key challenges brought to the convention floor concerned the South Carolina, California and Illinois delegations. The South Carolina challenge was brought by the National Women's Political Caucus in response to alleged underrepresentation of women in the delegation. Although the caucus' position was supposedly supported by the McGovern camp, votes were withheld to avoid jeopardizing McGovern's chances of winning the important California contest. The caucus' challenge lost 1,429.05 to 1,555.75. The California challenge was of crucial importance to McGovern, since it involved 151 delegates initially won by the South Dakota senator in the state's winner-take-all primary, but stripped from him by the credentials committee. By a vote of 1,618.28 to 1,238.22, McGovern regained the contested delegates, thereby nailing down his nomination. With victory in hand, the dominant McGovern camp sought a compromise on the Illinois case, which pitted a delegation headed by Chicago's powerful mayor Richard Daley against an insurgent delegation composed of party reformers. Compromise was unattainable and with the bulk of McGovern delegates voting for the reformers, a minority report to seat the Daley delegates was rejected.

# Major Platform Fights

**1860, Democratic.** A minority report on the slavery plank, stating that the decision on allowing slavery in the territories should be left to the Supreme Court, was approved, 165 to 138. The majority report (favored by the South) declared that no government — local, state or federal — could outlaw slavery in the territories. The acceptance of the minority report precipitated a walkout by several dozen Southern delegates and the eventual sectional split in the party.

**1896, Democratic.** The monetary plank of the platform committee, favoring free and unlimited coinage of silver at a ratio of 16 to 1 with gold, was accepted by the convention, which defeated a proposed gold plank, 626 to 303. During debate William Jennings Bryan made his famous "Cross of Gold" speech supporting the platform committee plank, bringing him to the attention of the convention and resulting in his nomination for president.

**1908, Republican.** A minority report, proposing a substitute platform, was presented by Sen. Robert M. LaFollette (Wis.). Minority proposals included increased antitrust activities, enactment of a law requiring publication of campaign expenditures and popular election of senators. All the proposed planks were defeated by wide margins; the closest vote, on direct election of senators, was 114 for, 866 against.

**1924, Democratic.** A minority plank was presented that condemned the activities of the Ku Klux Klan, then enjoying a resurgence in the South and some states in the Midwest. The plank was defeated 542-7/20 to 543-3/20, the closest vote in Democratic convention history.

**1932, Republican.** A minority plank favoring repeal of the 18th Amendment (Prohibition) in favor of a state-option arrangement was defeated, 460-2/9 to 690-19/36.

**1948, Democratic.** An amendment to the platform, strengthening the civil rights plank by guaranteeing full and equal political participation, equal employment opportunity, personal security and equal treatment in the military service, was accepted, 651-1/2 to 582-1/2.

**1964, Republican.** An amendment offered by Sen. Hugh Scott (Pa.) to strengthen the civil rights plank by including voting guarantees in state as well as in federal elections and by eliminating job bias was defeated, 409 to 897.

**1968, Democratic.** A minority report on Vietnam called for cessation of the bombing of North Vietnam, halting of offensive and search-and-destroy missions by American combat units, a negotiated withdrawal of American troops and establishment of a coalition government in South Vietnam. It was defeated, 1,041-1/4 to 1,567-3/4.

**1972, Democratic.** By a vote of 1,852.86 to 999.34, the convention rejected a minority report proposing a government guaranteed annual income of $6,500 for a family of four. By a vote of 1,101.37 to 1,572.80, a women's rights plank focusing on the issue of abortion was defeated.

**1980, Democratic.** The platform battle, one of the longest in party history, pitted President Jimmy Carter against his persistent rival, Sen. Edward M. Kennedy (Mass.). Stretching over 17 hours, the debate focused on Kennedy's economics plank, which finally was defeated by a voice vote. Yet Carter was forced to concede on so many specific points, including Kennedy's $12 billion anti-recession jobs programs, that the final document bore little resemblance to the draft initially drawn up by Carter's operatives.

**1992, Democratic.** A tax fairness plank offered by former senator Paul E. Tsongas (Mass.) was defeated by a vote of 953 to 2,287. The plank called for a delay in any middle-class tax cut and tax credit for families with children until the deficit was under control.

## Filling Vacancies

An important convention function that rarely has to be used is to anticipate possible vacancies at the top of the ticket. This happened in June 1912 when the Republicans renominated President William Howard Taft and Vice President James S. Sherman. Because Sherman was in failing health, the convention authorized the national committee to fill any vacancy that might occur.

When Sherman died before election day, on Oct. 30, the GOP national committee selected Nicholas Murray Butler, president of Columbia University, as Taft's running mate. Sherman's name remained on the ballot but the GOP lost to the Democratic ticket of Woodrow Wilson and Thomas R. Marshall in an election marked by a strong showing from former president Theodore Roosevelt running as a Progressive. The Electoral College subsequently awarded Sherman's eight votes to Butler.

Today standing rules of both major parties call for the national party committee to fill the vacancy if a nominee dies or resigns after the convention but before election day, or after the election but before Congress counts the electoral votes. *(Political Party Organization and Rules, p. 20)*

## Communications and the Media

Major changes in the national nominating convention have resulted from the massive advances in transportation and communication technologies during the 20th century.

The revolution in transportation has affected the scheduling of conventions. In the 19th century, conventions were sometimes held a year or more before the election and at the latest were completed by late spring of the election year. With the ability of people to assemble quickly, conventions in recent years have been held later in the election year, usually in July or August. Advances in transportation also have affected site location. Geographic centrality is no longer the primary consideration in the selection of a convention city. Increasingly, coastal cities have been chosen as convention hosts.

The invention of new means of communication, particularly television, has had a further impact on the convention system. The changes spurred by the media have been primarily cosmetic ones, designed to give the conven-

# Third Parties Usually Fade Rapidly

Most third party movements are like shooting stars, shining brightly in one election and then quickly disappearing. In the last century and a half, 10 third parties — plus independents John B. Anderson in 1980 and Ross Perot in 1992 — have drawn at least 5 percent of the popular vote in a presidential election. As of 1984 not one of the third parties was able to maintain its foothold in the electoral process. Four had disappeared by the next election, four others drew a smaller vote total and two merged with one of the major parties. It remained to be seen how Perot and his supporters would fare in the 1996 election.

Each of these significant third parties, except the Socialists in 1912, made its best showing in its first election. (The Socialists, led by Eugene V. Debs, first ran in 1900, winning just 0.62 percent of the vote.) The following chart lists each party's presidential candidate and the percentage of the vote the party received in its most successful race and in the following election. A dash (—) indicates that the party had disappeared.

| | Year | Percentage of Vote | Next Election |
|---|---|---|---|
| Anti-Mason (William Wirt) | 1832 | 7.8% | endorsed Whig |
| Free Soil (Martin Van Buren) | 1848 | 10.1 | 4.9% |
| Whig-American (Millard Fillmore) | 1856 | 21.5 | — |
| Southern Democrats (John C. Breckinridge) | 1860 | 18.1 | — |
| Constitutional Union (John Bell) | 1860 | 12.6 | — |
| Populist (James B. Weaver) | 1892 | 8.5 | endorsed Democrat |
| Progressive (Bull Moose) (Theodore Roosevelt) | 1912 | 27.4 | 0.2 |
| Socialist (Eugene V. Debs) | 1912 | 6.0 | 3.2 |
| Progressive (Robert M. La Follette) | 1924 | 16.6 | — |
| American Independent (George C. Wallace) | 1968 | 13.5 | 1.4 |
| John B. Anderson | 1980 | 6.6 | endorsed Democrat |
| Ross Perot | 1992 | 18.9 | [1] |

1. After the 1992 election, Perot supporters formed United We Stand, America, a nonpartisan organization designed to promote Perot's issues on the national agenda.

tion a look of efficiency that was not so necessary in earlier days. As the conduct of the convention has undergone closer scrutiny by the American electorate, both parties have made major efforts to cut back the frivolity and hoopla and to accentuate the more sober aspects of the convention process.

Radio coverage of conventions began in 1924, television coverage 16 years later. One of the first changes inspired by the media age was the termination of the custom that a presidential candidate not appear at the convention but accept his nomination in a ceremony several weeks later. Franklin D. Roosevelt was the first major party candidate to break this tradition when in 1932 he delivered his acceptance speech in person before the Democratic convention. Twelve years later Thomas E. Dewey became the first Republican nominee to give his acceptance speech to the convention. Since then the final activity of both the Democratic and Republican conventions has been the delivery of the acceptance speeches by the vice presidential and presidential nominees.

In addition to curbing the circus-like aspects of the convention, party leaders in recent years have streamlined the schedule, with the assumption that the interest level of most of the viewing public for politics is limited. The result has been shorter speeches and generally fewer roll calls than at those conventions in the pre-television era.

Party leaders desire to put on a good show for the viewing public with the hope of winning votes for their party in November. The convention is a showcase, designed to present the party as both a model of democracy and an efficient, harmonious body. The schedule of convention activities is drawn up with an eye on the peak evening television viewing hours. There is an attempt to put the party's major selling points — the highly partisan keynote speech, the nominating ballots, and the candidates' acceptance speeches — on in prime time. (The effort to put acceptance speeches on in prime time has been especially strong since 1972, when Democratic nominee George S. McGovern was forced to wait until 3 a.m. to make his speech.) Conversely, party leaders try to keep evidence of bitter party factionalism — such as explosive credentials and platform battles — out of the peak viewing period.

In the media age the appearance of fairness is important, and in a sense this need to look fair and open has assisted the movement for party reform. Some influential party leaders, skeptical of reform of the convention, have found resistance difficult in the glare of television.

Before the revolution in the means of transportation

# National Party Chairs

| Name | State | Years of Service | Name | State | Years of Service |
|------|-------|------------------|------|-------|------------------|
| **Democratic Party** | | | **Republican Party (continued)** | | |
| B. F. Hallett | Massachusetts | 1848-52 | D. M. Sabin | Minnesota | 1883-84 |
| Robert McLane | Maryland | 1852-56 | B. F. Jones | Pennsylvania | 1884-88 |
| David A. Smalley | Virginia | 1856-60 | Matthew S. Quay | Pennsylvania | 1888-91 |
| August Belmont | New York | 1860-72 | James S. Clarkson | Iowa | 1891-92 |
| Augustus Schell | New York | 1872-76 | Thomas H. Carter | Montana | 1892-96 |
| Abram S. Hewitt | New York | 1876-77 | Mark A. Hanna | Ohio | 1896-1904 |
| William H. Barnum | Connecticut | 1877-89 | Henry C. Payne | Wisconsin | 1904 |
| Calvin S. Brice | Ohio | 1889-92 | George B. Cortelyou | New York | 1904-07 |
| William F. Harrity | Pennsylvania | 1892-96 | Harry S. New | Indiana | 1907-08 |
| James K. Jones | Arkansas | 1896-1904 | Frank H. Hitchcock | Massachusetts | 1908-09 |
| Thomas Taggart | Indiana | 1904-08 | John F. Hill | Maine | 1909-12 |
| Norman E. Mack | New York | 1908-12 | Victor Rosewater | Nebraska | 1912 |
| William F. McCombs | New York | 1912-16 | Charles D. Hilles | New York | 1912-16 |
| Vance C. McCormick | Pennsylvania | 1916-19 | William R. Willcox | New York | 1916-18 |
| Homer S. Cummings | Connecticut | 1919-20 | Will Hays | Indiana | 1918-21 |
| George White | Ohio | 1920-21 | John T. Adams | Iowa | 1921-24 |
| Cordell Hull | Tennessee | 1921-24 | William M. Butler | Massachusetts | 1924-28 |
| Clem Shaver | West Virginia | 1924-28 | Hubert Work | Colorado | 1928-29 |
| John J. Raskob | Maryland | 1928-32 | Claudius H. Huston | Tennessee | 1929-30 |
| James A. Farley | New York | 1932-40 | Simeon D. Fess | Ohio | 1930-32 |
| Edward J. Flynn | New York | 1940-43 | Everett Sanders | Indiana | 1932-34 |
| Frank C. Walker | Pennsylvania | 1943-44 | Henry P. Fletcher | Pennsylvania | 1934-36 |
| Robert E. Hannegan | Missouri | 1944-47 | John Hamilton | Kansas | 1936-40 |
| J. Howard McGrath | Rhode Island | 1947-49 | Joseph W. Martin Jr. | Massachusetts | 1940-42 |
| William M. Boyle Jr. | Missouri | 1949-51 | Harrison E. Spangler | Iowa | 1942-44 |
| Frank E. McKinney | Indiana | 1951-52 | Herbert Brownell Jr. | New York | 1944-46 |
| Stephen A. Mitchell | Illinois | 1952-54 | B. Carroll Reece | Tennessee | 1946-48 |
| Paul M. Butler | Indiana | 1955-60 | Hugh D. Scott Jr. | Pennsylvania | 1948-49 |
| Henry M. Jackson | Washington | 1960-61 | Guy George Gabrielson | New Jersey | 1949-52 |
| John M. Bailey | Connecticut | 1961-68 | Arthur E. Summerfield | Michigan | 1952-53 |
| Lawrence F. O'Brien | Massachusetts | 1968-69 | C. Wesley Roberts | Kansas | 1953 |
| Fred Harris | Oklahoma | 1969-70 | Leonard W. Hall | New York | 1953-57 |
| Lawrence F. O'Brien | Massachusetts | 1970-72 | H. Meade Alcorn Jr. | Connecticut | 1957-59 |
| Jean Westwood | Utah | 1972 | Thruston B. Morton | Kentucky | 1959-61 |
| Robert Strauss | Texas | 1972-77 | William E. Miller | New York | 1961-64 |
| Kenneth Curtis | Maine | 1977-78 | Dean Burch | Arizona | 1964-65 |
| John White | Texas | 1978-81 | Ray C. Bliss | Ohio | 1965-69 |
| Charles Manatt | California | 1981-85 | Rogers C. B. Morton | Maryland | 1969-71 |
| Paul Kirk | Massachusetts | 1985-89 | Robert Dole | Kansas | 1971-73 |
| Ronald H. Brown | Washington, D.C. | 1989-93 | George Bush | Texas | 1973-74 |
| David Wilhelm | Illinois | 1993- | Mary Louise Smith | Iowa | 1974-77 |
| | | | William Brock | Tennessee | 1977-81 |
| **Republican Party** | | | Richard Richards | Utah | 1981-83 |
| Edwin D. Morgan | New York | 1856-64 | Paul Laxalt | | |
| Henry J. Raymond | New York | 1864-66 | (general chair) [1] | Nevada | 1983-86 |
| Marcus L. Ward | New Jersey | 1866-68 | Frank Fahrenkopf Jr. | Nevada | 1983-89 |
| William Claflin | Massachusetts | 1868-72 | Lee Atwater | South Carolina | 1989-91 |
| Edwin D. Morgan | New York | 1872-76 | Clayton Yeutter | Nebraska | 1991-92 |
| Zachariah Chandler | Michigan | 1876-79 | Rich Bond | New York | 1992-93 |
| J. Donald Cameron | Pennsylvania | 1879-80 | Haley Barbour | Mississippi | 1993- |
| Marshall Jewell | Connecticut | 1880-83 | | | |

1. In 1983 a new unsalaried position of general chair was created for Senator Laxalt in order to please President Reagan and skirt party rules that the national chair position be full time. Laxalt coordinated Republican congressional operations while Fahrenkopf managed party headquarters operations.

Sources: Hugh A. Bone, *Party Committees and National Politics* (Seattle: University of Washington Press, 1958), 241-243; *Congressional Quarterly's Guide to the Presidency,* ed. Michael Nelson (Washington, D.C.: Congressional Quarterly Inc., 1989), 604, 696; and *Congressional Quarterly Weekly Report,* January 16, 1992, 147-148; January 30, 1993, 232.

and communication, conventions met in relative anonymity. Today conventions are held in all the privacy of a fishbowl, with every action and every rumor closely scrutinized. They have become media events and as such are targets for

political demonstrations that can be not only an embarrassment to the party but a security problem as well.

In spite of its difficulties, the convention system has survived. As the nation has developed during the past century and a half, the convention has evolved as well, changing its form but retaining its variety of functions. Criticism has been leveled at the convention, but no substitute has yet been offered that would nominate a presidential ticket, adopt a party platform, act as the supreme governing body of the party and serve as a massive campaign rally and propaganda forum. In addition to these functions, a convention is a place where compromise can take place — compromise often mandatory in a major political party that combines varying viewpoints.

# Highlights of National Party Conventions, 1831-1992

**1831** First national political convention was held in Baltimore by Anti-Masonic Party. Second such convention was held several months later by National Republican Party (no relation to modern Republicans).

**1832** Democratic Party met in Baltimore for its first national political convention and nominated Andrew Jackson. The rule requiring a two-thirds majority for nominations was initiated.

**1835** President Jackson called his party's convention more than a year before the election to prevent buildup of opposition to his choice of successor, Martin Van Buren.

**1839** Whig Party held its first convention and chose the winning slate of William Henry Harrison and John Tyler. Party adopted unit rule for casting state delegations' votes.

**1840** To avoid bitter battle over vice presidential nomination, Democratic Party set up a committee to select nominees, subject to approval of convention. In accordance with committee recommendations, Van Buren was nominated for president and no one for vice president.

**1844** Democrats nominated James K. Polk — first "dark horse" or compromise candidate — after nine ballots. Silas Wright, convention's choice for vice president, declined the nomination. First time a convention nominee refused nomination. Convention subsequently nominated George M. Dallas.

**1848** Democratic convention voted to establish continuing committee, known as "Democratic National Committee."

**1852** Democrats and Whigs both adopted platforms before nominating candidates for president, setting precedent followed almost uniformly ever since.

**1854** First Republican state convention held in Jackson, Mich., to nominate candidate slate. Platform denounced slavery.

**1856** First Republican national convention held in Philadelphia. Kentucky sent the only Southern delegation. Nominated John C. Fremont for president.

**1860** One of the longest, most turbulent and mobile conventions in Democratic history. Democrats met in Charleston, S.C., April 23. After 10 days and no agreement on a presidential nominee, delegates adjourned and reconvened in Baltimore in mid-July, for what turned out to be another disorderly meeting. Delegates finally nominated Stephen A. Douglas for president.

Benjamin Fitzpatrick, the convention's choice for vice president, became the first candidate to withdraw after convention adjournment and be replaced by a selection of the national committee. Southern delegates who bolted the original convention later joined Baltimore dissidents to nominate Vice President John C. Breckinridge for president on the Southern Democrat ticket.

Republicans nominated Abraham Lincoln for the presidency. First Republican credentials dispute took place over seating delegates from slave states and voting strength of delegates from states where party was comparatively weak. Party rejected unit rule for first time.

Constitutional Union Party's platform of national unity nominated John Bell for president.

**1864** Civil War led to bitter debate within Democratic Party over candidates, including Gen. George B. McClellan, presidential nominee.

In attempt to close ranks during war, Republicans used the name "Union Party" at convention. Renominated Lincoln. Platform called for constitutional amendment outlawing slavery.

**1868** Susan B. Anthony urged Democratic support for women's suffrage.

For the first time, Republicans gave a candidate (Ulysses S. Grant) 100 percent of vote on first ballot. Incumbent Andrew Johnson, who succeeded the assassinated Lincoln, sought nomination unsuccessfully. First Republican convention with full Southern representation.

**1872** Republicans renominated Grant at Philadelphia. Dissident Liberal Republicans nominated Horace Greeley in Cincinnati. Democrats also nominated Greeley. Victoria Clafin Woodhull, nominated by the Equal Rights Party, was first woman presidential candidate. Black leader Frederick Douglass was her running mate.

**1876** First time either party nominated incumbent governor for president; both major parties did so that year with Rutherford B. Hayes, R-Ohio, and Samuel J. Tilden, D-N.Y. Republican convention rejected unit rule for second time.

**1880** Republicans nominated James A. Garfield for president on 36th ballot — party's all-time record number of ballots. Unit rule was rejected for third and final time. Republican convention passed loyalty pledge for nominee, binding each delegate to his support.

**1884** Democrats turned back Tammany Hall challenge to unit rule.

Republicans nominated James G. Blaine, Maine, for president and John Logan, Illinois, for vice president, reversing 24-year pattern of seeking presidential candidate from the Midwest and vice presidential candidate from the East. John Roy Lynch, three-term U.S. representative from Mississippi, became first black elected temporary chairman of national nominating convention.

**1888** Frederick Douglass was first black to receive a vote in presidential balloting at a major party political convention. He received one vote on fourth ballot at Republican convention. Nineteen names were entered into Republican balloting. Benjamin Harrison won nomination on eighth ballot.

**1892**  Democrat Grover Cleveland broke convention system tradition by receiving third presidential nomination. People's Party (Populists) held first national nominating convention in Omaha, Neb., and adopted first platform.

**1896**  Democrats, divided over silver-gold question, repudiated Cleveland administration and nominated William Jennings Bryan.

Thirty-four Republican delegates against free silver walked out of convention.

**1900**  Each party had one woman delegate.

**1904**  Florida Democrats elected national convention delegates in public primary, under first legislation permitting any recognized party to hold general primary elections.

Republicans nominated Theodore Roosevelt, first time a vice president who had succeeded a deceased president went on to be nominated in his own right.

**1908**  Democrats, calling for legislation terminating what they called "partnership" between Republicans and corporations, pledged to refuse campaign contributions from corporations.

Call to Republican convention provided for election of delegates by primary method introduced in some states for first time.

**1912**  Increasing numbers of delegates were selected in primaries held in 13 states.

First time Republicans renominated entire ticket — William Howard Taft and James S. Sherman. Malapportionment of convention seats as result of Republican decline in South killed Theodore Roosevelt's chances of nomination. Taft renominated but 349 delegates protested his nomination by refusing to vote. Roosevelt nominated for president on Progressive ticket at separate convention.

**1916**  Democrats renominated entire ticket — Woodrow Wilson and Thomas R. Marshall — for first time.

Hopes of reuniting Republicans diminished when Roosevelt could not secure their nomination and refused Progressive renomination.

**1920**  For first time, women attended conventions in significant numbers.

**1924**  Republicans adopted bonus votes for first time — three bonus delegates at large allotted to each state carried by party in preceding presidential election. Republican convention was first to be broadcast on radio.

John W. Davis was nominated by Democrats on record 103rd ballot.

Three Democratic women received one or more votes for presidential nomination.

**1928**  Democrat Alfred E. Smith, governor of New York, was first Roman Catholic nominated for president by a major party.

**1932**  Republicans began tradition of appointing party leader from House of Representatives as permanent convention chairman.

Franklin D. Roosevelt appeared before Democratic convention to accept presidential nomination, the first major party candidate to do so.

**1936**  Democratic Party voted to end requirement of two-thirds delegate majority for nomination, a rule adopted at party's first convention and one that sometimes had led to lengthy balloting and selection of dark-horse slates.

Republicans nominated Alfred M. Landon and Frank Knox in vain effort to break new Democratic coalition.

**1940**  Franklin D. Roosevelt was nominated for unprecedented third term. He then wrote out a refusal of his renomination because of opposition to his vice presidential choice, Henry A. Wallace. Opposition deferred and Wallace was nominated.

Republicans held first political convention to be televised.

**1944**  Franklin D. Roosevelt, already having broken tradition by winning third term, was nominated for fourth time. Democrats put system of bonus votes into effect for states that voted Democratic in previous presidential election.

Thomas E. Dewey became first Republican candidate to accept nomination in appearance before the convention.

**1948**  After Democratic convention adopted strong civil rights plank, entire Mississippi delegation and 13 of Alabama's 26 delegates walked out.

Dissidents from 13 Southern states met several days later and nominated Gov. Strom Thurmond of South Carolina for president on the States' Rights ticket.

Democrats began appointing Speaker of the House as permanent chairman. Practice followed through 1968, with exception of 1960, when Sam Rayburn declined. Since 1948 conventions, presidential nominees of both parties have appeared at their conventions. Republicans renominated Thomas E. Dewey — first time party renominated a defeated presidential candidate.

**1952**  Adlai E. Stevenson, who did not seek the nomination, was chosen as Democratic nominee in one of few genuine "drafts" in history of either political party.

Republicans nominated Dwight D. Eisenhower. Women delegates wanted to nominate Sen. Margaret Chase Smith, Maine, for vice president, but Smith requested her name not be put in nomination.

**1956**  Democratic nominee Adlai E. Stevenson left choice of running mate to convention. Winner of open race was Sen. Estes Kefauver of Tennessee. First time a party loyalty provision was put into effect during delegate selection.

Dwight D. Eisenhower renominated unanimously on first ballot at Republican convention.

**1960**  Democrats adopted civil rights plank that was strongest in party history. Presidential nominee Sen. John F. Kennedy of Massachusetts was second Catholic to receive presidential nomination of major party.

Republican nominee Richard Nixon was party's first vice president nominated for president at completion of his term.

**1964**  Democratic President Lyndon B. Johnson was nominated for second term by acclamation. Fight over credentials of Alabama and Mississippi delegations was overriding issue at the convention.

Sen. Margaret Chase Smith's name was placed in nomination for presidency at Republican convention — first time a woman placed in nomination by a major party. Sen. Barry Goldwater, Arizona, won the nomination.

**1968**  Democratic delegates voted to end unit rule and to eliminate it from all levels of party politics for 1972 convention. Vice President Hubert H. Humphrey of

Minnesota was nominated for president.

Republicans nominated Richard Nixon, who had made one of most remarkable political comebacks in American history.

**1972**    With newly adopted party reform guidelines, the Democratic convention included a record number of women, youth and minorities. Open debate on many issues occurred with an unprecedented 23 credentials challenges brought to the floor. Sen. George McGovern, of South Dakota, who built up following as an anti-war candidate, nominated for president on first ballot. His choice for vice president, Sen. Thomas F. Eagleton, Missouri, became second candidate in American history to withdraw. National committee chose R. Sargent Shriver as replacement.

In harmonious convention Republicans renominated Richard Nixon and Spiro T. Agnew with nearly unanimous votes.

**1976**    Democrats in unified convention nominated Gov. Jimmy Carter of Georgia and running mate Walter Mondale of Minnesota. Gathering was notable for lack of bitter floor fights and credentials challenges that had characterized some recent conventions.

Incumbent president Gerald R. Ford received Republican nomination, narrowly surviving a challenge from former governor of California, Ronald Reagan.

**1980**    Democrats renominated President Jimmy Carter in convention marked by bitter contests over party platform and rules binding delegates to vote on first ballot for candidates under whose banner they were elected. The struggle pitted Carter forces against supporters of Sen. Edward M. Kennedy, Massachusetts, who were trying to pry nomination away from the president and alter party platform. While the Carter camp prevailed on delegate-binding rule, Kennedy managed to force major concessions in Democratic platform.

In contrast, a harmonious and unified Republican convention nominated Ronald Reagan. Rumors abounded during convention that former president Gerald R. Ford would serve as Reagan's vice presiden-

tial candidate. After it became obvious that efforts to persuade Ford to join the ticket had failed, Reagan chose George Bush as his running mate.

**1984**    Democrats nominated Walter F. Mondale, Jimmy Carter's vice president, for presidential slot and in a historic move accepted Rep. Geraldine A. Ferraro of New York as his running mate. Ferraro was first woman placed on national ticket by a major party.

A jubilant Republican Party wound up its convention confident that President Ronald Reagan and Vice President George Bush would win in November. With the ticket's renomination certain beforehand, convention was more a celebration than a business meeting of GOP activists.

**1988**    Democrats rallied behind Gov. Michael S. Dukakis of Massachusetts and his running mate Sen. Lloyd Bentsen of Texas. The mood was one of unity and compromise, signaling a victory of pragmatism over idealism.

Vice President George Bush arrived at the Republican convention as its all-but-anointed standard-bearer. The four days of the convention were filled with unexpected drama as party members awaited news of Bush's running mate. When Sen. Dan Quayle of Indiana was announced, he quickly came under fire about his qualifications and background.

**1992**    Having secured the Democratic nomination in the primaries, Gov. Bill Clinton of Arkansas and running mate Sen. Al Gore of Tennessee led the appeal for change and new direction at a unified convention. The combination of two Southern moderates on the Democratic ticket was a sharp departure from previous elections.

Republicans renominated President George Bush and Vice President Dan Quayle with a platform that stressed family values and decentralized authority. The convention trumpeted Bush's international accomplishments while blaming a Democratic Congress for the nation's ills.

# Convention Chronology, 1831-1992

# Sources: Convention Chronology

This section (pages 35 to 189) contains brief descriptions of all presidential nominating conventions of major American political parties and excerpts from party platforms. The chronology begins in 1831, when the Anti-Masonic Party held the first nominating convention in American history, and concludes with the Democratic and Republican party conventions of 1992.

The narrative includes conventions for all parties receiving at least 2 percent of the popular vote in the presidential election *(see pages 429 to 468)*. Thus, conventions for the Socialist Party, which received at least 2 percent of the presidential popular vote in 1904, 1908, 1912, 1920 and 1932, are included. Socialist Party conventions for other presidential election years when the party received less than 2 percent of the popular vote do not appear.

The source most frequently consulted in preparing the narrative was *Convention Decisions and Voting Records*, Brookings Institution, Washington, D.C., 1973, by Richard C. Bain and Judith H. Parris.

## Ballot Vote Totals

Throughout the narrative, vote totals appear for significant ballots on platform disputes and procedural issues and for presidential and vice presidential balloting.

The source used for 1835-1972 vote totals was *Convention Decisions and Voting Records*. The sources for the 1976 through 1992 vote totals were *The Official Proceedings of the Democratic National Convention* and the Republican National Committee. Charts showing state-by-state voting on selected ballots appear in a separate section, "Key Convention Ballots," pages 193 to 256. *(See p. 192 for details on these charts.)*

## Platform Excerpts

The source for the party platform excerpts that appear in the convention chronology was *National Party Platforms, 1840-1968*, University of Illinois Press, 1972, compiled by Kirk H. Porter and Donald Bruce Johnson. For the Democratic and Republican platforms for 1972 to 1992, the official texts of the platforms adopted by the two parties were used.

In adopting the material from *National Party Platforms, 1840-1968*, Congressional Quarterly has added boldface subheadings to highlight the organization of the texts. For example, excerpts from the 1844 Democratic Party platform appear on page 40. The boldface headings — Appeal to the Masses, Internal Improvements, Government Spending, etc. — do not appear in the text of the party platform as it was published in *National Party Platforms, 1840-1968*. In all other respects, Congressional Quarterly has followed the style and typography of the platform texts appearing in *National Party Platforms, 1840-1968*.

# 1831-32 Conventions
## Presidential Candidates

**William Wirt**
**Anti-Mason**

**Henry Clay**
**National Republican**

**Andrew Jackson**
**Democrat**

### Anti-Masons

In September 1831, the Anti-Masonic Party held the first national nominating convention in American history. One hundred sixteen delegates from 13 states, none south of Maryland, gathered in Baltimore. They selected the party's presidential and vice presidential candidates, adopted an address to the people (a precursor of the party platform) and established a national corresponding committee that created the framework for a national campaign organization.

Ironically, the Anti-Masons, whose keystone was opposition to Masonry, nominated a former Mason, William Wirt of Maryland, as their presidential standard-bearer. In spite of a rule requiring a three-fourths nominating majority, Wirt was an easy first-ballot winner and the nearly unanimous nominee of the convention.

He was not, however, the first choice of party leaders, who had been rebuffed in their earlier efforts to persuade Henry Clay and later Supreme Court Justice John McLean to take the presidential nomination. Wirt himself was not an enthusiastic candidate, stating that he saw nothing repugnant about Masonry and that if his views did not suit the convention, he would willingly withdraw from the ticket. The delegates supported Wirt and chose Amos Ellmaker of Pennsylvania as his vice presidential running mate.

### National Republicans

In December 1831 the National Republicans held their national convention in Baltimore. The National Republicans were united primarily in their opposition to incumbent President Andrew Jackson. The idea of a convention had been proposed by an anti-Jackson committee in New York City and approved by the leading National Republican newspaper, the *National Intelligencer*. There was no uniform method of delegate selection, with state conventions, legislative caucuses and local meetings all being used.

One hundred sixty-eight delegates from 18 states attended the National Republican convention, although nearly one-quarter were late in arriving due to inclement winter weather. Without any pre-established rules, it was agreed that the roll calls would be taken by announcing each delegate's name. Henry Clay of Kentucky was the convention's unanimous choice for president, and former representative John Sergeant of Pennsylvania was selected without opposition for vice president. Letters accepting their nominations were received from both candidates.

There was no formal platform, although the convention adopted an address to the people that criticized Jackson for dividing a previously harmonious country.

In May 1832 a convention of young National Republicans met in Washington, D.C., and passed a series of resolutions calling for a protective tariff, federal support of internal improvements and recognition of the Supreme Court as the ultimate authority on constitutional questions. The last was a rebuke of Jackson for disregarding Supreme Court decisions concerning the Cherokee Indians. Other resolutions criticized Jackson's use of the spoils system in distributing patronage and his handling of foreign policy with Great Britain. Although not a formal platform, the resolutions adopted by the convention of young National Republicans were the most definitive discussion of issues during the 1832 campaign.

## Democrats

The Democrats held their first national convention in Baltimore in late May 1832. Representatives from 23 states attended. The call for a Democratic national convention had been made by Jacksonian members of the New Hampshire legislature, and their proposal was approved by prominent members of President Andrew Jackson's administration. The convention was called to order by a member of the New Hampshire legislature, who explained the intent of the gathering in these words:

> "...[The] object of the people of New Hampshire who called this convention was, not to impose on the people, as candidates for either of the two first offices of the government, any local favorite; but to concentrate the opinions of all the states.... They believed that the example of this convention would operate favorably in future elections; that

the people would be disposed, after seeing the good effects of this convention in conciliating the different and distant sections of the country, to continue this mode of nomination." *(Reprinted from* Convention Decisions and Voting Records, *by Richard C. Bain, p. 17.)*

The convention adopted two rules that Democratic conventions retained well into the 20th century. One based each state's convention vote on its electoral vote, an apportionment method unchanged until 1940.

A second rule established a two-thirds nominating majority, a controversial measure that remained a feature of Democratic conventions until 1936. The 1832 convention also adopted the procedure of having one person from each delegation announce the vote of his state.

The delegates did not formally nominate Jackson for the presidency. Instead they concurred in the various nominations he had received earlier from state legislatures. Jackson's choice for vice president, Martin Van Buren of New York, was easily nominated on the first ballot, receiving 208 of the 283 votes cast.

Instead of adopting a platform or address to the people, the convention decided that each state delegation should write its own report to its constituents. The convention also determined to establish in each state general corresponding committees that together would provide a nationwide organization for the campaign.

# 1835-36 Conventions

## Presidential Candidates

**Martin Van Buren**
**Democrat**

**William Henry Harrison**
**Whig**

**Daniel Webster**
**Whig**

**Hugh L. White**
**Whig**

## Democrats

The Democrats held their second national convention in Baltimore in May 1835. The early date had been set by President Jackson to prevent the emergence of opposition to his hand-picked successor, Vice President Martin Van Buren. Delegates from 22 states and two territories attended, and the size of the delegations was generally related to their distance from Baltimore. One hundred eighty-eight individuals were on hand from Maryland to cast the state's 10 votes, but only one person attended from Tennessee — a visiting businessman who cast 15 votes. Alabama, Illinois and South Carolina were unrepresented.

Two rival Pennsylvania delegations arrived, precipitating the first credentials dispute in convention history. It was decided to seat both delegations and let them share the Pennsylvania vote.

An effort to eliminate the rule requiring a two-thirds nominating majority initially passed by a margin of 231 to 210 (apparently counting individual delegates instead of state convention votes), but the two-thirds rule was reimposed by a voice vote. A question developed whether the nominating majority should be based on only the states represented or on all the states in the union. It was decided to base the majority on only those present.

Vice President Van Buren won the presidential nomination, winning all 265 votes. Richard M. Johnson of Kentucky barely reached the necessary two-thirds majority on the first vice presidential ballot, receiving 178 votes, just one vote more than the required minimum. *(Chart, p. 193)*

Johnson, famous as the alleged slayer of the Indian chief Tecumseh, had aroused some disapproval because of his personal life. Johnson had lived with a mulatto mistress by whom he had two daughters.

Once again the Democrats did not write a formal platform, although an address to the people was published in the party newspaper, *The Washington Globe.* Van Buren wrote a letter of acceptance in which he promised to "tread generally in the footsteps of President Jackson."

### Whigs

During Jackson's second term, a new party, the Whigs, emerged as the Democrats' primary opposition. It con-

tained remnants of the short-lived National Republican Party, as well as anti-Jackson elements in the Democratic and Anti-Masonic parties. Although the Whigs were a rising political force, the party lacked national cohesion in 1836. Instead of holding a convention and nominating national candidates, the Whigs ran regional candidates nominated by state legislatures. It was the hope of Whig strategists that the regional candidates would receive enough electoral votes to throw the election into the House of Representatives, where the party could unite behind the leading prospect.

Sen. Daniel Webster of New Hampshire ran as the Whig candidate in Massachusetts; Sen. Hugh L. White of Tennessee was the party standard-bearer in the South; Gen. William Henry Harrison of Ohio was the Whig candidate in the rest of the country. The Whigs chose Francis Granger of New York as Harrison and Webster's running mate and John Tyler of Virginia to run with White.

# 1839-40 Conventions

## Presidential Candidates

**William Henry Harrison**
**Whig**

**Martin Van Buren**
**Democrat**

### Whigs

By 1839 the Whigs had established themselves as a powerful opposition party, unified enough to run a national candidate against the Democratic president, Martin Van Buren. The call for the Whigs' first national convention was issued by a group of party members in Congress. Nearly 250 delegates responded, gathering in Harrisburg, Pa., in December 1839.

Three candidates were in contention for the presidential nomination: Generals William Henry Harrison of Ohio and Winfield Scott of Virginia and Sen. Henry Clay of Kentucky. After long debate, it was decided that each state would ballot separately, then select representatives who would meet and discuss the views and results of their delegation meetings with representatives of the other states. The unit rule would be in effect, binding the entire vote of each state to the candidate who received a majority of the state's delegates.

The nominating rules agreed to by the convention strongly favored the forces opposed to Clay. First, they negated substantial Clay strength in state delegations in

which he did not hold a majority of the vote. Second, they permitted balloting in relative anonymity, so that delegates would be more likely to defect from the popular Kentuckian than they would if the balloting were public.

Clay led on the first ballot, but switches by Scott delegates on subsequent roll calls gave the nomination to Harrison. On the final ballot, Harrison received 148 votes to 90 for Clay and 16 for Scott. Harrison's vote was short of a two-thirds majority, but under Whig rules only a simple majority was needed to nominate.

To give the ticket factional and geographic balance, a friend of Clay, former Democrat John Tyler of Virginia, was the unanimous selection for vice president. The convention did not risk destruction of the tenuous unity of its anti-Democratic coalition by adopting a party platform or statement of principles.

### Democrats

In May 1840 the Democrats held their national convention in Baltimore. The call once again was initiated by members of the New Hampshire legislature. Delegates from 21 states attended, while five states were unrepresented. Again, the size of the state delegations was largely determined by their distance from Baltimore. New Jersey sent 59 people to cast the state's eight votes, while only one delegate came from Massachusetts to decide that state's 14 votes.

To avoid a bitter dispute over the vice presidential nomination, the convention appointed a committee to recommend nominees for both spots on the ticket. The committee's recommendation that Van Buren be renominated for president was passed by acclamation. On the touchier problem of the vice presidency, the committee recommended that no nomination be made, a suggestion that was also agreed to by the convention. Dissatisfaction with the personal life of Vice President Johnson had increased, leading to the decision that state Democratic leaders determine who would run as the vice presidential candidate in their own states.

Before the nominating process had begun, the convention had approved the first party platform in American history. A platform committee was appointed "to prepare resolutions declaratory of the principles of the . . . party." The committee report was approved without discussion.

The first Democratic platform was a short document, fewer than 1,000 words long. Although brief by modern standards, the platform clearly emphasized the party's belief in a strict reading of the Constitution. It began by stating "that the federal government is one of limited powers" and spelled out in detail what the federal government could not do. The platform stated that the federal government did not have the power to finance internal improvements, assume state debts, charter a national bank or interfere with the rights of the states, especially relating to slavery. The platform criticized the abolitionists for stirring up the explosive slavery question. The Democrats urged the government to practice economy, supported President Van Buren's independent treasury plan and affirmed their belief in the principles expressed in the Declaration of Independence.

In addition to the platform, the convention adopted an address to the people, which was written by a separate committee. Much longer than the platform, the address discussed party principles, lauded Van Buren and Jackson for following these principles and warned of dire consequences if the opposition should be elected.

Following are excerpts from the Democratic platform of 1840:

**Strict Construction.** That the federal government is one of limited powers, derived solely from the constitution, and the grants of power shown therein, ought to be strictly construed by all the departments and agents of the government, and that it is inexpedient and dangerous to exercise doubtful constitutional powers.

**Internal Improvements.** That the constitution does not confer upon the general government the power to commence and carry on, a general system of internal improvements.

**State Debts.** That the constitution does not confer authority upon the federal government, directly or indirectly, to assume the debts of the several states, contracted for local internal improvements, or other state purposes; nor would such assumption be just or expedient.

**Equality of Rights.** That justice and sound policy forbid the federal government to foster one branch of industry to the detriment of another, or to cherish the interests of one portion to the injury of another portion of our common country — that every citizen and every section of the country, has a right to demand and insist upon an equality of rights and privileges, and to complete and ample protection of person and property from domestic violence, or foreign aggression.

**Government Spending.** That it is the duty of every branch of the government, to enforce and practice the most rigid economy, in conducting our public affairs, and that no more revenue ought to be raised, than is required to defray the necessary expenses of the government.

**National Bank.** That congress has no power to charter a national bank; that we believe such an institution one of deadly hostility to the best interests of the country, dangerous to our republican institutions and the liberties of the people, and calculated to place the business of the country within the control of a concentrated money power, and above the laws and the will of the people.

**States' Rights, Slavery.** That congress has no power, under the constitution, to interfere with or control the domestic institutions of the several states, and that such states are the sole and proper judges of everything appertaining to their own affairs, not prohibited by the constitution; that all efforts by abolitionists or others, made to induce congress to interfere with questions of slavery, or to take incipient steps in relation thereto, are calculated to lead to the most alarming and dangerous consequences, and that all such efforts have an inevitable tendency to diminish the happiness of the people, and endanger the stability and permanency of the union, and ought not to be countenanced by any friend to our political institutions.

**Independent Treasury.** That the separation of the moneys of the government from banking institutions, is indispensable for the safety of the funds of the government, and the rights of the people.

**Democratic Principles.** That the liberal principles embodied by Jefferson in the Declaration of Independence, and sanctioned in the constitution, which makes ours the land of liberty, and the asylum of the oppressed of every nation, have ever been cardinal principles in the democratic faith; and every attempt to abridge the present privilege of becoming citizens, and the owners of soil among us, ought to be resisted with the same spirit which swept the alien and sedition laws from our statute-book.

# 1843-44 Conventions

## Presidential Candidates

**James G. Birney**
**Liberty**

**Henry Clay**
**Whig**

**James K. Polk**
**Democrat**

### Liberty Party

The Liberty Party held its second national convention in Buffalo, N.Y., in August 1843. The party, born of the failure of the Whigs and the Democrats to make a strong appeal to abolitionist voters, had held its first national convention in April 1840 in Albany, N.Y. James G. Birney of Michigan, a former slave owner, was nominated for president and Thomas Earle of Ohio was chosen as his running mate. In the 1840 election the party polled 0.29 percent of the national popular vote.

At the 1843 convention, 148 delegates from 12 states assembled in Buffalo and renominated Birney for the presidency and chose Thomas Morris of Ohio as his running mate. The party platform was more than 3,000 words long, the lengthiest platform written by any party in the 19th century. In spite of its length, the platform discussed only one issue, slavery. In the 1844 election, the party received 2.3 percent of the national popular vote, its highest total in any presidential election. By 1848, most members of the party joined the newly formed Free Soil Party.

Following are excerpts from the Liberty Party platform of 1844:

*Resolved.* That the Liberty party ... will demand the absolute and unqualified divorce of the General Government from Slavery, and also the restoration of equality of rights, among men, in every State where the party exists, or may exist.

*Therefore, Resolved,* That we hereby give it to be distinctly understood, by this nation and the world, that, as abolitionists, considering that the strength of our cause lies in its righteousness — and our hope for it in our conformity to the LAWS of GOD, and our respect for the RIGHTS OF MAN, we owe it to the Sovereign Ruler of the Universe, as a proof of our allegiance to Him, in all our civil relations and offices, whether as private citizens, or as public functionaries sworn to support the Constitution of the United States, to regard and to treat the third clause of the second section of the fourth article of that instrument, whenever applied to the case of a fugitive slave, as utterly null and void, and consequently as forming no part of the Constitution of the United States, whenever we are called upon, or sworn, to support it.

### Whigs

In a harmonious one-day session, the Whigs' national convention nominated for the presidency the party's former leader in Congress, Henry Clay. It was a final rebuff for President John Tyler from the party that had nominated him for the second spot on its ticket in 1840. Three years of bickering between the White House and Whig leaders in Congress had made Tyler, former Democrat, persona non grata in the Whig Party.

Delegates from every state were represented at the Whig convention, held in Baltimore on May 1, 1844. Clay was the unanimous nominee, and it was proposed that he be invited to address the convention the next day. However, the Kentuckian declined this opportunity to make the first acceptance speech in American political history, stating in a letter that he was unable to reconcile an appearance with his "sense of delicacy and propriety." *(Chart, p. 193)*

Three potential candidates for the vice presidency sent letters of withdrawal before balloting for second place on the ticket began. Unlike the convention four years earlier, the Whigs abandoned their relatively secret state caucus method of voting and adopted a public roll call, with the chair calling the name of each delegate. Theodore Frelinghuysen of New Jersey won a plurality of the convention vote for vice president on the first ballot and went on to gain, on the third ballot, the required majority.

After the nominations, several resolutions were adopted, including one that defined Whig principles and served as the party's first platform. It was a brief document, fewer than 100 words long, and the only clear difference between it and the platform adopted later by the Democratic convention was on the issue of distributing proceeds from the sale of public land. The Whigs favored distribution of these revenues to the states; the Democrats opposed it believing the proceeds should be retained by the federal government. In a continued reaction to the Jackson administration, the Whigs criticized "executive usurpations" and proposed a single-term presidency. The rest of the Whig platform called for government efficiency, "a

39

well-regulated currency" and a tariff for revenue and the protection of American labor.

Westward territorial expansion, particularly the annexation of Texas, was not mentioned in the Whig platform, but it was an explosive issue by 1844 that made a significant impact on the Democratic convention.

Following are excerpts from the Whig platform of 1844:

*Resolved,* That these principles may be summed as comprising, a well-regulated currency; a tariff for revenue to defray the necessary expenses of the government, and discriminating with special reference to protection of the domestic labor of the country; the distribution of the proceeds of the sales of the public lands; a single term for the presidency; a reform of executive usurpations; — and, generally — such an administration of the affairs of the country as shall impart to every branch of the public service the greatest practicable efficiency, controlled by a well regulated and wise economy.

## Democrats

Delegates from every state except South Carolina assembled in Baltimore in late May 1844 for the Democratic convention. The front-runner for the presidential nomination was former president Martin Van Buren, whose status was threatened on the eve of the convention by his statement against the annexation of Texas. Van Buren's position jeopardized his support in the South, and with a two-thirds majority apparently necessary, dimmed his chances of obtaining the presidential nomination. The question of requiring a two-thirds nominating majority was debated in the early sessions of the convention, and by a vote of 148 to 118 the two-thirds majority rule, initially adopted by the party in 1832, was ratified. *(Chart, p. 194)*

Van Buren led the early presidential balloting, actually receiving a simple majority of the vote on the first ballot. On succeeding roll calls, however, his principal opponent, Lewis Cass of Michigan, gained strength and took the lead. But neither candidate approached the 178 votes needed for nomination.

With a deadlock developing, sentiment for a compromise candidate appeared. James K. Polk, former Speaker of the Tennessee House and former governor of Tennessee, emerged as an acceptable choice and won the nomination on the ninth ballot. It marked the first time in American history that a dark-horse candidate won a presidential nomination. *(Chart, p. 194)*

A friend of Van Buren, Sen. Silas Wright of New York, was the nearly unanimous nominee of the convention for vice president. But Wright refused the nomination, quickly notifying the delegates by way of Samuel Morse's new invention, the telegraph. After two more ballots, George M. Dallas of Pennsylvania was chosen as Polk's running mate.

Among its final actions, the convention appointed a central committee and recommended that a nationwide party organization be established — a forerunner of the national committee. The delegates did not adopt a platform but appointed a committee to draft resolutions.

The resulting document contained the same resolutions included in the party's 1840 platform, plus several new planks. The Democrats opposed the distribution of the proceeds from the sale of public lands; were against placing any restrictions on the executive veto power; and, to alleviate the sectional bitterness aroused by the prospect of Western expansion, recommended the annexation of both Texas and Oregon.

President Tyler, although abandoned by the major parties, wanted to remain in office. Friends and federal officeholders gathered in Baltimore at the same time as the Democrats and nominated Tyler. However, it became apparent that the president's national vote-getting appeal was limited, and he withdrew from the race in favor of the Democrat, Polk.

Following are excerpts from the Democratic resolutions of 1844:

**Appeal to the Masses.** That the American Democracy place their trust, not in factitious symbols, not in displays and appeals insulting to the judgment and subversive of the intellect of the people, but in a clear reliance upon the intelligence, patriotism, and the discriminating justice of the American masses.

That we regard this as a distinctive feature of our political creed, which we are proud to maintain before the world, as the great moral element in a form of government springing from and upheld by the popular will; and we contrast it with the creed and practice of Federalism, under whatever name or form, which seeks to palsy the will of the constituent, and which conceives no imposture too monstrous for the popular credulity.

**Internal Improvements.** That the Constitution does not confer upon the General Government the power to commence or carry on a general system of internal improvements.

**State Debts.** That the Constitution does not confer authority upon the Federal Government, directly or indirectly, to assume the debts of the several states.

**Government Spending.** That it is the duty of every branch of the government to enforce and practice the most rigid economy in conducting our public affairs, and that no more revenue ought to be raised than is required to defray the necessary expenses of the government.

**National Bank.** That Congress has no power to charter a United States Bank, that we believe such an institution one of deadly hostility to the best interests of the country, dangerous to our republican institutions and the liberties of the people.

**States' Rights.** That Congress has no power, under the Constitution, to interfere with or control the domestic institutions of the several States; and that such States are the sole and proper judges of everything pertaining to their own affairs, not prohibited by the Constitution; that all efforts, by abolitionists or others, made to induce Congress to interfere with questions of slavery, or to take incipient steps in relation thereto, are calculated to lead to the most alarming and dangerous consequences.

**Public Lands.** That the proceeds of the Public Lands ought to be sacredly applied to the national objects specified in the Constitution, and that we are opposed to the laws lately adopted, and to any law for the distribution of such proceeds among the States, as alike inexpedient in policy and repugnant to the Constitution.

**Executive Veto Power.** That we are decidedly opposed to taking from the President the qualified veto power by which he is enabled, under restrictions and responsibilities amply sufficient to guard the public interest.

**Western Expansion.** That our title to the whole of the Territory of Oregon is clear and unquestionable; that no portion of the same ought to be ceded to England or any other power, and that the reoccupation of Oregon and the reannexation of Texas at the earliest practicable period are great American measures, which this Convention recommends to the cordial support of the Democracy of the Union.

# 1848 Conventions

## Presidential Candidates

**Lewis Cass**
**Democrat**

**Zachary Taylor**
**Whig**

**Martin Van Buren**
**Free Soil**

### Democrats

Delegates from every state gathered in Baltimore in May 1848 for the Democratic Party's fifth national convention. A seating dispute between two rival New York delegations enlivened the early convention sessions. The conflict reflected a factional fight in the state Democratic Party between a more liberal anti-slavery faction, known as the Barnburners, and a more conservative faction, known as the Hunkers. By a vote of 126 to 125, the convention adopted a compromise by which both delegations were seated and shared New York's vote. However, this compromise satisfied neither of the contesting delegations. The Barnburners bolted the convention. The Hunkers remained but refused to vote. *(Chart, p. 194)*

Before the presidential balloting could begin, the convention had to decide whether to use the controversial two-thirds rule. Consideration of the rule preceded the credentials controversy, which brought an objection from New York delegates who wanted their seating dispute settled first. But, by a vote of 133 to 121, the convention refused to table the issue. A second vote on adoption of the two-thirds rule was approved, 176 to 78. *(Chart, p. 194)*

The front-runner for the presidential nomination was Sen. Lewis Cass of Michigan. Although Cass was from the North, his view that the existence of slavery in the territories should be determined by their inhabitants (a forerunner of Stephen Douglas' "popular sovereignty") was a position acceptable to the South.

Cass received 125 votes on the first ballot, more than double the total of his two principal rivals, James Buchanan of Pennsylvania and Levi Woodbury of New Hampshire. Cass' vote total steadily increased during the next three roll calls, and on the fourth ballot he received 179 votes and was nominated. His vote was actually short of a two-thirds majority of the allotted convention votes, but the chair ruled that, with New York not voting, the required majority was reduced. *(Chart, p. 194)*

The vice presidential nomination went on the second ballot to Gen. William O. Butler of Kentucky, who had 169 of the 253 votes cast. As in the earlier presidential balloting, Butler's two-thirds majority was based on votes cast

rather than votes allotted. Butler's primary rival for the nomination was a military colleague, Gen. John A. Quitman of Mississippi.

One of the most significant acts of the convention was the formation of a national committee, with one member from each state, that would handle party affairs until the next convention four years later.

As in 1840 and 1844, the heart of the Democratic platform was a series of resolutions describing the party's concept of a federal government with limited powers. New resolutions emphasized Democratic opposition to a national bank and the distribution of land sales to the states, while applauding the independent treasury plan, the lower tariff bill passed in 1846 and the successful war against Mexico. An effort by William L. Yancey of Alabama to insert in the platform a plank on slavery that would prevent interference with the rights of slaveholders in states or territories was defeated, 216 to 36. The slavery plank written in the platform had the same wording as earlier versions in the 1840 and 1844 Democratic platforms. The plank was milder than Yancey's proposal, stating simply that Congress did not have the power to interfere with slavery in the states. The convention adopted the complete platform by a vote of 247 to 0.

Following are excerpts from the 1848 Democratic platform:

**Mexican War.** That the war with Mexico, provoked on her part by years of insult and injury, was commenced by her army crossing the Rio Grande, attacking the American troops, and invading our sister State of Texas; and that, upon all the principles of patriotism and laws of nations, it is a just and necessary war on our part, in which every American citizen should have shown himself on the side of his country, and neither morally nor physically, by word or by deed, have given "aid and comfort to the enemy."

**Democratic Accomplishments.** That the fruits of the great political triumph of 1844, which elected James K. Polk and George M. Dallas President and Vice President of the United States, have fulfilled the hopes of the Democracy of the Union — in defeating the declared purposes of their opponents to create a national bank; in preventing the corrupt and unconstitutional distribution of the land proceeds, from the common treasury of the Union, for local purposes; in protecting the currency and the labor of the country from ruinous fluctuations, and guarding the money of the people for the use of the people, by the establishment of the constitutional treasury; in the noble impulse given to the cause of free trade, by the repeal of the tariff in 1842 and the creation of the more equal, honest, and productive tariff of 1846.

## Whigs

Whig delegates from every state except Texas gathered in Philadelphia in June 1848. Although the Lone Star state was unrepresented, a Texas Whig state convention had earlier given a proxy for its votes to the Louisiana delegates. There was debate in the convention about the legality of the proxy, but it was ultimately accepted by the delegates.

The battle for the Whig's presidential nomination involved three major contenders, the party's respected aging statesman, Henry Clay of Kentucky; and two generals — Zachary Taylor and Winfield Scott, both of Virginia — whose political appeal was significantly increased by their military exploits in the recently completed Mexican War. Taylor led throughout the balloting, taking the lead on the first ballot with 111 votes, compared with 97 for Clay and 43 for Scott. Taylor increased his lead on subsequent roll calls, winning the nomination on the fourth ballot with 171 of the 280 votes cast. *(Chart, p. 195)*

Millard Fillmore of New York and Abbott Lawrence of Massachusetts were the prime contenders for the vice presidential nomination. Fillmore led Lawrence, 115 to 109, on the first ballot and pulled away to win on the second ballot with 173 of the 266 votes cast.

A motion to make the presidential and vice presidential nominations unanimous failed when several delegates objected, doubting Taylor's support of Whig principles.

The Whig convention did not formally adopt a party platform, although a ratification meeting held in Philadelphia after the convention adopted a series of resolutions. The resolutions avoided a discussion of issues, instead lauding the party's presidential nominee, Zachary Taylor, and affirming his faithfulness to the tenets of the party.

## Free Soilers

Anti-slavery Whigs, New York Barnburners and members of the Liberty Party gathered in Buffalo, N.Y., in August 1848 to form a new third party, the Free Soilers. While opposition to slavery was a common denominator of the various elements in the new party, the dissident Democrats and Whigs also were attracted to the Free Soil Party by the lack of influence they exerted in their former parties. The call for a Free Soil convention was made by the New York Barnburners at their state conclave in June 1848 and by a non-partisan gathering in Columbus, Ohio, the same month. The latter assembly, organized by Salmon P. Chase, was entitled a People's Convention of Friends of Free Territory and was designed to set the stage for a national Free Soil convention.

Four hundred sixty-five delegates from 18 states (including representatives from the slave states of Delaware, Maryland and Virginia) assembled in Buffalo for the birth of the Free Soil Party. Because of the large number of delegates, convention leaders determined that delegates from each state would select several members to form a Committee on Conference, which would conduct conven-

tion business. The rest of the delegates would sit in a large tent and listen to campaign oratory.

Martin Van Buren, the former Democratic president and a favorite of the Barnburners, was chosen as the new party's standard-bearer on the first ballot. Van Buren received 244 votes to defeat John P. Hale of New Hampshire, who had 181 votes. Hale had been nominated by the Liberty Party in October 1847, but with Van Buren's nomination he withdrew from the race. The vice presidential nomination went to a former Whig, Charles Francis Adams of Massachusetts.

The platform adopted by the Free Soil Party focused on the slavery issue, but its opposition to slavery was milder than earlier Liberty Party platforms. The Free Soilers also declared themselves on other issues besides slavery, further distinguishing themselves from the single-minded Liberty Party.

While the Free Soilers opposed the extension of slavery into the territories, they did not feel the federal government had the power to interfere with slavery in the states. Although this position was significantly stronger than the position adopted by the Democrats, it was milder than the all-out opposition to slavery expressed by the Liberty Party four years earlier.

The Free Soilers also adopted positions on a variety of other issues, supporting free land for settlers, a tariff for revenue purposes, cheap postage and federal spending for river and harbor improvements. Basically, the Free Soil platform expressed belief in a federal government with broader powers than that conceived by the Democrats.

Following are excerpts from the 1848 Free Soil Party platform:

**Slavery.** That Slavery in the several States of this Union which recognize its existence, depends upon the State laws alone, which cannot be repealed or modified by the Federal Government, and for which laws that Government is not responsible. We therefore propose no interference by Congress with Slavery within the limits of any State.

*Resolved,* THAT IT IS THE DUTY OF THE FEDERAL GOVERNMENT TO RELIEVE ITSELF FROM ALL RESPONSIBILITY FOR THE EXISTENCE OR CONTINUANCE OF SLAVERY WHEREVER THAT GOVERNMENT POSSESS CONSTITUTIONAL POWER TO LEGISLATE ON THAT SUBJECT, AND IS THUS RESPONSIBLE FOR ITS EXISTENCE.

*Resolved,* That the true, and, in the judgment of this Convention, the *only* safe means of preventing the extension of Slavery into territory now free, is to prohibit its existence in all such territory by *an act of Congress.*

**Government Administration.** That we demand CHEAP POSTAGE for the people; a retrenchment of the expenses and patronage of the Federal Government; the *abolition* of all *unnecessary* offices and salaries; and the election by the People of all civil officers in the service of the Government, so far as the same may be practicable.

**Internal Improvements.** That *river and harbor improvements,* when demanded by the safety and convenience of commerce with foreign nations, or among the several States, are objects of *national concern;* and that it is the duty of Congress, in the exercise of its constitutional powers, to provide therefor.

**Homesteading.** That the FREE GRANT TO ACTUAL SETTLERS, in consideration of the expenses they incur in making settlements in the wilderness, which are usually fully equal to their actual cost, and of the public benefits resulting therefrom, of reasonable portions of the public lands, under suitable limitations, is a wise and just measure of public policy, which will promote, in various ways, the interest of all the States of this Union; and we therefore recommend it to the favorable consideration of the American People.

**Tariff.** That the obligations of honor and patriotism require the earliest practical payment of the national debt,

and we are therefore in favor of such a tariff of duties as will raise revenue adequate to defray the necessary expenses of the Federal Government, and to pay annual installments of our debt and the interest thereon.

**Party Motto.** *Resolved,* That we inscribe on our banner, "FREE SOIL, FREE SPEECH, FREE LABOR, AND FREE MEN."

# 1852 Conventions
## Presidential Candidates

**Franklin Pierce**
**Democrat**

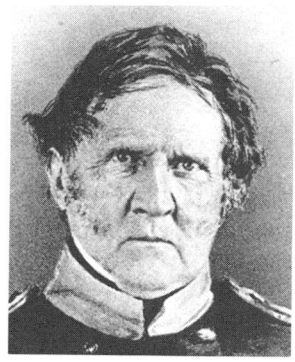

**Winfield Scott**
**Whig**

**John P. Hale**
**Free Soil**

### Democrats

In spite of the efforts of the major politicians of both parties, the explosive slavery question was fast becoming the dominant issue in American politics and was threatening the tenuous intersectional alliances that held together both the Democratic and Whig parties. Under the cloud of this volatile issue, the Democratic convention convened in Baltimore in June 1852.

The delegates were called to order by the party's first national chairman, Benjamin F. Hallett of Massachusetts. Hallett's first action was to limit the size of each state delegation to its electoral vote, dispatching members of oversized delegations to the rear of the hall. Retention of the two-thirds rule provoked little opposition, unlike the disputes at the 1844 and 1848 conventions, and an effort to table the rule was soundly beaten, 269 to 13.

With a degree of orderliness, the convention disposed of procedural matters, clearing the way for the presidential balloting. There were four major contenders for the nomination: Sen. Lewis Cass of Michigan, James Buchanan of Pennsylvania and William L. Marcy of New York — all three over 60 years old — and the rising young senator from Illinois, Stephen A. Douglas, 39. Each of the four challengers led at one point during the numerous ballots that followed.

Cass jumped in front initially, receiving 116 votes on the first ballot. Buchanan trailed with 93, while Marcy and Douglas were far back with 27 and 20 votes, respectively. Cass' vote dropped after the first few roll calls, but he was able to hold the lead until the 20th ballot, when Buchanan moved in front. Buchanan led for several roll calls, followed by Douglas, who edged into the lead on the 30th ballot,

only to be quickly displaced by Cass on the 32nd ballot. Marcy made his spurt between the 36th and 46th ballots, and took the lead on the 45th and 46th ballots. But in spite of the quick changes in fortune, none of the four contenders could win a simple majority of the votes, let alone the two-thirds required. *(Chart, p. 196)*

With a deadlock developing, on the 35th ballot the Virginia delegation introduced a new name, Franklin Pierce of New Hampshire. Although formerly a member of both houses of Congress, Pierce was little known nationally and not identified with any party faction. Pierce's relative anonymity made him an acceptable alternative in the volatile convention. Pierce received 15 votes on the 35th ballot and gradually gained strength on subsequent ballots, with the big break coming on the 49th roll call. Nearly unanimous votes for Pierce in the New England states created a bandwagon effect that resulted in his nomination on this ballot with 279 of the 288 votes cast. The 49 ballots took two days.

Beginning the vice presidential roll call, a spokesman for the Maine delegation suggested that second place on the ticket go to a representative of the South, specifically mentioning Sen. William R. King of Alabama. King moved into a strong lead on the first ballot with 125 votes and easily won nomination on the second roll call with 277 of the 288 votes cast.

The platform adopted by the Democratic convention contained the same nine resolutions that had been in all party platforms since 1840, detailing the Democratic concept of a limited federal government. The platform included a plank supporting the Compromise of 1850, the congressional solution to the slavery question. Actually, both the Whigs and Democrats endorsed the compromise of 1850. The major point of dispute between the two parties was over the issue of internal improvements, with the Whigs taking a broader view of federal power in this sphere.

Following are excerpts from the Democratic platform of 1852:

**Compromise of 1850.** *Resolved, ...* the democratic party of the Union, standing on this national platform, will abide by and adhere to a faithful execution of the acts known as the compromise measures settled by the last Congress — "the act for reclaiming fugitives from service or labor" included; which act, being designed to carry out an express provision of the constitution, cannot, with fidelity thereto be repealed nor so changed as to destroy or impair its efficiency.

*Resolved,* That the democratic party will resist all attempts at renewing, in congress or out of it, the agitation of the slavery question, under whatever shape or color the attempt may be made.

**Democratic Principles.** That, in view of the condition of popular institutions in the Old World, a high and sacred duty is devolved, with increased responsibility upon the democratic party of this country, as the party of the people, to uphold and maintain the rights of every State, and thereby the Union of the States, and to sustain and advance among us constitutional liberty, by continuing to resist all monopolies and exclusive legislation for the benefit of the few at the expense of the many, and by a vigilant and constant adherence to those principles and compromises of the constitution, which are broad enough and strong enough to embrace and uphold the Union as it was, the Union as it is, and the Union as it shall be, in the full expansion of the energies and capacity of this great and progressive people.

## Whigs

Although in control of the White House, the Whigs were more sharply divided by the Compromise of 1850 than were the Democrats. The majority of Northern Whigs in Congress opposed the Compromise, while most Southern members of the party favored it. Faced with widening division in their ranks, Whig delegates convened in Baltimore in June 1852. The call for this national convention had been issued by Whig members of Congress, and delegates from all 31 states attended.

The convention sessions were often lively and sometimes raucous. When asked to present its report the first day, the credentials committee responded that it was not ready to report and "didn't know when — maybe for days." A minister, invited to the hall to deliver a prayer to the convention, never had his chance. The delegates debated when the prayer should be delivered and finally decided to omit it.

A heated debate occurred on how many votes each state would be apportioned on the platform committee. By a vote of 149 to 144, the delegates adopted a plan whereby each state's vote on the committee would reflect its strength in the electoral college. Strong protests from Southern and small Northern states, however, brought a reversal of this decision, and although no formal vote was recorded, representation on the platform committee was changed so that each state received one vote.

The Northern and Southern wings of the Whig Party were nearly equally represented at the Baltimore convention, and the close split produced a prolonged battle for the party's presidential nomination. The two major rivals for the nomination, President Millard Fillmore and Winfield Scott, had nearly equal strength. Ironically, the basic appeal of Fillmore of New York was among Southern delegates, who appreciated his support of the Compromise of 1850.

Although a native of Virginia, Scott was not popular in the South because of his ambivalence on the Compromise and the active support given him by a leading anti-slavery Northerner, Sen. William H. Seward of New York. Scott's strength was in the Northern and Western states. A third candidate in the field was Daniel Webster, the party's elder statesman, whose appeal was centered in his native New England.

On the first ballot, Fillmore received 133 votes, Scott had 132 and Webster collected 29. This nearly equal distribution of the vote between Fillmore and Scott continued with little fluctuation through the first two days of balloting. Midway through the second day, after the 34th ballot, a motion was made to adjourn. Although it was defeated by a vote of 126 to 76, other motions were made to adjourn throughout the rest of the session. Finally, amid increasing confusion, after the 46th ballot, delegates voted by a margin of 176 to 116 to adjourn. *(Chart, p. 197)*

Commotion continued the next day, with Southern delegates trying unsuccessfully to expel Henry J. Raymond, the editor of the *New York Times,* who was also a delegate by proxy. In an article, Raymond had charged collusion between party managers and Southern delegates, with the South getting its way on the platform while Scott received the presidential nomination.

Amid this uproar, the leaders of the Fillmore and Webster forces were negotiating. Fillmore was willing to release his delegates to Webster, if Webster could muster 41 votes on his own. As the balloting continued, it was apparent that Webster could not; and enough delegates defected to Scott to give the Mexican War hero a simple majority and the nomination on the 53rd ballot. On the final roll call, Scott received 159 votes, compared with 112 for Fillmore and 21 for Webster.

Several individuals placed in nomination for the vice presidency refused it immediately. The chairman of the convention finally declared Secretary of the Navy William A. Graham of North Carolina to be the unanimous selection. No formal roll-call vote was recorded.

For only the second time in their history, the Whigs adopted a party platform. Like their Democratic adversaries, the Whigs supported the Compromise of 1850 and perceived the federal government as having limited powers. Additional planks called for a tariff on imports to raise revenue and for an isolationist foreign policy that avoided "entangling alliances." The platform was adopted by a vote of 227 to 66, with all the dissenting votes cast by delegates from the North and West.

Following are excerpts from the Whig platform of 1852:

**Strict Construction.** The Government of the United States is of a limited character, and it is confined to the exercise of powers expressly granted by the Constitution, and such as may be necessary and proper for carrying the granted powers into full execution, and that all powers not granted or necessarily implied are expressly reserved to the States respectively and to the people.

**Foreign Policy.** That while struggling freedom everywhere enlists the warmest sympathy of the Whig party, we still adhere to the doctrines of the Father of his Country, as announced in his Farewell Address, of keeping ourselves free from all entangling alliances with foreign countries, and of never quitting our own to stand upon foreign ground, that our mission as a republic is not to propagate our opinions, or impose on other countries our form of government by artifice or force; but to teach, by example, and show by our success, moderation and justice, the blessings of self-government, and the advantages of free institutions.

**Tariff.** Revenue sufficient for the expenses of an economical administration of the Government in time of peace ought to be derived from a duty on imports, and not from direct taxation.

**Internal Improvements.** The Constitution vests in Congress the power to open and repair harbors, and remove obstructions from navigable rivers, whenever such improvements are necessary for the common defense, and for the protection and facility of commerce with foreign nations, or among the States, said improvements being, in every instance, national and general in their character.

**Compromise of 1850.** That the series of acts of the Thirty-first Congress, — the act known as the Fugitive Slave Law, included — are received and acquiesced in by the Whig Party of the United States as a settlement in principle and substance, of the dangerous and exciting question which they embrace; and, so far as they are concerned, we will maintain them, and insist upon their strict enforcement, until time and experience shall demonstrate the necessity of further legislation.

## Free Democrats (Free Soilers)

After the 1848 election, the New York Barnburners returned to the Democratic Party, and the rest of the Free Soilers were ready to coalesce with either the Democrats or the Whigs. But the process of absorption was delayed by the Compromise of 1850. It was viewed as a solution to the slavery question by the two major parties but was regarded as a sellout by most anti-slavery groups.

Responding to a call for a national convention issued by a Cleveland, Ohio, anti-slavery meeting, delegates gathered in Pittsburgh in August 1852. Anti-slavery Whigs and remnants of the Liberty Party were in attendance at what was termed the Free Soil Democratic Convention.

John P. Hale of New Hampshire unanimously won the presidential nomination, and George W. Julian of Indiana was selected as his running mate.

Although the platform covered a number of issues, the document focused on the slavery question. The Free Soil Democrats opposed the Compromise of 1850 and called for the abolition of slavery. Like both major parties, the Free Democrats expressed the concept of a limited federal government, but they agreed with the Whigs that the government should undertake certain river and harbor improvements. The Free Democrats went beyond the other parties in advocating a homestead policy, extending a welcome to immigrants and voicing support for new republican governments in Europe and the Caribbean.

Following are excerpts from the Free Democratic platform of 1852:

**Strict Construction.** That the Federal Government is one of limited powers, derived solely from the Constitution, and the grants of power therein ought to be strictly construed by all the departments and agents of the Government, and it is inexpedient and dangerous to exercise doubtful constitutional powers.

**Compromise of 1850.** That, to the persevering and importunate demands of the slave power for more slave States, new slave Territories, and the nationalization of slavery, our distinct and final answer is — no more slave States, no slave Territory, no nationalized slavery, and no national legislation for the extradition of slaves.

That slavery is a sin against God and a crime against man, which no human enactment nor usage can make right; and that Christianity, humanity, and patriotism, alike demand its abolition.

That the Fugitive Slave Act of 1850 is repugnant to the Constitution, to the principles of the common law, to the spirit of Christianity, and to the sentiments of the civilized world. We therefore deny its binding force upon the American People, and demand its immediate and total repeal.

**Homesteading.** That the public lands of the United States belong to the people, and should not be sold to individuals nor granted to corporations, but should be held as a sacred trust for the benefit of the people, and should be granted in limited quantities, free of cost, to landless settlers.

**Internal Improvements.** That river and harbor improvements, when necessary to the safety and convenience of commerce with foreign nations or among the several States, are objects of national concern, and it is the duty of Congress in the exercise of its constitutional powers to provide for the same.

# 1856 Conventions

## Presidential Candidates

**John C. Fremont**
**Republican**

**Millard Fillmore**
**Know Nothing**

**James Buchanan**
**Democrat**

### Republicans

With the decline of the Whigs and the increasing importance of the slavery issue, there was room for a new political party. Officially born in 1854, the new Republican Party moved to fill the vacuum.

The party's first meeting was held in Pittsburgh in February 1856, with delegates from 24 states attending. United in their opposition to the extension of slavery and the policies of the Pierce administration, the gathering selected a national committee (with one representative from each state), which was empowered to call the party's first national convention.

The subsequent call was addressed not to Republicans but "to the people of the United States" who were opposed to the Pierce administration and the congressional compromises on slavery. Each state was allocated six delegates at the forthcoming convention, with three additional delegates for each congressional district.

When the first Republican National Convention assembled in Philadelphia in June 1856, the gathering was clearly sectional. There were nearly 600 delegates present, representing all the Northern states, the Border slave states of Delaware, Maryland, Virginia and Kentucky, and the District of Columbia. The territory of Kansas, symbolically important in the slavery struggle, was treated as a state and given full representation. There were no delegations from the remaining Southern slave states.

Under convention rules, the roll call was to proceed in alphabetical order, with each state allocated three times its electoral vote. In response to a question, the chair decided that a simple majority would be required and not the two-thirds majority mandated by the Democratic convention. This was an important rule that distinguished the conventions of the two major parties well into the 20th century.

Two major contenders for the Republican presidential nomination, Salmon P. Chase of Ohio and William H. Seward of New York, both withdrew before the balloting began. Another contender, Supreme Court Justice John McLean of Ohio, withdrew briefly, but then re-entered the race. However, McLean could not catch the front-runner, John C. Fremont of California. Although briefly a U.S.

senator, Fremont was most famous as an explorer, and he benefited from being free of any ideological identification.

The other contenders were all identified with one of the factions that had come to make up the new party. Fremont won a preliminary, informal ballot, receiving 359 votes to 190 for McLean. On the formal roll call, Fremont won easily, winning 520 of the 567 votes. *(Chart, p. 198)*

A preliminary, informal ballot was taken for the vice presidency as well. William L. Dayton, a former senator from New Jersey, led with 253 votes, more than twice the total received by an Illinois lawyer, Abraham Lincoln, who had served in the House of Representatives 1847-49. On the formal ballot, Dayton swept to victory with 523 votes. His nomination was quickly made unanimous.

The Republican platform was approved by a voice vote. It was a document with sectional appeal, written by Northern delegates for the North. Unlike the Democrats, the Republicans opposed the concept of popular sovereignty and believed that slavery should be prohibited in the territories. Specifically, the platform called for the admission of Kansas as a free state.

The Republicans also differed with the Democrats on the question of internal improvements, supporting the view that Congress should undertake river and harbor improvements. The Republican platform denounced the Ostend Manifesto, a document secretly drawn up by three of Pierce's ambassadors in Europe, that suggested the United States either buy or take Cuba from Spain. The Republicans termed the manifesto a "highwayman's plea, that 'might makes right.'"

Both parties advocated the building of a transcontinental transportation system, with the Republicans supporting the construction of a railroad.

Following are excerpts from the Republican platform of 1856:

> **Slavery.** This Convention of Delegates, assembled in pursuance of a call addressed to the people of the United States, without regard to past political differences or divisions, who are opposed to the repeal of the Missouri Compromise; to the policy of the present Administration; to the extension of Slavery into Free Territory; in favor of the

admission of Kansas as a Free State; of restoring the action of the Federal Government to the principles of Washington and Jefferson....

That the Constitution confers upon Congress sovereign powers over the Territories of the United States for their government; and that in the exercise of this power, it is both the right and the imperative duty of Congress to prohibit in the Territories those twin relics of barbarism — Polygamy, and Slavery.

**Cuba.** That the highwayman's plea, that "might makes right," embodied in the Ostend Circular, was in every respect unworthy of American diplomacy, and would bring shame and dishonor upon any Government or people that gave it their sanction.

**Transcontinental Railroad.** That a railroad to the Pacific Ocean by the most central and practicable route is imperatively demanded by the interests of the whole country.

**Internal Improvements.** That appropriations by Congress for the improvement of rivers and harbors, of a national character, required for the accommodation and security of our existing commerce, are authorized by the Constitution, and justified by the obligation of the Government to protect the lives and property of its citizens.

## American (Know-Nothings)

In addition to the Republicans, the American Party or Know-Nothings aspired to replace the Whigs as the nation's second major party. However, unlike the Republicans, the Know-Nothings were a national political organization, and the slavery issue that helped unite the Republicans divided the Know-Nothings. The main Know-Nothing concern was to place restrictions on the large number of European immigrants who arrived in the 1840s and 1850s.

The party held its first and only national convention in Philadelphia in February 1856. Several days before the convention began, the American Party's national council met and drew up the party platform. When the convention assembled, anti-slavery delegates objected to the platform, with its espousal of popular sovereignty, and called for the nomination of candidates who would outlaw slavery in the new territories. When their resolution was defeated, 141 to 59, these anti-slavery delegates — mainly from New England and Ohio — bolted the convention.

The remaining delegates nominated former president Millard Fillmore (1850-53) of New York for president. Fillmore was popular in the South for his support of compromise slavery measures during his administration and was nominated on the second ballot. Andrew Jackson Donelson of Tennessee was chosen as the vice presidential candidate.

In June 1856 several days before the Republican convention was scheduled to begin, the anti-slavery Know-Nothings assembled in New York and nominated Speaker of the House Nathaniel P. Banks of Massachusetts for the presidency and former governor William F. Johnston of Pennsylvania as his running mate. Banks, who actually favored Fremont's nomination, withdrew from the race when Fremont was chosen as the Republican candidate. Johnston bowed out in favor of Fremont's running mate, William L. Dayton, later in the campaign.

The Know-Nothing convention that had met earlier in Philadelphia adopted a platform similar to that of the Democrats on the slavery question. The document advocated non-interference in the affairs of the states and the concept of popular sovereignty for deciding slavery in the territories. Although also calling for economy in government spending, the bulk of the Know-Nothing platform dealt with restricting immigrants. Among the nativistic planks were proposals that native-born citizens be given the first chance for all government offices, that the naturalization period for immigrants be extended to 21 years and that paupers and convicted criminals be kept from entering the United States.

Following are excerpts from the Know-Nothing platform of 1856:

**Slavery, States' Rights.** The unequalled recognition and maintenance of the reserved rights of the several states, and the cultivation of harmony and fraternal good-will between the citizens of the several states, and to this end, non-interference by Congress with questions appertaining solely to the individual states, and non-intervention by each state with the affairs of any other state.

The recognition of the right of the native-born and naturalized citizens of the United States, permanently residing in any territory thereof, to frame their constitutions and laws, and to regulate their domestic and social affairs in their own mode, subject only to the provisions of the federal Constitution, with the right of admission into the Union whenever they have the requisite population for one representative in Congress.

**Nativism.** *Americans must rule America;* and to this end, *native*-born citizens should be selected for all state, federal, or municipal offices of government employment, in preference to naturalized citizens....

No person should be selected for political station (whether of native or foreign birth), who recognizes any alliance or obligation of any description to any foreign prince, potentate or power, who refuses to recognize the federal and state constitutions (each within its own sphere), as paramount to all other laws, as rules of particular [political] action.

A change in the laws of naturalization, making a continued residence of twenty-one years, of all not heretofore provided for, an indispensable requisite for citizenship hereafter, and excluding all paupers or persons convicted of crime from landing upon our shores.

## Democrats

In June 1856 delegates from all 31 states gathered in Cincinnati, Ohio, for the party's seventh quadrennial convention. It was the first Democratic convention to be held outside Baltimore.

Roll-call votes were taken during the first two days on the establishment of a platform committee and on the method of ticket allocation for the galleries. The first close vote came on the credentials committee report concerning the seating of two contesting New York delegations. By a vote of 136 to 123, the convention agreed to a minority report seating both contending factions and splitting the state's vote between them.

Three men were in contention for the party's presidential nomination: President Franklin Pierce of New Hampshire, James Buchanan of Pennsylvania and Sen. Stephen A. Douglas of Illinois. All three had actively sought the nomination before. Ironically, Buchanan, who had spent the previous three years as ambassador to Great Britain, was in the most enviable position. Having been abroad, Buchanan had largely avoided the increasing slavery controversy that bedeviled his major rivals.

Buchanan led on the first ballot with 135-1/2 votes, with Pierce receiving 122-1/2 and Douglas 33. As the balloting continued, Pierce lost strength, while both Buchanan and Douglas gained. After the 15th roll call, the vote stood:

Buchanan, 168-1/2, Douglas, 118-1/2, Pierce 3-1/2. *(Chart, p. 198)*

While the two front-runners had substantial strength, neither of them was a sectional candidate. Both received votes from Northern and Southern delegations. With the possibility of a stalemate looming, Douglas withdrew after the 16th ballot. On the 17th roll call, Buchanan received all 296 votes, and the nomination.

On the first ballot for the vice presidency, 11 different individuals received votes. Rep. John A. Quitman of Mississippi led with 59 votes, followed by Rep. John C. Breckinridge of Kentucky, with 50. At the beginning of the second ballot, the New England delegations cast a nearly unanimous vote for Breckinridge, creating a bandwagon effect that resulted in the nomination of the Kentuckian. Ironically, before the vice presidential balloting began, Breckinridge had asked that his name be withdrawn from consideration. Believing himself too young (he was 35), Breckinridge stated that "promotion should follow seniority."

In spite of his earlier demurrer, Breckinridge was in the convention hall and announced his acceptance of the nomination. It marked one of the few times in American political history that a candidate was present for his own nomination.

The party platform was considered in two segments, with the domestic and foreign policy sections debated separately. The theme of the domestic section, as in past platforms, was the Democrats' concept of a limited federal government. The unconstitutionality of a national bank, federal support for internal improvements and distribution of proceeds from the sale of public land were again mentioned.

Nearly one-third of the entire platform was devoted to the slavery question, with support for the various congressional compromise measures stressed. The Democratic position was underscored in a passage that was capitalized in the convention *Proceedings:* "non-interference by Congress with slavery in state and territory, or in the District of Columbia."

In another domestic area, the Democrats denounced the Know-Nothings for being un-American. The convention approved the domestic policy section of the platform by a vote of 261 to 35, with only the New York delegation voting in opposition.

The foreign policy section expressed a nationalistic and expansionist spirit that was absent from previous Democratic platforms.

There were six different foreign policy planks, each voted on separately. The first plank, calling for free trade, passed 210 to 29. The second, favoring implementation of the Monroe Doctrine, passed 240 to 21. The third plank, backing westward continental expansion, was approved 203 to 56. The fourth plank, which expressed sympathy with the people of Central America, grew out of the United States' dispute with Great Britain over control of that area. The plank was approved, 221 to 38. The fifth plank, calling for United States "ascendency in the Gulf of Mexico," passed 229 to 33. A final resolution, presented separately, called for the construction of roads to the Pacific Ocean. The resolution was at first tabled, 154 to 120, and a second vote to reconsider failed, 175 to 121. But when the resolution was raised a third time after the presidential nomination, it passed, 205 to 87.

Following are excerpts from the Democratic platform of 1856:

**Slavery.** That claiming fellowship with, and desiring the co-operation of all who regard the preservation of the Union under the Constitution as the paramount issue — and repudiating all sectional parties and platforms concerning domestic slavery, which seek to embroil the States and incite to treason and armed resistance to law in the Territories; and whose avowed purposes, if consummated, must end in civil war and disunion, the American Democracy recognize and adopt the principles contained in the organic laws establishing the Territories of Kansas and Nebraska as embodying the only sound and safe solution of the "slavery question" upon which the great national idea of the people of this whole country can repose in its determined conservatism of the Union — NON-INTERFERENCE BY CONGRESS WITH SLAVERY IN STATE AND TERRITORY, OR IN THE DISTRICT OF COLUMBIA.

**Know-Nothings.** ...the liberal principles embodied in the Declaration of Independence ... makes ours the land of liberty and the asylum of the oppressed ... every attempt to abridge the privilege of becoming citizens ... ought to be resisted. ...

Since the foregoing declaration was uniformly adopted by our predecessors in National Conventions, an adverse political and religious test has been secretly organized by a party claiming to be exclusively American, it is proper that the American Democracy should clearly define its relation thereto, and declare its determined opposition to all secret political societies, by whatever name they may be called.

**Free Trade.** That there are questions connected with the foreign policy of this country, which are inferior to no domestic question whatever. The time has come for the people of the United States to declare themselves in favor of free seas and progressive free trade. ...

**Latin America.** [W]e should hold as sacred the principles involved in the Monroe Doctrine: their bearing and import admit of no misconstruction; they should be applied with unbending rigidity.

**Gulf of Mexico.** That the Democratic party will expect of the next Administration that every proper effort be made to insure our ascendency in the Gulf of Mexico.

**Transcontinental Roads.** That the Democratic party recognizes the great importance, in a political and commercial point of view, of a safe and speedy communication, by military and postal roads, through our own territory, between the Atlantic and Pacific coasts. ...

## Whigs

On the verge of extinction, the Whig Party held its last national convention in September 1856. Delegates assembled in Baltimore from 21 states and endorsed the Know-Nothing ticket of Fillmore and Donelson.

However, the Whigs adopted their own platform. It avoided specific issues, instead calling for preservation of the Union. The platform criticized both the Democrats and Republicans for appealing to sectional passions and argued for the presidential candidacy of the former Whig, Millard Fillmore.

Following are excerpts from the Whig platform of 1856:

**Preserving the Union.** That the Whigs of the United States are assembled here by reverence for the Constitution, and unalterable attachment to the National Union, and a fixed determination to do all in their power to preserve it for themselves and posterity. They have no new principles to announce — no new platform to establish, but are content broadly to rest where their fathers have rested upon the Constitution of the United States, wishing no safer guide, no higher law.

# 1860 Conventions

## Presidential Candidates

**Stephen A. Douglas**
**Democrat**

**John C. Breckinridge**
**Southern Democrat**

**Abraham Lincoln**
**Republican**

**John Bell**
**Constitutional Union**

### Democrats

Rarely in American history has there been a convention as tumultuous as the one that assembled in Charleston, S.C., in April 1860. The Democrats met at a time when their party was threatened by sectional division, caused by the explosive slavery question. The issue had grown increasingly inflammatory during the 1850s, and, because of rising emotions, the chances of a successful compromise solution decreased.

From the outset of the convention, there was little visible effort to obtain party unity. Parliamentary squabbling with frequent appeals to the chair marked the early sessions. Before the presidential balloting even began, 27 separate roll calls on procedural and platform matters were taken.

A bitter dispute between Northern and Southern delegates over the wording of the platform's slavery plank precipitated a walkout by several dozen Southern delegates. Both the majority and minority reports submitted to the convention called for a reaffirmation of the Democratic platform of 1856. In addition, however, the majority report (favored by the South) declared that no government — local, state or federal — could outlaw slavery in the territories. The minority report took a more moderate position, stating that the decision on allowing slavery in the territories should be left to the Supreme Court.

After a day of debate, the convention agreed, by a vote of 152 to 151, to recommit both reports to the platform committee. Basically, the vote followed sectional lines, with Southern delegates approving recommittal. However, the revised majority and minority reports subsequently presented to the convention were similar to the originals.

An amendment by Benjamin F. Butler of Massachusetts, to endorse the 1856 platform without any mention of slavery, was defeated, 198 to 105. After two procedural roll calls, the delegates voted, 165 to 138, to accept the minority report. The vote followed sectional lines, with the Northern delegates victorious. *(Chart, p. 199)*

Unhappy with the platform and unwilling to accept it, 45 delegates from nine states bolted the convention. The majority of six Southern delegations withdrew (Alabama,

Mississippi, Florida, Texas, South Carolina and Louisiana), along with scattered delegates from three other states (Arkansas, Delaware and North Carolina).

With the size of the convention reduced, chairman Caleb Cushing of Massachusetts made an important decision. He ruled that the two-thirds nominating majority would be based on the total votes allocated (303) rather than the number of delegates present and voting. Although Cushing's ruling was approved by a vote of 141 to 112, it countered precedents established at the 1840 and 1848 Democratic conventions, when the nominating majority was based on those present and voting.

Cushing's ruling made it nearly impossible for any candidate to amass the necessary two-thirds majority. Particularly affected was the front-runner, Sen. Stephen A. Douglas of Illinois, whose standing in the South had diminished with his continued support of popular sovereignty. Douglas moved into a big lead on the first ballot, receiving 145-1/2 votes to 42 for Sen. Robert M. T. Hunter of Virginia and 35-1/2 for James Guthrie of Kentucky. Despite his large lead over the rest of the field, Douglas was well short of the 202 votes needed for nomination and, with his limited sectional appeal, had little chance of gaining the needed delegates.

After three days of balloting and 57 presidential roll calls, the standing of the three candidates had undergone little change. Douglas led with 151-1/2 votes, followed by Guthrie with 65-1/2 and Hunter with 16. The delegates, in session for 10 days and wearied by the presidential deadlock, voted 194-1/2 to 55-1/2 to recess for six weeks and reconvene in Baltimore. This marked the first and only time that a major party adjourned its convention and moved it from one city to another.

Reconvening in Baltimore in June, the delegates were faced with another sticky question: whether or not to seat the delegates who had bolted the Charleston convention. The majority report presented by the credentials committee reviewed each case individually and recommended that the bolting Southern delegates, except those from Alabama and Louisiana, be reseated. The minority report recommended that a larger majority of the withdrawing Charleston delegates be reseated. The minority report was defeated, 150 to 100-1/2. Ten more roll calls followed on various aspects of the credentials dispute, but they did not change the result of the first vote. *(Chart, p. 199)*

The convention vote on credentials produced a new walkout, involving the majority of delegates from Virginia, North Carolina, Tennessee, Maryland, Kentucky, Missouri, Arkansas, California and Oregon, and anti-Douglas delegates from Massachusetts. With the presidential balloting ready to resume, less than two-thirds of the original convention was present.

On the first ballot, Douglas received 173-1/2 of the 190-1/2 votes cast. On the second ballot, his total increased to 190-1/2, but it was obviously impossible for him to gain two-thirds (202) of the votes allocated (303). After the second roll call, a delegate moved that Douglas, having obtained a two-thirds majority of the votes cast, be declared the Democratic presidential nominee. The motion passed unanimously on a voice vote. *(Chart, p. 199)*

The convention left the selection of the vice presidential candidate to a caucus of the remaining Southern delegates. They chose Sen. Benjamin Fitzpatrick of Alabama, who received all 198-1/2 votes cast on the vice presidential roll call.

Shortly after the convention adjourned, Fitzpatrick declined the nomination. For the first time in American history, a national committee was called upon to fill a vacancy on the ticket. By a unanimous vote of committee members, the former governor of Georgia, Herschel V. Johnson, was chosen to be Douglas' running mate.

The Democratic platform, in addition to the controversial slavery plank, provided a reaffirmation of the 1856 platform, with its proposals for a limited federal government but an expansionist foreign policy. The 1860 platform added planks that continued the expansionist spirit, calling for the construction of a transcontinental railroad and acquisition of the island of Cuba.

Following are excerpts from the 1860 Democratic platform:

> **Slavery.** Inasmuch as difference of opinion exists in the Democratic party as to the nature and extent of the powers of a territorial legislature, and as to the powers and duties of Congress, under the Constitution of the United States, over the institution of slavery within the Territories,
>
> *Resolved,* That the Democratic party will abide by the decision of the Supreme Court of the United States upon these questions of Constitutional law.
>
> **Transcontinental Railroad.** That one of the necessities of the age, in a military, commercial, and postal point of view, is speedy communication between the Atlantic and Pacific States; and the Democratic party pledge such Constitutional Government aid as will insure the construction of a Railroad to the Pacific coast, at the earliest practicable period.
>
> **Cuba.** That the Democratic party are in favor of the acquisition of the Island of Cuba on such terms as shall be honorable to ourselves and just to Spain.

## Southern Democrats (Breckinridge Faction)

A small group of Southern delegates that bolted the Charleston convention met in Richmond, Va., in early June. They decided to delay action until after the resumed Democratic convention had concluded. In late June they met in Baltimore with bolters from the regular Democratic convention. There were representatives from 19 states among the more than 200 delegates attending, but most of

the 58 Northern delegates were officeholders in the Buchanan administration. Vice President John C. Breckinridge of Kentucky won the presidential nomination, and Sen. Joseph Lane of Oregon was chosen as his running mate.

The platform adopted by the Southern Democrats was similar to the one approved by the Democratic convention at Charleston. The bolters reaffirmed the Democrats' 1856 platform, which called for the construction of a transcontinental railroad and acquisition of Cuba. But on the controversial slavery issue, the rump assemblage adopted the Southerners' plank defeated at the Charleston convention. The failure to reach agreement on this one issue, the most disruptive sectional split in the history of American political parties, presaged the Civil War.

Following are excerpts from the platform adopted by the Southern (or Breckinridge faction) Democrats in 1860:

> *Resolved,* that the platform adopted by the Democratic party at Cincinnati be affirmed, with the following explanatory resolutions:
>
> 1. That the Government of a Territory organized by an act of Congress is provisional and temporary, and during its existence all citizens of the United States have an equal right to settle with their property in the Territory, without their rights, either of person or property, being destroyed or impaired by Congressional or Territorial legislation.
>
> 2. That it is the duty of the Federal Government, in all its departments, to protect, when necessary, the rights of persons and property in the Territories, and wherever else its constitutional authority extends.

## Republicans

With their major opposition split along sectional lines, the Republicans gathered for their convention in Chicago in a mood of optimism. The Democrats had already broken up at Charleston before the Republican delegates convened in May 1860.

The call for the convention was addressed not only to faithful party members but to other groups that shared the Republicans' dissatisfaction with the policies of the Buchanan administration. The call to the convention particularly emphasized the party's opposition to any extension of slavery into the territories.

Delegates from all the Northern states and the territories of Kansas and Nebraska, the District of Columbia, and the slave states of Maryland, Delaware, Virginia, Kentucky, Missouri and Texas assembled at Chicago's new 10,000-seat convention hall, known as the Wigwam. A carnival-like atmosphere enveloped Chicago, with bands marching through the streets and thousands of enthusiastic Republicans ringing the overcrowded convention hall.

Inside, the delegates' first debate concerned the credentials report. The question was raised whether the represented Southern states should be allocated votes reflecting their electoral college strength, when there were very few Republicans in these states. By a vote of 275-1/2 to 171-1/2, the convention recommitted the credentials report for the purpose of scaling down the vote allocation of the Southern states.

A second debate arose over what constituted a nominating majority. The rules committee recommended that the nominating majority reflect the total electoral vote of all the states in the Union. The minority report argued that, since all the states were not represented, the nominating majority suggested by the rules committee would in fact require nearly a two-thirds majority. The minority report recommended instead that nominations be based on a simple majority of votes allocated for the states represented. The minority report passed, 349-1/2 to 88-1/2.

Sen. William H. Seward of New York was the front-runner for the presidential nomination and led on the first ballot. Seward received 173-1/2 votes to lead runner-up Abraham Lincoln of Illinois, who had 102. Sen. Simon Cameron of Pennsylvania followed with 50-1/2 votes, Salmon P. Chase of Ohio with 49 and Edward Bates of Missouri with 48. *(Chart, p. 200)*

With the packed galleries cheering their native son, Lincoln closed the gap on the second roll call. After two ballots, the voting stood: Seward, 184-1/2; Lincoln, 181; Chase, 42-1/2; Bates, 35. Lincoln, who had gained national prominence two years earlier as a result of his debates on slavery with Democrat Stephen A. Douglas in the 1858 campaign for the U.S. Senate, emerged as the candidate of the anti-Seward forces. On the third ballot, he won the nomination. When the third roll call was completed, Lincoln's vote total stood at 231-1/2, 1-1/2 votes short of a majority. But Ohio quickly shifted four votes to Lincoln, giving him the nomination. After changes by other states, the final vote was Lincoln, 340; Seward, 121-1/2.

The primary contenders for the vice presidential nomination were Sen. Hannibal Hamlin of Maine and Cassius M. Clay of Kentucky. Hamlin assumed a strong lead on the first ballot, receiving 194 votes to 100-1/2 for Clay. On the second roll call, an increased vote for Hamlin from states in his native New England created a bandwagon for the Maine senator. Hamlin won the nomination on the second ballot with 367 votes, far outdistancing Clay, who received 86. After the roll call was completed, Hamlin's nomination was declared unanimous.

About half of the platform adopted by the Republican convention dealt with the slavery question. Unlike the Democrats, the Republicans clearly opposed the extension of slavery into the territories. However, the Republican platform also expressed support for states' rights, which served as a rebuke to radical abolitionism.

The Republican and Democratic platforms again were opposed on the question of internal improvements. The Republicans supported river and harbor improvements, while the Democrats, by reaffirming their 1856 platform, opposed any federal support for internal improvements. Both parties favored construction of a transcontinental railroad and opposed restrictions on immigration.

However, on two major issues, the Republicans went beyond the Democrats, advocating a protective tariff and homestead legislation.

Following are excerpts from the 1860 Republican platform:

**Slavery.** That the new dogma that the Constitution, of its own force, carries slavery into any or all of the territories of the United States, is a dangerous political heresy, at variance with the explicit provisions of that instrument itself, with contemporaneous exposition, and with legislative and judicial precedent; is revolutionary in its tendency, and subversive of the peace and harmony of the country.

That the normal condition of all the territory of the United States is that of freedom. . . . we deny the authority of Congress, of a territorial legislature, or of any individuals, to give legal existence to slavery in any territory of the United States.

**States' Rights.** That the maintenance inviolate of the rights of the states, and especially the right of each state to order and control its own domestic institutions according to its own judgment exclusively, is essential to that balance of powers on which the perfection and endurance of our political fabric depends; and we denounce the lawless invasion by armed force of the soil of any state or territory, no matter under what pretext, as among the gravest of crimes.

**Tariff.** That, while providing revenue for the support of the general government by duties upon imports, sound policy requires such an adjustment of these imports as to encourage the development of the industrial interests of the whole country.

**Transcontinental Railroad.** That a railroad to the Pacific Ocean is imperatively demanded by the interests of the whole country; that the federal government ought to render immediate and efficient aid in its construction; and that, as preliminary thereto, a daily overland mail should be promptly established.

## Constitutional Union

At the invitation of a group of Southern Know-Nothing congressmen, the remnants of the 1856 Fillmore campaign, conservative Whigs and Know-Nothings, met in Baltimore in May 1860 to form the Constitutional Union Party.

The chief rivals for the presidential nomination were former Sen. John Bell of Tennessee and Gov. Sam Houston of Texas. Bell won on the second ballot, and Edward Everett of Massachusetts was selected as his running mate.

The Constitutional Union Party saw itself as a national unifying force in a time of crisis. The brief platform did not discuss issues, instead denouncing the sectionalism of the existing parties and calling for national unity.

Following are excerpts from the 1860 Constitutional Union platform:

*Whereas,* Experience has demonstrated that Platforms adopted by the partisan Conventions of the country have had the effect to mislead and deceive the people, and at the same time to widen the political divisions of the country, by the creation and encouragement of geographical and sectional parties; therefore

*Resolved,* that it is both the part of patriotism and of duty to *recognize* no political principle other than THE CONSTITUTION OF THE COUNTRY, THE UNION OF THE STATES, AND THE ENFORCEMENT OF THE LAWS.

# 1864 Conventions

## Presidential Candidates

**Abraham Lincoln**
**Republican**

**George McClellan**
**Democrat**

### Republicans (Union Party)

Although elements in the Republican Party were dissatisfied with the conduct of the Civil War, President Lincoln was in firm control of his party's convention, which met in Baltimore in June 1864. As with previous Republican conventions, the call was not limited to the party faithful. Democrats in support of the Lincoln war policy were encouraged to attend, and the name "Union Party" was used to describe the wartime coalition.

Delegates were present from all the Northern states, the territories, the District of Columbia and the slave states of Arkansas, Florida, Louisiana, Tennessee, South Carolina and Virginia. Credentials disputes occupied the early sessions. The credentials committee recommended that all the Southern states except South Carolina be admitted, but denied the right to vote. A minority report, advocating voting privileges for the Tennessee delegation, was passed, 310 to 151. A second minority report favoring voting privileges for Arkansas and Louisiana was approved, 307 to 167. However, the credentials committee recommendation that Florida and Virginia be denied voting rights, and South Carolina be excluded entirely, were accepted without a roll call.

Although dissatisfaction with the administration's war policy had spawned opposition to Lincoln, the boomlets for such presidential hopefuls as Treasury Secretary Salmon P. Chase had petered out by convention time. The Lincoln forces controlled the convention, and the president was easily renominated on the first ballot. Lincoln received 494 of the 516 votes cast, losing only Missouri's 22 votes, which were committed to Gen. Ulysses S. Grant. After the roll call, Missouri moved that the vote be made unanimous.

Lincoln did not publicly declare his preference for a vice presidential running mate, leaving the selection to the convention. The main contenders included the incumbent vice president, Hannibal Hamlin of Maine; the former senator and military governor of Tennessee, Democrat Andrew Johnson; and former senator Daniel S. Dickinson of New York. Johnson led on the first ballot with 200 votes, followed by Hamlin with 150 and Dickinson with 108. After completion of the roll call, a switch to Johnson by the

Kentucky delegation ignited a surge to the Tennessean that delivered him 492 votes and the nomination.

The Republican (Union) platform was approved without debate. Unlike the Democrats, who criticized the war effort and called for a quick, negotiated peace, the Republicans favored a vigorous prosecution of the war until the South surrendered unconditionally. The Republicans called for the eradication of slavery, with its elimination embodied in a constitutional amendment.

Although the Republican document focused on the Civil War, it also included planks encouraging immigration, urging the speedy construction of a transcontinental railroad and reaffirming the Monroe Doctrine.

Following are excerpts from the Republican (Union) platform of 1864:

> *Resolved* ... we pledge ourselves, as Union men, animated by a common sentiment and aiming at a common object, to do everything in our power to aid the Government in quelling by force of arms the Rebellion now raging against its authority, and in bringing to the punishment due to their crimes the Rebels and traitors arrayed against it.
>
> *Resolved,* That we approve the determination of the Government of the United States not to compromise with Rebels, or to offer them any terms of peace, except such as may be based upon an unconditional surrender of their hostility and a return to their just allegiance to the Constitution and laws of the United States, and that we call upon the Government to maintain this position and to prosecute the war with the utmost possible vigor to the complete suppression of the Rebellion, in full reliance upon the self-sacrificing patriotism, the heroic valor and the undying devotion of the American people to the country and its free institutions.
>
> *Resolved,* That as slavery was the cause, and now constitutes the strength of this Rebellion, and as it must be, always and everywhere, hostile to the principles of Republican Government, justice and the National safety demand its utter and complete extirpation from the soil of the Republic ... we are in favor, furthermore, of such an amendment to the Constitution, to be made by the people in conformity with its provisions, as shall terminate and forever prohibit the existence of Slavery within the limits of the jurisdiction of the United States.

*Resolved,* That the thanks of the American people are due to the soldiers and sailors of the Army and Navy, who have periled their lives in defense of the country and in vindication of the honor of its flag.

## Democrats

The Democrats originally scheduled their convention for early summer but postponed it until late August to gauge the significance of military developments.

The party, badly split during the 1860 campaign, no longer had the Southern faction with which to contend. But while there was no longer a regional split, new divisions arose over the continuing war. There was a large peace faction, known as the Copperheads, that favored a quick, negotiated peace with the South. Another faction supported the war but criticized its handling by the Lincoln administration. A third faction supported Lincoln's conduct of the war and defected to support the Republican president.

Although factionalized, the Democratic delegates who assembled in Chicago were optimistic about their party's chances. The war-weary nation, they thought, was ready to vote out the Lincoln administration if there was not a quick change in Northern military fortunes.

Although the border states were represented at the Democratic convention, the territories and seceded Southern states were not. In spite of the party's internal divisions, there was little opposition to the presidential candidacy of Gen. George B. McClellan of New Jersey. The former commander of the Union Army won on the first ballot, receiving 174 of the 226 votes cast. Former governor Thomas H. Seymour of Connecticut trailed with 38 votes. A switch to McClellan by several Ohio delegates prompted shifts by other delegations and brought his total to 202-1/2. Clement Vallandigham, a leader of the Copperhead faction, moved that McClellan's nomination be made unanimous.

Eight candidates were placed in nomination for the vice presidency. James Guthrie of Kentucky led Rep. George H. Pendleton of Ohio, the favorite of the Copperheads, on the first ballot, 65-1/2 to 55. However, shifts to Pendleton by Illinois, Kentucky and New York after completion of the roll call created a bandwagon that led quickly to his unanimous nomination. In the convention hall at the time of his selection, Pendleton made a short speech of acceptance.

The platform adopted by the Democrats reflected the views of the Copperhead faction. The Lincoln administration's conduct of the Civil War was denounced, with particular criticism of the use of martial law and the abridgement of state and civil rights. The platform called for an immediate end to hostilities and a negotiated peace. The "sympathy" of the party was extended to soldiers and sailors involved in the war. Besides a criticism of the war and its conduct by the Lincoln administration, there were no other issues discussed in the platform.

Following are excerpts from the Democratic platform of 1864:

*Resolved,* That this convention does explicitly declare, as the sense of the American people, that after four years of failure to restore the Union by the experiment of war, during which, under the pretense of a military necessity of war-power higher than the Constitution, the Constitution itself has been disregarded in every part, and public liberty and private right alike trodden down, and the material prosperity of the country essentially impaired, justice, humanity, liberty, and the public welfare demand that immediate efforts be made for a cessation of hostilities, with a view of an ultimate convention of the States, or other peaceable means, to the end that, at the earliest practicable moment, peace may be restored on the basis of the Federal Union of the States.

*Resolved,* That the sympathy of the Democratic party is heartily and earnestly extended to the soldiery of our army and sailors of our navy, who are and have been in the field and on the sea under the flag of our country, and, in the events of its attaining power, they will receive all the care, protection, and regard that the brave soldiers and sailors of the republic have so nobly earned.

# 1868 Conventions
## Presidential Candidates

**Ulysses S. Grant**
**Republican**

**Horatio Seymour**
**Democrat**

### Republicans

The "National Union Republican Party," as the political organization was termed in its platform, held its first postwar convention in Chicago in May 1868. Delegations from the states of the old Confederacy were accepted; several included blacks.

The turbulent nature of postwar politics was evident in the fact that Gen. Ulysses S. Grant, the clear front-runner for the Republican nomination, had been considered a possible contender for the Democratic nomination barely a year earlier. Less than six months before the convention, the basically apolitical Grant had broken with Andrew Johnson, who had become president following the assassination of Abraham Lincoln in 1865.

Grant's was the only name placed in nomination, and on the ensuing roll call he received all 650 votes.

While the presidential race was cut and dried, the balloting for vice president was wide open, with 11 candidates receiving votes on the initial roll call. Sen. Benjamin F. Wade of Ohio led on the first ballot with 147 votes, followed by Gov. Reuben E. Fenton of New York with 126, Sen. Henry Wilson of Massachusetts with 119 and Speaker of the House Schuyler Colfax of Indiana with 115.

Over the next four ballots, Wade and Colfax were the front-runners, with Colfax finally moving ahead on the fifth ballot. His lead over Wade at this point was only 226 to 207, but numerous vote shifts after the roll call quickly pushed the Indiana representative over the top and gave him the nomination. After all the vote changes, Colfax's total stood at 541, followed by Fenton with 69 and Wade with 38.

Not surprisingly, the platform adopted by the Republicans differed sharply with the Democrats over reconstruction and Johnson's presidency. The Republican platform applauded the radical reconstruction program passed by Congress and denounced Johnson as "treacherous" and deserving of impeachment. The Republican platform approved of voting rights for black men in the South but determined that this was a subject for each state to decide in the rest of the nation.

The two parties also differed on their response to the currency question. While the Democrats favored a "soft-money" policy, the Republicans supported a continued "hard-money" approach, rejecting the Democratic proposal that the economic crisis could be eased by an increased supply of greenbacks.

Following are excerpts from the Republican platform of 1868:

> **Reconstruction.** We congratulate the country on the assured success of the reconstruction policy of Congress, as evinced by the adoption, in the majority of the States lately in rebellion, of constitutions securing equal civil and political rights to all, and regard it as the duty of the Government to sustain those constitutions, and to prevent the people of such States from being remitted to a state of anarchy or military rule.
>
> The guaranty by Congress of equal suffrage to all loyal men at the South was demanded by every consideration of public safety, of gratitude, and of justice, and must be maintained; while the question of suffrage in all the loyal States properly belongs to the people of those States.
>
> **President Andrew Johnson.** We profoundly deplore the untimely and tragic death of Abraham Lincoln, and regret the accession of Andrew Johnson to the Presidency, who has acted treacherously to the people who elected him and the cause he was pledged to support; has usurped high legislative and judicial functions; has refused to execute the laws; has used his high office to induce other officers to ignore and violate the laws; has employed his executive powers to render insecure the property, the peace, the liberty, and life of the citizen; has abused the pardoning power; has denounced the National Legislature as unconstitutional; has persistently and corruptly resisted, by every means in his power, every proper attempt at the reconstruction of the States lately in rebellion; has perverted the public patronage into an engine of wholesale corruption; and has been justly impeached for high crimes and misdemeanors, and properly pronounced guilty thereof by the vote of thirty-five senators.
>
> **Currency.** We denounce all forms of repudiation as a national crime; and national honor requires the payment of the public indebtedness in the utmost good faith to all creditors at home and abroad, not only according to the letter, but the spirit of the laws under which it was contracted.

## Democrats

Reunited after the Civil War, the Democratic Party held its first postwar convention in New York's newly constructed Tammany Hall. It was no accident that convention proceedings began on July 4, 1868. The Democratic National Committee had set the date, and its chairman, August Belmont of New York, opened the first session with a harsh criticism of Republican reconstruction policy and the abridgement of civil rights.

Delegates from Southern states were voting members of the convention, but an effort to extend representation to the territories was defeated, 184 to 106.

Before the presidential balloting began, the convention chairman ruled that, as at the 1860 Charleston assembly, a nominating majority would be based on two-thirds of the total votes allocated (317) and not votes cast. On the opening ballot, the party's vice presidential candidate four years earlier, George H. Pendleton of Ohio, took the lead. Pendleton, although popular in the economically depressed Midwest because of his plan to inflate the currency by printing more greenbacks, had little appeal in the Eastern states. Nonetheless, he led on the first ballot with 105 votes. President Andrew Johnson was next, with 65 votes. Johnson's vote was largely complimentary and declined after the first roll call. Pendleton, however, showed increased strength, rising to a peak of 156-1/2 votes on the eighth ballot. But Pendleton's total was well short of the 212 votes required to nominate, and his total steadily decreased after the eighth roll call. *(Chart, p. 202)*

The collapse of the Pendleton and Johnson candidacies produced a boom for Gen. Winfield Scott Hancock of Pennsylvania. Opponents of Hancock attempted to break his surge by calling for adjournment after the 16th ballot. Although the move for adjournment was defeated, 174-1/2 to 142-1/2, the Hancock boom began to lose momentum. The Civil War general peaked at 144-1/2 votes on the 18th ballot, well short of a two-thirds majority.

With Hancock stymied, a new contender, Sen. Thomas A. Hendricks of Indiana, gained strength. Hendricks' vote rose to 132 on the 21st ballot, and the trend to the Indiana senator continued on the 22nd ballot until the roll call reached Ohio. However, Ohio shifted its entire vote to Horatio Seymour, the permanent chairman of the convention and a former governor of New York. Seymour declined to be a candidate, and so announced to the convention, but Ohio did not change its vote, and friends of Seymour hustled the reluctant candidate from the hall. The bandwagon had begun, and when the vote switches were completed, Seymour had received all 317 votes.

The vice presidential nomination went to Gen. Francis P. Blair Jr. of Missouri, a former Republican, who was unanimously selected on the first ballot. The names of several other candidates were placed in nomination, but the announcement of Blair's candidacy created a bandwagon that led to the withdrawal of the others.

The Democratic platform was accepted by a voice vote without debate. The platform began by declaring the questions of slavery and secession to be permanently settled by the Civil War. Several planks criticized the Republican reconstruction program, passed by the party's Radical wing in Congress. The Radicals themselves were scathingly denounced for their "unparalleled oppression and tyranny." The Democratic platform expressed its support for Andrew Johnson's conduct as president and decried the attempts to impeach him.

For the first time, the question of the coinage and printing of money was discussed in the party platform. Two planks were included that could be generally interpreted as supporting Pendleton's inflationary greenback plan.

On the tariff issue, the Democrats called for a tariff that would primarily raise revenue but also protect American industry.

Following are excerpts from the Democratic platform of 1868:

**Reconstruction.** . . .we arraign the Radical party for its disregard of right, and the unparalleled oppression and tyranny which have marked its career.

Instead of restoring the Union, it has, so far as in its power, dissolved it, and subjected ten States, in time of profound peace, to military despotism and negro supremacy.

**President Andrew Johnson.** That the President of the United States, Andrew Johnson, in exercising the power of his high office in resisting the aggressions of Congress upon the Constitutional rights of the States and the people, is entitled to the gratitude of the whole American people; and in behalf of the Democratic party, we tender him our thanks for his patriotic efforts in that regard.

**Currency.** . . .where the obligations of the government do not expressly state upon their face, or the law under which they were issued does not provide, that they shall be paid in coin, they ought, in right and in justice, to be paid in the lawful money of the United States. . . . One currency for the government and the people, the laborer and the officeholder, the pensioner and the soldier, the producer and the bond-holder.

# 1872 Conventions
## Presidential Candidates

**Horace Greeley**
**Liberal Republican, Democrat**

**Ulysses S. Grant**
**Republican**

### Liberal Republicans

The short-lived Liberal Republican Party grew out of grievances that elements in the Republican Party had with the policies of the Grant administration. There was particular dissatisfaction with the "carpetbag" governments in the South, support for extensive civil service reform and a general distaste for the corrupt administration of President Ulysses S. Grant.

The idea for the Liberal Republican movement originated in Missouri, where, in the 1870 state elections, a coalition of reform Republicans and Democrats swept to victory. In January 1872 a state convention of this new coalition issued the call for a national convention to be held that May in Cincinnati, Ohio.

Without a formal, nationwide organization, the delegate selection process was haphazard. Some of the delegates were self-appointed, but generally the size of each delegation reflected twice a state's electoral vote.

Three separate groups — reformers, anti-Grant politicians and a coalition of four influential newspaper editors known as "the Quadrilateral" — vied for control of the convention. For the presidential nomination, the reformers favored either Charles Francis Adams of Massachusetts or Sen. Lyman Trumbull of Illinois. The professional politicians were inclined to Supreme Court Justice David Davis of Illinois or Horace Greeley of New York. The newspaper editors opposed Davis.

On the first ballot, Adams led with 203 votes, followed by Greeley with 147, Trumbull with 110, Gov. B. Gratz Brown of Missouri with 95 and Davis with 92-1/2. After the roll call, Brown announced his withdrawal from the race and his support for Greeley. For the next five ballots, Greeley and Adams battled for the lead. But on the sixth ballot, the professional politicians were able to ignite a stampede for Greeley that resulted in his nomination.

Many of the reform-minded delegates, disgusted with the selection of the New York editor, left the convention. The vice presidential nomination went on the second ballot to a Greeley supporter, Gov. Brown of Missouri.

The platform adopted by the Liberal Republicans differed with the one later accepted by the Republicans on three main points: reconstruction, civil service reform and the tariff.

The Liberal Republicans called for an end to reconstruction with its "carpetbag" governments, a grant of universal amnesty to southern citizens and a return to home rule in the South. The Liberal Republicans sharply criticized the corruption of civil service under the Grant administration and labeled its reform one of the leading issues of the day. The civil service plank advocated a one-term limit on the presidency.

The presence of delegates supporting both protection and free trade led to a tariff plank that frankly stated the party's position on the issue should be left to local determination.

Following are excerpts from the Liberal Republican platform of 1872:

**Reconstruction.** We demand the immediate and absolute removal of all disabilities imposed on account of the Rebellion, which was finally subdued seven years ago, believing that universal amnesty will result in complete pacification in all sections of the country.

Local self-government, with impartial suffrage, will guard the rights of all citizens more securely than any centralized power. The public welfare requires the supremacy of the civil over the military authority, and freedom of person under the protection of the *habeas corpus.*

**Civil Rights.** We recognize the equality of all men before the law, and hold that it is the duty of Government in its dealings with the people to mete out equal and exact justice to all of whatever nativity, race, color, or persuasion, religious or political.

**Civil Service Reform.** The Civil Service of the Government has become a mere instrument of partisan tyranny and personal ambition and an object of selfish greed. It is a scandal and reproach upon free institutions and breeds a demoralization dangerous to the perpetuity of republican government. We therefore regard such thorough reforms of the Civil Service as one of the most pressing necessities of the hour; that honesty, capacity, and fidelity constitute the only valid claim to public employment; that the offices of the Government cease to be a matter of arbitrary favoritism and patronage, and that public station become again a post of honor. To this end it is imperatively required that no President shall be a candidate for re-election.

**Tariff.** . . . recognizing that there are in our midst honest but irreconcilable differences of opinion with regard to the respective systems of Protection and Free Trade, we remit the discussion of the subject to the people in their Congress Districts, and to the decision of Congress thereon, wholly free of Executive interference or dictation.

**Homesteading.** We are opposed to all further grants of lands to railroads or other corporations. The public domain should be held sacred to actual settlers.

## Democrats

The Democratic convention that met in Baltimore in July 1872 was one of the most bizarre in American political history. In sessions totaling only six hours, the delegates endorsed the decisions on candidates and platform made at a convention one month earlier by the Liberal Republicans. The Democratic convention merely rubber-stamped the creation of a coalition of Liberal Republicans and the core of the Democratic Party. *(Chart, p. 204)*

This new coalition was established with little dissent. When it came time for the presidential balloting, nominating speeches were not allowed. On the subsequent roll call, Greeley, the nominee of the Liberal Republicans, received 686 of the allotted 732 votes. It was an ironic choice, because in earlier decades Greeley, as editor of *The New York Tribune,* had been a frequent critic of the Democratic Party. More than anything else, however, Greeley's selection underscored the lack of strong leadership in the post-Civil War Democratic Party.

In similar fashion, the convention endorsed the nomination of B. Gratz Brown for vice president. Brown, the governor of Missouri and the choice of the Liberal Republicans, was the early unanimous nominee of the Democrats, with 713 votes.

By a vote of 574 to 158, the delegates agreed to limit debate on the platform to one hour. Except for a brief introduction, the Democrats approved the same platform that had been adopted by the Liberal Republicans a month earlier. Key planks called for an end to reconstruction and complete amnesty for Southern citizens, a return to a federal government with limited powers, civil service reform and the halt of grants of public land to railroads and other corporations. Ironically, the platform also favored a hard-money policy, a reversal of the Democrats' soft-money stand in 1868. Although there was some objection to the point-by-point acceptance of the Liberal Republican platform, it was adopted by a vote of 671 to 62. *(For platform excerpts, see the Liberal Republicans section, p. 56)*

## Republicans

With the reform wing of the Republican Party already having bolted, the remaining elements of the party gathered in relative harmony in Philadelphia in June 1872. President Ulysses S. Grant was renominated without opposition, receiving all 752 votes cast. *(Chart, p. 204)*

The only contest at the convention centered around the vice presidential nomination, with the incumbent, Schuyler Colfax of Indiana, and Sen. Henry Wilson of Massachusetts the two major rivals. Wilson took a slim plurality over Colfax on the first roll call, 364-1/2 to 321-1/2, but a vote shift by Virginia after completion of the roll gave Wilson the necessary majority with 399-1/2 votes.

Without debate or opposition, the platform was adopted. It lauded the 11 years of Republican rule, noting the success of reconstruction, the hard-money policy and the homestead program. A tariff plank called for a duty on imports to raise revenue as well as to protect American business.

The platform also included several progressive planks, including a recommendation that the franking privilege be abolished, an extension of rights to women and a call for federal and state legislation that would ensure equal rights for all races throughout the nation. The last plank was a significant change from the 1868 platform, which called for black suffrage in the South but left the decision on black voting rights to the individual states elsewhere.

Following are excerpts from the Republican platform of 1872:

**Reconstruction.** We hold that Congress and the President have only fulfilled an imperative duty in their measures for the suppression of violent and treasonable organizations in certain lately rebellious regions, and for the protection of the ballot-box, and therefore they are entitled to the thanks of the nation.

**Civil Rights.** Complete liberty and exact equality in the enjoyment of all civil, political, and public rights should be established and effectually maintained throughout the Union, by efficient and appropriate State and Federal legislation. Neither the law nor its administration should admit any discrimination in respect of citizens by reason of race, creed, color, or previous condition of servitude.

**Civil Service Reform.** Any system of the civil service under which the subordinate positions of the government are considered rewards for mere party zeal is fatally demoralizing, and we therefore favor a reform of the system by laws which shall abolish the evils of patronage, and make honesty, efficiency, and fidelity the essential qualifications for public positions, without practically creating a life-tenure of office.

**Tariff.** . . . revenue . . . should be raised by duties upon importations, the details of which should be so adjusted as to aid in securing remunerative wages to labor, and to promote the industries, prosperity, and growth of the whole country.

**Homesteading.** We are opposed to further grants of the public lands to corporations and monopolies, and demand that the national domain be set apart for free homes for the people.

**Women's Rights.** The Republican party is mindful of its obligations to the loyal women of America for their noble devotion to the cause of freedom. Their admission to wider fields of usefulness is viewed with satisfaction, and the honest demand of any class of citizens for additional rights should be treated with respectful consideration.

# 1876 Conventions
## Presidential Candidates

**Rutherford B. Hayes**
**Republican**

**Samuel J. Tilden**
**Democrat**

### Republicans

The Republican convention assembled in Cincinnati, Ohio, in mid-June 1876. The call to the convention extended the olive branch to the dissident Liberal Republicans, who in large measure had rejoined their original party.

One of the highlights of the early sessions was a speech by the prominent black leader Frederick Douglass, who lambasted the Republicans for freeing the slaves without providing means for their economic or physical security.

A dispute developed over the seating of two contesting Alabama delegations. It was a candidate-oriented dispute, with the majority report favoring a delegation strongly for House Speaker James G. Blaine of Maine. The minority report supported a delegation pledged to Sen. Oliver P. Morton of Indiana. In the subsequent roll call, the convention decided in favor of the Blaine delegation by a vote of 369 to 360.

The presidential race was contested by the champions of the three nearly equal wings of the party. The Radicals were led by senators Roscoe Conkling of New York and Morton; the Half-Breeds, by Blaine; and the reformers, by former treasury secretary Benjamin H. Bristow of Kentucky.

A fiery nominating speech for Blaine, delivered by Col. Robert G. Ingersoll, referred to the House Speaker as the "plumed knight," an appellation that stuck with Blaine the rest of his political career. Although it was a compelling speech, its effect was reduced by a failure in the hall's lighting system, which forced an early adjournment.

Nonetheless, when balloting commenced the next morning, Blaine had a wide lead, receiving 285 votes on the first ballot, compared with 124 for Morton, 113 for Bristow and 99 for Conkling. *(Chart, p. 206)*

In the middle of the second ballot, a procedural dispute arose over the legality of the unit rule. Three delegates in the Pennsylvania delegation wished to vote for another candidate and appealed to the chair. The chair ruled that their votes should be counted, even though Pennsylvania was bound by the state convention to vote as a unit. The ruling of the chair was upheld on a voice vote, but subsequent debate brought a roll call on reconsidering

the decision. The motion to reconsider passed, 381 to 359. However, by a margin of 395 to 353, another roll call upheld the power of the convention chairman to abolish the unit rule.

Although the vote had long-range significance for future Republican conventions, in the short run it provided a slight boost for Blaine, who gained several delegates in Pennsylvania. On the next four ballots, Blaine retained his large lead but could not come close to the necessary 379 votes needed for nomination. The only candidate to show increased strength was Gov. Rutherford B. Hayes of Ohio, who jumped from 68 votes on the fourth roll call to 104 on the fifth.

On the sixth ballot, however, Blaine showed renewed strength, rising to 308 votes, while Hayes assumed second place with 113. The House Speaker continued to gain on the seventh ballot, but the anti-Blaine forces quickly and successfully united behind Hayes. The Ohio governor, a viable compromise choice who had not alienated any of the party factions, won the nomination with 384 votes to 351 for Blaine.

Five candidates were placed in nomination for the vice presidency. However, Rep. William A. Wheeler of New York was so far in the lead that the roll call was suspended after South Carolina voted, and Wheeler was declared the nominee by acclamation.

Platform debate centered on the party's immigration plank. A Massachusetts delegate proposed deletion of the plank, which called for a congressional investigation of oriental immigration. The delegate argued that the plank was inconsistent with the Republican principle that favored the equality of all races. However, by a vote of 518 to 229, the plank was retained as written.

The Republican platform included a scathing denunciation of the Democratic Party, but only on the issues of currency and tariff was it markedly different from the opposition. The Republicans, unlike the Democrats, favored complete payment of Civil War bonds in hard money as quickly as possible. While the Democrats supported a tariff for revenue purposes only, the Republicans implied that the tariff should protect American industry as well as raise revenue.

As in past platforms, the Republicans called for the extension of civil rights, civil service reform, increased rights for women, the abolition of polygamy and the distribution of public land to homesteaders. A new plank proposed that a constitutional amendment be passed forbidding the use of federal funds for non-public schools.

Following are excerpts from the Republican platform of 1876:

**Currency.** In the first act of congress, signed by President Grant, the national government ... solemnly pledged its faith "to make provisions at the earliest practicable period, for the redemption of the United States notes in coin." Commercial prosperity, public morals, and the national credit demand that this promise be fulfilled by a continuous and steady progress to specie payment.

**Tariff.** The revenue necessary for current expenditures and the obligations of the public debt must be largely derived from duties upon importations, which, so far as possible, should be so adjusted as to promote the interests of American labor and advance the prosperity of the whole country.

**Immigration.** It is the immediate duty of congress fully to investigate the effects of the immigration and importation of Mongolians on the moral and material interests of the country.

**Education.** The public school system of the several states is the bulwark of the American republic; and, with a view to its security and permanence, we recommend an amendment to the constitution of the United States, forbidding the application of any public funds or property for the benefit of any school or institution under sectarian control.

**Democratic Party.** We therefore note with deep solicitude that the Democratic party counts, as its chief hope of success, upon the electoral vote of a united South, secured through the efforts of those who were recently arrayed against the nation; and we invoke the earnest attention of the country to the grave truth, that a success thus achieved would reopen sectional strife and imperil national honor and human rights.

We charge the Democratic party with being the same in character and spirit as when it sympathized with treason; with making its control of the house of representatives the triumph and opportunity of the nation's recent foes; with reasserting and applauding in the national capitol the sentiments of unrepentant rebellion; with sending Union soldiers to the rear, and promoting Confederate soldiers to the front; with deliberately proposing to repudiate the plighted faith of the government; with being equally false and imbecile upon the over-shadowing financial question; with thwarting the ends of justice, by its partisan mismanagements and obstruction of investigation; with proving itself, through the period of its ascendency in the lower house of Congress, utterly incompetent to administer the government; — and we warn the country against trusting a party thus alike unworthy, recreant, and incapable.

## Democrats

America's rapid westward expansion was typified by the site of the Democratic Party's 1876 convention — St. Louis, Mo. It marked the first time that a national convention was held west of the Mississippi River.

The Democratic delegates assembled in late June. The one procedural matter debated was a proposal that the two-thirds rule be abolished at the 1880 convention and that the Democratic National Committee include such a recommendation in its next convention call. A move to table the proposal was defeated, 379 to 359. However, the national committee took no action on the proposal.

Two governors, Samuel J. Tilden of New York and Thomas A. Hendricks of Indiana, were the principal contenders for the presidential nomination, with Tilden having a substantial lead in delegates as the convention opened. Ironically, Tilden's most vocal opposition came from his own New York delegation, where John Kelly of Tammany Hall spearheaded an effort to undermine Tilden's candidacy. Tilden's reform moves as governor had alienated Tammany Hall, and several times during the convention, Kelly took the floor to denounce Tilden.

Nonetheless, Tilden had a substantial lead on the first ballot, receiving 401-1/2 votes to 140-1/2 for Hendricks. Although short of the 492 votes needed to nominate, Tilden moved closer when Missouri switched its votes to him after the first roll call. The movement to Tilden continued on the second ballot, and he finished the roll call with 535 votes, more than enough to assure his nomination. *(Chart, p. 205)*

Hendricks, the runner-up for the presidential nomination, was the nearly unanimous choice of the delegates for the vice presidency. Hendricks received 730 votes, with the other eight votes not being cast.

The Democratic platform was an unusual one. Rather than being arranged in usual fashion with a series of numbered planks, it was written in paragraph form in language unusually powerful for a party platform. The theme of the document was the need for reform, and nearly half the paragraphs began with the phrase, "Reform is necessary...."

Debate focused on the party's stand on the currency issue. The majority report proposed repeal of the Resumption Act of 1875, a hard-money measure that called for the payment of Civil War bonds in coin. A minority report sponsored by delegates from five eastern states proposing deletion of this position was defeated, 550 to 219. A second minority report, introduced by Midwestern delegates, favored a more strongly worded opposition to the Resumption Act. It too was defeated, 505 to 229, with Midwestern delegations providing the bulk of the minority vote. The platform as a whole was approved, 651 to 83, again with most of the dissenting votes coming from the Midwest.

Besides the currency proposal, the platform called for extensive civil service reform, a tariff for revenue purposes only, restrictions on Chinese immigration and a new policy on the distribution of public land that would benefit the homesteaders and not the railroads. In addition to its reform theme, the platform was filled with sharp criticisms of Republican rule.

Following are excerpts from the Democratic platform of 1876:

**Civil Service Reform.** Reform is necessary in the civil service. Experience proves that efficient economical conduct of the government is not possible if its civil service be subject to change at every election, be a prize fought for at the ballot-box, be an approved reward of party zeal instead of posts of honor assigned for proved competency and held for fidelity in the public employ; that the dispensing of patronage should neither be a tax upon the time of our public men nor an instrument of their ambition. Here again, profession falsified in the performance attest that the party in power can work out no practical or salutary reform. Reform is necessary even more in the higher grades of the public service. President, Vice-President, judges, senators, representatives, cabinet officers — these and all others in authority are the people's servants. Their offices are not a private perquisite; they are a public trust. When the annals of this Republic show disgrace and censure of a Vice-

President; a late Speaker of the House of Representatives marketing his rulings as a presiding officer; three Senators profiting secretly by their votes as law-makers; five chairmen of the leading committees of the late House of Representatives exposed in jobbery; a late Secretary of the Treasury forcing balances in the public accounts; a late Attorney-General misappropriating public funds; a Secretary of the Navy enriched and enriching friends by a percentage levied off the profits of contractors with his department; an Ambassador to England censured in a dishonorable speculation; the President's Private Secretary barely escaping conviction upon trial for guilty complicity in frauds upon the revenue; a Secretary of War impeached for high crimes and misdemeanors — the demonstration is complete, that the first step in reform must be the people's choice of honest men from another party, lest the disease of one political organization infect the body politic, and lest by making no change of men or parties, we get no change of measures and no real reform.

**Currency.** We denounce the improvidence which, in eleven years of peace, has taken from the people in Federal taxes thirteen times the whole amount of the legal-tender notes and squandered four times their sum in useless expense, without accumulating any reserve for their redemption. We denounce the financial imbecility and immorality of that party, which, during eleven years of peace, has made no advance toward resumption, no preparation for resumption, but instead has obstructed resumption by wasting our resources and exhausting all our surplus income, and while annually professing to intend a speedy return to specie payments, has annually enacted fresh hindrances thereto. As such hindrance we denounce the resumption clause of the act of 1875 and we here demand its repeal.

**Tariff.** We denounce the present tariff levied upon nearly four thousand articles as a masterpiece of injustice, inequality and false pretense, which yields a dwindling and not a yearly rising revenue, has impoverished many industries to subsidize a few.... We demand that all customhouse taxation shall be only for revenue.

**Homesteading.** Reform is necessary to put a stop to the profligate waste of public lands and their diversion from actual settlers by the party in power, which has squandered two hundred millions of acres upon railroads alone, and out of more than thrice that aggregate has disposed of less than a sixth directly to the tillers of the soil.

**Immigration.** ... we denounce the policy which thus discards the liberty-loving German and tolerates the revival of the coolie-trade in Mongolian women for immoral purposes, and Mongolian men held to perform servile labor contracts, and demand such modification of the treaty with the Chinese Empire, or such legislation within constitutional limitations, as shall prevent further importation or immigration of the Mongolian race.

# 1880 Conventions

## Presidential Candidates

**James A. Garfield**
**Republican**

**James B. Weaver**
**Greenback**

**Winfield Hancock**
**Democrat**

### Republicans

The Republicans gathered in Chicago beginning June 2, 1880, for their seventh quadrennial nominating convention. For the first time, the convention call was addressed only to Republicans and not more broadly to others who sympathized with party principles.

The convention was divided into two factions. One, headed by Sen. Roscoe Conkling of New York, favored the nomination of former president Ulysses S. Grant for a third term. The anti-Grant faction, although not united around one candidate, included the eventual nominee, Rep. James A. Garfield of Ohio, among its leaders.

Pre-convention skirmishing focused on the selection of a temporary chairman. The Grant forces desired one from their own ranks who would uphold the unit rule — a rule important to Grant, because he had the support of a majority of delegates in several large states. However, the Grant strategy was blocked, and a temporary chairman neutral to both sides was chosen by the Republican National Committee, leaving the ultimate decision on the unit rule to the convention.

A test of strength between the two factions came early in the convention on an amended motion by Conkling directing the credentials committee to report to the convention prior to the rules committee. Conkling's amended motion was defeated, 406 to 318.

In spite of the defeat of the amended motion, much time was spent debating delegate credentials. More than 50 cases were presented in committee, and seven of them came to the floor for a vote. Five of the cases featured seating disputes among delegates selected in district caucuses and those chosen for the same seats in state conventions. In each case — involving delegates from the states of Illinois, Kansas and West Virginia — the convention supported the claim of the delegates elected at the district level.

The Illinois credentials fight produced the only candidate-oriented division, with the Grant forces favoring the seating of the delegates selected at the state convention. But by a margin of 387 to 353, the convention voted to seat the delegates selected in the district caucuses. Three other votes were taken on disputed credentials from different Illinois districts, but all were decided in favor the anti-Grant forces by a similar margin. *(Chart, p. 208)*

The majority report of the rules committee advocated that the controversial unit rule not be used. A motion by the Grant forces that the presidential nominations begin without passage of the rules committee report was defeated, 479 to 276. The vote was a key setback for the supporters of the former president, as the majority report was subsequently adopted by acclamation.

While the Grant forces suffered defeat on adoption of the unit rule, their candidate assumed the lead on the first ballot for president, with 304 votes. Sen. James G. Blaine of Maine followed closely with 284, and Treasury Secretary John Sherman of Ohio, the candidate nominated by Rep. Garfield, trailed with 93 votes.

Ballot after ballot was taken throughout the day, but after the 28th roll call, the last of the night, there was little change in the vote totals of the leading candidates. Grant led with 307 votes; Blaine had 279, and Sherman, 91.

When balloting resumed the next morning, Sherman's vote total jumped to 116, the biggest gain among the contenders, but still well behind Grant and Blaine. Grant gained votes on the 34th ballot, rising to a new high of 312, but on the same roll call a boom for Garfield began, with the Ohio representative collecting 16 votes from Wisconsin. Garfield protested that he was not a candidate but was ruled out of order by the chairman.

The Ohio representative continued to gain on the 35th ballot, his vote total rising to 50. On the next ballot, Garfield won the nomination, receiving the votes of nearly all the anti-Grant delegates. At the end of the roll call, Garfield had 399 votes; Grant, 306, and Blaine, 42, with nine votes distributed among other candidates.

Four men were placed in nomination for the vice presidency, but Chester A. Arthur of New York was the easy winner on the first ballot. Arthur, the former collector of the port of New York, received 468 votes to 193 for former representative Elihu B. Washburne of Illinois. Most of Arthur's support came from delegates who had backed Grant.

The Republican platform was passed by a voice vote without debate. For the first time, the platform included planks that clearly called for the exercise of federal power, emphasizing that the Constitution was "a supreme law, and not a mere contract." This philosophy contrasted with the Democratic platform, which favored home rule and government decentralization.

The two parties also differed on the tariff issue. The Republicans favored a revenue tariff that would also protect American industry, while the Democrats explicitly called for a revenue tariff only.

In its original form, the Republican platform did not include a civil service plank. An amendment from the floor, however, calling for a "thorough, radical and complete" reform of the civil service, was passed by a voice vote.

Following are excerpts from the Republican platform of 1880:

**Federal Power.** The Constitution of the United States is a supreme law, and not a mere contract. Out of confederated States it made a sovereign nation. Some powers are denied to the Nation, while others are denied to the States; but the boundary between the powers delegated and those reserved is to be determined by the National and not by the State tribunal.

The work of popular education is one left to the care of the several States, but it is the duty of the National Government to aid that work to the extent of its constitutional power. The intelligence of the Nation is but the aggregate of the intelligence in the several States, and the destiny of the Nation must be guided, not by the genius of any one State, but by the aggregate genius of all.

**Tariff.** We affirm the belief, avowed in 1876, that the duties levied for the purpose of revenue should so discriminate as to favor American labor....

**Civil Service Reform.** The Republican party, ... adopts the declaration of President Hayes that the reform of the civil service should be thorough, radical and complete.

**Chinese Immigration.** ... the Republican party, regarding the unrestricted immigration of the Chinese as a matter of grave concernment ... would limit and restrict that immigration by the enactment of such just, humane and reasonable laws and treaties as will produce that result.

## Greenback Party

A coalition of farmer and labor groups met in Chicago beginning June 9, 1880, to hold the second national Greenback Party convention. The party's first convention was held four years earlier, but it was not until 1880 that the Greenback Party received more than 2 percent of the popular vote. The party held its third and final convention four years later, but was unable in 1884 to attain 2 percent of the popular vote.

The 1880 convention attracted representatives of the various Greenback Party factions, as well as 44 delegates from the Socialist Labor Party. Rep. James B. Weaver of Iowa was nominated for the presidency, and B. J. Chambers of Texas was chosen as his running mate.

The platform adopted was far broader than the one conceived by the Greenbacks at their first convention in 1876. That year they focused solely on the currency issue. For the agrarian interests, currency planks remained that called for the unlimited coinage of silver and gold and the issuance of currency by the federal government and not private banks. Also adopted for the farm elements were planks advocating increased public land for settlers, denouncing large monopolies and proposing that Congress control passenger and freight rates.

Included for the labor groups were proposals for an eight-hour day, the abolition of child labor, the improvement of working conditions and the curtailment of Chinese immigration.

The Greenback platform also included planks that favored a graduated income tax and women's suffrage.

Following are excerpts from the Greenback platform of 1880:

**Currency.** ... All money, whether metallic or paper, should be issued and its volume controlled by the Government, and not by or through banking corporations, and when so issued should be a full legal-tender for all debts, public and private.

That the bonds of the United States should not be refunded, but paid as rapidly as practicable, according to contract. To enable the Government to meet these obligations, legal-tender currency should be substituted for the notes of the National banks, the National banking system abolished, and the unlimited coinage of silver, as well as gold, established by law.

**Labor.** That labor should be so protected by National and State authority as to equalize the burdens and insure a just distribution of its results; the eight-hour law of Congress should be enforced, the sanitary condition of industrial establishments placed under rigid control; the competition of contract labor abolished, a bureau of labor statistics established, factories, mines, and workshops inspected, the employment of children under fourteen years of age forbidden, and wages paid in cash.

**Chinese Immigration.** Slavery being simply cheap labor, and cheap labor being simple slavery, the importation and presence of Chinese serfs necessarily tends to brutalize and degrade American labor.

**Homesteading.** Railroad and land grants forfeited by reason of non-fulfillment of contract should be immediately reclaimed by the Government, and henceforth the public domain reserved exclusively as homes for actual settlers.

**Regulation of Monopolies.** It is the duty of Congress to regulate inter-state commerce. All lines of communication and transportation should be brought under such legislative control as shall secure moderate, fair and uniform rates for passenger and freight traffic.

We denounce as destructive to prosperity and dangerous to liberty, the action of the old parties in fostering and sustaining gigantic land, railroad, and money corporations and monopolies, invested with, and exercising powers belonging to the Government, and yet not responsible to it for the manner of their exercise.

**Income Tax.** All property should bear its just proportion of taxation, and we demand a graduated income tax.

**Women's Suffrage.** That every citizen of due age, sound mind, and not a felon, be fully enfranchised, and that this resolution be referred to the States, with recommendation for their favorable consideration.

## Democrats

The Democrats held their 13th quadrennial nominating convention in Cincinnati, Ohio, in late June 1880. Credentials disputes enlivened the early sessions, with two competing New York delegations the focus of attention. The challenging group, controlled by Tammany Hall, requested 20 of New York's 70 votes. But by a margin of 457 to 205-1/2, the convention refused the request.

Samuel J. Tilden, the Democratic standard-bearer in 1876 and the narrow loser in that controversial election, was not a candidate in 1880, although he did not officially notify his supporters of this fact until the presidential balloting had begun. Tilden's indecision, however, had long before opened the door for other prospective candidates.

On the first ballot, Gen. Winfield Scott Hancock of Pennsylvania, a candidate for the nomination in both 1868 and 1876, led with 171 votes, followed by Sen. Thomas F. Bayard of Delaware with 153-1/2 and former representative Henry G. Payne of Ohio (who served as a stalking horse for the Tilden forces), with 81.

Tilden's declaration of non-candidacy was announced before the second ballot, and the Tilden forces shifted their strength to House Speaker Samuel J. Randall of Pennsylvania. Nonetheless, Hancock was the big gainer on the second ballot, his vote total jumping to 320. Randall followed with 128-1/2, and Bayard slipped to third place with 112. Although Hancock was well short of the 492 votes needed for nomination, Wisconsin began a string of vote switches to Hancock that resulted in the military leader's selection. After all the changes, Hancock received 705 of the 738 votes cast.

The vice presidential nomination went by acclamation to former representative William H. English of Indiana, the only candidate.

The platform was accepted without debate or opposition. Its style of short, sharp phrases contrasted with the 1876 platform, which was written in flowing sentences built around the theme of the necessity of reform.

The 1880 platform called for decentralization of the federal government with increased local government, currency based on hard money, a tariff for revenue only, civil service reform and an end to Chinese immigration. The platform saved its harshest language to describe the party's reaction to the controversial election of 1876, which it labeled "the great fraud."

Following are excerpts from the Democratic platform of 1880:

**Government Centralization.** Opposition to centralization and to that dangerous spirit of encroachment which tends to consolidate the powers of all departments in one, and thus to create whatever be the form of government, a real despotism. No sumptuary laws; separation of Church and State, for the good of each; common schools fostered and protected.

**Currency.** Home rule; honest money, consisting of gold and silver, and paper convertible into coin on demand.

**Tariff.** . . . a tariff for revenue only.

**Civil Service Reform.** We execrate the course of this administration in making places in the civil service a reward for political crime, and demand a reform by statute which shall make it forever impossible for a defeated candidate to bribe his way to the seat of the usurper by billeting villains upon the people.

**Chinese Immigration.** No more Chinese immigration, except for travel, education, and foreign commerce, and that even carefully guarded.

**Election of 1876.** The great fraud of 1876-77, by which, upon a false count of the electoral voters of two States, the candidate defeated at the polls was declared to be President, and for the first time in American history, the will of the people was set aside under a threat of military violence, struck a deadly blow at our system of representative government. The Democratic party, to preserve the country from the horrors of a civil war, submitted for the time in firm and patriotic faith that the people would punish this crime in 1880. This issue precedes and dwarfs every other. It imposes a more sacred duty upon the people of the Union than ever before addressed the conscience of a nation of free men.

# 1884 Conventions

## Presidential Candidates

**James G. Blaine**
**Republican**

**Grover Cleveland**
**Democrat**

### Republicans

The Republicans gathered in Chicago in June 1884 for their convention. For the first time, the call to the convention prescribed how and when delegates should be selected, an effort to avoid the credentials disputes that had besieged the convention four years earlier.

The assassination of President James A. Garfield three years earlier had opened up the Republican presidential race, and the party war horse, James G. Blaine of Maine, emerged as the front-runner for the nomination. However, there was strong opposition to Blaine from several candidates, including the incumbent president, Chester A. Arthur of New York.

The first test between the two sides was over the choice of a temporary chairman. The Blaine forces supported former senator Powell Clayton of Arkansas, while the anti-Blaine coalition favored a black delegate from Mississippi, John R. Lynch. Lynch won by a vote of 424 to 384.

A motion by the Blaine forces to adjourn after the presidential nominating speeches was also beaten, 412 to 391. But on the first ballot Blaine assumed the lead with 334-1/2 votes, followed by President Arthur with 278 and Sen. George F. Edmunds of Vermont with 93. Most of Arthur's strength was in the South, where the administration's patronage power had great effect.

Blaine gained votes on the next two ballots, his total rising to 375 on the third ballot, while Arthur dropped slightly to 274. After this roll call, the anti-Blaine forces tried to force adjournment but were defeated, 458 to 356. On the fourth ballot, Blaine received the nomination, winning 541 votes to 207 for Arthur and 41 for Edmunds.

Sen. John A. Logan of Illinois was the only person placed in nomination for vice president. Logan, who earlier had been in contention for the presidential nomination, received 779 of the 820 votes in the convention for second place on the ticket.

The party platform was adopted without dissent, and on major issues was little different from the planks presented by the Democrats. The Republicans proposed a tariff that would both protect American industry and raise revenue, called for civil service reform, advocated restric-

tions on Chinese immigration and favored increased availability of public lands for settlers. In addition, the Republicans adopted features of the Greenback Party platform, calling for government regulation of railroads and an eight-hour work day.

Following are excerpts from the Republican platform of 1884:

**Tariff.** We . . . demand that the imposition of duties on foreign imports shall be made, not "for revenue only," but that in raising the requisite revenues for the government, such duties shall be so levied as to afford security to our diversified industries and protection to the rights and wages of the laborer; to the end that active and intelligent labor, as well as capital, may have its just reward, and the laboring man his full share in the national prosperity.

**Chinese Immigration.** . . . we denounce the importation of contract labor, whether from Europe or Asia, as an offense against the spirit of American institutions; and we pledge ourselves to sustain the present law restricting Chinese immigration, and to provide such further legislation as is necessary to carry out its purposes.

**Labor.** We favor the establishment of a national bureau of labor; the enforcement of the eight hour law.

**Regulation of Railroads.** The principle of public regulation of railway corporations is a wise and salutary one for the protection of all classes of the people; and we favor legislation that shall prevent unjust discrimination and excessive charges for transportation, and that shall secure to the people, and the railways alike, the fair and equal protection of the laws.

### Democrats

The 1884 Democratic convention was held in Chicago in July. For the first time, the party extended delegate voting rights to the territories and the District of Columbia.

A debate over the unit rule highlighted the first day of the convention. Delegates from Tammany Hall, a minority of the New York delegation, presented an amendment to the temporary rules designed to abolish the unit rule. All the New York delegates were bound by their state convention to vote as a unit. However, the national convention defeated the amendment by a vote of 463 to 332, thus limiting the power of the Tammany delegates.

A resolution was passed opening the position of party chairman to individuals who were not members of the Democratic National Committee. Another resolution, to eliminate the two-thirds rule at future conventions, was put to a vote, but the roll call was suspended when it became apparent the resolution would not pass.

Several peculiarities were evident during the presidential nominating speeches. Sen. Thomas A. Hendricks of Indiana, the favorite of the Hoosier delegation, nominated former senator Joseph E. McDonald as the state's favorite son in a speech listing attributes that easily could have described Hendricks. Two seconding speeches for Gov. Grover Cleveland of New York were delivered by Tammany delegates who actually used the time to denounce him.

In spite of the opposition within his own delegation, Cleveland was the front-runner for the nomination and had a big lead on the first ballot. Cleveland received 392 votes, easily outdistancing Sen. Thomas F. Bayard of Delaware, who had 170. Former senator Allen G. Thurman of Ohio was next, with 88. Hendricks received one vote but protested to the convention that he was not a candidate.

A boom for Hendricks was undertaken on the second ballot, with the Indiana delegation shifting its support from McDonald to Hendricks. However, Cleveland also gained and continued to hold a large lead over the rest of the field. After two roll calls, these vote totals stood: Cleveland, 475; Bayard, 151-1/2; Hendricks, 123-1/2; Thurman, 60. With the New York governor holding a majority of the vote, North Carolina switched to Cleveland, and this started a bandwagon that gave him the required two-thirds majority. After the shifts, Cleveland received 683 of the 820 votes in the convention.

Over the objections of the Indiana delegation, Hendricks was nominated for the vice presidency. The Indiana leaders were a bit upset that Hendricks did not receive the presidential nomination but did contribute to his nearly unanimous total for second place on the ticket. When the roll call was completed, Hendricks had received all but four votes.

The Democratic platform of 1884 was one of the longest documents adopted by the party in the 19th century. The platform was about 3,000 words long, with the first third devoted to a description of alleged Republican failures.

The platform straddled the increasingly important tariff issue. In 1880 the Democrats clearly favored a revenue tariff only, but the 1884 document called for both revenue and protection of American industry.

A minority report introduced by Benjamin F. Butler, former governor of Massachusetts, focused on the tariff issue. Butler advocated a duty on imports that would hit harder at luxury items and less on necessities than the tariff favored by the majority report and would ensure more protection for American labor. The minority report was defeated, 721-1/2 to 96-1/2.

Butler, a former Republican and, earlier in 1884, nominated for president by the Greenback and Anti-Monopoly parties, also introduced substitute planks on labor, monopoly, public corporations, currency and civil service reform. These other planks were defeated by a voice vote, and the platform as written was adopted by acclamation.

Following are excerpts from the Democratic platform of 1884:

**Tariff.** Knowing full well, . . . that legislation affecting the operations of the people should be cautious and conservative in method, not in advance of public opinion, but reponsive to its demands, the Democratic party is pledged to revise the tariff in a spirit of fairness to all interests.

But in making reduction in taxes, it is not proposed to injure any domestic industries, but rather to promote their healthy growth. From the foundation of this Government, taxes collected at the Custom House have been the chief source of Federal Revenue. Such they must continue to be. Moreover, many industries have come to rely upon legislation for successful continuance, so that any change of law must be at every step regardful of the labor and capital thus involved. The process of reform must be subject in the execution to this plain dictate of justice. . . .

Sufficient revenue to pay all the expenses of the Federal Government . . . can be got, under our present system of taxation, from the custom house taxes on fewer imported articles, bearing heaviest on articles of luxury, and bearing lightest on articles of necessity.

**Civil Liberties — Civil Service Reform.** We oppose sumptuary laws which vex the citizen and interfere with individual liberty; we favor honest Civil Service Reform, and the compensation of all United States officers by fixed salaries; the separation of Church and State; and the diffusion of free education by common schools, so that every child in the land may be taught the rights and duties of citizenship.

**Chinese Immigration.** [W]e . . . do not sanction the importation of foreign labor, or the admission of servile races, unfitted by habits, training, religion, or kindred, for absorption into the great body of our people, or for the citizenship which our laws confer. American civilization demands that against the immigration or importation of Mongolians to these shores our gates be closed.

# 1888 Conventions

## Presidential Candidates

**Clinton B. Fisk**
**Prohibitionist**

**Grover Cleveland**
**Democrat**

**Benjamin Harrison**
**Republican**

### Prohibition

The Prohibition Party held its fifth national convention in Indianapolis in late May 1888. The party had held conventions since the 1872 campaign, but not until 1888 did the Prohibitionists receive at least 2 percent of the popular vote. *(Prohibition Party, p. 268)*

The 1888 convention selected Clinton B. Fisk of New Jersey for president and John A. Brooks of Missouri as his running mate. While the platform focused on the need for prohibition, planks were included that covered other issues. The Prohibition Party favored a tariff that would both protect American industry and raise revenue, supported the extension of voting rights, favored immigration restrictions and proposed the abolition of polygamy.

Following are excerpts from the Prohibition Party platform of 1888:

> **Prohibition.** That the manufacture, importation, exportation, transportation and sale of alcoholic beverages should be made public crimes, and prohibited as such.

> **Tariff.** That an adequate public revenue being necessary, it may properly be raised by import duties; but import duties should be so reduced that no surplus shall be accumulated in the Treasury, and that the burdens of taxation shall be removed from foods, clothing and other comforts and necessaries of life, and imposed on such articles of import as will give protection both to the manufacturing employer and producing laborer against the competition of the world.

### Democrats

When the Democratic convention assembled in St. Louis in early June 1888, the party, for the first time since the outset of the Civil War, was in control of the White House. There was no contest for the presidential nomination, with the incumbent, Grover Cleveland, renominated by acclamation. However, the death of Vice President Thomas A. Hendricks in 1885 left open the second place on the ticket.

Former senator Allen G. Thurman of Ohio was the favorite for the vice presidential nomination and won easily on the first ballot with 684 votes. Gov. Isaac P. Gray of

Indiana had 101 votes, and Gen. John C. Black of Illinois trailed with 36. After the nomination of the 75-year-old Thurman, red bandannas were strung up around the hall. The bandanna was Thurman's political symbol, used extensively in his public habit of pinching snuff.

The platform was adopted by acclamation. It reaffirmed the Democratic platform written four years earlier, but in addition lauded the policies of President Cleveland and the achievements of Democratic rule, opposed the existing protective tariff and supported legislation to modify it and proposed a reformation of tax laws. A plank introduced from the floor favoring Irish home rule was included in the platform.

Following are excerpts from the Democratic platform of 1888:

> **Tariff.** The Democratic party of the United States, in National Convention assembled, renews the pledge of its fidelity to Democratic faith and reaffirms the platform adopted by its representatives in the Convention of 1884, and indorses the views expressed by President Cleveland in his last annual message to Congress as the correct interpretation of that platform upon the question of Tariff reduction; and also indorses the efforts of our Democratic Representatives in Congress to secure a reduction of excessive taxation....
>
> *Resolved,* That this convention hereby indorses and recommends the early passage of the bill for the reduction of the revenue now pending in the House of Representatives.

> **Tax Reform.** All unnecessary taxation is unjust taxation.... Every Democratic rule of governmental action is violated when through unnecessary taxation a vast sum of money, far beyond the needs of an economical administration, is drawn from the people and the channels of trade, and accumulated as a demoralizing surplus in the National Treasury.... The Democratic remedy is to enforce frugality in public expense and abolish needless taxation.

> **Federal Power.** Chief among its principles of party faith are the maintenance of an indissoluble Union of free and indestructible States, now about to enter upon its second century of unexampled progress and renown; devotion to a plan of government regulated by a written Con-

stitution, strictly specifying every granted power and expressly reserving to the States or people the entire ungranted residue of power.

## Republicans

The Republicans assembled for their convention in Chicago in late June 1888. Not only was the party out of the White House for the first time since the Civil War, but a perennial contender for the presidential nomination, James G. Blaine, had taken himself out of the running. Although this encouraged a number of candidates to seek the nomination, none came near to mustering the needed majority as the balloting for president began.

The 832 convention votes were distributed among 14 candidates, with Sen. John Sherman of Ohio leading the field with 229 votes. Circuit Judge Walter Q. Gresham of Indiana followed with 107 votes, while four other candidates received more than 70 votes. During the rest of the day, two more ballots were taken, with little appreciable change in the strength of the candidates. After the third roll call, Sherman led with 244 votes, followed by Gresham with 123 and former governor Russell A. Alger of Michigan with 122.

The unexpected withdrawal from the race of Chauncey Depew of New York, the favorite of that state's delegation, prompted a call for adjournment after the third ballot. The motion passed, 531 to 287.

When balloting resumed the next morning, the biggest gainer was former Sen. Benjamin Harrison of Indiana. Although Sherman still held the lead with 235 votes on the fourth ballot, Harrison's vote total had leaped from 94 votes on the third to 216 on the fourth. There was little change on the fifth ballot, taken on a Saturday, and after the roll call the delegates approved, 492 to 320, a motion to adjourn until Monday. The motion was generally supported by delegates opposed to Harrison.

When the convention reconvened, both Sherman and Harrison showed small gains — Sherman rising to 244 votes and Harrison to 231. On the next roll call, the seventh, Harrison took the lead for the first time, thanks largely to a shift of votes from delegates previously holding out for Blaine. Harrison led, 279 to 230, and the trend to the Indianan accelerated to a bandwagon the next ballot. Harrison easily achieved a majority on the eighth roll call, winning 544 votes to 118 for Sherman.

Three individuals were placed in nomination for vice president, but former representative Levi P. Morton of New York was the runaway winner on the first ballot. Morton received 592 votes to easily outdistance Rep. William Walter Phelps of New Jersey, 119 votes, and William O. Bradley of Kentucky, 103.

The platform sharply differed from that of the Democrats on the important tariff issue, strongly supporting the protective tariff and opposing the legislation favored by the Democrats. Like the Democrats, the Republicans called for a reduction in taxes, specifically recommending repeal of taxes on tobacco and on alcohol used in the arts and for mechanical purposes. In other areas, the Republicans favored the use of both gold and silver as currency, strongly opposed the Mormon practice of polygamy and called for veterans' pensions.

Following are excerpts from the Republican platform of 1888:

**Tariff.** We are uncompromisingly in favor of the American system of protection; we protest against its destruction as proposed by the President and his party. They serve the interests of Europe; we will support the interests of America.... The protective system must be maintained. Its abandonment has always been followed by general disaster to all interests, except those of the usurer and the sheriff. We denounce the Mills bill as destructive to the general business, the labor and the farming interests of the country, and we heartily indorse the consistent and patriotic action of the Republican Representatives in Congress in opposing its passage.

**Tax Reform.** The Republican party would effect all needed reduction of the National revenue by repealing the taxes upon tobacco, which are an annoyance and burden to agriculture, and the tax upon spirits used in the arts, and for mechanical purposes, and by such revision of the tariff laws as will tend to check imports of such articles as are produced by our people, the production of which gives employment to our labor, and releases from import duties those articles of foreign production (except luxuries), the like of which cannot be produced at home. If there shall remain a larger revenue than is requisite for the wants of the government we favor the entire repeal of internal taxes rather than the surrender of any part of our protective system at the joint behests of the whiskey trusts and the agents of foreign manufacturers.

**Currency.** The Republican party is in favor of the use of both gold and silver as money, and condemns the policy of the Democratic Administration in its efforts to demonetize silver.

**Veterans' Benefits.** The gratitude of the Nation to the defenders of the Union cannot be measured by laws.... We denounce the hostile spirit shown by President Cleveland in his numerous vetoes of measures for pension relief, and the action of the Democratic House of Representatives in refusing even a consideration of general pension legislation.

**Polygamy.** The political power of the Mormon Church in the Territories as exercised in the past is a menace to free institutions too dangerous to be longer suffered. Therefore we pledge the Republican party to appropriate legislation asserting the sovereignty of the Nation in all Territories where the same is questioned, and in furtherance of that end to place upon the statute books legislation stringent enough to divorce the political from the ecclesiastical power, and thus stamp out the attendant wickedness of polygamy.

# 1892 Conventions

## Presidential Candidates

**Benjamin Harrison**
**Republican**

**Grover Cleveland**
**Democrat**

**James B. Weaver**
**Populist**

### Republicans

Although President Benjamin Harrison was unpopular with various elements in the Republican Party, administration forces were in control of the convention that assembled in early June 1892 in Minneapolis, Minn. A Harrison supporter, former representative William McKinley of Ohio, was elected without opposition as the convention's permanent chairman.

A question concerning the credentials of six Alabama delegates resulted in a protracted debate on whether the six delegates in question could vote on their own case. The situation was resolved when the Alabama delegates voluntarily abstained from voting. The minority report, which proposed seating the six Alabama delegates on the original roll, was defeated, 463 to 423-1/2, and the majority report was subsequently adopted, 476 to 365-1/2. The two votes were candidate-oriented, with the winning side in each case composed largely of Harrison voters.

Harrison's chances of renomination were so strong that two other possibilities, James G. Blaine and William McKinley, never publicly announced as candidates for the presidency. Harrison won easily on the first ballot, receiving 535-1/6 votes to 182-1/6 for Blaine and 182 for McKinley. McKinley was in the ironic position of presiding over the convention at the same time he was receiving votes on the presidential ballot. The Ohioan withdrew briefly as permanent chairman and moved that Harrison's nomination be made unanimous. The motion was withdrawn after objections but placed McKinley publicly on the Harrison bandwagon. *(Chart, p. 212)*

While the Republican Party had an incumbent vice president in Levi P. Morton, the New York delegation supported Whitelaw Reid, the former editor of *The New York Tribune* and ambassador to France. With Morton making little effort to retain his position, Reid was nominated by acclamation, the first time a Republican convention had dispensed with a roll call in choosing a member of its national ticket.

The platform was adopted by a voice vote, and on only two major issues did it differ from that of the Democrats. The Republicans supported a protective tariff, clearly diverging from the Democrats, who supported import duties for revenue only. The Republicans also included a plank that sympathized with the prohibition effort, while the Democrats announced their opposition "to all sumptuary laws."

Both parties favored a bimetallic currency, with gold and silver of equal value, and supported the construction of a canal across Nicaragua. In addition, the Republicans advocated an expansionist foreign policy.

Following are excerpts from the Republican platform of 1892:

**Tariff.** We reaffirm the American doctrine of protection. We call attention to its growth abroad. We maintain that the prosperous condition of our country is largely due to the wise revenue legislation of the Republican congress.

We believe that all articles which cannot be produced in the United States, except luxuries, should be admitted free of duty, and that on all imports coming into competition with the products of American labor, there should be levied duties equal to the difference between wages abroad and at home.

**Currency.** The American people, from tradition and interest, favor bi-metallism, and the Republican party demands the use of both gold and silver as standard money, with such restrictions and under such provisions, to be determined by legislation, as will secure the maintenance of the parity of values of the two metals so that the purchasing and debt-paying power of the dollar, whether of silver, gold, or paper, shall be at all times equal. The interests of the producers of the country, its farmers and its workingmen, demand that every dollar, paper or coin, issued by the government, shall be as good as any other.

**Foreign Policy.** We reaffirm our approval of the Monroe doctrine and believe in the achievement of the manifest destiny of the Republic in its broadest sense.

**Central American Canal.** The construction of the Nicaragua Canal is of the highest importance to the American people, both as a measure of National defense and to build up and maintain American commerce, and it should be controlled by the United States Government.

**Prohibition.** We sympathize with all wise and legitimate efforts to lessen and prevent the evils of intemperance and promote morality.

## Democrats

One of the strangest conventions in party annals was held by the Democrats in Chicago in late June 1892. Much of the disturbance was due to stormy weather, with the accompanying noise and leaks in the roof frequently interrupting the proceedings. Inside the hall, the discomfort of the delegates was increased by the vocal opposition of 600 Tammany Hall workers to the renomination of former president Grover Cleveland of New York.

Although Cleveland was a solid favorite for renomination, he was opposed by his home state delegation. The Tammany forces engineered an early state convention that chose a delegation committed to Gov. David B. Hill. But in spite of the hostility of the New York delegation, Cleveland was able to win renomination on the first ballot, receiving 617-1/3 votes to 114 for Hill and 103 for Gov. Horace Boies of Iowa. *(Chart, p. 212)*

Four individuals were placed in nomination for the vice presidency, with Adlai E. Stevenson of Illinois assuming the lead on the first ballot. Stevenson, a former representative and later assistant postmaster general during Cleveland's first administration, led former governor Isaac P. Gray of Indiana, 402 to 343. After the first roll call was completed, Iowa switched to Stevenson, starting a bandwagon that led quickly to his nomination. After all the switches had been tallied, Stevenson was the winner with 652 votes, followed by Gray with 185.

The platform debate centered around the tariff plank. The plank, as originally written, straddled the issue. But a sharply worded substitute proposed from the floor, calling for a tariff for revenue only, passed easily, 564 to 342. The currency section called for stable money, with the coinage of both gold and silver in equal amounts. The platform also included a plank that called for the construction of a canal through Nicaragua.

Following are excerpts from the Democratic platform of 1892:

**Tariff.** We denounce Republican protection as a fraud, a robbery of the great majority of the American people for the benefit of the few. We declare it to be a fundamental principle of the Democratic party that the Federal Government has no constitutional power to impose and collect tariff duties, except for the purpose of revenue only, and we demand that the collection of such taxes shall be limited to the necessities of the Government when honestly and economically administered.

**Currency.** ... We hold to the use of both gold and silver as the standard money of the country, and to the coinage of both gold and silver without discriminating against either metal or charge for mintage, but the dollar unit of coinage of both metals must be of equal intrinsic and exchangeable value, or be adjusted through international agreement or by such safeguards of legislation as shall insure the maintenance of the parity of the two metals and the equal power of every dollar at all times in the markets and in the payment of debts; and we demand that all paper currency shall be kept at par with and redeemable in such coin.

**Central American Canal.** For purposes of national defense and the promotion of commerce between the States, we recognize the early construction of the Nicaragua Canal and its protection against foreign control as of great importance to the United States.

**Prohibition.** We are opposed to all sumptuary laws, as an interference with the individual rights of the citizen.

**Federal Power.** ... we solemnly declare that the need of a return to these fundamental principles of free popular government, based on home rule and individual liberty, was never more urgent than now, when the tendency to centralize all power at the Federal capital has become a menace to the reserved rights of the States that strikes at the very roots of our Government under the Constitution as framed by the fathers of the Republic.

## Prohibition

The Prohibition Party's sixth convention was held in Cincinnati in late June 1892 and nominated John Bidwell of California for president and James B. Cranfill of Texas as his running mate. While the Prohibition Party continued to run a national ticket through the 1972 election, 1892 marked the last year that the party received more than 2 percent of the popular vote.

Although beginning and ending with calls for prohibition, the 1892 platform as a whole was a reform-minded document, favoring women's suffrage and equal wages for women, an inflated currency and the nationalization of railroad, telegraph, and other public corporations.

Following are excerpts from the Prohibition platform of 1892:

**Prohibition.** ... We declare anew for the entire suppression of the manufacture, sale, importation, exportation and transportation of alcoholic liquors as a beverage by Federal and State legislation, and the full powers of Government should be exerted to secure this result. Any party that fails to recognize the dominant nature of this issue in American politics is undeserving of the support of the people.

**Women's Rights.** No citizen should be denied the right to vote on account of sex, and equal labor should receive equal wages, without regard to sex.

**Currency.** The money of the country should consist of gold, silver, and paper, and be issued by the General Government only, and in sufficient quantity to meet the demands of business and give full opportunity for the employment of labor. To this end an increase in the volume of money is demanded, and no individual or corporation should be allowed to make any profit through its issue. It should be made a legal tender for the payment of all debts, public and private. Its volume should be fixed at a definite sum per capita and made to increase with our increase in population.

**Tariff.** Tariff should be levied only as a defense against foreign governments which levy tariff upon or bar out our products from their markets, revenue being incidental.

**Government Nationalization.** Railroad, telegraph, and other public corporations should be controlled by the Government in the interest of the people.

## People's Party (Populists)

The most successful of the 19th century farmer-labor coalitions was the People's Party, commonly known as the Populists, which formally organized as a political party at a convention in Cincinnati in May 1891. Further organization was accomplished at a convention in St. Louis the next February, from which emanated the call to the party's first national nominating convention, to be held that summer in Omaha, Neb. The election of 1892 was the only one in which the Populists received more than 2 percent of the national vote. Four years later the party endorsed the Democratic ticket, and from 1900 through 1908 the Populists ran separate tickets, but failed to receive 2 percent of the popular vote. *(Populist Party, p. 266)*

The call to the 1892 convention specified procedures

for the selection of delegates and set the size of the convention at 1,776 delegates. Thirteen hundred to fourteen hundred delegates actually assembled in Omaha for the Populist convention, which opened July 2. The field for the presidential nomination was reduced by the death early in 1892 of Southern agrarian leader Leonidas L. Polk of North Carolina and the refusal of Judge Walter Q. Gresham of Indiana to seek the nomination. First place on the ticket went to former representative James B. Weaver of Iowa, who defeated Sen. James H. Kyle of South Dakota, 995 to 275.

James G. Field of Virginia won the vice presidential nomination over Ben Terrell of Texas by a vote of 733 to 554. The ticket bridged any sectional division, pairing a former Union general (Weaver) with a former Confederate major (Field).

On July 4 the delegates enthusiastically adopted the platform. It contained few ideas that were not contained in the earlier platforms of other farmer-labor parties. But the document adopted by the Populists brought these proposals together into one forcefully written platform. More than half the platform was devoted to the preamble, which demanded widespread reform and sharply criticized the two major parties. It attacked the Democrats and Republicans for waging "a sham battle over the tariff," while ignoring more important issues.

The remainder of the platform was divided into three major parts that discussed finance, transportation and land policy. The Populists proposed that the currency be inflated, with the unlimited coinage of silver and a substantial increase in the circulating medium to at least $50 per capita. The Populists' currency plank was sharply different from those of the two major parties, which favored a stable, bimetallic currency.

The Populists also went well beyond the two major parties in advocating the nationalization of the railroads and telegraph and telephone companies. Both the Populists and Democrats advocated land reform, although the proposals received greater emphasis in the Populist platform.

The Populists included a call for a graduated income tax and expanded government power.

Although not considered part of the platform, supplementary resolutions were passed that favored the initiative and referendum, a limit of one term for the president, the direct election of senators, the secret ballot and additional labor-oriented proposals that called for improvement in working conditions.

Following are excerpts from the Populist platform of 1892:

**Preamble.** The conditions which surround us best justify our co-operation; we meet in the midst of a nation brought to the verge of moral, political, and material ruin. Corruption dominates the ballot-box, the Legislatures, the Congress, and touches even the ermine of the bench. The people are demoralized; most of the states have been compelled to isolate the voters at the polling places to prevent universal intimidation and bribery. The newspapers are largely subsidized or muzzled, public opinion silenced, business prostrated, homes covered with mortgages, labor impoverished, and the land concentrating in the hands of capitalists. The urban workmen are denied the right to organize for self-protection; imported pauperized labor beats down their wages, a hireling standing army, unrecognized by our laws, is established to shoot them down, and they are rapidly degenerating into European conditions. The fruits of the toil of millions are boldly stolen to build up colossal fortunes for a few, unprecedented in the history of mankind; and the possessors of these, in turn despise the Republic and endanger liberty. From the same prolific womb of governmental injustice we breed the two great classes — tramps and millionaires. . . .

We have witnessed for more than a quarter of a century the struggles of the two great political parties for power and plunder, while grievous wrongs have been inflicted upon the suffering people. We charge that the controlling influence dominating both these parties have permitted the existing dreadful conditions to develop without serious effort to prevent or restrain them. Neither do they now promise us any substantial reform. They have agreed together to ignore, in the coming campaign, every issue but one. They propose to drown the outcries of a plundered people with the uproar of a sham battle over the tariff, so that capitalists, corporations, national banks, rings, trusts, watered stock, the demonetization of silver and the oppressions of the usurers may all be lost sight of. They propose to sacrifice our homes, lives, and children on the altar of mammon; to destroy the multitude in order to secure corruption funds from the millionaires.

. . . We believe that the power of government — in other words, of the people — should be expanded (as in the case of the postal service) as rapidly and as far as the good sense of an intelligent people and the teachings of experience shall justify, to the end that oppression, injustice and poverty, shall eventually cease in the land.

While our sympathies as a party of reform are naturally upon the side of every proposition which will tend to make men intelligent, virtuous and temperate, we nevertheless regard these questions, important as they are, as secondary to the great issues now pressing for solution, and upon which not only our individual prosperity, but the very existence of free institutions depend; and we ask all men to first help us to determine whether we are to have a republic to administer, before we differ as to the conditions upon which it is to be administered, believing that the forces of reform this day organized will never cease to move forward, until every wrong is remedied, and equal rights and equal privileges securely established for all the men and women of this country.

**Currency.** We demand free and unlimited coinage of silver and gold at the present legal ratio of 16 to 1.

We demand that the amount of circulating medium be speedily increased to not less than $50 per capita.

We demand that postal savings banks be established by the government for the safe deposit of the earnings of the

---

**Explanatory Note**

This section on the history of party nominating conventions includes conventions for parties receiving at least 2 percent of the popular vote in the presidential election. The Socialist Party, for example, received at least 2 percent of the popular vote in 1904, 1908, 1912, 1916, 1920 and 1932; the Socialist Party conventions for these years are included in this section. The Socialist Party conventions for other years when the party received less than 2 percent of the vote are not included. (Additional details on this section, p. 34).

people and to facilitate exchange.

**Transportation.** Transportation being a means of exchange and a public necessity, the government should own and operate the railroads in the interest of the people. The telegraph and telephone, like the post office system, being a necessity for the transmission of news, should be owned and operated by the government in the interest of the people.

**Land.** The land, including all the natural sources of wealth, is the heritage of the people, and should not be monopolized for speculative purposes, and alien ownership of land should be prohibited. All land now held by railroad and other corporations in excess of their actual needs, and all lands now owned by aliens, should be reclaimed by the government and held for actual settlers only.

# 1896 Conventions

## Presidential Candidates

**William McKinley**
**Republican**

**William J. Bryan**
**Democrat**

### Republicans

The currency issue, which spawned several third-party efforts in the late 19th century, emerged as the dominant issue of contention between the Republican and Democratic parties in the campaign of 1896. The forces in favor of the gold standard were firmly in control of the Republican convention that was held in St. Louis in early June 1896.

Actually, the convention was less a forum for the discussion of issues than a showcase for the political acumen of Mark Hanna of Ohio. Hanna, William McKinley's campaign manager, had been intensely courting delegates across the country, especially in the South, for more than a year before the convention. Before the rap of the opening gavel, Hanna had amassed a majority of the delegates for the popular Ohio governor.

The first evidence of McKinley strength came on a credentials question. A minority report was introduced claiming the credentials committee had held hearings on only two of 160 cases and proposing that the committee resume hearings. A maneuver to squelch the minority report was made when a delegate moved to cut off debate. With the McKinley forces providing most of the majority, the motion passed, 551-1/2 to 359-1/2.

Four other candidates in addition to McKinley were in contention for the presidential nomination, but McKinley was the runaway winner on the first ballot. He received 661-1/2 votes to 84-1/2 for the runner-up, House Speaker Thomas B. Reed of Maine. *(Chart, p. 214)*

There were two serious contenders for the vice presidential nomination: Garret A. Hobart, a McKinley sup-

porter and former state legislator from New Jersey, and Henry Clay Evans, a former candidate for governor of Tennessee. Hobart won, winning 523-1/2 votes on the first ballot to 287-1/2 for Evans.

As at the Democratic convention, the platform debate centered around the currency issue. The gold forces, firmly in control of the Republican convention, produced a majority report that called for maintenance of the gold standard until the time when bimetallism could be effected by an international agreement. This plank did not satisfy the silver minority. Led by Sen. Henry M. Teller of Colorado, a minority plank was introduced favoring the unlimited coinage of silver and gold at the ratio of 16 to 1. Teller's plank, similar to the currency plank adopted later by the Democrats, was defeated, 818-1/2 to 105-1/2. A second roll call on adoption of the majority plank resulted in another decisive defeat for the silver forces. The majority plank carried, 812-1/2 to 110-1/2.

With the decisive defeat of the minority plank, Teller led a walkout by 24 silver delegates, including the entire Colorado and Idaho delegations and members of the Montana, South Dakota and Utah delegations. The rest of the platform was adopted by a voice vote.

The currency plank that caused the commotion was buried deep in the middle of the Republican platform. The document began with a denunciation of Democratic rule and proceeded into a discussion of the merits of a protective tariff. A tariff for revenue purposes only was advocated in the Democratic platform, but the issue in the Republican document was clearly considered to be of secondary importance.

The Republican platform was also distinguishable from that of the Democrats in recommending a more expansionistic foreign policy, proposing stricter immigration restrictions and, for the first time, specifically denouncing the practice of lynching.

Following are excerpts from the Republican platform of 1896:

**Currency.** The Republican party is unreservedly for sound money.... We are unalterably opposed to every measure calculated to debase our currency or impair the credit of our country. We are therefore opposed to the free coinage of silver, except by international agreement with the leading commercial nations of the earth, which agreement we pledge ourselves to promote, and until such agreement can be obtained the existing gold standard must be maintained.

**Tariff.** We renew and emphasize our allegiance to the policy of protection, as the bulwark of American industrial independence, and the foundation of American development and prosperity.... Protection and Reciprocity are twin measures of American policy and go hand in hand. Democratic rule has recklessly struck down both, and both must be re-established. Protection for what we produce; free admission for the necessaries of life which we do not produce; reciprocal agreement of mutual interests, which gain open markets for us in return for our open markets for others. Protection builds up domestic industry and trade and secures our own market for ourselves; reciprocity builds up foreign trade and finds an outlet for our surplus.

**Foreign Policy.** Our foreign policy should be at all times firm, vigorous and dignified, and all our interests in the western hemisphere should be carefully watched and guarded.

The Hawaiian Islands should be controlled by the United States, and no foreign power should be permitted to interfere with them. The Nicaragua Canal should be built, owned and operated by the United States. And, by the purchase of the Danish Islands we should secure a much needed Naval station in the West Indies.... We therefore, favor the continued enlargement of the navy, and a complete system of harbor and sea-coast defenses.

**Immigration.** For the protection of the equality of our American citizenship and of the wages of our workingmen, against the fatal competition of low priced labor, we demand that the immigration laws be thoroughly enforced, and so extended as to exclude from entrance to the United States those who can neither read nor write.

**Lynching.** We proclaim our unqualified condemnation of the uncivilized and preposterous [barbarous] practice well known as lynching, and the killing of human beings suspected or charged with crime without process of law.

## Democrats

The Democratic convention that assembled in Chicago in July 1896 was dominated by one issue — currency. A delegate's viewpoint on this single issue influenced his position on every vote taken. Generally, the party was split along regional lines, with Eastern delegations favoring a hard-money policy with maintenance of the gold standard, and most Southern and Western delegations supporting a soft-money policy with the unlimited coinage of silver.

Division in the convention was apparent on the first day, when the silver forces challenged the national committee's selection of Gov. David B. Hill of New York as temporary chairman. The pro-silver delegates put up Sen. John W. Daniel of Virginia for the post, and Daniel won easily, 556 to 349. His victory indicated the dominance of the silver forces and presaged their ability to control the convention.

Two sets of credentials challenges were next on the agenda. By a voice vote, the convention agreed to seat a Nebraska delegation headed by a young silver supporter, William Jennings Bryan. And, by a vote of 558 to 368, the convention defeated a recommendation to seat Michigan delegates supported by the hard-money-dominated national committee.

With their lack of strength apparent, the gold forces declined to run a candidate for president. However, the silver delegates could not initially coalesce behind one candidate, and 14 individuals received votes on the first ballot. Rep. Richard P. "Silver Dick" Bland of Missouri was the pacesetter, with 235 votes, followed by Bryan, a former House member, with 137 and Robert E. Pattison, former Pennsylvania governor, with 97. Bryan, 36 years old, earlier had electrified the convention during the platform debate on currency, with his memorable "Cross of Gold" speech, which had elevated him to the position of a major contender. *(Chart, p. 213)*

On the next two roll calls, both candidates showed gains. Bland's total climbed to 291 on the third ballot and Bryan's rose to 219. Bryan continued to gain on the next ballot and assumed the lead over Bland, 280 to 241. The movement to Bryan accelerated on the fifth ballot, and he won the nomination easily, receiving 652 of the 930 convention votes. Although Bryan was the nearly unanimous choice of the silver forces, 162 gold delegates indicated their dissatisfaction with the proceedings by refusing to vote.

With Bryan declining to indicate a preference for vice president, 16 candidates received votes for the office on the first ballot. The Nebraska delegation, following Bryan's example, declined to participate in the vice-presidential balloting.

Former representative John C. Sibley of Pennsylvania took the lead on the first ballot with 163 votes, followed by Ohio editor and publisher John R. McLean with 111, and Maine shipbuilder Arthur Sewall with 100.

Bland spurted into the lead on the second ballot with 294 votes, followed by McLean and Sibley. After the roll call, Sibley withdrew, and on the third ballot the race between Bland and McLean tightened. The Missourian led, 255 to 210, but he too withdrew after the roll call. Sewall emerged as McLean's major competitor on the fourth ballot, and with the withdrawal of the Ohio journalist from the race, the nomination was Sewall's on the fifth ballot. Actually, Sewall's vote total of 602 on the final roll call was less than two-thirds of the convention vote, but with 251 disgruntled gold delegates refusing to vote, the required majority was reduced to only those voting.

Not surprisingly, the platform debate centered around the currency plank. The Eastern delegations proposed that, until silver coinage could be arranged by international agreement, the gold standard should be maintained. The Southern and Western delegations countered by demanding that the unlimited coinage of silver should begin without requiring a delay to reach an international agreement. Bryan managed the platform debate for the silver forces and scheduled himself as the final speaker, an enviable position from which to make a deep impression on the emotion-packed convention.

Bryan made the most of his opportunity, ending his dramatic speech with the famous peroration: "You shall not press down upon the brow of labor this crown of thorns, you shall not crucify mankind upon a cross of gold." The gold plank was defeated, 626 to 303. Although the speech was a key factor in Bryan's nomination, it was not influential in defeating the gold plank, which was already doomed to defeat. *(Chart, p. 213)*

A resolution commending the Cleveland administration was also defeated, 564 to 357, and after several attempts to modify the currency plank were rejected by voice votes, the platform as a whole was adopted, 622 to 307.

Following are excerpts from the Democratic platform of 1896:

**Currency.** We demand the free and unlimited coinage of both silver and gold at the present legal ratio of 16 to 1 without waiting for the aid or consent of any other nation.

**Railroads.** The absorption of wealth by the few, the consolidation of our leading railroad systems, and the formation of trusts and pools require a stricter control by the Federal Government of those arteries of commerce. We demand the enlargement of the powers of the Interstate Commerce Commission and such restriction and guarantees in the control of railroads as will protect the people from robbery and oppression.

**No Third Term.** We declare it to be the unwritten law of this Republic, established by custom and usage of 100 years, and sanctioned by the examples of the greatest and wisest of those who founded and have maintained our Government that no man should be eligible for a third term of the Presidential office.

**Federal Power.** During all these years the Democratic Party has resisted the tendency of selfish interests to the centralization of governmental power, and steadfastly maintained the integrity of the dual scheme of government established by the founders of this Republic of republics. Under its guidance and teachings the great principle of local self-government has found its best expression in the maintenance of the rights of the States and in its assertion of the necessity of confining the general government to the exercise of the powers granted by the Constitution of the United States.

# 1900 Conventions

## Presidential Candidates

**William McKinley**
**Republican**

**William J. Bryan**
**Democrat**

### Republicans

Surface harmony was the hallmark of the Republican conclave held in Philadelphia in June 1900. The Colorado delegation, which had walked out of the 1896 convention, was honored by having one of its members, Sen. Edward O. Wolcott, chosen as temporary chairman.

There was no opposition to President William McKinley, and he won all 926 votes on the first roll call. However, the death of Vice President Garret A. Hobart in 1899 had left the second spot on the ticket open. McKinley did not have a preference and asked his campaign manager, Mark Hanna, not to influence the convention. McKinley's hands-off policy worked to the advantage of the popular governor of New York and hero of the Spanish-American War, Theodore Roosevelt, whom Hanna disliked. *(Chart, p. 215)*

Roosevelt's popularity, coupled with the desire of New York boss Thomas C. Platt to eliminate a powerful state rival, enabled the 41-year-old governor to clinch the nomination before balloting began. On the vice presidential roll call, Roosevelt received all but one vote. The single uncast vote came from Roosevelt's New York delegation, which cast 71 of its 72 votes for Roosevelt.

The Republicans adopted a platform that applauded the four years of Republican rule and credited McKinley's policies with improving business conditions and winning the Spanish-American War. The platform defended postwar expansionism and called for increased foreign trade and the creation of a Department of Commerce.

As in 1896, the Republican platform opposed the unlimited coinage of silver and supported maintenance of the gold standard. On the tariff issue, the Republicans continued to laud the protective duty on imports.

Following are excerpts from the Republican platform of 1900:

**Foreign Trade, Panama Canal.** We favor the construction, ownership, control and protection of an Isthmian Canal by the Government of the United States. New markets are necessary for the increasing surplus of our farm products. Every effort should be made to open and obtain new markets, especially in the Orient, and the Administration is warmly to be commended for its successful efforts to commit all trading and colonizing nations to the policy of the open door in China.

**International Expansion.** In accepting by the Treaty of Paris the just responsibility of our victories in the Spanish war, the President and the Senate won the undoubted approval of the American people. No other course was possible than to destroy Spain's sovereignty throughout the West Indies and in the Philippine Islands. That course created our responsibility before the world, and with the unorganized population whom our intervention had freed from Spain, to provide for the maintenance of law and order, and for the establishment of good government and for the performance of international obligations. Our authority could not be less than our responsibility; and whenever sovereign rights were extended it became the high duty of the Government to maintain its authority, to put down armed insurrection and to confer the blessings of liberty and civilization upon all the rescued peoples.

**Antitrust.** We recognize the necessity and propriety of the honest co-operation of capital to meet new business conditions and especially to extend our rapidly increasing foreign trade, but we condemn all conspiracies and combinations intended to restrict business, to create monopolies, to limit production, or to control prices; and favor such legislation as will effectively restrain and prevent all such abuses, protect and promote competition and secure the rights of producers, laborers, and all who are engaged in industry and commerce.

**Currency.** We renew our allegiance to the principle of the gold standard and declare our confidence in the wisdom of the legislation of the Fifty-sixth Congress, by which the parity of all our money and the stability of our currency upon a gold basis has been secured....

We declare our steadfast opposition to the free and unlimited coinage of silver.

**Tariff.** We renew our faith in the policy of Protection to American labor. In that policy our industries have been established, diversified and maintained. By protecting the home market competition has been stimulated and production cheapened.

## Democrats

The Democrats opened their 1900 convention in Kansas City, Mo., on July 4, and showed a degree of party harmony not evident at their convention four years earlier. After the party factionalism of 1896, the delegates made a conscious effort to display a unified front — an effort aided by the decline of the controversial silver issue. The discovery of new gold deposits in North America and the subsequent increase in currency had lessened the divisive impact of the silver issue.

William Jennings Bryan, the Democratic standard-bearer in 1896, was renominated without opposition, receiving all 936 votes. The harmony in the convention was evident when former New York senator David B. Hill, a leader of the gold forces four years earlier, gave a seconding speech for Bryan. *(Chart, p. 215)*

Seven names were placed in nomination for the vice presidency. However, two withdrew before the balloting began. Adlai E. Stevenson of Illinois, vice president under Grover Cleveland, led on the first roll call with 559-1/2 votes, followed by Hill, who received 200 votes in spite of withdrawing from the race before the voting started. After completion of the ballot, a series of vote switches resulted in Stevenson's unanimous nomination.

The platform was adopted without floor debate. The major theme of the document was anti-imperialism, although an attack on trusts and a discussion of the currency question also were emphasized.

The anti-imperialism section was placed at the beginning of the platform and was labeled the most important issue of the campaign. The delegates enthusiastically accepted the plank, which forcefully criticized American international expansion after the Spanish-American War. The platform asserted "that no nation can long endure half republic and half empire" and denounced increasing U.S. militarism. The Democratic position sharply differed from the one advocated by the Republicans, whose platform defended postwar expansionism.

After the anti-imperialism section was a sharp attack on monopolies, the most detailed antitrust section that had yet appeared in a Democratic platform. The plank called for more comprehensive antitrust legislation and more rigid enforcement of the laws already enacted. Although the Republicans also condemned monopolies, the issue received a mere one-sentence mention in their platform.

With the decline of the silver issue, the necessity of a pro-silver plank was a matter of debate in the resolutions committee. However, Bryan threatened to withdraw his candidacy if a plank calling for the unlimited coinage of silver was not included in the platform. By a majority of one vote, the resolutions committee included the silver plank, and it was accepted without dissent by the convention. The Democratic position set up another distinction with the Republicans, who, as four years earlier, favored maintenance of the gold standard.

In addition to the anti-imperialism, antitrust and currency sections of the platform, the Democrats proposed the creation of a Department of Labor, favored the direct election of senators and, unlike the Republicans, supported the construction and ownership of a Nicaraguan canal. The Republican platform advocated construction and ownership of a canal across the Isthmus of Panama.

Following are excerpts from the Democratic platform of 1900:

**Anti-imperialism.** We hold that the Constitution follows the flag, and denounce the doctrine that an Executive or Congress deriving their existence and their powers from the Constitution can exercise lawful authority beyond it or in violation of it. We assert that no nation can long endure half republic and half empire, and we warn the American people that imperialism abroad will lead quickly and inevitably to despotism at home....

We are not opposed to territorial expansion when it takes in desirable territory which can be erected into States in the Union, and whose people are willing and fit to become American citizens. We favor trade expansion by every peaceful and legitimate means. But we are unalterably opposed to seizing or purchasing distant islands to be governed outside the Constitution, and whose people can never become citizens....

The importance of other questions, now pending before the American people is no wise diminished and the Democratic party takes no backward step from its position on them, but the burning issue of imperialism growing out of the Spanish war involves the very existence of the Republic and the destruction of our free institutions. We regard it as the paramount issue of the campaign....

We oppose militarism. It means conquest abroad and intimidation and oppression at home. It means the strong arm which has ever been fatal to free institutions.... This republic has no place for a vast military establishment, a sure forerunner of compulsory military service and conscription. When the nation is in danger the volunteer soldier is his country's best defender.

**Antitrust.** We pledge the Democratic party to an unceasing warfare in nation, State and city against private monopoly in every form. Existing laws against trusts must be enforced and more stringent ones must be enacted....

Tariff laws should be amended by putting the products of trusts upon the free list, to prevent monopoly under the plea of protection.

**Currency.** We reaffirm and indorse the principles of the National Democratic Platform adopted at Chicago in 1896, and we reiterate the demand of that platform for an American financial system made by the American people for themselves, and which shall restore and maintain a bimetallic price-level, and as part of such system the immediate restoration of the free and unlimited coinage of silver and gold at the present legal ratio of 16 to 1, without waiting for the aid or consent of any other nation.

# 1904 Conventions

## Presidential Candidates

**Eugene V. Debs**
Socialist

**Theodore Roosevelt**
Republican

**Alton B. Parker**
Democrat

### Socialists

The Socialist Party held its first national nominating convention in Chicago in early May 1904 and nominated Eugene V. Debs of Indiana for president and Benjamin Hanford of New York as his running mate. Debs ran in 1900 as the presidential candidate of two socialist groups, the Social Democratic Party and a moderate faction of the Socialist Labor Party.

The bulk of the platform was devoted to the philosophy of the international Socialist movement, with its belief in the eventual demise of capitalism and the ultimate achievement of a classless, worker-oriented society. To hasten the creation of a Socialist society, the platform favored many reforms advocated by the Populists and earlier agrarian-labor movements: the initiative, referendum and recall; women's suffrage; tax reform, including the graduated income tax; the public ownership of transportation, communication and exchange; and various labor benefits, including higher wages and shorter hours.

Following are excerpts from the Socialist platform of 1904:

> To the end that the workers may seize every possible advantage that may strengthen them to gain complete control of the powers of government, and thereby the sooner establish the cooperative commonwealth, the Socialist Party pledges itself to watch and work, in both the economic and the political struggle, for each successive immediate interest of the working class; for shortened days of labor and increases of wages; for the insurance of the workers against accident, sickness and lack of employment; for pensions for aged and exhausted workers; for the public ownership of the means of transportation, communication and exchange; for the graduated taxation of incomes, inheritances, franchises and land values, the proceeds to be applied to the public employment and improvement of the conditions of the workers; for the complete education of children, and their freedom from the workshop; for the prevention of the use of the military against labor in the settlement of strikes; for the free administration of justice; for popular government, including initiative, referendum, proportional representation, equal suffrage of men and women, municipal home rule, and the recall of officers by their constituents; and for every gain or advantage for the workers that may be wrested from the capitalist system, and that may relieve the suffering and strengthen the hands of labor. We lay upon every man elected to any executive or legislative office the first duty of striving to procure whatever is for the workers' most immediate interest, and for whatever will lessen the economic and political powers of the capitalist, and increase the like powers of the worker.

### Republicans

President Theodore Roosevelt was totally in command of the Republican convention held in Chicago in June 1904. His most dangerous potential rival for the nomination, Sen. Mark Hanna of Ohio, had died in February, leaving the field clear for Roosevelt.

The rather trivial matter of most interest before the presidential balloting began was Hawaii's vote allocation. The rules committee recommended that the votes of the territory be reduced from six to two. A substitute amendment proposed that Hawaii retain its six votes for the 1904 convention but that its vote allocation be reviewed by the national committee for future conventions. The substitute was accepted by the narrow margin of 495 to 490.

Roosevelt's nomination caused less commotion. On the first ballot, he received all 994 votes. The party leadership favored Sen. Charles W. Fairbanks of Indiana for the vice presidency. Although the Georgia, Illinois, Missouri and

Nebraska delegations noted that they preferred other candidates, Fairbanks was nominated by acclamation.

The party platform was adopted without dissent. In the document the Republicans charted little new ground, instead detailing the benefits of Republican rule and restating old positions. America's expansionistic foreign policy was praised, as was the protective tariff and the gold standard.

A display of Roosevelt theatrics followed the adoption of the platform. The convention chairman was instructed to read a message from the secretary of state to the American consul in Morocco: "We want either Perdicaris alive or Raisuli dead." The message referred to an alleged American citizen, Ion Perdicaris, who had been captured by the Moroccan chieftain, Raisuli. The American ultimatum read to the convention followed the dispatch of several ships to Morocco. The reading of the message roused the delegates, as it was no doubt intended to do.

Following are excerpts from the Republican platform in 1904:

> **Shipbuilding.** We ... favor legislation which will encourage and build up the American merchant marine, and we cordially approve the legislation of the last Congress which created the Merchant Marine Commission to investigate and report upon this subject.

> **Monopoly.** Combinations of capital and of labor are the results of the economic movement of the age, but neither must be permitted to infringe upon the rights and interests of the people. Such combinations, when lawfully formed for lawful purposes, are alike entitled to the protection of the laws, but both are subject to the laws and neither can be permitted to break them.

## Democrats

William Jennings Bryan, after two unsuccessful campaigns for the presidency, was not a candidate for the Democratic nomination in 1904. However, he was present at the party's convention in St. Louis that July and was a prominent factor in the proceedings.

Bryan's first appearance before the convention came during a credentials dispute, featuring a challenge by Bryan supporters in Illinois to the state delegation approved by the credentials committee. Bryan spoke in behalf of his supporters, but their minority report was beaten, 647 to 299.

Bryan appeared again to second the presidential nomination of Sen. Francis M. Cockrell of Missouri, one of eight candidates nominated. Much of his speech, however, was devoted to criticizing the conservative front-runner, Alton B. Parker, chief justice of the New York Court of Appeals, while boosting more progressive candidates. In spite of Bryan's opposition, Parker came within nine votes of receiving the necessary two-thirds majority on the first ballot. Parker had 658 votes, followed by Rep. William Randolph Hearst of New York, with 200, and Cockrell, who trailed with 42. Although Hearst had progressive credentials, Bryan hesitated to support him and jeopardize his own leadership of the progressive wing of the party.

With Parker so close to victory, Idaho shifted its votes to the New York judge, prompting enough switches by other states to give Parker 679 votes and the nomination. Hearst, with his strength in the Middle West and West, finished with 181 votes. *(Chart, p. 216)*

With the nomination in hand, Parker stunned the convention by sending a telegram to the New York delega-

tion, announcing his support of the gold standard and advising the convention to select a new candidate if they found his position unacceptable. Parker supporters drafted a response stating that there was nothing to preclude his nomination, because the platform was silent on the currency issue.

Bryan, ill with a fever in his hotel but still a supporter of the silver cause, rose from his sickbed to join several Southern leaders on the floor of the convention in denouncing Parker's telegram and the drafted response. Nonetheless, the response recommended by the Parker forces was approved, 794 to 191, with opposition principally from the Middle West and West.

For vice president, the convention chose former West Virginia senator Henry G. Davis. He nearly achieved a two-thirds majority on the first ballot, receiving 654 votes. With Davis' nomination so near, a motion to declare him the vice presidential candidate was approved. Davis, at age 80, was the oldest candidate ever put on a national ticket by a major party. He was a man of great wealth, and the Democrats hoped that he would give freely to their campaign.

Although the platform was accepted without debate by a voice vote, there was maneuvering behind the scenes to meet the objections of Bryan. The initial platform draft before the resolutions committee included a plank that declared that recent gold discoveries had removed the currency question as a political issue. Bryan found this plank objectionable and successfully fought in the resolutions committee for its deletion. Bryan was less successful in having an income tax plank included but was able to get a more strongly worded antitrust resolution.

Unlike the Democratic platform of 1900, which focused on anti-imperialism, anti-monopoly and currency, the 1904 platform covered about two dozen topics with nearly equal emphasis.

The Democrats and Republicans disagreed on one new issue: federal support for private shipping firms. The Democrats opposed government assistance; the Republicans favored it. But on other issues the platform of the Democrats, like that of the Republicans, broke little new ground, instead restating positions that had been included in earlier Democratic platforms. There was a continued attack on American imperialism and a call for a smaller Army. There were planks that urged less international involvement and more emphasis on domestic improvements.

Following are excerpts from the Democratic platform of 1904:

> **Roosevelt Administration.** The existing Republican administration has been spasmodic, erratic, sensational, spectacular and arbitrary. It has made itself a satire upon the Congress, courts, and upon the settled practices and usages of national and international law ... the necessity of reform and the rescue of the administration of Government from the headstrong, arbitrary and spasmodic methods which distract business by uncertainty, and pervade the public mind with dread, distrust and perturbation.

> **Shipbuilding.** We denounce the ship subsidy bill recently passed by the United States Senate as an iniquitous appropriation of public funds for private purposes and a wasteful, illogical and useless attempt to overcome by subsidy the obstructions raised by Republican legislation to the growth and development of American commerce on the sea.
>
> We favor the upbuilding of a merchant marine without new or additional burdens upon the people and without bounties from the public treasury.

# 1908 Conventions

## Presidential Candidates

**Eugene V. Debs**
**Socialist**

**William H. Taft**
**Republican**

**William J. Bryan**
**Democrat**

### Socialists

The Socialists met in Chicago in May 1908 and re-nominated the ticket that had represented the party four years earlier: Eugene V. Debs of Indiana for president and Benjamin Hanford of New York as his running mate.

The platform was divided into several major sections, including a discussion of principles, and topics entitled general demands, industrial demands and political demands. The Socialists' goal was the creation of a classless society, and in pursuance of this goal the movement was identified as a party of the working class.

Among the general demands were proposals for public works programs to aid the unemployed and public ownership of land, means of transportation and communication and monopolies.

Industrial demands included calls for reduced working hours, the abolition of child labor and more effective inspections of working areas.

The section on political demands began with a restatement of earlier positions, with a call for tax reform, women's suffrage and the initiative, referendum and recall. However, the section also included more radical demands, such as the abolition of the Senate, the amendment of the Constitution by popular vote, the direct election of all judges and the removal of power from the Supreme Court to declare legislation passed by Congress unconstitutional.

Following are excerpts from the Socialist platform of 1908:

**Public Works Projects.** The immediate government relief for the unemployed workers by building schools, by reforesting of cutover and waste lands, by reclamation of arid tracts, and the building of canals, and by extending all other useful public works. All persons employed on such works shall be employed directly by the government under an eight hour work day and at the prevailing union wages. The government shall also loan money to states and municipalities without interest for the purpose of carrying on public works. It shall contribute to the funds of labor organizations for the purpose of assisting their unemployed members, and shall take such other measures within its power as will lessen the widespread misery of the workers caused by the misrule of the capitalist class.

**Public Ownership.** The collective ownership of railroads, telegraphs, telephones, steamship lines and all other means of social transportation and communication, and all land.

The collective ownership of all industries which are organized on a national scale and in which competition has virtually ceased to exist.

**Labor.** The improvement of the industrial condition of the workers.

(a) By shortening the workday in keeping with the increased productiveness of machinery.

(b) By securing to every worker a rest period of not less than a day and a half in each week.

(c) By securing a more effective inspection of workshops and factories.

(d) By forbidding the employment of children under sixteen years of age.

(e) By forbidding the interstate transportation of the products of child labor, of convict labor and of all uninspected factories.

(f) By abolishing official charity and substituting in its place compulsory insurance against unemployment, illness, accident, invalidism, old age and death.

**Tax Reform.** The extension of inheritance taxes, graduated in proportion to the amount of the bequests and the nearness of kin.

A graduated income tax.

**Women's Suffrage.** Unrestricted and equal suffrage for men and women....

**Senate.** The abolition of the senate.

**Constitutional and Judicial Reforms.** The abolition of the power usurped by the supreme court of the United States to pass upon the constitutionality of legislation enacted by Congress. National laws to be repealed or abrogated only by act of Congress or by a referendum of the whole people.

That the constitution be made amendable by majority vote.

That all judges be elected by the people for short terms, and that the power to issue injunctions shall be curbed by immediate legislation.

## Republicans

The Republicans held their convention in Chicago in June 1908. Although President Roosevelt declined to be a candidate for re-election, his choice for the presidency, Secretary of War William Howard Taft, was assured of nomination before the convention began.

Two hundred and twenty-three of the 980 seats at the convention were contested, but all the challenges were settled before the convention assembled. However, a dispute arose over the vote-allocation formula for the next convention. An amendment to the rules committee report proposed that the vote allocation be based on population rather than the electoral vote, as was currently in effect. Essentially, the amendment would have reduced the power of the Southern delegations. But a combination of Southern delegates and Taft supporters from other states defeated the amendment, 506 to 471. *(Chart, p. 218)*

Seven names were placed in nomination for the presidency, but Taft was a landslide winner on the first ballot, receiving 702 votes. Sen. Philander C. Knox of Pennsylvania was a distant runner-up with 68 votes.

For vice president, the convention selected Rep. James S. Sherman, a conservative New Yorker. Sherman won 816 votes on the first ballot, easily outdistancing former New Jersey governor Franklin Murphy, who had 77 votes.

The Wisconsin delegation, led by Sen. Robert M. La Follette, introduced a detailed minority report to the party platform. The Wisconsin proposals were considered in several separate sections. The first section included proposals for the establishment of a permanent tariff commission, the creation of a Department of Labor and the limitation of an eight-hour day for government workers. It was defeated, 952 to 28.

The second section recommended legislation to require the publication of campaign contributions. It was defeated, 880 to 94. Further sections of the minority report proposed the physical valuation of railroad property to help determine reasonable rates, and the direct election of senators. The railroad reform plank was beaten, 917 to 63, while the senatorial election plank was rejected, 866 to 114. After these votes, the majority report on the platform was adopted by a voice vote.

The platform approved by the delegates applauded the benefits of Republican rule, noting that under the party's guidance the United States had become the wealthiest nation on Earth. The principle of a protective tariff was applauded, as was the gold standard, an expansionist foreign policy and support for America's merchant marine.

Following are excerpts from the Republican platform of 1908:

**Party Differences.** In history, the difference between Democracy and Republicanism is that the one stood for debased currency, the other for honest currency; the one for free silver, the other for sound money; the one for free trade, the other for protection; the one for the contraction of American influence, the other for its expansion; the one has been forced to abandon every position taken on the great issues before the people, the other has held and vindicated all.

The present tendencies of the two parties are even more marked by inherent differences. The trend of Democracy is toward socialism, while the Republican party stands for a wise and regulated individualism. . . . Ultimately Democracy would have the nation own the people, while Republicanism would have the people own the nation.

## Democrats

The Democratic convention of 1908 was held in July in Denver, Colo. — the first convention held by a major party in a Western state. The convention was dominated by the Bryan forces, who regained control of the party after the conservative Alton B. Parker's landslide defeat in 1904.

Bryan's strength was evident on the first roll-call vote, concerning a Pennsylvania credentials dispute. The majority report claimed there were voting irregularities in five Philadelphia districts and urged the seating of Bryan delegates in place of those elected. By a vote of 604-1/2 to 386-1/2, the convention defeated the minority report, which argued for the delegates initially elected in the primary. The majority report then passed by a voice vote.

Bryan's presidential nomination was never in doubt. He was an easy winner on the first ballot, receiving 888-1/2 votes to 59-1/2 for Judge George Gray of Delaware and 46 for Gov. John A. Johnson of Minnesota. *(Chart, p. 217)*

Bryan left the choice of his running mate to the delegates. Although four names were placed in nomination, former Indiana gubernatorial candidate John W. Kern was chosen by acclamation. *The New York Times* sarcastically described the consistency of the Bryan-Kern ticket: "For a man twice defeated for the Presidency was at the head of it, and a man twice defeated for governor of his state was at the tail of it."

The platform adopted by the convention was tailored to Bryan's liking and had as its theme, "Shall the people rule?" The first portion of the document criticized Republican rule, specifically denouncing government overspending, a growing Republican-oriented bureaucracy and an unethical link between big business and the Republican Party characterized by large, unreported campaign contributions.

Meeting three weeks after the Republicans, the Democrats adopted most of the minority planks rejected earlier by the Republicans. Included in the Democratic platform were calls for the physical valuation of railroads, the creation of a Department of Labor, eight-hour work days for government employees, the direct election of senators and a prohibition against corporate campaign contributions and individual contributions over "a reasonable amount." The two parties continued to disagree on support of the American merchant marine, the nature of tariff revision and the direction of foreign policy, particularly regarding the lands acquired after the Spanish-American War.

The Democratic platform restated the party's support of a lower tariff, more extensive antitrust legislation with more rigid enforcement, a graduated income tax, increased power for the Interstate Commerce Commission to regulate railroads, telephone and telegraph companies, and a recommendation of prompt independence for the Philippines.

The Democrats included a plank abhorring Roosevelt's attempt to create a "dynasty," a direct reference to the outgoing president's hand-picking his war secretary, William Howard Taft, as the next Republican presidential candidate.

Following are excerpts from the Democratic platform of 1908:

**Appeal to the Masses.** The conscience of the nation is now aroused to free the Government from the grip of those who have made it a business asset of the favor-seeking corporations. It must become again a people's government, and be administered in all its departments according to the Jeffersonian maxim, "equal rights to all; special privileges to none."

"Shall the people rule?" is the overshadowing issue which manifests itself in all the questions now under discussion.

**Campaign Contributions.** We demand Federal legislation forever terminating the partnership which has existed between corporations of the country and the Republican party under the expressed or implied agreement that in return for the contribution of great sums of money wherewith to purchase elections, they should be allowed to continue substantially unmolested in their efforts to encroach upon the rights of the people. . . .

We pledge the Democratic party to the enactment of a law prohibiting any corporation from contributing to a campaign fund and any individual from contributing an amount above a reasonable maximum, and providing for the publication before election of all such contributions.

**Labor.** Questions of judicial practice have arisen especially in connection with industrial disputes. We deem that the parties to all judicial proceedings should be treated with rigid impartiality, and that injunctions should not be issued in any cases in which injunctions would not issue if no industrial dispute were involved. . . .

We favor the eight hour day on all Government work.

We pledge the Democratic party to the enactment of a law by Congress, as far as the Federal jurisdiction extends, for a general employer's liability act covering injury to body or loss of life of employes.

We pledge the Democratic party to the enactment of a law creating a Department of Labor, represented separately in the President's Cabinet, in which Department shall be included the subject of mines and mining.

# 1912 Conventions

## Presidential Candidates

**Eugene V. Debs**
**Socialist**

**William H. Taft**
**Republican**

**Woodrow Wilson**
**Democrat**

**Theodore Roosevelt**
**Progressive**

### Socialists

Eugene V. Debs of Indiana was nominated by the Socialists in 1912 to make his fourth run for the presidency. The convention, which met in Indianapolis in May, chose Emil Seidel of Wisconsin as his running mate.

The platform adopted by the Socialists was similar to the one written four years earlier, with calls for increased worker benefits, public works jobs for the unemployed, public ownership of land and the means of transportation and communication, tax reform, widespread political reform and a social insurance program.

The Socialists also added new proposals, advocating public ownership of the banking and currency system, the introduction of minimum wage scales, the elimination of the profit system in government contracts, an increase in corporation taxes and the direct election of the president and vice president.

Following are excerpts from the Socialist platform of 1912:

**Social Insurance.** By abolishing official charity and substituting a non-contributory system of old age pensions, a general system of insurance by the State of all its members against unemployment and invalidism and a system of compulsory insurance by employers of their workers, without cost to the latter, against industrial diseases, accidents and death.

**Government Contracts.** By abolishing the profit system in government work and substituting either the direct hire of labor or the awarding of contracts to cooperative groups of workers.

**Minimum Wage.** By establishing minimum wage scales.

**Tax Reform.** The adoption of a graduated income tax, the increase of the rates of the present corporation tax and the extension of inheritance taxes, graduated in proportion to the value of the estate and to nearness of kin — the proceeds of these taxes to be employed in the socialization of industry.

**Banking and Currency.** The collective ownership and democratic management of the banking and currency system.

**Direct Election of President.** The election of the President and Vice-President by direct vote of the people.

## Republicans

The 1912 Republican convention was one of the most tumultuous ever. It was held in Chicago in June and served as a fiery culmination to the bitter contest between President William Howard Taft and former president Theodore Roosevelt for the party's presidential nomination.

Roosevelt had overwhelmed Taft in the presidential primaries, but Roosevelt's popular strength was more than offset by Taft's control of the national committee and Southern delegations. Taft supporters held 37 of 53 seats on the national committee, an edge that the incumbent president's managers used to advantage in settling seating disputes. Two hundred and fifty-four of the 1,078 convention seats were contested before the national committee, and 235 were settled in favor of Taft delegates. Although a number of Roosevelt challenges were made with little justification, the dispensation of the challenges showed Taft's control of the convention organization.

With the conservative Republicans united behind Taft, Roosevelt faced the additional problem of sharing support from the progressive wing of the party with another candidate, Sen. Robert M. La Follette of Wisconsin. La Follette had only 41 delegates; but, angered by Roosevelt's bid to control the progressive forces, refused to withdraw as a candidate.

The first skirmish at the convention was over the choice of a temporary chairman. The Taft forces favored Sen. Elihu Root of New York, while the Roosevelt delegates supported Gov. Francis E. McGovern of Wisconsin.

On a prolonged roll call, during which the vote of each delegate was taken individually, Root defeated McGovern, 558 to 501. *(Chart, p. 220)*

With the contest for the temporary chairmanship settled, the battle shifted to credentials. Virtually shut out in the settlement of credentials cases by the national committee, the Roosevelt forces brought 72 delegate challenges to the floor of the convention. Before consideration of the cases, the Roosevelt leaders moved that none of the challenged delegates (favorable to Taft) be allowed to vote on any of the credentials contests. However, a motion to table this proposal carried, 567 to 507, and the challenged delegates were allowed to vote on all cases except their own. Although the Taft forces were clearly in control of the convention, four credentials cases were presented for a vote, and all were decided in favor of the Taft delegates. The rest of the contests were settled by voice votes.

At this point, Roosevelt, who had dramatically come to Chicago to direct his forces, advised his delegates to abstain from voting but to remain in the convention as a silent protest to what he regarded as steamroller tactics. In the convention hall itself, the pro-Roosevelt galleries emphasized the feelings of their leader by rubbing sandpaper and blowing horns to imitate the sounds of a steamroller.

Only two names were placed in nomination for the presidency — Taft's and La Follette's. Taft was nominated by Warren G. Harding of Ohio, who himself would be president less than a decade later but at the time was merely a former lieutenant governor. With most of the Roosevelt delegates abstaining, Taft won easily on the first ballot with 556 votes. Roosevelt received 107 votes and La Follette 41, while 348 delegates were present and did not vote.

Vice President James S. Sherman was easily renominated, collecting 596 votes to 21 for the runner-up, Sen. William E. Borah of Idaho. However, 352 delegates were present but refused to vote, and 72 others were absent. In recognition of Sherman's failing health, the convention passed a resolution empowering the national committee to fill any vacancy on the ticket that might occur.

Although the Roosevelt delegates had remained in the convention hall as a silent protest to the renomination of Taft and Sherman, the groundwork for the creation of a Roosevelt-led third party had begun as soon as the credentials contests were settled in favor of Taft. Before the Republican convention even began its presidential balloting, Roosevelt announced that he would accept the nomination of the "honestly elected majority" of the Republican convention or a new progressive party. The next day, June 22, after final adjournment of the Republican convention, many of the Roosevelt delegates assembled in a Chicago auditorium to hear their leader announce his availability as a candidate of an honestly elected progressive convention. Gov. Hiram Johnson of California was named temporary chairman of the new party, and planning was begun to hold a national convention later in the summer.

As in 1908, a progressive minority report to the platform was submitted. However, instead of taking individual votes on the various planks, the convention tabled the whole report by a voice vote. Subsequently, the majority report was accepted by a vote of 666 to 53, with 343 delegates present but not voting.

The platform lauded the accomplishments of the McKinley, Roosevelt and Taft administrations but contained few major positions different from the Democrats'. The Republican platform included, however, new planks favoring judicial reform and legislation publicizing campaign contributions and outlawing corporate campaign donations.

Following are excerpts from the Republican platform of 1912:

**Tariff.** The protective tariff is so woven into the fabric of our industrial and agricultural life that to substitute for it a tariff for revenue only would destroy many industries and throw millions of our people out of employment. The products of the farm and of the mine should receive the same measure of protection as other products of American labor.

**Campaign Contributions.** We favor such additional legislation as may be necessary more effectually to prohibit corporations from contributing funds, directly or indirectly, to campaigns for the nomination or election of the President, the Vice-President, Senators, and Representatives in Congress.

We heartily approve the recent Act of Congress requiring the fullest publicity in regard to all campaign contributions, whether made in connection with primaries, conventions, or elections.

**Judicial Reform.** That the Courts, both Federal and State, may bear the heavy burden laid upon them to the complete satisfaction of public opinion, we favor legislation to prevent long delays and the tedious and costly appeals which have so often amounted to a denial of justice in civil cases and to a failure to protect the public at large in criminal cases.

## Democrats

For the first time since 1872, the Democratic convention was held in Baltimore. The delegates, who assembled in the Maryland city in June, one week after the Republicans began their convention in Chicago, had a number of presidential candidates to choose from, although House Speaker Champ Clark of Missouri and Gov. Woodrow Wilson of New Jersey were the major contenders.

Once again, William Jennings Bryan had a major impact on the proceedings of a Democratic convention. His first appearance came in opposition to the national committee's selection of Judge Alton B. Parker of New York, the party's standard-bearer in 1904, as temporary chairman. Bryan nominated Sen. John W. Kern of Indiana for the post. In declining to be a candidate for temporary chairman, Kern recommended that Parker also withdraw as a candidate. But when Parker refused, Kern nominated Bryan for the post. Parker won on the roll call that followed, 579 to 508, with most of the Wilson delegates voting for Bryan, the Clark delegates splitting their support and delegates for other candidates favoring Parker. *(Chart, p. 219)*.

The defeat of Bryan produced an avalanche of telegrams from across the country, with a contemporary estimate of more than 100,000 flooding the delegates in Baltimore. Most of the telegrams were written by progressives and served to weaken the candidacy of the more conservative Clark.

In an attempt to appease Bryan, Parker urged members of the platform committee to select the Nebraskan as their chairman. Bryan, however, refused this overture. Subsequently, the platform committee announced that, by a margin of 41 to 11, the committee had voted to delay presentation of the platform until after selection of the candidates.

The Wilson forces won their first key vote on a question involving the unit rule. The vote specifically concerned the Ohio delegation, where district delegates, elected for Wilson, were bound by the state convention to vote for Gov. Judson Harmon of Ohio. By a vote of 565-1/2 to 491-1/3, the convention approved the right of the district delegates to vote for Wilson.

The Wilson forces won another test on a credentials dispute concerning the South Dakota delegation. The credentials committee recommended seating a delegation pledged to Clark; but the convention, by a vote of 639-1/2 to 437, supported the minority report, which called for seating delegates pledged to Wilson.

Bryan reappeared before the presidential balloting and introduced a resolution opposing the nomination of any candidate "who is the representative of or under obligation to J. Pierpont Morgan, Thomas F. Ryan, August Belmont, or any other member of the privilege-hunting and favor-seeking class." Bryan's resolution passed easily, 883 to 202-1/2.

Six names were placed in nomination for the presidency. Clark led on the first ballot with 440-1/2 votes, followed by Wilson with 324, Harmon with 148 and Rep. Oscar W. Underwood of Alabama with 117-1/2. Under the two-thirds rule, 730 votes were needed to nominate. *(Chart, p. 219)*

For nine ballots, there was little change in the vote totals, but on the 10th roll call New York shifted its 90 votes from Harmon to Clark. Expecting a quick triumph, the Clark forces unleashed an hour-long demonstration. However, their celebration was premature. While Clark had 556 votes, a majority, his total was well short of the two-thirds majority required by the rules.

The 10th ballot proved to be the high-water mark for Clark. On succeeding roll calls, he slowly began to lose strength. During the 14th ballot, Bryan received permission to address the convention again, this time to explain his vote. "The Great Commoner" announced that he could not support a candidate endorsed by the Tammany-con-

trolled New York delegation and, although bound earlier by state primary results to support Clark, was now switching his vote to Wilson. Most of the Nebraska delegation followed Bryan in voting for Wilson. After the 14th ballot, the vote totals stood: Clark, 553; Wilson, 361; Underwood, 111.

There were long intervals between other major vote switches. On the 20th ballot, Kansas shifted 20 of its votes from Clark to Wilson. On the 28th ballot, after a weekend recess, Indiana's favorite son, Gov. Thomas R. Marshall, withdrew in favor of Wilson. The slow trend in favor of the New Jersey governor finally enabled Wilson to pass Clark on the 30th roll call, 450 to 455; Underwood remained a distant third with 121-1/2 votes. *(Chart, p. 219)*

The convention adjourned for the evening after the 42nd ballot, but the Wilson momentum continued the next day. Illinois switched its 58 votes to Wilson on the 43rd ballot, giving him a simple majority with 602 votes. Clark continued to decline, slipping to 329 votes.

Wilson showed slight gains on the next two ballots, but the big break came on the 46th roll call, when Underwood withdrew. This was followed by the withdrawal of Clark and the other remaining candidates. Wilson received 990 votes on the 46th ballot, followed by Clark with 84.

Clark's failure to win the nomination marked the first occasion since 1844 that a candidate achieved a simple majority of the votes, without subsequently winning the necessary two-thirds majority. The 46 roll calls also represented the highest number of presidential ballots taken at any convention, Republican or Democratic, since 1860.

Wilson preferred Underwood as his running mate, but the Alabama representative was not interested in second place on the ticket. On the vice presidential roll call that followed, nine candidates received votes, led by Marshall with 389 votes and Gov. John Burke of North Dakota with 304-2/3. Marshall lengthened his lead over Burke on the second ballot, 644-1/2 to 386-1/3. After the roll call was completed, a New Jersey delegate moved that Marshall's nomination be made unanimous, and the motion passed.

The Democratic platform was approved without debate before selection of the vice presidential candidate. The platform restated a number of positions included in earlier party documents. It blamed the high cost of living on the protective tariff and the existence of trusts, and it called for a lower, revenue-only tariff and the passage of stronger antitrust legislation. The tariff issue was one of the major areas on which there was a marked difference between the parties, as the Republicans continued to support a protective tariff.

As in 1908, planks were included favoring the publicizing of campaign contributions and calling for the prohibition of corporate contributions and a limit on individual contributions.

The Democrats' labor plank was also virtually a restatement of the party's position four years earlier, supporting creation of a Department of Labor, a more limited use of injunctions, the guaranteed right of workers to organize and passage of an employees' compensation law. In contrast to the Democrats' support of employers' liability, the Republicans advocated workmen's compensation legislation.

Unlike the Republicans, the Democrats called for federal legislation to regulate the rates of railroad, telegraph, telephone and express companies based on valuation by the Interstate Commerce Commission. A plank was also included in the Democratic platform calling for the ratification of constitutional amendments establishing a graduated income tax and the direct election of senators — issues on which the Republican platform was silent. Imperialism was again denounced, as it had been in every Democratic platform since 1900.

New planks advocated a single-term presidency, the extension of presidential primaries to all states, reform of the judicial system to eliminate delays and cut expenses in court proceedings, and the strengthening of the government's pure food and public health agencies.

Following are excerpts from the Democratic platform of 1912:

**Single-term Presidency.** We favor a single Presidential term, and to that end urge the adoption of an amendment to the Constitution making the President of the United States ineligible to reelection, and we pledge the candidates of this Convention to this principle.

**Presidential Primaries.** The movement toward more popular government should be promoted through legislation in each State which will permit the expression of the preference of the electors for national candidates at presidential primaries.

**Judicial Reform.** We recognize the urgent need of reform in the administration of civil and criminal law in the United States, and we recommend the enactment of such legislation and the promotion of such measures as will rid the present legal system of the delays, expense, and uncertainties incident to the system as now administered.

**States' Rights.** Believing that the most efficient results under our system of government are to be attained by the full exercise by the States of their reserved sovereign powers, we denounce as usurpation the efforts of our opponents to deprive the States of any of the rights reserved to them, and to enlarge and magnify by indirection the powers of the Federal government.

## Progressives

Early in August 1912 the bolting Roosevelt forces assembled in Chicago and nominated their leader to guide a new party, the Progressives. More than 2,000 delegates, representing every state except South Carolina, gathered for the three-day convention. It was a diverse assembly that matched the Populists in crusading idealism and included, for the first time, women as well as men politicians and social workers as well as businessmen.

While the delegates enthusiastically sang "Onward, Christian Soldiers" and "The Battle Hymn of the Republic" and cheered the appearance of Roosevelt before the convention, there was some dissension caused by the party's racial policy.

During the campaign for the Republican presidential nomination, Taft had the support of party organizations in the South, which included blacks. As a result, Roosevelt directed his appeal strictly to white leaders in the region. Describing Southern black delegates as uneducated and purchasable, Roosevelt insisted that only "lily white" delegations from the South be seated at the Progressive convention, but he allowed blacks to be included in delegations from other states. Although there was no floor debate on this policy, a number of liberal delegates were dissatisfied with Roosevelt's decision.

Both Roosevelt and his handpicked choice for vice president, Gov. Hiram W. Johnson of California, were nominated by acclamation. Jane Addams, a Chicago social worker and leader in the women's rights movement, gave evidence of the role of women in the Progressive Party by delivering a seconding speech for Roosevelt.

Like the nominations of the Progressive standard-bearers, the party platform was adopted by acclamation. But the voice vote hid the dissatisfaction felt by Midwestern and Western Progressives over the antitrust plank. Most of the Progressives from these regions favored the busting of trusts through enforcement of the Sherman Anti-trust Act. Roosevelt, however, favored government regulation rather than trust-busting.

The platform approved by the convention included the trust-busting position. However, Roosevelt and his close advisers deleted the section in the official report. While there was obvious disagreement in the party on this issue, there was no floor debate or roll-call vote on the subject.

With the theme "A Covenant with the People," the platform argued for increased democratization coupled with more people-oriented federal programs. The party favored nationwide presidential primaries, the direct election of senators, the initiative, referendum and recall and women's suffrage. Additionally, the Progressives proposed that state laws ruled unconstitutional be submitted to a vote of the state electorate.

The platform also advocated congressional reforms: the registration of lobbyists, the publicizing of committee hearings except in foreign affairs, and the recording of committee votes.

Like the Democrats, the Progressives favored creation of a Department of Labor and a more limited use of labor injunctions, but additionally the new party called for a prohibition of child labor and convict contract labor.

The Progressives went beyond both major parties in proposing the union of government health agencies into a single national health service and the creation of a social insurance system that would assist both the elderly and workers who were ill or unemployed. To help support their proposed federal programs, the Progressives recommended passage of the income tax amendment and establishment of a graduated inheritance tax.

Having adopted their platform and selected their candidates, the delegates to the Progressive convention adjourned by singing the "Doxology."

Following are excerpts from the Progressive platform of 1912:

**Electoral Reform.** In particular, the party declares for direct primaries of the nomination of State and National officers, for nation-wide preferential primaries for candidates for the presidency; for the direct election of United States Senators by the people; and we urge on the States the policy of the short ballot, with responsibility to the people secured by the initiative, referendum and recall.

**Women's Suffrage.** The Progressive party, believing that no people can justly claim to be a true democracy which denies political rights on account of sex, pledges itself to the task of securing equal suffrage to men and women alike.

**Judicial Reform.** That when an Act, passed under the police power of the State, is held unconstitutional under the State Constitution, by the courts, the people, after an ample interval for deliberation, shall have an opportunity to vote on the question whether they desire the Act to become law, notwithstanding such decision.

**Campaign Contributions.** We pledge our party to legislation that will compel strict limitation of all campaign contributions and expenditures, and detailed publicity of both before as well as after primaries and elections.

**Congressional Reform.** We pledge our party to

legislation compelling the registration of lobbyists; publicity of committee hearings except on foreign affairs, and recording of all votes in committee....

**National Health Service.** We favor the union of all the existing agencies of the Federal Government dealing with the public health into a single national health service without discrimination against or for any one set of therapeutic methods, school of medicine, or school of healing with such additional powers as may be necessary to enable it to perform efficiently such duties in the protection of the public from preventable diseases as may be properly undertaken by the Federal authorities, including the executing of existing laws regarding pure food, quarantine and cognate subjects, the promotion of vital statistics and the extension of the registration area of such statistics, and cooperation with the health activities of the various States and cities of the Nation.

**Social Insurance.** The protection of home life against the hazards of sickness, irregular employment and old age through the adoption of a system of social insurance adapted to American use....

**Antitrust Action.** We therefore demand a strong National regulation of inter-State corporations ... we urge the establishment of a strong Federal administrative commission of high standing, which shall maintain permanent active supervision over industrial corporations engaged in inter-State commerce, or such of them as are of public importance, doing for them what the Government now does for the National banks, and what is now done for the railroads by the Inter-State Commerce Commission.

**Income and Inheritance Taxes.** We believe in a graduated inheritance tax as a National means of equalizing the obligations of holders of property to Government, and we hereby pledge our party to enact such a Federal law as will tax large inheritances, returning to the States an equitable percentage of all amounts collected.

We favor the ratification of the pending amendment to the Constitution giving the Government power to levy an income tax.

**Tariff.** We demand tariff revision because the present tariff is unjust to the people of the United States. Fair dealing toward the people requires an immediate downward revision of those schedules wherein duties are shown to be unjust or excessive....

The Democratic party is committed to the destruction of the protective system through a tariff for revenue only — a policy which would inevitably produce widespread industrial and commercial disaster.

**Republicans and Democrats.** Political parties exist to secure responsible government and to execute the will of the people.

From these great tasks both of the old parties have turned aside. Instead of instruments to promote the general welfare, they have become the tools of corrupt interests which use them impartially to serve their selfish purposes. Behind the ostensible government sits enthroned an invisible government owing no allegiance and acknowledging no responsibility to the people.

To destroy this invisible government, to dissolve the unholy alliance between corrupt business and corrupt politics is the first task of the statesmanship of the day.

**States' Rights.** The extreme insistence on States' rights by the Democratic party in the Baltimore platform demonstrates anew its ability to understand the world into which it has survived or to administer the affairs of a union of States which have in all essential respects become one people.

# 1916 Conventions

## Presidential Candidates

**Charles E. Hughes**
**Republican**

**Woodrow Wilson**
**Democrat**

### Republicans

The Republicans and Progressives both held their conventions in Chicago in early June 1916. Leaders of both parties were ready to negotiate to heal the split that had divided the Republican Party in 1912.

Before the convention began, the Republican National Committee already had effected reform in the vote-allocation formula. To meet the objection raised in 1912 that the South was overrepresented, the national committee adopted a new method of vote allocation that considered a state's Republican voting strength as well as its electoral vote. Under the new formula, the Southern states lost 78 delegate seats, or more than a third of their 1912 total.

But while the Republicans were willing to make some

internal reforms, most party leaders were adamantly opposed to nominating the hero of the Progressives, Theodore Roosevelt. Before the presidential balloting began, the Republican convention approved by voice vote the selection of a five-man committee to meet jointly with representatives of the Progressive convention, with the hope of finding a course of action that would unify the two parties.

However, the Republican representatives reported back that the Progressives, while desiring unity with the Republicans, firmly favored the nomination of Roosevelt. The Republican convention chairman, Sen. Warren G. Harding of Ohio, instructed the conferees to continue negotiations but allowed the presidential balloting to begin.

Charles Evans Hughes, a Supreme Court justice and former governor of New York, was the front-runner for the Republican nomination. Hughes did not actively seek the nomination and remained on the Supreme Court during the pre-convention period. But he was viewed by many party leaders as an ideal compromise candidate, because of his progressive credentials and lack of involvement in the divisive 1912 campaign.

However, some conservative party leaders felt Hughes was too progressive and sought other candidates. Seventeen men received votes on the first ballot, led by Hughes with 253-1/2. Next were Sen. John W. Weeks of Massachusetts with 105 votes and former senator Elihu Root of New York with 103. Five of the other vote recipients had at least 65 votes each. The justice widened his lead on the second ballot, receiving 328-1/2 votes to 98-1/2 for Root. After the second roll call the convention voted 694-1/2 to 286-1/2 to recess for the evening. Most of the votes for adjournment came from delegates outside the Hughes column. *(Chart, p. 222)*

While the Republican convention was in recess, the joint committee of Republicans and Progressives continued to negotiate. The Republican members proposed Hughes as a compromise candidate, but in a message from his home in Oyster Bay, N.Y., Roosevelt stunned both parties by suggesting the name of Henry Cabot Lodge, a conservative senator from Massachusetts.

The Progressive delegates reacted defiantly to this recommendation by nominating Roosevelt by acclamation and selecting John M. Parker of Louisiana as his running mate. Roosevelt, however, immediately scotched the enthusiasm of the Progressive delegates by conditionally declining the nomination. Roosevelt informed the convention that he would support Hughes if the latter's positions on major issues were acceptable.

When the Republican convention reconvened the next day, the opposition to Hughes had evaporated. The New Yorker received 949-1/2 of the 987 convention votes on the third ballot, and his nomination was subsequently declared unanimous.

Charles W. Fairbanks of Indiana, vice president under Roosevelt, was the convention's choice to fill out the Republican ticket. Fairbanks won on the first ballot by 863 votes to 108 for former Nebraska senator Elmer J. Burkett.

The Wisconsin delegation again presented its own minority platform report, which included planks that denounced "dollar diplomacy" and called for women's suffrage, a referendum before any declaration of war and constitutional amendments to establish the initiative, referendum and recall. The minority report was defeated and the majority report was approved by voice votes.

The adopted platform harshly criticized the policies of the Wilson administration. In foreign policy, the Republicans denounced the Wilson government for "shifty expedients" and "phrase making" and promised "strict and honest neutrality." The platform condemned the administration for its intervention in Mexico and non-involvement in the Philippines. The Republicans also called for a stronger national defense.

The two parties continued to disagree on the tariff issue, with the Republicans criticizing the lower (Democratic-passed) Underwood tariff and arguing for a higher, protective tariff. The Republican platform lauded the party's efforts in passing antitrust and transportation rate regulation, but it criticized the Democrats for harassing business.

Following are excerpts from the Republican platform of 1916:

**Foreign Policy.** We desire peace, the peace of justice and right, and believe in maintaining a strict and honest neutrality between the belligerents in the great war in Europe. We must perform all our duties and insist upon all our rights as neutrals without fear and without favor. We believe that peace and neutrality, as well as the dignity and influence of the United States, cannot be preserved by shifty expedients, by phrase making, by performances in language, or by attitudes ever changing in an effort to secure votes or voters.

**National Defense.** We must have a Navy so strong and so well proportioned and equipped, so thoroughly ready and prepared, that no enemy can gain command of the sea and effect a landing in force on either our Western or our Eastern coast. To secure these results we must have a coherent continuous policy of national defense, which even in these perilous days the Democratic party has utterly failed to develop, but which we promise to give to the country.

**Merchant Marine.** We are utterly opposed to the Government ownership of vessels as proposed by the Democratic party, because Government-owned ships, while effectively preventing the development of the American Merchant Marine by private capital, will be entirely unable to provide for the vast volume of American freights and will leave us more helpless than ever in the hard grip of foreign syndicates.

**Tariff.** The Republican party stands now, as always, in the fullest sense for the policy of tariff protection to American industries and American labor.

**Business.** The Republican party firmly believes that all who violate the laws in regulation of business, should be individually punished. But prosecution is very different from persecution, and business success, no matter how honestly attained, is apparently regarded by the Democratic party as in itself a crime. Such doctrines and beliefs choke enterprise and stifle prosperity. The Republican party believes in encouraging American business as it believes in and will seek to advance all American interests.

**Women's Suffrage.** The Republican party, reaffirming its faith in government of the people, by the people, for the people, as a measure of justice to one-half the adult people of this country, favors the extension of the suffrage to women, but recognizes the right of each state to settle this question for itself.

## Democrats

The Democratic convention of 1916 was held in St. Louis in mid-June. The delegates were nearly unanimous in their support for President Woodrow Wilson, who was renominated by the vote of 1,092 to 1 — the lone dissenting vote coming from an Illinois delegate who disapproved of a motion to nominate Wilson by acclamation. With Wilson's approval, Vice President Thomas R. Marshall was renominated by acclamation.

For the first time in more than two decades, William Jennings Bryan was not a major convention force. Bryan was defeated in his bid to be a delegate-at-large from Nebraska and attended the convention as a reporter. He was invited to address the delegates and echoed the theme stressed by other speakers, that Wilson would keep the nation out of war.

Wilson was the recognized leader of the Democratic Party, but the pacifistic theme, emphasized by Bryan and other convention orators, struck a responsive chord among the delegates that was mildly alarming to Wilson and his managers. They initially had planned to accent the theme of Americanism and national unity.

The wording of the national unity plank was a matter of debate within the platform committee. The Democratic senators from Missouri warned that Wilson's strongly worded plank might offend German-American citizens. Nonetheless, the Wilson plank was retained and placed prominently near the beginning of the platform.

The only section of the platform brought to a floor vote was the plank on women's suffrage. The majority plank favored extending the vote to women, while a minority plank advocated leaving the matter to the individual states. The minority plank was defeated, 888-1/2 to 181-1/2. The rest of the platform was then adopted by a voice vote. The Democratic position on women's suffrage contrasted with that of the Republicans, who proposed leaving the matter up to the individual states. *(Chart, p. 221)*

The platform's inclusion of national unity and military preparedness planks was a contrast with earlier Democratic platforms around the turn of the century, which had consistently denounced imperialism and denied the need for a stronger military. Even though spurred by the war in Europe, the new planks were a notable change.

The rest of the platform focused on the progressive reforms of the Wilson administration, particularly in tariff, banking, labor and agriculture. Wilson himself was lauded as "the greatest American of his generation."

Noticeably absent from the platform were two planks in the party's document four years earlier: a call for a single-term presidency and a defense of states' rights.

Following are excerpts from the Democratic platform of 1916:

**National Unity.** In this day of test, America must show itself not a nation of partisans but a nation of patriots. There is gathered here in America the best of the blood, the industry and the genius of the whole world, the elements of a great race and a magnificent society to be welded into a mighty and splendid Nation. Whoever, actuated by the purpose to promote the industry of a foreign power, in disregard of our own country's welfare or to injure this government in its foreign relations or cripple or destroy its industries at home, and whoever by arousing prejudices of a racial, religious or other nature creates discord and strife among our people so as to obstruct the wholesome process of unification, is faithless to the trust which the privileges of citizenship repose in him and is disloyal to his country.

**Military Preparedness.** We therefore favor the maintenance of an army fully adequate to the requirements of order, of safety, and of the protection of the nation's rights, the fullest development of modern methods of seacoast defence and the maintenance of an adequate reserve of citizens trained to arms and prepared to safeguard the people and territory of the United States against any danger of hostile action which may unexpectedly arise; and a fixed policy for the continuous development of a navy, worthy to support the great naval traditions of the United States and fully equal to the international tasks which this Nation hopes and expects to take a part in performing.

**Tariff.** We reaffirm our belief in the doctrine of a tariff for the purpose of providing sufficient revenue for the operation of the government economically administered, and unreservedly endorse the Underwood tariff law as truly exemplifying that doctrine.

**Women's Suffrage.** We recommend the extension of the franchise to the women of the country by the States upon the same terms as to men.

## Socialists

The Socialists did not hold a convention in 1916 but did nominate candidates and adopt a platform. The candidates were chosen in a unique mail referendum. With Eugene V. Debs' refusal to run, the presidential nomination went to Allan L. Benson of New York. George R. Kirkpatrick of New Jersey was selected as his running mate.

More than half of the Socialist platform was devoted to criticizing the United States' preparations for war. The Socialists opposed the war in Europe and viewed the American drive for preparedness as an effort by ruling capitalists to protect the system and their profits.

The Socialist platform specifically advocated no increase in military appropriations, a national referendum on any declaration of war, the shifting of the power to make foreign policy from the president to Congress, the abandonment of the Monroe Doctrine and immediate independence for the Philippines.

The rest of the platform was divided into sections entitled political demands, industrial demands and collective ownership. The proposals in these sections paralleled earlier Socialist platforms, although there was a new plank, advocating lending by the federal government to local governments, which was an early expression of the concept of revenue-sharing.

Following are excerpts from the Socialist platform of 1916:

**Militarism and Preparedness.** The working class must recognize militarism as the greatest menace to all efforts toward industrial freedom, and regardless of political or industrial affiliations must present a united front in the fight against preparedness and militarism.... The war in Europe, which diminished and is still diminishing the remote possibility of European attack upon the United States, was nevertheless seized upon by capitalists and by unscrupulous politicians as a means of spreading fear throughout the country, to the end that, by false pretenses, great military establishments might be obtained. We denounce such "preparedness" as both false in principle, unnecessary in character and dangerous in its plain tendencies toward militarism.

**Foreign Policy.** We, therefore, demand that the power to fix foreign policies and conduct diplomatic negotiations shall be lodged in congress and shall be exercised publicly, the people reserving the right to order congress, at any time, to change its foreign policy.

**Referendum on War.** That no war shall be declared or waged by the United States without a referendum vote of the entire people, except for the purpose of repelling invasion.

**Federal Loans to Local Governments.** The government shall lend money on bonds to counties and municipalities at a nominal rate of interest for the purpose of taking over or establishing public utilities and for building or maintaining public roads or highways and public schools.

# 1920 Conventions

## Presidential Candidates

**Eugene V. Debs**
Socialist

**Warren G. Harding**
Republican

**James M. Cox**
Democrat

## Socialists

The Socialists held their convention in New York in May and for the fifth time nominated Eugene V. Debs of Indiana for president. It was one of the strangest candidacies in American political history, because at the time Debs was serving a 10-year prison term in the Atlanta federal penitentiary for his outspoken opposition to the American war effort. Seymour Stedman of Ohio was chosen as his running mate.

The Socialist platform was again a distinctive document, going far beyond the platforms of the two major parties in the radical nature of the reforms proposed. The platform characterized the war policies and peace proposals of the Wilson administration as "despotism, reaction and oppression unsurpassed in the annals of the republic." It called for the replacement of the "mischievous" League of Nations with an international parliament. It favored recognition of both the newly established Irish Republic and the Soviet Union.

The Socialists continued to advocate extensive tax reform and included new calls for a tax on unused land and a progressive property tax on wartime profits that would help pay off government debts. The platform warned that the continuing militaristic mood of both major parties could lead to another war.

The Socialists continued to recommend extensive labor benefits, but for the first time they specifically mentioned migratory workers as needing government assistance.

Following are excerpts from the Socialist platform of 1920:

**League of Nations.** The Government of the United States should initiate a movement to dissolve the mischievous organization called the "League of Nations" and to create an international parliament, composed of democratically elected representatives of all nations of the world based upon the recognition of their equal rights, the principles of self determination, the right to national existence of colonies and other dependencies, freedom of international trade and trade routes by land and sea, and universal disarmament, and be charged with revising the Treaty of Peace on the principles of justice and conciliation.

**Labor.** Congress should enact effective laws to abolish child labor, to fix minimum wages, based on an ascertained cost of a decent standard of life, to protect migratory and unemployed workers from oppression, to abolish detective and strike-breaking agencies and to establish a shorter work-day in keeping with increased industrial productivity.

**Blacks.** Congress should enforce the provisions of the Thirteenth, Fourteenth and Fifteenth Amendments with reference to the Negroes, and effective federal legislation should be enacted to secure the Negroes full civil, political, industrial and educational rights.

## Republicans

In mid-June, Republicans met for the fifth straight time in Chicago for their quadrennial convention. For the first time, women were on the floor in large numbers as delegates. With the constitutional amendment granting women the vote on the verge of passage, Republicans, especially in the Midwest and West, were quick to include women in their delegations.

The Republicans, like the Democrats two weeks later, entered their convention with no clear front-runner for the presidential nomination. Three candidates were at the top of the list, but two of them, Maj. Gen. Leonard Wood of New Hampshire and Sen. Hiram Johnson of California, split the party's progressive wing, while the third entry, Gov. Frank Lowden of Illinois, ran poorly in the presidential primaries and was accused of campaign spending irregularities.

The names of 11 men were placed in nomination for the presidency, but none came close during the first day of balloting to the 493 votes needed to nominate. Wood led on the initial roll call with 287-1/2 votes, trailed by Lowden with 211-1/2 and Johnson with 133-1/2. Sen. Warren G. Harding of Ohio, who had not campaigned for the nomination as extensively as the three pacesetters, placed six with 65-1/2 votes. Wood, Lowden and Johnson all gained strength during the first three ballots. *(Chart, p. 224)*

After the third roll call, the Johnson delegates moved for adjournment but were defeated, 701-1/2 to 275-1/2. On the fourth ballot, Wood's vote total rose to 314-1/2, well short of a majority but the highest mark attained yet by any candidate. At this point, Harding stood in fifth place with 61-1/2 votes. Although a motion to adjourn had been soundly defeated after the previous roll call, the permanent chairman, Sen. Henry Cabot Lodge of Massachusetts, entertained a new motion to adjourn and declared it passed on a closely divided voice vote.

The adjournment gave Republican leaders a chance to confer and discuss the various presidential possibilities. Much is made in history books about Harding's selection that night in the legendary "smoke-filled room," when Harding was allegedly interviewed at 2 o'clock by Republican leaders and, answering their questions satisfactorily, was chosen as the nominee. The authenticity of the meeting has been questioned, as has the power of the politicians who made the designation. But, nonetheless, it was clear that Harding was a viable compromise choice who was both acceptable to the conservative party leadership and could be nominated by the delegates.

Harding's vote total rose slowly in the next day's balloting until the ninth ballot, when a large shift, primarily of Lowden delegates, boosted the Ohio senator's vote from 133 to 374-1/2. This was the highest total for any candidate to this point and started a bandwagon that produced Harding's nomination on the 10th ballot. After the various switches, the final vote stood: Harding, 692-1/5; Wood, 156, and Johnson, 80-4/5, with the rest of the vote scattered.

Immediately after Harding's nomination, the vice presidential balloting began. After the nomination of Sen. Irvine L. Lenroot of Wisconsin, a delegate from Oregon rose and, standing on his chair, nominated Gov. Calvin Coolidge of Massachusetts. An enthusiastic demonstration followed, showing the wide delegate support for Coolidge. The governor, who had risen to national prominence less than a year earlier with his handling of a Boston police strike, was a runaway winner on the one vice presidential ballot. Coolidge received 674-1/2 votes to Lenroot's 146-1/2.

The Wisconsin delegation again presented a detailed minority report to the platform. It included planks that opposed entry into the League of Nations under the terms of the proposed treaty, objected to compulsory military service, called for the quick conclusion of peace negotiations and normalization of foreign relations and recommended a bonus for servicemen to match the wages of wartime civilian workers.

In domestic reforms, the Wisconsin report advocated the election of federal judges and the passage of a constitutional amendment that would establish the initiative, referendum and recall. The entire minority report was rejected by a voice vote, and the platform as written was adopted in a similar manner.

The platform began by denouncing the Wilson administration for being completely unprepared for both war and peace. It went on to criticize Wilson for establishing an "executive autocracy" by arrogating to himself power that belonged to other branches of government.

The platform included a League of Nations plank that intentionally straddled the controversial issue, applauding the Republican-controlled Senate for defeating Wilson's League but pledging the party "to such agreements with the other nations of the world as shall meet the full duty of America to civilization and humanity."

To help cut federal spending, the Republicans favored consolidating some departments and bureaus and establishing an executive budget.

Both parties continued to differ on the tariff, with the Democrats reiterating their belief in a revenue tariff and the Republicans restating their support of a protective tariff.

Following are excerpts from the Republican platform of 1920:

> **League of Nations.** The Republican party stands for agreement among the nations to preserve the peace of the world. . . .
>
> The covenant signed by the President at Paris failed signally . . . and contains stipulations, not only intolerable for an independent people, but certain to produce the injustice, hostility and controversy among nations which it proposed to prevent.
>
> . . . we pledge the coming Republican administration to such agreements with the other nations of the world as shall meet the full duty of America to civilization and humanity, in accordance with American ideals, and without surrendering the right of the American people to exercise its judgment and its power in favor of justice and peace.

## Democrats

San Francisco was the host city for the 1920 Democratic convention, marking the first time a convention of one of the major parties was held west of the Rockies. Not only was the site a new one, but when the convention opened in late June, for the first time in a generation the Democratic Party had no recognized leader such as Cleveland, Bryan or Wilson.

President Woodrow Wilson had some hope of a third nomination, but his failing health and skidding popularity made this an unrealistic prospect. But Wilson's refusal to endorse another candidate prevented the emergence of any presidential hopeful as a front-runner for the nomination. In all, 24 candidates received votes on the first presidential roll call, but none approached the 729 votes needed for nomination. William Gibbs McAdoo, Wilson's son-in-law and former treasury secretary, led with 266 votes, in spite of having withdrawn from the race several days before the convention began. Attorney General A. Mitchell Palmer, famed for his efforts during the "Red Scare," followed closely with 254 votes. Two governors, Ohio's James M. Cox and New York's Alfred E. Smith, trailed with 134 and 109 votes, respectively. (Chart, p. 223)

Another ballot was taken before evening adjournment, with the top four candidates retaining the same order and nearly the same vote.

During the next day's balloting, Cox gained steadily and passed both McAdoo and Palmer. When the majority of McAdoo and Palmer delegates successfully carried a motion to recess after the 16th ballot, Cox held the lead with 454-1/2 votes. McAdoo was next with 337 votes and Palmer trailed with 164-1/2.

Six more ballots were taken during the evening session, and although Cox's lead narrowed, he still led McAdoo after the 22nd ballot, 430 to 372-1/2. In the next day's balloting, McAdoo gradually gained ground until he finally passed Cox on the 30th ballot, 403-1/2 to 400-1/2. After completion of the roll call, the motion was made to eliminate the lowest candidate on each succeeding ballot until a nominee had been selected. This drastic proposal to shorten the convention was defeated, 812-1/2 to 264.

Balloting continued without interruption through the 36th roll call. McAdoo still led with 399 votes, but his margin over Cox was reduced to 22 votes, and Palmer with 241 votes achieved his highest total since the 11th ballot.

A candidate was finally nominated during the evening session of the convention's third day of presidential balloting. The Palmer revival fizzled quickly, with most of his delegates going to either McAdoo or Cox. The Ohio governor regained the lead on the 39th ballot, when the majority of the Indiana delegation shifted from McAdoo to Cox. After this roll call, Cox led McAdoo, 468-1/2 to 440, Palmer having slipped to 74. Cox continued to gain, and a last-ditch effort by McAdoo delegates to force an adjournment failed, 637 to 406. Cox's vote total reached 699-1/2 votes on the 44th ballot, and, with victory imminent, a motion was adopted to declare the Ohio governor the unanimous nominee of the convention. *(Chart, p. 223)*

Cox's choice for the vice presidential nomination was Franklin Delano Roosevelt of New York, the 38-year-old assistant secretary of the Navy. Roosevelt was nominated by acclamation.

William Jennings Bryan attended the convention and proposed five planks as amendments to the platform. Only his plank endorsing prohibition, however, was submitted for a roll-call vote, and it was soundly beaten, 929-1/2 to 155-1/2. A counterproposal by a New York delegate, recognizing the legality of the prohibition amendment to the Constitution but favoring the manufacture of beer and light wines for home use, was also defeated, 724-1/2 to 356. The platform finally adopted did not discuss the prohibition question.

Bryan's four other planks covered a wide range of issues. He favored establishing a national newspaper, reducing from two-thirds to a simple majority the vote needed to approve treaties in the Senate, expressed opposition to peacetime universal compulsory military training and recommended that interstate companies reveal the difference between the cost and selling price of their products. All four planks were defeated by voice votes.

One other amendment, calling for the recognition of Irish independence, came to the floor for a roll-call vote. It was beaten, 674 to 402-1/2. Included instead was a milder plank sympathizing with the Irish struggle for indepen-

dence. Subsequently, the delegates approved by voice vote the entire platform as it was first written.

Although the delegates were unwilling to renominate Wilson, the platform was largely devoted to praise of his leadership and legislation passed during his presidency. The platform reflected Wilson's thinking by placing the League of Nations plank prominently at the beginning and supporting the president's call for American membership. The plank did allow for reservations to the treaty, but none that would prevent American participation in the League.

Following are excerpts from the Democratic platform of 1920:

**League of Nations.** The Democratic Party favors the League of Nations as the surest, if not the only, practicable means of maintaining the permanent peace of the world and terminating the insufferable burden of great military and naval establishments....

We commend the President for his courage and his high conception of good faith in steadfastly standing for the covenant agreed to by all the associated and allied nations at war with Germany, and we condemn the Republican Senate for its refusal to ratify the treaty merely because it was the product of Democratic statesmanship, thus interposing partisan envy and personal hatred in the way of the peace and renewed prosperity of the world....

We advocate the immediate ratification of the treaty without reservations which would impair its essential integrity, but do not oppose the acceptance of any reservations making clearer or more specific the obligations of the United States to the league associates.

**Irish Independence.** The great principle of national self-determination has received constant reiteration as one of the chief objectives for which this country entered the war and victory established this principle.

Within the limitations of international comity and usage, this Convention repeats the several previous expressions of the sympathy of the Democratic Party of the United States for the aspirations of Ireland for self-government.

# 1924 Conventions

## Presidential Candidates

**Calvin Coolidge**
**Republican**

**John W. Davis**
**Democrat**

**Robert M. La Follette**
**Progressive**

### Republicans

The Republicans gathered for their convention in Cleveland, Ohio, in June. For the first time, a convention was broadcast by radio. Also for the first time, Republican Party rules were changed to elect women to the national committee, with one man and one woman to be chosen from each state and territory.

Unlike the Democratic marathon that began two weeks later in New York, there was surface harmony at the Republican convention. President Calvin Coolidge's success in the spring primaries, and his ability to defuse the corruption issue, eliminated any major opposition. Coolidge was easily nominated on the first ballot, receiving 1,065 votes. Sen. Robert M. La Follette of Wisconsin was a distant second with 34 votes, while Sen. Hiram W. Johnson of California collected the remaining 10. *(Chart, p. 225)*

The vice presidential nomination was a confused matter. Eight candidates were nominated, and on the first ballot former Illinois governor Frank O. Lowden led with 222 votes. Although Lowden publicly stated that he would not accept the nomination, he received a majority of the vote on the second roll call. A recess was taken to see if Lowden had changed his mind, but when it was certain that he had not the delegates resumed balloting.

On the third roll call, former budget bureau director Charles G. Dawes received 682-1/2 votes to win nomination. Secretary of Commerce Herbert Hoover was second with 234-1/2 votes.

As was its custom throughout the early 20th century, the Wisconsin delegation proposed a detailed minority report to the platform. Proposals included government ownership of railroads and water power, an increased excess profits tax and reduced taxes on individuals with low incomes. The Wisconsin platform was rejected without a roll-call vote.

The platform that was adopted lauded the economy in government shown by the Republican administration and promised a reduction in taxes.

The Democrats and Republicans continued to differ on the tariff issue, with the Republicans again defending the protective tariff. The Ku Klux Klan was not mentioned in the Republican platform, nor was it discussed on the floor. The controversial organization was the subject of a divisive floor fight at the Democratic convention.

The Republican platform criticized the corruption found to exist in the Harding administration, but it also denounced efforts "to besmirch the names of the innocent and undermine the confidence of the people in the government under which they live."

In the area of foreign policy, the Republicans opposed membership in the League of Nations, although favoring participation in the World Court. While applauding the return of peace and reflecting the nation's increasing mood of isolationism, the Republicans opposed cutbacks in the Army and Navy.

Following are excerpts from the Republican platform of 1924:

**Corruption.** We demand the speedy, fearless and impartial prosecution of all wrong doers, without regard for political affiliations; but we declare no greater wrong can be committed against the people than the attempt to destroy their trust in the great body of their public servants. Admitting the deep humiliation which all good citizens share that our public life should have harbored some dishonest men, we assert that these undesirables do not represent the standard of our national integrity.

**Taxes.** We pledge ourselves to the progressive reduction of taxes of all the people as rapidly as may be done with due regard for the essential expenditures for the government administered with rigid economy and to place our tax system on a sound peace time basis.

**League of Nations.** This government has definitely refused membership in the league of nations or to assume any obligations under the covenant of the league. On this we stand.

**Military.** There must be no further weakening of our regular army and we advocate appropriations sufficient to provide for the training of all members of the national guard, the citizens' military training camps, the reserve officers' training camps and the reserves who may offer themselves for service. We pledge ourselves for service. We pledge ourselves to round out and maintain the navy to the full strength provided the United States by the letter and spirit of the limitation of armament conference.

**War Profiteering.** . . .should the United States ever again be called upon to defend itself by arms the president be empowered to draft such material resources and such services as may be required, and to stabilize the prices of services and essential commodities, whether used in actual warfare or private activities.

**Republican Philosophy.** The prosperity of the American nation rests on the vigor of private initiative which has bred a spirit of independence and self-reliance. The republican party stands now, as always, against all attempts to put the government into business.

American industry should not be compelled to struggle against government competition. The right of the government to regulate, supervise and control public utilities and public interests, we believe, should be strengthened, but we are firmly opposed to the nationalization or government ownership of public utilities.

## Democrats

The 1924 Democratic convention in New York's old Madison Square Garden was the longest in American history. From the opening gavel on June 24 through final adjournment on July 10, the convention spanned 17 days. The reason for the convention's unprecedented length was an almost unbreakable deadlock between the party's rural and urban factions that extended the presidential balloting for a record 103 roll calls. *(Chart, pp. 226-227)*

Gov. Alfred E. Smith of New York was the candidate of the urban delegates, while William Gibbs McAdoo of California led the rural forces. But beyond any ideological differences between the two candidates was a bitter struggle between the urban and rural wings for control of the party. Smith, a Roman Catholic of Irish ancestry and an opponent of Prohibition and the Ku Klux Klan, embodied characteristics loathed by the rural leaders. McAdoo, a Protestant, a supporter of Prohibition and tolerant of the Ku Klux Klan, was equally unacceptable to the urban forces. Without a strong leader to unite the two factions, and with the two-thirds rule in effect, a long deadlock was inevitable.

Besides Smith and McAdoo, 14 other candidates were nominated. The most memorable speech was delivered by Franklin Delano Roosevelt, who, in nominating Smith, referred to him as "the happy warrior," a description that remained with Smith the rest of his career.

Presidential balloting commenced on Monday, June 30. McAdoo led on the first roll call with 431-1/2 votes, followed by Smith with 241, with 733 votes needed for nomination. Through the week, 77 ballots were taken, but none of the candidates approached the required two-thirds majority. At the end of the week, after the 77th ballot, McAdoo led with 513 votes; Smith had 367; John W. Davis of New York, the eventual nominee, was a distant third with 76-1/2, an improvement of 45-1/2 votes over his first-ballot total. McAdoo had reached the highest total for any candidate, 530 votes, on the 69th ballot.

William Jennings Bryan, making his last appearance at a Democratic convention, as a delegate from Florida, was given permission to explain his opposition to Smith during the 38th ballot. But Bryan's final convention oration was lost in a chorus of boos from the urban forces who found his rural philosophy increasingly objectionable.

After the 66th ballot, the first of a series of proposals was introduced to break the deadlock. It was recommended that the convention meet in executive session and listen to each of the candidates. This received majority approval, 551 to 538, but a two-thirds majority was needed to change

the rules. A second proposal, to invite Smith alone to address the convention, also fell short of the necessary two-thirds, although achieving a majority, 604-1/2 to 473.

After the 73rd ballot, it was recommended that the lowest vote-getter be dropped after each roll call until only five candidates remained, a proposal to be in effect for one day only. This recommendation was defeated, 589-1/2 to 496. A more drastic motion, to adjourn after the 75th ballot and reconvene two weeks later in Kansas City, was decisively beaten, 1,007.3 to 82.7. The delegates did agree, however, to have representatives of each candidate hold a conference over the weekend.

Balloting resumed on Monday, July 7, with the 78th roll call. After the 82nd ballot, a resolution was passed, 985 to 105, releasing all delegates from their commitments.

McAdoo's vote dropped sharply as the balloting progressed, and for the first time, on the 86th roll call, Smith passed him, 360 to 353-1/2. A boom for Sen. Samuel M. Ralston of Indiana, which had begun on the 84th ballot, petered out on the 93rd roll call when Ralston quit the race. At the time of his withdrawal, Ralston was in third place with 196-1/4 votes.

After the ballot, Roosevelt announced that Smith was willing to withdraw from the race if McAdoo would also. McAdoo rejected this suggestion. McAdoo did regain the lead from Smith on the 94th ballot, 395 to 364-1/2, but with victory beyond reach, released his delegates after the 99th ballot.

Davis was the principal beneficiary of the McAdoo withdrawal, moving into second place on the 100th ballot and gaining the lead on the next roll call with 316 votes. Most of Smith's strength moved to Alabama's anti-Klan, anti-Prohibition senator, Oscar W. Underwood, who took second place on the 101st ballot with 229-1/2 votes. Underwood, however, could not keep pace with Davis, who stretched his lead on the next two ballots. After the 103rd ballot, Davis' total stood at 575-1/2 votes to 250-1/2 for the Alabama senator.

Before the next ballot could begin, Iowa switched its vote to Davis, causing other shifts that brought Davis the nomination. After the changes had been recorded, Davis had 844 votes to 102-1/2 for Underwood. The West Virginian's nomination was then declared unanimous.

The core of Davis' vote had come from the rural delegates; urban delegates gave him the necessary votes to win the nomination. After nine days of balloting, the Democrats had a presidential candidate.

The party leadership preferred Gov. Charles W. Bryan of Nebraska, William Jennings Bryan's younger brother, as Davis' running mate. Bryan trailed Tennessee labor leader George L. Berry on the first ballot, 263-1/2 to 238, but vote switches begun by Illinois after the roll call brought Bryan the nomination. After the changes Bryan had 740 votes, barely beyond the two-thirds majority necessary.

The discord evident in the presidential and vice presidential balloting had its roots in the spirited platform battle that preceded the nominations. The first subject of debate was the League of Nations, with the majority report recommending that American entry be determined by a national referendum. The minority plank argued that this was an unwieldy solution that would put the issue aside. Instead, the minority report favored entry into the League of Nations and World Court without reservation. The minority position was rejected, 742-1/2 to 353-1/2. Nonetheless, the Democrats differed markedly in their position from the Republicans, who flatly opposed membership in the League, although favoring participation in the World Court.

The League of Nations debate proved to be merely a warmup for the controversial religious liberties plank. The focus of debate was the Ku Klux Klan, which was opposed by name in the minority report but was not mentioned in the majority report. In one of the closest votes in convention history, the minority plank was defeated, 543-3/20 to 543-7/20. The vote closely followed factional lines, with most rural delegates opposing condemnation of the Klan and urban delegates supporting the minority plank.

The rest of the platform stressed Democratic accomplishments during the Wilson presidency, in contrast to Republican corruption. Democratic links with the common man were emphasized, while the Republicans were denounced as the party of the rich. The Democratic platform advocated increased taxes on the wealthy in contrast to the Republicans, who promised a reduction in taxes.

The Democrats continued to advocate a low tariff that would encourage competition. A plank demanding states' rights appeared in the platform, but there were also calls for government regulation of the anthracite coal industry, federal support of the American merchant marine and legislation that would restrict and publicize individual campaign contributions.

There were planks favoring a cutback in the American military, a national referendum before any declaration of war (except outright aggression against the United States) and the drafting of resources as well as men during wartime. The anti-militaristic planks were a return to the position the party had held earlier in the 20th century.

Following are excerpts from the Democratic platform of 1924:

**Republican Corruption.** Such are the exigencies of partisan politics that republican leaders are teaching the strange doctrine that public censure should be directed against those who expose crime rather than against criminals who have committed the offenses. If only three cabinet officers out of ten are disgraced, the country is asked to marvel at how many are free from taint. Long boastful that it was the only party "fit to govern," the republican party has proven its inability to govern even itself. It is at war with itself. As an agency of government it has ceased to function.

**Income Tax.** The income tax was intended as a tax upon wealth. It was not intended to take from the poor any part of the necessities of life. We hold that the fairest tax with which to raise revenue for the federal government is the income tax. We favor a graduated tax upon incomes, so adjusted as to lay the burdens of government upon the taxpayers in proportion to the benefits they enjoy and their ability to pay.

**Campaign Contributions.** We favor the prohibition of individual contributions, direct and indirect, to the campaign funds of congressmen, senators or presidential candidates, beyond a reasonable sum to be fixed in the law, for both individual contributions and total expenditures, with requirements for full publicity.

**States' Rights.** We demand that the states of the union shall be preserved in all their vigor and power. They constitute a bulwark against the centralizing and destructive tendencies of the republican party.

**Anti-militarism.** We demand a strict and sweeping reduction of armaments by land and sea, so that there shall be no competitive military program or naval building. Until international agreements to this end have been made we advocate an army and navy adequate for our national safety. . . .

War is a relic of barbarism and it is justifiable only as a measure of defense.

**War Profiteering.** In the event of war in which the manpower of the nation is drafted, all other resources should likewise be drafted. This will tend to discourage war by depriving it of its profits.

## Progressives

Under the sponsorship of the Conference of Progressive Political Action, representatives of various liberal, labor and agrarian groups met in Cleveland on July 4 to launch the Progressive Party and ratify the ticket of Wisconsin senator Robert M. La Follette for president and Montana senator Burton K. Wheeler for vice president. The conference earlier had designated La Follette as its presidential nominee and had given him the power to choose his running mate. The national ticket of the Progressives crossed party lines, joining a Republican, La Follette, with a Democrat, Wheeler. The ticket was endorsed by the Socialists, who supported the Progressive candidates rather than run a separate national ticket.

In large part the Progressive platform advocated measures that had been proposed earlier by the Populists, Socialists and Progressives before World War I. The key issue, as viewed by the La Follette Progressives, was "the control of government and industry by private monopoly." The platform favored the government ownership of railroads and water power, rigid federal control over natural resources, the outlawing of injunctions in labor disputes, a cutback in military spending, tax reform and political reform — including the direct election of the president, a national referendum before a declaration of war (except in cases of invasion), election of federal judges and congressional power to override the Supreme Court.

Following are excerpts from the Progressive platform of 1924:

**Anti-monopoly.** The great issue before the American people today is the control of government and industry by private monopoly.

For a generation the people have struggled patiently, in the face of repeated betrayals by successive administrations, to free themselves from this intolerable power which has been undermining representative government.

Through control of government, monopoly has steadily extended its absolute dominion to every basic industry.

In violation of law, monopoly has crushed competition, stifled private initiative and independent enterprise. . . .

The equality of opportunity proclaimed by the Declaration of Independence and asserted and defended by Jefferson and Lincoln as the heritage of every American citizen has been displaced by special privilege for the few, wrested from the government of the many.

**Tax Reform.** We . . . favor a taxation policy providing for immediate reductions upon moderate incomes, large increases in the inheritance tax rates upon large estates to prevent the indefinite accumulation by inheritance of great fortunes in a few hands, taxes upon excess profits to penalize profiteering, and complete publicity, under proper safeguards, of all Federal tax returns.

**Court Reform.** We favor submitting to the people, for their considerate judgment, a constitutional amendment providing that Congress may by enacting a statute make it effective over a judicial vote.

We favor such amendment to the constitution as may be necessary to provide for the election of all Federal

Judges, without party designation, for fixed terms not exceeding ten years, by direct vote of the people.

**National Referendums.** Over and above constitutions and statutes and greater than all is the supreme sovereignty of the people, and with them should rest the final decision of all great questions of national policy. We favor such amendments to the Federal Constitution as may be necessary to provide for the direct nomination and election of the President, to extend the initiative and referendum to the federal government, and to insure a popular referendum for or against war except in cases of actual invasion.

# 1928 Conventions

## Presidential Candidates

**Herbert Hoover**
**Republican**

**Alfred E. Smith**
**Democrat**

### Republicans

The Republicans held their convention in Kansas City, Mo., in mid-June 1928. Nearly a year earlier, President Calvin Coolidge had declared his intention not to seek reelection with a typically brief statement: "I do not choose to run for President in 1928." While some business leaders hoped that Coolidge would be open to a draft, the taciturn incumbent made no effort to encourage them. The vacuum caused by Coolidge's absence was quickly filled by Commerce Secretary Herbert Hoover of California, whose success in the spring primaries solidified his position as the front-runner.

Hoover's strength was evident on the first roll call of the convention, a credentials challenge to 18 Hoover delegates from Texas. In a vote that revealed candidate strength, the move to unseat the Hoover delegates was defeated, 659-1/2 to 399-1/2. In the presidential balloting that followed, he gained more votes to win the nomination easily on the first ballot. Hoover's vote total was swelled before the balloting began by the withdrawal of his principal opponent, former Illinois governor Frank O. Lowden, who declared in a letter that he could not accept the party platform's stand on agriculture. Six names were placed in nomination, but Hoover was a landslide winner, receiving 837 of the 1,089 convention votes. Lowden finished second with 74 votes. *(Chart, p. 228)*

Sen. Charles Curtis of Kansas was virtually unopposed for the vice presidential nomination, receiving 1,052 votes.

Although Wisconsin's prominent progressive leader, Robert M. La Follette, had died in 1925, his state's delegation again presented a minority platform. The report was presented by Sen. Robert M. La Follette Jr., who had taken over his father's Senate seat. Among the planks of the Wisconsin report were proposals favoring enactment of the McNary-Haugen farm bill, government operation of major water power projects, increased income taxes on the rich and liberalization of Prohibition. No vote was taken on the Wisconsin proposals.

A resolution favoring repeal of Prohibition was tabled by a voice vote.

A separate agricultural resolution was proposed that advocated the basic provisions of the McNary-Haugen bill (twice vetoed by Coolidge), without mentioning the controversial bill by name. On a roll-call vote, the resolution was defeated, 807 to 277, with support centered in the farm states but with most Hoover delegates voting against it.

The platform as originally written was adopted by a voice vote. The platform promised continued prosperity and government economy. The belief in a protective tariff was reiterated. The document concluded with a plank entitled "home rule," which expressed the party's belief in self-reliance and strong local government.

Following are excerpts from the Republican platform of 1928:

**Tariff.** We reaffirm our belief in the protective tariff as a fundamental and essential principle of the economic life of this nation.... However, we realize that there are certain industries which cannot now successfully compete with foreign producers because of lower foreign wages and a lower cost of living abroad, and we pledge the next Republican Congress to an examination and where necessary a revision of these schedules to the end that American labor in these industries may again command the home market, may maintain its standard of living, and may count upon steady employment in its accustomed field.

**Outlaw War.** We endorse the proposal of the Secretary of State for a multilateral treaty proposed to the principal powers of the world and open to the signatures of all nations, to renounce war as an instrument of national policy and declaring in favor of pacific settlement of international disputes, the first step in outlawing war.

**Agriculture.** We promise every assistance in the re-organization of the market system on sounder and more economical lines and, where diversification is needed, Government financial assistance during the period of transition.

The Republican Party pledges itself to the enactment of legislation creating a Federal Farm Board clothed with the necessary powers to promote the establishment of a farm marketing system of farmer-owned and controlled stabilization corporations or associations to prevent and control surpluses through orderly distribution. . . .

We favor, without putting the Government into business, the establishment of a Federal system of organization for co-operative and orderly marketing of farm products.

**Prohibition.** The people through the method provided by the Constitution have written the Eighteenth Amendment into the Constitution. The Republican Party pledges itself and its nominees to the observance and vigorous enforcement of this provision of the Constitution.

**Republican Philosophy.** There is a real need of restoring the individual and local sense of responsibility and self-reliance; there is a real need for the people once more to grasp the fundamental fact that under our system of government they are expected to solve many problems themselves through their municipal and State governments, and to combat the tendency that is all too common to turn to the Federal Government as the easiest and least burdensome method of lightening their own responsibilities.

## Democrats

The Democratic convention was held in late June in Houston, Texas, the first time since 1860 that the party's nominating convention had been conducted in a Southern city. The rural and urban wings of the party, which had produced the fiasco in Madison Square Garden four years earlier, wanted no more bloodletting. This explained the acceptance of Houston as the convention site by the urban forces, whose presidential candidate, Gov. Alfred E. Smith of New York, was the front-runner for the nomination. Smith's path to the nomination was largely unobstructed, thanks to the decision of William Gibbs McAdoo not to run. McAdoo, the rural favorite in 1924, feared the possibility of another bitter deadlock that would destroy party unity.

The convention broke with tradition by bypassing politicians and selecting Claude G. Bowers of Indiana, a historian and an editorial writer for *The New York World*, as temporary chairman.

When it came time for the selection of a presidential candidate, Franklin Delano Roosevelt once again placed Smith's name in nomination. On the roll call that followed, the New York governor came within 10 votes of the required two-thirds. Ohio quickly switched 44 of its votes to Smith, and the switch pushed "the happy warrior" over the top. When the vote switches were completed, Smith had received 849-1/6 of the 1,100 convention votes. No other candidate's vote had totaled more than 100. *(Chart, p. 228)*

Senate Minority Leader Joseph T. Robinson of Arkansas had little opposition for the vice presidency and was nominated on the first ballot with 914-1/6 votes. Sen. Alben W. Barkley of Kentucky finished a distant second with 77 votes. After a vote switch, Robinson had 1,035-1/6 votes. As a "dry" Protestant from the South, Robinson balanced the ticket. He was the first Southerner to be nominated for national office by either major party since the Civil War.

For the first time since 1912, there were no roll-call votes on amendments to the Democratic platform. A minority plank was introduced calling for the party's complete support of Prohibition, but there was no effort to force a roll-call vote. The platform included a milder Prohibition plank that promised "an honest effort to enforce the 18th Amendment (Prohibition)." On the surface there was little difference from the Republican plank, which pledged "vigorous enforcement" of Prohibition. But in a telegram read to the convention shortly before its final adjournment, Smith negated the effect of the milder plank by declaring there should be "fundamental changes in the present provisions for national Prohibition." Smith's statement was disappointing to many "dry" delegates and lessened whatever enthusiasm they felt for the New York governor. No other issues were discussed, and the platform as written was approved by a voice vote.

Agriculture, the most depressed part of the economy in the 1920s, received more space in the platform than any other issue. The Democrats opposed federal subsidies to farmers, but they advocated government loans to cooperatives and the creation of a federal farm board that would operate similarly to the Federal Reserve Board. While the Republican platform also favored creation of a farm board, as a whole it called for more initiative by the farmers themselves and less direct government help than did the Democratic platform.

Since the late 19th century, Democratic platforms had favored a low tariff. The 1928 tariff plank represented a change, expressing as much interest in ensuring competition and protecting the American wage-earner as in raising revenue. Instead of being consistently low, tariff rates were to be based on the difference between the cost of production in the United States and abroad. As a result of the Democrats' altered stand on the tariff, the positions of the two parties on this issue were the closest they had been in a generation.

The Democrats' 1928 platform did not mention the League of Nations, in contrast to the Republicans, who restated their opposition to the League. Both parties called for maintenance of American military strength until international disarmament agreements could be reached. A section of the Democratic foreign policy plank questioned the extent of presidential power in the area of international affairs. President Coolidge was specifically criticized for authorizing American military intervention in Nicaragua without congressional approval.

An unemployment plank was included in the Democratic platform that proposed the creation of public works jobs in times of economic hardship.

As was the case with most Democratic platforms since the early 19th century, there was a defense of states' rights and a plank that recognized education as an area of state responsibility. The Democrats made no mention of civil rights in contrast to the Republicans, who, as in 1920, proposed federal anti-lynching legislation.

Following are excerpts from the Democratic platform of 1928:

**Prohibition.** Speaking for the national Democracy, this convention pledges the party and its nominees to an honest effort to enforce the eighteenth amendment.

**Agriculture.** Farm relief must rest on the basis of an economic equality of agriculture with other industries. To give this equality a remedy must be found which will include among other things:

(a) Credit aid by loans to co-operatives on at least as

favorable a basis as the government aid to the merchant marine.

(b) Creation of a federal farm board to assist the farmer and stock raiser in the marketing of their products, as the Federal Reserve Board has done for the banker and business man.

**Presidential War Power.** Abolition of the practice of the president of entering into and carrying out agreements with a foreign government, either de facto or de jure, for the protection of such government against revolution or foreign attack, or for the supervision of its internal affairs, when such agreements have not been advised and consented to by the Senate, as provided in the Constitution of the United States, and we condemn the administration for carrying out such an unratified agreement that requires us to use our armed forces in Nicaragua.

**Tariff.** Duties that will permit effective competition, insure against monopoly and at the same time produce a fair revenue for the support of government. Actual difference between the cost of production at home and abroad, with adequate safeguard for the wage of the American laborer must be the extreme measure of every tariff rate.

**Unemployment and Public Works.** We favor the adoption by the government, after a study of this subject, of a scientific plan whereby during periods of unemployment appropriations shall be made available for the construction of necessary public works and the lessening, as far as consistent with public interests, of government construction work when labor is generally and satisfactorily employed in private enterprise.

**Education.** We believe with Jefferson and other founders of the Republic that ignorance is the enemy of freedom and that each state, being responsible for the intellectual and moral qualifications of its citizens and for the expenditure of the moneys collected by taxation for the support of its schools, shall use its sovereign right in all matters pertaining to education.

# 1932 Conventions

## Presidential Candidates

**Norman Thomas**
**Socialist**

**Herbert Hoover**
**Republican**

**Franklin D. Roosevelt**
**Democrat**

## Socialists

The Socialist Party held its convention in Milwaukee, Wis., in May and renominated the same ticket that had represented the party in 1928: Norman Thomas of New York for president and James H. Maurer of Pennsylvania for vice president. Aided by the deepening economic depression, the Socialists received more than 2 percent of the popular vote for the first time since 1920. The party continued to run a national ticket until 1956, but 1932 was the last election in which the Socialists received at least 2 percent of the vote.

By a vote of 117 to 64, the convention adopted a resolution supporting the efforts of the Soviet Union to create a Socialist society. An attempt to oust Morris Hillquit as national chairman of the party was beaten, 108 to 81.

The Socialist platform of 1932 contained a number of proposals that had been set forth in earlier party platforms, such as public ownership of natural resources and the means of transportation and communication, increased taxes on the wealthy, an end to the Supreme Court's power to rule congressional legislation unconstitutional and a reduction in the size and expenditures of the military.

The platform also advocated United States recognition of the Soviet Union and American entry into the League of Nations. Repeal of Prohibition was recommended, as was the creation of a federal marketing system that would buy and market farm commodities.

To meet the hardship of the Depression, the Socialists listed a series of proposals, which included the expenditure of $10 billion for unemployment relief and public works projects.

Following are excerpts from the Socialist platform of 1932:

**Unemployment Relief.** 1. A Federal appropriation of $5,000,000,000 for immediate relief for those in need to supplement State and local appropriations.

2. A Federal appropriation of $5,000,000,000 for public works and roads, reforestation, slum clearance, and decent homes for the workers, by Federal Government, States and cities.

3. Legislation providing for the acquisition of land, buildings, and equipment necessary to put the unemployed to work producing food, fuel, and clothing and for the erection of houses for their own use.

4. The 6-hour day and the 5-day week without reduction of wages.

5. A comprehensive and efficient system of free public employment agencies.

6. A compulsory system of unemployment compensation with adequate benefits, based on contributions by the Government and by employers.

7. Old-age pensions for men and women 60 years of age and over.

8. Health and maternity insurance.

## Republicans

As the incumbent party during the outset of the Depression, the Republicans bore the major political blame for the worsening economy. In a subdued mood, the party gathered in Chicago in June 1932 for its national convention.

Republican leaders did not view their electoral prospects optimistically for the fall election, but saw no realistic alternative to President Herbert Hoover.

Hoover was easily if unenthusiastically renominated, receiving 1,126-1/2 of the 1,154 convention votes. The highlight of the presidential balloting was the attempt by former Maryland senator Joseph I. France, who ran in several spring primaries, to gain the rostrum and nominate former president Coolidge. France's dramatic plan, however, was foiled by convention managers, who refused him permission to speak and had him escorted from the hall. *(Chart, p. 230)*

Vice President Charles Curtis had stiff opposition in his bid for renomination. The incumbent was seriously challenged by Maj. Gen. James G. Harbord of New York and the national commander of the American Legion, Hanford MacNider of Iowa. Curtis was short of a majority after the first ballot, but Pennsylvania quickly shifted its 75 votes to the vice president and this pushed him over the top. With the vote standing at Curtis, 634-1/4; MacNider, 182-3/4, and Harbord, 161-3/4, Curtis' renomination was made unanimous.

The major platform controversy surrounded the Prohibition plank. The majority plank, supported by Hoover, was ambiguous. It called for the enforcement of Prohibition but advocated a national referendum that would permit each state to determine whether or not it wanted Prohibition. A more clear-cut minority plank favored repeal of Prohibition. The minority proposal was defeated, however, 690-19/36 to 460-2/9. Following this roll call, the rest of the platform was approved by a voice vote.

The document approved by the Republicans was the longest in the party's history — nearly 9,000 words. It blamed the United States' continued economic problems on a worldwide depression, but lauded Hoover's leadership in meeting the crisis. The Republicans saw reduced government spending and a balanced budget as keys to ending the Depression. The party platform viewed unemployment relief as a matter for private agencies and local governments to handle.

The Republicans continued their support of a protective tariff. On the agricultural issue, the party proposed acreage controls to help balance supply and demand.

The final plank of the Republican platform urged party members in Congress to demonstrate party loyalty by supporting the Republican program. The plank warned that the party's strength was jeopardized by internal dissent.

Following are excerpts from the Republican platform of 1932:

**Unemployment Relief.** The people themselves, by their own courage, their own patient and resolute effort in the readjustments of their own affairs, can and will work out the cure. It is our task as a party, by leadership and a wise determination of policy, to assist that recovery. . . .

True to American traditions and principles of government, the administration has regarded the relief problem as one of State and local responsibility. The work of local agencies, public and private has been coordinated and enlarged on a nation-wide scale under the leadership of the President.

**Government Spending.** We urge prompt and drastic reduction of public expenditure and resistance to every appropriation not demonstrably necessary to the performance of government, national or local.

**Agriculture.** The fundamental problem of American agriculture is the control of production to such volume as will balance supply with demand. In the solution of this problem the cooperative organization of farmers to plan production, and the tariff, to hold the home market for American farmers, are vital elements. A third element equally as vital is the control of the acreage of land under cultivation, as an aid to the efforts of the farmer to balance production.

**Prohibition.** We . . . believe that the people should have an opportunity to pass upon a proposed amendment the provision of which, while retaining in the Federal Government power to preserve the gains already made in dealing with the evils inherent in the liquor traffic, shall allow the States to deal with the problem as their citizens may determine, but subject always to the power of the Federal Government to protect those States where prohibition may exist and safeguard our citizens everywhere from the return of the saloon and attendant abuses.

## Democrats

With the nation in the midst of the Great Depression, the Democratic Party had its best chance for victory since 1912. The delegates assembled in Chicago in late June 1932, confident that the convention's nominee would defeat President Hoover.

Gov. Franklin D. Roosevelt of New York entered the convention with a majority of the votes, but was well short of the two-thirds majority needed for nomination. Ironically, his principal opponent was the man he had nominated for the presidency three times, former New York governor Alfred E. Smith.

Roosevelt's strength was tested on several key roll calls before the presidential balloting began. Two of the votes involved credentials challenges to Roosevelt delegations from Louisiana and Minnesota. By a vote of 638-3/4 to 514-1/4, the delegates seated the Roosevelt forces from Louisiana, headed by Sen. Huey P. Long. And by a wider margin of 658-1/4 to 492-3/4 the convention seated the Roosevelt delegates from Minnesota. *(Chart, p. 229)*

After settlement of the credentials cases, the battleground shifted to the selection of the permanent convention chairman. The Roosevelt forces backed Sen. Thomas J. Walsh of Montana, who was recommended by the committee on permanent organization. The Smith and other anti-Roosevelt factions coalesced behind Jouett Shouse of Kansas, chairman of the executive committee of the Democratic National Committee, who was recommended for permanent chairman by the national committee. But by a vote of 626 to 528, the Roosevelt forces won again, and Walsh assumed the gavel as permanent chairman.

The Roosevelt managers considered challenging the two-thirds rule; but, realizing that a bruising fight could alienate some of their own delegates, particularly in the South, they dropped the idea. Instead, the report of the rules committee recommended that a change in the two-thirds rule be delayed until the 1936 convention.

The presidential balloting began in the middle of an all-night session. After a motion to adjourn was defeated, 863-1/2 to 281-1/2, the first roll call began at 4:30 a.m. Roosevelt received a clear majority of 666-1/4 votes on the first ballot, compared with 201-3/4 for Smith and 90-1/4 for House Speaker John Nance Garner of Texas. Seven hundred and seventy votes were necessary for nomination. *(Chart, p. 229)*

Roosevelt gained slightly on the second ballot, advancing to 677-3/4 votes, while Smith dropped to 194-1/4 and Garner remained constant. Of side interest was the shift of Oklahoma's votes from its governor to Will Rogers, the state's famous humorist.

There were few changes on the next roll call, and at 9:15 a.m. the delegates agreed to adjourn. The vote totals after three ballots: Roosevelt, 682.79; Smith, 190-1/4; Garner, 101-1/4.

When balloting resumed the next evening, William Gibbs McAdoo of California quickly launched the bandwagon for Roosevelt by announcing that his state's 44 votes were switching from Garner to the New York governor. Other states followed California's lead, and when the fourth ballot was completed Roosevelt had 945 votes and the nomination. With the Smith vote holding at 190-1/2, no effort was made to make the nomination unanimous.

Although it is not clear whether there was a formal deal struck before the fourth ballot between the Garner and Roosevelt forces, the Texas representative was the unanimous choice of the convention for vice president. Forty states seconded his nomination, and no roll call was taken.

In an effort to break what he described as "absurd traditions," Roosevelt flew from Albany to Chicago to accept the presidential nomination personally. (Previously, a major party candidate would be formally notified of his nomination in a ceremony several weeks after the convention.) In his speech of acceptance, Roosevelt struck a liberal tone and issued his memorable pledge of "a new deal for the American people."

The platform adopted by the convention was not a blueprint for the New Deal to follow. It was fewer than 2,000 words long, the party's shortest platform since 1888, and less than one-fourth as long as the document adopted by the Republicans. It blamed the Depression on the "disastrous policies" practiced by the Republicans but made few new proposals, instead forcefully restating positions that had appeared in earlier party platforms.

The Democrats advocated a balanced budget with a cut of at least 25 percent in federal spending and called for removal of the federal government from competition with private enterprise in all areas except public works and natural resources.

The Democratic platform, unlike its Republican counterpart, advocated extensive unemployment relief and public works projects, regulation of holding companies and securities exchanges, "a competitive tariff for revenue" and the extension of farm cooperatives.

The plank that sparked the most enthusiasm among the delegates was the call for the repeal of Prohibition. A milder plank favored by "dry" delegates was resoundingly defeated, 934-3/4 to 213-3/4.

The only measure added from the floor of the convention favored "continuous responsibility of government for human welfare, especially for the protection of children." It was approved by a standing vote.

Following are excerpts from the Democratic platform of 1932:

**Government Spending.** We advocate an immediate and drastic reduction of governmental expenditures by abolishing useless commissions and offices, consolidating departments and bureaus, and eliminating extravagance to accomplish a saving of not less than twenty-five percent in the cost of the Federal Government. And we call upon the Democratic Party in the states to make a zealous effort to achieve a proportionate result.

We favor maintenance of the national credit by a federal budget annually balanced on the basis of accurate executive estimates within revenues, raised by a system of taxation levied on the principle of ability to pay.

**Unemployment Relief, Public Works Projects.** We advocate the extension of federal credit to the states to provide unemployment relief wherever the diminishing resources of the states makes it impossible for them to provide for the needy; expansion of the federal program of necessary and useful construction effected with a public interest, such as adequate flood control and waterways.

We advocate the spread of employment by a substantial reduction in the hours of labor, the encouragement of the shorter week by applying that principle in government service; we advocate advance planning of public works.

We advocate unemployment and old-age insurance under state laws.

**Prohibition.** We advocate the repeal of the Eighteenth Amendment. To effect such repeal we demand that the Congress immediately propose a Constitutional Amendment to truly represent [sic] the conventions in the states called to act solely on that proposal; we urge the enactment of such measures by the several states as will actually promote temperance, effectively prevent the return of the saloon, and bring the liquor traffic into the open under complete supervision and control by the states.

**Agriculture.** Extension and development of the Farm Cooperative movement and effective control of crop surpluses so that our farmers may have the full benefit of the domestic market.

The enactment of every constitutional measure that will aid the farmers to receive for their basic farm commodities prices in excess of cost.

# 1936 Conventions

## Presidential Candidates

**Alfred M. Landon**
**Republican**

**Franklin D. Roosevelt**
**Democrat**

**William Lemke**
**Union**

### Republicans

The Republican convention, held in Cleveland in early June, was an unusually harmonious gathering for a party out of power. There were only two roll-call votes on the convention floor, for president and vice president, and both were one-sided.

The only matter of debate was the vote allocation for Alaska, Hawaii and the District of Columbia. By a voice vote, the convention approved the minority report of the rules committee, which sliced the vote for these three from six to three votes apiece.

Former president Herbert Hoover received an enthusiastic reception when he spoke, but by that time Kansas governor Alfred M. Landon had the presidential nomination sewed up. Landon, one of the few Republican governors to be re-elected during the Depression, received 984 votes on the first ballot, compared with 19 for Sen. William E. Borah of Idaho. *(Chart, p. 231)*

Before the balloting began, Landon had sent a telegram to the convention that expressed his agreement with the "word and spirit" of the party platform but elaborated his position on several points. The Kansan advocated the passage of a constitutional amendment to ensure women and children safe working conditions and to establish guidelines for wages and hours in the event that legislation passed by Congress was ruled unconstitutional. Landon's message also proposed extending the civil service to include all workers in federal departments and agencies below the rank of assistant secretary, and it defined "sound currency" as currency that could be exchanged for gold. Landon's pronouncements were met with 30 minutes of cheering.

For vice president, the convention selected Col. Frank Knox of Illinois, publisher of *The Chicago Daily News*. Knox, who earlier had campaigned energetically, if not successfully, for the presidential nomination, received all 1,003 votes on the first ballot.

The Republican platform, which began with the sentence, "America is in peril," focused on the alleged threat of New Deal policies to American constitutional government. The platform assailed the Roosevelt administration for "dishonoring American traditions" and promised to protect local self-government and the power of the Supreme Court.

The Republicans promised a balanced budget, reduced federal expenditures, a "sound currency," a more discriminating public works program and the administration of unemployment relief by "non-political local agencies" that would be financed jointly by the various states and the federal government.

The Republicans shared with the Democrats the belief in an isolationist foreign policy and the concepts of social security, unemployment insurance and crop control.

Following are excerpts from the Republican platform of 1936:

**Roosevelt's 'New Deal.'** America is in peril. The welfare of American men and women and the future of our youth are at stake. We dedicate ourselves to the preservation of their political liberty, their individual opportunity and their character as free citizens, which today for the first time are threatened by Government itself....

The powers of Congress have been usurped by the President.

The integrity and authority of the Supreme Court have been flouted.

The rights and liberties of American citizens have been violated.

Regulated monopoly has displaced free enterprise.

The New Deal Administration constantly seeks to usurp the rights reserved to the States and to the people.

**Unemployment Relief.** The return of responsibility for relief administration to nonpolitical local agencies familiar with community problems....

Undertaking of Federal public works only on their merits and separate from the administration of relief.

**Government Spending, Currency.** Balance the budget — not by increasing taxes but by cutting expenditures, drastically and immediately....

We advocate a sound currency to be preserved at all hazards.

The first requisite to a sound and stable currency is a balanced budget.

**Foreign Policy.** We pledge ourselves to promote and maintain peace by all honorable means not leading to foreign alliances or political commitments.

Obedient to the traditional foreign policy of America and to the repeatedly expressed will of the American people, we pledge that America shall not become a member of the League of Nations nor of the World Court nor shall America take on any entangling alliances in foreign affairs.

## Democrats

The 1936 Democratic convention, held in Philadelphia in late June, was one of the most harmonious in party history. There were no floor debates, and, for the first time since 1840, there were no roll-call votes.

The only matter that required discussion — elimination of the century-old two-thirds rule — was settled in the rules committee. There, by a vote of 36 to 13, the committee agreed to abrogate the rule, which had been a controversial part of Democratic conventions since 1832. To mollify the South, which was particularly threatened by elimination of the two-thirds rule, the rules committee added a provision that would include consideration of a state's Democratic voting strength in determining its future convention vote allocation. The rules committee report was approved by a voice vote.

Both President Franklin D. Roosevelt and Vice President John Nance Garner were renominated by acclamation, but more than a full day of oratory was expended in eulogizing the Democratic standard-bearers. Roosevelt was seconded by delegates from each of the states and territories — more than 50 separate speakers. Seventeen delegates spoke on behalf of Garner.

Both Roosevelt and Garner personally accepted their nominations in ceremonies at the University of Pennsylvania's Franklin Field. Before a crowd estimated as large as 100,000, Roosevelt electrified his listeners with a speech that blasted his adversaries among the rich as "economic royalists" and included the sentence: "This generation of Americans has a rendezvous with destiny."

As in 1932 the platform adopted by the Democrats was a short one, about 3,000 words. The document paid lip service to the concept of a balanced budget and reduced government spending, but it supported continuation of the extensive federal programs undertaken by the Roosevelt administration.

The platform did not, as many in past years had, mention states' rights; this reflected the party's changing view toward federal power. To counter what was viewed as obstructionism by the Supreme Court, the Democrats suggested the possibility of passing a "clarifying amendment" to the Constitution that would enable Congress and state legislatures to enact bills without the fear of an unfavorable decision from the Supreme Court.

The foreign policy plank recognized the isolationist mood of the period, calling for neutrality in foreign disputes and the avoidance of international commitments that would draw the United States into war.

Following are excerpts from the Democratic platform of 1936:

**Federal Power.** The Republican platform proposes to meet many pressing national problems solely by action of the separate States. We know that drought, dust storms, floods, minimum wages, maximum hours, child labor, and working conditions in industry, monopolistic and unfair business practices cannot be adequately handled exclusively by 48 separate State legislatures, 48 separate State administrations, and 48 separate State courts. Transactions and activities which inevitably overflow State boundaries call for both State and Federal treatment.

We have sought and will continue to seek to meet these problems through legislation within the Constitution.

If these problems cannot be effectively solved by legislation within the Constitution, we shall seek such clarifying amendment as will assure to the legislatures of the several States and to the Congress of the United States, each within its proper jurisdiction, the power to enact those laws which the State and Federal legislatures, within their respective spheres, shall find necessary, in order adequately to regulate commerce, protect public health and safety and safeguard economic security. Thus we propose to maintain the letter and spirit of the Constitution.

**Government Spending.** We are determined to reduce the expenses of government. We are being aided therein by the recession in unemployment. As the requirements of relief decline and national income advances, an increasing percentage of Federal expenditures can and will be met from current revenues, secured from taxes levied in accordance with ability to pay. Our retrenchment, tax and recovery programs thus reflect our firm determination to achieve a balanced budget and the reduction of the national debt at the earliest possible moment.

**Foreign Policy.** We reaffirm our opposition to war as an instrument of national policy, and declare that disputes between nations should be settled by peaceful means. We shall continue to observe a true neutrality in the disputes of others; to be prepared resolutely to resist aggression against ourselves; to work for peace and to take the profits out of war; to guard against being drawn, by political commitments, international banking or private trading, into any war which may develop anywhere.

## Union Party

With the support of Father Charles E. Coughlin and his National Union for Social Justice, on June 19, 1936, Rep. William Lemke of North Dakota, a Republican, declared his presidential candidacy on the newly formed Union Party ticket. Thomas O'Brien, a Boston railroad union lawyer, was announced as Lemke's running mate. The fledgling political organization had a brief existence, running a national ticket only in the 1936 election. *(Union Party profile, p. 271)*

The Union Party was basically an extension of Coughlin's organization, and the Lemke-O'Brien ticket was endorsed at the National Union for Social Justice convention in August by a vote of 8,152 to 1.

The Union Party platform reportedly was written by Coughlin, Lemke and O'Brien at the Roman Catholic priest's church in Royal Oak, Mich. It was a brief document, fewer than 1,000 words, that contained 15 points similar to the 16-point program favored by Coughlin's National Union. The primary distinctions between the Union Party and the two major parties were in currency expansion, civil service reform and restrictions on wealth. The Union Party called for the creation of a central bank, regulated by Congress, that would issue currency to help pay off the federal debt and refinance agricultural and home mortgage indebtedness. The Union Party platform also proposed extending the civil service to all levels of the federal government and advocated placing restrictions on annual individual income coupled with a ceiling on gifts and inheritances. The new party differed from the Socialists by emphasizing that private property should not be confiscated.

Following are excerpts from the Union Party platform of 1936:

**Currency Expansion.** Congress and Congress alone shall coin and issue the currency and regulate the value of all money and credit in the United States through a central bank of issue.

Immediately following the establishment of the central bank of issue Congress shall provide for the retirement of all tax-exempt, interest-bearing bonds and certificates of indebtedness of the Federal Government and shall refinance all the present agricultural mortgage indebtedness for the farmer and all the home mortgage indebtedness for the farmer and all the home mortgage indebtedness for the city owner by the use of its money and credit which it now gives to the private bankers.

**Civil Service Reform.** Congress shall so legislate that all Federal offices and positions of every nature shall be distributed through civil-service qualifications and not through a system of party spoils and corrupt patronage.

**Restrictions on Wealth.** Congress shall set a limitation upon the net income of any individual in any one year and a limitation of the amount that such an individual may receive as a gift or as an inheritance, which limitation shall be executed through taxation.

**Foreign Policy.** Congress shall establish an adequate and perfect defense for our country from foreign aggression either by air, by land, or by sea, but with the understanding that our naval, air, and military forces must not be used under any consideration in foreign fields or in foreign waters either alone or in conjunction with any foreign power. If there must be conscription, there shall be a conscription of wealth as well as a conscription of men.

# 1940 Conventions

## Presidential Candidates

**Wendell L. Willkie**
**Republican**

**Franklin D. Roosevelt**
**Democrat**

### Republicans

The Republican convention was held in Philadelphia in late June, and it culminated one of the most successful of all campaign blitzes. Wendell L. Willkie, an Indiana native who had never before run for public office, was nominated by the Republicans to run for president. A Democrat until 1938, Willkie had gained fame as a defender of private enterprise in opposition to Roosevelt's public power projects. Although Willkie had broad personal appeal, he and his well-financed group of political "amateurs" did not launch their presidential bid until late spring and missed the presidential primaries. Willkie's momentum came from his rapid rise in the Republican preference polls, as he soared from only 3 percent in early May to 29 percent six weeks later.

At the Republican convention, 10 names were placed in nomination for the presidency. Willkie's principal rivals were Manhattan District Attorney Thomas E. Dewey, making his first presidential bid at age 38, and Sen. Robert A. Taft of Ohio. On the first ballot, Dewey led with 360 votes, followed by Taft with 189 and Willkie with 105. Five hundred and one votes were needed for nomination. *(Chart, p. 232)*

After the first roll call, Dewey steadily lost strength, while Willkie and Taft gained. Willkie assumed the lead on the fourth ballot, passing both Dewey and Taft. Willkie's vote was 306, while Taft moved into second place with 254. Dewey dropped to third with 250.

On the fifth ballot, the contest narrowed to just Willkie and Taft, as both candidates continued to gain — Willkie jumping to 429 votes and Taft to 377. The shift of Michigan's votes to Willkie on the sixth ballot started a bandwagon for the Indianan that pushed him over the top. When the roll call was completed, Willkie was nominated with 655 votes, and a motion to make his nomination unanimous was adopted.

As his running mate, Willkie favored Senate Minority Leader Charles L. McNary of Oregon. McNary, a supporter of some New Deal measures, was opposed by Rep. Dewey Short of Missouri, a vocal anti-New Dealer. McNary, however, was able to win easily on a single ballot, receiving 890 votes to 108 for Short.

The Republican platform was adopted without debate, although an Illinois member of the platform committee commented that his state would have preferred a stronger anti-war plank. As it was, the Republican foreign policy plank sharply criticized the Roosevelt administration for not adequately preparing the nation's defense. However, the rest of the plank was similar to the one adopted three weeks later by the Democrats at the convention: opposing involvement in war but stressing national defense, and advocating aid to the Allies that would not be "inconsistent with the requirements of our own national defense."

In domestic affairs, the Republicans lambasted the extension of federal power under the New Deal and promised cuts in government spending and the reduction of federal competition with private enterprise. The Republican platform agreed with the concept of unemployment relief and social security initiated by the Roosevelt administration, but it proposed the administration of these programs by the states and not the federal government.

The Republicans attacked Roosevelt's monetary measures and advocated currency reforms that included congressional control.

The platform also proposed new amendments to the Constitution that would provide equal rights for men and women and would limit a president to two terms in office.

Following are excerpts from the Republican platform of 1940:

**Foreign Policy.** The Republican Party is firmly opposed to involving this Nation in foreign war....

The Republican Party stands for Americanism, preparedness and peace. We accordingly fasten upon the New Deal full responsibility for our unpreparedness and for the consequent danger of involvement in war....

Our sympathies have been profoundly stirred by invasion of unoffending countries and by disaster to nations whole [whose] ideals most closely resemble our own. We favor the extension to all peoples fighting for liberty, or whose liberty is threatened, of such aid as shall not be in violation of international law or inconsistent with the requirements of our own national defense.

**Unemployment Relief.** We shall remove waste, discrimination, and politics from relief — through administration by the States with federal grants-in-aid on a fair and nonpolitical basis, thus giving the man and woman on relief a larger share of the funds appropriated.

**Currency.** The Congress should reclaim its constitutional powers over money, and withdraw the President's arbitrary authority to manipulate the currency, establish bimetallism, issue irredeemable paper money, and debase the gold and silver coinage. We shall repeal the Thomas Inflation Amendment of 1933 and the (foreign) Silver Purchase Act of 1934, and take all possible steps to preserve the value of the Government's huge holdings of gold and reintroduce gold into circulation.

**Women's Rights.** We favor submission by Congress to the States of an amendment to the Constitution providing for equal rights for men and women.

**No Third Term.** To insure against the overthrow of our American system of government we favor an amendment to the Constitution providing that no person shall be President of the United States for more than two terms.

## Democrats

At the time of both major party conventions in the summer of 1940, Hitler's forces were moving quickly and relentlessly across Western Europe. International events assumed a major importance in political decisions. President Franklin D. Roosevelt, who gave evidence before 1940 that he would not seek a third term, became increasingly receptive to the idea of a draft as the Democratic convention drew nearer. The threat to American security caused by the awesomely successful Nazi military machine, coupled with Roosevelt's inability to find an adequate New Deal-style successor, seemed to spur F.D.R.'s decision to accept renomination.

The Democratic convention was held in Chicago in mid-July. On the second night of the convention, a message from Roosevelt was read stating that he did not desire to run for re-election and urging the delegates to vote for any candidate they wished. Although worded in a negative way, the message did not shut the door on a draft. The delegates reacted, however, by sitting in stunned silence until a Chicago city official began shouting over the public address system, "We want Roosevelt." The cheerleading galvanized the delegates into an hour-long demonstration.

Presidential balloting was held the next day. Roosevelt won easily on the first roll call, although two members of his administration, Vice President John Nance Garner and Postmaster General James A. Farley of New York, ran against him. Roosevelt received 945-13/30 of the 1,100 votes. Farley had 72-9/10 and Garner had 61. *(Chart, p. 231)*

While the delegates were satisfied to have Roosevelt at the top of the ticket again, many balked at his choice for vice president, Agriculture Secretary Henry A. Wallace of Iowa. Wallace, a leading liberal in the administration and a former Republican, was particularly distasteful to conservative Democrats. Many delegates were expecting Roosevelt to leave the vice presidential choice to the convention and were unhappy to have the candidate dictated to them.

It took a personal appearance at the convention by the president's wife, Eleanor Roosevelt, and a threat by F.D.R. that he would not accept the presidential nomination without his hand-picked running mate, to steer the delegates toward Wallace. In spite of the pressure by the Roosevelt forces, the vote was scattered among 13 candidates on the vice presidential ballot. Wallace, though, was able to obtain a slim majority, 626-11/30 votes to 329-3/5 for the runner-up, House Speaker William B. Bankhead of Alabama. Because of the displeasure of many of the delegates, Wallace was asked not to address the convention.

The convention closed by hearing a radio address by Roosevelt, who stated that he had not wanted the nomination but accepted it because the existing world crisis called for personal sacrifice.

The party platform was adopted without a roll call, although there was an amendment presented by a Minnesota representative that opposed any violation of the two-term tradition. It was rejected by a voice vote. The platform as adopted was divided into three sections. The first discussed American military preparedness and foreign policy; the second detailed the New Deal's benefits for various segments of the economy (agriculture, labor, business); the third listed New Deal welfare measures, ranging from unemployment relief to low-cost housing.

As a concession to the party's isolationist wing, the first section contained the administration's promise not to participate in foreign wars or fight in foreign lands, except in case of an attack on the United States. The plank stressed the need of a strong national defense to discourage aggression, but also pledged to provide to free nations (such as Great Britain) material aid "not inconsistent with the interests of our own national self-defense."

An electric power plank was included in the second section of the platform as a direct result of the Republicans' selection of Wendell L. Willkie, a former utilities executive, as their presidential candidate. The Democrats argued in favor of the massive public power projects constructed during the New Deal and criticized private utilities such as the one formerly headed by Willkie.

The third section of the platform drew a sharp distinction from the Republicans on the issue of unemployment relief, opposing any efforts to turn the administration of relief over to the states or local governments.

Following are excerpts from the Democratic platform of 1940:

**Democratic Achievements.** Toward the modern fulfillment of the American ideal, the Democratic Party, during the last seven years, has labored successfully:

1. *To strengthen democracy by defensive preparedness against aggression, whether by open attack or secret infiltration;*

2. *To strengthen democracy by increasing our economic efficiency; and*

3. *To strengthen democracy by improving the welfare of the people.*

**Foreign Policy.** We will not participate in foreign wars, and we will not send our army, naval or air forces to fight in foreign lands outside of the Americas, except in case of attack. . . .

Weakness and unpreparedness invite aggression. We must be so strong that no possible combination of powers would dare to attack us. We propose to provide America with an invincible air force, a navy strong enough to protect all our seacoasts and our national interests, and a fully-equipped and mechanized army.

**Unemployment Relief.** We shall continue to recognize the obligation of Government to provide work for deserving workers who cannot be absorbed by private industry.

We are opposed to vesting in the states and local authorities the control of Federally-financed work relief. We believe that this Republican proposal is a thinly disguised plan to put the unemployed back on the dole.

**Electric Power.** The nomination of a utility executive by the Republican Party as its presidential candidate raises squarely the issue, whether the nation's water power shall be used for all the people or for the selfish interests of a few. We accept that issue.

# 1944 Conventions

## Presidential Candidates

**Thomas E. Dewey**
**Republican**

**Franklin D. Roosevelt**
**Democrat**

### Republicans

For the first time since 1864, the nation was at war during a presidential election year. The Republicans held their convention first, meeting in Chicago in late June 1944. With a minimum of discord, the delegates selected a national ticket and adopted a platform. Gov. Thomas E. Dewey of New York, the front-runner for the presidential nomination, was the nearly unanimous selection when his last two rivals, Gov. John W. Bricker of Ohio and former Minnesota governor Harold E. Stassen, both withdrew from the race before the roll call. On the single ballot, Dewey received 1,056 of the 1,057 votes cast. The one dissenting vote was cast by a Wisconsin delegate for Gen. Douglas MacArthur. *(Chart, p. 233)*

As Dewey's running mate, the delegates unanimously selected Gov. Bricker, an isolationist and party regular, who received all 1,057 votes cast. During the nominating speeches, Rep. Charles A. Halleck of Indiana made the unusual move of recommending his state's first choice for vice president, William L. Hutcheson, for secretary of labor.

Dewey came to Chicago personally to accept the nomination, becoming the first Republican presidential candidate to break the tradition of waiting to accept the nomination in a formal notification ceremony. The thrust of Dewey's speech was an attack on the Roosevelt administration, which he referred to as "stubborn men grown old and tired and quarrelsome in office."

The platform was approved without dissent. The international section was written in a guarded tone. It favored "responsible participation by the United States in post-war cooperative organization" but declared that any agreement must be approved by a two-thirds vote of the Senate. The Republicans favored the establishment of a postwar Jewish state in Palestine.

The domestic section of the platform denounced the New Deal's centralization of power in the federal government, with its increased government spending and deficits. The Republicans proposed to stabilize the economy through the encouragement of private enterprise.

The platform restated several of the planks included four years earlier, among which were the call for an equal rights amendment, a two-term limitation on the president and the return of control over currency matters from the president to Congress.

The Republicans adopted a civil rights plank that

called for a congressional investigation of the treatment of blacks in the military, passage of a constitutional amendment to eliminate the poll tax and legislation that would outlaw lynching and permanently establish a Fair Employment Practice Commission.

Following are excerpts from the Republican platform of 1944:

**Postwar International Organization.** We favor responsible participation by the United States in post-war cooperative organization among sovereign nations to prevent military aggression and to attain permanent peace with organized justice in a free world.

Such organization should develop effective cooperative means to direct peace forces to prevent or repel military aggression. Pending this, we pledge continuing collaboration with the United Nations to assure these ultimate objectives. . . .

We shall sustain the Constitution of the United States in the attainment of our international aims; and pursuant to the Constitution of the United States any treaty or agreement to attain such aims made on behalf of the United States with any other nation or any association of nations, shall be made only by and with the advice and consent of the Senate of the United States provided two-thirds of the Senators present concur.

**Israel.** In order to give refuge to millions of distressed Jewish men, women and children driven from their homes by tyranny, we call for the opening of Palestine to their unrestricted immigration and land ownership, so that in accordance with the full intent and purpose of the Balfour Declaration of 1917 and the Resolution of a Republican Congress in 1922, Palestine may be constituted as a free and democratic Commonwealth. We condemn the failure of the President to insist that the mandatory of Palestine carry out the provision of the Balfour Declaration and of the mandate while he pretends to support them.

**New Deal.** Four more years of New Deal policy would centralize all power in the President, and would daily subject every act of every citizen to regulation by his henchmen; and this country could remain a Republic only in name. No problem exists which cannot be solved by American methods. We have no need of either the communistic or the fascist technique.

. . .The National Administration has become a sprawling, overlapping bureaucracy. It is undermined by executive abuse of power, confused lines of authority, duplication of effort, inadequate fiscal controls, loose personnel practices and an attitude of arrogance previously unknown in our history.

**Economy.** We reject the theory of restoring prosperity through government spending and deficit financing.

We shall promote the fullest stable employment through private enterprise.

**Civil Rights.** We pledge an immediate Congressional inquiry to ascertain the extent to which mistreatment, segregation and discrimination against Negroes who are in our armed forces are impairing morale and efficiency, and the adoption of corrective legislation.

We pledge the establishment by Federal legislation of a permanent Fair Employment Practice Commission.

The payment of any poll tax should not be a condition of voting in Federal elections and we favor immediate submission of a Constitutional amendment for its abolition.

We favor legislation against lynching and pledge our sincere efforts in behalf of its early enactment.

**Agriculture.** An American market price to the American farmer and the protection of such price by means of support prices, commodity loans, or a combination thereof, together with such other economic means as will assure an income to agriculture that is fair and equitable in comparison with labor, business and industry. We oppose subsidies as a substitute for fair markets.

Serious study of and search for a sound program of crop insurance with emphasis upon establishing a self-supporting program.

## Democrats

President Franklin Delano Roosevelt, who four years earlier did not make a final decision about accepting a third nomination until the last moment, clearly stated his intention to run for a fourth term a week before the 1944 convention was to open in Chicago. In a message to Democratic National Chairman Robert E. Hannegan of Missouri released July 11, Roosevelt declared that while he did not desire to run, he would accept renomination reluctantly as a "good soldier."

The early sessions of the convention were highlighted by approval of the rules committee report and settlement of a credentials challenge. The rules committee mandated the national committee to revamp the convention's vote-allocation formula in a way that would take into account Democratic voting strength. This measure was adopted to appease Southern delegates, who in 1936 were promised an increased proportion of the convention vote in return for elimination of the two-thirds rule. No action had been taken to implement the pledge in the intervening eight years.

The credentials dispute involved the Texas delegation, which was represented by two competing groups. By a voice vote, the convention agreed to seat both groups.

Vice President Henry A. Wallace enlivened the presidential nominations by appearing before the convention to urge Roosevelt's renomination. Wallace termed the president the "greatest liberal in the history of the U.S." In the balloting that followed, Roosevelt easily defeated Sen. Harry F. Byrd of Virginia, who was supported by some conservative Southern delegates unhappy with the domestic legislation favored by the New Deal. The final tally: Roosevelt, 1,086; Byrd, 89; former postmaster general James A. Farley, 1. *(Chart, p. 233)*

Roosevelt accepted the nomination in a radio address delivered from the San Diego Naval Base, where he had stopped off en route to a wartime conference.

The real drama of the convention, the selection of the vice presidential nominee, came next. Roosevelt had been ambivalent about the choice of his running mate, encouraging several people to run but not publicly endorsing any of them. The president wrote an ambiguous letter to the convention chairman, which was read to the delegates. Roosevelt stated that if he were a delegate himself he would vote for Wallace's renomination, but that the ultimate choice was the convention's and it must consider the pros and cons of its selection.

In another message, written privately for National Chairman Hannegan, Roosevelt declared that he would be happy to run with either Missouri senator Harry S. Truman or Supreme Court Justice William O. Douglas. Most of the party bosses preferred Truman to the more liberal alternatives, Wallace and Douglas. Truman originally was slated to nominate former South Carolina senator and Supreme Court Justice James F. Byrnes for vice president. But, spurred by his political advisers, Roosevelt telephoned Truman in Chicago and urged him to accept the nomination. Truman reluctantly agreed.

Roosevelt's final preference for Truman was not publicly announced, and 12 names were placed before the convention. Wallace led on the first roll call with 429-1/2 votes, followed by Truman with 319-1/2. Favorite sons and other hopefuls shared the remaining votes cast.

Truman passed Wallace on the second ballot, 477-1/2 to 473, and, immediately after completion of the roll call, Alabama began the bandwagon for the Missouri senator by switching its votes to him. When all the shifts had been made, Truman was an easy winner with 1,031 votes, while Wallace finished with 105.

The platform adopted by the convention was a short one, only 1,360 words. The first third of the platform lauded the accomplishments of Roosevelt's first three terms. The rest of the document outlined the party's proposals for the future. In foreign affairs, the Democrats advocated the creation of a postwar international organization that would have adequate forces available to prevent future wars. The party also called for American membership in an international court of justice. The Democrats joined their Republican opponents in favoring the establishment of an independent Jewish state in Palestine.

The domestic section of the platform proposed a continuation of New Deal liberalism, with passage of an equal rights amendment for women, price guarantees and crop insurance for farmers and the establishment of federal aid to education that would be administered by the states.

A minority report concerning foreign policy called for the establishment of an international air force to help keep peace. The proposal was rejected, however, when the platform committee chairman indicated that the existence of an air force was included in the majority report's call for "adequate forces" to be at the disposal of the proposed international organization.

Following are excerpts from the Democratic platform of 1944:

**Postwar International Organizations.** That the world may not again be drenched in blood by international outlaws and criminals, we pledge:

To join with the other United Nations in the establishment of an international organization based on the principle of the sovereign equality of all peace-loving states, open to membership by all such states, large and small, for the prevention of aggression and the maintenance of international peace and security.

To make all necessary and effective agreements and arrangements through which the nations would maintain adequate forces to meet the needs of preventing war and of making impossible the preparation for war and which would have such forces available for joint action when necessary.

Such organization must be endowed with power to employ armed forces when necessary to prevent aggression and preserve peace.

**Israel.** We favor the opening of Palestine to unrestricted Jewish immigration and colonization, and such a policy as to result in the establishment there of a free and democratic Jewish commonwealth.

**Women's Rights.** We favor legislation assuring equal pay for equal work, regardless of sex.

We recommend to Congress the submission of a Constitutional amendment on equal rights for women.

**Education.** We favor Federal aid to education administered by the states without interference by the Federal Government.

**Agriculture.** Price guarantees and crop insurance to farmers with all practical steps:

To keep agriculture on a parity with industry and labor.

To foster the success of the small independent farmer.

To aid the home ownership of family-sized farms.

To extend rural electrification and develop broader domestic and foreign markets for agricultural products.

**Civil Rights.** We believe that racial and religious minorities have the right to live, develop and vote equally with all citizens and share the rights that are guaranteed by our Constitution. Congress should exert its full constitutional powers to protect those rights.

# 1948 Conventions

## Presidential Candidates

**Thomas E. Dewey**
**Republican**

**Harry S. Truman**
**Democrat**

**J. Strom Thurmond**
**States' Rights**

**Henry A. Wallace**
**Progressive**

### Republicans

The Republican convention was held in Philadelphia in late June. As in 1944, New York governor Thomas E. Dewey entered the convention as the front-runner for the nomination. But unlike four years earlier, when he was virtually handed the nomination, Dewey was contested by several candidates, including Ohio senator Robert A. Taft and former Minnesota governor Harold E. Stassen.

In all, seven names were placed in nomination, with 548 votes needed to determine a winner. Dewey led on the first roll call with 434 votes, followed by Taft with 224 and Stassen with 157. Each of the other candidates received fewer than 100 votes. *(Chart, p. 235)*

On the second roll call, Dewey moved closer to the nomination, receiving 515 votes. Taft and Stassen continued to trail, with 274 and 149 votes respectively. At this point, the anti-Dewey forces requested a recess, which was agreed to by the confident Dewey organization.

Unable to form a coalition that could stop Dewey, all his opponents withdrew before the third ballot. On the subsequent roll call, the New York governor was the unanimous choice of the convention, receiving all 1,094 votes.

Dewey's choice for vice president was California governor Earl Warren, who was nominated by acclamation. Warren had been a favorite-son candidate for the presidency and agreed to take second place on the ticket only after receiving assurances that the responsibilities of the vice presidency would be increased if Dewey were elected.

The Republican platform was adopted without dissent. The wording of the platform was unusually positive for a party out of the White House. The failures of the Truman administration were dismissed in a short paragraph, with the rest of the document praising the accomplishments of the Republican 80th Congress and detailing the party's proposals for the future.

One of the major issues of the 1948 campaign was the controversial Taft-Hartley labor law, a measure supported by the Republicans, but which most Democratic leaders felt should be repealed. The Republicans were silent on national health insurance, and the party's housing position stressed private initiative rather than federal legislation. As in 1944

the Republicans opposed the poll tax and segregation in the military and favored legislation to outlaw lynching.

The Republican platform accepted the concept of a bipartisan foreign policy. Paragraphs were inserted that supported the Marshall Plan for European recovery, the United Nations and recognition of Israel.

Following are excerpts from the Republican platform of 1948:

**Civil Rights.** This right of equal opportunity to work and to advance in life should never be limited in any individual because of race, religion, color, or country of origin. We favor the enactment and just enforcement of such Federal legislation as may be necessary to maintain this right at all times in every part of this Republic....

Lynching or any other form of mob violence anywhere is a disgrace to any civilized state, and we favor the prompt enactment of legislation to end this infamy....

We favor the abolition of the poll tax as a requisite to voting.

We are opposed to the idea of racial segregation in the armed services of the United States.

**Housing.** Housing can best be supplied and financed by private enterprise; but government can and should encourage the building of better homes at less cost. We recommend Federal aid to the States for local slum clearance and low-rental housing programs only where there is a need that cannot be met either by private enterprise or by the States and localities.

**Labor.** Here are some of the accomplishments of this Republican Congress: a sensible reform of the labor law, protecting all rights of Labor while safeguarding the entire community, against those breakdowns in essential industries which endanger the health and livelihood of all....

We pledge continuing study to improve labor-management legislation in the light of experience and changing conditions....

We favor equal pay for equal work regardless of sex.

**Internal Security.** We pledge a vigorous enforcement of existing laws against Communists and enactment of such new legislation as may be necessary to expose the treasonable activities of Communists and defeat their objective of establishing here a godless dictatorship controlled from abroad.

**Foreign Policy.** We are proud of the part that Republicans have taken in those limited areas of foreign policy in which they have been permitted to participate. We shall invite the Minority Party to join us under the next Republican Administration in stopping partisan politics at the water's edge.

**United Nations.** We believe in collective security against aggression and in behalf of justice and freedom. We shall support the United Nations as the world's best hope in this direction, striving to strengthen it and promote its effective evolution and use. The United Nations should progressively establish international law, be freed of any veto in the peaceful settlement of international disputes, and be provided with the armed forces contemplated by the Charter.

**Israel.** We welcome Israel into the family of nations and take pride in the fact that the Republican Party was the first to call for the establishment of a free and independent Jewish Commonwealth.

## Democrats

The Democratic delegates were in a melancholy mood when they gathered in Philadelphia in mid-July 1948. Franklin D. Roosevelt was dead; the Republicans had regained control of Congress in 1946; Roosevelt's successor, Harry S. Truman, appeared unable to stem massive defections of liberals and Southern conservatives from the New Deal coalition.

The dissatisfaction of Southern delegates with policies of the national party was a prominent feature of the 1948 convention. Although the national committee had been mandated by the 1944 convention to devise a new vote allocation procedure that would appease the South, the redistribution of votes for the 1948 convention merely added two votes to each of the 36 states that backed Roosevelt in the 1944 election. This did not appreciably bolster Southern strength.

As the convention progressed, Southern displeasure focused on the civil rights issue. The Mississippi delegation included in its credentials anti-civil-rights resolutions that bound the delegation to bolt the convention if a states' rights plank was not included in the platform. The Mississippi resolutions also denied the power of the national convention to require the Democratic Party of Mississippi to support any candidate who favored President Truman's civil rights program or any candidate who failed to denounce that program.

A minority report was introduced that recommended the Mississippi delegation not be seated. This proposal was defeated by a voice vote, and, in the interest of party harmony, no roll-call vote was taken. However, in an unusual move, several delegations, including those of California and New York, asked that they be recorded in favor of the minority report.

Joined by several other Southern states, Texas presented a minority proposal to the rules committee report, which favored re-establishment of the two-thirds rule. The minority proposal, however, was beaten by a voice vote.

When the presidential balloting began, the entire Mississippi delegation and 13 members of the Alabama delegation withdrew in opposition to the convention's stand on civil rights. However, their withdrawal in no way jeopardized the nomination of Truman. Some party leaders had earlier flirted with the possibility of drafting Gen. Dwight D. Eisenhower or even Supreme Court Justice William O.

Douglas. But the lack of interest of these two men in the Democratic nomination left the field clear for Truman.

The incumbent won a clear majority on the first ballot, receiving 926 votes to 266 for Georgia senator Richard B. Russell, who received the votes of more than 90 percent of the remaining Southern delegates. Among the states of the Old Confederacy, Truman received only 13 votes, all from North Carolina. After several small vote switches, the final tally stood: Truman, 947-1/2; Russell, 263. *(Chart, p. 234)*

Veteran Kentucky senator Alben W. Barkley, the convention's keynoter, was nominated by acclamation for vice president.

Truman appeared before the convention to accept the nomination and aroused the dispirited delegates with a lively speech attacking the Republican Congress. Referring to it as the "worst 80th Congress," Truman announced that he would call a special session so that the Republicans could pass the legislation they said they favored in their platform.

The Democratic platform was adopted by a voice vote, after a heated discussion of the civil rights section. As presented to the convention by the platform committee, the plank favored equal rights for all citizens but was couched in generalities such as those in the 1944 plank. Southern delegates wanted a weaker commitment to civil rights, and various Southern delegations offered three different amendments.

One, presented by former governor Dan Moody of Texas and signed by 15 members of the platform committee, was a broadly worded statement that emphasized the power of the states. A second amendment, sponsored by two Tennessee members of the platform committee, was a brief, emphatic statement declaring the rights of the states. The third amendment, introduced by the Mississippi delegation as a substitute for the Moody amendment, specifically listed the powers of the states to maintain segregation. The Moody amendment was beaten, 924 to 310, with nearly all the support limited to the South. The other two amendments were rejected by voice vote. *(Chart, p. 234)*

Northern liberals countered by proposing to strengthen the civil rights plank. Introduced by former representative Andrew J. Biemiller of Wisconsin and championed by Mayor Hubert H. Humphrey of Minneapolis, the amendment commended Truman's civil rights program and called for congressional action to guarantee equal rights in voting participation, employment opportunity, personal security and military service. The Biemiller amendment was passed, 651-1/2 to 582-1/2, with delegations from the larger Northern states supporting it. Delegations from the South were in solid opposition and were joined by delegates from Border and small Northern states. *(Chart, p. 234).*

The rest of the platform lauded Truman's legislative program and blamed the Republican Congress for obstructing beneficial legislation. In the New Deal tradition, the platform advocated the extension of social security, raising of the minimum wage, establishment of national health insurance and the creation of a permanent flexible price support system for farmers. Congress was blamed for obstructing passage of federal aid to education, comprehensive housing legislation and funding for the Marshall Plan to help rebuild Europe. The Republicans were also criticized for crippling reciprocal trade agreements, passage of the Taft-Hartley Act and even the rising rate of inflation.

The development of the Cold War with the communist world produced a new issue, internal security, on which the two major parties differed sharply. While the Republican position stressed the pursuit of subversives, the Democrats placed more emphasis on the protection of individual rights.

In foreign affairs, the Democratic platform called for the establishment of a United Nations military force, international control of the atomic bomb and recognition of the state of Israel.

Following are excerpts from the Democratic platform of 1948:

**Civil Rights.** We highly commend President Harry S Truman for his courageous stand on the issue of civil rights.

We call upon the Congress to support our President in guaranteeing these basic and fundamental American Principles: (1) the right of full and equal political participation; (2) the right to equal opportunity of employment; (3) the right of security of person; (4) and the right of equal treatment in the service and defense of our nation.

**Housing.** We shall enact comprehensive housing legislation, including provisions for slum clearance and low-rent housing projects initiated by local agencies. This nation is shamed by the failure of the Republican 80th Congress to pass the vitally needed general housing legislation as recommended by the President. Adequate housing will end the need for rent control. Until then, it must be continued.

**Social Security, Health Insurance.** We favor the extension of the Social Security program established under Democratic leadership, to provide additional protection against the hazards of old age, disability, disease or death. We believe that this program should include:

Increases in old-age and survivors' insurance benefits by at least 50 percent, and reduction of the eligibility age for women from 65 to 60 years; extension of old-age and survivors' and unemployment insurance to all workers not now covered; insurance against loss of earnings on account of illness or disability; improved public assistance for the needy.

**Labor.** We advocate the repeal of the Taft-Hartley Act. It was enacted by the Republican 80th Congress over the President's veto....

We favor the extension of the coverage of the Fair Labor Standards Act as recommended by President Truman, and the adoption of a minimum wage of at least 75 cents an hour in place of the present obsolete and inadequate minimum of 40 cents an hour.

We favor legislation assuring that the workers of our nation receive equal pay for equal work, regardless of sex.

**United Nations.** We will continue to lead the way toward curtailment of the use of the veto. We shall favor such amendments and modifications of the charter as experience may justify. We will continue our efforts toward the establishment of an international armed force to aid its authority. We advocate the grant of a loan to the United Nations recommended by the President, but denied by the Republican Congress, for the construction of the United Nations headquarters in this country.

**Disarmament.** We advocate the effective international control of weapons of mass destruction, including the atomic bomb, and we approve continued and vigorous efforts within the United Nations to bring about the successful consummation of the proposals which our Government has advanced.

**Israel.** We pledge full recognition to the State of Israel. We affirm our pride that the United States under the leadership of President Truman played a leading role in the adoption of the resolution of November 29, 1947, by the United Nations General Assembly for the creation of a Jewish State.

**Internal Security.** We shall continue vigorously to enforce the laws against subversive activities, observing at all times the constitutional guarantees which protect free speech, the free press and honest political activity. We shall strengthen our laws against subversion to the full extent necessary, protecting at all times our traditional individual freedoms.

## States' Rights (Dixiecrats)

Provoked by the Democratic convention's adoption of a strong civil rights plank, Gov. Fielding L. Wright of Mississippi invited other Southern Democrats to meet in Birmingham, Ala., on July 17 to select a regional ticket that would reflect Southern views.

It was a disgruntled group that gathered in Birmingham, just three days after the close of the Democratic convention. Placards on the floor of the convention hall identified 13 states, yet there were no delegates from Georgia, Kentucky or North Carolina, and Virginia was represented by four University of Virginia students and an Alexandria woman who was returning home from a trip south. Most major Southern politicians shied away from the bolters, fearing that involvement would jeopardize their standing with the national party and their seniority in Congress.

Former Alabama governor Frank M. Dixon vocalized the anti-civil-rights mood of the gathering with a keynote address charging that Truman's civil rights program would "reduce us to the status of a mongrel, inferior race, mixed in blood, our Anglo-Saxon heritage a mockery."

As its standard-bearers, the convention chose Gov. J. Strom Thurmond of South Carolina for president and Gov. Wright for vice president. Thurmond's acceptance speech touched on another grievance of bolting Southern Democrats: their decreasing power within the Democratic Party. Thurmond warned: "If the South should vote for Truman this year, we might just as well petition the Government to give us a colonial status."

The platform adopted by the Dixiecrats was barely 1,000 words long, but it forcefully presented the case for states' rights. The platform warned that the tendency toward greater federal power ultimately would establish a totalitarian police state.

The Dixiecrats saved their most vitriolic passages to describe the civil rights plank adopted by the Democratic convention. They declared their support for segregation and charged that the plank adopted by the Democrats was meant "to embarrass and humiliate the South."

The platform also charged the national Democratic Party with ingratitude, claiming that the South had supported the Democratic ticket with "clock-like regularity" for nearly 100 years, but that now the national party was being dominated by states controlled by the Republicans.

Following are excerpts from the States' Rights platform of 1948:

**States' Rights.** We believe that the protection of the American people against the onward march of totalitarian government requires a faithful observance of Article X of the American Bill of Rights which provides that: "The powers not delegated to the United States by the Constitution, nor prohibited by it to the states, are reserved to the states respectively, or to the people."

**Civil Rights.** We stand for the segregation of the races and the racial integrity of each race; the constitutional right to choose one's associates; to accept private employment without governmental interference, and to earn one's living in any lawful way. We oppose the elimination of segregation employment by Federal bureaucrats called for by the misnamed civil rights program. We favor home rule, local self-government and a minimum interference with individual rights.

We oppose and condemn the action of the Democratic convention in sponsoring a civil rights program calling for the elimination of segregation, social equality by Federal fiat, regulation of private employment practices, voting and local law enforcement.

We affirm that the effective enforcement of such a program would be utterly destructive of the social, economic and political life of the Southern people, and of other localities in which there may be differences in race, creed or national origin in appreciable numbers.

## Progressives

On Dec. 29, 1947, former vice president Henry A. Wallace announced his presidential candidacy at the head of a new liberal party. Officially named the Progressive Party at its convention in Philadelphia in late July 1948, the new party was composed of some liberal Democrats as well as more radical groups and individuals that included some communists.

Nearly 3,200 delegates nominated Wallace for the presidency and Democratic senator Glen H. Taylor of Idaho as his running mate. The colorful Taylor and his family regaled the delegates with their rendition of "When You Were Sweet Sixteen."

On the final night of the convention, 32,000 spectators assembled to hear Wallace deliver his acceptance speech at Shibe Park. The Progressive standard-bearer expressed his belief in "progressive capitalism," which would place "human rights above property rights," and envisioned "a new frontier . . . across the wilderness of poverty and sickness."

Former Roosevelt associate Rexford G. Tugwell chaired the 74-member platform committee that drafted a detailed platform, about 9,000 words in length, that was adopted by the convention. The platform denounced the two major parties as champions of big business and claimed the new party to be the true "political heirs of Jefferson, Jackson and Lincoln." However, many political observers and opponents of the Progressives dismissed the new party as a Communist-front organization.

Although numerous positions taken by the Progressives in 1948 were considered radical, many were later adopted or seriously considered by the major parties.

The foreign policy plank advocated negotiations between the United States and the Soviet Union ultimately leading to a peace agreement, and it sharply criticized the "anti-Soviet hysteria" of the period. The platform called for repeal of the draft, repudiation of the Marshall Plan, worldwide disarmament featuring abolition of the atomic bomb, amnesty for conscientious objectors imprisoned in World War II, recognition and aid to Israel, extension of United Nations humanitarian programs and the establishment of a world legislature.

In the domestic area, the Progressives opposed internal security legislation, advocated the 18-year-old vote, favored the creation of a Department of Culture, called for food stamp and school hot lunch programs and proposed a federal housing plan that would build 25 million homes in 10 years and subsidize low-income housing.

The Progressives also reiterated the proposals of earlier third parties by favoring the direct election of the president and vice president, extensive tax reform, stricter control of monopolies and the nationalization of the principal means of communication, transportation and finance.

The Progressives joined the Democrats and Republicans in proposing strong civil rights legislation and an equal rights amendment for women.

Following are excerpts from the Progressive platform of 1948:

**Soviet Union.** The Progressive Party . . . demands negotiation and discussion with the Soviet Union to find areas of agreement to win the peace.

**Disarmament.** The Progressive Party will work through the United Nations for a world disarmament agreement to outlaw the atomic bomb, bacteriological warfare, and all other instruments of mass destruction; to destroy existing stockpiles of atomic bombs and to establish United Nations controls, including inspection, over the production of atomic energy; and to reduce conventional armaments drastically in accordance with resolutions already passed by the United Nations General Assembly.

**World Legislation.** The only ultimate alternative to war is the abandonment of the principle of the coercion of sovereignties by sovereignties and the adoption of the principle of the just enforcement upon individuals of world federal law, enacted by a world federal legislature with limited but adequate powers to safeguard the common defense and the general welfare of all mankind.

**Draft.** The Progressive Party calls for the repeal of the peacetime draft and the rejection of Universal Military Training.

**Amnesty.** We demand amnesty for conscientious objectors imprisoned in World War II.

**Internal Security.** We denounce anti-Soviet hysteria as a mask for monopoly, militarism, and reaction. . . .

The Progressive Party will fight for the constitutional rights of Communists and all other political groups to express their views as the first line in the defense of the liberties of a democratic people.

**Civil Rights.** The Progressive Party condemns segregation and discrimination in all its forms and in all places. . . .

We call for a Presidential proclamation ending segregation and all forms of discrimination in the armed services and Federal employment.

We demand Federal anti-lynch, anti-discrimination, and fair-employment-practices legislation, and legislation abolishing segregation in interstate travel.

We call for immediate passage of anti-poll tax legislation, enactment of a universal suffrage law to permit all citizens to vote in Federal elections, and the full use of Federal enforcement powers to assure free exercise of the right to franchise.

**Food Stamps, School Lunches.** We also call for assistance to low-income consumers through such programs as the food stamp plan and the school hot-lunch program.

**Housing.** We pledge an attack on the chronic housing shortage and the slums through a long-range program to build 25 million new homes during the next ten years. This program will include public subsidized housing for low-income families.

**Nationalization.** As a first step, the largest banks, the railroads, the merchant marine, the electric power and gas industry, and industries primarily dependent on government funds or government purchases such as the aircraft, the synthetic rubber and synthetic oil industries must be placed under public ownership.

**Youth Vote.** We call for the right to vote at eighteen.

# 1952 Conventions

## Presidential Candidates

**Dwight D. Eisenhower**
**Republican**

**Adlai E. Stevenson**
**Democrat**

### Republicans

For the third straight time, both major parties held their conventions in the same city. In 1952 the site was Chicago; the Republicans met there in early July two weeks before the Democrats. The battle for the presidential nomination pitted the hero of the party's conservative wing, Sen. Robert A. Taft of Ohio, against the favorite of most moderate and liberal Republicans, Gen. Dwight D. Eisenhower. The general, a Texas native, had resigned as supreme commander of the North Atlantic Treaty Organization (NATO) less than six weeks before the convention to pursue the nomination actively.

As in 1912, when Taft's father had engaged in a bitter struggle with Theodore Roosevelt for the nomination, the outcome of the presidential race was determined in preliminary battles over convention rules and credentials.

The first confrontation came on the issue of the voting rights of challenged delegates. The Taft forces proposed adoption of the 1948 rules, which would have allowed contested delegates to vote on all credentials challenges except their own. The Eisenhower forces countered by proposing what they called a "fair play amendment," which would seat only those contested delegates who were approved by at least a two-thirds vote of the national committee. At stake were a total of 68 delegates from Georgia, Louisiana and Texas, with the large majority of the challenged delegates in favor of Taft. The Taft forces introduced a substitute to the "fair play amendment," designed to exempt seven delegates from Louisiana. On the first test of strength between the two candidates, the Eisenhower forces were victorious, as the substitute amendment was defeated, 658 to 548. The "fair play amendment" was subsequently approved by a voice vote. *(Chart, p. 237)*

The second confrontation developed with the report of the credentials committee. The Eisenhower forces presented a minority report concerning the contested Georgia, Louisiana and Texas seats. After a bitter debate, a roll-call vote was taken on the Georgia challenge, with the Eisenhower forces winning again, 607 to 531.

The Louisiana and Texas challenges were settled in favor of the Eisenhower forces without a roll-call vote. The favorable settlement of the credentials challenges increased the momentum behind the Eisenhower candidacy.

Before the presidential balloting began, a non-partisan debate was held on a proposal to add state chairmen to the national committee from states recording Republican electoral majorities and to remove the requirement that women hold one of each state's seats on the national committee. The proposal was primarily intended to decrease Southern influence on the national committee. But the major opposition was raised by a number of women delegates who objected to the rule change; however, their effort to defeat it was rejected by voice vote.

Five men were nominated for the presidency, but on completion of the first roll call Eisenhower had 595 votes and was within nine votes of victory. Taft was a strong second with 500 votes. However, before a second ballot could begin, Minnesota switched 19 votes from favorite son Harold E. Stassen to Eisenhower, giving the latter the nomination. After a series of vote changes, the final tally stood: Eisenhower, 845; Taft, 280; other candidates, 81. The general's nomination was subsequently made unanimous.

Eisenhower's choice as a running mate, 39-year-old senator Richard M. Nixon of California, was nominated by acclamation. Eisenhower promised in his acceptance speech to lead a "crusade" against "a party too long in power."

The 6,000-word platform was adopted by a voice vote. The document included a sharp attack on the Democrats, charging the Roosevelt and Truman administrations with "violating our liberties ... by seizing powers never granted," "shielding traitors" and attempting to establish "national socialism." The foreign policy section, written by John Foster Dulles, supported the concept of collective security but denounced the Truman policy of containment and blamed the administration for the communist takeover of China. The Republican platform advocated increased national preparedness.

As well as castigating the Democrats for an incompetent foreign policy, the Republicans denounced their opposition for laxness in maintaining internal security. A plank asserted: "There are no Communists in the Republican Party."

On most domestic issues the platform advocated a reduction in federal power. The civil rights plank proposed federal action to outlaw lynching, poll taxes and discriminatory employment practices. However, unlike the plank four years earlier, the Republican position included a paragraph that declared the individual states had primary responsibility for their own domestic institutions. On a related issue of states' rights, the Republicans, as in 1948, favored state control of tideland resources.

Following are excerpts from the Republican platform of 1952:

**Democratic Failures.** We charge that they have arrogantly deprived our citizens of precious liberties by seizing powers never granted.

We charge that they work unceasingly to achieve their goal of national socialism....

We charge that they have shielded traitors to the Nation in high places, and that they have created enemies abroad where we should have friends.

We charge that they have violated our liberties by turning loose upon the country a swarm of arrogant bureaucrats and their agents who meddle intolerably in the lives and occupations of our citizens.

We charge that there has been corruption in high places, and that examples of dishonesty and dishonor have shamed the moral standards of the American people.

We charge that they have plunged us into war in Korea without the consent of our citizens through their authorized representatives in the Congress, and have carried on the war without will to victory....

Tehran, Yalta and Potsdam were the scenes of those tragic blunders with others to follow. The leaders of the Administration in power acted without the knowledge or consent of Congress or of the American people. They traded our overwhelming victory for a new enemy and for new oppressions and new wars which were quick to come.

...And finally they denied the military aid that had been authorized by Congress and which was crucially needed if China were to be saved. Thus they substituted on our Pacific flank a murderous enemy for an ally and friend.

**Internal Security.** By the Administration's appeasement of Communism at home and abroad it has permitted Communists and their fellow travelers to serve in many key agencies and to infiltrate our American life....

There are no Communists in the Republican Party. We have always recognized Communism to be a world conspiracy against freedom and religion. We never compromised with Communism and we have fought to expose it and to eliminate it in government and American life.

**Civil Rights.** We believe that it is the primary responsibility of each State to order and control its own domestic institutions, and this power, reserved to the states, is essential to the maintenance of our Federal Republic. However, we believe that the Federal Government should take supplemental action within its constitutional jurisdiction to oppose discrimination against race, religion or national origin.

We will prove our good faith by:

Appointing qualified persons, without distinction of race, religion or national origin, to responsible positions in the Government.

Federal action toward the elimination of lynching.

Federal action toward the elimination of poll taxes as a prerequisite to voting.

Appropriate action to end segregation in the District of Columbia.

Enacting Federal legislation to further just and equita-

ble treatment in the area of discriminatory employment practices. Federal action should not duplicate state efforts to end such practices; should not set up another huge bureaucracy.

**Labor.** We favor the retention of the Taft-Hartley Act.

...We urge the adoption of such amendments to the Taft-Hartley Act as time and experience show to be desirable, and which further protect the rights of labor, management and the public.

## Democrats

The Democrats held their 1952 convention in Chicago in late July. The convention lasted six days, the longest by either party in the post-World War II years. The proceedings were enlivened by disputes over credentials and a party loyalty pledge and a wide-open race for the presidential nomination.

The legitimately selected Texas delegation, dominated by the Dixiecrat wing of the state party, was challenged by a delegation loyal to the national party, but chosen in a rump assembly. Without a roll-call vote, the convention approved the credentials of the Dixiecrat-oriented delegates, although their seating was protested by Northern liberals.

The Dixiecrat bolt of 1948 resulted in the introduction of a party loyalty pledge at the 1952 convention. The resolution, introduced by Sen. Blair Moody of Michigan, proposed that no delegate be seated who would not assure the credentials committee that he would work to have the Democratic national ticket placed on the ballot in his state under the party's name. This resolution was aimed at several Southern states that had listed the Thurmond-Wright ticket under the Democratic Party label on their state ballots in 1948.

Sen. Spessard L. Holland of Florida introduced a substitute resolution that simply declared it would be "honorable" for each delegate to adhere to the decisions reached in the convention. Holland's resolution, however, was defeated and Moody's was approved, both by voice votes.

The report of the credentials committee listed three Southern states — Louisiana, South Carolina and Virginia — that declined to abide by the Moody resolution. The question of their seating rights came to a head during the roll call for presidential nominations, when Virginia questioned its own status in the convention. A motion to seat the Virginia delegation in spite of its non-observance of the resolution was presented for a vote. Although not agreeing to the pledge, the chairman of the Virginia delegation indicated that the problem prompting the Moody resolution was covered by state law. After a long, confusing roll call, interrupted frequently by demands to poll individual delegates, the motion to seat the Virginia delegation passed, 650-1/2 to 518. *(Chart, p. 236)*

After efforts to adjourn were defeated, the Louisiana and South Carolina delegations offered assurances similar to those presented by Virginia and were seated by a voice vote.

Eleven names were placed in nomination for the presidency, although the favorite of most party leaders, Illinois governor Adlai E. Stevenson, was a reluctant candidate. Stevenson expressed interest only in running for re-election as governor, but a draft-Stevenson movement developed and gained strength quickly as the convention proceeded.

Sen. Estes Kefauver of Tennessee, a powerful vote-getter in the primaries, was the leader on the first ballot, with 340 votes. He was followed by Stevenson with 273, Sen. Richard B. Russell of Georgia, the Southern favorite, with 268, and W. Averell Harriman of New York with 123-1/2.

The second ballot saw gains by the three front-runners, with Kefauver's vote rising to 362-1/2, Stevenson's to 324-1/2 and Russell's to 294. A recess was taken during which Harriman and Massachusetts' favorite son, Gov. Paul A. Dever, both withdrew in favor of Stevenson.

The Illinois governor won a narrow majority on the third ballot, receiving 617-1/2 of the 1,230 convention votes. Kefauver finished with 275-1/2 and Russell with 261. The selection of Stevenson represented the first success for a presidential draft movement of a reluctant candidate since the nomination of James A. Garfield by the Republicans in 1880. *(Chart, p. 236)*

For vice president, Stevenson chose Sen. John J. Sparkman of Alabama, who was nominated by acclamation.

Although a reluctant candidate, Stevenson promised the delegates a fighting campaign but warned: "Better we lose the election than mislead the people; and better we lose than misgovern the people."

The Democratic platform was adopted without the rancor that had accompanied consideration of the party platform four years earlier. The document was approved by a voice vote, although both the Georgia and Mississippi delegations asked that they be recorded in opposition.

The platform promised extension and improvement of New Deal and Fair Deal policies that had been proposed and enacted over the previous 20 years. The party's foremost goal was stated to be "peace with honor," which could be achieved by support for a strengthened United Nations, coupled with the policy of collective security in the form of American assistance for allies around the world. The peaceful use of atomic energy was pledged, as were efforts to establish an international control system. However, the platform also promised the use of atomic weapons, if needed, for national defense.

The civil rights plank was nearly identical to the one that appeared in the 1948 platform. Federal legislation was called for to guarantee equal rights in voting participation, employment opportunity and personal security.

The platform called for extending and changing the social security system. A plank favored elimination of the work clause so that the elderly could collect benefits and still work.

Political reform was recommended that would require the disclosure of campaign expenses in federal elections.

The Democrats and Republicans took different stands on several major domestic issues. The Democrats favored repeal of the Taft-Hartley Act; the Republicans proposed to retain the act but make modifications where necessary. The Democrats advocated closing tax loopholes and, after defense needs were met, reducing taxes. The Republicans called for tax reduction based on a cut in government spending. In education, the Democrats favored federal assistance to state and local units; the Republicans viewed education solely as the responsibility of local and state governments.

The Democrats favored continuation of federal power projects, while the Republicans opposed "all-powerful federal socialistic valley authorities."

Both parties favored a parity price program for farm-

ers. The Democrats advocated a mandatory price support program for basic agricultural products at not less than 90 percent of parity, and the Republicans proposing a program that would establish "full parity prices for all farm products."

Following are excerpts from the Democratic platform of 1952:

**Atomic Energy.** In the field of atomic energy, we pledge ourselves:

(1) to maintain vigorous and non-partisan civilian administrations, with adequate security safeguards;

(2) to promote the development of nuclear energy for peaceful purposes in the interests of America and mankind;

(3) to build all the atomic and hydrogen firepower needed to defend our country, deter aggression, and promote world peace;

(4) to exert every effort to bring about bona fide international control and inspection of all atomic weapons.

**Civil Rights.** We will continue our efforts to eradicate discrimination based on race, religion or national origin. . . .

We are proud of the progress that has been made in securing equality of treatment and opportunity in the Nation's armed forces and the civil service and all areas under Federal jurisdiction. . . .

At the same time, we favor Federal legislation effectively to secure these rights to everyone:

(1) the right to equal opportunity for employment;

(2) the right to security of persons;

(3) the right to full and equal participation in the Nation's political life, free from arbitrary restraints.

**Agriculture.** We will continue to protect the producers of basic agricultural commodities under the terms of a mandatory price support program at not less than ninety percent of parity. We continue to advocate practical methods for extending price supports to other storables and to the producers of perishable commodities, which account for three-fourths of all farm income.

**Campaign Finance.** We advocate new legislation to provide effective regulation and full disclosure of campaign expenditures in elections to Federal office, including political advertising from any source.

**Labor.** We strongly advocate the repeal of the Taft-Hartley Act.

**Tax Reform.** We believe in fair and equitable taxation. We oppose a Federal general sales tax. We adhere to the principle of ability to pay. We have enacted an emergency excess profits tax to prevent profiteering from the defense program and have vigorously attacked special tax privileges. . . . As rapidly as defense requirements permit, we favor reducing taxes, especially for people with lower incomes. . . .

Justice requires the elimination of tax loopholes which favor special groups. We pledge continued efforts to the elimination of remaining loopholes.

**Social Security.** We favor the complete elimination of the work clause for the reason that those contributing to the Social Security program should be permitted to draw benefits, upon reaching the age of eligibility, and still continue to work.

**Education.** Local, State and Federal governments have shared responsibility to contribute appropriately to the pressing needs of our educational system. We urge that Federal contributions be made available to State and local units which adhere to basic minimum standards.

The Federal Government should not dictate nor control educational policy.

# 1956 Conventions

## Presidential Candidates

**Adlai E. Stevenson**
**Democrat**

**Dwight D. Eisenhower**
**Republican**

### Democrats

Both parties held their conventions in August, the latest date ever for the Republicans and the latest for the Democrats since the wartime convention of 1864. For the first time since 1888 the date of the Democratic convention preceded that of the Republicans. The Democrats met in mid-August in Chicago with an allotment of 1,372 votes, the largest in party history. The increased allotment was the result of a new distribution formula, which for the first time rewarded states for electing Democratic governors and senators in addition to supporting the party's presidential candidate.

A provision of the convention call handled the party loyalty question, a thorny issue at the 1952 convention, by assuming that, in the absence of a challenge, any delegate would be understood to have the best interests of the party at heart. Another provision of the call threatened any national committeeman who did not support the party's national ticket with removal from the Democratic National Committee.

In an unusual occurrence, nominating speeches were delivered by a past and a future president for men who would not attain the office themselves. Sen. John F. Kennedy of Massachusetts placed Adlai E. Stevenson's name in nomination, while former president Harry S. Truman seconded the nomination of New York governor W. Averell Harriman. Truman criticized Stevenson as a "defeatist," but was countered by Eleanor Roosevelt, who appeared before the convention in support of the former Illinois governor.

In spite of the oratorical byplay, Stevenson was in good position to win the nomination before the convention even began, having eliminated his principal rival, Sen. Estes Kefauver of Tennessee, in the primaries. Stevenson won a majority on the first ballot, receiving 905-1/2 votes to easily defeat Harriman, who had 210. Sen. Lyndon B. Johnson of Texas finished third, with 80 votes. Upon completion of the roll call, a motion was approved to make Stevenson's nomination unanimous. *(Chart, p. 238)*

In an unusual move, Stevenson announced that he would not personally select his running mate but would leave the choice to the convention. Stevenson's desire for an open selection was designed to contrast with the expected cut-and-dried nature of the upcoming Republican convention. But the unusual move caught both delegates and prospective candidates off guard.

Numerous delegations passed on the first ballot, and upon completion of the roll call votes were scattered among 13 different candidates. When the vote totals were announced at the end of the roll call, Kefauver led with 483-1/2 votes, followed by Kennedy with 304, Sen. Albert A. Gore of Tennessee with 178, Mayor Robert F. Wagner of New York City with 162-1/2 and Sen. Hubert H. Humphrey of Minnesota with 134-1/2. Six hundred eighty-seven votes were needed to nominate.

With a coalition that included most of the Southern and Eastern delegates, Kennedy drew into the lead on the second ballot. After the roll call but before the chair recognized vote changes, the totals stood: Kennedy, 618; Kefauver, 551-1/2; Gore, 110-1/2. Kentucky, the first state to be recognized, shifted its 30 votes to Kennedy, leaving the 39-year-old senator fewer than 40 votes short of the nomination.

But Gore was recognized next and began a bandwagon for Kefauver by withdrawing in favor of his Tennessee colleague. Other states followed Gore's lead, and at the conclusion of the vote shifts Kefauver had a clear majority. The final tally was Kefauver, 755-1/2 and Kennedy, 589. Kennedy moved that his opponent's nomination be made unanimous.

Ironically, Kefauver won a majority of the votes in only two states in his home region, Tennessee and Florida. His strength lay in Midwestern and Western delegations.

As in 1948 platform debate focused on the civil rights issue. A Minnesota member of the platform committee introduced a minority report that advocated a civil rights plank stronger than that in the majority report. The plank presented by the platform committee pledged to carry out Supreme Court decisions on desegregation, but not through the use of force. The party promised to continue to work for equal rights in voting, employment, personal security and education. The Minnesota substitute was more specific, as it favored federal legislation to achieve equal voting rights and employment opportunities and to guarantee personal safety. The minority plank also favored more rigid enforcement of civil rights legislation. Although several states clamored for a roll-call vote, the chair took a voice vote, which went against the Minnesota substitute.

The entire platform was the longest yet approved by a Democratic convention, about 12,000 words. The document was divided into 11 sections, the first dealing with defense and foreign policy and the remainder with domestic issues.

The platform described President Eisenhower as a "political amateur . . . dominated . . . by special privilege." It applauded the legislative accomplishments of the Democratic Congress elected in 1954 and proposed a continuation of the social and economic legislation begun during the New Deal.

The foreign policy of the Eisenhower administration was criticized in a plank that accused the Republicans of cutting funds for the military in an attempt to balance the budget. The Democrats declared that the United States must have the strongest military in the world to discourage aggression by America's enemies. The foreign policy plank also pledged to strengthen the United Nations as a peace-keeping organization and promised to work diligently for worldwide disarmament.

The platform blamed the Republicans for allowing big business to dominate the economy and promised tax relief and other government assistance to help small business. The Democrats advocated repeal of the Taft-Hartley Act, as the party had done in every platform since 1948, and favored an increase in the minimum wage. Tax reductions were proposed for lower-income taxpayers, and an increase of at least $200 in the personal tax exemption was recommended.

For farmers, the Democrats proposed price supports at 90 percent of parity on basic crops, as opposed to the Republican program of flexible price supports.

For the first time since the beginning of the New Deal, the Democratic platform mentioned the importance of states' rights. The party also reiterated its position on education, which advocated federal assistance, but stated that ultimate control of the schools lay in the hands of state and local governments.

In political reform the platform proposed restrictions on government secrecy and repeated the party's call for the passage of an equal rights amendment.

Following are excerpts from the Democratic platform of 1956:

**Foreign Policy.** *The Failure at Home.* Political considerations of budget balancing and tax reduction now come before the wants of our national security and the needs of our Allies. The Republicans have slashed our own armed strength, weakened our capacity to deal with military threats, stifled our air force, starved our army and weakened our capacity to deal with aggression of any sort save by retreat or by the alternatives, "massive retaliation" and global atomic war. Yet, while our troubles mount, they tell us our prestige was never higher, they tell us we were never more secure.

**Disarmament.** To eliminate the danger of atomic war, a universal, effective and enforced disarmament system must be the goal of responsible men and women everywhere. So long as we lack enforceable international control of weapons, we must maintain armed strength to avoid war. But technological advances in the field of nuclear weapons make disarmament an ever more urgent problem. Time and distance can never again protect any nation of the world.

**Labor.** We unequivocally advocate repeal of the Taft-Hartley Act. The Act must be repealed because State "right-to-work" laws have their genesis in its discriminatory anti-labor provisions. . . .

The Taft-Hartley Act has been proven to be inadequate, unworkable and unfair. It interferes in an arbitrary manner with collective bargaining, causing imbalance in the relationship between management and labor.

**Agriculture.** Undertake immediately by appropriate action to endeavor to regain the full 100 percent of parity the farmers received under the Democratic Administrations. We will achieve this by means of supports on basic commodities at 90 percent of parity and by means of commodity loans, direct purchases, direct payments to producers, marketing agreements and orders, production adjustments, or a combination of these, including legislation, to bring order and stability into the relationship between the producer, the processor and the consumer.

**Education.** We are now faced with shortages of educational facilities that threaten national security, economic prosperity and human well-being. The resources of our States and localities are already strained to the limit. Federal aid and action should be provided, within the traditional framework of State and local control.

**Tax Reform.** We favor realistic tax adjustments, giving first consideration to small independent business and the small individual taxpayer. Lower-income families need tax relief; only a Democratic victory will assure this. We favor an increase in the present personal tax exemption of $600 to a minimum of at least $800.

**Government Secrecy.** *Freedom of Information.* During recent years there has developed a practice on the part of Federal agencies to delay and withhold information which is needed by Congress and the general public to make important decisions affecting their lives and destinies. We believe that this trend toward secrecy in Government should be reversed and that the Federal Government should return to its basic tradition of exchanging and promoting the freest flow of information possible in those unclassified areas where secrets involving weapons development and bona fide national security are not involved.

**States' Rights.** While we recognize the existence of honest differences of opinion as to the true location of a Constitutional line of demarcation between the Federal Government and the States, the Democratic Party expressly recognizes the vital importance of the respective States in our Federal Union. The Party of Jefferson and Jackson pledges itself to continued support of those sound principles of local government which will best serve the welfare of our people and the safety of our democratic rights.

**Civil Rights.** We are proud of the record of the Democratic Party in securing equality of treatment and opportunity in the nation's armed forces, the Civil Service, and in all areas under Federal jurisdiction. The Democratic Party pledges itself to continue its efforts to eliminate illegal discriminations of all kinds, in relation to (1) full rights to vote, (2) full rights to engage in gainful occupations, (3) full rights to enjoy security of the person, and (4) full rights to education in all publicly supported institutions.

Recent decisions of the Supreme Court of the United States relating to segregation in publicly supported schools and elsewhere have brought consequences of vast importance to our Nation as a whole and especially to communities directly affected. We reject all proposals for the use of force to interfere with the orderly determination of these matters by the courts.

## Republicans

The Republicans opened their convention in San Francisco three days after the close of the Democratic convention in Chicago. In contrast to the turbulent convention of their adversaries, the Republicans' renomination of Dwight D. Eisenhower and Richard M. Nixon was a formality. The only possible obstacle to Eisenhower's candidacy was his health, but by August 1956 his recovery from a heart attack and an ileitis operation was complete enough to allow him to seek a second term. On the convention's single roll call for president, Eisenhower received all 1,323 votes.

What drama occurred at the Republican convention surrounded the vice presidential nomination. Several weeks before the opening of the convention, former Minnesota governor Harold Stassen, the disarmament adviser to Eisenhower, had begun a movement to replace Vice President Nixon with Massachusetts governor Christian A. Herter. However, with lack of interest from party leaders, this movement petered out. At the convention both Herter and Stassen gave nominating speeches for Nixon. During the roll call, a commotion was caused by a Nebraska delegate, who attempted to nominate "Joe Smith." After some discussion, it was determined that "Joe Smith" was a fictitious individual, and the offending delegate was escorted from the hall. On the one ballot for vice president, a unanimous vote was recorded for Nixon.

While no opposition to the platform was expressed on the floor of the convention, several Southern delegates were unhappy with the civil rights plank and withdrew from the convention. The plank in question listed advances in desegregation under the Republican administration, voiced acceptance of the Supreme Court ruling on school desegregation and pledged to enforce existing civil rights statutes.

The platform as a whole was slightly longer than the Democratic document and was dedicated to Eisenhower and "the youth of America." Unlike the Democratic platform, which began with a discussion of foreign policy and national defense, the first issue pursued by the Republicans was the economy.

The Eisenhower administration was praised for balancing the budget, reducing taxes and halting inflation. The platform promised continued balanced budgets, gradual reduction of the national debt and cuts in government spending consistent with the maintenance of a strong military. Two measures favored by the Democrats, tax relief for small businesses and tax reductions for low-income and middle-income families, were both mentioned as secondary economic goals in the Republican platform.

The labor plank advocated revision but not repeal of the Taft-Hartley Act. The agricultural section favored elimination of price-depressing surpluses and continuation of the flexible price-support program. As they had for the past quarter century, the Republicans joined the Democrats in recommending passage of an equal rights amendment.

The foreign policy section of the Republican platform praised the Eisenhower administration for ending the Korean War, stemming the worldwide advance of communism and entering new collective security agreements. The plank also emphasized the necessity of a bipartisan foreign policy. The "preservation" of Israel was viewed as an "important tenet of American foreign policy," a notable difference from the Democratic platform, which took a more even-handed approach toward both Israel and the Arab states.

The national defense section emphasized the United States' possession of "the strongest striking force in the world," a rebuttal to Democratic charges that the Republicans had jeopardized the efficiency of the armed forces in an effort to balance the budget.

Following are excerpts from the Republican platform of 1956:

**Economy.** We pledge to pursue the following objectives:

Further reductions in Government spending as recommended in the Hoover Commission Report, without weakening the support of a superior defense program or depreciating the quality of essential services of government to our people.

Continued balancing of the budget, to assure the financial strength of the country which is so vital to the struggle of the free world in its battle against Communism; and to maintain the purchasing power of a sound dollar, and the value of savings, pensions and insurance.

Gradual reduction of the national debt.

Then, insofar as consistent with a balanced budget, we pledge to work toward these additional objectives:

Further reductions in taxes with particular consideration for low and middle income families.

Initiation of a sound policy of tax reductions which will encourage small independent businesses to modernize and progress.

**Labor.** Revise and improve the Taft-Hartley Act so as to protect more effectively the rights of labor unions, management, the individual worker, and the public. The protection of the right of workers to organize into unions and to bargain collectively is the firm and permanent policy of the Eisenhower Administration.

**Agriculture.** This program must be versatile and flexible to meet effectively the impact of rapidly changing conditions. It does not envision making farmers dependent upon direct governmental payments for their incomes. Our objective is markets which return full parity to our farm and ranch people when they sell their products.

**Civil Rights.** The Republican Party accepts the decision of the U.S. Supreme Court that racial discrimination in publicly supported schools must be progressively eliminated. We concur in the conclusion of the Supreme Court that its decision directing school desegregation should be accomplished with "all deliberate speed" locally through Federal District Courts. The implementation order of the Supreme Court recognizes the complex and acutely emotional problems created by its decision in certain sections of our country where racial patterns have been developed in accordance with prior and longstanding decisions of the same tribunal.

We believe that true progress can be attained through intelligent study, understanding, education and good will. Use of force or violence by any group or agency will tend only to worsen the many problems inherent in the situation. This progress must be encouraged and the work of the courts supported in every legal manner by all branches of the Federal Government to the end that the constitutional ideal of equality before the law, regardless of race, creed or color, will be steadily achieved.

**Foreign Policy.** The advance of Communism has been checked, and, at key points, thrown back. The once-monolithic structure of International Communism, denied the stimulant of successive conquests, has shown hesitancy both internally and abroad.

**National Defense.** We *have* the strongest striking force in the world — in the air — on the sea — and a magnificent supporting land force in our Army and Marine Corps.

**Israel.** We regard the preservation of Israel as an important tenet of American foreign policy. We are determined that the integrity of an independent Jewish State shall be maintained. We shall support the independence of

Israel against armed aggression. The best hope for peace in the Middle East lies in the United Nations. We pledge our continued efforts to eliminate the obstacles to a lasting peace in this area.

# 1960 Conventions

## Presidential Candidates

**John F. Kennedy**
**Democrat**

**Richard M. Nixon**
**Republican**

### Democrats

For the first time, a national political convention was held in Los Angeles. More than 4,000 delegates and alternates converged on the California metropolis in July to select the Democratic standard-bearers for 1960. The delegate allocation method had been changed since 1956 by the Democratic National Committee, from a formula that included Democratic voting strength to a system that emphasized population only. No states lost seats, but the new formula tended to strengthen populous Northern states.

The early sessions of the convention dealt with rules and credentials. The convention rules, approved without debate, included the compromise loyalty pledge adopted by the 1956 convention. The only credentials dispute involved two contesting delegations from the Commonwealth of Puerto Rico. By a voice vote, the convention agreed to seat both delegations while splitting the vote of the Commonwealth.

The front-runner for the presidential nomination was Massachusetts senator John F. Kennedy, whose success in the primaries and support from many of the party's urban leaders put him on the verge of a nominating majority. His principal rival was Senate Majority Leader Lyndon B. Johnson of Texas, although the favorite of the convention galleries was Adlai E. Stevenson, the party's unsuccessful standard-bearer in 1952 and 1956. Johnson challenged Kennedy to a debate, which was held before a joint gathering of the Massachusetts and Texas delegations. Coming the day before the balloting, the debate had little effect on the ultimate outcome.

Nine men were nominated, but Kennedy received a clear majority on the first ballot. At the end of the roll call, the Massachusetts senator had 806 votes, to easily outdistance Johnson, who received 409. Sen. Stuart Symington of Missouri was a distant third with 86 votes, and Stevenson followed with 79-1/2. A motion to make Kennedy's nomination unanimous was approved by a voice vote. Kennedy's selection marked the first time since 1920 that a senator had been nominated for the presidency by Democrats or Republicans and the first time since 1928 that a Roman Catholic had been represented on a national ticket of one of the two major parties. *(Chart, p. 239)*

Kennedy surprised some supporters and political observers by choosing his erstwhile adversary, Lyndon Johnson, as his running mate. A motion to nominate Johnson by acclamation was approved by a voice vote.

Kennedy delivered his acceptance speech to 80,000 spectators at the Los Angeles Coliseum. He envisioned the United States as "on the edge of a new frontier — the frontier of the 1960s — a frontier of unknown opportunities and perils — a frontier of unfulfilled hopes and threats," adding that this "new frontier . . . is not a set of promises — it is a set of challenges."

The Democratic platform was easily the longest yet written by the party, about 20,000 words. The platform itself was approved by a voice vote, although the civil rights and fiscal responsibility planks were debated on the convention floor, and roll-call votes had been taken in committee.

Regional hearings had been held by subcommittees of the 108-member platform committee in the spring, but votes on controversial issues were not taken by the full committee until the convention. A plank that urged elimination of the immigration quota system was approved, 66 to 28, with opposition led by Sen. James O. Eastland of Mississippi. An agricultural plank recommending price supports at 90 percent of parity was passed, 66 to 22, with opponents claiming that it was a restatement of the liberal program proposed by the National Farmers Union. A motion to reconsider the plank was defeated, 38 to 32. An Eastland motion to delete condemnation of "right-to-work" laws was defeated without a recorded vote.

The civil rights plank caused the greatest controversy. Sen. Sam J. Ervin Jr. of North Carolina introduced motions to delete portions that proposed establishing a Fair Employment Practices Commission, continuing the Civil

**113**

Rights Commission as a permanent agency, granting the attorney general the power to file civil injunction suits to prevent discrimination, and setting 1963 as the deadline for the initiation of school desegregation plans. Ervin's motions were defeated by a voice vote, and the entire plank was approved, 66 to 24.

Delegates from nine Southern states signed a statement that repudiated the civil rights plank. Led by Georgia Democratic Chairman James H. Gray and Ervin, these nine states introduced a minority report on the convention floor calling for elimination of the platform's civil rights plank. After an hour's debate, the minority report was rejected by a voice vote.

A minority amendment introduced by the Virginia delegation, proposing that the fiscal responsibility plank include a planned schedule for reduction of the national debt, also was rejected by a voice vote.

As approved by the convention, the platform began with a discussion of foreign policy. The Democrats blamed the Republican administration for allowing the United States military strength to deteriorate. The national defense plank declared there was a "missile gap, space gap, and limited-war gap," and promised to improve America's military position so that it would be second to none. The Democrats recommended creation of "a national peace agency for disarmament planning and research." The money saved by international disarmament, the plank stated, could be used to attack world poverty.

Foreign military aid was viewed as a short-range necessity that should be replaced by economic aid "as rapidly as security considerations permit." At the same time, the platform proposed that development programs be placed on a "long-term basis to permit more effective planning."

The Democrats' economic plank called for an average national growth rate of 5 percent annually. Economic growth at this rate would create needed tax revenue, the Democrats believed, which — coupled with cuts in government waste, closing of tax loopholes and more extensive efforts to catch tax evaders — would help balance the budget. The Democrats promised to use measures such as public works projects and temporary tax cuts to combat recessions or depressions.

The platform promised an increase in the minimum wage to $1.25 an hour and pledged to extend coverage to include more workers. There was a pledge to amend the Social Security program so the elderly could continue working without sacrificing basic benefits.

Equal rights legislation was favored, although the platform did not call for passage of a constitutional amendment of 1960.

Following are excerpts from the Democratic platform of 1960:

**National Defense.** Our military position today is measured in terms of gaps — missile gap, space gap, limited-war gap....

This is the strength that must be erected:

1. Deterrent military power such that the Soviet and Chinese leaders will have no doubt that an attack on the United States would surely be followed by their own destruction.

2. Balanced conventional military forces which will permit a response graded to the intensity of any threats of aggressive force.

3. Continuous modernization of these forces through intensified research and development, including essential programs now slowed down, terminated, suspended or neglected for lack of budgetary support.

**Disarmament.** This requires a national peace agency for disarmament planning and research to muster the scientific ingenuity, coordination, continuity, and seriousness of purpose which are now lacking in our arms control efforts....

As world-wide disarmament proceeds, it will free vast resources for a new international attack on the problem of world poverty.

**Immigration.** The national-origins quota system of limiting immigration contradicts the founding principles of this nation. It is inconsistent with our belief in the rights of man. This system was instituted after World War I as a policy of deliberate discrimination by a Republican Administration and Congress....

**Foreign Aid.** Where military assistance remains essential for the common defense, we shall see that the requirements are fully met. But as rapidly as security considerations permit, we will replace tanks with tractors, bombers with bulldozers, and tacticians with technicians.

**Civil Rights.** We believe that every school district affected by the Supreme Court's school desegregation decision should submit a plan providing for at least first-step compliance by 1963, the 100th anniversary of the Emancipation Proclamation....

For this and for the protection of all other Constitutional rights of Americans, the Attorney General should be empowered and directed to file civil injunction suits in Federal courts to prevent the denial of any civil right on grounds of race, creed or color.

**Economy.** We Democrats believe that our economy can and must grow at an average rate of 5 percent annually, almost twice as fast as our average annual rate since 1953. We pledge ourselves to policies that will achieve this goal without inflation....

The policies of a Democratic Administration to restore economic growth will reduce current unemployment to a minimum.

**Tax Reform.** We shall close the loopholes in the tax laws by which certain privileged groups legally escape their fair share of taxation.

Among the more conspicuous loopholes are depletion allowances which are inequitable, special consideration for recipients of dividend income, and deductions for extravagant "business expenses" which have reached scandalous proportions.

**Labor.** We pledge to raise the minimum wage to $1.25 an hour and to extend coverage to several million workers not now protected.

**Agriculture.** The Democratic Administration will work to bring about full parity income for farmers in all segments of agriculture by helping them to balance farm production with the expanding needs of the nation and the world.

Measures to this end include production and marketing quotas measured in terms of barrels, bushels and bales, loans on basic commodities at not less than 90 percent of parity, production payments, commodity purchases, and marketing orders and agreements.

**Government Spending.** The Democratic Party believes that state and local governments are strengthened — not weakened — by financial assistance from the Federal Government. We will extend such aid without impairing local administration through unnecessary Federal interference or red tape.

## Republicans

On July 25, 10 days after the close of the Democratic convention, the Republican convention opened in Chicago.

Although Vice President Richard M. Nixon had a lock on the presidential nomination, the party's two major figures four years later, Arizona senator Barry Goldwater and New York governor Nelson A. Rockefeller, both had major roles in convention activities.

Both Goldwater and Rockefeller announced that they did not want their names placed in nomination, but the Arizona delegation disregarded Goldwater's request and nominated him anyway. In a convention speech, the Arizona senator withdrew his name and went on to advise conservative Republicans to work within the party: "Let's grow up conservatives.... If we want to take this party back — and I think we can someday — let's get to work."

On the roll call that followed, Nixon was a nearly unanimous choice, receiving 1,321 votes to 10 for Goldwater (all from Louisiana). On a voice vote, Nixon's nomination was made unanimous.

Nixon reportedly wanted Rockefeller as his running mate, but was unable to persuade the New Yorker to join the ticket. The Republican standard-bearer subsequently turned to United Nations Ambassador Henry Cabot Lodge Jr., a former senator from Massachusetts who had been beaten for re-election by John Kennedy in 1952. On the vice presidential ballot, Lodge received all but one vote. The lone dissenter, a Texas delegate, initially abstained but switched his vote to Lodge at the end of the roll call.

In his acceptance speech, Nixon promised to campaign in all 50 states and rebutted a theme in Kennedy's acceptance speech. "Our primary aim must be not to help government, but to help people — to help people attain the life they deserve," said Nixon.

Much of the drama of the 1960 Republican convention surrounded the party platform. And the highlight of the platform maneuvering was a late-night meeting involving Nixon and Rockefeller, held at Rockefeller's New York City apartment two days before the opening of the convention. The meeting, a secret to most of Nixon's closest aides, resulted in a 14-point agreement between the two Republican leaders on major issues contained in the platform. The agreement, informally dubbed the "compact of Fifth Avenue," was issued by Rockefeller, who declared that the meeting was held at Nixon's insistence.

Half of the 14 points dealt with national security and foreign policy. The other half discussed domestic issues, including government reorganization, civil rights, agriculture, economic growth and medical care for the elderly. Although not markedly different in wording from the draft of the platform committee, the "compact" expressed a tone of urgency that was not evident in the draft.

The Nixon-Rockefeller agreement was made with the knowledge of the platform committee chairman, Charles H. Percy of Illinois, but was greeted with hostility by many members of the committee and by party conservatives. Goldwater termed the "compact" a "surrender" and the "Munich of the Republican Party" that would ensure the party's defeat that fall.

The two issues of greatest controversy were civil rights and national defense. The original civil rights plank, drafted by the platform committee, did not express support for civil rights demonstrations or promise federal efforts to gain job equality for blacks. The Nixon-Rockefeller agreement did both. Nixon threatened to wage a floor fight if the stronger civil rights plank was not inserted in the platform. By a vote of 50 to 35, the platform committee agreed to reconsider the original civil rights plank; by a margin of 56 to 28, the stronger plank was approved.

With the approval of both Rockefeller and President Dwight D. Eisenhower, several changes were made in the national security plank that emphasized the necessity of quickly upgrading America's armed forces. The platform committee approved reconsideration of the original defense plank by a voice vote, and the whole platform was adopted unanimously.

With disagreements resolved in the committee, there were neither minority reports nor floor fights. The convention approved the platform by a voice vote.

In its final form, the Republican platform was shorter than its Democratic counterpart, although still nearly 15,000 words in length. The foreign policy section asserted that the nation's greatest task was "to nullify the Soviet conspiracy." The platform claimed that America's military strength was second to none but, in line with the Nixon-Rockefeller "compact," indicated that improvements were needed in some parts of the armed forces.

The Republicans joined their Democratic opposition in favoring a workable disarmament program but did not advocate a phaseout of foreign military aid, as did the Democrats. However, the Republicans proposed a change in the funding of foreign aid that emphasized "the increasing use of private capital and government loans, rather than outright grants."

The Republicans agreed with the Democrats that the nation should experience more rapid economic growth but did not adopt the 5 percent annual growth rate favored by the Democrats. The Republicans stressed the virtues of a balanced budget and regarded free enterprise, rather than massive government programs, as the key to economic growth.

As in 1956, the two parties differed on farm price supports. The Republicans supported a program of flexible support payments, while the Democrats recommended setting price supports at 90 percent of parity.

Both parties proposed allowing individuals to work beyond their mandatory retirement age, although the Democrats tied their proposal to amendment of the Social Security program.

The Republicans did not urge elimination of the immigration quota system, as did their opponents, but they favored overhaul of the system to allow an increase in immigration.

On the issue of equal rights, the Republicans continued to favor passage of a constitutional amendment. The Democrats had backed away from this position, which they had held in earlier platforms, instead proposing the passage of equal rights legislation in Congress.

As they had since the beginning of the New Deal, the Republican and Democratic platforms differed noticeably as to the extent and desirability of federal spending. The Democrats viewed federal assistance to state and local governments as beneficial. The Republicans believed the federal government could help meet the problems of urban growth, but that state and local governments should administer all the programs they could best handle.

Following are excerpts from the Republican platform of 1960:

**National Defense.** The future of freedom depends heavily upon America's military might and that of her allies. Under the Eisenhower-Nixon Administration, our military might has been forged into a power second to none....
*The strategic imperatives of our national defense policy are these:*
A second-strike capability, that is, a nuclear retaliatory power that can survive surprise attack, strike back, and destroy any possible enemy.

Highly mobile and versatile forces, including forces deployed, to deter or check local aggressions and "brush fire wars" which might bring on all-out nuclear war.

National determination to employ all necessary military capabilities so as to render any level of aggression unprofitable. Deterrence of war since Korea, specifically, has been the result of our firm statement that we will never again permit a potential aggressor to set the ground rules for his aggression; that we will respond to aggression with the full means and weapons best suited to the situation....

**Disarmament.** We are similarly ready to negotiate and to institute realistic methods and safeguards for disarmament, and for the suspension of nuclear tests. We advocate an early agreement by all nations to forego nuclear tests in the atmosphere, and the suspension of other tests as verification techniques permit.

**Immigration.** The annual number of immigrants we accept be at least doubled.

Obsolete immigration laws be amended by abandoning the outdated 1920 census data as a base and substituting the 1960 census.

The guidelines of our immigration policy be based upon judgment of the individual merit of each applicant for admission and citizenship.

**Foreign Aid.** Agreeable to the developing nations, we would join with them in inviting countries with advanced economies to share with us a proportionate part of the capital and technical aid required. We would emphasize the increasing use of private capital and government loans, rather than outright grants, as a means of fostering independence and mutual respect.

**Civil Rights.** *Voting.* We pledge:

Continued vigorous enforcement of the civil rights laws to guarantee the right to vote to all citizens in all areas of the country....

*Public Schools.* We pledge:

The Department of Justice will continue its vigorous support of court orders for school desegregation....

We oppose the pretense of fixing a target date 3 years from now for the mere submission of plans for school desegregation. Slow-moving school districts would construe it as a three-year moratorium during which progress would cease, postponing until 1963 the legal process to enforce compliance. We believe that each of the pending court

actions should proceed as the Supreme Court has directed and that in no district should there be any such delay.

*Employment.* We pledge:

Continued support for legislation to establish a Commission on Equal Job Opportunity to make permanent and to expand with legislative backing the excellent work being performed by the President's Committee on Government Contracts....

*Housing.* We pledge:

Action to prohibit discrimination in housing constructed with the aid of federal subsidies.

*Public Facilities and Services.* We pledge:

Removal of any vestige of discrimination in the operation of federal facilities or procedures which may at any time be found....

**Economy.** We reject the concept of artificial growth forced by massive new federal spending and loose money policies. The only effective way to accelerate economic growth is to increase the traditional strengths of our free economy — initiative and investment, productivity and efficiency....

**Agriculture.** Use of price supports at levels best fitted to specific commodities, in order to widen markets, ease production controls, and help achieve increased farm family income.

**Government Reorganization.** The President must continue to be able to reorganize and streamline executive operations to keep the executive branch capable of responding effectively to rapidly changing conditions in both foreign and domestic fields....

Two top positions should be established to assist the President in, (1) the entire field of National Security and International Affairs, and (2) Governmental Planning and Management, particularly in domestic affairs.

**Government Spending.** Vigorous state and local governments are a vital part of our federal union. The federal government should leave to state and local governments those programs and problems which they can best handle and tax sources adequate to finance them. We must continue to improve liaison between federal, state and local governments. We believe that the federal government, when appropriate, should render significant assistance in dealing with our urgent problems of urban growth and change. No vast new bureaucracy is needed to achieve this objective.

# 1964 Conventions

## Presidential Candidates

**Barry Goldwater**
**Republican**

**Lyndon B. Johnson**
**Democrat**

## Republicans

Division between the party's conservative and moderate wings, muted during the Eisenhower administration, exploded at the Republicans' July 13-16 convention in San Francisco.

Although Sen. Barry Goldwater of Arizona, the hero of Republican conservatives, had a commanding lead as the convention opened, he was vigorously challenged by Pennsylvania governor William W. Scranton, the belated leader of the moderate forces. Two days before the presidential balloting, a letter in Scranton's name was sent to Goldwater. It charged the Goldwater organization with regarding the delegates as "little more than a flock of chickens whose necks will be wrung at will." The message continued, describing Goldwater's political philosophy as a "crazy-quilt collection of absurd and dangerous positions." The letter concluded by challenging the Arizona senator to a debate before the convention. Although the message was written by Scranton's staff without his knowledge, the Pennsylvania governor supported the substance of the letter. Goldwater declined the invitation to debate.

Although seven names were placed in nomination for the presidency, the outcome was a foregone conclusion. Goldwater was an easy winner on the first ballot, receiving 883 of the 1,308 votes. Scranton was a distant second with 214 votes; New York governor Nelson A. Rockefeller followed with 114. Scranton moved that Goldwater's nomination be made unanimous, and his motion was approved by a voice vote. Support for the major moderate candidates, Scranton and Rockefeller, was centered in the Northeast. Goldwater had an overwhelming majority of the delegates from other regions. *(Chart, p. 240)*

As his running mate, Goldwater selected the Republican national chairman, Rep. William E. Miller of New York. On disclosing his choice of Miller, Goldwater stated that "one of the reasons I chose Miller is that he drives Johnson nuts." On the vice presidential roll call, the conservative New York representative received 1,305 votes, with three delegates from Tennessee abstaining. A Roman Catholic, Miller became the first member of that faith ever to run on a Republican national ticket.

Goldwater's acceptance speech was uncompromising and did not attempt to dilute his conservatism in an effort to gain votes: "Anyone who joins us in all sincerity we welcome. Those who do not care for our cause, we don't expect to enter our ranks in any case. And let our Republicanism so focused and so dedicated not be made fuzzy and futile by unthinking and stupid labels. I would remind you that extremism in the defense of liberty is no vice. And let me remind you also that moderation in the pursuit of justice is no virtue."

By a voice vote, the convention adopted the party platform, but not before the moderate forces waged floor fights on three issues — extremism, civil rights and control of nuclear weapons. Within the platform committee, 70 to 80 different amendments were presented, but when the platform reached the floor the moderates concentrated on these three specific issues.

Extremism was the first issue considered, with Sen. Hugh Scott of Pennsylvania introducing an amendment that specifically denounced efforts of the John Birch Society, the Ku Klux Klan and the Communist Party to infiltrate the Republican Party. Rockefeller spoke on behalf of the amendment but was booed throughout his speech. Rockefeller argued that a "radical, high-financed, disciplined minority" was trying to take over the Republican Party, a minority "wholly alien to the middle course . . . the mainstream." The amendment was rejected on a standing vote, by a margin estimated at two to one.

A second amendment on extremism, proposed by Michigan governor George W. Romney, condemned extremist groups but not by name. The Romney amendment was similarly rejected on a standing vote by about the same margin. Scott introduced a civil rights amendment adding additional pledges to the existing plank, including more manpower for the Justice Department's Civil Rights Division; a statement of pride in Republican support of the 1964 Civil Rights Act; requirements for first-step compliance with school desegregation by all school districts in one year; voting guarantees to state as well as federal elections, and promises to eliminate job bias. The platform's brief plank on civil rights called for "full implementation and faithful execution" of the 1964 act, but it also stated that "the elimination of any such discrimination is a matter of heart, conscience and education as well as of equal rights under law." On a roll-call vote, the Scott amendment was defeated, 897 to 409. The pattern of the vote closely followed the presidential ballot, with support for the amendment centered in the Northeast. *(Chart, p. 240)*

Romney offered a brief, alternative civil rights plank that pledged action at the state, local and private levels to eliminate discrimination in all fields. It was defeated by a voice vote.

Scott proposed another amendment, declaring the president to have sole authority to control the use of nuclear weapons. This contrasted with Goldwater's position advocating that North Atlantic Treaty Organization (NATO) commanders be given greater authority in the use of tactical nuclear weapons. The Scott amendment was rejected on a standing vote.

In its final form, the Republican platform was barely half as long as its Democratic counterpart. The Republican platform was divided into four sections, the first two enumerating Democratic failures in foreign policy and domestic affairs. The last two sections detailed Republican proposals.

The Republicans were suspicious of any détente with the communist world, instead calling for "a dynamic strategy of victory ... for freedom." The platform contended that American military strength was deteriorating and promised the establishment of a military force superior to that of the nation's enemies. The Republicans expressed distrust of the 1963 nuclear test ban treaty and vowed to "never unilaterally disarm America." The platform promised to revitalize NATO, which was viewed as a keystone of Republican foreign policy.

Concerning specific trouble spots around the world, the platform demanded removal of the Berlin Wall, pledged to "move decisively to assure victory in South Vietnam" and promised to recognize a Cuban government in exile as well as to supply assistance to Cuban guerrilla freedom fighters.

Coupled with the anti-communism of the foreign policy sections was the central theme of the domestic sections — the need to trim the power of the federal government and to relocate it in state and local governments. This conservative philosophy was evident in various domestic planks.

The Republicans promised a reduction of at least $5 billion in federal spending and pledged to end budget deficits. A proposal was made to cut federal income taxes and to transfer the excise tax and several other federal tax sources from the federal government to state and local governments. The Republicans also recommended that state and local tax payments be credited against federal income taxes.

The platform favored a reduction of federal involvement in school financing and advocated passage of a constitutional amendment to allow prayer in public schools. A plank was included that urged passage of legislation to curb the flow of obscene materials through the mails.

The "one person, one vote" ruling of the Supreme Court brought the recommendation by the Republicans that a constitutional amendment be passed to allow states with bicameral legislatures to use a measurement other than population.

Following are excerpts from the Republican platform of 1964:

**Peace.** This Administration has sought accommodations with Communism without adequate safeguards and compensating gains for freedom. It has alienated proven allies by opening a "hot line" first with a sworn enemy rather than with a proven friend, and in general pursued a risky path such as began at Munich a quarter century ago....

The supreme challenge to this policy is an atheistic imperialism — Communism.

Our nation's leadership must be judged by — indeed, American independence and even survival are dependent upon — the stand it takes toward Communism.

That stand must be: victory for freedom. There can be no peace, there can be no security, until this goal is won.

**National Defense.** This Administration has adopted policies which will lead to a potentially fatal parity of power with Communism instead of continued military superiority for the United States.

It has permitted disarmament negotiations to proceed without adequate consideration of military judgment — a procedure which tends to bring about, in effect, a unilateral curtailment of American arms rendered the more dangerous by the Administration's discounting known Soviet advances in nuclear weaponry.

It has failed to take minimum safeguards against possible consequences of the limited nuclear test ban treaty, including advanced underground tests where permissible and full readiness to test elsewhere should the need arise....

... we will regularly review the status of nuclear weaponry under the limited nuclear test ban to assure this nation's protection. We shall also provide sensible, continuing reviews of the treaty itself....

We will maintain a superior, not merely equal, military capability as long as the Communist drive for world domination continues. It will be a capability of balanced force, superior in all its arms, maintaining flexibility for effective performance in the rapidly changing science of war.

Republicans will never unilaterally disarm America.

**Berlin.** We will demand that the Berlin Wall be taken down prior to the resumption of any negotiations with the Soviet Union on the status of forces in, or treaties affecting, Germany.

**Cuba.** We Republicans will recognize a Cuban government in exile; we will support its efforts to regain the independence of its homeland; we will assist Cuban freedom fighters in carrying on guerrilla warfare against the Communist regime; we will work for an economic boycott by all nations of the free world in trade with Cuba; and we will encourage free elections in Cuba after liberty and stability are restored.

**Vietnam.** We will move decisively to assure victory in South Vietnam. While confining the conflict as closely as possible, America must move to end the fighting in a reasonable time and provide guarantees against further aggression. We must make it clear to the Communist world that, when conflict is forced with America, it will end only in victory for freedom.

**United Nations.** This Administration has failed to provide forceful, effective leadership in the United Nations.

It has weakened the power and influence of this world organization by failing to demand basic improvements in its procedures and to guard against its becoming merely a form of anti-Western insult and abuse.

**Federal Power.** Humanity is tormented once again by an age-old issue — is man to live in dignity and freedom under God or to be enslaved — are men in government to serve, or are they to master, their fellow men? ...

1. Every person has the right to govern himself, to fix his own goals, and to make his own way with a minimum of governmental interference.

2. It is for government to foster and maintain an

environment of freedom encouraging every individual to develop to the fullest his God-given powers of mind, heart and body; and, beyond this, government should undertake only needful things, rightly of public concern, which the citizen cannot himself accomplish.

We Republicans hold that these two principles must regain their primacy in our government's relations, not only with the American people, but also with nations and peoples everywhere in the world.

**Economy.** In furtherance of our faith in the individual, we also pledge prudent, responsible management of the government's fiscal affairs to protect the individual against the evils of spendthrift government — protecting most of all the needy and fixed-income families against the cruelest tax, inflation — and protecting every citizen against the high taxes forced by excessive spending, in order that each individual may keep more of his earning for his own and his family's use.

**Tax Reform.** In furtherance of our faith in limited, frugal and efficient government we also pledge: credit against Federal taxes for specified State and local taxes paid, and a transfer to the States of excise and other Federal tax sources, to reinforce the fiscal strength of State and local governments so that they may better meet rising school costs and other pressing urban and suburban problems such as transportation, housing water systems and juvenile delinquency....

**Civil Rights.** Full implementation and faithful execution of the Civil Rights Act of 1964, and all other civil rights statutes, to assure equal rights and opportunities guaranteed by the Constitution to every citizen; ... continued opposition to discrimination based on race, creed, national origin or sex. We recognize that the elimination of any such discrimination is a matter of heart, conscience, and education, as well as of equal rights under law.

**Education.** To continue the advancement of education on all levels, through such programs as selective aid to higher education, strengthened State and local tax resources, including tax credits for college education, while resisting the Democratic efforts which endanger local control of schools; to help assure equal opportunity and a good education for all, while opposing Federally-sponsored "inverse discrimination," whether by the shifting of jobs, or the abandonment of neighborhood schools, for reasons of race;....

**School Prayer.** Support of a Constitutional amendment permitting those individuals and groups who choose to do so to exercise their religion freely in public places, provided religious exercises are not prepared or prescribed by the state or political subdivision thereof and no person's participation therein is coerced, thus preserving the traditional separation of church and state;....

**Obscenity.** Enactment of legislation, despite Democratic opposition, to curb the flow through the mails of obscene materials which has flourished into a multimillion dollar obscenity racket;....

**Medical Care for Elderly.** Full coverage of all medical and hospital costs for the needy elderly people, financed by general revenues through broader implementation of Federal-State plans, rather than the compulsory Democratic scheme covering only a small percentage of such costs, for everyone regardless of need;....

**Reapportionment.** Support of a Constitutional amendment, as well as legislation, enabling States having bicameral legislatures to apportion one House on bases of their choosing, including factors other than population;....

## Democrats

In late August in Atlantic City, N.J., the Democratic convention nominated President Lyndon B. Johnson for a full term in the White House. The proceedings were stage-managed by the president and were met with little visible dissent on the convention floor. The four-day event Aug. 24-27 was a political triumph for the veteran politician from Texas, who less than a year earlier had been the assassinated John F. Kennedy's vice president.

The Democratic convention was larger than any previous convention of an American political party, with 5,260 delegates and alternates. A new vote-allocation formula was in effect that combined consideration of a state's electoral vote with its support for the Kennedy-Johnson ticket in 1960. While no states lost votes from four years earlier, many of the larger states gained significantly. As a result, there were 2,316 votes at the 1964 convention, compared with 1,521 in 1960.

With no controversy surrounding either the party nominee or platform, attention focused on the credentials challenge brought by the integrated Mississippi Freedom Democratic Party against the all-white delegation sent by the regular state party. By a voice vote, the convention approved a compromise negotiated by Minnesota senator Hubert H. Humphrey. The settlement called for seating of the Mississippi regulars, provided they signed a written pledge to back the national ticket and urged the state's presidential electors to do likewise. It also proposed the seating of Democrats as delegates at large, and the remainder of the delegation as honored guests; and it stipulated that at future conventions delegations would be barred from states that allowed racial discrimination in voting. Although the convention approved this solution, the Freedom Democrats rejected the compromise, and all but four members of the regular Mississippi delegation refused to sign the pledge and left the convention.

The convention also approved a recommendation requiring the Alabama delegation to sign a personal loyalty oath, the result of the state party's placing "unpledged" (anti-Johnson) electors on the Alabama ballot. Eleven Alabama members signed the loyalty oath; the remaining 42 delegates and alternates withdrew from the convention.

The roll-call vote for president was dispensed with, and Johnson was nominated by acclamation. Immediately after his selection, Johnson made the unprecedented move of appearing before the delegates to announce his choice for vice president, Humphrey. Johnson had tried to make his selection as suspenseful and dramatic as possible. Although most observers felt Humphrey would be the choice, earlier that day Johnson had called both the Minnesota senator and Connecticut senator Thomas J. Dodd to the White House. However, at this meeting Johnson invited Humphrey to be on the ticket, and later that night the delegates nominated Humphrey by acclamation. (The 1964 Democratic convention was only the second in party history in which there were no roll-call votes — the other time was 1936.)

On the final day of the convention, the two nominees delivered their acceptance speeches. Humphrey frequently referred to the Republican candidate, Sen. Goldwater, as "the temporary Republican spokesman," and listed major legislation supported by a majority of both parties in the Senate, "but not Sen. Goldwater."

The emotional highlight of the convention was the appearance of Attorney General Robert F. Kennedy, who introduced a film about the presidency of his late brother.

By a voice vote, the convention approved the party platform. Following the trend toward longer and longer documents, the platform was 22,000 words in length. Although the document was adopted without debate on the convention floor, several roll-call votes were taken in the platform committee. By a vote of 53 to 16, the committee rejected a proposal by Sen. Joseph S. Clark of Pennsylvania to strengthen the disarmament plank. Clark's proposal called for further disarmament "under world law," wording that the committee majority did not want to include.

By a margin of 39 to 38, the platform committee pledged to support a constitutional amendment giving the District of Columbia representation in Congress. On another roll-call vote (52 to 19), the committee promised to repeal the Taft-Hartley Act provision permitting state right-to-work laws.

Without a recorded vote, the committee adopted another provision by Sen. Clark proposing revision of congressional rules and procedures to "assure majority rule after reasonable debate and to guarantee that major legislative proposals of the President can be brought to a vote after reasonable consideration in committee." The proposal was a reference to the Senate cloture rule, requiring a two-thirds vote to cut off debate, and to the power of the House Rules Committee to keep legislation from the floor.

The entire platform was a wide-ranging document designed to appeal to as many segments of the electorate as possible. Self-described as a "covenant of unity," the platform was written in a moderate tone to contrast with the unqualified conservatism expressed in the Republican platform.

The latter three-quarters of the Democratic platform was a section entitled "An Accounting of Stewardship, 1961-1964," which described the accomplishments of the Kennedy-Johnson administration in 38 areas of public policy. The first quarter of the platform discussed the party's position on major issues of the day, from peace and national defense to civil rights, the economy, agriculture, natural resources, urban affairs, federal power and government reform, and extremism.

In view of the militant anti-communism of Sen. Goldwater and the Republican platform, the Democrats viewed peace and national defense as winning issues with a majority of the electorate. The Democrats claimed that the world was closer to peace than in 1960, due in part to the United States' overwhelming nuclear superiority and internal splits in the communist world, as well as the success of international negotiations such as those resulting in the nuclear test ban treaty. But, in an allusion to Goldwater's stance, the platform warned that recklessness by a president in foreign policy could result in nuclear disaster. The Democratic platform included a provision rejected by the Republicans, insisting that control of nuclear weapons must be kept in the hands of the president.

While peace and national defense were stressed by the Democrats, the Republican platform concentrated on the need to limit the power of the federal government. On this issue, the Democratic platform contained a recommendation to help state and local governments develop new revenue sources. But the Democratic plank also included an assertion that contradicted the Republicans' criticism of expanding federal power: "No government at any level can properly complain of violation of its power, if it fails to meet its responsibilities."

Neither party had a civil rights plank containing specifics. The difference was wording, with the Democrats promising "fair, effective enforcement" of the 1964 Civil Rights Act, but precluding the use of quotas in combating racial discrimination. The Republicans pledged "full implementation and faithful execution" of civil rights laws.

An effort at the Republican convention to have the party platform condemn specific "extremist" groups failed, although the issue was hotly debated on the convention floor. Without dissent, the Democratic platform included a provision that condemned extremism of the right and left, especially the Communist Party, the Ku Klux Klan and the John Birch Society.

The two parties differed in their opinion of the health of the economy. The Republicans blamed their opposition for inflation and continuing unemployment and promised a reduction of at least $5 billion in federal spending. The Democrats countered by claiming the Kennedy-Johnson administration had engineered "the longest and strongest peacetime prosperity in modern history."

Following are excerpts from the Democratic platform of 1964:

**Peace.** At the start of the third decade of the nuclear age, the preservation of peace requires the strength to wage war and the wisdom to avoid it. The search for peace requires the utmost intelligence, the clearest vision, and a strong sense of reality.... Battered by economic failures, challenged by recent American achievements in space, torn by the Chinese-Russian rift, and faced with American strength and courage — international Communism has lost its unity and momentum.

**National Defense.** Specifically, we must and we will:
—Continue the overwhelming supremacy of our Strategic Nuclear Forces.
—Strengthen further our forces for discouraging limited wars and fighting subversion.
—Maintain the world's largest research and development effort, which has initiated more than 200 new programs since 1961, to ensure continued American leadership in weapons systems and equipment....
Control of the use of nuclear weapons must remain solely with the highest elected official in the country — the President of the United States....
The complications and dangers in our restless, constantly changing world require of us consummate understanding and experience. One rash act, one thoughtless decision, one unchecked reaction — and cities could become smouldering ruins and farms parched wasteland.

**Civil Rights.** The Civil Rights Act of 1964 deserves and requires full observance by every American and fair, effective enforcement if there is any default....
True democracy of opportunity will not be served by establishing quotas based on the same false distinctions we seek to erase, nor can the effects of prejudice be neutralized by the expedient of preferential practices.

**Extremism.** We condemn extremism, whether from the Right or Left, including the extreme tactics of such organizations as the Communist Party, the Ku Klux Klan and the John Birch Society.

**Federal Power.** The Democratic Party holds to the belief that government in the United States — local, state and federal — was created in order to serve the people. Each level of government has appropriate powers and each has specific responsibilities. The first responsibility of government at every level is to protect the basic freedoms of the people. No government at any level can properly complain of violation of its power, if it fails to meet its responsibilities.
The federal government exists not to grow larger, but to enlarge the individual potential and achievement of the people.
The federal government exists not to subordinate the states, but to support them.

**Economy.** In 42 months of uninterrupted expansion

under Presidents Kennedy and Johnson, we have achieved the longest and strongest peacetime prosperity in modern history. . . .

It is the national purpose, and our commitment, that every man or woman who is willing and able to work is entitled to a job and to a fair wage for doing it.

# 1968 Conventions
## Presidential Candidates

**Richard M. Nixon**
**Republican**

**Hubert H. Humphrey**
**Democrat**

**George C. Wallace**
**American Independent**

### Republicans

The Republican convention, held in Miami Beach, Fla., Aug. 5-8, had a surface tranquility that the later Democratic convention lacked. Only two roll-call votes were taken on the convention floor, to nominate presidential and vice presidential candidates.

There was only one challenge seriously considered by the credentials committee, and that involved a single delegate. By a 32-32 vote, the committee defeated an unexpectedly strong attempt to overturn the preconvention decision to seat Rep. H. R. Gross of Iowa rather than a Des Moines housewife. The full convention approved the report of the credentials committee without a roll-call vote.

The report of the rules committee was approved without comment. It contained recommendations to prohibit discrimination in the selection of future convention delegates and to add the Republican state chairmen as members of the Republican National Committee.

Twelve names were placed in nomination for the presidency, although the contest was clearly among three candidates: the front-runner, former vice president Richard M. Nixon, and two governors, Nelson A. Rockefeller of New York and Ronald Reagan of California. The ideological gulf between the more liberal Rockefeller and the more conservative Reagan made it difficult for them to agree on a common strategy to stop Nixon, even when Reagan abandoned his favorite-son status for active candidacy two days before the balloting.

To head off the defection to Reagan of his more conservative supporters, Nixon seemed to take a sharp tack to the right the day before the balloting. He told Southern delegations he would not run an administration that would "ram anything down your throats," that he opposed school busing, that he would appoint "strict constitutionalists" to the Supreme Court and that he was critical of federal intervention in local school board affairs.

Nixon won the nomination on the first ballot, receiving 692 votes (25 more than necessary) to easily outdistance

Rockefeller, who had 277, and Reagan, who had 182. After vote switches, the final totals were Nixon, 1,238, Rockefeller, 93, and Reagan, 2. In a brief speech to the convention, Reagan moved that Nixon's nomination be made unanimous, but his motion was never put to a vote. *(Chart, p. 242)*

In his selection of a running mate, Nixon surprised many observers by tapping Maryland governor Spiro T. Agnew. Agnew, who had delivered the major nominating speech for Nixon, had, ironically, been one of Rockefeller's earliest and strongest supporters. But the Maryland governor ceased his active support of Rockefeller in March, irked by the New York governor's indecision about entering the race, and, at the beginning of convention week, announced his support for Nixon.

In addition to Agnew, the name of Michigan governor George Romney also was placed in nomination for vice president. Agnew was an easy winner, receiving 1,119 votes to 186 for Romney, who made no effort to withdraw his name. After completion of the roll call, a Romney motion to make Agnew's nomination unanimous was approved.

The delegates approved without debate the 1968 Republican platform, which steered a careful middle course between conservatives and liberals on domestic policy and between "doves" and "hawks" on the touchy Vietnam issue. The 11,500-word document was somewhat more liberal in tone than that of 1960 and was far removed from the militantly conservative tone of the 1964 document.

A major floor fight on the platform was averted when platform committee members, led by Senate Minority Leader Everett McKinley Dirksen of Illinois, substituted for the original hard-line war plank new language stressing the need for de-Americanization of both the military and civilian efforts in Vietnam. Both "hawks" and "doves" decided to go along with the revised version.

As originally written, the plank criticized the Johnson administration for not leaving key Vietnam decisions to the military and for the administration's policy of military gradualism. Both Nixon and Rockefeller backers opposed the strong language, and a compromise Vietnam plank was accepted. As well as advocating the de-Americanization of the war, it proposed concentrating on protection of the South Vietnamese population rather than on capturing territory, and on efforts to strengthen local forces and responsibility.

While the platform endorsed continued negotiations with Hanoi, it remained silent on the important issues of a bombing pause and of a possible Saigon coalition that would include the communists. During platform committee deliberations, Sen. Jacob K. Javits of New York offered a plank to bring the National Liberation Front into the negotiations, but the suggestion was rejected overwhelmingly.

In its discussion of national defense, the platform criticized the administration for failure to develop superior new weaponry. The document indicated that, when the Vietnam War was over, a reduced defense budget might make possible increased federal spending on social welfare programs. But it neither suggested how much more spending nor recommended any substantial increases in the near future.

The platform treated rioting and crime in militant fashion: "We will not tolerate violence!" The crime plank criticized the Johnson administration for not taking effective action against crime and pledged "an all-out federal-state-local crusade."

It was in the cities plank that the party, in a short statement, mentioned civil rights legislation. The statement simply pledged: "Energetic, positive leadership to enforce statutory and constitutional protections to eliminate discrimination." It was seen as an endorsement of the recently enacted open housing law, in addition to other federal civil rights statutes. The platform did not endorse any new civil rights legislation. However, the Republicans endorsed high-priority objectives of civil rights groups, such as increased food for the poor and job-training programs.

In its youth plank, the Republicans made two specific proposals. First, the party urged the states to lower the voting age to 18 but did not endorse proposals for a constitutional amendment similarly to lower the federal voting age. Second, the plank advocated action to shorten the period in which young men were eligible for the draft and proposed to develop eventually a voluntary force.

Following are excerpts from the Republican platform of 1968:

**Vietnam.** The Administration's Vietnam policy has failed — militarily, politically, diplomatically, and with relation to our own people.

We condemn the Administration's breach of faith with the American people respecting our heavy involvement in Vietnam. Every citizen bitterly recalls the Democrat campaign oratory of 1964: "We are not about to send American boys 9-10,000 miles away from home to do what Asian boys ought to be doing for themselves." The Administration's failure to honor its own words has led millions of Americans to question its credibility.

The entire nation has been profoundly concerned by hastily-extemporized, undeclared land wars which embroil massive U.S. Army forces thousands of miles from our shores. It is time to realize that not every international conflict is susceptible of solution by American ground forces. . . .

We pledge to adopt a strategy relevant to the real problems of the war, concentrating on the security of the population, on developing a greater sense of nationhood,

and on strengthening the local forces. It will be a strategy permitting a progressive de-Americanization of the war, both military and civilian. . . .

We pledge a program for peace in Vietnam — neither peace at any price nor a camouflaged surrender of legitimate United States or allied interests — but a positive program that will offer a fair and equitable settlement to all, based on the principle of self-determination, our national interests and the cause of long-range world peace.

We will sincerely and vigorously pursue peace negotiations as long as they offer any reasonable prospect for a just peace. We pledge to develop a clear and purposeful negotiating position.

**National Defense.** Grave errors, many now irretrievable, have characterized the direction of our nation's defense.

A singular notion — that salvation for America lies in standing still — has pervaded the entire effort. Not retention of American superiority but parity with the Soviet Union has been made the controlling doctrine in many critical areas. We have frittered away superior military capabilities, enabling the Soviets to narrow their defense gap, in some areas to outstrip us, and to move to cancel our lead entirely by the early Seventies.

**China.** Improved relations with Communist nations can come only when they cease to endanger other states by force or threat. Under existing conditions, we cannot favor recognition of Communist China or its admission to the United Nations.

**Israel.** The fact of a growing menace to Israel is undeniable. Her forces must be kept at a commensurate strength both for her protection and to help keep the peace of the area. The United States, therefore, will provide countervailing help to Israel, such as supersonic fighters, as necessary for these purposes.

**Crime.** Fire and looting, causing millions of dollars of property damage, have brought great suffering to home owners and small businessmen, particularly in black communities least able to absorb catastrophic losses. The Republican Party strongly advocates measures to alleviate and remove the frustrations that contribute to riots. We simultaneously support decisive action to quell civil disorder, relying primarily on state and local governments to deal with these conditions.

America has adequate peaceful and lawful means for achieving even fundamental social change if the people wish it. *We will not tolerate violence!*

Lawlessness is crumbling the foundations of American society. . . .

We must re-establish the principle that men are accountable for what they do, that criminals are responsible for their crimes, that while the youth's environment may help to explain the man's crime, it does not excuse that crime.

The present Administration has:

—Refused to sanction the use of either the court-supervised wiretapping authority to combat organized crime or the revised rules of evidence, both made available by Congress.

—Failed to deal effectively with threats to the nation's internal security by not prosecuting identified subversives. . . .

For the future, we pledge an all-out, federal-state-local crusade against crime, including:

—Leadership by an Attorney General who will restore stature and respect to that office. . . .

—Enactment of legislation to control indiscriminate availability of firearms, safeguarding the right of responsible citizens to collect, own and use firearms for legitimate purposes, retaining primary responsibility at the state level, with such federal laws as necessary to better enable the states to meet their responsibilities.

**Economy.** Under the Johnson-Humphrey Administration we have had economic mismanagement of the highest order....

Such funds as become available with the termination of the Vietnam war and upon recovery from its impact on our national defense will be applied in a balanced way to critical domestic needs and to reduce the heavy tax burden.

## Democrats

While violence flared in the streets and thousands of police and guards imposed security precautions unprecedented at presidential nominating conventions, the 1968 Democratic convention met Aug. 26-29 in Chicago to nominate Hubert H. Humphrey of Minnesota for the presidency and to endorse the controversial Vietnam policies of the Johnson-Humphrey administration.

Twin themes — physical force to keep order and political force to overrule minority sentiment in the Democratic Party — were apparent throughout the convention.

The physical force, supplied by 11,900 Chicago police, 7,500 Army regulars, 7,500 Illinois National Guardsmen and 1,000 FBI and Secret Service agents, was exerted to keep vociferous Vietnam War critics away from the convention headquarters hotels and the International Amphitheatre where official sessions were held. A security ring several blocks wide guarded the amphitheatre, itself surrounded by a barbed wire fence and multiple security checkpoints for entering delegates, newsmen and guests. No violence erupted in the amphitheatre area, but near the downtown hotels there were days of bitter demonstrations that ended with repeated police use of tear gas. At the end of convention week, the Chicago police announced that 589 persons had been arrested during the disturbances, with more than 119 police and 100 demonstrators injured.

The political force was exerted by the Johnson administration organization backing Vice President Humphrey, whose supporters enjoyed clear control of convention proceedings from start to end. In a distinct minority were the anti-war factions that rallied around the candidacies of Senators Eugene J. McCarthy of Minnesota and George McGovern of South Dakota. The McCarthy forces mounted a series of challenges to the Humphrey faction — on credentials, rules, the platform and finally the nomination itself.

In the first business of the convention, the Humphrey and McCarthy forces joined to ban the unit rule, rejecting by voice vote a motion by the Texas delegation to retain the rule through the 1968 convention.

However, as expected, the brief moments of unity between the opposing sides ended when the convention moved on to consider credentials challenges. The two sides split on the question of adjournment, with the Humphrey forces defeating by a vote of 1,701-1/2 to 875 a motion to delay consideration of credentials until the second session.

The credentials committee had considered an unprecedented number of challenges, involving delegates from 15 states. Although McCarthy supported almost all the challenges, his candidacy was not always the paramount issue. In the case of the disputed Southern delegations, racial imbalance, the party loyalty issue, or a combination of both, were more important. Of the 17 different challenges, McCarthy supported all but one (in Wisconsin); McGovern backed all the Southern challenges; Humphrey supported only the Mississippi challenge publicly.

In a historic move, the convention by a voice vote seated a new loyalist Democratic faction from Mississippi and unseated the delegation of the traditionally segregationist, conservative regular party.

The credentials committee decided all other challenges in favor of the regular delegations, but minority reports were filed for the Alabama, Georgia, North Carolina and Texas challengers. The North Carolina case was decided by a voice vote supporting the regular delegation, but the other three cases were settled by roll-call votes.

The first state to be considered was Texas, and, by a vote of 2,368-1/4 to 956-3/4, the convention approved the seating of the regular delegation led by Gov. John B. Connally. The rival McCarthy-supported Texas faction was led by Sen. Ralph W. Yarborough. *(Chart, p. 241)*

The Georgia case was considered next, with the credentials committee recommending that both rival delegations be seated and the Georgia vote split evenly between them. However, both delegations found this to be an unsatisfactory solution and presented reports to have their entire delegation seated alone. A minority report to seat the challenging Loyal National Democrats, led by black state representative Julian Bond, was defeated 1,415.45 to 1,043.55. A minority report to seat the regular delegation, hand-picked by Gov. Lester G. Maddox and Democratic state chairman James H. Gray, was rejected by a voice vote. The solution recommended by the credentials committee was subsequently approved by a voice vote.

The Alabama case involved three competing factions: the regulars, the largely black National Democratic Party of Alabama (NDPA) and the integrated Alabama Independent Democratic Party (AIDP), created solely to run a slate of presidential electors loyal to the national party against the third-party candidacy of Alabama governor George C. Wallace. The credentials committee proposed seating all members of the regular delegation who would sign a loyalty pledge and replacing those who would not sign with loyal members of the AIDP delegation. However, the McCarthy-backed NDPA introduced a minority report to seat its entire delegation. By a vote of 1,607 to 880-3/4, the convention rejected this minority report and by a voice vote approved the recommendation of the credentials committee.

The remainder of the credentials committee report was approved, including a resolution instructing the Democratic National Committee to include, in the call for the 1972 convention, encouragement to state parties to ensure that all Democrats in each state have a "meaningful and timely" opportunity to participate in delegate selection.

McCarthy, McGovern and other liberal factions won their greatest breakthrough on convention rules, obtaining abolition of a mandatory unit rule for the 1968 convention, and, by a vote of 1,351-1/4 to 1,209, obtaining elimination of the unit rule at every level of party activity leading up to and including the 1972 convention. Many Humphrey-pledged delegates also backed the unit rule change. Also a part of this successful minority report was the requirement that the delegate-selection process in 1972 be public and held within the calendar year of the convention.

A proposal to add state chairmen and state Young Democratic presidents to the Democratic National Committee was defeated, 1,349-1/4 to 1,125-3/4.

On Wednesday night, on the third day of the convention, while nominations and balloting for president took place at the amphitheatre, the worst violence of the convention broke out downtown, and television screens carried pictures of phalanxes of Chicago police advancing on demonstrators.

At the same time, hundreds of Chicago mayor Richard

J. Daley's workers were brought into the galleries with apparent improper credentials. Some delegates, apparently refusing to show their credentials to the omnipresent security guards, were physically ejected from the convention floor. The McCarthy and McGovern forces charged "atrocities" and tried to adjourn the convention for two weeks. House Majority Leader Carl Albert of Oklahoma, the convention chairman, refused to accept their motions.

In addition to Humphrey, McCarthy and McGovern, only two other candidates were placed in nomination — the Rev. Channing E. Phillips of the District of Columbia, who became the first black ever nominated for the presidency at a national convention, and North Carolina governor Dan K. Moore. Telegrams were read from President Johnson and Massachusetts senator Edward M. Kennedy, each stating that he did not choose to be nominated.

The emotional highlight of the session was provided by McGovern's nominator, Connecticut senator Abraham A. Ribicoff, who charged that "with George McGovern as president of the United States we wouldn't have to have Gestapo tactics in the streets of Chicago."

Humphrey was an easy winner on the first ballot, receiving 1,759-1/4 votes to 601 for McCarthy, 146-1/2 for McGovern and 67-1/2 for Phillips. Humphrey's winning majority included the bulk of party moderates, big-city organizations of the North (including Daley's) and Southern conservatives. In a tumultuous ending to one of the wildest nights in American politics, Chairman Albert gaveled through a motion to make the nomination unanimous (despite major opposition on the floor) and adjourned the session. *(Chart, p. 241)*

As his running mate, Humphrey chose Maine senator Edmund S. Muskie. Julian Bond's name also was placed in nomination, but Bond, then 28, withdrew, explaining that he was under the "legal age" to be president (the constitutional minimum is 35). Before the end of the first ballot, Albert recognized Mayor Daley, who moved that Muskie be declared the vice presidential nominee by acclamation. With the convention in a particularly unruly state, the Daley motion was quickly adopted. At the time the roll call was suspended, Muskie already had received 1,942-1/2 votes, a majority. Bond was a distant second with 48-1/2.

A filmed tribute to the late New York senator Robert F. Kennedy preceded the vice presidential nomination. Kennedy had been a presidential candidate until his assassination in June after winning the California primary. The tribute to Kennedy evoked a long, standing ovation and the singing of "The Battle Hymn of the Republic."

The 18,000-word platform, adopted by a voice vote, was a document that met the demands of the Democratic Party's liberals word for word in almost every section except that which dealt with United States policy in Vietnam. At one point during the platform-writing sessions, it appeared that Humphrey might assent to a plank calling for a halt in U.S. bombing of North Vietnam. But President Johnson reportedly sent personal instructions that the plank should support administration policy.

The administration plank, approved by a 62-35 vote in the platform committee, supported a bombing halt only when it "would not endanger the lives of our troops in the field," did not call for a reduction in search-and-destroy missions or a withdrawal of troops until the end of the war, and advocated a new government in Saigon only after the war had ended. The minority plank, drafted by McCarthy and McGovern, called for an immediate halt to the bombing, reduction of offensive operations in the South Vietnamese countryside, a negotiated troop withdrawal and encouragement of the South Vietnamese government to negotiate with communist insurgents.

The bitterness created by the Vietnam issue and Humphrey's march toward the nomination finally erupted when the convention managers attempted to force debate and voting on the Vietnam plank at 2 a.m., when most television viewers were already asleep. Albert, in violation of convention rules, refused to recognize a motion from a McCarthy backer to adjourn. But a few minutes later, when the convention could not be brought to order, Albert recognized a similar motion from Mayor Daley.

Nearly three hours of debate were held the next afternoon. On the subsequent roll call, the minority plank was defeated, 1,567-3/4 to 1,041-1/4. After the result was announced, members of the New York delegation and others slipped on black armbands and sang "We Shall Overcome." *(Chart, p. 241)*

Unlike the Republican platform, which called for decreased United States involvement in Vietnam, Democrats adopted a plan that called for a continued strong American war effort. Although the Democrats agreed with Republicans that the South Vietnamese eventually should take over their nation's defense, they gave no indication that an expanded Vietnamese role could lead to U.S. troop reductions in the near future.

While promising to reduce waste in military spending, the Democrats stated that the nation "must and will maintain a strong and balanced defense establishment adequate to the task of security and peace." The platform said there "must be no doubt" about U.S. capability to meet either nuclear or more limited challenges.

Crime was one of the leading domestic issues. The platform contained a strongly worded but rather unspecific plank on crime, a plank containing fewer detailed proposals than its Republican counterpart. The Democratic crime plank was entitled "Justice and Law," in a deliberate effort to avoid use of such phrases as "law and order," which were in the Republican plank and which some observers felt had connotations of overly suppressive tactics, particularly in black ghettos.

The Democratic plank did not mention the role of the attorney general. The Republicans said they would seek an attorney general who would "restore stature and respect to that office." Nor did the Democrats, unlike the Republicans, mention implementation of the federal wiretapping authority granted by the Safe Streets Act, or prosecution of subversives.

Both parties pledged further efforts to control the indiscriminate sale of firearms, but neither party was specific. Democratic liberals had tried unsuccessfully within the platform committee to strengthen the gun control section.

The Democratic platform contained a more specific endorsement of open housing than did the Republican document. Both platforms urged better job opportunities, housing and food programs for the poor, and the Democrats also promised reforms in existing welfare programs.

The Democrats, like the Republicans, called for tax reform, but their goals were more pointed. The platform asked for a minimum income tax for wealthy persons based on total income regardless of source and committed the party to seeking decreased rates for lower-income families and an increase in the minimum standard deduction.

The Democrats supported a constitutional amendment to permit 18-year-old voting and recommended a draft lottery and better community representation on draft boards.

Reform of the electoral college was favored, so that it would accurately reflect the will of the voters.

Following are excerpts from the Democratic platform of 1968:

**Vietnam.** Recognizing that events in Vietnam and the negotiations in Paris may affect the timing and the actions we recommend we would support our Government in the following steps:

*Bombing* — Stop all bombing of North Vietnam when this action would not endanger the lives of our troops in the field; this action should take into account the response from Hanoi.

*Troop Withdrawal* — Negotiate with Hanoi an immediate end or limitation of hostilities and the withdrawal from South Vietnam of all foreign forces — both United States and allied forces, and forces infiltrated from North Vietnam.

*Election of Postwar Government* — Encourage all parties and interests to agree that the choice of the postwar government of South Vietnam should be determined by fair and safeguarded elections, open to all major political factions and parties prepared to accept peaceful political processes. We would favor an effective international presence to facilitate the transition from war to peace and to assure the protection of minorities against reprisal.

*Interim Defense and Development Measures* — Until the fighting stops, accelerate our efforts to train and equip the South Vietnamese army so that it can defend its own country and carry out cutbacks of U.S. military involvement as the South Vietnamese forces are able to take over their larger responsibilities. We should simultaneously do all in our power to support and encourage further economic, political and social development and reform in South Vietnam, including an extensive land reform program. We support President Johnson's repeated offer to provide a substantial U.S. contribution to the post-war reconstruction of South Vietnam as well as to the economic development of the entire region, including North Vietnam. Japan and the European industrial states should be urged to join in this post-war effort.

**National Defense.** We must and will maintain a strong and balanced defense establishment adequate to the task of security and peace. There must be no doubt about our strategic nuclear capacity, our capacity to meet limited challenges, and our willingness to act when our vital interests are threatened....

We face difficult and trying times in Asia and in Europe. We have responsibilities and commitments we cannot escape with honor.

**China.** The immediate prospects that China will emerge from its self-imposed isolation are dim. But both Asians and Americans will have to coexist with the 750 million Chinese on the mainland. We shall continue to make it clear that we are prepared to cooperate with China whenever it is ready to become a responsible member of the international community. We would actively encourage economic, social and cultural exchange with mainland China as a means of freeing that nation and her people from their narrow isolation.

**Israel.** As long as Israel is threatened by hostile and well-armed neighbors, we will assist her with essential military equipment needed for her defense, including the most advanced types of combat aircraft.

**Crime.** In fighting crime we must not foster injustice. Lawlessness cannot be ended by curtailing the hard-won liberties of all Americans. The right of privacy must be safeguarded. Court procedures must be expedited. Justice delayed is justice denied.

A respect for civil peace requires also a proper respect for the legitimate means of expressing dissent. A democratic society welcomes criticism within the limits of the law.

Freedom of speech, press, assembly and association, together with free exercise of the franchise, are among the legitimate means to achieve change in a democratic society. But when the dissenter resorts to violence, he erodes the institutions and values which are the underpinnings of our democratic society. We must not and will not tolerate violence.

**Tax Reform.** We support a proposal for a minimum income tax for persons of high income based on an individual's total income regardless of source, in order that wealthy persons will be required to make some kind of income tax contribution, no matter how many tax shelters they use to protect their incomes.

We also support a reduction of the tax burden on the poor by lowering the income tax rates at the bottom of the tax scale and increasing the minimum standard deduction. No person or family below the poverty level should be required to pay federal income taxes.

**Electoral Reform.** We fully recognize the principle of one man, one vote in all elections. We urge that due consideration be given to the question of Presidential primaries throughout the nation. We urge reform of the electoral college and election procedures to assure that the votes of the people are fully reflected.

## American Independent Party

Former Alabama governor George C. Wallace declared his third-party presidential candidacy on Feb. 8, 1968. The vehicle for his candidacy was his personally created American Independent Party. No convention was held by the party to ratify his selection. (A descendant of the 1968 Wallace campaign, the American Party ran a national ticket in 1972 but received less than 2 percent of the vote.)

On Feb. 14 Wallace announced the choice of former Georgia governor Marvin Griffin as his "interim" vice presidential running mate, but he made clear that an official candidate would be chosen later in the campaign. Griffin's tentative candidacy was necessary to allow the American Independent Party to get on the ballot in several states.

On Oct. 3 Wallace announced his choice of retired Air Force general Curtis E. LeMay, an Ohio native, as his official running mate.

Ten days later, Wallace released the text of his party's platform. The document generally took a harder line toward domestic and international problems than did the Democratic and Republican platforms.

Wallace favored termination of the Vietnam War through negotiations but added that, if negotiations failed, the United States should seek a military solution.

As expected, the emphasis of the platform on domestic issues centered on returning control of local affairs to the states and communities, with the federal government serving in an assisting role rather than an authoritarian manner.

To curb the interference of the federal government in local affairs, Wallace advocated adoption of a constitutional amendment under which federal district judges would stand for election periodically and higher judges, including Supreme Court justices, would be required to be periodically reconfirmed by the Senate. Wallace further proposed, in essence, repeal of the open housing provision of the 1968 Civil Rights Act and to "absolutely prohibit the agencies and agents of the Federal Government from intruding into and seeking to control the affairs of the local school systems of the states, counties and cities of the nation." He further pledged to "cooperate with the administrators of our institutions of higher learning now in the hands of revolutionaries. We must support these officials in the restoration of order on their campuses and we must assure that no assistance, financial or otherwise, from the federal level be given to those seeking to disrupt and destroy these great institutions."

In a section entitled "Crime and Disorder," Wallace pledged to give his full support to law enforcement agencies at every level of government, to "insist on fair and equal treatment for all persons before the bar of justice," to appoint an attorney general "interested in the enforcement rather than the disruption of the legal processes," and to oppose federal legislation requiring gun registration.

Wallace also promised to seek an immediate increase in Social Security benefits, to increase agricultural support prices to 90 percent of parity and to seek legislation increasing maximum support to 100 percent of parity.

Following are excerpts from the American Independent Party platform of 1968:

**Vietnam.** We earnestly desire that the conflict be terminated through peaceful negotiations and we will lend all aid, support, effort, sincerity and prayer to the efforts of our negotiators. Negotiation will be given every reasonable and logical chance for success and we will be patient to an extreme in seeking an end to the war through this means. If it becomes evident that the enemy does not desire to negotiate in good faith, that our hopes of termination of hostilities are not being realized and that the lives and safety of our committed troops are being further endangered, we must seek a military conclusion.

**National Defense.** We propose an intensive and immediate review of the policies, practices and capabilities of the Department of Defense with a view to reestablishing sound principles of logic and reasoning to the decisions and directives of that agency and to eliminating from its ranks all of those who have been party to the dissemination and promulgation of the false doctrines of security and the coercion, intimidation and punishment of all who would oppose or disagree with them.

**Middle East.** Should arms continue to be introduced . . . by foreign powers to such an extent as to endanger the peace in this part of the world, we must take steps to assure that a balance of force is brought to exist. We will join with other nations of the free world in providing the means whereby this balance of force will continue and the threat of aggression of one nation against another is made less likely.

**United Nations.** We will not abandon the United Nations Organization unless it first abandons us. It should be given fair opportunity at resolving international disputes, however, we will not subordinate the interest of our nation to the interest of any international organization. We feel that in this organization, as in any other, participating members should bear proportionate shares of the cost of operation and we will insist on financial responsibility on the part of the member nations.

**Crime.** Lawlessness has become commonplace in our present society. The permissive attitude of the executive and judiciary at the national level sets the tone for this moral decay. The criminal and anarchist who preys on the decent law abiding citizen is rewarded for his misconduct through never ending justification and platitudes from those in high places who seem to have lost their concern for that vast segment of America that so strongly believes in law and order. . . .

We will appoint as Attorney General a person interested in the enforcement rather than the disruption of legal processes and restore that office to the dignity and stature it deserves and requires.

**Economy.** We will review and propose revisions to our present tax structure so as to ease the load of the small income citizen and to place upon all their rightful share of the tax burden. . . .

We will eliminate the favorable treatment now accorded the giant, non-tax paying foundations and institutions and require these organizations to assume their rightful responsibility as to the operation of our government. . . .

We propose to rely heavily upon a competitive market structure rather than upon prices administered or fixed by bureaucratic procedures.

**Federal Power.** The Federal Government, in derogation and flagrant violation of this Article [X] of the Bill of Rights, has in the past three decades seized and usurped many powers not delegated to it, such as, among others: the operation and control of the public school system of the several states; the power to prescribe the eligibility and qualifications of those who would vote in our state and local elections; the power to intrude upon and control the farmer in the operation of his farm; the power to tell the property owner to whom he can and cannot sell or rent his property; and, many other rights and privileges of the individual citizen, which are properly subject to state or local control, as distinguished from federal control. The Federal Government has forced the states to reapportion their legislatures, a prerogative of the states alone. The Federal Government has attempted to take over and control the seniority and apprenticeship lists of the labor unions; the Federal Government has adopted so-called "Civil Rights Acts," particularly the one adopted in 1964, which have set race against race and class against class, all of which we condemn.

**The Judiciary.** In the period of the past three decades, we have seen the Federal judiciary, primarily the Supreme Court, transgress repeatedly upon the prerogatives of the Congress and exceed its authority by enacting judicial legislation, in the form of decisions based upon political and sociological considerations, which would never have been enacted by the Congress. We have seen them, in their solicitude for the criminal and lawless element of our society, shackle the police and other law enforcement agencies; and, as a result, they have made it increasingly difficult to protect the law-abiding citizen from crime and criminals. This is one of the principal reasons for the turmoil and the near revolutionary conditions which prevail in our country today, and particularly in our national capital. The Federal judiciary, feeling secure in their knowledge that their appointment is for life, have far exceeded their constitutional authority, which is limited to interpreting or construing the law.

It shall be our policy and our purpose, at the earliest possible time, to propose and advocate and urge the adoption of an amendment to the United States Constitution whereby members of the Federal judiciary at District level be required to face the electorate on his record at periodical intervals; and, in the event he receives a negative vote upon such election, his office shall thereupon become vacant, and a successor shall be appointed to succeed him.

With respect to the Supreme Court and the Courts of Appeals I [George Wallace] would propose that this amendment require reconfirmation of the office holder by the United States Senate at reasonable intervals.

# 1972 Conventions

## Presidential Candidates

George McGovern
Democrat

Richard M. Nixon
Republican

### Democrats

Massive reforms in convention rules and delegate selection procedures made the 1972 Democratic convention, held in Miami Beach, Fla., July 10-13, significantly different from the violence-plagued assembly in Chicago four years earlier.

Two special commissions created by the 1968 convention drafted the reforms. The Commission on Rules, chaired by Rep. James G. O'Hara of Michigan, composed the first set of rules ever written on Democratic convention procedure. Among the reforms that the Democratic National Committee adopted were:

• A new vote-allocation formula based nearly equally on electoral college strength and the Democratic vote in recent presidential elections.

• An expansion of the convention rules, platform and credentials committees so that their make-up would reflect state population differences rather than the previous method of allocating two seats to each state.

• The assurance that women and men be equally represented on committees and among convention officers.

• The requirement that the meetings and votes of all convention committees be open to the public.

• The requirement that the reports and minority views of all the committees be released at specified dates before the opening of the convention.

• The banning of floor demonstrations for candidates.

• The arrangement of the states and territories for roll calls in random sequence determined by lot rather than in the traditional alphabetical order.

The Commission on Party Structure and Delegate Selection, first chaired by Sen. George McGovern of South Dakota and later by Rep. Donald M. Fraser of Minnesota, formulated 18 guidelines to be met by the states in the delegate-selection process. With the approval of these guidelines by the Democratic National Committee, they became part of the 1972 convention call, thus requiring the states to be in full compliance with the guidelines before they would be seated.

Among the important features of the 18 guidelines were the elimination of the unit rule; the restriction that no

more than 10 percent of a state's delegation be named by its state committee; the requirement that all steps in the delegate-selection process be publicly advertised and held in easily accessible public places within the calendar year of the convention; the requirement that women, youth and minority groups be included in delegations "in reasonable relationship" to their presence in the state's population; and the establishment of a detailed, public method of hearing delegate challenges.

The reforms encouraged an unprecedented number of challenges. The credentials committee opened hearings in Washington, D.C., two weeks before the start of the convention, faced with 82 challenges from 30 states and one territory. A total of 1,289 delegates were challenged, representing more than 40 percent of the convention delegates. More than four-fifths of the challenges were filed on grounds of non-compliance with reform commission guidelines regarding adequate representation of women, youth and minorities.

The most controversial challenges involved the California delegation and the part of the Illinois delegation controlled by Mayor Richard J. Daley of Chicago.

The credentials committee, in a move that surprised supporters of McGovern, a candidate for the presidential nomination, upheld a challenge of California's winner-take-all primary law, stripping McGovern of 151 of the 271 delegate votes he had won in the primary.

The committee voted 72 to 66 to award the 151 convention seats to Sen. Hubert H. Humphrey of Minnesota and seven other candidates in proportion to their share of the popular ballots cast in the state's June primary. Although McGovern was clearly the front-runner for the nomination, the decision, if not overturned by the full convention, threatened his chances of being selected.

In a tense and dramatic balloting session the next day, the committee voted 71 to 61 to unseat Daley and 58 of his Chicago delegates. The committee decided to replace the 59 delegates on grounds that the procedures under which the Daley delegates had been selected violated five of the party's reform guidelines. Most of the Illinois delegates challenging Daley supported McGovern.

Although the losing sides in both the California and Illinois decisions appealed their cases, the courts ruled that the party conventions decide their claims.

The emotional credentials challenges were considered on the first night of the convention. Twenty-three challenges from 15 states were brought to the convention floor, but the spotlight was on the California and Illinois cases. A key preliminary vote took place on a challenge to the South Carolina delegation brought by the National Women's Political Caucus. The challenge, seeking to increase the number of women in the state delegation, was rejected by a vote of 1,555.75 to 1,429.05. *(Chart, pp. 244-245)*

The outcome of the vote could have set an important precedent on what constituted a majority on subsequent challenges. Anti-McGovern forces had hoped to get a ruling from the chair allowing an absolute majority of 1,509 delegates to prevail rather than a simple majority of delegates actually voting.

Convention Chairman Lawrence F. O'Brien (also chairman of the Democratic National Committee) had announced earlier that a majority would consist of one-half plus one of the number of eligible voters. The rules provided that no delegates could vote on their own credentials challenges.

Because the winning total on the South Carolina vote exceeded by a wide margin both the eligible majority and the absolute majority of the convention's 3,016 votes, the anti-McGovern coalition was unable to force a test of what constituted a majority. Thus the vote, although it rejected the position of South Carolina challengers favorable to McGovern, set the stage for returning the 151 California delegates to McGovern. The McGovern forces subsequently won the crucial California challenge, 1,618.28 to 1,238.22.

Immediately after the vote on the California challenge, a Wallace delegate from Florida appealed the ruling of the chair that allowed 120 McGovern delegates from California to vote on their state's other 151 delegates. The appeal was rejected, 1,689.52 to 1,162.23.

Former Nebraska governor Frank B. Morrison, a McGovern supporter, proposed a compromise solution for the Illinois case that would seat both the Daley delegates and the insurgent challengers, while splitting the vote between them. The Morrison proposal asked for suspension of the rules — a parliamentary procedure requiring a two-thirds majority. The motion to suspend the rules was rejected by 1,473.08 nays to 1,411.05 yeas.

The minority report, which asked for seating of the Daley delegates alone, was defeated 1,486.04 to 1,371.56. The vote seated a group, a majority of which supported McGovern, headed by Chicago alderman William Singer and black activist Jesse Jackson. *(Chart, pp. 244-245)*

No other roll-call votes were needed to resolve the remaining credentials challenges. After the settlement of all the delegate contests, the convention had a composition unlike that of any previous major party convention. The 1972 Democratic assembly was the largest in major party history, with 3,203 delegates casting 3,016 votes. Unlike the situation in 1968, most delegates were chosen in state primary elections rather than in state conventions or caucuses. Nearly two-thirds of the delegates to the 1972 convention were selected in primaries, while only 41 percent had been elected by the primary system four years earlier.

There were also large increases in the number of women, youth and racial minorities at the 1972 convention. The proportion of women delegates rose from 13 percent in 1968 to 40 percent in 1972; the number of youth delegates

(30 and under) dramatically jumped from 2.6 percent in 1968 to 21 percent four years later; and black delegates made up 15 percent of the 1972 convention, compared with 5.5 percent in 1968. But while women, youth and blacks were better represented than at earlier conventions, there was a lower level of participation by elected party officials. Only 30 of the 255 Democratic U.S. House members were present in Miami Beach.

The report of the rules committee was approved on the second day of the convention by a voice vote. The report proposed the abolition of winner-take-all primaries in 1976; the abolition of cross-over voting by Republicans in future Democratic presidential primaries; the selection of a woman as chairman of the 1976 convention, with the job rotating between the sexes thereafter; the creation of a special fund in the Democratic National Committee to subsidize the expenses of poor delegates at future national conventions and other party councils, and the appointment of a commission to make "appropriate revisions" in the reform guidelines.

Although the delegates overwhelmingly accepted these reforms, they balked at approving the party charter drafted by the rules committee. The new charter, the first ever written for a major party, was intended to free the national party of four-year presidential election cycles and to broaden public involvement in major national policy questions. But the charter was opposed by some party leaders, particularly members of Congress, who viewed the document as shifting power from elected politicians to the grass-roots level. By a vote of 2,408.45 to 195.10, the convention approved a compromise resolution to delay consideration of the charter until a proposed midterm policy conference in 1974. The compromise also enlarged the Democratic National Committee and revised its membership to reflect Democratic strength in the various states.

The settlement of the California challenge on the opening night of the convention in favor of the McGovern forces effectively locked up the presidential nomination for the South Dakota senator. The next day, two of his major rivals in the primaries, Senators Humphrey and Muskie, withdrew from the race. In the balloting on the third day of the convention, McGovern was an easy winner on the first roll call. Before switches, McGovern had received 1,728.35 votes to 525 for Sen. Henry M. Jackson of Washington, 381.7 for Gov. Wallace of Alabama and 151.95 for Rep. Shirley Chisholm of New York. After vote changes, McGovern's vote total rose to 1,864.95, but no attempt was made to make his nomination unanimous. *(Chart, pp. 244-245)*

With McGovern's first choice for vice president, Sen. Edward M. Kennedy of Massachusetts, rebuffing all overtures, McGovern selected Sen. Thomas F. Eagleton of Missouri. The vice presidential balloting was prolonged by the nomination of six other candidates, and, by the time the roll call was suspended, votes were distributed among more than 70 different "candidates." Eagleton received 1,741.81 votes, a majority. He was followed by Frances T. "Sissy" Farenthold, a women's rights leader from Texas, who had 404.04 votes, Sen. Mike Gravel of Alaska with 225.38 and former Massachusetts governor Endicott Peabody with 107.26. On the motion of Farenthold, the roll call was suspended and Eagleton was nominated by acclamation.

Because of the long vice presidential roll call, it was nearly 3 a.m. before McGovern was able to deliver his acceptance speech. In it he stressed the anti-war theme that was a basic part of his campaign and implored the nation to "come home" to its founding ideals.

Barely 10 days after selection of the Democratic ticket,

on July 25, Eagleton disclosed that he voluntarily had hospitalized himself three times between 1960 and 1966 for "nervous exhaustion and fatigue." McGovern strongly supported his running mate at the time, but in the following days, his support for the Missouri senator began to wane. After a meeting with McGovern on July 31, Eagleton withdrew from the ticket. It marked the first time since 1860 that a major party candidate had withdrawn from a national ticket after the convention had adjourned.

On Aug. 5 McGovern announced that his choice to replace Eagleton was R. Sargent Shriver of Maryland, U.S. ambassador to France and the former director of the Peace Corps and the Office of Economic Opportunity. The newly enlarged Democratic National Committee formally nominated Shriver in an Aug. 8 meeting in Washington. The new vice presidential candidate received 2,936 of the 3,013 votes cast, with the Missouri vote going to Eagleton and four of Oregon's votes to former senator Wayne Morse.

The 1972 Democratic platform was probably the most liberal and the longest (about 25,000 words) ever offered by a major political party. The platform was more a collection of independent reform proposals than a unified plan of action. Its recommendations, largely written by separate subject-area task forces, did not translate into a compact program for Congress to consider or for a president to propose. But the platform's common themes reflected the changes in the party since 1968 and set it off from all other Democratic platforms of the previous generation.

The convention made no concessions to the views of Wallace, even though he made a dramatic appearance at the podium in a wheelchair to urge adoption of minority planks his supporters had offered. Wallace was partially paralyzed from gunshot wounds he had received two months earlier in Laurel, Md., while campaigning for the Democratic presidential nomination.

The Wallace-supported planks called for a constitutional amendment to outlaw busing, tax reform, reintroduction of the death penalty, cutbacks in foreign aid, popular election of federal judges and Senate reconfirmation of Supreme Court justices, a school prayer amendment and support for the right to own guns. They were rejected by voice votes.

Twenty separate minority planks were considered by the convention, but only two were adopted, both by voice vote. One strengthened the American commitment to Israel by adding language promising "a military force in Europe and at sea in the Mediterranean ample to deter the Soviet Union from putting unbearable pressure on Israel." The second endorsed "allocation of federal surplus lands to American Indians on a priority basis."

Two roll-call votes were taken on other planks. The National Welfare Rights Organization sponsored a measure requiring the federal government to guarantee every family of four an annual income of $6,500. This proposal lost, 1,852.86 to 999.34. The other roll call was on a minority plank supporting the right of women to control their reproductive lives without legal interference. Offered by pro-abortion groups, it was defeated 1,572.80 to 1,101.37.

Two other significant minority planks were rejected by voice votes. One was a tax reform measure pushed by Sen. Fred Harris of Oklahoma, which had the slogan, "Take the rich off welfare." The other was a "gay rights" plank endorsing the repeal of all laws regarding voluntary sex acts performed by adults in private.

The platform session demonstrated the firm control McGovern had over the proceedings of the convention. The two minority planks added to the platform were the only proposed additions that McGovern did not specifically oppose. He asked his delegates to support the pro-Israel plank and told them to vote their consciences on the Indian issue.

Planks dealing with domestic issues composed more than four-fifths of the platform. The domestic planks recommended little significant expansion of the size and scope of the federal government. With the major exception of health insurance, the platform sought to restructure society by shifting money and political power to the underprivileged, not by developing federal agencies to alter their lives.

The platform endorsed income redistribution through tax reforms and a guaranteed annual income. It sought expansion of minority-group rights in all political and federal government affairs. To solve the financial crisis at local levels, it endorsed general revenue sharing with local control over use of the money. All this represented a departure from the statist liberalism that had dominated Democratic platforms since the New Deal of the 1930s.

The foreign policy planks broke with the Cold War rhetoric of 1968 and previous years. While endorsing the concept of a strong national defense, the platform devoted more space to peace in Indochina, improved relations with the communist world and less help for non-communist totalitarian regimes. Only four years earlier, the Democrats had given considerable space to warnings against Soviet and Chinese expansion and to praise for the North Atlantic Treaty Organization. The 1968 platform called for scrutiny of wasteful defense spending practices, but the 1972 document made military cuts a major campaign promise and a source of financing for domestic programs.

The platform's position on the Vietnam War was blunt and unequivocal. As "the first order of business" of a Democratic administration, the platform pledged "immediate and complete withdrawal of all U.S. forces in Indochina." The plank also promised an end to military aid to the Saigon regime but pledged economic assistance to Vietnam to help the nation emerge from the war. Amnesty for war resisters was recommended after the return of American prisoners of war.

Following are excerpts from the Democratic platform of 1972:

**Foreign Policy.** The next Democratic Administration should:

- End American participation in the war in Southeast Asia.
- Re-establish control over military activities and reduce military spending, where consistent with national security.
- Defend America's real interests and maintain our alliances, neither playing world policeman nor abandoning old and good friends.
- Not neglect America's relations with small third-world nations in placing reliance on great power relationships.
- Return to Congress, and to the people, a meaningful role in decisions on peace and war, and
- Make information public, except where real national defense interests are involved.

**Vietnam.** We believe that war is a waste of human life. We are determined to end forthwith a war which has cost 50,000 American lives, $150 billion of our resources, that has divided us from each other, drained our national will and inflicted incalculable damage to countless people. We will end that war by a simple plan that need not be kept secret: The immediate total withdrawal of all Americans from Southeast Asia.

**Military Spending.** Military strength remains an essential element of a responsible international policy.

America must have the strength required for effective deterrence.

But military defense cannot be treated in isolation from other vital national concerns. Spending for military purposes is greater by far than federal spending for education, housing, environmental protection, unemployment insurance or welfare. Unneeded dollars for the military at once add to the tax burden and pre-empt funds from programs of direct and immediate benefit to our people. Moreover, too much that is now spent on defense not only adds nothing to our strength but makes us less secure by stimulating other countries to respond.

**Vietnam Amnesty.** To those who for reasons of conscience refused to serve in this war and were prosecuted or sought refuge abroad, we state our firm intention to declare an amnesty, on an appropriate basis, when the fighting has ceased and our troops and prisoners of war have returned.

**Federal Power.** The new Democratic Administration can begin a fundamental re-examination of all federal domestic social programs and the patterns of service delivery they support. Simply advocating the expenditure of more funds is not enough, although funds are needed, for billions already have been poured into federal government programs like urban renewal, current welfare and aid to education, with meager results. The control, structure and effectiveness of every institution and government grant system must be fully examined and these institutions must be made accountable to those they are supposed to serve.

**Economy.** The heart of a program of economic security based on earned income must be creating jobs and training people to fill them. Millions of jobs — real jobs, not make-work — need to be provided. Public service employment must be greatly expanded in order to make the government the employer of last resort and guarantee a job for all.

**Tax Reform.** The cost of government must be distributed more fairly among income classes. We reaffirm the long-established principle of progressive taxation — allocating the burden according to ability to pay — which is all but a dead letter in the present tax code.

**Poverty.** The next Democratic Administration must end the present welfare system and replace it with an income security program which places cash assistance in an appropriate context with all of the measures outlined above, adding up to an earned income approach to ensure each family an income substantially more than the poverty level defined in the area. Federal income assistance will supplement the income of working poor people and assure an adequate income for those unable to work.

**Crime.** There must be laws to control the improper use of hand guns. Four years ago a candidate for the presidency was slain by a hand gun. Two months ago, another candidate for that office was gravely wounded. Three out of four police officers killed in the line of duty are slain with hand guns. Effective legislation must include a ban on sale of hand guns known as Saturday night specials which are unsuitable for sporting purposes.

**Free Expression and Privacy.** The new Democratic Administration should bring an end to the pattern of political persecution and investigation, the use of high office as a pulpit for unfair attack and intimidation and the blatant efforts to control the poor and to keep them from acquiring additional economic security or political power.

The epidemic of wiretapping and electronic surveillance engaged in by the Nixon Administration and the use of grand juries for purposes of political intimidation must be ended. The rule of law and the supremacy of the Constitution, as these concepts have traditionally been understood, must be restored.

**Rights of Women.** Women historically have been denied a full voice in the evolution of the political and social institutions of this country and are therefore allied with all underrepresented groups in a common desire to form a more humane and compassionate society. The Democratic Party pledges the following:

•A priority effort to ratify the Equal Rights Amendment. . . .

•Appointment of women to positions of top responsibilities in all branches of the federal government, to achieve an equitable ratio of women and men.

**School Busing.** We support the goal of desegregation as a means to achieve equal access to quality education for all our children. There are many ways to desegregate schools: School attendance lines may be redrawn; schools may be paired; larger physical facilities may be built to serve larger, more diverse enrollments; magnet schools or educational parks may be used. Transportation of students is another tool to accomplish desegregation. It must continue to be available according to Supreme Court decisions to eliminate legally imposed segregation and improve the quality of education for all children.

**Agriculture.** We will resist a price ceiling on agriculture products until farm prices reach 110 percent of parity, based on the 1910-14 ratios, and we will conduct a relationship between the prices of raw commodities and retail prices;

We will end farm program benefits to farm units larger than family-size. . . .

**Presidential Elections.** We favor a Constitutional change to abolish the Electoral College and to give every voter a direct and equal voice in Presidential elections. The amendment should provide for a runoff election, if no candidate received more than 40 percent of the popular vote.

## Republicans

Six weeks after the Democratic convention, the Republicans gathered in the same Miami Beach convention hall. The Aug. 21-23 convention, precisely programmed to make the most of free prime time, was a gigantic television spectacular from start to finish. The main business of the convention, the nomination of President Richard Nixon and Vice President Spiro T. Agnew to a second term, was a carefully planned ritual.

The selection of Miami Beach as the convention city provided as much drama as the convention itself. Initially the Republicans had chosen San Diego, Calif., as the host city, but the reluctance of that city to provide necessary facilities on schedule, coupled with the revelation that the International Telephone and Telegraph Corp. had pledged as much as $400,000 in local contributions, led the Republican National Committee to move the convention to Miami Beach.

Despite the preliminary organizational problems, the atmosphere of the convention itself was almost euphoric, and the sessions proceeded with dispatch. The five sessions lasted only 16 hours and 59 minutes, compared with the 32 hours and 18 minutes of the Democratic convention.

The one debate, which lasted only an hour, occurred over the adoption of new procedures for selecting national convention delegates. The Republican National Committee's preconvention rules committee approved a 1976 delegate-allocation plan initiated by Sen. John G. Tower of Texas and Rep. Jack F. Kemp of New York. The plan emphasized a state's Republican presidential vote in awarding bonus delegates. It was viewed as especially beneficial to small Southern and Western states. The convention rules committee amended the Tower-Kemp plan to make it more palatable to larger states by adding some bonus delegates for states electing Republican governors and members of Congress.

However, Rep. William A. Steiger of Wisconsin introduced a different plan, weighted more toward states electing Republican governors and members of Congress — a plan that would work to the advantage of the larger states. The debate on the contrasting plans focused on the question of whether states should be rewarded chiefly for delivering their electoral votes to a Republican presidential candidate or whether the bonus should be based to some extent on gubernatorial and congressional contests.

The dispute was in part a battle between liberals and conservatives. Final victory for the conservatives was achieved on a 910-to-434 roll-call vote that defeated the Steiger amendment. The reallocation formula adopted by the delegates would expand the 1976 convention to more than 2,000 delegates, compared with the 1,348 who went to Miami Beach in 1972.

The struggle over the delegate-allocation formula was the only sign of party division at the convention. Nixon was renominated on the third night of the convention, receiving 1,347 of the 1,348 votes. The only opposing vote was cast reluctantly by a delegate from New Mexico for Rep. Paul N. McCloskey Jr. of California, whose anti-war challenge of the president had fizzled after the year's first primary in New Hampshire. *(Chart, p. 243)*

One measure of the unity that surrounded the festive proceedings was the appearance of Gov. Nelson A. Rockefeller of New York to deliver Nixon's nominating speech. Rockefeller had become a loyal supporter of the president after having been his chief rival for the Republican nomination in 1960 and 1968.

Agnew was nominated the next night with 1,345 votes. There were two abstentions and one waggish vote for newscaster David Brinkley.

In his acceptance speech, Nixon combined a review of his first four years with promises for the next four and indirect but highly partisan attacks on his Democratic opponent, George McGovern. Nixon stressed that the choice in the upcoming election was "not between radical change and no change, the choice . . . is between change that works and change that won't work."

The Republican platform provoked little discussion on the convention floor and was approved by a voice vote. Two amendments were offered. The first, which would have pledged a prohibition on deficit federal spending, was defeated by voice vote. The second, advocating self-determination for American Indians, was approved by voice vote with the consent of the platform committee chairman, Rep. John J. Rhodes of Arizona.

The document, approximately 20,000 words long, was generally moderate in its proposals and conservative in language, in contrast to the Democrats' liberal platform.

The actual drafting of the Republican platform was heavily influenced by the White House, and platform committee sessions were held behind closed doors. In contrast, the Democrats held 10 regional hearings around the country, drafted their platform in public and were required by party rules to produce a final version at least 10 days before the convention opened.

The Republican platform was sharply critical not only of McGovern's new leadership of the Democratic Party but also of the Kennedy and Johnson administrations of the "nightmarish" 1960s.

The contrast with the Democratic platform on domestic affairs was stark. The Democrats advocated income redistribution through tax reform and a guaranteed annual income. The Republicans mentioned tax reform but did not include specifics. They rejected the guaranteed income plan.

Both parties called for a reduction in property taxes, although the Republicans made no mention of the value-added tax, a revenue measure the Nixon administration was said to be considering.

The Democrats advocated an immediate end to economic controls; the Republicans proposed to remove the controls "once the economic distortions spawned in the late 1960s are repaired."

The Democrats supported a federally financed and administered national health insurance system, while the Republicans supported a national health insurance plan financed by employers and employees as well as the federal government.

The Republicans opposed busing children to achieve racial balance in schools. The Democrats, however, viewed busing as "another tool" to bring about desegregation. The Republicans supported voluntary school prayer, an issue the Democrats did not mention.

The Republicans opposed legislation on gun control, while the Democrats endorsed a ban on the sale of handguns. The Republicans opposed the legalization of marijuana; the Democrats did not mention the subject in their platform.

Both parties took similar positions on several controversial social issues. The Republicans and Democrats both supported the Equal Rights Amendment to the Constitution, but neither platform specifically mentioned abortion or the rights of homosexuals.

Major differences between the parties were evident in national defense and foreign affairs. The Republicans chided the Democrats for proposing "meat-ax slashes" in the defense budget and charged that their proposals were "worse than misguided; they are dangerous." The Republicans rejected what they described as "a whimpering 'come back America' retreat to isolationism."

The continuing Vietnam War highlighted the foreign policy section. The Republican platform took a swipe at the Democrats by promising that the Nixon administration would not abandon the South Vietnamese or "go begging to Hanoi." If negotiations with North Vietnam failed, the platform promised continuation of the administration's Vietnamization program, gradually phasing out American involvement in the war. But before the remaining United States troops would be withdrawn, the Republicans declared, there must be a return of prisoners of war and an accounting of those missing in action. The Republicans opposed any form of amnesty.

The Republicans pledged to maintain an adequate nuclear deterrent, to help other nations develop the capability to defend themselves, to honor treaty commitments and to defend American interests but limit involvement when American interests were not at stake.

The Democrats had taken a stronger stand than in previous platforms against what they considered misguided American support for repressive regimes throughout the world. In addition, the Democrats argued for re-examination of the hostile United States policy toward Cuba.

Following are excerpts from the Republican platform of 1972:

**Foreign Policy.** Historians may well regard these years as a golden age of American diplomacy. Never before has our country negotiated with so many nations on so wide a range of subjects — and never with greater success.

**Vietnam.** We will continue to seek a settlement of the Vietnam War which will permit the people of Southeast Asia to live in peace under political arrangements of their own choosing. We take specific note of the remaining major obstacle to settlement — Hanoi's demand that the United States overthrow the Saigon government and impose a Communist-dominated government on the South Vietnamese. We stand unequivocally at the side of the President in his effort to negotiate honorable terms, and in his refusal to accept terms which would dishonor this country.

**Military Spending.** To the alarm of free nations everywhere, the New Democratic Left now would undercut our defenses and have America retreat into virtual isolation, leaving us weak in a world still not free of aggression and threats of aggression. We categorically reject this slash-now, beg-later approach to defense policy....

We draw a sharp distinction between prudent reductions in defense spending and the meat-ax slashes with which some Americans are not beguiled by the political opposition.

**Vietnam Amnesty.** We are proud of the men and women who wear our country's uniform, especially of those who have borne the burden of fighting a difficult and unpopular war. Here and now we reject all proposals to grant amnesty to those who have broken the law by evading military service. We reject the claim that those who fled are more deserving, or obeyed a higher morality, than those next in line who served in their places.

**Economy.** We have already removed some temporary controls on wages and prices and will remove them all once the economic distortions spawned in the late 1960s are repaired. We are determined to return to an unfettered economy at the earliest possible moment.

We affirm our support for the basic principles of capitalism which underline the private enterprise system of the United States. At a time when a small but dominant faction of the opposition Party is pressing for radical economic schemes which so often have failed around the world, we hold that nothing has done more to help the American people achieve their unmatched standard of living than the free enterprise system.

**Tax Reform.** We reject the deceitful tax "reform" cynically represented as one that would soak the rich, but in fact one that would sharply raise the taxes of millions of families in middle-income brackets as well. We reject as well the lavish spending promised by the opposition Party which would more than double the present budget of the United States Government. This, too, would cause runaway inflation or force heavy increases in personal taxes.

**Gun Control.** [We pledge to] safeguard the right of responsible citizens to collect, own and use firearms for legitimate purposes, including hunting, target shooting and self-defense. We will strongly support efforts of all law enforcement agencies to apprehend and prosecute to the limit of the law all those who use firearms in the commission of crimes.

**Women's Rights.** Continued ... support of the Equal Rights Amendment to the Constitution, our Party being the first national party to back this Amendment.

**School Busing.** We are irrevocably opposed to busing for racial balance. Such busing fails its stated objective — improved learning opportunities — while it achieves results no one wants — division within communities and hostility between classes and races. We regard it as unnecessary, counter-productive and wrong.

**School Prayer.** We reaffirm our view that voluntary prayer should be freely permitted in public places — particularly, by school children while attending public schools — provided that such prayers are not prepared or prescribed by the state or any of its political subdivisions and that no person's participation is coerced, thus preserving the traditional separation of church and state.

**Education.** Our efforts to remedy ancient neglect of disadvantaged groups will continue in universities as well as in society at large, but we distinguish between such efforts and quotas. We believe the imposition of arbitrary quotas in the hiring of faculties or the enrollment of students has no place in our universities; we believe quotas strike at the essence of the university.

**Health.** To assure access to basic medical care for all our people, we support a program financed by employers, employees and the Federal Government to provide comprehensive health insurance coverage, including insurance against the cost of long-term and catastrophic illnesses and accidents and renal failure which necessitates dialysis, at a cost which all Americans can afford....

We oppose nationalized compulsory health insurance. This approach would at least triple in taxes the amount the average citizen now pays for health and would deny families the right to choose the kind of care they prefer. Ultimately it would lower the overall quality of health care for all Americans.

**Welfare.** Perhaps nowhere else is there a greater contrast in policy and philosophy than between the Administration's remedy for the welfare ills and the financial orgy proposed by our political opposition.....

We flatly oppose programs or policies which embrace the principle of a government-guaranteed income. We reject as unconscionable the idea that all citizens have the right to be supported by the government, regardless of their ability or desire to support themselves and their families.

# 1976 Conventions

## Presidential Candidates

**Jimmy Carter**
**Democrat**

**Gerald R. Ford**
**Republican**

### Democrats

Jimmy Carter, whose presidential primary campaign flouted Democratic Party regulars, brought the party's diverse elements together July 12-15 in a show of unaccustomed unity.

The four-day 1976 convention in New York City was the party's most harmonious in 12 years and a stark contrast to the bitter and divisive conventions of 1968 and 1972.

The spirit of harmony was evident in the committee reports. No credentials challenges were carried to the convention floor and just one minority plank to the platform was offered. Only the rules committee report sparked much debate, and it was muted compared with the emotional struggles in the previous two conventions.

The lack of a spirited competition for the presidential nomination was an important factor in the absence of credentials challenges. However, the groundwork for the harmonious atmosphere had been established months earlier, when the Democratic National Committee adopted new delegate-selection and convention rules.

The delegate selection rules abolished the implicit quota system that had been the basis of most challenges in 1972. The only basis for a challenge in 1976 was the violation of a state's delegate selection or affirmative action plan to ensure the fair representation of minorities. Since all states had their plans approved by the national committee's Compliance Review Commission, the Credentials Committee was not weighing the fairness of the plan, but merely whether the state party had implemented it. In reverse of the 1972 system, the burden of proof was on the challenging individual or group, not on the state parties.

The task of challengers was further impeded by the action of the national committee in October 1975, raising the petition requirement for convention minority reports from 10 percent to 25 percent of Credentials Committee members.

The stringent new rules had an effect on the demographic composition of the convention. A post-convention survey by the national committee indicated that 36 percent of the delegates in 1976 were women, compared with 38

percent in 1972; 7 percent were black compared with 15 percent four years earlier and 14 percent were youths, compared with 21 percent in 1972.

The first roll call of the convention came on a Rules Committee minority report that would have permitted extended debate on the platform. The measure was promoted by party liberals, who complained that the restrictive convention rules cut off their chance for full debate. They urged platform debate on a maximum of three issues for a total of one hour, if at least 300 delegates from 10 states signed a petition for such issues. The proposal called for debate only; no votes would have been taken.

Carter delegates, though, were nearly unanimous in their opposition, fearing that adoption of the minority report would unduly lengthen the proceedings. The convention rejected the minority report by a vote of 735 to 1,957-1/2. *(Chart, p. 246)*

Liberals had better luck when the rules relating to future conventions were considered. By voice votes, they won approval of majority reports to establish the party's new Judicial Council as an arbiter of party rules and to eliminate the controversial loophole primary.

A loophole primary permitted election of delegates on a winner-take-all basis at the congressional district level. Carter and Democratic National Chairman Robert S. Strauss both favored the minority report, which called simply for review of the loophole primary by the newly established Commission on the Role and Future of Presidential Primaries, headed by Michigan state chairman Morley Winograd.

Liberals argued that this was not enough. They claimed that the loophole primary violated the party charter, which required proportional representation. Their position prevailed in the rules committee by a razor-thin margin of 58-1/2 to 58-1/4.

Although Carter managers were unhappy with the majority report, they did not press for a roll call and it was approved by voice vote.

But the convention rejected on roll-call votes liberal amendments to mandate the size and agenda of the party's

1978 mid-term conference and to lower the minority report requirement at future conventions.

The minority report on the 1978 conference would have required a prescribed agenda that included the discussion of policy matters. It also would have mandated a conference of at least 2,000 delegates, two-thirds of them elected at the congressional district level. On the roll call the proposal ran ahead 1,240 to 1,128, but it failed because of convention rules requiring a constitutional majority of 1,505 votes.

Another roll call came on the unsuccessful attempt by liberal delegates to have the minority report requirement at future conventions lowered from 25 percent to 15 percent of convention committee members. It was rejected, 1,249 to 1,354-1/2. *(Chart, p. 246)*

Potentially the most explosive of the rules issues, regarding a "female quota" at future conventions, was settled in behind-the-scenes meetings between Carter and representatives of the women's caucus.

At a Rules Committee meeting in Washington, D.C., in late June, the women's caucus had demanded equal representation with men in state delegations at future conventions. The Carter forces balked at this. Carter's views prevailed in the rules committee, which urged each state to promote equal division between the sexes but left the implementation of the rule to each state party. The women's caucus filed a minority report.

Both sides expressed a willingness to compromise, and in New York City July 11 and 12 Carter met with representatives of the women's caucus. They reached a compromise that encouraged — but did not require — equal representation for women at the party's mid-term conference and at future conventions. Language was inserted calling for the national committee to "encourage and assist" state parties in achieving equal division.

The compromise also included agreements between Carter and the women on other questions. Carter promised to establish an independent women's division in the party outside the realm of the chairman and pledged full party representation for women. The candidate promised to work for the ratification of the Equal Rights Amendment and pledged high government positions for women.

With acceptance of this compromise by the women's caucus, the minority report was withdrawn and the compromise language on equal division was worked into the majority report.

Balloting for president came on July 14, the third day of the convention, but it was merely a formality. Carter had locked up the nomination over a month earlier when he won the June 8 Ohio primary, a victory that prompted a cascade of endorsements and stymied his remaining opposition. Besides Carter, three other names were placed in nomination: Rep. Morris K. Udall of Arizona, Carter's most persistent primary challenger; Gov. Edmund G. Brown Jr. of California; and anti-abortion crusader Ellen McCormack. The proceedings, though, turned into a love-feast as Udall before the balloting and Brown afterwards appeared at the convention to declare their support for Carter.

On the presidential roll call, Carter received 2,238-1/2 of the convention's 3,008 votes, topping the needed majority little more than halfway through the balloting with the vote from Ohio. Udall finished second with 329-1/2 votes, followed by Brown with 300-1/2, Gov. George C. Wallace of Alabama with 57 and McCormack with 22. The rest of the vote was scattered. After completion of the roll call — and vote switches in California, Rhode Island and Louisiana —

a motion to make the nomination unanimous was approved by voice vote. *(Chart, p. 246)*

The following morning Carter announced that his choice for vice president was Sen. Walter F. Mondale of Minnesota. Carter noted that it was a difficult decision, admitting that he had changed his mind three times in the previous 30 days.

In explaining his choice, Carter cited Mondale's experience and political philosophy, his concept of the presidency and the preparation Mondale had made for his interview with Carter. Most of all, Carter emphasized compatibility, saying, "It's a very sure feeling that I have."

Mondale was one of seven prospective running mates Carter had personally interviewed. At his home in Plains, Ga., Carter had interviewed, besides Mondale, Sens. Edmund S. Muskie (Maine) and John Glenn (Ohio). At the New York convention he interviewed Sens. Henry M. Jackson (Wash.), Frank Church (Idaho) and Adlai E. Stevenson III (Ill.) and Rep. Peter W. Rodino Jr. (N.J.). Rodino withdrew his name from consideration shortly after his interview.

Like the presidential roll call the previous night, the balloting for vice president on July 15 was a formality. Mondale had only one declared opponent, Gary Benoit, a Massachusetts college student and a Wallace delegate. Two others were nominated but withdrew — Rep. Ronald V. Dellums of California and Vietnam War resister Fritz Efaw of Oklahoma.

Dellums, a black legislator from Oakland, appeared personally to withdraw his name and used the opportunity to plead with Carter to pay attention to the needs of minorities at home and to Third World aspirations abroad.

On the roll call, Mondale swamped his rivals, receiving 2,817 votes, more than 90 percent of the convention total. Retiring House Speaker Carl Albert (Okla.) finished a distant second with 36 votes, all cast as a complimentary gesture by his home state delegation. Rep. Barbara C. Jordan (Texas), the black congresswoman from Houston, followed with 28 votes, an apparent tribute to her dramatic keynote address.

Following the balloting, Mondale delivered his acceptance speech and succeeded in arousing the delegates with a partisan oratorical style reminiscent of his Minnesota mentor, Sen. Hubert H. Humphrey.

"We have just lived through the worst scandal in American history," Mondale declared, "and are now led by a president who pardoned the person who did it." His reference to the Watergate affair and to the Nixon pardon brought the delegates to their feet.

Carter's acceptance speech, unlike Mondale's, was not a rousing one in the traditional sense. But Carter was able to begin his address before 11 p.m., in the prime television slot that Strauss had promised as a contrast to George McGovern's nearly unheard 3 a.m. acceptance speech in 1972.

Like less-heralded Carter addresses earlier in the campaign, the acceptance speech ranged across a variety of issues and featured at least a few lines for those at different ends of the political spectrum. For the right, there were criticisms of wasteful federal bureaucracy, a call for a balanced budget and praise for business competition with "minimal intrusion of government in our free economic system."

For the left, there were endorsements of national health insurance, reform of the tax structure and further efforts to end discrimination by race and sex.

There was populism, with partisan overtones: "I see no reason why big-shot crooks should go free and the poor ones go to jail."

There were appeals to humanism: "We should make major investments in people, not in buildings and weapons. The poor, the aged, the weak and the afflicted must be treated with respect and with compassion and with love."

Throughout the speech was Carter's familiar emphasis on competence — a competent American people, a need for competence in the federal bureaucracy and derision for an incompetent Republican administration. "We can have an American government," Carter said, "that has turned away from scandal and corruption and official cynicism and is once again as decent and competent as our people."

"Love must be translated into simple justice," Carter said at one point, dropping his voice almost to a velvety whisper and holding the attention of the audience. A few moments later, he called for "full involvement by those who know what it is to suffer from discrimination," raising his voice almost to a shout and drawing loud applause. Then he added quietly, "and they'll be in the government if I'm elected."

Carter's speech ranged across a variety of issues and featured at least a few lines for those at different ends of the political spectrum.

The 1976 platform had been carefully constructed by the Carter forces at platform committee meetings in Washington, D.C., in June. The 90-page document was something of a throwback to earlier years — a broad statement of party goals rather than a list of legislative programs and controversial stands on issues.

The platform and the care with which it was written reflected the Democrats' determination to avoid the platform fights and issues that proved costly to the party in the previous two elections. The 1968 Vietnam plank approved on the convention floor had split the party so badly that many anti-war Democrats refused to support nominee Hubert H. Humphrey. The 1972 platform, probably the longest (about 25,000 words) and most liberal ever offered by a major party, covered too many issues in elaborate detail. It provided Republicans with free ammunition, such as the damaging charge that Democrats in 1972 favored "amnesty, acid and abortion."

Unlike 1972, when there was sharp, divisive debate on 20 minority planks, only one minority plank — on revising the 1939 Hatch Act to allow federal employees to run for political office and participate in partisan campaigns — was presented to the delegates in Madison Square Garden. It was approved by the Carter forces and was adopted by a voice vote after minimal debate.

Major goals outlined in the rest of the platform:

● A target of 3 percent unemployment within four years.

● A phased-in national health insurance system to be supported through payroll deductions and other federal tax revenues.

● Gradual replacement of federal-state welfare systems with a federal system of income maintenance for recipients who accepted jobs or job training.

● "Full and complete pardon" for Vietnam War resisters, and case-by-case judgment for military deserters.

● Prohibitions against control of multiple energy resources by major oil companies.

● Strategic arms limitation agreements with the Soviet Union "emphasizing mutual reductions."

Following are excerpts from the Democratic platform of 1976:

**Economy.** To meet our goals we must set annual targets for employment, production and price stability; the Federal Reserve must be made a full partner in national economic decisions and become responsive to the economic goals of Congress and the President; credit must be generally available at reasonable interest rates; tax spending and credit policies must be carefully coordinated with our economic goals, and coordinated within the framework of national economic planning.

**Full Employment.** We have met the goals of full employment with stable prices in the past and can do it again. The Democratic Party is committed to the right of all adult Americans willing, able and seeking work to have opportunities for useful jobs at living wages. To make that commitment meaningful, we pledge ourselves to the support of legislation that will make every responsible effort to reduce adult unemployment to 3 percent within 4 years.

Consistent and coherent economic policy required federal anti-recession grant programs to state and local government, accompanied by public employment, public works projects and direct stimulus to the private sector. In each case, the programs should be phased in automatically when unemployment rises and phased out as it declines.

**Inflation.** At times, direct government involvement in wage and price decisions may be required to ensure price stability. But we do not believe that such involvement requires a comprehensive system of mandatory controls at this time.

**Tax Reform.** We pledge the Democratic Party to a complete overhaul of the present tax system, which will review all special tax provisions to ensure that they are justified and distributed equitably among our citizens. A responsible Democratic tax reform program could save over $5 billion in the first year with larger savings in the future.

We will strengthen the internal revenue tax code so that high income citizens pay a reasonable tax on all economic income.

We will reduce the use of unjustified tax shelters in such areas as oil and gas, tax-loss farming, real estate and movies.

We will seek and eliminate provisions that encourage uneconomic corporate mergers and acquisitions.

**Government Reform.** The Democratic Party is committed to the adoption of reforms such as zero-based budgeting, mandatory reorganization timetables, and sunset laws which do not jeopardize the implementation of basic human and political rights.

An Office of Citizen Advocacy should be established as part of the executive branch, independent of any agency, with full access to agency records and with both the power and the responsibility to investigate complaints.

We support the revision of the Hatch Act so as to extend to federal workers the same political rights enjoyed by other Americans as a birthright, while still protecting the Civil Service from political abuse.

We call for legislative action to provide for partial public financing on a matching basis of the congressional elections, and the exploration of further reforms to insure the integrity of the electoral process.

**Health.** We need a comprehensive national health insurance system with universal and mandatory coverage. Such a national health insurance system should be financed by a combination of employer-employee shared payroll taxes and general tax revenues. Consideration should be given to developing a means of support for national health insurance that taxes all forms of economic income.

**Welfare Reform.** We should move toward replacement of our existing inadequate and wasteful system with a simplified system of income maintenance, substantially financed by the federal government, which includes a requirement that those able to work be provided with appropriate available jobs or job training opportunities. Those persons who are physically able to work (other than mothers with dependent children) should be required to accept appropriate available jobs or job training.

As an interim step, and as a means of providing immediate federal fiscal relief to state and local governments, local governments should no longer be required to bear the burden of welfare costs. Further, there should be a phased reduction in the states' share of welfare costs.

**Civil Rights and Liberties.** . . . [W]e pledge vigorous federal programs and policies of compensatory opportunity to remedy for many Americans the generations of injustice and deprivation; and full funding of programs to secure the implementation and enforcement of civil rights.

We seek ratification of the Equal Rights Amendment, to insure that sex discrimination in all its forms will be ended, implementation of Title IX, and elimination of discrimination against women in all federal programs.

We pledge effective and vigorous action to protect citizens' privacy from bureaucratic and technological intrusions, such as wiretapping and bugging without judicial scrutiny and supervision; and a full and complete pardon for those who are in legal or financial jeopardy because of their peaceful opposition to the Vietnam War, with deserters to be considered on a case-by-case basis.

We fully recognize the religious and ethical nature of the concerns which many Americans have on the subject of abortion. We feel, however, that it is undesirable to attempt to amend the U.S. Constitution to overturn the Supreme Court decision in this area.

**Education.** Mandatory transportation of students beyond their neighborhoods for the purpose of desegregation remains a judicial tool of last resort for the purpose of achieving school desegregation. The Democratic Party will be an active ally of those communities which seek to enhance the quality as well as the integration of educational opportunities. We encourage a variety of other measures, including the redrawing of attendance lines, pairing of schools, use of the "magnet school" concept, strong fair housing enforcement, and other techniques for the achievement of racial and economic integration.

The Party reaffirms its support of public school education. The Party also renews its commitment to the support of a constitutionally acceptable method of providing tax aid for the education of all pupils in non-segregated schools in order to insure parental freedom in choosing the best education for their children.

**Housing.** We support direct federal subsidies and low interest loans to encourage the construction of low and moderate income housing.

**Cities.** Federal policies and programs have inadvertently exacerbated the urban crisis. Within the framework of a new partnership of federal, state and local governments, and the private sector, the Democratic Party is pledged to the development of America's first national urban policy.

The Democratic Party recognizes that a number of major, older cities — including the nation's largest city — have been forced to undertake even greater social responsibilities, which have resulted in unprecedented fiscal crises. There is a national interest in helping such cities in their present travail, and a new Democratic President and the Congress shall undertake a massive effort to do so.

**Criminal Justice.** [W]e support a major reform of the criminal justice system, but we oppose any legislative effort to introduce repressive and anti-civil libertarian measures in the guise of reform of the criminal code.

**Gun Control.** Handguns simplify and intensify violent crime. Ways must be found to curtail the availability of these weapons. The Democratic Party must provide the leadership for a coordinated federal and state effort to strengthen the presently inadequate controls over the manufacture, assembly, distribution and possession of handguns and to ban Saturday night specials.

Furthermore, since people and not guns commit crimes, we support mandatory sentencing for individuals convicted of committing a felony with a gun.

The Democratic Party, however, affirms the right of sportsmen to possess guns for purely hunting and target-shooting purposes.

**Transportation.** . . . [W]e will work to expand substantially the discretion available to states and cities in the use of federal transportation money, for either operating expenses or capital programs on the modes of transportation which they choose. A greater share of Highway Trust Fund money should also be available on a flexible basis.

**Energy.** The Democratic energy platform begins with a recognition that the federal government has an important role to play in insuring the nation's energy future, and that it must be given the tools it needs to protect the economy and the nation's consumers from arbitrary and excessive energy price increases and help the nation embark on a massive domestic energy program focusing on conservation, coal conversion, exploration and development of new technologies to insure an adequate short-term and long-term supply of energy for the nation's needs.

The pricing of new natural gas is in need of reform. We should narrow the gap between oil and natural gas prices with new natural gas ceiling prices that maximize production and investment while protecting the economy and the consumer.

Strip mining legislation designed to protect and restore the environment, while ending the uncertainty over the rules governing future coal mining, must be enacted.

The huge reserves of oil, gas and coal on federal territory, including the outer continental shelf, belong to all the people. The Republicans have pursued leasing policies which give the public treasury the least benefit and the energy industry the most benefit from these public resources. Consistent with environmentally sound practices, new leasing procedures must be adopted to correct these policies, as well as insure the timely development of existing leases.

U.S. dependence on nuclear power should be kept to the minimum necessary to meet our needs. We should apply stronger safety standards as we regulate its use. And we must be honest with our people concerning its problems and dangers as well as its benefits.

When competition inadequate to insure free markets and maximum benefit to American consumers exists, we support effective restrictions on the right of major companies to own all phases of the oil industry.

We also support the legal prohibition against corporate ownership of competing types of energy, such as oil and coal. We believe such "horizontal" concentration of economic power to be dangerous both to the national interest and to the functioning of the competitive system.

Establishment of a more orderly system for setting energy goals and developing programs for reaching those goals should be undertaken. The current proliferation of energy jurisdictions among many executive agencies underscores the need for a more coordinated system. Such a system should be undertaken, and provide for centralization of overall energy planning in a specific executive agency and an assessment of the capital needs for all priority programs to increase production and conservation of energy.

**Environment.** The Democratic Party's strong commitment to environmental quality is based on its conviction that environmental protection is not simply an aesthetic goal, but is necessary to achieve a more just society. Cleaning up air and water supplies and controlling the proliferation of dangerous chemicals is a necessary part of a successful national health program. Protecting the worker from workplace hazards is a key element of our full employment program.

Federal environmental anti-pollution requirement programs should be as uniform as possible to eliminate economic discrimination. A vigorous program with national minimum environmental standards fully implemented, recognizing basic regional differences, will ensure that states and workers are not penalized by pursuing environmental programs.

**Foreign Policy.** Eight years of Nixon-Ford diplomacy have left our nation isolated abroad and divided at home. Policies have been developed and applied secretly and arbitrarily by the executive department from the time of secret bombing in Cambodia to recent covert assistance in Angola. They have been policies that relied on ad hoc, unilateral maneuvering, and a balance-of-power diplomacy suited better to the last century than to this one. They have disdained traditional American principles which once earned the respect of other peoples while inspiring our own. Instead of efforts to foster freedom and justice in the world, the Republican administration has built a sorry record of disregard for human rights, manipulative interference in the internal affairs of other nations, and, frequently, a greater concern for our relations with totalitarian adversaries than with our democratic allies...

We will...actively seek to limit the dangers inherent in the international development of atomic energy and in the proliferation of nuclear weapons.

The United States should not provide aid to any government — anywhere in the world — which uses secret police, detention without charges, and torture to enforce its powers. Exceptions to this policy should be rare, and the aid provided should be limited to that which is absolutely necessary. The United States should be open and unashamed in its exercise of diplomatic efforts to encourage the observance of human rights in countries which receive American aid.

**National Defense.** To this end, our strategic nuclear forces must provide a strong and credible deterrent to nuclear attack and nuclear blackmail. Our conventional forces must be strong enough to deter aggression in areas whose security is vital to our own. In a manner consistent with these objectives, we should seek those disarmament and arms control agreements which will contribute to mutual reductions in both nuclear and conventional arms.

...[W]ith the proper management, with the proper kind of investment of defense dollars, and with the proper choice of military programs, we believe we can reduce present defense spending by about $5-billion to $7-billion.

In order to provide for a comprehensive review of the B1 test and evaluation program, no decision regarding B-1 production should be made prior to February 1977.

**Détente.** Our task is to establish U.S.-U.S.S.R. relations on a stable basis, avoiding excesses of both hope and fear. Patience, a clear sense of our own priorities, and a willingness to negotiate specific firm agreements in areas of mutual interest can return balance to relations between the United States and the Soviet Union.

However, in the area of strategic arms limitation, the U.S. should accept only such agreements that would not over-all limit the U.S. to levels of intercontinental strategic forces inferior to the limits provided for the Soviet Union.

**United Nations.** The heat of debate at the General Assembly should not obscure the value of our supporting United Nations involvement in keeping the peace and in the increasingly complex technical and social problems — such as pollution, health, economic development and population growth — that challenge the world community.

**Middle East.** We shall continue to seek a just and lasting peace in the Middle East. The cornerstone of our policy is a firm commitment to the independence and security of the State of Israel.

We will continue our consistent support of Israel, including sufficient military and economic assistance to maintain Israel's deterrent strength in the region, and the maintenance of U.S. military forces in the Mediterranean adequate to deter military intervention by the Soviet Union.

We will avoid efforts to impose on the region an externally devised formula for settlement, and will provide support for initiatives toward settlement, based on direct face-to-face negotiation between the parties and normalization of relations and a full peace within secure and defensible boundaries.

**Asia.** We remain a Pacific power with important stakes and objectives in the region, but the Vietnam War has taught us the folly of becoming militarily involved where our vital interests were not at stake.

We reaffirm our commitment to the security of the Republic of Korea, both in itself and as a key to the security of Japan. However, on a prudent and carefully planned basis, we can redeploy, and gradually phase out, the U.S. ground forces, and can withdraw the nuclear weapons now stationed in Korea without endangering that support, as long as our tactical air and naval forces in the region remain strong.

**Latin America.** We must make clear our revulsion at the systematic violations of basic human rights that have occurred under some Latin American military regimes.

We pledge support for a new Panama Canal treaty, which insures the interests of the United States in that waterway, recognizes the principles already agreed upon, takes into account the interests of the Canal work force, and which will have wide hemispheric support.

Relations with Cuba can only be normalized if Cuba refrains from interference in the internal affairs of the United States, and releases all U.S. citizens currently detained in Cuban prisons and labor camps for political reasons. We can move towards such relations if Cuba abandons its provocative international actions and policies.

## Republicans

After four boisterous, raucous and sometimes tearful days, Republicans ended their 1976 national convention on a positive note absent during most of a gathering characterized by strident attacks on the Democrats and the Congress they controlled.

The Republican delegates arrived in Kansas City for the Aug. 16-19 convention more evenly split than they had been since 1952, when Dwight D. Eisenhower edged Sen. Robert A. Taft of Ohio (1939-53) for the GOP nomination. Both President Gerald R. Ford, breaking with tradition, and former California governor Ronald Reagan arrived in town three days before the balloting to continue their pursuit of delegates.

Ford, relying heavily on the prestige of the presidency that sometimes had failed to produce results during the seven-month campaign, invited a number of wavering delegates to his hotel suite in the new Crown Center Hotel while Reagan also courted delegates personally.

Campaign strategists and conservative supporters pursued other maneuvers that either fizzled or could not break Ford's scanty but solid delegate margin. Early in the week, conservative House members tried unsuccessfully to convince New York's senator James L. Buckley, Cons-R, to seek the nomination in an effort to draw off enough votes to deny Ford a first-ballot victory.

By a margin of 111 votes on Aug. 17, the Reagan forces

lost the first and probably the most important roll call of the convention. The vote came on a Reagan-sponsored amendment to the rules committee report that would have required all presidential candidates to name their running mates before the presidential balloting the next night.

The idea of a test vote on the vice presidential question was sprung by Reagan's campaign manager, John Sears, barely a week before the convention, when on Aug. 9 he appeared before the rules committee and urged that the proposal be included as Section C of Rule 16. The amendment was clearly aimed at throwing Ford on the defensive, because Reagan had designated Sen. Richard S. Schweiker of Pennsylvania as his running mate on July 26. Under the proposal, failure of a candidate to comply would have freed all delegates from any commitments to vote for him.

The Reagan proposal was handily defeated in the pre-convention rules committee, where Ford supporters predominated. But Sears was publicly confident that the Reagan forces could carry the issue on the convention floor. Victory on the rules question, he predicted, would be a steppingstone to Reagan's nomination.

The convention debate and vote on Rule 16C was the focal point of the Aug. 17 session and was treated as such by many in the gallery and on the floor, who interrupted the proceedings several times with loud chanting. Vociferous cheers and boos erupted from the Ford and Reagan sections of the hall as speeches were delivered for or against their positions.

Supporters of the proposals characterized it as a "right-to-know" amendment. "A presidential candidate must tell us who's on his team before we are expected to join him," argued former Missouri representative Thomas B. Curtis, the sponsor of the amendment. "The delegates have the right to be consulted for a day of decision that will have an impact for years to come."

Speakers against the amendment countered that it was solely a maneuver of the Reagan forces and that any vice presidential selection reform should be deliberately considered on its merits.

Reagan forces held the lead throughout the early going on the roll-call vote, but they lost the advantage about halfway through when New York voted against the amendment.

The deficit of the Reagan backers increased after Ohio went 7-90 against and Pennsylvania 14-89 against. The Pennsylvania result was a clear indication that state leaders in the Ford campaign remained in control of the delegation, despite Schweiker's effort to woo their support.

Reagan strength near the end of the roll call tightened the count, but Florida and Mississippi, which had passed when first called, cast heavy votes against the amendment. Florida's 28-38 vote against sealed the amendment's defeat. Mississippi, under the unit rule, cast its entire 30 votes against the Reagan proposal, padding the Ford margin.

The final count stood at 1,069 in favor of the amendment and 1,180 against, with 10 abstentions. The vote was the first tangible evidence of Ford strength at the convention and paved the way for his nomination. *(Chart, p. 247)*

None of the other parts of the rules committee report were debated, including the controversial "justice resolution" (Rule 18) that bound delegates elected in primary states according to state law. Fearing a defection of "closet" Reagan delegates in several primary-state delegations, Ford leaders had pushed for the amendment. In contrast to their attitude toward Rule 16C, the Reagan forces did not order a fight on the "justice resolution,"

although it was extensively debated in committee deliberations. After the roll-call vote on Rule 16C, the rules committee report was adopted by a voice vote.

Whatever enthusiasm the Reagan supporters had lost after their defeat on the vice presidential rule had returned by presidential nominating night, Aug. 18.

Two and one-half hours of the six-hour session were consumed in demonstrations. Reagan's supporters were by far the most boisterous. But it was the Californian's last hurrah.

On the presidential roll call, Reagan, bolstered by the votes in California and some Deep South states, took a healthy lead. But, as everyone expected, Ford's strength in the big Northeastern states — New York, New Jersey, Pennsylvania, Connecticut, Ohio — and others such as Minnesota and Illinois pushed Ford ahead.

There was a pause as the Virginia delegation was individually polled. Then West Virginia, voting 20 to 8 in favor of Ford, put the president over the top.

The final vote was 1,187 for Ford, 1,070 for Reagan, one vote from the New York delegation for Commerce Secretary Elliot L. Richardson and one abstention. *(Chart, p. 247)*

On a voice vote the convention made the nomination unanimous.

Ford added to the partisan style of the Republican ticket the next day by selecting Sen. Robert Dole of Kansas as his running mate after Reagan ruled out his acceptance of the second spot. While little mentioned during speculation about Ford's vice presidential choice, Dole, a former chairman of the Republican National Committee, was seen as an effective gut fighter who would allow Ford to keep his campaign style presidential in the battle against Carter.

Vice President Nelson A. Rockefeller nominated his own potential successor, telling the crowd that the Kansas senator not only could stand the heat of political battle, but also could "really dole it out." Rockefeller, unpopular with conservatives, had not sought to continue in the job he had gained through appointment in 1974.

On the vice presidential roll call, Dole received 1,921 of the convention's 2,259 votes. Sen. Jesse A. Helms of North Carolina, a hero of the conservatives, finished a distant second with 103 votes. The remaining votes were scattered among 29 other "candidates."

Ford's acceptance speech concentrated on his record since taking office in mid-1974. The president took credit for cutting inflation in half, increasing employment to a record level and bringing the country to peace.

He touched several times on the restoration of confidence in the White House and the return of personal integrity to the executive branch of government. His administration, Ford said, had been "open, candid and forthright" from the beginning.

Needling his Democratic challenger, Jimmy Carter, Ford asserted to applause: "My record is one of specifics, not smiles."

For the future, Ford promised continued economic recovery, less "impudence" from bureaucracy and a balanced federal budget by 1978. He listed a host of other proposals ranging from tax reform to a sane nuclear policy.

"We will build on performance, not promises; experiences, not expediency; real progress instead of mysterious plans to be revealed in some dim and distant future," Ford said in another reference to Carter.

While primarily positive in tone, Ford's speech did rebuke the Democratic Congress for its passage of bills he had vetoed and its obstruction of his proposals to revise tax rules, restrict busing and overhaul criminal laws.

"My friends, Washington is not the problem — their Congress is the problem," he argued.

Ford diverged from his prepared text to issue a direct challenge to Carter. "I'm ready, eager to go before the American people and debate the real issues face to face with Jimmy Carter," the president said. "The American people have the right to know first-hand exactly where both of us stand."

The 1976 Republican platform was a conservative document, combining restrained compliments toward the Ford administration with frequent and slashing attacks on the Democratic Congress.

Ford and Reagan both praised the platform. Although neither side was entirely happy with the final document, both were willing to compromise to avoid splitting the party.

By the time the convention got around to debating the platform the night of Aug. 17, an expected bitter struggle between Ford and Reagan forces had been deflated by the earlier vote on rules. The arena, which had been packed two hours earlier, held a somewhat smaller crowd after midnight. Many Ford delegates in particular, confident that they had won the main event, left while members of the platform committee presented the 65-page document.

Two minority planks were offered, in accordance with platform committee rules that required petitions signed by 25 percent of the members. The first, sponsored by Ann F. Peckham of Wisconsin, called for deleting all platform references to abortion. The committee-approved section supported a constitutional amendment "to restore protection of the right to life of unborn children."

The 12-minute debate on the abortion plank did not split along Ford-Reagan lines. Supporters of the minority report argued that abortion was not a suitable topic for a party document. Opponents insisted that the anti-abortion language should be retained. The minority report was defeated clearly by voice vote, and the language stayed in.

The second minority report, a six-paragraph addition to the foreign policy section, was sponsored by 34 Reagan supporters on the platform committee. Without mentioning names, it criticized President Ford and Secretary of State Henry A. Kissinger for losing public confidence, making secret international agreements and discouraging the hope of freedom for those who did not have it — presumably captive nations.

Many of Ford's supporters, including Rep. John B. Anderson of Illinois and Senate Minority Leader Hugh Scott of Pennsylvania, earlier had expressed strong opposition to the "morality in foreign policy" plank, as it came to be called. Ford's floor leader, Sen. Robert P. Griffin of Michigan, and Rep. David C. Treen of Louisiana sought compromise language in informal negotiations on the floor. But the Reagan forces, led by Sen. Helms, were adamant.

Not wishing to offend the Reagan contingent further, Ford's supporters decided not to fight. Sen. Roman L. Hruska of Nebraska, chairman of the foreign policy subcommittee, announced from the podium that there would be no organized opposition to the plank. It was passed by voice vote. The convention then approved the platform.

The document reflected the nearly equal influence of President Ford and Ronald Reagan at the convention. It was a traditional Republican blueprint for limited government — a clear contrast with the Democratic platform.

Ordinarily, the platform of the party holding the

White House heaps praise on the incumbent president and boasts of the way he has led the nation. This Republican platform did not. With Ford embroiled in a contest for the nomination, the platform writers chose to mention him by name only a few times. Richard Nixon was never mentioned. There were only vague references to Watergate.

The platform's foreign policy planks, over which Ford and Reagan clashed most strongly, praised the record of "two Republican administrations." But they also repeated some of Reagan's campaign criticisms of current foreign policy. Kissinger, a favorite target of the party's conservative wing, was not mentioned.

The domestic planks boasted of reductions in inflation and steered clear of direct government initiatives to reduce unemployment. The president was commended for vetoing 40 bills that would have increased federal spending.

The platform concentrated most of its fire on Congress. The Republicans barely acknowledged their opponent for national leadership, Jimmy Carter. The platform mentioned Carter only once, on the first page.

Following are excerpts from the Republican Party platform of 1976:

**Republican Philosophy.** — As a general rule we believe that government action should be taken first by the government that resides as close to you as possible. Governments tend to become less responsive to your needs the farther away they are from you. Thus, we prefer local and state government to national government, and decentralized national government wherever possible. The Democrats' Platform repeats the same thing on every page: More government, more spending, more inflation. Compare. This Republican Platform says exactly the opposite — less government, less spending, less inflation. In other words, we want you to retain more of your own money; money that represents the worth of your labors, to use as you see fit for the necessities and conveniences of life.

**Economy.** We believe it is of paramount importance that the American people understand that the number one destroyer of jobs is inflation.

Republicans hope every American realizes that if we are to permanently eliminate high unemployment, it is essential to protect the integrity of our money. That means putting an end to deficit spending.

Wage and price controls are not the solution to inflation. They attempt to treat only the symptom — rising prices — not the cause. Historically, controls have always been a dismal failure, and in the end they create only shortages, black markets and higher prices. For these reasons the Republican Party strongly opposes any reimposition of such controls, on a standby basis or otherwise.

Sound job creation can only be accomplished in the private sector of the economy. Americans must not be fooled into accepting government as the employer of last resort.

No nation can spend its way into prosperity; a nation can only spend its way into bankruptcy.

**Tax Reform.** Simplification should be a major goal of tax reform.

When balanced by expenditure reductions, the personal exemption should be raised to $1,000.

**Agriculture.** We oppose government-controlled grain reserves, just as we oppose federal regulations that are unrealistic in farm practices, such as those imposed by the Occupational Safety and Health Administration (OSHA) and the Environmental Protection Agency (EPA).

We firmly believe that when the nation asks our farmers to go all out to produce as much as possible for world-wide markets, the government should guarantee them unfettered access to those markets. Our farmers should not be singled out by export controls.

**Government Reform.** There must be functional re-alignment of government, instead of the current arrangement by subject areas or constituencies.

Revenue Sharing is an effort to reverse the trend toward centralization. Revenue Sharing must continue without unwarranted federal strictures and regulations.

Block grant programs should be extended to replace many existing categorical health, education, child nutrition and social programs.

While we oppose a uniform national primary, we encourage the concept of regional presidential primaries, which would group those states which voluntarily agree to have presidential primaries in a geographical area on a common date.

... [W]e oppose "federal post card registration." The possibilities could not only cheapen our ballot, but in fact threaten the entire electoral process.

We offer these proposals of far-reaching reform:

Public accountability demands that [congressmen] publicly vote on increases on the expenses of their office.

—Elimination of proxy voting which allows Members [of Congress] to record votes in committee without being present for the actual deliberations or vote on a measure.

—Full public disclosure of financial interests by Members [of Congress] and divestiture of those interests which present conflicts of interest.

—Improved lobby disclosure legislation so that the people will know how much money is being spent to influence public officials.

**Criminal Justice.** Each state should have the power to decide whether it wishes to impose the death penalty for certain crimes. All localities are urged to tighten their bail practices and to review their sentencing and parole procedures.

**Gun Control.** We support the right of citizens to keep and bear arms. We oppose federal registration of firearms. Mandatory sentences for crimes committed with a lethal weapon are the only effective solution to this problem.

**Education.** We believe that segregated schools are morally wrong and unconstitutional. However, we oppose forced busing to achieve racial balances in our schools. We believe there are educational advantages for children in attending schools in their own neighborhoods and that the Democrat-controlled Congress has failed to enact legislation to protect this concept.

If Congress continues to fail to act, we would favor consideration of an amendment to the Constitution forbidding the assignment of children to schools on the basis of race.

Local communities wishing to conduct non-sectarian prayers in their public schools should be able to do so. We favor a constitutional amendment to achieve this end.

**Health.** We support extension of catastrophic illness protection to all who cannot obtain it. We should utilize our private health insurance system to assure adequate protection for those who do not have it. Such an approach will eliminate the red tape and high bureaucratic costs inevitable in a comprehensive national program.

The Republican Party opposes compulsory national health insurance.

**Civil Rights and Liberties.** The Republican Party reaffirms its support for ratification of the Equal Rights Amendment. Our Party was the first national party to endorse the E.R.A. in 1940. We continue to believe its ratification is essential to insure equal rights for all Americans.

The Republican Party favors a continuance of the public dialogue on abortion and supports the efforts of those who seek enactment of a constitutional amendment to restore protection of the right to life for unborn children.

**Labor.** Union membership as a condition of employment has been regulated by state law under Section 14(b) of the Taft-Hartley Act. This basic right should continue to be determined by the states. We oppose strikes by federal employees, the unionization of our military forces and the legalization of common-situs picketing.

Employees of the federal government should not engage in partisan politics. The Civil Service System must remain nonpartisan and nonpolitical. The Hatch Act now protects federal employees; we insist that it be uniformly administered.

**Welfare Reform.** We oppose federalizing the welfare system; local levels of government are most aware of the needs of their communities.

We also oppose the guaranteed annual income concept or any programs that reduce the incentive to work.

Those features of the present law, particularly the food stamp program, that draw into assistance programs people who are capable of paying for their own needs should be corrected. The humanitarian purpose of such programs must not be corrupted by eligibility loopholes.

**Cities.** The Republican programs of revenue sharing and block grants for community development and manpower have already immensely helped our cities and counties. We favor extension of revenue sharing and the orderly conversion of categorical grants into block grants.

**Housing.** To continue to encourage home ownership which now encompasses 64 per cent of our families, we support the deductibility of interest on home mortgages and property taxes.

**Transportation.** In keeping with the local goal setting in transportation, the Republican Party applauds the system under which state and local governments can divert funds from interstate highway mileage not essential to interstate commerce or national defense to other, more pressing community needs, such as urban mass transit.

**Energy.** One fact should now be clear: We must reduce sharply our dependence on other nations for energy and strive to achieve energy independence at the earliest possible date. We cannot allow the economic destiny and international policy of the United States to be dictated by the sovereign powers that control major portions of the world's petroleum supplies.

We must immediately eliminate price controls on oil and newly-discovered natural gas in order to increase supply, and to provide the capital that is needed to finance further exploration and development of domestic hydrocarbon reserves.

At this critical time, the Democrats have characteristically resorted to political demagoguery seeking short-term political gain at the expense of the long-term national interest. They object to the petroleum industry making any profit. The petroleum industry is an important segment of our economy and is entitled to reasonable profits to permit further exploration and development.

Now, the Democrats proposed to dismember the American oil industry. We vigorously oppose such divestiture of oil companies — a move which would surely result in higher energy costs, inefficiency and under-capitalization of the industry.

The uncertainties of governmental regulation regarding the mining, transportation and use of coal must be removed and a policy established which will assure that governmental restraints, other than proper environmental controls, do not prevent the use of coal. Mined lands must be returned to beneficial use.

Uranium offers the best intermediate solution to America's energy crisis. We support accelerated use of nuclear energy through processes that have been proven safe.

**Environment.** We are in complete accord with the recent Supreme Court decision on air pollution that allows the level of government closest to the problem and the solution to establish and apply appropriate air quality standards.

We are determined to preserve land use planning as a unique responsibility of state and local government.

**Foreign Policy.** We recognize and commend that great beacon of human courage and morality, Alexander Solzhenitsyn, for his compelling message that we must face the world with no illusions about the nature of tyranny. Ours will be a foreign policy that keeps this ever in mind.

Ours will be a foreign policy which recognizes that in international negotiations we must make no undue concessions; that in pursuing détente we must not grant unilateral favors with only the hope of getting future favors in return.

Agreements that are negotiated, such as the one signed in Helsinki, must not take from those who do not have freedom the hope of one day gaining it.

Finally, we are firmly committed to a foreign policy in which secret agréements, hidden from our people, will have no part.

**National Defense.** A superior national defense is the fundamental condition for a secure America and for peace and freedom for the world. Military strength is the path to peace. A sound foreign policy must be rooted in a superior defense capability, and both must be perceived as a deterrent to aggression and supportive of our national interests.

As a necessary component of our long-range strategy, we will produce and deploy the B-1 bomber in a timely manner, allowing us to retain air superiority.

Security assistance programs are important to our allies and we will continue to strengthen their efforts at self-defense.

**Asia.** The United States is indisputably a Pacific power. Japan will remain the main pillar of our Asian policy. United States troops will be maintained in Korea so long as there exists the possibility of renewed aggression from North Korea.

We recognize that there is a wide divergence of opinion concerning Vietnam, but we pledge that American troops will never again be committed for the purpose of our own defense, or the defense of those to whom we are committed by treaty or other solemn agreements, without the clear purpose of achieving our stated diplomatic and military objectives.

The United States will fulfill and keep its commitments, such as the mutual defense treaty with the Republic of China.

**Latin America.** By continuing its policies of exporting subversion and violence, Cuba remains outside the Inter-American family of nations. We condemn attempts by the Cuban dictatorship to intervene in the affairs of other nations; and, as long as such conduct continues, it shall remain ineligible for admission to the Organization of American States.

The United States intends that the Panama Canal be preserved as an international waterway for the ships of all nations. This secure access is enhanced by a relationship which commands the respect of Americans and Panamanians and benefits the people of both countries. In any talks with Panama, however, the United States negotiators should in no way cede, dilute, forfeit, negotiate or transfer any rights, power, authority, jurisdiction, territory or property that are necessary for the protection and security of the United States and the entire Western Hemisphere.

**Middle East.** Our policy must remain one of decisive support for the security and integrity of Israel.

At the same time, Republican Administrations have succeeded in reestablishing communication with the Arab countries, and have made extensive progress in our diplomatic and commercial relations with the more moderate Arab nations.

Because we have such fundamental interests in the Middle East, it will be our policy to continue our efforts to maintain the balance of power in the Mediterranean region.

**Détente.** American foreign policy must be based upon a realistic assessment of the Communist challenge in the world. It is clear that the perimeters of freedom continue to shrink throughout the world in the face of the Communist challenge.

Thus our relations with the Soviet Union will be guided by solid principles. We will maintain our strategic and conventional forces; we will oppose the deployment of Soviet power for unilateral advantages or political and territorial expansion; we will never tolerate a shift against us in the strategic balance; and we will remain firm in the face of pressure, while at the same time expressing our willingness to work on the basis of strict reciprocity toward new agreements which will help achieve peace and stability.

**United Nations.** The political character of the United Nations has become complex. With 144 sovereign members, the U.N. experiences problems associated with a large, sometimes cumbersome and diverse body.

The United States does not wish to dictate to the U.N., yet we do have every right to expect and insist that scrupulous care be given to the rights of all members. Steamroller techniques for advancing discriminatory actions will be opposed.

The United States will continue to be a firm supporter and defender of any nation subjected to such outrageous assaults. We will not accept ideological abuses in the United States.

# 1980 Conventions

## Presidential Candidates

**Jimmy Carter**
**Democrat**

**Ronald Reagan**
**Republican**

**John B. Anderson**
**Independent**

### Republicans

Ronald Reagan, the 69-year-old former California governor, was installed as the Republican presidential nominee at the party's national convention in Detroit, but his moment of glory nearly was overshadowed by an unusual flap over the number-two spot. The choosing of Reagan's running mate provided the only suspense at the GOP convention, held July 14-17, 1980, in Detroit's Joe Louis Arena.

Who would fill the number-one spot had been determined long before when Reagan won 28 out of the 34 Republican presidential primaries and eliminated all of his major rivals. The last to withdraw — George Bush — was tapped by Reagan July 16 as his ticket mate in a dramatic post-midnight appearance before the delegates.

For most of the evening of July 16, it looked as though Gerald R. Ford would occupy the second spot on the ticket, which would have made him the first former president to run for vice president. Private polls reportedly had shown that Ford was the only Republican who would enhance Reagan's chances in November. And a number of Republicans had described the combination as a "dream ticket." Groups described as "friends of Ronald Reagan" and "friends of Gerald Ford" had met four times to "discuss" the possibility of forging a Reagan-Ford ticket.

The Ford group consisted of former secretary of state Henry A. Kissinger, former chairman of the Council of Economic Advisers Alan Greenspan, and Ford aides Robert Barnett and John Marsh. The Reagan group was the nucleus of his primary campaign staff: Edwin Meese, campaign director, and Richard Wirthlin, Reagan's pollster. Reagan and Ford first discussed Ford's joining the ticket at a meeting July 15, although no formal offer was made, according to a source close to Reagan. " 'I want you to think this over and then we'll discuss it tomorrow,' " the source quoted Reagan as telling Ford.

The pair met again the following day to continue their discussions, but nothing was resolved. When the convention reconvened at 6:30 p.m., reports began swirling about the floor, many of them spawned by Ford himself, who in two televised interviews gave strong indications that he would accept the second spot if certain conditions were met.

In an interview with Walter Cronkite of CBS about 7:30 p.m., Ford said, "I would not go to Washington and be a figurehead vice president. If I go to Washington I have to be there in the belief that I would play a meaningful role." Later, in an interview with Barbara Walters of ABC, Ford said he did not want the job unless his role would be "nonceremonial, constructive and responsive." Such an arrangement, he said, would require a "far different structure" from the duties performed by other vice presidents. Asked whether it would be difficult to be a vice president again after having had the top job, Ford said, "Not at all. I'd be more interested in substance than glamor."

Ford declined to spell out what his conditions for taking the job would be, but descriptions of his requirements would have made him in effect co-president with Reagan. The discussions reportedly centered around providing a role for Ford somewhat akin to the White House chief of staff's. In this kind of post he would have had responsibility for agencies such as the Office of Management and Budget, the National Security Council, the domestic policy staff and the Council of Economic Advisers.

Ford further fed the speculation, offering a simple solution to the temporary problem that would have been posed by the 12th Amendment to the Constitution. The amendment would have had the effect of prohibiting the members of the electoral college from California from voting for both Reagan and Ford because both were California residents. The amendment says that the electors from any state must vote for at least one person who is not from that state.

However, nothing in the Constitution would have excluded two residents of the same state from serving as president and vice president or prevented electors from states other than their home state from voting for those two individuals. Ford said Reagan's lawyers had researched the residency question and determined that legally there would be no problem if the former president changed his residence to Michigan, which he represented in the House for 25 years, or to Colorado, where he owned a home.

But Ford expressed reservations about how such a move might be interpreted. "I think it could create in the minds of the American people that we're trying to do something a little cute," he said. "Well, I've never done that in politics. I've got a good reputation and I'm worried about it.... I think it would be construed to be to some extent a gimmick."

As the evening of July 16 wore on, the speculation heightened. "The expectation, as it is presently being reported is it's going through," Gov. William G. Milliken of Michigan said of the Ford candidacy. "I have it on very reliable sources within the Ford camp that it is put together," said Gov. Pierre S. "Pete" du Pont of Delaware.

About 9:15 p.m. Reagan telephoned Ford to ask him to make up his mind whether he wanted the vice president's job. Meanwhile, convention officials proceeded to call the roll of the states. When Reagan received enough votes to become the official nominee, the arena erupted into a cheering, hornblowing, flag-waving, foot-stomping, band-playing demonstration. The noise abated a bit while the roll call was finished, but continued for more than an hour.

But at about 11:15 p.m. the Reagan-Ford arrangement fell apart. Ford went to Reagan's suite in the Detroit Plaza Hotel and the two men agreed that it would be better for Ford to campaign for the GOP ticket rather than be a member of it. "His [Ford's] instinct told him it was not the thing to do," Reagan said later.

When it became apparent that efforts to persuade Ford to join the ticket had failed, Reagan turned to Bush, a moderate with proven vote-getting ability. The Reagan camp refused to acknowledge that Bush was the second choice, even though it was widely perceived that way. "There was everybody else and then the Ford option," Edwin Meese, Reagan's chief of staff, said later.

Bush had been Reagan's most persistent competitor through the long primary season, but he won only six primaries — Michigan, Massachusetts, Connecticut, Pennsylvania, the District of Columbia and Puerto Rico. Bush was one of the vice presidential possibilities favored by those in the party who believed that Reagan had to reach outside the GOP's conservative wing if he were to have broad appeal in November.

Bush supporters said that his background would balance the ticket geographically and that his extensive government service would overcome criticism that Reagan did not have any Washington experience. Bush served from 1967 to 1971 in the U.S. House from Texas and had been ambassador to the United Nations, head of the U.S. liaison office in Peking and director of the Central Intelligence Agency.

Bush's first appearance at the convention earlier had produced a rousing demonstration from supporters throughout the hall, but his strongest support on the floor was in delegations from the Midwest and Northeast, such as New Jersey and the states where he won primary victories.

Reagan's choice of the moderate George Bush was viewed as his first major choice between political pragmatism and ideological purity. Throughout the primary season, Reagan had drawn a large measure of his support from the right wing of the Republican Party and had pledged himself to support conservative economic, social and defense policies. During the convention, Sen. Jesse Helms of North Carolina, the most vocal leader of the GOP's right wing, masterminded the rightward tilt of the party plat-

form to reflect conservative viewpoints. Helms, concerned about the nomination of a moderate such as Bush, threatened to place his own name in nomination to put pressure on the GOP standard-bearers to abide by conservative and "moral" principles. In the end, Helms supported the Reagan-Bush ticket but warned that it had better support the party's conservative platform. Though Helms was not nominated for vice president, his supporters nonetheless gave him 54 votes. He finished second behind Bush, who got 1,832 votes.

The Republican Party's 1980 platform was more a blueprint for victory in November than a definitive statement of party views. Rather than slug it out over specifics, the party's moderate and conservative wings agreed to blur their differences to appear united, to broaden the party's appeal and to smooth Reagan's way to the White House.

Platform writers veered from traditional Republican positions on a few issues. On others they went out of their way to embrace policies that meshed with Reagan's views more than their own. For the most part, they managed to fashion a policy statement that pleased no party faction entirely but with which all could live reasonably.

Overwhelmingly, platform committee members agreed the document should be consistent with Reagan's positions. Thus, though one media poll found delegates overwhelmingly in favor of resuming a peacetime draft, the platform bowed to the view of its nominee and stated its opposition to a renewal of the draft "at this time." In the same manner, the party's platform took no position on ratification of the Equal Rights Amendment (ERA) to the Constitution. Since 1940 Republican platforms had supported an ERA amendment. Reagan, however, opposed ratification, and ERA opponents far outnumbered the amendment's supporters on the platform committee. Yet Reagan, in a gesture to moderates, suggested that the platform not take a position on the issue, and the committee agreed.

Most of the platform document consisted of policy statements on which most Republicans agreed. There were calls for tax cuts, pleas for less government regulation and harsh criticisms of the Carter administration. In two areas, however, the platform took a particularly hard-line position. The platform supported a constitutional amendment that would outlaw abortion and called on a Reagan administration to appoint federal judges who opposed abortion. On defense, platform writers took an already hard-line plank that had been drafted by party staff and moved it sharply to the right. The platform called for massive increases in defense spending and scoffed at the Carter administration's proposed strategic arms limitation treaty (SALT II).

On the other hand, to pick up votes from organized labor, blacks and the poor, the platform made some new overtures to those traditionally non-Republican groups. It pledged to strengthen enforcement of the civil rights laws, made overtures to U.S. workers put out of their jobs by competition from foreign imports and promised to save America's inner cities.

The platform was adopted by the convention July 15 without change, but not before an attempt was made to reopen on the floor one of its more controversial sections. Although party moderates such as Sens. Charles H. Percy, Illinois, Charles McC. Mathias Jr., Maryland, and Jacob K. Javits, New York, made little secret of their unhappiness with the platform's failure to reaffirm the party's support for ratification of the ERA, they were particularly chagrined by the section suggesting that Reagan appoint federal judges who oppose abortion. Percy called the section "the worst plank I have ever seen in any platform by the Republican Party." The moderates July 14 sought to round up support for reopening the platform on the floor, but their efforts failed. In caucuses held early July 15, a number of state delegations including New York and Illinois voted down motions to change the platform's position on abortion.

Nonetheless, as Chairman John J. Rhodes, Ariz., proposed that the convention adopt the platform, Hawaii delegate John Leopold leaped onto a chair to seek Rhodes' recognition. When Rhodes ordered the Hawaii delegation's microphone turned on, Leopold said the group unanimously proposed a motion to suspend the convention rules to permit delegates to "discuss" the platform on the floor. If the rules were suspended, Leopold told reporters, he intended to propose that the language on federal judges be deleted. Not to allow floor discussion of the platform, he said, would be to "railroad" the document through the convention.

Rhodes explained that under convention rules a majority of the members of six state delegations was required to bring a motion to suspend the rules to a vote. He asked if a majority of the delegates from any other state supported Leopold's motion. Only Rep. Silvio O. Conte, chairman of the Massachusetts delegation, rose. But rather than announce support for Leopold's motion, Conte stated only that a majority of his delegation supported a recorded vote on the platform, something Leopold had not proposed. To the applause of many of the delegates, Rhodes then declared that Leopold's motion had failed. The platform subsequently was approved by voice vote.

Ronald Reagan received the Republican nomination on the first ballot. *(Chart, p. 249)*

In his acceptance speech, Reagan combined sharp jabs at the alleged shortcomings of the Carter administration with a reaffirmation of his own conservative credo. Reagan cited three grave threats to the nation's existence — "a disintegrating economy, a weakened defense and an energy policy based on the sharing of scarcity." The culprits, Reagan contended, were President Carter and the Democratic Congress. He said they had preached that the American people needed to tighten their belts. "I utterly reject that view," he declared. Reagan was especially critical of the Democratic administration's conduct of foreign policy. He ridiculed it as weak, vacillating and transparently hypocritical.

Following are excerpts from the Republican Party platform of 1980:

**Taxes.** . . . [W]e believe it is essential to cut personal tax rates out of fairness to the individual. . . .

Therefore, the Republican Party supports across-the-board reductions in personal income tax rates, phased in over three years, which will reduce tax rates from the range of 14 to 70 percent to a range of from 10 to 50 percent.

. . . Republicans will move to end tax bracket creep caused by inflation. We support tax indexing to protect taxpayers from the automatic tax increases caused when cost-of-living wage increases move them into higher tax brackets.

**Welfare.** We pledge a system that will:
- provide adequate living standards for the truly needy;
- end welfare fraud by removing ineligibles from the welfare rolls, tightening food stamp eligibility requirements, and ending aid to illegal aliens and the voluntarily unemployed;
- strengthen work incentives, particularly directed at the

productive involvement of able-bodied persons in useful community work projects;
- provide educational and vocational incentives to allow recipients to become self-supporting; and
- better coordinate federal efforts with local and state social welfare agencies and strengthen local and state administrative functions.

We oppose federalizing the welfare system; local levels of government are most aware of the needs in their communities. We support a block grant program that will help return control of welfare programs to the states.

**Black Americans.** During the next four years we are committed to policies that will:
- encourage local governments to designate specific enterprise zones within depressed areas that will promote new jobs, new and expanded businesses and new economic vitality;
- open new opportunities for black men and women to begin small businesses of their own by, among other steps, removing excessive regulations, disincentives for venture capital and other barriers erected by the government;
- bring strong, effective enforcement of federal civil rights statutes, especially those dealing with threats to physical safety and security which have recently been increasing; and
- ensure that the federal government follows a non-discriminatory system of appointments . . . with a careful eye for qualified minority aspirants.

**Women's Rights.** We acknowledge the legitimate efforts of those who support or oppose ratification of the Equal Rights Amendment.

We reaffirm our Party's historic commitment to equal rights and equality for women.

We support equal rights and equal opportunities for women, without taking away traditional rights of women such as exemption from the military draft. We support the enforcement of all equal opportunity laws and urge the elimination of discrimination against women.

We reaffirm our belief in the traditional role and values of the family in our society. . . . The importance of support for the mother and homemaker in maintaining the values of this country cannot be over-emphasized.

**Abortion.** While we recognize differing views on this question among Americans in general — and in our own Party — we affirm our support of a constitutional amendment to restore protection of the right to life for unborn children. We also support the Congressional efforts to restrict the use of taxpayers' dollars for abortion.

**Education.** . . . [T]he Republican Party supports deregulation by the federal government of public education, and encourages the elimination of the federal Department of Education.

We support Republican initiatives in the Congress to restore the right of individuals to participate in voluntary, non-denominational prayer in schools and other public facilities.

. . . [W]e condemn the forced busing of school children to achieve arbitrary racial quotas. . . . It [busing] has failed to improve the quality of education, while diverting funds from programs that could make the difference between success and failure for the poor, the disabled, and minority children.

[W]e reaffirm our support for a system of educational assistance based on tax credits that will in part compensate parents for their financial sacrifices in paying tuition at the elementary, secondary, and post-secondary level.

**Health.** Republicans unequivocally oppose socialized medicine, in whatever guise it is presented by the Democratic Party. We reject the creation of a national health service and all proposals for compulsory national health insurance.

**Older Americans.** Social Security is one of this nation's most vital commitments to our senior citizens. We commit the Republican Party to first save, and then strengthen, this fundamental contract between our government and its productive citizens.

... [W]e proudly reaffirm our opposition to mandatory retirement and our long-standing Republican commitment to end the Democrats' earnings limitation upon Social Security benefits. In addition, the Republican Party is strongly opposed to the taxation of Social Security benefits and we pledge to oppose any attempts to tax these benefits.

**Crime.** We believe that the death penalty serves as an effective deterrent to capital crime and should be applied by the federal government and by states which approve it as an appropriate penalty for certain major crimes.

We believe the right of citizens to keep and bear arms must be preserved. Accordingly, we oppose federal registration of firearms. Mandatory sentences for commission of armed felonies are the most effective means to deter abuse of this right.

**Foreign Competition.** The Republican Party recognizes the need to provide workers who have lost their jobs because of technological obsolescence or imports the opportunity to adjust to changing economic conditions. In particular, we will seek ways to assist workers threatened by foreign competition.

The Republican Party believes that protectionist tariffs and quotas are detrimental to our economic well-being. Nevertheless, we insist that our trading partners offer our nation the same level of equity, access, and fairness that we have shown them.

**Training and Skills.** ... [T]he success of federal employment efforts is dependent on private sector participation. It must be recognized as the ultimate location for unsubsidized jobs, as the provider of means to attain this end, and as an active participant in the formulation of employment and training policies on the local and national level.

We urge a reduction of payroll tax rates, a youth differential for the minimum wage, and alleviation of other costs of employment until a young person can be a productive employee.

**Fairness to the Employer.** The Republican Party declares war on government overregulation.

While we recognize the role of the federal government in establishing certain minimum standards designed to improve the quality of life in America, we reaffirm our conviction that these standards can best be attained through innovative efforts of American business without the federal government mandating the methods of attainment.

**OSHA.** OSHA should concentrate its resources on encouraging voluntary compliance by employers and monitoring situations where close federal supervision is needed and serious hazards are most likely to occur. OSHA should be required to consult with, advise, and assist businesses in coping with the regulatory burden before imposing any penalty for non-compliance. Small businesses and employers with good safety records should be exempt from safety inspections, and penalties should be increased for those with consistently poor performance.

**Agriculture.** Republicans will ensure that:

● international trade is conducted on the basis of fair and effective competition and that all imported agricultural products meet the same standards of quality that are required of American producers. ...

● the future of U.S. agricultural commodities is protected from the economic evils of predatory dumping by other producing nations and that the domestic production of these commodities ... is preserved.

... We believe that agricultural embargoes are only symbolic and are ineffective tools of foreign policy. ... The Carter grain embargo should be terminated immediately.

**Big Government.** The Republican Party reaffirms its belief in the decentralization of the federal government and in the traditional American principle that the best government is the one closest to the people. There, it is less costly, more accountable, and more responsive to people's needs. ...

**Energy.** We are committed to ... a strategy of aggressively boosting the nation's energy supplies; stimulating new energy technology and more efficient energy use; restoring maximum feasible choice and freedom in the marketplace for energy consumers and producers alike; and eliminating energy shortages and disruptions. ...

Republicans support a comprehensive program of regulatory reform, improved incentives, and revision of cumbersome and overly stringent Clean Air Act regulations.

We support accelerated use of nuclear energy through technologies that have been proven efficient and safe.

We reject unequivocally punitive gasoline and other energy taxes designed to artificially suppress energy consumption.

A Republican policy of decontrol, development of our domestic energy resources, and incentives for new supply and conservation technologies will substantially reduce our dependence on imported oil.

Republicans will move toward making available all suitable federal lands for multiple use purposes including exploration and production of energy resources.

**Environment.** We believe that a healthy environment is essential to the present and future well-being of our people, and to sustainable national growth.

At the same time, we believe that it is imperative that environmental laws and regulations be reviewed, and where necessary, reformed to ensure that the benefits achieved justify the costs imposed.

**Balanced Budget.** If federal spending is reduced as tax cuts are phased in, there will be sufficient budget surpluses to fund the tax cuts, and allow for reasonable growth in necessary program spending.

... We believe a Republican President and a Republican Congress can balance the budget and reduce spending through legislative actions, eliminating the necessity for a Constitutional amendment to compel it. However, if necessary, the Republican Party will seek to adopt a Constitutional amendment to limit federal spending and balance the budget, except in time of national emergency as determined by a two-thirds vote of Congress.

**Inflation.** The Republican Party believes inflation can be controlled only by fiscal and monetary restraint, combined with sharp reductions in the tax and regulatory disincentives for savings, investments, and productivity. Therefore, the Republican Party opposes the imposition of wage and price controls and credit controls.

**National Security.** Republicans commit themselves to an immediate increase in defense spending to be applied judiciously to critically needed programs. We will build toward a sustained defense expenditure sufficient to close the gap with the Soviets. Republicans approve and endorse a national strategy of peace through strength. ... The general principles and goals of this strategy would be:

● to inspire, focus, and unite the national will and determination to achieve peace and freedom;

● to achieve overall military and technological superiority over the Soviet Union;

● to create a strategic and civil defense which would protect the American people against nuclear war at least as well as the Soviet population is protected;

● to accept no arms control agreement which in any way jeopardizes the security of the United States or its allies, or which locks the United States into a position of military inferiority;

- to reestablish effective security and intelligence capabilities;
- to pursue positive nonmilitary means to roll back the growth of communism;
- to help our allies and other non-Communist countries defend themselves against Communist aggression; and
- to maintain a strong economy and protect our overseas sources of energy and . . . raw materials.

**Nuclear Forces.** . . . We reject the mutual-assured-destruction (MAD) strategy of the Carter Administration. . . . We propose, instead, a credible strategy which will deter a Soviet attack by the clear capability of our forces to survive and ultimately to destroy Soviet military targets.

A Republican Administration will strive for early modernization of our theater nuclear forces so that a seamless web of deterrence can be maintained against all levels of attack, and our credibility with our European allies is restored.

**National Intelligence.** A Republican Administration will seek adequate safeguards to ensure that past abuses will not recur, but we will seek the repeal of ill-considered restrictions sponsored by Democrats, which have debilitated U.S. intelligence capabilities while easing the intelligence collection and subversion efforts of our adversaries.

**Defense Manpower and the Draft.** The Republican Party is not prepared to accept a peacetime draft at this time. . . . We will not consider a peacetime draft unless a well-managed, Congressionally-funded, full-scale effort to improve the all-volunteer force does not meet expectations.

**Arms Control.** The Republican approach to arms control has been . . . based on three fundamental premises:

- first, before arms control negotiations may be undertaken, the security of the United States must be assured by the funding and deployment of strong military forces sufficient to deter conflict at any level or to prevail in battle should aggression occur;
- second, negotiations must be conducted on the basis of strict reciprocity of benefits — unilateral restraint by the U.S. has failed to bring reductions by the Soviet Union; and
- third, arms control negotiations, once entered, represent an important political and military undertaking that cannot be divorced from the broader political and military behavior of the parties.

**U.S.-Soviet Relations.** Republicans believe that the United States can only negotiate with the Soviet Union from a position of unquestioned principle and unquestioned strength.

A Republican Administration will continue to seek to negotiate arms reductions in Soviet strategic weapons, in Soviet bloc force levels in Central Europe, and in other areas that may be amenable to reductions or limitations. We will pursue hard bargaining for equitable, verifiable, and enforceable agreements.

We reaffirm our commitment to press the Soviet Union to implement the United Nations Declaration on Human Rights and the Helsinki Agreements which guarantee rights such as the free interchange of information and the right to emigrate.

**NATO and Western Europe.** A Republican Administration, as one of its highest priorities and in close concert with our NATO partners, will . . . ensure that the United States leads a concerted effort to rebuild a strong, confident Alliance. . . .

In pledging renewed United States leadership, cooperation, and consultation, Republicans assert their expectation that each of the allies will bear a fair share of the common defense effort and that they will work closely together in support of common Alliance goals.

**Middle East, Persian Gulf.** With respect to an ultimate peace settlement, Republicans reject any call for involvement of the PLO as not in keeping with the long-term interests of either Israel or the Palestinian Arabs. The imputation of legitimacy to organizations not yet willing to acknowledge the fundamental right to existence of the State of Israel is wrong.

The sovereignty, security, and integrity of the State of Israel is a moral imperative and serves the strategic interests of the United States. Republicans reaffirm our fundamental and enduring commitment to this principle.

While reemphasizing our commitment to Israel, a Republican Administration will pursue close ties and friendship with moderate Arab states.

**The Americas.** We deplore the Marxist Sandinista takeover of Nicaragua and the Marxist attempts to destabilize El Salvador, Guatemala, and Honduras. We do not support United States assistance to any Marxist government in this hemisphere and we oppose the Carter Administration aid program for the government of Nicaragua. However, we will support the efforts of the Nicaraguan people to establish a free and independent government.

**Asia and the Pacific.** A new Republican Administration will restore a strong American role in Asia and the Pacific. We will make it clear that any military action which threatens the independence of America's allies and friends will bring a response sufficient to make its cost prohibitive to potential adversaries.

**China.** We will strive for the creation of conditions that will foster the peaceful elaboration of our relationship with the People's Republic of China.

At the same time, we deplore the Carter Administration's treatment of Taiwan, our long-time ally and friend. We pledge that our concern for the safety and security of the 17 million people of Taiwan will be constant.

**Africa.** The Republican Party supports the principle and process of self-determination in Africa. We reaffirm our commitment to this principle and pledge our strong opposition to the effort of the Soviet Union . . . to subvert this process.

**Foreign Aid.** No longer should American foreign assistance programs seek to force acceptance of American governmental forms. The principal consideration should be whether or not extending assistance to a nation or group of nations will advance America's interests and objectives.

Decisions to provide military assistance should be made on the basis of U.S. foreign policy objectives. Such assistance to any nation need not imply complete approval of a regime's domestic policy.

**International Economic Policy.** Under a Republican Administration, our international economic policy will be harmonized with our foreign and defense policies to leave no doubt as to the strategy and purpose of American policy.

Republicans will conduct international economic policy in a manner that will stabilize the value of the dollar at home and abroad.

The Republican Party believes the United States must adopt an aggressive export policy. Trade, especially exporting, must be high on our list of national priorities. The Republicans will . . . promote trade to ensure the long-term health of the U.S. economy.

## Democrats

President Jimmy Carter emerged victorious from a deeply divided Democratic National Convention unsure whether his plea for unity to supporters of rival Sen. Edward M. Kennedy of Massachusetts had succeeded. Kennedy had been Carter's main opponent in his quest for renomination throughout the spring primary season. When it became apparent that Kennedy had not won in the primaries and caucuses the delegate support he needed, he turned his efforts to prying the nomination away from the president at the convention.

Kennedy's presence was strong throughout the convention week and expressions of support for the senator sometimes upstaged those for the incumbent president. Chants of "We want Ted" rocked off the walls of New York's Madison Square Garden during the convention's four days, Aug. 11-14. And their echo faintly followed the president as he left the podium following his acceptance speech. It was a stark reminder that Carter, even though he had captured the nomination and engaged in a series of reconciliation gestures with his rival, still faced the difficult task of rallying a divided party behind his candidacy.

Kennedy's efforts to wrest the nomination from Carter centered around a convention rule that bound delegates to vote on the first ballot for the candidates under whose banner they were elected. When the convention opened, Carter could count 315 more votes than he needed for the nomination — votes that he had won in nominating caucuses and presidential primaries. As a result, Kennedy's only chance to gain the nomination was to defeat the binding rule.

In the week before the convention, negotiators for Carter and Kennedy agreed to one hour of debate on the rules question to begin at 6:30 p.m. Monday, Aug. 11. Kennedy forces had wanted a Tuesday night rules vote, which would have given them an extra day to lobby delegates. But they settled instead for the Monday night debate, which enabled them to argue their case before a prime-time nationwide television audience.

Opponents of the binding rule tried to present a broad-based front. Arguing against the rule on the convention floor were a Carter delegate, two Kennedy backers and two leading uncommitted delegates — New York governor Hugh L. Carey and prominent Washington attorney Edward Bennett Williams, the chief spokesman of the Committee for an Open Convention.

They argued that political conditions had changed since the delegates were elected months earlier and that to bind them would break with a century and a half of Democratic tradition. "For the first time in 150 years, delegates to the national convention are being asked to deliver their final freedom of choice, and to vote themselves into bondage to a candidate," Williams contended. To adopt the binding rule, other speakers added, would make the delegates little more than robots.

But most Carter supporters scoffed at that contention, stressing that delegates were free to vote their conscience on all roll calls but the one for president. Passage of the rule was simply fair play, they added. It had been adopted in 1978 without opposition by the party's last rules review commission and the Democratic National Committee. Only when it was apparent that Carter was winning, claimed Atlanta mayor Maynard Jackson, did the Kennedy camp want to change the rules to allow a "fifth ball, a fourth out or a tenth inning."

When the measure finally came to a vote, Carter forces turned back the attempt to overturn the proposed rule. The vote was 1,390.580 to 1,936.418 against Kennedy's position. *(Chart, p. 248)*

Shortly after the vote, Kennedy ended his nine-month challenge to the president by announcing that his name would not be placed in nomination Aug. 13. Passage of the binding rule assured Carter's renomination.

In addition to its binding-rule objection, the Kennedy camp filed four other minority rules reports, but all were withdrawn before the Aug. 11 session. Three originally had been filed in response to Carter efforts to streamline the convention schedule. At its July meeting in Washington, D.C., the convention rules committee approved proposals to increase the number of signatures required on nominating petitions for president, vice president and convention chairman; to limit to two the number of speakers on each side of each issue of debate; and to allow every roll call, except for president and vice president, to be conducted by telephone while convention business proceeded.

In return for Kennedy's withdrawal of the minority reports, the Carter camp did consent to raise the number of speakers on each side of each issue to three. They also agreed to a Kennedy proposal to add a platform accountability rule that would require each presidential candidate to submit his written views on the party platform along with his pledge to carry it out. The statement would have to be presented shortly after convention consideration of the platform was completed. The Kennedy proposal also called for the candidates' statements to be distributed and read to the delegates.

Despite the loss on the binding rule, the Kennedy camp succeeded in molding the party platform more to their liking. The final document was filled with so many concessions to the Kennedy forces that it won only a half-hearted endorsement from the president. The platform battle, one of the longest in party history, filled 17 hours of debate and roll calls that stretched over two days, Aug. 12 and 13.

Most of Carter's concessions and outright defeats came on the economic and human needs sections of the 40,000-word document. It was these revisions that Carter rejected — as diplomatically as possible — in a statement issued several hours after the debate wound to a close.

In the debate on social issues, Carter lost two roll-call votes — one on adoption of Kennedy's plank calling for jobs to be "our single highest domestic priority," and the other supporting Medicaid funding for abortions. The president also lost a voice vote on a minority report to withhold all party funds and campaign assistance to candidates who did not support the then-pending Equal Rights Amendment to the Constitution.

The only victory posted by Carter in the human needs chapter was over a Kennedy minority report calling for a single, comprehensive national health insurance plan with gradually phased-in benefits. That report was defeated on a 1,409.9-to-1,623.8 vote that came at the start of the platform debate.

It had been clear since the platform was drafted in late June that the economic plank, which contained the major Carter-Kennedy differences, would be the focus of dispute. When the hour for debate arrived, it was evident that the control Carter had exercised the previous evening on the question of binding delegates had evaporated.

Before the convention began, Carter had yielded to Kennedy language on several issues, including one of the senator's four minority economic reports. That report asserted that a policy of high interest rates and unemployment should not be used to fight inflation. White House domestic affairs adviser Stuart E. Eizenstat announced Aug. 10 that Carter would go along with that amendment — but none of the others in the economy section — because it stated a broad goal while the others called for specific legislation.

The marathon platform debate reached its high point on Tuesday evening, Aug. 12, when Kennedy addressed the delegates on behalf of his minority report on the economic chapter. Kennedy's speech provided the Democratic convention with its most exciting moments. The address, which sparked a 40-minute emotional demonstration when it was over, called for Democratic unity and laced into the Republican nominee, Ronald Reagan.

Kennedy defended his liberal ideology, supporting national health insurance and federal spending to restore deteriorated urban areas. He lashed out at Reagan's proposal for a massive tax cut, labeling it as beneficial only to the wealthy. "For all those whose cares have been our concern the work goes on, the cause endures, the hope still lives and the dream shall never die," concluded Kennedy. Buoyed by the Kennedy oratory, the convention went on to pass by voice vote three liberal Kennedy platform planks on the economy, thereby rejecting the more moderate versions favored by Carter.

The first of the Kennedy-sponsored planks was a statement pledging that fairness would be the overriding principle of the Democrats' economic policy and that no actions would be taken that would "significantly increase" unemployment. The convention next approved a Kennedy plank seeking a $12 billion anti-recession jobs program, a $1 billion rail renewal plan and an expanded housing program for low- and moderate-income families. The final Kennedy economic plank was a statement of opposition to fighting inflation through a policy of high interest rates and unemployment. Carter had agreed to this plank the day before the convention opened.

Carter floor managers realized that it would be difficult to block passage of the Kennedy economic proposals. After the senator's emotion-filled speech, Carter advisers — realizing their position could not prevail — quickly sought to change from a roll call to a voice vote on the economic planks.

During the floor demonstration that followed Kennedy's speech, a series of telephone calls ricocheted between the podium and the senator's campaign trailer located off the convention floor. The negotiations involved how many elements of the Kennedy program would be accepted by voice vote. In the end, Carter prevailed on only one of Kennedy's economic minority reports, the call for an immediate wage and price freeze followed by controls.

Prior to the 1980 convention, Democratic presidential nominees had been able to gloss over their distaste for objectionable portions of the platform. But Kennedy made that difficult to do. In his carefully worded statement following the platform debate, Carter did not flatly reject any of Kennedy's amendments, but he did not embrace them either.

Of Kennedy's $12 billion anti-recession jobs program, Carter said he would "accept and support the intent" of the program but he refused to commit himself to a specific dollar amount. Responding to Kennedy language that placed a jobs program above all other domestic priorities, Carter wrote, "We must make it clear that to achieve full employment, we must also be successful in our fight against inflation."

Carter treated two women's issues the same way. Responding to adopted language that endorsed federal funding for abortion, the president repeated his personal opposition but said he would be guided by court decisions on the questions. He also reiterated his support for ratification of the Equal Rights Amendment but did not directly comment on the platform language adopted on the floor that prevented the Democratic Party from giving campaign funds to candidates who did not back the amendment.

Carter concluded his statement with the unity refrain that had become the hallmark of every official White House comment on the platform since the drafting process began: "The differences within our party on this platform are small in comparison with the differences between the Republican and Democratic Party platforms." Kennedy apparently agreed. And shortly after Carter's renomination Aug. 13, Kennedy issued a statement endorsing the platform and pledging his support for Carter. In the final moments before adjournment, Kennedy made a stiff and brief appearance on the platform with Carter, Vice President Walter F. Mondale and a host of Democratic officeholders. But the coolness of his appearance — accompanied by the warmest reception of the night — left questionable the commitment of the senator and his supporters to work strenuously for Carter's re-election.

Carter won the Democratic nomination with 2,123 votes compared with Kennedy's 1,150.5. Other candidates split 54.5 votes. *(Chart, p. 248)*

In his acceptance speech, Carter alluded to the convention's divisions. He led off with praise for Kennedy's tough campaign, thanks for his concessions during the convention and an appeal for future help. "Ted, your party needs — and I need — you, and your idealism and dedication working for us." Carter spent much of the speech characterizing Reagan's programs as a disastrous "fantasy world" of easy answers. He avoided detailed comments on the economic issues over which he and Kennedy had split, confining himself to statements that he wanted jobs for all who needed them.

As expected, Mondale was renominated for vice president. Two other party members had their names placed in nomination so they could raise the issues of homosexual rights and Carter's decision to reinstitute draft registration. Activist Patricia Simon of Newton, Mass., withdrew after delivering a plea that "we be known as a party of peace." The other candidate was Melvin Boozer of Washington, D.C. Boozer, a number of favorite sons and others received only a smattering of votes and Mondale was nominated by acclamation before that roll call had been completed.

The vice president's acceptance speech set delegates chanting "Not Ronald Reagan" as Mondale reeled off a list of liberal values and programs that, he said, most Americans agreed with. Mondale was one of the few speakers to unequivocally praise Carter's record, which he did at some length. The speech ended with a warning not to "let anyone make us less than what we can be."

Following are excerpts from the Democratic Party platform of 1980:

**Employment.** We specifically reaffirm our commitment to achieve all the goals of the Humphrey-Hawkins Full Employment Act within the currently prescribed dates in the Act, especially those relating to a joint reduction in unemployment and inflation. Full employment is important to the achievement of a rising standard of living, to the pursuit of sound justice, and to the strength and vitality of America.

**Anti-Recession Assistance.** A Democratic anti-recession program must recognize that Blacks, Hispanics, other minorities, women, and older workers bear the brunt of recession. We pledge a $12 billion anti-recession jobs program, providing at least 800,000 additional jobs, including full funding of the counter-cyclical assistance program for the cities, a major expansion of the youth employment and training program to give young people in our inner cities new hope, expanded training programs for women and displaced homemakers to give these workers a fair chance in the workplace, and new opportunities for the elderly to contribute their talents and skills.

**Tax Reductions.** We commit ourselves to targeted tax reductions designed to stimulate production and combat recession as soon as it appears so that tax reductions will not have a disproportionately inflationary effect. We must avoid untargeted tax cuts which would increase inflation.

**Federal Spending.** Spending restraint must be sensitive to those who look to the federal government for aid and assistance, especially to our nation's workers in times of high unemployment. At the same time, as long as inflationary pressures remain strong, fiscal prudence is essential to avoid destroying the progress made to date in reducing the inflation rate.

Fiscal policy must remain a flexible economic tool. We oppose a Constitutional amendment requiring a balanced budget.

**Interest Rates.** . . . [W]e must continue to pursue a tough anti-inflationary policy which will lead to an across-the-board reduction in interest rates on loans.

In using monetary policy to fight inflation, the government should be sensitive to the special needs of areas of our economy most affected by high interest rates.

**Expanding American Exports.** To create new markets for American products and strengthen the dollar, we must seek out new opportunities for American exports; help establish stable, long-term commercial relationships between nations; offer technical assistance to firms competing in world markets; promote reciprocal trading terms for nations doing business here; and help ensure that America's domestic retooling is consistent with new opportunities in foreign trade.

We must intensify our efforts to promote American exports and to ensure that our domestic industries and workers are not affected adversely by unfair trade practices, such as dumping. . . . We must ensure that our efforts to lower tariff barriers are reciprocated by our trading partners. We recognize the superior productivity of American agriculture and the importance of agricultural exports to the balance of trade.

**Worker Protection.** The Democratic Party will not pursue a policy of high interest rates and unemployment as the means to fight inflation. We will take no action whose effect will be a significant increase in unemployment, no fiscal action, no monetary action, no budgetary action. The Democratic Party remains committed to policies that will not produce high interest rates or high unemployment.

OSHA protections should be properly administered, with the concern of the worker being the highest priority; legislative or administrative efforts to weaken OSHA's basic worker protection responsibilities are unacceptable.

We will continue to oppose a sub-minimum wage for youth and other workers and to support increases in the minimum wage so as to ensure an adequate income for all workers.

**Small Business.** . . . [T]he Democratic Party commits itself to the first comprehensive program for small business in American history. That program will include the following measures:

. . . Allocation of a fair percentage of federal research funds to small business.

Protection of small and independent business against takeover by giant conglomerates.

Continued efforts to end federal regulations which reinforce barriers to entry by new and small firms, and which thereby entrench the dominance of market leaders.

A review of regulations and requirements which impose unnecessary burdens upon smaller firms. We will adopt regulatory requirements to meet the needs of smaller firms, where such action will not interfere with the objectives of the regulation.

**Minority Business.** The Democratic Party pledges itself to advance minority businesses, including Black, Hispanic, Asian/Pacific Americans, Native Americans and other minorities to:

● Increase the overall level of support and the overall level of federal procurement so that minority groups will receive additional benefits and opportunities.

● Triple the 1980 level of federal procurement from minority-owned firms as we have tripled the 1977 levels in the past three years.

● Increase substantially the targeting of Small Business Administration loans to minority-owned businesses.

● Increase ownership of small businesses by minorities, especially in those areas which have traditionally been closed to minorities, such as communications and newspapers.

● Expand management, technical, and training assistance for minority firms, and strengthen minority capital development. . . .

**Women and the Economy.** The Democratic Party . . . commits itself to strong steps to close the wage gap between men and women, to expand child care opportunities for families with working parents, to end the tax discrimination that penalizes married working couples, and to ensure that women can retire in dignity.

We will strictly enforce existing anti-discrimination laws with respect to hiring, pay and promotions. We will adopt a full employment policy, with increased possibilities for part-time work. . . . [W]e will ensure that women in both the public and private sectors are not only paid equally for work which is identical to that performed by men, but are also paid equally for work which is of comparable value to that performed by men.

**Consumer Protection.** Over the next four years, we must continue to guarantee and enhance the basic consumer rights to safety, to information, to choice and to a fair hearing.

We must continue our support of basic health, safety, environmental and consumer protection regulatory programs. . . .

**Human Needs.** While we recognize the need for fiscal restraint . . . we pledge as Democrats that for the sole and primary purpose of fiscal restraint alone, we will *not* support reductions in the funding of any program whose purpose is to serve the basic human needs of the most needy in our society — programs such as unemployment, income maintenance, food stamps, and efforts to enhance the educational, nutritional or health needs of children.

**Health.** The answer to runaway medical costs is not, as Republicans propose, to pour money into a wasteful and inefficient system. The answer is not to cut back on benefits for the elderly and eligibility for the poor. The answer is to enact a comprehensive, universal national health insurance plan.

To meet the goals of a program that will control costs and provide health coverage to every American, the Democratic Party pledges to seek a national health insurance program. . . .

**Social Security.** The Democratic Party will oppose any effort to tamper with the Social Security system by cutting or taxing benefits as a violation of the contract the

American government has made with its people. We hereby make a covenant with the elderly of America that as we have kept the Social Security trust fund sound and solvent in the past, we shall keep it sound and solvent in the years ahead.... We oppose efforts to raise the age at which Social Security benefits will be provided.

Finally, the Democratic Party vehemently opposes all forms of age discrimination and commits itself to eliminating mandatory retirement.

**Welfare Reform.** As a means of providing immediate federal fiscal relief to state and local governments, the federal government will assume the local government's burden of welfare costs. Further, there should be a phased reduction in the states' share of welfare costs in the immediate future.

We strongly reject the Republican Platform proposal to transfer the responsibility for funding welfare costs entirely to the states. Such a proposal would not only worsen the fiscal situation of state and local governments, but would also lead to reduced benefits and services to those dependent on welfare programs. The Democratic policy is exactly the opposite — to provide greater assistance to state and local governments for their welfare costs and to improve benefits and services....

**Education.** ... [W]e will continue to support the Department of Education and assist in its all-important educational enterprise....

... The federal government and the states should be encouraged to equalize or take over educational expenses, relieving the overburdened ... taxpayer.

The Democratic Party continues to support programs aimed at achieving communities integrated both in terms of race and economic class.... Mandatory transportation of students beyond their neighborhoods for the purpose of desegregation remains a judicial tool of last resort.

The Party reaffirms its support of public school education and would not support any program or legislation that would create or promote economic, sociological or racial segregation.

The Party accepts its commitment to the support of a constitutionally acceptable method of providing tax aid for the education of all pupils in schools which do not racially discriminate, and excluding so-called segregation academies.

**Equal Rights Amendment.** ... [T]he Democratic Party must ensure that ERA at last becomes the 27 Amendment to the Constitution. We oppose efforts to rescind ERA in states which have already ratified the amendment, and we shall insist that past recissions are invalid.

**Civil Rights and Liberties.** We oppose efforts to undermine the Supreme Court's historic mandate of school desegregation, and we support affirmative action goals to overturn patterns of discrimination in education and employment.

Our commitment to civil rights embraces not only a commitment to legal equality, but a commitment to economic justice as well. It embraces a recognition of the right of every citizen ... to a fair share in our economy.

We call for passage of legislation to charter the purposes, prerogatives, and restraints on the Federal Bureau of Investigation, the Central Intelligence Agency, and other intelligence agencies of government with full protection for the civil rights and liberties of American citizens living at home or abroad. Under no circumstances should American citizens be investigated because of their beliefs.

**Abortion.** The Democratic Party recognizes reproductive freedom as a fundamental human right. We therefore oppose government interference in the reproductive decisions of Americans, especially those government programs or legislative restrictions that deny poor Americans their

right to privacy by funding or advocating one or a limited number of reproductive choices only. Specifically, the Democratic Party opposes ... restrictions on funding for health services for the poor that deny poor women especially the right to exercise a constitutionally-guaranteed right to privacy.

**Tax Reform.** Capital formation is essential both to control inflation and to encourage growth. New tax reform efforts are needed to increase savings and investment, promote the principle of progressive taxation, close loopholes, and maintain adequate levels of federal revenue.

**Gun Control.** The Democratic Party affirms the right of sportsmen to possess guns for purely hunting and target-shooting purposes. However, handguns simplify and intensify violent crime.... The Democratic Party supports enactment of federal legislation to strengthen the presently inadequate regulations over the manufacture, assembly, distribution, and possession of handguns and to ban "Saturday night specials."

**Energy.** We must make energy conservation our highest priority, not only to reduce our dependence on foreign oil, but also to guarantee that our children and grandchildren have an adequate supply of energy.

Major new efforts must be launched to develop synthetic and alternative renewable energy sources.

The Democratic Party regards coal as our nation's greatest energy resource. It must play a decisive role in America's energy future.

Oil exploration on federal lands must be accelerated, consistent with environmental protections.

Offshore energy leasing and development should be conditioned on full protection of the environment and marine resources.

Solar energy use must be increased, and strong efforts, including continued financial support, must be undertaken to make certain that we achieve the goal of having solar energy account for 20% of our total energy by the year 2000.

A stand-by gasoline rationing plan must be adopted for use in the event of a serious energy supply interruption.

... Through the federal government's commitment to renewable energy sources and energy efficiency, and as alternative fuels become available in the future, we will retire nuclear power plants....

We must give the highest priority to dealing with the nuclear waste disposal problem.... [E]fforts to develop a safe, environmentally sound nuclear waste disposal plan must be continued and intensified.

**Environment.** We must move decisively to protect our countryside and our coastline from overdevelopment and mismanagement. ... [P]rotection must be balanced with the need to properly manage and utilize our land resources during the 1980s.

We must develop new and improved working relationships among federal, state, local, tribal, and territorial governments and private interests, to manage effectively our programs for increased domestic energy production and their impact on people, water, air, and the environment in general.

**Grain Embargo.** Recognizing the patriotic sacrifices made by the American farmer during the agricultural embargo protesting the invasion of Afghanistan, we commend the agricultural community's contribution in the field of foreign affairs. Except in time of war or grave threats to national security, the federal government should impose no future embargoes on agricultural products.

**Foreign Policy.** The Democratic Administration sought to reconcile ... two requirements of American foreign policy — principle and strength.... We have tried to make clear the continuing importance of American strength in a world of change. Without such strength, there is a genuine risk that global change will deteriorate into anarchy to be exploited by our adversaries' military power. Thus, the revival of American strength has been a central pre-occupation of the Democratic Administration.

The use of American power is necessary as a means of shaping not only a more secure, but also a more decent world. . . . [W]e must pursue objectives that are moral, that make clear our support for the aspirations of mankind and that are rooted in the ideals of the American people.

That is why the Democrats have stressed human rights. That is why America once again has supported the aspirations of the vast majority of the world's population for greater human justice and freedom.

. . . In meeting the dangers of the coming decade the United States will consult closely with our Allies to advance common security and political goals. As a result of annual summit meetings, coordinated economic policies and effective programs of international energy conservation have been fashioned.

. . . [W]e must continue to improve our relations with the Third World by being sensitive to their legitimate aspirations. The United States should be a positive force for peaceful change in responding to ferment in the Third World.

Our third objective must be peace in the Middle East. . . . Our nation feels a profound moral obligation to sustain and assure the security of Israel. . . . Israel is the single democracy, the most stable government, the most strategic asset and our closest ally in the region.

To fulfill this imperative, we must move towards peace in the Middle East. Without peace, there is a growing prospect, indeed inevitability, that this region will become radicalized, susceptible to foreign intrusion, and possibly involved in another war. Thus, peace in the Middle East also is vital for our national security interests. . . . Our goal is to make the Middle East an area of stability and progress in which the United States can play a full and constructive role.

**National Security.** Our fourth major objective is to strengthen the military security of the United States and our Allies at a time when trends in the military balance have become increasingly adverse. America is now, and will continue to be, the strongest power on earth. It was the Democratic Party's greatest hope that we could, in fact, reduce our military effort. But realities of the world situation, including the unremitting buildup of Soviet military forces, required that we begin early to reverse the decade-long decline in American defense efforts.

**Arms Control.** . . . [T]he Democrats have been and remain committed to arms control, especially to strategic arms limitations, and to maintain a firm and balanced relationship with the Soviet Union.

To avoid the danger to all mankind from an intensification of the strategic arms competition, and to curb a possible acceleration of the nuclear arms race while awaiting the ratification of the SALT II Treaty, we endorse the policy of continuing to take no action which would be inconsistent with its object and purpose, so long as the Soviet Union does likewise.

Arms control and strategic arms limitation are of crucial importance to us and to all other people. The SALT II Agreement is a major accomplishment of the Democratic Administration. It contributes directly to our national security, and we will seek its ratification at the earliest feasible time.

## National Unity Campaign

Rep. John B. Anderson of Illinois, a Republican, declared himself an independent candidate for the presidency April 24, 1980, after it became clear that he could not obtain his party's presidential nomination. Anderson cre-

ated the National Unity Campaign as the vehicle for his third-party candidacy. No party convention was held to select Anderson or to ratify the selection.

On Aug. 25 Anderson announced he had tapped former Wisconsin governor Patrick J. Lucey, a Democrat, to be his running mate. The selection of Lucey was seen as a move by Anderson to attract liberal Democrats disgruntled by President Jimmy Carter's renomination. Anderson's choice of a running mate and the Aug. 30 release of a National Unity Campaign platform helped establish him as a genuine contender in the presidential race.

The 317-page platform put forth specific proposals on a variety of national issues, emphasizing domestic questions. The positions taken generally were fiscally conservative and socially liberal, remaining true to Anderson's "wallet on the right, heart on the left" philosophy.

The platform made clear that Anderson's primary goal was to restore the nation's economic health by adopting fiscal and tax policies that would "generate a substantial pool of investment capital," which then would be used to increase productivity and create jobs. Anderson proposed countercyclical revenue sharing to direct federal funds to areas hardest hit by the election year recession. He rejected mandatory wage and price controls as a cure for inflation, proposing instead a program under which the government would encourage labor and management to work toward agreement on proper levels for wages and prices and use tax incentives to encourage compliance with the standards set. In contrast to both Carter and Reagan, Anderson opposed tax cuts for individuals. He also criticized constitutional amendments to balance the federal budget, saying that while the budget should be balanced "in ordinary times," it could be expected to run a deficit in times of "economic difficulty."

Anderson's energy policy made reducing oil imports the top priority. His platform proposed a 50-cent-a-gallon excise tax on gasoline to discourage consumption, with the revenue to be used to cut Social Security taxes. Anderson favored the decontrol of oil prices begun under Carter and proposed a 40-mile-per-gallon fuel economy standard for new autos.

For American cities, Anderson proposed using about 90 percent of alcohol and tobacco taxes to help build mass transit systems and fight deterioration of public facilities. He also favored offering tax incentives to encourage businesses to locate in blighted urban areas.

In foreign policy, Anderson emphasized strengthening alliances with Western Europe and Japan, resisting Soviet expansion while negotiating "whenever possible" and respecting the sovereignty of Third World nations. His platform supported human rights and humanitarian aid for refugees and disaster victims abroad. He pledged to support the Middle East peace process but opposed the creation of a Palestinian state between Israel and Jordan or U.S. recognition of the Palestine Liberation Organization until the PLO recognized Israel's right to exist.

On defense issues, Anderson opposed development of the MX missile, B-1 bomber and neutron bomb, criticized the arms race and opposed a peacetime draft registration. He pledged to seek ratification of the SALT II treaty negotiated with the Soviet Union, saying that "essential equivalence" existed between U.S. and Soviet missile forces. He opposed a strategy of nuclear superiority, emphasizing instead the beefing up of conventional military forces.

Anderson finished the 1980 presidential race a distant

third behind Jimmy Carter with 5,719,722 votes, 6.6 percent.

Following are excerpts from the National Unity Campaign platform of 1980:

**Economy.** We will construct a Wage-Price Incentives Program. Our administration will invite labor and management leaders to agree upon fair and realistic guidelines and to determine appropriate tax-based incentives to encourage compliance....

In the absence of sharp and prolonged increases in the rate of inflation, we will oppose mandatory wage and price standards.

**Youth Unemployment.** To deal with the critical problem of youth unemployment, particularly among minorities, we propose: enactment of the proposed Youth Act of 1980 to provide over $2 billion a year for job training and state and local educational programs designed to improve the employability of disadvantaged and out-of-school youth; increased funding for youth career intern programs; a youth opportunity wage incentive that would exempt eligible youths and employers from Social Security taxes during the first months of employment.

**Gasoline Tax.** We would couple decontrol of oil and gas prices with an excise tax of 50 cents per gallon on gasoline, the full revenues of that tax being returned to individuals through reductions in payroll taxes and increased Social Security benefits.... We will employ tax credits and other incentives to promote substitution of non-petroleum energy for oil, adoption of energy-efficient systems in industry and elsewhere, improvements in transportation and energy production technologies, and development of less wasteful structures for home and commerce.

**Nuclear Power.** ... [W]e will act on the recommendations of the Rogovin and Kemeny Commissions to make certain that installation of any future plants is preceded by demonstration of satisfactory standards and action on the nuclear waste question. We will assess nuclear power in light of its dependence on public subsidy and of the possibility that slower growth in demand may enable us to phase in other energy supplies in preference to nuclear systems.

**Cities.** ... [A]n Anderson-Lucey Administration will propose an Urban Reinvestment Trust Fund. Funded through ... revenues from the Federal alcohol and tobacco excise taxes and phased in over three years, it will disburse approximately $3.9 billion annually. It will be used for upgrading, repair and replacement of [urban] capital plant and equipment.

Within our distressed older cities, there are zones of devastation, blighted by crime, arson and population flight.... We favor legislation that would create "enterprise zones" in these areas, by lowering corporate, capital gains, payroll and property taxes and by furnishing new tax incentives....

**Environment.** We will guard and consolidate the achievements in every field of environmental protection and preservation. We will insist, however, that economic impact studies, assessing not only direct costs but employment and energy implications, accompany proposals for major changes in environmental standards.

**Social Issues.** We are committed to ratification of the Equal Rights Amendment. We oppose government intrusion in the most intimate of family decisions — the right to bear or not to bear children — and will fight against any constitutional amendment prohibiting abortion. We support public funding of family planning services and other efforts to enable women to find ... alternatives to abortion.

**National Defense and Arms Control.** In strategic forces, we will maintain a stable balance by preserving essential equivalence with the Soviet Union. To meet an evolving threat to our deterrent, we will modernize and diversify our strategic arsenal.

The growing concern over the threat to fixed, land-based missiles poses an urgent problem to both the United States and the Soviet Union. Economically, environmentally and strategically, the ... cure proposed by the Carter Administration — the MX system — is unsound.

Arms control agreements must enhance our basic security and must not compromise our ability to protect our national interests. Agreements must preserve and reinforce the stability of the strategic balance.... Arms control must be based on adequate, effective verification.

The Western alliance should proceed with its plans to modernize its theater nuclear arsenal; at the same time, we should keep open the possibility of negotiations with the Soviet Union to limit theater nuclear forces.

We favor ... a short-term ... nuclear test ban treaty between the United States, the Soviet Union and the United Kingdom....

For a more effective defense, we will rely heavily on collective security arrangements with our principal allies in NATO and Japan. We will work to reinforce and enhance our historic partnership with our Western European allies.

We will propose to Moscow supplementary measures that could make possible the ratification of the SALT II Treaty and the start of SALT III negotiations. These proposals will respond to concerns expressed in the U.S. Senate regarding such issues as verification and future force reductions.

**Middle East.** The establishment and maintenance of peace in the Middle East will be an urgent objective.... A lasting settlement must encompass the principles affirmed in the Camp David accords.

Our administration will support the recognition of Palestinian rights as embodied in the Camp David accords, but will oppose the creation of a Palestinian state between Israel and Jordan.

The United States will not recognize or negotiate with the Palestine Liberation Organization unless that organization repudiates terrorism, explicitly recognizes Israel's right to exist in peace and accepts U.N. Security Council Resolutions 242 and 338....

**China.** ... [T]he Anderson-Lucey Administration would work to discourage antagonism between Russia and China. We should not become an arms supplier to China. We should work for better understanding by China's leaders of the consequences of nuclear war, of measures that should be taken to guard against accidental war and of ways to make the nuclear balance more stable.

Finally, our administration would abide by both the letter and spirit of the Taiwan Relations Act. We would maintain our contacts with Taiwan but would not establish official relations with its government.

# 1984 Conventions
## Presidential Candidates

**Walter F. Mondale**
**Democrat**

**Ronald Reagan**
**Republican**

### Democrats

Ending a long and difficult nomination campaign with a display of party unity and a historic vice presidential choice, Walter F. Mondale used the 1984 Democratic convention to sound the opening themes of his challenge to President Ronald Reagan: family, fairness, the flag and the future.

Accepting their nominations July 19 before cheering, flag-waving delegates at the San Francisco convention, the presidential candidate and his running mate, Rep. Geraldine A. Ferraro of New York, served notice that they would hold Reagan to account for his policies in their uphill battle to capture the White House. "Here is the truth about the [nation's] future," Mondale told the Democrats as they wrapped up their four-day convention. "We are living on borrowed money and borrowed time."

The spectacle of Mondale and Ferraro, with their families, celebrating with delegates in the jammed Moscone Center capped a week in which the Democrats came together to choose their ticket and shore up party unity. Toward that end, the convention succeeded to a greater degree than had seemed possible when the former vice president was battling Sen. Gary Hart of Colorado and the Rev. Jesse Jackson in the primaries and caucuses. There was little acrimony over consideration of the party platform. And, once Mondale was nominated, the three rivals seemed to put aside their most visible differences.

The 56-year-old Minnesotan had been the apparent winner since the final round of primaries on June 5, when he took New Jersey, which gave him the 1,967 pledged delegates needed to take the nomination. Mondale finished the convention balloting with nearly 1,000 votes more than Hart, his closest competitor, yet he was by no means the overwhelming choice. He polled 2,191 votes — about 50 percent of a possible 3,933. *(Chart, p. 251)*

Fears that radical and homosexual elements in San Francisco would stage massive confrontations in the streets outside the convention center — evoking memories of the party's 1968 catastrophe in Chicago — did not materialize. Except for a few minor clashes between crowds and the police, there were no violent incidents. Several hundred thousand homosexuals and labor union members marched peacefully in separate demonstrations July 15, and protestors representing a variety of causes gathered throughout convention week in the giant parking lot across the street from the convention center.

The Democratic unity displayed in San Francisco — so different from the 1980 convention, when the struggle between President Jimmy Carter and Sen. Edward M. Kennedy of Massachusetts left the party torn and battered — was due largely to delegates' deeply felt antipathy to the policies of the Reagan administration. The unusual harmony was also due, at least in part, to Gov. Mario M. Cuomo of New York, who electrified delegates with his keynote address on the opening night, July 16. In an eloquent appeal for family values and compassion for the poor, he set the tone for the rest of the convention. His speech was rivaled in intensity only by Ferraro's nomination by acclamation July 19 and an impassioned speech given by Jackson on July 17.

Speaking forcefully but without dramatic oratorical flourishes, and repeatedly interrupted by emotional applause, Cuomo combined an appeal to Democratic traditions with specific attacks on the domestic and foreign policies of the Reagan administration. Noting Reagan's reference to America as "a shining city on a hill," Cuomo said that "the hard truth is that not everyone is sharing in this city's splendor and glory. There is despair, Mr. President, in the faces that you don't see, in the places that you don't visit in your shining city."

The product of weeks of intensive work by the candidate and a team of advisers, Mondale's acceptance speech July 19 was a carefully drawn outline for his campaign against Reagan. Although the former vice president had been criticized for lacking speech-making flair during the nomination campaign, he repeatedly brought delegates to their feet during his address.

To introduce Mondale, the party turned to Kennedy, one of its most effective practitioners of rousing oratory. Kennedy's booming voice filled the hall with denunciations of Reagan and the Republican Party, which he called a "cold citadel of privilege."

"By his choice of Geraldine Ferraro, Walter Mondale has already done more for this country in one short day than Ronald Reagan has done in four long years in office," he said, as delegates cheered and stomped their feet.

Shortly before Mondale's address, aides had passed out thousands of small American flags to delegates, so the crowd was a sea of red, white and blue when the former vice president arrived on the podium.

Pledging a government of "new realism" that would combine strong but conciliatory foreign policies with tough economic initiatives, Mondale vowed in his address to squeeze the budget and raise taxes to reduce soaring deficits, then approaching $200 billion a year. "Let's tell the truth. . . . Mr. Reagan will raise taxes, and so will I," Mondale said. "He won't tell you. I just did."

To Ferraro, the first woman put on the national ticket by a major party, her nomination by acclamation was a special honor. Quoting the late Rev. Martin Luther King Jr., she said that " 'Occasionally in life there are moments which cannot be completely explained in words. Their meaning can only be articulated by the inaudible language of the heart.' Tonight is such a moment for me: My heart is filled with pride."

The platform adopted at the convention created few divisions in the party, but few candidates were enthusiastic about using it in their fall campaigns. Adopted in an emphatic but seldom angry four-hour debate July 17, the platform drew heavily from Mondale's campaign themes. It also contained significant contributions from Hart and Jackson.

The process of assembling the platform was an important exercise for the party. In four months of hearings and drafting sessions, the Democrats invited dozens of interest groups to weave their goals and ideals into the platform. The variegated document became a symbol of the party's all-inclusive philosophy, as it grew to roughly 45,000 words after countless pressure groups had their say.

The final draft was loyal to traditional Democratic ideology, with commitments to unions, blacks, feminists, the poor, environmentalists and other liberal constituencies. But it also included new ideas from the party's younger generation, especially on economic policy. The platform did not call for major new social spending, making it economically more conservative than Democratic documents of the previous 50 years. But in its support for homosexual rights, the availability of abortions and other social issues, it was more liberal than earlier platforms.

The platform's central theme was an attack on the Reagan administration. The document indicted the president's record on topics ranging from budget deficits to civil rights to arms control, and it laid out what Democrats proposed as an alternative.

Besides giving a voice to the various interest groups that composed the Democratic Party, the 1984 platform also was a vehicle designed to unite the three presidential contenders. Negotiations continued up to the last minute on the five minority planks presented to the convention delegates July 17 by Jackson and Hart. But Mondale's forces demonstrated a firm grip on the delegates, soundly defeating Jackson planks on defense spending, "no first use" of nuclear weapons and runoff primaries. Mondale accepted Hart's plank restricting the use of U.S. troops overseas. Mondale also compromised on a Jackson plank outlining the party's affirmative action policy.

One person conspicuously absent from the convention platform debate was Ferraro, who chaired the committee that produced the document. Ferraro was to run the program July 17 — until Mondale asked her to be his running mate. When asked why Ferraro was not handling the plat-

form, Mondale quipped, "There's been a somewhat altered change in Mrs. Ferraro's professional plans over the next eight years."

The debate on the five minority planks was lackluster compared with the heated platform struggles between Carter and Kennedy at the 1980 convention. The first sign that Mondale would surmount the Jackson challenges came on the "no-first-use" plank. After a brief debate, it was defeated, with 1,405.7 delegates voting for it and 2,216.3 against. *(Chart, p. 250)*

As adopted by the platform committee June 23, the document said a Democratic president would "move toward" a policy in which the United States would not initiate a nuclear attack. Jackson supporters said it was "morally and militarily insane" even to consider using nuclear weapons, but Mondale's backers said the arms control language in the platform was strong enough. Also, Mondale argued that the North Atlantic Treaty Organization's conventional forces needed to be strengthened before the United States could adopt a "no-first-use" stance.

In contrast to the opposition to Jackson's national security planks, Hart's "peace plank" was readily accepted by Mondale. Delegates adopted it, 3,271.8 to 351.2. The plank delineated conditions under which a Democratic president would not "hazard American lives or engage in unilateral military involvement" abroad. It was dubbed the Persian Gulf — Central America plank, because the underlying message was that U.S. troops should not be sent to those regions unless American objectives were clear and diplomatic efforts had been exhausted.

Mondale's supporters opposed the plank when the platform committee considered it in June. At that time they said the plank would put a Democratic president "in a political or diplomatic straitjacket." But Mondale softened his stand in San Francisco. By accepting the plank, Mondale also hoped to distinguish Democratic foreign policy from Reagan's "saber-rattling" international agenda, as one Mondale supporter put it.

Jackson's two other minority reports dealt with issues of special interest to his black constituency: runoff primaries in the South and affirmative action. His call to abolish runoff primaries was defeated, but a compromise version of the affirmative action plank was accepted.

Ten Southern states used runoff primaries when no candidate received a majority in the first primary. Jackson claimed these second elections diluted minority voting strength because white voters often reverted to racial loyalty when a runoff choice was between a white and a black candidate. Supporters of second primaries argued that they prevented the nomination of fringe candidates who could receive a plurality in first-round primaries when more credible candidates split the vote. There also was strong sentiment against Jackson's plank from conservative Southerners who did not want the national party dictating their state election procedures.

Mondale's language pledged to eliminate discriminatory barriers to full voting rights. It also promised an in-depth study of runoff primaries and other voting practices that could discriminate against minorities.

The other dispute was whether the platform should reject the use of quotas to overturn discrimination in employment and education. As adopted in June, the platform specifically rejected quotas but called for affirmative action goals and timetables to end discrimination in hiring, promotions and education.

Following are excerpts from the Democratic platform of 1984:

**Budget Deficits.** ... The Democratic Party is pledged to reducing these intolerable deficits. We will reassess defense expenditures; create a tax system that is both adequate and fair; control skyrocketing health costs without sacrificing quality of care; and eliminate other unnecessary expenditures.

We oppose the artificial and rigid Constitutional restraint of a balanced budget amendment. Further we oppose efforts to call a federal constitutional convention for this purpose.

**Defense Spending.** ... As Democrats, we believe in devoting the needed resources to ensure our national security. But military might cannot be measured solely by dollars spent. American military strength must be secured at an affordable cost. We will reduce the rate of increase in defense spending. Through careful reevaluation of proposed and existing weapons, we will stop throwing away money on unworkable or unnecessary systems; through military reform we will focus defense expenditure on the most cost-effective military policies. We will insist that our allies contribute fairly to our collective security, and that the Department of Defense reduces its scandalous procurement waste.

**Tax Reform.** We will cap the effect of the Reagan tax cuts for wealthy Americans and enhance the progressivity of our personal income tax code, limiting the benefits of the third year of the Reagan tax cuts to the level of those with incomes of less than $60,000. We will partially defer indexation while protecting average Americans. We will close loopholes, eliminate the preferences and write-offs, exemptions, and deductions which skew the code toward the rich and toward unproductive tax shelters. Given the fact that there has been a veritable hemorrhage of capital out of the federal budget, reflected in part by the huge budget deficit, there must be a return to a fair tax on corporate income. Under the Reagan Administration, the rate of taxation on corporations has been so substantially reduced that they are not contributing their fair share to federal revenues. We believe there should be a 15% minimum corporate tax. In addition, our tax code has facilitated the transfer of capital from the United States to investments abroad, contributing to plant closing without notice in many communities and loss of millions of jobs. We will toughen compliance procedures to reduce the $100 billion annual tax evasion....

**Controlling Domestic Spending.** Social Security is one of the most important and successful initiatives in the history of our country, and it is an essential element of the social compact that binds us together as a community. There is no excuse — as the Reagan Administration has repeatedly suggested — for slashing Social Security to pay for excesses in other areas of the budget. We will steadfastly oppose such efforts, now and in the future.

It is rather in the area of health care costs that reform is urgently needed. By 1988, Medicare costs will rise to $106 billion; by the turn of the century, the debt of the trust fund may be as great as $1 trillion. In the Republican view, the problem is the level of benefits which senior citizens and the needy receive. As Democrats, we will protect the interests of health care beneficiaries. The real problem is the growing cost of health care services.

We propose to control these costs, and to demand that the health care industry become more efficient in providing care to all Americans, both young and old. We will limit what health care providers can receive as reimbursement, and spur innovation and competition in health care delivery....

**Education.** We call for the immediate restoration of the cuts in funding of education programs by the Reagan Administration, and for a major new commitment to education. We will create a partnership for excellence among federal, state and local governments. We will provide incentives to local school districts to concentrate on science, math, communications and computer literacy; to provide access to advanced technology....

Vocational education should be overhauled to bring instructional materials, equipment, and staff up to date with the technology and practices for the workplace and target assistance to areas with large numbers of disadvantaged youth. We will pay special attention to the needs of the handicapped....

Bilingual education enables children to achieve full competence in the English language and the academic success necessary to their full participation in the life of our nation....

We will make certain that higher education does not become a luxury affordable only by the children of the rich. In our America, no qualified student should be deprived of the ability to go on to college because of financial circumstance.

**Job Training.** The Democratic Party must give our young people new skills and new hope; we must work hand in hand with the private sector if job training is to lead to jobs. Specifically, targeted efforts are needed to address the urgent problem of unemployment among minority teenagers. We must provide job training for those who have dropped out of school, and take every step to expand educational opportunity for those still in school. We must recognize the special needs of the over-age 50 worker and the displaced homemaker. Through education, training and retraining we must reduce these dangerously high levels of unemployment.

We must provide an opportunity for workers, including those dislocated by changing technologies, to adapt to new opportunities; we must provide workers with choices as to which skills they wish to acquire. We know that Americans want to work. We are committed to ensuring that meaningful job training is available — for our students, for housewives returning to the workplace, and for those displaced by changing patterns of technology or trade....

**Housing.** First, we must intensify our commitment to the adequate operation, management, and rehabilitation of the current inventory of government-assisted housing. This housing stock is not one, but the only option for the least fortunate among our lower income families and senior citizens. It is the right thing to do and it makes economic sense to preserve our own economic investment.

Second, we must maintain and expand the flow of mortgage capital. The American dream of home ownership will fall beyond the reach of this generation and future ones if government fails to help attract new sources of capital for housing....

**Trade.** ... The reality of the 1980s is that the international economy is the arena in which we must compete. The world economy is an integrated economy; the challenge for our political leadership is to assure that the new arena is in fact a fair playing field for American businesses and consumers. We are committed to pursuing industrial strategies that effectively and imaginatively blend the genius of the free market with vital government partnership and leadership. As Democrats, we will be guided by the following principles and policies.

— We need a vigorous, open and fair trade policy that builds America's competitive strength and that allows our nation to remain an advanced, diversified economy while promoting full employment and raising living standards in the United States and other countries of the world; opens overseas markets for American products; strengthens the international economic system; assists adjustment to foreign competition; and recognizes the legitimate interests of American workers, farmers and businesses.

— We will pursue international negotiations to open markets and eliminate trade restrictions, recognizing that the growth and stability of the Third World depends on its ability to sell its products in international markets. High technology, agriculture and other industries should be brought under the General Agreement on Trade and Tariffs. Moreover, the developing world is a major market for U.S. exports, particularly capital goods. As a result, the U.S. has a major stake in international economic institutions that support growth in the developing world.

— We recognize that the growth and development of the Third World is vital both to global stability and to the continuing expansion of world trade. The U.S. presently sells more to the Third World than to the European Community and Japan combined. If we do not buy their goods, they cannot buy ours, nor can they service their debt. Consequently, it is important to be responsive to the issues of the North/South dialogue such as volatile commodity prices, inequities in the functioning of the international financial and monetary markets, and removal of barriers to the export of Third World goods.

— If trade has become big business for the country, exports have become critical to the economic health of a growing list of American industries. In the future, national economic policy will have to be set with an eye to its impact on U.S. exports. The strength of the dollar, the nature of the U.S. tax system, and the adequacy of export finance all play a role in making U.S. exports internationally competitive.

— The United States continues to struggle with trade barriers that affect its areas of international strength. Subsidized export financing on the part of Europe and Japan has also created problems for the United States, as has the use of industrial policies in Europe and Japan. In some cases, foreign governments target areas of America's competitive strength. In other cases, industrial targeting has been used to maintain industries that cannot meet international competition — often diverting exports to the American market and increasing the burden of adjustment for America's import-competing industries. We will ensure that timely and effective financing can be obtained by American businesses through the Export-Import Bank, so that they can compete effectively against subsidized competitors from abroad.

— A healthy U.S. auto industry is essential to a strong trade balance and economy. That industry generates a large number of American jobs and both develops and consumes new technology needed for economic vitality. We believe it is a sound principle of international trade for foreign automakers which enjoy substantial sales in the United States to invest here and create jobs where their markets are. We also believe U.S. automakers need to maintain high volume small car production in the U.S. With the U.S. auto companies' return to profitability (despite continued unemployment in the auto sector), we urge expanded domestic investment to supply consumers with a full range of competitive vehicles. We support efforts by management and labor to improve auto quality and productivity, and to restrain prices.

— Where foreign competition is fair, American industry should compete without government assistance. Where competition is unfair, we must respond powerfully. We will use trade law and international negotiations to aid U.S. workers, farmers, and business injured by unfair trade practices.

**Agriculture.** . . . The Democratic Party pledges action. We must solve the immediate farm crisis through a combination of humanitarian aid programs abroad, aggressive promotion of farm exports, and a fair moratorium on

farm debt and foreclosure by federal credit agencies to family farm borrowers being forced out of business through no fault of their own, until a long-term program addressing the farm credit crisis can be put into place. Beginning next January with the writing of a new long-term farm bill, the Democratic Party pledges to rebuild a prosperous system of family farms and ranches. We will forge a new agreement on a farm and food policy that assures a fair deal for family farmers, consumers, taxpayers, conservationists, and others with a direct stake in the organizational structure of the food economy. . . .

Finally, we must reverse the annual decrease in the value and volume of U.S. farm exports which has occurred in each year of Ronald Reagan's term. Our farm exports are vital to the nation's prosperity and provide a major part of total farm income. We must restore the ability of U.S. farm products to compete in world markets, and increase worldwide demand for American agricultural products. To do this, we must make major changes in Ronald Reagan's economic policies, and correct his grossly distorted currency exchange rates, which have caused American competitiveness in international trade to decline. We must also resist efforts to lower commodity price supports; such action would only lower farm income without addressing the economic policies which are the root cause of declining competitiveness of U.S. farm products in world markets.

**Energy.** . . . America is blessed with abundant coal and natural gas, substantial supplies of oil, and plentiful reserves of uranium. Although very costly to process, vast supplies of oil shales and tar sands represent future energy sources. Significant contributions to our energy supply can be made by utilizing renewable resources and indigenous energy, such as active and passive solar systems, windpower, geothermal and ocean thermal power, and the recovery of gas from agricultural waste, coal mines, and garbage dumps. These proven energy sources, as well as more experimental energy systems, should be encouraged for the positive environmental and economic contribution they can make to our energy security.

We will insist on the highest possible standards of safety and protection of public health with respect to nuclear power, including siting, design, operation, evacuation plans, and waste disposal procedures. We will require nuclear power to compete fairly in the marketplace. We will reexamine and review all federal subsidies to the nuclear industry, including the Price-Anderson Act's limits on the liability of the industry which will be considered for reauthorization in the next Congress. A Democratic Administration will give the Nuclear Regulatory Commission the integrity, competence, and credibility it needs to carry out its mandate to protect the public health and safety. We will expand the role of the public in NRC procedures.

We will ensure that no offshore oil and gas exploration will be taken up that is inconsistent with the protection of our fisheries and coastal resources.

**Hazardous Wastes.** Thousands of dump sites across America contain highly dangerous poisons that can threaten the health and safety of families who live nearby or who depend on water supplies that could be contaminated by the poisons. Although Congress has established the Superfund for emergency cleanup of these dangerous sites, President Reagan refuses to use it vigorously. The Democratic Party is committed to enforcing existing laws, to dramatically increasing Superfund resources to clean up all sites that threaten public health, and to assuring that everyone whose health or property is damaged has a fair opportunity to force the polluters to pay for the damage. This increased support should be financed at least in part through new taxes on the generation of hazardous wastes, so companies have an economic incentive to reduce the volume and toxicity of their dangerous wastes. . . .

**Clean Air and Water.** The Democratic Party supports a reauthorized and strengthened Clean Air Act. Statutory requirements for the control of toxic air pollutants should be strengthened, with the environmental agency required to identify and regulate within three years priority air pollutants known or anticipated to cause cancer and other serious diseases. The Democratic Party calls for an immediate program to reduce sulfur dioxide emissions by 50% from 1980 levels within the next decade. Our effort should be designed to reduce environmental and economic damage from acid rain while assuring such efforts do not cause regional economic dislocations....

The Democratic Party is committed to strengthening the Clean Water Act to curb both direct and indirect discharge of toxic pollutants into our nation's waters, and supports a strengthened Environmental Protection Agency to assure help to American cities in providing adequate supplies of drinking water free of toxic chemicals and other contaminants....

**Environmental Protection Agency.** The Democratic Party opposes the Reagan Administration's budget cuts, which have severely hampered the effectiveness of our environmental programs. The Environmental Protection Agency should receive a budget that exceeds in real dollars the agency's purchasing power when President Reagan took office, since the agency's workload has almost doubled in recent years.

**Public Lands.** The Democratic Party believes in retaining ownership and control of our public lands, and in managing those lands according to the principles of multiple use and sustained yield, with appropriate environmental standards and mitigation requirements to protect the public interest. The Democratic Party supports the substantial expansion of the National Wilderness Preservation System, with designations of all types of ecosystems, including coastal areas, deserts, and prairies as well as forest and alpine areas.

**Separation of Church and State.** The current Administration has consistently sought to reverse in the courts or overrule by constitutional amendment a long line of Supreme Court decisions that preserve our historic commitment to religious tolerance and church/state separation. The Democratic Platform affirms its support of the principles of religious liberty, religious tolerance and church/state separation and of the Supreme Court decisions forbidding violation of those principles. We pledge to resist all efforts to weaken those decisions....

**Affirmative Action.** The Democratic Party firmly commits itself to protect the civil rights of every citizen and to pursue justice and equal treatment under the law for all citizens. The Party reaffirms its longstanding commitment to the eradication of discrimination in all aspects of American life through the use of affirmative action goals, timetables, and other verifiable measurements to overturn historic patterns and historic burdens of discrimination in hiring, training, promotions, contract procurement, education, and the administration of all Federal programs....

**Equal Rights for Women.** A top priority of a Democratic Administration will be ratification of the unamended Equal Rights Amendment.... The Democratic Party defines nondiscrimination to encompass both equal pay for equal work *and* equal pay for work of comparable worth, and we pledge to take every step, including enforcement of current law and amending the Constitution to include the unamended ERA, to close the wage gap.

**Abortion.** The Democratic Party recognizes reproductive freedom as a fundamental human right. We therefore oppose government interference in the reproductive decisions of Americans, especially government interference which denies poor Americans their right to privacy by funding or advocating one or a limited number of reproductive choices only....

**Unions.** This nation established a labor policy more than a generation ago whose purpose is to encourage collective bargaining and the right of workers to organize to obtain this goal. The Democratic Party is committed to extending the benefit of this policy to all workers and to removing the barriers to its administration. To accomplish this, the Democratic Party supports: the repeal of Section 14B of the National Labor Relations Act; labor law reform legislation; a prohibition on the misuse of federal bankruptcy law to prevent the circumvention of the collective bargaining process and the destruction of labor-management contracts; and legislation to allow building trades workers the same peaceful picketing rights currently afforded industrial workers....

**Voting Rights Act.** A Democratic President and Administration pledge to eliminate any and all discriminatory barriers to full voting rights, whether they be at-large requirements, second-primaries, gerrymandering, annexation, dual registration, dual voting or other practices. Whatever law, practice, or regulation discriminates against the voting rights of minority citizens, a Democratic President and Administration will move to strike it down....

**Homosexual Rights.** ... All groups must be protected from discrimination based on race, color, sex, religion, national origin, language, age, or sexual orientation. We will support legislation to prohibit discrimination in the workplace based on sexual orientation. We will assure that sexual orientation *per se* does not serve as a bar to participation in the military....

**National Health Insurance.** ... As Democrats we believe that quality health care is a necessity for everyone. We reaffirm our commitment to the long-term goal of comprehensive national health insurance and view effective health care cost containment as an essential step toward that goal. Health cost containment must be based on a strong commitment to quality of service delivery and care. We also pledge to return to a proper emphasis on basic scientific research and meeting the need for health professionals — areas devastated by the Reagan Administration.

**Gun Control.** We support tough restraints on the manufacture, transportation, and sale of snubnosed handguns, which have no legitimate sporting use and are used in a high proportion of violent crimes.

**Arms Control.** ... A Democratic President will propose an early summit with regular, annual summits to follow, with the Soviet leaders, and meetings between senior civilian and military officials, in order to reduce tensions and explore possible formal agreements.... A new Democratic Administration will implement a strategy for peace which makes arms control an integral part of our national security policy. We must move the world back from the brink of nuclear holocaust and set a new direction toward an enduring peace, in which lower levels of military spending will be possible. Our ultimate aim must be to abolish all nuclear weapons in a world safe for peace and freedom....

The first practical step is to take the initiative, on January 20, 1985, to challenge the Soviets to halt the arms race quickly. As President Kennedy successfully did in stopping nuclear explosions above ground in 1963, a Democratic President will initiate temporary, verifiable, and mutual moratoria, to be maintained for a fixed period during negotiations so long as the Soviets do the same, on the testing of underground nuclear weapons and anti-satellite weapons; on the testing and deployment of all weapons in space; on the testing and deployment of new strategic ballistic missiles now under development; and on the deployment of nuclear-armed, sea-launched cruise missiles.

These steps should lead promptly to the negotiation of a comprehensive, mutual and verifiable freeze on the testing, production, and deployment of all nuclear weapons. Building on this initiative, the Democratic President will update and resubmit the SALT II Treaty to the Senate for its advice and consent. . . .

**Defense Policy.** The Reagan Administration measures military might by dollars spent. The Democratic Party seeks prudent defense based on sound planning and a realistic assessment of threats. In the field of defense policy, the Democratic Administration will work with our NATO and other allies to ensure our collective security, especially by strengthening our conventional defenses so as to reduce our need to rely on nuclear weapons, and to achieve this at increased spending levels, with funding to continue at levels appropriate to our collective security, with the firm hope that successful steps to reduce tensions and to obtain comprehensive and verifiable arms control agreements will guarantee our nation both military security and budgetary relief . . . [and] oppose a peacetime military draft or draft registration. . . .

A Democratic President will be prepared to apply military force when vital American interests are threatened, particularly in the event of an attack upon the United States or its immediate allies. But he or she will not hazard American lives or engage in unilateral military involvement:

- Where our objectives are not clear;
- Until all instruments of diplomacy and non-military leverage, as appropriate, have been exhausted;
- Where our objectives threaten unacceptable costs or unreasonable levels of military force;
- Where the local forces supported are not working to resolve the causes of conflict;
- Where multilateral or allied options for the resolution of conflict are available. . . .

**The Middle East.** The Democratic Party believes that the security of Israel and the pursuit of peace in the Middle East are fundamental priorities for American foreign policy. Israel remains more than a trusted friend, a steady ally, and a sister democracy. Israel is strategically important to the United States, and we must enter into meaningful strategic cooperation.

The Democratic Party opposes this Administration's sales of highly advanced weaponry to avowed enemies of Israel, such as AWACS aircraft and Stinger missiles to Saudi Arabia. While helping to meet the legitimate defensive needs of states aligned with our nation, we must ensure Israel's military edge over any combination of Middle East confrontation states. The Democratic Party opposes any consideration of negotiations with the PLO, unless the PLO abandons terrorism, recognizes the state of Israel, and adheres to U.N. Resolutions 242 and 338.

Jerusalem should remain forever undivided with free access to the holy places for people of all faiths. As stated in the 1976 and 1980 platforms, the Democratic Party recognizes and supports the established status of Jerusalem as the capital of Israel. As a symbol of this stand, the U.S. Embassy should be moved from Tel Aviv to Jerusalem.

**Central America.** A Democratic President . . . will approach Central American policy in the following terms:

— First, there must be unequivocal support for the Contadora process and for the efforts by those countries to achieve political solutions to the conflicts that plague the Central American region.

— Second, there must be a commitment on the part of the United States to reduce tensions in the region. We must terminate our support for the *contras* and other paramilitary groups fighting in Nicaragua. We must halt those U.S. military exercises in the region which are being conducted for no other real purpose than to intimidate or provoke the Nicaraguan government or which may be used as a pretext for deeper U.S. military involvement in the area. And, we must evidence our firm willingness to work for a demilitarized Central America, including the mutual withdrawal of all foreign forces and military advisers from the region. A Democratic President will

seek a multilateral framework to protect the security and independence of the region which will include regional agreements to bar new military bases, to restrict the numbers and sophistication of weapons being introduced into Central America, and to permit international inspection of borders. This diplomatic effort can succeed, however, only if all countries in Central America, including Nicaragua, will agree to respect the sovereignty and integrity of their neighbors, to limit their military forces, to reject foreign military bases (other than those provided for in the Panama Canal Treaties), and to deny any external force or power the use of their territories for purposes of subversion in the region. The viability of any security agreement for Central America would be enhanced by the progressive development of pluralism in Nicaragua. To this end, the elections proposed for November [1984] are important; how they are conducted will be an indication of Nicaragua's willingness to move in the direction of genuine democracy.

— Third, there must be a clear, concise signal to indicate that we are ready, willing and able to provide substantial economic resources, through the appropriate multilateral channels, to the nations of Central America, as soon as the Contadora process achieves a measure of success in restoring peace and stability in the region. In the meantime, of course, we will continue to provide humanitarian aid and refugee relief assistance. The Democratic Administration will work to help churches and universities which are providing sanctuary and assistance to Guatemalan, Haitian, and Salvadoran refugees, and will give all assistance to such refugees as is consistent with U.S. law.

— Fourth, a Democratic President will support the newly elected President of El Salvador in his efforts to establish civilian democratic control, by channeling U.S. aid through him and by conditioning it on the elimination of government-supported death squads and on progress toward his objectives of land reform, human rights, and serious negotiations with contending forces in El Salvador, in order to achieve a peaceful democratic political settlement of the Salvadoran conflict.

— Fifth, a Democratic President will not use U.S. armed forces in or over El Salvador or Nicaragua for the purpose of engaging in combat unless:

1) Congress has declared war or otherwise authorized the use of U.S. combat forces, or

2) the use of U.S. combat forces is necessary to meet a clear and present danger of attack upon the U.S., its territories or possessions or upon U.S. embassies or citizens, consistent with the War Powers Act.

## Republicans

A jubilant Republican Party wound up its Aug. 20-23 convention in Dallas, Texas, confident that President Ronald Reagan and Vice President George Bush would be the "winning team" in November. With the ticket's renomination certain beforehand, the 33rd Republican National Convention was more a celebration than a business meeting of GOP activists. Behind the cheering and display of party unity, however, ran a current of dissent: Moderates, who were greatly outnumbered, voiced unhappiness with the party's direction and its platform.

During convention week, speaker after speaker criticized the Democrats, saying they represented a legacy of "malaise" from Jimmy Carter's administration and promised only a future of fear. Reagan, too, emphasized that theme in his 55-minute acceptance speech. To repeated interruptions of applause and cheers, he drew sharp differences between Republicans and Democrats and between himself and the Democratic presidential nominee, Walter F. Mondale. "The choices this year are not just between two different personalities or between two political parties," Reagan said. "They are between two different visions of the future, two fundamentally different ways of governing — their government of pessimism, fear and limits . . . or ours of hope, confidence and growth."

In his acceptance speech, Bush vigorously touted the Reagan administration's record. "Under this president, more lands have been acquired for parks, more for wilderness," he said. "The quality of life is better — and that's a fact." In foreign affairs, Bush said, ". . . there is new confidence in the U.S. leadership around the world. . . . Because our president stood firm in defense of freedom, America has regained respect throughout the world. . . ."

Speakers in previous sessions had sought to make the same points. They tried to link former vice president Mondale to the policies and problems of the administration in which he had served. "Carter-Mondale" became their shorthand for a list of evils: inflation, high interest rates, foreign policy failures and sagging national spirit.

GOP leaders also were anxious to portray the Democratic ticket and the party's leadership as out of step with most Democrats. They gave the spotlight to Democrats-turned-Republicans and issued one of their warmest welcomes to Jeane J. Kirkpatrick, the U.S. representative to the United Nations, whom one party leader referred to as an "enlightened Democrat." Kirkpatrick delivered a foreign policy speech during the opening session.

Yet this convention was clearly a Republican event, with the administration firmly in control and many of its members on hand. The party's leaders also made clear they were making a pitch for women voters, in response to the candidacy of Rep. Geraldine A. Ferraro, D-N.Y., Mondale's running mate.

Conditions outside the hall were almost as controlled as events inside. Police were ever present, but demonstrations by and large were tepid. One major reason was the record-breaking heat: It prompted some protesters to leave town and delegates and the press to stay in the air-conditioned indoors.

The opening ceremonies Aug. 20 were a mix of the patriotic and the political. About 50 young people carrying flags and wearing smocks decorated with red, white and blue elephants lined the interior of the hall; delegates then sang "The Star-Spangled Banner" and recited the pledge of allegiance.

The evening session was the GOP's "ladies' night." Four of the six speakers were women, including Katherine D. Ortega, the U.S. treasurer, and Kirkpatrick. Although Ortega was billed as the keynote speaker, it was Democrat Kirkpatrick who received the most sustained and vigorous applause from the delegates. Kirkpatrick had harsh words for her fellow Democrats, charging that they "treat foreign affairs as an afterthought." She asserted that the Carter administration "did not seem to notice much, care much, or do much" about a host of international problems.

The highlight of the Aug. 21 evening session was a speech by former president Gerald R. Ford. Delegates gave Ford and his wife, Betty, a rousing welcome. Ford wasted no time attacking the Democratic nominee, telling delegates: "Mondale wants this election to be a 'referendum on the future.' I can't blame him for wanting to forget the past, the four years of Carter-Mondale from 1977 through 1980. Who wants to remember four years of roaring inflation, skyrocketing interest rates and so-called 'malaise'?"

Before Reagan and Bush were renominated on the evening of Aug. 22, Sen. Barry Goldwater of Arizona addressed the convention. Goldwater, the party's presidential nominee in 1964, said he wanted to talk to the delegates about "freedom." He opened his speech with a slogan from

his campaign 20 years earlier: "Let me remind you," he said, "extremism in the defense of liberty is no vice." Goldwater charged that the Democrats at their convention "turned their backs on our own heritage. Indeed, they would have us ashamed of our freedom and our ability to defend it. To me, the worst part was that they said nicer things about the Soviet Union than about our own military services."

The delegates moved to renominate Reagan and Bush. Although the outcome came as no surprise, there was an unusual joint roll call on the nominations, with Reagan receiving 2,233 votes and Bush, 2,231. *(Chart, p. 252)*

On the final night of the convention, Reagan and Bush came to the hall to claim their nominations. With standing room only in the 17,000-seat arena, guests were lined up three deep in some places for an evening of balloons, speeches and patriotic music.

Earlier, after spirited debate, the 106-member platform committee adopted a 1984 campaign document that conformed in virtually all respects to the themes Reagan had sounded during his first term in office. The convention itself ratified the 30,000-word platform with no debate Aug. 21. On almost every aspect of public policy, the document stood in stark contrast to the platform the Democrats had adopted in San Francisco.

However, in its strong stand against tax increases and its criticism of the independent Federal Reserve Board, the Republican platform went further than the White House wanted. Administration representatives led by former transportation secretary Drew Lewis sought to soften the tax plank, but, while they succeeded in modifying some of the language, they were unable to alter it substantially. The tax section of the Republican platform pledged that the party would continue efforts to lower tax rates and would support tax reform that "will lead to a fair and simple tax system." The platform said the party believed that a "modified flat tax — with specific exemptions for such items as mortgage interest — is a most promising approach."

Taxes had mushroomed as an election issue when Democratic presidential nominee Walter F. Mondale said in his acceptance speech at the Democratic National Convention that, regardless of who won in November, tax increases would be necessary in 1985 to combat record federal budget deficits. Mondale also accused Reagan of having a secret plan to raise taxes.

Despite an hour-long debate, the GOP platform committee had refused to endorse the proposed Equal Rights Amendment (ERA) — which Reagan opposed — or compromise language stating that the Republicans respected those who supported the amendment. The committee also turned aside challenges by party moderates to language endorsing voluntary prayer in public schools and opposing federal financing for abortions under any circumstances. Some moderate delegates had considered trying to offer a minority plank on the ERA stating respect for differing Republican views on the issue. But moderates determined that they lacked support to bring a floor challenge and did not pursue this.

The platform included the following major points:

● Unqualified opposition to tax increases, which were dismissed as a "misguided effort to balance the budget."

● A call for passage by Congress of a constitutional amendment to require a balanced federal budget.

● Support for a constitutional convention to write a balanced budget amendment if Congress failed to act on the issue.

● Criticism of Federal Reserve Board policies as "destabilizing," and a suggestion that the gold standard "may be a useful mechanism" for achieving the goal of stable prices.

● Support for the administration's policy in Central America, specifically its support of the government in El Salvador.

● A pledge of party support for putting the United States in a superior military position in the world, although the term "military superiority" that appeared in the 1980 platform was not used in 1984.

● A call for repealing the windfall profits tax on oil.

● Support for abolition of the Department of Energy.

● Opposition to quotas to remedy discrimination because they "are the most insidious form of discrimination against the innocent."

● Support for a constitutional amendment to ban abortion and reaffirmation of a statement in the 1980 platform that Reagan should appoint federal judges who opposed abortion.

● Support for the right of students to engage in voluntary school prayer.

A multi-section chapter entitled "Security for the Individual" covered the environment, education, individual rights and "our constitutional system." On the environment, the platform said the party "endorses a strong effort to control and clean up toxic wastes." It asserted further that the GOP "supports the continued commitment to clean air and clean water. This support includes the implementation of meaningful clean air and clean water acts."

The 1980 platform had called for abolition of the Department of Education, which Congress created in 1979 at the urging of President Carter. The 1984 GOP platform stated that education was a "local function, a state responsibility and a federal concern. The federal role should be limited." However, it stopped short of urging that the federal department be disbanded.

In the section on individual rights, the platform devoted several paragraphs to GOP support for women's rights. In one section, the document stated, "President Reagan believes, as do we, that all members of our party are free to work individually for women's progress." At another point, the platform called for "assuring that women have equal opportunity, security and real choices for the promising future." But while it called for "equal pay for equal work," the document said that "with equal emphasis, we oppose the concept of 'comparable worth.' We believe that the free-market system can determine the value of jobs better than any government authority."

On the issue of abortion, the platform picked up language from the 1980 document advocating a constitutional amendment to ban abortion and supporting a ban on federal funding for abortion. An amendment that called for support of federal funding for abortions in the case of rape or incest was rejected.

In the foreign affairs area, the Republicans took dead aim at the Democrats. The platform declared that the Soviet Union's "globalist ideology and its leadership obsessed with military power make it a threat to freedom and peace on every continent. The Carter-Mondale Administration ignored that threat, and the Democratic candidates underestimate it today. The Carter-Mondale illusion that the Soviet leaders share our ideals and aspirations is not only false but a profound danger to world peace." The platform added that Republicans "reaffirm our belief that

Soviet behavior at the negotiating table cannot be divorced from Soviet behavior elsewhere."

This section was similar in tone to the 1980 platform, which declared "the premier challenge facing the United States, its allies and the entire globe is to check the Soviet Union's global ambitions." Although the 1984 campaign document did not contain the call for outright U.S. "military superiority" that appeared in the 1980 platform, the notion that the United States should be the superior power in the world ran through the chapter. The platform also stated that the Republicans "enthusiastically" supported the development of "non-nuclear, space-based defensive systems" designed to protect the United States from incoming missiles, as proposed by Reagan in 1983.

Following are excerpts from the Republican platform of 1984:

**Economic Policy.** Our most important economic goal is to expand and continue the economic recovery and move the nation to full employment without inflation. We therefore oppose any attempts to increase taxes, which would harm the recovery and reverse the trend to restoring control of the economy to individual Americans. We favor reducing deficits by continuing and expanding the strong economic recovery brought about by the policies of this Administration and by eliminating wasteful and unnecessary government spending....

To assure workers and entrepreneurs the capital required to provide jobs and growth, we will further expand incentives for personal saving. We will expand coverage of the Individual Retirement Account, especially to homemakers, and increase and index the annual limits on IRA contributions. We will increase the incentives for savings by moving toward the reduction of taxation of interest income. We will work for indexation of capital assets and elimination of the double taxation of dividends to increase the attractiveness of equity investments for small investors.

We oppose withholding on dividend and interest income. It would discourage saving and investment, create needless paperwork, and rob savers of their due benefits. A higher personal savings rate is key to deficit control. We therefore oppose any disincentives to thrift.

History has proven again and again that wage and price controls will not stop inflation. Such controls only cause shortages, inequities, and ultimately high prices. We remain firmly opposed to the imposition of wage and price controls.

We are committed to bringing the benefits of economic growth to all Americans. Therefore, we support policies which will increase opportunities for the poorest in our society to climb the economic ladder. We will work to establish enterprise zones in urban and rural America; we will work to enable those living in government-owned or subsidized housing to purchase their homes....

**Tax Policy.** The Republican Party pledges to continue our efforts to lower tax rates, change and modernize the tax system, and eliminate the incentive-destroying effects of graduated tax rates. We therefore support tax reform that will lead to a fair and simple tax system and believe a modified flat tax — with specific exemptions for such items as mortgage interest — is a most promising approach.

For families, we will restore the value of personal exemptions, raising it to a minimum of $2,000 and indexing to prevent further erosion. We will preserve the deduction for mortgage interest payments. We will propose an employment income exclusion to assure that tax burdens are not shifted to the poor....

**Balancing the Budget.** The congressional budget process is bankrupt. Its implementation has not brought spending under control, and it must be thoroughly reformed. We will work for the constitutional amendment requiring a balanced federal budget passed by the Republican Senate but blocked by the Democrat-controlled House and denounced by the Democrat Platform. If Congress fails to act on this issue, a constitutional convention should be convened to address only this issue in order to bring deficit spending under control.

The President is denied proper control over the federal budget. To remedy this, we support enhanced authority to prevent wasteful spending, including a line-item veto....

**Monetary Policy.** Just as our tax policy has only laid the groundwork for a new era of prosperity, reducing inflation is only the first step in restoring a stable currency. A dollar now should be worth a dollar in the future. This allows real economic growth without inflation and is the primary goal of our monetary policy.

The Federal Reserve Board's destabilizing actions must therefore stop. We need coordination between fiscal and monetary policy, timely information about Fed decisions, and an end to the uncertainties people face in obtaining money and credit. The Gold Standard may be a useful mechanism for realizing the Federal Reserve's determination to adopt monetary policies needed to sustain price stability.

**Minimum Wage.** There are still federal statutes that keep Americans out of the workforce. Arbitrary minimum wage rates, for example, have eliminated hundreds of thousands of jobs and, with them, the opportunity for young people to get productive skills, good work habits, and a weekly paycheck. We encourage the adoption of a youth opportunity wage to encourage employers to hire and train inexperienced workers....

**Energy.** We will complete America's energy agenda. Natural gas should be responsibly decontrolled as rapidly as possible so that families and businesses can enjoy the full benefits of lower prices and greater production, as with decontrolled oil. We are committed to the repeal of the confiscatory windfall profits tax, which has forced the American consumer to pay more for less and left us vulnerable to the energy and economic stranglehold of foreign producers.

While protecting the environment, we should permit abundant American coal to be mined and consumed. Environmentally sound development of oil and natural gas on federal properties (which has brought the taxpayers $20 billion in revenue in the last four years) should continue. We believe that as controls have been lifted from the energy marketplace, conservation and alternative sources of energy, such as solar, wind, and geothermal, have become increasingly cost-effective....

We now have a sound, long-term program for disposal of nuclear waste. We will work to eliminate unnecessary regulatory procedures so that nuclear plants can be brought on line quickly, efficiently, and safely. We call for an energy policy, the stability and continuity of which will restore and encourage public confidence in the fiscal stability of the nuclear industry.

We are committed to the termination of the Department of Energy. President Reagan has succeeded in abolishing that part which was telling Americans what to buy, where to buy it, and at what price — the regulatory part of DOE. Then he reduced the number of bureaucrats by 25 percent. Now is the time to complete the job.

**Agriculture Policy.** ... Republicans are very much aware of the devastating impact which high interest rates have had, and continue to have, on the viability of America's farmers and ranchers. We also realize that, unless interest rates decline significantly in the near future, the character of American agriculture and rural life will be tragically changed. For these reasons, we pledge to pursue every possible course of action, including the consideration of temporary interest rate reductions, to ensure the Ameri-

can farmer or rancher is not a patient that dies in the course of a successful economic operation....

Republicans are cognizant that there are many well-managed, efficient, farm and ranch operations which face bankruptcy and foreclosure. The foreclosures and resulting land sales will jeopardize the equity positions of neighboring farms and ranches, compounding financial problems in agriculture. Republicans pledge to implement comprehensive Farmers Home Administration and commercial farm and ranch debt restructuring procedures, including the establishment of local community farm and ranch finance committees, which shall advise borrowers, lenders, and government officials regarding debt restructuring alternatives and farmer and rancher eligibility....

Our farmers and ranchers must have full access to world markets and should not have to face unfair export subsidies and predatory dumping by other producing nations without redress. Republicans believe that unfair trade practices and non-tariff barriers are so serious that a comprehensive renegotiation of multilateral trade arrangements must be undertaken to revitalize the free, fair, and open trade critical to worldwide economic growth.

The Republican Party is unalterably opposed to the use of embargoes of grain or other agricultural products as a tool of foreign policy....

**Trade Policy.**... We are committed to a free and open international trading system. All Americans benefit from the free flow of goods, services and capital, and the efficiencies of a vigorous international market. We will work with all of our international trading partners to eliminate barriers to trade, both tariff and non-tariff. As a first step, we call on our trading partners to join in a new round of trade negotiations to revise the General Agreement on Tariffs and Trade in order to strengthen it. And we further call on our trading partners to join us in reviewing trade with totalitarian regimes....

**Housing.** We reaffirm our commitment to the federal-tax deductibility of mortgage interest payments. In the States, we stand with those working to lower property taxes that strike hardest at the poor, the elderly, and large families. We stand, as well, with Americans earning possession of their homes through "sweat-equity" programs.

We will, over time, replace subsidies and welfare projects with a voucher system, returning public housing to the free market.

Despite billions of dollars poured into public housing developments, conditions remain deplorable for many low-income Americans who live in them. These projects have become breeding grounds for the very problems they were meant to eliminate. Their dilapidated and crumbling structures testify to decades of corrupt or incompetent management by poverty bureaucrats.

Some residents of public housing developments have reversed these conditions by successfully managing their own housing units through creative self-help efforts.... The Republican Party therefore supports the development of programs which will lead to homeownership of public housing developments by current residents.

We strongly believe in open housing. We will vigorously enforce all fair housing laws and will not tolerate their distortion into quotas and controls.

**Welfare.**...Because there are different reasons for poverty, our programs address different needs and must never be replaced with a unitary income guarantee. That would betray the interests of the poor and the taxpayers alike.

We will employ the latest technology to combat welfare fraud in order to protect the needy from the greedy.

Whenever possible, public assistance must be a transition to the world of work, except in cases, particularly with the aged and disabled, where that is not appropriate. In other cases, it is long overdue.

Remedying poverty requires that we sustain and broaden economic recovery, hold families together, get government's hand out of their pocketbooks, and restore the work ethic.

**Environment.** ... The Republican Party endorses a strong effort to control and clean up toxic wastes. We have already tripled funding to clean up hazardous waste dumps, quadrupled funding for acid rain research, and launched the rebirth of the Chesapeake Bay.

...The Republican Party supports the continued commitment to clean air and clean water. This support includes the implementation of meaningful clean air and clean water acts. We will continue to offer leadership to reduce the threat to our environment and our economy from acid rain, while at the same time preventing economic dislocation....

We will be responsible to future generations, but at the same time, we must remember that quality of life means more than protection and preservation. Quality of life also means a good job, a decent place to live, accommodation for a growing population, and the continued economic and technological development essential to our standard of living....

**Education.** We believe that education is a local function, a State responsibility, and a federal concern. The federal role in education should be limited. It includes helping parents and local authorities ensure high standards, protecting civil rights, and ensuring family rights....

We have enacted legislation to guarantee equal access to school facilities by student religious groups. Mindful of our religious diversity, we reaffirm our commitment to the freedoms of religion and speech guaranteed by the Constitution of the United States and firmly support the rights of students to openly practice the same, including the right to engage in voluntary prayer in schools....

While much has been accomplished, the agenda is only begun. We must complete the block-grant process begun in 1981. We will return revenue sources to State and local governments to make them independent of federal funds and of the control that inevitably follows.

The Republican Party believes that developing the individual dignity and potential of disabled Americans is an urgent responsibility. To this end, the Republican Party commits itself to prompt and vigorous enforcement of the rights of disabled citizens, particularly those rights established under the Education for All Handicapped Children Act, Section 504 of the Rehabilitation Act of 1973, and the Civil Rights of Institutionalized Persons Act. We insist on the highest standards of quality for services supported with federal funds.

In education, as in other activities, competition fosters excellence. We therefore support the President's proposal for tuition tax credits. We will convert the Chapter One grants to vouchers, thereby giving poor parents the ability to choose the best schooling available. Discrimination cannot be condoned, nor may public policies encourage its practice. Civil rights enforcement must not be twisted into excessive interference in the education process.

**Crime and Gun Control.** ... Republicans respect the authority of State and local law enforcement officials. The proper federal role is to provide strong support and coordination for their efforts and to vigorously enforce federal criminal laws. By concentrating on repeat offenders, we are determined to take career criminals off the street.

The best way to deter crime is to increase the probability of detection and to make punishment certain and swift. As a matter of basic philosophy, we advocate preventive rather than merely corrective measures. Republicans advocate sentencing reform and secure, adequate prison construction. We concur with the American people's approval of capital punishment where appropriate and will ensure that it is carried out humanely.

Republicans will continue to defend the constitutional right to keep and bear arms. When this right is abused and armed felonies are committed, we believe in stiff, mandatory sentencing....

**Discrimination.** Just as we must guarantee opportunity, we oppose attempts to dictate results. We will resist efforts to replace equal rights with discriminatory quota systems and preferential treatment. Quotas are the most insidious form of discrimination: reverse discrimination against the innocent. We must always remember that, in a free society, different individual goals will yield different results....

**Women's Rights.** The Republican Party has an historic commitment to equal rights for women. Republicans pioneered the right of women to vote, and our party was the first major party to advocate equal pay for equal work, regardless of sex.

President Reagan believes, as do we, that all members of our party are free to work individually for women's progress. As a party, we demand that there be no detriment to that progress or inhibition of women's rights to full opportunity and advancement within this society.

With women comprising an increasing share of the work force, it is essential that the employment opportunities created by our free market system be open to individuals without regard to their sex, race, religion, or ethnic origin. We firmly support an equal opportunity approach which gives women and minorities equal access to all jobs — including the traditionally higher-paying technical, managerial, and professional positions — and which guarantees that workers in those jobs will be compensated in accord with the laws requiring equal pay for equal work under Title VII of the Civil Rights Act.

We are creating an environment in which individual talents and creativity can be tapped to the fullest, while assuring that women have equal opportunity, security, and real choices for the promising future. For all Americans, we demand equal pay for equal work. With equal emphasis, we oppose the concept of "comparable worth." We believe that the free market system can determine the value of jobs better than any government authority.

**Protecting the Handicapped.** We are committed to enforcing statutory prohibitions barring discrimination against any otherwise qualified handicapped individuals, in any program receiving federal financial assistance, solely by reason of their handicap.

We recognize the need for watchful care regarding the procedural due process rights of persons with handicaps both to prevent their placement into inappropriate programs or settings and to ensure that their rights are represented by guardians or other advocates, if necessary.

For handicapped persons who need care, we favor family-based care where possible, supported by appropriate and adequate incentives. We increased the tax credit for caring for dependents or spouses physically or mentally unable to care for themselves. We also provided a deduction of up to $1,500 per year for adopting a child with special needs that may otherwise make adoption difficult.

**Labor Unions.** We reaffirm the right of all individuals freely to form, join, or assist labor organizations to bargain collectively, consistent with State laws and free from unnecessary government involvement. We support the fundamental principle of fairness in labor relations. We will continue the Reagan Administration's "open door" policy toward organized labor and its leaders. We reaffirm our long-standing support for the right of States to enact "Right-to-Work" laws under section 14(b) of the Taft-Hartley Act.

**Campaign Reform.** The holding of public office in our country demands the highest degree of commitment to integrity, openness, and honesty by candidates running for all elective offices. Without such a commitment, public confidence rapidly erodes. Republicans, therefore, reaffirm our commitment to the fair and consistent application of financial disclosure laws. We will continue our support for full disclosure by all high officials of the government and candidates in positions of public trust. This extends to the financial holdings of spouses or dependents, of which the official has knowledge, financial interest, or benefit. We will continue to hold all public officials to the highest ethical standards and will oppose the inconsistent application of those standards on the basis of gender....

...In light of the inhibiting role federal election laws and regulations have had, Congress should consider abolishing the Federal Election Commission....

**Abortion.** The unborn child has a fundamental individual right to life which cannot be infringed. We therefore reaffirm our support for a human life amendment to the Constitution, and we endorse legislation to make clear that the Fourteenth Amendment's protections apply to unborn children. We oppose the use of public revenues for abortion and will eliminate funding for organizations which advocate or support abortions....

We applaud President Reagan's fine record of judicial appointments, and we reaffirm our support for the appointment of judges at all levels of the judiciary who respect traditional family values and the sanctity of innocent human life....

**Foreign Policy.** The supreme purpose of our foreign policy must be to maintain our freedom in a peaceful international environment in which the United States and our allies and friends are secure against military threats, and democratic governments are flourishing in a world of increasing prosperity.

This we pledge to our people and to future generations: we shall keep the peace by keeping our country stronger than any potential adversary....

**Central America.** Today, democracy is under assault throughout [Central America]. Marxist Nicaragua threatens not only Costa Rica and Honduras, but also El Salvador and Guatemala. The Sandinista regime is building the largest military force in Central America, importing Soviet equipment, Eastern bloc and PLO advisers, and thousands of Cuban mercenaries. The Sandinista government has been increasingly brazen in its embrace of Marxism-Leninism. The Sandinistas have systematically persecuted free institutions, including synagogue and church, schools, the private sector, the free press, minorities, and families and tribes throughout Nicaragua. We support continued assistance to the democratic freedom fighters in Nicaragua. Nicaragua cannot be allowed to remain a Communist sanctuary, exporting terror and arms throughout the region. We condemn the Sandinista government's smuggling of illegal drugs into the United States as a crime against American society and international law.

The heroic effort to build democracy in El Salvador has been brutally attacked by Communist guerrillas supported by Cuba and the Sandinistas. Their violence jeopardizes improvements in human rights, delays economic growth, and impedes the consolidation of democracy. El Salvador is nearer to Texas than Texas is to New England, and we cannot be indifferent to its fate. In the tradition of President Truman's postwar aid to Europe, President Reagan has helped the people of El Salvador defend themselves. Our opponents object to that assistance, citing concern for human rights. We share that concern, and more than that, we have taken steps to help curb abuses. We have firmly and actively encouraged human rights reform, and results have been achieved. In judicial reform, the murderers of the American nuns in 1980 have been convicted and sentenced; and in political reform, the right to vote has been exercised by 80 percent of the voters in the fair, open elections of 1982 and 1984. Most important, if the Communists seize power there, human rights will be extinguished, and tens of thousands will be driven from their homes. We, therefore, support the President in his determination that the Salvadoran people will shape their own future.

**The Soviet Union.** Stable and peaceful relations with the Soviet Union are possible and desirable, but they depend upon the credibility of American strength and determination.... Our policy of peace through strength encourages freedom-loving people everywhere and provides hope for those who look forward one day to enjoying the fruits of self-government....

We hold a sober view of the Soviet Union. Its globalist ideology and its leadership obsessed with military power make it a threat to freedom and peace on every continent.... Republicans reaffirm our belief that Soviet behavior at the negotiating table cannot be divorced from Soviet behavior elsewhere. Over-eagerness to sign agreements with the Soviets at any price, fashionable in the Carter-Mondale Administration, should never blind us to this reality. Any future agreement with the Soviets must require full compliance, be fully verifiable, and contain suitable sanctions for non-compliance.... We insist on full Soviet compliance with all treaties and executive agreements.

We seek to deflect Soviet policy away from aggression and toward peaceful international conduct. To that end, we will seek substantial reductions in nuclear weapons, rather than merely freezing nuclear weapons at their present dangerous level. We will continue multilateral efforts to deny advanced Western technology to the Soviet war machine.

**Europe.** ... We would be in mortal danger were Western Europe to come under Soviet domination. Fragmenting NATO is the immediate objective of the Soviet military buildup and Soviet subversion.... To keep the peace, the Reagan-Bush Administration is offsetting the Soviet military threat with the defensive power of the Alliance. We are deploying Pershing II and Cruise missiles. Remembering the Nazi Reich, informed voters on both sides of the Atlantic know they cannot accept Soviet military superiority in Europe.

**The Middle East.** ... Lebanon is still in turmoil, despite our best efforts to foster stability in that unhappy country. With the Syrian leadership increasingly subject to Soviet influence, and the Palestine Liberation Organization and its homicidal subsidiaries taking up residence in Syria, U.S. policy toward the region must remain vigilant and strong. Republicans reaffirm that the United States should not recognize or negotiate with the PLO so long as that organization continues to promote terrorism, rejects Israel's right to exist, and refuses to accept U.N. Resolutions 242 and 338.

The bedrock of that protection remains, as it has for over three decades, our moral and strategic relationship with Israel. We are allies in the defense of freedom. Israel's strength, coupled with United States assistance, is the main obstacle to Soviet domination of the region. The sovereignty, security, and integrity of the state of Israel are moral imperatives. We pledge to help maintain Israel's qualitative military edge over its adversaries.

We recognize that attacks in the U.N. against Israel are but thinly disguised attacks against the United States, for it is our shared ideals and democratic way of life that are their true target. Thus, when a U.N. agency denied Israel's right to participate, we withheld our financial support until that action was corrected. And we have worked behind the scenes and in public in other international organizations to defeat discriminatory attacks against our ally.

...We pledge continued support to Egypt and other moderate regimes against Soviet and Libyan subversion, and we look to them to contribute to our efforts for a long-term settlement of the region's destructive disputes.

We believe that Jerusalem should remain an undivided

city with free and unimpeded access to all holy places by people of all faiths.

**China and Taiwan.** . . . In keeping with the pledge of the 1980 Platform, President Reagan has continued the process of developing our relationship with the People's Republic of China. We commend the President's initiatives to build a solid foundation for the long-term relations between the United States and the People's Republic, emphasizing peaceful trade and other policies to promote regional peace. Despite fundamental differences in many areas, both nations share an important common objective: opposition to Soviet expansionism.

At the same time, we specifically reaffirm our concern for, and our moral commitment to, the safety and security of the 18 million people on Taiwan. We pledge that this concern will be constant, and we will continue to regard any attempt to alter Taiwan's status by force as a threat to regional peace. We endorse, with enthusiasm, President Reagan's affirmation that it is the policy of the United States to support and fully implement the provisions of the Taiwan Relations Act. In addition, we fully support self determination for the people of Hong Kong.

**South Africa.** . . . We reaffirm our commitment to the rights of all South Africans. Apartheid is repugnant. In South Africa, as elsewhere on the continent, we support well-conceived efforts to foster peace, prosperity, and stability.

**International Organizations.** . . . We will not support international organizations inconsistent with our interests. In particular, we will work to eliminate their funding of Communist states.

Prominent among American ideals is the sanctity of the family. Decisions on family size should be made freely by each family. We support efforts to enhance the freedom of such family decisions. We will endeavor to assure that those who are responsible for our programs are more sensitive to the cultural needs of the countries to which we give assistance.

As part of our commitment to the family and our opposition to abortion, we will eliminate all U.S. funding for organizations which in any way support abortion or research on abortion methods. . . .

Americans cannot count on the international organizations to guarantee our security or adequately protect our interests. The United States hosts the headquarters of the United Nations, pays a fourth of its budget, and is proportionally the largest contributor to most international organizations; but many members consistently vote against us. As Soviet influence in these organizations has grown, cynicism and the double standard have become their way of life.

This is why President Reagan announced that we will leave the worst of these organizations, UNESCO. He has put the U.N. on notice that the U.S. will strongly oppose the use of the U.N. to foster anti-semitism, Soviet espionage, and hostility to the United States. The President decisively rejected the U.N. Convention on the Law of the Sea and embarked instead on a dynamic national oceans policy, animated by our traditional commitment to freedom of the seas. That pattern will be followed with regard to U.N. meddling in Antarctica and outer space. Enthusiastically endorsing those steps, we will apply the same standards to all international organizations. We will monitor their votes and activities, and particularly the votes of member states which receive U.S. aid. Americans will no longer silently suffer the hypocrisy of many of these organizations.

**Human Rights.** The American people believe that United States foreign policy should be animated by the cause of human rights for all the world's peoples.

A well-rounded human rights policy is concerned with specific individuals whose rights are denied by governments of the right or left, and with entire peoples whose Communist governments deny their claim to human rights as

individuals and acknowledge only the "rights" derived from membership in an economic class. Republicans support a human rights policy which includes both these concerns. . . .

By focusing solely on the shortcomings of non-Communist governments, Democrats have missed the forest for the trees, failing to recognize that the greatest threat to human rights is the Communist system itself. . . .

**Arms Control.** The prospect for peace is excellent because America is strong again. America's defenses have only one purpose: to assure that our people and free institutions survive and flourish.

Our security requires both the capability to defend against aggression and the will to do so. Together, will and capability deter aggression. That is why the danger of war has grown more remote under President Reagan. . . .

We are proud of a strong America. Our military strength exists for the high moral purpose of deterring conflict, not initiating war. The deterrence of aggression is ethically imperative. . . . We reaffirm the principle that the national security policy of the United States should be based upon a strategy of peace through strength, a goal of the 1980 Republican Platform.

Maintaining a technological superiority, the historical foundation of our policy of deterrence, remains essential. In other areas, such as our maritime forces, we should continue to strive for qualitative superiority.

President Reagan committed our nation to a modernized strategic and theater nuclear force sufficient to deter attack against the United States and our allies, while pursuing negotiations for balanced, verifiable reductions of nuclear weapons under arms control agreements. . . .

We will continue to modernize our deterrent capability while negotiating for verifiable arms control. We will continue the policies that have given fresh confidence and new hope to freedom-loving people everywhere. . . .

The Soviet Union has rejected every invitation by President Reagan to resume talks, refusing to return unless we remove the Pershing II and Cruise missiles which we have placed in Europe at the request of our NATO allies. Soviet intransigence is designed to force concessions from the United States even before negotiations begin. We will not succumb to this strategy. The Soviet Union will return to the bargaining table only when it recognizes that the United States will not make unilateral concessions or allow the Soviet Union to achieve nuclear superiority. . . .

To deter Soviet violations of arms control agreements, the United States must maintain the capability to verify, display a willingness to respond to Soviet violations which have military significance, and adopt a policy whereby the defense of the United States is not constrained by arms control agreements violated by the Soviet Union.

We support the President's efforts to curb the spread of nuclear weapons and to improve international controls and safeguards over sensitive nuclear technologies. The President's non-proliferation policy has emphasized results, rather than rhetoric, as symbolized by the successful meeting of nuclear supplier states in Luxembourg in July of this year. We endorse the President's initiative on comprehensive safeguards and his efforts to encourage other supplier states to support such measures.

The first duty of government is to provide for the common defense. . . . We must continue to devote the resources essential to deter a Soviet threat — a threat which has grown and should be met by an improved and modernized U.S. defense capability. . . .

We will continue to strengthen our intelligence services. We will remove statutory obstacles to the effective management, performance, and security of intelligence sources and methods. We will further improve our ability to influence international events in support of our foreign policy objectives, and we will strengthen our counterintelligence facilities. . . .

. . . Republicans understood that our nuclear deterrent

forces are the ultimate military guarantor of America's security and that of our allies. That is why we will continue to support the programs necessary to modernize our strategic forces and reduce the vulnerabilities. This includes the earliest possible deployment of a new small mobile ICBM. . . .

President Reagan has launched a bold new Strategic Defense Initiative to defend against nuclear attack. We enthusiastically support President Reagan's Strategic Defense Initiative. We enthusiastically support the development of non-nuclear, space-based defensive systems to protect the United States by destroying incoming missiles.

Recognizing the need for close consultation with our allies, we support a comprehensive and intensive effort to render obsolete the doctrine of Mutual Assured Destruction (MAD). The Democratic Party embraces Mutual Assured Destruction. The Republican Party rejects the strategy of despair and supports instead the strategy of hope and survival.

We will begin to eliminate the threat posed by strategic nuclear missiles as soon as possible. Our only purpose (one all people share) is to reduce the danger of nuclear war. To that end, we will use superior American technology to achieve space-based and ground-based defensive systems as soon as possible to protect the lives of the American people and our allies.

# 1988 Conventions

## Presidential Candidates

**Michael S. Dukakis**
**Democrat**

**George Bush**
**Republican**

## Democrats

After years of internal warfare, the Democrats staged a remarkable show of unity at their 1988 national convention, held July 18-21 in Atlanta, Ga. For once, the issue-oriented activists who dominated the Democratic nominating process for nearly two decades subordinated their agendas to the goal of party victory, thus avoiding the self-inflicted wounds that had marred so many conventions since the 1968 Chicago debacle.

Massachusetts governor Michael S. Dukakis arrived at the convention with enough delegate support to ensure his nomination as the Democratic presidential candidate. Earlier, on July 12, he had announced his choice of running mate, Sen. Lloyd Bentsen of Texas.

The only risk of serious political conflict at the convention came from Jesse Jackson, who finished second in the delegate race. The convention approached with some of Jackson's hard-core supporters threatening boycotts, protest marches and walkouts. Some saw Dukakis' selection of Bentsen as a snub to Jackson. A breakthrough, however, came at a three-hour morning meeting July 18 of Dukakis, Jackson and Bentsen.

At an ensuing news conference, Dukakis praised Jackson for his voter-registration accomplishments and for his efforts to reach out to constituent groups beyond his black base. He then stated, "I want Jesse Jackson to play a major role in this campaign. . . . He is going to be involved actively, and fully."

Jackson appeared to concur, though he said he would follow through on his plan to have his name placed in nomination the night of July 20 and even joked that he was still hoping for a "Chicago miracle." But he did agree that he and Dukakis had discussed "a relationship of substance . . . the commitment to help build a team that will expand our party and carry us to victory in November." In answer to a reporter's question, he said he no longer sought the vice presidency.

With the Dukakis-Jackson agreement reached, the atmosphere inside Atlanta's Omni Coliseum on opening night of the convention was remarkably fraternal. Democratic National Committee Chairman Paul G. Kirk Jr. persistently underlined the theme of unity, pointing to the fact that the credentials and rules reports — sources of numerous battles and test votes at past conventions — had been previously ratified by the Dukakis and Jackson campaigns. Both were adopted without discussion.

Texas state treasurer Ann Richards delivered the keynote address, which centered on a critique of the Republicans' alleged lack of concern for the interests of working

Americans. While Richards did not outline a bold new Democratic vision, she won widespread praise for her folksy, personalized delivery and her trademark sense of humor.

But any excitement that Richards generated was sapped by a series of less-than-enthralling events that followed, which culminated in an address by former president Jimmy Carter. Although the convention gave Carter an enthusiastic greeting — symbolic of the resurrection of his image within the party — many delegates became distracted during his litany of Democratic party virtues.

In the afternoon of the second day of the convention, the candidates' campaigns eliminated their last major grounds for argument — the minority planks of the Democratic platform — with a minimum of rancor.

In the debate on what the Jackson campaign called the "fair tax" plank, Manhattan Borough president David Dinkins said that "the rich and the corporations" received the bulk of the Reagan administration tax cuts, which he blamed for the large federal deficits. He echoed Jackson's line that, in closing the deficit, those tax-cut beneficiaries would now "have to pay for the party."

But Denver mayor Federico Pena called for delegates to reject the plank, warning that its passage would be campaign fodder for Republicans, who persistently portrayed the Democrats as the "tax-and-spend" party. The measure was defeated by a delegate vote of 1,091.5 to 2,499. *(Chart, p. 253)*

More emotion was expressed over the nuclear-strategy plank, with Jackson supporters waving placards and changing, "No first use!" Supporters of the plank said it would show Democratic commitment to world peace. But Dukakis supporters, while expressing solidarity with the cause of nuclear disarmament, said the defense strategy that called for use of nuclear weapons in the event of an invasion of Western Europe was a bedrock of the NATO alliance. They also said that, should Dukakis be elected president, the plank could deprive him of a key tool to force the Soviets to the bargaining table.

The minority plank was defeated, 1,220.59 to 2,474.13. *(Chart, p. 253)*

The most divisive issue was that of Palestinian rights. Arab-American activist James Zogby said that while they had agreed not to bring the subject to a vote, supporters of Palestinian self-determination had won a victory by getting the party to debate the issue openly.

Without debate the delegates adopted a compromise package of nine other amendments pressed by the Jackson camp and accepted by Dukakis. These embodied much of the spirit and some of the specifics that Jackson had tried to insert into the platform all along — a denunciation of aid to "irregular" forces in Central America, a national health program, sharply higher spending for education and a moratorium on missile flight testing.

Notwithstanding the compromise language inserted into the platform at Jackson's insistence, the overall platform debate represented a victory for the Dukakis forces. From the beginning, they had been bent on keeping the platform a document of general party themes, free of the kinds of commitments to programs and constituency groups that had aided past Republican efforts to label the Democrats the "party of special interests."

If the afternoon session was symbolic of the Democratic party's effort to moderate its national image, the evening session was a tribute to the liberalism that had been the dominant party thread for two decades. The schedule featured leading figures of the party's liberal wing and was capped by an electrifying speech by Jackson.

Edward M. Kennedy, introduced by his nephew John F. Kennedy Jr., warmed up the crowd with rousing political rhetoric. The Massachusetts senator accused Bush of "burying his head in his hands and hiding from the record of Reagan-Bush mistakes." Kennedy then listed a series of issues — Iran-contra, the Noriega drug connection, domestic budget cuts, civil rights — on which he said the Reagan administration had made wrong choices, following each example with the refrain, "Where was George?" The delegates spontaneously picked up the slogan as a chant.

In anticipation of Jackson's speech, delegates, guests, reporters and photographers filled the narrow aisles of the arena. The Omni was so packed that convention officials were compelled to close the doors at the suggestion of the fire marshal, shutting out a number of infuriated delegates and media representatives in the process.

Jackson entered the auditorium at 10:55 p.m. to a roaring ovation and a sea of red-and-white "Jesse!" placards. As an expression of unity, virtually all of the Dukakis delegates had kept their banners out of sight, and many had given up their passes so Jackson alternates could be on the floor to cheer.

Many party professionals had wondered whether Jackson's address might become a vehicle for venting whatever resentment lingered from the rift over the running-mate selection. But while his speech stopped short of an outright endorsement of Dukakis, Jackson expressed his solidarity with the Democratic effort to regain the White House. He praised Dukakis for resisting the "temptation to stoop to demagoguery" and said he had demonstrated "a good mind, fast at work, with steel nerves, guiding his campaign out of the crowded field without appeal to the worst in us."

In his 55-minute speech, Jackson invoked the heroes of the civil rights movement, including Martin Luther King Jr., and briefly shared the stage with Rosa Parks, heroine of the 1955 Montgomery, Ala., bus boycott. He said that his campaign was a historic culmination of earlier black struggles. "As a tribute to the endurance, the patience, the courage of our forefathers and mothers . . . tomorrow night my name will go into nomination for the presidency of the United States of America," Jackson declared.

Jackson called for liberal and conservative Democrats to find "common ground" of agreement on issues of social welfare, human rights and world peace; for U.S. allies to pay a greater share of their defense burden so that American resources could be shifted to housing, health care and other social needs; for the government to act to protect the family farm and to promote domestic oil production; and for youths to avoid the temptations of illegal drugs.

Jackson received the most emotional response with a paean to the struggles of the low-income working American. The speech was climaxed by Jackson's call for Americans to "never surrender" to poverty, drugs, malnutrition, inequality, disease or physical handicaps.

The evening session of the next day, July 20, featured the presidential nominating process and balloting. Jackson's name was placed in nomination by a trio intended to symbolize the candidate's concept of the "Rainbow Coalition." International Association of Machinists President William Winpisinger, who is white, made the nominating speech; he was seconded by state senator Olga Mendez of New York, a Puerto Rican, and by black state representative Maxine Waters of California.

Arkansas governor Bill Clinton was the personal choice

of Dukakis, his friend and fellow governor, to be his nominator. In a speech that will be remembered for its duration — 35 minutes — rather than its content, he emphasized Dukakis' personal qualities and praised Dukakis as a political leader, describing him as "a man with vision, a shining vision for this country."

The roll call, marked by the usual "Great State of ..." boosterism, went as predetermined by the primary-and-caucus process. The one surprise came from Minnesota, where three anti-abortion delegates registered support for Rep. Richard H. Stallings, Idaho, who shared their opposition to abortion.

The only apparent suspense was which state would put Dukakis over the 2,082-vote total he needed to clinch the nomination. But the Dukakis campaign — cognizant of California's importance in November — had even taken care of that detail. They arranged for several delegations to pass on the first call to ensure that California would have the honor. The final tally was Dukakis 2,876.25 delegate votes; Jackson, 1,218.5. *(Chart, p. 253)*

Following the roll call, Speaker Willie Brown Jr., of the California House and Jackson's national campaign chairman, announced that Jackson had phoned to ask that Dukakis be endorsed by acclamation. A near-unanimous chorus of "ayes" followed.

Party officials created a Hollywood-style show for the convention finale July 21. The schedule was crafted with prime-time television foremost in mind, and, in an unusual achievement for the traditionally unruly Democrats, the program went off like clockwork.

Rep. Dan Rostenkowski, Ill., gave a rousing nominating speech for Bentsen. He got his strongest response with a passage urging working-class Americans to "come home to your party ... the party that has contributed so much to our social progress."

Following Rostenkowski, Sen. Thomas A. Daschle, S.D., lauded Bentsen's commitment to rural America. The delegates then gave a long ovation to former Texas Rep. Barbara C. Jordan, a major figure in the 1974 Judiciary Committee impeachment hearings on President Richard Nixon and the 1976 Democratic convention keynoter.

Jordan praised her longtime ally Bentsen in remarks seemingly aimed at Jackson delegates. Saying that it was a mistake to label him a conservative, Jordan said, "Lloyd Bentsen ... believes in the principles of the Democratic party just like you do."

The compelling need for a defense of Bentsen already had been removed, though. Talk of a challenge to his nomination, so rife early in the week, had been silenced by the Dukakis-Jackson agreement and the ensuing push for unity. Jackson selected Rep. Mickey Leland of Texas to call for Bentsen's nomination by acclamation. The motion was passed overwhelmingly, with just a scattering of "no" votes.

Bentsen made a restrained address, true to his image as a dignified, formal and somewhat patrician figure. Shortly into his acceptance speech, Bentsen extended an olive branch to the Jackson supporters who had been deeply offended by Dukakis's vice presidential decision. He told the convention that "equality of opportunity is the ultimate civil right." He then hailed Jackson for "leadership and achievements [that] transcend pride of party and inspire a nation."

Bentsen received his strongest applause by calling for a plant-closing-notification law. He indicted the Reagan presidency as "an eight-year coma in which slogans were confused with solutions and rhetoric passed for reality."

Invoking a familiar Democratic theme, he said that many Americans had missed out on the prosperity of the Reagan years. He accused Reagan of financing prosperity by writing "hot checks for $200 billion a year." Dukakis, Bentsen said, was "talking about putting the American dream," including home ownership and a college education, "back in the reach of all the American people."

Though his speech was no rouser, Bentsen, who defeated Bush in a 1970 Senate contest, left the podium to a chant of "Beat Bush Again."

A series of theatrical touches primed the delegates for Dukakis. A specially commissioned musical piece, written by Boston Pops Orchestra Director John Williams and conducted by Dukakis's father-in-law, Harry Ellis Dickson, was performed. Dukakis was then introduced by his cousin, Olympia Dukakis, an Oscar-winning actress and New Jersey delegate.

Dukakis described himself as a product of the American dream. He paid tribute to his immigrant parents, and tears welled in his eyes when he talked about how proud his father would have been of his son, and of his adopted country. He cited individuals who represented America's cultural diversity, including Jackson.

Dukakis continued to feed the convention's celebratory mood, stating that "the Reagan era is over, and a new era is about to begin." He said it is time "to exchange voodoo economics for can-do economics," adding, "This election isn't about ideology. It's about competence."

Throughout the speech, Dukakis managed to hit buttons that energized the partisan audience, while avoiding contentious issues, such as tax increases and abortion, that had hurt the Democrats in recent presidential elections. The issues he emphasized were more popular Democratic stands on education, universal health care and plant-closing notification.

Dukakis's speech was interrupted several times by chants from the crowd. When he referred to Bush's failure to intercede to stop the Iran arms sales, the convention delegates reprised their "Where was George?" theme. And in a wave of optimism not seen since the post-Watergate 1976 convention, the delegates chanted, "We're gonna win."

Following are excerpts from the Democratic platform of 1988:

**Economy.** ... We believe that all Americans have a fundamental right to economic justice in a stronger, surer national economy, an economy that must grow steadily without inflation, that can generate a rising standard of living for all and fulfill the desire of all to work in dignity up to their full potential in good health with good jobs at good wages, an economy that is prosperous in every region, from coast to coast, including our rural towns and our older industrial communities, our mining towns, our energy producing areas and the urban areas that have been neglected for the past seven years.

**Employment, Child Care.** We believe that, as a first-rate world power moving into the 21st century, we can have a first-rate full employment economy, with an indexed minimum wage that can help lift and keep families out of poverty, with training and employment programs — including child care and health care — that can help people move from welfare to work, with portable pensions and an adequate Social Security System, safeguarded against emasculation and privatization, that can help assure a comfortable and fulfilling old age, with opportunities for voluntary national public service, above and beyond current services, that can enrich our communities, and with all workers assured the protection of an effective law that guarantees their rights to organize, join the union of their choice, and bargain collectively with their employer, free from anti-union tactics. . . .

We believe that Government should set the standard in recognizing that worker productivity is enhanced by the principle of pay equity for working women and no substandard wage competition for public contracts; by family leave policies that no longer force employees to choose between their jobs and their children or ailing parents; by safe and healthy work places, now jeopardized by seven callous years of lowered and unenforced occupational safety standards for American workers; and by major increases in assistance making child care more available and affordable to low and middle income families, helping states build a strong child care infrastructure, setting minimum standards for health, safety, and quality, and thereby enabling parents to work and their children to get an early start on their education and personal fulfillment. We believe that the strength of our families is enhanced by programs to prevent abuse and malnutrition among children, crime, dropouts and pregnancy among teenagers and violence in the family; by aggressive child support enforcement; and by emphasizing family preservation and quality foster care. We further believe that our nation faces a crisis of under-investment in our children, particularly in the early years of life. Strong, healthy babies with early opportunities that foster intellectual, emotional and physical growth begin school with an enhanced foundation for learning. There are few better investments for this country than prenatal care, infant nutrition and preschool education, and there are few more successful programs than WIC, Head Start, and prenatal care.

**Trade.** . . . America needs more trade, fair trade, an administration willing to use all the tools available to better manage our trade in order to export more American goods and fewer American jobs, an administration willing to recognize in the formulation and enforcement of our trade laws that workers' rights are important human rights abroad as well as at home, and that advance notice of plant closings and major layoffs is not only fundamentally right but also economically sound. . . . [W]e . . . can and must improve our competitiveness in the world economy, using our best minds to create the most advanced technology in the world through a greater commitment to civilian research and development and to science, engineering and mathematics training, through more public-private and business-labor cooperation and mutual respect, through more intergovernmental partnerships, and through a better balance between fiscal and monetary policy and between military and civilian research and development. We further believe in halting such irresponsible corporate conduct as unproductive takeovers, monopolistic mergers, insider trading, and golden parachutes for executives by reinvigorating our anti-trust and securities laws, reviewing large mergers, and discouraging short-term speculation taking place at the expense of long-term investment.

**Education.** . . . [T]he education of our citizens, from Head Start to institutions of higher learning, deserves our highest priority. . . . We pledge to better balance our national priorities by significantly increasing federal funding for education. We believe that this nation needs to invest in its children on the front side of life by expanding the availability of pre-school education for children at risk; to invest in its teachers through training and enrichment programs, including a National Teacher Corps to recruit teachers for tomorrow, especially minorities, with scholarships today; to commit itself for the first time to the principle that no one should be denied the opportunity to attend college for financial reasons; to ensure equal access to education by providing incentives and mechanisms for the equalization of financing among local school districts within each state; to reverse cuts made in compensatory reading, math and enrichment services to low income children; and to expand support for bilingual education, historically Black and Hispanic institutions, the education of those with special needs, the arts and humanities, and an aggressive campaign to end illiteracy.

**Drugs.** . . . [I]llegal drugs pose a direct threat to the security of our nation from coast to coast. . . . [E]very arm and agency of government at every federal, state and local level — including every useful diplomatic, military, educational, medical and law enforcement effort necessary — should at long last be mobilized and coordinated with private efforts under the direction of a National Drug "Czar" to halt both the international supply and the domestic demand for illegal drugs now ravaging our country; and that the legalization of illicit drugs would represent a tragic surrender in a war we intend to win. We believe that this effort should include comprehensive programs to educate our children at the earliest ages on the dangers of alcohol and drug abuse, readily available treatment and counseling for those who seek to address their dependency, the strengthening of vital interdiction agencies such as the U.S. Coast Guard and Customs, a summit of Western Hemispheric nations to coordinate efforts to cut off drugs at the source, and foreign development assistance to reform drug-based economies by promoting crop substitution.

**Criminal Justice.** . . . [T]he federal government should provide increased assistance to local criminal justice agencies, enforce a ban on "cop killer" bullets that have no purpose other than the killing and maiming of law enforcement officers, reinforce our commitment to help crime victims, and assume a leadership role in securing the safety of our neighborhoods and homes.

**Individual Rights.** . . . [W]e honor our multicultural heritage by assuring equal access to government services, employment, housing, business enterprise and education to every citizen regardless of race, sex, national origin, religion, age, handicapping condition or sexual orientation; that these rights are without exception too precious to be jeopardized by Federal Judges and Justice Department officials chosen during the past seven years — by a political party increasingly monolithic both racially and culturally — more for their unenlightened ideological views than for their respect for the rule of law. . . . [W]e must work for the adoption of the Equal Rights Amendment to the Constitution; that the fundamental right of reproductive choice should be guaranteed regardless of ability to pay; that our machinery for civil rights enforcement and legal services to the poor should be rebuilt and vigorously utilized; and that our immigration policy should be reformed to promote fairness, non-discrimination and family reunification and to reflect our constitutional freedoms of speech, association and travel. We further believe that the voting rights of all minorities should be protected, the recent surge in hate violence and negative stereotyping combatted, the discriminatory English-only pressure groups resisted, our treaty commitments with Native Americans enforced by culturally sensitive officials, and the lingering effects of past discrimination eliminated by affirmative action, including goals, timetables, and procurement set-asides.

**Housing.** . . . [T]he housing crisis of the 1980s must be halted — a crisis that has left this country battered by a rising tide of homelessness unprecedented since the Great Depression, by a tightening squeeze on low and moderate income families that is projected to leave seven million people without affordable housing by 1993, and by a bleak outlook for young working families who cannot afford to buy their first home. . . . We believe that homelessness — a national shame — should be ended in America; that the supply of affordable housing should be expanded in order to avoid the projected shortfall; that employer-assisted housing and development by community-based non-profit organizations should be encouraged; that the inventory of public and subsidized housing should be renovated, preserved and increased; that foreclosed government property should be restored to productive use; and that first-time home buyers should be assisted.

**Infrastructure.** . . . [W]e can rebuild America, creating jobs at good wages through a national reinvestment strategy to construct new housing, repair our sewers, rebuild our roads and replace our bridges. We believe that we must pursue needed investment through innovative partnerships and creative financing mechanisms such as a voluntary program to invest a portion of public and private pension funds as a steady source of investment capital by guaranteeing security and a fair rate of return and assuring sound project management.

**Health Care.** . . . We believe that all Americans should enjoy access to affordable, comprehensive health services for both the physically and mentally ill, from prenatal care for pregnant women at risk to more adequate care for our Vietnam and other veterans, from well-baby care to childhood immunization to Medicare; that a national health program providing federal coordination and leadership is necessary to restrain health care costs while assuring quality care and advanced medical research; that quality, affordable, long-term home and health care should be available to all senior and disabled citizens, allowing them to live with dignity in the most appropriate setting; that an important first step toward comprehensive health services is to ensure that every family should have the security of basic health insurance; and that the HIV/AIDS epidemic is an unprecedented public health emergency requiring increased support for accelerated research on, and expedited FDA approval of, treatments and vaccines, comprehensive education and prevention, compassionate patient care, adoption of the public health community consensus on voluntary and confidential testing and counseling, and protection of the civil rights of those suffering from AIDS or AIDS-Related Complex or testing positive for the HIV antibody.

**Environment.** . . . [P]ollution must be stopped at the source by shifting to new, environmentally sound manufacturing and farming technologies. . . . [T]he federal government must promote recycling as the best, least costly way to solve the trash crisis, aggressively enforce toxic waste laws and require polluters to be responsible for future clean-up costs. . . . [T]his nation must redouble its efforts to provide clean waterways, sound water management and safe drinkable ground water throughout the country. . . . [O]ur national parks, forests, wildlife refuges, and coastal zones must be protected and used only in an environmentally sound manner. . . . [A]ll offshore oil drilling in environmentally sensitive areas should be opposed. . . . [R]egular world environmental summits should be convened by the United States to address the depletion of the ozone layer, the "greenhouse effect," the destruction of tropical forests and other global threats and to create a global action plan for environmental restoration.

**Agriculture.** . . . [A]ll Americans, producers and consumers alike, benefit when food and fiber are produced not by a few large corporations and conglomerates but by hundreds of thousands of family farmers obtaining a fair price for their product. . . . [A] workable agricultural policy should include supply management, reasonable price supports, soil conservation and protection of rural water quality, credit and foreclosure relief, the return of federally held foreclosed lands to minority, beginning and restarting farmers, the development of new uses and markets for American farm products, improved disaster relief, and the revitalization of rural America through new sources of capital for rural business and new federal support for rural health care, housing, education, water supply and infrastructure. . . .

**Energy.** We believe that a balanced, coherent energy policy, based on dependable supplies at reasonable prices, is necessary to protect our national security, ensure a clean environment, and promote stable economic growth and prosperity, both nationally and in our energy producing regions; that the inevitable transition from our present, nearly total dependence on increasingly scarce and environmentally damaging non-renewable sources to renewable sources should begin now; that such a policy includes increased cooperation with our hemispheric neighbors, filling the Strategic Petroleum Reserve, promoting the use of natural gas, methanol and ethanol as alternative transportation fuels, encouraging the use of our vast natural gas and coal reserves while aggressively developing clean coal technology to combat acid rain, and providing targeted new incentives for new oil and gas drilling and development, for the development of renewable and alternative sources of energy, and for promotion of energy conservation. We believe that with these changes the country could reduce its reliance on nuclear power while insisting that all plants are safe, environmentally sound, and assured of safe waste disposal.

**Voting Rights.** . . . [T]his country's democratic processes must be revitalized: by securing universal, same day and mail-in voter registration as well as registration on the premises of appropriate government agencies; by preventing the misuse of at-large elections, the abuse of election day challenges and registration roll purges, any undercounting in the national census, and any dilution of the one-person, one-vote principle; by ending discrimination against public employees who are denied the right to full political participation; by supporting statehood for the District of Columbia; by treating the offshore territories under our flag equitably and sensitively under federal policies, assisting their economic and social development and respecting their right to decide their future in their relationship with the United States; by empowering the commonwealth of Puerto Rico with greater autonomy within its relationship with the United States to achieve the economic, social and political goals of its people, and by giving it just and fair participation in federal programs; by assuring and pledging the full and equal access of women and minorities to elective office and party endorsement; and by minimizing the domination and distortion of our elections by moneyed interests. . . .

**Foreign Policy.** We believe in a clear-headed, tough-minded, decisive American foreign policy that will reflect the changing nature of threats to our security and respond to them in a way that reflects our values and the support of our people, a foreign policy that will respect our Constitution, our Congress and our traditional democratic principles and will in turn be respected for its quiet strength, its bipartisan goals, and its steadfast attention to the concerns and contributions of our allies and international organizations. We believe that we must reassume a role of responsible active international leadership based upon our commitment to democracy, human rights and a more secure world; that this nation, as the world power with the broadest global interests and concerns, has a greater stake than any in building a world at peace and governed by law; that we can neither police the world nor retreat from it; and that to have reliable allies we must be a reliable ally.

**Defense.** We believe that our national strength has been sapped by a defense establishment wasting money on duplicative and dubious new weapons instead of investing more in readiness and mobility; that our national strength will be enhanced by more stable defense budgets and by a commitment from our allies to assume a greater share of the costs and responsibilities required to maintain peace and liberty; and that as military spending and priorities change, government should encourage the conversion of affected military facilities and the retraining of workers to facilitate the creation of new forms of communication, space development and new peacetime growth and productivity.

We believe in an America that will promote peace and prevent war ... by maintaining a stable nuclear deterrent sufficient to counter any Soviet threat, by standing up to any American adversary whenever necessary and sitting down with him whenever possible, by making clear our readiness to use force when force is required to protect our essential security commitments, by testing the intentions of the new Soviet leaders about arms control, emigration, human rights and other issues, and by matching them not merely in rhetoric but in reciprocal initiatives and innovation, which takes advantage of what may be the greatest opportunity of our lifetime to establish a new, mutually beneficial relationship with the Soviet Union, in which we engage in joint efforts to combat environmental threats, explore peaceful uses of space and eradicate disease and poverty in the developing world, and in a mutual effort to transform the arms race that neither side can win into a contest for people's minds, a contest we know our side will win.

**Arms Control.** We believe in following up the INF [intermediate-range nuclear force] Treaty, a commendable first step, with mutual, verifiable and enforceable agreements that will make significant reductions in strategic weapons in a way that diminishes the risk of nuclear attack by either superpower; reduce conventional forces to lower and equivalent levels in Europe, requiring deeper cuts on the Warsaw Pact side; ban chemical and space weapons in their entirety; promptly initiate a mutual moratorium on missile flight testing and halt all nuclear weapons testing while strengthening our efforts to prevent the spread of these weapons to other nations before the nightmare of nuclear terrorism engulfs us all.

**International Relations.** We believe in an America that recognizes not only the realities of East-West relations, but the challenges and opportunities of the developing world; that will support and strengthen international law and institutions, promote human and political rights and measure them by one yardstick, and work for economic growth and development. We believe that we must provide leadership, compassion and economic assistance to those nations stunted by overwhelming debt, deprivation and austerity, and that we must work to promote active agreements between developing and industrial countries, and the major public and commercial lenders, to provide debt relief and rekindle and sustain economic growth and democracy in Latin America, Asia, and the poorest continent, Africa, which deserves special attention. We further believe that we must enlist the trade surplus nations to join with us in supporting new aid initiatives to fuel growth in developing countries that, though economically depressed, are rich in human and natural potential.

We believe this country should work harder to stop the supplies of arms, from both East and West, that fuel conflict in regions such as the Persian Gulf and Angola.... [W]e believe that this country, maintaining the special relationship with Israel founded upon mutually shared values and strategic interests, should provide new leadership to deliver the promise of peace and security through negotiations that has been held out to Israel and its neighbors by the Camp David Accords. We support the sovereignty, independence, and territorial integrity of Lebanon with a central government strong enough to unite its people, maintain order and live in peace in the region. We are committed to Persian Gulf security and freedom of navigation of international waters, and to an end to the Iran-Iraq war by promoting United Nations efforts to achieve a ceasefire and a negotiated settlement, through an arms embargo on the combatants. We further believe that

the United States must fully support the Arias Peace Plan, which calls for an end to the fighting, national reconciliation, guarantees of justice, freedom, human rights and democracy, an end to support for irregular forces, and a commitment by the Central American governments to prevent the use of their territory to destabilize others in the region. Instead of the current emphasis on military solutions we will use negotiations and incentives to encourage free and fair elections and security for all nations in the region. We will cease dealing with drug smugglers and seek to reconcile our differences with countries in Central America, enabling the United States and other countries to focus on the pressing social and economic needs of the people of that region. We further believe in pursuing a policy of economic cooperation instead of confrontation with Mexico and our other hemispheric friends; in helping all developing countries build their own peaceful democratic institutions free from foreign troops, subversion and domination and free from domestic dictators and aggressors; in honoring our treaty obligations; and in using all the tools at our disposal, including diplomacy, trade, aid, food, ideas, and ideals, to defend and enlarge the horizons of freedom on this planet.

**Human Rights.** We believe in an America that will promote human rights, human dignity and human opportunity in every country on earth; that will fight discrimination, encourage free speech and association and decry oppression in nations friendly and unfriendly, communist and non-communist; that will encourage our European friends to respect human rights and resolve their long-standing differences over Northern Ireland and Cyprus; that will encourage wherever possible the forces of pluralism and democracy in Eastern Europe and that will support the struggle for human rights in Asia.

**South Africa.** We believe the apartheid regime in South Africa to be a uniquely repressive regime, ruthlessly deciding every aspect of public and private life by skin color, engaging in unrelenting violence against its citizens at home and promoting naked aggression against its neighbors in Africa. We believe the time has come to end all vestiges of the failed policy of constructive engagement, to declare South Africa a terrorist state, to impose comprehensive sanctions upon its economy, to lead the international community in participation in these actions, and to determine a certain date by which United States corporations must leave South Africa. We further believe that to achieve regional security in Southern Africa, we must press forcefully for Namibia's independence by calling for the end of South Africa's illegal occupation, a cease fire and elections, must end our counterproductive policy in Angola and must offer support and further assistance to Mozambique and other frontline states....

## Republicans

On the opening day of the Republican national convention, held Aug. 15-18 in New Orleans' Lousiana Superdome, the delegates hailed Ronald Reagan's valedictory, a swan song from a politician who had carried GOP conservatives to unprecedented levels of power. The delegates greeted Reagan as a conquering hero, and they cheered enthusiastically at many of his applause lines. But the mood was tempered by the poignancy of the moment — a realization that Reagan was making his last convention speech as leader of his party and his country, and that the future for Republicans was uncertain.

For his part, Reagan was firm if slightly subdued in his speech. He offered again his optimistic vision of America and took some predictable jabs at his Democratic critics. But the most pertinent symbol of Reagan's role in the 1988 campaign was his strong praise of Vice President George Bush as a key player in his administration. Stating that a regulatory task force headed by Bush had resulted in a reduction in bureaucratic paperwork, Reagan responded to the Democrats' "Where was George?" chant by intoning, "George was there." He also credited Bush with persuading NATO allies to accept American medium-range missiles, a move he said forced the Soviet Union to negotiate the intermediate-range nuclear force (INF) treaty.

Reagan's promise of campaign assistance and his call for Bush to "win one for the Gipper" was a lift for Bush supporters, who were disturbed by Reagan's previously pallid endorsement of their candidate. But the adulation afforded the president by the delegates was a reminder of why the party, fearing that the less charismatic Bush could be overshadowed, scheduled Reagan to speak on Aug. 15.

The Republicans had plenty of theater scheduled for Aug. 16, with an agenda that included New Jersey governor Thomas H. Kean's keynote address and speeches by evangelist and former GOP presidential candidate Pat Robertson, former United Nations Representative Jeane J. Kirkpatrick and former President Gerald R. Ford. But Bush himself stole the show with his midafternoon announcement that he had selected dark-horse prospect Sen. Dan Quayle of Indiana as his running mate.

Bush aides had said the candidate would not announce his choice until Aug. 18, to maintain some suspense and keep the television-viewing public focused on the convention. But after being greeted by the departing Reagan at the Belle Chasse Naval Air Station the morning of Aug. 16, Bush told reporters that he had settled on his choice.

Bush made the choice public at a welcoming ceremony on the New Orleans riverfront. He praised Quayle, who was a generation younger than Bush, as "a man of the future."

News reporters, meanwhile, had little to distract them from their rounds on the vice presidential rumor circuit as the reports of the credentials, rules, and platform committees were approved without debate in the morning session.

Though the delegates spent much of the evening session discussing what they knew about Quayle, a parade of speakers tried to engage their attention. A series of governors praised the GOP platform and compared its specifics with the generalities in the Democratic platform. The governors signaled the evening's theme, a portrayal of Massachusetts governor and Democratic presidential candidate Michael S. Dukakis and the Democrats as extreme liberals. California governor George Deukmejian, noting that Dukakis belonged to the American Civil Liberties Union (ACLU), said ACLU actually meant "Allowing Criminals to Leave Unsupervised" (a reference to a favorite GOP target, the longtime Massachusetts policy of prison furloughs).

Kirkpatrick's attack on Dukakis' foreign policy stances was warmly received. She said the contest between Dukakis and Bush was a choice between a "policy of unilateral concessions and wishful thinking or a policy of clarity and strength."

Much of keynoter speaker Kean's address was a traditional Republican assault on Democratic liberalism. Referring to the light shades of red, white, and blue used by the Democrats in Atlanta (lighting conditions at the Omni would have made bright colors look garish on television), Kean said that Americans "have no use for pastel patriotism."

Anti-abortion activists and religious conservatives, a large bloc within the Republican convention, had their moment with the appearance of Robertson. Insurgencies by Robertson supporters had led to intraparty divisions in several states. But Robertson officially released his delegates and pledged his support for the Republican ticket.

The session ended with Ford's speech. Ford hit hard at the Democrats for presenting themselves as the party of the American dream. He also reviewed Bush's extensive résumé, including his service as emissary to the People's Republic of China and CIA director under Ford.

There was no press "honeymoon" for the prospective vice presidential nominee. A series of tough questions about his background made Aug. 17 difficult for Quayle — and, by extension, for Bush.

At an afternoon news conference, their first formal appearance as the GOP team, Bush defended his choice of Quayle, who was much younger and had less government experience than many of the bypassed vice presidential prospects.

However, Quayle's answers to some of the questions he faced were not so deft. His first problem was with a question about a 1980 Florida incident in which Quayle, then a House member, and two colleagues were seen in the company of lobbyist Paula Parkinson, who later posed nude in *Playboy* magazine and said she had had sexual relationships with members of Congress. Quayle's defense at the time, that he had no involvement with Parkinson, never was refuted. But when asked if a version of the events that appeared to back up his story was true, he said, "No." When pressed, he said, "That has been covered, and there's nothing to it."

Quayle, a member of Indiana's Pulliam publishing family and one of the heirs to a family trust, also sought to deflect rumors about his wealth. He denied that his net worth was as high as $200 million.

The most potentially explosive issue raised at the news conference was whether Quayle had used family influence to gain enlistment in the Indiana National Guard in 1969 to avoid service in the Vietnam War. Quayle first referred to the question as "a cheap shot." But his answers did not defend his choice of the Guard over the combat services, and he said his thoughts at the time centered on plans for law school, marriage and family. He raised eyebrows with the off-the-cuff rejoinder, "I did not know in 1969 that I would be in this room today [as a vice presidential candidate], I confess."

The controversy, however, did not subdue the enthusiasm of convention delegates — for their soon-to-be presidential nominee George Bush or his choice of vice president.

In the evening session, Texas senator Phil Gramm took the podium to nominate Bush, lambasting the Democrats and praising Bush. The nomination was seconded by celebrities such as actress Helen Hayes, Pennsylvania State University football coach Joe Paterno, and Bush's Mexican-American daughter-in-law, Columba Bush.

The ensuing roll call turned into a frenzy of state self-promotion that took an hour and a half to complete. At 11:08 p.m. Central Daylight Time, George W. Bush announced the Texas delegation votes that put his father over the top. *(Chart, p. 253)*

With concerns about Quayle not abating, damage control became the major priority for Bush's new campaign chairman, James A. Baker III. Quayle was to address the Texas and Ohio delegations Aug. 18, but he canceled the campaign appearances, saying he had to rehearse his acceptance speech. That fueled rumors that he was to be dropped from the ticket. Late in the day, Baker, too, canceled several TV interviews. But he emerged early in the evening and trekked between network anchor booths to defend Quayle and roundly reject the rumors that the campaign considered dumping him.

During convention walk-throughs earlier in the day, Bush and Quayle had ignored a barrage of questions about the situation, allowing the convention proceedings to provide their response to the speculation. The answer came quickly. Shortly after a brief address by Barbara Bush, Quayle was placed in nomination and anointed with praise by a series of congressional colleagues, including several who had been considered for the vice presidential spot.

The Indiana senator was nominated by acclamation. A new party rule had eliminated the necessity of a roll call and made it difficult for dissident delegates to call for one if there was opposition to Bush's choice.

If Quayle was burdened with concerns over the military service issue, he checked those emotions backstage before giving his acceptance speech. The youthful-looking senator tackled his first appearance on the national stage with the cheerleader-like élan for which he was known.

Early on, Quayle confronted the National Guard issue briefly and with a somewhat defiant tone. After expressing pride in his congressional service, he said, "As a young man, I served six years in the National Guard, and like the millions of Americans who have served in the Guard . . . I am proud of it."

Stating that "the future under George Bush means peace and economic opportunity," Quayle lumped Dukakis in with other Democratic figures who were frequent targets of GOP criticism. "We do not need the future the Democratic party sees, the party of George McGovern, Jimmy Carter, Walter Mondale . . . Ted Kennedy, and his buddy, Michael Dukakis," Quayle said, as the delegates lustily booed each name.

Elucidating his own record, Quayle took credit for authoring the 1982 Job Training Partnership Act and discussed his membership on the Senate Armed Services Committee. He then proclaimed the "profound debt" that his generation — of which he was the first major-party national candidate — owed to Bush's generation "for bringing us to an era of peace and freedom and opportunity."

With Bush trailing Dukakis in public opinion polls, media commentators and Bush supporters alike said he had to make the "speech of his life" on the night of Aug. 18. Bush did not waste the opportunity.

"I mean to run hard, to fight hard, to stand on the issues — and I mean to win," Bush said early in his speech. And near its conclusion Bush said his experience as vice president had made him the candidate who was prepared to deal with the critical issues that came across the president's desk. "I am that man," Bush said emphatically, as the partisan crowd roared its approval.

Bush affirmed his vice presidential choice. "Born in the middle of the century, in the middle of America, and holding the promise of the future, I'm proud to have Dan Quayle at my side," Bush said.

Bush acknowledged the necessity of establishing his own identity. "Ronald Reagan asked for, and received, my candor; he never asked for, but he did receive, my loyalty," Bush said. "But now you must see me for what I am: the Republican candidate for president. . . . And now I turn to the American people to share my hopes and intentions, and why and where I wish to lead."

Bush hit on the conservative hot-button issues — the Pledge of Allegiance (Dukakis had vetoed, on constitutional grounds, a bill requiring Massachusetts public school students to recite the pledge), the death penalty, voluntary school prayer, gun ownership, opposition to abortion, prison furloughs — that had been raised by speaker after speaker during the convention.

But Bush prominently listed several social policy areas that had not ranked high in the conservative Republican rhetoric in the 1980s. He called for mainstreaming the disabled, ending ocean garbage-dumping, reducing acid rain, extending racial harmony and restoring pride and ethics to public service. He seemed to temper the anti-government sentiment so prominent in Reagan's politics.

While pledging "to be a patient friend to anyone . . . who will fight for freedom," he made no mention of aid to the Nicaraguan contras. He did not discuss the appointment of conservative judges to the federal judiciary.

Restating his promise not to raise taxes, which he said Dukakis would not rule out, Bush said he would tell persistent tax proponents to "Read my lips. 'No new taxes.' "

Like Reagan, who ended his 1980 acceptance speech with a moment of silent prayer, Bush finished with a flourish. He led the convention in the Pledge of Allegiance, ending a week in which a record may have been set for mentions of the pledge.

Following are excerpts from the Republican platform of 1988:

**Jobs.** . . . The Republican Party puts the creation of jobs and opportunity first. . . .

We will use new technologies, such as computer data bases and telecommunications, to strengthen and streamline job banks matching people who want work with available jobs.

We advocate incentives for educating, training, and retraining workers for new and better jobs — through programs like the Job Training Partnership Act, which provides for a public/private partnership. . . .

With its message of economic growth and opportunity, the GOP is the natural champion of blacks, minorities, women and ethnic Americans. . . .

We are the party of real social progress. Republicans welcome the millions of forward-looking Americans who want an "opportunity society," not a welfare state. . . .

● Families struggling near the poverty line are always hurt most by tax increases. . . . We will continue to reduce their burden.

● We advocate a youth training wage to expand opportunities and enable unskilled young people to enter the work force.

● As an alternative to inflationary — and job-destroying — increases in the minimum wage, we will work to boost the incomes of the working poor through the Earned Income Tax Credit. . . .

● We will reform welfare to encourage work as the ticket that guarantees full participation in American life.

● We will undertake a long overdue reform of the unemployment insurance program to reward workers who find new jobs quickly.

● We insist upon the right of Americans to work at home. The Home Work Rule, banning sale of certain items made at home, must go. . . .

● We will fight to end the Social Security earnings limitation for the elderly. . . . As a first step, we will remove the earnings limitation for those whose income is from child care.

We will continue our efforts . . . to revitalize our cities. We support, on the federal, State and local levels, enterprise zones to promote investment and job creation in beleaguered neighborhoods. . . .

**Small Business.** Republicans encourage the women and men in small businesses to think big. To help them create jobs, we will cut to 15% the current counterproductive capital gains tax. This will foster investment in new and untried ventures.... It will also build the retirement value of workers' pension funds and raise revenues for the federal government....

**Taxes.** *We oppose any attempts to increase taxes.* Tax increases harm the economic expansion and reverse the trend to restoring control of the economy to individual Americans.

We reject calls for higher taxes from all quarters — including "bipartisan commissions." The decisions of our government should not be left to a body of unelected officials....

Republicans know that sustaining the American economic miracle requires a growing pool of private savings.... To keep it going:

● We support incentives for private savings, such as our deductibility for IRA contributions.

● We oppose tax withholding on savings....

● We will reduce to 15 percent the tax rates for long-term capital gains to promote investment in jobs and to raise revenue for the federal government by touching off another surge of economic expansion....

**Public Services.** We resolve to defederalize, denationalize, and decentralize government monopolies that poorly serve the public and waste the taxpayer's dollars. To that end, we will foster competition wherever possible.

We advocate privatizing those government assets which would be more productive and better maintained in private ownership....

**Housing.** The best housing policy is sound economic policy. Low interest rates, low inflation rates, and the availability of a job with a good paycheck that makes a mortgage affordable are the best housing programs of all....

We want to foster greater choice in housing for all:

● First and foremost, Republicans stand united in defense of the homeowner's deduction for mortgage interest....

● We will continue our successful drive for lower interest rates.

● We support the efforts of those in the States who fight to lower property taxes that strike hardest at the poor, the elderly, large families, and family farmers.

● We support programs to allow low-income families to earn possession of their homes through urban and rural homesteading, cooperative ventures in construction and rehabilitation, and other pioneering projects that demonstrate the vitality of the private sector and individual initiative....

● We call for repeal of rent control laws....

**Federal Spending.** We call for structural changes to control government waste, including a two-year budget cycle, a super-majority requirement for raising taxes, a legislatively enacted line-item veto, individual transmission of spending bills, greater rescission authority for the chief executive and other reforms.

● We call for a flexible freeze on current government spending.... We oppose any increase in taxes....

● We believe the Grace Commission report to eliminate waste, inefficiency, and mismanagement in the federal government must be re-examined; its recommendations should be given a high profile by public policy officials.

● We call for a balanced budget amendment to the Constitution. If congressional Democrats continue to block it, we urge the States to renew their calls for a constitutional convention limited to consideration of such an amendment.

● We will use all constitutional authority to control congressional spending. This will include consideration of the inherent line-item veto power of the president....

**Trade.** We will not accept the loss of American jobs to nationalized, subsidized, protected foreign industries and will continue to negotiate assertively the destruction of trade barriers....

We will not tolerate unfair trade and will use free trade as a weapon against it. To ensure that rapid progress is forthcoming from our work through GATT [General Agreement on Tariffs and Trade], we stand ready to pursue special arrangements with nations which share our commitment to free trade.... We are prepared to negotiate free trade agreements with partners like the Republic of China on Taiwan and the Association of Southeast Asian Nations (ASEAN) countries if they are willing to open their markets to U.S. products....

We will use U.S. economic aid, whether bilateral or through international organizations, to promote free market reforms: lower marginal tax rates, less regulation, reduced trade barriers. We will work with developing nations to make their economies attractive to private investment — both domestic and foreign — the only lasting way to ensure that these nations can secure capital for growth. We support innovations to facilitate repayment of loans, including "debt for equity" swaps. We urge our representatives in all multilateral organizations such as the World Bank to support conditionality with all loans to encourage democracy, private sector development, and individual enterprise....

**Child Care.** The family's most important function is to raise the next generation of Americans, handing on to them the Judeo-Christian values of western civilization and our ideals of liberty....

Republicans affirm these commonsense principles of child care:

● The more options families have in child care, the better. Government must not constrain their decisions. Individual choice should determine child care arrangements for the family.

● The best care for most children, especially in the early years, is parental. Government must never hinder it.

● Public policy must acknowledge the full range of family situations. Mothers or fathers who stay at home, who work part-time, or who work full-time, should all receive the same respect and consideration in public policy.

● Child care by close relatives, religious organizations, and other community groups should never be inhibited by government programs or policies....

**Pornography.** We endorse legislative and regulatory efforts to anchor more securely a standard of decency in telecommunications and to prohibit the sale of sexually explicit materials in outlets operated on federal property. We commend those who refuse to sell pornographic material. We support the rigorous enforcement of "community standards" against pornography....

**Health.** Republicans believe in reduced government control of health care while maintaining an unequivocal commitment to quality health care....

● We will work for continuing progress in providing the most cost-effective, high-quality care.

● We will lead the fight for reform of medical malpractice laws to stop the intolerable escalation of malpractice insurance....

● We are opposed to the establishment of government mandated professional practice fees and services requirements as a condition of professional licensure or license renewal.

● We will continue to seek opportunities for private and public cooperation in support of hospices.

● We are committed to improving the quality and financing of long term care. We will remove regulatory and tax burdens to encourage private health insurance policies for acute or long term care. We will work for convertibility of savings, IRAs [Individual Retirement Accounts], life insurance, and pensions to pay for long term care.

● We will encourage the trend in the private sector to expand opportunities for home health care to protect the integrity of the family and to provide a less expensive alternative to hospital stays. We want to ensure flexibility for both Medicare and Medicaid in the provision of services to those who need them at home or elsewhere.

● We will foster employee choice in selecting health plans to promote personal responsibility for wellness.

● ... [W]e will work toward making catastrophic health care coverage available to our youngest citizens.

● Recognizing that inequities may exist in the current treatment of health insurance costs for those who are self employed, including farmers, we will study ways to more appropriately balance such costs....

● We will work to assure access to health care for all Americans through public and private initiatives....

**AIDS.** We will vigorously fight against AIDS.... Continued research on the virus is vital. We will continue as well to provide experimental drugs that may prolong life. We will establish within the Food and Drug Administration a process for expedited review of drugs which may benefit AIDS patients. We will allow supervised usage of experimental treatments.

We must not only marshal our scientific resources against AIDS, but must also protect those who do not have the disease. In this regard, education plays a critical role. AIDS education should emphasize that abstinence from drug abuse and sexual activity outside of marriage is the safest way to avoid infection with the AIDS virus. It is extremely important that testing and contact tracing measures be carried out and be appropriately confidential....

**Social Security.** We pledge to preserve the integrity of the Social Security trust funds. We encourage public officials at all levels to safeguard the integrity of public and private pension funds against raiding....

**Homeless.** Republicans are determined to help the homeless as a matter of ethical commitment, as well as sound public policy....

Republicans are ready to deal with the root causes of the problem:

● Our top priority must be homeless families. As part of an overall emphasis on family responsibility, we will strongly enforce child support laws. We call for development of a model divorce reform law that will adequately safeguard the economic and social interests of mothers and children while securing fairness to fathers in decisions concerning child custody and support....

● Rent controls promise housing below its market cost, but inevitably result in a shortage of decent homes. Our people should not have to underwrite any community which erodes its own housing supply by rent control....

**Equal Rights, Religious Rights, Abortion.** "Deep in our hearts, we do believe":

● That bigotry has no place in American life. We denounce those persons, organizations, publications and movements which practice or promote racism, anti-Semitism or religious intolerance.

● That the Pledge of Allegiance should be recited daily in schools in all States....

● In equal rights for all.

● In guaranteeing opportunity, not dictating the results of fair competition. We will resist efforts to replace equal rights with discriminatory quota systems and preferential treatment....

● In defending religious freedom. Mindful of our religious diversity, we firmly support the right of students to engage in voluntary prayer in schools. We call for full enforcement of the Republican legislation that now guarantees equal access to school facilities by student religious groups.

● That the unborn child has a fundamental right to life which cannot be infringed. We therefore reaffirm our support for a human life amendment to the Constitution, and we endorse legislation to make clear that the Fourteenth Amendment's protections apply to unborn children. We oppose the use of public revenues for abortion and will

eliminate funding for organizations which advocate or support abortion.

● We ... reaffirm our support for the appointment of judges at all levels of the judiciary who respect traditional family values and the sanctity of innocent human life.

● That churches, religious schools and any other religious institution should not be taxed....

**Disabled.** We support efforts to provide disabled voters full access to the polls and opportunity to participate in all aspects of the political process....

● We pledge to fight discrimination in health care.... [W]e insist upon full treatment for disabled infants....

● We will protect the rights established under the Education for All Handicapped Children Act, Section 504 of the Rehabilitation Act of 1973, and the Civil Rights of Institutionalized Persons Act. We will balance those rights against the public's right to be protected against diseases and conditions which threaten the health and safety of others....

**Native Americans.** We support self-determination for Indian Tribes in managing their own affairs and resources....

**Gun Ownership.** Republicans defend the constitutional right to keep and bear arms....

**Workers' Rights.** We affirm the right of all freely to form, join or assist labor organizations to bargain collectively, consistent with state laws.... We renew our long-standing support for the right of states to enact "Right-to-Work" laws. To protect the political rights of every worker, we oppose the use of compulsory dues or fees for partisan purposes....

The Republican Party supports legislation to amend the Hobbs Act, so that union officials, like all other Americans, are once again subject to the law's prohibition against extortion and violence in labor disputes.

We also support amendments to the National Labor Relations Act to provide greater protection from labor violence for workers who choose to work during strikes.

**Immigration.** We welcome those from other lands who bring to America their ideals and industry. At the same time, we insist upon our country's absolute right to control its borders....

**Education.** We will continue to ... expand horizons for learning, teaching, and mastering the future:

● We will use federal programs to foster excellence, rewarding "Merit Schools" which significantly improve education for their students.

● We will urge our local school districts to recognize the value of kindergarten and pre-kindergarten programs.

● We will direct federal matching funds to promote magnet schools that turn students toward the challenges of the future rather than the failures of the past.

● We will support laboratories of educational excellence in every State by refocusing federal funds for educational research.

● We will increase funding for the Head Start program....

● We will work with local schools and the private sector to develop models for evaluating teachers and other school officials.

● We will continue to support tuition tax credits for parents who choose to educate their children in private educational institutions....

In higher education, Republicans want to promote both opportunity and responsibility:

● We will keep resources focused on low-income students and address the barriers that discourage minority students from entering and succeeding in institutions of higher education....

● We will create a College Savings Bond program, with tax-exempt interest, to help families save for their children's higher education....

**Arts and Humanitites.** [W]e will:
- Continue the Republican economic renaissance which has made possible a tremendous outpouring of support for arts and humanities.
- Support full deductibility for donations to tax-exempt cultural institutions in order to encourage the private support of arts and humanities.
- Support the National Endowments for the Arts and Humanities and the Institute of Museum Services in their effort to support America's cultural institutions, artists, and scholars.
- Guard against the misuse of governmental grants by those who attack or derogate any race or creed and oppose the politicization of the National Endowments for the Arts and Humanities. . . .

**Science and Technology.** We will ensure that tax policy gives optimum incentive for the private sector to fund a high level of advanced research. Toward that end, we will make permanent the current tax credit for research and development and extend it to cooperative research ventures.
- We will strengthen the role of science and engineering in national policy by reinforcing the Office of the President's Science Advisor with the addition of a Science Advisory Council.
- We will encourage exchange of scientific information, especially between business and academic institutions, to speed up the application of research to benefit the public.
- We will improve the acquisition of scientific and technical information from other countries through expedited translation services and more aggressive outreach by federal agencies.
- We will include international technology flows as part of U.S. trade negotiations to ensure that the benefits of foreign advances are available to Americans.
- We will encourage innovation by strengthening protection for intellectual property at home and abroad. We will promote the public benefits that come from commercialization of research conducted under federal sponsorship by allowing private ownership of intellectual property developed in that manner.
- We will oppose regulation which stifles competition and hinders breakthroughs that can transform life for the better in areas like biotechnology. . . .

**Space.** The Republican Party will re-establish U.S. preeminence in space. It is our nation's frontier, our manifest destiny. . .

We support further development of the space station, the National Aerospace Plane, Project Pathfinder, a replacement shuttle, and the development of alternate launch vehicles. We endorse Mission to Planet Earth for space science to advance our understanding of environmental and climatic forces. . . .

We must commit to manned flight to Mars around the year 2000 and to continued exploration of the Moon. . . .

**Crime.** We will forge ahead with the Republican anti-crime agenda:
- . . . Republicans oppose furloughs for those criminals convicted of first degree murder and others who are serving a life sentence without possibility of parole. We believe that victims' rights should not be accorded less importance than those of convicted felons.
- We will re-establish the federal death penalty.
- We will reform the exclusionary rule, to prevent the release of guilty felons on technicalities.
- We will reform cumbersome habeas corpus procedures, used to delay cases and prevent punishment of the guilty.
- We support State laws implementing preventive detention to allow courts to deny bail to those considered dangerous and likely to commit additional crimes. . . .

**Drugs.** The Republican Party is committed to a drug-free America. Our policy is strict accountability, for users of illegal drugs as well as for those who profit by that usage. . . .
- The Republican Party unequivocally opposes legalizing or decriminalizing any illicit drug.
- We support strong penalties, including the death penalty for major drug traffickers. . . .
- Conviction for any drug crime should make the offender ineligible for discretionary federal assistance, grants, loans and contracts for a period of time.
- To impress young Americans with the seriousness of our fight against drugs, we urge States to suspend eligibility for a driver's license to anyone convicted of a drug offense. . . .
- We will strengthen interdiction of foreign drugs and expand the military's role in stopping traffickers.
- We will work with foreign governments to eradicate drug crops in their countries.
- In a summit of Western Hemisphere nations, we will seek total cooperation from other governments in wiping out the international drug empire. . . .
- [W]e encourage drug education in our schools. . . .
- We will encourage seizure and forfeiture programs by the Department of the Treasury and each State to take the profits out of illicit drug sales. . . .

We recognize the need to improve the availability of drug rehabilitation and treatment. . . .

**Agriculture.** Republicans will work to improve agricultural income through market returns at home and abroad, not government controls and subsidies:
- We pledge early action to renew and improve the successful farm programs set to expire in 1990.
- We pledge to continue international food assistance, including programs through the Eisenhower Food for Peace program, to feed the world's hungry and develop markets abroad.
- We will continue to provide leadership in the effort to improve standards of quality for grain and other agricultural products in order to meet international competition. . . .

**Oil.** We will set an energy policy for the United States to maintain a viable core industry and to ensure greater energy self sufficiency through private initiatives. We will adopt forceful initiatives to reverse the decline of our domestic oil production. Republicans support:
- Repeal of the counterproductive Windfall Profits Tax.
- Maintenance of our schedule for filling the Strategic Petroleum Reserve to reach 750 million barrels by 1993 and encouragement of our allies to maintain similar reserves.
- Tax incentives to save marginal wells, to encourage exploration for new oil, and to improve the recovery of oil still in place. . . .
- Exploration and development in promising areas, including federal lands and waters. . . in a manner that is protective of our environment and is in the best national interest. . . .

**Natural Gas.** More progress must be made in deregulation of natural gas:
- We support fully decontrolling prices and providing more open access to transportation.
- We also support the flexible use of natural gas to fuel automobiles and boilers. . . .

**Coal.** We should aggressively pursue the clean coal technology initiative. . . .
- A major effort should be made to encourage coal exports. . . .

**Nuclear Power.** We must preserve nuclear power as a safe and economic option to meet future electricity needs. . . . We will promote the adoption of standardized, cost-effective, and environmentally safe nuclear plant designs. We should enhance our efforts to manage nuclear waste and will insist on the highest standards of safety.

**Energy Alternatives, Conservation.** . . . We will set priorities and, where cost effective, support research and development for alternative fuels such as ethanol, methanol, and compressed natural gas. . . .

**Environment.** Republicans propose the following program for the environment in the 1990s:
- We will work for further reductions in air and water pollution and effective actions against the threats posed by acid rain. . . .
- A top priority of our country must be the continued improvement of our National Parks and wildlife areas. . . .
- We will fight to protect endangered species and to sustain biological diversity worldwide.
- We support federal, State, and local policies, including tax code provisions, which lead to the renewal and revitalization of our environment through restoration and which encourage scenic easements designed to preserve farmland and open spaces.
- We will protect the productive capacity of our lands by minimizing erosion. . . .

**Transportation.** [T]he Republican Party supports comprehensive efforts to curb drug and alcohol abuse in transportation, including drug and alcohol testing of all those in safety-related positions. . . .
- We advocate greater local autonomy in decision-making concerning the Highway Trust Fund and the Airport and Airway Trust Fund, and we oppose diversion of their resources to other purposes. . . .
- A new spirit of competitive enterprise in transportation throughout all levels of government should be encouraged. We will encourage both States and cities to utilize private companies, where effective, to operate commuter bus and transit services at substantial savings over what publicly funded systems cost. . . .
- We consider a privately owned merchant fleet and domestic shipbuilding capacity necessary to carry our nation's commerce in peace and to support our defense responsibilities. We will support programs to give the American maritime industry greater flexibility and freedom in meeting foreign competition. . . .

**Democracy Abroad.** [O]ur nation has a compelling interest to encourage and help actively to build the conditions of democracy wherever people strive for freedom. . . .

**The Americas.** The Republican party reaffirms its strong support of the Monroe Doctrine as the foundation for our policy throughout the Hemisphere, and pledges to conduct foreign policy in accord with its principles. . . .

Republicans will continue to oppose any normalization of relations with the government of Cuba as long as Fidel Castro continues to oppress the Cuban people at home and to support international terrorism and drug trafficking abroad. We will vigorously continue our support for establishment of a genuinely representative government directly elected by the Cuban people. We reiterate our support of Radio Marti and urge the creation of TV Marti to better reach the oppressed people of Cuba. . . .

Republicans view the Panama Canal as a critical, strategic artery connecting the Atlantic and Pacific. We believe that U.S. access to the Panama Canal must remain free and unencumbered consistent with the foremost principle of the Canal Treaty. . . .

**Soviet Union.** Steady American leadership is needed now more than ever to deal with the challenges posed by a rapidly changing Soviet Union. Americans cannot afford a future administration which eagerly attempts to embrace perceived, but as yet unproven, changes in Soviet policy. Nor can we indulge naive inexperience or an overly enthusiastic endorsement of current Soviet rhetoric. . . .

Republicans will continue to work with the new Soviet leadership. But the terms of the relationship will be based upon persistent and steady attention to certain fundamental principles:

- Human and religious rights in the Soviet Union.
- Economic reform in the Soviet Union.
- Cessation of Soviet support for communist regimes, radical groups, and terrorists.
- Verified full compliance with all arms control agreements.
- The right of free emigration for all Soviet citizens.
- Reduction in the Soviets' massive offensive strategic and conventional capability. . . .
- An end to untied credits. . . .

Republicans proudly reaffirm the Reagan Doctrine: America's commitment to aid freedom-fighters against the communist oppression which destroys freedom and the human spirit. . . .

We call on the Soviet government to release political prisoners, allow free emigration for "refuseniks" and others, and introduce full religious tolerance. . . .

We support the desire for freedom and self-determination of all those living in Captive Nations. . . .

**Europe, Defense of the West.** American aid and European industriousness have restored West Europe to a position of global strength. In accord with this, the Republican Party believes that all members of NATO should bear their fair share of the defense burden.

Republicans consider consultation and cooperation with our allies and friends to stop the proliferation of ballistic missile technology is a crucial allied goal. . . .

**Asia and the Pacific.** Japan has assumed the role earned by her people as a world economic power. The GOP believes that our relations can only be strengthened by attacking trade barriers, both tariff and nontariff, which not only hurt the U.S. now but also will eventually distort Japan's own economy. We believe that it is time for Japan to assume a greater role in this region and elsewhere. This should include a greater commitment to its own defense, commitment to leading the way in alleviating Third World debt, and fostering economic growth in fragile democracies. . . .

We pledge full cooperation in mutual defense of the Philippines and South Korea and the maintenance of our troops and bases vital for deterring aggression. . . . We reaffirm our commitment to the security of Taiwan and other key friends and allies in the region. . . .

[T]he Republican Party believes that we must continue to encourage the abandonment of political repression in the People's Republic of China and movement toward a free market. . . .

**The Middle East.** The foundation of our policy in the Middle East has been and must remain the promotion of a stable and lasting peace, recognizing our moral and strategic relationship with Israel. . . .

We will continue to maintain Israel's qualitative advantage over any adversary or coalition of adversaries.

We will continue to solidify our strategic relationship with Israel. . . .

We oppose the creation of an independent Palestinian state; its establishment is inimical to the security interests of Israel, Jordan and the U.S. . . .

Republicans see Egypt as a catalyst in the Arab world for advancing the cause of regional peace and security. For this reason, we believe that the United States has a significant stake in Egypt's continuing economic development and growth. . . .

**Africa.** Republicans have three priorities in our country's relations with Africa. The first is to oppose the forces of Marxist imperialism, which sustain the march of tyranny in Africa. . . .

Our second priority is the need to develop and sustain democracies in Africa. . . .

Our third area of concern is humanitarian assistance, especially food aid, to African nations. . . .

We believe that peace in southern Africa can best be achieved by the withdrawal of all foreign forces from Angola, complete independence and self-determination for the people of Namibia, a rapid process of internal reconciliation, and free and fair elections in both places....

Republicans deplore the apartheid system of South Africa and consider it morally repugnant.... Republicans call for an effective and coordinated policy that will promote equal rights and a peaceful transition to a truly representative constitutional form of government for all South Africans and the citizens of all nations throughout Africa....

**Terrorism.** The Republican Party believes that, in order to prevent terrorist attacks, the United States must maintain an unsurpassed intelligence capability. In cases of terrorism where prevention and deterrence are not enough, we believe that the United States must be prepared to use an appropriate mix of diplomatic, political, and military pressure and action to defeat the terrorist attack. The United States must continue to push for a Western commitment to a "no-concessions" policy on terrorism....

**Defense.** Republicans will ... advance the cause of world freedom and world peace by using our military credibility as a vehicle for security at home and peace abroad....

Even as we engage in dialogue with our adversaries to reduce the risks of war, we must continue to rely on nuclear weapons as our chief form of deterrence. This reliance will, however, move toward non-nuclear defensive weapon systems as we deploy the Strategic Defense System....

**Strategic Defense Initiative (SDI).** We are committed to rapid and certain deployment of SDI as technologies permit, and we will determine the exact architecture of the system as technologies are tested and proven....

**Strategic Forces.** Republicans will implement a strategic modernization program, emphasizing offensive and defensive strategic forces that are affordable and credible and that provide for a more stable balance....

In the conventional area, we need to ensure that our ground, naval, and air forces are outfitted with the finest equipment and weapons that modern technology can provide; we must also assure that they are fully capable of meeting any threats they may face. We put special emphasis on integrating the guard and reserves into effective combat forces. We must sustain and accelerate the progress we have already made to ensure that all of our forces are prepared for special operations warfare. In addition, advances in conventional weapons technology, specifically, "smart," highly accurate weaponry, must be accelerated....

**Arms Control.** Arms reduction can be an important aspect of our national policy only when agreements enhance the security of the United States and its allies. [T]rue arms reductions as a means to improve U.S. security, not just the perception of East-West detente....

● We will consistently undertake necessary improvements in our forces to maintain the effectiveness of our deterrent.

● We will not negotiate in areas which jeopardize our security. In particular, we will not compromise plans for the research, testing, or the rapid and certain deployment of SDI.

● We will insist on effective verification of compliance with any and all treaties and will take proportional, compensatory actions in cases of non-compliance....

● We will place special emphasis on negotiating asymmetrical Soviet cutbacks in those areas where a dangerous imbalance exists....

**Intelligence.** The Republican Party endorses covert action as one method of implementing U.S. national security policy. We reject legislative measures that impinge on the President's constitutional prerogatives....

# 1992 Conventions

## Presidential Candidates

**Bill Clinton**
**Democrat**

**George Bush**
**Republican**

### Democrats

The Democrats, meeting at Madison Square Garden in New York July 13-16, nominated a ticket consisting of two party moderates and adopted a platform heavily influenced by the centrist ideas of the Democratic Leadership Council (DLC) and its think tank, the Progressive Policy Institute. The convention stressed the themes Democrats planned to push in the fall campaign: redefining the party in the centrist vein, emphasizing youth, traditional family values and mainstream policy views — as desired by its nominee, Arkansas Gov. Bill Clinton. Every bit as unsubtle were the efforts to redefine his personal image. In appealing to youth, as in much else, Clinton, 45, was ably assisted by his running mate, Sen. Albert Gore, 44, of Tennessee, making their ticket the youngest in the twentieth century.

Despite former California governor Edmund G. "Jerry" Brown Jr.'s refusal to hop on the bandwagon or independent presidential candidate Ross Perot's stunning July 16 announcement from Dallas that he was bowing out (a decision he later reversed), Clinton controlled the focus and direction of the convention.

He declined to bow to the tough tactics of black activist and former presidential candidate Jesse L. Jackson, thus demonstrating a tough-mindedness and his own and signaling that he planed to put some distance between himself and Jackson's brand of urban liberalism.

There were reminders of Clinton's poor childhood, an effort to show he was in touch with the common people. There were clever and pointed attacks on President George Bush and Vice President Dan Quayle. There were consistent attempts to show that the Democratic Party had been unified and redefined in Clinton's centrist image. And there was a display of confidence, optimism and determination to end 12 years of GOP control of the White House.

The convention was marked by relatively few fractional disputes. Although Jesse Jackson was less than enthusiastic in his endorsement of the Arkansas governor, the important fact was that Clinton did not have to negotiate with Jackson the way his predecessors had. Brown remained the lone holdout, but Clinton's people never seemed overly upset by

that, and it did not prevent the Democrats from presenting an image of unity and harmony.

In their acceptance speeches, the final night, Clinton and Gore appealed to Perot supporters to recognize that Democrats could offer the change they wanted, but they otherwise stuck to the themes that had been stressed all week. Clinton used his speech to reintroduce himself to the voters. Recounting his fatherless childhood and stressing his small-town roots, Clinton summoned Americans to a "new covenant" of shared responsibility.

Controversy was almost entirely confined to the early part of the convention and involved primarily the question of whether Brown would be allowed to address the convention from the podium. Brown arrived with more than 600 delegates, enough to cause some disturbance. For most of the first session, they milled in the well beneath the main stage, heckling speakers and waving signs. Some covered their mouths with labels or duct tape.

The California delegation, although dominated by Clinton backers, united with the Brown delegates in support of their former governor's claim to address the convention from the podium. But neither Clinton nor DNC chair Ron Brown would relent in demanding an endorsement of the ticket as a condition for a prime-time speaking slot.

In the end, Jerry Brown was given the chance to give his own seconding speech on July 15. But that meant he spoke at shortly after 8 p.m. (5 p.m. in California), well before the commercial broadcast networks had switched from their regular programming to convention coverage. Gradually, the Brown delegates softened their protest and ended any serious attempt to disrupt the convention.

On July 13 a rousing welcome greeted Texas Gov. Ann W. Richards, the convention chair, who was best known nationally for her 1988 convention keynote address, in which she joked that Bush had been "born with a silver spoon in his mouth." She did not mention Bush by name this time, although she referred to her earlier speech and said: "I really hate to say it. But I told you so."

A large section of the opening program was designed to give exposure to six of the Democrats' leading female Senate candidates, all of whom spoke briefly from the convention floor. Dianne Feinstein of California, the last to speak, dismissed Republicans who referred to the wave of female candidates as "just gender politics." "It's not just about gender. It's about an agenda, an agenda of change," Feinstein said.

Heralding the "Year of the Woman," Democratic women played a major role at the convention, and issues women had highlighted — abortion rights, women's health care and the Clarence Thomas-Anita F. Hill hearings — were discussed from the podium, always to loud cheers from the floor.

Instead of the usual keynote speaker, the Democrats opted for three: Sen. Bill Bradley of New Jersey, Gov. Zell Miller of Georgia and former Texas representative Barbara Jordan. They stressed that the party had changed, blasted the Bush administration for economic policies that favored the rich and portrayed Clinton as a candidate from modest roots who was in touch with the people.

The Democrats later solidified their move to the center by adopting a platform devoid of many of the liberal planks and slogans that characterized previous documents. The debate over the party's manifesto was brief and uninspired. Clinton's overwhelming delegate strength and Democrats' frustration with three straight presidential losses helped mute any complaints over the centrist platform that clearly reflected the Clinton view of how the Democratic Party should present itself to voters.

The platform emphasized the need for economic growth, pledged to uphold law and order and to use military force overseas where necessary, called for a cutoff in welfare benefits after two years and supported the right of states to enact death penalty statutes. The platform did include more traditional Democratic viewpoints, such as protecting abortion rights, providing civil rights for homosexuals and taxing wealthy people at higher rates.

By prior agreement, delegates pledged to former senator Paul E. Tsongas of Massachusetts were allowed to offer and debate four minority planks. But it was a debate only in the loosest sense of the word. The speeches on both sides were brief, and most speakers for Clinton's position made little effort to engage in a point-by-point rebuttal.

Three of the planks ultimately were rejected by voice vote. One called for investment-related tax breaks. Another, on the deficit, called for limits on government spending, including Medicare and other politically sensitive entitlements. And a third proposed increasing the gasoline tax by 5 cents per gallon to benefit new spending on roads and bridges.

The hall's electronic voting system was to decide the fate of a fourth plank, which said that a middle-class tax cut and a tax credit for families with children ought to be delayed until the deficit was under control. This had a been a key difference between Tsongas and Clinton during the campaign. But the plank was defeated, 953 to 2,287. *(Chart, p. 255)*

The real drama came later, when two activists afflicted with the AIDS virus moved delegates to tears and when Jesse Jackson's rousing speech brought the convention to a fever pitch.

Former president Jimmy Carter was warmly received as he vouched for Clinton's character. He said he had known Clinton for more than 15 years and described him as "a friend and a fine governor" who had endured "false and misleading political attacks.... He is a man of honesty and integrity."

New York Gov. Mario M. Cuomo formally nominated Clinton, bringing the convention hall to a fever pitch with his denunciations of Bush and his salute to Clinton as the "Comeback Kid."

The final roll-call tally was Clinton, 3,372; Brown, 596; and Tsongas, 209, and subsequently the nomination was approved by acclamation. After the vote, the evening came to a dramatic and surprising end when the nominee answered chants of "we want Bill" by visiting the convention hall. Clinton, who had been watching the roll call two blocks away, walked most of the way to Madison Square Garden. His appearance a day early was unusual, but not unprecedented, and wildly welcomed by the delegates, who cheered, chanted and stomped in appreciation. Clinton likened his visit to the convention floor to that of John F. Kennedy in 1960, who he said "came to give a simple thank you."

On the fourth and final day of the convention — six months after the nation's first Democratic primary and more than four months before the election — Bill Clinton addressed the most pressing concern of his candidacy: How to define himself.

In his 54-minute speech, some 20 minutes longer than the seemingly interminable nominating speech he gave in 1988, Clinton zeroed in on the themes the campaign reflected in the party platform. He described himself as "a product of the American middle class" who would accept the nomination "in the name of all the people who do the work, pay the taxes, raise the kids and play by the rules — the hard-working Americans who make up our forgotten middle class." He talked about his own family and an "America where 'family values' live in our actions, not just our speeches."

Clinton and Gore paid respect to the intensity of women's political feeling. They endorsed abortion rights and equal rights in the workplace. Both lavished praise on their wives, receiving roars of approval from the audience. And when Clinton talked of a notional child "somewhere at this very moment ... born in America," he deliberately used female pronouns to refer to her.

Clinton often referred to himself as "the comeback kid." He claimed the title after rebounding from damaging stories about his alleged relationship with a singer and about the means by which he avoided the Vietnam War draft.

Clinton's acceptance speech was rife with references to God and faith, home and family. He twice quoted from Scripture. And a "New Covenant" was the Arkansan's successor phrase to the New Frontier and the New Deal.

Following are excerpts from the Democratic platform of 1992:

**Economic Opportunity.** Our party's first priority is opportunity — broad-based, non-inflationary economic growth and the opportunity that flows from it. Democrats in 1992 hold nothing more important for America than an economy that offers growth and jobs for all....

We reject both the do-nothing government of the last 12 years and the big government theory that says we can hamstring business and tax and spend our way to prosperity. Instead we offer a third way. Just as we have always viewed working men and women as the bedrock of our economy, we honor business as a noble endeavor and vow to create a far better climate for firms and independent contractors of all sizes that empower their workers, revolutionize their workplaces, respect the environment, and serve their communities well.

**Investment in America.** The only way to lay the foundation for renewed American prosperity is to spur both public and private investment. We must strive to close both the budget deficit and the investment gap. Our major competitors invest far more than we do in roads, bridges, and the information networks and technologies of the future. We will rebuild America by investing more in transportation, environmental technologies, defense conversion and a national information network.

To begin making our economy grow, the president and Congress should agree that savings from defense must be reinvested productively at home, including research, education and training, and other productive investments. This will sharply increase the meager 9 percent of the national budget now devoted to the future. We will create a "future budget" for investments that make us richer, to be kept separate from those parts of the budget that pay for the past and present. For the private sector, instead of a sweeping capital gains windfall to the wealthy and those who speculate, we will create an investment tax credit and a capital gains reduction for patient investors in emerging technologies and new business.

**Technological Innovation.** We will take back the advantage now ceded to Japan and Germany, which invest in new technologies at higher rates than the U.S. and have the growth to show for it. We will make the R&D tax credit permanent, double basic research in the key technologies for our future and create a civilian research agency to fast-forward their development.

**The Deficit.** Addressing the deficit requires fair and shared sacrifice of all Americans for the common good. . . . In place of the Republican supply side disaster, the Democratic investment, economic conversion and growth strategy will generate more revenues from a growing economy. We must also tackle spending by putting everything on the table; eliminate non-productive programs; achieve defense savings; reform entitlement programs to control soaring health-care costs; cut federal administrative costs by 3 percent annually for four years; limit increases in the "present budget" to the rate of growth in the average American's paycheck; apply a strict "pay as you go" rule to new non-investment spending; and make the rich pay their fair share in taxes. These choices will be made while protecting senior citizens and without further victimizing the poor. . . .

**Defense Conversion.** Our economy needs both the people and the funds released from defense at the Cold War's end. We will help the stalwarts of that struggle — the men and women who served in our armed forces and who work in our defense industries — make the most of a new era. We will provide early notice of program changes to give communities, business and workers enough time to plan. We will honor and support our veterans. Departing military personnel, defense workers and defense support personnel will have access to job retraining, continuing education, placement and relocation assistance, early retirement benefits for military personnel, and incentives to enter teaching, law enforcement and other vital civilian fields. Redirected national laboratories and a new civilian research agency will put defense scientists, engineers and technicians to work at critical civilian technologies. Small business defense firms will have technical assistance and transition grants and loans to help convert to civilian markets, and defense-dependent communities will have similar aid in planning and implementing conversion. We will strongly support our civilian space program, particularly environmental missions.

**Cities.** Only a robust economy will revitalize our cities. It is in all Americans' interest that the cities once again be places where hard-working families can put down roots and find good jobs, quality health care, affordable housing and decent schools. Democrats will create a new partnership to rebuild America's cities after 12 years of Republican neglect. This partnership will include consideration of the seven economic growth initiatives set forth by our nation's mayors. We will create jobs by investing significant resources to put people back to work, beginning with a summer jobs initiative and training programs for inner-city youth. We support a stronger community development program and targeted fis-

cal assistance to cities that need it most. A national public works investment and infrastructure program will provide jobs and strengthen our cities, suburbs, rural communities and country. We will encourage the flow of investment to inner-city development and housing through targeted enterprise zones and incentives for private and public pension funds to invest in urban and rural projects. While cracking down on redlining and housing discrimination, we also support and will enforce a revitalized Community Reinvestment Act that challenges banks to lend to entrepreneurs and development projects; a national network of Community Development Banks to invest in urban and rural small businesses; and microenterprise lending for poor people seeking self-employment as an alternative to welfare.

**Agriculture.** A sufficient and sustainable agricultural economy can be achieved through fiscally responsible programs. It is time to re-establish the private/public partnership to ensure that family farmers get a fair return for their labor and investment, that consumers receive safe and nutritious foods, and that needed investments are made in basic research, education, rural business development, market development and infrastructure to sustain rural communities.

**Workers' Rights.** Our workplaces must be revolutionized to make them more flexible and productive. We will reform the job safety laws to empower workers with greater rights and to hold employers accountable for dangers on the job. We will act against sexual harassment in the workplace. We will honor the work ethic — by expanding the earned-income tax credit so no one with children at home who works full time is still in poverty, by fighting on the side of family farmers to ensure they get a fair price for their hard work and working to sustain rural communities; by making work more valuable than welfare; and by supporting the right of workers to organize and bargain collectively without fear of intimidation or permanent replacement during labor disputes.

**Education.** A competitive American economy requires the global market's best-educated, best-trained, most flexible work force. It's not enough to spend more on our schools; we must insist on results. We oppose the Bush administration's efforts to bankrupt the public school system — the bedrock of democracy — through private school vouchers. To help children reach school ready to learn, we will expand child health and nutrition programs and extend Head Start to all eligible children, and guarantee all children access to quality, affordable child care. We deplore the savage inequalities among public schools across the land and believe every child deserves an equal chance to a world-class education. Reallocating resources toward this goal must be a priority. We support education reforms such as site-based decision-making and public school choice, with strong protections against discrimination. We support the goal of a 90 percent graduation rate and programs to end dropouts. We will invest in educational technology and establish world-class standards in math, science and other core subjects, and support effective tests of progress to meet them. In areas where there are no registered apprenticeship programs, we will adopt a national apprenticeship-style program to ease the transition from school to work for non-college-bound students, so they can acquire skills that lead to high-wage jobs. In the new economy, opportunity will depend on lifelong learning. We will support the goal of literacy for all Americans. We will ask firms to invest in the training of all workers, not just corporate management.

**A Domestic GI Bill.** It is time to revolutionize the way student loan programs are run. We will make college affordable to *all* students who are qualified to attend, *regardless of family income*. A Domestic GI Bill will enable all Americans to borrow money for college, so long as they are willing to pay it back as a percentage of their income over time or through national service addressing unmet community needs.

**Health Care.** All Americans should have universal access to quality, affordable health care — not as a privilege but as a right. That requires tough controls on health costs, which are rising at two to three times the rate of inflation, terrorizing American families and businesses and depriving millions of the care they need. We will enact a uniquely American reform of the health-care system to control costs and make health care affordable; ensure quality and choice of health-care providers; cover all Americans regardless of pre-existing conditions; squeeze out waste, bureaucracy and abuse; improve primary and preventive care including child immunization and prevention of diseases like tuberculosis now becoming rampant in our cities; provide expanded education on the relationship between diet and health; expand access to mental health treatment services; provide a safety net through support of public hospitals; provide for the full range of reproductive choice — education, counseling, access to contraceptives and the right to a safe, legal abortion; expand medical research; and provide more long-term care, including home health care. We will make ending the epidemic in breast cancer a major priority, and expand reproductive health services and other special health needs of women. We must be united in declaring war on AIDS and HIV disease, implement the recommendations of the National Commission on AIDS and fully fund the Ryan White Care Act; provide targeted and honest prevention campaigns; combat HIV-related discrimination; make drug treatment available for all addicts who seek it; guarantee access to quality care; expand clinical trials for treatments and vaccines; and speed up the FDA [Food and Drug Administration] drug approval process.

**Energy.** We reject the Republican myth that energy efficiency and environmental protection are enemies of economic growth. We will make our economy more efficient, using less energy, reducing our dependence on foreign oil, and producing less solid and toxic waste. We will adopt a coordinated transportation policy, with a strong commitment to mass transit; encourage efficient alternative-fueled vehicles; increase our reliance on clean natural gas; promote clean coal technology; invest in R&D [research and development] on renewable energy sources; strengthen efforts to prevent air and water pollution; support incentives for domestic oil and gas operations; and push for revenue-neutral incentives that reward conservation, prevent pollution and encourage recycling.

**Civil and Equal Rights.** We don't have an American to waste. Democrats will continue to lead the fight to ensure that no Americans suffer discrimination or deprivation of rights on the basis of race, gender, language, national origin, religion, age, disability, sexual orientation or other characteristics irrelevant to ability. We support ratification of the Equal Rights Amendment, affirmative action, stronger protection of voting rights for racial and ethnic minorities, including language access to voting, and continued resistance to discriminatory English-only pressure groups. We will reverse the Bush administration's assault on civil rights enforcement, and instead work to rebuild and vigorously use machinery for civil rights enforcement; support comparable remedies for women; aggressively prosecute hate crimes; strengthen legal services for the poor; deal with other nations in a way that Americans of any origin do not become scapegoats or victims of foreign policy disputes; provide civil rights protection for gay men and lesbians and an end to Defense Department discrimination; respect Native American culture and our treaty commitments; require the United States government to recognize its trustee obligations to the inhabitants of Hawaii generally and to Native Hawaiians in particular; and fully enforce the Americans with Disability Act to enable people with disabilities to achieve independence and function at their highest possible level.

**Strengthening the Family.** Governments don't raise children, people do. People who bring children into this world have a responsibility to care for them and give them values, motivation and discipline. Children should not have children. We need a national crackdown on deadbeat parents, an effective system of child-support enforcement nationwide and a systematic effort to establish paternity for every child. We must also make it easier for parents to build strong families through pay equity. Family and medical leave will ensure that workers don't have to choose between family and work. We support a family preservation program to reduce child and spousal abuse by providing preventive services and foster care to families in crisis. We favor ensuring quality and affordable child-care opportunities for working parents, and a fair and healthy start for every child, including essential prenatal and well-baby care. We support the needs of our senior citizens for productive and healthy lives including hunger prevention, income adequacy, transportation access and abuse prevention.

**Welfare Reform.** Welfare should be a second chance, not a way of life. We want to break the cycle of welfare by adhering to two simple principles: No one who is able to work can stay on welfare forever, and no one who works should live in poverty. We will continue to help those who cannot help themselves. We will offer people on welfare a new social contract. We'll invest in education and job training, and provide the child care and health care they need to go to work and achieve long-term self-sufficiency. We will give them the help they need to make the transition from welfare to work, and require people who can work to go to work within two years in available jobs either in the private sector or in community service to meet unmet needs. That will restore the covenant that welfare was meant to be: A promise of temporary help for people who have fallen on hard times.

**Abortion.** Democrats stand behind the right of every woman to choose, consistent with *Roe v. Wade*, regardless of ability to pay, and support a national law to protect that right. It is a fundamental constitutional liberty that individual Americans — not government — can best take responsibility for making the most difficult and intensely personal decisions regarding reproduction. The goal of our nation must be to make abortion less necessary, not more difficult or more dangerous. We pledge to support contraceptive research, family planning, comprehensive family life education, and policies that support healthy childbearing and enable parents to care most effectively for their children.

**Management and Labor.** The private sector is the engine of our economy and the main source of national wealth. . . . America's corporate leaders have a responsibility to invest in their country. . . . If a company wants to overpay its executives and underinvest in the future or transfer jobs overseas, it shouldn't get special treatment and tax breaks from the Treasury. Managers must work with employees to make the workplace safer, more satisfying and more efficient.

Workers must also accept added responsibilities in the new economy. In return for an increased voice and a greater stake in the success of their enterprises, workers should be prepared to join in cooperative efforts to increase productivity, flexibility and quality. Government's neutrality between labor and management cannot mean neutrality about the collective bargaining process, which has been purposely crippled by Republican administrations. Our economic growth depends on processes, including collective bargaining, that permit labor and management to work together on their common interests, even as they work out their conflicts.

**Environment.** For ourselves and future generations, we must protect our environment. We will protect our old-growth forests, preserve critical habitats, provide a genuine "no net loss" policy on wetlands, conserve the critical resources of soil, water and air, oppose new offshore oil drilling and mineral exploration and production in our nation's many environmentally critical areas, and address ocean pollution by reducing oil and toxic waste spills at sea. We believe America's youth can serve their country well through a civilian conservation corps. To protect the public health, we will clean up the environmental horrors at federal facilities, insist that private polluters clean up their toxic and hazardous wastes, and vigorously prosecute environmental criminals. We will oppose Republican efforts to gut the Clean Air Act in the guise of competitiveness. We will reduce the volume of solid waste and encourage the use of recycled materials while discouraging excess packaging. To avoid the mistakes of the past, we will actively support energy efficiency, recycling and pollution-prevention strategies.

**Government Reform.** Democrats in 1992 intend to lead a revolution in government, challenging it to act responsibly and be accountable, starting with the hardest and most urgent problems of the deficit and economic growth. Rather than throwing money at obsolete programs, we will eliminate unnecessary layers of management, cut administrative costs, give people more choices in the service they get and empower them to make those choices. To foster greater responsibility in government at every level, we support giving greater flexibility to our cities, counties and states in achieving federal mandates and carrying out existing programs.

All branches of government must live by the laws the rest of us obey, determine their pay in an open manner that builds public trust and eliminate special privileges. People in public office need to be accessible to the people they represent. It's time to reform the campaign finance system, to get big money out of our politics and let the people back in. We must limit overall campaign spending and limit the disproportionate and excessive role of PACs [political action committees]. We need new voter registration laws that expand the electorate, such as universal same-day registration, along with full political rights and protections for public employees and new regulations to ensure that the airwaves truly help citizens make informed choices among candidates and policies. And we need fair political representation for all sectors of our country — including the District of Columbia, which deserves and must get statehood status.

**Crime and Drugs.** To empower America's communities, Democrats pledge to restore government as upholder of basic law and order for crime-ravaged communities. The simplest and most direct way to restore order in our cities is to put more police on the streets. America's police are locked in an unequal struggle with crime: Since 1951 the ratio of police officers to reported crimes has reversed, from 3-to-1 to 1-to-3. We will create a Police Corps, in which participants will receive college aid in return for several years of service after graduation in a state or local police department. As we shift people and resources from defense to the civilian economy, we will create new jobs in law enforcement for those leaving the military.

We will expand drug counseling and treatment for those who need it, intensify efforts to educate our children at the earliest ages to the dangers of drug and alcohol abuse, and curb demand from the street corner to the penthouse suite, so that the United States, with 5 percent of the world's population, no longer consumes 50 percent of the world's illegal drugs.

Neighborhoods and police should be partners in the war on crime. Democrats support more community policing, which uses foot patrols and storefront offices to make police officers visible fixtures in urban neighborhoods. We will combat street violence, and emphasize building trust and solving the problems that breed crime.

It is time to shut down the weapons bazaars in our cities. We support a reasonable waiting period to permit background checks for purchases of handguns, as well as assault weapons controls to ban the possession, sale, importation and manufacture of the most deadly assault weapons. We do not support efforts to restrict weapons used for legitimate hunt-

ing and sporting purposes. We will work for swift and certain punishment of all people who violate the country's gun laws and for stronger sentences for criminals who use guns. We will also seek to shut down the black market for guns and impose severe penalties on people who sell guns to children....

Democrats also favor innovative sentencing and punishment options, including community service and boot camps for first-time offenders; tougher penalties for rapists; victim-impact statements and restitution to ensure that crime victims will not be lost in the complexities of the criminal justice system; and initiatives to make our schools safe, including alternative schools for disruptive children.

**Social Services.** We must further the new direction set in the Family Support Act of 1988, away from subsistence and dependence and toward work, family and personal initiative and responsibility. We advocate slower phasing out of Medicaid and other benefits to encourage work; special savings accounts to help low-income families build assets; fair lending; an indexed minimum wage; an expanded Job Corps; and an end to welfare rules that encourage family breakup and penalize individual initiative, such as the $1,000 limit on personal savings.

**Immigration.** Our nation of immigrants has been invigorated repeatedly as new people, ideas and ways of life have become part of the American tapestry. Democrats support immigration policies that promote fairness, non-discrimination and family reunification and that reflect our constitutional freedoms of speech, association and travel.

**Housing.** Safe, secure housing is essential to the institutions of community and family. We support homeownership for working families and will honor that commitment through policies to encourage affordable mortgage credit. We must also confront homelessness by renovating, preserving and expanding the stock of affordable low-income housing. We support tenant management and ownership, so public housing residents can manage their own affairs and acquire property worth protecting.

**National Service.** We will create new opportunities for citizens to serve each other, their communities and their country. By mobilizing hundreds of thousands of volunteers, national service will enhance the role of ordinary citizens in solving unresolved community problems.

**The Arts.** We believe in public support for the arts, including a National Endowment for the Arts that is free from political manipulation and firmly rooted in the First Amendment's freedom of expression guarantee.

**Defense.** America is the world's strongest military power, and we must remain so. A post-Cold War restructuring of American forces will produce substantial savings beyond those promised by the Bush administration, but that restructuring must be achieved without undermining our ability to meet future threats to our security. A military structure for the 1990s and beyond must be built on four pillars: *First,* a survivable nuclear force to deter any conceivable threat as we reduce our nuclear arsenals through arms control negotiations and other reciprocal action. *Second,* conventional forces shifted toward projecting power wherever our vital national interests are threatened. This means reducing the size of our forces in Europe while meeting our obligations to NATO and strengthening our rapid deployment capabilities to deal with new threats to our security posed by renegade dictators, terrorists, international drug traffickers and the local armed conflicts that can threaten the peace of entire regions. *Third,* maintenance of the two qualities that make America's military the best in the world — the superiority of our military personnel and of our technology. These qualities are vital to shortening any conflict and saving American lives. *Fourth,* intelligence capabilities redirected to develop far more sophisticated, timely and accurate analyses of the economic and political conditions that can fuel new conflicts.

The United States must be prepared to use military force decisively when necessary to defend our vital interests. The burdens of collective security in a new era must be shared fairly, and we should encourage multilateral peace-keeping through the United Nations and other international efforts.

American policy must be focused on averting military threats as well as meeting them. To halt the spread of nuclear and other weapons of mass destruction, we must lead a renewed international effort to get tough with companies that peddle nuclear and chemical warfare technologies, strengthen the International Atomic Energy Agency and enforce strong sanctions against governments that violate international restraints. A Comprehensive Test Ban would strengthen our ability to stop the spread of nuclear weapons to other countries, which may be our greatest future security threat. We must press for strong international limits on the dangerous and wasteful flow of conventional arms to troubled regions. A U.S. troop presence should be maintained in Korea as long as North Korea presents a threat to South Korea.

**International Trade.** The United States cannot be strong abroad if it is weak at home. Restoring America's global economic leadership must become a central element of our national security policies. The strength of nations, once defined in military terms, now is measured also by the skill of their workers, the imagination of their managers and the power of their technologies.

Either we develop and pursue a national plan for restoring our economy through a partnership of government, labor and business, or we slip behind the nations that are competing with us and growing. At stake are American jobs, our standard of living and the quality of life for ourselves and our children.

Economic strength — indeed our national security — is grounded on a healthy domestic economy. But we cannot be strong at home unless we are part of a vibrant and expanding global economy that recognizes human rights and seeks to improve the living standards of all the world's people. This is vital to achieving good quality, high-paying jobs for Americans.

Our government must work to expand trade while insisting that the conduct of world trade is fair. It must fight to uphold American interests — promoting exports, expanding trade in agricultural and other products, opening markets in major product and service sectors with our principal competitors, achieving reciprocal access. This should include renewed authority to use America's trading leverage against the most serious problems. The U.S. government also must firmly enforce U.S. laws against unfair trade.

Multilateral trade agreements can advance our economic interests by expanding the global economy. Whether negotiating the North American Free Trade Area (NAFTA) or completing the GATT [General Agreement on Tariffs and Trade] negotiations, our government must assure that our legitimate concerns about environmental, health and safety, and labor standards are included. Those American workers whose jobs are affected must have the benefit of effective adjustment assistance.

**Emerging Democracies.** Helping to lead an international effort to assist the emerging — and still fragile — democracies in Eastern Europe and the former Soviet Union build democratic institutions in free market settings, demilitarize their societies and integrate their economies into the world trading system. Unlike the Bush administration, which waited too long to recognize the new democratic governments in the Baltic countries and the nations of the former Soviet Union, we must act decisively with our European allies to support freedom, diminish ethnic tensions, and oppose aggression in the former communist countries, such as Bosnia-Herzegovina, which are struggling to make the transition from communism to democracy. As change sweeps through the Balkans, the United States must be sensitive to the concerns of Greece regarding the use of the name Macedonia. And in the post-Cold War era, our foreign assistance programs in Africa, the Caribbean, Latin America and elsewhere should be targeted at helping democracies rather than tyrants.

**Democracy Corps.** Promoting democratic institutions by creating a Democracy Corps to send American volunteers to countries that seek legal, financial and political expertise to build democratic institutions, and support groups like the National Endowment for Democracy and Asia Foundation and others.

**China.** Conditioning of favorable trade terms for China on respect for human rights in China and Tibet, greater market access for U.S. goods, and responsible conduct on weapons proliferation.

**South Africa.** Maintenance of state and local sanctions against South Africa in support of an investment code of conduct, existing limits on deductibility of taxes paid to South Africa and diplomatic pressure until there is an irreversible, full and fair accommodation with the black majority to create a democratic government with full rights for all its citizens....

**Middle East Peace.** Support for the peace process now under way in the Middle East, rooted in the tradition of the Camp David accords. Direct negotiations between Israel, her Arab neighbors and Palestinians, with no imposed solutions, are the only way to achieve enduring security for Israel and full peace for all parties in the region. The end of the Cold War does not alter America's deep interest in our longstanding special relationship with Israel, based on shared values, a mutual commitment to democracy and a strategic alliance that benefits both nations....

**Human Rights.** Standing everywhere for the rights of individuals and respect for ethnic minorities against the repressive acts of governments — against torture, political imprisonment and all attacks on civilized standards of human freedom. This is a proud tradition of the Democratic Party, which has stood for freedom in South Africa and continues to resist oppression in Cuba. Our nation should once again promote the principle of sanctuary for politically oppressed people everywhere, be they Haitian refugees, Soviet Jews seeking U.S. help in their successful absorption into Israeli society or Vietnamese fleeing communism. Forcible return of anyone fleeing political repression is a betrayal of American values.

**Human Needs.** Support for the struggle against poverty and disease in the developing world, including the heartbreaking famine in Africa. We must not replace the East-West conflict with one between North and South, a growing divide between the industrialized and developing world. Our development programs must be re-examined and restructured to assure that their benefits truly help those most in need to help themselves. At stake are the lives of millions of human beings who live in hunger, uprooted from their homes, too often without hope. The United States should work to establish a specific plan and timetable for the elimination of world hunger.

**Global Environment.** As the threat of nuclear holocaust recedes, the future of the Earth is challenged by gathering environmental crises. As governments around the world have sought the path to concerted action, the Bush administration — despite its alleged foreign policy expertise — has been more of an obstacle to progress than a leader for change, practicing isolationism on an issue that affects us all. Democrats know we must act now to save the health of the Earth and the health of our children for generations to come.

The United States must become a leader, not an impediment, in the fight against global warming. We should join our European allies in agreeing to limit carbon dioxide emissions to 1990 levels by the year 2000.

The United States must be a world leader in finding replacements for CFCs [chlorofluorocarbons] and other ozone-depleting substances.

We must work actively to protect the planet's biodiversity and preserve its forests....

We must fashion imaginative ways of engaging governments and business in the effort to encourage developing nations to preserve their environmental heritage.

Explosive population growth must be controlled by working closely with other industrialized and developing nations and private organizations to fund greater family-planning efforts.

## Republicans

Five weeks after the Democratic convention, the Republicans convened in Houston Aug. 17-20 and did their best to persuade voters to remember the past and trust in experience. From the rousing opening night performance of former president Ronald Reagan to the repeated calls to honor traditional family values, the Republican National Convention looked backward as much as it looked ahead.

There were frequent references to having defeated communism and having won the Persian Gulf War. Voters were asked to ignore the Democrats' attempt to remake themselves in a more moderate image and to remember instead what life was like under Jimmy Carter, the most recent Democratic president.

There was little moderation evident in the party platform adopted for George Bush's second term. The GOP approved a hard-line approach opposing abortion rights and any attempt to increase taxes. On the social issues front, there were planks favoring school choice, school prayer and family unity.

Finally, the delegates needed little prompting to vent their frustrations at the "liberal media" for praising Democratic nominee Bill Clinton, dwelling on dissension over the GOP's anti-abortion stance and overemphasizing the weak economy. Bush sought to link Clinton to the Democratic Congress, which he blamed for the nation's problems — a refrain that would be played over and over throughout the week.

This was a homecoming of sorts for Bush. A New Englander by birth who went to Texas to work in the oil business, he retained his residency at a Houston hotel.

Party activists also sought a fresh start for Dan Quayle, widely perceived as being bumbling, gaffe-prone and ineffective. But many conservatives still viewed the vice president as a hero, and because Quayle survived attempts to dump him from the ticket during the weeks leading up to the convention, GOP strategists looked forward to remaking his image as a thoughtful, middle-class American fighting for family values.

Recognizing that a vacuum of leadership would exist after 16 years of nominating Reagan and Bush, a host of potential presidential candidates in 1996 looked forward to Houston as a place to make their mark.

By week's end, Jack F. Kemp, secretary of Housing and Urban Development, seemed to draw the widest support among the class of 1996. Television commentator and 1992 candidate Patrick J. Buchanan was the most combative and divisive. And Massachusetts governor William F. Weld, a social and economic libertarian, became the most sought-after voice for the party's moderate wing.

When the convention opened it already had become clear that efforts to force a debate on abortion had fallen short. A majority in six delegations was required to challenge the platform's call for a constitutional ban on all abortions, but abortion rights supporters said they could muster majorities in only four delegations — Maine, Massachusetts, New Mexico and the Virgin Islands. The reason, they said, was that delegates felt it was more important to avoid embarrassing Bush than to force an open debate.

In the end the platform was approved by voice vote. There were cries of "no!" when the document was put to delegates, but no public challenge.

In his speech Buchanan, who had unsuccessfully challenged Bush in the primaries, appealed to his supporters to throw their support to the president. He acknowledged the disagreements that led him to challenge Bush but said the convention marked the time to unite.

"The right place for us to be now in this presidential campaign is right beside George Bush," Buchanan said.

Buchanan had whipped the crowd into a frenzy with a bitter, scathing attack on Clinton, attacking his patriotism and charging that his view of change for America would mean abortion on demand, a litmus test for the Supreme Court, homosexual rights, women in combat and discrimination against religious schools. "That's change, all right," said Buchanan, but "it's not the kind of change we can abide in a nation that we still call God's country."

Buchanan's remarks were enthusiastically received in the hall, but the biggest response came for President Reagan, who described his speech as the "last chapter" in his political career. At 81, the grand patriarch of the Republican Party showed all the oratorical skills and political spirit that had made him the hero of GOP conservatives.

"We stood tall and proclaimed that communism was destined for the ash heap of history," he said. "We never heard so much ridicule from our liberal friends. But we knew then what the liberal Democrat leaders just couldn't figure out: The sky would not fall if America restored her strength and resolve. The sky would not fall if an American president spoke the truth. The only thing that would fall was the Berlin Wall."

House Minority Leader Robert H. Michel of Illinois, the convention chair, set the blistering tone against Congressional Democrats.

"We are here to tell the American people that this election is just as much about the Congress as it is about the presidency," he said. "The Democrats have controlled the House of Representatives now for 38 straight years, and that has to change." The Democrats "alone ... are responsible for the unholy mess Congress is in."

Congressional Democrats were used throughout as a foil to highlight the president's domestic agenda and the change he sought to implement. "The Constitution makes the president commander in chief of the Army but not commander in chief of the Congress," said keynote speaker Sen. Phil Gramm of Texas. "The Democrats who control Congress by overwhelming margins have used their majority to throttle the president's program and strangle the nation's economy in a partisan gridlock the likes of which we have not seen in this century."

Delegates heard from three governors whose successes at home had thrust them into the national spotlight and fueled speculation about a future spot on the national ticket. Tommy G. Thompson of Wisconsin and John Engler of Michigan delivered unemotional speeches, but Gov. William F. Weld of Massachusetts highlighted divisions between moderates and conservatives on abortion and homosexual rights. He said, "I happen to think that individual freedom should extend to a woman's right to choose. I want the government out of your pocketbook and your bedroom." Crowd reaction was a mixed bag of boos and cheers.

Kemp got an enthusiastic response when he credited Reagan and Bush for their roles in the demise of communism. "Ladies and gentleman," he told the assembled, "communism didn't fall. It was pushed. It was our ideas that did the pushing and our Republican presidents, Ronald Reagan and George Bush, that helped change the world."

Wednesday was family night at the Astrodome. The delegates heard from the candidates' wives, Barbara Bush and Marilyn Quayle, and speakers throughout the evening discussed family values. The evening's high point came when the entire Bush clan gathered at the podium, and the president made a cameo appearance.

Many delegates were milling about during speeches by television evangelist Pat Robertson and others; they did not settle in until the address by Mary Fisher, a victim of HIV, the virus that causes AIDS. The crowd hushed as Fisher, 44, the daughter of a Detroit multimillionaire and longtime GOP fundraiser, spoke about the AIDS virus, which she had contracted from her ex-husband.

Imploring the delegates to show people with AIDS the same sort of compassion that the president and Mrs. Bush had shown her, she said, ". . . [W]e do the president's cause no good if we praise the American family but ignore a virus that destroys it."

The mood turned more combative when Marilyn Quayle said that she and her husband, like the Democratic standard-bearers, were members of the baby boom generation, but "not everyone demonstrated, dropped out, took drugs, joined in the sexual revolution or dodged the draft."

Barbara Bush adopted a gentler theme, praising her husband as "the strongest, the most decent, the most caring, the wisest, yes, and the healthiest man I know."

Leading off the nomination speakers, Labor Secretary Lynn Martin called Democrats "whimpering naysayers" who peddle "the crass politics of fear and the false promise of change," while describing their congressmen as "aging punjabs."

The roll call was arranged so that Texas, the convention's host state and technically Bush's home, put him over the top. The final tally was 2,166 votes for Bush, 18 for Buchanan and three for others, before the nomination was approved by acclamation. New Hampshire never cast its 23 votes. (*Chart, p. 256*)

The first three days of convention week were little more than prelude for the critical closing night when Bush and Quayle would make their acceptance speeches and the convention would be pronounced a success or failure. The buildup for both addresses had been intense. Quayle's was seen as his big chance to redefine his political persona. Bush had an even greater task — to give "the speech of his life."

Neither quite lived up to the advance billing, but both delivered effective addresses that lifted the voices and spirits of the convention hall, and when both left town Friday morning, they could point to significantly better opinion polls as a sign of success. Speaking first, Quayle defiantly answered his legion of detractors. "I know my critics wish I were not standing here tonight, "he said." They don't like our values. They look down on our beliefs. They're afraid of our ideas. And they know the American people stand on our side."

Bush came out fighting against the Democratic-controlled Congress and Clinton. Responding to the concerns of delegates still angry over his broken "no-new-taxes" pledge, Bush admitted that it had been a mistake but posed a question to the electorate. "Who do you trust in this election — the candidate who has raised taxes one time and regrets it, or the other candidate who raised taxes and fees 128 times and enjoyed it every time?"

Trust was again the issue as Bush highlighted his role as commander in chief in what was widely considered to be his strength — foreign policy. He spoke of Cold War triumph yet warned that "the Soviet bear may be gone, but there are still wolves in the woods."

These existing threats allowed Bush to tout his stewardship in the Persian Gulf War and raise questions about what his opponent would have done.

Quayle's entrance was preceded by a short biographical video, similar to the one that introduced Clinton to the Democratic convention.

Following are excerpts form the Republican platform of 1992:

**Family Values.** Our greatness starts at home — literally. So Republicans believe government should strengthen families, not replace them. Today, more than ever, the traditional family is under assault. We believe our laws should reflect what makes our nation prosperous and wholesome: faith in God, hard work, service to others and limited government. . . .

The Republican Party responds, as it has since 1980, with an unabashed commitment to the family's economic liberty and moral rights. Republicans trust parents and believe they, not courts and lawyers, know what is best for their children. That is why we will work to ensure that the Congress and the states shall enact no law abridging the rights of the family formed by blood, marriage, adoption or legal custody — rights that are anterior and superior to those of government. . . .

The demands of employment and commuting often make it hard for parents to spend time with their children. Republicans advocate maximum flexibility in working and child-care arrangements so that families can make the most of their schedules. We support pro-family policies: job-sharing, telecommuting, compressed workweeks, parental leave negotiated between employer and employees, and flextime. . . .

Most parents prefer in-home care of their children but often encounter government obstacles. Republicans will promote in-home care by allowing payment annually, instead of quarterly, of income taxes by employees and withholding taxes by employers. . . .

[W]e want to expand the Young Child Tax Credit to $500 per child and make it available to all families with children under the age of 10. . . .

**Education.** The Republican strategy is based on sound principle. Parents have the right to choose the best school for their children. Schools should teach right from wrong. Schools should reinforce parental authority, not replace it. We should increase flexibility from federal regulation. We should explore a new generation of break-the-mold New American Schools. Standards and assessments should be raised, not reduced to a lowest common denominator. Communities should be empowered to find what works. The pursuit of excellence in education is a fundamental goal. Good teachers should be rewarded for teaching well. Alternative certification can bring desperately needed new people into the teaching profession. America needs public, private and parochial schools. . . .

The president's proposed "GI Bill for Children" will provide $1,000 scholarships to middle- and low-income families, enabling their children to attend the school of their choice. This innovative plan will not only drive schools to excel as they compete, but will also give every parent consumer power to obtain an excellent education for his or her child. . . .

The president has proposed allowing families to deduct the interest they pay on student loans, and penalty-free withdrawal of IRA [individual retirement account] funds for educational expenses. . . .

We strongly support youth apprenticeships that include a year of college, to encourage a lifetime of learning and opportunity for students. . . .

[W]e support the right of students to engage in voluntary prayer in schools and the right of the community to do so at commencements or other occasions. We will strongly enforce the law guaranteeing equal access to school facilities. We also advocate recitation of the Pledge of Allegiance in schools as a reminder of the principles that sustain us as one nation under God. . . .

**Health Care.** Republicans believe government control of health care is irresponsible and ineffective. We believe health-care choices should remain in the hands of the people, not government bureaucrats. This issue truly represents a fundamental difference between the two parties.

We endorse President Bush's comprehensive health-care plan, which solves the two major problems of the current system — access and affordability — while preserving the high-quality care Americans now enjoy. The president's plan will make health care *more affordable* through tax credits and deductions that will offset insurance costs for 95 million Americans; and make health care *more accessible,* especially for small businesses, by reducing insurance costs and eliminating workers' worries of losing insurance if they change jobs. This plan will expand access to health care by:

● Creating new tax credits and deductions to help low- and middle-income Americans. These tax credits would be available in the form of vouchers for low-income people who work.

● Providing insurance security for working Americans by requiring insurers to cover pre-existing conditions.

● Making health insurance premiums fully deductible for the self-employed.

● Making it easier for small firms to purchase coverage for their employees. . . .

● Addressing the medical malpractice problem by a cap on non-economic damage recoveries in malpractice claims and an alternative dispute resolution before going to court.

In short, the president aims to make coverage available to all, guaranteed, renewable, with no preconditions. Under his plan, no one will have to go broke to get well. . . .

**AIDS.** We are committed to ensure that our nation's response to AIDS is shaped by compassion, not fear or ignorance and will oppose, as a matter of decency and honor, any discrimination against Americans who are its victims. . . .

Above all, a cure must be found. We have committed enormous resources — $4.2 billion over the past four years for research alone, more than for any disease except cancer. . . .

**The Homeless.** The Bush administration has worked vigorously to address this tragedy, believing that involuntary homelessness in America is unacceptable. Accordingly, the administration has proposed $4 billion in homeless assistance, an amount cut back by the Democrat-controlled Congress. We have also implemented a Shelter Plus Care program designed to assist homeless persons who are mentally ill, chemically dependent or stricken with AIDS. . . .

**Social Security.** We reaffirm our commitment to a strong Social Security system. To stop penalizing grandparents and other seniors who care for children, we pledge to continue the Republican crusade to end the earnings limitation for Social Security recipients. More than ever, our nation needs older Americans in its schools and workplaces. There should be no barriers to their full participation in our country's future. We pledge support for greater availability of long-term care and for research to combat Alzheimer's disease. Republicans also took the lead in expanding home health care in government programs, and we want to build on that accomplishment.

**Cultural Values.** We oppose any legislation or law that legally recognizes same-sex marriages and allows such couples to adopt children or provide foster care.

We must recognize that the time has come for a national crusade against pornography. . . . We call on federal agencies to halt the sale, under government auspices, of pornographic materials. We endorse Republican legislation, the Pornography Victims Compensation Act, allowing victims of pornography to seek damages from those who make or sell it. . . .

Government has a responsibility, as well, to ensure that it promotes the common moral values that bind us together as a nation. We therefore condemn the use of public funds to subsidize obscenity and blasphemy masquerading as art. . . .

**Welfare Reform.** Today's welfare system is anti-work and anti-marriage. It taxes families to subsidize illegitimacy. It rewards unethical behavior and penalizes initiative. It cannot be merely tinkered with by Congress; it must be re-created by states and localities. Republican governors and legislators in several states have already launched dramatic reforms, especially with workfare and learnfare. Welfare can no longer be a check in the mail with no responsibility.

We believe fathers and mothers must be held responsible for their children. We support stronger enforcement of child support laws. We call for strong enforcement and tough penalties against welfare fraud and insist that work must be a mandatory part of public assistance for all who are able to work. Because divorce, desertion and illegitimacy account for almost all the increase in child poverty over the last 20 years, we put the highest priority upon enforcement of family rights and responsibilities. . . .

**Crime.** We believe in giving police the resources to do their job. Law enforcement must remain primarily a state and local responsibility. With 95 percent of all violent crimes within the jurisdiction of the states, we have led efforts to increase the number of police protecting our citizens. We also support incentives to encourage personnel leaving the armed forces to continue to defend their country — against the enemy within — by entering the law enforcement profession. . . .

We . . . support the stiffest penalties, including the death penalty, for major drug traffickers. . . . Drug users must face punishment, including fines and imprisionment. . . .

**Illegal Immigration.** We will build on the already announced strengthening of the Border Patrol to better coordinate interdiction of illegal entrants through greater cross-border cooperation. Specifically, we will increase the size of the Border Patrol in order to meet the increasing need to stop illegal immigration and we will equip the Border Patrol with the tools, technologies and structures necessary to secure the border. . . .

**Individual Rights.** The protection of individual rights is the foundation for opportunity and security. . . .

[W]e declare that bigotry and prejudice have no place in American life. We denounce all who practice or promote racism, anti-Semitism or religious intolerance. We believe churches and religious schools should not be taxed; we defend the right of religious leaders to speak out on public issues; and we condemn the cowardly desecration of places of worship that has shocked our country in recent years. . . .

We renew the historic Republican commitment to the rights of women from the early days of the suffragist movement to the present. Because legal rights mean little without opportunity, we assert economic growth as the key to the continued progress of women in all fields of American life.

We believe the unborn child has a fundamental individual right to life that cannot be infringed. We therefore reaffirm our support for a human life amendment to the Constitution, and we endorse legislation to make clear that the 14th Amendment's protections apply to unborn children. We oppose using public revenues for abortion and will not fund organizations that advocate it. . . .

We reaffirm our commitment to the Fifth Amendment to the Constitution: "No person shall be . . . deprived of life, liberty, or property, without due process of law; nor shall private property be taken for public use, without just compensation." We support strong enforcement of this Takings Clause to keep citizens secure in the use and development of their property. We also seek to reduce the amount of land owned or controlled by the government, especially in the Western states. We insist upon prompt payment for private lands certified as critical for preserving essential parks and preserves.

Republicans defend the constitutional right to keep and bear arms. We call for stiff mandatory sentences for those who use firearms in a crime. . . .

We affirm the right of individuals to form, join or assist labor organizations to bargain collectively, consistent with state laws. We support the right of states to enact right-to-work laws.

A Republican Congress will amend the Hobbs Act, so that union officials will not be exempt from the law's prohibition against extortion and violence. We call for greater legal protection from violence for workers who stay on the job during strikes.

We support self-determination for Indian tribes in managing their own affairs and resources. . . . Reservations and tribal lands held in trust should be free to become enterprise zones so their people can fully share in the nation's prosperity. We will work with tribal governments to improve education, health, economic opportunity and environmental conditions. . . .

**Taxes.** We will oppose any attempt to increase taxes. . . . We believe the tax increases of 1990 should ultimately be repealed. . . .

As the deficit comes under control, we aspire to further tax rate cuts, strengthening incentives to work, save, invest and innovate. We also support President Bush's efforts to reduce federal spending and to cap the growth of non-Social Security entitlements. . . .

We support further tax simplification. . . .

**Business Deregulation.** We support President Bush's freeze on new regulations. . . . We call for a permanent moratorium until our regulatory reforms are fully in place. They include market-based regulation, cost-benefit analysis of all new rule-making, and a regulatory budget that will make Congress admit — and correct — the harm it does by legislation that destroys jobs and competitiveness. . . .

**Homeownership.** The best housing policy is a non-inflationary, growing economy that has produced low mortgage rates and has made housing more affordable.

We demand Congress enact President's Bush's housing program introduced as part of his pro-growth package in January.

Provide a $5,000 tax credit for first-time home buyers and allow them penalty-free IRA withdrawals.

Set a modified "passive loss rule" for active real estate investors.

Extend tax preferences for mortgage revenue bonds and low-income housing.

And allow deductions for losses on personal residences.

The average American's home is his or her primary asset. That asset should be completely shielded from federal taxation, allowing the homeowner to maintain it or access it

as he or she sees fit. We call for the complete elimination of the capital gains tax on the sale of a principal residence. . . .

**Enterprise Zones.** The Republican Party enthusiastically encourages the passage of federal enterprise zones. Enterprise zones have been effective programs for promoting growth in urban and rural America. Republicans believe that the concept of enterprise zones is based on unyielding faith in the entrepreneurial spirit of all Americans. Enterprise zones foster individual initiative and government deregulation. . . .

**Technology.** We believe America must make technological development one of its highest priorities. We therefore support efforts to promote science and technology — providing funding for basic research, supporting investment in emerging technologies, improving education in science and engineering, enhancing tax credits for research and development, eliminating unnecessary regulation to create competitive markets, and protecting intellectual property. . . .

**Space.** Republicans . . . are determined to complete space station *Freedom* within this decade. Our agenda is to lower the cost of access to space, and to broaden that access to the private sector, with a family of new launchers; to build and fly sensors for the global environment; and to advance cutting-edge capabilities like the National Aerospace Plane and single stage-to-orbit rockets, so technological breakthroughs can be quickly exploited. We will promote space-based industry and ensure that space remains a frontier for private enterprise, not a restricted preserve for government. . . .

**International Trade.** Economic freedom is an essential link to our foreign policy. It means expanded trade, but it also means dynamic growth based on shared values — a coming together of nations in the commonwealth of peaceful progress. To that end, U.S. aid, whether bilateral or through international organizations, should promote market reforms, limit regulation and encourage free trade.

Chief among these market reforms should be the privatization of state-owned industries such as telecommunications, power, mining and refining. . . .

We will work with developing nations to make their economies attractive to private investment and will support innovations to guarantee repayment of their loans, including debt for equity swaps. Our experience can help them develop environmentally rational strategies for growth. . . .

**Government Reform.** We reaffirm our support for a constitutional amendment to limit the number of terms House members and senators may serve. . . .

Congress must stop exempting itself from laws such as the minimum wage and the civil rights statutes, as well as laws that apply to the executive branch. The Independent Counsel Act is a case in point. . . . If that act is reauthorized, it must be extended to Congress as well. Safety and health regulations, civil rights and minimum wage laws are further examples of areas where Congress has set itself apart from the people. This practice must end.

Congress must slash its own bureaucracy. . . .

We support state-level appointment of nonpartisan redistricting commissions to apply clear standards for compactness of districts, competitiveness between the parties and protection of community interests.

**Budget Reform.** Republicans vigorously support a balanced budget, a balanced-budget constitutional amendment and a line-item veto for the president.

Republicans believe this balancing of the budget should be achieved, not by increasing taxes to match spending, but by cutting spending to current levels of revenue. We prefer a balanced-budget amendment that contains a supermajority requirement to raise taxes.

We also propose procedural reforms. We support legislation that would require Congress to pass a legally binding budget before it can consider spending bills. The budget's spending ceilings shall not be exceeded without a supermajority vote of both chambers. If Congress fails to pass any appropriation bill, funding for its programs will automatically be frozen at the previous year's level. The key to prosperity for the rest of this century and for the next generation of Americans is a budget strategy that restores sanity to the budget process and checks the growth of government.

**Campaign Reform.** We will require congressional candidates to raise most of their funds from individuals within their home constituencies. This will limit outside special-interest money and result in less expensive campaigns, with less padding for incumbents. To the same end, we will strengthen the role of political parties to remove pressure on candidates to spend so much time soliciting funds. We will eliminate political action committees supported by corporations, unions or trade associations, and restrict the practice of bundling.

To restore competition in elections by attacking the unfair advantages of incumbency, we will stop incumbents from warding off challengers merely by amassing huge war chests. Congressional candidates will be forbidden from carrying campaign funds from one election to the next. We will oppose arbitrary spending limits — cynical devices which hobble challengers to keep politicians in office.

**Privatization.** Privatization is an important alternative to higher taxes and reduced services. If private enterprise can perform better and more cheaply than government, let it do so....

Where it advances both efficiency and safety, we will advocate privatization of airport operation and management.

We deplore the blatant political bias of the government-sponsored radio and television networks. It is especially outrageous that taxpayers are now forced to underwrite this biased broadcasting through the Corporation for Public Broadcasting (CPB). We call for sweeping reform of CPB....

We will not initiate any federal activity that can be conducted better on the state or local level. In doing so, we reassert the crucial importance of the 10th Amendment. We oppose costly federal mandates that stifle innovation and force tax hikes upon states and localities. We require that Congress calculate the cost of mandated initiatives upon communities affected and provide adequate financial support for mandates invoked. We will continue the process of returning power to local voters by replacing federal programs with block grants.

**Legal Reform.** We support the Fairness Rule, to allow the winning party to a lawsuit to recover the costs of litigation from the losing party....

We believe complainants should have a choice of ways to settle problems through alternative dispute programs that will permit parties to pursue less costly and less complicated ways to resolve conflicts. We also call for greater use of judicial sanctions to stop frivolous lawsuits. We call for changes to the federal Racketeer Influenced and Corrupt Organizations (RICO) law to limit its use in civil litigation by requiring proof of all elements by clear and convincing proof.

We seek to restore fairness and predictability to punitive damages by placing appropriate limits on them, dividing trials into two phases to determine liability separately from damages and requiring clear proof of wrongdoing....

Because four-fifths of the time and cost of a lawsuit involves discovery — pretrial investigation of the facts — we will require automatic disclosure, by both sides, of basic information....

We will fight rising health-care costs — and equally important, help dedicated doctors to keep practicing in critical areas like obstetrics — by providing incentives for states to reform their liability laws. This will reduce the practice of "defensive medicine," requiring patients to be tested for every conceivable ailment at their own enormous expense to guard against the mere possibility of a lawsuit.

Recognizing that legal reform can solve only parts of the larger problem, we support a federal product liability law. The cost of product liability protection is a great expense to the American consumer and seriously impedes our international competitiveness....

**Washington, D.C.** We call for closer and responsible congressional scrutiny of the city, federal oversight of its law enforcement and courts, and tighter fiscal restraints over its expenditures. We oppose statehood as inconsistent with the original intent of the framers of the Constitution and with the need for a federal city belonging to all the people as our nation's capital.

**Agriculture.** Agricultural prosperity is essential to the nation's global competitiveness. We will continue to expand the growth of American agriculture through exports, development of new products and new markets....

We pledge to fight unfair competition and to bring down the walls of protectionism around the world that unfairly inhibit competitiveness of U.S. farm exports. We pledge continued pressure to open world markets through the Uruguay Round, the North American Free Trade Agreement and bilateral negotiations.

We affirm that there will be no GATT agreement unless it improves opportunities for U.S. farmers to compete in world markets. We repeat our demands for cutbacks in export subsidies by the European Community and elsewhere, and we will fight the use of arbitrary health and sanitation standards to sabotage U.S. exports....

We support the widest possible use of ethanol in the U.S. motor fuel market, including in oxygenated fuels programs and as ethanol blends in reformulated gasolines.

In addition, the Republican Party supports increased research and development to reduce ethanol production costs and expand its use in motor fuel markets....

We value our nation's real wetlands habitat and the diversity of our native animal and plant life. We oppose, however, bureaucratic harassment of farm, ranch and timber families under statutes regarding endangered species and wetlands. When actions are required to protect an endangered species, we recognize that jobs can be lost, communities displaced and economic progress for all denied. Accordingly, prior to the implementation of a recovery plan for a species declared to be endangered, we will require the Congress to affirm the priority of the species on the endangered list and the specific measures to be taken in any recovery plan....

**Energy.** We will ... [allow] access, under environmental safeguards, to the coastal plain of the Arctic National Wildlife Refuge, possibly one of the largest petroleum reserves in our country, and to selected areas of the outer continental shelf (OCS). We support incentives to encourage domestic investment for onshore and OCS oil and gas exploration and development, including relief from the alternative minimum tax, credits for enhanced oil recovery and geological exploration under known geological oil fields and producing geological structures, and modified percentage depletion rules to benefit marginal production....

We endorse major national projects, like the superconducting super collider, which offer the promise of developing more efficient ways to store, transport and use energy.

We will hasten development of the next generation of nuclear power plants — one of the cleanest, safest energy sources of all....

We endorse development of renewable energy sources and research on fuel cells, conservation, hydro, solar, hydrogen and wind power as components of our overall plan for energy security and environmental quality.

**Public Lands.** The millions of acres that constitute this nation's public lands must continue to provide for a number of uses. We are committed to the multiple use of our public lands. We believe that recreation, forestry, ranching, mining, oil and gas exploration, and production on our public lands can be conducted in a way compatible with their conservation. . . .

**Transportation.** To keep America on the move, we assert the same principle that guides us in all other sectors of the economy: consumers benefit through competition within the private sector. That is why we will complete the job of trucking deregulation. We will also abolish the Interstate Commerce Commission, finally freeing shippers and consumers from horse-and-buggy regulation. . . .

**Environment.** Clearly we have led the world in investment in environmental protection. We have taught the world three vital lessons. First, environmental progress is integrally related to economic advancement. Second, economic growth generates the capital to pay for environmental gains. Third, private ownership and economic freedom are the best security against environmental degradation. . . .

However, with billions of dollars at stake in national production and jobs, not to mention our quality of life, our decisions to spend on environmental protection must not be determined by the politics of the moment. We will use scientifically respectable risk-benefit assessments to settle environmental controversies. . . .

We will legislatively overhaul the "superfund" program to speed the cleanup of hazardous waste and more efficiently use superfund dollars. . . .

**NATO.** [W]e reaffirm the NATO alliance. . . . The United States must remain a European power in the broadest sense, able to influence the policies and events that affect the livelihood and security of future generations of Americans. . . .

**Israel.** Consistent with our strategic relationship, the United States should continue to provide large-scale security assistance to Israel, maintaining Israel's qualitative military advantage over any adversary or coalition of adversaries. We also will continue to negotiate with the major arms supplying nations to reach an agreement on limiting arms sales to the Middle East and preventing the proliferation of non-conventional weapons. . . .

**Middle East Peace.** The basis for negotiations must be U.N. Security Council Resolutions 242 and 338. Peace must come from direct negotiations.

A meaningful peace must assure Israel's security while recognizing the legitimate rights of the Palestinian people. We oppose the creation of an independent Palestinian state. Nor will we support the creation of any political entity that would jeopardize Israel's security. . . .

**Foreign Aid.** We recognize that foreign aid must have a reasonable relationship to our national interests. We therefore support an ongoing review of such programs so that they can be both effectual and justified. We promote financial contribution from other democracies of the world to share the cost of the American burden for peacekeeping and foreign aid. . . .

**Disarmament.** We will banish the threat of nuclear annihilation from the face of the earth — not by savaging our military, as some Democrats might insist but by building on the historic diplomatic achievements of Presidents Bush and Reagan.

This means ensuring stable command and control of the former Soviet arsenal, complete acceptance and verified implementation of all treaty obligations by the successor states to the Soviet Union, and achieving the additional 50 percent reduction in strategic forces now agreed upon. We must assist in dismantling weapons, transforming the massive Soviet war machine into an engine of peace and civilian revival. We will cooperate with our former adversaries both to curtail proliferation and to move beyond the ABM Treaty toward effective ballistic missile defenses.

We will not permit the Soviet nuclear nightmare to be replaced by another one. Outlaw nations — North Korea, Iran, Iraq, Libya and others — lust for weapons of mass destruction. This is the nightmare of proliferation: nuclear, chemical and biological weapons that, together with ballistic missiles, can deliver death across whole continents, including our own.

We will renew and strengthen the Nuclear Nonproliferation Treaty. We will design security policies to counter proliferation dangers. We will reinforce multilateral accords like the Missile Technology Control Regime. And most important, we will develop and deploy global defenses against ballistic missiles. Despite the opposition of the Democratic Party and congressional Democrats, we will deploy an effective strategic defense system for the American people.

**Defense.** Republicans call for a controlled defense drawdown, not a free fall. That is why President Bush proposes to carefully reduce defense spending over the next four years by an additional $34 billion, including $18 billion in outlays, with a 25 percent reduction in personnel. He has already eliminated over 100 weapon systems. Around the world, American forces are coming home from the frontiers of the Cold War. More than 550 overseas bases are being closed or realigned. Yet U.S. forces retain the ability to meet the challenge of another Desert Storm with equal success. . . .

Because the United States will rely on a smaller force of offensive nuclear weapons to deter aggression in the post-Cold War era, we will maintain the triad of land, sea, and air-based strategic forces. We will continue to test the safety, reliability and effectiveness of our nuclear weapons. . . .

We will upgrade existing weapons and selectively procure those that hold the promise of dramatic forward leaps in capability. Under no circumstances will we yield our technological superiority. . . .

We applaud the president's efforts to assist all individuals and communities adversely affected by the ongoing defense build-down, with more than 30 defense adjustment programs already in place and more than $7 billion committed to the effort in just the next two years. . . .

However, we oppose liberal Democrat attempts to place women in combat positions just to make an ideological point. Unlike the Democratic Party and its candidate, we support the continued exclusion of homosexuals from the military as a matter of good order and discipline. . . .

# Key Convention Ballots

# Sources: Key Convention Ballots

This section (pages 193 to 256) presents the results of important balloting from the presidential nominating conventions of three major American political parties 1835 to 1988. The balloting results are arranged in chronological order by convention year. Major contenders for the respective party nominations appear in the tables by last name only. Full names and other detailed descriptions of each convention can be found in the preceding section, "Convention Chronology." Each table contains a reference indicating the page where this information appears.

The source for the balloting results for the 1835-1972 conventions is *Convention Decisions and Voting Records,* Brookings Institution, Washington, D.C., 1973, by Richard C. Bain and Judith H. Parris. Permission to use this material was granted by the Brookings Institution, which holds the copyright. The sources for the 1976 to 1992 vote totals are *The Official Proceedings of the Democratic National Convention* and the Republican National Committee.

*Convention Decisions and Voting Records* contains ballots for three major parties in American history — the Democrats, the Whigs and the modern Republicans. This section includes ballots from conventions of these three parties alone.

In selecting ballots to include in *National Party Conventions 1831-1988,* Congressional Quarterly followed several criteria:

● To include nominating ballots and selected other critical presidential ballots. The Democratic Party conventions of 1832, 1840, 1888, 1916, 1936 and 1964 nominated presidential candidates by acclamation without balloting.

● To include key ballots on important procedural issues, credentials contests and platform disputes.

● To exclude all ballots for vice presidential candidates.

## Vote Total Discrepancies

Bain and Parris note frequent discrepancies between totals given in the published proceedings of the party conventions and the totals reached by adding up the state-by-state delegation votes. They state: "Wherever the discrepancy was obvious and the correct figure could be clearly derived, the record has been printed in corrected form. When the added totals of detailed figures listed differ from the sums printed in the proceedings, both totals are given."

Congressional Quarterly has followed this same procedure. For example, on page 196, the 49th presidential ballot of the 1852 Democratic Party convention appears. Franklin Pierce is listed as receiving 279 votes, the sum of the column. A footnote, however, indicates that the convention proceedings recorded Pierce as receiving 283 votes. Similar examples appear on pages 199, 200 and 241.

# 1844 Democratic

*(Narrative, p. 40)*

# 1835 Democratic

*(Narrative, p. 36)*

| Delegation | Total Votes | First Pres. Ballot Van Buren |
|---|---|---|
| Connecticut | 8 | 8 |
| Delaware | 3 | 3 |
| Georgia | 11 | 11 |
| Indiana | 9 | 9 |
| Kentucky | 15 | 15 |
| Louisiana | 5 | 5 |
| Maine | 10 | 10 |
| Maryland | 10 | 10 |
| Massachusetts | 14 | 14 |
| Mississippi | 4 | 4 |
| Missouri | 4 | 4 |
| New Hampshire | 7 | 7 |
| New Jersey | 8 | 8 |
| New York | 42 | 42 |
| North Carolina | 15 | 15 |
| Ohio | 21 | 21 |
| Pennsylvania | 30 | 30 |
| Rhode Island | 4 | 4 |
| Tennessee | 15 | 15 |
| Vermont | 7 | 7 |
| Virginia | 23 | 23 |
| **Total** | **265** | **265** |

| Delegation | Total Votes | Amendment Ratifying Two-Thirds Rule | | First Pres. Ballot[1] | | Fifth Pres. Ballot[2] | | Ninth Pres. Ballot (Before shift)[3] | | Ninth Pres. Ballot (After shift) |
|---|---|---|---|---|---|---|---|---|---|---|
| | | Yea | Nay | Van Buren | Cass | Van Buren | Cass | Polk | Cass | Polk |
| Alabama | 9 | 9 | — | 1 | 8 | 1 | 8 | 9 | — | 9 |
| Arkansas | 3 | 3 | — | — | — | — | — | 3 | — | 3 |
| Connecticut | 6 | 3 | 3 | 6 | — | — | — | 6 | — | 6 |
| Delaware | 3 | 3 | — | — | 3 | — | 3 | 3 | — | 3 |
| Georgia | 10 | 10 | — | — | 9 | — | 9 | 9 | — | 10 |
| Illinois | 9 | 9 | — | 5 | 2 | 2 | 4 | 9 | — | 9 |
| Indiana | 12 | 12 | — | 3 | 9 | 1 | 11 | 12 | — | 12 |
| Kentucky | 12 | 12 | — | — | — | — | — | 12 | — | 12 |
| Louisiana | 6 | 6 | — | — | — | — | — | 6 | — | 6 |
| Maine | 9 | — | 9 | 8 | — | 8 | 1 | 7 | 1 | 9 |
| Maryland | 8 | 6 | 2 | 2 | 4 | 2 | 6 | 7 | 1 | 8 |
| Massachusetts | 12 | 5 | 7 | 8 | 1 | 7 | 3 | 10 | 2 | 12 |
| Michigan | 5 | 5 | — | 1 | 4 | — | 5 | — | 5 | 5 |
| Mississippi | 6 | 6 | — | — | 6 | — | 6 | 6 | — | 6 |
| Missouri | 7 | — | 7 | 7 | — | 7 | — | 7 | — | 7 |
| New Hampshire | 6 | — | 6 | 6 | — | 2 | — | 6 | — | 6 |
| New Jersey | 7 | 7 | — | 3 | 2 | — | 4 | 2 | 5 | 7 |
| New York | 36 | — | 36 | 36 | — | 36 | — | 35 | — | 36 |
| North Carolina | 11 | 5 | 5 | 2 | 4 | — | 7 | 11 | — | 11 |
| Ohio | 23 | — | 23 | 23 | — | 20 | 3 | 18 | 2 | 23 |
| Pennsylvania | 26 | 12 | 13 | 26 | — | 16 | — | 19 | 7 | 26 |
| Rhode Island | 4 | 2 | 2 | 4 | — | 1 | 1 | 4 | — | 4 |
| Tennessee | 13 | 13 | — | — | 13 | — | 13 | 13 | — | 13 |
| Vermont | 6 | 3 | 3 | 5 | 1 | — | 6 | — | 6 | 6 |
| Virginia | 17 | 17 | — | — | 17 | — | 17 | 17 | — | 17 |
| **Total** | **266** | **148** | **118** | **146** | **83** | **103** | **107** | **231** | **29** | **266** |

1. *Other candidates: Richard M. Johnson, 24; John C. Calhoun, 6; James Buchanan, 4; Levi Woodbury, 2; Commodore Stewart, 1.*
2. *Other candidates: Johnson, 29; Buchanan, 26; not voting, 1.*
3. *Not voting, 6.*

# 1844 Whig

*(Narrative, p. 39)*

| Delegation | Total Votes | First Pres. Ballot Clay |
|---|---|---|
| Alabama | 9 | 9 |
| Arkansas | 3 | 3 |
| Connecticut | 6 | 6 |
| Delaware | 3 | 3 |
| Georgia | 10 | 10 |
| Illinois | 9 | 9 |
| Indiana | 12 | 12 |
| Kentucky | 12 | 12 |
| Louisiana | 6 | 6 |
| Maine | 9 | 9 |
| Maryland | 8 | 8 |
| Massachusetts | 12 | 12 |
| Michigan | 5 | 5 |
| Mississippi | 6 | 6 |
| Missouri | 7 | 7 |
| New Hampshire | 6 | 6 |
| New Jersey | 7 | 7 |
| New York | 36 | 36 |
| North Carolina | 11 | 11 |
| Ohio | 23 | 23 |
| Pennsylvania | 26 | 26 |
| Rhode Island | 4 | 4 |
| South Carolina | 9 | 9 |
| Tennessee | 13 | 13 |
| Vermont | 6 | 6 |
| Virginia | 17 | 17 |
| Total | 275 | 275 |

# 1848 Democratic

*(Narrative, p. 41)*

| Delegation | Total Votes | Adoption of Two-Thirds Rule | | | Amendment on N.Y. Credentials | | | First Pres. Ballot[1] | | | Fourth Pres. Ballot[2] | | |
|---|---|---|---|---|---|---|---|---|---|---|---|---|---|
| | | Yea | Nay | Not Voting | Yea | Nay | Not Voting | Cass | Buchanan | Woodbury | Cass | Buchanan | Woodbury |
| Alabama | 9 | 9 | — | — | — | 9 | — | — | 4 | 5 | — | 4 | 5 |
| Arkansas | 3 | 3 | — | — | — | 3 | — | 3 | — | — | 3 | — | — |
| Connecticut | 6 | 6 | — | — | 6 | — | — | — | — | 6 | — | — | 6 |
| Delaware | 3 | 2 | 1 | — | 1 | 2 | — | 3 | — | — | 3 | — | — |
| Florida | 3 | 3 | — | — | — | 3 | — | — | — | — | — | — | 3 |
| Georgia | 10 | 10 | — | — | — | 10 | — | — | 2 | 5 | 10 | — | — |
| Illinois | 9 | 9 | — | — | 9 | — | — | 9 | — | — | 9 | — | — |
| Indiana | 12 | 3 | 9 | — | 7 | 5 | — | 12 | — | — | 12 | — | — |
| Iowa | 4 | 4 | — | — | 4 | — | — | 1 | 3 | — | 4 | — | — |
| Kentucky | 12 | 12 | — | — | 10 | 2 | — | 7 | 1 | 1 | 8 | 1 | 1 |
| Louisiana | 6 | 6 | — | — | — | 6 | — | 6 | — | — | 6 | — | — |
| Maine | 9 | 9 | — | — | 9 | — | — | — | — | 9 | — | — | 9 |
| Maryland | 8 | 7 | 1 | — | 2 | 5 | 1 | 6 | — | 2 | 6 | — | 2 |
| Massachusetts | 12 | 10 | 2 | — | 11 | 1 | — | — | — | 12 | 8 | — | 4 |
| Michigan | 5 | 5 | — | — | — | 5 | — | 5 | — | — | 5 | — | — |
| Mississippi | 6 | 6 | — | — | — | 6 | — | 6 | — | — | 6 | — | — |
| Missouri | 7 | 1 | 6 | — | 1 | 4 | 2 | 7 | — | — | 7 | — | — |
| New Hampshire | 6 | 6 | — | — | 6 | — | — | — | — | 6 | — | — | 6 |
| New Jersey | 7 | 7 | — | — | 7 | — | — | — | 7 | — | 7 | — | — |
| New York | 36 | — | — | 36 | — | — | 36 | — | — | — | — | — | — |
| North Carolina | 11 | 11 | — | — | — | 11 | — | — | 10 | 1 | 11 | — | — |
| Ohio | 23 | — | 23 | — | 14 | 9 | — | 23 | — | — | 23 | — | — |
| Pennsylvania | 26 | — | 26 | — | 19 | 7 | — | — | 26 | — | — | 26 | — |
| Rhode Island | 4 | 3 | 1 | — | 2 | 2 | — | 1 | — | 3 | 4 | — | — |
| South Carolina | 9 | 9 | — | — | — | 9 | — | — | — | — | 9 | — | — |
| Tennessee | 13 | 13 | — | — | 9 | 4 | — | 7 | 2 | 1 | 7 | 2 | 2 |
| Texas | 4 | 4 | — | — | 4 | — | — | 4 | — | — | 4 | — | — |
| Vermont | 6 | 1 | 5 | — | 5 | 1 | — | 4 | — | 2 | 6 | — | — |
| Virginia | 17 | 17 | — | — | — | 17 | — | 17 | — | — | 17 | — | — |
| Wisconsin | 4 | — | 4 | — | — | 4 | — | 4 | — | — | 4 | — | — |
| Total | 290 | 176 | 78 | 36 | 126 | 125 | 39 | 125 | 55 | 53 | 179 | 33 | 38 |

1. Other candidates: John C. Calhoun, 9; W. J. Worth, 6; George M. Dallas, 3; not voting, 39.
2. Other candidates: William O. Butler, 4; Worth, 1; not voting, 35.

# 1848 Whig

*(Narrative, p. 42)*

| Delegation | Total Votes | First Pres. Ballot[1] | | | Fourth Pres. Ballot[2] | | |
|---|---|---|---|---|---|---|---|
| | | Taylor | Clay | Scott | Taylor | Clay | Scott |
| Alabama | 7 | 6 | 1 | — | 6 | 1 | — |
| Arkansas | 3 | 3 | — | — | 3 | — | — |
| Connecticut | 6 | — | 6 | — | 3 | 3 | — |
| Delaware | 3 | — | — | — | 2 | — | 1 |
| Florida | 3 | 3 | — | — | 3 | — | — |
| Georgia | 10 | 10 | — | — | 10 | — | — |
| Illinois | 8 | 4 | 3 | 1 | 8 | — | — |
| Indiana | 12 | 1 | 2 | 9 | 7 | 1 | 4 |
| Iowa | 4 | 2 | 1 | — | 4 | — | — |
| Kentucky | 12 | 7 | 5 | — | 11 | 1 | — |
| Louisiana | 6 | 5 | 1 | — | 6 | — | — |
| Maine | 9 | 5 | 1 | — | 5 | — | 3 |
| Maryland | 8 | — | 8 | — | 8 | — | — |
| Massachusetts | 12 | — | — | — | 1 | — | 2 |
| Michigan | 5 | — | 3 | 2 | 2 | — | 3 |
| Mississippi | 6 | 6 | — | — | 6 | — | — |
| Missouri | 7 | 6 | — | — | 7 | — | — |
| New Hampshire | 6 | — | — | — | 2 | — | — |
| New Jersey | 7 | 3 | 4 | — | 4 | 3 | — |
| New York | 36 | — | 29 | 5 | 6 | 13 | 17 |
| North Carolina | 11 | 6 | 5 | — | 10 | 1 | — |
| Ohio | 23 | 1 | 1 | 20 | 1 | 1 | 21 |
| Pennsylvania | 26 | 8 | 12 | 6 | 12 | 4 | 10 |
| Rhode Island | 4 | — | 4 | — | 4 | — | — |
| South Carolina | 2 | 1 | 1 | — | 1 | 1 | — |
| Tennessee | 13 | 13 | — | — | 13 | — | — |
| Texas | 4 | 4 | — | — | 4 | — | — |
| Vermont | 6 | 1 | 5 | — | 2 | 2 | 2 |
| Virginia | 17 | 15 | 2 | — | 16 | 1 | — |
| Wisconsin | 4 | 1 | 3 | — | 4 | — | — |
| **Total** | 280 | 111 | 97 | 43 | 171 | 32 | 63 |

1. Other candidates: Daniel Webster, 22; John McLean, 2; John M. Clayton, 4.
2. Other candidate: Webster, 14.

# 1852 Democratic

*(Narrative, p. 43)*

| Delegation | Total Votes | First Pres. Ballot[1] | | Twentieth Pres. Ballot[2] | | | Thirtieth Pres. Ballot[3] | | | Thirty-Fifth Pres. Ballot[4] | | | | Forty-Eighth Pres. Ballot[5] | | | | Forty-ninth Pres. Ballot[6] |
|---|---|---|---|---|---|---|---|---|---|---|---|---|---|---|---|---|---|---|
| | | Cass | Buchanan | Buchanan | Cass | Douglas | Douglas | Buchanan | Cass | Cass | Douglas | Marcy | Buchanan | Marcy | Cass | Pierce | Douglas | Pierce |
| Alabama | 9 | — | 9 | 9 | — | — | — | 9 | — | — | — | — | 9 | 9 | — | — | — | 9 |
| Arkansas | 4 | — | 4 | — | — | 4 | 4 | — | — | — | 4 | — | — | — | — | — | 4 | 4 |
| California | 4 | — | — | 1 | — | 3 | 3 | 1 | — | 2 | 1 | — | 1 | — | 4 | — | — | 4 |
| Connecticut | 6 | 2 | 2 | 2 | 2 | 1 | 6 | — | — | 3 | 3 | — | — | 6 | — | — | — | 6 |
| Delaware | 3 | 3 | — | — | 3 | — | — | — | — | 3 | — | — | — | — | 3 | — | — | 3 |
| Florida | 3 | — | — | — | — | 2 | 2 | — | — | — | 2 | — | — | — | — | — | 2 | 3 |
| Georgia | 10 | — | 10 | 10 | — | — | — | 10 | — | — | 10 | — | — | 10 | — | — | — | 10 |
| Illinois | 11 | — | — | — | — | 11 | 11 | — | — | — | 11 | — | — | — | — | — | 11 | 11 |
| Indiana | 13 | — | — | — | — | — | — | — | — | 13 | — | — | — | — | 13 | — | — | 13 |
| Iowa | 4 | 2 | — | — | 1 | 3 | 4 | — | — | 2 | 2 | — | — | — | 2 | — | 2 | 4 |
| Kentucky | 12 | 12 | — | — | 12 | — | — | — | — | 12 | — | — | — | — | — | 12 | — | 12 |
| Louisiana | 6 | 6 | — | — | 6 | — | 6 | — | — | 6 | — | — | — | — | 6 | — | — | 6 |
| Maine | 8 | 5 | 3 | 1 | 4 | 3 | 5 | 2 | — | 2 | 5 | — | 1 | — | — | 8 | — | 8 |
| Maryland | 8 | 8 | — | — | 8 | — | — | — | 8 | 8 | — | — | — | 1 | 1 | 5 | — | 5 |
| Massachusetts | 13 | 9 | — | — | 1 | 7 | 7 | — | 1 | 7 | 1 | 5 | — | 6 | — | 6 | 1 | 13 |
| Michigan | 6 | 6 | — | — | 6 | — | — | — | 6 | 6 | — | — | — | — | 6 | — | — | 6 |
| Mississippi | 7 | — | 7 | 7 | — | — | — | 7 | — | — | — | 7 | — | 7 | — | — | — | 7 |
| Missouri | 9 | 9 | — | — | — | 9 | 9 | — | — | 9 | — | — | — | — | 9 | — | — | 9 |
| New Hampshire | 5 | 4 | — | — | 5 | — | — | 2 | — | 5 | — | — | — | — | — | 5 | — | 5 |
| New Jersey | 7 | 7 | — | 7 | — | — | — | 7 | — | 7 | — | — | — | 7 | — | — | — | 7 |
| New York | 35 | 11 | — | — | 12 | — | 1 | — | 11 | 12 | 1 | 22 | — | 24 | 10 | — | 1 | 35 |
| North Carolina | 10 | — | 10 | 9 | — | 1 | 4 | 6 | — | — | — | 10 | — | 10 | — | — | — | 10 |
| Ohio | 23 | 16 | — | — | 13 | 6 | 9 | — | 7 | 18 | 3 | — | — | — | 15 | — | 4 | 17 |
| Pennsylvania | 27 | — | 27 | 27 | — | — | — | 27 | — | — | — | — | 27 | — | — | — | — | 27 |
| Rhode Island | 4 | 3 | — | — | — | 4 | 4 | — | — | 4 | — | — | — | — | — | 4 | — | 4 |
| Tennessee | 12 | 6 | 6 | 4 | 5 | 3 | 7 | 5 | — | 9 | 2 | — | 1 | 9 | — | — | 1 | 12 |
| Texas | 4 | — | — | — | — | — | — | — | — | — | — | — | — | — | — | — | — | 4 |
| Vermont | 5 | 5 | — | — | — | 5 | 5 | — | — | — | 5 | — | — | — | — | — | 5 | 5 |
| Virginia | 15 | — | 15 | 15 | — | — | — | 15 | — | — | — | — | — | — | — | 15 | — | 15 |
| Wisconsin | 5 | 2 | — | — | 3 | 2 | 5 | — | — | 3 | 2 | — | — | — | 3 | — | 2 | 5 |
| **Total** | 288 | 116 | 93 | 92 | 81 | 64 | 92 | 91 | 33 | 131 | 52 | 44 | 39 | 89 | 72 | 55 | 33 | 279[a] |

1. Other candidates: William L. Marcy, 27; Stephen A. Douglas, 20; Joseph Lane, 13; Samuel Houston, 8; J. B. Weller, 4; Henry Dodge, 3; William O. Butler, 2; Daniel S. Dickinson, 1; not voting, 1.
2. Other candidates: Marcy, 26; Lane, 13; Houston, 10; Butler, 1; Dickinson, 1.
3. Other candidates: Marcy, 26; Butler, 20; Lane, 13; Houston, 12; Dickinson, 1.
4. Other candidates: Franklin Pierce, 15; Houston, 5; Butler, 1; Dickinson, 1.
5. Other candidates: Buchanan, 28; Houston, 6; Linn Boyd, 2; Butler, 1; R. J. Ingersoll, 1; Dickinson, 1.
6. Other candidates: Cass, 2; Douglas, 2; Butler, 1; Houston, 1; not voting, 3.
a. Sum of column; proceedings record 283.

# 1852 Whig

*(Narrative, p. 44)*

| Delegation | Total Votes | First Pres. Ballot | | | 50th Pres. Ballot | | | 52nd Pres. Ballot | | | 53rd Pres. Ballot | | |
|---|---|---|---|---|---|---|---|---|---|---|---|---|---|
| | | Scott | Fillmore | Webster | Scott | Fillmore | Webster | Scott | Fillmore | Webster | Scott | Fillmore | Webster |
| Alabama | 9 | — | 9 | — | — | 9 | — | — | 9 | — | — | 9 | — |
| Arkansas | 4 | — | 4 | — | — | 4 | — | — | 4 | — | — | 4 | — |
| California | 4 | 2 | 1 | 1 | 3 | 1 | — | 3 | — | 1 | 3 | — | 1 |
| Connecticut | 6 | 2 | 1 | 3 | 2 | 1 | 3 | 2 | 1 | 3 | 2 | 1 | 3 |
| Delaware | 3 | 3 | — | — | 3 | — | — | 3 | — | — | 3 | — | — |
| Florida | 3 | — | 3 | — | — | 3 | — | — | 3 | — | — | 3 | — |
| Georgia | 10 | — | 10 | — | — | 10 | — | — | 10 | — | — | 10 | — |
| Illinois | 11 | 11 | — | — | 11 | — | — | 11 | — | — | 11 | — | — |
| Indiana | 13 | 13 | — | — | 13 | — | — | 13 | — | — | 13 | — | — |
| Iowa | 4 | — | 4 | — | 1 | 3 | — | 1 | 3 | — | 1 | 3 | — |
| Kentucky | 12 | — | 12 | — | — | 12 | — | — | 12 | — | — | 11 | — |
| Louisiana | 6 | — | 6 | — | — | 6 | — | — | 6 | — | — | 6 | — |
| Maine | 8 | 8 | — | — | 8 | — | — | 8 | — | — | 8 | — | — |
| Maryland | 8 | — | 8 | — | — | 8 | — | — | 8 | — | — | 8 | — |
| Massachusetts | 13 | 2 | — | 11 | 2 | — | 11 | 2 | — | 11 | 2 | — | 11 |
| Michigan | 6 | 6 | — | — | 6 | — | — | 6 | — | — | 6 | — | — |
| Mississippi | 7 | — | 7 | — | — | 7 | — | — | 7 | — | — | 7 | — |
| Missouri | 9 | — | 9 | — | 3 | 6 | — | 1 | 6 | — | 3 | 6 | — |
| New Hampshire | 5 | 1 | — | 4 | 1 | — | 4 | 1 | — | 4 | 5 | — | — |
| New Jersey | 7 | 7 | — | — | 7 | — | — | 7 | — | — | 7 | — | — |
| New York | 35 | 24 | 7 | 2 | 25 | 7 | 1 | 25 | 7 | 1 | 25 | 7 | 1 |
| North Carolina | 10 | — | 10 | — | — | 10 | — | — | 10 | — | — | 10 | — |
| Ohio | 23 | 22 | 1 | — | 23 | — | — | 23 | — | — | 23 | — | — |
| Pennsylvania | 27 | 26 | 1 | — | 26 | 1 | — | 27 | — | — | 27 | — | — |
| Rhode Island | 4 | 1 | 1 | 2 | 2 | — | 2 | 2 | — | 2 | 3 | — | 1 |
| South Carolina | 8 | — | 8 | — | — | 8 | — | — | 8 | — | — | 8 | — |
| Tennessee | 12 | — | 12 | — | — | 12 | — | 4 | 8 | — | 3 | 9 | — |
| Texas | 4 | — | 4 | — | — | 4 | — | — | 4 | — | — | 4 | — |
| Vermont | 5 | 1 | 1 | 3 | 2 | — | 3 | 2 | 2 | 1 | 5 | — | — |
| Virginia | 15 | 1 | 13 | — | 3 | 10 | — | 3 | 10 | — | 8 | 6 | — |
| Wisconsin | 5 | 1 | 1 | 3 | 1 | 1 | 3 | 2 | — | 2 | 1 | — | 4 |
| **Total** | 296 | 132[a] | 133 | 29 | 142 | 122[a] | 27 | 148[a] | 118 | 25 | 159 | 112 | 21 |

a. The sum of the column for Scott on the first ballot is 131 votes, for Fillmore on the 50th ballot 123 votes and for Scott on the 52nd ballot is 146 votes. The source for these discrepancies is the Baltimore Sun for June 19, 1852, and June 22, 1852. The Sun reported June 19, 1852, total votes for Scott on the first ballot as 132 votes; however, the column of figures for the state-by-state ballots reported in the Sun add up to 131 votes. Similarly, on June 22, 1852, the Sun reported 122 votes for Fillmore on the 50th ballot and 148 for Scott on the 52nd ballot, but the state-by-state ballots reported in the Sun add up to 123 votes and 146 votes, respectively. Bain's Convention Decisions and Voting Records used the Baltimore Sun as its source for the 1852 Whig convention ballots.

# 1856 Democratic

(Narrative, p. 47)

| Delegation | Total Votes | First Pres. Ballot Buchanan | Pierce | Douglas | Other | Tenth Pres. Ballot Buchanan | Pierce | Douglas | Other | Fifteenth Pres. Ballot Buchanan | Douglas | Other | 17th Pres. Ballot Buchanan |
|---|---|---|---|---|---|---|---|---|---|---|---|---|---|
| Alabama | 9 | — | 9 | — | — | — | 9 | — | — | — | 9 | — | 9 |
| Arkansas | 4 | — | 4 | — | — | — | — | 4 | — | — | 4 | — | 4 |
| California | 4 | — | — | — | 4 | — | — | — | 4 | — | — | 4 | 4 |
| Connecticut | 3 | 6 | — | — | — | 6 | — | — | — | 6 | — | — | 6 |
| Delaware | 3 | 3 | — | — | — | 3 | — | — | — | 3 | — | — | 3 |
| Florida | 3 | — | 3 | — | — | — | 3 | — | — | — | 3 | — | 3 |
| Georgia | 10 | — | 10 | — | — | 3 | — | 7 | — | 3 | 7 | — | 10 |
| Illinois | 11 | — | — | 11 | — | — | — | 11 | — | — | 11 | — | 11 |
| Indiana | 13 | 13 | — | — | — | 13 | — | — | — | 13 | — | — | 13 |
| Iowa | 4 | — | — | 4 | — | 2 | — | 2 | — | 2 | 2 | — | 4 |
| Kentucky | 12 | 4 | 5 | 3 | — | 4½ | — | 7½ | — | 4 | 7 | 1 | 12 |
| Louisiana | 6 | 6 | — | — | — | 6 | — | — | — | 6 | — | — | 6 |
| Maine | 8 | 5 | 3 | — | — | 6 | 2 | — | — | 7 | — | 1 | 8 |
| Maryland | 8 | 6 | 2 | — | — | 7 | 1 | — | — | 8 | — | — | 8 |
| Massachusetts | 13 | 4 | 9 | — | — | 6 | 7 | — | — | 10 | 3 | — | 13 |
| Michigan | 6 | 6 | — | — | — | 6 | — | — | — | 6 | — | — | 6 |
| Mississippi | 7 | — | 7 | — | — | — | 7 | — | — | — | 7 | — | 7 |
| Missouri | 9 | — | — | 9 | — | — | — | 9 | — | — | 9 | — | 9 |
| New Hampshire | 5 | — | 5 | — | — | — | 5 | — | — | — | 5 | — | 5 |
| New Jersey | 7 | 7 | — | — | — | 7 | — | — | — | 7 | — | — | 7 |
| New York | 35 | 17 | 18 | — | — | 18 | 17 | — | — | 17 | 18 | — | 35 |
| North Carolina | 10 | — | 10 | — | — | — | 10 | — | — | — | 10 | — | 10 |
| Ohio | 23 | 13½ | 4½ | 4 | 1 | 13 | 3½ | 5 | 1½ | 13½ | 6½ | 3 | 23 |
| Pennsylvania | 27 | 27 | — | — | — | 27 | — | — | — | 27 | — | — | 27 |
| Rhode Island | 4 | — | 4 | — | — | — | 4 | — | — | 4 | — | — | 4 |
| South Carolina | 8 | — | 8 | — | — | — | 8 | — | — | — | 8 | — | 8 |
| Tennessee | 12 | — | 12 | — | — | — | — | 12 | — | 12 | — | — | 12 |
| Texas | 4 | — | 4 | — | — | — | 4 | — | — | — | 4 | — | 4 |
| Vermont | 5 | — | 5 | — | — | — | — | 5 | — | — | 5 | — | 5 |
| Virginia | 15 | 15 | — | — | — | 15 | — | — | — | 15 | — | — | 15 |
| Wisconsin | 5 | 3 | — | 2 | — | 5 | — | — | — | 5 | — | — | 5 |
| **Total** | **296** | **135½** | **122½** | **33** | **5[1]** | **147½** | **80½** | **62½** | **5½[2]** | **168½** | **118½** | **9[3]** | **296** |

1. Other candidate: Lewis Cass, 5.
2. Other candidate: Cass, 5½.
3. Other candidates: Cass, 4½; Franklin Pierce, 3½; not voting, 1.

# 1856 Republican

(Narrative, p. 46)

| Delegation | Total Votes | Informal Pres. Ballot[1] Fremont | McLean | Formal Pres. Ballot[2] Fremont |
|---|---|---|---|---|
| California | 12 | 12 | — | 12 |
| Connecticut | 18 | 18 | — | 18 |
| Delaware | 9 | — | 9 | 9 |
| Illinois | 34 | 14 | 19 | 33 |
| Indiana | 39 | 18 | 21 | 39 |
| Iowa | 12 | 12 | — | 12 |
| Kansas | 10 | 9 | — | 9 |
| Kentucky | 5 | 5 | — | 5 |
| Maine | 24 | 13 | 11 | 24 |
| Maryland | 9 | 4 | 3 | 7 |
| Massachusetts | 39 | 39 | — | 39 |
| Michigan | 18 | 18 | — | 18 |
| Minnesota | 2 | — | — | — |
| New Hampshire | 15 | 15 | — | 15 |
| New Jersey | 21 | 7 | 14 | 21 |
| New York | 105 | 93 | 3 | 105 |
| Ohio | 69 | 30 | 39 | 55 |
| Pennsylvania | 81 | 10 | 71 | 57 |
| Rhode Island | 12 | 12 | — | 12 |
| Vermont | 15 | 15 | — | 15 |
| Wisconsin | 15 | 15 | — | 15 |
| District of Columbia | 3 | — | — | — |
| **Total** | **567** | **359** | **190** | **520** |

1. Other candidates: Nathaniel Banks, 1; Charles Sumner, 2; William Seward, 1; absent or not voting, 14.
2. Other candidates: John McLean, 37; Seward, 1; absent or not voting, 9.

# 1860 Democratic

*(Narrative, p. 49)*

| Delegation | Total Votes | Charleston Convention — Butler Amend. on 1856 platform Yea | Nay | Minority Report on platform Yea | Nay | First Pres. Ballot¹ Douglas | Hunter | Guthrie | 57th Pres. Ballot² Douglas | Guthrie | Baltimore Convention — Minority Report on Credentials Yea | Nay | Not Voting | Reconsider Louisiana Credentials Yea | Nay | Not Voting | First Pres. Ballot³ Douglas | Second Pres. Ballot⁴ Douglas |
|---|---|---|---|---|---|---|---|---|---|---|---|---|---|---|---|---|---|---|
| Alabama | 9 | — | 9 | — | 9 | — | — | — | — | — | — | — | 9 | — | — | 9 | 9 | 9 |
| Arkansas | 4 | — | 4 | — | 4 | — | 1 | — | — | — | ½ | ½ | 3 | ½ | ½ | 3 | 1 | 1½ |
| California | 4 | — | 4 | — | 4 | — | — | — | — | — | 4 | — | — | — | 4 | — | — | — |
| Connecticut | 6 | 2½ | 3½ | 6 | — | 3½ | — | — | 3½ | 2½ | 2½ | 3½ | — | 3½ | 2½ | — | 3½ | 3½ |
| Delaware | 3 | 3 | — | — | 3 | — | 2 | — | — | — | 2 | — | 1 | — | 2 | 1 | — | — |
| Florida | 3 | — | 3 | — | 3 | — | — | — | — | — | — | — | 3 | — | — | 3 | — | — |
| Georgia | 10 | 10 | — | — | 10 | — | — | — | — | — | — | — | 10 | — | — | 10 | — | — |
| Illinois | 11 | — | 11 | 11 | — | 11 | — | — | 11 | — | — | 11 | — | 11 | — | — | 11 | 11 |
| Indiana | 13 | — | 13 | 13 | — | 13 | — | — | 13 | — | — | 13 | — | 13 | — | — | 13 | 13 |
| Iowa | 4 | — | 4 | 4 | — | 4 | — | — | 4 | — | — | 4 | — | 4 | — | — | 4 | 4 |
| Kentucky | 12 | 9 | 3 | 2½ | 9½ | — | — | 12 | — | 12 | 10 | 2 | — | 2 | 10 | — | — | 3 |
| Louisiana | 6 | — | 6 | — | 6 | — | — | — | — | — | — | — | 6 | — | — | 6 | 6 | 6 |
| Maine | 8 | 3 | 5 | 8 | — | 5 | — | 3 | 5 | 3 | 2½ | 5½ | — | 5½ | 2½ | — | 5½ | 7 |
| Maryland | 8 | 5½ | 2½ | 3½ | 4½ | 2 | 5 | — | 4 | 4 | 5½ | 2 | ½ | 2 | 6 | — | 2½ | 2½ |
| Massachusetts | 13 | 8 | 5 | 7 | 6 | 5½ | 6 | — | 6 | 6 | 8 | 5 | — | 5 | 8 | — | 10 | 10 |
| Michigan | 6 | — | 6 | 6 | — | 6 | — | — | 6 | — | — | 6 | — | 6 | — | — | 6 | 6 |
| Minnesota | 4 | 1½ | 2½ | 4 | — | 4 | — | — | 3 | — | 1½ | 2½ | — | 2½ | 1½ | — | 2½ | 4 |
| Mississippi | 7 | — | 7 | — | 7 | — | — | — | — | — | — | — | 7 | — | — | 7 | — | — |
| Missouri | 9 | 4½ | 4½ | 4 | 5 | 4½ | — | 4½ | 4½ | 4½ | 5 | 4 | — | 4½ | 4½ | — | 4½ | 4½ |
| New Hampshire | 5 | — | 5 | 5 | — | 5 | — | — | 5 | — | ½ | 4½ | — | 4½ | ½ | — | 5 | 5 |
| New Jersey | 7 | 5 | 2 | 5 | 2 | — | — | 7 | 2 | 5 | 4 | 3 | — | 2½ | 4½ | — | 2½ | 2½ |
| New York | 35 | — | 35 | 35 | — | 35 | — | — | 35 | — | — | 35 | — | 35 | — | — | 35 | 35 |
| North Carolina | 10 | 10 | — | — | 10 | 1 | 9 | — | 1 | — | 9 | 1 | — | 1 | 8½ | ½ | 1 | 1 |
| Ohio | 23 | — | 23 | 23 | — | 23 | — | — | 23 | — | — | 23 | — | 23 | — | — | 23 | 23 |
| Oregon | 3 | 3 | — | — | 3 | — | — | — | — | — | 3 | — | — | — | 3 | — | — | — |
| Pennsylvania | 27 | 16½ | 10½ | 12 | 15 | 9 | 3 | 9 | 9½ | 17½ | 17 | 10 | — | 10 | 17 | — | 10 | 19 |
| Rhode Island | 4 | — | 4 | 4 | — | 4 | — | — | 4 | — | — | 4 | — | 4 | — | — | 4 | 4 |
| South Carolina | 8 | — | 8 | — | 8 | — | 1 | — | — | — | — | — | 8 | — | — | 8 | — | — |
| Tennessee | 12 | 11 | 1 | 1 | 11 | — | — | — | 1 | 11 | 10 | 1 | 1 | 2 | 10 | — | 3 | 3 |
| Texas | 4 | — | 4 | — | 4 | — | — | — | — | — | — | — | 4 | — | — | 4 | — | — |
| Vermont | 5 | — | 5 | 5 | — | 5 | — | — | 5 | — | 1½ | 3½ | — | 4½ | ½ | — | 5 | 5 |
| Virginia | 15 | 12½ | 2½ | 1 | 14 | — | 15 | — | 1 | — | 14 | 1 | — | — | 15 | — | 1½ | 3 |
| Wisconsin | 5 | -- | 5 | 5 | — | 5 | — | — | 5 | — | — | 5 | — | 5 | — | — | 5 | 5 |
| **Total** | 303 | 105 | 198 | 165 | 138 | 145½ | 42 | 35½ᵃ | 151½ | 65½ | 100½ | 150 | 52½ | 151ᵇ | 100½ᶜ | 51½ | 173½ | 190½ᵈ |

1. Other candidates: Andrew Johnson, 12; Daniel S. Dickinson, 7; Joseph Lane, 6; Isaac Toucey, 2½; Jefferson Davis, 1½; James A. Pearce, 1; not voting, 50.
2. Other candidates: Robert M. T. Hunter, 16; Lane, 14; Dickinson, 4; Davis, 1; not voting, 51.
3. Other candidates: James Guthrie, 9; John C. Breckinridge, 5; Thomas S. Bocock, 1; Horatio Seymour, 1; Henry A. Wise, ½; Dickinson, ½; not voting, 112½.
4. Other candidates: Breckinridge, 7½; Guthrie, 5½; not voting, 99½.
a. Sum of column; proceedings record 35.
b. Sum of column; proceedings record 150½.
c. Sum of column; proceedings record 99.
d. Sum of column; proceedings record 181½.

# 1860 Republican

*(Narrative, p. 50)*

| Delegation | Total Votes | First Pres. Ballot[1] | | | | | Second Pres. Ballot[2] | | Third Pres. Ballot[3] (Before shift) | | Third Pres. Ballot[4] (After shift) | |
|---|---|---|---|---|---|---|---|---|---|---|---|---|
| | | Seward | Lincoln | Cameron | Bates | Chase | Seward | Lincoln | Seward | Lincoln | Seward | Lincoln |
| California | 8 | 8 | — | — | — | — | 8 | — | 8 | — | 3 | 5 |
| Connecticut | 12 | — | 2 | — | 7 | 2 | — | 4 | 1 | 4 | 1 | 8 |
| Delaware | 6 | — | — | — | 6 | — | — | 6 | — | 6 | — | 6 |
| Illinois | 22 | — | 22 | — | — | — | — | 22 | — | 22 | — | 22 |
| Indiana | 26 | — | 26 | — | — | — | — | 26 | — | 26 | — | 26 |
| Iowa | 8 | 2 | 2 | 1 | 1 | 1 | 2 | 5 | 2 | 5½ | — | 8 |
| Kansas | 6 | 6 | — | — | — | — | 6 | — | 6 | — | — | 6 |
| Kentucky | 23 | 5 | 6 | — | — | 8 | 7 | 9 | 6 | 13 | — | 23 |
| Maine | 16 | 10 | 6 | — | — | — | 10 | 6 | 10 | 6 | — | 16 |
| Maryland | 11 | 3 | — | — | 8 | — | 3 | — | 2 | 9 | 2 | 9 |
| Massachusetts | 26 | 21 | 4 | — | — | — | 22 | 4 | 18 | 8 | 18 | 8 |
| Michigan | 12 | 12 | — | — | — | — | 12 | — | 12 | — | 12 | — |
| Minnesota | 8 | 8 | — | — | — | — | 8 | — | 8 | — | — | 8 |
| Missouri | 18 | — | — | — | 18 | — | — | — | — | — | — | 18 |
| Nebraska | 6 | 2 | 1 | 1 | — | 2 | 3 | 1 | 3 | 1 | — | 6 |
| New Hampshire | 10 | — | — | — | — | 1 | 1 | 9 | 1 | 9 | — | 10 |
| New Jersey | 14 | 1 | 7 | — | — | — | 4 | — | 5 | 8 | 5 | 8 |
| New York | 70 | 70 | — | — | — | — | 70 | — | 70 | — | 70 | — |
| Ohio | 46 | — | 8 | — | — | 34 | — | 14 | — | 29 | — | 46 |
| Oregon | 5 | — | — | — | 5 | — | — | — | 1 | 4 | — | 5 |
| Pennsylvania | 54 | 1½ | 4 | 47½ | — | — | 2½ | 48 | — | 52 | ½ | 53 |
| Rhode Island | 8 | — | — | — | 1 | 1 | — | 3 | 1 | 5 | — | 8 |
| Texas | 6 | 4 | — | — | 2 | — | 6 | — | 6 | — | — | 6 |
| Vermont | 10 | — | — | — | — | — | — | 10 | — | 10 | — | 10 |
| Virginia | 23 | 8 | 14 | 1 | — | — | 8 | 14 | 8 | 14 | — | 23 |
| Wisconsin | 10 | 10 | — | — | — | — | 10 | — | 10 | -- | 10 | — |
| District of Columbia | 2 | 2 | — | — | — | — | 2 | — | 2 | — | — | 2 |
| **Total** | 466 | 173½ | 102 | 50½ | 48 | 49 | 184½ | 181 | 180 | 231½ | 121½ | 340[a] |

1. *Other candidates: Benjamin F. Wade, 3; John McLean, 12; John M. Reed, 1; William L. Dayton, 14; Charles Sumner, 1; John C. Fremont, 1; Jacob Collamer, 10; absent and not voting, 1.*
2. *Other candidates: Edward Bates, 35; Simon Cameron, 2; McLean, 8; Salmon P. Chase, 42½; Dayton, 10; Cassius M. Clay, 2; absent and not voting, 1.*
3. *Other candidates: Edward Bates, 22; Chase, 24½; McLean, 5; Dayton, 1; Clay, 1; absent and not voting, 1.*
4. *Other candidates: Chase, 2; Dayton, 1; Clay, 1; McLean, ½.*
a. *Sum of column; proceedings record 364.*

# 1864 Democratic

*(Narrative, p. 53)*

| Delegation | Total Votes | First Pres. Ballot[1] (Before shift) | | First Pres. Ballot (After shift) | |
|---|---|---|---|---|---|
| | | McClellan | Seymour | McClellan | Seymour |
| California | 5 | 2½ | 2½ | 5 | — |
| Connecticut | 6 | 5½ | — | 6 | — |
| Delaware | 3 | — | 3 | — | 3 |
| Illinois | 16 | 16 | — | 16 | — |
| Indiana | 13 | 9½ | 3½ | 9½ | 3½ |
| Iowa | 8 | 3 | — | 8 | — |
| Kansas | 3 | 3 | — | 3 | — |
| Kentucky | 11 | 5½ | 5½ | 11 | — |
| Maine | 7 | 4 | 3 | 7 | — |
| Maryland | 7 | — | 7 | — | 7 |
| Massachusetts | 12 | 11½ | — | 12 | — |
| Michigan | 8 | 6½ | — | 8 | — |
| Minnesota | 4 | 4 | — | 4 | — |
| Missouri | 11 | 6½ | — | 7 | 4 |
| New Hampshire | 5 | 5 | — | 5 | — |
| New Jersey | 7 | 7 | — | 7 | — |
| New York | 33 | 33 | — | 33 | — |
| Ohio | 21 | 8½ | 10½ | 15 | 6 |
| Oregon | 3 | 2 | 1 | 3 | — |
| Pennsylvania | 26 | 26 | — | 26 | — |
| Rhode Island | 4 | 4 | — | 4 | — |
| Vermont | 5 | 4 | 1 | 5 | — |
| Wisconsin | 8 | 7 | 1 | 8 | — |
| **Total** | **226** | **174** | **38** | **202½** | **23½[a]** |

1. Other candidates: Horatio Seymour, 12; Charles O'Connor, ½; blank, 1½.
a. Sum of column; proceedings record 28½.

# 1864 Republican

*(Narrative, p. 52)*

| Delegation | Total Votes | First Pres. Ballot[1] | |
|---|---|---|---|
| | | Lincoln | Grant |
| Arkansas | 10 | 10 | — |
| California | 10 | 7 | — |
| Colorado | 6 | 6 | — |
| Connecticut | 12 | 12 | — |
| Delaware | 6 | 6 | — |
| Illinois | 32 | 32 | — |
| Indiana | 26 | 26 | — |
| Iowa | 16 | 16 | — |
| Kansas | 6 | 6 | — |
| Kentucky | 22 | 22 | — |
| Louisiana | 14 | 14 | — |
| Maine | 14 | 14 | — |
| Maryland | 14 | 14 | — |
| Massachusetts | 24 | 24 | — |
| Michigan | 16 | 16 | — |
| Minnesota | 8 | 8 | — |
| Missouri | 22 | — | 22 |
| Nebraska | 6 | 6 | — |
| Nevada | 6 | 6 | — |
| New Hampshire | 10 | 10 | — |
| New Jersey | 14 | 14 | — |
| New York | 66 | 66 | — |
| Ohio | 42 | 42 | — |
| Oregon | 6 | 6 | — |
| Pennsylvania | 52 | 52 | — |
| Rhode Island | 8 | 8 | — |
| Tennessee | 15 | 15 | — |
| Vermont | 10 | 10 | — |
| West Virginia | 10 | 10 | — |
| Wisconsin | 16 | 16 | — |
| **Total** | **519** | **494[a]** | **22** |

1. Not voting, 3.
a. Sum of column; proceedings record 484.

# 1868 Democratic

*(Narrative, p. 55)*

| Delegation | Total Votes | First Pres. Ballot[1] | | | | 22nd Pres. Ballot[2] (Before shift) | | 22nd Pres. Ballot (After shift) |
|---|---|---|---|---|---|---|---|---|
| | | Pendleton | Hancock | Church | Johnson | Hancock | Hendricks | Seymour |
| Alabama | 8 | — | — | — | 8 | 8 | — | 8 |
| Arkansas | 5 | — | — | — | — | — | 5 | 5 |
| California | 5 | 2 | — | — | — | — | 5 | 5 |
| Connecticut | 6 | — | — | — | — | — | — | 6 |
| Delaware | 3 | 3 | — | — | — | 3 | — | 3 |
| Florida | 3 | — | — | — | 3 | — | 3 | 3 |
| Georgia | 9 | — | — | — | 9 | 9 | — | 9 |
| Illinois | 16 | 16 | — | — | — | — | 16 | 16 |
| Indiana | 13 | 13 | — | — | — | — | 13 | 13 |
| Iowa | 8 | 8 | — | — | — | — | 8 | 8 |
| Kansas | 3 | 2 | — | — | — | 1 | 2 | 3 |
| Kentucky | 11 | 11 | — | — | — | — | — | 11 |
| Louisiana | 7 | — | 7 | — | — | 7 | — | 7 |
| Maine | 7 | 1½ | 4½ | — | 1 | 4½ | 2½ | 7 |
| Maryland | 7 | 4½ | — | — | 2½ | 6 | 1 | 7 |
| Massachusetts | 12 | 1 | 11 | — | — | — | — | 12 |
| Michigan | 8 | — | — | — | — | — | 8 | 8 |
| Minnesota | 4 | 4 | — | — | — | — | 4 | 4 |
| Mississippi | 7 | — | 7 | — | — | 7 | — | 7 |
| Missouri | 11 | 5 | 2 | 1 | ½ | 2 | 8 | 11 |
| Nebraska | 3 | 3 | — | — | — | — | 3 | 3 |
| Nevada | 3 | — | — | — | — | — | 3 | 3 |
| New Hampshire | 5 | 2 | 2 | — | — | 4½ | ½ | 5 |
| New Jersey | 7 | — | — | — | — | — | 7 | 7 |
| New York | 33 | — | — | 33 | — | — | 33 | 33 |
| North Carolina | 9 | — | — | — | 9 | — | 9 | 9 |
| Ohio | 21 | 21 | — | — | — | — | — | 21 |
| Oregon | 3 | 3 | — | — | — | — | 3 | 3 |
| Pennsylvania | 26 | — | — | — | — | 26 | — | 26 |
| Rhode Island | 4 | — | — | — | — | — | — | 4 |
| South Carolina | 6 | — | — | — | 6 | 6 | — | 6 |
| Tennessee | 10 | — | — | — | 10 | 3½ | 1½ | 10 |
| Texas | 6 | — | — | — | 6 | 6 | — | 6 |
| Vermont | 5 | — | — | — | — | — | 5 | 5 |
| Virginia | 10 | — | — | — | 10 | 10 | — | 10 |
| West Virginia | 5 | 5 | — | — | — | — | 5 | 5 |
| Wisconsin | 8 | — | — | — | — | — | — | 8 |
| **Total** | 317 | 105 | 33½ | 34 | 65 | 103½ | 145½ | 317 |

1. Other candidates: James E. English, 16; Joel Parker, 13; Asa Packer, 26; James R. Doolittle, 13; Thomas A. Hendricks, 2½; Frank P. Blair, ½; Reverdy Johnson, 8½.
2. Other candidates: Horatio Seymour, 22; English, 7; Doolittle, 4; Johnson, 4; not voting, 31.

# 1868 Republican

*(Narrative, p. 54)*

| Delegation | Total Votes | First Pres. Ballot Grant |
|---|---|---|
| Alabama | 18 | 18 |
| Arkansas | 10 | 10 |
| California | 10 | 10 |
| Colorado | 6 | 6 |
| Connecticut | 12 | 12 |
| Delaware | 6 | 6 |
| Florida | 6 | 6 |
| Georgia | 18 | 18 |
| Idaho | 2 | 2 |
| Illinois | 32 | 32 |
| Indiana | 26 | 26 |
| Iowa | 16 | 16 |
| Kansas | 6 | 6 |
| Kentucky | 22 | 22 |
| Louisiana | 14 | 14 |
| Maine | 14 | 14 |
| Maryland | 14 | 14 |
| Massachusetts | 24 | 24 |
| Michigan | 16 | 16 |
| Minnesota | 8 | 8 |
| Mississippi | 14 | 14 |
| Missouri | 22 | 22 |
| Montana | 2 | 2 |
| Nebraska | 6 | 6 |
| Nevada | 6 | 6 |
| New Hampshire | 10 | 10 |
| New Jersey | 14 | 14 |
| New York | 66 | 66 |
| North Carolina | 18 | 18 |
| Dakota[a] | 2 | 2 |
| Ohio | 42 | 42 |
| Oregon | 6 | 6 |
| Pennsylvania | 52 | 52 |
| Rhode Island | 8 | 8 |
| South Carolina | 12 | 12 |
| Tennessee | 20 | 20 |
| Texas | 12 | 12 |
| Vermont | 10 | 10 |
| Virginia | 20 | 20 |
| West Virginia | 10 | 10 |
| Wisconsin | 16 | 16 |
| District of Columbia | 2 | 2 |
| **Total** | **650** | **650** |

a. *Dakota Territory, includes North and South Dakota.*

# 1872 Democratic

*(Narrative, p. 57)*

| Delegation | Total Votes | First Pres. Ballot[1] Greeley |
|---|---|---|
| Alabama | 20 | 20 |
| Arkansas | 12 | 12 |
| California | 12 | 12 |
| Connecticut | 12 | 12 |
| Delaware | 6 | — |
| Florida | 8 | 6 |
| Georgia | 22 | 18 |
| Illinois | 42 | 42 |
| Indiana | 30 | 30 |
| Iowa | 22 | 22 |
| Kansas | 10 | 10 |
| Kentucky | 24 | 24 |
| Louisiana | 16 | 16 |
| Maine | 14 | 14 |
| Maryland | 16 | 16 |
| Massachusetts | 26 | 26 |
| Michigan | 22 | 22 |
| Minnesota | 10 | 10 |
| Mississippi | 16 | 16 |
| Missouri | 30 | 30 |
| Nebraska | 6 | 6 |
| Nevada | 6 | 6 |
| New Hampshire | 10 | 10 |
| New Jersey | 18 | 9 |
| New York | 70 | 70 |
| North Carolina | 20 | 20 |
| Ohio | 44 | 44 |
| Oregon | 6 | 6 |
| Pennsylvania | 58 | 35 |
| Rhode Island | 8 | 8 |
| South Carolina | 14 | 14 |
| Tennessee | 24 | 24 |
| Texas | 16 | 16 |
| Vermont | 10 | 10 |
| Virginia | 22 | 22 |
| West Virginia | 10 | 8 |
| Wisconsin | 20 | 20 |
| **Total** | **732** | **686** |

1. Other candidates: Thomas F. Bayard, 15; Jeremiah S. Black, 21; William S. Groesbeck, 2; blank, 8.

# 1872 Republican

*(Narrative, p. 57)*

| Delegation | Total Votes | First Pres. Ballot Grant |
|---|---|---|
| Alabama | 20 | 20 |
| Arizona | 2 | 2 |
| Arkansas | 12 | 12 |
| California | 12 | 12 |
| Colorado | 2 | 2 |
| Connecticut | 12 | 12 |
| Delaware | 6 | 6 |
| Florida | 8 | 8 |
| Georgia | 22 | 22 |
| Idaho | 2 | 2 |
| Illinois | 42 | 42 |
| Indiana | 30 | 30 |
| Iowa | 22 | 22 |
| Kansas | 10 | 10 |
| Kentucky | 24 | 24 |
| Louisiana | 16 | 16 |
| Maine | 14 | 14 |
| Maryland | 16 | 16 |
| Massachusetts | 26 | 26 |
| Michigan | 22 | 22 |
| Minnesota | 10 | 10 |
| Mississippi | 16 | 16 |
| Missouri | 30 | 30 |
| Montana | 2 | 2 |
| Nebraska | 6 | 6 |
| Nevada | 6 | 6 |
| New Hampshire | 10 | 10 |
| New Jersey | 18 | 18 |
| New Mexico | 2 | 2 |
| New York | 70 | 70 |
| North Carolina | 20 | 20 |
| Dakota[a] | 2 | 2 |
| Ohio | 44 | 44 |
| Oregon | 6 | 6 |
| Pennsylvania | 58 | 58 |
| Rhode Island | 8 | 8 |
| South Carolina | 14 | 14 |
| Tennessee | 24 | 24 |
| Texas | 16 | 16 |
| Utah | 2 | 2 |
| Vermont | 10 | 10 |
| Virginia | 22 | 22 |
| Washington | 2 | 2 |
| West Virginia | 10 | 10 |
| Wisconsin | 20 | 20 |
| Wyoming | 2 | 2 |
| District of Columbia | 2 | 2 |
| **Total** | **752** | **752** |

a. Dakota Territory, includes North and South Dakota.

# 1876 Democratic

*(Narrative, p. 59)*

| Delegation | Total Votes | First Pres. Ballot[1] | | | Second Pres. Ballot[2] | |
|---|---|---|---|---|---|---|
| | | Tilden | Hendricks | Hancock | Tilden | Hendricks |
| Alabama | 20 | 13 | 5 | 2 | 20 | — |
| Arkansas | 12 | 12 | — | — | 12 | — |
| California | 12 | 12 | — | — | 12 | — |
| Colorado | 6 | — | 6 | — | 6 | — |
| Connecticut | 12 | 12 | — | — | 12 | — |
| Delaware | 6 | — | — | — | 6 | — |
| Florida | 8 | 8 | — | — | 8 | — |
| Georgia | 22 | 5 | — | 1 | 22 | — |
| Illinois | 42 | 19 | 23 | — | 26 | 16 |
| Indiana | 30 | — | 30 | — | — | 30 |
| Iowa | 22 | 14 | 6 | 2 | 22 | — |
| Kansas | 10 | — | 10 | — | 2 | 8 |
| Kentucky | 24 | 24 | — | — | 24 | — |
| Louisiana | 16 | 9 | — | 5 | 16 | — |
| Maine | 14 | 14 | — | — | 14 | — |
| Maryland | 16 | 11 | 3 | — | 14 | 2 |
| Massachusetts | 26 | 26 | — | — | 26 | — |
| Michigan | 22 | 14 | 8 | — | 19 | 3 |
| Minnesota | 10 | 10 | — | — | 10 | — |
| Mississippi | 16 | 16 | — | — | 16 | — |
| Missouri | 30 | — | 14 | — | 30 | — |
| Nebraska | 6 | 6 | — | — | 6 | — |
| Nevada | 6 | 3 | 3 | — | 4 | — |
| New Hampshire | 10 | 10 | — | — | 10 | — |
| New Jersey | 18 | — | — | — | 18 | — |
| New York | 70 | 70 | — | — | 70 | — |
| North Carolina | 20 | 9 | 4 | 5 | 20 | — |
| Ohio | 44 | — | — | — | — | — |
| Oregon | 6 | 6 | — | — | 6 | — |
| Pennsylvania | 58 | — | — | 58 | — | — |
| Rhode Island | 8 | 8 | — | — | 8 | — |
| South Carolina | 14 | 14 | — | — | 14 | — |
| Tennessee | 24 | — | 24 | — | — | 24 |
| Texas | 16 | 10½ | 2½ | 2 | 16 | — |
| Vermont | 10 | 10 | — | — | 10 | — |
| Virginia | 22 | 17 | 1 | — | 17 | 1 |
| West Virginia | 10 | — | — | — | — | — |
| Wisconsin | 20 | 19 | 1 | — | 19 | 1 |
| **Total** | **738** | **401½[a]** | **140½** | **75** | **535** | **85** |

1. Other candidates: William Allen, 54; Allen G. Thurman, 3; Thomas F. Bayard, 33; Joel Parker, 18; James O. Broadhead, 16.
2. Other candidates: Allen, 54; Bayard, 4; Winfield Scott Hancock, 58; Thurman, 2.
a. Sum of column; proceedings record 404½.

# 1876 Republican

(Narrative, p. 58)

| Delegation | Total Votes | First Pres. Ballot[1] Blaine | Morton | Conkling | Bristow | Abolish Unit Rule Yea | Nay | Not Voting | Fifth Pres. Ballot[2] Blaine | Bristow | Conkling | Hayes | Morton | Sixth Pres. Ballot[3] Blaine | Morton | Conkling | Bristow | Hayes | Seventh Pres. Ballot[4] Blaine | Hayes |
|---|---|---|---|---|---|---|---|---|---|---|---|---|---|---|---|---|---|---|---|---|
| Ala. | 20 | 10 | — | — | 7 | 20 | — | — | 16 | 4 | — | — | — | 15 | — | — | 4 | 1 | 17 | — |
| Ariz. | 2 | 2 | — | — | — | 2 | — | — | 2 | — | — | — | — | 2 | — | — | — | — | 2 | — |
| Ark. | 12 | — | 12 | — | — | 4 | 8 | — | 1 | — | — | — | 11 | 1 | 11 | — | — | — | 11 | 1 |
| Calif. | 12 | 9 | — | 1 | 2 | 11 | 1 | — | 6 | — | 3 | 3 | — | 6 | — | 2 | — | 4 | 6 | 6 |
| Colo. | 6 | 6 | — | — | — | 6 | — | — | 6 | — | — | — | — | 6 | — | — | — | — | 6 | — |
| Conn. | 12 | — | — | — | 2 | 3 | 9 | — | 2 | 8 | — | 2 | — | 2 | — | — | 7 | 3 | 2 | 3 |
| Del. | 6 | 6 | — | — | — | 5 | 1 | — | 6 | — | — | — | — | 6 | — | — | — | — | 6 | — |
| Fla. | 8 | 1 | 4 | 3 | — | 4 | 4 | — | 2 | — | — | — | 3 | 4 | 4 | — | — | — | 8 | — |
| Ga. | 22 | 5 | 6 | 8 | 3 | 9 | 13 | — | 8 | 2 | 6 | — | 5 | 9 | 4 | 6 | 2 | — | 14 | 7 |
| Idaho | 2 | 2 | — | — | — | 2 | — | — | 2 | — | — | — | — | 2 | — | — | — | — | 2 | — |
| Ill. | 42 | 38 | — | — | 3 | 38 | 4 | — | 33 | 5 | — | 3 | — | 32 | — | — | 5 | 3 | 35 | 2 |
| Ind. | 30 | — | 30 | — | — | 1 | 29 | — | — | — | — | — | 30 | — | 30 | — | — | — | — | 25 |
| Iowa | 22 | 22 | — | — | — | 22 | — | — | 21 | — | 1 | — | — | 21 | — | — | — | 1 | 22 | — |
| Kan. | 10 | 10 | — | — | — | 10 | — | — | 10 | — | — | — | — | 10 | — | — | — | — | 10 | — |
| Ky. | 24 | — | — | — | 24 | 1 | 23 | — | — | 24 | — | — | — | — | — | — | 24 | — | — | 24 |
| La. | 16 | 2 | 14 | — | — | 6 | 10 | — | 5 | — | — | — | 11 | 6 | 10 | — | — | — | 14 | 2 |
| Maine | 14 | 14 | — | — | — | 14 | — | — | 14 | — | — | — | — | 14 | — | — | — | — | 14 | — |
| Md. | 16 | 16 | — | — | — | 16 | — | — | 16 | — | — | — | — | 16 | — | — | — | — | 16 | — |
| Mass. | 26 | 6 | — | — | 17 | 15 | 7 | 4 | 5 | 19 | — | — | — | 5 | — | — | 19 | — | 5 | 21 |
| Mich. | 22 | 8 | — | 1 | 9 | 3 | 19 | — | — | — | — | 22 | — | — | — | — | — | 22 | — | 22 |
| Minn. | 10 | 10 | — | — | — | 7 | 3 | — | 9 | — | — | — | — | 9 | — | — | — | — | 9 | 1 |
| Miss. | 16 | — | 11 | 1 | 3 | 9 | 6 | 1 | — | 8 | 2 | 2 | 4 | 1 | 5 | 2 | 4 | 4 | — | 16 |
| Mo. | 30 | 14 | 12 | 1 | 2 | 25 | 5 | — | 20 | 3 | — | 2 | 5 | 18 | 7 | — | 3 | 2 | 20 | 10 |
| Mont. | 2 | 2 | — | — | — | 2 | — | — | 1 | — | — | 1 | — | 1 | — | — | — | 1 | — | 2 |
| Neb. | 6 | 6 | — | — | — | 6 | — | — | 6 | — | — | — | — | 6 | — | — | — | — | 6 | — |
| Nev. | 6 | — | — | 2 | 3 | — | 6 | — | — | 1 | 2 | 1 | — | — | — | 2 | 2 | 1 | — | 6 |
| N.H. | 10 | 7 | — | — | 3 | 10 | — | — | 7 | 3 | — | — | — | 7 | — | — | 3 | — | 7 | 3 |
| N.J. | 18 | 13 | — | — | — | 15 | 3 | — | 12 | — | — | 6 | — | 12 | — | — | — | 6 | 12 | 6 |
| N.M. | 2 | 2 | — | — | — | 2 | — | — | 2 | — | — | — | — | 2 | — | — | — | 1 | 2 | — |
| N.Y. | 70 | — | — | 69 | 1 | 15 | 54 | 1 | — | 2 | 68 | — | — | — | — | 68 | 2 | — | 9 | 61 |
| N.C. | 20 | 9 | 2 | 7 | 1 | 6 | 13 | 1 | — | — | — | 12 | 1 | 12 | 1 | — | — | 1 | — | 20 |
| Dak.ª | 2 | 2 | — | — | — | 2 | — | — | 2 | — | — | — | — | 2 | — | — | — | — | 2 | — |
| Ohio | 44 | — | — | — | — | 14 | 30 | — | — | — | — | 44 | — | — | — | — | — | 44 | — | 44 |
| Ore. | 6 | 6 | — | — | — | 6 | — | — | 6 | — | — | — | — | 6 | — | — | — | — | 6 | — |
| Pa. | 58 | — | — | — | — | 1 | 57 | — | 5 | — | — | — | — | 14 | — | — | — | — | 30 | 28 |
| R.I. | 8 | 2 | — | — | 6 | 1 | 7 | — | 2 | 6 | — | — | — | 2 | — | — | 6 | — | 2 | 6 |
| S.C. | 14 | — | 13 | — | 1 | 2 | 12 | — | 5 | 3 | — | 1 | 5 | 10 | 2 | — | 1 | 1 | 7 | 7 |
| Tenn. | 24 | 4 | 10 | — | 10 | 19 | 5 | — | 7 | 10 | — | — | 7 | 7 | 1 | — | 12 | 4 | 6 | 18 |
| Texas | 16 | 2 | 5 | 3 | 6 | 4 | 12 | — | 3 | 3 | — | 1 | 8 | 2 | 4 | 1 | 1 | 7 | 1 | 15 |
| Utah | 2 | 2 | — | — | — | 2 | — | — | 2 | — | — | — | — | 2 | — | — | — | — | 2 | — |
| Vt. | 10 | 1 | — | — | 8 | 5 | 5 | — | — | 8 | — | 2 | — | — | — | — | 8 | 2 | — | 10 |
| Va. | 22 | 16 | 3 | 3 | — | 19 | 2 | 1 | 16 | — | — | — | 3 | 13 | 4 | — | 3 | 2 | 14 | 8 |
| Wash. | 2 | 2 | — | — | — | 2 | — | — | 2 | — | — | — | — | 2 | — | — | — | — | 2 | — |
| W.Va. | 10 | 8 | — | — | — | 10 | — | — | 7 | — | — | 2 | — | 6 | — | — | — | 4 | 6 | 4 |
| Wis. | 20 | 20 | — | — | — | 17 | 3 | — | 16 | 3 | — | — | 1 | 16 | 1 | — | 3 | — | 16 | 4 |
| Wyo. | 2 | — | — | — | 2 | — | 2 | — | — | 2 | — | — | — | — | — | — | 2 | — | — | 2 |
| D.C. | 2 | — | 2 | — | — | 2 | — | — | 1 | — | — | — | 1 | 1 | 1 | — | — | — | 2 | — |
| **Total** | 756 | 285 | 124 | 99 | 113 | 395 | 353 | 8 | 286 | 114 | 82 | 104 | 95 | 308 | 85 | 81 | 111 | 113 | 351 | 384 |

1. Other candidates: Rutherford B. Hayes, 61; John F. Hartranft, 58; Marshall Jewell, 11; William A. Wheeler, 3; not voting, 2.
2. Other candidates: Hartranft, 69; Elihu B. Washburne, 3; Wheeler, 2; not voting, 2.
3. Other candidates: Hartranft, 50; Washburne, 4; Wheeler, 2; not voting, 2.
4. Other candidate: Benjamin H. Bristow, 21.
a. Dakota Territory, includes North and South Dakota.

# 1880 Democratic

*(Narrative, p. 62)*

| Delegation | Total Votes | First Pres. Ballot[1] | | | Second Pres. Ballot[2] (Before shift) | | | Second Pres. Ballot[3] (After shift) |
|---|---|---|---|---|---|---|---|---|
| | | Bayard | Hancock | Payne | Hancock | Bayard | Randall | Hancock |
| Alabama | 20 | 7 | 7 | — | 11 | 5 | — | 20 |
| Arkansas | 12 | — | — | — | — | — | — | 12 |
| California | 12 | — | — | — | 5 | — | — | 12 |
| Colorado | 6 | — | — | — | — | — | — | 6 |
| Connecticut | 12 | 4 | — | 2 | — | 1 | — | 12 |
| Delaware | 6 | 6 | — | — | — | 6 | — | 6 |
| Florida | 8 | 8 | — | — | — | 8 | — | 8 |
| Georgia | 22 | 5 | 8 | — | 7 | 5 | — | 22 |
| Illinois | 42 | — | — | — | 42 | — | — | 42 |
| Indiana | 30 | — | — | — | — | — | — | — |
| Iowa | 22 | 3 | 7 | 2 | 9 | 1 | 12 | 21 |
| Kansas | 10 | — | — | — | 10 | — | — | 10 |
| Kentucky | 24 | 6 | 1 | — | 8 | 7 | — | 24 |
| Louisiana | 16 | — | 16 | — | 16 | — | — | 16 |
| Maine | 14 | — | 14 | — | 14 | — | — | 14 |
| Maryland | 16 | 16 | — | — | — | 16 | — | 14 |
| Massachusetts | 26 | 11½ | 6 | — | 11 | 7 | 3½ | 26 |
| Michigan | 22 | 2 | 5 | 1 | 14 | 4 | 1 | 22 |
| Minnesota | 10 | — | 10 | — | 10 | — | — | 10 |
| Mississippi | 16 | 8 | 5 | — | 6 | 8 | — | 16 |
| Missouri | 30 | 4 | 12 | — | 28 | 2 | — | 30 |
| Nebraska | 6 | — | — | 6 | — | — | 6 | 6 |
| Nevada | 6 | — | — | — | — | — | 1 | 6 |
| New Hampshire | 10 | 3 | 4 | — | 5 | — | 5 | 10 |
| New Jersey | 18 | 10 | — | — | 7 | 4 | 4 | 18 |
| New York | 70 | — | — | 70 | — | — | 70 | 70 |
| North Carolina | 20 | 7 | 9 | — | 20 | — | — | 20 |
| Ohio | 44 | — | — | — | — | — | — | 44 |
| Oregon | 6 | — | — | — | — | — | — | 6 |
| Pennsylvania | 58 | 7 | 28 | — | 32 | — | 25 | 58 |
| Rhode Island | 8 | 2 | 2 | — | 6 | — | 1 | 8 |
| South Carolina | 14 | 14 | — | — | — | 14 | — | 14 |
| Tennessee | 24 | 9 | 11 | — | 14 | 8 | — | 24 |
| Texas | 16 | 5 | 9 | — | 11 | 5 | — | 16 |
| Vermont | 10 | — | 10 | — | 10 | — | — | 10 |
| Virginia | 22 | 10 | 3 | — | 7 | 8 | — | 22 |
| West Virginia | 10 | — | 3 | — | 7 | 1 | — | 10 |
| Wisconsin | 20 | 6 | 1 | — | 10 | 2 | — | 20 |
| **Total** | **738** | **153½** | **171** | **81** | **320** | **112** | **128½** | **705** |

1. Other candidates: Allen G. Thurman, 68½; Stephen J. Field, 65; William R. Morrison, 62; Thomas A. Hendricks, 49½; Samuel J. Tilden, 38; Horatio Seymour, 8; W. A. H. Loveland, 5; Samuel J. Randall, 6; Thomas Ewing, 10; Joseph E. McDonald, 3; George B. McClellan, 2; Joel Parker, 1; Jeremiah Black, 1; Hugh J. Jewett, 1; James E. English, 1; Lothrop, 1; not voting, 10½.
2. Other candidates: Hendricks, 31; English, 19; Tilden, 6; Thurman, 50; Parker, 2; Field, 65½; Jewett, 1; not voting, 3.
3. Other candidates: Hendricks, 30; Bayard, 2; Tilden, 1.

# 1880 Republican

(Narrative, p. 60)

| Delegation | Total Votes | Minority Report Illinois 1st Dist. | | | First Pres. Ballot[1] | | | | 34th Pres. Ballot[2] | | | | 35th Pres. Ballot[3] | | | | | 36th Pres. Ballot[4] | | | |
|---|---|---|---|---|---|---|---|---|---|---|---|---|---|---|---|---|---|---|---|---|---|
| | | Yea | Nay | Not Voting | Grant | Blaine | Sherman | Other | Grant | Blaine | Sherman | Other | Grant | Blaine | Sherman | Garfield | Other | Grant | Blaine | Garfield | Other |
| Ala. | 20 | 16 | 4 | — | 16 | 1 | 3 | — | 16 | 4 | — | — | 16 | 4 | — | — | — | 16 | 4 | — | — |
| Ariz. | 2 | — | 2 | — | — | 2 | — | — | — | 2 | — | — | — | 2 | — | — | — | — | — | 2 | — |
| Ark. | 12 | 12 | — | — | 12 | — | — | — | 12 | — | — | — | 12 | — | — | — | — | 12 | — | — | — |
| Calif. | 12 | — | 12 | — | — | 12 | — | — | — | 12 | — | — | — | 12 | — | — | — | — | 12 | — | — |
| Colo. | 6 | 6 | — | — | 6 | — | — | — | 6 | — | — | — | 6 | — | — | — | — | 6 | — | — | — |
| Conn. | 12 | — | 10 | 2 | — | 3 | — | 9 | — | 3 | — | 9 | — | 3 | — | — | 9 | — | 1 | 11 | — |
| Del. | 6 | — | 6 | — | — | 6 | — | — | — | 6 | — | — | — | 6 | — | — | — | — | 6 | — | — |
| Fla. | 8 | 8 | — | — | 8 | — | — | — | 8 | — | — | — | 8 | — | — | — | — | 8 | — | — | — |
| Ga. | 22 | 6 | 16 | — | 6 | 8 | 8 | — | 8 | 9 | 5 | — | 8 | 9 | 5 | — | — | 8 | 10 | 1 | 3 |
| Idaho | 2 | — | 2 | — | — | 2 | — | — | — | 2 | — | — | — | 2 | — | — | — | — | 2 | — | — |
| Ill. | 42 | 40 | — | 2 | 24 | 10 | — | 8 | 24 | 10 | — | 8 | 24 | 10 | — | — | 8 | 24 | 6 | 7 | 5 |
| Ind. | 30 | 5 | 25 | — | 1 | 26 | 2 | 1 | 2 | 20 | 2 | 6 | 1 | 2 | — | 27 | — | 1 | — | 29 | — |
| Iowa | 22 | — | 22 | — | — | 22 | — | — | — | 22 | — | — | — | 22 | — | — | — | — | 22 | — | — |
| Kan. | 10 | — | — | 10 | 4 | 6 | — | — | 4 | 6 | — | — | 4 | 6 | — | — | — | 4 | 6 | — | — |
| Ky. | 24 | 21 | 3 | — | 20 | 1 | 3 | — | 20 | 1 | 3 | — | 20 | 1 | 3 | — | — | 20 | 1 | 3 | — |
| La. | 16 | 8 | 8 | — | 8 | 2 | 6 | — | 8 | 4 | 4 | — | 8 | 4 | 4 | — | — | 8 | — | 8 | — |
| Maine | 14 | — | 14 | — | — | 14 | — | — | — | 14 | — | — | — | 14 | — | — | — | — | — | 14 | — |
| Md. | 16 | 8 | 8 | — | 7 | 7 | 2 | — | 7 | 2 | 7 | — | 7 | 3 | 2 | 4 | — | 6 | — | 10 | — |
| Mass. | 26 | 4 | 22 | — | 3 | — | 2 | 21 | 4 | — | 21 | 1 | 4 | — | 21 | — | 1 | 4 | — | 22 | — |
| Mich. | 22 | 1 | 21 | — | 1 | 21 | — | — | 1 | 21 | — | — | 1 | 21 | — | — | — | 1 | — | 21 | — |
| Minn. | 10 | 4 | 6 | — | — | — | — | 10 | — | 6 | — | 4 | 1 | 6 | — | — | 3 | 2 | — | 8 | — |
| Miss. | 16 | 11 | 5 | — | 6 | 4 | 6 | — | 8 | 4 | 3 | 1 | 8 | 4 | 3 | 1 | — | 7 | — | 9 | — |
| Mo. | 30 | 29 | 1 | — | 29 | — | — | 1 | 29 | — | — | 1 | 29 | — | — | — | 1 | 29 | — | 1 | — |
| Mont. | 2 | — | 2 | — | — | 2 | — | — | — | 2 | — | — | — | 2 | — | — | — | — | — | 2 | — |
| Neb. | 6 | — | 6 | — | — | 6 | — | — | — | 6 | — | — | — | 6 | — | — | — | 2 | 1 | 3 | — |
| Nev. | 6 | — | 6 | — | — | 6 | — | — | — | 6 | — | — | — | 6 | — | — | — | — | — | 6 | — |
| N.H. | 10 | — | 10 | — | — | 10 | — | — | — | 10 | — | — | — | 10 | — | — | — | — | — | 10 | — |
| N.J. | 18 | — | 18 | — | — | 16 | — | 2 | — | 14 | 2 | 2 | — | 14 | 2 | — | 2 | — | — | 18 | — |
| N.M. | 2 | — | 2 | — | — | 2 | — | — | — | 2 | — | — | — | 2 | — | — | — | — | — | 2 | — |
| N.Y. | 70 | 47 | 22 | 1 | 51 | 17 | 2 | — | 50 | 18 | 2 | — | 50 | 18 | 2 | — | — | 50 | — | 20 | — |
| N.C. | 20 | 19 | 1 | — | 6 | — | 14 | — | 6 | — | 14 | — | 6 | — | 13 | 1 | — | 5 | — | 15 | — |
| Dak.[a] | 2 | 1 | 1 | — | 1 | 1 | — | — | 1 | 1 | — | — | 1 | 1 | — | — | — | — | — | 2 | — |
| Ohio | 44 | 16 | 28 | — | — | 9 | 34 | 1 | — | 9 | 34 | 1 | — | 9 | 34 | — | 1 | — | — | 43 | 1 |
| Ore. | 6 | — | 6 | — | — | 6 | — | — | — | 6 | — | — | — | 6 | — | — | — | — | — | 6 | — |
| Pa. | 58 | 34 | 24 | — | 32 | 23 | 3 | — | 35 | 22 | — | 1 | 36 | 20 | — | 1 | 1 | 37 | — | 21 | — |
| R.I. | 8 | — | 8 | — | — | 8 | — | — | — | 8 | — | — | — | 8 | — | — | — | — | — | 8 | — |
| S.C. | 14 | 10 | 4 | — | 13 | — | 1 | — | 11 | 1 | 2 | — | 11 | 1 | 2 | — | — | 8 | — | 6 | — |
| Tenn. | 24 | 16 | 8 | — | 16 | 6 | 1 | 1 | 17 | 4 | 3 | — | 17 | 4 | 3 | — | — | 15 | 1 | 8 | — |
| Texas | 16 | 11 | 4 | 1 | 11 | 2 | 2 | 1 | 13 | 1 | 1 | 1 | 13 | 1 | 1 | — | 1 | 13 | — | 3 | — |
| Utah | 2 | — | 2 | — | 1 | 1 | — | — | 1 | 1 | — | — | 1 | 1 | — | — | — | — | — | 2 | — |
| Vt. | 10 | 4 | 6 | — | — | — | — | 10 | — | — | — | 10 | — | — | — | — | 10 | — | — | 10 | — |
| Va. | 22 | 13 | 9 | — | 18 | 3 | 1 | — | 16 | 3 | 3 | — | 16 | 3 | 3 | — | — | 19 | — | 3 | — |
| Wash. | 2 | — | 2 | — | — | 2 | — | — | — | 2 | — | — | — | 2 | — | — | — | — | — | 2 | — |
| W.Va. | 10 | — | 10 | — | 1 | 8 | — | 1 | 1 | 8 | 1 | — | 1 | 8 | 1 | — | — | 1 | — | 9 | — |
| Wis. | 20 | 1 | 19 | — | 1 | 7 | 3 | 9 | 2 | 1 | — | 17 | 2 | 2 | — | 16 | — | — | — | 20 | — |
| Wyo. | 2 | 1 | 1 | — | 1 | 1 | — | — | 1 | 1 | — | — | 1 | 1 | — | — | — | — | — | 2 | — |
| D.C. | 2 | 1 | 1 | — | 1 | 1 | — | — | 1 | 1 | — | — | 1 | 1 | — | — | — | — | — | 2 | — |
| **Total** | 756 | 353 | 387 | 16 | 304 | 284 | 93 | 75 | 312 | 275 | 107 | 62 | 313 | 257 | 99 | 50 | 37 | 306 | 42 | 399 | 9 |

1. Other candidates: George F. Edmunds, 34; Elihu B. Washburne, 30; William Windom, 10; not voting. 1.
2. Other candidates: Washburne, 30; James A. Garfield, 17; Edmunds, 11; Windom, 4.
3. Other candidates: Washburne, 23; Edmunds, 11; Windom, 3.
4. Other candidates: Washburne, 5; John Sherman, 3; not voting, 1.
a. Dakota Territory, includes North and South Dakota.

# 1884 Democratic

*(Narrative, p. 63)*

| Delegation | Total Votes | Unit Rule: Amendment to Permit Polling of Delegates | | | First Pres. Ballot[1] | | | Second Pres. Ballot[2] (Before shift) | | | Second Pres. Ballot[3] (After shift) | |
|---|---|---|---|---|---|---|---|---|---|---|---|---|
| | | Yea | Nay | Not Voting | Cleveland | Bayard | Thurman | Cleveland | Bayard | Hendricks | Cleveland | Bayard |
| Alabama | 20 | 15 | 5 | — | 4 | 14 | 1 | 5 | 14 | — | 5 | 14 |
| Arizona | 2 | — | — | 2 | 2 | — | — | 2 | — | — | 2 | — |
| Arkansas | 14 | — | 14 | — | 14 | — | — | 14 | — | — | 14 | — |
| California | 16 | 16 | — | — | — | — | 16 | 6 | — | — | 16 | — |
| Colorado | 6 | 4 | 2 | — | — | — | 1 | 6 | — | — | 6 | — |
| Connecticut | 12 | 2 | 10 | — | 12 | — | — | 12 | — | — | 12 | — |
| Delaware | 6 | 6 | — | — | — | 6 | — | — | 6 | — | — | 6 |
| Florida | 8 | 2 | 6 | — | 8 | — | — | 6 | 2 | — | 8 | — |
| Georgia | 24 | 12 | 12 | — | 10 | 12 | — | 14 | 10 | — | 22 | 2 |
| Idaho | 2 | — | — | 2 | 2 | — | — | 2 | — | — | 2 | — |
| Illinois | 44 | 22 | 22 | — | 28 | 2 | 1 | 38 | 3 | 1 | 43 | — |
| Indiana | 30 | 30 | — | — | — | — | — | — | — | 30 | 30 | — |
| Iowa | 26 | 6 | 20 | — | 23 | 1 | 1 | 22 | — | 4 | 26 | — |
| Kansas | 18 | 3 | 15 | — | 11 | 5 | 2 | 12 | 4 | — | 17 | 1 |
| Kentucky | 26 | 20 | 6 | — | — | — | — | 3 | 7 | 15 | 4 | 21 |
| Louisiana | 16 | — | 16 | — | 13 | 1 | 1 | 15 | — | — | 15 | — |
| Maine | 12 | 2 | 10 | — | 12 | — | — | 12 | — | — | 12 | — |
| Maryland | 16 | — | 16 | — | 6 | 10 | — | 10 | 6 | — | 16 | — |
| Massachusetts | 28 | 21 | 7 | — | 5 | 21 | 2 | 8 | 7½ | 12½ | 8 | 7½ |
| Michigan | 26 | 12 | 12 | 2 | 14 | 1 | 11 | 13 | — | 13 | 23 | — |
| Minnesota | 14 | — | 14 | — | 14 | — | — | 14 | — | — | 14 | — |
| Mississippi | 18 | 18 | — | — | 1 | 15 | 1 | 2 | 14 | 2 | 2 | 14 |
| Missouri | 32 | 8 | 24 | — | 15 | 10 | 3 | 21 | 5 | 6 | 32 | — |
| Montana | 2 | — | — | 2 | 2 | — | — | 2 | — | — | 2 | — |
| Nebraska | 10 | 5 | 5 | — | 8 | 1 | 1 | 9 | 1 | — | 9 | 1 |
| Nevada | 6 | 6 | — | — | — | — | 6 | — | — | 5 | — | — |
| New Hampshire | 8 | — | 8 | — | 8 | — | — | 8 | — | — | 8 | — |
| New Jersey | 18 | 14 | 4 | — | 4 | 3 | — | 5 | 2 | 11 | 5 | 2 |
| New Mexico | 2 | — | — | 2 | 2 | — | — | 1 | — | — | 2 | — |
| New York | 72 | — | 72 | — | 72 | — | — | 72 | — | — | 72 | — |
| North Carolina | 22 | 10 | 12 | — | — | 22 | — | — | 22 | — | 22 | — |
| Dakota[a] | 2 | — | — | 2 | 2 | — | — | 2 | — | — | 2 | — |
| Ohio | 46 | 25 | 21 | — | 21 | — | 23 | 21 | — | 1 | 46 | — |
| Oregon | 6 | — | 6 | — | 2 | 4 | — | 2 | 2 | 2 | 6 | — |
| Pennsylvania | 60 | 21 | 39 | — | 5 | — | — | 42 | 2 | 11 | 42 | 2 |
| Rhode Island | 8 | — | 8 | — | 6 | 2 | — | 6 | 2 | — | 7 | 1 |
| South Carolina | 18 | 3 | 14 | 1 | 8 | 10 | — | 8 | 9 | 1 | 10 | 8 |
| Tennessee | 24 | 17 | 7 | — | 2 | 8 | 9 | 2 | 10 | 1 | 24 | — |
| Texas | 26 | 12 | 10 | 4 | 11 | 10 | 4 | 12 | 12 | 1 | 26 | — |
| Utah | 2 | — | — | 2 | — | — | — | 1 | — | 1 | 2 | — |
| Vermont | 8 | — | 8 | — | 8 | — | — | 8 | — | — | 8 | — |
| Virginia | 24 | 6 | 18 | — | 13 | 9 | 1 | 13 | 8 | 2 | 23 | — |
| Washington | 2 | — | — | 2 | 1 | — | — | 2 | — | — | 2 | — |
| West Virginia | 12 | 9 | 3 | — | 7 | 2 | 2 | 6 | 3 | — | 10 | 2 |
| Wisconsin | 22 | 5 | 17 | — | 12 | 1 | 2 | 20 | — | 2 | 22 | — |
| Wyoming | 2 | — | — | 2 | 2 | — | — | 2 | — | — | 2 | — |
| District of Columbia | 2 | — | — | 2 | 2 | — | — | — | — | 2 | 2 | — |
| **Total** | 820 | 332 | 463 | 25 | 392 | 170 | 88 | 475 | 151½ | 123½ | 683 | 81½ |

1. Other candidates: Joseph E. McDonald, 56; Samuel J. Randall, 78; John G. Carlisle, 27; George Hoadly, 3; Thomas A. Hendricks, 1; Samuel J. Tilden, 1; Roswell P. Flower, 4.
2. Other candidates: Allen G. Thurman, 60; Randall, 5; McDonald, 2; Tilden, 2; not voting, 1.
3. Other candidates: Hendricks, 45½; Thurman, 4; Randall, 4; McDonald, 2.
a. Dakota Territory, includes North and South Dakota.

# 1884 Republican

(Narrative, p. 63)

| Delegation | Total Votes | Temporary Chairman[1] | | First Pres. Ballot[2] | | | Third Pres. Ballot[3] | | Fourth Pres. Ballot[4] | |
|---|---|---|---|---|---|---|---|---|---|---|
| | | Lynch | Clayton | Arthur | Blaine | Edmunds | Arthur | Blaine | Arthur | Blaine |
| Alabama | 20 | 19 | 1 | 17 | 1 | — | 17 | 2 | 12 | 8 |
| Arizona | 2 | — | 2 | — | 2 | — | — | 2 | — | 2 |
| Arkansas | 14 | 1 | 13 | 4 | 8 | 2 | 3 | 11 | 3 | 11 |
| California | 16 | — | 16 | — | 16 | — | — | 16 | — | 16 |
| Colorado | 6 | — | 6 | — | 6 | — | — | 6 | — | 6 |
| Connecticut | 12 | 6 | 6 | — | — | — | — | — | — | — |
| Delaware | 6 | 1 | 5 | 1 | 5 | — | 1 | 5 | 1 | 5 |
| Florida | 8 | 7 | 1 | 7 | 1 | — | 7 | 1 | 5 | 3 |
| Georgia | 24 | 24 | — | 24 | — | — | 24 | — | 24 | — |
| Idaho | 2 | 2 | — | 2 | — | — | 1 | 1 | — | 2 |
| Illinois | 44 | 16 | 28 | 1 | 3 | — | 1 | 3 | 3 | 34 |
| Indiana | 30 | 10 | 20 | 9 | 18 | 1 | 10 | 18 | — | 30 |
| Iowa | 26 | 3 | 23 | — | 26 | — | — | 26 | 2 | 24 |
| Kansas | 18 | 4 | 14 | 4 | 12 | — | — | 15 | — | 18 |
| Kentucky | 26 | 20 | 6 | 16 | 5½ | — | 16 | 6 | 15 | 9 |
| Louisiana | 16 | 11 | 4 | 10 | 2 | — | 9 | 4 | 7 | 9 |
| Maine | 12 | — | 12 | — | 12 | — | — | 12 | — | 12 |
| Maryland | 16 | 6 | 10 | 6 | 10 | — | 4 | 12 | 1 | 15 |
| Massachusetts | 28 | 24 | 4 | 2 | 1 | 25 | 3 | 1 | 7 | 3 |
| Michigan | 26 | 12 | 14 | 2 | 15 | 7 | 4 | 18 | — | 26 |
| Minnesota | 14 | 6 | 8 | 1 | 7 | 6 | 2 | 7 | — | 14 |
| Mississippi | 18 | 16 | 2 | 17 | 1 | — | 16 | 1 | 16 | 2 |
| Missouri | 32 | 14 | 16 | 10 | 5 | 6 | 11 | 12 | — | 32 |
| Montana | 2 | 1 | 1 | — | 1 | 1 | — | 1 | — | 2 |
| Nebraska | 10 | 2 | 8 | 2 | 8 | — | — | 10 | — | 10 |
| Nevada | 6 | — | 6 | — | 6 | — | — | 6 | — | 6 |
| New Hampshire | 8 | 8 | — | 4 | — | 4 | 5 | — | 2 | 3 |
| New Jersey | 18 | 9 | 9 | — | 9 | 6 | 1 | 11 | — | 17 |
| New Mexico | 2 | 2 | — | 2 | — | — | 2 | — | 2 | — |
| New York | 72 | 46 | 26 | 31 | 28 | 12 | 32 | 28 | 30 | 29 |
| North Carolina | 22 | 17 | 3 | 19 | 2 | — | 18 | 4 | 12 | 8 |
| Dakota[a] | 2 | — | 2 | — | 2 | — | — | 2 | — | 2 |
| Ohio | 46 | 22 | 23 | — | 21 | — | — | 25 | — | 46 |
| Oregon | 6 | — | 6 | — | 6 | — | — | 6 | — | 6 |
| Pennsylvania | 60 | 13 | 45 | 11 | 47 | 1 | 8 | 50 | 8 | 51 |
| Rhode Island | 8 | 8 | — | — | — | 8 | — | — | 1 | 7 |
| South Carolina | 18 | 18 | — | 17 | 1 | — | 16 | 2 | 15 | 2 |
| Tennessee | 24 | 21 | 2 | 16 | 7 | — | 17 | 7 | 12 | 11 |
| Texas | 26 | 12 | 12 | 11 | 13 | — | 11 | 14 | 8 | 15 |
| Utah | 2 | — | 2 | 2 | — | — | 2 | — | — | 2 |
| Vermont | 8 | 8 | — | — | — | 8 | — | — | — | — |
| Virginia | 24 | 20 | 4 | 21 | 2 | — | 20 | 4 | 20 | 4 |
| Washington | 2 | 1 | 1 | — | 2 | — | — | 2 | — | 2 |
| West Virginia | 12 | — | 12 | — | 12 | — | — | 12 | — | 12 |
| Wisconsin | 22 | 11 | 10 | 6 | 10 | 6 | 10 | 11 | — | 22 |
| Wyoming | 2 | 2 | — | 2 | — | — | 2 | — | — | 2 |
| District of Columbia | 2 | 1 | 1 | 1 | 1 | — | 1 | 1 | 1 | 1 |
| **Total** | **820** | **424** | **384** | **278** | **334½** | **93** | **274** | **375** | **207** | **541** |

1. Not voting, 12.
2. Other candidates: John A. Logan, 63½; John Sherman, 30; Joseph R. Hawley, 13; Robert T. Lincoln, 4; William T. Sherman, 2; not voting, 2.
3. Other candidates: George F. Edmunds, 69; Logan, 53; John Sherman, 25; Hawley, 13; Lincoln, 8; William T. Sherman, 3; not voting, 1.
4. Other candidates: Edmunds, 41; Hawley, 15; Logan, 7; Lincoln, 2; not voting, 7.
a. Dakota Territory, includes North and South Dakota.

# 1888 Republican

(Narrative, p. 66)

| Delegation | Total Votes | First Pres. Ballot[1] | | | | | | Sixth Pres. Ballot[2] | | | | | Seventh Pres. Ballot[3] | | | | | Eighth Pres. Ballot[4] | | | |
| --- | --- | --- | --- | --- | --- | --- | --- | --- | --- | --- | --- | --- | --- | --- | --- | --- | --- | --- | --- | --- | --- |
| | | Alger | Allison | Depew | Gresham | Harrison | Sherman | Alger | Allison | Gresham | Harrison | Sherman | Alger | Allison | Gresham | Harrison | Sherman | Alger | Gresham | Harrison | Sherman |
| Ala. | 20 | 6 | — | 1 | — | 1 | 12 | 6 | — | — | 1 | 12 | 6 | — | — | 12 | — | 10 | — | 3 | 5 |
| Ariz. | 2 | 2 | — | — | — | — | — | 2 | — | — | — | — | 2 | — | — | — | — | — | — | 2 | — |
| Ark. | 14 | — | — | — | 1 | 1 | 2 | 14 | — | — | — | — | 14 | — | — | — | — | 14 | — | — | — |
| Calif. | 16 | — | — | — | — | — | — | — | — | — | — | — | 1 | — | — | 15 | — | — | — | 15 | — |
| Colo. | 6 | — | 1 | — | 3 | 2 | — | — | — | — | 5 | — | — | 6 | — | — | — | — | — | 6 | — |
| Conn. | 12 | — | — | — | — | — | — | 2 | 4 | — | — | 6 | 2 | — | — | 4 | 5 | — | — | 12 | — |
| Del. | 6 | — | — | — | — | 6 | — | — | — | 1 | 5 | — | — | — | 1 | 5 | — | — | — | 6 | — |
| Fla. | 8 | — | — | — | — | 1 | 4 | 5 | — | — | 1 | 1 | 3 | — | — | 4 | 1 | 4 | — | 2 | 2 |
| Ga. | 24 | — | — | — | 1 | 2 | 19 | — | — | 1 | 2 | 19 | 1 | — | 1 | 3 | 17 | 3 | 1 | 10 | 9 |
| Idaho | 2 | — | 1 | — | 1 | — | — | — | — | 2 | — | — | — | — | 2 | — | — | — | — | 2 | — |
| Ill. | 44 | — | — | — | 44 | — | — | — | — | 41 | 3 | — | 1 | — | 40 | 3 | — | — | 40 | 4 | — |
| Ind. | 30 | — | — | — | 1 | 29 | — | — | — | 1 | 29 | — | — | — | 1 | 29 | — | — | 1 | 29 | — |
| Iowa | 26 | — | 26 | — | — | — | — | — | 26 | — | — | — | — | 26 | — | — | — | 1 | 3 | 22 | — |
| Kan. | 18 | — | — | — | — | — | — | 2 | 3 | 3 | 6 | 1 | 1 | 3 | — | 12 | 1 | 1 | — | 16 | — |
| Ky. | 26 | 4 | — | 1 | 5 | 4 | 12 | 6 | — | 2 | 7 | 9 | 3 | — | 2 | 10 | 9 | 1 | 2 | 15 | 7 |
| La. | 16 | 2 | 3 | 1 | 1 | — | 9 | 3 | 2 | 2 | — | 9 | 3 | 2 | 2 | — | 9 | 4 | — | 9 | 3 |
| Maine | 12 | 3 | 2 | 3 | 1 | 2 | 1 | 2 | 1 | 2 | 1 | 3 | 1 | 2 | 2 | 2 | 1 | — | 1 | 5 | 3 |
| Md. | 16 | — | 2 | 1 | 1 | 5 | 5 | — | 1 | — | 6 | 6 | — | — | — | 9 | 6 | — | — | 11 | 4 |
| Mass. | 28 | 6 | 2 | 1 | 2 | 4 | 9 | 8 | 2 | 1 | 5 | 11 | 2 | 3 | 1 | 9 | 11 | 1 | — | 25 | 2 |
| Mich. | 26 | 26 | — | — | — | — | — | 26 | — | — | — | — | 26 | — | — | — | — | 26 | — | — | — |
| Minn. | 14 | 1 | — | 2 | 11 | — | — | 3 | — | 5 | 6 | — | 2 | — | 4 | 8 | — | 1 | — | 13 | — |
| Miss. | 18 | — | — | 1 | 3 | — | 14 | — | — | 3 | — | 14 | — | — | 3 | — | 14 | — | 3 | 4 | 11 |
| Mo. | 32 | 6 | 3 | 2 | 11 | 3 | 6 | 15 | 1 | 11 | 2 | 2 | 14 | — | 12 | 3 | 2 | 15 | 8 | 7 | 2 |
| Mont. | 2 | — | 1 | — | 1 | — | — | — | 1 | 1 | — | — | — | 1 | 1 | — | — | — | — | 2 | — |
| Neb. | 10 | 2 | 3 | — | 1 | — | 3 | 2 | 5 | — | — | 3 | 2 | 5 | — | 2 | 1 | 1 | — | 9 | — |
| Nev. | 6 | 3 | 3 | — | — | — | — | 5 | — | — | — | — | — | 6 | — | — | — | 2 | — | 4 | — |
| N.H. | 8 | — | — | 4 | — | 4 | — | — | 1 | — | 6 | 1 | — | — | — | 8 | — | — | — | 8 | — |
| N.J. | 18 | — | — | — | — | — | — | — | — | 1 | 14 | — | 1 | — | 1 | 10 | 1 | — | — | 18 | — |
| N.M. | 2 | 1 | — | — | — | — | — | 1 | — | — | — | — | 1 | — | — | — | — | — | — | 2 | — |
| N.Y. | 72 | — | — | 71 | — | — | 1 | — | — | — | 72 | — | — | — | — | 72 | — | — | — | 72 | — |
| N.C. | 22 | 2 | — | 1 | 2 | 1 | 15 | 9 | — | — | 2 | 11 | 7 | — | — | 3 | 12 | 3 | — | 8 | 11 |
| Dak.[a] | 10 | 1 | 1 | 2 | 1 | 1 | 1 | — | — | — | 10 | — | — | — | — | 10 | — | — | — | 10 | — |
| Ohio | 46 | — | — | — | — | — | 46 | — | — | — | 1 | 45 | — | — | — | 1 | 45 | — | — | 1 | 45 |
| Ore. | 6 | — | — | — | 4 | 1 | — | — | 5 | — | — | — | — | — | 6 | — | — | — | — | 6 | — |
| Pa. | 60 | 1 | — | 5 | — | — | 29 | — | — | — | 6 | 54 | — | — | — | 9 | 51 | — | — | 59 | 1 |
| R.I. | 8 | — | 8 | — | — | — | — | — | 8 | — | — | — | — | 6 | — | 2 | — | — | — | 8 | — |
| S.C. | 18 | 3 | — | 1 | — | — | 11 | 11 | — | — | 1 | 6 | 11 | — | — | 1 | 6 | 10 | — | 4 | 4 |
| Tenn. | 24 | 9 | 1 | 2 | 1 | 1 | 7 | 6 | 1 | — | 1 | 8 | 9 | 1 | — | 3 | 5 | 3 | — | 20 | — |
| Texas | 26 | 2 | 7 | — | 5 | 1 | 7 | 3 | 8 | 3 | 1 | 7 | 2 | 8 | 1 | 3 | 7 | — | — | 26 | — |
| Utah | 2 | — | 2 | — | — | — | — | — | 2 | — | — | — | — | 2 | — | — | — | — | — | 2 | — |
| Vt. | 8 | — | — | — | 8 | — | — | — | — | 8 | — | — | — | — | 8 | — | — | — | 8 | — | — |
| Va. | 24 | 3 | 3 | — | 1 | 5 | 11 | 3 | 5 | — | 6 | 10 | 3 | 5 | — | 6 | 10 | — | — | 15 | 9 |
| Wash. | 6 | — | 1 | — | 3 | 1 | — | 1 | — | 4 | 1 | — | 1 | — | 4 | 1 | — | — | — | 6 | — |
| W.Va. | 12 | 1 | — | — | 2 | 2 | 5 | 1 | — | 1 | 2 | 5 | — | — | 5 | 3 | 1 | — | — | 12 | — |
| Wis. | 22 | — | — | — | — | — | — | — | — | 1 | 21 | — | — | — | 2 | 20 | — | — | — | 22 | — |
| Wyo. | 2 | — | 2 | — | — | — | — | — | 2 | — | — | — | — | — | — | — | 2 | — | — | 2 | — |
| D.C. | 2 | — | — | — | — | — | — | 1 | — | — | — | — | 1 | — | — | — | — | — | — | 2 | — |
| **Total** | 832 | 84 | 72 | 99 | 107 | 85 | 229 | 137 | 73 | 91 | 231 | 244 | 120 | 76 | 91 | 279 | 230 | 100 | 59 | 544 | 118 |

1. Other candidates: James G. Blaine, 35; John J. Ingalls, 28; William W. Phelps, 25; Jeremiah M. Rusk, 25; Edwin H. Fitler, 24; Joseph R. Hawley, 13; Robert T. Lincoln, 3; William McKinley, 2; not voting, 1.
2. Other candidates: Blaine, 40; McKinley, 12; Foraker, 1; Frederick D. Grant, 1; not voting, 2.
3. Other candidates: McKinley, 16; Blaine, 15; Lincoln, 2; Joseph B. Foraker, 1; Creed Haymond, 1; not voting, 1.
4. Other candidates: Blaine, 5; McKinley, 4; not voting, 2.
a. Dakota Territory, includes North and South Dakota.

# 1892 Democratic

*(Narrative, p. 68)*

### First Pres. Ballot[1]

| Delegation | Total Votes | Cleveland | Boies | Hill |
|---|---|---|---|---|
| Alabama | 22 | 14 | 1 | 2 |
| Arizona | 6 | 5 | — | — |
| Arkansas | 16 | 16 | — | — |
| California | 18 | 18 | — | — |
| Colorado | 8 | — | 5 | 3 |
| Connecticut | 12 | 12 | — | — |
| Delaware | 6 | 6 | — | — |
| Florida | 8 | 5 | — | — |
| Georgia | 26 | 17 | — | 5 |
| Idaho | 6 | — | 6 | — |
| Illinois | 48 | 48 | — | — |
| Indiana | 30 | 30 | — | — |
| Iowa | 26 | — | 26 | — |
| Kansas | 20 | 20 | — | — |
| Kentucky | 26 | 18 | 2 | — |
| Louisiana | 16 | 3 | 11 | 1 |
| Maine | 12 | 9 | — | 1 |
| Maryland | 16 | 6 | — | — |
| Massachusetts | 30 | 24 | 1 | 4 |
| Michigan | 28 | 28 | — | — |
| Minnesota | 18 | 18 | — | — |
| Mississippi | 18 | 8 | 3 | 3 |
| Missouri | 34 | 34 | — | — |
| Montana | 6 | — | 6 | — |
| Nebraska | 16 | 15 | — | — |
| Nevada | 6 | — | 4 | — |
| New Hampshire | 8 | 8 | — | — |
| New Jersey | 20 | 20 | — | — |
| New Mexico | 6 | 4 | 1 | 1 |
| New York | 72 | — | — | 72 |
| North Carolina | 22 | 3 1/3 | 1 | — |
| North Dakota | 6 | 6 | — | — |
| Ohio | 46 | 14 | 16 | 6 |
| Oklahoma[a] | 4 | 4 | — | — |
| Oregon | 8 | 8 | — | — |
| Pennsylvania | 64 | 64 | — | — |
| Rhode Island | 8 | 8 | — | — |
| South Carolina | 18 | 2 | 13 | 3 |
| South Dakota | 8 | 7 | 1 | — |
| Tennessee | 24 | 24 | — | — |
| Texas | 30 | 23 | 6 | 1 |
| Utah | 2 | 2 | — | — |
| Vermont | 8 | 8 | — | — |
| Virginia | 24 | 12 | — | 11 |
| Washington | 8 | 8 | — | — |
| West Virginia | 12 | 7 | — | 1 |
| Wisconsin | 24 | 24 | — | — |
| Wyoming | 6 | 3 | — | — |
| Alaska | 2 | 2 | — | — |
| District of Columbia | 2 | 2 | — | — |
| **Total** | 910 | 617 1/3 | 103 | 114 |

1. *Other candidates: Arthur P. Gorman, 36 1/2; John G. Carlisle, 14; Adlai E. Stevenson, 16 2/3; James E. Campbell, 2; William R. Morrison, 3; William E. Russell, 1; William C. Whitney, 1; Robert E. Pattison, 1; not voting, 1/2.*
a. *Including Indian Territory, 2 votes.*

# 1892 Republican*

*(Narrative, p. 67)*

### First Pres. Ballot[1]

| Delegation | Total Votes | Harrison | Blaine | McKinley |
|---|---|---|---|---|
| Alabama | 22 | 15 | — | 7 |
| Arizona | 2 | 1 | 1 | — |
| Arkansas | 16 | 15 | — | 1 |
| California | 18 | 8 | 9 | 1 |
| Colorado | 8 | — | 8 | — |
| Connecticut | 12 | 4 | — | 8 |
| Delaware | 6 | 4 | 1 | 1 |
| Florida | 8 | 8 | — | — |
| Georgia | 26 | 26 | — | — |
| Idaho | 6 | — | 6 | — |
| Illinois | 48 | 34 | 14 | — |
| Indiana | 30 | 30 | — | — |
| Iowa | 26 | 20 | 5 | 1 |
| Kansas | 20 | 11 | — | 9 |
| Kentucky | 26 | 22 | 2 | 1 |
| Louisiana | 16 | 8 | 8 | — |
| Maine | 12 | — | 12 | — |
| Maryland | 16 | 14 | — | 2 |
| Massachusetts | 30 | 18 | 1 | 11 |
| Michigan | 28 | 7 | 2 | 19 |
| Minnesota | 18 | 8 | 9 | 1 |
| Mississippi | 18 | 13 1/2 | 4 1/2 | — |
| Missouri | 34 | 28 | 4 | 2 |
| Montana | 6 | 5 | 1 | — |
| Nebraska | 16 | 15 | — | 1 |
| Nevada | 6 | — | 6 | — |
| New Hampshire | 8 | 4 | 2 | — |
| New Jersey | 20 | 18 | 2 | — |
| New Mexico | 6 | 6 | — | — |
| New York | 72 | 27 | 35 | 10 |
| North Carolina | 22 | 17 2/3 | 2 2/3 | 1 |
| North Dakota | 6 | 2 | 4 | — |
| Ohio | 46 | 1 | — | 45 |
| Oklahoma | 2 | 2 | — | — |
| Oregon | 8 | 1 | — | 7 |
| Pennsylvania | 64 | 19 | 3 | 42 |
| Rhode Island | 8 | 5 | 1 | 1 |
| South Carolina | 18 | 13 | 3 | 2 |
| South Dakota | 8 | 8 | — | — |
| Tennessee | 24 | 17 | 4 | 3 |
| Texas | 30 | 22 | 6 | — |
| Utah | 2 | 2 | — | — |
| Vermont | 8 | 8 | — | — |
| Virginia | 24 | 9 | 13 | 2 |
| Washington | 8 | 1 | 6 | 1 |
| West Virginia | 12 | 12 | — | — |
| Wisconsin | 24 | 19 | 2 | 3 |
| Wyoming | 6 | 4 | 2 | — |
| Alaska | 2 | 2 | — | — |
| District of Columbia | 2 | — | 2 | — |
| Indian Territory | 2 | 1 | 1 | — |
| **Total** | 906 | 535 1/6 | 182 1/6 | 182 |

1. *Other candidates: Thomas B. Reed, 4; Robert T. Lincoln, 1; not voting, 1 2/3.*
* *Source: Official Proceeding, 10th Republican Convention.*

# 1896 Democratic

*(Narrative, p. 71)*

| Delegation | Total Votes | Minority Gold Standard Plank | | | First Pres. Ballot[1] | | | Fourth Pres. Ballot[2] | | | Fifth Pres. Ballot[3] | |
|---|---|---|---|---|---|---|---|---|---|---|---|---|
| | | Yea | Nay | Not Voting | Bryan | Bland | Pattison | Bryan | Bland | Pattison | Bryan | Pattison |
| Alabama | 22 | — | 22 | — | — | — | — | 22 | — | — | 22 | — |
| Arizona | 6 | — | 6 | — | — | 6 | — | — | 6 | — | 6 | — |
| Arkansas | 16 | — | 16 | — | — | 16 | — | — | 16 | — | 16 | — |
| California | 18 | — | 18 | — | 4 | — | — | 12 | 2 | — | 18 | — |
| Colorado | 8 | — | 8 | — | — | — | — | 8 | — | — | 8 | — |
| Connecticut | 12 | 12 | — | — | — | — | — | — | — | 2 | — | 2 |
| Delaware | 6 | 5 | 1 | — | 1 | — | 3 | 1 | — | 3 | 1 | 3 |
| Florida | 8 | 3 | 5 | — | 1 | 2 | 1 | 5 | — | — | 8 | — |
| Georgia | 26 | — | 26 | — | 26 | — | — | 26 | — | — | 26 | — |
| Idaho | 6 | — | 6 | — | — | 6 | — | 6 | — | — | 6 | — |
| Illinois | 48 | — | 48 | — | — | 48 | — | — | 48 | — | 48 | — |
| Indiana | 30 | — | 30 | — | — | — | — | — | — | — | 30 | — |
| Iowa | 26 | — | 26 | — | — | — | — | — | — | — | 26 | — |
| Kansas | 20 | — | 20 | — | — | 20 | — | 20 | — | — | 20 | — |
| Kentucky | 26 | — | 26 | — | — | — | — | — | — | — | 26 | — |
| Louisiana | 16 | — | 16 | — | 16 | — | — | 16 | — | — | 16 | — |
| Maine | 12 | 10 | 2 | — | 2 | 2 | 5 | 2 | 2 | 5 | 4 | 4 |
| Maryland | 16 | 12 | 4 | — | 4 | — | 11 | 5 | — | 10 | 5 | 10 |
| Massachusetts | 30 | 27 | 3 | — | 1 | 2 | 3 | 1 | 2 | 3 | 6 | 3 |
| Michigan | 28 | — | 28 | — | 9 | 4 | — | 28 | — | — | 28 | — |
| Minnesota | 18 | 11 | 6 | 1 | 2 | — | 2 | 10 | 1 | — | 11 | — |
| Mississippi | 18 | — | 18 | — | 18 | — | — | 18 | — | — | 18 | — |
| Missouri | 34 | — | 34 | — | — | 34 | — | — | 34 | — | 34 | — |
| Montana | 6 | — | 6 | — | — | 4 | — | — | 6 | — | 6 | — |
| Nebraska | 16 | — | 16 | — | 16 | — | — | 16 | — | — | 16 | — |
| Nevada | 6 | — | 6 | — | — | — | — | 6 | — | — | 6 | — |
| New Hampshire | 8 | 8 | — | — | — | — | 1 | — | — | 1 | — | 1 |
| New Jersey | 20 | 20 | — | — | — | — | — | — | — | 2 | — | 2 |
| New Mexico | 6 | — | 6 | — | — | 6 | — | — | 6 | — | 6 | — |
| New York | 72 | 72 | — | — | — | — | — | — | — | — | — | — |
| North Carolina | 22 | — | 22 | — | 22 | — | — | 22 | — | — | 22 | — |
| North Dakota | 6 | — | 6 | — | — | — | — | — | — | — | 4 | — |
| Ohio | 46 | — | 46 | — | — | — | — | — | — | — | 46 | — |
| Oklahoma | 12 | — | 12 | — | — | 12 | — | — | 12 | — | 12 | — |
| Oregon | 8 | — | 8 | — | — | — | — | 8 | — | — | 8 | — |
| Pennsylvania | 64 | 64 | — | — | — | — | 64 | — | — | 64 | — | 64 |
| Rhode Island | 8 | 8 | — | — | — | — | 6 | — | — | 6 | — | 6 |
| South Carolina | 18 | — | 18 | — | — | — | — | 18 | — | — | 18 | — |
| South Dakota | 8 | 8 | — | — | 6 | — | 1 | 7 | — | 1 | 8 | — |
| Tennessee | 24 | — | 24 | — | — | 24 | — | — | 24 | — | 24 | — |
| Texas | 30 | — | 30 | — | — | 30 | — | — | 30 | — | 30 | — |
| Utah | 6 | — | 6 | — | — | 6 | — | — | 6 | — | 6 | — |
| Vermont | 8 | 8 | — | — | 4 | — | — | 4 | — | — | 4 | — |
| Virginia | 24 | — | 24 | — | — | — | — | — | 24 | — | 24 | — |
| Washington | 8 | 3 | 5 | — | 1 | 7 | — | 2 | 6 | — | 4 | — |
| West Virginia | 12 | — | 12 | — | — | — | — | 1 | 10 | — | 2 | — |
| Wisconsin | 24 | 24 | — | — | 4 | — | — | 5 | — | — | 5 | — |
| Wyoming | 6 | — | 6 | — | — | — | — | 6 | — | — | 6 | — |
| Alaska | 6 | 6 | — | — | — | 6 | — | — | 6 | — | 6 | — |
| District of Columbia | 6 | 2 | 4 | — | — | — | — | 5 | — | — | 6 | — |
| **Total** | **930** | **303** | **626** | **1** | **137** | **235** | **97** | **280** | **241** | **97** | **652** | **95** |

1. Other candidates: Horace Boies, 67; Claude Matthews, 37; John R. McLean, 54; Joseph S. C. Blackburn, 82; Adlai E. Stevenson, 6; Henry M. Teller, 8; William E. Russell, 2; Benjamin R. Tillman, 17; James E. Campbell, 1; Sylvester Pennoyer, 8; David B. Hill, 1; not voting, 178.
2. Other candidates: Boies, 33; Mathews, 36; Blackburn, 27; McLean, 46; Stevenson, 8; Hill, 1; not voting, 161.
3. Other candidates: Richard P. Bland, 11; Stevenson, 8; Hill, 1; David Turpie, 1; not voting, 162.
a. Including Indian Territory, 6 votes.

# 1896 Republican

*(Narrative, p. 70)*

| Delegation | Total Votes | First Pres. Ballot[1] | | | | |
|---|---|---|---|---|---|---|
| | | McKinley | Reed | Morton | Allison | Quay |
| Alabama | 22 | 19 | 2 | 1 | — | — |
| Arizona | 6 | 6 | — | — | — | — |
| Arkansas | 16 | 16 | — | — | — | — |
| California | 18 | 18 | — | — | — | — |
| Colorado | 8 | — | — | — | — | — |
| Connecticut | 12 | 7 | 5 | — | — | — |
| Delaware | 6 | 6 | — | — | — | — |
| Florida | 8 | 6 | — | 2 | — | — |
| Georgia | 26 | 22 | 2 | — | — | 2 |
| Idaho | 6 | — | — | — | — | — |
| Illinois | 48 | 46 | 2 | — | — | — |
| Indiana | 30 | 30 | — | — | — | — |
| Iowa | 26 | — | — | — | 26 | — |
| Kansas | 20 | 20 | — | — | — | — |
| Kentucky | 26 | 26 | — | — | — | — |
| Louisiana | 16 | 11 | 4 | — | ½ | ½ |
| Maine | 12 | — | 12 | — | — | — |
| Maryland | 16 | 15 | 1 | — | — | — |
| Massachusetts | 30 | 1 | 29 | — | — | — |
| Michigan | 28 | 28 | — | — | — | — |
| Minnesota | 18 | 18 | — | — | — | — |
| Mississippi | 18 | 17 | — | — | — | 1 |
| Missouri | 34 | 34 | — | — | — | — |
| Montana | 6 | 1 | — | — | — | — |
| Nebraska | 16 | 16 | — | — | — | — |
| Nevada | 6 | 3 | — | — | — | — |
| New Hampshire | 8 | — | 8 | — | — | — |
| New Jersey | 20 | 19 | 1 | — | — | — |
| New Mexico | 6 | 5 | — | — | 1 | — |
| New York | 72 | 17 | — | 55 | — | — |
| North Carolina | 22 | 19½ | 2½ | — | — | — |
| North Dakota | 6 | 6 | — | — | — | — |
| Ohio | 46 | 46 | — | — | — | — |
| Oklahoma[a] | 12 | 10 | 1 | — | 1 | — |
| Oregon | 8 | 8 | — | — | — | — |
| Pennsylvania | 64 | 6 | — | — | — | 58 |
| Rhode Island | 8 | — | 8 | — | — | — |
| South Carolina | 18 | 18 | — | — | — | — |
| South Dakota | 8 | 8 | — | — | — | — |
| Tennessee | 24 | 24 | — | — | — | — |
| Texas | 30 | 21 | 5 | — | 3 | — |
| Utah | 6 | 3 | — | — | 3 | — |
| Vermont | 8 | 8 | — | — | — | — |
| Virginia | 24 | 23 | 1 | — | — | — |
| Washington | 8 | 8 | — | — | — | — |
| West Virginia | 12 | 12 | — | — | — | — |
| Wisconsin | 24 | 24 | — | — | — | — |
| Wyoming | 6 | 6 | — | — | — | — |
| Alaska | 4 | 4 | — | — | — | — |
| District of Columbia | 2 | — | 1 | — | 1 | — |
| **Total** | **924** | **661½** | **84½** | **58** | **35½** | **61½** |

1. Other candidates: J. Donald Cameron, 1; not voting, 22.
a. Including Indian Territory, 6 votes.

# 1900 Democratic

(Narrative, p. 73)

| Delegation | Total Votes | First Pres. Ballot Bryan |
|---|---|---|
| Alabama | 22 | 22 |
| Arizona | 6 | 6 |
| Arkansas | 16 | 16 |
| California | 18 | 18 |
| Colorado | 8 | 8 |
| Connecticut | 12 | 12 |
| Delaware | 6 | 6 |
| Florida | 8 | 8 |
| Georgia | 26 | 26 |
| Idaho | 6 | 6 |
| Illinois | 48 | 48 |
| Indiana | 30 | 30 |
| Iowa | 26 | 26 |
| Kansas | 20 | 20 |
| Kentucky | 26 | 26 |
| Louisiana | 16 | 16 |
| Maine | 12 | 12 |
| Maryland | 16 | 16 |
| Massachusetts | 30 | 30 |
| Michigan | 28 | 28 |
| Minnesota | 18 | 18 |
| Mississippi | 18 | 18 |
| Missouri | 34 | 34 |
| Montana | 6 | 6 |
| Nebraska | 16 | 16 |
| Nevada | 6 | 6 |
| New Hampshire | 8 | 8 |
| New Jersey | 20 | 20 |
| New Mexico | 6 | 6 |
| New York | 72 | 72 |
| North Carolina | 22 | 22 |
| North Dakota | 6 | 6 |
| Ohio | 46 | 46 |
| Oklahoma[a] | 12 | 12 |
| Oregon | 8 | 8 |
| Pennsylvania | 64 | 64 |
| Rhode Island | 8 | 8 |
| South Carolina | 18 | 18 |
| South Dakota | 8 | 8 |
| Tennessee | 24 | 24 |
| Texas | 30 | 30 |
| Utah | 6 | 6 |
| Vermont | 8 | 8 |
| Virginia | 24 | 24 |
| Washington | 8 | 8 |
| West Virginia | 12 | 12 |
| Wisconsin | 24 | 24 |
| Wyoming | 6 | 6 |
| Alaska | 6 | 6 |
| District of Columbia | 6 | 6 |
| Hawaii | 6 | 6 |
| **Total** | **936** | **936** |

a. Including Indian Territory, 6 votes.

# 1900 Republican

(Narrative, p. 72)

| Delegation | Total Votes | First Pres. Ballot McKinley |
|---|---|---|
| Alabama | 22 | 22 |
| Arizona | 6 | 6 |
| Arkansas | 16 | 16 |
| California | 18 | 18 |
| Colorado | 8 | 8 |
| Connecticut | 12 | 12 |
| Delaware | 6 | 6 |
| Florida | 8 | 8 |
| Georgia | 26 | 26 |
| Idaho | 6 | 6 |
| Illinois | 48 | 48 |
| Indiana | 30 | 30 |
| Iowa | 26 | 26 |
| Kansas | 20 | 20 |
| Kentucky | 26 | 26 |
| Louisiana | 16 | 16 |
| Maine | 12 | 12 |
| Maryland | 16 | 16 |
| Massachusetts | 30 | 30 |
| Michigan | 28 | 28 |
| Minnesota | 18 | 18 |
| Mississippi | 18 | 18 |
| Missouri | 34 | 34 |
| Montana | 6 | 6 |
| Nebraska | 16 | 16 |
| Nevada | 6 | 6 |
| New Hampshire | 8 | 8 |
| New Jersey | 20 | 20 |
| New Mexico | 6 | 6 |
| New York | 72 | 72 |
| North Carolina | 22 | 22 |
| North Dakota | 6 | 6 |
| Ohio | 46 | 46 |
| Oklahoma[a] | 12 | 12 |
| Oregon | 8 | 8 |
| Pennsylvania | 64 | 64 |
| Rhode Island | 8 | 8 |
| South Carolina | 18 | 18 |
| South Dakota | 8 | 8 |
| Tennessee | 24 | 24 |
| Texas | 30 | 30 |
| Utah | 6 | 6 |
| Vermont | 8 | 8 |
| Virginia | 24 | 24 |
| Washington | 8 | 8 |
| West Virginia | 12 | 12 |
| Wisconsin | 24 | 24 |
| Wyoming | 6 | 6 |
| Alaska | 4 | 4 |
| District of Columbia | 2 | 2 |
| Hawaii | 2 | 2 |
| **Total** | **926** | **926** |

a. Including Indian Territory, 6 votes.

# 1904 Democratic

*(Narrative, p. 75)*

| Delegation | Total Votes | First Pres. Ballot[1] (Before shift) Parker | First Pres. Ballot[1] (Before shift) Hearst | First Pres. Ballot[2] (After shift) Parker | First Pres. Ballot[2] (After shift) Hearst | Sending Telegram to Parker Yea | Sending Telegram to Parker Nay | Sending Telegram to Parker Not Voting |
|---|---|---|---|---|---|---|---|---|
| Alabama | 22 | 22 | — | 22 | — | 22 | — | — |
| Arizona | 6 | — | 6 | — | 6 | — | 6 | — |
| Arkansas | 18 | 18 | — | 18 | — | 18 | — | — |
| California | 20 | — | 20 | — | 20 | 16 | 4 | — |
| Colorado | 10 | 4 | 5 | 4 | 5 | 4 | 6 | — |
| Connecticut | 14 | 14 | — | 14 | — | 14 | — | — |
| Delaware | 6 | — | — | — | — | 6 | — | — |
| Florida | 10 | 6 | 4 | 6 | 4 | 6 | 4 | — |
| Georgia | 26 | 26 | — | 26 | — | 26 | — | — |
| Idaho | 6 | — | 6 | 6 | — | — | 6 | — |
| Illinois | 54 | — | 54 | — | 54 | 54 | — | — |
| Indiana | 30 | 30 | — | 30 | — | 30 | — | — |
| Iowa | 26 | — | 26 | — | 26 | — | 26 | — |
| Kansas | 20 | 7 | 10 | 7 | 10 | — | 20 | — |
| Kentucky | 26 | 26 | — | 26 | — | 26 | — | — |
| Louisiana | 18 | 18 | — | 18 | — | 18 | — | — |
| Maine | 12 | 7 | 1 | 7 | 1 | 7 | 2 | 3 |
| Maryland | 16 | 16 | — | 16 | — | 16 | — | — |
| Massachusetts | 32 | — | — | — | — | 32 | — | — |
| Michigan | 28 | 28 | — | 28 | — | 28 | — | — |
| Minnesota | 22 | 9 | 9 | 9 | 9 | 9 | 13 | — |
| Mississippi | 20 | 20 | — | 20 | — | 20 | — | — |
| Missouri | 36 | — | — | — | — | — | 36 | — |
| Montana | 6 | 6 | — | 6 | — | — | 6 | — |
| Nebraska | 16 | — | 4 | — | 4 | — | 16 | — |
| Nevada | 6 | — | 6 | 2 | 4 | 2 | 4 | — |
| New Hampshire | 8 | 8 | — | 8 | — | 8 | — | — |
| New Jersey | 24 | 24 | — | 24 | — | 24 | — | — |
| New Mexico | 6 | — | 6 | — | 6 | 6 | — | — |
| New York | 78 | 78 | — | 78 | — | 78 | — | — |
| North Carolina | 24 | 24 | — | 24 | — | 24 | — | — |
| North Dakota | 8 | — | — | — | — | — | 8 | — |
| Ohio | 46 | 46 | — | 46 | — | 31 | 6 | 9 |
| Oklahoma[a] | 12 | 7 | 3 | 7 | 3 | 7 | 5 | — |
| Oregon | 8 | 4 | 2 | 4 | 2 | 4 | 4 | — |
| Pennsylvania | 68 | 68 | — | 68 | — | 68 | — | — |
| Rhode Island | 8 | 2 | 6 | 2 | 6 | 2 | 5 | 1 |
| South Carolina | 18 | 18 | — | 18 | — | 18 | — | — |
| South Dakota | 8 | — | 8 | — | 8 | — | 8 | — |
| Tennessee | 24 | 24 | — | 24 | — | 24 | — | — |
| Texas | 36 | 36 | — | 36 | — | 36 | — | — |
| Utah | 6 | 6 | — | 6 | — | 6 | — | — |
| Vermont | 8 | 8 | — | 8 | — | 8 | — | — |
| Virginia | 24 | 24 | — | 24 | — | 24 | — | — |
| Washington | 10 | — | 10 | 10 | — | 10 | — | — |
| West Virginia | 14 | 10 | 2 | 13 | 1 | 14 | — | — |
| Wisconsin | 26 | — | — | — | — | 26 | — | — |
| Wyoming | 6 | — | 6 | — | 6 | 2 | 2 | 2 |
| Alaska | 6 | 6 | — | 6 | — | 6 | — | — |
| District of Columbia | 6 | 6 | — | 6 | — | 6 | — | — |
| Hawaii | 6 | — | 6 | — | 6 | 2 | 4 | — |
| Puerto Rico | 6 | 2 | — | 2 | — | 6 | — | — |
| **Total** | **1000** | **658** | **200** | **679** | **181** | **794** | **191** | **15** |

1. Other candidates: George Gray, 12; Nelson A. Miles, 3; Francis M. Cockrell, 42; Richard Olney, 38; Edward C. Wall, 27; George B. McClellan, 3; Charles A. Towne, 2; Robert E. Pattison, 4; John S. Williams, 8; Bird S. Coler, 1; Arthur P. Gorman, 2.
2. Other candidates: Gray, 12; Miles, 3; Cockrell, 42; Olney, 38; Wall, 27; McClellan, 3; Towne, 2; Pattison, 4; Williams, 8; Coler, 1.
a. Including Indian Territory, 6 votes.

# 1904 Republican

*(Narrative, p. 74)*

| Delegation | Total Votes | First Pres. Ballot Roosevelt |
|---|---|---|
| Alabama | 22 | 22 |
| Arizona | 6 | 6 |
| Arkansas | 18 | 18 |
| California | 20 | 20 |
| Colorado | 10 | 10 |
| Connecticut | 14 | 14 |
| Delaware | 6 | 6 |
| Florida | 10 | 10 |
| Georgia | 26 | 26 |
| Idaho | 6 | 6 |
| Illinois | 54 | 54 |
| Indiana | 30 | 30 |
| Iowa | 26 | 26 |
| Kansas | 20 | 20 |
| Kentucky | 26 | 26 |
| Louisiana | 18 | 18 |
| Maine | 12 | 12 |
| Maryland | 16 | 16 |
| Massachusetts | 32 | 32 |
| Michigan | 28 | 28 |
| Minnesota | 22 | 22 |
| Mississippi | 20 | 20 |
| Missouri | 36 | 36 |
| Montana | 6 | 6 |
| Nebraska | 16 | 16 |
| Nevada | 6 | 6 |
| New Hampshire | 8 | 8 |
| New Jersey | 24 | 24 |
| New Mexico | 6 | 6 |
| New York | 78 | 78 |
| North Carolina | 24 | 24 |
| North Dakota | 8 | 8 |
| Ohio | 46 | 46 |
| Oklahomaa | 12 | 12 |
| Oregon | 8 | 8 |
| Pennsylvania | 68 | 68 |
| Rhode Island | 8 | 8 |
| South Carolina | 18 | 18 |
| South Dakota | 8 | 8 |
| Tennessee | 24 | 24 |
| Texas | 36 | 36 |
| Utah | 6 | 6 |
| Vermont | 8 | 8 |
| Virginia | 24 | 24 |
| Washington | 10 | 10 |
| West Virginia | 14 | 14 |
| Wisconsin | 26 | 26 |
| Wyoming | 6 | 6 |
| Alaska | 6 | 6 |
| District of Columbia | 2 | 2 |
| Hawaii | 6 | 6 |
| Philippine Islands | 2 | 2 |
| Puerto Rico | 2 | 2 |
| **Total** | **994** | **994** |

a. Including Indian Territory, 6 votes.

# 1908 Democratic

*(Narrative, p. 77)*

| Delegation | Total Votes | First Pres. Ballot[1] Bryan |
|---|---|---|
| Alabama | 22 | 22 |
| Arizona | 6 | 6 |
| Arkansas | 18 | 18 |
| California | 20 | 20 |
| Colorado | 10 | 10 |
| Connecticut | 14 | 9 |
| Delaware | 6 | — |
| Florida | 10 | 10 |
| Georgia | 26 | 4 |
| Idaho | 6 | 6 |
| Illinois | 54 | 54 |
| Indiana | 30 | 30 |
| Iowa | 26 | 26 |
| Kansas | 20 | 20 |
| Kentucky | 26 | 26 |
| Louisiana | 18 | 18 |
| Maine | 12 | 10 |
| Maryland | 16 | 7 |
| Massachusetts | 32 | 32 |
| Michigan | 28 | 28 |
| Minnesota | 22 | — |
| Mississippi | 20 | 20 |
| Missouri | 36 | 36 |
| Montana | 6 | 6 |
| Nebraska | 16 | 16 |
| Nevada | 6 | 6 |
| New Hampshire | 8 | 7 |
| New Jersey | 24 | — |
| New Mexico | 6 | 6 |
| New York | 78 | 78 |
| North Carolina | 24 | 24 |
| North Dakota | 8 | 8 |
| Ohio | 46 | 46 |
| Oklahoma | 14 | 14 |
| Oregon | 8 | 8 |
| Pennsylvania | 68 | 49½ |
| Rhode Island | 8 | 5 |
| South Carolina | 18 | 18 |
| South Dakota | 8 | 8 |
| Tennessee | 24 | 24 |
| Texas | 36 | 36 |
| Utah | 6 | 6 |
| Vermont | 8 | 7 |
| Virginia | 24 | 24 |
| Washington | 10 | 10 |
| West Virginia | 14 | 14 |
| Wisconsin | 26 | 26 |
| Wyoming | 6 | 6 |
| Alaska | 6 | 6 |
| District of Columbia | 6 | 6 |
| Hawaii | 6 | 6 |
| Puerto Rico | 6 | 6 |
| **Total** | **1002** | **888½** |

1. *Other candidates: John A. Johnson, 46; George Gray, 59½; not voting, 8.*

# 1908 Republican

(Narrative, p. 77)

| Delegation | Total Votes | Minority Report on Changing Delegate Apportionment Formula | | | Minority Plank for Direct Election of Senators | | First Pres. Ballot[1] |
|---|---|---|---|---|---|---|---|
| | | Yea | Nay | Not Voting | Yea | Nay | Taft |
| Alabama | 22 | — | 22 | — | — | 22 | 22 |
| Arizona | 2 | — | 2 | — | — | 2 | 2 |
| Arkansas | 18 | — | 18 | — | — | 18 | 18 |
| California | 20 | — | 20 | — | — | 20 | 20 |
| Colorado | 10 | 10 | — | — | — | 10 | 10 |
| Connecticut | 14 | 14 | — | — | — | 14 | 14 |
| Delaware | 6 | — | 6 | — | — | 6 | 6 |
| Florida | 10 | — | 10 | — | — | 10 | 10 |
| Georgia | 26 | — | 26 | — | — | 26 | 17 |
| Idaho | 6 | — | 6 | — | 3 | 3 | 6 |
| Illinois | 54 | 54 | — | — | 1 | 53 | 3 |
| Indiana | 30 | 30 | — | — | 11 | 19 | — |
| Iowa | 26 | 6 | 20 | — | 1 | 25 | 26 |
| Kansas | 20 | — | 20 | — | — | 20 | 20 |
| Kentucky | 26 | 1 | 25 | — | 2 | 24 | 24 |
| Louisiana | 18 | — | 18 | — | — | 18 | 18 |
| Maine | 12 | 12 | — | — | — | 12 | 12 |
| Maryland | 16 | — | 16 | — | 1 | 15 | 16 |
| Massachusetts | 32 | 32 | — | — | — | 32 | 32 |
| Michigan | 28 | 18 | 10 | — | 5 | 23 | 27 |
| Minnesota | 22 | 10 | 11 | 1 | — | 22 | 22 |
| Mississippi | 20 | — | 20 | — | — | 20 | 20 |
| Missouri | 36 | 12 | 24 | — | 4 | 32 | 36 |
| Montana | 6 | — | 6 | — | — | 6 | 6 |
| Nebraska | 16 | 7 | 9 | — | 16 | — | 16 |
| Nevada | 6 | — | 6 | — | — | 6 | 6 |
| New Hampshire | 8 | 8 | — | — | — | 8 | 5 |
| New Jersey | 24 | 23 | 1 | — | — | 24 | 15 |
| New Mexico | 2 | — | — | 2 | — | 2 | 2 |
| New York | 78 | 78 | — | — | — | 78 | 10 |
| North Carolina | 24 | — | 24 | — | — | 24 | 24 |
| North Dakota | 8 | — | 8 | — | — | 8 | 8 |
| Ohio | 46 | 8 | 38 | — | 2 | 44 | 42 |
| Oklahoma | 14 | — | 14 | — | 14 | — | 14 |
| Oregon | 8 | 3 | 5 | — | — | 8 | 8 |
| Pennsylvania | 68 | 68 | — | — | 13 | 55 | 1 |
| Rhode Island | 8 | 8 | — | — | — | 8 | 8 |
| South Carolina | 18 | — | 18 | — | — | 18 | 13 |
| South Dakota | 8 | 8 | — | — | 8 | — | 8 |
| Tennessee | 24 | — | 24 | — | — | 24 | 24 |
| Texas | 36 | — | 36 | — | — | 36 | 36 |
| Utah | 6 | 6 | — | — | 2 | 4 | 6 |
| Vermont | 8 | 8 | — | — | — | 8 | 8 |
| Virginia | 24 | — | 24 | — | — | 24 | 21 |
| Washington | 10 | 4 | 6 | — | — | 10 | 10 |
| West Virginia | 14 | 14 | — | — | 5 | 9 | 14 |
| Wisconsin | 26 | 26 | — | — | 25 | 1 | 1 |
| Wyoming | 6 | — | 6 | — | — | 6 | 6 |
| Alaska | 2 | 2 | — | — | — | 2 | 2 |
| District of Columbia | 2 | 1 | 1 | — | — | 2 | 1 |
| Hawaii | 2 | — | 2 | — | 1 | 1 | 2 |
| Philippine Islands | 2 | — | 2 | — | — | 2 | 2 |
| Puerto Rico | 2 | — | 2 | — | — | 2 | 2 |
| **Total** | 980 | 471 | 506 | 3 | 114 | 866 | 702 |

1. Other candidates: Philander C. Knox, 68; Charles E. Hughes, 67; Joseph G. Cannon, 58; Charles W. Fairbanks, 40; Robert M. LaFollette, 25; Joseph B. Foraker, 16; Theodore Roosevelt, 3; not voting, 1.

# 1912 Democratic

(Narrative, p. 79)

| Delegation | Total Votes | Temporary Chairman[1] | | First Pres. Ballot[2] | | | | Tenth Pres. Ballot[3] | | | Thirtieth Pres. Ballot[4] | | | 43rd Pres. Ballot[5] | | 45th Pres. Ballot[6] | | 46th Pres. Ballot[7] |
|---|---|---|---|---|---|---|---|---|---|---|---|---|---|---|---|---|---|---|
| | | Bryan | Parker | Clark | Wilson | Harmon | Underwood | Clark | Wilson | Underwood | Clark | Wilson | Underwood | Clark | wilson | Clark | Wilson | Wilson |
| Ala. | 24 | 1½ | 22½ | — | — | — | 24 | — | — | 24 | — | — | 24 | — | — | — | — | 24 |
| Ariz. | 6 | 4 | 2 | 6 | — | — | — | 6 | — | — | 4 | 2 | — | 3 | 2 | 3 | 3 | 6 |
| Ark. | 18 | — | 18 | 18 | — | — | — | 18 | — | — | 18 | — | — | 18 | — | 18 | — | 18 |
| Calif. | 26 | 7 | 18 | 26 | — | — | — | 26 | — | — | 26 | — | — | 26 | — | 26 | — | 2 |
| Colo. | 12 | 6 | 6 | 12 | — | — | — | 12 | — | — | 12 | — | — | 11 | 1 | 2 | 10 | 12 |
| Conn. | 14 | 2 | 12 | — | — | — | — | 7 | — | 7 | 7 | 3 | 4 | 1 | 5 | 2 | 5 | 14 |
| Del. | 6 | 6 | — | — | 6 | — | — | — | 6 | — | — | 6 | — | — | 6 | — | 6 | 6 |
| Fla. | 12 | 1 | 11 | — | — | — | 12 | — | — | 12 | — | — | 12 | — | 2 | — | 3 | 7 |
| Ga. | 28 | — | 28 | — | — | — | 28 | — | — | 28 | — | — | 28 | — | — | — | — | 28 |
| Idaho | 8 | 8 | — | 8 | — | — | — | 8 | — | — | 2½ | 5½ | — | 1 | 7 | 1½ | 6½ | 8 |
| Ill. | 58 | — | 58 | 58 | — | — | — | 58 | — | — | 58 | — | — | — | 58 | — | 58 | 58 |
| Ind. | 30 | 8 | 21 | — | — | — | — | — | — | — | 1 | 28 | — | 1 | 28 | — | 30 | 30 |
| Iowa | 26 | 13 | 13 | 26 | — | — | — | 26 | — | — | 12 | 14 | — | 11½ | 14½ | 9 | 17 | 26 |
| Kan. | 20 | 20 | — | 20 | — | — | — | 20 | — | — | — | 20 | — | — | 20 | — | 20 | 20 |
| Ky. | 26 | 7½ | 17½ | 26 | — | — | — | 26 | — | — | 26 | — | — | 26 | — | 26 | — | 26 |
| La. | 20 | 10 | 10 | 11 | 9 | — | — | 10 | 10 | — | 7 | 12 | — | 6 | 14 | 5 | 15 | 18 |
| Maine | 12 | 1 | 11 | 1 | 9 | — | 2 | 1 | 11 | — | 1 | 9 | 2 | 1 | 11 | 1 | 11 | 12 |
| Md. | 16 | 1½ | 14½ | 16 | — | — | — | 16 | — | — | 11 | 4½ | — | 9 | 5½ | 8½ | 7 | 16 |
| Mass. | 36 | 18 | 15 | 36 | — | — | — | 33 | 1 | 2 | — | 7 | — | — | 9 | — | 9 | 36 |
| Mich. | 30 | 9 | 21 | 12 | 10 | 7 | — | 18 | 9 | — | 18 | 12 | — | 2 | 28 | 2 | 28 | 30 |
| Minn. | 24 | 24 | — | — | 24 | — | — | — | 24 | — | — | 24 | — | — | 24 | — | 24 | 24 |
| Miss. | 20 | — | 20 | — | — | — | 20 | — | — | 20 | — | — | 20 | — | — | — | — | 20 |
| Mo. | 36 | 14 | 22 | 36 | — | — | — | 36 | — | — | 36 | — | — | 36 | — | 36 | — | — |
| Mont. | 8 | 7 | 1 | 8 | — | — | — | 8 | — | — | 2 | 6 | — | 1 | 7 | 1 | 7 | 8 |
| Neb. | 16 | 13 | 3 | 12 | — | 4 | — | 13 | 3 | — | 3 | 13 | — | 3 | 13 | 3 | 13 | 16 |
| Nev. | 6 | 6 | — | 6 | — | — | — | 6 | — | — | 6 | — | — | 6 | — | 6 | — | — |
| N.H. | 8 | 5 | 3 | 8 | — | — | — | 5 | 3 | — | 3 | 5 | — | 3 | 5 | 3 | 5 | 8 |
| N.J. | 28 | 24 | 4 | 2 | 24 | — | 2 | 4 | 24 | — | 4 | 24 | — | 4 | 24 | 4 | 24 | 24 |
| N.M. | 8 | 8 | — | 8 | — | — | — | 8 | — | — | 8 | — | — | 8 | — | 8 | — | 8 |
| N.Y. | 90 | — | 90 | — | — | 90 | — | 90 | — | — | 90 | — | — | 90 | — | 90 | — | 90 |
| N.C. | 24 | 9 | 15 | — | 16½ | ½ | 7 | — | 18 | 6 | — | 17½ | 6½ | — | 22 | — | 22 | 24 |
| N.D. | 10 | 10 | — | — | 10 | — | — | — | 10 | — | — | 10 | — | — | 10 | — | 10 | 10 |
| Ohio | 48 | 19 | 29 | 1 | 10 | 35 | — | 6 | 11 | — | — | 19 | 10 | — | 20 | — | 23 | 33 |
| Okla. | 20 | 20 | — | 10 | 10 | — | — | 10 | 10 | — | 10 | 10 | — | 10 | 10 | 10 | 10 | 20 |
| Ore. | 10 | 9 | 1 | — | 10 | — | — | — | 10 | — | — | 10 | — | — | 10 | — | 10 | 10 |
| Pa. | 76 | 67 | 9 | — | 71 | 5 | — | 5 | 71 | — | 4 | 72 | — | 2 | 74 | — | 76 | 76 |
| R.I. | 10 | — | 10 | 10 | — | — | — | 10 | — | — | 10 | — | — | 10 | — | 10 | — | 10 |
| S.C. | 18 | 18 | — | — | 18 | — | — | — | 18 | — | — | 18 | — | — | 18 | — | 18 | 18 |
| S.D. | 10 | 10 | — | — | 10 | — | — | — | 10 | — | — | 10 | — | — | 10 | — | 10 | 10 |
| Tenn. | 24 | 7 | 17 | 6 | 6 | 6 | 6 | 13 | 7½ | 3½ | 13½ | 8 | 2½ | 10 | 8 | 8 | 10 | 24 |
| Texas | 40 | 40 | — | — | 40 | — | — | — | 40 | — | — | 40 | — | — | 40 | — | 40 | 40 |
| Utah | 8 | 4 | 4 | 1½ | 6 | ½ | — | 1½ | 6½ | — | 1½ | 6½ | — | 1½ | 6½ | — | 8 | 8 |
| Vt. | 8 | — | 8 | — | — | — | — | — | 8 | — | — | 8 | — | — | 8 | — | 8 | 8 |
| Va. | 24 | 10 | 14 | — | 9½ | — | 14½ | ½ | 9½ | 14 | 3 | 9½ | 11½ | — | 24 | — | 24 | 24 |
| Wash. | 14 | 14 | — | 14 | — | — | — | 14 | — | — | 14 | — | — | 14 | — | 14 | — | 14 |
| W.Va. | 16 | 4½ | 10½ | 16 | — | — | — | 16 | — | — | 16 | — | — | 16 | — | — | 16 | 16 |
| Wis. | 26 | 26 | — | 6 | 19 | — | — | 6 | 20 | — | 6 | 19 | — | 4 | 22 | — | 26 | 26 |
| Wyo. | 6 | 6 | — | 6 | — | — | — | 6 | — | — | 6 | — | — | — | 6 | — | 6 | 6 |
| Alaska | 6 | 2 | 4 | 4 | — | — | — | 3 | 3 | — | 6 | — | — | 1 | 5 | — | 6 | 6 |
| D.C. | 6 | — | 6 | 6 | — | — | — | 6 | — | — | 6 | — | — | 6 | — | 6 | — | 6 |
| Hawaii | 6 | 2 | 4 | 2 | 3 | — | 1 | 2 | 3 | 1 | 2 | 3 | 1 | 2 | 4 | 2 | 4 | 6 |
| Phil. Is. | 6 | 2 | 4 | — | — | — | — | — | — | — | — | — | — | — | — | — | — | — |
| P.R. | 6 | 4 | 2 | 2 | 3 | — | 1 | 2 | 4 | — | 1½ | 4½ | — | 1 | 4½ | 1 | 4½ | 6 |
| **Total** | 1094 | 508 | 579 | 440½ | 324 | 148 | 117½ | 556 | 350½ | 117½ | 455 | 460 | 121½ | 329 | 602 | 306 | 633 | 990 |

1. Other candidates: James A. O'Gorman, 4; John W. Kern, 1; not voting, 2.
2. Other candidates: Simeon E. Baldwin, 22; Thomas R. Marshall, 31; William J. Bryan, 1; William Sulzer, 2; not voting, 8.
3. Other candidates: Judson Harmon, 31; Marshall, 31; Kern, 1; Bryan, 1; not voting, 6.
4. Other candidates: Eugene N. Foss, 30; Harmon, 19; Kern, 2; not voting ½.
5. Other candidates: Oscar W. Underwood, 98½; Harmon, 28; Foss, 27; Bryan, 1; Kern, 1; not voting, 7½.
6. Other candidates: Underwood, 97; Foss, 27; Harmon, 25; not voting, 6.
7. Other candidates: Champ Clark, 84; Harmon, 12; not voting, 8.

# 1912 Republican

(Narrative, p. 79)

| Delegation | Total Votes | Temporary Chairman[1] | | Table Motion Prohibiting Challenged Taft Delegates from Voting | | | First Pres. Ballot[2] | | |
|---|---|---|---|---|---|---|---|---|---|
| | | Root | McGovern | Yea | Nay | Not Voting | Taft | Roosevelt | Present, Not Voting |
| Alabama | 24 | 22 | 2 | 22 | 2 | — | 22 | — | 2 |
| Arizona | 6 | 6 | — | 6 | — | — | 6 | — | — |
| Arkansas | 18 | 17 | 1 | 17 | 1 | — | 17 | — | 1 |
| California | 26 | 2 | 24 | 2 | 24 | — | 2 | — | 24 |
| Colorado | 12 | 12 | — | 12 | — | — | 12 | — | — |
| Connecticut | 14 | 14 | — | 14 | — | — | 14 | — | — |
| Delaware | 6 | 6 | — | 6 | — | — | 6 | — | — |
| Florida | 12 | 12 | — | 12 | — | — | 12 | — | — |
| Georgia | 28 | 22 | 6 | 24 | 4 | — | 28 | — | — |
| Idaho | 8 | — | 8 | — | 8 | — | 1 | — | — |
| Illinois | 58 | 9 | 49 | 7 | 51 | — | 2 | 53 | 1 |
| Indiana | 30 | 20 | 10 | 20 | 9 | 1 | 20 | 3 | 7 |
| Iowa | 26 | 16 | 10 | 16 | 10 | — | 16 | — | — |
| Kansas | 20 | 2 | 18 | 2 | 18 | — | 2 | — | 18 |
| Kentucky | 26 | 23 | 3 | 24 | 2 | — | 24 | 2 | — |
| Louisiana | 20 | 20 | — | 20 | — | — | 20 | — | — |
| Maine | 12 | — | 12 | — | 12 | — | — | — | 12 |
| Maryland | 16 | 8 | 8 | 9 | 7 | — | 1 | 9 | 5 |
| Massachusetts | 36 | 18 | 18 | 18 | 18 | — | 15 | — | 21 |
| Michigan | 30 | 19 | 10 | 20 | 10 | — | 20 | 9 | 1 |
| Minnesota | 24 | — | 24 | — | 24 | — | — | — | 24 |
| Mississippi | 20 | 16 | 4 | 16 | 4 | — | 17 | — | 3 |
| Missouri | 36 | 16 | 20 | 16 | 20 | — | 16 | — | 20 |
| Montana | 8 | 8 | — | 8 | — | — | 8 | — | — |
| Nebraska | 16 | — | 16 | — | 16 | — | — | 2 | 14 |
| Nevada | 6 | 6 | — | 6 | — | — | 6 | — | — |
| New Hampshire | 8 | 8 | — | 8 | — | — | 8 | — | — |
| New Jersey | 28 | — | 28 | — | 28 | — | — | 2 | 26 |
| New Mexico | 8 | 6 | 2 | 7 | 1 | — | 7 | 1 | — |
| New York | 90 | 76 | 13 | 75 | 15 | — | 76 | 8 | 6 |
| North Carolina | 24 | 3 | 21 | 2 | 22 | — | 1 | 1 | 22 |
| North Dakota | 10 | — | 9 | 2 | 8 | — | — | — | — |
| Ohio | 48 | 14 | 34 | 14 | 34 | — | 14 | — | 34 |
| Oklahoma | 20 | 4 | 16 | 4 | 16 | — | 4 | 1 | 15 |
| Oregon | 10 | 3 | 6 | 5 | 5 | — | — | 8 | 2 |
| Pennsylvania | 76 | 12 | 64 | 12 | 64 | — | 9 | 2 | 62 |
| Rhode Island | 10 | 10 | — | 10 | — | — | 10 | — | — |
| South Carolina | 18 | 11 | 7 | 11 | 6 | 1 | 16 | — | 1 |
| South Dakota | 10 | — | 10 | — | 10 | — | — | 5 | — |
| Tennessee | 24 | 23 | 1 | 23 | 1 | — | 23 | 1 | — |
| Texas | 40 | 31 | 8 | 29 | 9 | 2 | 31 | — | 8 |
| Utah | 8 | 7 | 1 | 7 | 1 | — | 8 | — | — |
| Vermont | 8 | 6 | 2 | 6 | 2 | — | 6 | — | 2 |
| Virginia | 24 | 22 | 2 | 21 | 3 | — | 22 | — | 1 |
| Washington | 14 | 14 | — | 14 | — | — | 14 | — | — |
| West Virginia | 16 | — | 16 | — | 16 | — | — | — | 16 |
| Wisconsin | 26 | — | 12 | — | 26 | — | 6 | — | — |
| Wyoming | 6 | 6 | — | 6 | — | — | 6 | — | — |
| Alaska | 2 | 2 | — | 2 | — | — | 2 | — | — |
| District of Columbia | 2 | 2 | — | 2 | — | — | 2 | — | — |
| Hawaii | 6 | — | 6 | 6 | — | — | 6 | — | — |
| Philippine Islands | 2 | 2 | — | 2 | — | — | 2 | — | — |
| Puerto Rico | 2 | 2 | — | 2 | — | — | 2 | — | — |
| Total | 1078 | 558 | 501 | 567 | 507 | 4 | 556[a] | 107 | 348[b] |

1. Other candidates: W. S. Lauder, 12; Asle J. Gronna, 1; not voting, 6.
2. Other candidates: Robert M. LaFollette, 41; Albert B. Cummins, 17; Charles E. Hughes, 2; absent and not voting, 7.
a. Sum of column; proceedings record 561.
b. Sum of column; proceedings record 349.

# 1916 Democratic

*(Narrative, p. 83)*

| Delegation | Total Votes | Minority Plank on Women's Suffrage | | |
|---|---|---|---|---|
| | | Yea | Nay | Not Voting |
| Alabama | 24 | 1 | 23 | — |
| Arizona | 6 | — | 6 | — |
| Arkansas | 18 | — | 18 | — |
| California | 26 | — | 26 | — |
| Colorado | 12 | — | 12 | — |
| Connecticut | 14 | 1 | 13 | — |
| Delaware | 6 | — | 6 | — |
| Florida | 12 | 4 | 8 | |
| Georgia | 28 | 23½ | 4½ | — |
| Idaho | 8 | — | 8 | — |
| Illinois | 58 | 1 | 57 | — |
| Indiana | 30 | 24 | 6 | — |
| Iowa | 26 | — | 26 | — |
| Kansas | 20 | — | 20 | — |
| Kentucky | 26 | — | 26 | — |
| Louisiana | 20 | 8 | 12 | — |
| Maine | 12 | — | 6 | 6 |
| Maryland | 16 | 16 | — | — |
| Massachusetts | 36 | 6 | 30 | — |
| Michigan | 30 | — | 30 | — |
| Minnesota | 24 | 9 | 15 | — |
| Mississippi | 20 | — | 20 | — |
| Missouri | 36 | 4 | 24 | 8 |
| Montana | 8 | — | 8 | — |
| Nebraska | 16 | — | 16 | — |
| Nevada | 6 | — | 6 | — |
| New Hampshire | 8 | 1 | 7 | — |
| New Jersey | 28 | 10 | 11 | 7 |
| New Mexico | 6 | — | 6 | — |
| New York | 90 | — | 90 | — |
| North Carolina | 24 | 11 | 13 | — |
| North Dakota | 10 | — | 10 | — |
| Ohio | 48 | 20 | 28 | — |
| Oklahoma | 20 | — | 20 | — |
| Oregon | 10 | — | 10 | — |
| Pennsylvania | 76 | — | 76 | — |
| Rhode Island | 10 | 1 | 9 | — |
| South Carolina | 18 | — | 18 | — |
| South Dakota | 10 | — | 10 | — |
| Tennessee | 24 | — | 24 | — |
| Texas | 40 | 32 | 8 | — |
| Utah | 8 | — | 8 | — |
| Vermont | 8 | — | 8 | — |
| Virginia | 24 | — | 24 | — |
| Washington | 14 | — | 14 | — |
| West Virginia | 16 | 8 | 8 | — |
| Wisconsin | 26 | — | 26 | — |
| Wyoming | 6 | — | 6 | — |
| Alaska | 6 | — | 6 | — |
| District of Columbia | 6 | — | 6 | — |
| Hawaii | 6 | — | 6 | — |
| Philippine Islands | 6 | 1 | 4 | 1 |
| Puerto Rico | 6 | — | 6 | — |
| Total | 1092 | 181½ | 888½ | 22 |

# 1916 Republican

*(Narrative, p. 82)*

| Delegation | Total Votes | First Pres. Ballot[1] | | | Second Pres. Ballot[2] | | Third Pres. Ballot[3] |
|---|---|---|---|---|---|---|---|
| | | Hughes | Root | Weeks | Hughes | Root | Hughes |
| Alabama | 16 | 8 | — | 3 | 9 | — | 16 |
| Arizona | 6 | 4 | — | — | 4 | — | 6 |
| Arkansas | 15 | 1 | 3 | 3 | — | 2 | 15 |
| California | 26 | 9 | 8 | 3 | 11 | 12 | 26 |
| Colorado | 12 | — | 5 | — | — | 5 | 12 |
| Connecticut | 14 | 5 | 5 | 1 | 5 | 7 | 14 |
| Delaware | 6 | — | — | — | — | — | 6 |
| Florida | 8 | 8 | — | — | 8 | — | 8 |
| Georgia | 17 | 5 | — | 6 | 6 | — | 17 |
| Idaho | 8 | 4 | — | — | 4 | 1 | 8 |
| Illinois | 58 | — | — | — | — | — | 58 |
| Indiana | 30 | — | — | — | — | — | 30 |
| Iowa | 26 | — | — | — | — | — | 26 |
| Kansas | 20 | 10 | 2 | 3 | 10 | 2 | 20 |
| Kentucky | 26 | 10 | — | — | 11 | — | 26 |
| Louisiana | 12 | 4 | 1 | 3 | 6 | 1 | 12 |
| Maine | 12 | 6 | 1 | 3 | 8 | 1 | 12 |
| Maryland | 16 | 7 | 1 | 5 | 7 | 1 | 15 |
| Massachusetts | 36 | 4 | — | 28 | 12 | — | 32 |
| Michigan | 30 | — | — | — | 28 | — | 30 |
| Minnesota | 24 | — | — | — | — | — | 24 |
| Mississippi | 12 | 4 | — | 1½ | 4 | — | 8½ |
| Missouri | 36 | 18 | — | 8 | 22 | — | 34 |
| Montana | 8 | — | — | — | — | — | 7 |
| Nebraska | 16 | — | — | — | 2 | — | 16 |
| Nevada | 6 | 4 | 2 | — | 4 | 2 | 6 |
| New Hampshire | 8 | — | — | 8 | 3 | 3 | 8 |
| New Jersey | 28 | 12 | 12 | 1 | 16 | 3 | 27 |
| New Mexico | 6 | 2 | — | 2 | 2 | — | 5 |
| New York | 87 | 42 | 43 | — | 43 | 42 | 87 |
| North Carolina | 21 | 6 | 2 | 3 | 6 | 2 | 14 |
| North Dakota | 10 | — | — | — | — | — | 10 |
| Ohio | 48 | — | — | — | — | — | 48 |
| Oklahoma | 20 | 5 | 1 | 6 | 5 | 1 | 19 |
| Oregon | 10 | 10 | — | — | 10 | — | 10 |
| Pennsylvania | 76 | 2 | — | — | 8 | 1 | 72 |
| Rhode Island | 10 | 10 | — | — | 10 | — | 10 |
| South Carolina | 11 | 2 | 1 | 3 | 4 | — | 6 |
| South Dakota | 10 | — | — | — | — | — | 10 |
| Tennessee | 21 | 9 | — | 3½ | 8 | ½ | 18 |
| Texas | 26 | 1 | 1 | 1 | 3 | 3 | 26 |
| Utah | 8 | 4 | 3 | — | 5 | 2 | 7 |
| Vermont | 8 | 8 | — | — | 8 | — | 8 |
| Virginia | 15 | 5½ | 3 | 3 | 8½ | 5 | 15 |
| Washington | 14 | 5 | 8 | — | 5 | — | 14 |
| West Virginia | 16 | 1 | — | 5 | 4 | 1 | 16 |
| Wisconsin | 26 | 11 | — | — | 11 | — | 23 |
| Wyoming | 6 | 6 | — | — | 6 | — | 6 |
| Alaska | 2 | 1 | — | 1 | 1 | — | 2 |
| Hawaii | 2 | — | — | 1 | 1 | — | 2 |
| Philippine Islands | 2 | — | 1 | — | — | 1 | 2 |
| **Total** | 987 | 253½ | 103 | 105 | 328½ | 98½ | 949½ |

1. *Other candidates: Albert B. Cummins, 85; Theodore E. Burton, 77½; Charles W. Fairbanks, 74½; Lawrence Y. Sherman, 66; Theodore Roosevelt, 65; Philander C. Knox, 36; Henry Ford, 32; Martin G. Brumbaugh, 29; Robert M. La Follette, 25; William H. Taft, 14; Coleman du Pont, 12; Frank B. Willis, 4; William E. Borah, 2; Samuel W. McCall, 1; not voting, 2½.*
2. *Other candidates: Fairbanks, 88½; Cummins, 85; Roosevelt, 81; John W. Weeks, 79; Burton, 76½; Sherman, 65; Knox, 36; La Follette, 25; du Pont, 13; John Wanamaker, 5; Willis, 1; Leonard Wood, 1; Warren G. Harding, 1; McCall, 1; not voting, 2.*
3. *Other candidates: Roosevelt, 18½; La Follette, 3; du Pont, 5; Henry Cabot Lodge, 7; Weeks, 3; not voting, 1.*

# 1920 Democratic

*(Narrative, p. 86)*

| Delegation | Total Votes | First Pres. Ballot[1] | | | | Thirtieth Pres. Ballot[2] | | | 39th Pres. Ballot[3] | | 44th Pres. Ballot[4] | |
|---|---|---|---|---|---|---|---|---|---|---|---|---|
| | | McAdoo | Cox | Palmer | Smith | McAdoo | Cox | Palmer | McAdoo | Cox | McAdoo | Cox |
| Alabama | 24 | 9 | 3 | 6 | 2 | 12 | 7 | — | 8 | — | 8 | 13 |
| Arizona | 6 | 4 | 1 | — | — | 3 | 2 | — | 4 | 2 | 2½ | 3½ |
| Arkansas | 18 | 3 | 7 | 2 | — | 3 | 14 | 1 | 4 | 14 | — | 18 |
| California | 26 | 10 | 4 | 3 | 1 | 10 | 13 | 1 | 14 | 12 | 13 | 13 |
| Colorado | 12 | 3 | — | 8 | — | 5 | 6 | — | 4 | 7 | 3 | 9 |
| Connecticut | 14 | — | — | — | — | I | 6 | 4 | 3 | 10 | 2 | 12 |
| Delaware | 6 | 4 | — | — | — | 4 | 2 | — | 4 | 2 | 3 | 3 |
| Florida | 12 | 1 | — | 8 | — | 3 | 9 | — | 3 | 9 | — | 12 |
| Georgia | 28 | — | — | 28 | — | — | — | 28 | 28 | — | — | 28 |
| Idaho | 8 | 8 | — | — | — | 8 | — | — | 8 | — | 8 | — |
| Illinois | 58 | 9 | 9 | 35 | 5 | 21 | 36 | 1 | 18 | 38 | 13 | 44 |
| Indiana | 30 | — | — | — | — | 29 | — | — | 11 | 19 | — | 30 |
| Iowa | 26 | — | — | — | — | — | 26 | — | — | 26 | — | 26 |
| Kansas | 20 | 20 | — | — | — | 20 | — | — | 20 | — | 20 | — |
| Kentucky | 26 | 3 | 23 | — | — | 5 | 20 | — | 5 | 20 | — | 26 |
| Louisiana | 20 | 5 | 2 | 2 | — | 4 | 14 | — | 7 | 12 | — | 20 |
| Maine | 12 | 5 | — | 5 | — | 7 | — | 5 | 12 | — | 5 | 5 |
| Maryland | 16 | 5½ | 5½ | — | — | 5½ | 8½ | — | 5½ | 8½ | — | 13½ |
| Massachusetts | 36 | 4 | 4 | 17 | 7 | 2 | 15 | 16 | 1 | 33 | — | 35 |
| Michigan | 30 | 15 | — | 12 | — | 15 | 6 | 9 | 14 | 12 | — | — |
| Minnesota | 24 | 10 | 2 | 7 | — | 14 | 4 | 4 | 16 | 7 | 15 | 8 |
| Mississippi | 20 | — | — | — | — | — | 20 | — | — | 20 | — | 20 |
| Missouri | 36 | 15½ | 2½ | 10 | — | 18 | 6 | 5 | 20½ | 11½ | 17 | 18 |
| Montana | 8 | 1 | — | — | — | 8 | — | — | 8 | — | 2 | 6 |
| Nebraska | 16 | — | — | — | — | 7 | — | — | 7 | — | 2 | 5 |
| Nevada | 6 | — | 6 | — | — | — | 6 | — | — | 6 | — | 6 |
| New Hampshire | 8 | 4 | — | 1 | — | 5 | 2 | 1 | 5 | 2 | 6 | 2 |
| New Jersey | 28 | — | — | — | — | — | 28 | — | — | 28 | — | 28 |
| New Mexico | 6 | 2 | — | 1 | — | 6 | — | — | 6 | — | 6 | — |
| New York | 90 | — | — | — | 90 | 20 | 70 | — | 20 | 70 | 20 | 70 |
| North Carolina | 24 | — | — | — | — | 24 | — | — | 24 | — | 24 | — |
| North Dakota | 10 | 6 | 1 | 2 | — | 8 | 2 | — | 9 | 1 | 4 | 2 |
| Ohio | 48 | — | 48 | — | — | — | 48 | — | — | 48 | — | 48 |
| Oklahoma | 20 | — | — | — | — | — | — | — | — | — | — | — |
| Oregon | 10 | 10 | — | — | — | 10 | — | — | 10 | — | 10 | — |
| Pennsylvania | 76 | 2 | — | 73 | — | 2 | 1 | 73 | 2 | 1 | 4 | 68 |
| Rhode Island | 10 | 2 | — | 5 | 2 | 3 | 4 | 3 | 1 | 7 | 1 | 9 |
| South Carolina | 18 | 18 | — | — | — | 18 | — | — | 18 | — | 18 | — |
| South Dakota | 10 | — | — | — | — | 6 | 4 | — | 6 | 3 | 3 | 5 |
| Tennessee | 24 | 2 | 8 | 9 | — | — | — | — | — | — | — | — |
| Texas | 40 | 40 | — | — | — | 40 | — | — | 40 | — | 40 | — |
| Utah | 8 | 8 | — | — | — | 8 | — | — | 8 | — | 7 | 1 |
| Vermont | 8 | 4 | 2 | 1 | 1 | 1 | 6 | 1 | 4 | 4 | — | 8 |
| Virginia | 24 | — | — | — | — | — | — | — | 10 | 11 | 2½ | 18½ |
| Washington | 14 | 10 | — | — | — | 14 | — | — | 11 | 2½ | — | 13 |
| West Virginia | 16 | — | — | — | — | — | — | — | — | — | — | — |
| Wisconsin | 26 | 11 | 5 | 3 | 1 | 19 | 7 | — | 19 | 7 | 3 | 23 |
| Wyoming | 6 | 6 | — | — | — | 6 | — | — | 6 | — | 3 | 3 |
| Alaska | 6 | 2 | 1 | 3 | — | 2 | 1 | 3 | 4 | 2 | — | 6 |
| Canal Zone | 2 | 1 | — | 1 | — | 1 | — | 1 | 2 | — | 2 | — |
| District of Columbia | 6 | — | — | 6 | — | — | — | 6 | — | 6 | — | 6 |
| Hawaii | 6 | 2 | — | 4 | — | 1 | 5 | — | 1 | 5 | — | 6 |
| Philippine Islands | 6 | — | — | — | — | 3 | 2 | 1 | 3 | 2 | 2 | 4 |
| Puerto Rico | 6 | 1 | — | 2 | — | 2 | — | 2 | 6 | — | 1 | 5 |
| **Total** | 1094 | 266 | 134 | 254[a] | 109 | 403½ | 400½ | 165 | 440 | 468½ | 270 | 699½ |

1. *Other candidates: Homer S. Cummings, 25; James W. Gerard, 21; Robert L. Owen, 33; Gilbert M. Hitchcock, 18; Edwin T. Meredith, 27; Edward I. Edwards, 42; John W. Davis, 32; Carter Glass, 26½; Furnifold M. Simmons, 24; Francis B. Harrison, 6; John S. Williams, 20; Thomas R. Marshall, 37; Champ Clark, 9; Oscar W. Underwood, ½; William R. Hearst, 1; William J. Bryan, 1; Bainbridge Colby, 1; Josephus Daniels, 1; Wood, 4.*
2. *Other candidates: Cummings, 4; Owen, 33; Davis, 58; Glass, 24; Clark, 2; Underwood, 2; not voting, 2.*
3. *Other candidates: A. Mitchell Palmer, 74; Davis, 71½; Owen, 32; Cummings, 2; Clark, 2; Colby, 1; not voting, 3.*
4. *Other candidates: Palmer, 1; Davis, 52; Owen, 34; Glass, 1½; Colby, 1; not voting, 36.*
a. *Sum of column; proceedings record 256.*

# 1920 Republican

(Narrative, p. 85)

| Delegation | Total Votes | First Pres. Ballot[1] | | | Fourth Pres. Ballot[2] | | | Eighth Pres. Ballot[3] | | | Ninth Pres. Ballot[4] | | | Tenth Pres. Ballot[5] (Before shift) | | Tenth Pres. Ballot[6] (After shift) | |
|---|---|---|---|---|---|---|---|---|---|---|---|---|---|---|---|---|---|
| | | Wood | Lowden | Johnson | Wood | Lowden | Johnson | Wood | Lowden | Harding | Wood | Lowden | Harding | Wood | Harding | Wood | Harding |
| Alabama | 14 | 4 | 6 | 3 | 4 | 6 | 4 | 4 | 6 | 4 | 4 | 6 | 4 | 3 | 8 | 3 | 8 |
| Arizona | 6 | 6 | — | — | 6 | — | — | 6 | — | — | 6 | — | — | 6 | — | — | 6 |
| Arkansas | 13 | 6 | 6 | — | 2½ | 10½ | — | 1½ | 11½ | — | 1½ | 10½ | 1 | — | 13 | — | 13 |
| California | 26 | — | — | 26 | — | — | 26 | — | — | — | — | — | — | — | — | — | — |
| Colorado | 12 | 9 | 2 | — | 9 | 2 | — | 6 | 3 | 3 | 6 | 1 | 5 | 6 | 5 | — | 12 |
| Connecticut | 14 | — | 14 | — | — | 13 | 1 | 1 | 11 | — | — | — | 13 | — | 13 | — | 13 |
| Delaware | 6 | — | — | — | — | 2 | — | — | — | 3 | — | — | 3 | — | 6 | — | 6 |
| Florida | 8 | 4½ | 2½ | — | 6½ | 1½ | — | 7 | 1 | — | 1 | — | 7 | ½ | 7½ | ½ | 7½ |
| Georgia | 17 | 8 | 9 | — | 8 | 9 | — | 8 | 9 | — | 8 | 8 | 1 | 7 | 10 | 7 | 10 |
| Idaho | 8 | 5 | — | 1 | 5 | 1 | 1 | 4 | 2 | 1 | 5 | 1 | 1 | 3 | 2 | 3 | 2 |
| Illinois | 58 | 14 | 41 | 3 | — | 41 | 17 | — | 41 | — | — | 41 | — | — | 22.2 | — | 38.2 |
| Indiana | 30 | 22 | — | 8 | 18 | 3 | 6 | 15 | 4 | 11 | 15 | 4 | 11 | 8 | 20 | 9 | 21 |
| Iowa | 26 | — | 26 | — | — | 26 | — | — | 26 | — | — | 26 | — | — | 26 | — | 26 |
| Kansas | 20 | 14 | 6 | — | 14 | 6 | — | 10 | 6 | 4 | — | — | 20 | 1 | 18 | 1 | 18 |
| Kentucky | 26 | — | 20 | 1 | — | 26 | — | — | 26 | — | — | — | 26 | — | 26 | — | 26 |
| Louisiana | 12 | 3 | 3 | 1 | 3 | 6 | — | 3 | 7 | 2 | — | — | 12 | — | 12 | — | 12 |
| Maine | 12 | 11 | — | — | 11 | — | — | 12 | — | — | 12 | — | — | 12 | — | 12 | — |
| Maryland | 16 | 16 | — | — | 16 | — | — | 16 | — | — | 16 | — | — | 10 | 5 | 10 | 5 |
| Massachusetts | 35 | 7 | — | — | 16 | — | — | 11 | — | — | 11 | 1 | 1 | 17 | 17 | 17 | 17 |
| Michigan | 30 | — | — | 30 | — | — | 30 | 13 | 7 | — | 15 | 6 | 1 | 1 | 25 | 1 | 25 |
| Minnesota | 24 | 19 | 3 | 2 | 17 | 5 | 2 | 16 | 5 | — | 17 | 5 | — | 21 | 2 | 21 | 2 |
| Mississippi | 12 | 4½ | 2 | 2 | 7½ | 2½ | — | 8½ | 1½ | 2 | 7½ | — | 4½ | 2½ | 9½ | — | 12 |
| Missouri | 36 | 4½ | 18 | 3 | 8½ | 19 | 1 | 2½ | 15½ | 17 | — | — | 36 | — | 36 | — | 36 |
| Montana | 8 | — | — | 8 | — | — | 8 | — | — | — | — | — | — | — | — | — | — |
| Nebraska | 16 | 3 | — | 13 | 6 | — | 10 | 14 | — | — | 16 | — | — | 5 | 4 | 5 | 4 |
| Nevada | 6 | 2 | 1½ | 2 | 2½ | 2 | 1½ | 1½ | — | 3½ | 1½ | — | 3½ | — | 3½ | — | 3½ |
| New Hampshire | 8 | 8 | — | — | 8 | — | — | 8 | — | — | 8 | — | — | 8 | — | 8 | — |
| New Jersey | 28 | 17 | — | 11 | 17 | — | 11 | 16 | — | 2 | 15 | — | 4 | 15 | 5 | 15 | 5 |
| New Mexico | 6 | 6 | — | — | 6 | — | — | 6 | — | — | 6 | — | — | 6 | — | — | 6 |
| New York | 88 | 10 | 2 | — | 20 | 32 | 5 | 23 | 45 | 8 | 5 | 4 | 66 | 6 | 68 | 6 | 68 |
| North Carolina | 22 | — | — | 1 | 3 | 15 | 2 | 2 | 16 | 4 | 3 | — | 18 | 2 | 20 | 2 | 20 |
| North Dakota | 10 | 2 | — | 8 | 3 | 1 | 6 | 3 | 4 | — | 3 | 4 | — | 1 | 9 | — | 10 |
| Ohio | 48 | 9 | — | — | 9 | — | — | 9 | — | 39 | 9 | — | 39 | — | 48 | — | 48 |
| Oklahoma | 20 | 1½ | 18½ | — | 2 | 18 | — | 2 | 18 | — | ½ | — | 18 | 3 | 2 | 3 | 2 |
| Oregon | 10 | 1 | — | 9 | 5 | — | 5 | 4 | — | 1 | 4 | — | 1 | — | — | — | — |
| Pennsylvania | 76 | — | — | — | — | — | — | — | — | — | — | — | — | 14 | 60 | 14 | 60 |
| Rhode Island | 10 | 10 | — | — | 10 | — | — | 10 | — | — | 10 | — | — | — | 10 | — | 10 |
| South Carolina | 11 | — | 8 | — | — | 11 | — | — | 11 | — | — | — | 11 | — | 11 | — | 11 |
| South Dakota | 10 | 10 | — | — | 10 | — | — | 10 | — | — | 10 | — | — | 6 | 4 | 6 | 4 |
| Tennessee | 20 | 20 | — | — | 19 | 1 | — | 10 | 7 | 3 | 6 | 1 | 13 | — | 20 | — | 20 |
| Texas | 23 | 8½ | 5 | 1½ | 8 | 9½ | 1 | 5 | 8½ | 8½ | 1 | 1 | 19½ | 1 | 23 | 1 | 23 |
| Utah | 8 | 5 | 2 | — | 5 | 2 | — | 4 | 2 | 2 | 2 | 2 | 4 | 8 | — | 8 | — |
| Vermont | 8 | 8 | — | — | 8 | — | — | 8 | — | — | 8 | — | — | 8 | — | 8 | — |
| Virginia | 15 | 3 | 12 | — | 3 | 12 | — | 3 | 10 | 2 | 4 | — | 11 | 1 | 14 | 1 | 14 |
| Washington | 14 | — | — | — | — | — | — | — | — | — | — | — | — | 5 | 6 | — | 14 |
| West Virginia | 16 | — | — | — | 8 | — | 1 | 9 | — | 7 | 8 | — | 7 | — | 16 | — | 16 |
| Wisconsin | 26 | 1 | — | — | 1 | — | 2 | 1 | — | — | 1 | — | — | — | 1 | — | 1 |
| Wyoming | 6 | — | 3 | — | 3 | 3 | — | — | — | — | — | — | 6 | — | 6 | — | 6 |
| Alaska | 2 | — | — | — | 1 | — | — | 1 | — | — | 1 | — | — | — | 2 | — | 2 |
| District of Columbia | 2 | 2 | — | — | 2 | — | — | 2 | — | — | — | — | — | — | 2 | — | 2 |
| Hawaii | 2 | — | — | — | — | 2 | — | -- | 2 | — | — | — | — | — | 2 | — | 2 |
| Philippine Islands | 2 | 2 | — | — | 2 | — | — | 2 | — | — | 2 | — | — | 2 | — | 2 | — |
| Puerto Rico | 2 | 1 | — | 1 | 1 | 1 | — | 1 | 1 | — | — | — | 2 | — | 2 | — | 2 |
| **Total** | **984** | **287½** | **211½** | **133½** | **314½** | **289** | **140½** | **299** | **307** | **133[a]** | **249** | **121½** | **374½** | **181½** | **644.7** | **156** | **692.2** |

1. Other candidates: Warren G. Harding, 65½; William C. Sproul, 84; Calvin Coolidge, 34; Herbert Hoover, 5½; Coleman du Pont, 7; Jeter C. Pritchard, 21; Robert M. La Follette, 24; Howard Sutherland, 17; William E. Borah, 2; Charles B. Warren, 1; Miles Poindexter, 20; Nicholas M. Butler, 69½; not voting, 1.
2. Other candidates: Harding, 61½; Sproul, 79½; Coolidge, 25; Hoover, 5; du Pont, 3; La Follette, 22; Sutherland, 3; Borah, 1; Poindexter, 15; Butler, 20; James E. Watson, 4; Knox, 2.
3. Other candidates: Haram W. Johnson, 87; Coolidge, 30; du Pont, 3; Frank B. Kellogg, 1; La Follette, 24; Poindexter, 15; Irving L. Lenroot, 1; Hoover, 5; Butler, 2; Knox, 1; Sproul, 76.
4. Other candidates: Johnson, 82; Sproul, 78; Coolidge, 28; Hoover, 6; Lenroot, 1; Butler, 2; Knox, 1; La Follette, 24; Poindexter, 14; Will H. Hays, 1; H. F. MacGregor, 1; not voting, 1.
5. Other candidates: Frank Lowden, 28; Johnson, 80 4/5; Hoover, 10½; Coolidge, 5; Butler, 2; Lenroot, 1; Hays, 1; Knox, 1; La Follette, 24; Poindexter, 2; not voting, 2½.
6. Other candidates: Lowden, 11; Johnson, 80 4/5; Hoover, 9½; Coolidge, 5; Butler, 2; Lenroot, 1; Hays, 1; Knox, 1; La Follette, 24; not voting, ½.
a. Sum of column; proceedings record 133½.

# 1924 Republican

*(Narrative, p. 88)*

| Delegation | Total Votes | First Pres. Ballot[1] Coolidge |
|---|---|---|
| Alabama | 16 | 16 |
| Arizona | 9 | 9 |
| Arkansas | 14 | 14 |
| California | 29 | 29 |
| Colorado | 15 | 15 |
| Connecticut | 17 | 17 |
| Delaware | 9 | 9 |
| Florida | 10 | 10 |
| Georgia | 18 | 18 |
| Idaho | 11 | 11 |
| Illinois | 61 | 61 |
| Indiana | 33 | 33 |
| Iowa | 29 | 29 |
| Kansas | 23 | 23 |
| Kentucky | 26 | 26 |
| Louisiana | 13 | 13 |
| Maine | 15 | 15 |
| Maryland | 19 | 19 |
| Massachusetts | 39 | 39 |
| Michigan | 33 | 33 |
| Minnesota | 27 | 27 |
| Mississippi | 12 | 12 |
| Missouri | 39 | 39 |
| Montana | 11 | 11 |
| Nebraska | 19 | 19 |
| Nevada | 9 | 9 |
| New Hampshire | 11 | 11 |
| New Jersey | 31 | 31 |
| New Mexico | 9 | 9 |
| New York | 91 | 91 |
| North Carolina | 22 | 22 |
| North Dakota | 13 | 7 |
| Ohio | 51 | 51 |
| Oklahoma | 23 | 23 |
| Oregon | 13 | 13 |
| Pennsylvania | 79 | 79 |
| Rhode Island | 13 | 13 |
| South Carolina | 11 | 11 |
| South Dakota | 13 | 3 |
| Tennessee | 27 | 27 |
| Texas | 23 | 23 |
| Utah | 11 | 11 |
| Vermont | 11 | 11 |
| Virginia | 17 | 17 |
| Washington | 17 | 17 |
| West Virginia | 19 | 19 |
| Wisconsin | 29 | 1 |
| Wyoming | 9 | 9 |
| Alaska | 2 | 2 |
| District of Columbia | 2 | 2 |
| Hawaii | 2 | 2 |
| Philippine Islands | 2 | 2 |
| Puerto Rico | 2 | 2 |
| **Total** | **1109** | **1065** |

1. Other candidates: Robert M. La Follette, 34; Hiram W. Johnson, 10.

# 1924 Democratic

*(Narrative, p. 89)*

| Delegation | Total Votes | Minority Report on League of Nations | | | Minority Report on Ku Klux Klan | | | First Pres. Ballot[1] | | Fiftieth Pres. Ballot[2] | | Ninetieth Pres. Ballot[3] | | |
|---|---|---|---|---|---|---|---|---|---|---|---|---|---|---|
| | | Yea | Nay | Not Voting | Yea | Nay | Not Voting | McAdoo | Smith | McAdoo | Smith | McAdoo | Smith | Ralston |
| Alabama | 24 | 12½ | 11½ | — | 24 | — | — | — | — | — | — | — | — | — |
| Arizona | 6 | 1½ | 4½ | — | 1 | 5 | — | 4½ | — | 3½ | — | 3½ | — | — |
| Arkansas | 18 | 3 | 15 | — | — | 18 | — | — | — | — | — | — | — | — |
| California | 26 | 4 | 22 | — | 7 | 19 | — | 26 | — | 26 | — | 26 | — | — |
| Colorado | 12 | 9½ | 2½ | — | 6 | 6 | — | — | — | 4 | 3 | 1 | 3 | ½ |
| Connecticut | 14 | 5 | 9 | — | 13 | 1 | — | — | 6 | 4 | 10 | 2 | 12 | — |
| Delaware | 6 | 6 | — | — | 6 | — | — | — | — | — | — | — | — | — |
| Florida | 12 | 5 | 7 | — | 1 | 11 | — | 12 | — | 10 | 1 | 9 | — | 3 |
| Georgia | 28 | — | 28 | — | 1 | 19½ | 7½ | 28 | — | 28 | — | 28 | — | — |
| Idaho | 8 | 8 | — | — | — | 8 | — | 8 | — | 8 | — | 8 | — | — |
| Illinois | 58 | 10 | 48 | — | 45 | 13 | — | 12 | 15 | 13 | 20 | 12 | 36 | 6 |
| Indiana | 30 | — | 30 | — | 5 | 25 | — | — | — | — | — | — | — | 30 |
| Iowa | 26 | — | 26 | — | 13½ | 12½ | — | 26 | — | 26 | — | — | — | — |
| Kansas | 20 | — | 20 | — | — | 20 | — | — | — | 20 | — | — | — | — |
| Kentucky | 26 | 9½ | 16½ | — | 9½ | 16½ | — | 26 | — | 26 | — | 26 | — | — |
| Louisiana | 20 | — | 20 | — | — | 20 | — | — | — | — | — | — | — | — |
| Maine | 12 | 11 | 1 | — | 8 | 4 | — | 2 | 3½ | 2½ | 4½ | 1½ | 4½ | — |
| Maryland | 16 | — | 16 | — | 16 | — | — | — | — | — | — | — | — | — |
| Massachusetts | 36 | 8 | 28 | — | 35½ | ½ | — | 1½ | 33 | 2½ | 33½ | 2½ | 33½ | — |
| Michigan | 30 | 6 | 24 | — | 12½ | 16½ | 1 | — | — | 15 | 15 | — | 10 | 20 |
| Minnesota | 24 | 10 | 14 | — | 17 | 7 | — | 5 | 10 | 6 | 15 | 6 | 15 | — |
| Mississippi | 20 | — | 20 | — | — | 20 | — | — | — | — | — | — | — | 20 |
| Missouri | 36 | 2 | 34 | — | 10½ | 25½ | — | 36 | — | 36 | — | — | — | 36 |
| Montana | 8 | — | 8 | — | 1 | 7 | — | 7 | 1 | 7 | — | 7 | 1 | — |
| Nebraska | 16 | — | 16 | — | 3 | 13 | — | 1 | — | 13 | 3 | 1 | — | — |
| Nevada | 6 | — | 6 | — | — | 6 | — | 6 | — | 6 | — | — | — | 6 |
| New Hampshire | 8 | 8 | — | — | 2½ | 5½ | — | — | — | 4½ | 3½ | 3 | 3½ | — |
| New Jersey | 28 | — | 28 | — | 28 | — | — | — | — | — | 28 | — | 28 | — |
| New Mexico | 6 | — | 6 | — | 1 | 5 | — | 6 | — | 6 | — | 6 | — | — |
| New York | 90 | 35 | 55 | — | 90 | — | — | — | 90 | 2 | 88 | 2 | 88 | — |
| North Carolina | 24 | 6 | 18 | — | 3 17/20 | 20 3/20 | — | 24 | — | 17 | — | 3 | — | — |
| North Dakota | 10 | 1 | 9 | — | 10 | — | — | 10 | — | 5 | 5 | 5 | 5 | — |
| Ohio | 48 | 48 | — | — | 32½ | 15½ | — | — | — | — | — | — | 20½ | 17 |
| Oklahoma | 20 | — | 20 | — | — | 20 | — | 20 | — | 10 | — | — | — | 20 |
| Oregon | 10 | 1 | 9 | — | — | 10 | — | 10 | — | 10 | — | 10 | — | — |
| Pennsylvania | 76 | 52 | 22 | 2 | 49½ | 24½ | 2 | 25½ | 35½ | 25½ | 38½ | 25½ | 39½ | — |
| Rhode Island | 10 | — | 10 | — | 10 | — | — | — | 10 | — | 10 | — | 10 | — |
| South Carolina | 18 | 18 | — | — | — | 18 | — | 18 | — | 18 | — | 18 | — | — |
| South Dakota | 10 | — | 10 | — | 6 | 4 | — | 10 | — | 9 | — | 9 | — | — |
| Tennessee | 24 | 15 | 9 | — | 3 | 21 | — | 24 | — | 24 | — | 24 | — | — |
| Texas | 40 | — | 40 | — | — | 40 | — | 40 | — | 40 | — | 40 | — | — |
| Utah | 8 | 5½ | 2½ | — | 4 | 4 | — | 8 | — | 8 | — | 8 | — | — |
| Vermont | 8 | 2 | 6 | — | 8 | — | — | 1 | 7 | 1 | 7 | — | 8 | — |
| Virginia | 24 | 24 | — | — | 2½ | 21½ | — | 14 | — | 14 | — | 14 | — | — |
| Washington | 14 | — | 14 | — | — | 14 | — | 14 | — | 14 | — | 14 | — | — |
| West Virginia | 16 | 16 | — | — | 7 | 9 | — | — | — | — | — | — | — | 1 |
| Wisconsin | 26 | 4 | 22 | — | 25 | 1 | — | 3 | 23 | 3 | 23 | 1 | 23 | — |
| Wyoming | 6 | 3 | 3 | — | 2 | 4 | — | — | — | 1 | 4½ | — | 3 | — |
| Alaska | 6 | — | 5 | — | 6 | — | — | 1 | 3 | 1 | 3 | — | 5 | — |
| Canal Zone | 6 | — | 6 | — | 2 | 2 | 2 | 6 | — | 6 | — | 3 | 3 | — |
| District of Columbia | 6 | — | 6 | — | 6 | — | — | 6 | — | 6 | — | 6 | — | — |
| Hawaii | 6 | — | 6 | — | 4 | 2 | — | 1 | 1 | 1 | 1 | 1 | — | — |
| Philippine Islands | 6 | 2 | 4 | — | 2 | 2 | 2 | 3 | 3 | 3 | 3 | 2 | 2 | — |
| Puerto Rico | 6 | 1 | 5 | — | 2 | 4 | — | — | — | — | — | — | 1 | — |
| Virgin Islands | — | — | — | — | — | — | — | — | — | — | — | — | — | — |
| **Total** | **1098** | **353½** | **742½** | **2** | **542 7/20** | **543 3/20** | **12½** | **431½** | **241** | **461½** | **320½** | **314** | **354½** | **159½** |

1. *Other candidates: Oscar W. Underwood, 42½; Joseph T. Rominson, 21; Willard Saulsbury, 7; Samuel M. Ralston, 30; Jonathan M. Davis, 20; Albert C. Ritchie, 22½; Woodbridge N. Ferris, 30; James M. Cox, 59; Charles W. Bryan, 18; Fred H. Brown, 17; George S. Silzer, 38; Carter Glass, 25; John W. Davis, 31; William E. Sweet, 12; Partick Harrison, 43½; Houston Thompson, 1; John B. Kendrick, 6.*
2. *Other candidates: John W. Davis, 64; Ralston, 58; Underwood, 42½; Robinson, 44; Glass, 24; Cox, 54; Ritchie, 16½; Saulsbury, 6; Thomas J. Walsh, 1; Jonathan M. Davis, 2; Owen, 4.*
3. *Other candidates: Underwood, 42½; Robinson, 20; John W. Davis, 65½; Glass, 30½; Ritchie, 16½; Saulsbury, 6; Walsh, 5; Bryan, 15; Jonathan M. Davis, 22; Josephus Daniels, 19; Edwin T. Meredith, 26; not voting, 2.*

# 1924 Democratic

(Narrative, p. 89)

| Delegation | 100th Pres. Ballot[4] | | | 101st Pres. Ballot[5] | | | | 102nd Pres. Ballot[6] | | | 103rd Pres. Ballot[7] (Before shift) | | 103rd Pres. Ballot[8] (After shift) | |
|---|---|---|---|---|---|---|---|---|---|---|---|---|---|---|
| | McAdoo | Smith | Davis | Underwood | Smith | Davis | Meredith | Underwood | Davis | Walsh | Underwood | Davis | Underwood | Davis |
| Alabama | — | — | — | 24 | — | — | — | 24 | — | — | 24 | — | — | 24 |
| Arizona | 3 | — | — | 3 | — | — | — | 3 | — | — | 3 | — | 3 | — |
| Arkansas | — | — | — | — | — | — | — | — | — | — | — | — | — | — |
| California | 16½ | — | — | — | 1 | — | 3 | — | — | 26 | 2 | 2 | — | 26 |
| Colorado | ½ | 3½ | 1½ | 1 | 3 | 2½ | 1 | 6½ | 1½ | — | 5 | 3 | 5 | 3 |
| Connecticut | 2 | 12 | — | 11 | — | 1 | — | 11 | — | 3 | 11 | — | — | 14 |
| Delaware | — | — | — | — | — | 6 | — | — | — | — | 6 | — | 6 | — |
| Florida | 9 | — | 3 | — | — | 3 | — | — | 5 | 4 | — | 6 | — | 6 |
| Georgia | 28 | — | — | — | — | 5 | 12 | 1 | 13 | — | — | 27 | — | 27 |
| Idaho | — | — | — | — | — | — | — | — | — | 8 | — | 8 | — | 8 |
| Illinois | — | 35 | 6 | 20 | — | 4 | 13 | 20 | 3 | 13 | 19 | 19 | — | 58 |
| Indiana | — | — | 14 | 3 | — | 10 | 6 | 10 | 10 | — | 5 | 25 | 5 | 25 |
| Iowa | — | — | — | — | — | — | 26 | — | — | — | — | — | — | 26 |
| Kansas | — | — | 20 | — | 20 | — | — | — | 20 | — | — | 20 | — | 20 |
| Kentucky | 12 | — | 8½ | 1 | 1 | 9 | ½ | 1 | 9 | 6½ | 1 | 22½ | — | 26 |
| Louisiana | — | — | 20 | — | — | 20 | — | — | 20 | — | — | 20 | — | 20 |
| Maine | 1 | 2 | 8 | 5 | — | 6 | — | 8 | 4 | — | 10 | 2 | 10 | 2 |
| Maryland | — | — | — | — | — | 16 | — | — | 16 | — | — | 16 | — | 16 |
| Massachusetts | 2½ | 33½ | — | — | 33 | — | — | 8 | ½ | 2 | 23½ | 2 | 23½ | 2 |
| Michigan | — | 10 | 15 | 10 | — | 12 | 1 | 14 | 16 | — | — | 29½ | — | 29½ |
| Minnesota | 6 | 15 | 1 | — | 15 | 1 | — | 14 | 2 | 1 | 16 | 3 | 16 | 3 |
| Mississippi | — | — | — | — | — | 20 | — | — | 20 | — | — | 20 | — | 20 |
| Missouri | — | — | 36 | — | — | 36 | — | — | 36 | — | — | 36 | — | 36 |
| Montana | 1 | — | — | — | — | — | — | — | — | 8 | — | — | — | — |
| Nebraska | — | 2 | — | — | 1 | — | 11 | 2 | — | 4 | 2 | 1 | 2 | 1 |
| Nevada | — | 6 | — | — | — | — | — | — | — | 6 | — | 6 | — | 6 |
| New Hampshire | — | 1 | 2 | — | 1 | 1 | 1½ | — | 3½ | 4½ | — | 3½ | — | 3½ |
| New Jersey | — | 28 | — | 16 | — | — | — | 16 | 2 | — | 16 | 1 | 16 | 1 |
| New Mexico | 6 | — | — | — | 1½ | 1 | 1 | — | 2½ | — | — | 2 | — | 2 |
| New York | 2 | 88 | — | 86½ | — | — | — | 84 | 1 | 1 | 44 | 4 | — | 60 |
| North Carolina | — | — | — | 1 | — | 20 | 1 | — | 23 | — | 5½ | 18½ | — | 24 |
| North Dakota | 3 | 5 | — | — | 5 | — | 1 | 5 | — | 5 | — | — | — | — |
| Ohio | — | 15 | 23 | 5 | 10 | 23 | 5 | 7 | 25 | — | 4 | 41 | 1 | 46 |
| Oklahoma | — | — | — | — | — | — | — | — | 20 | — | — | 20 | — | 20 |
| Oregon | 10 | — | — | 1 | — | 2 | 1 | 1 | 2 | — | 1 | 5 | 1 | 5 |
| Pennsylvania | 17½ | 39½ | 9 | 6 | 36½ | 19½ | 1 | 32½ | 29½ | 4 | 31½ | 37½ | — | 76 |
| Rhode Island | — | 10 | — | 10 | — | — | — | 10 | — | — | — | 10 | — | 10 |
| South Carolina | 18 | — | — | — | — | 18 | — | — | 18 | — | — | 18 | — | 18 |
| South Dakota | — | — | — | — | — | — | — | 2 | — | — | 2 | — | 2 | — |
| Tennessee | 6 | — | 8 | 1 | — | 15 | — | — | 19 | — | — | 19 | — | 19 |
| Texas | 40 | — | — | — | — | — | — | — | 40 | — | — | 40 | — | 40 |
| Utah | — | — | 4 | — | — | — | — | — | 4 | 4 | — | 8 | — | 8 |
| Vermont | — | 8 | — | 4 | — | 4 | — | 4 | 4 | — | — | 8 | — | 8 |
| Virginia | — | — | — | — | — | 12 | — | — | 12 | — | — | 12 | — | 24 |
| Washington | — | — | — | — | — | — | — | — | — | 14 | — | 14 | — | 14 |
| West Virginia | — | — | 16 | — | — | 16 | — | — | 16 | — | — | 16 | — | 16 |
| Wisconsin | — | 22 | — | 8 | 9 | — | 1 | 11 | — | 9 | 8 | 1 | 1 | 22 |
| Wyoming | — | 3 | ½ | — | 3 | 3 | — | — | 6 | — | — | 6 | — | 6 |
| Alaska | — | 6 | — | 6 | — | — | — | 6 | — | — | 2 | 4 | 2 | 4 |
| Canal Zone | 3 | 3 | — | — | — | 1 | 3 | 3 | 3 | — | — | 6 | — | 6 |
| District of Columbia | — | — | — | — | — | — | — | — | 6 | — | 6 | — | 6 | — |
| Hawaii | 1 | 1 | 3 | 1 | 1 | 4 | — | 1 | 4 | — | 1 | 4 | 1 | 4 |
| Philippine Islands | 2 | 2 | — | 5 | — | — | 1 | 5 | — | — | 1 | 4 | 1 | 4 |
| Puerto Rico | — | 1 | 5 | 1 | — | 5 | — | 1 | 5 | — | 1 | 5 | 1 | 5 |
| Virgin Islands | — | — | — | — | — | — | — | — | — | — | — | — | — | — |
| **Total** | 190 | 351½ | 203½ | 229½ | 121 | 316 | 130 | 317 | 415½ | 123 | 250½ | 575½ | 102½ | 844 |

4. Other candidates: Underwood, 41½; Robinson, 46; Bryan, 2; Saulsbury, 6; Walsh, 52½; Owen, 20; Ritchie, 17½; Meredith, 75½; David F. Houston, 9; Glass, 35; Daniels, 24; Newton D. Baker, 4; George L. Berry, 1; James W. Gerard, 19; not voting, 9.

5. Other candidates: Robinson, 22½; McAdoo, 52; Walsh, 98; Ritchie, ½; Berry, 1; A. A. Murphree, 4; Houston, 9; Owen, 23; Cummings, 9; Glass, 59; Gerard, 16; Baker, 1; Daniels, 24; Cordell Hull, 2; not voting, 3½.

6. Other candidates: Robinson, 21; William Gibbs Mcadoo, 21; Alfred E. Smith, 44; Thompson, 1; Ritchie, ½; Bryan, 1; Gerard, 7; Glass, 67; Cordell Daniels, 2; Berry, 1½; Meredith, 66½; Henry T. Allen, 1; Hull, 1; not voting, 9.

7. Other candidates: McAdoo, 14½; Robinson, 21; Meredith, 42½; Glass, 79; Hull, 1; Smith, 10½; Daniels, 1; Gerard, 8; Thompson, 1; Walsh, 84½; not voting, 9.

8. Other candidates: Robinson, 20; McAdoo, 11½; Smith, 7½; Walsh, 58; Meredith, 15½; Glass, 23; Gerard, 7; Hull, 1; not voting, 8.

# 1928 Democratic

*(Narrative, p. 92)*

| Delegation | Total Votes | First Pres. Ballot[1] (Before shift) Smith | First Pres. Ballot[2] (After shift) Smith |
|---|---|---|---|
| Alabama | 24 | 1 | 1 |
| Arizona | 6 | 6 | 6 |
| Arkansas | 17 | 17 | 17 |
| California | 26 | 26 | 26 |
| Colorado | 12 | 12 | 12 |
| Connecticut | 14 | 14 | 14 |
| Delaware | 6 | 6 | 6 |
| Florida | 12 | — | — |
| Georgia | 28 | — | — |
| Idaho | 8 | 8 | 8 |
| Illinois | 58 | 56 | 56 |
| Indiana | 30 | — | 25 |
| Iowa | 26 | 26 | 26 |
| Kansas | 20 | — | 11½ |
| Kentucky | 26 | 26 | 26 |
| Louisiana | 20 | 20 | 20 |
| Maine | 12 | 12 | 12 |
| Maryland | 16 | 16 | 16 |
| Massachusetts | 36 | 36 | 36 |
| Michigan | 30 | 30 | 30 |
| Minnesota | 24 | 24 | 24 |
| Mississippi | 20 | — | 9½ |
| Missouri | 36 | — | — |
| Montana | 8 | 8 | 8 |
| Nebraska | 16 | — | 12 |
| Nevada | 6 | 6 | 6 |
| New Hampshire | 8 | 8 | 8 |
| New Jersey | 28 | 28 | 28 |
| New Mexico | 6 | 6 | 6 |
| New York | 90 | 90 | 90 |
| North Carolina | 24 | 4 2/3 | 4 2/3 |
| North Dakota | 10 | 10 | 10 |
| Ohio | 48 | 1 | 45 |
| Oklahoma | 20 | 10 | 10 |
| Oregon | 10 | 10 | 10 |
| Pennsylvania | 76 | 70½ | 70½ |
| Rhode Island | 10 | 10 | 10 |
| South Carolina | 18 | — | — |
| South Dakota | 10 | 10 | 10 |
| Tennessee | 24 | — | 23 |
| Texas | 40 | — | — |
| Utah | 8 | 8 | 8 |
| Vermont | 8 | 8 | 8 |
| Virginia | 24 | 6 | 6 |
| Washington | 14 | 14 | 14 |
| West Virginia | 16 | 10½ | 10½ |
| Wisconsin | 26 | 26 | 26 |
| Wyoming | 6 | 6 | 6 |
| Alaska | 6 | 6 | 6 |
| Canal Zone | 6 | 6 | 6 |
| District of Columbia | 6 | 6 | 6 |
| Hawaii | 6 | 6 | 6 |
| Philippine Islands | 6 | 6 | 6 |
| Puerto Rico | 6 | 6 | 6 |
| Virgin Islands | 2 | 2 | 2 |
| **Total** | 1100 | 724 2/3 | 849 1/6 |

1. Other candidates: Cordell Hull, 71 5/6; Walter F. George, 52½; James A. Reed, 48; Atlee Pomerene, 47; Jesse H. Jones, 43; Evans Woollen, 32; Patrick Harrison, 20; William A. Ayres, 20; Richard C. Watts, 18; Gilbert M. Hitchcock, 16; Vic Donahey, 5; Houston Thompson, 2.
2. Other candidates: George, 52½; Reed, 52; Hull, 50 5/6; Jones, 43; Watts, 18; Harrison, 8½; Woollen, 7; Donahey, 5; Ayres, 3; Pomerene, 3; Hitchcock, 2; Thompson, 2; Theodore G. Bilbo, 1; not voting, 2½.

# 1928 Republican

*(Narrative, p. 91)*

| Delegation | Total Votes | First Pres. Ballot[1] Hoover |
|---|---|---|
| Alabama | 15 | 15 |
| Arizona | 9 | 9 |
| Arkansas | 11 | 11 |
| California | 29 | 29 |
| Colorado | 15 | 15 |
| Connecticut | 17 | 17 |
| Delaware | 9 | 9 |
| Florida | 10 | 9 |
| Georgia | 16 | 15 |
| Idaho | 11 | 11 |
| Illinois | 61 | 24 |
| Indiana | 33 | — |
| Iowa | 29 | 7 |
| Kansas | 23 | — |
| Kentucky | 29 | 29 |
| Louisiana | 12 | 11 |
| Maine | 15 | 15 |
| Maryland | 19 | 19 |
| Massachusetts | 39 | 39 |
| Michigan | 33 | 33 |
| Minnesota | 27 | 11 |
| Mississippi | 12 | 12 |
| Missouri | 39 | 28 |
| Montana | 11 | 10 |
| Nebraska | 19 | 11 |
| Nevada | 9 | 9 |
| New Hampshire | 11 | 11 |
| New Jersey | 31 | 31 |
| New Mexico | 9 | 7 |
| New York | 90 | 90 |
| North Carolina | 20 | 17 |
| North Dakota | 13 | 4 |
| Ohio | 51 | 36 |
| Oklahoma | 20 | — |
| Oregon | 13 | 13 |
| Pennsylvania | 79 | 79 |
| Rhode Island | 13 | 12 |
| South Carolina | 11 | 11 |
| South Dakota | 13 | 2 |
| Tennessee | 19 | 19 |
| Texas | 26 | 26 |
| Utah | 11 | 9 |
| Vermont | 11 | 11 |
| Virginia | 15 | 15 |
| Washington | 17 | 17 |
| West Virginia | 19 | 1 |
| Wisconsin | 26 | 9 |
| Wyoming | 9 | 9 |
| Alaska | 2 | 2 |
| District of Columbia | 2 | 2 |
| Hawaii | 2 | 2 |
| Philippine Islands | 2 | 2 |
| Puerto Rico | 2 | 2 |
| **Total** | 1089 | 837 |

1. Other candidates: Frank O. Lowden, 74; Charles Curtis, 64; James E. Watson, 45; George W. Norris, 24; Guy D. Goff, 18; Calvin Coolidge, 17; Charles G. Dawes, 4; Charles E. Hughes, 1; not voting, 5.

# 1932 Democratic

(Narrative, p. 94)

| Delegation | Total Votes | Louisiana Credentials Yea | Nay | Not Voting | Minnesota Credentials Yea | Nay | Not Voting | Permanent Organization Yea | Nay | First Pres. Ballot[1] Roosevelt | Smith | Second Pres. Ballot[2] Roosevelt | Smith | Third Pres. Ballot[3] Roosevelt | Smith | Fourth Pres. Ballot[4] Roosevelt | Smith |
|---|---|---|---|---|---|---|---|---|---|---|---|---|---|---|---|---|---|
| Ala. | 24 | — | 24 | — | — | 24 | — | 4½ | 19½ | 24 | — | 24 | — | 24 | — | 24 | — |
| Ariz. | 6 | — | 6 | — | — | 6 | — | — | 6 | 6 | — | 6 | — | 6 | — | 6 | — |
| Ark. | 18 | — | 18 | — | — | 18 | — | — | 18 | 18 | — | 18 | — | 18 | — | 18 | — |
| Calif. | 44 | 44 | — | — | 44 | — | — | 44 | — | — | — | — | — | — | — | 44 | — |
| Colo. | 12 | — | 12 | — | — | 12 | — | — | 12 | 12 | — | 12 | — | 12 | — | 12 | — |
| Conn. | 16 | 9½ | 6½ | — | 9¼ | 6¾ | — | 9½ | 6½ | — | 16 | — | 16 | — | 16 | — | 16 |
| Del. | 6 | 1 | 5 | — | — | 6 | — | 1 | 5 | 6 | — | 6 | — | 6 | — | 6 | — |
| Fla. | 14 | 3 | 11 | — | — | 14 | — | — | 14 | 14 | — | 14 | — | 14 | — | 14 | — |
| Ga. | 28 | — | 28 | — | — | 28 | — | — | 28 | 28 | — | 28 | — | 28 | — | 28 | — |
| Idaho | 8 | — | 8 | — | — | 8 | — | — | 8 | 8 | — | 8 | — | 8 | — | 8 | — |
| Ill. | 58 | 50¼ | 7¾ | — | 48 | 10 | — | 42 | 16 | 15¼ | 2¼ | 15¼ | 2¼ | 15¼ | 2¼ | 58 | — |
| Ind. | 30 | 30 | — | — | 30 | — | — | 30 | — | 14 | 2 | 16 | 2 | 16 | 2 | 30 | — |
| Iowa | 26 | 13 | 13 | — | — | 26 | — | 10 | 16 | 26 | — | 26 | — | 26 | — | 26 | — |
| Kan. | 20 | — | 20 | — | — | 20 | — | 6½ | 13½ | 20 | — | 20 | — | 20 | — | 20 | — |
| Ky. | 26 | — | 26 | — | — | 26 | — | — | 26 | 26 | — | 26 | — | 26 | — | 26 | — |
| La. | 20 | — | 20 | — | — | 20 | — | — | 20 | 20 | — | 20 | — | 20 | — | 20 | — |
| Maine | 12 | 6 | 6 | — | 6 | 6 | — | 7 | 5 | 12 | — | 12 | — | 12 | — | 12 | — |
| Md. | 16 | 16 | — | — | 16 | — | — | 16 | — | — | — | — | — | — | — | 16 | — |
| Mass. | 36 | 36 | — | — | 36 | — | — | 36 | — | — | 36 | — | 36 | — | 36 | — | 36 |
| Mich. | 38 | — | 38 | — | — | 38 | — | — | 38 | 38 | — | 38 | — | 38 | — | 38 | — |
| Minn. | 24 | 1 | 23 | — | 1 | 23 | — | 3 | 21 | 24 | — | 24 | — | 24 | — | 24 | — |
| Miss. | 20 | — | 20 | — | — | 20 | — | — | 20 | 20 | — | 20 | — | 20 | — | 20 | — |
| Mo. | 36 | 19½ | 19½ | — | 16½ | 19½ | — | 16½ | 10½ | 12 | — | 18 | — | 20½ | — | 36 | — |
| Mont. | 8 | — | 8 | — | — | 8 | — | — | 8 | 8 | — | 8 | — | 8 | — | 8 | — |
| Neb. | 16 | — | 16 | — | — | 16 | — | 1 | 15 | 16 | — | 16 | — | 16 | — | 16 | — |
| Nev. | 6 | — | 6 | — | — | 6 | — | — | 6 | 6 | — | 6 | — | 6 | — | 6 | — |
| N.H. | 8 | — | 8 | — | — | 8 | — | — | 8 | 8 | — | 8 | — | 8 | — | 8 | — |
| N.J. | 32 | 32 | — | — | 32 | — | — | 32 | — | — | 32 | — | 32 | — | 32 | — | 32 |
| N.M. | 6 | — | 6 | — | — | 6 | — | 3 | 3 | 6 | — | 6 | — | 6 | — | 6 | — |
| N.Y. | 94 | 65 | 29 | — | 65 | 29 | — | 67 | 27 | 28½ | 65½ | 29½ | 64½ | 31 | 63 | 31 | 63 |
| N.C. | 26 | 20½ | 5½ | — | — | 26 | — | 4 | 22 | 26 | — | 26 | — | 25 4/100 | — | 26 | — |
| N.D. | 10 | — | 10 | — | 2½ | 7½ | — | 1 | 9 | 9 | — | 10 | — | 9 | — | 10 | — |
| Ohio | 52 | 40 | 11 | 1 | 48½ | 2½ | 1 | 49½ | 2½ | — | — | ½ | — | 2½ | — | 29 | 17 |
| Okla. | 22 | 22 | — | — | 22 | — | — | 22 | — | — | — | — | — | — | — | 22 | — |
| Ore. | 10 | — | 10 | — | — | 10 | — | 1 | 9 | 10 | — | 10 | — | 10 | — | 10 | — |
| Pa. | 76 | 20½ | 55½ | — | 25 | 49 | 2 | 27½ | 48½ | 44½ | 30 | 44½ | 23½ | 45½ | 21 | 49 | 14½ |
| R.I. | 10 | 10 | — | — | 10 | — | — | 10 | — | — | 10 | — | 10 | — | 10 | — | 10 |
| S.C. | 18 | — | 18 | — | — | 18 | — | — | 18 | 18 | — | 18 | — | 18 | — | 18 | — |
| S.D. | 10 | — | 10 | — | — | 10 | — | — | 10 | 10 | — | 10 | — | 10 | — | 10 | — |
| Tenn. | 24 | — | 24 | — | — | 24 | — | — | 24 | 24 | — | 24 | — | 24 | — | 24 | — |
| Texas | 46 | 46 | — | — | 46 | — | — | 46 | — | — | — | — | — | — | — | 46 | — |
| Utah | 8 | — | 8 | — | — | 8 | — | — | 8 | 8 | — | 8 | — | 8 | — | 8 | — |
| Vt. | 8 | — | 8 | — | — | 8 | — | — | 8 | 8 | — | 8 | — | 8 | — | 8 | — |
| Va. | 24 | 24 | — | — | 24 | — | — | 24 | — | — | — | — | — | — | — | 24 | — |
| Wash. | 16 | — | 16 | — | — | 16 | — | — | 16 | 16 | — | 16 | — | 16 | — | 16 | — |
| W.Va. | 16 | — | 16 | — | 3 | 13 | — | — | 16 | 16 | — | 16 | — | 16 | — | 16 | — |
| Wis. | 26 | 2 | 24 | — | 2 | 24 | — | 2 | 24 | 24 | 2 | 24 | 2 | 24 | 2 | 24 | 2 |
| Wyo. | 6 | — | 6 | — | — | 6 | — | — | 6 | 6 | — | 6 | — | 6 | — | 6 | — |
| Alaska | 6 | — | 6 | — | — | 6 | — | 6 | — | — | 5 | 6 | — | 6 | — | 6 | — |
| Canal Z. | 6 | — | 6 | — | — | 6 | — | — | 6 | 6 | — | 6 | — | 6 | — | 6 | — |
| D.C. | 6 | — | 6 | — | — | 6 | — | — | 6 | 6 | — | 6 | — | 6 | — | 6 | — |
| Hawaii | 6 | — | 6 | — | — | 6 | — | — | 6 | 6 | — | 6 | — | 6 | — | 6 | — |
| Phil. Is. | 6 | 6 | — | — | 6 | — | — | 6 | — | — | 6 | — | 6 | — | 6 | 6 | — |
| P.R. | 6 | — | 6 | — | — | 6 | — | — | 6 | 6 | — | 6 | — | 6 | — | 6 | — |
| Vir. Is. | 2 | — | 2 | — | — | 2 | — | — | 2 | 2 | — | 2 | — | 2 | — | 2 | — |
| **Total** | 1154 | 514¼ | 638¾ | 1 | 492¾ | 658¼ | 3 | 528 | 626 | 666¼ | 201¾ | 677¾ | 194¼ | 682 79/100 | 190¼ | 945 | 190½ |

1. Other candidates: John N. Garner, 90¼; Harry F. Byrd, 25; Melvin A. Traylor, 42¼; Albert C. Ritchie, 21; James A. Reed, 24; George White, 52; William H. Murray, 23; Newton D. Baker, 8½.
2. Other candidates: Garner, 90¼; Byrd, 24; Traylor, 40¼; Ritchie, 23½; Reed, 18; White, 50½; Baker, 8; Will Rogers, 22; not voting, 5½.
3. Other candidates: Garner, 101¼; Byrd, 24 96/100; Traylor, 40¼; Ritchie, 23½; Reed, 27½; White, 52½; Baker, 8½; not voting, 2½.
4. Other candidates: Ritchie, 3½; White, 3; Baker, 5½; James M. Cox, 1; not voting, 5½.

# 1932 Republican

*(Narrative, p. 94)*

| Delegation | Total Votes | Repeal of Prohibition Plank | | First Pres. Ballot[1] |
|---|---|---|---|---|
| | | Yea | Nay | Hoover |
| Alabama | 19 | — | 19 | 19 |
| Arizona | 9 | 9 | — | 9 |
| Arkansas | 15 | — | 15 | 15 |
| California | 47 | 6 | 41 | 47 |
| Colorado | 15 | 1 | 14 | 15 |
| Connecticut | 19 | 19 | — | 19 |
| Delaware | 9 | — | 9 | 9 |
| Florida | 16 | — | 16 | 16 |
| Georgia | 16 | 2 | 14 | 16 |
| Idaho | 11 | — | 11 | 11 |
| Illinois | 61 | 45 | 15½ | 54½ |
| Indiana | 31 | 28 | 3 | 31 |
| Iowa | 25 | 3 | 22 | 25 |
| Kansas | 21 | 4 | 17 | 21 |
| Kentucky | 25 | 15 | 10 | 25 |
| Louisiana | 12 | — | 12 | 12 |
| Maine | 13 | 5 | 8 | 13 |
| Maryland | 19 | — | 19 | 19 |
| Massachusetts | 34 | 16 | 17 | 34 |
| Michigan | 41 | 25½ | 15½ | 41 |
| Minnesota | 25 | — | 25 | 25 |
| Mississippi | 11 | 11 | — | 11 |
| Missouri | 33 | 8½ | 23¾ | 33 |
| Montana | 11 | — | 11 | 11 |
| Nebraska | 17 | 1 | 16 | 17 |
| Nevada | 9 | 8 | 1 | 9 |
| New Hampshire | 11 | — | 11 | 11 |
| New Jersey | 35 | 35 | — | 35 |
| New Mexico | 9 | 2 | 7 | 8 |
| New York | 97 | 76 | 21 | 97 |
| North Carolina | 28 | 3 | 25 | 28 |
| North Dakota | 11 | — | 11 | 9 |
| Ohio | 55 | 12 2/9 | 42 2/9 | 55 |
| Oklahoma | 25 | — | 25 | 25 |
| Oregon | 13 | 3 | 10 | 9 |
| Pennsylvania | 75 | 51 | 23 | 73 |
| Rhode Island | 8 | 8 | — | 8 |
| South Carolina | 10 | — | 10 | 10 |
| South Dakota | 11 | 3 | 8 | 11 |
| Tennessee | 24 | 1 | 23 | 24 |
| Texas | 49 | — | 49 | 49 |
| Utah | 11 | 1 | 10 | 11 |
| Vermont | 9 | 9 | — | 9 |
| Virginia | 25 | — | 25 | 25 |
| Washington | 19 | 11 | 8 | 19 |
| West Virginia | 19 | 4 | 15 | 19 |
| Wisconsin | 27 | 22 | 5 | 15 |
| Wyoming | 9 | 9 | — | 9 |
| Alaska | 2 | — | 2 | 2 |
| District of Columbia | 2 | — | 2 | 2 |
| Hawaii | 2 | 2 | — | 2 |
| Philippine Islands | 2 | 1 | 1 | 2 |
| Puerto Rico | 2 | — | 2 | 2 |
| Total | 1154 | 460 2/9 | 690 19/36 | 1126½ |

1. *Other candidates: John J. Blaine, 13; Calvin Coolidge, 4½; Joseph I. France, 4; Charles G. Dawes, 1; James W. Wadsworth, 1; not voting, 4.*

# 1936 Republican

*(Narrative, p. 96)*

| Delegation | Total Votes | First Pres. Ballot[1] Landon |
|---|---|---|
| Alabama | 13 | 13 |
| Arizona | 6 | 6 |
| Arkansas | 11 | 11 |
| California | 44 | 44 |
| Colorado | 12 | 12 |
| Connecticut | 19 | 19 |
| Delaware | 9 | 9 |
| Florida | 12 | 12 |
| Georgia | 14 | 14 |
| Idaho | 8 | 8 |
| Illinois | 57 | 57 |
| Indiana | 28 | 28 |
| Iowa | 22 | 22 |
| Kansas | 18 | 18 |
| Kentucky | 22 | 22 |
| Louisiana | 12 | 12 |
| Maine | 13 | 13 |
| Maryland | 16 | 16 |
| Massachusetts | 33 | 33 |
| Michigan | 38 | 38 |
| Minnesota | 22 | 22 |
| Mississippi | 11 | 11 |
| Missouri | 30 | 30 |
| Montana | 8 | 8 |
| Nebraska | 14 | 14 |
| Nevada | 6 | 6 |
| New Hampshire | 11 | 11 |
| New Jersey | 32 | 32 |
| New Mexico | 6 | 6 |
| New York | 90 | 90 |
| North Carolina | 23 | 23 |
| North Dakota | 8 | 8 |
| Ohio | 52 | 52 |
| Oklahoma | 21 | 21 |
| Oregon | 10 | 10 |
| Pennsylvania | 75 | 75 |
| Rhode Island | 8 | 8 |
| South Carolina | 10 | 10 |
| South Dakota | 8 | 8 |
| Tennessee | 17 | 17 |
| Texas | 25 | 25 |
| Utah | 8 | 8 |
| Vermont | 9 | 9 |
| Virginia | 17 | 17 |
| Washington | 16 | 16 |
| West Virginia | 16 | 15 |
| Wisconsin | 24 | 6 |
| Wyoming | 6 | 6 |
| Alaska | 3 | 3 |
| District of Columbia | 3 | 3 |
| Hawaii | 3 | 3 |
| Philippine Islands | 2 | 2 |
| Puerto Rico | 2 | 2 |
| **Total** | **1003** | **984** |

1. Other candidates: William E. Borah, 19.

# 1940 Democratic

*(Narrative, p. 98)*

| Delegation | Total Votes | First Pres. Ballot[1] Roosevelt |
|---|---|---|
| Alabama | 22 | 20 |
| Arizona | 6 | 6 |
| Arkansas | 18 | 18 |
| California | 44 | 43 |
| Colorado | 12 | 12 |
| Connecticut | 16 | 16 |
| Delaware | 6 | 6 |
| Florida | 14 | 12½ |
| Georgia | 24 | 24 |
| Idaho | 8 | 8 |
| Illinois | 58 | 58 |
| Indiana | 28 | 28 |
| Iowa | 22 | 22 |
| Kansas | 18 | 18 |
| Kentucky | 22 | 22 |
| Louisiana | 20 | 20 |
| Maine | 10 | 10 |
| Maryland | 16 | 7½ |
| Massachusetts | 34 | 21½ |
| Michigan | 38 | 38 |
| Minnesota | 22 | 22 |
| Mississippi | 18 | 18 |
| Missouri | 30 | 26½ |
| Montana | 8 | 8 |
| Nebraska | 14 | 13 |
| Nevada | 6 | 2 |
| New Hampshire | 8 | 8 |
| New Jersey | 32 | 32 |
| New Mexico | 6 | 6 |
| New York | 94 | 64½ |
| North Carolina | 26 | 26 |
| North Dakota | 8 | 8 |
| Ohio | 52 | 52 |
| Oklahoma | 22 | 22 |
| Oregon | 10 | 10 |
| Pennsylvania | 72 | 72 |
| Rhode Island | 8 | 8 |
| South Carolina | 16 | 16 |
| South Dakota | 8 | 3 |
| Tennessee | 22 | 22 |
| Texas | 46 | — |
| Utah | 8 | 8 |
| Vermont | 6 | 6 |
| Virginia | 22 | 5 14/15 |
| Washington | 16 | 15 |
| West Virginia | 16 | 12 |
| Wisconsin | 24 | 21 |
| Wyoming | 6 | 6 |
| Alaska | 6 | — |
| Canal Zone | 6 | — |
| District of Columbia | 6 | 6 |
| Hawaii | 6 | 6 |
| Philippine Islands | 6 | 6 |
| Puerto Rico | 6 | 3 |
| Virgin Islands | 2 | 2 |
| **Total** | **1100** | **946 13/30** |

1. Other candidates: James A. Farley, 72 9/10; John N. Garner; 61; Millard E. Tydings, 9½; Cordell Hull, 5 2/3; not voting, 4½.

# 1940 Republican

*(Narrative, p. 98)*

| Delegation | Total Votes | First Pres. Ballot[1] | | | Fourth Pres. Ballot[2] | | | Fifth Pres. Ballot[3] | | Sixth (before shift)[4] | | Sixth (after shift)[5] |
|---|---|---|---|---|---|---|---|---|---|---|---|---|
| | | Dewey | Taft | Willkie | Dewey | Taft | Willkie | Taft | Willkie | Taft | Willkie | Willkie |
| Alabama | 13 | 7 | 6 | — | 7 | 5 | 1 | 7 | 5 | 7 | 6 | 13 |
| Arizona | 6 | — | — | — | — | — | 6 | — | 6 | — | 6 | 6 |
| Arkansas | 12 | 2 | 7 | 2 | 3 | 7 | 2 | 10 | 2 | 10 | 2 | 12 |
| California | 44 | 7 | 7 | 7 | 9 | 11 | 10 | 12 | 9 | 22 | 17 | 44 |
| Colorado | 12 | 1 | 4 | 3 | 1 | 4 | 3 | 4 | 4 | 6 | 5 | 12 |
| Connecticut | 16 | — | — | 16 | — | — | 16 | — | 16 | — | 16 | 16 |
| Delaware | 6 | — | 1 | 3 | — | — | 6 | — | 6 | — | 6 | 6 |
| Florida | 12 | 6 | 1 | — | 9 | 2 | — | 3 | 7 | 2 | 10 | 12 |
| Georgia | 14 | 7 | 3 | — | 6 | 3 | 2 | 7 | 6 | 7 | 6 | 14 |
| Idaho | 8 | 8 | — | — | 8 | — | — | 7 | — | 6 | 2 | 8 |
| Illinois | 58 | 52 | 2 | 4 | 17 | 27 | 10 | 30 | 17 | 33 | 24 | 58 |
| Indiana | 28 | 7 | 7 | 9 | 5 | 6 | 15 | 7 | 20 | 5 | 23 | 28 |
| Iowa | 22 | — | — | — | 2 | — | — | 13 | 7 | 15 | 7 | 22 |
| Kansas | 18 | — | — | — | 11 | 2 | 5 | — | 18 | — | 18 | 18 |
| Kentucky | 22 | 12 | 8 | — | 9 | 13 | — | 22 | — | 22 | — | 22 |
| Louisiana | 12 | 5 | 5 | — | 6 | 6 | — | 12 | — | 12 | — | 12 |
| Maine | 13 | — | — | — | 2 | 2 | 9 | — | 13 | — | 13 | 13 |
| Maryland | 16 | 16 | — | — | — | — | 14 | 1 | 14 | 1 | 15 | 16 |
| Massachusetts | 34 | — | — | 1 | — | 2 | 28 | 2 | 28 | 2 | 30 | 34 |
| Michigan | 38 | — | — | — | 2 | — | — | — | — | 2 | 35 | 38 |
| Minnesota | 22 | 3 | 4 | 6 | 2 | 9 | 9 | 12 | 9 | 11 | 10 | 22 |
| Mississippi | 11 | 3 | 8 | — | 2 | 9 | — | 11 | — | 9 | 2 | 11 |
| Missouri | 30 | 10 | 3 | 6 | 4 | 3 | 18 | 7 | 21 | 4 | 26 | 30 |
| Montana | 8 | 8 | — | — | 3 | 3 | 2 | 4 | 4 | 4 | 4 | 8 |
| Nebraska | 14 | 14 | — | — | 2 | 5 | 5 | 9 | 5 | 6 | 8 | 14 |
| Nevada | 6 | — | 2 | 2 | — | 1 | 4 | 2 | 4 | 2 | 4 | 6 |
| New Hampshire | 8 | — | — | — | — | — | 4 | 2 | 6 | 2 | 6 | 8 |
| New Jersey | 32 | 20 | — | 12 | 6 | 1 | 23 | 1 | 26 | — | 32 | 32 |
| New Mexico | 6 | 3 | 1 | 2 | 1 | 1 | 4 | 2 | 4 | 1 | 5 | 6 |
| New York | 92 | 61 | — | 8 | 48 | 5 | 35 | 10 | 75 | 7 | 78 | 92 |
| North Carolina | 23 | 9 | 7 | 2 | 6 | 6 | 9 | 11 | 12 | 8 | 15 | 23 |
| North Dakota | 8 | 2 | 1 | 1 | 2 | 1 | 3 | 4 | 4 | 4 | 4 | 8 |
| Ohio | 52 | — | 52 | — | — | 52 | — | 52 | — | 52 | — | 52 |
| Oklahoma | 22 | 22 | — | — | 10 | 6 | 3 | 18 | 4 | 5 | 17 | 22 |
| Oregon | 10 | — | — | — | 1 | — | 1 | — | 1 | 3 | 7 | 10 |
| Pennsylvania | 72 | 1 | — | 1 | — | — | 19 | — | 21 | — | 72 | 72 |
| Rhode Island | 8 | 1 | 3 | 3 | — | 4 | 4 | 4 | 4 | 3 | 5 | 8 |
| South Carolina | 10 | 10 | — | — | 8 | — | 2 | — | 9 | — | 10 | 10 |
| South Dakota | 8 | — | — | — | 4 | 1 | — | 7 | 1 | 2 | 6 | 8 |
| Tennessee | 18 | 8 | 3 | 2 | 5 | 6 | 5 | 9 | 6 | 5 | 10 | 17 |
| Texas | 26 | — | 26 | — | — | 26 | — | 26 | — | 26 | — | 26 |
| Utah | 8 | 2 | 2 | 1 | 2 | 2 | 1 | 3 | 5 | 1 | 7 | 8 |
| Vermont | 9 | 1 | 3 | 3 | 1 | 3 | 5 | 3 | 6 | 2 | 7 | 9 |
| Virginia | 18 | 2 | 9 | 5 | — | 7 | 11 | 7 | 11 | 2 | 16 | 18 |
| Washington | 16 | 13 | 3 | — | 12 | 3 | — | 16 | — | 4 | 10 | 16 |
| West Virginia | 16 | 8 | 5 | 3 | 6 | 3 | 7 | 9 | 6 | — | 15 | 15 |
| Wisconsin | 24 | 24 | — | — | 24 | — | — | — | — | 2 | 20 | 24 |
| Wyoming | 6 | 1 | 1 | 2 | 3 | 2 | 1 | 3 | 3 | — | 6 | 6 |
| Alaska | 3 | 1 | 2 | — | — | 2 | 1 | 3 | — | 1 | 2 | 3 |
| District of Columbia | 3 | 2 | 1 | — | — | 1 | 2 | 1 | 2 | — | 3 | 3 |
| Hawaii | 3 | — | — | — | — | — | — | 1 | 1 | — | 3 | 3 |
| Philippine Islands | 2 | — | 1 | 1 | — | 1 | 1 | 1 | 1 | — | 2 | 2 |
| Puerto Rico | 2 | 1 | 1 | — | 1 | 1 | — | 2 | — | — | 2 | 2 |
| Total | 1000 | 360 | 189 | 105 | 250 | 254 | 306 | 377 | 429 | 318 | 655 | 998 |

1. *Other candidate: Arthur H. Vandenberg, 76; Arthur H. James, 74; Joseph W. Martin, 44; Hanford MacNider, 34; Frank E. Gannett, 33; H. Styles Bridges, 28; Arthur Capper, 18; Herbert Hoover, 17; Charles L. McNary, 13; Harlan J. Bushfield, 9.*
2. *Other candidates: Vandenberg, 61; James, 56; Hoover, 31; NacMider, 26; McNary, 8; Gannett, 4; Bridges, 1; not voting, 3.*
3. *Other candidates: James, 59; Thomas E. Dewey, 57; Vandenberg, 42; Hoover, 20; McNary, 9; MacNider, 4; Gannett, 1; not voting, 2.*
4. *Other candidates: Dewey, 11; Hoover, 10; Gannett, 1; McNary, 1; not voting, 4.*
5. *Not voting, 2.*

# 1944 Democratic

*(Narrative, p. 101)*

| Delegation | Total Votes | First Pres. Ballot[1] Roosevelt |
|---|---|---|
| Alabama | 24 | 22 |
| Arizona | 10 | 10 |
| Arkansas | 20 | 20 |
| California | 52 | 52 |
| Colorado | 12 | 12 |
| Connecticut | 18 | 18 |
| Delaware | 8 | 8 |
| Florida | 18 | 14 |
| Georgia | 26 | 26 |
| Idaho | 10 | 10 |
| Illinois | 58 | 58 |
| Indiana | 26 | 26 |
| Iowa | 20 | 20 |
| Kansas | 16 | 16 |
| Kentucky | 24 | 24 |
| Louisiana | 22 | — |
| Maine | 10 | 10 |
| Maryland | 18 | 18 |
| Massachusetts | 34 | 34 |
| Michigan | 38 | 38 |
| Minnesota | 24 | 24 |
| Mississippi | 20 | — |
| Missouri | 32 | 32 |
| Montana | 10 | 10 |
| Nebraska | 12 | 12 |
| Nevada | 8 | 8 |
| New Hampshire | 10 | 10 |
| New Jersey | 34 | 34 |
| New Mexico | 10 | 10 |
| New York | 96 | 94½ |
| North Carolina | 30 | 30 |
| North Dakota | 8 | 8 |
| Ohio | 52 | 52 |
| Oklahoma | 22 | 22 |
| Oregon | 14 | 14 |
| Pennsylvania | 72 | 72 |
| Rhode Island | 10 | 10 |
| South Carolina | 18 | 14½ |
| South Dakota | 8 | 8 |
| Tennessee | 26 | 26 |
| Texas | 48 | 36 |
| Utah | 10 | 10 |
| Vermont | 6 | 6 |
| Virginia | 24 | — |
| Washington | 18 | 18 |
| West Virginia | 18 | 17 |
| Wisconsin | 26 | 26 |
| Wyoming | 8 | 8 |
| Alaska | 6 | 6 |
| Canal Zone | 6 | 6 |
| District of Columbia | 6 | 6 |
| Hawaii | 6 | 6 |
| Philippine Islands | 6 | 6 |
| Puerto Rico | 6 | 6 |
| Virgin Islands | 2 | 2 |
| **Total** | **1176** | **1086** |

1. *Other candidates: Harry F. Byrd, 89; James A. Farley, 1.*

# 1944 Republican

*(Narrative, p. 100)*

| Delegation | Total Votes | First Pres. Ballot[1] Dewey |
|---|---|---|
| Alabama | 14 | 14 |
| Arizona | 8 | 8 |
| Arkansas | 12 | 12 |
| California | 50 | 50 |
| Colorado | 15 | 15 |
| Connecticut | 16 | 16 |
| Delaware | 9 | 9 |
| Florida | 15 | 15 |
| Georgia | 14 | 14 |
| Idaho | 11 | 11 |
| Illinois | 59 | 59 |
| Indiana | 29 | 29 |
| Iowa | 23 | 23 |
| Kansas | 19 | 19 |
| Kentucky | 22 | 22 |
| Louisiana | 13 | 13 |
| Maine | 13 | 13 |
| Maryland | 16 | 16 |
| Massachusetts | 35 | 35 |
| Michigan | 41 | 41 |
| Minnesota | 25 | 25 |
| Mississippi | 6 | 6 |
| Missouri | 30 | 30 |
| Montana | 8 | 8 |
| Nebraska | 15 | 15 |
| Nevada | 6 | 6 |
| New Hampshire | 11 | 11 |
| New Jersey | 35 | 35 |
| New Mexico | 8 | 8 |
| New York | 93 | 93 |
| North Carolina | 25 | 25 |
| North Dakota | 11 | 11 |
| Ohio | 50 | 50 |
| Oklahoma | 23 | 23 |
| Oregon | 15 | 15 |
| Pennsylvania | 70 | 70 |
| Rhode Island | 8 | 8 |
| South Carolina | 4 | 4 |
| South Dakota | 11 | 11 |
| Tennessee | 19 | 19 |
| Texas | 33 | 33 |
| Utah | 8 | 8 |
| Vermont | 9 | 9 |
| Virginia | 19 | 19 |
| Washington | 16 | 16 |
| West Virginia | 19 | 19 |
| Wisconsin | 24 | 23 |
| Wyoming | 9 | 9 |
| Alaska | 3 | 3 |
| District of Columbia | 3 | 3 |
| Hawaii | 5 | 5 |
| Philippine Islands | 2 | — |
| Puerto Rico | 2 | 2 |
| **Total** | **1059** | **1056** |

1. *Other candidates: Douglas MacArthur, 1; absent, 2.*

# 1948 Democratic

*(Narrative, p. 104)*

| Delegation | Total Votes | Pro-Southern Amendment to Civil Rights Plank | | Plank Endorsing Truman's Civil Rights Policy | | First Pres. Ballot[1] (Before shift) | | First Pres. Ballot[2] (After shift) | |
|---|---|---|---|---|---|---|---|---|---|
| | | Yea | Nay | Yea | Nay | Truman | Russell | Truman | Russell |
| Alabama | 26 | 26 | — | — | 26 | — | 26 | — | 26 |
| Arizona | 12 | — | 12 | — | 12 | 12 | — | 12 | — |
| Arkansas | 22 | 22 | — | — | 22 | — | 22 | — | 22 |
| California | 54 | 1½ | 52½ | 53 | 1 | 53½ | — | 54 | — |
| Colorado | 12 | 3 | 9 | 10 | 2 | 12 | — | 12 | — |
| Connecticut | 20 | — | 20 | 20 | — | 20 | — | 20 | — |
| Delaware | 10 | — | 10 | — | 10 | 10 | — | 10 | — |
| Florida | 20 | 20 | — | — | 20 | — | 19 | — | 20 |
| Georgia | 28 | 28 | — | — | 28 | — | 28 | — | 28 |
| Idaho | 12 | — | 12 | — | 12 | 12 | — | 12 | — |
| Illinois | 60 | — | 60 | 60 | — | 60 | — | 60 | — |
| Indiana | 26 | — | 26 | 17 | 9 | 25 | — | 26 | — |
| Iowa | 20 | — | 20 | 18 | 2 | 20 | — | 20 | — |
| Kansas | 16 | — | 16 | 16 | — | 16 | — | 16 | — |
| Kentucky | 26 | — | 26 | — | 26 | 26 | — | 26 | — |
| Louisiana | 24 | 24 | — | — | 24 | — | 24 | — | 24 |
| Maine | 10 | — | 10 | 3 | 7 | 10 | — | 10 | — |
| Maryland | 20 | — | 20 | — | 20 | 20 | — | 20 | — |
| Massachusetts | 36 | — | 36 | 36 | — | 36 | — | 36 | — |
| Michigan | 42 | — | 42 | 42 | — | 42 | — | 42 | — |
| Minnesota | 26 | — | 26 | 26 | — | 26 | — | 26 | — |
| Mississippi | 22 | 22 | — | — | 22 | — | — | — | — |
| Missouri | 34 | — | 34 | — | 34 | 34 | — | 34 | — |
| Montana | 12 | — | 12 | 1½ | 10½ | 12 | — | 12 | — |
| Nebraska | 12 | — | 12 | 3 | 9 | 12 | — | 12 | — |
| Nevada | 10 | — | 10 | — | 10 | 10 | — | 10 | — |
| New Hampshire | 12 | — | 12 | 1 | 11 | 11 | — | 11 | — |
| New Jersey | 36 | — | 36 | 36 | — | 36 | — | 36 | — |
| New Mexico | 12 | — | 12 | — | 12 | 12 | — | 12 | — |
| New York | 98 | — | 98 | 98 | — | 83 | — | 98 | — |
| North Carolina | 32 | 32 | — | — | 32 | 13 | 19 | 13 | 19 |
| North Dakota | 8 | — | 8 | — | 8 | 8 | — | 8 | — |
| Ohio | 50 | — | 50 | 39 | 11 | 50 | — | 50 | — |
| Oklahoma | 24 | — | 24 | — | 24 | 24 | — | 24 | — |
| Oregon | 16 | 3 | 13 | 7 | 9 | 16 | — | 16 | — |
| Pennsylvania | 74 | — | 74 | 74 | — | 74 | — | 74 | — |
| Rhode Island | 12 | — | 12 | — | 12 | 12 | — | 12 | — |
| South Carolina | 20 | 20 | — | — | 20 | — | 20 | — | 20 |
| South Dakota | 8 | — | 8 | 8 | — | 8 | — | 8 | — |
| Tennessee | 28 | 28 | — | — | 28 | — | 28 | — | 28 |
| Texas | 50 | 50 | — | — | 50 | — | 50 | — | 50 |
| Utah | 12 | — | 12 | — | 12 | 12 | — | 12 | — |
| Vermont | 6 | — | 6 | 6 | — | 5½ | — | 5½ | — |
| Virginia | 26 | 26 | — | — | 26 | — | 26 | — | 26 |
| Washington | 20 | — | 20 | 20 | — | 20 | — | 20 | — |
| West Virginia | 20 | — | 20 | 7 | 13 | 15 | 4 | 20 | — |
| Wisconsin | 24 | — | 24 | 24 | — | 24 | — | 24 | — |
| Wyoming | 6 | 1½ | 4½ | 4 | 2 | 6 | — | 6 | — |
| Alaska | 6 | 3 | 3 | 2 | 4 | 6 | — | 6 | — |
| Canal Zone | 2 | — | 2 | — | 2 | 2 | — | 2 | — |
| District of Columbia | 6 | — | 6 | 6 | — | 6 | — | 6 | — |
| Hawaii | 6 | — | 6 | 6 | — | 6 | — | 6 | — |
| Puerto Rico | 6 | — | 6 | 6 | — | 6 | — | 6 | — |
| Virgin Islands | 2 | — | 2 | 2 | — | 2 | — | 2 | — |
| Total | 1234 | 310[a] | 924[b] | 651½ | 582½ | 926 | 266 | 947½ | 263 |

1. *Other candidates: Paul V. McNutt, 2½; James A. Roe, 15; Alben W. Barkley, 1; not voting, 23½.*
2. *Other candidates: McNutt, ½; not voting, 23.*
a. *Sum of column; proceedings record 309.*
b. *Sum of column; proceedings record 925.*

# 1948 Republican

*(Narrative, p. 103)*

| Delegation | Total Votes | First Pres. Ballot[1] | | | Second Pres. Ballot[2] | | | Third Pres. Ballot |
|---|---|---|---|---|---|---|---|---|
| | | Dewey | Stassen | Taft | Dewey | Stassen | Taft | Dewey |
| Alabama | 14 | 9 | — | 5 | 9 | — | 5 | 14 |
| Arizona | 8 | 3 | 2 | 3 | 4 | 2 | 2 | 8 |
| Arkansas | 14 | 3 | 4 | 7 | 3 | 4 | 7 | 14 |
| California | 53 | — | — | — | — | — | — | 53 |
| Colorado | 15 | 3 | 5 | 7 | 3 | 8 | 4 | 15 |
| Connecticut | 19 | — | — | — | — | — | — | 19 |
| Delaware | 9 | 5 | 1 | 2 | 6 | 1 | 2 | 9 |
| Florida | 16 | 6 | 4 | 6 | 6 | 4 | 6 | 16 |
| Georgia | 16 | 12 | 1 | — | 13 | 1 | — | 16 |
| Idaho | 11 | 11 | — | — | 11 | — | — | 11 |
| Illinois | 56 | — | — | — | 5 | — | 50 | 56 |
| Indiana | 29 | 29 | — | — | 29 | — | — | 29 |
| Iowa | 23 | 3 | 13 | 5 | 13 | 7 | 2 | 23 |
| Kansas | 19 | 12 | 1 | 2 | 14 | 1 | 2 | 19 |
| Kentucky | 25 | 10 | 1 | 11 | 11 | 1 | 11 | 25 |
| Louisiana | 13 | 6 | — | 7 | 6 | — | 7 | 13 |
| Maine | 13 | 5 | 4 | 1 | 5 | 7 | — | 13 |
| Maryland | 16 | 8 | 3 | 5 | 13 | — | 3 | 16 |
| Massachusetts | 35 | 17 | 1 | 2 | 18 | 1 | 3 | 35 |
| Michigan | 41 | — | — | — | — | — | — | 41 |
| Minnesota | 25 | — | 25 | — | — | 25 | — | 25 |
| Mississippi | 8 | — | — | 8 | — | — | 8 | 8 |
| Missouri | 33 | 17 | 6 | 8 | 18 | 6 | 7 | 33 |
| Montana | 11 | 5 | 3 | 3 | 6 | 2 | 3 | 11 |
| Nebraska | 15 | 2 | 13 | — | 6 | 9 | — | 15 |
| Nevada | 9 | 6 | 1 | 2 | 6 | 1 | 2 | 9 |
| New Hampshire | 8 | 6 | 2 | — | 6 | 2 | — | 8 |
| New Jersey | 35 | — | — | — | 24 | 6 | 2 | 35 |
| New Mexico | 8 | 3 | 2 | 3 | 3 | 2 | 3 | 8 |
| New York | 97 | 96 | — | 1 | 96 | — | 1 | 97 |
| North Carolina | 26 | 16 | 2 | 5 | 17 | 2 | 4 | 26 |
| North Dakota | 11 | — | 11 | — | — | 11 | — | 11 |
| Ohio | 53 | — | 9 | 44 | 1 | 8 | 44 | 53 |
| Oklahoma | 20 | 18 | — | 1 | 19 | — | 1 | 20 |
| Oregon | 12 | 12 | — | — | 12 | — | — | 12 |
| Pennsylvania | 73 | 41 | 1 | 28 | 40 | 1 | 29 | 73 |
| Rhode Island | 8 | 1 | — | 1 | 4 | — | 2 | 8 |
| South Carolina | 6 | — | — | 6 | — | — | 6 | 6 |
| South Dakota | 11 | 3 | 8 | — | 7 | 4 | — | 11 |
| Tennessee | 22 | 6 | — | — | 8 | — | 13 | 22 |
| Texas | 33 | 2 | 1 | 30 | 2 | 2 | 29 | 33 |
| Utah | 11 | 5 | 2 | 4 | 6 | 2 | 3 | 11 |
| Vermont | 9 | 7 | 2 | — | 7 | 2 | — | 9 |
| Virginia | 21 | 10 | — | 10 | 13 | — | 7 | 21 |
| Washington | 19 | 14 | 2 | 1 | 14 | 2 | 3 | 19 |
| West Virginia | 16 | 11 | 5 | — | 13 | 3 | — | 16 |
| Wisconsin | 27 | — | 19 | — | 2 | 19 | — | 27 |
| Wyoming | 9 | 4 | 3 | 2 | 6 | 3 | — | 9 |
| Alaska | 3 | 2 | — | 1 | 3 | — | — | 3 |
| District of Columbia | 3 | 2 | — | — | 3 | — | — | 3 |
| Hawaii | 5 | 3 | — | 1 | 3 | — | 2 | 5 |
| Puerto Rico | 2 | — | — | 2 | 1 | — | 1 | 2 |
| **Total** | **1094** | **434** | **157** | **224** | **515** | **149** | **274** | **1094** |

1. *Other candidates: Arthur H. Vandenberg, 62; Earl Warren, 59; Dwight H. Green, 56; Alfred E. Driscoll, 35; Raymond E. Baldwin, 19; Joseph W. Martin, 18; B. Carroll Reece, 15; Douglas MacArthur, 11; Everett M. Dirksen, 1; not voting, 3.*
2. *Other candidates: Vandenberg, 62; Warren, 57; Baldwin, 19; Martin, 10; MacArthur, 7; Reece, 1.*

# 1952 Democratic

*(Narrative, p. 108)*

| | | Seating Virginia Delegation | | | Table Motion to Adjourn | | | First Pres. Ballot[1] | | | | Second Pres. Ballot[2] | | | | Third Pres. Ballot[3] | | |
|---|---|---|---|---|---|---|---|---|---|---|---|---|---|---|---|---|---|---|
| Delegation | Total Votes | Yea | Nay | Not Voting | Yea | Nay | Not Voting | Harriman | Kefauver | Russell | Stevenson | Harriman | Kefauver | Russell | Stevenson | Kefauver | Russell | Stevenson |
| Alabama | 22 | 22 | — | — | 13½ | 8½ | — | — | 8 | 13 | ½ | — | 7½ | 14 | ½ | 7½ | 14 | ½ |
| Arizona | 12 | 12 | — | — | 12 | — | — | — | — | — | — | — | — | 12 | — | — | 12 | — |
| Arkansas | 22 | 22 | — | — | 19 | 3 | — | — | — | — | — | 1 | 1½ | 18 | 1½ | 1½ | — | 20½ |
| California | 68 | 4 | 61 | 3 | — | 68 | — | — | 68 | — | — | — | 68 | — | — | 68 | — | — |
| Colorado | 16 | 4½ | 11½ | — | 4 | 12 | — | 5 | 2 | 8½ | ½ | 5 | 5 | 2½ | 3½ | 4 | 3½ | 8½ |
| Connecticut | 16 | — | 16 | — | 16 | — | — | — | — | — | 16 | — | — | — | 16 | — | — | 16 |
| Delaware | 6 | 6 | — | — | 6 | — | — | — | — | — | 6 | — | — | — | 6 | — | — | 6 |
| Florida | 24 | 24 | — | — | 19 | 5 | — | — | 5 | 19 | — | — | 5 | 19 | — | 5 | 19 | — |
| Georgia | 28 | 28 | — | — | 28 | — | — | — | — | 28 | — | — | — | 28 | — | — | 28 | — |
| Idaho | 12 | 12 | — | — | — | 12 | — | 3½ | 3 | 1 | 1½ | — | — | — | 12 | — | — | 12 |
| Illinois | 60 | 52 | 8 | — | 53 | 7 | — | 1 | 3 | — | 53 | — | 3 | — | 54 | 3 | — | 54 |
| Indiana | 25 | 14½ | 6½ | 5 | 25 | 1 | — | — | 1 | — | 25 | — | 1 | — | 25 | 1 | — | 25 |
| Iowa | 24 | 17 | 7 | — | 8 | 15 | 1 | ½ | 8 | 2 | 8 | ½ | 8½ | 3 | 9½ | 8 | 3 | 10 |
| Kansas | 16 | — | 16 | — | 16 | — | — | — | — | — | 16 | — | — | — | 16 | — | — | 16 |
| Kentucky | 26 | 26 | — | — | 26 | — | — | — | — | — | — | — | — | — | — | — | — | — |
| Louisiana | 20 | 20 | — | — | 20 | — | — | — | — | 20 | — | — | — | 20 | — | — | 20 | — |
| Maine | 10 | 2½ | 7½ | — | 4½ | 5½ | — | 1½ | 1½ | 2½ | 3½ | 1 | 1 | 2½ | 4½ | ½ | 2½ | 7 |
| Maryland | 18 | 18 | — | — | 18 | — | — | — | 18 | — | — | — | 15½ | 2 | — | 8½ | 2½ | 6 |
| Massachusetts | 36 | 16 | 19 | 1 | 30 | 4½ | 1½ | — | — | — | — | — | 2½ | — | — | 5 | 1 | 25 |
| Michigan | 40 | — | 40 | — | — | 40 | — | — | 40 | — | — | — | 40 | — | — | — | — | 40 |
| Minnesota | 26 | — | 26 | — | — | 26 | — | — | — | — | — | 1½ | 17 | — | 7½ | 13 | — | 13 |
| Mississippi | 18 | 18 | — | — | 18 | — | — | — | — | 18 | — | — | — | 18 | — | — | 18 | — |
| Missouri | 34 | 34 | — | — | 29 | 5 | — | 1½ | 2 | — | 18 | 1½ | 2 | — | 19½ | 2 | — | 22 |
| Montana | 12 | — | 12 | — | 12 | — | — | — | — | — | — | 3 | 3 | 3 | — | — | — | 12 |
| Nebraska | 12 | 8 | 3 | 1 | — | 12 | — | — | 5 | 1 | 2 | — | 5 | 1 | 2 | 3 | 1 | 8 |
| Nevada | 10 | 10 | — | — | 9½ | ½ | — | — | ½ | 8 | 1 | — | ½ | 7½ | 2 | ½ | 7½ | 2 |
| New Hampshire | 8 | 1 | 7 | — | — | 8 | — | — | 8 | — | — | — | 8 | — | — | 8 | — | — |
| New Jersey | 32 | — | 32 | — | 24 | 8 | — | 1 | 3 | — | 28 | — | 4 | — | 28 | 4 | — | 28 |
| New Mexico | 12 | 12 | — | — | 12 | — | — | 1 | 1½ | 4 | 1 | — | 1½ | 6 | 4½ | 1½ | 3½ | 7 |
| New York | 94 | 7 | 87 | — | 5 | 89 | — | 83½ | 1 | — | 6½ | 84½ | — | 1 | 6½ | 4 | — | 86½ |
| North Carolina | 32 | 32 | — | — | 32 | — | — | — | — | 26 | 5½ | — | — | 24 | 7 | — | 24 | 7½ |
| North Dakota | 8 | 8 | — | — | 8 | — | — | — | 2 | 2 | 2 | — | — | — | — | — | — | 8 |
| Ohio | 54 | 33½ | 14½ | 6 | 26 | 28 | — | 1 | 29½ | 7 | 13 | 1 | 27½ | 8 | 17½ | 27 | 1 | 26 |
| Oklahoma | 24 | 24 | — | — | 24 | — | — | — | — | — | — | — | — | — | — | — | — | — |
| Oregon | 12 | 4 | 8 | — | — | 12 | — | — | 12 | — | — | — | 12 | — | — | 11 | — | 1 |
| Pennsylvania | 70 | 57 | 13 | — | 35 | 35 | — | 4½ | 22½ | — | 36 | 2½ | 21½ | — | 40 | — | — | 70 |
| Rhode Island | 12 | 10 | 2 | — | 10 | 2 | — | 1½ | 3½ | — | 5½ | — | 4 | — | 8 | — | — | 12 |
| South Carolina | 16 | — | — | 16 | — | — | 16 | — | — | 16 | — | — | — | 16 | — | — | 16 | — |
| South Dakota | 8 | — | 8 | — | — | 8 | — | — | 8 | — | — | — | 8 | — | — | 8 | — | — |
| Tennessee | 28 | — | 28 | — | — | 28 | — | — | 28 | — | — | — | 28 | — | — | 28 | — | — |
| Texas | 52 | 52 | — | — | 52 | — | — | — | — | 52 | — | — | — | 52 | — | — | 52 | — |
| Utah | 12 | 3 | 9 | — | — | 12 | — | 6½ | ½ | 2 | ½ | 9 | 1½ | — | ½ | — | — | 12 |
| Vermont | 6 | — | 6 | — | 6 | — | — | — | ½ | — | 5 | — | ½ | ½ | 5 | — | ½ | 5½ |
| Virginia | 28 | — | — | 28 | 28 | — | — | — | — | 28 | — | — | — | 28 | — | — | 28 | — |
| Washington | 22 | 12½ | 9½ | — | 3 | 10 | — | — | 12 | ½ | 6 | 2 | 12½ | ½ | 6 | 11 | ½ | 10½ |
| West Virginia | 20 | 13½ | 5 | 1½ | 10 | 9 | 1 | — | 5½ | 7 | 1 | — | 7½ | 6½ | 5½ | 7½ | 3½ | 9 |
| Wisconsin | 28 | 1 | 27 | — | — | 28 | — | — | 28 | — | — | — | 28 | — | — | 28 | — | — |
| Wyoming | 10 | 5½ | 4½ | — | 2½ | 7½ | — | 3½ | 1½ | ½ | 3 | 2½ | 3 | — | 4½ | — | — | 10 |
| Alaska | 6 | — | 6 | — | — | 6 | — | — | 6 | — | — | — | 6 | — | — | 6 | — | — |
| Canal Zone | 2 | 2 | — | — | 2 | — | — | — | — | 2 | — | — | — | 2 | — | — | — | 2 |
| D.C. | 6 | — | 6 | — | — | 6 | — | 6 | — | — | — | 6 | — | — | — | — | — | 6 |
| Hawaii | 6 | — | 6 | — | 4 | 2 | — | 1 | 1 | — | 2 | — | 1 | — | 5 | 1 | — | 5 |
| Puerto Rico | 6 | 2 | 4 | — | 1 | 5 | — | — | — | — | 6 | — | — | — | 6 | — | — | 6 |
| Virgin Islands | 2 | — | 2 | — | — | 2 | — | — | 1 | — | 1 | — | 1 | — | 1 | — | — | 2 |
| Total | 1230 | 650½ | 518 | 61½ | 671 | 539½[a] | 19½ | 123½ | 340 | 268 | 273 | 121 | 362½ | 294 | 324½ | 275½ | 261 | 617½ |

1. *Other candidates: Alben W. Barkley, 48½; Robert S. Kerr, 65; J. William Fulbright, 22; Paul H. Douglas, 3; Oscar R. Ewing, 4; Paul A. Dever, 37½; Hubert H. Humphrey, 26; James E. Murray, 12; Harry S. Truman, 6; William O. Douglas, ½; not voting, 1.*
2. *Other candidates: Barkley, 78½; Paul H. Douglas, 3; Kerr, 5½; Ewing, 3; Dever, 30½; Truman, 6; not voting, 1½.*
3. *Other candidates: Barkley, 67½; Paul H. Douglas, 3; Dever, ½; Ewing, 3; not voting, 2.*

a. *Sum of column; proceedings record 534.*

# 1952 Republican

*(Narrative, p. 107)*

| Delegation | Total Votes | Pro-Taft Amendment on Louisiana Delegates Yea | Nay | Pro-Eisenhower Report on Georgia Delegates Yea | Nay | First Pres. Ballot[1] (Before shift) Eisenhower | Taft | First Pres. Ballot[2] (After shift) Eisenhower | Taft |
|---|---|---|---|---|---|---|---|---|---|
| Alabama | 14 | 9 | 5 | 5 | 9 | 5 | 9 | 14 | — |
| Arizona | 14 | 12 | 2 | 3 | 11 | 4 | 10 | 4 | 10 |
| Arkansas | 11 | 11 | — | 3 | 8 | 4 | 6 | 11 | — |
| California | 70 | — | 70 | 62 | 8 | — | — | — | — |
| Colorado | 18 | 1 | 17 | 17 | 1 | 15 | 2 | 17 | 1 |
| Connecticut | 22 | 2 | 20 | 21 | 1 | 21 | 1 | 22 | — |
| Delaware | 12 | 5 | 7 | 8 | 4 | 7 | 5 | 12 | — |
| Florida | 18 | 15 | 3 | 5 | 13 | 6 | 12 | 18 | — |
| Georgia | 17 | 17 | — | — | — | 14 | 2 | 16 | 1 |
| Idaho | 14 | 14 | — | — | 14 | — | 14 | 14 | — |
| Illinois | 60 | 58 | 2 | 1 | 59 | 1 | 59 | 1 | 59 |
| Indiana | 32 | 31 | 1 | 3 | 29 | 2 | 30 | 2 | 30 |
| Iowa | 26 | 11 | 15 | 16 | 10 | 16 | 10 | 20 | 6 |
| Kansas | 22 | 2 | 20 | 20 | 2 | 20 | 2 | 22 | — |
| Kentucky | 20 | 18 | 2 | 2 | 18 | 1 | 19 | 13 | 7 |
| Louisiana | 15 | 13 | 2 | — | 2 | 13 | 2 | 15 | — |
| Maine | 16 | 5 | 11 | 11 | 5 | 11 | 5 | 15 | 1 |
| Maryland | 24 | 5 | 19 | 15 | 9 | 16 | 8 | 24 | — |
| Massachusetts | 38 | 5 | 33 | 33 | 5 | 34 | 4 | 38 | — |
| Michigan | 46 | 1 | 45 | 32 | 14 | 35 | 11 | 35 | 11 |
| Minnesota | 28 | — | 28 | 28 | — | 9 | — | 28 | — |
| Mississippi | 5 | 5 | — | — | 5 | — | 5 | 5 | — |
| Missouri | 26 | 4 | 22 | 21 | 5 | 21 | 5 | 26 | — |
| Montana | 8 | 7 | 1 | 1 | 7 | 1 | 7 | 1 | 7 |
| Nebraska | 18 | 13 | 5 | 7 | 11 | 4 | 13 | 7 | 11 |
| Nevada | 12 | 7 | 5 | 2 | 10 | 5 | 7 | 10 | 2 |
| New Hampshire | 14 | — | 14 | 14 | — | 14 | — | 14 | — |
| New Jersey | 38 | 5 | 33 | 32 | 6 | 33 | 5 | 38 | — |
| New Mexico | 14 | 8 | 6 | 5 | 9 | 6 | 8 | 6 | 8 |
| New York | 96 | 1 | 95 | 92 | 4 | 92 | 4 | 95 | 1 |
| North Carolina | 26 | 14 | 12 | 10 | 16 | 12 | 14 | 26 | — |
| North Dakota | 14 | 11 | 3 | 3 | 11 | 4 | 8 | 5 | 8 |
| Ohio | 56 | 56 | — | — | 56 | — | 56 | — | 56 |
| Oklahoma | 16 | 10 | 6 | 4 | 12 | 4 | 7 | 8 | 4 |
| Oregon | 18 | — | 18 | 18 | — | 18 | — | 18 | — |
| Pennsylvania | 70 | 13 | 57 | 52 | 18 | 53 | 15 | 70 | — |
| Rhode Island | 8 | 2 | 6 | 6 | 2 | 6 | 1 | 8 | — |
| South Carolina | 6 | 5 | 1 | 1 | 5 | 2 | 4 | 6 | — |
| South Dakota | 14 | 14 | — | — | 14 | — | 14 | 7 | 7 |
| Tennessee | 20 | 20 | — | — | 20 | — | 20 | 20 | — |
| Texas | 38 | 22 | 16 | — | — | 33 | 5 | 38 | — |
| Utah | 14 | 14 | — | — | 14 | — | 14 | 14 | — |
| Vermont | 12 | — | 12 | 12 | — | 12 | — | 12 | — |
| Virginia | 23 | 13 | 10 | 7 | 16 | 9 | 14 | 19 | 4 |
| Washington | 24 | 4 | 20 | 19 | 5 | 20 | 4 | 21 | 3 |
| West Virginia | 16 | 15 | 1 | 1 | 15 | 1 | 14 | 3 | 13 |
| Wisconsin | 30 | 24 | 6 | 6 | 24 | — | 24 | — | 24 |
| Wyoming | 12 | 8 | 4 | 4 | 8 | 6 | 6 | 12 | — |
| Alaska | 3 | 3 | — | — | 3 | 1 | 2 | 3 | — |
| Canal Zone | — | — | — | — | — | — | — | — | — |
| District of Columbia | 6 | 6 | — | — | 6 | — | 6 | 6 | — |
| Hawaii | 8 | 7 | 1 | 3 | 5 | 3 | 4 | 4 | 4 |
| Puerto Rico | 3 | 2 | 1 | 1 | 2 | — | 3 | 1 | 2 |
| Virgin Islands | 1 | — | 1 | 1 | — | 1 | — | 1 | — |
| **Total** | **1206** | **548** | **658** | **607** | **531** | **595** | **500** | **845** | **280** |

1. Other candidates: Earl Warren, 81; Harold E. Stassen, 20; Douglas MacArthur, 10.
2. Other candidates: Warren, 77; MacArthur, 4.

# 1956 Democratic

(Narrative, p. 110)

| | Total Votes | First Pres. Ballot[1] | | |
| Delegation | | Stevenson | Harriman | Other |
| --- | --- | --- | --- | --- |
| Alabama | 26 | 15½ | — | 10½ |
| Arizona | 16 | 16 | — | — |
| Arkansas | 26 | 26 | — | — |
| California | 68 | 68 | — | — |
| Colorado | 20 | 13½ | 6 | ½ |
| Connecticut | 20 | 20 | — | — |
| Delaware | 10 | 10 | — | — |
| Florida | 28 | 25 | — | 3 |
| Georgia | 32 | — | — | 32 |
| Idaho | 12 | 12 | — | — |
| Illinois | 64 | 53½ | 8½ | 2 |
| Indiana | 26 | 21½ | 3 | 1½ |
| Iowa | 24 | 16½ | 7 | ½ |
| Kansas | 16 | 16 | — | — |
| Kentucky | 30 | — | — | 30 |
| Louisiana | 24 | 24 | — | — |
| Maine | 14 | 10½ | 3½ | — |
| Maryland | 18 | 18 | — | — |
| Massachusetts | 40 | 32 | 7½ | ½ |
| Michigan | 44 | 39 | 5 | — |
| Minnesota | 30 | 19 | 11 | — |
| Mississippi | 22 | — | — | 22 |
| Missouri | 38 | — | — | 38 |
| Montana | 16 | 10 | 6 | — |
| Nebraska | 12 | 12 | — | — |
| Nevada | 14 | 5½ | 7 | 1½ |
| New Hampshire | 8 | 5½ | 1½ | 1 |
| New Jersey | 36 | 36 | — | — |
| New Mexico | 16 | 12 | 3½ | ½ |
| New York | 98 | 5½ | 92½ | — |
| North Carolina | 36 | 34½ | 1 | ½ |
| North Dakota | 8 | 8 | — | — |
| Ohio | 58 | 52 | ½ | 5½ |
| Oklahoma | 28 | — | 28 | — |
| Oregon | 16 | 16 | — | — |
| Pennsylvania | 74 | 67 | 7 | — |
| Rhode Island | 16 | 16 | — | — |
| South Carolina | 20 | 2 | — | 18 |
| South Dakota | 8 | 8 | — | — |
| Tennessee | 32 | 32 | — | — |
| Texas | 56 | — | — | 56 |
| Utah | 12 | 12 | — | — |
| Vermont | 6 | 5½ | ½ | — |
| Virginia | 32 | — | — | 32 |
| Washington | 26 | 19½ | 6 | ½ |
| West Virginia | 24 | 24 | — | — |
| Wisconsin | 28 | 22½ | 5 | ½ |
| Wyoming | 14 | 14 | — | — |
| Alaska | 6 | 6 | — | — |
| Canal Zone | 3 | 3 | — | — |
| District of Columbia | 6 | 6 | — | — |
| Hawaii | 6 | 6 | — | — |
| Puerto Rico | 6 | 6 | — | — |
| Virgin Islands | 3 | 3 | — | — |
| Total | 1372 | 905½ | 210 | 256½ |

1. Other candidates: Lyndon B. Johnson, 80; James C. Davis, 33; Albert B. Chandler, 36½; John S. Battle, 32½; George B. Timmerman, 23½; W. Stuart Symington, 45½; Frank Lausche, 5½.

# 1956 Republican

(Narrative, p. 111)

| Delegation | Total Votes | First Pres. Ballot Eisenhower |
| --- | --- | --- |
| Alabama | 21 | 21 |
| Arizona | 14 | 14 |
| Arkansas | 16 | 16 |
| California | 70 | 70 |
| Colorado | 18 | 18 |
| Connecticut | 22 | 22 |
| Delaware | 12 | 12 |
| Florida | 26 | 26 |
| Georgia | 23 | 23 |
| Idaho | 14 | 14 |
| Illinois | 60 | 60 |
| Indiana | 32 | 32 |
| Iowa | 26 | 26 |
| Kansas | 22 | 22 |
| Kentucky | 26 | 26 |
| Louisiana | 20 | 20 |
| Maine | 16 | 16 |
| Maryland | 24 | 24 |
| Massachusetts | 38 | 38 |
| Michigan | 46 | 46 |
| Minnesota | 28 | 28 |
| Mississippi | 15 | 15 |
| Missouri | 32 | 32 |
| Montana | 14 | 14 |
| Nebraska | 18 | 18 |
| Nevada | 12 | 12 |
| New Hampshire | 14 | 14 |
| New Jersey | 38 | 38 |
| New Mexico | 14 | 14 |
| New York | 96 | 96 |
| North Carolina | 28 | 28 |
| North Dakota | 14 | 14 |
| Ohio | 56 | 56 |
| Oklahoma | 22 | 22 |
| Oregon | 18 | 18 |
| Pennsylvania | 70 | 70 |
| Rhode Island | 14 | 14 |
| South Carolina | 16 | 16 |
| South Dakota | 14 | 14 |
| Tennessee | 28 | 28 |
| Texas | 54 | 54 |
| Utah | 14 | 14 |
| Vermont | 12 | 12 |
| Virginia | 30 | 30 |
| Washington | 24 | 24 |
| West Virginia | 16 | 16 |
| Wisconsin | 30 | 30 |
| Wyoming | 12 | 12 |
| Alaska | 4 | 4 |
| District of Columbia | 6 | 6 |
| Hawaii | 10 | 10 |
| Puerto Rico | 3 | 3 |
| Virgin Islands | 1 | 1 |
| Total | 1323 | 1323 |

# 1960 Democratic

*(Narrative, p. 113)*

# 1960 Republican

*(Narrative, p. 114)*

### First Pres. Ballot[1]

| Delegation | Total Votes | Kennedy | Johnson | Stevenson | Symington |
|---|---|---|---|---|---|
| Alabama | 29 | 3 | 20 | ½ | 3½ |
| Alaska | 9 | 9 | — | — | — |
| Arizona | 17 | 17 | — | — | — |
| Arkansas | 27 | — | 27 | — | — |
| California | 81 | 33½ | 7½ | 31½ | 8 |
| Colorado | 21 | 13½ | — | 5½ | 2 |
| Connecticut | 21 | 21 | — | — | — |
| Delaware | 11 | — | 11 | — | — |
| Florida | 29 | — | — | — | — |
| Georgia | 33 | — | 33 | — | — |
| Hawaii | 9 | 1½ | 3 | 3½ | 1 |
| Idaho | 13 | 6 | 4½ | ½ | 2 |
| Illinois | 69 | 61½ | — | 2 | 5½ |
| Indiana | 34 | 34 | — | — | — |
| Iowa | 26 | 21½ | ½ | 2 | ½ |
| Kansas | 21 | 21 | — | — | — |
| Kentucky | 31 | 3½ | 25½ | 1½ | ½ |
| Louisiana | 26 | — | 26 | — | — |
| Maine | 15 | 15 | — | — | — |
| Maryland | 24 | 24 | — | — | — |
| Massachusetts | 41 | 41 | — | — | — |
| Michigan | 51 | 42½ | — | 2½ | 6 |
| Minnesota | 31 | — | — | — | — |
| Mississippi | 23 | — | — | — | — |
| Missouri | 39 | — | — | — | 39 |
| Montana | 17 | 10 | 2 | 2½ | 2½ |
| Nebraska | 16 | 11 | ½ | — | 4 |
| Nevada | 15 | 5½ | 6½ | 2½ | ½ |
| New Hampshire | 11 | 11 | — | — | — |
| New Jersey | 41 | — | — | — | — |
| New Mexico | 17 | 4 | 13 | — | — |
| New York | 114 | 104½ | 3½ | 3½ | 2½ |
| North Carolina | 37 | 6 | 27½ | 3 | — |
| North Dakota | 11 | 11 | — | — | — |
| Ohio | 64 | 64 | — | — | — |
| Oklahoma | 29 | — | 29 | — | — |
| Oregon | 17 | 16½ | — | ½ | — |
| Pennsylvania | 81 | 68 | 4 | 7½ | — |
| Rhode Island | 17 | 17 | — | — | — |
| South Carolina | 21 | — | 21 | — | — |
| South Dakota | 11 | 4 | 2 | 1 | 2½ |
| Tennessee | 33 | — | 33 | — | — |
| Texas | 61 | — | 61 | — | — |
| Utah | 13 | 8 | 3 | — | 1½ |
| Vermont | 9 | 9 | — | — | — |
| Virginia | 33 | — | 33 | — | — |
| Washington | 27 | 14½ | 2½ | 6½ | 3 |
| West Virginia | 25 | 15 | 5½ | 3 | 1½ |
| Wisconsin | 31 | 23 | — | — | — |
| Wyoming | 15 | 15 | — | — | — |
| Canal Zone | 4 | — | 4 | — | — |
| District of Columbia | 9 | 9 | — | — | — |
| Puerto Rico | 7 | 7 | — | — | — |
| Virgin Islands | 4 | 4 | — | — | — |
| **Total** | **1521** | **806** | **409** | **79½** | **86** |

### First Pres. Ballot

| Delegation | Total Votes | Nixon | Goldwater |
|---|---|---|---|
| Alabama | 22 | 22 | — |
| Alaska | 6 | 6 | — |
| Arizona | 14 | 14 | — |
| Arkansas | 16 | 16 | — |
| California | 70 | 70 | — |
| Colorado | 18 | 18 | — |
| Connecticut | 22 | 22 | — |
| Delaware | 12 | 12 | — |
| Florida | 26 | 26 | — |
| Georgia | 24 | 24 | — |
| Hawaii | 12 | 12 | — |
| Idaho | 14 | 14 | — |
| Illinois | 60 | 60 | — |
| Indiana | 32 | 32 | — |
| Iowa | 26 | 26 | — |
| Kansas | 22 | 22 | — |
| Kentucky | 26 | 26 | — |
| Louisiana | 26 | 16 | 10 |
| Maine | 16 | 16 | — |
| Maryland | 24 | 24 | — |
| Massachusetts | 38 | 38 | — |
| Michigan | 46 | 46 | — |
| Minnesota | 28 | 28 | — |
| Mississippi | 12 | 12 | — |
| Missouri | 26 | 26 | — |
| Montana | 14 | 14 | — |
| Nebraska | 18 | 18 | — |
| Nevada | 12 | 12 | — |
| New Hampshire | 14 | 14 | — |
| New Jersey | 38 | 38 | — |
| New Mexico | 14 | 14 | — |
| New York | 96 | 96 | — |
| North Carolina | 28 | 28 | — |
| North Dakota | 14 | 14 | — |
| Ohio | 56 | 56 | — |
| Oklahoma | 22 | 22 | — |
| Oregon | 18 | 18 | — |
| Pennsylvania | 70 | 70 | — |
| Rhode Island | 14 | 14 | — |
| South Carolina | 13 | 13 | — |
| South Dakota | 14 | 14 | — |
| Tennessee | 28 | 28 | — |
| Texas | 54 | 54 | — |
| Utah | 14 | 14 | — |
| Vermont | 12 | 12 | — |
| Virginia | 30 | 30 | — |
| Washington | 24 | 24 | — |
| West Virginia | 22 | 22 | — |
| Wisconsin | 30 | 30 | — |
| Wyoming | 12 | 12 | — |
| District of Columbia | 8 | 8 | — |
| Puerto Rico | 3 | 3 | — |
| Virgin Islands | 1 | 1 | — |
| **Total** | **1331** | **1321** | **10** |

1. *Other candidates: Ross R. Barnett, 23 (Mississippi); George A. Smathers, 30 (29 in Florida, ½ in Alabama, ½ in North Carolina); Hubert H. Humphrey, 42½ (31 in Minnesota, 8 in Wisconsin, 1½ in South Dakota, ½ in Nebraska, ½ in Utah); Robert B. Meyner, 43 (41 in New Jersey, 1½ in Pennsylvania, ½ in Alabama); Herschel C. Loveless, 1½ (Iowa); Faubus, ½ (Alabama); Edmund G. Brown, ½ (California); Albert Dean Rosellini, ½ (Washington).*

# 1964 Republican

*(Narrative, p. 117)*

| Delegation | Total Votes | Minority Amendment on Civil Rights[1] | | First Pres. Ballot[2] (Before shift) | | | First Pres. Ballot[3] (After shift) | | |
|---|---|---|---|---|---|---|---|---|---|
| | | Yea | Nay | Goldwater | Rockefeller | Scranton | Goldwater | Rockefeller | Scranton |
| Alabama | 20 | — | 20 | 20 | — | — | 20 | — | — |
| Alaska | 12 | 12 | — | — | — | 8 | — | — | 8 |
| Arizona | 16 | — | 16 | 16 | — | — | 16 | — | — |
| Arkansas | 12 | — | 12 | 9 | 1 | 2 | 12 | — | — |
| California | 86 | — | 86 | 86 | — | — | 86 | — | — |
| Colorado | 18 | — | 18 | 15 | — | 3 | 18 | — | — |
| Connecticut | 16 | 11 | 5 | 4 | — | 12 | 16 | — | — |
| Delaware | 12 | 11 | 1 | 7 | — | 5 | 10 | — | 2 |
| Florida | 34 | — | 34 | 34 | — | 2 | 34 | — | — |
| Georgia | 24 | — | 24 | 22 | — | 2 | 24 | — | — |
| Hawaii | 8 | 4 | 4 | 4 | — | — | 8 | — | — |
| Idaho | 14 | — | 14 | 14 | — | — | 14 | — | — |
| Illinois | 58 | 4 | 54 | 56 | 2 | — | 56 | 2 | — |
| Indiana | 32 | — | 32 | 32 | — | — | 32 | — | — |
| Iowa | 24 | 2 | 22 | 14 | — | 10 | 24 | — | — |
| Kansas | 20 | 2 | 18 | 18 | — | 1 | 18 | — | 1 |
| Kentucky | 24 | 1 | 23 | 21 | — | 3 | 22 | — | 2 |
| Louisiana | 20 | — | 20 | 20 | — | — | 20 | — | — |
| Maine | 14 | 11 | 3 | — | — | — | — | — | — |
| Maryland | 20 | 17 | 3 | 6 | 1 | 13 | 7 | 1 | 12 |
| Massachusetts | 34 | 27 | 7 | 5 | — | 26 | 34 | — | — |
| Michigan | 48 | 37 | 9 | 8 | — | — | 48 | — | — |
| Minnesota | 26 | 17 | 9 | 8 | — | — | 26 | — | — |
| Mississippi | 13 | — | 13 | 13 | — | — | 13 | — | — |
| Missouri | 24 | 1 | 23 | 23 | — | 1 | 24 | — | — |
| Montana | 14 | — | 14 | 14 | — | — | 14 | — | — |
| Nebraska | 16 | — | 16 | 16 | — | — | 16 | — | — |
| Nevada | 6 | — | 6 | 6 | — | — | 6 | — | — |
| New Hampshire | 14 | 14 | — | — | — | 14 | — | — | 14 |
| New Jersey | 40 | 40 | — | 20 | — | 20 | 38 | — | 2 |
| New Mexico | 14 | — | 14 | 14 | — | — | 14 | — | — |
| New York | 92 | 86 | 6 | 5 | 87 | — | 87 | — | — |
| North Carolina | 26 | — | 26 | 26 | — | — | 26 | — | — |
| North Dakota | 14 | 1 | 13 | 7 | 1 | — | 14 | — | — |
| Ohio | 58 | — | 58 | 57 | — | — | 58 | — | — |
| Oklahoma | 22 | — | 22 | 22 | — | — | 22 | — | — |
| Oregon | 18 | 10 | 8 | — | 18 | — | 16 | — | — |
| Pennsylvania | 64 | 62 | 2 | 4 | — | 60 | 64 | — | — |
| Rhode Island | 14 | 11 | 3 | 3 | — | 11 | 14 | — | — |
| South Carolina | 16 | — | 16 | 16 | — | — | 16 | — | — |
| South Dakota | 14 | — | 14 | 12 | — | 2 | 14 | — | — |
| Tennessee | 28 | — | 28 | 28 | — | — | 28 | — | — |
| Texas | 56 | — | 56 | 56 | — | — | 56 | — | — |
| Utah | 14 | — | 14 | 14 | — | — | 14 | — | — |
| Vermont | 12 | 8 | 4 | 3 | 2 | 2 | 3 | 2 | 2 |
| Virginia | 30 | — | 30 | 29 | — | 1 | 30 | — | — |
| Washington | 24 | 1 | 23 | 22 | — | 1 | 22 | — | 1 |
| West Virginia | 14 | 4 | 10 | 10 | 2 | 2 | 12 | 1 | 1 |
| Wisconsin | 30 | — | 30 | 30 | — | — | 30 | — | — |
| Wyoming | 12 | — | 12 | 12 | — | — | 12 | — | — |
| District of Columbia | 9 | 7 | 2 | 4 | — | 5 | 4 | — | 5 |
| Puerto Rico | 5 | 5 | — | — | — | 5 | 5 | — | — |
| Virgin Islands | 3 | 3 | — | — | — | 3 | 3 | — | — |
| Total | 1308 | 409 | 897 | 883 | 114 | 214 | 1220 | 6 | 50 |

1. *Not voting, 2.*
2. *Other candidates: George Romney, 41 (40 in Michigan, 1 in Kansas); Margaret C. Smith, 27 (14 in Maine, 5 in Vermont, 3 in North Dakota, 2 in Alaska, 1 in Massachusetts, 1 in Ohio, 1 in Washington); Walter H. Judd, 22 (18 in Minnesota, 3 in North Dakota, 1 in Alaska); Hiram L. Fong, 5 (4 in Hawaii, 1 in Alaska); Henry C. Lodge, 2 (Massachusetts).*
3. *Other candidates: Smith, 22 (14 in Maine, 5 in Vermont, 2 in Alaska, 1 in Washington); Fong, 1 (Alaska); Judd, 1 (Alaska); Romney, 1 (Kansas); not voting, 7 (5 in New York, 2 in Oregon).*

# 1968 Democratic

*(Narrative, p. 123)*

| Delegation | Total Votes | Texas Credentials[1] Yea | Nay | Georgia Credentials[2] Yea | Nay | Alabama Credentials[3] Yea | Nay | End Unit Rule[4] Yea | Nay | Report on Vietnam[5] Yea | Nay | First Pres. Ballot[6] Humphrey | McCarthy | McGovern | Phillips |
|---|---|---|---|---|---|---|---|---|---|---|---|---|---|---|---|
| Ala. | 32 | 32 | — | 10 | 22 | — | — | 5½ | 24½ | 1½ | 30½ | 23 | — | — | — |
| Alaska | 22 | 17 | 5 | 5 | 17 | 14 | 8 | 22 | — | 10 | 12 | 17 | 2 | 3 | — |
| Ariz. | 19 | 1½ | 17 | 17 | 2 | 7½ | 11½ | — | 19 | 6½ | 12½ | 14½ | 2½ | 2 | — |
| Ark. | 33 | 33 | — | 3 | 29 | 8 | 23 | — | 32 | 7 | 25 | 30 | 2 | — | — |
| Calif. | 174 | 1 | 173 | 173 | 1 | 173 | 1 | 173 | 1 | 166 | 6 | 14 | 91 | 51 | 17 |
| Colo. | 35 | — | 35 | 30 | 5 | 34 | 1 | 35 | — | 21 | 14 | 16½ | 10 | 5½ | 3 |
| Conn. | 44 | 30 | 12 | 13 | 27 | 21 | 21 | 9 | 30 | 13 | 30 | 35 | 8 | — | 1 |
| Del. | 22 | 21 | — | 3 | 18 | 2 | 19 | — | 21 | — | 21 | 21 | — | — | — |
| Fla. | 63 | 58 | 4 | 9 | 54 | 6 | 57 | 11 | 52 | 7 | 56 | 58 | 5 | — | — |
| Ga. | 43 | — | — | — | — | 25 | 17½ | 39 | 4 | 19½ | 23½ | 19½ | 13½ | 1 | 3 |
| Hawaii | 26 | 26 | — | 4 | 22 | — | 26 | 3 | 23 | — | 26 | 26 | — | — | — |
| Idaho | 25 | 22½ | 2½ | 4½ | 20½ | 2 | 23 | 1 | 24 | 10 | 15 | 21 | 3½ | ½ | — |
| Ill. | 118 | 114 | 4 | 12 | 83 | 18 | 100 | 3 | 115 | 13 | 105 | 112 | 3 | 3 | — |
| Ind. | 63 | 34 | 10 | 25 | 38 | 13 | 41½ | 63 | — | 15 | 47½ | 49 | 11 | 2 | 1 |
| Iowa | 46 | 37½ | 8½ | 32 | 12 | 24½ | 21½ | 46 | — | 36 | 10 | 18½ | 19½ | 5 | — |
| Kan. | 38 | 38 | — | 3½ | 34½ | 5½ | 31½ | 6 | 20 | 4½ | 33½ | 34 | 1 | 3 | — |
| Ky. | 46 | 40½ | 5½ | 6 | 40 | 6½ | 39½ | 6½ | 39½ | 7 | 39 | 41 | 5 | — | — |
| La. | 36 | 32 | 4 | 7 | 29 | — | 36 | — | 36 | 2½ | 33½ | 35 | — | — | — |
| Maine | 27 | 25 | 1 | 5 | 22 | — | 26 | 27 | — | 4½ | 22½ | 23 | 4 | — | — |
| Md. | 49 | 46 | 3 | 3 | 46 | 2 | 47 | 49 | — | 12 | 37 | 45 | 2 | 2 | — |
| Mass. | 72 | 16 | 47 | 39 | 24 | 29 | 29 | 37 | 31 | 56 | 16 | 2 | 70 | — | — |
| Mich. | 96 | 70 | 23 | 35 | 58 | 26 | 67 | 43½ | 44½ | 52 | 44 | 72½ | 9½ | 7½ | 6½ |
| Minn. | 52 | 34½ | 14½ | 16 | 33 | 23½ | 28½ | 16 | 33½ | 16½ | 34½ | 38 | 11½ | — | 2½ |
| Miss. | 24 | 2 | 18½ | 18 | 2 | 12½ | 8½ | 21½ | ½ | 19½ | 2½ | 9½ | 6½ | 4 | 2 |
| Mo. | 60 | 48 | 12 | 12 | 48 | 8 | 52 | 60 | — | 10 | 50 | 56 | 3½ | — | ½ |
| Mont. | 26 | 20 | 4 | 2½ | 21½ | 3½ | 22½ | 12½ | 12 | 6 | 20 | 23½ | 2½ | — | — |
| Neb. | 30 | 12 | 16 | 11 | 18 | 13 | 15 | 26 | 2 | 19 | 11 | 15 | 6 | 9 | — |
| Nev. | 22 | 13 | 7 | 14 | 8 | 12½ | 9½ | 22 | — | 3½ | 18½ | 18½ | 2½ | 1 | — |
| N.H. | 26 | 6 | 20 | 23 | 2 | 25 | — | 23 | 3 | 23 | 3 | 6 | 20 | — | — |
| N.J. | 82 | 43 | 25 | 22 | 51 | 21 | 61 | 21 | 61 | 24 | 57 | 62 | 19 | — | 1 |
| N.M. | 26 | 13 | 13 | 11 | 15 | 11 | 15 | 11 | 15 | 11½ | 14½ | 15 | 11 | — | — |
| N.Y. | 190 | — | 190 | 190 | — | 80e | 82e | 190 | — | 148 | 42 | 96½ | 87 | 1½ | 2 |
| N.C. | 59 | 54½ | 4½ | 3½ | 55½ | 1 | 58 | 2 | 57 | 7 | 51 | 44½ | 2 | ½ | — |
| N.D. | 25 | 17 | 5 | 5 | 17 | 7 | 18 | 17 | 5 | 6 | 19 | 18 | 7 | — | — |
| Ohio | 115 | 37½ | 27 | 21 | 80 | 30½ | 65 | 23 | 92 | 48 | 67 | 94 | 18 | 2 | — |
| Okla. | 41 | 40 | 1 | 1 | 40 | 6½ | 34 | 6 | 35 | 4 | 37 | 37½ | 2½ | ½ | ½ |
| Ore. | 35 | 10 | 23 | 32 | — | 31 | 3 | 31 | — | 29 | 6 | — | 35 | — | — |
| Pa. | 130 | 80¾ | 42¼ | 31½ | 90½ | 22¼ | 100½ | 39¾ | 79½ | 35¼ | 92¼ | 103¾ | 21½ | 2½ | 1½ |
| R.I. | 27 | 24½ | 2½ | 12 | 11 | 2½ | 24½ | 3½ | 23½ | 5 | 22 | 23½ | 2½ | — | — |
| S.C. | 28 | 28 | — | 4 | 22 | — | 28 | 4½ | 23½ | 1 | 27 | 28 | — | — | — |
| S.D. | 26 | 1 | 25 | 26 | — | 24 | 2 | 26 | — | 26 | — | 2 | — | 24 | — |
| Tenn. | 51 | 48½ | 1 | — | 51 | ½ | 49½ | 2½ | 46½ | 2 | 49 | 49½ | ½ | 1 | — |
| Texas | 104 | — | — | 2.55 | 101.45 | — | 104 | 5 | 99 | — | 104 | 100½ | 2½ | — | 1 |
| Utah | 26 | 18 | 8 | 7 | 19 | 5 | 21 | 26 | — | 6 | 20 | 23 | 2 | — | 1 |
| Vt. | 22 | 5 | 13 | 17 | 4 | 14 | 7 | 22 | — | 17 | 5 | 8 | 6 | 7 | — |
| Va. | 54 | 21½ | 22½ | 8½ | 35½ | 1 | 53 | 9½ | 43½ | 8 | 46 | 42½ | 5½ | — | 2 |
| Wash. | 47 | 31½ | 15½ | 18 | 29 | 16 | 28 | 21½ | 25½ | 15½ | 31½ | 32½ | 8½ | 6 | — |
| W.Va. | 38 | 19 | 12 | 8 | 22 | 9 | 29 | 38 | — | 8 | 30 | 34 | 3 | — | — |
| Wis. | 59 | 5 | 54 | 52 | 7 | 54 | 4 | 58 | 1 | 52 | 7 | 8 | 49 | 1 | 1 |
| Wyo. | 22 | 18½ | 3½ | 2 | 20 | 6½ | 15½ | 3 | 19 | 3½ | 18½ | 18½ | 3½ | — | — |
| Canal Z. | 5 | 4 | — | 2 | 3 | — | 4 | 1 | 4 | 1½ | 3½ | 4 | — | 1 | — |
| D.C. | 23 | — | 22 | 22 | — | 23 | — | 23 | — | 21 | 2 | 2 | — | — | 21 |
| Guam | 5 | 4½ | ½ | — | 5 | — | 5 | ½ | 4½ | ½ | 4½ | 5 | — | — | — |
| P.R. | 8 | 8 | — | 7½ | — | — | 8 | 1 | 7 | — | 8 | 8 | — | — | — |
| Vir. Is. | 5 | 5 | — | 2½ | — | — | 5 | 5 | — | — | 8 | 5 | — | — | — |
| **Total** | **2622** | **1368¼a** | **956¾b** | **1043.55c** | **1415.45d** | **880¾f** | **1607g** | **1351¼h** | **1209** | **1041¼** | **1567¾** | **1759¼j** | **601** | **146½** | **67½** |

1. Not voting, 297.
2. Not voting, 163.
3. Not voting, 134½.
4. Not voting, 61¾.
5. Not voting, 13.
6. Other candidates: Dan K. Moore, 17½ (12 in North Carolina, 3 in Virginia, 2 in Georgia, ½ in Alabama); Edward M. Kennedy, 12¾ (proceedings record, 12½) (3½ in Alabama, 3 in Iowa, 3 in New York, 1 in Ohio, 1 in West Virginia, ¾ in Pennsylvania; ½ in Georgia); Bryant, 1½ (Alabama); George C. Wallace, ½ (Alabama); James H. Gray, ½ (Georgia); not voting, 15 (3 in Alabama, 3 in Georgia, 2 in Mississippi, 1 in Arkansas, 1 in California, 1 in Delaware, 1 in Louisiana, 1 in Rhode Island, 1 in Vermont, 1 in Virginia).

a. Sum of column; proceedings record, 1368.
b. Sum of column; proceedings record, 955.
c. Sum of column; proceedings record, 1041½.
d. Sum of column; proceedings record, 1413.
e. New York vote announced after outcome of roll call.
f. Sum of column; proceedings record (without New York vote), 801½.
g. Sum of column; proceedings record (without New York), 1525.
h. Sum of column; proceedings record, 1350.
i. Sum of column; proceedings record, 1206.
j. Sum of column; proceedings record, 1761¾.

# 1968 Republican

*(Narrative, p. 121)*

| Delegation | Total Votes | First Pres. Ballot[1] (Before shift) | | | First Pres. Ballot (After shift) | | |
|---|---|---|---|---|---|---|---|
| | | Nixon | Rockefeller | Reagan | Nixon | Rockefeller | Reagan |
| Alabama | 26 | 14 | — | 12 | 26 | — | — |
| Alaska | 12 | 11 | 1 | — | 12 | — | — |
| Arizona | 16 | 16 | — | — | 16 | — | — |
| Arkansas | 18 | — | — | — | 18 | — | — |
| California | 86 | — | — | 86 | 86 | — | — |
| Colorado | 18 | 14 | 3 | 1 | 18 | — | — |
| Connecticut | 16 | 4 | 12 | — | 16 | — | — |
| Delaware | 12 | 9 | 3 | — | 12 | — | — |
| Florida | 34 | 32 | 1 | 1 | 34 | — | — |
| Georgia | 30 | 21 | 2 | 7 | 30 | — | — |
| Hawaii | 14 | — | — | — | 14 | — | — |
| Idaho | 14 | 9 | — | 5 | 14 | — | — |
| Illinois | 58 | 50 | 5 | 3 | 58 | — | — |
| Indiana | 26 | 26 | — | — | 26 | — | — |
| Iowa | 24 | 13 | 8 | 3 | 24 | — | — |
| Kansas | 20 | — | — | — | 19 | 1 | — |
| Kentucky | 24 | 22 | 2 | — | 24 | — | — |
| Louisiana | 26 | 19 | — | 7 | 26 | — | — |
| Maine | 14 | 7 | 7 | — | 14 | — | — |
| Maryland | 26 | 18 | 8 | — | 26 | — | — |
| Massachusetts | 34 | — | 34 | — | 34 | — | — |
| Michigan | 48 | 4 | — | — | 48 | — | — |
| Minnesota | 26 | 9 | 15 | — | 26 | — | — |
| Mississippi | 20 | 20 | — | — | 20 | — | — |
| Missouri | 24 | 16 | 5 | 3 | 24 | — | — |
| Montana | 14 | 11 | — | 3 | 14 | — | — |
| Nebraska | 16 | 16 | — | — | 16 | — | — |
| Nevada | 12 | 9 | 3 | — | 12 | — | — |
| New Hampshire | 8 | 8 | — | — | 8 | — | — |
| New Jersey | 40 | 18 | — | — | 40 | — | — |
| New Mexico | 14 | 8 | 1 | 5 | 14 | — | — |
| New York | 92 | 4 | 88 | — | 4 | 88 | — |
| North Carolina | 26 | 9 | 1 | 16 | 26 | — | — |
| North Dakota | 8 | 5 | 2 | 1 | 8 | — | — |
| Ohio | 58 | 2 | — | — | 58 | — | — |
| Oklahoma | 22 | 14 | 1 | 7 | 22 | — | — |
| Oregon | 18 | 18 | — | — | 18 | — | — |
| Pennsylvania | 64 | 22 | 41 | 1 | 64 | — | — |
| Rhode Island | 14 | — | 14 | — | 14 | — | — |
| South Carolina | 22 | 22 | — | — | 22 | — | — |
| South Dakota | 14 | 14 | — | — | 14 | — | — |
| Tennessee | 28 | 28 | — | — | 28 | — | — |
| Texas | 56 | 41 | — | 15 | 54 | — | 2 |
| Utah | 8 | 2 | — | — | 8 | — | — |
| Vermont | 12 | 9 | 3 | — | 12 | — | — |
| Virginia | 24 | 22 | 2 | — | 24 | — | — |
| Washington | 24 | 15 | 3 | 6 | 24 | — | — |
| West Virginia | 14 | 11 | 3 | — | 13 | 1 | — |
| Wisconsin | 30 | 30 | — | — | 30 | — | — |
| Wyoming | 12 | 12 | — | — | 12 | — | — |
| District of Columbia | 9 | 6 | 3 | — | 6 | 3 | — |
| Puerto Rico | 5 | — | 5 | — | 5 | — | — |
| Virgin Islands | 3 | 2 | 1 | — | 3 | — | — |
| **Total** | 1333 | 692 | 277 | 182 | 1238 | 93 | 2 |

1. Other candidates: James A. Rhodes, 55 (Ohio); George Romney, 50 (44 in Michigan, 6 in Utah); Clifford P. Case, 22 (New Jersey); Frank Carlson, 20 (Kansas); Winthrop Rockefeller, 18 (Arkansas); Hiram L. Fong, 14 (Hawaii); Harold Stassen, 2 (1 in Minnesota, 1 in Ohio); John V. Lindsay, 1 (Minnesota).

# 1972 Republican

*(Narrative, p. 130)*

| Delegation | Total Votes | First Pres. Ballot | |
|---|---|---|---|
| | | Nixon | McCloskey |
| Alabama | 18 | 18 | — |
| Alaska | 12 | 12 | — |
| Arizona | 18 | 18 | — |
| Arkansas | 18 | 18 | — |
| California | 96 | 96 | — |
| Colorado | 20 | 20 | — |
| Connecticut | 22 | 22 | — |
| Delaware | 12 | 12 | — |
| Florida | 40 | 40 | — |
| Georgia | 24 | 24 | — |
| Hawaii | 14 | 14 | — |
| Idaho | 14 | 14 | — |
| Illinois | 58 | 58 | — |
| Indiana | 32 | 32 | — |
| Iowa | 22 | 22 | — |
| Kansas | 20 | 20 | — |
| Kentucky | 24 | 24 | — |
| Louisiana | 20 | 20 | — |
| Maine | 8 | 8 | — |
| Maryland | 26 | 26 | — |
| Massachusetts | 34 | 34 | — |
| Michigan | 48 | 48 | — |
| Minnesota | 26 | 26 | — |
| Mississippi | 14 | 14 | — |
| Missouri | 30 | 30 | — |
| Montana | 14 | 14 | — |
| Nebraska | 16 | 16 | — |
| Nevada | 12 | 12 | — |
| New Hampshire | 14 | 14 | — |
| New Jersey | 40 | 40 | — |
| New Mexico | 14 | 13 | 1 |
| New York | 88 | 88 | — |
| North Carolina | 32 | 32 | — |
| North Dakota | 12 | 12 | — |
| Ohio | 56 | 56 | — |
| Oklahoma | 22 | 22 | — |
| Oregon | 18 | 18 | — |
| Pennsylvania | 60 | 60 | — |
| Rhode Island | 8 | 8 | — |
| South Carolina | 22 | 22 | — |
| South Dakota | 14 | 14 | — |
| Tennessee | 26 | 26 | — |
| Texas | 52 | 52 | — |
| Utah | 14 | 14 | — |
| Vermont | 12 | 12 | — |
| Virginia | 30 | 30 | — |
| Washington | 24 | 24 | — |
| West Virginia | 18 | 18 | — |
| Wisconsin | 28 | 28 | — |
| Wyoming | 12 | 12 | — |
| District of Columbia | 9 | 9 | — |
| Guam | 3 | 3 | — |
| Puerto Rico | 5 | 5 | — |
| Virgin Islands | 3 | 3 | — |
| Total | 1348 | 1347 | 1 |

# 1972 Democratic

(Narrative, p. 127)

| Delegation[1] | Total Votes | Minority Report South Carolina Credentials | | | Minority Report California Credentials | | | Minority Report Illinois Credentials | | |
|---|---|---|---|---|---|---|---|---|---|---|
| | | Yea | Nay | Not Voting | Yea | Nay | Not Voting | Yea | Nay | Not Voting |
| California | 271 | 120 | 151 | — | 120 | — | 151 | 84 | 136 | 51 |
| South Carolina | 32 | — | 9 | 23 | 3 | 29 | — | 31 | 1 | — |
| Ohio | 153 | 63 | 87 | 3 | 75 | 78 | — | 69 | 70 | 14 |
| Canal Zone | 3 | 1.50 | 1.50 | — | 3 | — | — | 1 | 2 | — |
| Utah | 19 | 10 | 8 | 1 | 13 | 6 | — | 5 | 14 | — |
| Delaware | 13 | 5.85 | 7.15 | — | 6.50 | 6.50 | — | 6.50 | 6.50 | — |
| Rhode Island | 22 | 20 | 2 | — | 22 | — | — | 7.09 | 14.91 | — |
| Texas | 130 | 34 | 96 | — | 34 | 96 | — | 96 | 34 | — |
| West Virginia | 35 | 13 | 22 | — | 15 | 20 | — | 24 | 11 | — |
| South Dakota | 17 | 17 | — | — | 17 | — | — | — | 17 | — |
| Kansas | 35 | 17 | 18 | — | 18 | 17 | — | 18 | 17 | — |
| New York | 278 | 269 | 9 | — | 267 | 11 | — | 20 | 256 | 2 |
| Virginia | 53 | 34.50 | 18.50 | — | 38.50 | 14.50 | — | 16.50 | 35.50 | 1 |
| Wyoming | 11 | 2.20 | 8.80 | — | 4.40 | 6.60 | — | 7.70 | 3.30 | — |
| Arkansas | 27 | 13 | 14 | — | 8 | 19 | — | 13 | 14 | — |
| Indiana | 76 | 18 | 58 | — | 33 | 43 | — | 53 | 23 | — |
| Puerto Rico | 7 | 6.50 | 0.50 | — | 6.50 | 0.50 | — | 0.50 | 6.50 | — |
| Tennessee | 49 | 22 | 27 | — | 23 | 26 | — | 20 | 29 | — |
| Pennsylvania | 182 | 55.50 | 126 | 0.50 | 72 | 105 | 5 | 106.50 | 62 | 13.50 |
| Mississippi | 25 | 20 | 5 | — | 19 | 6 | — | — | 25 | — |
| Wisconsin | 67 | 39 | 28 | — | 55 | 12 | — | 12 | 55 | — |
| Illinois | 170 | 79 | 90 | 1 | 114.50 | 55.50 | — | 76 | 30 | 64 |
| Maine | 20 | 1 | 19 | — | — | 20 | — | 13 | 7 | — |
| Florida | 81 | 1 | 80 | — | 3 | 78 | — | 80 | 1 | — |
| New Hampshire | 18 | 13.50 | 4.50 | — | 9.90 | 8.10 | — | 9 | 8.10 | 0.90 |
| Arizona | 25 | 15 | 10 | — | 12 | 13 | — | 4 | 21 | — |
| North Carolina | 64 | 6 | 58 | — | 21 | 43 | — | 39 | 23 | 2 |
| Massachusetts | 102 | 97 | 5 | — | 97 | 5 | — | 11 | 91 | — |
| Nebraska | 24 | 14 | 9 | 1 | 20 | 4 | — | 13 | 11 | — |
| Georgia | 53 | 5.50 | 47.50 | — | 21.75 | 31.25 | — | 24 | 27.50 | 1.50 |
| North Dakota | 14 | 7 | 6.30 | 0.70 | 8.40 | 5.60 | — | 2.10 | 11.90 | — |
| Maryland | 53 | 24 | 29 | — | 27.83 | 25.17 | — | 28.67 | 24.33 | — |
| New Jersey | 109 | 79 | 29 | 1 | 85.50 | 22.50 | 1 | 30 | 75.50 | 3.50 |
| Vermont | 12 | 7 | 5 | — | 11 | 1 | — | 2 | 10 | — |
| Nevada | 11 | 5.75 | 5.25 | — | 5.75 | 5.25 | — | 6.75 | 4.25 | — |
| Michigan | 132 | 51 | 81 | — | 55 | 76 | 1 | 85 | 47 | — |
| Iowa | 46 | 23 | 23 | — | 27 | 19 | — | 20 | 26 | — |
| Colorado | 36 | 23 | 13 | — | 27 | 9 | — | 5 | 31 | — |
| Alabama | 37 | 1 | 36 | — | 1 | 36 | — | 32 | 5 | — |
| Alaska | 10 | 6.75 | 3.25 | — | 7.25 | 2.75 | — | 4.75 | 5.25 | — |
| Hawaii | 17 | 2 | 15 | — | 7 | 10 | — | 17 | — | — |
| Washington | 52 | — | 52 | — | — | 52 | — | 52 | — | — |
| Minnesota | 64 | 56 | 8 | — | 29 | 35 | — | 32 | 32 | — |
| Louisiana | 44 | 25 | 19 | — | 22.50 | 21.50 | — | 9.50 | 32.50 | 2 |
| Idaho | 17 | 12.50 | 4.50 | — | 11.50 | 5.50 | — | 4 | 13 | — |
| Montana | 17 | 10 | 7 | — | 14.50 | 1 | 1.50 | 2.50 | 14.50 | — |
| Connecticut | 51 | 8 | 43 | — | 21 | 30 | — | 40 | 11 | — |
| District of Columbia | 15 | 12 | 3 | — | 13.50 | 1.50 | — | 1.50 | 13.50 | — |
| Virgin Islands | 3 | 1 | 2 | — | 2.50 | 0.50 | — | 3 | — | — |
| Kentucky | 47 | 10 | 37 | — | 11 | 36 | — | 36 | 10 | 1 |
| Missouri | 73 | 13.50 | 59.50 | — | 22.50 | 50.50 | — | 59 | 13 | 1 |
| New Mexico | 18 | 10 | 8 | — | 10 | 8 | — | 8 | 10 | — |
| Guam | 3 | 1.50 | 1.50 | — | 1.50 | 1.50 | — | — | 3 | — |
| Oregon | 34 | 16 | 18 | — | 33 | 1 | — | 2 | 32 | — |
| Oklahoma | 39 | 11 | 28 | — | 11 | 28 | — | 29 | 9 | 1 |
| Total | 3016 | 1429.05 | 1555.75 | 31.20 | 1618.28 | 1238.22 | 159.50 | 1371.56[a] | 1486.04[b] | 158.40 |

1. Delegations at this convention are listed in the order in which they voted. All fractional votes are expressed in decimals for consistency.
a. Sum of column; proceedings record, 1371.55.
b. Sum of column; proceedings record, 1486.05.

# 1972 Democratic

(Narrative, p. 127)

| Minority Report Guaranteed Income | | | First Presidential[2] (Before shift) | | | | | First Presidential[3] (After shift) | | | | |
|---|---|---|---|---|---|---|---|---|---|---|---|---|
| Yea | Nay | Not Voting | McGovern | Jackson | Wallace | Chisholm | Sanford | McGovern | Jackson | Wallace | Chisholm | Sanford |
| 131 | 114 | 26 | 271 | — | — | — | — | 271 | — | — | — | — |
| 4 | 21 | 7 | 6 | 10 | 6 | 4 | 6 | 10 | 9 | 6 | — | 6 |
| 39 | 86 | 28 | 77 | 39 | — | 23 | 3 | 77 | 39 | — | 23 | 3 |
| 2.50 | 0.50 | — | 3 | — | — | — | — | 3 | — | — | — | — |
| 8 | 11 | — | 14 | 1 | — | — | 3 | 14 | 1 | — | — | 3 |
| 4.55 | 8.45 | — | 5.85 | 6.50 | — | 0.65 | — | 5.85 | 5.85 | — | 0.65 | — |
| 10.86 | 11.14 | — | 22 | — | — | — | — | 22 | — | — | — | — |
| 15 | 115 | — | 54 | 23 | 48 | 4 | — | 54 | 23 | 48 | 4 | — |
| 3 | 32 | — | 16 | 14 | 1 | — | 4 | 16 | 14 | 1 | — | 4 |
| 1 | 16 | — | 17 | — | — | — | — | 17 | — | — | — | — |
| 5 | 30 | — | 20 | 10 | — | 2 | 1 | 20 | 10 | — | 2 | 1 |
| 152 | 118 | 8 | 263 | 9 | — | 6 | — | 278 | — | — | — | — |
| 30 | 21 | 2 | 33.50 | 4 | 1 | 5.50 | 9 | 37 | 5 | — | 2.50 | 8.50 |
| 0.55 | 10.45 | — | 3.30 | 6.05 | — | 1.10 | — | 3.30 | 6.05 | — | 1.10 | — |
| 10 | 16 | 1 | 1 | 1 | — | — | — | 1 | 1 | — | — | — |
| 17 | 56 | 3 | 26 | 20 | 26 | 1 | — | 28 | 19 | 25 | — | — |
| 4 | 3 | — | 7 | — | — | — | — | 7 | — | — | — | — |
| 21 | 27 | 1 | — | — | 33 | 10 | — | 5 | — | 32 | 7 | — |
| 49.50 | 117.50 | 15 | 81 | 86.50 | 2 | 9.50 | 1 | 81 | 86.50 | 2 | 9.50 | 1 |
| 22 | — | 3 | 10 | — | — | 12 | 3 | 23 | — | — | 2 | — |
| 29 | 38 | — | 55 | 3 | — | 5 | — | 55 | 3 | — | 5 | — |
| 59 | 95 | 16 | 119 | 30.50 | 0.50 | 4.50 | 2 | 155 | 6 | — | 1 | — |
| 1 | 19 | — | 5 | — | — | — | — | 5 | — | — | — | — |
| 4 | 77 | — | 2 | — | 75 | 2 | — | 4 | — | 75 | 1 | — |
| 0.90 | 14.40 | 2.70 | 10.80 | 5.40 | — | — | — | 10.80 | 5.40 | — | — | — |
| 6 | 19 | — | 21 | 3 | — | — | 1 | 22 | 3 | — | — | — |
| 17 | 47 | — | — | — | 37 | — | 27 | — | — | 37 | — | 27 |
| 60 | 40 | 2 | 102 | — | — | — | — | 102 | — | — | — | — |
| 2 | 22 | — | 21 | 3 | — | — | — | 21 | 3 | — | — | — |
| 10.50 | 34 | 8.50 | 14.50 | 14.50 | 11 | 12 | 1 | 14.50 | 14.50 | 11 | 12 | 1 |
| 1.40 | 10.50 | 2.10 | 8.40 | 2.80 | 0.70 | 0.70 | — | 10.50 | 2.10 | — | 0.70 | — |
| 14.33 | 38.67 | — | 13 | — | 38 | 2 | — | 13 | — | 38 | 2 | — |
| 61.50 | 35.50 | 12 | 89 | 11.50 | — | 4 | 1.50 | 92.50 | 11 | — | 3.50 | — |
| 4 | 8 | — | 12 | — | — | — | — | 12 | — | — | — | — |
| 2.75 | 8.25 | — | 5.75 | 5.25 | — | — | — | 5.75 | 5.25 | — | — | — |
| 30.50 | 96.50 | 5 | 50.50 | 7 | 67.50 | 3 | 1 | 51.50 | 7 | 67.50 | 2 | 1 |
| 6 | 39 | 1 | 35 | — | — | 3 | 4 | 35 | — | — | 3 | 4 |
| 15 | 21 | — | 27 | — | — | 7 | — | 29 | 2 | — | 5 | — |
| 10 | 27 | — | 9 | 1 | 24 | — | 1 | 9 | 1 | 24 | — | 1 |
| 3 | 5.50 | 1.50 | 6.50 | 3.25 | — | — | — | 6.50 | 3.25 | — | — | — |
| 1.50 | 15.50 | — | 6.50 | 8.50 | — | 1 | — | 6.50 | 8.50 | — | 1 | — |
| 1 | 51 | — | — | 52 | — | — | — | — | 52 | — | — | — |
| 28 | 33 | 3 | 11 | — | — | 6 | — | 43 | — | — | 4 | 1 |
| 22 | 20 | 2 | 10.25 | 10.25 | 3 | 18.50 | 2 | 25.75 | 5.25 | 3 | 4 | 1 |
| 5 | 12 | — | 12.50 | 2.50 | — | 2 | — | 12.50 | 2.50 | — | 2 | — |
| 2 | 14 | 1 | 16 | — | — | 1 | — | 16 | — | — | 1 | — |
| 22 | 29 | — | 30 | 20 | — | — | 1 | 30 | 20 | — | — | 1 |
| 15 | — | — | 13.50 | 1.50 | — | — | — | 13.50 | 1.50 | — | — | — |
| 2.50 | 0.50 | — | 1 | 1.50 | — | 0.50 | — | 1 | 1.50 | — | 0.50 | — |
| 1 | 41 | 5 | 10 | 35 | — | — | 2 | 10 | 35 | — | — | 2 |
| 12 | 55 | 6 | 24.50 | 48.50 | — | — | — | 24.50 | 48.50 | — | — | — |
| 3 | 15 | — | 10 | — | 8 | — | — | 10 | — | 8 | — | — |
| — | 3 | — | 1.50 | 1.50 | — | — | — | 1.50 | 1.50 | — | — | — |
| 11 | 23 | — | 34 | — | — | — | — | 34 | — | — | — | — |
| 5.50 | 31.50 | 2 | 10.50 | 23.50 | — | 1 | 4 | 9.50 | 23.50 | — | 2 | 4 |
| 999.34 | 1852.86 | 163.80 | 1728.35 | 525.00 | 381.70 | 151.95 | 77.50 | 1864.95 | 485.65 | 377.50 | 101.45 | 69.50 |

2. *Other candidates: Hubert H. Humphrey, 66.70 (46 in Minnesota, 4 in Ohio, 4 in Wisconsin, 3 in Michigan, 2 in Indiana, 2 in Pennsylvania, 2 in Florida, 1 in Utah, 1 in Colorado, 1 in Hawaii, 0.70 in North Dakota); Wilbur D. Mills, 33.80 (25 in Arkansas, 3 in Illinois, 3 in New Jersey, 2 in Alabama, 0.55 in Wyoming, 0.25 in Alaska); Edmund S. Muskie, 24.30 (15 in Maine, 5.50 in Illinois, 1.80 in New Hampshire, 1 in Texas, 1 in Colorado); Edward M. Kennedy, 12.70 (4 in Iowa, 3 in Illinois, 2 in Ohio, 1 in Kansas, 1 in Indiana, 1 in Tennessee, 0.70 in North Dakota); Wayne L. Hays, 5 (Ohio); Eugene J. McCarthy, 2 (Illinois); Mondale, 1 (Kansas); Clark, 1 (Minnesota); not voting, 5 (Tennessee).*

3. *Humphrey, 35 (16 in Minnesota, 4 in Ohio, 4 in Wisconsin, 3 in Indiana, 3 in Michigan, 2 in Pennsylvania, 1 in Utah, 1 in Florida, 1 in Hawaii); Mills, 32.80 (25 in Arkansas, 2 in Illinois, 2 in New Jersey, 2 in Alabama, 1 in South Carolina, 0.55 in Wyoming, 0.25 in Alaska); Muskie, 20.80 (15 in Maine, 3 in Illinois, 1.80 in New Hampshire, 1 in Texas); Kennedy, 10.65 (4 in Iowa, 2 in Ohio, 1 in Kansas, 1 in Indiana, 1 in Tennessee, 1 in Illinois, 0.65 in Delaware); Hays, 5 (Ohio); McCarthy, 2 (Illinois); Mondale, 1 (Kansas).*

# 1976 Democratic

*(Narrative, p. 133)*

| Delegation | Total Votes | First Pres. Ballot[1] (Before shift) | | | | First Pres. Ballot[2] (After shift) | | | |
|---|---|---|---|---|---|---|---|---|---|
| | | Carter | Udall | Brown | Wallace | Carter | Udall | Brown | Wallace |
| Alabama | 35 | 30 | — | — | 5 | 30 | — | — | 5 |
| Alaska | 10 | 10 | — | — | — | 10 | — | — | — |
| Arizona | 25 | 6 | 19 | — | — | 6 | 19 | — | — |
| Arkansas | 26 | 25 | 1 | — | — | 25 | 1 | — | — |
| California | 280 | 73 | 2 | 205 | — | 278 | 2 | — | — |
| Colorado | 35 | 15 | 6 | 11 | — | 15 | 6 | 11 | — |
| Connecticut | 51 | 35 | 16 | — | — | 35 | 16 | — | — |
| Delaware | 12 | 10.50 | — | 1.50 | — | 10.50 | — | 1.50 | — |
| Florida | 81 | 70 | — | 1 | 10 | 70 | — | 1 | 10 |
| Georgia | 50 | 50 | — | — | — | 50 | — | — | — |
| Hawaii | 17 | 17 | — | — | — | 17 | — | — | — |
| Idaho | 16 | 16 | — | — | — | 16 | — | — | — |
| Illinois | 169 | 164 | 1 | 2 | 1 | 164 | 1 | 2 | 1 |
| Indiana | 75 | 72 | — | — | 3 | 72 | — | – | 3 |
| Iowa | 47 | 25 | 20 | 1 | — | 25 | 20 | 1 | — |
| Kansas | 34 | 32 | 2 | — | — | 32 | 2 | — | — |
| Kentucky | 46 | 39 | 2 | — | 5 | 29 | 2 | — | 5 |
| Louisiana | 41 | 18 | — | 18 | 5 | 35 | — | 1 | 5 |
| Maine | 20 | 15 | 5 | — | — | 15 | 5 | — | — |
| Maryland | 53 | 44 | 6 | 3 | — | 44 | 6 | 3 | — |
| Massachusetts[3] | 104 | 65 | 21 | — | 11 | 65 | 21 | — | 11 |
| Michigan | 133 | 75 | 58 | — | — | 75 | 58 | — | — |
| Minnesota | 65 | 37 | 2 | 1 | — | 37 | 2 | 1 | — |
| Mississippi | 24 | 23 | — | — | — | 23 | — | — | — |
| Missouri | 71 | 58 | 4 | 2 | — | 58 | 4 | 2 | — |
| Montana | 17 | 11 | 2 | — | — | 11 | 2 | — | — |
| Nebraska | 23 | 20 | — | 3 | — | 20 | — | 3 | — |
| Nevada | 11 | 3 | — | 6.50 | — | 3 | — | 6.50 | — |
| New Hampshire | 17 | 15 | 2 | — | — | 15 | 2 | — | — |
| New Jersey | 108 | 108 | — | — | — | 108 | — | — | — |
| New Mexico | 18 | 14 | 4 | — | — | 14 | 4 | — | — |
| New York | 274 | 209.50 | 56.50 | 4 | — | 209.50 | 56.50 | 4 | — |
| North Carolina | 61 | 56 | — | — | 3 | 56 | — | — | 3 |
| North Dakota | 13 | 13 | — | — | — | 13 | — | — | — |
| Ohio | 152 | 132 | 20 | — | — | 132 | 20 | — | — |
| Oklahoma | 37 | 32 | 1 | — | — | 32 | 1 | — | — |
| Oregon | 34 | 16 | — | 10 | — | 16 | — | 10 | — |
| Pennsylvania | 178 | 151 | 21 | 6 | — | 151 | 21 | 6 | — |
| Rhode Island | 22 | 14 | — | 8 | — | 22 | — | — | — |
| South Carolina | 31 | 28 | — | 1 | 2 | 28 | — | 1 | 2 |
| South Dakota | 17 | 11 | 5 | — | — | 11 | 5 | — | — |
| Tennessee | 46 | 45 | — | — | 1 | 45 | — | — | 1 |
| Texas | 130 | 124 | — | 4 | 1 | 124 | — | 4 | 1 |
| Utah | 18 | 10 | — | 5 | — | 10 | — | 5 | — |
| Vermont | 12 | 5 | 4 | 3 | — | 5 | 4 | 3 | — |
| Virginia | 54 | 48 | 6 | — | — | 48 | 6 | — | — |
| Washington | 53 | 36 | 11 | 3 | — | 36 | 11 | 3 | — |
| West Virginia | 33 | 30 | 1 | — | — | 30 | 1 | — | — |
| Wisconsin | 68 | 29 | 25 | — | 10 | 29 | 25 | — | 10 |
| Wyoming | 10 | 8 | 1 | 1 | — | 8 | 1 | 1 | — |
| District of Columbia | 17 | 12 | 5 | — | — | 12 | 5 | — | — |
| Puerto Rico | 22 | 22 | — | — | — | 22 | — | — | — |
| Canal Zone | 3 | 3 | — | — | — | 3 | — | — | — |
| Guam | 3 | 3 | — | — | — | 3 | — | — | — |
| Virgin Islands | 3 | 3 | — | — | — | 3 | — | — | — |
| Democrats Abroad | 3 | 2.50 | — | 0.50 | — | 2.50 | — | 0.50 | — |
| **Total** | **3008** | **2238.50** | **329.50** | **300.50** | **57.00** | **2468.50** | **329.50** | **70.50** | **57.00** |

1. *Other candidates: Ellen McCormack, 22 (1 in Illinois, 2 in Massachusetts, 11 in Minnesota, 7 in Missouri, 1 in Wisconsin); Frank Church, 19 (3 in Colorado, 4 in Montana, 1 in Nevada, 8 in Oregon, 1 in Utah, 2 in Washington); Hubert H. Humphrey, 10 (9 in Minnesota, 1 in South Dakota); Henry M. Jackson, 10 (2 in Massachusetts, 4 in New York, 1 in Washington, 3 in Wisconsin); Fred Harris, 9 (2 in Massachusetts, 4 in Minnesota, 3 in Oklahoma); Milton J. Shapp, 2 (1 in Massachusetts, 1 in Utah); receiving one vote each Robert C. Byrd (West Virginia); Cesar Chavez (Utah); Leon Jaworski (Texas); Barbara C. Jordan (Oklahoma); Edward M. Kennedy (Iowa); Jennings Randolph (West Virginia); Fred Stover (Minnesota); "nobody" (0.5 in Nevada); not voting, 3 (1 in Mississippi, 2 in North Carolina).*
2. *The rules were suspended after the switches and Carter was nominated by acclamation.*
3. *Massachusetts passed when originally called on and cast its votes at the end of the roll call, after vote switches.*

# 1976 Republican

*(Narrative, p. 137)*

| Delegation | Total Votes | Rule 16C[1] | | First Pres. Ballot[2] | |
|---|---|---|---|---|---|
| | | Yes | Nay | Ford | Reagan |
| Alabama | 37 | 37 | — | — | 37 |
| Alaska | 19 | 2 | 17 | 17 | 2 |
| Arizona | 29 | 25 | 4 | 2 | 27 |
| Arkansas | 27 | 17 | 10 | 10 | 17 |
| California | 167 | 166 | 1 | — | 167 |
| Colorado | 31 | 26 | 5 | 5 | 26 |
| Connecticut | 35 | — | 35 | 35 | — |
| Delaware | 17 | 1 | 16 | 15 | 2 |
| Florida | 66 | 28 | 38 | 43 | 23 |
| Georgia | 48 | 39 | 7 | — | 48 |
| Hawaii | 19 | 1 | 18 | 18 | 1 |
| Idaho | 21 | 17 | 4 | 4 | 17 |
| Illinois | 101 | 20 | 79 | 86 | 14 |
| Indiana | 54 | 27 | 27 | 9 | 45 |
| Iowa | 36 | 18 | 18 | 19 | 17 |
| Kansas | 34 | 4 | 30 | 30 | 4 |
| Kentucky | 37 | 26 | 10 | 19 | 18 |
| Louisiana | 41 | 34 | 6 | 5 | 36 |
| Maine | 20 | 5 | 15 | 15 | 5 |
| Maryland | 43 | 8 | 35 | 43 | — |
| Massachusetts | 43 | 15 | 28 | 28 | 15 |
| Michigan | 84 | 29 | 55 | 55 | 29 |
| Minnesota | 42 | 5 | 35 | 32 | 10 |
| Mississippi | 30 | — | 30 | 16 | 14 |
| Missouri | 49 | 30 | 18 | 18 | 31 |
| Montana | 20 | 20 | — | — | 20 |
| Nebraska | 25 | 18 | 7 | 7 | 18 |
| Nevada | 18 | 15 | 3 | 5 | 13 |
| New Hampshire | 21 | 3 | 18 | 18 | 3 |
| New Jersey | 67 | 4 | 62 | 63 | 4 |
| New Mexico | 21 | 20 | 1 | — | 21 |
| New York | 154 | 20 | 134 | 133 | 20 |
| North Carolina | 54 | 51 | 3 | 25 | 29 |
| North Dakota | 18 | 6 | 12 | 11 | 7 |
| Ohio | 97 | 7 | 90 | 91 | 6 |
| Oklahoma | 36 | 36 | — | — | 36 |
| Oregon | 30 | 14 | 16 | 16 | 14 |
| Pennsylvania | 103 | 14 | 89 | 93 | 10 |
| Rhode Island | 19 | — | 19 | 19 | — |
| South Carolina | 36 | 25 | 11 | 9 | 27 |
| South Dakota | 20 | 11 | 9 | 9 | 11 |
| Tennessee | 43 | 17 | 26 | 21 | 22 |
| Texas | 100 | 100 | — | — | 100 |
| Utah | 20 | 20 | — | — | 20 |
| Vermont | 18 | — | 18 | 18 | — |
| Virginia | 51 | 36 | 15 | 16 | 35 |
| Washington | 38 | 31 | 7 | 7 | 31 |
| West Virginia | 28 | 12 | 16 | 20 | 8 |
| Wisconsin | 45 | — | 45 | 45 | — |
| Wyoming | 17 | 9 | 8 | 7 | 10 |
| District of Columbia | 14 | — | 14 | 14 | — |
| Puerto Rico | 8 | — | 8 | 8 | — |
| Guam | 4 | — | 4 | 4 | — |
| Virgin Islands | 4 | — | 4 | 4 | — |
| **Total** | 2259 | 1069 | 1180 | 1187 | 1070 |

1. Not voting, 10.
2. Other candidate: Elliot L. Richardson, 1 (New York); not voting, 1 (Illinois). The nomination was made unanimous at the end of the balloting.

# 1980 Democratic

*(Narrative, p. 146)*

| Delegation | Total Votes | Minority Rule #5[1] | | First Pres. Ballot[3] (Before shift) | | First Pres. Ballot[4] (After shift) | |
|---|---|---|---|---|---|---|---|
| | | Yea | Nay | Carter | Kennedy | Carter | Kennedy |
| Alabama | 45 | 3 | 42 | 43 | 2 | 43 | 2 |
| Alaska | 11 | 6.11 | 4.89 | 8.40 | 2.60 | 8.40 | 2.60 |
| Arizona | 29 | 16 | 13 | 13 | 16 | 13 | 16 |
| Arkansas | 33 | 9 | 24 | 25 | 6 | 25 | 6 |
| California | 306 | 171 | 132[2] | 140 | 166 | 140 | 166 |
| Colorado | 40 | 24 | 16 | 27 | 10 | 27 | 10 |
| Connecticut | 54 | 28 | 26 | 26 | 28 | 26 | 28 |
| Delaware | 14 | 6.50 | 7.50 | 10 | 4 | 14 | — |
| District of Columbia | 19 | 12 | 7 | 12 | 5 | 12 | 5 |
| Florida | 100 | 25 | 75 | 75 | 25 | 75 | 25 |
| Georgia | 63 | 1 | 62 | 62 | — | 62 | — |
| Hawaii | 19 | 4 | 15 | 16 | 2 | 16 | 2 |
| Idaho | 17 | 9 | 8 | 9 | 7 | 9 | 7 |
| Illinois | 179 | 26 | 153 | 163 | 16 | 163 | 16 |
| Indiana | 80 | 27 | 53 | 53 | 27 | 53 | 27 |
| Iowa | 50 | 21 | 29 | 31 | 17 | 33 | 17 |
| Kansas | 37 | 17 | 20 | 23 | 14 | 23 | 14 |
| Kentucky | 50 | 12 | 38 | 45 | 5 | 45 | 5 |
| Louisiana | 51 | 15 | 36 | 50 | 1 | 50 | 1 |
| Maine | 22 | 12 | 10 | 11 | 11 | 11 | 11 |
| Maryland | 59 | 27 | 32 | 34 | 24 | 34 | 24 |
| Massachusetts | 111 | 81 | 30 | 34 | 77 | 34 | 77 |
| Michigan | 141 | 71 | 70 | 102 | 38 | 102 | 38 |
| Minnesota | 75 | 30 | 45 | 41 | 14 | 41 | 14 |
| Mississippi | 32 | — | 32 | 32 | — | 32 | — |
| Missouri | 77 | 20 | 57 | 58 | 19 | 58 | 19 |
| Montana | 19 | 9 | 10 | 13 | 6 | 13 | 6 |
| Nebraska | 24 | 11 | 13 | 14 | 10 | 14 | 10 |
| Nevada | 12 | 6.47 | 5.53 | 8.12 | 3.88 | 8.12 | 3.88 |
| New Hampshire | 19 | 9 | 10 | 10 | 9 | 10 | 9 |
| New Jersey | 113 | 68 | 45 | 45 | 68 | 45 | 68 |
| New Mexico | 20 | 11 | 9 | 10 | 10 | 10 | 10 |
| New York | 282 | 163 | 118 | 129 | 151 | 129 | 151 |
| North Carolina | 69 | 13 | 56 | 66 | 3 | 66 | 3 |
| North Dakota | 14 | 10 | 4 | 5 | 7 | 5 | 7 |
| Ohio | 161 | 81 | 80 | 89 | 72 | 89 | 72 |
| Oklahoma | 42 | 9 | 33 | 36 | 3 | 36 | 3 |
| Oregon | 39 | 14 | 25 | 26 | 13 | 26 | 13 |
| Pennsylvania | 185 | 102 | 83 | 95 | 90 | 95 | 90 |
| Puerto Rico | 41 | 20 | 21 | 21 | 20 | 21 | 20 |
| Rhode Island | 23 | 17 | 6 | 6 | 17 | 6 | 17 |
| South Carolina | 37 | 6 | 31 | 37 | — | 37 | — |
| South Dakota | 19 | 10 | 9 | 9 | 10 | 9 | 10 |
| Tennessee | 55 | 8 | 47 | 51 | 4 | 51 | 4 |
| Texas | 152 | 47 | 105 | 108 | 38 | 108 | 38 |
| Utah | 20 | 12 | 8 | 11 | 4 | 11 | 4 |
| Vermont | 12 | 7.50 | 4.50 | 5 | 7 | 5 | 7 |
| Virginia | 64 | 7 | 57 | 59 | 5 | 59 | 5 |
| Washington | 58 | 24 | 34 | 36 | 22 | 36 | 22 |
| West Virginia | 35 | 16 | 19 | 21 | 10 | 21 | 10 |
| Wisconsin | 75 | 26 | 49 | 48 | 26 | 48 | 26 |
| Wyoming | 11 | 3.50 | 7.50 | 8 | 3 | 8 | 3 |
| Virgin Islands | 4 | — | 4 | 4 | — | 4 | — |
| Guam | 4 | — | 4 | 4 | — | 4 | — |
| Latin America | 4 | 4 | — | 4 | — | 4 | — |
| Democrats Abroad | 4 | 2.50 | 1.50 | 1.50 | 2 | 1.50 | 2 |
| **Total** | **3331** | **1390.58** | **1936.42** | **2123.02** | **1150.48** | **2129.02** | **1150.48** |

1. The vote was on a minority report by supporters of Sen. Edward M. Kennedy to overturn a proposed rule that would bind all delegates to vote on the first ballot for the presidential candidate under whose banner they were elected. A "yes" vote supported the Kennedy position while a "no" supported the Carter view that delegates should be bound.

2. Not voting, 1.

3. Other candidates: William Proxmire, 10 (Minnesota); Scott M. Matheson, 5 (Utah); Koryne Horbal, 5 (Minnesota); Ronald V. Dellums, 2.5 (2 in New York, 0.5 from Democrats Abroad); receiving 2 votes each: John C. Culver (Iowa); Warren Spannous (Minnesota); Alice Tripp (Minnesota); Kent Hance (Texas); Robert C. Byrd (West Virginia); receiving 1 vote each: Dale Bumpers (Arkansas); Edmund S. Muskie (Colorado); Walter F. Mondale (Minnesota); Hugh L. Carey (Oklahoma); Tom Steed (Oklahoma); Edmund G. Brown (Wisconsin); uncommitted, 10; not voting, 5; absent, 2.

4. Votes for other candidates remained the same except that Iowa switched its 2 votes for Culver to Carter. After the switches Carter was nominated by acclamation.

# 1980 Republican

(*Narrative, p. 142*)

| Delegation | Total Votes | First Pres. Ballot[1] | | |
| --- | --- | --- | --- | --- |
| | | Reagan | Anderson | Bush |
| Alabama | 27 | 27 | — | — |
| Alaska | 19 | 19 | — | — |
| Arizona | 28 | 28 | — | — |
| Arkansas | 19 | 19 | — | — |
| California | 168 | 168 | — | — |
| Colorado | 31 | 31 | — | — |
| Connecticut | 35 | 35 | — | — |
| Delaware | 12 | 12 | — | — |
| District of Columbia | 14 | 14 | — | — |
| Florida | 51 | 51 | — | — |
| Georgia | 36 | 36 | — | — |
| Guam | 4 | 4 | — | — |
| Hawaii | 14 | 14 | — | — |
| Idaho | 21 | 21 | — | — |
| Illinois | 102 | 81 | 21 | — |
| Indiana | 54 | 54 | — | — |
| Iowa | 37 | 37 | — | — |
| Kansas | 32 | 32 | — | — |
| Kentucky | 27 | 27 | — | — |
| Louisiana | 31 | 31 | — | — |
| Maine | 21 | 21 | — | — |
| Maryland | 30 | 30 | — | — |
| Massachusetts | 42 | 33 | 9 | — |
| Michigan | 82 | 67 | — | 13 |
| Minnesota | 34 | 33 | — | — |
| Mississippi | 22 | 22 | — | — |
| Missouri | 37 | 37 | — | — |
| Montana | 20 | 20 | — | — |
| Nebraska | 25 | 25 | — | — |
| Nevada | 17 | 17 | — | — |
| New Hampshire | 22 | 22 | — | — |
| New Jersey | 66 | 66 | — | — |
| New Mexico | 22 | 22 | — | — |
| New York | 123 | 121 | — | — |
| North Carolina | 40 | 40 | — | — |
| North Dakota | 17 | 17 | — | — |
| Ohio | 77 | 77 | — | — |
| Oklahoma | 34 | 34 | — | — |
| Oregon | 29 | 29 | — | — |
| Pennsylvania | 83 | 83 | — | — |
| Puerto Rico | 14 | 14 | — | — |
| Rhode Island | 13 | 13 | — | — |
| South Carolina | 25 | 25 | — | — |
| South Dakota | 22 | 22 | — | — |
| Tennessee | 32 | 32 | — | — |
| Texas | 80 | 80 | — | — |
| Utah | 21 | 21 | — | — |
| Vermont | 19 | 19 | — | — |
| Virginia | 51 | 51 | — | — |
| Virgin Islands | 4 | 4 | — | — |
| Washington | 37 | 36 | 1 | — |
| West Virginia | 18 | 18 | — | — |
| Wisconsin | 34 | 28 | 6 | — |
| Wyoming | 19 | 19 | — | — |
| Total | 1994 | 1939 | 37 | 13 |

1. Other candidates: Anne Armstrong, 1 (Michigan); not voting, 4.

# 1984 Democratic

(Narrative, p. 153)

| Delegation | Total Votes | No First Use of Nuclear Weapons | | | Defense Spending | | | Dual Primaries | | | Military Force Restrictions | | |
|---|---|---|---|---|---|---|---|---|---|---|---|---|---|
| | | Yea | Nay | Not Voting | Yea | Nay | Not Voting | Yea | Nay | Not Voting | Yea | Nay | Not Voting |
| Alabama | 62 | 15 | 46 | 1 | 11 | 49 | 2 | 13 | 49 | — | 61 | 1 | — |
| Alaska | 14 | 7 | 7 | — | 1 | 13 | — | 2 | 12 | — | 13 | 1 | — |
| Arizona | 40 | 20 | 19 | — | 18 | 21 | — | 20 | 19 | — | 39 | — | — |
| Arkansas | 42 | 13 | 29 | — | 12 | 30 | — | 7 | 33 | 2 | 39 | 2 | 1 |
| California | 345 | 149 | 84 | — | 99 | 170 | — | 129 | 128 | — | 285 | 31 | — |
| Colorado | 51 | 31 | 16 | 4 | 5 | 45 | 1 | 26 | 24 | 1 | 51 | — | — |
| Connecticut | 60 | 28 | 24 | 8 | 32 | 27 | 1 | 27 | 33 | — | 60 | — | — |
| Delaware | 18 | 1 | 17 | — | 1 | 17 | — | 1 | 17 | — | 18 | — | — |
| D.C. | 19 | 15 | 4 | — | 17 | 2 | — | 14 | 5 | — | 6 | 12 | — |
| Florida | 143 | 47 | 76 | 20 | 42 | 81 | 20 | 27 | 110 | 6 | 95 | 25 | 23 |
| Georgia | 84 | 40 | 33 | — | 38 | 45 | — | 39 | 42 | — | 67 | 1 | 2 |
| Hawaii | 27 | 1 | 26 | — | — | 27 | — | — | 27 | — | — | — | — |
| Idaho | 22 | 9 | — | — | 10 | 11 | — | 9 | 13 | — | 22 | — | — |
| Illinois | 194 | 42 | 145 | — | 40 | 147 | — | 48 | 143 | — | 191 | — | 3 |
| Indiana | 88 | 31 | 46 | — | 18 | 64 | — | 23 | 64 | — | 88 | — | — |
| Iowa | 58 | 22 | 36 | — | 7 | 51 | — | 5 | 53 | — | 58 | — | — |
| Kansas | 44 | 14 | 29 | 1 | 6 | 38 | — | 10 | 34 | — | 44 | — | — |
| Kentucky | 63 | 14 | 48 | — | 10 | 52 | — | 15 | 47 | — | 55 | 8 | — |
| Louisiana | 69 | 24 | 32 | — | 30 | 39 | — | 44 | 22 | — | 44 | 22 | — |
| Maine | 27 | 7 | 16 | — | 3 | 23 | — | 10 | 16 | — | 23 | 1 | — |
| Maryland | 74 | 20 | 51 | 3 | 20 | 54 | — | 18 | 56 | — | 51 | 19 | 4 |
| Massachusetts | 116 | 89 | 24 | — | 69 | 43 | 1 | 82 | 31 | 1 | 112 | — | — |
| Michigan | 155 | 43 | 105 | 7 | 32 | 118 | 5 | 37 | 111 | 7 | 137 | — | 18 |
| Minnesota | 86 | 37 | 41 | 8 | 30 | 48 | 8 | 25 | 57 | 4 | 73 | 2 | 11 |
| Mississippi | 43 | 15 | 26 | 2 | 16 | 26 | 1 | 13 | 29 | 1 | 33 | 8 | 2 |
| Missouri | 86 | 20 | 62 | 4 | 22 | 62 | 2 | 24 | 61 | 1 | 70 | — | 16 |
| Montana | 25 | 8 | 15 | 2 | 4 | 21 | — | 5 | 20 | — | 25 | — | — |
| Nebraska | 30 | 2 | 25 | 3 | 2 | 25 | 3 | 10 | 17 | 3 | 24 | — | 6 |
| Nevada | 20 | 6 | 14 | — | 3 | 17 | — | 5 | 15 | — | 19 | — | — |
| New Hampshire | 22 | 10 | 12 | — | 5 | 17 | — | 1 | 21 | — | 22 | — | — |
| New Jersey | 122 | 9 | 113 | — | 9 | 113 | — | 7 | 115 | — | 116 | 6 | — |
| New Mexico | 28 | 7 | 19 | 2 | 2 | 26 | — | 3 | 25 | — | 27 | 1 | — |
| New York | 285 | 134 | 140 | — | 131 | 139 | 7 | 125 | 146 | 3 | 196 | 57 | — |
| North Carolina | 88 | 28 | 56 | — | 19 | 66 | — | 32 | 55 | — | 73 | 3 | — |
| North Dakota | 18 | 13 | 5 | — | 8 | 10 | — | 8 | 10 | — | 18 | — | — |
| Ohio | 175 | 71 | 103 | — | 47 | 122 | 6 | 40 | 133 | 2 | 173 | — | 2 |
| Oklahoma | 53 | 16 | 35 | 2 | 3 | 47 | 3 | 3 | 49 | 1 | 49 | 3 | 1 |
| Oregon | 50 | 32 | 13 | 5 | 26 | 21 | 3 | 24 | 24 | 2 | 49 | — | 1 |
| Pennsylvania | 195 | 42 | 153 | — | 39 | 156 | — | 53 | 142 | — | 195 | — | — |
| Puerto Rico | 53 | — | 53 | — | — | 53 | — | — | 53 | — | 10 | 43 | — |
| Rhode Island | 27 | 11 | 15 | 1 | 11 | 15 | 1 | 8 | 18 | 1 | 24 | — | 2 |
| South Carolina | 48 | 21 | 23 | 4 | 23 | 19 | 6 | 21 | 25 | 2 | 21 | 19 | 8 |
| South Dakota | 19 | 7 | 12 | — | 7 | 12 | — | 7 | 12 | — | — | 6 | — |
| Tennessee | 76 | 31 | 41 | 4 | 29 | 41 | 6 | 34 | 39 | 3 | 72 | 1 | 3 |
| Texas | 200 | 53 | 137 | 10 | 47 | 141 | 12 | 39 | 150 | 11 | 152 | 38 | 10 |
| Utah | 27 | 17 | 10 | — | 11 | 15 | 1 | 13 | 14 | — | 19 | 7 | 1 |
| Vermont | 17 | 11 | 4 | — | 10 | 4 | — | 10 | 4 | — | 12 | 3 | — |
| Virginia | 78 | 29 | 48 | — | 29 | 48 | — | 33 | 43 | — | 50 | 23 | 4 |
| Washington | 70 | 49 | 18 | — | 29 | 39 | 1 | 35 | 35 | — | 67 | — | — |
| West Virginia | 44 | 12 | 27 | 5 | 12 | 29 | 3 | 17 | 24 | 3 | — | — | — |
| Wisconsin | 89 | 28 | 45 | 16 | 26 | 57 | 6 | 31 | 54 | 4 | 83 | 6 | — |
| Wyoming | 15 | 2 | 12 | — | 2 | 12 | — | 13 | 1 | — | 13 | 1 | — |
| Latin America | 5 | — | 5 | — | .5 | 4.5 | — | — | 5 | — | 5 | — | — |
| Democrats Abroad | 5 | 1.5 | 3.5 | — | 1.5 | 3.5 | — | — | 5 | — | 5 | — | — |
| Virgin Islands | 6 | 1.2 | 4.8 | — | 2.6 | 2.6 | .6 | 1.2 | 4.8 | — | 4.8 | 1.2 | — |
| American Samoa | 6 | — | 6 | — | — | 6 | — | — | 6 | — | 6 | — | — |
| Guam | 7 | — | 7 | — | — | 7 | — | 7 | — | — | 7 | — | — |
| **Total** | 3933 | 1405.7 | 2216.3 | 112 | 1127.6 | 2591.6 | 99.6 | 1253.2 | 2500.8 | 58 | 3271.8 | 351.2 | 118 |

# 1984 Democratic

*(Narrative, p. 153)*

| Delegation | Total Votes | First Pres. Ballot[1] | | |
|---|---|---|---|---|
| | | Mondale | Hart | Jackson |
| Alabama | 62 | 39 | 13 | 9 |
| Alaska | 14 | 9 | 4 | 1 |
| Arizona | 40 | 20 | 16 | 2 |
| Arkansas | 42 | 26 | 9 | 7 |
| California | 345 | 95 | 190 | 33 |
| Colorado | 51 | 1 | 42 | 1 |
| Connecticut | 60 | 23 | 36 | 1 |
| Delaware | 18 | 13 | 5 | 0 |
| D.C. | 19 | 5 | — | 14 |
| Florida | 143 | 82 | 55 | 3 |
| Georgia | 84 | 40 | 24 | 20 |
| Hawaii | 27 | 27 | — | 0 |
| Idaho | 22 | 10 | 12 | 0 |
| Illinois | 194 | 114 | 41 | 39 |
| Indiana | 88 | 42 | 38 | 8 |
| Iowa | 58 | 37 | 18 | 2 |
| Kansas | 44 | 25 | 16 | 3 |
| Kentucky | 63 | 51 | 5 | 7 |
| Louisiana | 69 | 26 | 19 | 24 |
| Maine | 27 | 13 | 13 | 0 |
| Maryland | 74 | 54 | 3 | 17 |
| Massachusetts | 116 | 59 | 49 | 5 |
| Michigan | 155 | 96 | 49 | 10 |
| Minnesota | 86 | 63 | 3 | 4 |
| Mississippi | 43 | 26 | 4 | 13 |
| Missouri | 86 | 55 | 14 | 16 |
| Montana | 25 | 11 | 13 | 1 |
| Nebraska | 30 | 12 | 17 | 1 |
| Nevada | 20 | 9 | 10 | 1 |
| New Hampshire | 22 | 12 | 10 | 0 |
| New Jersey | 122 | 115 | — | 7 |
| New Mexico | 28 | 13 | 13 | 2 |
| New York | 285 | 156 | 75 | 52 |
| North Carolina | 88 | 53 | 19 | 16 |
| North Dakota | 18 | 10 | 5 | 1 |
| Ohio | 175 | 84 | 80 | 11 |
| Oklahoma | 53 | 24 | 26 | 3 |
| Oregon | 50 | 16 | 31 | 2 |
| Pennsylvania | 195 | 177 | — | 18 |
| Puerto Rico | 53 | 53 | — | 0 |
| Rhode Island | 27 | 14 | 12 | 0 |
| South Carolina | 48 | 16 | 13 | 19 |
| South Dakota | 19 | 9 | 10 | 0 |
| Tennessee | 76 | 39 | 20 | 17 |
| Texas | 200 | 119 | 40 | 36 |
| Utah | 27 | 8 | 19 | 0 |
| Vermont | 17 | 5 | 8 | 3 |
| Virginia | 78 | 34 | 18 | 25 |
| Washington | 70 | 31 | 36 | 3 |
| West Virginia | 44 | 30 | 14 | 0 |
| Wisconsin | 89 | 58 | 25 | 6 |
| Wyoming | 15 | 7 | 7 | 0 |
| Latin America | 5 | 5 | — | 0 |
| Democrats Abroad | 5 | 3 | 1.5 | 0.5 |
| Virgin Islands | 6 | 4 | — | 2 |
| American Samoa | 6 | 6 | — | 0 |
| Guam | 7 | 7 | — | 0 |
| **Total** | **3933** | **2191** | **1200.5** | **465.5** |

1. *Other candidates: Thomas F. Eagleton, 18 (16 in Minnesota, 2 in North Dakota); George McGovern, 4 (3 in Massachusetts, 1 in Iowa); John Glenn, 2 (Texas); Joseph R. Biden Jr., 1 (Maine); Martha Kirkland, 1 (Alabama); not voting, 40 (27 in California, 7 in Connecticut, 2 in Arizona, 2 in Florida, 1 in Vermont, 1 in Wyoming); absent, 10.*

# 1984 Republican

*(Narrative, p. 158)*

| Delegation | Total Votes | First Pres. Ballot[1] Reagan |
|---|---|---|
| Alabama | 38 | 38 |
| Alaska | 18 | 18 |
| Arizona | 32 | 32 |
| Arkansas | 29 | 29 |
| California | 176 | 176 |
| Colorado | 35 | 35 |
| Connecticut | 35 | 35 |
| Delaware | 19 | 19 |
| District of Columbia | 14 | 14 |
| Florida | 82 | 82 |
| Georgia | 37 | 37 |
| Guam | 4 | 4 |
| Hawaii | 14 | 14 |
| Idaho | 21 | 21 |
| Illinois | 93 | 92 |
| Indiana | 52 | 52 |
| Iowa | 37 | 37 |
| Kansas | 32 | 32 |
| Kentucky | 37 | 37 |
| Louisiana | 41 | 41 |
| Maine | 20 | 20 |
| Maryland | 31 | 31 |
| Massachusetts | 52 | 52 |
| Michigan | 77 | 77 |
| Minnesota | 32 | 32 |
| Mississippi | 30 | 30 |
| Missouri | 47 | 47 |
| Montana | 20 | 20 |
| Nebraska | 24 | 24 |
| Nevada | 22 | 22 |
| New Hampshire | 22 | 22 |
| New Jersey | 64 | 64 |
| New Mexico | 24 | 24 |
| New York | 136 | 136 |
| North Carolina | 53 | 53 |
| North Dakota | 18 | 18 |
| Ohio | 89 | 89 |
| Oklahoma | 35 | 35 |
| Oregon | 32 | 32 |
| Pennsylvania | 98 | 97 |
| Puerto Rico | 14 | 14 |
| Rhode Island | 14 | 14 |
| South Carolina | 35 | 35 |
| South Dakota | 19 | 19 |
| Tennessee | 46 | 46 |
| Texas | 109 | 109 |
| Utah | 26 | 26 |
| Vermont | 19 | 19 |
| Virginia | 50 | 50 |
| Virgin Islands | 4 | 4 |
| Washington | 44 | 44 |
| West Virginia | 19 | 19 |
| Wisconsin | 46 | 46 |
| Wyoming | 18 | 18 |
| **Total** | 2235 | 2233 |

1. Not voting, 2.

# 1988 Democratic

*(Narrative, p. 165)*

| Delegation | Total Votes | Fair Tax[1] | | No First Use of Nuclear Weapons[2] | | First Pres. Ballot[3] | |
|---|---|---|---|---|---|---|---|
| | | Yea | Nay | Yea | Nay | Dukakis | Jackson |
| Alabama | 65 | 14 | 35 | 19 | 38 | 37 | 28 |
| Alaska | 17 | 5 | 7 | 8 | 8 | 9 | 7 |
| Arizona | 43 | 15 | 21 | 15 | 25 | 28 | 14 |
| Arkansas | 48 | 11 | 27 | 9 | 25 | 31 | 11 |
| California | 363 | 104 | 240 | 119.09 | 192.63 | 235 | 122 |
| Colorado | 55 | 20 | 31 | 20 | 32 | 37 | 18 |
| Connecticut | 63 | 16 | 42 | 21 | 39 | 47 | 16 |
| Delaware | 19 | 8 | 11 | 8 | 11 | 9 | 7 |
| Florida | 154 | 33 | 89 | 33 | 100 | 116 | 35 |
| Georgia | 94 | 30 | 43 | 36 | 43 | 50 | 42 |
| Hawaii | 28 | 8 | 19 | 8 | 19 | 19 | 8 |
| Idaho | 24 | 3 | 18 | 3 | 18 | 20 | 3 |
| Illinois | 200 | 28 | 75 | 40 | 62 | 138 | 57 |
| Indiana | 89 | 18 | 68 | 19 | 66 | 69.50 | 18 |
| Iowa | 61 | 11 | 48 | 21 | 38 | 49 | 12 |
| Kansas | 45 | 12 | 29.50 | 14.50 | 28.50 | 30 | 15 |
| Kentucky | 65 | 6 | 43 | 6 | 46 | 59 | 6 |
| Louisiana | 76 | 23 | 11 | 26 | 13 | 41 | 33 |
| Maine | 29 | 11 | 15 | 11 | 14 | 17 | 12 |
| Maryland | 84 | 21 | 58 | 21 | 58 | 59 | 25 |
| Massachusetts | 119 | 20 | 79 | 23 | 86 | 99 | 19 |
| Michigan | 162 | 78 | 77 | 78 | 77 | 80 | 80 |
| Minnesota | 91 | 36 | 45 | 42 | 46 | 57 | 29 |
| Mississippi | 47 | 24 | 15 | 27 | 16 | 19 | 26 |
| Missouri | 88 | 31 | 49 | 33 | 50 | 50 | 37 |
| Montana | 28 | 5 | 21 | 7 | 19 | 22 | 5 |
| Nebraska | 30 | 7 | 23 | 7 | 23 | 22 | 8 |
| Nevada | 23 | 5 | 15 | 6 | 15 | 16 | 5 |
| New Hampshire | 22 | 0 | 22 | 1 | 21 | 22 | 0 |
| New Jersey | 126 | 19 | 39 | 19 | 64 | 107 | 19 |
| New Mexico | 30 | 7 | 19 | 7 | 20 | 22 | 8 |
| New York | 292 | 90 | 181 | 108 | 173 | 194 | 97 |
| North Carolina | 95 | 36 | 51 | 37 | 51 | 58 | 35 |
| North Dakota | 22 | 46 | 131 | 5 | 11 | 17 | 3 |
| Ohio | 183 | 46 | 131 | 48 | 132 | 136 | 46 |
| Oklahoma | 56 | 4 | 44 | 4 | 46 | 52 | 4 |
| Oregon | 54 | 18 | 31 | 18 | 34 | 35 | 18 |
| Pennsylvania | 202 | 22 | 177 | 22 | 179 | 179 | 23 |
| Rhode Island | 28 | 3 | 15 | 4 | 16 | 24 | 3 |
| South Carolina | 53 | 29 | 19 | 30 | 23 | 22 | 31 |
| South Dakota | 20 | 2 | 16 | 2 | 17 | 19 | 1 |
| Tennessee | 84 | 12 | 54 | 15 | 57 | 63 | 20 |
| Texas | 211 | 72 | 123 | 72 | 121 | 135 | 71 |
| Utah | 28 | 3 | 18 | 5 | 20 | 25 | 3 |
| Vermont | 20 | 10 | 9 | 11 | 9 | 9 | 9 |
| Virginia | 86 | 37 | 46 | 41 | 44 | 42 | 42 |
| Washington | 77 | 27 | 46 | 29 | 42 | 50 | 27 |
| West Virginia | 47 | 0 | 44 | 1 | 43 | 47 | 0 |
| Wisconsin | 91 | 24 | 59 | 25 | 59 | 65 | 25 |
| Wyoming | 18 | 4 | 12 | 6 | 10 | 14 | 4 |
| District of Columbia | 25 | 13 | 6 | 16 | 8 | 7 | 18 |
| Puerto Rico | 57 | 3 | 53 | 8 | 48 | 48.50 | 8 |
| Virgin Islands | 5 | 5 | 0 | 5 | 0 | 0 | 5 |
| American Samoa | 6 | 0 | 6 | 0 | 6 | 6 | 0 |
| Guam | 4 | 0 | 4 | 0 | 4 | 4 | 0 |
| Democrats Abroad | 9 | 0.50 | 8.50 | 1 | 8 | 8.25 | 0.50 |
| Total | 4,162 | 1,091.50 | 2,499.00 | 1,220.59 | 2,474.13 | 2,876.25 | 1,218.50 |

1. Not voting, 90.
2. Not voting, 67.
3. Other candidates: Lloyd Bentsen, 1 (Alaska); Joseph R. Biden Jr., 2 (Delaware); Richard A. Gephardt, 2 (1 in Louisiana, 1 in Texas); Richard H. Stallings, 3 (Minnesota); Gary Hart, 1 (Vermont), absent, 44.25.

# 1988 Republican

*(Narrative, p. 170)*

| Delegation | Total Votes | First Pres. Ballot Bush |
|---|---|---|
| Alabama | 38 | 38 |
| Alaska | 19 | 19 |
| Arizona | 33 | 33 |
| Arkansas | 27 | 27 |
| California | 175 | 175 |
| Colorado | 36 | 36 |
| Connecticut | 35 | 35 |
| Delaware | 17 | 17 |
| Florida | 82 | 82 |
| Georgia | 48 | 48 |
| Hawaii | 20 | 20 |
| Idaho | 22 | 22 |
| Illinois | 92 | 92 |
| Indiana | 51 | 51 |
| Iowa | 37 | 37 |
| Kansas | 34 | 34 |
| Kentucky | 38 | 38 |
| Louisiana | 41 | 41 |
| Maine | 22 | 22 |
| Maryland | 41 | 41 |
| Massachusetts | 52 | 52 |
| Michigan | 77 | 77 |
| Minnesota | 31 | 31 |
| Mississippi | 31 | 31 |
| Missouri | 47 | 47 |
| Montana | 20 | 20 |
| Nebraska | 25 | 25 |
| Nevada | 20 | 20 |
| New Hampshire | 23 | 23 |
| New Jersey | 64 | 64 |
| New Mexico | 26 | 26 |
| New York | 136 | 136 |
| North Carolina | 54 | 54 |
| North Dakota | 16 | 16 |
| Ohio | 88 | 88 |
| Oklahoma | 36 | 36 |
| Oregon | 32 | 32 |
| Pennsylvania | 96 | 96 |
| Rhode Island | 21 | 21 |
| South Carolina | 37 | 37 |
| South Dakota | 18 | 18 |
| Tennessee | 45 | 45 |
| Texas | 111 | 111 |
| Utah | 26 | 26 |
| Vermont | 17 | 17 |
| Virginia | 50 | 50 |
| Washington | 41 | 41 |
| West Virginia | 28 | 28 |
| Wisconsin | 47 | 47 |
| Wyoming | 18 | 18 |
| District of Columbia | 14 | 14 |
| Puerto Rico | 14 | 14 |
| Virgin Islands | 4 | 4 |
| Guam | 4 | 4 |
| Total | 2,277 | 2,277 |

# 1992 Democratic

*(Narrative, p. 178)*

| Delegation | Total Votes | Tax Fairness [1] | | First Pres. Ballot [2] | | |
|---|---|---|---|---|---|---|
| | | Yes | Nay | Clinton | Brown | Tsongas |
| Alabama | 67 | 0 | 67 | 67 | 0 | 0 |
| Alaska | 18 | 0 | 16 | 18 | 0 | 0 |
| Arizona | 49 | 29 | 15 | 23 | 12 | 14 |
| Arkansas | 48 | 0 | 48 | 48 | 0 | 0 |
| California | 406 | 96 | 176 | 211 | 160 | 0 |
| Colorado | 58 | 31 | 23 | 26 | 19 | 13 |
| Connecticut | 66 | 23 | 30 | 45 | 21 | 0 |
| Delaware | 21 | 8 | 8 | 17 | 3 | 1 |
| Florida | 167 | 50 | 71 | 141 | 3 | 15 |
| Georgia | 96 | 14 | 50 | 96 | 0 | 0 |
| Hawaii | 28 | 5 | 17 | 24 | 2 | 0 |
| Idaho | 26 | 5 | 17 | 22 | 0 | 1 |
| Illinois | 195 | 51 | 76 | 155 | 9 | 29 |
| Indiana | 93 | 21 | 68 | 73 | 20 | 0 |
| Iowa | 59 | 7 | 43 | 55 | 2 | 0 |
| Kansas | 44 | 5 | 38 | 43 | 0 | 0 |
| Kentucky | 64 | 3 | 53 | 63 | 0 | 0 |
| Louisiana | 75 | 0 | 75 | 75 | 0 | 0 |
| Maine | 31 | 18 | 2 | 14 | 13 | 4 |
| Maryland | 85 | 27 | 23 | 83 | 0 | 2 |
| Massachusetts | 119 | 97 | 0 | 109 | 6 | 1 |
| Michigan | 159 | 43 | 82 | 120 | 35 | 0 |
| Minnesota | 92 | 23 | 43 | 61 | 8 | 2 |
| Mississippi | 46 | 0 | 46 | 46 | 0 | 0 |
| Missouri | 92 | 6 | 46 | 91 | 1 | 0 |
| Montana | 24 | 0 | 19 | 21 | 2 | 0 |
| Nebraska | 33 | 10 | 14 | 24 | 9 | 0 |
| Nevada | 27 | 0 | 25 | 23 | 4 | 0 |
| New Hampshire | 24 | 10 | 10 | 17 | 0 | 7 |
| New Jersey | 126 | 12 | 76 | 102 | 24 | 0 |
| New Mexico | 34 | 3 | 27 | 30 | 3 | 0 |
| New York | 290 | 116 | 109 | 155 | 67 | 64 |
| North Carolina | 99 | 0 | 64 | 95 | 1 | 0 |
| North Dakota | 22 | 3 | 14 | 18 | 0 | 0 |
| Ohio | 178 | 37 | 141 | 144 | 34 | 0 |
| Oklahoma | 58 | 0 | 53 | 56 | 2 | 0 |
| Oregon | 57 | 14 | 38 | 38 | 19 | 0 |
| Pennsylvania | 194 | 21 | 78 | 139 | 43 | 4 |
| Rhode Island | 29 | 7 | 9 | 27 | 2 | 0 |
| South Carolina | 54 | 7 | 40 | 54 | 0 | 0 |
| South Dakota | 21 | 1 | 16 | 21 | 0 | 0 |
| Tennessee | 85 | 6 | 38 | 85 | 0 | 0 |
| Texas | 232 | 33 | 112 | 204 | 4 | 20 |
| Utah | 29 | 25 | 0 | 20 | 9 | 0 |
| Vermont | 21 | 11 | 6 | 14 | 7 | 0 |
| Virginia | 97 | 11 | 43 | 94 | 3 | 0 |
| Washington | 84 | 30 | 29 | 49 | 18 | 14 |
| West Virginia | 41 | 0 | 13 | 41 | 0 | 0 |
| Wisconsin | 94 | 29 | 61 | 46 | 30 | 18 |
| Wyoming | 19 | 5 | 8 | 18 | 1 | 0 |
| District of Columbia | 31 | 0 | 30 | 31 | 0 | 0 |
| Puerto Rico | 58 | 0 | 58 | 57 | 0 | 0 |
| Virgin Islands | 5 | 0 | 5 | 5 | 0 | 0 |
| American Samoa | 5 | 0 | 5 | 5 | 0 | 0 |
| Guam | 4 | 0 | 4 | 4 | 0 | 0 |
| Democrats Abroad | 9 | 0 | 8.75 | 9 | 0 | 0 |
| Total | 4,288 | 953.00 | 2,286.75 | 3,372 | 596 | 209 |

1. Not voting, 177.
2. Other candidates: Larry Agran, 3 (1 in Idaho, 2 in Minnesota); Robert P. Casey, 10 (Minnesota); Patricia Schroeder, 8 (Colorado); Albert Gore Jr., 1 (Pennsylvania); Joseph Simonetti, 1 (Pennsylvania); Others, 2 (1 in New Mexico, 1 in North Dakota). Not voting, 86.

# 1992 Republican

(Narrative, p. 184)

| Delegation | Total Votes | First Pres. Ballot [1] | |
| --- | --- | --- | --- |
| | | Bush | Buchanan |
| Alabama | 38 | 38 | 0 |
| Alaska | 19 | 19 | 0 |
| Arizona | 37 | 37 | 0 |
| Arkansas | 27 | 27 | 0 |
| California | 201 | 201 | 0 |
| Colorado | 37 | 31 | 5 |
| Connecticut | 35 | 35 | 0 |
| Delaware | 19 | 19 | 0 |
| Florida | 97 | 97 | 0 |
| Georgia | 52 | 52 | 0 |
| Hawaii | 14 | 14 | 0 |
| Idaho | 22 | 22 | 0 |
| Illinois | 85 | 85 | 0 |
| Indiana | 51 | 51 | 0 |
| Iowa | 23 | 23 | 0 |
| Kansas | 30 | 30 | 0 |
| Kentucky | 35 | 35 | 0 |
| Louisiana | 38 | 38 | 0 |
| Maine | 22 | 22 | 0 |
| Maryland | 42 | 42 | 0 |
| Massachusetts | 38 | 35 | 1 |
| Michigan | 72 | 72 | 0 |
| Minnesota | 32 | 32 | 0 |
| Mississippi | 34 | 34 | 0 |
| Missouri | 47 | 47 | 0 |
| Montana | 20 | 20 | 0 |
| Nebraska | 24 | 24 | 0 |
| Nevada | 21 | 21 | 0 |
| New Hampshire [2] | 23 | — | 0 |
| New Jersey | 60 | 60 | 0 |
| New Mexico | 25 | 25 | 0 |
| New York | 100 | 100 | 0 |
| North Carolina | 57 | 57 | 0 |
| North Dakota | 17 | 17 | 0 |
| Ohio | 83 | 83 | 0 |
| Oklahoma | 34 | 34 | 0 |
| Oregon | 23 | 23 | 0 |
| Pennsylvania | 91 | 90 | 1 |
| Rhode Island | 15 | 15 | 0 |
| South Carolina | 36 | 36 | 0 |
| South Dakota | 19 | 19 | 0 |
| Tennessee | 45 | 34 | 11 |
| Texas | 121 | 121 | 0 |
| Utah | 27 | 27 | 0 |
| Vermont | 19 | 19 | 0 |
| Virginia | 55 | 55 | 0 |
| Washington | 35 | 35 | 0 |
| West Virginia | 18 | 18 | 0 |
| Wisconsin | 35 | 35 | 0 |
| Wyoming | 20 | 20 | 0 |
| District of Columbia | 14 | 14 | 0 |
| Puerto Rico | 14 | 14 | 0 |
| Virgin Islands | 4 | 4 | 0 |
| American Samoa | 4 | 4 | 0 |
| Guam | 4 | 4 | 0 |
| Total | 2,210 | 2,166 | 18 |

1. Other candidates: Howard Phillips, 2 (1 in Colorado; 1 in Massachusetts), Alan Keyes, 1 (Massachusetts).
2. Never voted.

# Profiles of American
# Political Parties

# American Political Parties since 1789

## Major Parties

Federalist

Democratic-Republican

National Republican

Democratic

Whig

Republican

## Third Parties

Anti-Mason

Liberty

Free Soil

American (Know-Nothing)

Constitutional Union

Southern Democrats

Prohibition

Liberal

Greenback

Socialist Labor

Populist

National Democratic

Socialist

Bull Moose Progressive

La Follette Progressive

Communist

Union

Socialist Workers

States' Rights Democratic

Henry Wallace Progressive

Workers World

George Wallace American Independent

Libertarian

People's

U.S. Labor

Citizen's

National Unity

New Alliance

Ross Perot United We Stand

1789 1792 1796 1800 1804 1808 1812 1816 1820 1824 1828 1832 1836 1840 1844 1848 1852 1856 1860 1864 1868 1872 1876 1880 1884 1888 1892 1896 1900 1904 1908 1912 1916 1920 1924 1928 1932 1936 1940 1944 1948 1952 1956 1960 1964 1968 1972 1976 1980 1984 1988 1992

# Historical Profiles
# Of American Political Parties

## American Independent Party (1968-   ) and American Party (1972-   )

Both the American Party and the American Independent Party descended from the American Independent Party that served as the vehicle for George C. Wallace's third party presidential candidacy in 1968.

Wallace, governor of Alabama (1963-67; 1971-79), burst onto the national scene in 1964 as a Democratic presidential candidate opposed to the 1964 Civil Rights Act. Entering three Northern primaries — Wisconsin, Indiana and Maryland — he surprised political observers by winning between 30 percent and 43 percent of the popular vote in the three primaries. His unexpectedly strong showing brought the term "white backlash" into the political vocabulary as a description of the racial undertone of the Wallace vote.

In 1968 Wallace broke with the Democrats and embarked on his second presidential campaign as a third party candidate under the American Independent Party label. His candidacy capitalized on the bitter reactions of millions of voters, especially whites and blue-collar workers, to the civil rights activism, urban riots, anti-war demonstrations and heavy federal spending on Johnson administration "Great Society" programs that marked the mid-1960s. With the help of his Alabama advisers and volunteer groups, Wallace was able to get his party on the ballot in all 50 states.

The former governor did not hold a convention for his party, but in October he announced his vice presidential running mate (retired Air Force General Curtis LeMay) and released a platform. In the November election the Wallace ticket received 9,906,473 votes (13.5 percent of the popular vote), carried five Southern states and won 46 electoral votes. The party's showing was the best by a third party since 1924, when Robert M. La Follette collected 16.6 percent of the vote on the Progressive Party ticket.

After his defeat in that election, Wallace returned to the Democratic Party, competing in Democratic presidential primaries in 1972 and 1976. Wallace's American Independent Party began to break into factions after the 1968 election but in 1972 united behind John G. Schmitz, a Republican U.S. representative from Southern California (1970-73), as its presidential nominee. Thomas J. Anderson, a farm magazine and syndicated news features publisher from Tennessee, was the candidate for vice president. In many states, the party shortened its name to American Party. In the November election, the Schmitz ticket won 1,099,482 votes (1.4 percent of the popular vote) but failed to win any electoral votes.

In December 1972 a bitter fight occurred for the chairmanship of the American Independent Party between Anderson and William K. Shearer, the California chairman of the party. Anderson defeated Shearer, retaining control of the party but renaming it the American Party. Shearer, over the following four years, expanded his California-based group into a new national party. He had kept the name American Independent Party in California and made that the name of the new nationwide group.

Thus, by 1976, there were two distinct entities — the American Party headed by Anderson and the American Independent Party headed by Shearer.

The 1976 American Party convention was held in Salt Lake City, Utah, from June 17 to 20. Anderson was nominated for president and Rufus Shackleford of Florida for vice president.

The party's nomination of Anderson followed its failure to enlist a prominent conservative to lead the ticket. Both Gov. Meldrim Thomson Jr. of New Hampshire and Sen. Jesse Helms of North Carolina were approached, but both decided to remain in the Republican Party. With well-known conservatives declining the party's overtures, the convention turned to Anderson. He easily won the nomination on the first ballot by defeating six party workers.

Anderson's campaign stressed the "permanent principles" of the party, augmented by the 1976 platform. These principles included opposition to foreign aid, U.S. withdrawal from the United Nations and an end to trade with or recognition of communist nations. The platform included planks opposing abortion, gun control, the Equal Rights Amendment and government-sponsored health care and welfare programs. In general, the party favored limits on federal power and was against budget deficits except in wartime.

The American Party was on the ballot in 18 states, including eight states where the American Independent Party was also. In seven of those eight states, Anderson ran ahead of the American Independent Party ticket. Anderson's strength was spread fairly evenly across the country. His best showings were in Utah (2.5 percent of the vote) and Montana (1.8 percent). He received more than 0.5 percent of the vote in Virginia (1.0), Mississippi (0.9), Minnesota (0.7) and Kentucky (0.7). Anderson's total of 160,773 popular votes (0.2 percent) placed him almost 10,000 votes behind the American Independent Party candidate nationally.

## Sources

Congressional Quarterly. *Congressional Quarterly Weekly Report.* Washington, D.C.: Congressional Quarterly.

*Dictionary of American History.* 8 vols. New York: Charles Scribner's Sons, 1976.

*Encyclopaedia Britannica.* Chicago: Encyclopaedia Britannica, 1980.

*Encyclopedia Americana.* 30 vols. Danbury, Conn.: Grolier Education, 1982.

Schlesinger, Arthur M. Jr. *History of U.S. Political Parties.* 1973. Reprint. New York: Chelsea House, 1981.

Stimpson, George W. *A Book About American Politics.* New York: Harper, 1952.

The American Independent Party convention met in Chicago, Aug. 24-27, 1976, and chose former Georgia governor Lester Maddox (1967-71), a Democrat, as its presidential nominee and former Madison, Wis., mayor William Dyke, a Republican, as its vice presidential candidate. Maddox won a first-ballot nomination over Dallas columnist Robert Morris and former representative John R. Rarick, a Democrat of Louisiana (1967-75).

At the convention, a group of nationally prominent conservatives made a bid to take over the party and use it as a vehicle to build a new conservative coalition. Richard Viguerie, a fund raiser for Wallace and a nationally known direct mail expert, was the leader of the group. He was joined at the convention by two leading conservatives — William Rusher, publisher of the *National Review,* and Howard Phillips, the former head of the Office of Economic Opportunity (1973) and leader of the Conservative Caucus, an activist conservative group. Viguerie, Phillips and Rusher all argued that the American Independent Party should be overhauled, changed from a fringe group to a philosophical home for believers in free enterprise and traditional moral values. They also hoped they could attract Sen. Helms, Gov. Thomson or Rep. Philip M. Crane, R-Ill. When none of these men agreed to run on the American Independent Party ticket, Viguerie and his allies found themselves unable to promote Morris, a lesser-known substitute, successfully.

Many American Independent Party members favored Maddox because they saw him as a colorful personality, one capable of drawing media attention and perhaps of picking up the 5 percent of the national vote needed to qualify the party for federal funding. Maddox never came close to that goal, however, achieving only 0.2 percent of the national vote (170,531). It was 51,098 votes in California, where American Party nominee Anderson was not on the ballot, that enabled Maddox to run slightly ahead of Anderson nationally.

Despite the power struggle between Anderson and Shearer, there was little difference between their two party platforms. Like the American Party, the American Independent Party opposed abortion, gun control, forced busing, foreign aid and membership in the United Nations.

By 1980 neither party was much of a force in American politics. Both retained the same basic platforms, but each was on the ballot in only a handful of states. The American Independent Party's nominee, former Democratic representative Rarick, ran in only eight states. Economist Percy L. Greaves Jr., the American Party candidate, was listed in just seven.

The American Independent Party did not field candidates in 1984, while the American Party placed Delmar Dennis, a book publisher from Pigeon Forge, Tenn., on the ballot in six states.

Dennis also ran under the American Party banner in 1988 and, with his running mate, Earl Jeppson, received 3,475 votes. The American Independent Party did better with their candidates, presidential nominee James C. Griffin and vice presidential nominee Charles J. Morsa, receiving 27,818 votes.

By 1992 fortunes for both parties had dwindled. American Party presidential nominee Robert J. Smith and running mate Doris Feimer were only on the ballot in Utah, where they received 292 votes. The American Independent Party did not appear on any presidential ballots.

## American Party-'Know-Nothings' (1856)

The American Party politicized the nativist, anti-immigrant movement in the mid-1850s, a peak period of European immigration to the United States in the pre-Civil War years. In the decade before the rise of a formal party, the movement took the form of local, secret organizations whose members were sworn to secrecy about their elaborate rituals. To questions about their affiliation, they pleaded ignorance. Hence, the party's popular name: the Know-Nothings.

Many of the millions of immigrants in the mid-19th century were Catholic, and the Know-Nothings were hostile to Catholics. They advocated nominating only native American Protestants for political office and requiring a 21-year waiting period before naturalization.

In addition to the great waves of immigrants, the party's meteoric rise was spurred by the increasing polarization of the Democrats and Whigs over the volatile slavery issue. The Know-Nothings benefited from the political situation and attracted members from both of the older parties. In the party's peak years 1854 and 1855, the Know-Nothings elected governors in California, Connecticut, Delaware, Kentucky, Massachusetts, New Hampshire and Rhode Island, and elected five senators and 43 members of the House.

But as a national party the Know-Nothings, like the Democrats and Whigs, were split eventually by the slavery issue. When a party convention in June 1855 adopted a pro-Southern position on slavery, anti-slavery elements bolted, dividing the party and setting the stage for its downfall.

The Know-Nothings held their first and only national nominating convention in February 1856 and selected as their candidate the former Whig, President Millard Fillmore (1850-53). The anti-slavery wing of the party convened separately and endorsed the Republican nominee, John C. Fremont. Fillmore finished third in the three-way race, receiving 21.5 percent of the popular vote and carrying only one state, Maryland.

Within a year, the bulk of the Northern Know-Nothings had joined the Republican Party. By the end of the decade, the party existed only in the Border states, where it formed the basis for the unsuccessful, anti-war Constitutional Union Party. (*Constitutional Union Party,* p. 261)

## Anti-Federalists (1789-96)

Never a formal party, the Anti-Federalists were a loosely organized group opposed to ratification of the Constitution. With the adoption of the Constitution in 1788, the Anti-Federalists served as the opposition to the Federalists in the early years of Congress.

Anti-Federalists were primarily rural, agrarian interests from inland regions, who favored individual freedom and states' rights, which they felt would be jeopardized by the new Constitution. After ratification, the efforts of the Anti-Federalists led to adoption of the first 10 amendments, the Bill of Rights, which spelled out the major limitations of federal power.

As the opposition faction in Congress during the formative years of the Republic, the Anti-Federalists basically held to a strict interpretation of the Constitution, particularly in regard to the various economic proposals of Treasury Secretary Alexander Hamilton to centralize more power in the federal government.

Although never the majority faction in Congress, the Anti-Federalists were a forerunner of Jefferson's Democratic-Republican Party, which came into existence in the 1790s and dominated American politics for the first quarter of the 19th century. (*Democratic-Republican Party, p. 263*)

## Anti-Masonic Party (1832-36)

Born in the late 1820s in upstate New York, the Anti-Masonic Party focused the strong, anti-elitist mood of the period on a conspicuous symbol of privilege, the Masons. The Masons were a secret fraternal organization with membership drawn largely from the upper class. Conversely, the appeal of the Anti-Masonic movement was to the common man — poor farmers and laborers especially — who resented the secrecy and privilege of the Masons.

The spark that created the party came in 1826, when William Morgan, a dissident Mason from Batavia, N.Y., allegedly on the verge of exposing the inner workings of the order, mysteriously disappeared and never was seen again. Refusal of Masonic leaders to cooperate in the inconclusive investigation of Morgan's disappearance led to suspicions that Masons had kidnapped and murdered him and were suppressing the inquiry.

From 1828 through 1831, the new Anti-Masonic Party spread through New England and the Middle Atlantic states, in many places establishing itself as the primary opposition to the Democrats. In addition to its appeal to the working classes, particularly in Northern rural areas, and its opposition to Masonry, the Anti-Masons displayed a fervor against immorality, as seen not only in secret societies but also in slavery, intemperance and urban life.

In September 1831 the party held the first national nominating convention in American history. One hundred and sixteen delegates from 13 states gathered in Baltimore, Maryland, and nominated former attorney general William Wirt of Maryland for the presidency. While Wirt received only 100,715 votes (7.8 percent of the popular vote) and carried just one state, Vermont, the Anti-Masons did reasonably well at other levels, winning two governorships and 53 House seats.

But the decline of Masonry, especially in New York, where the number of lodges dropped from 507 in 1826 to 48 six years later, robbed the Anti-Masons of an emotional issue and hastened their decline. The 1832 election was the high point for the Anti-Masons as a national party. In the 1836 campaign the party endorsed Whig candidate William Henry Harrison. Subsequently, the bulk of the Anti-Masonic constituency moved into the Whig Party.

## Citizens Party (1979-84)

Organized in 1979 as a coalition of dissident liberals and populists, the first Citizens Party convention chose author and environmental scientist Barry Commoner as its 1980 presidential candidate and La Donna Harris, wife of former Democratic senator Fred R. Harris of Oklahoma, as his running mate. The Citizens Party ticket ran on the central theme that major decisions in America were made to benefit corporations and not the average citizen. The party proposed public control of energy industries and multinational corporations, a halt to the use of nuclear power, a sharp cut in military spending and price controls on food, fuel, housing and health care.

Commoner ran in all of the large electoral vote states except Florida and Texas. He made his biggest push in California, Illinois, Michigan, New York and Pennsylvania, where party leaders believed they could tap a "sophisticated working-class population" and appeal to political activists who had been involved in the environmental and antinuclear movements that sprang up in the late 1970s.

The Commoner/Harris ticket was on the ballot in 29 states and the District of Columbia in 1980. Party leaders asserted that it was the largest number of ballot positions attained by any third party in its first campaign. In addition to its presidential ticket, the Citizens Party also fielded 22 candidates for other offices, including two for the U.S. Senate and seven for the House.

The Citizens Party won 234,294 votes in the 1980 presidential election, or 0.3 percent of the vote.

As its 1984 presidential nominee the Citizens Party chose outspoken feminist Sonia Johnson of Virginia. Johnson first attracted national attention in 1979, when the Mormon Church excommunicated her for supporting the Equal Rights Amendment. In 1982 she staged a 37-day hunger strike in an unsuccessful effort to pressure the Illinois Legislature to approve the ERA. The Citizens Party selected party activist Richard J. Walton of Rhode Island to accompany Johnson on the ticket. Winning 72,200 votes in 1984, the ticket garnered 0.1 percent of the vote.

## Communist Party (1924- )

In 1919, shortly after the Russian Revolution, Soviet communists encouraged American left-wing groups to withdraw from the Socialist Party and to form a Communist Party in the United States. After several years of internal dissension, a new political organization named the Workers' Party of America was established in 1921 at the insistence of Moscow. The goal of the new party was revolutionary — to overthrow capitalism and to create a communist state ruled by the working classes.

William Z. Foster, a labor organizer, was the party's first presidential candidate, in 1924. National tickets were run every four years through 1940 and from 1968 through 1984, but the party's peak year at the polls was 1932, when Foster received 103,253 votes (0.3 percent of the popular vote).

The Communists have a distinctive place in American political history as the only party to have had international ties. In 1929 a party split brought the formal creation of the Communist Party of the United States, with acknowledged status as a part of the worldwide communist movement (the Communist International).

The Communist International terminated during World War II, and in 1944 the party's leader in America, Earl Browder, dissolved the party and committed the movement to operate within the two-party system. In the 1944 campaign the communists endorsed President Franklin D. Roosevelt, who repudiated their support.

However, with the breakup of the U.S.-Soviet alliance after World War II, the Communists reconstituted themselves as a political party. They supported Henry Wallace's Progressive Party candidacy in 1948, but they were limited in the Cold War period of the 1950s by restrictive federal and state legislation that virtually outlawed the party.

With the gradual easing of restrictive measures, the Communist Party resumed electoral activities in the late 1960s. In a policy statement written in 1966, the party described itself as "a revolutionary party whose aim is the fundamental transformation of society."

The party's success at the polls, however, continued to be minimal. Its presidential candidates in 1968, 1972, 1976, 1980 and 1984 each received less than one-tenth of 1 percent of the vote. The party did not appear on any presidential ballots in 1988 or 1992.

## Constitutional Union Party (1860)

The short-lived Constitutional Union Party was formed in 1859 to promote national conciliation in the face of rampant sectionalism, which included Southern threats of secession. The party appealed to conservative remnants of the American (Know-Nothing) and Whig parties, who viewed preservation of the Union as their primary goal.

The Constitutional Union Party held its first and only national convention in Baltimore in May 1860. For president the party nominated John Bell of Tennessee, a former senator and Speaker of the House of Representatives, who previously had been both a Democrat and a Whig. The convention adopted a short platform, which intentionally avoided controversial subjects, most notably the divisive slavery issue. Instead, the platform simply urged support for "the Constitution, the Union and the Laws."

In the fall election, Bell received 590,901 votes (12.6 percent of the popular vote) and won Kentucky, Tennessee and Virginia. However, the Bell ticket finished last in the four-way presidential race and, together with the sectional split in the Democratic Party, was a prominent factor in the victory of Republican Abraham Lincoln.

In the months after the 1860 election the Constitutional Union Party continued to urge national conciliation, but with the outbreak of the Civil War the party disappeared.

## Democratic Party (1832- )

There is no precise birth date for the Democratic Party. It developed as an outgrowth of Thomas Jefferson's Democratic-Republican Party, which splintered into factions in the 1820s. The faction led by Andrew Jackson took the name Democratic-Republican, but after 1830 dropped the last half of this label and became simply the Democratic Party. The new party encouraged and benefited from the increasing democratization of American politics that began in the 1820s. Andrew Jackson became a symbol of this mass democracy, and when he was elected in 1828 a period of Democratic dominance began that lasted until the Civil War.

The Democrats were a national party, with a particular appeal among workingmen, immigrants and settlers west of the Alleghenies. The success of the party in the pre-Civil War period was due in part to a national organization stronger than that of its rivals. In 1832 the Democrats were the first major party to hold a national nominating convention, and they in 1848 became the first party to establish an ongoing national committee.

Between 1828 and 1860, the party held the White House for 24 years, controlled the Senate for 26 years and controlled the House of Representatives for 24 years. Leadership in the party generally resided in Congress. The Democrats' two-thirds nominating rule, adopted at the 1832 convention and retained for a century, gave the South veto power over the choice of a national ticket. The result, not only in the pre-Civil War years but until the rule was eliminated in 1936, was the frequent selection of conservative candidates for president.

The early philosophy of the Democratic Party stressed a belief in a strict interpretation of the Constitution, states' rights and limited spending by the federal government. While party members throughout the nation accepted these basic tenets, there was no national consensus on the volatile slavery issue, which strained the party in the mid-19th century and finally divided it geographically in 1860. Two separate Democratic tickets were run in the 1860 election — one Northern, one Southern. The party division aided the election of the candidate of the new anti-slavery Republican Party, Abraham Lincoln, who received less than 40 percent of the popular vote.

During the Civil War the Northern wing of the party was factionalized, with one wing, the Copperheads, hostile to the Union war effort and favoring a negotiated peace with the Confederacy. The stance of the Copperheads, coupled with the involvement of many Southern Democrats in the Confederate government, enabled the Republicans for a generation after the Civil War to denounce the reunified Democratic Party as the "party of treason."

The Democrats were a national party after the Civil War, but they were displaced as the majority party by the Republicans. The strength of the Democrats was in the South, which voted in large majorities for Democratic candidates. Party strength outside the South was scattered, being most noticeable among urban ethnics and voters in the Border States. The period of Republican dominance lasted for nearly three-quarters of a century, 1860 to 1932. The Democrats occupied the White House for 16 of these 72 years, controlled the House of Representatives for 26 years and controlled the Senate for 10 years.

The Depression, which began in 1929, dramatically altered American politics and provided the opportunity for the Democrats to re-emerge as the majority party. The Democrats swept to victory behind Franklin D. Roosevelt in 1932 and with widespread popular acceptance of his New Deal programs a new coalition was formed, which has remained largely intact. The new majority coalition combined the bulk of the black electorate, the academic community and organized labor with the party's core strength among urban ethnic and Southern voters.

Between 1932 and 1980, the Democrats occupied the presidency 32 of 48 years and controlled both houses of Congress for 44 years. The acceptance of Roosevelt's New Deal, coupled with the abolition of the two-thirds rule for nominating candidates and the decline of Southern power, resulted in more liberal party leadership. The liberal stance of most party leaders included belief in a broad interpretation of the Constitution, increased use of federal power and government spending to combat the problems of society. This basic philosophy has been maintained by Democratic presidential candidates since 1932.

While the years since 1932 have been the longest period of Democratic control in American history, the party's unity at times has been threatened. The party includes diverse elements across the political spectrum, and its strength at the congressional level frequently has been undermined by a loose alliance of Republicans and Southern Democrats. At the national level the party has been internally divided by explosive, controversial issues — most notably in the late 1960s and early 1970s — such as the war in Vietnam.

In spite of the impact of divisive issues and inroads in the conservative sector of the party by the Republicans, particularly in presidential elections, the Roosevelt coalition continued basically intact and the Democrats remained the majority party in the 1970s. The 1980 election brought signs of a power shift, however, as the Republicans regained the presidency and won control of the Senate for the first time in 28 years. The 1982 mid-term elections swept 26 new Democrats into the House and strengthened the Democrats' control of that chamber. According to a Gallup Poll taken in spring 1983, when the nation was beginning to recover from the most serious recession since the Great Depression of the 1930s, more than twice as many people described themselves as Democrats (46 percent) than as Republicans (23 percent).

As the economy rebounded under the leadership of Republican president Ronald Reagan, the Democratic Party lost ground, according to a Gallup Poll taken in August 1984. By this time the percentage of people who identified themselves as Democrats had dropped to 42 percent, while the Republican share increased to 28 percent. In the 1984 election, Democratic presidential nominee Walter F. Mondale won 40.6 percent of the popular vote and only 13 of the 538 electoral votes. Mondale's running mate, Rep. Geraldine A. Ferraro, N.Y., was the first woman to receive a major party nomination for national office.

By late 1986 the Democratic Party rejuvenated. Congressional elections gave the Senate back to the Democrats with a 55-45 majority. Some experts speculated that the "forgotten middle class" and other groups that suffered from federal budget cuts voted Democratic in hope of finding a voice there. A Democratic Congress paired with a Republican president limited the GOP's power.

The Democrats were not able to rally enough support in 1988 to usher their presidential and vice presidential candidates — Michael S. Dukakis and Lloyd Bentsen — into the White House. The Democratic ticket received 45.6 percent of the popular vote and 111 electoral votes. In Congress, meanwhile, the Democrats held on to their majority. In the mid-term elections of 1990, they even picked up eight seats in the House and one seat in the Senate.

In 1992, the Democrats for the first time paired two Southern moderates, Bill Clinton of Arkansas and Albert Gore Jr. of Tennessee, on the presidential ticket. Widespread dissatisfaction with government and the lingering effects of the recession of 1990-91 helped the Democrats regain the presidency after 12 years. The presence of a major third party candidate, Ross Perot, although not substantially affecting the outcome, did result in Clinton's being elected without a majority. The Clinton-Gore ticket took 43 percent of the popular vote and received 370 electoral votes. In the 1992 congressional elections the Democrats lost 10 seats in the House, while party strength in the Senate remained unchanged.

## Democratic-Republican Party (1796-1828)

The Democratic-Republican Party developed in the early 1790s as the organized opposition to the incumbent Federalists and successor to the Anti-Federalists, who were a loose alliance of elements initially opposed to the ratification of the Constitution and subsequently to the policies of the Washington administration, which were designed to centralize power in the federal government.

Thomas Jefferson was the leader of the new party, whose members as early as 1792 referred to themselves as Republicans. This remained their primary name throughout the party's history, although in some states they became known as Democratic-Republicans, the label used frequently by historians to avoid confusing Jefferson's party with the later Republican Party, which began in 1854. Party members were called Jeffersonian Republicans as well.

The Democratic-Republicans favored states' rights, a literal interpretation of the Constitution and expanded democracy through extension of suffrage and popular control of the government. The party was dominated by rural, agrarian interests, intent on maintaining their dominance over the growing commercial and industrial interests of the Northeast. The principal strength of the party came from the Southern and Middle Atlantic states.

The Democratic-Republicans first gained control of the federal government in 1800, when Jefferson was elected president and the party won majorities in both houses of Congress. For the next 24 years the party controlled both the White House and Congress, the last eight years virtually without opposition. For all but four years during this 24-year period, there was a Virginia-New York alliance controlling the executive branch, with all three presidents from Virginia — Jefferson, James Madison and James Monroe — and three of the four vice presidents from New York. Lacking an opposition party, the Democratic-Republicans in the 1820s became increasingly divided. In 1824, when four party leaders ran for president, John Quincy Adams won the election in the House of Representatives, although Andrew Jackson had received more popular votes.

The deep factionalism evident in the 1824 election doomed the Democratic-Republican Party. The two-party system revived shortly thereafter with the emergence of the National Republican Party, an outgrowth of the Adams faction, and the Democratic-Republican Party, the political organization of the Jackson faction. After 1830 the Jacksonians adopted the name Democratic Party.

## Federalist Party (1789-1816)

The Federalist Party grew out of the movement that drafted and worked for the ratification of the Constitution of 1787, which established a stronger national government than that in operation under the existing Articles of Confederation. Supporters of the new constitutional government were known as Federalists, and in the formative first decade of the Republic they controlled the national government. With President George Washington staying aloof from the development of political parties, leadership of the Federalists was exercised by Alexander Hamilton and John Adams. The party's basic strength was among urban, commercial interests, who were particularly drawn to the Federalists by the party's belief in a strong federal economic policy and the maintenance of domestic order — viewpoints based on a broad interpretation of the Constitution.

The Federalists were perceived widely as a party of the aristocracy, a decided liability in the late 18th and early 19th centuries when the right to vote was being widely extended to members of the middle and lower classes. Never as well organized as the Democratic-Republicans, the Federalists were unable to compete for support of the important rural, agrarian elements that composed a majority of the electorate.

The election of Jefferson in 1800 ended Federalist control of both the White House and Congress. After 1800 the Federalists did not elect a president or win a majority in either house of Congress. The party's strength was largely limited to commercial New England, where Federalists advocated states' rights and were involved in threats of regional secession in 1808 and again during the War of 1812.

The party soon began to lose its energy, and in 1812 the Federalists held their last meeting of party leaders to field a presidential ticket. Four years later there were no nominations, but Federalist electors were chosen in three states. Although this marked the last appearance of the party at the national level, the Federalists remained in existence at the local level until the mid-1820s.

## Free Soil Party (1848-52)

Born as a result of opposition to the extension of slavery into the newly acquired Southwest territories, the Free Soil Party was launched formally at a convention in Buffalo, N.Y., in August 1848. The Free Soilers were composed of anti-slavery elements from the Democratic and Whig parties as well as remnants of the Liberal Party. Representatives from all the Northern states and three Border states attended the Buffalo convention, where the slogan "free soil, free speech, free labor and free men" was adopted. This slogan expressed the anti-slavery sentiment of the Free Soilers as well as the desire for cheap Western land.

Former Democratic president Martin Van Buren (1837-41) was selected by the convention as the party's presidential candidate and Charles Francis Adams, the son of President John Quincy Adams (1825-29), was chosen as his running mate.

In the 1848 election the Free Soil ticket received 291,501 votes (10.1 percent of the popular vote) but was unable to carry a single state. The party did better at the congressional level, winning nine House seats and holding the balance of power in the organization of the closely divided new Congress.

The 1848 election marked the peak of the party's influence. With the passage of compromise legislation on slavery in 1850, the Free Soilers lost their basic issue and began a rapid decline. The party ran its second and last national ticket in 1852, headed by John Hale, who received 155,210 votes (4.9 percent of the popular vote). As in 1848 the Free Soil national ticket failed to carry a single state.

Although the party went out of existence shortly thereafter, its program and constituency were absorbed by the Republican Party, whose birth and growth dramatically paralleled the resurgence of the slavery issue in the mid-1850s.

## Greenback Party (1876-84)

The National Independent or Greenback-Labor Party, commonly known as the Greenback Party, was launched in Indianapolis, Ind., in November 1874 at a meeting organized by the Indiana Grange. The party grew out of the Panic of 1873, a post-Civil War economic depression, which hit farmers and industrial workers particularly hard. Currency was the basic issue of the new party, which opposed return to the gold standard and favored retention of the inflationary paper money (known as greenbacks), first introduced as an emergency measure during the Civil War.

In the 1876 presidential election the party ran Peter Cooper, a New York philanthropist, and drafted a platform that focused entirely on the currency issue. Cooper received 75,973 votes (0.9 percent of the popular vote), mainly from agrarian voters. Aided by the continuing depression, a Greenback national convention in 1878 effected the merger of the party with various labor reform groups and adopted a platform that addressed labor and currency issues. Showing voting strength in the industrial East as well as in the agrarian South and Midwest, the Greenbacks polled more than one million votes in the 1878 congressional races and won 14 seats in the U.S. House of Representatives. This marked the high point of the party's strength.

Returning prosperity, the prospect of fusion with one of the major parties and a split between the party's agrarian and labor leadership served to undermine the Greenback Party. In the 1880 election the party elected only eight representatives and its presidential candidate, Rep. James B. Weaver of Iowa, received 305,997 votes (3.3 percent of the popular vote), far less than party leaders expected.

The party slipped further four years later, when the Greenbacks' candidate for president, former Massachusetts governor Benjamin F. Butler, received 175,096 votes (1.7 percent of the popular vote). With the demise of the Greenbacks, most of the party's constituency moved into the Populist Party, the agrarian reform movement that swept the South and Midwest in the 1890s.

## Liberal Republican Party (1872)

A faction of the Republican Party, dissatisfied with President Ulysses S. Grant's first term in office, withdrew from the party in 1872 to form its own party. Composed of party reformers, as well as anti-Grant politicians and newspaper editors, the new party focused on the corruption of the Grant administration and the need for civil service reform and for an end to the Reconstruction policy in the South.

The call for the Liberal Republican national convention came from the state party in Missouri, the birthplace of the reform movement. The convention, meeting in Cincinnati, Ohio, in May 1872, nominated Horace Greeley, editor of the *New York Tribune,* for president and Missouri governor B. Gratz Brown as his running mate. Greeley, the choice of anti-Grant politicians but suspect among reformers, was not popular among many Democrats either, who recalled his longtime criticism of the Democratic Party.

However, with the hope of victory in the fall election, the Democratic national convention, meeting in July, endorsed the Liberal Republican ticket and platform. The coalition was an unsuccessful one, as many Democrats refused to vote for Greeley. He received 2,834,761 votes (43.8 percent of the popular vote) but carried only six states and lost to Grant by more than 750,000 votes out of nearly 6.5 million cast. Greeley died shortly after the election.

Underfinanced, poorly organized and dependent on the Democrats for their success, the Liberal Republicans went out of existence after the 1872 election.

## Libertarian Party (1971-  )

In the brief period of four years, the Libertarian Party leaped from a fledgling organization on the presidential ballot in only two states to the nation's largest third party. As of 1994 the Libertarians remained the largest third party in the United States.

Formed in Colorado in 1971, the party nominated John Hospers of California for president in 1972. On the ballot only in Colorado and Washington, Hospers garnered 3,673 votes (including write-in votes from other states). But he received a measure of national attention when a Republican presidential elector from Virginia, Roger MacBride, cast his electoral vote for the Libertarian presidential nominee.

MacBride's action made him a hero in Libertarian circles, and the party chose him as its 1976 standard-bearer at its August 1975 convention in New York City. MacBride had served in the Vermont legislature in the 1960s and was defeated for the Republican gubernatorial nomination in that state in 1964. In the 1970s he settled on a farm near Charlottesville, Va., and devoted himself to writing and party affairs. He was co-creator of the television series "Little House on the Prairie."

Making a major effort in 1976, the Libertarians got on the ballot in 32 states, more than Eugene J. McCarthy — who ran independent of any political party — or any other third party candidate. The reward was a vote of 173,011, more than any other minor party candidate, but far below McCarthy's total and only 0.2 percent of the national vote. MacBride's strength was centered in the West; he received 5.5 percent of the vote in Alaska and 1.0 percent or more in Arizona, Hawaii and Idaho. He also ran well ahead of his national average in California (0.7 percent) and Nevada (0.8 percent). His running mate was David P. Bergland, a California lawyer.

In 1980 the Libertarian Party appeared on the ballot in all 50 states and the District of Columbia for the first time.

The party also fielded about 550 candidates for other offices, a number that dwarfed other third-party efforts. The party nominees, Edward E. Clark of California for president and David Koch of New York for vice president, garnered 921,299 votes or 1.1 percent of the vote nationwide. As in previous elections, the major support for the Libertarians came from Western states.

Of all minor party presidential candidates running in 1984, the Libertarians appeared on the greatest number of ballots: 38 states and the District of Columbia. Bergland, who had run in 1976 for the second slot, was the party's presidential candidate, and Jim Lewis, a Connecticut business executive, his running mate. In 1988 the Libertarian presidential and vice presidential nominees — Ron Paul and Andre V. Marrou, respectively — were on the ballot in all 51 jurisdictions save four and received 432,179 votes.

In 1992 Nevada real estate broker Marrou was the presidential nominee with running mate Nancy Lord, a lawyer from Georgia. The pair was on the ballot in all 50 states and the District of Columbia and had a campaign budget of $1 million. Marrou received 291,627 votes in a fourth-place finish behind Ross Perot, who stole most of the third party candidates' thunder that year. The Libertarians maintained their strong base in the West, especially in California, Nevada and Hawaii, where they also ran candidates in 1992 for most House seats.

Individual responsibility and minimal government interference were the hallmarks of the Libertarian philosophy. The party favored repeal of laws against so-called victimless crimes — such as pornography, drug use and homosexual activity — the abolition of all federal police agencies, and the elimination of all government subsidies to private enterprise. In foreign and military affairs, the Libertarians advocated the removal of U.S. troops from abroad, a cut in the defense budget and the emergence of the United States as a "giant Switzerland," with no international treaty obligations. MacBride commented that it was his party's intention to "reduce the Pentagon to a trigon."

Libertarians also favored repeal of legislation that they believe hindered individual or corporate action. They opposed gun control, civil rights laws, price controls on oil and gas, labor protection laws, federal welfare and poverty programs, forced busing, compulsory education, Social Security, national medical care, federal land-use restrictions and the 55-miles-per-hour speed limit.

## Liberty Party (1840-48)

Born in 1839, the Liberty Party was the product of a split in the anti-slavery movement between a faction led by William Lloyd Garrison that favored action outside the political process and a second led by James G. Birney that proposed action within the political system through the establishment of an independent anti-slavery party. The Birney faction launched the Liberty Party in November 1839. The following April a national convention with delegates from six states nominated Birney for the presidency.

Although the Liberty Party was the first political party to take an anti-slavery position, and the only one at the time to do so, most abolitionist voters in the 1840 election supported the Democratic or Whig presidential candidates. Birney received only 6,797 votes (0.3 percent of the popular vote).

Aided by the controversy over the annexation of slaveholding Texas, the Liberty Party's popularity increased in 1844. Birney, again the party's presidential nominee, re-

ceived 62,103 votes (2.3 percent of the popular vote) but again as in 1840 carried no states. The peak strength of the party was reached two years later in 1846, when in various state elections Liberty Party candidates received 74,017 votes.

In October 1847 the party nominated New Hampshire senator John P. Hale for the presidency, but his candidacy was withdrawn the following year when the Liberty Party joined the broader-based Free Soil Party. *(Free Soil Party, p. 263)*

## National Democratic Party (1896)

A conservative faction in favor of the gold standard, the National Democrats bolted from the Democratic Party after the 1896 convention adopted a pro-silver platform and nominated William Jennings Bryan. With the nation in the midst of a depression and the Populists in the agrarian Midwest and South demanding monetary reform, currency was the dominant issue of the 1896 campaign. This produced a brief realignment in American politics.

The Republican Party was controlled by leaders who favored maintenance of the gold standard, a non-inflationary currency. Agrarian Midwestern and Southern Democrats, reflecting a Populist philosophy, gained control of the Democratic Party in 1896 and committed it to the free coinage of silver, an inflationary currency demanded by rural elements threatened by debts. The Democrats attracted pro-silver bolters from the Republican Party, but gold standard Democrats, opposed to the Republicans' protectionist position on the tariff issue, established an independent party.

Meeting in Indianapolis, Ind., in September 1896, the National Democrats adopted a platform favoring maintenance of the gold standard and selected a ticket headed by 79-year-old Illinois senator John M. Palmer.

Democratic president Grover Cleveland and leading members of his administration, repudiated by the convention that chose Bryan, supported the National Democrats. During the campaign the National Democrats encouraged conservative Democrats to vote either for the National Democratic ticket or for the Republican candidate, William McKinley. The Palmer ticket received 133,435 votes (1.0 percent of the popular vote), and McKinley defeated Bryan.

In the 1890s returning prosperity and the Spanish-American War overshadowed the currency issue, and the intense Democratic Party factionalism that produced the National Democratic Party ended.

## National Republican Party (1828-32)

The Democratic-Republican Party splintered after the 1824 election into two factions. The group led by Andrew Jackson retained the name Democratic-Republicans, which eventually was shortened to Democrats; the other faction, headed by President John Quincy Adams, assumed the name National Republicans. Reflecting the belief of President Adams in the establishment of a national policy by the federal government, the new party supported a protective tariff, the Bank of the United States, federal administration of public lands and national programs of internal improvements. However, Adams' belief in a strong national government contrasted with the period's prevailing mood of populism and states' rights.

The Adams forces controlled Congress for two years, 1825 to 1827, but as party structures formalized the National Republicans became a minority in Congress and suffered a decisive loss in the 1828 presidential election. Running for re-election, Adams was beaten by Jackson. Adams received 43.6 percent of the popular vote and carried eight states, none in the South. Henry Clay, the party's candidate against Jackson four years later, had even less success. He received only 37.4 percent of the popular vote and carried just six states, none of which, again, were in the South.

Poorly organized, with dwindling support and a heritage of defeat, the National Republicans went out of existence after the 1832 election, but their members provided the base for a new anti-Jackson party, the Whigs, which came into being in 1834. *(Whig Party, p. 272)*

## National Unity Party
## (Independent John B. Anderson) (1980-88)

Republican representative John B. Anderson of Illinois formed the National Unity Campaign as the vehicle for his independent presidential campaign in 1980. Anderson began his quest for the presidency by trying to win the Republican Party nomination. But, as a liberal in a party coming under conservative control, he won no primaries and could claim only 57 convention delegates by April 1980. Anderson withdrew from the Republican race and declared his independent candidacy.

Anderson focused his campaign on the need to establish a viable third party as an alternative to domination of the political scene by the Republican and Democratic parties. The National Unity Campaign platform touted the Anderson program as a "new public philosophy" — more innovative than that of the Democrats, who "cling to the policies of the New Deal," and more enlightened than that of the Republicans, who talk "incessantly about freedom, but hardly ever about justice." Generally the group took positions that were fiscally conservative and socially liberal. Anderson and his running mate, former Democratic Wisconsin governor Patrick J. Lucey, tried to appeal to Republican and Democratic voters disenchanted with their parties and to the growing bloc of voters who classified themselves as independents.

The National Unity Campaign ticket was on the ballot in all 50 states in 1980, although Anderson had to wage costly legal battles in some states to ensure that result. In the end, the party won 6.6 percent of the presidential vote, well over the 5 percent necessary to qualify for retroactive federal campaign funding.

In April 1984 Anderson announced that he would not seek the presidency in that year. He said that instead he would focus his energies on building the National Unity Party, which he established officially in December 1983. He planned to concentrate initially on running candidates at the local level. On Aug. 28 Anderson endorsed Walter F. Mondale, the Democratic nominee for president, and his running mate, Geraldine A. Ferraro.

The National Unity Party did not run a presidential candidate in the 1988 race, and by 1992 was no longer a political party.

## New Alliance Party (1988- )

The New Alliance Party formed in the late 1980s to promote a combination of minority interests. Self-described as "black-led, multiracial, pro-gay and pro-socialist," the party has been aggressive in filing lawsuits to attain ballot access. In 1988 presidential candidate Lenora B. Fulani, a New York psychologist, drew 217,219 votes nationwide for a fourth-place finish. Her best showing was in the District of Columbia, where she received more than 1 percent of the vote.

In 1992, with the party qualifying for $1.8 million in federal matching funds, Fulani ran again, this time with California teacher Maria Munoz as a running mate. Fulani campaigned for equal employment for all. "I believe that a job at a union wage is the right of all Americans," she said. The New Alliance ticket appeared on the ballot in 39 states and the District of Columbia and received 73,714 votes, slightly less than 0.1 percent nationwide.

## People's Party (1971- )

Delegates from activist and peace groups established the People's Party at a November 1971 convention held in Dallas, Texas. The initial co-chairmen were pediatrician Dr. Benjamin Spock and author Gore Vidal.

The People's Party first ran a presidential candidate in 1972. They chose Dr. Spock for president and black activist Julius Hobson of Washington, D.C., for vice president. Despite hopes for widespread backing from the poor and social activists, the ticket received only 78,756 votes, 0.1 percent of the national total. A total of 55,167 of those votes came from California alone.

At its convention, held in St. Louis, Mo., Aug. 31, 1975, the People's Party chose black civil rights activist Margaret Wright of California for president and Maggie Kuhn of Pennsylvania, a leader in the Gray Panthers movement for rights for the elderly, for vice president. Kuhn, however, declined the nomination and was replaced on the ticket by Spock.

The party platform focused on cutting the defense budget, closing tax loopholes and making that money available for social programs. Other planks included redistribution of land and wealth; unconditional amnesty for war objectors; and free health care. In her campaign, Wright stressed the necessity for active participation by citizens in the governmental process, so that institutions and programs could be run from the roots up rather than from the top down.

As in 1972 the party's main backing came in California, where it was supported by the state Peace and Freedom Party. Wright's total national vote in 1976 was 49,024, and 85.1 percent (41,731 votes) of those votes came from California. The party has not fielded presidential candidates since 1976.

## People's Party-Populists (1892-1908, 1983- )

The People's Party, also called the Populist Party, was organized at a convention in Cincinnati, Ohio, in May 1891 and climaxed several decades of farm protest against deteriorating economic conditions. Chronically depressed commodity prices, caused by over-production and world competition, had spurred the politicization of farmers.

Most of the Populist leaders came from the defunct Greenback movement and Southern and Midwestern farm cooperative associations. The Populists tended to blame their problems on the most visible causes, primarily the high railroad rates and shrinking currency supply, but the platform they adopted at their first national nominating convention in 1892 was a wide-reaching one. As well as advocating the government ownership of railroads and the free coinage of silver, the Populists proposed institution of a graduated income tax and the direct election of senators. Although the Populists proposed labor reforms, such as reducing the working day to eight hours, the party never gained appreciable support among industrial workers.

The Populists ran James B. Weaver, the former Greenback candidate, as their presidential nominee in 1892. Weaver received 1,024,280 votes (8.5 percent of the popular vote) and carried five states in the Midwest and West. Increasingly tied to the silver issue, the party showed growing strength in the 1894 congressional races. Especially strong west of the Mississippi River, party congressional candidates polled nearly 1.5 million votes. After the election the Populists had six senators and seven representatives in Congress.

The Democrats surprised Populist leaders in 1896 by writing a free silver platform and nominating a free silver candidate, William Jennings Bryan. The Populists were faced with the dilemma of either endorsing Bryan and losing their party identity or running a separate ticket and splitting the free silver vote. The Populist convention endorsed Bryan but ran a separate candidate for vice president, Thomas E. Watson.

After this initial fusion with the Democrats, most Populists remained within the Democratic Party after the 1896 election. The Populist Party remained in existence, running presidential candidates until 1908, but never received more than 0.8 percent of the popular vote. The party did not expand its voter appeal beyond an agrarian reform movement, but many of its proposals, particularly in the areas of government and electoral reform, were espoused by progressive politicians in the early 20th century and enacted into law.

After being absent from the political scene for nearly three-quarters of a century, the Populist Party revived in early 1984 to place former Olympic pole vaulter Bob Richards as a candidate on the presidential ballot in 14 states. Backers of the new party advocated wiping out the Federal Reserve System, repealing the federal income tax and protecting U.S. industry from imports. Richards received 66,336 votes. In 1988 the Populists nominated David Duke, a former member of the Ku Klux Klan, who received 47,047 votes nationwide.

In 1992 the Populist Party nominated former Green Beret commander James "Bo" Gritz for president and Cyril Minett for vice president. On the ballot in 18 states, the Populists received 107,014 votes or 0.1 percent nationwide. Gritz performed especially well in the West, where he received 3.8 percent of the vote in Utah and 2.1 percent in Idaho.

## Progressive Party-Bull Moose (1912)

A split in Republican ranks, spurred by the bitter personal and ideological dispute between President William Howard Taft (1909-13) and former president Theodore Roosevelt (1901-09), resulted in the withdrawal of the Roosevelt forces from the Republican Party after the June 1912 convention and the creation of the Progressive Party two months later. The new party was known popularly as the Bull Moose Party, a name resulting from Roosevelt's assertion early in the campaign that he felt as fit as a bull moose. While the Taft-Roosevelt split was the immediate reason for the new party, the Bull Moosers were an outgrowth of the progressive movement that was a powerful force in both major parties in the early years of the 20th century.

Although in 1908 Roosevelt had handpicked Taft as his successor, his disillusionment with Taft's conservative philosophy came quickly, and with the support of progressive Republicans Roosevelt challenged the incumbent for the 1912 Republican presidential nomination. Roosevelt outpolled Taft in the presidential primary states. Taft nevertheless won the nomination with nearly solid support in the South and among party conservatives, providing the narrow majority of delegates that enabled him to win the bulk of the key credentials challenges.

Although few Republican politicians followed Roosevelt in his bolt, the new party demonstrated a popular base at its convention in Chicago in August 1912. Thousands of delegates, basically middle- and upper-class reformers from small towns and cities, attended the convention that launched the party and nominated Roosevelt for president and California governor Hiram Johnson as his running mate. Roosevelt appeared in person to deliver his "Confession of Faith," a speech detailing his nationalistic philosophy and progressive reform ideas. The Bull Moose platform reflected key tenets of the Progressive movement, calling for more extensive government antitrust action and labor, social, government and electoral reform.

Roosevelt was wounded in an assassination attempt while campaigning in Milwaukee, Wis., in October, but he finished the campaign. In the general election Roosevelt received more than 4 million votes (27.4 percent of the popular vote) and carried six states. His percentage of the vote was the highest ever received by a third party candidate in American history, but his candidacy split the Republican vote and enabled the Democrats' nominee, Woodrow Wilson, to win the election. The Progressive Party had minimal success at the state and local levels, winning approximately 13 House seats but electing no senators or governors.

Roosevelt declined the Progressive nomination in 1916 and endorsed the Republican candidate, Charles Evans Hughes. With the defection of its leader, the decline of the progressive movement, and the lack of an effective party organization, the Bull Moose Party ceased to exist.

## Progressive Party (1924)

Like the Bull Moose Party of Theodore Roosevelt, the Progressive Party that emerged in the mid-1920s was a reform effort led by a Republican. Wisconsin senator Robert M. La Follette led the new Progressive Party, a separate entity from the Bull Moosers, which, unlike the middle- and upper-class Roosevelt party of the previous decade, had its greatest appeal among farmers and organized labor.

The La Follette Progressive Party grew out of the Conference for Progressive Political Action (CPPA), a coalition of railway union leaders and a remnant of the Bull Moose effort that was formed in 1922. The Socialist Party joined the coalition the following year. Throughout 1923 the Socialists and labor unions argued over whether their coalition should form a third party, with the Socialists in favor and the labor unions against it. It was finally decided to run an independent presidential candidate, La Follette, in the 1924 election but not to field candidates at the state and local levels. La Follette was given the power to choose his own running mate and selected Montana senator Burton K. Wheeler, a Democrat.

Opposition to corporate monopolies was the major issue of the La Follette campaign, although the party advocated various other reforms, particularly aimed at farmers and workers, which were proposed earlier by either the Populists or Bull Moosers. But the Progressive Party itself was a major issue in the 1924 campaign, as the Republicans attacked the alleged radicalism of the party.

Although La Follette had its endorsement, the American Federation of Labor (AFL) provided minimal support.

The basic strength of the Progressives, like that of the Populists in the 1890s, derived from agrarian voters west of the Mississippi River. La Follette received 4,832,532 votes (16.6 percent of the popular vote) but carried just one state, his native Wisconsin. When La Follette died in 1925, the party collapsed as a national force. It was revived by La Follette's sons on a statewide level in Wisconsin in the mid-1930s.

## Progressive Party (1948)

Henry A. Wallace's Progressive Party resulted from the dissatisfaction of liberal elements in the Democratic Party with the leadership of President Harry S. Truman, particularly in the realm of foreign policy. The Progressive Party was one of two bolting groups from the Democratic Party in 1948; conservative Southern elements withdrew to form the States' Rights Party.

Henry Wallace, the founder of the Progressive Party, was secretary of agriculture, vice president and finally secretary of commerce under President Franklin D. Roosevelt. He carried the reputation of one of the most liberal idealists in the Roosevelt administration. Fired from the Truman Cabinet in 1946 after breaking with administration policy and publicly advocating peaceful coexistence with the Soviet Union, Wallace began to consider the idea of a liberal third party candidacy. Supported by the American Labor Party, the Progressive Citizens of America and other progressive organizations in California and Illinois, Wallace announced his third party candidacy in December 1947.

The Progressive Party was launched formally the following July at a convention in Philadelphia, which ratified the selection of Wallace for president and Sen. Glen H. Taylor, D-Idaho, as his running mate. The party adopted a platform that emphasized foreign policy — opposing the Cold War anti-communism of the Truman administration and specifically urging abandonment of the Truman Doctrine and the Marshall Plan. These measures were designed to contain the spread of communism and bolster non-communist nations. On domestic issues the Progressives stressed humanitarian concerns and equal rights for both sexes and all races.

Minority groups — women, youth, blacks, Jews, Hispanic-Americans — were active in the new party, but the openness of the Progressives brought Wallace a damaging endorsement from the Communist Party. Believing the two parties could work together, Wallace accepted the endorsement while characterizing his own philosophy as "progressive capitalism."

In 1948 the Progressives appeared on the presidential ballot in 45 states, but the Communist endorsement helped keep the party on the defensive the entire campaign. In the November election Wallace received only 1,157,326 votes (2.4 percent of the national popular vote), with nearly half of the votes from the state of New York. Not only were the Progressives unable to carry a single state, but in spite of their defection from the Democratic Party President Truman won re-election. The Progressives had poor results in the congressional races, failing to elect one representative or senator.

The Progressive Party's opposition to the Korean War in 1950 drove many moderate elements out of the party, including Henry Wallace. The party ran a national ticket in 1952, but received only 140,023 votes nationwide or 0.2 percent of the national popular vote. The party crumbled completely after the election.

## Prohibition Party (1869-   )

The Prohibition Party existed longer than any third party in American history. It was formed in September 1869 at a convention in Chicago, which attracted approximately 500 delegates from 20 states. For the first time in U.S. politics, women had equal status with men as delegates. By a narrow majority the convention decided to form an independent party, and three years later the new party put forth its first national ticket. The party's basic goal was enactment of laws prohibiting the manufacture and sale of intoxicating liquor, but its platforms have included other reform proposals. The 1872 Prohibition Party platform included the first women's suffrage plank.

For all but one election between 1884 and 1916, the party's presidential candidate received at least 1 percent of the popular vote. The party's best showing came in 1892, when its presidential nominee, John Bidwell, received 270,770 votes (2.2 percent of the popular vote). The party has run a national ticket in every presidential election since 1872, but its candidates have never carried a single state. After the 1976 election the Prohibitionist Party changed its name to the National Statesman Party, and its 1980 candidate registered using that party name. The 1984 candidate, Earl F. Dodge of Colorado, emphasized that his party — on the ballots once again as Prohibitionists — no longer focused on a single issue: the party backed religious liberty and an anti-abortion amendment. Dodge again was the party's standard-bearer in 1988 and 1992. In 1992 the party could only muster 961 votes nationwide.

The temperance movement succeeded in gaining prohibition legislation in numerous states in the late 19th and early 20th centuries, and its efforts were capped in 1919 by passage of national prohibition legislation (the 18th Amendment to the U.S. Constitution, repealed 14 years later by the 21st Amendment). The achievements of the temperance movement were due as much to independent organizations, such as the Women's Christian Temperance Union (WCTU) and the Anti-Saloon League, as to the Prohibition Party, which had limited success at the polls. These organizations allowed active Democrats and Republicans to remain in their own parties while working for prohibition.

## Republican Party (1854-   )

Born in 1854 in the upper Midwest, the Republican Party grew out of the anti-slavery forces' bitter dissatisfaction with the Kansas-Nebraska Act. The bill overturned earlier legislation (the Missouri Compromise of 1820 and the Compromise of 1850), limiting the extension of slavery into the territories, and instituted the concept of popular sovereignty, by which each territory decided its own position on slavery. While historians generally credit residents of Ripon, Wis., with holding the party's first organizational meeting in March 1854 and citizens of Jackson, Mich., with running the party's first electoral ticket in July 1854, the birth of the party was nearly simultaneous in many communities throughout the Northern states. The volatile slavery issue was the catalyst that brought the party's birth, but the political vacuum caused by the decline of the Whigs and the failure of the Know-Nothing and Free Soil parties to gain a stable national following allowed the Republicans to grow with dramatic rapidity.

The constituency of the new party was limited to the Northern states, since opposition to slavery was the basic issue of the Republicans. But the party did attract diverse elements in the political spectrum — former Whigs, Know-Nothings, Free Soilers and dissident Democrats.

In its first year the party took the name Republican. Horace Greeley is credited with initiating the name in a June 1854 issue of his newspaper, the *New York Tribune*. In pushing the name, he referred to the Jeffersonian Republicans of the early 19th century and Henry Clay's National Republican Party of the 1830s, which was an early rival of the Democrats.

The Republicans ran candidates throughout the North in 1854, and in combination with other candidates opposed to the Kansas-Nebraska Act won a majority in the House of Representatives. Two years later the Republicans ran their first national ticket. Although their presidential candidate, John C. Fremont, did not win, he polled one-third of the vote in a three-man race and carried 11 states. The Republicans were established as a major party.

While the party was built on the slavery question, the Republicans were far from a one-issue party. They presented a nationalistic platform with appeal to business and commercial interests as well as rural anti-slavery elements. The Republicans proposed legislation for homesteading (free land), the construction of a transcontinental railroad and the institution of a protective tariff.

Firmly established by the late 1850s, the Republican Party benefited from the increasing sectional factionalism in the Democratic Party over the slavery issue. In 1858 the party won control of the House of Representatives. Two years later, with Abraham Lincoln as its candidate, the Republicans won the White House and retained control of the House. Lincoln, benefiting from a sectional split in the Democratic Party, won an unusual four-way race and captured the presidency with 39.9 percent of the popular vote.

Lincoln was a wartime president, and his success in preserving the Union helped the party for the next generation. After the Civil War the Republicans projected a patriotic image, which, coupled with the party's belief in national expansion and limited federal involvement in the free enterprise system, helped make it the dominant party over the next three-quarters of a century. For most of the 72 years between 1860 and 1932, the Republicans were the majority party, occupying the White House for 56 years, controlling the Senate for 60 years and controlling the House for 50 years. Except for the South, where the party basically was limited to the small number of black voters, the Republicans were strong throughout the nation.

Congressional leaders exercised the dominant power during this period of Republican hegemony. Presidents had little success in challenging the authority wielded by the GOP's congressional leadership.

Just as the party vaulted to power on the divisive slavery issue, its history was altered by another traumatic event — the Great Depression, which began in 1929. As the incumbent party during the economic collapse, the Republicans suffered the political blame; their fall from power was rapid. In 1928 the Republican presidential candidate (Herbert Hoover) carried 40 states; in 1936, during Franklin D. Roosevelt's New Deal days, the Republican standard-bearer (Alfred M. Landon) won just two states. In 1928 the party held a clear majority of seats in both the House and Senate, 267 and 56 respectively; but eight years later the party's numbers had shrunk dramatically, the Republicans holding only 89 seats in the House and 17 in the Senate.

The party eventually made a comeback from this low point but remained the minority party in Congress through the 1980 elections. Between 1932 and 1988 the Republicans

won seven of 15 presidential elections but controlled both chambers of Congress for just four years.

While the Republicans struggled to find the formula for a new majority, the party's basic conservatism made it increasingly appealing, especially in presidential races, to segments of the electorate that previously were firm parts of the Democratic coalition — notably blue-collar workers and the once-Democratic South. Beginning in 1952, the party was able to attract a winning combination when it ran presidential candidates with a moderate conservative image, such as Dwight D. Eisenhower, Richard Nixon or Ronald Reagan. However, the GOP enjoyed less success at the state and local levels where Democratic majorities, established during the New Deal, remained largely intact.

The Republican difficulties in establishing a new majority were compounded after the 1972 election by the Watergate scandal, which brought down the Nixon administration. Gerald R. Ford, who became president after Nixon resigned Aug. 9, 1974, lost his 1976 election bid to former Georgia governor Jimmy Carter, giving the Democrats control of the White House as well as Congress.

Republican fortunes improved dramatically in 1980 when former California governor Reagan won a landslide electoral vote victory over Carter. Republicans also took control of the Senate for the first time in 28 years and made substantial gains in the House. Although a resurgence of Democratic political strength in the 1982 mid-term elections swept more Democrats into the House, the Republicans retained control of the Senate.

In a Gallup Poll taken shortly before the 1984 national elections, 28 percent of the respondents identified themselves as Republicans. Although Republicans remained the minority party (the Democrats had captured 42 percent of the voters in this survey), the party clearly was recovering from the lows it had experienced during the Watergate era. Not since the Eisenhower presidency had more voters identified themselves as Republicans. The party enjoyed a second landslide victory for Reagan, gaining even more strength and making Reagan one of the most popular presidents of this century.

But the Republicans' cycle of misfortune repeated itself in late 1986. Congressional elections saw the Democrats regain control of the Senate — despite a nationwide campaign by Reagan to promote Republican senatorial candidates — giving the Democrats full control of Congress and the GOP a sizable obstacle in policy making. A few weeks later the Iran-contra scandal broke. A special prosecutor was appointed, and congressional investigations, including months of public hearings, lasted for almost all of 1987.

The setback to the party, if any, did not keep Reagan's vice president, George Bush, from winning big in 1988 — 53.4 percent of the vote and 426 electoral votes. Bush became the first sitting vice president to win the White House since Martin Van Buren in 1836. Bush also was the first candidate since John F. Kennedy to win the presidential election while his party lost seats in the House. His inability to carry others into office may have been partly due to his message, which was essentially a call to "stay the course" set by Reagan.

In seeking a second term in 1992, Bush was burdened with a slow-recovering economy brought on by the recession of 1990-91. The Republican platform also had little that was new to offer to disgruntled voters. Bush took only 37.4 percent of the nationwide vote and received 168 electoral votes. But while the Democrats regained the White House after 12 years, the Republicans posted victories elsewhere, gaining 10 seats in the House in 1992 and one Senate seat and two gubernatorial seats in 1993.

## Socialist Labor Party (1888-  )

The Socialist Labor Party, the first national Socialist party in the United States, ranks second only to the Prohibitionists among third parties in longevity. Formed in 1874 by elements of the Socialist International in New York, it was first known as the Social Democratic Workingmen's Party. In 1877 the group adopted the name Socialist Labor Party. Throughout the 1880s the party worked in concert with other left-wing third parties, including the Greenbacks.

The Socialist Labor Party ran national tickets in every presidential election from 1892 through 1976. The party collected its highest proportion of the national vote in 1896, when its candidate received 36,356 votes (0.3 percent of the popular vote).

Led by the autocratic Daniel DeLeon (1852-1914), a former Columbia University law lecturer, the Socialist Labor Party became increasingly militant and made its best showing in local races in 1898. But DeLeon's insistence on rigid party discipline and his opposition to the organized labor movement created a feeling of alienation among many members. Moderate elements in the party bolted, eventually joining the Socialist Party of Eugene V. Debs, which formed in 1901.

The Socialist Labor Party continued as a small, tightly organized far-left group bound to DeLeon's uncompromising belief in revolution. As late as 1970 the party advocated direct worker action to take over control of production and claimed 5,000 members nationwide.

## Socialist Party (1901-  )

The Socialist Party was born officially in July 1901 at a convention in Indianapolis, Ind., which joined together former American Railway Union president Eugene V. Debs' Social Democratic Party with a moderate faction of the Socialist Labor Party. The two groups had begun discussions a year before and in the 1900 presidential campaign jointly supported a ticket headed by Debs that received 86,935 votes (0.6 percent of the popular vote).

The 1901 unity convention identified the new Socialist Party with the working class and described the party's goal as "collective ownership . . . of the means of production and distribution." The party grew rapidly in the early 20th century, reaching a peak membership of approximately 118,000 in 1912. That year also proved to be the party's best at the polls. Debs, a presidential candidate five times between 1900 and 1920, received 900,369 votes (6.0 percent of the popular vote). The Socialists elected 1,200 candidates to local offices, including 79 candidates for mayor.

With the outbreak of World War I, the party became a vehicle for anti-war protest. In 1917 pacifist Socialists converted a number of mayoral elections into referendums on the war, winning 34 percent of the vote in Chicago, more than 25 percent in Buffalo and 22 percent in New York City.

The following year Debs was convicted of sedition for making an anti-war speech and was sentenced to a term in the Atlanta federal penitentiary, from which he ran for president in 1920 and received 915,490 votes (3.4 percent of the popular vote).

Four years later the Socialists endorsed Wisconsin senator Robert M. La Follette's presidential candidacy, an unsuccessful attempt to establish a farm-labor coalition. In 1928 the Socialists resumed running their own presidential ticket. With the death of Debs in 1926, the party selected Norman Thomas, a former minister and social worker, to be the party's standard-bearer for the next six elections. The Depression brought a brief surge for the Socialists in 1932, with Thomas polling 884,649 votes (2.2 percent of the popular vote).

But 1932 proved to be only a temporary revival for the Socialists. Roosevelt's New Deal stole their thunder, and the Socialist Party failed to attract even one-half of 1 percent of the vote in any succeeding presidential election. In 1976 the party ran its first presidential ticket in two decades. The candidates received 6,038 votes, 0.01 percent of the popular vote. Although Socialist Party candidates received a few more votes in the 1980 elections, 6,898, their percentage share of the total vote remained 0.01 percent. The old-line Socialist Party faded again from the presidential candidate scene in 1984 but made a reappearance in 1988. The Socialist candidates, Willa Kenoyer and Ron Ehrenreich, however, experienced a precipitous drop in support, receiving only 3,882 nationwide votes.

## Socialist Workers Party (1938-  )

The Socialist Workers Party was formed in 1938 by followers of the Russian revolutionary Leon Trotsky. Originally a faction within the U.S. Communist Party, the Trotskyites were expelled in 1936 on instructions from Soviet leader Joseph Stalin. A brief Trotskyite coalition with the Socialist Party ended in 1938 when the dissidents decided to organize independently as the Socialist Workers Party. Through its youth arm, the Young Socialist Alliance, the Socialist Workers Party was active in the anti-Vietnam War movement and contributed activists to civil rights protests.

Since 1948 the party has run a presidential candidate, but its entries have never received more than 0.1 percent of the popular vote. In 1992 presidential candidate James Warren was on the ballot in 13 states and the District of Columbia and drew 23,096 votes nationwide.

## Southern Democrats (1860)

Agitation over the slavery issue, building for a generation, reached a climax in 1860 and produced a sectional split in the Democratic Party. Throughout the mid-19th century, the Democrats had remained unified by supporting the various pieces of compromise legislation that both protected slavery in the Southern states and endorsed the policy of popular sovereignty in the territories. But in 1860 Southern Democrats wanted the Democratic convention (meeting in Charleston, S.C.) to insert a plank specifically protecting slavery in the territories. When their plank was defeated, delegates from most of the Southern states walked out.

The Charleston convention stalemated over a presidential choice and, after recessing for six weeks, reconvened in Baltimore, where Illinois senator Stephen A. Douglas was nominated. Most of the Southern delegates, plus those from California and Oregon, bolted the convention and nominated their own ticket in a rump convention held after Douglas' selection. Vice President John C. Breckinridge of Kentucky was chosen for president, and Joseph Lane, a states' rights advocate from Oregon, was selected as his running mate. A platform was adopted that recognized the right of slavery to exist in the territories. After the formation of the two sectional tickets, two separate Democratic national committees operated in Washington, D.C., to oversee their campaigns.

Although in the 1860 election the combined Douglas-Breckinridge vote comprised a majority of the ballots cast, the split in Democratic ranks was a boon to the campaign of the Republican candidate, Abraham Lincoln, who won with a plurality of the vote. The Breckinridge ticket received 848,019 votes (18.1 percent of the popular vote) and carried nine Southern and Border states.

During the Civil War the Southern Democrats provided much of the leadership for the Confederate government, including its president, Jefferson Davis. At the end of the conflict the Southern Democrats made no attempt to continue as a separate sectional entity and rejoined the national Democratic Party.

### States' Rights Democratic Party (1948)

The States' Rights Democratic Party was a conservative Southern faction that bolted from the Democrats in 1948. The immediate reason for the new party, popularly known as the Dixiecrats, was dissatisfaction with President Harry S. Truman's civil rights program. But the Dixiecrat effort to maintain a segregated way of life was also an attempt to demonstrate the political power of the 20th century Southern Democrats and to re-establish their importance in the Democratic Party.

The Mississippi Democratic Party's state executive committee met in Jackson in May 1948 to lay the groundwork for the Dixiecrat secession. The meeting called for a bolt by Southern delegates if the Democratic National Convention endorsed Truman's civil rights program. When the convention did approve a strong civil rights plank, the entire Mississippi delegation and half the Alabama delegation left the convention. Gov. Fielding L. Wright of Mississippi invited all anti-Truman delegates to meet in Birmingham three days after the close of the Democratic convention to select a states' rights ticket.

Most Southern Democrats with something at stake — national prominence, seniority in Congress, patronage privileges — shunned the new Dixiecrat Party. The party's leaders came from the ranks of Southern governors and other state and local officials. The Birmingham convention chose two governors to lead the party: J. Strom Thurmond of South Carolina for president and Wright of Mississippi for vice president.

Other than the presidential ticket, the Dixiecrats did not run candidates for any office. Rather than try to develop an independent party organization, the Dixiecrats, whenever possible, used existing Democratic Party apparatus.

The party was on the ballot in only one state outside the South and in the November election received only 1,157,326 votes (2.4 percent of the popular vote). The Thurmond ticket carried four Deep South states where it ran under the Democratic Party label, but it failed in its basic objective to prevent the re-election of President Truman.

After the election the party ceased to exist almost as abruptly as it had begun, with most of its members returning to the Democratic Party. In a statement upon re-entering the Democratic fold, Thurmond characterized the Dixiecrat episode as "a fight within our family." (While serving in the U.S. Senate 16 years later, Thurmond switched to the Republican Party.)

### Union Party (1936)

Advocating more radical economic measures due to the Great Depression, several early supporters of President Franklin D. Roosevelt broke with him and ran their own ticket in 1936 under the Union Party label. Largely an outgrowth of the Rev. Charles E. Coughlin's National Union

for Social Justice, the new party also had the support of Dr. Francis E. Townsend, leader of a movement for government-supported old-age pensions, and Gerald L. K. Smith, self-appointed heir of Louisiana senator Huey P. Long's share-the-wealth program.

Father Coughlin was the keystone of the Union Party and was instrumental in choosing its presidential ticket in June 1936 — Rep. William Lemke, R-N.D., for president and Thomas O'Brien, a Massachusetts railroad union lawyer, for vice president. The new party did not hold a convention. The party's platform reportedly was written by Coughlin, Lemke and O'Brien and was similar to the program espoused by Coughlin's National Union. Among the features of the Union Party platform were proposals for banking and currency reform, a guaranteed income for workers, restrictions on wealth and an isolationist foreign policy.

Lacking organization and finances during the campaign, the party further suffered from the increasingly violent and often anti-Semitic tone of the oratory of both Coughlin and Smith.

The Union Party failed miserably in its primary goal of defeating Roosevelt. Roosevelt won a landslide victory and the Lemke ticket received only 892,267 votes (2 percent of the popular vote). The party standard-bearers were unable to carry a single state, and the Union Party's candidates for the House and Senate all were defeated. The party continued on a local level until it was finally dissolved in 1939.

### United We Stand, America (Independent Ross Perot) (1992- )

The presidential campaign of Texas billionaire Ross Perot in 1992 drew the highest vote share of any independent or third party candidate in 80 years. Relying heavily on his own wealth and on grass-roots volunteer efforts to get his name on the ballot in all 50 states and the District of Columbia, Perot received 19,741,657 votes or 19 percent of the nationwide vote. He did not win any sizable constituency or receive any electoral votes, but he drew a respectable 10 percent to 30 percent in popular voting across the nation. He ran best in the West, New England, the Plains states, around his Dallas base, in economically distressed parts of the Rust Belt and in high-growth districts on Florida's coasts.

Perot, who announced the possibility of his candidacy in February 1992, ran his early unofficial campaign mainly on one issue — eliminating the federal deficit. He had the luxury of funding his entire campaign, which included buying huge amounts of television time. Drawing on the disenchantment of voters, Perot and his folksy, no-nonsense approach to government reform struck a populist chord. But he also demonstrated his quirkiness by bizarrely withdrawing from the presidential race in mid-July and then reversing himself and re-entering in October.

United We Stand, America (UWSA), formed from the ashes of Perot's candidacy, did not bill itself as an official political party. Promoting itself instead as a non-partisan educational organization, UWSA called for a balanced budget, government reform and health care reform. While the group's leaders did not endorse candidates or offer them financial assistance, the leaders planned to try to influence elections and hold incumbents accountable through election forums and voter guides ranking candidates on selected issues. Some state UWSA leaders suggested they would recruit candidates if incumbents were unopposed, or if the candidates from both parties got poor grades on United We Stand issues.

In 1993 Ross Perot, rather than UWSA, commanded a lot of attention on Capitol Hill. From marshaling grass-roots support on congressional reform to unsuccessfully opposing the North American Free Trade Agreement (NAFTA), Perot remained highly visible on the political scene. Democrats and Republicans were unable to co-opt his following as they had those of major third-party movements in the past. And Perot continued to use his supporters' anger with government and the political process to sustain himself as an independent political force. For the most part, UWSA remained a party in waiting for Perot to decide again to run for president.

## U.S. Labor Party
### (Independent Lyndon LaRouche) (1973-    )

Formed in 1973 as the political arm of the National Caucus of Labor Committees (NCLC), the U.S. Labor Party made its debut in national politics in 1976. The NCLC was organized in 1968 by splinters of the radical movements of the 1960s. It is a Marxist group. New Yorker Lyndon LaRouche, the party's chairman and a self-taught economist who worked in the management and computer fields, became its 1976 presidential nominee and Wayne Evans, a Detroit steelworker, his running mate.

The party directed much of its fire at the Rockefeller family. It charged that banks controlled by the Rockefellers were strangling the U.S. and world economies. In an apocalyptic vein, the party predicted a world monetary collapse by Election Day and the destruction of the country by thermonuclear war by the summer of 1977.

LaRouche's party developed a reputation for harassment because of its shouted interruptions and demonstrations against its political foes, including the Communist Party and the United Auto Workers. It accused some left-wing organizations and individuals, such as linguist Noam Chomsky and Marcus Raskin and his Institute for Policy Studies, of conspiring with the Rockefellers and the Central Intelligence Agency.

During the 1976 campaign, LaRouche was more critical of Carter than Ford. He depicted Ford as a well-meaning man out of his depth in the presidency, but Carter as a pawn of nuclear war advocates and a disgracefully unqualified presidential candidate. LaRouche captured only 40,043 votes, less than 0.1 percent of the national vote. He was on the ballot in 23 states and the District of Columbia.

Although the U.S. Labor Party did not run a presidential candidate in the 1980 election, LaRouche ran a strident campaign — as a Democrat. By this time, LaRouche's politics had shifted to the right, and his speeches were fraught with warnings of conspiracy.

He continued his crusade in 1984 but as an "independent Democrat," dismissing Democratic presidential nominee Walter F. Mondale as an "agent of Soviet influence." LaRouche received 78,807 votes, or 0.1 percent of the vote.

In 1988 LaRouche again attempted to run as a Democrat but, failing the nomination, garnered 25,562 votes under the banner of the National Economic Recovery Party. On Dec. 16, 1988, LaRouche and six of his associates were convicted on 47 counts of mail fraud and conspiracy to commit mail fraud. LaRouche was sentenced to 15 years in prison.

In 1992 the unflagging LaRouche ran again for president from his jail cell. As a convicted felon, he no longer had the right to vote himself. LaRouche ran as an independent although his name appeared on several state ballots under various party names. His supporters, experienced in winning

ballot access, placed him on the ballot in 17 states and the District of Columbia. He received 26,333 votes nationwide.

## Whig Party (1834-1856)

Organized in 1834 during the administration of President Andrew Jackson, the Whig Party was an amalgam of forces opposed to Jackson administration policies. Even the name "Whig" was symbolic of the intense anti-Jackson feeling among the party's adherents. The name was taken from the earlier British Whig Party, founded in the 17th century in opposition to the tyranny of the Stuart monarchs. Likewise, the term was popular during the American Revolution, as the colonists opposed what they considered the tyranny of King George III. The new Whig Party was opposed to "King Andrew," the Whig characterization of President Jackson and his strong executive actions.

Southerners, enraged over Jackson's stand against states' rights in the South Carolina nullification dispute, joined the coalition early. Then came businessmen, merchants and conservatives, shocked and fearful of Jackson's war on the Bank of the United States. This group, basically a remnant of the National Republican Party, espoused Henry Clay's American Plan, a program of federal action to aid the economy and tie together the sections of the country. The plan included tariff protection for business, a national bank, public works and distribution to the states of money received for the sale of public lands. The Clay plan became the basis for the Whigs' nationalistic economic program.

Another influential group joining the Whig coalition was the Anti-Masons, an egalitarian movement strong in parts of New England, New York and Pennsylvania.

Throughout its life, the Whig Party was plagued by factionalism and disunity. In 1836, the first presidential election in which the Whigs took part, the party had no national presidential candidate. Rather, three different candidates ran in different parts of the country — Gen. William Henry Harrison, Hugh L. White and Daniel Webster — each hoping to carry Whig electors in states where they were popular. Then the Whig electors, if a majority, could combine in the Electoral College on one candidate or, if that proved impossible, throw the election into the House. But Van Buren, the Democratic nominee, won a majority of the electors.

Befitting their lack of unity, the Whigs adopted no platform in 1840 and nominated Harrison, a military hero, for the presidency. His campaign, emphasizing an apocryphal log cabin and hard cider home life in Ohio, resulted in a landslide victory.

But Harrison died only a month after taking office (April 4, 1841). The new president, John Tyler of Virginia, proceeded to veto most elements of the Whig economic program, including the tariff and re-establishment of the national bank. Given Tyler's well-known states' rights position — ignored by the Whigs in 1840 when they capitalized on his Southern appeal — the vetoes were inevitable. Tyler's outraged Cabinet resigned, and for the rest of his term he remained a president without a party. Since his first two years in office were the only ones in which the Whigs controlled the presidency and both houses of Congress, Tyler's vetoes spoiled the only chance the Whigs ever had of implementing their program.

The Whigs won the White House for the second and last time in 1848 by running another military hero, Gen. Zachary Taylor. Like Harrison, Taylor was a non-ideological candidate who died in office. He was succeeded by Vice President Millard Fillmore.

The development of the slavery question in the 1840s and its intensification in the 1850s proved to be the death knell for the Whig Party. A party containing anti-slavery New Englanders and Southern plantation owners was simply unable to bridge the gap between them. The Compromise of 1850, forged by Clay, only briefly allayed the controversy over extension of slavery into the Western territories. Many Southern Whigs gravitated toward the Democrats, whom they believed more responsive to their interests. In the North, new parties specifically dedicated to opposing the expansion of slavery (Free Soilers, Anti-Nebraskans, Republicans) attracted Whig voters.

The last Whig national convention, in 1856, adopted a platform but endorsed former president Millard Fillmore, already the nominee of the Know-Nothing Party. The Whig platform deplored sectional strife and called for compromise to save the Union. But it was a futile campaign, with Fillmore carrying only Maryland and winning only 21.5 percent of the national vote.

## Workers World Party (1959-    )

With the Hungarian citizen revolt and other developments in Eastern Europe providing some impetus, the Workers World Party in 1959 split off from the Socialist Workers Party. The party theoretically supports worker uprisings in all parts of the world. Yet it backed the communist governments that put down rebellions in Hungary during the 1950s, Czechoslovakia in the 1960s and Poland in the 1980s. Workers World is an activist revolutionary group that, up until 1980, concentrated its efforts on specific issues, such as the anti-war and civil rights demonstrations during the 1960s and 1970s. The party has an active youth organization, Youth Against War and Fascism.

In 1980 party leaders saw an opportunity, created by the weakness of the U.S. economy and the related high unemployment, to interest voters in its revolutionary ideas. That year it placed Deirdre Griswold, the editor of the party's newspaper and one of its founding members, on the presidential ballot in 10 states. Together with her running mate Larry Holmes, a 27-year-old black activist, Griswold received 13,300 votes. In 1984 Holmes ran as the presidential candidate, getting on the ballot in eight states and receiving 15,329 votes. In 1988 Holmes ran with Gloria LaRiva, and they garnered 7,846 votes. LaRiva ran as the presidential candidate in 1992 and was only on the ballot in New Mexico, where she received 181 votes.

# Political Party Nominees, 1831-1992

Following is a comprehensive list of major and minor party nominees for president and vice president since 1831 when the first nominating convention was held by the Anti-Masonic party.

In many cases, minor parties made only token efforts at a presidential campaign. Often, third party candidates declined to run after being nominated by the convention, or their names appeared on the ballots of only a few states. In some cases the names of minor candidates did not appear on any state ballots and they received only a scattering of write-in-votes, if any.

The basic source used to compile the list was Joseph Nathan Kane, *Facts About the Presidents,* 6th edition, The H. W. Wilson Co., New York, 1993. To verify the names appearing in Kane, Congressional Quarterly consulted the following additional sources: Richard M. Scammon, *America at the Polls,* University of Pittsburgh Press, Pittsburgh, 1965; *America Votes 8* (1968 election), Congressional Quar-

terly, Washington, 1969; *America Votes 10* (1972 election), Congressional Quarterly, Washington, 1973; *Encyclopedia of American History,* edited by Richard B. Morris, Harper and Row, New York, 1965; *Dictionary of American Biography,* Charles Scribner's Sons, New York, 1928-1936; *Facts on File,* Facts on File Inc., New York 1945-75; *History of U.S. Political Parties,* Vols. I-IV, edited by Arthur M. Schlesinger, McGraw Hill, New York, 1971; and *Who Was Who in America,* Vol. I-V (1607-1968), Marquis Who's Who, Chicago. The sources for the 1976 to 1992 elections were Richard M. Scammon, *America Votes 12* (1977), *America Votes 14* (1981), *America Votes 16* (1985), *America Votes 18* (1989), and *America Votes 20* (1993).

When these sources contained information in conflict with Kane, the conflicting information is included in a footnote. Where a candidate appears in Kane, *but could not be verified in another source,* an asterisk appears beside the candidate's name on the list.

### 1832 Election

**Democratic Party**
President: Andrew Jackson, Tennessee
Vice President: Martin Van Buren, New York
**National Republican Party**
President: Henry Clay, Kentucky
Vice President: John Sergeant, Pennsylvania
**Anti-Masonic Party**
President: William Wirt, Maryland
Vice President: Amos Ellmaker, Pennsylvania
**Independent Party**
President: John Floyd, Virginia
Vice President: Henry Lee, Massachusetts

### 1836 Election

**Democratic Party**
President: Martin Van Buren, New York
Vice President: Richard Mentor Johnson, Kentucky
**Whig Party**
  President: William Henry Harrison, Hugh Lawson White, Daniel Webster
Vice President: Francis Granger, John Tyler.
  The Whigs nominated regional candidates in 1836 hoping that each candidate would carry his region and deny Democrat Van Buren an electoral vote majority. Webster was the Whig candidate in Massachusetts; Harrison in the rest of New England, the middle Atlantic states, and the West; and White in the South.
  Granger was the running mate of Harrison and Webster. Tyler was White's running mate.

### 1840 Election

**Whig Party**
  President: William Henry Harrison, Ohio
Vice President: John Tyler, Virginia

**Democratic Party**
  President: Martin Van Buren, New York
  The Democratic convention adopted a resolution that left the choice of vice presidential candidates to the states. Democratic electors divided their vice presidential votes among incumbent Richard M. Johnson (48 votes), Littleton W. Tazewell (11 votes), and James K. Polk (1 vote).
**Liberty Party**
  President: James Gillespie Birney, New York
  Vice President: Thomas Earle, Pennsylvania

### 1844 Election

**Democratic Party**
  President: James Knox Polk, Tennessee
  Vice President: George Mifflin Dallas, Pennsylvania
**Whig Party**
  President: Henry Clay, Kentucky
  Vice President: Theodore Frelinghuysen, New Jersey
**Liberty Party**
  President: James Gillespie Birney, New York
  Vice President: Thomas Morris, Ohio
**National Democratic**
  President: John Tyler, Virginia
  Vice President: None
  Tyler withdrew from the race in favor of the Democrat, Polk.

### 1848 Election

**Whig Party**
  President: Zachary Taylor, Louisiana
  Vice President: Millard Fillmore, New York
**Democratic Party**
  President: Lewis Cass, Michigan
  Vice President: William Orlando Butler, Kentucky
**Free Soil Party**
  President: Martin Van Buren, New York
  Vice President: Charles Francis Adams, Massachusetts

## Political Parties

**Free Soil (Barnburners—Liberty Party)**
President: John Parker Hale, New Hampshire
Vice President: Leicester King, Ohio
Later John Parker Hale relinquished the nomination.
**National Liberty Party**
President: Gerrit Smith, New York
Vice President: Charles C. Foote, Michigan

### 1852 Election

**Democratic Party**
President: Franklin Pierce, New Hampshire
Vice President: William R. King, Alabama
**Whig Party**
President: Winfield Scott, New Jersey
Vice President: William Alexander Graham, North Carolina
**Free Soil**
President: John Parker Hale, New Hampshire
Vice President: George Washington Julian, Indiana

### 1856 Election

**Democratic Party**
President: James Buchanan, Pennsylvania
Vice President: John Cabell Breckinridge, Kentucky
**Republican Party**
President: John Charles Fremont, California
Vice President: William Lewis Dayton, New Jersey
**American (Know-Nothing) Party**
President: Millard Fillmore, New York
Vice President: Andrew Jackson Donelson, Tennessee
**Whig Party (the 'Silver Grays')**
President: Millard Fillmore, New York
Vice President: Andrew Jackson Donelson, Tennessee
**North American Party**
President: Nathaniel Prentice Banks, Massachusetts
Vice President: William Freame Johnston, Pennsylvania
Banks and Johnson declined the nominations and gave their support to the Republicans.

### 1860 Election

**Republican Party**
President: Abraham Lincoln, Illinois
Vice President: Hannibal Hamlin, Maine
**Democratic Party**
President: Stephen Arnold Douglas, Illinois
Vice President: Herschel Vespasian Johnson, Georgia
**Southern Democratic Party**
President: John Cabell Breckinridge, Kentucky
Vice President: Joseph Lane, Oregon
**Constitutional Union Party**
President: John Bell, Tennessee
Vice President: Edward Everett, Massachusetts

### 1864 Election

**Republican Party**
President: Abraham Lincoln, Illinois
Vice President: Andrew Johnson, Tennessee
**Democratic Party**
President: George Brinton McClellan, New York
Vice President: George Hunt Pendleton, Ohio
**Independent Republican Party**
President: John Charles Fremont, California
Vice President: John Cochrane, New York
Fremont and Cochrane declined and gave their support to the Republican party nominees.

### 1868 Election

**Republican Party**
President: Ulysses Simpson Grant, Illinois
Vice President: Schuyler Colfax, Indiana
**Democratic Party**
President: Horatio Seymour, New York
Vice President: Francis Preston Blair Jr., Missouri

### 1872 Election

**Republican Party**
President: Ulysses Simpson Grant, Illinois
Vice President: Henry Wilson, Massachusetts
**Liberal Republican Party**
President: Horace Greeley, New York
Vice President: Benjamin Gratz Brown, Missouri
**Straight-Out Democratic Party**
President: Charles O'Conor, New York
Vice President: John Quincy Adams, Massachusetts
**Independent Liberal Republican Party (Opposition Party)**
President: William Slocum Groesbeck, Ohio
Vice President: Frederick Law Olmsted, New York
**Democratic Party**
President: Horace Greeley, New York
Vice President: Benjamin Gratz Brown, Missouri
**Prohibition Party**
President: James Black, Pennsylvania
Vice President: John Russell, Michigan
**People's Party (Equal Rights Party)**
President: Victoria Claflin Woodhull, New York
Vice President: Frederick Douglass
**Labor Reform Party**
President: David Davis, Illinois
Vice President: Joel Parker, New Jersey
**Liberal Republican Party of Colored Men**
President: Horace Greeley, New York
Vice President: Benjamin Gratz Brown, Missouri
**National Working Men's Party**
President: Ulysses Simpson Grant, Illinois
Vice President: Henry Wilson, Massachusetts

### 1876 Election

**Republican Party**
President: Rutherford Birchard Hayes, Ohio
Vice President: William Almon Wheeler, New York
**Democratic Party**
President: Samuel Jones Tilden, New York
Vice President: Thomas Andrews Hendricks, Indiana
**Greenback Party**
President: Peter Cooper, New York
Vice President: Samuel Fenton Cary, Ohio
**Prohibition Party**
President: Green Clay Smith, Kentucky
Vice President: Gideon Tabor Stewart, Ohio
**American National Party**
President: James B. Walker, Illinois
Vice President: Donald Kirkpatrick, New York

### 1880 Election

**Republican Party**
President: James Abram Garfield, Ohio
Vice President: Chester Alan Arthur, New York
**Democratic Party**
President: Winfield Scott Hancock, Pennsylvania
Vice President: William Hayden English, Indiana
**Greenback Labor Party**
President: James Baird Weaver, Iowa
Vice President: Benjamin J. Chambers, Texas

**Prohibition Party**
President: Neal Dow, Maine
Vice President: Henry Adams Thompson, Ohio
**American Party**
President: John Wolcott Phelps, Vermont
Vice President: Samuel Clarke Pomeroy, Kansas *

## 1884 Election

**Democratic Party**
President: Grover Cleveland, New York
Vice President: Thomas Andrews Hendricks, Indiana
**Republican Party**
President: James Gillespie Blaine, Maine
Vice President: John Alexander Logan, Illinois
**Greenback Party**
President: Benjamin Franklin Butler, Massachusetts
Vice President: Absolom Madden West, Mississippi
**Anti-Monopoly Party**
President: Benjamin Franklin Butler, Massachusetts
Vice President: Absolom Madden West, Mississippi
**Prohibition Party**
President: John Pierce St. John, Kansas
Vice President: William Daniel, Maryland
**American Prohibition Party**
President: Samuel Clark Pomeroy, Kansas
Vice President: John A. Conant, Connecticut
**Equal Rights Party**
President: Belva Ann Bennett Lockwood, District of Columbia
Vice President: Marietta Lizzie Bell Stow, California

## 1888 Election

**Republican Party**
President: Benjamin Harrison, Indiana
Vice President: Levi Parsons Morton, New York
**Democratic Party**
President: Grover Cleveland, New York
Vice President: Allen Granberry Thurman, Ohio
**Prohibition Party**
President: Clinton Bowen Fisk, New Jersey
Vice President: John Anderson Brooks, Missouri *
**Union Labor Party**
President: Alson Jenness Streeter, Illinois
Vice President: Charles E. Cunningham, Arkansas *
**United Labor Party**
President: Robert Hall Cowdrey, Illinois
Vice President: William H. T. Wakefield, Kansas *
**American Party**
President: James Langdon Curtis, New York
Vice President: Peter Dinwiddie Wigginton, California *
**Equal Rights Party**
President: Belva Ann Bennett Lockwood, District of Columbia
Vice President: Alfred Henry Love, Pennsylvania *
**Industrial Reform Party**
President: Albert E. Redstone, California *
Vice President: John Colvin, Kansas *

## 1892 Election

**Democratic Party**
President: Grover Cleveland, New York
Vice President: Adlai Ewing Stevenson, Illinois
**Republican Party**
President: Benjamin Harrison, Indiana
Vice President: Whitelaw Reid, New York
**People's Party of America**
President: James Baird Weaver, Iowa
Vice President: James Gaven Field, Virginia
**Prohibition Party**
President: John Bidwell, California
Vice President: James Britton Cranfill, Texas

**Socialist Labor Party**
President: Simon Wing, Massachusetts
Vice President: Charles Horatio Matchett, New York *

## 1896 Election

**Republican Party**
President: William McKinley, Ohio
Vice President: Garret Augustus Hobart, New Jersey
**Democratic Party**
President: William Jennings Bryan, Nebraska
Vice President: Arthur Sewall, Maine
**People's Party (Populist)**
President: William Jennings Bryan, Nebraska
Vice President: Thomas Edward Watson, Georgia
**National Democratic Party**
President: John McAuley Palmer, Illinois
Vice President: Simon Bolivar Buckner, Kentucky
**Prohibition Party**
President: Joshua Levering, Maryland
Vice President: Hale Johnson, Illinois *
**Socialist Labor Party**
President: Charles Horatio Matchett, New York
Vice President: Matthew Maguire, New Jersey
**National Party**
President: Charles Eugene Bentley, Nebraska
Vice President: James Haywood Southgate, North Carolina *
**National Silver Party (Bi-Metallic League)**
President: William Jennings Bryan, Nebraska
Vice President: Arthur Sewall, Maine

## 1900 Election

**Republican Party**
President: William McKinley, Ohio
Vice President: Theodore Roosevelt, New York
**Democratic Party**
President: William Jennings Bryan, Nebraska
Vice President: Adlai Ewing Stevenson, Illinois
**Prohibition Party**
President: John Granville Wooley, Illinois
Vice President: Henry Brewer Metcalf, Rhode Island
**Social-Democratic Party**
President: Eugene Victor Debs, Indiana
Vice President: Job Harriman, California
**People's Party (Populist—Anti-Fusionist faction)**
President: Wharton Barker, Pennsylvania
Vice President: Ignatius Donnelly, Minnesota
**Socialist Labor Party**
President: Joseph Francis Malloney, Massachusetts
Vice President: Valentine Remmel, Pennsylvania
**Union Reform Party**
President: Seth Hockett Ellis, Ohio
Vice President: Samuel T. Nicholson, Pennsylvania
**United Christian Party**
President: Jonah Fitz Randolph Leonard, Iowa
Vice President: David H. Martin, Pennsylvania
**People's Party (Populist—Fusionist faction)**
President: William Jennings Bryan, Nebraska
Vice President: Adlai Ewing Stevenson, Illinois
**Silver Republican Party**
President: William Jennings Bryan, Nebraska
Vice President: Adlai Ewing Stevenson, Illinois
**National Party**
President: Donelson Caffery, Louisiana
Vice President: Archibald Murray Howe, Massachusetts *

## 1904 Election

**Republican Party**
President: Theodore Roosevelt, New York
Vice President: Charles Warren Fairbanks, Indiana

**Democratic Party**
President: Alton Brooks Parker, New York
Vice President: Henry Gassaway Davis, West Virginia
**Socialist Party**
President: Eugene Victor Debs, Indiana
Vice President: Benjamin Hanford, New York
**Prohibition Party**
President: Silas Comfort Swallow, Pennsylvania
Vice President: George W. Carroll, Texas
**People's Party (Populists)**
President: Thomas Edward Watson, Georgia
Vice President: Thomas Henry Tibbles, Nebraska
**Socialist Labor Party**
President: Charles Hunter Corregan, New York
Vice President: William Wesley Cox, Illinois
**Continental Party**
President: Austin Holcomb
Vice President: A. King, Missouri

### 1908 Election

**Republican Party**
President: William Howard Taft, Ohio
Vice President: James Schoolcraft Sherman, New York
**Democratic Party**
President: William Jennings Bryan, Nebraska
Vice President: John Worth Kern, Indiana
**Socialist Party**
President: Eugene Victor Debs
Vice President: Benjamin Hanford
**Prohibition Party**
President: Eugene Wilder Chafin, Illinois
Vice President: Aaron Sherman Watkins, Ohio
**Independence Party**
President: Thomas Louis Hisgen, Massachusetts
Vice President: John Temple Graves, Georgia
**People's Party (Populist)**
President: Thomas Edward Watson, Georgia
Vice President: Samuel Williams, Indiana
**Socialist Labor Party**
President: August Gillhaus, New York
Vice President: Donald L. Munro, Virginia
**United Christian Party**
President: Daniel Braxton Turney, Illinois
Vice President: Lorenzo S. Coffin, Iowa

### 1912 Election

**Democratic Party**
President: Woodrow Wilson, New Jersey
Vice President: Thomas Riley Marshall, Indiana
**Progressive Party ('Bull Moose' Party)**
President: Theodore Roosevelt, New York
Vice President: Hiram Warren Johnson, California
**Republican Party**
President: William Howard Taft, Ohio
Vice President: James Schoolcraft Sherman, New York
Sherman died Oct. 30; replaced by Nicholas Murray Butler,
New York
**Socialist Party**
President: Eugene Victor Debs, Indiana
Vice President: Emil Seidel, Wisconsin
**Prohibition Party**
President: Eugene Wilder Chafin, Illinois
Vice President: Aaron Sherman Watkins, Ohio
**Socialist Labor Party**
President: Arthur Elmer Reimer, Massachusetts
Vice President: August Gillhaus, New York [1]

### 1916 Election

**Democratic Party**
President: Woodrow Wilson, New Jersey
Vice President: Thomas Riley Marshall, Indiana
**Republican Party**
President: Charles Evans Hughes, New York
Vice President: Charles Warren Fairbanks, Indiana
**Socialist Party**
President: Allan Louis Benson, New York
Vice President: George Ross Kirkpatrick, New Jersey
**Prohibition Party**
President: James Franklin Hanly, Indiana
Vice President: Ira Landrith, Tennessee
**Socialist Labor Party**
President: Arthur Elmer Reimer, Massachusetts *
Vice President: Caleb Harrison, Illinois *
**Progressive Party**
President: Theodore Roosevelt, New York
Vice President: John Milliken Parker, Louisiana

### 1920 Election

**Republican Party**
President: Warren Gamaliel Harding, Ohio
Vice President: Calvin Coolidge, Massachusetts
**Democratic Party**
President: James Middleton Cox, Ohio
Vice President: Franklin Delano Roosevelt, New York
**Socialist Party**
President: Eugene Victor Debs, Indiana
Vice President: Seymour Stedman, Illinois
**Farmer Labor Party**
President: Parley Parker Christensen, Utah
Vice President: Maximilian Sebastian Hayes, Ohio
**Prohibition Party**
President: Aaron Sherman Watkins, Ohio
Vice President: David Leigh Colvin, New York
**American Party**
President: James Edward Ferguson, Texas
Vice President: William J. Hough
**Socialist Labor Party**
President: William Wesley Cox, Missouri
Vice President: August Gillhaus, New York
**Single Tax Party**
President: Robert Colvin Macauley, Pennsylvania
Vice President: R. G. Barnum, Ohio

### 1924 Election

**Republican Party**
President: Calvin Coolidge, Massachusetts
Vice President: Charles Gates Dawes, Illinois
**Democratic Party**
President: John William Davis, New York
Vice President: Charles Wayland Bryan, Nebraska
**Progressive Party**
President: Robert La Follette, Wisconsin
Vice President: Burton Kendall Wheeler, Montana
**Prohibition Party**
President: Herman Preston Faris, Missouri
Vice President: Marie Caroline Brehm, California
**Socialist Labor Party**
President: Frank T. Johns, Oregon
Vice President: Verne L. Reynolds, New York
**Socialist Party**
President: Robert La Follette, New York
Vice President: Burton Kendall Wheeler, Montana
**Workers Party (Communist Party)**
President: William Zebulon Foster, Illinois
Vice President: Benjamin Gitlow, New York

**American Party**
President: Gilbert Owen Nations, District of Columbia
Vice President: Charles Hiram Randall, California ²
**Commonwealth Land Party**
President: William J. Wallace, New Jersey
Vice President: John Cromwell Lincoln, Ohio
**Farmer Labor Party**
President: Duncan McDonald, Illinois *
Vice President: William Bouck, Washington *
**Greenback Party**
President: John Zahnd, Indiana *
Vice President: Roy M. Harrop, Nebraska *

## 1928 Election

**Republican Party**
President: Herbert Clark Hoover, California
Vice President: Charles Curtis, Kansas
**Democratic Party**
President: Alfred Emanuel Smith, New York
Vice President: Joseph Taylor Robinson, Arkansas
**Socialist Party**
President: Norman Mattoon Thomas, New York
Vice President: James Hudson Maurer, Pennsylvania
**Workers Party (Communist Party)**
President: William Zebulon Foster, Illinois
Vice President: Benjamin Gitlow, New York
**Socialist Labor Party**
President: Verne L. Reynolds, Michigan
Vice President: Jeremiah D. Crowley, New York
**Prohibition Party**
President: William Frederick Varney, New York
Vice President: James Arthur Edgerton, Virginia
**Farmer Labor Party**
President: Frank Elbridge Webb, California
Vice President: Will Vereen, Georgia ³
**Greenback Party**
President: John Zahnd, Indiana *
Vice President: Wesley Henry Bennington, Ohio *

## 1932 Election

**Democratic Party**
President: Franklin Delano Roosevelt, New York
Vice President: John Nance Garner, Texas
**Republican Party**
President: Herbert Clark Hoover, California
Vice President: Charles Curtis, Kansas
**Socialist Party**
President: Norman Mattoon Thomas, New York
Vice President: James Hudson Maurer, Pennsylvania
**Communist Party**
President: William Zebulon Foster, Illinois
Vice President: James William Ford, New York
**Prohibition Party**
President: William David Upshaw, Georgia
Vice President: Frank Stewart Regan, Illinois
**Liberty Party**
President: William Hope Harvey, Arkansas
Vice President: Frank B. Hemenway, Washington
**Socialist Labor Party**
President: Verne L. Reynolds, New York
Vice President: John W. Aiken, Massachusetts
**Farmer Labor Party**
President: Jacob Sechler Coxey, Ohio
Vice President: Julius J. Reiter, Minnesota
**Jobless Party**
President: James Renshaw Cox, Pennsylvania
Vice President: V. C. Tisdal, Oklahoma
**National Party**
President: Seymour E. Allen, Massachusetts

## 1936 Election

**Democratic Party**
President: Franklin Delano Roosevelt, New York
Vice President: John Nance Garner, Texas
**Republican Party**
President: Alfred Mossman Landon, Kansas
Vice President: Frank Knox, Illinois
**Union Party**
President: William Lemke, North Dakota
Vice President: Thomas Charles O'Brien, Massachusetts
**Socialist Party**
President: Norman Mattoon Thomas, New York
Vice President: George A. Nelson, Wisconsin
**Communist Party**
President: Earl Russell Browder, Kansas
Vice President: James William Ford, New York
**Prohibition Party**
President: David Leigh Colvin, New York
Vice President: Alvin York, Tennessee
**Socialist Labor Party**
President: John W. Aiken, Massachusetts
Vice President: Emil F. Teichert, New York
**National Greenback Party**
President: John Zahnd, Indiana *
Vice President: Florence Garvin, Rhode Island *

## 1940 Election

**Democratic Party**
President: Franklin Delano Roosevelt, New York
Vice President: Henry Agard Wallace, Iowa
**Republican Party**
President: Wendell Lewis Willkie, New York
Vice President: Charles Linza McNary, Oregon
**Socialist Party**
President: Norman Mattoon Thomas, New York
Vice President: Maynard C. Krueger, Illinois
**Prohibition Party**
President: Roger Ward Babson, Massachusetts
Vice President: Edgar V. Moorman, Illinois
**Communist Party (Workers Party)**
President: Earl Russell Browder, Kansas
Vice President: James William Ford, New York
**Socialist Labor Party**
President: John W. Aiken, Massachusetts
Vice President: Aaron M. Orange, New York
**Greenback Party**
President: John Zahnd, Indiana *
Vice President: James Elmer Yates, Arizona *

## 1944 Election

**Democratic Party**
President: Franklin Delano Roosevelt, New York
Vice President: Harry S. Truman, Missouri
**Republican Party**
President: Thomas Edmund Dewey, New York
Vice President: John William Bricker, Ohio
**Socialist Party**
President: Norman Mattoon Thomas, New York
Vice President: Darlington Hoopes, Pennsylvania
**Prohibition Party**
President: Claude A. Watson, California
Vice President: Andrew Johnson, Kentucky
**Socialist Labor Party**
President: Edward A. Teichert, Pennsylvania
Vice President: Arla A. Albaugh, Ohio
**America First Party**
President: Gerald Lyman Kenneth Smith, Michigan
Vice President: Henry A. Romer, Ohio

## 1948 Election

**Democratic Party**
President: Harry S. Truman, Missouri
Vice President: Alben William Barkley, Kentucky
**Republican Party**
President: Thomas Edmund Dewey, New York
Vice President: Earl Warren, California
**States' Rights Democratic Party**
President: James Strom Thurmond, South Carolina
Vice President: Fielding Lewis Wright, Mississippi
**Progressive Party**
President: Henry Agard Wallace, Iowa
Vice President: Glen Hearst Taylor, Idaho
**Socialist Party**
President: Norman Mattoon Thomas, New York
Vice President: Tucker Powell Smith, Michigan
**Prohibition Party**
President: Claude A. Watson, California
Vice President: Dale Learn, Pennsylvania
**Socialist Labor Party**
President: Edward A. Teichert, Pennsylvania
Vice President: Stephen Emery, New York
**Socialist Workers Party**
President: Farrell Dobbs, New York
Vice President: Grace Carlson, Minnesota
**Christian Nationalist Party**
President: Gerald Lyman Kenneth Smith, Missouri
Vice President: Henry A. Romer, Ohio
**Greenback Party**
President: John G. Scott, New York
Vice President: Granville B. Leeke, Indiana *
**Vegetarian Party**
President: John Maxwell, Illinois
Vice President: Symon Gould, New York *

## 1952 Election

**Republican Party**
President: Dwight David Eisenhower, New York
Vice President: Richard Milhous Nixon, California
**Democratic Party**
President: Adlai Ewing Stevenson, Illinois
Vice President: John Jackson Sparkman, Alabama
**Progressive Party**
President: Vincent William Hallinan, California
Vice President: Charlotta A. Bass, New York
**Prohibition Party**
President: Stuart Hamblen, California
Vice President: Enoch Arden Holtwick, Illinois
**Socialist Labor Party**
President: Eric Hass, New York
Vice President: Stephen Emery, New York
**Socialist Party**
President: Darlington Hoopes, Pennsylvania
Vice President: Samuel Herman Friedman, New York
**America First Party**
President: Douglas MacArthur, Wisconsin
Vice President: Harry Flood Byrd, Virginia
**Socialist Workers Party**
President: Farrell Dobbs, New York
Vice President: Myra Tanner Weiss, New York
**Poor Man's Party**
President: Henry B. Krajewski, New Jersey
Vice President: Frank Jenkins, New Jersey
**American Labor Party**
President: Vincent William Hallinan, California
Vice President: Charlotta A. Bass, New York
**American Vegetarian Party**
President: Daniel J. Murphy, California
Vice President: Symon Gould, New York *

**Church of God Party**
President: Homer Aubrey Tomlinson, New York
Vice President: Willie Isaac Bass, North Carolina *
**Constitution Party**
President: Douglas MacArthur, Wisconsin
Vice President: Harry Flood Byrd, Virginia
**Greenback Party**
President: Frederick C. Proehl, Washington
Vice President: Edward J. Bedell, Indiana

## 1956 Election

**Republican Party**
President: Dwight David Eisenhower, Pennsylvania
Vice President: Richard Milhous Nixon, California
**Democratic Party**
President: Adlai Ewing Stevenson, Illinois
Vice President: Estes Kefauver, Tennessee
**States' Rights Party**
President: Thomas Coleman Andrews, Virginia
Vice President: Thomas Harold Werdel, California
Ticket also favored by Constitution Party.
**Socialist Labor Party**
President: Eric Hass, New York
Vice President: Georgia Cozzini, Wisconsin
**Prohibition Party**
President: Enoch Arden Holtwick, Illinois
Vice President: Edward M. Cooper, California
**Socialist Workers Party**
President: Farrell Dobbs, New York
Vice President: Myra Tanner Weiss, New York
**States' Rights Party of Kentucky**
President: Harry Flood Byrd, Virginia
Vice President: William Ezra Jenner, Indiana
**South Carolinians for Independent Electors**
President: Harry Flood Byrd, Virginia
**Texas Constitution Party**
President: William Ezra Jenner, Indiana *
Vice President: Joseph Bracken Lee, Utah *
**Socialist Party**
President: Darlington Hoopes, Pennsylvania
Vice President: Samuel Herman Friedman, New York
**American Third Party**
President: Henry Krajewski, New Jersey
Vice President: Ann Marie Yezo, New Jersey
**Pioneer Party**
President: William Langer, North Dakota *
Vice President: Burr McCloskey, Illinois *
**American Vegetarian Party**
President: Herbert M. Shelton, California *
Vice President: Symon Gould, New York *
**Greenback Party**
President: Frederick C. Proehl, Washington
Vice President: Edward Kirby Meador, Massachusetts *
**Christian National Party**
President: Gerald Lyman Kenneth Smith
Vice President: Charles I. Robertson

## 1960 Election

**Democratic Party**
President: John Fitzgerald Kennedy, Massachusetts
Vice President: Lyndon Baines Johnson, Texas
**Republican Party**
President: Richard Milhous Nixon, California
Vice President: Henry Cabot Lodge, Massachusetts
**Socialist Labor Party**
President: Eric Hass, New York
Vice President: Georgia Cozzini, Wisconsin
**National States' Rights Party**
President: Orval Eugene Faubus, Arkansas
Vice President: John Geraerdt Crommelin, Alabama

**Prohibition Party**
President: Rutherford Losey Decker, Missouri
Vice President: Earle Harold Munn, Michigan
**Socialist Workers Party**
President: Farrell Dobbs, New York
Vice President: Myra Tanner Weiss, New York
**Constitution Party (Texas)**
President: Charles Loten Sullivan, Mississippi
Vice President: Merritt B. Curtis, District of Columbia
**Conservative Party of New Jersey**
President: Joseph Bracken Lee, Utah
Vice President: Kent H. Courtney, Louisiana
**Conservative Party of Virginia**
President: C. Benton Coiner, Virginia
Vice President: Edward M. Silverman, Virginia
**Greenback Party**
President: Whitney Hart Slocomb, California *
Vice President: Edward Kirby Meador, Massachusetts *
**Tax Cut Party (America First Party; American Party)**
President: Lar Daly, Illinois
Vice President: Merritt Barton Curtis, District of Columbia
**Independent Afro-American Party**
President: Clennon King, Georgia
Vice President: Reginald Carter
**Constitution Party (Washington)**
President: Merritt B. Curtis, District of Columbia
Vice President: B. N. Miller
**Theocratic Party**
President: Homer Aubrey Tomlinson, New York
Vice President: Raymond L. Teague, Alaska *
**Vegetarian Party**
President: Symon Gould, New York
Vice President: Christopher Gian-Cursio, Florida

### 1964 Election

**Democratic Party**
President: Lyndon Baines Johnson, Texas
Vice President: Hubert Horatio Humphrey, Minnesota
**Republican Party**
President: Barry Morris Goldwater, Arizona
Vice President: William Edward Miller, New York
**Socialist Labor Party**
President: Eric Hass, New York
Vice President: Henning A. Blomen, Massachusetts
**Socialist Workers Party**
President: Clifton DeBerry, New York
Vice President: Edward Shaw, New York
**Prohibition Party**
President: Earle Harold Munn, Michigan
Vice President: Mark Shaw, Massachusetts
**National States' Rights Party**
President: John Kasper, Tennessee
Vice President: J. B. Stoner, Georgia
**Constitution Party**
President: Joseph B. Lightburn, West Virginia
Vice President: Theodore C. Billings, Colorado
**Independent States' Rights Party**
President: Thomas Coleman Andrews, Virginia
Vice President: Thomas H. Werdel, California *
**Theocratic Party**
President: Homer Aubrey Tomlinson, New York
Vice President: William R. Rogers, Missouri *
**Universal Party**
President: Kirby James Hensley, California
Vice President: John O. Hopkins, Iowa

### 1968 Election

**Republican Party**
President: Richard Milhous Nixon, New York
Vice President: Spiro Theodore Agnew, Maryland

**Democratic Party**
President: Hubert Horatio Humphrey, Minnesota
Vice President: Edmund Sixtus Muskie, Maine
**American Independent Party**
President: George Corley Wallace, Alabama
Vice President: Curtis Emerson LeMay, Ohio
LeMay replaced S. Marvin Griffin, who originally had been selected.
**Socialist Labor Party**
President: Henning A. Blomen, Massachusetts
Vice President: George Sam Taylor, Pennsylvania
**Freedom and Peace Party**
President: Richard C. (Dick) Gregory, Illinois
Vice President: Mark Lane, New York
**Socialist Workers Party**
President: Fred Halstead, New York
Vice President: Paul Boutelle, New Jersey
**Peace and Freedom Party**
President: Eldridge Cleaver
Vice President: Judith Mage, New York
**Prohibition Party**
President: Earle Harold Munn, Sr., Michigan
Vice President: Rolland E. Fisher, Kansas
**Communist Party**
President: Charlene Mitchell, California
Vice President: Michael Zagarell, New York
**Constitution Party**
President: Richard K. Troxell, Texas
Vice President: Merle Thayer, Iowa
**Patriotic Party**
President: George Corley Wallace, Alabama
Vice President: William Penn Patrick, California
**Theocratic Party**
President: William R. Rogers, Missouri
**Universal Party**
President: Kirby James Hensley, California
Vice President: Roscoe B. MacKenna

### 1972 Election

**Republican Party**
President: Richard Milhous Nixon, California
Vice President: Spiro Theodore Agnew, Maryland
**Democratic Party**
President: George Stanley McGovern, South Dakota
Vice President: Thomas Francis Eagleton, Missouri
Eagleton resigned and was replaced on August 8, 1972, by Robert Sargent Shriver, Maryland, selected by the Democratic National Committee.
**American Independent Party**
President: John George Schmitz, California
Vice President: Thomas Jefferson Anderson, Tennessee
**Socialist Workers Party**
President: Louis Fisher, Illinois
Vice President: Genevieve Gunderson, Minnesota
**People's Party**
President: Benjamin McLane Spock
Vice President: Julius Hobson, District of Columbia
**Socialist Labor Party**
President: Linda Jenness, Georgia
Vice President: Andrew Pulley, Illinois
**Communist Party**
President: Gus Hall, New York
Vice President: Jarvis Tyner
**Prohibition Party**
President: Earle Harold Munn, Sr., Michigan
Vice President: Marshall Uncapher
**Libertarian Party**
President: John Hospers, California
Vice President: Theodora Nathan, Oregon
**America First Party**
President: John V. Mahalchik
Vice President: Irving Homer

**Political Parties**

**Universal Party**
President: Gabriel Green
Vice President: Daniel Fry

## 1976 Election

**Democratic Party**
President: Jimmy Carter, Georgia
Vice President: Walter F. Mondale, Minnesota
**Republican Party**
President: Gerald R. Ford, Michigan
Vice President: Robert Dole, Kansas
**Independent Candidate**
President: Eugene J. McCarthy, Minnesota
Vice President: none [4]
**Libertarian Party**
President: Roger MacBride, Virginia
Vice President: David P. Bergland, California
**American Independent Party**
President: Lester Maddox, Georgia
Vice President: William Dyke, Wisconsin
**American Party**
President: Thomas J. Anderson, Tennessee
Vice President: Rufus Shackleford, Florida
**Socialist Workers Party**
President: Peter Camejo, California
Vice President: Willie Mae Reid, California
**Communist Party**
President: Gus Hall, New York
Vice President: Jarvis Tyner, New York
**People's Party**
President: Margaret Wright, California
Vice President: Benjamin Spock, New York
**U.S. Labor Party**
President: Lyndon H. LaRouche Jr., New York
Vice President: R. W. Evans, Michigan
**Prohibition Party**
President: Benjamin C. Bubar, Maine
Vice President: Earl F. Dodge, Colorado
**Socialist Labor Party**
President: Jules Levin, New Jersey
Vice President: Constance Blomen, Massachusetts
**Socialist Party**
President: Frank P. Zeidler, Wisconsin
Vice President: J. Quinn Brisben, Illinois
**Restoration Party**
President: Ernest L. Miller
Vice President: Roy N. Eddy
**United American Party**
President: Frank Taylor
Vice President: Henry Swan

## 1980 Election [5]

**Republican Party**
President: Ronald Reagan, California
Vice President: George Bush, Texas
**Democratic Party**
President: Jimmy Carter, Georgia
Vice President: Walter F. Mondale, Minnesota
**National Unity Campaign**
President: John B. Anderson, Illinois
Vice President: Patrick J. Lucey, Wisconsin
**Libertarian Party**
President: Edward E. Clark, California
Vice President: David Koch, New York
**Citizens Party**
President: Barry Commoner, New York
Vice President: LaDonna Harris, New Mexico
**Communist Party**
President: Gus Hall, New York
Vice President: Angela Davis, California

**American Independent Party**
President: John R. Rarick, Louisiana
Vice President: Eileen M. Shearer, California
**Socialist Workers Party**
President: Clifton DeBerry, California
Vice President: Matilde Zimmermann

President: Andrew Pulley, Illinois
Vice President: Matilde Zimmermann

President: Richard Congress, Ohio
Vice President: Matilde Zimmermann
**Right to Life Party**
President: Ellen McCormack, New York
Vice President: Carroll Driscoll, New Jersey
**Peace and Freedom Party**
President: Maureen Smith, California
Vice President: Elizabeth Barron
**Workers World Party**
President: Deirdre Griswold, New Jersey
Vice President: Larry Holmes, New York
**Statesman Party**
President: Benjamin C. Bubar, Maine
Vice President: Earl F. Dodge, Colorado
**Socialist Party**
President: David McReynolds, New York
Vice President: Diane Drufenbrock, Wisconsin
**American Party**
President: Percy L. Greaves, New York
Vice President: Frank L. Varnum, California

President: Frank W. Shelton, Utah
Vice President: George E. Jackson
**Middle Class Party**
President: Kurt Lynen, New Jersey
Vice President: Harry Kieve, New Jersey
**Down With Lawyers Party**
President: Bill Gahres, New Jersey
Vice President: J. F. Loghlin, New Jersey
**Independent Party**
President: Martin E. Wendelken
**Natural Peoples Party**
President: Harley McLain, North Dakota
Vice President: Jewelie Goeller, North Dakota

## 1984 Election [6]

**Republican Party**
President: Ronald Reagan, California
Vice President: George Bush, Texas
**Democratic Party**
President: Walter F. Mondale, Minnesota
Vice President: Geraldine A. Ferraro, New York
**Libertarian Party**
President: David Bergland, California
Vice President: Jim Lewis, Connecticut
**Independent Party**
President: Lyndon H. LaRouche Jr., Virginia
Vice President: Billy Davis, Mississippi
**Citizens Party**
President: Sonia Johnson, Virginia
Vice President: Richard Walton, Rhode Island
**Populist Party**
President: Bob Richards, Texas
Vice President: Maureen Kennedy Salaman, California
**Independent Alliance Party**
President: Dennis L. Serrette, New Jersey
Vice President: Nancy Ross, New York
**Communist Party**
President: Gus Hall, New York
Vice President: Angela Davis, California
**Socialist Workers Party**
President: Mel Mason, California
Vice President: Andrea Gonzalez, New York

**Workers World Party**
President: Larry Holmes, New York
Vice President: Gloria La Riva, California
President: Gavrielle Holmes, New York
Vice President: Milton Vera
**American Party**
President: Delmar Dennis, Tennessee
Vice President: Traves Brownlee, Delaware
**Workers League Party**
President: Ed Winn, New York
Vice Presidents: Jean T. Brust, Helen Halyard, Edward Bergonzi
**Prohibition Party**
President: Earl F. Dodge, Colorado
Vice President: Warren C. Martin, Kansas

### 1988 Election [7]

**Republican Party**
President: George Bush, Texas
Vice President: Dan Quayle, Indiana
**Democratic Party**
President: Michael Stanley Dukakis, Massachusetts
Vice President: Lloyd Millard Bentsen Jr., Texas
**Libertarian Party**
President: Ronald Ernest Paul, Texas
Vice President: Andre V. Marrou, Nevada
**New Alliance Party**
President: Lenora B. Fulani, New York
Vice President: Joyce Dattner
**Populist Party**
President: David E. Duke, Louisiana
Vice President: Floyd C. Parker
**Consumer Party**
President: Eugene Joseph McCarthy, Minnesota
Vice President: Florence Rice
**American Independent Party**
President: James C. Griffin, California
Vice President: Charles J. Morsa
**National Economic Recovery Party**
President: Lyndon H. LaRouche Jr., Virginia
Vice President: Debra H. Freeman
**Right to Life Party**
President: William A. Marra, New Jersey
Vice President: Joan Andrews
**Workers League Party**
President: Edward Winn, New York
Vice President: Barry Porster
**Socialist Workers Party**
President: James Warren, New Jersey
Vice President: Kathleen Mickells
**Peace and Freedom Party**
President: Herbert Lewin
Vice President: Vikki Murdock
**Prohibition Party**
President: Earl F. Dodge, Colorado
Vice President: George D. Ormsby
**Workers World Party**
President: Larry Holmes, New York
Vice President: Gloria La Riva, California
**Socialist Party**
President: Willa Kenoyer, Minnesota
Vice President: Ron Ehrenreich
**American Party**
President: Delmar Dennis, Tennessee
Vice President: Earl Jepson
**Grassroots Party**
President: Jack E. Herer
Vice President: Dana Beal
**Independent Party**
President: Louie Youngkeit, Utah
**Third World Assembly Party**
President: John G. Martin, District of Columbia
Vice President: Cleveland Sparrow

### 1992 Election [8]

**Democratic Party**
President: Bill Clinton, Arkansas
Vice President: Albert Gore Jr., Tennessee
**Republican Party**
President: George Bush, Texas
Vice President: Dan Quayle, Indiana
**Independent**
President: Ross Perot, Texas
Vice President: James Stockdale, California
**Libertarian Party**
President: Andre V. Marrou, Nevada
Vice President: Nancy Lord, Georgia
**America First Party (Populist)**
President: James "Bo" Gritz
Vice President: Cyril Minett
**New Alliance Party**
President: Lenora B. Fulani, New York
Vice President: Maria E. Munoz, California
**Taxpayers Party**
President: Howard Phillips, Virginia
Vice President: Albion W. Knight, Maryland
**Natural Law Party**
President: John Hagelin, Iowa
Vice President: Mike Tompkins, Iowa
**Peace and Freedom Party**
President: Ron Daniels
Vice President: Asiba Tupahache
**Independent**
President: Lyndon H. LaRouche Jr., Virginia
Vice President: James L. Bevel
**Socialist Workers Party**
President: James Warren, New Jersey
Vice President: Willie Mae Reid
**Independent**
President: Drew Bradford
**Grassroots Party**
President: Jack E. Herer
Vice President: Derrick P. Grimmer
**Socialist Party**
President: J. Quinn Brisben
Vice President: Barbara Garson
**Workers League Party**
President: Helen Halyard
Vice President: Fred Mazelis
**Take Back America Party**
President: John Yiamouyiannas
Vice President: Allen C. McCone
**Independent**
President: Delbert L. Ehlers
Vice President: Rick Wendt
**Prohibition Party**
President: Earl F. Dodge, Colorado
Vice President: George D. Ormsby
**Apathy Party**
President: Jim Boren
Vice President: Will Weidman
**Third Party**
President: Eugene A. Hem
Vice President: Joanne Roland
**Looking Back Party**
President: Isabell Masters
Vice President: Walter Masters
**American Party**
President: Robert J. Smith
Vice President: Doris Feimer
**Workers World Party**
President: Gloria La Riva, California
Vice President: Larry Holmes, New York

*Notes*
  * Candidates appeared in Kane's Facts About the Presidents *but could not be verified in another source.*

*1. 1912: Schlesinger's* History of Presidential Elections *lists the Socialist Labor party vice presidential candidate as Francis. No first name is given.*

*2. 1924: Scammon's* America at the Polls *lists the American party vice presidential candidate as Leander L. Pickett.*

*3. 1928:* America at the Polls *lists the Farmer Labor party vice presidential candidate as L. R. Tillman.*

*4. 1976: McCarthy, who ran as an independent with no party designation, had no national running mate, favoring the elimination of the office. But as various state laws required a running mate, he had different ones in different states, amounting to nearly two dozen, all political unknowns.*

*5. 1980: In several cases vice presidential nominees were different from those listed for most states, and the Socialist Workers and American party nominees for president varied from state to state. For example, because Pulley, the major standard-bearer for the Socialist Workers party was only 29 years old, his name was not allowed on the ballot on some states (the Constitution requires presidential candidates to be at least 35 years old). Hence, the party ran other candidates in those states. In a number of states candidates appeared on the ballot with variants of the party designations listed, without any party designation, or with entirely different party names.*

*6. 1984: Both Larry Holmes and Gavrielle Holmes were standard-bearers of the Workers World party. Of the two, Larry Holmes was listed on more state ballots. Milton Vera was Gavrielle Holmes's vice presidential running mate in Ohio and Rhode Island. The Workers League party had three vice presidential running mates: Jean T. Brust in Illinois; Helen Halyard in Michigan, New Jersey and Pennsylvania; and Edward Bergonzi in Minnesota and Ohio.*

*7. 1988: The candidates listed include all those who appeared on the ballot in at least one state. In some cases a party's vice presidential candidate varied from state to state. Candidates' states were not available from some parties.*

*8. 1992: The candidates listed include all those who appeared on the ballot in at least one state. In some cases a party's vice presidential candidate varied from state to state. Candidates' states were not available from some parties.*

# Presidential Elections

**"The Republican National Convention in Session in the
Auditorium Building, Chicago."** *Harper's*, **June 30, 1888.**

# Chronology of Presidential Elections

The American people and their leaders were ambivalent about the concept of democracy in the early years of the Republic. This ambivalence was evident in the compromise for presidential selection worked out at the Constitutional Convention in 1787 and in the halting steps the nation took toward party competition.

The presidential selection process has changed significantly since George Washington was elected to his first term in 1789. The Electoral College is still the center of the system, but all the related institutions and processes have changed dramatically. In part, this is because the constitutional provisions for presidential selection are so vague.

The major features of the electoral system developed over time, as a process of trial and error. The Constitution contains no provisions for organizing political parties, nominating candidates or campaigning for office. The Framers assumed, incorrectly, that the selection process would be a reasoned one that would transcend petty partisanship. The original provision for balloting by the Electoral College was flawed and had to be superseded by the 12th Amendment in 1804.

Until the 17th century, elections with opposition were rare. The nation's first legislative body, the Virginia House of Burgesses, usually had uncontested elections until the 1700s. Even when the states' elections involved opponents, there was little active campaigning. Only with the decline of homogenous communities and the end of elite control over politics did contested elections occur. Many elections into the 1790s were uncontested or focused on personalities.

The very concept of the party—the most fundamental way of organizing electoral coalitions—was viewed with distrust by the nation's early leaders. George Washington described the dangers of parties in a letter: "A fire not to be quenched; it demands a uniform vigilance to prevent its bursting into a flame, lest instead of warming it should consume." [1] Only with experience of factional debate in Congress did the idea of parties seem necessary and capable of control.

The method of choosing presidential and vice presidential candidates has moved through several distinct phases. Political scientist Richard P. McCormick has identified four phases. [2]

The first phase was a period marked by uncertain and hazardous rules that lasted until the 12th Amendment was ratified in 1804. The second phase, continuing through 1820, saw the decline of the Federalists as a national force and the dominance of the Democratic-Republicans. This phase is associated with "King Caucus"—the nomination of candidates by congressional caucus. In the third phase, King Caucus was replaced by factional politics and unsettled rules for selecting candidates.

The fourth phase—ongoing today—evolved between 1832 and 1844. It is characterized by a two-party system that nominates candidates by national conventions. In recent years, the conventions have been rendered obsolete by mass politics—mass media presentations of candidates to the public and mass participation of party members in primary elections.

## Washington's First Election

The establishment of the rules for democratic decision making in the United States took place inauspiciously.

The states completed their separate ratifications of the Constitution in July 1788—nearly nine months after the close of the Constitutional Convention in Philadelphia. The Continental Congress then decided that the seat of government would be New York City. There, on September 13, 1788, Congress passed a resolution that the states should appoint electors on the first Wednesday in January, that those electors would assemble and vote in their respective states on the first Wednesday in February and that the new government would convene on the first Wednesday in March.

The method of choosing electors was left up to the individual state legislatures. *(See Methods of Choosing Electors, p. 345)* The requirement that all electors be chosen on the same day proved to be troublesome for the states. Some did not have time to call elections. In New York, for example, where electors were to have been chosen by the legislature, dissension between the two houses led to stalemate and prevented the state from participating in the election.

No formal nomination of candidates took place in 1788. Since the Constitutional Convention the previous year, all knew that George Washington of Virginia, the reluctant hero of the Revolutionary War, would be president. The only real question was who would be his vice president. Federalist leaders ultimately decided to support John Adams of Massachusetts.

The inherent flaws of the electoral system came to light right away. Under the Constitution, each elector cast two votes. The two votes had to be for different persons, and these two candidates could not both be from the same home state as the elector. The individual receiving the votes of a majority of the electors was named president, and the person receiving the second highest total was named vice president. Since no distinction was made between balloting for president and vice president, it was possible for both candidates to receive an equal number of votes, thus throwing the election to the House of Representatives. It also was possible that the candidate for vice president—through fluke or machination—actually could end up with the most votes and become president.

The Federalist leader Alexander Hamilton recognized the danger. Hamilton's personal animosity toward Adams aggravated his concern. He plotted to siphon away votes from Adams. In a letter to James Wilson of Pennsylvania, Hamilton wrote: "Everybody is aware of that defect in the constitution which renders it possible that the man intended for vice president may in fact turn up president." To prevent such a crisis, Hamilton recommended that several votes that would otherwise have gone to Adams be thrown away on other candidates: "I have proposed to friends in Connecticut to throw away 2 [votes], to others in New Jersey to throw away an equal number and I submit to you whether it would not be well to lose three or four in Pennsylvania. . . ." [3]

Hamilton's efforts were successful. Washington was unanimously elected president with 69 electoral votes. Adams, however, won the vice presidency with only 34 electoral votes. Only two states—New Hampshire and his own Massachusetts—voted solidly for Adams. In other states, Federalist leaders withheld support from Adams and sometimes worked against him. Adams did not receive *any* votes from Delaware, Georgia, Maryland or South Carolina, and he received only one vote from New Jersey. The remaining votes were spread among 10 other candidates, including John Jay, John Hancock, Robert Harrison, John Rutledge and George Clinton.

Although the new government was supposed to begin on March 4, 1789, not enough members of Congress had arrived in New York City by that date to have a quorum. The Senate did not convene until April 6 to count the electoral votes. A messenger was dispatched on horseback to deliver the news to president-elect Washington at Mount Vernon. He received the news on April 14. Washington then set out for New York, where he was sworn in on April 30.

Before the end of Washington's first term as president, political divisions developed that would lead to a party system. James Madison emerged as a *de facto* opposition leader in Congress. Seventeen members of the House of Representatives regularly sided with Madison, while another bloc of 15 supported the Washington administration. The rest of the House switched back and forth between the administration and Madison's faction. [4]

The election of 1789 demonstrated the potential for partisanship and intrigue in presidential contests. It also pointed out the weaknesses of the existing election calendar (which had made it difficult for New York to participate in the election) and reminded participants of the danger of the constitutional "defect" in the selection process that made it possible for the person intended to be vice president to become president.

## Washington's Reelection: 1792

George Washington remained first in the hearts of his nation when his first term as president drew to a close in 1792. But the facade of national unity showed signs of crumbling. The development of bitter oppositional factions eventually brought on the system of electoral competition.

President Washington won a second unanimous presidential election in 1792, but the election did produce competition for vice president. An overtly partisan contest broke out when the Democratic-Republicans decided to challenge the Federalist John Adams. Some of Adams' approving statements about the British angered populists, who campaigned against him behind the scenes. Adams managed to win, but not before bitter partisan identities had developed.

The election was different in another way as well. The election calendar was changed and made more flexible by an act of Congress. That law, which remained in effect until 1845, allowed states to choose electors within a 34-day span before the first Wednesday in December, when the electors met to vote.

Thomas Jefferson, the leader of the Democratic-Republicans, chose not to run for vice president, in part because he came from the same state as President Washington. Since electors could vote for only one candidate from their own state, Jefferson was tacitly precluded from receiving the large electoral vote of Virginia. Besides, a "balanced ticket" required a regional diversity.

Instead, Democratic-Republican leaders from New York, Pennsylvania, Virginia and South Carolina chose New York governor George Clinton as their candidate at a meeting in Philadelphia in October 1792. The endorsement of Clinton was a milestone in the evolution of the presidential nominating process and a step away from the Framers' original understanding of the selection process.

Both Washington and Adams were reelected, although Clinton scored well in the Electoral College. Adams received 77 electoral votes to Clinton's 50 (with 4 votes going to Jefferson and 1 to Aaron Burr), and Washington was reelected president by a unanimous electoral vote of 132.

The political tensions brought out by the Adams-Clinton contest developed more strongly over policy controversies. Thomas Jefferson resigned as secretary of state in 1793 in protest over Secretary of the Treasury Alexander Hamilton's growing influence in foreign affairs. Jefferson complained: "In place of that noble love of liberty and Republican government which carried us triumphantly through the war, an Anglican, Monarchical, and Aristocratical party has sprung up, whose avowed subject is to draw over us the substance as they have already done the forms of the British government." Even George Washington was subject to attacks. A Pennsylvania politician wondered aloud if Washington had not "become the tyrant instead of the saviour of his country." [5]

News of the French Revolution's period of terror divided the nation's elitist and populist leaders. Federalists recoiled in horror with the news of a democratic revolution gone awry, while democrats like Thomas Jefferson expressed empathy with France's struggle. The government's use of troops to suppress the Whiskey Rebellion of 1794, approval of the Jay Treaty of 1795 and maneuvering between the warring French and British also polarized the young nation into factions. State-level Democratic and Republican societies formed during this period in opposition to the Federalists.

## The First Succession: 1796

George Washington decided not to run for president again in 1796, even though the Constitution did not bar a third term and public sentiment supported it. With Washington out of the race, the United States witnessed its first partisan contest for president. Washington's farewell address, published in the summer, was "a signal, like dropping a hat, for the party racers to start." [6]

On the Democratic-Republican side, Thomas Jefferson faced no opposition as the presidential candidate. A consensus of party leaders selected him to run in 1796. A caucus of Democratic-Republican senators was unable, however, to agree on a running mate, producing a tie vote for Sen. Aaron Burr of New York and Sen. Pierce Butler of South Carolina that ended with a walkout by Butler's supporters. As a result, there was no formal Democratic-Republican candidate to run with Jefferson.

The Federalists, by contrast, held what historian Roy F. Nichols described as a "quasi caucus" of the party's members of Congress in Philadelphia in May 1796.[7] The gathering chose Vice President Adams and Minister to Great Britain Thomas Pinckney of South Carolina as the Federalist candidates. The choice of Adams was all but obligatory given that he was Washington's vice president. Nonetheless, Adams was unpopular in the South, and he continued to be disliked by Hamilton. As a result, Hamilton tried to use the "defect" in the Constitution to make Pinckney president instead of Adams. He urged northern electors to give equal support to Adams and Pinckney in the hopes that the South would not vote for Adams and that Pinckney would therefore win the most votes.

Had northern electors followed Hamilton's advice, Pinckney might have won the presidency. Instead, 18 votes were thrown to other Federalists. As a result, Adams won the presidency with 71 electoral votes, but Pinckney—with 59 votes—was not even able to win the vice presidency.

Jefferson—the candidate of the opposing Democratic-Republican ticket—came in second with 68 votes and became Adams' vice president. Although the results again played up the defects in the constitutional procedure for electing presidents, Federalists and Democratic-Republicans did not seem unduly concerned that the president and vice president were of opposing parties. Both sides felt that they had prevented the opposition from gaining total victory.

For the first and last time, a foreign figure played a prominent public role in the election. French Ambassador Pierre Adet promoted Jefferson's campaign in appearances and in written statements. Whether the Adet effort helped or hurt Jefferson is uncertain. The effort aroused supporters of France but angered others who favored Great Britain or resented outside interference.

# Jefferson's Revenge

The election of 1800 was the first in which both parties used congressional caucuses to nominate candidates for their tickets. Such caucuses were an important innovation in the presidential selection process. They mobilized partisan alignments in Congress and demonstrated the emergence of organized political parties.

President Adams was bitterly hated by farmers, populists and states' rights advocates. In one of the nation's first professionally run smear campaigns, Adams was denounced as a "hideous hermaphroditical character which has neither the force and firmness of a man, nor the gentleness and sensibility of a woman." [8]

Federalist members of Congress met in the Senate chamber in Philadelphia on May 3, 1800, to choose their candidates. As in previous presidential election years, Feder-

alists were divided in their support of Adams. Nonetheless, Federalists felt that they had to nominate Adams since he was the incumbent president. Because of their ambivalence toward Adams, they nominated both Adams and Maj. Gen. Charles Cotesworth Pinckney of South Carolina without giving preference to one or the other for president. Pinckney was the elder brother of the Federalist vice presidential candidate in 1796.

The choice of Pinckney was made at Hamilton's insistence. Once again Hamilton was plotting to use the constitutional defect against Adams. In 1796, South Carolina had voted for an all-southern ticket—Jefferson and Thomas Pinckney—even though the two were of opposing parties. Hamilton hoped that South Carolina would vote the same way in 1800, and that all other Federalist electors could be persuaded to vote for Adams and Charles Pinckney. That would give Pinckney more votes than Adams, thus making him president.

Although the deliberations of the Federalist caucus were secret, the fact that it was meeting was not. It was described by the local Democratic-Republican paper, the Philadelphia *Aurora*, as a "Jacobinical conclave." Further denunciations by the paper's editor, Benjamin F. Bache, earned him a personal rebuke from the U.S. Senate.

The Democratic-Republicans once again chose Jefferson as the presidential candidate by consensus. On May 11, a caucus of Democratic-Republican members of Congress met at Marache's boarding house in Philadelphia to choose a running mate. Their unanimous choice was Aaron Burr.

Although there was no such thing as a formal party platform in 1800, Jefferson wrote fairly detailed statements of principle in letters to various correspondents. Among other things, the Democratic-Republicans believed in states' rights, a small national government and a relatively weak executive. They opposed standing armies in peacetime, a large naval force and alliances with other countries. And they denounced the Alien and Sedition Acts, which had been passed by the Federalists in 1798 for the ostensible purpose of protecting the nation from subversives given the threat of war with France.

The 1800 election saw other signs of formal public campaigning. Tickets listing the names of Democratic-Republican electors were printed and distributed in a number of states, including New York, Massachusetts, Pennsylvania and Delaware. Speeches on behalf of the candidates increased markedly. Partisan newspapers also helped to spread the party positions. The number of newspapers in the United States had grown dramatically in the last decade of the century, from 91 to 234.[9] Despite attempts by the Federalists to muzzle the opposition press with the passage of the Sedition Act of 1798, partisan newspapers on both sides actively defamed the opposition. Ultimately, the Sedition Act worked against the Federalists by turning the Democratic-Republicans into champions of a free press.

Increased partisan activity spurred voter participation. Since electors still were chosen indirectly in 12 of the 16 states, voters often expressed themselves through state legislative elections as a means of influencing future presidential elections.[10] The seeds were being sowed for a new phase in the development of the presidential election process.

A harbinger of Democratic-Republican success came in May, when the party won state legislative elections. Burr managed the campaign in the states, building a machine with ward and precinct organizations. Burr's efforts showed the importance of large-scale mobilization—a lesson that would not be lost on the party in future years.

When the electors voted in December, the constitutional defect did not work as Hamilton had hoped. Instead of resulting in a Pinckney victory, the defect produced an unexpected tie vote between the two Democratic-Republican candidates, Jefferson and Burr—each of whom had 73 electoral votes. Adams came in third with 65, and Pinckney followed with 64. In accord with the constitutional provision, the election was thrown to the Federalist-controlled House of Representatives.

Some Federalists felt that Burr was the lesser of the two evils and plotted to elect him president instead of Jefferson—even though Jefferson was clearly the presidential candidate. Hamilton helped to squelch the idea. After 36 ballots, Jefferson received a majority in the House of Representatives. The crisis—which could have fatally wounded the nation by calling into question the legitimacy of the new president—was over. Jefferson was elected president and Burr, vice president.

The near disaster brought about by the constitutional defect led to the passage of the 12th Amendment to the Constitution in September 1804. It called for electors to vote for president and vice president on separate ballots, thereby clarifying who was the presidential candidate and eliminating the possibility of a tie between the principal candidate and the running mate.

## Jefferson's Reelection: 1804

By the time of the 1804 election, President Jefferson had grudgingly accepted the emergence of a party system. In a letter that year, the president wrote: "The party division in this country is certainly not among its pleasant features. To a certain degree it will always exist." [11]

Jefferson's record—lower taxes, a reduced national debt, repeal of the Alien and Sedition Acts and purchase of the Louisiana Territory from France—ensured him a second term. Particularly important was Jefferson's willingness to expand the nation's reach and power with the Louisiana Purchase, which compromised his philosophical preference for a small republic. The opposition's case against Jefferson was personal, but the voters were not persuaded to make a change.

The 1804 election was the first one held after the 12th Amendment to the Constitution went into effect, requiring electors to cast separate votes for president and vice president. With ratification of the amendment, parties in 1804 and thereafter specifically designated their presidential and vice presidential candidates.

The Democratic-Republicans retained the caucus system of nomination in 1804, as they did for the next two decades, and for the first time they publicly reported their deliberations. The party caucus met on Feb. 25, 1804, and attracted 108 of the party's senators and representatives.

President Jefferson was renominated by acclamation, but Vice President Burr, who had fallen out with his party, was not considered for a second term. On the first nominating roll call publicly reported in U.S. political history, New York governor George Clinton was chosen by the caucus to run for vice president. He received 67 votes and easily defeated Sen. John Breckinridge of Kentucky, who collected 20 votes. To "avoid unpleasant discussions" no names were placed in nomination, and the vote was taken by written ballot.

Before adjourning, the caucus appointed a 13-member committee to conduct the campaign and promote the success of Democratic-Republican candidates. A forerunner of party national committees, the new campaign group included members of both the House and Senate, but with no two persons from the same state. Since the 12th Amendment had not yet been passed when the caucus met, the committee was designed to "manage" the vote of Democratic-Republican electors to make sure that the events of 1800 were not repeated. In fact, that precaution was not necessary since the 12th Amendment was ratified in September—well before the electors voted.

By 1804, the Federalist party had deteriorated badly. The new era of dominance by the Virginia-led Democratic-Republicans had begun. The Federalists did not even hold a congressional caucus to select their nominees. Instead, Federalist leaders in 1804 informally chose Charles Cotesworth Pinckney for president and Rufus King of New York for vice president. The exact details of how Federalists formulated this ticket are not clear. There is no record of any formal meeting to nominate Federalist candidates in 1804.

The Federalists mounted a disorganized and dispirited national campaign. Despite concerted efforts to win at least the votes of New England, the Federalists failed miserably. Pinckney received only 14 electoral votes—those of Connecticut and Delaware, plus 2 from Maryland. Jefferson, the Democratic-Republican candidate, was the overwhelming victor with 162 electoral votes.

## Madison's 1808 Victory

Following George Washington's precedent, Thomas Jefferson refused to seek a third term of office. The nation was bitterly divided over Jefferson's policy toward France and Britain. In an attempt to stay out of their war, Jefferson pushed an embargo of trade so that they would not seize American ships. But the embargo only undermined American business interests. Under attack, Jefferson decided to return to his beloved home of Charlottesville, Virginia.

Despite the unpopularity of the administration's European policy, Jefferson's secretary of state and chosen successor, James Madison, won the presidency in 1808.

Jefferson's retirement provided a serious test to the authority of the Democratic-Republican congressional caucus to select presidential candidates. The caucus met on Jan. 23, 1808. For the first time a formal call was issued. Sen. Stephen R. Bradley of Vermont, chairman of the 1804 caucus, issued the call to all 146 Democratic-Republicans in Congress and several Federalists sympathetic to the Democratic-Republican cause. Several party leaders questioned Bradley's authority to call the caucus, but various reports indicate that 89 to 94 members of Congress attended.

As in 1804, the balloting took place without the formal placing of names in nomination. Madison easily won the presidential nomination with 83 votes. Despite earlier support for James Monroe among Democratic-Republicans in Virginia, and Vice President Clinton's own desire to be president, each won only three votes at the caucus. For vice president, the caucus overwhelmingly renominated Clinton. He received 79 votes, while runner-up John Langdon of New Hampshire collected five.

The Democratic-Republican caucus also repeated its practice of appointing a committee to conduct the campaign. Membership was expanded to 15 House and Senate members, and it was formally called the "committee of correspondence and arrangement." The committee was authorized to fill any vacancies on the national ticket, should any occur. Before the caucus adjourned, it passed a resolution defending the caucus system as "the most practicable mode of consulting and respecting the interest and wishes of all." Later caucuses adopted similar resolutions throughout the history of the system.

Still, the Democratic-Republicans suffered divisions. Forty percent of the Democratic-Republican members of Congress refused to attend the nominating caucus. Monroe refused to withdraw from the presidential race even after his defeat in the caucus. Even Clinton, although he was nominated for vice president, was angry at not being nominated for president. Clinton publicly denounced the caucus, as did Monroe's supporters. Pro-Clinton newspapers in New York launched harsh attacks on Madison and even suggested a Clinton-Monroe ticket. Some Clinton supporters went so far as to hope that Federalists would nominate Clinton for president later in the year. Such a thought was unpalatable to the Federalists, who ultimately nominated Charles Cotesworth Pinckney.

The Federalists chose their ticket at a secret meeting of party leaders in New York City in August 1808. The meeting was initially called by the Federalist members of the Massachusetts legislature. Twenty-five to 30 party leaders from seven states, all north of the Potomac River except South Carolina, attended the national meeting. Despite the suggestion from Massachusetts representatives that Clinton be nominated, the gathering decided to run the same ticket they had chosen in 1804—Pinckney and King. Federalists did not actively publicize their ticket. The party itself was divided and devoid of leadership. Many Virginia Federalists formally endorsed Monroe, even though he was a Democratic-Republican. Others preferred to align themselves with Clinton. In the end, Madison achieved a wide margin of victory with 122 electoral votes. For the sake of future party unity, Democratic-Republicans retained Clinton as their vice presidential nominee even though he had tried to subvert Madison's candidacy. Clinton received 113 electoral votes for vice president, thus winning that office; he received six electoral votes from New York for president. Pinckney came in second for president with 47 electoral votes. Monroe received no electoral votes.

## Madison's Reelection

The winds of war swept through presidential politics when James Madison sought a second term in 1812. In response to constant agitation by "war hawks," the President on June 1 asked Congress for a declaration of war against Great Britain. Madison swept to a second term. The Federalists did not field a candidate but supported a dissident from Madison's own party.

The possibility of war had hung over the United States for years. Great Britain had taken American ships captive for years—boarding the vessels, taking cargo and intimidating seamen. Anti-British forces also charged that the British encouraged Native Americans in their attacks against Americans in the North and West.

The Democratic-Republican party held its quadrennial nominating caucus on May 18, 1812. Only 83 of the 178 Democratic-Republicans in Congress participated. New England and New York delegations in particular were poorly represented. Many of the New Yorkers supported the candidacy of their state's lieutenant governor, De Witt Clinton (George Clinton's nephew), who also was maneuvering for the Federalist nomination. New England was noticeably upset with Madison's foreign policy, which was leading to war with England. Others did not attend the caucus because they opposed the system in principle.

Madison won a near-unanimous renomination in the caucus, receiving 82 votes. John Langdon of New Hampshire got the vice presidential nomination by a wide margin, collecting 64 votes to 16 for Gov. Elbridge Gerry of Massachusetts. But Langdon declined the nomination, citing his age (70) as the reason. The Democratic-Republicans held a second caucus on June 8 to select another vice presidential candidate. Gerry was the clear winner with 74 votes. He responded with a formal letter of acceptance. Ten members of Congress who had not been present at the first caucus also took the opportunity to endorse the presidential candidacy of Madison.

Democratic-Republicans from New York were unwilling to accept the choice of Madison. They held their own caucus, consisting of nearly all party members from the New York state legislature. They unanimously nominated Clinton, who responded with a written "Address" that was a precursor to party platforms. Clinton won the endorsement of the Federalists as well.

As they had four years earlier, Federalists convened a three-day secret meeting in New York City. The September meeting was more than twice the size of the 1808 gathering, with 70 representatives from 11 states attending. Delegates were sent to the conference by Federalist general committees, with all but nine of the delegates coming from the New England and Middle Atlantic states.

Debate centered on whether to run a separate Federalist ticket or to endorse the candidacy of Clinton. After much debate, they decided to endorse Clinton. They nominated Jared Ingersoll of Pennsylvania as vice president. Originally, the caucus's decision was meant to be kept a secret, but leaks eventually were reported by Democratic-Republican newspapers.

The presidential election of 1812 was the first wartime contest for power in the United States. Federalists—calling Madison a dupe of French emperor Napoleon Bonaparte—aligned themselves with the cause of peace and unimpeded commerce. In some northern states, the Federalists even adopted the Peace Party label.

Despite all the opposition to President Madison, he beat Clinton by an electoral vote count of 128 to 89. The vote reflected the growing split between Southern agricultural states, which supported Madison, and Northern commercial states, which supported Clinton. Indeed, the common bond that held the Clinton coalition together was a hatred of Virginia—the kingmaker of the Democratic-Republican party.

The 1812 race was the last real campaign by the Federalists. Disgraced by their obstructionist tactics during the war, isolated by their talk of secession from the union and unable to coordinate a national campaign, the Federalists faded from a system increasingly marked by permanent party competition.

## Monroe's 1816 Victory

An old foe of President Madison who left the Democratic-Republican Party in 1808 might seem like an unlikely presidential candidate for the party in 1820. Given the bitter taste from the War of 1812, the governing party's victory might seem more unlikely. But not only did James Monroe return to the Democratic-Republican fold. He won the White House without any opposition.

The inconclusive War of 1812 colored American politics for years. The United States and Great Britain fought to a stalemate. Both sides offered conditions for ending the war that the other would not accept. The British, for example, demanded control over the Great Lakes and Mississippi River for commerce, as well as creation of an Indian state in the Northwest. In the end, both parties simply accepted the end of hostilities. An American representative said the treaty was "a truce rather than a peace." [12] Inconclusive or not, the war sparked a generation of nationalism. Rufus King tried to revive the Federalist Party in 1816 with his race for the governorship of New York. But he lost the race and found maintaining the party a "fruitless struggle" afterwards. Despite Federalist efforts to convene another secret meeting in Philadelphia to nominate candidates for president and vice president, the party held no such meeting. With the Federalists not running candidates, nomination by the Democratic-Republican caucus was tantamount to election.

Despite his opposition to Madison in 1808, Monroe had been accepted back into the Democratic-Republican fold in the years that followed. In 1811, Madison named him secretary of state. By 1816, he was Madison's heir apparent, but many states were increasingly jealous of the Virginia dynasty that had held a grip on the presidency since 1804. Democratic-Republicans in such states opposed Monroe (himself a Virginian) and favored Secretary of War William H. Crawford of Georgia.

A Democratic-Republican caucus met in the House chamber on March 12, 1816, but only 58 members of Congress—mostly Crawford supporters—attended. With the expectation of better attendance, a second caucus was held on March 16. It drew 119 of the 141 Democratic-Republicans in Congress. There, Monroe narrowly defeated Crawford by a vote of 65-54. Forty of Crawford's votes came from five states: Georgia, Kentucky, New Jersey, New York and North Carolina. The vice presidential nomination went to New York governor Daniel D. Tompkins, who easily outdistanced Pennsylvania governor Simon Snyder, 85-30.

The nominations of Monroe and Tompkins revived a Virginia-New York alliance that extended back to the late 18th century. With the lone exception of 1812, every Democratic-Republican ticket from 1800 to 1824 was composed of a presidential candidate from Virginia and a vice presidential candidate from New York.

With the Federalist party in disarray, the Democratic-Republican ticket won easily. Monroe received 183 electoral votes. Three states—Connecticut, Delaware and Massachusetts—chose Federalist electors, who cast their 34 electoral votes for Rufus King.

Although the collapse of the Federalists ensured Democratic-Republican rule, it also increased intraparty friction and spurred further attacks on the caucus system. Twenty-two Democratic-Republican members of Congress were absent from the second party caucus, and at least 15 were known to be opposed to the system. Mass meetings around the country protested the caucus system.[13] Opponents asserted that the writers of the Constitution did not envision the caucus, that presidential nominating should not be a function of Congress and that the caucus system encouraged candidates to curry the favor of Congress.

## Monroe's Reelection: 1820

The 1820 election took place during the "Era of Good Feelings," a phrase coined by a Boston publication, the *Columbian Centinel*, to describe a brief period of virtual one-party rule in the United States. But that phrase glosses over serious sectional divisions that were growing during Monroe's presidency. The divisions did not prevent Monroe from winning another term, however.

Sectional strife was on the brink of explosion during Monroe's first term over the admission of Missouri as a new state. Tensions between Northern and Southern states simmered for years. The emotional core of the struggle was slavery. Whichever region controlled Congress might decide whether slavery was extended into new territories—and the shape of the nation's economy and culture for years to come.

The Senate held a tenuous balance between the two regions, with 11 free states and 11 slave states. The admission of Missouri threatened that balance. The two sides finally agreed to a compromise in which both Missouri and Maine would apply for statehood at the same time. Maine would apply as a free state and Missouri as a slave state. Monroe remained neutral in the debate leading up to the compromise. Despite a financial panic in 1819, he retained overwhelming popular support, bolstered by peace and a wave of nationalistic feeling that overshadowed any partisan divisions.

While the United States struggled over the slavery issue, President Monroe embarked on a bold new foreign policy. Still smarting over the British presence in North America that had resulted in the War of 1812, the president declared that the United States would view any European attempts to colonize the Western Hemisphere as acts of hostility. The Monroe Doctrine claimed the hemisphere as the preserve of the United States. It was the boldest venture of the nation into foreign policy and permanently defined America's role in world affairs.

Although several rival Democratic-Republican candidates aspired to win the presidency when Monroe retired in 1824, none wanted to challenge his reelection in 1820. A nominating caucus was called for early March, but fewer than 40 members of Congress showed up. The caucus voted unanimously to make no nominations and passed a resolution explaining that it was inexpedient to do so. Although Monroe and Tompkins were not formally renominated, electoral slates were filed on their behalf.

Because the Federalist party was dead, Monroe ran virtually unopposed. Even John Adams, the last Federalist president, voted for Monroe as an elector from Massachusetts. Only one elector, a Democratic-Republican from New Hampshire, cast a vote against Monroe, supporting instead the young John Quincy Adams, son of the former president.

## Last of the Old Order

The 1824 election, in an odd way, represented everything that the Framers of the Constitution had hoped to see. Without a permanent party system, a number of candidates vied for the presidency. Unable to win an electoral majority, the names of the top three finishers went to the House of Representatives for a final decision. The elite candidate with House ties won.

But if the 1824 election of John Quincy Adams represented something old, it also represented something new. The popular winner and House loser, Andrew Jackson, screamed that the election had been stolen from the people. Jackson would soon mobilize the Democratic Party around a populist rally cry. American politics would never be the same.

In 1824, as in 1820, only one working party existed in the United States. But that party had an abundance of candidates competing for the presidency: Secretary of State John Quincy Adams of Massachusetts, Sen. Andrew Jackson of Tennessee, Secretary of War John C. Calhoun of South

Carolina, House Speaker Henry Clay of Kentucky, and Secretary of the Treasury William H. Crawford. The number of candidates, coupled with the growing democratization of the U.S. political system, led to the demise of King Caucus in 1824.

Early on, Crawford was the leading candidate. He had strong Southern support and appeared likely to win the support of New York Democratic-Republicans. Since it was assumed that he would win a caucus if one were held, Crawford's opponents joined the growing list of caucus opponents. But Crawford's apparent invincibility suddenly ended in September 1823, when he suffered a paralytic stroke. Nearly blind and unable even to sign his name, he was kept in seclusion for months.

In early February 1824, 11 Democratic-Republican members of Congress issued a call for a caucus to be held in the middle of the month. Their call was countered by 24 other members of Congress from 15 states who deemed it "inexpedient under existing circumstances" to hold a caucus. They claimed that 181 members of Congress were resolved not to attend if a caucus were held.

The caucus convened in mid-February, but only 66 members of Congress showed up. Three-quarters of those attending came from just four states—Georgia, New York, North Carolina and Virginia. Despite his illness, Crawford won the caucus nomination with 64 votes. Albert Gallatin of Pennsylvania was selected for vice president with 57 votes. The caucus adopted a resolution defending its actions as "the best means of collecting and concentrating the feelings and wishes of the people of the Union upon this important subject." The caucus also appointed a committee to write an address to the people. As written, the text of the address viewed with alarm the "dismemberment" of the Democratic-Republican party.

In fact, the action of the caucus just aggravated splits in the party. Since so few members of Congress attended the caucus—almost all of them Crawford supporters—opponents could argue that the choice was not even representative of the Democratic-Republican faction in Congress. Crawford was roundly criticized as being an illegitimate candidate. His opponents derided King Caucus, and Crawford's physical condition made it even easier for them to reject his nomination. As it stood, other candidates simply refused to follow the caucus' decision. Never again were candidates chosen by the caucus system.

With the caucus devoid of power and the party lacking unity or leadership, there was no chance of rallying behind a single ticket. In addition, many political issues proved to be divisive. Western expansion and protective tariffs, for example, benefited some parts of the country but hurt others. Thus, the various candidates came to represent sectional interests.

The candidates themselves recognized that such a crowded field was dangerous. The election would be thrown to the House of Representatives if no candidate received a majority. The candidates therefore made efforts to join forces. Adams tried to lure Jackson to be his running mate. Adams was a short, stocky, aloof, well-educated New Englander who came from a family of Federalists, while Jackson was a tall, thin, hot-tempered war hero with little education who came to epitomize a new brand of populist democracy. In trying to lure Jackson onto their team, Adams supporters envisaged a ticket of "the writer and the fighter." Jackson would have nothing of it.

In the meantime, Crawford dropped Gallatin as his vice presidential running mate. His supporters then tried to get Clay to drop his own quest for the presidency and join the Crawford team. They hinted that Crawford's physical condition was such that he would probably not finish out a term of office if elected (in fact, he lived 10 more years). But Clay was not swayed. Instead, Calhoun dropped his race for the presidency and joined efforts with Crawford.

Four candidates remained in the field and each collected electoral votes. None, however, received a majority. Jackson received a plurality with 99 votes, followed by Adams with 84, Crawford with 41, and Clay with 37. Thus, the election was thrown to the House of Representatives.

In accordance with the 12th Amendment, the names of the top three candidates—Jackson, Adams and Crawford—were placed before the House. Clay, who had come in fourth place and was Speaker of the House, would play a major role in tipping the balance in favor of one of the candidates.

In contrast to Jackson, Adams actively lobbied for support, and Washington rocked with rumors of corruption. Clay informed Adams in January that he would support Adams in the House election—a major blow to Jackson. Shortly thereafter, a letter in a Philadelphia newspaper alleged that Adams had offered Clay the post of secretary of state in return for his support. Adams went on to win the House election narrowly. Each state delegation had one vote, and Adams won the vote of 13 out of 24 states. Jackson came in second with seven, and Crawford third with the remaining four. Thus, the candidate who won the most electoral votes and the most popular votes did not win the presidency.

Jackson was furious at what he considered unfair bargaining between Adams and Clay. He felt that the will of the people had been thwarted, and he seethed when President Adams proceeded to name Clay secretary of state as rumor had indicated he would. The events of 1824 kindled the flame of popular democracy. The stage was set for a rematch between Adams and Jackson in 1828.

## The Age of Jackson

Andrew Jackson was in many ways the perfect man to usher in an age of popular politics, although his rhetoric was more populist than his true style of governing. The textbook version of U.S. history depicts Jackson as a coarse man of the frontier, a war hero, a battler of banks and moneyed interests and a leader of the unschooled and exploited men who built a mass party on patronage and charismatic leadership. Jackson was the first politician to break the Virginia dynasty that had governed the country since the Revolution. After his bitter defeat in the 1824 election, Jackson fought back and grabbed the reins of government in a turbulent election in 1828. These two elections signaled the passing of elite politics and the rise of popular politics. In 1828 Jackson roused the people to turn Adams and his aristocratic clique out of office.

But the Jacksonian folklore has serious flaws. Jackson traveled in elite business circles, for example, and one of his greatest contributions as president was the creation of a more rationally organized bureaucracy.[14] Still, the textbook depiction suffices to show some trends in U.S. politics, including the development of a stable mass party system, sectionalism, urbanization and shifts in the debate about U.S. expansionism.

As President Adams struggled with the factions and turf battles in Washington, an opposition force gathered strength. The opposition was able to deal the president a number of humiliating defeats. Adams' desire for a national program of roads and canals, education and research in the arts and sciences antagonized even the most nationalistic groups in the country. U.S. participation in a conference of countries from the Western Hemisphere and the imposition of a tariff (a tax on imported goods designed either to raise revenues or to protect domestic industries from foreign competition) were also divisive issues. But even though Adams was under constant personal attack, the opposition was divided on the same issues. The opposition was united, however, behind Old Hickory.[15]

Jackson, the Battle of New Orleans hero in the War of 1812, had a strong appeal to the common man even though he traveled in the circles of Southern gentlemen. People who met with Jackson talked of his unerring "intuition." Jackson's decision to push for reforms of the punishment of debtors was an important gesture to small business owners and workers who were held to a kind of indentured servitude. Martin Van Buren said the people "were his blood relations—the only blood relations he had."[16]

## Jackson's 1828 Victory

Jackson and his running mate, John C. Calhoun, easily beat Adams in their 1828 rematch; Jackson won 178 electoral votes, and Adams won 83. (Calhoun also had been vice president under John Quincy Adams.) Of the popular vote, Jackson received 643,000 votes (56.0 percent) to Adams' 501,000 (43.6 percent). Sectional splits showed in the vote distribution. Adams held all but 1 of New England's electoral votes, all of Delaware's and New Jersey's, 16 of New York's 36 votes, and 6 of Maryland's 11 votes. Jackson took all the rest—the South and the West. The election was decided by the thousands of votes from newly enfranchised voters in the burgeoning regions of the country. The U.S. electorate was expanding not only in the West but also in the original states. Voter participation grew from 3.8 percent to 16.7 percent of the total population between 1824 and 1856.[17]

Jackson had only begun to exert his electoral influence with his revenge victory over Adams. The expanded pool of politically involved citizens that brought Jackson victory also brought him demands for patronage jobs with the federal government. Van Buren, a master machine politician from New York, tutored the beleaguered new president on dealing with the office seekers. Jackson replaced fewer than one-fifth of the government's employees, which he defended as a perfectly reasonable "rotation in office" that would keep the ranks of the bureaucracy fresh. But the effect of his system was greater. Appointees of previous administrations were able to retain their jobs only when they expressed loyalty to Jackson and his party. Far more important than any government turnover, Jackson's spoils system inaugurated an age in which mass party loyalty was a paramount concern in politics.

The central element of the Jacksonian program was expansion. Much as 20th-century politicians would talk about economic growth as the key to opportunity, Jackson maintained that movement West "enlarg[ed] the area of freedom."[18] The administration fought to decentralize the management of expansion. Jackson railed against the "corrupt bargain" between the government and banks, joint-stock companies and monopolies, which, he said, were squeezing out the average person seeking opportunity. Jackson opposed the Bank of the United States and promoted state banks because of his desire to free finance capital from central control.

The increased importance of loyalty, to the president and to the party, became clear with Jackson's dispute with Vice President Calhoun and the subsequent purging of the cabinet. A growing feud between Jackson and Calhoun came to a head when a personal letter by Calhoun became public. The letter criticized Jackson's conduct of the Seminole Indian campaign and the 1818 invasion of Florida. In a letter to Calhoun during the crisis, Jackson wrote: "Et tu, Brute." A purge of Calhoun men in the cabinet followed the incident. Secretary of State Van Buren enabled the president to make the purge when he and Secretary of War John Eaton, both Jackson allies, resigned their posts; the president then called on the whole cabinet to quit.

Jackson's political strength was further underscored with the introduction of a quintessentially party-oriented institution: the national party convention. *(See Nominating Conventions, p. 13)* Jacksonians from New Hampshire proposed the Democratic convention of 1832, and the president and his advisers jumped at the opportunity. The only previous national convention had been held by the Anti-Masonic Party in 1831. Conventions had been the principal means of selecting candidates for local offices since the early part of the century. Especially compared with the caucus system that preceded it, the convention system was a democratic leap forward.

The convention system enabled the parties to gather partisans from all geographic areas, and it welded them together as a cohesive unit that ultimately was accountable to the electorate, if only in a plebiscitary way. Voters had the opportunity to give approval or disapproval to a party program with one vote. Historian Eugene H. Roseboom has written: "It was representative in character; it divorced nominations from congressional control and added to the independence of the executive; it permitted an authoritative formulation of a party program; and it concentrated the party's strength behind a single ticket, the product of compromise of personal rivalries and group or sectional interests."[19]

Jackson's presidency was activist from the beginning. The president in his first term carried on a long-running battle with Nicholas Biddle, the head of the Bank of the United States, and with Congress over the status of the bank. Alexander Hamilton created the bank to manage the nation's monetary policy and investment but Jackson opposed it as a tool of the Eastern financial establishment. Jackson failed to close the bank but neutered it when he placed its deposits in a number of regional institutions.

The Jackson administration also negotiated treaties with France, the Ottoman Empire, Russia and Mexico. Jackson established a distinctive system of federalism when he vetoed a number of public improvements bills as unconstitutional infringements of local affairs. Jackson also called for a tariff that would yield revenues for disbursement to the states for their own public projects—an early form of "revenue sharing." Jackson signed the Indian Removal Act of 1830, which provided for settlement of the territory west of the Mississippi River. Late in his first term, Jackson's strong stand defeated the South Carolina legislature's claim to "nullify," or declare "null and void," federal tariff legislation that the state disliked.

## Jackson's 1832 Victory

There was never any doubt that Jackson would be renominated in 1832; in fact, several state legislatures endorsed him before the convention. The purpose of the convention was to rally behind the president and select a new vice presidential candidate. Van Buren got the nomination, despite lingering resistance from Calhoun supporters and various "favorite sons" (prominent state and local figures).

Jackson's opposition was fragmented as usual. The Whigs—the opposition party that developed from grass-roots protests in the North and West against Jackson's tariff and development policies—met in convention in Baltimore in December 1831, and unanimously nominated Henry Clay of Kentucky. Eighteen states used a variety of selection procedures to determine who would be their convention delegates. The party's platform sharply criticized the administration's patronage practices, relations with Great Britain, criticism of Supreme Court decisions and ill-tempered congressional relations.

The incumbent easily dispatched the opposition in 1832. "The news from the voting states blows over us like a great cold storm," wrote Rufus Choate, a prominent lawyer, to a friend.[20] Despite last-minute maneuvering to unite the opposition to Jackson and a well-financed campaign by the National Bank, the president won 219 electoral votes to Clay's 49, Independent John Floyd's 11, and Anti-Mason William Wirt's 7. Jackson won all but seven states. Clay won Kentucky, Massachusetts, Rhode Island, Connecticut and Delaware, plus five electors from Maryland. Jackson won 702,000 popular votes to Clay's 484,000 and Wirt's 101,000.[21]

Before Jackson finally left the political stage in 1837, he had changed the face of U.S. politics. Even if his pretensions to being an everyman were overstated, he did open up the system to mass participation and force politicians to listen to popular demands. He developed the notion of a strong party organization. He fought, and eventually defeated, the National Bank by withdrawing its funds and placing them in state banks. He strongly opposed two forces that could have torn the nation apart—the nullification principle of state sovereignty and the Supreme Court's bid for broader discretion over political issues—by simply proclaiming the law to be "unauthorized by the Constitution" and "therefore null and void."

## Van Buren's 1836 Win

Many historians consider the election of 1836 to be the most important event in the development of the party system. Van Buren, a Democratic follower of Jackson and a theorist on the role of political parties in a democratic system, easily won the election over an uncoordinated Whig party. The defeat eventually convinced Whig leaders of the need for a permanent organization for political competition. The emergence of two permanent parties extinguished the American suspicion of the morality of a party system based upon unabashed competition for the levers of power.

Van Buren, who had allied with Jackson during the cabinet controversies and promoted his philosophy of parties and patronage, received the Democratic nomination in 1836 at a convention packed with Jackson administration appointees. The vice presidential nomination of Richard M. Johnson of Kentucky, whose past relationship with a mulatto woman caused controversy, damaged the ticket in the South, but the Democrats won anyway.

The Whigs' campaign strategy was to run several favorite sons to prevent any candidate from getting a majority of the electoral votes, thereby throwing the election into the House of Representatives. As one Whig put the matter: "The disease [Democratic rule] is to be treated as a local disorder—apply local remedies." [22] The Whig expectation

was that Gen. William Henry Harrison of Ohio or Hugh Lawson White of Tennessee would be selected by the House after the Electoral College vote proved inconclusive.

Van Buren, however, had Jackson's machine and his personal backing and was able to overcome the Whigs' local strategy. In the last race for the White House before presidential elections became dominated by two national parties, Van Buren took 170 electoral votes—22 more than he needed for election. Of the Whig candidates, Harrison received 73 electoral votes; White, 26; and Daniel Webster of Massachusetts, 14. Willie Mangum, an Independent Democrat from North Carolina, received 11 electoral votes from the South Carolina legislature, which was hostile to White because of his role in nullification politics. Van Buren won 764,000 popular votes (50.8 percent); Harrison, 551,000 (36.6 percent); White, 146,000 (9.7 percent); and Webster, 41,000 (2.7 percent). For the only time in history, the Senate selected the vice president, Richard M. Johnson, who fell one vote shy of election by the Electoral College and defeated Francis Granger by a 33-16 Senate vote.

Van Buren was besieged practically from the minute he took the oath of office in March 1837. The economy crashed after years of feverish business growth, overspeculation in land and business, huge private debt accumulation and unregulated financial and trade practices. Van Buren's approach to the economic crisis was either stubborn refusal to fix a mess that he had not created or action that was guaranteed to antagonize key interest groups.

When Van Buren moved to create an independent treasury to give the federal government insulation from state financial institutions, he was opposed by conservative Democrats who were supporters of the state financial institutions that Jackson had promoted in his legendary National Bank battles. When Van Buren was not hit from the right, he was hit from the left. The nascent labor movement called for protection of jobs and wages and made protests against monopoly and privilege.

## The Idea of a Party System

Whatever problems Van Buren had in governing, he can receive credit at least for helping to establish the principle of party government in the United States. That principle—much derided in the early days of the nation's history—has come to enjoy unquestioned allegiance in the United States.

Van Buren's arguments on behalf of a party system—contained in his 1867 book, *An Inquiry into the Origin and Course of Political Parties in the United States*—are similar to the economic principle of Adam Smith that the pursuit of selfish ends redounds to the good of the entire community. American leaders from George Washington through John Quincy Adams had stated that self-interested factions endangered the functioning and virtue of the Republic. These leaders also warned against the dangers of democracy, which they often called "mob rule." The worst of all possible scenarios pictured permanent parties with strong ideological stances appealing to the mass public for support. Most of the Framers feared that democratic institutions would undermine the ability of national leaders to guide public virtue.[23]

The basic tension that Van Buren had to resolve was the system's need for stability and responsible leadership and the party system's imperative to gain office. How could a party's selfish desire to run the government and award patronage and contracts to political allies benefit the whole system?

Van Buren argued that the absence of parties—collections of people from disparate backgrounds—resulted in a system of personal politics that fueled demagogy, perpetual campaigns and a lack of accountability. Personal presidential politics was more polarizing than the politics of consensus or of coalition building. Presidents should be able to do their job without constant carping from outsiders who fancy themselves to be prospective presidents. Mass parties with certain partisan principles would enable presidents to get the backing they needed to do their work.

The existence of two parties would enable the nation to move beyond its many cleavages—toward the general interest and away from simple clashes of particular interests. Competition among parties, like competition among economic enterprises, would bring about a situation in which disparate demands are promoted by a party. The key is to achieve a balance of competing forces. Political scientist James W. Ceaser has written:

> Established parties ... may stand 'over' the raw electoral cleavages, possessing some leeway or discretion about which potential issues and electoral divisions will be emphasized and which will be suppressed or kept at the fringes. This discretion is exercised according to the interests of the organizations and the judgement of their leaders. But it is important to keep in mind that the degree of this discretion is limited.... Their discretion is always threatened or held in check by the possibility that they might be displaced by a new party having as its goal the advancement of a certain policy.... When a sufficiently powerful and enduring issue exists, an impartial reading of American party history suggests that the party system in the end will have to respond to it, regardless of how the established parties initially react.[24]

The Age of Jackson brought a fundamental shift from republican to democratic values as the nation's territory and activities expanded. Republicanism was the product of a variety of strains of thought—from the Romans Cicero and Tacitus and the Greek Polybius to the Frenchman Montesquieu—that stressed the need for a balancing of interests to produce public virtue. Republicans worried about excess in any single form of governance. Of particular concern was "mob rule"—the excess of democracy. *Democracy* was a term of derision. The Constitution contained many buffers against this and other forms of excess.

Republicanism declined in many stages. A greater stress on the individual's role in society, embodied in the work of Adam Smith and David Hume, reduced the sphere open to public pursuits.

The pace of economic change undermined established patterns. As the nation demanded large-scale projects, and as rival factions looked to the mobilization of larger and larger parts of the electorate to augment their strength, democratic rhetoric gained respectability. Mass party participation became a vehicle for pursuing civic virtue and balance. The notion of a constant opposition party gained strength. If the democratic process had enough "checks," political thinkers now reasoned, the harmful "mob" aspects of democracy could be tempered. The development of the Jacksonian party as a way of arbitrating interests was the final stage in republican decline and democratic ascendance.

Political scientist Russell Hanson has noted that the new democratic ethos sprang from one of the same goals as the old republican ethos: development of a public spirit by rising above particular restraints. "Support for popular sovereignty became the lowest common denominator for a Democratic Party composed of interests seeking liberation from a variety of sectionally specific restraints on the 'will of the people.' "[25]

A two-party system persisted as the nation drifted toward civil war, but it was not a simple two-party system. The Democrats and Whigs competed for the presidency and other political offices until 1856, when the Republican Party fielded its first national ticket and made the Whigs obsolete. But the parties were so unstable that their many elements were constantly forming and breaking up coalitions—and threatening to bolt from the system itself. A series of third parties entered the national electoral arena for short periods, applying or relieving pressures on the two major parties.[26]

Only by examining the parties and their various factions and struggles can one understand the presidential contests in the years before the Civil War, and the way that the Civil War revealed the basic fault lines of U.S. politics.

# The Whigs' 1840 Victory

The Whigs developed to fill the role of their British namesake, which had been to mount a republican opposition to the royal ruling power. The rise of Andrew Jackson and his supposedly imperial presidency threatened the "balance" of the United States, and the Whigs rose to restore that balance. The Whigs saw Jackson's Democrats as a faction of the most dangerous variety—a majority faction that had the ability to trample liberties in its mad scramble for spoils.

The key to Whiggery was the notion of balanced development. The Whigs opposed the war with Mexico and other expansionist programs because they feared the perils of overextending the nation's abilities and getting entangled with foreign powers. The Whigs favored internal improvements, but only as a way of maintaining balance and staving off the corruption of the Jackson era. The protective tariff was central to the Whigs' program of internal development and protection from outsiders. Political scientist Russell Hanson has described the Whig philosophy:

> Even in America, which was uniquely blessed by an abundance of natural resources and a citizenry of hardy stock, there was need for informed guidance and direction of progress. For the Whigs, government was the primary agent of this progress. Government represented a strong and positive force to be used in calling forth a richer society from the unsettled possibilities of America. In the economic realm this meant that government was responsible for providing the essential conditions for a sound economy, namely, a reliable currency, ample credit, and the impetus for internal improvements. And in the social realm, the government was responsible for promoting virtue in its citizenry through education and exhortation.[27]

The Whig desire for balance and compromise was intended to give the party a national rather than a sectional identity. A series of Senate battles with President Jackson, especially the tariff battles of 1833, which resulted in an unsatisfying compromise, gave impetus to grass-roots organizations in the North and West and to Southern Democratic opponents. The tendency of the Whigs to nominate widely popular military heroes helped create at least the illusion of a party of national dimensions. The Whigs developed first in the South, where voters were dissatisfied with Jackson's selection of Van Buren as his running mate. Loose coalitions elected candidates in the 1834 and 1835 state and congressional elections in the South. Westerners also organized to oppose the Democratic Party, which was headed by a New Yorker.

The first serious Whig presidential contest was a loss, but an encouraging one. In 1836, the Whig ticket headed by Harrison showed surprising appeal in the loss to the Democrat Van Buren. The Whig strategy was to run a number of favorite sons and produce inconclusive results in the Electoral College, sending the contest to the House of Representatives for resolution. The Whigs won Jackson's home state of Tennessee and the neighboring Georgia, as well as three Border slave states, and were strong competitors elsewhere. Harrison carried the old Northwest (now the Midwest) and came close in Northern states like Pennsylvania.

Because of the rise of the antislavery "conscience Whigs," the Whigs eventually moved to a completely different base of support—the North rather than the South and West—but their early organizing at least broke the Democratic stranglehold on the latter two regions. The Whigs nominated Harrison in 1840 after a nomination struggle with Clay. A Clay supporter, John Tyler of Virginia, was the vice presidential nominee. This time, the popular if politically inexperienced hero of the War of 1812 won his ticket to the White House. Harrison defeated the incumbent Van Buren in an electoral vote landslide, receiving 234 of the 294 electoral votes—all the states except Alabama, Arkansas, Illinois, Missouri, New Hampshire, South Carolina and Virginia. Harrison won 1.3 million popular votes (52.9 percent) to Van Buren's 1.1 million (46.8 percent).

According to Richard P. McCormick:

> The campaign of 1840 brought the American party system at last to fruition. In every region of the country, and indeed in every state, politics was conducted within the framework of a two party system, and in all but a handful of states the parties were so closely balanced as to be competitive. In broad terms, it was the contest for the presidency that shaped this party system and defined its essential purpose.[28]

Harrison's campaign was as vague as his government experience was unimpressive. The image of Harrison as a sort of frontier everyman—which received its popular expression when a Baltimore newspaper mocked him as a sedentary man who would sit in a log cabin and drink cider rather than perform great deeds of leadership—was the theme of numerous parades and mass meetings. On issues from banking and currency to slavery, Harrison spoke in generalities. Harrison's strategist acknowledged that he advised the candidate to "say not a single word about his principles or creed. Let him say nothing—promise nothing."[29]

Harrison did not have an opportunity to do much as president besides discipline the aggressive Clay. Clay assumed that he and the rest of the congressional leadership would play the leading role in the government, and Harrison wrote a quick note rebuking him. But one month after his inauguration, the 68-year-old Harrison, physically weakened by the pressures of office, developed pneumonia and died. On April 6, 1841, the burdens of the presidency fell upon Vice President John Tyler.

The rift between the White House and Congress widened under Tyler. Clay acted as if he were prime minister during a special session of Congress, pushing through a legislative program that included a recharter of the long-controversial National Bank, higher import taxes and distribution of proceeds from land sales to the states. Tyler, a lifetime states' rights advocate, vetoed two bills for a national bank, and the Whigs in Congress and his own cabinet entered a bitter feud with the president. In 1842 Clay left the Senate to promote his presidential aspirations, and everyone in the cabinet except Secretary of State Daniel Webster quit. Tyler was all alone, but he did manage to defeat the Whig program in his four years as president.

## Polk's Dark-Horse Victory in 1844

The Democrats were transformed into a well-organized mass by Andrew Jackson and Martin Van Buren between 1828 and 1836. But, like the Whigs, the Democratic Party became vulnerable because of the irreconcilable differences among many of its parts.

From the beginning, the Democratic Party had contained contradictory elements. According to Sundquist: "The party had been formed originally as an alliance between Southern planters and New Yorkers and had always spanned both regions. Northern men of abolitionist sympathies were accustomed to sitting with slaveholders in presidential cabinets and collaborating with them in the halls of Congress."[30] Northerners went so far as to organize antiabolitionist rallies in their cities and towns, and newspapers and churches also defended slavery.

The deepest Democratic divisions—which eventually would lead to the failure not only of the party but also of the nation—were the regional differences based on slavery. Although slavery and the regional split it engendered were a constant and growing theme in U.S. politics, other, more complex divisions also affected the operation of the Democratic Party. When the party was able to reconcile or even delay action on the divisive issues, it won. When the divisions burst into the open, the party was in trouble.

James K. Polk of Tennessee, the first "dark-horse" candidate in history, defeated the Whig Henry Clay in 1844 by supporting an expansionist program and winning the support of the solid South. One of the key issues in the campaign was whether Texas should be admitted to the Union and, if so, whether it should be slave or free. President Van Buren in 1840 opposed annexation—opposition that might have cost him the presidency—and the Democrats and Whigs hedged on the issue for the next eight years. In 1844, Polk endorsed the annexation of Texas as a slave state; that was enough for him to lock up the South.

During the 1844 nominating convention, the Democrats finessed the sectional dangers of the Texas issue by combining it with a call for occupying Oregon and for eventually bringing that state into the Union. The Democrats also appealed to Pennsylvania and the rest of the Northeast by supporting a high tariff. Both parties spoke out against the growing foreign elements in the cities, but the Whigs were more effective because of the Democrats' swelling immigrant ranks.

Polk defeated Clay, winning 1.34 million votes (49.5 percent) to Clay's 1.30 million (48.1 percent) and 170 electoral votes to Clay's 105. Clay received his strongest support from five northeastern states and five Border slave states. Of the expansionist Northwest, only Ohio fell in the Clay column.

The Liberty Party's abolitionist campaign may have been the deciding factor in the 1844 race. Although it received only 2.3 percent of the popular vote and no electoral votes, the Liberty Party was strong enough in New York to prevent the Whigs from winning that state's crucial 36 electoral votes. Those votes went to the Democrat Polk rather than to the Whig Clay.

The depth of the Democrats' divisions were agonizingly evident even when the party won elections and started to pass out spoils and make policy. Like Harrison, the Whig who had won the presidency four years before, President Polk faced the antagonisms of party factions when he began making appointments after his 1844 win. Westerners were angry when they were shut out of the cabinet and Polk vetoed a rivers and harbors bill. Supporters of both Van Buren and John Calhoun were angry that their faction did not win more prominent positions. Northeasterners were upset at tariff cuts. The New York split between the reformist "Barnburners" and the party-regular "Hunkers"—who disagreed on every issue, including banks, currency, internal improvements and political reforms—also disrupted the administration.

Creating still more dissension was the war with Mexico (1846-1848), fought because of the dispute over the Texas border and the possible annexation of California. Patronage was intensely controversial, and Northerners resented the country's fighting Mexico over a slave state. Among the war's more prominent opponents was Henry David Thoreau.

# Whig Success under Taylor in 1848

In 1848 the Whigs recaptured the White House behind another military hero, Gen. Zachary Taylor, who was vague on most political issues. Taylor defeated the irrepressible Clay and Gen. Winfield Scott for the nomination on the fourth convention ballot. Clay mounted an impressive public campaign that drew large crowds, but the Whigs had lost too many times with Clay. The Whig ticket was headed by the Louisiana slave-owning Taylor, and his running mate was New Yorker Millard Fillmore.

The Whigs were so determined to avoid sectional and other issue splits that they not only nominated the popular Taylor but also eschewed writing a platform. Despite such extreme measures to maintain unity, the convention was disturbed by squabbles between pro- and antislavery forces on the question of the Wilmot Proviso, which would ban slavery in any territory obtained from Mexico.

Sen. Lewis Cass of Michigan defeated Sen. James Buchanan of Pennsylvania and Supreme Court Justice Levi Woodbury for the Democratic nomination, and Gen. William Butler was picked as his running mate. But the convention experienced splits between the New York factions of the Barnburners, who were part of the antislavery movement, and the Hunkers, who had ties to Southerners. The Barnburners defected from the party to become part of the Free Soil party.

The Democrats behind Cass praised the administration of the beleaguered Polk, defended the war with Mexico, congratulated the French Republic that emerged from the wave of revolution in Europe, and did everything it could to avoid the nasty slavery issue. The nomination of Cass—a "doughface," or Northerner with Southern principles—was expected to appeal to both sides of the simmering issue.

Taylor defeated Cass, winning 1.4 million popular votes (47.3 percent) to Cass's 1.2 million (42.5 percent). New York Democrat Martin Van Buren, the former president, running on the Free Soil ticket, won 291,500 votes (10 percent) but no electoral votes. Taylor received 163 electoral votes to Cass's 127, with a strong showing in the North. Taylor won Connecticut, Massachusetts, New Jersey, New York, Pennsylvania, Rhode Island and Vermont in the North; Delaware, Kentucky, Maryland, North Carolina and Tennessee in the Border states; and Florida, Georgia and Louisiana in

the Deep South. This combination was enough to beat Cass's coalition of seven slave states, six northwestern states, and two New England states.

On July 10, 1850, Fillmore succeeded to the presidency when President Taylor suddenly died. After consuming too many refreshments at a Fourth of July celebration, Taylor developed cramps, then a fatal illness, probably typhoid fever. Fillmore, however, was unable to secure the party nomination in 1852 despite an early lead in convention polling. General Scott won the nomination, and the Whigs entered into permanent decline.

## Slavery Divides the Whigs

Try as they might with the selection of military heroes as candidates and vague issue statements, the Whigs could not cover over the nation's disagreements forever. When divisive issues burst into the open, the party was in trouble. The tariff issue and their mildly probusiness stance gave the Whigs strength in the North. But the Whigs, like the Democrats, needed to attract support also in the South; so they tried to keep the slavery question out of their rhetoric. The Whigs could count on being competitive in the Border slave states, but not in the rest of Dixie. In 1844, Clay had won only the northern rim of slave states (Delaware, Kentucky, Maryland, North Carolina and Tennessee).

As political scientist James L. Sundquist has noted, both the Whig and Democratic parties in the pre-Civil War era attempted to ignore the slavery issue, but the Whigs had less room to maneuver. The Democrats' agrarian and populist position gave them the solid South as a foundation, and they could make a variety of antiabolitionist appeals to the rest of the electorate. Democrats could argue that their support for slavery in the South was compatible with many "moderate" positions. The appeal of Stephen Douglas and Buchanan rested on such a coalition-building strategy. The Whigs, however, included vociferous opponents of slavery that could not be reconciled easily with "moderate" positions. Abolitionism had upper-class and religious roots that were difficult to use as a foundation. The support the Whigs were able to retain in the South was based on their positions on local issues. In sum, the Whigs did not have the same potential to build a national party organization as the Democrats.

Both parties contained slavery sympathizers and opponents; neither was willing to make a principled stand against the institution, particularly where it already existed. The parties were more competitive over issues such as westward expansion, banking questions, public improvements, the tariff and foreign relations. It was up to third parties such as the Liberty and Free Soil Parties to press the slavery issue. Sectional cleavages were so strong that Congress in 1836 passed a "gag rule" that forbade the reading of antislavery statements in Congress. Such attempts to silence abolitionist fervor were in vain, however, as politics was entering an age of mass communication and organization. The slavery issue would become irrepressible.

The beginning of the abolitionist movement, which may be dated to the founding of William Lloyd Garrison's newspaper, *The Liberator*, in 1831, posed problems for the Whigs that eventually proved fatal. The antislavery belt developed in the Whigs' strongest territory—New England—and westward into what today would be called the Midwest. Abolitionism was largely an upper- or middle-class and religious cause. But it also was a partisan issue: the Whigs, the party out of power for years, needed an issue with which to confront the Democrats. Slavery was a useful issue, even if the Whigs' antislavery stance in the North contradicted their accommodating stance in the South.

The slavery issue split the Whigs badly with the controversy over the admission of Texas to the Union in 1845. A splinter group of young party members calling themselves the "Conscience Whigs" argued for a straightforward statement of principle against slavery. An opposition group called the "Cotton Whigs" wanted to defuse the slavery issue by ignoring moral arguments and simply calling for a halt to annexation. The party split became complete with Clay's Compromise of 1850, which admitted California as a free state, ended slave trade in the District of Columbia and admitted Texas but reduced its size by splitting off the New Mexico territory. After agitation from Conscience Whigs and General Scott's nomination in 1852, the party was irreparably rent by the slavery issue.

The Whigs attempted to make concessions to the South, but many of their efforts only antagonized Northern supporters. The 1852 Whig convention platform contained several statements supporting states' rights and the principles behind Clay's compromise.[31] Northern Whigs made these concessions to win Southern support for their presidential favorite, General Scott. When no Whigs voted for the Kansas-Nebraska Act in 1854, which permitted state determination of the slavery question, the Whigs' remaining ties to Dixie were severed.

The Whigs' support in the Northwest was almost nonexistent. Only Ohio, in 1844, went for the Whigs even once over the course of the 1844, 1848 and 1852 presidential elections. Previously strong ties between the "lake region" and the South deteriorated as immigrants and others moved from the Northeast to the Northwest and, after the completion of railroad links, the two regions developed strong economic ties.

The Whigs' last gasp came in 1852, when Scott was demolished by Democrat Franklin Pierce. Pierce won all the states except two in New England (Massachusetts and Vermont) and two Border states (Kentucky and Tennessee). Pierce won 27 states and 254 electoral votes to Scott's four states and 42 electoral votes.

Whig divisions were most evident in 1856 as the Whigs split their votes among the Democrat Buchanan, the former Whig Fillmore and the Republican John C. Fremont. Not all Whigs were ready yet to join the nascent Republican Party, because of the extremism of some of the party's abolitionists. The majority of Whigs folded into the Republicans in 1860 when Abraham Lincoln avoided a white "backlash" by insisting that he supported slavery where it existed and opposed its spread only because of how it would affect the economic fortunes of poor Northern whites.

## Slavery Divides the Democrats

The Democrats suffered a North-South cleavage that Lincoln exploited against Stephen Douglas in the 1860 election. Southern Democrats were intent on protecting slavery, and they felt that control of Congress was necessary to their strategy. Extension of slavery to the new states joining the Union was necessary to maintain congressional strength.

Northern Democrats were willing to allow Dixie to maintain its peculiar institution but were scared about their own electoral prospects if slavery should expand. Northern Democrats at first rallied to Douglas' doctrine of "popular sovereignty" (under which the people of new states could decide whether to adopt slavery), but they got nervous when Lincoln hammered away at his argument that any unchecked slavery threatened the freedom of whites as well as blacks. Lincoln argued that Democrats such as Douglas wanted to make slavery a nationwide, rather than a selective state-by-state, institution.

Lincoln planted seeds of doubt about partial solutions to the slavery question by asserting that slavery could extend to whites if it were nationalized: "If free negroes should be made *things,* how long, think you, before they will begin to make *things* out of poor white men?"[32] Lincoln also maintained that the extension of slavery into new territories would close off the territories for whites seeking upward mobility: "The whole nation is interested that the best use be made of these Territories. We want them for homes of free white people. This they cannot be, to any considerable extent, if slavery shall be planted within them."[33]

The growing movement against the extension of slavery was based on a concern for the upward mobility of labor. Rather than stressing the common interests of blacks and poor white Northern laborers, the antiextension movement followed Lincoln's lead in playing up the competition between the two groups. Horace Greeley's vision of the frontier as "the great regulator of the relations of Labor and Capital, the safety valve of our industrial and social engine"[34] left little room for the extension of slavery into the new territories. The extension of slavery was the issue that most divided the Democratic Party.

## Democrat Pierce's Victory in 1852

Clay's congressional compromise on slavery in the territories, known as the Compromise of 1850, turned out to be the major reason for the Democrats' 1852 victory. President Taylor stalled action for months and even suggested that California and New Mexico might become independent nations. But his successor, Fillmore, threw his support behind the compromise. The Whigs were divided on the proposal. The compromise addressed the slavery question in all the new U.S. territories by making concessions to both sides of the struggle. For the North, California would be admitted as a free state, and the slave trade (but not slavery itself) would be abolished in the District of Columbia. For the South, fugitive slave laws would be strengthened, and the New Mexico territory would be divided into two states where popular sovereignty would decide the slave issue.

The compromise was designed to settle the issue of slavery in new territories once and for all. But the slavery issue could not be contained by region; it had an increasingly important "spillover" effect. Because of concerns for the congressional balance of power and the difficulties of enforcing slavery provisions such as the fugitive-slave law in states that opposed slavery, it was impossible to isolate the slavery question into particular regions as Clay intended.

General Scott won the Whig nomination in 1852 after platform concessions to the party's Southern delegation. Scott's appeal was always limited to the North, while Fillmore appealed to the South and Daniel Webster appealed to New England. Scott won on the 53rd ballot.

Franklin Pierce of New Hampshire, a dark horse who gained fame with his Mexican War record, won the Democratic nomination in 1852. The vice presidential candidate was Sen. William Rufus de Vane King of Alabama. The party held together a coalition of groups with contradictory positions on the slavery issue and regional affairs. The convention, meeting in Baltimore, pledged to "abide by, and adhere to" Clay's compromise and to do what it could to smother the slavery issue.

Attempts to inject issues of economics and foreign affairs into the election failed, and the campaign degenerated into squabbles over personalities. Pierce easily won with 1.6 million popular votes (50.4 percent) to Scott's 1.4 million (43.9 percent). Pierce had 27 states and 254 electoral votes to Scott's four states and 42 electoral votes.

# The Democrats' Bruising 1856 Victory

By 1856, the North-South split had eliminated the Whigs as a national party and fatally damaged the Democrats' chances for winning a national election for decades.

Congress opened the slavery issue by passing the Kansas-Nebraska Act of 1854. The act declared "null and void" the Missouri Compromise, which prohibited slavery in new territories north of the 36°30' parallel except in Missouri. The 1854 legislation created two territories (Kansas and Nebraska) from the original Nebraska territory and left the slavery issue to be determined by popular sovereignty there and in the Utah and New Mexico territories.

The Kansas-Nebraska Act was a vehicle to spur the development of the West. Such development was part of a longstanding American approach to creating opportunity and freedom via growth. Sen. Stephen A. Douglas of Illinois—the promoter of the law and the main advocate of popular sovereignty—held that the law was necessary if the country was to be bound together by rail and telegraph lines and was to drive Great Britain off the continent. The latter goal was intertwined with a widely held suspicion that Britain was exploiting the slavery issue to distract American politics and stunt American growth.

Whatever the economic motives for unification, the Kansas-Nebraska Act was bitterly divisive. Northern state legislatures passed resolutions denouncing the law. The development of sectional parties continued.

A flood of new settlers into Kansas, and the terror-filled balloting over whether Kansas was to be a free or a slave state, further inflamed passions. Neighboring Missourians took part in the controversy, arguing that their status as slave owners would be undermined if Kansas voted to be free. Especially with the Supreme Court's infamous 1857 *Dred Scott* decision, which defined slaves as property, and the Lincoln-Douglas debates in Illinois in 1858, the slavery question was becoming decisive in American politics.

The Democrats won the White House in 1856 when the party endorsed the Kansas-Nebraska Act and nominated the pro-Southern James Buchanan as its presidential candidate. John Breckinridge of Kentucky, who later served in the Confederate Army, was Buchanan's running mate. The Democrats, who were becoming almost exclusively a Southern party, benefited from close wins in Buchanan's home state of Pennsylvania and in New Jersey, and in western states such as Illinois, Indiana and California. But the only strong region for the Democrats was the South. Buchanan won all the slave states except Maryland. Overall, Buchanan won 1.8 million popular votes (45.3 percent) to Fremont's 1.3 million (33.1 percent). The Electoral College gave Buchanan a 174-114 victory.

The nativist American Party—or the "Know-Nothings," as they were called—nominated former Whig president Millard Fillmore, but the party was never able to move beyond an urban strength based on parochial resistance to immigration and Catholicism. Fillmore won only the state of Maryland; overall, he got 873,000 popular votes (21.5 percent) and 8 electoral votes.

After an 1854 meeting in Ripon, Wisconsin, where a new national party was first proposed, the Republican Party developed quickly. The Republicans had a strong grass-roots organization in the Northwest after the Kansas-Nebraska Act and attracted Whigs, Know-Nothings and Northern Democrats who were troubled by the possible extension of slavery. Uncertainty about how the extension of slavery would affect laborers who sought opportunity in the territories also helped unite the new coalition.

The first Republican presidential convention met in Philadelphia in 1856 with delegates from all the free states, four Border states, three territories and the District of Columbia. The party's opposition to slavery was far from unanimous, but its willingness to address rather than suppress the issue enabled it to redefine the political dialogue. Besides strong antislavery statements, the party platform contained proposals for several internal improvements advantageous to the North. The party did not offer anything to the solidly Democratic South. To win a national election, it would have to sweep the North. Col. John Charles Fremont was named the Republicans' first presidential candidate. Former Whig senator William Dayton of New Jersey received the vice presidential nomination.

In 1860, the Democratic split was complete when the party's Southern elements supported Vice President Breckinridge and Northerners backed Stephen Douglas. The Buchanan administration earlier had waged war on Douglas by ousting Douglas allies from the federal bureaucracy for opposing the administration's pro-Southern stance on the Kansas issue.

When the time came for the 1860 presidential campaign, the Democrats were hopelessly split over slavery. The biggest sticking point was the *Dred Scott* decision, which held that Congress had no power to prohibit the slave trade in a territory. The decision was just what Southerners favoring popular sovereignty wanted, but it also created uncertainty about any legislature's authority over slavery. If the federal legislature could not regulate slavery, could state legislatures? The Republicans were able to use the decision as a rallying point for popular control of government; the Democrats were in the uncustomary position of defending the Supreme Court, which since Thomas Jefferson they had pictured as elitist. Douglas, the eventual Democratic nominee and architect of the platform, insisted on state resolution of the issue. Jefferson Davis of Mississippi, the eventual president of the Confederate States of America, fought in Congress for the right of Congress to promote and protect slavery in new territories.

Eventually, the Davis Democrats held their own convention and nominated Vice President Breckinridge for the presidency. Although these "Dixiecrats"—a term used to distinguish Southern from Northern Democrats—insisted that they were the backbone of the party and had been strong enough to elect Buchanan four years before, the party divided would not be able to win a national election.

Democratic Party splits enabled Lincoln to win the 1860 election, resulting in the secession of seven Southern states from the Union even before his inauguration. (The remaining four states forming the Confederacy seceded after the fall of Fort Sumter, April 13, 1861.)

# The Fateful Election of 1860

The regional splits that had been tearing the nation apart for decades reached their peak in 1860. None of the four major candidates who sought the presidency could compete seriously throughout the nation. The winner would probably be a candidate from the North, the region with the most electoral votes. The two Northern candidates were former U.S. representative Abraham Lincoln of Illinois and Stephen Douglas, a Democrat, who defeated Lincoln for the Illinois Senate seat in 1858. Moderate Constitutional Union nominee John Bell of Tennessee and Democrat John Breckinridge of Kentucky were the candidates competing in the South.

The Republican Party developed out of disgruntled elements of the Whigs, the Know-Nothings, abolitionists, members of the Liberty and Free-Soil parties, anti-imperialists, high-tariff supporters, temperance activists and states' rights advocates. The Republicans succeeded in 1860 because they were able to pull together a variety of potentially warring factions. Above all else, the Republicans stood against the extension of slavery into new territories. By accepting slavery where it already existed but warning against the nationalization of the system, the Republicans divided the Democrats and picked up support from a diverse array of otherwise contentious factions—abolitionists, moderate abolitionists and whites who feared for their position in the economy.

The *Dred Scott* decision enabled the Republicans to rail publicly against the high court in the tradition of Jefferson and Jackson. While opposing the Democratic doctrine of popular sovereignty, the Republicans picked up some states' rights sympathizers.

Lincoln won the nomination at a frenzied convention in Chicago. After the convention blocked several radical candidates, Lincoln emerged as the consensus compromise choice. Lincoln was known widely throughout Illinois, which improved his chances at the Chicago convention.

Among the Democrats, Douglas was Lincoln's principal rival. Douglas managed several moderate platform victories at the Democratic convention in Charleston, S.C., defeating resolutions that called for acceptance of the *Dred Scott* decision and protection of slavery in the territories. But Douglas' success prompted delegates from 10 Southern states to bolt the convention. After disputes over quorum rules and 57 ballots, the Democrats were unable to muster the necessary two-thirds majority for Douglas. The convention adjourned, reassembled at Baltimore and faced disputes about the seating of delegates that caused further defections from the South. With Southern radicals effectively eliminated from the convention, Douglas swept to a unanimous nomination victory.

The Democratic defectors named Vice President Breckinridge to run for president in the South. The Constitutional Union Party, which developed as a futile attempt to repair the nation's geographic divisions, nominated Bell to oppose Breckinridge.

These two candidates were doomed from the start, however, since the South's electoral vote total was significantly below that of just a few major Northern states.

The Republicans assembled the wide-ranging coalition that eluded the Whigs in their last years of existence. Lincoln could count on strength in the areas that Fremont had won in 1856—New England and the upper Northwest, as well as New York and Ohio. The Republicans offered an internal-improvements program to attract settlers in the frontier. Lincoln's local ties would help him in Illinois and Indiana, and his Whig background was a plus in the Ohio valley. The coal and iron regions of Pennsylvania and Ohio were attracted to the party's high-tariff policy. Urban immigrants, particularly Germans, were attracted by Republican support of homestead (that is, frontier settlement) legislation and the Lincoln campaign's "Vote Yourself a Farm" appeal.[35] The vice presidential selection of Hannibal Hamlin of Maine, a former Democrat, broadened the coalition beyond partisan lines. Lincoln's oft-stated desire to protect slavery where it then existed was an appeal to Border states.

Lincoln easily won with a total of 180 electoral votes to Breckinridge's 72, Bell's 39 and Douglas' 12. Lincoln's closest competitor in the popular vote was Douglas. Lincoln had 1.9 million popular votes (40.0 percent); Douglas had 1.4 million (29.5 percent) spread out geographically. The two other principal candidates received much less support, which was concentrated in the South: Breckinridge won 848,000 popular votes (18.1 percent); Bell, 591,000 (12.6 percent).

Southerners had vowed to secede from the Union if Lincoln won the election. In the period before Lincoln's inauguration, congressional committees sought to put together a compromise that would save the nation from civil war, but they always failed because of Lincoln's refusal to abandon his policy of containment of slavery. Lincoln rejected proposals for popular sovereignty or a slave-free geographic division of Western states. Lincoln would not comment on proposals for constitutional amendments or popular referenda on the issue.

After Lincoln was elected, South Carolina, Louisiana, Mississippi, Alabama, Georgia, Texas and Florida seceded from the Union and on February 7, 1861, adopted a constitution forming the Confederate States of America. After a protracted standoff between Union soldiers who held Fort Sumter and the Confederate soldiers who controlled South Carolina, the Confederates fired on the fort. Virginia, Arkansas, North Carolina and Tennessee then joined the Confederacy, and the Civil War was under way.

# The Civil War Election: 1864

The Union's military difficulties in 1861 and 1862 created resentment and impatience with President Lincoln, and splits that developed in the Republican Party seemed to imperil his chances for renomination and reelection.

From the very beginning of his administration Lincoln suffered because of the difficulty he had finding a general who could successfully prosecute the war. Repeated military setbacks and stalemates—such as the battles of Fredericksburg and Chancellorsville, Confederate general Robert E. Lee's escape after the battle of Antietam (Sharpsburg) and heavy casualties in the drive to Richmond—hurt the Republicans. Publicized conflicts with generals such as George McClellan caused further damage. In addition to the military problems, the president's announcement of the emancipation of slaves in rebellious states in September 1862 (the Emancipation Proclamation) created legal and political controversy.

The Republicans experienced widespread losses in congressional and state elections in the 1862 midterm elections. Among the more bitter defeats for Lincoln was John Stuart's victory in the president's old congressional district in Illinois. By the time of the election, Stuart, a former law partner of the president, was an ardent political foe.

The military frustrations gave rise to deep divisions within Lincoln's own cabinet. Treasury Secretary Salmon P. Chase led a radical faction of the administration, and Philadelphia banker Jay Gould briefly led a movement for Chase's nomination for president in 1864. Chase withdrew only after the Lincoln forces dealt him a severe blow at the party caucus in his home state of Ohio. Other radicals met in Cleveland in May 1864 and named John Fremont to run against Lincoln in the fall. Fremont withdrew only after a series of Union military victories strengthened Lincoln's political standing.

The president manipulated the Republican convention in Baltimore brilliantly, ensuring not only his own renomination but also the selection of pro-Union governor Andrew Johnson of Tennessee as the vice presidential candidate. Lincoln professed indifference about a possible running mate. "Wish not to interfere about V.P. Cannot interfere about platform," he said in a letter. "Convention must judge for itself." [36] Nonetheless, he maneuvered to build support for Johnson. Johnson's selection was in accord with the desire of the party, which called itself the Union Party as a way to attract Democrats and to develop nationwide unity. Yet Lincoln's reelection drive was so uncertain that he obliged his cabinet in August 1864 to sign a statement pledging an orderly transition of power if he lost. The statement read: "This morning, as for some days past, it seems exceedingly probable that this Administration will not be reelected. Then it will be my duty to so cooperate with the President-elect, as to save the Union between the election and the inauguration; as he will have secured his election on such ground that he cannot possibly save it afterwards." [37]

The man for whom Lincoln anticipated arranging a wartime transition was General McClellan, the Democratic nominee whom Lincoln had fired as general in January 1863. McClellan had won the Democratic nomination with the strong backing of "peace Democrats" such as Clement L. Vallandigham of Ohio, who was arrested by Union general Ambrose E. Burnside after making a series of antiwar speeches. (Vallandigham later took up exile in Canada.) McClellan's running mate was Rep. George Pendleton of Ohio, who would later sponsor landmark civil-service reform legislation.

McClellan was a vocal critic of the administration. The general did not win a single major battle despite constant infusions of extra troops, but he blamed Lincoln for the losses. McClellan was popular with the soldiers, and his campaign was built around a call for a cease-fire and a convention to restore the Union. McClellan and other peace Democrats also criticized the administration's violation of civil liberties and other unconstitutional actions.

Lincoln's fortunes improved in the two months before the election. When Gen. William Tecumseh Sherman took Atlanta after a scorched-earth march through the South, the Confederacy was left badly divided geographically. The military victory cut off Gulf states from the Confederate capital of Richmond. Gen. Philip Sheridan had important successes in the Shenandoah Valley, and Gen. Ulysses Grant did well in Virginia.

Not only did the Democrats face a Republican Party reconstituted for the war election as the Union Party and united by recent military victories, but McClellan also had a difficult time developing consistent campaign themes. He was at various times conciliatory toward the Confederacy and solicitous of the soldiers who fought for the Union. The balancing problem was underscored by the inclusion of both war and peace songs in the *McClellan Campaign Songster*, a piece of campaign literature.[38] McClellan also had a difficult time selling his message to Northern industrialists who profited from munitions procurement.

Not until the arrival of election results from three state elections on October 11 were Lincoln and the Unionists confident that they would win the national election in November. Republican victories in Indiana, Ohio and Pennsylvania were the first concrete indications that Lincoln's fortunes had turned around.

Lincoln overwhelmed McClellan by winning all of the loyal states except Delaware, Kentucky and New Jersey for a 212-21 electoral vote victory. Lincoln garnered 2.2 million popular votes (55.0 percent) to McClellan's 1.8 million (45.0 percent). The electoral votes of Louisiana and Tennessee, the first Confederate states to return to the Union, were not accepted by Congress.

## Postwar Radicalism

The Civil War's end left the nation almost as divided as it had been in the antebellum years. Concerns about punishment of the rebel states, the status of the freedmen and economic development replaced slavery as the principal sources of disagreement

The nation undoubtedly would have experienced bitter splits no matter who served as chief executive, but the assassination of President Lincoln on April 14, 1865, shortly after the Confederate surrender, created a crisis of leadership. Lincoln's vice president, Andrew Johnson, ascended to the presidency and immediately came into conflict with the radical Northern Republicans who controlled Congress. Johnson, a Democrat from Tennessee, was stubborn, which only aggravated the troubles that were inevitable anyway because of his party and regional background.

Johnson intended to continue Lincoln's plans for a reconstruction of North and South "with malice toward none," but the Congress was intent on establishing political institutions that would respect the rights of former slaves and promote economic growth.[39] A states' rights politician, Johnson attempted to put together a coalition of moderates from all parts of the country that would bring about a quick reconciliation. He chafed at the notion of the South as a conquered territory. Johnson and Congress fought over bills that would extend the life of the Freedmen's Bureau and guarantee the franchise and equal protection to blacks. Johnson vetoed both bills. Johnson also opposed the 14th Amendment, which guaranteed equal protection, as well as the stipulation that Confederate states approve the amendment as a condition of their readmission to the Union.

When the Radicals took over Congress in the 1866 midterm elections, the war with Johnson began in earnest. In March 1867 Congress established limited military rule in recalcitrant Southern states and passed the Tenure of Office Act limiting the president's right to dismiss his appointees. Johnson contemptuously disregarded the tenure act and fired Edwin Stanton, his secretary of war. For this action Johnson was impeached by the House and tried by the Senate. When the Senate voted in May 1868, he avoided conviction by a single vote (35-19).

## The Grant Years, 1869-1877

Ulysses S. Grant was more than a concerned citizen during the dispute between Johnson and Congress. Despite its portrayal in many history books as a clear instance of congressional abuse of power, the affair was more complicated. All of the players in the drama negotiated their way with care, and almost none of them escaped without major scars. Grant was a central figure, and his style of maneuvering was dictated by his ambition to succeed Johnson as president.

Radical Republicans in Congress achieved a lasting victory when they secured passage of the Civil Rights Act of 1866 over President Johnson's veto, but they were increasingly disturbed by reports that the statute was not being enforced. A congressional investigation of violence against blacks in Memphis concluded that the Freedmen's Bureau could not enforce civil rights without help. Radicals began to look to Secretary of War Stanton to enforce the law that the president clearly disliked and repeatedly subverted.

Stanton indicated that he would carry out the law in the Confederacy as Congress intended, and Johnson began to think about replacing him. Congress passed the Tenure of Office Act over Johnson's veto in May 1867, reasoning that its constitutional "advise and consent" powers over appointments extended to removal as well. Johnson decided to test the law's constitutionality. Johnson's concern—and indeed the concern of all involved—was who could be given the post with minimal threat to his own position. Johnson first considered General Sherman but decided to appoint Grant on a temporary basis. Originally a Democrat and supporter of moderate Southern policies, Grant worried about appearing too close to the unpopular president. After vaguely assuring Johnson that he would accept a temporary appointment, Grant hedged. He increasingly expressed support for the notion that appointees should interpret and obey laws according to congressional intent. Eventually, Grant told the president in a letter that he could not accept the appointment.

After the drama of impeachment, Grant was in a good position to seek the White House. He had avoided allying himself with controversy both during Johnson's search for a replacement for Stanton and in the ensuing impeachment battle. Everyone but Grant and Chief Justice Salmon Chase was tainted by the affair. Grant even managed to maintain his public posture of disinterested duty. Thus during one of the nation's ugliest political episodes, Grant looked clean. He was ready for a presidential campaign.

As Johnson endured his Senate impeachment trial in March, Grant won his first electoral victory. A New Hampshire congressional campaign, which normally would favor the Democrat, became an early Grant referendum when Republican candidate Donald Sickles told voters that a vote for a Republican was a vote for Grant; Sickles won. Just before the Republican convention in May, a Soldiers and Sailors Convention "nominated" Grant. Grant avoided an excessively military image when he vowed to reduce the size of the standing army. He was on his way.

Grant won the nomination without opposition. The real battle at the 1868 Republican convention was for the vice-presidential nomination. Schuyler Colfax of Indiana, the Speaker of the House, won on the sixth ballot.

The Democrats had a difficult time finding a nominee. Johnson sought the Democratic nomination, but his appeal was to the South; and, because many Southern states were still outside the Union, Northern politicians were selecting the nominee. Chase, highly regarded for his fairness during Johnson's Senate trial, was a possibility, but his strong stand for black suffrage was a barrier. Thomas Hendricks of Indiana was strong in the East, and George Pendleton of Ohio was strong in the West. Gen. Winfield Hancock of Pennsylvania presented the opportunity of running one military hero against another.

After 23 bitter ballots in a sweltering New York City, Horatio Seymour, the party chair and popular war governor of New York, accepted the Democratic nomination against his will. Gen. Francis P. Blair, Jr., of Missouri was the vice-presidential nominee. The party platform called for a rapid reentry of Confederate states to the Union, state authority over suffrage questions, and the "Ohio Idea," which set an inflationary money supply and helped the indebted South.

Both sides were well-financed in the election, but the Republicans had the edge. Their positions on the tariff, railroad grants, and the currency attracted millions of dollars. Newspapers and magazines tended to be pro-Republican.

Grant ran his campaign from his home in Galena, Illinois. He was vague about issues ranging from the currency to voting rights. Appearances in Colorado with fellow generals Sherman and Sheridan were taken to be endorsements. Everything seemed to go Grant's way. Even the traditional campaign gossip about the sexual activities of candidates did not hurt him. Charges that Grant was excessively pro-black—"I am Captain Grant of the Black Marines, The stupidest man that was ever seen" were the lyrics of one ditty[40]—helped him with the recently enfranchised citizens. Without the black vote, Grant probably would have lost the popular vote and maybe the electoral vote. Results from October state elections that favored the Republicans created a brief movement for Seymour and Blair to quit the contest so that the Democrats could name a new ticket. Seymour instead took the October results as an incentive to get to the campaign stump. Seymour was a good speaker, but nothing he could do could help the Democrats.

Grant defeated Seymour by 3.0 million (52.7 percent) to 2.7 million votes (47.3 percent). The electoral vote tally was 214 for Grant and 80 for Seymour. Grant won all but 8 of the 34 states taking part in the election. He benefited from Radical Republican reconstructionist sentiment in the North and newly enfranchised blacks in the South.

With Grant's ascension to the presidency in 1869, the Republican Party entered a new era—what the German sociologist Max Weber would call a shift from "charismatic" to "rational" institutional authority. The party shifted its devotion from a great moral cause to its own survival as an organization. The party began as a coalition of activists fervently opposed to the expansion of slavery (many opposed to slavery itself) and to the rebellion of Southern states against the Union. The Republicans' 1868 victory under Grant was the first not dominated wholly by crisis conditions.

The Republicans had a strong base of support: Eastern bankers, manufacturers, railroads and land speculators. With the old Confederacy under the control of military governments and with blacks given the franchise, the Republicans had strength in the South. The West was restive, however, because of depressed farm prices, high taxes and debt. The industrial-agrarian split between North and South before the Civil War would be resumed as an East-West split in the years after the war.

Republican leadership was turning over to new hands. Age was claiming a number of the early Republican leaders, such as Thaddeus Stevens, William Seward, Benjamin Wade, Charles Sumner, James Grimes, Stanton and Chase. New party leaders included Senators Roscoe Conkling of New York, Oliver Morton of Indiana, Simon Cameron of Pennsylvania and Zachariah Chandler of Michigan, and

Representatives Benjamin Butler of Massachusetts, John Logan of Illinois, James Garfield of Ohio and James G. Blaine of Maine.

The Grant administration was undistinguished. The new president's inaugural address—spoken without the traditional company of the outgoing president, since Grant neglected to respond to Johnson's polite letters—was decent but uninspiring. Grant vowed that "all laws will be faithfully executed, whether they meet my approval or not," that debtors would not be tolerated, and that blacks should get the vote throughout the country, and Indians should be offered "civilization and ultimate citizenship." [41] With a few important exceptions, cabinet positions went to old Grant cronies.

The nation experienced a financial panic when financiers Jay Gould and Jim Fisk attempted to corner the world's gold market. Their scheme led to "Black Friday," September 24, 1869. Gould and Fisk met with President Grant and urged him not to sell government gold—therefore keeping the price of gold high. At the last minute, however, Grant decided to reject their advice and dumped $4 million worth of gold on the market. That dumping caused a severe drop in gold prices, breaking up the Gould-Fisk conspiracy but also causing tremendous losses for thousands of speculators. It was the worst disaster on Wall Street up to that time. Although it did not cause a depression, the South and West were hard hit by the financial retrenchment program that followed. Tariff rates remained high on most manufactured goods, despite tentative efforts to reform the system. The spoils system was in full swing during the Grant years. Grant himself was not involved in the scramble for booty, but his family and aides were often shameless in their greed. When Grant learned that liberal Republicans were planning an independent presidential campaign against him in 1872, he took the edge off the spoils issue by creating the Civil Service Reform Commission, but his neglect of the commission made it ineffective.

Before the 1872 election, the *New York Sun* exposed the Crédit Mobilier scandal. The newspaper reported that the firm's board of directors had many of the same members as the Union Pacific Railroad Company, which hired it to build a transcontinental route, and that Crédit Mobilier had paid its board exorbitant profits. To avoid a public investigation, Crédit Mobilier offered stock to Vice President Colfax and Rep. James Garfield (later president). Colfax lost his place on the Republican ticket for his role in the scandal; Sen. Henry Wilson of New Hampshire took his position as the vice-presidential candidate in 1872.

Liberal Republicans, discontented with protective tariffs, spoils and uneven administration of the Southern states, bolted the party in 1872. The group was interested in policies such as civil service reform and free trade that would promote individual virtue in a laissez-faire economic system. The reformers thought they had a chance to win. German-born senator Carl Schurz of Missouri wrote to a friend, "[T]he administration with its train of offices and officemongers [is] the great incubus pressing upon the party.... The superstition that Grant is the necessary man is rapidly giving way. The spell is broken, and we have only to push through the breach." [42]

Candidates for the nomination from this group of Republicans included former ambassador to Great Britain Charles Francis Adams, son of President John Quincy Adams and grandson of President John Adams; Supreme Court Justice David Davis; Salmon Chase; Sen. Lyman Trumbull of Illinois; and Horace Greeley, editor of the *New York Tribune*. Greeley won the nomination on the sixth ballot. The Democrats were so weak that they did not field a candidate of their own. They endorsed the Greeley ticket.

Since his early days as a newspaper reporter, when he described President Van Buren as an effeminate failure, Greeley won fame as a pungent social critic. He was a crusading abolitionist editor and a dedicated reformer, but his rumpled appearance and unpolished speaking style made him appear "unpresidential." Greeley was unable to parlay an amalgam of promises to various interest groups—blacks, soldiers, immigrants and laborers—into a victory over Grant. Groups that Greeley actively courted found him wanting for a variety of reasons, and even though Greeley advocated the tariff favored by the North, he could not cut into Grant's northeastern strength. A Republican cartoon showed Greeley's difficult task: Sitting on the fence are a laborer, skeptical because of Greeley's stand against strikes, and a black, concerned because of Greeley's advocacy of amnesty for Confederates. Sitting on the sidelines is a German upset because of Greeley's prohibitionist stance. He says: "Oh! Yaw! You would take my Lager away, den you must get widout me along!" [43]

Even though he went on the stump and delivered a series of impressive speeches, Greeley never had a chance. Republican gubernatorial victories in North Carolina in August and in Pennsylvania, Ohio and Indiana in October were clear harbingers that the party would do well in November. Grant took the entire North and the newly admitted South with 3.6 million popular votes (55.6 percent). Greeley won three Border states, as well as Tennessee, Texas and Georgia, with 2.8 million popular votes (43.9 percent). Less than a month after the election, Greeley died. Of the electoral votes, which were cast after Greeley's death, Grant received 286; the Democrats' 63 electoral votes were scattered among various candidates, and 17 Democratic electoral votes were not cast.

# The Compromise of 1876

The pattern of Republican, Northern and business domination of presidential politics was institutionalized in the 1876 election. Republican Rutherford B. Hayes, the three-time governor of Ohio, lost the popular vote and had a questionable hold on the Electoral College vote, but he managed to beat Democrat Samuel J. Tilden for the presidency when the election was settled by a special commission created by Congress. (Hayes won 4.0 million votes, or 48 percent, to Tilden's 4.3 million, or 51 percent.) Some feared that this election outcome, perhaps the most controversial election outcome in history, would set off a second civil war.

The problem arose when the vote tallies in Florida, South Carolina and Louisiana were called into question. Violence attended the voting in all three states, but President Grant did not send in federal troops to ensure fair balloting. On those states hung the electoral outcome. There was good reason to be suspicious of any vote count in those and other Southern states. While the Republicans controlled the balloting places and mounted vigorous drives to get blacks to the polls, the Democrats used physical intimidation and bribery to keep blacks away. The bitterness between Northern interests and Southern whites was apparent in the violence that often took place at polls.

State election board recounts and investigations did not settle the question, and Congress took it up. An electoral commission made up of five senators (three majority party Republicans, two minority Democrats), five representatives (three majority party Democrats, two minority Republicans), and five Supreme Court justices (two from each party, one independent) assembled to hear complaints about the disputed states. At the last minute the independent justice could not serve; his place was taken by a Republican who was accepted by Democrats because they considered him to be the most independent of possibilities. Weeks of bargaining followed, during which the Republican vote totals of the disputed states were confirmed, and the Southern Democrats extracted promises of financial aid and political independence from the federal government.

When the validity of the Florida vote count for Hayes was challenged, the commission responded that it did not have the capacity to judge the actual conduct of the balloting, only the validity of the certificates presented to Congress. That decision gave the state to Hayes. Challenges to the vote counts of Louisiana, South Carolina and Oregon were dismissed in a similar way, so Hayes was awarded the presidency.

The compromise not only settled the partisan dispute between Hayes and Tilden; it also established a rigid alignment of political interests that would dominate U.S. politics for the next half-century. Although Democrats won occasional victories, the Republican, Eastern, conservative, business-oriented establishment held sway over the system until Franklin Roosevelt's election in 1932. The institutional form of the regional splits created by the compromise remained much longer.

Historian C. Vann Woodward has argued that secret wheeling and dealing among congressional and party leaders institutionally divided the political system by party, region, economic interest and governmental branches. Northern Republican industrial interests were given control of the presidential election process, and Southern Democratic agricultural interests were given autonomy over their regional politics which led to their domination of Congress.[44] This alignment was not completely dislodged until the passage of important civil rights legislation in the 1960s. In return for throwing the election to the Republican Hayes, Northern politicians agreed to pull federal troops out of the South and to allow Southern whites to take over the system. Within months, Southern states were erecting a powerful edifice of racial discrimination that would last until the 1960s. Former South Carolina governor Daniel H. Chamberlain later summed up the deal:

> What is the president's Southern policy? [I]t consists in the abandonment of Southern Republicans and especially the colored race, to the control and rule not only of the Democratic Party, but of that class of the South which regarded slavery as a Divine Institution, which waged four years of destructive war for its perpetuation, which steadily opposed citizenship and suffrage for the negro—in a word, a class whose traditions, principles, and history are opposed to every step and feature of what Republicans call our national progress since 1860.[45]

## The Age of Republicanism

From 1860 until 1908, the Republicans won nine elections; the Democrats won only two. Only Grover Cleveland could put together a Democratic win, and he was as conservative on most issues as the Republicans of the period. Presidential election winners after the Great Compromise were Hayes (1876), James Garfield (1880), Cleveland (1884), Benjamin Harrison (1888), Cleveland (1892), William Mc-

Kinley (1896 and 1900), Theodore Roosevelt (1904) and William Howard Taft (1908).

The political aspirants of the day were required to adhere to the religion of high tariffs, laissez-faire economics and tight money. Tight money policies—the restricted issuance of currency, which favored bankers and other established interests but hurt debtors and those seeking more rapid expansion of some kinds of investment and spending—provided openings for resistance to Republican hegemony. Resistance also developed when the scramble for tariff protections created obvious inequities among businesses and hardships for the consumer. Populist uprisings such as Democrat William Jennings Bryan's 1896 campaign faltered, however, because of strong mobilization by the Republicans and divisions within the Democratic ranks. Bryan failed to bring a likely Democratic constituency—the worker—into the fold. Eastern businessmen were able to portray their interest in industrial growth as a common concern with labor and Bryan's western agrarian alliance as a danger to that growth.

While the GOP dominated presidential politics, the parties were well-balanced in Congress and in state governments until the class and sectional cleavages of the 1890s. The Senate was split in 1881, 37-37, and two years later the Republicans had a 38-36 edge. Democrats made gains in Northern congressional races, and Republicans were making smaller gains in the South. The House tended to provide a majority for the presidential party in power.

## Garfield Carries the GOP Banner

Hayes honored his pledge to serve only one term, setting off a scramble for the parties' nominations in 1880. When the momentum for a third term for Grant faltered, the Republican contest became a battle between Grant, House Speaker James Blaine and General John Sherman. Grant was able to muster a first-ballot plurality but could not attract new supporters as the balloting proceeded. A stalemate between Blaine and Sherman ensued.

Rep. James Garfield of Ohio, a former preacher who was impressive in his oratory and organization for Sherman, was the compromise choice for the nomination. He selected as his running mate Chester A. Arthur, the collector of the Port of New York, an important patronage job.

The Democrats named Gen. Winfield Hancock and former representative William English to head their ticket. The Democrats' platform advocated the gold standard, a tariff to raise revenue, civil service reform, restrictions on Chinese immigration and a belated criticism of the 1876 deal that gave the presidency to Hayes. Except for the tariff and 1876 questions, the Democrats' platform was close to the Republicans' statement of principles.

The regional breakdown of support, with most of the North and West falling in Garfield's camp and the South lining up behind Hancock, gave the presidency to Garfield. The popular vote was close—4.45 million (48.27 percent) to 4.44 million (48.25 percent)—but Garfield won a 214-155 electoral-vote victory.

The festering issue of patronage and civil service came to a head shortly after Garfield's inauguration. On July 2, 1881, Charles Guiteau, a man history textbooks have described as a "disappointed office-seeker," shot Garfield in a railroad depot while the president was traveling to Williams College to deliver a commencement address. Garfield died in September, and Arthur became president. The outstanding feature of Arthur's presidency was the easy passage of the

Pendleton Act, which set up a commission to regulate the provision of federal jobs and the behavior of civil servants. The number of federal workers removed from the patronage system was small at first, but successive presidents widened the coverage of nonpartisan workers so that today less than 1 percent of all federal workers are appointed by the White House.[46]

The tariff question also emerged as crucial. The Tariff Act of 1883 "gave little or no relief to the consumer and took care of every important industrial interest."[47] The Democrats opposed the bill and later worked for gradual lowering of rates, but failed. The tariff would be a major issue in later elections.

The next three elections, 1884, 1888 and 1892, revolved around Democrat Grover Cleveland of New York, a city politician who worked his way up to the governorship. Cleveland defeated Blaine for the presidency in 1884, lost to Harrison in 1888, then came back to defeat Harrison in 1892. Even after his two staggered terms, Cleveland remained involved in Democratic presidential politics. He emerged as the chief foe of Bryan in 1896 and was even considered for the presidency in 1900.

## Democrat Cleveland Wins: 1884

Arthur wanted the Republican nomination in 1884, and his record as stand-in for the assassinated Garfield arguably should have earned him the nomination. Not only was he an important player in the civil service reform and the tariff issue, but he began the modernization of the navy and vetoed the Chinese Exclusion Act of 1883. He was a model of fiscal probity with his veto of the $19 million river and harbor bill.

James G. Blaine of Maine—secretary of state in Arthur's own administration—stood in Arthur's way. After months of public appeals by old-line Republicans interested in stronger leadership and more generous patronage from their own party, Blaine quit his administration position and opposed Arthur for the nomination.

Blaine was the most charismatic figure of the period. A former teacher, editor, state legislator and member of Congress, he captured the imagination of the political establishment with his firey oratory. He had made a national name for himself when he opposed an 1876 congressional resolution extending forgiveness to Civil War rebels including the Confederate president, Jefferson Davis. Col. Robert G. Ingersoll, a rising political figure in the Republican Party, said of Blaine: "Like an armed warrior, like a plumed knight, James G. Blaine marched down the halls of the American Congress and threw his shining lance full and fair against the brazen forehead of every traitor to his country."[48]

The Republican convention in Chicago praised Arthur's administration and fudged the tariff issue. The tariff that passed in 1883 was the product of swarms of lobbyists for private interests. The GOP platform promised better protection for raw wool interests, angered by their treatment in 1883, and a generally protective stance for domestic industry. The platform also called for an international currency conference, railway regulation, a national agency for labor affairs and further improvements in the navy.

At a frenzied convention, Blaine took the lead over Arthur on the first ballot. Old-line party leaders quickly united behind Blaine, while Arthur was unable to consolidate the support of reform Republicans still skeptical of his leadership abilities from his days as a patronage politician

and collector of the Port of New York. Blaine won the nomination on the fourth ballot. Gen. John Logan of Illinois received the vice presidential nomination.

The Democrats nominated Grover Cleveland after skirmishes with Sen. Thomas Bayard of Delaware and Sen. Thomas Hendricks of Indiana. Hendricks, whose liberal expansionist currency stance would balance the more conservative stance of Cleveland, was named the vice presidential candidate. The Democratic platform vaguely promised reform of the tariff laws to make them more fair and, even more vaguely, promised a more honest and efficient administration.

Cleveland was a former teacher, lawyer, assistant district attorney and reform mayor of Buffalo who had won the governorship of New York only two years before. Members of both parties consistently underestimated Cleveland's intellect and resolve. As governor, he made enemies through vetoes of low public-transit fares and aid to sectarian schools. He also defied Tammany Hall, the Democratic Party organization that dominated New York politics, especially in New York City.

Cleveland's nomination signaled a triumph for the "educational politics" characteristic of urban progressivism. In a move away from the highly partisan and vitriolic campaigns of the post-Civil War era, Cleveland and other disciples of former New York governor Samuel Tilden promoted their program through a "literary bureau" that distributed pamphlets describing the party's policy positions. Campaign themes were developed at the national level and disseminated via the mails and meetings with the many professional and community organizations. The educational style was adopted by Republican Harrison in 1888.[49]

Blaine's campaign was one of the dirtiest in U.S. history. Blaine first attempted to spark sectional antagonisms with his "bloody shirt" warnings that the South was trying to reassert its rebel ways through Cleveland. Blaine also tried to rouse business fears with claims that Cleveland would institute free trade policies damaging to domestic industries. That appeal failed because the Democratic platform's plank on the tariff laws specifically supported protection of those interests. Finally, Blaine tried to make a scandal of Cleveland's fathering of a child out of wedlock years before. Among the charges against Cleveland was that he kidnapped and immured both the mother and child to cover up the story.

The campaign eventually turned on Cleveland's victory in New York, which resulted from a number of blunders by Blaine. One blunder had occurred years before, when Blaine mocked New York party boss Roscoe Conkling: "The contempt of that large-minded gentleman is so wilted, his haughty disdain, his grandiloquent swell, his majestic, supereminent, overpowering, turkey-gobbler strut, has been so crushing to myself that I know it was an act of the greatest temerity to venture upon a controversy with him."[50] Conkling was so peeved by the turkey image that he spent his whole career battling Blaine, including the presidential campaign of 1884. Blaine's own running mate, Logan, sympathized with Conkling in the dispute.

The other Blaine faux pas occurred a week before the election when a Protestant minister praised Blaine and proclaimed, "We are Republicans, and do not propose to leave our party and identify ourselves with the party whose antecedents have been rum, Romanism, and rebellion." Blaine did not separate himself from the remark, which angered New York Democrats and cost him votes. Later the same day, Blaine attended a formal dinner with a number of wealthy persons that became known as "the millionaires dinner"; the event belied Blaine's claims to speak for ordinary people.

Blaine, of Irish background, appealed to Irish immigrants in New York for their votes. But Cleveland countered Blaine's Irish tactic with the last-minute endorsement of the powerful Tammany leader Edward Kelly. Cleveland made two campaign speeches and attended a public rally in Buffalo. On the Saturday before the election, he attended a parade in New York City that attracted 40,000 people chanting: "Blaine, Blaine, James G. Blaine, the Monumental Liar from the State of Maine!" With the help of an economic downturn and the "Mugwumps"—independents and liberal Republicans offended by Blaine—Cleveland won the presidency.

The race, however, was close. Cleveland received 4.9 million votes (48.5 percent) to Blaine's 4.8 million (48.3 percent). He won the solid South, Indiana, Connecticut, New Jersey and, most important, New York (although by only 1,047 out of 1.13 million votes cast). Still, the election controversy did not end with the balloting. The *New York Tribune* reported that Blaine won the race, fueling fears about an election deadlock similar to the Hayes-Tilden contest of 1876. But Cleveland received 219 electoral votes to Blaine's 182, making the Democrat the clear winner.

Cleveland's first two years in the White House were productive. His inaugural address and cabinet selections won wide praise. His style of leadership—examined closely in the newspapers—appeared refreshingly unassuming. The Cleveland agenda included issues like tariff reform (cutting rates on the "necessaries of life"), navy modernization, civil service, expansion and land law reform. The president oversaw passage of the Presidential Succession Act and the Electoral Count Act, changes in currency policy and labor controversies.

As during his terms as mayor of Buffalo and governor of New York, Cleveland icily refused to compromise his values. But when he became party leader, this steadfastness proved to be a problem. Thousands of Democratic Party workers went to Washington seeking jobs in the new administration only to be disappointed. "Ah, I suppose you mean that I should appoint two horse thieves a day instead of one," Cleveland said in response to one party leader.[51] In vetoing pension bills, Cleveland called their sponsors "blood-suckers," "coffee-boilers," "pension leeches," and "bums."[52] The president appeared just as aloof to labor when a record number of strikes and disturbances swept the nation in 1886; the federal troops that Cleveland sent to the Haymarket riot in Chicago killed thirty people.

When Cleveland did bend to political realities, his timing was off. After standing firm against patronage when party enthusiasm was at its height, Cleveland disappointed reformers when he allowed lieutenants such as First Assistant Postmaster Adlai E. Stevenson to distribute favors.

The biggest controversy of the Cleveland administration involved tariffs. Concerned about federal budget surpluses that threatened to stall economic activity, Cleveland prodded the House of Representatives to pass tariff reductions. The Senate responded with a highly protective tariff measure. The unpopular tariff issue propelled the two parties into the 1888 election. The Democrats nominated Cleveland by acclamation and chose 75-year-old judge Allen G. Thurman of Ohio for the vice presidency. The Democrats tried to soften their low-tariff image by promising that domestic industries would get larger markets. Lower tariffs were said to be necessary for avoiding disastrous federal budget surpluses, preventing the development of monopolies and ensuring consumers reasonable prices for basic goods.

## The 1888 Republican Recovery

A politics-weary James Blaine sent word from Florence and Paris that he would not be a candidate in 1888. The race was left open to some lesser lights, including Sen. John Sherman of Ohio, Gov. Russell Alger of Michigan, Sen. William Allison of Iowa and Sen. Benjamin Harrison of Indiana. Sherman led the early balloting but quickly lost ground to Alger and Harrison. After extensive back-room maneuvering, including a last-minute plea to Blaine to accept the nomination, Harrison, who had the backing of state party bosses, won on the ninth ballot. Levi Morton, a banker, got the vice presidential nomination.

Harrison, a senator from Indiana, was a former Civil War brigadier and the grandson of President William Henry Harrison with a scandal-free if colorless demeanor. Harrison was a good speaker, but often appeared aloof. One historian wrote: "Those who talked with him were met with a frigid look from two expressionless steel grey eyes; and their remarks were sometimes answered in a few chill monosyllables devoid of the slightest note of interest."[53] Harrison pledged a modernized navy, civil service reforms and traditional Republican protective trust and trade policies.

The election turned, as in 1884, on New York and Indiana—both states with extensive evidence of voter intimidation and manipulation of counting. Harrison won the two states narrowly—New York by only 14,373 votes—and won the White House. Except for Connecticut and New Jersey, Harrison swept the North and West. Cleveland won the South. Overall, Harrison won 5.4 million popular votes (47.8 percent) and 233 electoral votes; Cleveland won 5.5 million popular votes (48.6 percent) and 168 electoral votes.

Cleveland left the White House with an unusual amount of good will among the public because of his honest tariff campaign. His popularity increased during the next four years as the economy hit slumps and as the former president, while practicing law, delivered speeches calling for a more egalitarian brand of politics. Cleveland would be back in 1892 for vindication.

With the first one-party majority in both the executive and legislative branches in a dozen years, the Republicans went about their business briskly after the election. Postmaster General John Wanamaker dispensed patronage with zeal. President Harrison signed into law the McKinley Tariff Act and the Sherman Silver Purchase Act. The former raised duties on manufactured goods to their highest level ever but also included provisions for negotiating with other countries to bring the rates down. The silver act loosened the money supply, which stimulated economic activity (but angered creditors and bankers since money, when it is more readily available, is worthless).

## Cleveland's Comeback, 1892

The 1890 midterm elections brought huge Democratic gains. Voters all over the country—but especially in the depressed farm belt—rebelled against the inflation that high tariffs brought. The Republicans held on to the Senate, but the new House of Representatives had 235 Democrats, 88 Republicans, and 9 Farmers' Alliance members. The brief experiment in one-party government ended with two years of stalemate.

President Harrison evoked widespread discontent in 1892 both for his demeanor and policies, but no Republican could mount an effective challenge. Through their strong party government, Republicans had cast their lot with Harrison and had few places to turn for an alternative. Political wizard Mark Hanna, a wealthy coal magnate who became a powerful behind-the-scenes political strategist, promoted William McKinley, and Secretary of State Blaine became an alternative when he abruptly quit the administration just before the GOP convention. But Harrison received a first-ballot nomination. Former minister to France Whitelaw Reid of New York got the vice presidential nomination.

Cleveland enjoyed widespread backing among rank-and-file voters, but party leaders were suspicious. New York governor David B. Hill got a head start when he called a "snap" state convention and won the delegation. An "anti-snapper" convention from New York sent a rival delegation to the national party convention. Democrats across the country rebelled at Hill's move and rapidly switched their support to Cleveland.

Another problem for Cleveland was the rising sentiment in agrarian states for free and unlimited coinage of silver—a way of boosting sagging farm prices by inducing inflation in the overall economy. Cleveland always had opposed this solution. The former president's consistent, principled stance on the issue not only added to his reputation for integrity but kept business- and finance-dominated states in the Northeast in the Democratic camp. Cleveland defeated Hill for the nomination on the first ballot and selected Stevenson of Illinois as his running mate.

The fall campaign was uneventful. Historian Eugene Roseboom wrote: "Honest bearded Benjamin Harrison confronting honest mustached Grover Cleveland in a tariff debate was a repeat performance that did not inspire parades with torches or the chanting of campaign ditties.... Democrats, out of power, could assail Republican tariff policy without clarifying their own position." [54]

Cleveland won easily. He received 5.6 million popular votes (46.1 percent) to Harrison's 5.2 million (43.0 percent) and 277 electoral votes to Harrison's 145. Populist general James B. Weaver, advocating expansion of currency and limits on interest rates, won 1.0 million popular votes (8.5 percent) and 32 electoral votes.

# The Age of Reform

Throughout the period dominated by Republican conservatism—from Grant's election in 1868 until William C. McKinley's 1896 win—movements for reform of political and economic institutions gathered strength at all levels of the American political system. The so-called Populists and progressives did not overturn the system, as their rhetoric sometimes suggested, but over time they made major changes in the operation and discourse of U.S. politics.

Depending on the time and place, people who called themselves "Populists" and "progressives" promoted such contradictory ideas as strict morals and free spirits, tight money and loose money, redistribution to the masses and control of the economy by elites, federal intervention and local control of politics, the opening and closing of electoral participation, technological progress and a return to a pastoral ideal long gone, individualism and community action, ethnic celebration and immigration barriers, scientific investigation and religion and internationalism and isolationism.

Reformism was the response to the pressures of national expansion, urban development and growth. Both major parties had adopted probusiness, laissez-faire policies in the latter part of the 19th century; the parties existed to make sure the terrain was suitable for economic expansion. But the lack of any program to deal with the undesired consequences of explosive growth led to an accumulation of problems that demanded attention. The most obvious problems evolved on the opposite ends of the rural-urban continuum: on the farms and in the cities.

The farm problem developed as the United States became a major economic power in the world. Agriculture expanded on a vast scale to feed the booming cities and, with international trade, to bring foreign capital to the United States. By 1880, the value of U.S. wheat and flour exports nearly equaled that of cotton exports.[55] As agriculture became part of the international market, farmers became dependent not only on the vagaries of the weather but also on the fluctuations of currency in the larger economy.

In the 30 years after the Civil War, prices for farm staples fell steadily. A debt that could have been paid by producing 1,000 bushels of grain immediately after the war required 3,000 bushels in 1895. The more farmers produced to meet their obligations, the more prices fell to exacerbate their problems. Confronting the problem required attention to a wide array of issues, including tight money, bankers who charged 20 percent interest for loans, monopolies among farm-equipment producers, high tariffs, railroad gouging, shipping inflation, warehouse monopolies and land speculation. Throughout the farm belt, particularly in the West, tens of thousands of farmers developed an "intense class consciousness." [56]

All of these issues received attention from a variety of third parties and independent organizations, but the two major parties were usually inattentive. The Granger Movement of the 1870s, for example, took hold in several farm states and elected new legislatures and high state officials. The Greenback Party attempted to merge a labor-farmer alliance with a doctrine of silver use for public debts. Later, the Farmers' Alliance politicized the same issues. In 1892, the Populist Party won 8.5 percent of the vote on a platform calling for free coinage of silver.

Another site of growing reformist strength was the city. The dominance of machines of both parties in the cities established an electoral system based on patronage but stubbornly opposed to any coherent program for addressing urban ills, such as poverty, poor housing, unsanitary conditions, transportation, education and unfair workplace practices. Electoral fraud spurred mostly middle-class reformers to devise new electoral and city government machinery, while social problems spurred some insurgent class politics.[57] The labor movement developed strength during this period.[58]

Other parts of the progressive agenda developed with a greater understanding of the nationalization of the economic and political systems. The wider sphere of economic activities created calls for regulation of economic corporations, railroads and banks; attention to health and environmental concerns; and product safety.

Until the ascendance of William Jennings Bryan, the Democratic presidential nominee in 1896, 1900 and 1908, the reformers were unable to capture a major party. Partly because political activism was based at the state and local levels, neither national party adopted the reformers' widely variegated program as its own. The depression of

1888 caused the Populist forces to pull together more than they had during previous economic downturns, probably because of the accumulated effects of inaction. The panic of 1873 created a sectional rather than a party split, with the Democrats eventually adopting a conservative stance on the debate over whether the currency should be expanded to spur economic activity and redistribute social burdens.[59]

The Republican presidential candidates steadfastly opposed the class-oriented proposals of the progressive movement, especially the loose-money demands.

The only Democrat to win the presidency since the Civil War was Cleveland, a stubborn advocate of hard money and other conservative economic policies, in 1884 and 1892. President Cleveland vetoed dozens of private pension bills, only grudgingly accepted railroad regulation and did not address domestic problems in any comprehensive way. Cleveland's public statements on the currency question were especially strong. He called the use of silver "a dangerous and reckless experiment" that was "unpatriotic."[60] On the question of labor, Cleveland was just as conservative: he called out federal troops to put down the Pullman strike of 1894 and regularly preached about the evils of disorder that the labor movement seemed to foster.

Despite the complexity of the agriculture issue, the most concerted Populist action concentrated on the currency question alone. The drive to overturn the prevailing conventional economic thought by moving from a gold (tight) to a gold and silver (loose) money standard captured the imagination of the entire farm belt stretching from the Southeast to the prairie and the silver-producing states of the West. The silver standard was a very simple answer to the problem of farm prices: "If money was scarce, the farmer reasoned, then the logical thing was to increase the money supply."[61]

Gold-runs on banks, manipulation of the gold crisis by J. P. Morgan and other leading financiers, procorporation Supreme Court decisions and antilabor actions all stirred up resentment in the South and West. Silver sentiment escalated. The Democratic convention in 1896 called for the issuance of silver and rejected a resolution praising President Cleveland.[62] The movement for a silver currency found an eloquent advocate in Bryan, a member of the House of Representatives from Nebraska, who defeated Richard P. Bland of Missouri for the 1896 Democratic presidential nomination on the strength of his fiery "Cross of Gold" speech.

That speech was one of the most emotional and successful in U.S. history. Bryan attacked Eastern financiers and businessmen who exploited farmers. In an important theme to which his fall campaign would return, Bryan sought to expand the traditional Democratic conception of the independent working man to include farmers and factory workers.[63] In his speech's fortissimo, Bryan declared: "You shall not press down upon the brow of labor this crown of thorns, you shall not crucify mankind upon a cross of gold."[64]

In 1896 the Republicans nominated Ohio governor William McKinley after brilliant maneuvering by his manager, Mark Hanna. Hanna's chief strengths were fund raising and his mastery over state party organizations.

McKinley had little difficulty defeating Bryan. McKinley outspent the prairie populist by as much as ten to one, and he attracted the disaffected progold wing of the Democratic Party.[65] The GOP platform called for retention of the gold standard unless international negotiations could produce a bimetallic (that is, silver and gold) currency system.

The platform also called for restored tariff protections and an aggressive foreign policy in the Western Hemisphere.

Bryan's campaign was a political hurricane. He spent just $650,000, most of it donated by silver interests, compared with the millions McKinley spent. But Bryan traveled 18,000 miles and gave some 600 speeches, and his campaign staffers put out an impressive quantity of literature. Several million copies of *Coin's Financial School,* a prosilver pamphlet, were distributed during the fall of 1896. Other silverites also maintained busy speaking schedules in the fall.

Bryan's appeal to industrial workers to join his coalition of independent businessmen failed, largely because they depended for their livelihoods on the very Eastern interests that Bryan attacked. McKinley won not only the East but also the small cities and towns in Bryan's Southern and Western belt of support. Bryan was unable to win rural areas of the East. McKinley won the popular vote 7.1 million (51.0 percent) to 6.5 million (46.7 percent) and the electoral vote 271-176.

The effect of the 1896 presidential election was lasting. Political scientist James Sundquist wrote: "For 20 years the two-party system had been based on dead issues of the past. It had offered the voters no means of expressing a choice on the crucial issues of domestic policy around which the country had been polarizing.... Then suddenly, with the nomination of Bryan in 1896, the party system took on meaning once again."[66]

The new Republican coalition included residents of cities, where capital and labor were both reasonably content with the economic growth that the GOP tariff policy promoted; farmers in the East and Midwest, who had strong ties to the "party of Lincoln" and who came to favor high tariffs; Catholic, German Lutheran and other liturgical Christian denominations; and some border states. Sundquist noted: "It was the persistence of the Civil War attachments that made the realignment of the North so largely a one-way movement—pro-Republican."[67]

After 1896, the competitive party balance that had prevailed for years gave way to lopsided party strength according to region—Democrats in the South, Republicans in the North. Strong opposition parties disappeared in all regions of the country, vesting political power in the hands of those already part of the system.

As political scientist E. E. Schattschneider has observed:

> The 1896 party cleavage resulted from the tremendous reaction of conservatives in both major parties to the Populist movement.... [S]outhern conservatives reacted so strongly that they were willing to revive the tensions and animosities of the Civil War and the Reconstruction in order to set up a one-party sectional southern political monopoly in which nearly all Negroes and many poor whites were disenfranchised. One of the most important consequences of the creation of the Solid South was that it severed permanently the connection between the western and the southern wings of the Populist movement.[68]

Conservative Republicans won the White House in all but two (1912 and 1916) of the nine elections from 1896 to 1928.

The country experienced economic prosperity that blunted the possible activism of workers and the previous activism of farmers. With good harvests and rising commodity prices, the agrarian revolt fizzled. The development of new ore extraction methods and discovery of new gold deposits made calls for silver to expand the currency supply superfluous. The war with Spain, which McKinley reluctantly entered and the burgeoning mass media publicized, created a patriotic fervor.

McKinley's reelection in 1900 was even stronger than his 1896 election. He won 7.2 million popular votes (51.7 percent) to Bryan's 6.4 million (45.5 percent), and 292 electoral votes to Bryan's 155. McKinley swept to victory with all states except the silver states of the West (Colorado, Montana, Idaho and Nevada).

## The Rise of Theodore Roosevelt

Since Vice President Garret A. Hobart died in office in 1899, the Republicans selected New York's Progressive governor Theodore Roosevelt to run with McKinley. Roosevelt, an independent-minded environmentalist and trust-buster, was promoted for vice president by New York GOP boss Thomas Platt to rid the state of progressive politics. Roosevelt was reluctant to take the job—"I am a comparatively young man yet and I like to work. . . . It would not entertain me to preside in the Senate" [69]—but accepted when a convention movement and McKinley prevailed upon him.

When McKinley was assassinated in 1901 and Roosevelt became president, U.S. presidential politics came under the influence of a variant of the progressive movement. As Gabriel Kolko and other historians have demonstrated, Roosevelt's administration was friendly to many of the Republicans' traditional conservative allies. But Roosevelt's rhetoric and his legacy of regulation and conservation had strong progressive or reformist elements.[70]

Roosevelt's leadership of progressives is an example of generational politics. The new president grew up in an era in which economic expansion strained the nation's fabric, causing political figures to seek idealistic but pragmatic solutions to a wide variety of problems. The previous generation had grown up in a simpler age when "politics were devoid of substance, built around appeals to tradition and old loyalties and aimed at patronage." [71]

Roosevelt steered his party toward conservation of natural resources, enforcement of antitrust laws, promotion of the concerns of labor and railroad regulation. The government's suit to dissolve the Northern Securities Company under the Sherman Anti-Trust Act and Roosevelt's intervention in the anthracite coal miners' strike, both in 1902, established the tenor for an activist presidency. TR (the first president identified by his initials) also used his office as a "bully pulpit" to promote his increasingly sophisticated progressive ideology.

Roosevelt had no trouble winning nomination for election as president in his own right in 1904. The Republican convention, arranged in advance at the White House, unanimously voted for Roosevelt and his platform of trust-busting, tariffs, labor relations and activist foreign policy. Sen. Charles W. Fairbanks of Indiana was the GOP vice presidential nominee.

To oppose the rambunctious Roosevelt, the Democrats selected a sober-visaged judge. Alton Parker, the chief justice of the New York State Court of Appeals, received the backing of the Democratic Party's conservative establishment when former president Cleveland turned down entreaties to make a fourth presidential run. Parker was opposed by William Randolph Hearst, a member of Congress and newspaper magnate. Bryan forced the party to adopt a liberal platform, as a balance to the conservative judge.

The Roosevelt victory was a landslide. He won 7.6 million votes (56.4 percent) to Parker's 5.1 million (37.6 percent) and won all but the Southern states. Roosevelt won 336 electoral votes to Parker's 140. Both houses of Congress were overwhelmingly Republican.

President Roosevelt pledged not to seek a second term of his own because he had served most of McKinley's second term. He occupied himself with his progressive agenda and groomed his secretary of war, William Howard Taft, as his successor.

## Roosevelt Picks Taft

Roosevelt appeared to be genuinely dismayed by talk in 1907 of a possible third term, so he made public shows of support for Taft. Roosevelt was able to line up state delegations for Taft, and the nomination was never in doubt. Taft, through Roosevelt, was particularly strong among Republicans in the South. Attempts to restrict Southern representation and pass a more liberal party platform were defeated.

Taft had impressive government experience. Before joining Roosevelt's cabinet, he had been a Cincinnati judge, U.S. solicitor general, federal circuit judge, head of the U.S. Commission on the Philippines and the first civil governor of the Philippines.

Roosevelt's only problem in pushing Taft at the convention was avoiding a stampede in his own favor. Despite a highly disciplined convention, the galleries demonstrated wildly for Roosevelt. But Taft—a newcomer to electoral politics—easily won the nomination on the first ballot. He had 702 votes to the runner-up's 68. Rep. James S. Sherman of New York was selected as his running mate.

The Democrats nominated Bryan for the third time. The electoral disaster that befell Judge Parker in 1904 was said to be evidence that the party needed an aggressive challenger to the Republicans rather than another conservative candidate. The Democrats were bereft of new talent, especially in close states in the East and Midwest, and turned to Bryan despite his disastrous campaign record and the warnings of former president Cleveland.

The campaign was void of serious discussion. Taft campaigned on the Roosevelt record. Bryan called for government ownership of railroads and other liberal measures—such as a lower tariff, campaign finance reform, a graduated income tax, labor reforms and greater enforcement of antitrust and other business regulations.

With Roosevelt and Taft promoting much of the progressive agenda, Bryan's message was no longer distinctive. Taft easily won. He gathered 7.7 million popular votes (51.6 percent) to Bryan's 6.4 million (43.1 percent) and 321 electoral votes to Bryan's 162. The North, most of the West and the border states went into the Republican column.

## Wilson and the Divided Republicans

Taft was not, by temperament, an ideal executive. His lifelong ambition had been to serve on the Supreme Court, and his disciplined legal mind and collegial nature eventually would enable Taft to become one of the high court's most able chief justices. But Taft foundered in the presidency. He carried out Roosevelt's program of business regulation and conservation, yet Roosevelt responded not with gratitude but with a series of nasty statements and plans for a campaign against Taft.

The tariff issue proved to be Taft's early trouble spot. Taft was committed to reducing tariffs—he was less political than Roosevelt, who fudged the divisive issue—and quickly became embroiled in a fight with Congress, which wanted to raise tariffs. The Senate remolded House legislation to push up various duties, and Taft publicly promoted the legislation after he managed to secure new corporate taxes and tariff reductions for raw materials. Taft proved ineffective and indecisive on the tariff issue and, as a consequence, began losing the party.

The Glavis-Ballinger affair further muddied the image of the administration. The scandal broke when the chief forester of the Interior Department, Gifford Pinchot, charged that Secretary Richard A. Ballinger had betrayed the cause of conservation and had even engaged in corrupt practices regarding minerals and water power. Pinchot also charged that Ballinger had wrongly fired another Interior official, Louis Glavis, for trying to expose the scandal. Pinchot took his complaints directly to Taft, but Taft sided with Ballinger and urged Pinchot to drop the matter. After an indignant Pinchot went public with the issue, Taft fired him, fueling suspicion of a coverup at Interior. The incident was a major embarrassment to Taft because of the priority that conservation had received under Roosevelt and because of the inevitable complaints that Taft was betraying his mentor on the issue.[72]

Divisions within the Republican Party eventually created the movement toward rival Taft and Roosevelt factions. Tariffs, Arizona's new state constitution (which included a provision that Taft opposed for recall of the governor), treaties, and antitrust issues split the former president and the sitting president. In many ways, the dispute was over personalities. Taft carried out Roosevelt's program, but lacked his evangelical fervor and decisiveness. In a still conservative age, progressives felt they needed more aggressive leadership than the judicially tempered Taft would ever give them.

Roosevelt spent more than a year of Taft's term hunting in Africa, but he was an active speaker and campaigner when he returned to the United States. He gave a detailed accounting of his philosophy of government at a 1912 speech in Columbus, Ohio, calling for voter referenda and initiatives, recall of elected officials and curbs on judicial power. When a dump-Taft movement decided that Wisconsin's Sen. Robert La Follette had no chance to defeat the president for the GOP nomination, party discontents turned to the energetic and still young (at 50) Roosevelt.

Roosevelt made an all-out effort for the Republican nomination, entering twelve primaries and winning all but three. Roosevelt won 278 delegates in states with primaries to Taft's 48 and La Follette's 36. In today's system, Roosevelt probably would have marched to a first-ballot nomination (because today more delegates are allocated by popular votes than by the party organizations, which then dominated the process). Three crucial Republican states—Pennsylvania, Illinois and Ohio—went for Roosevelt. Roosevelt clearly had great popular appeal and vote-getting ability—perhaps more than ever.

But Taft won the nomination. The president controlled the party machinery, and most of the convention's delegates were sent by the state machines. Roosevelt challenged the credentials of Taft delegates at the Chicago convention, and the nomination's outcome turned on battles over almost one-fourth of the delegates. The fight went to the floor of the convention, but Taft's smooth operation defeated Roosevelt. Roosevelt appeared at the convention to buoy his forces and cry foul.

When Roosevelt, after the defeat, urged his supporters to continue their fight, some bolting progressive delegates organized a convention in August to mount a third party effort. The bolters formed the Progressive Party. When Roosevelt remarked to a reporter during the GOP convention, "I'm feeling like a bull moose," his vigorous campaign had a symbol. With the Republicans divided, the Democrats saw their first opportunity to win the presidency since Cleveland.

As the 1912 Democratic convention in Baltimore neared, several national candidates and favorite sons were vying for the nomination. The front-runner was House Speaker James Beauchamp (Champ) Clark of Missouri, a party regular who had party organization support and years of experience to recommend him.

Gov. Woodrow Wilson of New Jersey—who held a doctorate in political science and moved into politics after a distinguished career as professor and president at Princeton University—was another strong candidate. Wilson's virtues were the opposite of Clark's. He did not have an extensive record for opponents to attack, and he was supported enthusiastically because of his dynamic presence and reformist rhetoric rather than a long political apprenticeship. The New Jersey machine had brought Wilson into politics, but he quickly asserted his independence and became something of a crusader. Wilson had guided an election bill, an anticorruption act, public utilities regulation and worker's compensation legislation through the state legislature. Although he had dealt with the state's party bosses, he also put a distance between himself and the machine.

A newcomer to national politics, Wilson both refreshed and alienated Democratic crowds in speeches before the convention. He came out strongly for the "radical" platform of referendum, initiative and recall, prompting a newspaper to report: "The boldness, the directness, the incisiveness, the fearlessness, and the force of the 'Virginian-Jerseyan's' words crashed at times through the throng like a series of thunderbolt jolts." [73] But Wilson's embrace of the progressive agenda and attacks on business alienated many southerners; Wilson's own home delegates of Virginia opposed him at the convention.

Other Democratic candidates were the conservative Rep. Oscar Underwood of Alabama, author of a historic tariff act; another conservative, Gov. Judson Harmon of Ohio; and four favorite-son governors. Clark appeared to have won the nomination when a Tammany bloc of delegates moved to support him after he won a tenth-ballot majority. The requirement for a two-thirds majority, however, gave other candidates time to maneuver. Wilson almost dropped out of the race, but Bryan's late transfer of his support from Clark to Wilson created a bandwagon effect for Wilson. On the 46th ballot, Wilson accumulated the necessary two-thirds of delegates for the nomination. Gov. Thomas Marshall of Indiana, one of the favorite-son candidates, was picked to be the vice presidential candidate because Underwood, Wilson's choice, would not accept.

The Democratic platform was progressive. It called for tariff reduction, utility regulation, banking reforms, legislation to curb monopolies, a national income tax, direct election of senators, campaign finance reforms and a national presidential primary.

Theodore Roosevelt actually praised Wilson as "an able man" in the early fall and said he might not have started a third party effort if he had known Wilson would be the Democrats' candidate. But Wilson and Roosevelt eventually criticized each other's approach to government, especially after Wilson expressed reservations about government activism.[74]

Wilson easily won the election, receiving 435 electoral votes to Roosevelt's 88 and Taft's 8. The Republican splits obviously helped Wilson; if Roosevelt and Taft had combined their totals of 4.1 million votes (27.4 percent) and 3.5 million votes (23.2 percent), they would have topped Wilson's 6.3 million (41.8 percent). But even though Wilson was a minority president, there was a clear Democratic trend, since the Democrats had taken over the House and replaced several Republican governors in the 1910 midterm elections. It was the worst showing ever for an incumbent president—third place with only two states.

Whatever the strength of Wilson's "mandate," he acted as though he had won by a landslide. His first term was one of the most productive in U.S. history. With the Democrats in control of Congress, and with a shrewd political adviser in Col. Edward M. House, Wilson adopted a reform agenda that had been percolating at various levels of government for years. He broke precedent by delivering his first State of the Union message to Congress in person. At the center of the message was a call for reductions in tariff rates. After a bitter fight raged for a month, Wilson went public with a demand that members of Congress reveal their property holdings. The revelations showed close links between their holdings and the kinds of tariff protections on the books. Congress soon was shamed into passing tariff cuts of 15 percent. Some one hundred items were placed on a free-trade list for the first time.

Wilson also addressed other areas successfully: taxes (institution of a graduated income tax in 1913); banking regulation (the Glass-Owen Act of 1913, which created the Federal Reserve System); antitrust legislation (the Clayton Anti-Trust Act of 1914, creation of the Federal Trade Commission in 1914); labor relations (Section 6 of the Sherman Anti-Trust Act, which exempted unions from antitrust strictures); agriculture (the Smith-Lever Act of 1914, the Federal Farm Loan Act of 1916); environmentalism (creation of the National Park Service in 1916); and the judiciary (the appointment of Louis Brandeis to the Supreme Court).

Despite his strong leadership—highlighted by his stirring oratory—Wilson still faced the prospect of a tough reelection. He had won the presidency in 1912 with only 41.8 percent of the popular vote, and the growing war in Europe was beginning to disturb the American process of contented economic growth.

Public opinion on the war was volatile, largely because more than a third of the U.S. population was either foreign-born or offspring of foreign-born parents. Some 11 million Americans surveyed in the 1910 census were of direct German or Austrian descent, and another 5 million were from Ireland. Other immigrants were Russian, Italian, Hungarian, British and French. Wilson sought to defuse feelings for the immigrants' native lands when he denounced "hyphenism"—the tendency of many citizens to identify themselves with appellations that linked their ethnic origins and American status—but politicians at lower levels tailored their campaigns to specific nationality voting blocs.[75]

Wilson and Vice President Marshall won renomination without any opposition. The most significant event of the Democratic convention was the passage of the platform, which indicated the party's main campaign theme. By calling for national universal suffrage, Wilson helped himself in the 11 Western states where women had already won the vote. The platform praised "the splendid diplomatic victories of our great president, who has preserved the vital interests of our government and its citizens, and kept us out of war." The latter phrase would be repeated endlessly during the fall.[76]

The Republicans nominated Supreme Court Justice Charles Evans Hughes. Hughes was silent in the months before the convention, but a number of party leaders lined up enough delegates for him to win a third-ballot nomination. Other potential candidates that year included former president Roosevelt, former senator Elihu Root of New York, former vice president Fairbanks and senators John Weeks, Albert Cummins and Lawrence Sherman. Fairbanks won the vice presidential nomination.

Prosperity and reformism limited the campaign themes of the Republicans. The GOP railed against Wilson's foreign policy as "shifty expedients" and "phrasemaking" that put the United States in danger of entering the war. Hughes turned out to be a bad campaigner, but he bridged the gap between conservative and progressive Republicans that cost the party the 1912 election. Wilson was occupied with Congress throughout the summer of 1916, but he emerged to give a series of speeches in the fall. Democratic strategists, meanwhile, conceived and executed a masterful strategy to return Wilson to the White House. The Democrats concentrated all their resources on "swing states" and ignored states they thought Wilson was sure to lose. Illinois, for example, was ignored since it was a certain Republican state. Bryan, Wilson's secretary of state, toured the West.

Wilson won one of the closest elections in history. California, an uncertain state, ensured Wilson's victory when, because of the urban vote, it went the president's way late in the campaign. The margin of victory was 3,420 votes in that state. The president defeated Hughes by a margin of 9.1 million (49.2 percent) to 8.5 million popular votes (46.1 percent). The Electoral College gave Wilson 277 votes and Hughes 254.

## The "Return to Normalcy" and the Roaring Twenties

After the tumult of Woodrow Wilson's domestic reforms, the First World War and the divisive battle over the Versailles treaty, the time was ripe for a period of conservatism and Republican government. Deep resentments developed toward Wilson and the Democratic Party, and the Democrats were divided over many issues, including economic regulation, Prohibition and race relations.

Blessed with good luck, strong financial backing and a strong trend toward split-ticket voting, the Republicans were able to resume their dominance over national politics with three successful presidential campaigns. Warren G. Harding was elected in 1920, Calvin Coolidge in 1924 and Herbert C. Hoover in 1928.

The 1920s are usually pictured as a time of steady, unexciting politics. The conservatives dominated the federal government, and occupying the White House were men who spoke of "normalcy" and a noninterventionist brand of politics in both domestic and foreign affairs. One of the symbols of the age is President Coolidge's program of tax cuts, which reduced the rates on the wealthy. The wartime Revenue Act of 1918 had driven tax rates to the highest point in U.S. history. The total tax rate in the highest brackets was 77 percent. In 1921, 1923 and 1926, Secretary of the Treasury Andrew Mellon presented to Congress proposals to cut taxes, the most controversial being the reduction in the maximum surtax from 77 to 25 percent.

Congress eventually cut the surtax to 40 percent in 1924 and 20 percent in 1926.[77]

But the three sober men who filled the presidency met challenges from progressives of both parties in Congress and in the state governments. On a wide range of issues—including relief of the poor, subsidies for the depressed farm sector, regulation of utilities, immigration, race relations, states' rights, tax cuts and Prohibition—the conservative presidents encountered strong challenges. They frequently responded by vetoing legislation, but such an expedient would not prevent the pressures for a more activist government from developing.

## Harding and "Normalcy"

Sen. Warren Harding, a product of the GOP machine of Ohio, emerged from a crowded and largely unknown pack to win the Republican nomination in 1920 at a convention dominated by economic interests such as oil, railroads and steel.

The early candidates were Gen. Leonard Wood, an old Roosevelt ally; Gov. Frank Lowden of Illinois, who married into the Pullman family and therefore had ample financing for a campaign; and Sen. Hiram Johnson of California, whose progressive and isolationist stances put him in good stead with voters in many states. A dozen favorite sons hoped that a deadlocked convention might bring the nomination their way. All the candidates were on hand in Chicago to maneuver for the nomination.

While Wood, Johnson and Lowden performed reasonably well in the primaries, Harding won only his home state of Ohio and did not arouse much popular enthusiasm. Under the direction of a shrewd campaign manager, Harry Daugherty, Harding gained the support of the party's bosses and won the nomination on the tenth ballot after a brief interview in the "smoke-filled room" that was synonymous with boss control. Gov. Calvin Coolidge of Massachusetts, a favorite-son contender for president, became Harding's vice presidential candidate.

The Democrats selected Gov. James Cox, also from Ohio, after lengthy platform battles and balloting for the nomination. Early balloting put former Treasury secretary William McAdoo and Attorney General Mitchell Palmer in the lead, but Cox gained steadily and had the nomination by the 44th roll call. Franklin D. Roosevelt of New York, the assistant secretary of the Navy, was the quick selection for Cox's running mate.

The image of Woodrow Wilson hung over the convention and would hang over the fall campaign. The Democratic platform praised Wilson's conduct of the war and his domestic reform program. The results in the November election indicated deep unease over the Democratic administration, however. Harding's landslide victory was termed "election by disgust" by political analysts.

Harding amassed 16.1 million popular votes (60.3 percent) to Cox's 9.1 million (34.2 percent), and 404 electoral votes to Cox's 127. Harding carried the North and West including Oklahoma and all of the Southern and Border states except Tennessee and Kentucky.

The sacrifices demanded under Wilson were widely perceived as the cause of Harding's victory rather than a desire for the ideology or policy proposals that Harding offered. The *New York Post* editorialized: "We are in the backwash from the mighty spiritual and physical effort to which America girded herself when she won the war for the Allies.... The war has not been repudiated, though the administration that fought it has been overwhelmed.

We are now in the chill that comes with the doctor's bills."[78]

The electorate's ability to shift allegiances from the Republicans to the Democrats and back again—from one period to the next, and from one level of government to the next—suggested a dissolution of partisan alignments. The addition of women to the electorate after passage of the 19th Amendment in 1920 and increasing independence among all voters added uncertainty. Apathy resulted from the national exhaustion from the war and the lack of sharp ideological differences between the candidates. The electorate's instability was suggested by the divisions within both parties on high-profile issues such as Prohibition, the League of Nations and agricultural policies, as well as on other social and economic issues such as technical assistance and trust busting. The appearance of numerous "blocs" in both parties represented "little if anything more than a transitory alignment upon a particular vote or issue."[79]

The shifts in control of congressional and state offices also indicated electoral instability. The Democrats had comfortable control of Congress under Wilson, but in 1920 the Republicans gained a majority of 301 to 131 in the House and 59 to 37 in the Senate. Impressive liberal gains in congressional and state elections in 1922 appeared to be a slap at the Harding administration. The high turnover of votes also indicates unstable party affiliations: the 14.2 percentage point increase in the Republican vote between the 1916 and 1920 presidential elections was the largest since the Civil War, obviously a time of turmoil.[80]

President Harding died on August 2, 1923, of a heart attack, just as revelations of kickbacks and favoritism in the administration began to surface. Several members of the administration quit and two committed suicide. The investigation into the so-called Teapot Dome scandal—named after the site of naval oil reserves that were transferred to private hands in exchange for bribes—would last five years. The Democrats hoped to make the scandal a major issue in 1924, but Democratic complicity in the wrongdoing and the integrity of Harding's successor, Calvin Coolidge, defused the issue.

## Coolidge Cleans Up: 1924

President Coolidge fired Attorney General Harry M. Daugherty and other members of Harding's clique and projected an image of puritan cleanliness. Coolidge—a taciturn man who had slowly climbed the political ladder in Massachusetts from city council member, city solicitor, mayor, state legislator, lieutenant governor and governor before he became vice president—expounded a deeply individualistic Yankee philosophy that helped to separate him from the corrupt men in the Harding White House.

Except for appointing as attorney general Harlan Fiske Stone, former dean of the Columbia University School of Law, Coolidge allowed others to clean up the mess left behind by Harding. The new president was concerned about unnecessarily alienating himself from party leaders.

By the time Coolidge sought the presidency in his own right in 1924, the economy had rebounded. The Republican platform called for additional tax cuts but said nothing substantive about the increasingly salient agriculture and labor issues. Coolidge, one of the most conservative presidents ever, also pushed an isolationist foreign policy plank. He won the nomination on the first ballot.

While the Republicans were able to "Keep Cool with Coolidge," the Democrats spent 16 days in a seemingly endless attempt to pick a nominee in New York's sweltering

Madison Square Garden. The fight developed because the party was badly split between its Northeastern urban bloc and its more conservative Southern and Western rural bloc. New York governor Alfred Smith and former Treasury secretary William McAdoo of California were the key combatants at the convention until the delegates were freed from boss instructions on the 100th ballot.

Suspicions between the North and South were intense. A platform plank denouncing the Ku Klux Klan created the most controversy. Northerners wanted an explicit repudiation of the society, which preached hatred of Catholics, Jews and blacks; in the end, southerners would settle only for a vaguely worded rebuke. The Klan infiltrated the party in many rural areas. Another divisive issue was Prohibition, with northerners attacking the initiative and southerners supporting it. These sectional splits would cripple the Democrats in the next two elections.

After the delegates were freed from instructions, a stampede developed for John W. Davis of West Virginia, a lawyer with Wall Street connections. The ticket was balanced with the vice presidential selection of Charles Bryan of Nebraska, the younger brother of three-time presidential candidate William Jennings Bryan.

The Progressive candidacy of Robert La Follette complicated the calculations of voters, particularly those on the liberal end of the spectrum. Since the Democrats had a nearly impenetrable hold on the South, La Follette was not given a reasonable chance of winning. But the conservatism of both Coolidge and Davis meant that La Follette was the only genuine liberal in the race. Still, many liberals voted for Davis or even Coolidge because of the fear of an inconclusive election that would have to be resolved in the House of Representatives.

Coolidge won the election easily, with the Democrats polling their smallest percentage ever. Coolidge won 54.1 percent of the vote, Davis won 28.8 percent, and La Follette won 16.6 percent. Coolidge attracted 15.7 million popular votes and 382 electoral votes; Davis, 8.4 million and 136; and La Follette, 4.8 million and 13.

On August 2, 1927, when Coolidge announced his decision not to seek reelection by passing out a brief note to reporters and then refusing further comment, the Republicans began jockeying for the nomination for the 1928 election.

## The Hoover Succession

Secretary of Commerce Herbert Hoover was the obvious choice to replace Coolidge at the head of the GOP ticket. A native of Iowa who learned mining engineering at Stanford University, Hoover was immensely popular with most of the party. His administration of Belgian relief and food distribution programs during World War I had earned him the status of statesman and humanitarian.

Hoover began working for the nomination soon after Coolidge dropped out, spending $400,000 in the nomination phase of the election. He won the nomination on the first ballot over Lowden and Gov. Charles Curtis of Kansas. Curtis was named Hoover's running mate.

Hoover was religious in his zeal for what he called "the American system" of free enterprise and individualism. He did not see any inconsistency in having the government vigorously support businesses with tax breaks, tariffs, public provision of infrastructure and police protection, while at the same time denying relief to people in need. Hoover appeared to be less rigid than Coolidge, however. He proposed creation of a special farm board and said he would consider legislation to protect labor unions from abuses in the use of court injunctions.

Al Smith, the Tammany-schooled governor of New York, was the Democratic nominee. Smith had the support of all the party's Northern states, and he won a first-ballot nomination. Sen. Joseph Robinson of Arkansas was the vice presidential candidate.

Smith's candidacy polarized the electorate, particularly in the South. He was the first Catholic to be nominated for president by a major party, and he endured religious slurs throughout the fall. He favored repeal of Prohibition, still a divisive issue. He was an urbanite, a problem for a nation that had nurtured a rural ideal since Thomas Jefferson. He was a machine politician, a problem for anyone outside (and many people inside) the nation's great cities. He was a strong opponent of the Klan, which put him in trouble in the South. Finally, he was an unabashed liberal who proposed public works, farm relief programs, stronger protection of workers and regulation of banking and industry.

During the fall campaign, Hoover acted like the incumbent and Smith barnstormed the country, trying in vain to pick up support in the South and West. The 1928 campaign was the first with extensive radio coverage, and Hoover generally fared better than Smith on the airwaves. Hoover, the small-town boy who made good, represented fulfillment of the American Dream; Smith, the inner-city boy who made good, also embodied that ideal, but he had too many alien traits for much of the nation to realize it.

The November election produced another Republican landslide. Hoover carried 40 states with 21.4 million popular votes (58.2 percent) and 444 electoral votes, while Smith carried only eight states with 15.0 million popular votes (40.8 percent) and 87 electoral votes. As disastrous as the election appeared to be for the Democrats, it put them in position to build a wide-ranging coalition in future years.

Smith carried only six Southern states, but the defection of the others was temporary. More important to the Democrats' long-range fortunes was the movement of cities into the Democratic column, probably for the rest of the century. In all, Smith diverted 122 Northern counties from the GOP to the Democratic Party. Catholics, whose turnout previously was low, turned out in record numbers. Immigrants in cities also expanded their vision from local politics to the national stage for the first time. Smith also seemed to pick up some of the Progressive farm vote that La Follette had tapped before. In Wisconsin, for example, the Democratic vote jumped from 68,000 in 1924 to 450,000 in 1928. Smith's candidacy also put the Democrats solidly in the "wet" column, just as the national temper began to resent Prohibition.

President Hoover impressed political observers with his managerial skills and "coordinating mind." With passage of the Agricultural Marketing Act in June 1929, the administration appeared to address the most pressing economic problem for the business-minded president. He met some legislative setbacks, but overall the Great Engineer appeared to be in good political condition as the nation looked back over his record when Congress began its recess in the summer of 1929.

The national economic and social fiesta that began at the close of World War I came to an abrupt end on October 29, 1929. After climbing to dizzying new heights for months, the stock market crashed. First described by economists and politicians as a temporary interruption of the good times, the crash quickly led to a wave of business and bank failures, mortgage foreclosures, wage cuts, layoffs and a crisis of political leadership. By the end of Hoover's term in 1932, more than 12 million workers had lost their jobs; the unemployment rate was approximately 25 percent. An October 1931 advertisement for 6,000 jobs in the Soviet Union brought 100,000 American applications.[81]

President Hoover, who had celebrated his inauguration with a prediction that poverty and hunger were near an end, did not know how to cope with the crisis. In a special session that Hoover called, Congress created the Federal Farm Board to coordinate marketing of agricultural products, but Hoover steadfastly opposed further moves, especially subsidies. Hoover also signed the Smoot-Hawley tariff bill to protect manufacturers, but, true to the predictions of economists and bankers, the tariff only aggravated economic conditions by hurting foreign trade.

Hoover later approved agricultural relief and public works programs and established the Reconstruction Finance Corporation. The president refused to approve direct relief to the unemployed and businesses, but he did approve some loans and aid to specific sectors of the economy.

Despite his earnest and tireless efforts, Hoover became a target of widespread enmity. The low point of his distinguished career came when World War I veterans petitioned for early receipt of their service bonuses, which, by contract, were not to be paid until 1945. They set up camp in Washington, singing old war songs and carrying placards that bore their pleas. The "Bonus Army" numbered 20,000 at its height. When Hoover feared a protracted protest, he ordered federal troops to take buildings over where some veterans were camping. In two skirmishes, two veterans were killed. The president then sent in Gen. Douglas MacArthur with tanks, infantry and calvary soldiers. (MacArthur's junior officers included Dwight D. Eisenhower and George Patton.) After successfully removing the veterans, the military forces overran nearby veterans' camps in a rain of fire and tear gas. Thousands of veterans and their families fled the burning district.

The administration's tough stance against a defeated, ragtag band of former war heroes shocked and embittered the nation. The barricaded White House and administration statements about "insurrectionists" symbolized a dangerous gulf between the government and the people.

Partly because of the economic crisis he did not create, but also because of a dour and unimaginative demeanor, Hoover probably never had a chance to win reelection. The 1930 midterm elections indicated a loss of confidence in the administration. The House went Democratic, 219 to 214, and the Senate came within a seat of going Democratic as well.

Those election results did not convey the bitterness and despair that the Depression would aggravate before the next presidential campaign. Hoover was mercilessly ridiculed in newspapers and in Democratic speeches. The Democratic Party coordinated a comprehensive anti-Hoover campaign that made the president politically impotent.

# Election of 1932

Franklin D. Roosevelt, fifth cousin to Theodore Roosevelt, was the perfect candidate to oppose Hoover. The New York governor had been an activist in state politics, first opposing the state's Tammany machine and then pioneering many relief and reconstruction programs that Hoover refused to expand to the national scale. Roosevelt had been the party's vice presidential candidate 12 years before, and he had served in the federal government as assistant secretary of the Navy.

Perhaps more important than any of his political accomplishments was FDR's image of strength and optimism and his deft handling of hot issues and disparate members of the potential Democratic coalition. Although he was a polio victim, Roosevelt often smiled—a devastating contrast to Hoover. (Gutzon Borglum, the sculptor, wrote: "If you put a rose in Hoover's hand, it would wilt." [82]) Roosevelt was able to campaign for the presidency without putting forth a comprehensive program; the simple promise of a change in leadership was enough.

Some observers found the man from Hyde Park wanting. Journalist Walter Lippmann, for example, complained that Roosevelt was "a pleasant man who, without any important qualifications for the office, would like very much to be president." [83] But those detractors and a large field of Democrats were not able to keep Roosevelt from his "rendezvous with destiny." [84]

The Democratic field included the 1928 Democratic standard-bearer, Al Smith; John Nance Garner, the Speaker of the House; Gov. Albert Ritchie of Maryland; Gov. George White of Ohio; Gov. Harry Byrd of Virginia; and Sen. James Reed of Mississippi. Most considered Smith more of a "stalking horse" for the anti-FDR forces than a serious candidate in his own right. Garner had impressive backing from newspaper magnate William Randolph Hearst and former Democratic candidate William G. McAdoo.

The many favorite sons in the race threatened to deadlock the convention and deny the nomination to the front-runner, as they had done so often in the past. Roosevelt had difficulty with his own region of the country because of his opposition to the Tammany machine in New York. Winning the two-thirds majority required for the nomination was difficult for Roosevelt or any other candidate, but FDR eventually won on the fourth ballot when he promised the vice presidential slot to Garner.

Franklin Roosevelt was the first candidate to appear before the convention that nominated him. In an acceptance speech to the conventioneers who had staged wild rallies in his support, Roosevelt made passing reference to a "new deal" that his administration would offer Americans. That phrase, picked up in a newspaper cartoon the following day, would symbolize the renewal that Americans yearned for as riots and radicalism seemed to threaten the nation's spirit and the legitimacy of its institutions.

Roosevelt conducted an active fall campaign, traveling 23,000 miles in all but seven states to quell suspicions that his physical handicaps would deter him from performing his job. Besides barnstorming the nation, Roosevelt also took to the radio airwaves—he was the first sophisticated electronic media candidate—and conveyed a sense of warmth and confidence. He also showed an intellectual bent and an open mind when he called on academics and professionals—the famed "brains trust"—for their expert advice on the issues. Roosevelt won 22.8 million votes (57.4 percent) to Hoover's 15.8 million (39.6 percent). Forty-two of the 48 states and 472 of the 531 electoral votes went for Roosevelt. The election was a landslide and a realignment of the major forces in U.S. politics.

# The New Deal Coalition

The profound effect of Roosevelt's victory on U.S. politics can hardly be overstated. The New Deal coalition that Roosevelt assembled shaped the political discourse and electoral competition of the United States until the late

1960s. In many respects, that coalition is a central element of politics today.

The new Democratic coalition brought together a disparate group of interests: southerners, blacks, immigrants, farmers, capital-intensive producers, international businessmen, financiers, urbanites, trade unions, Catholics and Jews. Rexford Tugwell called it "the most miscellaneous coalition in history."[85] These blocs were not always in perfect harmony—for example, the Democrats juggled the demands of blacks and white southerners with great difficulty—but they were solid building blocks for national political dominance.

The dominance was impressive. Between 1932 and 1964, the Democrats won seven of nine presidential elections. The only successful Republican, Eisenhower, could just as easily have run as a Democrat. Party leaders in fact asked him to run as a Democrat in 1948 and 1952, and his name was entered in some Democratic primaries in 1952.

The strength of the Roosevelt rule is attributable partly to the president's personality. He could be soothing. When he gave his first "fireside chat" about the banking crisis, the nation responded with cooperation; the raids and violence at banks ended in a matter of weeks. More important than his soothing nature was his ability to experiment and shift gears. Professor James David Barber described Roosevelt's many public postures:

> Founder of the New Deal, modern American democracy's closest approximation to a common political philosophy, Roosevelt came on the scene as the least philosophical of men—"a chameleon in plaid," Hoover called him. Firm fighter of yet another Great War, Roosevelt appeared to H.L. Mencken in 1932 as "far too feeble and wishy-washy a fellow to make a really effective fight." Architect of world organization, he introduced himself as totally concerned with America's domestic drama. His name is inseparable from his generation's great social revolution; in 1932, nearly all the heavy thinkers scoffed at him as just another placebo politician—a "pill to cure an earthquake," said Professor [Harold] Laski.[86]

More important than personality was what Roosevelt had to offer the many groups in his coalition. As historian Richard Hofstadter has noted, the New Deal was "a series of improvisations, many adopted very suddenly, many contradictory."[87] The Roosevelt credo was: "Save the people and the nation, and if we have to change our minds twice a day to accomplish that end, we should do it."[88]

Until the vast expenditures of World War II, there was not enough pump-priming to end the Depression, but Roosevelt's initiatives touched almost everyone affected by the slump.[89] For the jobless, there were unemployment insurance and public works programs like the Works Progress Administration and the Civilian Conservation Corps. For the poor, there were categorical aid programs. For westerners, there were conservation measures. For the banks, there was the famous holiday that stopped runs on holdings, and there were currency and securities reforms. For farmers, there were incentives and price supports and cooperatives. For the aged, there was Social Security. For the southeasterners, there was the Tennessee Valley Authority. For Southern whites, there was a hands-off policy on race matters. For blacks, there was sympathy. For those living in rural areas, there was electrification. For families, there were home loans. For the weary worker eager for a few rounds at the local pub, there was the repeal of Prohibition. For laborers, there was acknowledgment of the right to negotiate for their share of the national wealth. For business, there were the Federal Emergency Relief Act and the National

Industrial Recovery Act, as well as negotiation to reduce trade barriers.

The remarkably divergent interests in the coalition were underscored by the politics of race. Blacks moved en masse to the Democratic Party from their traditional position in the "Party of Lincoln," partly because of Hoover's failure but also because of the inclusive rhetoric of the New Deal. Yet Roosevelt was too concerned about his bloc of Southern support even to accept antilynching legislation.

Scholars have argued that the New Deal coalition did not indicate a wholesale shift in existing political loyalties, but rather that new forces had joined an already stable alliance to tip the competitive balance of U.S. parties. The political discourse in the United States changed not because all or even most groups changed their behavior, but because new groups and issues became involved.[90]

The core of Roosevelt's winning coalition is easy to describe: "Southern white Protestants, Catholics and non-Southern white Protestants of the lowest socioeconomic stratum together accounted for roughly three-fourths of all Americans of voting age in 1940 who thought of themselves as Democrats. By way of contrast, these three groups provided only about 40 percent of the smaller cadre of Republican identifiers."[91] Within this coalition, there were both new and old elements.

Although the Democratic Party encompassed new constituencies and addressed new issues, it retained many of its traditional supporters. The "Jim Crow" South had consistently been in the Democratic column; in 1896, for example, the South's percentage support for Democrat William Jennings Bryan exceeded that of the rest of the nation by 15.3 points. Even in 1928, when Al Smith's Catholicism brought Democratic support for the Democrats below 50 percent for the only time, the Deep South supported the Democrats more than the Border South.[92] To the South, the Democrats were reliably the party of white supremacy and agricultural interests, while Republicans favored the industrial interests of the North.

Outside the South, the Democrats were the party of immigrants and Catholics. Since Andrew Jackson's day, the overwhelming monolithic Democratic voting patterns of Catholics contrasted with the split vote of Protestants in the United States. The Catholic-Protestant divisions "represent not so much religious as more general ethnocultural traditions."[93] The Democratic hold on the Catholic vote was reinforced by the heavy immigration into Northern cities in the last half of the 19th century. While the anti-Catholic Ku Klux Klan received Democratic backing in the South, it received Republican backing in the North, pushing Catholics decisively into the Democratic Party.

A steady base in the Democratic Party consisted of laborers and the poor. From the first party machines in the early 19th century to William Jennings Bryan's campaign on behalf of the depressed farm belt in 1896 to Woodrow Wilson's acceptance of labor bargaining in 1914, the Democrats had shown sympathy for the less privileged classes. Such sympathies were often constricted by prejudice, but the Democrats offered more hope of representation than the business-oriented Republicans. Roosevelt solidified the support of the poor and laboring classes.[94] Sundquist has written: "The party system undoubtedly reflected some degree of class before the realignment, but there can be little doubt that it was accentuated by the event. It was in the New Deal era that tight bonds were formed between organized labor and the Democratic Party, that ties equally close if less formal and overt were formed between business and the GOP, and that politics for the first time since 1896 sharply accented class issues." [95] Roosevelt consistently received the support of more than two-thirds of the voters of low socioeconomic status.[96]

New converts to the Democratic Party included blacks and Jews. The inclusion of blacks into the New Deal coalition underscores a "multiplier effect" at work with thriving interest-group politics. The Republicans received the black vote in the seventeen elections from Reconstruction to 1932. Roosevelt received 35 percent of the black vote in 1932, and his black support was as low as 23 percent in Chicago and 29 percent in Cincinnati.[97] Even though Roosevelt did little to promote black interests in the South, where most blacks lived, the black vote for him increased to 70 percent in 1936 and 1940. Migration of blacks to the North and spillover effects of Roosevelt's many domestic programs brought blacks to the Democratic Party.

Jews, who had voted Republican since their numbers swelled during immigration around the turn of the century, turned to the Democrats as they became the more liberal party. Roosevelt got 85 percent of the Jewish vote in 1936 and 84 percent in 1940. New Deal assistance programs and Roosevelt's efforts to fight Nazism appealed to Jews, but perhaps more important was "the historic pattern of discrimination which forced or disposed Jews to oppose conservative parties." [98] The class division that split other social groups was absent in the Jewish population.

In many ways, the whole of the New Deal was greater than the sum of its parts. Political scientist Samuel Beer has argued that two long-competing visions of U.S. politics—the national idea and the democratic idea—at last came together during Roosevelt's administration. With the New Deal, the Democratic Party was able to combine its traditional concern for local, individualistic interests with a national vision. By bringing "locked-out" groups into the system, the Democrats enhanced both nation building and individual freedoms. The parts, put together, created a stronger whole. Beer quotes the French sociologist Emile Durkheim: "The image of the one who completes us becomes inseparable from ours. . . . It thus becomes an integral and permanent part of our conscience. . . ." [99]

The political genius of "interest-group liberalism" [100] was not just that it offered something to everyone, but that it created a new age of consumerism in which everyone's interest was in growth rather than structural change. The general good was defined as growth. The potentially divisive competition over restricted and unequally distributed resources was avoided with a general acceptance of growth as the common goal. When there was growth, everyone could get a little more. That public philosophy became a permanent part of American political discourse.

## The Four-term President

Roosevelt's coalition and leadership were so strong that he became the only president to win more than two elections. He won four elections and served a little more than 12 years in the White House before dying in office.

Roosevelt's four electoral triumphs caused Republicans to fume about his "imperial" presidency; all they could do in response to FDR was promote a constitutional amendment to limit presidents to two terms. More important was the way Roosevelt shaped the American political agenda. For many people of the time, it was difficult to imagine the United States under any other leadership. It is possible that Roosevelt could have forged an even stronger liberal coalition than he did. But Roosevelt was a pragmatist above all else and alternately angered and wooed groups like business, labor, farmers and the military. For example, Roosevelt kept a distance from Upton Sinclair's populist campaign for governor of California in 1934. Sinclair was the target of a sustained personal attack by business and other conservative forces in the state in what one authority has called the first media campaign in American history. Sinclair's losing effort, historian Greg Mitchell argues, undermined the power of reformers nationally.[101]

Roosevelt's three successful reelection drives evoked a changing response from Republicans. Roosevelt's first reelection opponent, in 1936, was Gov. Alfred M. Landon of Kansas, who strongly criticized every aspect of the New Deal. After 1936, Republican candidates did not criticize federal intervention in economic and social affairs but rather the speed and the skill of Democratic intervention. In the third election, the Republicans argued that Roosevelt was a "warmonger" because he tilted toward Great Britain in World War II. The GOP argued in the third and fourth elections that Roosevelt threatened to become a "dictator" by breaking the traditional two-term limit.

Landon was the early favorite for the Republican nomination in 1936. Sen. Charles McNary of Oregon, Sen. Arthur Vandenberg of Michigan and *Chicago Daily News* publisher Frank Knox provided weak opposition. Landon was attached to neither the old-guard nor the younger liberal Republicans. A Republican bolter for Theodore Roosevelt's "Bull Moose" candidacy in 1912, Landon was consistently to the left of the GOP. Historian James MacGregor Burns observed: "Landon had just the qualities of common sense, homely competence, cautious liberalism and rocklike 'soundness' that the Republicans hoped would appeal to a people tiring, it was hoped, of the antics and heroics in the White House." [102]

In 1936 the Republicans could not have stated their opposition to the popular New Deal in any stronger terms. The platform read: "America is in peril. The welfare of American men and women and the future of our youth are at stake. We dedicate ourselves to the preservation of their political liberty, their individual opportunity, and their character as free citizens, which today for the first time are threatened by government itself." [103]

The Republicans called for ending a wide range of government regulations, returning relief to state and local governments, replacing Social Security, balancing the budget and changing tariff and currency policies. Landon's only innovation was a call for a constitutional amendment allowing the states to regulate the labor of women and children; the Supreme Court had struck down a New York minimum-wage law. After Landon won the nomination on the first ballot, he selected Knox as his running mate.

The only time the two presidential candidates met was at a meeting Roosevelt called with state governors to discuss farm relief and a recent drought. The candidates sparred inconclusively.

Assisting in Landon's campaign were a lavish war chest of $9 million, the defections of Democratic stalwarts such as Al Smith and John Davis, well-coordinated campaign work by business lobbies, and smear campaigns that portrayed Social Security as a simple "pay reduction" measure and Roosevelt as physically and mentally ill. Landon argued that New Deal spending was just another form of spoils politics, a charge Roosevelt addressed by folding postmasters into the civil service system.

The only important departure at the Democratic convention was the repeal of the party's requirement that a candidate receive two-thirds of the delegates to win the nomination. After some arm twisting, Southern delegates backed the change, but the governor of Texas wondered aloud if the change was designed for a third Roosevelt run in 1940. Roosevelt was renominated without opposition. He asked Garner to run with him a second time.

In response to Landon's GOP nomination and agitation by leaders of the left—including Huey Long of Louisiana, Father Charles Coughlin of Detroit, Dr. Francis Townsend of California (who espoused a federal pension plan for senior citizens) and the Socialist Norman Thomas of New York— President Roosevelt in his acceptance speech launched a rhetorical war against "economic royalists" who opposed his programs. He dropped the idea of a "unity" campaign in favor of a partisan ideological attack intended to gain a mandate for a variety of stalled programs rather than a personal vote of confidence.[104]

Roosevelt at first had planned a low-key campaign of "conciliation" but decided to wage the more aggressive campaign when Landon got the GOP nomination. Landon had run an impressive nomination campaign and was thought to appeal to American pinings for governmental stability. In the early stages of the fall campaign, Roosevelt pretended not to be a partisan politician. He moved around the country to make "official" inspections of drought states and public works programs and to deliver speeches on electrical power, conservation, and social welfare programs, among other topics. Roosevelt assigned Postmaster General James Farley the task of addressing party rifts and Republican charges of spoils.

At the end of September, Roosevelt returned to his role as partisan leader. The president answered Republican charges point by point, then lashed out at the Republicans in biting, sarcastic terms. As the campaign progressed and Roosevelt sensed a strong response from the large crowds to his attacks, the attacks became stronger. At the close of the campaign, he said:

> We have not come this far without a struggle and I assure you that we cannot go further without a struggle. For 12 years, our nation was afflicted with a hear-nothing, see-nothing, do-nothing government. The nation looked to the government but the government looked away. Nine mocking years with the golden calf and three long years of the scourge! Nine crazy years at the ticker and three long years at the breadlines! Nine mad years of mirage and three long years of despair! And, my friends, powerful influences strive today to restore that kind of government with its doctrine that that government is best which is most indifferent to mankind.... Never before in all of our history have these forces been so united against one candidate as they stand today. They are unanimous in their hate for me—and I welcome their hatred.[105]

Especially to sophisticated campaign technicians of the modern age, a poll that predicted a big Landon victory provides some amusement. The *Literary Digest,* which had predicted past elections with accuracy, conducted a postcard poll that pointed toward a Landon landslide. The heavy middle- and upper-class bias of the magazine's readership meant that the views of the voters on the lower rungs of the economic ladder were left out of the sample. To this day, the poll is cited as the prime example of bad survey-group selection.

The failure of the *Literary Digest*'s survey pointed to the most salient aspect of the election results: the heavy class divisions among the voters. Polls show that class divisions widened starting around the midpoint of Roose-

velt's first term. The broad support FDR had enjoyed because of a common economic disaster hardened along class lines by 1936. Roosevelt won 27.7 million popular votes (60.8 percent) to Landon's 16.7 million (36.5 percent). Roosevelt won all but two of the 48 states, and he took 523 of the 531 electoral votes. In addition, the Senate's Democratic majority increased to 75 of 96 seats, and the House majority increased to 333 of 435 seats. Roosevelt ran ahead of candidates such as gubernatorial candidate Herbert Lehman of New York, who had been recruited to boost his vote totals in various states. The Democratic victory was almost too overwhelming, Roosevelt suggested, because it would encourage Democrats to fight among themselves rather than with Republicans.

# The Third Term

Soon after his landslide, Roosevelt tempted fate with a proposal that would have increased the size of the Supreme Court from 9 to 15 members in order to "pack" the Court with justices closer to the president's political philosophy. The high court had constantly struck down important New Deal initiatives such as the Agriculture Adjustment Act, the National Recovery Administration and the tax on food processing.

Roosevelt shrouded his proposal in statements of concern for the capacities of some of the Court's older and more conservative justices. In a fireside speech, Roosevelt said the Court's failure to keep pace with the other "horses" in the "three-horse team" of the federal government constituted a "quiet crisis." [106] The elderly chief justice Charles Evans Hughes belied that charge with the energy he brought to the tribunal. Roosevelt refused to compromise on the bill, and it became an executive-legislative dispute. The proposal was widely seen as a brazen power play, and by the summer Congress had defeated it.

President Roosevelt eventually got the judicial approval he wanted for his initiatives—what wags called "the switch in time that saved nine." The Court appeared to shift its philosophy during the court-packing affair, and, before long, enough justices had retired so that Roosevelt could put his own appointees on the Court.

Other problems awaited Roosevelt in the second term. Splits in the labor movement gave rise to violence during organizing drives, and the president responded haltingly. After his rift with business over the full range of New Deal policies, Roosevelt appeared to be drifting. Conservatives in Congress were more assertive than ever in opposing the "socialist" measures of the Roosevelt years. The only major New Deal legislation in the second term was the Fair Labor Standards Act of 1938, which abolished child labor and set a minimum wage and an official rate of time-and-a-half for overtime.

As Roosevelt looked toward a third term in 1940, the widening war in Europe posed a difficult problem. Nazi Germany had invaded the Rhineland, Poland, France, Norway, Denmark, Holland, Belgium and Luxembourg and had made alliances with Italy and the Soviet Union, while Japan invaded China. Adolf Hitler launched the Battle of Britain in the summer of 1940 and all-night air raids of London soon afterwards.

British prime minister Winston Churchill desperately petitioned President Roosevelt to provide 50 destroyers. Britain's need for the destroyers was so great that Roosevelt balked at asking Congress for help. He reasoned that congressional action probably would take three months, and isolationists might even block action—dealing a crippling blow to Britain. After lengthy administration debate, Roosevelt agreed to send Churchill the destroyers as part of a "lend-lease" agreement. The United States would receive bases in the Caribbean as part of the deal.

A favorite parlor game as the 1940 election approached was guessing whom Roosevelt might tap as his successor. Roosevelt publicly maintained that he did not want another term, but he refused to issue a definitive statement begging off the race. Despite the historic precedent against third terms, however, Roosevelt wanted to remain president. To avoid the appearance of overzealousness, Roosevelt wanted the Democrats to draft him in 1940.

While the nation waited for Roosevelt to act, Vice President Garner announced his candidacy. Postmaster General Farley and Secretary of State Cordell Hull also wanted to be president, and Roosevelt gave both vague assurances of support. Roosevelt, whose relations with Garner had been sour for years, simply watched the vice president struggle to gain a respectable public profile. The Farley and Hull prospects withered without the help of the old master.

From a distance, Roosevelt watched state Democratic delegations declare their support. Polls showed Roosevelt's fortunes rising with the deepening European crisis. Just before the GOP convention, Roosevelt appointed Republicans Henry Stimson and Frank Knox to his cabinet. Roosevelt did not reveal his plans even to his closest aides. The president did not forbid aides such as Harry Hopkins to work on a draft, but he did not get involved because he wanted the Democrats to call on him and not the other way round.

At the Chicago convention, Sen. Alben Barkley told the convention: "The president has never had, and has not today, any desire or purpose to continue in the office of president. . . . He wishes in all earnestness and sincerity to make it clear that all the delegates of this convention are free to vote for any candidate."[107] The statement was followed by an hour-long demonstration and Roosevelt's first-ballot nomination.

The convention mood turned sour, however, when Roosevelt announced that he wanted the liberal secretary of agriculture, Henry Wallace, as his running mate. The announcement disgruntled delegates who had already lined up behind other candidates. Wallace eventually beat Alabama representative William Bankhead, his strongest opponent for the nomination.

The Republicans mounted their strongest challenge to Roosevelt in 1940, largely on their charge that Roosevelt was moving the United States toward involvement in the world war. Several moves toward military preparedness had failed at the hands of isolationists in Congress. When Roosevelt asked for increases in defense spending after Gen. Francisco Franco's victory in Spain and Hitler's invasion of Austria in 1938, critics asserted that the president was attempting to cover up domestic failures with foreign adventures. Roosevelt pressed on, however, and Congress passed the Selective Service Act and increases in military spending in 1940.

The Republican field in 1940 included several fresh faces—Sen. Robert A. Taft of Ohio, son of the former president; District Attorney Thomas E. Dewey of New York City; and Sen. Charles L. McNary of Oregon and Sen. Arthur H. Vandenberg of Michigan who had sought the Republican nomination in 1936. The freshest face of all was Wendell L. Willkie, a utility executive who had never run for political office. A large and affable man, former Democrat Willkie had barnstormed the country for seven years speak-

ing in opposition to the New Deal.[108] Hundreds of "Willkie clubs" sprang up in the summer of 1940, and a number of publications including Henry Luce's *Time* magazine chronicled Willkie's career and encouraged the Willkie groundswell. Despite concern about Willkie's lack of political experience that led to a "stop Willkie" movement, the Indianan won a sixth-ballot nomination by acclamation. Senator McNary, the Republicans' Senate floor leader, reluctantly accepted the vice presidential nomination.

Traveling 30,000 miles in 34 states, Willkie gave some 540 speeches. By the time his campaign ended, his already husky voice turned hoarse. The Republicans spent lavishly and organized grass-roots clubs for Willkie across the country. Charges against Roosevelt of managerial incompetence, "warmongering," and imperial ambitions punctuated the Willkie effort. A dramatic moment came when labor leader John L. Lewis called on workers to back Willkie.

After a period of strictly "presidential" behavior, Roosevelt took to the campaign trail with partisan vigor. He answered Willkie's warmongering charges with a promise never to involve the United States in "foreign wars" (which left Roosevelt free to respond to a direct attack).

The alienation of some Democratic and independent voters was symbolized by Vice President Garner, who did not even vote. Roosevelt won, but by the slimmest margin of any race since 1912. Roosevelt received 27.3 million popular votes (54.7 percent) to Willkie's 22.3 million (44.8 percent). The electoral vote tally was 449-82.

## The War and Its Legacy

Roosevelt's third term and fourth election were dominated by the Second World War. Japan attacked U.S. bases at Pearl Harbor, Hawaii, on December 7, 1941. The president, speaking before Congress, declared the date of the surprise attack "a day that will live in infamy." Congress shook off its isolationist inclinations and declared war.

The war did for the economy what the New Deal, by itself, could not: it brought economic prosperity. The number of unemployed workers fell from eight million to one million between 1940 and 1944. The boom brought seven million more people, half of them women, into the job market. Inflation, worker shortages and occasional shortages in raw materials posed problems for wartime agencies. The number of U.S. families paying taxes quadrupled, and by 1945 tax revenues were 20 times their 1940 level. Budget deficits reached new heights.[109]

The war effort was grim for two years of the president's new term. Isolationist sentiment built up in Congress, with the Midwest proving the region most resistant to Roosevelt's foreign policy. Criticism of war administration was rampant. The administration won key congressional votes on the war but faced stubborn resistance on domestic measures. In the 1942 midterm elections, the Republicans gained 10 seats in the Senate and 47 seats in the House—a major repudiation of Roosevelt.

After several setbacks, the Allied forces won impressive victories. Roosevelt and Churchill worked together closely. Allied forces led by Gen. Dwight D. Eisenhower routed the Axis powers in North Africa in 1942. The Soviet Union beat back a Nazi assault on Stalingrad in the winter of 1942-43. The Allies took over Italy in 1943 and struggled with the Nazis in France. By September 1944, British and American troops entered Germany. In the Pacific war, American offensives secured Australia in 1942 and the Philippines in 1944.

Despite the bitterness that prevailed through much of his administration, Roosevelt had no trouble winning a fourth term in 1944. The Allies found greater success on the battlefield and on the sea, and the nation did not appear willing to risk untested leadership to prosecute the war. The Republicans turned to the smooth governor of New York, Thomas Dewey. Willkie wanted another shot at the White House, and his best-selling book *One World* put him in the public eye, but old-line conservatives blamed him for the 1944 election defeat. Governors John Bricker of Ohio and Harold Stassen of Minnesota and Gen. MacArthur were the other hopefuls.

Dewey's primary victories over Willkie in the Wisconsin, Nebraska and Oregon primaries finished Willkie's public career. Dewey was too far in front to stop. At the convention, he won a nearly unanimous, first-ballot nomination after Bricker and Stassen dropped out. After Gov. Earl Warren of California refused the vice presidential nomination, Bricker accepted it.

The party platform extolled the virtues of free enterprise but did not criticize the concept of the New Deal and even made bids for the votes of blacks and women. In his acceptance speech, Dewey criticized "stubborn men grown old and tired and quarrelsome in office." [110]

The 1944 election marked the early resistance of the South to the modern Democratic party. Roosevelt was a shoo-in for the nomination, but southerners wanted a replacement for Wallace as vice president, restoration of the two-thirds nominating rule and a platform declaration of white supremacy. Unsatisfied Dixiecrats threatened to bolt the party in November, but when the party adopted only a vague civil rights plank in its platform, Southern discontent dissipated. The rest of the platform called for an internationalist thrust in foreign policy and further New Deal-style reforms domestically.

Roosevelt expressed support for Wallace but said he would allow the convention to pick his running mate. Wallace gave a stirring convention speech but disturbed conservatives with his stand against the poll tax and for equal opportunity for all "regardless of race or sex." Sen. Harry S. Truman of Missouri, who had won fame as a critic of defense spending, beat Wallace for the vice presidential nomination on the second ballot.

The Democratic campaign was dominated by references to the need for wartime unity and reminders of the Republican rule under Hoover. One leaflet bore the words "Lest We Forget" and a photograph of an unemployed man selling apples in front of a "Hoover Club"; an inset photograph showed Dewey conferring with former president Hoover. The Republicans spent nearly as much money as they had in the record-setting 1936 election.

Roosevelt won with 25.6 million popular votes (53.4 percent) to Dewey's 22.0 million (45.9 percent). The electoral vote score was 432-99. President Roosevelt—who reshaped U.S. politics at all levels—did not have the opportunity to see the end of the war or to participate in the making of the postwar world. On April 12, 1945, less than two months after his fourth inauguration, Roosevelt collapsed while sitting for a portrait in Warm Springs, Georgia.

# The Truman Presidency

The shock of President Roosevelt's death was perhaps greatest for the former haberdasher and machine politician who succeeded him. Truman had been a last-minute choice as FDR's running mate the previous year, and he never became a part of Roosevelt's inner circle. Truman did not have any knowledge of the most important military program of the age—the Manhattan Project, which, in a race with the Nazis, was developing a nuclear bomb in the secrecy of the brand-new town of Oak Ridge, Tennessee.

Truman also faced a problem of stature. Roosevelt had done nothing less than redefine the presidency in his 12 years in office. He not only effected the longest-lasting partisan realignment in U.S. history, but he changed the very scope of government activity. As would become clear during the Eisenhower presidency, even conservative Republicans came to accept, grudgingly, the notion that government ought to play an active role in stimulating the economy and addressing the needs of specific constituency groups. Many people could not fathom a presidency without Roosevelt. One member of the White House staff said later: "It was all so sudden, I had completely forgotten about Mr. Truman. Stunned, I realized that I simply couldn't comprehend the presidency as something separate from Roosevelt. The presidency, the White House, the war, our lives—they were all Roosevelt." [111] Other aides could not bring themselves to call Truman "Mr. President," as if so doing would dishonor the late president.

Truman's personality could not have presented a greater contrast to Roosevelt's. Plain-speaking, blunt, middle-class, Midwestern, not college-educated, wheeling-and-dealing and surrounded by old pals from the Pendergast machine of Missouri (the Democratic organization that dominated politics in the state), Truman offended people who had been accustomed to the charisma of Roosevelt. Truman's wife, Bess, also paled in comparison to the dynamic, more public Eleanor Roosevelt as First Lady. Truman showed absolute loyalty to the New Deal, but that would never be enough for many old Roosevelt hands and a nation entering a difficult period of postwar readjustment.

By the time the 1948 elections neared, Truman was in grave political shape. He brought former president Hoover back from exile for special projects—one of the many ways he rankled the sensibilities of former Roosevelt aides and Mrs. Roosevelt. Truman professed a desire to "keep my feet on the ground" and avoid the "crackpots and lunatic fringe" that had surrounded FDR.[112] Toward that end, Truman got rid of Commerce Secretary Henry Wallace and others. Independent journalist I. F. Stone wrote of Truman's personnel moves: "The little nameplates outside the little doors ... began to change. In Justice, Treasury, Commerce and elsewhere, the New Dealers began to be replaced by the kind of men one was accustomed to meeting in county courthouses." [113]

The politics of postwar adjustment were difficult. The Republican Congress elected in 1946 sought to dismantle many New Deal programs, and it frustrated anti-inflation efforts. Truman duelled with Congress, vetoing 250 bills (11 of these vetoes were overridden). Tentative civil rights initiatives disgruntled the South. Labor unrest was on the rise. Postwar mapmaking and subsequent efforts to "contain" Soviet geopolitical ambitions not only created splits among Democrats but also brought attacks from Republican isolationists. Truman also was said to have performed inadequately at Potsdam, the summer 1945 conference of World War II victors that established many geographic borders in Europe.

The situation was so bad that Roosevelt's own son promoted General Eisenhower and Supreme Court Justice William O. Douglas for a 1948 run for the Democratic nomination against Truman. Truman, in other words, was doing a good job antagonizing both the left and the right. The Democratic convention in August 1948 appeared to show a dangerously polarized nation. The convention began with a feeling of desperation when Eisenhower and Douglas refused to run. Then a "states' rights" plank offered by Southern delegates was defeated, and, after strong speeches by Minneapolis mayor Hubert H. Humphrey and others, a strong Northern plank passed. The party's New Deal and Northern machine elements decided that Southern defection would be less damaging than Northern defection. Defect is just what the southerners did. The Dixiecrats, under the leadership of South Carolina's governor J. Strom Thurmond, left the convention to conduct their own fall campaign. Thurmond ran under the Democratic Party label in four states (Alabama, Louisiana, Mississippi and South Carolina) and under the States' Rights Party elsewhere in the South. Meanwhile, the party's left wing, behind Henry Wallace, protested Truman's Marshall Plan, military buildup and confrontational stance toward the Soviet Union. It, too, ran its own fall campaign under the banner of the Progressive Citizens of America (the Progressive Party).

The seeds of Dixie defection were planted long before the convention. In 1947 the President's Committee on Civil Rights issued a report calling for the protection of the rights of all minorities. It was just the kind of spark Southern segregationists needed to begin a dump-Truman drive and to organize their own campaign in 1948. The Southern Governors Conference in March 1948 recommended that Southern states send delegates to the Democratic convention and electors to the Electoral College who would refuse to back a pro-civil rights candidate.

As political scientist V. O. Key, Jr., has shown, the degree of resistance to civil rights in Southern states depended on two basic factors: the proportion of blacks and the strength of the two-party system. Key argued that the existence of a large black population led to stronger Democratic measures against black enfranchisement and led whites to support the party in greater numbers. "To them [the whites in such districts], a single Negro vote threatened the whole caste system." [114] Alabama, Louisiana, Mississippi and South Carolina ended up voting for the Thurmond ticket. Other Southern states found broader economic and political issues more compelling than race.[115]

Many of FDR's old political allies eventually got behind the new man, but Truman's election prospects looked bleak. Some support was grudging—Mrs. Roosevelt offered a straightforward endorsement only to rebut newspaper reports that she favored the Republicans. While the Democratic Party was badly fractured, the Republican Party united behind Dewey.

Dewey was part of a new breed of Republican leaders—pragmatic and accepting of the New Deal and the international role that the United States would play in the postwar era. He expressed support for the basic tenets of postwar liberalism, including Social Security, civil rights and the United Nations. In the 1948 campaign, Dewey planned to put himself above the slashing attack style of President Truman. His constant calls for national unity—spoken in a baritone voice and perfect English—expressed acceptance of the vast changes in U.S. politics over the previous 20 years.

Dewey, the 1944 GOP candidate, survived a large field in 1948 to become the nominee once again. Senator Taft of Ohio was the main threat, but his isolationism and dull public demeanor were liabilities. The most spirited opposi-

tion came from Governor Stassen of Minnesota, who appealed to the more liberal and internationalist wing of the party. An anathema to party bosses, Stassen proved his strength in a series of primary victories. Other candidates or potential convention contenders included generals Eisenhower and MacArthur, Governor Warren and Senator Vandenberg. Polls showed all the Republicans but Taft beating Truman.[116]

Dewey gained the preconvention momentum he needed with an impressive primary victory over Stassen in Oregon. Dewey spent three weeks in the state, while Stassen frittered away his time and resources with a hopeless challenge to Taft in the Ohio primary. Dewey was especially tough in a primary debate about Communism. He also had impressive organizational strength and mastery over convention mechanics, and he won the nomination on the third ballot. Warren was selected as the vice presidential nominee.

From the beginning of the campaign, the media and professional politicians gave Truman little chance of retaining the White House. Early polls showed Dewey with such a strong lead that pollsters simply stopped surveying voters. But the polls failed because of a bias in the way the questions were asked and a presumption that the large bloc of undecided voters would cast their ballots in the same way as the rest of the population, when in fact they heavily favored Truman.[117]

Dewey was so certain of victory that he ran as if he were the incumbent. He made a series of bland, almost diplomatic statements rather than energetic campaign speeches. Dewey appeared confident that his advice to one audience—"Vote your own interests"—would attract an amalgam of disaffected groups. Never even mentioning the president's name, Dewey calmly canvassed the country and just smiled when people called him "President Dewey." He was careful to avoid the overaggressive posture that he thought ruined his 1944 campaign against Roosevelt. He even made some initial cabinet and policy decisions.

From the beginning, Truman's strategy was simply to mobilize the New Deal coalition. The biggest danger was apathy, he and campaign aide Clark Clifford reasoned, so the best strategy was to give the voters a reason to go to the polling booths. Since the Democrats were the majority party, they had to concentrate mainly on getting their longtime supporters to the polls.

Truman ran a scrappy and blunt underdog campaign that could have been mistaken for an outsider's effort. Truman was the president, but he ran against the Washington establishment. Crisscrossing the nation on a "whistlestop" train tour, Truman traveled some 31,000 miles and spoke before 6 million people. He turned his record of vetoes into an asset, claiming that the "do nothing" Republican 80th Congress made him do it. He assailed the conservative Republican record on inflation, housing, labor, farm issues and foreign affairs. The president drew large crowds—sometimes many times the size of Dewey's crowds—but he was the only political professional who thought he would win.

Truman himself predicted in October that he had 229 solid electoral votes to Dewey's 109 and Thurmond's 9; he said 189 votes could go either way. The best anyone would say about the Truman campaign was that its fighting spirit improved the Democrats' chances to win the Senate. Truman answered the Republicans' claims of liberalism and reformism by criticizing the GOP for obstruction of his policies. Truman's outsider taunt was constant: "that no-account, do-nothing, Republican 80th Congress!"[118]

Despite the *Chicago Tribune*'s now famous headline—

"Dewey Defeats Truman"—President Truman prevailed. Early returns put Truman in front, but it was expected that the later-reporting Western states would give Dewey the win. When California and Ohio went into the Truman column mid-morning Wednesday, Dewey conceded defeat. Especially considering the Democratic defections, Truman's appeal was widespread. Truman won 28 states with 24.11 million votes (49.51 percent) and might have won more in the South and North with a united party. Thurmond won 22 percent of the vote in the South. Dewey won 21.97 million votes (45.12 percent), and Thurmond polled 1.17 million votes (2.40 percent). Henry Wallace won some 1.16 million votes (2.38 percent) but no electoral votes. Wallace's candidacy may have cost Truman New York, Michigan and Maryland. On the other hand, Wallace may have done Truman a favor by freeing him from the taint of being the most liberal candidate in a time when the electorate was weary of liberalism. Particularly because the Republicans did not have a Midwesterner on their ticket and talked about cutting back agricultural subsidies, farmers felt safer with Truman. In all, Truman won 303 electoral votes, Dewey 189 and Thurmond 39.

The Democratic defections might have helped Truman by making him the candidate of the center. The Wallace campaign freed the president from suspicions on the right, and the Thurmond defection strengthened Truman's more liberal Northern constituency. In addition, the defections might have inspired Democratic voters to turn out in larger numbers than they would have had victory seemed certain.

In the end, the election merely confirmed long-held partisan allegiances. In the words of political scientist Angus Campbell and his colleagues, it was a "maintaining" election: "The electorate responded to current elements in politics very much in terms of its existing partisan loyalties. Apparently very little of the political landscape attracted strong feeling in that year. But what feeling there was seemed to be governed largely by antecedent attachments to one of the two major parties." [119]

# The Eisenhower Years

Truman's political fortunes worsened during his second term to the extent that he belatedly decided against making a bid for the Democratic nomination. In 1952, for the first time in 24 years, neither party had an incumbent president as its nominee.

### Election of 1952

The Democrats suffered from a weariness that is bound to affect any party that has been in power for 20 years. Problems and opponents' frustrated ambitions were piling up, and in Dwight Eisenhower the Republicans were able to recruit a candidate with universal appeal who was coveted by both parties. The national mood in the years before the 1952 election was sour. The nation was tiring of the Korean War, which the administration had entered in 1950 but did not appear interested in winning or leaving; price controls; and recurring scandals among members of the White House staff. The Republicans asked for a chance to "clean up the mess" in Washington and punctuated their appeals with the question: "Had Enough?"

The Truman administration met with repeated frustration in dealing with the Congress that the president ran against in 1948. On civil rights, tariffs, taxes, labor reform and the sensationalized question of Communist sympathizers in the government, Truman met a stubborn Democratic Congress—which became more stubborn after Republican gains in the 1950 midterm elections. When Truman seized control of the steel mills because he said the steelworkers' strike threatened the nation's security, he was rebuffed by the Supreme Court.[120]

Truman's biggest problems, however, concerned cronyism and war. Republicans in congressional investigations and on the stump hammered away at conflict-of-interest scandals in Truman's administration—creating nationwide sentiment to "clean up" Washington with a new administration. Meanwhile, the United States was mired in a stalemate in Korea—a distant war that was being fought inconclusively under the aegis of the United Nations, with uncertain goals (was it to protect South Korea or replace North Korea as well?) and uncertain enemies (was the People's Republic of China an opponent as well as North Korea?). Truman evoked ire with his firing of General MacArthur, who wanted to take the war into China, and with the slow movement toward a settlement. Just as the nation tired of sacrifices in World War I under Woodrow Wilson, it tired of sacrifices under Truman.

General Eisenhower—who had just left the presidency of Columbia University to take charge of the forces of the North Atlantic Treaty Organization (NATO)—was recruited by Republicans to run when it appeared that other GOP candidates lacked the national appeal to win the White House. Senator Taft was again running, but his isolationism was considered a liability in the postwar age of internationalism. Stassen, MacArthur and Warren were other likely Republican candidates.

Eisenhower's popular appeal was revealed when he attracted 50.4 percent of the vote in the New Hampshire primary to Taft's 38.7 percent and Stassen's 7.1 percent. Eisenhower performed well in the Northeast, and Taft generally performed well in the Midwest. A write-in campaign for Eisenhower almost upset Stassen in his home state of Minnesota.

When the GOP convention finally met in Chicago, Taft had the lead in convention delegates. In crucial delegate-seating contests, many of them played out on national television, Eisenhower defeated Taft and won the right to seat pro-Eisenhower insurgents from the South. Taft had relied on the old strategy of mobilizing state machines, but such tactics looked unsavory on television. Eisenhower had undisputed popular appeal, and he won on the first ballot after his early lead turned into a stampede.

Eisenhower selected Sen. Richard Nixon of California as his running mate. The 39-year-old conservative had won national recognition with his activities on the controversial House Committee on Un-American Activities, which investigated the alleged Soviet ties of Alger Hiss, a former State Department official. Hiss served time for a perjury conviction.

The Democrats moved haltingly toward putting together a ticket. Truman did not announce his decision to stay out of the race until April, after two primary losses. Sen. Estes Kefauver of Tennessee, who gained fame with his televised hearings of organized crime, ran an aggressive primary campaign and entered the convention with the lead in delegates. Other candidates included Gov. Averell Harriman of New York, Vice President Alben Barkley, Sen. Robert Kerr of Oklahoma and Sen. Richard Russell of Georgia.

The eventual nominee was Gov. Adlai Stevenson of Illinois, grandson of Grover Cleveland's second vice president. Stevenson had experience in the Navy and State departments before running for governor. President Truman privately recruited Stevenson for the race—at first unsuccessfully. Truman and Illinois backers set up a draft movement for Stevenson, which the governor disavowed until the last minute. Kefauver was the early leader in convention balloting, but Stevenson was always close, and he pulled into the lead on the third ballot.

Stevenson's campaign was an eloquent call to arms for liberals and reformers. Years later, Democrats would recall that the campaign had inspired the generation that would take the reins of power under John F. Kennedy. Democratic politics at all levels in subsequent years would revolve around battles of party regulars and reformers.

Stevenson did not have a chance, however, against the popular Eisenhower. Some Southern states bolted the party in response to Stevenson's pro-civil rights stance. While the Republicans had them as a gift, they hammered away at the misdeeds of the Democratic administration under Truman. Issues like the Communist revolution in China of 1949 ("Who lost China?"), the protracted Korean War, administration corruption and the alleged Communist infiltration of the government captured the nation's attention more than Stevenson's oratory.

More than anything, however, the desire for party change rather than policy change determined the election. The Republican evocation of the theme of "Corruption, Korea and Communism" did not challenge the policies that the Democrats offered the nation as much as the way they executed those policies. Eisenhower was a proven administrator and was free of the taint of everyday U.S. politics. Stevenson was a reformer himself, but his campaign had the conspicuous backing of President Truman. Stevenson's divorce and public support of Hiss were constant if only vaguely stated issues.

The campaign's biggest controversy developed when newspaper reports alleged that Nixon used a "secret fund" provided by California millionaires to pay for travel and other expenses. To a Democratic Party weary of charges of impropriety, the revelation offered an opportunity to charge that Nixon was beholden to special interests. Nixon admitted the existence of the fund but maintained that he used the money solely for travel and that his family did not accept personal gifts.

Nixon originally reacted to the story by asserting that it was a Communist smear. When Eisenhower would not publicly back his running mate, speculation developed that Ike would ask him to leave the ticket—and the Republican *New York Herald-Tribune* openly called for him to drop out. When Nixon decided to confront his accusers with a television speech, campaign aides told him he would be dropped if the public reaction was not favorable.

Nixon's speech was remarkable. He denied any impropriety and stated that the Stevenson campaign was hypocritical in its criticisms because it had similar funds. He denied that he accepted gifts such as a mink coat for his wife, Pat; he said that his wife wore a "Republican cloth coat." Nixon acknowledged receiving a pet dog named Checkers from a Texas admirer: "And you know, the kids love that dog, and I just want to say this right now, that regardless of what they say about it, we're going to keep it." [121] His folksy message and appeal for telegrams created a wave of sympathy, which Eisenhower rewarded with a pledge of support. The crisis was over.

In a personal victory—surveys showed that the nation still favored the programs of the New Deal and simply wanted to put the cronyism, sacrifices and Korean War behind it—Eisenhower swept to the White House. Ike won the entire North and West, parts of the South and some Border states—a total of 39 states to Stevenson's nine. Eisenhower's 442 electoral votes and 33.9 million popular votes (55.1 percent) overwhelmed Stevenson's 89 electoral votes and 27.3 million popular votes (44.4 percent). The election of 1956 would bring more of the same.

## Election of 1956

Despite his age and a heart attack in 1955, Eisenhower was the strong favorite to be the GOP nominee for another term. Close cooperation with the congressional leadership and a "hidden-hand" leadership style seemed to comport with the electorate's wishes for normalcy. [122] The White House apparatus was ably run by the chief of staff, Sherman Adams, and foreign policy was supervised by Secretary of State John Foster Dulles. The genius of Eisenhower's management style was the use of aides as "lightning rods" for unpopular policies.

Even without lightning rods, Eisenhower probably would have fared well. The economy was booming, and Eisenhower quickly brought the Korean War to a close. His nuclear policy gave the nation a "bigger bang for the buck" in defense spending and kept the troop requirements low. Federal housing and highway programs gave impetus to suburbanization, now considered part of the middle-class American Dream. Issues that would in the future become divisive, such as civil rights, were muffled.

The only unsettled Republican issue was whether Nixon would again be the vice presidential candidate. Eisenhower offered him a cabinet post, and Stassen mounted a campaign to replace Nixon with Massachusetts governor Christian Herter. After some hesitation, however, Eisenhower stood by his controversial running mate.

Kefauver challenged Stevenson for the right to face Eisenhower in the fall. After impressive primary victories in New Hampshire and Minnesota, the Stevenson campaign fought back with a string of primary wins in states as varied as California, Florida and Oregon.

Former president Truman continued his stormy relationship with Stevenson when he endorsed New York governor Harriman at the opening of the Democratic convention. A variety of other favorite sons entered the race. With the help of Eleanor Roosevelt and with careful campaigning among the convention's delegations, Stevenson was able to win the nomination for a second time. He won on the first ballot.

Stevenson left the vice presidential slot open to the convention delegates. Kefauver, after battling senators John Kennedy, Albert Gore and Hubert Humphrey and New York mayor Robert Wagner, eventually won. The open contest highlighted the future potential of Kennedy, who, according to later accounts, mainly intended not to win the second spot but to gain visibility for a 1960 presidential run.

The campaign was bereft of real issues. Eisenhower's campaigning was a tempered appeal to American values and bipartisan consensus. To Nixon was left the job of hacking away at the opposition; he called Stevenson "Adlai the Appeaser" and a "Ph.D. graduate of Dean Acheson's cowardly College of Communist Containment." [123] Overall, however, the campaign was an example of what James David Barber calls "the politics of conciliation," with little conflict or desire for change. Whether or not the electorate was "asleep," as frustrated critics charged, Eisenhower won another strong victory. He won 42 states, 457 electoral votes, and 35.6 million popular votes (57.4 percent), compared with Stevenson's six states, 73 electoral votes, and 26.0 million popular votes (42.0 percent). In an unprecedented development, however, both houses of Congress went to the opposition.

# Kennedy and the Politics of Change

The periodic national desire for change came at the expense of the Republicans in 1960, when Sen. John F. Kennedy of Massachusetts became the youngest person elected president by defeating Vice President Richard Nixon in the tightest election in history.

The presidential election took shape in the 1958 midterm election, when the Democrats made impressive gains in Congress. An economic recession and generational politics created the first major shift toward liberalism since the administration of Franklin D. Roosevelt. The "Class of '58" decisively changed the discourse of U.S. politics. After the election the Democrats held 64 of 98 Senate seats and 283 of 435 House seats, and 35 states had Democratic governors. The time appeared ripe for reopening issues that had long been stifled.[124]

The 1960 Democratic field was dominated by senators—Kennedy, Lyndon B. Johnson of Texas, Hubert H. Humphrey of Minnesota and Stuart Symington of Missouri. Each had important advantages and disadvantages. Kennedy was from a wealthy and politically minded family, but his Catholicism and undistinguished Senate record were liabilities. Johnson was a masterful majority leader, but no southerner had won the White House since James K. Polk in 1844. Humphrey was popular in the Midwest, but he lacked financial backing and was considered too loquacious and liberal. Symington had a strong Senate record and Harry S. Truman's backing, but he was considered colorless, and Truman's backing carried liabilities.

Former Illinois governor Adlai E. Stevenson, the party's nominee in 1952 and 1956, and Sen. Estes Kefauver of Tennessee stood on the sidelines, hoping that a convention deadlock or draft movement would finally bring them a ticket to the White House. Early speculation was that the convention would be deadlocked and a compromise candidate would have to emerge. It appeared likely that the nomination would go to Symington, Johnson, Humphrey or one of the two senior candidates, Stevenson and Kefauver; the other candidates were good bets for the vice presidential slot.

Kennedy presented the most intriguing candidacy. He was the son of Joseph P. Kennedy, the millionaire who had been Franklin Roosevelt's ambassador to Britain before their bitter break over U.S. involvement in World War II. John Kennedy was also an Ivy League graduate (of Harvard University), a war hero and a Pulitzer Prize-winner. With an experienced campaign staff, he had won an overwhelming reelection to the Senate in 1958. Moreover, he had been planning a run for the White House for years.

There were Kennedy skeptics, however. No Catholic since Alfred Smith had been a major-party nominee. Smith's bitter loss and the anti-Catholic sentiments he aroused made political professionals wary of naming another Catholic. Others focused on the influence of Joseph Kennedy, who bankrolled his sons' political careers.[125] Some considered Kennedy, at age 43, to be too young. Truman's comment captured the crux of Kennedy's liabilities: "It's not the Pope I'm afraid of, it's the Pop."[126]

To address the doubts, Kennedy entered political primaries that would enable him to demonstrate vote-getting ability and to confront the religion problem. The two key primaries were Wisconsin and West Virginia. In Wisconsin, Kennedy would answer the charge that he was too conservative and uncommitted to expanding the New Deal. The Kennedy strategists were divided about whether to oppose Senator Humphrey of nearby Minnesota; Wisconsin's growing independence in party politics eventually convinced them it would present a low risk in exchange for the possibility of beating Humphrey in his native region. In West Virginia, Kennedy would attempt to blunt the religion issue by attracting the votes of an overwhelmingly Protestant electorate.

Kennedy defeated Humphrey in Wisconsin, a state close to Humphrey's home state of Minnesota not only geographically but also culturally and ideologically. Kennedy's impressive campaign treasury enabled him to staff offices in eight of the ten congressional districts in the state; Humphrey had only two offices. Humphrey maintained that the defeat stemmed from crossover Republican Catholic votes and was therefore illegitimate. (Most of the state's Catholics, 31 percent of the population, belonged to the GOP.) But to Kennedy and many political observers, it was still an important victory.

Humphrey wanted to even the score in West Virginia. If Humphrey had quit the campaign and left Kennedy with no opponents, as many advised him to do, a Kennedy victory would have attracted little attention.[127] But Kennedy was able to use the Appalachian state as a way to deflect the religion issue as well as the "can't win" problem. Kennedy had a thorough organization in the state, and he worked hard. He had commissioned polls in the state as far back as 1958 in anticipation of the presidential race.

Kennedy's handling of the religion question in the primaries was shrewd and would be repeated in the fall campaign. He framed the question as one of tolerance—which put Humphrey on the defensive since he had never tried to exploit the religion issue. Kennedy had his campaign workers plant questions about how his religious beliefs would affect his loyalty to the nation, to which the candidate replied with a stock answer: "When any man stands on the steps of the Capitol and takes the oath of office as president, he is swearing to uphold the separation of church and state; he puts one hand on the Bible and raises the other hand to God as he takes the oath. And if he breaks the oath, he is not only committing a crime against the Constitution, for which the Congress can impeach him—but he is committing a sin against God."[128]

Kennedy's direct confrontation of the religion issue worked to his benefit. Kennedy had the money to get his message across: his television expenditures alone in the state totaled $34,000, while Humphrey had only $25,000 for the whole primary campaign in West Virginia.[129] Early polls gave Humphrey wide leads, and interviews elicited strong reservations about Kennedy's Catholicism. As the commercials aired and the primary neared, the lead became smaller, and voters privately said they would vote for Kennedy.

JFK, as he asked headline writers to call him instead of the youthful-sounding "Jack," easily won the primary. He was on his way to a first-ballot nomination.

The Kennedy campaign staffers managed the convention with consummate skill. Had they failed to gain a majority by the first ballot, pressure might have developed for another candidate. But the Kennedy team efficiently lobbied delegations to augment support; the vice presidential slot was vaguely offered to several politicians. In the end, Johnson was the surprise choice for running mate. Even

Kennedy supporters had doubts about Johnson, but the selection of the southerner was a classic ticket-balancing move.[130]

Central to Kennedy's winning campaign was his younger brother Robert F. Kennedy. A former counsel to Republican senator Joseph McCarthy, Robert developed into the consummate political operative. He was JFK's confidant, chief strategist, delegate counter, fund-raiser, taskmaster and persuader. Biographer Arthur M. Schlesinger Jr., wrote that Robert Kennedy's strength "lay in his capacity to address a specific situation, to assemble an able staff, to inspire and flog them into exceptional deeds, and to prevail through sheer force of momentum."[131]

Vice President Richard Nixon was the overwhelming choice for the Republican nomination. Nelson A. Rockefeller, elected governor of New York in 1958, was a liberal alternative, but he announced in 1959 that he would not run. There was a brief surge for Rockefeller when he criticized the party and its "leading candidate," but meetings with Nixon settled the differences. Some conservatives were disgruntled with Nixon, but their efforts for Sen. Barry Goldwater of Arizona would have to wait until 1964.

Nixon selected United Nations Ambassador Henry Cabot Lodge as his running mate, and the party platform and rhetoric stressed the need for experience in a dangerous world. Nixon promised to continue President Dwight D. Eisenhower's policies. He attempted to portray Kennedy as an inexperienced upstart, even though he was Kennedy's senior by only four years and the two had entered Congress the same year. Nixon led in the polls at the traditional Labor Day start of the fall campaign.

Kennedy's campaign was based on a promise to "get the nation moving again" after eight years of calm Republican rule. Specifically, he assured voters he would lead the nation out of a recession. The real gross national product increased at a rate of only 2.25 percent annually between 1955 and 1959. Economists puzzled over the simultaneously high unemployment and high inflation rates.[132] Kennedy repeatedly called for two related changes in national policy: pumping up the economy and increasing defense spending dramatically.

The Democrat faced up to the religion issue again with an eloquent speech before the Greater Houston Ministerial Association, and he attracted attention from civil rights leaders when he offered moral and legal support to the Rev. Martin Luther King Jr., after King was arrested for taking part in a sit-in at an Atlanta restaurant. While Kennedy appealed to the party's more liberal and moderate wing, Johnson toured the South to appeal to regional pride and to assuage fears about an activist government.

The high point of the campaign came on September 26, 1960, when the candidates debated on national television before 70 million viewers. Kennedy was well-rested and tanned and spent the week before the debate with friends and associates. Nixon was tired from two solid weeks of campaigning, and he spent the preparation period by himself. Their appearances alone greatly influenced the outcome of the debates.

Kennedy's main objective had been simply to look relaxed and "up to" the presidency. He had little to lose. Nixon was always confident of his debating skills, and he performed well in the give-and-take of the debate. But the rules of debating—the way "points" are allocated—are different in formal debating from what they are in televised encounters. Kennedy's managers prepared their candidate better for the staging of the debate. Nixon's five-o'clock

shadow reinforced the cartoon image of him as darkly sinister. Polls of radio listeners found that Nixon had "won" the debate, but polls of television viewers found that Kennedy had "won" the debate. Historian Theodore H. White wrote: "It was the picture image that had done it—and in 1960 it was television that had won the nation away from sound to images, and that was that."[133]

While Kennedy called for a more activist and imaginative approach to world problems, Nixon stressed the candidates' similarities so much that their differences paled into insignificance. Kennedy called for a crusade to eliminate want and to confront tyranny. Nixon responded: "I can subscribe completely to the spirit that Sen. Kennedy has expressed tonight."[134] With ideology an unimportant part of the debate, the images of personal character the candidates were able to project gained in importance.

The candidates held three more debates and addressed issues including Fidel Castro's Cuba, the Chinese offshore islands of Quemoy and Matsu and relations with Nikita Khrushchev's Soviet Union. None of the debates had the effect of the first, which neutralized Nixon's incumbency advantage. Nor was Nixon greatly helped by President Eisenhower, who did not campaign for his protégé until late in the campaign.

The election results were so close that Nixon did not concede his defeat until the afternoon of the day following the election. Nixon later said he considered contesting some returns more than a week after the election. After a vacation in Florida and Nassau, Nixon returned to Washington on November 19 to consider a series of charges that voter fraud had cost him the election. A shift of between 11,000 and 13,000 votes in a total of five or six states could have given Nixon the electoral vote triumph. Nixon said he decided against demanding a recount because it would take "at least a year and a half" and would throw the federal government into turmoil.[135]

When the Electoral College voted, Kennedy won 303 electoral votes to Nixon's 219. Democratic senator Harry F. Byrd of Virginia attracted 15 electoral votes. Kennedy won 23 states to Nixon's 26. (A slate of eight independent electors won Mississippi; these eight, plus six from Alabama and one from Oklahoma voted for Byrd.) The overall popular vote went 34.2 million for Kennedy and 34.1 million for Nixon. The margin was about one-tenth of 1 percent, or 115,000 votes. The margins in many states were very close. Kennedy won Illinois by 8,858 votes and Texas by 46,242 votes. Despite statements that the religion question would hurt Kennedy, it probably helped him by mobilizing Catholics on his behalf. Gallup polls showed that 78 percent of Catholics voted for JFK. Although Catholics were a traditional Democratic constituent group—by margins of three or four to one—they had voted for Eisenhower by large margins.[136] In addition, Kennedy put together a predictable coalition: he won the support of voters in the Northeast, in most of the South, and in cities, plus blacks and union workers. Upper New England, the Midwest and the West went primarily to Nixon.

In an informal way, Kennedy and Goldwater discussed the way they would conduct their campaigns for the presidency in 1964. The two expected to win their party nominations easily, and they talked about crisscrossing the nation in head-to-head debates, which would set a new standard for national campaigns.[137]

The Kennedy-Goldwater campaign never came. On November 22, 1963, while riding in a motorcade in Dallas, Texas, President Kennedy was assassinated by a gunman named Lee Harvey Oswald.[138] Vice President Johnson assumed the presidency.[139]

In his brief administration, Kennedy had compiled a record disappointing even to many of his supporters. The Bay of Pigs fiasco in which a CIA plan to overthrow the Cuban government failed miserably, the inability to obtain passage of landmark civil rights legislation, budget deficits and a drain of gold supplies from the United States, confrontations with the Soviet Union in Cuba, Hungary and Berlin, and the nascent U.S. involvement in the Vietnam War created doubts about the young president's control of the government.

Still, Kennedy had made a start on many important issues. Arms control initiatives such as the test-ban treaty, economic growth through tax cuts, modernization of the military, the successful management of the Cuban missile crisis, civil rights and other domestic initiatives, the Peace Corps and Alliance for Progress and growing world stature all offered hope for the second term. It would fall to Johnson, the legendary former Senate majority leader, to bring the Kennedy plans to fruition. First acting as the loyal servant of the slain president, then as his own man, Johnson was able to bring to legislative enactment many of the long-cherished initiatives of the U.S. liberal establishment—most notably the Civil Rights Act of 1964, which was considerably stronger than the Kennedy bill that had stalled in Congress.

# "All the Way with LBJ"

From the time of his sad but graceful ascension to the White House, Johnson was never in doubt as the Democrats' 1964 nominee. He was expected to select an Eastern or Midwestern liberal as his running mate, and he did so when he tapped Senator Humphrey of Minnesota at the convention, which his campaign organization stage-managed to the last detail. The only dissent from the Democratic unity was provided by Gov. George C. Wallace of Alabama, whose segregationist campaign took advantage of a backlash against the civil rights movement. Wallace entered three primaries against Johnson-allied favorite sons. He polled 43 percent of the vote in Maryland. Wallace talked about mounting a third party bid in the fall, but he backed off.

The Republicans were divided into two bitter camps led by Senator Goldwater of Arizona, the eventual nominee, and Governor Rockefeller of New York. The nomination contest was a struggle for the soul of the party. Other active and inactive candidates included Ambassador to Vietnam Henry Cabot Lodge, former vice president Nixon and Gov. William Scranton of Pennsylvania. After a New Hampshire primary victory by Lodge, achieved through a well-organized write-in drive while he was still ambassador to Vietnam, Goldwater and Rockefeller scrapped through a series of primaries. The moderate Lodge eventually helped Scranton in an effort to recruit uncommitted delegates to stop Goldwater, but by then it was too late. Goldwater lined up strong delegate support to get the nomination before the primary season even began, but he needed to use the primaries to show that he had vote-getting ability. The state organizations that backed him needed evidence that his conservative message would find popular acceptance.

In the "mixed" system then in place, candidates were able to pick and choose the primaries that best suited their strategy. Front-runners avoided risks, and long shots entered high-visibility and often risky contests as a way to attract the attention of party professionals. As expected, Goldwater won widespread support in the Southern state conventions and had strong primary showings in Illinois and Indiana. Rocke-

feller beat Lodge in Oregon, but the decisive test came when Goldwater narrowly upset Rockefeller in California.

More important than the confusing preconvention contests was the rhetoric. Both the conservative Goldwater and the liberal Rockefeller vowed to save the party from the other's ideology. Goldwater, who rode the bestseller success of his *Conscience of a Conservative* to hero worship among conservatives, made a vigorous case against New Deal politics and for American sway in world politics: "I don't give a tinker's damn what the rest of the world thinks about the United States, as long as we keep strong militarily." [140] Rockefeller implied that Goldwater risked nuclear war and would recklessly dismantle basic social programs.

The nomination contest was a regional as well as an ideological struggle. The westerner Goldwater—backed by labor-intensive manufacturers, small business and agricultural enterprises and oil producers—opposed internationalist banking and commercial interests.[141] Goldwater made Eastern media the objects of scorn. Rockefeller and his family represented the apex of the Eastern establishment. Because of his strategy, Goldwater made himself an outsider to the growth-oriented consumer politics of the period.

Bitter battles over the party platform and unseemly heckling of Rockefeller displayed the party's divisions at the convention. When the conservatives won the nomination and the platform, there was no reconciliation. Goldwater selected Rep. William Miller of New York, another conservative, as his running mate and vowed to purify the party of liberal and moderate elements.

In a defiant acceptance speech, Goldwater painted a picture of the United States as inept in international affairs and morally corrupt in domestic pursuits, and he vowed an all-out crusade to change the situation: "Tonight there is violence in our streets, corruption in our highest offices, aimlessness among our youth, anxiety among our elderly, and there's a virtual despair among the many who look beyond the material successes toward the inner meaning of their lives.... Extremism in defense of liberty is no vice; moderation in pursuit of justice is no virtue." [142]

To a nation experiencing prosperity and unaware of the true proportions of its involvement in Vietnam, the "choice, not an echo" that Goldwater offered was a moral crusade. But the American consensus was built on material, consumer foundations and an "outsider" appeal would have to wait until the system's foundations became unstable.

The divided GOP made for easy pickings for Johnson. The fall campaign was dominated by Goldwater's gaffes, which started long before the campaign began. He said, for example, that troops committed to the North Atlantic Treaty Organization (NATO) in Europe "probably" could be cut by "at least one-third" if NATO "commanders" had the authority to use tactical nuclear weapons in an emergency.[143] Goldwater also proposed a number of changes in the Social Security system, called for selling off the Tennessee Valley Authority, criticized the civil rights movement and denounced the Supreme Court, the National Labor Relations Board and the federal bureaucracy. Except for use of nuclear weapons and changes in Social Security, most of Goldwater's proposals when taken alone were not shocking. But the sum of his proposals—and his sometimes halting explanations—scared many voters.

President Johnson campaigned very actively to win a mandate for an activist new term. He traveled throughout the country to build a consensus for his domestic programs as well as his reelection. Johnson resisted Goldwater's constant calls for televised debates. The nation's prosperity was probably enough to keep the president in the White House.[144]

Johnson desperately wanted a personal mandate to pursue a variety of domestic programs that fell under the rubric "the Great Society"—a term that Johnson used in a 1964 commencement address (borrowed from a book of the same title by British socialist Graham Wallas). The desired landslide—underscored by his campaign slogan, "All the Way with LBJ"—was essential to initiatives in civil rights, health care, community action, education, welfare, housing and creation of jobs. Central to the landslide was not only economic prosperity but also peace in the world's trouble spots. Johnson therefore ran as a "peace" candidate.

But while he was trying to build a coalition that would sustain his domestic initiatives, Johnson faced an increasingly difficult dilemma about U.S. involvement in Vietnam. The United States opposed Ho Chi Minh's revolution against French colonial rule in the 1940s and 1950s, and under presidents Eisenhower and Kennedy the United States had made a commitment to South Vietnam (created after the failure of the 1954 Geneva accord) as a bastion against Communist expansion in Asia. But talk of war would likely imperil the domestic initiatives of the Great Society.

So while Johnson was campaigning as the peace candidate in 1964, he also was preparing for a major increase in U.S. involvement in Vietnam. As early as February 1964 the administration began elaborate covert operations in Southeast Asia and prepared a resolution to give the president a "blank check" in Vietnam.[145] By June the resolution was ready, and the Pentagon had chosen 94 bombing targets in North Vietnam and made provisions for bombing support systems. But on June 15, Johnson decided to delay major offensives until after the election.[146] In August Johnson sent to Congress what would be known as the Tonkin Gulf Resolution, which passed quickly and nearly unanimously. The president instructed congressional leaders to get an overwhelming majority so his policy would be bipartisan.

Johnson also seized on Rockefeller's use of the peace issue during the Republican primaries against Goldwater. Alluding to some of Goldwater's scarier statements about war, and he pledged, "[W]e are not about to send American boys nine or ten thousand miles away from home to do what Asian boys ought to be doing for themselves."[147] A week before the election, Johnson said: "The only real issue in this campaign, the only one you ought to get concerned about, is who can best keep the peace."[148]

Johnson's landslide was the largest in U.S. history. He won 61 percent of the popular vote to Goldwater's 38 percent (or 43.1 million to 27.2 million votes). In the Electoral College Johnson received 486 votes to Goldwater's 52, and he carried 44 states—all but Goldwater's home state of Arizona and five Southern states. In addition, the Democratic Party amassed huge majorities in both the Senate (67-33) and the House of Representatives (295-140).

On election day Johnson created a working group to study "immediately and intensively" the U.S. options in Southeast Asia.[149] The war was increasing far beyond what most supporters of the Tonkin Gulf Resolution or "peace" supporters of the president imagined. In 1965 alone the number of U.S. troops in Vietnam increased from 15,000 to nearly 200,000.[150]

## The Breakup of Consensus

A long period of uncertainty in American politics began sometime after Johnson's landslide victory over Goldwater.

By 1968, some 30,000 Americans had been killed in action, and television was bringing the war into the living rooms of American families. Despite repeated assertions that the United States was defeating the North Vietnamese enemy, U.S. bombing efforts and ground troops did not break the resolve of the Communists in the North or their sympathizers who had infiltrated the South. The corrupt South Vietnamese government and army appeared to lack the resolve to fight the war on their own.

The opposition to the war developed as the casualties mounted, and the administration experienced a "credibility gap" because of its statements about the war. Before the United States left Vietnam in 1975, 55,000 Americans had died in combat. Perhaps more important than the number of casualties—about the same as in the Korean War—was the long-term commitment that the United States appeared to make with little evidence of progress. The "quagmire," as *New York Times* reporter David Halberstam called the war, was perhaps typified by the program of intense U.S. bombing raids that were judged by many experts to be ineffectual against the North's guerrilla warfare strategy.[151]

As opposition to the war grew among an increasingly vocal and well-organized minority, strains developed in Johnson's economic and domestic programs. Starting with the Watts riots in Los Angeles in 1965, urban areas sizzled with resentment of the mainstream liberal establishment. Detroit, Newark and other U.S. cities erupted in riots that burned miles of city streets and caused millions of dollars in damage. The assassination of civil rights leader Martin Luther King, Jr., in Memphis April 4, 1968, led to riots throughout the nation. Even before the riots, however, a conservative reaction against the Great Society had developed.

The activities of the Great Society were many and varied: the Civil Rights Act of 1964, the Voting Rights Act of 1965, Head Start, Model Cities, mass transit legislation, food stamps, Medicaid, the Elementary and Secondary Education Act, college loans, housing programs that included subsidies for the poor, to name just the most prominent programs.

The conservative backlash was apparent before many programs had time to do their work. Efforts such as the Model Cities program and the Community Action Program, which mandated that poverty programs promote "maximum feasible participation" by the poor themselves, were often badly organized. They also were the source of additional struggles over jurisdiction in cities that already were notorious for divisive politics. Liberal efforts that predated the Great Society, such as school desegregation, created other tensions in cities.

One of the greatest sources of backlash in the late 1960s was an alarming increase in street crime. Even though blacks and the poor were the chief victims of the increase, the issue was most salient for conservative whites. Many tied the breakdown in order to the growth of the welfare state inspired by the Great Society. The crime rate seemed to many to be nothing less than ingratitude on the part of the poor. James Sundquist writes: "While increasing millions were supported by welfare, rising state and local taxes made the citizen more and more aware of who paid the bill. And while he armed himself for protection against thieves or militants, the liberals were trying to pass legislation to take away his guns."[152]

The crime problem was an important element in both national and metropolitan politics. Polls showed that half the women and a fifth of the men in the country were afraid to walk alone in their own neighborhoods at night.[153] In Alabama, Gov. George Wallace was whipping up his supporters in a frenzy of prejudice and resentment. The fear of crime also would be an important element in Richard Nixon's 1968 campaign.

# 'Nixon Now': 1968

With the nation divided over the war and domestic policy, the Democrats entered the 1968 campaign in an increasingly perilous state. In December 1967, Sen. Eugene McCarthy of Minnesota challenged President Johnson for the Democratic nomination, a move based almost entirely on McCarthy's anti-war stance. The senator did unexpectedly well against Johnson's write-in candidacy in the New Hampshire primary on March 12, 1968, drawing 42.4 percent of the vote to Johnson's 49.5 percent. Anticipating a devastating defeat in the Wisconsin primary April 2, Johnson dramatically announced his withdrawal from the campaign in a televised address March 31.

After the New Hampshire primary, New York senator Robert F. Kennedy declared his anti-war candidacy, which put in place all the elements for a Democratic fight of historic proportions. Vice President Humphrey took Johnson's place as the administration's candidate; he eschewed the primaries but eventually won the nomination on the strength of endorsements from state party organizations.

McCarthy and Kennedy fought each other in the primaries, and Kennedy appeared to have the upper hand when he closed the primary season with a victory in California on June 5. But after making his acceptance speech, he was assassinated, and the party was in greater turmoil than ever.

At the party convention in Chicago, a site Johnson had chosen for what he thought would be his own nomination, Humphrey became the Democratic Party's candidate. The vice president took the nomination on the first ballot after Mayor Richard Daley of Chicago committed the Illinois delegation to his effort. Humphrey won with support from the traditional elements of the Democratic coalition—labor, blacks, urban voters—plus the backers of President Johnson. Humphrey appealed to many of the party's "moderates" on the Vietnam War. Preliminary battles over rules and delegate seating, the representativeness of the party and Vietnam War policies caused ugly skirmishes on the convention floor. The party's platform eventually endorsed the administration's war policy, including bombing, but strong opposition to this plank left the party divided.[154]

Outside the convention halls, demonstrations for civil rights and an end to the war met brutal rejection from the police. After three days of sometimes harsh verbal and physical battles with anti-war demonstrators in parks, the police charged a group of protesters that planned a march on the convention. Theodore H. White described the scene that played on national television:

> Like a fist jolting, like a piston exploding from its chamber, comes a hurtling column of police from off Balbo into the intersection, and all things happen too fast: first the charge as the police wedge cleaves through the mob; then screams, whistles, confusion, people running off into Grant Park, across bridges, into hotel lobbies. And as the scene clears, there are little knots in the open clearing—police clubbing youngsters, police dragging youngsters, police rushing them by their elbows, their heels dragging, to patrol wagons, prodding recalcitrants who refuse to enter quietly.[155]

Humphrey and his running mate, Sen. Edmund Muskie of Maine, faced an uphill fight. The Republicans united behind Richard Nixon, the 1960 nominee whose political career seemed at an end after a loss in the 1962 California gubernatorial election. The GOP did not have to deal with any of the divisiveness of the 1964 Goldwater-Rockefeller battle. Nixon outspent Humphrey two-to-one and followed a carefully devised script, avoiding the exhausting schedule of his 1960 campaign. He capitalized on the national discontent created by the Vietnam War, urban riots, political assassinations and general concern about the speed of change wrought by the Great Society. Nixon traveled the high road in his own campaign by calling for the nation to unite and heal its wounds. While he promised an "open administration," Nixon's main offer was change. "I must say the man who helped us get into trouble is not the man to get us out." [156] To avoid scrutiny by the national media, Nixon gave few major addresses, preferring instead a series of interviews with local newspapers and broadcasters.

As President Johnson resisted calls for a halt in the bombing of North Vietnam, Nixon said he had a "secret plan" to end the war. He appealed to weary Democrats with his pledge of an activist administration and alternative approaches to dealing with some of the problems the Great Society addressed. Nixon promised to give blacks, in his words, "a piece of the action with a program to encourage entrepreneurial activity in cities." The "new Nixon" appeared willing to deal with the Soviet Union, which he had scorned earlier in his career. Meanwhile, his vice presidential nominee, Gov. Spiro T. Agnew of Maryland, offered a slashing critique of the Democrats to middle-class and blue-collar Americans who resented the civil rights laws, government bureaucracy, Vietnam War protesters and the young protest generation.

Governor Wallace of Alabama ran one of the strongest third party campaigns in U.S. history. He ran as an anti-establishment conservative, railing away at desegregation, crime, taxes, opponents of the war in Vietnam, social programs and "pointy-head" bureaucrats and "intellectual morons." His American Independent Party was the strongest effort since Theodore Roosevelt's Bull Moose campaign in 1912 and Robert La Follette's Progressive run in 1924. Like the earlier third party campaigns, the Wallace run caused concern about the soundness of the Electoral College system. Because the race was so close, it was conceivable that no candidate would win an Electoral College victory. In that event, Wallace could have held the balance of power.[157]

Despite the early disadvantage, Humphrey made steady inroads into Nixon's support by disassociating himself from Johnson's Vietnam policies. When Johnson on November 1 ordered a halt to all bombing of North Vietnam, Humphrey appeared to be free at last from the stigma of the administration. But this change in administration policy was not enough to win the election for Humphrey.

The 1968 election was one of the closest in U.S. history. Nixon's victory was not confirmed until the day after the election when California, Ohio and Illinois—each with very close counts—finally went into the Nixon column. Nixon attracted 31.8 million votes (43.4 percent of all votes cast); Humphrey, 31.3 million votes (42.7 percent); and Wallace, 9.9 million votes (13.5 percent). Nixon won 32 states and 301 electoral votes, compared with Humphrey's 13 states and 191 electoral votes. Nixon won six Southern states (Wallace won five others), all of the West except Texas, Washington and Hawaii, and all the Midwestern states except Michigan and Minnesota. Humphrey won all of the East except New

Hampshire, Vermont, New Jersey and Delaware, plus West Virginia, Maryland and the District of Columbia.

One long-lasting effect of 1968 was a transformation of the nomination process. In response to the bitter complaints about the 1968 Democratic convention, the party adopted rules that would make the primaries the center of the nomination process. The Chicago convention, dominated by party professionals at the expense of many important constituencies—blacks, women, youths—nominated a candidate who did not compete in any primaries. The key reform was a limit on the number of delegates that state committees could choose—after 1968, no more than 10 percent of the delegation.

# Nixon's Reelection: 1972

Sen. George McGovern of South Dakota was the miracle candidate of 1972, but his miracle did not last long enough.

Edmund Muskie, a veteran of the U.S. Senate and the vice presidential nominee in 1968, was the early favorite to win the Democratic nomination. But because of party reforms enacted in response to the disastrous 1968 convention, the nomination process was bound to create surprises and confusion.

No fewer than 15 contenders announced their candidacies, 12 with serious hopes of winning or influencing the final selection. Some 22 primaries to choose 60 percent of the party's delegates—a third more than in 1968—were to take place over four months. The marathon would be decided by accidents, media strategy and a confusing array of voter choices that changed with each new development.

Muskie was badly damaged before the primary when he appeared to cry while lashing back at the *Manchester Union Leader*'s vicious and unrelenting attacks on his campaign and on his outspoken wife, Jane. The *Union Leader* had printed a series of attacks on Jane, then falsely reported that Muskie had laughed at a derogatory joke about French Canadians. Muskie later said of the incident: "It changed people's minds about me, of what kind of a guy I was. They were looking for a strong, steady man, and here I was weak." [158]

Muskie won the first-in-the-nation New Hampshire primary, but his 46.4 percent of the vote was considered a "disappointing" showing. McGovern, the anti-war candidate who won 37.1 percent of the vote, was pronounced the real winner by media and pundits. His strong showing — engineered by imaginative young political operatives, such as Gary Hart and Patrick Caddell, and a corps of youthful volunteers—was a surprise. After New Hampshire, the Democrats battled through the summer. Wallace parlayed his anti-busing rhetoric into an impressive victory in the Florida primary. Better organized than the others, McGovern swept the Wisconsin delegation by winning 29.6 percent of the state vote. McGovern then won an easy Massachusetts victory with 52.7 percent of the vote to Muskie's 21.3 percent. Humphrey edged McGovern in Ohio by 41.2 to 39.6 percent, but McGovern claimed a moral victory.

In the popular primary vote before the late summer California primary, McGovern actually stood in third place behind Wallace and Humphrey. But the delegate allocation rules gave the edge to the candidate who could squeeze out narrow victories in congressional districts, and that was McGovern. McGovern had 560 delegates to Humphrey's 311. Wallace had 324 delegates, but he was paralyzed after being shot in a Maryland shopping center and therefore no longer appeared to have a chance at the nomination.

The big McGovern-Humphrey showdown was in California, which offered 271 delegates to the winner. The spirited campaign included a head-to-head debate and strong Humphrey assaults on McGovern's positions on welfare and defense spending. McGovern went on to beat Humphrey by five percentage points in the winner-take-all primary. McGovern also won a majority of the delegates in New Jersey, South Dakota and New Mexico in the last day of the primary season. [159]

After platform battles over welfare, busing and the Vietnam War, McGovern won the nomination handily. He then selected Sen. Thomas Eagleton of Missouri as his running mate after several others declined. McGovern did not get to deliver his acceptance speech—perhaps the best speech of his career—until 2:48 a.m., when most television viewers were already in bed.

President Nixon and Vice President Agnew were renominated with barely a peep out of other Republicans. Rep. Paul N. (Pete) McCloskey of California opposed Nixon in the primaries but won only one delegate (from New Mexico).

McGovern would have been an underdog in the best of circumstances, but his chances were badly damaged by what came to be known as the "Eagleton affair." As the McGovernites celebrated their hard-won nomination, rumors circulated that Eagleton had been hospitalized for exhaustion after the 1960 campaign. Eagleton finally told McGovern operatives that he had been hospitalized three times for nervous exhaustion and fatigue, and his treatment included electroshock therapy. Despite McGovern's public statement that he was "1,000 percent for Tom Eagleton, and I have no intention of dropping him," Eagleton left the ticket less than two weeks after his nomination.

McGovern eventually replaced Eagleton with his sixth choice, R. Sargent Shriver, the former Peace Corps and Office of Economic Opportunity executive. But the aura of confusion that surrounded the Eagleton affair and the search for a new vice presidential candidate hurt the campaign badly. Columnist Tom Braden likened it to a school teacher who could not control the class: "Nice people, too. One looks back with sympathy and a sense of shame. But at the time—was it that they were too nice?—their classes were a shambles. The erasers flew when they turned their backs." [160]

Nixon was in command of the fall campaign. He paraded a litany of accomplishments—the Paris peace talks over the Vietnam War, the diplomatic opening to China, the arms limitation treaty with the Soviet Union and a number of domestic initiatives. Most of all, he was a strong figure; and if he still aroused suspicion, he was at least a known commodity.

Nixon won all but Massachusetts and the District of Columbia in the fall election. His popular vote margin was 47.2 million to McGovern's 29.2 million; the Electoral College cast 521 votes for Nixon and only 17 for McGovern. Nixon's 60.7 percent share of the popular vote stood second only to Johnson's 61.1 percent in 1964.

# Nixon's Downfall: The Watergate Scandals

On the surface, it appeared in 1972 that American politics was entering an age of calm consensus. At the time of the election, the economy was temporarily strong: opposition to the Vietnam War had faded as the two sides negotiated in Paris for an end to the war; the United States had signed an important nuclear arms treaty with the Soviet Union and had made important diplomatic moves with that country and the People's Republic of China. Nixon's landslide victory appeared to be a mandate and a vote of confidence.

But trouble loomed behind the apparent stability and consensus. The war in Vietnam continued, as did the antiwar protests, and generational cleavages remained. The economy experienced the first of many "shocks" in 1973 when the Organization of Petroleum Exporting Countries agreed to increases in the world prices of oil. The economic turmoil was topped off with a wage and price freeze. In addition, a warlike atmosphere between the White House and the media (as well as other perceived enemies of the administration that appeared on Nixon's "enemies list") and the mushrooming Watergate scandal combined to create a dark side to U.S. politics in the 1970s.[161]

The Watergate affair was perhaps the greatest political scandal in U.S. history. For the first time, a president was forced to leave office before his term expired. President Nixon resigned on August 9, 1974, when it became apparent that the House of Representatives would impeach him for "high crimes and misdemeanors" and the Senate would convict him. In addition, a number of Nixon aides, including his first attorney general and campaign manager, John Mitchell, would spend time in jail because of the scandal.

At its simplest level, the Watergate affair was "a third-rate burglary" and a subsequent coverup by President Nixon and his aides. In the summer of 1972, several employees of the Committee to Re-elect the President were arrested after they were discovered breaking into and bugging the Democratic National Committee's offices at the posh Watergate complex in Washington. The break-in was not a major issue in the 1972 election, but the next year congressional committees began an investigation.

During the investigation, a presidential aide revealed that Nixon had secretly taped Oval Office conversations with aides. When the Watergate special prosecutor, Archibald Cox, ordered Nixon to surrender the tapes in October 1973, Nixon ordered Cox fired. Nixon's attorney general and assistant attorney general refused to fire Cox; eventually, the solicitor general, Robert Bork, fired Cox, and a constitutional crisis dubbed the "Saturday night massacre" ensued. Nixon soon handed over the tapes Cox sought. In the summer of 1974, the Supreme Court ruled that Nixon had to surrender even more tapes, which indicated that he had played an active role in covering up the Watergate scandal. Nixon resigned the presidency when his impeachment and conviction appeared certain. The impeachment articles charged him with obstruction of justice, abuse of presidential powers and contempt of Congress.

Many students of the Watergate affair maintain that the illegal campaign activities were just part of a tapestry of illegal activities in the Nixon administration—including secretly bombing Cambodia, accepting millions of dollars of illegal campaign contributions, offering government favors in return for contributions, "laundering" money through third parties, wiretapping and burglarizing a wide variety of people thought to be unsupportive of the president, offering executive clemency to convicted campaign workers, engaging in "dirty tricks" to discredit other political figures, compromising criminal investigations by giving information to the people under scrutiny and using government funds to renovate the president's private residence.[162]

The decade saw other political scandals as well. In 1973, Nixon's vice president, Spiro T. Agnew, resigned after pleading "no contest" to charges of bribe-taking while he was governor of Maryland. Members of Congress became enmeshed in the "Koreagate" and "Abscam" influence-peddling scandals. Congressional investigations uncovered massive abuses by the Federal Bureau of Investigation and the CIA reaching back into the 1950s.

After Agnew's resignation on October 10, 1973, Nixon named House Minority Leader Gerald Ford, a longtime GOP stalwart, to become vice president under the 25th Amendment for presidential succession.

Ford, who had never entered a national election, became president upon Nixon's resignation and quickly attracted the support of the American public with his modest, earnest disposition. Ford responded to the widespread feeling that Nixon's isolation in the Oval Office contributed to his downfall by promising to work closely with Congress and to meet with the press regularly.

Less than two months after becoming president, however, Ford ignited a firestorm of criticism with his full pardon of Nixon for crimes he may have committed while president. Ford testified before Congress that he believed Nixon had suffered enough and that the nation would have been badly torn if a former president were brought to court to face criminal charges. Critics asserted that Ford had made a "deal" in which Nixon resigned the presidency in exchange for the pardon.[163]

Ford selected former New York governor Nelson Rockefeller to be his vice president. Rockefeller received Senate and House confirmation on December 10 and 19, respectively, after long and difficult hearings that centered on his financial dealings.

# Jimmy Who?

With the benefit of the Watergate scandal and Ford's pardon of Nixon, the Democrats won resounding victories in the 1974 midterm elections. The Democrats' gains of 52 House seats and four Senate seats not only created stronger majorities but also cut the number of members with allegiance to the old system of organizing congressional business.

The moralistic zeal of the "Watergate class" forced major changes on Congress that affected not only the legislative process but also the presidency and the nation's process of pluralistic political bargaining. The new crop of legislators was so large that it was able to undermine the seniority system that had ordered the way Congress had operated for years. The new system of committee assignments led to a proliferation of subcommittees on which most members had prominent roles. That, in turn, created a fragmented policy-making process—less susceptible to coercion by presidents and party leaders and more susceptible to interest group politics.[164]

The 1976 campaign was the first governed by campaign finance reform legislation enacted in 1971 and 1974. The Federal Election Campaign Act (FECA) of 1971 limited campaign expenditures and required disclosure of campaign receipts and expenditures. The Revenue Act of 1971 created a tax check-off in which taxpayers could designate $1.00 of their taxes to be allocated for public financing of elections. The FECA amendments of 1974 limited spending and donations for both primary and general election campaigns, established a system of partial public funding of elections and created the Federal Election Commission to monitor campaign activities.

The Democrats and their eventual nominee, Jimmy Carter, were able to continue exploiting the nation's discontent through the 1976 election. Ronald Reagan, the former movie actor and California governor, added to the Republican Party's vulnerability by waging a a stubborn primary campaign against President Ford.

The Democrats appeared headed for a long and bitter nomination struggle for the third time in a row. A few candidates—such as senators Henry Jackson of Washington, Birch Bayh of Indiana and Governor Wallace of Alabama—had greater stature than others, but their appeal was limited to specific factions of the Democratic coalition. Other candidates included Rep. Morris Udall of Arizona, Sen. Fred Harris of Oklahoma, Sen. Frank Church of Idaho and Gov. Edmund G. Brown Jr., of California. Church and Brown entered the race late, and senators Humphrey of Minnesota and Edward M. Kennedy of Massachusetts awaited a draft in the event of a deadlocked convention.

The moderate Carter, whose name recognition in polls stood in single figures as the campaign began, executed a brilliant campaign strategy to win the nomination on the first ballot. Constructing strong organizations for the Iowa caucus and the New Hampshire primary, Carter won both contests by slim margins. Although liberal candidates Udall and Bayh together polled better than Carter, it was Carter who received cover billings on national magazines and live interviews on morning television talk shows.[165] Within a matter of days, Carter changed from long shot to front-runner.

Udall performed well in the primaries but never won a single state. He and other liberals constantly split their vote; Udall's chance for a Wisconsin primary win fizzled when Harris refused to back out to create a one-on-one matchup of a liberal with Carter.[166] Carter ran into strong challenges from Church and Brown in later primaries, but by the time of the Democratic convention in New York he had the delegates and endorsements for a first-ballot nomination.

The Democratic convention was a "love-feast" with the Democrats united behind Carter and his running mate, Sen. Walter F. Mondale of Minnesota.

The GOP was divided between Ford and Reagan. Ford won the early contests, but Reagan scored big wins in the North Carolina and Texas primaries. Reagan was put on the defensive with his proposals for transferring welfare obligations to the states, but when he focused on foreign policy issues he had success. He attacked Ford for his policy of détente with the Soviet Union and his negotiation of a treaty that would forfeit U.S. control of the Panama Canal.

With Ford and Reagan locked in a close contest for delegates in the late summer, Reagan tried to gain advantage by breaking precedent and naming his vice presidential candidate before the convention. Reagan's choice was Sen. Richard Schweicker of Pennsylvania, a moderate who widened Reagan's ideological appeal but angered many of his conservative supporters. Reagan tried to force Ford to name a vice presidential candidate in advance, and the convention vote on the issue was a crucial test of the candidates' delegate strength. Ford won that test and the nomination. He selected the acerbic senator Robert Dole of Kansas as his running mate as a consolation prize for disappointed conservatives.

Carter emerged from the Democratic convention with a wide lead over Ford, but the race was too close to call by election day. A number of gaffes—such as Carter's interview with *Playboy* magazine, his ambiguous statements about abortion and his confused observations on tax reform—hurt the Democratic contender.[167] Ford also gained in the polls when he began to use the patronage powers of the presi-

dency and effectively contrasted his 27 years of Washington experience to Carter's four years as governor of Georgia.

For the first time since 1960, the major candidates took part in televised debates. As the outsider, Carter helped himself by demonstrating a good grasp of national issues and by appealing to Democrats to vote the party line. Ford hurt himself with a claim that Eastern European nations did not consider themselves to be under the control of the Soviet Union.[168] The remark was intended to be testimony to the Europeans' sense of national identity, but it was interpreted as evidence of the president's naiveté. Carter's main advantage was regional pride. The Democrats had long since lost their hold over the South, but Carter gained widespread support as the first candidate nominated from the region on his own in more than a century. The Democratic Party's many factions—including big-city mayors such as Daley of Chicago and Abraham Beame of New York, civil rights activists and organized labor—put on a rare display of unity.

Carter defeated Ford by a slim margin, winning 40.8 million votes (50.1 percent) to Ford's 39.1 million (48.0 percent). In the Electoral College, 297 votes went to Carter, 240 to Ford. Carter won by pulling together the frazzled New Deal coalition of industrial and urban voters, blacks, Jews and southerners. Ford won the West, and Carter won the South, except Virginia. Ford won all the states from the Mississippi River westward except Texas and Hawaii, plus states in his native Midwest like Iowa, Illinois, Michigan and Indiana. Ford also won Connecticut and the three northernmost New England states—New Hampshire, Vermont and Maine.

## Carter's Uncertain Leadership

After his election, President Carter's ability to hold the coalition together was limited. The growing influence of nationalized media politics and interest group politics, poor relations with Congress and difficult "crosscutting" issues—inflation and unemployment, oil shocks and the more general energy crisis, the Iran hostage crisis, relations with the Soviet Union and budget austerity moves such as proposed cutbacks in water projects and social welfare—all damaged Carter's governing ability.

As the 1980 election approached, Carter appeared to have lost all but his institutional strength and the reluctance of voters to reject a president for the fourth time in a row. Carter controlled party processes, such as the primary schedule; he had access to key financial support and skilled political operatives; and he shaped much of the political agenda. But Kennedy hit him hard from the left, and Reagan and others hit him hard from the right. Carter was unable to forge a lasting consensus on important issues. Kennedy led Carter in polls by a two-to-one margin when he announced his challenge to Carter in November 1979. But Carter overcame that lead by the start of the nominating season when the seizure of American hostages in Iran rallied the nation around the president and Kennedy made a series of political mistakes. Kennedy was unable to develop campaign themes or answer questions about his personal conduct in the 1969 Chappaquiddick incident, in which a woman died after a car he was driving went off a bridge. Other "character" issues, such as Kennedy's alleged "womanizing," and more substantive issues, such as his liberal voting record, also hurt him in a year dominated by conservative themes. Kennedy's campaign also was in financial jeopardy early because of lavish spending on transportation, headquarters and other expenses.

The campaign of Governor Brown of California was unable to find much support for his appeal for recognition of economic and environmental limits. He dropped out of the race on April 1, 1980.

The president was able to manipulate the primary and caucus schedule to bunch states favorable to him and to match pro-Kennedy states with pro-Carter states. The result was an early, strong Carter lead in delegates. Kennedy came back with some strong primary wins in New York and Pennsylvania, but his campaign by then was reduced to a vehicle for anti-Carter expressions. Many Kennedy voters hoped for a deadlocked convention at which a third candidate could win the nomination.

Carter won the nomination on the first ballot despite a variety of stop-Carter efforts and Kennedy's attempt to free delegates to vote for any candidate. When Carter won the crucial floor vote on the "open convention" question, Kennedy did not have a chance. The Carter-Mondale ticket entered the fall campaign as a wounded army with little enthusiasm from the troops.

The Republicans united early behind Reagan. By April 22, 1980, less than two months after the New Hampshire primary, six candidates had dropped out of the race, and George Bush, Reagan's only surviving competitor, was desperately behind in the delegate count. Reagan's campaign experienced an early scare when Bush beat Reagan in the Iowa caucus; but Reagan rebounded, changed campaign managers and tactics and won a string of primaries and caucuses. By the time of the convention, Reagan was the consensus candidate, and he improved party unity by adding Bush to the fall ticket.

Reagan called for the electorate to replace politics that he said were marked by "pastels," or compromising and uncertain policies, with "bold colors." Reagan's proposed bold strokes included a 30 percent reduction in marginal tax rates based on a "supply-side" economic theory—which even some Republicans said was a dangerous kind of "voodoo economics"—and massive increases in military expenditures. At the same time, Reagan criticized Carter's alleged vacillation and his commitment to liberal policies.

President Carter—vulnerable as the hostage crisis neared its first anniversary (which was November 4, election day) and high inflation and unemployment rates persisted—attempted to portray Reagan as a dangerous, heartless and inexperienced amateur. Reagan managed to use Carter's attacks to his own advantage by assuming a posture of hurt feelings at the unfair criticism. When in a televised debate Carter attacked Reagan's previous opposition to social welfare programs, Reagan cut him off with a line, "There you go again," that suggested Carter was unfairly and relentlessly distorting Reagan's record. The greatest controversy of the campaign did not emerge until years later. Books published after the Reagan years charged that the Reagan-Bush campaign negotiated a deal with Iran to delay release of the hostages until after the campaign to embarrass President Carter. Gary Sick, a national security aide for Carter, charged that Reagan campaign officials met with Iranian officials in Europe in the summer of 1980 to arrange weapons sales in exchange for holding the hostages. If true, the deal could have cost Carter the presidency.[169]

Carter strategists also were concerned about the independent candidacy of Rep. John B. Anderson of Illinois, a moderate who dropped out of the Republican race when it became clear that conservatives would dominate that party. After some stronger support in the polls, Anderson stood at about 10 percent for the final two months of the campaign.

Carter was concerned that Anderson would take more votes from him than from Reagan, even though analysis of Anderson support suggested otherwise.[170]

Private money almost doubled the amount that Reagan was legally entitled to spend under the federal financing system. Well-organized groups on the "new right" that opposed abortion, gun control, détente and many social welfare programs spent lavishly on television commercials and efforts to register like-minded voters. These groups also made a "hit list" of leading liberals in Congress; these candidates were so weakened by the new right's attacks that they put a local and regional drag on an already dragging Democratic ticket.[171]

Polls before election day predicted a close race. Reagan, however, won all but six states and took the White House in an electoral landslide, 489 electoral votes to 49. Reagan won 51 percent of the vote, while Carter managed 41 percent and Anderson 7 percent. Carter ran tight races in ten additional states that could have gone his way with a shift of less than one and a half percentage points. In 21 states, Anderson's vote totals made up most or all of the difference between Reagan and Carter. Despite these factors and polls that regularly showed preference for Carter's policy positions, Reagan's victory was impressive. He beat Carter by better than a two-to-one margin in nine states.

Even more surprising than Reagan's electoral landslide was the Republican takeover of the Senate. The new right's targeting of several Senate liberals—such as McGovern, Bayh, Gaylord Nelson of Wisconsin, John Tunney of California and John Culver of Iowa—created the biggest Senate turnover since 1958. The Republicans now held the Senate by a 53-to-46 margin.

President Reagan was able to parlay his claims of an electoral mandate into wide-ranging changes in tax, budget and military policies. Reagan won passage of a three-year, 25 percent cut in tax rates that would reduce federal revenues by $196 billion annually by the time the three-stage program was in place. He also secured omnibus legislation that cut the domestic budget by $140 billion over four years and increases in defense spending of $181 billion over the same period. The media hailed Reagan as the most successful handler of Congress since Lyndon Johnson.

## Reagan's 1984 Landslide

Reagan's popularity dipped to 44 percent in 1983—about the average for modern presidents—but rebounded when the economy later picked up.[172] As the 1984 election approached, Reagan faced no opposition from Republicans, but a large field of Democrats sought the right to oppose him in the fall.

The Democrats' early front-runner was former vice president Mondale, who accumulated a wide range of endorsements (AFL-CIO, National Education Association, United Mine Workers and the National Organization for Women) and an impressive campaign treasury. The more conservative senator John Glenn of Ohio, the first American to orbit Earth, was considered a strong challenger. Other candidates included senators Gary Hart of Colorado, Alan Cranston of California and Ernest Hollings of South Carolina, civil rights leader Jesse Jackson, former presidential candidate George McGovern and former governor Reubin Askew of Florida.

The early results eliminated all but Mondale, Hart and Jackson just 16 days after the New Hampshire primary. Hart became the serious challenger to Mondale when he finished second in Iowa and first in New Hampshire, creating an explosion of media coverage. Mondale recovered, and the two fought head-to-head until the convention. Jackson, the second black to run, stayed in the race to promote his liberal party agenda.[173]

After interviewing a wide range of candidates, Mondale selected Rep. Geraldine Ferraro of New York as his running mate—the first woman ever to receive a major-party nomination for national office. Representative Ferraro's vice presidential candidacy probably was a drag on the ticket, not so much because she was a woman but because the controversies created by her husband's finances and her stand on the abortion question hindered the Democratic campaign's effort to articulate its own vision for the nation.[174] Ferraro appeared knowledgeable and strong in her debate with Vice President Bush, and she often drew large and enthusiastic crowds. But she was stuck in controversy when details of her husband's questionable real estate, trusteeship and tax practices became public. Opponents of abortion held prominent and often loud protests at the sites of her speeches, and she got involved in a lengthy public dispute over abortion with Catholic archbishop John O'Connor. Ferraro also did not help the ticket in regions where the Democrats were weak, such as the South and West.

Mondale ran a generally conservative campaign, concentrating on a proposed tax increase to address the unprecedented budget deficit of over $200 billion and proposing no new social programs. Mondale criticized Reagan's record on the arms race, but did not outline basic disagreements on other foreign affairs issues. He charged that Reagan, the oldest president in history, was lazy and out of touch. Only late in the campaign, when his speeches became unabashedly liberal and combative, did Mondale create any excitement.

Just once—in the period after the first presidential debate—did Mondale appear to have a chance to defeat President Reagan. Political pundits had marked Mondale as a poor television performer, but the challenger outfoxed Reagan in the debate and afterwards appeared to be gaining ground for a few days. Before the debate, Mondale aides leaked erroneous information that suggested he would make a slashing attack. But Mondale surprised Reagan. At the advice of strategist Patrick Caddell, Mondale adopted a "gold-watch approach" suitable to a family business retiring an oldtimer—"sort of embracing a grandfather, and gently pushing him aside."[175] Mondale gave the president credit for helping to restore national patriotism and beginning a national debate on education reform, but he said it was time for new leadership. Reagan appeared confused and, in the rush to demonstrate statistical knowledge of policies, he failed to outline broad themes.

Although the first debate boosted the Mondale campaign's morale, it never brought Mondale within striking range of Reagan. He never came within 10 percentage points of Reagan in the polls. Reagan's campaign was a series of rallies with masses of colorful balloons and confident talk about the United States "standing tall" in domestic and world affairs. Reagan was so sure of victory that he made a last-minute trip to Mondale's home state of Minnesota with the hope of completing a 50-state sweep of the nation.

Reagan's triumph was resounding almost everywhere. He won 54.5 million votes (58.8 percent) to Mondale's 37.6 million (40.6 percent). In the Electoral College, he received 525 votes to Mondale's 13 votes. Reagan won 49 states, with 2-to-1 margins in eight states. Idaho, Nebraska and Utah each gave Reagan more than 70 percent of the vote.

Mondale won only the District of Columbia and his home state of Minnesota, where he beat Reagan by only two-tenths of 1 percent.

Reagan's two landslides and the conservative discourse of his administration led many experts to wonder if they were witnessing a "realignment"—that is, a major shift in political alliances among a variety of social, economic and ethnic groups.[176] The noteworthy aspect of U.S. politics in the last two decades appeared to be the Democratic hold on congressional and state elections and the Republican dominance of presidential elections. Some experts pointed to the electorate's ticket-splitting tendencies as evidence of "dealignment"—that is, breakdown of the old system without development of an entirely new system.[177]

Perhaps the most noteworthy development of recent years, which fits the dealignment thesis, has been the convergence of the appeal of the two parties. Michael Barone, in *The Almanac of American Politics,* wrote:

> Political preferences in the America of the 1940's correlated to a fair degree with income. Republican strength was greater than average in high income states . . . , while Roosevelt and Truman carried virtually every state with incomes below the national average. But today there is virtually no correlation between income level and political preference. Utah, with one of the lowest per capita incomes, was one of the nation's most Republican states in 1980. . . . In the Midwest, high income Illinois is more Democratic than low income Indiana.[178]

## The New Conservative Discourse

Reagan's rise ushered in a new age of conservatism in the American political discourse. The vigorous conservative campaigns for the presidency and Congress were accompanied by a host of new "think tanks" and publications with a restyled set of philosophical and policy pronouncements.

The most celebrated event of the conservative revival was the publication of George Gilder's *Wealth and Poverty,* a far-reaching attack on welfare state policies that rested on supply-side economic theory. Gilder argued that free markets and low taxes promoted not only economic efficiency and growth but also other benefits such as family strength and artistic creativity. Gilder's book was a central element of Reagan's campaign for major tax cuts.[179] But the supply-side tracts of Gilder and others were only the most prominent signs of the conservative movement. Reagan's criticism of the Supreme Court decisions on abortion and school prayer helped to bring evangelical Christians into the political process. Businesses and conservative philanthropists, meanwhile, sponsored an unprecedented level of public policy research that shaped the debate of elections and government policy.[180]

Reagan's political appeal, according to scholar Garry Wills, turned on his ability to blend contradictory elements of American culture such as capitalism, conservatism and individualism. While Reagan decried the decline of "traditional American values," for example, he extolled the dynamic economic system that demanded constant change. Wills writes: "There are so many contradictions in this larger construct that one cannot risk entertaining serious challenge to any of its details. In Reagan, luckily, all these clashes are resolved. He is the ideal past, the successful present, the hopeful future all in one."[181]

Using the "bully pulpit" of the presidency, Reagan was able to overwhelm his opponents with his vision. When Democrats criticized specific Reagan policies, Reagan deflated them with expressions of disdain for "little men with loud voices [that] cry doom." [182] Jeane Kirkpatrick's depiction of Democrats as the "blame America first crowd" neatly expressed the way the Reagan rhetoric foreclosed debate on major policy issues such as the budget and trade deficits, military spending, the U.S. role in the Third World and U.S.-Soviet relations. By the time the 1984 campaign took place, much of the nation had adopted Reagan's terms of debate. Mondale's strongest performance, in fact, was in the first debate when he congratulated Reagan for restoring national pride and suggested not that Reagan should be ousted but rather given a graceful retirement. Mondale's campaign was basically conservative: he did not propose a single new social program and called the federal budget deficit the nation's top problem.

# The Post-Reagan Era

The election of 1988 was the first since 1968 in which an incumbent president did not run. With no major figure and no major issues, the campaign was a tumultuous affair. As 14 candidates struggled to develop an identity with the voters, the campaign lurched from one symbolic issue to the next and never developed the overarching themes of previous campaigns.

In the absence of any major new issues, and in a time of general peace and prosperity, Republican vice president George Bush won the presidency. Bush defeated Democratic Massachusetts governor Michael S. Dukakis by a margin of 54 percent to 46 percent—47.9 million votes to 41.0 million votes. Bush's electoral vote margin was more impressive, 426-112. A negative campaign and limited voter-registration efforts resulted in the lowest voter turnout in modern times. Just more than 50 percent of all eligible citizens voted for president.

Bush won with the Nixon-Reagan presidential coalition. He won all the states of the old Confederacy, the entire West except Oregon and Washington, and several Northern industrial states. Dukakis originally hoped to crack the South by selecting a favorite son, Sen. Lloyd M. Bentsen Jr. of Texas, as his running mate; but that failed. Dukakis lost crucial states that he fought for to the end, such as California, Pennsylvania, Illinois, Ohio and Missouri. He won New York, Massachusetts, Wisconsin, Minnesota, Oregon, Washington, West Virginia, Iowa, Rhode Island, Hawaii and the District of Columbia.

President Ronald Reagan's retirement after two full terms created a void as the campaign began. By most accounts, Reagan was the most popular president since Dwight D. Eisenhower. His dominance of national politics left little room for other figures to establish presidential stature.

Reagan's fiscal and social policies reduced the possibility for candidates to offer ambitious new programs. The national government's huge budget deficits—which exceeded $200 billion, compared with about $73 billion in the last year of the Carter administration—checked any grandiose new spending plans. The Reagan debt exceeded the debt of the previous 39 presidents.

President Reagan also reshaped the dialogue on foreign affairs. He maintained strong opposition to the Soviet Union and other "Marxist" nations with his policies in Nicaragua, Afghanistan and Angola. He also projected an image of strength with military action in Libya and Grenada. At the same time, however, he co-opted critics by meeting Soviet leader Mikhail Gorbachev several times and signing a nu-

clear arms control agreement. Reagan even asserted that the Gorbachev regime was fundamentally different from previous Soviet regimes, which he had called the "evil empire."

The early Republican front-runners were Bush and Sen. Robert J. Dole of Kansas; former senator Gary Hart of Colorado was considered the early Democratic leader. The campaign got scrambled before it began, however. Hart left the race in 1987 when the Miami *Herald* augmented rumors of Hart's infidelity with a report that he had spent the night with a young model. The newspaper staked out Hart's Washington townhouse with two reporters, two editors and a photographer. The investigators sat in a rental car, loitered nearby and jogged down the street. Hart, considered by many to be the brightest and most issue-oriented candidate, had long faced criticism about his "character." The Hart story dominated the political news in 1987. Network news programs devoted 132 minutes to Hart, mostly in the first half of the year and, on the GOP side, 32 minutes to the longshot televangelist Marion G. "Pat" Robertson. The two front-runners and eventual nominees, Bush and Dukakis, got 28 and 20 minutes, respectively.[183] Sen. Joseph R. Biden Jr. of Delaware was the next casualty of the media's 1987 concern with character issues.[184] Media reports that he had committed plagiarism on a law school paper and in campaign speeches led to Biden's early exit from the campaign. Biden had been considered a leading candidate because of his experience and strong speaking style.

With Hart and Biden out of the race, the Democrats were in disarray. Dubbed "dwarfs," the remaining candidates—Rev. Jesse Jackson of Illinois, Gov. Dukakis, Rep. Richard A. Gephardt of Missouri, Sen. Albert A. Gore Jr. of Tennessee, Sen. Paul M. Simon of Illinois and former Arizona governor Bruce Babbitt—lacked the combination of extensive government experience and strong national bases many observers thought necessary to win the presidency.

The Republicans had problems of their own. Vice President Bush was the early favorite, and he benefited from his association with President Reagan. But Bush's public fealty to Reagan created a problem: he was considered a "wimp," unable to stand on his own. Every major position Bush had held in his political career was the result of appointment: ambassador to the United Nations, chairman of the Republican National Committee, envoy to China, director of the Central Intelligence Agency and vice president. Bush had represented Texas for two terms in the House and lost two Senate races.

Dole, too, was considered strong at the outset of the race. As Republican leader in the Senate, he had a high profile in national politics and proven fund-raising abilities. His wife, Elizabeth, was prominent as secretary of transportation. Dole also had an acerbic wit, which gave spark to his campaigning style but also irritated some voters. Other GOP candidates were Rep. Jack Kemp of New York, former secretary of state Alexander M. Haig Jr. of Pennsylvania, former Delaware governor Pierre S. "Pete" du Pont IV, and television minister Robertson of Virginia.

The marathon campaign for the nomination began with the Iowa caucuses, a significant event only because of intense media attention. Gephardt barely edged Simon in the Democratic contests, and Dole won the Republican race. The big story was just how badly Bush performed: he finished third behind Dole and Robertson.

The Iowa loss caused the Bush campaign to emerge from its isolation. Bush had been the most restrained and cautious candidate as he tried to benefit from the prestige of the White House. But in the New Hampshire primary Bush beat Dole. Bush won with a series of television advertisements charging that Dole would raise taxes. Bush also was more animated on the campaign trail than he had been before. Dole failed to respond quickly to the Bush offensive, and when he snapped on national television about Bush's "lying about my record," he reinforced his image as a mean-spirited candidate.

Among the Democrats, Governor Dukakis easily won the New Hampshire primary. Capitalizing on his regional popularity, Dukakis beat Gephardt and Simon. Most of the Democratic fire in that race took place between the two runners-up. Dukakis escaped without any major criticism, and his already strong fund-raising machine went into high gear.

The decisive stage of the GOP campaign was Super Tuesday—March 8—when 22 states held presidential primaries or caucuses. Benefiting from a well-organized campaign, Bush won 17 of the 18 GOP contests. Dole staked his campaign on the ensuing Illinois primary, but he lost badly, and Bush was virtually ensured the Republican nomination.

The one issue that threatened Bush throughout 1988 was the Iran-contra scandal. Revelations that the Reagan administration had traded arms to Iran in exchange for the release of hostages, then used the proceeds illegally to fund the war in Nicaragua, raised questions about Bush's role. Administration officials admitted lying to Congress, destroying evidence and operating outside normal government channels; one top official even attempted suicide. But the question of Bush's involvement fizzled after months of inconclusive questioning of Bush.

The Democrats sorted things out slowly on Super Tuesday. Dukakis won Texas and Florida and five Northern states and confirmed his shaky front-runner status. Civil rights leader Jesse Jackson was the big surprise, however, winning five Southern states. Gore won seven states. Even though it was designed to help conservative candidates, Super Tuesday fit Jackson's strengths. Six of the nine states here Jackson scored best in 1984 held their contests on Super Tuesday in 1988. Super Tuesday was also supposed to put the South in the national spotlight, but the region received only a few more candidate visits in 1988 (149) than it had in 1976 (145).[185]

The Democratic marathon continued into Illinois, Michigan and New York. Dukakis took and maintained the lead in delegates with steady wins over Jackson and Gore. Gore dropped out after finishing third in a divisive New York primary, and the rest of the campaign was a one-on-one race between Dukakis and Jackson. Only once—after his victory over Dukakis in the Michigan caucuses—did Jackson appear to have a chance to win the Democratic nomination.

Jackson was a mixed blessing for the party. An energetic campaigner, he attracted support from blacks and from farmers and blue-collar workers who were disgruntled by the uneven rewards of economic growth. But Jackson was considerably to the left of the rest of the party and never had held any government office. Race also was a factor: no political professional believed that a black could be elected president.

Dukakis practically clinched the nomination with his victory over Jackson in the New York primary. The issue of race was at the center of the campaign. New York City mayor Edward I. Koch, a Gore supporter, called Jackson a "radical" and said Jews would be "crazy" to vote for him. Such remarks aggravated tensions between blacks and Jews that had festered since the 1960s. Dukakis avoided the race issue and won the primary.

As the summer conventions approached, Bush and Dukakis each had the full support of his party. The parties' internal divisions were on display as the prospective nominees considered possible vice presidential candidates. Blacks lobbied for Jackson's selection by Dukakis, while "New Right" GOP leaders lobbied against a "moderate" running mate.

Dukakis selected conservative senator Lloyd Bentsen of Texas as his running mate before the Atlanta Democratic convention. Jackson complained publicly and privately, but he eventually embraced Bentsen for the sake of party unity. Dukakis hoped Bentsen would be able to help carry Texas: no Democrat has won the presidency without winning Texas since the state became part of the nation in 1845.

The July convention was a success for the Democrats. After a week of Bush-bashing and Democratic conciliation, Dukakis gave an effective acceptance speech peppered with statements in Spanish and Greek. Dukakis left the convention with a double-digit lead over Bush in the polls.

The Republican convention in August did not start out as well. Bush announced his selection of Sen. Dan Quayle of Indiana as he arrived in New Orleans. After revelations that Quayle had avoided military service in the Vietnam War by enlisting in the Indiana National Guard, many Republicans criticized Bush's choice. Some even said Quayle might have to be dropped from the ticket.[186] By the end of the convention, however, the Republicans had weathered the storm. Bush delivered a crisp address, which provided the self-portrait that the vice president needed, and moved into the fall campaign for a close battle with Dukakis.

Bush took the offensive immediately after the August GOP convention and hit Dukakis as a "liberal" out of touch with American "values." Bush attacked Dukakis for his membership in the American Civil Liberties Union, his veto of a bill requiring Massachusetts teachers to lead children in the Pledge of Allegiance and a Massachusetts program allowing prisoners time off for weekends. As he pounded away at these symbolic issues, Dukakis' "negative" ratings with voters soared. Not believing the attacks would affect his standing with undecided voters—and believing they might even hurt Bush—Dukakis did not respond forcefully to the attacks until October. By then, however, Bush had effectively defined Dukakis, a newcomer to national politics. Dukakis' counteroffensive in the last two weeks of the campaign came too late.

Roger Ailes, Bush's media adviser, said: "We always knew we would have to define Dukakis. . . . You've got to understand that the media has no interest in substance. . . . There are three ways to get on the air: pictures, attacks, and mistakes, so what you do is spend your time avoiding mistakes, staying on the attack, and giving them pictures."[187] Other major national issues—the national debt, the trade deficit, housing, education, U.S.-Soviet relations, the environment and ethics in government—were drowned out by the emphasis on symbolic issues.

As Dukakis fell behind Bush, his campaign pinned its hopes on two nationally televised debates. Dukakis performed well in the first debate, but Bush appeared to "win" the second debate. Dukakis failed to gain on Bush.

The only major problem for Bush was Quayle. Most political professionals considered Quayle a "lightweight." The 41-year-old Quayle was a poor student and marginal member of Congress.[188]

Dukakis said Bush's selection of Quayle amounted to failure in his "first presidential decision." Dukakis compared Quayle with the more experienced Bentsen, who performed much better in a vice presidential debate. Public polls revealed that most voters thought that Quayle was a bad choice.

The Bush campaign minimized the damage by limiting Quayle's public exposure and carefully scripting his statements. Quayle rarely spoke in major media markets; many of his campaign stops were accessible only by bus. While Bush delivered speeches in several states each day, Quayle often made just one speech before schoolchildren or partisan audiences.

After months of inconsistent and confusing strategy, Dukakis finally developed a strong appeal in the last two weeks of the campaign. He told voters he was "on your side" and portrayed Bush as a toady to the wealthy. Dukakis said the middle class was "squeezed" by the policies of the Reagan administration and that the Democrats would provide good jobs, affordable housing and health care, and tough enforcement of environmental protection laws.

It was not enough. Bush, who had made a fortune in the oil business before entering politics and was the son of a former U.S. senator, persuaded more voters that his experience and values were what they wanted in the very personal choice of a president.

# The End of Republican Rule

In March 1991, in the aftermath of the U.S.-led victory over Iraq in the Persian Gulf War, President George Bush received the highest approval ratings since opinion polling began. Some 91 percent of people said they approved of his performance as president. But just a year later, Bush struggled to keep his job. He failed.

Bill Clinton's victory over Bush in 1992 might be viewed as a dramatic shift in American politics. Clinton's constant campaign slogan was "change." The 46-year-old Arkansas governor repeatedly blasted the Republican White House for inattention to domestic problems such as the budget deficit, health care, welfare, civil rights, crime, trade and economic investment. President Bush, Clinton said, was too obsessed with foreign policy and unconcerned with domestic affairs.

But Clinton's election could be viewed as an aberration. Only the second Democrat elected president since 1968, Clinton got only 43 percent of the vote in a three-man race. Voters said they voted against Bush, not for Clinton. The independent candidacy of Texas billionaire H. Ross Perot might have cost Bush the election, as much by tarnishing his reputation as taking away the votes of the angry middle class. Even people who supported Clinton expressed reservations about his character. Voters reacted warily to reports of Clinton's avoidance of military service in Vietnam, marital infidelity, and conflict of interest while governor, and to his evasiveness about smoking marijuana as a student. On policy questions, Clinton was well-informed but also appeared insincere. A label pinned on Clinton in Arkansas—"Slick Willie"—stuck.

President Bush began the election cycle looking unbeatable. With his leadership during the Gulf War, Bush appeared to have the strength to lead the United States into what he called the "new world order." In 1989 the countries of the so-called Soviet bloc—East Germany, Poland, Czechoslovakia, Romania, Yugoslavia—broke from Communist rule in a series of non-violent revolutions. In August 1991 an attempted coup against Mikhail Gorbachev's "perestroika" government in the Soviet Union failed. Afterward, the Soviet regime—Communist Party and all—collapsed. Bush was president during the most remarkable realignment of world politics since World War II.

Bush took credit for presiding over these dramatic changes, but those American "victories" also undermined his position. The Republican Party dominated presidential politics at least partly because of its hawkish policies during the Cold War. With the end of the Soviet threat, the GOP no longer had a "gut" issue to use against the Democrats. Journalist Sidney Blumenthal wrote: "The Cold War's end was not a photo opportunity, a sound bite, a revelation of 'character,' a political consultant's tactic, or even a theme. It was a global sea change as profound as the Cold War's beginning." [189] Bush had a hard time adjusting.

For a while, President Bush looked so strong that leading Democrats were reluctant to take him on. The party's leading figures—Gov. Mario Cuomo of New York; senators Bill Bradley of New Jersey, Al Gore of Tennessee and Jay Rockefeller of West Virginia; and Rep. Richard Gephardt of Missouri—announced they would not run. Only former senator Paul Tsongas of Massachusetts, recently recovered from a bout with cancer, announced his candidacy.

Notwithstanding his numbers, President Bush might have been doomed from the start. Historically, "understudy" presidents do not win reelection. Presidents who gain their office by carrying the legacy of their mentors have a hard time developing their own program or strategy. In addition, the tensions within their party coalitions burst into the open. John Adams, James Madison, Martin Van Buren, William Howard Taft, Herbert Hoover, as well as Bush, all fit this description. [190]

Despite three decades in public life, Bush never conveyed a coherent identity or campaign theme. His advisers planned to "narrowcast" messages to selected groups until the summer, when Bush would deliver his big "what-do-I-stand-for" speech. But by that time, Bush's opponents had defined him as weak and unprincipled. His attempt to divert attention to Clinton's foibles only intensified Bush's image as uncertain of his own values and goals. [191]

Bush's base crumbled by 1992. The president decided to "sit" on his high popularity ratings and win reelection by avoiding mistakes. Bush's chief of staff, John Sununu, summed up the strategy: "There's not another single piece of legislation that needs to be passed in the next two years for this president. In fact, if Congress wants to come together, adjourn, and leave, it's all right with us." [192] The results were devastating. By May of 1992 a poll found that 76 percent of the public disapproved of the way Bush handled the economy. [193] His overall approval rating dropped an unprecedented 57 points from the end of the Gulf War to the beginning of the 1992 GOP convention.

A bitter anti-incumbent mood dominated the new campaign year. Nationwide, reformers promoted the idea of term limits for elected officials as a way of sweeping out career politicians. [194] Perot, who parlayed his wealth into a number of headline-grabbing exploits over the years, became a viable independent candidate. [195] His pithy statements about how to "fix" government captured the imagination of the public.

Pennsylvania voters sent a warning shot to the White House when they rejected the 1991 Senate candidacy of Bush's friend and first attorney general, Richard Thornburgh. Democrat Harris Wofford, appointed to the seat that opened with the death of John Heinz, won on a platform of national health care and a return to domestic priorities—themes that Bill Clinton reprised in 1992.

Wofford, a former college president and Kennedy administration official, came from 30 points behind in the polls to win with 55 percent of the vote. It was the highest percentage that any Democrat had received in Pennsylvania senatorial elections. Wofford's campaign was run by a young operative named James Carville.

Bush's major domestic initiative—the budget law passed in October 1990—angered the Republican Party's right wing. Conservatives had long distrusted Bush because of his past moderate positions on taxes, abortion, civil rights and social programs. The budget act, which increased taxes by $150 billion, broke Bush's "no new taxes" pledge.

As the recession and other domestic crises deepened, the president seemed increasingly out of touch. Bush's reported confusion over the use of bar codes at a grocery store symbolized his elite background and isolation. After race riots in Los Angeles drew the nation's attention to the severity of poverty, Bush was photographed teaching baffled-looking urban youths how to use a fishing pole. In a politics driven by symbolism, these images were ruinous.

Since the Democrats controlled the Senate by 10 seats and the House by 85 seats, Bush began his term with less party support than any president in history. Bush's legislative initiatives routinely were called "dead on arrival." For the first time, the Senate rejected an incoming president's Cabinet nominee when it voted down John Tower's bid to be secretary of defense. In his dealings with Capitol Hill, Bush vacillated between confrontation and compromise. Bush regularly tussled with Congress, vetoing 44 bills.

The Democratic field grew slowly. Besides Clinton and Tsongas, the field included former governor Edmund G. "Jerry" Brown Jr. of California, senators Thomas Harkin of Iowa and Robert Kerrey of Nebraska, and Gov. L. Douglas Wilder of Virginia. Wilder dropped out before the first contest.

Clinton won the "invisible primaries" before the formal balloting began. He attracted $3.3 million in contributions by the end of 1991. Harkin was second best with a little more than $2 million.[196] Clinton organized supporters in most states holding early contests. Clinton also won the favor of opinion-makers because of his grasp of issues, as well as an engaging personality.

By calling himself a "new Democrat," Clinton hoped to separate himself from rejected candidates such as Jimmy Carter, Walter Mondale and Michael Dukakis. Clinton promised to move beyond liberal orthodoxy and "reinvent government."[197] His record in Arkansas suggested a willingness to oppose liberal nostrums on issues such as the death penalty, economic growth and public education.

The centerpiece of Clinton's strategy was to appeal to the "forgotten middle class." Suburbanites, the working class and Southerners and Westerners had abandoned the Democratic Party since the late 1960s. Unfortunately for the Democrats, these groups comprised a growing part of the electorate. Many pundits argued that these groups gave the Republicans a "lock" on the presidency.[198] Clinton's goal was to forge a new ideological center and "pick" the lock.

As expected, "favorite son" Harkin won the Iowa caucuses, winning 76.4 percent of the delegates selected on Feb. 10. Clinton led the polling in New Hampshire early but ran into trouble when media questioned his character. A woman claimed that she and Clinton had an affair and Clinton helped her get a state job. Meanwhile, Clinton was reported to have misled an Army Reserves recruiter as part of a scheme to avoid service in Vietnam.

At one point, Clinton's campaign was almost broke. Clinton hit back. He and his wife appeared on the television news magazine "60 Minutes" after the Super Bowl game. Clinton admitted he had "caused pain" in his marriage but said he and his wife solved their problems. Hillary Clinton's appearance seemed to close the matter. Skeptics should vote against Clinton, she said, but also drop the character charges.

Tsongas won the New Hampshire primary on Feb. 18 with 33.2 percent of the vote to Clinton's 24.7 percent. Tsongas offered the policy equivalent of castor oil. He said the nation needed to make difficult economic choices such as higher taxes and program cutbacks. He called Clinton, who spoke in favor of a tax cut and the costly Connecticut-built Polaris Navy submarine, a "pander bear."

Clinton, who fell some 20 points in polls in a month, exuberantly called his second-place finish a victory by noting Tsongas' regional ties and declaring himself the "Comeback Kid." His campaign was out of money, though, and was rescued by a $3.5 million line of credit from the well-connected Worthen Bank in Arkansas.

Tsongas and Brown won scattered contests after New Hampshire, but Clinton rolled to the nomination starting with his March 3 victory in the Georgia primary. Kerrey and Harkin dropped out in early March. Clinton's sweep of Southern states on "Super Tuesday," March 10, and his decisive wins in Michigan and Illinois on March 17 practically clinched the nomination. Clinton had a scare when Brown beat him in Connecticut on March 24, but he beat Brown decisively in New York on April 7. Tsongas, by that time an inactive candidate, finished ahead of Brown in New York.

Clinton won 32 state primaries with 51.8 percent of the vote; Tsongas won four states with 18.1 percent and Brown won two states with 20.1 percent.[199]

Even as Clinton won state after state, Democratic leaders searched for an alternative. Bush plummeted in the polls, but Democrats grew nervous about Clinton's ability to confront the character issue. In March, almost half of Democratic voters in Connecticut's primary said Clinton lacked the "honesty or integrity" to be president.[200] Former governor Brown fed the uncertainty with his relentless attacks on Clinton's ties to special interests. Talk of drafting another candidate developed regularly, but party professionals became resigned to Clinton's nomination.

President Bush faced an unusually pointed challenge from conservative columnist and former White House aide Patrick J. Buchanan, who charged that Bush betrayed the conservative faith. Buchanan's main point of attack was the 1990 tax increase. But he also criticized Bush's activism in world affairs, federal support of arts projects that he called "blasphemous" and the nationwide recession.

Buchanan's campaign in New Hampshire, run by his sister, was simple. Buchanan wrote his own speeches. Roughly designed television ads showed people mimicking Bush's "no new taxes" pledge. Buchanan mocked Bush's superior campaign organization and resources. He said that the "Buchanan brigades" would defeat "King George and his armies." Bush ignored Buchanan's campaign, sending his wife and other administration representatives to campaign in New Hampshire.

Bush won New Hampshire, but media focused on the 37 percent of the vote that the underdog Buchanan received. Buchanan continued his campaign until June. He was guaranteed media attention by virtue of his quixotic quest and uncompromising rhetoric. In the final analysis,

Buchanan did not win any states with his 22 percent of the total primary vote.[201]

Buchanan made a vigorous effort to win some of the Southern contests in early March but never matched his New Hampshire numbers. Despite his hard hits at Bush, he may have helped to neutralize another protest candidate, former Ku Klux Klan leader David Duke, who finished second in the Louisiana gubernatorial contest in 1991. Republican leaders were embarrassed by Duke's GOP membership, but he disappeared after a poor showing in New Hampshire.

Ross Perot's on-and-off campaign unsettled Republicans' plans to build on their base in the South and West. Perot's folksy anti-government rhetoric appealed to voters in suburbs and high-growth areas of the 1980s—the heart of the GOP base since Richard Nixon's 1968 campaign.

Perot's campaign began where much of the 1992 campaign was waged: on the television talk-show circuit. On the cable TV show "Larry King Live," Perot said in February that he would run for president if volunteers put him on the ballot in all 50 states. He said he would spend up to $100 million of his own money to fund a "world class campaign." At one point, Perot appeared to have a chance to win the presidency. Polls in May showed him in second place nationally behind President Bush and winning some Southern and Western states outright.

As Perot's unofficial campaign progressed, the media raised doubts about his background and grasp of government. Perot made his fortune by gaining rights to a computer accounting system for government health programs. His lobbying behind the scenes prompted the Nixon administration to drop a government battle for control of the computer system. Perot's conspiracy theories about issues such as prisoners of war in Vietnam and political opponents created the image of paranoia. When asked about details for his plans to address the budget deficit, improve government efficiency, improve U.S. trade and address foreign affairs, Perot appeared ill-informed and irritable. By summer, more people viewed Perot unfavorably than favorably.

Perot dropped out of the campaign before he had a chance to announce his entry. He said that Clinton's selection of Gore indicated that the Democrats were "getting their act together." He said his campaign would split the vote badly and send the election into the House of Representatives.

Perot resumed his campaign in the fall, blaming his temporary exit on a Republican "dirty tricks" effort to smear his family. By then the critical reporting had faded. But it was too late for Perot because his erratic behavior had driven away supporters and curious voters alike. Perot also had difficulty finding a credible running mate. His selection of retired admiral James Stockdale became the subject of parody when Stockdale appeared confused and poorly informed at a debate of vice presidential candidates.

Even though Perot had no real chance to win, his campaign was significant. He spent $60 million of his own money, mostly to purchase television advertisements. Some of the ads, dubbed "infomercials," won critical acclaim for their plain talk about the dangers of the federal budget deficit. Perot's bluntness lent credibility to his relentless attacks on Bush.

The communications revolution changed the way that candidates reached voters. Candidates appeared in settings once considered undignified for potential presidents. Television talk shows such as "Larry King Live" and "The Arsenio Hall Show," as well as radio programs like "Imus in the Morning," provided a way for candidates to bypass the establishment media. The blurred lines between news and entertainment were perhaps clearest on cable in the rock music MTV channel's ongoing coverage and interviews. New outlets were especially important for candidates facing credibility problems in mainstream media, such as Bill Clinton and insurgents Ross Perot and Jerry Brown.

Bush's campaign was on the defensive early for "dirty" campaign tactics. Democrats cited Bush's 1988 "Willie Horton" commercials—which told of a black prisoner raping a woman while out on a weekend release program—as evidence of a Republican willingness to appeal to racism and fear. Newspaper citations of the Horton campaign were greater in 1992 than 1988, suggesting that Democrats eventually got more from the ad's backlash than Republicans got from the original campaign.

Clinton parroted Perot's rhetoric about the evils of special-interest influence in Washington and promised reforms of the campaign finance system. But he also raised money aggressively. The Democrats raised $71 million in 1992, $9 million more than the Republicans.[202] Clinton's selection of moderate senator Al Gore of Tennessee as a running mate was central to his fall strategy. Gore's service in Vietnam and military expertise countered Clinton's suspect status in foreign policy. Gore's Washington experience going back to 1976 helped Clinton to compensate for lack of experience. Gore's reputation as an intellectual—he wrote an acclaimed book about the environment in 1992[203]—contrasted with Vice President Quayle's lightweight reputation.

Clinton benefited from the "year of the woman." Women supported Democratic candidates in greater numbers than men since the Republican Party dropped its support for the Equal Rights Amendment and abortion rights in 1980. But the Democrats could not exploit the "gender gap" until 1992. The galvanizing issue was the allegation that Clarence Thomas, Bush's appointee to the Supreme Court, had sexually harassed a former colleague named Anita Hill. Women were outraged with the Senate Judiciary Committee's handling of the matter and feminist groups mobilized to increase female representation in politics. The issue put President Bush on the defensive, while Clinton rallied liberals and libertarians alike with his calls for equal opportunity and abortion rights.

The Republican convention in Houston was a turning point. Strategists decided to shore up Bush's right-wing support and raise doubts about Clinton's character. The party's platform committee was dominated by the right-wing Christian Coalition. Speeches by Patrick Buchanan, Pat Robertson and Marilyn Quayle, questioning the Democrats' patriotism and raising the specter of a rollback of civil liberties, played badly. Bush's lost convention opportunity was apparent in the meager 3 percent "bounce" in poll support, compared with Clinton's 17-to-20-percent increase.[204]

Clinton ran a sophisticated campaign, coordinated from the "War Room" in Little Rock. Strategists led by James Carville choreographed every aspect of the campaign, from television commercials to talk-show appearances to speechwriting to the bus tours of small towns. The campaign professionals were especially adept at answering charges from the opposition. When Bush attacked, Clintonites issued instant, detailed responses. The quick response prevented Bush's charges from dominating the news cycle.

The Bush-Quayle fall campaign was erratic. Early on, it focused on "family values," critiquing the Democrats as elitists out of touch with ordinary people. Then Bush used the powers of incumbency by announcing billions of dollars in grants to different states. All along, Bush criticized Clinton's character and experience. The personal attacks often appeared shrill; at one point, he called Clinton and Gore "bozos" and said "my dog Millie" would be better at foreign policy. Bush criticized Clinton's visit to the Soviet Union as a student and suggested that he wanted to import British-style socialism to the United States.

Bush's own credibility came under fire in the campaign's final days when a special prosecutor indicted former defense secretary Caspar Weinberger and released a memorandum that indicated Bush had participated in the Iran-contra scandal more more actively than he had acknowledged.

The Clinton-Gore ticket gave the Democrats a strong base in the Border states to build on. With Arkansas and Tennessee strongly in the Democratic camp, the Democrats could build outward into the old Confederacy (Louisiana, Kentucky, Georgia), north into industrial states (Illinois, Ohio, Michigan) and west and north into farm states (Iowa, Wisconsin, Minnesota). Democrats consistently lost those states in presidential elections in the past generation, despite strong support in congressional and statewide races.

The Democrats also built on their core of support in the Northeast (winning all the states from Maine to Virginia) and capitalized on disgruntlement with Bush in the West (California, Washington, Oregon, Nevada, Montana, Colorado, New Mexico, Hawaii). That was enough to "pick" the Republican "lock" on the Electoral College.

Clinton took only 43 percent of the vote but won 370 electoral votes, compared with Bush's 38 percent and 168 electoral votes. Perot's 19 percent share of the vote did not win any states.

The hard anti-incumbent mood of the electorate, stoked by Perot, helped to produce the highest voter turnout since 1960. Some 55 percent of eligible voters participated in the election. That participation rate was a far cry from rates of other countries and earlier periods in U.S. history. But it seemed to stem, momentarily, the apathy and resignation of American politics.

## Notes

1. Quoted in A. James Reichley, *The Life of the Parties: A History of American Political Parties* (New York: The Free Press, 1992), 17.
2. Richard P. McCormick, *The Presidential Game: The Origins of American Presidential Politics* (New York: Oxford University Press, 1982), chap. 1.
3. Quoted in McCormick, 33-34.
4. Reichley, *Life of the Parties,* 42.
5. Quoted in Reichley, 49.
6. Robert J. Dinkin, *Campaigning in America: A History of Election Practices* (New York: Greenwood Press, 1989), 18.
7. Roy F. Nichols, *The Invention of the American Political Parties* (New York: Macmillan, 1967), 192.
8. Quoted in Bruce L. Felkner, *Political Mischief: Smear, Sabotage, and Reform in U.S. Elections* (New York: Praeger, 1992), 31.
9. Dinkin, *Campaigning in America,* 15, 18.
10. Edward Stanwood, *A History of the Presidency* (Boston: Houghton Mifflin, 1898), 63.
11. Quoted in John F. Hoadley, *Origins of American Party Politics, 1789-1803* (Lexington: University Press of Kentucky, 1986), 191.
12. Quoted in T. Harry Williams, *The History of American Wars: From Colonial Times to World War I* (New York: Alfred A. Knopf, 1981), 134.
13. Quoted in Stanwood, *A History of the Presidency,* 110.
14. Matthew A. Crenson, *The Federal Machine* (Baltimore: Johns Hopkins University Press, 1971), 11-30.
15. Jackson biographer Robert V. Remini explains the nickname "Old Hickory." In an arduous, five-hundred-mile march, Jackson gave his three horses to wounded soldiers and marched on foot with his troops to give them moral support. The soldiers serving under him agreed that their general was as tough as hickory. "Not much later," Remini writes, "they started calling him 'Hickory' as a sign of their respect and regard; then the affectionate 'Old' was added to give Jackson a nickname ... that admirably served him thereafter throughout his military and political wars" (Robert V. Remini, *Andrew Jackson* [New York: Harper and Row, 1969], 54).
16. Quoted in Arthur M. Schlesinger, Jr., *The Age of Jackson* (New York: New American Library, 1945), 34.
17. *Guide to Congress,* 2d ed. (Washington, D.C.: Congressional Quarterly Inc., 1982), 613.
18. Russell L. Hanson, *The Democratic Imagination in America: Conversations with Our Past* (Princeton, N.J.: Princeton University Press, 1985), 125.
19. Eugene H. Roseboom, *A History of Presidential Elections* (New York: Macmillan, 1970), 106.
20. Quoted in Schlesinger, *Jackson,* 55.
21. Estimates of vote totals vary, especially in the years before standardized methods of balloting. Discrepancies developed because of disputes about stuffing ballot boxes, the eligibility of some voters, absentee ballots, and simple counting and reporting difficulties in the pre-media age.
22. Quoted in Roseboom, *Presidential Elections,* 112.
23. Hanson, *Democratic Imagination,* 54-120.
24. Quoted in Hanson, 140-141.
25. Hanson, 136.
26. See Albert O. Hirschman, *Exit, Voice, and Loyalty* (Cambridge: Harvard University Press, 1970).
27. Hanson, *Democratic Imagination,* 138.
28. Richard P. McCormick, "Political Development and the Second Party System," in *The American Party Systems: Stages of Development,* ed. William Nisbet Chambers and Walter Dean Burnham (New York: Oxford University Press, 1967), 102.
29. Quoted in Paul Taylor, *See How They Run: Electing a President in the Age of Mediaocracy* (New York: Alfred A. Knopf, 1991), 4.
30. James L. Sundquist, *Dynamics of the Party System,* rev. ed. (Washington, D.C.: Brookings, 1983), 51.
31. Roseboom, *Presidential Elections,* 143.
32. Quoted in Richard Hofstadter, *The American Political Tradition* (New York: Vintage, 1948), 113.
33. Ibid.
34. Quoted in Hanson, *Democratic Imagination,* 176.
35. Quoted in Roseboom, *Presidential Elections,* 177-181.
36. Paul N. Angle, ed., *The Lincoln Reader* (New York: Pocket Books, 1954), 523.
37. Ibid., 531.
38. Roseboom, *Presidential Elections,* 201.
39. Eric Foner, *Reconstruction: America's Unfinished Revolution, 1863-1877* (New York: Harper and Row, 1988).
40. Quoted in William S. McFeely, *Grant* (New York: Norton, 1981), 283.
41. McFeely, 288-289.
42. Quoted in McFeely, 381.
43. Bernhard Bailyn et al., *The Great Republic: A History of the American People* (Boston: Little, Brown, 1977), 802.
44. C. Vann Woodward, *Reunion and Reaction* (New York: Doubleday Anchor Books, 1951).
45. Quoted in Kenneth M. Stampp, *The Era of Reconstruction, 1865-1877* (New York: Vintage, 1965), 210-211.
46. Michael Nelson, "A Short, Ironic History of American National Bureaucracy," *Journal of Politics* 44 (Winter 1982): 747-777.
47. Roseboom, *Presidential Elections,* 264.
48. Quoted in Harry Thurston Peck, *Twenty Years of the Repub-*

tional Bureaucracy," *Journal of Politics* 44 (Winter 1982): 747-777.

47. Roseboom, *Presidential Elections*, 264.
48. Quoted in Harry Thurston Peck, *Twenty Years of the Republic, 1885-1905* (New York: Dodd, Mead, 1906), 20.
49. Michael E. McGerr, *The Decline of Popular Politics: The American North, 1865-1928* (New York: Oxford University Press, 1986), 82-106.
50. Quoted in Peck, *Twenty Years of the Republic*, 41.
51. Ibid., 78.
52. Ibid., 144.
53. Ibid., 169.
54. Roseboom, *Presidential Elections*, 290.
55. Bailyn et al., *Great Republic*, 786.
56. Sundquist, *Party System*, 107.
57. For a concise account of the machine-reform struggle, see Dennis R. Judd, *The Politics of American Cities* (Boston: Little, Brown, 1984), 50-110.
58. See David Montgomery, *The Fall of the House of Labor* (New York: Cambridge University Press, 1987).
59. Sundquist, *Party System*, 116-118.
60. Quoted in Sundquist, 143, 152.
61. Hofstadter, *American Political Tradition*, 187.
62. Sundquist, *Party System*, 149-152.
63. Hofstadter, *American Political Tradition*, 192-193.
64. See "William Jennings Bryan, Cross of Gold Speech," in *Great Issues in American History: From Reconstruction to the Present Day, 1864-1969*, ed. Richard Hofstadter (New York: Vintage, 1969), 166-173.
65. Jasper B. Shannon, *Money and Politics* (New York: Random House, 1959), 30-32.
66. Sundquist, *Party System*, 158.
67. Ibid., 169; for a general discussion of the 1896 election's resulting realignment, see pp. 160-169.
68. E. E. Schattschneider, *The Semisovereign People* (Hinsdale, Ill.: Dryden Press, 1975), 76-77.
69. Quoted in Edmund Morris, *The Rise of Theodore Roosevelt* (New York: Ballantine, 1979), 718.
70. See Gabriel Kolko, *The Triumph of Conservatism* (New York: Free Press, 1963).
71. Sundquist, *Party System*, 176.
72. See Alpheus I. Mason, *Bureaucracy Convicts Itself* (New York: Viking Press, 1941); and James Penick, Jr., *Progressive Politics and Conservation* (Chicago: University of Chicago Press, 1968).
73. Quoted in August Heckscher, *Woodrow Wilson* (New York: Charles Scribner's Sons, 1991), 231-232.
74. Hecksher, 259.
75. J. Leonard Bates, *The United States, 1898-1928* (New York: McGraw-Hill, 1976), 187.
76. Roseboom, *Presidential Elections*, 384.
77. John L. Shover, ed., *Politics of the Nineteen Twenties* (Waltham, Mass.: Ginn-Blaisdell, 1970), 148.
78. Quoted in Shover, 4.
79. Shover, 12.
80. Ibid., 10.
81. James David Barber, *The Pulse of Politics* (New York: Norton, 1980), 239.
82. Quoted in William E. Leuchtenberg, *Franklin D. Roosevelt and the New Deal* (New York: Harper and Row, 1963), 13.
83. Quoted in Frank Friedel, *Franklin D. Roosevelt: The Triumph* (Boston: Little, Brown, 1956), 248-249.
84. Barber, *Pulse of Politics*, 243.
85. Quoted in Barber, 244.
86. Barber, 238.
87. Hofstadter, *American Political Tradition*, 332.
88. Barber, *Pulse of Politics*, 244.
89. See Robert Lekachman, *The Age of Keynes* (New York: Random, 1966).
90. Schattschneider argues in *The Semisovereign People* that the key element of any conflict is the extent to which the protagonists are able to control how many people get involved. Every "scope of conflict" has a bias. The size of the group involved in the conflict is almost always open to change. Schattschneider writes: "A look at political literature shows that there has indeed been a long-standing struggle between the conflicting tendencies toward the privatization and socialization of conflict" (p. 7). The New Deal was a stage of socialization of conflict.
91. Everett Carll Ladd, Jr., and Charles D. Hadley, *Transformations of the American Party System* (New York: Norton, 1978), 86.
92. Ibid., 43.
93. Ibid., 46.
94. Ibid., 64-74, 112; Sundquist, *Party System*, 214-224.
95. Sundquist, *Party System*, 217.
96. Ladd and Hadley, *American Party System*, 82.
97. Ibid., 58-59.
98. Ibid., 63.
99. Samuel H. Beer, "Liberalism and the National Interest," *The Public Interest*, no. 1 (Fall 1966): 81.
100. Theodore J. Lowi, *The End of Liberalism* (New York: Norton, 1969). See also Hanson, *Democratic Imagination*, 257-292.
101. Greg Mitchell, *The Campaign of the Century: Upton Sinclair's Race for Governor of California and the Birth of Modern Media Politics* (New York: Random House, 1992).
102. James MacGregor Burns, *Roosevelt: The Lion and the Fox* (New York: Harcourt, Brace, and World, 1956), 282-283.
103. Quoted in Roseboom, *Presidential Elections*, 447.
104. Burns, *Roosevelt*, 269-271.
105. Quoted in Burns, 282-283.
106. Burns, 300.
107. Quoted in Burns, 427.
108. Quoted in James David Barber, *The Pulse of Politics* (New York: W. W. Norton, 1980) tells the story behind the Willkie movement and the role played by Henry R. Luce, the founder of Time, Inc.
109. See Lekachman, *Age of Keynes*, esp. chaps. 5 and 6.
110. Quoted in Roseboom, *Presidential Elections*, 483.
111. Quoted in William E. Leuchtenberg, *In the Shadow of F.D.R.: From Harry Truman to Ronald Reagan* (Ithaca, N.Y.: Cornell University Press, 1983), 1-2.
112. Leuchtenberg, 15.
113. Quoted in Leuchtenberg, 21.
114. V. O. Key, *Southern Politics in State and Nation* (Knoxville: University of Tennessee Press, 1984), 649.
115. Ibid., 330-344.
116. Barber, *Pulse of Politics*, 50.
117. Nelson W. Polsby and Aaron Wildavsky, *Presidential Elections* (New York: Scribner's, 1984), 205-206.
118. Quoted in Barber, *Pulse of Politics*, 61.
119. Angus Campbell, Gerald Gurin, and Warren E. Miller, *The American Voter* (New York: Wiley, 1960), 532.
120. Richard Neustadt, *Presidential Power* (New York: Wiley, 1980), 10, 12-14, 16, 18, 19, 22-25, 43, 67-68, 178.
121. Quoted in Garry Wills, *Nixon Agonistes* (New York: New American Library, 1969), 91.
122. Fred Greenstein, *The Hidden-Hand Presidency* (New York: Basic Books, 1982).
123. Quoted in Barber, *Pulse of Politics*, 269.
124. Eric F. Goldman quipped, "The returns, as the gangsters said, made even Alf Landon look good" (*The Crucial Decade* [New York: Vintage, 1960], 326).
125. The elder Kennedy always planned for his sons to enter national politics. He originally pushed his eldest son, Joseph, Jr., who died in combat in World War II. John was next; he ran for Congress in 1946. Robert, the third Kennedy son, served as an aide to Sen. Joseph McCarthy before managing John's 1960 presidential campaign and serving as his attorney general. Edward, the youngest, worked on the 1960 campaign and won a Senate seat in 1962.
126. Quoted in Merle Miller, *Plain Speaking* (New York: Berkley, 1974), 199.
127. Theodore H. White, *The Making of the President 1960* (New York: Atheneum, 1961), 114-116.
128. Quoted in White, 128.

129. White, 130.

130. Ibid., 198-204.

131. Arthur M. Schlesinger, Jr., *Robert F. Kennedy and His Times* (Boston: Houghton Mifflin, 1978), 193.

132. Henry Fairlie, *The Kennedy Promise* (New York: Dell, 1972), 30-31.

133. White, *Making of the President 1960*, 329.

134. Ibid., 327.

135. Richard M. Nixon, *Six Crises* (Garden City, N.Y.: Doubleday, 1962), 412.

136. White, *Making of the President 1960*, 397-401.

137. Sen. Barry Goldwater, letter to the author, January 25, 1988.

138. The Warren Commission, appointed by Johnson, concluded that Oswald acted alone, but Oswald himself was killed before he had a chance to give full testimony. Many experts dispute the Warren Commission conclusion.

139. The Kennedy assassination fomented passage of the 25th Amendment, which provides for a more orderly system of replacement. Previously, when a vice president ascended to the White House after the death or removal of a president, the vice presidency was left vacant. The amendment provides for presidential appointment of a vice president to fill the vacant spot. It also provides for at least temporary replacement of the president in the case of disability. The latter provision developed out of a concern that the country could have become leaderless had Kennedy been physically or mentally impaired but not killed.

140. Quoted in Barber, *Pulse of Politics*, 167.

141. Thomas Ferguson and Joel Rogers, *Right Turn: The Decline of the Democrats and the Future of American Politics* (New York: Hill and Wang, 1986), 53.

142. Quoted in Theodore H. White, *The Making of the President 1964* (New York: New American Library, 1965), 261.

143. Ibid., 353.

144. The central importance of economic conditions to electoral politics is widely documented. See, for example, Stanley Kelley, Jr., *Interpreting Elections* (Princeton, N.J.: Princeton University Press, 1983); Edward R. Tufte, *Political Control of the Economy* (Princeton, N.J.: Princeton University Press, 1978); and Angus Campbell, Gerald Gurin, and Warren E. Miller, *The American Voter*. On the link between economic conditions and the 1964 election, see Kelley, *Interpreting Elections*, 194.

145. Stanley Karnow, *Vietnam: A History* (New York: Viking, 1983), 358.

146. Ibid., 362.

147. Quoted in Karnow, 395.

148. Quoted in James David Barber, *The Presidential Character* (Englewood Cliffs, N.J.: Prentice-Hall, 1972), 34.

149. Karnow, *Vietnam*, 403.

150. Ibid., 479.

151. David Halberstam, *The Best and the Brightest* (New York: Random, 1969).

152. Sundquist, *Party System*, 384.

153. Ibid., 383.

154. The administration plank supported a bombing halt only when it "would not endanger the lives of our troops in the field," did not call for a reduction in search-and-destroy missions or a withdrawal of troops until the end of the war, and advocated a new government in Saigon only after the war had ended. The minority plank, drafted by McCarthy and McGovern, called for an immediate halt to the bombing, reduction of offensive operations in the South Vietnamese countryside, a negotiated troop withdrawal, and encouragement of the South Vietnamese government to negotiate with Communist insurgents. After nearly three hours of debate, the minority plank was defeated, 1,567-3/4 to 1,041-1/4.

155. White, *Making of the President 1968*, 371.

156. Quoted in Roseboom, *Presidential Elections*, 603.

157. See Russell Baker, *The Next President* (New York: Dell, 1968).

158. Quoted in David Broder, "The Story That Still Nags at Me," *Washington Monthly*, February 1987, 29-32; see also White, *Making of the President 1972*, 82.

159. White, *Making of the President 1972*, 129.

160. Quoted in White, *Making of the President, 1972*, 207.

161. On the politics of the period, see Sundquist, *Party System*, 393-411; and Theodore H. White, *America in Search of Itself* (New York: Harper and Row, 1981). Good accounts of the Watergate scandal include Theodore H. White, *Breach of Faith* (New York: Atheneum, 1975); Jonathan Schell, *The Time of Illusion* (New York: Knopf, 1976); and Lewis Chester et al., *Watergate* (New York: Ballantine, 1973).

162. See Bruce Odes, ed., *From: The President: Richard Nixon's Secret Files* (New York: Harper and Row, 1989).

163. Seymour Hersch, "The Pardon," *Atlantic*, August 1983, 55-78.

164. David J. Vogler, *The Politics of Congress* (Boston: Allyn and Bacon, 1977), 15-20, 25-26, 34, 147-155, 243-245.

165. For a good account of Jimmy Carter's 1976 Iowa victory, see Hugh Winebrenner, *The Iowa Precinct Caucuses* (Ames: University of Iowa Press, 1987), 67-93.

166. Jules Witcover, *Marathon* (New York: Viking, 1977), 274-288.

167. Ibid., 545-560.

168. Responding to a question during a debate, Ford said: "There is no Soviet domination of Eastern Europe, and there never will be under a Ford administration. . . . I don't believe . . . that the Yugoslavians consider themselves dominated by the Soviet Union. I don't believe that the Rumanians consider themselves dominated by the Soviet Union. I don't believe that the Poles consider themselves dominated by the Soviet Union" (Quoted in Witcover, 597, 598).

169. See Gary Sick, *October Surprise: America's Hostages in Iran and the Election of Ronald Reagan* (New York: Times Books, 1992).

170. Richard Harwood, ed., *The Pursuit of the Presidency 1980* (New York: Berkley, 1980), 305-307.

171. Thomas Byrne Edsall, *The New Politics of Inequality* (New York: Norton, 1984), 77-78.

172. Thomas Ferguson and Joel Rogers, *Right Turn* (New York: Hall and Wang, 1986), 26.

173. Rep. Shirley Chisholm of Brooklyn, New York, was the first black to seek a major-party nomination. Her participation in the 1972 Democratic primaries won 151 delegates.

174. Geraldine Ferraro, with Linda Bird Francke, *Ferraro: My Story* (New York: Bantam, 1985), 164.

175. Paul R. Abramson, John H. Aldrich, and David W. Rohde, *Change and Continuity in the 1984 Elections*, rev. ed. (Washington, D.C.: CQ Press, 1986), 58.

176. V. O. Key, Jr., "A Theory of Critical Elections," *Journal of Politics* 17 (February 1955): 3-18.

177. Abramson, Aldrich, and Rohde, *Change and Continuity*, 286-287.

178. Michael Barone and Grant Ujifusa, *The Almanac of American Politics: 1984* (Washington, D.C.: National Journal, 1983), xiv. See also Ladd and Hadley, *American Party System*, 237-249.

179. George Gilder, *Wealth and Poverty* (New York: Basic Books, 1980). Another prominent supply-side tract is Jude Wanniski, *The Way the World Works* (New York: Basic Books, 1978). A sympathetic summary of the whole movement can be found in Robert Craig Paul, *The Supply-Side Revolution* (Cambridge, Mass.: Harvard University Press, 1984).

180. Ferguson and Rogers, *Right Turn*, 86-88, n. 245.

181. Garry Wills, *Reagan's America: Innocents at Home* (Garden City, N.Y.: Doubleday, 1987), 387.

182. Quoted in Wills, 385.

183. Taylor, *See How They Run*, 76.

184. Also that year, two Supreme Court nominees, Robert H. Bork and Douglas H. Ginsburg, failed to win Senate confirmation. Bork lost because of his views on a wide variety of social issues, but many criticisms focused on his personality. Ginsburg withdrew from consideration after revelations that he had smoked marijuana as a student and law school professor.

185. Barbara Norrander, *Super Tuesday: Regional Politics and Presidential Primaries* (Lexington: University Press of Kentucky, 1992), 101.

**341**

186. In the 12 days after Bush picked Quayle, ABC, CBS, and NBC aired 93 stories about him — more than Michael Dukakis received during the whole primary season. Two-thirds of the stories were negative. See Taylor, 162.

187. Quoted in Nelson W. Polsby and Aaron Wildavsky, *Presidential Elections: Contemporary Strategies of American Electoral Politics*, 8th. ed. (New York: Basic Books, 1991), 248.

188. Quayle did not meet the requirements set for political science majors and failed the first general examination at DePauw University in Indiana. He also failed to gain admission to law school under the usual application procedure. A study of Quayle's congressional career concludes that Quayle had no policy achievements in the House of Representatives but mastered some policy issues in the Senate. See Anthony Lewis, "The Intimidated Press," *New York Times*, January 19, 1989, 27, and Richard F. Fenno, Jr., *The Making of a Senator: Dan Quayle* (Washington, D.C.: CQ Press, 1988).

189. Sidney Blumenthal, *Pledging Allegiance: The Last Campaign of the Cold War* (New York: HarperCollins, 1990), 317.

190. See Walter Dean Burnham, "The Legacy of George Bush: Travails of an Understudy," in Gerald M. Pomper, ed., *The Election of 1992* (Chatham, N.J.: Chatham House Publishers, 1993), 1-38.

191. Michael Duffy and Dan Goodgame, *Marching in Place: The Status Quo Presidency of George Bush* (New York: Simon and Schuster, 1992), 267-268.

192. Quoted in Michael Nelson, "The Presidency: Clinton and the Cycle of Politics and Policy," in *The Elections of 1992*, ed. Michael Nelson (Washington, D.C.: CQ Press, 1993), 144.

193. Paul J. Quirk and Jon K. Dalager, "The Election: A 'New Democrat' and a New Kind of Presidential Campaign," *Elections of 1992*, ed. Nelson, 61.

194. The unofficial manifesto of this movement is George F. Will, *Restoration: Congress, Term Limits, and the Recovery of Deliberative Democracy* (New York: Free Press, 1993).

195. Perot's rescue of employees from Tehran during the 1979 Iranian revolution, for example, resulted in a bestselling book—Ken Follett's *On Wings of Eagles* (New York: William Morrow, 1983)—and a made-for-TV movie. Earlier he founded a national organization to support President Nixon's Vietnam policy. Later his company's merger with General Motors provoked a public dispute that cast him as the problem solver and G.M. officials as entrenched bureaucrats.

196. Ryan J. Barilleaux and Randall E. Adkins, "The Nominations: Process and Patterns," in Nelson, ed., *Elections of 1992*, 38-39.

197. See David Osborne and Ted Gaebler, *Reinventing Government: How the Entreprenurial Spirit is Transforming the Public Sector* (Reading, Mass.: Addison-Wesley, 1992) for a manifesto of Clinton's approach to government reform.

198. For an excellent treatment of the importance of the middle class and suburbanism on modern American politics, see Thomas Byrne Edsall and Mary D. Edsall, *Chain Reaction: The Impact of Race, Rights, and Taxes on American Politics* (New York: W.W. Norton, 1991).

199. Barilleaux and Adkins, "The Nominations," in Nelson, ed., *Elections of 1992*, 48-49.

200. Duffy and Goodgame, *Marching in Place*.

201. *Congressional Quarterly Weekly Report* Suppements, 50, July 4, 1992, 71, and August 8, 1992, 67.

202. Daniel Hellinger and Dennis R. Judd, *The Democratic Facade* (Belmont, Calif.: Wadsworth Publishing Company, 1994), 180.

203. Al Gore, *Earth in the Balance: Ecology and the Human Spirit* (Boston: Houghton Mifflin, 1992).

204. Ross K. Barker, "Sorting Out and Suiting Up: The Presidential Nominations," in Pomper, ed., *Election of 1992*, 67.

# The Electoral College

For more than two centuries, Americans have been electing their presidents through the Electoral College. Created by the Framers of the Constitution as a compromise between electing presidents by Congress or by direct popular vote, the system has continued to function even though the United States has undergone radical transformation from an agricultural seaboard nation to a world power.

Under the Electoral College system, each state is entitled to electoral votes equal in number to its congressional delegation — that is, the number of representatives from the state, plus two for the state's two senators. Under the system as it works today, the party that receives a plurality of the popular vote in a state is virtually assured of receiving that state's electoral votes. But in the past there were variations of that procedure including choosing electors by congressional district, statewide votes for each individual elector and selection of electors by state legislatures. There also have been cases of a so-called faithless elector, who cast his or her electoral vote for the candidate of the defeated party. (Splitting of States' Electoral Votes, box, p. 350)

## Constitutional Background

The method of selecting a president was the subject of long debate at the Constitutional Convention of 1787. Several plans were proposed and rejected before a compromise solution, which was modified only slightly in later years, was adopted (Article II, Section I, Clause 2).

Facing the convention when it convened May 25 was the question of whether the chief executive should be chosen by direct popular election, by the Congress, by state legislatures or by intermediate electors. Direct election was opposed because it was felt generally that the people lacked sufficient knowledge of the character and qualifications of possible candidates to make an intelligent choice. Many delegates also feared that the people of the various states would be unlikely to agree on a single person, usually casting their votes for favorite-son candidates well known to them.

The possibility of giving Congress the power to choose the president also received consideration. This plan was rejected, however, largely because of fear that it would jeopardize the principle of executive independence. Similarly, a plan favored by many delegates, to let state legislatures choose the president, was turned down because the delegates thought the president might feel so indebted to the states as to allow them to encroach on federal authority.

Unable to agree on a plan, the convention Aug. 31 appointed a "Committee of 11" to solve the problem. On Sept. 4 it suggested a compromise under which each state would appoint presidential electors equal to the total number of its representatives and senators. The electors, chosen in a manner set forth by each state legislature, would meet in their own states and each cast votes for two persons. The votes would be counted in Congress, with the candidate receiving a majority elected president and the second-highest candidate becoming vice president.

No distinction was made between ballots for president and vice president. Moreover, the development of national political parties and the nomination of tickets for president and vice president created further confusion in the electoral system. All the electors of one party tended to cast ballots for their two party nominees. But with no distinction between the presidential and vice presidential nominees, the danger arose of a tie vote between the two. That actually happened in 1800, leading to a change in the original electoral system with ratification of the 12th Amendment in 1804.

The committee's compromise plan constituted a great concession to the less populous states, since they were assured of three votes (two for their two senators and at least one for their representative) however small their populations might be. The plan also left important powers with the states by giving complete discretion to state legislatures to determine the method of choosing electors.

---

## Sources

Petersen, Svend. *A Statistical History of the American Presidential Elections.* Westport, Conn.: Greenwood Press, 1981.

Schlesinger, Arthur M., Jr., ed. *History of American Presidential Elections.* 4 vols. New York: McGraw-Hill, 1971.

Stanwood, Edward. *History of the Presidency, 1788-1916.* 2 vols. rev. ed. New York: Kelley, 1921.

U.S. Bureau of the Census. *Historical Statistics of the United States, Colonial Times to 1970.* 2 vols. Washington, D.C.: Government Printing Office, 1975.

# U.S. Presidents and Vice Presidents

| President and Political Party | Born | Died | Age at Inauguration | Native of | Elected from | Term of Service | Vice President |
|---|---|---|---|---|---|---|---|
| George Washington (F) | 1732 | 1799 | 57 | Va. | Va. | April 30, 1789-March 4, 1793 | John Adams |
| George Washington (F) | | | 61 | | | March 4, 1793-March 4, 1797 | John Adams |
| John Adams (F) | 1735 | 1826 | 61 | Mass. | Mass. | March 4, 1797-March 4, 1801 | Thomas Jefferson |
| Thomas Jefferson (D-R) | 1743 | 1826 | 57 | Va. | Va. | March 4, 1801-March 4, 1805 | Aaron Burr |
| Thomas Jefferson (D-R) | | | 61 | | | March 4, 1805-March 4, 1809 | George Clinton |
| James Madison (D-R) | 1751 | 1836 | 57 | Va. | Va. | March 4, 1809-March 4, 1813 | George Clinton |
| James Madison (D-R) | | | 61 | | | March 4, 1813-March 4, 1817 | Elbridge Gerry |
| James Monroe (D-R) | 1758 | 1831 | 58 | Va. | Va. | March 4, 1817-March 4, 1821 | Daniel D. Tompkins |
| James Monroe (D-R) | | | 62 | | | March 4, 1821-March 4, 1825 | Daniel D. Tompkins |
| John Q. Adams (D-R) | 1767 | 1848 | 57 | Mass. | Mass. | March 4, 1825-March 4, 1829 | John C. Calhoun |
| Andrew Jackson (D) | 1767 | 1845 | 61 | S.C. | Tenn. | March 4, 1829-March 4, 1833 | John C. Calhoun |
| Andrew Jackson (D) | | | 65 | | | March 4, 1833-March 4, 1837 | Martin Van Buren |
| Martin Van Buren (D) | 1782 | 1862 | 54 | N.Y. | N.Y. | March 4, 1837-March 4, 1841 | Richard M. Johnson |
| W. H. Harrison (W) | 1773 | 1841 | 68 | Va. | Ohio | March 4, 1841-April 4, 1841 | John Tyler |
| John Tyler (W) | 1790 | 1862 | 51 | Va. | Va. | April 6, 1841-March 4, 1845 | |
| James K. Polk (D) | 1795 | 1849 | 49 | N.C. | Tenn. | March 4, 1845-March 4, 1849 | George M. Dallas |
| Zachary Taylor (W) | 1784 | 1850 | 64 | Va. | La. | March 4, 1849-July 9, 1850 | Millard Fillmore |
| Millard Fillmore (W) | 1800 | 1874 | 50 | N.Y. | N.Y. | July 10, 1850-March 4, 1853 | |
| Franklin Pierce (D) | 1804 | 1869 | 48 | N.H. | N.H. | March 4, 1853-March 4, 1857 | William R. King |
| James Buchanan (D) | 1791 | 1868 | 65 | Pa. | Pa. | March 4, 1857-March 4, 1861 | John C. Breckinridge |
| Abraham Lincoln (R) | 1809 | 1865 | 52 | Ky. | Ill. | March 4, 1861-March 4, 1865 | Hannibal Hamlin |
| Abraham Lincoln (R) | | | 56 | | | March 4, 1865-April 15, 1865 | Andrew Johnson |
| Andrew Johnson (R) | 1808 | 1875 | 56 | N.C. | Tenn. | April 15, 1865-March 4, 1869 | |
| Ulysses S. Grant (R) | 1822 | 1885 | 46 | Ohio | Ill. | March 4, 1869-March 4, 1873 | Schuyler Colfax |
| Ulysses S. Grant (R) | | | 50 | | | March 4, 1873-March 4, 1877 | Henry Wilson |
| Rutherford B. Hayes (R) | 1822 | 1893 | 54 | Ohio | Ohio | March 4, 1877-March 4, 1881 | William A. Wheeler |
| James A. Garfield (R) | 1831 | 1881 | 49 | Ohio | Ohio | March 4, 1881-Sept. 19, 1881 | Chester A. Arthur |
| Chester A. Arthur (R) | 1830 | 1886 | 50 | Vt. | N.Y. | Sept. 20, 1881-March 4, 1885 | |
| Grover Cleveland (D) | 1837 | 1908 | 47 | N.J. | N.Y. | March 4, 1885-March 4, 1889 | Thomas A. Hendricks |
| Benjamin Harrison (R) | 1833 | 1901 | 55 | Ohio | Ind. | March 4, 1889-March 4, 1893 | Levi P. Morton |
| Grover Cleveland (D) | 1837 | 1908 | 55 | | | March 4, 1893-March 4, 1897 | Adlai E. Stevenson |
| William McKinley (R) | 1843 | 1901 | 54 | Ohio | Ohio | March 4, 1897-March 4, 1901 | Garret A. Hobart |
| William McKinley (R) | | | 58 | | | March 4, 1901-Sept. 14, 1901 | Theodore Roosevelt |
| Theodore Roosevelt (R) | 1858 | 1919 | 42 | N.Y. | N.Y. | Sept. 14, 1901-March 4, 1905 | |
| Theodore Roosevelt (R) | | | 46 | | | March 4, 1905-March 4, 1909 | Charles W. Fairbanks |
| William H. Taft (R) | 1857 | 1930 | 51 | Ohio | Ohio | March 4, 1909-March 4, 1913 | James S. Sherman |
| Woodrow Wilson (D) | 1856 | 1924 | 56 | Va. | N.J. | March 4, 1913-March 4, 1917 | Thomas R. Marshall |
| Woodrow Wilson (D) | | | 60 | | | March 4, 1917-March 4, 1921 | Thomas R. Marshall |
| Warren G. Harding (R) | 1865 | 1923 | 55 | Ohio | Ohio | March 4, 1921-Aug. 2, 1923 | Calvin Coolidge |
| Calvin Coolidge (R) | 1872 | 1933 | 51 | Vt. | Mass. | Aug. 3, 1923-March 4, 1925 | |
| Calvin Coolidge (R) | | | 52 | | | March 4, 1925-March 4, 1929 | Charles G. Dawes |
| Herbert Hoover (R) | 1874 | 1964 | 54 | Iowa | Calif. | March 4, 1929-March 4, 1933 | Charles Curtis |
| Franklin D. Roosevelt (D) | 1882 | 1945 | 51 | N.Y. | N.Y. | March 4, 1933-Jan. 20, 1937 | John N. Garner |
| Franklin D. Roosevelt (D) | | | 55 | | | Jan. 20, 1937-Jan. 20, 1941 | John N. Garner |
| Franklin D. Roosevelt (D) | | | 59 | | | Jan. 20, 1941-Jan. 20, 1945 | Henry A. Wallace |
| Franklin D. Roosevelt (D) | | | 63 | | | Jan. 20, 1945-April 12, 1945 | Harry S. Truman |
| Harry S. Truman (D) | 1884 | 1972 | 60 | Mo. | Mo. | April 12, 1945-Jan. 20, 1949 | |
| Harry S. Truman (D) | | | 64 | | | Jan. 20, 1949-Jan. 20, 1953 | Alben W. Barkley |
| Dwight D. Eisenhower (R) | 1890 | 1969 | 62 | Texas | N.Y. | Jan. 20, 1953-Jan. 20, 1957 | Richard Nixon |
| Dwight D. Eisenhower (R) | | | 66 | | Pa. | Jan. 20, 1957-Jan. 20, 1961 | Richard Nixon |
| John F. Kennedy (D) | 1917 | 1963 | 43 | Mass. | Mass. | Jan. 20, 1961-Nov. 22, 1963 | Lyndon B. Johnson |
| Lyndon B. Johnson (D) | 1908 | 1973 | 55 | Texas | Texas | Nov. 22, 1963-Jan. 20, 1965 | |
| Lyndon B. Johnson (D) | | | 56 | | | Jan. 20, 1965-Jan. 20, 1969 | Hubert H. Humphrey |
| Richard Nixon (R) | 1913 | 1994 | 56 | Calif. | N.Y. | Jan. 20, 1969-Jan. 20, 1973 | Spiro T. Agnew |
| Richard Nixon (R) | | | 60 | | Calif. | Jan. 20, 1973-Aug. 9, 1974 | Spiro T. Agnew / Gerald R. Ford |
| Gerald R. Ford (R) | 1913 | | 61 | Neb. | Mich. | Aug. 9, 1974-Jan. 20, 1977 | Nelson A. Rockefeller |
| Jimmy Carter (D) | 1924 | | 52 | Ga. | Ga. | Jan. 20, 1977-Jan. 20, 1981 | Walter F. Mondale |
| Ronald Reagan (R) | 1911 | | 69 | Ill. | Calif. | Jan. 20, 1981-Jan. 20, 1985 | George Bush |
| Ronald Reagan (R) | | | 73 | | | Jan. 20, 1985-Jan. 20, 1989 | George Bush |
| George Bush (R) | 1924 | | 64 | Mass. | Texas | Jan. 20, 1989-Jan. 20, 1993 | Dan Quayle |
| Bill Clinton (D) | 1946 | | 46 | Ark. | Ark. | Jan. 20, 1993- | Albert Gore Jr. |

Abbreviations: (D) Democrat, (D-R) Democratic-Republican, (F) Federalist, (R) Republican, (W) Whig

The only part of the committee's plan that aroused serious opposition was a provision giving the Senate the right to decide presidential elections in which no candidate received a majority of electoral votes. Some delegates feared that the Senate, which already had been given treaty ratification powers and the responsibility to "advise and consent" on all important executive appointments, might become too powerful. A proposal was made and accepted to let the House of Representatives decide the winner in instances when the electors failed to give a majority of their votes to a single candidate. The interests of the small states were preserved by giving each state's delegation only one vote in the House on roll calls to elect a president.

The system adopted by the Constitutional Convention was a compromise born out of problems involved in diverse state voting requirements, the slavery problem, big-state versus small-state rivalries and the complexities of the balance of power among different branches of the government. Moreover, it was probably as close to a direct popular election as the men who wrote the Constitution thought possible and appropriate at the time.

The term *electoral college* itself does not appear in the Constitution. It was first used unofficially in the early 1800s and became the official designation for the electoral body in 1845.

### The 12th Amendment

Only once since ratification of the Constitution has an amendment been adopted that substantially altered the method of electing the president. In the 1800 presidential election, the Democratic-Republican electors inadvertently caused a tie in the Electoral College by casting equal numbers of votes for Thomas Jefferson, whom they wished to be elected president, and Aaron Burr, whom they wished to elect vice president. The election was thrown into the House, and 36 ballots were required before Jefferson was finally elected president. The 12th Amendment, ratified in 1804, sought to prevent a recurrence of this incident by providing that the electors should vote separately for president and vice president. *(Jefferson's Revenge, Election Chronology, p. 289; 12th Amendment text, Appendix, p. 1347)*

Other changes in the system evolved over the years. The authors of the Constitution, for example, had intended that each state should choose its most distinguished citizens as electors and that they would deliberate and vote as individuals in electing the president. But as strong political parties began to appear, the electors came to be chosen merely as representatives of the parties; independent voting by electors disappeared almost entirely.

# Methods of Choosing Electors

In the early years of the Republic, states used a variety of methods to select presidential electors. For the first presidential election, in 1789, four states held direct popular elections to choose their electors: Pennsylvania and Maryland (at large) as well as Virginia and Delaware (by district). In five states — Connecticut, Georgia, New Jersey, New York and South Carolina — the state legislatures were to make the choice.

New Hampshire and Massachusetts adopted a combination of the legislative and popular methods. New Hampshire held a statewide popular vote for presidential electors with the stipulation that any elector would have to win a majority of the popular vote to be elected; otherwise,

---

## Methods of Selecting Electors: Sources

Information on the methods of selecting presidential electors for the period 1789-1836 appears in several sources, and the sources in a number of instances are in conflict. Among the sources are *Historical Statistics of the United States, Colonial Times to 1970,* prepared by the Bureau of the Census with the cooperation of the Social Science Research Council, Washington, D.C.: Government Printing Office, 1975; Edward Stanwood, *A History of the Presidency, 1788-1916,* 2 vols. rev. ed. New York: Kelley, 1921; Svend Petersen, *A Statistical History of the American Presidential Elections,* Westport, Conn.: Greenwood Press, 1981; and Neal R. Peirce and Lawrence D. Longley, *The People's President: The Electoral College in American History and the Direct Vote Alternative,* New York: Simon and Schuster, 1968.

Congressional Quarterly used the Census Bureau's *Historical Statistics of the United States* as its basic source.

---

the legislature would choose. In Massachusetts the arrangement was for the voters in each congressional district to vote for the two persons they wanted to be presidential electors. From the two individuals in each district receiving the highest number of votes, the legislature, by joint ballot of both houses, was to choose one. In addition, the legislature was to choose two electors at large.

Because of a dispute between the two chambers, the New York legislature failed to choose electors. The state Senate insisted on full equality with the Assembly (lower house); that is, the Senate wanted each house to take a separate ballot and to resolve any differences between them by agreement rather than by having one house impose its will on the other. The Assembly, on the other hand, wanted a joint ballot, on which the lower house's larger numbers would prevail, or it was willing to divide the electors with the Senate. The failure to compromise cost the state its vote in the first presidential election.

The 12th and 13th states — North Carolina and Rhode Island — had not ratified the Constitution by the time the electors were chosen, and so they did not participate.

Generally similar arrangements prevailed for the election of 1792. Massachusetts, while continuing to choose electors by district, changed the system somewhat to provide for automatic election of any candidate for elector who received a majority of the popular vote. New Hampshire continued the system of popular election at large, but substituted a popular runoff election in place of legislative choice, if no candidate received a majority of the popular vote.

Besides Massachusetts and New Hampshire, electors were chosen in 1792 by popular vote in Maryland and Pennsylvania (at large) and Virginia and Kentucky (by district). State legislatures chose electors in Connecticut, Delaware, Georgia, New Jersey, New York, North Carolina, Rhode Island, South Carolina and Vermont.

By 1796 several changes had occurred. New Hampshire switched back to legislative choice for those electors who failed to receive a majority of the popular vote. Tennessee entered the Union (1796) with a unique system for choosing presidential electors: the state legislature appointed three persons in each county, who in turn chose the presidential electors. Massachusetts retained the system used in 1792. Other states chose their electors as follows: at-large popular vote: Georgia, Pennsylvania; district popular vote: Kentucky, Maryland, North Carolina, Virginia; state legislature: Connecticut, Delaware, New Jersey, New York, Rhode Island, South Carolina, Vermont.

## Political Parties and Electors: 1800

As political parties gained power, manipulation of the system of choosing electors became increasingly widespread. For example, in 1800 Massachusetts switched from popular voting to legislative selection of electors because of recent successes by the Democratic-Republican Party in that state. The Federalists, still in firm control of the legislature, sought to secure the state's entire electoral vote for its presidential candidate, native son John Adams. New Hampshire did likewise.

The Democratic-Republicans were not innocent of this kind of political maneuver. In Virginia, where that party was in control, the legislature changed the system for choosing electors from districts to a statewide at-large ballot. That way, the expected statewide Democratic-Republican majority could overcome Federalist control in some districts and garner a unanimous vote for Jefferson, the Democratic-Republican presidential candidate.

In Pennsylvania the two houses of the state legislature could not agree on legislation providing for popular ballots, the system used in the first three elections, so the legislature itself chose the electors, dividing them between the parties.

In other changes in 1800, Rhode Island switched to popular election and Georgia reverted to legislative elections. The 16 states thus used the following methods of choosing presidential electors in 1800:

● By popular vote: Kentucky, Maryland, North Carolina (by district); Rhode Island, Virginia (at large).

● By the legislature: Connecticut, Delaware, Georgia, Massachusetts, New Hampshire, New Jersey, New York, Pennsylvania, South Carolina, Tennessee (indirectly, as in 1796), Vermont.

## Trend to Winner-Take-All System

For the next third of a century, the states moved slowly but inexorably toward a standard system of choosing presidential electors — the statewide, winner-take-all popular ballot. The development of political parties resulted in the adoption of slates of electors pledged to vote for the parties' presidential candidates. Each party organization saw a statewide ballot as being in its best interest, with the hope of sweeping in all its electors and preventing the opposition group from capitalizing on local areas of strength (which could result in winning only part of the electoral vote under the districting system).

*From 1804 to 1832 the states used three basic methods of choosing presidential electors — at-large popular vote, district popular vote and election by the state legislature. The following list shows the changing methods of choosing presidential electors for each state from 1804 to 1832:*

### 1804

Popular vote, at large: New Hampshire, New Jersey, Ohio, Pennsylvania, Rhode Island, Virginia.

Popular vote, by district: Kentucky, Maryland, Massachusetts, North Carolina, Tennessee.

State legislature: Connecticut, Delaware, Georgia, New York, South Carolina, Vermont.

### 1808

Popular vote, at large: New Hampshire, New Jersey, Ohio, Pennsylvania, Rhode Island, Virginia.

Popular vote, by district: Kentucky, Maryland, North Carolina, Tennessee.

State legislature: Connecticut, Delaware, Georgia, Massachusetts, New York, South Carolina, Vermont.

### 1812

Popular vote, at large: New Hampshire, Ohio, Pennsylvania, Rhode Island, Virginia.

Popular vote, by district: Kentucky, Maryland, Massachusetts, Tennessee.

State legislature: Connecticut, Delaware, Georgia, Louisiana, New Jersey, New York, North Carolina, South Carolina, Vermont.

### 1816

Popular vote, at large: New Hampshire, New Jersey, North Carolina, Ohio, Pennsylvania, Rhode Island, Virginia.

Popular vote, by district: Kentucky, Maryland, Tennessee.

State legislature: Connecticut, Delaware, Georgia, Indiana, Louisiana, Massachusetts, New York, South Carolina, Vermont.

### 1820

Popular vote, at large: Connecticut, Mississippi, New Hampshire, New Jersey, North Carolina, Ohio, Pennsylvania, Rhode Island, Virginia.

Popular vote, by district: Illinois, Kentucky, Maine, Maryland, Massachusetts, Tennessee.

State legislature: Alabama, Delaware, Georgia, Indiana, Louisiana, Missouri, New York, South Carolina, Vermont.

### 1824

Popular vote, at large: Alabama, Connecticut, Indiana, Massachusetts, Mississippi, New Hampshire, New Jersey, North Carolina, Ohio, Pennsylvania, Rhode Island, Virginia.

Popular vote, by district: Illinois, Kentucky, Maine, Maryland, Missouri, Tennessee.

State legislature: Delaware, Georgia, Louisiana, New York, South Carolina, Vermont.

### 1828

Popular vote, at large: Alabama, Connecticut, Georgia, Illinois, Indiana, Kentucky, Louisiana, Massachusetts, Mississippi, Missouri, New Hampshire, New Jersey, North Carolina, Ohio, Pennsylvania, Rhode Island, Vermont, Virginia.

Popular vote, by district: Maine, Maryland, New York, Tennessee.

State legislature: Delaware, South Carolina.

### 1832

Popular vote, at large: All states except Maryland and South Carolina.

Popular vote, by district: Maryland.

State legislature: South Carolina.

By 1836 Maryland switched to the system of choosing its electors by statewide popular vote. This left only South Carolina selecting its electors through the state legislature. The state continued this practice through the election of

1860. Only after the Civil War was popular voting for presidential electors instituted in South Carolina.

Thus, since 1836 the statewide, winner-take-all popular vote for electors has been the almost universal practice. Exceptions include the following:

*Massachusetts, 1848.* Three slates of electors ran — Whig, Democratic, and Free Soil — none of which received a majority of the popular vote. Under the law then in force, the state legislature was to choose in such a case. It chose the Whig electors.

*Florida, 1868.* The state legislature chose the electors.

*Colorado, 1876.* The state legislature chose the electors because the state had just been admitted to the Union, had held state elections in August and did not want to go to the trouble and expense of holding a popular vote for the presidential election so soon thereafter.

*Michigan, 1892.* Republicans had been predominant in the state since the 1850s. However, in 1890 the Democrats gained control of the legislature and the governorship and enacted a districting system of choosing presidential electors in the expectation that the Democrats could carry some districts and thus some electoral votes in 1892. They were correct; the Republicans won nine and the Democrats five electoral votes that year. But the Republicans soon regained control of the state and reenacted the at-large system for the 1896 election.

*Maine, 1972.* In 1969 the Maine legislature enacted a district system for choosing presidential electors. Two of the state's four electors were selected on the basis of the statewide vote, and the other two were determined by which party carried each of the state's two congressional districts. The system is still in force.

## Historical Anomalies

The complicated and indirect system of electing the president has led to anomalies from time to time. In 1836, for example, the Whigs sought to take advantage of the electoral system by running different presidential candidates in different parts of the country. William Henry Harrison ran in most of New England, the mid-Atlantic states and the Midwest; Daniel Webster ran in Massachusetts; Hugh White of Tennessee ran in the South.

The theory was that each candidate could capture electoral votes for the Whig Party in the region where he was strongest. Then the Whig electors could combine on one candidate or, alternatively, throw the election into the House, whichever seemed to their advantage. However, the scheme did not work because Martin Van Buren, the Democratic nominee, captured a majority of the electoral vote.

Another quirk in the system surfaced in 1872. The Democratic presidential nominee, Horace Greeley, died between the time of the popular vote and the meeting of the presidential electors. The Democratic electors had no party nominee to vote for, and each was left to his own judgment. Forty-two of the 66 Democratic electors chose to vote for the Democratic governor-elect of Indiana, Thomas Hendricks. The rest of the electors split their votes among three other politicians: 18 for B. Gratz Brown of Missouri, the Democratic vice presidential nominee; two for Charles J. Jenkins of Georgia, and one for David Davis of Illinois. Three Georgia electors insisted on casting their votes for Greeley, but Congress refused to count them.

In three elections the Electoral College has chosen presidents who ran behind their opponents in the popular vote. In two of these instances — Republican Rutherford B.

Hayes in 1876 and Republican Benjamin Harrison in 1888 — the winning candidate carried a number of key states by close margins, while losing other states by wide margins. In the third instance — Democratic-Republican John Quincy Adams in 1824 — the House chose the new president after no candidate had achieved a majority in the Electoral College. *("Minority" Presidents, box, p. 417; Last of the Old Order, Election Chronology, p. 292)*

## Election by Congress

Under the Constitution, Congress has two major responsibilities relating to the election of the president and vice president. First, it is directed to receive and, in joint session, count the electoral votes certified by the states. Second, if no candidate has a majority of the electoral vote, the House of Representatives must elect the president and the Senate the vice president.

Although many of the Framers of the Constitution apparently thought that most elections would be decided by Congress, the House actually has chosen a president only twice, in 1801 and 1825. But a number of campaigns have been deliberately designed to throw elections into the House, where each state has one vote and a majority of states is needed to elect.

In modern times the formal counting of electoral votes has been largely a ceremonial function, but the congressional role can be decisive when votes are contested. The preeminent example is the Hayes-Tilden contest of 1876, when congressional decisions on disputed electoral votes from four states gave the election to Republican Hayes despite the fact that Democrat Samuel J. Tilden had a majority of the popular vote. *(Hayes-Tilden election, p. 352)* From the beginning, the constitutional provisions governing the selection of the president have had few defenders, and many efforts at Electoral College reform have been undertaken. Although prospects for reform seemed favorable after the close 1968 presidential election, the 91st Congress (1969-1971) did not take final action on a proposed constitutional amendment that would have provided for direct popular election of the president and eliminated the existing provision for contingent election by the House. Reform legislation was reintroduced in the Senate during the 94th Congress (1975-1977) and 95th Congress (1977-1979).

In addition to its role in electing the president, Congress bears responsibility in the related areas of presidential succession and disability. The 12th Amendment empowers Congress to decide what to do if the president-elect and the vice president-elect both fail to qualify by the date prescribed for commencement of their terms; it also gives Congress authority to settle problems arising from the death of candidates in cases where the election devolves upon Congress. Under the 25th Amendment, Congress has ultimate responsibility for resolving disputes over presidential disability. It also must confirm presidential nominations to fill a vacancy in the vice presidency.

### Jefferson-Burr Deadlock

The election of 1800 was the first in which the contingent election procedures of the Constitution were put to the test and the president was elected by the House.

The Federalists, a declining but still potent political force, nominated John Adams for a second term and chose Charles Cotesworth Pinckney as his running mate. A Democratic-Republican congressional caucus chose Vice President

# Presidential Election by the House

*The following rules, reprinted from Hinds' Prece-dents of the House of Representatives, were adopted by the House in 1825 for use in deciding the presidential election of 1824. They would provide a precedent for any future House election of a president, although the House could change them.*

1. In the event of its appearing, on opening all the certificates, and counting the votes given by the electors of the several States for President, that no person has a majority of the votes of the whole number of electors appointed, the same shall be entered on the Journals of this House.

2. The roll of the House shall then be called by States; and, on its appearing that a Member or Members from two-thirds of the States are present, the House shall immediately proceed, by ballot, to choose a President from the persons having the highest numbers, not ex-ceeding three, on the list of those voted for as President; and, in case neither of those persons shall receive the votes of a majority of all the states on the first ballot, the House shall continue to ballot for a President, without interruption by other business, until a President be chosen.

3. The doors of the Hall shall be closed during the balloting, except against the Members of the Senate, stenographers, and the officers of the House.

4. From the commencement of the balloting until an election is made no proposition to adjourn shall be received, unless on the motion of one State, seconded by another State, and the question shall be decided by States. The same rule shall be observed in regard to any motion to change the usual hour for the meeting of the House.

5. In balloting the following mode shall be observed, to wit:

The Representatives of each State shall be arranged and seated together, beginning with the seats at the right hand of the Speaker's chair, with the Members from the State of Maine; thence, proceeding with the Members from the States, in the order the States are usually named for receiving petitions[1] around the Hall of the House, until all are seated.

A ballot box shall be provided for each State.

The Representatives of each State shall, in the first instance, ballot among themselves, in order to ascertain the vote of their State; and they may, if necessary, appoint tellers of their ballots.

After the vote of each State is ascertained, dupli-cates thereof shall be made out; and in case any one of the persons from whom the choice is to be made shall receive a majority of the votes given, on any one balloting by the Representatives of a State, the name of that person shall be written on each of the duplicates; and in case the votes so given shall be divided so that neither of said persons shall have a majority of the whole number of votes given by such State, on any one balloting, then the word "divided" shall be written on each duplicate.

After the delegation from each State shall have ascertained the vote of their State, the Clerk shall name the States in the order they are usually named for receiving petitions; and as the name of each is called the Sergeant-at-Arms shall present to the delegation of each two ballot boxes, in each of which shall be deposited, by some Representative of the State, one of the duplicates made as aforesaid of the vote of said State, in the presence and subject to the examination of all the Members from said State then present; and where there is more than one Representative from a State, the duplicates shall not both be deposited by the same person.

When the votes of the States are thus all taken in, the Sergeant-at-Arms shall carry one of said ballot boxes to one table and the other to a separate and distinct table.

One person from each State represented in the balloting shall be appointed by the Representatives to tell off said ballots; but, in case the Representatives fail to appoint a teller, the Speaker shall appoint.

The said tellers shall divide themselves into two sets, as nearly equal in number as can be, and one of the said sets of tellers shall proceed to count the votes in one of said boxes, and the other set the votes in the other box.

When the votes are counted by the different sets of tellers, the result shall be reported to the House; and if the reports agree, the same shall be accepted as the true votes of the States; but if the reports disagree, the States shall proceed, in the same manner as before, to a new ballot.

6. All questions arising after the balloting com-mences, requiring the decision of the House, which shall be decided by the House, voting per capita, to be incidental to the power of choosing a President, shall be decided by States without debate; and in case of an equal division of the votes of States, the question shall be lost.

7. When either of the persons from whom the choice is to be made shall have received a majority of all the States, the Speaker shall declare the same, and that that person is elected President of the United States.

8. The result shall be immediately communicated to the Senate by message, and a committee of three persons shall be appointed to inform the President of the United States and the President-elect of said election.

On Feb. 9, 1825, the election of John Quincy Adams took place in accordance with these rules.

---

*1. Petitions are no longer introduced in this way. This old procedure of calling the states beginning with Maine proceeded through the original 13 states and then through the remaining states in the order of their admission to the Union.*

Jefferson for president and Burr, who had been instrumental in winning the New York legislature for the Democratic-Republicans earlier in 1800, for vice president.

The electors met in each state on December 4, with the following results: Jefferson and Burr, 73 electoral votes each; Adams, 65; Pinckney, 64; and John Jay, 1. The Federalists had lost, but because the Democratic-Republicans had neglected to withhold one electoral vote from Burr, their presidential and vice presidential candidates were tied, and the election was thrown into the House.

The lame-duck Congress, with a partisan Federalist majority, was still in office for the electoral count, and the possibilities for intrigue were only too apparent. After toying with and rejecting a proposal to block any election until March 4, when Adams' term expired, the Federalists decided to support Burr and thus elect a relatively pliant politician over a man they considered a "dangerous radical." Alexander Hamilton opposed this move. "I trust the Federalists will not finally be so mad as to vote for Burr," he wrote. "I speak with intimate and accurate knowledge of his character. His elevation can only promote the purposes of the desperate and the profligate. If there be a man in the world I ought to hate, it is Jefferson. With Burr I have always been personally well. But the public good must be paramount to every private consideration."

On Feb. 11, 1801, Congress met in joint session — with Jefferson, the outgoing vice president, in the chair — to count the electoral vote. This ritual ended, the House retired to its own chamber to elect a president. When the House met, it became apparent that Hamilton's advice had been rejected; a majority of Federalists insisted on backing Burr over Jefferson, the man they despised more. Indeed, if Burr had given clear assurances that he would run the country as a Federalist, he might have been elected. But Burr was unwilling to make those assurances; and, as one chronicler put it, "No one knows whether it was honor or a wretched indecision which gagged Burr's lips."

In all, there were 106 members of the House at the time, 58 Federalists and 48 Democratic-Republicans. If the ballots had been cast per capita Burr would have been elected, but the Constitution provided that each state should cast a single vote and that a majority of states was necessary for election.

On the first ballot Jefferson received the votes of eight states, one short of a majority of the 16 states then in the Union. Six states backed Burr. The representatives of Vermont and Maryland were equally divided and, therefore, could not cast their states' votes. By midnight of the first day of voting, 19 ballots had been taken, and the deadlock remained.

In all, 36 ballots were taken before the House came to a decision on February 17. Predictably, there were men who sought to exploit the situation for personal gain. Jefferson wrote: "Many attempts have been made to obtain terms and promises from me. I have declared to them unequivocally that I would not receive the Government on capitulation; that I would not go in with my hands tied."

The impasse was broken finally when Vermont and Maryland switched to support Jefferson. Delaware and South Carolina also withdrew their support from Burr by casting blank ballots. The final vote: 10 states for Jefferson, four (all in New England) for Burr. Jefferson became president, and Burr, under the Constitution as it then stood, automatically became vice president.

Federalist James A. Bayard of Delaware, who had played an important role in breaking the deadlock, wrote to Hamilton: "The means existed of electing Burr, but this required his cooperation. By deceiving one man (a great blockhead) and tempting two (not incorruptible), he might have secured a majority of the states. He will never have another chance of being president of the United States; and the little use he has made of the one which has occurred gives me but an humble opinion of the talents of an unprincipled man."

The Jefferson-Burr contest clearly illustrated the dangers of the double-balloting system established by the original Constitution, and pressure began to build for an amendment requiring separate votes for president and vice president. Congress approved the 12th Amendment in December 1803, and the states — acting with unexpected speed — ratified it in time for the 1804 election.

## John Quincy Adams Election

The only other time the House of Representatives elected a president was in 1825. There were many contenders in the 1824 election, but four predominated: John Quincy Adams, Henry Clay, William H. Crawford and Andrew Jackson. Crawford, secretary of the Treasury under President James Monroe, was the early frontrunner, but his candidacy faltered after he suffered an incapacitating illness in 1823.

When the electoral votes were counted, Jackson had 99, Adams 84, Crawford 41 and Clay 37. With 18 of the 24 states choosing their electors by popular vote, Jackson also led in the popular voting, although the significance of the popular vote was open to challenge. Under the 12th Amendment, the names of the three top contenders — Jackson, Adams and the ailing Crawford — were placed before the House. Clay's support was vital to either of the two front-runners.

From the start, Clay apparently intended to support Adams as the lesser of two evils. But before the House voted, a great scandal erupted. A Philadelphia newspaper published an anonymous letter alleging that Clay had agreed to support Adams in return for being made secretary of state. The letter alleged also that Clay would have been willing to make the same deal with Jackson. Clay immediately denied the charge and pronounced the writer of the letter "a base and infamous character, a dastard and a liar."

When the House met to vote, Adams was supported by the six New England states and New York and, in large part through Clay's backing, by Maryland, Ohio, Kentucky, Illinois, Missouri and Louisiana. Thus a majority of 13 delegations voted for him — the bare minimum he needed for election, since there were 24 states in the Union at the time. The election was accomplished on the first ballot, but Adams took office under a cloud from which his administration never emerged.

Jackson had believed the charges and found his suspicions vindicated when Adams, after the election, did appoint Clay as secretary of state. "Was there ever witnessed such a bare-faced corruption in any country before?" Jackson wrote to a friend. Jackson's successful 1828 campaign made much of his contention that the House of Representatives had thwarted the will of the people by denying him the presidency in 1825, even though he had been the leader in the popular and electoral votes.

## Other Anomalies

The Senate has chosen the vice president only once. That was in 1837, when Van Buren was elected president with 170 of the 294 electoral votes while his vice presidential running mate, Richard M. Johnson, received only 147 elec-

# Splitting of States' Electoral Votes . . .

Throughout the history of presidential elections, there have been numerous cases where the electoral votes of a state have been divided between two candidates. The split electoral votes occurred for a variety of reasons.

## Electoral Vote Splits, 1789-1836

Splits of a state's electoral votes cast for president before 1836 occurred for these reasons:

● For the first four presidential elections (1789-1800) held under Article II, Section 1 of the Constitution, each elector cast two votes without designating which vote was for president and which for vice president. As a result, electoral votes for each state were often scattered among several candidates. The 12th Amendment, ratified in 1804, required electors to vote separately for president and vice president.

● The district system of choosing electors, in which different candidates each could carry several districts. This system is the explanation for the split electoral votes in Maryland in 1804, 1808, 1812, 1824, 1828 and 1832; North Carolina in 1808; Illinois in 1824; Maine in 1828; and New York in 1828.

● The selection of electors by the legislatures of some states. This system sometimes led to party factionalism or political deals that resulted in the choice of electors loyal to more than one candidate. This was the cause for the division of electoral votes in New York in 1808 and 1824, Delaware in 1824 and Louisiana in 1824.

● The vote of an individual elector for someone other than his party's candidate. This happened in New Hampshire in 1820 when one Democratic-Republican elector voted for John Quincy Adams instead of the party nominee, James Monroe.

## Voting for Individual Electors

By 1836 all states except South Carolina, which selected its electors by the state legislature until after the Civil War, had established a system of statewide popular election of electors. The new system limited the frequency of electoral vote splits. Nevertheless, a few states on occasion still divided their electoral votes among different presidential candidates. This occurred because of the practice of listing on the ballot the names of all electors and allowing voters to cross off the names of any particular electors they did not like, or, alternatively, requiring voters to vote for each individual elector. In a close election, electors of different parties sometimes were chosen. An example occurred in California in 1880, when one Democratic elector ran behind the Republican thus:

| Winning Votes | Party | Losing Electors | Party |
|---|---|---|---|
| 80,443 | Democratic | 80,282 | Republican |
| 80,426 | Democratic | 80,252 | Republican |
| 80,420 | Democratic | 80,242 | Republican |
| 80,413 | Democratic | 80,228 | Republican |
| 80,348 | Republican | 79,885 | Democratic |

Other similar occurrences include the following:

*New Jersey, 1860.* Four Republican and three Douglas Democratic electors won.

*California, 1892.* Eight Democratic electors and one Republican won.

---

toral votes — 1 less than a majority. This discrepancy occurred because Van Buren electors from Virginia boycotted Johnson, reportedly in protest against his social behavior. The Senate elected Johnson, 33-16, over Francis Granger of New York, the runner-up in the electoral vote for vice president.

Although only two presidential elections actually have been decided by the House, a number of others — including those of 1836, 1856, 1860, 1892, 1948, 1960 and 1968 — could have been thrown into the House by only a small shift in the popular vote.

The threat of House election was most clearly evident in 1968, when Democrat George C. Wallace of Alabama ran as a strong third-party candidate. Wallace frequently asserted that he could win an outright majority in the Electoral College by the addition of key Midwestern and Mountain states to his hoped-for base in the South and Border states. In reality, the Wallace campaign had a narrower goal: to win the balance of power in Electoral College voting, thus depriving either major party of the clear electoral majority required for election. Wallace made it clear that he then would expect one of the major party candidates to make concessions in return for enough votes from Wallace electors to win the election. Wallace indicated that he expected the

election to be settled in the Electoral College and not in the House of Representatives. At the end of the campaign it was disclosed that Wallace had obtained written affidavits from all of his electors in which they promised to vote for Wallace "or whomsoever he may direct" in the Electoral College.

In response to the Wallace challenge, both major party candidates, Republican Richard Nixon and Democrat Hubert H. Humphrey, maintained that they would refuse to bargain with Wallace for his electoral votes. Nixon asserted that the House, if the decision rested there, should elect the popular-vote winner. Humphrey said the representatives should select "the president they believe would be best for the country." Bipartisan efforts to obtain advance agreements from House candidates to vote for the national popular-vote winner if the election should go to the House ended in failure. Neither Nixon nor Humphrey replied to suggestions that they pledge before the election to swing enough electoral votes to the popular-vote winner to ensure his election without help from Wallace.

In the end Wallace received only 13.5 percent of the popular vote and 46 electoral votes (including the vote of one Republican defector), all from Southern states. He failed to win the balance of power in the Electoral College, which he had hoped to use to wring policy concessions from

# ... Factionalism and ''Faithless Electors''

*North Dakota, 1892.* Two Fusionists (Democrats and Populists) and one Republican won. One of the Fusion electors voted for Democrat Grover Cleveland, and the other voted for Populist James B. Weaver, while the Republican elector voted for Benjamin Harrison, thus splitting the state's electoral vote three ways.

*Ohio, 1892.* Twenty-two Republicans and one Democratic elector won.

*Oregon, 1892.* Three Republicans and one Populist with Democratic support won.

*California, 1896.* Eight Republicans and one Democratic elector won.

*Kentucky, 1896.* Twelve Republicans and one Democratic elector won.

*Maryland, 1904.* Seven Democratic electors and one Republican won.

*Maryland, 1908.* Six Democratic and two Republican electors won.

*California, 1912.* Eleven Progressive and two Democratic electors won.

*West Virginia, 1916.* Seven Republicans and one Democratic elector won.

The increasing use of voting machines and straight-ticket voting — where the pull of a lever or the marking of an "X" results in automatically casting a vote for every elector — led to the decline in split electoral votes.

## 'Faithless Electors'

Yet another cause for occasional splits in a state's electoral vote is the so-called "faithless elector." Legally, electors are not bound to vote for any particular candidate; they may cast their ballots any way they wish. But in reality electors are almost always faithful to the candidate of the party with which they are affiliated.

But at times in American political history electors have broken ranks to vote for candidates not supported by their parties. In 1796 a Pennsylvania Federalist elector voted for Democratic-Republican Thomas Jefferson instead of Federalist John Adams. And some historians and political scientists claim that three Democratic-Republican electors voted for Adams. However, the fluidity of political party lines at that early date and the well-known personal friendship between Adams and at least one of the electors make the claim of their being faithless electors one of continuing controversy. In 1820 a New Hampshire Democratic-Republican elector voted for John Quincy Adams instead of the party nominee, James Monroe.

There was no further occurrence until 1948, when Preston Parks, a Truman elector in Tennessee, voted for Gov. Strom Thurmond of South Carolina, the States Rights Democratic Party (Dixiecrat) presidential nominee. Since then, there have been the following instances:

- In 1956 W. F. Turner, a Stevenson elector in Alabama, voted for a local judge, Walter B. Jones.
- In 1960 Henry D. Irwin, a Nixon elector in Oklahoma, voted for Sen. Harry F. Byrd, D-Va.
- In 1968 Dr. Lloyd W. Bailey, a Nixon elector in North Carolina, voted for George C. Wallace, the American Independent Party candidate.
- In 1972 Roger L. MacBride, a Nixon elector in Virginia, voted for John Hospers, the Libertarian Party candidate.
- In 1976 Mike Padden, a Ford elector in the state of Washington, voted for former governor Ronald Reagan of California.
- In 1988 Margaret Leach, a Dukakis elector in West Virginia, voted for Dukakis's running mate, Sen. Lloyd Bentsen of Texas.

---

one of the major party candidates. If Wallace had won a few Border states, or if a few thousand more Democratic votes had been cast in Northern states barely carried by Nixon, thus reducing Nixon's electoral vote below 270, Wallace would have been in a position to bargain off his electoral votes or to throw the election into the House for final settlement.

## Counting the Electoral Vote

Over the years Congress has mandated a variety of dates for the casting of popular votes, the meeting of the electors to cast ballots in the various states and the official counting of the electoral votes before both houses of Congress.

The Continental Congress made the provisions for the first election. On Sept. 13, 1788, it directed that each state choose its electors on the first Wednesday in January 1789. It further directed these electors to cast their ballots on the first Wednesday in February 1789.

In 1792 the Second Congress passed legislation setting up a permanent calendar for choosing electors. Allowing some flexibility in dates, the law directed that states choose their electors within the 34 days preceding the first Wednes-

day in December of each presidential election year. Then the electors would meet in their various states and cast their ballots on the first Wednesday in December. On the second Wednesday of the following February, the votes were to be opened and counted before a joint session of Congress. Provision also was made for a special presidential election in case of the removal, death, resignation or disability of both the president and vice president.

Under that system, states chose presidential electors at various times. For instance, in 1840 the popular balloting for electors began in Pennsylvania and Ohio on Oct. 30 and ended in North Carolina on Nov. 12. South Carolina, the only state still choosing presidential electors through its state legislature, appointed its electors on Nov. 26.

Congress modified the system in 1845, providing that each state choose its electors on the same day — the Tuesday next after the first Monday in November — a provision that still remains in force. Otherwise, the days for casting and counting the electoral votes remained the same.

The next change occurred in 1887, when Congress provided that electors were to meet and cast their ballots on the second Monday in January instead of the first Wednesday in December. Congress also dropped the provision for a special presidential election.

In 1934 Congress again revised the law. The new arrangements, still in force, directed the electors to meet on the first Monday after the second Wednesday in December. The ballots are opened and counted before Congress on Jan. 6 (the next day if Jan. 6 falls on a Sunday).

The Constitution states: "The President of the Senate shall, in the presence of the Senate and House of Representatives, open all the certificates, and the votes shall then be counted." It gives no guidance on disputed ballots.

Before counting the electoral votes in 1865, Congress adopted the 22nd Joint Rule, which provided that no electoral votes objected to in joint session could be counted except by the concurrent votes of both the Senate and House. The rule was pushed by congressional Republicans to ensure rejection of the electoral votes from the newly reconstructed states of Louisiana and Tennessee. Under this rule, Congress in 1873 also threw out the electoral votes of Louisiana and Arkansas and three from Georgia.

However, the rule lapsed at the beginning of 1876, when the Senate refused to readopt it because the House was under Democratic control. Thus, following the 1876 Hayes-Tilden election, when it became apparent that for the first time the outcome of an election would be determined by decisions on disputed electoral votes, Congress had no rules to guide it.

## Hayes-Tilden Contest

The 1876 campaign pitted Republican Hayes against Democrat Tilden. Early returns indicated that Tilden had been elected. He had won the swing states of Indiana, New York, Connecticut and New Jersey; those states plus his expected Southern support would give him the election. However, by the following morning it became apparent that if the Republicans could hold South Carolina, Florida and Louisiana, Hayes would be elected with 185 electoral votes to 184 for Tilden. But if a single elector in any of these states voted for Tilden, he would throw the election to the Democrats. Tilden led in the popular-vote count by more than a quarter million votes.

The situation was much the same in each of the three contested states. Historian Eugene H. Roseboom described it as follows: "The Republicans controlled the state governments and the election machinery, had relied upon the Negro masses for votes, and had practiced frauds as in the past. The Democrats used threats, intimidation, and even violence when necessary, to keep Negroes from the polls; and where they were in a position to do so they resorted to fraud also. The firm determination of the whites to overthrow carpetbag rule contributed to make a full and fair vote impossible; carpetbag hold on the state governments made a fair count impossible. Radical reconstruction was reaping its final harvest."

Both parties pursued the votes of the three states with a fine disregard for propriety or legality, and in the end double sets of elector returns were sent to Congress from all three. Oregon also sent two sets of returns. Although Hayes carried that state, the Democratic governor discovered that one of the Hayes electors was a postmaster and therefore ineligible under the Constitution, so he certified the election of the top-polling Democratic elector. However, the Republican electors met, received the resignation of their ineligible colleague, then reappointed him to the vacancy because he had in the meantime resigned his postmastership.

Had the 22nd Joint Rule remained in effect, the Democratic House of Representatives could have objected to any of Hayes' disputed votes. But since the rule had lapsed, Con-

gress had to find a new method of resolving electoral disputes. A joint committee was created to work out a plan, and the resulting Electoral Commission Law was approved by large majorities and signed into law Jan. 29, 1877 — only days before the date scheduled for counting the electoral votes.

The law, which applied only to the 1876 electoral vote count, established a 15-member commission that was to have final authority over disputed electoral votes, unless both houses of Congress agreed to overrule it. The commission was to consist of five senators, five representatives and five Supreme Court justices. Each chamber was to appoint its own members of the commission, with the understanding that the majority party would have three members and the minority two. Four justices, two from each party, were named in the bill, and these four were to select the fifth. It was expected that they would choose Justice David Davis, who was considered a political independent, but he disqualified himself when the Illinois legislature named him to a seat in the Senate. Justice Joseph P. Bradley, a Republican, then was named to the fifteenth seat. The Democrats supported his selection because they considered him the most independent of the remaining justices, all of whom were Republicans. However, he was to vote with the Republicans on every dispute and thus ensure the victory of Hayes.

The electoral count began in Congress Feb. 1 (moved up from the second Wednesday in February for this one election), and the proceedings continued until March 2. States were called in alphabetical order, and as each disputed state was reached objections were raised to both the Hayes and Tilden electors. The question was then referred to the electoral commission, which in every case voted 8-7 for Hayes. In each case, the Democratic House rejected the commission's decision, but the Republican Senate upheld it, so the decision stood.

As the count went on, Democrats in the House threatened to launch a filibuster to block resumption of joint sessions so that the count could not be completed before Inauguration Day. The threat was never carried out because of an agreement reached between the Hayes forces and Southern conservatives. The southerners agreed to let the electoral count continue without obstruction. In return Hayes agreed that, as president, he would withdraw federal troops from the South, end Reconstruction and make other concessions. The southerners, for their part, pledged to respect Negro rights, a pledge they did not carry out.

Thus, at 4 a.m. March 2, 1877, the president of the Senate was able to announce that Hayes had been elected president with 185 electoral votes, as against 184 for Tilden. Later that day Hayes arrived in Washington. The next evening he took the oath of office privately at the White House, because March 4 fell on a Sunday. His formal inauguration followed on Monday. The country acquiesced. Thus ended a crisis that could have resulted in civil war.

Not until 1887 did Congress enact permanent legislation on the handling of disputed electoral votes. The Electoral Count Act of that year gave each state final authority in determining the legality of its choice of electors and required a concurrent majority of both the Senate and House to reject any electoral votes. It also established procedures for counting electoral votes in Congress. (*Law for Counting Electoral Votes in Congress, box, p. 353*)

## Application of 1887 Law in 1969

The procedures relating to disputed electoral votes were used for the first time after the election of 1968. When Congress met in joint session Jan. 6, 1969, to count the

# Law for Counting Electoral Votes in Congress

*Following is the complete text of Title 3, section 15 of the U.S. Code, enacted originally in 1887, governing the counting of electoral votes in Congress:*

Congress shall be in session on the sixth day of January succeeding every meeting of the electors. The Senate and House of Representatives shall meet in the Hall of the House of Representatives at the hour of 1 o'clock in the afternoon on that day, and the President of the Senate shall be their presiding officer. Two tellers shall be previously appointed on the part of the Senate and two on the part of the House of Representatives, to whom shall be handed, as they are opened by the President of the Senate, all the certificates and papers purporting to be certificates of the electoral votes, which certificates and papers shall be opened, presented, and acted upon in the alphabetical order of the States, beginning with the letter A; and said tellers, having then read the same in the presence and hearing of the two Houses, shall make a list of the votes as they shall appear from the said certificates; and the votes having been ascertained and counted according to the rules in this subchapter provided, the result of the same shall be delivered to the President of the Senate, who shall thereupon announce the state of the vote, which announcement shall be deemed a sufficient declaration of the persons, if any, elected President and Vice President of the United States, and, together with a list of votes, be entered on the Journals of the two Houses. Upon such reading of any such certificate or paper, the President of the Senate shall call for objections, if any. Every objection shall be made in writing, and shall state clearly and concisely, and without argument, the ground thereof, and shall be signed by at least one Senator and one Member of the House of Representatives before the same shall be received. When all objections so made to any vote or paper from a State shall have been received and read, the Senate shall thereupon withdraw, and such objections shall be submitted to the Senate for its decision; and the Speaker of the House of Representatives shall, in like manner, submit such objections to the House of Representatives for its decision; and no electoral vote or votes from any State which shall have been regularly given by electors whose appointment has been lawfully certified to according to section 6* of this title from which but one return has been received shall be rejected, but the two Houses concurrently may reject the vote or votes when they agree that such vote or votes have not been so regularly given by electors whose appointment has been so certified. If more than one return or paper purporting to be a return from a State shall have been received by the President of the Senate, those votes, and those only, shall be counted which shall have been regularly given by the electors who are shown by the determination mentioned in section 5† of this title to have been appointed, if the determination in said section provided for shall have been made, or by such successors or substitutes, in case of a vacancy in the board of electors so ascertained, as have been appointed to fill such vacancy in the mode provided by the laws of the State; but in case there shall arise the question which of two or more of such State authorities determining what electors have been appointed, as mentioned in section 5 of this title, is the lawful tribunal of such State, the votes regularly given of those electors, and those only, of such State shall be counted whose title as electors the two Houses, acting separately, shall concurrently decide is supported by the decision of such State so authorized by its law; and in such case of more than one return or paper purporting to be a return from a State, if there shall have been no such determination of the question in the State aforesaid, then those votes, and those only, shall be counted which the two Houses shall concurrently decide were cast by lawful electors appointed in accordance with the laws of the State, unless the two Houses, acting separately, shall concurrently decide such votes not to be the lawful votes of the legally appointed electors of such State. But if the two Houses shall disagree in respect of the counting of such votes, then, and in that case, the votes of the electors whose appointment shall have been certified by the executive of the State, under the seal thereof, shall be counted. When the two Houses have voted, they shall immediately again meet, and the presiding officer shall then announce the decision of the questions submitted. No votes or papers from any other State shall be acted upon until the objections previously made to the votes or papers from any State shall have been finally disposed of.

*Section 6 provides for certification of votes by electors by state governors.*

*†Section 5 provides that if state law specifies a method for resolving disputes concerning the vote for presidential electors, Congress must respect any determination so made by a state.*

electoral votes, Sen. Edmund S. Muskie, D-Maine, and Rep. James G. O'Hara, D-Mich., joined by six other senators and 37 other representatives, filed a written objection to the vote cast by a North Carolina elector, Lloyd W. Bailey of Rocky Mount. He had been elected as a Republican but chose to vote for George Wallace and Curtis LeMay, the candidates of the American Independent party, instead of Republican Nixon and his running mate, Spiro T. Agnew.

Acting under the 1887 law, Muskie and O'Hara objected to Bailey's vote on the grounds that it was "not properly given" because a plurality of the popular votes in North Carolina were cast for Nixon-Agnew and the state's voters had chosen electors to vote for Nixon and Agnew only.

Muskie and O'Hara asked that Bailey's vote not be counted at all by Congress.

The 1887 statute stipulated that "no electoral vote or votes from any state which shall have been regularly given by electors whose appointment has been lawfully certified ... from which but one return has been received shall be rejected, but the two Houses concurrently may reject the vote or votes when they agree that such vote or votes have not been so regularly given by electors whose appointment has been so certified." The statute did not define the term "regularly given," although at the time of its adoption chief concern centered on problems of dual sets of electoral vote returns from a state, votes cast on an improper day, or votes disputed because of uncertainty about whether a state lawfully was in the Union when the vote was cast.

The 1887 statute provided that if written objection to any state's vote was received from at least one member of both the Senate and House, the two legislative bodies were to retire immediately to separate sessions, debate for two hours with a five-minute limitation on speeches, and each decide the issue by vote before resuming the joint session. The statute made clear that both the Senate and House had to reject a challenged electoral vote (or votes) for such action to prevail.

At the Jan. 6 joint session, with Senate President Pro Tempore Richard B. Russell, D-Ga., presiding, the counting of the electoral vote proceeded smoothly through the alphabetical order of states until the North Carolina result was announced, at which time O'Hara rose to announce filing of the complaint. The two houses then reassembled in joint session at which the results of the separate deliberations were announced and the count of the electoral vote by state proceeded without event. At the conclusion, Russell announced the vote and declared Nixon and Agnew elected.

# Reform Proposals

Since Jan. 6, 1797, when Rep. William L. Smith, F-S.C., introduced in Congress the first proposed constitutional amendment for reform of the Electoral College system, hardly a session of Congress has passed without the introduction of one or more resolutions of this nature. But only one — the 12th Amendment, ratified in 1804 — ever has been approved.

In recent years, public interest in a change in the Electoral College system was spurred by the close 1960 and 1968 elections, by a series of Supreme Court rulings relating to apportionment and districting and by introduction of unpledged elector systems in the Southern states.

## House Approval of Amendment

Early in 1969, President Nixon asked Congress to take prompt action on Electoral College reform. He said he would support any plan that would eliminate individual electors and distribute among the presidential candidates the electoral vote of every state and the District of Columbia in a manner more closely approximating the popular vote.

Later that year the House approved, 338-70, a resolution proposing a constitutional amendment to eliminate the Electoral College and to provide instead for direct popular election of the president and vice president. The measure set a minimum of 40 percent of the popular vote as sufficient for election and provided for a runoff election between the two top candidates for the presidency if no candidate received 40 percent. Under this plan the House of Representatives could no longer be called upon to select a president. The proposed amendment also authorized Congress to provide a method of filling vacancies caused by the death, resignation or disability of presidential nominees before the election and a method of filling post-election vacancies caused by the death of the president-elect or vice president-elect.

Nixon, who previously had favored a proportional plan of allocating each state's electoral votes, endorsed the House resolution and urged the Senate to adopt it. To become effective, the proposed amendment had to be approved by a two-thirds majority in both the Senate and House and be ratified by the legislatures of three-fourths of the states. When the proposal reached the Senate floor in September

1970, senators from small states and the South succeeded in blocking final action. The resolution was laid aside Oct. 5, after two unsuccessful efforts to cut off debate by invoking cloture.

## Carter Endorsement of Plan

Another major effort to eliminate the Electoral College occurred in 1977, when President Jimmy Carter included such a proposal in his election reform package, unveiled March 22. Carter endorsed the amendment approved by the House in 1969 to replace the Electoral College with direct popular election of the president and vice president, and provide for a runoff if no candidate received at least 40 percent of the vote. Because the Senate again was seen as the major stumbling block, the House waited to see what the Senate would do before beginning any deliberation of its own.

After several months of deadlock, the Senate Judiciary Committee approved Sept. 15 the direct presidential election plan by a 9-8 vote. But Senate opponents threatened a filibuster, and the Senate leadership decided it could not spare the time or effort to try to break it. The measure was never brought to the floor and died when the 95th Congress adjourned in 1978.

On Jan. 15, 1979, the opening day of the 96th Congress, Sen. Birch Bayh, D-Ind., began another effort to abolish the Electoral College through a constitutional amendment. In putting off action in the previous Congress, Senate leaders had agreed to try for early action in the 96th.

A proposed constitutional amendment to abolish the Electoral College and elect the president by popular vote did reach the Senate floor in July 1979. The Senate voted in favor of the measure, 51-48 — 15 votes short of the required two-thirds majority of those present and voting needed to approve a constitutional amendment.

Supporters of the resolution blamed defections by several Northern liberals for the margin of defeat. Major Jewish and black groups extensively lobbied the Northern senators, arguing that the voting strength of black and Jewish voters is maximized under the Electoral College system because both groups are concentrated in urban areas of the large electoral vote states.

# Presidential Disability

A decade of congressional concern over the question of presidential disability was eased in 1967 by ratification of the 25th Amendment to the Constitution. The amendment for the first time provided for continuity in carrying out the functions of the presidency in the event of presidential disability and for filling a vacancy in the vice presidency. The amendment was approved by the Senate and House in 1965 and took effect Feb. 10, 1967, after ratification by 38 states. *(Text, Appendix, p. 1348)* Congressional consideration of the problem of presidential disability had been prompted by President Dwight D. Eisenhower's heart attack in 1955. The ambiguity of the language of the disability clause (Article II, Section 1, Clause 5) of the Constitution had provoked occasional debate ever since the Constitutional Convention of 1787. But it never had been decided how far the term *disability* extended or who would be the judge of it.

Clause 5 provided that Congress should decide who was to succeed to the presidency if both the president and the vice president died, resigned, or became disabled. Congress enacted succession laws three times. By the Act of March 1,

1792, it provided for succession (after the vice president) of the president pro tempore of the Senate, then of the House Speaker; if those offices were vacant, states were to send electors to Washington to choose a new president.

That law stood until passage of the Presidential Succession Act of Jan. 19, 1886, which changed the line of succession to run from the vice president to the secretary of state, secretary of the Treasury and so on through the cabinet in order of rank. Sixty-one years later the Presidential Succession Act of July 18, 1947, (still in force) placed the Speaker of the House and the president pro tempore of the Senate ahead of cabinet officers in succession after the vice president.

Before ratification of the 25th Amendment, no procedures had been laid down to govern situations arising in the event of presidential incapacity or of a vacancy in the office of vice president. Two presidents had had serious disabilities — James A. Garfield, shot in 1881 and confined to his bed until he died two and a half months later, and Woodrow Wilson, who suffered a stroke in 1919. In each case the vice president did not assume any duties of the presidency for fear he would appear to be usurping the powers of that office. As for a vice presidential vacancy, the United States has been without a vice president 18 times for a total of 40 years through 1980, after the elected vice president succeeded to the presidency, died or resigned.

Ratification of the 25th Amendment established procedures that clarified these areas of uncertainty in the Constitution. The amendment provided that the vice president should become acting president under either one of two circumstances: (1) if the president informed Congress that he was unable to perform his duties, the vice president would become acting president until the president could resume his responsibilities; (2) if the vice president and a majority of the cabinet, or another body designated by Congress, found the president to be incapacitated, the vice president would become acting president until the president informed Congress that his disability had ended. Congress was given 21 days to resolve any dispute over the president's disability; a two-thirds vote of both chambers was required to overrule the president's declaration that he was no longer incapacitated.

## Vacancy in the Vice Presidency

Whenever a vacancy occurred in the office of the vice president, either by death, succession to the presidency or resignation, the president was to nominate a vice president, and the nomination was to be confirmed by a majority vote of both houses of Congress.

Within only eight years, the power of the president to appoint a new vice president under the terms of the 25th Amendment was used twice. In 1973 when Vice President Agnew resigned, President Nixon nominated Gerald R. Ford as the new vice president. Ford was confirmed by both houses of Congress and sworn in Dec. 6, 1973. On Nixon's resignation Aug. 9, 1974, Ford succeeded to the presidency, becoming the first president in American history who was elected neither to the presidency nor to the vice presidency. President Ford chose as his new vice president Nelson A. Rockefeller, former governor of New York, who was sworn in Dec. 19, 1974.

With both the president and vice president holding office through appointment rather than election, members of Congress and the public expressed concern about the power of a president to appoint, in effect, his own successor. Accordingly, Sen. John O. Pastore, D-R.I., introduced a proposed constitutional amendment Feb. 3, 1975, to provide for a special national election for president when more than one year remained in a presidential term. Hearings were held before the Senate Judiciary Subcommittee on Constitutional Amendments, but no action was taken.

## Confusion After Reagan Shooting

In the aftermath of the attempted assassination of President Ronald Reagan in 1981, there was no need to invoke the presidential disability provisions of the 25th Amendment. However, some of the public statements made by administration officials immediately after the president was shot by John W. Hinckley Jr., reflected continuing confusion over the issue of who is in charge when the president temporarily is unable to function. Soon after news of the shooting became known, the members of the Reagan cabinet gathered in the White House, ready to invoke the amendment's procedures, if necessary. Vice President George Bush was on an Air Force jet returning to Washington from Texas.

At a televised press briefing later that afternoon, Secretary of State Alexander M. Haig Jr., confirmed that Reagan was in surgery and under anesthesia. It was clear that he temporarily was unable to make presidential decisions should the occasion — such as a foreign attack or other national emergency — require them. Attempting to reassure the country, Haig stated that he was in control in the White House pending the return of Vice President Bush, with whom he was in contact.

This assertion was followed by a question from the press about who was making administration decisions. Haig responded, "Constitutionally, gentlemen, you have the president, the vice president and the secretary of state in that order, and should the president decide he wants to transfer the helm to the vice president, he will do so. He has not done that." Haig's response reflected the law in effect before the Presidential Succession Act of 1947. The law applicable in the 1981 shooting incident was the 1947 act, which specifies that the line of succession is the vice president, the Speaker of the House, the president pro tempore of the Senate and then the cabinet officials in order of rank.

# Electoral Votes for President, 1789-1992

# Sources: Electoral College Votes

Electoral votes cast for presidential candidates were listed in the *Senate Manual,* Washington, D.C., U.S. Government Printing Office, 1994, pp. 961-1008.

Total electoral votes for each state through the 1970 census were compiled from a chart of each apportionment of the House of Representatives, published in the *Biographical Directory of the United States Congress, 1774-1989,* Washington, D.C., U.S. Government Printing Office, 1989, p. 47. The source for apportionment after the 1990 census was the Bureau of the Census.

Article II, Section 1 of the Constitution gives each state a number of electors equal to the number of senators and representatives to which it is entitled.

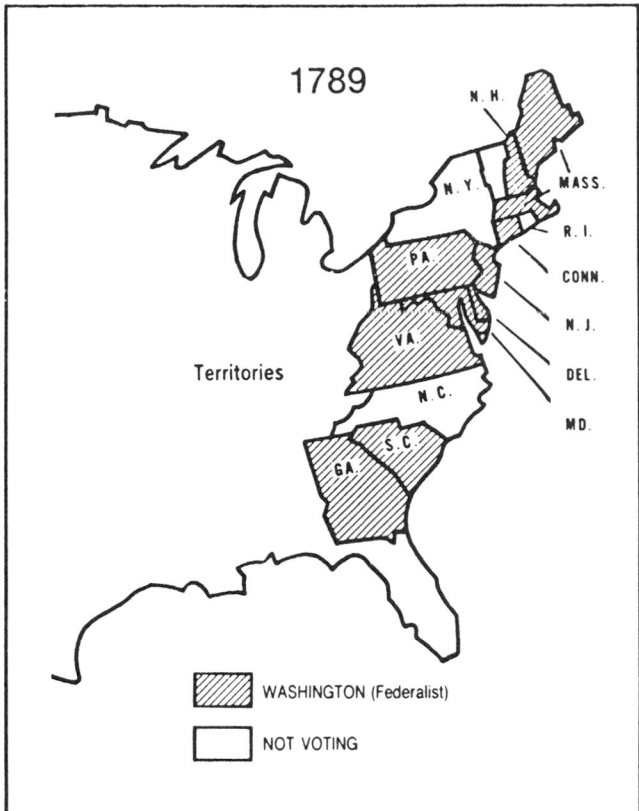

WASHINGTON (Federalist)

NOT VOTING

### Electoral Votes 1789-1992

Under Article II, Section 1, of the Constitution, each presidential elector had two votes and was required to cast each vote for a different person. The person receiving the highest number of votes from a majority of electors was elected president; the person receiving the second highest total became vice president. Since there were 69 electors in 1789, Washington's 69 votes constituted a unanimous election. After ratification of the 12th Amendment in 1804, electors were required to designate which of their two votes was for president and which was for vice president. The Electoral College tables on pages 359-410 show *all* electoral votes cast in the elections of 1798, 1792, 1796 and 1800; the charts for 1894 and thereafter show electoral votes cast only for president. For electoral votes totals for vice president, see table page 411.

| States | Electoral Votes [1] | Washington | Adams | Jay | Harrison | Rutledge | Hancock | Clinton | Huntington | Milton | Armstrong | Lincoln | Telfair |
|---|---|---|---|---|---|---|---|---|---|---|---|---|---|
| Connecticut [2] | (14) | 7 | 5 | - | - | - | - | - | 2 | - | - | - | - |
| Delaware | (6) | 3 | - | 3 | - | - | - | - | - | - | - | - | - |
| Georgia [2] | (10) | 5 | - | - | - | - | - | - | - | 2 | 1 | 1 | 1 |
| Maryland [3] | (16) | 6 | - | - | 6 | - | - | - | - | - | - | - | - |
| Massachusetts | (20) | 10 | 10 | - | - | - | - | - | - | - | - | - | - |
| New Hampshire | (10) | 5 | 5 | - | - | - | - | - | - | - | - | - | - |
| New Jersey [2] | (12) | 6 | 1 | 5 | - | - | - | - | - | - | - | - | - |
| New York [4] | (16) | - | - | - | - | - | - | - | - | - | - | - | - |
| North Carolina [5] | (14) | - | - | - | - | - | - | - | - | - | - | - | - |
| Pennsylvania [2] | (20) | 10 | 8 | - | - | - | 2 | - | - | - | - | - | - |
| Rhode Island [5] | (6) | - | - | - | - | - | - | - | - | - | - | - | - |
| South Carolina [2] | (14) | 7 | - | - | - | 6 | 1 | - | - | - | - | - | - |
| Virginia [6] | (24) | 10 | 5 | 1 | - | - | 1 | 3 | - | - | - | - | - |
| **Totals** | (182) | 69 | 34 | 9 | 6 | 6 | 4 | 3 | 2 | 2 | 1 | 1 | 1 |

1. Two votes for each elector; see text above.
2. For explanation of split electoral votes, see p. 350.
3. Two Maryland electors did not vote.
4. Not voting. For explanation, see p. 345.

5. Not voting because had not yet ratified Constitution.
6. Two Virginia electors did not vote. For explanation of split electoral votes, see p. 350.

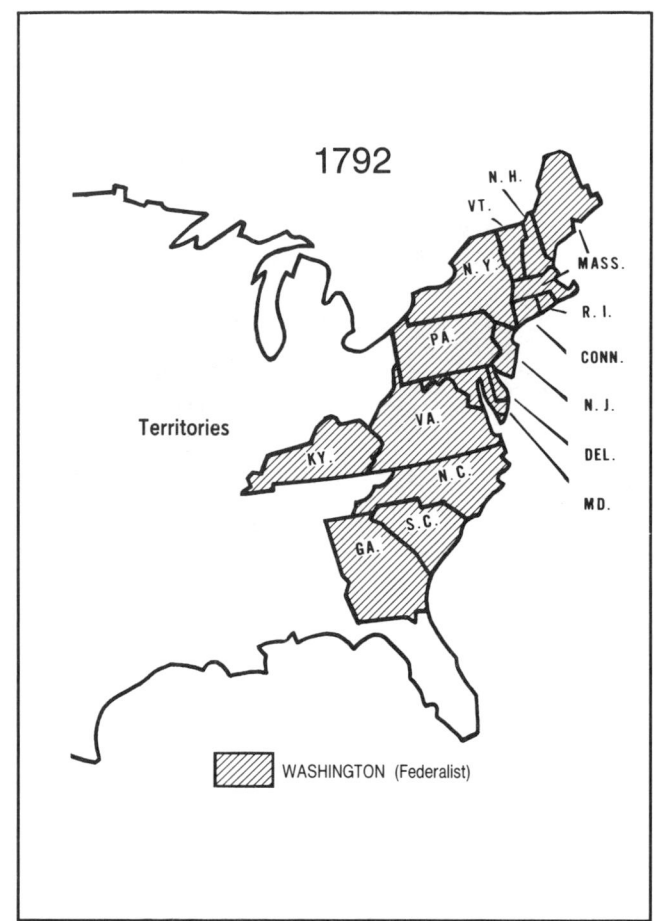

1792

WASHINGTON (Federalist)

| States | Electoral Votes [1] | Washington | Adams | Clinton | Jefferson | Burr |
|---|---|---|---|---|---|---|
| Connecticut | (18) | 9 | 9 | - | - | - |
| Delaware | (6) | 3 | 3 | - | - | - |
| Georgia | (8) | 4 | - | 4 | - | - |
| Kentucky | (8) | 4 | - | - | 4 | - |
| Maryland [2] | (20) | 8 | 8 | - | - | - |
| Massachusetts | (32) | 16 | 16 | - | - | - |
| New Hampshire | (12) | 6 | 6 | - | - | - |
| New Jersey | (14) | 7 | 7 | - | - | - |
| New York | (24) | 12 | - | 12 | - | - |
| North Carolina | (24) | 12 | - | 12 | - | - |
| Pennsylvania [3] | (30) | 15 | 14 | 1 | - | - |
| Rhode Island | (8) | 4 | 4 | - | - | - |
| South Carolina [3] | (16) | 8 | 7 | - | - | 1 |
| Vermont [2] | (8) | 3 | 3 | - | - | - |
| Virginia | (42) | 21 | - | 21 | - | - |
| **Totals** | **(270)** | **132** | **77** | **50** | **4** | **1** |

1. Two votes for each elector; see page 359.
2. Two Maryland electors and one Vermont elector did not vote.
3. For explanation of split electoral votes, see p. 350.

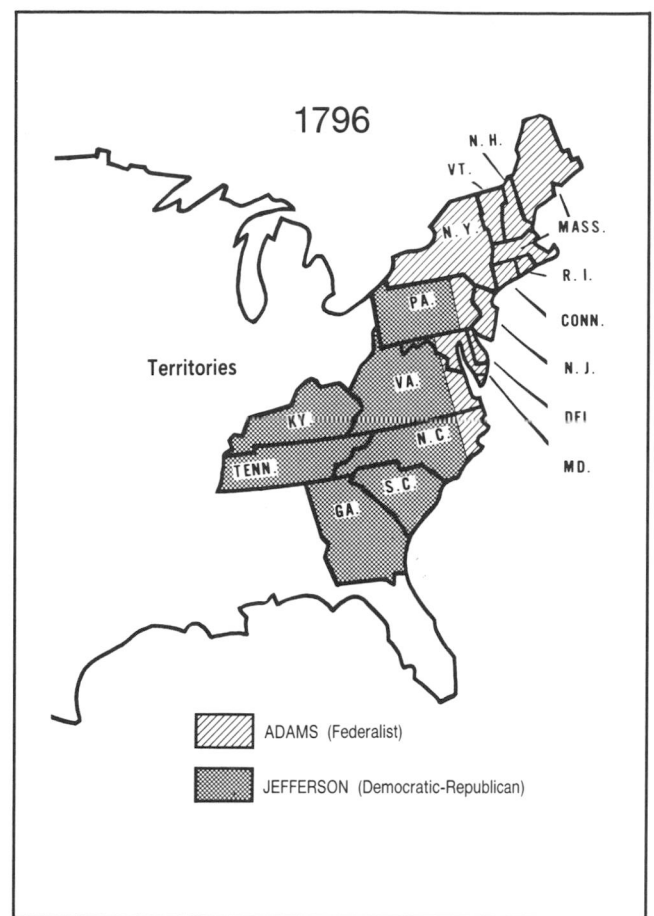

1796

Territories

ADAMS (Federalist)

JEFFERSON (Democratic-Republican)

| States | Electoral Votes [1] | J. Adams | Jefferson | T. Pinckney | Burr | S. Adams | Ellsworth | Clinton | Jay | Iredell | Henry | Johnston | Washington | C. Pinckney |
|---|---|---|---|---|---|---|---|---|---|---|---|---|---|---|
| **Connecticut** [2] | (18) | 9 | - | 4 | - | - | - | - | 5 | - | - | - | - | - |
| **Delaware** | (6) | 3 | - | 3 | - | - | - | - | - | - | - | - | - | - |
| **Georgia** | (8) | - | 4 | - | - | - | - | 4 | - | - | - | - | - | - |
| **Kentucky** | (8) | - | 4 | - | 4 | - | - | - | - | - | - | - | - | - |
| **Maryland** [2] | (20) | 7 | 4 | 4 | 3 | - | - | - | - | - | 2 | - | - | - |
| **Massachusetts** [2] | (32) | 16 | - | 13 | - | - | 1 | - | - | - | - | 2 | - | - |
| **New Hampshire** | (12) | 6 | - | - | - | - | 6 | - | - | - | - | - | - | - |
| **New Jersey** | (14) | 7 | - | 7 | - | - | - | - | - | - | - | - | - | - |
| **New York** | (24) | 12 | - | 12 | - | - | - | - | - | - | - | - | - | - |
| **North Carolina** [2] | (24) | 1 | 11 | 1 | 6 | - | - | - | - | 3 | - | - | 1 | 1 |
| **Pennsylvania** [2] | (30) | 1 | 14 | 2 | 13 | - | - | - | - | - | - | - | - | - |
| **Rhode Island** | (8) | 4 | - | - | - | - | 4 | - | - | - | - | - | - | - |
| **South Carolina** | (16) | - | 8 | 8 | - | - | - | - | - | - | - | - | - | - |
| **Tennessee** | (6) | - | 3 | - | 3 | - | - | - | - | - | - | - | - | - |
| **Vermont** | (8) | 4 | - | 4 | - | - | - | - | - | - | - | - | - | - |
| **Virginia** [2] | (42) | 1 | 20 | 1 | 1 | 15 | - | 3 | - | - | - | - | 1 | - |
| **Totals** | **(276)** | **71** | **68** | **59** | **30** | **15** | **11** | **7** | **5** | **3** | **2** | **2** | **2** | **1** |

1. *Two votes for each elector; see page 359.*
2. *For explanation of split electoral votes, see p. 350.*

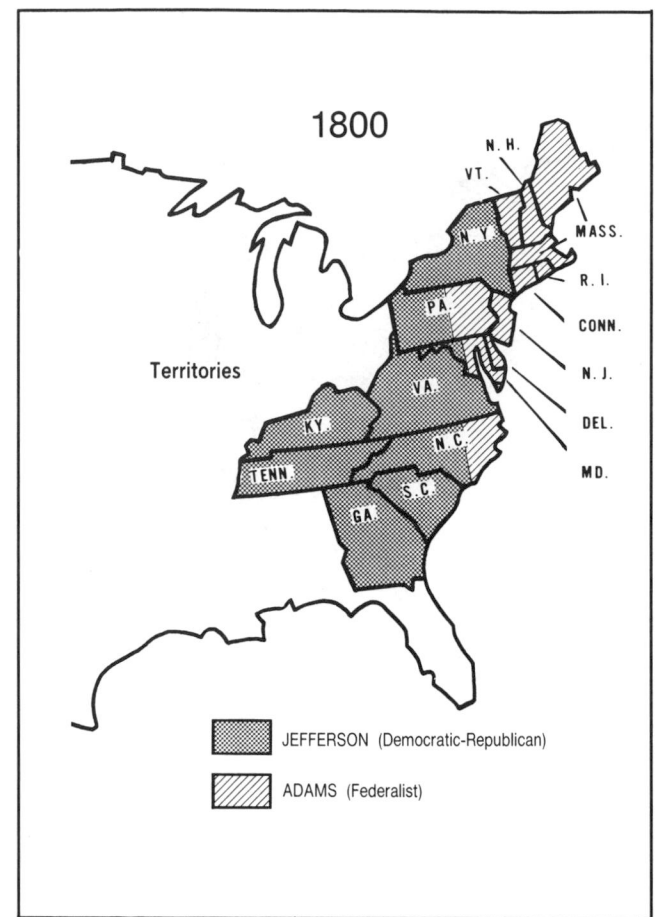

1800

JEFFERSON (Democratic-Republican)

ADAMS (Federalist)

| States | Electoral Votes [1] | Jefferson [2] | Burr [2] | Adams | Pinckney | Jay |
|---|---|---|---|---|---|---|
| Connecticut | (18) | - | - | 9 | 9 | - |
| Delaware | (6) | - | - | 3 | 3 | - |
| Georgia | (8) | 4 | 4 | - | - | - |
| Kentucky | (8) | 4 | 4 | - | - | - |
| Maryland [3] | (20) | 5 | 5 | 5 | 5 | - |
| Massachusetts | (32) | - | - | 16 | 16 | - |
| New Hampshire | (12) | - | - | 6 | 6 | - |
| New Jersey | (14) | - | - | 7 | 7 | - |
| New York | (24) | 12 | 12 | - | - | - |
| North Carolina [3] | (24) | 8 | 8 | 4 | 4 | - |
| Pennsylvania [3] | (30) | 8 | 8 | 7 | 7 | - |
| Rhode Island [3] | (8) | - | - | 4 | 3 | 1 |
| South Carolina [1] | (16) | 8 | 8 | - | - | - |
| Tennessee | (6) | 3 | 3 | - | - | - |
| Vermont | (8) | - | - | 4 | 4 | - |
| Virginia | (42) | 21 | 21 | - | - | - |
| **Totals** | **(276)** | **73** | **73** | **65** | **64** | **1** |

1. *Two votes for each elector; see page 359.*
2. *For explanation and result of tie vote, see p. 347.*
3. *For explanation of split electoral votes, see p. 350.*

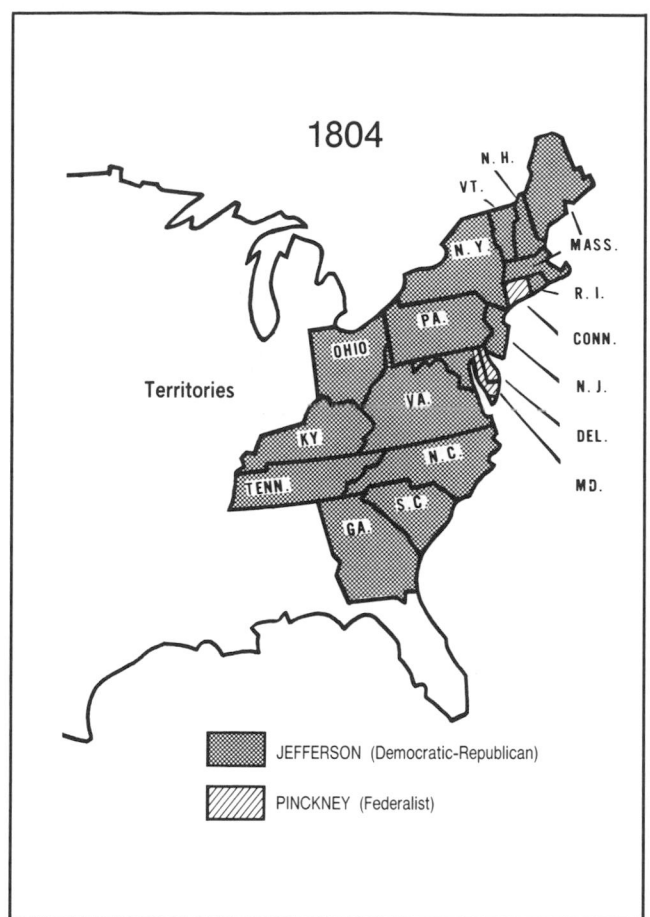

1804

Territories

N.H.
VT.
N.Y.
MASS.
R.I.
CONN.
N.J.
DEL.
MD.
P.A.
OHIO
VA.
KY.
N.C.
TENN.
S.C.
GA.

JEFFERSON (Democratic-Republican)

PINCKNEY (Federalist)

| States | Electoral Votes | Jefferson | Pinckney |
|--------|:-:|:-:|:-:|
| Connecticut | (9) | - | 9 |
| Delaware | (3) | - | 3 |
| Georgia | (6) | 6 | - |
| Kentucky | (8) | 8 | - |
| Maryland [1] | (11) | 9 | 2 |
| Massachusetts | (19) | 19 | - |
| New Hampshire | (7) | 7 | - |
| New Jersey | (8) | 8 | - |
| New York | (19) | 19 | - |
| North Carolina | (14) | 14 | - |
| Ohio | (3) | 3 | - |
| Pennsylvania | (20) | 20 | - |
| Rhode Island | (4) | 4 | - |
| South Carolina | (10) | 10 | - |
| Tennessee | (5) | 5 | - |
| Vermont | (6) | 6 | - |
| Virginia | (24) | 24 | - |
| **Totals** | **(176)** | **162** | **14** |

1. *For explanation of split electoral votes, see p. 350.*

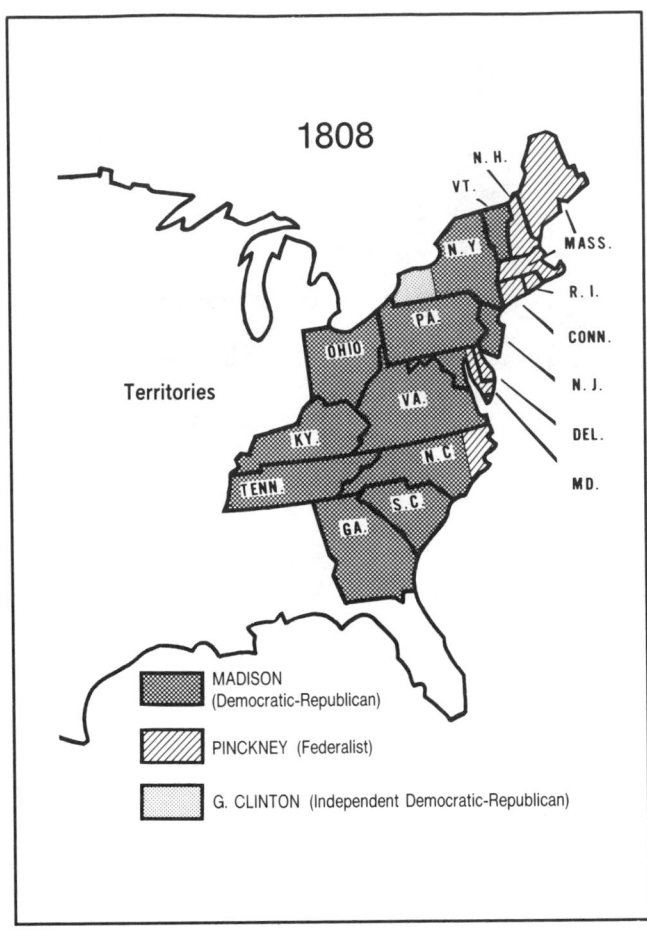

1808

MADISON
(Democratic-Republican)

PINCKNEY (Federalist)

G. CLINTON (Independent Democratic-Republican)

| States | Electoral Votes | Madison | Pinckney | Clinton |
|---|---|---|---|---|
| Connecticut | (9) | - | 9 | - |
| Delaware | (3) | - | 3 | - |
| Georgia | (6) | 6 | - | - |
| Kentucky [1] | (8) | 7 | - | - |
| Maryland [2] | (11) | 9 | 2 | - |
| Massachusetts | (19) | - | 19 | - |
| New Hampshire | (7) | - | 7 | - |
| New Jersey | (8) | 8 | - | - |
| New York [2] | (19) | 13 | - | 6 |
| North Carolina [2] | (14) | 11 | 3 | - |
| Ohio | (3) | 3 | - | - |
| Pennsylvania | (20) | 20 | - | - |
| Rhode Island | (4) | - | 4 | - |
| South Carolina | (10) | 10 | - | - |
| Tennessee | (5) | 5 | - | - |
| Vermont | (6) | 6 | - | - |
| Virginia | (24) | 24 | - | - |
| **Totals** | **(176)** | **122** | **47** | **6** |

1. One Kentucky elector did not vote.
2. For explanation of split electoral votes, see p. 350.

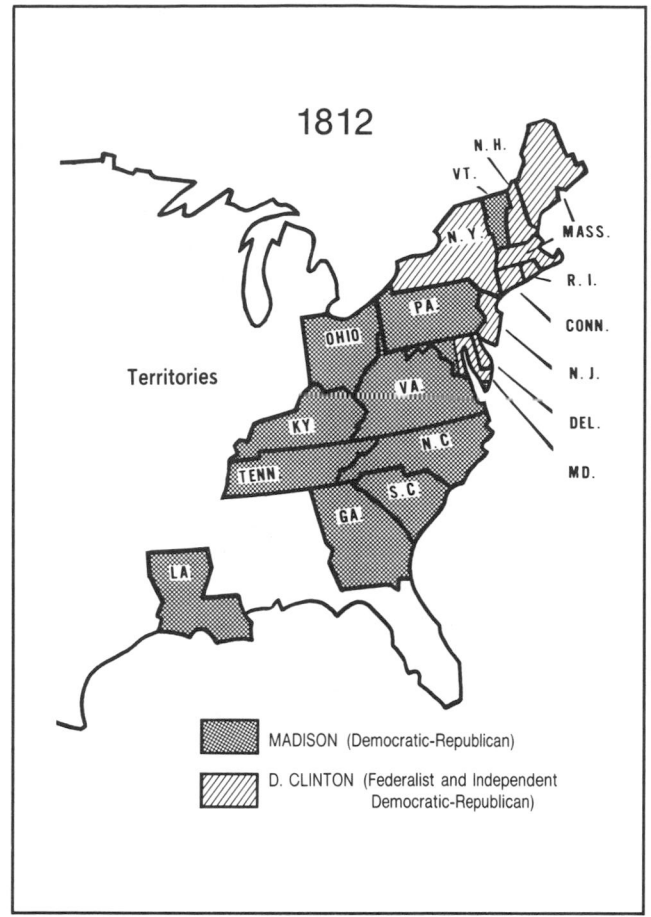

1812

MADISON (Democratic-Republican)

D. CLINTON (Federalist and Independent
Democratic-Republican)

| States | Electoral Votes | Madison | Clinton |
|---|---|---|---|
| Connecticut | (9) | - | 9 |
| Delaware | (4) | - | 4 |
| Georgia | (8) | 8 | - |
| Kentucky | (12) | 12 | - |
| Louisiana | (3) | 3 | - |
| Maryland [1] | (11) | 6 | 5 |
| Massachusetts | (22) | - | 22 |
| New Hampshire | (8) | - | 8 |
| New Jersey | (8) | - | 8 |
| New York | (29) | - | 29 |
| North Carolina | (15) | 15 | - |
| Ohio [2] | (8) | 7 | - |
| Pennsylvania | (25) | 25 | - |
| Rhode Island | (4) | - | 4 |
| South Carolina | (11) | 11 | - |
| Tennessee | (8) | 8 | - |
| Vermont | (8) | 8 | - |
| Virginia | (25) | 25 | - |
| **Totals** | **(218)** | **128** | **89** |

1. For explanation of split electoral votes, see p. 350.
2. One Ohio elector did not vote.

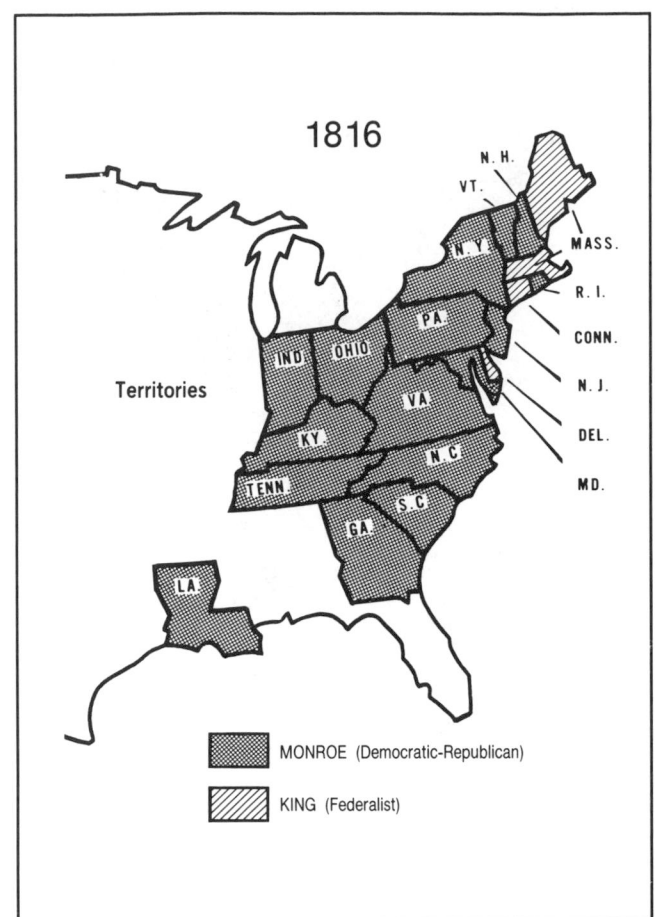

1816

MONROE (Democratic-Republican)

KING (Federalist)

| States | Electoral Votes | Monroe | King |
|---|---|---|---|
| Connecticut | (9) | - | 9 |
| Delaware [1] | (4) | - | 3 |
| Georgia | (8) | 8 | - |
| Indiana | (3) | 3 | - |
| Kentucky | (12) | 12 | - |
| Louisiana | (3) | 3 | - |
| Maryland [1] | (11) | 8 | - |
| Massachusetts | (22) | - | 22 |
| New Hampshire | (8) | 8 | - |
| New Jersey | (8) | 8 | - |
| New York | (29) | 29 | - |
| North Carolina | (15) | 15 | - |
| Ohio | (8) | 8 | - |
| Pennsylvania | (25) | 25 | - |
| Rhode Island | (4) | 4 | - |
| South Carolina | (11) | 11 | - |
| Tennessee | (8) | 8 | - |
| Vermont | (8) | 8 | - |
| Virginia | (25) | 25 | - |
| **Totals** | **(221)** | **183** | **34** |

1. One Delaware and three Maryland electors did not vote.

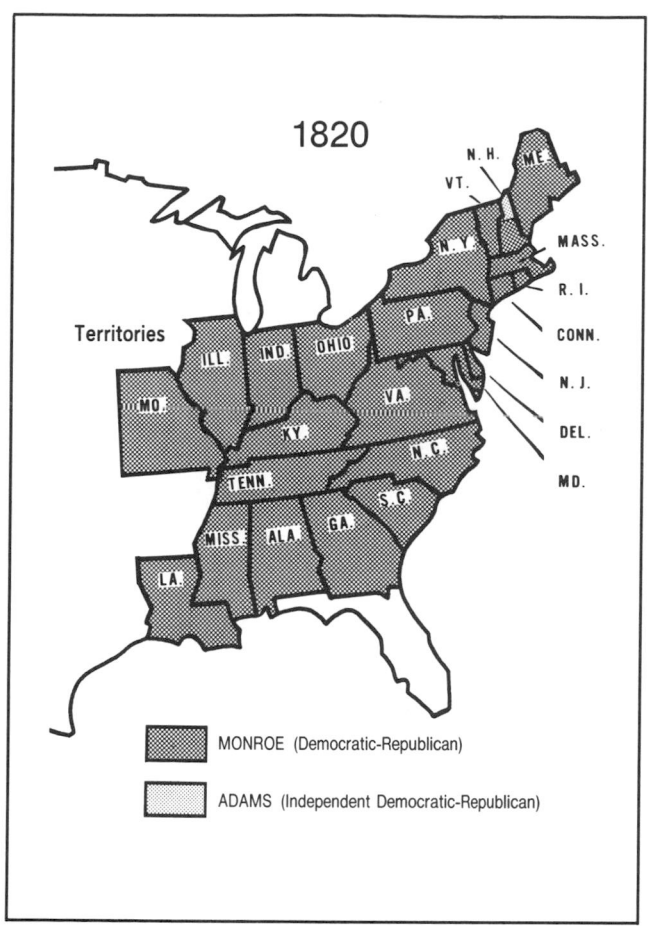

1820

MONROE (Democratic-Republican)

ADAMS (Independent Democratic-Republican)

| States | Electoral Votes | Monroe | Adams |
|---|---|---|---|
| Alabama | (3) | 3 | - |
| Connecticut | (9) | 9 | - |
| Delaware | (4) | 4 | - |
| Georgia | (8) | 8 | - |
| Illinois | (3) | 3 | - |
| Indiana | (3) | 3 | - |
| Kentucky | (12) | 12 | - |
| Louisiana | (3) | 3 | - |
| Maine | (9) | 9 | - |
| Maryland | (11) | 11 | - |
| Massachusetts | (15) | 15 | - |
| Mississippi [1] | (3) | 2 | - |
| Missouri | (3) | 3 | - |
| New Hampshire [2] | (8) | 7 | 1 |
| New Jersey | (8) | 8 | - |
| New York | (29) | 29 | - |
| North Carolina | (15) | 15 | - |
| Ohio | (8) | 8 | - |
| Pennsylvania [1] | (25) | 24 | - |
| Rhode Island | (4) | 4 | - |
| South Carolina | (11) | 11 | - |
| Tennessee [1] | (8) | 7 | - |
| Vermont | (8) | 8 | - |
| Virginia | (25) | 25 | - |
| **Totals** | **(235)** | **231** | **1** |

1. One elector each from Mississippi, Pennsylvania and Tennessee did not vote.
2. For explanation of split electoral votes, see p. 350.

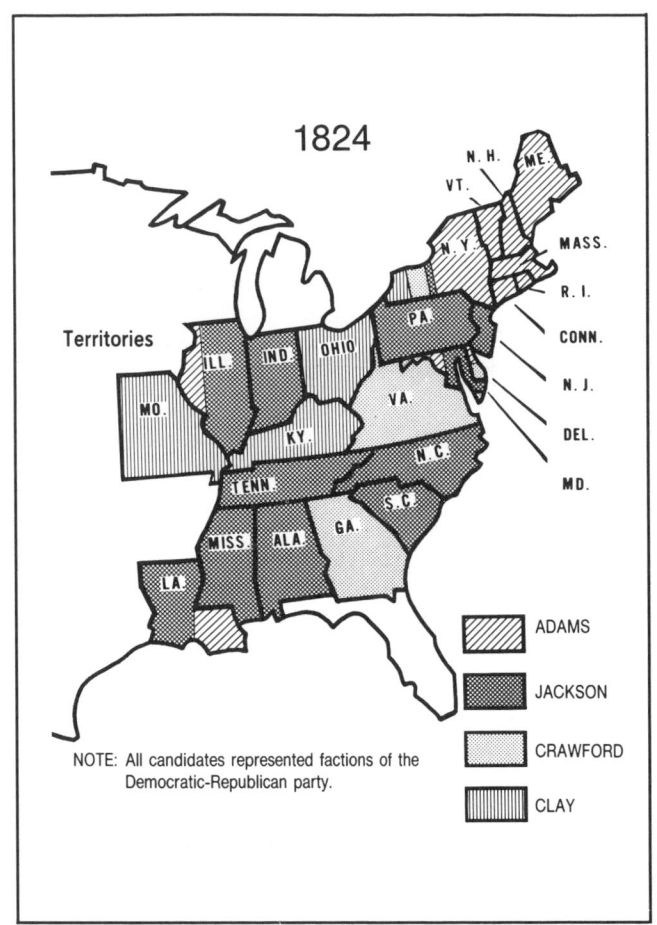

1824

Territories

ADAMS

JACKSON

CRAWFORD

CLAY

NOTE: All candidates represented factions of the Democratic-Republican party.

| States | Electoral Votes | Jackson | Adams | Crawford | Clay |
|---|---|---|---|---|---|
| Alabama | (5) | 5 | - | - | - |
| Connecticut | (8) | - | 8 | - | - |
| Delaware [1] | (3) | - | 1 | 2 | - |
| Georgia | (9) | - | - | 9 | - |
| Illinois [1] | (3) | 2 | 1 | - | - |
| Indiana | (5) | 5 | - | - | - |
| Kentucky | (14) | - | - | - | 14 |
| Louisiana [1] | (5) | 3 | 2 | - | - |
| Maine | (9) | - | 9 | - | - |
| Maryland [1] | (11) | 7 | 3 | 1 | - |
| Massachusetts | (15) | - | 15 | - | - |
| Mississippi | (3) | 3 | - | - | - |
| Missouri | (3) | - | - | - | 3 |
| New Hampshire | (8) | - | 8 | - | - |
| New Jersey | (8) | 8 | - | - | - |
| New York [1] | (36) | 1 | 26 | 5 | 4 |
| North Carolina | (15) | 15 | - | - | - |
| Ohio | (16) | - | - | - | 16 |
| Pennsylvania | (28) | 28 | - | - | - |
| Rhode Island | (4) | - | 4 | - | - |
| South Carolina | (11) | 11 | - | - | - |
| Tennessee | (11) | 11 | - | - | - |
| Vermont | (7) | - | 7 | - | - |
| Virginia | (24) | - | - | 24 | - |
| **Totals** | **(261)** | **99** [2] | **84** | **41** | **37** |

1. For explanation of split electoral votes, see p. 350.
2. As no candidate received a majority of the electoral votes, the election was decided by the House of Representatives. See p. 349.

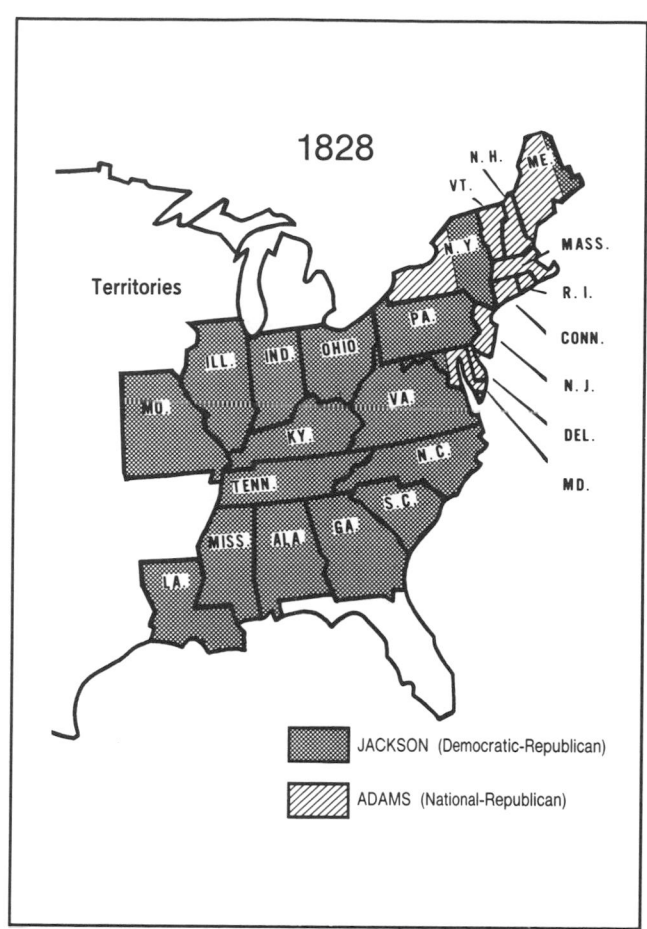

| States | Electoral Votes | Jackson | Adams |
|---|---|---|---|
| Alabama | (5) | 5 | - |
| Connecticut | (8) | - | 8 |
| Delaware | (3) | - | 3 |
| Georgia | (9) | 9 | - |
| Illinois | (3) | 3 | - |
| Indiana | (5) | 5 | - |
| Kentucky | (14) | 14 | - |
| Louisiana | (5) | 5 | - |
| Maine [1] | (9) | 1 | 8 |
| Maryland [1] | (11) | 5 | 6 |
| Massachusetts | (15) | - | 15 |
| Mississippi | (3) | 3 | - |
| Missouri | (3) | 3 | - |
| New Hampshire | (8) | - | 8 |
| New Jersey | (8) | - | 8 |
| New York [1] | (36) | 20 | 16 |
| North Carolina | (15) | 15 | - |
| Ohio | (16) | 16 | - |
| Pennsylvania | (28) | 28 | - |
| Rhode Island | (4) | - | 4 |
| South Carolina | (11) | 11 | - |
| Tennessee | (11) | 11 | - |
| Vermont | (7) | - | 7 |
| Virginia | (24) | 24 | - |
| **Totals** | **(261)** | **178** | **83** |

1. For explanation of split electoral votes, see p. 350.

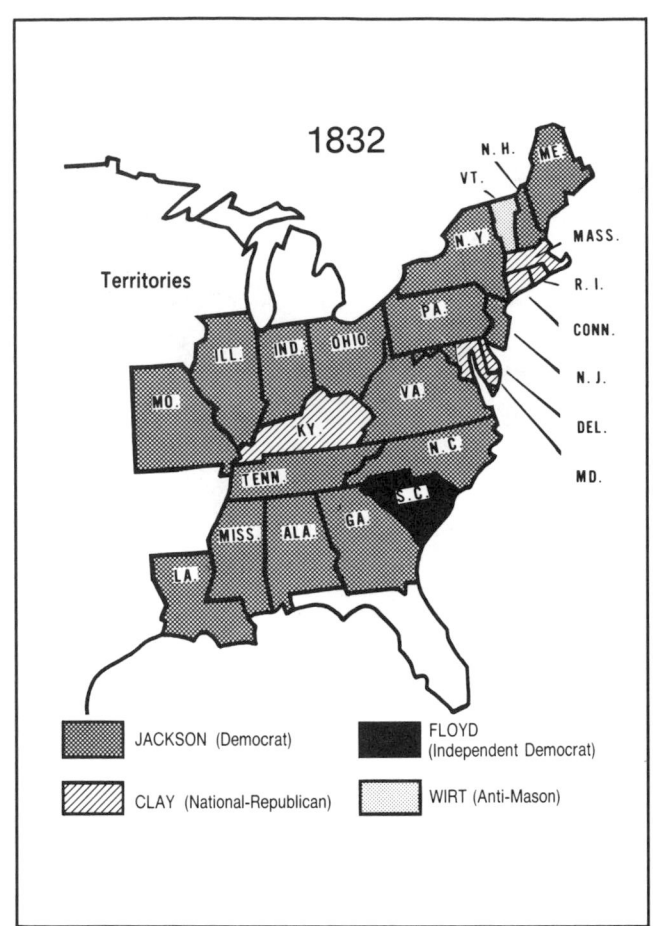

| States | Electoral Votes | Jackson | Clay | Floyd | Wirt |
|---|---|---|---|---|---|
| **Alabama** | (7) | 7 | - | - | - |
| **Connecticut** | (8) | - | 8 | - | - |
| **Delaware** | (3) | - | 3 | - | - |
| **Georgia** | (11) | 11 | - | - | - |
| **Illinois** | (5) | 5 | - | - | - |
| **Indiana** | (9) | 9 | - | - | - |
| **Kentucky** | (15) | - | 15 | - | - |
| **Louisiana** | (5) | 5 | - | - | - |
| **Maine** | (10) | 10 | - | - | - |
| **Maryland** [1] | (10) | 3 | 5 | - | - |
| **Massachusetts** | (14) | - | 14 | - | - |
| **Mississippi** | (4) | 4 | - | - | - |
| **Missouri** | (4) | 4 | - | - | - |
| **New Hampshire** | (7) | 7 | - | - | - |
| **New Jersey** | (8) | 8 | - | - | - |
| **New York** | (42) | 42 | - | - | - |
| **North Carolina** | (15) | 15 | - | - | - |
| **Ohio** | (21) | 21 | - | - | - |
| **Pennsylvania** | (30) | 30 | - | - | - |
| **Rhode Island** | (4) | - | 4 | - | - |
| **South Carolina** | (11) | - | - | 11 | - |
| **Tennessee** | (15) | 15 | - | - | - |
| **Vermont** | (7) | - | - | - | 7 |
| **Virginia** | (23) | 23 | - | - | - |
| **Totals** | **(288)** | **219** | **49** | **11** | **7** |

*1. Two Maryland electors did not vote. For explanation of split electoral votes, see p. 350.*

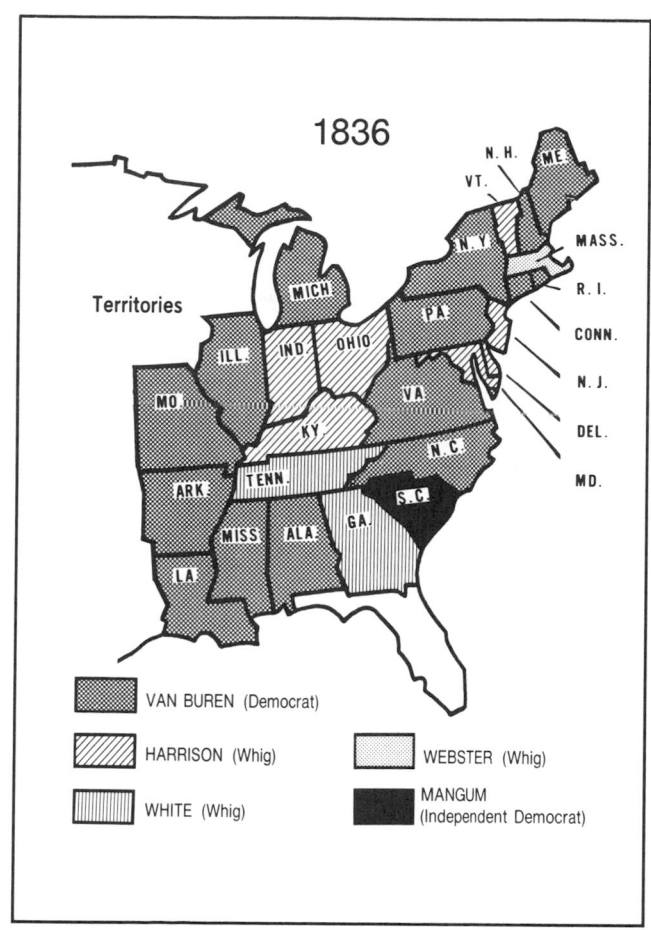

| States | Electoral Votes | Van Buren | Harrison [1] | White [1] | Webster [1] | Mangum |
|---|---|---|---|---|---|---|
| Alabama | (7) | 7 | - | - | - | - |
| Arkansas | (3) | 3 | - | - | - | - |
| Connecticut | (8) | 8 | - | - | - | - |
| Delaware | (3) | - | 3 | - | - | - |
| Georgia | (11) | - | - | 11 | - | - |
| Illinois | (5) | 5 | - | - | - | - |
| Indiana | (9) | - | 9 | - | - | - |
| Kentucky | (15) | - | 15 | - | - | - |
| Louisiana | (5) | 5 | - | - | - | - |
| Maine | (10) | 10 | - | - | - | - |
| Maryland | (10) | - | 10 | - | - | - |
| Massachusetts | (14) | - | - | - | 14 | - |
| Michigan | (3) | 3 | - | - | - | - |
| Mississippi | (4) | 4 | - | - | - | - |
| Missouri | (4) | 4 | - | - | - | - |
| New Hampshire | (7) | 7 | - | - | - | - |
| New Jersey | (8) | - | 8 | - | - | - |
| New York | (42) | 42 | - | - | - | - |
| North Carolina | (15) | 15 | - | - | - | - |
| Ohio | (21) | - | 21 | - | - | - |
| Pennsylvania | (30) | 30 | - | - | - | - |
| Rhode Island | (4) | 4 | - | - | - | - |
| South Carolina | (11) | - | - | - | - | 11 |
| Tennessee | (15) | - | - | 15 | - | - |
| Vermont | (7) | - | 7 | - | - | - |
| Virginia | (23) | 23 | - | - | - | - |
| **Totals** | **(294)** | **170** | **73** | **26** | **14** | **11** |

1. *For explanation of three Whig presidential candidates, see p. 347.*

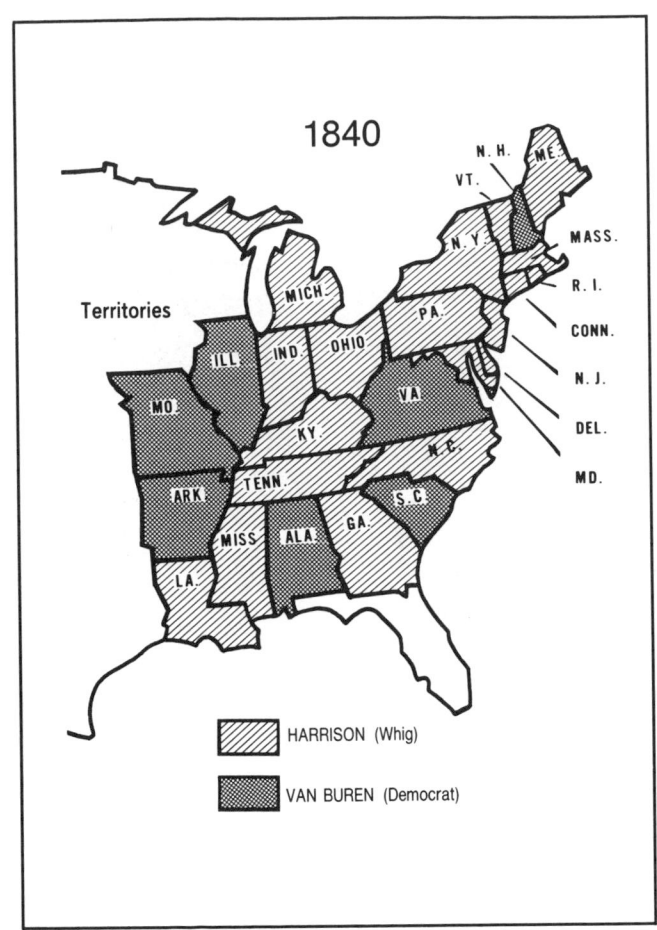

1840

Territories

HARRISON (Whig)

VAN BUREN (Democrat)

| States | Electoral Votes | Harrison | Van Buren |
|---|---|---|---|
| Alabama | (7) | - | 7 |
| Arkansas | (3) | - | 3 |
| Connecticut | (8) | 8 | - |
| Delaware | (3) | 3 | - |
| Georgia | (11) | 11 | - |
| Illinois | (5) | - | 5 |
| Indiana | (9) | 9 | - |
| Kentucky | (15) | 15 | - |
| Louisiana | (5) | 5 | - |
| Maine | (10) | 10 | - |
| Maryland | (10) | 10 | - |
| Massachusetts | (14) | 14 | - |
| Michigan | (3) | 3 | - |
| Mississippi | (4) | 4 | - |
| Missouri | (4) | - | 4 |
| New Hampshire | (7) | - | 7 |
| New Jersey | (8) | 8 | - |
| New York | (42) | 42 | - |
| North Carolina | (15) | 15 | - |
| Ohio | (21) | 21 | - |
| Pennsylvania | (30) | 30 | - |
| Rhode Island | (4) | 4 | - |
| South Carolina | (11) | - | 11 |
| Tennessee | (15) | 15 | - |
| Vermont | (7) | 7 | - |
| Virginia | (23) | - | 23 |
| **Totals** | **(294)** | **234** | **60** |

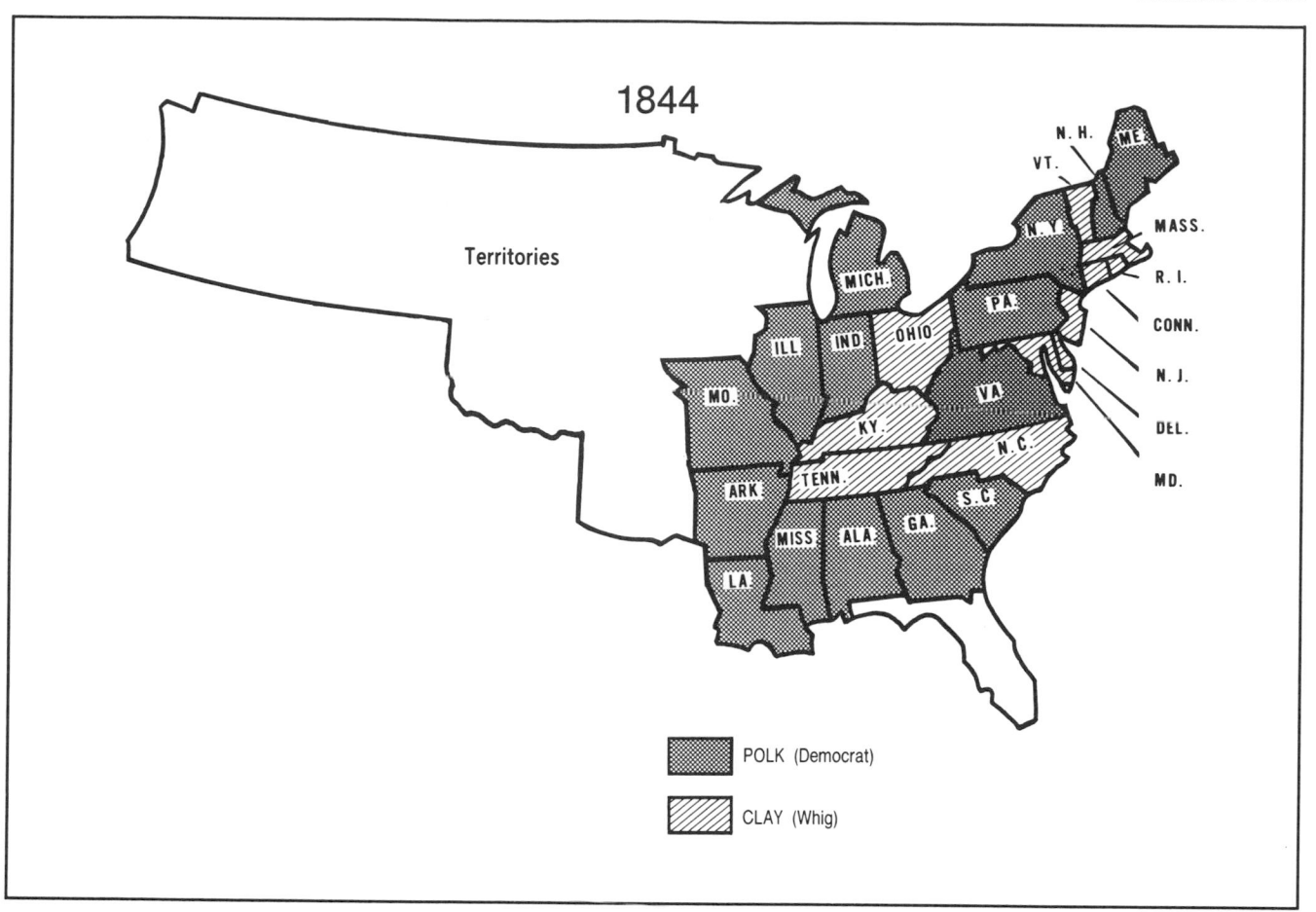

1844

Territories

POLK (Democrat)

CLAY (Whig)

| States | Electoral Votes | Polk | Clay |
|---|---|---|---|
| Alabama | (9) | 9 | - |
| Arkansas | (3) | 3 | - |
| Connecticut | (6) | - | 6 |
| Delaware | (3) | - | 3 |
| Georgia | (10) | 10 | - |
| Illinois | (9) | 9 | - |
| Indiana | (12) | 12 | - |
| Kentucky | (12) | - | 12 |
| Louisiana | (6) | 6 | - |
| Maine | (9) | 9 | - |
| Maryland | (8) | - | 8 |
| Massachusetts | (12) | - | 12 |
| Michigan | (5) | 5 | - |
| Mississippi | (6) | 6 | - |
| Missouri | (7) | 7 | - |
| New Hampshire | (6) | 6 | - |
| New Jersey | (7) | - | 7 |
| New York | (36) | 36 | - |
| North Carolina | (11) | - | 11 |
| Ohio | (23) | - | 23 |
| Pennsylvania | (26) | 26 | - |
| Rhode Island | (4) | - | 4 |
| South Carolina | (9) | 9 | - |
| Tennessee | (13) | - | 13 |
| Vermont | (6) | - | 6 |
| Virginia | (17) | 17 | - |
| **Totals** | **(275)** | **170** | **105** |

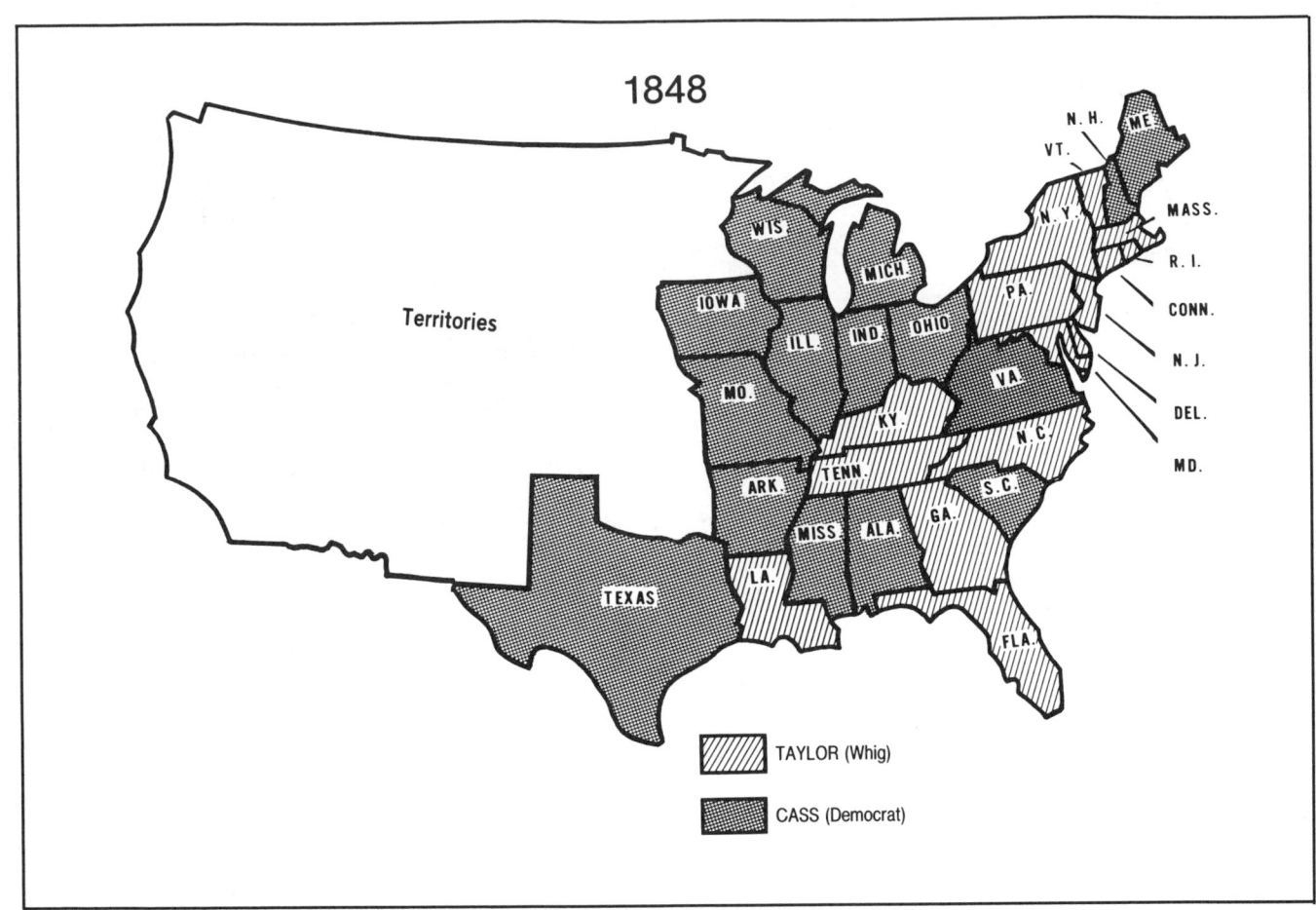

1848

Territories

TAYLOR (Whig)

CASS (Democrat)

| States | Electoral Votes | Taylor | Cass | States | Electoral Votes | Taylor | Cass |
|---|---|---|---|---|---|---|---|
| **Alabama** | (9) | - | 9 | **Mississippi** | (6) | - | 6 |
| **Arkansas** | (3) | - | 3 | **Missouri** | (7) | - | 7 |
| **Connecticut** | (6) | 6 | - | **New Hampshire** | (6) | - | 6 |
| **Delaware** | (3) | 3 | - | **New Jersey** | (7) | 7 | - |
| **Florida** | (3) | 3 | - | **New York** | (36) | 36 | - |
| **Georgia** | (10) | 10 | - | **North Carolina** | (11) | 11 | - |
| **Illinois** | (9) | - | 9 | **Ohio** | (23) | - | 23 |
| **Indiana** | (12) | - | 12 | **Pennsylvania** | (26) | 26 | - |
| **Iowa** | (4) | - | 4 | **Rhode Island** | (4) | 4 | - |
| **Kentucky** | (12) | 12 | - | **South Carolina** | (9) | - | 9 |
| **Louisiana** | (6) | 6 | - | **Tennessee** | (13) | 13 | - |
| **Maine** | (9) | - | 9 | **Texas** | (4) | - | 4 |
| **Maryland** | (8) | 8 | - | **Vermont** | (6) | 6 | - |
| **Massachusetts** | (12) | 12 | - | **Virginia** | (17) | - | 17 |
| **Michigan** | (5) | - | 5 | **Wisconsin** | (4) | - | 4 |
| | | | | **Totals** | (290) | 163 | 127 |

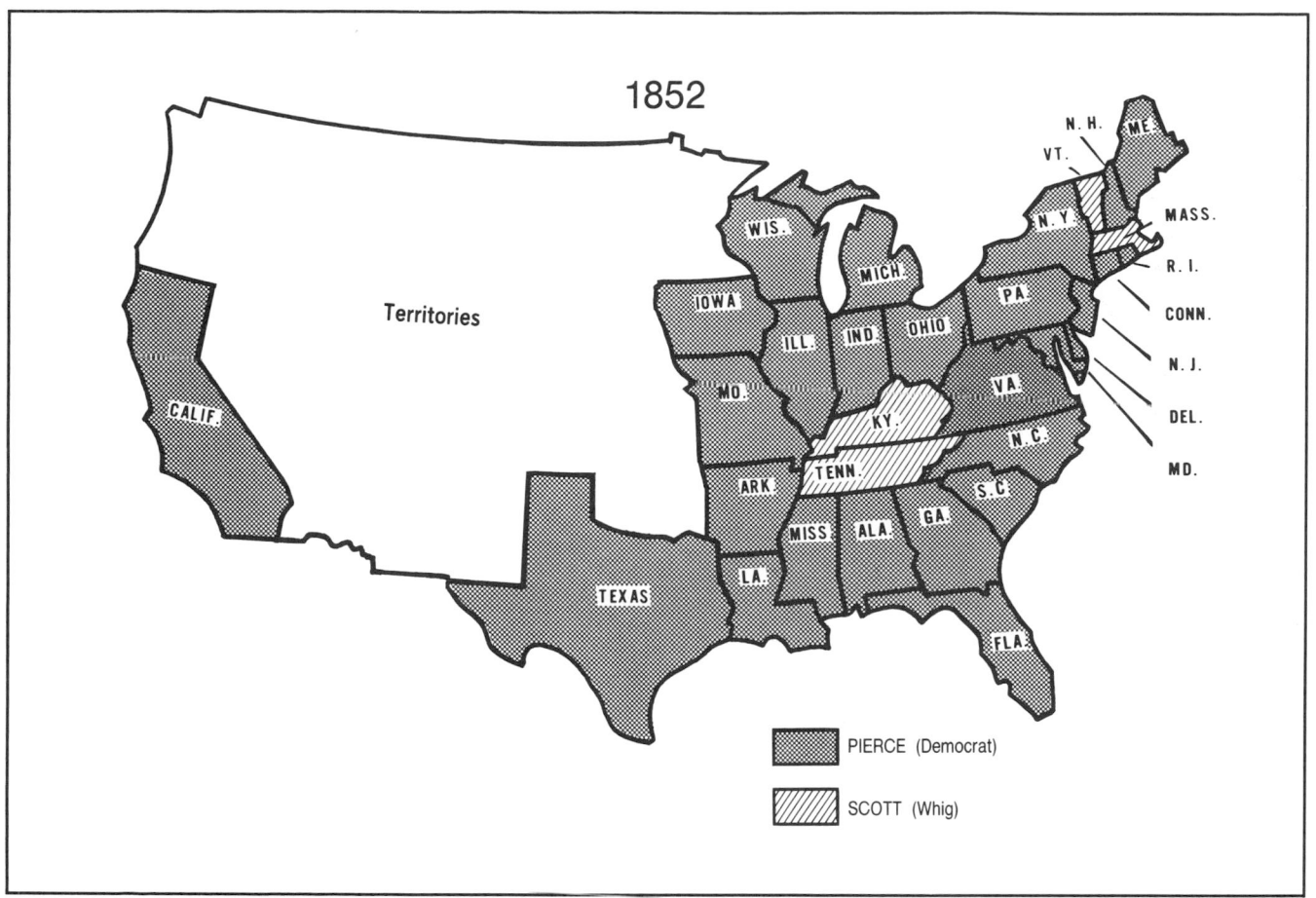

1852

Territories

PIERCE (Democrat)

SCOTT (Whig)

| States | Electoral Votes | Pierce | Scott | States | Electoral Votes | Pierce | Scott |
|--------|-----------------|--------|-------|--------|-----------------|--------|-------|
| Alabama | (9) | 9 | - | Mississippi | (7) | 7 | - |
| Arkansas | (4) | 4 | - | Missouri | (9) | 9 | - |
| California | (4) | 4 | - | New Hampshire | (5) | 5 | - |
| Connecticut | (6) | 6 | - | New Jersey | (7) | 7 | - |
| Delaware | (3) | 3 | - | New York | (35) | 35 | - |
| Florida | (3) | 3 | - | North Carolina | (10) | 10 | - |
| Georgia | (10) | 10 | - | Ohio | (23) | 23 | - |
| Illinois | (11) | 11 | - | Pennsylvania | (27) | 27 | - |
| Indiana | (13) | 13 | - | Rhode Island | (4) | 4 | - |
| Iowa | (4) | 4 | - | South Carolina | (8) | 8 | - |
| Kentucky | (12) | - | 12 | Tennessee | (12) | - | 12 |
| Louisiana | (6) | 6 | - | Texas | (4) | 4 | - |
| Maine | (8) | 8 | - | Vermont | (5) | - | 5 |
| Maryland | (8) | 8 | - | Virginia | (15) | 15 | - |
| Massachusetts | (13) | - | 13 | Wisconsin | (5) | 5 | - |
| Michigan | (6) | 6 | - | **Totals** | **(296)** | **254** | **42** |

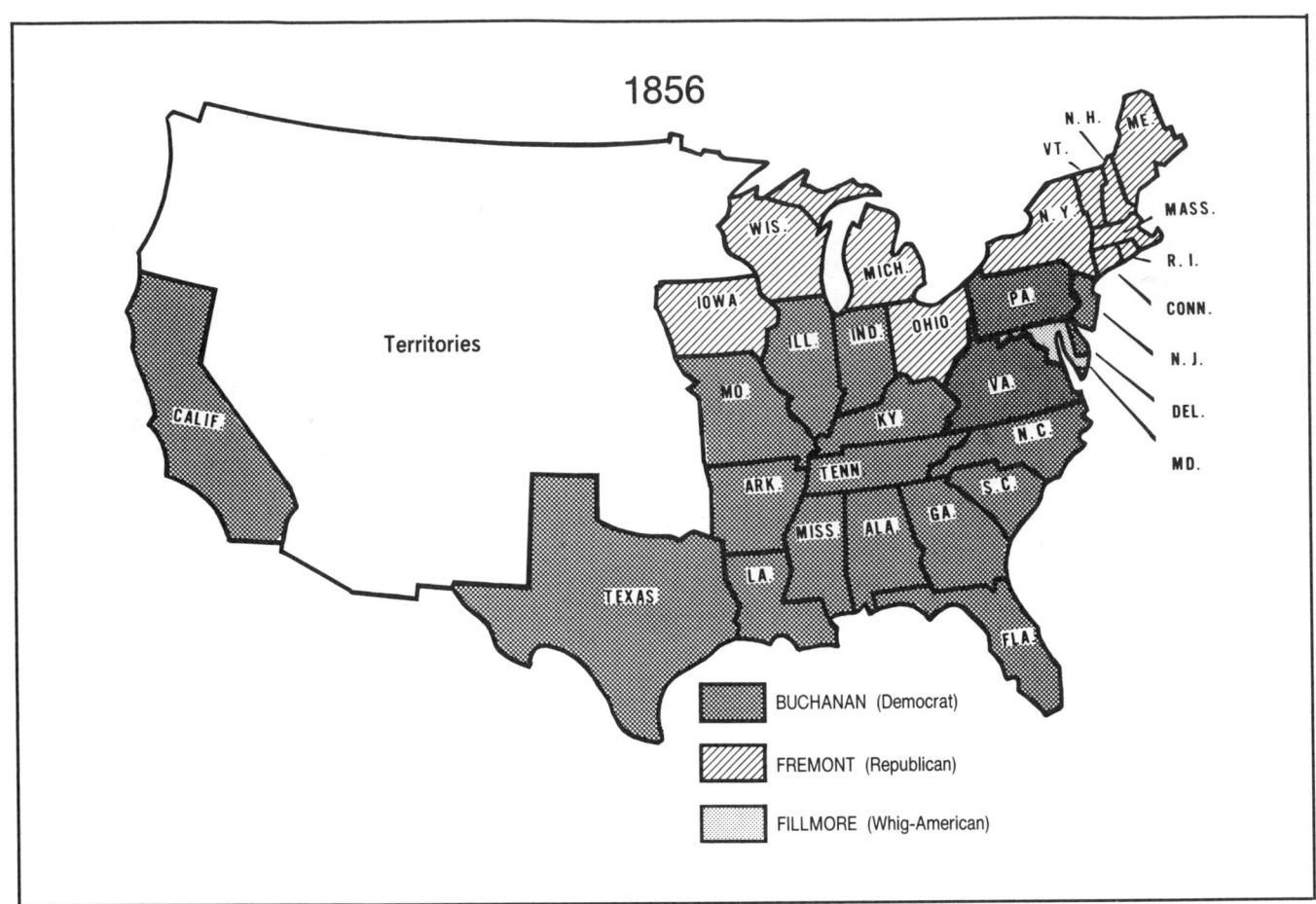

1856

| States | Electoral Votes | Buchanan | Fremont | Fillmore |
|--------|-----------------|----------|---------|----------|
| **Alabama** | (9) | 9 | - | - |
| **Arkansas** | (4) | 4 | - | - |
| **California** | (4) | 4 | - | - |
| **Connecticut** | (6) | - | 6 | - |
| **Delaware** | (3) | 3 | - | - |
| **Florida** | (3) | 3 | - | - |
| **Georgia** | (10) | 10 | - | - |
| **Illinois** | (11) | 11 | - | - |
| **Indiana** | (13) | 13 | - | - |
| **Iowa** | (4) | - | 4 | - |
| **Kentucky** | (12) | 12 | - | - |
| **Louisiana** | (6) | 6 | - | - |
| **Maine** | (8) | - | 8 | - |
| **Maryland** | (8) | - | - | 8 |
| **Massachusetts** | (13) | - | 13 | - |
| **Michigan** | (6) | - | 6 | - |
| **Mississippi** | (7) | 7 | - | - |
| **Missouri** | (9) | 9 | - | - |
| **New Hampshire** | (5) | - | 5 | - |
| **New Jersey** | (7) | 7 | - | - |
| **New York** | (35) | - | 35 | - |
| **North Carolina** | (10) | 10 | - | - |
| **Ohio** | (23) | - | 23 | - |
| **Pennsylvania** | (27) | 27 | - | - |
| **Rhode Island** | (4) | - | 4 | - |
| **South Carolina** | (8) | 8 | - | - |
| **Tennessee** | (12) | 12 | - | - |
| **Texas** | (4) | 4 | - | - |
| **Vermont** | (5) | - | 5 | - |
| **Virginia** | (15) | 15 | - | - |
| **Wisconsin** | (5) | - | 5 | - |
| **Totals** | (296) | 174 | 114 | 8 |

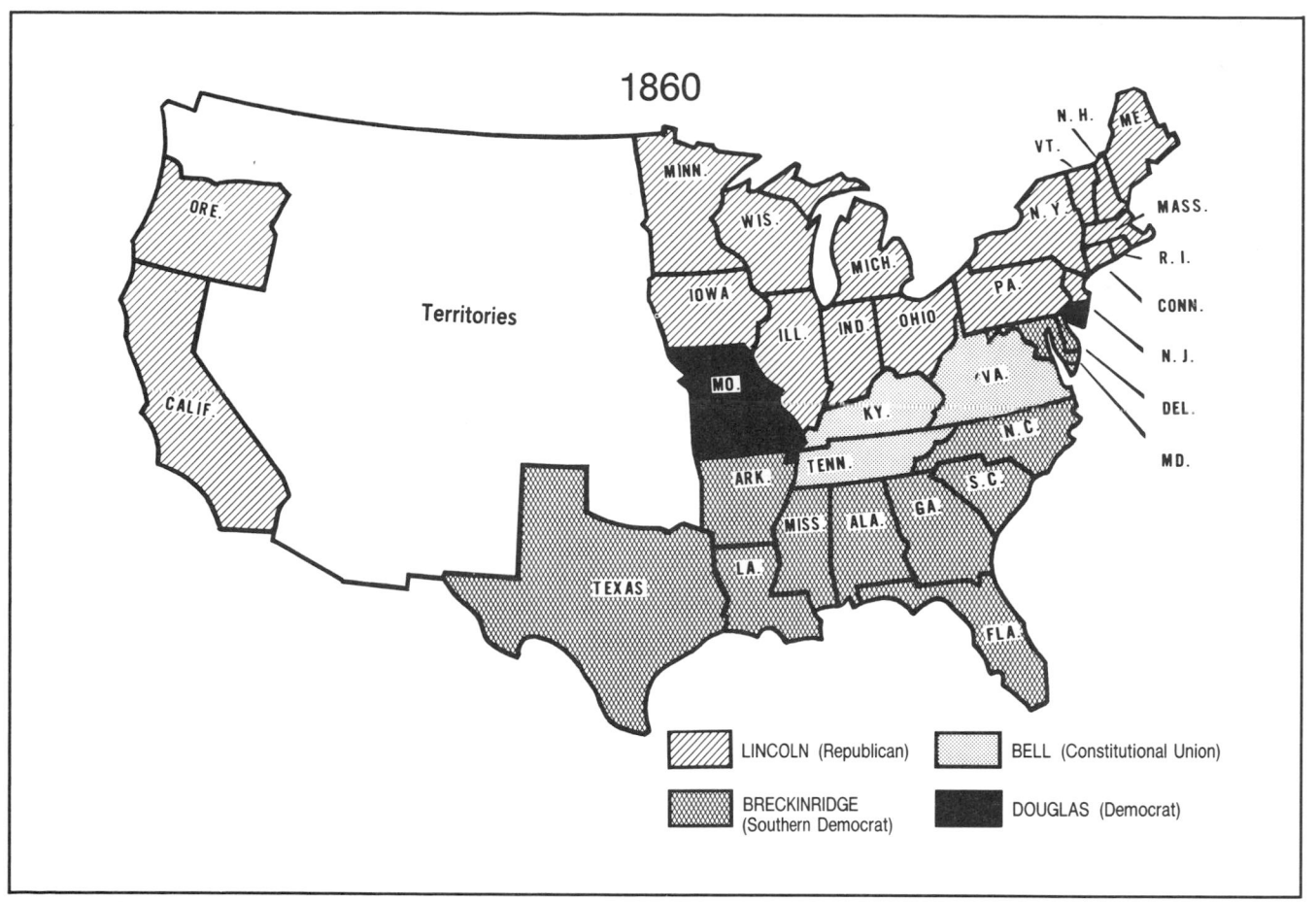

1860

| States | Electoral Votes | Lincoln | Breckinridge | Bell | Douglas |
|---|---|---|---|---|---|
| **Alabama** | (9) | - | 9 | - | - |
| **Arkansas** | (4) | - | 4 | - | - |
| **California** | (4) | 4 | - | - | - |
| **Connecticut** | (6) | 6 | - | - | - |
| **Delaware** | (3) | - | 3 | - | - |
| **Florida** | (3) | - | 3 | - | - |
| **Georgia** | (10) | - | 10 | - | - |
| **Illinois** | (11) | 11 | - | - | - |
| **Indiana** | (13) | 13 | - | - | - |
| **Iowa** | (4) | 4 | - | - | - |
| **Kentucky** | (12) | - | - | 12 | - |
| **Louisiana** | (6) | - | 6 | - | - |
| **Maine** | (8) | 8 | - | - | - |
| **Maryland** | (8) | - | 8 | - | - |
| **Massachusetts** | (13) | 13 | - | - | - |
| **Michigan** | (6) | 6 | - | - | - |
| **Minnesota** | (4) | 4 | - | - | - |

| States | Electoral Votes | Lincoln | Breckinridge | Bell | Douglas |
|---|---|---|---|---|---|
| **Mississippi** | (7) | - | 7 | - | - |
| **Missouri** | (9) | - | - | - | 9 |
| **New Hampshire** | (5) | 5 | - | - | - |
| **New Jersey** [1] | (7) | 4 | - | - | 3 |
| **New York** | (35) | 35 | - | - | - |
| **North Carolina** | (10) | - | 10 | - | - |
| **Ohio** | (23) | 23 | - | - | - |
| **Oregon** | (3) | 3 | - | - | - |
| **Pennsylvania** | (27) | 27 | - | - | - |
| **Rhode Island** | (4) | 4 | - | - | - |
| **South Carolina** | (8) | - | 8 | - | - |
| **Tennessee** | (12) | - | - | 12 | - |
| **Texas** | (4) | - | 4 | - | - |
| **Vermont** | (5) | 5 | - | - | - |
| **Virginia** | (15) | - | - | 15 | - |
| **Wisconsin** | (5) | 5 | - | - | - |
| **Totals** | (303) | 180 | 72 | 39 | 12 |

1. For explanation of split electoral votes, see p. 350.

377

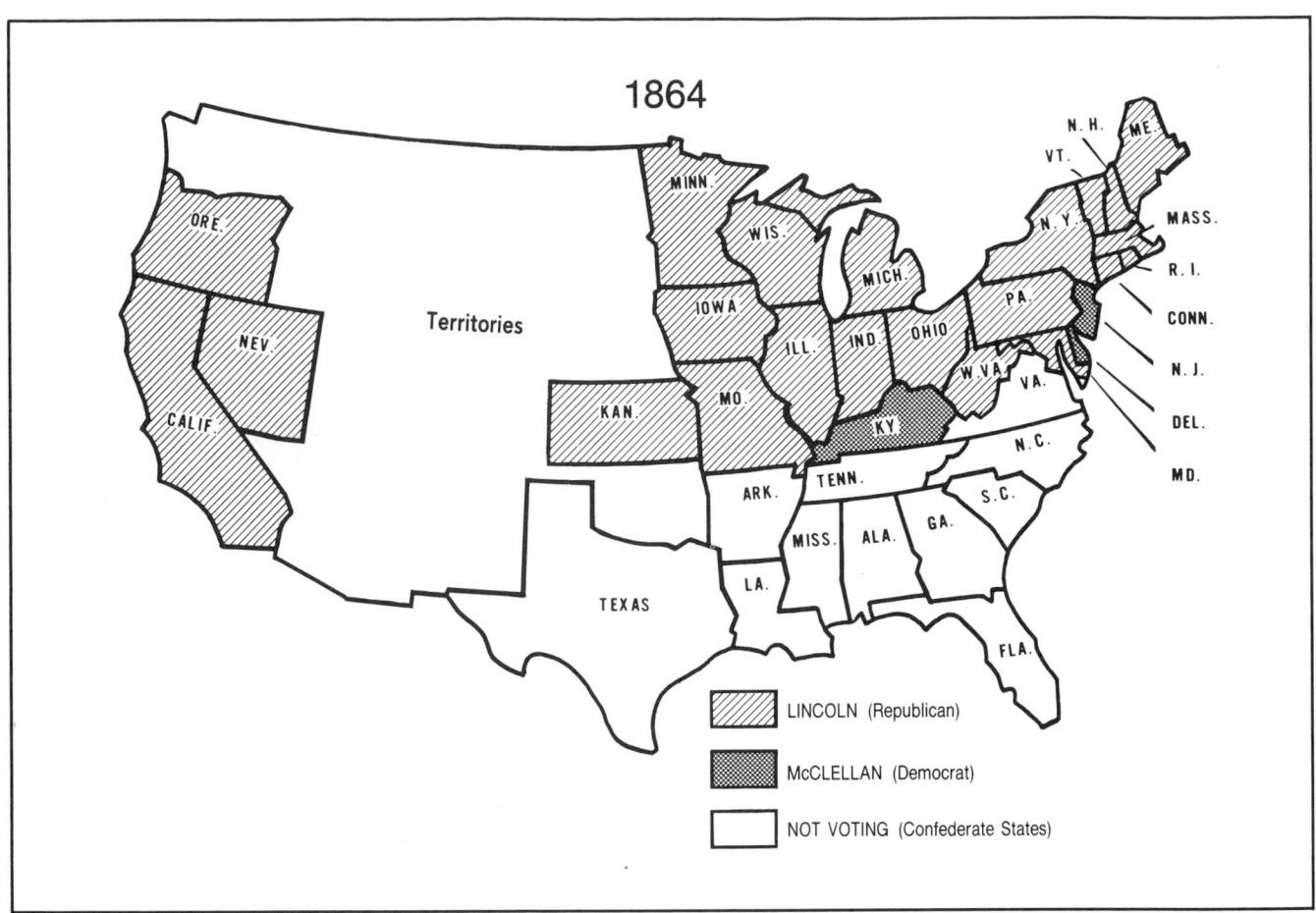

1864

LINCOLN (Republican)

McCLELLAN (Democrat)

NOT VOTING (Confederate States)

| States [1] | Electoral Votes | Lincoln | McClellan | States [1] | Electoral Votes | Lincoln | McClellan |
|---|---|---|---|---|---|---|---|
| California | (5) | 5 | - | Missouri | (11) | 11 | - |
| Connecticut | (6) | 6 | - | Nevada [2] | (3) | 2 | - |
| Delaware | (3) | - | 3 | New Hampshire | (5) | 5 | - |
| Illinois | (16) | 16 | - | New Jersey | (7) | - | 7 |
| Indiana | (13) | 13 | - | New York | (33) | 33 | - |
| Iowa | (8) | 8 | - | Ohio | (21) | 21 | - |
| Kansas | (3) | 3 | - | Oregon | (3) | 3 | - |
| Kentucky | (11) | - | 11 | Pennsylvania | (26) | 26 | - |
| Maine | (7) | 7 | - | Rhode Island | (4) | 4 | - |
| Maryland | (7) | 7 | - | Vermont | (5) | 5 | - |
| Massachusetts | (12) | 12 | - | West Virginia | (5) | 5 | - |
| Michigan | (8) | 8 | - | Wisconsin | (8) | 8 | - |
| Minnesota | (4) | 4 | - | **Totals** | **(234)** | **212** | **21** |

1. Eleven Southern States — Alabama, Arkansas, Florida, Georgia, Louisiana, Mississippi, North Carolina, South Carolina, Tennessee, Texas and Virginia — had seceded from the Union and did not vote.
2. One Nevada elector did not vote.

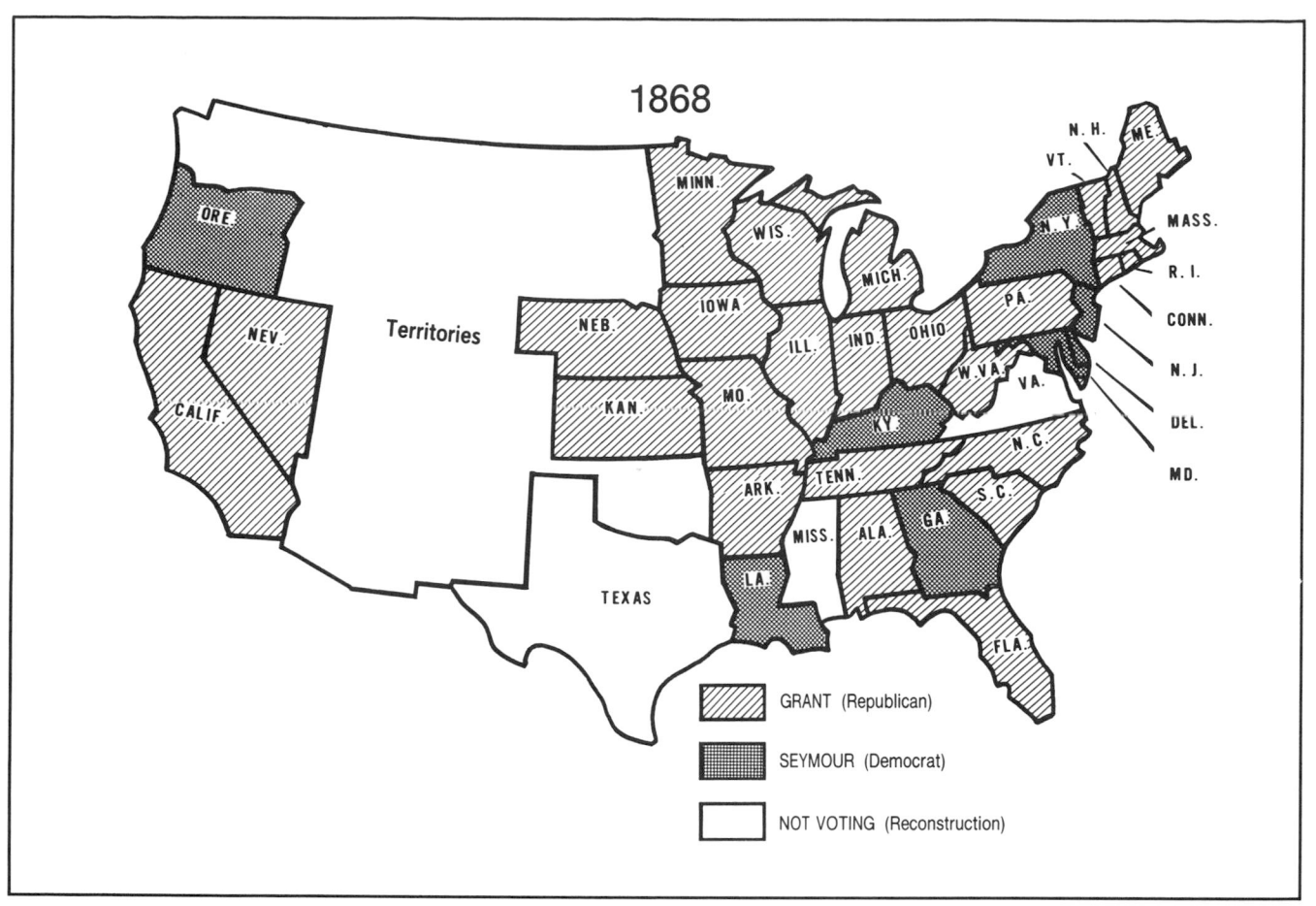

| States [1] | Electoral Votes | Grant | Seymour | States [1] | Electoral Votes | Grant | Seymour |
|---|---|---|---|---|---|---|---|
| Alabama | (8) | 8 | - | Missouri | (11) | 11 | - |
| Arkansas | (5) | 5 | - | Nebraska | (3) | 3 | - |
| California | (5) | 5 | - | Nevada | (3) | 3 | - |
| Connecticut | (6) | 6 | - | New Hampshire | (5) | 5 | - |
| Delaware | (3) | - | 3 | New Jersey | (7) | - | 7 |
| Florida | (3) | 3 | - | New York | (33) | - | 33 |
| Georgia | (9) | - | 9 | North Carolina | (9) | 9 | - |
| Illinois | (16) | 16 | - | Ohio | (21) | 21 | - |
| Indiana | (13) | 13 | - | Oregon | (3) | - | 3 |
| Iowa | (8) | 8 | - | Pennsylvania | (26) | 26 | - |
| Kansas | (3) | 3 | - | Rhode Island | (4) | 4 | - |
| Kentucky | (11) | - | 11 | South Carolina | (6) | 6 | - |
| Louisiana | (7) | - | 7 | Tennessee | (10) | 10 | - |
| Maine | (7) | 7 | - | Vermont | (5) | 5 | - |
| Maryland | (7) | - | 7 | West Virginia | (5) | 5 | - |
| Massachusetts | (12) | 12 | - | Wisconsin | (8) | 8 | - |
| Michigan | (8) | 8 | - | **Totals** | **(294)** | **214** | **80** |
| Minnesota | (4) | 4 | - | | | | |

1. *Mississippi, Texas, and Virginia were not yet readmitted to the Union and did not participate in the election.*

379

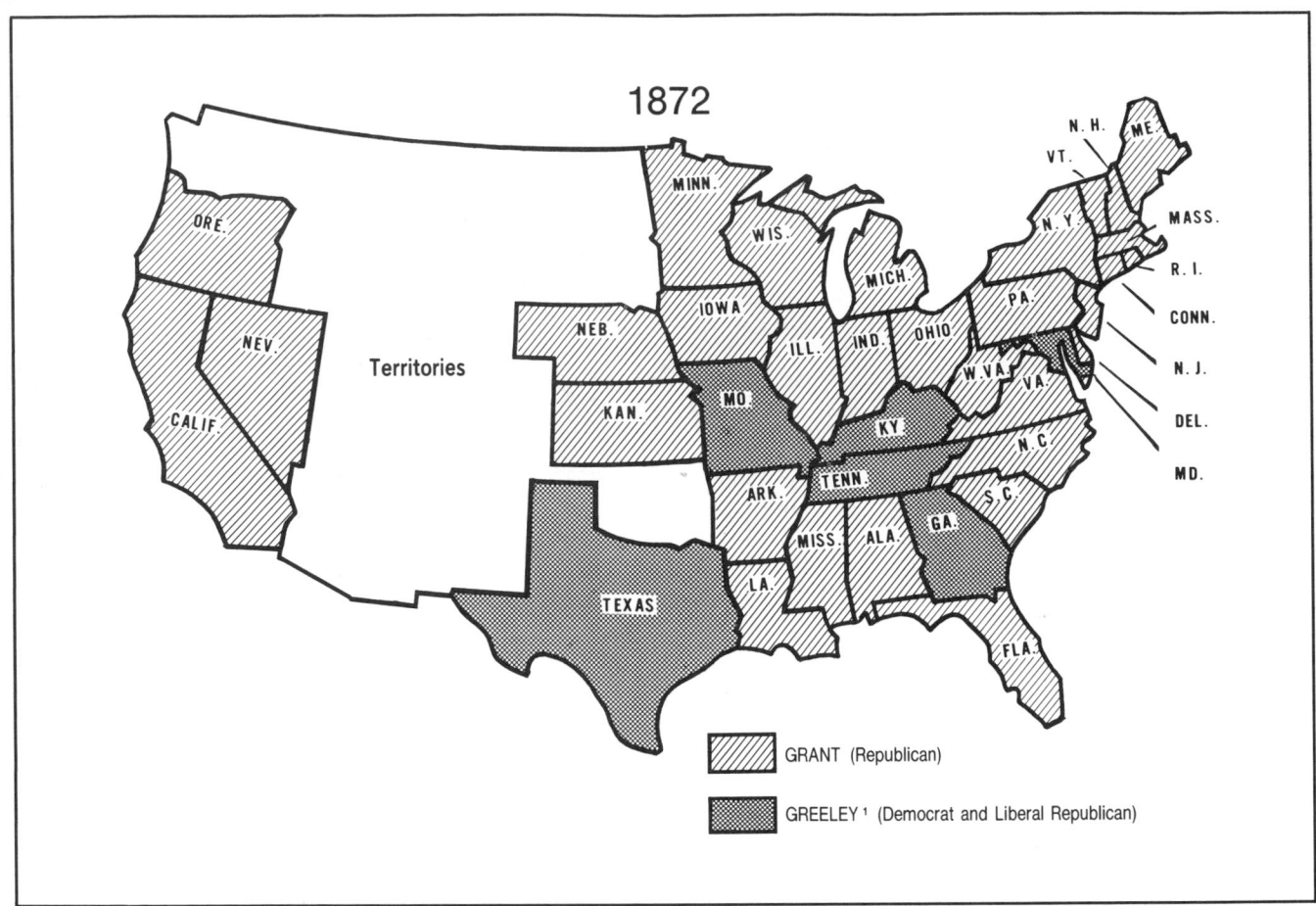

1872

GRANT (Republican)

GREELEY [1] (Democrat and Liberal Republican)

| States | Electoral Votes | Grant | Hendricks [1] | Brown [1] | Jenkins [1] | Davis [1] | States | Electoral Votes | Grant | Hendricks [1] | Brown [1] | Jenkins [1] | Davis [1] |
|---|---|---|---|---|---|---|---|---|---|---|---|---|---|
| **Alabama** | (10) | 10 | - | - | - | - | **Nebraska** | (3) | 3 | - | - | - | - |
| **Arkansas** [2] | (6) | - | - | - | - | - | **Nevada** | (3) | 3 | - | - | - | - |
| **California** | (6) | 6 | - | - | - | - | **New Hampshire** | (5) | 5 | - | - | - | - |
| **Connecticut** | (6) | 6 | - | - | - | - | **New Jersey** | (9) | 9 | - | - | - | - |
| **Delaware** | (3) | 3 | - | - | - | - | **New York** | (35) | 35 | - | - | - | - |
| **Florida** | (4) | 4 | - | - | - | - | **North Carolina** | (10) | 10 | - | - | - | - |
| **Georgia** [3] | (11) | - | - | 6 | 2 | - | **Ohio** | (22) | 22 | - | - | - | - |
| **Illinois** | (21) | 21 | - | - | - | - | **Oregon** | (3) | 3 | - | - | - | - |
| **Indiana** | (15) | 15 | - | - | - | - | **Pennsylvania** | (29) | 29 | - | - | - | - |
| **Iowa** | (11) | 11 | - | - | - | - | **Rhode Island** | (4) | 4 | - | - | - | - |
| **Kansas** | (5) | 5 | - | - | - | - | **South Carolina** | (7) | 7 | - | - | - | - |
| **Kentucky** | (12) | - | 8 | 4 | - | - | **Tennessee** | (12) | - | 12 | - | - | - |
| **Louisiana** [2] | (8) | - | - | - | - | - | **Texas** | (8) | - | 8 | - | - | - |
| **Maine** | (7) | 7 | - | - | - | - | **Vermont** | (5) | 5 | - | - | - | - |
| **Maryland** | (8) | - | 8 | - | - | - | **Virginia** | (11) | 11 | - | - | - | - |
| **Massachusetts** | (13) | 13 | - | - | - | - | **West Virginia** | (5) | 5 | - | - | - | - |
| **Michigan** | (11) | 11 | - | - | - | - | **Wisconsin** | (10) | 10 | - | - | - | - |
| **Minnesota** | (5) | 5 | - | - | - | - | **Totals** | (366) | 286 | 42 | 18 | 2 | 1 |
| **Mississippi** | (8) | 8 | - | - | - | - | | | | | | | |
| **Missouri** | (15) | - | 6 | 8 | - | 1 | | | | | | | |

1. *For explanation of Democratic electoral vote, cast after Greeley's death, see p. 347.*
2. *Congress refused to accept electoral votes of Arkansas and Louisiana because of disruptive conditions during Reconstruction.*
3. *Three Georgia electoral votes cast for Greeley were not counted.*

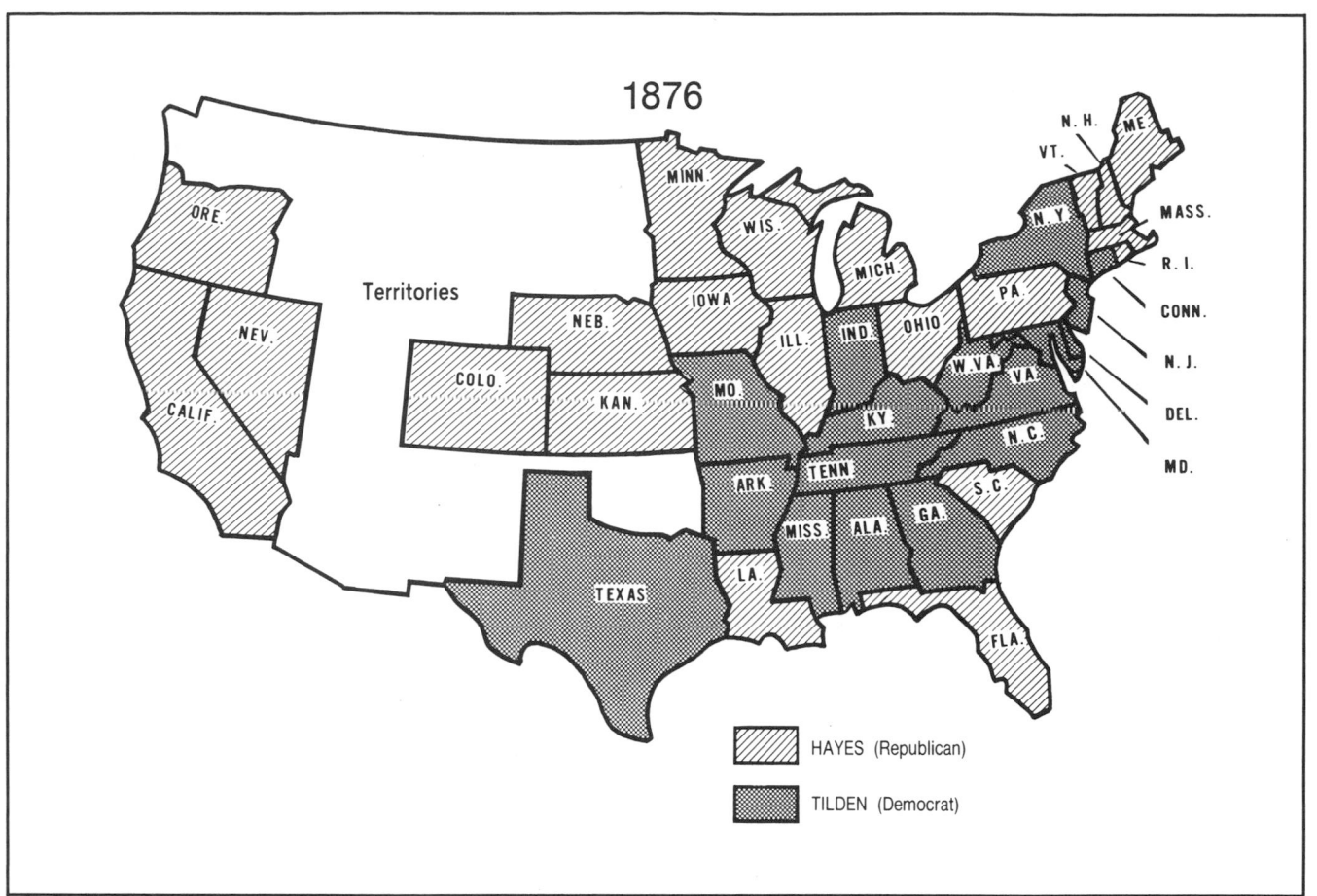

1876

HAYES (Republican)

TILDEN (Democrat)

| States | Electoral Votes | Hayes | Tilden | States | Electoral Votes | Hayes | Tilden |
|--------|-----------------|-------|--------|--------|-----------------|-------|--------|
| Alabama | (10) | - | 10 | Missouri | (15) | - | 15 |
| Arkansas | (6) | - | 6 | Nebraska | (3) | 3 | - |
| California | (6) | 6 | - | Nevada | (3) | 3 | - |
| Colorado | (3) | 3 | - | New Hampshire | (5) | 5 | - |
| Connecticut | (6) | - | 6 | New Jersey | (9) | - | 9 |
| Delaware | (3) | - | 3 | New York | (35) | - | 35 |
| Florida [1] | (4) | 4 | - | North Carolina | (10) | - | 10 |
| Georgia | (11) | - | 11 | Ohio | (22) | 22 | - |
| Illinois | (21) | 21 | - | Oregon [1] | (3) | 3 | - |
| Indiana | (15) | - | 15 | Pennsylvania | (29) | 29 | - |
| Iowa | (11) | 11 | - | Rhode Island | (4) | 4 | - |
| Kansas | (5) | 5 | - | South Carolina [1] | (7) | 7 | - |
| Kentucky | (12) | - | 12 | Tennessee | (12) | - | 12 |
| Louisiana [1] | (8) | 8 | - | Texas | (8) | - | 8 |
| Maine | (7) | 7 | - | Vermont | (5) | 5 | - |
| Maryland | (8) | - | 8 | Virginia | (11) | - | 11 |
| Massachusetts | (13) | 13 | - | West Virginia | (5) | - | 5 |
| Michigan | (11) | 11 | - | Wisconsin | (10) | 10 | - |
| Minnesota | (5) | 5 | - | **Totals** | **(369)** | **185** | **184** |
| Mississippi | (8) | - | 8 | | | | |

1. For explanation of disputed electoral votes of Florida, Louisiana, Oregon and South Carolina, see p. 352.

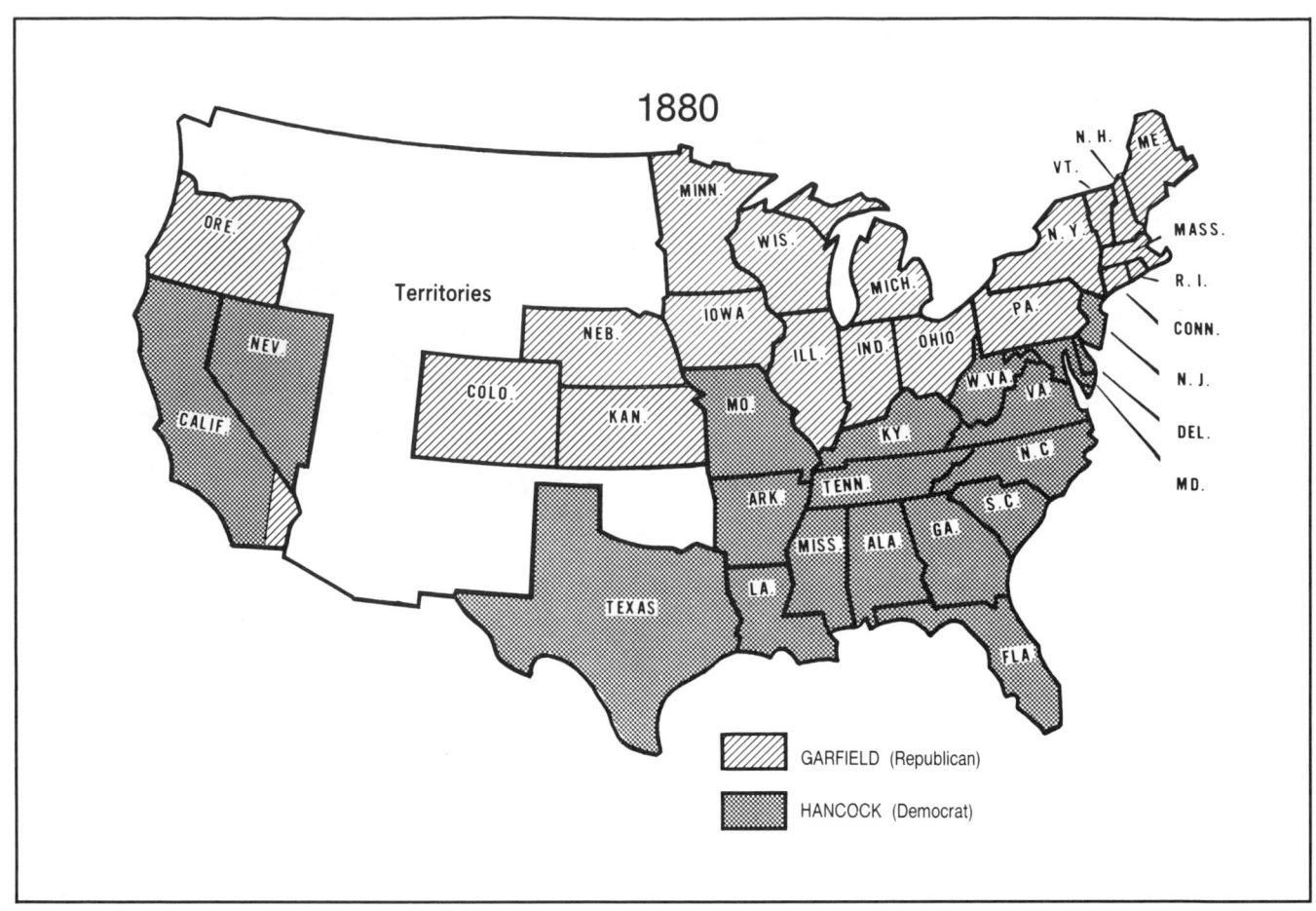

1880

GARFIELD (Republican)

HANCOCK (Democrat)

| States | Electoral Votes | Garfield | Hancock | States | Electoral Votes | Garfield | Hancock |
|---|---|---|---|---|---|---|---|
| Alabama | (10) | - | 10 | Mississippi | (8) | - | 8 |
| Arkansas | (6) | - | 6 | Missouri | (15) | - | 15 |
| California [1] | (6) | 1 | 5 | Nebraska | (3) | 3 | - |
| Colorado | (3) | 3 | - | Nevada | (3) | - | 3 |
| Connecticut | (6) | 6 | - | New Hampshire | (5) | 5 | - |
| Delaware | (3) | - | 3 | New Jersey | (9) | - | 9 |
| Florida | (4) | - | 4 | New York | (35) | 35 | - |
| Georgia | (11) | - | 11 | North Carolina | (10) | - | 10 |
| Illinois | (21) | 21 | - | Ohio | (22) | 22 | - |
| Indiana | (15) | 15 | - | Oregon | (3) | 3 | - |
| Iowa | (11) | 11 | - | Pennsylvania | (29) | 29 | - |
| Kansas | (5) | 5 | - | Rhode Island | (4) | 4 | - |
| Kentucky | (12) | - | 12 | South Carolina | (7) | - | 7 |
| Louisiana | (8) | - | 8 | Tennessee | (12) | - | 12 |
| Maine | (7) | 7 | - | Texas | (8) | - | 8 |
| Maryland | (8) | - | 8 | Vermont | (5) | 5 | - |
| Massachusetts | (13) | 13 | - | Virginia | (11) | - | 11 |
| Michigan | (11) | 11 | - | West Virginia | (5) | - | 5 |
| Minnesota | (5) | 5 | - | Wisconsin | (10) | 10 | - |
| | | | | **Totals** | **(369)** | **214** | **155** |

1. For explanation of split electoral votes, see p. 350.

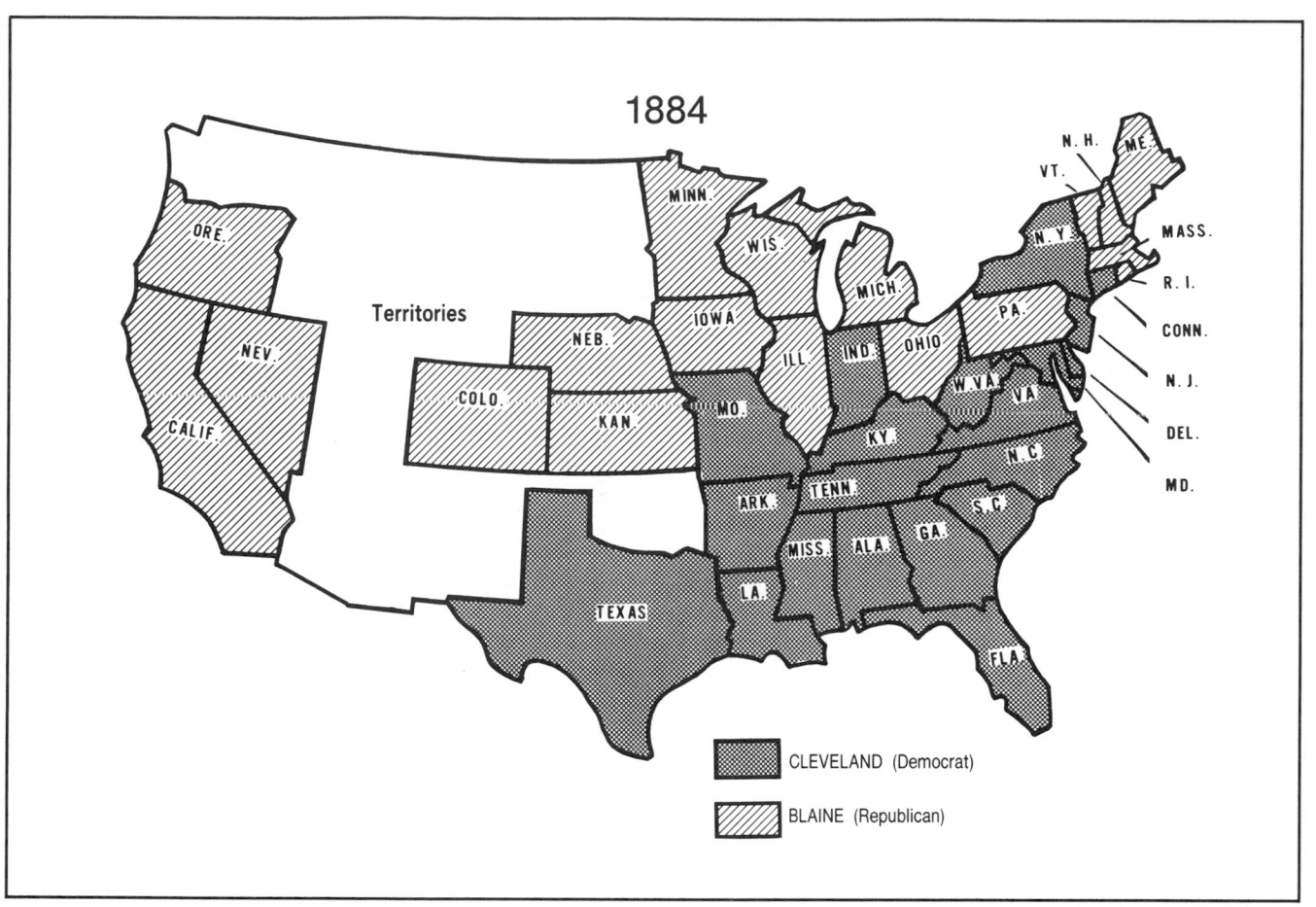

1884

CLEVELAND (Democrat)

BLAINE (Republican)

| States | Electoral Votes | Cleveland | Blaine | States | Electoral Votes | Cleveland | Blaine |
|--------|-----------------|-----------|--------|--------|-----------------|-----------|--------|
| Alabama | (10) | 10 | - | Mississippi | (9) | 9 | - |
| Arkansas | (7) | 7 | - | Missouri | (16) | 16 | - |
| California | (8) | - | 8 | Nebraska | (5) | - | 5 |
| Colorado | (3) | - | 3 | Nevada | (3) | - | 3 |
| Connecticut | (6) | 6 | - | New Hampshire | (4) | - | 4 |
| Delaware | (3) | 3 | - | New Jersey | (9) | 9 | - |
| Florida | (4) | 4 | - | New York | (36) | 36 | - |
| Georgia | (12) | 12 | - | North Carolina | (11) | 11 | - |
| Illinois | (22) | - | 22 | Ohio | (23) | - | 23 |
| Indiana | (15) | 15 | - | Oregon | (3) | - | 3 |
| Iowa | (13) | - | 13 | Pennsylvania | (30) | - | 30 |
| Kansas | (9) | - | 9 | Rhode Island | (4) | - | 4 |
| Kentucky | (13) | 13 | - | South Carolina | (9) | 9 | - |
| Louisiana | (8) | 8 | - | Tennessee | (12) | 12 | - |
| Maine | (6) | - | 6 | Texas | (13) | 13 | - |
| Maryland | (8) | 8 | - | Vermont | (4) | - | 4 |
| Massachusetts | (14) | - | 14 | Virginia | (12) | 12 | - |
| Michigan | (13) | - | 13 | West Virginia | (6) | 6 | - |
| Minnesota | (7) | - | 7 | Wisconsin | (11) | - | 11 |
| | | | | **Totals** | **(401)** | **219** | **182** |

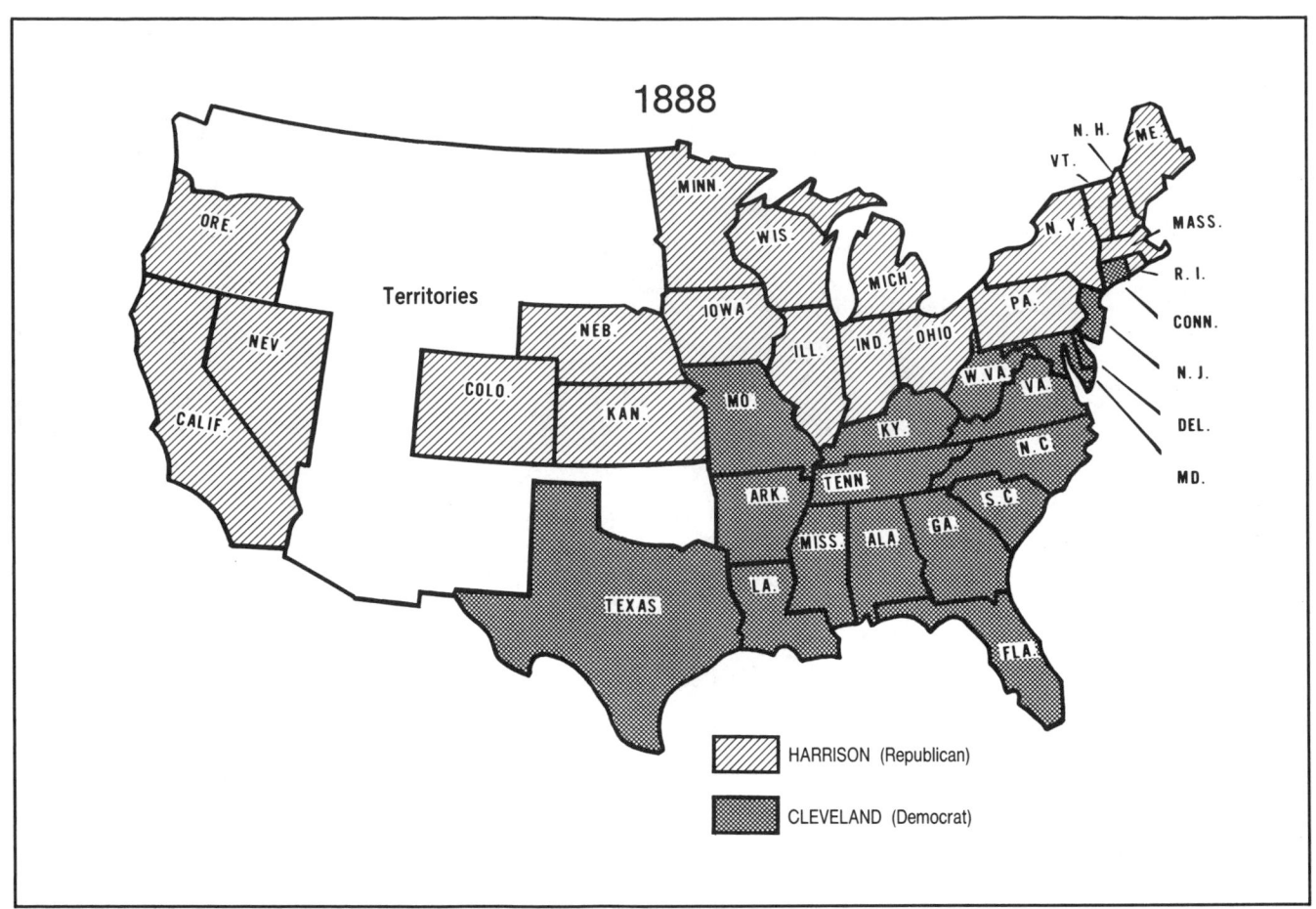

1888

Territories

HARRISON (Republican)

CLEVELAND (Democrat)

| States | Electoral Votes | Harrison | Cleveland | States | Electoral Votes | Harrison | Cleveland |
|---|---|---|---|---|---|---|---|
| Alabama | (10) | - | 10 | Mississippi | (9) | - | 9 |
| Arkansas | (7) | - | 7 | Missouri | (16) | - | 16 |
| California | (8) | 8 | - | Nebraska | (5) | 5 | - |
| Colorado | (3) | 3 | - | Nevada | (3) | 3 | - |
| Connecticut | (6) | - | 6 | New Hampshire | (4) | 4 | - |
| Delaware | (3) | - | 3 | New Jersey | (9) | - | 9 |
| Florida | (4) | - | 4 | New York | (36) | 36 | - |
| Georgia | (12) | - | 12 | North Carolina | (11) | - | 11 |
| Illinois | (22) | 22 | - | Ohio | (23) | 23 | - |
| Indiana | (15) | 15 | - | Oregon | (3) | 3 | - |
| Iowa | (13) | 13 | - | Pennsylvania | (30) | 30 | - |
| Kansas | (9) | 9 | - | Rhode Island | (4) | 4 | - |
| Kentucky | (13) | - | 13 | South Carolina | (9) | - | 9 |
| Louisiana | (8) | - | 8 | Tennessee | (12) | - | 12 |
| Maine | (6) | 6 | - | Texas | (13) | - | 13 |
| Maryland | (8) | - | 8 | Vermont | (4) | 4 | - |
| Massachusetts | (14) | 14 | - | Virginia | (12) | - | 12 |
| Michigan | (13) | 13 | - | West Virginia | (6) | - | 6 |
| Minnesota | (7) | 7 | - | Wisconsin | (11) | 11 | - |
| | | | | **Totals** | **(401)** | **233** | **168** |

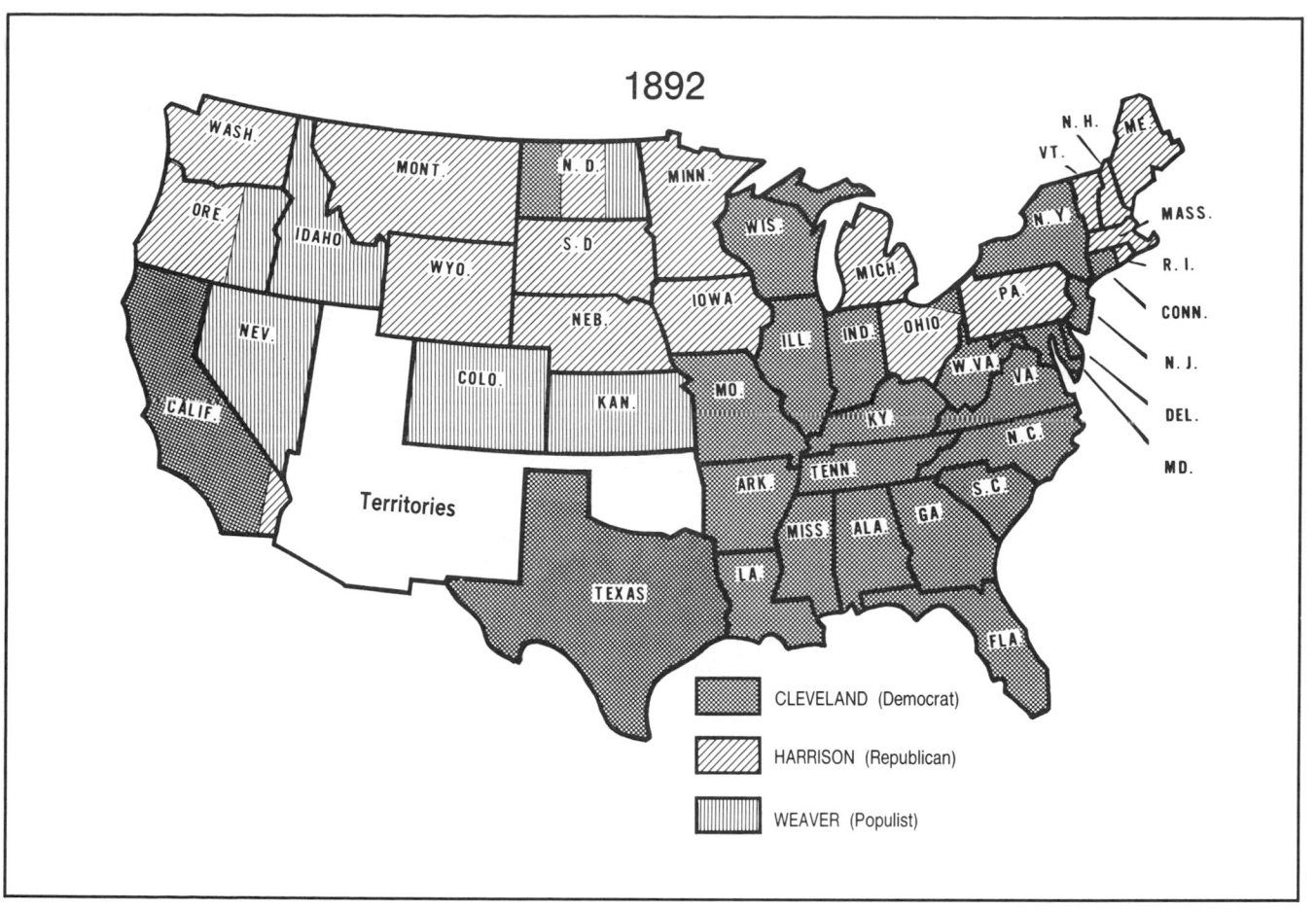

1892

CLEVELAND (Democrat)

HARRISON (Republican)

WEAVER (Populist)

| States | Electoral Votes | Cleveland | Harrison | Weaver | States | Electoral Votes | Cleveland | Harrison | Weaver |
|---|---|---|---|---|---|---|---|---|---|
| Alabama | (11) | 11 | - | - | Montana | (3) | - | 3 | - |
| Arkansas | (8) | 8 | - | - | Nebraska | (8) | - | 8 | - |
| California[1] | (9) | 8 | 1 | - | Nevada | (3) | - | - | 3 |
| Colorado | (4) | - | - | 4 | New Hampshire | (4) | - | 4 | - |
| Connecticut | (6) | 6 | - | - | New Jersey | (10) | 10 | - | - |
| Delaware | (3) | 3 | - | - | New York | (36) | 36 | - | - |
| Florida | (4) | 4 | - | - | North Carolina | (11) | 11 | - | - |
| Georgia | (13) | 13 | - | - | North Dakota[1] | (3) | 1 | 1 | 1 |
| Idaho | (3) | - | - | 3 | Ohio[1] | (23) | 1 | 22 | - |
| Illinois | (24) | 24 | - | - | Oregon[1] | (4) | - | 3 | 1 |
| Indiana | (15) | 15 | - | - | Pennsylvania | (32) | - | 32 | - |
| Iowa | (13) | - | 13 | - | Rhode Island | (4) | - | 4 | - |
| Kansas | (10) | - | - | 10 | South Carolina | (9) | 9 | - | - |
| Kentucky | (13) | 13 | - | - | South Dakota | (4) | - | 4 | - |
| Louisiana | (8) | 8 | - | - | Tennessee | (12) | 12 | - | - |
| Maine | (6) | - | 6 | - | Texas | (15) | 15 | - | - |
| Maryland | (8) | 8 | - | - | Vermont | (4) | - | 4 | - |
| Massachusetts | (15) | - | 15 | - | Virginia | (12) | 12 | - | - |
| Michigan[1] | (14) | 5 | 9 | - | Washington | (4) | - | 4 | - |
| Minnesota | (9) | - | 9 | - | West Virginia | (6) | 6 | - | - |
| Mississippi | (9) | 9 | - | - | Wisconsin | (12) | 12 | - | - |
| Missouri | (17) | 17 | - | - | Wyoming | (3) | - | 3 | - |
| | | | | | **Totals** | **(444)** | **277** | **145** | **22** |

1. For explanation of split electoral votes, see p. 350.

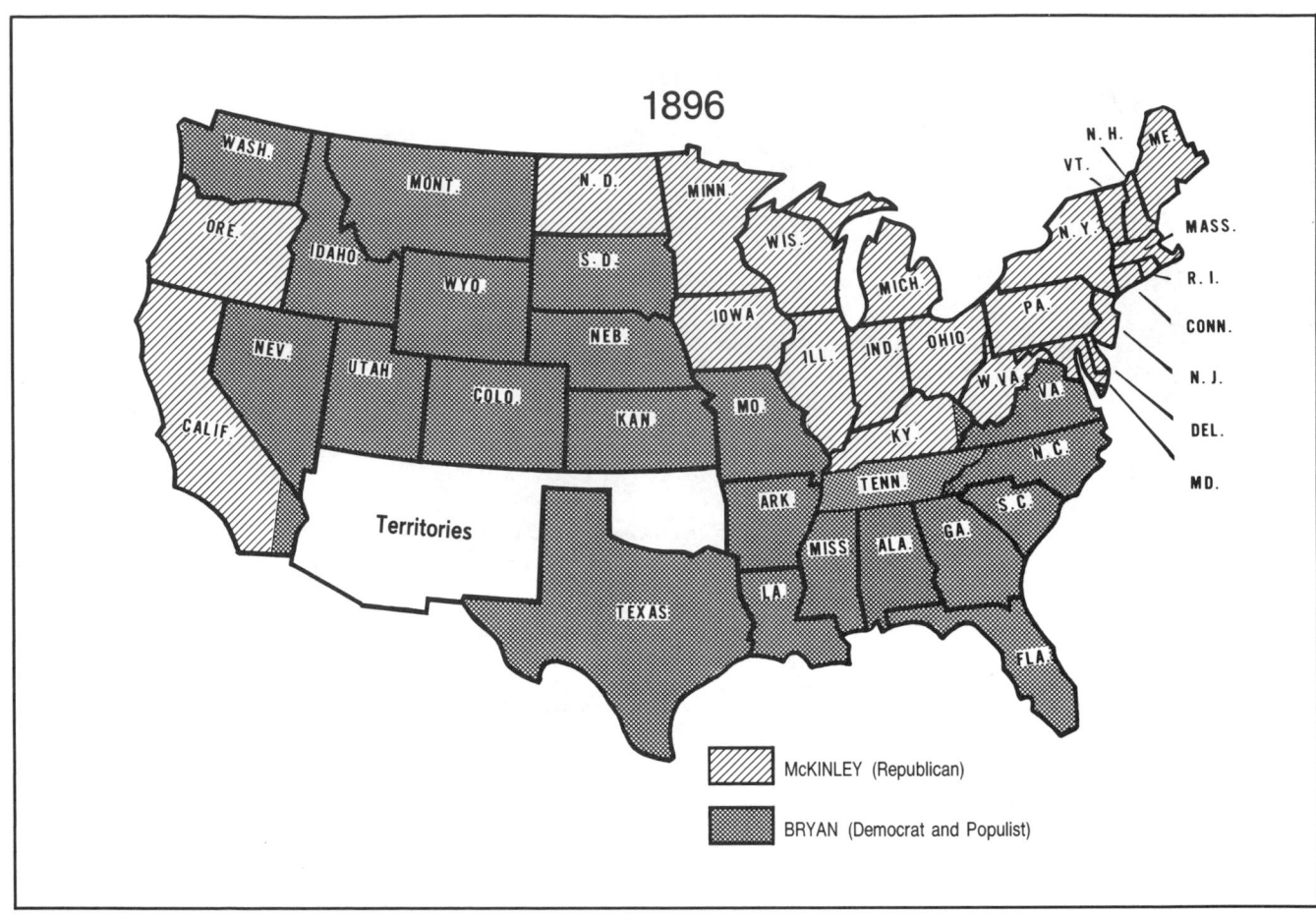

1896

McKINLEY (Republican)

BRYAN (Democrat and Populist)

| States | Electoral Votes | McKinley | Bryan | States | Electoral Votes | McKinley | Bryan |
|--------|-----------------|----------|-------|--------|-----------------|----------|-------|
| Alabama | (11) | - | 11 | Nebraska | (8) | - | 8 |
| Arkansas | (8) | - | 8 | Nevada | (3) | - | 3 |
| California [1] | (9) | 8 | 1 | New Hampshire | (4) | 4 | - |
| Colorado | (4) | - | 4 | New Jersey | (10) | 10 | - |
| Connecticut | (6) | 6 | - | New York | (36) | 36 | - |
| Delaware | (3) | 3 | - | North Carolina | (11) | - | 11 |
| Florida | (4) | - | 4 | North Dakota | (3) | 3 | - |
| Georgia | (13) | - | 13 | Ohio | (23) | 23 | - |
| Idaho | (3) | - | 3 | Oregon | (4) | 4 | - |
| Illinois | (24) | 24 | - | Pennsylvania | (32) | 32 | - |
| Indiana | (15) | 15 | - | Rhode Island | (4) | 4 | - |
| Iowa | (13) | 13 | - | South Carolina | (9) | - | 9 |
| Kansas | (10) | - | 10 | South Dakota | (4) | - | 4 |
| Kentucky [1] | (13) | 12 | 1 | Tennessee | (12) | - | 12 |
| Louisiana | (8) | - | 8 | Texas | (15) | - | 15 |
| Maine | (6) | 6 | - | Utah | (3) | - | 3 |
| Maryland | (8) | 8 | - | Vermont | (4) | 4 | - |
| Massachusetts | (15) | 15 | - | Virginia | (12) | - | 12 |
| Michigan | (14) | 14 | - | Washington | (4) | - | 4 |
| Minnesota | (9) | 9 | - | West Virginia | (6) | 6 | - |
| Mississippi | (9) | - | 9 | Wisconsin | (12) | 12 | - |
| Missouri | (17) | - | 17 | Wyoming | (3) | - | 3 |
| Montana | (3) | - | 3 | **Totals** | **(447)** | **271** | **176** |

1. *For explanation of split electoral votes, see p. 350.*

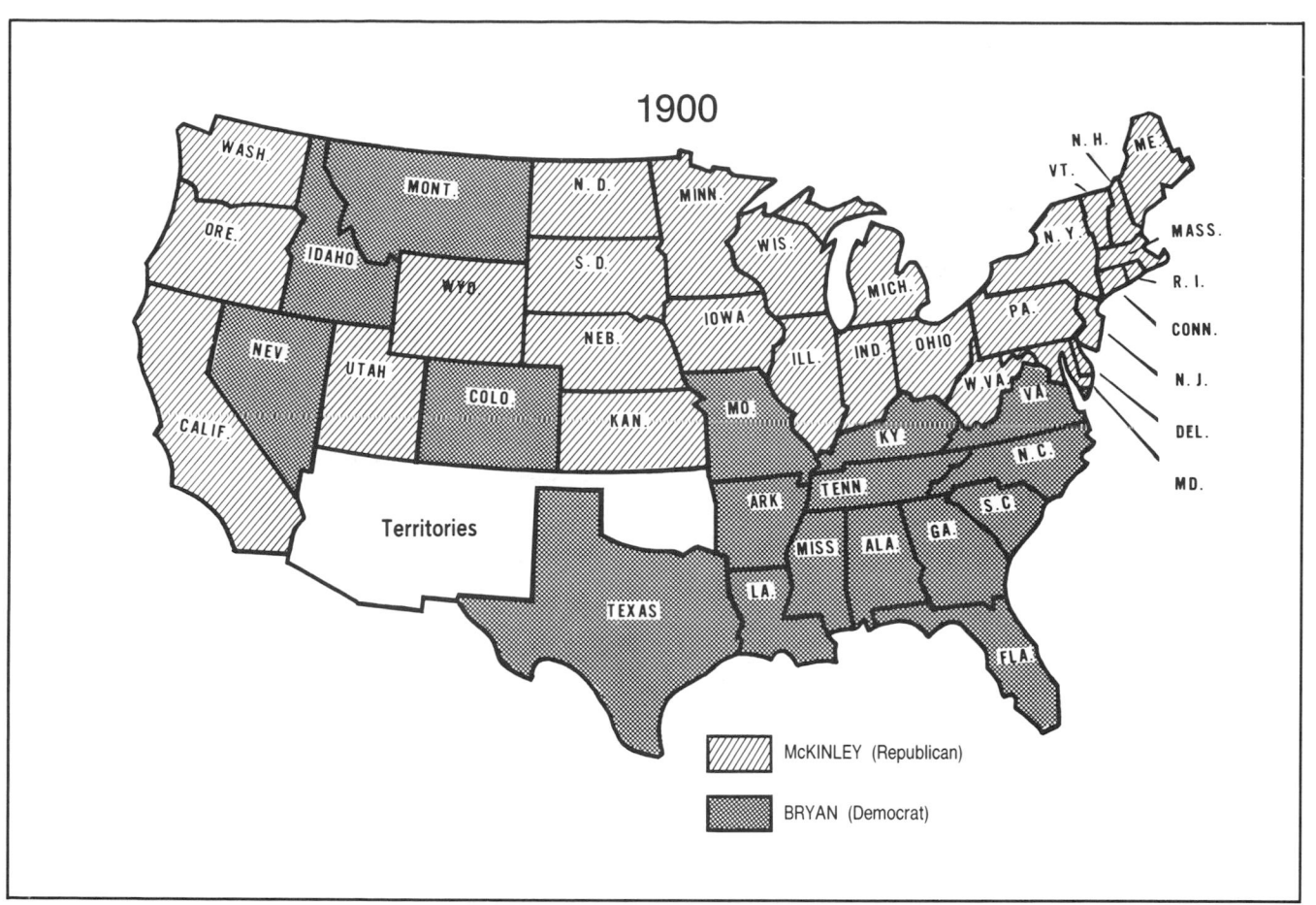

1900

McKINLEY (Republican)

BRYAN (Democrat)

| States | Electoral Votes | McKinley | Bryan | States | Electoral Votes | McKinley | Bryan |
|---|---|---|---|---|---|---|---|
| Alabama | (11) | - | 11 | Nebraska | (8) | 8 | - |
| Arkansas | (8) | - | 8 | Nevada | (3) | - | 3 |
| California | (9) | 9 | - | New Hampshire | (4) | 4 | - |
| Colorado | (4) | - | 4 | New Jersey | (10) | 10 | - |
| Connecticut | (6) | 6 | - | New York | (36) | 36 | - |
| Delaware | (3) | 3 | - | North Carolina | (11) | - | 11 |
| Florida | (4) | - | 4 | North Dakota | (3) | 3 | - |
| Georgia | (13) | - | 13 | Ohio | (23) | 23 | - |
| Idaho | (3) | - | 3 | Oregon | (4) | 4 | - |
| Illinois | (24) | 24 | - | Pennsylvania | (32) | 32 | - |
| Indiana | (15) | 15 | - | Rhode Island | (4) | 4 | - |
| Iowa | (13) | 13 | - | South Carolina | (9) | - | 9 |
| Kansas | (10) | 10 | - | South Dakota | (4) | 4 | - |
| Kentucky | (13) | - | 13 | Tennessee | (12) | - | 12 |
| Louisiana | (8) | - | 8 | Texas | (15) | - | 15 |
| Maine | (6) | 6 | - | Utah | (3) | 3 | - |
| Maryland | (8) | 8 | - | Vermont | (4) | 4 | - |
| Massachusetts | (15) | 15 | - | Virginia | (12) | - | 12 |
| Michigan | (14) | 14 | - | Washington | (4) | 4 | - |
| Minnesota | (9) | 9 | - | West Virginia | (6) | 6 | - |
| Mississippi | (9) | - | 9 | Wisconsin | (12) | 12 | - |
| Missouri | (17) | - | 17 | Wyoming | (3) | 3 | - |
| Montana | (3) | - | 3 | **Totals** | **(447)** | **292** | **155** |

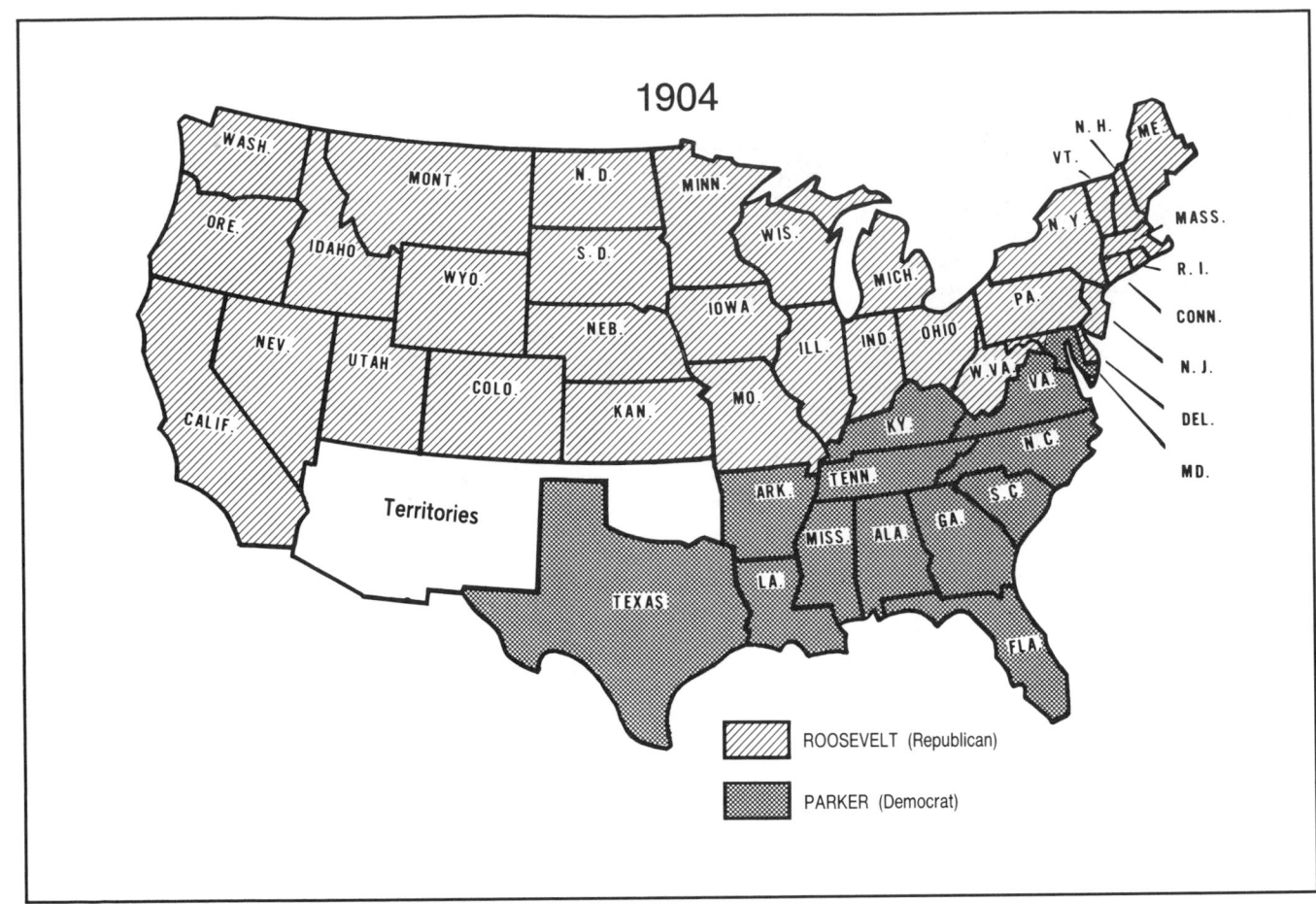

| States | Electoral Votes | Roosevelt | Parker | States | Electoral Votes | Roosevelt | Parker |
|---|---|---|---|---|---|---|---|
| **Alabama** | (11) | - | 11 | **Nebraska** | (8) | 8 | - |
| **Arkansas** | (9) | - | 9 | **Nevada** | (3) | 3 | - |
| **California** | (10) | 10 | - | **New Hampshire** | (4) | 4 | - |
| **Colorado** | (5) | 5 | - | **New Jersey** | (12) | 12 | - |
| **Connecticut** | (7) | 7 | - | **New York** | (39) | 39 | - |
| **Delaware** | (3) | 3 | - | **North Carolina** | (12) | - | 12 |
| **Florida** | (5) | - | 5 | **North Dakota** | (4) | 4 | - |
| **Georgia** | (13) | - | 13 | **Ohio** | (23) | 23 | - |
| **Idaho** | (3) | 3 | - | **Oregon** | (4) | 4 | - |
| **Illinois** | (27) | 27 | - | **Pennsylvania** | (34) | 34 | - |
| **Indiana** | (15) | 15 | - | **Rhode Island** | (4) | 4 | - |
| **Iowa** | (13) | 13 | - | **South Carolina** | (9) | - | 9 |
| **Kansas** | (10) | 10 | - | **South Dakota** | (4) | 4 | - |
| **Kentucky** | (13) | - | 13 | **Tennessee** | (12) | - | 12 |
| **Louisiana** | (9) | - | 9 | **Texas** | (18) | - | 18 |
| **Maine** | (6) | 6 | - | **Utah** | (3) | 3 | - |
| **Maryland** [1] | (8) | 1 | 7 | **Vermont** | (4) | 4 | - |
| **Massachusetts** | (16) | 16 | - | **Virginia** | (12) | - | 12 |
| **Michigan** | (14) | 14 | - | **Washington** | (5) | 5 | - |
| **Minnesota** | (11) | 11 | - | **West Virginia** | (7) | 7 | - |
| **Mississippi** | (10) | - | 10 | **Wisconsin** | (13) | 13 | - |
| **Missouri** | (18) | 18 | - | **Wyoming** | (3) | 3 | - |
| **Montana** | (3) | 3 | - | **Totals** | (476) | 336 | 140 |

1. For explanation of split electoral votes, see p. 350.

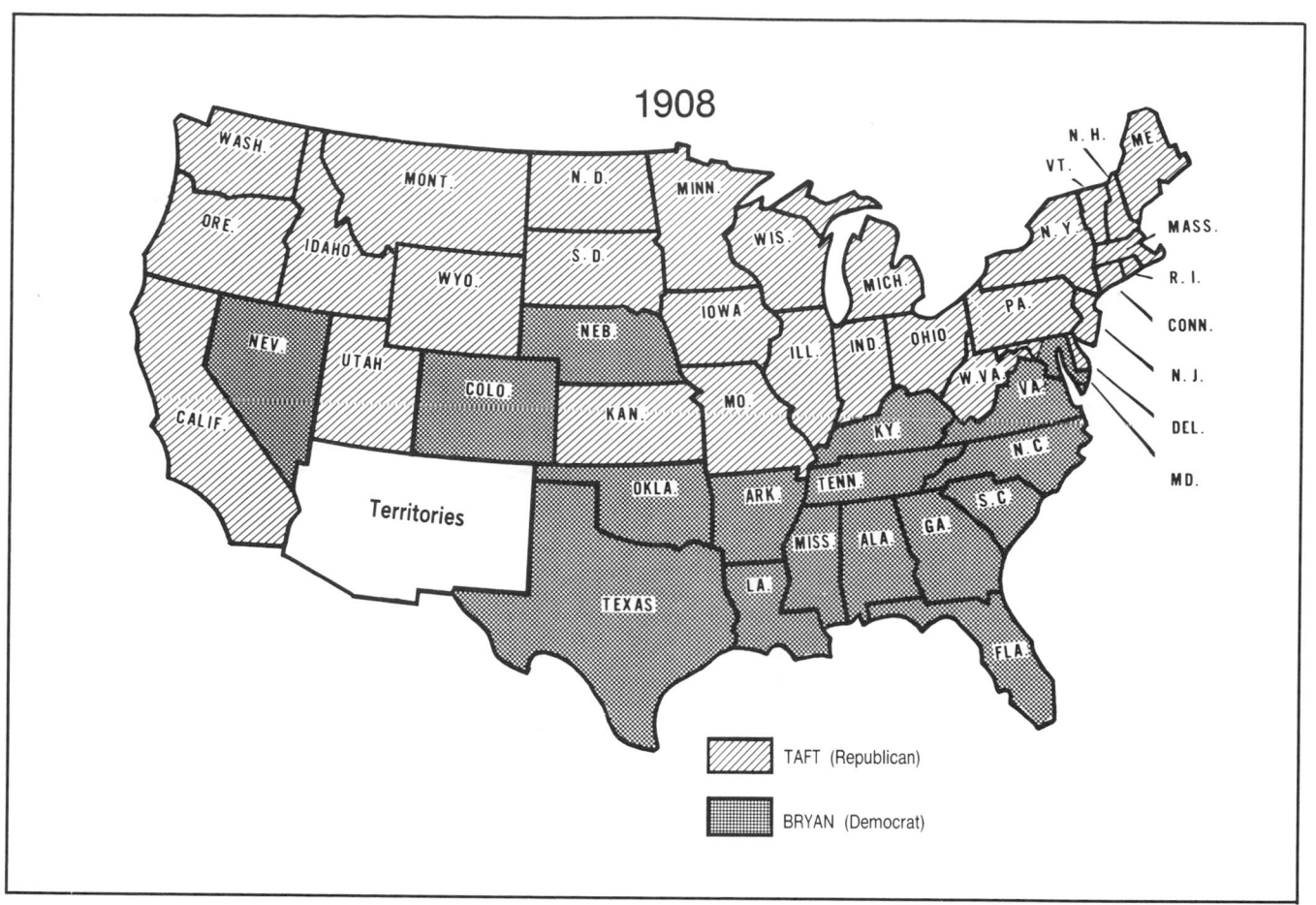

| States | Electoral Votes | Taft | Bryan | States | Electoral Votes | Taft | Bryan |
|---|---|---|---|---|---|---|---|
| **Alabama** | (11) | - | 11 | **Nebraska** | (8) | - | 8 |
| **Arkansas** | (9) | - | 9 | **Nevada** | (3) | - | 3 |
| **California** | (10) | 10 | - | **New Hampshire** | (4) | 4 | - |
| **Colorado** | (5) | - | 5 | **New Jersey** | (12) | 12 | - |
| **Connecticut** | (7) | 7 | - | **New York** | (39) | 39 | - |
| **Delaware** | (3) | 3 | - | **North Carolina** | (12) | - | 12 |
| **Florida** | (5) | - | 5 | **North Dakota** | (4) | 4 | - |
| **Georgia** | (13) | - | 13 | **Ohio** | (23) | 23 | - |
| **Idaho** | (3) | 3 | - | **Oklahoma** | (7) | - | 7 |
| **Illinois** | (27) | 27 | - | **Oregon** | (4) | 4 | - |
| **Indiana** | (15) | 15 | - | **Pennsylvania** | (34) | 34 | - |
| **Iowa** | (13) | 13 | - | **Rhode Island** | (4) | 4 | - |
| **Kansas** | (10) | 10 | - | **South Carolina** | (9) | - | 9 |
| **Kentucky** | (13) | - | 13 | **South Dakota** | (4) | 4 | - |
| **Louisiana** | (9) | - | 9 | **Tennessee** | (12) | - | 12 |
| **Maine** | (6) | 6 | - | **Texas** | (18) | - | 18 |
| **Maryland** [1] | (8) | 2 | 6 | **Utah** | (3) | 3 | - |
| **Massachusetts** | (16) | 16 | - | **Vermont** | (4) | 4 | - |
| **Michigan** | (14) | 14 | - | **Virginia** | (12) | - | 12 |
| **Minnesota** | (11) | 11 | - | **Washington** | (5) | 5 | - |
| **Mississippi** | (10) | - | 10 | **West Virginia** | (7) | 7 | - |
| **Missouri** | (18) | 18 | - | **Wisconsin** | (13) | 13 | - |
| **Montana** | (3) | 3 | - | **Wyoming** | (3) | 3 | - |
| | | | | **Totals** | **(483)** | 321 | 162 |

1. *For explanation of split electoral votes, see p. 350.*

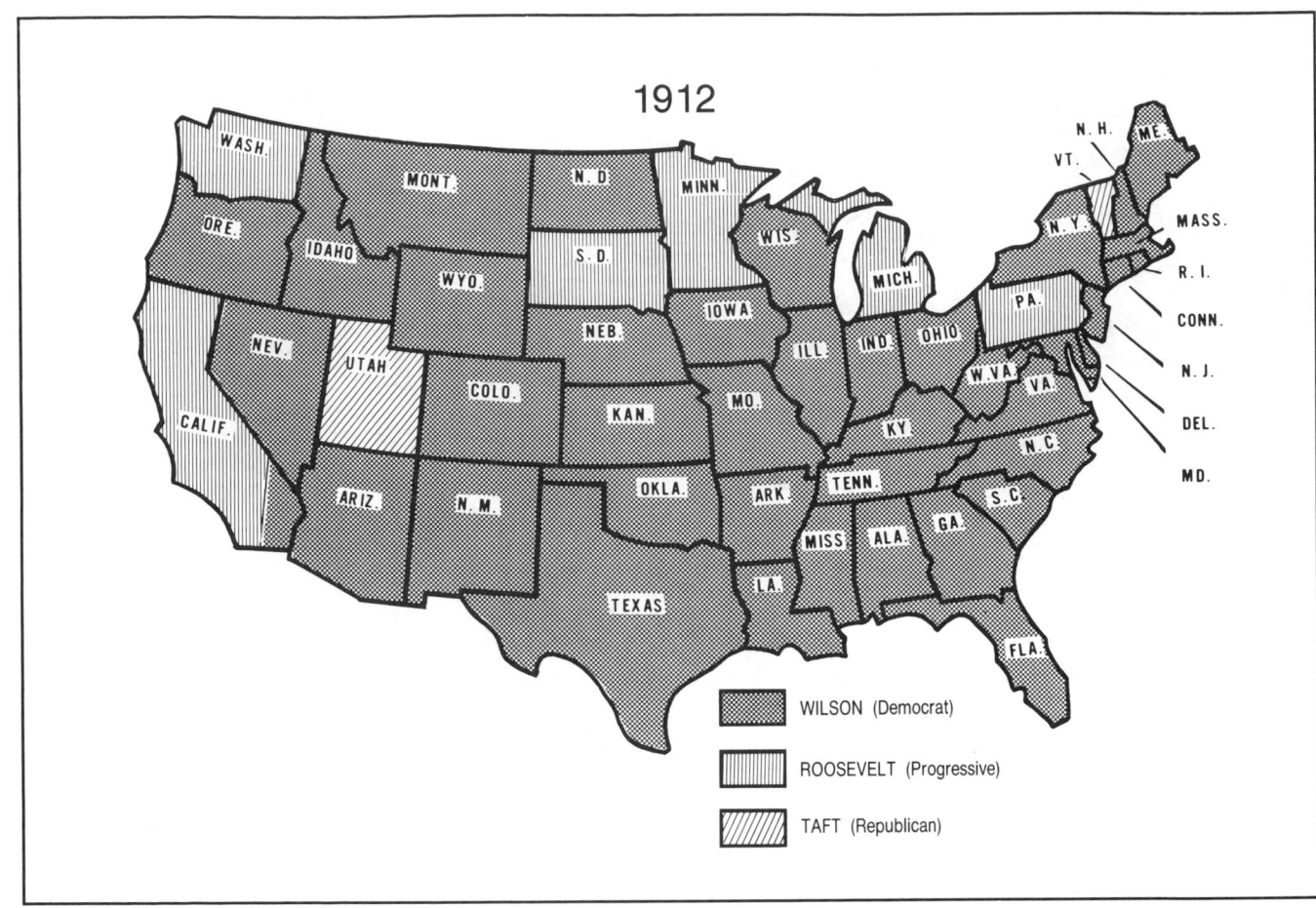

1912

WILSON (Democrat)

ROOSEVELT (Progressive)

TAFT (Republican)

| States | Electoral Votes | Wilson | Roosevelt | Taft | States | Electoral Votes | Wilson | Roosevelt | Taft |
|--------|-----------------|--------|-----------|------|--------|-----------------|--------|-----------|------|
| Alabama | (12) | 12 | - | - | Nebraska | (8) | 8 | - | - |
| Arizona | (3) | 3 | - | - | Nevada | (3) | 3 | - | - |
| Arkansas | (9) | 9 | - | - | New Hampshire | (4) | 4 | - | - |
| California [1] | (13) | 2 | 11 | - | New Jersey | (14) | 14 | - | - |
| Colorado | (6) | 6 | - | - | New Mexico | (3) | 3 | - | - |
| Connecticut | (7) | 7 | - | - | New York | (45) | 45 | - | - |
| Delaware | (3) | 3 | - | - | North Carolina | (12) | 12 | - | - |
| Florida | (6) | 6 | - | - | North Dakota | (5) | 5 | - | - |
| Georgia | (14) | 14 | - | - | Ohio | (24) | 24 | - | - |
| Idaho | (4) | 4 | - | - | Oklahoma | (10) | 10 | - | - |
| Illinois | (29) | 29 | - | - | Oregon | (5) | 5 | - | - |
| Indiana | (15) | 15 | - | - | Pennsylvania | (38) | - | 38 | - |
| Iowa | (13) | 13 | - | - | Rhode Island | (5) | 5 | - | - |
| Kansas | (10) | 10 | - | - | South Carolina | (9) | 9 | - | - |
| Kentucky | (13) | 13 | - | - | South Dakota | (5) | - | 5 | - |
| Louisiana | (10) | 10 | - | - | Tennessee | (12) | 12 | - | - |
| Maine | (6) | 6 | - | - | Texas | (20) | 20 | - | - |
| Maryland | (8) | 8 | - | - | Utah | (4) | - | - | 4 |
| Massachusetts | (18) | 18 | - | - | Vermont | (4) | - | - | 4 |
| Michigan | (15) | - | 15 | - | Virginia | (12) | 12 | - | - |
| Minnesota | (12) | - | 12 | - | Washington | (7) | - | 7 | - |
| Mississippi | (10) | 10 | - | - | West Virginia | (8) | 8 | - | - |
| Missouri | (18) | 18 | - | - | Wisconsin | (13) | 13 | - | - |
| Montana | (4) | 4 | - | - | Wyoming | (3) | 3 | - | - |
| | | | | | **Totals** | **(531)** | **435** | **88** | **8** |

1. For explanation of split electoral votes, see p. 350.

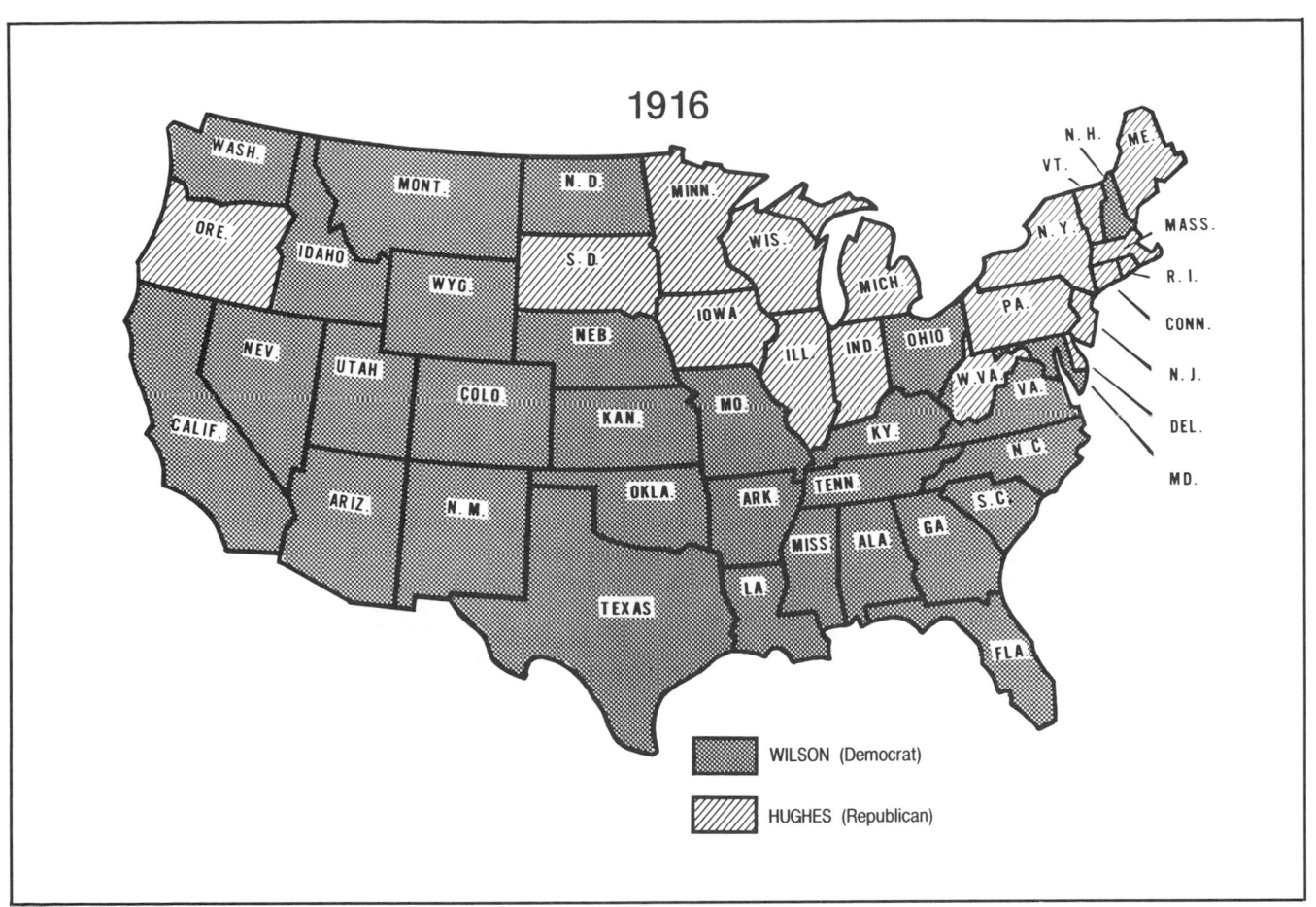

# 1916

WILSON (Democrat)

HUGHES (Republican)

| States | Electoral Votes | Wilson | Hughes | States | Electoral Votes | Wilson | Hughes |
|--------|-----------------|--------|--------|--------|-----------------|--------|--------|
| **Alabama** | (12) | 12 | - | **Nebraska** | (8) | 8 | - |
| **Arizona** | (3) | 3 | - | **Nevada** | (3) | 3 | - |
| **Arkansas** | (9) | 9 | - | **New Hampshire** | (4) | 4 | - |
| **California** | (13) | 13 | - | **New Jersey** | (14) | - | 14 |
| **Colorado** | (6) | 6 | - | **New Mexico** | (3) | 3 | - |
| **Connecticut** | (7) | - | 7 | **New York** | (45) | - | 45 |
| **Delaware** | (3) | - | 3 | **North Carolina** | (12) | 12 | - |
| **Florida** | (6) | 6 | - | **North Dakota** | (5) | 5 | - |
| **Georgia** | (14) | 14 | - | **Ohio** | (24) | 24 | - |
| **Idaho** | (4) | 4 | - | **Oklahoma** | (10) | 10 | - |
| **Illinois** | (29) | - | 29 | **Oregon** | (5) | - | 5 |
| **Indiana** | (15) | - | 15 | **Pennsylvania** | (38) | - | 38 |
| **Iowa** | (13) | - | 13 | **Rhode Island** | (5) | - | 5 |
| **Kansas** | (10) | 10 | - | **South Carolina** | (9) | 9 | - |
| **Kentucky** | (13) | 13 | - | **South Dakota** | (5) | - | 5 |
| **Louisiana** | (10) | 10 | - | **Tennessee** | (12) | 12 | - |
| **Maine** | (6) | - | 6 | **Texas** | (20) | 20 | - |
| **Maryland** | (8) | 8 | - | **Utah** | (4) | 4 | - |
| **Massachusetts** | (18) | - | 18 | **Vermont** | (4) | - | 4 |
| **Michigan** | (15) | - | 15 | **Virginia** | (12) | 12 | - |
| **Minnesota** | (12) | - | 12 | **Washington** | (7) | 7 | - |
| **Mississippi** | (10) | 10 | - | **West Virginia** [1] | (8) | 1 | 7 |
| **Missouri** | (18) | 18 | - | **Wisconsin** | (13) | - | 13 |
| **Montana** | (4) | 4 | - | **Wyoming** | (3) | 3 | - |
| | | | | **Totals** | (531) | 277 | 254 |

1. For explanation of split electoral votes, see p. 350.

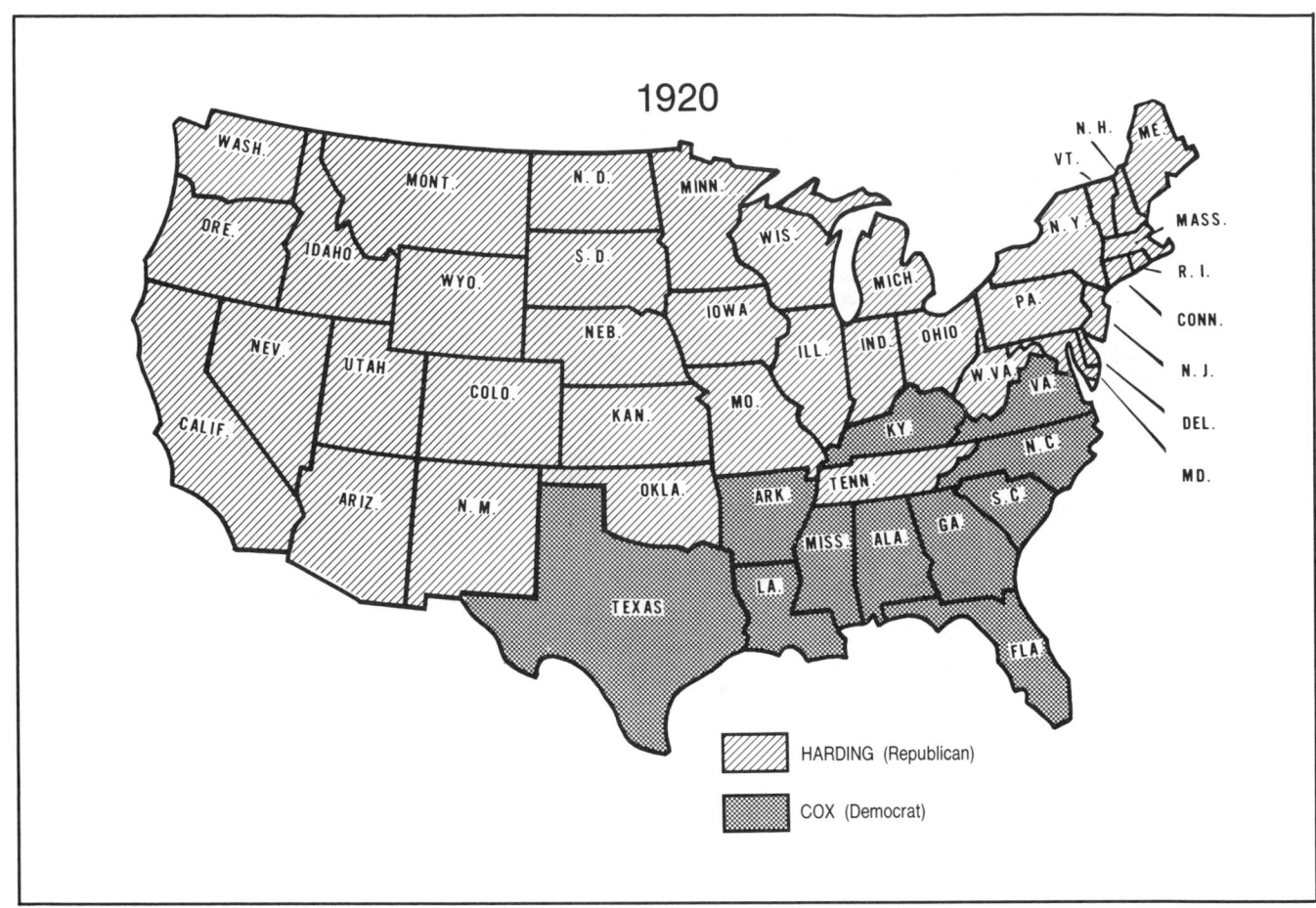

1920

HARDING (Republican)

COX (Democrat)

| States | Electoral Votes | Harding | Cox | States | Electoral Votes | Harding | Cox |
|---|---|---|---|---|---|---|---|
| Alabama | (12) | - | 12 | Nebraska | (8) | 8 | - |
| Arizona | (3) | 3 | - | Nevada | (3) | 3 | - |
| Arkansas | (9) | - | 9 | New Hampshire | (4) | 4 | - |
| California | (13) | 13 | - | New Jersey | (14) | 14 | - |
| Colorado | (6) | 6 | - | New Mexico | (3) | 3 | - |
| Connecticut | (7) | 7 | - | New York | (45) | 45 | - |
| Delaware | (3) | 3 | - | North Carolina | (12) | - | 12 |
| Florida | (6) | - | 6 | North Dakota | (5) | 5 | - |
| Georgia | (14) | - | 14 | Ohio | (24) | 24 | - |
| Idaho | (4) | 4 | - | Oklahoma | (10) | 10 | - |
| Illinois | (29) | 29 | - | Oregon | (5) | 5 | - |
| Indiana | (15) | 15 | - | Pennsylvania | (38) | 38 | - |
| Iowa | (13) | 13 | - | Rhode Island | (5) | 5 | - |
| Kansas | (10) | 10 | - | South Carolina | (9) | - | 9 |
| Kentucky | (13) | - | 13 | South Dakota | (5) | 5 | - |
| Louisiana | (10) | - | 10 | Tennessee | (12) | 12 | - |
| Maine | (6) | 6 | - | Texas | (20) | - | 20 |
| Maryland | (8) | 8 | - | Utah | (4) | 4 | - |
| Massachusetts | (18) | 18 | - | Vermont | (4) | 4 | - |
| Michigan | (15) | 15 | - | Virginia | (12) | - | 12 |
| Minnesota | (12) | 12 | - | Washington | (7) | 7 | - |
| Mississippi | (10) | - | 10 | West Virginia | (8) | 8 | - |
| Missouri | (18) | 18 | - | Wisconsin | (13) | 13 | - |
| Montana | (4) | 4 | - | Wyoming | (3) | 3 | - |
| | | | | **Totals** | **(531)** | **404** | **127** |

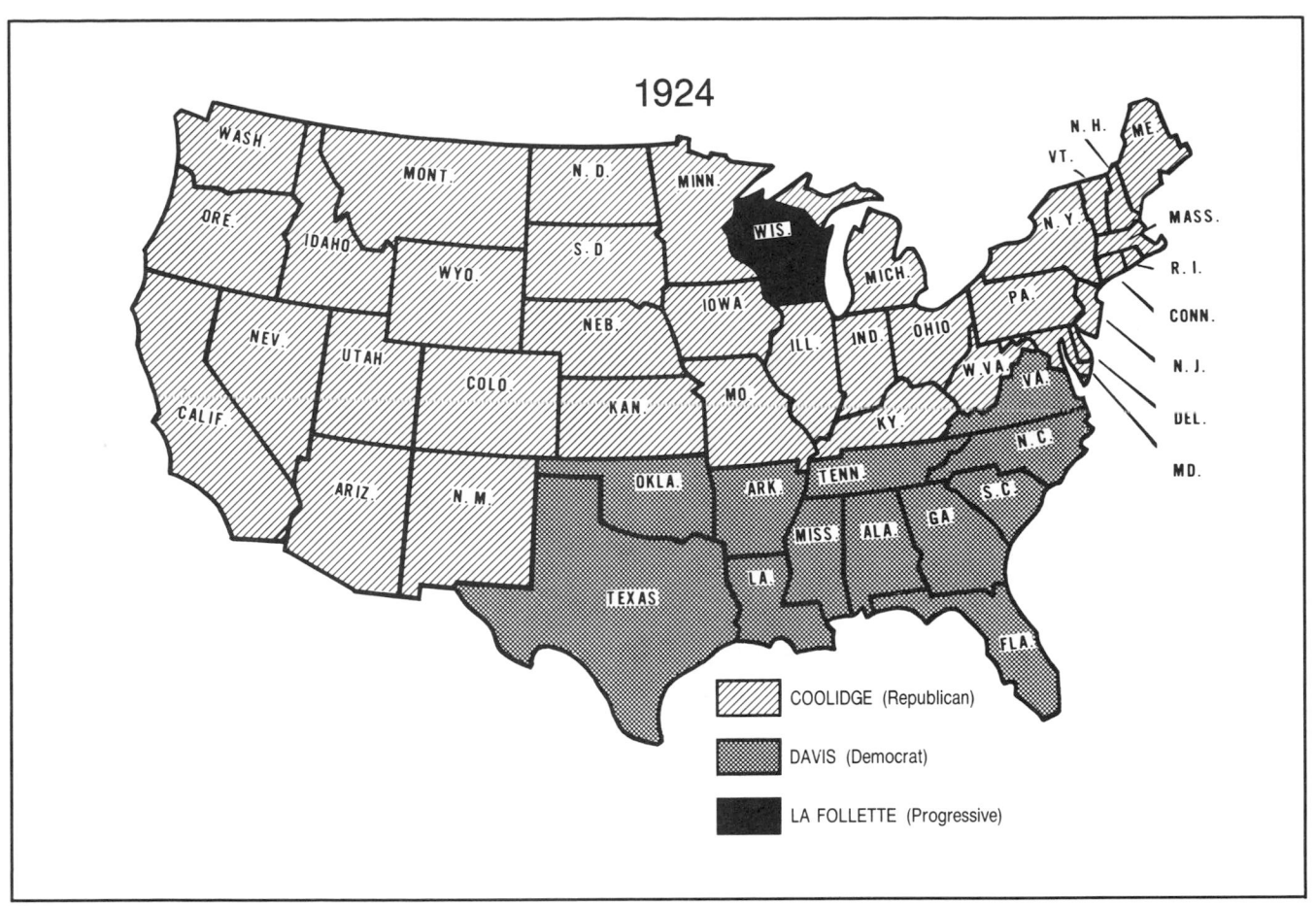

1924

COOLIDGE (Republican)

DAVIS (Democrat)

LA FOLLETTE (Progressive)

| States | Electoral Votes | Coolidge | Davis | La Follette | States | Electoral Votes | Coolidge | Davis | La Follette |
|---|---|---|---|---|---|---|---|---|---|
| **Alabama** | (12) | - | 12 | - | **Nebraska** | (8) | 8 | - | - |
| **Arizona** | (3) | 3 | - | - | **Nevada** | (3) | 3 | - | - |
| **Arkansas** | (9) | - | 9 | - | **New Hampshire** | (4) | 4 | - | - |
| **California** | (13) | 13 | - | - | **New Jersey** | (14) | 14 | - | - |
| **Colorado** | (6) | 6 | - | - | **New Mexico** | (3) | 3 | - | - |
| **Connecticut** | (7) | 7 | - | - | **New York** | (45) | 45 | - | - |
| **Delaware** | (3) | 3 | - | - | **North Carolina** | (12) | - | 12 | - |
| **Florida** | (6) | - | 6 | - | **North Dakota** | (5) | 5 | - | - |
| **Georgia** | (14) | - | 14 | - | **Ohio** | (24) | 24 | - | - |
| **Idaho** | (4) | 4 | - | - | **Oklahoma** | (10) | - | 10 | - |
| **Illinois** | (29) | 29 | - | - | **Oregon** | (5) | 5 | - | - |
| **Indiana** | (15) | 15 | - | - | **Pennsylvania** | (38) | 38 | - | - |
| **Iowa** | (13) | 13 | - | - | **Rhode Island** | (5) | 5 | - | - |
| **Kansas** | (10) | 10 | - | - | **South Carolina** | (9) | - | 9 | - |
| **Kentucky** | (13) | 13 | - | - | **South Dakota** | (5) | 5 | - | - |
| **Louisiana** | (10) | - | 10 | - | **Tennessee** | (12) | - | 12 | - |
| **Maine** | (6) | 6 | - | - | **Texas** | (20) | - | 20 | - |
| **Maryland** | (8) | 8 | - | - | **Utah** | (4) | 4 | - | - |
| **Massachusetts** | (18) | 18 | - | - | **Vermont** | (4) | 4 | - | - |
| **Michigan** | (15) | 15 | - | - | **Virginia** | (12) | - | 12 | - |
| **Minnesota** | (12) | 12 | - | - | **Washington** | (7) | 7 | - | - |
| **Mississippi** | (10) | - | 10 | - | **West Virginia** | (8) | 8 | - | - |
| **Missouri** | (18) | 18 | - | - | **Wisconsin** | (13) | - | - | 13 |
| **Montana** | (4) | 4 | - | - | **Wyoming** | (3) | 3 | - | - |
| | | | | | **Totals** | (531) | 382 | 136 | 13 |

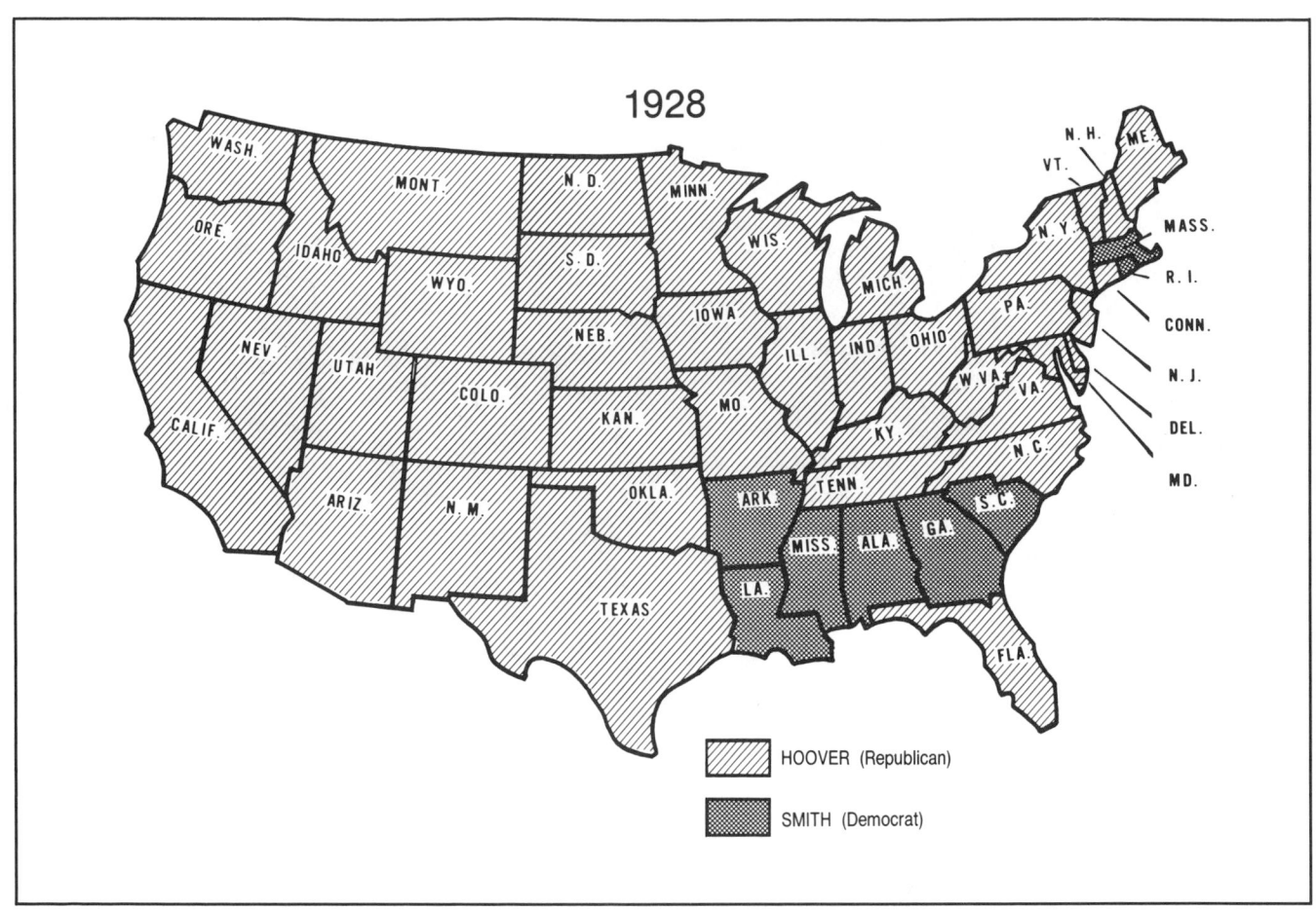

1928

HOOVER (Republican)

SMITH (Democrat)

| States | Electoral Votes | Hoover | Smith | States | Electoral Votes | Hoover | Smith |
|--------|----------------|--------|-------|--------|----------------|--------|-------|
| **Alabama** | (12) | - | 12 | **Nebraska** | (8) | 8 | - |
| **Arizona** | (3) | 3 | - | **Nevada** | (3) | 3 | - |
| **Arkansas** | (9) | - | 9 | **New Hampshire** | (4) | 4 | - |
| **California** | (13) | 13 | - | **New Jersey** | (14) | 14 | - |
| **Colorado** | (6) | 6 | - | **New Mexico** | (3) | 3 | - |
| **Connecticut** | (7) | 7 | - | **New York** | (45) | 45 | - |
| **Delaware** | (3) | 3 | - | **North Carolina** | (12) | 12 | - |
| **Florida** | (6) | 6 | - | **North Dakota** | (5) | 5 | - |
| **Georgia** | (14) | - | 14 | **Ohio** | (24) | 24 | - |
| **Idaho** | (4) | 4 | - | **Oklahoma** | (10) | 10 | - |
| **Illinois** | (29) | 29 | - | **Oregon** | (5) | 5 | - |
| **Indiana** | (15) | 15 | - | **Pennsylvania** | (38) | 38 | - |
| **Iowa** | (13) | 13 | - | **Rhode Island** | (5) | - | 5 |
| **Kansas** | (10) | 10 | - | **South Carolina** | (9) | - | 9 |
| **Kentucky** | (13) | 13 | - | **South Dakota** | (5) | 5 | - |
| **Louisiana** | (10) | - | 10 | **Tennessee** | (12) | 12 | - |
| **Maine** | (6) | 6 | - | **Texas** | (20) | 20 | - |
| **Maryland** | (8) | 8 | - | **Utah** | (4) | 4 | - |
| **Massachusetts** | (18) | - | 18 | **Vermont** | (4) | 4 | - |
| **Michigan** | (15) | 15 | - | **Virginia** | (12) | 12 | - |
| **Minnesota** | (12) | 12 | - | **Washington** | (7) | 7 | - |
| **Mississippi** | (10) | - | 10 | **West Virginia** | (8) | 8 | - |
| **Missouri** | (18) | 18 | - | **Wisconsin** | (13) | 13 | - |
| **Montana** | (4) | 4 | - | **Wyoming** | (3) | 3 | - |
| | | | | **Totals** | (531) | 444 | 87 |

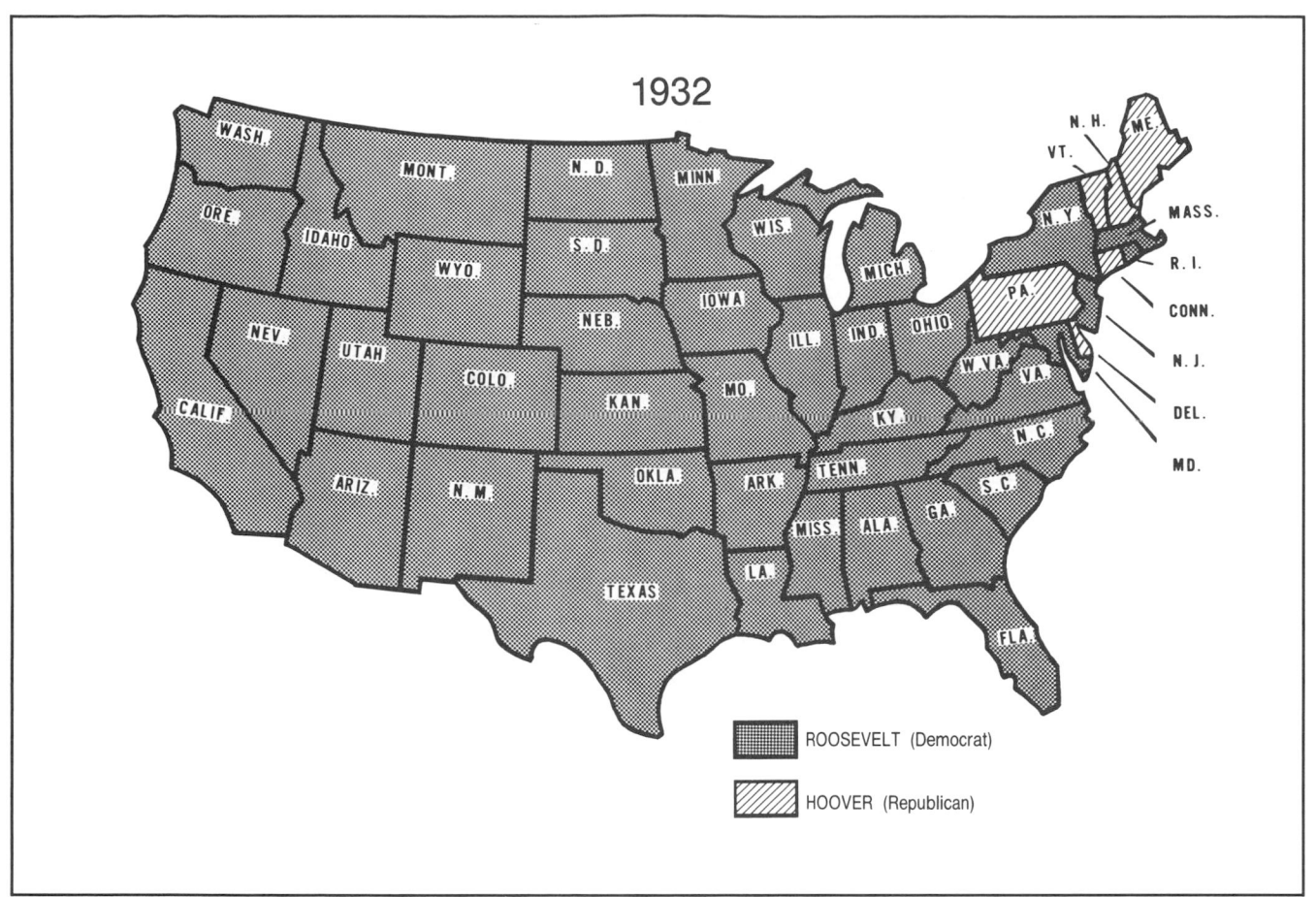

## 1932

ROOSEVELT (Democrat)

HOOVER (Republican)

| States | Electoral Votes | Roosevelt | Hoover | States | Electoral Votes | Roosevelt | Hoover |
|---|---|---|---|---|---|---|---|
| Alabama | (11) | 11 | - | Nebraska | (7) | 7 | - |
| Arizona | (3) | 3 | - | Nevada | (3) | 3 | - |
| Arkansas | (9) | 9 | - | New Hampshire | (4) | - | 4 |
| California | (22) | 22 | - | New Jersey | (16) | 16 | - |
| Colorado | (6) | 6 | - | New Mexico | (3) | 3 | - |
| Connecticut | (8) | - | 8 | New York | (47) | 47 | - |
| Delaware | (3) | - | 3 | North Carolina | (13) | 13 | - |
| Florida | (7) | 7 | - | North Dakota | (4) | 4 | - |
| Georgia | (12) | 12 | - | Ohio | (26) | 26 | - |
| Idaho | (4) | 4 | - | Oklahoma | (11) | 11 | - |
| Illinois | (29) | 29 | - | Oregon | (5) | 5 | - |
| Indiana | (14) | 14 | - | Pennsylvania | (36) | - | 36 |
| Iowa | (11) | 11 | - | Rhode Island | (4) | 4 | - |
| Kansas | (9) | 9 | - | South Carolina | (8) | 8 | - |
| Kentucky | (11) | 11 | - | South Dakota | (4) | 4 | - |
| Louisiana | (10) | 10 | - | Tennessee | (11) | 11 | - |
| Maine | (5) | - | 5 | Texas | (23) | 23 | - |
| Maryland | (8) | 8 | - | Utah | (4) | 4 | - |
| Massachusetts | (17) | 17 | - | Vermont | (3) | - | 3 |
| Michigan | (19) | 19 | - | Virginia | (11) | 11 | - |
| Minnesota | (11) | 11 | - | Washington | (8) | 8 | - |
| Mississippi | (9) | 9 | - | West Virginia | (8) | 8 | - |
| Missouri | (15) | 15 | - | Wisconsin | (12) | 12 | - |
| Montana | (4) | 4 | - | Wyoming | (3) | 3 | - |
| | | | | **Totals** | **(531)** | **472** | **59** |

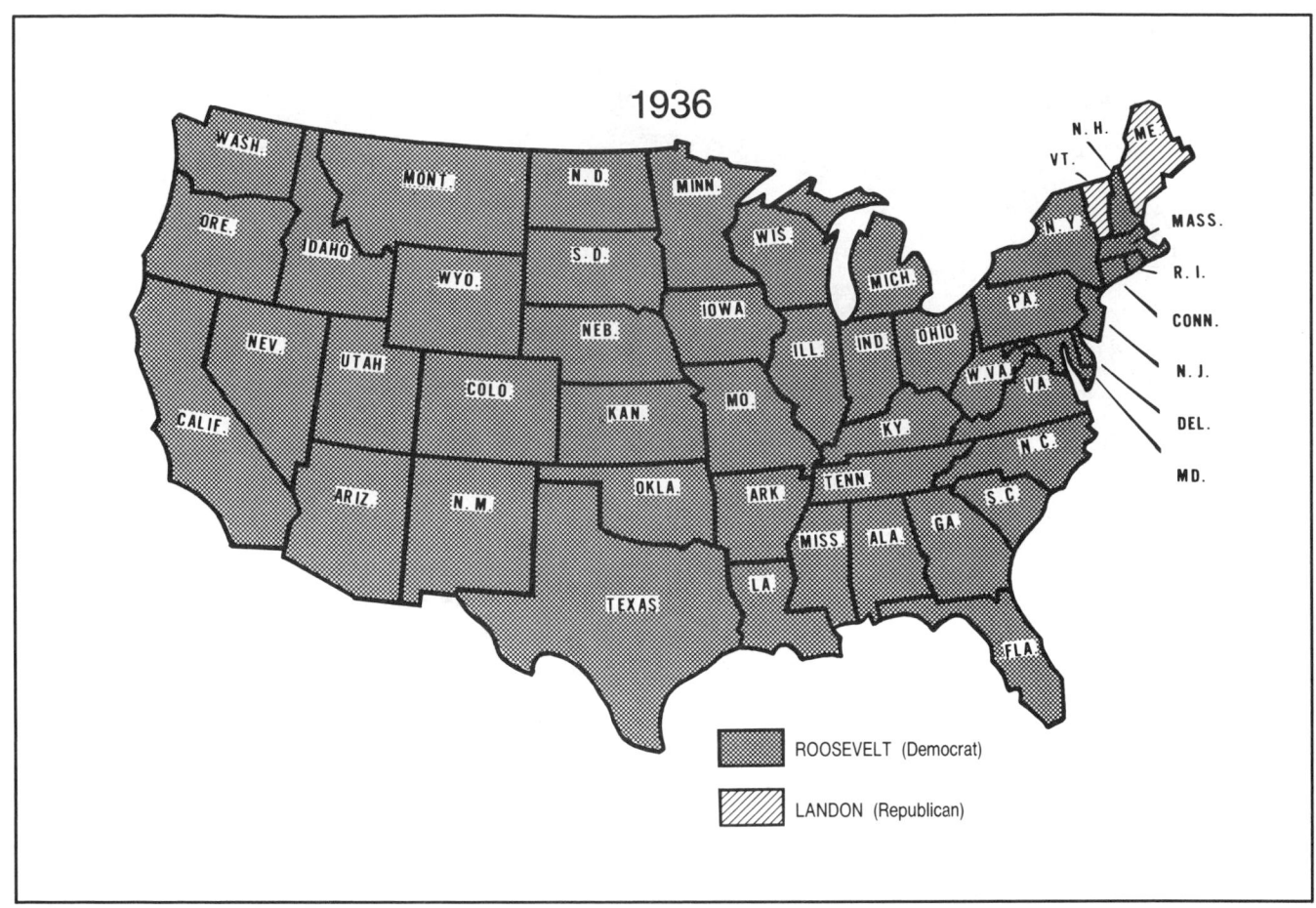

1936

ROOSEVELT (Democrat)

LANDON (Republican)

| States | Electoral Votes | Roosevelt | Landon | States | Electoral Votes | Roosevelt | Landon |
|---|---|---|---|---|---|---|---|
| Alabama | (11) | 11 | - | Nebraska | (7) | 7 | - |
| Arizona | (3) | 3 | - | Nevada | (3) | 3 | - |
| Arkansas | (9) | 9 | - | New Hampshire | (4) | 4 | - |
| California | (22) | 22 | - | New Jersey | (16) | 16 | - |
| Colorado | (6) | 6 | - | New Mexico | (3) | 3 | - |
| Connecticut | (8) | 8 | - | New York | (47) | 47 | - |
| Delaware | (3) | 3 | - | North Carolina | (13) | 13 | - |
| Florida | (7) | 7 | - | North Dakota | (4) | 4 | - |
| Georgia | (12) | 12 | - | Ohio | (26) | 26 | - |
| Idaho | (4) | 4 | - | Oklahoma | (11) | 11 | - |
| Illinois | (29) | 29 | - | Oregon | (5) | 5 | - |
| Indiana | (14) | 14 | - | Pennsylvania | (36) | 36 | - |
| Iowa | (11) | 11 | - | Rhode Island | (4) | 4 | - |
| Kansas | (9) | 9 | - | South Carolina | (8) | 8 | - |
| Kentucky | (11) | 11 | - | South Dakota | (4) | 4 | - |
| Louisiana | (10) | 10 | - | Tennessee | (11) | 11 | - |
| Maine | (5) | - | 5 | Texas | (23) | 23 | - |
| Maryland | (8) | 8 | - | Utah | (4) | 4 | - |
| Massachusetts | (17) | 17 | - | Vermont | (3) | - | 3 |
| Michigan | (19) | 19 | - | Virginia | (11) | 11 | - |
| Minnesota | (11) | 11 | - | Washington | (8) | 8 | - |
| Mississippi | (9) | 9 | - | West Virginia | (8) | 8 | - |
| Missouri | (15) | 15 | - | Wisconsin | (12) | 12 | - |
| Montana | (4) | 4 | - | Wyoming | (3) | 3 | - |
| | | | | **Totals** | **(531)** | **523** | **8** |

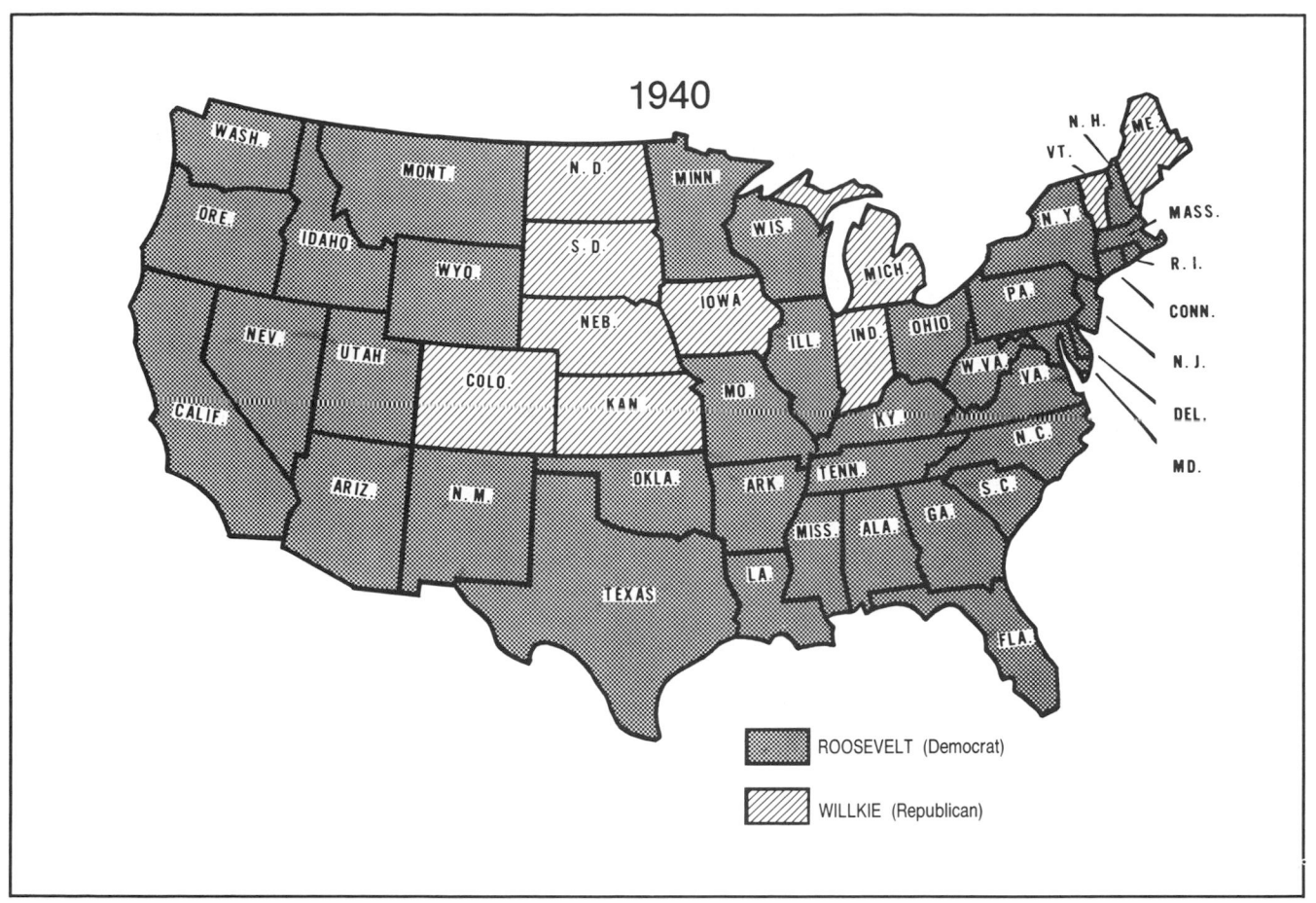

1940

ROOSEVELT (Democrat)

WILLKIE (Republican)

| States | Electoral Votes | Roosevelt | Willkie | States | Electoral Votes | Roosevelt | Willkie |
|--------|-----------------|-----------|---------|--------|-----------------|-----------|---------|
| Alabama | (11) | 11 | - | Nebraska | (7) | - | 7 |
| Arizona | (3) | 3 | - | Nevada | (3) | 3 | - |
| Arkansas | (9) | 9 | - | New Hampshire | (4) | 4 | - |
| California | (22) | 22 | - | New Jersey | (16) | 16 | - |
| Colorado | (6) | - | 6 | New Mexico | (3) | 3 | - |
| Connecticut | (8) | 8 | - | New York | (47) | 47 | - |
| Delaware | (3) | 3 | - | North Carolina | (13) | 13 | - |
| Florida | (7) | 7 | - | North Dakota | (4) | - | 4 |
| Georgia | (12) | 12 | - | Ohio | (26) | 26 | - |
| Idaho | (4) | 4 | - | Oklahoma | (11) | 11 | - |
| Illinois | (29) | 29 | - | Oregon | (5) | 5 | - |
| Indiana | (14) | - | 14 | Pennsylvania | (36) | 36 | - |
| Iowa | (11) | - | 11 | Rhode Island | (4) | 4 | - |
| Kansas | (9) | - | 9 | South Carolina | (8) | 8 | - |
| Kentucky | (11) | 11 | - | South Dakota | (4) | - | 4 |
| Louisiana | (10) | 10 | - | Tennessee | (11) | 11 | - |
| Maine | (5) | - | 5 | Texas | (23) | 23 | - |
| Maryland | (8) | 8 | - | Utah | (4) | 4 | - |
| Massachusetts | (17) | 17 | - | Vermont | (3) | - | 3 |
| Michigan | (19) | - | 19 | Virginia | (11) | 11 | - |
| Minnesota | (11) | 11 | - | Washington | (8) | 8 | - |
| Mississippi | (9) | 9 | - | West Virginia | (8) | 8 | - |
| Missouri | (15) | 15 | - | Wisconsin | (12) | 12 | - |
| Montana | (4) | 4 | - | Wyoming | (3) | 3 | - |
| | | | | **Totals** | **(531)** | **449** | **82** |

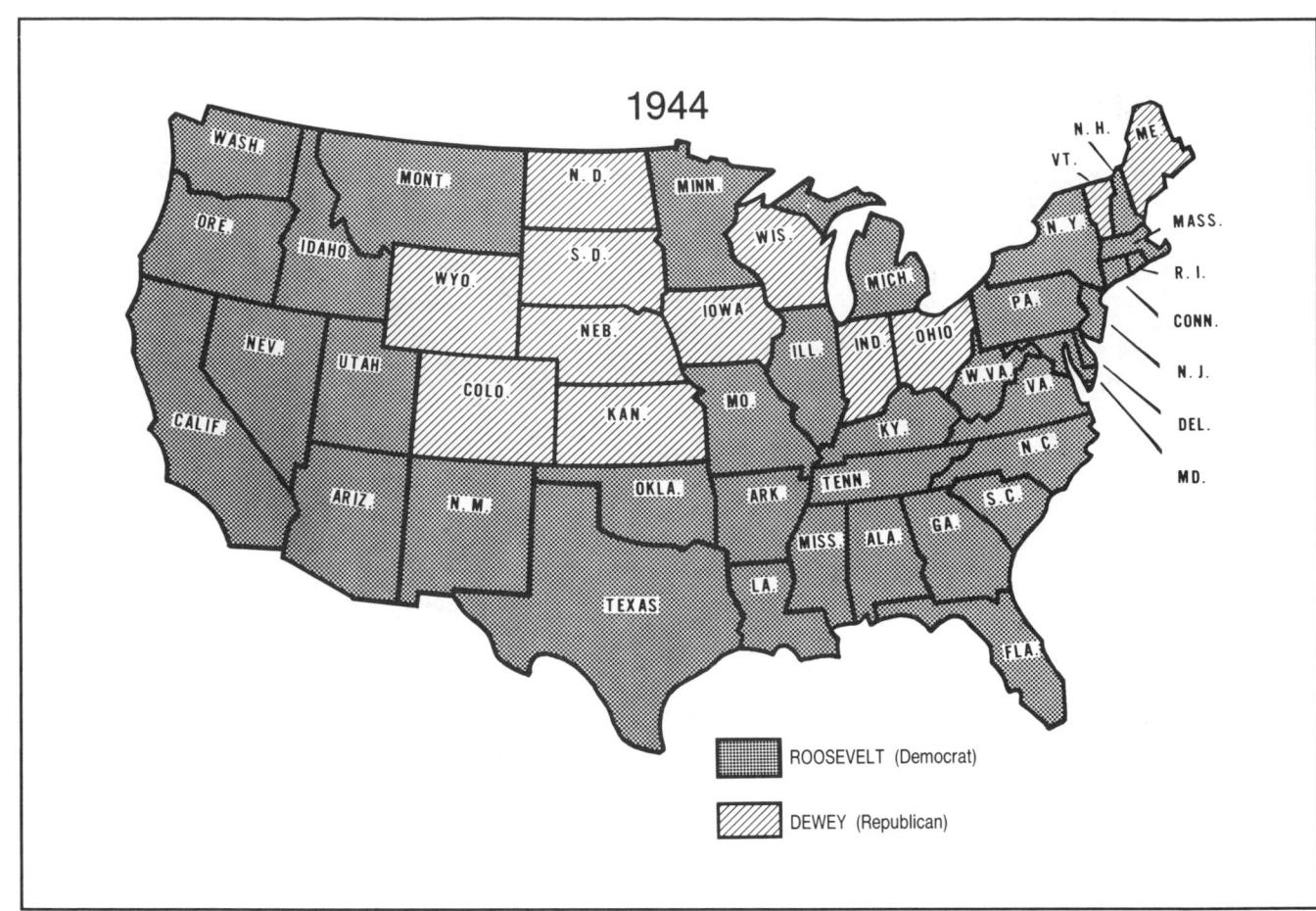

1944

ROOSEVELT (Democrat)

DEWEY (Republican)

| States | Electoral Votes | Roosevelt | Dewey | States | Electoral Votes | Roosevelt | Dewey |
|--------|-----------------|-----------|-------|--------|-----------------|-----------|-------|
| Alabama | (11) | 11 | - | Nebraska | (6) | - | 6 |
| Arizona | (4) | 4 | - | Nevada | (3) | 3 | - |
| Arkansas | (9) | 9 | - | New Hampshire | (4) | 4 | - |
| California | (25) | 25 | - | New Jersey | (16) | 16 | - |
| Colorado | (6) | - | 6 | New Mexico | (4) | 4 | - |
| Connecticut | (8) | 8 | - | New York | (47) | 47 | - |
| Delaware | (3) | 3 | - | North Carolina | (14) | 14 | - |
| Florida | (8) | 8 | - | North Dakota | (4) | - | 4 |
| Georgia | (12) | 12 | - | Ohio | (25) | - | 25 |
| Idaho | (4) | 4 | - | Oklahoma | (10) | 10 | - |
| Illinois | (28) | 28 | - | Oregon | (6) | 6 | - |
| Indiana | (13) | - | 13 | Pennsylvania | (35) | 35 | - |
| Iowa | (10) | - | 10 | Rhode Island | (4) | 4 | - |
| Kansas | (8) | - | 8 | South Carolina | (8) | 8 | - |
| Kentucky | (11) | 11 | - | South Dakota | (4) | - | 4 |
| Louisiana | (10) | 10 | - | Tennessee | (12) | 12 | - |
| Maine | (5) | - | 5 | Texas | (23) | 23 | - |
| Maryland | (8) | 8 | - | Utah | (4) | 4 | - |
| Massachusetts | (16) | 16 | - | Vermont | (3) | - | 3 |
| Michigan | (19) | 19 | - | Virginia | (11) | 11 | - |
| Minnesota | (11) | 11 | - | Washington | (8) | 8 | - |
| Mississippi | (9) | 9 | - | West Virginia | (8) | 8 | - |
| Missouri | (15) | 15 | - | Wisconsin | (12) | - | 12 |
| Montana | (4) | 4 | - | Wyoming | (3) | - | 3 |
| | | | | **Totals** | **(531)** | **432** | **99** |

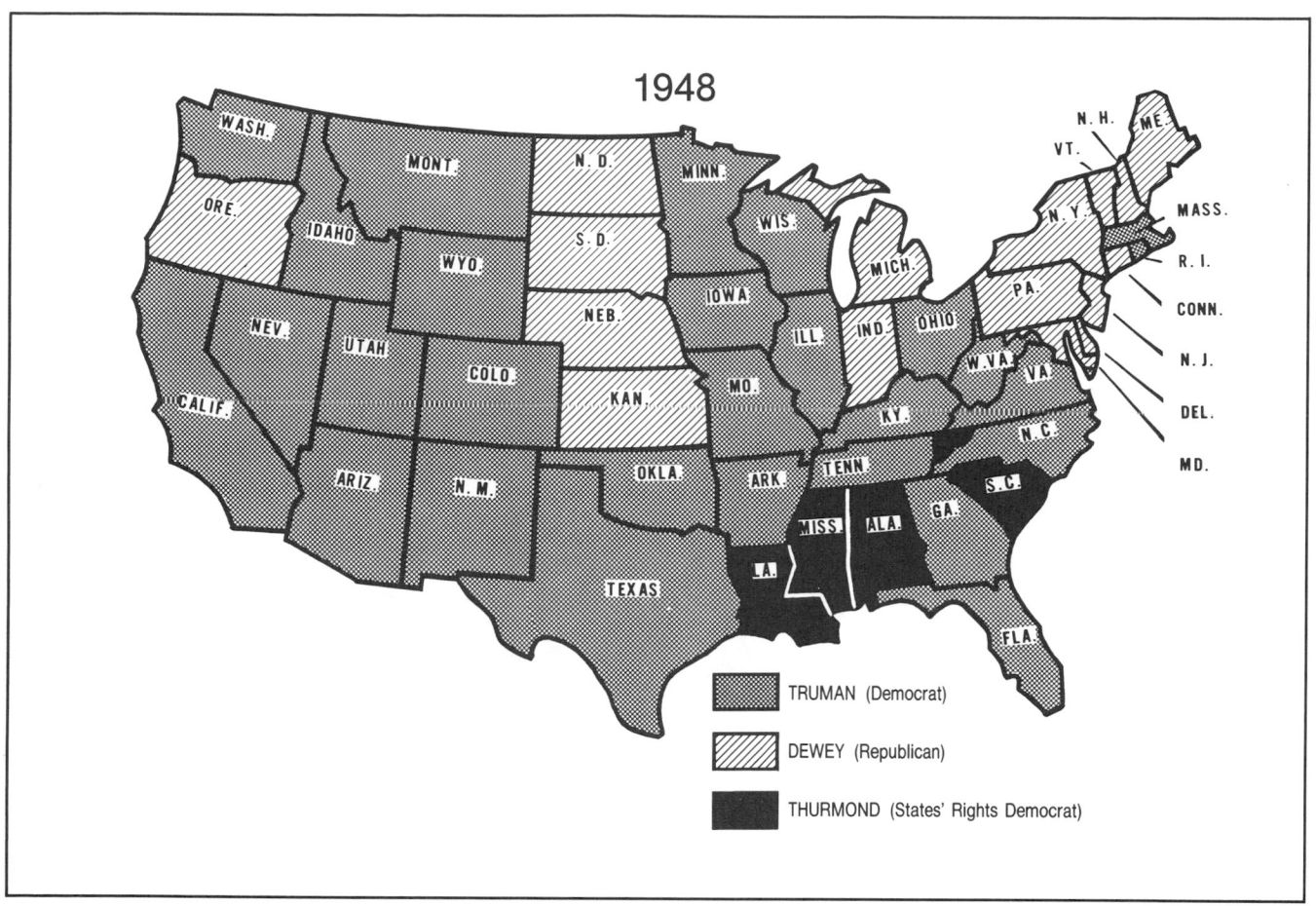

1948

TRUMAN (Democrat)

DEWEY (Republican)

THURMOND (States' Rights Democrat)

| States | Electoral Votes | Truman | Dewey | Thurmond | States | Electoral Votes | Truman | Dewey | Thurmond |
|---|---|---|---|---|---|---|---|---|---|
| Alabama | (11) | - | - | 11 | Nebraska | (6) | - | 6 | - |
| Arizona | (4) | 4 | - | - | Nevada | (3) | 3 | - | - |
| Arkansas | (9) | 9 | - | - | New Hampshire | (4) | - | 4 | - |
| California | (25) | 25 | - | - | New Jersey | (16) | - | 16 | - |
| Colorado | (6) | 6 | - | - | New Mexico | (4) | 4 | - | - |
| Connecticut | (8) | - | 8 | - | New York | (47) | - | 47 | - |
| Delaware | (3) | - | 3 | - | North Carolina | (14) | 14 | - | - |
| Florida | (8) | 8 | - | - | North Dakota | (4) | - | 4 | - |
| Georgia | (12) | 12 | - | - | Ohio | (25) | 25 | - | - |
| Idaho | (4) | 4 | - | - | Oklahoma | (10) | 10 | - | - |
| Illinois | (28) | 28 | - | - | Oregon | (6) | - | 6 | - |
| Indiana | (13) | - | 13 | - | Pennsylvania | (35) | - | 35 | - |
| Iowa | (10) | 10 | - | - | Rhode Island | (4) | 4 | - | - |
| Kansas | (8) | - | 8 | - | South Carolina | (8) | - | - | 8 |
| Kentucky | (11) | 11 | - | - | South Dakota | (4) | - | 4 | - |
| Louisiana | (10) | - | - | 10 | Tennessee [1] | (12) | 11 | - | 1 |
| Maine | (5) | - | 5 | - | Texas | (23) | 23 | - | - |
| Maryland | (8) | - | 8 | - | Utah | (4) | 4 | - | - |
| Massachusetts | (16) | 16 | - | - | Vermont | (3) | - | 3 | - |
| Michigan | (19) | - | 19 | - | Virginia | (11) | 11 | - | - |
| Minnesota | (11) | 11 | - | - | Washington | (8) | 8 | - | - |
| Mississippi | (9) | - | - | 9 | West Virginia | (8) | 8 | - | - |
| Missouri | (15) | 15 | - | - | Wisconsin | (12) | 12 | - | - |
| Montana | (4) | 4 | - | - | Wyoming | (3) | 3 | - | - |
| | | | | | **Totals** | **(531)** | **303** | **189** | **39** |

1. For explanation of split electoral votes, see p. 350.

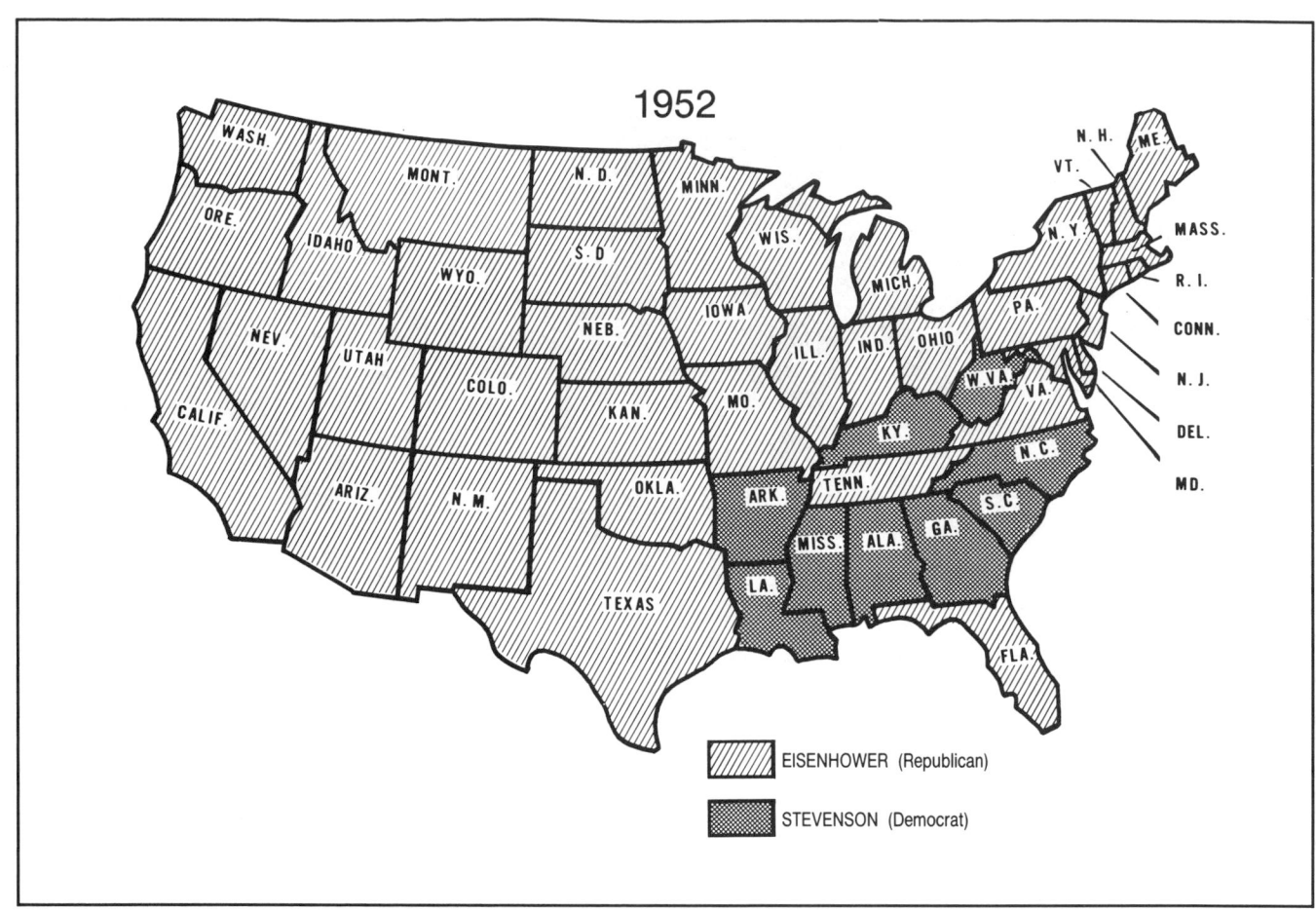

1952

EISENHOWER (Republican)

STEVENSON (Democrat)

| States | Electoral Votes | Eisenhower | Stevenson | States | Electoral Votes | Eisenhower | Stevenson |
|---|---|---|---|---|---|---|---|
| Alabama | (11) | - | 11 | Nebraska | (6) | 6 | - |
| Arizona | (4) | 4 | - | Nevada | (3) | 3 | - |
| Arkansas | (8) | - | 8 | New Hampshire | (4) | 4 | - |
| California | (32) | 32 | - | New Jersey | (16) | 16 | - |
| Colorado | (6) | 6 | - | New Mexico | (4) | 4 | - |
| Connecticut | (8) | 8 | - | New York | (45) | 45 | - |
| Delaware | (3) | 3 | - | North Carolina | (14) | - | 14 |
| Florida | (10) | 10 | - | North Dakota | (4) | 4 | - |
| Georgia | (12) | - | 12 | Ohio | (25) | 25 | - |
| Idaho | (4) | 4 | - | Oklahoma | (8) | 8 | - |
| Illinois | (27) | 27 | - | Oregon | (6) | 6 | - |
| Indiana | (13) | 13 | - | Pennsylvania | (32) | 32 | - |
| Iowa | (10) | 10 | - | Rhode Island | (4) | 4 | - |
| Kansas | (8) | 8 | - | South Carolina | (8) | - | 8 |
| Kentucky | (10) | - | 10 | South Dakota | (4) | 4 | - |
| Louisiana | (10) | - | 10 | Tennessee | (11) | 11 | - |
| Maine | (5) | 5 | - | Texas | (24) | 24 | - |
| Maryland | (9) | 9 | - | Utah | (4) | 4 | - |
| Massachusetts | (16) | 16 | - | Vermont | (3) | 3 | - |
| Michigan | (20) | 20 | - | Virginia | (12) | 12 | - |
| Minnesota | (11) | 11 | - | Washington | (9) | 9 | - |
| Mississippi | (8) | - | 8 | West Virginia | (8) | - | 8 |
| Missouri | (13) | 13 | - | Wisconsin | (12) | 12 | - |
| Montana | (4) | 4 | - | Wyoming | (3) | 3 | - |
| | | | | **Totals** | **(531)** | **442** | **89** |

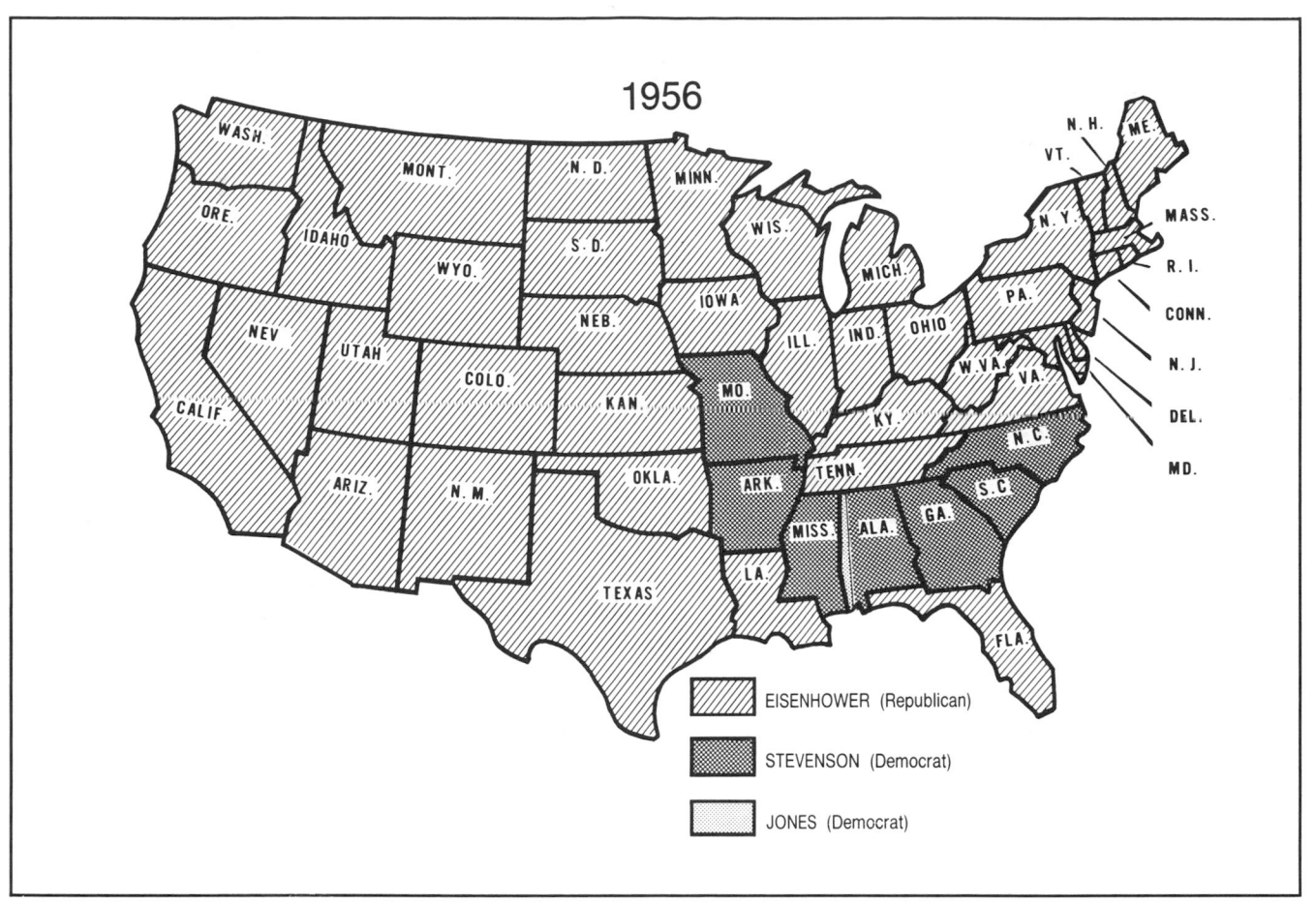

1956

| | EISENHOWER (Republican) |
| | STEVENSON (Democrat) |
| | JONES (Democrat) |

| States | Electoral Votes | Eisenhower | Stevenson | Jones | States | Electoral Votes | Eisenhower | Stevenson | Jones |
|---|---|---|---|---|---|---|---|---|---|
| Alabama [1] | (11) | - | 10 | 1 | Nebraska | (6) | 6 | - | - |
| Arizona | (4) | 4 | - | - | Nevada | (3) | 3 | - | - |
| Arkansas | (8) | - | 8 | - | New Hampshire | (4) | 4 | - | - |
| California | (32) | 32 | - | - | New Jersey | (16) | 16 | - | - |
| Colorado | (6) | 6 | - | - | New Mexico | (4) | 4 | - | - |
| Connecticut | (8) | 8 | - | - | New York | (45) | 45 | - | - |
| Delaware | (3) | 3 | - | - | North Carolina | (14) | - | 14 | - |
| Florida | (10) | 10 | - | - | North Dakota | (4) | 4 | - | - |
| Georgia | (12) | - | 12 | - | Ohio | (25) | 25 | - | - |
| Idaho | (4) | 4 | - | - | Oklahoma | (8) | 8 | - | - |
| Illinois | (27) | 27 | - | - | Oregon | (6) | 6 | - | - |
| Indiana | (13) | 13 | - | - | Pennsylvania | (32) | 32 | - | - |
| Iowa | (10) | 10 | - | - | Rhode Island | (4) | 4 | - | - |
| Kansas | (8) | 8 | - | - | South Carolina | (8) | - | 8 | - |
| Kentucky | (10) | 10 | - | - | South Dakota | (4) | 4 | - | - |
| Louisiana | (10) | 10 | - | - | Tennessee | (11) | 11 | - | - |
| Maine | (5) | 5 | - | - | Texas | (24) | 24 | - | - |
| Maryland | (9) | 9 | - | - | Utah | (4) | 4 | - | - |
| Massachusetts | (16) | 16 | - | - | Vermont | (3) | 3 | - | - |
| Michigan | (20) | 20 | - | - | Virginia | (12) | 12 | - | - |
| Minnesota | (11) | 11 | - | - | Washington | (9) | 9 | - | - |
| Mississippi | (8) | - | 8 | - | West Virginia | (8) | 8 | - | - |
| Missouri | (13) | - | 13 | - | Wisconsin | (12) | 12 | - | - |
| Montana | (4) | 4 | - | - | Wyoming | (3) | 3 | - | - |
| | | | | | **Totals** | **(531)** | **457** | **73** | **1** |

1. For explanation of split electoral votes, see p. 350.

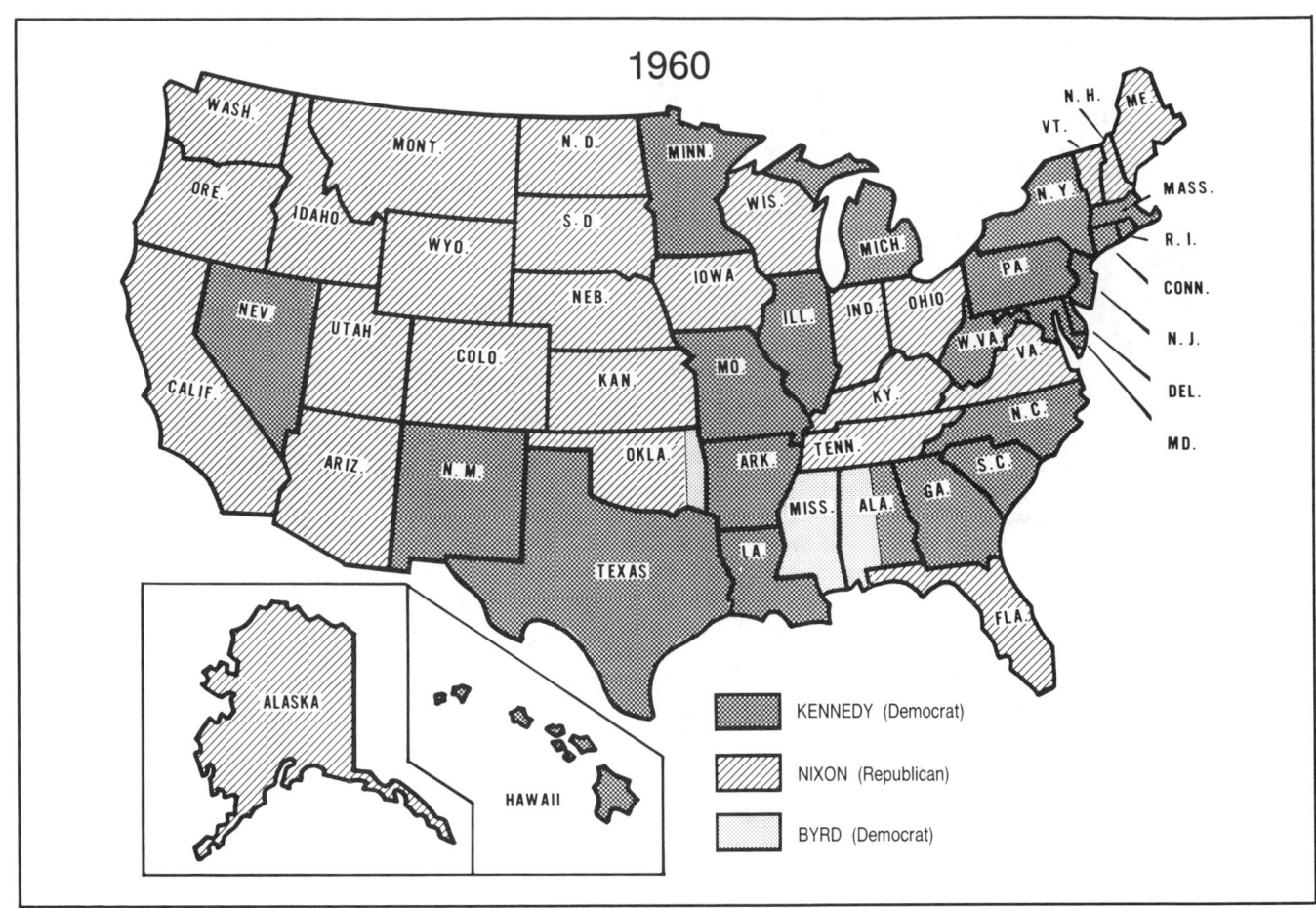

1960

KENNEDY (Democrat)

NIXON (Republican)

BYRD (Democrat)

| States | Electoral Votes | Kennedy | Nixon | Byrd | States | Electoral Votes | Kennedy | Nixon | Byrd |
|---|---|---|---|---|---|---|---|---|---|
| **Alabama** [1] | (11) | 5 | - | 6 | **Montana** | (4) | - | 4 | - |
| **Alaska** | (3) | - | 3 | - | **Nebraska** | (6) | - | 6 | - |
| **Arizona** | (4) | - | 4 | - | **Nevada** | (3) | 3 | - | - |
| **Arkansas** | (8) | 8 | - | - | **New Hampshire** | (4) | - | 4 | - |
| **California** | (32) | - | 32 | - | **New Jersey** | (16) | 16 | - | - |
| **Colorado** | (6) | - | 6 | - | **New Mexico** | (4) | 4 | - | - |
| **Connecticut** | (8) | 8 | - | - | **New York** | (45) | 45 | - | - |
| **Delaware** | (3) | 3 | - | - | **North Carolina** | (14) | 14 | - | - |
| **Florida** | (10) | - | 10 | - | **North Dakota** | (4) | - | 4 | - |
| **Georgia** | (12) | 12 | - | - | **Ohio** | (25) | - | 25 | - |
| **Hawaii** | (3) | 3 | - | - | **Oklahoma** [2] | (8) | - | 7 | 1 |
| **Idaho** | (4) | - | 4 | - | **Oregon** | (6) | - | 6 | - |
| **Illinois** | (27) | 27 | - | - | **Pennsylvania** | (32) | 32 | - | - |
| **Indiana** | (13) | - | 13 | - | **Rhode Island** | (4) | 4 | - | - |
| **Iowa** | (10) | - | 10 | - | **South Carolina** | (8) | 8 | - | - |
| **Kansas** | (8) | - | 8 | - | **South Dakota** | (4) | - | 4 | - |
| **Kentucky** | (10) | - | 10 | - | **Tennessee** | (11) | - | 11 | - |
| **Louisiana** | (10) | 10 | - | - | **Texas** | (24) | 24 | - | - |
| **Maine** | (5) | - | 5 | - | **Utah** | (4) | - | 4 | - |
| **Maryland** | (9) | 9 | - | - | **Vermont** | (3) | - | 3 | - |
| **Massachusetts** | (16) | 16 | - | - | **Virginia** | (12) | - | 12 | - |
| **Michigan** | (20) | 20 | - | - | **Washington** | (9) | - | 9 | - |
| **Minnesota** | (11) | 11 | - | - | **West Virginia** | (8) | 8 | - | - |
| **Mississippi** [1] | (8) | - | - | 8 | **Wisconsin** | (12) | - | 12 | - |
| **Missouri** | (13) | 13 | - | - | **Wyoming** | (3) | - | 3 | - |
| | | | | | **Totals** | (537) | 303 | 219 | 15 |

1. Six Alabama electors and all eight Mississippi electors, elected as "unpledged Democrats," cast their votes for Byrd.
2. One Republican elector voted for Byrd.

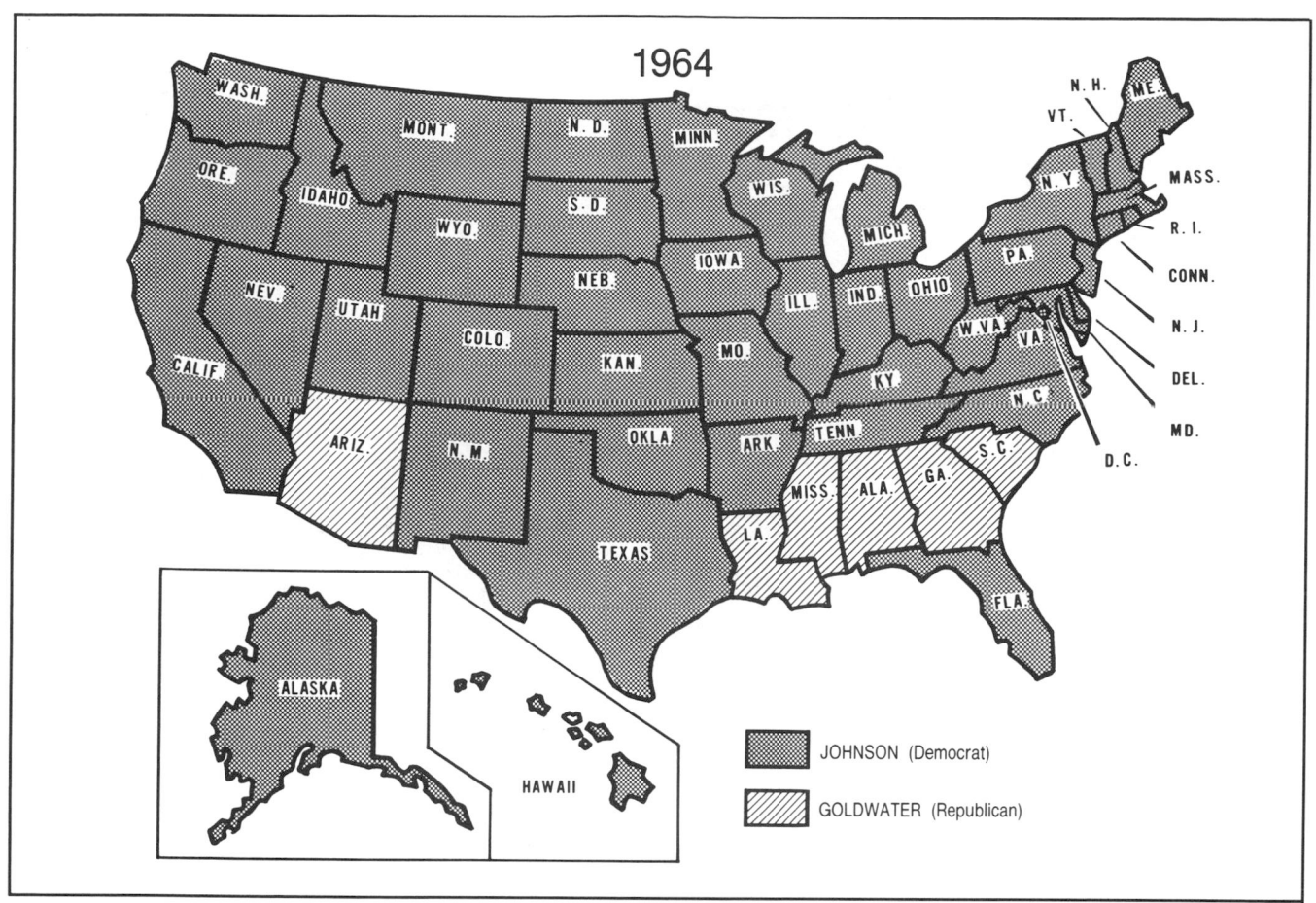

1964

JOHNSON (Democrat)

GOLDWATER (Republican)

| States | Electoral Votes | Johnson | Goldwater | States | Electoral Votes | Johnson | Goldwater |
|---|---|---|---|---|---|---|---|
| Alabama | (10) | - | 10 | Montana | (4) | 4 | - |
| Alaska | (3) | 3 | - | Nebraska | (5) | 5 | - |
| Arizona | (5) | - | 5 | Nevada | (3) | 3 | - |
| Arkansas | (6) | 6 | - | New Hampshire | (4) | 4 | - |
| California | (40) | 40 | - | New Jersey | (17) | 17 | - |
| Colorado | (6) | 6 | - | New Mexico | (4) | 4 | - |
| Connecticut | (8) | 8 | - | New York | (43) | 43 | - |
| Delaware | (3) | 3 | - | North Carolina | (13) | 13 | - |
| District of Columbia | (3) | 3 | - | North Dakota | (4) | 4 | - |
| Florida | (14) | 14 | - | Ohio | (26) | 26 | - |
| Georgia | (12) | - | 12 | Oklahoma | (8) | 8 | - |
| Hawaii | (4) | 4 | - | Oregon | (6) | 6 | - |
| Idaho | (4) | 4 | - | Pennsylvania | (29) | 29 | - |
| Illinois | (26) | 26 | - | Rhode Island | (4) | 4 | - |
| Indiana | (13) | 13 | - | South Carolina | (8) | - | 8 |
| Iowa | (9) | 9 | - | South Dakota | (4) | 4 | - |
| Kansas | (7) | 7 | - | Tennessee | (11) | 11 | - |
| Kentucky | (9) | 9 | - | Texas | (25) | 25 | - |
| Louisiana | (10) | - | 10 | Utah | (4) | 4 | - |
| Maine | (4) | 4 | - | Vermont | (3) | 3 | - |
| Maryland | (10) | 10 | - | Virginia | (12) | 12 | - |
| Massachusetts | (14) | 14 | - | Washington | (9) | 9 | - |
| Michigan | (21) | 21 | - | West Virginia | (7) | 7 | - |
| Minnesota | (10) | 10 | - | Wisconsin | (12) | 12 | - |
| Mississippi | (7) | - | 7 | Wyoming | (3) | 3 | - |
| Missouri | (12) | 12 | - | **Totals** | **(538)** | **486** | **52** |

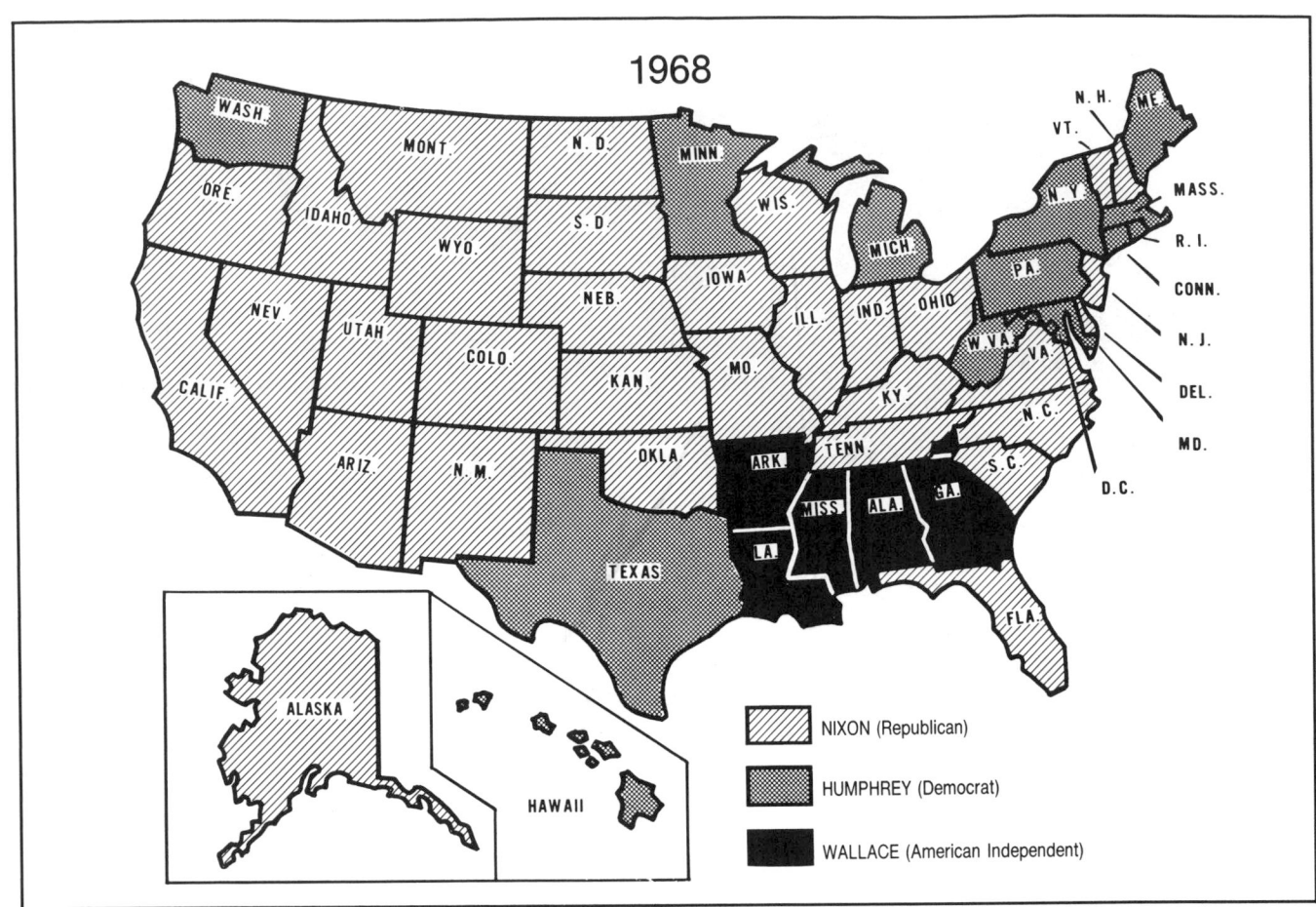

## 1968

| | NIXON (Republican) |
| | HUMPHREY (Democrat) |
| | WALLACE (American Independent) |

| States | Electoral Votes | Nixon | Humphrey | Wallace | States | Electoral Votes | Nixon | Humphrey | Wallace |
|---|---|---|---|---|---|---|---|---|---|
| Alabama | (10) | - | - | 10 | Montana | (4) | 4 | - | - |
| Alaska | (3) | 3 | - | - | Nebraska | (5) | 5 | - | - |
| Arizona | (5) | 5 | - | - | Nevada | (3) | 3 | - | - |
| Arkansas | (6) | - | - | 6 | New Hampshire | (4) | 4 | - | - |
| California | (40) | 40 | - | - | New Jersey | (17) | 17 | - | - |
| Colorado | (6) | 6 | - | - | New Mexico | (4) | 4 | - | - |
| Connecticut | (8) | - | 8 | - | New York | (43) | - | 43 | - |
| Delaware | (3) | 3 | - | - | North Carolina [1] | (13) | 12 | - | 1 |
| District of Columbia | (3) | - | 3 | - | North Dakota | (4) | 4 | - | - |
| Florida | (14) | 14 | - | - | Ohio | (26) | 26 | - | - |
| Georgia | (12) | - | - | 12 | Oklahoma | (8) | 8 | - | - |
| Hawaii | (4) | - | 4 | - | Oregon | (6) | 6 | - | - |
| Idaho | (4) | 4 | - | - | Pennsylvania | (29) | - | 29 | - |
| Illinois | (26) | 26 | - | - | Rhode Island | (4) | - | 4 | - |
| Indiana | (13) | 13 | - | - | South Carolina | (8) | 8 | - | - |
| Iowa | (9) | 9 | - | - | South Dakota | (4) | 4 | - | - |
| Kansas | (7) | 7 | - | - | Tennessee | (11) | 11 | - | - |
| Kentucky | (9) | 9 | - | - | Texas | (25) | - | 25 | - |
| Louisiana | (10) | - | - | 10 | Utah | (4) | 4 | - | - |
| Maine | (4) | - | 4 | - | Vermont | (3) | 3 | - | - |
| Maryland | (10) | - | 10 | - | Virginia | (12) | 12 | - | - |
| Massachusetts | (14) | - | 14 | - | Washington | (9) | - | 9 | - |
| Michigan | (21) | - | 21 | - | West Virginia | (7) | - | 7 | - |
| Minnesota | (10) | - | 10 | - | Wisconsin | (12) | 12 | - | - |
| Mississippi | (7) | - | - | 7 | Wyoming | (3) | 3 | - | - |
| Missouri | (12) | 12 | - | - | **Totals** | **(538)** | **301** | **191** | **46** |

1. For explanation of split electoral votes, see p. 350.

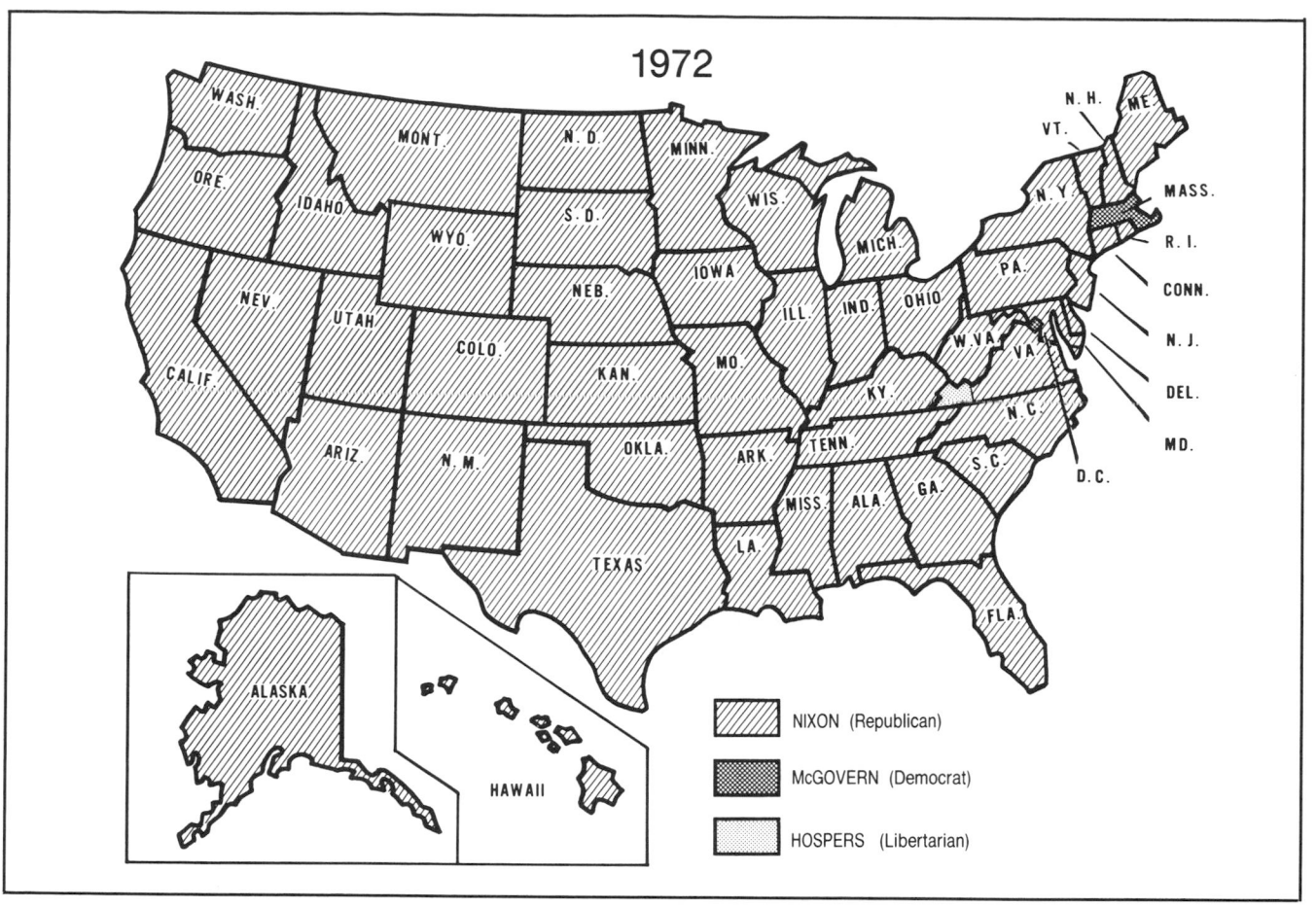

## 1972

| | NIXON (Republican) |
| | McGOVERN (Democrat) |
| | HOSPERS (Libertarian) |

| States | Electoral Votes | Nixon | McGovern | Hospers | States | Electoral Votes | Nixon | McGovern | Hospers |
|---|---|---|---|---|---|---|---|---|---|
| **Alabama** | (9) | 9 | – | – | **Montana** | (4) | 4 | – | – |
| **Alaska** | (3) | 3 | – | – | **Nebraska** | (5) | 5 | – | – |
| **Arizona** | (6) | 6 | – | – | **Nevada** | (3) | 3 | – | – |
| **Arkansas** | (6) | 6 | – | – | **New Hampshire** | (4) | 4 | – | – |
| **California** | (45) | 45 | – | – | **New Jersey** | (17) | 17 | – | – |
| **Colorado** | (7) | 7 | – | – | **New Mexico** | (4) | 4 | – | – |
| **Connecticut** | (8) | 8 | – | – | **New York** | (41) | 41 | – | – |
| **Delaware** | (3) | 3 | – | – | **North Carolina** | (13) | 13 | – | – |
| **District of Columbia** | (3) | – | 3 | – | **North Dakota** | (3) | 3 | – | – |
| **Florida** | (17) | 17 | – | – | **Ohio** | (25) | 25 | – | – |
| **Georgia** | (12) | 12 | – | – | **Oklahoma** | (8) | 8 | – | – |
| **Hawaii** | (4) | 4 | – | – | **Oregon** | (6) | 6 | – | – |
| **Idaho** | (4) | 4 | – | – | **Pennsylvania** | (27) | 27 | – | – |
| **Illinois** | (26) | 26 | – | – | **Rhode Island** | (4) | 4 | – | – |
| **Indiana** | (13) | 13 | – | – | **South Carolina** | (8) | 8 | – | – |
| **Iowa** | (8) | 8 | – | – | **South Dakota** | (4) | 4 | – | – |
| **Kansas** | (7) | 7 | – | – | **Tennessee** | (10) | 10 | – | – |
| **Kentucky** | (9) | 9 | – | – | **Texas** | (26) | 26 | – | – |
| **Louisiana** | (10) | 10 | – | – | **Utah** | (4) | 4 | – | – |
| **Maine** | (4) | 4 | – | – | **Vermont** | (3) | 3 | – | – |
| **Maryland** | (10) | 10 | – | – | **Virginia** [1] | (12) | 11 | – | 1 |
| **Massachusetts** | (14) | – | 14 | – | **Washington** | (9) | 9 | – | – |
| **Michigan** | (21) | 21 | – | – | **West Virginia** | (6) | 6 | – | – |
| **Minnesota** | (10) | 10 | – | – | **Wisconsin** | (11) | 11 | – | – |
| **Mississippi** | (7) | 7 | – | – | **Wyoming** | (3) | 3 | – | – |
| **Missouri** | (12) | 12 | – | – | **Totals** | (538) | 520 | 17 | 1 |

1. For explanation of split electoral votes, see p. 350.

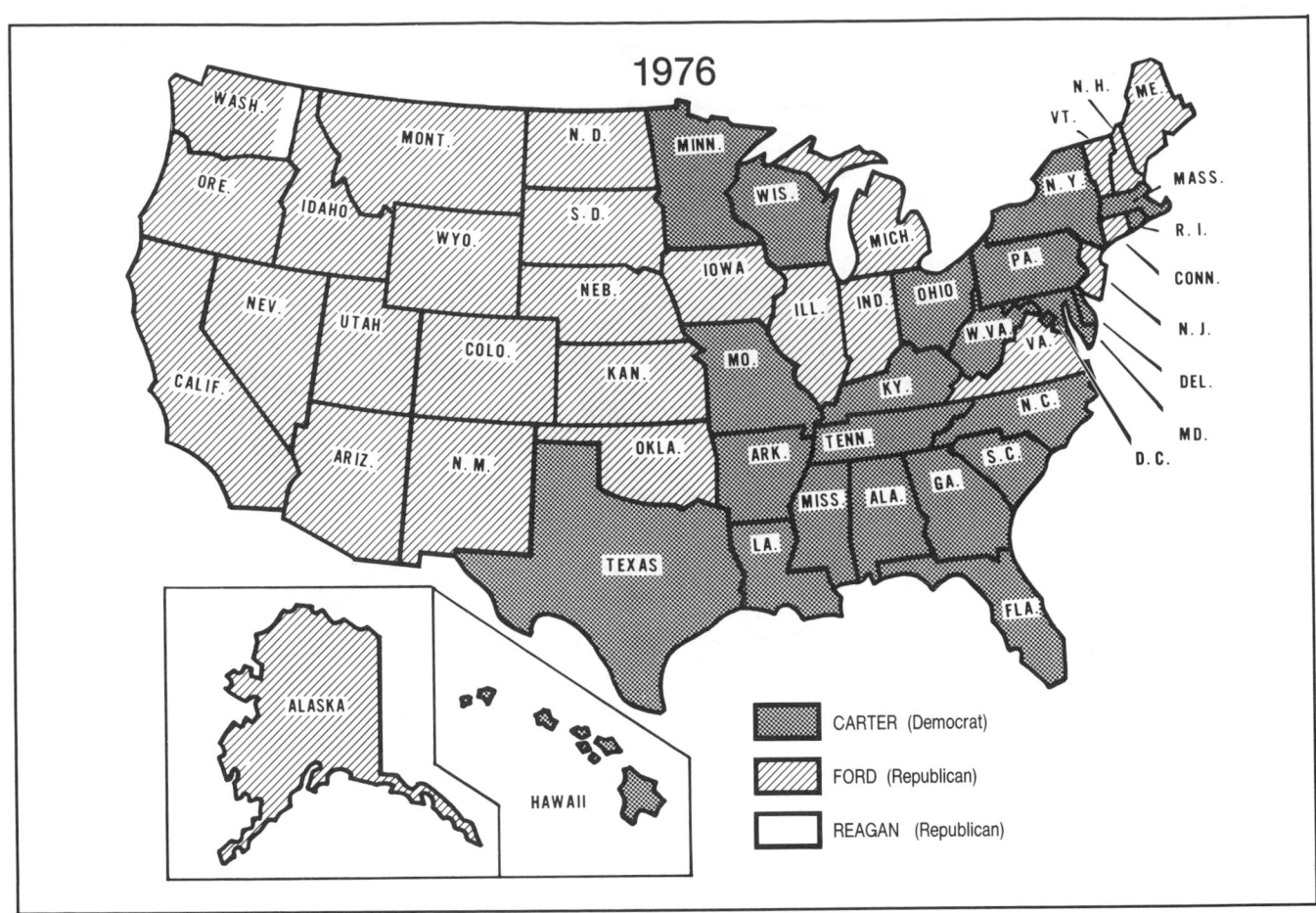

## 1976

| States | Electoral Votes | Carter | Ford | Reagan |
|---|---|---|---|---|
| **Alabama** | (9) | 9 | – | – |
| **Alaska** | (3) | – | 3 | – |
| **Arizona** | (6) | – | 6 | – |
| **Arkansas** | (6) | 6 | – | – |
| **California** | (45) | – | 45 | – |
| **Colorado** | (7) | – | 7 | – |
| **Connecticut** | (8) | – | 8 | – |
| **Delaware** | (3) | 3 | – | – |
| **District of Columbia** | (3) | 3 | – | – |
| **Florida** | (17) | 17 | – | – |
| **Georgia** | (12) | 12 | – | – |
| **Hawaii** | (4) | 4 | – | – |
| **Idaho** | (4) | – | 4 | – |
| **Illinois** | (26) | – | 26 | – |
| **Indiana** | (13) | – | 13 | – |
| **Iowa** | (8) | – | 8 | – |
| **Kansas** | (7) | – | 7 | – |
| **Kentucky** | (9) | 9 | – | – |
| **Louisiana** | (10) | 10 | – | – |
| **Maine** | (4) | – | 4 | – |
| **Maryland** | (10) | 10 | – | – |
| **Massachusetts** | (14) | 14 | – | – |
| **Michigan** | (21) | – | 21 | – |
| **Minnesota** | (10) | 10 | – | – |
| **Mississippi** | (7) | 7 | – | – |
| **Missouri** | (12) | 12 | – | – |
| **Montana** | (4) | – | 4 | – |
| **Nebraska** | (5) | – | 5 | – |
| **Nevada** | (3) | – | 3 | – |
| **New Hampshire** | (4) | – | 4 | – |
| **New Jersey** | (17) | – | 17 | – |
| **New Mexico** | (4) | – | 4 | – |
| **New York** | (41) | 41 | – | – |
| **North Carolina** | (13) | 13 | – | – |
| **North Dakota** | (3) | – | 3 | – |
| **Ohio** | (25) | 25 | – | – |
| **Oklahoma** | (8) | – | 8 | – |
| **Oregon** | (6) | – | 6 | – |
| **Pennsylvania** | (27) | 27 | – | – |
| **Rhode Island** | (4) | 4 | – | – |
| **South Carolina** | (8) | 8 | – | – |
| **South Dakota** | (4) | – | 4 | – |
| **Tennessee** | (10) | 10 | – | – |
| **Texas** | (26) | 26 | – | – |
| **Utah** | (4) | – | 4 | – |
| **Vermont** | (3) | – | 3 | – |
| **Virginia** | (12) | – | 12 | – |
| **Washington** [1] | (9) | – | 8 | 1 |
| **West Virginia** | (6) | 6 | – | – |
| **Wisconsin** | (11) | 11 | – | – |
| **Wyoming** | (3) | – | 3 | – |
| **Totals** | (538) | 297 | 240 | 1 |

1. For explanation of split electoral votes, see p. 350.

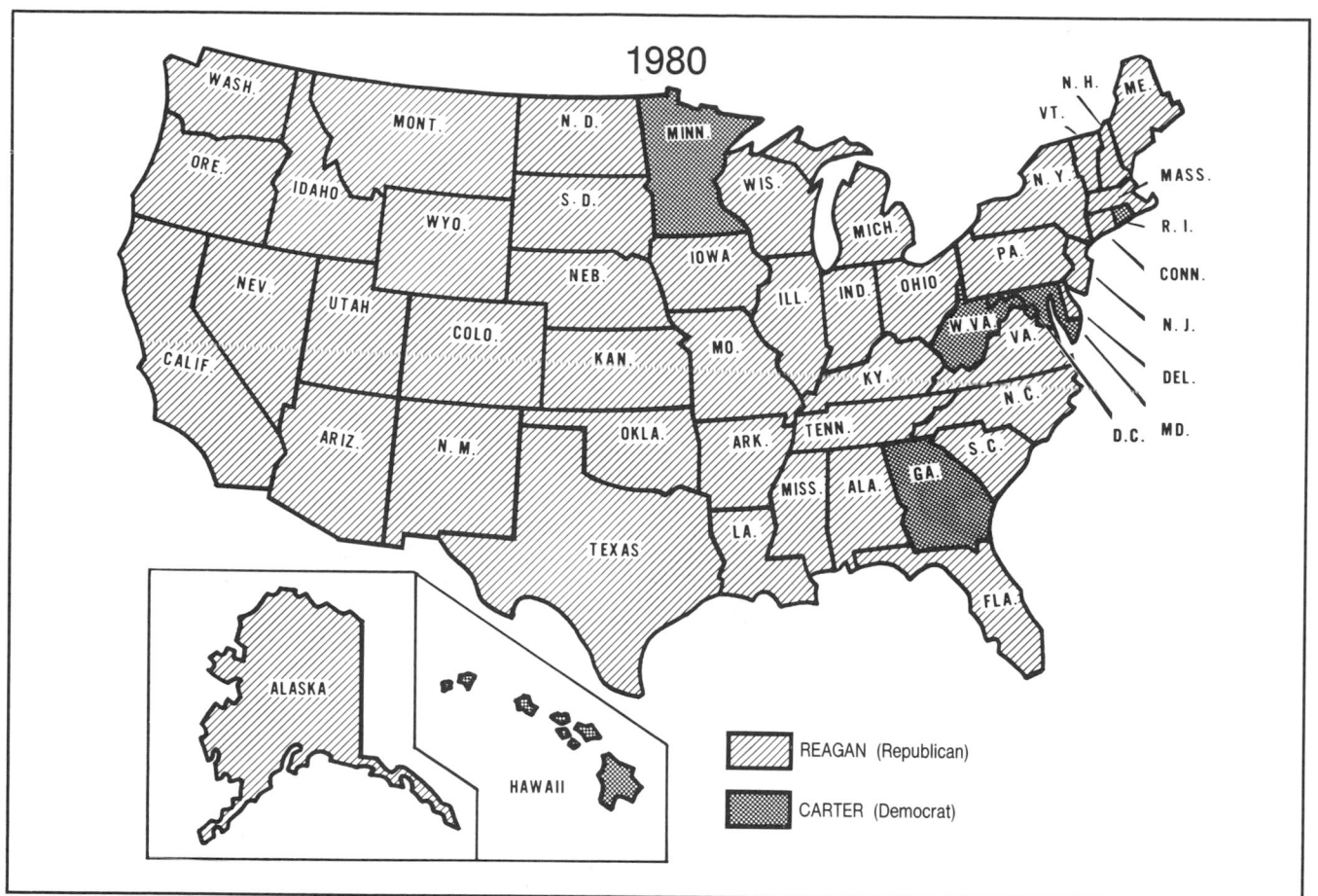

1980

REAGAN (Republican)

CARTER (Democrat)

| States | Electoral Votes | Reagan | Carter | States | Electoral Votes | Reagan | Carter |
|---|---|---|---|---|---|---|---|
| Alabama | (9) | 9 | - | Montana | (4) | 4 | - |
| Alaska | (3) | 3 | - | Nebraska | (5) | 5 | - |
| Arizona | (6) | 6 | - | Nevada | (3) | 3 | - |
| Arkansas | (6) | 6 | - | New Hampshire | (4) | 4 | - |
| California | (45) | 45 | - | New Jersey | (17) | 17 | - |
| Colorado | (7) | 7 | - | New Mexico | (4) | 4 | - |
| Connecticut | (8) | 8 | - | New York | (41) | 41 | - |
| Delaware | (3) | 3 | - | North Carolina | (13) | 13 | - |
| District of Columbia | (3) | - | 3 | North Dakota | (3) | 3 | - |
| Florida | (17) | 17 | - | Ohio | (25) | 25 | - |
| Georgia | (12) | - | 12 | Oklahoma | (8) | 8 | - |
| Hawaii | (4) | - | 4 | Oregon | (6) | 6 | - |
| Idaho | (4) | 4 | - | Pennsylvania | (27) | 27 | - |
| Illinois | (26) | 26 | - | Rhode Island | (4) | - | 4 |
| Indiana | (13) | 13 | - | South Carolina | (8) | 8 | - |
| Iowa | (8) | 8 | - | South Dakota | (4) | 4 | - |
| Kansas | (7) | 7 | - | Tennessee | (10) | 10 | - |
| Kentucky | (9) | 9 | - | Texas | (26) | 26 | - |
| Louisiana | (10) | 10 | - | Utah | (4) | 4 | - |
| Maine | (4) | 4 | - | Vermont | (3) | 3 | - |
| Maryland | (10) | - | 10 | Virginia | (12) | 12 | - |
| Massachusetts | (14) | 14 | - | Washington | (9) | 9 | - |
| Michigan | (21) | 21 | - | West Virginia | (6) | - | 6 |
| Minnesota | (10) | - | 10 | Wisconsin | (11) | 11 | - |
| Mississippi | (7) | 7 | - | Wyoming | (3) | 3 | - |
| Missouri | (12) | 12 | - | **Totals** | **(538)** | **489** | **49** |

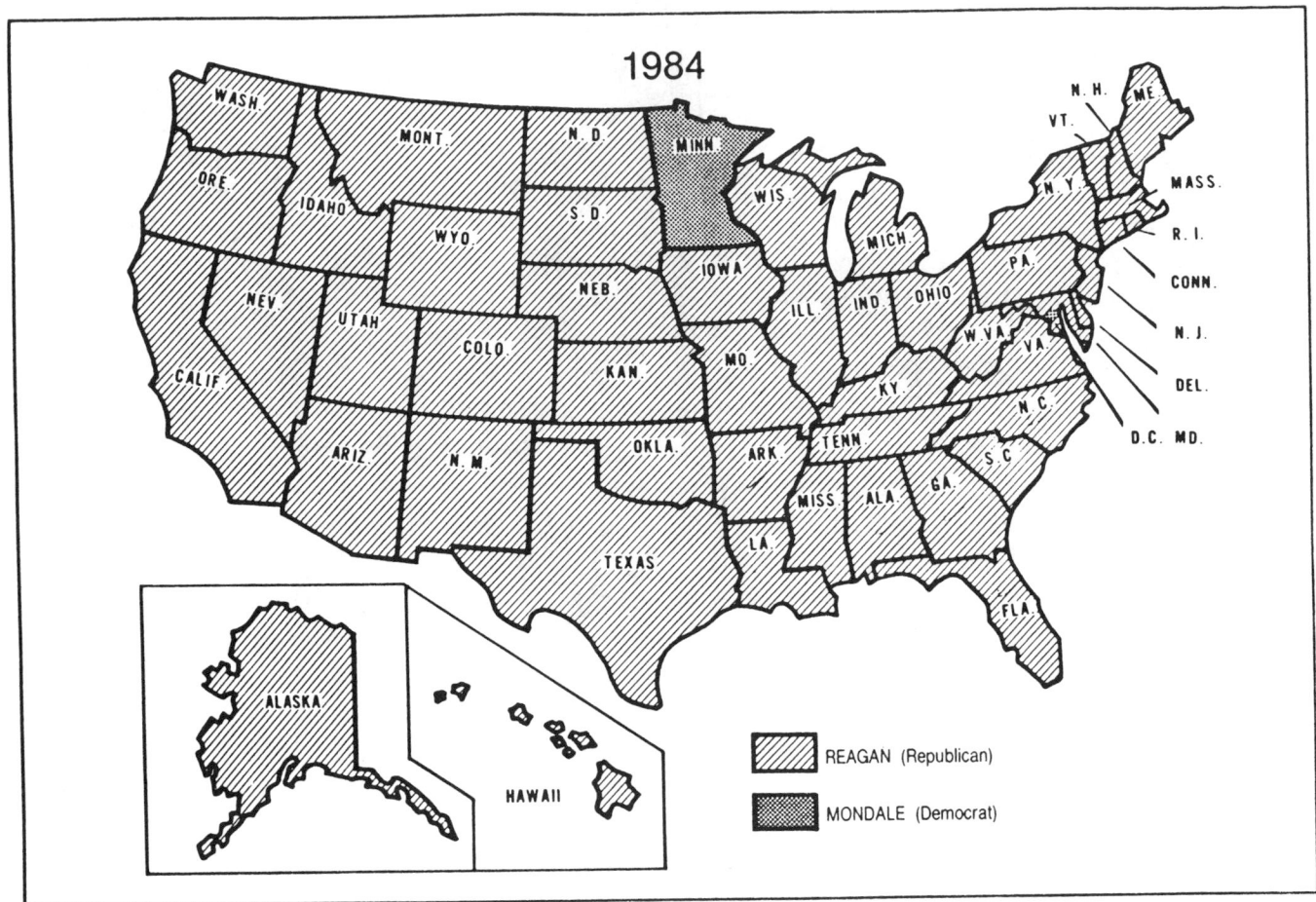

1984

REAGAN (Republican)

MONDALE (Democrat)

| States | Electoral Votes | Reagan | Mondale | States | Electoral Votes | Reagan | Mondale |
|---|---|---|---|---|---|---|---|
| Alabama | (9) | 9 | - | Montana | (4) | 4 | - |
| Alaska | (3) | 3 | - | Nebraska | (5) | 5 | - |
| Arizona | (7) | 7 | - | Nevada | (4) | 4 | - |
| Arkansas | (6) | 6 | - | New Hampshire | (4) | 4 | - |
| California | (47) | 47 | - | New Jersey | (16) | 16 | - |
| Colorado | (8) | 8 | - | New Mexico | (5) | 5 | - |
| Connecticut | (8) | 8 | - | New York | (36) | 36 | - |
| Delaware | (3) | 3 | - | North Carolina | (13) | 13 | - |
| District of Columbia | (3) | - | 3 | North Dakota | (3) | 3 | - |
| Florida | (21) | 21 | - | Ohio | (23) | 23 | - |
| Georgia | (12) | 12 | - | Oklahoma | (8) | 8 | - |
| Hawaii | (4) | 4 | - | Oregon | (7) | 7 | - |
| Idaho | (4) | 4 | - | Pennsylvania | (25) | 25 | - |
| Illinois | (24) | 24 | - | Rhode Island | (4) | 4 | - |
| Indiana | (12) | 12 | - | South Carolina | (8) | 8 | - |
| Iowa | (8) | 8 | - | South Dakota | (3) | 3 | - |
| Kansas | (7) | 7 | - | Tennessee | (11) | 11 | - |
| Kentucky | (9) | 9 | - | Texas | (29) | 29 | - |
| Louisiana | (10) | 10 | - | Utah | (5) | 5 | - |
| Maine | (4) | 4 | - | Vermont | (3) | 3 | - |
| Maryland | (10) | 10 | - | Virginia | (12) | 12 | - |
| Massachusetts | (13) | 13 | - | Washington | (10) | 10 | - |
| Michigan | (20) | 20 | - | West Virginia | (6) | 6 | - |
| Minnesota | (10) | - | 10 | Wisconsin | (11) | 11 | - |
| Mississippi | (7) | 7 | - | Wyoming | (3) | 3 | - |
| Missouri | (11) | 11 | - | **Totals** | **(538)** | **525** | **13** |

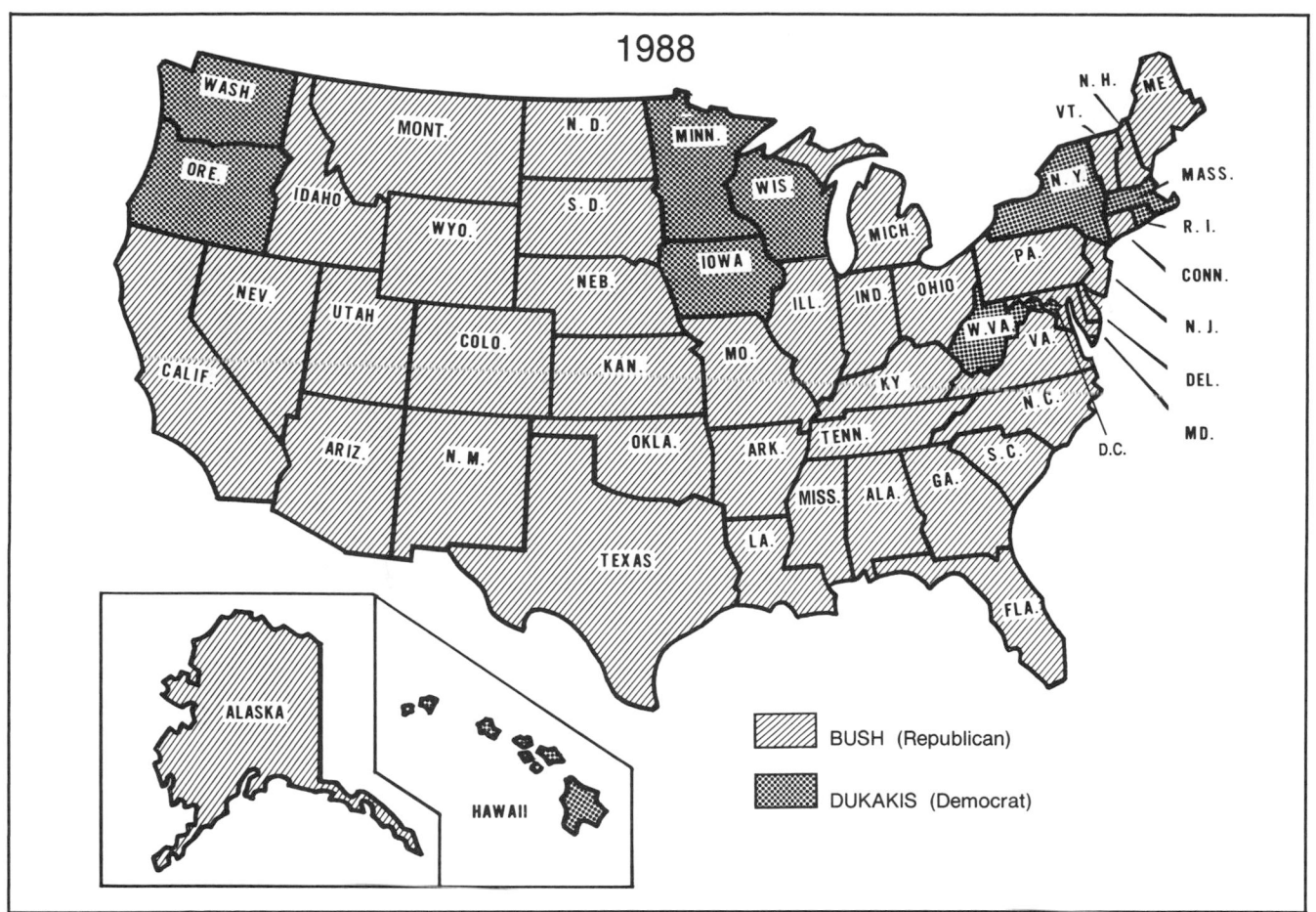

| States | Electoral Votes | Bush | Dukakis | Bentsen | States | Electoral Votes | Bush | Dukakis | Bentsen |
|---|---|---|---|---|---|---|---|---|---|
| **Alabama** | (9) | 9 | - | - | **Montana** | (4) | 4 | - | - |
| **Alaska** | (3) | 3 | - | - | **Nebraska** | (5) | 5 | - | - |
| **Arizona** | (7) | 7 | - | - | **Nevada** | (4) | 4 | - | - |
| **Arkansas** | (6) | 6 | - | - | **New Hampshire** | (4) | 4 | - | - |
| **California** | (47) | 47 | - | - | **New Jersey** | (16) | 16 | - | - |
| **Colorado** | (8) | 8 | - | - | **New Mexico** | (5) | 5 | - | - |
| **Connecticut** | (8) | 8 | - | - | **New York** | (36) | - | 36 | - |
| **Delaware** | (3) | 3 | - | - | **North Carolina** | (13) | 13 | - | - |
| **District of Columbia** | (3) | - | 3 | - | **North Dakota** | (3) | 3 | - | - |
| **Florida** | (21) | 21 | - | - | **Ohio** | (23) | 23 | - | - |
| **Georgia** | (12) | 12 | - | - | **Oklahoma** | (8) | 8 | - | - |
| **Hawaii** | (4) | - | 4 | - | **Oregon** | (7) | - | 7 | - |
| **Idaho** | (4) | 4 | - | - | **Pennsylvania** | (25) | 25 | - | - |
| **Illinois** | (24) | 24 | - | - | **Rhode Island** | (4) | - | 4 | - |
| **Indiana** | (12) | 12 | - | - | **South Carolina** | (8) | 8 | - | - |
| **Iowa** | (8) | - | 8 | - | **South Dakota** | (3) | 3 | - | - |
| **Kansas** | (7) | 7 | - | - | **Tennessee** | (11) | 11 | - | - |
| **Kentucky** | (9) | 9 | - | - | **Texas** | (29) | 29 | - | - |
| **Louisiana** | (10) | 10 | - | - | **Utah** | (5) | 5 | - | - |
| **Maine** | (4) | 4 | - | - | **Vermont** | (3) | 3 | - | - |
| **Maryland** | (10) | 10 | - | - | **Virginia** | (12) | 12 | - | - |
| **Massachusetts** | (13) | - | 13 | - | **Washington** | (10) | - | 10 | - |
| **Michigan** | (20) | 20 | - | - | **West Virginia** [1] | (6) | - | 5 | 1 |
| **Minnesota** | (10) | - | 10 | - | **Wisconsin** | (11) | - | 11 | - |
| **Mississippi** | (7) | 7 | - | - | **Wyoming** | (3) | 3 | - | - |
| **Missouri** | (11) | 11 | - | - | **Totals** | (538) | 426 | 111 | 1 |

1. *Margaret Leach, a Dukakis elector, voted for Dukakis's running mate, Sen. Lloyd Bentsen of Texas.*

# 1992

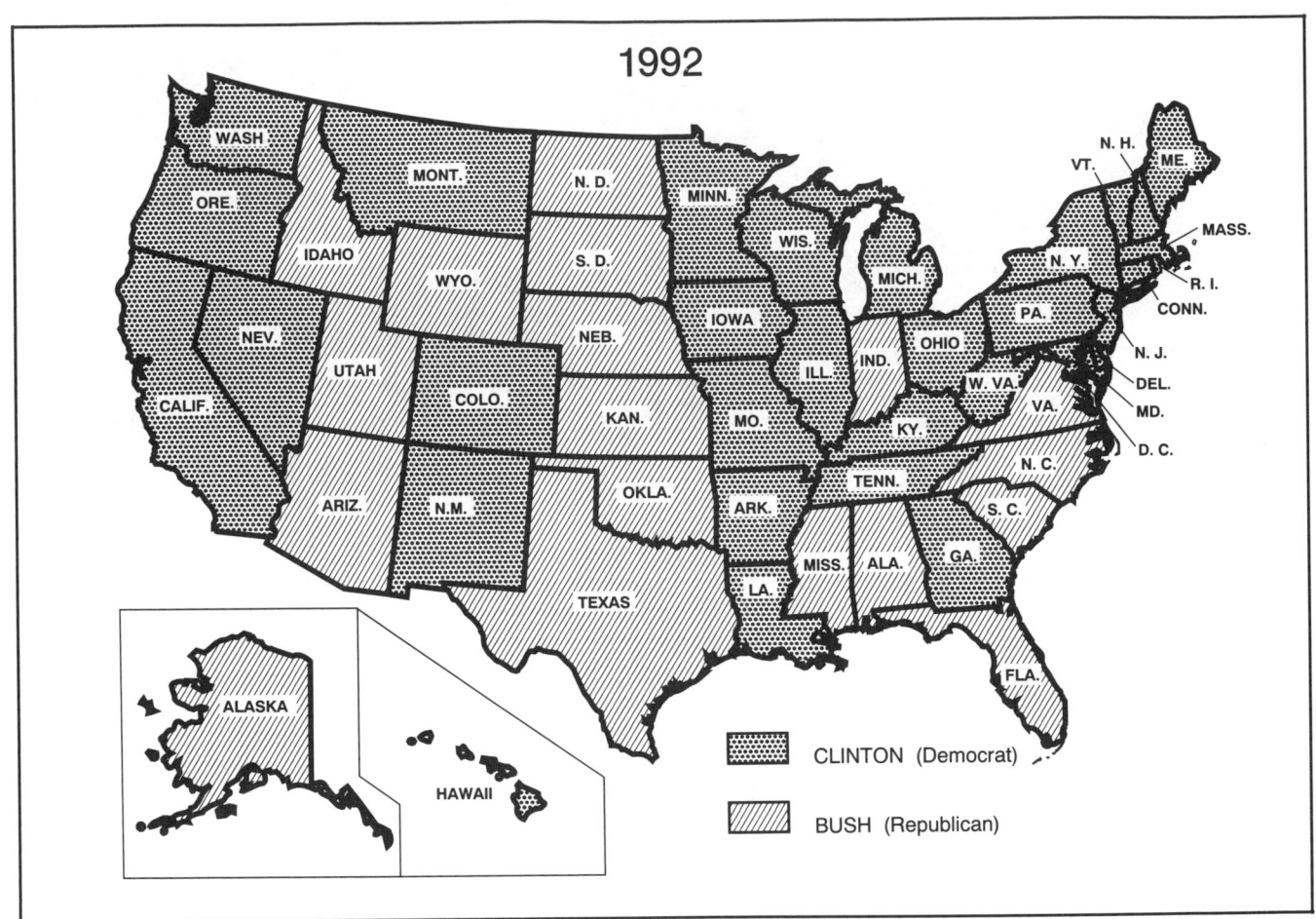

| | CLINTON (Democrat) |
| | BUSH (Republican) |

| States | Electoral Votes | Clinton | Bush | States | Electoral Votes | Clinton | Bush |
|--------|:---------------:|:-------:|:----:|--------|:---------------:|:-------:|:----:|
| Alabama | (9) | – | 9 | Montana | (3) | 3 | – |
| Alaska | (3) | – | 3 | Nebraska | (5) | – | 5 |
| Arizona | (8) | – | 8 | Nevada | (4) | 4 | – |
| Arkansas | (6) | 6 | – | New Hampshire | (4) | 4 | – |
| California | (54) | 54 | – | New Jersey | (15) | 15 | – |
| Colorado | (8) | 8 | – | New Mexico | (5) | 5 | – |
| Connecticut | (8) | 8 | – | New York | (33) | 33 | – |
| Delaware | (3) | 3 | – | North Carolina | (14) | – | 14 |
| District of Columbia | (3) | 3 | – | North Dakota | (3) | – | 3 |
| Florida | (25) | – | 25 | Ohio | (21) | 21 | – |
| Georgia | (13) | 13 | – | Oklahoma | (8) | – | 8 |
| Hawaii | (4) | 4 | – | Oregon | (7) | 7 | – |
| Idaho | (4) | – | 4 | Pennsylvania | (23) | 23 | – |
| Illinois | (22) | 22 | – | Rhode Island | (4) | 4 | – |
| Indiana | (12) | – | 12 | South Carolina | (8) | – | 8 |
| Iowa | (7) | 7 | – | South Dakota | (3) | – | 3 |
| Kansas | (6) | – | 6 | Tennessee | (11) | 11 | – |
| Kentucky | (8) | 8 | – | Texas | (32) | – | 32 |
| Louisiana | (9) | 9 | – | Utah | (5) | – | 5 |
| Maine | (4) | 4 | – | Vermont | (3) | 3 | – |
| Maryland | (10) | 10 | – | Virginia | (13) | – | 13 |
| Massachusetts | (12) | 12 | – | Washington | (11) | 11 | – |
| Michigan | (18) | 18 | – | West Virginia | (5) | 5 | – |
| Minnesota | (10) | 10 | – | Wisconsin | (11) | 11 | – |
| Mississippi | (7) | – | 7 | Wyoming | (3) | – | 3 |
| Missouri | (11) | 11 | – | **Totals** | **(538)** | **370** | **168** |

# Electoral Votes for Vice President, 1804-1992

The following list gives the electoral votes for vice president from 1804 to 1992. Unless indicated by a note, the state-by-state breakdown of electoral votes for each vice presidential candidate was the same as for his or her party's presidential candidate.

Prior to 1804, under Article II, Section 1 of the Constitution, each elector cast two votes — each vote for a different person. The electors did not distinguish between votes for president and vice president. The candidate receiving the second highest total became vice president. The 12th Amendment, ratified in 1804, required electors to vote separately for president and vice president.

In some cases, persons had received electoral votes although they had never been formally nominated. The word *candidate* is used in this section to designate persons receiving electoral votes.

The *Senate Manual* (Washington, D.C.: Government Printing Office, 1994) was the source used for vice presidential electoral votes.

For political party designation, the basic source was Svend Petersen, *A Statistical History of the American Presidential Elections* (Westport, Conn.: Greenwood Press, 1981). Petersen gives the party designation of *presidential candidates only.* Congressional Quarterly adopted Petersen's party designations for the running mates of presidential candidates.

To supplement Petersen, Congressional Quarterly consulted the *Biographical Directory of the United States Congress, 1774-1989* (Washington, D.C.: Government Printing Office, 1989); the *Dictionary of American Biography* (New York: Charles Scribner's Sons, 1928-36); the *Encyclopedia of American Biography* (New York: Harper and Row, 1974); and *Who Was Who in America, 1607-1968* (Chicago: Marquis Co., 1943-68).

| Year | Candidate | Electoral Votes |
|------|-----------|-----------------|
| 1804 | George Clinton (Democratic-Republican) | 162 |
|      | Rufus King (Federalist) | 14 |
| 1808 | George Clinton (Democratic-Republican) [1] | 113 |
|      | John Langdon (Democratic-Republican) | 9 |
|      | James Madison (Democratic-Republican) | 3 |
|      | James Monroe (Democratic-Republican) | 3 |
|      | Rufus King (Federalist) | 47 |
| 1812 | Elbridge Gerry (Democratic-Republican) [2] | 131 |
|      | Jared Ingersoll (Federalist) | 86 |
| 1816 | Daniel D. Tompkins (Democratic-Republican) | 183 |
|      | John E. Howard (Federalist) [3] | 22 |
|      | James Ross (Federalist) | 5 |
|      | John Marshall (Federalist) | 4 |
|      | Robert G. Harper (Federalist) | 3 |
| 1820 | Daniel D. Tompkins (Democratic-Republican) [4] | 218 |
|      | Richard Rush (Democratic-Republican) | 1 |
|      | Richard Stockton (Federalist) | 8 |
|      | Daniel Rodney (Federalist) | 4 |
|      | Robert G. Harper (Federalist) | 1 |
| 1824 | John C. Calhoun (Democratic-Republican) [5] | 182 |
|      | Nathan Sanford (Democratic-Republican) | 30 |
|      | Nathaniel Macon (Democratic-Republican) | 24 |
|      | Andrew Jackson (Democratic-Republican) | 13 |
|      | Martin Van Buren (Democratic-Republican) | 9 |
|      | Henry Clay (Democratic-Republican) | 2 |
| 1828 | John C. Calhoun (Democratic-Republican) [6] | 171 |
|      | William Smith (Independent Democratic-Republican) | 7 |
|      | Richard Rush (National Republican) | 83 |
| 1832 | Martin Van Buren (Democrat) [7] | 189 |
|      | William Wilkins (Democrat) | 30 |
|      | Henry Lee (Independent Democrat) | 11 |
|      | John Sergeant (National Republican) | 49 |
|      | Amos Ellmaker (Anti-Mason) | 7 |
| 1836 | Richard M. Johnson (Democrat) [8] | 147 |
|      | William Smith (Independent Democrat) | 23 |
|      | Francis Granger (Whig) | 77 |
|      | John Tyler (Whig) | 47 |
| 1840 | John Tyler (Whig) | 234 |
|      | Richard M. Johnson (Democrat) [9] | 48 |
|      | L. W. Tazewell (Democrat) | 11 |
|      | James K. Polk (Democrat) | 1 |
| 1844 | George M. Dallas (Democrat) | 170 |
|      | Theodore Frelinghuysen (Whig) | 105 |
| 1848 | Millard Fillmore (Whig) | 163 |
|      | William Orlando Butler (Democrat) | 127 |
| 1852 | William R. King (Democrat) | 254 |
|      | William Alexander Graham (Whig) | 42 |
| 1856 | John C. Breckinridge (Democrat) | 174 |
|      | William L. Dayton (Republican) | 114 |
|      | Andrew Jackson Donelson (Whig-American) | 8 |
| 1860 | Hannibal Hamlin (Republican) | 180 |
|      | Joseph Lane (Southern Democrat) | 72 |
|      | Edward Everett (Constitutional Union) | 39 |
|      | Herschel V. Johnson (Democrat) | 12 |
| 1864 | Andrew Johnson (Republican) | 212 |
|      | George H. Pendleton (Democrat) | 21 |
| 1868 | Schuyler Colfax (Republican) | 214 |
|      | Francis P. Blair (Democrat) | 80 |
| 1872 | Henry Wilson (Republican) | 286 |
|      | Benjamin Gratz Brown (Democrat) [10] | 47 |
|      | Alfred H. Colquitt (Democrat) | 5 |
|      | John M. Palmer (Democrat) | 3 |
|      | Thomas E. Bramlette (Democrat) | 3 |
|      | William S. Groesbeck (Democrat) | 1 |
|      | Willis B. Machen (Democrat) | 1 |
|      | George W. Julian (Liberal Republican) | 5 |
|      | Nathaniel P. Banks (Liberal Republican) | 1 |
| 1876 | William A. Wheeler (Republican) | 185 |
|      | Thomas A. Hendricks (Democrat) | 184 |
| 1880 | Chester A. Arthur (Republican) | 214 |
|      | William H. English (Democrat) | 155 |
| 1884 | Thomas A. Hendricks (Democrat) | 219 |
|      | John A. Logan (Republican) | 182 |
| 1888 | Levi P. Morton (Republican) | 233 |
|      | Allen G. Thurman (Democrat) | 168 |

| Year | Candidate | Electoral Votes |
|------|-----------|----------------:|
| 1892 | Adlai E. Stevenson (Democrat) | 277 |
|      | Whitelaw Reid (Republican) | 145 |
|      | James G. Field (Populist) | 22 |
| 1896 | Garret A. Hobart (Republican) | 271 |
|      | Arthur Sewall (Democrat) [11] | 149 |
|      | Thomas E. Watson (Populist) | 27 |
| 1900 | Theodore Roosevelt (Republican) | 292 |
|      | Adlai E. Stevenson (Democrat) | 155 |
| 1904 | Charles W. Fairbanks (Republican) | 336 |
|      | Henry G. Davis (Democrat) | 140 |
| 1908 | James S. Sherman (Republican) | 321 |
|      | John W. Kern (Democrat) | 162 |
| 1912 | Thomas R. Marshall (Democrat) | 435 |
|      | Hiram W. Johnson (Progressive) | 88 |
|      | Nicholas Murray Butler (Republican) [12] | 8 |
| 1916 | Thomas R. Marshall (Democrat) | 277 |
|      | Charles W. Fairbanks (Republican) | 254 |
| 1920 | Calvin Coolidge (Republican) | 404 |
|      | Franklin D. Roosevelt (Democrat) | 127 |
| 1924 | Charles G. Dawes (Republican) | 382 |
|      | Charles W. Bryan (Democrat) | 136 |
|      | Burton K. Wheeler (Progressive) | 13 |
| 1928 | Charles Curtis (Republican) | 444 |
|      | Joseph T. Robinson (Democrat) | 87 |
| 1932 | John N. Garner (Democrat) | 472 |
|      | Charles Curtis (Republican) | 59 |
| 1936 | John N. Garner (Democrat) | 523 |
|      | Frank Knox (Republican) | 8 |
| 1940 | Henry A. Wallace (Democrat) | 449 |
|      | Charles L. McNary (Republican) | 82 |
| 1944 | Harry S. Truman (Democrat) | 432 |
|      | John W. Bricker (Republican) | 99 |

| Year | Candidate | Electoral Votes |
|------|-----------|----------------:|
| 1948 | Alben W. Barkley (Democrat) | 303 |
|      | Earl Warren (Republican) | 189 |
|      | Fielding L. Wright (States' Rights Democrat) | 39 |
| 1952 | Richard Nixon (Republican) | 442 |
|      | John J. Sparkman (Democrat) | 89 |
| 1956 | Richard Nixon (Republican) | 457 |
|      | Estes Kefauver (Democrat) | 73 |
|      | Herman Talmadge (Democrat) | 1 |
| 1960 | Lyndon B. Johnson (Democrat) | 303 |
|      | Strom Thurmond (Democrat) [13] | 14 |
|      | Henry Cabot Lodge (Republican) | 219 |
|      | Barry Goldwater (Republican) | 1 |
| 1964 | Hubert H. Humphrey (Democrat) | 486 |
|      | William E. Miller (Republican) | 52 |
| 1968 | Spiro T. Agnew (Republican) | 301 |
|      | Edmund S. Muskie (Democrat) | 191 |
|      | Curtis E. LeMay (American Independent) | 46 |
| 1972 | Spiro T. Agnew (Republican) | 520 |
|      | R. Sargent Shriver (Democrat) | 17 |
|      | Theodora Nathan (Libertarian) | 1 |
| 1976 | Walter F. Mondale (Democrat) | 297 |
|      | Robert Dole (Republican) [14] | 241 |
| 1980 | George Bush (Republican) | 489 |
|      | Walter F. Mondale (Democrat) | 49 |
| 1984 | George Bush (Republican) | 525 |
|      | Geraldine A. Ferraro (Democrat) | 13 |
| 1988 | Dan Quayle (Republican) | 426 |
|      | Lloyd Bentsen (Democrat) [15] | 111 |
|      | Michael S. Dukakis (Democrat) | 1 |
| 1992 | Al Gore (Democrat) | 370 |
|      | Dan Quayle (Republican) | 168 |

## Notes

1. New York cast 13 presidential electoral votes for Democratic-Republican James Madison and 6 votes for Clinton; for vice president, New York cast 13 votes for Clinton, 3 votes for Madison, and 3 votes for Monroe.
Langdon received Ohio's 3 votes and Vermont's 6 votes.

2. The state-by-state vote for Gerry was the same as for Democratic-Republican presidential candidate Madison, except for Massachusetts and New Hampshire. Massachusetts cast 2 votes for Gerry and 20 votes for Ingersoll; New Hampshire cast 1 vote for Gerry and 7 votes for Ingersoll.

3. Four Federalists received vice-presidential electoral votes: Howard — Massachusetts, 22 votes; Ross — Connecticut, 5 votes; Marshall — Connecticut, 4 votes; Harper — Delaware, 3 votes.

4. The state-by-state vote for Tompkins was the same as for Democratic-Republican presidential candidate Monroe, except for Delaware, Maryland, and Massachusetts. Delaware cast 4 votes for Rodney; Maryland cast 10 votes for Tompkins and 1 for Harper; Massachusetts cast 7 votes for Tompkins and 8 for Stockton.

New Hampshire, which cast 7 presidential electoral votes for Monroe and 1 vote for John Quincy Adams, cast 7 vice-presidential electoral votes for Tompkins and 1 vote for Rush.

5. The state-by-state vice-presidential electoral vote was as follows:

Calhoun — Alabama, 5 votes; Delaware, 1 vote; Illinois, 3 votes; Indiana, 5 votes; Kentucky, 7 votes; Louisiana, 5 votes; Maine, 9 votes; Maryland, 10 votes; Massachusetts, 15 votes; Mississippi, 3 votes; New Hampshire, 7 votes; New Jersey, 8 votes; New York, 29 votes; North Carolina, 15 votes; Pennsylvania, 28 votes; Rhode Island, 3 votes; South Carolina, 11 votes; Tennessee, 11 votes; Vermont, 7 votes.

Sanford — Kentucky, 7 votes; New York, 7 votes; Ohio, 16 votes.

Macon — Virginia, 24 votes.

Jackson — Connecticut, 8 votes; Maryland, 1 vote; Missouri, 3 votes; New Hampshire, 1 vote.

Van Buren — Georgia, 9 votes.

Clay — Delaware, 2 votes.

6. The state-by-state vote for Calhoun was the same as for Democratic-Republican presidential candidate Jackson, except for Georgia, which cast 2 votes for Calhoun and 7 votes for Smith.

7. The state-by-state vote for Van Buren was the same as for Democratic-Republican presidential candidate Jackson, except for Pennsylvania, which cast 30 votes for Wilkins.

South Carolina cast 11 presidential electoral votes for Independent Democratic presidential candidate Floyd and 11 votes for Independent Democratic vice-presidential candidate Lee.

Vermont cast 7 presidential electoral votes for Anti-Masonic candidate Wirt and 7 vice-presidential electoral votes for Wirt's running mate, Ellmaker.

8. The state-by-state vote for Johnson was the same as for Democratic presidential candidate Van Buren, except for Virginia, which cast 23 votes for Smith.

Granger's state-by-state vote was the same as for Whig presidential candidate Harrison, except for Maryland and Massachusetts. Maryland cast 10 presidential electoral votes for Harrison and 10 vice-presidential electoral votes for Tyler; Massachusetts cast 14 presidential electoral votes for Whig candidate Webster and 14 vice-presidential votes over Granger.

Tyler received 11 votes from Georgia, 10 from Maryland, 11 from South Carolina, and 15 from Tennessee.

No vice-presidential candidate received a majority of the electoral vote. As a result the Senate, for the only time in history, selected the vice president under the provisions of the Twelfth Amendment. Johnson was elected vice president by a vote of 33 to 16 over Granger.

9. The Democratic party did not nominate a vice-presidential candidate in 1840. Johnson's state-by-state vote was the same as for presidential candidate Van Buren, except for South Carolina and Virginia. South Carolina cast 11 votes for Tazewell. Virginia cast 23 presidential electoral votes for Van Buren, 22 vice-presidential votes for Johnson, and 1 vice-presidential vote for Polk.

10. Liberal Republican and Democratic presidential candidate Horace Greeley died November 29, 1872. As a result eighteen electors pledged to Greeley cast their presidential electoral votes for Brown, Greeley's running mate.

The vice-presidential vote was as follows:

Brown — Georgia, 5 votes; Kentucky, 8 votes; Maryland, 8 votes; Missouri, 6 votes; Tennessee, 12 votes; Texas, 8 votes.

Colquitt — Georgia, 5 votes.

Palmer — Missouri, 3 votes.

Bramlette — Kentucky, 3 votes.

Groesbeck — Missouri, 1 vote.

Machen — Kentucky, 1 vote.

Julian — Missouri, 5 votes.

Banks — Georgia, 1 vote.

11. The state-by-state vote for Sewall was the same as for Democratic-Populist candidate William Jennings Bryan, except for the following states, which cast electoral votes for Watson: Arkansas, 3 votes; Louisiana, 4; Missouri, 4; Montana, 1; Nebraska, 4; North Carolina, 5; South Dakota, 2; Utah, 1; Washington, 2; Wyoming, 1.

12. Butler received the 8 electoral votes of Vice President James Sherman, who died Oct. 30, 1912, after being renominated on the Republican ticket. Butler was named as the substitute candidate.

13. Democratic electors carried Alabama's 11 electoral votes. Five of the electors were pledged to the national Democratic ticket of Kennedy and Johnson. Six electors ran unpledged and voted for Harry F. Byrd for president and Strom Thurmond for vice president.

Mississippi's eight electors voted for Byrd and Thurmond.

In Oklahoma the Republican ticket of Nixon and Lodge carried the state, but Henry D. Irwin, 1 of the state's 8 electors voted for Byrd for president and Goldwater for vice president.

14. Mike Padden, a Republican elector from the state of Washington cast his presidential electoral vote for Reagan instead of the Republican nominee, Ford. But he voted for Dole, Ford's running mate, for vice president. Dole thus received one more electoral vote than Ford.

15. Margaret Leach, a Democratic elector from West Virginia, cast her vice presidential electoral vote for Dukakis, the Democratic nominee for president, and her presidential vote for his running mate, Bentsen.

# The Popular Vote

Few elements of the American political system have changed so markedly over the years as has the electorate. Since the early days of the nation, when the voting privilege was limited to the upper economic class of males, one voting barrier after another has fallen to pressures for wider suffrage. First non-property-holding males, then women, then African Americans and finally young people pushed for the franchise. By the early 1970s almost every restriction on voting had been removed, and virtually every adult citizen 18 years of age and older had won the right to vote.

Actions to expand the electorate have taken place at both the state and federal levels. Voting qualifications have varied widely because the federal Constitution (Article I, Section 2) permits the states to set their own voting standards. Early in the nation's history, the states dropped their property qualifications for voting, but some retained literacy tests as late as 1970.

On the federal level the Constitution has been amended five times to circumvent state qualifications denying the franchise to certain categories of people. The 14th Amendment, ratified in 1868, directed Congress to reduce the number of representatives from any state that disfranchised adult male citizens for any reason other than commission of a crime. However, no such reduction was ever made. The 15th Amendment, ratified in 1870, prohibited denial of the right to vote "on account of race, color or previous condition of servitude," and the 19th Amendment in 1920 prohibited denial of that right "on account of sex." The 24th Amendment, which came into effect in 1964, barred denial of the right to vote in any federal election "by reason of failure to pay any poll tax or other tax." Finally, in 1971 the 26th Amendment lowered the voting age to 18 in federal, state and local elections.

Congress in the 1950s and 1960s enacted a series of statutes to enforce the 15th Amendment's guarantee against racial discrimination in voting. A law passed in 1970 nullified state residence requirements of longer than 30 days for voting in presidential elections, suspended literacy tests for a five-year period (the suspension was made permanent in 1975) and lowered the minimum voting age to 18 years from 21, the requirement then in effect in most states. A 1970 Supreme Court ruling upheld the voting-age change for federal elections but invalidated it for state and local elections. In the same decision the Court upheld the provision on residence requirements and sustained the suspension of literacy tests with respect to both state and local

elections. The 26th Amendment was ratified six months after the Court's decision.

The right to vote in presidential elections was extended to citizens of the District of Columbia by the 23rd Amendment, ratified in 1961. District residents had been disfranchised from national elections except for a brief period in the 1870s when they elected a non-voting delegate to the House of Representatives. In 1970 Congress took another step toward full suffrage for District residents by again authorizing the election of a non-voting delegate to the House.

In the 103rd Congress, 1993-95, District residents moved another step closer to full representation in Congress when the House voted to allow delegates to vote in the Committee of the Whole, a device the House uses to expedite consideration of amendments to legislation. The delegates could not vote, however, on final action when the House reconvened as itself. The change, instigated by District delegate Eleanor Holmes Norton, Democrat, also applied to delegates from American Samoa, Guam, Puerto Rico and the Virgin Islands.

## Voting Trends

Statistics show that each major liberalization of election laws resulted in a sharp increase in the number of people voting. From 1824 to 1856, a period in which states gradually relaxed their property and taxpaying qualifications, voter participation in presidential elections increased from 3.8 percent to 16.7 percent of the total population. In 1920, when the 19th Amendment giving women the franchise went into effect, voter participation increased to 25.1 percent.

Between 1932 and 1976 both the voting-age population and the number of voters in presidential elections almost doubled. Except for the 1948 presidential election, when just a little over half of the voting-age population was estimated to have gone to the polls, the turnout in the postwar years through 1968 was approximately 60 percent, according to Census Bureau surveys. This relatively high percentage was due largely to passage of new civil rights laws encouraging blacks to vote.

Despite a steady increase in the number of persons voting in the 1970s, voter turnout actually declined as a percentage of eligible voters. Voter participation reached a modern peak of 62.8 percent in the 1960 presidential election. It declined steadily over the next decade, falling to

# Growing Franchise in the United States, 1930-92

| Year | Estimated Population of Voting Age | Vote Cast for Presidential Electors | | Vote Cast for U.S. Representatives | |
|---|---|---|---|---|---|
| | | Number | Percent | Number | Percent |
| 1930 | 73,623,000 | — | — | 24,777,000 | 33.7 |
| 1932 | 75,768,000 | 39,758,759 | 52.5 | 37,657,000 | 49.7 |
| 1934 | 77,997,000 | — | — | 32,256,000 | 41.4 |
| 1936 | 80,174,000 | 45,654,763 | 56.9 | 42,886,000 | 53.5 |
| 1938 | 82,354,000 | — | — | 36,236,000 | 44.0 |
| 1940 | 84,728,000 | 49,900,418 | 58.9 | 46,951,000 | 55.4 |
| 1942 | 86,465,000 | — | — | 28,074,000 | 32.5 |
| 1944 | 85,654,000 | 47,976,670 | 56.0 | 45,103,000 | 52.7 |
| 1946 | 92,659,000 | — | — | 34,398,000 | 37.1 |
| 1948 | 95,573,000 | 48,793,826 | 51.1 | 45,933,000 | 48.1 |
| 1950 | 98,134,000 | — | — | 40,342,000 | 41.1 |
| 1952 | 99,929,000 | 61,550,918 | 61.6 | 57,571,000 | 57.6 |
| 1954 | 102,075,000 | — | — | 42,580,000 | 41.7 |
| 1956 | 104,515,000 | 62,026,908 | 59.3 | 58,426,000 | 55.9 |
| 1958 | 106,447,000 | — | — | 45,818,000 | 43.0 |
| 1960 | 109,672,000 | 68,838,219 | 62.8 | 64,133,000 | 58.5 |
| 1962 | 112,952,000 | — | — | 51,267,000 | 45.4 |
| 1964 | 114,090,000 | 70,644,592 | 61.9 | 65,895,000 | 57.8 |
| 1966 | 116,638,000 | — | — | 52,908,000 | 45.4 |
| 1968 | 120,285,000 | 73,211,875 | 60.9 | 66,288,000 | 55.1 |
| 1970 | 124,498,000 | — | — | 54,173,000 | 43.5 |
| 1972 | 140,777,000 | 77,718,554 | 55.2 | 71,430,000 | 50.7 |
| 1974 | 146,338,000 | — | — | 52,495,000 | 35.9 |
| 1976 | 152,308,000 | 81,555,889 | 53.5 | 74,422,000 | 48.9 |
| 1978 | 158,369,000 | — | — | 55,332,000 | 34.9 |
| 1980 | 164,595,000 | 86,515,221 | 52.6 | 77,995,000 | 47.4 |
| 1982 | 169,936,000 | — | — | 64,514,000 | 38.0 |
| 1984 | 174,468,000 | 92,652,842 | 53.1 | 83,231,000 | 47.7 |
| 1986 | 178,566,000 | — | — | 56,619,000 | 33.4 |
| 1988 | 182,779,000 | 91,594,809 | 50.1 | 81,786,000 | 44.7 |
| 1990 | 185,812,000 | — | — | 61,513,000 | 33.1 |
| 1992 | 189,044,000 | 104,425,014 | 55.2 | 96,239,000 | 50.9 |

Source: Bureau of the Census, *Statistical Abstracts of the United States 1993;* Elections Research Center, Chevy Chase, Md.

61.9 percent in 1964, 60.9 percent in 1968 and 55.2 percent in 1972. Voting in the off-year congressional elections, always lower than in presidential years, also declined during this period.

According to the Census Bureau, 59.2 percent of adults eligible to vote reported that they went to the polls in 1976 and 1980. In 1984, 59.9 percent reported that they voted, but the number of ballots cast indicates that only 53.1 percent actually voted. For the 1988 election, 57.4 reported voting. Polling data show, however, that only 50.1 percent of the voting age population went to the polls. Census Bureau surveys, it should be pointed out, are based on *polls* of eligible voters rather than on actual vote counts.

The bureau surveys a cross section of eligible voters, defined as all adult civilians of voting age — 18 and older, registered and unregistered — except those confined in penal or other institutions. The number of registered voters nationwide at any given time is impossible to calculate. States have different registration deadlines before an election. People who move may be registered in more than one state at the same time or may not be recorded in any state. Moreover, a few states permit registration on election day, and others do not require towns and municipalities to keep registration records. Thus in states without registration requirements the Census Bureau considers all eligible voters as registered.

Changes in the age distribution of the electorate figured prominently in the decline during the 1970s. Since the surge in the birth rate beginning in 1947, youth has been the most rapidly growing group. However, young adults have tended to vote in much smaller proportions than the rest of the voting-age population. Approximately 11 million young vot-

# "Minority" Presidents

Under the U.S. electoral system, 16 presidents have been elected, either by the Electoral College itself or by the House of Representatives, who did not receive a majority of the popular votes cast in the election. Three of these future presidents — John Quincy Adams in 1824, Rutherford B. Hayes in 1876 and Benjamin Harrison in 1888 — actually trailed their opponents in the popular vote.

The following table shows the percentage of the popular vote received by candidates in the 16 elections in which a "minority" president (designated by boldface type) was elected:

| Year Elected | Candidate | Percentage of Popular Vote | Candidate | Percentage of Popular Vote | Candidate | Percentage of Popular Vote | Candidate | Percentage of Popular Vote |
|---|---|---|---|---|---|---|---|---|
| 1824 | Jackson | 41.34 | **Adams** | 30.92 | Clay | 12.99 | Crawford | 11.17 |
| 1844 | **Polk** | 49.54 | Clay | 48.08 | Birney | 2.30 | | |
| 1848 | **Taylor** | 47.28 | Cass | 42.49 | Van Buren | 10.12 | | |
| 1856 | **Buchanan** | 45.28 | Fremont | 33.11 | Fillmore | 21.53 | | |
| 1860 | **Lincoln** | 39.82 | Douglas | 29.46 | Breckenridge | 18.09 | Bell | 12.61 |
| 1876 | Tilden | 50.97 | **Hayes** | 47.95 | Cooper | .97 | | |
| 1880 | **Garfield** | 48.27 | Hancock | 48.25 | Weaver | 3.32 | Others | .15 |
| 1884 | **Cleveland** | 48.50 | Blaine | 48.25 | Butler | 1.74 | St. John | 1.47 |
| 1888 | Cleveland | 48.62 | **Harrison** | 47.82 | Fisk | 2.19 | Streeter | 1.29 |
| 1892 | **Cleveland** | 46.05 | Harrison | 42.96 | Weaver | 8.50 | Others | 2.25 |
| 1912 | **Wilson** | 41.84 | T. Roosevelt | 27.39 | Taft | 23.18 | Debs | 5.99 |
| 1916 | **Wilson** | 49.24 | Hughes | 46.11 | Benson | 3.18 | Others | 1.46 |
| 1948 | **Truman** | 49.52 | Dewey | 45.12 | Thurmond | 2.40 | Wallace | 2.38 |
| 1960 | **Kennedy** | 49.72 | Nixon | 49.55 | Others | .72 | | |
| 1968 | **Nixon** | 43.42 | Humphrey | 42.72 | Wallace | 13.53 | Others | .33 |
| 1992 | **Clinton** | 43.01 | Bush | 37.45 | Perot | 18.91 | Others | .64 |

ers entered the electorate in 1972 when the voting age was lowered to 18; even though the total number of voters who cast ballots for president rose to 77,625,000, 4.4 million more than in 1968, the percentage of eligible Americans who voted dropped sharply. (*Growing Franchise in the United States, 1930-92, table, p. 416*)

In addition to changes in the composition of the electorate, political scientists have attributed the decline in the percentage of Americans voting to several factors: long periods of political stability, the predictable outcome of many races and the lack of appeal of some candidates.

Studies by the Census Bureau have shown a marked difference in participation among various groups of voters. In general, the studies have found higher participation rates among whites, people 45 to 65 years of age, non-southerners, people with higher family incomes, white-collar workers and professionals. Those with higher levels of education also had higher turnout rates.

Political parties grew increasingly important in the electoral process in the 19th century. As the voting population grew, the power of each vote became more and more diluted, and voters found parties a convenient mechanism for defining political issues and mobilizing the strength to push a particular policy through to enactment and execution. After the rise and fall of numerous political parties during the first half of the 19th century, two major parties emerged — the Republican and the Democratic. This changed somewhat during the early years of the 20th century when the Progressive movement won a sizable following. After World War II the numbers of independent voters — those who choose not to register in either of the major parties — increased appreciably.

## Broadening the Franchise

During the first few decades of the Republic, all 13 of the original states limited the franchise to property holders and taxpayers. Seven of the states required ownership of land or a life estate as opposed to a leased estate as a qualification for voting, and the other six permitted persons to qualify by substituting either evidence of ownership of certain amounts of personal property or payment of taxes.

The Framers of the Constitution apparently were content to have the states limit the right to vote to adult males who had a real stake in good government. This meant, in most cases, persons in the upper economic levels. Not wishing to discriminate against any particular type of property owner (uniform federal voting standards inevitably would have conflicted with some of the state standards), the Constitutional Convention adopted without dissent the recommendation of its Committee of Detail providing that qualifications for the electors of the House of Representatives "shall be the same . . . as those of the electors in the several states of the most numerous branch of their own legislatures."

Under this provision fewer than half of the adult white men in the United States were eligible to vote in federal elections. Because no state made women eligible (although states were not forbidden to do so), only one white adult in four qualified to go to the polls. Slaves and most blacks and Indians were ineligible, and they formed almost one-fifth of

# Statesmen, Military Leaders Displaced . . .

As a nation the United States has never made up its mind what background a president ought to have. Most presidents have come to the White House with long careers of public service behind them. Yet there have been notable exceptions. A look back to the 18th century shows just how often the fashion has changed.

The earliest tradition developed around the secretary of state, who was considered the pre-eminent Cabinet officer and thus the most important man in the executive branch after the president. Washington's first secretary of state was Thomas Jefferson. Although Jefferson left the Cabinet early in Washington's second term, he went on to become leader of the newly formed Democratic-Republican Party and its candidate for president in 1796, 1800 and 1804. Losing to John Adams in 1796, Jefferson came back to win four years later.

In turn, Jefferson's secretary of state for two terms, James Madison, won the presidency in 1808. During his first term, President Madison appointed fellow Virginian James Monroe as his secretary of state. And following in what was rapidly becoming a tradition, Monroe went on to the presidency in 1816, serving two terms (1817-25).

Throughout Monroe's terms, the secretary of state was John Quincy Adams, son of former President John Adams. When Monroe's second term was nearing its end, five major candidates, including Adams, entered the race to succeed him. None of the candidates managed to acquire a majority in the Electoral College, and the House then chose Secretary of State Adams.

Adams was the last secretary of state to go directly from his Cabinet post to the White House. After him, only two secretaries of state made it to the White House at all — Martin Van Buren and James Buchanan.

Another institution died at approximately the same time as the Cabinet tradition. "King Caucus" was a derogatory reference to the congressional party caucuses that met throughout the early 1800s to designate presidential nominees. During its heyday, the Washington-centered mentality of the caucus had virtually guaranteed that Cabinet officers should be among those most often nominated by the party in power. But the caucus came under attack as being undemocratic and unrepresentative and ceased to function as a presidential nominating mechanism after 1824. It was replaced by the national conventions, bodies that are not connected with Congress and that as of 1992 had never met in the national capital.

## Men on Horseback

The next cycle of American politics, from the presidency of Andrew Jackson (1829-37) to the Civil War, saw a variety of backgrounds qualify candidates for the presidency. One of the most prevalent was the military. Andrew Jackson, who ran in 1824 (unsuccessfully), 1828 and 1832, was a general in the War of 1812, gaining near-heroic stature by his defeat of the British at the Battle of New Orleans in January 1815. Like most military officers who have risen to the presidency, however, Jackson was only a part-time military man.

Other candidates during this era who were or had been military officers included William Henry Harrison, a Whig candidate in 1836 and 1840; Zachary Taylor, the Whig candidate in 1848; Winfield Scott, the 1852 Whig candidate; Franklin Pierce, the Democratic nominee in 1852; and John Charles Fremont in 1856, the Republican Party's first presidential candidate. Thus, from 1824 through 1856, all but one presidential election featured a major candidate with a military background.

The smoldering political conflicts of the 1840s and 1850s probably contributed to the naming of military men for the presidency. Generals had usually escaped involvement in national politics and had avoided taking stands on the issues that divided the country — slavery, expansion, the currency and the tariff.

Later on, the nature of the Civil War almost automatically led at least one of the parties to choose a military officer as presidential standard-bearer every four years. To have been on the "right" side during the war — fighting to save the Union and destroy slavery — was a major political asset in the North and Middle West, where tens of thousands of war veterans were effectively organized in the Grand Army of the Republic (GAR). The GAR became part of the backbone of the Republican Party during the last third of the 19th century.

Consequently, it became customary for Republicans to have a Civil War officer at the head of their ticket. Except for James G. Blaine in 1884, every Republican presidential nominee from 1868 to 1900 had served as an officer in the Union Army during the Civil War. Of all the Republican nominees, however, only Ulysses S. Grant, who was elected president in 1868 and 1872, was a professional military man. The others — Rutherford B. Hayes in 1876, James A. Garfield in 1880, Benjamin Harrison in 1888 and 1892 and William McKinley in 1896 and 1900 — were civilians who volunteered for service in the Civil War.

The Democrats, who had been split over the war, had few prominent military veterans to choose from. Only twice between 1860 and 1900 did the Democrats pick a Civil War officer as their nominee. In 1864, during the Civil War, the Democrats nominated Gen. George B. McClellan, the Union military commander who had fallen out with President Abraham Lincoln. And in 1880 Gen. Winfield Scott Hancock of Pennsylvania was the Democrats' choice.

## The Empire State

Otherwise, Democrats tended to favor governors or former governors of New York. Their 1868 nominee was Horatio Seymour, who had been governor of New York in 1853-55 and again in 1863-65. In 1876 they chose Samuel J. Tilden, New York's reform governor who was battling Tammany Hall. And in 1884 Grover Cleveland, another New York reform governor, captured the Democratic nomination. He went on to become the first Democrat to win the White House in 28 years. Cleveland was again the Democratic nominee in 1888 and 1892.

# . . . At Head of Long Road to Presidency

Besides being the most populous state, New York was a swing state in presidential politics. During the period from Reconstruction through the turn of the century, most Southern states voted Democratic, while the Republicans usually carried Pennsylvania, the Midwest and New England. A New Yorker appeared as the nominee for president or vice president of at least one of the major parties in every election from 1868 through 1892.

This general tradition was maintained through the candidacy of Thomas E. Dewey, Republican governor of New York, in 1948. Only twice between 1868 and 1948 was there no New Yorker on the national ticket of at least one of the major parties — for president or vice president. Once, in 1944, both major party presidential nominees, Democrat Franklin D. Roosevelt and Republican Dewey, were selected from New York.

From 1952 to 1992, however, no New Yorkers were nominated by a major party for president and only two for vice president. The latter two were Rep. William E. Miller, R, in 1964 and Rep. Geraldine A. Ferraro, D, in 1984. Eisenhower in 1952 and Richard Nixon in 1968 were technically residents of New York, but they were generally identified with other states. Gerald R. Ford's vice president, Nelson Rockefeller, was a former governor of New York, but he was appointed to the vice presidency. He was not asked to be on the ticket when Ford ran in 1976.

Another major swing state in the years from the Civil War through World War I was Indiana. And, in most elections, a prominent Indianan found his way onto one of the major party's national tickets. In the 13 presidential elections between 1868 and 1916, an Indianan appeared 10 times on at least one of the major parties' national tickets. However, since 1916 only two Indianans, Wendell Willkie in 1940 and Dan Quayle in 1988 and 1992, have been major party nominees.

## The Governors

From 1900 to 1956, Democrats tended to favor governors for the presidential nomination. Democratic governors who received their party's presidential nomination included Woodrow Wilson of New Jersey in 1912, James M. Cox of Ohio in 1920, Alfred E. Smith of New York in 1928, Franklin D. Roosevelt of New York in 1932 and Adlai E. Stevenson of Illinois in 1952.

During the same period, 1900 to 1956, Republican presidential nominees had a wide variety of backgrounds. There were two Cabinet officers, a Supreme Court justice, a U.S. senator, two governors, a private lawyer and a general. Calvin Coolidge of Massachusetts, the 1924 nominee, and Theodore Roosevelt of New York, the 1904 nominee, both of whom succeeded to the presidency from the vice presidency, had been governors of their respective states.

## Former Vice Presidents

A sudden change took place in 1960 with the nomination of John F. Kennedy, a senator, and Nixon, a former senator and sitting vice president. It was the first time

since 1860 and only the second time in the history of party nominating conventions that an incumbent vice president was chosen for the presidency. And it was only the second time in the 20th century that an incumbent U.S. senator was nominated for the presidency. The first time was in 1920 when the Republicans nominated Ohio senator Warren G. Harding. In the 19th century the phenomenon was also rare, with National-Republican Henry Clay in 1832, Democrat Lewis Cass in 1848 and Democrat Stephen A. Douglas in 1860 the only incumbent senators nominated for president by official party conventions. Republican James A. Garfield was a senator-elect at the time of his election in 1880.

The nomination of Nixon, like the nomination of Kennedy, was a sign of things to come. Beginning in 1960 the vice presidency, like the Senate, became a presidential training ground. Vice President Hubert H. Humphrey was chosen by the Democrats for president in 1968. That same year the Republicans renominated Nixon, who went on to win the presidency eight years after being vice president. In 1984 former vice president Walter F. Mondale, who had served under Jimmy Carter, emerged as the Democratic choice for the presidential nomination. When Republican George Bush won the presidency in 1988, after filling the second spot under Ronald Reagan for eight years, it marked the first time a sitting vice president had been elected president since Martin Van Buren in 1836.

Even defeated vice presidential nominees have been considered for the nomination — witness Henry Cabot Lodge Jr. of Massachusetts in 1964, Edmund S. Muskie of Maine in 1972, Sargent Shriver of Maryland in 1976 and Robert Dole of Kansas in 1980 and 1988.

## Governors Making a Comeback

The field of candidates for the 1980 presidential nomination continued a trend that first appeared in the 1976 campaign — the re-emergence of governors as leading contenders in the nomination sweepstakes. For 16 years, beginning with Kennedy's ascension from the Senate to the White House in 1960 until 1976, senators dominated presidential campaigns. During that time every single major party nominee was a senator or former senator.

Yet, while there was no shortage of senators in the 1976 campaign, it was the governors who attracted the most attention. Former California governor Reagan came close to depriving incumbent Ford of the Republican presidential nomination. The Democratic nominee and eventual winner, former Georgia governor Jimmy Carter, faced a dramatic last-minute challenge from the governor of California at the time, Jerry Brown. Reagan (successfully), Carter and Brown were candidates again in 1980; Reagan again in 1984.

In 1988 and 1992 the Democrats nominated governors for president: Massachusetts governor Michael S. Dukakis, who lost to Bush in 1988, and Arkansas governor Bill Clinton, who defeated Bush in 1992.

# Presidents' Re-election Chances

The record of 20th century U.S. presidential elections indicates that a smooth path to renomination is essential for incumbents seeking re-election.

Every president who actively sought renomination this century was successful. And those who were virtually unopposed within their own party won another term. But all the presidents who faced significant opposition for renomination ended up losing in the general election.

The following chart shows the presidents who sought re-election to a second term since 1900, whether they had "clear sailing" or "tough sledding" for renomination and their fate in the general election.

A president with an asterisk (*) next to his name was, like Ronald Reagan in 1984, completing his first full four-year term when he sought re-election. A dash (—) indicates there were no presidential preference primaries. The primary vote for President Lyndon B. Johnson in 1964 included the vote for favorite sons and uncommitted delegate slates. George Bush in 1992 had to fight off a significant challenge by Patrick J. Buchanan in the primaries before he went on to win 95 percent of the convention delegates.

| | Incumbent's Percentage of: | | |
| --- | --- | --- | --- |
| | Primary Vote | Convention Delegates | General Election Result |
| **'Clear Sailing'** | | | |
| William McKinley (1900) * | — | 100% | Won |
| Theodore Roosevelt (1904) | — | 100 | Won |
| Woodrow Wilson (1916) * | 99% | 99 | Won |
| Calvin Coolidge (1924) | 68 | 96 | Won |
| Franklin D. Roosevelt (1936) * | 93 | 100 | Won |
| Franklin D. Roosevelt (1940) | 72 | 86 | Won |
| Franklin D. Roosevelt (1944) | 71 | 92 | Won |
| Harry S. Truman (1948) | 64 | 75 | Won |
| Dwight D. Eisenhower (1956) * | 86 | 100 | Won |
| Lyndon B. Johnson (1964) | 88 | 100 | Won |
| Richard Nixon (1972) * | 87 | 99 | Won |
| Ronald Reagan (1984) * | 99 | 100 | Won |
| **'Tough Sledding'** | | | |
| William H. Taft (1912) * | 34% | 52% | Lost |
| Herbert Hoover (1932) * | 33 | 98 | Lost |
| Gerald R. Ford (1976) | 53 | 53 | Lost |
| Jimmy Carter (1980) * | 51 | 64 | Lost |
| George Bush (1992) * | 73 | 95 | Lost |

ownership a condition for voting substituted a taxpaying requirement: Delaware in 1792, Maryland in 1810, Connecticut in 1818, Massachusetts in 1821, New York in 1821, Rhode Island in 1842 and Virginia in 1850. By the middle of the 19th century most states had removed even the taxpaying qualifications, although some jurisdictions persisted in this practice into the 20th century.

Another 19th century development, one that made it easier to vote, was the introduction of the *Australian ballot,* which is produced by the government and lists candidates from all parties. Previously, parties offered their own ballots listing only their own candidates. Introduced in the United States in 1888, the Australian ballot was adopted by almost all states by 1896. Variations introduced later were the *Indiana ballot,* which facilitates straight-ticket voting by listing candidates under their party name, and the *Massachusetts ballot,* which lists candidates of all parties under the office they are seeking.

The trend toward a broadened franchise continued in the 20th century with women obtaining the vote and with barriers to black voting slowly falling. Once Congress acted, the Supreme Court steadily backed its power to ensure the right to vote. In general, by the 200th anniversary of the nation, the only remaining restrictions prevented voting by the insane, convicted felons and otherwise eligible voters who were unable to meet short residence requirements.

# Voting Behavior

A precise breakdown that shows which groups of voters (such as African Americans or women) have higher turnout rates has never been possible. It would require an elaborate questionnaire for every eligible voter asking whether the person had participated in the election as well as an honest answer from the voter.

In place of a complete survey, the Census Bureau attempts to measure voting behavior by taking a random sample of the electorate in every election year, a practice the bureau began in 1964. The Survey Research Center-Center for Political Studies at the University of Michigan also analyzes voting behavior in surveys referred to as the National Election Studies (NES). Again, these surveys cannot be precise because they are based on people's responses. Estimates made from the survey differ from the actual ballot count because people frequently report that they or members of their families voted when in fact they did not.

Despite the get-out-the-vote drives in 1984, voter participation rose only half a percentage point. In 1988 both parties cut back their voter registration drives, and experts thought that turnout would decline, but few expected the 3 point drop that occurred. Between 1960 and 1988, the turnout of those eligible to vote declined 12.4 points. If turnout of the politically eligible population had been as high in 1988 as it was in 1960, an additional 21 million people would have voted, a number three times greater than George Bush's popular vote margin over Michael Dukakis.

Bush won the presidency by garnering the votes of 26.8 percent of the voting age population, about 3 percentage points below the average turnout for winners in the eighteen presidential elections held 1920-88. Lyndon B. Johnson won the highest percentage of the voting age population in these elections with 37.8 percent in 1964. Calvin Coolidge, with just 23.7 of the voting age population, won with the least support. In 1988, 49.8 percent of the voting age population stayed home, compared with an average non-participation rate of 45.3 percent in the previous elections since 1920.

the American population as enumerated in the census of 1790. Also ineligible were white indentured servants, whose status was little better than that of the slaves.

Actually, these early state practices represented a liberalization of restrictions on voting that had prevailed at one time in the colonial period. Roman Catholics had been disfranchised in almost every colony, Jews in most colonies, Quakers and Baptists in some. In Rhode Island Jews remained legally ineligible to vote until 1842.

For half a century before the Civil War there was a steady broadening of the electorate. The new Western settlements supplied a stimulus to the principle of universal male suffrage, and Jacksonian democracy encouraged its acceptance. Gradually, the seven states making property

# Voter Turnout, 1992 Presidential Election

| State | Resident Voting Age Population | November 1992 Registration | Total Valid Vote President | Percentage Voting Age Registered | Percentage Voting Age Voted [1] | Percentage Registered Voted |
|---|---|---|---|---|---|---|
| Alabama | 3,056,000 | 2,367,972 | 1,688,060 | 77.5 | 55.2 | 71.3 |
| Alaska | 395,000 | 315,058 | 258,506 | 79.8 | 65.4 | 82.1 |
| Arizona | 2,749,000 | 1,964,949 | 1,486,975 | 71.5 | 54.1 | 75.7 |
| Arkansas | 1,768,000 | 1,317,944 | 950,653 | 74.5 | 53.8 | 72.1 |
| California | 22,668,000 | 15,101,473 | 11,131,721 | 66.6 | 49.1 | 73.7 |
| Colorado | 2,501,000 | 2,003,375 | 1,569,180 | 80.1 | 62.7 | 78.3 |
| Connecticut | 2,535,000 | 1,955,268 | 1,616,332 | 77.1 | 63.8 | 82.7 |
| Delaware | 525,000 | 342,088 | 289,735 | 65.2 | 55.2 | 84.7 |
| Florida | 10,586,000 | 6,541,825 | 5,314,392 | 61.8 | 50.2 | 81.2 |
| Georgia | 4,950,000 | 3,177,061 | 2,321,125 | 64.2 | 46.9 | 73.1 |
| Hawaii | 889,000 | 464,495 | 372,842 | 52.2 | 41.9 | 80.3 |
| Idaho | 740,000 | 611,121 | 482,142 | 82.6 | 65.2 | 78.9 |
| Illinois | 8,568,000 | 6,600,358 | 5,050,157 | 77.0 | 58.9 | 76.5 |
| Indiana | 4,176,000 | 3,180,157 | 2,305,871 | 76.2 | 55.2 | 72.5 |
| Iowa | 2,075,000 | 1,703,532 | 1,354,607 | 82.1 | 65.3 | 79.5 |
| Kansas | 1,836,000 | 1,365,849 | 1,157,335 | 74.4 | 63.0 | 84.7 |
| Kentucky | 2,779,000 | 2,076,263 | 1,492,900 | 74.7 | 53.7 | 71.9 |
| Louisiana | 2,992,000 | 2,292,129 | 1,790,017 | 76.6 | 59.8 | 78.1 |
| Maine | 944,000 | 974,605 | 679,499 | 103.2 | 72.0 | 69.7 |
| Maryland | 3,719,000 | 2,463,010 | 1,985,046 | 66.2 | 53.4 | 80.6 |
| Massachusetts | 4,607,000 | 3,351,918 | 2,773,700 | 72.8 | 60.2 | 82.7 |
| Michigan | 6,923,000 | 6,147,083 | 4,274,673 | 88.8 | 61.7 | 69.5 |
| Minnesota | 3,278,000 | 3,138,901 | 2,347,948 | 95.8 | 71.6 | 74.8 |
| Mississippi | 1,861,000 | 1,640,150 | 981,793 | 88.1 | 52.8 | 59.9 |
| Missouri | 3,858,000 | 3,067,955 | 2,391,565 | 79.5 | 62.0 | 78.0 |
| Montana | 586,000 | 529,822 | 410,611 | 90.4 | 70.1 | 77.5 |
| Nebraska | 1,167,000 | 951,395 | 737,546 | 81.5 | 63.2 | 77.5 |
| Nevada | 1,013,000 | 649,913 | 506,318 | 64.2 | 50.0 | 77.9 |
| New Hampshire | 852,000 | 660,985 | 537,943 | 77.6 | 63.1 | 81.4 |
| New Jersey | 5,943,000 | 4,059,472 | 3,343,594 | 68.3 | 56.3 | 82.4 |
| New Mexico | 1,104,000 | 706,966 | 569,986 | 64.0 | 51.6 | 80.6 |
| New York | 13,609,000 | 9,193,391 | 6,926,925 | 67.6 | 50.9 | 75.3 |
| North Carolina | 5,217,000 | 3,817,380 | 2,611,850 | 73.2 | 50.1 | 68.4 |
| North Dakota [2] | 458,000 | — | 308,133 | — | 67.3 | — |
| Ohio | 8,146,000 | 6,542,931 | 4,939,967 | 80.3 | 60.6 | 75.5 |
| Oklahoma | 2,328,000 | 2,302,279 | 1,390,359 | 98.9 | 59.7 | 60.4 |
| Oregon | 2,226,000 | 1,774,449 | 1,462,643 | 79.7 | 65.7 | 82.4 |
| Pennsylvania | 9,129,000 | 5,993,002 | 4,959,810 | 65.6 | 54.3 | 82.8 |
| Rhode Island | 776,000 | 554,664 | 453,477 | 71.5 | 58.4 | 81.8 |
| South Carolina | 2,672,000 | 1,537,140 | 1,202,527 | 57.5 | 45.0 | 78.2 |
| South Dakota | 502,000 | 448,292 | 336,254 | 89.3 | 67.0 | 75.0 |
| Tennessee | 3,783,000 | 2,726,449 | 1,982,638 | 72.1 | 52.4 | 72.7 |
| Texas | 12,524,000 | 8,440,143 | 6,154,018 | 67.4 | 49.1 | 72.9 |
| Utah | 1,142,000 | 965,211 | 743,999 | 84.5 | 65.1 | 77.1 |
| Vermont | 429,000 | 383,371 | 289,701 | 89.4 | 67.5 | 75.6 |
| Virginia | 4,842,000 | 3,054,662 | 2,558,665 | 63.1 | 52.8 | 83.8 |
| Washington | 3,818,000 | 2,814,680 | 2,288,230 | 73.7 | 59.9 | 81.3 |
| West Virginia | 1,350,000 | 956,172 | 683,762 | 70.8 | 50.6 | 71.5 |
| Wisconsin [2] | 3,669,000 | — | 2,531,114 | — | 69.0 | — |
| Wyoming | 322,000 | 234,260 | 200,598 | 72.8 | 62.3 | 85.6 |
| Dist. of Col. | 459,000 | 340,953 | 227,572 | 74.3 | 49.6 | 66.7 |
| **United States** | 189,044,000 | 133,802,521 | 104,425,014 | 70.8 | 55.2 | 78.0 |

1. Based on actual votes cast as opposed to Census Bureau estimates, which are based on polls.
2. North Dakota has no formal registration system; Wisconsin has no statewide registration system.

Source: Richard M. Scammon and Alice V. McGillivray, *America Votes 20.* (Washington, D.C.: Congressional Quarterly, 1993.)

In the *Statistical Abstract of the United States, 1990,* the Census Bureau reported that 66.6 percent of the voting-age population said they were registered to vote in 1988, which is 1.7 points lower than in 1984. Of the white voting-age population, 59.1 percent reported they voted in 1988 (61.4 in 1984), compared with 51.5 percent (55.8 percent in 1984) of the black population, and 28.8 percent (32.6 percent in 1984) of the Hispanic population.

Women outvoted men by almost 2 percentage points in 1988. Of the male voting-age population, 65.4 percent voted, while 58.3 percent of the females voted. The Census Bureau reported 9.1 million more females than males of voting age, however. The youngest group of voters continued to lag far behind others in participation. Only 33.2 percent of voters aged 18 to 20 reported voting in 1984. That figure was lower than the 36.7 percent that voted in 1988. The oldest voters (over age 65) had the best participation rate with 68.8 percent, beating the 45-64 age group (67.9 percent). In 1984 the rates were 69.8 percent for the 45-64 age group and 67.7 percent for the oldest voters.

The Midwest led the rest of the country in 1988 as it had in 1984, with reported turnouts of 62.9 percent and 65.7 percent respectively. The South, with 54.5 percent in 1988 and 56.8 percent in 1984, had the lowest rate, according to the Census Bureau. In the West 55.6 percent voted in 1988 as compared with 58.5 percent in 1984. In the Northeast the figures were 57.4 percent for 1988 and 59.7 percent for 1984.

Turnout in 1988 was highest among the best-educated Americans, but the rate was still lower than in 1984. Of those with four or more years of college, 77.6 percent voted in 1988, and 79.1 voted in 1984. The numbers declined with fewer years of education; 36.7 percent (42.9 percent, 1984) of those with less than an eighth grade education reported voting.

A total of 104.4 million voters cast ballots in the 1992 presidential election, easily surpassing the previous record of 92.7 million in 1984. Turnout was 55.2 percent of the estimated voting age population of 189 million, the highest turnout rate for any national election since 1968. (Census Bureau surveys placed the 1992 turnout at 61.3 percent of a lower estimated voting age population, 185.7 million.)

The 44.9 million votes cast for Bill Clinton were the most that a Democratic candidate had ever received, surpassing the 43.1 million cast for Lyndon B. Johnson in 1964. But Clinton's 43.0 percent share of the popular vote was the fourth lowest for anyone elected president. Only John Quincy Adams (1824), Abraham Lincoln (1860) and Wood-row Wilson (1912) won with lower percentages. *("Minority" Presidents, table, p. 417)*

The 39.1 million votes for President George Bush were 15.4 million fewer than the record 54.5 million won in 1984 by Republican Ronald Reagan, the first presidential candidate to receive more than 50 million votes.

Independent candidate Ross Perot received 19.7 million votes, nearly twice the previous total for any third-party candidate. His 18.9 percent share of the total was the highest for any third-party candidate since former president Theodore Roosevelt ran in 1912.

With one of the youngest tickets on record challenging an older incumbent president, young people turned out in bigger numbers for the 1992 election. The 18-20 youth vote showed a 5-point increase over the 33.2 percent turnout in 1988. The peak was 48.0 percent in 1972, the first year that persons under 21 could vote. For voters 18 to 24, the 1992 rate was 42.8 percent compared with 36.2 percent in 1988, according to the Census Bureau.

In most other respects, the 1992 turnout pattern was consistent with 1988's: women (62.3 percent) took part more than men (60.2 percent); the Midwest had the highest voting rate (67.2 percent) and the South (59.0 percent) and West (58.5 percent), the lowest; whites had the highest turnout (63.6 percent) and persons of Hispanic origin (who may be of any race), the lowest (28.9 percent); voters 45 or older had the highest participation rate (70.0 percent), while those 18-24, despite the increase, still had the lowest (42.8 percent).

About 40 percent of Hispanics in the United States are not citizens. Omitting non-citizens raises the Hispanic turnout rate to about 48 percent. In 1992 for the first time the Census Bureau tabulated voting among Asians and Pacific Islanders, about 45 percent of whom are not citizens. Their turnout rates were 27.3 percent overall and about 50 percent with non-citizens omitted.

College-educated voters again had a higher turnout rate (81.0 percent) than those with less education, as did employed persons (63.8 percent), compared with the unemployed (46.2 percent).

Several reasons have been advanced to explain the generally lower turnout in modern elections. Various surveys pointed to a growing sense of powerlessness among the electorate, a feeling that one vote was not important and that it made no difference which party won. Another reason that has been suggested is the weakness of party identification for much of the electorate. The lack of party loyalty makes voting decisions more difficult and time-consuming.

# Victorious Party in Presidential Races, 1860-1992

| State | 1860 | 1864 | 1868 | 1872 | 1876 | 1880 | 1884 | 1888 | 1892 | 1896 | 1900 | 1904 | 1908 | 1912 | 1916 | 1920 | 1924 | 1928 | 1932 | 1936 | 1940 | 1944 | 1948 | 1952 | 1956 | 1960 | 1964 | 1968 | 1972 | 1976 | 1980 | 1984 | 1988 | 1992 | Dem. | Rep. | Other |
|---|---|---|---|---|---|---|---|---|---|---|---|---|---|---|---|---|---|---|---|---|---|---|---|---|---|---|---|---|---|---|---|---|---|---|---|---|---|
| Ala. | SD | [b] | R | R | D | D | D | D | D | D | D | D | D | D | D | D | D | D | D | D | D | D | SR | D | D[r] | D[s] | R | AI | R | D | R | R | R | R | 22 | 8 | 3 |
| Alaska | | | | | | | | | | | | | | | | | | | | | | | | | | R | D | R | R | R | R | R | R | R | 1 | 8 | 0 |
| Ariz. | | | | | | | | | | | | | | D | D | R | R | R | D | D | D | D | D | R | R | R | R | R | R | R | R | R | R | R | 7 | 14 | 0 |
| Ark. | SD | [b] | R | [d] | D | D | D | D | D | D | D | D | D | D | D | D | D | D | D | D | D | D | D | D | D | D | D | AI | R | D | R | R | R | D | 25 | 5 | 2 |
| Calif. | R | R | R | R | R | D[f] | R | R | D[g] | R[l] | R | R | R | PR | D | R | R | R | D | D | D | D | D | R | R | R | D | R | R | R | R | R | R | D | 10 | 23 | 1 |
| Colo. | | | | | R | R | R | R | PP | D | D | R | D | D | D | R | R | R | D | D | R | R | D | R | R | R | D | R | R | R | R | R | R | D | 10 | 19 | 1 |
| Conn. | R | R | R | R | D | R | D | D | D | R | R | R | R | D | R | R | R | R | D | D | D | D | D | R | R | D | R | R | R | R | R | R | R | D | 12 | 22 | 0 |
| Del. | SD | D | D | R | D | D | D | D | D | R | R | R | R | R | D | R | R | R | R | D | D | D | R | R | R | D | D | R | R | D | R | R | R | D | 15 | 18 | 1 |
| D.C. | | | | | | | | | | | | | | | | | | | | | | | | | | | D | D | D | D | D | D | D | D | 8 | 0 | 0 |
| Fla. | SD | [b] | R | R | R | D | D | D | D | D | D | D | D | D | D | D | D | R | D | D | D | D | D | R | R | R | D | R | R | D | R | R | R | R | 19 | 13 | 1 |
| Ga. | SD | [b] | D | D[e] | D | D | D | D | D | D | D | D | D | D | D | D | D | D | D | D | D | D | D | D | D | D | R | AI | R | D | D | R | R | D | 27 | 4 | 2 |
| Hawaii | | | | | | | | | | | | | | | | | | | | | | | | | | D | D | D | R | D | D | R | D | D | 7 | 2 | 0 |
| Idaho | | | | | | | | | PP | D | D | R | R | D | D | R | R | R | D | D | D | D | D | R | R | R | D | R | R | R | R | R | R | R | 10 | 15 | 1 |
| Ill. | R | R | R | R | R | R | R | R | D | R | R | R | R | D | R | R | R | R | D | D | D | D | D | R | R | D | D | R | R | R | R | R | R | D | 10 | 24 | 0 |
| Ind. | R | R | R | R | D | R | D | R | D | R | R | R | R | D | R | R | R | R | D | D | R | R | R | R | R | R | D | R | R | R | R | R | R | R | 7 | 27 | 0 |
| Iowa | R | R | R | R | R | R | R | R | R | R | R | R | R | D | R | R | R | R | D | D | R | R | D | R | R | R | D | R | R | R | R | R | D | D | 7 | 27 | 0 |
| Kan. | | R | R | R | R | R | R | R | PP | D | R | R | R | D | D | R | R | R | D | D | R | R | R | R | R | R | D | R | R | R | R | R | R | R | 6 | 26 | 1 |
| Ky. | CU | D | D | D | D | D | D | D | D | R[m] | D | D | D | D | D | R | D | R | D | D | D | D | D | D | R | R | D | R | R | D | R | R | R | D | 23 | 10 | 1 |
| La. | SD | [b] | D | [d] | R | D | D | D | D | D | D | D | D | D | D | D | D | D | D | D | D | D | SR | D | R | D | R | AI | R | D | R | R | R | D | 22 | 7 | 3 |
| Maine | R | R | R | R | R | R | R | R | R | R | R | R | R | D | R | R | R | R | R | R | R | R | R | R | R | R | D | D | R | R | R | R | R | D | 4 | 30 | 0 |
| Md. | SD | R | D | D | D | D | D | D | D | R | R | D[n] | D[o] | D | D | R | R | R | D | D | D | D | R | R | R | D | D | D | R | D | D | R | R | D | 21 | 12 | 1 |
| Mass. | R | R | R | R | R | R | R | R | R | R | R | R | R | D | R | R | R | D | D | D | D | D | D | R | R | D | D | D | D | D | R | R | D | D | 14 | 20 | 0 |
| Mich. | R | R | R | R | R | R | R | R | R[h] | R | R | R | R | PR | R | R | R | R | D | D | R | D | R | R | R | D | D | D | R | R | R | R | R | D | 7 | 26 | 1 |
| Minn. | R | R | R | R | R | R | R | R | R | R | R | R | R | PR | R | R | R | R | D | D | D | D | D | R | R | D | D | D | R | D | D | D | D | D | 13 | 20 | 1 |
| Miss. | SD | [b] | [c] | R | D | D | D | D | D | D | D | D | D | D | D | D | D | D | D | D | D | D | SR | D | D | D[t] | R | AI | R | D | R | R | R | R | 21 | 7 | 3 |
| Mo. | D | R | R | D | D | D | D | D | D | D | D | R | R | D | D | R | R | R | D | D | D | D | D | R | D | D | D | R | R | D | R | R | R | D | 21 | 13 | 0 |
| Mont. | | | | | | | | | R | D | D | R | D | D | D | R | R | R | D | D | D | D | D | R | R | R | D | R | R | R | R | R | R | R | 11 | 15 | 0 |
| Neb. | | | R | R | R | R | R | R | R | D | R | R | D | D | D | R | R | R | D | D | R | R | R | R | R | R | D | R | R | R | R | R | R | R | 7 | 25 | 0 |
| Nev. | | R | R | R | R | D | R | R | PP | D | D | R | D | D | D | R | R | R | D | D | D | D | D | R | R | D | D | R | R | R | R | R | R | D | 14 | 18 | 1 |
| N.H. | R | R | R | R | R | R | R | R | R | R | R | R | R | D | D | R | R | R | R | D | D | D | R | R | R | R | D | R | R | R | R | R | R | D | 7 | 27 | 0 |
| N.J. | R[a] | D | D | R | D | D | D | D | D | R | R | R | R | D | R | R | R | R | D | D | D | D | R | R | R | D | D | R | R | R | R | R | R | D | 15 | 19 | 0 |
| N.M. | | | | | | | | | | | | | | D | D | R | R | R | D | D | D | D | D | R | R | D | D | R | R | R | R | R | R | D | 10 | 11 | 0 |
| N.Y. | R | R | D | R | D | R | D | R | D | R | R | R | R | D | R | R | R | R | D | D | D | D | R | R | R | D | D | D | R | D | R | R | D | D | 15 | 19 | 0 |
| N.C. | SD | [b] | R | R | D | D | D | D | D | D | D | D | D | D | D | D | D | R | D | D | D | D | D | D | D | D | D | R[v] | R | D | R | R | R | R | 23 | 9 | 1 |
| N.D. | | | | | | | | | [i] | R | R | R | R | D | D | R | R | R | D | D | R | R | R | R | R | R | D | R | R | R | R | R | R | R | 5 | 20 | 1 |
| Ohio | R | R | R | R | R | R | R | R | R[j] | R | R | R | R | D | D | R | R | R | D | D | D | R | D | R | R | R | D | R | R | D | R | R | R | D | 9 | 25 | 0 |
| Okla. | | | | | | | | | | | | | D | D | D | R | D | R | D | D | D | D | D | R | R | R[u] | D | R | R | R | R | R | R | R | 10 | 12 | 0 |
| Ore. | R | R | D | R | R | R | R | R | R[k] | R | R | R | R | D | R | R | R | R | D | D | D | D | R | R | R | R | D | R | R | R | R | R | D | D | 9 | 25 | 0 |
| Pa. | R | R | R | R | R | R | R | R | R | R | R | R | R | PR | R | R | R | R | R | D | D | D | R | R | R | D | D | D | R | D | R | R | R | D | 8 | 25 | 1 |
| R.I. | R | R | R | R | R | R | R | R | R | R | R | R | R | D | R | R | R | D | D | D | D | D | D | R | R | D | D | D | R | D | D | R | D | D | 14 | 20 | 0 |
| S.C. | SD | [b] | R | R | R | D | D | D | D | D | D | D | D | D | D | D | D | D | D | D | D | D | SR | D | D | D | R | R | R | D | R | R | R | R | 21 | 10 | 2 |
| S.D. | | | | | | | | | R | D | R | R | R | PR | R | R | R | R | D | D | R | R | R | R | R | R | D | R | R | R | R | R | R | R | 4 | 21 | 1 |
| Tenn. | CU | [b] | R | D | D | D | D | D | D | D | D | D | D | D | D | R | D | R | D | D | D | D | D[q] | R | R | R | D | R | R | D | R | R | R | D | 21 | 11 | 1 |
| Texas | SD | [b] | [c] | D | D | D | D | D | D | D | D | D | D | D | D | D | D | R | D | D | D | D | D | R | R | D | D | D | R | D | R | R | R | R | 23 | 8 | 1 |
| Utah | | | | | | | | | | D | R | R | R | R | D | R | R | R | D | D | D | D | D | R | R | R | D | R | R | R | R | R | R | R | 8 | 17 | 0 |
| Vt. | R | R | R | R | R | R | R | R | R | R | R | R | R | R | R | R | R | R | R | R | R | R | R | R | R | R | D | R | R | R | R | R | R | D | 2 | 32 | 0 |
| Va. | CU | [b] | [c] | R | D | D | D | D | D | D | D | D | D | D | D | D | D | R | D | D | D | D | D | R | R | R | D | R | R[w] | R | R | R | R | R | 19 | 12 | 1 |
| Wash. | | | | | | | | | R | D | R | R | R | PR | D | R | R | R | D | D | D | D | D | R | R | R | D | D | R | R[x] | R | R | D | D | 11 | 14 | 1 |
| W.Va. | | R | R | D | D | D | D | D | D | D | R | R | R | D | R[p] | R | R | R | D | D | D | D | D | R | R | D | D | D | R | D | R | R | D[y] | D | 19 | 14 | 1 |
| Wis. | R | R | R | R | R | R | R | R | D | R | R | R | R | D | R | R | PR | R | D | D | D | R | D | R | R | R | D | R | R | D | R | R | D | D | 10 | 23 | 1 |
| Wyo. | | | | | | | | | R | D | R | R | R | D | D | R | R | R | D | D | D | R | D | R | R | R | D | R | R | R | R | R | R | R | 8 | 18 | 0 |
| Winning Party | R | R | R | R | R | R | D | R | D | R | R | R | R | D | D | R | R | R | D | D | D | D | D | R | R | D | D | R | R | D | R | R | R | D | 13 | 21 | 0 |

Note: With the exception of the District of Columbia, blanks indicate states not yet admitted to the Union. The District of Columbia received the presidential vote in 1961.

Key: AI—American Independent Party; CU—Constitutional Union Party; D—Democratic Party; PP—People's Party; PR—Progressive Party; R—Republican Party; SD—Southern Democratic Party; SR—States' Rights Democratic Party.

[a] Four electors voted Republican; three, Democratic.
[b] Confederate states did not vote in 1864.
[c] Did not vote in 1868.
[d] Votes were not counted.
[e] Three votes for Greeley not counted.
[f] Five electors voted Democratic; one, Republican.
[g] Eight electors voted Democratic; one, Republican.
[h] Nine electors voted Republican; five, Democratic.
[i] One vote each for Democratic, Republican and People's party.
[j] Twenty-two electors voted Republican; one, Democratic.
[k] Three electors voted Republican; one, People's Party.
[l] Eight electors voted Republican; one, Democratic.
[m] Twelve electors voted Republican; one, Democratic.
[n] Seven electors voted Democratic; one, Republican.
[o] Six electors voted Democratic; two, Republican.
[p] Seven electors voted Republican; one, Democratic.
[q] Eleven electors voted Democratic; one, States' Rights.
[r] One elector voted for Walter B. Jones.
[s] Six of eleven electors voted for Harry F. Byrd.
[t] Eight independent electors voted for Byrd.
[u] One vote cast for Byrd.
[v] Twelve electors voted Republican; one, American Independent.
[w] One elector voted Libertarian.
[x] One elector voted for Ronald Reagan.
[y] One elector voted for Lloyd Bentsen.

# What They Did Before They Became President

This list gives the terms of office for each president and the public jobs each held before becoming president.

**George Washington.** 1759-74, Virginia House of Burgesses; 1774-75, delegate to Continental Congress; 1775-83, commanding general of Continental Army; 1787, president, Constitutional Convention; 1789-97, president.

**John Adams.** 1771, Massachusetts colonial legislature; 1774-75, Continental Congress; 1778, minister to France; 1779, delegate to Massachusetts constitutional convention; 1780, minister to the Netherlands; 1785, minister to Great Britain; 1789-97, vice president; 1797-1801, president.

**Thomas Jefferson.** 1769-74, Virginia House of Burgesses; 1775, delegate to Continental Congress; 1775, delegate to Virginia convention; 1776, delegate to Continental Congress; 1776-79, Virginia House of Delegates; 1779-81, governor of Virginia; 1784-89, envoy and minister to France; 1789-93, secretary of state; 1797-1801, vice president; 1801-09, president.

**James Madison.** 1774, Colonial Committee of Safety; 1776, delegate to Virginia convention; 1776-77, Virginia House of Delegates; 1777, Virginia State Council; 1778, Virginia Executive Council; 1779-83, Continental Congress; 1784-86, Virginia House of Delegates; 1786-88, Continental Congress; 1787, delegate to Constitutional Convention; 1789-97, U.S. House (Va.); 1801-09, secretary of state; 1809-17, president.

**James Monroe.** 1780, Virginia House of Delegates; 1781-83, governor's council; 1783-86, Continental Congress; 1786, Virginia House of Delegates; 1787, delegate to Constitutional Convention; 1790-94, U.S. Senate (Va.); 1794-96, minister to France; 1799-1803, governor of Virginia; 1803, minister to England and France; 1804, minister to Spain; 1810, Virginia House of Delegates; 1811-17, secretary of state; 1814-15, secretary of war; 1817-25, president.

**John Quincy Adams.** 1794, minister to Netherlands; 1796, minister to Portugal; 1797, minister to Prussia; 1802, Massachusetts Senate; 1803-08, U.S. Senate (Mass.); 1809-14, minister to Russia; 1815-17, minister to Great Britain; 1817-25, secretary of state; 1825-29, president.

**Andrew Jackson.** 1788, solicitor for western North Carolina; 1796, delegate to Tennessee constitutional convention; 1796-97, U.S. House (Tenn.); 1797-98, U.S. Senate (Tenn.); 1798-1804, Tennessee Supreme Court; 1807, Tennessee Senate; 1812, commander, U.S. militia; 1814, general U.S. Army; 1821, governor of Florida; 1823-25, U.S. Senate (Tenn.); 1829-37, president.

**Martin Van Buren.** 1813-20, New York Senate; 1815-19, New York attorney general; 1821-28, U.S. Senate; 1829, governor of New York; 1829, secretary of state; 1831, minister to Great Britain; 1833-37, vice president; 1837-41, president.

**William Henry Harrison.** 1798-99, secretary of Northwest Territory; 1799-1800, U.S. House (territorial delegate); 1801-13, territorial governor of Indiana; 1812-14, general, U.S. Army; 1816-19, U.S. House (Ohio); 1819-21, Ohio Senate; 1825-28, minister to Colombia; 1841, president.

**John Tyler.** 1811-16, Virginia House of Delegates; 1816, Virginia State Council; 1817-21, U.S. House (Va.); 1823-25, Virginia House of Delegates; 1825-27, governor of Virginia; 1827-36, U.S. Senate (Va.); 1829, Virginia House of Delegates; 1841, vice president; 1841-45, president.

**James Knox Polk.** 1821-23, chief clerk, Tennessee Senate; 1823-25, Tennessee House; 1825-39, U.S. House (Tenn.); 1839-41, governor of Tennessee; 1845-49, president.

**Zachary Taylor.** 1808-49, U.S. Army; 1849-50, president.

**Millard Fillmore.** 1828-31, New York Assembly; 1833-35, U.S. House (N.Y.); 1837-43, U.S. House (N.Y.); 1848-49, New York controller; 1849-50, vice president; 1850-53, president.

**Franklin Pierce.** 1829-33, New Hampshire House; 1833-37, U.S. House (N.H.); 1837-42, U.S. Senate (N.H.); 1850, New Hampshire constitutional convention; 1853-57, president.

**James Buchanan.** 1814-15, Pennsylvania House; 1821-31, U.S. House (Pa.); 1832-33, minister to Russia; 1834-45, U.S. Senate (Pa.); 1845-49, secretary of state; 1853, minister to Great Britain; 1857-61, president.

**Abraham Lincoln.** 1833, postmaster, New Salem, Illinois; 1835-36, Illinois General Assembly; 1847-49, U.S. House (Ill.); 1861-65, president.

**Andrew Johnson.** 1828-29, alderman, Greeneville, Tenn.; 1830-33, mayor, Greeneville, Tenn.; 1835-37, Tennessee House; 1839-41, Tennessee House; 1841, Tennessee Senate; 1843-53, U.S. House (Tenn.); 1853-57, governor of Tennessee; 1857-62, U.S. Senate (Tenn.); 1862-65, military governor of Tennessee; 1865, vice president; 1865-69, president.

**Ulysses S. Grant.** 1843-54, U.S. Army; 1861-65, general, U.S. Army; 1867-68, secretary of war; 1869-77, president.

**Rutherford B. Hayes.** 1857-59, Cincinnati city solicitor; 1865-67, U.S. House (Ohio); 1868, governor of Ohio; 1876-77, governor of Ohio; 1877-81, president.

**James A. Garfield.** 1859, Ohio Senate; 1863-80, U.S. House (Ohio); 1881, president.

**Chester A. Arthur.** 1871-78, collector for Port of New York; 1881, vice president; 1881-85, president.

**Grover Cleveland.** 1863-65, assistant district attorney of Erie County, N.Y.; 1871-73, sheriff of Erie County, N.Y.; 1882, mayor of Buffalo, N.Y.; 1883-85, governor of New York; 1885-89, president; 1893-97, president.

**Benjamin Harrison.** 1864-68, reporter of decisions, Indiana Supreme Court; 1879, member, Mississippi River Commission; 1881-87, U.S. Senate (Ind.); 1889-93, president.

**William McKinley.** 1869-71, prosecutor, Stark County, Ohio; 1877-83, U.S. House (Ohio); 1885-91, U.S. House (Ohio); 1892-96, governor of Ohio; 1897-1901, president.

**Theodore Roosevelt.** 1882-84, New York State Assembly; 1889-95, U.S. Civil Service Commission; 1895, president of New York City board of police commissioners; 1897, assistant secretary of the Navy; 1898, U.S. Army; 1899-1901, governor of New York; 1901, vice president; 1901-09, president.

**William Howard Taft.** 1881-82, assistant prosecutor, Cincinnati; 1887, assistant city solicitor, Cincinnati; 1887-90, Cincinnati Superior Court; 1890-92, U.S. solicitor general; 1892-1900, U.S. Circuit Court; 1900-01, president of Philippines Commission; 1901, governor general, Philippine Islands; 1904-08, secretary of war; 1907, provisional governor of Cuba; 1909-13, president.

**Woodrow Wilson.** 1911-13, governor of New Jersey; 1913-21, president.

**Warren G. Harding.** 1895, auditor of Marion County, Ohio; 1899-1903, Ohio Senate; 1904-05, lieutenant governor of Ohio; 1915-21, U.S. Senate (Ohio); 1921-23, president.

**Calvin Coolidge.** 1899, city council of Northampton, Mass.; 1900-01, city solicitor of Northampton, Mass.; 1903-04, clerk of the courts, Hampshire County, Mass.; 1907-08, Massachusetts House; 1910-11, mayor of Northampton, Mass.; 1912-15, Massachusetts Senate; 1916-18, lieutenant governor of Massachusetts; 1919-20, governor of Massachusetts; 1921-23, vice president; 1923-29, president.

**Herbert Hoover.** 1914-15, chairman of American Committee in London; 1915-18, chairman, Commission for the Relief of Belgium; 1917-19, U.S. food administrator; 1919, chairman, Supreme Economic Conference in Paris; 1920, chairman, European Relief Council; 1921-28, secretary of commerce; 1929-33, president.

**Franklin D. Roosevelt.** 1911-13, New York Senate; 1913-20, assistant secretary of the Navy; 1929-33, governor of New York; 1933-45, president.

**Harry S. Truman.** 1926-34, administrative judge, court of Jackson County, Missouri; 1935-45, U.S. Senate (Mo.); 1945, vice president; 1945-53, president.

**Dwight D. Eisenhower.** 1915-48, U.S. Army; 1950-52, commander of NATO forces in Europe; 1953-61, president.

**John F. Kennedy.** 1947-53, U.S. House (Mass.); 1953-61, U.S. Senate (Mass.); 1961-63, president.

**Lyndon B. Johnson.** 1935-37, Texas director of National Youth Administration; 1937-48, U.S. House (Texas); 1949-61, U.S. Senate (Texas); 1961-63, vice president; 1963-69, president.

**Richard M. Nixon.** 1947-51, U.S. House (Calif.); 1951-53, U.S. Senate (Calif.); 1953-61, vice president; 1969-74, president.

**Gerald R. Ford.** 1949-73, U.S. House (Mich.); 1973-74, vice president; 1974-77, president.

**Jimmy Carter.** 1955-62, chairman, Sumter County (Ga.) Board of Education; 1963-67, Georgia Senate; 1971-75, governor of Georgia; 1977-81, president.

**Ronald Reagan.** 1967-75, governor of California; 1981-89, president.

**George Bush.** 1967-71, U.S. House (Texas); 1971-73, ambassador to the United Nations; 1974-75, chief of U.S. Liaison Office, Beijing, People's Republic of China; 1976-77, director of Central Intelligence Agency; 1981-88, vice president; 1989-93, president.

**Bill Clinton.** 1977-79, attorney general of Arkansas; 1979-81, governor of Arkansas; 1983-93, governor of Arkansas; 1993- president.

# Popular Vote Returns for President, 1824-1992

# Sources for Presidential Returns

The presidential election popular returns presented in this section (pages 429-468), except where indicated by a footnote, were obtained from two sources. The returns for 1824 to 1916 are from Inter-University Consortium for Political and Social Research (ICPSR) at the University of Michigan. The returns from 1920 to 1992 are from Richard M. Scammon and Alice V. McGillivray, *America at the Polls* (Washington, D.C.: Congressional Quarterly, 1994).

The 1824 starting date for the ICPSR collection was based on factors such as the pronounced trend by 1824 for the election of presidential electors by popular vote, as well as the availability, accessibility and quality of the returns. The bulk of the ICPSR election data collection consists of returns at the county level in computer-readable form.

The collection of ICPSR presidential returns — part of a larger project involving gubernatorial, House and Senate returns — began in 1962 under grants from the Social Science Research Council and the National Science Foundation. Scholars searched state and local archives, newspaper files and other sources for the data. In as many cases as possible, multiple sources were consulted. Although general preference was given to official sources, these scholars were charged with evaluating the quality and completeness of all available sources.

## Table Organization

For each presidential election from 1824 to 1992, the following information is provided in the tables for the popular returns:

- Names and party affiliations of major candidates.
- Total state-by-state popular vote for president.
- State-by-state breakdown of the popular vote and the percentage of the vote received by each candidate.
- The aggregate vote and percentage of the total vote received in each state by minor party candidates, minor parties running unpledged electors or unidentified votes. These figures appear in the column designated "Other"; a complete breakdown of these votes appears on pages 469-478. The presidential index contains entries for all candidates.
- The plurality received by the candidate who carried each state, along with the candidate's party designation.
- The total national popular vote for president, the total national popular vote and percentage of the vote received by each candidate and the nationwide plurality of the candidate who received the greatest number of votes.

The omission of popular vote returns for a state *after 1824* indicates an absence of popular voting for that election. The South Carolina legislature, for example, chose the state's presidential electors until 1860, and the state did not participate in the 1864 presidential election because of the Civil War. Thus, the first popular vote returns shown for South Carolina are for the 1868 election.

## Party Designation

In many cases presidential candidates appeared on state ballots under different, even *multiple* party designations. Thus, in the returns for 1968, George C. Wallace ran for president under a variety of party designations in different states: Democratic, American, American Independent, Independent, George Wallace Party, Conservative, American Party of Missouri, Independent American, Courage, and George Wallace and Independent.

To provide one party designation for presidential candidates for the elections 1824 through 1916, Congressional Quarterly has aggregated under a single party designation the votes of candidates who are listed in the ICPSR data as receiving votes under more than one party designation. The source used for assigning party designation for these years is Svend Petersen, *A Statistical History of the American Presidential Elections* (Westport, Conn.: Greenwood Press, 1981). For the 1920 to 1992 elections, the sources for party designation are Scammon and McGillivray, *America at the Polls,* (Washington, D.C.: Congressional Quarterly, 1994). For 1968, Scammon lists Wallace as an American Independent, and Congressional Quarterly follows this usage.

## Vote Totals and Percentages

The total popular vote for each candidate in a given election was determined by adding the votes received by that candidate in each state (including write-in votes where available), even though the vote totals for some states may have come from sources other than ICPSR or Scammon.

The percentages of the vote received in each state and nationally by any candidate or party has been calculated to two decimal places and rounded to one place; thus, 0.05 percent is listed as 0.1 percent. Due to rounding, state and national percentages do not always equal 100 percent.

## Pluralities

The plurality column represents the differences between the vote received by the first- and second-place finishers in each state and in the nation. In most cases, most notably in 1912 and 1924, a losing major party candidate finished in third place in a state. In those few cases where votes from the "Other" column were needed to calculate the plurarity, a footnote provides an explanation. (For a breakdown of "Other" votes, see Popular Returns: Minor Candidates and Parties, pp. 469-478.)

# 1824 Presidential Election

| STATE | TOTAL VOTE | JOHN Q. ADAMS (Democratic-Republican) Votes | % | ANDREW JACKSON (Democratic-Republican) Votes | % | HENRY CLAY (Democratic-Republican) Votes | % | WILLIAM H. CRAWFORD (Democratic-Republican) Votes | % | OTHER [1] Votes | % | PLURALITY [2] | |
|---|---|---|---|---|---|---|---|---|---|---|---|---|---|
| Alabama | 13,603 | 2,422 | 17.8 | 9,429 | 69.3 | 96 | 0.7 | 1,656 | 12.2 | — | | 7,007 | AJ |
| Connecticut | 10,647 | 7,494 | 70.4 | — | | — | | 1,965 | 18.5 | 1,188 | 11.2 | 5,529 | JQA |
| Illinois | 4,671 | 1,516 | 32.5 | 1,272 | 27.2 | 1,036 | 22.2 | 847 | 18.1 | — | | 244 | JQA |
| Indiana | 15,838 | 3,071 | 19.4 | 7,444 | 47.0 | 5,316 | 33.6 | — | | 7 | | 2,128 | AJ |
| Kentucky | 23,338 | — | | 6,356 | 27.2 | 16,982 | 72.8 | — | | — | | 10,626 | HC |
| Maine [3] | 12,625 | 10,289 | 81.5 | — | | — | | 2,336 | 18.5 | — | | 7,953 | JQA |
| Maryland [3] | 33,214 | 14,632 | 44.1 | 14,523 | 43.7 | 695 | 2.1 | 3,364 | 10.1 | — | | 109 | JQA |
| Massachusetts | 42,056 | 30,687 | 73.0 | — | | — | | — | | 11,369 | 27.0 | 24,071 | JQA [4] |
| Mississippi | 4,894 | 1,654 | 33.8 | 3,121 | 63.8 | — | | 119 | 2.4 | — | | 1,467 | AJ |
| Missouri | 3,432 | 159 | 4.6 | 1,166 | 34.0 | 2,042 | 59.5 | 32 | 0.9 | 33 | 1.0 | 876 | HC |
| New Hampshire [3] | 10,032 | 9,389 | 93.6 | — | | — | | 643 | 6.4 | — | | 8,746 | JQA |
| New Jersey | 19,837 | 8,309 | 41.9 | 10,332 | 52.1 | — | | 1,196 | 6.0 | — | | 2,023 | AJ |
| North Carolina | 36,109 | — | | 20,231 | 56.0 | — | | 15,622 | 43.3 | 256 | 0.7 | 4,609 | AJ |
| Ohio [3] | 50,024 | 12,280 | 24.5 | 18,489 | 37.0 | 19,255 | 38.5 | — | | — | | 766 | HC |
| Pennsylvania | 47,073 | 5,441 | 11.6 | 35,736 | 75.9 | 1,690 | 3.6 | 4,206 | 8.9 | — | | 30,295 | AJ |
| Rhode Island | 2,344 | 2,144 | 91.5 | — | | — | | — | | 200 | 8.5 | 1,944 | JQA |
| Tennessee [3] | 20,725 | 216 | 1.0 | 20,197 | 97.5 | — | | 312 | 1.5 | — | | 19,885 | AJ |
| Virginia | 15,371 | 3,419 | 22.2 | 2,975 | 19.4 | 419 | 2.7 | 8,558 | 55.7 | — | | 5,139 | WHC |
| **Totals** | **365,833** | **113,122** | **30.9** | **151,271** | **41.3** | **47,531** | **13.0** | **40,856** | **11.2** | **13,053** | **3.6** | **38,149** | **AJ** |

# 1828 Presidential Election

| STATE | TOTAL VOTE | ANDREW JACKSON (Democratic-Republican) Votes | % | JOHN Q. ADAMS (National-Republican) Votes | % | OTHER [1] Votes | % | PLURALITY | |
|---|---|---|---|---|---|---|---|---|---|
| Alabama | 18,618 | 16,736 | 89.9 | 1,878 | 10.1 | 4 | | 14,858 | DR |
| Connecticut | 19,378 | 4,448 | 23.0 | 13,829 | 71.4 | 1,101 | 5.7 | 9,381 | NR |
| Georgia [5] | 20,004 | 19,362 | 96.8 | 642 | 3.2 | — | | 18,720 | DR |
| Illinois | 14,222 | 9,560 | 67.2 | 4,662 | 32.8 | — | | 4,898 | DR |
| Indiana | 39,210 | 22,201 | 56.6 | 17,009 | 43.4 | — | | 5,192 | DR |
| Kentucky | 70,776 | 39,308 | 55.5 | 31,468 | 44.5 | — | | 7,840 | DR |
| Louisiana | 8,687 | 4,605 | 53.0 | 4,082 | 47.0 | — | | 523 | DR |
| Maine | 34,789 | 13,927 | 40.0 | 20,773 | 59.7 | 89 | 0.3 | 6,846 | NR |
| Maryland | 45,796 | 22,782 | 49.7 | 23,014 | 50.3 | — | | 232 | NR |
| Massachusetts | 39,074 | 6,012 | 15.4 | 29,836 | 76.4 | 3,226 | 8.3 | 23,824 | NR |
| Mississippi | 8,344 | 6,763 | 81.1 | 1,581 | 18.9 | — | | 5,182 | DR |
| Missouri | 11,654 | 8,232 | 70.6 | 3,422 | 29.4 | — | | 4,810 | DR |
| New Hampshire | 44,035 | 20,212 | 45.9 | 23,823 | 54.1 | — | | 3,611 | NR |
| New Jersey | 45,570 | 21,809 | 47.9 | 23,753 | 52.1 | 8 | | 1,944 | NR |
| New York | 270,975 | 139,412 | 51.4 | 131,563 | 48.6 | — | | 7,849 | DR |
| North Carolina | 51,747 | 37,814 | 73.1 | 13,918 | 26.9 | 15 | | 23,896 | DR |
| Ohio | 131,049 | 67,596 | 51.6 | 63,453 | 48.4 | — | | 4,143 | DR |
| Pennsylvania | 152,220 | 101,457 | 66.7 | 50,763 | 33.3 | — | | 50,694 | DR |
| Rhode Island | 3,580 | 820 | 22.9 | 2,755 | 77.0 | 5 | 0.1 | 1,935 | NR |
| Tennessee [5] | 46,533 | 44,293 | 95.2 | 2,240 | 4.8 | — | | 42,053 | DR |
| Vermont | 32,833 | 8,350 | 25.4 | 24,363 | 74.2 | 120 | 0.4 | 16,013 | NR |
| Virginia | 38,924 | 26,854 | 69.0 | 12,070 | 31.0 | — | | 14,784 | DR |
| **Totals** | **1,148,018** | **642,553** | **56.0** | **500,897** | **43.6** | **4,568** | **0.4** | **141,656** | **DR** |

1. For breakdown of "Other" votes, see minor candidate vote totals, p. 469.
2. For the 1824 plurality winner the designations are JQA (John Quincy Adams), AJ (Andrew Jackson), WHC (William H. Crawford) and HC (Henry Clay). Adams was elected president by the House of Representatives. See p. 292.
3. Figures from Svend Petersen, A Statistical History of the American Presidential Elections, (Westport, Conn. 1981), p. 18.
4. Plurality of 24,071 votes is calculated on the basis of 6,616 for unpledged electors.
5. Figures from Petersen, op. cit., p. 20.

# 1832 Presidential Election

| STATE | TOTAL VOTE | ANDREW JACKSON (Democrat) | | HENRY CLAY (National-Republican) | | WILLIAM WIRT (Anti-Mason) | | OTHER [1] | | PLURALITY | |
|---|---|---|---|---|---|---|---|---|---|---|---|
| | | Votes | % | Votes | % | Votes | % | Votes | % | | |
| Alabama | 14,291 | 14,286 | 100.0 | 5 | | — | | — | | 14,281 | D |
| Connecticut | 32,833 | 11,269 | 34.3 | 18,155 | 55.3 | 3,409 | 10.4 | — | | 6,886 | NR |
| Delaware | 8,386 | 4,110 | 49.0 | 4,276 | 51.0 | — | | — | | 166 | NR |
| Georgia [2] | 20,750 | 20,750 | 100.0 | — | | — | | — | | 20,750 | D |
| Illinois | 21,481 | 14,609 | 68.0 | 6,745 | 31.4 | 97 | 0.5 | 30 | 0.1 | 7,864 | D |
| Indiana | 57,152 | 31,652 | 55.4 | 25,473 | 44.6 | 27 | | — | | 6,179 | D |
| Kentucky | 79,741 | 36,292 | 45.5 | 43,449 | 54.5 | — | | — | | 7,157 | NR |
| Louisiana | 6,337 | 3,908 | 61.7 | 2,429 | 38.3 | — | | — | | 1,479 | D |
| Maine | 62,153 | 33,978 | 54.7 | 27,331 | 44.0 | 844 | 1.4 | — | | 6,647 | D |
| Maryland | 38,316 | 19,156 | 50.0 | 19,160 | 50.0 | — | | — | | 4 | NR |
| Massachusetts | 67,619 | 13,933 | 20.6 | 31,963 | 47.3 | 14,692 | 21.7 | 7,031 | 10.4 | 17,271 | NR |
| Mississippi | 5,750 | 5,750 | 100.0 | — | | — | | — | | 5,750 | D |
| Missouri [2] | 5,192 | 5,192 | 100.0 | — | | — | | — | | 5,192 | D |
| New Hampshire | 43,793 | 24,855 | 56.8 | 18,938 | 43.2 | — | | — | | 5,917 | D |
| New Jersey | 47,760 | 23,826 | 49.9 | 23,466 | 49.1 | 468 | 1.0 | — | | 360 | D |
| New York | 323,393 | 168,497 | 52.1 | 154,896 | 47.9 | — | | — | | 13,601 | D |
| North Carolina | 29,799 | 25,261 | 84.8 | 4,538 | 15.2 | — | | — | | 20,723 | D |
| Ohio | 158,350 | 81,246 | 51.3 | 76,566 | 48.4 | 538 | 0.3 | — | | 4,680 | D |
| Pennsylvania | 157,679 | 90,973 | 57.7 | — | | 66,706 | 42.3 | — | | 24,267 | D |
| Rhode Island | 5,747 | 2,051 | 35.7 | 2,871 | 50.0 | 819 | 14.3 | 6 | 0.1 | 820 | NR |
| Tennessee | 29,425 | 28,078 | 95.4 | 1,347 | 4.6 | — | | — | | 26,731 | D |
| Vermont | 32,344 | 7,865 | 24.3 | 11,161 | 34.5 | 13,112 | 40.5 | 206 | 0.6 | 1,951 | AM |
| Virginia | 45,682 | 34,243 | 75.0 | 11,436 | 25.0 | 3 | | — | | 22,807 | D |
| **Totals** | **1,293,973** | **701,780** | **54.2** | **484,205** | **37.4** | **100,715** | **7.8** | **7,273** | **0.6** | **217,575** | **D** |

# 1836 Presidential Election

| STATE | TOTAL VOTE | MARTIN VAN BUREN (Democrat) | | WILLIAM H. HARRISON (Whig) | | HUGH L. WHITE (Whig) | | DANIEL WEBSTER (Whig) | | OTHER [1] | | PLURALITY [3] | |
|---|---|---|---|---|---|---|---|---|---|---|---|---|---|
| | | Votes | % | Votes | % | Votes | % | Votes | % | Votes | % | | |
| Alabama | 37,296 | 20,638 | 55.3 | — | | 16,658 | 44.7 | — | | — | | 3,980 | MBV |
| Arkansas | 3,714 | 2,380 | 64.1 | — | | 1,334 | 35.9 | — | | — | | 1,046 | MBV |
| Connecticut | 38,093 | 19,294 | 50.6 | 18,799 | 49.4 | — | | — | | — | | 495 | MBV |
| Delaware | 8,895 | 4,154 | 46.7 | 4,736 | 53.2 | — | | — | | 5 | 0.1 | 582 | WHH |
| Georgia | 47,259 | 22,778 | 48.2 | — | | 24,481 | 51.8 | — | | — | | 1,703 | HLW |
| Illinois | 33,589 | 18,369 | 54.7 | 15,220 | 45.3 | — | | — | | — | | 3,149 | MBV |
| Indiana | 74,423 | 33,084 | 44.5 | 41,339 | 55.5 | — | | — | | — | | 8,255 | WHH |
| Kentucky | 70,090 | 33,229 | 47.4 | 36,861 | 52.6 | — | | — | | — | | 3,632 | WHH |
| Louisiana | 7,425 | 3,842 | 51.7 | — | | 3,583 | 48.3 | — | | — | | 259 | MBV |
| Maine | 38,740 | 22,825 | 58.9 | 14,803 | 38.2 | — | | — | | 1,112 | 2.9 | 8,022 | MBV |
| Maryland | 48,119 | 22,267 | 46.3 | 25,852 | 53.7 | — | | — | | — | | 3,585 | WHH |
| Massachusetts | 74,732 | 33,486 | 44.8 | — | | — | | 41,201 | 55.1 | 45 | 0.1 | 33,486 | DW |
| Michigan | 12,052 | 6,507 | 54.0 | 5,545 | 46.0 | — | | — | | — | | 962 | MBV |
| Mississippi | 20,079 | 10,297 | 51.3 | — | | 9,782 | 48.7 | — | | — | | 515 | MBV |
| Missouri [4] | 18,332 | 10,995 | 60.0 | — | | 7,337 | 40.0 | — | | — | | 3,658 | MBV |
| New Hampshire | 24,925 | 18,697 | 75.0 | 6,228 | 25.0 | — | | — | | — | | 12,469 | MBV |
| New Jersey | 51,729 | 25,592 | 49.5 | 26,137 | 50.5 | — | | — | | — | | 545 | WHH |
| New York | 305,343 | 166,795 | 54.6 | 138,548 | 45.4 | — | | — | | — | | 28,247 | MBV |
| North Carolina | 50,153 | 26,631 | 53.1 | — | | 23,521 | 46.9 | — | | 1 | | 3,110 | MBV |
| Ohio | 202,931 | 97,122 | 47.9 | 105,809 | 52.1 | — | | — | | — | | 8,687 | WHH |
| Pennsylvania | 178,701 | 91,466 | 51.2 | 87,235 | 48.8 | — | | — | | — | | 4,231 | MBV |
| Rhode Island | 5,673 | 2,962 | 52.2 | 2,710 | 47.8 | — | | — | | 1 | | 252 | MBV |
| Tennessee | 62,197 | 26,170 | 42.1 | — | | 36,027 | 57.9 | — | | — | | 9,857 | HLW |
| Vermont | 35,099 | 14,040 | 4 | 20,994 | 59.8 | — | | — | | 65 | 0.2 | 6,954 | WHH |
| Virginia | 53,945 | 30,556 | 56.6 | — | | 23,384 | 43.3 | — | | 5 | | 7,172 | MBV |
| **Totals** | **1,503,534** | **764,176** | **50.8** | **550,816** | **36.6** | **146,107** | **9.7** | **41,201** | **2.7** | **1,234** | **0.1** | **213,360** | **MBV** |

*1. For breakdown of "Other" vote, see minor candidate vote totals, p. 467.*
*2. Figures from Petersen, op. cit., p. 21.*
*3. For the 1836 plurality winner, the designations are MVB (Martin Van Buren), WHH (William Henry Harrison), HLW (Hugh L. White) and DW (Daniel Webster).*
*4. Figures from Petersen, op. cit., p. 22.*

# 1840 Presidential Election

| STATE | TOTAL VOTE | WILLIAM H. HARRISON (Whig) | | MARTIN VAN BUREN (Democrat) | | JAMES G. BIRNEY (Liberty) | | OTHER [1] | | PLURALITY | |
|---|---|---|---|---|---|---|---|---|---|---|---|
| | | Votes | % | Votes | % | Votes | % | Votes | % | | |
| Alabama | 62,511 | 28,515 | *45.6* | 33,996 | *54.4* | — | | — | | 5,481 | D |
| Arkansas | 11,839 | 5,160 | *43.6* | 6,679 | *56.4* | — | | — | | 1,519 | D |
| Connecticut | 56,879 | 31,598 | *55.6* | 25,281 | *44.4* | — | | — | | 6,317 | W |
| Delaware | 10,852 | 5,967 | *55.0* | 4,872 | *44.9* | — | | 13 | *0.1* | 1,095 | W |
| Georgia | 72,322 | 40,339 | *55.8* | 31,983 | *44.2* | — | | — | | 8,356 | W |
| Illinois | 93,175 | 45,574 | *48.9* | 47,441 | *50.9* | 160 | *0.2* | — | | 1,867 | D |
| Indiana | 117,605 | 65,280 | *55.5* | 51,696 | *44.0* | 30 | | 599 | *0.5* | 13,584 | W |
| Kentucky | 91,104 | 58,400 | *64.2* | 32,616 | *35.8* | — | | — | | 25,872 | W |
| Louisiana | 18,912 | 11,296 | *59.7* | 7,616 | *40.3* | — | | — | | 3,680 | W |
| Maine | 92,802 | 46,612 | *50.2* | 46,190 | *49.8* | — | | — | | 422 | W |
| Maryland | 62,280 | 33,528 | *53.8* | 28,752 | *46.2* | — | | — | | 4,776 | W |
| Massachusetts | 126,825 | 72,852 | *57.4* | 52,355 | *41.3* | 1,618 | *1.3* | — | | 20,497 | W |
| Michigan | 44,029 | 22,933 | *52.1* | 21,096 | *47.9* | — | | — | | 1,837 | W |
| Mississippi | 36,525 | 19,515 | *53.4* | 17,010 | *46.6* | — | | — | | 2,505 | W |
| Missouri | 52,923 | 22,954 | *43.4* | 29,969 | *56.6* | — | | — | | 7,015 | D |
| New Hampshire | 59,956 | 26,310 | *43.9* | 32,774 | *54.7* | 872 | *1.5* | — | | 6,464 | D |
| New Jersey | 64,454 | 33,351 | *51.7* | 31,034 | *48.1* | 69 | *0.1* | — | | 2,317 | W |
| New York | 441,543 | 226,001 | *51.2* | 212,733 | *48.2* | 2,809 | *0.6* | — | | 13,268 | W |
| North Carolina | 80,735 | 46,567 | *57.7* | 34,168 | *42.3* | — | | — | | 12,399 | W |
| Ohio | 272,890 | 148,043 | *54.3* | 123,944 | *45.4* | 903 | *0.3* | — | | 24,099 | W |
| Pennsylvania | 287,695 | 144,023 | *50.1* | 143,672 | *49.9* | — | | — | | 351 | W |
| Rhode Island | 8,631 | 5,213 | *60.4* | 3,263 | *37.8* | 19 | *0.2* | 136 | *1.6* | 1,950 | W |
| Tennessee | 108,145 | 60,194 | *55.7* | 47,951 | *44.3* | — | | — | | 12,243 | W |
| Vermont | 50,782 | 32,440 | *63.9* | 18,006 | *35.5* | 317 | *0.6* | 19 | | 14,434 | W |
| Virginia | 86,394 | 42,637 | *49.4* | 43,757 | *50.6* | — | | — | | 1,120 | D |
| **Totals** | **2,411,808** | **1,275,390** | ***52.9*** | **1,128,854** | ***46.8*** | **6,797** | ***0.3*** | **767** | | **146,536** | **W** |

# 1844 Presidential Election

| STATE | TOTAL VOTE | JAMES K. POLK (Democrat) | | HENRY CLAY (Whig) | | JAMES G. BIRNEY (Liberty) | | OTHER [1] | | PLURALITY | |
|---|---|---|---|---|---|---|---|---|---|---|---|
| | | Votes | % | Votes | % | Votes | % | Votes | % | | |
| Alabama | 63,403 | 37,401 | *59.0* | 26,002 | *41.0* | — | | — | | 11,399 | D |
| Arkansas | 15,150 | 9,546 | *63.0* | 5,604 | *37.0* | — | | — | | 3,942 | D |
| Connecticut | 64,616 | 29,841 | *46.2* | 32,832 | *50.8* | 1,943 | *3.0* | — | | 2,991 | W |
| Delaware | 12,247 | 5,970 | *48.7* | 6,271 | *51.2* | — | | 6 | | 301 | W |
| Georgia | 86,247 | 44,147 | *51.2* | 42,100 | *48.8* | — | | — | | 2,047 | D |
| Illinois | 109,057 | 58,795 | *53.9* | 45,854 | *42.0* | 3,469 | *3.2* | 939 | *0.9* | 12,941 | D |
| Indiana | 140,157 | 70,183 | *50.1* | 67,866 | *48.4* | 2,108 | *1.5* | — | | 2,317 | D |
| Kentucky | 113,237 | 51,988 | *45.9* | 61,249 | *54.1* | — | | — | | 9,261 | W |
| Louisiana | 26,865 | 13,782 | *51.3* | 13,083 | *48.7* | — | | — | | 699 | D |
| Maine | 84,933 | 45,719 | *53.8* | 34,378 | *40.5* | 4,836 | *5.7* | — | | 11,341 | D |
| Maryland | 68,690 | 32,706 | *47.6* | 35,984 | *52.4* | — | | — | | 3,278 | W |
| Massachusetts | 132,037 | 53,039 | *40.2* | 67,062 | *50.8* | 10,830 | *8.2* | 1,106 | *0.8* | 14,023 | W |
| Michigan | 55,560 | 27,737 | *49.9* | 24,185 | *43.5* | 3,638 | *6.5* | — | | 3,552 | D |
| Mississippi | 45,004 | 25,846 | *57.4* | 19,158 | *42.6* | — | | — | | 6,688 | D |
| Missouri | 72,522 | 41,322 | *57.0* | 31,200 | *43.0* | — | | — | | 10,122 | D |
| New Hampshire | 49,187 | 27,160 | *55.2* | 17,866 | *36.3* | 4,161 | *8.5* | — | | 9,294 | D |
| New Jersey | 75,944 | 37,495 | *49.4* | 38,318 | *50.5* | 131 | *0.2* | — | | 823 | W |
| New York | 485,882 | 237,588 | *48.9* | 232,482 | *47.8* | 15,812 | *3.3* | — | | 5,106 | D |
| North Carolina | 82,521 | 39,287 | *47.6* | 43,232 | *52.4* | — | | 2 | | 3,945 | W |
| Ohio | 312,300 | 149,127 | *47.8* | 155,091 | *49.7* | 8,082 | *2.6* | — | | 5,964 | W |
| Pennsylvania | 331,645 | 167,311 | *50.4* | 161,195 | *48.6* | 3,139 | *0.9* | — | | 6,116 | D |
| Rhode Island | 12,194 | 4,867 | *39.9* | 7,322 | *60.0* | — | | 5 | | 2,455 | W |
| Tennessee | 119,957 | 59,917 | *49.9* | 60,040 | *50.1* | — | | — | | 123 | W |
| Vermont | 48,765 | 18,041 | *37.0* | 26,770 | *54.9* | 3,954 | *8.1* | — | | 8,729 | W |
| Virginia | 95,539 | 50,679 | *53.0* | 44,860 | *47.0* | — | | — | | 5,819 | D |
| **Totals** | **2,703,659** | **1,339,494** | ***49.5*** | **1,300,004** | ***48.1*** | **62,103** | ***2.3*** | **2,058** | ***0.1*** | **39,490** | **D** |

*1. For breakdown of "Other" vote, see minor candidate vote totals, p. 469.*

# 1848 Presidential Election

| STATE | TOTAL VOTE | ZACHARY TAYLOR (Whig) | | LEWIS CASS (Democrat) | | MARTIN VAN BUREN (Free Soil) | | OTHER [1] | | PLURALITY | |
|---|---|---|---|---|---|---|---|---|---|---|---|
| | | Votes | % | Votes | % | Votes | % | Votes | % | | |
| Alabama | 61,659 | 30,482 | 49.4 | 31,173 | 50.6 | — | | 4 | | 691 | D |
| Arkansas | 16,888 | 7,587 | 44.9 | 9,301 | 55.1 | — | | — | | 1,714 | D |
| Connecticut | 62,398 | 30,318 | 48.6 | 27,051 | 43.4 | 5,005 | 8.0 | 24 | | 3,267 | W |
| Delaware | 12,432 | 6,440 | 51.8 | 5,910 | 47.5 | 82 | 0.7 | — | | 530 | W |
| Florida | 7,203 | 4,120 | 57.2 | 3,083 | 42.8 | — | | — | | 1,037 | W |
| Georgia | 92,317 | 47,532 | 51.5 | 44,785 | 48.5 | — | | — | | 2,747 | W |
| Illinois | 124,596 | 52,853 | 42.4 | 55,952 | 44.9 | 15,702 | 12.6 | 89 | 0.1 | 3,099 | D |
| Indiana | 152,394 | 69,668 | 45.7 | 74,695 | 49.0 | 8,031 | 5.3 | — | | 5,027 | D |
| Iowa | 22,271 | 9,930 | 44.6 | 11,238 | 50.5 | 1,103 | 5.0 | — | | 1,308 | D |
| Kentucky | 116,865 | 67,145 | 57.5 | 49,720 | 42.5 | — | | — | | 17,425 | W |
| Louisiana | 33,866 | 18,487 | 54.6 | 15,379 | 45.4 | — | | — | | 3,108 | W |
| Maine | 87,625 | 35,273 | 40.3 | 40,195 | 45.9 | 12,157 | 13.9 | — | | 4,922 | D |
| Maryland | 72,359 | 37,702 | 52.1 | 34,528 | 47.7 | 129 | 0.2 | — | | 3,174 | W |
| Massachusetts | 134,748 | 61,072 | 45.3 | 35,281 | 26.2 | 38,333 | 28.4 | 62 | | 22,739 | W |
| Michigan | 65,082 | 23,947 | 36.8 | 30,742 | 47.2 | 10,393 | 16.0 | — | | 6,795 | D |
| Mississippi | 52,456 | 25,911 | 49.4 | 26,545 | 50.6 | — | | — | | 634 | D |
| Missouri | 72,748 | 32,671 | 44.9 | 40,077 | 55.1 | — | | — | | 7,406 | D |
| New Hampshire | 50,104 | 14,781 | 29.5 | 27,763 | 55.4 | 7,560 | 15.1 | — | | 12,982 | D |
| New Jersey | 77,745 | 40,015 | 51.5 | 36,901 | 47.5 | 829 | 1.1 | — | | 3,114 | W |
| New York | 455,944 | 218,583 | 47.9 | 114,319 | 25.1 | 120,497 | 26.4 | 2,545 | 0.6 | 98,086 | W |
| North Carolina | 79,826 | 44,054 | 55.2 | 35,772 | 44.8 | — | | — | | 8,282 | W |
| Ohio | 328,987 | 138,656 | 42.1 | 154,782 | 47.0 | 35,523 | 10.8 | 26 | | 16,126 | D |
| Pennsylvania | 369,092 | 185,730 | 50.3 | 172,186 | 46.7 | 11,176 | 3.0 | — | | 13,544 | W |
| Rhode Island | 11,049 | 6,705 | 60.7 | 3,613 | 32.7 | 726 | 6.6 | 5 | | 3,092 | W |
| Tennessee | 122,463 | 64,321 | 52.5 | 58,142 | 47.5 | — | | — | | 6,179 | W |
| Texas | 17,000 | 5,281 | 31.1 | 11,644 | 68.5 | — | | 75 | 0.4 | 6,363 | D |
| Vermont | 47,897 | 23,117 | 48.3 | 10,943 | 22.8 | 13,837 | 28.9 | — | | 9,280 | W |
| Virginia | 92,004 | 45,265 | 49.2 | 46,739 | 50.8 | — | | — | | 1,474 | D |
| Wisconsin | 39,166 | 13,747 | 35.1 | 15,001 | 38.3 | 10,418 | 26.6 | — | | 1,254 | D |
| Totals | 2,879,184 | 1,361,393 | 47.3 | 1,223,460 | 42.5 | 291,501 | 10.1 | 2,830 | 0.1 | 137,933 | W |

1. *For breakdown of "Other" vote, see minor candidate vote totals, p. 469.*

# 1852 Presidential Election

| STATE | TOTAL VOTE | FRANKLIN PIERCE (Democrat) | | WINFIELD SCOTT (Whig) | | JOHN P. HALE (Free Soil) | | OTHER [1] | | PLURALITY | |
|---|---|---|---|---|---|---|---|---|---|---|---|
| | | Votes | % | Votes | % | Votes | % | Votes | % | | |
| Alabama | 44,147 | 26,881 | 60.9 | 15,061 | 34.1 | — | | 2,205 | 5.0 | 11,820 | D |
| Arkansas | 19,577 | 12,173 | 62.2 | 7,404 | 37.8 | — | | — | | 4,769 | D |
| California | 76,810 | 40,721 | 53.0 | 35,972 | 46.8 | 61 | 0.1 | 56 | 0.1 | 4,749 | D |
| Connecticut | 66,781 | 33,249 | 49.8 | 30,359 | 45.5 | 3,161 | 4.7 | 12 | | 2,890 | D |
| Delaware | 12,673 | 6,318 | 49.9 | 6,293 | 49.7 | 62 | 0.5 | — | | 25 | D |
| Florida | 7,193 | 4,318 | 60.0 | 2,875 | 40.0 | — | | — | | 1,443 | D |
| Georgia [2] | 62,626 | 40,516 | 64.7 | 16,660 | 26.6 | — | | 5,450 | 8.7 | 23,856 | D |
| Illinois | 154,974 | 80,378 | 51.9 | 64,733 | 41.8 | 9,863 | 6.4 | — | | 15,645 | D |
| Indiana | 183,176 | 95,340 | 52.0 | 80,907 | 44.2 | 6,929 | 3.8 | — | | 14,433 | D |
| Iowa | 35,364 | 17,763 | 50.2 | 15,856 | 44.8 | 1,606 | 4.5 | 139 | 0.4 | 1,907 | D |
| Kentucky | 111,643 | 53,949 | 48.3 | 57,428 | 51.4 | 266 | 0.2 | — | | 3,479 | W |
| Louisiana | 35,902 | 18,647 | 51.9 | 17,255 | 48.1 | — | | — | | 1,392 | D |
| Maine | 82,182 | 41,609 | 50.6 | 32,543 | 39.6 | 8,030 | 9.8 | — | | 9,066 | D |
| Maryland | 75,120 | 40,022 | 53.3 | 35,077 | 46.7 | 21 | | — | | 4,945 | D |
| Massachusetts | 127,103 | 44,569 | 35.1 | 52,683 | 41.4 | 28,023 | 22.0 | 1,828 | 1.4 | 8,114 | W |
| Michigan | 82,939 | 41,842 | 50.4 | 33,860 | 40.8 | 7,237 | 8.7 | — | | 7,982 | D |
| Mississippi | 44,454 | 26,896 | 60.5 | 17,558 | 39.5 | — | | — | | 9,338 | D |
| Missouri | 68,801 | 38,817 | 56.4 | 29,984 | 43.6 | — | | — | | 8,833 | D |
| New Hampshire | 50,535 | 28,503 | 56.4 | 15,486 | 30.6 | 6,546 | 13.0 | — | | 13,017 | D |
| New Jersey | 83,926 | 44,301 | 52.8 | 38,551 | 45.9 | 336 | 0.4 | 738 | 0.9 | 5,750 | D |
| New York | 522,294 | 262,083 | 50.2 | 234,882 | 45.0 | 25,329 | 4.8 | — | | 27,201 | D |
| North Carolina | 78,891 | 39,788 | 50.4 | 39,043 | 49.5 | — | | 60 | 0.1 | 745 | D |
| Ohio | 352,903 | 169,193 | 47.9 | 152,577 | 43.2 | 31,133 | 8.8 | — | | 16,616 | D |
| Pennsylvania | 387,920 | 198,568 | 51.2 | 179,182 | 46.2 | 8,500 | 2.2 | 1,670 | 0.4 | 19,386 | D |
| Rhode Island | 17,005 | 8,735 | 51.4 | 7,626 | 44.8 | 644 | 3.8 | — | | 1,109 | D |
| Tennessee | 115,486 | 56,900 | 49.3 | 58,586 | 50.7 | — | | — | | 1,686 | W |
| Texas | 20,223 | 14,857 | 73.5 | 5,356 | 26.5 | — | | 10 | | 9,501 | D |
| Vermont | 43,838 | 13,044 | 29.8 | 22,173 | 50.6 | 8,621 | 19.7 | — | | 9,129 | W |
| Virginia | 132,604 | 73,872 | 55.7 | 58,732 | 44.3 | — | | — | | 15,140 | D |
| Wisconsin | 64,740 | 33,658 | 52.0 | 22,240 | 34.4 | 8,842 | 13.7 | — | | 11,418 | D |
| Totals | 3,161,830 | 1,607,510 | 50.8 | 1,386,942 | 43.9 | 155,210 | 4.9 | 12,168 | 0.4 | 220,568 | D |

1. For breakdown of "Other" vote, see minor candidate vote totals, p. 469.
2. Figures from Petersen, op. cit., 31.

# 1856 Presidential Election

| STATE | TOTAL VOTE | JAMES BUCHANAN (Democrat) | | JOHN C. FREMONT (Republican) | | MILLARD FILLMORE (Whig-American) | | OTHER [1] | | PLURALITY | |
|---|---|---|---|---|---|---|---|---|---|---|---|
| | | Votes | % | Votes | % | Votes | % | Votes | % | | |
| Alabama | 75,291 | 46,739 | 62.1 | — | | 28,552 | 37.9 | — | | 18,187 | D |
| Arkansas | 32,642 | 21,910 | 67.1 | — | | 10,732 | 32.9 | — | | 11,178 | D |
| California | 110,255 | 53,342 | 48.4 | 20,704 | 18.8 | 36,195 | 32.8 | 14 | | 17,147 | D |
| Connecticut | 80,360 | 35,028 | 43.6 | 42,717 | 53.2 | 2,615 | 3.3 | — | | 7,689 | R |
| Delaware | 14,598 | 8,004 | 54.8 | 310 | 2.1 | 6,275 | 43.0 | 9 | 0.1 | 1,729 | D |
| Florida | 11,191 | 6,358 | 56.8 | — | | 4,833 | 43.2 | — | | 1,525 | D |
| Georgia | 99,020 | 56,581 | 57.1 | — | | 42,439 | 42.9 | — | | 14,142 | D |
| Illinois | 239,334 | 105,528 | 44.1 | 96,275 | 40.2 | 37,531 | 15.7 | — | | 9,253 | D |
| Indiana | 235,401 | 118,670 | 50.4 | 94,375 | 40.1 | 22,356 | 9.5 | — | | 24,295 | D |
| Iowa | 92,310 | 37,568 | 40.7 | 45,073 | 48.8 | 9,669 | 10.5 | — | | 7,505 | R |
| Kentucky | 142,058 | 74,642 | 52.5 | — | | 67,416 | 47.5 | — | | 7,226 | D |
| Louisiana | 42,873 | 22,164 | 51.7 | — | | 20,709 | 48.3 | — | | 1,455 | D |
| Maine | 109,689 | 39,140 | 35.7 | 67,279 | 61.3 | 3,270 | 3.0 | — | | 28,139 | R |
| Maryland | 86,860 | 39,123 | 45.0 | 285 | 0.3 | 47,452 | 54.6 | — | | 8,329 | WA |
| Massachusetts | 170,048 | 39,244 | 23.1 | 108,172 | 63.6 | 19,626 | 11.5 | 3,006 | 1.8 | 68,928 | R |
| Michigan | 125,558 | 52,136 | 41.5 | 71,762 | 57.2 | 1,660 | 1.3 | — | | 19,626 | R |
| Mississippi | 59,647 | 35,456 | 59.4 | — | | 24,191 | 40.6 | — | | 11,265 | D |
| Missouri | 106,486 | 57,964 | 54.4 | — | | 48,522 | 45.6 | — | | 9,442 | D |
| New Hampshire | 69,774 | 31,891 | 45.7 | 37,473 | 53.7 | 410 | 0.6 | — | | 5,582 | R |
| New Jersey | 99,396 | 46,943 | 47.2 | 28,338 | 28.5 | 24,115 | 24.3 | — | | 18,605 | D |
| New York | 596,486 | 195,878 | 32.8 | 276,004 | 46.3 | 124,604 | 20.9 | — | | 80,126 | R |
| North Carolina | 84,963 | 48,243 | 56.8 | — | | 36,720 | 43.2 | — | | 11,523 | D |
| Ohio | 386,640 | 170,874 | 44.2 | 187,497 | 48.5 | 28,121 | 7.3 | 148 | | 16,623 | R |
| Pennsylvania | 460,937 | 230,772 | 50.1 | 147,963 | 32.1 | 82,202 | 17.8 | — | | 82,809 | D |
| Rhode Island | 19,822 | 6,680 | 33.7 | 11,467 | 57.8 | 1,675 | 8.5 | — | | 4,787 | R |
| Tennessee | 133,582 | 69,704 | 52.2 | — | | 63,878 | 47.8 | — | | 5,826 | D |
| Texas | 48,005 | 31,995 | 66.6 | — | | 16,010 | 33.4 | — | | 15,985 | D |
| Vermont | 50,675 | 10,569 | 20.9 | 39,561 | 78.1 | 545 | 1.1 | — | | 28,992 | R |
| Virginia | 150,233 | 90,083 | 60.0 | — | | 60,150 | 40.0 | — | | 29,933 | D |
| Wisconsin | 120,513 | 52,843 | 43.8 | 67,090 | 55.7 | 580 | 0.5 | — | | 14,247 | R |
| **Totals** | **4,054,647** | **1,836,072** | **45.3** | **1,342,345** | **33.1** | **873,053** | **21.5** | **3,177** | **0.1** | **493,727** | **D** |

1. For breakdown of "Other" vote, see minor candidate vote totals, p. 470.

# 1860 Presidential Election

| STATE | TOTAL VOTE | ABRAHAM LINCOLN (Republican) | | STEPHEN A. DOUGLAS (Democrat) | | JOHN C. BRECKINRIDGE (Southern Democrat) | | JOHN BELL (Constitutional Union) | | OTHER [1] | | PLURALITY | |
|---|---|---|---|---|---|---|---|---|---|---|---|---|---|
| | | Votes | % | Votes | % | Votes | % | Votes | % | Votes | % | | |
| Alabama | 90,122 | — | | 13,618 | 15.1 | 48,669 | 54.0 | 27,835 | 30.9 | — | | 20,834 | SD |
| Arkansas | 54,152 | — | | 5,357 | 9.9 | 28,732 | 53.1 | 20,063 | 37.0 | — | | 8,669 | SD |
| California | 119,827 | 38,733 | 32.3 | 37,999 | 31.7 | 33,969 | 28.3 | 9,111 | 7.6 | 15 | | 734 | R |
| Connecticut | 74,819 | 43,488 | 58.1 | 15,431 | 20.6 | 14,372 | 19.2 | 1,528 | 2.0 | — | | 28,057 | R |
| Delaware | 16,115 | 3,822 | 23.7 | 1,066 | 6.6 | 7,339 | 45.5 | 3,888 | 24.1 | — | | 3,451 | SD |
| Florida | 13,301 | — | | 223 | 1.7 | 8,277 | 62.2 | 4,801 | 36.1 | — | | 3,476 | SD |
| Georgia | 106,717 | — | | 11,581 | 10.9 | 52,176 | 48.9 | 42,960 | 40.3 | — | | 9,216 | SD |
| Illinois | 339,666 | 172,171 | 50.7 | 160,215 | 47.2 | 2,331 | 0.7 | 4,914 | 1.4 | 35 | | 11,956 | R |
| Indiana | 272,143 | 139,033 | 51.1 | 115,509 | 42.4 | 12,295 | 4.5 | 5,306 | 1.9 | — | | 23,524 | R |
| Iowa | 128,739 | 70,302 | 54.6 | 55,639 | 43.2 | 1,035 | 0.8 | 1,763 | 1.4 | — | | 14,663 | R |
| Kentucky [2] | 146,216 | 1,364 | 0.9 | 25,651 | 17.5 | 53,143 | 36.3 | 66,058 | 45.2 | — | | 12,915 | CU |
| Louisiana | 50,510 | — | | 7,625 | 15.1 | 22,681 | 44.9 | 20,204 | 40.0 | — | | 2,477 | SD |
| Maine | 100,918 | 62,811 | 62.2 | 29,693 | 29.4 | 6,368 | 6.3 | 2,046 | 2.0 | — | | 33,118 | R |
| Maryland | 92,502 | 2,294 | 2.5 | 5,966 | 6.4 | 42,482 | 45.9 | 41,760 | 45.1 | — | | 722 | SD |
| Massachusetts | 169,876 | 106,684 | 62.8 | 34,370 | 20.2 | 6,163 | 3.6 | 22,331 | 13.1 | 328 | 0.2 | 72,314 | R |
| Michigan | 154,758 | 88,481 | 57.2 | 65,057 | 42.0 | 805 | 0.5 | 415 | 0.3 | — | | 23,424 | R |
| Minnesota | 34,804 | 22,069 | 63.4 | 11,920 | 34.2 | 748 | 2.1 | 50 | 0.1 | 17 | | 10,149 | R |
| Mississippi | 69,095 | — | | 3,282 | 4.7 | 40,768 | 59.0 | 25,045 | 36.2 | — | | 15,723 | SD |
| Missouri | 165,563 | 17,028 | 10.3 | 58,801 | 35.5 | 31,362 | 18.9 | 58,372 | 35.3 | — | | 429 | D |
| New Hampshire | 65,943 | 37,519 | 56.9 | 25,887 | 39.3 | 2,125 | 3.2 | 412 | 0.6 | — | | 11,632 | R |
| New Jersey [2] | 121,215 | 58,346 | 48.1 | 62,869 | 51.9 | — | | — | | — | | 4,523 | D |
| New York | 675,156 | 362,646 | 53.7 | 312,510 | 46.3 | — | | — | | — | | 50,136 | R |
| North Carolina | 96,712 | — | | 2,737 | 2.8 | 48,846 | 50.5 | 45,129 | 46.7 | — | | 3,717 | SD |
| Ohio | 442,866 | 231,709 | 52.3 | 187,421 | 42.3 | 11,406 | 2.6 | 12,194 | 2.8 | 136 | | 44,288 | R |
| Oregon | 14,758 | 5,329 | 36.1 | 4,136 | 28.0 | 5,075 | 34.4 | 218 | 1.5 | — | | 254 | R |
| Pennsylvania | 476,442 | 268,030 | 56.3 | 16,765 | 3.5 | 178,871 | 37.5 | 12,776 | 2.7 | — | | 89,159 | R |
| Rhode Island | 19,951 | 12,244 | 61.4 | 7,707 | 38.6 | — | | — | | — | | 4,537 | R |
| Tennessee | 146,106 | — | | 11,281 | 7.7 | 65,097 | 44.6 | 69,728 | 47.7 | — | | 4,631 | CU |
| Texas | 62,855 | — | | 18 | | 47,454 | 75.5 | 15,383 | 24.5 | — | | 32,071 | SD |
| Vermont | 44,644 | 33,808 | 75.7 | 8,649 | 19.4 | 218 | 0.5 | 1,969 | 4.4 | — | | 25,159 | R |
| Virginia | 166,891 | 1,887 | 1.1 | 16,198 | 9.7 | 74,325 | 44.5 | 74,481 | 44.6 | — | | 156 | CU |
| Wisconsin | 152,179 | 86,110 | 56.6 | 65,021 | 42.7 | 887 | 0.6 | 161 | 0.1 | — | | 21,089 | R |
| **Totals** | **4,685,561** | **1,865,908** | **39.9** | **1,380,202** | **29.5** | **848,019** | **18.1** | **590,901** | **12.6** | **531** | | **485,706** | **R** |

*1. For breakdown of "Other" vote, see minor candidate vote totals, p. 470.*
*2. Figures from Petersen, op. cit., p. 37.*

# 1864 Presidential Election

| STATE [1] | TOTAL VOTE | ABRAHAM LINCOLN (Republican) | | GEORGE B. McCLELLAN (Democrat) | | OTHER [2] | | PLURALITY | |
|---|---|---|---|---|---|---|---|---|---|
| | | Votes | % | Votes | % | Votes | % | | |
| California | 105,890 | 62,053 | 58.6 | 43,837 | 41.4 | — | | 18,216 | R |
| Connecticut | 86,958 | 44,673 | 51.4 | 42,285 | 48.6 | — | | 2,388 | R |
| Delaware | 16,922 | 8,155 | 48.2 | 8,767 | 51.8 | — | | 612 | D |
| Illinois | 348,236 | 189,512 | 54.4 | 158,724 | 45.6 | — | | 30,788 | R |
| Indiana | 280,117 | 149,887 | 53.5 | 130,230 | 46.5 | — | | 19,657 | R |
| Iowa | 132,947 | 83,858 | 63.1 | 49,089 | 36.9 | — | | 34,769 | R |
| Kansas | 21,580 | 17,089 | 79.2 | 3,836 | 17.8 | 655 | 3.0 | 13,253 | R |
| Kentucky | 92,088 | 27,787 | 30.2 | 64,301 | 69.8 | — | | 36,514 | D |
| Maine | 114,797 | 67,805 | 59.1 | 46,992 | 40.9 | — | | 20,813 | R |
| Maryland | 72,892 | 40,153 | 55.1 | 32,739 | 44.9 | — | | 7,414 | R |
| Massachusetts | 175,493 | 126,742 | 72.2 | 48,745 | 27.8 | 6 | | 77,997 | R |
| Michigan | 165,279 | 91,133 | 55.1 | 74,146 | 44.9 | — | | 16,987 | R |
| Minnesota | 42,433 | 25,031 | 59.0 | 17,376 | 40.9 | 26 | 0.1 | 7,655 | R |
| Missouri | 104,346 | 72,750 | 69.7 | 31,596 | 30.3 | — | | 41,154 | R |
| Nevada | 16,420 | 9,826 | 59.8 | 6,594 | 40.2 | — | | 3,232 | R |
| New Hampshire | 69,630 | 36,596 | 52.6 | 33,034 | 47.4 | — | | 3,562 | R |
| New Jersey | 128,744 | 60,724 | 47.2 | 68,020 | 52.8 | — | | 7,296 | D |
| New York | 730,721 | 368,735 | 50.5 | 361,986 | 49.5 | — | | 6,749 | R |
| Ohio | 471,283 | 265,674 | 56.4 | 205,609 | 43.6 | — | | 60,065 | R |
| Oregon | 18,350 | 9,888 | 53.9 | 8,457 | 46.1 | 5 | | 1,431 | R |
| Pennsylvania | 573,735 | 296,292 | 51.6 | 277,443 | 48.4 | — | | 18,849 | R |
| Rhode Island | 23,067 | 14,349 | 62.2 | 8,718 | 37.8 | — | | 5,631 | R |
| Vermont | 55,740 | 42,419 | 76.1 | 13,321 | 23.9 | — | | 29,098 | R |
| West Virginia | 34,877 | 23,799 | 68.2 | 11,078 | 31.8 | — | | 12,721 | R |
| Wisconsin | 149,342 | 83,458 | 55.9 | 65,884 | 44.1 | — | | 17,574 | R |
| **Totals** | **4,031,887** | **2,218,388** | **55.0** | **1,812,807** | **45.0** | **692** | | **405,581** | **R** |

1. Eleven Confederate states did not participate in election because of the Civil War.
2. For breakdown of "Other" vote, see minor candidate vote totals, p. 470.

# 1868 Presidential Election

| STATE [1] | TOTAL VOTE | ULYSSES S. GRANT (Republican) | | HORATIO SEYMOUR (Democrat) | | OTHER [2] | | PLURALITY | |
|---|---|---|---|---|---|---|---|---|---|
| | | Votes | % | Votes | % | Votes | % | | |
| Alabama | 149,594 | 76,667 | 51.3 | 72,921 | 48.7 | 6 | | 3,746 | R |
| Arkansas | 41,190 | 22,112 | 53.7 | 19,078 | 46.3 | — | | 3,034 | R |
| California | 108,656 | 54,588 | 50.2 | 54,068 | 49.8 | — | | 520 | R |
| Connecticut | 98,570 | 50,789 | 51.5 | 47,781 | 48.5 | — | | 3,008 | R |
| Delaware | 18,571 | 7,614 | 41.0 | 10,957 | 59.0 | — | | 3,343 | D |
| Georgia | 159,816 | 57,109 | 35.7 | 102,707 | 64.3 | — | | 45,598 | D |
| Illinois | 449,420 | 250,304 | 55.7 | 199,116 | 44.3 | — | | 51,188 | R |
| Indiana | 343,528 | 176,548 | 51.4 | 166,980 | 48.6 | — | | 9,568 | R |
| Iowa | 194,439 | 120,399 | 61.9 | 74,040 | 38.1 | — | | 46,359 | R |
| Kansas | 43,630 | 30,027 | 68.8 | 13,600 | 31.2 | 3 | | 16,427 | R |
| Kentucky | 155,455 | 39,566 | 25.5 | 115,889 | 74.5 | — | | 76,323 | D |
| Louisiana | 113,488 | 33,263 | 29.3 | 80,225 | 70.7 | — | | 46,962 | D |
| Maine | 112,962 | 70,502 | 62.4 | 42,460 | 37.6 | — | | 28,042 | R |
| Maryland | 92,795 | 30,438 | 32.8 | 62,357 | 67.2 | — | | 31,919 | D |
| Massachusetts | 195,508 | 136,379 | 69.8 | 59,103 | 30.2 | 26 | | 77,276 | R |
| Michigan | 225,632 | 128,563 | 57.0 | 97,069 | 43.0 | — | | 31,494 | R |
| Minnesota | 71,620 | 43,545 | 60.8 | 28,075 | 39.2 | — | | 15,470 | R |
| Missouri | 152,488 | 86,860 | 57.0 | 65,628 | 43.0 | — | | 21,232 | R |
| Nebraska | 15,291 | 9,772 | 63.9 | 5,519 | 36.1 | — | | 4,253 | R |
| Nevada | 11,689 | 6,474 | 55.4 | 5,215 | 44.6 | — | | 1,259 | R |
| New Hampshire | 68,304 | 37,718 | 55.2 | 30,575 | 44.8 | 11 | | 7,143 | R |
| New Jersey | 163,133 | 80,132 | 49.1 | 83,001 | 50.9 | — | | 2,869 | D |
| New York | 849,771 | 419,888 | 49.4 | 429,883 | 50.6 | — | | 9,995 | D |
| North Carolina | 181,498 | 96,939 | 53.4 | 84,559 | 46.6 | — | | 12,380 | R |
| Ohio | 518,665 | 280,159 | 54.0 | 238,506 | 46.0 | — | | 41,653 | R |
| Oregon | 22,086 | 10,961 | 49.6 | 11,125 | 50.4 | — | | 164 | D |
| Pennsylvania | 655,662 | 342,280 | 52.2 | 313,382 | 47.8 | — | | 28,898 | R |
| Rhode Island | 19,511 | 13,017 | 66.7 | 6,494 | 33.3 | — | | 6,523 | R |
| South Carolina | 107,538 | 62,301 | 57.9 | 45,237 | 42.1 | — | | 17,064 | R |
| Tennessee | 82,757 | 56,628 | 68.4 | 26,129 | 31.6 | — | | 30,499 | R |
| Vermont | 56,224 | 44,173 | 78.6 | 12,051 | 21.4 | — | | 32,122 | R |
| West Virginia | 49,321 | 29,015 | 58.8 | 20,306 | 41.2 | — | | 8,709 | R |
| Wisconsin | 193,628 | 108,920 | 56.3 | 84,708 | 43.7 | — | | 24,212 | R |
| Totals | 5,722,440 | 3,013,650 | 52.7 | 2,708,744 | 47.3 | 46 | | 304,906 | R |

1. Mississippi, Texas and Virginia did not participate in the election due to Reconstruction. In Florida the state legislature cast the electoral vote.
2. For breakdown of "Other" vote, see minor candidate vote totals, p. 470.

# 1872 Presidential Election

| STATE | TOTAL VOTE | ULYSSES S. GRANT (Republican) | | HORACE GREELEY (Democrat, Liberal Republican) | | CHARLES O'CONOR (Straight Out Democrat) | | OTHER [1] | | PLURALITY | |
|---|---|---|---|---|---|---|---|---|---|---|---|
| | | Votes | % | Votes | % | Votes | % | Votes | % | | |
| Alabama | 169,716 | 90,272 | 53.2 | 79,444 | 46.8 | — | | — | | 10,828 | R |
| Arkansas | 79,300 | 41,373 | 52.2 | 37,927 | 47.8 | — | | — | | 3,446 | R |
| California | 95,785 | 54,007 | 56.4 | 40,717 | 42.5 | 1,061 | 1.1 | — | | 13,290 | R |
| Connecticut | 95,992 | 50,307 | 52.4 | 45,685 | 47.6 | — | | — | | 4,622 | R |
| Delaware | 21,822 | 11,129 | 51.0 | 10,205 | 46.8 | 488 | 2.2 | — | | 924 | R |
| Florida | 33,190 | 17,763 | 53.5 | 15,427 | 46.5 | — | | — | | 2,336 | R |
| Georgia | 138,906 | 62,550 | 45.0 | 76,356 | 55.0 | — | | — | | 13,806 | D |
| Illinois | 429,971 | 241,936 | 56.3 | 184,884 | 43.0 | 3,151 | 0.7 | — | | 57,052 | R |
| Indiana | 349,779 | 186,147 | 53.2 | 163,632 | 46.8 | — | | — | | 22,515 | R |
| Iowa | 216,365 | 131,566 | 60.8 | 71,189 | 32.9 | 2,221 | 1.0 | 11,389 | 5.3 | 60,377 | R |
| Kansas | 100,512 | 66,805 | 66.5 | 32,970 | 32.8 | 156 | 0.2 | 581 | 0.6 | 33,835 | R |
| Kentucky | 191,135 | 88,766 | 46.4 | 99,995 | 52.3 | 2,374 | 1.2 | — | | 11,229 | D |
| Louisiana | 128,692 | 71,663 | 55.7 | 57,029 | 44.3 | — | | — | | 14,634 | R |
| Maine | 90,523 | 61,426 | 67.9 | 29,097 | 32.1 | — | | — | | 32,329 | R |
| Maryland | 134,447 | 66,760 | 49.7 | 67,687 | 50.3 | — | | — | | 927 | D |
| Massachusetts | 192,650 | 133,455 | 69.3 | 59,195 | 30.7 | — | | — | | 74,260 | R |
| Michigan | 221,569 | 138,768 | 62.6 | 78,651 | 35.5 | 2,879 | 1.3 | 1,271 | 0.6 | 60,117 | R |
| Minnesota | 91,339 | 56,040 | 61.4 | 35,131 | 38.5 | — | | 168 | 0.2 | 20,909 | R |
| Mississippi | 129,457 | 82,175 | 63.5 | 47,282 | 36.5 | — | | — | | 34,893 | R |
| Missouri | 273,059 | 119,196 | 43.7 | 151,434 | 55.5 | 2,429 | 0.9 | — | | 32,238 | D |
| Nebraska | 25,932 | 18,329 | 70.7 | 7,603 | 29.3 | — | | — | | 10,726 | R |
| Nevada | 14,649 | 8,413 | 57.4 | 6,236 | 42.6 | — | | — | | 2,177 | R |
| New Hampshire | 68,906 | 37,168 | 53.9 | 31,425 | 45.6 | — | | 313 | 0.5 | 5,743 | R |
| New Jersey | 168,112 | 91,656 | 54.5 | 76,456 | 45.5 | — | | — | | 15,200 | R |
| New York | 828,020 | 440,738 | 53.2 | 387,282 | 46.8 | — | | — | | 53,456 | R |
| North Carolina | 165,163 | 94,772 | 57.4 | 70,130 | 42.5 | 261 | 0.2 | — | | 24,642 | R |
| Ohio | 529,435 | 281,852 | 53.2 | 244,320 | 46.1 | 1,163 | 0.2 | 2,100 | 0.4 | 37,532 | R |
| Oregon | 20,107 | 11,818 | 58.8 | 7,742 | 38.5 | 547 | 2.7 | — | | 4,076 | R |
| Pennsylvania | 561,629 | 349,589 | 62.2 | 212,040 | 37.8 | — | | — | | 137,549 | R |
| Rhode Island | 18,994 | 13,665 | 71.9 | 5,329 | 28.1 | — | | — | | 8,336 | R |
| South Carolina | 95,452 | 72,290 | 75.7 | 22,699 | 23.8 | 204 | 0.2 | 259 | 0.3 | 49,591 | R |
| Tennessee | 179,046 | 85,655 | 47.8 | 93,391 | 52.2 | — | | — | | 7,736 | D |
| Texas | 115,700 | 47,910 | 41.4 | 67,675 | 58.5 | 115 | 0.1 | — | | 19,765 | D |
| Vermont | 52,408 | 41,481 | 79.2 | 10,927 | 20.8 | — | | — | | 30,554 | R |
| Virginia | 185,195 | 93,463 | 50.5 | 91,647 | 49.5 | 85 | | — | | 1,816 | R |
| West Virginia | 62,467 | 32,320 | 51.7 | 29,532 | 47.3 | 615 | 1.0 | — | | 2,788 | R |
| Wisconsin | 192,255 | 105,012 | 54.6 | 86,390 | 44.9 | 853 | 0.4 | — | | 18,622 | R |
| **Totals** | **6,467,679** | **3,598,235** | **55.6** | **2,834,761** | **43.8** | **18,602** | **0.3** | **16,081** | **0.3** | **763,474** | **R** |

1. *For breakdown of "Other" vote, see minor candidate vote totals, p. 470.*

# 1876 Presidential Election

| STATE | TOTAL VOTE | RUTHERFORD B. HAYES [1] (Republican) | | SAMUEL J. TILDEN [1] (Democrat) | | PETER COOPER (Greenback) | | OTHER [2] | | PLURALITY | |
|---|---|---|---|---|---|---|---|---|---|---|---|
| | | Votes | % | Votes | % | Votes | % | Votes | % | | |
| Alabama | 171,699 | 68,708 | 40.0 | 102,989 | 60.0 | — | | 2 | | 34,281 | D |
| Arkansas | 96,946 | 38,649 | 39.9 | 58,086 | 59.9 | 211 | 0.2 | — | | 19,437 | D |
| California | 155,784 | 79,258 | 50.9 | 76,460 | 49.1 | 47 | | 19 | | 2,798 | R |
| Connecticut | 122,134 | 59,033 | 48.3 | 61,927 | 50.7 | 774 | 0.6 | 400 | 0.3 | 2,894 | D |
| Delaware | 24,133 | 10,752 | 44.6 | 13,381 | 55.4 | — | | — | | 2,629 | D |
| Florida | 46,776 | 23,849 | 51.0 | 22,927 | 49.0 | — | | — | | 922 | R |
| Georgia | 180,690 | 50,533 | 28.0 | 130,157 | 72.0 | — | | — | | 79,624 | D |
| Illinois | 554,368 | 278,232 | 50.2 | 258,611 | 46.6 | 17,207 | 3.1 | 318 | 0.1 | 19,621 | R |
| Indiana | 431,073 | 208,011 | 48.3 | 213,529 | 49.5 | 9,533 | 2.2 | — | | 5,518 | D |
| Iowa | 293,398 | 171,326 | 58.4 | 112,121 | 38.2 | 9,431 | 3.2 | 520 | 0.2 | 59,205 | R |
| Kansas | 124,134 | 78,324 | 63.1 | 37,902 | 30.5 | 7,770 | 6.3 | 138 | 0.1 | 40,422 | R |
| Kentucky | 260,626 | 97,568 | 37.4 | 160,060 | 61.4 | — | | 2,998 | 1.2 | 62,492 | D |
| Louisiana | 145,823 | 75,315 | 51.6 | 70,508 | 48.4 | — | | — | | 4,807 | R |
| Maine | 117,045 | 66,300 | 56.6 | 49,917 | 42.6 | — | | 828 | 0.7 | 16,383 | R |
| Maryland | 163,759 | 71,980 | 44.0 | 91,779 | 56.0 | — | | — | | 19,799 | D |
| Massachusetts | 259,619 | 150,063 | 57.8 | 108,777 | 41.9 | — | | 779 | 0.3 | 41,286 | R |
| Michigan | 318,426 | 166,901 | 52.4 | 141,665 | 44.5 | 9,023 | 2.8 | 837 | 0.3 | 25,236 | R |
| Minnesota | 124,160 | 72,962 | 58.8 | 48,799 | 39.3 | 2,399 | 1.9 | — | | 24,163 | R |
| Mississippi | 164,776 | 52,603 | 31.9 | 112,173 | 68.1 | — | | — | | 59,570 | D |
| Missouri | 350,610 | 145,027 | 41.4 | 202,086 | 57.6 | 3,497 | 1.0 | — | | 57,059 | D |
| Nebraska | 49,258 | 31,915 | 64.8 | 17,343 | 35.2 | — | | — | | 14,572 | R |
| Nevada | 19,691 | 10,383 | 52.7 | 9,308 | 47.3 | — | | — | | 1,075 | R |
| New Hampshire | 80,143 | 41,540 | 51.8 | 38,510 | 48.1 | — | | 93 | 0.1 | 3,030 | R |
| New Jersey | 220,193 | 103,517 | 47.0 | 115,962 | 52.7 | 714 | 0.3 | — | | 12,445 | D |
| New York | 1,015,503 | 489,207 | 48.2 | 521,949 | 51.4 | 1,978 | 0.2 | 2,369 | 0.2 | 32,742 | D |
| North Carolina | 233,911 | 108,484 | 46.4 | 125,427 | 53.6 | — | | — | | 16,943 | D |
| Ohio | 658,650 | 330,698 | 50.2 | 323,182 | 49.1 | 3,058 | 0.5 | 1,712 | 0.3 | 7,516 | R |
| Oregon | 29,873 | 15,207 | 50.9 | 14,157 | 47.4 | 509 | 1.7 | — | | 1,050 | R |
| Pennsylvania | 758,973 | 384,157 | 50.6 | 366,204 | 48.2 | 7,209 | 0.9 | 1,403 | 0.2 | 17,953 | R |
| Rhode Island | 26,499 | 15,787 | 59.6 | 10,712 | 40.4 | — | | — | | 5,075 | R |
| South Carolina | 182,683 | 91,786 | 50.2 | 90,897 | 49.8 | — | | — | | 889 | R |
| Tennessee | 222,743 | 89,566 | 40.2 | 133,177 | 59.8 | — | | — | | 43,611 | D |
| Texas | 151,431 | 45,013 | 29.7 | 106,372 | 70.2 | — | | 46 | | 61,359 | D |
| Vermont | 64,460 | 44,092 | 68.4 | 20,254 | 31.4 | — | | 114 | 0.2 | 23,838 | R |
| Virginia | 236,288 | 95,518 | 40.4 | 140,770 | 59.6 | — | | — | | 45,252 | D |
| West Virginia | 99,647 | 41,997 | 42.1 | 56,546 | 56.7 | 1,104 | 1.1 | — | | 14,549 | D |
| Wisconsin | 257,176 | 130,050 | 50.6 | 123,922 | 48.2 | 1,509 | 0.6 | 1,695 | 0.7 | 6,128 | R |
| Totals | 8,413,101 | 4,034,311 | 48.0 | 4,288,546 | 51.0 | 75,973 | 0.9 | 14,271 | 0.2 | 254,235 | D |

1. Hayes won the election. For resolution of disputed 1876 election, see p. 304.
2. For breakdown of "Other" vote, see minor candidate vote totals, p. 470.

# 1880 Presidential Election

| STATE | TOTAL VOTE | JAMES A. GARFIELD (Republican) | | WINFIELD S. HANCOCK (Democrat) | | JAMES B. WEAVER (Greenback) | | OTHER [1] | | PLURALITY | |
|---|---|---|---|---|---|---|---|---|---|---|---|
| | | Votes | % | Votes | % | Votes | % | Votes | % | | |
| Alabama | 151,902 | 56,350 | 37.1 | 91,130 | 60.0 | 4,422 | 2.9 | — | | 34,780 | D |
| Arkansas | 107,772 | 41,661 | 38.7 | 60,489 | 56.1 | 4,079 | 3.8 | 1,543 | 1.4 | 18,828 | D |
| California | 164,218 | 80,282 | 48.9 | 80,426 | 49.0 | 3,381 | 2.1 | 129 | 0.1 | 144 | D |
| Colorado | 53,546 | 27,450 | 51.3 | 24,647 | 46.0 | 1,435 | 2.7 | 14 | | 2,803 | R |
| Connecticut | 132,798 | 67,071 | 50.5 | 64,411 | 48.5 | 868 | 0.7 | 448 | 0.3 | 2,660 | R |
| Delaware | 29,458 | 14,148 | 48.0 | 15,181 | 51.5 | 129 | 0.4 | — | | 1,033 | D |
| Florida | 51,618 | 23,654 | 45.8 | 27,964 | 54.2 | — | | — | | 4,310 | D |
| Georgia | 157,451 | 54,470 | 34.6 | 102,981 | 65.4 | — | | — | | 48,511 | D |
| Illinois | 622,305 | 318,036 | 51.1 | 277,321 | 44.6 | 26,358 | 4.2 | 590 | 0.1 | 40,715 | R |
| Indiana | 470,758 | 232,169 | 49.3 | 225,523 | 47.9 | 13,066 | 2.8 | — | | 6,646 | R |
| Iowa | 323,140 | 183,904 | 56.9 | 105,845 | 32.8 | 32,327 | 10.0 | 1,064 | 0.3 | 78,059 | R |
| Kansas | 201,054 | 121,520 | 60.4 | 59,789 | 29.7 | 19,710 | 9.8 | 35 | | 61,731 | R |
| Kentucky | 267,104 | 106,490 | 39.9 | 148,875 | 55.7 | 11,506 | 4.3 | 233 | 0.1 | 42,385 | D |
| Louisiana | 104,462 | 38,978 | 37.3 | 65,047 | 62.3 | 437 | 0.4 | — | | 26,069 | D |
| Maine | 143,903 | 74,052 | 51.5 | 65,211 | 45.3 | 4,409 | 3.1 | 231 | 0.2 | 8,841 | R |
| Maryland | 172,221 | 78,515 | 45.6 | 93,706 | 54.4 | — | | — | | 15,191 | D |
| Massachusetts | 282,505 | 165,198 | 58.5 | 111,960 | 39.6 | 4,548 | 1.6 | 799 | 0.3 | 53,238 | R |
| Michigan | 353,076 | 185,335 | 52.5 | 131,596 | 37.3 | 34,895 | 9.9 | 1,250 | 0.4 | 53,739 | R |
| Minnesota | 150,806 | 93,939 | 62.3 | 53,314 | 35.4 | 3,267 | 2.2 | 286 | 0.2 | 40,625 | R |
| Mississippi | 117,068 | 34,844 | 29.8 | 75,750 | 64.7 | 5,797 | 5.0 | 677 | 0.6 | 40,906 | D |
| Missouri | 397,289 | 153,647 | 38.7 | 208,600 | 52.5 | 35,042 | 8.8 | — | | 54,953 | D |
| Nebraska | 87,355 | 54,979 | 62.9 | 28,523 | 32.7 | 3,853 | 4.4 | — | | 26,456 | R |
| Nevada | 18,343 | 8,732 | 47.6 | 9,611 | 52.4 | — | | — | | 879 | D |
| New Hampshire | 86,361 | 44,856 | 51.9 | 40,797 | 47.2 | 528 | 0.6 | 180 | 0.2 | 4,059 | R |
| New Jersey | 245,928 | 120,555 | 49.0 | 122,565 | 49.8 | 2,617 | 1.1 | 191 | 0.1 | 2,010 | D |
| New York | 1,103,945 | 555,544 | 50.3 | 534,511 | 48.4 | 12,373 | 1.1 | 1,517 | 0.1 | 21,033 | R |
| North Carolina | 240,946 | 115,616 | 48.0 | 124,204 | 51.5 | 1,126 | 0.5 | — | | 8,588 | D |
| Ohio | 724,984 | 375,048 | 51.7 | 340,867 | 47.0 | 6,456 | 0.9 | 2,613 | 0.4 | 34,181 | R |
| Oregon | 40,841 | 20,619 | 50.5 | 19,955 | 48.9 | 267 | 0.7 | — | | 664 | R |
| Pennsylvania | 874,783 | 444,704 | 50.8 | 407,428 | 46.6 | 20,667 | 2.4 | 1,984 | 0.2 | 37,276 | R |
| Rhode Island | 29,235 | 18,195 | 62.2 | 10,779 | 36.9 | 236 | 0.8 | 25 | 0.1 | 7,416 | R |
| South Carolina | 169,793 | 57,954 | 34.1 | 111,236 | 65.5 | 567 | 0.3 | 36 | | 53,282 | D |
| Tennessee | 243,263 | 107,677 | 44.3 | 129,569 | 53.3 | 6,017 | 2.5 | — | | 21,892 | D |
| Texas | 233,632 | 50,217 | 21.5 | 156,010 | 66.8 | 27,405 | 11.7 | — | | 105,793 | D |
| Vermont | 65,098 | 45,567 | 70.0 | 18,316 | 28.1 | 1,215 | 1.9 | — | | 27,251 | R |
| Virginia | 211,616 | 83,533 | 39.5 | 128,083 | 60.5 | — | | — | | 44,550 | D |
| West Virginia | 112,641 | 46,243 | 41.1 | 57,390 | 50.9 | 9,008 | 8.0 | — | | 11,147 | D |
| Wisconsin | 267,202 | 144,406 | 54.0 | 114,650 | 42.9 | 7,986 | 3.0 | 160 | 0.1 | 29,756 | R |
| Totals | 9,210,420 | 4,446,158 | 48.3 | 4,444,260 | 48.3 | 305,997 | 3.3 | 14,005 | 0.2 | 1,898 | R |

1. For breakdown of "Other" vote, see minor candidate vote totals, p. 470.

# 1884 Presidential Election

| STATE | TOTAL VOTE | GROVER CLEVELAND (Democrat) | | JAMES G. BLAINE (Republican) | | BENJAMIN F. BUTLER (Greenback) | | JOHN P. ST. JOHN (Prohibition) | | OTHER [1] | | PLURALITY | |
|---|---|---|---|---|---|---|---|---|---|---|---|---|---|
| | | Votes | % | Votes | % | Votes | % | Votes | % | Votes | % | | |
| Alabama | 153,624 | 92,736 | 60.4 | 59,444 | 38.7 | 762 | 0.5 | 610 | 0.4 | 72 | | 33,292 | D |
| Arkansas | 125,779 | 72,734 | 57.8 | 51,198 | 40.7 | 1,847 | 1.5 | — | | — | | 21,536 | D |
| California | 196,988 | 89,288 | 45.3 | 102,369 | 52.0 | 2,037 | 1.0 | 2,965 | 1.5 | 329 | 0.2 | 13,081 | R |
| Colorado | 66,519 | 27,723 | 41.7 | 36,084 | 54.2 | 1,956 | 2.9 | 756 | 1.1 | — | | 8,361 | R |
| Connecticut | 137,221 | 67,167 | 48.9 | 65,879 | 48.0 | 1,682 | 1.2 | 2,493 | 1.8 | — | | 1,288 | D |
| Delaware | 29,984 | 16,957 | 56.6 | 12,953 | 43.2 | 10 | | 64 | 0.2 | — | | 4,004 | D |
| Florida | 59,990 | 31,769 | 53.0 | 28,031 | 46.7 | — | | 72 | 0.1 | 118 | 0.2 | 3,738 | D |
| Georgia | 143,610 | 94,667 | 65.9 | 48,603 | 33.8 | 145 | 0.1 | 195 | 0.1 | — | | 46,064 | D |
| Illinois | 672,670 | 312,351 | 46.4 | 337,469 | 50.2 | 10,776 | 1.6 | 12,074 | 1.8 | — | | 25,118 | R |
| Indiana | 491,649 | 244,989 | 49.8 | 238,466 | 48.5 | 8,194 | 1.7 | — | | — | | 6,523 | D |
| Iowa | 393,542 | 177,316 | 45.1 | 197,089 | 50.1 | 16,341 | 4.2 | 1,499 | 0.4 | 1,297 | 0.3 | 19,773 | R |
| Kansas | 250,991 | 90,111 | 35.9 | 154,410 | 61.5 | 1,691 | 0.7 | 4,311 | 1.7 | 468 | 0.2 | 64,299 | R |
| Kentucky | 274,910 | 152,961 | 55.6 | 118,690 | 43.2 | 120 | | 3,139 | 1.1 | — | | 34,271 | D |
| Louisiana | 113,234 | 62,594 | 55.3 | 46,347 | 40.9 | 3,955 | 3.5 | 338 | 0.3 | — | | 16,247 | D |
| Maine | 127,114 | 52,153 | 41.0 | 72,217 | 56.8 | 578 | 0.5 | 2,160 | 1.7 | 6 | | 20,064 | R |
| Maryland | 209,823 | 96,866 | 46.2 | 85,748 | 40.9 | 24,382 | 11.6 | 2,827 | 1.3 | — | | 11,118 | D |
| Massachusetts | 321,253 | 122,352 | 38.1 | 146,724 | 45.7 | 42,252 | 13.2 | 9,923 | 3.1 | 2 | | 24,372 | R |
| Michigan | 364,490 | 149,835 | 41.1 | 192,669 | 52.9 | 3,583 | 1.0 | 18,403 | 5.0 | — | | 42,834 | R |
| Minnesota | 186,434 | 70,065 | 37.6 | 111,685 | 59.9 | — | | 4,684 | 2.5 | — | | 41,620 | R |
| Mississippi | 120,688 | 77,653 | 64.3 | 43,035 | 35.7 | — | | — | | — | | 34,618 | D |
| Missouri | 441,268 | 236,023 | 53.5 | 203,081 | 46.0 | — | | 2,164 | 0.5 | — | | 32,942 | D |
| Nebraska | 134,202 | 54,391 | 40.5 | 76,912 | 57.3 | — | | 2,899 | 2.2 | — | | 22,521 | R |
| Nevada | 12,779 | 5,577 | 43.6 | 7,176 | 56.2 | 26 | 0.2 | — | | — | | 1,599 | R |
| New Hampshire | 84,586 | 39,198 | 46.3 | 43,254 | 51.1 | 554 | 0.7 | 1,580 | 1.9 | — | | 4,056 | R |
| New Jersey | 260,853 | 127,747 | 49.0 | 123,436 | 47.3 | 3,486 | 1.3 | 6,156 | 2.4 | 28 | | 4,311 | D |
| New York | 1,167,003 | 563,048 | 48.2 | 562,001 | 48.2 | 16,955 | 1.5 | 24,999 | 2.1 | — | | 1,047 | D |
| North Carolina | 268,356 | 142,905 | 53.3 | 125,021 | 46.6 | — | | 430 | 0.2 | — | | 17,884 | D |
| Ohio | 784,620 | 368,280 | 46.9 | 400,092 | 51.0 | 5,179 | 0.7 | 11,069 | 1.4 | — | | 31,812 | R |
| Oregon | 52,683 | 24,598 | 46.7 | 26,845 | 51.0 | 726 | 1.4 | 479 | 0.9 | 35 | 0.1 | 2,247 | R |
| Pennsylvania | 899,710 | 394,772 | 43.9 | 472,792 | 52.5 | 16,992 | 1.9 | 15,154 | 1.7 | — | | 78,020 | R |
| Rhode Island | 32,771 | 12,391 | 37.8 | 19,030 | 58.1 | 422 | 1.3 | 928 | 2.8 | — | | 6,639 | R |
| South Carolina | 92,812 | 69,845 | 75.3 | 21,730 | 23.4 | — | | — | | 1,237 | 1.3 | 48,115 | D |
| Tennessee | 259,978 | 133,770 | 51.5 | 124,101 | 47.7 | 957 | 0.4 | 1,150 | 0.4 | — | | 9,669 | D |
| Texas | 321,242 | 223,209 | 69.5 | 91,234 | 28.4 | 3,310 | 1.0 | 3,489 | 1.1 | — | | 131,975 | D |
| Vermont | 59,409 | 17,331 | 29.2 | 39,514 | 66.5 | 785 | 1.3 | 1,752 | 2.9 | 27 | | 22,183 | R |
| Virginia | 284,977 | 145,491 | 51.1 | 139,356 | 48.9 | — | | 130 | | — | | 6,135 | D |
| West Virginia | 132,145 | 67,311 | 50.9 | 63,096 | 47.7 | 799 | 0.6 | 939 | 0.7 | — | | 4,215 | D |
| Wisconsin | 319,847 | 146,447 | 45.8 | 161,155 | 50.4 | 4,594 | 1.4 | 7,651 | 2.4 | — | | 14,708 | R |
| **Totals** | **10,049,754** | **4,874,621** | **48.5** | **4,848,936** | **48.2** | **175,096** | **1.7** | **147,482** | **1.5** | **3,619** | | **25,685** | **D** |

1. For breakdown of "Other" vote, see minor candidate vote totals, p. 470.

# 1888 Presidential Election

| STATE | TOTAL VOTE | BENJAMIN HARRISON [1] (Republican) | | GROVER CLEVELAND [1] (Democrat) | | CLINTON B. FISK (Prohibition) | | ALSON J. STREETER (Union Labor) | | OTHER [2] | | PLURALITY | |
|---|---|---|---|---|---|---|---|---|---|---|---|---|---|
| | | Votes | % | Votes | % | Votes | % | Votes | % | Votes | % | | |
| Alabama | 175,085 | 57,177 | 32.7 | 117,314 | 67.0 | 594 | 0.3 | — | | — | | 60,137 | D |
| Arkansas | 157,058 | 59,752 | 38.0 | 86,062 | 54.8 | 614 | 0.4 | 10,630 | 6.8 | — | | 26,310 | D |
| California | 251,339 | 124,816 | 49.7 | 117,729 | 46.8 | 5,761 | 2.3 | — | | 3,033 | 1.2 | 7,087 | R |
| Colorado | 91,946 | 50,772 | 55.2 | 37,549 | 40.8 | 2,182 | 2.4 | 1,266 | 1.4 | 177 | 0.2 | 13,223 | R |
| Connecticut | 153,978 | 74,584 | 48.4 | 74,920 | 48.7 | 4,234 | 2.7 | 240 | 0.2 | — | | 336 | D |
| Delaware | 29,764 | 12,950 | 43.5 | 16,414 | 55.1 | 399 | 1.3 | — | | 1 | | 3,464 | D |
| Florida | 66,500 | 26,529 | 39.9 | 39,557 | 59.5 | 414 | 0.6 | — | | — | | 13,028 | D |
| Georgia | 142,936 | 40,499 | 28.3 | 100,493 | 70.3 | 1,808 | 1.3 | 136 | 0.1 | — | | 59,994 | D |
| Illinois | 747,813 | 370,475 | 49.5 | 348,351 | 46.6 | 21,703 | 2.9 | 7,134 | 1.0 | 150 | | 22,124 | R |
| Indiana | 536,988 | 263,366 | 49.0 | 260,990 | 48.6 | 9,939 | 1.9 | 2,693 | 0.5 | — | | 2,376 | R |
| Iowa | 404,694 | 211,607 | 52.3 | 179,876 | 44.4 | 3,550 | 0.9 | 9,105 | 2.2 | 556 | 0.1 | 31,731 | R |
| Kansas | 331,133 | 182,845 | 55.2 | 102,739 | 31.0 | 6,774 | 2.0 | 37,838 | 11.4 | 937 | 0.3 | 80,106 | R |
| Kentucky | 344,868 | 155,138 | 45.0 | 183,830 | 53.3 | 5,223 | 1.5 | 677 | 0.2 | — | | 28,692 | D |
| Louisiana | 115,891 | 30,660 | 26.5 | 85,032 | 73.4 | 160 | 0.1 | 39 | | — | | 54,372 | D |
| Maine | 128,253 | 73,730 | 57.5 | 50,472 | 39.4 | 2,691 | 2.1 | 1,344 | 1.0 | 16 | | 23,258 | R |
| Maryland | 210,941 | 99,986 | 47.4 | 106,188 | 50.3 | 4,767 | 2.3 | — | | — | | 6,202 | D |
| Massachusetts | 344,243 | 183,892 | 53.4 | 151,590 | 44.0 | 8,701 | 2.5 | — | | 60 | | 32,302 | R |
| Michigan | 475,356 | 236,387 | 49.7 | 213,469 | 44.9 | 20,945 | 4.4 | 4,555 | 1.0 | — | | 22,918 | R |
| Minnesota | 263,162 | 142,492 | 54.1 | 104,372 | 39.7 | 15,201 | 5.8 | 1,097 | 0.4 | — | | 38,120 | R |
| Mississippi | 115,786 | 30,095 | 26.0 | 85,451 | 73.8 | 240 | 0.2 | — | | — | | 55,356 | D |
| Missouri | 521,359 | 236,252 | 45.3 | 261,943 | 50.2 | 4,539 | 0.9 | 18,625 | 3.6 | — | | 25,691 | D |
| Nebraska | 202,630 | 108,417 | 53.5 | 80,552 | 39.8 | 9,435 | 4.7 | 4,226 | 2.1 | — | | 27,865 | R |
| Nevada | 12,573 | 7,229 | 57.5 | 5,303 | 42.2 | 41 | 0.3 | — | | — | | 1,926 | R |
| New Hampshire | 90,770 | 45,734 | 50.4 | 43,382 | 47.8 | 1,596 | 1.8 | — | | 58 | 0.1 | 2,352 | R |
| New Jersey | 303,634 | 144,347 | 47.5 | 151,493 | 49.9 | 7,794 | 2.6 | — | | — | | 7,146 | D |
| New York | 1,319,748 | 650,338 | 49.3 | 635,965 | 48.2 | 30,231 | 2.3 | 627 | | 2,587 | 0.2 | 14,373 | R |
| North Carolina | 285,563 | 134,784 | 47.2 | 147,902 | 51.8 | 2,840 | 1.0 | — | | 37 | | 13,118 | D |
| Ohio | 839,357 | 416,054 | 49.6 | 395,456 | 47.1 | 24,356 | 2.9 | 3,491 | 0.4 | — | | 20,598 | R |
| Oregon | 61,889 | 33,291 | 53.8 | 26,518 | 42.8 | 1,676 | 2.7 | — | | 404 | 0.7 | 6,773 | R |
| Pennsylvania | 997,568 | 526,091 | 52.7 | 446,633 | 44.8 | 20,947 | 2.1 | 3,873 | 0.4 | 24 | | 79,458 | R |
| Rhode Island | 40,775 | 21,969 | 53.9 | 17,530 | 43.0 | 1,251 | 3.1 | 18 | | 7 | | 4,439 | R |
| South Carolina | 79,997 | 13,736 | 17.2 | 65,824 | 82.3 | — | | — | | 437 | 0.5 | 52,088 | D |
| Tennessee | 303,694 | 138,978 | 45.8 | 158,699 | 52.3 | 5,969 | 2.0 | 48 | | — | | 19,721 | D |
| Texas | 354,412 | 88,604 | 25.0 | 232,189 | 65.5 | 4,739 | 1.3 | 28,880 | 8.1 | — | | 143,585 | D |
| Vermont | 63,476 | 45,193 | 71.2 | 16,788 | 26.4 | 1,460 | 2.3 | — | | 35 | 0.1 | 28,405 | R |
| Virginia | 304,087 | 150,399 | 49.5 | 152,004 | 50.0 | 1,684 | 0.6 | — | | — | | 1,605 | D |
| West Virginia | 159,440 | 78,171 | 49.0 | 78,677 | 49.3 | 1,084 | 0.7 | 1,508 | 0.9 | — | | 506 | D |
| Wisconsin | 354,614 | 176,553 | 49.8 | 155,232 | 43.8 | 14,277 | 4.0 | 8,552 | 2.4 | — | | 21,321 | R |
| Totals | 11,383,320 | 5,443,892 | 47.8 | 5,534,488 | 48.6 | 249,819 | 2.2 | 146,602 | 1.3 | 8,519 | 0.1 | 90,596 | D |

1. Harrison won the election. See p. 307.
2. For breakdown of "Other" vote, see minor candidate vote totals, p. 470.

# 1892 Presidential Election

| STATE | TOTAL VOTE | GROVER CLEVELAND (Democrat) | | BENJAMIN HARRISON (Republican) | | JAMES B. WEAVER (Populist) | | JOHN BIDWELL (Prohibition) | | OTHER [1] | | PLURALITY | |
|---|---|---|---|---|---|---|---|---|---|---|---|---|---|
| | | Votes | % | Votes | % | Votes | % | Votes | % | Votes | % | | |
| Alabama | 232,543 | 138,135 | 59.4 | 9,184 | 3.9 | 84,984 | 36.5 | 240 | 0.1 | — | | 53,151 | D |
| Arkansas | 148,117 | 87,834 | 59.3 | 47,072 | 31.8 | 11,831 | 8.0 | 113 | 0.1 | 1,267 | 0.9 | 40,762 | D |
| California | 269,585 | 118,151 | 43.8 | 118,027 | 43.8 | 25,311 | 9.4 | 8,096 | 3.0 | — | | 124 | D |
| Colorado | 93,881 | — | | 38,620 | 41.1 | 53,584 | 57.1 | 1,677 | 1.8 | — | | 14,964 | POP |
| Connecticut | 164,593 | 82,395 | 50.1 | 77,030 | 46.8 | 809 | 0.5 | 4,026 | 2.4 | 333 | 0.2 | 5,365 | D |
| Delaware | 37,235 | 18,581 | 49.9 | 18,077 | 48.5 | — | | 564 | 1.5 | 13 | | 504 | D |
| Florida | 35,471 | 30,153 | 85.0 | — | | 4,843 | 13.7 | 475 | 1.3 | — | | 25,310 | D |
| Georgia | 223,126 | 129,446 | 58.0 | 48,408 | 21.7 | 41,939 | 18.8 | 988 | 0.4 | 2,345 | 1.1 | 81,038 | D |
| Idaho | 19,407 | — | | 8,599 | 44.3 | 10,520 | 54.2 | 288 | 1.5 | — | | 1,921 | POP |
| Illinois | 873,667 | 426,281 | 48.8 | 399,308 | 45.7 | 22,207 | 2.5 | 25,871 | 3.0 | — | | 26,973 | D |
| Indiana | 553,613 | 262,740 | 47.5 | 255,615 | 46.2 | 22,208 | 4.0 | 13,050 | 2.4 | — | | 7,125 | D |
| Iowa | 443,159 | 196,367 | 44.3 | 219,795 | 49.6 | 20,595 | 4.6 | 6,402 | 1.4 | — | | 23,428 | R |
| Kansas | 323,591 | — | | 156,134 | 48.3 | 162,888 | 50.3 | 4,569 | 1.4 | — | | 6,754 | POP |
| Kentucky | 340,864 | 175,461 | 51.5 | 135,462 | 39.7 | 23,500 | 6.9 | 6,441 | 1.9 | — | | 39,999 | D |
| Louisiana | 114,889 | 87,926 | 76.5 | 26,963 | 23.5 | — | | — | | — | | 60,963 | D |
| Maine | 116,451 | 48,049 | 41.3 | 62,936 | 54.0 | 2,396 | 2.1 | 3,066 | 2.6 | 4 | | 14,887 | R |
| Maryland | 213,275 | 113,866 | 53.4 | 92,736 | 43.5 | 796 | 0.4 | 5,877 | 2.8 | — | | 21,130 | D |
| Massachusetts | 391,028 | 176,813 | 45.2 | 202,814 | 51.9 | 3,210 | 0.8 | 7,539 | 1.9 | 652 | 0.2 | 26,001 | R |
| Michigan | 466,917 | 202,396 | 43.3 | 222,708 | 47.7 | 20,031 | 4.3 | 20,857 | 4.5 | 925 | 0.2 | 20,312 | R |
| Minnesota | 267,841 | 100,589 | 37.6 | 122,736 | 45.8 | 30,399 | 11.3 | 14,117 | 5.3 | — | | 22,147 | R |
| Mississippi | 52,519 | 40,030 | 76.2 | 1,398 | 2.7 | 10,118 | 19.3 | 973 | 1.9 | — | | 29,912 | D |
| Missouri | 541,583 | 268,400 | 49.6 | 227,646 | 42.0 | 41,204 | 7.6 | 4,333 | 0.8 | — | | 40,754 | D |
| Montana | 44,461 | 17,690 | 39.8 | 18,871 | 42.4 | 7,338 | 16.5 | 562 | 1.3 | — | | 1,181 | R |
| Nebraska | 200,205 | 24,956 | 12.5 | 87,213 | 43.6 | 83,134 | 41.5 | 4,902 | 2.4 | — | | 4,079 | R |
| Nevada | 10,826 | 703 | 6.5 | 2,811 | 26.0 | 7,226 | 66.7 | 86 | 0.8 | — | | 4,415 | POP |
| New Hampshire | 89,328 | 42,081 | 47.1 | 45,658 | 51.1 | 292 | 0.3 | 1,297 | 1.5 | — | | 3,577 | R |
| New Jersey | 337,485 | 170,987 | 50.7 | 156,059 | 46.2 | 969 | 0.3 | 8,133 | 2.4 | 1,337 | 0.4 | 14,928 | D |
| New York | 1,336,793 | 654,868 | 49.0 | 609,350 | 45.6 | 16,429 | 1.2 | 38,190 | 2.9 | 17,956 | 1.3 | 45,518 | D |
| North Carolina | 280,270 | 132,951 | 47.4 | 100,346 | 35.8 | 44,336 | 15.8 | 2,637 | 0.9 | — | | 32,805 | D |
| North Dakota [2] | 36,118 | — | | 17,519 | 48.5 | 17,700 | 49.0 | 899 | 2.5 | — | | 181 | POP |
| Ohio | 850,164 | 404,115 | 47.5 | 405,187 | 47.7 | 14,850 | 1.7 | 26,012 | 3.1 | — | | 1,072 | R |
| Oregon | 78,378 | 14,243 | 18.2 | 35,002 | 44.7 | 26,875 | 34.3 | 2,258 | 2.9 | — | | 8,127 | R |
| Pennsylvania | 1,003,000 | 452,264 | 45.1 | 516,011 | 51.4 | 8,714 | 0.9 | 25,123 | 2.5 | 888 | 0.1 | 63,747 | R |
| Rhode Island | 53,196 | 24,336 | 45.7 | 26,975 | 50.7 | 228 | 0.4 | 1,654 | 3.1 | 3 | | 2,639 | R |
| South Carolina | 70,504 | 54,680 | 77.6 | 13,345 | 18.9 | 2,407 | 3.4 | — | | 72 | 0.1 | 41,335 | D |
| South Dakota | 70,160 | 8,894 | 12.7 | 34,714 | 49.5 | 26,552 | 37.8 | — | | — | | 8,162 | R |
| Tennessee | 265,732 | 136,468 | 51.4 | 100,537 | 37.8 | 23,918 | 9.0 | 4,809 | 1.8 | — | | 35,931 | D |
| Texas | 410,860 | 236,979 | 57.7 | 70,982 | 17.3 | 96,649 | 23.5 | 2,164 | 0.5 | 4,086 | 1.0 | 140,330 | D |
| Vermont | 55,793 | 16,325 | 29.3 | 37,992 | 68.1 | 42 | 0.1 | 1,424 | 2.6 | 10 | | 21,667 | R |
| Virginia | 292,238 | 164,136 | 56.2 | 113,098 | 38.7 | 12,275 | 4.2 | 2,729 | 0.9 | — | | 51,038 | D |
| Washington | 87,968 | 29,802 | 33.9 | 36,459 | 41.4 | 19,165 | 21.8 | 2,542 | 2.9 | — | | 6,657 | R |
| West Virginia | 171,079 | 84,467 | 49.4 | 80,292 | 46.9 | 4,167 | 2.4 | 2,153 | 1.3 | — | | 4,175 | D |
| Wisconsin | 371,481 | 177,325 | 47.7 | 171,101 | 46.1 | 9,919 | 2.7 | 13,136 | 3.5 | — | | 6,224 | D |
| Wyoming | 16,703 | — | | 8,454 | 50.6 | 7,722 | 46.2 | 498 | 3.0 | 29 | 0.2 | 732 | R |
| Totals | 12,056,097 | 5,551,883 | 46.1 | 5,179,244 | 43.0 | 1,024,280 | 8.5 | 270,770 | 2.2 | 29,920 | 0.2 | 372,639 | D |

1. For breakdown of "Other" vote, see minor candidate vote totals, p. 470.
2. Figures from Petersen, op. cit., p. 60.

# 1896 Presidential Election

| STATE | TOTAL VOTE | WILLIAM McKINLEY (Republican) | | WILLIAM J. BRYAN (Democrat, Populist) | | JOHN M. PALMER (National Democrat) | | JOSHUA LEVERING (Prohibition) | | OTHER [1] | | PLURALITY | |
|---|---|---|---|---|---|---|---|---|---|---|---|---|---|
| | | Votes | % | Votes | % | Votes | % | Votes | % | Votes | % | | |
| Alabama | 194,580 | 55,673 | 28.6 | 130,298 | 67.0 | 6,375 | 3.3 | 2,234 | 1.1 | — | | 74,625 | D |
| Arkansas | 149,396 | 37,512 | 25.1 | 110,103 | 73.7 | — | | 889 | 0.6 | 892 | 0.6 | 72,591 | D |
| California | 298,598 | 146,756 | 49.1 | 144,877 | 48.5 | 1,730 | 0.6 | 2,573 | 0.9 | 2,662 | 0.9 | 1,879 | R |
| Colorado | 189,539 | 26,271 | 13.9 | 161,005 | 84.9 | 1 | | 1,717 | 0.9 | 545 | 0.3 | 134,734 | D |
| Connecticut | 174,394 | 110,285 | 63.2 | 56,740 | 32.5 | 4,336 | 2.5 | 1,806 | 1.0 | 1,227 | 0.7 | 53,545 | R |
| Delaware | 38,456 | 20,450 | 53.2 | 16,574 | 43.1 | 966 | 2.5 | 466 | 1.2 | — | | 3,876 | R |
| Florida | 46,488 | 11,298 | 24.3 | 32,756 | 70.5 | 1,778 | 3.8 | 656 | 1.4 | — | | 21,458 | D |
| Georgia | 162,480 | 59,395 | 36.6 | 93,885 | 57.8 | 3,670 | 2.3 | 5,483 | 3.4 | 47 | | 34,490 | D |
| Idaho | 29,631 | 6,324 | 21.3 | 23,135 | 78.1 | — | | 172 | 0.6 | | | 16,811 | D |
| Illinois | 1,090,766 | 607,130 | 55.7 | 465,593 | 42.7 | 6,307 | 0.6 | 9,796 | 0.9 | 1,940 | 0.2 | 141,537 | R |
| Indiana | 637,089 | 323,754 | 50.8 | 305,538 | 48.0 | 2,145 | 0.3 | 3,061 | 0.5 | 2,591 | 0.4 | 18,216 | R |
| Iowa | 521,550 | 289,293 | 55.5 | 223,744 | 42.9 | 4,516 | 0.9 | 3,192 | 0.6 | 805 | 0.2 | 65,549 | R |
| Kansas | 336,085 | 159,484 | 47.5 | 173,049 | 51.5 | 1,209 | 0.4 | 1,723 | 0.5 | 620 | 0.2 | 13,565 | D |
| Kentucky | 445,928 | 218,171 | 48.9 | 217,894 | 48.9 | 5,084 | 1.1 | 4,779 | 1.1 | — | | 277 | R |
| Louisiana | 101,046 | 22,037 | 21.8 | 77,175 | 76.4 | 1,834 | 1.8 | — | | — | | 55,138 | D |
| Maine | 118,419 | 80,403 | 67.9 | 34,587 | 29.2 | 1,867 | 1.6 | 1,562 | 1.3 | — | | 45,816 | R |
| Maryland | 250,249 | 136,959 | 54.7 | 104,150 | 41.6 | 2,499 | 1.0 | 5,918 | 2.4 | 723 | 0.3 | 32,809 | R |
| Massachusetts | 401,269 | 278,976 | 69.5 | 105,414 | 26.3 | 11,749 | 2.9 | 2,998 | 0.7 | 2,132 | 0.5 | 173,562 | R |
| Michigan | 545,583 | 293,336 | 53.8 | 237,164 | 43.5 | 6,923 | 1.3 | 4,978 | 0.9 | 3,182 | 0.6 | 56,172 | R |
| Minnesota | 341,762 | 193,503 | 56.6 | 139,735 | 40.9 | 3,222 | 0.9 | 4,348 | 1.3 | 954 | 0.3 | 53,768 | R |
| Mississippi | 69,591 | 4,819 | 6.9 | 63,355 | 91.0 | 1,021 | 1.5 | 396 | 0.6 | — | | 58,536 | D |
| Missouri | 674,032 | 304,940 | 45.2 | 363,667 | 54.0 | 2,365 | 0.4 | 2,169 | 0.3 | 891 | 0.1 | 58,727 | D |
| Montana | 53,330 | 10,509 | 19.7 | 42,628 | 79.9 | — | | 193 | 0.4 | — | | 32,119 | D |
| Nebraska | 223,181 | 103,064 | 46.2 | 115,007 | 51.5 | 2,885 | 1.3 | 1,242 | 0.6 | 983 | 0.4 | 11,943 | D |
| Nevada | 10,286 | 1,938 | 18.8 | 8,348 | 81.2 | — | | — | | — | | 6,410 | D |
| New Hampshire | 83,670 | 57,444 | 68.7 | 21,650 | 25.9 | 3,520 | 4.2 | 779 | 0.9 | 277 | 0.3 | 35,794 | R |
| New Jersey | 371,014 | 221,367 | 59.7 | 133,675 | 36.0 | 6,373 | 1.7 | — | | 9,599 | 2.6 | 87,692 | R |
| New York | 1,423,876 | 819,838 | 57.6 | 551,369 | 38.7 | 18,950 | 1.3 | 16,052 | 1.1 | 17,667 | 1.2 | 268,469 | R |
| North Carolina | 331,337 | 155,122 | 46.8 | 174,408 | 52.6 | 578 | 0.2 | 635 | 0.2 | 594 | 0.2 | 19,286 | D |
| North Dakota | 47,391 | 26,335 | 55.6 | 20,686 | 43.6 | — | | 358 | 0.8 | 12 | | 5,649 | R |
| Ohio | 1,014,295 | 525,991 | 51.9 | 477,497 | 47.1 | 1,858 | 0.2 | 5,068 | 0.5 | 3,881 | 0.4 | 48,494 | R |
| Oregon | 97,335 | 48,700 | 50.0 | 46,739 | 48.0 | 977 | 1.0 | 919 | 0.9 | — | | 1,961 | R |
| Pennsylvania | 1,194,355 | 728,300 | 61.0 | 433,228 | 36.3 | 11,000 | 0.9 | 19,274 | 1.6 | 2,553 | 0.2 | 295,072 | R |
| Rhode Island | 54,785 | 37,437 | 68.3 | 14,459 | 26.4 | 1,166 | 2.1 | 1,160 | 2.1 | 563 | 1.0 | 22,978 | R |
| South Carolina | 68,938 | 9,313 | 13.5 | 58,801 | 85.3 | 824 | 1.2 | — | | — | | 49,488 | D |
| South Dakota | 82,937 | 41,040 | 49.5 | 41,225 | 49.7 | — | | 672 | 0.8 | — | | 185 | D |
| Tennessee | 320,903 | 148,683 | 46.3 | 167,168 | 52.1 | 1,953 | 0.6 | 3,099 | 1.0 | — | | 18,485 | D |
| Texas | 541,018 | 163,894 | 30.3 | 370,308 | 68.4 | 5,022 | 0.9 | 1,794 | 0.3 | — | | 206,414 | D |
| Utah | 78,098 | 13,491 | 17.3 | 64,607 | 82.7 | — | | — | | — | | 51,116 | D |
| Vermont | 63,568 | 51,127 | 80.4 | 10,367 | 16.3 | 1,341 | 2.1 | 733 | 1.2 | — | | 40,760 | R |
| Virginia | 294,674 | 135,379 | 45.9 | 154,708 | 52.5 | 2,129 | 0.7 | 2,350 | 0.8 | 108 | | 19,329 | D |
| Washington | 93,583 | 39,153 | 41.8 | 53,314 | 57.0 | — | | 968 | 1.0 | 148 | 0.2 | 14,161 | D |
| West Virginia | 201,757 | 105,379 | 52.2 | 94,480 | 46.8 | 678 | 0.3 | 1,220 | 0.6 | — | | 10,899 | R |
| Wisconsin | 447,409 | 268,135 | 59.9 | 165,523 | 37.0 | 4,584 | 1.0 | 7,507 | 1.7 | 1,660 | 0.4 | 102,612 | R |
| Wyoming | 21,067 | 10,072 | 47.8 | 10,862 | 51.6 | — | | 133 | 0.6 | — | | 790 | D |
| Totals | 13,935,738 | 7,108,480 | 51.0 | 6,511,495 | 46.7 | 133,435 | 1.0 | 125,072 | 0.9 | 57,256 | 0.4 | 596,985 | R |

1. For breakdown of "Other" vote, see minor candidate vote totals, p. 470.

# 1900 Presidential Election

| STATE | TOTAL VOTE | WILLIAM McKINLEY (Republican) | | WILLIAM J. BRYAN (Democrat) | | JOHN G. WOOLEY (Prohibition) | | EUGENE V. DEBS (Socialist) | | OTHER [1] | | PLURALITY | |
|---|---|---|---|---|---|---|---|---|---|---|---|---|---|
| | | Votes | % | Votes | % | Votes | % | Votes | % | Votes | % | | |
| Alabama | 159,692 | 55,612 | 34.8 | 97,129 | 60.8 | 2,763 | 1.7 | — | | 4,188 | 2.6 | 41,517 | D |
| Arkansas | 127,966 | 44,800 | 35.0 | 81,242 | 63.5 | 584 | 0.5 | — | | 1,340 | 1.0 | 36,442 | D |
| California | 302,318 | 164,755 | 54.5 | 124,985 | 41.3 | 5,024 | 1.7 | — | | 7,554 | 2.5 | 39,770 | R |
| Colorado | 220,895 | 92,701 | 42.0 | 122,705 | 55.5 | 3,790 | 1.7 | 686 | 0.3 | 1,013 | 0.5 | 30,004 | D |
| Connecticut | 180,195 | 102,572 | 56.9 | 74,014 | 41.1 | 1,617 | 0.9 | 1,029 | 0.6 | 963 | 0.5 | 28,558 | R |
| Delaware | 41,989 | 22,535 | 53.7 | 18,852 | 44.9 | 546 | 1.3 | 56 | 0.1 | — | | 3,683 | R |
| Florida | 39,649 | 7,355 | 18.6 | 28,273 | 71.3 | 2,244 | 5.7 | 634 | 1.6 | 1,143 | 2.9 | 20,918 | D |
| Georgia | 121,410 | 34,260 | 28.2 | 81,180 | 66.9 | 1,402 | 1.2 | — | | 4,568 | 3.8 | 46,920 | D |
| Idaho | 57,984 | 27,198 | 46.9 | 29,484 | 50.8 | 857 | 1.5 | — | | 445 | 0.8 | 2,286 | D |
| Illinois | 1,131,898 | 597,985 | 52.8 | 503,061 | 44.4 | 17,626 | 1.6 | 9,687 | 0.9 | 3,539 | 0.3 | 94,924 | R |
| Indiana | 664,094 | 336,063 | 50.6 | 309,584 | 46.6 | 13,718 | 2.1 | 2,374 | 0.4 | 2,355 | 0.4 | 26,479 | R |
| Iowa | 530,345 | 307,799 | 58.0 | 209,261 | 39.5 | 9,502 | 1.8 | 2,743 | 0.5 | 1,040 | 0.2 | 98,538 | R |
| Kansas [2] | 353,766 | 185,955 | 52.6 | 162,601 | 46.0 | 3,605 | 1.0 | 1,605 | 0.5 | — | | 23,354 | R |
| Kentucky | 468,265 | 227,132 | 48.5 | 235,126 | 50.2 | 2,890 | 0.6 | 766 | 0.2 | 2,351 | 0.5 | 7,994 | D |
| Louisiana | 67,906 | 14,234 | 21.0 | 53,668 | 79.0 | — | | — | | 4 | | 39,434 | D |
| Maine | 105,693 | 65,412 | 61.9 | 36,822 | 34.8 | 2,581 | 2.4 | 878 | 0.8 | — | | 28,590 | R |
| Maryland | 264,386 | 136,151 | 51.5 | 122,237 | 46.2 | 4,574 | 1.7 | 900 | 0.3 | 524 | 0.2 | 13,914 | R |
| Massachusetts | 414,804 | 238,866 | 57.6 | 156,997 | 37.8 | 6,202 | 1.5 | 9,607 | 2.3 | 3,132 | 0.8 | 81,869 | R |
| Michigan | 543,789 | 316,014 | 58.1 | 211,432 | 38.9 | 11,804 | 2.2 | 2,820 | 0.5 | 1,719 | 0.3 | 104,582 | R |
| Minnesota | 316,311 | 190,461 | 60.2 | 112,901 | 35.7 | 8,555 | 2.7 | 3,065 | 1.0 | 1,329 | 0.4 | 77,560 | R |
| Mississippi | 59,055 | 5,707 | 9.7 | 51,706 | 87.6 | — | | — | | 1,642 | 2.8 | 45,999 | D |
| Missouri | 683,658 | 314,092 | 45.9 | 351,922 | 51.5 | 5,965 | 0.9 | 6,139 | 0.9 | 5,540 | 0.8 | 37,830 | D |
| Montana | 63,856 | 25,409 | 39.8 | 37,311 | 58.4 | 306 | 0.5 | 711 | 1.1 | 119 | 0.2 | 11,902 | D |
| Nebraska | 241,430 | 121,835 | 50.5 | 114,013 | 47.2 | 3,655 | 1.5 | 823 | 0.3 | 1,104 | 0.5 | 7,822 | R |
| Nevada | 10,196 | 3,849 | 37.8 | 6,347 | 62.2 | — | | — | | — | | 2,498 | D |
| New Hampshire | 92,364 | 54,799 | 59.3 | 35,489 | 38.4 | 1,270 | 1.4 | 790 | 0.9 | 16 | | 19,310 | R |
| New Jersey | 401,050 | 221,707 | 55.3 | 164,808 | 41.1 | 7,183 | 1.8 | 4,609 | 1.1 | 2,743 | 0.7 | 56,899 | R |
| New York | 1,548,043 | 822,013 | 53.1 | 678,462 | 43.8 | 22,077 | 1.4 | 12,869 | 0.8 | 12,622 | 0.8 | 143,551 | R |
| North Carolina | 292,518 | 132,997 | 45.5 | 157,733 | 53.9 | 990 | 0.3 | — | | 798 | 0.3 | 24,736 | D |
| North Dakota | 57,783 | 35,898 | 62.1 | 20,524 | 35.5 | 735 | 1.3 | 517 | 0.9 | 109 | 0.2 | 15,374 | R |
| Ohio | 1,040,073 | 543,918 | 52.3 | 474,882 | 45.7 | 10,203 | 1.0 | 4,847 | 0.5 | 6,223 | 0.6 | 69,036 | R |
| Oregon | 83,251 | 46,172 | 55.5 | 32,810 | 39.4 | 2,536 | 3.0 | 1,464 | 1.8 | 269 | 0.3 | 13,362 | R |
| Pennsylvania | 1,173,210 | 712,665 | 60.7 | 424,232 | 36.2 | 27,908 | 2.4 | 4,831 | 0.4 | 3,574 | 0.3 | 288,433 | R |
| Rhode Island | 56,548 | 33,784 | 59.7 | 19,812 | 35.0 | 1,529 | 2.7 | — | | 1,423 | 2.5 | 13,972 | R |
| South Carolina | 50,698 | 3,525 | 7.0 | 47,173 | 93.0 | — | | — | | — | | 43,648 | D |
| South Dakota | 96,169 | 54,574 | 56.7 | 39,538 | 41.1 | 1,541 | 1.6 | 176 | 0.2 | 340 | 0.4 | 15,036 | R |
| Tennessee | 273,860 | 123,108 | 45.0 | 145,240 | 53.0 | 3,844 | 1.4 | 346 | 0.1 | 1,322 | 0.5 | 22,132 | D |
| Texas | 424,334 | 131,174 | 30.9 | 267,945 | 63.1 | 2,642 | 0.6 | 1,846 | 0.4 | 20,727 | 4.9 | 136,771 | D |
| Utah | 93,071 | 47,089 | 50.6 | 44,949 | 48.3 | 205 | 0.2 | 717 | 0.8 | 111 | 0.1 | 2,140 | R |
| Vermont | 56,212 | 42,569 | 75.7 | 12,849 | 22.9 | 383 | 0.7 | 39 | 0.1 | 372 | 0.7 | 29,720 | R |
| Virginia | 264,208 | 115,769 | 43.8 | 146,079 | 55.3 | 2,130 | 0.8 | — | | 230 | 0.1 | 30,310 | D |
| Washington | 107,523 | 57,455 | 53.4 | 44,833 | 41.7 | 2,363 | 2.2 | 2,006 | 1.9 | 866 | 0.8 | 12,622 | R |
| West Virginia | 220,796 | 119,829 | 54.3 | 98,807 | 44.8 | 1,628 | 0.7 | 286 | 0.1 | 246 | 0.1 | 21,022 | R |
| Wisconsin | 442,501 | 265,760 | 60.1 | 159,163 | 36.0 | 10,027 | 2.3 | 7,048 | 1.6 | 503 | 0.1 | 106,597 | R |
| Wyoming | 24,708 | 14,482 | 58.6 | 10,164 | 41.1 | — | | 21 | 0.1 | 41 | 0.2 | 4,318 | R |
| Totals | 13,970,470 | 7,218,039 | 51.7 | 6,358,345 | 45.5 | 209,004 | 1.5 | 86,935 | 0.6 | 98,147 | 0.7 | 859,694 | R |

1. For breakdown of "Other" vote, see minor candidate vote totals, p. 471.
2. Figures from Petersen, op. cit., p. 67.

# 1904 Presidential Election

| STATE | TOTAL VOTE | THEODORE ROOSEVELT (Republican) | | ALTON B. PARKER (Democrat) | | EUGENE V. DEBS (Socialist) | | SILAS C. SWALLOW (Prohibition) | | OTHER [1] | | PLURALITY | |
|---|---|---|---|---|---|---|---|---|---|---|---|---|---|
| | | Votes | % | Votes | % | Votes | % | Votes | % | Votes | % | | |
| Alabama | 108,785 | 22,472 | 20.7 | 79,797 | 73.4 | 853 | 0.8 | 612 | 0.6 | 5,051 | 4.6 | 57,325 | D |
| Arkansas | 116,328 | 46,760 | 40.2 | 64,434 | 55.4 | 1,816 | 1.6 | 992 | 0.9 | 2,326 | 2.0 | 17,674 | D |
| California | 331,768 | 205,226 | 61.9 | 89,294 | 26.9 | 29,535 | 8.9 | 7,380 | 2.2 | 333 | 0.1 | 115,932 | R |
| Colorado | 243,667 | 134,661 | 55.3 | 100,105 | 41.1 | 4,304 | 1.8 | 3,438 | 1.4 | 1,159 | 0.5 | 34,556 | R |
| Connecticut | 191,136 | 111,089 | 58.1 | 72,909 | 38.1 | 4,543 | 2.4 | 1,506 | 0.8 | 1,089 | 0.6 | 38,180 | R |
| Delaware | 43,856 | 23,705 | 54.1 | 19,347 | 44.1 | 146 | 0.3 | 607 | 1.4 | 51 | 0.1 | 4,358 | R |
| Florida | 38,705 | 8,314 | 21.5 | 26,449 | 68.3 | 2,337 | 6.0 | — | | 1,605 | 4.1 | 18,135 | D |
| Georgia | 130,986 | 24,004 | 18.3 | 83,466 | 63.7 | 196 | 0.1 | 685 | 0.5 | 22,635 | 17.3 | 59,462 | D |
| Idaho | 72,577 | 47,783 | 65.8 | 18,480 | 25.5 | 4,949 | 6.8 | 1,013 | 1.4 | 352 | 0.5 | 29,303 | R |
| Illinois | 1,076,495 | 632,645 | 58.8 | 327,606 | 30.4 | 69,225 | 6.4 | 34,770 | 3.2 | 12,249 | 1.1 | 305,039 | R |
| Indiana | 682,206 | 368,289 | 54.0 | 274,356 | 40.2 | 12,023 | 1.8 | 23,496 | 3.4 | 4,042 | 0.6 | 93,933 | R |
| Iowa | 485,703 | 307,907 | 63.4 | 149,141 | 30.7 | 14,847 | 3.1 | 11,601 | 2.4 | 2,207 | 0.5 | 158,766 | R |
| Kansas | 329,047 | 213,455 | 64.9 | 86,164 | 26.2 | 15,869 | 4.8 | 7,306 | 2.2 | 6,253 | 1.9 | 127,291 | R |
| Kentucky | 435,946 | 205,457 | 47.1 | 217,170 | 49.8 | 3,599 | 0.8 | 6,603 | 1.5 | 3,117 | 0.7 | 11,713 | D |
| Louisiana | 53,908 | 5,205 | 9.7 | 47,708 | 88.5 | 995 | 1.8 | — | | — | | 42,503 | D |
| Maine | 97,023 | 65,432 | 67.4 | 27,642 | 28.5 | 2,102 | 2.2 | 1,510 | 1.6 | 337 | 0.3 | 37,790 | R |
| Maryland | 224,229 | 109,497 | 48.8 | 109,446 | 48.8 | 2,247 | 1.0 | 3,034 | 1.4 | 5 | | 51 | R |
| Massachusetts | 445,100 | 257,813 | 57.9 | 165,746 | 37.2 | 13,604 | 3.1 | 4,279 | 1.0 | 3,658 | 0.8 | 92,067 | R |
| Michigan | 520,443 | 361,863 | 69.5 | 134,163 | 25.8 | 8,942 | 1.7 | 13,312 | 2.6 | 2,163 | 0.4 | 227,700 | R |
| Minnesota | 292,860 | 216,651 | 74.0 | 55,187 | 18.8 | 11,692 | 4.0 | 6,253 | 2.1 | 3,077 | 1.1 | 161,464 | R |
| Mississippi | 58,721 | 3,280 | 5.6 | 53,480 | 91.1 | 462 | 0.8 | — | | 1,499 | 2.6 | 50,200 | D |
| Missouri | 643,861 | 321,449 | 49.9 | 296,312 | 46.0 | 13,009 | 2.0 | 7,191 | 1.1 | 5,900 | 0.9 | 25,137 | R |
| Montana | 63,568 | 33,994 | 53.5 | 21,816 | 34.3 | 5,675 | 8.9 | 339 | 0.5 | 1,744 | 2.7 | 12,178 | R |
| Nebraska | 225,732 | 138,558 | 61.4 | 52,921 | 23.4 | 7,412 | 3.3 | 6,323 | 2.8 | 20,518 | 9.1 | 85,637 | R |
| Nevada | 12,115 | 6,864 | 56.7 | 3,982 | 32.9 | 925 | 7.6 | — | | 344 | 2.8 | 2,882 | R |
| New Hampshire | 90,151 | 54,157 | 60.1 | 34,071 | 37.8 | 1,090 | 1.2 | 750 | 0.8 | 83 | 0.1 | 20,086 | R |
| New Jersey | 432,247 | 245,164 | 56.7 | 164,566 | 38.1 | 9,587 | 2.2 | 6,845 | 1.6 | 6,085 | 1.4 | 80,598 | R |
| New York | 1,617,765 | 859,533 | 53.1 | 683,981 | 42.3 | 36,883 | 2.3 | 20,787 | 1.3 | 16,581 | 1.0 | 175,552 | R |
| North Carolina | 207,818 | 82,442 | 39.7 | 124,091 | 59.7 | 124 | 0.1 | 342 | 0.2 | 819 | 0.4 | 41,649 | D |
| North Dakota | 70,014 | 52,595 | 75.1 | 14,273 | 20.4 | 2,009 | 2.9 | 1,137 | 1.6 | — | | 38,322 | R |
| Ohio | 1,004,395 | 600,095 | 59.7 | 344,674 | 34.3 | 36,260 | 3.6 | 19,339 | 1.9 | 4,027 | 0.4 | 255,421 | R |
| Oregon | 89,656 | 60,309 | 67.3 | 17,327 | 19.3 | 7,479 | 8.3 | 3,795 | 4.2 | 746 | 0.8 | 42,982 | R |
| Pennsylvania | 1,236,738 | 840,949 | 68.0 | 337,998 | 27.3 | 21,863 | 1.8 | 33,717 | 2.7 | 2,211 | 0.2 | 502,951 | R |
| Rhode Island | 68,656 | 41,605 | 60.6 | 24,839 | 36.2 | 956 | 1.4 | 768 | 1.1 | 488 | 0.7 | 16,766 | R |
| South Carolina | 55,890 | 2,570 | 4.6 | 53,320 | 95.4 | — | | — | | — | | 50,750 | D |
| South Dakota | 101,395 | 72,083 | 71.1 | 21,969 | 21.7 | 3,138 | 3.1 | 2,965 | 2.9 | 1,240 | 1.2 | 50,114 | R |
| Tennessee | 242,750 | 105,363 | 43.4 | 131,653 | 54.2 | 1,354 | 0.6 | 1,889 | 0.8 | 2,491 | 1.0 | 26,290 | D |
| Texas | 233,609 | 51,307 | 22.0 | 167,088 | 71.5 | 2,788 | 1.2 | 3,933 | 1.7 | 8,493 | 3.6 | 115,781 | D |
| Utah | 101,626 | 62,446 | 61.4 | 33,413 | 32.9 | 5,767 | 5.7 | — | | — | | 29,033 | R |
| Vermont | 51,888 | 40,459 | 78.0 | 9,777 | 18.8 | 859 | 1.7 | 792 | 1.5 | 1 | | 30,682 | R |
| Virginia | 130,410 | 48,180 | 36.9 | 80,649 | 61.8 | 202 | 0.2 | 1,379 | 1.1 | — | | 32,469 | D |
| Washington | 145,151 | 101,540 | 70.0 | 28,098 | 19.4 | 10,023 | 6.9 | 3,229 | 2.2 | 2,261 | 1.6 | 73,442 | R |
| West Virginia | 239,986 | 132,620 | 55.3 | 100,855 | 42.0 | 1,573 | 0.7 | 4,599 | 1.9 | 339 | 0.1 | 31,765 | R |
| Wisconsin | 443,440 | 280,314 | 63.2 | 124,205 | 28.0 | 28,240 | 6.4 | 9,872 | 2.2 | 809 | 0.2 | 156,109 | R |
| Wyoming | 30,614 | 20,489 | 66.9 | 8,930 | 29.2 | 987 | 3.2 | 208 | 0.7 | — | | 11,559 | R |
| Totals | 13,518,964 | 7,626,593 | 56.4 | 5,082,898 | 37.6 | 402,489 | 3.0 | 258,596 | 1.9 | 148,388 | 1.1 | 2,543,695 | R |

1. For breakdown of "Other" vote, see minor candidate vote totals, p. 471.

# 1908 Presidential Election

| STATE | TOTAL VOTE | WILLIAM H. TAFT (Republican) | | WILLIAM J. BRYAN (Democrat) | | EUGENE V. DEBS (Socialist) | | EUGENE W. CHAFIN (Prohibition) | | OTHER [1] | | PLURALITY | |
|---|---|---|---|---|---|---|---|---|---|---|---|---|---|
| | | Votes | % | Votes | % | Votes | % | Votes | % | Votes | % | | |
| Alabama | 105,152 | 25,561 | 24.3 | 74,391 | 70.7 | 1,450 | 1.4 | 690 | 0.7 | 3,060 | 2.9 | 48,830 | D |
| Arkansas | 151,845 | 56,684 | 37.3 | 87,020 | 57.3 | 5,842 | 3.8 | 1,026 | 0.7 | 1,273 | 0.8 | 30,336 | D |
| California | 386,625 | 214,398 | 55.5 | 127,492 | 33.0 | 28,659 | 7.4 | 11,770 | 3.0 | 4,306 | 1.1 | 86,906 | R |
| Colorado | 263,858 | 123,693 | 46.9 | 126,644 | 48.0 | 7,960 | 3.0 | 5,559 | 2.1 | 2 | | 2,951 | D |
| Connecticut | 189,903 | 112,815 | 59.4 | 68,255 | 35.9 | 5,113 | 2.7 | 2,380 | 1.3 | 1,340 | 0.7 | 44,560 | R |
| Delaware | 48,007 | 25,014 | 52.1 | 22,055 | 45.9 | 239 | 0.5 | 670 | 1.4 | 29 | 0.1 | 2,959 | R |
| Florida | 49,360 | 10,654 | 21.6 | 31,104 | 63.0 | 3,747 | 7.6 | 1,356 | 2.7 | 2,499 | 5.1 | 20,450 | D |
| Georgia | 132,504 | 41,355 | 31.2 | 72,350 | 54.6 | 584 | 0.4 | 1,452 | 1.1 | 16,763 | 12.7 | 30,995 | D |
| Idaho | 97,293 | 52,621 | 54.1 | 36,162 | 37.2 | 6,400 | 6.6 | 1,986 | 2.0 | 124 | 0.1 | 16,459 | R |
| Illinois | 1,155,254 | 629,932 | 54.5 | 450,810 | 39.0 | 34,711 | 3.0 | 29,364 | 2.5 | 10,437 | 0.9 | 179,122 | R |
| Indiana | 721,117 | 348,993 | 48.4 | 338,262 | 46.9 | 13,476 | 1.9 | 18,036 | 2.5 | 2,350 | 0.3 | 10,731 | R |
| Iowa | 494,770 | 275,210 | 55.6 | 200,771 | 40.6 | 8,287 | 1.7 | 9,837 | 2.0 | 665 | 0.1 | 74,439 | R |
| Kansas | 376,043 | 197,316 | 52.5 | 161,209 | 42.9 | 12,420 | 3.3 | 5,030 | 1.3 | 68 | | 36,107 | R |
| Kentucky | 490,719 | 235,711 | 48.0 | 244,092 | 49.7 | 4,093 | 0.8 | 5,885 | 1.2 | 938 | 0.2 | 8,381 | D |
| Louisiana | 75,117 | 8,958 | 11.9 | 63,568 | 84.6 | 2,514 | 3.3 | — | | 77 | 0.1 | 54,610 | D |
| Maine | 106,335 | 66,987 | 63.0 | 35,403 | 33.3 | 1,758 | 1.7 | 1,487 | 1.4 | 700 | 0.7 | 31,584 | R |
| Maryland | 238,531 | 116,513 | 48.8 | 115,908 | 48.6 | 2,323 | 1.0 | 3,302 | 1.4 | 485 | 0.2 | 605 | R |
| Massachusetts | 456,905 | 265,966 | 58.2 | 155,533 | 34.0 | 10,778 | 2.4 | 4,373 | 1.0 | 20,255 | 4.4 | 110,433 | R |
| Michigan | 538,124 | 333,313 | 61.9 | 174,619 | 32.4 | 11,527 | 2.1 | 16,785 | 3.1 | 1,880 | 0.3 | 158,694 | R |
| Minnesota | 330,254 | 195,843 | 59.3 | 109,401 | 33.1 | 14,472 | 4.4 | 10,114 | 3.1 | 424 | 0.1 | 86,442 | R |
| Mississippi | 66,904 | 4,363 | 6.5 | 60,287 | 90.1 | 978 | 1.5 | — | | 1,276 | 1.9 | 55,924 | D |
| Missouri | 715,841 | 347,203 | 48.5 | 346,574 | 48.4 | 15,431 | 2.2 | 4,209 | 0.6 | 2,424 | 0.3 | 629 | R |
| Montana | 69,233 | 32,471 | 46.9 | 29,511 | 42.6 | 5,920 | 8.6 | 838 | 1.2 | 493 | 0.7 | 2,960 | R |
| Nebraska | 266,799 | 126,997 | 47.6 | 131,099 | 49.1 | 3,524 | 1.3 | 5,179 | 1.9 | — | | 4,102 | D |
| Nevada | 24,526 | 10,775 | 43.9 | 11,212 | 45.7 | 2,103 | 8.6 | — | | 436 | 1.8 | 437 | D |
| New Hampshire | 89,595 | 53,144 | 59.3 | 33,655 | 37.6 | 1,299 | 1.4 | 905 | 1.0 | 592 | 0.7 | 19,489 | R |
| New Jersey | 467,111 | 265,298 | 56.8 | 182,522 | 39.1 | 10,249 | 2.2 | 4,930 | 1.1 | 4,112 | 0.9 | 82,776 | R |
| New York | 1,638,350 | 870,070 | 53.1 | 667,468 | 40.7 | 38,451 | 2.3 | 22,667 | 1.4 | 39,694 | 2.4 | 202,602 | R |
| North Carolina | 252,554 | 114,887 | 45.5 | 136,928 | 54.2 | 372 | 0.1 | 354 | 0.1 | 13 | | 22,041 | D |
| North Dakota | 94,524 | 57,680 | 61.0 | 32,884 | 34.8 | 2,421 | 2.6 | 1,496 | 1.6 | 43 | | 24,796 | R |
| Ohio | 1,121,552 | 572,312 | 51.0 | 502,721 | 44.8 | 33,795 | 3.0 | 11,402 | 1.0 | 1,322 | 0.1 | 69,591 | R |
| Oklahoma | 254,260 | 110,473 | 43.4 | 122,362 | 48.1 | 21,425 | 8.4 | — | | — | | 11,889 | D |
| Oregon | 110,539 | 62,454 | 56.5 | 37,792 | 34.2 | 7,322 | 6.6 | 2,682 | 2.4 | 289 | 0.3 | 24,662 | R |
| Pennvylvania | 1,267,450 | 745,779 | 58.8 | 448,782 | 35.4 | 33,914 | 2.7 | 36,694 | 2.9 | 2,281 | 0.2 | 296,997 | R |
| Rhode Island | 72,317 | 43,942 | 60.8 | 24,706 | 34.2 | 1,365 | 1.9 | 1,016 | 1.4 | 1,288 | 1.8 | 19,236 | R |
| South Carolina | 66,379 | 3,945 | 5.9 | 62,288 | 93.8 | 100 | 0.2 | — | | 46 | 0.1 | 58,343 | D |
| South Dakota | 114,775 | 67,536 | 58.8 | 40,266 | 35.1 | 2,846 | 2.5 | 4,039 | 3.5 | 88 | 0.1 | 27,270 | R |
| Tennessee | 257,180 | 117,977 | 45.9 | 135,608 | 52.7 | 1,870 | 0.7 | 301 | 0.1 | 1,424 | 0.6 | 17,631 | D |
| Texas | 292,913 | 65,605 | 22.4 | 216,662 | 74.0 | 7,779 | 2.7 | 1,626 | 0.6 | 1,241 | 0.4 | 151,057 | D |
| Utah | 108,757 | 61,165 | 56.2 | 42,610 | 39.2 | 4,890 | 4.5 | — | | 92 | 0.1 | 18,555 | R |
| Vermont | 52,680 | 39,552 | 75.1 | 11,496 | 21.8 | — | | 799 | 1.5 | 833 | 1.6 | 28,056 | R |
| Virginia | 137,065 | 52,572 | 38.4 | 82,946 | 60.5 | 255 | 0.2 | 1,111 | 0.8 | 181 | 0.1 | 30,374 | D |
| Washington | 183,570 | 106,062 | 57.8 | 58,383 | 31.8 | 14,177 | 7.7 | 4,700 | 2.6 | 248 | 0.1 | 47,679 | R |
| West Virginia | 258,098 | 137,869 | 53.4 | 111,410 | 43.2 | 3,679 | 1.4 | 5,140 | 2.0 | — | | 26,459 | R |
| Wisconsin | 454,438 | 247,744 | 54.5 | 166,662 | 36.7 | 28,147 | 6.2 | 11,565 | 2.5 | 320 | 0.1 | 81,082 | R |
| Wyoming | 37,608 | 20,846 | 55.4 | 14,918 | 39.7 | 1,715 | 4.6 | 66 | 0.2 | 63 | 0.2 | 5,928 | R |
| Totals | 14,882,734 | 7,676,258 | 51.6 | 6,406,801 | 43.0 | 420,380 | 2.8 | 252,821 | 1.7 | 126,474 | 0.8 | 1,269,457 | R |

1. For breakdown of "Other" vote, see minor candidate vote totals, p. 471.

# 1912 Presidential Election

| STATE | TOTAL VOTE | WOODROW WILSON (Democrat) | | THEODORE ROOSEVELT (Progressive) | | WILLIAM H. TAFT (Republican) | | EUGENE V. DEBS (Socialist) | | OTHER [1] | | PLURALITY |
|---|---|---|---|---|---|---|---|---|---|---|---|---|
| | | Votes | % | Votes | % | Votes | % | Votes | % | Votes | % | |
| Alabama | 117,959 | 82,438 | 69.9 | 22,680 | 19.2 | 9,807 | 8.3 | 3,029 | 2.6 | 5 | | 59,758 D |
| Arizona | 23,687 | 10,324 | 43.6 | 6,949 | 29.3 | 2,986 | 12.6 | 3,163 | 13.4 | 265 | 1.1 | 3,375 D |
| Arkansas | 125,104 | 68,814 | 55.0 | 21,644 | 17.3 | 25,585 | 20.5 | 8,153 | 6.5 | 908 | 0.7 | 43,229 D |
| California | 677,877 | 283,436 | 41.8 | 283,610 | 41.8 | 3,847 | 0.6 | 79,201 | 11.7 | 27,783 | 4.1 | 174 PR |
| Colorado | 265,954 | 113,912 | 42.8 | 71,752 | 27.0 | 58,386 | 22.0 | 16,366 | 6.2 | 5,538 | 2.1 | 42,160 D |
| Connecticut | 190,404 | 74,561 | 39.2 | 34,129 | 17.9 | 68,324 | 35.9 | 10,056 | 5.3 | 3,334 | 1.8 | 6,237 D |
| Delaware | 48,690 | 22,631 | 46.5 | 8,886 | 18.3 | 15,997 | 32.9 | 556 | 1.1 | 620 | 1.3 | 6,634 D |
| Florida | 50,837 | 35,343 | 69.5 | 4,555 | 9.0 | 4,279 | 8.4 | 4,806 | 9.5 | 1,854 | 3.6 | 30,788 D |
| Georgia | 121,470 | 93,087 | 76.6 | 21,985 | 18.1 | 5,191 | 4.3 | 1,058 | 0.9 | 149 | 0.1 | 71,102 D |
| Idaho | 105,754 | 33,921 | 32.1 | 25,527 | 24.1 | 32,810 | 31.0 | 11,960 | 11.3 | 1,536 | 1.5 | 1,111 D |
| Illinois | 1,146,173 | 405,048 | 35.3 | 386,478 | 33.7 | 253,593 | 22.1 | 81,278 | 7.1 | 19,776 | 1.7 | 18,570 D |
| Indiana | 654,474 | 281,890 | 43.1 | 162,007 | 24.8 | 151,267 | 23.1 | 36,931 | 5.6 | 22,379 | 3.4 | 119,883 D |
| Iowa | 492,353 | 185,322 | 37.6 | 161,819 | 32.9 | 119,805 | 24.3 | 16,967 | 3.4 | 8,440 | 1.7 | 23,503 D |
| Kansas | 365,560 | 143,663 | 39.3 | 120,210 | 32.9 | 74,845 | 20.5 | 26,779 | 7.3 | 63 | | 23,453 D |
| Kentucky | 452,714 | 219,484 | 48.5 | 101,766 | 22.5 | 115,510 | 25.5 | 11,646 | 2.6 | 4,308 | 1.0 | 103,974 D |
| Louisiana | 79,248 | 60,871 | 76.8 | 9,283 | 11.7 | 3,833 | 4.8 | 5,261 | 6.6 | — | | 51,588 D |
| Maine | 129,641 | 51,113 | 39.4 | 48,495 | 37.4 | 26,545 | 20.5 | 2,541 | 2.0 | 947 | 0.7 | 2,618 D |
| Maryland | 231,981 | 112,674 | 48.6 | 57,789 | 24.9 | 54,956 | 23.7 | 3,996 | 1.7 | 2,566 | 1.1 | 54,885 D |
| Massachusetts | 488,056 | 173,408 | 35.5 | 142,228 | 29.1 | 155,948 | 32.0 | 12,616 | 2.6 | 3,856 | 0.8 | 17,460 D |
| Michigan | 547,971 | 150,201 | 27.4 | 213,243 | 38.9 | 151,434 | 27.6 | 23,060 | 4.2 | 10,033 | 1.8 | 61,809 PR |
| Minnesota | 334,219 | 106,426 | 31.8 | 125,856 | 37.7 | 64,334 | 19.2 | 27,505 | 8.2 | 10,098 | 3.0 | 19,430 PR |
| Mississippi | 64,483 | 57,324 | 88.9 | 3,549 | 5.5 | 1,560 | 2.4 | 2,050 | 3.2 | — | | 53,775 D |
| Missouri | 698,566 | 330,746 | 47.3 | 124,375 | 17.8 | 207,821 | 29.7 | 28,466 | 4.1 | 7,158 | 1.0 | 122,925 D |
| Montana | 80,256 | 28,129 | 35.0 | 22,709 | 28.3 | 18,575 | 23.1 | 10,811 | 13.5 | 32 | | 5,420 D |
| Nebraska | 249,483 | 109,008 | 43.7 | 72,681 | 29.1 | 54,226 | 21.7 | 10,185 | 4.1 | 3,383 | 1.4 | 36,327 D |
| Nevada | 20,115 | 7,986 | 39.7 | 5,620 | 27.9 | 3,196 | 15.9 | 3,313 | 16.5 | — | | 2,366 D |
| New Hampshire | 87,961 | 34,724 | 39.5 | 17,794 | 20.2 | 32,927 | 37.4 | 1,981 | 2.3 | 535 | 0.6 | 1,797 D |
| New Jersey | 433,663 | 178,638 | 41.2 | 145,679 | 33.6 | 89,066 | 20.5 | 15,948 | 3.7 | 4,332 | 1.0 | 32,959 D |
| New Mexico | 48,807 | 20,437 | 41.9 | 8,347 | 17.1 | 17,164 | 35.2 | 2,859 | 5.9 | — | | 3,273 D |
| New York | 1,588,315 | 655,573 | 41.3 | 390,093 | 24.6 | 455,487 | 28.7 | 63,434 | 4.0 | 23,728 | 1.5 | 200,086 D |
| North Carolina | 243,776 | 144,407 | 59.2 | 69,135 | 28.4 | 29,129 | 11.9 | 987 | 0.4 | 118 | | 75,272 D |
| North Dakota | 86,474 | 29,549 | 34.2 | 25,726 | 29.7 | 22,990 | 26.6 | 6,966 | 8.1 | 1,243 | 1.4 | 3,823 D |
| Ohio | 1,037,114 | 424,834 | 41.0 | 229,807 | 22.2 | 278,168 | 26.8 | 90,164 | 8.7 | 14,141 | 1.4 | 146,666 D |
| Oklahoma | 253,694 | 119,143 | 47.0 | — | | 90,726 | 35.8 | 41,630 | 16.4 | 2,195 | 0.9 | 28,417 D |
| Oregon | 137,040 | 47,064 | 34.3 | 37,600 | 27.4 | 34,673 | 25.3 | 13,343 | 9.7 | 4,360 | 3.2 | 9,464 D |
| Pennsylvania | 1,217,736 | 395,637 | 32.5 | 444,894 | 36.5 | 273,360 | 22.4 | 83,614 | 6.9 | 20,231 | 1.7 | 49,257 PR |
| Rhode Island | 77,894 | 30,412 | 39.0 | 16,878 | 21.7 | 27,703 | 35.6 | 2,049 | 2.6 | 852 | 1.1 | 2,709 D |
| South Carolina | 50,403 | 48,355 | 95.9 | 1,293 | 2.6 | 536 | 1.1 | 164 | 0.3 | 55 | 0.1 | 47,062 D |
| South Dakota | 116,327 | 48,942 | 42.1 | 58,811 | 50.6 | — | | 4,664 | 4.0 | 3,910 | 3.4 | 9,869 PR |
| Tennessee | 251,933 | 133,021 | 52.8 | 54,041 | 21.5 | 60,475 | 24.0 | 3,564 | 1.4 | 832 | 0.3 | 72,546 D |
| Texas | 300,961 | 218,921 | 72.7 | 26,715 | 8.9 | 28,310 | 9.4 | 24,884 | 8.3 | 2,131 | 0.7 | 190,611 D |
| Utah | 112,272 | 36,576 | 32.6 | 24,174 | 21.5 | 42,013 | 37.4 | 8,999 | 8.0 | 510 | 0.5 | 5,437 R |
| Vermont | 62,804 | 15,350 | 24.4 | 22,129 | 35.2 | 23,303 | 37.1 | 928 | 1.5 | 1,094 | 1.7 | 1,174 R |
| Virginia | 136,975 | 90,332 | 65.9 | 21,776 | 15.9 | 23,288 | 17.0 | 820 | 0.6 | 759 | 0.6 | 67,044 D |
| Washington | 322,799 | 86,840 | 26.9 | 113,698 | 35.2 | 70,445 | 21.8 | 40,134 | 12.4 | 11,682 | 3.6 | 26,858 PR |
| West Virginia | 268,728 | 113,097 | 42.1 | 79,112 | 29.4 | 56,754 | 21.1 | 15,248 | 5.7 | 4,517 | 1.7 | 33,985 D |
| Wisconsin | 399,975 | 164,230 | 41.1 | 62,448 | 15.6 | 130,596 | 32.7 | 33,476 | 8.4 | 9,225 | 2.3 | 33,634 D |
| Wyoming | 42,283 | 15,310 | 36.2 | 9,232 | 21.8 | 14,560 | 34.4 | 2,760 | 6.5 | 421 | 1.0 | 750 D |
| **Totals** | **15,040,963** | **6,293,152** | **41.8** | **4,119,207** | **27.4** | **3,486,333** | **23.2** | **900,369** | **6.0** | **241,902** | **1.6** | **2,173,945 D** |

1. For breakdown of "Other" vote, see minor candidate vote totals, p. 471.

# 1916 Presidential Election

| STATE | TOTAL VOTE | WOODROW WILSON (Democrat) | | CHARLES E. HUGHES (Republican) | | ALLAN L. BENSON (Socialist) | | J. FRANK HANLY (Prohibition) | | OTHER [1] | | PLURALITY | |
|---|---|---|---|---|---|---|---|---|---|---|---|---|---|
| | | Votes | % | Votes | % | Votes | % | Votes | % | Votes | % | | |
| Alabama | 130,435 | 99,116 | 76.0 | 28,662 | 22.0 | 1,916 | 1.5 | 741 | 0.6 | — | | 70,454 | D |
| Arizona | 58,019 | 33,170 | 57.2 | 20,522 | 35.4 | 3,174 | 5.5 | 1,153 | 2.0 | — | | 12,648 | D |
| Arkansas | 170,104 | 112,211 | 66.0 | 48,879 | 28.7 | 6,999 | 4.1 | 2,015 | 1.2 | — | | 63,332 | D |
| California | 999,250 | 465,936 | 46.6 | 462,516 | 46.3 | 42,898 | 4.3 | 27,713 | 2.8 | 187 | | 3,420 | D |
| Colorado | 292,037 | 177,496 | 60.8 | 101,388 | 34.7 | 9,951 | 3.4 | 2,793 | 1.0 | 409 | 0.1 | 76,108 | D |
| Connecticut | 213,874 | 99,786 | 46.7 | 106,514 | 49.8 | 5,179 | 2.4 | 1,789 | 0.8 | 606 | 0.3 | 6,728 | R |
| Delaware | 51,810 | 24,753 | 47.8 | 26,011 | 50.2 | 480 | 0.9 | 566 | 1.1 | — | | 1,258 | R |
| Florida | 80,734 | 55,984 | 69.3 | 14,611 | 18.1 | 5,353 | 6.6 | 4,786 | 5.9 | — | | 41,373 | D |
| Georgia | 160,681 | 127,754 | 79.5 | 11,294 | 7.0 | 941 | 0.6 | — | | 20,692 | 12.9 | 107,062 | D [2] |
| Idaho | 134,615 | 70,054 | 52.0 | 55,368 | 41.1 | 8,066 | 6.0 | 1,127 | 0.8 | — | | 14,686 | D |
| Illinois | 2,192,707 | 950,229 | 43.3 | 1,152,549 | 52.6 | 61,394 | 2.8 | 26,047 | 1.2 | 2,488 | 0.1 | 202,320 | R |
| Indiana | 718,853 | 334,063 | 46.5 | 341,005 | 47.4 | 21,860 | 3.0 | 16,368 | 2.3 | 5,557 | 0.8 | 6,942 | R |
| Iowa | 518,738 | 221,699 | 42.7 | 280,439 | 54.1 | 10,976 | 2.1 | 3,371 | 0.6 | 2,253 | 0.4 | 58,740 | R |
| Kansas | 629,813 | 314,588 | 49.9 | 277,658 | 44.1 | 24,685 | 3.9 | 12,882 | 2.0 | — | | 36,930 | D |
| Kentucky | 520,078 | 269,990 | 51.9 | 241,854 | 46.5 | 4,734 | 0.9 | 3,039 | 0.6 | 461 | 0.1 | 28,136 | D |
| Louisiana | 92,974 | 79,875 | 85.9 | 6,466 | 7.0 | 284 | 0.3 | — | | 6,349 | 6.8 | 73,409 | D |
| Maine | 136,314 | 64,033 | 47.0 | 69,508 | 51.0 | 2,177 | 1.6 | 596 | 0.4 | — | | 5,475 | R |
| Maryland | 262,039 | 138,359 | 52.8 | 117,347 | 44.8 | 2,674 | 1.0 | 2,903 | 1.1 | 756 | 0.3 | 21,012 | D |
| Massachusetts | 531,822 | 247,885 | 46.6 | 268,784 | 50.5 | 11,058 | 2.1 | 2,993 | 0.6 | 1,102 | 0.2 | 20,899 | R |
| Michigan | 646,873 | 283,993 | 43.9 | 337,952 | 52.2 | 16,012 | 2.5 | 8,085 | 1.2 | 831 | 0.1 | 53,959 | R |
| Minnesota | 387,367 | 179,155 | 46.2 | 179,544 | 46.3 | 20,117 | 5.2 | 7,793 | 2.0 | 758 | 0.2 | 389 | R |
| Mississippi | 86,679 | 80,422 | 92.8 | 4,253 | 4.9 | 1,484 | 1.7 | — | | 520 | 0.6 | 76,169 | D |
| Missouri | 786,773 | 398,032 | 50.6 | 369,339 | 46.9 | 14,612 | 1.9 | 3,887 | 0.5 | 903 | 0.1 | 28,693 | D |
| Montana | 178,009 | 101,104 | 56.8 | 66,933 | 37.6 | 9,634 | 5.4 | — | | 338 | 0.2 | 34,171 | D |
| Nebraska | 287,315 | 158,827 | 55.3 | 117,771 | 41.0 | 7,141 | 2.5 | 2,952 | 1.0 | 624 | 0.2 | 41,056 | D |
| Nevada | 33,314 | 17,776 | 53.4 | 12,127 | 36.4 | 3,065 | 9.2 | 346 | 1.0 | — | | 5,649 | D |
| New Hampshire | 89,127 | 43,781 | 49.1 | 43,725 | 49.1 | 1,318 | 1.5 | 303 | 0.3 | — | | 56 | D |
| New Jersey | 494,442 | 211,018 | 42.7 | 268,982 | 54.4 | 10,405 | 2.1 | 3,182 | 0.6 | 855 | 0.2. | 57,964 | R |
| New Mexico | 66,879 | 33,693 | 50.4 | 31,097 | 46.5 | 1,977 | 3.0 | 112 | 0.2 | — | | 2,596 | D |
| New York | 1,706,305 | 759,426 | 44.5 | 879,238 | 51.5 | 45,944 | 2.7 | 19,031 | 1.1 | 2,666 | 0.2 | 119,812 | R |
| North Carolina | 289,837 | 168,383 | 58.1 | 120,890 | 41.7 | 509 | 0.2 | 55 | | — | | 47,493 | D |
| North Dakota | 115,390 | 55,206 | 47.8 | 53,471 | 46.3 | 5,716 | 5.0 | 997 | 0.9 | — | | 1,735 | D |
| Ohio | 1,165,091 | 604,161 | 51.9 | 514,753 | 44.2 | 38,092 | 3.3 | 8,085 | 0.7 | — | | 89,408 | D |
| Oklahoma | 292,327 | 148,123 | 50.7 | 97,233 | 33.3 | 45,091 | 15.4 | 1,646 | 0.6 | 234 | 0.1 | 50,890 | D |
| Oregon | 261,650 | 120,087 | 45.9 | 126,813 | 48.5 | 9,711 | 3.7 | 4,729 | 1.8 | 310 | 0.1 | 6,726 | R |
| Pennsylvania | 1,297,189 | 521,784 | 40.2 | 703,823 | 54.3 | 42,638 | 3.3 | 28,525 | 2.2 | 419 | | 182,039 | R |
| Rhode Island | 87,816 | 40,394 | 46.0 | 44,858 | 51.1 | 1,914 | 2.2 | 470 | 0.5 | 180 | 0.2 | 4,464 | R |
| South Carolina | 63,950 | 61,845 | 96.7 | 1,550 | 2.4 | 135 | 0.2 | — | | 420 | 0.7 | 60,295 | D |
| South Dakota | 128,942 | 59,191 | 45.9 | 64,217 | 49.8 | 3,760 | 2.9 | 1,774 | 1.4 | — | | 5,026 | R |
| Tennessee | 272,190 | 153,280 | 56.3 | 116,223 | 42.7 | 2,542 | 0.9 | 145 | 0.1 | — | | 37,057 | D |
| Texas | 373,310 | 287,415 | 77.0 | 64,999 | 17.4 | 18,960 | 5.1 | 1,936 | 0.5 | — | | 222,416 | D |
| Utah | 143,145 | 84,145 | 58.8 | 54,137 | 37.8 | 4,460 | 3.1 | 149 | 0.1 | 254 | 0.2 | 30,008 | D |
| Vermont | 64,475 | 22,708 | 35.2 | 40,250 | 62.4 | 798 | 1.2 | 709 | 1.1 | 10 | | 17,542 | R |
| Virginia | 152,025 | 101,840 | 67.0 | 48,384 | 31.8 | 1,056 | 0.7 | 678 | 0.4 | 67 | | 53,456 | D |
| Washington | 380,994 | 183,388 | 48.1 | 167,208 | 43.9 | 22,800 | 6.0 | 6,868 | 1.8 | 730 | 0.2 | 16,180 | D |
| West Virginia | 289,671 | 140,403 | 48.5 | 143,124 | 49.4 | 6,144 | 2.1 | — | | — | | 2,721 | R |
| Wisconsin | 447,134 | 191,363 | 42.8 | 220,822 | 49.4 | 27,631 | 6.2 | 7,318 | 1.6 | — | | 29,459 | R |
| Wyoming | 51,906 | 28,376 | 54.7 | 21,698 | 41.8 | 1,459 | 2.8 | 373 | 0.7 | — | | 6,678 | D |
| **Totals** | **18,535,022** | **9,126,300** | **49.2** | **8,546,789** | **46.1** | **589,924** | **3.2** | **221,030** | **1.2** | **50,979** | **0.3** | **579,511** | **D** |

1. For breakdown of "Other" vote, see minor candidate vote totals, p. 471.
2. Plurality of 107,062 votes is calculated on the basis of 20,692 votes cast for the Progressive Party.

# 1920 Presidential Election

| STATE | TOTAL VOTE | WARREN G. HARDING (Republican) | | JAMES M. COX (Democrat) | | EUGENE V. DEBS (Socialist) | | PARLEY P. CHRISTENSEN (Farmer-Labor) | | OTHER [1] | | PLURALITY | |
|---|---|---|---|---|---|---|---|---|---|---|---|---|---|
| | | Votes | % | Votes | % | Votes | % | Votes | % | Votes | % | | |
| Alabama | 233,951 | 74,719 | 31.9 | 156,064 | 66.7 | 2,402 | 1.0 | — | | 766 | 0.3 | 81,345 | D |
| Arizona | 66,803 | 37,016 | 55.4 | 29,546 | 44.2 | 222 | 0.3 | 15 | | 4 | | 7,470 | R |
| Arkansas | 183,871 | 72,316 | 39.3 | 106,427 | 57.9 | 5,128 | 2.8 | — | | — | | 34,111 | D |
| California | 943,463 | 624,992 | 66.2 | 229,191 | 24.3 | 64,076 | 6.8 | — | | 25,204 | 2.7 | 395,801 | R |
| Colorado | 292,053 | 173,248 | 59.3 | 104,936 | 35.9 | 8,046 | 2.8 | 3,016 | 1.0 | 2,807 | 1.0 | 68,312 | R |
| Connecticut | 365,518 | 229,238 | 62.7 | 120,721 | 33.0 | 10,350 | 2.8 | 1,947 | 0.5 | 3,262 | 0.9 | 108,517 | R |
| Delaware | 94,875 | 52,858 | 55.7 | 39,911 | 42.1 | 988 | 1.0 | 93 | 0.1 | 1,025 | 1.1 | 12,947 | R |
| Florida | 145,684 | 44,853 | 30.8 | 90,515 | 62.1 | 5,189 | 3.6 | — | | 5,127 | 3.5 | 45,662 | D |
| Georgia | 149,558 | 42,981 | 28.7 | 106,112 | 71.0 | 465 | 0.3 | — | | — | | 63,131 | D |
| Idaho | 138,281 | 91,351 | 66.1 | 46,930 | 33.9 | — | | — | | — | | 44,421 | R |
| Illinois | 2,094,714 | 1,420,480 | 67.8 | 534,395 | 25.5 | 74,747 | 3.6 | 49,630 | 2.4 | 15,462 | 0.7 | 886,085 | R |
| Indiana | 1,262,974 | 696,370 | 55.1 | 511,364 | 40.5 | 24,713 | 2.0 | 16,499 | 1.3 | 14,028 | 1.1 | 185,006 | R |
| Iowa | 894,959 | 634,674 | 70.9 | 227,804 | 25.5 | 16,981 | 1.9 | 10,321 | 1.2 | 5,179 | 0.6 | 406,870 | R |
| Kansas | 570,243 | 369,268 | 64.8 | 185,464 | 32.5 | 15,511 | 2.7 | — | | — | | 183,804 | R |
| Kentucky | 918,636 | 452,480 | 49.3 | 456,497 | 49.7 | 6,409 | 0.7 | — | | 3,250 | 0.4 | 4,017 | D |
| Louisiana | 126,397 | 38,539 | 30.5 | 87,519 | 69.2 | — | | — | | 339 | 0.3 | 48,980 | D |
| Maine | 197,840 | 136,355 | 68.9 | 58,961 | 29.8 | 2,214 | 1.1 | — | | 310 | 0.2 | 77,394 | R |
| Maryland | 428,443 | 236,117 | 55.1 | 180,626 | 42.2 | 8,876 | 2.1 | 1,645 | 0.4 | 1,179 | 0.3 | 55,491 | R |
| Massachusetts | 993,718 | 681,153 | 68.5 | 276,691 | 27.8 | 32,267 | 3.2 | — | | 3,607 | 0.4 | 404,462 | R |
| Michigan | 1,048,411 | 762,865 | 72.8 | 233,450 | 22.3 | 28,947 | 2.8 | 10,480 | 1.0 | 12,669 | 1.2 | 529,415 | R |
| Minnesota | 735,838 | 519,421 | 70.6 | 142,994 | 19.4 | 56,106 | 7.6 | — | | 17,317 | 2.4 | 376,427 | R |
| Mississippi | 82,351 | 11,576 | 14.1 | 69,136 | 84.0 | 1,639 | 2.0 | — | | — | | 57,560 | D |
| Missouri | 1,332,140 | 727,252 | 54.6 | 574,699 | 43.1 | 20,342 | 1.5 | 3,108 | 0.2 | 6,739 | 0.5 | 152,553 | R |
| Montana | 179,006 | 109,430 | 61.1 | 57,372 | 32.1 | — | | 12,204 | 6.8 | — | | 52,058 | R |
| Nebraska | 382,743 | 247,498 | 64.7 | 119,608 | 31.3 | 9,600 | 2.5 | — | | 6,037 | 1.6 | 127,890 | R |
| Nevada | 27,194 | 15,479 | 56.9 | 9,851 | 36.2 | 1,864 | 6.9 | — | | — | | 5,628 | R |
| New Hampshire | 159,092 | 95,196 | 59.8 | 62,662 | 39.4 | 1,234 | 0.8 | — | | — | | 32,534 | R |
| New Jersey | 910,251 | 615,333 | 67.6 | 258,761 | 28.4 | 27,385 | 3.0 | 2,264 | 0.2 | 6,508 | 0.7 | 356,572 | R |
| New Mexico | 105,412 | 57,634 | 54.7 | 46,668 | 44.3 | 2 | | 1,104 | 1.0 | 4 | | 10,966 | R |
| New York | 2,898,513 | 1,871,167 | 64.6 | 781,238 | 27.0 | 203,201 | 7.0 | 18,413 | 0.6 | 24,494 | 0.8 | 1,089,929 | R |
| North Carolina | 538,649 | 232,819 | 43.2 | 305,367 | 56.7 | 446 | 0.1 | — | | 17 | | 72,548 | D |
| North Dakota | 205,786 | 160,082 | 77.8 | 37,422 | 18.2 | 8,282 | 4.0 | — | | — | | 122,660 | R |
| Ohio | 2,021,653 | 1,182,022 | 58.5 | 780,037 | 38.6 | 57,147 | 2.8 | — | | 2,447 | 0.1 | 401,985 | R |
| Oklahoma | 485,678 | 243,840 | 50.2 | 216,122 | 44.5 | 25,716 | 5.3 | — | | — | | 27,718 | R |
| Oregon | 238,522 | 143,592 | 60.2 | 80,019 | 33.5 | 9,801 | 4.1 | — | | 5,110 | 2.1 | 63,573 | R |
| Pennsylvania | 1,851,248 | 1,218,215 | 65.8 | 503,202 | 27.2 | 70,021 | 3.8 | 15,642 | 0.8 | 44,168 | 2.4 | 715,013 | R |
| Rhode Island | 167,981 | 107,463 | 64.0 | 55,062 | 32.8 | 4,351 | 2.6 | — | | 1,105 | 0.7 | 52,401 | R |
| South Carolina | 66,808 | 2,610 | 3.9 | 64,170 | 96.1 | 28 | | — | | — | | 61,560 | D |
| South Dakota | 182,237 | 110,692 | 60.7 | 35,938 | 19.7 | — | | 34,707 | 19.0 | 900 | 0.5 | 74,754 | R |
| Tennessee | 428,036 | 219,229 | 51.2 | 206,558 | 48.3 | 2,249 | 0.5 | — | | — | | 12,671 | R |
| Texas | 486,109 | 114,658 | 23.6 | 287,920 | 59.2 | 8,124 | 1.7 | — | | 75,407 | 15.5 | 173,262 | D |
| Utah | 145,828 | 81,555 | 55.9 | 56,639 | 38.8 | 3,159 | 2.2 | 4,475 | 3.1 | — | | 24,916 | R |
| Vermont | 89,961 | 68,212 | 75.8 | 20,919 | 23.3 | — | | — | | 830 | 0.9 | 47,293 | R |
| Virginia | 231,000 | 87,456 | 37.9 | 141,670 | 61.3 | 808 | 0.3 | 240 | 0.1 | 826 | 0.4 | 54,214 | D |
| Washington | 398,715 | 223,137 | 56.0 | 84,298 | 21.1 | 8,913 | 2.2 | 77,246 | 19.4 | 5,121 | 1.3 | 138,839 | R |
| West Virginia | 509,936 | 282,007 | 55.3 | 220,785 | 43.3 | 5,618 | 1.1 | — | | 1,526 | 0.3 | 61,222 | R |
| Wisconsin | 701,281 | 498,576 | 71.1 | 113,422 | 16.2 | 80,635 | 11.5 | — | | 8,648 | 1.2 | 385,154 | R |
| Wyoming | 56,253 | 35,091 | 62.4 | 17,429 | 31.0 | 1,288 | 2.3 | 2,180 | 3.9 | 265 | 0.5 | 17,662 | R |
| Totals | 26,768,613 | 16,153,115 | 60.3 | 9,133,092 | 34.1 | 915,490 | 3.4 | 265,229 | 1.0 | 301,687 | 1.1 | 7,020,023 | R |

1. For breakdown of "Other" vote, see minor candidate vote totals, p. 472.

# 1924 Presidential Election

| STATE | TOTAL VOTE | CALVIN COOLIDGE (Republican) | | JOHN W. DAVIS (Democrat) | | ROBERT M. LA FOLLETTE (Progressive) | | HERMAN P. FARIS (Prohibition) | | OTHER [1] | | PLURALITY | |
|---|---|---|---|---|---|---|---|---|---|---|---|---|---|
| | | Votes | % | Votes | % | Votes | % | Votes | % | Votes | % | | |
| Alabama | 164,563 | 42,823 | 26.0 | 113,138 | 68.8 | 8,040 | 4.9 | 562 | 0.3 | — | | 70,315 | D |
| Arizona | 73,961 | 30,516 | 41.3 | 26,235 | 35.5 | 17,210 | 23.3 | — | | — | | 4,281 | R |
| Arkansas | 138,540 | 40,583 | 29.3 | 84,790 | 61.2 | 13,167 | 9.5 | — | | — | | 44,207 | D |
| California | 1,281,778 | 733,250 | 57.2 | 105,514 | 8.2 | 424,649 | 33.1 | 18,365 | 1.4 | — | | 308,601 | R |
| Colorado | 342,261 | 195,171 | 57.0 | 75,238 | 22.0 | 69,946 | 20.4 | 966 | 0.3 | 940 | 0.3 | 119,933 | R |
| Connecticut | 400,306 | 246,322 | 61.5 | 110,184 | 27.5 | 42,416 | 10.6 | — | | 1,474 | 0.4 | 136,138 | R |
| Delaware | 90,885 | 52,441 | 57.7 | 33,445 | 36.8 | 4,979 | 5.5 | — | | 20 | | 18,996 | R |
| Florida | 109,158 | 30,633 | 28.1 | 62,083 | 56.9 | 8,625 | 7.9 | 5,498 | 5.0 | 2,319 | 2.1 | 31,450 | D |
| Georgia | 166,635 | 30,300 | 18.2 | 123,262 | 74.0 | 12,687 | 7.6 | 231 | 0.1 | 155 | 0.1 | 92,962 | D |
| Idaho | 147,690 | 69,791 | 47.3 | 23,951 | 16.2 | 53,948 | 36.5 | — | | — | | 15,843 | R |
| Illinois | 2,470,067 | 1,453,321 | 58.8 | 576,975 | 23.4 | 432,027 | 17.5 | 2,367 | 0.1 | 5,377 | 0.2 | 876,346 | R |
| Indiana | 1,272,390 | 703,042 | 55.3 | 492,245 | 38.7 | 71,700 | 5.6 | 4,416 | 0.3 | 987 | 0.1 | 210,797 | R |
| Iowa | 976,770 | 537,458 | 55.0 | 160,382 | 16.4 | 274,448 | 28.1 | — | | 4,482 | 0.5 | 263,010 | R |
| Kansas | 662,456 | 407,671 | 61.5 | 156,320 | 23.6 | 98,461 | 14.9 | — | | 4 | | 251,351 | R |
| Kentucky | 813,843 | 396,758 | 48.8 | 375,593 | 46.2 | 38,465 | 4.7 | — | | 3,027 | 0.4 | 21,165 | R |
| Louisiana | 121,951 | 24,670 | 20.2 | 93,218 | 76.4 | — | | — | | 4,063 | 3.3 | 68,548 | D |
| Maine | 192,192 | 138,440 | 72.0 | 41,964 | 21.8 | 11,382 | 5.9 | — | | 406 | 0.2 | 96,476 | R |
| Maryland | 358,630 | 162,414 | 45.3 | 148,072 | 41.3 | 47,157 | 13.1 | — | | 987 | 0.3 | 14,342 | R |
| Massachusetts | 1,129,837 | 703,476 | 62.3 | 280,831 | 24.9 | 141,225 | 12.5 | — | | 4,305 | 0.4 | 422,645 | R |
| Michigan | 1,160,419 | 874,631 | 75.4 | 152,359 | 13.1 | 122,014 | 10.5 | 6,085 | 0.5 | 5,330 | 0.5 | 722,272 | R |
| Minnesota | 822,146 | 420,759 | 51.2 | 55,913 | 6.8 | 339,192 | 41.3 | — | | 6,282 | 0.8 | 81,567 | R |
| Mississippi | 112,442 | 8,494 | 7.6 | 100,474 | 89.4 | 3,474 | 3.1 | — | | — | | 91,980 | D |
| Missouri | 1,310,095 | 648,488 | 49.5 | 574,962 | 43.9 | 83,996 | 6.4 | 1,418 | 0.1 | 1,231 | 0.1 | 73,526 | R |
| Montana | 174,425 | 74,138 | 42.5 | 33,805 | 19.4 | 66,124 | 37.9 | — | | 358 | 0.2 | 8,014 | R |
| Nebraska | 463,559 | 218,985 | 47.2 | 137,299 | 29.6 | 105,681 | 22.8 | 1,594 | 0.3 | — | | 81,686 | R |
| Nevada | 26,921 | 11,243 | 41.8 | 5,909 | 21.9 | 9,769 | 36.3 | — | | — | | 1,474 | R |
| New Hampshire | 164,769 | 98,575 | 59.8 | 57,201 | 34.7 | 8,993 | 5.5 | — | | — | | 41,374 | R |
| New Jersey | 1,088,054 | 676,277 | 62.2 | 298,043 | 27.4 | 109,028 | 10.0 | 1,660 | 0.2 | 3,046 | 0.3 | 378,234 | R |
| New Mexico | 112,830 | 54,745 | 48.5 | 48,542 | 43.0 | 9,543 | 8.5 | — | | — | | 6,203 | R |
| New York | 3,263,939 | 1,820,058 | 55.8 | 950,796 | 29.1 | 474,913 | 14.6 | — | | 18,172 | 0.6 | 869,262 | R |
| North Carolina | 481,608 | 190,754 | 39.6 | 284,190 | 59.0 | 6,651 | 1.4 | 13 | | — | | 93,436 | D |
| North Dakota | 199,081 | 94,931 | 47.7 | 13,858 | 7.0 | 89,922 | 45.2 | — | | 370 | 0.2 | 5,009 | R |
| Ohio | 2,016,296 | 1,176,130 | 58.3 | 477,887 | 23.7 | 358,008 | 17.8 | — | | 4,271 | 0.2 | 698,243 | R |
| Oklahoma | 527,828 | 225,756 | 42.8 | 255,798 | 48.5 | 46,274 | 8.8 | — | | — | | 30,042 | D |
| Oregon | 279,488 | 142,579 | 51.0 | 67,589 | 24.2 | 68,403 | 24.5 | — | | 917 | 0.3 | 74,176 | R |
| Pennsylvania | 2,144,850 | 1,401,481 | 65.3 | 409,192 | 19.1 | 307,567 | 14.3 | 9,779 | 0.5 | 16,831 | 0.8 | 992,289 | R |
| Rhode Island | 210,115 | 125,286 | 59.6 | 76,606 | 36.5 | 7,628 | 3.6 | — | | 595 | 0.3 | 48,680 | R |
| South Carolina | 50,755 | 1,123 | 2.2 | 49,008 | 96.6 | 623 | 1.2 | — | | 1 | | 47,885 | D |
| South Dakota | 203,868 | 101,299 | 49.7 | 27,214 | 13.3 | 75,355 | 37.0 | — | | — | | 25,944 | R |
| Tennessee | 301,030 | 130,831 | 43.5 | 159,339 | 52.9 | 10,666 | 3.5 | 94 | | 100 | | 28,508 | D |
| Texas | 657,054 | 130,794 | 19.9 | 483,381 | 73.6 | 42,879 | 6.5 | — | | — | | 352,587 | D |
| Utah | 156,990 | 77,327 | 49.3 | 47,001 | 29.9 | 32,662 | 20.8 | — | | — | | 30,326 | R |
| Vermont | 102,917 | 80,498 | 78.2 | 16,124 | 15.7 | 5,964 | 5.8 | 326 | 0.3 | 5 | | 64,374 | R |
| Virginia | 223,603 | 73,328 | 32.8 | 139,717 | 62.5 | 10,369 | 4.6 | — | | 189 | 0.1 | 66,389 | D |
| Washington | 421,549 | 220,224 | 52.2 | 42,842 | 10.2 | 150,727 | 35.8 | — | | 7,756 | 1.8 | 69,497 | R |
| West Virginia | 583,662 | 288,635 | 49.5 | 257,232 | 44.1 | 36,723 | 6.3 | — | | 1,072 | 0.2 | 31,403 | R |
| Wisconsin | 840,827 | 311,614 | 37.1 | 68,115 | 8.1 | 453,678 | 54.0 | 2,918 | 0.3 | 4,502 | 0.5 | 142,064 | P |
| Wyoming | 79,900 | 41,858 | 52.4 | 12,868 | 16.1 | 25,174 | 31.5 | — | | — | | 16,684 | R |
| Totals | 29,095,023 | 15,719,921 | 54.0 | 8,386,704 | 28.8 | 4,832,532 | 16.6 | 56,292 | 0.2 | 99,574 | 0.3 | 7,333,217 | R |

1. For breakdown of "Other" vote, see minor candidate vote totals, p. 472.

# 1928 Presidential Election

| STATE | TOTAL VOTE | HERBERT C. HOOVER (Republican) | | ALFRED E. SMITH (Democrat) | | NORMAN M. THOMAS (Socialist) | | WILLIAM Z. FOSTER (Communist) | | OTHER [1] | | PLURALITY | |
|---|---|---|---|---|---|---|---|---|---|---|---|---|---|
| | | Votes | % | Votes | % | Votes | % | Votes | % | Votes | % | | |
| Alabama | 248,981 | 120,725 | 48.5 | 127,796 | 51.3 | 460 | 0.2 | — | | — | | 7,071 | D |
| Arizona | 91,254 | 52,533 | 57.6 | 38,537 | 42.2 | — | | 184 | 0.2 | — | | 13,996 | R |
| Arkansas | 197,726 | 77,784 | 39.3 | 119,196 | 60.3 | 429 | 0.2 | 317 | 0.2 | — | | 41,412 | D |
| California | 1,796,656 | 1,162,323 | 64.7 | 614,365 | 34.2 | 19,595 | 1.1 | — | | 373 | | 547,958 | R |
| Colorado | 392,242 | 253,872 | 64.7 | 133,131 | 33.9 | 3,472 | 0.9 | 675 | 0.2 | 1,092 | 0.3 | 120,741 | R |
| Connecticut | 553,118 | 296,641 | 53.6 | 252,085 | 45.6 | 3,029 | 0.5 | 738 | 0.1 | 625 | 0.1 | 44,556 | R |
| Delaware | 104,602 | 68,860 | 65.8 | 35,354 | 33.8 | 329 | 0.3 | 59 | 0.1 | — | | 33,506 | R |
| Florida | 252,068 | 145,860 | 57.9 | 101,764 | 40.4 | 2,284 | 0.9 | 2,160 | 0.9 | — | | 44,096 | R |
| Georgia | 231,592 | 101,800 | 44.0 | 129,604 | 56.0 | 124 | 0.1 | 64 | | — | | 27,804 | D |
| Idaho | 151,541 | 97,322 | 64.2 | 52,926 | 34.9 | 1,293 | 0.9 | — | | — | | 44,396 | R |
| Illinois | 3,107,489 | 1,769,141 | 56.9 | 1,313,817 | 42.3 | 19,138 | 0.6 | 3,581 | 0.1 | 1,812 | 0.1 | 455,324 | R |
| Indiana | 1,421,314 | 848,290 | 59.7 | 562,691 | 39.6 | 3,871 | 0.3 | 321 | | 6,141 | 0.4 | 285,599 | R |
| Iowa | 1,009,189 | 623,570 | 61.8 | 379,011 | 37.6 | 2,960 | 0.3 | 328 | | 3,320 | 0.3 | 244,559 | R |
| Kansas | 713,200 | 513,672 | 72.0 | 193,003 | 27.1 | 6,205 | 0.9 | 320 | | — | | 320,669 | R |
| Kentucky | 940,521 | 558,064 | 59.3 | 381,070 | 40.5 | 783 | 0.1 | 288 | | 316 | | 176,994 | R |
| Louisiana | 215,833 | 51,160 | 23.7 | 164,655 | 76.3 | — | | — | | 18 | | 113,495 | D |
| Maine | 262,170 | 179,923 | 68.6 | 81,179 | 31.0 | 1,068 | 0.4 | — | | — | | 98,744 | R |
| Maryland | 528,348 | 301,479 | 57.1 | 223,626 | 42.3 | 1,701 | 0.3 | 636 | 0.1 | 906 | 0.2 | 77,853 | R |
| Massachusetts | 1,577,823 | 775,566 | 49.2 | 792,758 | 50.2 | 6,262 | 0.4 | 2,461 | 0.2 | 776 | | 17,192 | D |
| Michigan | 1,372,082 | 965,396 | 70.4 | 396,762 | 28.9 | 3,516 | 0.3 | 2,881 | 0.2 | 3,527 | 0.3 | 568,634 | R |
| Minnesota | 970,976 | 560,977 | 57.8 | 396,451 | 40.8 | 6,774 | 0.7 | 4,853 | 0.5 | 1,921 | 0.2 | 164,526 | R |
| Mississippi | 151,568 | 27,030 | 17.8 | 124,538 | 82.2 | — | | — | | — | | 97,508 | D |
| Missouri | 1,500,845 | 834,080 | 55.6 | 662,684 | 44.2 | 3,739 | 0.2 | — | | 342 | | 171,396 | R |
| Montana | 194,108 | 113,300 | 58.4 | 78,578 | 40.5 | 1,667 | 0.9 | 563 | 0.3 | — | | 34,722 | R |
| Nebraska | 547,128 | 345,745 | 63.2 | 197,950 | 36.2 | 3,433 | 0.6 | — | | — | | 147,795 | R |
| Nevada | 32,417 | 18,327 | 56.5 | 14,090 | 43.5 | — | | — | | — | | 4,237 | R |
| New Hampshire | 196,757 | 115,404 | 58.7 | 80,715 | 41.0 | 465 | 0.2 | 173 | 0.1 | — | | 34,689 | R |
| New Jersey | 1,549,381 | 926,050 | 59.8 | 616,517 | 39.8 | 4,897 | 0.3 | 1,257 | 0.1 | 660 | | 309,533 | R |
| New Mexico | 118,077 | 69,708 | 59.0 | 48,211 | 40.8 | — | | 158 | 0.1 | — | | 21,497 | R |
| New York | 4,405,626 | 2,193,344 | 49.8 | 2,089,863 | 47.4 | 107,332 | 2.4 | 10,876 | 0.2 | 4,211 | 0.1 | 103,481 | R |
| North Carolina | 635,150 | 348,923 | 54.9 | 286,227 | 45.1 | — | | — | | — | | 62,696 | R |
| North Dakota | 239,845 | 131,419 | 54.8 | 106,648 | 44.5 | 936 | 0.4 | 842 | 0.4 | — | | 24,771 | R |
| Ohio | 2,508,346 | 1,627,546 | 64.9 | 864,210 | 34.5 | 8,683 | 0.3 | 2,836 | 0.1 | 5,071 | 0.2 | 763,336 | R |
| Oklahoma | 618,427 | 394,046 | 63.7 | 219,174 | 35.4 | 3,924 | 0.6 | — | | 1,283 | 0.2 | 174,872 | R |
| Oregon | 319,942 | 205,341 | 64.2 | 109,223 | 34.1 | 2,720 | 0.9 | 1,094 | 0.3 | 1,564 | 0.5 | 96,118 | R |
| Pennsylvania | 3,150,612 | 2,055,382 | 65.2 | 1,067,586 | 33.9 | 18,647 | 0.6 | 4,726 | 0.2 | 4,271 | 0.1 | 987,796 | R |
| Rhode Island | 237,194 | 117,522 | 49.5 | 118,973 | 50.2 | — | | 283 | 0.1 | 416 | 0.2 | 1,451 | D |
| South Carolina | 68,605 | 5,858 | 8.5 | 62,700 | 91.4 | 47 | 0.1 | — | | — | | 56,842 | D |
| South Dakota | 261,857 | 157,603 | 60.2 | 102,660 | 39.2 | 443 | 0.2 | 224 | 0.1 | 927 | 0.4 | 54,943 | R |
| Tennessee | 353,192 | 195,388 | 55.3 | 157,143 | 44.5 | 567 | 0.2 | 94 | | — | | 38,245 | R |
| Texas | 717,733 | 372,324 | 51.9 | 344,542 | 48.0 | 658 | 0.1 | 209 | | — | | 27,782 | R |
| Utah | 176,603 | 94,618 | 53.6 | 80,985 | 45.9 | 954 | 0.5 | 46 | | — | | 13,633 | R |
| Vermont | 135,191 | 90,404 | 66.9 | 44,440 | 32.9 | — | | — | | 347 | 0.3 | 45,964 | R |
| Virginia | 305,364 | 164,609 | 53.9 | 140,146 | 45.9 | 249 | 0.1 | 179 | 0.1 | 181 | 0.1 | 24,463 | R |
| Washington | 500,840 | 335,844 | 67.1 | 156,772 | 31.3 | 2,615 | 0.5 | 1,541 | 0.3 | 4,068 | 0.8 | 179,072 | R |
| West Virginia | 642,752 | 375,551 | 58.4 | 263,784 | 41.0 | 1,313 | 0.2 | 401 | 0.1 | 1,703 | 0.3 | 111,767 | R |
| Wisconsin | 1,016,831 | 544,205 | 53.5 | 450,259 | 44.3 | 18,213 | 1.8 | 1,528 | 0.2 | 2,626 | 0.3 | 93,946 | R |
| Wyoming | 82,835 | 52,748 | 63.7 | 29,299 | 35.4 | 788 | 1.0 | — | | — | | 23,449 | R |
| Totals | 36,805,951 | 21,437,277 | 58.2 | 15,007,698 | 40.8 | 265,583 | 0.7 | 46,896 | 0.1 | 48,497 | 0.1 | 6,429,579 | R |

1. For breakdown of "Other" vote see minor candidate vote totals, p. 472.

# 1932 Presidential Election

| STATE | TOTAL VOTE | FRANKLIN D. ROOSEVELT (Democrat) Votes | % | HERBERT C. HOOVER (Republican) Votes | % | NORMAN M. THOMAS (Socialist) Votes | % | WILLIAM Z. FOSTER (Communist) Votes | % | OTHER [1] Votes | % | PLURALITY |
|---|---|---|---|---|---|---|---|---|---|---|---|---|
| Alabama | 245,303 | 207,910 | 84.8 | 34,675 | 14.1 | 2,030 | 0.8 | 675 | 0.3 | 13 | | 173,235 D |
| Arizona | 118,251 | 79,264 | 67.0 | 36,104 | 30.5 | 2,618 | 2.2 | 256 | 0.2 | 9 | | 43,160 D |
| Arkansas | 216,569 | 186,829 | 86.3 | 27,465 | 12.7 | 1,166 | 0.5 | 157 | 0.1 | 952 | 0.4 | 159,364 D |
| California | 2,266,972 | 1,324,157 | 58.4 | 847,902 | 37.4 | 63,299 | 2.8 | 1,023 | | 30,591 | 1.3 | 476,255 D |
| Colorado | 457,696 | 250,877 | 54.8 | 189,617 | 41.4 | 13,591 | 3.0 | 787 | 0.2 | 2,824 | 0.6 | 61,260 D |
| Connecticut | 594,183 | 281,632 | 47.4 | 288,420 | 48.5 | 20,480 | 3.4 | 1,364 | 0.2 | 2,287 | 0.4 | 6,788 R |
| Delaware | 112,901 | 54,319 | 48.1 | 57,073 | 50.6 | 1,376 | 1.2 | 133 | 0.1 | — | | 2,754 R |
| Florida | 276,943 | 206,307 | 74.5 | 69,170 | 25.0 | 775 | 0.3 | — | | 691 | 0.2 | 137,137 D |
| Georgia | 255,590 | 234,118 | 91.6 | 19,863 | 7.8 | 461 | 0.2 | 23 | | 1,125 | 0.4 | 214,255 D |
| Idaho | 186,520 | 109,479 | 58.7 | 71,312 | 38.2 | 526 | 0.3 | 491 | 0.3 | 4,712 | 2.5 | 38,167 D |
| Illinois | 3,407,926 | 1,882,304 | 55.2 | 1,432,756 | 42.0 | 67,258 | 2.0 | 15,582 | 0.5 | 10,026 | 0.3 | 449,548 D |
| Indiana | 1,576,927 | 862,054 | 54.7 | 677,184 | 42.9 | 21,388 | 1.4 | 2,187 | 0.1 | 14,114 | 0.9 | 184,870 D |
| Iowa | 1,036,687 | 598,019 | 57.7 | 414,433 | 40.0 | 20,467 | 2.0 | 559 | 0.1 | 3,209 | 0.3 | 183,586 D |
| Kansas | 791,978 | 424,204 | 53.6 | 349,498 | 44.1 | 18,276 | 2.3 | — | | — | | 74,706 D |
| Kentucky | 983,059 | 580,574 | 59.1 | 394,716 | 40.2 | 3,853 | 0.4 | 271 | | 3,645 | 0.4 | 185,858 D |
| Louisiana | 268,804 | 249,418 | 92.8 | 18,853 | 7.0 | — | | — | | 533 | 0.2 | 230,565 D |
| Maine | 298,444 | 128,907 | 43.2 | 166,631 | 55.8 | 2,489 | 0.8 | 162 | 0.1 | 255 | 0.1 | 37,724 R |
| Maryland | 511,054 | 314,314 | 61.5 | 184,184 | 36.0 | 10,489 | 2.1 | 1,031 | 0.2 | 1,036 | 0.2 | 130,130 D |
| Massachusetts | 1,580,114 | 800,148 | 50.6 | 736,959 | 46.6 | 34,305 | 2.2 | 4,821 | 0.3 | 3,881 | 0.2 | 63,189 D |
| Michigan | 1,664,765 | 871,700 | 52.4 | 739,894 | 44.4 | 39,205 | 2.4 | 9,318 | 0.6 | 4,648 | 0.3 | 131,806 D |
| Minnesota | 1,002,843 | 600,806 | 59.9 | 363,959 | 36.3 | 25,476 | 2.5 | 6,101 | 0.6 | 6,501 | 0.6 | 236,847 D |
| Mississippi | 146,034 | 140,168 | 96.0 | 5,180 | 3.5 | 686 | 0.5 | — | | — | | 134,988 D |
| Missouri | 1,609,894 | 1,025,406 | 63.7 | 564,713 | 35.1 | 16,374 | 1.0 | 568 | | 2,833 | 0.2 | 460,693 D |
| Montana | 216,479 | 127,286 | 58.8 | 78,078 | 36.1 | 7,891 | 3.6 | 1,775 | 0.8 | 1,449 | 0.7 | 49,208 D |
| Nebraska | 570,135 | 359,082 | 63.0 | 201,177 | 35.3 | 9,876 | 1.7 | — | | — | | 157,905 D |
| Nevada | 41,430 | 28,756 | 69.4 | 12,674 | 30.6 | — | | — | | — | | 16,082 D |
| New Hampshire | 205,520 | 100,680 | 49.0 | 103,629 | 50.4 | 947 | 0.5 | 264 | 0.1 | — | | 2,949 R |
| New Jersey | 1,630,063 | 806,630 | 49.5 | 775,684 | 47.6 | 42,998 | 2.6 | 2,915 | 0.2 | 1,836 | 0.1 | 30,946 D |
| New Mexico | 151,606 | 95,089 | 62.7 | 54,217 | 35.8 | 1,776 | 1.2 | 135 | 0.1 | 389 | 0.3 | 40,872 D |
| New York | 4,688,614 | 2,534,959 | 54.1 | 1,937,963 | 41.3 | 177,397 | 3.8 | 27,956 | 0.6 | 10,339 | 0.2 | 596,996 D |
| North Carolina | 711,498 | 497,566 | 69.9 | 208,344 | 29.3 | 5,588 | 0.8 | — | | — | | 289,222 D |
| North Dakota | 256,290 | 178,350 | 69.6 | 71,772 | 28.0 | 3,521 | 1.4 | 830 | 0.3 | 1,817 | 0.7 | 106,578 D |
| Ohio | 2,609,728 | 1,301,695 | 49.9 | 1,227,319 | 47.0 | 64,094 | 2.5 | 7,231 | 0.3 | 9,389 | 0.4 | 74,376 D |
| Oklahoma | 704,633 | 516,468 | 73.3 | 188,165 | 26.7 | — | | — | | — | | 328,303 D |
| Oregon | 368,751 | 213,871 | 58.0 | 136,019 | 36.9 | 15,450 | 4.2 | 1,681 | 0.5 | 1,730 | 0.5 | 77,852 D |
| Pennsylvania | 2,859,021 | 1,295,948 | 45.3 | 1,453,540 | 50.8 | 91,119 | 3.2 | 5,658 | 0.2 | 12,756 | 0.4 | 157,592 R |
| Rhode Island | 266,170 | 146,604 | 55.1 | 115,266 | 43.3 | 3,138 | 1.2 | 546 | 0.2 | 616 | 0.2 | 31,338 D |
| South Carolina | 104,407 | 102,347 | 98.0 | 1,978 | 1.9 | 82 | 0.1 | — | | — | | 100,369 D |
| South Dakota | 288,438 | 183,515 | 63.6 | 99,212 | 34.4 | 1,551 | 0.5 | 364 | 0.1 | 3,796 | 1.3 | 84,303 D |
| Tennessee | 390,273 | 259,473 | 66.5 | 126,752 | 32.5 | 1,796 | 0.5 | 254 | 0.1 | 1,998 | 0.5 | 132,721 D |
| Texas | 874,382 | 771,109 | 88.2 | 98,218 | 11.2 | 4,414 | 0.5 | 207 | | 434 | | 672,891 D |
| Utah | 206,578 | 116,750 | 56.5 | 84,795 | 41.0 | 4,087 | 2.0 | 946 | 0.5 | — | | 31,955 D |
| Vermont | 136,980 | 56,266 | 41.1 | 78,984 | 57.7 | 1,533 | 1.1 | 195 | 0.1 | 2 | | 22,718 R |
| Virginia | 297,942 | 203,979 | 68.5 | 89,637 | 30.1 | 2,382 | 0.8 | 86 | | 1,858 | 0.6 | 114,342 D |
| Washington | 614,814 | 353,260 | 57.5 | 208,645 | 33.9 | 17,080 | 2.8 | 2,972 | 0.5 | 32,857 | 5.3 | 144,615 D |
| West Virginia | 743,774 | 405,124 | 54.5 | 330,731 | 44.5 | 5,133 | 0.7 | 444 | 0.1 | 2,342 | 0.3 | 74,393 D |
| Wisconsin | 1,114,814 | 707,410 | 63.5 | 347,741 | 31.2 | 53,379 | 4.8 | 3,105 | 0.3 | 3,179 | 0.3 | 359,669 D |
| Wyoming | 96,962 | 54,370 | 56.1 | 39,583 | 40.8 | 2,829 | 2.9 | 180 | 0.2 | — | | 14,787 D |
| **Totals** | **39,758,759** | **22,829,501** | **57.4** | **15,760,684** | **39.6** | **884,649** | **2.2** | **103,253** | **0.3** | **180,672** | **0.5** | **7,068,817 D** |

1. For breakdown of "Other" vote, see minor candidate vote totals, p. 472.

# 1936 Presidential Election

| STATE | TOTAL VOTE | FRANKLIN D. ROOSEVELT (Democrat) | | ALFRED M. LANDON (Republican) | | WILLIAM LEMKE (Union) | | NORMAN M. THOMAS (Socialist) | | OTHER [1] | | PLURALITY |
|---|---|---|---|---|---|---|---|---|---|---|---|---|
| | | Votes | % | Votes | % | Votes | % | Votes | % | Votes | % | |
| Alabama | 275,744 | 238,196 | 86.4 | 35,358 | 12.8 | 551 | 0.2 | 242 | 0.1 | 1,397 | 0.5 | 202,838 D |
| Arizona | 124,163 | 86,722 | 69.8 | 33,433 | 26.9 | 3,307 | 2.7 | 317 | 0.3 | 384 | 0.3 | 53,289 D |
| Arkansas | 179,431 | 146,765 | 81.8 | 32,049 | 17.9 | 4 | | 446 | 0.2 | 167 | 0.1 | 114,716 D |
| California | 2,638,882 | 1,766,836 | 67.0 | 836,431 | 31.7 | — | | 11,331 | 0.4 | 24,284 | 0.9 | 930,405 D |
| Colorado | 488,685 | 295,021 | 60.4 | 181,267 | 37.1 | 9,962 | 2.0 | 1,594 | 0.3 | 841 | 0.2 | 113,754 D |
| Connecticut | 690,723 | 382,129 | 55.3 | 278,685 | 40.3 | 21,805 | 3.2 | 5,683 | 0.8 | 2,421 | 0.4 | 103,444 D |
| Delaware | 127,603 | 69,702 | 54.6 | 57,236 | 44.9 | 442 | 0.3 | 172 | 0.1 | 51 | | 12,466 D |
| Florida | 327,436 | 249,117 | 76.1 | 78,248 | 23.9 | — | | — | | 71 | | 170,869 D |
| Georgia | 293,170 | 255,363 | 87.1 | 36,943 | 12.6 | 136 | | 68 | | 660 | 0.2 | 218,420 D |
| Idaho | 199,617 | 125,683 | 63.0 | 66,256 | 33.2 | 7,678 | 3.8 | — | | — | | 59,427 D |
| Illinois | 3,956,522 | 2,282,999 | 57.7 | 1,570,393 | 39.7 | 89,439 | 2.3 | 7,530 | 0.2 | 6,161 | 0.2 | 712,606 D |
| Indiana | 1,650,897 | 934,974 | 56.6 | 691,570 | 41.9 | 19,407 | 1.2 | 3,856 | 0.2 | 1,090 | 0.1 | 243,404 D |
| Iowa | 1,142,737 | 621,756 | 54.4 | 487,977 | 42.7 | 29,687 | 2.6 | 1,373 | 0.1 | 1,944 | 0.2 | 133,779 D |
| Kansas | 865,507 | 464,520 | 53.7 | 397,727 | 46.0 | 494 | 0.1 | 2,766 | 0.3 | — | | 66,793 D |
| Kentucky | 926,214 | 541,944 | 58.5 | 369,702 | 39.9 | 12,501 | 1.3 | 627 | 0.1 | 1,440 | 0.2 | 172,242 D |
| Louisiana | 329,778 | 292,894 | 88.8 | 36,791 | 11.2 | — | | — | | 93 | | 256,103 D |
| Maine | 304,240 | 126,333 | 41.5 | 168,823 | 55.5 | 7,581 | 2.5 | 783 | 0.3 | 720 | 0.2 | 42,490 R |
| Maryland | 624,896 | 389,612 | 62.3 | 231,435 | 37.0 | — | | 1,629 | 0.3 | 2,220 | 0.4 | 158,177 D |
| Massachusetts | 1,840,357 | 942,716 | 51.2 | 768,613 | 41.8 | 118,639 | 6.4 | 5,111 | 0.3 | 5,278 | 0.3 | 174,103 D |
| Michigan | 1,805,098 | 1,016,794 | 56.3 | 699,733 | 38.8 | 75,795 | 4.2 | 8,208 | 0.5 | 4,568 | 0.3 | 317,061 D |
| Minnesota | 1,129,975 | 698,811 | 61.8 | 350,461 | 31.0 | 74,296 | 6.6 | 2,872 | 0.3 | 3,535 | 0.3 | 348,350 D |
| Mississippi | 162,142 | 157,333 | 97.0 | 4,467 | 2.8 | — | | 342 | 0.2 | — | | 152,866 D |
| Missouri | 1,828,635 | 1,111,043 | 60.8 | 697,891 | 38.2 | 14,630 | 0.8 | 3,454 | 0.2 | 1,617 | 0.1 | 413,152 D |
| Montana | 230,502 | 159,690 | 69.3 | 63,598 | 27.6 | 5,539 | 2.4 | 1,066 | 0.5 | 609 | 0.3 | 96,092 D |
| Nebraska | 608,023 | 347,445 | 57.1 | 247,731 | 40.7 | 12,847 | 2.1 | — | | — | | 99,714 D |
| Nevada | 43,848 | 31,925 | 72.8 | 11,923 | 27.2 | — | | — | | — | | 20,002 D |
| New Hampshire | 218,114 | 108,460 | 49.7 | 104,642 | 48.0 | 4,819 | 2.2 | — | | 193 | 0.1 | 3,818 D |
| New Jersey | 1,820,437 | 1,083,850 | 59.5 | 720,322 | 39.6 | 9,407 | 0.5 | 3,931 | 0.2 | 2,927 | 0.2 | 363,528 D |
| New Mexico | 169,135 | 106,037 | 62.7 | 61,727 | 36.5 | 924 | 0.5 | 343 | 0.2 | 104 | 0.1 | 44,310 D |
| New York | 5,596,398 | 3,293,222 | 58.8 | 2,180,670 | 39.0 | — | | 86,897 | 1.6 | 35,609 | 0.6 | 1,112,552 D |
| North Carolina | 839,475 | 616,141 | 73.4 | 223,294 | 26.6 | 2 | | 21 | | 17 | | 392,847 D |
| North Dakota | 273,716 | 163,148 | 59.6 | 72,751 | 26.6 | 36,708 | 13.4 | 552 | 0.2 | 557 | 0.2 | 90,397 D |
| Ohio | 3,012,660 | 1,747,140 | 58.0 | 1,127,855 | 37.4 | 132,212 | 4.4 | 167 | | 5,286 | 0.2 | 619,285 D |
| Oklahoma | 749,740 | 501,069 | 66.8 | 245,122 | 32.7 | — | | 2,221 | 0.3 | 1,328 | 0.2 | 255,947 D |
| Oregon | 414,021 | 266,733 | 64.4 | 122,706 | 29.6 | 21,831 | 5.3 | 2,143 | 0.5 | 608 | 0.1 | 144,027 D |
| Pennsylvania | 4,138,105 | 2,353,788 | 56.9 | 1,690,300 | 40.8 | 67,467 | 1.6 | 14,375 | 0.3 | 12,175 | 0.3 | 663,488 D |
| Rhode Island | 310,278 | 164,338 | 53.0 | 125,031 | 40.3 | 19,569 | 6.3 | — | | 1,340 | 0.4 | 39,307 D |
| South Carolina | 115,437 | 113,791 | 98.6 | 1,646 | 1.4 | — | | — | | — | | 112,145 D |
| South Dakota | 296,452 | 160,137 | 54.0 | 125,977 | 42.5 | 10,338 | 3.5 | — | | — | | 34,160 D |
| Tennessee | 477,086 | 328,083 | 68.8 | 147,055 | 30.8 | 296 | 0.1 | 692 | 0.1 | 960 | 0.2 | 181,028 D |
| Texas | 849,701 | 739,952 | 87.1 | 104,661 | 12.3 | 3,187 | 0.4 | 1,122 | 0.1 | 779 | 0.1 | 635,291 D |
| Utah | 216,679 | 150,248 | 69.3 | 64,555 | 29.8 | 1,121 | 0.5 | 432 | 0.2 | 323 | 0.1 | 85,693 D |
| Vermont | 143,689 | 62,124 | 43.2 | 81,023 | 56.4 | — | | — | | 542 | 0.4 | 18,899 R |
| Virginia | 334,590 | 234,980 | 70.2 | 98,336 | 29.4 | 233 | 0.1 | 313 | 0.1 | 728 | 0.2 | 136,644 D |
| Washington | 692,338 | 459,579 | 66.4 | 206,892 | 29.9 | 17,463 | 2.5 | 3,496 | 0.5 | 4,908 | 0.7 | 252,687 D |
| West Virginia | 829,945 | 502,582 | 60.6 | 325,358 | 39.2 | — | | 832 | 0.1 | 1,173 | 0.1 | 177,224 D |
| Wisconsin | 1,258,560 | 802,984 | 63.8 | 380,828 | 30.3 | 60,297 | 4.8 | 10,626 | 0.8 | 3,825 | 0.3 | 422,156 D |
| Wyoming | 103,382 | 62,624 | 60.6 | 38,739 | 37.5 | 1,653 | 1.6 | 200 | 0.2 | 166 | 0.2 | 23,885 D |
| Totals | 45,654,763 | 27,757,333 | 60.8 | 16,684,231 | 36.5 | 892,267 | 2.0 | 187,833 | 0.4 | 133,099 | 0.3 | 11,073,102 D |

1. For breakdown of "Other" vote, see minor candidate vote totals, p. 472.

# 1940 Presidential Election

| STATE | TOTAL VOTE | FRANKLIN D. ROOSEVELT (Democrat) | | WENDELL WILLKIE (Republican) | | NORMAN M. THOMAS (Socialist) | | ROGER W. BABSON (Prohibition) | | OTHER [1] | | PLURALITY | |
|---|---|---|---|---|---|---|---|---|---|---|---|---|---|
| | | Votes | % | Votes | % | Votes | % | Votes | % | Votes | % | | |
| Alabama | 294,219 | 250,726 | 85.2 | 42,184 | 14.3 | 100 | | 700 | 0.2 | 509 | 0.2 | 208,542 | D |
| Arizona | 150,039 | 95,267 | 63.5 | 54,030 | 36.0 | — | | 742 | 0.5 | — | | 41,237 | D |
| Arkansas | 200,429 | 157,213 | 78.4 | 42,122 | 21.0 | 301 | 0.2 | 793 | 0.4 | — | | 115,091 | D |
| California | 3,268,791 | 1,877,618 | 57.4 | 1,351,419 | 41.3 | 16,506 | 0.5 | 9,400 | 0.3 | 13,848 | 0.4 | 526,199 | D |
| Colorado | 549,004 | 265,554 | 48.4 | 279,576 | 50.9 | 1,899 | 0.3 | 1,597 | 0.3 | 378 | 0.1 | 14,022 | R |
| Connecticut | 781,502 | 417,621 | 53.4 | 361,819 | 46.3 | — | | — | | 2,062 | 0.3 | 55,802 | D |
| Delaware | 136,374 | 74,599 | 54.7 | 61,440 | 45.1 | 115 | 0.1 | 220 | 0.2 | — | | 13,159 | D |
| Florida | 485,640 | 359,334 | 74.0 | 126,158 | 26.0 | — | | — | | 148 | | 233,176 | D |
| Georgia | 312,686 | 265,194 | 84.8 | 46,495 | 14.9 | — | | 983 | 0.3 | 14 | | 218,699 | D |
| Idaho | 235,168 | 127,842 | 54.4 | 106,553 | 45.3 | 497 | 0.2 | — | | 276 | 0.1 | 21,289 | D |
| Illinois | 4,217,935 | 2,149,934 | 51.0 | 2,047,240 | 48.5 | 10,914 | 0.3 | 9,190 | 0.2 | 657 | | 102,694 | D |
| Indiana | 1,782,747 | 874,063 | 49.0 | 899,466 | 50.5 | 2,075 | 0.1 | 6,437 | 0.4 | 706 | | 25,403 | R |
| Iowa | 1,215,432 | 578,802 | 47.6 | 632,370 | 52.0 | — | | 2,284 | 0.2 | 1,976 | 0.2 | 53,568 | R |
| Kansas | 860,297 | 364,725 | 42.4 | 489,169 | 56.9 | 2,347 | 0.3 | 4,056 | 0.5 | — | | 124,444 | R |
| Kentucky | 970,163 | 557,322 | 57.4 | 410,384 | 42.3 | 1,014 | 0.1 | 1,443 | 0.1 | — | | 146,938 | D |
| Louisiana | 372,305 | 319,751 | 85.9 | 52,446 | 14.1 | — | | — | | 108 | | 267,305 | D |
| Maine | 320,840 | 156,478 | 48.8 | 163,951 | 51.1 | — | | — | | 411 | 0.1 | 7,473 | R |
| Maryland | 660,104 | 384,546 | 58.3 | 269,534 | 40.8 | 4,093 | 0.6 | — | | 1,931 | 0.3 | 115,012 | D |
| Massachusetts | 2,026,993 | 1,076,522 | 53.1 | 939,700 | 46.4 | 4,091 | 0.2 | 1,370 | 0.1 | 5,310 | 0.3 | 136,822 | D |
| Michigan | 2,085,929 | 1,032,991 | 49.5 | 1,039,917 | 49.9 | 7,593 | 0.4 | 1,795 | 0.1 | 3,633 | 0.2 | 6,926 | R |
| Minnesota | 1,251,188 | 644,196 | 51.5 | 596,274 | 47.7 | 5,454 | 0.4 | — | | 5,264 | 0.4 | 47,922 | D |
| Mississippi | 175,824 | 168,267 | 95.7 | 7,364 | 4.2 | 193 | 0.1 | — | | — | | 160,903 | D |
| Missouri | 1,833,729 | 958,476 | 52.3 | 871,009 | 47.5 | 2,226 | 0.1 | 1,809 | 0.1 | 209 | | 87,467 | D |
| Montana | 247,873 | 145,698 | 58.8 | 99,579 | 40.2 | 1,443 | 0.6 | 664 | 0.3 | 489 | 0.2 | 46,119 | D |
| Nebraska | 615,878 | 263,677 | 42.8 | 352,201 | 57.2 | — | | — | | — | | 88,524 | R |
| Nevada | 53,174 | 31,945 | 60.1 | 21,229 | 39.9 | — | | — | | — | | 10,716 | D |
| New Hampshire | 235,419 | 125,292 | 53.2 | 110,127 | 46.8 | — | | — | | — | | 15,165 | D |
| New Jersey | 1,972,552 | 1,016,808 | 51.5 | 945,475 | 47.9 | 2,433 | 0.1 | 873 | | 6,963 | 0.4 | 71,333 | D |
| New Mexico | 183,258 | 103,699 | 56.6 | 79,315 | 43.3 | 144 | 0.1 | 100 | 0.1 | — | | 24,384 | D |
| New York | 6,301,596 | 3,251,918 | 51.6 | 3,027,478 | 48.0 | 18,950 | 0.3 | 3,250 | 0.1 | — | | 224,440 | D |
| North Carolina | 822,648 | 609,015 | 74.0 | 213,633 | 26.0 | — | | — | | — | | 395,382 | D |
| North Dakota | 280,775 | 124,036 | 44.2 | 154,590 | 55.1 | 1,279 | 0.5 | 325 | 0.1 | 545 | 0.2 | 30,554 | R |
| Ohio | 3,319,912 | 1,733,139 | 52.2 | 1,586,773 | 47.8 | — | | — | | — | | 146,366 | D |
| Oklahoma | 826,212 | 474,313 | 57.4 | 348,872 | 42.2 | — | | 3,027 | 0.4 | — | | 125,441 | D |
| Oregon | 481,240 | 258,415 | 53.7 | 219,555 | 45.6 | 398 | 0.1 | 154 | | 2,718 | 0.6 | 38,860 | D |
| Pennsylvania | 4,078,714 | 2,171,035 | 53.2 | 1,889,848 | 46.3 | 10,967 | 0.3 | — | | 6,864 | 0.2 | 281,187 | D |
| Rhode Island | 321,152 | 182,181 | 56.7 | 138,654 | 43.2 | — | | 74 | | 243 | 0.1 | 43,527 | D |
| South Carolina | 99,830 | 95,470 | 95.6 | 4,360 | 4.4 | — | | — | | — | | 91,110 | D |
| South Dakota | 308,427 | 131,362 | 42.6 | 177,065 | 57.4 | — | | — | | — | | 45,703 | R |
| Tennessee | 522,823 | 351,601 | 67.3 | 169,153 | 32.4 | 463 | 0.1 | 1,606 | 0.3 | — | | 182,448 | D |
| Texas | 1,124,437 | 909,974 | 80.9 | 212,692 | 18.9 | 628 | 0.1 | 928 | 0.1 | 215 | | 697,282 | D |
| Utah | 247,819 | 154,277 | 62.3 | 93,151 | 37.6 | 200 | 0.1 | — | | 191 | 0.1 | 61,126 | D |
| Vermont | 143,062 | 64,269 | 44.9 | 78,371 | 54.8 | — | | — | | 422 | 0.3 | 14,102 | R |
| Virginia | 346,608 | 235,961 | 68.1 | 109,363 | 31.6 | 282 | 0.1 | 882 | 0.3 | 120 | | 126,598 | D |
| Washington | 793,833 | 462,145 | 58.2 | 322,123 | 40.6 | 4,586 | 0.6 | 1,686 | 0.2 | 3,293 | 0.4 | 140,022 | D |
| West Virginia | 868,076 | 495,662 | 57.1 | 372,414 | 42.9 | — | | — | | — | | 123,248 | D |
| Wisconsin | 1,405,522 | 704,821 | 50.1 | 679,206 | 48.3 | 15,071 | 1.1 | 2,148 | 0.2 | 4,276 | 0.3 | 25,615 | D |
| Wyoming | 112,240 | 59,287 | 52.8 | 52,633 | 46.9 | 148 | 0.1 | 172 | 0.2 | — | | 6,654 | D |
| **Totals** | **49,900,418** | **27,313,041** | **54.7** | **22,348,480** | **44.8** | **116,410** | **0.2** | **58,708** | **0.1** | **63,779** | **0.1** | **4,964,561** | **D** |

1. For breakdown of "Other" vote see minor candidate vote totals, p. 473.

# 1944 Presidential Election

| STATE | TOTAL VOTE | FRANKLIN D. ROOSEVELT (Democrat) | | THOMAS E. DEWEY (Republican) | | NORMAN M. THOMAS (Socialist) | | CLAUDE A. WATSON (Prohibition) | | OTHER [1] | | PLURALITY | |
|---|---|---|---|---|---|---|---|---|---|---|---|---|---|
| | | Votes | % | Votes | % | Votes | % | Votes | % | Votes | % | | |
| Alabama | 244,743 | 198,918 | 81.3 | 44,540 | 18.2 | 190 | 0.1 | 1,095 | 0.4 | — | | 154,378 | D |
| Arizona | 137,634 | 80,926 | 58.8 | 56,287 | 40.9 | — | | 421 | 0.3 | — | | 24,639 | D |
| Arkansas | 212,954 | 148,965 | 70.0 | 63,551 | 29.8 | 438 | 0.2 | — | | — | | 85,414 | D |
| California | 3,520,875 | 1,988,564 | 56.5 | 1,512,965 | 43.0 | 2,515 | 0.1 | 14,770 | 0.4 | 2,061 | 0.1 | 475,599 | D |
| Colorado | 505,039 | 234,331 | 46.4 | 268,731 | 53.2 | 1,977 | 0.4 | — | | — | | 34,400 | R |
| Connecticut | 831,990 | 435,146 | 52.3 | 390,527 | 46.9 | 5,097 | 0.6 | — | | 1,220 | 0.1 | 44,619 | D |
| Delaware | 125,361 | 68,166 | 54.4 | 56,747 | 45.3 | 154 | 0.1 | 294 | 0.2 | — | | 11,419 | D |
| Florida | 482,803 | 339,377 | 70.3 | 143,215 | 29.7 | — | | — | | 211 | | 196,162 | D |
| Georgia | 328,129 | 268,187 | 81.7 | 59,900 | 18.3 | 6 | | 36 | | — | | 208,287 | D |
| Idaho | 208,321 | 107,399 | 51.6 | 100,137 | 48.1 | 282 | 0.1 | 503 | 0.2 | — | | 7,262 | D |
| Illinois | 4,036,061 | 2,079,479 | 51.5 | 1,939,314 | 48.0 | 180 | | 7,411 | 0.2 | 9,677 | 0.2 | 140,165 | D |
| Indiana | 1,672,091 | 781,403 | 46.7 | 875,891 | 52.4 | 2,223 | 0.1 | 12,574 | 0.8 | — | | 94,488 | R |
| Iowa | 1,052,599 | 499,876 | 47.5 | 547,267 | 52.0 | 1,511 | 0.1 | 3,752 | 0.4 | 193 | | 47,391 | R |
| Kansas | 733,776 | 287,458 | 39.2 | 442,096 | 60.2 | 1,613 | 0.2 | 2,609 | 0.4 | — | | 154,638 | R |
| Kentucky | 867,924 | 472,589 | 54.5 | 392,448 | 45.2 | 535 | 0.1 | 2,023 | 0.2 | 329 | | 80,141 | D |
| Louisiana | 349,383 | 281,564 | 80.6 | 67,750 | 19.4 | — | | — | | 69 | | 213,814 | D |
| Maine | 296,400 | 140,631 | 47.4 | 155,434 | 52.4 | — | | — | | 335 | 0.1 | 14,803 | R |
| Maryland | 608,439 | 315,490 | 51.9 | 292,949 | 48.1 | — | | — | | — | | 22,541 | D |
| Massachusetts | 1,960,665 | 1,035,296 | 52.8 | 921,350 | 47.0 | — | | 973 | | 3,046 | 0.2 | 113,946 | D |
| Michigan | 2,205,223 | 1,106,899 | 50.2 | 1,084,423 | 49.2 | 4,598 | 0.2 | 6,503 | 0.3 | 2,800 | 0.1 | 22,476 | D |
| Minnesota | 1,125,504 | 589,864 | 52.4 | 527,416 | 46.9 | 5,048 | 0.4 | — | | 3,176 | 0.3 | 62,448 | D |
| Mississippi | 180,234 | 168,621 | 93.6 | 11,613 | 6.4 | — | | — | | — | | 157,008 | D |
| Missouri | 1,571,697 | 807,356 | 51.4 | 761,175 | 48.4 | 1,751 | 0.1 | 1,195 | 0.1 | 220 | | 46,181 | D |
| Montana | 207,355 | 112,556 | 54.3 | 93,163 | 44.9 | 1,296 | 0.6 | 340 | 0.2 | — | | 19,393 | D |
| Nebraska | 563,126 | 233,246 | 41.4 | 329,880 | 58.6 | — | | — | | — | | 96,634 | R |
| Nevada | 54,234 | 29,623 | 54.6 | 24,611 | 45.4 | — | | — | | — | | 5,012 | D |
| New Hampshire | 229,625 | 119,663 | 52.1 | 109,916 | 47.9 | 46 | | — | | — | | 9,747 | D |
| New Jersey | 1,963,761 | 987,874 | 50.3 | 961,335 | 49.0 | 3,358 | 0.2 | 4,255 | 0.2 | 6,939 | 0.4 | 26,539 | D |
| New Mexico | 152,225 | 81,389 | 53.5 | 70,688 | 46.4 | — | | 148 | 0.1 | — | | 10,701 | D |
| New York | 6,316,790 | 3,304,238 | 52.3 | 2,987,647 | 47.3 | 10,553 | 0.2 | — | | 14,352 | 0.2 | 316,591 | D |
| North Carolina | 790,554 | 527,399 | 66.7 | 263,155 | 33.3 | — | | — | | — | | 264,244 | D |
| North Dakota | 220,182 | 100,144 | 45.5 | 118,535 | 53.8 | 954 | 0.4 | 549 | 0.2 | — | | 18,391 | R |
| Ohio | 3,153,056 | 1,570,763 | 49.8 | 1,582,293 | 50.2 | — | | — | | — | | 11,530 | R |
| Oklahoma | 722,636 | 401,549 | 55.6 | 319,424 | 44.2 | — | | 1,663 | 0.2 | — | | 82,125 | D |
| Oregon | 480,147 | 248,635 | 51.8 | 225,365 | 46.9 | 3,785 | 0.8 | 2,362 | 0.5 | — | | 23,270 | D |
| Pennsylvania | 3,794,793 | 1,940,479 | 51.1 | 1,835,054 | 48.4 | 11,721 | 0.3 | 5,750 | 0.2 | 1,789 | | 105,425 | D |
| Rhode Island | 299,276 | 175,356 | 58.6 | 123,487 | 41.3 | — | | 433 | 0.1 | — | | 51,869 | D |
| South Carolina | 103,382 | 90,601 | 87.6 | 4,617 | 4.5 | — | | 365 | 0.4 | 7,799 | 7.5 | 82,802 | D [2] |
| South Dakota | 232,076 | 96,711 | 41.7 | 135,365 | 58.3 | — | | — | | — | | 38,654 | R |
| Tennessee | 510,692 | 308,707 | 60.4 | 200,311 | 39.2 | 792 | 0.2 | 882 | 0.2 | — | | 108,396 | D |
| Texas | 1,150,334 | 821,605 | 71.4 | 191,423 | 16.6 | 594 | 0.1 | 1,018 | 0.1 | 135,694 | 11.8 | 630,182 | D |
| Utah | 248,319 | 150,088 | 60.4 | 97,891 | 39.4 | 340 | 0.1 | — | | — | | 52,197 | D |
| Vermont | 125,361 | 53,820 | 42.9 | 71,527 | 57.1 | — | | — | | 14 | | 17,707 | R |
| Virginia | 388,485 | 242,276 | 62.4 | 145,243 | 37.4 | 417 | 0.1 | 459 | 0.1 | 90 | | 97,033 | D |
| Washington | 856,328 | 486,774 | 56.8 | 361,689 | 42.2 | 3,824 | 0.4 | 2,396 | 0.3 | 1,645 | 0.2 | 125,085 | D |
| West Virginia | 715,596 | 392,777 | 54.9 | 322,819 | 45.1 | — | | — | | — | | 69,958 | D |
| Wisconsin | 1,339,152 | 650,413 | 48.6 | 674,532 | 50.4 | 13,205 | 1.0 | — | | 1,002 | 0.1 | 24,119 | R |
| Wyoming | 101,340 | 49,419 | 48.8 | 51,921 | 51.2 | — | | — | | — | | 2,502 | R |
| Totals | 47,976,670 | 25,612,610 | 53.4 | 22,017,617 | 45.9 | 79,003 | 0.2 | 74,779 | 0.2 | 192,661 | 0.4 | 3,594,993 | D |

1. For breakdown of "Other" vote see minor candidate vote totals, p. 473.
2. Plurality of 82,802 votes is calculated on the basis of 7,799 votes cast for Southern Democratic electors.

# 1948 Presidential Election

| STATE | TOTAL VOTE | HARRY S. TRUMAN (Democrat) | | THOMAS E. DEWEY (Republican) | | J. STROM THURMOND (States' Rights Democrat) | | HENRY A. WALLACE (Progressive) | | OTHER [1] | | PLURALITY | |
|---|---|---|---|---|---|---|---|---|---|---|---|---|---|
| | | Votes | % | Votes | % | Votes | % | Votes | % | Votes | % | | |
| Alabama | 214,980 | — | | 40,930 | 19.0 | 171,443 | 79.7 | 1,522 | 0.7 | 1,085 | 0.5 | 130,513 | SR |
| Arizona | 177,065 | 95,251 | 53.8 | 77,597 | 43.8 | — | | 3,310 | 1.9 | 907 | 0.5 | 17,654 | D |
| Arkansas | 242,475 | 149,659 | 61.7 | 50,959 | 21.0 | 40,068 | 16.5 | 751 | 0.3 | 1,038 | 0.4 | 98,700 | D |
| California | 4,021,538 | 1,913,134 | 47.6 | 1,895,269 | 47.1 | 1,228 | | 190,381 | 4.7 | 21,526 | 0.5 | 17,865 | D |
| Colorado | 515,237 | 267,288 | 51.9 | 239,714 | 46.5 | — | | 6,115 | 1.2 | 2,120 | 0.4 | 27,574 | D |
| Connecticut | 883,518 | 423,297 | 47.9 | 437,754 | 49.5 | — | | 13,713 | 1.6 | 8,754 | 1.0 | 14,457 | R |
| Delaware | 139,073 | 67,813 | 48.8 | 69,588 | 50.0 | — | | 1,050 | 0.8 | 622 | 0.4 | 1,775 | R |
| Florida | 577,643 | 281,988 | 48.8 | 194,280 | 33.6 | 89,755 | 15.5 | 11,620 | 2.0 | — | | 87,708 | D |
| Georgia | 418,844 | 254,646 | 60.8 | 76,691 | 18.3 | 85,135 | 20.3 | 1,636 | 0.4 | 736 | 0.2 | 169,511 | D |
| Idaho | 214,816 | 107,370 | 50.0 | 101,514 | 47.3 | — | | 4,972 | 2.3 | 960 | 0.4 | 5,856 | D |
| Illinois | 3,984,046 | 1,994,715 | 50.1 | 1,961,103 | 49.2 | — | | — | | 28,228 | 0.7 | 33,612 | D |
| Indiana | 1,656,212 | 807,831 | 48.8 | 821,079 | 49.6 | — | | 9,649 | 0.6 | 17,653 | 1.1 | 13,248 | R |
| Iowa | 1,038,264 | 522,380 | 50.3 | 494,018 | 47.6 | — | | 12,125 | 1.2 | 9,741 | 0.9 | 28,362 | D |
| Kansas | 788,819 | 351,902 | 44.6 | 423,039 | 53.6 | — | | 4,603 | 0.6 | 9,275 | 1.2 | 71,137 | R |
| Kentucky | 822,658 | 466,756 | 56.7 | 341,210 | 41.5 | 10,411 | 1.3 | 1,567 | 0.2 | 2,714 | 0.3 | 125,546 | D |
| Louisiana | 416,336 | 136,344 | 32.7 | 72,657 | 17.5 | 204,290 | 49.1 | 3,035 | 0.7 | 10 | | 67,946 | SR |
| Maine | 264,787 | 111,916 | 42.3 | 150,234 | 56.7 | — | | 1,884 | 0.7 | 753 | 0.3 | 38,318 | R |
| Maryland | 596,748 | 286,521 | 48.0 | 294,814 | 49.4 | 2,489 | 0.4 | 9,983 | 1.7 | 2,941 | 0.5 | 8,293 | R |
| Massachusetts | 2,107,146 | 1,151,788 | 54.7 | 909,370 | 43.2 | — | | 38,157 | 1.8 | 7,831 | 0.4 | 242,418 | D |
| Michigan | 2,109,609 | 1,003,448 | 47.6 | 1,038,595 | 49.2 | — | | 46,515 | 2.2 | 21,051 | 1.0 | 35,147 | R |
| Minnesota | 1,212,226 | 692,966 | 57.2 | 483,617 | 39.9 | — | | 27,866 | 2.3 | 7,777 | 0.6 | 209,349 | D |
| Mississippi | 192,190 | 19,384 | 10.1 | 5,043 | 2.6 | 167,538 | 87.2 | 225 | 0.1 | — | | 148,154 | SR |
| Missouri | 1,578,628 | 917,315 | 58.1 | 655,039 | 41.5 | — | | 3,998 | 0.3 | 2,276 | 0.1 | 262,276 | D |
| Montana | 224,278 | 119,071 | 53.1 | 96,770 | 43.1 | — | | 7,313 | 3.3 | 1,124 | 0.5 | 22,301 | D |
| Nebraska | 488,940 | 224,165 | 45.8 | 264,774 | 54.2 | — | | — | | 1 | | 40,609 | R |
| Nevada | 62,117 | 31,291 | 50.4 | 29,357 | 47.3 | — | | 1,469 | 2.4 | — | | 1,934 | D |
| New Hampshire | 231,440 | 107,995 | 46.7 | 121,299 | 52.4 | 7 | | 1,970 | 0.9 | 169 | 0.1 | 13,304 | R |
| New Jersey | 1,949,555 | 895,455 | 45.9 | 981,124 | 50.3 | — | | 42,683 | 2.2 | 30,293 | 1.6 | 85,669 | R |
| New Mexico | 187,063 | 105,464 | 56.4 | 80,303 | 42.9 | — | | 1,037 | 0.6 | 259 | 0.1 | 25,161 | D |
| New York | 6,177,337 | 2,780,204 | 45.0 | 2,841,163 | 46.0 | — | | 509,559 | 8.2 | 46,411 | 0.8 | 60,959 | R |
| North Carolina | 791,209 | 459,070 | 58.0 | 258,572 | 32.7 | 69,652 | 8.8 | 3,915 | 0.5 | — | | 200,498 | D |
| North Dakota | 220,716 | 95,812 | 43.4 | 115,139 | 52.2 | 374 | 0.2 | 8,391 | 3.8 | 1,000 | 0.5 | 19,327 | R |
| Ohio | 2,936,071 | 1,452,791 | 49.5 | 1,445,684 | 49.2 | — | | 37,596 | 1.3 | — | | 7,107 | D |
| Oklahoma | 721,599 | 452,782 | 62.7 | 268,817 | 37.3 | — | | — | | — | | 183,965 | D |
| Oregon | 524,080 | 243,147 | 46.4 | 260,904 | 49.8 | — | | 14,978 | 2.9 | 5,051 | 1.0 | 17,757 | R |
| Pennsylvania | 3,735,348 | 1,752,426 | 46.9 | 1,902,197 | 50.9 | — | | 55,161 | 1.5 | 25,564 | 0.7 | 149,771 | R |
| Rhode Island | 327,702 | 188,736 | 57.6 | 135,787 | 41.4 | — | | 2,619 | 0.8 | 560 | 0.2 | 52,949 | D |
| South Carolina | 142,571 | 34,423 | 24.1 | 5,386 | 3.8 | 102,607 | 72.0 | 154 | 0.1 | 1 | | 68,184 | SR |
| South Dakota | 250,105 | 117,653 | 47.0 | 129,651 | 51.8 | — | | 2,801 | 1.1 | — | | 11,998 | R |
| Tennessee | 550,283 | 270,402 | 49.1 | 202,914 | 36.9 | 73,815 | 13.4 | 1,864 | 0.3 | 1,288 | 0.2 | 67,488 | D |
| Texas | 1,249,577 | 824,235 | 66.0 | 303,467 | 24.3 | 113,920 | 9.1 | 3,918 | 0.3 | 4,037 | 0.3 | 520,768 | D |
| Utah | 276,306 | 149,151 | 54.0 | 124,402 | 45.0 | — | | 2,679 | 1.0 | 74 | | 24,749 | D |
| Vermont | 123,382 | 45,557 | 36.9 | 75,926 | 61.5 | — | | 1,279 | 1.0 | 620 | 0.5 | 30,369 | R |
| Virginia | 419,256 | 200,786 | 47.9 | 172,070 | 41.0 | 43,393 | 10.4 | 2,047 | 0.5 | 960 | 0.2 | 28,716 | D |
| Washington | 905,058 | 476,165 | 52.6 | 386,314 | 42.7 | — | | 31,692 | 3.5 | 10,887 | 1.2 | 89,851 | D |
| West Virginia | 748,750 | 429,188 | 57.3 | 316,251 | 42.2 | — | | 3,311 | 0.4 | — | | 112,937 | D |
| Wisconsin | 1,276,800 | 647,310 | 50.7 | 590,959 | 46.3 | — | | 25,282 | 2.0 | 13,249 | 1.0 | 56,351 | D |
| Wyoming | 101,425 | 52,354 | 51.6 | 47,947 | 47.3 | — | | 931 | 0.9 | 193 | 0.2 | 4,407 | D |
| **Totals** | **48,793,826** | **24,179,345** | **49.6** | **21,991,291** | **45.1** | **1,176,125** | **2.4** | **1,157,326** | **2.4** | **289,739** | **0.6** | **2,188,054** | **D** |

*1. For breakdown of "Other" vote, see minor candidate vote totals, p. 473.*

# 1952 Presidential Election

| STATE | TOTAL VOTE | DWIGHT D. EISENHOWER (Republican) | | ADLAI E. STEVENSON (Democrat) | | VINCENT HALLINAN (Progressive) | | STUART HAMBLEN (Prohibition) | | OTHER [1] | | PLURALITY | |
|---|---|---|---|---|---|---|---|---|---|---|---|---|---|
| | | Votes | % | Votes | % | Votes | % | Votes | % | Votes | % | | |
| Alabama | 426,120 | 149,231 | 35.0 | 275,075 | 64.6 | — | | 1,814 | 0.4 | — | | 125,844 | D |
| Arizona | 260,570 | 152,042 | 58.3 | 108,528 | 41.7 | — | | — | | — | | 43,514 | R |
| Arkansas | 404,800 | 177,155 | 43.8 | 226,300 | 55.9 | — | | 886 | 0.2 | 459 | 0.1 | 49,145 | D |
| California | 5,141,849 | 2,897,310 | 56.3 | 2,197,548 | 42.7 | 24,106 | 0.5 | 15,653 | 0.3 | 7,232 | 0.1 | 699,762 | R |
| Colorado | 630,103 | 379,782 | 60.3 | 245,504 | 39.0 | 1,919 | 0.3 | — | | 2,898 | 0.5 | 134,278 | R |
| Connecticut | 1,096,911 | 611,012 | 55.7 | 481,649 | 43.9 | 1,466 | 0.1 | — | | 2,784 | 0.3 | 129,363 | R |
| Delaware | 174,025 | 90,059 | 51.8 | 83,315 | 47.9 | 155 | 0.1 | 234 | 0.1 | 262 | 0.2 | 6,744 | R |
| Florida | 989,337 | 544,036 | 55.0 | 444,950 | 45.0 | — | | — | | 351 | | 99,086 | R |
| Georgia | 655,785 | 198,961 | 30.3 | 456,823 | 69.7 | — | | — | | 1 | | 257,862 | D |
| Idaho | 276,254 | 180,707 | 65.4 | 95,081 | 34.4 | 443 | 0.2 | — | | 23 | | 85,626 | R |
| Illinois | 4,481,058 | 2,457,327 | 54.8 | 2,013,920 | 44.9 | — | | — | | 9,811 | 0.2 | 443,407 | R |
| Indiana | 1,955,049 | 1,136,259 | 58.1 | 801,530 | 41.0 | 1,085 | 0.1 | 15,335 | 0.8 | 840 | | 334,729 | R |
| Iowa | 1,268,773 | 808,906 | 63.8 | 451,513 | 35.6 | 5,085 | 0.4 | 2,882 | 0.2 | 387 | | 357,393 | R |
| Kansas | 896,166 | 616,302 | 68.8 | 273,296 | 30.5 | — | | 6,038 | 0.7 | 530 | 0.1 | 343,006 | R |
| Kentucky | 993,148 | 495,029 | 49.8 | 495,729 | 49.9 | 336 | | 1,161 | 0.1 | 893 | 0.1 | 700 | D |
| Louisiana | 651,952 | 306,925 | 47.1 | 345,027 | 52.9 | — | | — | | — | | 38,102 | D |
| Maine | 351,786 | 232,353 | 66.0 | 118,806 | 33.8 | 332 | 0.1 | — | | 295 | 0.1 | 113,547 | R |
| Maryland | 902,074 | 499,424 | 55.4 | 395,337 | 43.8 | 7,313 | 0.8 | — | | — | | 104,087 | R |
| Massachusetts | 2,383,398 | 1,292,325 | 54.2 | 1,083,525 | 45.5 | 4,636 | 0.2 | 886 | | 2,026 | 0.1 | 208,800 | R |
| Michigan | 2,798,592 | 1,551,529 | 55.4 | 1,230,657 | 44.0 | 3,922 | 0.1 | 10,331 | 0.4 | 2,153 | 0.1 | 320,872 | R |
| Minnesota | 1,379,483 | 763,211 | 55.3 | 608,458 | 44.1 | 2,666 | 0.2 | 2,147 | 0.2 | 3,001 | 0.2 | 154,753 | R |
| Mississippi | 285,532 | 112,966 | 39.6 | 172,566 | 60.4 | — | | — | | — | | 59,600 | D |
| Missouri | 1,892,062 | 959,429 | 50.7 | 929,830 | 49.1 | 987 | 0.1 | 885 | | 931 | | 29,599 | R |
| Montana | 265,037 | 157,394 | 59.4 | 106,213 | 40.1 | 723 | 0.3 | 548 | 0.2 | 159 | 0.1 | 51,181 | R |
| Nebraska | 609,660 | 421,603 | 69.2 | 188,057 | 30.8 | — | | — | | — | | 233,546 | R |
| Nevada | 82,190 | 50,502 | 61.4 | 31,688 | 38.6 | — | | — | | — | | 18,814 | R |
| New Hampshire | 272,950 | 166,287 | 60.9 | 106,663 | 39.1 | — | | — | | — | | 59,624 | R |
| New Jersey | 2,418,554 | 1,373,613 | 56.8 | 1,015,902 | 42.0 | 5,589 | 0.2 | 989 | | 22,461 | 0.9 | 357,711 | R |
| New Mexico | 238,608 | 132,170 | 55.4 | 105,661 | 44.3 | 225 | 0.1 | 297 | 0.1 | 255 | 0.1 | 26,509 | R |
| New York | 7,128,239 | 3,952,813 | 55.5 | 3,104,601 | 43.6 | 64,211 | 0.9 | — | | 6,614 | 0.1 | 848,212 | R |
| North Carolina | 1,210,910 | 558,107 | 46.1 | 652,803 | 53.9 | — | | — | | — | | 94,696 | D |
| North Dakota | 270,127 | 191,712 | 71.0 | 76,694 | 28.4 | 344 | 0.1 | 302 | 0.1 | 1,075 | 0.4 | 115,018 | R |
| Ohio | 3,700,758 | 2,100,391 | 56.8 | 1,600,367 | 43.2 | — | | — | | — | | 500,024 | R |
| Oklahoma | 948,984 | 518,045 | 54.6 | 430,939 | 45.4 | — | | — | | — | | 87,106 | R |
| Oregon | 695,059 | 420,815 | 60.5 | 270,579 | 38.9 | 3,665 | 0.5 | — | | — | | 150,236 | R |
| Pennsylvania | 4,580,969 | 2,415,789 | 52.7 | 2,146,269 | 46.9 | 4,222 | 0.1 | 8,951 | 0.2 | 5,738 | 0.1 | 269,520 | R |
| Rhode Island | 414,498 | 210,935 | 50.9 | 203,293 | 49.0 | 187 | | — | | 83 | | 7,642 | R |
| South Carolina | 341,087 | 168,082 | 49.3 | 173,004 | 50.7 | — | | 1 | | — | | 4,922 | D |
| South Dakota | 294,283 | 203,857 | 69.3 | 90,426 | 30.7 | — | | — | | — | | 113,431 | R |
| Tennessee | 892,553 | 446,147 | 50.0 | 443,710 | 49.7 | 885 | 0.1 | 1,432 | 0.2 | 379 | | 2,437 | R |
| Texas | 2,075,946 | 1,102,878 | 53.1 | 969,228 | 46.7 | 294 | | 1,983 | 0.1 | 1,563 | 0.1 | 133,650 | R |
| Utah | 329,554 | 194,190 | 58.9 | 135,364 | 41.1 | — | | — | | — | | 58,826 | R |
| Vermont | 153,557 | 109,717 | 71.5 | 43,355 | 28.2 | 282 | 0.2 | — | | 203 | 0.1 | 66,362 | R |
| Virginia | 619,689 | 349,037 | 56.3 | 268,677 | 43.4 | 311 | 0.1 | — | | 1,664 | 0.3 | 80,360 | R |
| Washington | 1,102,708 | 599,107 | 54.3 | 492,845 | 44.7 | 2,460 | 0.2 | — | | 8,296 | 0.8 | 106,262 | R |
| West Virginia | 873,548 | 419,970 | 48.1 | 453,578 | 51.9 | — | | — | | — | | 33,608 | D |
| Wisconsin | 1,607,370 | 979,744 | 61.0 | 622,175 | 38.7 | 2,174 | 0.1 | — | | 3,277 | 0.2 | 357,569 | R |
| Wyoming | 129,253 | 81,049 | 62.7 | 47,934 | 37.1 | — | | 194 | 0.2 | 76 | 0.1 | 33,115 | R |
| Totals | 61,550,918 | 33,936,234 | 55.1 | 27,314,992 | 44.4 | 140,023 | 0.2 | 72,949 | 0.1 | 86,720 | 0.1 | 6,621,242 | R |

1. For breakdown of "Other" vote, see minor candidate vote totals, p. 473.

# 1956 Presidential Election

| STATE | TOTAL VOTE | DWIGHT D. EISENHOWER (Republican) | | ADLAI E. STEVENSON (Democrat) | | T. COLEMAN ANDREWS (Constitution) | | ERIC HASS (Socialist Labor) | | OTHER [1] | | PLURALITY | |
|---|---|---|---|---|---|---|---|---|---|---|---|---|---|
| | | Votes | % | Votes | % | Votes | % | Votes | % | Votes | % | | |
| Alabama | 496,861 | 195,694 | 39.4 | 280,844 | 56.5 | — | | — | | 20,323 | 4.1 | 85,150 | D |
| Arizona | 290,173 | 176,990 | 61.0 | 112,880 | 38.9 | 303 | 0.1 | — | | — | | 64,110 | R |
| Arkansas | 406,572 | 186,287 | 45.8 | 213,277 | 52.5 | 7,008 | 1.7 | — | | — | | 26,990 | D |
| California | 5,466,355 | 3,027,668 | 55.4 | 2,420,135 | 44.3 | 6,087 | 0.1 | 300 | | 12,165 | 0.2 | 607,533 | R |
| Colorado | 657,074 | 394,479 | 60.0 | 257,997 | 39.3 | 759 | 0.1 | 3,308 | 0.5 | 531 | 0.1 | 136,482 | R |
| Connecticut | 1,117,121 | 711,837 | 63.7 | 405,079 | 36.3 | — | | — | | 205 | | 306,758 | R |
| Delaware | 177,988 | 98,057 | 55.1 | 79,421 | 44.6 | | | 110 | 0.1 | 400 | 0.2 | 18,636 | R |
| Florida | 1,125,762 | 643,849 | 57.2 | 480,371 | 42.7 | — | | — | | 1,542 | 0.1 | 163,478 | R |
| Georgia | 669,655 | 222,778 | 33.3 | 444,688 | 66.4 | 2,096 | 0.3 | — | | 93 | | 221,910 | D |
| Idaho | 272,989 | 166,979 | 61.2 | 105,868 | 38.8 | 126 | | — | | 16 | | 61,111 | R |
| Illinois | 4,407,407 | 2,623,327 | 59.5 | 1,775,682 | 40.3 | — | | 8,342 | 0.2 | 56 | | 847,645 | R |
| Indiana | 1,974,607 | 1,182,811 | 59.9 | 783,908 | 39.7 | — | | 1,334 | 0.1 | 6,554 | 0.3 | 398,903 | R |
| Iowa | 1,234,564 | 729,187 | 59.1 | 501,858 | 40.7 | 3,202 | 0.3 | 125 | | 192 | | 227,329 | R |
| Kansas | 866,243 | 566,878 | 65.4 | 296,317 | 34.2 | — | | — | | 3,048 | 0.4 | 270,561 | R |
| Kentucky | 1,053,805 | 572,192 | 54.3 | 476,453 | 45.2 | — | | 358 | | 4,802 | 0.5 | 95,739 | R |
| Louisiana | 617,544 | 329,047 | 53.3 | 243,977 | 39.5 | — | | — | | 44,520 | 7.2 | 85,070 | R |
| Maine | 351,706 | 249,238 | 70.9 | 102,468 | 29.1 | — | | — | | — | | 146,770 | R |
| Maryland | 932,827 | 559,738 | 60.0 | 372,613 | 39.9 | — | | — | | 476 | 0.1 | 187,125 | R |
| Massachusetts | 2,348,506 | 1,393,197 | 59.3 | 948,190 | 40.4 | — | | 5,573 | 0.2 | 1,546 | 0.1 | 445,007 | R |
| Michigan | 3,080,468 | 1,713,647 | 55.6 | 1,359,898 | 44.1 | — | | — | | 6,923 | 0.2 | 353,749 | R |
| Minnesota | 1,340,005 | 719,302 | 53.7 | 617,525 | 46.1 | — | | 2,080 | 0.2 | 1,098 | 0.1 | 101,777 | R |
| Mississippi | 248,104 | 60,685 | 24.5 | 144,453 | 58.2 | — | | — | | 42,966 | 17.3 | 83,768 | D |
| Missouri | 1,832,562 | 914,289 | 49.9 | 918,273 | 50.1 | — | | — | | — | | 3,984 | D |
| Montana | 271,171 | 154,933 | 57.1 | 116,238 | 42.9 | — | | — | | — | | 38,695 | R |
| Nebraska | 577,137 | 378,108 | 65.5 | 199,029 | 34.5 | — | | — | | — | | 179,079 | R |
| Nevada | 96,689 | 56,049 | 58.0 | 40,640 | 42.0 | — | | — | | — | | 15,409 | R |
| New Hampshire | 266,994 | 176,519 | 66.1 | 90,364 | 33.8 | 111 | | — | | — | | 86,155 | R |
| New Jersey | 2,484,312 | 1,606,942 | 64.7 | 850,337 | 34.2 | 5,317 | 0.2 | 6,736 | 0.3 | 14,980 | 0.6 | 756,605 | R |
| New Mexico | 253,926 | 146,788 | 57.8 | 106,098 | 41.8 | 364 | 0.1 | 69 | | 607 | 0.2 | 40,690 | R |
| New York | 7,095,971 | 4,345,506 | 61.2 | 2,747,944 | 38.7 | 1,027 | | 150 | | 1,344 | | 1,597,562 | R |
| North Carolina | 1,165,592 | 575,062 | 49.3 | 590,530 | 50.7 | — | | — | | — | | 15,468 | D |
| North Dakota | 253,991 | 156,766 | 61.7 | 96,742 | 38.1 | 483 | 0.2 | — | | — | | 60,024 | R |
| Ohio | 3,702,265 | 2,262,610 | 61.1 | 1,439,655 | 38.9 | — | | — | | — | | 822,955 | R |
| Oklahoma | 859,350 | 473,769 | 55.1 | 385,581 | 44.9 | — | | — | | — | | 88,188 | R |
| Oregon | 736,132 | 406,393 | 55.2 | 329,204 | 44.7 | — | | — | | 535 | 0.1 | 77,189 | R |
| Pennsylvania | 4,576,503 | 2,585,252 | 56.5 | 1,981,769 | 43.3 | — | | 7,447 | 0.2 | 2,035 | | 603,483 | R |
| Rhode Island | 387,609 | 225,819 | 58.3 | 161,790 | 41.7 | — | | — | | — | | 64,029 | R |
| South Carolina | 300,583 | 75,700 | 25.2 | 136,372 | 45.4 | 2 | | — | | 88,509 | 29.4 | 47,863 | D [2] |
| South Dakota | 293,857 | 171,569 | 58.4 | 122,288 | 41.6 | — | | — | | — | | 49,281 | R |
| Tennessee | 939,404 | 462,288 | 49.2 | 456,507 | 48.6 | 19,820 | 2.1 | — | | 789 | 0.1 | 5,781 | R |
| Texas | 1,955,168 | 1,080,619 | 55.3 | 859,958 | 44.0 | 14,591 | 0.7 | — | | — | | 220,661 | R |
| Utah | 333,995 | 215,631 | 64.6 | 118,364 | 35.4 | — | | — | | — | | 97,267 | R |
| Vermont | 152,978 | 110,390 | 72.2 | 42,549 | 27.8 | — | | — | | 39 | | 67,841 | R |
| Virginia | 697,978 | 386,459 | 55.4 | 267,760 | 38.4 | 42,964 | 6.2 | 351 | 0.1 | 444 | 0.1 | 118,699 | R |
| Washington | 1,150,889 | 620,430 | 53.9 | 523,002 | 45.4 | — | | 7,457 | 0.6 | — | | 97,428 | R |
| West Virginia | 830,831 | 449,297 | 54.1 | 381,534 | 45.9 | — | | — | | — | | 67,763 | R |
| Wisconsin | 1,550,558 | 954,844 | 61.6 | 586,768 | 37.8 | 6,918 | 0.4 | 710 | | 1,318 | 0.1 | 368,076 | R |
| Wyoming | 124,127 | 74,573 | 60.1 | 49,554 | 39.9 | — | | — | | — | | 25,019 | R |
| **Totals** | **62,026,908** | **35,590,472** | **57.4** | **26,022,752** | **42.0** | **111,178** | **0.2** | **44,450** | **0.1** | **258,056** | **0.4** | **9,567,720** | **R** |

1. For breakdown of "Other" vote, see minor candidate vote totals, p. 474.
2. Plurality of 47,863 votes is calculated on the basis of Stevenson's vote and the 88,509 votes cast for unpledged electors.

# 1960 Presidential Election

| STATE | TOTAL VOTE | JOHN F. KENNEDY (Democrat) | | RICHARD M. NIXON (Republican) | | ERIC HASS (Socialist Labor) | | UNPLEDGED | | OTHER [1] | | PLURALITY | |
|---|---|---|---|---|---|---|---|---|---|---|---|---|---|
| | | Votes | % | Votes | % | Votes | % | Votes | % | Votes | % | | |
| Alabama | 570,225 | 324,050 | 56.8 | 237,981 | 41.7 | — | | — | | 8,194 | 1.4 | 86,069 | D |
| Alaska | 60,762 | 29,809 | 49.1 | 30,953 | 50.9 | — | | — | | — | | 1,144 | R |
| Arizona | 398,491 | 176,781 | 44.4 | 221,241 | 55.5 | 469 | 0.1 | — | | — | | 44,460 | R |
| Arkansas | 428,509 | 215,049 | 50.2 | 184,508 | 43.1 | — | | — | | 28,952 | 6.8 | 30,541 | D |
| California | 6,506,578 | 3,224,099 | 49.6 | 3,259,722 | 50.1 | 1,051 | | — | | 21,706 | 0.3 | 35,623 | R |
| Colorado | 736,236 | 330,629 | 44.9 | 402,242 | 54.6 | 2,803 | 0.4 | — | | 562 | 0.1 | 71,613 | R |
| Connecticut | 1,222,883 | 657,055 | 53.7 | 565,813 | 46.3 | — | | — | | 15 | | 91,242 | D |
| Delaware | 196,683 | 99,590 | 50.6 | 96,373 | 49.0 | 82 | | — | | 638 | 0.3 | 3,217 | D |
| Florida | 1,544,176 | 748,700 | 48.5 | 795,476 | 51.5 | — | | — | | — | | 46,776 | R |
| Georgia | 733,349 | 458,638 | 62.5 | 274,472 | 37.4 | — | | — | | 239 | | 184,166 | D |
| Hawaii | 184,705 | 92,410 | 50.0 | 92,295 | 50.0 | — | | — | | — | | 115 | D |
| Idaho | 300,450 | 138,853 | 46.2 | 161,597 | 53.8 | — | | — | | — | | 22,744 | R |
| Illinois | 4,757,409 | 2,377,846 | 50.0 | 2,368,988 | 49.8 | 10,560 | 0.2 | — | | 15 | | 8,858 | D |
| Indiana | 2,135,360 | 952,358 | 44.6 | 1,175,120 | 55.0 | 1,136 | 0.1 | — | | 6,746 | 0.3 | 222,762 | R |
| Iowa | 1,273,810 | 550,565 | 43.2 | 722,381 | 56.7 | 230 | | — | | 634 | | 171,816 | R |
| Kansas | 928,825 | 363,213 | 39.1 | 561,474 | 60.4 | — | | — | | 4,138 | 0.4 | 198,261 | R |
| Kentucky | 1,124,462 | 521,855 | 46.4 | 602,607 | 53.6 | — | | — | | — | | 80,752 | R |
| Louisiana | 807,891 | 407,339 | 50.4 | 230,980 | 28.6 | — | | — | | 169,572 | 21.0 | 176,359 | D |
| Maine | 421,767 | 181,159 | 43.0 | 240,608 | 57.0 | — | | — | | — | | 59,449 | R |
| Maryland | 1,055,349 | 565,808 | 53.6 | 489,538 | 46.4 | — | | — | | 3 | | 76,270 | D |
| Massachusetts | 2,469,480 | 1,487,174 | 60.2 | 976,750 | 39.6 | 3,892 | 0.2 | — | | 1,664 | 0.1 | 510,424 | D |
| Michigan | 3,318,097 | 1,687,269 | 50.9 | 1,620,428 | 48.8 | 1,718 | 0.1 | — | | 8,682 | 0.3 | 66,841 | D |
| Minnesota | 1,541,887 | 779,933 | 50.6 | 757,915 | 49.2 | 962 | 0.1 | — | | 3,077 | 0.2 | 22,018 | D |
| Mississippi | 298,171 | 108,362 | 36.3 | 73,561 | 24.7 | — | | 116,248 [2] | 39.0 | — | | 7,886 | U |
| Missouri | 1,934,422 | 972,201 | 50.3 | 962,221 | 49.7 | — | | — | | — | | 9,980 | D |
| Montana | 277,579 | 134,891 | 48.6 | 141,841 | 51.1 | — | | — | | 847 | 0.3 | 6,950 | R |
| Nebraska | 613,095 | 232,542 | 37.9 | 380,553 | 62.1 | — | | — | | — | | 148,011 | R |
| Nevada | 107,267 | 54,880 | 51.2 | 52,387 | 48.8 | — | | — | | — | | 2,493 | D |
| New Hampshire | 295,761 | 137,772 | 46.6 | 157,989 | 53.4 | — | | — | | — | | 20,217 | R |
| New Jersey | 2,773,111 | 1,385,415 | 50.0 | 1,363,324 | 49.2 | 4,262 | 0.2 | — | | 20,110 | 0.7 | 22,091 | D |
| New Mexico | 311,107 | 156,027 | 50.2 | 153,733 | 49.4 | 570 | 0.2 | — | | 777 | 0.2 | 2,294 | D |
| New York | 7,291,079 | 3,830,085 | 52.5 | 3,446,419 | 47.3 | — | | — | | 14,575 | 0.2 | 383,666 | D |
| North Carolina | 1,368,556 | 713,136 | 52.1 | 655,420 | 47.9 | — | | — | | — | | 57,716 | D |
| North Dakota | 278,431 | 123,963 | 44.5 | 154,310 | 55.4 | — | | — | | 158 | 0.1 | 30,347 | R |
| Ohio | 4,161,859 | 1,944,248 | 46.7 | 2,217,611 | 53.3 | — | | — | | — | | 273,363 | R |
| Oklahoma | 903,150 | 370,111 | 41.0 | 533,039 | 59.0 | — | | — | | — | | 162,928 | R |
| Oregon | 776,421 | 367,402 | 47.3 | 408,060 | 52.6 | — | | — | | 959 | 0.1 | 40,658 | R |
| Pennsylvania | 5,006,541 | 2,556,282 | 51.1 | 2,439,956 | 48.7 | 7,185 | 0.1 | — | | 3,118 | 0.1 | 116,326 | D |
| Rhode Island | 405,535 | 258,032 | 63.6 | 147,502 | 36.4 | — | | — | | 1 | | 110,530 | D |
| South Carolina | 386,688 | 198,129 | 51.2 | 188,558 | 48.8 | — | | — | | 1 | | 9,571 | D |
| South Dakota | 306,487 | 128,070 | 41.8 | 178,417 | 58.2 | — | | — | | — | | 50,347 | R |
| Tennessee | 1,051,792 | 481,453 | 45.8 | 556,577 | 52.9 | — | | — | | 13,762 | 1.3 | 75,124 | R |
| Texas | 2,311,084 | 1,167,567 | 50.5 | 1,121,310 | 48.5 | — | | — | | 22,207 | 1.0 | 46,257 | D |
| Utah | 374,709 | 169,248 | 45.2 | 205,361 | 54.8 | — | | — | | 100 | | 36,113 | R |
| Vermont | 167,324 | 69,186 | 41.3 | 98,131 | 58.6 | — | | — | | 7 | | 28,945 | R |
| Virginia | 771,449 | 362,327 | 47.0 | 404,521 | 52.4 | 397 | 0.1 | — | | 4,204 | 0.5 | 42,194 | R |
| Washington | 1,241,572 | 599,298 | 48.3 | 629,273 | 50.7 | 10,895 | 0.9 | — | | 2,106 | 0.2 | 29,975 | R |
| West Virginia | 837,781 | 441,786 | 52.7 | 395,995 | 47.3 | — | | — | | — | | 45,791 | D |
| Wisconsin | 1,729,082 | 830,805 | 48.0 | 895,175 | 51.8 | 1,310 | 0.1 | — | | 1,792 | 0.1 | 64,370 | R |
| Wyoming | 140,782 | 63,331 | 45.0 | 77,451 | 55.0 | — | | — | | — | | 14,120 | R |
| Totals | 68,838,219 | 34,226,731 | 49.7 | 34,108,157 | 49.5 | 47,522 | 0.1 | 116,248 | 0.2 | 339,561 | 0.5 | 118,574 | D |

1. For breakdown of "Other" vote, see minor candidate vote totals, p. 474.
2. Votes for unpledged electors who carried the state and cast electoral votes for Harry F. Byrd (D Va.).

# 1964 Presidential Election

| STATE | TOTAL VOTE | LYNDON B. JOHNSON (Democrat) | | BARRY M. GOLDWATER (Republican) | | ERIC HASS (Socialist Labor) | | CLIFTON DeBERRY (Socialist Workers) | | OTHER [1] | | PLURALITY | |
|---|---|---|---|---|---|---|---|---|---|---|---|---|---|
| | | Votes | % | Votes | % | Votes | % | Votes | % | Votes | % | | |
| Alabama | 689,818 | — | | 479,085 | 69.5 | — | | — | | 210,733 | 30.5 | 268,353 | R [2] |
| Alaska | 67,259 | 44,329 | 65.9 | 22,930 | 34.1 | — | | — | | — | | 21,399 | D |
| Arizona | 480,770 | 237,753 | 49.5 | 242,535 | 50.4 | 482 | 0.1 | — | | — | | 4,782 | R |
| Arkansas | 560,426 | 314,197 | 56.1 | 243,264 | 43.4 | — | | — | | 2,965 | 0.5 | 70,933 | D |
| California | 7,057,586 | 4,171,877 | 59.1 | 2,879,108 | 40.8 | 489 | | 378 | | 5,734 | 0.1 | 1,292,769 | D |
| Colorado | 776,986 | 476,024 | 61.3 | 296,767 | 38.2 | 302 | | 2,537 | 0.3 | 1,356 | 0.2 | 179,257 | D |
| Connecticut | 1,218,578 | 826,269 | 67.8 | 390,996 | 32.1 | — | | — | | 1,313 | 0.1 | 435,273 | D |
| Delaware | 201,320 | 122,704 | 60.9 | 78,078 | 38.8 | 113 | 0.1 | — | | 425 | 0.2 | 44,626 | D |
| Florida | 1,854,481 | 948,540 | 51.1 | 905,941 | 48.9 | — | | — | | — | | 42,599 | D |
| Georgia | 1,139,335 | 522,556 | 45.9 | 616,584 | 54.1 | — | | — | | 195 | | 94,028 | R |
| Hawaii | 207,271 | 163,249 | 78.8 | 44,022 | 21.2 | — | | — | | — | | 119,227 | D |
| Idaho | 292,477 | 148,920 | 50.9 | 143,557 | 49.1 | — | | — | | — | | 5,363 | D |
| Illinois | 4,702,841 | 2,796,833 | 59.5 | 1,905,946 | 40.5 | — | | — | | 62 | | 890,887 | D |
| Indiana | 2,091,606 | 1,170,848 | 56.0 | 911,118 | 43.6 | 1,374 | 0.1 | — | | 8,266 | 0.4 | 259,730 | D |
| Iowa | 1,184,539 | 733,030 | 61.9 | 449,148 | 37.9 | 182 | | 159 | | 2,020 | 0.2 | 283,882 | D |
| Kansas | 857,901 | 464,028 | 54.1 | 386,579 | 45.1 | 1,901 | 0.2 | — | | 5,393 | 0.6 | 77,449 | D |
| Kentucky | 1,046,105 | 669,659 | 64.0 | 372,977 | 35.7 | — | | — | | 3,469 | 0.3 | 296,682 | D |
| Louisiana | 896,293 | 387,068 | 43.2 | 509,225 | 56.8 | — | | — | | — | | 122,157 | R |
| Maine | 380,965 | 262,264 | 68.8 | 118,701 | 31.2 | — | | — | | — | | 143,563 | D |
| Maryland | 1,116,457 | 730,912 | 65.5 | 385,495 | 34.5 | — | | — | | 50 | | 345,417 | D |
| Massachusetts | 2,344,798 | 1,786,422 | 76.2 | 549,727 | 23.4 | 4,755 | 0.2 | — | | 3,894 | 0.2 | 1,236,695 | D |
| Michigan | 3,203,102 | 2,136,615 | 66.7 | 1,060,152 | 33.1 | 1,704 | 0.1 | 3,817 | 0.1 | 814 | | 1,076,463 | D |
| Minnesota | 1,554,462 | 991,117 | 63.8 | 559,624 | 36.0 | 2,544 | 0.2 | 1,177 | 0.1 | — | | 431,493 | D |
| Mississippi | 409,146 | 52,618 | 12.9 | 356,528 | 87.1 | — | | — | | — | | 303,910 | R |
| Missouri | 1,817,879 | 1,164,344 | 64.0 | 653,535 | 36.0 | — | | — | | — | | 510,809 | D |
| Montana | 278,628 | 164,246 | 58.9 | 113,032 | 40.6 | — | | 332 | 0.1 | 1,018 | 0.4 | 51,214 | D |
| Nebraska | 584,154 | 307,307 | 52.6 | 276,847 | 47.4 | — | | — | | — | | 30,460 | D |
| Nevada | 135,433 | 79,339 | 58.6 | 56,094 | 41.4 | — | | — | | — | | 23,245 | D |
| New Hampshire | 288,093 | 184,064 | 63.9 | 104,029 | 36.1 | — | | — | | — | | 80,035 | D |
| New Jersey | 2,847,663 | 1,868,231 | 65.6 | 964,174 | 33.9 | 7,075 | 0.2 | 8,183 | 0.3 | — | | 904,057 | D |
| New Mexico | 328,645 | 194,015 | 59.0 | 132,838 | 40.4 | 1,217 | 0.4 | — | | 575 | 0.2 | 61,177 | D |
| New York | 7,166,275 | 4,913,102 | 68.6 | 2,243,559 | 31.3 | 6,118 | 0.1 | 3,228 | | 268 | | 2,669,543 | D |
| North Carolina | 1,424,983 | 800,139 | 56.2 | 624,844 | 43.8 | — | | — | | — | | 175,295 | D |
| North Dakota | 258,389 | 149,784 | 58.0 | 108,207 | 41.9 | — | | 224 | 0.1 | 174 | 0.1 | 41,577 | D |
| Ohio | 3,969,196 | 2,498,331 | 62.9 | 1,470,865 | 37.1 | — | | — | | — | | 1,027,466 | D |
| Oklahoma | 932,499 | 519,834 | 55.7 | 412,665 | 44.3 | — | | — | | — | | 107,169 | D |
| Oregon | 786,305 | 501,017 | 63.7 | 282,779 | 36.0 | — | | — | | 2,509 | 0.3 | 218,238 | D |
| Pennsylvania | 4,822,690 | 3,130,954 | 64.9 | 1,673,657 | 34.7 | 5,092 | 0.1 | 10,456 | 0.2 | 2,531 | 0.1 | 1,457,297 | D |
| Rhode Island | 390,091 | 315,463 | 80.9 | 74,615 | 19.1 | — | | — | | 13 | | 240,848 | D |
| South Carolina | 524,779 | 215,723 | 41.1 | 309,048 | 58.9 | — | | — | | 8 | | 93,325 | R |
| South Dakota | 293,118 | 163,010 | 55.6 | 130,108 | 44.4 | — | | — | | — | | 32,902 | D |
| Tennessee | 1,143,946 | 634,947 | 55.5 | 508,965 | 44.5 | — | | — | | 34 | | 125,982 | D |
| Texas | 2,626,811 | 1,663,185 | 63.3 | 958,566 | 36.5 | — | | — | | 5,060 | 0.2 | 704,619 | D |
| Utah | 401,413 | 219,628 | 54.7 | 181,785 | 45.3 | — | | — | | — | | 37,843 | D |
| Vermont | 163,089 | 108,127 | 66.3 | 54,942 | 33.7 | — | | — | | 20 | | 53,185 | D |
| Virginia | 1,042,267 | 558,038 | 53.5 | 481,334 | 46.2 | 2,895 | 0.3 | — | | — | | 76,704 | D |
| Washington | 1,258,556 | 779,881 | 62.0 | 470,366 | 37.4 | 7,772 | 0.6 | 537 | | — | | 309,515 | D |
| West Virginia | 792,040 | 538,087 | 67.9 | 253,953 | 32.1 | — | | — | | — | | 284,134 | D |
| Wisconsin | 1,691,815 | 1,050,424 | 62.1 | 638,495 | 37.7 | 1,204 | 0.1 | 1,692 | 0.1 | — | | 411,929 | D |
| Wyoming | 142,716 | 80,718 | 56.6 | 61,998 | 43.4 | — | | — | | — | | 18,720 | D |
| Dist. of Col. | 198,597 | 169,796 | 85.5 | 28,801 | 14.5 | — | | — | | — | | 140,995 | D |
| Totals | 70,644,592 | 43,129,566 | 61.1 | 27,178,188 | 38.5 | 45,219 | 0.1 | 32,720 | | 258,899 | 0.4 | 15,951,378 | D |

1. For breakdown of "Other" vote, see minor candidate vote totals, p. 474.
2. Plurality of 268,353 votes is calculated on the basis of Goldwater's vote and the 210,732 votes cast for the unpledged Democratic elector ticket.

# 1968 Presidential Election

| STATE | TOTAL VOTE | RICHARD M. NIXON (Republican) Votes | % | HUBERT H. HUMPHREY (Democrat) Votes | % | GEORGE C. WALLACE (American Independent) Votes | % | HENNING A. BLOMEN (Socialist Labor) Votes | % | OTHER [1] Votes | % | PLURALITY | |
|---|---|---|---|---|---|---|---|---|---|---|---|---|---|
| Alabama | 1,049,922 | 146,923 | 14.0 | 196,579 | 18.7 | 691,425 | 65.9 | — | | 14,995 | 1.4 | 494,846 | A |
| Alaska | 83,035 | 37,600 | 45.3 | 35,411 | 42.6 | 10,024 | 12.1 | — | | — | | 2,189 | R |
| Arizona | 486,936 | 266,721 | 54.8 | 170,514 | 35.0 | 46,573 | 9.6 | 75 | | 3,053 | 0.6 | 96,207 | R |
| Arkansas | 619,969 | 190,759 | 30.8 | 188,228 | 30.4 | 240,982 | 38.9 | — | | — | | 50,223 | A |
| California | 7,251,587 | 3,467,664 | 47.8 | 3,244,318 | 44.7 | 487,270 | 6.7 | 341 | | 51,994 | 0.7 | 223,346 | R |
| Colorado | 811,199 | 409,345 | 50.5 | 335,174 | 41.3 | 60,813 | 7.5 | 3,016 | 0.4 | 2,851 | 0.4 | 74,171 | R |
| Connecticut | 1,256,232 | 556,721 | 44.3 | 621,561 | 49.5 | 76,650 | 6.1 | — | | 1,300 | 0.1 | 64,840 | D |
| Delaware | 214,367 | 96,714 | 45.1 | 89,194 | 41.6 | 28,459 | 13.3 | — | | — | | 7,520 | R |
| Florida | 2,187,805 | 886,804 | 40.5 | 676,794 | 30.9 | 624,207 | 28.5 | — | | — | | 210,010 | R |
| Georgia | 1,250,266 | 380,111 | 30.4 | 334,424 | 26.7 | 535,550 | 42.8 | — | | 165 | | 155,439 | A |
| Hawaii | 236,218 | 91,425 | 38.7 | 141,324 | 59.8 | 3,469 | 1.5 | — | | — | | 49,899 | D |
| Idaho | 291,183 | 165,369 | 56.8 | 89,273 | 30.7 | 36,541 | 12.5 | — | | — | | 76,096 | R |
| Illinois | 4,619,749 | 2,174,774 | 47.1 | 2,039,814 | 44.2 | 390,958 | 8.5 | 13,878 | 0.3 | 325 | | 134,960 | R |
| Indiana | 2,123,597 | 1,067,885 | 50.3 | 806,659 | 38.0 | 243,108 | 11.4 | — | | 5,945 | 0.3 | 261,226 | R |
| Iowa | 1,167,931 | 619,106 | 53.0 | 476,699 | 40.8 | 66,422 | 5.7 | 241 | | 5,463 | 0.5 | 142,407 | R |
| Kansas | 872,783 | 478,674 | 54.8 | 302,996 | 34.7 | 88,921 | 10.2 | — | | 2,192 | 0.3 | 175,678 | R |
| Kentucky | 1,055,893 | 462,411 | 43.8 | 397,541 | 37.6 | 193,098 | 18.3 | — | | 2,843 | 0.3 | 64,870 | R |
| Louisiana | 1,097,450 | 257,535 | 23.5 | 309,615 | 28.2 | 530,300 | 48.3 | — | | — | | 220,685 | A |
| Maine | 392,936 | 169,254 | 43.1 | 217,312 | 55.3 | 6,370 | 1.6 | — | | — | | 48,058 | D |
| Maryland | 1,235,039 | 517,995 | 41.9 | 538,310 | 43.6 | 178,734 | 14.5 | — | | — | | 20,315 | D |
| Massachusetts | 2,331,752 | 766,844 | 32.9 | 1,469,218 | 63.0 | 87,088 | 3.7 | 6,180 | 0.3 | 2,422 | 0.1 | 702,374 | D |
| Michigan | 3,306,250 | 1,370,665 | 41.5 | 1,593,082 | 48.2 | 331,968 | 10.0 | 1,762 | 0.1 | 8,773 | 0.3 | 222,417 | D |
| Minnesota | 1,588,506 | 658,643 | 41.5 | 857,738 | 54.0 | 68,931 | 4.3 | 285 | | 2,909 | 0.2 | 199,095 | D |
| Mississippi | 654,509 | 88,516 | 13.5 | 150,644 | 23.0 | 415,349 | 63.5 | — | | — | | 264,705 | A |
| Missouri | 1,809,502 | 811,932 | 44.9 | 791,444 | 43.7 | 206,126 | 11.4 | — | | — | | 20,488 | R |
| Montana | 274,404 | 138,835 | 50.6 | 114,117 | 41.6 | 20,015 | 7.3 | — | | 1,437 | 0.5 | 24,718 | R |
| Nebraska | 536,851 | 321,163 | 59.8 | 170,784 | 31.8 | 44,904 | 8.4 | — | | — | | 150,379 | R |
| Nevada | 154,218 | 73,188 | 47.5 | 60,598 | 39.3 | 20,432 | 13.2 | — | | — | | 12,590 | R |
| New Hampshire | 297,298 | 154,903 | 52.1 | 130,589 | 43.9 | 11,173 | 3.8 | — | | 633 | 0.2 | 24,314 | R |
| New Jersey | 2,875,395 | 1,325,467 | 46.1 | 1,264,206 | 44.0 | 262,187 | 9.1 | 6,784 | 0.2 | 16,751 | 0.6 | 61,261 | R |
| New Mexico | 327,350 | 169,692 | 51.8 | 130,081 | 39.7 | 25,737 | 7.9 | — | | 1,840 | 0.6 | 39,611 | R |
| New York | 6,791,688 | 3,007,932 | 44.3 | 3,378,470 | 49.7 | 358,864 | 5.3 | 8,432 | 0.1 | 37,990 | 0.6 | 370,538 | D |
| North Carolina | 1,587,493 | 627,192 | 39.5 | 464,113 | 29.2 | 496,188 | 31.3 | — | | — | | 131,004 | R |
| North Dakota | 247,882 | 138,669 | 55.9 | 94,769 | 38.2 | 14,244 | 5.7 | — | | 200 | 0.1 | 43,900 | R |
| Ohio | 3,959,698 | 1,791,014 | 45.2 | 1,700,586 | 42.9 | 467,495 | 11.8 | 120 | | 483 | | 90,428 | R |
| Oklahoma | 943,086 | 449,697 | 47.7 | 301,658 | 32.0 | 191,731 | 20.3 | — | | — | | 148,039 | R |
| Oregon | 819,622 | 408,433 | 49.8 | 358,866 | 43.8 | 49,683 | 6.1 | — | | 2,640 | 0.3 | 49,567 | R |
| Pennsylvania | 4,747,928 | 2,090,017 | 44.0 | 2,259,405 | 47.6 | 378,582 | 8.0 | 4,977 | 0.1 | 14,947 | 0.3 | 169,388 | D |
| Rhode Island | 385,000 | 122,359 | 31.8 | 246,518 | 64.0 | 15,678 | 4.1 | — | | 445 | 0.1 | 124,159 | D |
| South Carolina | 666,978 | 254,062 | 38.1 | 197,486 | 29.6 | 215,430 | 32.3 | — | | — | | 38,632 | R |
| South Dakota | 281,264 | 149,841 | 53.3 | 118,023 | 42.0 | 13,400 | 4.8 | — | | — | | 31,818 | R |
| Tennessee | 1,248,617 | 472,592 | 37.8 | 351,233 | 28.1 | 424,792 | 34.0 | — | | — | | 47,800 | R |
| Texas | 3,079,216 | 1,227,844 | 39.9 | 1,266,804 | 41.1 | 584,269 | 19.0 | — | | 299 | | 38,960 | D |
| Utah | 422,568 | 238,728 | 56.5 | 156,665 | 37.1 | 26,906 | 6.4 | — | | 269 | 0.1 | 82,063 | R |
| Vermont | 161,404 | 85,142 | 52.8 | 70,255 | 43.5 | 5,104 | 3.2 | — | | 903 | 0.6 | 14,887 | R |
| Virginia | 1,361,491 | 590,319 | 43.4 | 442,387 | 32.5 | 321,833 | 23.6 | 4,671 | 0.3 | 2,281 | 0.2 | 147,932 | R |
| Washington | 1,304,281 | 588,510 | 45.1 | 616,037 | 47.2 | 96,990 | 7.4 | 488 | | 2,256 | 0.2 | 27,527 | D |
| West Virginia | 754,206 | 307,555 | 40.8 | 374,091 | 49.6 | 72,560 | 9.6 | — | | — | | 66,536 | D |
| Wisconsin | 1,691,538 | 809,997 | 47.9 | 748,804 | 44.3 | 127,835 | 7.6 | 1,338 | 0.1 | 3,564 | 0.2 | 61,193 | R |
| Wyoming | 127,205 | 70,927 | 55.8 | 45,173 | 35.5 | 11,105 | 8.7 | — | | — | | 25,754 | R |
| Dist. of Col. | 170,578 | 31,012 | 18.2 | 139,566 | 81.8 | — | | — | | — | | 108,554 | D |
| Totals | 73,211,875 | 31,785,480 | 43.4 | 31,275,166 | 42.7 | 9,906,473 | 13.5 | 52,588 | 0.1 | 192,168 | 0.3 | 510,314 | R |

1. For breakdown of "Other" vote, see minor candidate vote totals, p. 474.

# 1972 Presidential Election

| STATE | TOTAL VOTE | RICHARD M. NIXON (Republican) | | GEORGE S. McGOVERN (Democrat) | | JOHN G. SCHMITZ (American) | | BENJAMIN SPOCK (People's) | | OTHER [1] | | PLURALITY | |
|---|---|---|---|---|---|---|---|---|---|---|---|---|---|
| | | Votes | % | Votes | % | Votes | % | Votes | % | Votes | % | | |
| Alabama | 1,006,111 | 728,701 | 72.4 | 256,923 | 25.5 | 11,928 | 1.2 | — | | 8,559 | 0.9 | 471,778 | R |
| Alaska | 95,219 | 55,349 | 58.1 | 32,967 | 34.6 | 6,903 | 7.2 | — | | — | | 22,382 | R |
| Arizona | 622,926 | 402,812 | 64.7 | 198,540 | 31.9 | 21,208 | 3.4 | — | | 366 | 0.1 | 204,272 | R |
| Arkansas | 651,320 | 448,541 | 68.9 | 199,892 | 30.7 | 2,887 | 0.4 | — | | — | | 248,649 | R |
| California | 8,367,862 | 4,602,096 | 55.0 | 3,475,847 | 41.5 | 232,554 | 2.8 | 55,167 | 0.7 | 2,198 | | 1,126,249 | R |
| Colorado | 953,884 | 597,189 | 62.6 | 329,980 | 34.6 | 17,269 | 1.8 | 2,403 | 0.3 | 7,043 | 0.7 | 267,209 | R |
| Connecticut | 1,384,277 | 810,763 | 58.6 | 555,498 | 40.1 | 17,239 | 1.2 | — | | 777 | 0.1 | 255,265 | R |
| Delaware | 235,516 | 140,357 | 59.6 | 92,283 | 39.2 | 2,638 | 1.1 | — | | 238 | 0.1 | 48,074 | R |
| Florida | 2,583,283 | 1,857,759 | 71.9 | 718,117 | 27.8 | — | | — | | 7,407 | 0.3 | 1,139,642 | R |
| Georgia | 1,174,772 | 881,496 | 75.0 | 289,529 | 24.6 | 812 | 0.1 | — | | 2,935 | 0.2 | 591,967 | R |
| Hawaii | 270,274 | 168,865 | 62.5 | 101,409 | 37.5 | — | | — | | — | | 67,456 | R |
| Idaho | 310,379 | 199,384 | 64.2 | 80,826 | 26.0 | 28,869 | 9.3 | 903 | 0.3 | 397 | 0.1 | 118,558 | R |
| Illinois | 4,723,236 | 2,788,179 | 59.0 | 1,913,472 | 40.5 | 2,471 | 0.1 | — | | 19,114 | 0.4 | 874,707 | R |
| Indiana | 2,125,529 | 1,405,154 | 66.1 | 708,568 | 33.3 | — | | 4,544 | 0.2 | 7,263 | 0.3 | 696,586 | R |
| Iowa | 1,225,944 | 706,207 | 57.6 | 496,206 | 40.5 | 22,056 | 1.8 | — | | 1,475 | 0.1 | 210,001 | R |
| Kansas | 916,095 | 619,812 | 67.7 | 270,287 | 29.5 | 21,808 | 2.4 | — | | 4,188 | 0.5 | 349,525 | R |
| Kentucky | 1,067,499 | 676,446 | 63.4 | 371,159 | 34.8 | 17,627 | 1.7 | 1,118 | 0.1 | 1,149 | 0.1 | 305,287 | R |
| Louisiana | 1,051,491 | 686,852 | 65.3 | 298,142 | 28.4 | 52,099 | 5.0 | — | | 14,398 | 1.4 | 388,710 | R |
| Maine | 417,042 | 256,458 | 61.5 | 160,584 | 38.5 | — | | — | | — | | 95,874 | R |
| Maryland | 1,353,812 | 829,305 | 61.3 | 505,781 | 37.4 | 18,726 | 1.4 | — | | — | | 323,524 | R |
| Massachusetts | 2,458,756 | 1,112,078 | 45.2 | 1,332,540 | 54.2 | 2,877 | 0.1 | 101 | | 11,160 | 0.5 | 220,462 | D |
| Michigan | 3,489,727 | 1,961,721 | 56.2 | 1,459,435 | 41.8 | 63,321 | 1.8 | — | | 5,250 | 0.2 | 502,286 | R |
| Minnesota | 1,741,652 | 898,269 | 51.6 | 802,346 | 46.1 | 31,407 | 1.8 | 2,805 | 0.2 | 6,825 | 0.4 | 95,923 | R |
| Mississippi | 645,963 | 505,125 | 78.2 | 126,782 | 19.6 | 11,598 | 1.8 | — | | 2,458 | 0.4 | 378,343 | R |
| Missouri | 1,855,803 | 1,153,852 | 62.2 | 697,147 | 37.6 | — | | — | | 4,804 | 0.3 | 456,705 | R |
| Montana | 317,603 | 183,976 | 57.9 | 120,197 | 37.8 | 13,430 | 4.2 | — | | — | | 63,779 | R |
| Nebraska | 576,289 | 406,298 | 70.5 | 169,991 | 29.5 | — | | — | | — | | 236,307 | R |
| Nevada | 181,766 | 115,750 | 63.7 | 66,016 | 36.3 | — | | — | | — | | 49,734 | R |
| New Hampshire | 334,055 | 213,724 | 64.0 | 116,435 | 34.9 | 3,386 | 1.0 | — | | 510 | 0.2 | 97,289 | R |
| New Jersey | 2,997,229 | 1,845,502 | 61.6 | 1,102,211 | 36.8 | 34,378 | 1.1 | 5,355 | 0.2 | 9,783 | 0.3 | 743,291 | R |
| New Mexico | 386,241 | 235,606 | 61.0 | 141,084 | 36.5 | 8,767 | 2.3 | — | | 784 | 0.2 | 94,522 | R |
| New York | 7,165,919 | 4,192,778 | 58.5 | 2,951,084 | 41.2 | — | | — | | 22,057 | 0.3 | 1,241,694 | R |
| North Carolina | 1,518,612 | 1,054,889 | 69.5 | 438,705 | 28.9 | 25,018 | 1.6 | — | | — | | 616,184 | R |
| North Dakota | 280,514 | 174,109 | 62.1 | 100,384 | 35.8 | 5,646 | 2.0 | — | | 375 | 0.1 | 73,725 | R |
| Ohio | 4,094,787 | 2,441,827 | 59.6 | 1,558,889 | 38.1 | 80,067 | 2.0 | — | | 14,004 | 0.3 | 882,938 | R |
| Oklahoma | 1,029,900 | 759,025 | 73.7 | 247,147 | 24.0 | 23,728 | 2.3 | — | | — | | 511,878 | R |
| Oregon | 927,946 | 486,686 | 52.4 | 392,760 | 42.3 | 46,211 | 5.0 | — | | 2,289 | 0.2 | 93,926 | R |
| Pennsylvania | 4,592,106 | 2,714,521 | 59.1 | 1,796,951 | 39.1 | 70,593 | 1.5 | — | | 10,041 | 0.2 | 917,570 | R |
| Rhode Island | 415,808 | 220,383 | 53.0 | 194,645 | 46.8 | 25 | | 5 | | 750 | 0.2 | 25,738 | R |
| South Carolina | 673,960 | 477,044 | 70.8 | 186,824 | 27.7 | 10,075 | 1.5 | — | | 17 | | 290,220 | R |
| South Dakota | 307,415 | 166,476 | 54.2 | 139,945 | 45.5 | — | | — | | 994 | 0.3 | 26,531 | R |
| Tennessee | 1,201,182 | 813,147 | 67.7 | 357,293 | 29.7 | 30,373 | 2.5 | — | | 369 | | 455,854 | R |
| Texas | 3,471,281 | 2,298,896 | 66.2 | 1,154,289 | 33.3 | 6,039 | 0.2 | — | | 12,057 | 0.3 | 1,144,607 | R |
| Utah | 478,476 | 323,643 | 67.6 | 126,284 | 26.4 | 28,549 | 6.0 | — | | — | | 197,359 | R |
| Vermont | 186,947 | 117,149 | 62.7 | 68,174 | 36.5 | — | | 1,010 | 0.5 | 614 | 0.3 | 48,975 | R |
| Virginia | 1,457,019 | 988,493 | 67.8 | 438,887 | 30.1 | 19,721 | 1.4 | — | | 9,918 | 0.7 | 549,606 | R |
| Washington | 1,470,847 | 837,135 | 56.9 | 568,334 | 38.6 | 58,906 | 4.0 | 2,644 | 0.2 | 3,828 | 0.3 | 268,801 | R |
| West Virginia | 762,399 | 484,964 | 63.6 | 277,435 | 36.4 | — | | — | | — | | 207,529 | R |
| Wisconsin | 1,852,890 | 989,430 | 53.4 | 810,174 | 43.7 | 47,525 | 2.6 | 2,701 | 0.1 | 3,060 | 0.2 | 179,256 | R |
| Wyoming | 145,570 | 100,464 | 69.0 | 44,358 | 30.5 | 748 | 0.5 | — | | — | | 56,106 | R |
| Dist. of Col. | 163,421 | 35,226 | 21.6 | 127,627 | 78.1 | — | | — | | 568 | 0.3 | 92,401 | D |
| Totals | 77,718,554 | 47,169,911 | 60.7 | 29,170,383 | 37.5 | 1,099,482 | 1.4 | 78,756 | 0.1 | 200,022 | 0.3 | 17,999,528 | R |

1. For breakdown of "Other" vote, see minor candidate vote totals, p. 475.

# 1976 Presidential Election

| STATE | TOTAL VOTE | JIMMY CARTER (Democrat) Votes | % | GERALD R. FORD (Republican) Votes | % | EUGENE J. McCARTHY (Independent) Votes | % | ROGER MacBRIDE (Libertarian) Votes | % | OTHER [1] Votes | % | PLURALITY | |
|---|---|---|---|---|---|---|---|---|---|---|---|---|---|
| Alabama | 1,182,850 | 659,170 | 55.7 | 504,070 | 42.6 | 99 | | 1,481 | 0.1 | 18,030 | 1.5 | 155,100 | D |
| Alaska | 123,574 | 44,058 | 35.7 | 71,555 | 57.9 | — | | 6,785 | 5.5 | 1,176 | 1.0 | 27,497 | R |
| Arizona | 742,719 | 295,602 | 39.8 | 418,642 | 56.4 | 19,229 | 2.6 | 7,647 | 1.0 | 1,599 | 0.2 | 123,040 | R |
| Arkansas | 767,535 | 498,604 | 65.0 | 267,903 | 34.9 | 639 | 0.1 | — | | 389 | 0.1 | 230,701 | D |
| California | 7,867,117 | 3,742,284 | 47.6 | 3,882,244 | 49.3 | 58,412 | 0.7 | 56,388 | 0.7 | 127,789 | 1.6 | 139,960 | R |
| Colorado | 1,081,554 | 460,353 | 42.6 | 584,367 | 54.0 | 26,107 | 2.4 | 5,330 | 0.5 | 5,397 | 0.5 | 124,014 | R |
| Connecticut | 1,381,526 | 647,895 | 46.9 | 719,261 | 52.1 | 3,759 | 0.3 | 209 | | 10,402 | 0.8 | 71,366 | R |
| Delaware | 235,834 | 122,596 | 52.0 | 109,831 | 46.6 | 2,437 | 1.0 | — | | 970 | 0.4 | 12,765 | D |
| Florida | 3,150,631 | 1,636,000 | 51.9 | 1,469,531 | 46.6 | 23,643 | 0.8 | 103 | | 21,354 | 0.7 | 166,469 | D |
| Georgia | 1,467,458 | 979,409 | 66.7 | 483,743 | 33.0 | 991 | 0.1 | 175 | | 3,140 | 0.2 | 495,666 | D |
| Hawaii | 291,301 | 147,375 | 50.6 | 140,003 | 48.1 | — | | 3,923 | 1.3 | — | | 7,372 | D |
| Idaho | 344,071 | 126,549 | 36.8 | 204,151 | 59.3 | 1,194 | 0.3 | 3,558 | 1.0 | 8,619 | 2.5 | 77,602 | R |
| Illinois | 4,718,914 | 2,271,295 | 48.1 | 2,364,269 | 50.1 | 55,939 | 1.2 | 8,057 | 0.2 | 19,354 | 0.4 | 92,974 | R |
| Indiana | 2,220,362 | 1,014,714 | 45.7 | 1,183,958 | 53.3 | — | | — | | 21,690 | 1.0 | 169,244 | R |
| Iowa | 1,279,306 | 619,931 | 48.5 | 632,863 | 49.5 | 20,051 | 1.6 | 1,452 | 0.1 | 5,009 | 0.4 | 12,932 | R |
| Kansas | 957,845 | 430,421 | 44.9 | 502,752 | 52.5 | 13,185 | 1.4 | 3,242 | 0.3 | 8,245 | 0.9 | 72,331 | R |
| Kentucky | 1,167,142 | 615,717 | 52.8 | 531,852 | 45.6 | 6,837 | 0.6 | 814 | 0.1 | 11,922 | 1.0 | 83,865 | D |
| Louisiana | 1,278,439 | 661,365 | 51.7 | 587,446 | 46.0 | 6,588 | 0.5 | 3,325 | 0.3 | 19,715 | 1.5 | 73,919 | D |
| Maine | 483,216 | 232,279 | 48.1 | 236,320 | 48.9 | 10,874 | 2.3 | 11 | | 3,732 | 0.8 | 4,041 | R |
| Maryland | 1,439,897 | 759,612 | 52.8 | 672,661 | 46.7 | 4,541 | 0.3 | 255 | | 2,828 | 0.2 | 86,951 | D |
| Massachusetts | 2,547,558 | 1,429,475 | 56.1 | 1,030,276 | 40.4 | 65,637 | 2.6 | 135 | | 22,035 | 0.9 | 399,199 | D |
| Michigan | 3,653,749 | 1,696,714 | 46.4 | 1,893,742 | 51.8 | 47,905 | 1.3 | 5,406 | 0.1 | 9,982 | 0.3 | 197,028 | R |
| Minnesota | 1,949,931 | 1,070,440 | 54.9 | 819,395 | 42.0 | 35,490 | 1.8 | 3,529 | 0.2 | 21,077 | 1.1 | 251,045 | D |
| Mississippi | 769,361 | 381,309 | 49.6 | 366,846 | 47.7 | 4,074 | 0.5 | 2,788 | 0.4 | 14,344 | 1.9 | 14,463 | D |
| Missouri | 1,953,600 | 998,387 | 51.1 | 927,443 | 47.5 | 24,029 | 1.2 | — | | 3,741 | 0.2 | 70,944 | D |
| Montana | 328,734 | 149,259 | 45.4 | 173,703 | 52.8 | — | | — | | 5,772 | 1.8 | 24,444 | R |
| Nebraska | 607,668 | 233,692 | 38.5 | 359,705 | 59.2 | 9,409 | 1.5 | 1,482 | 0.2 | 3,380 | 0.6 | 126,013 | R |
| Nevada | 201,876 | 92,479 | 45.8 | 101,273 | 50.2 | — | | 1,519 | 0.8 | 6,605 | 3.3 | 8,794 | R |
| New Hampshire | 339,618 | 147,635 | 43.5 | 185,935 | 54.7 | 4,095 | 1.2 | 936 | 0.3 | 1,017 | 0.3 | 38,300 | R |
| New Jersey | 3,014,472 | 1,444,653 | 47.9 | 1,509,688 | 50.1 | 32,717 | 1.1 | 9,449 | 0.3 | 17,965 | 0.6 | 65,035 | R |
| New Mexico | 418,409 | 201,148 | 48.1 | 211,419 | 50.5 | 1,161 | 0.3 | 1,110 | 0.3 | 3,571 | 0.9 | 10,271 | R |
| New York | 6,534,170 | 3,389,558 | 51.9 | 3,100,791 | 47.5 | 4,303 | 0.1 | 12,197 | 0.2 | 27,321 | 0.4 | 288,767 | D |
| North Carolina | 1,678,914 | 927,365 | 55.2 | 741,960 | 44.2 | 780 | | 2,219 | 0.1 | 6,590 | 0.4 | 185,405 | D |
| North Dakota | 297,188 | 136,078 | 45.8 | 153,470 | 51.6 | 2,952 | 1.0 | 253 | 0.1 | 4,435 | 1.5 | 17,392 | R |
| Ohio | 4,111,873 | 2,011,621 | 48.9 | 2,000,505 | 48.7 | 58,258 | 1.4 | 8,961 | 0.2 | 32,528 | 0.8 | 11,116 | D |
| Oklahoma | 1,092,251 | 532,442 | 48.7 | 545,708 | 50.0 | 14,101 | 1.3 | — | | — | | 13,266 | R |
| Oregon | 1,029,876 | 490,407 | 47.6 | 492,120 | 47.8 | 40,207 | 3.9 | — | | 7,142 | 0.7 | 1,713 | R |
| Pennsylvania | 4,620,787 | 2,328,677 | 50.4 | 2,205,604 | 47.7 | 50,584 | 1.1 | — | | 35,922 | 0.8 | 123,073 | D |
| Rhode Island | 411,170 | 227,636 | 55.4 | 181,249 | 44.1 | 479 | 0.1 | 715 | 0.2 | 1,091 | 0.3 | 46,387 | D |
| South Carolina | 802,583 | 450,807 | 56.2 | 346,149 | 43.1 | 289 | | 53 | | 5,285 | 0.7 | 104,658 | D |
| South Dakota | 300,678 | 147,068 | 48.9 | 151,505 | 50.4 | — | | 1,619 | 0.5 | 486 | 0.2 | 4,437 | R |
| Tennessee | 1,476,345 | 825,879 | 55.9 | 633,969 | 42.9 | 5,004 | 0.3 | 1,375 | 0.1 | 10,118 | 0.7 | 191,910 | D |
| Texas | 4,071,884 | 2,082,319 | 51.1 | 1,953,300 | 48.0 | 20,118 | 0.5 | 189 | | 15,958 | 0.4 | 129,019 | D |
| Utah | 541,198 | 182,110 | 33.6 | 337,908 | 62.4 | 3,907 | 0.7 | 2,438 | 0.5 | 14,835 | 2.7 | 155,798 | R |
| Vermont | 187,765 | 80,954 | 43.1 | 102,085 | 54.4 | 4,001 | 2.1 | — | | 725 | 0.4 | 21,131 | R |
| Virginia | 1,697,094 | 813,896 | 48.0 | 836,554 | 49.3 | — | | 4,648 | 0.3 | 41,996 | 2.5 | 22,658 | R |
| Washington | 1,555,534 | 717,323 | 46.1 | 777,732 | 50.0 | 36,986 | 2.4 | 5,042 | 0.3 | 18,451 | 1.2 | 60,409 | R |
| West Virginia | 750,964 | 435,914 | 58.0 | 314,760 | 41.9 | 113 | | 16 | | 161 | | 121,154 | D |
| Wisconsin | 2,104,175 | 1,040,232 | 49.4 | 1,004,987 | 47.8 | 34,943 | 1.7 | 3,814 | 0.2 | 20,199 | 1.0 | 35,245 | D |
| Wyoming | 156,343 | 62,239 | 39.8 | 92,717 | 59.3 | 624 | 0.4 | 89 | 0.1 | 674 | 0.4 | 30,478 | R |
| Dist. of Col. | 168,830 | 137,818 | 81.6 | 27,873 | 16.5 | — | | 274 | 0.2 | 2,865 | 1.7 | 109,945 | D |
| Totals | 81,555,889 | 40,830,763 | 50.1 | 39,147,793 | 48.0 | 756,691 | 0.9 | 173,011 | 0.2 | 647,631 | 0.8 | 1,682,970 | D |

1. For breakdown of "Other" vote, see minor candidate vote totals, p. 475.

# 1980 Presidential Election

| STATE | TOTAL VOTE | RONALD REAGAN (Republican) | | JIMMY CARTER (Democrat) | | JOHN B. ANDERSON (Independent) | | ED CLARK (Libertarian) | | OTHER [1] | | PLURALITY | |
|---|---|---|---|---|---|---|---|---|---|---|---|---|---|
| | | Votes | % | Votes | % | Votes | % | Votes | % | Votes | % | | |
| Alabama | 1,341,929 | 654,192 | 48.8 | 636,730 | 47.4 | 16,481 | 1.2 | 13,318 | 1.0 | 21,208 | 1.6 | 17,462 | R |
| Alaska | 158,445 | 86,112 | 54.3 | 41,842 | 26.4 | 11,155 | 7.0 | 18,479 | 11.7 | 857 | 0.5 | 44,270 | R |
| Arizona | 873,945 | 529,688 | 60.6 | 246,843 | 28.2 | 76,952 | 8.8 | 18,784 | 2.1 | 1,678 | 0.2 | 282,845 | R |
| Arkansas | 837,582 | 403,164 | 48.1 | 398,041 | 47.5 | 22,468 | 2.7 | 8,970 | 1.1 | 4,939 | 0.6 | 5,123 | R |
| California | 8,587,063 | 4,524,858 | 52.7 | 3,083,661 | 35.9 | 739,833 | 8.6 | 148,434 | 1.7 | 90,277 | 1.1 | 1,441,197 | R |
| Colorado | 1,184,415 | 652,264 | 55.1 | 367,973 | 31.1 | 130,633 | 11.0 | 25,744 | 2.2 | 7,801 | 0.7 | 284,291 | R |
| Connecticut | 1,406,285 | 677,210 | 48.2 | 541,732 | 38.5 | 171,807 | 12.2 | 8,570 | 0.6 | 6,966 | 0.5 | 135,478 | R |
| Delaware | 235,900 | 111,252 | 47.2 | 105,754 | 44.8 | 16,288 | 6.9 | 1,974 | 0.8 | 632 | 0.3 | 5,498 | R |
| Florida | 3,686,930 | 2,046,951 | 55.5 | 1,419,475 | 38.5 | 189,692 | 5.1 | 30,524 | 0.8 | 288 | | 627,476 | R |
| Georgia | 1,596,695 | 654,168 | 41.0 | 890,733 | 55.8 | 36,055 | 2.3 | 15,627 | 1.0 | 112 | | 236,565 | D |
| Hawaii | 303,287 | 130,112 | 42.9 | 135,879 | 44.8 | 32,021 | 10.6 | 3,269 | 1.1 | 2,006 | 0.7 | 5,767 | D |
| Idaho | 437,431 | 290,699 | 66.5 | 110,192 | 25.2 | 27,058 | 6.2 | 8,425 | 1.9 | 1,057 | 0.2 | 180,507 | R |
| Illinois | 4,749,721 | 2,358,049 | 49.6 | 1,981,413 | 41.7 | 346,754 | 7.3 | 38,939 | 0.8 | 24,566 | 0.5 | 376,636 | R |
| Indiana | 2,242,033 | 1,255,656 | 56.0 | 844,197 | 37.7 | 111,639 | 5.0 | 19,627 | 0.9 | 10,914 | 0.5 | 411,459 | R |
| Iowa | 1,317,661 | 676,026 | 51.3 | 508,672 | 38.6 | 115,633 | 8.8 | 13,123 | 1.0 | 4,207 | 0.3 | 167,354 | R |
| Kansas | 979,795 | 566,812 | 57.9 | 326,150 | 33.3 | 68,231 | 7.0 | 14,470 | 1.5 | 4,132 | 0.4 | 240,662 | R |
| Kentucky | 1,294,627 | 635,274 | 49.1 | 616,417 | 47.6 | 31,127 | 2.4 | 5,531 | 0.4 | 6,278 | 0.5 | 18,857 | R |
| Louisiana | 1,548,591 | 792,853 | 51.2 | 708,453 | 45.7 | 26,345 | 1.7 | 8,240 | 0.5 | 12,700 | 0.8 | 84,400 | R |
| Maine | 523,011 | 238,522 | 45.6 | 220,974 | 42.3 | 53,327 | 10.2 | 5,119 | 1.0 | 5,069 | 1.0 | 17,548 | R |
| Maryland | 1,540,496 | 680,606 | 44.2 | 726,161 | 47.1 | 119,537 | 7.8 | 14,192 | 0.9 | — | | 45,555 | D |
| Massachusetts | 2,524,298 | 1,057,631 | 41.9 | 1,053,802 | 41.7 | 382,539 | 15.2 | 22,038 | 0.9 | 8,288 | 0.3 | 3,829 | R |
| Michigan | 3,909,725 | 1,915,225 | 49.0 | 1,661,532 | 42.5 | 275,223 | 7.0 | 41,597 | 1.1 | 16,148 | 0.4 | 253,693 | R |
| Minnesota | 2,051,980 | 873,268 | 42.6 | 954,174 | 46.5 | 174,990 | 8.5 | 31,592 | 1.5 | 17,956 | 0.9 | 80,906 | D |
| Mississippi | 892,620 | 441,089 | 49.4 | 429,281 | 48.1 | 12,036 | 1.3 | 5,465 | 0.6 | 4,749 | 0.5 | 11,808 | R |
| Missouri | 2,099,824 | 1,074,181 | 51.2 | 931,182 | 44.3 | 77,920 | 3.7 | 14,422 | 0.7 | 2,119 | 0.1 | 142,999 | R |
| Montana | 363,952 | 206,814 | 56.8 | 118,032 | 32.4 | 29,281 | 8.0 | 9,825 | 2.7 | — | | 88,782 | R |
| Nebraska | 640,854 | 419,937 | 65.5 | 166,851 | 26.0 | 44,993 | 7.0 | 9,073 | 1.4 | — | | 253,086 | R |
| Nevada | 247,885 | 155,017 | 62.5 | 66,666 | 26.9 | 17,651 | 7.1 | 4,358 | 1.8 | 4,193 | 1.7 | 88,351 | R |
| New Hampshire | 383,990 | 221,705 | 57.7 | 108,864 | 28.4 | 49,693 | 12.9 | 2,064 | 0.5 | 1,664 | 0.4 | 112,841 | R |
| New Jersey | 2,975,684 | 1,546,557 | 52.0 | 1,147,364 | 38.6 | 234,632 | 7.9 | 20,652 | 0.7 | 26,479 | 0.9 | 399,193 | R |
| New Mexico | 456,971 | 250,779 | 54.9 | 167,826 | 36.7 | 29,459 | 6.4 | 4,365 | 1.0 | 4,542 | 1.0 | 82,953 | R |
| New York | 6,201,959 | 2,893,831 | 46.7 | 2,728,372 | 44.0 | 467,801 | 7.5 | 52,648 | 0.8 | 59,307 | 1.0 | 165,459 | R |
| North Carolina | 1,855,833 | 915,018 | 49.3 | 875,635 | 47.2 | 52,800 | 2.8 | 9,677 | 0.5 | 2,703 | 0.1 | 39,383 | R |
| North Dakota | 301,545 | 193,695 | 64.2 | 79,189 | 26.3 | 23,640 | 7.8 | 3,743 | 1.2 | 1,278 | 0.4 | 114,506 | R |
| Ohio | 4,283,603 | 2,206,545 | 51.5 | 1,752,414 | 40.9 | 254,472 | 5.9 | 49,033 | 1.1 | 21,139 | 0.5 | 454,131 | R |
| Oklahoma | 1,149,708 | 695,570 | 60.5 | 402,026 | 35.0 | 38,284 | 3.3 | 13,828 | 1.2 | — | | 293,544 | R |
| Oregon | 1,181,516 | 571,044 | 48.3 | 456,890 | 38.7 | 112,389 | 9.5 | 25,838 | 2.2 | 15,355 | 1.3 | 114,154 | R |
| Pennsylvania | 4,561,501 | 2,261,872 | 49.6 | 1,937,540 | 42.5 | 292,921 | 6.4 | 33,263 | 0.7 | 35,905 | 0.8 | 324,332 | R |
| Rhode Island | 416,072 | 154,793 | 37.2 | 198,342 | 47.7 | 59,819 | 14.4 | 2,458 | 0.6 | 660 | 0.2 | 43,549 | D |
| South Carolina | 894,071 | 441,841 | 49.4 | 430,385 | 48.1 | 14,153 | 1.6 | 5,139 | 0.6 | 2,553 | 0.3 | 11,456 | R |
| South Dakota | 327,703 | 198,343 | 60.5 | 103,855 | 31.7 | 21,431 | 6.5 | 3,824 | 1.2 | 250 | 0.1 | 94,488 | R |
| Tennessee | 1,617,616 | 787,761 | 48.7 | 783,051 | 48.4 | 35,991 | 2.2 | 7,116 | 0.4 | 3,697 | 0.2 | 4,710 | R |
| Texas | 4,541,636 | 2,510,705 | 55.3 | 1,881,147 | 41.4 | 111,613 | 2.5 | 37,643 | 0.8 | 528 | | 629,558 | R |
| Utah | 604,222 | 439,687 | 72.8 | 124,266 | 20.6 | 30,284 | 5.0 | 7,226 | 1.2 | 2,759 | 0.5 | 315,421 | R |
| Vermont | 213,299 | 94,628 | 44.4 | 81,952 | 38.4 | 31,761 | 14.9 | 1,900 | 0.9 | 3,058 | 1.4 | 12,676 | R |
| Virginia | 1,866,032 | 989,609 | 53.0 | 752,174 | 40.3 | 95,418 | 5.1 | 12,821 | 0.7 | 16,010 | 0.9 | 237,435 | R |
| Washington | 1,742,394 | 865,244 | 49.7 | 650,193 | 37.3 | 185,073 | 10.6 | 29,213 | 1.7 | 12,671 | 0.7 | 215,051 | R |
| West Virginia | 737,715 | 334,206 | 45.3 | 367,462 | 49.8 | 31,691 | 4.3 | 4,356 | 0.6 | — | | 33,256 | D |
| Wisconsin | 2,273,221 | 1,088,845 | 47.9 | 981,584 | 43.2 | 160,657 | 7.1 | 29,135 | 1.3 | 13,000 | 0.6 | 107,261 | R |
| Wyoming | 176,713 | 110,700 | 62.6 | 49,427 | 28.0 | 12,072 | 6.8 | 4,514 | 2.6 | — | | 61,273 | R |
| Dist. of Col. | 175,237 | 23,545 | 13.4 | 131,113 | 74.8 | 16,337 | 9.3 | 1,114 | 0.6 | 3,128 | 1.8 | 107,568 | D |
| **Totals** | **86,515,221** | **43,904,153** | **50.7** | **35,483,883** | **41.0** | **5,720,060** | **6.6** | **921,299** | **1.1** | **485,826** | **0.6** | **8,420,270** | **R** |

1. For breakdown of "Other" vote, see minor candidate vote totals, p. 476.

# 1984 Presidential Election

| STATE | TOTAL VOTE | RONALD REAGAN (Republican) | | WALTER F. MONDALE (Democrat) | | DAVID BERGLAND (Libertarian) | | LYNDON H. LaROUCHE JR. (Independent) | | OTHER [1] | | PLURALITY | |
|---|---|---|---|---|---|---|---|---|---|---|---|---|---|
| | | Votes | % | Votes | % | Votes | % | Votes | % | Votes | % | | |
| Alabama | 1,441,713 | 872,849 | 60.5 | 551,899 | 38.3 | 9,504 | 0.7 | — | | 7,461 | 0.5 | 320,950 | R |
| Alaska | 207,605 | 138,377 | 66.7 | 62,007 | 29.9 | 6,378 | 3.1 | — | | 843 | 0.4 | 76,370 | R |
| Arizona | 1,025,897 | 681,416 | 66.4 | 333,854 | 32.5 | 10,585 | 1.0 | — | | 42 | | 347,562 | R |
| Arkansas | 884,406 | 534,774 | 60.5 | 338,646 | 38.3 | 2,221 | 0.3 | 1,890 | 0.2 | 6,875 | 0.8 | 196,128 | R |
| California | 9,505,423 | 5,467,009 | 57.5 | 3,922,519 | 41.3 | 49,951 | 0.5 | — | | 65,944 | 0.7 | 1,544,490 | R |
| Colorado | 1,295,380 | 821,817 | 63.4 | 454,975 | 35.1 | 11,257 | 0.9 | 4,662 | 0.4 | 2,669 | 0.2 | 366,842 | R |
| Connecticut | 1,466,900 | 890,877 | 60.7 | 569,597 | 38.8 | 204 | | — | | 6,222 | 0.4 | 321,280 | R |
| Delaware | 254,572 | 152,190 | 59.8 | 101,656 | 39.9 | 268 | 0.1 | — | | 458 | 0.2 | 50,534 | R |
| Florida | 4,180,051 | 2,730,350 | 65.3 | 1,448,816 | 34.7 | 754 | | — | | 131 | | 1,281,534 | R |
| Georgia | 1,776,120 | 1,068,722 | 60.2 | 706,628 | 39.8 | 152 | | 34 | | 584 | | 362,094 | R |
| Hawaii | 335,846 | 185,050 | 55.1 | 147,154 | 43.8 | 2,167 | 0.6 | 654 | 0.2 | 821 | 0.2 | 37,896 | R |
| Idaho | 411,144 | 297,523 | 72.4 | 108,510 | 26.4 | 2,823 | 0.7 | — | | 2,288 | 0.6 | 189,013 | R |
| Illinois | 4,819,088 | 2,707,103 | 56.2 | 2,086,499 | 43.3 | 10,086 | 0.2 | — | | 15,400 | 0.3 | 620,604 | R |
| Indiana | 2,233,069 | 1,377,230 | 61.7 | 841,481 | 37.7 | 6,741 | 0.3 | — | | 7,617 | 0.3 | 535,749 | R |
| Iowa | 1,319,805 | 703,088 | 53.3 | 605,620 | 45.9 | 1,844 | 0.1 | 6,248 | 0.5 | 3,005 | 0.2 | 97,468 | R |
| Kansas | 1,021,991 | 677,296 | 66.3 | 333,149 | 32.6 | 3,329 | 0.3 | — | | 8,217 | 0.8 | 344,147 | R |
| Kentucky | 1,369,345 | 821,702 | 60.0 | 539,539 | 39.4 | — | | 1,776 | 0.1 | 6,328 | 0.5 | 282,163 | R |
| Louisiana | 1,706,822 | 1,037,299 | 60.8 | 651,586 | 38.2 | 1,876 | 0.1 | 3,552 | 0.2 | 12,509 | 0.7 | 385,713 | R |
| Maine | 553,144 | 336,500 | 60.8 | 214,515 | 38.8 | — | | — | | 2,129 | 0.4 | 121,985 | R |
| Maryland | 1,675,873 | 879,918 | 52.5 | 787,935 | 47.0 | 5,721 | 0.3 | — | | 2,299 | 0.1 | 91,983 | R |
| Massachusetts | 2,559,453 | 1,310,936 | 51.2 | 1,239,606 | 48.4 | — | | — | | 8,911 | 0.3 | 71,330 | R |
| Michigan | 3,801,658 | 2,251,571 | 59.2 | 1,529,638 | 40.2 | 10,055 | 0.3 | 3,862 | 0.1 | 6,532 | 0.2 | 721,933 | R |
| Minnesota | 2,084,449 | 1,032,603 | 49.5 | 1,036,364 | 49.7 | 2,996 | 0.1 | 3,865 | 0.2 | 8,621 | 0.4 | 3,761 | D |
| Mississippi | 941,104 | 582,377 | 61.9 | 352,192 | 37.4 | 2,336 | 0.2 | 1,001 | 0.1 | 3,198 | 0.3 | 230,185 | R |
| Missouri | 2,122,783 | 1,274,188 | 60.0 | 848,583 | 40.0 | — | | — | | 12 | | 425,605 | R |
| Montana | 384,377 | 232,450 | 60.5 | 146,742 | 38.2 | 5,185 | 1.3 | — | | — | | 85,708 | R |
| Nebraska | 652,090 | 460,054 | 70.6 | 187,866 | 28.8 | 2,079 | 0.3 | — | | 2,091 | 0.3 | 272,188 | R |
| Nevada | 286,667 | 188,770 | 65.8 | 91,655 | 32.0 | 2,292 | 0.8 | — | | 3,950 | 1.4 | 97,115 | R |
| New Hampshire | 389,066 | 267,051 | 68.6 | 120,395 | 30.9 | 735 | 0.2 | 467 | 0.1 | 418 | 0.1 | 146,656 | R |
| New Jersey | 3,217,862 | 1,933,630 | 60.1 | 1,261,323 | 39.2 | 6,416 | 0.2 | — | | 16,493 | 0.5 | 672,307 | R |
| New Mexico | 514,370 | 307,101 | 59.7 | 201,769 | 39.2 | 4,459 | 0.9 | — | | 1,041 | 0.2 | 105,332 | R |
| New York | 6,806,810 | 3,664,763 | 53.8 | 3,119,609 | 45.8 | 11,949 | 0.2 | — | | 10,489 | 0.2 | 545,154 | R |
| North Carolina | 2,175,361 | 1,346,481 | 61.9 | 824,287 | 37.9 | 3,794 | 0.2 | — | | 799 | | 522,194 | R |
| North Dakota | 308,971 | 200,336 | 64.8 | 104,429 | 33.8 | 703 | 0.2 | 1,278 | 0.4 | 2,225 | 0.7 | 95,907 | R |
| Ohio | 4,547,619 | 2,678,560 | 58.9 | 1,825,440 | 40.1 | 5,886 | 0.1 | 10,693 | 0.2 | 27,040 | 0.6 | 853,120 | R |
| Oklahoma | 1,255,676 | 861,530 | 68.6 | 385,080 | 30.7 | 9,066 | 0.7 | — | | — | | 476,450 | R |
| Oregon | 1,226,527 | 685,700 | 55.9 | 536,479 | 43.7 | — | | — | | 4,348 | 0.4 | 149,221 | R |
| Pennsylvania | 4,844,903 | 2,584,323 | 53.3 | 2,228,131 | 46.0 | 6,982 | 0.1 | — | | 25,467 | 0.5 | 356,192 | R |
| Rhode Island | 410,492 | 212,080 | 51.7 | 197,106 | 48.0 | 277 | 0.1 | — | | 1,029 | 0.3 | 14,974 | R |
| South Carolina | 968,529 | 615,539 | 63.6 | 344,459 | 35.6 | 4,359 | 0.5 | — | | 4,172 | 0.4 | 271,080 | R |
| South Dakota | 317,867 | 200,267 | 63.0 | 116,113 | 36.5 | — | | — | | 1,487 | 0.5 | 84,154 | R |
| Tennessee | 1,711,994 | 990,212 | 57.8 | 711,714 | 41.6 | 3,072 | 0.2 | 1,852 | 0.1 | 5,144 | 0.3 | 278,498 | R |
| Texas | 5,397,571 | 3,433,428 | 63.6 | 1,949,276 | 36.1 | — | | 14,613 | 0.3 | 254 | | 1,484,152 | R |
| Utah | 629,656 | 469,105 | 74.5 | 155,369 | 24.7 | 2,447 | 0.4 | — | | 2,735 | 0.4 | 313,736 | R |
| Vermont | 234,561 | 135,865 | 57.9 | 95,730 | 40.8 | 1,002 | 0.4 | 423 | 0.2 | 1,541 | 0.7 | 40,135 | R |
| Virginia | 2,146,635 | 1,337,078 | 62.3 | 796,250 | 37.1 | — | | 13,307 | 0.6 | — | | 540,828 | R |
| Washington | 1,883,910 | 1,051,670 | 55.8 | 807,352 | 42.9 | 8,844 | 0.5 | 4,712 | 0.3 | 11,332 | 0.6 | 244,318 | R |
| West Virginia | 735,742 | 405,483 | 55.1 | 328,125 | 44.6 | — | | — | | 2,134 | 0.3 | 77,358 | R |
| Wisconsin | 2,211,689 | 1,198,584 | 54.2 | 995,740 | 45.0 | 4,883 | 0.2 | 3,791 | 0.2 | 8,691 | 0.4 | 202,844 | R |
| Wyoming | 188,968 | 133,241 | 70.5 | 53,370 | 28.2 | 2,357 | 1.2 | — | | — | | 79,871 | R |
| Dist. of Col. | 211,288 | 29,009 | 13.7 | 180,408 | 85.4 | 279 | 0.1 | 127 | 0.1 | 1,465 | 0.7 | 151,399 | D |
| Totals | 92,652,842 | 54,455,075 | 58.8 | 37,577,185 | 40.6 | 228,314 | 0.2 | 78,807 | 0.1 | 313,461 | 0.3 | 16,877,890 | R |

1. For breakdown of "Other" vote, see minor candidate vote totals, p. 476.

# 1988 Presidential Election

| STATE | TOTAL VOTE | GEORGE BUSH (Republican) | | MICHAEL S. DUKAKIS (Democrat) | | RON PAUL (Libertarian) | | LENORA B. FULANI (New Alliance) | | OTHER [1] | | PLURALITY | |
|---|---|---|---|---|---|---|---|---|---|---|---|---|---|
| | | Votes | % | Votes | % | Votes | % | Votes | % | Votes | % | | |
| Alabama | 1,378,476 | 815,576 | 59.2 | 549,506 | 39.9 | 8,460 | 0.6 | 3,311 | 0.2 | 1,623 | 0.1 | 266,070 | R |
| Alaska | 200,116 | 119,251 | 59.6 | 72,584 | 36.3 | 5,484 | 2.7 | 1,024 | 0.5 | 1,773 | 0.9 | 46,667 | R |
| Arizona | 1,171,873 | 702,541 | 60.0 | 454,029 | 38.7 | 13,351 | 1.1 | 1,662 | 0.1 | 290 | | 248,512 | R |
| Arkansas | 827,738 | 466,578 | 56.4 | 349,237 | 42.2 | 3,297 | 0.4 | 2,161 | 0.3 | 6,465 | 0.8 | 117,341 | R |
| California | 9,887,065 | 5,054,917 | 51.1 | 4,702,233 | 47.6 | 70,105 | 0.7 | 31,181 | 0.3 | 28,629 | 0.3 | 352,684 | R |
| Colorado | 1,372,394 | 728,177 | 53.1 | 621,453 | 45.3 | 15,482 | 1.1 | 2,539 | 0.2 | 4,743 | 0.3 | 106,724 | R |
| Connecticut | 1,443,394 | 750,241 | 52.0 | 676,584 | 46.9 | 14,071 | 1.0 | 2,491 | 0.2 | 7 | | 73,657 | R |
| Delaware | 249,891 | 139,639 | 55.9 | 108,647 | 43.5 | 1,162 | 0.5 | 443 | 0.2 | — | | 30,992 | R |
| Florida | 4,302,313 | 2,618,885 | 60.9 | 1,656,701 | 38.5 | 19,796 | 0.5 | 6,655 | 0.2 | 276 | | 962,184 | R |
| Georgia | 1,809,672 | 1,081,331 | 59.8 | 714,792 | 39.5 | 8,435 | 0.5 | 5,099 | 0.3 | 15 | | 366,539 | R |
| Hawaii | 354,461 | 158,625 | 44.8 | 192,364 | 54.3 | 1,999 | 0.6 | 1,003 | 0.3 | 470 | 0.1 | 33,739 | D |
| Idaho | 408,968 | 253,881 | 62.1 | 147,272 | 36.0 | 5,313 | 1.3 | 2,502 | 0.6 | — | | 106,609 | R |
| Illinois | 4,559,120 | 2,310,939 | 50.7 | 2,215,940 | 48.6 | 14,944 | 0.3 | 10,276 | 0.2 | 7,021 | 0.2 | 94,999 | R |
| Indiana | 2,168,621 | 1,297,763 | 59.8 | 860,643 | 39.7 | — | | 10,215 | 0.5 | — | | 437,120 | R |
| Iowa | 1,225,614 | 545,355 | 44.5 | 670,557 | 54.7 | 2,494 | 0.2 | 540 | | 6,668 | 0.5 | 125,202 | D |
| Kansas | 993,044 | 554,049 | 55.8 | 422,636 | 42.6 | 12,553 | 1.3 | 3,806 | 0.4 | — | | 131,413 | R |
| Kentucky | 1,322,517 | 734,281 | 55.5 | 580,368 | 43.9 | 2,118 | 0.2 | 1,256 | 0.1 | 4,494 | 0.3 | 153,913 | R |
| Louisiana | 1,628,202 | 883,702 | 54.3 | 717,460 | 44.1 | 4,115 | 0.3 | 2,355 | 0.1 | 20,570 | 1.3 | 166,242 | R |
| Maine | 555,035 | 307,131 | 55.3 | 243,569 | 43.9 | 2,700 | 0.5 | 1,405 | 0.3 | 230 | | 63,562 | R |
| Maryland | 1,714,358 | 876,167 | 51.1 | 826,304 | 48.2 | 6,748 | 0.4 | 5,115 | 0.3 | 24 | | 49,863 | R |
| Massachusetts | 2,632,805 | 1,194,635 | 45.4 | 1,401,415 | 53.2 | 24,251 | 0.9 | 9,561 | 0.4 | 2,943 | 0.1 | 206,780 | D |
| Michigan | 3,669,163 | 1,965,486 | 53.6 | 1,675,783 | 45.7 | 18,336 | 0.5 | 2,513 | 0.1 | 7,045 | 0.2 | 289,703 | R |
| Minnesota | 2,096,790 | 962,337 | 45.9 | 1,109,471 | 52.9 | 5,109 | 0.2 | 1,734 | 0.1 | 18,139 | 0.9 | 147,134 | D |
| Mississippi | 931,527 | 557,890 | 59.9 | 363,921 | 39.1 | 3,329 | 0.4 | 2,155 | 0.2 | 4,232 | 0.5 | 193,969 | R |
| Missouri | 2,093,713 | 1,084,953 | 51.8 | 1,001,619 | 47.8 | 434 | | 6,656 | 0.3 | 51 | | 83,334 | R |
| Montana | 365,674 | 190,412 | 52.1 | 168,936 | 46.2 | 5,047 | 1.4 | 1,279 | 0.3 | — | | 21,476 | R |
| Nebraska | 661,465 | 397,956 | 60.2 | 259,235 | 39.2 | 2,534 | 0.4 | 1,740 | 0.3 | — | | 138,721 | R |
| Nevada | 350,067 | 206,040 | 58.9 | 132,738 | 37.9 | 3,520 | 1.0 | 835 | 0.2 | 6,934 | 2.0 | 73,302 | R |
| New Hampshire | 451,074 | 281,537 | 62.4 | 163,696 | 36.3 | 4,502 | 1.0 | 790 | 0.2 | 549 | 0.1 | 117,841 | R |
| New Jersey | 3,099,553 | 1,743,192 | 56.2 | 1,320,352 | 42.6 | 8,421 | 0.3 | 5,139 | 0.2 | 22,449 | 0.7 | 422,840 | R |
| New Mexico | 521,287 | 270,341 | 51.9 | 244,497 | 46.9 | 3,268 | 0.6 | 2,237 | 0.4 | 944 | 0.2 | 25,844 | R |
| New York | 6,485,683 | 3,081,871 | 47.5 | 3,347,882 | 51.6 | 12,109 | 0.2 | 15,845 | 0.2 | 27,976 | 0.4 | 266,011 | D |
| North Carolina | 2,134,370 | 1,237,258 | 58.0 | 890,167 | 41.7 | 1,263 | 0.1 | 5,682 | 0.3 | — | | 347,091 | R |
| North Dakota | 297,261 | 166,559 | 56.0 | 127,739 | 43.0 | 1,315 | 0.4 | 396 | 0.1 | 1,252 | 0.4 | 38,820 | R |
| Ohio | 4,393,699 | 2,416,549 | 55.0 | 1,939,629 | 44.1 | 11,989 | 0.3 | 12,017 | 0.3 | 13,515 | 0.3 | 476,920 | R |
| Oklahoma | 1,171,036 | 678,367 | 57.9 | 483,423 | 41.3 | 6,261 | 0.5 | 2,985 | 0.3 | — | | 194,944 | R |
| Oregon | 1,201,694 | 560,126 | 46.6 | 616,206 | 51.3 | 14,811 | 1.2 | 6,487 | 0.5 | 4,064 | 0.3 | 56,080 | D |
| Pennsylvania | 4,536,251 | 2,300,087 | 50.7 | 2,194,944 | 48.4 | 12,051 | 0.3 | 4,379 | 0.1 | 24,790 | 0.5 | 105,143 | R |
| Rhode Island | 404,620 | 177,761 | 43.9 | 225,123 | 55.6 | 825 | 0.2 | 280 | 0.1 | 631 | 0.2 | 47,362 | D |
| South Carolina | 986,009 | 606,443 | 61.5 | 370,554 | 37.6 | 4,935 | 0.5 | 4,077 | 0.4 | — | | 235,889 | R |
| South Dakota | 312,991 | 165,415 | 52.8 | 145,560 | 46.5 | 1,060 | 0.3 | 730 | 0.2 | 226 | 0.1 | 19,855 | R |
| Tennessee | 1,636,250 | 947,233 | 57.9 | 679,794 | 41.5 | 2,041 | 0.1 | 1,334 | 0.1 | 5,848 | 0.4 | 267,439 | R |
| Texas | 5,427,410 | 3,036,829 | 56.0 | 2,352,748 | 43.3 | 30,355 | 0.6 | 7,208 | 0.1 | 270 | | 684,081 | R |
| Utah | 647,008 | 428,442 | 66.2 | 207,343 | 32.0 | 7,473 | 1.2 | 455 | 0.1 | 3,295 | 0.5 | 221,099 | R |
| Vermont | 243,328 | 124,331 | 51.1 | 115,775 | 47.6 | 1,000 | 0.4 | 205 | 0.1 | 2,017 | 0.8 | 8,556 | R |
| Virginia | 2,191,609 | 1,309,162 | 59.7 | 859,799 | 39.2 | 8,336 | 0.4 | 14,312 | 0.7 | — | | 449,363 | R |
| Washington | 1,865,253 | 903,835 | 48.5 | 933,516 | 50.0 | 17,240 | 0.9 | 3,520 | 0.2 | 7,142 | 0.4 | 29,681 | D |
| West Virginia | 653,311 | 310,065 | 47.5 | 341,016 | 52.2 | — | | 2,230 | 0.3 | — | | 30,951 | D |
| Wisconsin | 2,191,608 | 1,047,499 | 47.8 | 1,126,794 | 51.4 | 5,157 | 0.2 | 1,953 | 0.1 | 10,205 | 0.5 | 79,295 | D |
| Wyoming | 176,551 | 106,867 | 60.5 | 67,113 | 38.0 | 2,026 | 1.1 | 545 | 0.3 | — | | 39,754 | R |
| Dist. of Col. | 192,877 | 27,590 | 14.3 | 159,407 | 82.6 | 554 | 0.3 | 2,901 | 1.5 | 2,425 | 1.3 | 131,817 | D |
| Totals | 91,594,809 | 48,886,097 | 53.4 | 41,809,074 | 45.6 | 432,179 | 0.5 | 217,219 | 0.2 | 250,240 | 0.3 | 7,077,023 | R |

1. For breakdown of "Other" vote, see minor candidate vote totals, p. 477.

# 1992 Presidential Election

| STATE | TOTAL VOTE | BILL CLINTON (Democrat) | | GEORGE BUSH (Republican) | | ROSS PEROT (Independent) | | ANDRE V. MARROU (Libertarian) | | OTHER [1] | | PLURALITY | |
|---|---|---|---|---|---|---|---|---|---|---|---|---|---|
| | | Votes | % | Votes | % | Votes | % | Votes | % | Votes | % | | |
| Alabama | 1,688,060 | 690,080 | 40.9 | 804,283 | 47.6 | 183,109 | 10.8 | 5,737 | 0.3 | 4,851 | 0.3 | 114,203 | R |
| Alaska | 258,506 | 78,294 | 30.3 | 102,000 | 39.5 | 73,481 | 28.4 | 1,378 | 0.5 | 3,353 | 1.3 | 23,706 | R |
| Arizona | 1,486,975 | 543,050 | 36.5 | 572,086 | 38.5 | 353,741 | 23.8 | 6,759 | 0.5 | 11,339 | 0.8 | 29,036 | R |
| Arkansas | 950,653 | 505,823 | 53.2 | 337,324 | 35.5 | 99,132 | 10.4 | 1,261 | 0.1 | 7,113 | 0.7 | 168,499 | D |
| California | 11,131,721 | 5,121,325 | 46.0 | 3,630,574 | 32.6 | 2,296,006 | 20.6 | 48,139 | 0.4 | 35,677 | 0.3 | 1,490,751 | D |
| Colorado | 1,569,180 | 629,681 | 40.1 | 562,850 | 35.9 | 366,010 | 23.3 | 8,669 | 0.6 | 1,970 | 0.1 | 66,831 | D |
| Connecticut | 1,616,332 | 682,318 | 42.2 | 578,313 | 35.8 | 348,771 | 21.6 | 5,391 | 0.3 | 1,539 | 0.1 | 104,005 | D |
| Delaware | 289,735 | 126,054 | 43.5 | 102,313 | 35.3 | 59,213 | 20.4 | 935 | 0.3 | 1,220 | 0.4 | 23,741 | D |
| Florida | 5,314,392 | 2,072,698 | 39.0 | 2,173,310 | 40.9 | 1,053,067 | 19.8 | 15,079 | 0.3 | 238 | | 100,612 | R |
| Georgia | 2,321,125 | 1,008,966 | 43.5 | 995,252 | 42.9 | 309,657 | 13.3 | 7,110 | 0.3 | 140 | | 13,714 | D |
| Hawaii | 372,842 | 179,310 | 48.1 | 136,822 | 36.7 | 53,003 | 14.2 | 1,119 | 0.3 | 2,588 | 0.7 | 42,488 | D |
| Idaho | 482,142 | 137,013 | 28.4 | 202,645 | 42.0 | 130,395 | 27.0 | 1,167 | 0.2 | 10,922 | 2.3 | 65,632 | R |
| Illinois | 5,050,157 | 2,453,350 | 48.6 | 1,734,096 | 34.3 | 840,515 | 16.6 | 9,218 | 0.2 | 12,978 | 0.3 | 719,254 | D |
| Indiana | 2,305,871 | 848,420 | 36.8 | 989,375 | 42.9 | 455,934 | 19.8 | 7,936 | 0.3 | 4,206 | 0.2 | 140,955 | R |
| Iowa | 1,354,607 | 586,353 | 43.3 | 504,891 | 37.3 | 253,468 | 18.7 | 1,076 | 0.1 | 8,819 | 0.7 | 81,462 | D |
| Kansas | 1,157,335 | 390,434 | 33.7 | 449,951 | 38.9 | 312,358 | 27.0 | 4,314 | 0.4 | 278 | | 59,517 | R |
| Kentucky | 1,492,900 | 665,104 | 44.6 | 617,178 | 41.3 | 203,944 | 13.7 | 4,513 | 0.3 | 2,161 | 0.1 | 47,926 | D |
| Louisiana | 1,790,017 | 815,971 | 45.6 | 733,386 | 41.0 | 211,478 | 11.8 | 3,155 | 0.2 | 26,027 | 1.5 | 82,585 | D |
| Maine | 679,499 | 263,420 | 38.8 | 206,504 | 30.4 | 206,820 | 30.4 | 1,681 | 0.2 | 1,074 | 0.2 | 56,600 | D |
| Maryland | 1,985,046 | 988,571 | 49.8 | 707,094 | 35.6 | 281,414 | 14.2 | 4,715 | 0.2 | 3,252 | 0.2 | 281,477 | D |
| Massachusetts | 2,773,700 | 1,318,662 | 47.5 | 805,049 | 29.0 | 630,731 | 22.7 | 9,024 | 0.3 | 10,234 | 0.4 | 513,613 | D |
| Michigan | 4,274,673 | 1,871,182 | 43.8 | 1,554,940 | 36.4 | 824,813 | 19.3 | 10,175 | 0.2 | 13,563 | 0.3 | 316,242 | D |
| Minnesota | 2,347,948 | 1,020,997 | 43.5 | 747,841 | 31.9 | 562,506 | 24.0 | 3,374 | 0.1 | 13,230 | 0.6 | 273,156 | D |
| Mississippi | 981,793 | 400,258 | 40.8 | 487,793 | 49.7 | 85,626 | 8.7 | 2,154 | 0.2 | 5,962 | 0.6 | 87,535 | R |
| Missouri | 2,391,565 | 1,053,873 | 44.1 | 811,159 | 33.9 | 518,741 | 21.7 | 7,497 | 0.3 | 295 | | 242,714 | D |
| Montana | 410,611 | 154,507 | 37.6 | 144,207 | 35.1 | 107,225 | 26.1 | 986 | 0.2 | 3,686 | 0.9 | 10,300 | D |
| Nebraska | 737,546 | 216,864 | 29.4 | 343,678 | 46.6 | 174,104 | 23.6 | 1,340 | 0.2 | 1,560 | 0.2 | 126,814 | R |
| Nevada | 506,318 | 189,148 | 37.4 | 175,828 | 34.7 | 132,580 | 26.2 | 1,835 | 0.4 | 6,927 | 1.4 | 13,320 | D |
| New Hampshire | 537,943 | 209,040 | 38.9 | 202,484 | 37.6 | 121,337 | 22.6 | 3,548 | 0.7 | 1,534 | 0.3 | 6,556 | D |
| New Jersey | 3,343,594 | 1,436,206 | 43.0 | 1,356,865 | 40.6 | 521,829 | 15.6 | 6,822 | 0.2 | 21,872 | 0.7 | 79,341 | D |
| New Mexico | 569,986 | 261,617 | 45.9 | 212,824 | 37.3 | 91,895 | 16.1 | 1,615 | 0.3 | 2,035 | 0.4 | 48,793 | D |
| New York | 6,926,925 | 3,444,450 | 49.7 | 2,346,649 | 33.9 | 1,090,721 | 15.7 | 13,451 | 0.2 | 31,654 | 0.5 | 1,097,801 | D |
| North Carolina | 2,611,850 | 1,114,042 | 42.7 | 1,134,661 | 43.4 | 357,864 | 13.7 | 5,171 | 0.2 | 112 | | 20,619 | R |
| North Dakota | 308,133 | 99,168 | 32.2 | 136,244 | 44.2 | 71,084 | 23.1 | 416 | 0.1 | 1,221 | 0.4 | 37,076 | R |
| Ohio | 4,939,967 | 1,984,942 | 40.2 | 1,894,310 | 38.3 | 1,036,426 | 21.0 | 7,252 | 0.1 | 17,037 | 0.3 | 90,632 | D |
| Oklahoma | 1,390,359 | 473,066 | 34.0 | 592,929 | 42.6 | 319,878 | 23.0 | 4,486 | 0.3 | — | | 119,863 | R |
| Oregon | 1,462,643 | 621,314 | 42.5 | 475,757 | 32.5 | 354,091 | 24.2 | 4,277 | 0.3 | 7,204 | 0.5 | 145,557 | D |
| Pennsylvania | 4,959,810 | 2,239,164 | 45.1 | 1,791,841 | 36.1 | 902,667 | 18.2 | 21,477 | 0.4 | 4,661 | 0.1 | 447,323 | D |
| Rhode Island | 453,477 | 213,299 | 47.0 | 131,601 | 29.0 | 105,045 | 23.2 | 571 | 0.1 | 2,961 | 0.7 | 81,698 | D |
| South Carolina | 1,202,527 | 479,514 | 39.9 | 577,507 | 48.0 | 138,872 | 11.5 | 2,719 | 0.2 | 3,915 | 0.3 | 97,993 | R |
| South Dakota | 336,254 | 124,888 | 37.1 | 136,718 | 40.7 | 73,295 | 21.8 | 814 | 0.2 | 539 | 0.2 | 11,830 | R |
| Tennessee | 1,982,638 | 933,521 | 47.1 | 841,300 | 42.4 | 199,968 | 10.1 | 1,847 | 0.1 | 6,002 | 0.3 | 92,221 | D |
| Texas | 6,154,018 | 2,281,815 | 37.1 | 2,496,071 | 40.6 | 1,354,781 | 22.0 | 19,699 | 0.3 | 1,652 | | 214,256 | R |
| Utah | 743,999 | 183,429 | 24.7 | 322,632 | 43.4 | 203,400 | 27.3 | 1,900 | 0.3 | 32,638 | 4.4 | 119,232 | R |
| Vermont | 289,701 | 133,592 | 46.1 | 88,122 | 30.4 | 65,991 | 22.8 | 501 | 0.2 | 1,495 | 0.5 | 45,470 | D |
| Virginia | 2,558,665 | 1,038,650 | 40.6 | 1,150,517 | 45.0 | 348,639 | 13.6 | 5,730 | 0.2 | 15,129 | 0.6 | 111,867 | R |
| Washington | 2,288,230 | 993,037 | 43.4 | 731,234 | 32.0 | 541,780 | 23.7 | 7,533 | 0.3 | 14,646 | 0.6 | 261,803 | D |
| West Virginia | 683,762 | 331,001 | 48.4 | 241,974 | 35.4 | 108,829 | 15.9 | 1,873 | 0.3 | 85 | | 89,027 | D |
| Wisconsin | 2,531,114 | 1,041,066 | 41.1 | 930,855 | 36.8 | 544,479 | 21.5 | 2,877 | 0.1 | 11,837 | 0.5 | 110,211 | D |
| Wyoming | 200,598 | 68,160 | 34.0 | 79,347 | 39.6 | 51,263 | 25.6 | 844 | 0.4 | 984 | 0.5 | 11,187 | R |
| Dist. of Col. | 227,572 | 192,619 | 84.6 | 20,698 | 9.1 | 9,681 | 4.3 | 467 | 0.2 | 4,107 | 1.8 | 171,921 | D |
| Totals | 104,425,014 | 44,909,326 | 43.0 | 39,103,882 | 37.4 | 19,741,657 | 18.9 | 291,627 | 0.3 | 378,522 | 0.4 | 5,805,444 | D |

1. For breakdown of "Other" votes, see minor candidate vote totals, p. 477.

# Popular Returns: Minor Candidates and Parties

This section contains popular vote returns for all minor candidates and parties that were aggregated in the columns labeled "Other" in the presidential election returns found on pages 429-468. The source for these data for 1824-1916, except where indicated by a footnote, is the Inter-University Consortium for Political and Social Research (ICPSR). For 1920-92 the source was Scammon and McGillivray's *America at the Polls*. Footnotes are on page 478.

The material is presented in the following order:
- Year of presidential election.
- Name of candidate and party, if available from the ICPSR and Scammon data. "Scattered write-ins" is used where votes were recorded but neither the candidate nor a party was known. In nearly all cases, these figures were the total write-in vote.
- State name and number of votes. Percentages may be calculated by using the state vote totals from the presidential election tables found on pages 429-468.
- Nationwide vote totals. Percentages may be calculated by using the national vote total from the presidential election tables.

In the ICPSR data, the distinct party designations appearing in the original sources are preserved. Thus, in the ICPSR returns for 1880, John W. Phelps received votes under the following four party designations: "Anti-Masonic" — California, 5 votes, Illinois, 150 votes, and Pennsylvania, 44 votes; "Anti-Secret" — Kansas, 25 votes; "National American" — Michigan, 312 votes; and "American" — Rhode Island, 4 votes, and Wisconsin, 91 votes.

To provide one party designation for each minor candidate for the elections 1824 to 1916, Congressional Quarterly has aggregated under a single party designation the votes of minor candidates who are listed in the ICPSR data as receiving votes under more than one party designation. The source used for assigning party designations for these years is Svend Petersen, *A Statistical History of the American Presidential Elections* (Westport, Conn.: Greenwood Press, 1981) where Petersen gives a party designation. In the 1880 election cited above, Peterson lists John W. Phelps as an American Party candidate. Where Petersen lists no party designation, Congressional Quarterly selected the party designation for a candidate that appeared most frequently in the ICPSR returns. For the 1920 to 1992 elections, the sources for party designation are Scammon and McGillivray, *America at the Polls* (Washington, D.C.: Congressional Quarterly, 1994).

## 1824 Election

**Unpledged Republican**
Massachusetts, 6,616 votes.
**Scattered write-ins**
Connecticut, 1,188 votes; Indiana, 7; Massachusetts, 4,753; Missouri, 33; North Carolina, 256; Rhode Island, 200.
Total: 6,437

## 1828 Election

**Scattered write-ins**
Alabama, 4 votes; Connecticut, 1,101; Maine, 89; Massachusetts, 3,226; New Jersey, 8; North Carolina, 15; Rhode Island, 5; Vermont, 120.
Total: 4,568

## 1832 Election

**Scattered write-ins**
Illinois, 30 votes; Massachusetts, 7,031; Rhode Island, 6; Vermont, 206.
Total: 7,273

## 1836 Election

**Scattered write-ins**
Delaware, 5 votes; Maine, 1,112; Massachusetts, 45; North Carolina, 1; Rhode Island, 1; Vermont, 65; Virginia, 5.
Total: 1,234

## 1840 Election

**Scattered write-ins**
Delaware, 13 votes; Indiana, 599; Rhode Island, 136; Vermont, 19.
Total: 767

## 1844 Election

**Scattered write-ins**
Delaware, 6 votes; Illinois, 939; Massachusetts, 1,106; North Carolina, 2; Rhode Island, 5.
Total: 2,058

## 1848 Election

**Gerrit Smith (Liberty)**
New York, 2,545 votes.
**Henry Clay (Clay Whig)**
Illinois, 89 votes.
**Scattered write-ins**
Alabama, 4 votes; Connecticut, 24; Massachusetts, 62; North Carolina, 26; Rhode Island, 5; Texas, 75.
Total: 196

## 1852 Election

**Daniel Webster (Whig)** [1]
Georgia, 5,324 votes; Massachusetts, 1,670.
Total: 6,994
**—Broome (Native American)**
Massachusetts, 158 votes; New Jersey, 738; Pennsylvania, 1,670.
Total: 2,566
**George Michael Troup (Southern Rights)** [2]
Alabama, 2,205 votes; Georgia, 126.
Total: 2,331
**Scattered write-ins**
California, 56 votes; Connecticut, 12; Iowa, 139; North Carolina, 60; Texas, 10.
Total: 272

### 1856 Election

**Scattered write-ins**
California, 14 votes; Delaware, 9; Massachusetts, 3,006; Ohio, 148.
Total: 3,177

### 1860 Election

**Gerrit Smith (Union)**
Illinois, 35 votes; Ohio, 136.
**Scattered write-ins**
California, 15 votes; Massachusetts, 328; Minnesota, 17.
Total: 360

### 1864 Election

**E. Cheeseborough**
Kansas, 543 votes.
**Scattered write-ins**
Kansas, 112 votes; Massachusetts, 6; Minnesota, 26; Oregon, 5.
Total: 149

### 1868 Election

**Scattered write-ins**
Alabama, 6 votes; Kansas, 3; Massachusetts, 26; New Hampshire, 11.
Total: 46

### 1872 Election

**James Black (Prohibition)**
Michigan, 1,271 votes; Ohio, 2,100.
Total: 3,371
**Liberal Republican Elector**
Iowa, 10,447 votes.
**Scattered write-ins**
Iowa, 942 votes; Kansas, 581; Minnesota, 168; New Hampshire, 313; South Carolina, 259.
Total: 2,263

### 1876 Election

**Green Clay Smith (Prohibition)**
Connecticut, 374 votes; Illinois, 141; Kansas, 110; Michigan, 766; New York, 2,369; Ohio, 1,636; Pennsylvania, 1,320; Wisconsin, 27.
Total: 6,743
**James B. Walker (American)**
Illinois, 177 votes; Kansas, 23; Michigan, 71; Ohio, 76; Pennsylvania, 83; Wisconsin, 29.
Total: 459
**Communist**
Wisconsin, 32 votes.
**Scattered write-ins**
Alabama, 2 votes; California, 19; Connecticut, 26; Iowa, 520; Kansas, 5; Kentucky, 2,998; Maine, 828; Massachusetts, 779; New Hampshire, 93; Texas, 46; Vermont, 114; Wisconsin, 1,607.
Total: 7,037

### 1880 Election

**Neal Dow (Prohibition)**
California, 54 votes; Connecticut, 409; Illinois, 440; Kansas, 10; Kentucky, 233; Maine, 92; Massachusetts, 682; Michigan, 938; Minnesota, 286; New Hampshire, 180; New Jersey, 191; New York, 1,517; Ohio, 2,613; Pennsylvania, 1,940; Rhode Island, 20; Wisconsin, 69.
Total: 9,674
**John W. Phelps (American)**
California, 5 votes; Illinois, 150; Kansas, 25; Michigan, 312; Pennsylvania, 44; Rhode Island, 4; Wisconsin, 91.
Total: 631
**A. C. Brewer (Independent Democrat)**
Arkansas, 322 votes.
**Scattered write-ins**
Arkansas, 1,221 votes; California, 70; Colorado, 14; Connecticut, 39; Iowa, 1,064; Maine, 139; Massachusetts, 117; Mississippi, 677; Rhode Island, 1; South Carolina, 36.
Total: 3,378

### 1884 Election

**Scattered write-ins**
Alabama, 72 votes; California, 329; Florida, 118; Iowa, 1,297; Kansas, 468; Maine, 6; Massachusetts, 2; New Jersey, 28; Oregon, 35; South Carolina, 1,237; Vermont, 27.
Total: 3,619

### 1888 Election

**Robert H. Cowdrey (United Labor)**
Illinois, 150 votes; New York, 519; Oregon, 351.
Total: 1,020
**Socialist Labor**
New York, 2,068 votes.
Total: 2,068
**James Langdon Curtis (American)**
California, 1,591 votes; Pennsylvania, 24.
Total: 1,615
**Scattered write-ins**
California, 1,442 votes; Colorado, 177; Delaware, 1; Iowa, 556; Kansas, 937; Maine, 16; Massachusetts, 60; New Hampshire, 58; North Carolina, 37; Oregon, 53; Rhode Island, 7; South Carolina, 437; Vermont, 35.
Total: 3,816

### 1892 Election

**Simon Wing (Socialist Labor)**
Connecticut, 333 votes; Massachusetts, 649; New Jersey, 1,337; New York, 17,956; Pennsylvania, 888.
Total: 21,163
**Scattered write-ins**
Arkansas, 1,267 votes; Delaware, 13; Georgia, 2,345; Maine, 4; Massachusetts, 3; Michigan, 925; Rhode Island, 3; South Carolina, 72; Texas, 4,086; Vermont, 10; Wyoming, 29.
Total: 8,757

### 1896 Election

**Charles Horatio Matchett (Socialist Labor)**
California, 1,611 votes; Colorado, 159; Connecticut, 1,223; Illinois, 1,147; Indiana, 324; Iowa, 453; Maryland, 587; Massachusetts, 2,112; Michigan, 293; Minnesota, 954; Missouri, 599; Nebraska, 186; New Hampshire, 228; New Jersey, 3,985; New York, 17,667; Ohio, 1,165; Pennsylvania, 1,683; Rhode Island, 558; Virginia, 108; Wisconsin, 1,314
Total: 36,356
**Charles Eugene Bentley (National Prohibition)**
Arkansas, 892 votes; California, 1,047; Colorado, 386; Illinois, 793; Indiana, 2,267; Iowa, 352; Kansas, 620; Maryland, 136; Michigan, 1,816; Missouri, 292; Nebraska, 797; New Hampshire, 49; New Jersey, 5,614; North Carolina, 222; Ohio, 2,716; Pennsylvania, 870; Washington, 148; Wisconsin, 346.
Total: 19,363

**Scattered write-ins**

California, 4 votes; Connecticut, 4; Georgia, 47; Massachusetts, 20; Michigan, 1,073; North Carolina, 372; North Dakota, 12; Rhode Island, 5.

Total: 1,537

## 1900 Election

**Wharton Barker (Populist)**

Alabama, 4,188 votes; Arkansas, 972; Colorado, 333; Florida, 1,143; Georgia, 4,568; Idaho, 445; Illinois, 1,141; Indiana, 1,438; Iowa, 615; Kentucky, 1,961; Michigan, 889; Mississippi, 1,642; Missouri, 4,244; Nebraska, 1,104; New Jersey, 669; North Carolina, 798; North Dakota, 109; Ohio, 251; Oregon, 269; Pennsylvania, 638; South Dakota, 340; Tennessee, 1,322; Texas, 20,565; Vermont, 367; Virginia, 63; West Virginia, 246; Wyoming, 20.

Total: 50,340

**Joseph P. Malloney (Socialist Labor)**

California, 7,554 votes; Colorado, 654; Connecticut, 908; Illinois, 1,374; Indiana, 663; Iowa, 259; Kentucky, 390; Maryland, 382; Massachusetts, 2,599; Michigan, 830; Minnesota, 1,329; Missouri, 1,296; Montana, 119; New Jersey, 2,074; New York, 12,622; Ohio, 1,688; Pennsylvania, 2,936; Rhode Island, 1,423; Texas, 162; Utah, 102; Virginia, 167; Washington, 866; Wisconsin, 503.

Total: 40,900

**Seth Hockett Ellis (Union Reform)**

Arkansas, 341 votes; Illinois, 672; Indiana, 254; Maryland, 142; Ohio, 4,284.

Total: 5,693

**Jonah Fitz Randolph Leonard (United Christian)**

Illinois, 352 votes; Iowa, 166.

Total: 518

**Anti-Imperialist**

Connecticut, 45 votes.

**Scattered write-ins**

Arkansas, 27 votes; Colorado, 26; Connecticut, 10; Louisiana, 4; Massachusetts, 533, New Hampshire, 16; Utah, 9; Vermont, 5; Wyoming, 21.

Total: 651

## 1904 Election

**Thomas E. Watson (Populist)**

Alabama, 5,051 votes; Arkansas, 2,326; Colorado, 824; Connecticut, 495; Delaware, 51; Florida, 1,605; Georgia, 22,635; Idaho, 352; Illinois, 6,725; Indiana, 2,444; Iowa, 2,207; Kansas, 6,253; Kentucky, 2,521; Maine, 337; Maryland, 1; Massachusetts, 1,294; Michigan, 1,145; Minnesota, 2,103; Mississippi, 1,499; Missouri, 4,226; Montana, 1,531; Nebraska, 20,518; Nevada, 344; New Hampshire, 82; New Jersey, 3,705; New York, 7,459; North Carolina, 819; Ohio, 1,392; Oregon, 746; South Dakota, 1,240; Tennessee, 2,491; Texas, 8,062; Washington, 669; West Virginia, 339; Wisconsin, 560.

Total: 114,051

**Charles Hunter Corregan (Socialist Labor)**

Colorado, 335 votes; Connecticut, 583; Illinois, 4,698; Indiana, 1,598; Kentucky, 596; Massachusetts, 2,359; Michigan, 1,018; Minnesota, 974; Missouri, 1,674; Montana, 213; New Jersey, 2,380; New York, 9,122; Ohio, 2,635; Pennsylvania, 2,211; Rhode Island, 488; Texas, 431; Washington, 1,592; Wisconsin, 249.

Total: 33,156

**Austin Holcomb (Continental)**

Illinois, 826 votes.

**Scattered write-ins**

California, 333 votes; Connecticut, 11; Maryland, 4; Massachusetts, 5; New Hampshire, 1; Vermont, 1.

Total: 355

## 1908 Election

**Thomas L. Hisgen (Independence)**

Alabama, 497 votes; Arkansas, 286; California, 4,278; Connecticut, 728; Delaware, 29; Florida, 553; Georgia, 76; Idaho, 124; Illinois, 7,724; Indiana, 514; Iowa, 404; Kansas, 68; Kentucky, 200; Louisiana, 77; Maine, 700; Maryland, 485; Massachusetts, 19,235; Michigan, 734; Minnesota, 424; Missouri, 392; Montana, 493; Nevada, 436; New Hampshire, 584; New Jersey, 2,916; New York, 35,817; North Dakota, 43; Ohio, 439; Oregon, 289; Pennsylvania, 1,057; Rhode Island, 1,105; South Carolina, 46; South Dakota, 88; Tennessee, 332; Texas, 106; Utah, 92; Vermont, 804; Virginia, 51; Washington, 248; Wyoming, 63.

Total: 82,537

**Thomas E. Watson (Populist)**

Alabama, 1,576 votes; Arkansas, 987; Florida, 1,946; Georgia, 16,687; Illinois, 633; Indiana, 1,193; Iowa, 261; Kentucky, 333; Mississippi, 1,276; Missouri, 1,165; Ohio, 162; Tennessee, 1,092; Texas, 960; Virginia, 105.

Total: 28,376

**August Gillhaus (Socialist Labor)**

Connecticut, 608 votes; Illinois, 1,680; Indiana, 643; Kentucky, 405; Massachusetts, 1,011; Michigan, 1,085; Missouri, 867; New Jersey, 1,196; New York, 3,877; Ohio, 721; Pennsylvania, 1,224; Rhode Island, 183; Texas, 175; Virginia, 25; Wisconsin, 318.

Total: 14,018

**Daniel Braxton Turney (United Christian)**

Illinois, 400 votes; Michigan, 61.

**Republican (Davidson Faction)**

Alabama, 987 votes.

**Scattered write-ins**

California, 28 votes; Colorado, 2; Connecticut, 4; Massachusetts, 9; New Hampshire, 8; North Carolina, 13; Vermont, 29; Wisconsin, 2.

Total: 95

## 1912 Election

**Eugene W. Chafin (Prohibition)**

Arizona, 265 votes; Arkansas, 908; California, 23,366; Colorado, 5,063; Connecticut, 2,068; Delaware, 620; Florida, 1,854; Georgia, 149; Idaho, 1,536; Illinois, 15,710; Indiana, 19,249; Iowa, 8,440; Kentucky, 3,253; Maine, 947; Maryland, 2,244; Massachusetts, 2,753; Michigan, 8,794; Minnesota, 7,886; Missouri, 5,380; Montana, 32; Nebraska, 3,383; New Hampshire, 535; New Jersey, 2,936; New York, 19,455; North Carolina, 118; North Dakota, 1,243; Ohio, 11,511; Oklahoma, 2,195; Oregon, 4,360; Pennsylvania, 19,525; Rhode Island, 616; South Dakota, 3,910; Tennessee, 832; Texas, 1,701; Vermont, 1,094; Virginia, 709; Washington, 9,810; West Virginia, 4,517; Wisconsin, 8,584; Wyoming, 421.

Total: 207,972

**Arthur E. Reimer (Socialist Labor)**

Colorado, 475 votes; Connecticut, 1,260; Illinois, 4,066; Indiana, 3,130; Kentucky, 1,055; Maryland, 322; Massachusetts, 1,102; Michigan, 1,239; Minnesota, 2,212; Missouri, 1,778; New Jersey, 1,396; New York, 4,273; Ohio, 2,630; Pennsylvania, 706; Rhode Island, 236; Texas, 430; Utah, 510; Virginia, 50; Washington, 1,872; Wisconsin, 632.

Total: 29,374

**Scattered write-ins**

Alabama, 5 votes; California, 4,417; Connecticut, 6; Kansas, 63; Massachusetts, 1; South Carolina, 55; Wisconsin, 9.

Total: 4,556

## 1916 Election

**Arthur E. Reimer (Socialist Labor)**

Connecticut, 606 votes; Illinois, 2,488; Indiana, 1,659; Iowa, 460; Kentucky, 332; Maryland, 756; Massachusetts, 1,096; Michigan, 831; Minnesota, 468; Missouri, 903; Nebraska, 624; New Jersey, 855; New York, 2,666; Pennsylvania, 419; Rhode Island, 180; Utah, 144; Virginia, 67; Washington, 730.

Total: 15,284

**Progressive** [3]

Colorado, 409 votes; Georgia, 20,692; Indiana, 3,898; Iowa, 1,793; Kentucky, 129; Louisiana, 6,349; Minnesota, 290; Missis-

sippi, 520; Montana, 338; Oklahoma, 234; Oregon, 310; South Carolina, 162; Utah, 110.
Total: 35,234

**Scattered write-ins**
California, 187 votes; Massachusetts, 6; South Carolina, 258; Vermont, 10.
Total: 461

## 1920 Election

**Aaron Sherman Watkins (Prohibition)**
Alabama, 766 votes; Arizona, 4; California, 25,204; Colorado, 2,807; Connecticut, 1,771; Delaware, 986; Florida, 5,127; Illinois, 11,216; Indiana, 13,462; Iowa, 4,197; Kentucky, 3,250; Michigan, 9,646; Minnesota, 11,489; Missouri, 5,152; Nebraska, 5,947; New Jersey, 4,895; New York, 19,653; North Carolina, 17; Ohio, 294; Oregon, 3,595; Pennsylvania, 42,612; Rhode Island, 510; South Dakota, 900; Vermont, 774; Virginia, 826; Washington, 3,800; West Virginia, 1,526; Wisconsin, 8,648; Wyoming, 265.
Total: 189,339

**James Edward Ferguson (American)**
Texas, 48,098 votes.

**William W. Cox (Socialist Labor)**
Connecticut, 1,491 votes; Illinois, 3,471; Iowa, 982; Maryland, 1,178; Massachusetts, 3,583; Michigan, 2,539; Minnesota, 5,828; Missouri, 1,587; New Jersey, 1,010; New York, 4,841; Oregon, 1,515; Pennsylvania, 753; Rhode Island, 495; Washington, 1,321.
Total: 30,594

**Robert Colvin Macauley (Single Tax)**
Delaware, 39 votes; Illinois, 775; Indiana, 566; Maine, 310; Michigan, 484; New Jersey, 603; Ohio, 2,153; Pennsylvania, 803; Rhode Island, 100.
Total: 5,833

**Black and Tan Republican**
Texas, 27,309 votes.

**Scattered write-ins**
Louisiana, 339 votes; Maryland, 1; Massachusetts, 24; Nebraska, 90; New Mexico, 4; Vermont, 56.
Total: 514

## 1924 Election

**Frank T. Johns (Socialist Labor)**
Colorado, 378 votes; Connecticut, 1,373; Illinois, 2,334; Kentucky, 1,501; Maine, 406; Maryland, 987; Massachusetts, 1,668; Michigan, 5,330; Minnesota, 1,855; Missouri, 1,066; New Jersey, 853; New York, 9,928; Ohio, 3,025; Oregon, 917; Pennsylvania, 634; Rhode Island, 268; Virginia, 189; Washington, 1,004; Wisconsin, 458.
Total: 34,174

**William Z. Foster (Communist)**
Colorado, 562 votes; Illinois, 2,622; Indiana, 987; Iowa, 4,037; Massachusetts, 2,635; Minnesota, 4,427; Montana, 358; New Jersey, 1,560; New York, 8,244; North Dakota, 370; Pennsylvania, 2,735; Rhode Island, 289; Washington, 761; Wisconsin, 3,773.
Total: 33,360

**Gilbert Owen Nations (American)**
Florida, 2,319 votes; Georgia, 155; Kentucky, 1,300; New Jersey, 368; Pennsylvania, 13,035; Tennessee, 100; Washington, 5,991; West Virginia, 1,072.
Total: 24,340

**William J. Wallace (Commonwealth Land)**
Delaware, 20 votes; Illinois, 421; Kentucky, 226; Missouri, 165; New Jersey, 265; Ohio, 1,246, Pennsylvania, 296; Rhode Island, 38; Wisconsin, 271.
Total: 2,948

**Scattered write-ins**
Connecticut, 101 votes; Iowa, 445; Kansas, 4; Louisiana, 4,063; Pennsylvania, 131; South Carolina, 1; Vermont, 5.
Total: 4,752

## 1928 Election

**Verne L. Reynolds (Socialist Labor)**
Connecticut, 625 votes; Illinois, 1,812; Indiana, 645; Iowa, 230; Kentucky, 316; Maryland, 906; Massachusetts, 772; Michigan, 799; Minnesota, 1,921; Missouri, 342; New Jersey, 500; New York, 4,211; Ohio, 1,515; Oregon, 1,564; Pennsylvania, 382; Rhode Island, 416; Virginia, 181; Washington, 4,068; Wisconsin, 381.
Total: 21,586

**William Frederick Varney (Prohibition)**
Indiana, 5,496 votes; Michigan, 2,728; New Jersey, 160; Ohio, 3,556; Pennsylvania, 3,875; Vermont, 338; West Virginia, 1,703; Wisconsin, 2,245.
Total: 20,101

**Frank Elbridge Webb (Farmer Labor)**
Colorado, 1,092 votes; Iowa, 3,088; Oklahoma, 1,283; South Dakota, 927.
Total: 6,390

**Scattered write-ins**
California, 373 votes; Iowa, 2; Massachusetts, 4; Pennsylvania, 14; Vermont, 9.
Total: 420

## 1932 Election

**William David Upshaw (Prohibition)**
Alabama, 13 votes; California, 20,637; Colorado, 1,928; Georgia, 1,125; Illinois, 6,388; Indiana, 10,399; Iowa, 2,111; Kentucky, 2,252; Massachusetts, 1,142; Michigan, 2,893; Missouri, 2,429; New Jersey, 774; Ohio, 7,421; Pennsylvania, 11,319; Rhode Island, 183; South Dakota, 463; Tennessee, 1,998; Virginia, 1,843; Washington, 1,540; West Virginia, 2,342; Wisconsin, 2,672.
Total: 81,872

**William Hope Harvey (Liberty)**
Arkansas, 952 votes; California, 9,827; Idaho, 4,712; Michigan, 217; Montana, 1,449; New Mexico, 389; North Dakota, 1,817; South Dakota, 3,333; Texas, 243; Washington, 30,308.
Total: 53,247

**Verne L. Reynolds (Socialist Labor)**
Colorado, 427 votes; Connecticut, 2,287; Illinois, 3,638; Indiana, 2,070; Kentucky, 1,393; Maine, 255; Maryland, 1,036; Massachusetts, 2,668; Michigan, 1,401; Minnesota, 770; Missouri, 404; New Jersey, 1,062; New York, 10,339; Ohio, 1,968; Oregon, 1,730; Pennsylvania, 659; Rhode Island, 433; Washington, 1,009; Wisconsin, 494.
Total: 34,043

**Jacob S. Coxey (Farmer Labor)**
Colorado, 469 votes; Iowa, 1,094; Michigan, 137; Minnesota, 5,731.
Total: 7,431

**John Zahnd (National)**
Indiana, 1,645 votes.

**James R. Cox (Jobless)**
Pennsylvania, 725 votes; Virginia, 15.
Total: 740.

**Jacksonian**
Texas, 157 votes.

**Arizona Progressive Democrat**
Arizona, 9 votes.

**Scattered write-ins**
California, 127 votes; Florida, 691; Iowa, 4; Louisiana, 533; Massachusetts, 71; Pennsylvania, 53; Texas, 34; Vermont, 2; Wisconsin, 13.
Total: 1,528

## 1936 Election

**Earl Browder (Communist)**
Alabama, 678 votes; Arkansas, 167; California, 10,877; Colorado, 497; Connecticut, 1,193; Delaware, 51; Illinois, 801; Indiana, 1,090; Iowa, 506; Kentucky, 207; Maine, 257; Maryland, 915; Massachusetts, 2,930; Michigan, 3,384; Minnesota, 2,574; Missouri,

417; Montana, 385; New Hampshire, 193; New Jersey, 1,639; New Mexico, 43; New York, 35,609; North Carolina, 11; North Dakota, 360; Ohio, 5,251; Oregon, 104; Pennsylvania, 4,060; Rhode Island, 411; Tennessee, 326; Texas, 257; Utah, 280; Vermont, 405; Virginia, 98; Washington, 1,907; Wisconsin, 2,197; Wyoming, 91.

Total: 80,171

**D. Leigh Colvin (Prohibition)**

Alabama, 719 votes; Arizona, 384; California, 12,917; Georgia, 660; Illinois, 3,439; Iowa, 1,182; Kentucky, 939; Maine, 334; Massachusetts, 1,032; Michigan, 579; Missouri, 908; Montana, 224; New Jersey, 926; New Mexico, 61; North Dakota, 197; Oklahoma, 1,328; Oregon, 4; Pennsylvania, 6,691; Tennessee, 634; Texas, 522; Utah, 43; Virginia, 594; Washington, 1,041; West Virginia, 1,173; Wisconsin, 1,071; Wyoming, 75.

Total: 37,677

**John W. Aiken (Socialist Labor)**

Colorado, 344 votes; Connecticut, 1,228; Illinois, 1,921; Iowa, 252; Kentucky, 294; Maine, 129; Maryland, 1,305; Massachusetts, 1,305; Michigan, 600; Minnesota, 961; Missouri, 292; New Jersey, 362; Ohio, 28; Oregon, 500; Pennsylvania, 1,424; Rhode Island, 929; Virginia, 36; Washington, 362; Wisconsin, 557.

Total: 12,829

**William Dudley Pelley (Christian)**

Washington, 1,598 votes.

**Scattered write-ins**

California, 490 votes; Florida, 71; Iowa, 4; Louisiana, 93; Massachusetts, 11; Michigan, 5; North Carolina, 6; Ohio, 7; Oregon, 108; Vermont, 137.

Total: 824

## 1940 Election

**Earl Browder (Communist)**

Alabama, 509 votes; California, 13,586; Colorado, 378; Connecticut, 1,091; Idaho, 276; Iowa, 1,524; Maine, 411; Maryland, 1,274; Massachusetts, 3,806; Michigan, 2,834; Minnesota, 2,711; Montana, 489; New Jersey, 6,508; Oregon, 191; Pennsylvania, 4,519; Rhode Island, 243; Texas, 215; Utah, 191; Vermont, 411; Virginia, 72; Washington, 2,626; Wisconsin, 2,394.

Total: 46,259

**John W. Aiken (Socialist Labor)**

Connecticut, 971 votes; Indiana, 706; Iowa, 452; Maryland, 657; Massachusetts, 1,492; Michigan, 795; Minnesota, 2,553; Missouri, 209; New Jersey, 455; Oregon, 2,487; Pennsylvania, 1,518; Virginia, 48; Washington, 667; Wisconsin, 1,882.

Total: 14,892

**Alfred Knutson (Independent)**

North Dakota, 545 votes.

**Scattered write-ins**

California, 262 votes; Florida, 148; Georgia, 14; Illinois, 657; Louisiana, 108; Massachusetts, 12; Michigan, 4; Oregon, 40: Pennsylvania, 827; Vermont, 11.

Total: 2,083

## 1944 Election

**Edward A. Teichert (Socialist Labor)**

California, 180 votes; Connecticut, 1,220; Illinois, 9,677; Iowa, 193; Kentucky, 329; Maine, 335; Massachusetts, 2,780; Michigan, 1,264; Minnesota, 3,176; Missouri, 220; New Jersey, 6,939; New York, 14,352; Pennsylvania, 1,789; Virginia, 90; Washington, 1,645; Wisconsin, 1,002.

Total: 45,191

**Gerald L. K. Smith (America First)**

Michigan, 1,530 votes; Texas, 250.

Total: 1,780

**Texas Regulars**

Texas, 135,444 votes.

**Southern Democrat**

South Carolina, 7,799.

**Scattered write-ins**

California, 1,881 votes; Florida, 211; Louisiana, 69; Massachusetts, 266; Michigan, 6; Vermont, 14.

Total: 2,447

## 1948 Election

**Norman M. Thomas (Socialist)**

Arkansas, 1,037 votes; California, 3,459; Colorado, 1,678; Connecticut, 6,964; Delaware, 250; Georgia, 3; Idaho, 332; Illinois, 11,522; Indiana, 2,179; Iowa, 1,829; Kansas, 2,807; Kentucky, 1,284; Maine, 547; Maryland, 2,941; Michigan, 6,063; Minnesota, 4,646; Missouri, 2,222; Montana, 695; New Hampshire, 86; New Jersey, 10,521; New Mexico, 83; New York, 40,879; North Dakota, 1,000; Oregon, 5,051; Pennsylvania, 11,325; Rhode Island, 429; South Carolina, 1; Tennessee, 1,288; Texas, 922; Vermont, 585; Virginia, 726; Washington, 3,534; Wisconsin, 12,547; Wyoming, 137.

Total: 139,572

**Claude A. Watson (Prohibition)**

Alabama, 1,085 votes; Arizona, 786; Arkansas, 1; California, 16,926; Delaware, 343; Georgia, 732; Idaho, 628; Illinois, 11,959; Indiana, 14,711; Iowa, 3,382; Kansas, 6,468; Kentucky, 1,245; Massachusetts, 1,663; Michigan, 13,052; Montana, 429; New Jersey, 10,593; New Mexico, 127; Pennsylvania, 10,538; Texas, 3,115; Washington, 6,117.

Total: 103,900

**Edward A. Teichert (Socialist Labor)**

Arizona, 121 votes; California, 195; Colorado, 214; Connecticut, 1,184; Delaware, 29; Illinois, 3,118; Indiana, 763; Iowa, 4,274; Kentucky, 185; Maine, 206; Massachusetts, 5,535; Michigan, 1,263; Minnesota, 2,525; New Hampshire, 83; New Jersey, 3,354; New Mexico, 49; New York, 2,729; Pennsylvania, 1,461; Rhode Island, 131; Virginia, 234; Washington, 1,133; Wisconsin, 399; Wyoming, 56.

Total: 29,241

**Farrell Dobbs (Socialist Workers)**

California, 133 votes; Colorado, 228; Connecticut, 606; Iowa, 256; Michigan, 672; Minnesota, 606; New Jersey, 5,825; New York, 2,675; Pennsylvania, 2,133; Utah, 74; Washington, 103; Wisconsin, 303.

Total: 13,614

**Scattered write-ins**

California, 813 votes; Geoergia, 1; Illinois, 1,629; Louisiana, 10; Massachusetts, 633; Michigan, 1; Missouri, 54; Nebraska, 1; New York, 128; Pennsylvania, 107; Vermont, 35.

Total: 3,412

## 1952 Election

**Eric Hass (Socialist Labor)**

Arkansas, 1 vote; California, 273; Colorado, 352; Connecticut, 535; Delaware, 242; Illinois, 9,363; Indiana, 840; Iowa, 139; Kentucky, 893; Maine, 156; Massachusetts, 1,957; Michigan, 1,495; Minnesota, 2,383; Missouri, 169; New Jersey, 5,815; New Mexico, 35; New York, 1,560; Pennsylvania, 1,377; Rhode Island, 83; Virginia, 1,160; Washington, 633; Wisconsin, 770; Wyoming, 36.

Total: 30,267

**Darlington Hoopes (Socialist)**

California, 206 votes; Colorado, 365; Connecticut, 2,244; Delaware, 20; Iowa, 219; Kansas, 530; Maine, 138; Missouri, 227; Montana, 159; New Jersey, 8,593; New York, 2,664; Pennsylvania, 2,698; Vermont, 185; Virginia, 504; Washington, 254; Wisconsin, 1,157; Wyoming, 40.

Total: 20,203

**Douglas MacArthur (Constitution)** [4]

Arkansas, 458 votes; California, 3,504; Colorado, 2,181; Missouri, 535; New Mexico; 220; North Dakota, 1,075; Tennessee, 379; Texas, 1,563; Washington, 7,290.

Total: 17,205

**Farrell Dobbs (Socialist Workers)**
Michigan, 655 votes; Minnesota, 618; New Jersey, 3,850; New York, 2,212; Pennsylvania, 1,508; Washington, 119; Wisconsin, 1,350.
Total: 10,312

**Henry Krajewski (Poor Man's)**
New Jersey, 4,203 votes.

**Scattered write-ins**
California, 3,249 votes; Connecticut, 5; Florida, 351; Georgia, 1; Idaho, 23; Illinois, 448; Iowa, 29; Maine, 1; Massachusetts, 69; Michigan, 3; New York, 178; Pennsylvania, 155; Vermont, 18.
Total: 4,530

## 1956 Election

**Enoch A. Holtwick (Prohibition)**
California, 11,119 votes; Delaware, 400; Indiana, 6,554; Kansas, 3,048; Kentucky, 2,145; Massachusetts, 1,205; Michigan, 6,923; New Jersey, 9,147; New Mexico, 607; Tennessee, 789.
Total: 41,937

**Farrell Dobbs (Socialist Workers)**
California, 96 votes; Minnesota, 1,098; New Jersey, 4,004; Pennsylvania, 2,035; Wisconsin, 564.
Total: 7,797

**Harry F. Byrd (States' Rights)**
Kentucky, 2,657 votes.

**Darlington Hoopes (Socialist)**
California, 123 votes; Colorado, 531; Iowa, 192; New York, 82; Virginia, 444; Wisconsin, 754.
Total: 2,126

**Henry Krajewski (American Third Party)**
New Jersey, 1,829 votes.

**Gerald L. K. Smith (Christian Nationalist)**
California, 8 votes.

**Independent Electors**
Alabama, 20,323 votes; Louisiana, 44,520; Mississippi, 42,966; South Carolina, 88,509.
Total: 196,318

**Scattered write-ins**
California, 819 votes; Connecticut, 205; Florida, 1,542; Georgia, 93; Idaho, 16; Illinois, 56; Maryland, 476; Massachusetts, 341; New York, 1,262; Oregon, 535; Vermont, 39.
Total: 5,384

## 1960 Election

**Rutherford L. Decker (Prohibition)**
Alabama, 2,106 votes; California, 21,706; Delaware, 284; Indiana, 6,746; Kansas, 4,138; Massachusetts, 1,633; Michigan, 2,029; Montana, 456; New Mexico, 777; Tennessee, 2,458; Texas, 3,870.
Total: 46,203

**Orval E. Faubus (National States' Rights)**
Alabama, 4,367 votes; Arkansas, 28,952; Delaware, 354; Tennessee, 11,296.
Total: 44,977

**Farrell Dobbs (Socialist Workers)**
Colorado, 562 votes; Iowa, 634; Michigan, 4,347; Minnesota, 3,077; Montana, 391; New Jersey, 11,402; New York, 14,319; North Dakota, 158; Pennsylvania, 2,678; Utah, 100; Washington, 705; Wisconsin, 1,792.
Total: 40,165

**Charles L. Sullivan (Constitutional)**
Texas, 18,162 votes.

**J. Bracken Lee (Conservative)**
New Jersey, 8,708 votes.

**C. Benton Coiner (Virginia Conservative)**
Virginia, 4,204 votes.

**Lar Daly (Tax Cut)**
Michigan, 1,767 votes.

**Clennon King (Independent Afro-American Unity)**
Alabama, 1,485 votes.

**Merritt B. Curtis (Constitution)**
Washington, 1,401 votes.

**Independent Electors**
Louisiana, 169,572 votes; Michigan, 539.
Total: 170,111

**Scattered write-ins**
Alabama, 236 votes; Connecticut, 15; Georgia, 239; Illinois, 15; Maryland, 3; Massachusetts, 31; Oregon, 959; Pennsylvania, 440; South Carolina, 1; Texas, 175; Vermont, 7.
Total: 2,378

## 1964 Election

**E. Harold Munn (Prohibition)**
California, 305 votes; Colorado, 1,356; Delaware, 425; Indiana, 8,266; Iowa, 1,902; Kansas, 5,393; Massachusetts, 3,735; Michigan, 669; Montana, 499; New Mexico, 543; North Dakota, 174.
Total: 23,267

**John Kasper (National States' Rights)**
Arkansas, 2,965 votes; Kentucky, 3,469; Montana, 519.
Total: 6,953

**Joseph B. Lightburn (Constitution)**
Texas, 5,060 votes.

**James Hensley (Universal Party)**
California, 19 votes.

**Unpledged Democrat**
Alabama, 210,732 votes.

**Scattered write-ins**
Alabama, 1 vote; California, 5,410; Connecticut, 1,313; Georgia, 195; Illinois, 62; Iowa, 118; Maryland, 50; Massachusetts, 159; Michigan, 145; New York, 268; Oregon, 2,509; Pennsylvania, 2,531; Rhode Island, 13; South Carolina, 8; Tennessee, 34; Vermont, 20.
Total: 12,868

## 1968 Election

**Dick Gregory (Freedom and Peace)**
California, 3,230 votes; Colorado, 1,393; Indiana, 36; New Jersey, 8,084; New York, 24,517; Ohio, 372; Pennsylvania, 7,821; Virginia, 1,680.
Total: 47,133

**Fred Halstead (Socialist Workers)**
Arizona, 85 votes; Colorado, 235; Indiana, 1,293; Iowa, 3,377; Kentucky, 2,843; Michigan, 4,099; Minnesota, 807; Montana, 457; New Hampshire, 104; New Jersey, 8,667; New Mexico, 252; New York, 11,851; North Dakota, 128; Ohio, 69; Pennsylvania, 4,862; Rhode Island, 383; Utah, 89; Vermont, 295; Washington, 270; Wisconsin, 1,222.
Total: 41,388

**Eldridge Cleaver (Peace and Freedom)**
Arizona, 217 votes; California, 27,707; Iowa, 1,332; Michigan, 4,585; Minnesota, 933; Utah, 180; Washington, 1,609.
Total: 36,563

**Eugene J. McCarthy**
Arizona, 2,751 votes; California, 20,721; Minnesota, 584; Oregon, 1,496.
Total: 25,552

**E. Harold Munn (Prohibition)**
Alabama, 4,022 votes; California, 59; Colorado, 275; Indiana, 4,616; Iowa, 362; Kansas, 2,192; Massachusetts, 2,369; Michigan, 60; Montana, 510; North Dakota, 38; Ohio, 19; Virginia, 601.
Total: 15,123

**Ventura Chavez (People's Constitution)**
New Mexico, 1,519 votes.

**Charlene Mitchell (Communist)**
California, 260 votes; Minnesota, 415; Ohio, 23; Washington, 377.
Total: 1,075

**James Hensley (Universal)**
Iowa, 142 votes.

**Richard K. Troxell (Constitution)**
North Dakota, 34 votes.

**Kent M. Soeters (Berkeley Defense Group)**
California, 17 votes.
**American Independent Democrat**
Alabama, 10,960 votes.
**New Party**
New Hampshire, 421 votes; Vermont, 579.
Total: 1,000
**New Reform**
Montana, 470 votes.
**Scattered write-ins**
Alabama, 13 votes; Colorado, 948; Connecticut, 1,300; Georgia, 165; Illinois, 325; Iowa, 250; Massachusetts, 53; Michigan, 29; Minnesota, 170; New Hampshire, 108; New Mexico, 69; New York, 1,622; Oregon, 1,144; Pennsylvania, 2,264; Rhode Island, 62; Texas, 299; Vermont, 29; Wisconsin, 2,342.
Total: 11,192

## 1972 Election

**Louis Fisher (Socialist Labor)**
California, 197 votes; Colorado, 4,361; Georgia, 3; Illinois, 12,344; Indiana, 1,688; Iowa, 195; Massachusetts, 129; Michigan, 2,437; Minnesota, 4,261; New Jersey, 4,544; New York, 4,530; Ohio, 7,107; Virginia, 9,918; Washington, 1,102; Wisconsin, 998.
Total: 53,814
**Linda Jenness (Socialist Workers)**
Arizona, 366 votes; California, 574; Colorado, 666; District of Columbia, 316; Idaho, 397; Iowa, 488; Kentucky, 685; Louisiana, 14,398; Massachusetts, 10,600; Michigan, 1,603; Minnesota, 940; Mississippi, 2,458; New Hampshire, 368; New Jersey, 2,233; New Mexico, 474; North Dakota, 288; Pennsylvania, 4,639; Rhode Island, 729; South Dakota, 994; Texas, 8,664; Vermont, 296; Washington, 623.
Total: 52,799
**Gus Hall (Communist)**
California, 373 votes; Colorado, 432; District of Columbia, 252; Illinois, 4,541; Iowa, 272; Kentucky, 464; Massachusetts, 46; Michigan, 1,210; Minnesota, 662; New Jersey, 1,263; New York, 5,641; North Dakota, 87; Ohio, 6,437; Pennsylvania, 2,686; Washington, 566; Wisconsin, 663.
Total: 25,595
**Evelyn Reed (Socialist Workers)**
Indiana, 5,575 votes; New York, 7,797; Wisconsin, 506.
Total: 13,878
**E. Harold Munn (Prohibition)**
Alabama, 8,559 votes; California, 53; Colorado, 467; Delaware, 238; Kansas, 4,188.
Total: 13,505
**John Hospers (Libertarian)**
California, 980 votes; Colorado, 1,111; Massachusetts, 43; Rhode Island, 2; Washington, 1,537.
Total: 3,673
**John V. Mahalchik (America First)**
New Jersey, 1,743 votes.
**Gabriel Green (Universal)**
California, 21 votes; Iowa, 199.
Total: 220
**Scattered write-ins**
Colorado, 6 votes; Connecticut, 777; Florida, 7,407; Georgia, 2,932; Illinois, 2,229; Iowa, 321; Massachusetts, 342; Minnesota, 962; Missouri, 4,804; New Hampshire, 142; New Mexico, 310; New York, 4,089; Ohio, 460; Oregon, 2,289; Pennsylvania, 2,716; Rhode Island, 19; South Carolina, 17; Tennessee, 369; Texas, 3,393; Vermont, 318; Wisconsin, 893.
Total: 34,795

## 1976 Election

**Lester Maddox (American Independent)**
Alabama, 9,198 votes; Arizona, 85; California, 51,098; Connecticut, 7,101; Georgia, 1,071; Idaho, 5,935; Kansas, 2,118; Kentucky, 2,328; Louisiana, 10,058; Maine, 8; Maryland, 171; Mis-

sissippi, 4,861; Nebraska, 3,380; Nevada, 1,497; New Jersey, 7,716; New Mexico, 31; New York, 97; North Dakota, 269; Ohio, 15,529; Pennsylvania, 25,344; Rhode Island, 1; South Carolina, 1,950; Tennessee, 2,303; Texas, 41; Utah, 1,162; Washington, 8,585; West Virginia, 12; Wisconsin, 8,552; Wyoming; 30.
Total: 170,531

**Thomas J. Anderson (American)**
Alabama, 70 votes; Arizona, 564; Arkansas, 389; California, 4,565; Colorado, 397; Connecticut, 155; Delaware, 645; Florida, 21,325; Georgia, 1,168; Idaho, 493; Illinois, 387; Indiana, 14,048; Iowa, 3,040; Kansas, 4,724; Kentucky, 8,308; Maine, 28; Maryland, 321; Massachusetts, 7,555; Minnesota, 13,592; Mississippi, 6,678; Montana, 5,772; New Mexico, 106; New York, 451; North Carolina, 5,607; North Dakota, 3,796; Oregon, 1,035; Rhode Island, 24; South Carolina, 2,996; Tennessee, 5,769; Texas, 11,442; Utah, 13,284; Virginia, 16,686; Washington, 5,046; West Virginia, 17; Wyoming, 290.
Total: 160,773

**Peter Camejo (Socialist Workers)**
Alabama, 1 vote; Arizona, 928; California, 17,259; Colorado, 1,126; Connecticut, 42; District of Columbia, 545; Georgia, 43; Idaho, 14; Illinois, 3,615; Indiana, 5,695; Iowa, 267; Kentucky, 350; Louisiana, 2,240; Maine, 1; Maryland, 261; Massachusetts, 8,138; Michigan, 1,804; Minnesota, 4,149; Mississippi, 2,805; New Hampshire, 161; New Jersey, 1,184; New Mexico, 2,462; New York, 6,996; North Dakota, 43; Ohio, 4,717; Pennsylvania, 3,009; Rhode Island, 462; South Carolina, 8; South Dakota, 168; Texas, 1,723; Utah, 268; Vermont, 430; Virginia, 17,802; Washington, 905; West Virginia, 2; Wisconsin, 1,691.
Total: 91,314

**Gus Hall (Communist)**
Alabama, 1,954 votes; California, 12,766; Colorado, 403; Connecticut, 186; District of Columbia, 219; Georgia, 3; Idaho, 5; Illinois, 9,250; Iowa, 554; Kentucky, 426; Louisiana, 7,417; Maine, 14; Maryland, 68; Minnesota, 1,092; New Jersey, 1,662; New Mexico, 19; New York, 10,270; North Dakota, 84; Ohio, 7,817; Pennsylvania, 1,891; Rhode Island, 334; South Carolina, 1; South Dakota, 318; Tennessee, 547; Utah, 121; Washington, 817; West Virginia, 5; Wisconsin, 749.
Total: 58,992

**Margaret Wright (People's Party)**
California, 41,731 votes; Connecticut, 1; Idaho, 1; Maryland, 8; Massachusetts, 33; Michigan, 3,504; Minnesota, 635; New Jersey, 1,044; Washington, 1,124; Wisconsin, 943.
Total: 49,024

**Lyndon H. LaRouche Jr. (U.S. Labor)**
Alabama, 1 vote; Colorado, 567; Connecticut, 1,789; Delaware, 136; District of Columbia, 157; Georgia, 1; Idaho, 739; Illinois, 2,018; Indiana, 1,947; Iowa, 241; Kentucky, 510; Maryland, 21; Massachusetts, 4,922; Michigan, 1,366; Minnesota, 543; New Hampshire, 186; New Jersey, 1,650; New Mexico, 1; New York, 5,413; North Carolina, 755; North Dakota, 142; Ohio, 4,335; Pennsylvania, 2,744; South Carolina, 2; Tennessee, 512; Vermont, 196; Virginia, 7,508; Washington, 903; Wisconsin, 738.
Total: 40,043

**Benjamin C. Bubar (Prohibition)**
Alabama, 6,669 votes; California, 34; Colorado, 2,882; Delaware, 103; Kansas, 1,403; Maine, 3,495; Maryland, 2; Massachusetts, 14;
New Jersey, 554; New Mexico, 211; North Dakota, 63; Ohio, 62; Tennessee, 442.
Total: 15,934
**Jules Levin (Socialist Labor)**
California, 222 votes; Colorado, 14; Connecticut, 1; Delaware, 86; Florida, 19; Georgia, 2; Illinois, 2,422; Iowa, 167; Maine, 1; Maryland, 7; Massachusetts, 19; Michigan, 1,148; Minnesota, 370; New Hampshire, 66; New Jersey, 3,686; New York, 28; Ohio, 68; Rhode Island, 188; Washington, 713; Wisconsin, 389.
Total: 9,616

**Frank P. Zeidler (Socialist)**

Connecticut, 5 votes; Florida, 8; Georgia, 2; Idaho, 2; Iowa, 234; Maryland, 16; Minnesota, 354; New Jersey, 469; New Mexico, 240; New York, 14; North Dakota, 38; Washington, 358; Wisconsin, 4,298.

Total: 6,038

**Ernest L. Miller (Restoration)**

California, 26 votes; Colorado, 6; Florida, 2; Georgia, 3; Maryland, 8; Tennessee, 316.

Total: 361

**Frank Taylor (United American)**

Arizona, 22 votes; California, 14.

Total: 36

**Scattered write-ins**

Alabama, 137 votes; Alaska, 1,176; California, 74; Colorado, 2; Connecticut, 1,122; District of Columbia, 1,944, 1.2; Georgia, 847; Idaho, 1,430; Illinois, 1,662; Iowa, 506; Maine, 185; Maryland, 1,945; Massachusetts, 1,354; Michigan, 2,160; Minnesota, 342; Missouri, 3,741; Nevada, 5,108 (none of the above), 2.5; New Hampshire, 604; New Mexico, 501; New York, 4,052; North Carolina, 228; Oregon, 6,107; Pennsylvania, 2,934; Rhode Island, 82; South Carolina, 328; Tennessee, 229; Texas, 2,752; Vermont, 99; West Virginia, 125; Wisconsin, 2,839; Wyoming, 354.

Total: 44,969

## 1980 Election

**Barry Commoner (Citizens)**

Alabama, 517 votes; Arizona, 551; Arkansas, 2,345; California, 61,063; Colorado, 5,614; Connecticut, 6,130; Delaware, 103; District of Columbia, 1,840; Georgia, 104; Hawaii, 1,548; Illinois, 10,692; Indiana, 4,852; Iowa, 2,273; Kentucky, 1,304; Louisiana, 1,584; Maine, 4,394; Massachusetts, 2,056; Michigan, 11,930; Minnesota, 8,407; Missouri, 573; New Hampshire, 1,320; New Jersey, 8,203; New Mexico, 2,202; New York, 23,186; North Carolina, 2,287; North Dakota, 429; Ohio, 8,564; Oregon, 13,642; Pennsylvania, 10,430; Rhode Island, 67; Tennessee, 1,112; Texas, 453; Utah, 1,009; Vermont, 2,316; Virginia, 14,024; Washington, 9,403; Wisconsin, 7,767.

Total: 234,294

**Gus Hall (Communist)**

Alabama, 1,629 votes; Arizona, 25; Arkansas, 1,244; California, 847; Colorado, 487; Delaware, 13; District of Columbia, 371; Florida, 123; Hawaii, 458; Illinois, 9,711; Indiana, 702; Iowa, 298; Kansas, 967; Kentucky, 348; Maine, 591; Michigan, 3,262; Minnesota, 1,184; Missouri, 26; New Hampshire, 129; New Jersey, 2,555; New York, 7,414; North Dakota, 93; Pennsylvania, 5,184; Rhode Island, 218; Tennessee, 503; Texas, 49; Utah, 139; Vermont, 118; Washington, 834; Wisconsin, 772.

Total: 45,023

**John R. Rarick (American Independent)**

Alabama, 15,010 votes; California, 9,856; Idaho, 1,057; Kansas, 789; Louisiana, 10,333; Michigan, 5; South Carolina, 2,177; Utah, 522; Wisconsin, 1,519.

Total: 41,268

**Clifton DeBerry (Socialist Workers)**

Alabama, 1,303 votes; Arizona, 1,100; District of Columbia, 173; Florida, 41; Illinois, 1,302; Indiana, 610; Iowa, 244; Louisiana, 783; Massachusetts, 5,143; Minnesota, 711; Missouri, 1,515; New Hampshire, 71; New York, 2,068; North Carolina, 416; North Dakota, 89; Pennsylvania, 20,291; Rhode Island, 90; Tennessee, 490; Utah, 124; Vermont, 75; Virginia, 1,986; Washington, 1,137.

Total: 38,737

**Ellen McCormack (Right to Life)**

Delaware, 3 votes; Kentucky, 4,233; Missouri, 5; New Jersey, 3,927; New York, 24,159; Rhode Island, 1.

Total: 32,327

**Maureen Smith (Peace and Freedom)**

California, 18,116 votes.

**Deirdre Griswold (Workers World)**

California, 15 votes; Delaware, 3; District of Columbia, 52; Florida, 8; Georgia, 1; Illinois, 2,257; Massachusetts, 19; Michigan, 30; Minnesota, 698; Mississippi, 2,402; New Hampshire, 76; New Jersey, 1,288; Ohio, 3,790; Rhode Island, 77; Tennessee, 400; Texas, 11; Washington, 341; Wisconsin, 414.

Total: 13,300

**Benjamin C. Bubar (Statesman)**

Alabama, 1,743 votes; Arkansas, 1,350; California, 36; Colorado, 1,180; Delaware, 6; Iowa, 150; Kansas, 821; Massachusetts, 34; Michigan, 9; New Mexico, 1,281; North Dakota, 54; Ohio, 27; Tennessee, 521.

Total: 7,212

**David McReynolds (Socialist)**

Alabama, 1,006 votes; Florida, 116; Iowa, 534; Massachusetts, 62; Minnesota, 536; New Jersey, 1,973; North Dakota, 82; Rhode Island, 170; Tennessee, 519; Vermont, 136; Washington, 956; Wisconsin, 808.

Total: 6,898

**Percy L. Greaves (American)**

California, 87 votes, Delaware, 400; Indiana, 4,750; Iowa, 189; Michigan, 21; North Dakota, 235; Utah, 965.

Total: 6,647

**Andrew Pulley (Socialist Workers)**

California, 231 votes; Colorado, 520; Delaware, 4; Georgia, 4; Kentucky, 393; Mississippi, 2,347; New Jersey, 2,198; New Mexico, 325; South Dakota, 250.

Total: 6,272

**Richard Congress (Socialist Workers)**

Ohio, 4,029 votes.

**Kurt Lynen (Middle Class)**

New Jersey, 3,694 votes.

**Bill Gahres (Down With Lawyers)**

New Jersey, 1,718 votes.

**Frank W. Shelton (American)**

Kansas, 1,555 votes.

**Martin E. Wendelken, (Independent)**

New Jersey, 923 votes.

**Harley McLain (Natural Peoples League)**

North Dakota, 296 votes.

**Scattered write-ins**

Alaska, 857 votes; California, 1,242; Connecticut, 836; Delaware, 101; District of Columbia, 690; Georgia, 112; Illinois, 604; Iowa, 519; Maine, 84; Massachusetts, 2,382; Michigan, 891; Minnesota, 6,139 (American Party, with no candidate specified); Missouri, 604; Nevada, 4,193 (none of the above); New Hampshire, 68; New Mexico, 734; New York, 1,064; Oregon, 1,713; Rhode Island, 37; South Carolina, 376; Tennessee, 152; Vermont, 413; Wisconsin, 1,337.

Total: 23,517

## 1984 Election

**Sonia Johnson (Citizens)**

Arizona, 18 votes; Arkansas, 960; California, 26,297; Colorado, 23; Connecticut, 14; Delaware, 121; Florida, 58; Georgia, 4; Illinois, 2,716; Kentucky, 599; Louisiana, 9,502; Massachusetts, 18; Michigan, 1,191; Minnesota, 1,219; Missouri, 2; New Jersey, 1,247; New Mexico, 455; North Dakota, 368; Pennsylvania, 21,628; Rhode Island, 240; Tennessee, 978; Texas, 87; Utah, 844; Vermont, 264; Washington, 1,891; Wisconsin, 1,456.

Total: 72,200

**Bob Richards (Populist)**

Alabama, 1,401 votes; Arkansas, 1,461; California, 39,265; Georgia, 95; Idaho, 2,288; Kansas, 3,564; Louisiana, 1,310; Minnesota, 2,377; Mississippi, 641; North Dakota, 1,077; Rhode Island, 510; Tennessee, 1,763; Washington, 5,724; West Virginia, 996; Wisconsin, 3,864.

Total: 66,336

**Dennis L. Serrette (Independent Alliance)**

Alabama, 659 votes; Arkansas, 1,291; California, 16; Colorado, 978; Connecticut, 1,374; Delaware, 68; District of Columbia, 165; Georgia, 2; Illinois, 2,386; Iowa, 463; Kansas, 2,544; Kentucky, 365; Louisiana, 533; Maine, 755; Maryland, 656; Massachusetts, 7,998; Michigan, 665; Minnesota, 232; Mississippi, 356; Nebraska, 1,025; New Hampshire, 305; New Jersey, 2,293; New Mexico, 155; New

York, 3,200; North Dakota, 152; Ohio, 12,090; Rhode Island, 49; South Carolina, 682; South Dakota, 1,150; Tennessee, 524; Texas, 41; Utah, 220; Vermont, 323; Washington, 1,654; West Virginia, 493; Wisconsin, 1,006.

Total: 46,868

**Gus Hall (Communist)**

Alabama, 4,671 votes; Arkansas, 1,499; Connecticut, 4,826; District of Columbia, 257; Georgia, 1; Hawaii, 821; Illinois, 4,672; Iowa, 286; Kentucky, 328; Maine, 1,292; Maryland, 898; Michigan, 1,048; Minnesota, 630; New Jersey, 1,564; New York, 4,226; North Dakota, 169; Ohio, 4,438; Pennsylvania, 1,780; Rhode Island, 75; Tennessee, 1,036; Texas, 126; Utah, 184; Vermont, 115; Washington, 814; Wisconsin, 596.

Total: 36,386

**Mel Mason (Socialist Workers)**

Alabama, 730 votes; Colorado, 810; District of Columbia, 127; Florida, 7; Georgia, 10; Illinois, 2,132; Iowa, 313; Kentucky, 3,129; Louisiana, 1,164; Michigan, 1,049; Minnesota, 3,180; Mississippi, 1,032; Missouri, 8; Nebraska, 1,066; New Jersey, 1,264; New Mexico, 224; North Carolina, 799; North Dakota, 239; Ohio, 4,344; Rhode Island, 61; South Dakota, 337; Tennessee, 715; Utah, 142; Vermont, 127; Washington, 608; West Virginia, 645; Wisconsin, 444.

Total: 24,706

**Larry Holmes (Workers World)**

District of Columbia, 107 votes; Georgia, 2; Maryland, 745; Michigan, 1,416; Mississippi, 1,169; New Jersey, 8,404; New York, 2,226; Washington, 641; Wisconsin, 619.

Total: 15,329

**Delmar Dennis (American)**

Delaware, 269 votes; Georgia, 4; Indiana, 7,617; Kentucky, 428; Missouri, 1; South Carolina, 3,490; Tennessee, 7; Utah, 1,345.

Total: 13,161

**Ed Winn (Workers League)**

Arizona, 3 votes; Illinois, 2,632 ; Michigan, 561; Minnesota, 260; New Jersey, 1,721; Ohio, 3,565; Pennsylvania, 2,059.

Total: 10,801

**Earl F. Dodge (Prohibition)**

Arkansas, 842 votes; Colorado, 858; Kansas, 2,109; Massachusetts, 3; New Mexico, 206; North Dakota, 220; Ohio, 4.

Total: 4,242

**Gavrielle Holmes (Workers World)**

Ohio, 2,565 votes; Rhode Island, 91.

Total: 2,656

**John B. Anderson (National Unity Party of Kentucky)**

Georgia, 3 votes; Kentucky, 1,479; Tennessee, 4.

Total: 1,486

**Gerald Baker (Big Deal)**

Iowa, 892 votes.

**Arthur J. Lowery (United Sovereign Citizens)**

Arkansas, 822 votes; Georgia, 3.

Total: 825

**Scattered write-ins**

Alaska, 843 votes; Arizona, 21; California, 366; Connecticut, 8; District of Columbia, 809; Florida, 32; Georgia, 460; Illinois, 862; Iowa, 1,051; Maine, 82; Massachusetts, 892; Michigan, 602; Minnesota, 1; Montana, 1; Nevada, 3,950 (none of the above); New Hampshire, 113; New Mexico, 1; New York, 837; Ohio, 34; Oregon, 4,348; Rhode Island, 3; Tennessee, 117; Vermont, 712; Wisconsin, 706.

Total: 17,573

## 1988 Election

**David E. Duke (Populist)**

Arizona, 113 votes; Arkansas, 5,146; California, 483; Colorado, 139; Florida, 249; Iowa, 755; Kentucky, 4,494; Louisiana, 18,612; Michigan, 60; Minnesota, 1,529; Mississippi, 4,232; Missouri, 44; New Jersey, 2,446; Oregon, 90; Pennsylvania, 3,444; Rhode Island, 159; Tennessee, 1,807; Vermont, 189; Wisconsin, 3,056.

Total: 47,047

**Eugene J. McCarthy (Consumer)**

Arizona, 159 votes; California, 234; Michigan, 2,497; Minnesota, 5,403; New Jersey, 3,454; Pennsylvania, 19,158.

Total: 30,905

**James C. Griffin (American Independent)**

California, 27,818 votes.

**Lyndon H. LaRouche Jr. (National Economic Recovery)**

Alaska, 816 votes; Hawaii, 470; Iowa, 3,526; Louisiana, 1,958; Minnesota, 1,702; North Dakota, 905; Ohio, 7,733; Tennessee, 873; Utah, 427; Vermont, 275; Washington, 4,412; Wisconsin, 2,302; District of Columbia, 163.

Total: 25,562

**William A. Marra (Right to Life)**

Connecticut, 7 votes; New York, 20,497.

Total: 20,504

**Ed Winn (Workers League)**

Alabama, 461 votes; Illinois, 7,021; Iowa, 235; Michigan, 1,958; Minnesota, 489; New Jersey, 691; New York, 10; Ohio, 5,432; Pennsylvania, 2,188; District of Columbia, 208.

Total: 18,693

**James Warren (Socialist Workers)**

Alabama, 656 votes; Iowa, 205; Michigan, 819; Minnesota, 2,155; New Jersey, 2,298; New Mexico, 344; New York, 3,287 0.1; North Dakota, 347; Rhode Island, 130; South Dakota, 226; Tennessee, 718; Texas, 110; Utah, 209; Vermont, 113; Washington, 1,290; Wisconsin, 2,574; District of Columbia, 123.

Total: 15,604

**Herbert Lewin (Peace and Freedom)**

California, 58 votes; New Jersey, 9,953; Rhode Island, 195; Vermont, 164.

Total: 10,370

**Earl F. Dodge (Prohibition)**

Arkansas, 1,319 votes; Colorado, 4,604; Massachusetts, 18; Michigan, 5; New Mexico, 249; Tennessee, 1,807.

Total: 8,002

**Larry Holmes (Workers World)**

California, 11 votes; Michigan, 804; New Jersey, 1,020; New Mexico, 258; New York 4,179; Ohio, 134; Washington, 1,440.

Total: 7,846

**Willa Kenoyer (Socialist)**

Florida, 14 votes; Iowa, 334; Massachusetts, 15; New Jersey, 2,587; New York, 3; Rhode Island, 96; Tennessee, 358; Texas, 62; Utah, 129; Vermont, 142; District of Columbia, 142.

Total: 3,882

**Delmar Dennis (American)**

Arizona, 18 votes; Minnesota, 1,298; Missouri, 1; Utah, 2,158.

Total: 3,475

**Jack E. Herer (Grassroots)**

Minnesota, 1,949 votes.

**Louie G. Youngkeit (Independent)**

Utah, 372 votes.

**John G. Martin (Third World Assembly)**

District of Columbia, 236 votes.

**Scattered write-ins**

Alabama, 506 votes; Alaska, 957; California, 25; Florida, 13; Georgia, 15; Iowa, 1,613; Maine, 230; Maryland, 24; Massachusetts, 2,910; Michigan, 902; Minnesota, 3,614; Missouri, 6; Nevada, 6,934 (none of the above); New Hampshire, 549; New Mexico, 93; Ohio, 216; Oregon, 3,974; Rhode Island, 51; Tennessee, 285; Texas, 98; Vermont, 1,134; Wisconsin, 2,273; District of Columbia, 1,553.

Total: 27,975

## 1992 Election

**James "Bo" Gritz (Populist)**

Alaska, 1,379 votes; Arizona, 8,141; Arkansas, 819; California, 3,077; Colorado, 274; Connecticut, 72; Delaware, 9; Georgia, 78; Hawaii, 1,452; Idaho, 10,281; Illinois, 3,577; Indiana, 1,467; Iowa, 1,177; Kansas, 79; Kentucky, 47; Louisiana, 18,545; Maryland, 41; Michigan, 168; Minnesota, 3,363; Mississippi, 545; Missouri, 180; Montana, 3,658; Nevada, 2,892; New Jersey, 1,867; New York, 23; Ohio, 4,699; Oregon, 1,470; Rhode Island, 3; Tennessee, 756;

Texas, 505; Utah, 28,602, 3.8; Washington, 4,854; West Virginia, 34; Wisconsin, 2,311; Wyoming, 569.

Total: 107,014

**Lenora B. Fulani (New Alliance)**

Alabama, 2,161 votes; Alaska, 330; Arizona, 923; Arkansas, 1,022; Colorado, 1,608; Connecticut, 1,363; Delaware, 1,105; District of Columbia, 1,459; Georgia, 44; Hawaii, 720; Idaho, 613; Illinois, 5,267; Indiana, 2,583; Iowa, 197; Kansas, 10; Kentucky, 430; Louisiana, 1,434; Maine, 519; Maryland, 2,786; Massachusetts, 3,172; Michigan, 21; Minnesota, 958; Mississippi, 2,625; Missouri, 17; Montana, 8; Nebraska, 846; Nevada, 483; New Hampshire, 512; New Jersey, 3,513; New Mexico, 369; New York, 11,318; North Carolina, 59; North Dakota, 143; Ohio, 6,413; Oregon, 3,030; Pennsylvania, 4,661; Rhode Island, 1,878; South Carolina, 1,235; South Dakota, 110; Tennessee, 727; Texas, 301; Utah, 414; Vermont, 429; Virginia, 3,192; Washington, 1,776; West Virginia, 6; Wisconsin, 654; Wyoming, 270.

Total: 73,714

**Howard Phillips (U.S. Taxpayers)**

Alaska, 377 votes; Arkansas, 1,437; California, 12,711; Connecticut, 20; Delaware, 2; Georgia, 7; Iowa, 480; Kansas, 55; Kentucky, 989; Louisiana, 1,552; Maine, 464; Maryland, 22; Massachusetts, 2,218; Michigan, 8,263; Minnesota, 733; Mississippi, 1,652; Nevada, 677; New Jersey, 2,670; New Mexico, 620; Rhode Island, 215; South Carolina, 2,680; Tennessee, 579; Texas, 359; Utah, 393; Vermont, 124; Washington, 2,354; West Virginia, 2; Wisconsin, 1,772; Wyoming, 7.

Total: 43,434

**John Hagelin (Natural Law)**

Alabama, 495 votes; Alaska, 433; Arizona, 2,267; Arkansas, 764; California, 836; Colorado, 47; Connecticut, 75; Delaware, 6; District of Columbia, 230; Florida, 214; Hawaii, 416; Idaho, 24; Illinois, 2,751; Indiana, 126; Iowa, 3,079; Kansas, 77; Kentucky, 695; Louisiana, 889; Maryland, 191; Massachusetts, 1,812; Michigan, 2,954; Minnesota, 1,406; Mississippi, 1,140; Missouri, 64; Montana, 20; Nebraska, 714; Nevada, 338; New Hampshire, 292; New Jersey, 1,353; New Mexico, 562; New York, 4,420; North Carolina, 41; North Dakota, 240; Ohio, 3,437; Oregon, 91; Rhode Island, 262; South Dakota, 429; Tennessee, 599; Texas, 217; Utah, 1,319; Vermont, 315; Washington, 2,456; West Virginia, 2; Wisconsin, 1,070; Wyoming, 11.

Total: 39,179

**Ron Daniels (Peace and Freedom)**

California, 18,597 votes; District of Columbia, 1,186; Iowa, 212; Louisiana, 1,663; Maryland, 167; Missouri, 12; New Jersey, 1,996; New York, 385; Rhode Island, 1; Tennessee, 511; Utah, 177; Washington, 1,171; Wisconsin, 1,883.

Total: 27,961

**Lyndon H. LaRouche Jr. (Economic Recovery)**

Alabama, 641 votes; Alaska, 469; Arizona, 8; Arkansas, 762; California, 180; Colorado, 20; Connecticut, 4; Delaware, 9; District of Columbia, 260; Idaho, 1; Indiana, 14; Iowa, 238; Louisiana, 1,136; Maryland, 18; Massachusetts, 1,027; Michigan, 14; Minnesota, 622; Missouri, 13; New Jersey, 2,095; New York, 20; North Dakota, 642; Ohio, 2,446; Rhode Island, 494; Tennessee, 460; Texas, 169; Utah, 1,089; Vermont, 57; Virginia, 11,937; Washington, 855; Wisconsin, 633.

Total: 26,333

**James Warren (Socialist Workers)**

Alabama, 831 votes; California, 115; Connecticut, 5; Delaware, 3; District of Columbia, 105; Georgia, 9; Illinois, 1,361; Iowa, 273; Maryland, 25; Minnesota, 990; Missouri, 6; New Jersey, 2,011; New Mexico, 183; New York, 15,472; North Carolina, 12; North Dakota, 193; Ohio, 32; Tennessee, 277; Utah, 200; Vermont, 82; Washington, 515; West Virginia, 6; Wisconsin, 390.

Total: 23,096

**Drew Bradford (Independent)**

New Jersey, 4,749 votes.

**Jack E. Herer (Grassroots)**

Iowa, 669 votes; Minnesota, 2,659; Wisconsin, 547.

Total: 3,875

**J. Quinn Brisben (Socialist)**

District of Columbia, 191 votes; Florida, 16; Idaho, 3; Indiana, 16; Massachusetts, 13; New York, 16; Oregon, 4; Rhode Island, 2; Tennessee, 1,356; Texas, 78; Utah, 151; Wisconsin, 1,211.

Total: 3,057

**Helen Halyard (Workers League)**

Michigan, 1,432 votes; New Jersey, 1,618.

Total: 3,050

**John Yiamouyiannas (Take Back America)**

Arkansas, 554 votes; Iowa, 604; Louisiana, 808; Tennessee, 233.

Total: 2,199

**Delbert L. Ehlers (Independent)**

Iowa, 1,149 votes.

**Earl F. Dodge (Prohibition)**

Arkansas, 472 votes; Colorado, 21; Massachusetts, 2; New Mexico, 120; North Dakota, 3; Tennessee, 343.

Total: 961

**Jim Boren (Apathy)**

Arkansas, 956 votes.

**Eugene A. Hem (Third)**

Wisconsin, 405 votes.

**Isabell Masters (Looking Back)**

Arkansas, 327 votes; California, 12.

Total: 339

**Robert J. Smith (American)**

Utah, 292 votes.

**Gloria LaRiva (Workers World)**

New Mexico, 181 votes.

**Scattered write-ins**

Alabama, 723 votes; Alaska, 365; California, 149; Delaware, 86; District of Columbia, 676; Florida, 8; Georgia, 2; Illinois, 22; Iowa, 741; Kansas, 57; Maine, 91; Maryland, 2; Massachusetts, 1,990; Michigan, 711; Minnesota, 2,499; Missouri, 3; Nevada (None of these candidates), 2,537; New Hampshire, 730; Ohio, 10; Oregon, 2,609; Rhode Island, 106; Tennessee, 161; Texas, 23; Utah, 1; Vermont, 488; Washington, 665; West Virginia, 35; Wisconsin, 961; Wyoming, 127.

Total: 16,578

---

1. *Georgia figures for Webster obtained from Svend Petersen, A Statistical History of the American Presidential Elections, Westport, Conn.: Greenwood Press, 1981, p. 31.*

2. *Troup figures obtained from Petersen, A Statistical History, p. 31.*

3. *Iowa and Mississippi figures from Petersen, A Statistical History, p. 81. Petersen lists these votes, as well as Progressive votes in all other states, for Theodore Roosevelt. In the ICPSR data for 1916, votes are listed for*

*Progressive electors; Roosevelt's name does not appear. Since Roosevelt declined to be a candidate, Congressional Quarterly followed ICPSR in listing these votes as Progressive.*

4. *MacArthur ran under a variety of party designations: Christian Nationalist in Arkansas, New Mexico, Tennessee, North Dakota and Washington; Christian Nationalist—Constitution in California and Texas; Constitution in Colorado; and Christian Nationalist—America First in Missouri.*

# Presidential Primaries

After temporarily losing some popularity in the mid-1980s, presidential primaries stood undisputed a decade later as the favored method of showing voter preferences among candidates for the major party nominations. Both parties held record numbers of primaries in 1992 — 40 Democratic and 39 Republican — and both used primaries to select more than 85 percent of their national convention delegates. The remainder were chosen in statewide party caucuses.

In most cases, the convention delegates were bound to vote for the candidates who received the most votes in their states, thus giving primary voters a direct and important role in the nominating of American presidential candidates. Not since George S. McGovern won the Democratic nomination in 1972 has a candidate obtained a major party nomination without first winning at least a plurality in the party's total primary vote.

Yet, entrenched as they now are in the electoral process, primaries are still relatively recent replacements for the old smoke-filled rooms where party bosses once dictated the choice of presidential nominees.

Presidential primaries originated as an outgrowth of the Progressive movement in the early 20th century. Progressives, populists and reformers in general were fighting state and municipal corruption. They objected to the links between political bosses and big business and advocated returning the government to the people.

Part of this "return to the people" was a turn away from what were looked upon as boss-dominated conventions. It was only a matter of time before the primary idea spread from state and local elections to presidential contests. Because there was no provision for a nationwide primary, state primaries were initiated to choose delegates to the national party conventions (delegate-selection primaries) and to register voters' preferences on their parties' eventual presidential nominees (preference primaries).

Florida enacted the first presidential primary law in 1901. The law gave party officials an option of holding a party primary to choose any party candidate for public office, as well as delegates to the national conventions. However, there was no provision for placing names of presidential candidates on the ballot — either in the form of a preference vote or with information indicating the presidential preference of the candidates for convention delegates.

## Impact of Progressives

Wisconsin's Progressive Republican politician, Gov. Robert M. La Follette, gave a major boost to the presidential primary following the 1904 Republican National Convention. It was at that convention that the credentials of La Follette's Progressive delegation were rejected and a regular Republican delegation from Wisconsin was seated. Angered by what he considered his unfair treatment, La Follette returned to his home state and began pushing for a presidential primary law. The result was the Wisconsin law of 1905 mandating the direct election of national convention delegates. The law, however, did not include a provision for indicating the delegates' presidential preference.

Pennsylvania closely followed Wisconsin (in 1906) with a statute providing that each candidate for delegate to a national convention could have printed beside his name on the official primary ballot the name of the presidential candidate he would support at the convention. However, no member of either party exercised this option in the 1908 primary.

La Follette's sponsorship of the delegate-selection primary helped make the concept a part of the Progressive political program. The growth of the Progressive movement rapidly resulted in the enactment of presidential primary laws in other states.

## Sources

Davis, James W. *Presidential Primaries: Road to the White House.* 1967. Reprint. Westport, Conn.: Greenwood Press, 1980.

Scammon, Richard M. *America Votes 1956-57.* New York: Macmillan, 1958. *America Votes 4.* Pittsburgh: University of Pittsburgh Press, 1962. *America Votes 6, America Votes 8, America Votes 10.* Washington, D.C.: Congressional Quarterly, 1966, 1970, 1973.

Scammon, Richard M. and Alice V. McGillivray. *America Votes* series, vols. 12-20. Washington, D.C.: Congressional Quarterly, 1977, 1981.

# Types of Primaries and Procedures

There are two basic types of presidential primaries. One is the presidential preference primary in which voters vote directly for the person they wish to be nominated for president. The second is the type in which voters elect delegates to the national conventions.

States may use combinations of these methods:

● A state may have a preference vote but choose delegates at party conventions. The preference vote may or may not be binding on the delegates.

● A state may combine the preference and delegate-selection primaries by electing delegates pledged or favorable to a candidate named on the ballot. Under this system, however, state party organizations may run unpledged slates of delegates.

● A state may have an advisory preference vote and a separate delegate-selection vote in which delegates may be listed three ways: pledged to a candidate, favorable to a candidate or unpledged.

● A state may have a mandatory preference vote with a separate delegate-selection vote. In these cases, the delegates are required to reflect the preference primary vote.

For those primaries in which the preference vote is binding upon delegates, state laws may vary as to the number of ballots through which delegates at the convention must remain committed.

Most primary states hold presidential preference votes, in which voters choose among the candidates who have qualified for the ballot in their states. Although preference votes may be binding or non-binding, in most states the vote is binding on the delegates, who are elected in the primary itself or chosen outside of it by a caucus process, by a state committee or by the candidates who have qualified to win delegates.

Delegates may be bound for as short as one ballot or as long as a candidate remains in the race. National Democratic rules in effect in 1980 required delegates to be bound for one ballot unless released by the candidate they were elected to support. The rule was not in effect in subsequent elections.

Until 1980 the Republicans had a rule requiring delegates bound to a specific candidate by state law in primary states to vote for that candidate at the convention regardless of their personal presidential preferences. That rule was repealed at the July 1980 convention.

Delegates from primary states are allocated to candidates in various ways. Most of the methods are based on the preference vote — proportional representation, statewide winner-take-all (in which the candidate winning the most votes statewide wins all the delegates), congressional district and statewide winner-take-all (in which the high vote-getter in a district wins that district's delegates and the high vote-getter statewide wins all the at-large delegates), or some combination of the three. Still another method is the selection of individual delegates in a "loophole," or direct election, primary. Then the preference vote is either non-binding or there is no preference vote at all.

In the proportional representation system, the qualifying threshold for candidates to win delegates can vary. After a decade of intensive debate, Democratic leaders voted to require proportional representation in all primary and caucus states in 1980. This was made optional in 1984 and 1988, with qualifying thresholds of 20 percent and 15 percent, respectively. For 1992 the Democrats again made proportional allocation mandatory, with candidates awarded delegates if they received 15 percent of the vote. Along with winner-take-all systems, the Democrats also banned winner-reward systems that gave extra delegates to primary or caucus victors.

The Republicans allow the primary states to set their own thresholds, which in many states were lower than the Democrats'. In Massachusetts, for example, a GOP candidate in 1992 had to receive only 2.631 percent of the vote to win a delegate.

In nearly half the primary states, major candidates are placed on the ballot by the secretary of state or a special nominating committee. The consent of the candidate is required in only three states — Kentucky, Michigan and North Carolina. Elsewhere, candidates must take the initiative to get on the ballot. The filing requirements range from sending a letter of candidacy to election officials — the case in Puerto Rico — to filing petitions signed by a specified number of registered voters and paying a filing fee — the case in Alabama.

On many primary ballots, voters have the opportunity to mark a line labeled "uncommitted" if they do not prefer any of the candidates.

---

The next step in presidential primaries — the preferential vote for president — took place in Oregon. There, in 1910, Sen. Jonathan Bourne, a Progressive Republican colleague of La Follette (then a senator), sponsored a referendum to establish a presidential preference primary, with delegates legally bound to support the winner of the preference primary.

By 1912, with Oregon in the lead, 12 states had enacted presidential primary laws that provided for either direct election of delegates, a preferential vote, or both. The number had expanded to 26 states by 1916.

## Primaries and Conventions

The first major test of the impact of presidential primary laws — in 1912 — demonstrated that victories in the primaries did not ensure a candidate's nomination. Former president Theodore Roosevelt, campaigning in 12 Republican primaries, won nine of them, including a defeat of incumbent Republican president William Howard Taft in Ohio, Taft's home state. Roosevelt lost to Taft by a narrow margin in Massachusetts and to La Follette in North Dakota and Wisconsin.

Despite this impressive string of primary victories, the convention rejected Roosevelt in favor of Taft. Taft supporters dominated the Republican National Committee, which ran the convention, and the convention's credentials committee, which ruled on contested delegates. Moreover, Taft was backed by many state organizations, especially in the South, where most delegates were chosen by caucuses or conventions dominated by party leaders.

# Votes Cast and Delegates Selected in Presidential Primaries, 1912-92

| | Democratic Party | | | Republican Party | | | Total | |
| --- | --- | --- | --- | --- | --- | --- | --- | --- |
| Year | Number of Primaries | Votes Cast | Delegates Selected Through Primaries (%) | Number of Primaries | Votes Cast | Delegates Selected Through Primaries (%) | Votes Cast | Delegates Selected Through Primaries (%) |
| 1912 | 12 | 974,775 | 32.9 | 13 | 2,261,240 | 41.7 | 3,236,015 | 37.3 |
| 1916 | 20 | 1,187,691 | 53.5 | 20 | 1,923,374 | 58.9 | 3,111,065 | 56.2 |
| 1920 | 16 | 571,671 | 44.6 | 20 | 3,186,248 | 57.8 | 3,757,919 | 51.2 |
| 1924 | 14 | 763,858 | 35.5 | 17 | 3,525,185 | 45.3 | 4,289,043 | 40.4 |
| 1928 | 16 | 1,264,220 | 42.2 | 15 | 4,110,288 | 44.9 | 5,374,508 | 43.5 |
| 1932 | 16 | 2,952,933 | 40.0 | 14 | 2,346,996 | 37.7 | 5,299,929 | 38.8 |
| 1936 | 14 | 5,181,808 | 36.5 | 12 | 3,319,810 | 37.5 | 8,501,618 | 37.0 |
| 1940 | 13 | 4,468,631 | 35.8 | 13 | 3,227,875 | 38.8 | 7,696,506 | 37.3 |
| 1944 | 14 | 1,867,609 | 36.7 | 13 | 2,271,605 | 38.7 | 4,139,214 | 37.7 |
| 1948 | 14 | 2,151,865 | 36.3 | 12 | 2,653,255 | 36.0 | 4,805,120 | 36.1 |
| 1952 | 16 | 4,928,006 | 38.7 | 13 | 7,801,413 | 39.0 | 12,729,419 | 38.8 |
| 1956 | 19 | 5,832,592 | 42.7 | 19 | 5,828,272 | 44.8 | 11,660,864 | 43.7 |
| 1960 | 16 | 5,686,664 | 38.3 | 15 | 5,537,967 | 38.6 | 11,224,631 | 38.5 |
| 1964 | 16 | 6,247,435 | 45.7 | 16 | 5,935,339 | 45.6 | 12,182,774 | 45.6 |
| 1968 | 15 | 7,535,069 | 40.2 | 15 | 4,473,551 | 38.1 | 12,008,620 | 39.1 |
| 1972 | 21 | 15,993,965 | 65.3 | 20 | 6,188,281 | 56.8 | 22,182,246 | 61.0 |
| 1976 | 27 | 16,052,652 | 76.0 | 26 | 10,374,125 | 71.0 | 26,426,777 | 73.5 |
| 1980 | 35 | 18,747,825 | 71.8 | 35 | 12,690,451 | 76.0 | 31,438,276 | 73.7 |
| 1984 | 30 | 18,009,217 | 52.4 | 25 | 6,575,651 | 71.0 | 24,584,868 | 59.6 |
| 1988 | 37 | 22,961,936 | 66.6 | 37 | 12,165,115 | 76.9 | 35,127,051 | 70.2 |
| 1992 | 40 | 20,239,385 | 66.9 | 39 | 12,696,547 | 83.9 | 32,935,932 | 72.7 |

Sources: Percentages of delegates selected are from Michael Nelson, *Congressional Quarterly's Guide to the Presidency,* (Washington, D.C.: Congressional Quarterly Inc., 1989). 1992 figures are from Richard M. Scammon and Alice V. McGillivray, *America Votes* 20 (Washington, D.C.: Congressional Quarterly Inc., 1993) and *Congressional Quarterly Weekly Report.*

On the Democratic side, the convention more closely reflected the results of the primaries. Gov. Woodrow Wilson of New Jersey and Speaker of the House Champ Clark of Missouri were closely matched in total primary votes, with Wilson only 29,632 votes ahead of Clark. Wilson emerged with the nomination after a long struggle with Clark at the convention.

Likewise, in 1916 Democratic primary results foreshadowed the winner of the nomination, although Wilson, who was then the incumbent, had no major opposition for renomination. But once again Republican presidential primaries had little impact upon the nominating process at the convention. The eventual nominee, Supreme Court justice Charles Evans Hughes, had won only two primaries.

In 1920 presidential primaries did not play a major role in determining the winner of either party's nomination. Democrat James M. Cox, the eventual nominee, ran in only one primary, his home state of Ohio. Most of the Democratic primaries featured favorite-son candidates or write-in votes. And at the convention Democrats took 44 ballots to make their choice.

Similarly, the main entrants in the Republican presidential primaries that year failed to capture their party's nomination. Sen. Warren G. Harding of Ohio, the compromise choice, won the primary in his home state but lost badly in Indiana and garnered only a handful of votes elsewhere. The three primary leaders — Sen. Hiram Johnson of California, Gen. Leonard Wood of New Hampshire and Gov. Frank O. Lowden of Illinois — lost out in the end.

After the first wave of enthusiasm for presidential primaries in the early years of the century, interest in them waned. By 1935, eight states had repealed their presidential primary laws. The diminution of reform zeal during the 1920s and the preoccupation of the country with the Great Depression in the 1930s and war in the 1940s appeared to have been leading factors in this decline. Also, party leaders were not enthusiastic about primaries; the cost of conducting them was relatively high, both for the candidates and the states. Many presidential candidates ignored the primaries, and voter participation often was low.

But after World War II interest picked up again. Some politicians with presidential ambitions, knowing the party leadership was not enthusiastic about their candidacies, entered the primaries to try to generate a bandwagon effect. In 1948 Harold Stassen, Republican governor of Minnesota from 1939 to 1943, entered presidential primaries in opposition to the Republican organization and made some headway before losing in Oregon to Gov. Thomas E. Dewey of New York. And in 1952 senator Estes Kefauver, D-Tenn., riding a wave of public recognition as head of the Senate Organized Crime Investigating Committee, challenged Democratic Party leaders by winning several primaries, including an upset of President Harry S. Truman in New Hampshire. The Eisenhower-Taft struggle for the Republican Party nomination that year also stimulated interest in the primaries.

With the growing demand for political reform in the 1960s and early 1970s, the presidential primaries became more attractive as a path to the nomination. John F. Kennedy, then a relatively obscure U.S. senator from Massachusetts, helped to popularize that route with his successful uphill fight for the Democratic nomination in 1960. An unbroken string of Kennedy victories persuaded his chief rival in the primaries, Sen. Hubert H. Humphrey of Minnesota, to withdraw.

Similarly, Sen. Barry M. Goldwater, R-Ariz., in 1964, former vice president Richard Nixon, R-Calif., in 1968 and Sen. George S. McGovern, D-S.D., in 1972 — all party presidential nominees — were able to use the primaries to show their vote-getting and organizational abilities.

### The Democrats Begin to Tinker

Despite the Progressive reforms, party leaders until 1968 remained in firm control of the nominating process. With only a handful of the 15 to 20 primaries regularly contested, candidates could count on a short primary season. They began in New Hampshire in March, then tested their appeal during the spring in Wisconsin, Nebraska, Oregon and California before resuming their courtship of party leaders.

But in 1968 the Democrats began tinkering with the nominating rules, resulting in presidential nominating campaigns that were predictable only in their unpredictability. The reforms were launched in an effort to reduce the alienation of liberals and minorities from the Democratic nominating system and to allow the people to choose their own leaders. The Republicans seldom made any changes in their rules. *(GOP rules, box, p. 22; Democratic rules, box, p. 23)*

This era of grass-roots control produced for the Democrats presidential candidates such as McGovern, a liberal from South Dakota who lost in a landslide to Nixon in 1972, and Jimmy Carter, who beat incumbent president Gerald R. Ford in 1976 but lost to Ronald Reagan in 1980.

With a then-record high of 37 primaries held in 1980, the opportunity for mass participation in the nominating process was greater than ever before. President Carter and Republican nominee Reagan were the clear winners of the long 1980 primary season. Although Carter received a bare majority of the cumulative Democratic primary vote, he amassed a plurality of nearly 2.7 million votes over his major rival, Sen. Edward M. Kennedy of Massachusetts. With no opposition in the late primary contests, Reagan emerged as a more one-sided choice of GOP primary voters. He finished nearly 4.8 million votes ahead of George Bush, who eventually withdrew from the race.

Disheartened by their nominee's massive defeat in 1980, the Democrats revised their nominating rules for the 1984 election. The party created the so-called superdelegates; that is, delegate seats were reserved for party leaders who were not formally committed to any presidential candidate. This reform had two main goals. First, Democratic leaders wanted to ensure that the party's elected and appointed officials would participate at the convention. Second, they wanted to ensure that these uncommitted party leaders could play a major role in selecting the presidential nominee if no candidate was a clear front-runner.

While the reforms of the 1970s were designed to give more influence to grass-roots activists and less to party regulars, these revisions were intended to bring about a deliberative process in which experienced party leaders could help select a consensus Democratic nominee with a strong chance to win the presidency.

The Democrats' new rules had some expected, as well as unexpected, results. For the first time since 1968, the number of primaries declined and the number of caucuses increased. The Democrats held only 30 primaries in 1984. Yet, like McGovern in 1972 and Carter in 1976, Colorado senator Gary Hart used the primaries to pull ahead (temporarily) of former vice president Walter F. Mondale, an early front-runner whose strongest ties were to the party leadership and its traditional core elements. In 1984 the presence of superdelegates was important because about four out of five backed Mondale.

Some critics regarded the seating of superdelegates as undemocratic, and there were calls for reducing their numbers. Instead, by adding 75 superdelegate seats, the Democratic National Committee (DNC) increased their numbers from 14 percent of the delegates in 1984 to 15 percent for 1988. Moreover, another 150 new delegate seats were set aside for party leaders. All members of the DNC are guaranteed seats, as are all Democratic governors. About 80 percent of the Democrats in Congress also are guaranteed seats.

Still more superdelegate seats were added in 1992, bringing the total to 772 or 18 percent of the 4,288 delegates to the Democratic convention in New York City.

Having won 51.8 percent of the Democratic primary vote, Arkansas governor Bill Clinton went to the convention with the nomination virtually ensured. He was nominated by acclamation after receiving 3,372 votes on the first ballot.

The Republican Party does not guarantee delegate seats to its leaders, nor has the party created superdelegates. However, its rules permit less rigid pledging of delegates and generally have led to substantial participation by Republican leaders, despite the absence of such guarantees.

## Regional Primaries and Super Tuesday

In addition to the Democrats' internal party concerns with the nominating process, other critics often cited the length of the primary season (nearly twice as long as the general election campaign), the expense, the physical strain on the candidates and the variations and complexities of state laws as problems of presidential primaries.

To deal with these problems, several states in 1974 and 1975 discussed the feasibility of creating regional primaries, in which individual states within a geographical region would hold their primaries on the same day. Supporters of the concept believed it would reduce candidate expenses and strain and would permit concentration on regional issues.

The idea achieved some limited success in 1976 when two groups of states — one in the West and the other in the South — decided to organize regional primaries in each of their areas. However, the two groups both chose May 25 to hold their primaries, thus defeating one of the main purposes of the plan by forcing candidates to shuttle across the country to cover both areas. The Western states participating in the grouping were Idaho, Nevada and Oregon; the Southern states were Arkansas, Kentucky and Tennessee.

Attempts also were made in New England to construct a regional primary. But New Hampshire could not participate because its law requires the state to hold its primary at

# Selection by Caucus Method

In the current primary-dominated era of presidential politics, which began two decades ago, caucuses have survived in the quiet backwater of the Democratic nominating process.

The impact of caucuses decreased in the 1970s as the number of primaries grew dramatically. During the 1960s a candidate sought to run well in primary states mainly to have a bargaining chip with which to deal with powerful leaders in the caucus states. Republicans Barry M. Goldwater in 1964 and Richard Nixon in 1968 and Democrat Hubert H. Humphrey in 1968 all built up solid majorities among caucus state delegates that carried them to their parties' nominations. Humphrey did not even enter a primary in 1968.

After 1968 candidates placed their principal emphasis on primaries. First George McGovern in 1972 — and then incumbent Republican president Gerald R. Ford and Democratic challenger Jimmy Carter in 1976 — won nomination by securing large majorities of the primary state delegates. Neither McGovern nor Ford won a majority of the caucus state delegates. Carter was able to win a majority only after his opponents' campaigns collapsed.

## Complex Method

Compared with a primary, the caucus system is complicated. Instead of focusing on a single primary election ballot, the caucus presents a multi-tiered system that involves meetings scheduled over several weeks, sometimes even months. There is mass participation at the first level only, with meetings often lasting several hours and attracting only the most enthusiastic and dedicated party members.

The operation of the caucus varies from state to state, and each party has its own set of rules. Most begin with precinct caucuses or some other type of local mass meeting open to all party voters. Participants, often publicly declaring their votes, elect delegates to the next stage in the process.

In smaller states such as Delaware and Hawaii, delegates are elected directly to a state convention, where the national convention delegates are chosen. In larger states such as Iowa, there is at least one more step. Most frequently, delegates are elected at the precinct caucuses to county conventions, where the national convention delegates are chosen.

Participation, even at the first level of the caucus process, is much lower than in primaries. Caucus participants usually are local party leaders and activists. Many rank-and-file voters find a caucus complex, confusing, or intimidating.

In a caucus state the focus is on one-on-one campaigning. Time, not money, is the most valuable resource. Because organization and personal campaigning are so important, an early start is far more crucial in a caucus state than in a primary. And because only a small segment of the electorate is targeted in most caucus states, candidates usually use media advertising sparingly.

Although the basic steps in the caucus process are the same for both parties, the rules that govern them are vastly different. Democratic rules have been revamped substantially since 1968, establishing national standards for grass-roots participation. Republican rules have remained largely unchanged, with the states given wide latitude in drawing up their delegate-selection plans.

## Caucuses

For both the Republican and Democratic parties, the percentage of delegates elected from caucus states was on a sharp decline throughout the 1970s. But the Democrats broke the downward trend and elected more delegates by the caucus process in 1980 than in 1976.

Between 1980 and 1984 six states switched from a primary to a caucus system; none the other way. Since 1984 the trend has turned back toward primaries. In 1992 primaries were held in 38 states, the District of Columbia and Puerto Rico. The Democrats elected 66.9 percent of their national convention delegates in primaries, against only 15.1 percent in caucuses. (The remaining 18.0 percent were "superdelegate" party and elected officials.) The Republicans in 1992 chose 83.9 percent of delegates in primaries and the rest in caucuses, with no superdelegates.

A strong showing in the caucuses by Walter F. Mondale in 1984 led many Democrats — and not only supporters of his chief rivals — to conclude that caucuses are inherently unfair. The mainstream Democratic coalition of party activists, labor union members and teachers dominated the caucuses in Mondale's behalf.

The caucus also came in for criticism in 1988. The Iowa Democratic caucuses were seen as an unrepresentative test dominated by liberal interest groups. And the credibility of the caucuses was shaken by the withdrawal from the race of the two winners — Democrat Richard A. Gephardt and Republican Robert Dole — within a month after the caucuses were held. Furthermore, several other state caucuses featured vicious infighting between supporters of various candidates.

In 1992 the presence of a favorite son, Sen. Tom Harkin, among the leading Democratic candidates for president further diminished the Iowa caucus' significance as a rival to the New Hampshire primary as an early indicator of the candidate to beat for the nomination. Harkin easily won his state's party caucus, but he soon dropped out after fading in the primaries elsewhere. By contrast, 20 years earlier, a surprise win in Iowa helped to propel Sen. George McGovern of South Dakota toward the Democratic nomination.

The major complaint about the caucus process is that it does not involve enough voters, and that the low turnouts are not so representative of voter sentiment as a higher-turnout primary.

Staunch defenders, however, believe a caucus has party-building attributes a primary cannot match. They note that several hours at a caucus can involve voters in a way that quickly casting a primary ballot does not. Following caucus meetings, the state party comes away with lists of thousands of voters who can be tapped to volunteer time or money, or even to run for local office. And, while the multi-tiered caucus process is often a chore for the state party to organize, a primary is substantially more expensive.

# Choosing a Running Mate: The Balancing Act

In modern times veteran political convention-watchers have come to look forward to the almost-traditional night of uncertainty as the new presidential nominee tries to come up with a running mate. But this hectic process is a recent one. During the country's first years, the runner-up for the presidency automatically took the second slot.

That system did not last long. In 1800 Thomas Jefferson and Aaron Burr found themselves in a tie for electoral votes. Neither man's supporters were willing to settle for the lesser office. The deadlock went to the House of Representatives, where Jefferson needed 36 ballots to clinch the presidency. It also led to the 12th Amendment to the U.S. Constitution, ratified in 1804, providing for separate Electoral College balloting for president and vice president. With the emergence of political parties after 1800, candidates ran as teams. Once party conventions began in 1831, delegates, with the guidance of party bosses, began to do the choosing.

In fact, it was only in 1940 that presidential nominees began regularly hand-picking their running mates. That year, after failing to persuade Secretary of State Cordell Hull to accept the vice presidency, Franklin D. Roosevelt forced Henry A. Wallace on a reluctant Democratic convention by threatening to refuse his own nomination if Wallace was rejected. The only exception to the practice Roosevelt established came in 1956, when Democrat Adlai E. Stevenson left the choice up to the convention.

If the selection of a running mate often has seemed like something of an afterthought, it could be because the position itself is not especially coveted. John Adams, the first man to hold the job, once complained, "My country has in its wisdom contrived for me the most insignificant office that ever the intention of man contrived or his imagination conceived." More than a century later Thomas R. Marshall, Woodrow Wilson's vice president, expressed a similarly dismal view: "Once there were two brothers. One ran away to sea; the other was elected Vice President. And nothing was ever heard of either of them again."

Writing in *Atlantic* in 1974, historian Arthur Schlesinger Jr. suggested the office be done away with. "It is a doomed office," he commented. "The Vice President has only one serious thing to do: that is, to wait around for the President to die." But there is a reasonable chance that whoever fills the position will get a chance to move up, either by succession or election. As of 1994, 14 presidents had held the second-ranking post, seven in the 20th century.

Also, since the 1970s the vice presidency has evolved from the somnolent office it once was; during this period four vice presidents enjoyed responsibility their predecessors did not. Nelson A. Rockefeller, who served under Gerald R. Ford, was given considerable authority in domestic policy coordination. Walter F. Mondale and George Bush helped to set policy for their respective presidents. And Bill Clinton placed Al Gore in charge of a "reinventing government" task force.

Yet whoever is selected is scrutinized not so much as a policy maker, but for how well the choice balances (or unbalances) the ticket. One important factor is geography, which Clinton of Arkansas used unconventionally in choosing Gore of Tennessee to form the first successful all-Southern ticket in 164 years. Other traditional factors weighed by nominees are religion and ethnicity. In modern national politics, however, those considerations seemed to be losing their place to race, gender and age. In 1984, for example, the Democrats chose Rep. Geraldine A. Ferraro of New York to be their vice presidential candidate, the first woman to receive a major party nomination.

Although no black has so far been selected by either party, many Democrats thought that Jesse L. Jackson deserved second place on the ticket in 1988. Jackson had received 29 percent of the primary vote to 43 percent for Michael Dukakis. Instead, the 54-year-old Dukakis chose Sen. Lloyd Bentsen of Texas, then 67, balancing the Democratic ticket by age as well as geographically and philosophically.

George Bush selected Sen. Dan Quayle of Indiana, a choice that proved extremely controversial, even among Republicans. Quayle, born in 1947, had served two terms in the House of Representatives before his election to the Senate in 1980. His brief career in politics, as well as some disturbing revelations about his education and service in the Indiana National Guard, fostered doubts that he was qualified to serve as president, should that become necessary.

Because of Quayle's youth and good looks, it was even suggested by some critics that Bush had selected him to appeal to young voters and women. Moreover, Quayle seemed ill at ease before the television camera and often misspoke when giving a speech or answering questions. But Bush vigorously defended his choice of running mate, and the two swept to victory in November.

For his running mate, the 46-year-old Clinton, in another unbalancing act, selected someone in his own age group (Gore, 44) rather than an elder statesman like Bentsen, who became secretary of the Treasury in the Clinton administration.

least one week before any other state. Hesitancy by the other New England state legislatures defeated the idea. Only Vermont joined Massachusetts, on March 2, in holding a simultaneous presidential primary, although New Hampshire voted only one week earlier.

In 1980 limited regional primaries were held again in several areas of the country — on March 4 in New England (Massachusetts and Vermont), on March 11 in the Southeast (Alabama, Florida and Georgia) and on May 27 in the South (Arkansas and Kentucky) and the West (Idaho and Nevada). In 1984 the so-called Super Tuesday, March 13, produced small regional primaries in New England (Massachusetts and Rhode Island) and in the South (Alabama, Florida and Georgia).

In 1988, 36 states and the District of Columbia held presidential primaries. More and more states, hoping to increase their impact on the presidential campaign, decided to hold their primaries early. When South Dakota announced its Feb. 23 primary date, New Hampshire moved its date to Feb. 16.

Sixteen states — Alabama, Arkansas, Florida, Georgia, Kentucky, Louisiana, Maryland, Massachusetts, Mississippi, Missouri, North Carolina, Oklahoma, Rhode Island, Tennessee, Texas and Virginia — held primaries on Super Tuesday, March 8. The parties' long-held goal of a regional Southern primary was finally realized. (South Carolina held its Republican primary a few days earlier on Saturday, March 5.) In New England, only two states, Massachusetts and Rhode Island, held their primaries on Super Tuesday. Vermont, which in 1976 and 1980 had joined with Massachusetts, this time held its primary a week before, on March 1.

The Democrats selected nearly 67 percent of their convention delegates through primaries in 1988. That figure was up from 52 percent in 1984, but nine percentage points less than the 76 percent set in 1976, the record to that time. The Republicans chose 77 percent of their delegates via primaries, up six points from 1984.

George Bush's win in New Hampshire proved to be the turning point in his campaign, and because most Republican primaries were the winner-take-all kind, Bush had the Republican nomination all but locked up by Super Tuesday. He went over the top with the Pennsylvania primary, April 26. In contrast, the Democratic candidates were awarded delegates based on the proportion of votes cast for them in each primary. Democrat Michael S. Dukakis won enough delegates to become his party's nominee June 7.

## 'March Madness'

By 1992 Super Tuesday had become part of a general rush among states to hold their primaries as early as possible and thus help to determine the ultimate nominees. Dubbed "March Madness," the early clustering of primaries was viewed with dismay by some political analysts. They said it could lead to nominees being locked in before most voters knew what was happening, resulting in less informed and deliberative voting in the general election.

As winners in the eight Super Tuesday primaries March 10, President Bush and Bill Clinton were already well on their way to nomination. Bush had half the delegates he needed for renomination, and Clinton with 707 delegates held a commanding lead over his nearest rival, former senator Paul Tsongas of Massachusetts.

In all, roughly half the states held their primaries before the end of March 1992. With California and Ohio moving their primaries from June, and other states also considering March dates, 1996 was shaping up as even more heavily weighted toward early primaries. It was likely that both parties' nominations would be wrapped up within a few weeks of the February start in New Hampshire and Iowa.

While it was too late to do anything about 1996, some observers were pushing reforms to spread out the primary schedule in 2000 and future presidential election years.

## Ballot Access

The two major political parties have a virtual lock on the presidential nomination system and other aspects of the U.S. electoral system. Since the advent of the so-called Australian ballot in the late 1800s, states — not parties — have compiled the official election ballots. Democratic and

### Fourteen VPs Became President

Fourteen men who served as vice president have become president: John Adams, Thomas Jefferson, Martin Van Buren, John Tyler, Millard Fillmore, Andrew Johnson, Chester A. Arthur, Theodore Roosevelt, Calvin Coolidge, Harry S. Truman, Richard Nixon, Lyndon B. Johnson, Gerald R. Ford and George Bush.

Of those, all but Adams, Jefferson, Van Buren, Nixon and Bush first became president on the death or resignation of their predecessor. Eight vice presidents since 1900 have run unsuccessfully for president:

● Thomas R. Marshall, Democratic vice president under Woodrow Wilson from 1913 to 1921, failed to win the nomination in 1920.

● Charles G. Dawes, Republican vice president under Coolidge from 1925 to 1929, unsuccessfully sought the nomination in 1928 and 1932.

● John Nance Garner, Democratic vice president under Franklin D. Roosevelt from 1933 to 1941, ran unsuccessfully for the nomination in 1940.

● Henry A. Wallace, Democratic vice president under Roosevelt from 1941 to 1945, was Progressive Party nominee in 1948.

● Alben W. Barkley, Democratic vice president under Truman from 1949 to 1953, failed to win the 1952 nomination.

● Nixon, Republican vice president under Dwight D. Eisenhower from 1953 to 1961, was the GOP nominee in 1960. (He won in 1968 and 1972.)

● Hubert H. Humphrey, Democratic vice president under Lyndon Johnson from 1965 to 1969, was the Democratic nominee in 1968.

● Walter F. Mondale, Democratic vice president under Jimmy Carter from 1977 to 1981, was the Democratic nominee in 1984.

Republican candidates are automatically listed, but for third party or independent candidates, getting on the ballot is an arduous and costly process.

The restrictions vary from state to state, but all states have requirements to keep the ballot from becoming unwieldy and to discourage frivolous or non-serious candidates. Usually the third party or independent must submit petitions with valid voters' signatures, which can vary from as few as 25 in Tennessee to 3 to 5 percent of the state's registered voters, which can run into several hundred thousand.

In Florida, for example, a third party or independent candidate for governor or U.S. Senate needs petitions from 3 percent of the voters registered in the previous election, which for 1992 meant at least 196,000. And since many signatures are likely to be invalid, the candidate must round up several thousand more than the minimum to ensure placement on the ballot.

No independent candidate has ever achieved the 196,000 signatures, according to Ronald Cole, chairman of the Fair Ballot Access Committee in Florida. The committee is fighting what it calls "Florida's unfair and restrictive election laws" and is gathering petitions to have an amendment to the state constitution placed on the ballot.

Third parties also complain that in many states they are forced to file too early, weeks or months before they know who their candidates will be.

# Approaches to Reform

In the past, various approaches to changing the primary system have been attempted at the national level. One suggested change was to establish a direct national primary. But a Democratic study commission as well as several academic groups that examined the idea rejected it. The consensus was that such a process would strip the party leadership of any role in the nominating process, enable presidential candidates to run factional or regional campaigns and increase the primacy of media "image" over serious discussion of the issues. "If you go to a national primary," said Ann Lewis, who served as the political director of the Democratic National Committee, "you don't have a political process anymore, you have the 'Battle of the Network Stars.'"

Some political scientists longed for the days when the nominees were chosen in large measure by the party leaders. In 1980 Jeane J. Kirkpatrick, then a Georgetown University professor and later the U.S. representative to the United Nations in the Reagan administration, called for the abolition of primaries and creation of a decision-making process restricted to party and elected leaders.

Political scientist Austin Ranney also felt that the power of the party leaders should be restored: "In the old smoke-filled-room days, the people who really chose the presidential nominee were people who knew [the candidates] and saw them in action and had some idea of what they were like."

Ranney did not go so far as Kirkpatrick. Instead, he advocated a process in which the consensus of political leaders would be the deciding influence in national conventions. Ranney, however, thought it unlikely that either party would return to the smoke-filled rooms. "I think it's against the whole ethos of our times," he said.

Since 1911 hundreds of bills have been introduced in Congress to reform the presidential primary system. Most of them appeared during sessions after the 1912, 1952 and 1968 nominating campaigns. These three campaigns produced the feeling among many voters that the will of the electorate, as expressed in the primaries, had been thwarted by national conventions. But since 1911 the only legislation enacted by Congress concerned the presidential primary in the District of Columbia.

# Presidential Primary Returns
# 1912-92

# Sources: Presidential Primary Returns

The main source for the primary returns from 1912 through 1952 was James W. Davis, *Presidential Primaries: Road to the White House,* Westport, Conn.: Greenwood Press, 1980.

Congressional Quarterly has supplemented Davis' material with the following sources: Louise Overacker, *The Presidential Primary,* the source used by Davis for the 1912-24 returns; Walter Kravitz, "Presidential Preference Primaries, 1928-56," a 1960 Library of Congress study; Paul Davis, Malcolm Moos and Ralph Goldman, *Presidential Nominating Politics in 1952,* Johns Hopkins Press, 1954; the offices of the secretaries of state; and state handbooks and newspapers. All statistics and footnotes are from Davis, unless otherwise indicated.

The basic source for the primary returns from 1956-92 was the *America Votes* series compiled by Richard M. Scammon and Alice V. McGillivray. All statistics and footnotes are from Scammon-McGillivray, unless otherwise indicated.

Figures in the following charts represent one of three types of votes:

- Votes cast directly for a presidential candidate.
- Votes cast for delegates whose candidate preference was indicated on the ballot.
- Votes cast for unpledged delegates. (Included in the "unpledged" category were delegates designated on the ballot as "uninstructed" and "no preference.")

For the delegate-at-large vote in 1912-24 primaries, Overacker listed the average vote for delegates at large. For the 1928-52 delegate-at-large vote, Davis listed the highest vote received by any one delegate at large. Congressional Quarterly followed Davis' style for subsequent years.

Percentages in the following tables have been calculated to two decimal points and then rounded; 0.05 percent appears as 0.1 percent. Therefore, columns of percentages do not always total 100 percent. Presidential candidates, primary winners, favorite sons, members of Congress and prominent national and state political figures are included in the state-by-state primary results; others receiving votes are listed in the footnotes.

# 1912 Primaries

| Republican | | | Democratic | | |
|---|---|---|---|---|---|
| | | | | Votes | % |

**March 19   North Dakota**

| | | | | | |
|---|---|---|---|---|---|
| Robert M. LaFollette (Wis.) | 34,123 | *57.2* | John Burke (N.D.)[1] | 9,357 | *100.0* |
| Theodore Roosevelt (N.Y.) | 23,669 | *39.7* | | | |
| William H. Taft (Ohio) | 1,876 | *3.1* | | | |

**March 26   New York** [2]

**April 2   Wisconsin**

| | | | | | |
|---|---|---|---|---|---|
| LaFollette | 133,354 | *73.2* | Woodrow Wilson (N.J.) | 45,945 | *55.7* |
| Taft | 47,514 | *26.1* | Champ Clark (Mo.) | 36,464 | *44.2* |
| Roosevelt | 628 | *.3* | Others | 148 | *.2* |
| Others | 643 | *.4* | | | |

**April 9   Illinois**

| | | | | | |
|---|---|---|---|---|---|
| Roosevelt | 266,917 | *61.1* | Clark | 218,483 | *74.3* |
| Taft | 127,481 | *29.2* | Wilson | 75,527 | *25.7* |
| LaFollette | 42,692 | *9.8* | | | |

**April 13   Pennsylvania**

| | | | | | |
|---|---|---|---|---|---|
| Roosevelt | 282,853[3] | *59.7* | Wilson | 98,000[3] | *100.0* |
| Taft | 191,179[3] | *40.3* | | | |

**April 19   Nebraska**

| | | | | | |
|---|---|---|---|---|---|
| Roosevelt | 45,795 | *58.7* | Clark | 21,027 | *41.0* |
| LaFollette | 16,785 | *21.5* | Wilson | 14,289 | *27.9* |
| Taft | 13,341 | *17.1* | Judson Harmon (Ohio) | 12,454 | *24.3* |
| Others | 2,036 | *2.6* | Others | 3,499 | *6.8* |

**April 19   Oregon**

| | | | | | |
|---|---|---|---|---|---|
| Roosevelt | 28,905 | *40.2* | Wilson | 9,588 | *53.0* |
| LaFollette | 22,491 | *31.3* | Clark | 7,857 | *43.4* |
| Taft | 20,517 | *28.5* | Harmon | 606 | *3.3* |
| Others | 14 | — | Others | 49 | *.3* |

**April 30   Massachusetts**

| | | | | | |
|---|---|---|---|---|---|
| Taft | 86,722 | *50.4* | Clark | 34,575 | *68.9* |
| Roosevelt | 83,099 | *48.3* | Wilson | 15,002 | *29.9* |
| LaFollette | 2,058 | *1.2* | Others | 627 | *1.2* |
| Others | 99 | *.1* | | | |

**May 6   Maryland**

| | | | | | |
|---|---|---|---|---|---|
| Roosevelt | 29,124 | *52.8* | Clark | 34,021 | *54.4* |
| Taft | 25,995 | *47.2* | Wilson | 21,490 | *34.3* |
| | | | Harmon | 7,070 | *11.3* |

**May 14   California**

| | | | | | |
|---|---|---|---|---|---|
| Roosevelt | 138,563 | *54.6* | Clark | 43,163 | *71.5* |
| Taft | 69,345 | *27.3* | Wilson | 17,214 | *28.5* |
| LaFollette | 45,876 | *18.1* | | | |

**May 21   Ohio**

| | | | | | |
|---|---|---|---|---|---|
| Roosevelt | 165,809 | *55.3* | Harmon | 96,164 | *51.7* |
| Taft | 118,362 | *39.5* | Wilson | 85,084 | *45.7* |
| LaFollette | 15,570 | *5.2* | Clark | 2,428 | *1.3* |
| | | | Others | 2,440 | *1.3* |

# Republican                                                                          # Democratic

|  | Votes | % |  | Votes | % |
|---|---|---|---|---|---|

### May 28   **New Jersey**

| Roosevelt | 61,297 | 56.3 | Wilson | 48,336 | 98.9 |
| Taft | 44,034 | 40.5 | Clark[4] | 522 | 1.1 |
| LaFollette | 3,464 | 3.2 |  |  |  |

### June 4   **South Dakota**

| Roosevelt | 38,106 | 55.2 | Wilson[5] | 4,694 | 35.2 |
| Taft | 19,960 | 28.9 | Clark[5] | 4,275 | 32.0 |
| LaFollette | 10,944 | 15.9 | Clark[5] | 2,722 | 20.4 |
|  |  |  | Others | 1,655 | 12.4 |

| **TOTALS** |  |  |  |  |  |
| Roosevelt | 1,164,765 | 51.5 | Wilson | 435,169 | 44.6 |
| Taft | 766,326 | 33.9 | Clark | 405,537 | 41.6 |
| LaFollette | 327,357 | 14.5 | Harmon | 116,294 | 11.9 |
| Others | 2,792 | .1 | Burke | 9,357 | 1.0 |
|  |  |  | Others | 8,418 | .9 |
|  | 2,261,240 |  |  |  |  |
|  |  |  |  | 974,775 |  |

1. Burke was the "favorite son" candidate, according to the North Dakota secretary of state.
2. Primary law optional in 1912. Republicans elected pledged delegates but figures not available.
3. Unofficial figures.
4. Write-in.

5. No presidential preference. Three sets of delegates ran: one labelled "Wilson-Bryan" which came out openly for Wilson; one "Wilson-Clark-Bryan" which became identified with Clark; one Champ Clark which was accused by the Clark people of being a scheme to split the Clark vote. The "Wilson-Clark-Bryan" list polled 4,275 and the Champ Clark list 2,722. The delegates were given to Wilson by the convention.

# 1916 Primaries

| Republican | | | Democratic | | |
|---|---|---|---|---|---|
| | Votes | % | | Votes | % |

**March 7   Indiana**

| | | | | | |
|---|---|---|---|---|---|
| Charles W. Fairbanks (Ind.)[1] | 176,078 | 100.0 | Woodrow Wilson (N.J.) | 160,423 | 100.0 |

**March 14   Minnesota**

| | | | | | |
|---|---|---|---|---|---|
| Albert B. Cummins (Iowa) | 54,214 | 76.8 | Wilson | 45,136 | 100.0 |
| Others | 16,403 | 23.2 | | | |

**March 14   New Hampshire**

| | | | | | |
|---|---|---|---|---|---|
| Unpledged delegates | 9,687 | 100.0 | Wilson | 5,684 | 100.0 |

**March 21   North Dakota**

| | | | | | |
|---|---|---|---|---|---|
| Robert M. LaFollette (Wis.) | 23,374[2] | 70.4 | Wilson | 12,341 | 100.0 |
| Others | 9,851[2] | 29.6 | | | |

**April 3   Michigan**

| | | | | | |
|---|---|---|---|---|---|
| Henry Ford (Mich.) | 83,057 | 47.4 | Wilson | 84,972 | 100.0 |
| William A. Smith (Mich.) | 77,872 | 44.4 | | | |
| William O. Simpson (Mich.) | 14,365 | 8.2 | | | |

**April 4   New York**

| | | | | | |
|---|---|---|---|---|---|
| Unpledged delegates | 147,038 | 100.0 | Wilson | 112,538 | 100.0 |

**April 4   Wisconsin**

| | | | | | |
|---|---|---|---|---|---|
| LaFollette[1] | 110,052 | 98.8 | Wilson | 109,462 | 99.8 |
| Others | 1,347 | 1.2 | Others | 231 | .2 |

**April 11   Illinois**

| | | | | | |
|---|---|---|---|---|---|
| Lawrence Y. Sherman (Ill.)[1] | 155,945 | 90.2 | Wilson | 136,839 | 99.8 |
| Theodore Roosevelt (N.Y.)[3] | 15,348 | 8.9 | Others | 219 | .2 |
| Others | 1,689 | 1.0 | | | |

**April 18   Nebraska**

| | | | | | |
|---|---|---|---|---|---|
| Cummins | 29,850 | 33.7 | Wilson | 69,506 | 87.7 |
| Ford | 26,884 | 30.3 | Others | 9,744 | 12.3 |
| Charles E. Hughes (N.Y.)[3] | 15,837 | 17.9 | | | |
| Roosevelt[3] | 2,256 | 2.5 | | | |
| Others | 13,780 | 15.6 | | | |

**April 21   Montana**

| | | | | | |
|---|---|---|---|---|---|
| Cummins | 10,415 | 89.9 | Wilson | 17,960 | 100.0 |
| Others | 1,173 | 10.1 | | | |

**April 25   Iowa**

| | | | | | |
|---|---|---|---|---|---|
| Cummins | 40,257 | 100.0 | Wilson | 31,447 | 100.0 |

**April 25   Massachusetts**

| | | | | | |
|---|---|---|---|---|---|
| Unpledged delegates at large[4] | 60,462 | 57.3 | Wilson | 19,580 | 100.0 |
| Roosevelt[4] | 45,117 | 42.7 | | | |

**April 25   New Jersey**

| | | | | | |
|---|---|---|---|---|---|
| Roosevelt[3] | 1,076 | 73.7 | Wilson | 25,407 | 100.0 |
| Hughes[3] | 383 | 26.3 | | | |

# Republican

# Democratic

| | Votes | % | | Votes | % |
|---|---|---|---|---|---|

**April 25  Ohio**

| | Votes | % | | Votes | % |
|---|---|---|---|---|---|
| Theodore E. Burton (Ohio)[1] | 122,165 | 86.8 | Wilson | 82,688 | 97.2 |
| Roosevelt[3] | 1,932 | 1.4 | Others | 2,415 | 2.8 |
| Ford[3] | 1,683 | 1.2 | | | |
| Hughes[3] | 469 | .3 | | | |
| Others | 14,428 | 10.3 | | | |

**May 2  California**

| | Votes | % | | Votes | % |
|---|---|---|---|---|---|
| Unpledged delegates | 236,277 | 100.0 | Wilson | 75,085 | 100.0 |

**May 16  Pennsylvania**

| | Votes | % | | Votes | % |
|---|---|---|---|---|---|
| Martin G. Brumbaugh (Pa.)[1] | 233,095 | 86.3 | Wilson | 142,202 | 98.7 |
| Ford[3] | 20,265 | 7.5 | Others | 1,839 | 1.3 |
| Roosevelt[3] | 12,359 | 4.6 | | | |
| Hughes[3] | 1,804 | .7 | | | |
| Others | 2,682 | 1.0 | | | |

**May 16  Vermont**

| | Votes | % | | Votes | % |
|---|---|---|---|---|---|
| Hughes[3] | 5,480 | 70.0 | Wilson | 3,711 | 99.4 |
| Roosevelt[3] | 1,931 | 24.6 | Others | 23 | .6 |
| Others | 423 | 5.4 | | | |

**May 19  Oregon**

| | Votes | % | | Votes | % |
|---|---|---|---|---|---|
| Hughes | 56,764 | 59.8 | Wilson | 27,898 | 100.0 |
| Cummins | 27,558 | 29.0 | | | |
| Others | 10,593 | 11.2 | | | |

**May 23  South Dakota**

| | Votes | % | | Votes | % |
|---|---|---|---|---|---|
| Cummins | 29,656 | 100.0 | Wilson | 10,341 | 100.0 |

**June 6  West Virginia**

| | | | | |
|---|---|---|---|---|
| 5 | | | 5 | |

**TOTALS**

| | Votes | % | | Votes | % |
|---|---|---|---|---|---|
| Unpledged delegates | 453,464 | 23.6 | Wilson | 1,173,220 | 98.8 |
| Brumbaugh | 233,095 | 12.1 | Others | 14,471 | 1.2 |
| Cummins | 191,950 | 10.0 | | | |
| Fairbanks | 176,078 | 9.2 | | 1,187,691 | |
| Sherman | 155,945 | 8.1 | | | |
| LaFollette | 133,426 | 6.9 | | | |
| Ford | 131,889 | 6.9 | | | |
| Burton | 122,165 | 6.4 | | | |
| Hughes | 80,737 | 4.2 | | | |
| Roosevelt | 80,019 | 4.2 | | | |
| Smith | 77,872 | 4.0 | | | |
| Simpson | 14,365 | .7 | | | |
| Others[6] | 72,369 | 3.8 | | | |
| | 1,923,374 | | | | |

1. *Source for names of "favorite son" candidates: The New York Times.*
2. *Source for vote breakdown: North Dakota secretary of state.*
3. *Write-in.*
4. *No presidential preference vote but one set of delegates at large was for Roosevelt and the other set unpledged.*

5. *Figures not available. Republican winner was Sen. Theodore E. Burton (R Ohio) and Democratic winner was Woodrow Wilson, according to The New York Times.*
6. *In addition to scattered votes, "others" includes Robert G. Ross who received 5,-506 votes in the Nebraska primary; Henry D. Estabrook who received 9,851 in the North Dakota primary and 8,132 in the Nebraska primary.*

# 1920 Primaries

| Republican | | | Democratic | | |
|---|---|---|---|---|---|
| | Votes | % | | Votes | % |

**March 9  New Hampshire**

| Republican | | | Democratic | | |
|---|---|---|---|---|---|
| Leonard Wood (N.H.)[1] | 8,591 | 53.0 | Unpledged delegates[1] | 7,103 | 100.0 |
| Unpledged delegates | 5,604 | 34.6 | | | |
| Hiram Johnson (Calif.)[1] | 2,000 | 12.3 | | | |

**March 16  North Dakota**

| Republican | | | Democratic | | |
|---|---|---|---|---|---|
| Johnson | 30,573 | 96.1 | William G. McAdoo (N.Y.)[2] | 49 | 12.6 |
| Leonard Wood[2] | 987 | 3.1 | Others[2] | 340 | 87.4 |
| Frank O. Lowden (Ill.)[2] | 265 | .8 | | | |

**March 23  South Dakota**

| Republican | | | Democratic | | |
|---|---|---|---|---|---|
| Leonard Wood | 31,265 | 36.5 | Others | 6,612 | 100.0 |
| Lowden | 26,981 | 31.5 | | | |
| Johnson | 26,301 | 30.7 | | | |
| Others | 1,144 | 1.3 | | | |

**April 5  Michigan**

| Republican | | | Democratic | | |
|---|---|---|---|---|---|
| Johnson | 156,939 | 38.4 | McAdoo | 18,665 | 21.1 |
| Leonard Wood | 112,568[3] | 27.5 | Edward I. Edwards (N.J.) | 16,642 | 18.8 |
| Lowden | 62,418 | 15.3 | A. Mitchell Palmer (Pa.) | 11,187 | 12.6 |
| Herbert C. Hoover (Calif.) | 52,503 | 12.8 | Others | 42,000 | 47.5 |
| Others | 24,729 | 6.0 | | | |

**April 6  New York**

| Republican | | | Democratic | | |
|---|---|---|---|---|---|
| Unpledged delegates | 199,149 | 100.0 | Unpledged delegates | 113,300 | 100.0 |

**April 6  Wisconsin** [4]

| Republican | | | Democratic | | |
|---|---|---|---|---|---|
| Leonard Wood[2] | 4,505 | 15.0 | James M. Cox (Ohio)[2] | 76 | 2.2 |
| Hoover[2] | 3,910 | 13.0 | Others | 3,391 | 97.8 |
| Johnson[2] | 2,413 | 8.0 | | | |
| Lowden[2] | 921 | 3.1 | | | |
| Others | 18,350 | 60.9 | | | |

**April 13  Illinois**

| Republican | | | Democratic | | |
|---|---|---|---|---|---|
| Lowden | 236,802 | 51.1 | Edwards[2] | 6,933 | 32.3 |
| Leonard Wood | 156,719 | 33.8 | McAdoo[2] | 3,838 | 17.9 |
| Johnson | 64,201 | 13.8 | Cox[2] | 266 | 1.2 |
| Hoover[2] | 3,401 | .7 | Others | 10,418 | 48.6 |
| Others | 2,674 | .6 | | | |

**April 20  Nebraska**

| Republican | | | Democratic | | |
|---|---|---|---|---|---|
| Johnson | 63,161 | 46.2 | Gilbert M. Hitchcock (Neb.) | 37,452 | 67.3 |
| Leonard Wood | 42,385 | 31.0 | Others | 18,230 | 32.7 |
| John J. Pershing (Mo.) | 27,669 | 20.3 | | | |
| Others | 3,432 | 2.5 | | | |

**April 23  Montana**

| Republican | | | Democratic | | |
|---|---|---|---|---|---|
| Johnson | 21,034 | 52.4 | Others[2] | 2,994 | 100.0 |
| Leonard Wood | 6,804 | 17.0 | | | |
| Lowden | 6,503 | 16.2 | | | |
| Hoover | 5,076 | 12.6 | | | |
| Warren G. Harding (Ohio) | 723 | 1.8 | | | |

**April 27  Massachusetts**

| Republican | | | Democratic | | |
|---|---|---|---|---|---|
| Unpledged delegates | 93,356 | 100.0 | Unpledged delegates | 21,226 | 100.0 |

# Republican

# Democratic

|  | Votes | % |  | Votes | % |
|---|---|---|---|---|---|

**April 27   New Jersey**

| Leonard Wood | 52,909 | 50.2 | Edwards | 4,163 | 91.4 |
| Johnson | 51,685 | 49.0 | McAdoo[2] | 180 | 4.0 |
| Hoover | 900 | .9 | Others | 213 | 4.7 |

**April 27   Ohio**

| Harding | 123,257 | 47.6 | Cox | 85,838 | 97.8 |
| Leonard Wood | 108,565 | 41.9 | McAdoo[2] | 292 | .3 |
| Johnson[2] | 16,783 | 6.5 | Others | 1,647 | 1.9 |
| Hoover[2] | 10,467 | 4.0 |  |  |  |

**May 3   Maryland**

| Leonard Wood | 15,900 | 66.4 | [5] |  |  |
| Johnson | 8,059 | 33.6 |  |  |  |

**May 4   California**

| Johnson | 369,853 | 63.9 | Unpledged delegates | 23,831 | 100.0 |
| Hoover | 209,009 | 36.1 |  |  |  |

**May 4   Indiana**

| Leonard Wood | 85,708 | 37.9 | [5] |  |  |
| Johnson | 79,840 | 35.3 |  |  |  |
| Lowden | 39,627 | 17.5 |  |  |  |
| Harding | 20,782 | 9.2 |  |  |  |

**May 18   Pennsylvania**

| Edward R. Wood (Pa.) | 257,841 | 92.3 | Palmer[6] | 80,356 | 73.7 |
| Johnson[2] | 10,869 | 3.8 | McAdoo | 26,875 | 24.6 |
| Leonard Wood[2] | 3,878 | 1.4 | Edwards[2] | 674 | .6 |
| Hoover[2] | 2,825 | 1.0 | Others | 1,132 | 1.0 |
| Others[2] | 4,059 | 1.5 |  |  |  |

**May 18   Vermont**

| Leonard Wood | 3,451 | 66.1 | McAdoo[2] | 137 | 31.4 |
| Hoover[2] | 564 | 10.8 | Edwards[2] | 58 | 13.3 |
| Johnson[2] | 402 | 7.7 | Cox[2] | 14 | 3.2 |
| Lowden[2] | 29 | .5 | Others | 227 | 52.1 |
| Others | 777 | 14.9 |  |  |  |

**May 21   Oregon**

| Johnson | 46,163 | 38.4 | McAdoo | 24,951 | 98.6 |
| Leonard Wood | 43,770 | 36.5 | Others | 361 | 1.4 |
| Lowden | 15,581 | 13.0 |  |  |  |
| Hoover | 14,557 | 12.1 |  |  |  |

**May 25   West Virginia**

| Leonard Wood | 27,255 | 44.6 | [5] |  |  |
| Others | 33,849 [7] | 55.4 |  |  |  |

## Republican

| | Votes | % |
|---|---|---|
| | | |

## Democratic

| | Votes | % |
|---|---|---|

### June 5   **North Carolina**

| | | | |
|---|---|---|---|
| Johnson | 15,375 | 73.3 | 5 |
| Leonard Wood | 5,603 | 26.7 | |

| **TOTALS** | | | | | | |
|---|---|---|---|---|---|---|
| Johnson | 965,651 | 30.3 | Unpledged delegates | 165,460 | 28.9 |
| Leonard Wood | 710,863 | 22.3 | Palmer | 91,543 | 16.0 |
| Lowden | 389,127 | 12.2 | Cox | 86,194 | 15.0 |
| Hoover | 303,212 | 9.5 | McAdoo | 74,987 | 13.1 |
| Unpledged delegates | 298,109 | 9.4 | Hitchcock | 37,452 | 6.6 |
| Edward R. Wood | 257,841 | 8.1 | Edwards | 28,470 | 5.0 |
| Harding | 144,762 | 4.5 | Others [9] | 87,565 | 15.3 |
| Pershing | 27,669 | .9 | | | |
| Others [8] | 89,014 | 2.8 | | 571,671 | |
| | 3,186,248 | | | | |

1. Source: Louise Overacker, The Presidential Primaries (1926), p. 238-39. There was no preference vote. In the Republican primary, figures given were for delegates at large favoring Wood and Johnson. In the Democratic primary, although delegates were unpledged, the organization (Robert Charles Murchie) group was understood to be for Hoover. The highest Democratic Hoover delegate received 3,714 votes.

2. Write-in.

3. Source: Overacker, op. cit., p. 238.

4. No names entered for presidential preference in the Republican primary. The real contest lay between two lists of delegates, one headed by Robert M. La Follette and the other by Emanuel L. Philipp.

5. No names entered and no preference vote recorded.

6. Source for name of "favorite son" candidate: The New York Times.

7. Most of these votes were received by Sen. Howard Sutherland (R W.Va.). The figure is unofficial.

8. In addition to scattered votes, "others" includes Robert G. Ross who received 1,698 votes in the Nebraska primary.

9. In addition to scattered votes, "others" includes Robert G. Ross who received 13,179 in the Nebraska primary.

# 1924 Primaries

| **Republican** | Votes | % | **Democratic** | Votes | % |
|---|---|---|---|---|---|

**March 11  New Hampshire**

| | | | | | |
|---|---|---|---|---|---|
| Calvin Coolidge (Mass.) | 17,170 | 100.0 | Unpledged delegates | 6,687 | 100.0 |

**March 18  North Dakota**

| | | | | | |
|---|---|---|---|---|---|
| Coolidge | 52,815 | 42.1 | William G. McAdoo (Calif.) | 11,273 | 100.0 |
| Robert M. LaFollette (Wis.) | 40,252 | 32.1 | | | |
| Hiram Johnson (Calif.) | 32,363 | 25.8 | | | |

**March 25  South Dakota**

| | | | | | |
|---|---|---|---|---|---|
| Johnson | 40,935 | 50.7 | McAdoo[1] | 6,983 | 77.4 |
| Coolidge | 39,791 | 49.3 | Unpledged delegates[1] | 2,040 | 22.6 |

**April 1  Wisconsin [2]**

| | | | | | |
|---|---|---|---|---|---|
| LaFollette[3] | 40,738 | 62.5 | McAdoo | 54,922 | 68.2 |
| Coolidge[3] | 23,324 | 35.8 | Alfred E. Smith (N.Y.)[3] | 5,774 | 7.2 |
| Johnson[3] | 411 | .6 | Others | 19,827 | 24.6 |
| Others | 688 | 1.1 | | | |

**April 7  Michigan**

| | | | | | |
|---|---|---|---|---|---|
| Coolidge | 236,191 | 67.2 | Henry Ford (Mich.)[4] | 48,567 | 53.4 |
| Johnson | 103,739 | 29.5 | Woodbridge N. Ferris (Mich.)[4] | 42,028 | 46.2 |
| Others | 11,312 | 3.2 | Others | 435 | .5 |

**April 8  Illinois**

| | | | | | |
|---|---|---|---|---|---|
| Coolidge | 533,193 | 58.0 | McAdoo | 180,544 | 98.9 |
| Johnson | 385,590 | 42.0 | Smith[3] | 235 | .1 |
| LaFollette[3] | 278 | — | Others | 1,724 | .9 |
| Others | 21 | — | | | |

**April 8  Nebraska**

| | | | | | |
|---|---|---|---|---|---|
| Coolidge | 79,676 | 63.6 | McAdoo[3] | 9,342 | 57.3 |
| Johnson | 45,032 | 35.9 | Smith[3] | 700 | 4.3 |
| Others | 627 | .5 | Others[3] | 6,268 | 38.4 |

**April 22  New Jersey**

| | | | | | |
|---|---|---|---|---|---|
| Coolidge | 111,739 | 89.1 | George S. Silzer (N.J.)[5] | 35,601 | 97.7 |
| Johnson | 13,626 | 10.9 | Smith[3] | 721 | 2.0 |
| | | | McAdoo[3] | 69 | .2 |
| | | | Others | 38 | .1 |

**April 22  Pennsylvania**

| | | | | | |
|---|---|---|---|---|---|
| Coolidge[3] | 117,262 | 87.9 | McAdoo[3] | 10,376 | 43.7 |
| Johnson[3] | 4,345 | 3.3 | Smith[3] | 9,029 | 38.0 |
| LaFollette[3] | 1,224 | .9 | Others[3] | 4,341 | 18.3 |
| Others | 10,523 | 7.9 | | | |

**April 29  Massachusetts**

| | | | | | |
|---|---|---|---|---|---|
| Coolidge | 84,840 | 100.0 | Unpledged delegates at large[6] | 30,341 | 100.0 |

**April 29  Ohio**

| | | | | | |
|---|---|---|---|---|---|
| Coolidge | 173,613 | 86.3 | James M. Cox (Ohio)[5] | 74,183 | 71.7 |
| Johnson | 27,578 | 13.7 | McAdoo | 29,267 | 28.3 |

| | Republican | | | Democratic | | |
|---|---|---|---|---|---|---|
| | Votes | % | | | Votes | % |
| **May 5   Maryland** | | | | | | |
| Coolidge | 19,657 | 93.7 | 7 | | | |
| Unpledged delegates | 1,326 | 6.3 | | | | |
| Johnson [3] | 3 | — | | | | |
| **May 6   California** | | | | | | |
| Coolidge | 310,618 | 54.3 | McAdoo | | 110,235 | 85.6 |
| Johnson | 261,566 | 45.7 | Unpledged delegates | | 18,586 | 14.4 |
| **May 6   Indiana** | | | | | | |
| Coolidge | 330,045 | 84.1 | 7 | | | |
| Johnson | 62,603 | 15.9 | | | | |
| **May 16   Oregon** | | | | | | |
| Coolidge | 99,187 | 76.8 | McAdoo | | 33,664 | 100.0 |
| Johnson | 30,042 | 23.2 | | | | |
| **May 27   West Virginia** | | | | | | |
| Coolidge | 162,042 | 100.0 | 7 | | | |
| **May 28   Montana** | | | | | | |
| Coolidge | 19,200 | 100.0 | McAdoo | | 10,058 | 100.0 |
| **TOTALS** | | | | | | |
| Coolidge | 2,410,363 | 68.4 | McAdoo | | 456,733 | 59.8 |
| Johnson | 1,007,833 | 28.6 | Cox | | 74,183 | 9.7 |
| LaFollette | 82,492 | 2.3 | Unpledged delegates | | 57,654 | 7.5 |
| Unpledged delegates | 1,326 | — | Ford | | 48,567 | 6.4 |
| Others | 23,171 | .7 | Ferris | | 42,028 | 5.5 |
| | | | Silzer | | 35,601 | 4.7 |
| | 3,525,185 | | Smith | | 16,459 | 2.2 |
| | | | Others | | 32,633 | 4.3 |
| | | | | | 763,858 | |

*1. No presidential preference vote, as McAdoo's was the only name entered, but a contest developed between "McAdoo" and "anti-McAdoo" lists of delegates. Figures are average votes cast for these lists.*

*2. In Wisconsin the real contest in the Republican primary was between two lists of delegates, one led by La Follette and one by Emanuel L. Philipp. In the Democratic primary, the real contest was between two lists of delegates, one favoring Smith and one favoring McAdoo.*

*3. Write-in.*

*4. Source for names of "favorite son" candidates: Michigan Manual, 1925.*

*5. Source for names of "favorite son" candidates: The New York Times.*

*6. No presidential preference vote provided for. There were nine candidates for the eight places as delegates at large, one of whom announced his preference for Smith during the campaign and received the second highest number of votes.*

*7. No names entered and no presidential preference vote taken.*

# 1928 Primaries

| | Republican | | | Democratic | | |
|---|---|---|---|---|---|---|
| | Votes | % | | | Votes | % |
| **March 13 New Hampshire** | | | | | | |
| Unpledged delegates at large[1] | 25,603 | 100.0 | Unpledged delegates at large[1] | | 9,716 | 100.0 |
| **March 20 North Dakota** | | | | | | |
| Frank O. Lowden (Ill.) | 95,857 | 100.0 | Alfred E. Smith (N.Y.) | | 10,822 | 100.0 |
| **April 2 Michigan** | | | | | | |
| Herbert C. Hoover (Calif.) | 282,809 | 97.6 | Smith | | 77,276 | 98.3 |
| Lowden | 5,349 | 1.8 | Thomas Walsh (Mont.) | | 1,034 | 1.3 |
| Calvin Coolidge (Mass.) | 1,666 | .6 | James A. Reed (Mo.) | | 324 | .4 |
| **April 3 Wisconsin** | | | | | | |
| George W. Norris (Neb.) | 162,822 | 87.1 | Reed | | 61,097 | 75.0 |
| Hoover | 17,659 | 9.4 | Smith | | 19,781 | 24.3 |
| Lowden | 3,302 | 1.8 | Walsh | | 541 | .7 |
| Coolidge | 680 | .4 | | | | |
| Charles G. Dawes (Ill.) | 505 | .3 | | | | |
| Others | 1,894 | 1.0 | | | | |
| **April 10 Illinois** | | | | | | |
| Lowden | 1,172,278 | 99.3 | Smith | | 44,212 | 91.7 |
| Hoover | 4,368 | .4 | Reed | | 3,786 | 7.9 |
| Coolidge | 2,420 | .2 | William G. McAdoo (Calif.) | | 213 | .4 |
| Dawes | 756 | .1 | | | | |
| Others | 946 | .1 | | | | |
| **April 10 Nebraska** | | | | | | |
| Norris | 96,726 | 91.8 | Gilbert M. Hitchcock (Neb.) | | 51,019 | 91.5 |
| Hoover | 6,815 | 6.5 | Smith | | 4,755 | 8.5 |
| Lowden | 711 | .7 | | | | |
| Dawes | 679 | .7 | | | | |
| Coolidge | 452 | .4 | | | | |
| **April 24 Ohio** | | | | | | |
| Hoover | 217,430 | 68.1 | Smith | | 42,365 | 65.9 |
| Frank B. Willis (Ohio) | 84,461 | 26.5 | Atlee Pomerene (Ohio) | | 13,957 | 21.7 |
| Dawes | 4,311 | 1.4 | Victor Donahey (Ohio) | | 7,935 | 12.3 |
| Lowden | 3,676 | 1.2 | | | | |
| Others | 9,190 | 2.9 | | | | |
| **April 24 Pennsylvania** | | | | | | |
| [2] | | | [2] | | | |
| **April 28 Massachusetts** | | | | | | |
| Hoover[3] | 100,279 | 85.2 | Smith | | 38,081 | 98.1 |
| Coolidge[3] | 7,767 | 6.6 | Walsh | | 254 | .7 |
| Alvan Fuller (Mass.) | 1,686 | 1.4 | Others | | 478 | 1.2 |
| Lowden[3] | 1,040 | .9 | | | | |
| Others | 6,950 | 5.9 | | | | |
| **May 1 California** | | | | | | |
| Hoover | 567,219 | 100.0 | Smith | | 134,471 | 54.1 |
| | | | Reed | | 60,004 | 24.1 |
| | | | Walsh | | 46,770 | 18.8 |
| | | | Others | | 7,263 | 2.9 |

## Republican          ## Democratic

| | Votes | % | | Votes | % |
|---|---|---|---|---|---|
| **May 7   Indiana** | | | | | |
| James E. Watson (Ind.) | 228,795 | 53.0 | Evans Woollen (Ind.) | 146,934 | 100.0 |
| Hoover | 203,279 | 47.0 | | | |
| **May 7   Maryland[4]** | | | | | |
| Hoover | 27,128 | 83.3 | [5] | | |
| Unpledged delegates | 5,426 | 16.7 | | | |
| **May 8   Alabama** | | | | | |
| [5] | | | Unpledged delegates at large[6] | 138,957 | 100.0 |
| **May 15   New Jersey** | | | | | |
| Hoover | 382,907 | 100.0 | Smith[3] | 28,506 | 100.0 |
| **May 18   Oregon** | | | | | |
| Hoover | 101,129 | 98.7 | Smith | 17,444 | 48.5 |
| Lowden | 1,322 | 1.3 | Walsh | 11,272 | 31.3 |
| | | | Reed | 6,360 | 17.7 |
| | | | Others | 881 | 2.5 |
| **May 22   South Dakota** | | | | | |
| Unpledged delegates at large[7] | 34,264 | 100.0 | Unpledged delegates at large[7] | 6,221 | 100.0 |
| **May 29   West Virginia** | | | | | |
| Guy D. Goff (W.Va.) | 128,429 | 54.0 | Smith | 81,739 | 50.0 |
| Hoover | 109,303 | 46.0 | Reed | 75,796 | 46.4 |
| | | | Others | 5,789 | 3.5 |
| **June 5   Florida** | | | | | |
| [5] | | | Unpledged delegates at large[8] | 108,167 | 100.00 |
| | | | | | |
| **TOTALS** | | | | | |
| Hoover | 2,020,325 | 49.2 | Smith | 499,452 | 39.5 |
| Lowden | 1,283,535 | 31.2 | Unpledged delegates | 263,061 | 20.8 |
| Norris | 259,548 | 6.3 | Reed | 207,367 | 16.4 |
| Watson | 228,795 | 5.6 | Woollen | 146,934 | 11.6 |
| Goff | 128,429 | 3.1 | Walsh | 59,871 | 4.7 |
| Willis | 84,461 | 2.1 | Hitchcock | 51,019 | 4.0 |
| Unpledged delegates | 65,293 | 1.6 | Pomerene | 13,957 | 1.1 |
| Coolidge | 12,985 | .3 | Donahey | 7,935 | .6 |
| Dawes | 6,251 | .2 | McAdoo | 213 | — |
| Fuller | 1,686 | — | Others[10] | 14,411 | 1.1 |
| Others[9] | 18,980 | .5 | | 1,264,220 | |
| | 4,110,288 | | | | |

1. *Winning Republican delegates were unofficially pledged to Hoover and winning Democratic delegates were unofficially pledged to Smith, according to Walter Kravitz, "Presidential Preferential Primaries: Results 1928-1956" (1960), p. 4.*
2. *No figures available.*
3. *Write-in.*
4. *Source: Kravitz, op. cit., p. 5.*
5. *No primary.*
6. *The* Montgomery Advertiser *of May 3, 1928, described the delegates as independent and anti-Smith.*

7. *Winning Republican delegates favored Lowden and winning Democratic delegates favored Smith, according to Kravitz, op. cit., p. 5.*
8. *The Miami Herald of June 6, 1928, described the delegates as unpledged and anti-Smith.*
9. *In addition to scattered votes, "others" includes Robert G. Ross who received 8,280 votes in the Ohio primary.*
10. *In addition to scattered votes, "others" includes Poling who received 7,263 votes in the California primary; and Workman who received 881 in the Oregon primary and 5,789 in the West Virginia primary.*

# 1932 Primaries

| | Republican | | | Democratic | | |
|---|---|---|---|---|---|---|
| | | Votes | % | | Votes | % |
| **March 8   New Hampshire** | | | | | | |
| | Unpledged delegates at large[1] | 22,903 | 100.0 | Unpledged delegates at large[1] | 15,401 | 100.0 |
| **March 15   North Dakota** | | | | | | |
| | Joseph I. France (Md.) | 36,000[2] | 59.0 | Franklin D. Roosevelt (N.Y.) | 52,000[2] | 61.9 |
| | Jacob S. Coxey (Ohio) | 25,000[2] | 41.0 | William H. Murray (Okla.) | 32,000[2] | 38.1 |
| **March 23   Georgia** | | | | | | |
| | [3] | | | Roosevelt | 51,498 | 90.3 |
| | | | | Others | 5,541 | 9.7 |
| **April 5   Wisconsin** | | | | | | |
| | George W. Norris (Neb.) | 139,514 | 95.5 | Roosevelt | 241,742 | 98.6 |
| | Herbert C. Hoover (Calif.) | 6,588 | 4.5 | Alfred E. Smith (N.Y.)[4] | 3,502 | 1.4 |
| **April 12   Nebraska** | | | | | | |
| | France | 40,481 | 74.4 | Roosevelt | 91,393 | 63.5 |
| | Hoover | 13,934 | 25.6 | John N. Garner (Texas) | 27,359 | 19.0 |
| | | | | Murray | 25,214 | 17.5 |
| **April 13   Illinois** | | | | | | |
| | France | 345,498 | 98.7 | James H. Lewis (Ill.) | 590,130 | 99.8 |
| | Hoover | 4,368 | 1.2 | Roosevelt | 1,084 | .2 |
| | Charles G. Dawes (Ill.) | 129 | — | Smith | 266 | — |
| | | | | Others[4] | 72 | — |
| **April 26   Massachusetts** | | | | | | |
| | Unpledged delegates at large[5] | 57,534 | 100.0 | Smith[5] | 153,465 | 73.1 |
| | | | | Roosevelt[5] | 56,454 | 26.9 |
| **April 26   Pennsylvania** | | | | | | |
| | France | 352,092 | 92.9 | Roosevelt | 133,002 | 56.6 |
| | Hoover | 20,662 | 5.5 | Smith | 101,227 | 43.1 |
| | Others | 6,126 | 1.6 | Others | 563 | .2 |
| **May 2   Maryland** | | | | | | |
| | Hoover | 27,324 | 60.0 | [6] | | |
| | France | 17,008 | 37.3 | | | |
| | Unpledged delegates | 1,236 | 2.7 | | | |
| **May 3   Alabama** | | | | | | |
| | [3] | | | Unpledged delegates[7] | 134,781 | 100.0 |
| **May 3   California** | | | | | | |
| | Hoover | 657,420 | 100.0 | Garner | 222,385 | 41.3 |
| | | | | Roosevelt | 175,008 | 32.5 |
| | | | | Smith | 141,517 | 26.3 |
| **May 3   South Dakota** | | | | | | |
| | Johnson[8] | 64,464 | 64.7 | Roosevelt | 35,370 | 100.0 |
| | Others | 35,133 | 35.3 | | | |

## Republican                                    ## Democratic

|  | Votes | % |  | Votes | % |
|---|---|---|---|---|---|
| **May 10  Ohio** | | | | | |
| Coxey | 75,844 | 58.9 | Murray | 112,512 | 96.4 |
| France | 44,853 | 34.8 | Roosevelt[4] | 1,999 | 1.7 |
| Hoover | 8,154 | 6.3 | Smith[4] | 951 | .8 |
| | | | George White (Ohio) | 834 | .7 |
| | | | Newton D. Baker (Ohio) | 289 | .2 |
| | | | Garner[4] | 72 | — |
| **May 10  West Virginia** | | | | | |
| France | 88,005 | 100.0 | Roosevelt | 219,671 | 90.3 |
| | | | Murray | 19,826 | 8.2 |
| | | | Others | 3,727 | 1.5 |
| **May 17  New Jersey** | | | | | |
| France | 141,330 | 93.3 | Smith | 5,234 | 61.9 |
| Hoover | 10,116 | 6.7 | Roosevelt | 3,219 | 38.1 |
| **May 20  Oregon** | | | | | |
| France | 72,681 | 69.0 | Roosevelt | 48,554 | 78.6 |
| Hoover | 32,599 | 31.0 | Murray | 11,993 | 19.4 |
| | | | Others | 1,214 | 2.0 |
| **June 7  Florida** | | | | | |
| 3 | | | Roosevelt | 203,372 | 87.7 |
| | | | Murray | 24,847 | 10.7 |
| | | | Others | 3,645 | 1.6 |
| **TOTALS** | | | | | |
| France | 1,137,948 | 48.5 | Roosevelt | 1,314,366 | 44.5 |
| Hoover | 781,165 | 33.3 | Lewis | 590,130 | 20.0 |
| Norris | 139,514 | 5.9 | Smith | 406,162 | 13.8 |
| Coxey | 100,844 | 4.3 | Garner | 249,816 | 8.5 |
| Unpledged delegates | 81,673 | 3.5 | Murray | 226,392 | 7.7 |
| Johnson | 64,464 | 2.7 | Unpledged delegates | 150,182 | 5.1 |
| Dawes | 129 | — | White | 834 | — |
| Others[9] | 41,259 | 1.8 | Baker | 289 | — |
| | | | Others[10] | 14,762 | .5 |
| | 2,346,996 | | | 2,952,933 | |

1. *Hoover delegates won the Republican primary and Roosevelt delegates won the Democratic primary, according to Kravitz, op. cit., p. 6.*
2. *Unofficial figures.*
3. *No primary.*
4. *Write-in.*
5. *Delegate-at-large vote in Republican and Democratic primaries. Hoover delegates won the Republican primary, according to Kravitz, op. cit., p. 6. The New York Times of April 28, 1932, also reported that the Republican delegates were pledged to Hoover.*
6. *No names entered, according to the Maryland Record of Election Returns.*

7. *These were unpledged delegates who favored Roosevelt, according to Kravitz, op. cit., p. 6.*
8. *The winning Republican delegation supported Hoover, according to Kravitz, op. cit., p. 7.*
9. *In addition to scattered votes, "others" includes Bogue who received 35,133 in the South Dakota primary.*
10. *In addition to scattered votes, "others" includes Leo J. Chassee who received 3,645 in the Florida primary and 3,727 in the West Virginia primary; and Howard who received 5,541 votes in the Georgia primary.*

# 1936 Primaries

| | **Republican** | | | **Democratic** | | |
|---|---|---|---|---|---|---|
| | Votes | % | | Votes | % |

**March 10  New Hampshire**

| Unpledged delegates at large[1] | 32,992 | 100.0 | Unpledged delegates at large[1] | 15,752 | 100.0 |
|---|---|---|---|---|---|

**April 7  Wisconsin**

| William E. Borah (Idaho) | 187,334 | 98.2 | Franklin D. Roosevelt (N.Y.) | 401,773 | 100.0 |
|---|---|---|---|---|---|
| Alfred M. Landon (Kan.) | 3,360 | 1.8 | John N. Garner (Texas) | 108 | — |
| | | | Alfred E. Smith (N.Y.) | 46 | — |

**April 14  Illinois**

| Frank Knox (Ill.) | 491,575 | 53.7 | Roosevelt | 1,416,411 | 100.0 |
|---|---|---|---|---|---|
| Borah | 419,220 | 45.8 | Others[2] | 411 | — |
| Landon | 3,775 | .4 | | | |
| Others[2] | 205 | — | | | |

**April 14  Nebraska**

| Borah | 70,240 | 74.5 | Roosevelt | 139,743 | 100.0 |
|---|---|---|---|---|---|
| Landon | 23,117 | 24.5 | | | |
| Others | 973 | 1.0 | | | |

**April 28  Massachusetts**

| Landon[2] | 76,862 | 80.6 | Roosevelt[2] | 51,924 | 85.9 |
|---|---|---|---|---|---|
| Herbert C. Hoover (Calif.)[2] | 7,276 | 7.6 | Smith[2] | 2,928 | 4.8 |
| Borah[2] | 4,259 | 4.5 | Charles E. Coughlin (Mich.)[2] | 2,854 | 4.7 |
| Knox[2] | 1,987 | 2.1 | Others[2] | 2,774 | 4.6 |
| Others[2] | 5,032 | 5.3 | | | |

**April 28  Pennsylvania**

| Borah | 459,982 | 100.0 | Roosevelt | 720,309 | 95.3 |
|---|---|---|---|---|---|
| | | | Henry Breckinridge (N.Y.) | 35,351 | 4.7 |

**May 4  Maryland**

| [3] | | | Roosevelt | 100,269 | 83.4 |
|---|---|---|---|---|---|
| | | | Breckinridge | 18,150 | 15.1 |
| | | | Unpledged delegates | 1,739 | 1.4 |

**May 5  California**

| Earl Warren (Calif.) | 350,917 | 57.4 | Roosevelt | 790,235 | 82.5 |
|---|---|---|---|---|---|
| Landon | 260,170 | 42.6 | Upton Sinclair (Calif.) | 106,068 | 11.1 |
| | | | John S. McGroarty (Calif.) | 61,391 | 6.4 |

**May 5  South Dakota**

| Warren E. Green[4] | 44,518 | 50.1 | Roosevelt | 48,262 | 100.0 |
|---|---|---|---|---|---|
| Borah | 44,261 | 49.9 | | | |

**May 12  Ohio**

| Stephen A. Day (Ohio) | 155,732 | 93.4 | Roosevelt | 514,366 | 94.0 |
|---|---|---|---|---|---|
| Landon | 11,015 | 6.6 | Breckinridge | 32,950 | 6.0 |

**May 12  West Virginia**

| Borah | 105,855 | 84.8 | Roosevelt | 288,799 | 97.3 |
|---|---|---|---|---|---|
| Others | 18,986 | 15.2 | Others | 8,162 | 2.7 |

## Republican                          ## Democratic

| May 15 | **Oregon** | | | | | |
|---|---|---|---|---|---|---|

| Borah | 91,949 | 90.2 | Roosevelt | 88,305 | 99.8 |
|---|---|---|---|---|---|
| Landon | 4,467 | 4.4 | Others | 208 | .2 |
| Others | 5,557 | 5.4 | | | |

| May 19 | **New Jersey** |
|---|---|

| Landon | 347,142 | 79.2 | Breckinridge | 49,956 | 81.1 |
|---|---|---|---|---|---|
| Borah | 91,052 | 20.8 | Roosevelt[2] | 11,676 | 18.9 |

| June 6 | **Florida** |
|---|---|

[3]

| | | | Roosevelt | 242,906 | 89.7 |
|---|---|---|---|---|---|
| | | | Others | 27,982 | 10.3 |

**TOTALS**

| Borah | 1,474,152 | 44.4 | Roosevelt | 4,814,978 | 92.9 |
|---|---|---|---|---|---|
| Landon | 729,908 | 22.0 | Breckinridge | 136,407 | 2.6 |
| Knox | 493,562 | 14.9 | Sinclair | 106,068 | 2.0 |
| Warren | 350,917 | 10.6 | McGroarty | 61,391 | 1.2 |
| Day | 155,732 | 4.7 | Unpledged delegates | 17,491 | .3 |
| Green | 44,518 | 1.3 | Smith | 2,974 | .1 |
| Unpledged delegates | 32,992 | 1.0 | Coughlin | 2,854 | .1 |
| Hoover | 7,276 | .2 | Garner | 108 | — |
| Others[5] | 30,753 | .9 | Others[6] | 39,537 | .8 |
| | 3,319,810 | | | 5,181,808 | |

1. *Delegates favorable to Knox won the Republican primary and Roosevelt delegates won the Democratic primary, according to Kravitz, op. cit., p. 8.*
2. *Write-in.*
3. *No preferential primary held.*
4. *These delegates were unpledged but favored Landon, according to Kravitz, op. cit., p. 9.*

5. *In addition to scattered votes, "others" includes Leo J. Chassee who received 18,986 votes in the West Virginia primary.*
6. *In addition to scattered votes, "others" includes Joseph A. Coutremarsh who received 27,982 votes in the Florida primary and 8,162 votes in the West Virginia primary.*

# 1940 Primaries

| Republican | | | Democratic | | |
|---|---|---|---|---|---|

**March 12   New Hampshire**

| Unpledged delegates at large | 34,616 | *100.0* | Unpledged delegates at large [1] | 10,501 | *100.0* |
|---|---|---|---|---|---|

**April 2   Wisconsin**

| Thomas E. Dewey (N.Y.) | 70,168 | *72.6* | Franklin D. Roosevelt (N.Y.) | 322,991 | *75.4* |
|---|---|---|---|---|---|
| Arthur Vandenberg (Mich.) | 26,182 | *27.1* | John N. Garner (Texas) | 105,662 | *24.6* |
| Robert A. Taft (Ohio) | 341 | *.4* | | | |

**April 9   Illinois**

| Dewey | 977,225 | *99.9* | Roosevelt | 1,176,531 | *86.0* |
|---|---|---|---|---|---|
| Others [2] | 552 | *.1* | Garner | 190,801 | *14.0* |
| | | | Others [2] | 35 | — |

**April 9   Nebraska**

| Dewey | 102,915 | *58.9* | Roosevelt | 111,902 | *100.0* |
|---|---|---|---|---|---|
| Vandenberg | 71,798 | *41.1* | | | |

**April 23   Pennsylvania**

| Dewey | 52,661 | *66.7* | Roosevelt | 724,657 | *100.0* |
|---|---|---|---|---|---|
| Franklin D. Roosevelt (N.Y.) | 8,294 | *10.5* | | | |
| Arthur H. James (Pa.) | 8,172 | *10.3* | | | |
| Taft | 5,213 | *6.6* | | | |
| Vandenberg | 2,384 | *3.0* | | | |
| Herbert C. Hoover (Calif.) | 1,082 | *1.4* | | | |
| Wendell Willkie (N.Y.) | 707 | *.9* | | | |
| Others | 463 | *.6* | | | |

**April 30   Massachusetts**

| Unpledged delegates at large [3] | 98,975 | *100.0* | Unpledged delegates at large [3] | 76,919 | *100.0* |
|---|---|---|---|---|---|

**May 5   South Dakota**

| Unpledged delegates | 52,566 | *100.0* | Unpledged delegates | 27,636 | *100.0* |
|---|---|---|---|---|---|

**May 6   Maryland**

| Dewey | 54,802 | *100.0* | [4] | | |
|---|---|---|---|---|---|

**May 7   Alabama**

| [4] | | | Unpledged delegates at large [5] | 196,508 | *100.0* |
|---|---|---|---|---|---|

**May 7   California**

| Jerrold L. Seawell [6] | 538,112 | *100.0* | Roosevelt | 723,782 | *74.0* |
|---|---|---|---|---|---|
| | | | Garner | 114,594 | *11.7* |
| | | | Unpledged delegates [6] | 139,055 | *14.2* |

**May 14   Ohio**

| Taft | 510,025 | *99.5* | Unpledged delegates at large [7] | 283,952 | *100.0* |
|---|---|---|---|---|---|
| Dewey [2] | 2,059 | *.4* | | | |
| John W. Bricker (Ohio) | 188 | — | | | |
| Vandenberg [2] | 83 | — | | | |
| Willkie | 53 | — | | | |
| Others | 69 | — | | | |

<table>
<thead>
<tr><th></th><th colspan="2">Republican</th><th></th><th colspan="2">Democratic</th></tr>
<tr><th></th><th>Votes</th><th>%</th><th></th><th>Votes</th><th>%</th></tr>
</thead>
<tbody>
<tr><td colspan="6">May 14 **West Virginia**</td></tr>
<tr><td>R. N. Davis (W.Va.)</td><td>106,123</td><td>*100.0*</td><td>H. C. Allen (W.Va.)</td><td>102,729</td><td>*100.0*</td></tr>
<tr><td colspan="6">May 17 **Oregon**</td></tr>
<tr><td>Charles L. McNary (Ore.)</td><td>133,488</td><td>*95.9*</td><td>Roosevelt</td><td>109,913</td><td>*87.2*</td></tr>
<tr><td>Dewey</td><td>5,190</td><td>*3.7*</td><td>Garner</td><td>15,584</td><td>*12.4*</td></tr>
<tr><td>Taft</td><td>254</td><td>*.2*</td><td>Others</td><td>601</td><td>*.5*</td></tr>
<tr><td>Willkie</td><td>237</td><td>*.2*</td><td></td><td></td><td></td></tr>
<tr><td>Vandenberg</td><td>36</td><td>—</td><td></td><td></td><td></td></tr>
<tr><td colspan="6">May 21 **New Jersey**</td></tr>
<tr><td>Dewey</td><td>340,734</td><td>*93.9*</td><td>Roosevelt[2]</td><td>34,278</td><td>*100.0*</td></tr>
<tr><td>Willkie[2]</td><td>20,143</td><td>*5.6*</td><td></td><td></td><td></td></tr>
<tr><td>Roosevelt[2]</td><td>1,202</td><td>*.3*</td><td></td><td></td><td></td></tr>
<tr><td>Taft[2]</td><td>595</td><td>*.2*</td><td></td><td></td><td></td></tr>
<tr><td>Vandenberg[2]</td><td>168</td><td>—</td><td></td><td></td><td></td></tr>
<tr><td>**TOTALS**</td><td></td><td></td><td></td><td></td><td></td></tr>
<tr><td>Dewey</td><td>1,605,754</td><td>*49.7*</td><td>Roosevelt</td><td>3,240,054</td><td>*71.7*</td></tr>
<tr><td>Seawell</td><td>538,112</td><td>*16.7*</td><td>Unpledged delegates</td><td>734,571</td><td>*16.4*</td></tr>
<tr><td>Taft</td><td>516,428</td><td>*16.0*</td><td>Garner</td><td>426,641</td><td>*9.5*</td></tr>
<tr><td>Unpledged delegates</td><td>186,157</td><td>*5.8*</td><td>Allen</td><td>102,729</td><td>*2.3*</td></tr>
<tr><td>McNary</td><td>133,488</td><td>*4.1*</td><td>Others</td><td>636</td><td>—</td></tr>
<tr><td>Davis</td><td>106,123</td><td>*3.3*</td><td></td><td></td><td></td></tr>
<tr><td>Vandenberg</td><td>100,651</td><td>*3.1*</td><td></td><td>4,468,631</td><td></td></tr>
<tr><td>Willkie</td><td>21,140</td><td>*.7*</td><td></td><td></td><td></td></tr>
<tr><td>Roosevelt</td><td>9,496</td><td>*.3*</td><td></td><td></td><td></td></tr>
<tr><td>James</td><td>8,172</td><td>*.3*</td><td></td><td></td><td></td></tr>
<tr><td>Hoover</td><td>1,082</td><td>—</td><td></td><td></td><td></td></tr>
<tr><td>Bricker</td><td>188</td><td>—</td><td></td><td></td><td></td></tr>
<tr><td>Others</td><td>1,084</td><td>—</td><td></td><td></td><td></td></tr>
<tr><td></td><td>3,227,875</td><td></td><td></td><td></td><td></td></tr>
</tbody>
</table>

1. Roosevelt delegates won, according to Kravitz, op. cit., p. 10.
2. Write-in.
3. An unpledged Republican slate defeated a slate of delegates pledged to Dewey, according to Kravitz, op. cit., p. 10. Sixty-nine James A. Farley delegates and three unpledged delegates won in the Democratic primary, according to Kravitz, ibid. The New York Times of May 1, 1940, also reported that most Democratic delegates favored Farley.
4. No primary.
5. Winning delegates were pledged to "favorite son" candidate William B. Bankhead,

then Speaker of the U.S. House of Representatives, according to Kravitz, op. cit., p. 10, and the Montgomery Advertiser of May 8, 1940.
6. The Los Angeles Times of May 8, 1940, reported that the Republican delegation was unpledged. In the Democratic primary, according to Davis, p. 293, unpledged slates were headed by Willis Allen, head of the California "Ham and Eggs" pension ticket which received 90,718 votes; and by Lt. Gov. Ellis E. Patterson, whose slate, backed by Labor's Non-Partisan League, received 48,337 votes.
7. Democratic delegates were pledged to Charles Sawyer (Ohio), according to Ohio Election Statistics, 1940, and Kravitz, op. cit., p. 10.

# 1944 Primaries

| | Republican | | | Democratic | | |
|---|---|---|---|---|---|---|
| | Votes | % | | | Votes | % |
| **March 14 New Hampshire** | | | | | | |
| Unpledged delegates at large[1] | 16,723 | 100.0 | | Unpledged delegates at large[1] | 6,772 | 100.0 |
| **April 5 Wisconsin** | | | | | | |
| Douglas MacArthur (Wis.) | 102,421 | 72.6 | | Franklin D. Roosevelt (N.Y.) | 49,632 | 94.3 |
| Thomas E. Dewey (N.Y.) | 21,036 | 14.9 | | Others | 3,014 | 5.7 |
| Harold E. Stassen (Minn.) | 7,928 | 5.6 | | | | |
| Wendell Willkie (N.Y.) | 6,439 | 4.6 | | | | |
| Others | 3,307 | 2.3 | | | | |
| **April 11 Illinois** | | | | | | |
| MacArthur | 550,354 | 92.0 | | Roosevelt | 47,561 | 99.3 |
| Dewey | 9,192 | 1.5 | | Others | 343 | .7 |
| Everett M. Dirksen (Ill.) | 581 | .1 | | | | |
| John W. Bricker (Ohio) | 148 | — | | | | |
| Stassen | 111 | — | | | | |
| Willkie | 107 | — | | | | |
| Others | 37,575 | 6.3 | | | | |
| **April 11 Nebraska** | | | | | | |
| Stassen | 51,800 | 65.7 | | Roosevelt | 37,405 | 99.2 |
| Dewey | 18,418 | 23.3 | | Others | 319 | .8 |
| Willkie | 8,249 | 10.5 | | | | |
| Others | 432 | .5 | | | | |
| **April 25 Massachusetts** | | | | | | |
| Unpledged delegates at large | 53,511 | 100.0 | | Unpledged delegates at large | 57,299 | 100.0 |
| **April 25 Pennsylvania** | | | | | | |
| Dewey[2] | 146,706 | 83.8 | | Roosevelt | 322,469 | 99.7 |
| MacArthur[2] | 9,032 | 5.2 | | Others | 961 | .3 |
| Franklin D. Roosevelt (N.Y.) | 8,815 | 5.0 | | | | |
| Willkie[2] | 3,650 | 2.1 | | | | |
| Bricker[2] | 2,936 | 1.7 | | | | |
| Edward Martin (Pa.) | 2,406 | 1.4 | | | | |
| Stassen[2] | 1,502 | .9 | | | | |
| **May 1 Maryland** | | | | | | |
| Unpledged delegates | 17,600 | 78.9 | | [3] | | |
| Willkie | 4,701 | 21.1 | | | | |
| **May 2 Alabama** | | | | | | |
| [3] | | | | Unpledged delegates at large[4] | 116,922 | 100.0 |
| **May 2 Florida** | | | | | | |
| [3] | | | | Unpledged delegates at large[5] | 118,518 | 100.0 |
| **May 2 South Dakota** | | | | | | |
| Charles A. Christopherson[6] | 33,497 | 60.2 | | Fred Hildebrandt (S.D.)[6] | 7,414 | 52.4 |
| Others[6] | 22,135 | 39.8 | | Others[6] | 6,727 | 47.6 |

| | Republican | | | | Democratic | | |
|---|---|---|---|---|---|---|---|
| | | Votes | % | | | Votes | % |

**May 9   Ohio**

| Unpledged delegates at large [7] | 360,139 | *100.0* | Unpledged delegates at large [7] | 164,915 | *100.0* |
|---|---|---|---|---|---|

**May 9   West Virginia**

| Unpledged delegates at large | 91,602 | *100.0* | Claude R. Linger (W.Va.) | 59,282 | *100.0* |
|---|---|---|---|---|---|

**May 16   California**

| Carl Warren (Calif.) | 594,439 | *100.0* | Roosevelt | 770,222 | *100.0* |
|---|---|---|---|---|---|

**May 16   New Jersey**

| Dewey | 17,393 | *86.2* | Roosevelt | 16,884 | *99.6* |
|---|---|---|---|---|---|
| Roosevelt [2] | 1,720 | *8.5* | Thomas E. Dewey (N.Y.) | 60 | *.4* |
| Willkie | 618 | *3.1* | | | |
| Bricker | 203 | *1.0* | | | |
| MacArthur | 129 | *.6* | | | |
| Stassen | 106 | *.5* | | | |

**May 19   Oregon**

| Dewey [2] | 50,001 | *78.2* | Roosevelt | 79,833 | *98.7* |
|---|---|---|---|---|---|
| Stassen [2] | 6,061 | *9.5* | Others | 1,057 | *1.3* |
| Willkie [2] | 3,333 | *5.2* | | | |
| Bricker [2] | 3,018 | *4.7* | | | |
| MacArthur [2] | 191 | *.3* | | | |
| Others | 1,340 | *2.1* | | | |

**TOTALS**

| MacArthur | 662,127 | *29.1* | Roosevelt | 1,324,006 | *70.9* |
|---|---|---|---|---|---|
| Warren | 594,439 | *26.2* | Unpledged delegates | 464,426 | *24.9* |
| Unpledged delegates | 539,575 | *23.8* | Linger | 59,282 | *3.2* |
| Dewey | 262,746 | *11.6* | Hildebrandt | 7,414 | *.4* |
| Stassen | 67,508 | *3.0* | Dewey | 60 | *—* |
| Christopherson | 33,497 | *1.5* | Others [9] | 12,421 | *.7* |
| Willkie | 27,097 | *1.2* | | | |
| Roosevelt | 10,535 | *.5* | | 1,867,609 | |
| Bricker | 6,305 | *.3* | | | |
| Martin | 2,406 | *.1* | | | |
| Dirksen | 581 | *—* | | | |
| Others [8] | 64,789 | *2.9* | | | |
| | 2,271,605 | | | | |

1. Nine unpledged and two Dewey delegates won the Republican primary, and Roosevelt delegates won the Democratic primary, according to Kravitz, op. cit., p. 12.
2. Write-in.
3. No primary.
4. The Montgomery Advertiser of May 3, 1944, reported that these delegates were pro-Roosevelt but uninstructed.
5. The New York Times of May 3, 1944, reported that a contest for delegates took place between supporters of Roosevelt and supporters of Sen. Harry F. Byrd (D Va.). A vote breakdown showing Roosevelt and Byrd strength is unavailable.

6. The winning Republican slate was pledged to Stassen, the losing Republican slate to Dewey and the two Democratic slates to Roosevelt, according to the office of the South Dakota secretary of state and Kravitz, op. cit., p. 12.
7. Bricker delegates won the Republican primary and Joseph T. Ferguson delegates won the Democratic primary, according to Kravitz, op. cit., p. 13.
8. In addition to scattered votes, "others" includes Riley A. Bender who received 37,575 votes in the Illinois primary and Joe H. Bottum who received 22,135 in the South Dakota primary.
9. In addition to scattered votes, "others" includes Powell who received 6,727 votes in the South Dakota primary.

# 1948 Primaries

| Republican | | | Democratic | | |
|---|---|---|---|---|---|
| | Votes | % | | Votes | % |

**March 9   New Hampshire**

| | | | | | |
|---|---|---|---|---|---|
| Unpledged delegates at large[1] | 28,854 | 100.0 | Unpledged delegates at large[1] | 4,409 | 100.0 |

**April 6   Wisconsin**

| | | | | | |
|---|---|---|---|---|---|
| Harold E. Stassen (Minn.) | 64,076 | 39.4 | Harry S Truman (Mo.) | 25,415 | 83.8 |
| Douglas MacArthur (Wis.) | 55,302 | 34.0 | Others | 4,906 | 16.2 |
| Thomas E. Dewey (N.Y.) | 40,943 | 25.2 | | | |
| Others | 2,429 | 1.5 | | | |

**April 13   Illinois**

| | | | | | |
|---|---|---|---|---|---|
| Riley A. Bender (Ill.) | 324,029 | 96.9 | Truman | 16,299 | 81.7 |
| MacArthur | 6,672 | 2.0 | Dwight D. Eisenhower (N.Y.) | 1,709 | 8.6 |
| Stassen | 1,572 | .5 | Scott Lucas (Ill.) | 427 | 2.1 |
| Dewey | 953 | .3 | Others[2] | 1,513 | 7.6 |
| Robert A. Taft (Ohio) | 705 | .2 | | | |
| Others[2] | 475 | .1 | | | |

**April 13   Nebraska**

| | | | | | |
|---|---|---|---|---|---|
| Stassen | 80,979 | 43.5 | Truman | 67,672 | 98.7 |
| Dewey | 64,242 | 34.5 | Others | 894 | 1.3 |
| Taft | 21,608 | 11.6 | | | |
| Arthur Vandenberg (Mich.) | 9,590 | 5.2 | | | |
| MacArthur | 6,893 | 3.7 | | | |
| Earl Warren (Calif.) | 1,761 | .9 | | | |
| Joseph W. Martin (Mass.) | 910 | .5 | | | |
| Others | 24 | — | | | |

**April 20   New Jersey[3]**

| | | | | | |
|---|---|---|---|---|---|
| Dewey | 3,714 | 41.4 | Truman | 1,100 | 92.5 |
| Stassen | 3,123 | 34.8 | Henry A. Wallace (Iowa) | 87 | 7.3 |
| MacArthur | 718 | 8.0 | Others | 2 | .2 |
| Vandenberg | 516 | 5.8 | | | |
| Taft | 495 | 5.5 | | | |
| Dwight D. Eisenhower (N.Y.) | 288 | 3.2 | | | |
| Joseph W. Martin | 64 | .7 | | | |
| Alfred E. Driscoll (N.J.) | 44 | — | | | |
| Warren | 14 | .2 | | | |

**April 27   Massachusetts**

| | | | | | |
|---|---|---|---|---|---|
| Unpledged delegates at large[4] | 72,191 | 100.0 | Unpledged delegates at large[4] | 51,207 | 100.0 |

**April 27   Pennsylvania**

| | | | | | |
|---|---|---|---|---|---|
| Stassen[2] | 81,242 | 31.5 | Truman | 328,891 | 96.0 |
| Dewey[2] | 76,988 | 29.8 | Eisenhower | 4,502 | 1.3 |
| Edward Martin (Pa.) | 45,072 | 17.5 | Wallace | 4,329 | 1.3 |
| MacArthur[2] | 18,254 | 7.1 | Harold E. Stassen (Minn.) | 1,301 | .4 |
| Taft[2] | 15,166 | 5.9 | Douglas MacArthur (Wis.) | 1,220 | .4 |
| Vandenberg | 8,818 | 3.4 | Others | 2,409 | .7 |
| Harry S Truman (Mo.) | 4,907 | 1.9 | | | |
| Eisenhower | 4,726 | 1.8 | | | |
| Henry A. Wallace (Iowa) | 1,452 | .6 | | | |
| Others | 1,537 | .6 | | | |

**May 4   Alabama**

| | | | | | |
|---|---|---|---|---|---|
| [5] | | | Unpledged delegates at large[6] | 161,629 | 100.0 |

## Republican

| | Votes | % |
|---|---|---|

## Democratic

| | Votes | % |
|---|---|---|

**May 4  Florida**

| Republican | Votes | % | Democratic | Votes | % |
|---|---|---|---|---|---|
| 5 | | | Others [7] | 92,169 | 100.0 |

**May 4  Ohio**

| Republican | Votes | % | Democratic | Votes | % |
|---|---|---|---|---|---|
| Unpledged delegates at large [8] | 426,767 | 100.0 | Unpledged delegates at large [8] | 271,146 | 100.0 |

**May 11  West Virginia**

| Republican | Votes | % | Democratic | Votes | % |
|---|---|---|---|---|---|
| Stassen | 110,775 | 83.2 | Unpledged delegates at large | 157,102 | 100.0 |
| Others | 22,410 | 16.8 | | | |

**May 21  Oregon**

| Republican | Votes | % | Democratic | Votes | % |
|---|---|---|---|---|---|
| Dewey | 117,554 | 51.8 | Truman | 112,962 | 93.8 |
| Stassen | 107,946 | 47.6 | Others | 7,436 | 6.2 |
| Others | 1,474 | .6 | | | |

**June 1  California**

| Republican | Votes | % | Democratic | Votes | % |
|---|---|---|---|---|---|
| Warren | 769,520 | 100.0 | Truman | 811,920 | 100.0 |

**June 1  South Dakota**

| Republican | Votes | % | Democratic | Votes | % |
|---|---|---|---|---|---|
| Hitchcock [9] | 45,463 | 100.0 | Truman [9] | 11,193 | 58.3 |
| | | | Unpledged Delegates [9] | 8,016 | 41.7 |

**TOTALS**

| Republican | Votes | % | Democratic | Votes | % |
|---|---|---|---|---|---|
| Warren | 771,295 | 29.1 | Truman | 1,375,452 | 63.9 |
| Unpledged delegates | 527,812 | 19.9 | Unpledged delegates | 653,509 | 30.4 |
| Stassen | 449,713 | 16.9 | Eisenhower | 6,211 | .3 |
| Bender | 324,029 | 12.2 | Wallace | 4,416 | .2 |
| Dewey | 304,394 | 11.5 | Stassen | 1,301 | .1 |
| MacArthur | 87,839 | 3.3 | MacArthur | 1,220 | .1 |
| Hitchcock | 45,463 | 1.7 | Lucas | 427 | — |
| Edward Martin | 45,072 | 1.7 | Others | 109,329 | 5.1 |
| Taft | 37,974 | 1.4 | | | |
| Vandenberg | 18,924 | .7 | | 2,151,865 | |
| Eisenhower | 5,014 | .2 | | | |
| Truman | 4,907 | .2 | | | |
| Wallace | 1,452 | .1 | | | |
| Joseph W. Martin | 974 | — | | | |
| Driscoll | 44 | — | | | |
| Others [10] | 28,349 | 1.1 | | | |
| | 2,653,255 | | | | |

1. Six unpledged and two Dewey delegates won in the Republican primary, and Truman delegates won in the Democratic primary, according to Kravitz, op. cit., p. 14.
2. Write-in.
3. Source: Kravitz, op. cit., p. 14.
4. The Boston Globe of April 28, 1948, reported that the Republican delegation was "generally unpledged" but was expected to support the "favorite son" candidacy of Sen. Leverett Saltonstall (R Mass.) on the first convention ballot. The Globe reported that Democratic delegates were presumed to favor Truman's nomination.
5. No primary.

6. Unpledged, anti-Truman slate, according to Kravitz, op. cit., p. 15.
7. Unpledged slate, according to Kravitz, ibid.
8. Taft won 44 delegates and Stassen nine in the Republican primary, and W.A. Julian won 55 delegates and Bixler one in the Democratic primary, according to Kravitz., ibid.
9. Republican delegates were unpledged, according to Kravitz, op. cit., p. 15. In the Democratic primary, according to Davis, p. 297, the slate led by South Dakota Democratic Party Chairman Lynn Fellows endorsed Truman and the slate headed by former Rep. Fred Hildebrandt (D S.D.) ran uninstructed.
10. In addition to scattered votes, "others" includes Byer who received 15,675 votes and Vander Pyl who received 6,735 votes in the West Virginia primary.

# 1952 Primaries

| Republican | Votes | % | Democratic | Votes | % |
|---|---|---|---|---|---|

**March 11  New Hampshire**

| | | | | | |
|---|---|---|---|---|---|
| Dwight D. Eisenhower (N.Y.) | 46,661 | 50.4 | Estes Kefauver (Tenn.) | 19,800 | 55.0 |
| Robert A. Taft (Ohio) | 35,838 | 38.7 | Harry S Truman (Mo.) | 15,927 | 44.2 |
| Harold E. Stassen (Minn.) | 6,574 | 7.1 | Douglas MacArthur (Wis.) | 151 | .4 |
| Douglas MacArthur (Wis.)[1] | 3,227 | 3.5 | James A. Farley (N.Y.) | 77 | .2 |
| Others | 230 | .3 | Adlai E. Stevenson (Ill.) | 40 | .1 |

**March 18  Minnesota**

| | | | | | |
|---|---|---|---|---|---|
| Stassen | 129,706 | 44.4 | Hubert H. Humphrey (Minn.) | 102,527 | 80.0 |
| Eisenhower[1] | 108,692 | 37.2 | Kefauver[1] | 20,182 | 15.8 |
| Taft[1] | 24,093 | 8.2 | Truman[1] | 3,634 | 2.8 |
| Earl Warren (Calif.)[1] | 5,365 | 1.8 | Dwight D. Eisenhower (N.Y.) | 1,753 | 1.4 |
| MacArthur[1] | 1,369 | .5 | | | |
| Estes Kefauver (Tenn.) | 386 | .1 | | | |
| Others | 22,712 | 7.8 | | | |

**April 1  Nebraska**

| | | | | | |
|---|---|---|---|---|---|
| Taft[1] | 79,357 | 36.2 | Kefauver | 64,531 | 60.3 |
| Eisenhower[1] | 66,078 | 30.1 | Robert S. Kerr (Okla.) | 42,467 | 39.7 |
| Stassen | 53,238 | 24.3 | | | |
| MacArthur[1] | 7,478 | 3.4 | | | |
| Warren[1] | 1,872 | .9 | | | |
| Others | 11,178 | 5.1 | | | |

**April 1  Wisconsin**

| | | | | | |
|---|---|---|---|---|---|
| Taft | 315,541 | 40.6 | Kefauver | 207,520 | 85.9 |
| Warren | 262,271 | 33.8 | Others | 34,005 | 14.1 |
| Stassen | 169,679 | 21.8 | | | |
| Others | 29,133 | 3.8 | | | |

**April 8  Illinois**

| | | | | | |
|---|---|---|---|---|---|
| Taft | 935,867 | 73.6 | Kefauver | 526,301 | 87.7 |
| Stassen | 155,041 | 12.2 | Stevenson | 54,336 | 9.1 |
| Eisenhower[1] | 147,518 | 11.6 | Truman | 9,024 | 1.5 |
| MacArthur[1] | 7,504 | .6 | Eisenhower | 6,655 | 1.1 |
| Warren | 2,841 | .2 | Others[1] | 3,798 | .6 |
| Others | 23,550 | 1.9 | | | |

**April 15  New Jersey**

| | | | | | |
|---|---|---|---|---|---|
| Eisenhower | 390,591 | 60.7 | Kefauver | 154,964 | 100.0 |
| Taft | 228,916 | 35.6 | | | |
| Stassen | 23,559 | 3.7 | | | |

**April 22  Pennsylvania**

| | | | | | |
|---|---|---|---|---|---|
| Eisenhower | 863,785 | 73.6 | Kefauver[1] | 93,160 | 53.3 |
| Taft[1] | 178,629 | 15.2 | Eisenhower[1] | 28,660 | 16.4 |
| Stassen | 120,305 | 10.3 | Truman[1] | 26,504 | 15.2 |
| MacArthur[1] | 6,028 | .5 | Robert A. Taft (Ohio) | 8,311 | 4.8 |
| Warren | 3,158 | .3 | Averell Harriman (N.Y.)[1] | 3,745 | 2.1 |
| Harry S Truman (Mo.) | 267 | — | Stevenson[1] | 3,678 | 2.1 |
| Others | 1,121 | .1 | Richard B. Russell (Ga.)[1] | 1,691 | 1.0 |
| | | | Others | 9,026 | 5.2 |

**April 29  Massachusetts**

| | | | | | |
|---|---|---|---|---|---|
| Eisenhower[1] | 254,898 | 69.8 | Kefauver | 29,287 | 55.7 |
| Taft[1] | 110,188 | 30.2 | Eisenhower | 16,007 | 30.5 |
| | | | Truman | 7,256 | 13.8 |

| | Republican | | | Democratic | | |
|---|---|---|---|---|---|---|
| | **Votes** | **%** | | | **Votes** | **%** |
| **May 5    Maryland**[2] | | | | | | |
| [3] | | | | Kefauver | 137,885 | 74.8 |
| | | | | Unpledged delegates | 46,361 | 25.2 |
| **May 6    Florida** | | | | | | |
| [3] | | | | Russell | 367,980 | 54.5 |
| | | | | Kefauver | 285,358 | 42.3 |
| | | | | Others | 21,296 | 3.2 |
| **May 6    Ohio** | | | | | | |
| Taft[4] | 663,791 | 78.8 | | Kefauver [4] | 305,992 | 62.3 |
| Stassen[4] | 178,739 | 21.2 | | Robert J. Bulkley (Ohio) [4] | 184,880 | 37.7 |
| **May 13    West Virginia** | | | | | | |
| Taft | 139,812 | 78.5 | | Unpledged delegates at large | 191,471 | 100.0 |
| Stassen | 38,251 | 21.5 | | | | |
| **May 16    Oregon** | | | | | | |
| Eisenhower | 172,486 | 64.6 | | Kefauver | 142,440 | 72.3 |
| Warren | 44,034 | 16.5 | | William O. Douglas (Wash.) | 29,532 | 15.0 |
| MacArthur | 18,603 | 7.0 | | Stevenson | 20,353 | 10.3 |
| Taft[1] | 18,009 | 6.7 | | Eisenhower[1] | 4,690 | 2.4 |
| Wayne L. Morse (Ore.) | 7,105 | 2.7 | | | | |
| Stassen | 6,610 | 2.5 | | | | |
| Others | 350 | .1 | | | | |
| **June 3    California** | | | | | | |
| Warren | 1,029,495 | 66.4 | | Kefauver | 1,155,839 | 70.4 |
| Thomas H. Werdel (Calif.) | 521,110 | 33.6 | | Edmund G. Brown (Calif.) | 485,578 | 29.6 |
| **June 3    South Dakota** | | | | | | |
| Taft | 64,695 | 50.3 | | Kefauver | 22,812 | 66.0 |
| Eisenhower | 63,879 | 49.7 | | Others [5] | 11,741 | 34.0 |
| **June 17    District of Columbia**[6] | | | | | | |
| [3] | | | | Harriman | 14,075 | 74.9 |
| | | | | Kefauver | 3,377 | 18.0 |
| | | | | Others[1] | 1,329 | 7.1 |
| **TOTALS** | | | | | | |
| Taft | 2,794,736 | 35.8 | | Kefauver | 3,169,448 | 64.3 |
| Eisenhower | 2,114,588 | 27.1 | | Brown | 485,578 | 9.9 |
| Warren | 1,349,036 | 17.3 | | Russell | 369,671 | 7.5 |
| Stassen | 881,702 | 11.3 | | Unpledged delegates | 237,832 | 4.8 |
| Werdel | 521,110 | 6.7 | | Bulkley | 184,880 | 3.8 |
| MacArthur | 44,209 | .6 | | Humphrey | 102,527 | 2.1 |
| Morse | 7,105 | .1 | | Stevenson | 78,583 | 1.6 |
| Kefauver | 386 | — | | Truman | 62,345 | 1.3 |
| Truman | 267 | — | | Eisenhower | 57,765 | 1.2 |
| Others | 88,274 | 1.1 | | Kerr | 42,467 | .9 |
| | | | | Douglas | 29,532 | .6 |
| | 7,801,413 | | | Harriman | 17,820 | .4 |
| | | | | Taft | 8,311 | .2 |
| | | | | MacArthur | 151 | — |
| | | | | Farley | 77 | — |
| | | | | Others[8] | 81,019 | 1.6 |
| | | | | | 4,928,006 | |

1. Write-in.
2. Source: Kravitz, op. cit., p. 18, and the office of the Maryland secretary of state.
3. No primary.
4. Delegate-at-large vote.
5. These delegates ran on an uninstructed slate, according to Kravitz, op. cit., p. 19.
6. Source: David, Moos, and Goldman, Nominating Politics in 1952, Vol. 2, p. 331-332.
7. In addition to scattered votes, "others" includes Schneider who received 230

received 10,411 in the Nebraska primary; Ritter who received 26,208 and Stearns who received 2,925 in the Wisconsin primary; Slettendahl who received 22,712 in the Minnesota primary and Riley Bender who received 22,321 votes in the Illinois primary.
8. In addition to scattered votes, "others" includes Fox who received 18,322 votes and Charles Broughton who received 15,683 votes in the Wisconsin primary; Compton who received 11,331 and Shaw who received 9,965 in the Florida primary.

# 1956 Primaries

| | Republican | | | Democratic | | |
|---|---|---|---|---|---|---|
| | Votes | % | | | Votes | % |
| **March 13 New Hampshire** | | | | | | |
| Dwight D. Eisenhower (Pa.) | 56,464 | 98.9 | Estes Kefauver (Tenn.) | | 21,701 | 84.6 |
| Others | 600 | 1.1 | Others | | 3,945 | 15.4 |
| **March 20 Minnesota** | | | | | | |
| Eisenhower | 198,111 | 98.4 | Kefauver | | 245,885 | 56.8 |
| William F. Knowland (Calif.) | 3,209 | 1.6 | Adlai E. Stevenson (Ill.) | | 186,723 | 43.2 |
| Others | 51 | — | Others | | 48 | — |
| **April 3 Wisconsin** | | | | | | |
| Eisenhower | 437,089 | 95.9 | Kefauver | | 330,665[1] | 100.0 |
| Others | 18,743 | 4.1 | | | | |
| **April 10 Illinois** | | | | | | |
| Eisenhower | 781,710 | 94.9 | Stevenson | | 717,742 | 95.3 |
| Knowland | 33,534 | 4.1 | Kefauver[2] | | 34,092 | 4.5 |
| Others | 8,455 | 1.0 | Others | | 1,640 | .2 |
| **April 17 New Jersey** | | | | | | |
| Eisenhower | 357,066 | 100.0 | Kefauver | | 117,056 | 95.7 |
| Others | 23 | — | Others | | 5,230 | 4.3 |
| **April 24 Alaska** (Territory) | | | | | | |
| Eisenhower | 8,291 | 94.4 | Stevenson | | 7,123 | 61.1 |
| Knowland | 488 | 5.6 | Kefauver | | 4,536 | 38.9 |
| **April 24 Massachusetts** | | | | | | |
| Eisenhower[2] | 51,951 | 95.1 | John W. McCormack (Mass.)[2] | | 26,128 | 47.9 |
| Adlai E. Stevenson (Ill.)[2] | 604 | 1.1 | Stevenson[2] | | 19,024 | 34.9 |
| Christian A. Herter (Mass.)[2] | 550 | 1.0 | Kefauver[2] | | 4,547 | 8.3 |
| Richard M. Nixon (N.Y.)[2] | 316 | .6 | Dwight D. Eisenhower (Pa.)[2] | | 1,850 | 3.4 |
| John W. McCormack (Mass.)[2] | 268 | .5 | John F. Kennedy (Mass.)[2] | | 949 | 1.7 |
| Knowland[2] | 250 | .5 | Averell Harriman (N.Y.)[2] | | 394 | .7 |
| Others[2] | 700 | 1.3 | Frank J. Lausche (Ohio)[2] | | 253 | .5 |
| | | | Others[2] | | 1,379 | 2.5 |
| **April 24 Pennsylvania** | | | | | | |
| Eisenhower | 951,932 | 95.5 | Stevenson | | 642,172 | 93.6 |
| Knowland | 43,508 | 4.4 | Kefauver[2] | | 36,552 | 5.3 |
| Others | 976 | .1 | Others | | 7,482 | 1.1 |
| **May 1 District of Columbia**[3] | | | | | | |
| Eisenhower | 18,101 | 100.0 | Stevenson | | 17,306 | 66.2 |
| | | | Kefauver | | 8,837 | 33.8 |
| **May 7 Maryland** | | | | | | |
| Eisenhower | 66,904 | 95.5 | Kefauver | | 112,768 | 65.9 |
| Unpledged delegates | 3,131 | 4.5 | Unpledged delegates | | 58,366 | 34.1 |
| **May 8 Indiana** | | | | | | |
| Eisenhower | 351,903 | 96.4 | Kefauver | | 242,842[1] | 100.0 |
| Others | 13,320 | 3.6 | | | | |

# Republican                                  # Democratic

|  | Votes | % |  | Votes | % |
|---|---|---|---|---|---|
| **May 8   Ohio** | | | | | |
| John W. Bricker (Ohio) | 478,453[1] | 100.0 | Lausche | 276,670[1] | 100.0 |
| **May 8   West Virginia** | | | | | |
| Unpledged delegates at large | 111,883[1] | 100.0 | Unpledged delegates at large | 112,832[1] | 100.0 |
| **May 15   Nebraska** | | | | | |
| Eisenhower | 102,576 | 99.8 | Kefauver | 55,265 | 94.0 |
| Others | 230 | .2 | Others | 3,556 | 6.0 |
| **May 18   Oregon** | | | | | |
| Eisenhower | 231,418[1] | 100.0 | Stevenson[2] | 98,131 | 60.2 |
|  | | | Kefauver[2] | 62,987 | 38.6 |
|  | | | Harriman[2] | 1,887 | 1.2 |
| **May 29   Florida** | | | | | |
| Eisenhower | 39,690 | 92.0 | Stevenson | 230,285 | 51.5 |
| Knowland | 3,457 | 8.0 | Kefauver | 216,549 | 48.5 |
| **June 5   California** | | | | | |
| Eisenhower | 1,354,764[1] | 100.0 | Stevenson | 1,139,964 | 62.6 |
|  | | | Kefauver | 680,722 | 37.4 |
| **June 5   Montana** | | | | | |
| S.C. Arnold[4] | 32,732 | 85.7 | Kefauver | 77,228[1] | 100.0 |
| Others | 5,447 | 14.3 | | | |
| **June 5   South Dakota** | | | | | |
| Unpledged delegates[5] | 59,374[1] | 100.0 | Kefauver | 30,940[1] | 100.0 |

| **TOTALS** | | | | | |
|---|---|---|---|---|---|
| Eisenhower | 5,007,970 | 85.9 | Stevenson | 3,051,347 | 52.3 |
| Bricker | 478,453 | 8.2 | Kefauver | 2,278,636 | 39.1 |
| Unpledged delegates | 174,388 | 3.0 | Lausche | 276,923 | 4.7 |
| Knowland | 84,446 | 1.4 | Unpledged delegates | 171,198 | 2.9 |
| S.C. Arnold | 32,732 | .6 | McCormack | 26,128 | .4 |
| Stevenson | 604 | — | Harriman | 2,281 | — |
| Herter | 550 | — | Eisenhower | 1,850 | — |
| Nixon | 316 | — | Kennedy | 949 | — |
| McCormack | 268 | — | Others | 23,280 | .4 |
| Others[6] | 48,545 | .8 | | | |
|  | 5,828,272 | | | 5,832,592 | |

1. *Figures obtained from Scammon's office. In* America Votes, *Scammon did not record vote totals if a candidate was unopposed or if the primary was strictly for delegate selection.*
2. *Write-in.*
3. *Source: Davis, op. cit., pp. 300-301.*
4. *Voters cast their ballots for S. C. Arnold, "stand-in" candidate for Eisenhower.*

5. *Slate unofficially pledged to Eisenhower but appeared on the ballot as "No preference."*
6. *In addition to scattered votes, "others" includes Lar Daly who received 8,364 votes in the Illinois primary, 13,320 votes in the Indiana primary and 5,447 votes in the Montana primary; and John Bowman Chapple who received 18,743 votes in the Wisconsin primary.*

# 1960 Primaries

| | Republican | | | Democratic | | |
|---|---|---|---|---|---|---|
| | Votes | % | | | Votes | % |

### March 8   New Hampshire

| | Republican | | | Democratic | | |
|---|---|---|---|---|---|---|
| Richard M. Nixon (N.Y.) | 65,204 | 89.3 | John F. Kennedy (Mass.) | | 43,372 | 85.2 |
| Nelson A. Rockefeller (N.Y.)[1] | 2,745 | 3.8 | Others | | 7,527 | 14.8 |
| John F. Kennedy (Mass.)[1] | 2,196 | 3.0 | | | | |
| Others | 2,886 | 4.0 | | | | |

### April 5   Wisconsin

| | Republican | | | Democratic | | |
|---|---|---|---|---|---|---|
| Nixon | 339,383[2] | 100.0 | Kennedy | | 476,024 | 56.5 |
| | | | Hubert H. Humphrey (Minn.) | | 366,753 | 43.5 |

### April 12   Illinois

| | Republican | | | Democratic | | |
|---|---|---|---|---|---|---|
| Nixon | 782,849[2] | 99.9 | Kennedy[1] | | 34,332 | 64.6 |
| Others[1] | 442[2] | .1 | Adlai E. Stevenson (Ill.)[1] | | 8,029 | 15.1 |
| | | | Stuart Symington (Mo.)[1] | | 5,744 | 10.8 |
| | | | Humphrey[1] | | 4,283 | 8.1 |
| | | | Lyndon B. Johnson (Texas)[1] | | 442 | .8 |
| | | | Others[1] | | 337 | .6 |

### April 19   New Jersey

| | Republican | | | Democratic | | |
|---|---|---|---|---|---|---|
| Unpledged delegates at large | 304,766[2] | 100.0 | Unpledged delegates at large | | 217,608[2] | 100.0 |

### April 26   Massachusetts

| | Republican | | | Democratic | | |
|---|---|---|---|---|---|---|
| Nixon[1] | 53,164 | 86.0 | Kennedy[1] | | 91,607 | 92.4 |
| Rockefeller[1] | 4,068 | 6.6 | Stevenson[1] | | 4,684 | 4.7 |
| Kennedy[1] | 2,989 | 4.8 | Humphrey[1] | | 794 | .8 |
| Henry Cabot Lodge (Mass.)[1] | 373 | .6 | Richard M. Nixon (Calif.)[1] | | 646 | .7 |
| Adlai E. Stevenson (Ill.)[1] | 266 | .4 | Symington[1] | | 443 | .4 |
| Barry Goldwater (Ariz.)[1] | 221 | .4 | Johnson[1] | | 268 | .3 |
| Dwight D. Eisenhower (Pa.)[1] | 172 | .3 | Others[1] | | 721 | .7 |
| Others[1] | 592 | 1.0 | | | | |

### April 26   Pennsylvania

| | Republican | | | Democratic | | |
|---|---|---|---|---|---|---|
| Nixon | 968,538 | 98.1 | Kennedy[1] | | 183,073 | 71.3 |
| Rockefeller[1] | 12,491 | 1.3 | Stevenson[1] | | 29,660 | 11.5 |
| Kennedy[1] | 3,886 | .4 | Nixon[1] | | 15,136 | 5.9 |
| Stevenson[1] | 428 | — | Humphrey[1] | | 13,860 | 5.4 |
| Goldwater[1] | 286 | — | Symington[1] | | 6,791 | 2.6 |
| Others[1] | 1,202 | .1 | Johnson[1] | | 2,918 | 1.1 |
| | | | Rockefeller[1] | | 1,078 | .4 |
| | | | Others[1] | | 4,297 | 1.7 |

### May 3   District of Columbia[3]

| | Republican | | | Democratic | | |
|---|---|---|---|---|---|---|
| Unpledged delegates | 9,468 | 100.0 | Humphrey | | 8,239 | 57.4 |
| | | | Wayne L. Morse (Ore.) | | 6,127 | 42.6 |

### May 3   Indiana

| | Republican | | | Democratic | | |
|---|---|---|---|---|---|---|
| Nixon | 408,408 | 95.4 | Kennedy | | 353,832 | 81.0 |
| Others | 19,677 | 4.6 | Others | | 82,937 | 19.0 |

### May 3   Ohio

| | Republican | | | Democratic | | |
|---|---|---|---|---|---|---|
| Nixon | 504,072[2] | 100.0 | Michael V. DiSalle (Ohio) | | 315,312[2] | 100.0 |

# Republican | Democratic

| | Votes | % | | Votes | % |
|---|---|---|---|---|---|
| **May 10   Nebraska** | | | | | |
| Nixon | 74,356 | 93.8 | Kennedy | 80,408 | 88.7 |
| Rockefeller[1] | 2,028 | 2.6 | Symington[1] | 4,083 | 4.5 |
| Goldwater[1] | 1,068 | 1.3 | Humphrey[1] | 3,202 | 3.5 |
| Others[1] | 1,805 | 2.3 | Stevenson[1] | 1,368 | 1.5 |
| | | | Johnson[1] | 962 | 1.1 |
| | | | Others[1] | 669 | .7 |
| **May 10   West Virginia** | | | | | |
| Unpledged delegates at large | 123,756[2] | 100.0 | Kennedy | 236,510 | 60.8 |
| | | | Humphrey | 152,187 | 39.2 |
| **May 17   Maryland** | | | | | |
| [4] | | | Kennedy | 201,769 | 70.3 |
| | | | Morse | 49,420 | 17.2 |
| | | | Unpledged delegates | 24,350 | 8.5 |
| | | | Others | 11,417 | 4.0 |
| **May 20   Oregon** | | | | | |
| Nixon | 211,276 | 93.1 | Kennedy | 146,332 | 51.0 |
| Rockefeller[1] | 9,307 | 4.1 | Morse | 91,715 | 31.9 |
| Kennedy[1] | 2,864 | 1.3 | Humphrey | 16,319 | 5.7 |
| Goldwater[1] | 1,571 | .7 | Symington | 12,496 | 4.4 |
| Others[1] | 2,015 | .9 | Johnson | 11,101 | 3.9 |
| | | | Stevenson[1] | 7,924 | 2.8 |
| | | | Others[1] | 1,210 | .4 |
| **May 24   Florida** | | | | | |
| Nixon | 51,036[2] | 100.0 | George A. Smathers (Fla.) | 322,235[2] | 100.0 |
| **June 7   California** | | | | | |
| Nixon | 1,517,652[2] | 100.0 | Edmund G. Brown (Calif.) | 1,354,031 | 67.7 |
| | | | George H. McLain (Calif.) | 646,387 | 32.3 |
| **June 7   South Dakota** | | | | | |
| Unpledged delegates | 48,461[2] | 100.0 | Humphrey | 24,773[2] | 100.0 |
| **TOTALS** | | | | | |
| Nixon | 4,975,938 | 89.9 | Kennedy | 1,847,259 | 32.5 |
| Unpledged delegates | 486,451 | 8.8 | Brown | 1,354,031 | 23.8 |
| Rockefeller | 30,639 | .6 | McLain | 646,387 | 11.4 |
| Kennedy | 11,935 | .2 | Humphrey | 590,410 | 10.4 |
| Goldwater | 3,146 | .1 | Smathers | 322,235 | 5.7 |
| Stevenson | 694 | — | DiSalle | 315,312 | 5.5 |
| Lodge | 373 | — | Unpledged delegates | 241,958 | 4.3 |
| Eisenhower | 172 | — | Morse | 147,262 | 2.6 |
| Others[5] | 28,619 | .5 | Stevenson | 51,665 | .9 |
| | | | Symington | 29,557 | .5 |
| | 5,537,967 | | Nixon | 15,782 | .3 |
| | | | Johnson | 15,691 | .3 |
| | | | Others[6] | 110,192 | 1.9 |
| | | | | 5,687,742 | |

1. Write-in.
2. Figures obtained from Scammon's office. In America Votes, Scammon did not record vote totals if a candidate was unopposed or if the primary was strictly for delegate selection.
3. Source: District of Columbia Board of Elections.
4. No primary.
5. In addition to scattered votes, "others" includes Paul C. Fisher who received 2,388 votes in the New Hampshire primary and Frank R. Beckwith who received 19,677 in the Indiana primary.
6. In addition to scattered votes, "others" includes Lar Daly who received 40,853 votes in the Indiana primary and 7,536 in the Maryland primary; Paul C. Fisher who received 6,853 votes in the New Hampshire primary; John H. Latham who received 42,084 in the Indiana primary and Andrew J. Easter who received 3,881 votes in the Maryland primary.

# 1964 Primaries

| Republican | Votes | % | Democratic | Votes | % |
|---|---|---|---|---|---|

**March 10   New Hampshire**

| | | | | | |
|---|---|---|---|---|---|
| Henry Cabot Lodge (Mass.)[1] | 33,007 | 35.5 | Lyndon B. Johnson (Texas)[1] | 29,317 | 95.3 |
| Barry M. Goldwater (Ariz.) | 20,692 | 22.3 | Robert F. Kennedy (N.Y.)[1] | 487 | 1.6 |
| Nelson A. Rockefeller (N.Y.) | 19,504 | 21.0 | Henry Cabot Lodge (Mass.)* | 280 | .9 |
| Richard M. Nixon (Calif.)[1] | 15,587 | 16.8 | Richard M. Nixon (Calif.)[1] | 232 | .8 |
| Margaret Chase Smith (Maine) | 2,120 | 2.3 | Barry M. Goldwater (Ariz.)[1] | 193 | .6 |
| Harold E. Stassen (Pa.) | 1,373 | 1.5 | Nelson A. Rockefeller (N.Y.)[1] | 109 | .4 |
| William W. Scranton (Pa.)[1] | 105 | .1 | Others[1] | 159 | .5 |
| Others | 465 | .5 | | | |

**April 7   Wisconsin**

| | | | | | |
|---|---|---|---|---|---|
| John W. Byrnes (Wis.) | 299,612 | 99.7 | John W. Reynolds (Wis.) | 522,405 | 66.2 |
| Unpledged delegate | 816 | .3 | George C. Wallace (Ala.) | 266,136 | 33.8 |

**April 14   Illinois**

| | | | | | |
|---|---|---|---|---|---|
| Goldwater | 512,840 | 62.0 | Johnson[1] | 82,027 | 91.6 |
| Smith | 209,521 | 25.3 | Wallace[1] | 3,761 | 4.2 |
| Henry Cabot Lodge[1] | 68,122 | 8.2 | Robert F. Kennedy[1] | 2,894 | 3.2 |
| Nixon[1] | 30,313 | 3.7 | Others[1] | 841 | .9 |
| George C. Wallace (Ala.)[1] | 2,203 | .3 | | | |
| Rockefeller[1] | 2,048 | .2 | | | |
| Scranton[1] | 1,842 | .2 | | | |
| George W. Romney (Mich.)[1] | 465 | .1 | | | |
| Others[1] | 437 | .1 | | | |

**April 21   New Jersey**

| | | | | | |
|---|---|---|---|---|---|
| Henry Cabot Lodge[1] | 7,896 | 41.7 | Johnson[1] | 4,863 | 82.3 |
| Goldwater[1] | 5,309 | 28.0 | Wallace[1] | 491 | 8.3 |
| Nixon[1] | 4,179 | 22.1 | Robert F. Kennedy[1] | 431 | 7.3 |
| Scranton[1] | 633 | 3.3 | Others[1] | 124 | 2.1 |
| Rockefeller[1] | 612 | 3.2 | | | |
| Others[1] | 304 | 1.6 | | | |

**April 28   Massachusetts**

| | | | | | |
|---|---|---|---|---|---|
| Henry Cabot Lodge[1] | 70,809 | 76.9 | Johnson[1] | 61,035 | 73.4 |
| Goldwater[1] | 9,338 | 10.1 | Robert F. Kennedy[1] | 15,870 | 19.1 |
| Nixon[1] | 5,460 | 5.9 | Lodge[1] | 2,269 | 2.7 |
| Rockefeller[1] | 2,454 | 2.7 | Edward M. Kennedy (Mass.)[1] | 1,259 | 1.5 |
| Scranton[1] | 1,709 | 1.9 | Wallace[1] | 565 | .7 |
| Lyndon B. Johnson (Texas)[1] | 600 | .7 | Adlai E. Stevenson (Ill.)[1] | 452 | .5 |
| Smith[1] | 426 | .5 | Hubert H. Humphrey (Minn.)[1] | 323 | .4 |
| George C. Lodge (Mass.)[1] | 365 | .4 | Others[1] | 1,436 | 1.7 |
| Romney[1] | 262 | .3 | | | |
| Others[1] | 711 | .8 | | | |

**April 28   Pennsylvania**

| | | | | | |
|---|---|---|---|---|---|
| Scranton[1] | 235,222 | 51.9 | Johnson[1] | 209,606 | 82.8 |
| Henry Cabot Lodge[1] | 92,712 | 20.5 | Wallace[1] | 12,104 | 4.8 |
| Nixon[1] | 44,396 | 9.8 | Robert F. Kennedy[1] | 12,029 | 4.8 |
| Goldwater[1] | 38,669 | 8.5 | William W. Scranton (Pa.)[1] | 8,156 | 3.2 |
| Johnson[1] | 22,372 | 4.9 | Lodge[1] | 4,895 | 1.9 |
| Rockefeller[1] | 9,123 | 2.0 | Others[1] | 6,438 | 2.5 |
| Wallace[1] | 5,105 | 1.1 | | | |
| Others[1] | 5,269 | 1.2 | | | |

**May 2   Texas**

| | | | | | |
|---|---|---|---|---|---|
| Goldwater | 104,137 | 74.7 | [2] | | |
| Henry Cabot Lodge[1] | 12,324 | 8.8 | | | |
| Rockefeller | 6,207 | 4.5 | | | |
| Nixon[1] | 5,390 | 3.9 | | | |
| Stassen | 5,273 | 3.8 | | | |
| Smith | 4,816 | 3.5 | | | |
| Scranton[1] | 803 | .6 | | | |
| Others[1] | 373 | .3 | | | |

## Republican

## Democratic

| | Votes | % | | Votes | % |
|---|---|---|---|---|---|
| **May 5  District of Columbia**[3] | | | | | |
| [3] | | | Unpledged delegates | 41,095 | 100.0 |
| **May 5  Indiana** | | | | | |
| Goldwater | 267,935 | 67.0 | Matthew E. Welsh (Ind.) | 376,023 | 64.9 |
| Stassen | 107,157 | 26.8 | Wallace | 172,646 | 29.8 |
| Others | 24,588 | 6.2 | Others | 30,367 | 5.2 |
| **May 5  Ohio** | | | | | |
| James A. Rhodes (Ohio) | 615,754[4] | 100.0 | Albert S. Porter (Ohio) | 493,619[4] | 100.0 |
| **May 12  Nebraska** | | | | | |
| Goldwater | 68,050 | 49.1 | Johnson[1] | 54,713 | 89.3 |
| Nixon[1] | 43,613 | 31.5 | Robert F. Kennedy[1] | 2,099 | 3.4 |
| Henry Cabot Lodge[1] | 22,622 | 16.3 | Wallace[1] | 1,067 | 1.7 |
| Rockefeller[1] | 2,333 | 1.7 | Lodge[1] | 1,051 | 1.7 |
| Scranton[1] | 578 | .4 | Nixon[1] | 833 | 1.4 |
| Johnson[1] | 316 | .2 | Goldwater[1] | 603 | 1.0 |
| Others[1] | 1,010 | .7 | Others[1] | 904 | 1.5 |
| **May 12  West Virginia** | | | | | |
| Rockefeller | 115,680[4] | 100.0 | Unpledged delegates at large | 131,432[4] | 100.0 |
| **May 15  Oregon** | | | | | |
| Rockefeller | 94,190 | 33.0 | Johnson | 272,099[4] | 99.5 |
| Henry Cabot Lodge | 79,169 | 27.7 | Wallace[1] | 1,365[4] | .5 |
| Goldwater | 50,105 | 17.6 | | | |
| Nixon | 48,274 | 16.9 | | | |
| Smith | 8,087 | 2.8 | | | |
| Scranton | 4,509 | 1.6 | | | |
| Others | 1,152 | .4 | | | |
| **May 19  Maryland** | | | | | |
| Unpledged delegates | 57,004 | 58.2 | Daniel B. Brewster (Md.) | 267,106 | 53.1 |
| Others | 40,994 | 41.8 | Wallace | 214,849 | 42.7 |
| | | | Unpledged delegates | 12,377 | 2.5 |
| | | | Others | 8,275 | 1.6 |
| **May 26  Florida** | | | | | |
| Unpledged delegates | 58,179 | 57.8 | Johnson | 393,339[4] | 100.0 |
| Goldwater | 42,525 | 42.2 | | | |
| **June 2  California** | | | | | |
| Goldwater | 1,120,403 | 51.6 | Unpledged delegates[5] | 1,693,813 | 68.0 |
| Rockefeller | 1,052,053 | 48.4 | Unpledged delegates[5] | 798,431 | 32.0 |
| **June 2  South Dakota** | | | | | |
| Unpledged delegates | 57,653 | 68.0 | Unpledged delegates | 28,142[4] | 100.0 |
| Goldwater | 27,076 | 32.0 | | | |

# Republican

# Democratic

**TOTALS**

| Republican | | | Democratic | | |
|---|---:|---:|---|---:|---:|
| Goldwater | 2,267,079 | 38.2 | Unpledged delegates | 2,705,290 | 43.3 |
| Rockefeller | 1,304,204 | 22.0 | Johnson | 1,106,999 | 17.7 |
| Rhodes | 615,754 | 10.4 | Wallace | 672,984 | 10.8 |
| Henry Cabot Lodge | 386,661 | 6.5 | Reynolds | 522,405 | 8.4 |
| Byrnes | 299,612 | 5.0 | Porter | 493,619 | 7.9 |
| Scranton | 245,401 | 4.1 | Welsh | 376,023 | 6.0 |
| Smith | 224,970 | 3.8 | Brewster | 267,106 | 4.3 |
| Nixon | 197,212 | 3.3 | Robert F. Kennedy | 33,810 | .5 |
| Unpledged delegates | 173,652 | 2.9 | Henry Cabot Lodge | 8,495 | .1 |
| Stassen | 113,803 | 1.9 | Scranton | 8,156 | .1 |
| Johnson | 23,288 | .4 | Edward M. Kennedy | 1,259 | — |
| Wallace | 7,308 | .1 | Nixon | 1,065 | — |
| Romney | 727 | — | Goldwater | 796 | — |
| George C. Lodge | 365 | — | Stevenson | 452 | — |
| Others[6] | 75,303 | 1.3 | Humphrey | 323 | — |
| | | | Rockefeller | 109 | — |
| | | | Others[7] | 48,544 | .8 |
| | 5,935,339 | | | 6,247,435 | |

1. Write-in.
2. No primary authorized.
3. Source: *District of Columbia Board of Elections. No figures available for vote for delegates to Republican convention.*
4. *Figures obtained from Scammon's office. In* America Votes, *Scammon did not record vote totals if a candidate was unopposed or if the primary was strictly for delegate selection.*
5. *Gov. Edmund G. Brown (D Calif.) headed the winning slate of delegates and Mayor Sam Yorty of Los Angeles headed the losing slate.*

6. *In addition to scattered votes, "others" includes Norman LePage who received 82 votes in the New Hampshire primary; Frank R. Beckwith who received 17,884 votes and Joseph G. Ettl who received 6,704 votes in the Indiana primary; John W. Steffey who received 22,135 votes and Robert E. Ennis who received 18,859 votes in the Maryland primary.*
7. *In addition to scattered votes, "others" includes Lar Daly who received 15,160 votes, John H. Latham who received 8,067 votes and Fay T. Carpenter Swain who received 7,140 votes in the Indiana primary; and Andrew J. Easter who received 8,275 votes in the Maryland primary.*

# 1968 Primaries*

| | Republican | | | Democratic | |
|---|---|---|---|---|---|
| | Votes | % | | Votes | % |

## March 12  New Hampshire

| | Votes | % | | Votes | % |
|---|---|---|---|---|---|
| Richard M. Nixon (N.Y.) | 80,666 | 77.6 | Lyndon B. Johnson (Texas)[1] | 27,520 | 49.6 |
| Nelson A. Rockefeller (N.Y.)[1] | 11,241 | 10.8 | Eugene J. McCarthy (Minn.) | 23,263 | 41.9 |
| Eugene J. McCarthy (Minn.)[1] | 5,511 | 5.3 | Richard M. Nixon (N.Y.)[1] | 2,532 | 4.6 |
| Lyndon B. Johnson (Texas)[1] | 1,778 | 1.7 | Others | 2,149 | 3.9 |
| George W. Romney (Mich.) | 1,743 | 1.7 | | | |
| Harold E. Stassen (Pa.) | 429 | .4 | | | |
| Others | 2,570 | 2.5 | | | |

## April 2  Wisconsin

| | Votes | % | | Votes | % |
|---|---|---|---|---|---|
| Nixon | 390,368 | 79.7 | McCarthy | 412,160 | 56.2 |
| Ronald Reagan (Calif.) | 50,727 | 10.4 | Johnson | 253,696 | 34.6 |
| Stassen | 28,531 | 5.8 | Robert F. Kennedy (N.Y.)[1] | 46,507 | 6.3 |
| Rockefeller[1] | 7,995 | 1.6 | Unpledged delegates | 11,861 | 1.6 |
| Unpledged delegates | 6,763 | 1.4 | George C. Wallace (Ala.)[1] | 4,031 | .5 |
| Romney[1] | 2,087 | .4 | Hubert H. Humphrey (Minn.)[1] | 3,605 | .5 |
| Others | 3,382 | .7 | Others | 1,142 | .2 |

## April 23  Pennsylvania

| | Votes | % | | Votes | % |
|---|---|---|---|---|---|
| Nixon[1] | 171,815 | 59.7 | McCarthy | 428,259 | 71.7 |
| Rockefeller[1] | 52,915 | 18.4 | Robert F. Kennedy[1] | 65,430 | 11.0 |
| McCarthy[1] | 18,800 | 6.5 | Humphrey[1] | 51,998 | 8.7 |
| George C. Wallace (Ala.)[1] | 13,290 | 4.6 | Wallace[1] | 24,147 | 4.0 |
| Robert F. Kennedy (N.Y.)[1] | 10,431 | 3.6 | Johnson[1] | 21,265 | 3.6 |
| Reagan[1] | 7,934 | 2.8 | Nixon[1] | 3,434 | .6 |
| Hubert H. Humphrey (Minn.)[1] | 4,651 | 1.6 | Others[1] | 2,556 | .4 |
| Johnson[1] | 3,027 | 1.1 | | | |
| Raymond P. Shafer (Pa.)[1] | 1,223 | .4 | | | |
| Others[1] | 3,487 | 1.2 | | | |

## April 30  Massachusetts

| | Votes | % | | Votes | % |
|---|---|---|---|---|---|
| Rockefeller[1] | 31,964 | 30.0 | McCarthy | 122,697 | 49.3 |
| John A. Volpe (Mass.) | 31,465 | 29.5 | Robert F. Kennedy[1] | 68,604 | 27.6 |
| Nixon[1] | 27,447 | 25.8 | Humphrey[1] | 44,156 | 17.7 |
| McCarthy[1] | 9,758 | 9.2 | Johnson[1] | 6,890 | 2.8 |
| Reagan[1] | 1,770 | 1.7 | Nelson A. Rockefeller (N.Y.)[1] | 2,275 | 1.0 |
| Kennedy[1] | 1,184 | 1.1 | Wallace[1] | 1,688 | .7 |
| Others[1] | 2,933 | 2.8 | Others[1] | 2,593 | 1.0 |

## May 7  District of Columbia

| | Votes | % | | Votes | % |
|---|---|---|---|---|---|
| Nixon-Rockefeller[2] | 12,102 | 90.1 | Robert F. Kennedy[3] | 57,555 | 62.5 |
| Unpledged delegates[2] | 1,328 | 9.9 | Humphrey[3] | 32,309 | 35.1 |
| | | | Humphrey[3] | 2,250 | 2.4 |

## May 7  Indiana

| | Votes | % | | Votes | % |
|---|---|---|---|---|---|
| Nixon | 508,362[4] | 100.0 | Robert F. Kennedy | 328,118 | 42.3 |
| | | | Roger D. Branigin (Ind.) | 238,700 | 30.7 |
| | | | McCarthy | 209,695 | 27.0 |

## May 7  Ohio

| | Votes | % | | Votes | % |
|---|---|---|---|---|---|
| James A. Rhodes (Ohio) | 614,492[4] | 100.0 | Stephen M. Young (Ohio) | 549,140[4] | 100.0 |

## Republican

## Democratic

| May 14 | **Nebraska**[5] | | | | | |
|---|---|---|---|---|---|---|
| Nixon | 140,336 | *70.0* | Robert F. Kennedy | 84,102 | *51.7* |
| Reagan | 42,703 | *21.3* | McCarthy | 50,655 | *31.2* |
| Rockefeller[1] | 10,225 | *5.1* | Humphrey[1] | 12,087 | *7.4* |
| Stassen | 2,638 | *1.3* | Johnson | 9,187 | *5.6* |
| McCarthy[1] | 1,544 | *.8* | Nixon[1] | 2,731 | *1.7* |
| Others | 3,030 | *1.5* | Ronald Reagan (Calif.)[1] | 1,905 | *1.2* |
| | | | Wallace[1] | 1,298 | *.8* |
| | | | Others | 646 | *.4* |

| May 14 | **West Virginia** | | | | |
|---|---|---|---|---|---|
| Unpledged delegates at large | 81,039[4] | *100.0* | Unpledged delegates at large | 149,282[4] | *100.0* |

| May 28 | **Florida** | | | | |
|---|---|---|---|---|---|
| Unpledged delegates | 51,509[4] | *100.0* | George A. Smathers (Fla.) | 236,242 | *46.1* |
| | | | McCarthy | 147,216 | *28.7* |
| | | | Unpledged delegates | 128,899 | *25.2* |

| May 28 | **Oregon** | | | | |
|---|---|---|---|---|---|
| Nixon | 203,037 | *65.0* | McCarthy | 163,990 | *44.0* |
| Reagan | 63,707 | *20.4* | Robert F. Kennedy | 141,631 | *38.0* |
| Rockefeller[1] | 36,305 | *11.6* | Johnson | 45,174 | *12.1* |
| McCarthy[1] | 7,387 | *2.4* | Humphrey[1] | 12,421 | *3.3* |
| Kennedy[1] | 1,723 | *.6* | Reagan[1] | 3,082 | *.8* |
| | | | Nixon[1] | 2,974 | *.8* |
| | | | Rockefeller[1] | 2,841 | *.8* |
| | | | Wallace[1] | 957 | *.3* |

| June 4 | **California** | | | | |
|---|---|---|---|---|---|
| Reagan | 1,525,091[4] | *100.0* | Robert F. Kennedy | 1,472,166 | *46.3* |
| | | | McCarthy | 1,329,301 | *41.8* |
| | | | Unpledged delegates | 380,286 | *12.0* |

| June 4 | **New Jersey** | | | | |
|---|---|---|---|---|---|
| Nixon[1] | 71,809 | *81.1* | McCarthy[1] | 9,906 | *36.1* |
| Rockefeller[1] | 11,530 | *13.0* | Robert F. Kennedy[1] | 8,603 | *31.3* |
| Reagan[1] | 2,737 | *3.1* | Humphrey[1] | 5,578 | *20.3* |
| McCarthy[1] | 1,358 | *1.5* | Wallace[1] | 1,399 | *5.1* |
| Others[1] | 1,158 | *1.3* | Nixon[1] | 1,364 | *5.0* |
| | | | Others[1] | 596 | *2.2* |

| June 4 | **South Dakota** | | | | |
|---|---|---|---|---|---|
| Nixon | 68,113[4] | *100.0* | Robert F. Kennedy | 31,826 | *49.5* |
| | | | Johnson | 19,316 | *30.0* |
| | | | McCarthy | 13,145 | *20.4* |

| June 11 | **Illinois** | | | | |
|---|---|---|---|---|---|
| Nixon[1] | 17,490 | *78.1* | McCarthy[1] | 4,646 | *38.6* |
| Rockefeller[1] | 2,165 | *9.7* | Edward M. Kennedy (Mass.)[1] | 4,052 | *33.7* |
| Reagan[1] | 1,601 | *7.1* | Humphrey[1] | 2,059 | *17.1* |
| Others[1] | 1,147 | *5.1* | Others[1] | 1,281 | *10.6* |

## Republican

| | Votes | % |
|---|---|---|
| Reagan | 1,696,270 | 37.9 |
| Nixon | 1,679,443 | 37.5 |
| Rhodes | 614,492 | 13.7 |
| Rockefeller | 164,340 | 3.7 |
| Unpledged delegates | 140,639 | 3.1 |
| McCarthy | 44,358 | 1.0 |
| Stassen | 31,598 | .7 |
| Volpe | 31,465 | .7 |
| Robert F. Kennedy | 13,338 | .3 |
| Wallace | 13,290 | .3 |
| Nixon-Rockefeller[2] | 12,102 | .3 |
| Johnson | 4,805 | .1 |
| Humphrey | 4,651 | .1 |
| Romney | 3,830 | .1 |
| Shafer | 1,223 | — |
| Others[6] | 17,707 | .4 |
| | 4,473,551 | |

## Democratic

| | Votes | % |
|---|---|---|
| McCarthy | 2,914,933 | 38.7 |
| Robert F. Kennedy | 2,304,542 | 30.6 |
| Unpledged delegates | 670,328 | 8.9 |
| Young | 549,140 | 7.3 |
| Johnson | 383,048 | 5.1 |
| Branigin | 238,700 | 3.2 |
| Smathers | 236,242 | 3.1 |
| Humphrey | 166,463 | 2.2 |
| Wallace | 33,520 | .4 |
| Nixon | 13,035 | .2 |
| Rockefeller | 5,116 | .1 |
| Reagan | 4,987 | .1 |
| Edward M. Kennedy | 4,052 | .1 |
| Others[7] | 10,963 | .1 |
| | 7,535,069 | |

---

* Delegate selection primaries were held in Alabama and New York. In America Votes, Scammon did not record vote totals if the primary was strictly for delegate selection and there was no presidential preference voting.

1. Write-in.

2. Prior to the primary, the District Republican organization agreed to divide the nine delegate votes, with six going to Nixon and three going to Rockefeller, according to the 1968 Congressional Quarterly Almanac, Vol. XXIV. Figures obtained from Scammon's office.

3. Figures obtained from Scammon's office. Two slates favored Humphrey; a member of an "independent" Humphrey slate received 2,250 votes.

4. Figures obtained from Scammon's office. In America Votes, Scammon did not record vote totals if a candidate was unopposed or if the primary was strictly for delegate selection.

5. In the American Party presidential primary, Wallace received 493 of the 504 votes cast, or 97.8% of the vote, according to the office of the Nebraska secretary of state.

6. In addition to scattered votes, "others includes Willis E. Stone who received 527 votes, Herbert F. Hoover who received 247 votes, David Watumull who received 161 votes, William W. Evans who received 151 votes, Elmer W. Coy who received 73 votes and Don DuMont who received 39 votes in the New Hampshire primary; and Americus Liberator who received 1,302 votes in the Nebraska primary.

7. In addition to scattered votes, "others" includes John G. Crommelin who received 186 votes, Richard E. Lee who received 170 votes and Jacob J. Gordon who received 77 votes in the New Hampshire primary.

# 1972 Primaries*

| Republican | Votes | % | Democratic | Votes | % |
|---|---|---|---|---|---|

### March 7 New Hampshire

| Republican | Votes | % | Democratic | Votes | % |
|---|---|---|---|---|---|
| Richard M. Nixon (Calif.) | 79,239 | 67.6 | Edmund S. Muskie (Maine) | 41,235 | 46.4 |
| Paul N. McCloskey (Calif.) | 23,190 | 19.8 | George S. McGovern (S.D.) | 33,007 | 37.1 |
| John M. Ashbrook (Ohio) | 11,362 | 9.7 | Sam Yorty (Calif.) | 5,401 | 6.1 |
| Others | 3,417 | 2.9 | Wilbur D. Mills (Ark.)[1] | 3,563 | 4.0 |
| | | | Vance Hartke (Ind.) | 2,417 | 2.7 |
| | | | Edward M. Kennedy (Mass.)[1] | 954 | 1.1 |
| | | | Hubert H. Humphrey (Minn.)[1] | 348 | .4 |
| | | | Henry M. Jackson (Wash.)[1] | 197 | .2 |
| | | | George C. Wallace (Ala.)[1] | 175 | .2 |
| | | | Others | 1,557 | 1.8 |

### March 14 Florida

| Republican | Votes | % | Democratic | Votes | % |
|---|---|---|---|---|---|
| Nixon | 360,278 | 87.0 | Wallace | 526,651 | 41.6 |
| Ashbrook | 36,617 | 8.8 | Humphrey | 234,658 | 18.6 |
| McCloskey | 17,312 | 4.2 | Jackson | 170,156 | 13.5 |
| | | | Muskie | 112,523 | 8.9 |
| | | | John V. Lindsay (N.Y.) | 82,386 | 6.5 |
| | | | McGovern | 78,232 | 6.2 |
| | | | Shirley Chisholm (N.Y.) | 43,989 | 3.5 |
| | | | Eugene J. McCarthy (Minn.) | 5,847 | .5 |
| | | | Mills | 4,539 | .4 |
| | | | Hartke | 3,009 | .2 |
| | | | Yorty | 2,564 | .2 |

### March 21 Illinois

| Republican | Votes | % | Democratic | Votes | % |
|---|---|---|---|---|---|
| Nixon[1] | 32,550 | 97.0 | Muskie | 766,914 | 62.6 |
| Ashbrook[1] | 170 | .5 | McCarthy | 444,260 | 36.3 |
| McCloskey[1] | 47 | .1 | Wallace[1] | 7,017 | .6 |
| Others[1] | 802 | 2.4 | McGovern[1] | 3,687 | .3 |
| | | | Humphrey[1] | 1,476 | .1 |
| | | | Chisholm[1] | 777 | .1 |
| | | | Jackson[1] | 442 | — |
| | | | Kennedy[1] | 242 | — |
| | | | Lindsay[1] | 118 | — |
| | | | Others | 211 | — |

### April 4 Wisconsin

| Republican | Votes | % | Democratic | Votes | % |
|---|---|---|---|---|---|
| Nixon | 277,601 | 96.9 | McGovern | 333,528 | 29.6 |
| McCloskey | 3,651 | 1.3 | Wallace | 248,676 | 22.0 |
| Ashbrook | 2,604 | .9 | Humphrey | 233,748 | 20.7 |
| None of the names shown | 2,315 | .8 | Muskie | 115,811 | 10.3 |
| Others | 273 | .1 | Jackson | 88,068 | 7.8 |
| | | | Lindsay | 75,579 | 6.7 |
| | | | McCarthy | 15,543 | 1.4 |
| | | | Chisholm | 9,198 | .8 |
| | | | None of the names shown | 2,450 | .2 |
| | | | Yorty | 2,349 | .2 |
| | | | Patsy T. Mink (Hawaii) | 1,213 | .1 |
| | | | Mills | 913 | .1 |
| | | | Hartke | 766 | .1 |
| | | | Kennedy[1] | 183 | — |
| | | | Others | 559 | — |

# Republican                                                     # Democratic

|  | Votes | % |  | Votes | % |
|---|---|---|---|---|---|

### April 25  **Massachusetts**

| | | | | | |
|---|---|---|---|---|---|
| Nixon | 99,150 | 81.2 | McGovern | 325,673 | 52.7 |
| McCloskey | 16,435 | 13.5 | Muskie | 131,709 | 21.3 |
| Ashbrook | 4,864 | 4.0 | Humphrey | 48,929 | 7.9 |
| Others | 1,690 | 1.4 | Wallace | 45,807 | 7.4 |
| | | | Chisholm | 22,398 | 3.6 |
| | | | Mills | 19,441 | 3.1 |
| | | | McCarthy | 8,736 | 1.4 |
| | | | Jackson | 8,499 | 1.4 |
| | | | Kennedy[1] | 2,348 | .4 |
| | | | Lindsay | 2,107 | .3 |
| | | | Hartke | 874 | .1 |
| | | | Yorty | 646 | .1 |
| | | | Others | 1,349 | .2 |

### April 25  **Pennsylvania**

| | | | | | |
|---|---|---|---|---|---|
| Nixon[1] | 153,886 | 83.3 | Humphrey | 481,900 | 35.1 |
| George C. Wallace (Ala.)[1] | 20,472 | 11.1 | Wallace | 292,437 | 21.3 |
| Others[1] | 10,443 | 5.7 | McGovern | 280,861 | 20.4 |
| | | | Muskie | 279,983 | 20.4 |
| | | | Jackson | 38,767 | 2.8 |
| | | | Chisholm[1] | 306 | — |
| | | | Others | 585 | — |

### May 2  **District of Columbia**

| | | | | | |
|---|---|---|---|---|---|
| [2] | | | Walter E. Fauntroy (D.C.) | 21,217 | 71.8 |
| | | | Unpledged delegates | 8,343 | 28.2 |

### May 2  **Indiana**

| | | | | | |
|---|---|---|---|---|---|
| Nixon | 417,069 | 100.0 | Humphrey | 354,244 | 47.1 |
| | | | Wallace | 309,495 | 41.2 |
| | | | Muskie | 87,719 | 11.7 |

### May 2  **Ohio**

| | | | | | |
|---|---|---|---|---|---|
| Nixon | 692,828 | 100.0 | Humphrey | 499,680 | 41.2 |
| | | | McGovern | 480,320 | 39.6 |
| | | | Muskie | 107,806 | 8.9 |
| | | | Jackson | 98,498 | 8.1 |
| | | | McCarthy | 26,026 | 2.1 |

### May 4  **Tennessee**

| | | | | | |
|---|---|---|---|---|---|
| Nixon | 109,696 | 95.8 | Wallace | 335,858 | 68.2 |
| Ashbrook | 2,419 | 2.1 | Humphrey | 78,350 | 15.9 |
| McCloskey | 2,370 | 2.1 | McGovern | 35,551 | 7.2 |
| Others | 4 | — | Chisholm | 18,809 | 3.8 |
| | | | Muskie | 9,634 | 2.0 |
| | | | Jackson | 5,896 | 1.2 |
| | | | Mills | 2,543 | .5 |
| | | | McCarthy | 2,267 | .5 |
| | | | Hartke | 1,621 | .3 |
| | | | Lindsay | 1,476 | .3 |
| | | | Yorty | 692 | .1 |
| | | | Others | 24 | — |

# Republican                    # Democratic

### May 6    North Carolina

| | | | | | |
|---|---|---|---|---|---|
| Nixon | 159,167 | *94.8* | Wallace | 413,518 | *50.3* |
| McCloskey | 8,732 | *5.2* | Terry Sanford (N.C.) | 306,014 | *37.3* |
| | | | Chisholm | 61,723 | *7.5* |
| | | | Muskie | 30,739 | *3.7* |
| | | | Jackson | 9,416 | *1.1* |

### May 9    Nebraska

| | | | | | |
|---|---|---|---|---|---|
| Nixon | 179,464 | *92.4* | McGovern | 79,309 | *41.3* |
| McCloskey | 9,011 | *4.6* | Humphrey | 65,968 | *34.3* |
| Ashbrook | 4,996 | *2.6* | Wallace | 23,912 | *12.4* |
| Others | 801 | *.4* | Muskie | 6,886 | *3.6* |
| | | | Jackson | 5,276 | *2.7* |
| | | | Yorty | 3,459 | *1.8* |
| | | | McCarthy | 3,194 | *1.7* |
| | | | Chisholm | 1,763 | *.9* |
| | | | Lindsay | 1,244 | *.6* |
| | | | Mills | 377 | *.2* |
| | | | Kennedy[1] | 293 | *.2* |
| | | | Hartke | 249 | *.1* |
| | | | Others | 207 | *.1* |

### May 9    West Virginia

| | | | | | |
|---|---|---|---|---|---|
| Unpledged delegates at large | 95,813[3] | *100.0* | Humphrey | 246,596 | *66.9* |
| | | | Wallace | 121,888 | *33.1* |

### May 16    Maryland

| | | | | | |
|---|---|---|---|---|---|
| Nixon | 99,308 | *86.2* | Wallace | 219,687 | *38.7* |
| McCloskey | 9,223 | *8.0* | Humphrey | 151,981 | *26.8* |
| Ashbrook | 6,718 | *5.8* | McGovern | 126,978 | *22.4* |
| | | | Jackson | 17,728 | *3.1* |
| | | | Yorty | 13,584 | *2.4* |
| | | | Muskie | 13,363 | *2.4* |
| | | | Chisholm | 12,602 | *2.2* |
| | | | Mills | 4,776 | *.8* |
| | | | McCarthy | 4,691 | *.8* |
| | | | Lindsay | 2,168 | *.4* |
| | | | Mink | 573 | *.1* |

### May 16    Michigan

| | | | | | |
|---|---|---|---|---|---|
| Nixon | 321,652 | *95.5* | Wallace | 809,239 | *51.0* |
| McCloskey | 9,691 | *2.9* | McGovern | 425,694 | *26.8* |
| Unpledged delegates | 5,370 | *1.6* | Humphrey | 249,798 | *15.7* |
| Others | 30 | — | Chisholm | 44,090 | *2.8* |
| | | | Muskie | 38,701 | *2.4* |
| | | | Unpledged delegates | 10,700 | *.7* |
| | | | Jackson | 6,938 | *.4* |
| | | | Hartke | 2,862 | *.2* |
| | | | Others | 51 | — |

### May 23    Oregon

| | | | | | |
|---|---|---|---|---|---|
| Nixon | 231,151 | *82.0* | McGovern | 205,328 | *50.2* |
| McCloskey | 29,365 | *10.4* | Wallace | 81,868 | *20.0* |
| Ashbrook | 16,696 | *5.9* | Humphrey | 51,163 | *12.5* |
| Others | 4,798 | *1.7* | Jackson | 22,042 | *5.4* |
| | | | Kennedy | 12,673 | *3.1* |
| | | | Muskie | 10,244 | *2.5* |
| | | | McCarthy | 8,943 | *2.2* |
| | | | Mink | 6,500 | *1.6* |
| | | | Lindsay | 5,082 | *1.2* |
| | | | Chisholm | 2,975 | *.7* |
| | | | Mills | 1,208 | *.3* |
| | | | Others | 618 | *.2* |

# Republican                              # Democratic

| May 23  **Rhode Island** | Votes | % | | Votes | % |
|---|---|---|---|---|---|
| Nixon | 4,953 | 88.3 | McGovern | 15,603 | 41.2 |
| McCloskey | 337 | 6.0 | Muskie | 7,838 | 20.7 |
| Ashbrook | 175 | 3.1 | Humphrey | 7,701 | 20.3 |
| Unpledged delegates | 146 | 2.6 | Wallace | 5,802 | 15.3 |
| | | | Unpledged delegates | 490 | 1.3 |
| | | | McCarthy | 245 | .6 |
| | | | Jackson | 138 | .4 |
| | | | Mills | 41 | .1 |
| | | | Yorty | 6 | — |
| June 6  **California** | | | | | |
| Nixon | 2,058,825 | 90.1 | McGovern | 1,550,652 | 43.5 |
| Ashbrook | 224,922 | 9.8 | Humphrey | 1,375,064 | 38.6 |
| Others | 175 | — | Wallace[1] | 268,551 | 7.5 |
| | | | Chisholm | 157,435 | 4.4 |
| | | | Muskie | 72,701 | 2.0 |
| | | | Yorty | 50,745 | 1.4 |
| | | | McCarthy | 34,203 | 1.0 |
| | | | Jackson | 28,901 | .8 |
| | | | Lindsay | 26,246 | .7 |
| | | | Others | 20 | — |
| June 6  **New Jersey** | | | | | |
| Unpledged delegates at large | 215,719[3] | 100.0 | Chisholm | 51,433 | 66.9 |
| | | | Sanford | 25,401 | 33.1 |
| June 6  **New Mexico** | | | | | |
| Nixon | 49,067 | 88.5 | McGovern | 51,011 | 33.3 |
| McCloskey | 3,367 | 6.1 | Wallace | 44,843 | 29.3 |
| None of the names shown | 3,035 | 5.5 | Humphrey | 39,768 | 25.9 |
| | | | Muskie | 6,411 | 4.2 |
| | | | Jackson | 4,236 | 2.8 |
| | | | None of the names shown | 3,819 | 2.5 |
| | | | Chisholm | 3,205 | 2.1 |
| June 6  **South Dakota** | | | | | |
| Nixon | 52,820 | 100.0 | McGovern | 28,017 | 100.0 |

| **TOTALS** | | | | | |
|---|---|---|---|---|---|
| Nixon | 5,378,704 | 86.9 | Humphrey | 4,121,372 | 25.8 |
| Unpledged delegates | 317,048 | 5.1 | McGovern | 4,053,451 | 25.3 |
| Ashbrook | 311,543 | 5.0 | Wallace | 3,755,424 | 23.5 |
| McCloskey | 132,731 | 2.1 | Muskie | 1,840,217 | 11.5 |
| Wallace | 20,472 | .3 | McCarthy | 553,955 | 3.5 |
| None of the names shown | 5,350 | .1 | Jackson | 505,198 | 3.2 |
| Others[4] | 22,433 | .4 | Chisholm | 430,703 | 2.7 |
| | | | Sanford | 331,415 | 2.1 |
| | 6,188,281 | | Lindsay | 196,406 | 1.2 |
| | | | Yorty | 79,446 | .5 |
| | | | Mills | 37,401 | .2 |
| | | | Fauntroy | 21,217 | .1 |
| | | | Unpledged delegates | 19,533 | .1 |
| | | | Kennedy | 16,693 | .1 |
| | | | Hartke | 11,798 | .1 |
| | | | Mink | 8,286 | .1 |
| | | | None of the names shown | 6,269 | — |
| | | | Others[5] | 5,181 | — |
| | | | | 15,993,965 | |

*Delegate selection primaries were held in Alabama and New York. In* America Votes, *Scammon did not record vote totals if the primary was strictly for delegate selection and there was no presidential preference voting.*

1. Write-in.
2. No Republican primary in 1972.

3. Figures obtained from Scammon's office. In America Votes, Scammon did not record vote totals if the primary was strictly for delegate selection.
4. In addition to scattered votes, "others" includes Patrick Paulsen, who received 1,211 votes in the New Hampshire primary.
5. In addition to scattered votes, "others" includes Edward T. Coll, who received 280 votes in the New Hampshire primary and 589 votes in the Massachusetts primary.

# 1976 Primaries*

| Republican | | | Democratic | | |
|---|---|---|---|---|---|
| | Votes | % | | Votes | % |

**February 24  New Hampshire**

| Republican | | | Democratic | | |
|---|---|---|---|---|---|
| Gerald R. Ford (Mich.) | 55,156 | 49.4 | Jimmy Carter (Ga.) | 23,373 | 28.4 |
| Ronald Reagan (Calif.) | 53,569 | 48.0 | Morris K. Udall (Ariz.) | 18,710 | 22.7 |
| Others[1] | 2,949 | 2.6 | Birch Bayh (Ind.) | 12,510 | 15.2 |
| | | | Fred R. Harris (Okla.) | 8,863 | 10.8 |
| | | | Sargent Shriver (Md.) | 6,743 | 8.2 |
| | | | Hubert H. Humphrey (Minn.) | 4,596 | 5.6 |
| | | | Henry M. Jackson (Wash.) | 1,857 | 2.3 |
| | | | George C. Wallace (Ala.) | 1,061 | 1.3 |
| | | | Ellen McCormack (N.Y.) | 1,007 | 1.2 |
| | | | Others | 3,661 | 4.8 |

**March 2  Massachusetts**

| Republican | | | Democratic | | |
|---|---|---|---|---|---|
| Ford | 115,375 | 61.2 | Jackson | 164,393 | 22.3 |
| Reagan | 63,555 | 33.7 | Udall | 130,440 | 17.7 |
| None of the names shown | 6,000 | 3.2 | Wallace | 123,112 | 16.7 |
| Others[1] | 3,519 | 1.8 | Carter | 101,948 | 13.9 |
| | | | Harris | 55,701 | 7.6 |
| | | | Shriver | 53,252 | 7.2 |
| | | | Bayh | 34,963 | 4.8 |
| | | | McCormack | 25,772 | 3.5 |
| | | | Milton J. Shapp (Pa.) | 21,693 | 2.9 |
| | | | None of the names shown | 9,804 | 1.3 |
| | | | Humphrey[1] | 7,851 | 1.1 |
| | | | Edward M. Kennedy (Mass.)[1] | 1,623 | 0.2 |
| | | | Lloyd Bentsen (Texas) | 364 | — |
| | | | Others | 4,905 | 0.7 |

**March 2  Vermont**

| Republican | | | Democratic | | |
|---|---|---|---|---|---|
| Ford | 27,014 | 84.0 | Carter | 16,335 | 42.2 |
| Reagan[1] | 4,892 | 15.2 | Shriver | 10,699 | 27.6 |
| Others[1] | 251 | — | Harris | 4,893 | 12.6 |
| | | | McCormack | 3,324 | 8.6 |
| | | | Others | 3,463 | 9.0 |

**March 9  Florida**

| Republican | | | Democratic | | |
|---|---|---|---|---|---|
| Ford | 321,982 | 52.8 | Carter | 448,844 | 34.5 |
| Reagan | 287,837 | 47.2 | Wallace | 396,820 | 30.5 |
| | | | Jackson | 310,944 | 23.9 |
| | | | None of the names shown | 37,626 | 2.9 |
| | | | Shapp | 32,198 | 2.5 |
| | | | Udall | 27,235 | 2.1 |
| | | | Bayh | 8,750 | .7 |
| | | | McCormack | 7,595 | .6 |
| | | | Shriver | 7,084 | .5 |
| | | | Harris | 5,397 | .4 |
| | | | Robert C. Byrd (W.Va.) | 5,042 | .4 |
| | | | Frank Church (Idaho) | 4,906 | .4 |
| | | | Others | 7,889 | .6 |

**March 16  Illinois**

| Republican | | | Democratic | | |
|---|---|---|---|---|---|
| Ford | 456,750 | 58.9 | Carter | 630,915 | 48.1 |
| Reagan | 311,295 | 40.1 | Wallace | 361,798 | 27.6 |
| Lar Daly (Ill.) | 7,582 | 1.0 | Shriver | 214,024 | 16.3 |
| Others[1] | 266 | — | Harris | 98,862 | 7.5 |
| | | | Others[1] | 6,315 | .5 |

## Republican

| | Votes | % |
|---|---|---|
| **March 23  North Carolina** | | |
| Reagan | 101,468 | 52.4 |
| Ford | 88,897 | 45.9 |
| None of the names shown | 3,362 | 1.7 |
| **April 6  Wisconsin** | | |
| Ford | 326,869 | 55.2 |
| Reagan | 262,126 | 44.3 |
| None of the names shown | 2,234 | .3 |
| Others[1] | 583 | — |
| **April 27  Pennsylvania** | | |
| Ford | 733,472 | 92.1 |
| Reagan[1] | 40,510 | 5.1 |
| Others[1] | 22,678 | 2.8 |
| **May 4  District of Columbia** | | |
| [2] | | |
| **May 4  Georgia** | | |
| Reagan | 128,671 | 68.3 |
| Ford | 59,801 | 31.7 |

## Democratic

| | Votes | % |
|---|---|---|
| **March 23  North Carolina** | | |
| Carter | 324,437 | 53.6 |
| Wallace | 210,166 | 34.7 |
| Jackson | 25,749 | 4.3 |
| None of the names shown | 22,850 | 3.8 |
| Udall | 14,032 | 2.3 |
| Harris | 5,923 | 1.0 |
| Bentsen | 1,675 | .3 |
| **April 6  Wisconsin** | | |
| Carter | 271,220 | 36.6 |
| Udall | 263,771 | 35.6 |
| Wallace | 92,460 | 12.5 |
| Jackson | 47,605 | 6.4 |
| McCormack | 26,982 | 3.6 |
| Harris | 8,185 | 1.1 |
| None of the names shown | 7,154 | 1.0 |
| Shriver | 5,097 | .7 |
| Bentsen | 1,730 | .2 |
| Bayh | 1,255 | .2 |
| Shapp | 596 | .1 |
| Others[1] | 14,473 | 2.0 |
| **April 27  Pennsylvania** | | |
| Carter | 511,905 | 37.0 |
| Jackson | 340,340 | 24.6 |
| Udall | 259,166 | 18.7 |
| Wallace | 155,902 | 11.3 |
| McCormack | 38,800 | 2.8 |
| Shapp | 32,947 | 2.4 |
| Bayh | 15,320 | 1.1 |
| Harris | 13,067 | .9 |
| Humphrey[1] | 12,563 | .9 |
| Others | 5,032 | .3 |
| **May 4  District of Columbia** | | |
| Carter | 10,521 | 31.6 |
| Walter E. Fauntroy (unpledged delegates) | 10,149 | 30.5 |
| Udall | 6,999 | 21.0 |
| Walter E. Washington (unpledged delegates) | 5,161 | 15.5 |
| Harris | 461 | 1.4 |
| **May 4  Georgia** | | |
| Carter | 419,272 | 83.4 |
| Wallace | 57,594 | 11.5 |
| Udall | 9,755 | 1.9 |
| Byrd | 3,628 | .7 |
| Jackson | 3,358 | .7 |
| Church | 2,477 | .5 |
| Shriver | 1,378 | .3 |
| Bayh | 824 | .2 |
| Harris | 699 | .1 |
| McCormack | 635 | .1 |
| Bentsen | 277 | .1 |
| Shapp | 181 | — |
| Others | 2,393 | .5 |

# Republican

# Democratic

| | Votes | % | | Votes | % |
|---|---|---|---|---|---|
| **May 4** **Indiana** | | | | | |
| Reagan | 323,779 | *51.3* | Carter | 417,480 | *68.0* |
| Ford | 307,513 | *48.7* | Wallace | 93,121 | *15.2* |
| | | | Jackson | 72,080 | *11.7* |
| | | | McCormack | 31,708 | *5.2* |
| **May 11** **Nebraska** | | | | | |
| Reagan | 113,493 | *54.5* | Church | 67,297 | *38.5* |
| Ford | 94,542 | *45.4* | Carter | 65,833 | *37.6* |
| Others | 379 | *.1* | Humphrey | 12,685 | *7.2* |
| | | | Kennedy | 7,199 | *4.1* |
| | | | McCormack | 6,033 | *3.4* |
| | | | Wallace | 5,567 | *3.2* |
| | | | Udall | 4,688 | *2.7* |
| | | | Jackson | 2,642 | *1.5* |
| | | | Harris | 811 | *.5* |
| | | | Bayh | 407 | *.2* |
| | | | Shriver | 384 | *.2* |
| | | | Others[1] | 1,467 | *.8* |
| **May 11** **West Virginia** | | | | | |
| Ford | 88,386 | *56.8* | Byrd | 331,639 | *89.0* |
| Reagan | 67,306 | *43.2* | Wallace | 40,938 | *11.0* |
| **May 18** **Maryland** | | | | | |
| Ford | 96,291 | *58.0* | Edmund G. Brown Jr. (Calif.) | 286,672 | *48.4* |
| Reagan | 69,680 | *42.0* | Carter | 219,404 | *37.1* |
| | | | Udall | 32,790 | *5.5* |
| | | | Wallace | 24,176 | *4.1* |
| | | | Jackson | 13,956 | *2.4* |
| | | | McCormack | 7,907 | *1.3* |
| | | | Harris | 6,841 | *1.2* |
| **May 18** **Michigan** | | | | | |
| Ford | 690,180 | *64.9* | Carter | 307,559 | *43.4* |
| Reagan | 364,052 | *34.3* | Udall | 305,134 | *43.1* |
| Unpledged delegates | 8,473 | *.8* | Wallace | 49,204 | *6.9* |
| Others[1] | 109 | — | Unpledged delegates | 15,853 | *2.2* |
| | | | Jackson | 10,332 | *1.5* |
| | | | McCormack | 7,623 | *1.1* |
| | | | Shriver | 5,738 | *.8* |
| | | | Harris | 4,081 | *.6* |
| | | | Others[1] | 3,142 | *.4* |
| **May 25** **Arkansas** | | | | | |
| Reagan | 20,628 | *63.4* | Carter | 314,306 | *62.6* |
| Ford | 11,430 | *35.1* | Wallace | 83,005 | *16.5* |
| Unpledged delegates | 483 | *1.5* | Unpledged delegates | 57,152 | *11.4* |
| | | | Udall | 37,783 | *7.5* |
| | | | Jackson | 9,554 | *1.9* |
| **May 25** **Idaho** | | | | | |
| Reagan | 66,743 | *74.3* | Church | 58,570 | *78.7* |
| Ford | 22,323 | *24.9* | Carter | 8,818 | *11.9* |
| Unpledged delegates | 727 | *.8* | Humphrey | 1,700 | *2.3* |
| | | | Brown[1] | 1,453 | *2.0* |
| | | | Wallace | 1,115 | *1.5* |
| | | | Udall | 981 | *1.3* |
| | | | Unpledged delegates | 964 | *1.3* |
| | | | Jackson | 485 | *.7* |
| | | | Harris | 319 | *.4* |

|  | **Republican** | | | **Democratic** | |
| --- | --- | --- | --- | --- | --- |
|  | Votes | % |  | Votes | % |

**May 25    Kentucky**

| | Republican | | | Democratic | |
| --- | --- | --- | --- | --- | --- |
| Ford | 67,976 | 50.9 | Carter | 181,690 | 59.4 |
| Reagan | 62,683 | 46.9 | Wallace | 51,540 | 16.8 |
| Unpledged delegates | 1,781 | 1.3 | Udall | 33,262 | 10.9 |
| Others | 1,088 | .8 | McCormack | 17,061 | 5.6 |
|  |  |  | Unpledged delegates | 11,962 | 3.9 |
|  |  |  | Jackson | 8,186 | 2.7 |
|  |  |  | Others | 2,305 | .8 |

**May 25    Nevada**

| | Republican | | | Democratic | |
| --- | --- | --- | --- | --- | --- |
| Reagan | 31,637 | 66.3 | Brown | 39,671 | 52.7 |
| Ford | 13,747 | 28.8 | Carter | 17,567 | 23.3 |
| None of the names shown | 2,365 | 5.0 | Church | 6,778 | 9.0 |
|  |  |  | None of the names shown | 4,603 | 6.1 |
|  |  |  | Wallace | 2,490 | 3.3 |
|  |  |  | Udall | 2,237 | 3.0 |
|  |  |  | Jackson | 1,896 | 2.5 |

**May 25    Oregon**

| | Republican | | | Democratic | |
| --- | --- | --- | --- | --- | --- |
| Ford | 150,181 | 50.3 | Church | 145,394 | 33.6 |
| Reagan | 136,691 | 45.8 | Carter | 115,310 | 26.7 |
| Others[1] | 11,663 | 3.9 | Brown[1] | 106,812 | 24.7 |
|  |  |  | Humphrey | 22,488 | 5.2 |
|  |  |  | Udall | 11,747 | 2.7 |
|  |  |  | Kennedy | 10,983 | 2.5 |
|  |  |  | Wallace | 5,797 | 1.3 |
|  |  |  | Jackson | 5,298 | 1.2 |
|  |  |  | McCormack | 3,753 | .9 |
|  |  |  | Harris | 1,344 | .3 |
|  |  |  | Bayh | 743 | .2 |
|  |  |  | Others[1] | 2,963 | .7 |

**May 25    Tennessee**

| | Republican | | | Democratic | |
| --- | --- | --- | --- | --- | --- |
| Ford | 120,685 | 49.8 | Carter | 259,243 | 77.6 |
| Reagan | 118,997 | 49.1 | Wallace | 36,495 | 10.9 |
| Unpledged delegates | 2,756 | 1.1 | Udall | 12,420 | 3.7 |
| Others[1] | 97 | — | Church | 8,026 | 2.4 |
|  |  |  | Unpledged delegates | 6,148 | 1.8 |
|  |  |  | Jackson | 5,672 | 1.7 |
|  |  |  | McCormack | 1,782 | .5 |
|  |  |  | Harris | 1,628 | .5 |
|  |  |  | Brown[1] | 1,556 | .5 |
|  |  |  | Shapp | 507 | .2 |
|  |  |  | Humphrey[1] | 109 | — |
|  |  |  | Others[1] | 492 | .1 |

**June 1    Montana**

| | Republican | | | Democratic | |
| --- | --- | --- | --- | --- | --- |
| Reagan | 56,683 | 63.1 | Church | 63,448 | 59.4 |
| Ford | 31,100 | 34.6 | Carter | 26,329 | 24.6 |
| None of the names shown | 1,996 | 2.2 | Udall | 6,708 | 6.3 |
|  |  |  | None of the names shown | 3,820 | 3.6 |
|  |  |  | Wallace | 3,680 | 3.4 |
|  |  |  | Jackson | 2,856 | 2.7 |

**June 1    Rhode Island**

| | Republican | | | Democratic | |
| --- | --- | --- | --- | --- | --- |
| Ford | 9,365 | 65.3 | Unpledged delegates | 19,035 | 31.5 |
| Reagan | 4,480 | 31.2 | Carter | 18,237 | 30.2 |
| Unpledged delegates | 507 | 3.5 | Church | 16,423 | 27.2 |
|  |  |  | Udall | 2,543 | 4.2 |
|  |  |  | McCormack | 2,468 | 4.1 |
|  |  |  | Jackson | 756 | 1.3 |
|  |  |  | Wallace | 507 | .8 |
|  |  |  | Bayh | 247 | .4 |
|  |  |  | Shapp | 132 | .2 |

# Republican

# Democratic

| | Votes | % | | Votes | % |
|---|---|---|---|---|---|
| **June 1  South Dakota** | | | | | |
| Reagan | 43,068 | 51.2 | Carter | 24,186 | 41.2 |
| Ford | 36,976 | 44.0 | Udall | 19,510 | 33.3 |
| None of the names shown | 4,033 | 4.8 | None of the names shown | 7,871 | 13.4 |
| | | | McCormack | 4,561 | 7.8 |
| | | | Wallace | 1,412 | 2.4 |
| | | | Harris | 573 | 1.0 |
| | | | Jackson | 558 | 1.0 |
| **June 8  California** | | | | | |
| Reagan | 1,604,836 | 65.5 | Brown | 2,013,210 | 59.0 |
| Ford | 845,655 | 34.5 | Carter | 697,092 | 20.4 |
| Others[1] | 20 | — | Church | 250,581 | 7.3 |
| | | | Udall | 171,501 | 5.0 |
| | | | Wallace | 102,292 | 3.0 |
| | | | Unpledged delegates | 78,595 | 2.3 |
| | | | Jackson | 38,634 | 1.1 |
| | | | McCormack | 29,242 | .9 |
| | | | Harris | 16,920 | .5 |
| | | | Bayh | 11,419 | .3 |
| | | | Others[1] | 215 | — |
| **June 8  New Jersey** | | | | | |
| Ford | 242,122 | 100.00 | Carter | 210,655 | 58.4 |
| | | | Church | 49,034 | 13.6 |
| | | | Jackson | 31,820 | 8.8 |
| | | | Wallace | 31,183 | 8.6 |
| | | | McCormack | 21,774 | 6.0 |
| | | | Others | 16,373 | 4.5 |
| **June 8  Ohio** | | | | | |
| Ford | 516,111 | 55.2 | Carter | 593,130 | 52.3 |
| Reagan | 419,646 | 44.8 | Udall | 240,342 | 21.2 |
| | | | Church | 157,884 | 13.9 |
| | | | Wallace | 63,953 | 5.6 |
| | | | Gertrude W. Donahey (unpledged delegates) | 43,661 | 3.9 |
| | | | Jackson | 35,404 | 3.1 |

| **TOTALS** | | | | | |
|---|---|---|---|---|---|
| Ford | 5,529,899 | 53.3 | Carter | 6,235,609 | 38.8 |
| Reagan | 4,758,325 | 45.9 | Brown | 2,449,374 | 15.3 |
| None of the names shown | 19,990 | 0.2 | Wallace | 1,995,388 | 12.4 |
| Unpledged delegates | 14,727 | 0.1 | Udall | 1,611,754 | 10.0 |
| Daly | 7,582 | 0.1 | Jackson | 1,134,375 | 7.1 |
| Others[3] | 43,602 | 0.4 | Church | 830,818 | 5.2 |
| | | | Byrd | 340,309 | 2.1 |
| | 10,374,125 | | Shriver | 304,399 | 1.9 |
| | | | Unpledged delegates | 248,680 | 1.5 |
| | | | McCormack | 238,027 | 1.5 |
| | | | Harris | 234,568 | 1.5 |
| | | | None of the names shown | 93,728 | 0.6 |
| | | | Shapp | 88,254 | 0.5 |
| | | | Bayh | 86,438 | 0.5 |
| | | | Humphrey | 61,992 | 0.4 |
| | | | Kennedy | 19,805 | 0.1 |
| | | | Bentsen | 4,046 | — |
| | | | Others[4] | 75,088 | 0.5 |
| | | | | 16,052,652 | |

*Delegate selection primaries were held in Alabama, New York and Texas. In America Votes, Scammon did not record vote totals if the primary was strictly for delegate selection and there was no presidential preference voting.*

*1. Write-in.*

*2. Ford unopposed. No primary held.*

*3. In addition to scattered write-in votes, "others" include Tommy Klein, who received 1,088 votes in Kentucky.*

*4. In addition to scattered write-in votes, "others" include Frank Ahern who received 1,487 votes in Georgia; Stanley Arnold, 371 votes in New Hampshire; Arthur O. Blessitt, 828 votes in New Hampshire and 7,889 in Georgia; Frank Bona, 135 votes in New Hampshire and 263 in Georgia; Billy Joe Clegg, 174 votes in New Hampshire; Abram Eisenman, 351 votes in Georgia; John S. Gonas, 2,288 votes in New Jersey; Jesse Gray, 3,574 votes in New Jersey; Robert L. Kelleher, 87 votes in New Hampshire, 1,603 in Massachusetts and 139 in Georgia; Rick Loewenherz, 49 votes in New Hampshire; Frank Lomento, 3,555 votes in New Jersey; Floyd L. Lunger, 3,935 votes in New Jersey; H. R. H. "Fifi" Rockefeller, 2,305 votes in Kentucky; George Roden, 153 votes in Georgia; Ray Rollinson, 3,021 votes in New Jersey; Terry Sanford, 53 votes in New Hampshire and 351 votes in Massachusetts; Bernard B. Schechter, 173 votes in New Hampshire.*

# 1980 Primaries[1]

## Republican

| | Votes | % |
|---|---|---|

## Democratic

| | Votes | % |
|---|---|---|

**February 17   Puerto Rico**

| | Votes | % | March 16 | Votes | % |
|---|---|---|---|---|---|
| George Bush (Texas)[2] | 111,940 | 60.1 | Jimmy Carter (Ga.) | 449,681 | 51.7 |
| Howard H. Baker Jr. (Tenn.)[3] | 68,934 | 37.0 | Edward M. Kennedy (Mass.) | 418,068 | 48.0 |
| Benjamin Fernandez (Calif.) | 2,097 | 1.1 | Edmund G. Brown Jr. (Calif.)[5] | 1,660 | 0.2 |
| John B. Connally (Texas)[4] | 1,964 | 1.1 | Others | 826 | 0.1 |
| Harold Stassen (N.Y.) | 672 | 0.4 | | | |
| Robert Dole (Kan.) | 483 | 0.3 | | | |
| Others | 281 | 0.1 | | | |

**February 26   New Hampshire**

| | Votes | % | | Votes | % |
|---|---|---|---|---|---|
| Ronald Reagan (Calif.) | 72,983 | 49.6 | Carter | 52,692 | 47.1 |
| Bush | 33,443 | 22.7 | Kennedy | 41,745 | 37.3 |
| Baker | 18,943 | 12.1 | Brown | 10,743 | 9.6 |
| John B. Anderson (Ill.)[6] | 14,458 | 9.8 | Lyndon LaRouche (N.Y.) | 2,326 | 2.1 |
| Philip M. Crane (Ill.) | 2,618 | 1.8 | Richard Kay (Ohio) | 566 | 0.5 |
| Connally | 2,239 | 1.5 | Others[7] | 3,858 | 3.4 |
| Dole | 597 | — | | | |
| Others[7] | 1,876 | 1.3 | | | |

**March 4   Massachusetts**

| | Votes | % | | Votes | % |
|---|---|---|---|---|---|
| Bush | 124,365 | 31.0 | Kennedy | 590,393 | 65.1 |
| Anderson | 122,987 | 30.7 | Carter | 260,401 | 28.7 |
| Reagan | 115,334 | 28.8 | Brown | 31,498 | 3.5 |
| Baker | 19,366 | 4.8 | Others[7] | 5,368 | 0.6 |
| Connally | 4,714 | 1.2 | No preference | 19,663 | 2.2 |
| Crane | 4,669 | 1.2 | | | |
| Gerald R. Ford (Mich.)[7] | 3,398 | 0.8 | | | |
| Dole | 577 | — | | | |
| Fernandez | 374 | 0.1 | | | |
| Stassen | 218 | 0.1 | | | |
| Others[7] | 2,581 | 0.6 | | | |
| No preference | 2,243 | 0.6 | | | |

**March 4   Vermont**

| | Votes | % | | Votes | % |
|---|---|---|---|---|---|
| Reagan | 19,720 | 30.1 | Carter | 29,015 | 73.1 |
| Anderson | 19,030 | 29.0 | Kennedy | 10,135 | 25.5 |
| Bush | 14,226 | 21.7 | Brown[7] | 358 | 0.9 |
| Baker | 8,055 | 12.3 | LaRouche[7] | 6 | — |
| Ford[7] | 2,300 | 3.5 | Others | 189 | 0.5 |
| Crane | 1,238 | 1.9 | | | |
| Connally | 884 | 1.3 | | | |
| Stassen | 105 | 0.2 | | | |
| Others[7] | 53 | — | | | |

**March 8   South Carolina**

| | Votes | % |
|---|---|---|
| Reagan | 79,549 | 54.7 |
| Connally | 43,113 | 29.6 |
| Bush | 21,569 | 14.8 |
| Baker | 773 | 0.5 |
| Fernandez | 171 | 0.1 |
| Stassen | 150 | 0.1 |
| Dole | 117 | 0.1 |
| Nick Belluso | 59 | — |

# Republican           Democratic

| | Votes | % | | Votes | % |
|---|---|---|---|---|---|

**March 11 Alabama**

| | Votes | % | | Votes | % |
|---|---|---|---|---|---|
| Reagan | 147,352 | 69.7 | Carter | 193,734 | 81.6 |
| Bush | 54,730 | 25.9 | Kennedy | 31,382 | 13.2 |
| Crane | 5,099 | 2.4 | Brown | 9,529 | 4.0 |
| Baker | 1,963 | 0.9 | William L. Nuckols | 609 | — |
| Connally | 1,077 | 0.5 | Bob Maddox | 540 | — |
| Stassen | 544 | 0.3 | Unpledged delegates | 1,670 | 0.7 |
| Dole | 447 | 0.2 | | | |
| Belluso | 141 | — | | | |

**March 11 Florida**

| | Votes | % | | Votes | % |
|---|---|---|---|---|---|
| Reagan | 345,699 | 56.2 | Carter | 666,321 | 60.7 |
| Bush | 185,996 | 30.2 | Kennedy | 254,727 | 23.2 |
| Anderson | 56,636 | 9.2 | Brown | 53,474 | 4.9 |
| Crane | 12,000 | 2.0 | Kay | 19,160 | 1.7 |
| Baker | 6,345 | 1.0 | No preference | 104,321 | 9.5 |
| Connally | 4,958 | 0.8 | | | |
| Stassen | 1,377 | 0.2 | | | |
| Dole | 1,086 | 0.2 | | | |
| Fernandez | 898 | 0.1 | | | |

**March 11 Georgia**

| | Votes | % | | Votes | % |
|---|---|---|---|---|---|
| Reagan | 146,500 | 73.2 | Carter | 338,772 | 88.0 |
| Bush | 25,293 | 12.6 | Kennedy | 32,315 | 8.4 |
| Anderson | 16,853 | 8.4 | Brown | 7,255 | 1.9 |
| Crane | 6,308 | 3.2 | Cliff Finch (Miss.) | 1,378 | 0.4 |
| Connally | 2,388 | 1.2 | Kay | 840 | 0.2 |
| Baker | 1,571 | 0.8 | LaRouche | 513 | 0.1 |
| Fernandez | 809 | 0.4 | Unpledged delegates | 3,707 | 1.0 |
| Dole | 249 | 0.1 | | | |
| Stassen | 200 | 0.1 | | | |

**March 18 Illinois**

| | Votes | % | | Votes | % |
|---|---|---|---|---|---|
| Reagan | 547,355 | 48.4 | Carter | 780,787 | 65.0 |
| Anderson | 415,193 | 36.7 | Kennedy | 359,875 | 30.0 |
| Bush | 124,057 | 11.0 | Brown | 39,168 | 3.3 |
| Crane | 24,865 | 2.2 | LaRouche | 19,192 | 1.6 |
| Baker | 7,051 | 0.6 | Anderson [7] | 1,643 | 0.1 |
| Connally | 4,548 | 0.4 | Others [7] | 402 | — |
| V. A. Kelley | 3,757 | 0.3 | | | |
| Dole | 1,843 | 0.2 | | | |
| Ford [7] | 1,106 | 0.1 | | | |
| Others | 306 | — | | | |

**March 25 Connecticut**

| | Votes | % | | Votes | % |
|---|---|---|---|---|---|
| Bush | 70,367 | 38.6 | Kennedy | 98,662 | 46.9 |
| Reagan | 61,735 | 33.9 | Carter | 87,207 | 41.5 |
| Anderson | 40,354 | 22.1 | LaRouche | 5,617 | 2.7 |
| Baker | 2,446 | 1.3 | Brown | 5,386 | 2.6 |
| Crane | 1,887 | 1.0 | Unpledged delegates | 13,403 | 6.4 |
| Connally | 598 | 0.3 | | | |
| Dole | 333 | 0.2 | | | |
| Fernandez | 308 | 0.2 | | | |
| Unpledged delegates | 4,256 | 2.3 | | | |

| Republican | Votes | % | Democratic | Votes | % |
|---|---|---|---|---|---|

**March 25  New York**

| | | | | | |
|---|---|---|---|---|---|
| | | | Kennedy | 582,757 | 58.9 |
| | | | Carter | 406,305 | 41.1 |

**April 1  Kansas**

| | | | | | |
|---|---|---|---|---|---|
| Reagan | 179,739 | 63.0 | Carter | 109,807 | 56.6 |
| Anderson | 51,924 | 18.2 | Kennedy | 61,318 | 31.6 |
| Bush | 35,838 | 12.6 | Brown | 9,434 | 4.9 |
| Baker | 3,603 | 1.3 | Finch | 629 | 0.3 |
| Connally | 2,067 | 0.7 | Maddox | 632 | 0.3 |
| Fernandez | 1,650 | 0.6 | Frank Ahern | 571 | 0.2 |
| Crane | 1,367 | 0.5 | Ray Rollinson | 364 | — |
| R. W. Yeager | 1,063 | 0.4 | None of the names shown | 11,163 | 5.8 |
| Alvin G. Carris | 483 | 0.2 | | | |
| Stassen | 383 | 0.1 | | | |
| William E. Carlson | 311 | — | | | |
| Donald Badgley | 244 | — | | | |
| None of the names shown | 6,726 | 2.4 | | | |

**April 1  Wisconsin**

| | | | | | |
|---|---|---|---|---|---|
| Reagan | 364,898 | 40.2 | Carter | 353,662 | 56.2 |
| Bush | 276,164 | 30.4 | Kennedy | 189,520 | 30.1 |
| Anderson | 248,623 | 27.4 | Brown | 74,496 | 11.8 |
| Baker | 3,298 | 0.4 | LaRouche | 6,896 | 1.1 |
| Crane | 2,951 | 0.3 | Finch | 1,842 | 0.3 |
| Connally | 2,312 | 0.3 | Others [7] | 509 | 0.1 |
| Fernandez | 1,051 | 0.1 | None of the names shown | 2,694 | 0.4 |
| Stassen | 1,010 | 0.1 | | | |
| Others [7] | 4,951 | 0.5 | | | |
| None of the names shown | 2,595 | 0.3 | | | |

**April 5  Louisiana**

| | | | | | |
|---|---|---|---|---|---|
| Reagan | 31,212 | 74.9 | Carter | 199,956 | 55.7 |
| Bush | 7,818 | 18.8 | Kennedy | 80,797 | 22.5 |
| Stassen | 126 | 0.3 | Brown | 16,774 | 4.7 |
| Belluso | 155 | 0.3 | Finch | 11,153 | 3.1 |
| Fernandez | 84 | 0.2 | Kay | 3,362 | 0.9 |
| C. Leon Pickett | 67 | — | Maddox | 2,830 | 0.8 |
| None of the names shown | 2,221 | 5.3 | Don Reaux | 2,255 | 0.6 |
| | | | Unpledged delegates | 41,614 | 11.6 |

**April 22  Pennsylvania**

| | | | | | |
|---|---|---|---|---|---|
| Bush | 626,759 | 50.5 | Kennedy | 736,854 | 45.7 |
| Reagan | 527,916 | 42.5 | Carter | 732,332 | 45.4 |
| Baker | 30,846 | 2.5 | Brown | 37,669 | 2.3 |
| Anderson | 26,890 | 2.1 | Anderson [7] | 9,182 | 0.6 |
| Connally | 10,656 | 0.9 | Bush [7] | 2,074 | 0.1 |
| Stassen | 6,767 | 0.5 | Reagan [7] | 1,097 | 0.1 |
| Alvin J. Jacobson | 4,357 | 0.4 | Ford [7] | 150 | — |
| Fernandez | 2,521 | 0.2 | No preference | 93,865 | 5.8 |
| Others | 4,699 | 0.4 | | | |

**May 3  Texas**

| | | | | | |
|---|---|---|---|---|---|
| Reagan | 268,798 | 51.0 | Carter | 770,390 | 55.9 |
| Bush | 249,819 | 47.4 | Kennedy | 314,129 | 22.8 |
| Unpledged delegates | 8,152 | 1.5 | Brown | 35,585 | 2.6 |
| | | | Unpledged delegates | 257,250 | 18.7 |

# Republican                                    # Democratic

|  | Votes | % |  | Votes | % |
|---|---|---|---|---|---|

### May 6  District of Columbia

| Bush | 4,973 | 66.1 | Kennedy | 39,561 | 61.7 |
| Anderson | 2,025 | 26.9 | Carter | 23,697 | 36.9 |
| Crane | 270 | 3.6 | LaRouche | 892 | 1.4 |
| Stassen | 201 | 2.7 |  |  |  |
| Fernandez | 60 | 0.8 |  |  |  |

### May 6  Indiana

| Reagan | 419,016 | 73.7 | Carter | 398,949 | 67.7 |
| Bush | 92,955 | 16.4 | Kennedy | 190,492 | 32.3 |
| Anderson | 56,342 | 9.9 |  |  |  |

### May 6  North Carolina

| Reagan | 113,854 | 67.6 | Carter | 516,778 | 70.1 |
| Bush | 36,631 | 21.8 | Kennedy | 130,684 | 17.7 |
| Anderson | 8,542 | 5.1 | Brown | 21,420 | 2.9 |
| Baker | 2,543 | 1.5 | No preference | 68,380 | 9.3 |
| Connally | 1,107 | 0.7 |  |  |  |
| Dole | 629 | 0.4 |  |  |  |
| Crane | 547 | 0.3 |  |  |  |
| No preference | 4,538 | 2.7 |  |  |  |

### May 6  Tennessee

| Reagan | 144,625 | 74.1 | Carter | 221,658 | 75.2 |
| Bush | 35,274 | 18.1 | Kennedy | 53,258 | 18.1 |
| Anderson | 8,722 | 4.5 | Brown | 5,612 | 1.9 |
| Crane | 1,574 | 0.8 | Finch | 1,663 | 0.6 |
| Baker [7] | 16 | — | LaRouche | 925 | 0.3 |
| Ford [7] | 14 | — | Others [7] | 49 | — |
| Connally [7] | 1 | — | Unpledged delegates | 11,515 | 3.9 |
| Others [7] | 8 | — |  |  |  |
| Unpledged delegates | 4,976 | 2.5 |  |  |  |

### May 13  Maryland

| Reagan | 80,557 | 48.2 | Carter | 226,528 | 47.5 |
| Bush | 68,389 | 40.9 | Kennedy | 181,091 | 38.0 |
| Anderson | 16,244 | 9.7 | Brown | 14,313 | 3.0 |
| Crane | 2,113 | 1.3 | Finch | 4,891 | 1.0 |
|  |  |  | LaRouche | 4,388 | 0.9 |
|  |  |  | Unpledged delegates | 45,879 | 9.6 |

### May 13  Nebraska

| Reagan | 155,995 | 76.0 | Carter | 72,120 | 46.9 |
| Bush | 31,380 | 15.3 | Kennedy | 57,826 | 37.6 |
| Anderson | 11,879 | 5.8 | Brown | 5,478 | 3.6 |
| Dole | 1,420 | 0.7 | LaRouche | 1,169 | 0.8 |
| Crane | 1,062 | 0.5 | Others [7] | 1,247 | 0.8 |
| Stassen | 799 | 0.4 | Unpledged delegates | 16,041 | 10.4 |
| Fernandez | 400 | 0.2 |  |  |  |
| Others [7] | 2,268 | 1.1 |  |  |  |

## Republican | | | Democratic

| | Votes | % | | Votes | % |
|---|---|---|---|---|---|

**May 20  Michigan**

| Bush | 341,998 | 57.5 | Brown | 23,043 | 29.4 |
| Reagan | 189,184 | 31.8 | LaRouche | 8,948 | 11.4 |
| Anderson | 48,947 | 8.2 | Others [7] | 10,048 | 12.8 |
| Fernandez | 2,248 | 0.4 | Unpledged delegates | 36,385 | 46.4 |
| Stassen | 1,938 | 0.3 | | | |
| Others [7] | 596 | 0.1 | | | |
| Unpledged delegates | 10,265 | 1.7 | | | |

**May 20  Oregon**

| Reagan | 170,449 | 54.0 | Carter | 208,693 | 56.7 |
| Bush | 109,210 | 34.6 | Kennedy | 114,651 | 31.1 |
| Anderson | 32,118 | 10.2 | Brown | 34,409 | 9.3 |
| Crane | 2,324 | 0.7 | Anderson [7] | 5,407 | 1.5 |
| Others [7] | 1,265 | 0.4 | Reagan [7] | 2,206 | 0.6 |
| | | | Bush [7] | 1,838 | 0.5 |

**May 27  Arkansas**

| | | | Carter | 269,375 | 60.1 |
| | | | Kennedy | 78,542 | 17.5 |
| | | | Finch | 19,469 | 4.3 |
| | | | Unpledged delegates | 80,904 | 18.0 |

**May 27  Idaho**

| Reagan | 111,868 | 82.9 | Carter | 31,383 | 62.2 |
| Anderson | 13,130 | 9.7 | Kennedy | 11,087 | 22.0 |
| Bush | 5,416 | 4.0 | Brown | 2,078 | 4.1 |
| Crane | 1,024 | 0.8 | Unpledged delegates | 5,934 | 11.8 |
| Unpledged delegates | 3,441 | 2.6 | | | |

**May 27  Kentucky**

| Reagan | 78,072 | 82.4 | Carter | 160,819 | 66.9 |
| Bush | 6,861 | 7.2 | Kennedy | 55,167 | 23.0 |
| Anderson | 4,791 | 5.1 | Kay | 2,609 | 1.1 |
| Stassen | 1,223 | 1.3 | Finch | 2,517 | 1.0 |
| Fernandez | 764 | 0.8 | Unpledged delegates | 19,219 | 8.0 |
| Unpledged delegates | 3,084 | 3.3 | | | |

**May 27  Nevada**

| Reagan | 39,352 | 83.0 | Carter | 25,159 | 37.6 |
| Bush | 3,078 | 6.5 | Kennedy | 19,296 | 28.8 |
| None of the names shown | 4,965 | 10.5 | None of the names shown | 22,493 | 33.6 |

**June 3  California**

| Reagan | 2,057,923 | 80.3 | Kennedy slate | 1,507,142 | 44.8 |
| Anderson | 349,315 | 13.6 | Carter slate | 1,266,276 | 37.6 |
| Bush | 125,113 | 4.9 | Brown slate | 135,962 | 4.0 |
| Crane | 21,465 | 0.8 | LaRouche slate | 71,779 | 2.1 |
| Fernandez | 10,242 | 0.4 | Others [7] | 51 | — |
| Others [7] | 14 | — | Unpledged slate | 382,759 | 11.4 |

# Republican

# Democratic

| | Votes | % | | Votes | % |
|---|---|---|---|---|---|

**June 3 New Mexico**

| | Votes | % | | Votes | % |
|---|---|---|---|---|---|
| Reagan | 37,982 | 63.8 | Kennedy | 73,721 | 46.3 |
| Anderson | 7,171 | 12.0 | Carter | 66,621 | 41.8 |
| Bush | 5,892 | 9.9 | LaRouche | 4,798 | 3.0 |
| Crane | 4,412 | 7.4 | Finch | 4,490 | 2.8 |
| Fernandez | 1,795 | 3.0 | Unpledged delegates | 9,734 | 6.1 |
| Stassen | 947 | 1.6 | | | |
| Unpledged delegates | 1,347 | 2.3 | | | |

**June 3 New Jersey**

| | Votes | % | | Votes | % |
|---|---|---|---|---|---|
| Reagan | 225,959 | 81.3 | Kennedy | 315,109 | 56.2 |
| Bush | 47,447 | 17.1 | Carter | 212,387 | 37.9 |
| Stassen | 4,571 | 1.6 | LaRouche | 13,913 | 2.5 |
| | | | Unpledged delegates | 19,499 | 3.5 |

**June 3 Montana**

| | Votes | % | | Votes | % |
|---|---|---|---|---|---|
| Reagan | 68,744 | 86.6 | Carter | 66,922 | 51.5 |
| Bush | 7,665 | 9.7 | Kennedy | 47,671 | 36.7 |
| No preference | 3,014 | 3.8 | No preference | 15,466 | 11.9 |

**June 3 Ohio**

| | Votes | % | | Votes | % |
|---|---|---|---|---|---|
| Reagan | 692,288 | 80.8 | Carter | 605,744 | 51.1 |
| Bush | 164,485 | 19.2 | Kennedy | 523,874 | 44.4 |
| | | | LaRouche | 35,268 | 3.0 |
| | | | Kay | 21,524 | 1.8 |

**June 3 Rhode Island**

| | Votes | % | | Votes | % |
|---|---|---|---|---|---|
| Reagan | 3,839 | 72.0 | Kennedy | 26,179 | 68.3 |
| Bush | 993 | 18.6 | Carter | 9,907 | 25.8 |
| Stassen | 107 | 2.0 | LaRouche | 1,160 | 3.0 |
| Fernandez | 48 | 0.9 | Brown | 310 | 0.8 |
| Unpledged delegates | 348 | 6.5 | Unpledged delegates | 771 | 2.0 |

**June 3 South Dakota**

| | Votes | % | | Votes | % |
|---|---|---|---|---|---|
| Reagan slate | 72,861 | 82.2 | Kennedy slate | 33,418 | 48.6 |
| Bush | 3,691 | 4.2 | Carter slate | 31,251 | 45.4 |
| Stassen | 987 | 1.1 | Uncommitted slate | 4,094 | 6.0 |
| No preference | 5,366 | 6.1 | | | |

**June 3 West Virginia**

| | Votes | % | | Votes | % |
|---|---|---|---|---|---|
| Reagan | 115,407 | 83.6 | Carter | 197,687 | 62.2 |
| Bush | 19,509 | 14.1 | Kennedy | 120,247 | 37.8 |
| Stassen | 3,100 | 2.2 | | | |

**June 3 Mississippi**

| | Votes | % |
|---|---|---|
| Reagan slate | 23,028 | 89.4 |
| Bush slate | 2,105 | 8.2 |
| Unslated | 618 | 2.4 |

# Republican

|  | Votes | % |
|---|---|---|
| **TOTALS** [8] | | |
| Reagan | 7,709,793 | *60.8* |
| Bush | 2,958,093 | *23.3* |
| Anderson | 1,572,174 | *12.4* |
| Baker | 112,219 | *0.9* |
| Crane | 97,793 | *0.8* |
| Connally | 80,661 | *0.6* |
| Stassen | 24,753 | *0.2* |
| Fernandez | 23,423 | *0.2* |
| Dole | 7,298 | *0.1* |
| Jacobsen | 4,357 | — |
| Kelley | 3,757 | — |
| Yeager | 1,063 | — |
| Carris | 483 | — |
| Belluso | 355 | — |
| Carlson | 311 | — |
| Badgley | 244 | — |
| Pickett | 67 | — |
| Unpledged delegates | 38,708 | *0.3* |
| No preference | 15,161 | *0.1* |
| None of the names shown | 14,286 | *0.1* |
| Others | 25,452 | *0.2* |
| | 12,690,451 | |

# Democratic

|  | Votes | % |
|---|---|---|
| Carter | 9,593,335 | *51.2* |
| Kennedy | 6,963,625 | *37.1* |
| Brown | 573,636 | *3.1* |
| LaRouche | 177,784 | *1.0* |
| Kay | 48,061 | *0.3* |
| Finch | 48,032 | *0.3* |
| Maddox | 4,002 | — |
| Reaux | 2,255 | — |
| Nuckols | 609 | — |
| Ahern | 571 | — |
| Rollinson | 364 | — |
| Unpledged delegates | 950,378 | *5.1* |
| No preference | 301,695 | *1.6* |
| None of the names shown | 36,350 | *0.1* |
| Others | 47,128 | *0.2* |
| | 18,747,825 | |

*1. In 1980, 35 states, the District of Columbia and Puerto Rico held presidential primaries. California Democrats and South Dakota Republicans and Democrats held state-type preference primaries. In New York, Democrats had a presidential preference, but Republicans held primaries for the selection of delegates only, without indication of presidential preference. In Mississippi, Republicans elected delegates by congressional districts pledged to candidates and the vote indicated is for the highest of each slate's candidates in each congressional district. In Arkansas, the Republicans did not hold a primary although Democrats did. In South Carolina, the Democrats did not hold a primary but Republicans did. The vote in Ohio is for at-large delegates pledged to specific candidates and elected as a group. The Republican and Democratic primaries in Puerto Rico were held on two different dates: February 17 and March 16, respectively.*

*2. Bush withdrew May 26.*

*3. Baker withdrew March 5.*

*4. Connally withdrew March 9.*

*5. Brown withdrew April 1.*

*6. Anderson withdrew April 24.*

*7. Write-in vote.*

*8. Totals exclude Puerto Rico, where citizens are unable to vote in the general election.*

# 1984 Primaries

| | Republican | | | Democratic | | |
|---|---|---|---|---|---|---|
| | Votes | % | | Votes | % |

**February 28  New Hampshire**

| Republican | Votes | % | Democratic | Votes | % |
|---|---|---|---|---|---|
| Ronald Reagan (Calif.) | 65,033 | 86.1 | Gary Hart (Colo.) | 37,702 | 37.3 |
| Harold E. Stassen (Pa.) | 1,543 | 2.0 | Walter F. Mondale (Minn.) | 28,173 | 27.9 |
| David Kelly (La.) | 360 | 0.5 | John Glenn (Ohio) | 12,088 | 12.0 |
| Gary Arnold (Minn.) | 252 | 0.3 | Jesse Jackson (Ill.) | 5,311 | 5.3 |
| Benjamin Fernandez (Calif.) | 202 | 0.3 | George McGovern (S.D.) | 5,217 | 5.2 |
| Others [1] | 8,180 | 10.8 | Ernest F. Hollings (S.C.) | 3,583 | 3.5 |
| | | | Alan Cranston (Calif.) | 2,136 | 2.1 |
| | | | Reubin Askew (Fla.) | 1,025 | 1.0 |
| | | | Stephen A. Koczak (D.C.) | 155 | 0.2 |
| | | | Gerald Willis (Ala.) | 50 | — |
| | | | Richard B. Kay (Fla.) | 27 | — |
| | | | Others [1] | 5,664 | 5.6 |

**March 6  Vermont [2]**

| Republican | Votes | % | Democratic | Votes | % |
|---|---|---|---|---|---|
| Reagan | 33,218 | 98.7 | Hart | 51,873 | 70.0 |
| Others | 425 | 1.3 | Mondale | 14,834 | 20.0 |
| | | | Jackson | 5,761 | 7.8 |
| | | | Askew | 444 | 0.6 |
| | | | Others | 1,147 | 1.5 |

**March 13  Alabama**

[3]

| Democratic | Votes | % |
|---|---|---|
| Mondale | 148,165 | 34.6 |
| Glenn | 89,286 | 20.8 |
| Hart | 88,465 | 20.7 |
| Jackson | 83,787 | 19.6 |
| Willis | 6,153 | 1.4 |
| Hollings | 4,759 | 1.1 |
| Unpledged delegates | 4,464 | 1.0 |
| Askew | 1,827 | 0.4 |
| Cranston | 1,377 | 0.3 |

**March 13  Florida**

| Republican | Votes | % | Democratic | Votes | % |
|---|---|---|---|---|---|
| Reagan | 344,150 | 100.0 | Hart | 463,799 | 39.2 |
| | | | Mondale | 394,350 | 33.4 |
| | | | Jackson | 144,263 | 12.2 |
| | | | Glenn | 128,209 | 10.8 |
| | | | Askew | 26,258 | 2.2 |
| | | | McGovern | 17,614 | 1.5 |
| | | | Hollings | 3,115 | 0.3 |
| | | | Cranston | 2,097 | 0.2 |
| | | | Kay | 1,328 | 0.1 |
| | | | Koczak | 1,157 | 0.1 |

## Republican                    ## Democratic

|  | Votes | % |  | Votes | % |
|---|---|---|---|---|---|
| **March 13  Georgia** | | | | | |
| Reagan | 50,793 | *100.0* | Mondale | 208,588 | *30.5* |
| | | | Hart | 186,903 | *27.3* |
| | | | Jackson | 143,730 | *21.0* |
| | | | Glenn | 122,744 | *17.9* |
| | | | McGovern | 11,321 | *1.7* |
| | | | Hollings | 3,800 | *0.6* |
| | | | Unpledged delegates | 3,068 | *0.4* |
| | | | Willis | 1,804 | *0.3* |
| | | | Askew | 1,660 | *0.2* |
| | | | Cranston | 923 | *0.1* |
| **March 13  Massachusetts** | | | | | |
| Reagan | 58,996 | *89.5* | Hart | 245,943 | *39.0* |
| No preference | 5,005 | *7.6* | Mondale | 160,893 | *25.5* |
| Others | 1,936 | *2.9* | McGovern | 134,341 | *21.3* |
| | | | Glenn | 45,456 | *7.2* |
| | | | Jackson | 31,824 | *5.0* |
| | | | No preference | 5,080 | *0.8* |
| | | | Askew | 1,394 | *0.2* |
| | | | Hollings | 1,203 | *0.2* |
| | | | Cranston | 853 | *0.1* |
| | | | Others | 3,975 | *0.6* |
| **March 13  Rhode Island** | | | | | |
| Reagan | 2,028 | *90.7* | Hart | 20,011 | *45.0* |
| Unpledged delegates | 207 | *9.3* | Mondale | 15,338 | *34.5* |
| | | | Jackson | 3,875 | *8.7* |
| | | | Glenn | 2,249 | *5.0* |
| | | | McGovern | 2,146 | *4.8* |
| | | | Unpledged delegates | 439 | *1.0* |
| | | | Cranston | 273 | *0.6* |
| | | | Askew | 96 | *0.2* |
| | | | Hollings | 84 | *0.2* |
| **March 18  Puerto Rico** | | | | | |
| [3] | | | Mondale | 141,698 | *99.1* |
| | | | Hart | 874 | *0.6* |
| | | | Glenn | 436 | *0.3* |
| | | | Sterling P. Davis (Miss.) | 31 | — |
| **March 20  Illinois** | | | | | |
| Reagan | 594,742 | *99.9* | Mondale | 670,951 | *40.4* |
| Others | 336 | *0.1* | Hart | 584,579 | *35.2* |
| | | | Jackson | 348,843 | *21.0* |
| | | | McGovern | 25,336 | *1.5* |
| | | | Glenn | 19,800 | *1.2* |
| | | | Betty Jean Williams (Ill.) | 4,797 | *0.3* |
| | | | Cranston | 2,786 | *0.2* |
| | | | Askew | 2,182 | *0.1* |
| | | | Others | 151 | — |

**539**

| | Republican | | | Democratic | |
|---|---|---|---|---|---|
| | Votes | % | | Votes | % |

**March 27 Connecticut**

[3]

| | | | | | |
|---|---|---|---|---|---|
| | | | Hart | 116,286 | 52.7 |
| | | | Mondale | 64,230 | 29.1 |
| | | | Jackson | 26,395 | 12.0 |
| | | | Askew | 6,098 | 2.8 |
| | | | McGovern | 2,426 | 1.1 |
| | | | Hollings | 2,283 | 1.0 |
| | | | Unpledged delegates | 1,973 | 0.9 |
| | | | Glenn | 955 | 0.4 |
| | | | Cranston | 196 | 0.1 |

**April 3 New York**

[3]

| | | | | | |
|---|---|---|---|---|---|
| | | | Mondale | 621,581 | 44.8 |
| | | | Hart | 380,564 | 27.4 |
| | | | Jackson | 355,541 | 25.6 |
| | | | Glenn | 15,941 | 1.1 |
| | | | Cranston | 6,815 | 0.5 |
| | | | McGovern | 4,547 | 0.3 |
| | | | Askew | 2,877 | 0.2 |
| | | | Others | 84 | — |

**April 3 Wisconsin [4]**

| | | | | | |
|---|---|---|---|---|---|
| "Ronald Reagan Yes" | 280,608 | 95.2 | Hart | 282,435 | 44.4 |
| "Ronald Reagan No" | 14,047 | 4.7 | Mondale | 261,374 | 41.1 |
| Others [1] | 158 | 0.1 | Jackson | 62,524 | 9.8 |
| | | | McGovern | 10,166 | 1.6 |
| | | | "None of the names shown" | 7,036 | 1.1 |
| | | | Glenn | 6,398 | 1.0 |
| | | | Cranston | 2,984 | 0.5 |
| | | | Hollings | 1,650 | 0.3 |
| | | | Askew | 683 | 0.1 |
| | | | Others | 518 | 0.1 |

**April 10 Pennsylvania**

| | | | | | |
|---|---|---|---|---|---|
| Reagan | 616,916 | 99.3 | Mondale | 747,267 | 45.1 |
| Others | 4,290 | 0.7 | Hart | 551,335 | 33.3 |
| | | | Jackson | 264,463 | 16.0 |
| | | | Cranston | 22,829 | 1.4 |
| | | | Glenn | 22,605 | 1.4 |
| | | | Lyndon H. LaRouche Jr. (Va.) | 19,180 | 1.2 |
| | | | McGovern | 13,139 | 0.8 |
| | | | Robert K. Griser (Pa.) | 6,090 | 0.4 |
| | | | Askew | 5,071 | 0.3 |
| | | | Hollings | 2,972 | 0.2 |
| | | | Others | 1,343 | 0.1 |

**May 1 District of Columbia**

| | | | | | |
|---|---|---|---|---|---|
| Reagan | 5,692 | 100.0 | Jackson | 69,106 | 67.3 |
| | | | Mondale | 26,320 | 25.6 |
| | | | Hart | 7,305 | 7.1 |

| Republican | | | Democratic | | |
|---|---|---|---|---|---|
| | Votes | % | | Votes | % |

**May 1   Tennessee**

| Republican | | | Democratic | | |
|---|---|---|---|---|---|
| Reagan | 75,367 | 90.9 | Mondale | 132,201 | 41.0 |
| Unpledged delegates | 7,546 | 9.1 | Hart | 93,710 | 29.1 |
| Others | 8 | — | Jackson | 81,418 | 25.3 |
| | | | Unpledged delegates | 6,682 | 2.1 |
| | | | Glenn | 4,198 | 1.3 |
| | | | McGovern | 3,824 | 1.2 |
| | | | Others | 30 | — |

**May 5   Louisiana**

| Republican | | | Democratic | | |
|---|---|---|---|---|---|
| Reagan | 14,964 | 89.7 | Jackson | 136,707 | 42.9 |
| Unpledged delegates | 1,723 | 10.3 | Hart | 79,593 | 25.0 |
| | | | Mondale | 71,162 | 22.3 |
| | | | Unpledged delegates | 19,409 | 6.1 |
| | | | LaRouche | 4,970 | 1.6 |
| | | | McGovern | 3,158 | 1.0 |
| | | | Griser | 1,924 | 0.6 |
| | | | Kay | 1,344 | 0.4 |
| | | | Koczak | 543 | 0.2 |

**May 5   Texas**

| Republican | | | Democratic | | |
|---|---|---|---|---|---|
| Reagan | 308,713 | 96.5 | 3 | | |
| Unpledged delegates | 11,126 | 3.5 | | | |

**May 8   Indiana**

| Republican | | | Democratic | | |
|---|---|---|---|---|---|
| Reagan | 428,559 | 100.0 | Hart | 299,491 | 41.8 |
| | | | Mondale | 293,413 | 40.9 |
| | | | Jackson | 98,190 | 13.7 |
| | | | Glenn | 16,046 | 2.2 |
| | | | Bob Brewster (Fla.) | 9,815 | 1.4 |

**May 8   Maryland**

| Republican | | | Democratic | | |
|---|---|---|---|---|---|
| Reagan | 73,663 | 100.0 | Mondale | 215,222 | 42.5 |
| | | | Jackson | 129,387 | 25.5 |
| | | | Hart | 123,365 | 24.3 |
| | | | Unpledged delegates | 15,807 | 3.1 |
| | | | LaRouche | 7,836 | 1.5 |
| | | | Glenn | 6,238 | 1.2 |
| | | | McGovern | 5,796 | 1.1 |
| | | | Cranston | 1,768 | 0.3 |
| | | | Hollings | 1,467 | 0.3 |

**May 8   North Carolina**

| Republican | | | Democratic | | |
|---|---|---|---|---|---|
| 3 | | | Mondale | 342,324 | 35.6 |
| | | | Hart | 289,877 | 30.2 |
| | | | Jackson | 243,945 | 25.4 |
| | | | No preference | 44,232 | 4.6 |
| | | | Glenn | 17,659 | 1.8 |
| | | | McGovern | 10,149 | 1.1 |
| | | | Hollings | 8,318 | 0.9 |
| | | | Askew | 3,144 | 0.3 |
| | | | Cranston | 1,209 | 0.1 |

<table>
<tr><td colspan="3" align="center">**Republican**</td><td colspan="3" align="center">**Democratic**</td></tr>
<tr><td></td><td>Votes</td><td>%</td><td></td><td>Votes</td><td>%</td></tr>
</table>

**May 8  Ohio**

| | Votes | % | | Votes | % |
|---|---|---|---|---|---|
| Reagan | 658,169 | 100.0 | Hart | 608,528 | 42.0 |
| | | | Mondale | 583,595 | 40.3 |
| | | | Jackson | 237,133 | 16.4 |
| | | | McGovern | 8,991 | 0.6 |
| | | | Cranston | 4,653 | 0.3 |
| | | | LaRouche | 4,336 | 0.3 |

**May 15  Nebraska**

| | Votes | % | | Votes | % |
|---|---|---|---|---|---|
| Reagan | 145,245 | 99.9 | Hart | 86,582 | 58.2 |
| Others | 1,403 | 1.0 | Mondale | 39,635 | 26.6 |
| | | | Jackson | 13,495 | 9.1 |
| | | | Unpledged delegates | 4,631 | 3.1 |
| | | | McGovern | 1,561 | 1.0 |
| | | | LaRouche | 1,227 | 0.8 |
| | | | Cranston | 538 | 0.4 |
| | | | Hollings | 450 | 0.3 |
| | | | Others | 736 | 0.5 |

**May 15  Oregon**

| | Votes | % | | Votes | % |
|---|---|---|---|---|---|
| Reagan | 238,594 | 98.0 | Hart | 233,638 | 58.5 |
| Others [1] | 4,752 | 2.0 | Mondale | 110,374 | 27.6 |
| | | | Jackson | 37,106 | 9.3 |
| | | | Glenn | 10,831 | 2.7 |
| | | | LaRouche | 5,943 | 1.5 |
| | | | Others | 1,787 | 0.5 |

**May 15  Idaho**

| | Votes | % | | Votes | % |
|---|---|---|---|---|---|
| Reagan | 97,450 | 92.2 | Hart | 31,737 | 58.0 |
| "None of the names shown" | 8,237 | 7.8 | Mondale | 16,460 | 30.1 |
| | | | Jackson | 3,104 | 5.7 |
| | | | "None of the names shown" | 2,225 | 4.1 |
| | | | LaRouche | 1,196 | 2.2 |

**June 5  California**

| | Votes | % | | Votes | % |
|---|---|---|---|---|---|
| Reagan | 1,874,897 | 100.0 | Hart | 1,155,499 | 38.9 |
| Others [1] | 78 | | Mondale | 1,049,342 | 35.3 |
| | | | Jackson | 546,693 | 18.4 |
| | | | Glenn | 96,770 | 3.3 |
| | | | McGovern | 69,926 | 2.4 |
| | | | LaRouche | 52,647 | 1.8 |
| | | | Others [1] | 26 | — |

**June 5  Montana**

| | Votes | % | | Votes | % |
|---|---|---|---|---|---|
| Reagan | 66,432 | 92.4 | No preference | 28,385 | 83.0 |
| No preference | 5,378 | 7.5 | Hart [1] | 3,080 | 9.0 |
| Others | 77 | 0.1 | Mondale [1] | 2,026 | 5.9 |
| | | | Jackson [1] | 388 | 1.1 |
| | | | Others | 335 | 1.0 |

**June 5  New Jersey**

| | Votes | % | | Votes | % |
|---|---|---|---|---|---|
| Reagan | 240,054 | 100.0 | Mondale | 305,516 | 45.2 |
| | | | Hart | 200,948 | 29.7 |
| | | | Jackson | 159,788 | 23.6 |
| | | | LaRouche | 10,309 | 1.5 |

## Republican

## Democratic

| | Votes | % | | Votes | % |
|---|---|---|---|---|---|
| **June 5  New Mexico** | | | | | |
| Reagan | 40,805 | 94.9 | Hart | 87,610 | 46.7 |
| Unpledged delegates | 2,189 | 5.1 | Mondale | 67,675 | 36.1 |
| | | | Jackson | 22,168 | 11.8 |
| | | | McGovern | 5,143 | 2.7 |
| | | | LaRouche | 3,330 | 1.8 |
| | | | Unpledged delegates | 1,477 | 0.8 |
| **June 5  South Dakota** | | | | | |
| 3 | | | Hart | 26,641 | 50.7 |
| | | | Mondale | 20,495 | 39.0 |
| | | | Jackson | 2,738 | 5.2 |
| | | | LaRouche | 1,383 | 2.6 |
| | | | Unpledged delegates | 1,304 | 2.5 |
| **June 5  West Virginia** | | | | | |
| Reagan | 125,790 | 91.8 | Mondale | 198,776 | 53.8 |
| Stassen | 11,206 | 8.2 | Hart | 137,866 | 37.3 |
| | | | Jackson | 24,697 | 6.7 |
| | | | LaRouche | 7,274 | 2.0 |
| | | | Alfred Timinski (N.J.) | 632 | 0.2 |
| **June 12  North Dakota** | | | | | |
| Reagan | 44,109 | 100.0 | Hart | 28,603 | 85.1 |
| | | | LaRouche | 4,018 | 12.0 |
| | | | Mondale [1] | 934 | 2.8 |

| **TOTALS** [5] | | | | | |
|---|---|---|---|---|---|
| Reagan | 6,484,987 | 98.6 | Mondale | 6,811,214 | 37.8 |
| "Ronald Reagan No" | 14,047 | 0.2 | Hart | 6,503,968 | 36.1 |
| Stassen | 12,749 | 0.2 | Jackson | 3,282,431 | 18.2 |
| Kelly | 360 | — | Glenn | 617,380 | 3.4 |
| Arnold | 252 | — | McGovern | 334,801 | 1.9 |
| Fernandez | 202 | — | LaRouche | 123,649 | 0.7 |
| Uncommitted | 41,411 | 0.6 | Askew | 52,759 | 0.3 |
| Others | 21,643 | 0.3 | Cranston | 51,437 | 0.3 |
| | 6,575,651 | | Hollings | 33,684 | 0.2 |
| | | | Brewster | 9,815 | 0.1 |
| | | | Griser | 8,014 | — |
| | | | Willis | 8,007 | — |
| | | | Williams | 4,797 | — |
| | | | Kay | 2,699 | — |
| | | | Koczak | 1,855 | — |
| | | | Timinski | 632 | — |
| | | | Uncommitted | 146,212 | 0.8 |
| | | | Others | 15,796 | 0.1 |
| | | | | 18,009,217 | |

1. Write-in vote.
2. In Vermont's Liberty Union presidential primary, Dennis L. Serrette received 276 of the 309 votes cast, or 89.3 percent of the vote.
3. No primary.
4. Delegates could vote for or against Reagan within the Republican ticket.

5. Totals exclude Puerto Rico, where citizens are unable to vote in the general election.
6. The Uncommitted category includes votes cast on the following ballot lines: No preference, Unpledged delegates and "None of the names shown."

# 1988 Primaries

| **Republican** | Votes | % | **Democratic** | Votes | % |
|---|---|---|---|---|---|

**February 16   New Hampshire**

| Republican | Votes | % | Democratic | Votes | % |
|---|---|---|---|---|---|
| George Bush (Maine) | 59,290 | 37.6 | Michael S. Dukakis (Mass.) | 44,112 | 35.7 |
| Robert Dole (Kan.) | 44,797 | 28.4 | Richard A. Gephardt (Mo.) | 24,513 | 19.8 |
| Jack F. Kemp (N.Y.) | 20,114 | 12.8 | Paul Simon (Ill.) | 21,094 | 17.1 |
| Pierre S. du Pont IV (Del.) | 15,885 | 10.1 | Jesse Jackson (Ill.) | 9,615 | 7.8 |
| Pat Robertson (Va.) | 14,775 | 9.4 | Albert Gore Jr. (Tenn.) | 8,400 | 6.8 |
| Alexander M. Haig Jr. (Pa.) | 481 | 0.3 | Bruce Babbitt (Ariz.) | 5,644 | 4.6 |
| Harold E. Stassen (Pa.) | 130 | — | Gary Hart (Colo.) | 4,888 | 4.0 |
| Paul B. Conley (N.Y.) | 107 | — | William J. du Pont IV (Ill.) | 1,349 | 1.1 |
| Mary Jane Rachner (Minn.) | 107 | — | David E. Duke (D.C.) | 264 | 0.2 |
| Robert F. Drucker | 83 | — | Lyndon H. LaRouche Jr. (Va.) | 188 | 0.2 |
| William Horrigan (Conn.) | 76 | — | William A. Marra (N.J.) | 142 | 0.1 |
| Michael S. Levinson (N.Y.) | 43 | — | Conrad W. Roy | 122 | 0.1 |
| Others [1] | 1,756 | 1.1 | Florenzo Di Donato | 84 | 0.1 |
| | | | Anthony R. Martin-Trigona (Conn.) | 61 | — |
| | | | Stephen A. Koczak (D.C.) | 47 | — |
| | | | William King (Fla.) | 36 | — |
| | | | Edward T. O'Donnell | 33 | — |
| | | | Cyril E. Sagan (Pa.) | 33 | — |
| | | | Frank L. Thomas | 28 | — |
| | | | Claude R. Kirk (Fla.) | 25 | — |
| | | | Irwin Zucker | 22 | — |
| | | | Norbert G. Dennerll (Ohio) | 18 | — |
| | | | Osie Thorpe (D.C.) | 16 | — |
| | | | A. A. Van Petten (Calif.) | 10 | — |
| | | | Stanley Lock (Mich.) | 9 | — |
| | | | Others [1] | 2,759 | 2.2 |

**February 23   South Dakota**

| Republican | Votes | % | Democratic | Votes | % |
|---|---|---|---|---|---|
| Dole slate | 51,599 | 55.2 | Gephardt | 31,184 | 43.6 |
| Robertson slate | 18,310 | 19.6 | Dukakis | 22,349 | 31.2 |
| Bush slate | 17,404 | 18.6 | Gore | 5,993 | 8.4 |
| Kemp slate | 4,290 | 4.6 | Simon | 3,992 | 5.6 |
| Unpledged delegates slate | 1,226 | 1.3 | Hart | 3,875 | 5.4 |
| du Pont slate | 576 | 0.6 | Jackson | 3,867 | 5.4 |
| | | | Babbitt | 346 | 0.5 |

**March 1   Vermont [2]**

| Republican | Votes | % | Democratic | Votes | % |
|---|---|---|---|---|---|
| Bush | 23,565 | 49.3 | Dukakis | 28,353 | 55.8 |
| Dole | 18,655 | 39.0 | Jackson | 13,044 | 25.7 |
| Robertson | 2,452 | 5.1 | Gephardt | 3,910 | 7.7 |
| Kemp | 1,877 | 3.9 | Simon | 2,620 | 5.2 |
| du Pont | 808 | 1.7 | Hart | 2,055 | 4.0 |
| Haig | 324 | 0.7 | Others [1] | 809 | 1.6 |
| Others [1] | 151 | 0.3 | | | |

**March 5   South Carolina**

| Republican | Votes | % | Democratic |
|---|---|---|---|
| Bush | 94,738 | 48.5 | [3] |
| Dole | 40,265 | 20.6 | |
| Robertson | 37,261 | 19.1 | |
| Kemp | 22,431 | 11.5 | |
| du Pont | 316 | 0.2 | |
| Haig | 177 | 0.1 | |
| Stassen | 104 | 0.1 | |

## Republican                                                    ## Democratic

| | Votes | % | | Votes | % |
|---|---|---|---|---|---|

### March 8  **Alabama**

| Republican | Votes | % | Democratic | Votes | % |
|---|---|---|---|---|---|
| Bush | 137,807 | 64.5 | Jackson | 176,764 | 43.6 |
| Dole | 34,733 | 16.2 | Gore | 151,739 | 37.4 |
| Robertson | 29,772 | 13.9 | Dukakis | 31,306 | 7.7 |
| Kemp | 10,557 | 4.9 | Gephardt | 30,214 | 7.4 |
| du Pont | 392 | 0.2 | Hart | 7,530 | 1.9 |
| Haig | 300 | 0.1 | Simon | 3,063 | 0.8 |
| | | | Babbitt | 2,410 | 0.6 |
| | | | Unpledged delegates | 1,771 | 0.4 |
| | | | LaRouche | 845 | 0.2 |

### March 8  **Arkansas**

| Republican | Votes | % | Democratic | Votes | % |
|---|---|---|---|---|---|
| Bush | 32,114 | 47.0 | Gore | 185,758 | 37.3 |
| Dole | 17,667 | 25.9 | Dukakis | 94,103 | 18.9 |
| Robertson | 12,918 | 18.9 | Jackson | 85,003 | 17.1 |
| Kemp | 3,499 | 5.1 | Gephardt | 59,711 | 12.0 |
| Unpledged delegates | 1,402 | 2.1 | Unpledged delegates | 35,553 | 7.1 |
| du Pont | 359 | 0.5 | Hart | 18,630 | 3.7 |
| Haig | 346 | 0.5 | Simon | 9,020 | 1.8 |
| | | | Duke | 4,805 | 1.0 |
| | | | Babbitt | 2,614 | 0.5 |
| | | | LaRouche | 2,347 | 0.5 |

### March 8  **Florida**

| Republican | Votes | % | Democratic | Votes | % |
|---|---|---|---|---|---|
| Bush | 559,820 | 62.1 | Dukakis | 521,041 | 40.9 |
| Dole | 191,197 | 21.2 | Jackson | 254,912 | 20.0 |
| Robertson | 95,826 | 10.6 | Gephardt | 182,861 | 14.4 |
| Kemp | 41,795 | 4.6 | Gore | 161,165 | 12.7 |
| du Pont | 6,726 | 0.7 | Undecided | 79,088 | 6.2 |
| Haig | 5,858 | 0.7 | Hart | 36,315 | 2.9 |
| | | | Simon | 27,620 | 2.2 |
| | | | Babbitt | 10,296 | 0.8 |

### March 8  **Georgia**

| Republican | Votes | % | Democratic | Votes | % |
|---|---|---|---|---|---|
| Bush | 215,516 | 53.8 | Jackson | 247,831 | 39.8 |
| Dole | 94,749 | 23.6 | Gore | 201,490 | 32.6 |
| Robertson | 65,163 | 16.3 | Dukakis | 97,179 | 15.6 |
| Kemp | 23,409 | 5.8 | Gephardt | 41,489 | 6.7 |
| du Pont | 1,309 | 0.3 | Hart | 15,852 | 2.5 |
| Haig | 782 | 0.2 | Simon | 8,388 | 1.3 |
| | | | Unpledged delegates | 7,276 | 1.2 |
| | | | Babbitt | 3,247 | 0.5 |

### March 8  **Kentucky**

| Republican | Votes | % | Democratic | Votes | % |
|---|---|---|---|---|---|
| Bush | 72,020 | 59.3 | Gore | 145,988 | 45.8 |
| Dole | 27,868 | 23.0 | Dukakis | 59,433 | 18.6 |
| Robertson | 13,526 | 11.1 | Jackson | 49,667 | 15.6 |
| Kemp | 4,020 | 3.3 | Gephardt | 28,982 | 9.1 |
| Unpledged delegates | 2,245 | 1.8 | Hart | 11,798 | 3.7 |
| Stassen | 844 | 0.7 | Unpledged delegates | 10,465 | 3.3 |
| du Pont | 457 | 0.4 | Simon | 9,393 | 2.9 |
| Haig | 422 | 0.3 | Babbitt | 1,290 | 0.4 |
| | | | LaRouche | 681 | 0.2 |
| | | | Martin-Trigona | 537 | 0.2 |
| | | | Richard B. Kay (Fla.) | 487 | 0.2 |

**545**

# Republican                                      # Democratic

|  | Votes | % |  | Votes | % |
|---|---|---|---|---|---|

**March 8  Louisiana**

| Bush | 83,687 | 57.8 | Jackson | 221,532 | 35.5 |
| Robertson | 26,295 | 18.2 | Gore | 174,974 | 28.0 |
| Dole | 25,626 | 17.7 | Dukakis | 95,667 | 15.3 |
| Kemp | 7,722 | 5.3 | Gephardt | 66,434 | 10.6 |
| du Pont | 853 | 0.6 | Hart | 26,442 | 4.2 |
| Haig | 598 | 0.4 | Duke | 23,390 | 3.7 |
|  |  |  | Simon | 5,155 | 0.8 |
|  |  |  | Frank Ahern (La.) | 3,701 | 0.6 |
|  |  |  | Babbitt | 3,076 | 0.5 |
|  |  |  | LaRouche | 1,681 | 0.3 |
|  |  |  | Dennerll | 1,575 | 0.3 |
|  |  |  | Kay | 823 | 0.1 |

**March 8  Maryland**

| Bush | 107,026 | 53.3 | Dukakis | 242,479 | 45.6 |
| Dole | 64,987 | 32.8 | Jackson | 152,642 | 28.7 |
| Robertson | 12,860 | 6.5 | Gore | 46,063 | 8.7 |
| Kemp | 11,909 | 5.9 | Gephardt | 42,059 | 8.0 |
| du Pont | 2,551 | 1.8 | Simon | 16,513 | 3.1 |
| Haig | 1,421 | 0.7 | Unpledged delegates | 14,948 | 2.8 |
|  |  |  | Hart | 9,732 | 1.8 |
|  |  |  | Babbitt | 4,750 | 0.9 |
|  |  |  | LaRouche | 2,149 | 0.4 |

**March 8  Massachusetts**

| Bush | 141,113 | 58.6 | Dukakis | 418,256 | 58.6 |
| Dole | 63,392 | 26.3 | Jackson | 133,141 | 18.7 |
| Kemp | 16,791 | 7.0 | Gephardt | 72,944 | 10.2 |
| Robertson | 10,891 | 4.5 | Gore | 31,631 | 4.4 |
| du Pont | 3,522 | 1.5 | Simon | 26,176 | 3.6 |
| No preference | 3,416 | 1.4 | No preference | 11,866 | 1.7 |
| Haig | 1,705 | 0.7 | Hart | 10,837 | 1.5 |
| Others [1] | 351 | 0.1 | Babbitt | 4,222 | 0.6 |
|  |  |  | DiDonato | 1,971 | 0.3 |
|  |  |  | LaRouche | 998 | 0.1 |
|  |  |  | Others [1] | 1,405 | 0.2 |

**March 8  Mississippi**

| Bush | 104,814 | 66.1 | Jackson | 160,651 | 44.7 |
| Dole | 26,855 | 16.9 | Gore | 120,364 | 33.5 |
| Robertson | 21,378 | 13.5 | Dukakis | 29,941 | 8.3 |
| Kemp | 5,479 | 3.5 | Gephardt | 19,693 | 5.5 |
|  |  |  | Hart | 13,934 | 3.9 |
|  |  |  | Unpledged delegates | 9,384 | 2.6 |
|  |  |  | Simon | 2,118 | 0.6 |
|  |  |  | Babbitt | 2,037 | 0.6 |
|  |  |  | LaRouche | 1,295 | 0.4 |

**March 8  Missouri**

| Bush | 168,812 | 42.2 | Gephardt | 305,287 | 57.8 |
| Dole | 164,394 | 41.1 | Jackson | 106,386 | 20.2 |
| Robertson | 44,705 | 11.2 | Dukakis | 61,303 | 11.7 |
| Kemp | 14,180 | 3.5 | Simon | 21,433 | 4.1 |
| Unpledged delegates | 5,563 | 1.4 | Gore | 14,549 | 2.8 |
| du Pont | 1,788 | 0.4 | Hart | 7,607 | 1.4 |
| Haig | 858 | 0.2 | Unpledged delegates | 6,635 | 1.3 |
|  |  |  | Duke | 1,760 | 0.3 |
|  |  |  | Babbitt | 1,377 | 0.3 |
|  |  |  | LaRouche | 664 | 0.1 |
|  |  |  | Kay | 372 | — |
|  |  |  | Koczak | 241 | — |
|  |  |  | Dennerll | 191 | — |

# Republican

# Democratic

|  | Votes | % |  | Votes | % |
|---|---|---|---|---|---|

## March 8  North Carolina

| Bush | 124,260 | 45.4 | Gore | 235,669 | 34.7 |
|---|---|---|---|---|---|
| Dole | 107,032 | 39.1 | Jackson | 224,177 | 33.0 |
| Robertson | 26,861 | 9.8 | Dukakis | 137,993 | 20.3 |
| Kemp | 11,361 | 4.1 | Gephardt | 37,553 | 5.5 |
| No preference | 2,797 | 1.0 | Hart | 16,381 | 2.4 |
| du Pont | 944 | 0.3 | No preference | 16,337 | 2.4 |
| Haig | 546 | 0.2 | Simon | 8,032 | 1.2 |
|  |  |  | Babbitt | 3,816 | 0.6 |

## March 8  Oklahoma

| Bush | 78,224 | 37.4 | Gore | 162,584 | 41.4 |
|---|---|---|---|---|---|
| Dole | 73,016 | 34.9 | Gephardt | 82,596 | 21.0 |
| Robertson | 44,067 | 21.0 | Dukakis | 66,278 | 16.9 |
| Kemp | 11,439 | 5.5 | Jackson | 52,417 | 13.3 |
| du Pont | 938 | 0.4 | Hart | 14,336 | 3.7 |
| Haig | 715 | 0.3 | Simon | 6,901 | 1.8 |
| Isabell Masters (Kan.) | 539 | 0.3 | Duke | 2,388 | 0.6 |
|  |  |  | Babbitt | 1,601 | 0.4 |
|  |  |  | LaRouche | 1,078 | 0.3 |
|  |  |  | Koczak | 1,068 | 0.3 |
|  |  |  | Charles R. Doty (Okla.) | 1,005 | 0.3 |
|  |  |  | DennerlI | 475 | 0.1 |

## March 8  Rhode Island

| Bush | 10,401 | 64.9 | Dukakis | 34,211 | 69.7 |
|---|---|---|---|---|---|
| Dole | 3,628 | 22.6 | Jackson | 7,445 | 15.2 |
| Robertson | 911 | 5.7 | Gephardt | 2,028 | 4.1 |
| Kemp | 792 | 4.9 | Gore | 1,939 | 4.0 |
| Unpledged delegates | 174 | 1.1 | Simon | 1,395 | 2.8 |
| du Pont | 80 | 0.5 | Unpledged delegates | 809 | 1.7 |
| Haig | 49 | 0.3 | Hart | 733 | 1.5 |
|  |  |  | Babbitt | 469 | 1.0 |

## March 8  Tennessee

| Bush | 152,515 | 60.0 | Gore | 416,861 | 72.3 |
|---|---|---|---|---|---|
| Dole | 55,027 | 21.6 | Jackson | 119,248 | 20.7 |
| Robertson | 32,015 | 12.6 | Dukakis | 19,348 | 3.3 |
| Kemp | 10,911 | 4.3 | Gephardt | 8,470 | 1.5 |
| Unpledged delegates | 2,340 | 0.9 | Hart | 4,706 | 0.8 |
| Haig | 777 | 0.3 | Unpledged delegates | 3,032 | 0.5 |
| du Pont | 646 | 0.3 | Simon | 2,647 | 0.5 |
| Others [1] | 21 | — | Babbitt | 1,946 | 0.3 |
|  |  |  | Others [1] | 56 | — |

## March 8  Texas

| Bush | 648,178 | 63.9 | Dukakis | 579,713 | 32.8 |
|---|---|---|---|---|---|
| Robertson | 155,449 | 15.3 | Jackson | 433,335 | 24.5 |
| Dole | 140,795 | 13.9 | Gore | 357,764 | 20.2 |
| Kemp | 50,586 | 5.0 | Gephardt | 240,158 | 13.6 |
| Unpledged delegates | 12,563 | 1.2 | Hart | 82,199 | 4.7 |
| du Pont | 4,245 | 0.4 | Simon | 34,499 | 1.9 |
| Haig | 3,140 | 0.3 | Babbitt | 11,618 | 0.7 |
|  |  |  | LaRouche | 9,013 | 0.5 |
|  |  |  | Duke | 8,808 | 0.5 |
|  |  |  | W. A. Williams | 6,238 | 0.4 |
|  |  |  | DennerlI | 3,700 | 0.2 |

# Republican          Democratic

| | Votes | % | | Votes | % |
|---|---|---|---|---|---|

**March 8   Virginia**

| Republican | Votes | % | Democratic | Votes | % |
|---|---|---|---|---|---|
| Bush | 124,738 | 53.7 | Jackson | 164,709 | 45.1 |
| Dole | 60,921 | 26.0 | Gore | 81,419 | 22.3 |
| Robertson | 32,173 | 13.7 | Dukakis | 80,183 | 22.0 |
| Kemp | 10,809 | 4.6 | Gephardt | 15,935 | 4.4 |
| Unpledged delegates | 3,675 | 1.6 | Simon | 7,045 | 1.9 |
| du Pont | 1,229 | 0.5 | Hart | 6,266 | 1.7 |
| Haig | 597 | 0.3 | Unpledged delegates | 6,142 | 1.7 |
| | | | Babbitt | 2,454 | 0.7 |
| | | | LaRouche | 746 | 0.2 |

**March 15   Illinois [4]**

| Republican | Votes | % | Democratic | Votes | % |
|---|---|---|---|---|---|
| Bush | 469,151 | 54.6 | Simon | 635,219 | 42.3 |
| Dole | 309,253 | 36.0 | Jackson | 484,233 | 32.3 |
| Robertson | 59,087 | 6.9 | Dukakis | 245,289 | 16.3 |
| Kemp | 12,687 | 1.5 | Gore | 77,265 | 5.1 |
| du Pont | 4,653 | 0.5 | Gephardt | 35,108 | 2.3 |
| Haig | 3,806 | 0.4 | Hart | 12,769 | 0.9 |
| | | | LaRouche | 6,094 | 0.4 |
| | | | Babbitt | 4,953 | 0.3 |

**March 29   Connecticut**

| Republican | Votes | % | Democratic | Votes | % |
|---|---|---|---|---|---|
| Bush | 73,501 | 70.6 | Dukakis | 140,291 | 58.1 |
| Dole | 21,005 | 20.2 | Jackson | 68,372 | 28.3 |
| Kemp | 3,281 | 3.1 | Gore | 18,501 | 7.7 |
| Unpledged delegates | 3,193 | 3.1 | Hart | 5,761 | 2.4 |
| Robertson | 3,191 | 3.1 | Simon | 3,140 | 1.3 |
| | | | Babbitt | 2,370 | 1.0 |
| | | | Unpledged delegates | 1,951 | 0.8 |
| | | | Gephardt | 1,009 | 0.4 |

**April 5   Wisconsin**

| Republican | Votes | % | Democratic | Votes | % |
|---|---|---|---|---|---|
| Bush | 295,295 | 82.2 | Dukakis | 483,172 | 47.6 |
| Dole | 28,460 | 7.9 | Jackson | 285,995 | 28.2 |
| Robertson | 24,798 | 6.9 | Gore | 176,712 | 17.4 |
| Kemp | 4,915 | 1.4 | Simon | 48,419 | 4.8 |
| Uninstructed delegation | 2,372 | 0.7 | Gephardt | 7,996 | 0.8 |
| Haig | 1,554 | 0.4 | Hart | 7,068 | 0.7 |
| du Pont | 1,504 | 0.4 | Uninstructed delegation | 2,554 | 0.3 |
| Others [1] | 396 | 0.1 | Babbitt | 2,353 | 0.2 |
| | | | Others [1] | 513 | 0.1 |

**April 19   New York [3]**

| Republican | Votes | % | Democratic | Votes | % |
|---|---|---|---|---|---|
| | | | Dukakis | 801,457 | 50.9 |
| | | | Jackson | 585,076 | 37.1 |
| | | | Gore | 157,559 | 10.0 |
| | | | Simon | 17,011 | 1.1 |
| | | | Unpledged delegates | 10,258 | 0.7 |
| | | | Gephardt | 2,672 | 0.2 |
| | | | LaRouche | 1,153 | 0.1 |

**April 26   Pennsylvania**

| Republican | Votes | % | Democratic | Votes | % |
|---|---|---|---|---|---|
| Bush | 687,323 | 79.0 | Dukakis | 1,002,480 | 66.5 |
| Dole | 103,763 | 11.9 | Jackson | 411,260 | 27.3 |
| Robertson | 79,463 | 9.1 | Gore | 44,542 | 3.0 |
| | | | Hart | 20,473 | 1.4 |
| | | | Simon | 9,692 | 0.6 |
| | | | Jennifer Alden Wesner (Pa.) | 7,546 | 0.5 |
| | | | Gephardt | 7,254 | 0.5 |
| | | | LaRouche | 4,443 | 0.3 |

## Republican

## Democratic

| | Votes | % | | Votes | % |
|---|---|---|---|---|---|

**May 3   District of Columbia**

| | | | | | |
|---|---|---|---|---|---|
| Bush | 5,890 | 87.6 | Jackson | 68,840 | 80.0 |
| Dole | 469 | 7.0 | Dukakis | 15,415 | 17.9 |
| Robertson | 268 | 4.0 | Simon | 769 | 0.9 |
| Others [1] | 93 | 1.4 | Gore | 648 | 0.8 |
| | | | Gephardt | 300 | 0.3 |
| | | | Thorpe | 80 | 0.1 |

**May 3   Indiana**

| | | | | | |
|---|---|---|---|---|---|
| Bush | 351,829 | 80.4 | Dukakis | 449,495 | 69.6 |
| Dole | 42,878 | 9.8 | Jackson | 145,021 | 22.5 |
| Robertson | 28,712 | 6.6 | Gore | 21,865 | 3.4 |
| Kemp | 14,236 | 3.6 | Gephardt | 16,777 | 2.6 |
| | | | Simon | 12,550 | 1.9 |

**May 3   Ohio**

| | | | | | |
|---|---|---|---|---|---|
| Bush slate | 643,907 | 81.0 | Dukakis slate | 869,792 | 62.9 |
| Dole slate | 94,650 | 11.9 | Jackson slate | 378,866 | 27.4 |
| Robertson slate | 56,347 | 7.1 | Gore slate | 29,931 | 2.2 |
| | | | James A. Traficant slate (Ohio) | 29,912 | 2.2 |
| | | | Hart slate | 28,414 | 2.1 |
| | | | Douglas Applegate slate (Ohio) | 25,068 | 1.8 |
| | | | Simon slate | 15,524 | 1.1 |
| | | | LaRouche slate | 6,065 | 0.4 |

**May 10   Nebraska [5]**

| | | | | | |
|---|---|---|---|---|---|
| Bush | 138,784 | 68.0 | Dukakis | 106,334 | 62.9 |
| Dole | 45,572 | 22.3 | Jackson | 43,380 | 25.7 |
| Robertson | 10,334 | 5.1 | Gephardt | 4,948 | 2.9 |
| Kemp | 8,423 | 4.1 | Unpledged delegates | 4,763 | 2.8 |
| Others [1] | 936 | 0.5 | Hart | 4,220 | 2.5 |
| | | | Gore | 2,519 | 1.5 |
| | | | Simon | 2,104 | 1.2 |
| | | | LaRouche | 416 | 0.2 |
| | | | Others [1] | 324 | 0.2 |

**May 10   West Virginia**

| | | | | | |
|---|---|---|---|---|---|
| Bush | 110,705 | 77.3 | Dukakis | 254,289 | 74.8 |
| Dole | 15,600 | 10.9 | Jackson | 45,788 | 13.5 |
| Robertson | 10,417 | 7.3 | Gore | 11,573 | 3.4 |
| Kemp | 3,820 | 2.7 | Hart | 9,284 | 2.7 |
| Stassen | 1,604 | 1.1 | Gephardt | 6,130 | 1.8 |
| Conley | 994 | 0.7 | Angus W. McDonald (W.Va.) | 3,604 | 1.1 |
| | | | Simon | 2,280 | 0.7 |
| | | | Babbitt | 1,978 | 0.6 |
| | | | LaRouche | 1,482 | 0.4 |
| | | | Duke | 1,383 | 0.4 |
| | | | Dennerll | 1,339 | 0.4 |
| | | | Traficant | 967 | 0.3 |

**May 17   Oregon**

| | | | | | |
|---|---|---|---|---|---|
| Bush | 199,938 | 72.8 | Dukakis | 221,048 | 56.8 |
| Dole | 49,128 | 17.9 | Jackson | 148,207 | 38.1 |
| Robertson | 21,212 | 7.7 | Gephardt | 6,772 | 1.7 |
| Others [1] | 4,208 | 1.5 | Gore | 5,445 | 1.4 |
| | | | Simon | 4,757 | 1.2 |
| | | | LaRouche | 1,562 | 0.4 |
| | | | Others [1] | 1,141 | 0.3 |

<table>
<tr><td colspan="3" align="center">**Republican**</td><td colspan="3" align="center">**Democratic**</td></tr>
<tr><td></td><td>Votes</td><td>%</td><td></td><td>Votes</td><td>%</td></tr>
</table>

**May 24  Idaho**

| Republican | Votes | % | Democratic | Votes | % |
|---|---|---|---|---|---|
| Bush | 55,464 | 81.2 | Dukakis | 37,696 | 73.4 |
| "None of the names shown" | 6,935 | 10.2 | Jackson | 8,066 | 15.7 |
| Robertson | 5,876 | 8.6 | "None of the names shown" | 2,308 | 4.5 |
| | | | Gore | 1,891 | 3.7 |
| | | | Simon | 1,409 | 2.7 |

**June 7  California [6]**

| Republican | Votes | % | Democratic | Votes | % |
|---|---|---|---|---|---|
| Bush | 1,856,273 | 82.9 | Dukakis | 1,910,808 | 60.9 |
| Dole | 289,220 | 12.9 | Jackson | 1,102,093 | 35.1 |
| Robertson | 94,779 | 4.2 | Gore | 56,645 | 1.8 |
| Others [1] | 115 | — | Simon | 43,771 | 1.4 |
| | | | LaRouche | 25,417 | 0.8 |

**June 7  Montana**

| Republican | Votes | % | Democratic | Votes | % |
|---|---|---|---|---|---|
| Bush | 63,098 | 73.0 | Dukakis | 83,684 | 68.7 |
| Dole | 16,762 | 19.4 | Jackson | 26,908 | 22.1 |
| No preference | 6,520 | 7.5 | No preference | 4,083 | 3.4 |
| | | | Gephardt | 3,369 | 2.8 |
| | | | Gore | 2,261 | 1.9 |
| | | | Simon | 1,566 | 1.3 |

**June 7  New Jersey**

| Republican | Votes | % | Democratic | Votes | % |
|---|---|---|---|---|---|
| Bush | 241,033 | 100.0 | Dukakis | 414,829 | 63.4 |
| | | | Jackson | 213,705 | 32.7 |
| | | | Gore | 18,062 | 2.8 |
| | | | LaRouche | 2,621 | 0.4 |
| | | | Marra | 2,594 | 0.4 |
| | | | Duke | 2,491 | 0.4 |

**June 7  New Mexico**

| Republican | Votes | % | Democratic | Votes | % |
|---|---|---|---|---|---|
| Bush | 69,359 | 78.2 | Dukakis | 114,968 | 61.0 |
| Dole | 9,305 | 10.5 | Jackson | 52,988 | 28.1 |
| Robertson | 5,350 | 6.0 | Hart | 6,898 | 3.7 |
| Unpledged delegates | 2,569 | 2.9 | Gore | 4,747 | 2.6 |
| Haig | 2,161 | 2.4 | Unpledged delegates | 3,275 | 1.7 |
| | | | Babbitt | 2,913 | 1.5 |
| | | | Simon | 2,821 | 1.5 |

**June 14  North Dakota**

| Republican | Votes | % | |
|---|---|---|---|
| Bush | 37,062 | 94.0 | [7] |
| Rachner | 2,372 | 6.0 | |

| | **Republican** | | | **Democratic** | | |
|---|---|---|---|---|---|---|
| | Votes | % | | | Votes | % |
| **TOTALS** | | | | | | |
| Bush | 8,254,654 | 67.9 | Dukakis | | 9,817,185 | 42.8 |
| Dole | 2,333,268 | 19.2 | Jackson | | 6,685,699 | 29.1 |
| Robertson | 1,097,442 | 9.0 | Gore | | 3,134,516 | 13.7 |
| Kemp | 331,333 | 2.7 | Gephardt | | 1,388,356 | 6.0 |
| du Pont | 49,781 | 0.4 | Simon | | 1,018,136 | 4.4 |
| Haig | 26,617 | 0.2 | Hart | | 389,003 | 1.7 |
| Stassen | 2,682 | — | Babbitt | | 77,780 | 0.3 |
| Rachner | 2,479 | — | LaRouche | | 70,938 | 0.3 |
| Conley | 1,101 | — | Duke | | 45,289 | 0.2 |
| Masters | 539 | — | Traficant | | 30,879 | 0.1 |
| Drucker | 83 | — | Applegate | | 25,068 | 0.1 |
| Horrigan | 76 | — | Dennerll | | 7,298 | — |
| Levinson | 43 | — | Wesner | | 7,546 | — |
| Uncommitted [8] | 57,990 | 0.5 | Williams | | 6,238 | — |
| Others [1] | 8,027 | 0.1 | Ahern | | 3,701 | — |
| | 12,165,115 | | McDonald | | 3,604 | — |
| | | | Marra | | 2,736 | — |
| | | | Di Nonato | | 2,055 | — |
| | | | Kay | | 1,682 | — |
| | | | Koczak | | 1,356 | — |
| | | | du Pont | | 1,349 | — |
| | | | Doty | | 1,005 | — |
| | | | Martin-Trigona | | 598 | — |
| | | | Roy | | 122 | — |
| | | | Thorpe | | 96 | — |
| | | | King | | 36 | — |
| | | | O'Donnell | | 33 | — |
| | | | Sagan | | 33 | — |
| | | | Thomas | | 28 | — |
| | | | Kirk | | 25 | — |
| | | | Zucker | | 22 | — |
| | | | Van Petten | | 10 | — |
| | | | Lock | | 9 | — |
| | | | Uncommitted [8] | | 232,498 | 1.0 |
| | | | Others [1] | | 7,007 | — |
| | | | | | 22,961,936 | |

1. Write-in votes.
2. In Vermont's Liberty Union presidential primary, Willa Kenoyer received 199 votes (68.9 percent), Herb Lewin received 65 votes (22.5 percent), and there were 25 scattered write-in votes (8.7 percent).
3. No primary.
4. In Illinois's Solidarity presidential primary, Lenora B. Fulani received 170 votes (100 percent).
5. In Nebraska's New Alliance presidential primary, Lenora B. Fulani received 10 votes (100 percent).
6. In California's American Independent presidential primary, James C. Griffin received 9,762 votes (64.4 percent), James Gritz received 5,401 votes (35.6 percent), and

there were 3 scattered write-in votes (0.0 percent). In the Peace and Freedom presidential primary, Lenora B. Fulani received 2,117 votes (35.7 percent), Shirley Isaacson received 1,222 votes (20.6 percent), Larry Holmes received 1,042 votes (17.6 percent), Herb Lewin received 778 votes (13.1 percent), Willa Kenoyer received 411 votes (6.9 percent), Al Hamburg received 353 votes (6.0 percent), and there were 6 scattered write-in votes (0.1 percent).
7. No candidates' names appeared on the Democratic ballot. Tallied write-in votes were for Dukakis (2,890) and Jackson (515).
8. The Uncommitted category includes votes cast on the following ballot lines: Unpledged delegates, Undecided, No preference, Uninstructed delegation and "None of the names shown."

# 1992 Primaries

| Republican | Votes | % | Democratic | Votes | % |
|---|---|---|---|---|---|

### February 18  New Hampshire [1]

| Republican | Votes | % | Democratic | Votes | % |
|---|---|---|---|---|---|
| George Bush (Texas) | 92,233 | 53.0 | Paul E. Tsongas (Mass.) | 55,638 | 33.2 |
| Patrick J. Buchanan (Va.) | 65,087 | 37.4 | Bill Clinton (Ark.) | 41,522 | 24.7 |
| James P. Lennane (Fla.) | 1,684 | 1.0 | Bob Kerrey (Neb.) | 18,575 | 11.1 |
| Pat Paulsen (Calif.) | 600 | 0.3 | Tom Harkin (Iowa) | 17,057 | 10.2 |
| Richard P. Bosa (N.H.) | 349 | 0.2 | Edmund G. Brown (Calif.) | 13,654 | 8.1 |
| John D. Merwin (N.H.) | 223 | 0.1 | Tom Laughlin (Calif.) | 3,251 | 1.9 |
| Harold E. Stassen (Minn.) | 206 | 0.1 | Charles Woods (Nev.) | 2,862 | 1.7 |
| Paul B. Conley (N.Y.) | 115 | 0.1 | Lenora B. Fulani (N.Y.) | 402 | 0.2 |
| Billy Joe Clegg (Miss.) | 110 | 0.1 | Lawrence A. Agran (Calif.) | 332 | 0.2 |
| Georgiana Doerschuck (Fla.) | 57 | — | Patrick J. Mahoney (Fla.) | 303 | 0.2 |
| Paul C. Daugherty (S.C.) | 53 | — | Eugene J. McCarthy (Va.) | 211 | 0.1 |
| Michael Levinson (N.Y.) | 44 | — | John D. Rigazio (N.H.) | 186 | 0.1 |
| Jack Fellure (W.Va.) | 36 | — | Curly Thornton (Mont.) | 125 | 0.1 |
| Vincent Latchford (N.J.) | 32 | — | Lyndon H. LaRouche Jr. (Va.) | 115 | 0.1 |
| Hubert D. Patty (Tenn.) | 31 | — | L. Douglas Wilder (Va.) | 103 | 0.1 |
| George Zimmermann (Texas) | 31 | — | Caroline P. Killeen (Ariz.) | 93 | 0.1 |
| Stephen A. Koczak (D.C.) | 29 | — | John P. Cahill (N.Y.) | 83 | — |
| Thomas S. Fabish (Calif.) | 25 | — | Paul Fisher (Ill.) | 82 | — |
| F. Dean Johnson (Calif.) | 24 | — | Frank J. Bona (Fla.) | 65 | — |
| Norm Bertasavage (Pa.) | 23 | — | Karl J. Hegger (Ill.) | 61 | — |
| Jack Trinsey (Pa.) | 22 | — | William Horrigan (Conn.) | 53 | — |
| Tennie Rogers (Calif.) | 20 | — | Dean A. Curtis (Calif.) | 43 | — |
| Conrad A. Ryden (N.C.) | 20 | — | Stephen Burke (N.Y.) | 39 | — |
| Oscar A. Erickson (Calif.) | 16 | — | Gilbert H. Holmes (D.C.) | 39 | — |
| Richard F. Reber (Ga.) | 14 | — | Ron Kovic (Calif.) | 36 | — |
| Others [2] | 13,081 | 7.5 | Rufus T. Higginbotham (Texas) | 31 | — |
| | | | Chris Norton (N.Y.) | 31 | — |
| | | | Fanny R.Z. Monyek (Fla.) | 29 | — |
| | | | James B. Gay (Texas) | 28 | — |
| | | | Barry J. Deutsch (N.Y.) | 26 | — |
| | | | Cyril E. Sagan (Pa.) | 26 | — |
| | | | Edward T. O'Donnell (Del.) | 24 | — |
| | | | Tom Shiekman (Fla.) | 23 | — |
| | | | Stephen H. Schwartz (N.Y.) | 17 | — |
| | | | George W. Benns (N.Y.) | 11 | — |
| | | | Nathan Averick (Ill.) | 7 | — |
| | | | Others [2] | 12,636 | 7.5 |

### February 25  South Dakota

| Republican | Votes | % | Democratic | Votes | % |
|---|---|---|---|---|---|
| Bush | 30,964 | 69.3 | Kerrey | 23,892 | 40.2 |
| Uncommitted | 13,707 | 30.7 | Harkin | 15,023 | 25.2 |
| | | | Clinton | 11,375 | 19.1 |
| | | | Tsongas | 5,729 | 9.6 |
| | | | Brown | 2,300 | 3.9 |
| | | | Agran | 606 | 1.0 |
| | | | LaRouche | 441 | 0.7 |
| | | | Wilder | 137 | 0.2 |

## Republican                                 ## Democratic

|  | Votes | % |  | Votes | % |
|---|---|---|---|---|---|

**March 3  Colorado**

| Bush | 132,100 | 67.5 | Brown | 69,073 | 28.8 |
|---|---|---|---|---|---|
| Buchanan | 58,753 | 30.0 | Clinton | 64,470 | 26.9 |
| Zimmermann | 1,592 | 0.8 | Tsongas | 61,360 | 25.6 |
| Paul S. Jensen (Colo.) | 1,332 | 0.7 | Kerrey | 29,572 | 12.3 |
| Terrance R. Scott (Colo.) | 719 | 0.4 | Harkin | 5,866 | 2.4 |
| Koczak | 659 | 0.3 | Noncommitted | 5,356 | 2.2 |
| Rogers | 535 | 0.3 | Woods | 1,051 | 0.4 |
|  |  |  | Agran | 672 | 0.3 |
|  |  |  | Burke | 532 | 0.2 |
|  |  |  | McCarthy | 488 | 0.2 |
|  |  |  | LaRouche | 328 | 0.1 |
|  |  |  | Jim Hayes | 279 | 0.1 |
|  |  |  | Leonard Talbow | 202 | 0.1 |
|  |  |  | Tod H. Hawks | 165 | 0.1 |
|  |  |  | Shiekman | 76 | — |
|  |  |  | Jeffrey Marsh | 59 | — |
|  |  |  | Louis McAlpine | 48 | — |
|  |  |  | Ray Rollinson | 46 | — |

**March 3  Georgia**

| Bush | 291,905 | 64.3 | Clinton | 259,907 | 57.2 |
|---|---|---|---|---|---|
| Buchanan | 162,085 | 35.7 | Tsongas | 109,148 | 24.0 |
|  |  |  | Brown | 36,808 | 8.1 |
|  |  |  | Kerrey | 22,033 | 4.8 |
|  |  |  | Uncommitted | 17,256 | 3.8 |
|  |  |  | Harkin | 9,479 | 2.1 |

**March 3  Maryland**

| Bush | 168,374 | 70.1 | Tsongas | 230,490 | 40.6 |
|---|---|---|---|---|---|
| Buchanan | 71,647 | 29.9 | Clinton | 189,905 | 33.5 |
|  |  |  | Brown | 46,500 | 8.2 |
|  |  |  | Uncommitted | 36,155 | 6.4 |
|  |  |  | Harkin | 32,899 | 5.8 |
|  |  |  | Kerrey | 27,035 | 4.8 |
|  |  |  | LaRouche | 4,259 | 0.8 |

**March 7  South Carolina**

| Bush | 99,558 | 66.9 | Clinton | 73,221 | 62.9 |
|---|---|---|---|---|---|
| Buchanan | 38,247 | 25.7 | Tsongas | 21,338 | 18.3 |
| David Duke (La.) | 10,553 | 7.1 | Harkin | 7,657 | 6.6 |
| Daugherty | 482 | 0.3 | Brown | 6,961 | 6.0 |
|  |  |  | Uncommitted | 3,640 | 3.1 |
|  |  |  | Bob Cunningham | 1,369 | 1.2 |
|  |  |  | Woods | 854 | 0.7 |
|  |  |  | Kerrey | 566 | 0.5 |
|  |  |  | William P. Kreml | 336 | 0.3 |
|  |  |  | Angus W. McDonald | 268 | 0.2 |
|  |  |  | LaRouche | 204 | 0.2 |

**March 10  Florida**

| Bush | 608,077 | 68.1 | Clinton | 570,566 | 50.8 |
|---|---|---|---|---|---|
| Buchanan | 285,386 | 31.9 | Tsongas | 388,124 | 34.5 |
|  |  |  | Brown | 139,569 | 12.4 |
|  |  |  | Harkin | 13,587 | 1.2 |
|  |  |  | Kerrey | 12,011 | 1.1 |

# Republican                                    # Democratic

|  | Votes | % |  |  | Votes | % |
|---|---|---|---|---|---|---|

**March 10  Louisiana**

| Bush | 83,744 | 62.0 | Clinton | 267,002 | 69.5 |
|---|---|---|---|---|---|
| Buchanan | 36,525 | 27.0 | Tsongas | 42,508 | 11.1 |
| Duke | 11,955 | 8.8 | Brown | 25,480 | 6.6 |
| Paulsen | 1,186 | 0.9 | McCarthy | 15,129 | 3.9 |
| Rogers | 1,111 | 0.8 | Woods | 8,989 | 2.3 |
| Zimmermann | 474 | 0.4 | Burke | 4,294 | 1.1 |
| Fabish | 114 | 0.1 | Harkin | 4,033 | 1.0 |
|  |  |  | Agran | 3,511 | 0.9 |
|  |  |  | LaRouche | 3,082 | 0.8 |
|  |  |  | Kerrey | 2,984 | 0.8 |
|  |  |  | Marsh | 2,120 | 0.6 |
|  |  |  | Laughlin | 1,857 | 0.5 |
|  |  |  | Hawks | 1,469 | 0.4 |
|  |  |  | Rollinson | 1,069 | 0.3 |
|  |  |  | McAlpine | 870 | 0.2 |

**March 10  Massachusetts [3]**

| Bush | 176,868 | 65.6 | Tsongas | 526,297 | 66.4 |
|---|---|---|---|---|---|
| Buchanan | 74,797 | 27.7 | Brown | 115,746 | 14.6 |
| No preference | 10,132 | 3.8 | Clinton | 86,817 | 10.9 |
| Duke | 5,557 | 2.1 | Ralph Nader | 32,881 | 4.1 |
| Others [2] | 2,347 | 0.9 | No preference | 12,198 | 1.5 |
|  |  |  | Kerrey | 5,409 | 0.7 |
|  |  |  | Harkin | 3,764 | 0.5 |
|  |  |  | McCarthy | 3,127 | 0.4 |
|  |  |  | Agran | 2,224 | 0.3 |
|  |  |  | LaRouche | 2,167 | 0.3 |
|  |  |  | Others [2] | 2,255 | 0.3 |

**March 10  Mississippi**

| Bush | 111,794 | 72.3 | Clinton | 139,893 | 73.1 |
|---|---|---|---|---|---|
| Buchanan | 25,891 | 16.7 | Brown | 18,396 | 9.6 |
| Duke | 16,426 | 10.6 | Tsongas | 15,538 | 8.1 |
| Clegg | 408 | 0.3 | Uncommitted | 11,796 | 6.2 |
| Rogers | 189 | 0.1 | Harkin | 2,509 | 1.3 |
|  |  |  | Kerrey | 1,660 | 0.9 |
|  |  |  | LaRouche | 1,394 | 0.7 |
|  |  |  | Others [2] | 171 | 0.1 |

**March 10  Oklahoma**

| Bush | 151,612 | 69.6 | Clinton | 293,266 | 70.5 |
|---|---|---|---|---|---|
| Buchanan | 57,933 | 26.6 | Brown | 69,624 | 16.7 |
| Duke | 5,672 | 2.6 | Woods | 16,828 | 4.0 |
| Isabell Masters (Kan.) | 1,830 | 0.8 | Harkin | 14,015 | 3.4 |
| Rogers | 674 | 0.3 | Kerrey | 13,252 | 3.2 |
|  |  |  | LaRouche | 6,474 | 1.6 |
|  |  |  | McAlpine | 2,670 | 0.6 |

## Republican                                    ## Democratic

| | Votes | % | | Votes | % |
|---|---|---|---|---|---|

**March 10   Rhode Island**

| | Votes | % | | Votes | % |
|---|---|---|---|---|---|
| Bush | 9,853 | 63.0 | Tsongas | 26,825 | 52.9 |
| Buchanan | 4,967 | 31.8 | Clinton | 10,762 | 21.2 |
| Uncommitted | 444 | 2.8 | Brown | 9,541 | 18.8 |
| Duke | 326 | 2.1 | Uncommitted | 703 | 1.4 |
| Others [2] | 46 | 0.3 | Kerrey | 469 | 0.9 |
| | | | Woods | 408 | 0.8 |
| | | | Harkin | 319 | 0.6 |
| | | | Susan C. Fey | 308 | 0.6 |
| | | | LaRouche | 300 | 0.6 |
| | | | McCarthy | 235 | 0.5 |
| | | | John J. Staradumsky | 168 | 0.3 |
| | | | Laughlin | 94 | 0.2 |
| | | | Rollinson | 91 | 0.2 |
| | | | Agran | 79 | 0.2 |
| | | | Thornton | 52 | 0.1 |
| | | | Burke | 48 | 0.1 |
| | | | Others [2] | 307 | 0.6 |

**March 10   Tennessee**

| | Votes | % | | Votes | % |
|---|---|---|---|---|---|
| Bush | 178,219 | 72.5 | Clinton | 214,485 | 67.3 |
| Buchanan | 54,585 | 22.2 | Tsongas | 61,717 | 19.4 |
| Duke | 7,709 | 3.1 | Brown | 25,560 | 8.0 |
| Uncommitted | 5,022 | 2.0 | Uncommitted | 12,551 | 3.9 |
| Others [2] | 118 | — | Harkin | 2,099 | 0.7 |
| | | | Kerrey | 1,638 | 0.5 |
| | | | Others [2] | 432 | 0.1 |

**March 10   Texas**

| | Votes | % | | Votes | % |
|---|---|---|---|---|---|
| Bush | 556,280 | 69.8 | Clinton | 972,151 | 65.6 |
| Buchanan | 190,572 | 23.9 | Tsongas | 285,191 | 19.2 |
| Uncommitted | 27,936 | 3.5 | Brown | 118,923 | 8.0 |
| Duke | 20,255 | 2.5 | Woods | 30,092 | 2.0 |
| Zimmermann | 1,349 | 0.2 | Kerrey | 20,298 | 1.4 |
| Rogers | 754 | 0.1 | Harkin | 19,617 | 1.3 |
| | | | LaRouche | 12,220 | 0.8 |
| | | | Benns | 7,876 | 0.5 |
| | | | Higginbotham | 7,674 | 0.5 |
| | | | Hawks | 4,924 | 0.3 |
| | | | McAlpine | 4,009 | 0.3 |

**March 17   Illinois**

| | Votes | % | | Votes | % |
|---|---|---|---|---|---|
| Bush | 634,588 | 76.4 | Clinton | 776,829 | 51.6 |
| Buchanan | 186,915 | 22.5 | Tsongas | 387,891 | 25.8 |
| Maurice Horton (Ill.) | 9,637 | 1.2 | Brown | 220,346 | 14.6 |
| | | | Uncommitted | 67,612 | 4.5 |
| | | | Harkin | 30,710 | 2.0 |
| | | | Kerrey | 10,916 | 0.7 |
| | | | LaRouche | 6,599 | 0.4 |
| | | | Agran | 3,227 | 0.2 |

**March 17   Michigan**

| | Votes | % | | Votes | % |
|---|---|---|---|---|---|
| Bush | 301,948 | 67.2 | Clinton | 297,280 | 50.7 |
| Buchanan | 112,122 | 25.0 | Brown | 151,400 | 25.8 |
| Uncommitted | 23,809 | 5.3 | Tsongas | 97,017 | 16.6 |
| Duke | 10,688 | 2.4 | Uncommitted | 27,836 | 4.8 |
| Others [2] | 566 | 0.1 | Harkin | 6,265 | 1.1 |
| | | | Kerrey | 3,219 | 0.5 |
| | | | LaRouche | 2,049 | 0.3 |
| | | | Others [2] | 906 | 0.2 |

| Republican | | | Democratic | | |
|---|---|---|---|---|---|
| | Votes | % | | Votes | % |

### March 24  Connecticut

| Republican | Votes | % | Democratic | Votes | % |
|---|---|---|---|---|---|
| Bush | 66,356 | 66.7 | Brown | 64,472 | 37.2 |
| Buchanan | 21,815 | 21.9 | Clinton | 61,698 | 35.6 |
| Uncommitted | 9,008 | 9.1 | Tsongas | 33,811 | 19.5 |
| Duke | 2,294 | 2.3 | Uncommitted | 5,430 | 3.1 |
| | | | Agran | 2,688 | 1.6 |
| | | | Harkin | 1,919 | 1.1 |
| | | | Kerrey | 1,169 | 0.7 |
| | | | McCarthy | 1,036 | 0.6 |
| | | | LaRouche | 896 | 0.5 |

### April 7  Kansas

| Republican | Votes | % | Democratic | Votes | % |
|---|---|---|---|---|---|
| Bush | 132,131 | 62.0 | Clinton | 82,145 | 51.3 |
| "None of the names shown" | 35,450 | 16.6 | Tsongas | 24,413 | 15.2 |
| Buchanan | 31,494 | 14.8 | "None of the names shown" | 22,159 | 13.8 |
| Paulsen | 5,105 | 2.4 | Brown | 20,811 | 13.0 |
| Duke | 3,837 | 1.8 | Kerrey | 2,215 | 1.4 |
| Masters | 1,303 | 0.6 | Gary Hauptli | 1,303 | 0.8 |
| Philip Skow | 1,105 | 0.5 | Woods | 1,119 | 0.7 |
| Zimmermann | 766 | 0.4 | Don Beamgard | 1,009 | 0.6 |
| Jack J.H. Beemont | 735 | 0.3 | Harkin | 940 | 0.6 |
| Charles Doty (Okla.) | 417 | 0.2 | John A. Barnes | 892 | 0.6 |
| Koczak | 262 | 0.1 | Hawks | 765 | 0.5 |
| Daugherty | 236 | 0.1 | LaRouche | 631 | 0.4 |
| Fellure | 164 | 0.1 | Ralph Spelbring | 537 | 0.3 |
| Rogers | 85 | — | Raymond Vanskiver | 510 | 0.3 |
| Patty | 62 | — | William D. Pawley | 364 | 0.2 |
| Fabish | 44 | — | Marsh | 160 | 0.1 |
| | | | Agran | 147 | 0.1 |
| | | | McAlpine | 131 | 0.1 |

### April 7  Minnesota

| Republican | Votes | % | Democratic | Votes | % |
|---|---|---|---|---|---|
| Bush | 84,841 | 63.9 | Clinton | 63,584 | 31.1 |
| Buchanan | 32,094 | 24.2 | Brown | 62,474 | 30.6 |
| Uncommitted | 4,098 | 3.1 | Tsongas | 43,588 | 21.3 |
| Stassen | 4,074 | 3.1 | Uncommitted | 11,366 | 5.6 |
| Ross Perot [2] (Texas) | 3,558 | 2.7 | Ross Perot (Texas) [2] | 4,250 | 2.1 |
| Sharon Anderson | 300 | 0.2 | Harkin | 4,077 | 2.0 |
| Beatrice Mooney | 196 | 0.1 | McCarthy | 3,704 | 1.8 |
| Zimmermann | 135 | 0.1 | Kerrey | 1,191 | 0.6 |
| Rogers | 61 | — | Agran | 1,042 | 0.5 |
| Others [2] | 3,399 | 2.6 | Woods | 990 | 0.5 |
| | | | Mary Jane Rachner (Minn.) | 620 | 0.3 |
| | | | LaRouche | 532 | 0.3 |
| | | | Burke | 348 | 0.2 |
| | | | McAlpine | 183 | 0.1 |
| | | | Hawks | 111 | 0.1 |
| | | | Marsh | 106 | 0.1 |
| | | | Averick | 105 | 0.1 |
| | | | Others [2] | 5,899 | 2.9 |

### April 7  New York

[4]

| Democratic | Votes | % |
|---|---|---|
| Clinton | 412,349 | 40.9 |
| Tsongas | 288,330 | 28.6 |
| Brown | 264,278 | 26.2 |
| Harkin | 11,535 | 1.1 |
| Kerrey | 11,147 | 1.1 |
| Agran | 10,733 | 1.1 |
| McCarthy | 9,354 | 0.9 |

## Republican                                    ## Democratic

| | Votes | % | | Votes | % |
|---|---|---|---|---|---|

**April 7  Wisconsin**

| Republican | Votes | % | Democratic | Votes | % |
|---|---|---|---|---|---|
| Bush | 364,507 | 75.6 | Clinton | 287,356 | 37.2 |
| Buchanan | 78,516 | 16.3 | Brown | 266,207 | 34.5 |
| Duke | 12,867 | 2.7 | Tsongas | 168,619 | 21.8 |
| Uninstructed | 8,725 | 1.8 | Uninstructed | 15,487 | 2.0 |
| Stassen | 3,819 | 0.8 | McCarthy | 6,525 | 0.8 |
| Emmanuel L. Branch | 1,013 | 0.2 | Harkin | 5,395 | 0.7 |
| Others [2] | 12,801 | 2.7 | Agran | 3,193 | 0.4 |
| | | | LaRouche | 3,120 | 0.4 |
| | | | Kerrey | 3,044 | 0.4 |
| | | | Others [2] | 13,650 | 1.8 |

**April 28  Pennsylvania**

| Republican | Votes | % | Democratic | Votes | % |
|---|---|---|---|---|---|
| Bush | 774,865 | 76.8 | Clinton | 715,031 | 56.5 |
| Buchanan | 233,912 | 23.2 | Brown | 325,543 | 25.7 |
| | | | Tsongas | 161,572 | 12.8 |
| | | | LaRouche | 21,534 | 1.7 |
| | | | Harkin | 21,013 | 1.7 |
| | | | Kerrey | 20,802 | 1.6 |

**May 5  District of Columbia**

| Republican | Votes | % | Democratic | Votes | % |
|---|---|---|---|---|---|
| Bush | 4,265 | 81.5 | Clinton | 45,716 | 73.8 |
| Buchanan | 970 | 18.5 | Tsongas | 6,452 | 10.4 |
| | | | Uncommitted | 5,292 | 8.5 |
| | | | Brown | 4,444 | 7.2 |

**May 5  Indiana**

| Republican | Votes | % | Democratic | Votes | % |
|---|---|---|---|---|---|
| Bush | 374,666 | 80.1 | Clinton | 301,905 | 63.3 |
| Buchanan | 92,949 | 19.9 | Brown | 102,379 | 21.5 |
| | | | Tsongas | 58,215 | 12.2 |
| | | | Kerrey | 14,350 | 3.0 |

**May 5  North Carolina**

| Republican | Votes | % | Democratic | Votes | % |
|---|---|---|---|---|---|
| Bush | 200,387 | 70.7 | Clinton | 443,498 | 64.1 |
| Buchanan | 55,420 | 19.5 | No preference | 106,697 | 15.4 |
| No preference | 27,764 | 9.8 | Brown | 71,984 | 10.4 |
| | | | Tsongas | 57,589 | 8.3 |
| | | | Kerrey | 6,216 | 0.9 |
| | | | Harkin | 5,891 | 0.9 |

**May 12  Nebraska**

| Republican | Votes | % | Democratic | Votes | % |
|---|---|---|---|---|---|
| Bush | 156,346 | 81.4 | Clinton | 68,562 | 45.5 |
| Buchanan | 25,847 | 13.5 | Brown | 31,673 | 21.0 |
| Duke | 2,808 | 1.5 | Uncommitted | 24,714 | 16.4 |
| Zimmermann | 1,313 | 0.7 | Tsongas | 10,707 | 7.1 |
| Rogers | 751 | 0.4 | Harkin | 4,239 | 2.8 |
| Others [2] | 5,033 | 2.6 | McCarthy | 1,520 | 1.0 |
| | | | LaRouche | 1,148 | 0.8 |
| | | | Woods | 485 | 0.3 |
| | | | Agran | 280 | 0.2 |
| | | | Others [2] | 7,259 | 4.8 |

# Republican

| | Votes | % |
|---|---|---|

# Democratic

| | Votes | % |
|---|---|---|

### May 12  West Virginia

| Republican | Votes | % | Democratic | Votes | % |
|---|---|---|---|---|---|
| Bush | 99,994 | 80.5 | Clinton | 227,815 | 74.2 |
| Buchanan | 18,067 | 14.6 | Brown | 36,505 | 11.9 |
| Fellure | 6,096 | 4.9 | Tsongas | 21,271 | 6.9 |
| | | | McDonald | 9,632 | 3.1 |
| | | | Kerrey | 3,152 | 1.0 |
| | | | LaRouche | 3,141 | 1.0 |
| | | | Harkin | 2,774 | 0.9 |
| | | | Woods | 1,487 | 0.5 |
| | | | Spelbring | 1,089 | 0.4 |

### May 19  Oregon

| Republican | Votes | % | Democratic | Votes | % |
|---|---|---|---|---|---|
| Bush | 203,957 | 67.1 | Clinton | 159,802 | 45.1 |
| Buchanan | 57,730 | 19.0 | Brown | 110,494 | 31.2 |
| Duke | 6,667 | 2.2 | Tsongas | 37,139 | 10.5 |
| Others [2] | 35,805 | 11.8 | McCarthy | 6,714 | 1.9 |
| | | | LaRouche | 3,096 | 0.9 |
| | | | Woods | 1,895 | 0.5 |
| | | | Agran | 1,652 | 0.5 |
| | | | Others [2] | 33,540 | 9.5 |

### May 19  Washington

| Republican | Votes | % | Democratic | Votes | % |
|---|---|---|---|---|---|
| Bush | 86,839 | 67.0 | Clinton | 62,171 | 42.0 |
| Perot [2] | 25,423 | 19.6 | Brown | 34,111 | 23.1 |
| Buchanan | 13,273 | 10.2 | Perot [2] | 28,311 | 19.1 |
| Stephen D. Michael | 2,619 | 2.0 | Tsongas | 18,981 | 12.8 |
| Duke | 1,501 | 1.2 | Harkin | 1,858 | 1.3 |
| | | | Kerrey | 1,489 | 1.0 |
| | | | LaRouche | 1,060 | 0.7 |

### May 26  Arkansas

| Republican | Votes | % | Democratic | Votes | % |
|---|---|---|---|---|---|
| Bush | 45,590 | 87.4 | Clinton | 342,017 | 68.0 |
| Buchanan | 6,551 | 12.6 | Uncommitted | 90,710 | 18.0 |
| | | | Brown | 55,234 | 11.0 |
| | | | LaRouche | 14,656 | 2.9 |

### May 26  Idaho

| Republican | Votes | % | Democratic | Votes | % |
|---|---|---|---|---|---|
| Bush | 73,297 | 63.5 | Clinton | 27,004 | 49.0 |
| "None of the names shown" | 27,038 | 23.4 | "None of the names shown" | 16,029 | 29.1 |
| Buchanan | 15,167 | 13.1 | Brown | 9,212 | 16.7 |
| | | | LaRouche | 2,011 | 3.6 |
| | | | Agran | 868 | 1.6 |

### May 26  Kentucky

| Republican | Votes | % | Democratic | Votes | % |
|---|---|---|---|---|---|
| Bush | 75,371 | 74.5 | Clinton | 207,804 | 56.1 |
| Uncommitted | 25,748 | 25.5 | Uncommitted | 103,590 | 28.0 |
| | | | Brown | 30,709 | 8.3 |
| | | | Tsongas | 18,097 | 4.9 |
| | | | Harkin | 7,136 | 1.9 |
| | | | Kerrey | 3,242 | 0.9 |

### June 2  Alabama

| Republican | Votes | % | Democratic | Votes | % |
|---|---|---|---|---|---|
| Bush | 122,703 | 74.3 | Clinton | 307,621 | 68.2 |
| Uncommitted | 29,830 | 18.1 | Uncommitted | 90,863 | 20.2 |
| Buchanan | 12,588 | 7.6 | Brown | 30,626 | 6.8 |
| | | | Woods | 15,247 | 3.4 |
| | | | LaRouche | 6,542 | 1.4 |

|  | **Republican** | | |  | **Democratic** | |
|---|---|---|---|---|---|---|
|  | Votes | % |  |  | Votes | % |
| **June 2   California** [5] | | | | | | |
| Bush | 1,587,369 | *73.6* |  | Clinton | 1,359,112 | *47.5* |
| Buchanan | 568,892 | *26.4* |  | Brown | 1,150,460 | *40.2* |
| Others [2] | 203 | *—* |  | Tsongas | 212,522 | *7.4* |
|  | | | | McCarthy | 60,635 | *2.1* |
|  | | | | Kerrey | 33,935 | *1.2* |
|  | | | | Agran | 24,784 | *0.9* |
|  | | | | LaRouche | 21,971 | *0.8* |
|  | | | | Others [2] | 190 | *—* |
| **June 2   Montana** | | | | | | |
| Bush | 65,176 | *71.6* |  | Clinton | 54,989 | *46.8* |
| No preference | 15,098 | *16.6* |  | No preference | 28,164 | *24.0* |
| Buchanan | 10,701 | *11.8* |  | Brown | 21,704 | *18.5* |
|  | | | | Tsongas | 12,614 | *10.7* |
| **June 2   New Jersey** | | | | | | |
| Bush | 240,535 | *77.5* |  | Clinton | 243,741 | *62.1* |
| Buchanan | 46,432 | *15.0* |  | Brown | 79,877 | *20.3* |
| Perot [2] | 23,303 | *7.5* |  | Tsongas | 45,191 | *11.5* |
|  | | | | Perot [2] | 12,478 | *3.2* |
|  | | | | LaRouche | 7,799 | *2.0* |
|  | | | | George H. Ballard | 2,067 | *0.5* |
|  | | | | Robert F. Hanson | 1,473 | *0.4* |
| **June 2   New Mexico** | | | | | | |
| Bush | 55,522 | *63.8* |  | Clinton | 95,933 | *52.9* |
| Uncommitted | 23,574 | *27.1* |  | Uncommitted | 35,269 | *19.4* |
| Buchanan | 7,871 | *9.1* |  | Brown | 30,705 | *16.9* |
|  | | | | Tsongas | 11,315 | *6.2* |
|  | | | | Harkin | 3,233 | *1.8* |
|  | | | | Agran | 2,573 | *1.4* |
|  | | | | LaRouche | 2,415 | *1.3* |
| **June 2   Ohio** | | | | | | |
| Bush | 716,766 | *83.3* |  | Clinton | 638,347 | *61.2* |
| Buchanan | 143,687 | *16.7* |  | Brown | 197,449 | *18.9* |
|  | | | | Tsongas | 110,773 | *10.6* |
|  | | | | Louis Stokes (Ohio) | 29,983 | *2.9* |
|  | | | | Harkin | 25,395 | *2.4* |
|  | | | | Kerrey | 22,976 | *2.2* |
|  | | | | LaRouche | 17,412 | *1.7* |
| **June 9   North Dakota** | | | | | | |
| Bush | 39,863 | *83.4* |  | Perot [2] | 9,516 | *29.0* |
| Paulsen | 4,093 | *8.6* |  | LaRouche | 7,003 | *21.4* |
| Perot [2] | 3,852 | *8.1* |  | Woods | 6,641 | *20.3* |
|  | | | | Shiekman | 4,866 | *14.8* |
|  | | | | Clinton [2] | 4,760 | *14.5* |

| Republican | Votes | % | Democratic | Votes | % |
|---|---|---|---|---|---|
| **TOTALS** | | | **TOTALS** | | |
| Bush | 9,199,463 | 72.5 | Clinton | 10,482,411 | 51.8 |
| Buchanan | 2,899,488 | 22.8 | Brown | 4,071,232 | 20.1 |
| Duke | 119,115 | 0.9 | Tsongas | 3,656,010 | 18.1 |
| Perot [2] | 56,136 | 0.4 | Kerry | 318,457 | 1.6 |
| Paulsen | 10,984 | 0.1 | Harkin | 280,304 | 1.4 |
| Horton | 9,637 | 0.1 | LaRouche | 154,599 | 0.8 |
| Stassen | 8,099 | 0.1 | McCarthy | 108,678 | 0.5 |
| Fellure | 6,296 | — | Woods | 88,948 | 0.4 |
| Zimmermann | 5,660 | — | Agran | 58,611 | 0.3 |
| Rogers | 4,180 | — | Perot [2] | 54,755 | 0.3 |
| Masters | 3,133 | — | Nader | 32,881 | 0.2 |
| Michael | 2,619 | — | Stokes | 29,983 | 0.1 |
| Lennane | 1,684 | — | McDonald | 9,900 | — |
| Jensen | 1,332 | — | McAlpine | 7,911 | — |
| Skow | 1,105 | — | Benns | 7,887 | — |
| Branch | 1,013 | — | Higginbotham | 7,705 | — |
| Koczak | 950 | — | Hawks | 7,434 | — |
| Daugherty | 771 | — | Burke | 5,261 | — |
| Beemont | 735 | — | Laughlin | 5,202 | — |
| Scott | 719 | — | Shiekman | 4,965 | — |
| Clegg | 518 | — | Marsh | 2,445 | — |
| Doty | 417 | — | Ballard | 2,067 | — |
| Bosa | 349 | — | Spelbring | 1,626 | — |
| Anderson | 300 | — | Hanson | 1,473 | — |
| Merwin | 223 | — | Cunningham | 1,369 | — |
| Mooney | 196 | — | Hauptli | 1,303 | — |
| Fabish | 183 | — | Rollinson | 1,206 | — |
| Conley | 115 | — | Beamgard | 1,009 | — |
| Patty | 93 | — | Barnes | 892 | — |
| Doerschuck | 57 | — | Rachner | 620 | — |
| Levinson | 44 | — | Vanskiver | 510 | — |
| Latchford | 32 | — | Fulani | 402 | — |
| Johnson | 24 | — | Pawley | 364 | — |
| Bertasavage | 23 | — | Kreml | 336 | — |
| Trinsey | 22 | — | Fey | 308 | — |
| Ryden | 20 | — | Mahoney | 303 | — |
| Erickson | 16 | — | Hayes | 279 | — |
| Reber | 14 | — | Wilder | 240 | — |
| Uncommitted [6] | 287,383 | 2.3 | Talbow | 202 | — |
| Others [2] | 73,399 | 0.6 | Rigazio | 186 | — |
| | 12,696,547 | | Thornton | 177 | — |
| | | | Staradumsky | 168 | — |
| | | | Averick | 112 | — |
| | | | Killeen | 93 | — |
| | | | Cahill | 83 | — |
| | | | Fisher | 82 | — |
| | | | Bona | 65 | — |
| | | | Hegger | 61 | — |
| | | | Horrigan | 53 | — |
| | | | Curtis | 43 | — |
| | | | Holmes | 39 | — |
| | | | Kovic | 36 | — |
| | | | Norton | 31 | — |
| | | | Monyek | 29 | — |
| | | | Gay | 28 | — |
| | | | Deutsch | 26 | — |
| | | | Sagan | 26 | — |
| | | | O'Donnell | 24 | — |
| | | | Schwartz | 17 | — |
| | | | Others [2] | 77,045 | 0.4 |
| | | | Uncommitted [6] | 750,873 | 3.7 |
| | | | | 20,239,385 | |

*1. In New Hampshire's Libertarian presidential primary, Andre V. Marrou received 3,219 votes (95.0 percent) and there were 168 scattered write-in votes (5.0 percent).*
*2. Write-in votes.*

*3. In Massachusetts' independent presidential primary, Howard Phillips received 352 votes (25.4 percent), "No preference" received 269 votes (19.4 percent), James Gritz received 177 votes (12.8 percent), Robert J. Smith received 54 votes (3.9 percent), Darcy*

G. Richardson received 36 votes (2.6 percent), Erik Thompson received 35 votes (2.5 percent), Earl F. Dodge received 26 votes (1.9 percent), J. Quinn Brisben received 24 votes (1.7 percent), Michael S. Levinson received 21 votes (1.5 percent), and there were 391 scattered write-in votes (28.2 percent).

4. No primary.

5. In California's American Independent presidential primary, Howard Phillips received 15,456 votes (99.9 percent) and there were 13 scattered write-in votes. In the Libertarian presidential primary, Andre V. Marrou received 15,002 votes (99.9 percent) and there were 12 scattered write-in votes. In the Peace & Freedom presidential primary, Lenora B. Fulani received 4,586 votes (51.6 percent), Ron Daniels received 2;868 votes (32.2 percent), R. Alison Star-Martinez received 1,434 votes (16.1 percent), and there were 6 scattered write-in votes.

6. The Uncommitted category includes votes cast on the following ballot lines: Uncommitted, Noncommitted, No preference, Uninstructed and "None of the names shown."

# Presidential Nomination Campaigns, 1976–92

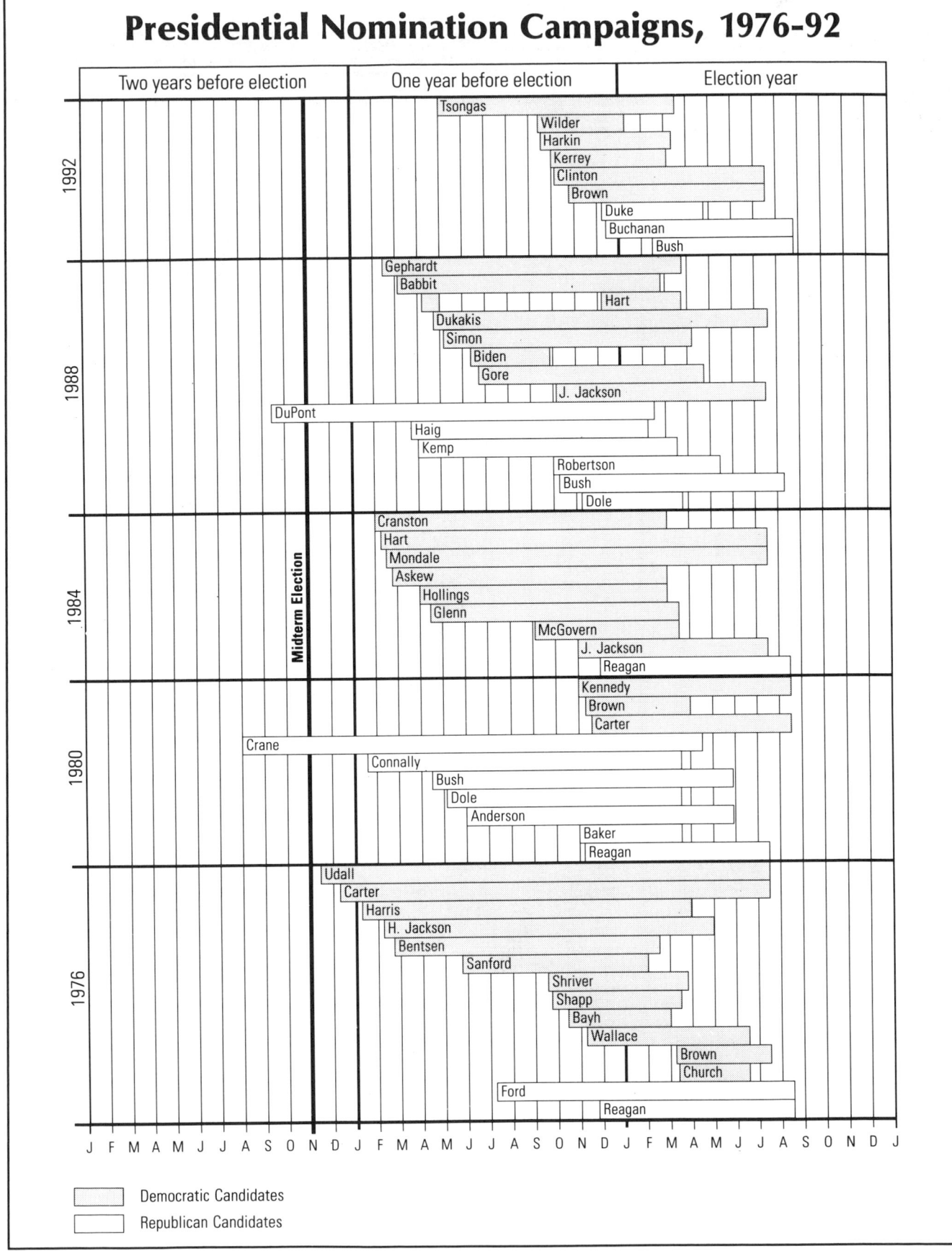

| Two years before election | One year before election | Election year |
|---|---|---|

**1992**
- Tsongas
- Wilder
- Harkin
- Kerrey
- Clinton
- Brown
- Duke
- Buchanan
- Bush

**1988**
- Gephardt
- Babbit
- Hart
- Dukakis
- Simon
- Biden
- Gore
- J. Jackson
- DuPont
- Haig
- Kemp
- Robertson
- Bush
- Dole

**1984**
- Cranston
- Hart
- Mondale
- Askew
- Hollings
- Glenn
- McGovern
- J. Jackson
- Reagan

**Midterm Election**

**1980**
- Kennedy
- Brown
- Carter
- Crane
- Connally
- Bush
- Dole
- Anderson
- Baker
- Reagan

**1976**
- Udall
- Carter
- Harris
- H. Jackson
- Bentsen
- Sanford
- Shriver
- Shapp
- Bayh
- Wallace
- Brown
- Church
- Ford
- Reagan

J F M A M J J A S O N D J F M A M J J A S O N D J F M A M J J A S O N D J

- Democratic Candidates
- Republican Candidates

# Biographical Directory of Presidential and Vice Presidential Candidates

The names in the directory include all persons who have received electoral votes for president or vice president since 1789. Also included are prominent third party candidates who received popular votes but no electoral votes, and Nelson Aldrich Rockefeller, appointed vice president by Gerald R. Ford, who became president following the resignation of Richard M. Nixon.

The material is organized as follows: name, state of residence in the year(s) the individual received electoral votes, party or parties with which the individual identified when he or she received electoral votes, date of birth, date of death (where applicable), major offices held, and the year(s) of candidacy.

For the elections of 1789 through 1800, presidential electors did not vote separately for president or vice president. It was, therefore, difficult in many cases to determine if an individual receiving electoral votes in these elections was a candidate for the office of president or vice president. Where no determination could be made from the sources consulted by Congressional Quarterly, the year in which the individual received electoral votes is given with no specification as to whether the individual was a candidate for president or vice president.

The following sources were used: *American Leaders, 1789-1994: A Biographical Summary*, Congressional Quarterly, Washington, D.C., 1994; *Biographical Directory of the United States Congress, 1774-1989*, Government Printing Office, Washington, D.C., 1989; *Dictionary of American Biography*, Charles Scribner's Sons, New York, 1928-36; *Encyclopedia of American Biography*, John A. Garraty, editor, Harper and Row, New York, 1974; *Who's Who in American Politics*, 6th edition, 1977-78, edited by Jaques Cattell Press, R. R. Bowker, New York, 1977; *Who Was Who in America, 1607-1968*, Marquis, Chicago, 1943-68; Svend Petersen, *A Statistical History of the American Presidential Elections*, Greenwood Press, Westport, Conn., 1981; Richard M. Scammon, *America Votes 10* (1972), Governmental Affairs Institute, Congressional Quarterly, Washington, D.C., 1973; Richard M. Scammon and Alice V. McGillivray, *America Votes 12* (1976), Governmental Affairs Institute, Congressional Quarterly, Washington, D.C., 1977; *America Votes 14* (1980), Elections Research Center, Washington, D.C., 1981; *America Votes 18* (1988), Elections Research Center, Washington, D.C., 1989; *America Votes 20* (1992), Elections Research Center, Washington, D.C., 1993.

---

**ADAMS,** Charles Francis - Mass. (Free Soil) Aug. 18, 1807 - Nov. 21, 1886; House, 1859-61; minister to Great Britain, 1861-68. Candidacy: VP - 1848.

**ADAMS,** John - Mass. (Federalist) Oct. 30, 1735 - July 4, 1826; Continental Congress, 1774; signer of Declaration of Independence, 1776; minister to Great Britain, 1785; U.S. vice president, 1789-97; U.S. president, 1797-1801. Candidacies: VP - 1789, 1792; P - 1796, 1800.

**ADAMS,** John Quincy - Mass. (Democratic-Republican, National Republican) July 11, 1767 - Feb. 23, 1848; Senate, 1803-08; minister to Russia, 1809-14; minister to Great Britain, 1815-17; secretary of state, 1817-25; U.S. president, 1825-29; House, 1831-48. Candidacies: P - 1820, 1824, 1828.

**ADAMS,** Samuel - Mass. (Federalist) Sept. 27, 1722 - Oct. 2, 1803; Continental Congress, 1774-81; signer of Declaration of Independence; governor, 1793-97. Candidacy: 1796.

**AGNEW,** Spiro Theodore - Md. (Republican) Nov. 9, 1918—; governor, 1967-69; U.S. vice president, 1969-73 (resigned Oct. 10, 1973). Candidacies: VP - 1968, 1972.

**ANDERSON,** John B. - Ill. (Republican, Independent) Feb. 15, 1922—; state's attorney, 1956-60; House, 1961-81. Candidacy: P - 1980.

**ARMSTRONG,** James - Pa. (Federalist) Aug. 29, 1748 - May 6, 1828; House, 1793-95. Candidacy: 1789.

**ARTHUR,** Chester Alan - N.Y. (Republican) Oct. 5, 1830 - Nov. 18, 1886; collector, Port of N.Y., 1871-78; U.S. vice president, 1881; U.S. president, 1881-85 (succeeded James A. Garfield, who was assassinated). Candidacy: VP - 1880.

**BANKS,** Nathaniel Prentice - Mass. (Liberal Republican) Jan. 30, 1816 - Sept. 1, 1894; House, 1853-57, 1865-73, 1875-79, 1889-91; governor, 1858-61. Candidacy: VP - 1872.

**BARKLEY,** Alben William - Ky. (Democratic) Nov. 24, 1877 - April 30, 1956; House, 1913-27; Senate, 1927-49, 1955-56; Senate majority leader, 1937-47; Senate minority leader, 1947-49; U.S. vice president, 1949-53. Candidacy: VP - 1948.

**BELL,** John - Tenn. (Constitutional Union) Feb. 15, 1797 - Sept. 10, 1869; House, 1827-41; Speaker of the House, 1834-35; secretary of war, 1841; Senate, 1847-59. Candidacy: P - 1860.

**BENSON,** Allan Louis - N.Y. (Socialist) Nov. 6, 1871 - Aug. 19, 1940; writer, editor; founder of *Reconstruction Magazine*, 1918. Candidacy: P - 1916.

**BENTSEN,** Lloyd Millard Jr. - Texas (Democratic) Feb. 11, 1921—; House 1948-55; Senate 1971-93. Candidacy: VP - 1988.

**BIDWELL,** John - Calif. (Prohibition) Aug. 5, 1819 - April 4, 1900; California pioneer; major in Mexican War; House, 1865-67. Candidacy: P - 1892.

**BIRNEY,** James Gillespie - N.Y. (Liberty) Feb. 4, 1792 - Nov. 25, 1857; Kentucky Legislature, 1816-17; Alabama Legislature, 1819-20. Candidacies: P - 1840, 1844.

**BLAINE,** James Gillespie - Maine (Republican) Jan. 31, 1830 - Jan. 27, 1893; House, 1863-76; Speaker of the House, 1869-75; Senate, 1876-81; secretary of state, 1881, 1889-92; president, first Pan American Congress, 1889. Candidacy: P - 1884.

**BLAIR,** Francis Preston Jr. - Mo. (Democratic) Feb. 19, 1821 - July 8, 1875; House, 1857-59, 1860, 1861-62, 1863-64; Senate, 1871-73. Candidacy: VP - 1868.

**BRAMLETTE,** Thomas E. - Ky. (Democratic) Jan. 3, 1817 - Jan. 12, 1875; governor, 1863-67. Candidacy: VP - 1872.

**BRECKINRIDGE,** John Cabell - Ky. (Democratic, Southern Democratic) Jan. 21, 1821 - May 17, 1875; House, 1851-55; U.S. vice president, 1857-61; Senate, 1861; major general, Confederacy, 1861-65; secretary of war, Confederacy, 1865. Candidacies: VP - 1856; P - 1860.

**BRICKER,** John William - Ohio (Republican) Sept. 6, 1893 - March 22, 1986; attorney general of Ohio, 1933-37; governor, 1939-45; Senate, 1947-59. Candidacy: VP - 1944.

**BROWN,** Benjamin Gratz - Mo. (Democratic) May 28, 1826 - Dec. 13, 1885; Senate, 1863-67; governor, 1871-73. Candidacy: VP - 1872.

**BRYAN,** Charles Wayland - Neb. (Democratic) Feb. 10, 1867 - March 4, 1945; governor, 1923-25, 1931-35; Candidacy: VP - 1924.

**BRYAN,** William Jennings - Neb. (Democratic, Populist) March 19, 1860 - July 26, 1925; House, 1891-95; secretary of state, 1913-15. Candidacies: P - 1896, 1900, 1908.

**BUCHANAN,** James - Pa. (Democratic) April 23, 1791 - June 1, 1868; House, 1821-31; minister to Russia, 1832-34; Senate, 1834-45; secretary of state, 1845-49; minister to Great Britain, 1853-56; U.S. president, 1857-61. Candidacy: P - 1856.

**BURR,** Aaron - N.Y. (Democratic-Republican) Feb. 6, 1756 - Sept. 14, 1836; attorney general of N.Y., 1789-90; Senate, 1791-97; U.S. vice president, 1801-05. Candidacies: 1792, 1796, 1800.

**BUSH,** George - Texas (Republican) June 12, 1924—; House, 1967-70; ambassador to the United Nations, 1971-73; chairman of the Republican National Committee, 1973-74; head of the U.S. liaison office in Peking, 1974-75; director of the Central Intelligence Agency, 1976-77; U.S. vice president, 1981-89; U.S. president, 1989-93. Candidacies: VP - 1980, 1984; P - 1988, 1992.

**BUTLER,** Benjamin Franklin - Mass. (Greenback, Anti-Monopoly) Nov. 5, 1818 - Jan. 11, 1893; House, 1867-75, 1877-79; governor, 1883-84. Candidacy: P - 1884.

**BUTLER,** Nicholas Murray - N.Y. (Republican) April 2, 1862 - Dec. 7, 1947; president, Columbia University, 1901-45; president, Carnegie Endowment for International Peace, 1925-45. Candidacy: VP - 1912. (Substituted as candidate after Oct. 30 death of nominee James S. Sherman.)

**BUTLER,** William Orlando - Ky. (Democratic) April 19, 1791 - Aug. 6, 1880; House, 1939-43. Candidacy: VP - 1848.

**BYRD,** Harry Flood - Va. (States' Rights Democratic, Independent Democratic) June 10, 1887 - Oct. 20, 1966; governor, 1926-30; Senate, 1933-65. Candidacies: P - 1956, 1960.

**CALHOUN,** John Caldwell - S.C. (Democratic-Republican, Democratic) March 18, 1782 - March 31, 1850; House, 1811-17; secretary of war, 1817-25; U.S. vice president, 1825-32; Senate, 1832-43, 1845-50; secretary of state, 1844-45. Candidacies: VP - 1824, 1828.

**CARTER,** James Earl Jr. - Ga. (Democratic) Oct. 1, 1924—; Georgia Legislature, 1963-67; governor, 1971-75; U.S. president, 1977-81. Candidacies: P - 1976, 1980.

**CASS,** Lewis - Mich. (Democratic) Oct. 9, 1782 - June 17, 1866; military and civil governor of Michigan Territory, 1813-31; secretary of war, 1831-36; minister to France, 1836-42; Senate, 1845-48, 1849-57; secretary of state, 1857-60. Candidacy: P - 1848.

**CLAY,** Henry - Ky. (Democratic-Republican, National Republican, Whig) April 12, 1777 - June 29, 1852; Senate, 1806-07, 1810-11, 1831-42, 1849-52; House, 1811-14, 1815-21, 1823-25; Speaker of the House, 1811-14, 1815-20, 1823-25; secretary of state, 1825-29. Candidacies: P - 1824, 1832, 1844.

**CLEVELAND,** Stephen Grover - N.Y. (Democratic) March 18, 1837 - June 24, 1908; mayor of Buffalo, 1882; governor, 1883-85; U.S. president, 1885-89, 1893-97. Candidacies: P - 1884, 1888, 1892.

**CLINTON,** Bill - Ark. (Democrat) Aug. 19, 1946—; attorney general of Arkansas, 1977-79; governor, 1979-81, 1983-92; U.S. president, 1993—. Candidacy: P - 1992.

**CLINTON,** De Witt - N.Y. (Independent Democratic-Republican, Federalist) March 2, 1769 - Feb. 11, 1828; Senate, 1802-03; mayor of New York, 1803-07, 1810, 1811, 1813, 1814; governor, 1817-23, 1825-28. Candidacy: P - 1812.

**CLINTON,** George - N.Y. (Democratic-Republican) July 26, 1739 - April 20, 1812; Continental Congress, 1775-76; governor, 1777-95, 1801-04; U.S. vice president, 1805-12. Candidacies: VP - 1789, 1792, 1796, 1804, 1808.

**COLFAX,** Schuyler - Ind. (Republican) March 23, 1823 - Jan. 13, 1885; House, 1855-69; Speaker of the House, 1863-69; U.S. vice president, 1869-73. Candidacy: VP - 1868.

**COLQUITT,** Alfred Holt - Ga. (Democratic) April 20, 1824 - March 26, 1894; House, 1853-55; governor, 1877-82; Senate, 1883-94. Candidacy: VP - 1872.

**COOLIDGE,** Calvin - Mass. (Republican) July 4, 1872 - Jan. 5, 1933; governor, 1919-21; U.S. vice president, 1921-23; U.S. president, 1923-29. Candidacies: VP - 1920; P - 1924.

**COX,** James Middleton - Ohio (Democratic) March 31, 1870 - July 15, 1957; House, 1909-13; governor, 1913-15, 1917-21. Candidacy: P - 1920.

**CRAWFORD,** William Harris - Ga. (Democratic-Republican) Feb. 24, 1772 - Sept. 15, 1834; Senate, 1807-13; president pro tempore of the Senate, 1812-13; secretary of war, 1815-16; secretary of the treasury, 1816-25. Candidacy: P - 1824.

**CURTIS,** Charles - Kan. (Republican) Jan. 25, 1860 - Feb. 8, 1936; House, 1893-1907; Senate, 1907-13, 1915-29; president pro tempore of the Senate, 1911; Senate majority leader, 1925-29; U.S. vice president, 1929-33. Candidacies: VP - 1928, 1932.

**DALLAS,** George Mifflin - Pa. (Democratic) July 10, 1792 - Dec. 31, 1864; Senate, 1831-33; minister to Russia, 1837-39; U.S. vice president, 1845-49; minister to Great Britain, 1856-61. Candidacy: VP - 1844.

**DAVIS,** David - Ill. (Democratic) March 9, 1815 - June 26, 1886; associate justice of U.S. Supreme Court, 1862-77; Senate, 1877-83; president pro tempore of the Senate, 1881. Candidacy: P - 1872.

**DAVIS,** Henry Gassaway - W.Va. (Democratic) Nov. 16, 1823 - March 11, 1916; Senate, 1871-83; chairman of Pan American Railway Committee, 1901-16. Candidacy: VP - 1904.

**DAVIS,** John William - W.Va., N.Y. (Democratic) April 13, 1873 - March 24, 1955; House, 1911-13; solicitor general, 1913-18; ambassador to Great Britain, 1918-21. Candidacy: P - 1924.

**DAWES,** Charles Gates - Ill. (Republican) Aug. 27, 1865 - April 3, 1951; U.S. comptroller of the currency, 1898-1901; first director of Bureau of the Budget, 1921-22; U.S. vice president, 1925-29; ambassador to Great Britain, 1929-32. Candidacy: VP - 1924.

**DAYTON,** William Lewis - N.J. (Republican) Feb. 17, 1807 - Dec. 1, 1864; Senate, 1842-51; minister to France, 1861-64. Candidacy: VP - 1856.

**DEBS,** Eugene Victor - Ind. (Socialist) Nov. 5, 1855 - Oct. 20, 1926; Indiana Legislature, 1885; president, American Railway

Union, 1893-97. Candidacies: P - 1900, 1904, 1908, 1912, 1920.

**DEWEY,** Thomas Edmund - N.Y. (Republican) March 24, 1902 - March 16, 1971; district attorney, New York County, 1937-41; governor, 1943-55. Candidacies: P - 1944, 1948.

**DOLE,** Robert Joseph - Kan. (Republican) July 22, 1923—; House, 1961-69; Senate, 1969—; Senate majority leader, 1985-87; Senate minority leader, 1987—; chairman of the Republican National Committee, 1971-73. Candidacy: VP - 1976.

**DONELSON,** Andrew Jackson - Tenn. (American "Know-Nothing") Aug. 25, 1799 - June 26, 1871; minister to Prussia, 1846-48; minister to Germany, 1848-49. Candidacy: VP - 1856.

**DOUGLAS,** Stephen Arnold - Ill. (Democratic) April 23, 1813 - June 3, 1861; House, 1843-47; Senate, 1847-61. Candidacy: P - 1860.

**DUKAKIS,** Michael Stanley - Mass. (Democratic) Nov. 3, 1933—; governor, 1975-79, 1983-91. Candidacy: P - 1988.

**EAGLETON,** Thomas Francis - Mo. (Democratic) Sept. 4, 1929—; attorney general of Missouri, 1961-65; lieutenant governor, 1965-68; Senate, 1968-87. Candidacy: VP - 1972. (Resigned from Democratic ticket July 31; replaced by R. Sargent Shriver Jr.)

**EISENHOWER,** Dwight David - N.Y., Pa. (Republican) Oct. 14, 1890 - March 28, 1969; general of U.S. Army, 1943-48; Army chief of staff, 1945-48; president of Columbia University, 1948-51; commander of North Atlantic Treaty Organization, 1951-52; U.S. president, 1953-61. Candidacies: P - 1952, 1956.

**ELLMAKER,** Amos - Pa. (Anti-Masonic) Feb. 2, 1787 - Nov. 28, 1851; elected to the House for the term beginning in 1815 but did not qualify; attorney general of Pennsylvania, 1816-19, 1828-29. Candidacy: VP - 1832.

**ELLSWORTH,** Oliver - Conn. (Federalist) April 29, 1745 - Nov. 26, 1807; Continental Congress, 1778-83; Senate, 1789-96; chief justice of United States, 1796-1800; minister to France, 1799. Candidacy: 1796.

**ENGLISH,** William Hayden - Ind. (Democratic) Aug. 27, 1822 - Feb. 7, 1896; House, 1853-61. Candidacy: VP - 1880.

**EVERETT,** Edward - Mass. (Constitutional Union) April 11, 1794 - Jan. 15, 1865; House, 1825-35; governor, 1836-40; minister to Great Britain, 1841-45; president of Harvard University, 1846-49;

secretary of state, 1852-53; Senate, 1853-54. Candidacy: VP - 1860.

**FAIRBANKS,** Charles Warren - Ind. (Republican) May 11, 1852 - June 4, 1918; Senate, 1897-1905; U.S. vice president, 1905-09. Candidacies: VP - 1904, 1916.

**FERRARO,** Geraldine Anne - N.Y. (Democratic) Aug. 26, 1935—; assistant district attorney, Queens County, 1974-78; House, 1979-85. Candidacy: VP - 1984.

**FIELD,** James Gaven - Va. (Populist) Feb. 24, 1826 - Oct. 12, 1901; major in the Confederate Army, 1861-65; attorney general of Virginia, 1877-82. Candidacy: VP - 1892.

**FILLMORE,** Millard - N.Y. (Whig, American "Know-Nothing") Jan. 7, 1800 - March 8, 1874; House, 1833-35, 1837-43; N.Y. comptroller, 1847-49; U.S. vice president, 1849-50; U.S. president, 1850-53. Candidacies: VP - 1848; P - 1856.

**FISK,** Clinton Bowen - N.J. (Prohibition) Dec. 8, 1828 - July 9, 1890; Civil War brevet major general; founder of Fisk University, 1866; member, Board of Indian Commissioners, 1874, president, 1881-90. Candidacy: P - 1888.

**FLOYD,** John - Va. (Independent Democratic) April 24, 1783 - Aug. 17, 1837; House, 1817-29; governor, 1830-34. Candidacy: P - 1832.

**FORD,** Gerald Rudolph Jr. - Mich. (Republican) July 14, 1913—; House, 1949-73; House minority leader, 1965-73; U.S. vice president, 1973-74; U.S. president, 1974-77. Candidacy: P - 1976.

**FRELINGHUYSEN,** Theodore - N.J. (Whig) March 28, 1787 - April 12, 1862; attorney general of New Jersey, 1817-29; Senate, 1829-35; president of Rutgers College, 1850-62. Candidacy: VP - 1844.

**FREMONT,** John Charles - Calif. (Republican) Jan. 21, 1813 - July 13, 1890; explorer and Army officer in West before 1847; Senate, 1850-51; governor of Arizona Territory, 1878-81. Candidacy: P - 1856.

**GARFIELD,** James Abram - Ohio (Republican) Nov. 19, 1831 - Sept. 19, 1881; major general in Union Army during Civil War; House, 1863-80; U.S. president, 1881. Candidacy: P - 1880.

**GARNER,** John Nance - Texas (Democratic) Nov. 22, 1868 - Nov. 7, 1967; House, 1903-33; House minority leader, 1929-31; Speaker of the House, 1931-33; U.S. vice president, 1933-41. Candidacies: VP - 1932, 1936.

**GERRY,** Elbridge - Mass. (Democratic-Republican) July 17, 1744 - Nov. 23, 1814; Continental Congress, 1776-80, 1783-

85; signer of Declaration of Independence; Constitutional Convention, 1787; House, 1789-93; governor, 1810-12; U.S. vice president, 1813-14. Candidacy: VP - 1812.

**GOLDWATER,** Barry Morris - Ariz. (Republican) Jan. 1, 1909—; Senate, 1953-65, 1969-87. Candidacies: VP - 1960; P - 1964.

**GORE,** Albert Jr. - Tenn. (Democrat) March 31, 1948—; House, 1977-85; Senate, 1985-93; U.S. vice president, 1993—. Candidacy: VP - 1992.

**GRAHAM,** William Alexander - N.C. (Whig) Sept. 5, 1804 - Aug. 11, 1875; Senate, 1840-43; governor, 1845-49; secretary of the Navy, 1850-52; Confederate Senate, 1864. Candidacy: VP - 1852.

**GRANGER,** Francis - N.Y (Whig) Dec. 1, 1792 - Aug. 31, 1868; House, 1835-37, 1839-41, 1841-43; postmaster general, 1841. Candidacy: VP - 1836.

**GRANT,** Ulysses Simpson - Ill. (Republican) April 27, 1822 - July 23, 1885; commander-in-chief, Union Army during Civil War; U.S. president, 1869-77. Candidacies: P - 1868, 1872.

**GREELEY,** Horace - N.Y. (Liberal Republican, Democratic) Feb. 3, 1811 - Nov. 29, 1872; founder and editor, *New York Tribune*, 1841-72; House, 1848-49. Candidacy: P - 1872.

**GRIFFIN,** S. Marvin - Ga. (American Independent) Sept. 4, 1907 - June 13, 1982; governor, 1955-59. Candidacy: VP - 1968. (Substituted as candidate until permanent candidate Curtis LeMay was chosen.)

**GROESBECK,** William Slocum - Ohio (Democratic) July 24, 1815 - July 7, 1897; House, 1857-59; delegate to International Monetary Conference in Paris, 1878. Candidacy: VP - 1872.

**HALE,** John Parker - N.H. (Free Soil) March 31, 1806 - Nov. 19, 1873; House, 1843-45; Senate, 1847-53, 1855-65; minister to Spain, 1865-69. Candidacy: P - 1852.

**HAMLIN,** Hannibal - Maine (Republican) Aug. 27, 1809 - July 4, 1891; House, 1843-47; Senate, 1848-57, 1857-61, 1869-81; governor, 1857; U.S. vice president, 1861-65. Candidacy: VP - 1860.

**HANCOCK,** John - Mass. (Federalist) Jan. 23, 1737 - Oct. 8, 1793; Continental Congress, 1775-78, 1785-86; president of Continental Congress, 1775-77; governor, 1780-85, 1787-93. Candidacy: 1789.

**HANCOCK,** Winfield Scott - Pa. (Democratic) Feb. 14, 1824 - Feb. 9, 1886; brigadier general, commander of II

Army Corps, Civil War. Candidacy: P - 1880.

**HARDING,** Warren Gamaliel - Ohio (Republican) Nov. 2, 1865 - Aug. 2, 1923; lieutenant governor, 1904-05; Senate, 1915-21; U.S. president, 1921-23. Candidacy: P - 1920.

**HARPER,** Robert Goodloe - Md. (Federalist) January 1765 - Jan. 14, 1825; House, 1795-1801; Senate, 1816. Candidacies: VP - 1816, 1820.

**HARRISON,** Benjamin - Ind. (Republican) Aug. 20, 1833 - March 13, 1901; Union officer in Civil War; Senate, 1881-87; U.S. president, 1889-93. Candidacies: P - 1888, 1892.

**HARRISON,** Robert H. - Md. 1745 - 1790; chief justice, General Court of Maryland, 1781. Candidacy: 1789.

**HARRISON,** William Henry - Ohio (Whig) Feb. 9, 1773 - April 4, 1841; delegate to Congress from the Northwest Territory, 1799-1800; territorial governor of Indiana, 1801-13; House, 1816-19; Senate, 1825-28; U.S. president, 1841. Candidacies: P - 1836, 1840.

**HAYES,** Rutherford Birchard - Ohio (Republican) Oct. 4, 1822 - Jan. 17, 1893; major general in Union Army during Civil War; House, 1865-67; governor, 1868-72, 1876-77; U.S. president, 1877-81. Candidacy: P - 1876.

**HENDRICKS,** Thomas Andrews - Ind. (Democratic) Sept. 7, 1819 - Nov. 25, 1885; House, 1851-55; Senate, 1863-69; governor, 1873-77; U.S. vice president, 1885. Candidacies: P - 1872; VP - 1876, 1884.

**HENRY,** John - Md. (Democratic-Republican) Nov. 1750 - Dec. 16, 1798; Continental Congress, 1778-80, 1785-86; Senate, 1789-97; governor, 1797-98. Candidacy - 1796.

**HOBART,** Garret Augustus - N.J. (Republican) June 3, 1844 - Nov. 21, 1899; New Jersey Senate, 1876-82; president of New Jersey Senate, 1881-82; Republican National Committee, 1884-96; U.S. vice president, 1897-99. Candidacy: VP - 1896

**HOOVER,** Herbert Clark - Calif. (Republican) Aug. 10, 1874 - Oct. 20, 1964; U.S. food administrator, 1917-19; secretary of commerce, 1921-28; U.S. president, 1929-33; chairman, Commission on Organization of the Executive Branch of Government, 1947-49, 1953-55. Candidacies: P - 1928, 1932.

**HOSPERS,** John - Calif. (Libertarian) June 9, 1918—; director of school of philosophy at University of Southern California. Candidacy: P - 1972.

**HOWARD,** John Eager - Md. (Federalist) June 4, 1752 - Oct. 12, 1827; Continental Congress, 1788; governor, 1788-91; Senate, 1796-1803. Candidacy: VP - 1816.

**HUGHES,** Charles Evans - N.Y. (Republican) April 11, 1862 - Aug. 27, 1948; governor, 1907-10; associate justice of U.S. Supreme Court, 1910-16; secretary of state, 1921-25; chief justice of United States, 1930-41. Candidacy: P - 1916.

**HUMPHREY,** Hubert Horatio Jr. - Minn. (Democratic) May 27, 1911 - Jan. 13, 1978; mayor of Minneapolis, 1945-48; Senate, 1949-64, 1971-78; U.S. vice president, 1965-69. Candidacies: VP - 1964; P - 1968.

**HUNTINGTON,** Samuel - Conn., July 3, 1731 - Jan. 5, 1796; Continental Congress, 1776, 1778-81, 1783; president of the Continental Congress, 1779-81; governor, 1786-96. Candidacy: 1789.

**INGERSOLL,** Jared - Pa. (Federalist) Oct. 24, 1749 - Oct. 31, 1822; Continental Congress, 1780-81; Constitutional Convention, 1787. Candidacy: VP - 1812.

**IREDELL,** James - N.C. (Federalist) Oct. 5, 1751 - Oct. 20, 1799; associate justice of U.S. Supreme Court, 1790-99. Candidacy: 1796.

**JACKSON,** Andrew - Tenn. (Democratic-Republican, Democratic) March 15, 1767 - June 8, 1845; House, 1796-97; Senate, 1797-98, 1823-25; territorial governor of Florida, 1821; U.S. president, 1829-37. Candidacies: P - 1824, 1828, 1832.

**JAY,** John - N.Y. (Federalist) Dec. 12, 1745 - May 17, 1829; Continental Congress, 1774-76, 1778-79; president of Continental Congress, 1778-79; minister to Spain, 1779; chief justice of United States, 1789-95; governor, 1795-1801. Candidacies: 1789, 1796, 1800.

**JEFFERSON,** Thomas - Va. (Democratic-Republican) April 13, 1743 - July 4, 1826; Continental Congress, 1775-76, 1783-84; author and signer of Declaration of Independence, 1776; governor, 1779-81; minister to France, 1784-89; secretary of state, 1790-93; U.S. vice president, 1797-1801; U.S. president, 1801-09. Candidacies: VP - 1792; P - 1796, 1800, 1804.

**JENKINS,** Charles Jones - Ga. (Democratic) Jan. 6, 1805 - June 14, 1883; governor, 1865-68. Candidacy: P - 1872.

**JOHNSON,** Andrew - Tenn. (Republican) Dec. 29, 1808 - July 31, 1875; House, 1843-53; governor, 1853-57; Senate, 1857-62, 1875; U.S. vice president, 1865; U.S. president, 1865-69. Candidacy: VP - 1864.

**JOHNSON,** Herschel Vespasian - Ga. (Democratic) Sept. 18, 1812 - Aug. 16, 1880; Senate, 1848-49; governor, 1853-57; senator, Confederate Congress, 1862-65. Candidacy: VP - 1860.

**JOHNSON,** Hiram Warren - Calif. (Progressive) Sept. 2, 1866 - Aug. 6, 1945; governor, 1911-17; Senate, 1917-45. Candidacy: VP - 1912.

**JOHNSON,** Lyndon Baines - Texas (Democratic) Aug. 27, 1908 - Jan. 22, 1973; House, 1937-49; Senate, 1949-61; Senate minority leader, 1953-55; Senate majority leader, 1955-61; U.S. vice president, 1961-63; U.S. president, 1963-69. Candidacies: VP - 1960; P - 1964.

**JOHNSON,** Richard Mentor - Ky. (Democratic) Oct. 17, 1780 - Nov. 19, 1850; House, 1807-19, 1829-37; Senate, 1819-29; U.S. vice president, 1837-41. Candidacies: VP - 1836, 1840.

**JOHNSTON,** Samuel - N.C. (Federalist) Dec. 15, 1733 - Aug. 17, 1816; Continental Congress, 1780-81; governor, 1787-89; Senate, 1789-93. Candidacy: 1796.

**JONES,** Walter Burgwyn - Ala. (Independent Democratic) Oct. 16, 1888 - Aug. 1, 1963; Alabama Legislature, 1919-20; Alabama circuit court judge, 1920-35; presiding judge, 1935-63. Candidacy: P - 1956.

**JULIAN,** George Washington - Ind. (Free Soil, Liberal Republican) May 5, 1817 - July 7, 1899; House, 1849-51, 1861-71. Candidacies: VP - 1852, 1872.

**KEFAUVER,** Estes - Tenn. (Democratic) July 26, 1903 - Aug. 10, 1963; House, 1939-49; Senate, 1949-63. Candidacy: VP - 1956.

**KENNEDY,** John Fitzgerald - Mass. (Democratic) May 29, 1917 - Nov. 22, 1963; House, 1947-53; Senate, 1953-60; U.S. president, 1961-63. Candidacy: P - 1960.

**KERN,** John Worth - Ind. (Democratic) Dec. 20, 1849 - Aug. 17, 1917; Senate, 1911-17; Senate majority leader, 1913-17. Candidacy: VP - 1908.

**KING,** Rufus - N.Y. (Federalist) March 24, 1755 - April 29, 1827; Continental Congress, 1784-87; Constitutional Convention, 1787; Senate, 1789-96, 1813-25; minister to Great Britain, 1796-1803, 1825-26. Candidacies: VP - 1804, 1808; P - 1816.

**KING,** William Rufus de Vane - Ala. (Democratic) April 7, 1786 - April 18, 1853; House, 1811-16; Senate, 1819-44, 1848-52; president pro tempore of the Senate, 1836, 1837, 1838, 1839, 1840, 1841, 1850; minister to France, 1844-46; U.S.

vice president, 1853. Candidacy: VP - 1852.

**KNOX,** Franklin - Ill. (Republican) Jan. 1, 1874 - April 28, 1944; secretary of the Navy, 1940-44. Candidacy: VP - 1936.

**LA FOLLETTE,** Robert Marion - Wis. (Progressive) June 14, 1855 - June 18, 1925; House, 1885-91; governor, 1901-06; Senate, 1906-25. Candidacy: P - 1924.

**LANDON,** Alfred Mossman - Kan. (Republican) Sept. 9, 1887 - Oct. 12, 1987; governor, 1933-37. Candidacy: P - 1936.

**LANE,** Joseph - Ore. (Southern Democratic) Dec. 14, 1801 - April 19, 1881; governor of Oregon Territory, 1849-50, 1853; House (territorial delegate), 1851-59; Senate, 1859-61. Candidacy: VP - 1860.

**LANGDON,** John - N.H. (Democratic-Republican) June 26, 1741 - Sept. 18, 1819; Continental Congress, 1775-76, 1787; governor, 1805-09, 1810-12; Senate, 1789-1801; first president pro tempore of the Senate, 1789. Candidacy: VP - 1808.

**LEE,** Henry - Mass. (Independent Democratic) Feb. 4, 1782 - Feb. 6, 1867; merchant and publicist. Candidacy: VP - 1832.

**LeMAY,** Curtis Emerson - Ohio (American Independent) Nov. 15, 1906 - Oct. 1, 1990; Air Force chief of staff, 1961-65. Candidacy: VP - 1968.

**LEMKE,** William - N.D. (Union) Aug. 13, 1878 - May 30, 1950; House, 1933-41, 1943-50. Candidacy: P - 1936.

**LINCOLN,** Abraham - Ill. (Republican) Feb. 12, 1809 - April 15, 1865; House, 1847-49; U.S. president, 1861-65. Candidacies: P - 1860, 1864.

**LINCOLN,** Benjamin - Mass. (Federalist) Jan. 24, 1733 - May 9, 1810; major general in Continental Army, 1777-81. Candidacy: 1789.

**LODGE,** Henry Cabot Jr. - Mass. (Republican) July 5, 1902 - Feb. 27, 1985; Senate, 1937-44, 1947-53; ambassador to United Nations, 1953-60; ambassador to Republic of Vietnam, 1963-64, 1965-67. Candidacy: VP - 1960.

**LOGAN,** John Alexander - Ill. (Republican) Feb. 9, 1826 - Dec. 26, 1886; House, 1859-62, 1867-71; Senate, 1871-77, 1879-86. Candidacy: VP - 1884.

**MACHEN,** Willis Benson - Ky. (Democratic) April 10, 1810 - Sept. 29, 1893; Confederate Congress, 1861-65; Senate, 1872-73. Candidacy: VP - 1872.

**MACON,** Nathaniel - N.C. (Democratic-Republican) Dec. 17, 1757 - June 29, 1837;

House, 1791-1815; Speaker of the House, 1801-07; Senate, 1815-28; president pro tempore of the Senate, 1826, 1827. Candidacy: VP - 1824.

**MADISON,** James - Va. (Democratic-Republican) March 16, 1751 - June 28, 1836; Continental Congress, 1780-83, 1787-88; Constitutional Convention, 1787; House, 1789-97; secretary of state, 1801-09; U.S. president, 1809-17. Candidacies: P - 1808, 1812.

**MANGUM,** Willie Person - N.C. (Independent Democrat) May 10, 1792 - Sept. 7, 1861; House, 1823-26; Senate, 1831-36, 1840-53. Candidacy: P - 1836.

**MARSHALL,** John - Va. (Federalist) Sept. 24, 1755 - July 6, 1835; House 1799-1800; secretary of state, 1800-01; chief justice of United States, 1801-35. Candidacy: VP - 1816.

**MARSHALL,** Thomas Riley - Ind. (Democratic) March 14, 1854 - June 1, 1925; governor, 1909-13; U.S. vice president, 1913-21. Candidacies: VP - 1912, 1916.

**McCARTHY,** Eugene Joseph - Minn. (Independent) March 29, 1916—; House, 1949-59; Senate, 1959-71. Candidacy: P - 1976.

**McCLELLAN,** George Brinton - N.J. (Democratic) Dec. 3, 1826 - Oct. 29, 1885; general-in-chief of Army of the Potomac, 1861; governor, 1878-81. Candidacy: P - 1864.

**McGOVERN,** George Stanley - S.D. (Democratic) July 19, 1922—; House, 1957-61; Senate, 1963-81. Candidacy: P - 1972.

**McKINLEY,** William Jr. - Ohio (Republican) Jan. 29, 1843 - Sept. 14, 1901; House, 1877, 1885-91; governor, 1892-96; U.S. president, 1897-1901. Candidacies: P - 1896, 1900.

**McNARY,** Charles Linza - Ore. (Republican) June 12, 1874 - Feb. 25, 1944; state Supreme Court judge, 1913-15; Senate, 1917-18, 1918-44; Senate minority leader, 1933-44. Candidacy: VP - 1940.

**MILLER,** William Edward - N.Y. (Republican) March 22, 1914 - June 24, 1983; House, 1951-65; chairman of Republican National Committee, 1960-64. Candidacy: VP - 1964.

**MILTON,** John - Ga. circa 1740 - circa 1804; secretary of state, Georgia, circa 1778, 1781, 1783. Candidacy: 1789.

**MONDALE,** Walter Frederick - Minn. (Democratic) Jan. 5, 1928—; Senate, 1964-76; U.S. vice president, 1977-81. Candidacies: VP - 1976, 1980; P - 1984.

**MONROE,** James - Va. (Democratic-Republican) April 28, 1758 - July 4, 1831; Continental Congress, 1783-86; Senate, 1790-94; minister to France, 1794-96, 1803; minister to England, 1803-07; governor, 1799-1802, 1811; secretary of state, 1811-14, 1815-17; U.S. president, 1817-25. Candidacies: VP - 1808; P - 1816, 1820.

**MORTON,** Levi Parsons - N.Y. (Republican) May 16, 1824 - May 16, 1920; House, 1879-81; minister to France, 1881-85; U.S. vice president, 1889-93; governor, 1895-97. Candidacy: VP - 1888.

**MUSKIE,** Edmund Sixtus - Maine (Democratic) March 28, 1914—; governor, 1955-59; Senate, 1959-80; secretary of state, 1980-81. Candidacy: VP - 1968.

**NATHAN,** Theodora Nathalia - Ore. (Libertarian) Feb. 9, 1923—; broadcast journalist; National Judiciary Committee, Libertarian Party, 1972-75; vice chairperson, Oregon Libertarian Party, 1974-75. Candidacy: VP - 1972.

**NIXON,** Richard Milhous - Calif., N.Y. (Republican) Jan. 9, 1913 - April 22, 1994; House, 1947-50; Senate, 1950-53; U.S. vice president, 1953-61; U.S. president, 1969-74. Candidacies: VP - 1952, 1956; P - 1960, 1968, 1972.

**PALMER,** John McAuley - Ill. (Democratic, National Democratic) Sept. 13, 1817 - Sept. 25, 1900; governor, 1869-73; Senate, 1891-97. Candidacies: VP - 1872; P - 1896.

**PARKER,** Alton Brooks - N.Y. (Democratic) May 14, 1852 - May 10, 1926; chief justice of N.Y. Court of Appeals, 1898-1904. Candidacy: P - 1904.

**PENDLETON,** George Hunt - Ohio (Democratic) July 19, 1825 - Nov. 24, 1889; House, 1857-65; Senate, 1879-85; minister to Germany, 1885-89. Candidacy: VP - 1864.

**PEROT,** Ross - Texas (Independent) June 27, 1930—; business executive and owner. Candidacy: P - 1992.

**PIERCE,** Franklin - N.H. (Democratic) Nov. 23, 1804 - Oct. 8, 1869; House, 1833-37; Senate, 1837-42; U.S. president, 1853-57. Candidacy: P - 1852.

**PINCKNEY,** Charles Cotesworth - S.C. (Federalist) Feb. 25, 1746 - Aug. 16, 1825; president, state senate, 1779; minister to France, 1796. Candidacies: VP - 1800; P - 1804, 1808.

**PINCKNEY,** Thomas - S.C. (Federalist) Oct. 23, 1750 - Nov. 2, 1828; governor, 1787-89; minister to Great Britain, 1792-96; envoy to Spain, 1794-95; House, 1797-1801. Candidacy: 1796.

**POLK,** James Knox - Tenn. (Democratic) Nov. 2, 1795 - June 15, 1849; House, 1825-39; Speaker of the House, 1835-39; governor, 1839-41; U.S. president, 1845-49. Candidacies: VP - 1840; P - 1844.

**QUAYLE,** Dan - Ind. (Republican) Feb. 4, 1947—; House, 1977-81; Senate, 1981-89; U.S. vice president, 1989-93. Candidacies: VP - 1988, 1992.

**REAGAN,** Ronald Wilson - Calif. (Democratic, Republican) Feb. 6, 1911—; governor, 1967-75; U.S. president, 1981-89. Candidacies: P - 1980, 1984.

**REID,** Whitelaw - N.Y. (Republican) Oct. 27, 1837 - Dec. 15, 1912; minister to France, 1889-92; editor-in-chief, *New York Tribune,* 1872-1905. Candidacy: VP - 1892.

**ROBINSON,** Joseph Taylor - Ark. (Democratic) Aug. 26, 1872 - July 14, 1937; House, 1903-13; governor, 1913; Senate, 1913-37; Senate minority leader, 1923-33; Senate majority leader, 1933-37. Candidacy: VP - 1928.

**ROCKEFELLER,** Nelson Aldrich - N.Y. (Republican) July 8, 1908 - Jan. 26, 1979; governor, 1959-73; U.S. vice president, 1974-77 (nominated under the provisions of the 25th Amendment)..

**RODNEY,** Daniel - Del. (Federalist) Sept. 10, 1764 - Sept. 2, 1846; governor, 1814-17; House, 1822-23; Senate, 1826-27. Candidacy: VP - 1820.

**ROOSEVELT,** Franklin Delano - N.Y. (Democratic) Jan. 30, 1882 - April 12, 1945; assistant secretary of the Navy, 1913-20; governor, 1929-33; U.S. president, 1933-45. Candidacies: VP - 1920; P - 1932, 1936, 1940, 1944.

**ROOSEVELT,** Theodore - N.Y. (Republican, Progressive) Oct. 27, 1858 - Jan. 6, 1919; assistant secretary of the Navy, 1897-98; governor, 1899-1901; U.S. vice president, 1901; U.S. president, 1901-09. Candidacies: VP - 1900; P - 1904, 1912.

**ROSS,** James - Pa. (Federalist) July 12, 1762 - Nov. 27, 1847; Senate, 1794-1803. Candidacy: VP - 1816.

**RUSH,** Richard - Pa. (Democratic-Republican, National-Republican) Aug. 29, 1780 - July 30, 1859; attorney general, 1814-17; minister to Great Britain, 1817-24; secretary of the Treasury, 1825-29. Candidacies: VP - 1820, 1828.

**RUTLEDGE,** John - S.C. (Federalist) Sept. 1739 - July 23, 1800; Continental Congress, 1774-75, 1782-83; governor, 1779-82; Constitutional Convention, 1787; associate justice of U.S. Supreme Court, 1789-91; chief justice of United States, 1795. Candidacy: 1789.

**SANFORD,** Nathan - N.Y. (Democratic-Republican) Nov. 5, 1777 - Oct. 17, 1838; Senate, 1815-21, 1826-31. Candidacy: VP - 1824.

**SCHMITZ,** John George - Calif. (American Independent) Aug. 12, 1930—; House, 1970-73. Candidacy: P - 1972.

**SCOTT,** Winfield - N.J. (Whig) June 13, 1786 - May 29, 1866; general-in-chief of U.S. Army, 1841-61. Candidacy: P - 1852.

**SERGEANT,** John - Pa. (National-Republican) Dec. 5, 1779 - Nov. 23, 1852; House, 1815-23, 1827-29, 1837-41. Candidacy: VP - 1832.

**SEWALL,** Arthur - Maine (Democratic) Nov. 25, 1835 - Sept. 5, 1900; Democratic National Committee member, 1888-96. Candidacy: VP - 1896.

**SEYMOUR,** Horatio - N.Y. (Democratic) May 31, 1810 - Feb. 12, 1886; governor, 1853-55, 1863-65. Candidacy: P - 1868.

**SHERMAN,** James Schoolcraft - N.Y. (Republican) Oct. 24, 1855 - Oct. 30, 1912; House, 1887-91, 1893-1909; U.S. vice president, 1909-12. Candidacies: VP - 1908, 1912. (Died during 1912 campaign; Nicholas Murray Butler replaced Sherman on the Republican ticket.)

**SHRIVER,** Robert Sargent Jr. - Md. (Democratic) Nov. 9, 1915—; director, Peace Corps, 1961-66; director, Office of Economic Opportunity, 1964-68; ambassador to France, 1968-70. Candidacy: VP - 1972. (Replaced Thomas F. Eagleton on Democratic ticket Aug. 8.)

**SMITH,** Alfred Emanuel - N.Y. (Democratic) Dec. 30, 1873 - Oct. 4, 1944; governor, 1919-21, 1923-29. Candidacy: P - 1928.

**SMITH,** William - S.C., Ala. (Independent Democratic-Republican) Sept. 6, 1762 - June 26, 1840; Senate, 1816-23, 1826-31. Candidacies: VP - 1828, 1836.

**SPARKMAN,** John Jackson - Ala. (Democratic) Dec. 20, 1899 - Nov. 16, 1985; House, 1937-46; Senate, 1946-79. Candidacy: VP - 1952.

**STEVENSON,** Adlai Ewing - Ill. (Democratic) Oct. 23, 1835 - June 14, 1914; House, 1875-77, 1879-81; assistant postmaster general, 1885-89; U.S. vice president, 1893-97. Candidacies: VP - 1892, 1900.

**STEVENSON,** Adlai Ewing II - Ill. (Democratic) Feb. 5, 1900 - July 14, 1965; assistant to the secretary of Navy, 1941-44; assistant to the secretary of state, 1945; governor, 1949-53; ambassador to United Nations, 1961-65. Candidacies: P - 1952, 1956.

**STOCKTON,** Richard - N.J. (Federalist) April 17, 1764 - March 7, 1828; Senate, 1796-99; House, 1813-15. Candidacy: VP - 1820.

**TAFT,** William Howard - Ohio (Republican) Sept. 15, 1857 - March 8, 1930; secretary of war, 1904-08; U.S. president, 1909-13; chief justice of United States, 1921-30. Candidacies: P - 1908, 1912.

**TALMADGE,** Herman Eugene - Ga. (Independent Democratic) Aug. 9, 1913—; governor, 1947, 1948-55; Senate, 1957-81. Candidacy: VP - 1956.

**TAYLOR,** Glen Hearst - Idaho (Progressive) April 12, 1904 - April 28, 1984; Senate, 1945-51. Candidacy: VP - 1948.

**TAYLOR,** Zachary - La. (Whig) Nov. 24, 1784 - July 9, 1850; major general, U.S. Army; U.S. president, 1849-50. Candidacy: P - 1848.

**TAZEWELL,** Littleton Waller - Va. (Democratic) Dec. 17, 1774 - May 6, 1860; House, 1800-01; Senate, 1824-32; president pro tempore of the Senate, 1832; governor, 1834-36. Candidacy: VP - 1840.

**TELFAIR,** Edward - Ga. (Democratic-Republican) 1735 - Sept. 17, 1807; Continental Congress, 1778, 1780-82; governor, 1789-93. Candidacy: 1789.

**THOMAS,** Norman Mattoon - N.Y. (Socialist) Nov. 20, 1884 - Dec. 19, 1968; Presbyterian minister, 1911-31; author and editor. Candidacies: P - 1928, 1932, 1936, 1940, 1944, 1948.

**THURMAN,** Allen Granberry - Ohio (Democratic) Nov. 13, 1813 - Dec. 12, 1895; House, 1845-47; Ohio Supreme Court, 1851-56; Senate, 1869-81; president pro tempore of the Senate, 1879, 1880. Candidacy: VP - 1888.

**THURMOND,** James Strom - S.C. (States' Rights Democrat, Democratic, Republican) Dec. 5, 1902—; governor, 1947-51; Senate, 1954-56, 1956—; president pro tempore of the Senate, 1981-87. Candidacies: P - 1948; VP - 1960.

**TILDEN,** Samuel Jones - N.Y. (Democratic) Feb. 9, 1814 - Aug. 4, 1886; governor, 1875-77. Candidacy: P - 1876.

**TOMPKINS,** Daniel D. - N.Y. (Democratic-Republican) June 21, 1774 - June 11, 1825; elected to the House for the term beginning in 1805 but resigned before taking seat; governor, 1807-17; U.S. vice president, 1817-25. Candidacies: VP - 1816, 1820.

**TRUMAN,** Harry S. - Mo. (Democratic) May 8, 1884 - Dec. 26, 1972; Senate, 1935-45; U.S. vice president, 1945; U.S. president, 1945-53. Candidacies: VP - 1944; P - 1948.

**TYLER,** John - Va. (Whig) March 29, 1790 - Jan. 18, 1862; governor, 1825-27; Senate, 1827-36; U.S. vice president, 1841; U.S. president, 1841-45. Candidacies: VP - 1836, 1840.

**VAN BUREN,** Martin - N.Y. (Democratic, Free Soil) Dec. 5, 1782 - July 24, 1862; Senate, 1821-28; governor, 1829; secretary of state, 1829-31; U.S. vice president, 1833-37; U.S. president, 1837-41. Candidacies: VP - 1824, 1832; P - 1836, 1840, 1848.

**WALLACE,** George Corley - Ala. (American Independent) Aug. 25, 1919—; governor, 1963-67, 1971-79, 1983-89. Candidacy: P - 1968.

**WALLACE,** Henry Agard - Iowa (Democratic, Progressive) Oct. 7, 1888 - Nov. 18, 1965; secretary of agriculture, 1933-40; U.S. vice president, 1941-45; secretary of commerce, 1945-46. Candidacies: VP - 1940; P - 1948.

**WARREN,** Earl - Calif. (Republican) March 19, 1891 - July 9, 1974; governor, 1943-53; chief justice of United States, 1953-69. Candidacy: VP - 1948.

**WASHINGTON,** George - Va. (Federalist) Feb. 22, 1732 - Dec. 14, 1799; First and Second Continental Congresses, 1774, 1775; commander-in-chief of armed forces, 1775-83; president of Constitutional Convention, 1787; U.S. president, 1789-97. Candidacies: P - 1789, 1792, 1796.

**WATSON,** Thomas Edward - Ga. (Populist) Sept. 5, 1856 - Sept. 26, 1922; House, 1891-93; Senate, 1921-22. Candidacies: VP - 1896; P - 1904, 1908.

**WEAVER,** James Baird - Iowa (Greenback, Populist) June 12, 1833 - Feb. 6, 1912; House, 1879-81, 1885-89; Candidacies: P - 1880, 1892.

**WEBSTER,** Daniel - Mass. (Whig) Jan. 18, 1782 - Oct. 24, 1852; House, 1813-17, 1823-27; Senate, 1827-41, 1845-50; secretary of state, 1841-43, 1850-52. Candidacy: P - 1836.

**WHEELER,** Burton Kendall - Mont. (Progressive) Feb. 27, 1882 - Jan. 6, 1975; Senate, 1923-47. Candidacy: VP - 1924.

**WHEELER,** William Almon - N.Y. (Republican) June 30, 1819 - June 4, 1887; House, 1861-63, 1869-77; U.S. vice president, 1877-81. Candidacy: VP - 1876.

**WHITE,** Hugh Lawson - Tenn. (Whig) Oct. 30, 1773 - April 10, 1840; Senate, 1825-35, 1835-40. Candidacy: P - 1836.

**WILKINS,** William - Pa. (Democratic) Dec. 20, 1779 - June 23, 1865; Senate, 1831-34; minister to Russia, 1834-35; House, 1843-44; secretary of war, 1844-45. Candidacy: VP - 1832.

**WILLKIE,** Wendell Lewis - N.Y. (Republican) Feb. 18, 1892 - Oct. 8, 1944; utility executive, 1933-40. Candidacy: P - 1940.

**WILSON,** Henry - Mass. (Republican) Feb. 16, 1812 - Nov. 22, 1875; Senate, 1855-73; U.S. vice president, 1873-75. Candidacy: VP - 1872.

**WILSON,** Woodrow - N.J. (Democratic) Dec. 28, 1856 - Feb. 3, 1924; governor, 1911-13; U.S. president, 1913-21. Candidacies: P - 1912, 1916.

**WIRT,** William - Md. (Anti-Masonic) Nov. 8, 1772 - Feb. 18, 1834; attorney general, 1817-29. Candidacy: P - 1832.

**WRIGHT,** Fielding Lewis - Miss. (States' Rights Democratic) May 16, 1895 - May 4, 1956; governor, 1946-52. Candidacy: VP - 1948.

# Gubernatorial and Congressional Elections

**"Counting the Vote on November 7th at 'Elephant Johnnie's.'" From a sketch by S. W. Bennett.**

# Politics and Issues, 1945-92

Following is a narrative chronology of the political and legislative events of the years after World War II, putting in perspective the national and state elections that took place during that period.

## The Postwar Years

By the end of World War II the American people had come to two fundamental decisions that would have a deep influence on the political life of the nation in the postwar years from 1945 through the mid-1960s. In domestic affairs Americans in general had concluded that the social and economic reforms of the New Deal years ought to be preserved and that government had a legitimate role in protecting the individual against economic disaster. On the international front isolationism clearly was rejected in favor of acceptance of a role of active leadership for the United States in world affairs.

These two decisions paved the way for a politics of national consensus in the postwar years. The ideological conflicts of the 1930s were softened, and it was possible for the two major political parties to argue more about means and less about basic national aims.

The main issue usually was which party could best provide for the needs of the people in a steadily expanding economy and at the same time provide firm, reliable leadership for the United States and the free world in a protracted cold war with the Communist bloc. Implicit in both parties' appeals were two basic elements: an acceptance of government's role in the social welfare field and close industry-government ties at home, coupled with a desire to avoid nuclear confrontation with the Soviet Union abroad. When, in 1964, one of the two major national parties sought to deny this postwar consensus in both its domestic and foreign aspects, it encountered the most sweeping electoral repudiation in a quarter-century.

By and large the Democratic Party was more successful than the Republican in presenting itself as the party better able to carry out the national consensus in the postwar years. Three Democrats were elected to the presidency—Harry S. Truman, John F. Kennedy and Lyndon B. Johnson—while only one Republican, Dwight D. Eisenhower, was successful, and then largely because of his status as a hero of World War II. Of the ten Congresses elected in the postwar period, eight had Democratic and only two had Republican majorities. Except for brief periods in 1947-48 and 1951-54

the Democrats held a majority of the state governorships. Democrats maintained regular majorities in most state legislatures. Even the eight-year incumbency of a Republican president failed to strengthen the Republican Party appreciably.

The frequent Democratic victories, however, did not reflect the depth of loyalty to the Democratic Party that had existed in the 1930s, when the fresh recollection of the Great Depression maintained an unwavering Democratic mandate. In fact, the political movements of the postwar period demonstrated a rapidly changing and ambiguous electoral mandate: Republicans scored major victories in 1946 and 1952, but the Democrats achieved significant and far-reaching success in 1948, 1958 and 1964.

Even in the years of party sweeps voters showed an increasing tendency to vote for the candidate rather than the party. The trend toward split tickets was especially evident in 1956, when Eisenhower was reelected by a landslide but the Democrats held Congress, and in 1964, when numerous Republican candidates eked out narrow victories despite the massive national vote for Johnson. Part of the trend toward split tickets could be attributed to an increasingly well educated electorate. But it also seemed to reflect a willingness among the voters to support superior candidates of either party—candidates who represented, in large part, the domestic and foreign policy consensus of the postwar era.

In the early 1960s a new awareness emerged on the issue of civil rights. Civil rights for black citizens had divided Northern and Southern Democrats in Congress for decades and had even caused a rump Southern Dixiecrat Party in the 1948 presidential election. But pressures for equal rights for blacks continued to increase and reached a climax with a series of nationwide demonstrations in 1963. Many white Americans, with church and union groups at the fore, joined the fight for legislative action for equal rights. The result was the comprehensive, bipartisanly sponsored Civil Rights Act of 1964.

Throughout the postwar period Congress was slower to reflect the national consensus on major issues than was the president or the judicial branch of the government. As a rule it was the executive branch that proposed major new programs in fields such as education, welfare and domestic aid—programs that Congress accepted slowly if at all. And it was the Supreme Court that, with its 1954 decision outlawing segregation in the public schools, sparked the movement toward bringing blacks into the mainstream of American life. Other decisions of the Court on constitutional rights, ranging from legislative apportionment to the rights of witnesses and the accused, far outstripped anything Congress was willing to consider.

When Congress did assume a more central role—helping, for instance, to formulate and develop foreign aid programs from the mid-1940s on, pushing aggressively for broader domestic programs while Eisenhower was in the White House, or remolding and expanding the scope of the 1964 Civil Rights Act—its actions stood out as exceptions to the pattern of executive or judicial initiative.

Congress' conservatism and its reticence in initiating programs were based in large part on the committee seniority system and restrictive legislative rules. Committee chairmen often were Southern Democrats or Midwestern Republicans, representing the most rigidly held districts and states. The congressional representatives least able to build up seniority, and thus the least likely to head committees, were those from the politically volatile suburbs and city fringe areas where the major new population movements—and many major problems—of the postwar era occurred.

During this period the House, intended by the Framers of the Constitution to be the chamber closest to the people, actually was the more conservative body, blocking a substantial amount of legislation approved by the Senate. The Senate, especially after the liberal Democratic sweep of 1958, became markedly liberal in its orientation. A principal explanation for the Senate's position was that metropolitan centers, with their pressing demands, had sprung up in virtually every state, prompting senators to be responsive to their needs.

The postwar era might be remembered as one in which both American parties became truly national. Democrats extended their power and influence into Midwestern and northern New England territory that had been unwaveringly Republican in the past. Republicans made significant new breakthroughs in the growing industrial South and in their best years won the votes of millions of Americans who had never voted Republican before.

The 1964 election, at the end of the era, left the Democratic Party in control of most of the power centers, from the presidency to the state legislatures. But many Republicans, noting the somber outcome of an election in which their party had moved far to the right and by implication had repudiated the national stance on most matters, began to work to return the party to a central course. The 1964 election, by underlining the strength of the American consensus on vital issues of domestic economy, civil rights and foreign policy, had demonstrated anew the broad opportunities for a party willing to offer solutions to national needs.

# 1945-47:
# The 79th Congress

The death of a president who had led his country through 12 years of economic and military crisis, the end of the greatest war in history and the inauguration of the atomic age all took place in the two-year interval between Franklin D. Roosevelt's election to a fourth term in 1944 and the 1946 midterm congressional elections.

The president died April 12, 1945, of a cerebral hemorrhage. Two weeks later, on April 25, delegates from Allied powers gathered in San Francisco to write the United Nations charter. (The U.S. Senate ratified the charter July 28, a contrast to the unwillingness of the Senate in 1919 to join the League of Nations.) On April 28 Italian partisans captured and butchered dictator Benito Mussolini. Adolf Hitler was reported to have committed suicide April 29 in his ruined Berlin chancery while Soviet troops poured into the city. Germany surrendered unconditionally on May 7.

In the Pacific, American airplanes administered the coup de grace to the tottering Japanese empire by dropping the first atomic bomb on Hiroshima Aug. 6, 1945; another was used on Nagasaki Aug. 9. World War II ended with the unconditional surrender of Japan on Aug. 14.

In 1944, running on the theme that the nation shouldn't "change horses in the middle of the stream," President Roosevelt had won an unprecedented fourth term with a national vote plurality of 3,594,993 (of 47,976,670 cast) and a total of 432 (of 531) electoral votes. Reversing Democratic losses in the 1942 midterm elections, Congress went heavily Democratic. After the 1944 election 57 Democrats and 38 Republicans were in the Senate, and the House was balanced 243-190 in favor of the Democrats. Less than three months later Roosevelt was dead.

Roosevelt's successor, Harry S. Truman, took office April 12. He faced a perplexing task as he sought to hold together the coalition of big-city machines, organized labor, conservative Southern Democrats, farmers, minority groups, ethnic and religious blocs and intellectual liberals, which FDR had brought together for his successive electoral victories.

Pent-up tensions erupted with the end of World War II. The country was hit by strikes, climaxed in June 1946 by a nationwide rail strike, which President Truman tried to break with a "labor draft," thus incurring deep resentment in the ranks of organized labor. On the right wing Southern Democrats continued to bolt the administration on almost every item of domestic legislation as they had since 1938. Conservative forces in Congress pressed for a relaxation of wartime price controls far more rapidly than Truman thought advisable.

Despite its failure to reach agreement on such basic issues as labor-management relations, a national housing program, federal aid to schools and national health insurance, the 79th Congress produced some notable legislation, including the Atomic Energy Act of 1946, which transferred control over all aspects of atomic energy development from the War Department to a civilian Atomic Energy Commission.

The Employment Act of 1946, considerably weaker than the "Full Employment" bill first proposed—which bordered on a government guarantee of jobs for all—nevertheless broke new ground in fixing responsibility for national economic policies. The Hospital Survey and Construction Act of 1946 authorized a program of matching federal grants to state and local health bodies for hospital construction. The Legislative Reorganization Act of 1946 cut the number of standing committees in the House and the Senate, provided for preparation of an annual legislative budget to complement the president's budget and raised the salaries of senators and representatives from $10,000 to $12,500, plus a $2,500 tax-free expense account. Included in the law, as a separate title, was the Federal Regulation of Lobbying Act, requiring lobbyists to register and report their lobbying expenses.

Congress also authorized a 50-year loan of $3.75 billion to Great Britain, intended to assist the British in removing trade and currency exchange restrictions hampering postwar programs for economic reconstruction and trade liberalization.

## 1946 Midterm Elections

The 1946 congressional election campaign was marked by two events disadvantageous to the administration. First, President Truman on Sept. 20, 1946, dismissed Secretary of Commerce Henry A. Wallace, former vice president (1941-45) and only original New Dealer still remaining in the cabinet and a spokesperson of labor and progressive groups. The dismissal followed a speech Wallace gave—which Wallace had read to Truman in advance—criticizing the allegedly anti-Soviet tone of the foreign policy of Under Secretary of State James F. Byrnes. The incident encouraged Republicans to pin the "red" label on all candidates for whom Wallace subsequently spoke during the campaign.

A second bad break for the administration came in a seven-week national meat shortage just before the election. Truman was forced to issue an order, Oct. 14, ending all meat price controls. His action drew sharp criticism from organized labor and a charge by the Republican national chairman, Rep. B. Carroll Reece of Tennessee, that he was taking action "after the horse has gone to the butcher shop." The mood of the country was clearly in favor of an early end to all remaining wartime controls. The pent-up frustrations of wartime were directly appealed to in the Republican slogans—"Had enough?" and "It's time for a change." Reece promised that a Republican Congress would restore "orderly, capable and honest government in Washington and replace controls, confusion, corruption and communism."

Symptomatic of the tone of the times—pictured by contemporary observers as a desire to return to "normalcy"—were two election-morning newspaper headlines. One read, "Gay Crowd Hails Return of National Horse Show." A second read, "Crackers, Sugar Back in Stores."

The Democratic congressional campaign was lackadaisical. Democratic national Chairman Robert E. Hannegan did warn the country that a GOP victory would be a "surrender to the will of a few who want only large profits for themselves." But Truman failed to hit the campaign trail and offered scarcely any comment on the important races and issues.

The Democrats appeared to depend in large measure on frequent radio broadcasts of the late president Roosevelt's campaign addresses recorded in earlier years. The most publicized activity for Democratic candidates was carried out by the political action committee of the CIO (Congress of Industrial Organizations), headed by the controversial Sidney Hillman.

## Results of the 1946 Elections

The 1946 campaign proved to be the most successful for the Republicans since the 1920s—and the best year they would have for many years to come. Across the nation Republicans swept Senate, House and gubernatorial contests. The Republicans increased their Senate membership from 38 to 51 seats, while the Democrats slipped from 57 to 45 seats.

Among the new Republican senators were John W. Bricker of Ohio, Irving M. Ives of New York, William E. Jenner of Indiana, William F. Knowland of California (who had been appointed to the Senate in 1945), George W. Malone of Nevada, Arthur V. Watkins of Utah and John J. Williams of Delaware. The Progressive candidate, Robert La Follette Jr. of Wisconsin, lost to Republican Joseph R. McCarthy. With the exception of Ives, all represented their party's most conservative wing.

The House Republican delegation rose from 190 seats to 246 seats, while the Democratic delegation dropped from 243 to 188; this was the lowest figure since the 1928 elections. The ratio among the nation's governorships changed from 26-22 in favor of the Democrats to 25-23 in favor of the Republicans.

Important Republican gubernatorial victories included the reelection of Thomas E. Dewey of New York and Earl Warren of California and the elections of Robert F. Bradford of Massachusetts, Alfred E. Driscoll of New Jersey, James H. Duff of Pennsylvania, Thomas J. Herbert of Ohio, Kim Sigler of Michigan and L. W. Youngdahl of Minnesota. The only Democrats to win in generally two-party states were William L. Knous of Colorado, William P. Lane Jr. of Maryland and Lester C. Hunt of Wyoming.

# 1947-49: The 80th Congress

In 1947 and 1948 the nation proceeded to shake off most of the remaining wartime economic controls and to enjoy an economic boom marred somewhat by substantial inflation and the beginnings of the first postwar recession in late 1948. Americans began to realize that the postwar period would be one of continuing international tensions rather than a return to "normalcy."

The foreign scene was darkened by increasing Soviet intransigence at the United Nations; by the civil war in Greece and Communist pressures on Turkey, which led to announcement of the Truman Doctrine in 1947; by the ouster of non-Communists from the Hungarian government in May 1947; by the Communist coup d'état in Czechoslovakia in Feb. 1948; and by the beginning of the Soviet blockade of Berlin in April 1948. Faced with the responsibility of formulating new solutions for the new problems of the postwar era, the Republican-controlled 80th Congress wrote some basic laws that governed domestic and foreign policy for many years to come.

On May 15, 1947, Congress approved the Greek-Turkish aid program requested by President Truman (the Truman Doctrine). The concept of massive economic aid to European countries to assist them in their postwar recovery, suggested by Secretary of State George C. Marshall, received final congressional approval in passage of the European Recovery Program (Marshall Plan) April 2, 1948. International tensions paved the way for congressional approval of a peacetime draft law June 19, 1948.

The legislation that placed the most strain on bipartisan foreign policy was extension of the Reciprocal Trade Agreements Act. Congress in 1948 turned down presidential requests for a three-year extension, granting only a single year's extension in a limited form.

During its first session the 80th Congress approved legislation for unifying the armed forces under a single Department of Defense with separate Army, Navy and Air Force departments under the secretary of defense, and for forming the Central Intelligence Agency.

In domestic affairs the Democratic president and Republican Congress generally were at loggerheads. Presidential recommendations to extend New Deal social welfare concepts were largely ignored by Congress. The most significant single piece of domestic legislation approved by the Congress was the Taft-Hartley Labor-Management Relations Act, passed over President Truman's veto June 23, 1947. The bill outlawed the closed shop, jurisdictional strikes and secondary boycotts and was bitterly opposed by organized labor. Its chief provisions were to remain on the statute books throughout the postwar period.

The 80th Congress completed two significant actions concerning the office of president: it passed a bill, approved by Truman on July 18, 1947, making the Speaker and the president pro tempore of the Senate the next two in line of succession to the presidency after the vice president, ahead of the secretary of state and other cabinet members. In a slap at President Roosevelt's four terms, it sent to the states a constitutional amendment limiting the tenure of future presidents to two terms. The 22nd Amendment became law in February 1951. The communist issue monopolized national attention in the summer of 1948, as Elizabeth Bentley and Whittaker Chambers, self-confessed former Communist Party members, spread before the House Un-American Activities Committee charges that numerous high administration officials during the 1930s and war years had been members of communist spy rings. Chambers' Aug. 3 testimony that former State Department aide Alger Hiss had been a communist spy became the most celebrated case of all. It was highly dramatized on nationwide television on Aug. 25, when Hiss and Chambers confronted each other at a hearing of the committee.

## The 1948 Campaigns

Truman's underdog victory in the 1948 presidential election set the pattern of rapid and startling reversals in domestic political trends during the postwar years. His victory was accompanied by a Democratic congressional and gubernatorial sweep that reversed, in overwhelming measure, the Republican triumph of 1946.

The year 1947 had appeared to be a favorable one for Truman. The Marshall Plan, his "get-tough-with-Russia" policy, his advocacy of government action to curb rising prices, and his willingness to deal firmly with labor leader John L. Lewis had all increased the president's popularity in sharp contrast to its nadir at the time of the 1946 elections. In November 1947 elections the Democrats were especially successful, electing a governor in Kentucky and winning other important races.

By the late spring of 1948, however, Truman's popularity had plummeted to such depths that leaders of his own party cast about for another nominee to head the Democratic ticket. Several developments contributed to the sharp dip in presidential popularity. Reacting in part to Henry A. Wallace's December 1947 announcement that he was forming a third party, Truman included in his 1948 State of the Union address requests for new social welfare legislation plus a call for a straight $40 tax cut for each individual in the nation. Even some liberal Democrats accused the president of having made a "political harangue" in the most partisan spirit.

In February the president's advocacy of a far-sweeping civil rights program, based on recommendations of his civil rights commission, created a predictably bitter reaction in the Southern wing of his party. The stage was set for the States' Rights ticket, putting four parties in the upcoming presidential campaign. Truman's reelection in the face of open revolts on the left wing (Wallaceites) and the right wing (Dixiecrats) seemed almost impossible.

Fearing defeat for the party in the November elections, an unusual coalition of Democrats began to press in late spring for General Dwight D. Eisenhower's nomination by the Democratic National Convention. The coalition included states' rights southerners, big-city bosses from the North and party liberals. In statements on June 5 and 9,

however, Eisenhower made clear his refusal to consider seeking or accepting the nomination. Neither Eisenhower's political philosophy nor his party were known; it was not until 1952 that he identified himself as a Republican.

A brief effort to draft Supreme Court Justice William O. Douglas also collapsed. No further obstacle remained to Truman's renomination when the Democrats assembled gloomily in Philadelphia July 12 for their 30th national convention.

Truman was nominated on the first ballot on July 15, receiving 947-1/2 votes to 263 for Sen. Richard Russell of Georgia. Senate Democratic leader Alben W. Barkley of Kentucky, who had roused the delegates with a fiery key-note speech July 12, was later nominated for vice president.

Truman's acceptance speech created a sensation. Lashing into the Republicans as "the party of special interests," he called for repeal of the Taft-Hartley Act, criticized Congress for its failure to control prices or pass a housing bill, and said that the tax reduction measure approved was a "Republican rich-man's tax bill." He then announced it was his duty to call Congress back into session on July 26 to act on anti-inflation legislation, housing, aid to education, a national health program, civil rights, an increase in the minimum wage from 40 cents to 75 cents hourly, extension of Social Security, public power and cheaper electricity projects and a new "adequate" displaced-persons bill.

The closing day of the Democratic convention was marked by a walkout of delegations from Mississippi and Alabama, when the convention, at the instigation of Minneapolis mayor Hubert H. Humphrey and other party liberals, adopted a tough substitute civil rights plank. Following an impassioned speech by Humphrey in behalf of the stronger plank, the convention approved it by a 651-1/2 to 582-1/2 vote, substituting it for a noncontroversial plank recommended by the Resolutions (Platform) Committee.

Rebellious southerners from 13 states convened in Birmingham, Alabama, on July 17 as the States' Rights Party and nominated Gov. J. Strom Thurmond, D-S.C., for president and Gov. Fielding L. Wright, D-Miss., for vice president. They urged Southern Democratic parties to substitute Thurmond and Wright for Truman and Barkley as the Democratic candidates on the ballot. The convention adopted a platform terming the national Democratic civil rights plank "this infamous and iniquitous program" that would mean a "police state in a totalitarian, centralized, bureaucratic government." The platform stated, "We stand for the segregation of the races and the integrity of each race."

Another group met in Philadelphia in July. Calling itself the Progressive Party, it nominated Henry A. Wallace for president and Sen. Glen H. Taylor, D-Idaho, for vice president. Party leaders denied that the party was communist-dominated, though most observers considered it heavily influenced by the extreme left. In his acceptance speech Wallace blamed Truman for the Berlin crisis. He said there had been a "great betrayal" following President Roosevelt's death in which the administration inaugurated its "get tough" policy, thus "slamming the door" on peace talks with the Soviet Union. The Progressive platform called for a program of U.S. disarmament, a conciliatory policy toward the Soviet Union, an end to segregation, nationalization of key industries, repeal of Taft-Hartley, high farm price supports and the Townsend plan, giving a $100 monthly pension to everyone at the age of 60.

Scenting victory, Republicans engaged in a lively contest for their party's presidential nomination. The three chief candidates were New York governor Thomas E. Dewey, former Minnesota governor Harold E. Stassen and Sen. Robert A. Taft of Ohio. Taft enjoyed the support of most of the more conservative party regulars.

As the primaries developed during the spring, it first appeared that Stassen might be on his way to the nomination. After losing to Dewey in New Hampshire, he won an overwhelming victory in Wisconsin over Dewey and native son Gen. Douglas MacArthur, who had been considered the strong favorite. Stassen won 19 delegates to eight for Mac-Arthur and none for Dewey. In the Nebraska primary Stassen again won against Dewey, Taft and several other candidates whose names were placed on the ballot.

Observers began to predict Stassen's nomination, but he then made what later appeared to be a serious error. He entered the May 4 Ohio primary, bluntly antagonizing the Taft wing of the party. (He won only nine of the 23 contested delegate spots, the rest going to Taft.) In Oregon, where Stassen had been an early favorite, he lost to Dewey in the May 21 primary (117,554 votes to 107,946), after a radio debate between the two men in which Stassen endorsed and Dewey opposed outlawing the Communist Party. Observers believe the debate and primary returns effectively finished Stassen's chances.

When the 24th Republican National Convention opened in Philadelphia June 21, the Dewey victory already seemed probable. Taft was handicapped because many conservatives considered his stands for federal aid to education and housing too liberal, while many party professionals feared his co-authorship of the Taft-Hartley Act might harm the party among union voters. California governor Earl Warren and Michigan senator Arthur Vandenberg both had hopes that a convention deadlock might turn the delegates toward them, but neither ambition was justified. Dewey began with the solid bloc of New York State and enjoyed substantial support in delegations from every part of the country.

In first ballot voting June 24, with 547 needed to win, Dewey received 434 votes to 224 for Taft and 157 for Stassen. Favorite-son candidates shared the rest. On the second ballot Dewey's total rose to 515 against 274 for Taft and 149 for Stassen. Following this, the other candidates quickly fell behind Dewey. His nomination on the third roll call was merely a formality.

During the following night Dewey conferred with influential party leaders and decided on Governor Warren as his running mate. The party adopted a platform backing a "bipartisan" foreign policy, foreign aid to anti-Communist countries, "full" recognition of Israel, housing, anti-inflation and civil rights legislation, and promised a fight against communists inside and outside government.

The Truman and Dewey campaigns became historic examples. The Truman effort showed how a determined candidate can win by going to the people, even with the odds against him; the Dewey performance was an example of how a supposedly sure candidate can lose by waging a lackluster campaign of overconfidence.

Truman undertook a 31,000-mile "barnstorming" whistle-stop tour by train, appearing before an estimated 6 million persons. At each opportunity the president would appear to give one of his "give-'em-hell" attacks on the Republicans. The "do-nothing Republican 80th Congress" was Mr. Truman's chief target: "When I called them back into session what did they do? Nothing. Nothing. That Congress never did anything the whole time it was in session." If the Republicans win, "they'll tear you apart."

---

# Actions of the ''Do-Nothing'' 80th Congress

The 80th Congress (1947-48), characterized by a hard-campaigning President Truman as the "do-nothing Republican 80th Congress," actually produced a great deal of legislation, some of which Truman wanted, some over his serious objections. A partial list of 80th Congress actions:

- Truman doctrine of aid to Greece and Turkey.
- Marshall Plan for aid to Europe.
- Peace treaties ratified with Italy, Hungary, Bulgaria, and Romania.
- Inter-American Treaty of Mutual Assistance ratified.
- Vandenberg Resolution favoring collective and regional mutual assistance pacts.
- Unification of armed forces under Department of Defense; creation of Central Intelligence Agency.
- $65 million building loan for UN headquarters.
- Peacetime draft law.
- Passage of Taft-Hartley Act, over veto.
- Presidential succession change.
- Constitutional amendment to limit presidential tenure to two terms.
- Hope-Aiken flexible price support bill.
- Newsboys excluded from Social Security system, over veto.
- A tax-reduction bill, over veto.
- Liberalized housing credit terms.
- Extended rent control.

---

The Republicans are "predatory animals who don't care if you people are thrown into a depression.... They like runaway prices."

Toward the end of the campaign Truman began a special appeal to minority racial and religious groups, calling for strong civil rights legislation and condemning Republican leaders for passing the Displaced Persons Act, which he said discriminated against Catholics and Jews.

Dewey's campaign was characterized by his aloofness and cool manner, his skirting of issues and his diffuse, repetitive calls for "national unity." Dewey called the 80th Congress "one of the best," but he failed to come to the defense of its individual programs even when they were under direct attack from Truman. Assured by the pollsters, campaign strategists, advertising consultants and reporters that he had the election well in hand, Dewey refrained from direct or forceful answers to any of the Truman attacks. Even more than Dewey, vice presidential candidate Warren disdained to enter the partisan fray.

The Dewey program was particularly vague on farm legislation, which was a new field to him as a New York governor. "There are some people who would like to inject politics into the necessities of food raising in our country. I don't believe in that," Dewey said. He expressed a general support for price supports, not indicating whether they should be at parity or close to it or on a flexible or rigid scale. Meanwhile, farm prices were taking a nosedive that was concerning farmers across the Midwest. Also, storage capacity in grain elevators was short, adding to rural dissatisfaction.

Both the Progressive and Dixiecrat movements, meanwhile, were faltering. Wallace became increasingly identified with the communists and few "liberal" leaders joined his cause. His campaign crowds dwindled to a fraction of their size earlier in the year.

The Dixiecrat ticket failed to make substantial headway as most Southern governors and senators—including some who had been most vociferous in denouncing Truman's civil rights proposals—chose the route of party regularity and backed the president. Only four Southern Democratic parties—those in Alabama, Mississippi, South Carolina and Louisiana—followed through on the plea of the Birmingham convention to put Thurmond and Wright on the ballot as the regular Democratic nominees. They went on the ballot as States' Rights Party candidates in ten other states: Arkansas, California, Florida, Georgia, Kentucky, North Carolina, North Dakota, Tennessee, Texas and Virginia.

With the first election eve returns from the Northeastern states, Truman took a lead that he never lost despite the closeness of the election. As the night wore on state after state considered "safe Republican" moved into the Truman column. Dewey carried Pennsylvania, New Jersey, Indiana, Maryland, Michigan and New York (the last three evidently because of usual Democratic voters defecting to Wallace). But the president carried Massachusetts, won the Border states, took all but four Southern states (Alabama, Louisiana, Mississippi and South Carolina) that were in the Dixiecrat column and carried the farm belt. Finally California fell in his column. When Ohio conclusively went for Truman at 11 o'clock Wednesday morning, Nov. 3, Dewey conceded.

The election returns seemed to indicate that the Democratic New Deal philosophy was so generally accepted by the electorate that the president's warnings of a return to "Republican" depression days remained a telling point. On a less philosophical level many observers felt the Truman "Mr. Average" approach, compared to Dewey's "Olympian airs," drew a large sympathy vote from the average people in the street for the conceded "underdog."

### Results of the 1948 Elections

With the Truman victory the Democrats took control of Congress with commanding majorities in both the Senate and the House. The Democrats picked up nine Senate seats to make the new balance 54-42 in their favor. Among the new Democratic senators were Lyndon B. Johnson (Texas), Paul H. Douglas (Illinois), Hubert H. Humphrey (Minnesota), Estes Kefauver (Tennessee), Robert S. Kerr (Oklahoma) and Clinton P. Anderson (New Mexico). Republican Margaret Chase Smith was elected senator from Maine. And in House elections Democrats made a net gain of 75 seats; the new total was 263 Democrats and 171 Republicans.

The Democrats also ran strong in gubernatorial contests, winning 20 of the 32 seats up for election and reversing the Republican trend of the immediate past years. The new totals were 30 Democratic and 18 Republican governorships. Among the new Democratic governors were Chester Bowles (Connecticut), Adlai E. Stevenson (Illinois) and G. Mennen Williams (Michigan).

# 1949-1951:
# The 81st Congress

The international situation in the years 1949 and 1950 was marked by stabilization and cooling of tensions in Europe, in sharp contrast to renewed Communist conquest and the threat of nuclear war in Asia. In April 1949 the North Atlantic Treaty was signed by the United States, Canada and 10 European nations, agreeing that "an armed attack against any one or more of them in Europe and North America shall be considered an attack against all." A direct reaction to Communist power moves, which included the 1948 takeover of Czechoslovakia, the NATO treaty laid down a policy of containment of Soviet expansionist ambitions that helped to preserve a territorial status quo on the European continent for years to come. On Sept. 30, 1949, the Soviets lifted a blockade of Berlin, which had been in effect since April 1, 1948.

In Asia, however, the Western position was disintegrating rapidly. On Jan. 22, 1949, the Chinese Communists took Beijing. On April 23 they crossed the Yangtze and captured Nanjing. On Aug. 6 Secretary of State Dean Acheson blamed Generalissimo Chiang Kai-shek's "reactionary" clique for the Communist victory and gave notice that no further aid would be given Chiang's government. On Dec. 7, 1949, the Nationalist Chinese government fled to Formosa.

The takeover of mainland China by a hostile Communist power did not shake the Western world, however, as did the surprise attack of Communist North Korean troops on South Korea June 25, 1950. The UN Security Council immediately ordered a cease-fire. Two days later President Truman ordered U.S. forces under Gen. Douglas MacArthur to repel the North Koreans. This became a UN "peace action" but was largely an American venture. U.S. involvement in Korea led to a near-wartime mobilization of the U.S. economy. It also led to President Truman's dispute with General MacArthur over the proposed bombing of Manchuria, which in turn led to MacArthur's dismissal in April 1951. As the war dragged on for two years with heavy U.S. casualties, it became a source of great frustration for the American people.

In other important developments the Soviet Union in September 1949 exploded its first atomic bomb, ending the U.S. atomic monopoly; India was proclaimed independent in January 1950; Alger Hiss was found guilty of perjury on Jan. 21, 1950; and Truman, in January 1950, authorized the Atomic Energy Commission to produce the hydrogen bomb.

In his inaugural address Jan. 20, 1949, President Truman included a "Point IV" proposal of American foreign policy for "a bold new program for making the benefits of our scientific advances and industrial progress available for the improvement and growth of underdeveloped areas." Over the succeeding years, foreign aid assistance for capital investment to build up the economies of fledgling nations of Africa, Asia and Latin America became a cornerstone of U.S. foreign policy.

When the heavily Democratic 81st Congress assembled in Washington Jan. 3, 1949, liberals had high hopes that it would enact a new body of social welfare legislation such as that proposed by Truman in the 1948 campaign. The first signs for the Truman program seemed bright as the House on Jan. 3 adopted a new rule to break the power of its Rules Committee to bottle up legislation indefinitely. The "21-day rule" provided that if the Rules Committee failed to clear a bill after 21 legislative days the chairman of the legislative committee that originally approved it could ask the House to vote on whether to consider the measure or not, with a majority vote required to bring the bill to the floor. The rule lasted only through the 81st Congress and was rejected by the House when the 82nd Congress organized in 1951.

On Jan. 5 Truman appeared before Congress to urge a sweeping new Fair Deal program of social reform. But Congress in general proved to be a disappointment to the liberal camp on domestic issues. Approval was given to a long-range housing bill providing for expanded federal programs in slum clearance, public housing and farm improvement programs, which Truman signed into law July 15, 1949, "with deep satisfaction." The administration also scored an important victory in passage of the Social Security Expansion Act of 1950 and a limited victory in a 1949 minimum wage increase. But otherwise the Fair Deal program hit formidable obstacles.

Legislation to continue the Marshall Plan, military assistance to friendly foreign nations and a two-year extension of the Trade Agreements Act cleared Congress with some bipartisan support. The Senate on July 21, 1949, ratified the North Atlantic Treaty by a 2-1 margin. In domestic affairs important steps toward streamlining the executive branch of the government were made in the Government Reorganization Act of 1949.

An explosive new issue, meanwhile, had developed on the domestic scene. In a Feb. 11, 1950, speech in Wheeling, W.Va., Sen. Joseph R. McCarthy, R-Wis., charged that there were 57 communists working in the State Department, a charge promptly denied by the department. Until his formal censure by the Senate in 1954, McCarthy and his freewheeling accusations of communist sympathies among high- and low-placed government officials absorbed much of the public attention. The phenomenon of McCarthyism had a major effect on the psychological climate of the early 1950s.

### The 1950 Midterm Elections

The liberal Democratic trend apparent in Truman's surprise 1948 victory was sharply reversed in the 1950 elections as Republicans exploited the issues of inflation, Korea, communism and corruption, to make strong comebacks in congressional and gubernatorial elections.

Truman, delivering his only major speech of the campaign Nov. 4, 1950, sought to bolster the Democratic effort with charges similar to those he leveled against the Republicans in 1948: that they were captives of "special interests," that they would undo the country's progress toward peace and prosperity if they gained control of the national government. Truman said the Republicans were "isolationists" and that "any farmer who votes for the Republican Party ought to have his head examined."

The Republican campaign assumed a far more aggressive tone than it had in 1948. Sen. Robert A. Taft, R-Ohio, said the administration was responsible for high prices, high taxes, the loss of China to the Communists and the Korean conflict. (Republicans pointed frequently to a Jan. 12, 1950, speech by Secretary of State Dean Acheson before the National Press Club in which Acheson described the U.S. defensive line in the Far East in such a way as to exclude Korea.)

Typical of other Republican attacks was a Nov. 4 reply to Truman by Harold Stassen, charging that the "blinded, blundering, bewildering" Far East policy of the "spy-riddled" Truman administration was directly to blame for American casualties in Korea.

McCarthy's charges of communism in high places in the government played an important part in the campaign. Whether or not the voters believed all of McCarthy's charges, many seemed to accept the thesis that there was something drastically wrong with U.S. foreign policy and that Acheson was a likely villain.

In Maryland the prominent veteran Democratic senator Millard E. Tydings was defeated by John Marshall Butler, an obscure Republican, after a campaign in which Tydings was accused of having "whitewashed" the State Department as head of a Senate committee investigating McCarthy's charges of communism in the department. Butler was later accused of countenancing distribution of a campaign leaflet with a doctored photograph showing Tydings with U.S. Communist leader Earl Browder.

In California Republican representative Richard M. Nixon ran for the Senate against Rep. Helen Gahagan Douglas, a prominent liberal Democrat. Nixon's charges that Douglas voted frequently with New York representative Vito Marcantonio, a member of the American Labor Party, whose voting record was often depicted as pro-communist, established the image of Nixon as a ruthless campaigner, an image that would harm him in future races.

Another Senate contest with communism as the chief issue took place in North Carolina, where Willis Smith defeated incumbent Frank P. Graham in a June 24 Democratic primary runoff. Smith charged that Graham was badly tainted with socialism because of his alleged "associations with communism."

Among major issues stressed by the Republicans was Truman's program for compulsory health insurance for all, termed "socialized medicine" by doctors who fought it both in the primaries and in the general elections. The issue was thought to have contributed to the defeat of several Democratic senators, including Claude Pepper of Florida and Graham of North Carolina in primaries and Elbert D. Thomas of Utah and Glen H. Taylor of Idaho in the general election. But in each one of these cases and in the California Senate race the "soft-on-communism" issue, at its peak in 1950, played a more important role.

### Results of the 1950 Elections

The two most closely watched Senate battles were in Ohio, where Republican senator Robert Taft was the target of an all-out attempt by organized labor to defeat him because of his co-authorship of the Taft-Hartley Act, and in Illinois, where Senate majority leader Scott W. Lucas was challenged by former Republican representative Everett McKinley Dirksen, who campaigned as a conservative near-isolationist. The election returns showed Taft the winner in Ohio by a gigantic 431,184 vote margin (57.5 percent), while Dirksen upset Lucas with 294,354 votes to spare (53.9 percent). Both men later became their party's Senate leader.

Assessment of the election returns showed that, while the Democrats retained nominal control of Congress (the Senate by 2 votes, the House by 35), the Truman-Fair Deal influence on Congress had been virtually nullified. Outside the conservative Southern states, the Democrats elected only 126 House members to 196 for the Republicans.

On the Senate side the Republicans won 18 and the Democrats 9 of the non-Southern contests. Among the new senators were Richard M. Nixon, R-Calif.; George A. Smathers, D-Fla.; Everett McKinley Dirksen, R-Ill.; A. S. Mike Monroney, D-Okla.; and James H. Duff, R-Pa., who was one of the prime movers for the nomination of Eisenhower in 1952.

# 1951-53:
# The 82nd Congress

The Korean conflict continued to dominate American life in 1951 and 1952 and led directly to the defeat of the

Democrats in the 1952 elections. On April 11, 1951, President Truman removed General of the Army Douglas MacArthur from his command of UN and U.S. forces in the Far East. MacArthur had wanted to pursue the Chinese Communists across the Yalu River to their sanctuary in Manchuria in order to destroy the air depots and lines of supply being used to sustain their war effort in Korea. On March 25 MacArthur had threatened Communist China with air and naval attack. These steps, running contrary to the Truman administration policy under Secretary of State Dean Acheson, led to MacArthur's removal. Negotiations for a truce along the 38th parallel began July 10, 1951, but the fighting continued for another two years.

In other international developments the Japanese peace treaty was signed in San Francisco on Sept. 8, 1951. War between Germany and the United States was formally ended Oct. 19. On May 26, 1952, a peace contract between Germany and the Western allies was signed. In Nov. 1952 the first hydrogen bomb was exploded by the United States.

A major domestic controversy developed in 1952 when Truman on April 8 ordered seizure of the nation's steel mills to avert a strike by 600,000 CIO steel workers. On June 2, however, the Supreme Court ruled the seizure illegal. The workers struck from June 3 to July 25.

The 82nd Congress accomplished very little outside the realm of foreign and military affairs. None of the Fair Deal proposals expounded by the president and the Democratic leadership in 1948 and 1950—national health insurance, aid to education and increased public health benefits—was enacted into law.

In 1951 the nation's interest was captured by the televised crime hearings of a Senate subcommittee chaired by Sen. Estes Kefauver, D-Tenn. The hearings exposed nationwide criminal organizations that reaped huge illegal profits, influencing local politicians and buying protection.

## The 1952 Campaigns

President Truman ended any speculation about his third-term ambitions by announcing March 29 that he would not be a candidate for reelection. The field of possible Democratic nominees included Senator Kefauver; Gov. Adlai E. Stevenson, D-Ill.; W. Averell Harriman of New York; Vice President Alben W. Barkley of Kentucky; Sen. Robert S. Kerr, D-Okla.; and Sen. Richard B. Russell, D-Ga. Stevenson was Truman's personal choice for the nomination and was offered presidential support as early as January. Truman was willing to back Barkley after Stevenson's repeated disavowals of interest in the nomination; however, influential labor leaders vetoed Barkley's nomination, forcing him to withdraw on the eve of the convention.

Stevenson consistently professed his disinterest in the nomination and only submitted to a draft movement in his behalf while the 1952 Democratic convention, which convened in Chicago July 21, was in progress. The support for Stevenson, already strong, began to snowball with the July 24 announcement of Thomas J. Gavin, President Truman's alternate as a delegate from Missouri, that he would vote for Stevenson on Truman's instructions. Stevenson ran second to Kefauver in both the first and second ballots.

Only on the third ballot, not completed until 12:25 a.m. on July 26, did Stevenson move close to nomination as Harriman withdrew in his favor. A unanimous nomination by acclamation was then moved and carried. Following a conference with President Truman, Stevenson chose Sen. John J. Sparkman, D-Ala., a backer of the national Democratic Party on most issues except civil rights, as his running

mate. The convention then confirmed his choice by acclamation.

The contest for the Republican presidential nomination, despite other entries in the field, was fought out between the supporters of two relatively clearly defined groups within the party: Sen. Robert A. Taft of Ohio represented the conservative Midwestern and Southern wing of the party, and Gen. Dwight D. Eisenhower became the candidate of the "internationalist" wing of the party centered on the East and West coasts. Other announcements of candidacy were made by California governor Earl Warren and by Harold E. Stassen.

Eisenhower in early 1952 was on duty in Paris as commanding general of the new North Atlantic Treaty Organization. The major political question as 1952 began was whether he would permit his name to be put forth for the Republican nomination. Previously he had always rejected talk of his running for president, and he had declined to make his political affiliations known. The mystery ended on Jan. 7 when Sen. Henry Cabot Lodge, R-Mass., announced that he was entering Eisenhower's name in the March 11 New Hampshire primary after having received assurances from the general that he was a Republican. In a Jan. 8 statement from Paris, Eisenhower confirmed his Republican loyalties and said he would run for president if he received a "clear-cut call to political duty." Eisenhower said, however, that he would not actively seek the nomination. Despite his refusal to campaign, Eisenhower ran strongly in most of the primaries where his name was entered.

When the 25th Republican National Convention opened in Chicago on July 7, the delegate issue was the hottest—and one of the first—items of business. In a preliminary test the convention voted 658-548 against allowing delegates with disputed seats to vote on other delegate contests until their own credentials were accepted. This resolution, which had been endorsed by 25 of the nation's Republican governors, prevented disputed Taft delegates from the South from voting for each other's seating. The victory of the Eisenhower forces on this issue foreshadowed the general's eventual nomination.

Korea, foreign affairs, corruption in government, internal communism and the domestic economy were the major issues of the 1952 campaign. Of these, only the domestic economy—booming through the stimulation of the Korean War—proved to be in any way a plus for the Democrats. The other issues aided the Republican campaign.

The most dramatic episode of the campaign opened Sept. 18 with an article in the *New York Post,* charging that GOP vice presidential nominee Nixon had been the beneficiary of an allegedly secret fund financed by California businesses. For a week controversy raged with many demands that Nixon resign from the ticket so that the corruption issue against the Democrats would not be diluted.

Eisenhower declined to take a firm stand on Nixon's continuance on the ticket. Finally, Nixon on Sept. 23 went on nationwide television for a melodramatic defense of the moral rectitude of the fund and to make a complete accounting of his own relatively limited personal assets. In this speech Nixon referred to his wife's "respectable Republican cloth coat" and the gift dog, Checkers—"regardless of what they say about it, we're going to keep it."

Response to Nixon's speech overwhelmingly favored keeping him on the ticket. Eisenhower immediately issued a statement lauding Nixon for his bravery in a "tough situation." At a Sept. 24 meeting between the two men in

Wheeling, W.Va., Eisenhower announced that Nixon had completely "vindicated himself."

## Results of the 1952 Elections

In contrast to 1948, when the pollsters and commentators had all foreseen a sweeping Dewey victory, there was a marked reluctance to make a firm prediction on the outcome of the 1952 campaign. But when the returns started to roll in election eve, it was clear that Eisenhower had won by a landslide and that his victory had probably never been in doubt.

Only nine of the 48 states went for Stevenson, and they were in the South or Border areas (West Virginia, Kentucky, Alabama, Arkansas, Georgia, Louisiana, Mississippi, North Carolina and South Carolina). Every state across the East, Midwest and Far West went for Eisenhower. And the tide rolled on into many parts of the South, with the Eisenhower-Nixon ticket carrying Texas, Oklahoma, Florida, Virginia and Tennessee.

The electoral vote count was 442 for Eisenhower, 89 for Stevenson. In popular votes Eisenhower won a 6,621,242-vote plurality. He polled 33,936,234 votes, the highest number of votes ever received by a presidential candidate. But in defeat Stevenson won 27,314,992 votes, the highest number ever received by a losing candidate.

Seeking explanations for the Eisenhower landslide, observers found a multitude of reasons. The doubts, fears and frustrations stemming from the stalemated Korean War, the Hiss case and the communist spy trials, revelations of corruption in the federal government, rising prices and high taxes—all contributed to a strong desire for a change in executive leadership. Stevenson's divorce and wit were thought to be unpopular with many voters. Sparkman's identification with the white supremacy views of the Alabama Democratic Party harmed the ticket among black voters.

The lack of enthusiasm for the Republican congressional leadership, the memory of the depression and fear of reversal of social-economic gains of the Democratic years might have nullified these Republican advantages, however, if the Republicans had not found in Eisenhower an ideal candidate to allay such fears. A national hero, a man whose leadership had already been proven in World War II and in laying the groundwork for the North Atlantic Alliance, Eisenhower also had the invaluable asset of a magic personality that charmed voters and the image of being "above politics." Few could seriously believe that "Ike" would scuttle the New Deal reforms.

The uniquely personal aspect of Eisenhower's victory was underlined by the narrow margins with which Republicans moved into control of Congress, despite the presidential landslide. Republicans made a net gain of 22 House seats to a new total of 221, only three more than the 218 needed to give them control. The Democratic House total slipped from 235 to 213. In Senate elections the Republicans made a net gain of only one seat, just enough to give them a one-seat edge in the new Senate. The new Senate totals were 48 Republicans, 47 Democrats and one Independent (Wayne Morse of Oregon, formerly a Republican).

In what proved to be a significant Senate race 35-year-old Democratic representative John F. Kennedy defeated Republican Henry Cabot Lodge Jr., a top leader in the Eisenhower drive for the GOP presidential nomination, by a 70,737-vote margin in Massachusetts. Other newly elected senators included Barry Goldwater, R-Ariz.; Stuart Symington, D-Mo.; Mike Mansfield, D-Mont.; Henry M. Jackson, D-Wash.; and Albert Gore, D-Tenn.

On the gubernatorial level Republicans solidified the national lead they had achieved in 1950 by winning five new seats. The winners were Christian A. Herter, R-Mass.; William G. Stratton, R-Ill.; J. Caleb Boggs, R-Del.; George N. Craig, R-Ind.; and Hugo Aronson, R-Mont. The new governorship totals were 30 Republicans and 18 Democrats.

# 1953-55:
# The 83rd Congress

Many Americans had hoped that Eisenhower's election to the presidency would usher in an era of domestic tranquillity and international stability. In some respects these wishes were fulfilled. There was a more harmonious relationship between the president and Congress than at any time since World War II. A Korean armistice was finally signed July 27, 1953, with prisoner repatriation following shortly thereafter.

Republicans claimed that President Eisenhower's action in instructing the U.S. Seventh Fleet to stop shielding Communist China from any possible Nationalist Chinese attacks, combined with information relayed to the Chinese that the United States would resort to full-scale war in Korea if the Communists refused to come to peace terms, were decisive factors in persuading the Communists to come to terms. Democrats replied that the terms of the armistice were no better than those the Truman administration had previously rejected.

Even with a return to relative stability in Korea, however, the international situation remained in flux on other fronts. Soviet Premier Joseph Stalin died March 5, setting off a contest for succession in the USSR. On July 7, 1953, an uprising that broke out in Communist-held East Germany was quelled when the Communists called in Soviet troops and tanks, which mowed down civilians revolting in the streets of East Berlin. The United States did not intervene, drawing into question the wisdom of the "liberation" policy spelled out by Republican campaigners in 1952.

On Aug. 20, 1953, the Soviet Union announced the successful testing of its first hydrogen bomb. President Eisenhower went before the United Nations on Dec. 8 to urge the major powers to cooperate in developing the peaceful uses of atomic energy. The United States on Jan. 21, 1954, launched the *Nautilus,* the first atomic-powered submarine.

The curtain began to go down on France's colonial empire as she admitted defeat in the seven-and-a-half-year war against Communist infiltration in Indo-China and submitted to a partition of Vietnam at the spring 1953 Geneva conference on Far Eastern affairs; France subsequently withdrew forces from Vietnam, Cambodia and Laos. Threatened Communist inroads in Central America were reversed, however, by U.S.-supported anti-Communist forces, which invaded Guatemala and overthrew the Communist-oriented government of President Jacobo Arbenz Guzman in June 1954.

The 83rd Congress produced few innovations in domestic or foreign policy, but neither did it reverse New Deal social reforms. During the first session (1953), foreign aid and military appropriations were pared, the controversial Reconstruction Finance Corp. was abolished, legislation was passed giving the states title to the oil-rich coastal lands previously claimed by the federal government, and Congress permitted the president to carry out a governmental reorganization creating a new Department of Health, Education, and Welfare, which it had denied President Truman in 1949 and 1950.

Sen. Joseph R. McCarthy and his unrestrained accusations of communist influence throughout the government remained a domestic issue. Taking over chairmanship of the Senate Government Operations Committee in 1953, McCarthy conducted hearings and investigated the State Department, Voice of America, Department of the Army and other agencies. An opinion-stifling "climate of fear" in many government agencies was said to be one of the results of his probes. The Army-McCarthy hearings, televised in the spring of 1954, were the climax of McCarthy's career and led finally to his censure by the Senate on Dec. 2, 1954. McCarthy's influence waned steadily thereafter. He died May 2, 1957.

The Supreme Court on May 17, 1954, handed down a unanimous decision declaring racial segregation in the public schools to be unconstitutional. The opinion, written by Chief Justice Earl Warren (whom Eisenhower had appointed on the death of Chief Justice Fred M. Vinson in 1953), began a major movement toward racial desegregation across the nation. It inspired bitter hostility in the Southern states.

A potential Democratic comeback with the nation's voters was presaged by special elections held during 1953. The traditional Republican hold on New Jersey was broken by the election of Democrat Robert B. Meyner to the governorship. Special elections in the New Jersey 6th and Wisconsin 9th Districts resulted in the election of two Democrats, Harrison A. Williams Jr. in New Jersey and Lester Johnson in Wisconsin. They were the first members of their party ever to win in either of these districts.

### The 1954 Midterm Elections

The Republican success under Eisenhower in winning both houses of Congress in 1952 was not repeated in 1954. Democrats made significant comebacks, recapturing control of both House and Senate and reversing the Republican gubernatorial trend of recent years. But the swing back to the Democrats, while it indicated that the Republican Party was probably much weaker than its popular president, was by no means strong enough to spell a major change in the nation's mood. Although it was in the majority, much of the Democratic Party strength was concentrated in the conservative South.

President Eisenhower appealed to the voters to return a Republican Congress and he campaigned harder and longer than any other president had ever done in a midterm election. He claimed that Congress had enacted 54 of 64 legislative proposals he had submitted and that this "batting average of .830" was "pretty good in any league." (Congressional Quarterly figures showed Congress had approved 150 of 232 specific Eisenhower requests for a batting average of .647.)

In an Oct. 8 televised address he warned that a Democratic congressional victory would start "a cold war of partisan politics between the Congress and the Executive Branch," which would block "the great work" his administration had "begun so well." Congressional Democratic leaders Sam Rayburn and Lyndon B. Johnson, both of Texas, replied in a joint telegram to the president that "there will be no cold war conducted against you by the Democrats" and complained that the president had made an "unjust attack on the many Democrats who have done so much to cooperate with your Administration and to defend your program against attacks by members of your own party."

In a last-minute effort to bolster the Republican vote in critical states, Eisenhower made an unprecedented one-day,

1,521-mile flying trip on Oct. 29, 1954, to address crowds in Cleveland, Detroit, Louisville and Wilmington, Del. In these speeches he implied that Democratic administrations had been able to boast of full employment and prosperity only during war. Following the campaign some observers speculated that Eisenhower may have kept many women's votes by reminding them that the Republicans had put an end to the "futile casualties" in Korea. There was general agreement that his campaign activities averted a still stronger Democratic trend, especially in congressional elections.

Vice President Nixon played a controversial role in the campaign, charging that the Democrats were unfit to govern because of their record on the communist issue.

On the issue of mounting unemployment in several areas of the country, Democrats charged Republicans with a "callous" attitude toward the problem, while Republicans replied that they had provided jobs without war. Public power was also an issue, with Democrats accusing Republicans of "give-aways" to private interests, while Republicans replied that Democratic public power policy had tended toward socialism and government monopoly.

### Results of the 1954 Elections

Democrats moved into control of the Senate by a 48-47-1 margin as compared with the 49-46-1 Republican edge before the election. Among the new senators were Richard L. Neuberger, D-Ore., former vice president Alben W. Barkley, D-Ky. and Clifford P. Case, R-N.J.

In the House the new lineup was 232 Democrats and 203 Republicans, a net Democratic gain of 19 seats over the previous Congress, which had had 221 Republicans and 213 Democrats.

The Democratic congressional majorities grew throughout the remainder of the Eisenhower years. Sam Rayburn, D-Texas, again became Speaker of the House, and Lyndon B. Johnson, D-Texas, Senate majority leader—posts they held through the rest of the decade.

Republicans fared even worse in the governorship races. Including the Democratic victory of Edmund S. Muskie in the September 13 Maine election, the Democrats ousted Republicans from eight state governments, and the Republicans failed to take a single Democratic seat. The gubernatorial balance shifted from 29-19 in favor of the Republicans to 27-21 in favor of the Democrats. In the New York governorship election to succeed retiring three-term governor Thomas E. Dewey, a Republican, Democrat Averell Harriman won a narrow 11,125-vote plurality over Republican senator Irving M. Ives. Other Democratic gubernatorial winners included Abraham Ribicoff in Connecticut, Orville Freeman in Minnesota and George M. Leader in Pennsylvania.

# 1955-57: The 84th Congress

Cooperation between a middle-of-the-road president and a middle-of-the-road Congress, tension in the Formosa Strait, growing pressures in Africa and Asia for independence from colonial rule, the Geneva "summit" conference, presidential illnesses, "de-Stalinization" in the Soviet empire, revolt in Poland and Hungary, war over the Suez Canal—these events were highlights of the last half of President Eisenhower's first term in office.

Divided responsibility for government brought unexpectedly harmonious sessions of Congress, with nothing resembling the "cold war of partisan politics" predicted in 1954 by Eisenhower if the Democrats were to take control of

Congress. Administration measures fared almost as well as they had during the Republican 83rd Congress, again with substantial aid from Democrats.

Especially in foreign affairs the Democratic leadership cooperated substantially with the president. Early in 1955 Congress approved the resolution Eisenhower had requested to give him authority to employ U.S. armed forces to defend Formosa. Prompted by Communist Chinese bombardment of the off-shore islands of Quemoy and Matsu, the resolution also gave the president authority to defend, in addition to Formosa, "related positions and territories now in friendly hands," an evident reference to Quemoy and Matsu. Senate moves to delete this authority were overwhelmingly rejected.

The Senate ratified, by almost unanimous votes, the Southeast Asia Collective Defense Treaty (which created the Southeast Asia Defense Organization—SEATO), plus protocols ending the occupation of Germany, restoring sovereignty to West Germany and permitting West German rearmament and NATO membership. The peace treaty with Austria, creating an independent, neutral state, was signed in Vienna on May 15 and was ratified by the Senate June 7, 1955. The controversial constitutional amendment offered by Sen. John W. Bricker, R-Ohio, to trim the president's treaty-making powers was reported out of the Senate Foreign Relations Committee in 1956, but it was not brought up for Senate debate because of the president's firm opposition. In 1955 the Reciprocal Trade Agreements Act was extended for three years, the longest single extension since 1945. Foreign aid appropriations came fairly close to matching presidential requests.

Domestic enactments by the politically divided government were less impressive. The two most important measures approved by Congress appeared to be the multibillion dollar federal highway program, providing for a 41,000-mile interstate superhighway program as part of the most extensive public works project in the nation's history, and the Agricultural Act of 1956, which included the soil bank program that supporters hoped would limit farm surpluses and raise farmers' incomes. Congress also voted an increase in the minimum wage to $1 an hour (as opposed to the 90-cent figure recommended by the administration).

On the international scene the first conference of Asian-African countries met April 18-27, 1955, in Bandung, Indonesia. Delegates endorsed an end to colonialism, called for national independence and demanded UN membership for all states qualified in terms of the UN charter (including Communist China). In the following month the Warsaw Treaty, counterpart to NATO for the Communist satellites of Eastern Europe, was ratified.

At the 20th Congress of the Soviet Communist Party in Moscow, Feb. 14-25, 1956, Nikita Khrushchev proclaimed a new party line, which included destruction of Joseph Stalin as a national idol. The rush to "de-Stalinize" however, loosed forces in the Communist world that the Soviet Union was able to control only by bloody repressions of the June 28, 1956, workers revolt in Poznan, Poland, and the revolt of Hungarians in October and November of 1956.

Reacting adversely to Egyptian president Gamal Abdel Nasser's acceptance of Soviet-bloc arms and economic agreements with the Communist world, the United States on July 19, 1956, informed Egypt that it was withdrawing its offer to aid in construction of the Aswan Dam on the Nile River. Britain on July 20 announced it was also withdrawing from the project. On July 26 Egypt seized the British-held Suez Canal and denounced the Western powers. Prolonged

negotiations during the summer and fall failed to persuade Egypt to modify its decision on nationalizing the canal, and on Oct. 29 Israel launched an invasion of Egypt. The move was coordinated with the British and French governments, which attacked Egypt on Oct. 31. The Suez Canal was blocked by sunken and scuttled ships. The Soviet Union stepped into the controversy, threatening atomic war if Britain and France refused to retreat. The United Nations, led by the United States, condemned the French, British and Israeli moves. A UN cease-fire ended the fighting Nov. 7, and a UN international peace force moved in to enforce the peace, the terms of which allowed Egypt to regain control of the canal and forced Israeli withdrawal.

The question of President Eisenhower's health hung over the nation for a year before the November 1956 election. On Sept. 24, 1955, the 64-year-old president was stricken by a heart attack, which totally incapacitated him for a period of days and necessitated his hospitalization for almost two months. Republican leaders, who had confidently expected Eisenhower to seek (and easily win) reelection in 1956, suddenly faced the possibility that he might not be available. As the president gradually improved, party leaders, particularly GOP national chairman Leonard W. Hall, repeatedly urged him to run again despite his illness. After thorough physical examinations Eisenhower on Feb. 29, 1956, announced that he was convinced that his health would permit him to carry the "burdens of the Presidency" under a reduced work schedule and that he would seek reelection.

On June 8 the president was again hospitalized, this time with ileitis. He underwent successful surgery on June 9 and was once more hospitalized for several weeks. Again the possibility arose that he might not seek reelection. But on July 10 Eisenhower made it clear he would go ahead with his campaign for reelection.

Without the question of presidential illness, there would probably have been little doubt, at any time, that Ike could achieve reelection. The presidential illness, however, added an element of uncertainty to the entire campaign and made the Democratic nomination appear far more "worth having" than might otherwise have been the case.

## The 1956 Campaigns

A familiar cast stepped forward to seek the Democratic presidential nomination: Adlai E. Stevenson, the 1952 nominee; Tennessee senator Estes Kefauver, the popular primary choice of 1952; and New York governor Averell Harriman. Senate majority leader Lyndon B. Johnson of Texas was supported for the nomination by several Southern leaders, but he had little backing outside the South.

Early in the spring it appeared that Kefauver might again sweep the primaries. After winning the New Hampshire Democratic primary without opposition on March 13, he went on to pick up 56 percent of the vote in the March 20 Minnesota primary against Stevenson. The decisive contest came on June 5 in California, where both men had waged vigorous campaigns. The results: Stevenson, 1,139,964; Kefauver, 680,722. The Kefauver campaign limped along for a few more weeks. On July 26 Kefauver announced his withdrawal in favor of Stevenson.

When the Democratic National Convention met in Chicago on Aug. 13, Stevenson and Harriman were the only two serious candidates for the nomination. Harriman's candidacy, discounted by most observers, received a boost when former president Truman on Aug. 11 endorsed him. But in the vital contest for actual delegate votes, Stevenson, with

Kefauver's support, was too far ahead to be stopped. On the first ballot on Aug. 16 Stevenson was nominated with 905-1/2 votes to 210 for Harriman, 80 for Johnson, and the remainder scattered.

Historically, the most significant event at the 1956 convention was the cliff-hanging decision about the Democratic vice-presidential nominee. Following his nomination Stevenson made a brief appearance before the convention to tell the delegates he had decided "to depart from the precedents of the past." He said "the selection of the Vice Presidential nominee should be made through the free processes of this convention."

After a stiff two-ballot contest, Kefauver, on Aug. 17, narrowly won the vice presidential nomination over Massachusetts senator John F. Kennedy. With 686-1/2 votes required for nomination, Kennedy's total moved as high as 648 at one point during the second ballot. But a series of vote switches gave the nomination to Kefauver, who had 755-1/2 votes against 589 for Kennedy and 27-1/2 scattered. Other unsuccessful aspirants for the vice presidential nomination, all of whom received substantial first-ballot votes, were Sen. Hubert H. Humphrey of Minnesota, Sen. Albert Gore of Tennessee and New York mayor Robert F. Wagner.

The vice presidential fight marked Kennedy's entry into presidential politics. The good showing that Kennedy had made, particularly in Southern delegations, convinced his backers that despite his Roman Catholic faith Kennedy could be elected president.

The convention on Aug. 16 adopted a platform including a compromise civil rights plank. It termed Supreme Court rulings "the law of the land" but made no specific pledge to apply the Court's decisions and denounced the use of force to implement them. A move by a Northern liberal group led by Gov. G. Mennen Williams of Michigan, Sen. Paul H. Douglas of Illinois and Sen. Herbert H. Lehman of New York to insert a pledge to "carry out" the Court's decisions, was defeated by voice vote on the convention floor.

On the Republican side from Feb. 29, when Eisenhower announced he would seek a second term, there was no visible opposition to his renomination. Senate minority leader William F. Knowland, R-Calif., had previously announced his "provisional" candidacy, if Eisenhower were not to run, but he quickly withdrew it. The president swept all the primaries where his name was entered.

With the GOP presidential nomination a foregone conclusion, interest centered on the Republican vice presidential nomination. Eisenhower declined to make an early clear-cut endorsement of Richard M. Nixon for renomination as vice president and was reported to have suggested to Nixon that he consider a cabinet assignment or another government post, if Nixon planned to seek the GOP presidential nomination at a later date.

Presidential disarmament adviser Harold E. Stassen on July 25 attempted to spark a "stop Nixon" movement, claiming that Nixon's presence on the ticket might cost Eisenhower as much as 6 percent of the vote in the fall and endanger Republican congressional campaigns. No major Republican leaders came forward to support Stassen and the stop-Nixon move quickly faded. At Eisenhower's request Stassen actually ended by making a seconding speech for Nixon at the convention, which met in San Francisco Aug. 20-23.

The convention adopted without dissent a platform pledging a "continuation of peace, prosperity and progress." Threatened opposition to the civil rights plank evaporated after the Resolutions Committee modified an earlier and "stronger" version and proposed a plank acceptable to both Northern and Southern delegates.

The attack on Egypt and uprisings in Hungary and Poland dominated the news during the last weeks of the 1956 campaign, eclipsing domestic issues and changing the emphasis in international policy debates.

Early in the campaign Eisenhower boasted that his administration had offered, "in all levels of government," an "honest" regime of "good judgment," "tolerance" and "conciliation." The voters were asked to reelect him in order to keep the country "going down the straight road of prosperity and peace." Vice President Nixon, answering Democratic criticisms of Eisenhower administration foreign policy, said the families of "157,000 Americans who were killed, wounded or missing in Korea" could testify "whether we have peace today." Nixon said "the great majority of the American people have enjoyed the best four years of their lives under the Eisenhower Administration."

Stevenson's first approach was to challenge the effectiveness of Eisenhower's executive leadership, putting forth his own gospel of "the New America" under a Democratic Party that "can build as we have to build." He criticized the administration for failing to pass school aid legislation and other vitally needed domestic programs. He said the administration had "pilloried innocent men and women under the pretense of conducting loyalty and security investigations."

The tone of the campaign began to change as debate mounted over Stevenson's proposals to end the draft and stop U.S. testing of hydrogen bombs. The Stevenson proposal to end the draft drew the reply from Eisenhower that he saw "no chance of ending the draft and carrying out the responsibilities for the security of the country."

The debate was disturbed, however, by the beginning of the Hungarian uprising on Oct. 23 and the Israeli attack on Egypt on Oct. 29. Whatever the merits of the Stevenson proposals, they appeared to be badly timed in view of the international situation. Eisenhower again stressed that "we need our military draft for the safety of our nation" and that the country must have the "most advanced military weapons." With war threatening both in the Mideast and in Eastern Europe, the general public reaction seemed to be that it was a bad time to change leaders, especially considering the president's military background.

## Results of the 1956 Elections

President Eisenhower was reelected with the largest popular vote in history and a plurality second only to that of Franklin D. Roosevelt in 1936. Eisenhower came out with 35,590,472 votes (457 electoral votes) and Stevenson with 26,022,752 (73 electoral votes). Eisenhower's plurality was 9,567,720 votes.

In the North the president carried or ran unusually well in many urban areas formerly considered safe Democratic areas. More blacks voted Republican than in any election since pre-New Deal days. The only states where Eisenhower pluralities dropped from 1952 were several farm states where Secretary of Agriculture Ezra Taft Benson and administration agricultural policies were highly unpopular.

The presidential election did not have the necessary coattail effect to give Republicans control of Congress. Although the returns indicated Ike's tremendous popularity with voters, the outcome for other offices made it clear that most citizens still identified their interests with those of the Democratic Party. For the first time since 1848 the winning presidential candidate was unable to carry at least one house of Congress for his party.

The Democrats amazingly maintained their 49-47 lead in the Senate, taking Republican seats in Colorado, Idaho, Ohio and Pennsylvania to make up for their losses in New York, West Virginia and Kentucky. Democratic senator Wayne Morse, the man whom the Republicans had wanted most to defeat, won over former secretary of the interior Douglas McKay. Newly elected senators included Thruston B. Morton, R-Ky.; Joseph S. Clark, D-Pa.; Jacob K. Javits, R-N.Y.; Frank Church, D-Idaho; and Frank J. Lausche, D-Ohio.

In the House the Democrats added to the 29-seat margin they had achieved in 1954, bringing their ranks to 234 as against 201 Republicans.

The Democrats made a net gain of one new governorship for a new 28-20 balance in their favor. Important Democratic gubernatorial victories included two in normally Republican farm states: Herschel C. Loveless in Iowa and George Docking in Kansas. Other Democrats winning previously held Republican governorships were Foster Furcolo in Massachusetts and Robert D. Holmes in Oregon. Republicans winning Democratic gubernatorial seats were C. William O'Neill in Ohio, Cecil Underwood in West Virginia and Edwin L. Mechem in New Mexico.

# 1957-59:
# The 85th Congress

The first two years of Eisenhower's second term in office were marked by two major events, one domestic and one foreign, in the fall of 1957.

On Sept. 4 a controversy over admission of black students to the previously all-white Central High School in Little Rock, Arkansas, reached a showdown as the National Guard, ordered out by Gov. Orval Faubus, prevented the black students from entering the school. A federal court on Sept. 21 ordered removal of the National Guard. But when the black students reentered the school two days later, they were ordered to leave by local authorities because of fear of mob violence. Eisenhower then ordered federal troops sent into Little Rock to enforce the court's order, and the school began operation on an integrated basis.

The spectacle of angry, racist crowds in the face of fixed bayonets rioting to prevent black children from entering the school shocked the world. The scene was offset in part by the use of federal troops to enforce the constitutional rights of U.S. citizens. Throughout the South, however, the reaction was one of bitterness toward Eisenhower for using troops to enforce a deeply resented Supreme Court decision.

The second major event in the fall of 1957 was the Soviet Union's successful launching, on Oct. 4, of the first manufactured satellite, Sputnik I, into an orbit around the world. Congress and the nation responded with anger, frustration and alarm, directed chiefly at the Eisenhower administration because it had not pressed the U.S. effort to beat the Soviets into outer space and because it showed, at least initially, little concern about the Soviet achievement. More profound concern developed about the quality of U.S. education, especially in scientific fields. The first successful U.S. satellite, Explorer I, was launched by the Army from Cape Canaveral, Florida, on Jan. 31, 1958.

Other major international events in 1957 and 1958 were the following:

● On March 25, 1957, the Common Market (European Economic Community) and Euratom (European Atomic Energy Community) treaties among six Western European powers were signed in Rome. (The countries were France, Belgium, Netherlands, Luxembourg, Italy and West Germany.) These treaties were significant steps toward the U.S.-supported goal of a united Europe.

● Vice President and Mrs. Nixon narrowly escaped injury from Communist-inspired riots while on a good-will tour in Caracas, Venezuela, on May 13, 1957.

● Great Britain exploded its first hydrogen bomb, May 15, 1957.

● Former premier Georgii M. Malenkov, former foreign minister V. M. Molotov and L. M. Kaganovich were purged by the Soviet Presidium under Nikita Khrushchev's leadership, July 3-4, 1957, for alleged pro-Stalinist activities. On March 27, 1958, Chairman Khrushchev completed solidification of power by succeeding Nikolai A. Bulganin as premier.

● Charles de Gaulle became head of the French government on June 1, 1958, averting threatened civil war.

● At the request of the Lebanese government, U.S. Marines were dispatched to Lebanon on July 15, 1958, to forestall a threatened effort by Egyptian president Gamal Abdel Nasser's United Arab Republic and the Soviet Union to overthrow Lebanon's pro-Western regime. U.S. troops withdrew in August after calm was restored.

● In the fall of 1958 the United States and the Soviet Union began a three-and-one-half-year unpoliced moratorium on nuclear weapons tests.

Major domestic events included the development of the most serious postwar recession, in mid-1957 lasting through 1958; a stroke suffered by President Eisenhower Nov. 25, 1957, from which he was pronounced "completely recovered" on March 1, 1958; and the resignation of Sherman Adams, assistant to the president. Adams' resignation in Sept. 1958 followed revelations before a House subcommittee that he had interceded with various federal agencies in behalf of his friend, Boston industrialist Bernard Goldfine, and that he had received gifts from Goldfine. The Goldfine-Adams episode hurt the Eisenhower administration on the corruption-in-government issue and was one of several elements contributing to the Democratic sweep in the 1958 congressional and gubernatorial elections.

The 85th Congress established a record of moderate productivity, all its chief enactments bearing the "middle-of-the-road" stamp that was the natural result of compromise between a "mildly conservative" president and the "mildly liberal" congressional leadership of House Speaker Sam Rayburn and Senate majority leader Lyndon B. Johnson, both of Texas.

The mounting recession pushed the federal budget increasingly into the red, with a $2.8 billion deficit in fiscal 1958 and a $12.4 billion deficit for the fiscal 1959 budget, approved in mid-1958.

In foreign policy the Senate in 1957 approved the International Atomic Energy treaty (stemming from President Eisenhower's Atoms for Peace program). During its first session Congress approved the Mideast Resolution (Eisenhower Doctrine), in response to the president's request for advance authority to use U.S. troops to protect free Middle East nations from "overt armed aggression" by "power hungry Communists." During the second session Congress acceded readily to the president's request for authority to extend financial aid and technical assistance to the newly formed European Atomic Energy Community.

A military reorganization bill was approved by Congress in 1958. This bill eliminated the "separately administered" provision for Army, Navy and Air Force written into the

1947 National Security Act and made it clear that the three military departments were to operate under the direction and control of the secretary of defense. Legislation passed in July 1958 established a civilian-controlled National Aeronautics and Space Administration. Both houses organized permanent standing committees on space matters.

The major domestic bill passed in 1957 was the Civil Rights Act. The bill created the executive Commission on Civil Rights and empowered the attorney general to seek injunctions when individuals are denied the right to vote. With strengthening amendments in succeeding years, this legislation gave more and more black citizens the power of the ballot, viewed by the bill's advocates as the foundation of most other civil liberties.

The most notable accomplishment of Congress' 1958 session was passage and signature by the president of the Alaska statehood bill, culminating decades of pressure to admit the territory to the Union.

Other important actions of the second session included emergency housing and highway construction legislation to help stem the recession; passage of the National Defense Education Act of 1958, including $295 million for loans to needy college students; the Transportation Act of 1958, designed to revive the failing railroads; and passage of a low-support farm bill with few controls generally in line with administration proposals.

Under the leadership of Democratic national chairman Paul M. Butler, a policy-making Democratic Advisory Committee was organized in November 1956 and became the chief voice for the militantly liberal Democratic point of view. It made sharp partisan attacks on the Eisenhower administration. Democratic congressional leaders Rayburn and Johnson had been asked to join but instead actively opposed it, expressing a preference for policy formulation through regular Democratic congressional leadership channels. Many of the committee's statements reflected severe criticism of the Democratic congressional leadership for alleged lack of sufficiently aggressive opposition to the Eisenhower administration. (The committee was eventually abolished in March 1961 after the Democratic takeover of the executive office. The new Democratic National Chairman, John M. Bailey, said the committee had "served a function" only when the party was out of power.)

## The 1958 Midterm Elections

The swing of the political pendulum against the Republicans and in favor of the Democrats was apparent as early as mid-1957. It ended Nov. 25, 1958, with a clean Democratic sweep in Alaska's first election as a state. The over-all national result was the most thorough Democratic victory since the Roosevelt landslide year of 1936.

In August 1957 Democrat William Proxmire easily won the Wisconsin Senate seat of the late Republican senator Joseph R. McCarthy, who had died May 2 of the same year. In the November 1957 off-year elections the Democrats reelected New Jersey Democratic governor Robert B. Meyner by a plurality of nearly 200,000 votes, also scoring important victories in Virginia and New York. In the Sept. 8, 1958, Maine elections the Democrats swept that normally Republican state, electing a Democratic governor, a Democratic senator and two Democratic representatives.

The Republicans began the 1958 campaign with a number of handicaps. The Adams-Goldfine incident had been a source of profound embarrassment for the Eisenhower administration, only partly relieved by Adams' resignation in September. Although recovery from the 1957-58 recession was already under way, the recession had served to weaken seriously voter confidence in the Eisenhower prosperity formula. Another crisis in the Formosa Strait, with renewed Communist shelling of Quemoy and Matsu, reminded voters that the administration had yet to find a solution for the China problem. Sputnik had weakened voter confidence in the Eisenhower administration's defense and space programs.

In many states the Republicans backed ballot initiative proposals for right-to-work laws that were bitterly opposed by organized labor. This inspired labor to work particularly hard to get its members out to vote: against right-to-work and for Democrats. A major portion of the blame for Republican debacles in states such as Ohio and California was attributed to GOP right-to-work stands. Still another incident harming the Republicans was deep Southern resentment against Eisenhower's ordering of paratroops into Little Rock in 1957. This effectively curtailed Republican efforts for new inroads in the South.

In the campaign the Democrats charged that the Republicans had callously allowed the country to slip into a serious recession, showing little regard for the interests of the unemployed. Adlai Stevenson on Oct. 18 said that the crises over Quemoy, desegregation, education and recession "could have been avoided if we had an administration which thought in advance instead of waiting placidly on the fairways until the mortal danger is upon us and then angrily calling out the Marines." "The tragedy of the Eisenhower Administration," Stevenson said, "is that its only weapons seem to be platitudes or paratroops."

Alarmed by the apparent Democratic inroads, the Republicans held an Oct. 6 White House strategy session that produced a manifesto declaring that if a new Democratic Congress were elected, "we are certain to go down the left lane which leads inseparably to socialism." In Baltimore, on Oct. 31, Eisenhower used such terms as "political free spenders," "gloomdoggler," and "extremist" to describe his Democratic opponents.

House Speaker Rayburn on Nov. 1 predicted that a new Democratic-controlled Congress would not fight the president despite "desperation" oratory in which Rayburn said Eisenhower went "pretty far in accusing us of being radicals and left-wingers." Rayburn said that "in the past about 85 percent of the time Eisenhower's programs were just an extension of Democratic principles.... We're not going to hate Eisenhower bad enough for us to change our principles."

Much of the hard campaigning for Republican candidates throughout the country was done by Vice President Nixon. On Oct. 21 Nixon said that the Democratic Party was split between "essentially moderate" Democratic leaders in Congress and the group "which presently controls the Democratic National Committee, which is radical in its approach to economic problems (and) bitterly partisan in its criticism of the Eisenhower foreign policy."

As the campaign progressed, the Republicans came under increasingly heavy Democratic fire for being anti-labor. Eisenhower and Nixon refused to endorse the right-to-work laws, but the president called for legislation to let workers "free themselves of their corrupt labor bosses who have betrayed their trust."

In reply to the potent Democratic "missile gap" issue of allegedly slow U.S. progress in rockets and missiles, Eisenhower repeatedly declared that no more than $1 million had been spent on development of long-range missiles in any year before he became president, but that "the so-called missile gap is being rapidly filled."

**Results of the 1958 Elections**

As election returns poured in during the evening of Nov. 4, it was clear that the Democratic tide had engulfed Republicans in virtually every area of the nation. Including the Nov. 25 Alaska election, the results showed a new Senate of 64 Democrats and 34 Republicans, a Democratic gain of 15 seats and a Republican loss of 13 from the 49-47 Democratic edge in 1956. Democrats gained seats in California (where Republicans were embroiled in internecine fights and the right-to-work issue), Connecticut, Indiana, Maine, Michigan, Minnesota, Nevada, New Jersey, Ohio, Utah, West Virginia (two seats) and Wyoming and took the two new seats from Alaska.

The new Democratic senators included Eugene J. McCarthy of Minnesota, Thomas J. Dodd of Connecticut, Clair Engle of California and Harrison A. Williams Jr. of New Jersey. New Republicans elected to the Senate were Kenneth B. Keating of New York and Hugh Scott of Pennsylvania.

In the House there were 282 Democrats, 48 more than the previous Congress' total and the highest figure since the 1936 elections. Republicans slipped from 201 to 154 seats. Republican House losses were heaviest in the Midwest, where 23 seats were lost (many in the traditional Republican heartland), and in the East, where 20 were lost. Only two incumbent Democratic House members were defeated: Rep. Coya Knutson of Minnesota, evidently as a result of her marital difficulties, and Rep. Brooks Hays of Arkansas, a moderate on racial issues defeated on a write-in vote by Dale Alford, a Democratic archsegregationist in Arkansas's 5th (Little Rock) District.

In gubernatorial races there was a net switch of five governorships, plus the new Alaska governorship, to the Democrats for a new total of 35 Democratic and 14 Republican governors. Important Democratic gubernatorial victories included Edmund G. Brown in California (over Senate minority leader William F. Knowland); Michael V. DiSalle, Ohio; Ralph G. Brooks, Nebraska; Ralph Herseth, South Dakota; Gaylord A. Nelson, Wisconsin; and J. Millard Tawes, Maryland. Democrats also reelected Gov. Abraham A. Ribicoff in Connecticut by a record majority and reelected Democratic governor George Docking in traditionally Republican Kansas.

The brightest spot in the entire picture for the Republicans was Nelson A. Rockefeller's New York victory over incumbent governor Averell Harriman by a 573,034-vote margin. Republicans also won the Oregon governorship with Mark Hatfield and the Rhode Island governorship with Christopher Del Sesto.

# 1959-61:
# The 86th Congress

Relations between the United States and the Soviet Union dominated the international news, running the gamut from cordial to extremely bitter during 1959-60.

In November 1958 Soviet premier Nikita S. Khrushchev had demanded an end to the four-power occupation of Berlin and threatened to turn control of Allied supply lines to West Berlin over to East Germany, asking that Berlin be made into a demilitarized "free city." The Soviet Union set May 27, 1959, as the deadline for the end of the occupation of Berlin. An international crisis, threatening atomic war, appeared to develop over the ensuing months. But when the Big Four foreign ministers sat down for consultations in Paris the following May, the Soviet deadline had been lifted and no changes in the Berlin status quo evolved.

Meanwhile, President Eisenhower had lost his key foreign policy adviser when Secretary of State John Foster Dulles was stricken by cancer early in 1959. Dulles resigned by April 15 and died on May 24. Under Secretary Christian A. Herter, former Massachusetts congressman and governor, succeeded Dulles.

A period of moderation in U.S.-Soviet relations followed. Vice President Richard Nixon on July 22 left for a 13-day tour of the Soviet Union. Nixon received a friendly reception by Russian crowds. In September, at Eisenhower's invitation, Khrushchev visited the United States for consultations with the president and a transcontinental tour. But the 1959 "spirit of Camp David" failed to result in a lasting thaw in the cold war.

In May 1960, just before a scheduled Big Four summit conference in Paris, the Soviet Union announced that an American plane had been shot down over its territory. The United States at first said no violation of Soviet air space had been intended. After Khrushchev revealed that the pilot of the U-2 reconnaissance plane had confessed being on an intelligence-gathering flight for the U.S. Central Intelligence Agency, Secretary of State Herter admitted that the United States had engaged in "extensive aerial surveillance of the USSR." President Eisenhower took full responsibility for the flights, terming them a "distasteful but vital necessity."

When the Big Four met May 16, Khrushchev denounced the "spy flight" and demanded a U.S. apology and punishment of responsible officials before the summit conference could continue. He withdrew an already-accepted invitation to Eisenhower to visit the Soviet Union in June 1960. Eisenhower said the flights had been discontinued and would not begin again, but he refused to accept Khrushchev's ultimatum. The conference collapsed, and leaders withdrew to their capitals amid mutual recriminations.

The incident weakened the confidence of many voters in the Republicans' skill in handling foreign affairs. Some observers later speculated that if there had been no U-2 incident, and if the summit conference and the Eisenhower trip to the Soviet Union had proceeded as planned, the country might have been in no mood to replace the Republican hold on the White House in the November elections.

Other important international developments in 1959 and 1960 included the following:

● Fidel Castro assumed power in Cuba after collapse of the Batista dictatorship on Jan. 1, 1959. Communist influence and control over the Castro revolution became increasingly evident in the succeeding years.

● A revolt by the Tibetan people against Chinese Communist rule was crushed in March 1959.

● Eisenhower made good-will visits to Europe, Asia and Africa in December 1959, to Latin America in February-March 1960, and to the Far East in early summer 1960. Leftist riots in Japan protesting the new U.S.-Japanese treaty of mutual security and cooperation forced Eisenhower to cancel plans to include that country in his Far Eastern tour.

● The French tested their first nuclear device in the Sahara, Feb. 13, 1960.

● The Belgian Congo gained independence, becoming the Republic of the Congo on June 30, 1960; soon thereafter the country was plunged into civil war, resulting in UN intervention in July 1960.

On the domestic front heavy Democratic majorities in the 86th Congress failed to produce the kind of prolabor, liberal legislation for which many observers had seen a mandate in the 1958 election returns. The two major accomplishments of Congress—Hawaiian statehood and a labor reform law—were in fact just as much administration as Democratic bills.

Statehood for Hawaii, signed into law March 18, 1959, after 59 years of territorial status for the one-time island kingdom, added a 50th state to the Union. The new state elected the nation's first two representatives of Chinese and Japanese ancestry: Sen. Hiram L. Fong, a Republican, and Rep. Daniel K. Inouye, a Democrat.

In the waning days of the 1959 session Congress passed a "strong" labor regulation law (the Landrum-Griffin bill), which contained major Taft-Hartley Act amendments favored by business and opposed by organized labor. The continuing exposure of union corruption and labor-management collusion by the Senate Select Committee on Improper Activities in the Labor or Management Field had produced a deluge of letters, telegrams and editorials calling for action.

The relatively mild Kennedy bill for labor regulation was passed by the Senate April 25. The House, on Aug. 13, by a 229-201 roll call, approved a tougher measure, the Landrum-Griffin bill, which incorporated important Taft-Hartley reforms sought by President Eisenhower. The vote was a major victory for Eisenhower and the House Republican leadership under the newly chosen minority leader, Charles A. Halleck, R-Ind. It was a defeat for House Speaker Sam Rayburn, who preferred a milder measure. Most of Landrum-Griffin was incorporated in the conference committee compromise.

Determined to prevent adoption of expensive domestic programs suggested by liberal Democrats, Eisenhower sought to dramatize the issue of "spending" in his press conferences and other public utterances. Grass-roots response was so positive that he was able to galvanize the Republican minority and invigorate the Republican-Southern Democratic coalition, preventing passage of most liberal measures and rallying sufficient strength to sustain his vetoes of all but a handful of those that did pass. Thus Democratic proposals for a wide program of aid for school construction and teachers' salaries, for a massive area redevelopment program, for an increased minimum wage and for medical care for the aged under Social Security all came to naught.

During 1960, however, the liberals found a new issue on which to base their call for increased social welfare legislation: the need for a rapid rate of growth in the national economy. The issue of economic growth developed too late to assist in passage of liberal measures in the 86th Congress, but it provided campaign fodder for Democratic nominee John F. Kennedy in the 1960 presidential campaign.

The failure of many important domestic bills to clear Congress was largely attributed to the continuing party division between the executive and legislative branches and the approaching presidential elections. In 1959, for instance, the Senate took time out for a long and bitter debate that ended in rejection of the president's nomination of Lewis L. Strauss to be secretary of commerce. In 1960 a $750 million pay raise for federal employees was passed over the president's veto. Scenting victory in the upcoming elections, Democrats refused to pass a bill creating 35 badly needed new federal judgeships.

After long debate over the "missile gap" and the general adequacy of the nation's defense effort, Congress passed the president's defense budget with few overall changes in 1959 but in 1960 added $600 million more than Eisenhower had requested. The missile gap became a major issue in the 1960 presidential campaign, only to recede as an apparent mirage early in 1961.

During the postconventions session of Congress that began Aug. 8, 1960, Democratic presidential candidate John F. Kennedy, a Massachusetts senator, and his running mate, Senate majority leader Lyndon B. Johnson, failed in their efforts to complete action on major Democratic legislation planks. The Senate approved the Kennedy minimum wage bill, but the measure died when House conferees refused to budge from their own truncated version. Medical care for the aged under the Social Security system—a second "must" bill—was rejected by the Senate, and a school construction bill expired when the House Rules Committee refused to send it to conference. As Congress adjourned Sept. 1 and the campaign began in earnest, Republicans made the most of their opponents' plight.

## The 1960 Campaigns

The 22nd Amendment to the Constitution, placing a two-term limitation on the presidency, meant that Eisenhower was ineligible to seek reelection in 1960. Adlai E. Stevenson's record of two defeats for the presidency appeared to preclude him from choice as the Democrats' candidate, barring a convention deadlock. Thus both parties were faced with the prospect of coming up with new nominees in 1960. For the Republicans the choice appeared relatively easy since Vice President Richard Nixon had been in the public eye for eight full years. Nixon had been an extremely active vice president, he was a tireless campaigner for GOP candidates, and he had strong support in Republican organizations throughout the country. For the Democrats the choice was more difficult because no members of the party had clearly established themselves as leaders of presidential stature.

In a departure from the American tendency to select governors for presidential nominees, all four chief contenders for the Democratic nomination were senators. In order of their announcements they were Hubert H. Humphrey of Minnesota, John F. Kennedy of Massachusetts, Stuart Symington of Missouri and Majority Leader Lyndon B. Johnson of Texas. Of these four only Kennedy and Humphrey chose to campaign in the primaries. In the end the primaries were the decisive factor in Kennedy's victory.

Symington dismissed primary contests as useless and Johnson maintained that he could not carry out his Senate duties properly and simultaneously run in numerous individual primaries. (CQ 1960 Senate Voting Participation scores showed an average of 80 percent for all Democrats. Kennedy scored 35 percent, Humphrey 49 percent; both campaigned extensively during the session. Symington scored 58 percent, and Johnson, 95 percent.)

The issue of Kennedy's religion dominated much of the preconvention and general-election debate and speculation about his chances. Not since 1928, when the Democrats nominated Alfred E. Smith of New York for the presidency, had a Roman Catholic headed a national ticket. Smith had been resoundingly defeated, with many normally Democratic but heavily Protestant states going against him, although other considerations than religion, perhaps equally important, ran against Smith. In the intervening years Roman Catholics had become a far larger segment of the population than before (16 percent in 1928; 22.8 percent by 1960, with especially large concentrations in the urban areas in the biggest states). The consensus was that the nation had become far more tolerant in its religious outlook.

The spring primaries produced a string of unbroken victories for Kennedy. Unopposed, he piled up an impressive 43,372 vote total in the early-bird New Hampshire primary March 8. In May Humphrey withdrew after the West Virginia primary, leaving Symington and Johnson as opponents for Kennedy. Just before the convention it appeared that Stevenson might reenter the race.

At the Democratic National Convention, which opened in Los Angeles on July 11, Kennedy won on the first ballot. After conferring with Democratic leaders, he announced that Lyndon B. Johnson would be his running mate. Most observers were surprised that Johnson, powerful Senate majority leader and almost 10 years Kennedy's senior, would accept the nomination. Most party liberals expressed consternation at Kennedy's selection. Later it became evident that Johnson's presence on the ticket was probably an essential element in holding most of the South behind Kennedy and achieving Democratic victory in one of the closest presidential elections in U.S. history.

Without any significant opposition, Nixon breezed through the primaries and at the Republican National Convention was nominated July 27, receiving 1,321 votes to 10 for Barry Goldwater. He selected UN ambassador and former Massachusetts senator Henry Cabot Lodge as his running mate.

By election day, Nov. 8, Kennedy had covered 75,000 miles and visited 46 states, while Nixon had traveled more than 60,000 miles and appeared in all 50 states. Speaking as often as a dozen times a day, both candidates were seen and heard by millions of voters, in person as well as on radio and television, in what may have been the most talkative as well as the most expensive campaign on record.

The central issue, Kennedy asserted time and again, was the need for strong presidential leadership to reverse the nation's declining prestige abroad and lagging economy at home. Arguing that the position of the United States relative to that of the Soviets had deteriorated under the Eisenhower administration, he called for a stepped-up defense effort and an enlarged federal role in a wide variety of fields at home and abroad "to get America moving again."

In an unprecedented series of face-to-face encounters, candidates Kennedy and Nixon appeared on four nationally televised, hour-long programs during which they were questioned by panels of journalists and permitted to rebut each other's answers. The time was provided free of charge by the networks when Congress suspended the equal time provision of the Communications Act for the duration of the 1960 campaign. The audiences for the four debates were estimated by the Arbitron rating service at 70 to 75 million, 61 million, 65 million and 64 million, respectively.

Republicans generally were dismayed by Nixon's appearance on the first debate, blaming it on poor lighting and their candidate's unaggressive stance, but they found little fault with the remaining three programs. Democrats regarded all the debates as highly successful on grounds that they served to demolish the GOP theme of Kennedy's "immaturity" and to project his personality to millions of undecided voters, many of whom were disturbed by his Catholic faith.

## Results of the 1960 Elections

On election day 68,838,219 Americans—the largest number in history—cast ballots for president. Kennedy emerged the victor with a solid majority in the Electoral College. But his popular-vote plurality over Nixon was only 118,574 votes, the smallest vote margin of the 20th century. In 11 states—eight won by Kennedy, three by Nixon—a shift of less than 1 percent of the vote would have switched the state's electoral votes.

The Kennedy-Johnson ticket carried 23 states with 303 electoral votes. They put together a coalition of Eastern states (including New York, Pennsylvania and New Jersey), central industrial states (Illinois, Michigan and Minnesota) and several of the traditionally Democratic Southern states (including Johnson's own Texas) that was sufficient to win, despite loss of almost the entire West and farm belt and several Southern states.

Democrats maintained their heavy majorities in Congress and among the nation's governors in 1960, but Republicans were able to make some important gains, especially in the House of Representatives. Republican gains, taking place in the face of a victory for Democratic candidate Kennedy, appeared due in part to the return of normally Republican seats to the GOP to offset the serious losses suffered by Republicans in the 1958 Democratic sweep.

The continued heavy Democratic congressional majority, especially in the Senate, made it appear unlikely that Republicans would be able to regain control of Congress at any time during President-elect Kennedy's first term in the White House.

The Republicans made a gain of two Senate seats, replacing Democrats in Delaware and Wyoming. Despite advance predictions of possible trouble for Republican Senate incumbents in Massachusetts and New Jersey, both were able to withstand the Kennedy tide in those states. Democrats held their seats in Minnesota, Missouri, Michigan and Montana, where Republican challengers ran energetic campaigns. The new Senate balance was 64 Democrats and 36 Republicans.

The Republican Senate gain was reduced when Senator-elect Keith Thomson, R-Wyo., died on Dec. 9 and was replaced by Democrat J. J. Hickey. But the Senate balance returned to 64-36 in May 1961, when Republican John Tower won the Texas Senate seat vacated by Lyndon B. Johnson, the new vice president.

In House elections Republicans made a net gain of 20 seats. The new House had 263 Democrats and 174 Republicans, as compared to a 283-154 balance in the previous Congress.

In contrast to most presidential elections, the victory of the national Democratic ticket did not appear to play an important part in most congressional contests. If Kennedy coattails existed at all, they were probably evident in New York State, which he carried by a wide margin and where three incumbent GOP congressmen were defeated; in Connecticut, where Democrats held two close seats; and in New Jersey, where one Republican seat went Democratic. All other Democratic House gains appeared to be the result of special local conditions.

The most important Republican congressional gains came in the Midwest, where Nixon ran a strong race. Widespread and deep-seated anti-Catholic sentiment, combined with a marked cooling off of the farm issue, which hurt midwestern Republicans so badly in 1958, appeared to form the basis of much of the increased Republican Midwestern strength in both presidential and local races.

Many Republican gains, through Midwestern farm states but also in Connecticut, Maine, Ohio, Vermont, Oregon and Pennsylvania, seemed to mark the return to the GOP fold of traditionally Republican congressional districts,

## Members of Congress Who Became President

From James Madison to George Bush, 24 presidents have served previously in the House of Representatives, or the Senate, or both.

Following is a list of these presidents and the chambers in which they served. Three other presidents — George Washington, John Adams and Thomas Jefferson — had served in the Continental Congress, as had James Madison and James Monroe.

James A. Garfield was elected to the Senate in January 1880 for a term beginning March 4, 1881, but declined to accept in December 1880 because he had been elected president. John Quincy Adams served in the House for 17 years after his term as president, and Andrew Johnson returned to the Senate five months before he died.

### House Only

James Madison
James K. Polk
Millard Fillmore
Abraham Lincoln
Rutherford B. Hayes
James A. Garfield
William McKinley
Gerald R. Ford
George Bush

### Senate Only

James Monroe
John Quincy Adams
Martin Van Buren
Benjamin Harrison
Warren G. Harding
Harry S. Truman

### Both Chambers

Andrew Jackson
William Henry Harrison
John Tyler
Franklin Pierce
James Buchanan

Andrew Johnson
John F. Kennedy
Lyndon B. Johnson
Richard Nixon

Sources: *Biographical Directory of the United States Congress, 1774-1989.* Washington, D.C.: Government Printing Office, 1989; *American Leaders 1789-1994.* Washington, D.C.: Congressional Quarterly Inc., 1994.

which had gone Democratic in 1958 in a temporary protest against Republican policies.

In gubernatorial races the Democrats captured seven seats from the Republicans, and the Republicans captured six from the Democrats. The new lineup was 34 Democrats to 16 Republicans, a net gain of one for the Democrats. Among the governors elected were Democrats Otto Kerner of Illinois, Matthew E. Welsh of Indiana, John B. Swainson of Michigan and Frank B. Morrison of Nebraska. Republican governors elected included John A. Volpe of Massachusetts, Elmer L. Andersen of Minnesota, Norman A. Erbe of Iowa and John Anderson Jr. of Kansas.

## 1961-63: The 87th Congress

Hopes were high, both in America and abroad, when John F. Kennedy took office as president Jan. 20, 1961. In his inaugural address Kennedy called on Americans and all free people "to bear the burden of a long twilight struggle . . .

against the common enemies of man: tyranny, poverty, disease and war itself." Kennedy urged Americans: "Ask not what your country can do for you—ask what you can do for your country."

Some of this idealism was translated into specific programs and action during the next two years. A Peace Corps was established, sending young Americans to underdeveloped nations, to provide trained personnel for development projects. Fulfilling another campaign promise, Kennedy got congressional approval of a U.S. Arms Control and Disarmament Agency. On March 14, 1961, the president announced an Alliance for Progress with the countries of Latin America, under which the United States would step up aid to the other Americas but expect to see political and social reforms to guarantee true democracy and promote stability and progress in those countries.

In the domestic field several items of "liberal" legislation that had failed passage because of a stalemate between President Eisenhower and a Democratic Congress were enacted into law. Chief among these were a hike in the minimum wage to $1.25, a subsidy program for economically distressed areas in the United States, widening of Social Security benefits, a $4.88 billion omnibus housing bill, stepped-up federal aid to localities to battle water pollution and a vastly increased public works program.

The first two years of Kennedy's term, however, contained disappointments, both foreign and domestic. In January 1961 the administration had high hopes of a period of relaxed tensions with the Soviet world. Congratulating Kennedy on his election, Soviet premier Nikita S. Khrushchev had expressed the "hope that while you are at this post the relations between our countries will again follow the line along which they were developing in Franklin Roosevelt's time." Khrushchev made specific mention of chances for early conclusion of a nuclear test ban treaty and a German peace treaty. During the first week of Kennedy's presidency the Soviet government freed two U.S. Air Force RB-47 pilots who had been held in the USSR since their plane was downed off Soviet shores in July 1960. But the optimism of January 1961 seemed more like overconfidence by late 1961 as the tide of events continued to run almost consistently against the nation's foreign policy objectives.

On April 17, 1961, 1,200 Cuban refugees—recruited, trained and supplied by the U.S. Central Intelligence Agency—landed 90 miles south of Havana; their announced goal was to overthrow the Communist-oriented regime of Fidel Castro. Within three days the invasion had been crushed, inflicting a disastrous blow to American prestige and to that of the new president.

Kennedy met with Khrushchev June 3-4, 1961, in Vienna. At this summit conference Khrushchev made clear his determination to sign a peace treaty with the East German Communist regime, a move long interpreted in the West as part of the effort to force the Western powers out of West Berlin. The Vienna confrontation convinced Kennedy that it was time to muster public support in behalf of a "firm stand" in Berlin. In a July 25 televised report to the nation, he called for an immediate buildup of U.S. and NATO forces along with an extra $3.5 billion in U.S. defense funds. Congress promptly granted his requests.

Khrushchev's reply was to threaten Soviet mobilization and to boast that the Soviets could build a hundred-megaton nuclear warhead. Much more damaging to the West, however, was the Communists' unexpected action on Aug. 13 in sealing off the border between East and West Berlin. The wall virtually stopped the large flow of refugees from East to West that had bled the Communist regime of much of its most valuable personnel during the postwar years.

Adding immeasurably to the tension over Berlin was the Soviet announcement on Aug. 30, 1961, that it would break the three-year voluntary moratorium on testing of nuclear weapons because of the "ever increasing aggressiveness of the policy of the NATO military bloc." The Soviet test series began Sept. 1 and concluded in Nov. 1961. Their tests completed, the Soviets returned to the test ban negotiations in Geneva on Nov. 28. The United States, however, refused to reimpose an uncontrolled moratorium on itself and, between April 25 and Nov. 4, 1962, carried out a series of tests underground and in the atmosphere.

Two Southeast Asian nations, Laos and Vietnam, were thorny problems for the new administration. Fearful that a Communist takeover of Laos would make the Western position in Vietnam untenable, the administration supported establishment of a "neutral" government in Laos, in the hope that the tiny kingdom could serve as a buffer. In Vietnam increased Communist guerrilla activity forced increased commitment of U.S. military "advisers," who soon found themselves in the thick of military engagements.

Cuba, however, remained the chief foreign policy problem of the administration. The Castro regime became increasingly identified as a Soviet satellite and was expelled from the Organization of American States. During the summer of 1962 Soviet arms began to pour into Cuba. On Oct. 22 President Kennedy told the American people in a radio-television address that U.S. aerial surveillance of the Soviet military buildup in Cuba had produced "unmistakable evidence" that "a series of offensive missile sites is now in preparation on that imprisoned island. The purpose of these bases can be none other than to provide a nuclear strike capacity against the Western Hemisphere."

As countermeasures the president announced "a strict quarantine on all offensive military equipment under shipment to Cuba" and said that U.S. ships would begin checking incoming shipments to the island. He called on the Soviet leader to withdraw his offensive weapons from Cuba.

For several days the Soviets continued preparation of their missile sites, and the world wondered whether it might be plunged into war. On Oct. 27 Khrushchev, apparently unwilling to take the ultimate risk, sent a note to Kennedy in which he agreed to remove the offensive weapons systems from Cuba under UN observation and supervision in return for removal of the U.S. quarantine and agreement not to launch an invasion of the islands.

In succeeding weeks the removal of the bases took place at a relatively rapid rate. Castro, however, blocked UN inspection, and the United States never formalized its agreement not to invade Cuba. Thousands of Soviet troops and technical personnel remained on the island, along with a heavy array of "defensive" weapons.

Kennedy's chief domestic problem during his first two years in office was the lagging condition of the U.S. economy. The new administration made clear its commitment to a general monetary and fiscal policy aimed at the inducement of economic growth, even at the price of heavy federal budget deficits. Federal expenditures rose from $81.5 billion in fiscal 1961 to $87.8 billion in fiscal 1962 and $94.3 billion in estimated figures for fiscal 1963. The federal deficit rose from $3.8 billion in 1961 to $6.4 billion in 1962 and dropped slightly to $6.2 billion for fiscal 1963.

Aided in part by the sharply increased federal expenditures under Kennedy, the 1960 recession tapered off by mid-1961. But the basic underlying problems remained.

Although President Kennedy had himself served in the House for six years and in the Senate for eight, relations between his administration and Congress were far from ideal. The change in Democratic leadership in both houses, some congressional apprehension about use of political power by the new administration and a continuing "conservative coalition" between Republicans and Southern Democrats all tended to slow down if not wreck parts of the Kennedy program.

Most apparent and serious was the shift in leadership. The elevation of Lyndon B. Johnson to the vice presidency removed one of the strongest majority leaders in the history of the Senate. He was succeeded by Sen. Mike Mansfield, D-Mont., a mild-mannered man who lacked Johnson's drive.

On Nov. 16, 1961, House Speaker Sam Rayburn, D-Texas, died of cancer. Rayburn had been a member of the House for almost 49 years and had served as Speaker for 17 years (twice interrupted by brief periods of Republican majorities). Any successor would have faced difficulties in filling the shoes of "Mr. Sam," a man who understood the House and, until his later years, could draw together the disparate elements of his party with remarkable success. John W. McCormack of Massachusetts, elevated from the majority leadership to be Speaker, faced the unenviable task of succeeding Rayburn. His first year in office was considered a qualified success.

The 87th Congress ended on an acrimonious note. A year-long feud between the House and Senate on procedural issues regarding appropriation bills was symptomatic of a broader rift between the two chambers that had been growing for several years. The dispute held up several fund bills for months (well beyond July 1, the start of the new fiscal year) and helped prolong the 1962 session to Oct. 13. Not since the Korean War year of 1951 had a session lasted until so late in the autumn.

During the ensuing months increasing discussion was heard of the need to modernize and streamline congressional procedures.

## The 1962 Midterm Elections

The Kennedy administration entered the 1962 campaign determined to reinforce the narrow margin by which the president had been elected in 1960 and to prevent serious losses in Democratic congressional strength. The off-year elections of 1961 had produced mixed results. In a May 1961 special election in Texas the Democrats had lost the Senate seat vacated by Vice President Johnson to Republican John Tower. Not since Reconstruction days had Texas sent a Republican to the Senate.

But in the November 1961 elections, Democrat Richard J. Hughes, aided by a personal appearance on his behalf by President Kennedy, won the New Jersey governorship against no less an opponent than Republican James P. Mitchell, secretary of labor in the Eisenhower administration.

Mayor Robert F. Wagner, a political ally of the president, easily won reelection in New York City. The administration felt confident that with sufficient presidential campaigning, the party could fare well in the 1962 elections.

Kennedy set the tone for the 1962 battle in a July 23 press conference. Declaring that the congressional Republicans were almost wholly negative on domestic social legislation, he said that he would go all-out to defeat them in the fall campaign. Kennedy said a Democratic gain of one or two Senate seats and five or ten House seats would make it possible to enact controversial administration bills in such fields as Medicare, public works, mass transit and urban affairs. He said the 1962 elections would give the American people a "clear" choice: to "anchor down" by voting Republican or to "sail" by voting Democratic.

In midsummer the president began to make flying campaign trips to various states every weekend and some weekdays. Until halted by the Cuban crisis Oct. 20, the president's campaigning promised to be the most vigorous of any U.S. president in a midterm election. In every appearance he went down the line for all Democratic candidates. The president was accorded a warm personal reception in most cities, confirming the high degree of personal popularity with the people that had been recorded in Gallup polls. Whether his plea to elect "more Democrats" was making a serious impression remained in doubt, however.

By October public uneasiness over the Communist arms buildup in Cuba was growing. Republicans made a central campaign issue of Cuba, and most observers thought the GOP would make some gains. But the president's Oct. 22 announcement of a naval quarantine of Cuba and his ultimatum to Khrushchev blunted the Republican arguments and rallied the country behind him.

The Republicans began the 1962 campaign in hopes they could win important congressional and gubernatorial gains and thereby increase their effectiveness as an opposition party in Washington and prepare for a possible presidential comeback. They counted on the traditional pattern of midterm gains for the party out of power to help them in the congressional elections.

The party, however, was suffering from image problems. The congressional wing of the GOP, headed by Senate minority leader Everett Dirksen, R-Ill., and House minority leader Charles Halleck, R-Ind., had dominated the news of Republican activity in Washington since Eisenhower's retirement. Deprived of the expertise of the executive branch, Hill Republicans came up with few legislative initiatives and had few counterproposals to the stream of legislative requests that flowed from the White House. The only serious competition to Dirksen and Halleck for the Republican spotlight was Sen. Barry Goldwater of Arizona, whose outspoken conservatism made him the favorite of the right wing throughout the country. Moderate and liberal Republicans received scant attention. Eisenhower had retired; Nixon was embroiled in California politics; New York governor Nelson A. Rockefeller was busy preparing for his own reelection campaign in New York and wrestling with possible adverse effects of his divorce announced late in 1961.

The Republicans waged the 1962 campaign with familiar issues: the need for fiscal responsibility in government, calls for a balanced budget and warnings of the dangers of encroaching federal (especially executive) power. But the GOP lacked any single strong issue, such as the demand for an end to wartime controls in 1946 or alleged Democratic responsibility for the Korean War in 1950, with which to rout the Democrats. For a while they hoped Cuba would be that issue, but the president's firm action in late October effectively deprived them of it. In the end improved Republican organizations, especially in the big cities, helped the party to some victories. But the only region of the country in which they made any significant congressional gains was the South, where they jumped from nine to 14 seats.

## Results of the 1962 Elections

The Democratic Party confirmed its heavy majorities in both houses of Congress and among the states' governors. Democrats avoided "normal" midterm losses of the party in power by gaining four Senate seats and suffering only a nominal loss in the House. Not since 1934 had the presidential party fared so well in a midterm election. Democrats said that, in contrast to the familiar patterns of major midterm loses by the presidential party, the 1962 results constituted a real vote of confidence in the administration.

Republicans replied that they saw "no endorsement of the New Frontier and its policies." They pointed out that President Kennedy had not carried Democrats into office with him in 1960, actually losing 20 House seats that year, so that there were fewer vulnerable seats for the GOP to pick off in 1962. The Republicans argued that the national House vote for the GOP had actually risen to 47.7 percent, 4.0 points higher than 1958 and 2.7 points higher than 1960. Privately, however, Republicans expressed deep disappointment that they had not been able to register important gains, especially in the House.

Congressional reapportionment after the 1960 census had caused major shifts in the distribution of seats in the House. The Eastern states lost a net of seven seats; the South, one; and the Midwest, four. The Western states were the beneficiaries, picking up ten new seats; eight of them went to California.

Democrats controlled the California legislature, which redistricted in 1961. As a result they gained eight seats from California in the 1962 elections. A similar Republican gerrymander in New York State misfired, and Republican gains in other areas barely balanced the Democratic bonus from California.

Republicans were especially disappointed by their net loss of four Senate seats. The new Senate was so heavily Democratic that the Republicans had no real hope of regaining control until 1968 or later.

Despite a heavy turnover in the governorship elections (Democrats took seven from the Republicans and lost a like number), the gubernatorial party balance remained 34-16 in favor of the Democrats. The Republicans, however, did seize control of several important state governorships including those of Pennsylvania, Ohio and Michigan.

The most devastating defeat of the year was suffered by former vice president Richard M. Nixon, who was soundly defeated for governor of California only two years after barely missing election to the presidency. Other political veterans retired by the voters included longtime senators Homer E. Capehart, R-Ind. and Alexander Wiley, R-Wis.; Rep. Walter H. Judd, R-Minn.; and Gov. Michael V. DiSalle, D-Ohio.

The potential national leaders elected in 1962 included Republican representative William W. Scranton, elected governor of Pennsylvania by a 486,651-vote majority; former auto maker George W. Romney, a Republican who ended 14 years of Democratic control of the Michigan governorship; youthful Democratic state representative Birch Bayh, who toppled Homer Earl Capehart in the Indiana Senate race; Edward M. "Ted" Kennedy, youngest brother of the president, who was elected U.S. senator from Massachusetts; and Robert Taft Jr., a Republican who was elected congressman at large from Ohio.

Among the new senators elected in 1962 was Democrat Abraham A. Ribicoff, former governor of Connecticut and first secretary of Health, Education, and Welfare in the Kennedy administration. Hawaiian voters sent Rep. Daniel K. Inouye, a Democrat, to the Senate. He was the first U.S. senator of Japanese ancestry. The new governorship roster included James A. Rhodes, R-Ohio; John A. Love, R-Colo.;

Karl Rolvaag, D-Minn.; John B. Connally, D-Texas; and John A. Burns, D-Hawaii.

Among the "miracle men" of 1962 were Philip H. Hoff, who became the first Democratic governor of Vermont in more than a century, and Henry L. Bellmon, who became Oklahoma's first Republican governor since the state joined the Union.

Incumbents who won impressive victories included Sen. Jacob K. Javits, R-N.Y., reelected by a plurality of almost one million; Republican Senate whip Thomas H. Kuchel, R-Calif., reelected by a quarter-million vote margin despite the 296,758-vote triumph of Democratic governor Edmund G. "Pat" Brown over Nixon in the same state's balloting; Sen. Thruston B. Morton, former national chairman of the Republican Party, reelected against powerful Democratic opposition in Kentucky; and New York governor Nelson A. Rockefeller, whose plurality was down slightly from its 1958 level but still big enough to make him appear the top contender for the 1964 Republican presidential nomination.

Across the nation, voters showed a continuing tendency to disregard traditional party lines in choosing people for high office. The success of Democrats in the traditional Republican states of northern New England and breakthroughs for the Republicans in the South—including a near miss in the Alabama Senate race—attested to the possible development of significant new voting patterns.

# 1963-65:
# The 88th Congress

The years 1963-64 were good years for most Americans as the nation enjoyed continued economic prosperity and international affairs remained relatively tranquil. These same years, however, witnessed the assassination of a president, the launching of the most profound equal rights drive since the Civil War and seizure of control of one of the major American political parties by a right-wing faction.

John F. Kennedy was shot on Nov. 22, 1963, as his motorcade moved through cheering crowds in downtown Dallas. Approximately one-half hour later the president was pronounced dead. A special presidential commission, headed by Chief Justice Earl Warren, reported Sept. 27, 1964, that Lee Harvey Oswald, "acting alone and without advice or assistance," had shot the president. The report said Jack Ruby was on his own in killing Oswald and that neither was part of "any conspiracy, domestic or foreign," to kill President Kennedy. The report called for an overhauling and modernization of the Secret Service, the group entrusted with physical protection of the president, and of FBI procedures.

At 1:39 p.m., Nov. 22, Vice President Lyndon B. Johnson took the oath of office as the 36th president aboard the presidential jet plane just before its departure from Dallas to Washington. The next few days witnessed President Kennedy's funeral; the confluence in Washington of heads of state, dignitaries and emissaries from governments all over the world to pay their respects to the dead president; and the resolute grasp of the reins of power by Lyndon Johnson.

The new president's political roots reached into the liberalism of the New Deal on the one hand and into the conservatism of political life in his native Texas on the other. His wealth of experience in American political life, especially in Congress, served him well as he moved into the presidency. He quickly embraced the salient features of President Kennedy's program, especially the tax cut bill and

## Governors Who Became President

When Bill Clinton was elected president in 1992, he continued the trend in recent years of governors advancing to the White House. Between 1976 and 1992, former governors won four out of five presidential elections. Bill Clinton was the first sitting governor to be elected president since Franklin Roosevelt in 1932. Over the course of U.S. history, 16 presidents have served previously as state governors.

Following is a list of these presidents and the states in which they served as governor. Thomas Jefferson's term of governor of Virginia was during the Revolutionary War. Two other presidents served as governors of territories: Andrew Jackson was the territorial governor of Florida and William Henry Harrison was the territorial governor of Indiana.

| President | State |
| --- | --- |
| Thomas Jefferson | Virginia |
| James Monroe | Virginia |
| Martin Van Buren | New York |
| John Tyler | Virginia |
| James K. Polk | Tennessee |
| Andrew Johnson | Tennessee |
| Rutherford B. Hayes | Ohio |
| Grover Cleveland | New York |
| William McKinley | Ohio |
| Theodore Roosevelt | New York |
| Woodrow Wilson | New Jersey |
| Calvin Coolidge | Massachusetts |
| Franklin D. Roosevelt | New York |
| Jimmy Carter | Georgia |
| Ronald Reagan | California |
| Bill Clinton | Arkansas |

Source: *American Leaders 1789-1994.* Washington, D.C.: Congressional Quarterly Inc., 1994.

civil rights legislation; moved to win the confidence of the liberal community by a well-publicized "war on poverty" in America; and won the confidence of the business community and many conservatives by ordering strict economies in federal spending. Johnson's foes accused him of political sleight-of-hand in being both liberal and conservative at the same time, but opinion polls—and the 1964 elections—indicated the American people approved wholeheartedly.

The issue of civil rights produced a profound domestic crisis for the United States in 1963 and 1964. Discontented with the pace of their advances in all spheres of life, black Americans pressed for full rights in every field from voting to employment, from education to housing.

President Kennedy, in February 1963, had sent his first civil rights legislative program to Congress—one characterized by liberals of both parties as "thin." On April 3 mass demonstrations for equal rights began in Birmingham, Ala. Dramatized by the use of children in the demonstrations and the use of dogs and hoses by the police against the blacks, events in Birmingham sparked a determined nationwide series of protests. By the end of 1963 demonstrations had taken place in more than 800 cities and towns, climaxed by a gigantic but orderly "March on Washington for Jobs and Freedom" in which more than 200,000 persons participated on Aug. 28.

The demonstrations began primarily with black protesters, but millions of white Americans—most noticeably church groups and college students—took interest in the lot of black Americans. At the same time, however, many Northern whites showed their hostility to the civil rights drive because it appeared to threaten de facto segregation in housing, employment and education. Capitalizing on white Northern fears, Alabama's segregationist governor, George C. Wallace, entered spring 1964 Democratic presidential primaries in Wisconsin, Indiana and Maryland and won 33.8, 29.8 and 42.8 percent of the vote in the respective races. But when the new Republican national leadership sought to cultivate the "white backlash" vote in the 1964 presidential campaign, the effort proved singularly unsuccessful outside a few Deep South states.

In early June 1963 congressional Republicans and liberal Democrats began to press for strong civil rights legislation, and on June 11 President Kennedy told the nation: "We cannot say to 10 percent of the population that . . . the only way they are going to get their rights is to go into the streets and demonstrate." A week later he submitted a new and broadened civil rights program to combat discrimination in public accommodations, schools, jobs and voting, which he urged Congress to enact.

For a while it appeared the bill might go aground, but in November the House Judiciary Committee reported a bipartisan civil rights measure, the fruit of conferences between administration leaders and Republican congressional civil rights advocates. Working under cloture the Senate passed the bill June 19, 1964, by a 73-27 vote. The House passed the amended bill July 2, and President Johnson signed it into law a few hours later. Among other things the bill expanded federal power to protect voting rights; guaranteed access to all public accommodations and public facilities for all races, with federal power to back up the pledge; gave the federal government power to sue for school desegregation; outlawed denial of equal job opportunities in businesses or unions with 25 or more workers; and authorized the federal government to intervene in any court suit alleging denial of equal protection of the laws. It was the most sweeping civil rights measure in American history.

Determined to prevent economic stagnation and give the country's economy a major boost forward, President Kennedy in January 1963 proposed a $10.3 billion personal and corporate income tax cut to take effect July 1, 1963. After protracted hearings in the House and Senate, the final version, reducing taxes $11.5 billion annually, was signed into law by President Johnson Feb. 26, 1964.

In the meantime the economy, which the tax bill had been designed to help, was doing surprisingly well on its own. The 1963 gross national product reached $585 billion, and the Council of Economic Advisers predicted a $623 billion level in 1964. With the exception of unemployment, which remained above 5 percent of the work force, most economic indicators continued a gradual upward rise during 1963 and 1964. In October 1964, 71.2 million Americans were employed. Despite the rise in the economy, only a few economists saw any serious threat of inflation.

In his State of the Union message Jan. 8, 1964, Johnson called for an "unconditional" declaration of "war on poverty in America." The poverty program constituted the chief innovation in the president's legislative proposals. Submitting his specific program to Congress March 16, he called for

a fiscal 1965 outlay of $962.5 million to fight poverty. When Congress finished action on his request in August, it had authorized $947.5 million, only $15 million less than the draft proposal, with approval of almost all the president's requests. As enacted, the bill authorized ten separate programs under the supervision of the Office of Economic Opportunity, created by the bill. Major sections authorized a Job Corps to provide youths with work experience and training in conservation camps and in residential training centers, a work-training program to employ youths locally, a community action program under which the government would assist a variety of local efforts to combat poverty, an adult education program and a "domestic peace corps" program.

The years 1963 and 1964 witnessed a steady relaxation in the tensions of the cold war, perhaps the closest approximation to an East-West detente since 1945. At the beginning of 1963 U.S.-Soviet relations were at a standoff, produced by Russian withdrawal of missiles from Cuba in October 1962. By mid-1963 a Soviet-Chinese rift had deepened, and a lessening of U.S.-Soviet tensions was evident.

In a speech on June 10, 1963, Kennedy announced that the United States, the Soviet Union and Great Britain would begin talks on a partial test ban, apart from the 17-nation Geneva talks that had dragged on intermittently without much hope since 1958. Then, before many realized that progress was at last to be made, a limited treaty was initialed in Moscow July 25. The Senate consented to ratification Sept. 24.

A moderately optimistic tone pervaded U.S.-Soviet relations in 1964. On April 20 both the United States and the Soviet Union announced they were going to cut back their production of nuclear materials for weapons use. The growing tensions between China and the Soviet Union caused the Soviets to turn their attention more and more inward. On Oct. 16 the Western world was shocked to hear that Nikita S. Khrushchev had been ousted from his duties as premier and also as first secretary of the Soviet Communist Party. He was replaced as premier by Aleksei N. Kosygin and as party secretary by Leonid Brezhnev, possibly presaging a prolonged struggle for power within the Soviet hierarchy. The new Soviet leaders quickly made it clear they would follow Khrushchev's policy of "peaceful coexistence" with the West.

The Kennedy-Johnson administration's Alliance for Progress suffered as democratically elected regimes were deposed in Ecuador, Guatemala, Honduras, the Dominican Republic and Bolivia. The Johnson administration faced its first major foreign policy crisis in January 1964 when large-scale violence broke out in Central America as Panamanians protested the 1903 treaty under which the United States administered the Panama Canal and Americans enjoyed special privileges in the Canal Zone. The United States was encouraged, however, when President Joao Goulart of Brazil, accused of conducting a leftist and chaotic administration, was deposed in a bloodless coup on April 1, 1964.

Apparently upset by Vietnam government moves against Buddhists, suicidal burnings by Buddhist monks, corruption within the government and inadequate military success against the Communist Viet Cong, the State Department in 1963 gradually curtailed aid to the Vietnamese regime of Catholic president Ngo Dinh Diem. On Nov. 1 a military coup ended the Diem regime. The State Department denied participation in the coup, but unofficially it admitted that it might have encouraged the "proper climate" for such a revolt. The new ruling junta in Vietnam was itself overturned by a coup in January 1964, starting a series of bewildering governmental shifts that lasted through 1964 as the military situation continued to deteriorate.

The off-year elections of November 1963 provided no definite clue to possible trends for 1964. Democrats maintained control of the Kentucky and Mississippi governorships and the Philadelphia mayoralty in the top three races, but the GOP vote was up sharply in all three areas.

Top Republican takeovers of the year were scored in New Jersey, where the Assembly reverted to GOP hands to give the Republicans majorities in both houses, and in Indiana, where the GOP elected 25 new mayors. The Republicans also scored gains in Virginia and Mississippi legislative elections. Democratic Representative John F. Shelley won election as mayor of San Francisco, ending 55 years of GOP control in technically nonpartisan elections. Suburban New York also showed some Democratic gains.

## The 1964 Campaigns

From the beginning of 1964 it was apparent that President Johnson was the strong favorite to win a full four-year White House term in his own right. As the Democrats gathered in Atlantic City for their convention on Aug. 24, Johnson kept silence about his final decision for a running mate. In a move unprecedented in American politics, he appeared before the Democratic National Convention just before his own nomination the same evening to announce to the delegates that Sen. Hubert H. Humphrey of Minnesota was his choice for the vice presidential slot.

The most fascinating story of the 1964 presidential campaign, however, lay in the opposition party. Throughout the postwar years, the Republican Party, despite its conservative inclinations, had generally embraced the wide consensus of U.S. politics: agreement on basic social welfare responsibilities of the government together with a firm but not bellicose policy toward the Communist world. But in 1964 the Republican Party turned abruptly from the moderate course. For president it nominated a militantly conservative two-term Arizona senator, Barry Goldwater, known for his hostile views toward the power of the federal government and his apparent willingness to risk nuclear confrontation with the Soviets to advance the Western cause. The course set by Goldwater brought the Republican Party its most devastating defeat in more than a quarter-century. Republican ranks in Congress and the state legislatures were greatly reduced. Even worse, national confidence in the party was so badly shaken that it might take years to recoup.

Early in 1964, however, only one Republican of national stature was willing to speak out on the possible dangers of Goldwater and his philosophy for the Republican Party. That man was New York governor Nelson A. Rockefeller, who had entered the race for the GOP nomination Nov. 7, 1963. Rockefeller symbolized the Eastern progressive wing of the Republican Party that had dominated Republican National Conventions since 1940. The other leaders of the Republican Party's moderate wing—governors William W. Scranton of Pennsylvania and George W. Romney of Michigan, Ambassador Henry Cabot Lodge and former vice president Richard M. Nixon—all were thought to harbor some presidential ambitions, but none was willing to take the plunge in the presidential primaries or to risk an open challenge to the Goldwater wing of the party.

The "National Draft Goldwater Committee," which organized formally in the spring of 1963, aimed both at nominating Goldwater and at remaking the entire Republican Party into a vehicle for militant conservatism. Their aim

appeared to be the reforming of two U.S. political parties along straight liberal versus conservative lines. By the autumn of 1963 the years of Goldwater stewardship within the ranks of the Republican Party had begun to bear fruit. Goldwater supporters held important positions in the Republican Party apparatus. Rep. William E. Miller, R-N.Y., who would later become Goldwater's vice presidential running mate, was the Republican national chairman.

The Republican National Convention, meeting in San Francisco July 13-16, turned sharply to the right, rejecting the party's moderate tone of the postwar years and substituting instead an unabashed conservatism in domestic affairs and all-out nationalism in foreign policy.

Goldwater's controversial stands and his failure to advance meaningful alternative solutions to national problems relieved Johnson of having to spell out in any substantial detail what his plans for the "great society" were. For the most part Johnson confined himself to calls for national unity and remarks aimed at broadening the breach between Goldwater and the bulk of moderate and liberal Republicans. Johnson was so successful in preempting the vital "middle ground" of American politics that a Democratic victory was assured long before election day.

## Results of the 1964 Elections

In the Nov. 3 elections President Johnson led the Democratic Party to its greatest national victory since 1936. Not only did Johnson win a four-year White House term in his own right, amassing the largest vote of any presidential candidate in history, but his broad coattails helped the Democrats score major gains in the House of Representatives and increase their already heavy majority in the Senate.

The Johnson-Humphrey ticket ran 15,951,378 votes ahead of the Goldwater-Miller ticket, easily exceeding the record national popular vote plurality of 11,073,102 by which Franklin D. Roosevelt defeated Alfred M. Landon in 1936. The final, official vote for Johnson-Humphrey was 43,129,566; for Goldwater-Miller, 27,178,188.

Johnson won 44 states and the District of Columbia (which voted for the first time for president, under the terms of the 23rd Amendment to the Constitution). His electoral vote total was 486. Goldwater won six states with a total of 52 electoral votes. The Democratic presidential victory began in New England and the East, where Johnson carried every state and chalked up a better than 2-1 majority.

The Democratic sweep continued through the Republican Midwestern heartland, where every state also cast its electoral vote for Johnson. The president was the winner in every mountain and Pacific state except Arizona, Goldwater's home state. California, which had boosted Goldwater to the Republican nomination in the June primary, went for Johnson by over a million votes.

Only an unusual degree of ticket splitting saved the Republican Party from almost total annihilation in races for congressional and state posts. As it was, the Republicans were reduced to their lowest congressional levels since depression days. In elections to the House the Republicans suffered a net loss of 38 seats. The new House balance was 295 Democrats and 140 Republicans, the lowest GOP membership figure since the 1936 elections. Among the more serious Republican House losses were seven seats in New York, five in Iowa and four each in New Jersey, Michigan, Ohio and Washington. Many of the Northern Republican representatives defeated were among their party's most conservative, representing formerly "safe Republican" seats. For example, 54 Republican House members had backed Goldwater's nomination drive in June by signing a statement saying his nomination would "result in substantial increases in Republican membership in both houses of Congress." Of these, 17 were defeated, another three retired but saw their districts go Democratic and all but six saw their winning percentages dwindle. Of the 21 Northern Republicans who had voted with Goldwater against the 1964 Civil Rights Act, 11 were defeated. Republicans who disassociated themselves from Goldwater and his policies were generally more successful. The most spectacular Republican House victory of the year was scored by Rep. John V. Lindsay of New York, who refused to endorse Goldwater but won a 71.5 percent victory in his district, while Johnson was carrying it by more than 2-1.

The only area of significant Republican House gains was the deep South, where Goldwater coattails helped the party elect five new representatives in Alabama and one each in Georgia and Mississippi. They were the first Republican House members from these states since Reconstruction. But at the same time three conservative GOP Southern House members—two in Texas, one in Kentucky—were going down to defeat.

One result of the election was to erode the power base of the "conservative coalition" between Republicans and Southern Democrats. Not only would there be less conservative representation in the House, but the relative strength of Northern liberals in the Democratic House Caucus would be increased substantially.

The Senate elections resulted in a net Democratic gain of two seats, making the new balance 68 Democrats and 32 Republicans. Not since the elections of 1940 had the Democrats held such a heavy majority. But the major story was not the new Democratic Senate gains of 1964 but the fact that the members of the liberal Democratic class of 1958 were all reelected to office. The Democrats' gain of 13 formerly Republican seats in 1958 had effected a basic realignment of power within the Senate, giving it a much more liberal orientation than the House. The Republicans had long looked forward to 1964 as the year when they would win back many of the class of 1958 seats.

The Democrats actually won three GOP Senate seats in 1964: Kenneth Keating's seat in New York, taken by Robert F. Kennedy (thus making Kennedy a potential future contender for the Democratic presidential nomination); J. Glenn Beall's seat in Maryland, won by Democrat Joseph D. Tydings; and the New Mexico seat of interim senator Edwin L. Mechem, won by Rep. Joseph M. Montoya. The sole GOP gain was in California, where George Murphy scored an upset victory over interim senator Pierre Salinger, former presidential press secretary.

A major blow to the GOP was the defeat in Ohio of Robert Taft Jr., who was challenging Democratic senator Stephen M. Young. Before the election Taft had been looked to as a major future leader of his party. But the Goldwater "drag"—Johnson won Ohio by 1,027,466 votes—was too much for Taft to overcome.

In gubernatorial elections the Republicans scored gains in Washington, Wisconsin and Massachusetts and lost seats they had held in Arizona and Utah. The result was a net gain of one for the GOP. But the already heavy Democratic majority was not weakened significantly. The new lineup was 33 Democrats and 17 Republicans.

Without Goldwater at the head of the ticket the Republicans might have scored much better. Their most disap-

pointing defeat came in Illinois, where Charles H. Percy, who had been regarded as a possible future presidential candidate, went down to defeat in the Democratic landslide.

The most spectacular GOP governorship win was scored by Michigan governor George R. Romney, seeking reelection. He withstood a Johnson landslide of more than 2-1 to win reelection. The outcome established Romney, who had refused to endorse Goldwater's candidacy, as a powerful future leader of his party.

Among the new governors elected were Samuel P. Goddard, D-Ariz.; Roger D. Branigin, D-Ind.; Daniel J. Evans, R-Wash.; and Warren P. Knowles, R-Wis.

Democratic governors who won substantial reelection victories despite the Republican complexion of their states included Frank B. Morrison of Nebraska, Harold E. Hughes of Iowa, John W. King of New Hampshire, and Philip H. Hoff of Vermont. But in normally Democratic Rhode Island, Republican governor John H. Chaffee won reelection with 61.3 percent of the vote, while Goldwater received only 19.1 percent of the state's vote.

# The Vietnam War Years

The years of the 1960s and 1970s were some of the most turbulent in the nation's history. The seeds of the great upheavals ahead were already sprouting even before President Kennedy's death in November 1963. The country's role in the Vietnam War was inching upward. Black Americans were becoming ever more insistent in demanding an end to all forms of racial discrimination. A huge generation of teenagers, born in the post-World War II baby boom, were reaching college age and were preparing to challenge authority on a scale unprecedented in American history. And there were growing indications of conservative political strength, especially within the Republican Party.

In the late 1960s the nation experienced a series of cataclysmic changes that, while they did not appear to endanger the basic economic health of the nation, did jeopardize the postwar politics of consensus and promise as yet unpredictable changes in the social and political climate of American life. Only when the nation found itself entangled in a seemingly endless and unwinnable war in Vietnam in the mid-1960s did the first major cracks appear in the general national consensus behind U.S. foreign policy. For the first time serious doubts were raised about the role of the nation as a global policeman, and there were indications that a period of limited isolationism might come in the wake of any Vietnam settlement.

Through the 1964 election the United States had enjoyed remarkably stable two-party politics in the postwar years. No major ideological gulfs existed between the parties, and although the Democrats were more frequently victorious at the polls than the Republicans (an apparent legacy of Franklin Roosevelt's New Deal), few Americans were deeply concerned when the party in power changed in Washington or the state capitals. Indeed, two-party politics infused virtually every region of the country for the first time in its history. And as the parties became more competitive, personal allegiances shifted more frequently and ticket splitting became an American electoral pastime.

When Barry Goldwater was repudiated at the polls in 1964, the post-New Deal consensus seemed to have been reaffirmed. Indeed, the year 1965 saw the last major burst of legislative accomplishments and national optimism that the country was to witness for some time. With the large Democratic majorities created by the Johnson landslide,

Congress enacted federal aid to education, a national health insurance program and a voting rights act.

But the Johnson administration's fortunes soon changed. The decision to commit massive American ground forces to Vietnam resulted in increased opposition at home to American participation in the war. The war further stimulated student unrest on the campuses resulting in siege conditions at some universities. Blacks burst forth in anger and destroyed large sections of American cities. And the Rev. Martin Luther King Jr. and Sen. Robert F. Kennedy were assassinated in 1968.

The Democratic Party coalition broke open under these strains in 1968, with the challenge to President Johnson's renomination and the Independent candidacy of Alabama governor George C. Wallace. The result was that Republican Richard Nixon was elected to the presidency.

At the end of the 1960s both parties were clearly in transition. The Democrats, in order to hold their solid base among low-income voters and minorities, would be obliged to remain strong advocates of wide-ranging social reform. But that very course could possibly seal their eventual downfall in the South, even if an increased black vote in that region compensated for some of that loss. And while organized labor had turned out a strong Democratic vote in 1968, its leaders were having increasing difficulty in convincing workers that they should remain unswervingly loyal to the Democratic Party.

The Republicans, even in winning the presidential election of 1968, received only 43 percent of the national vote and had to recognize that in their major base of support—the predominantly white, middle-class rural areas and small cities—they faced a diminishing asset in overall population terms. It was clear that the Republicans' growing strength in the burgeoning white suburban areas of America would hold solidly only as long as the party maintained domestic prosperity and found a way to calm inner-city tensions.

During his first term President Nixon too had to deal with anti-war demonstrations. But his policy of gradual withdrawal of American troops, climaxing with the peace settlement of January 1973, finally removed the war from the top of the American political agenda.

At the same time, with the passage of the baby-boom generation out of college and into the labor market, the nation's campuses became more peaceful. And the movement of many blacks onto the voter rolls, into public office and into more jobs and better housing seemed to relieve some of the racial tension.

But at the very moment when things began looking better, the nation was hit by a fresh series of calamities. Throughout 1973 and 1974 the Watergate scandal implicated several top public officials, including the president himself, in illegal activities. The immediate result was the first presidential resignation in U.S. history, but the deeper ramifications could be found in the weakening of the confidence of the people in their government and leaders.

While the revelations were continuing, the United States was hit with an energy crisis when the Arab states cut off the flow of oil during the October 1973 war in the Middle East. Even when the flow was resumed, the price had been jacked up more than 300 percent, and this increase, combined with other trends in the economy, produced some of the worst inflation in the nation's history. Buffeted by these forces, seemingly beyond their control, many Americans wondered about the future of their country and the stability of their economic and political system.

President Gerald Ford, with his low-key personality and image of personal integrity, helped calm the country after these misfortunes. But he was not seen by many as a strong leader and was almost defeated for the presidential nomination of his own party in the 1976 primaries.

# 1965-67:
# The 89th Congress

Buoyed by the largest party majorities enjoyed by any president in three decades, Lyndon Johnson led the 89th Congress in an amazingly productive 1965 session. The scope of the legislation was even more impressive than the number of major new laws. In the course of the year Congress approved programs that had long been on the agenda of the Democratic Party—in the case of medical care for the aged under Social Security, for as long as 20 years. Other longstanding objectives were met by enactment of aid to primary and secondary schools, college scholarships and immigration reform.

The pace of the 1965 session was so breathless as to cause a major revision of the image, widely prevalent in preceding years, of Congress as structurally incapable of swift decision. The change was because of three primary elements not always present in past years: the decisive Democratic majorities elected in 1965, the personal leadership of President Johnson and the shaping of legislation to obtain maximum political support in Congress.

The expanded Democratic pluralities were most significant in the House, where the Democrats had not only scored a 38-seat net gain over the Republicans in the 1964 elections but had also traded a number of conservative Democratic votes in the South for liberal Democratic votes in the North. The new liberal strength in the House showed itself most dramatically in passage of the aid to education and medical care (Medicare) bills. The Senate had passed similar measures in previous years only to see them blocked by the hitherto powerful coalition of Republicans and conservative Southern Democrats in the House. But the "conservative coalition," where it did appear in House roll call votes, was victorious only 25 percent of the time in 1965, compared with 67 percent in 1962 and 1964 and 74 percent in 1961, the first year of President Kennedy's term.

The president gained maximum political effect from his efforts to build a broad consensus of support. An excise tax cut, designed to keep the economy growing steadily, appealed to business and consumer interests alike. Lack of strong opposition from business circles made it easier for Democrats to mount the Great Society program of greatly increased civil benefits and tended to smother Republican protests that Congress was merely rubber stamping ill-conceived administration proposals.

The Voting Rights Act of 1965, the most comprehensive legislation to ensure the right to vote in 90 years, was prompted by the brutal suppression of demonstrations in Selma, Ala. and other parts of the South. The bill went beyond the milder courtroom remedies of earlier civil rights acts. In the wake of this legislation an additional 500,000 Southern blacks were registered by the time of the 1966 elections.

Other legislation included a housing bill authorizing $7.8 billion to fund new and existing housing programs through 1969 and a bill establishing a cabinet-level Department of Housing and Urban Development.

The year 1965 was punctuated by major crises in Vietnam. Faced with the threat of success by the Viet Cong Communist insurgents in South Vietnam, President Johnson initiated large-scale bombing raids in North Vietnam, which was giving major aid to the Viet Cong. When this tactic failed to turn the unfavorable course of the war, he ordered a vast increase—from about 20,000 to eventually more than 140,000—in American troop strength in the South and an aggressive prosecution of the land war. Both steps required new outlays for personnel and materiel. Despite highly vocal criticism of his Vietnam policy by a small band of senators, Congress overwhelmingly approved Johnson's special request for funds.

The Vietnam budget pressures soon had serious effects on the domestic economy. As 1966 began the U.S. economy was already strained to its noninflationary limit. After 59 months of stable economic growth, it was near full employment. Plant capacity was in full use. Any sizable increase in demand under these conditions would be bound to result in inflation. This is precisely what occurred as the defense budget shot upward, without any significant offsetting measures to cut back on other purchasing power. The cost-of-living index jumped from 111.0 percent in January to 113.8 percent in August. The president early in the year asked and received congressional approval of a $5.9 billion bill to accelerate certain types of tax payments and reimpose 1965 excise tax levies, but the measure was hardly adequate to counter the Vietnam spending boom. Almost every leading economist in the nation called for a general tax increase, but President Johnson refused.

With the public increasingly concerned with inflation and the Vietnam War, congressional Republicans found new Democratic allies in the effort to curb the Great Society—not only its spending programs but almost any measure providing social reform. Despite strong persuasive efforts by the president, the administration was rebuffed on many major bills.

An important reason for the defeat of the administration's new civil rights proposals was a wave of summertime riots in black "ghetto" areas of the large cities. In August 1965 a six-day disturbance had erupted in Los Angeles's 95 percent black Watts area, with about 7,000 youths participating in rioting, looting and arson. The National Guard finally restored order, but only after 34 deaths. In the summer of 1966 other riots followed in the black areas of several other American cities. The 1966 riots were attributed not only to decades of frustration among urban blacks in education, housing and employment fields but to the growth of a new philosophy of "black power," expounded by extremist civil rights groups such as the Congress of Racial Equality (CORE) and the Student Nonviolent Coordinating Committee (SNCC).

In the House, Rep. John William McCormack of Massachusetts continued as Speaker. Sen. Mike Mansfield of Montana remained as Senate majority leader, with Sen. Everett Dirksen of Illinois his Republican counterpart. House minority leader Charles Halleck of Indiana was defeated for reelection to his leadership post by Rep. Gerald R. Ford of Michigan, just before formal opening of the 89th Congress. Ford's election as minority leader was a continuation of the revolt of younger House Republicans that had begun with Ford's election as House GOP Conference chairman two years before. As in 1963 the leadership struggle seemed to be based less on ideological differences than on the question of which representative could give the most forceful leadership to the depleted Republican House ranks.

The 1964 elections had left the Republicans at such a low point that some resurgence seemed inevitable. In 1965 it

began in a spectacular way as Republican-Liberal John V. Lindsay won election as mayor in heavily Democratic New York City. Lindsay's victory, combined with the victories of liberally inclined Republican candidates for district attorney in Philadelphia and mayor in Louisville, Ky., signaled a potential Republican resurgence on the left in the very areas where Goldwater had been weakest—in the major cities and especially among blacks and other minority groups.

In New Jersey, however, the Republican gubernatorial candidate took a conservative tack similar to that of the 1964 Goldwater campaign and found himself defeated by Democratic governor Richard J. Hughes by a record 363,572-vote margin. Democrats also held the Virginia governorship and legislature and easily maintained control of the mayors' offices in major cities such as New Haven, St. Louis, Pittsburgh and Detroit. In Cleveland a black state legislator running as an Independent came within 2,143 votes of upsetting the incumbent Democratic mayor. In the smaller cities some of the most interesting contests took place on June 8 in Hattiesburg and Columbus, Miss., where the first Republicans of the 20th century—all staunch conservatives—were elected mayors.

## The 1966 Midterm Elections

From the beginning of the 1966 campaign the Democrats realized that they faced formidable odds if they hoped to maintain their overwhelming margins of control in Congress and in the state governorships and legislatures. Yet at the end of 1965 it looked as if the minority Republicans might be held to minimal gains. The first session of the 89th Congress had passed laws with benefits for almost every segment of the population. President Johnson still enjoyed the wide "consensus" support he had enjoyed in 1964, from every group from organized labor to big business and minorities. And the economy was booming on virtually every front.

By the beginning of the 1966 campaign, however, it was apparent that the odds had shifted significantly to the benefit of the Republicans. Behind the change was the escalation of the Vietnam War, with its heavy toll both in American lives and dollars. The conflict in Vietnam, because of its limited nature, increased frustrations across the country and began to undermine public support of the administration in power.

The war effort generated inflationary pressures that were being felt throughout the country by mid-1966. The Republicans were able to argue with some effectiveness that the Johnson administration should be cutting down, rather than increasing, national expenditures for a wide variety of Great Society programs. Moreover, those very social welfare programs that had looked so politically attractive at the end of 1965 were beginning to encounter serious administrative difficulties, with wide gaps between the administration's promises to improve educational standards, end conditions of poverty and ensure racial peace and its ability to deliver on those promises.

President Johnson's own popularity plummeted during the year; wide splits appeared in the Democratic Party in many important states; and at the same time several attractive Republican candidates appeared to lead the GOP in critical states—in sharp contrast to the unpopularity of Goldwater, the party's 1964 standard bearer.

Early in 1965 the Democrats had launched an ambitious Operation Support from within the Democratic National Committee, designed to reelect a large portion of the 71 freshman Democratic representatives who came into office in the 1964 Democratic sweep—38 of them from formerly Republican districts. But while Operation Support functioned smoothly in 1965, it tended to fall off in 1966 as the national committee obeyed presidential orders to cut back on its activities in order to pay off a heavy debt left from the 1964 campaign.

The Republican congressional effort, on the other hand, was bolstered by a massive fund-raising campaign that made it possible to funnel thousands of dollars into every doubtful congressional district in the country. Reports just before the elections showed national-level gifts of $1.6 million to GOP congressional candidates from their party headquarters, compared with only $250,000 from national-level Democratic committees.

The primary season indicated some significant shifts in the political landscape. In California, long a bastion of liberal Republicanism, actor Ronald Reagan, an outspoken conservative, won a sweeping primary victory over more liberal opposition. In the Virginia primary two aging representatives of traditional conservative Southern Democracy were defeated by younger men of more moderate persuasion. In Florida the mayor of Miami, Robert King High, won the Democratic gubernatorial primary with liberal support over the more conservative incumbent governor. Staunch segregationist candidates, on the other hand, won Democratic gubernatorial primaries in the Deep South: Jim Johnson in Arkansas, Lester Maddox in Georgia and Lurleen Wallace, wife of outgoing governor George C. Wallace (who was ineligible to succeed himself), in Alabama.

As the campaign gathered steam in the fall, the Republicans concentrated their fire increasingly on the issues of inflation, Vietnam, crime and the alleged credibility gap between what President Johnson and his administration said they were doing and their actual performance.

### Results of the 1966 Elections

The Republican Party reasserted itself as a major force in American politics by capturing eight new governorships, three new seats in the Senate and 47 additional House seats in the Nov. 8 elections. In a striking comeback from its devastating defeat of 1964, the GOP elected enough new governors to give it control of 25 of the 50 states with a substantial majority of the nation's population. The Senate and House gains left the party still short of a majority but in a position of new power and relevance on the national scene.

A new vigor shown by Republican candidates across the country marked a return to more competitive two-party politics and the possibility that the 1968 presidential election could be closely contested. The vast majority of successful Republican candidates, both for congressional and state offices, appeared to have rejected the ultraconservative ideology espoused by former senator Barry Goldwater. But the winning Republicans did represent a somewhat more conservative philosophy than that of the president and his administration, reflecting a national movement to the right, which many observers felt was reflected in the slowdown on major domestic reforms in the closing session of the 89th Congress. The 1966 elections appeared to lay the groundwork for a strong moderate Republican challenge to Johnson in 1968.

The party control among the state governorships shifted from 33-17 in favor of the Democrats to 25-25, the greatest Republican strength since the early 1950s. The Republicans gained California and held New York, Pennsylvania, Ohio and Michigan to give them control of five of the nation's seven largest states. In addition to California, the

Republicans added Alaska, Arizona, Arkansas, Florida, Maryland, Minnesota, Nebraska, Nevada and New Mexico to the list of governorships under their control. Among the new Republican governors were Winthrop Rockefeller of Arkansas; Claude R. Kirk Jr. (in traditionally Democratic Florida); and Spiro T. Agnew of Maryland, a political moderate who defeated George P. Mahoney, the narrow victor in a three-way Democratic primary who had pitched his campaign to the "white backlash" vote. (In general, "backlash" candidates were unsuccessful in the elections.) Republican gubernatorial candidate Howard Callaway won a plurality of the votes in the one-time impregnable Democratic stronghold of Georgia. But Callaway failed to poll an absolute majority, and under the Georgia constitution, the election was thrown into the state legislature, which chose the Democratic runner-up, Lester Maddox.

The Republicans' most spectacular gain was in the House, where they picked up 52 seats and lost only five to the Democrats. The new party lineup in the House would be 248 Democrats and 187 Republicans. The Republican total in the thirteen Southern states rose to 28 seats, compared with only 14 in 1962. In Senate elections Republicans gained seats in Illinois, Oregon and Tennessee, giving them 36 seats to the Democrats' 64. Democrats failed to take any Senate seats from the Republicans.

In the state legislatures the Republicans scored net gains of 156 senate seats and 401 seats in the lower houses, reflecting not only the strong party trend running in the Republicans' favor but the fact that reapportionment, by adding seats in suburban areas, was helping them as much as it helped the Democrats, if not more.

# 1967-69:
# The 90th Congress

The United States in 1967-68 underwent two of the most trying years in its history as a rising wave of rioting and looting swept over its largely black central cities, the Vietnam War continued to build in human and dollar costs, inflationary pressures mounted and two major national leaders were assassinated. President Johnson, recognizing the inability of his administration to command continued strong popular support, announced in March 1968 that he would not seek reelection to a second full term in the White House.

The Vietnam War became increasingly troublesome. It often overshadowed civil rights and city problems, distorted the U.S. economy and loomed over U.S. foreign policy. Its cost soared to more than $2 billion a month. Reflecting the expense of the war, the federal budget by fiscal 1969 was at a record $186 billion, with $80 billion of that for defense.

Hopes for a political settlement in Vietnam were buoyed on Oct. 31, when President Johnson announced he was ordering a complete halt to all American bombing of the North. Though not officially confirmed, it was believed that the bombing halt was undertaken with tacit agreement that it would last only so long as the North Vietnamese did not use it to their military advantage. A new and complicated round of negotiations then began in Paris on the means and protocol for substantive peace negotiations.

The patterns of violence in American life reasserted themselves when two prominent Americans became victims of assassins' bullets. The first was the Rev. Martin Luther King Jr., who was shot and killed April 4, 1968, in Memphis, Tenn. Following his death, rioting, looting and burning broke out in black districts in more than one hundred cities.

On June 5 another apostle of social progress and reconciliation between the races was struck down. Leaving the Los Angeles hotel ballroom in which he had made his California presidential primary victory statement, Sen. Robert F. Kennedy was shot in the head and died 25 hours later.

## The 1968 Campaigns

Few presidential election years in the history of the nation brought as many surprising developments as 1968. Just a year before the election, it appeared likely that the two candidates might be President Johnson for the Democrats and Michigan's governor George W. Romney for the Republicans. But by late winter 1968 both Johnson and Romney were out of the picture, and each of the major parties was plunged into spirited fights for their presidential nominations. During 1968 continued racial tensions in the nation led to fears that Alabama's former governor George C. Wallace, running as the candidate of his own American Independent Party, might win a major share of the national vote or at least cause deadlock in the Electoral College.

For the Democrats the year of surprises began Nov. 30, 1967, when Minnesota's Eugene McCarthy announced that he would enter four 1968 presidential primaries to demonstrate opposition to the Johnson policies. McCarthy's candidacy struck an immediate chord of response, especially among younger Americans who shared his fervent distaste for the war in Vietnam. Most political observers discounted the seriousness of McCarthy's candidacy, but in the March 12 presidential primary in New Hampshire, McCarthy scored an amazing "moral" victory by gathering 42 percent of the vote against the president's 49 percent.

The McCarthy vote in New Hampshire then triggered another major surprise: the entry of Robert Kennedy into the Democratic presidential race, announced March 16. And on March 31 President Johnson stunned the nation by announcing, at the end of a lengthy radio and television address on Vietnam policy, that he would not seek reelection in 1968.

After Johnson withdrew, the race for the Democratic nomination turned into a three-way affair: McCarthy, Kennedy and Vice President Hubert Humphrey, who entered the fray in April. On June 4, in the conclusive California primary, Kennedy emerged the narrow victor over McCarthy, only to be assassinated as he left the hotel ballroom where he had claimed victory.

The death of Kennedy, who had shared McCarthy's Vietnam views while taking a far more aggressive stance on urban and minority problems, was followed by an eerie moratorium in Democratic politics as the shaken party factions sought to decide on their next move. But within weeks Humphrey emerged as the odds-on favorite for the nomination.

While violence flared in the city streets and thousands of police and guards imposed security precautions unprecedented in the annals of American presidential conventions, the 35th Democratic National Convention met Aug. 26-29 in Chicago to nominate Hubert H. Humphrey of Minnesota for the presidency and to endorse the controversial Vietnam policies of the Johnson-Humphrey administration. Humphrey's selection as running mate was Maine's Sen. Edmund S. Muskie. In the campaign that followed Muskie's calm-voiced appeals for understanding between the groups in American society would prove an asset for the Democratic ticket.

In a minority were the anti-war factions that rallied around the candidacies of McCarthy and McGovern. The McCarthy forces mounted a series of challenges to the Humphrey faction, on credentials, rules, the platform and the nomination itself. An unprecedented number of credentials were challenged. McCarthy, McGovern and other liberal factions won their greatest breakthrough on convention rules, obtaining abolition of a mandatory unit rule for the 1968 convention and at every level of party activity leading up to and including the 1972 convention. Many Humphrey-pledged delegates also backed the move. For the first time in recent party history, the functioning of party machinery at every level had been questioned. Humphrey won his party's nomination, but he would lead a bitterly divided party into the autumn campaign.

In the Republican Party George Romney had established himself as the early leader in the race for the nomination, but his liberalism was distasteful to many orthodox Republicans. He was followed into the GOP race by Richard Nixon, who made his long-anticipated candidacy formal on Feb. 1. The two front-runners entered the New Hampshire presidential primary, but it soon became apparent to Romney that he faced a likely loss, and on Feb. 28 he surprised the nation by withdrawing from the contest. Nixon won an overwhelming victory in the March 12 New Hampshire GOP primary. Moderate and liberal Republicans hoped that New York's Gov. Nelson A. Rockefeller would step into the void created by Romney's withdrawal, but Rockefeller declared on March 21 that he would not run because "the majority of (Republican) leaders want the candidacy of Richard Nixon."

Without significant opposition Nixon swept the Wisconsin, Indiana, Nebraska, Oregon and South Dakota primaries, shedding most of the "loser" image he had acquired from his 1960 defeat for president and 1962 defeat for governor of California. Rockefeller reversed his ground once again by entering the race on April 30, but even in the primaries where write-ins were permitted, the vote for him was generally low.

The Republican National Convention, meeting in Miami Beach Aug. 5-8, wrote a moderately progressive party platform and then chose candidates for president and vice president who, at the moment of their selection, seemed to be taking increasingly restrictive attitudes on the sensitive national issues of law, order and civil rights.

Nixon won nomination for the presidency on the first ballot, bearing out the predictions of his campaign organization. For vice president, at Nixon's suggestion, the Republicans selected Spiro T. Agnew, governor of Maryland since his election in 1966. The selection of Agnew, one of the major surprises of the year, was announced by Nixon the morning after his own nomination, and in the wake of almost-solid all-night conferences with Republican leaders, chiefly those of a conservative bent. Liberal Republicans were outraged at Agnew's designation.

Nixon seemed to represent the middle ground of the Republican Party of 1968, substantially to the right of Governor Rockefeller and well to the center of the road compared to the conservative Ronald Reagan. The Republican platform of 1968, adopted by the Convention Aug. 6 without a floor fight or any amendments, was generally moderate in tone and contained a preamble calling for a major national effort to rebuild urban and rural slums and attack the root causes of poverty, including racism.

To conduct his second campaign for the presidency, Nixon assembled a massive—and doubtless the best financed—campaign organization in U.S. history. Nixon was intent on avoiding the mistakes of his 1960 campaign, when a frenetic campaign pace resulted in exhaustion and snap decisions.

A central theme of Nixon's campaign was an appeal to a group he called the "forgotten Americans," whom Nixon defined as "the nonshouters," those who "work in America's factories, run America's business, serve in Government, provide most of the soldiers who died to keep us free." By suggesting that his administration would look chiefly to the interest of this group, Nixon was able to make a strong bid for the support of white suburban and small-town America, the traditional heartland of GOP strength in the nation.

Humphrey's bid for the presidency got off to a depressing start in September 1968 with sparse crowds, disordered schedules and vicious heckling by left-wing, anti-war elements virtually everywhere he sought to speak. Humphrey's first task was to establish some measure of independence from the vastly unpopular Johnson administration. A significant step to win some of the anti-war Democrats to his side came in a Sept. 30 televised address from Salt Lake City, when he said he would stop the bombing of North Vietnam "as an acceptable risk for peace." When President Johnson actually took that step on Oct. 31, Humphrey could hardly restrain his glee. The combination of his own softened stand and the presidential position won him, at least at the last moment, the support of many of the Democrats who had been most disaffected at Chicago.

Humphrey endorsed virtually all the social advances of the Kennedy-Johnson years but called for a substantial broadening of domestic efforts to solve the problems of cities and minorities. He charged that Nixon's economic policies would bring America "back to McKinley," with recessions and unemployment like those the country experienced during the Eisenhower years.

George Wallace had announced on Feb. 8, 1968, that he would run for president as a third party candidate under the banner of the American Independent Party. His campaign had a narrower goal: to win the balance of power in Electoral College voting, thus depriving either major party of the clear electoral majority required for election. Wallace made it clear that he would then expect one of the major party candidates to make concessions in return for sufficient support from the Wallace supporters to win election. Wallace indicated he expected the election to be resolved in the Electoral College and not go to the House of Representatives for resolution. At the end of the campaign, it was revealed that he had obtained affidavits from all his electors in which they promised to vote for Wallace "or whomsoever he may direct" in the Electoral College.

## Results of the 1968 Elections

In one of the closest elections of the century Richard Nixon on Nov. 5 was elected president. In percentage terms Nixon had 43.4 percent of the popular vote, the lowest winning percentage for a winning presidential candidate since 1912, when Woodrow Wilson won by 41.9 percent. Humphrey's percentage was 42.7; Wallace's was 13.5.

For the Republican Party Nixon's victory had special significance. He was the first successful GOP presidential contender since the 1920s who was closely identified with the party organization. The victories of Dwight D. Eisenhower in the 1950s, followed by Nixon's defeat in 1960, had raised the possibility that the Republicans might lack the broad appeal ever to win a presidential victory unless their candidate possessed special nonparty appeal.

The Democrats had feared that the election would bring a final dissolution of the grand Democratic coalition that had controlled the federal government in most elections since the 1930s. The election returns did show the South deserting the Democratic Party in presidential voting, the Deep South to Wallace, the border South to Nixon. But the other elements of the Democratic coalition held together remarkably well, helping the party to win the electoral votes of several major states and to return a high proportion of its congressional incumbents.

Preelection surveys of Wallace voters had indicated that if they had been obliged to choose between Nixon and Humphrey, about twice as many would have preferred Nixon as Humphrey. If Wallace had not been on the ballot, Nixon would very possibly have carried some of the five Deep South states that went for Wallace, possibly building up a stronger national vote lead in the process. But it was difficult to tell from the election returns whether Wallace had hurt Nixon or Humphrey the more in the non-Southern states.

Another bright spot for the Republicans was on the governorship level, where the GOP added five seats for a new total of 31. But the Democrats retained control of both houses of the Congress.

In the Senate Republicans gained five new seats, for a total of 42, the largest number they had held since 1956. The gain was a major accomplishment for the GOP. It was the biggest gain since 1950, when the Republicans also won five new seats. The breakdown for the new Senate was 58 Democrats and 42 Republicans. In the 90th Congress, there had been 63 Democrats and 37 Republicans. Republicans actually won seven seats previously held by Democrats, but since Democrats won two seats previously held by Republicans, the net gain for the Republicans was five. No incumbent Republican standing for reelection was defeated, while four incumbent Democrats lost their bids for additional terms.

The makeup of the new Senate was expected to result in a shift, although not a dramatic one, to the right. While liberal strength remained the same as in the 90th Congress, strength among moderate senators dropped and strength among conservative senators rose correspondingly.

The seven Republicans who captured Senate seats previously held by Democrats included Barry Goldwater, former senator from Arizona and unsuccessful Republican presidential candidate in 1964. Goldwater, whose previous service gave him seniority over the other Republican freshmen, replaced retiring Carl Hayden, president pro tempore of the Senate.

Three Republican representatives also won Senate seats previously held by Democrats. They were Edward J. Gurney of Florida, Charles McC. Mathias Jr. of Maryland and Richard S. Schweiker of Pennsylvania. Other Republicans winning seats previously held by Democrats were Henry L. Bellmon of Oklahoma and William B. Saxbe of Ohio. The other two freshman Republicans were Marlow W. Cook of Kentucky and Rep. Robert Dole of Kansas. The two Democrats who won seats previously held by Republicans were Alan Cranston of California and Iowa governor Harold E. Hughes.

In the House the party breakdown when the 91st Congress convened was 243 Democrats and 192 Republicans. In all Republicans took nine seats from the Democrats and lost five of their own for a four-seat net gain. Republicans had scored a net gain of 47 seats in the 1966 elections and had won a special election to fill a Democratic vacancy earlier in 1968. The Republicans had lost 38 seats in the 1964 elections.

Of the 435 representatives elected in November 396 were incumbents (223 Democrats and 173 Republicans), and only 39 (20 Democrats and 19 Republicans) were newcomers. The new winners included two former representatives, one a Democrat and the other a Republican.

The new Congress would have the smallest crop of freshman members in years. Between 1940 and 1948 an average of 96 newcomers were elected to each new House. The average dropped to 68 between 1950 and 1958 but rose to 72 between 1960 and 1966. In 1964 there were 91 newcomers elected and in 1966, 73.

In gubernatorial races the Republican Party, winning 13 of the year's 21 races and capturing seven seats held by Democrats, increased its control of the nation's statehouses from 26 to 31. Even after the selection of a Democrat to succeed Vice President-elect Agnew, the GOP would boast 30 governors, equaling its holdings after the Eisenhower sweep of 1952, when there were two fewer states.

In light of the extremely close presidential race and the continuing, though narrowed, control of Congress by the Democrats, the Republican margin of 10 governorships gave the party its most broad-based mandate for leadership. The GOP scored a net gain of three seats each in the East and the Midwest and lost one in the West. There were no party changes in the South.

Nixon's coattails had a less decisive effect than did Eisenhower's four national elections earlier. Nixon did carry six of the seven states in which Republicans took governorships formerly held by Democrats (including two incumbents). But it was far from clear who helped whom in several of those races. In Montana an easy Nixon win failed to save Gov. Tim M. Babcock, an early Nixon backer. In Rhode Island, the only other race in which a Republican incumbent was beaten, Gov. John H. Chaffee's advocacy of a state income tax appeared to be the major factor in his defeat.

Battling for seats vacated by Democratic incumbents, Republicans won in Indiana, Iowa, West Virginia, New Hampshire and Vermont. State matters, primarily fiscal, were the main issues in all five states. The Democrats suffered particularly through the voluntary retirement of their popular governors in normally Republican Iowa, New Hampshire and Vermont. Except for Montana and Rhode Island the Democrats picked up no seats formerly held by Republicans.

Republicans scored minimal gains in the contests for state legislature seats around the country. As a result of the elections, they would control 20 legislatures, the same number controlled by the Democrats. (The other 10 were split in control or nonpartisan.) The GOP rose in strength from 41.8 to 43.4 percent of the seats in all senate chambers around the country but held static at just over 42 percent of all seats in lower houses.

# 1969-71:
# The 91st Congress

The 91st Congress, which adjourned on Jan. 2, 1971, compiled a substantial record of domestic accomplishments despite drawn-out disputes with President Nixon over foreign policy and spending.

The Senate made the first substantial attempt since World War II to challenge the president's authority on foreign policy and military involvement. Although the House generally agreed to uphold President Nixon's requests to finance new weapons systems and to send money

and troops into Southeast Asia, the Senate engaged in numerous long debates on those issues.

It was in domestic legislation, however, that Congress compiled its most substantial record of accomplishment. This legislation included major air and water pollution control measures, a $25-billion education authorization and a bill extending the 1965 Voting Rights Act and allowing 18-year-olds to vote in national elections. In the final days of the 1970 session Congress completed action on a bill extending the food stamp program that, for the first time, provided free food stamps for the poorest families.

Congress and the administration worked to establish new federal agencies. Foremost among these was the government-owned postal corporation to replace the Post Office Department. Congress also agreed to the president's reorganization plans to set up an independent Environmental Protection Agency and a National Atmospheric and Oceanic Administration in the Commerce Department.

Problems concerning the economy dominated Nixon's first two years in office, and Congress attempted periodically to deal with these problems. In 1969 it enacted a major overhaul of the tax code. It sliced funds from military, foreign aid and space requests and added money to numerous domestic programs, notably education, health, training and pollution control. Congress enacted a federal spending ceiling for fiscal 1971, as it had for fiscal years 1969 and 1970.

Congress engaged in debates over the Vietnam War in attempts to limit deployment of troops and reduce spending. The Senate voted twice to repeal the 1964 Tonkin Gulf resolution, and the House eventually agreed to repeal the resolution.

### The 1970 Midterm Elections

Despite the unprecedented off-year campaign efforts of President Nixon and Vice President Agnew, most observers felt the Republicans suffered a net loss in the elections of Nov. 3, 1970. In their drive to improve the Republican position in Congress and in state capitals, the president campaigned for candidates in 23 states during the weeks preceding the election, and the vice president visited 29 states.

Although the effect of a presidential appearance for a candidate was unclear, Nixon and Agnew could point to victories in several states where they campaigned: Senate victories in Maryland, Connecticut, Ohio and Tennessee, for example, and gubernatorial victories in Connecticut, Tennessee, California, Arizona, Iowa, Vermont and Wyoming. Administration efforts failed to pay off in other states on the Republican target list. Democratic candidates were elected to the Senate in Utah, New Mexico, Wyoming, Nevada, North Dakota and Indiana, despite the high-level administration campaigning. And Nixon or Agnew visits failed to persuade voters to elect Republican senators in California, Texas, Illinois, or Florida.

The most spectacular third party victory of the year was that of James L. Buckley of New York, a Conservative who was elected to the Senate with a minority of the votes. Buckley's election was made possible by a division of the votes for the Republican-Liberal incumbent, Charles E. Goodell, and the Democratic candidate, Rep. Richard L. Ottinger.

Another third party success belonged to Sen. Harry F. Byrd Jr of Virginia. In March 1970 the veteran Democrat announced that he would not run as a Democrat because of a party "loyalty oath" that he claimed would force him to commit himself to the Democratic presidential candidate in

1972. Byrd ran as an Independent, easily defeating the Democratic and Republican candidates.

A second incumbent Democratic senator who ran as an Independent was Thomas J. Dodd of Connecticut. Dodd had been censured by the Senate in 1967 for diverting testimonial funds to his personal use. He was regarded as unlikely to win the Senate nomination in a Democratic primary. His Independent candidacy divided the Democratic vote and helped elect a Republican, Rep. Lowell P. Weicker Jr., to his seat.

## Results of the 1970 Elections

Republicans registered a net gain of two Senate seats in the Nov. 3 elections, leaving Democrats with a majority of 55 to 45 in the 92nd Congress. Of the 35 Senate seats being contested, 11 were won by Republicans, 22 by Democrats, one by a Conservative Party candidate and one by an Independent. Democrats had held 25 of the seats and Republicans, 10. Republicans who captured Democratic seats were Rep. Weicker, Rep. J. Glenn Beall Jr. of Maryland, Rep. Robert Taft Jr. of Ohio and Rep. W. E. Brock III of Tennessee.

In Minnesota Hubert H. Humphrey won back a seat in the Senate, where he had served from 1949 to 1965, when he became vice president. He defeated Republican representative Clark MacGregor for the seat of retiring Democrat Eugene J. McCarthy. In Texas former Democratic representative Lloyd M. Bentsen Jr. defeated Rep. George Bush for the seat held by Ralph W. Yarborough, a Democrat defeated in the May 2 primary.

The Democratic Party showed renewed strength in the Great Plains and the Far West in the 1970 elections as it gained nine House seats to open up a 255-180 margin for the 92nd Congress. Republicans claimed success in limiting Democratic gains to less than the 38-seat average pickup recorded by the nonpresidential party in off-year elections during this century. Democrats said their gains were significant because President Nixon's 1968 victory carried in few of the marginal candidates, who are normally easy prey to the party out of power in off-year contests.

Registering the most impressive net gain in statehouses by any party since 1938, Democrats in 1970 took 13 governorships from Republican control, while losing only two, in Tennessee and Connecticut. The balance of state power shifted dramatically from 18 Democratic and 32 Republican governors before the election to 29 Democratic and 21 Republican governors.

State-level gains were doubly significant in 1970. Democratic control of a majority of the states furnished vital power bases for the 1972 presidential elections. Democrats won Ohio and Pennsylvania and held Texas, thus controlling three of the most populous states. Democrats also wrested from Republican control Alaska, Florida, Arkansas and Oklahoma and the Western and Midwestern states of Idaho, Minnesota, Nebraska, Nevada, New Mexico, South Dakota and Wisconsin. Republicans continued to hold New York, California, Michigan and Illinois.

Republicans went into the 1970 elections holding 51 of the 99 state legislative bodies (Nebraska has a unicameral legislature). This figure included the two nominally nonpartisan legislatures of Minnesota and Nebraska, which were controlled by conservative, Republican-oriented majorities. Democrats held the other 48 chambers. Following the 1970 elections Democrats gained control of eight new legislative bodies, giving them control of 56.

# 1971-73:
# The 92nd Congress

The years 1971-73 saw some of the boldest and most dramatic presidential initiatives in years. In the summer of 1971 President Nixon imposed wage and price controls on the economy, announced that he would visit Communist China and planned a summit meeting with Soviet leaders. His visits to China and the Soviet Union in 1972 gave Nixon a strong boost in his campaign for reelection.

Dissent over the Vietnam War, which seemed on the rise in the spring of 1971, had waned by midyear following troop withdrawal announcements by Nixon. At year's end 45,000 additional troops were scheduled for withdrawal, practically bringing to an end the offensive combat involvement of U.S. ground forces. By late 1972 it appeared that a settlement of the Vietnam War, or at least a cease-fire and return of U.S. prisoners, was imminent. Presidential aide Henry Kissinger and North Vietnamese officials had hammered out a nine-point agreement, but the Saigon government balked, and the elusive peace had to await a final agreement in January 1973.

In October 1972 Congress gave President Nixon a major legislative victory: passage of a general revenue-sharing measure. The bill was the only one of the president's "six great goals" to pass during the 92nd Congress. In 1972 Congress also approved the Equal Rights Amendment, 49 years after it was introduced. The amendment was sent to the states for ratification March 22 after the Senate passed it 84-8.

On June 17, 1972, five men were arrested in the Democratic national headquarters at the Watergate building in Washington, D.C. This incident was the beginning of a process that was to continue over the next two years and destroy a presidency. The break-in was immediately tagged the "Watergate caper" by the press. But by the time the election arrived it had become the "Watergate affair," and it was being examined seriously. In the months following the celebrated break-in, allegations of a widespread network of political espionage and sabotage engineered by the Republicans were carried in the news media. Charges of involvement were leveled by the Democrats and the press against persons in high positions in the White House and the Committee for the Reelection of the President.

Seven men were indicted on criminal charges, three civil suits were filed and one man was found guilty in a Florida court on a minor charge related to Watergate. Two congressional committees initiated staff investigations of the allegations. And Watergate repeatedly surfaced in the presidential campaign, with Democratic nominee George McGovern and his campaign pursuing the charges and President Nixon and his staff denouncing them. Investigators and reporters began to backtrack: meetings, phone calls, financial transactions and other related events were traced back months before the incident.

## The 1972 Campaigns

President Nixon was in a strong position to seek another term as the 1972 presidential election year opened. His wage and price control system had curbed the inflationary spiral, while increased federal spending cut into the unemployment rate. His scheduled trips to Beijing and Moscow promised widespread publicity and a focus on the "peace" half of a peace and prosperity theme. And although he had alienated small groups of Republicans on the left and right wings of his party, Nixon could count on being renominated without much trouble.

The Democrats, meanwhile, headed toward a bruising battle for the nomination that would rip their party apart. Although Maine senator Edmund S. Muskie looked like a strong possibility for the nomination in late 1971, his centrist liberal political stance was not enough to hold the party together. His candidacy soon collapsed in the rush of primary voters toward the left or right wings of the party. Still angry over the Vietnam War, left-wing party activists gathered behind Sen. George McGovern of South Dakota. On the right Alabama governor George C. Wallace gathered voters angry with busing and the rapid pace of social change in general.

Other well-known candidates who entered the fray for the Democratic presidential nomination were Sen. Henry M. Jackson of Washington and Sen. Hubert H. Humphrey of Minnesota. Several other hopefuls failed to gain any significant momentum; among them were former senator Eugene J. McCarthy of Minnesota and Rep. Shirley Chisholm of New York. Chisholm was the first black to run in a series of presidential primaries.

McGovern began his upward climb to the nomination by a stronger than expected showing in the New Hampshire primary. Although Muskie won the popular vote there, he was labeled a loser because he received far fewer votes than expected. From there it was downhill for Muskie, and after he ran fourth in the Pennsylvania primary on April 25, he ceased active campaigning. McGovern, meanwhile, ran first in Wisconsin on April 4, then won Massachusetts, Nebraska, Oregon, and beat Humphrey in a June 6 showdown in California. From there on he was practically assured of the nomination, although there was a last-minute effort at the convention to stop him.

McGovern's highly vocal and longstanding opposition to the Vietnam War caused many political analysts to look on him as a one-issue candidate. But his major problem was one of recognition. Public opinion polls indicated that he had only 2 percent support from the voters in the field of prospective Democratic nominees. By mid-March, after two months of extensive campaigning, McGovern had gained only 3 percentage points in the polls.

Beyond any doubt the reform commission that McGovern had headed after the disastrous Democratic convention of 1968 had changed the face of the Democratic Party. And beyond any doubt the changes favored McGovern's candidacy by expanding the party's base and bringing more women, minorities and youths into the process.

At the convention, McGovern's winning of the nomination was never really in doubt, even before the balloting began, and he moved steadily toward his goal. The Democrats chose Sen. Thomas F. Eagleton of Missouri as their nominee for vice president. But on July 25 Eagleton disclosed that he had voluntarily hospitalized himself three times between 1960 and 1966 for "nervous exhaustion and fatigue." Since 1966, said the candidate, he had "experienced good, solid, sound health." But Eagleton's statement, culminating an investigation by reporters of his past difficulties under stress, started a sequence of developments that included increasing pressure for Eagleton to withdraw from the ticket. After a meeting with McGovern on July 31, Eagleton withdrew from the ticket.

His presidential campaign sidetracked, McGovern announced Aug. 5 that his choice to replace Eagleton was R. Sargent Shriver, former director of the Peace Corps and the Office of Economic Opportunity and U.S. ambassador to France. In a display of unity and anti-Nixon oratory, the newly enlarged Democratic National Committee at an Aug. 8 meeting in Washington nominated Shriver with 2,936 of the 3,013 votes cast.

In the Republican camp the renomination of President Nixon did not go completely unchallenged. He had opposition from both the left and the right. Assailing the president from the left was California representative Paul N. McCloskey Jr., who based his campaign on opposition to administration policies and its deception of the news media. McCloskey withdrew six days after the New Hampshire primary because of insufficient funds, but his name remained on the ballot in 12 other states as a symbolic protest. Nixon's opponent on the right was Ohio representative John M. Ashbrook, who attacked the president for what he called his failure to live up to 1968 promises in fiscal matters, foreign affairs and defense posture. Ashbrook's name was on the ballot in 11 state presidential primaries.

The Republican National Convention was a gigantic television spectacular from start to finish. The main business of the convention, the nomination of President Nixon and Vice President Agnew to a second term, was a preordained ritual.

Nixon did little campaigning for his second term. Because of his strong lead in the polls and lack of speech making, the president also was in the enviable position of making few, if any, concrete campaign pledges to the electorate. He enunciated the major themes of the campaign in his acceptance speech before the Republican convention, emphasizing the divisions in the Democratic Party and urging dissatisfied Democrats to downplay traditional party loyalty.

From almost every standpoint the Democratic campaign contrasted sharply with that of the Republicans. McGovern and his running mate were on the road incessantly from Labor Day until election day. McGovern tried in vain to draw Nixon into debate. His initial tax and welfare reform proposals attracted widespread criticism and helped alienate several traditional sources of Democratic strength, such as ethnic groups and blue-collar workers. When he substituted Shriver for Eagleton, he was attacked for poor judgment and vacillation. His chief issue, administration conduct of the Vietnam War, lost whatever remaining effect it might have had when an administration-negotiated peace appeared to be in sight during the last days of the campaign.

Rather than moving into the offensive against the administration, McGovern was kept on the defensive throughout the campaign, constantly forced to explain earlier positions and rebut Republican charges. The break-in at Democratic headquarters at Watergate in June and ensuing disclosures of the alleged involvement of administration officials in espionage and sabotage directed against the Democrats was potentially damaging, but the charge failed to excite the voters enough to head off the Nixon sweep.

## Results of the 1972 Elections

Nixon swept back into the White House on Nov. 7 with a devastating landslide victory over McGovern. He carried a record of 49 states for a total of 520 electoral votes. Only Massachusetts and the District of Columbia, with a meager 17 electoral votes between them, went for McGovern.

The Nixon landslide was the first Republican sweep since Reconstruction of the once solid Democratic South. By runaway margins Nixon took all 11 states of the old Confederacy, plus all the border states.

Americans engaged in massive ticket splitting in the 1972 election. Nixon's landslide victory was not reflected in significant Republican gains in Congress or in governorships. Despite the avalanche of votes for Nixon, the Democrats scored a net gain of two seats in the Senate, thereby increasing their majority to 57-43 in the 93rd Congress. Of the 33 seats contested, the Democrats won 16 and the Republicans won 17. Nineteen of those seats had been controlled by the Republicans in the 92nd Congress, 14 by the Democrats.

The most significant, and surprising, element of the Democratic gain was the upset of four seemingly well entrenched Republican incumbents: Gordon Allott of Colorado, J. Caleb Boggs of Delaware, Jack Miller of Iowa and Margaret Chase Smith of Maine. If it had not been for Republican gains in three Southern states (North Carolina, Oklahoma and Virginia), the Democratic majority in the Senate would have been much larger.

Half of the eight new Democrats were considered significantly more liberal than the incumbent Republicans they upset. In this category were Floyd K. Haskell, who beat Allott in Colorado; Joseph R. Biden Jr., who defeated Boggs in Delaware; Dick Clark, who retired Miller in Iowa; and Rep. William D. Hathaway, who upset Smith in Maine. A fifth Democrat, Rep. James Abourezk, defeated Republican Robert W. Hirsch in South Dakota to take the seat of retiring Republican incumbent Karl E. Mundt. Abourezk was considered far more liberal than the conservative Mundt.

Two more Democrats were conservatives who replaced conservatives. Sam Nunn of Georgia and J. Bennett Johnston Jr. of Louisiana defeated Republican opponents to fill the seats of Democratic incumbents David H. Gambrell of Georgia and the late Allen J. Ellender of Louisiana. The remaining Democrat, Walter "Dee" Huddleston, defied the Southern election trend by winning his race against Republican Louie B. Nunn in Kentucky for the seat of retiring Republican John Sherman Cooper. Both the incumbent and his successor were moderates.

Final returns showed that Republicans gained 13 House seats in the 1972 elections, far short of the number they needed to win control of the House. The 13-seat pickup was slightly more than the four House seats gained when President Nixon first was elected in 1968, but it was far less than the winning party usually has gained in a presidential landslide. A close look at the House figures showed that the president not only lacked coattails, but appeared to have little if any perceptible effect on House races.

The only semblance of coattail effects in the election was in the South, where the Republicans took seven House seats out of Democratic hands. For several states the election of Republican representatives meant drastic breaks with tradition.

The 1972 election was the first to take place after the reapportionment and redistricting that followed the 1970 census. More than a dozen entirely new districts were created, and others had major changes in their boundary lines. Most of these changes tended to favor the Republicans, because many new districts were placed in fast-growing Republican suburbs and because legislatures in several key states drew the lines to partisan Republican advantage.

Redistricting also played a significant part in the defeat of House incumbents. Thirteen incumbents, eight Democrats and five Republicans, were defeated. For nine of these incumbents, seven of them Democrats, redistricting was the

dominant factor in their defeat. Three lost because redistricting forced them to run against other incumbents.

The House of Representatives in the 93rd Congress looked quite a bit different from its predecessor, but the reasons were mainly because of redistricting and retirement, not election defeats. The new count was 243 Democrats and 192 Republicans.

Chalking up a net gain of one, the Democrats in 1972 retained the wide margin of statehouse control they won in 1970, holding 31 governorships to the Republicans' 19. (Democrats had gained the Kentucky governorship in the 1971 off-year elections.) Of the 18 seats up for election in 1972, Democrats won 11 and Republicans won seven. Despite upsets in several states, the net result was only a minimal change in party power.

Republicans lost governorships in Delaware, Illinois, and Vermont, while ousting Democrats in Missouri and North Carolina. Close races in New Hampshire, North Carolina, Washington and West Virginia were won by Republicans, who also upset a favored Democratic candidate in Indiana. As expected, Republicans won gubernatorial contests in Iowa and Missouri.

Incumbent or favored Republicans were upset by Democrats in Illinois, North Dakota, Rhode Island and Vermont, while Democratic incumbents were reelected in Arkansas, Kansas, South Dakota and Utah. In Montana and Texas, Democrats were elected to succeed retiring Democratic governors. As expected, the Democratic challenger unseated Delaware's Republican incumbent by capitalizing on the issue of taxes.

In West Virginia's gubernatorial race, which drew national attention, Republican governor Arch A. Moore Jr. put together his general popularity and campaigning ability with Nixon's strong showing in the state—and the obvious incongruity of a millionaire populist candidate running in one of the nation's poorest states—to defeat Democratic challenger John D. "Jay" Rockefeller, the secretary of state.

# 1973-75: The 93rd Congress

The legislative activities of the 93rd Congress were overshadowed by one of the nation's greatest political crises: Watergate. Watergate dominated the news from the beginning of the second Nixon administration in January 1973 until the president's resignation on Aug. 9, 1974. The year 1973 opened with the trial of the seven Watergate burglars beginning Jan. 8. Five of the seven defendants pleaded guilty a few days after the trial opened, while the remaining two stood trial and were found guilty by the end of the month. Sentencing was March 23.

From mid-May until early August 1973 American television screens were filled with politicians and former government officials testifying before the Senate Select Committee on Presidential Campaign Activities—the Watergate committee. Most important of all information produced by the hearings was the revelation that tape recordings had been made of many presidential conversations in the White House during the period in which the break-in occurred and the cover-up began. The tapes contained evidence that ultimately led to Nixon's resignation.

Immediately after the existence of the tapes was made public on July 16, a struggle for the recordings began. The legal battle would last a year, from July 23, 1973, to July 24, 1974, when the Supreme Court ruled that Nixon had to turn over the tapes to U.S. District Judge John J. Sirica for use as evidence in the Watergate cover-up trial.

In the midst of the tapes battle, Spiro Agnew, on Oct. 10, 1973, became the second vice president in American history to resign. Under investigation for multiple charges of alleged conspiracy, extortion and bribery, Agnew agreed to resign and avoided imprisonment by pleading nolo contendere to charges of income tax evasion.

Two days after Agnew's resignation President Nixon nominated House Minority Leader Gerald R. Ford of Michigan as his successor. Ford became the 40th vice president of the United States on Dec. 6, 1973.

While Americans were reeling from these events, they were overtaken by an energy crisis, as a result of the Arab oil embargo, and some of the worst inflation to hit the economy in peacetime history.

But even as public attention focused on the presidency and the economic problems of the country, Congress was passing landmark legislation representing an attempt to change the balance of power between the presidency and Congress. Among measures enacted were limits on a president's right to impound money, the establishment of a more thorough method for Congress to consider the federal budget and restrictions on the president's war-making powers.

Investigation of Watergate continued. After two months of closed congressional hearings beginning May 9, 1974, and a series of televised debates beginning July 24, the House Judiciary Committee voted to recommend three articles of impeachment.

On Aug. 5 Nixon released three previously undisclosed transcripts. The conversations showed clearly Nixon's participation in the cover-up. In a written statement the president acknowledged that he had withheld the contents of the tapes despite the fact that they contradicted his previous declarations that he had not known of or participated in the cover-up. These admissions destroyed almost all of Nixon's remaining support in Congress. On Aug. 8 Nixon announced his resignation, to be effective at noon the next day, and Vice President Ford became the nation's 38th president.

A month after assuming office, Ford pardoned Nixon "for all offenses against the United States which he, Richard Nixon, has committed or may have committed" during his years as president.

Ford was succeeded in the vice presidency by Nelson A. Rockefeller, who became vice president Dec. 19, 1974, after the House confirmed his nomination by President Ford, 287-128. The Senate had given its approval Dec. 10, 90-7. Thus the nation for the first time had both a president and a vice president chosen under the 25th Amendment to the Constitution rather than by a national election.

Reacting to presidential campaign abuses, Congress in 1974 enacted a landmark campaign reform bill that radically overhauled the existing system of financing election campaigns. The new measure cleared Congress Oct. 10, 1974, and was signed into law five days later by President Ford. It established the first spending limits ever for candidates in presidential primary and general elections and in primary campaigns for the House and Senate.

Although the Arab nations had lifted their oil embargo, they and other oil producing states refused to lower the posted price for oil. The energy situation became intertwined with the grave economic problems President Ford inherited on taking office. Within months, he and Congress were trying to get together on an economic-energy package that reflected the inseparability of the two crises. The

continuing high oil prices played havoc with the international monetary system and contributed heavily to the deepening worldwide recession.

## The 1974 Midterm Elections

Republicans paid the bill in November 1974 for two years of scandal and economic decline, losing heavily in congressional and gubernatorial elections throughout the country and slipping deeper into a minority status. Democrats gained 43 seats in the House, three seats in the Senate and four new governorships.

As soon as the Nov. 5 election returns were in, Republicans began looking for comfort in the fact that parties holding the White House normally lose heavily in midterm elections. But it was a small comfort. Democrats went into the 1974 election with nearly 60 percent of the seats in the Senate and House. For the most part the Democratic gains in the House were not marginal seats won by Republicans in a previous presidential sweep but solid Republican districts.

If there was one region that disappointed Republicans the most, it was the South. Shortly before the election the South was thought to be the one Republican bright spot. Losses were expected to be lightest in that area, and there was a good chance for the party to gain half a dozen House seats. As it turned out Republicans lost 10 House seats in the South and won only 2 Democratic ones.

The Midwest proved even more disastrous for Republicans. Before the election the Midwest had been the only region of the country in which Republicans held a majority of the House seats. But with a net Democratic gain of 14 seats there, that was no longer true.

A look at the demographics of the election yielded another interesting conclusion: Republicans suffered badly in the suburbs, where much of the so-called emerging Republican majority was supposed to lie. The striking fact about these suburban districts was that they were not marginal. In many cases the suburban districts that went Democratic contained thousands of former Democrats who left their party behind as they became prosperous enough to move outside the city limits. The new suburban middle class had been hard hit by recession and inflation, and Republicans may have paid the price.

Perhaps more important, however, was the prevalence in the suburbs of independent and ticket-splitting voters. Surveys had consistently shown a clear majority of independent voters favoring Democratic congressional candidates in 1974, and the switch in the independent vote probably was concentrated in the suburbs.

The heavy turnover decreed by the election—11 new senators, 92 new representatives, 40 incumbent representatives defeated—broke one of the most consistent political patterns of previous years. The tendency since World War II had been for incumbents to seek reelection as long as they were physically able to serve and for nearly all of them to win.

In 1974 that changed. Thanks to the combination of retirement and defeat, there were more first termers elected to the 94th House than to any other since 1949. More than one-third of the new House was elected either in 1972 or 1974.

## Results of the 1974 Elections

The Democrats scored a net gain of three Senate seats in the Nov. 5 elections. A fourth gain came later in New Hampshire, where the state ballot law commission had at first declared Republican Louis C. Wyman the winner by two votes. But the Senate refused to seat Wyman, eventually declaring a vacancy which Democrat John Durkin won in a special election in September 1975. In addition, the Democrats had gained a seat in Ohio by appointment early in 1974, which they held in the November balloting.

Two incumbents, both Republicans, were defeated in the election. Marlow W. Cook of Kentucky lost by a substantial margin to Democratic governor Wendell H. Ford. In Colorado, Republican Peter H. Dominick was swamped by Democrat Gary W. Hart.

Democrats also captured two seats from which incumbent Republicans were retiring. In a major upset in Vermont Patrick J. Leahy beat Rep. Richard W. Mallary in a close race and became the first Democratic senator in the state's history. Leahy replaced retiring George D. Aiken, the Senate's senior Republican.

The Republicans' only Senate gain was in Nevada, where former governor Paul Laxalt was the winner by 624 votes.

In other races for vacant seats there were no shifts in party lineup. Democratic representative John C. Culver won the seat of retiring Harold E. Hughes in Iowa. In North Carolina former state attorney general Robert B. Morgan easily held the seat of Sam J. Ervin Jr. Two Democrats who defeated incumbents in primaries, former astronaut John H. Glenn Jr. of Ohio and Gov. Dale Bumpers of Arkansas, won landslide victories over weak Republican opposition.

Republicans, while losing Aiken's seat, held onto the Utah Senate seat of Wallace F. Bennett, who retired. Salt Lake City mayor Jake Garn won easily over Democratic representative Wayne Owens.

The Democratic gain was kept modest because the Republicans managed to hold their vulnerable Utah seat and to reelect three incumbents who had been in serious trouble: Senators Robert Dole of Kansas, Henry L. Bellmon of Oklahoma and Milton R. Young of North Dakota.

Three Democratic incumbents in difficult races won reelection. They were Birch Bayh of Indiana, George McGovern of South Dakota and Mike Gravel of Alaska. Other incumbents in both parties won easily.

In the House Democrats gained 43 seats, pushing their number just above the two-thirds mark. They had already made a net gain of five seats in special elections and a party switch, raising their total in the last days of the 93rd Congress to 248. Thus, after the elections, they had won 291 seats.

The Democratic trend was as broad as it was deep. It took away four Republican seats in New Jersey and four in California. It took five in Indiana, five in New York, three in Illinois, and two in Michigan. In nearly all cases the change to a new member of the House appeared to mean at least a slight shift to the left. There were a few new conservative Democratic representatives in the new House, such as John Birch Society member Lawrence P. McDonald of Georgia, but they were exceptions. For the most part liberal Democrats who retired were replaced by persons of similar persuasion, and conservative Republicans were replaced by Democrats who ran against them from the left.

The Republican group in the House was also expected to shift slightly toward liberalism even as it shrank by 43 members. Nearly every House Republican beaten Nov. 5 was counted among the conservatives; the liberal and moderate Republicans generally had little trouble winning reelection. The only serious casualty among the Republican moderates was John Dellenback of Oregon. Moderates such as John B. Anderson of Illinois and Paul N. McCloskey Jr. of California won without serious contest.

Election night was not pleasant for Republicans who remained loyal to President Nixon in the days just before his resignation. Four Republicans who supported Nixon during the House Judiciary Committee's impeachment inquiry were beaten decisively. They were David W. Dennis of Indiana, Wiley Mayne of Iowa and Joseph J. Maraziti and Charles W. Sandman Jr. of New Jersey. Harold V. Froehlich of Wisconsin, who supported two articles of impeachment against Nixon but opposed the third, also was defeated. All the Republicans on the Judiciary Committee who consistently voted to impeach Nixon were reelected, as were several Nixon defenders.

Democrats increased their firm hold on the nation's governorships from 32 to 36. Of the 35 seats up for election Democrats won 27, Republicans won seven, and an Independent was elected in Maine. The new lineup of governorships was 36 Democrats, 13 Republicans, and one Independent. Not since the 1930s had the Democrats—or any party—held as many as 36 of the nation's governorships.

Republicans lost governorships in three of the nation's ten largest states—New York, California and Massachusetts. They suffered three losses in the mountain states—Wyoming, Colorado and Arizona. Besides these states Republicans also lost control of governorships in Oregon, Connecticut and Tennessee, for a total loss of nine.

The Democrats also suffered some gubernatorial reverses, despite their overall net gain. In Alaska, Ohio, Kansas and South Carolina, Republicans picked up state capitols held by Democrats, leaving the Republicans with a net loss of five. Democrats also lost Maine to an Independent.

Perhaps the two greatest upsets in the gubernatorial races occurred in Maine and Ohio. In Maine voters rejected both major political parties, choosing instead James B. Longley, who ran as an Independent. Longley was the first Independent to be elected governor of any state since 1930. In Ohio, Democratic governor John J. Gilligan lost to former Republican governor James A. Rhodes.

Minority groups fared well in gubernatorial contests. Both Arizona and New Mexico elected Spanish-surnamed governors, Arizona for the first time in history and New Mexico for the first time in 56 years. In Hawaii Democrat George R. Ariyoshi became the first Japanese-American to hold the governorship of any state.

There were 15 other newcomers, for a total of 19 new governors. Among them were Edmund G. Brown Jr., D-Calif.; Ella T. Grasso, D-Conn.; Michael S. Dukakis, D-Mass.; David L. Boren, D-Okla.; James B. Edwards, R-S.C.; and Jay Hammond, R-Alaska.

# Years of Uneasy Peace

By the time Jimmy Carter took the oath as president in January 1977, America's confidence had been shaken by almost a decade and a half of violence and scandal. The country had in effect lost its first war; had gone through a series of political assassinations and its first case of presidential resignation; had been besieged by urban, campus and racial violence; and had experienced the strains of an energy crisis and rampant inflation. In large part Carter's victory stemmed from the weariness of the voters with the normal political leadership of the country and their search for a new start. But however great the hopes, President Carter soon became embroiled in national problems and Washington politics. Critics charged him with inflexibility and lack of leadership. His energy bill was stalled and dismantled in Congress. And inflation resumed its seemingly inexorable rise. By mid-1979 few were optimistic that the nation's energy shortages and economic ills would be resolved any time soon. The debate over solutions continued to preoccupy the nation and its leaders.

The Democrats saw a reversal of fortunes in the 1980 election when conservative Ronald Reagan swept Carter from office. Reagan was the first GOP president since Dwight D. Eisenhower to have his party in a majority position in either chamber. The election gave conservatives a chance to control or influence national policy in the executive and legislative branches of government.

In line with his conservative ideology, President Reagan instigated huge tax cuts, which were largely credited with moving the country from recession to prosperity. The president came into office speaking in a traditional Republican manner, calling for a balanced budget. But he presided over the biggest deficits in American history, transforming the United States from the world's biggest creditor nation to the world's biggest debtor nation. During his tenure the national debt increased nearly threefold, from $931 billion to $2.69 trillion.

The Reagan foreign policy took many turns, gradually toning down an early ideological bent and a tendency to exert military muscle—such as in the 1983 invasion of Grenada and the 1986 bombing of Libya. But the focus always was on the Soviet Union. Over the years the United States had grown accustomed to dealing with a Soviet Union that was predictable. Kremlin leaders came and went, but the fundamental Soviet policies remained the same, and Washington did not have to be particularly creative in responding to them. Gorbachev, who came to power in March 1985, during the early stage of Reagan's second term, upset many of the underlying assumptions about Soviet behavior.

At the outset President Reagan vested much of his energy in strengthening the armed forces. He left the presidency as an apostle of superpower disarmament, welcoming U.S.-Soviet summitry that he had once disdained and discarding his earlier belief that the Soviet Union was an "evil empire." Reagan had vowed never to deal with terrorists, but he suffered the humiliation of a White House scandal that involved the secret sale of arms to Iran in an attempt to release American hostages in Lebanon—and the illegal siphoning of the sale proceeds to Central American contra guerrillas.

President Reagan's final year in office was one of warming relations between Washington and Moscow. He took his unique brand of politicking to Moscow May 29-June 2, 1988, for an upbeat summit meeting at which he and Gorbachev exchanged documents ratifying an arms control treaty they had signed the previous December in Washington. It was the first arms treaty ratified by the two countries since 1972 and the first to ban an entire class of nuclear weapons—ground-launched intermediate-range nuclear-force missiles.

Perhaps Reagan's ultimate accolade from the nation's voters was their elevation of his vice president and preferred successor, George Bush, to the Oval Office. In winning the party's nomination and then the presidency in 1988, Bush portrayed himself as the rightful heir to the Reagan legacy.

# 1975-77:
# The 94th Congress

The years 1975-76 gave America a significant respite from the high political temperature of the previous several years. With Richard Nixon gone and the Vietnam War over,

the two great issues that had convulsed the country for so long were gone. But even as the country was cooling off, it found itself stalemated on the prime issues facing it. Congress and the president failed to agree on a workable energy program. A strategic arms limitation treaty with the Soviet Union was put off. And while inflation lessened, unemployment jumped to alarming heights.

As the 94th Congress opened, there were clear differences over what steps to take to cure the continuing economic ills of inflation and recession. The Democrats were calling for a massive tax cut, emergency jobs for the unemployed, housing construction subsidies, an end to certain tax shelters and other proposals aimed at closing tax loopholes.

Ford, who in late 1974 had called for a tax increase to combat inflation, in March 1975 reluctantly agreed to a tax cut package drafted by the Democrats that was retroactive to Jan. 1. He and his advisers insisted that it was just as important to fight inflation as to reduce taxes. For this reason, he vetoed as too inflationary the Democrats' bill to create more than one million jobs; the veto was sustained by Congress even though the national unemployment rate was climbing to its high of 9.2 percent in May. Ford subsequently made an about-face and agreed to a compromise version that had a lower price tag but contained many of the same jobs programs.

No subject consumed more time during the first session of the 94th Congress than energy legislation. But despite the amount of time expended in debate and hearings on energy issues, the legislation enacted fell far short of setting a national energy policy. Congress and the White House were deadlocked on fundamental energy questions, with Ford unable to sell his programs and the Democratic majority unable to draft viable alternatives. After a temporary compromise allowed extension of energy controls until mid-December, a more lasting resolution was attained under which controls would continue until early 1979.

In 1976 Congress generally agreed with the administration's request for increased defense spending. Impressed by evidence of a Soviet military buildup, Congress gave the Defense Department virtually all Ford had requested and accepted the principle that defense spending must continue to grow beyond the amount needed to cover inflation.

## The 1976 Campaigns

Both parties witnessed an intense struggle for the presidential nominations in 1976, with President Ford barely surviving an effort by former California governor Ronald Reagan to deny him the Republican nomination and the Democrats selecting an obscure former governor of Georgia, Jimmy Carter.

Because of the scandals of the Nixon regime and the perceived weakness of the Ford administration, Carter was heavily favored to take the presidency at the beginning of the fall campaign. But the race gradually narrowed, until on election day Carter won by only 2.1 percentage points.

Carter's nomination represented a repudiation of the political establishment by Democratic primary voters. Such well-known names as Sen. Henry M. Jackson of Washington, Gov. George C. Wallace of Alabama, 1972 vice presidential nominee Sargent Shriver and Rep. Morris K. Udall of Arizona, all fell before the little-known Georgian who espoused an anti-Washington rhetoric combined with an appeal to the old virtues. Tired of political corruption and what they perceived as too much government interference in their lives, voters responded positively to Carter's appeal, despite his lack of experience in the federal government.

On Dec. 2, 1974, Carter announced his candidacy for the 1976 presidential nomination. His speech before the National Press Club included most of the themes of his campaign: restoration of public trust in government; reforms to make government more open and more efficient; comprehensive energy policy; thorough tax reform; "a simplified, fair, and compassionate welfare program"; and a comprehensive national health program.

Carter won the New Hampshire primary Feb. 24 with 28.4 percent in a field of nine candidates, including write-ins. In Massachusetts on March 2, Carter ran behind Jackson, Udall and Wallace but picked up 16 delegates. The same day he won Vermont's advisory primary with more than 42 percent against three other candidates. His next major test came March 9 in Florida, where he had vowed to defeat Wallace. When all the votes were counted, Carter had beaten Wallace 34.5 to 30.5 percent. Jackson was third with 23.9. Most observers felt that if Jackson had stayed out of the race Carter's victory over Wallace would have been much stronger.

Carter ended the longest primary season ever with 38.8 percent of all votes cast. Of the 27 presidential preference primaries, Carter finished first in 17 and second in eight. On the way to the nomination, he eliminated a dozen candidates who entered the campaign and showed enough strength to block his greatest potential rival, Sen. Hubert H. Humphrey.

Jimmy Carter brought the Democratic Party's diverse elements together in July at its national convention. The four-day convention in New York City was the party's most harmonious in 12 years and a stark contrast to the bitter and divisive conventions of 1968 and 1972.

Balloting for president was merely a formality. Besides Carter, three other names were placed in nomination: Udall, California governor Jerry Brown and anti-abortion crusader Ellen McCormack. The proceedings, however, turned into a love-feast as Udall before the balloting and Brown afterwards appeared at the convention to declare their support for Carter. On the presidential roll call Carter received 2,238½ of the convention's 3,008 votes, topping the needed majority little more than halfway through the balloting with the vote from Ohio. The following morning Carter announced that his choice for vice president was Minnesota senator Walter F. Mondale.

Gerald Ford ran his campaign on his two-year performance record as president. The plan was to cultivate the image of an America healed of its divisive internal wounds, involved in a promising economic recovery, and at peace both at home and abroad. In doing this Ford had many of the incumbent's powers of policy making, media access and patronage. All of these were to be used against Ronald Reagan, who announced his candidacy Nov. 20, 1975.

Ford began early to capitalize on his position, spending considerable time in the fall of 1975 traveling across the country. Knowing that Reagan would have to make bold stands on key issues, Ford hoped to remain presidential in his own low-key manner.

At first the plan seemed to work. Ford won New Hampshire by about 1,500 votes. In Florida, where he was once thought far behind, the president was helped by older voters' fears that Reagan would alter the Social Security system. Ford scored a convincing victory. Following a big win in Illinois March 16, Ford strategists hoped to build a party consensus that would force Reagan to withdraw and support the president's nomination before the campaign moved into Reagan's Sun Belt strongholds. As they had

done privately before the campaign had begun, Ford's supporters began publicly urging Reagan to pull out of the race in the name of party unity. It was at that point that the plan, as scheduled, began to bog down.

Reagan scored a series of important victories in the South and Southwest. By mid-May the Ford candidacy had fallen behind in the convention delegate count. Ford survived with a large victory in his home state of Michigan on May 18, breaking Reagan's momentum. Added to that victory were stepped-up efforts to cash in on Ford's incumbency with a flurry of patronage in key primary states and more effective usage of Ford's access to the press. The two candidates split the six May 25 primaries evenly, with Ford taking Kentucky, Tennessee and Oregon. The Border state wins were interpreted as a success for Ford, showing he could compete with Reagan for conservative votes.

The president finally regained the edge in the delegate count in late May by persuading his technically uncommitted supporters in New York and Pennsylvania to declare for him. Ford ended the primary season with an easy win in New Jersey and a hefty margin in Ohio. Reagan kept close with a landslide victory in California, ensuring that the nomination would turn on the status of the uncommitted delegates to the convention.

The Republican delegates arrived in Kansas City for their convention in August more evenly split than they had been since 1952. Both President Ford, breaking with tradition, and Ronald Reagan arrived in town three days before the balloting to continue their pursuit of delegates.

On the presidential roll call, Reagan, bolstered by the votes in California and some Deep South states, took a healthy lead. But Ford's strength in the big Northeastern states—New York, New Jersey, Pennsylvania, Connecticut, Ohio—and others such as Minnesota and Illinois pushed Ford ahead. There was a pause as the Virginia delegation was individually polled. And then West Virginia put the president over the top.

The final vote was 1,187 for Ford, 1,070 for Reagan, one vote from the New York delegation for Commerce Secretary Elliot L. Richardson and one abstention. On a voice vote the convention made the nomination unanimous.

Ford the next day selected Sen. Robert Dole of Kansas as his running mate after Reagan ruled out his acceptance of the second spot. Dole was seen as an effective gut fighter against the Carter forces who would allow Ford to keep his campaign style presidential.

Ford's basic campaign strategy was to portray himself as an experienced leader, a calm and reasonable man who had restored openness and respect to the presidency. Carter's strategy was to attack Ford as an inept leader who lacked the imagination and instincts to move the country forward.

Also campaigning was Eugene J. McCarthy, who ran as an Independent, unaffiliated with any party. The McCarthy campaign was aimed at people who had been frequent nonvoters in the past, a group making up nearly half the potential electorate. The Democrats, however, saw the McCarthy voter as a liberal Democrat who would choose Carter over Ford in a two-way race.

## Results of the 1976 Elections

On Nov. 2 Jimmy Carter swept the South, took a majority in the East and did well enough in the Midwest to struggle home with a victory. But it was not easy. Carter's win in Ohio by 11,000 votes still left him with the smallest Electoral College margin since Woodrow Wilson won reelection in 1916. Without Ohio's 25 electoral votes, Carter's total would have dropped to 272, giving him the smallest edge in a hundred years.

In several states McCarthy's Independent candidacy appeared to have tipped the balance to Ford, although in the national popular vote count McCarthy made little impact, receiving less than 1 percent of the total.

Carter won by welding together varying proportions of Roosevelt's New Deal coalition: the South, the industrial Northeast, organized labor, minorities and the liberal community. Carter won majorities in each of these regions and voting groups and made a better than usual showing for a Democratic candidate in the rural Midwest.

Ford made his best showing in the West, winning 53 percent of the popular vote and carrying all but one state, Hawaii. Neither Ford nor Carter ran well in the region during the primaries, but the president benefited from traditional Republican strength and the absence of an intensive Carter effort in the region to score a series of one-sided victories.

An unusual number of new people were elected to the Senate in 1976, but it changed little in ideology and none at all in party lineup. Voters turned nine incumbent senators out of office, more than in any year since 1958. But they took care to treat both parties about the same way, and when the 95th Congress convened in January, there were 62 Senate Democrats and 38 Republicans, just as there were in the Senate that had left in October.

It was an extraordinarily large freshman class—18, including the replacement for Vice President-elect Mondale. Ten of the first-termers were Democrats; eight were Republicans. The large-scale rejection of incumbents had not been expected. The nine who lost represented more than one-third of all the incumbents seeking reelection. By some stroke of challengers' luck virtually every senator who found himself in a difficult race lost.

Three Democratic senators in the "class of 1958"—Vance Hartke of Indiana, Gale W. McGee of Wyoming and Frank E. Moss of Utah—lost decisively. The other four were easy winners. They were Robert C. Byrd of West Virginia, Harrison A. Williams Jr. of New Jersey, Howard W. Cannon of Nevada and Edmund S. Muskie of Maine.

But the group of senators that did worst in 1976 was the Republican "class of 1970," who had won their first terms six years earlier with Nixon administration help. All six senators ran for second terms in 1976, and four were beaten: J. Glenn Beall Jr. of Maryland, Bill Brock of Tennessee, James L. Buckley of New York (elected as a Conservative) and Robert Taft Jr. of Ohio.

The classes of 1958 and 1970 thus accounted for seven of the nine incumbent defeats on Nov. 2. The other two beaten incumbents were Democrats John V. Tunney of California and Joseph M. Montoya of New Mexico.

The ten new Democrats were Dennis DeConcini of Arizona, Spark M. Matsunaga of Hawaii, John Melcher of Montana, Howard M. Metzenbaum of Ohio, Daniel Patrick Moynihan of New York, Donald W. Riegle Jr. of Michigan, Paul S. Sarbanes of Maryland, Jim Sasser of Tennessee, Edward Zorinsky of Nebraska and Wendell R. Anderson, appointed from Minnesota.

The eight new Republicans were John H. Chafee of Rhode Island, John C. Danforth of Missouri, Orrin G. Hatch of Utah, S. I. "Sam" Hayakawa of California, John Heinz of Pennsylvania, Richard G. Lugar of Indiana, Harrison "Jack" Schmitt of New Mexico and Malcolm Wallop of Wyoming.

In the House the Democratic freshmen taught the Republicans a lesson in the power of incumbency, winning reelection almost unanimously to ensure a Democratic majority by the same 2-1 margin the party held in the 94th Congress. Democrats won 292 House seats, and the Republicans, 143.

The Democratic freshmen used the perquisites of office with consummate skill to build political strength and resist close identification with the rest of Congress and the federal bureaucracy. The nationwide Republican effort to brand them as big-spending radicals flopped and left the House GOP in the same minority status as before the elections.

Only 13 House incumbents—eight Democrats and five Republicans—lost their seats. This was far below the number retired by the voters in 1974, when 36 Republicans and four Democrats were defeated in the Watergate landslide that raised the Democrats to overwhelming dominance in the chamber.

The majority of the Democratic seats were safe, while most of the Republican ones were up for grabs, and many were won by the Democrats. The GOP held onto only nine of its 17 seats while winning three held by Democrats, for a net loss of five in this open category.

In gubernatorial races the Democrats gained one more governorship, defeating Republican candidates in 9 states out of the 14. The new lineup was 37 Democrats, 12 Republicans and one Independent, James B. Longley of Maine. Most of the races for governor ended as expected. Voters reelected five incumbents, defeated two others and elected nine new governors.

The one real upset was in Missouri, where Democrat Joseph P. Teasdale defeated Republican governor Christopher S. "Kit" Bond by 13,000 votes. Bond, Missouri's first GOP governor since World War II, was expected to win a second term.

Four states—Montana, North Dakota, Utah and Washington—chose Ford over Carter but elected Democratic governors. Delaware voted for Carter but elected a Republican as governor.

# 1977-79:
# The 95th Congress

With a new and unknown president taking office in January 1977, Congress and the nation waited expectantly to see how Carter would tackle the intractable problems of energy and the economy. In addition, the new president would have to work out a constructive relationship with a Congress that had asserted its power after a long period of presidential dominance. It was also a Congress that had selected new Democratic leadership on both sides of the Capitol, caused by the retirement of Senate Majority Leader Mike Mansfield, D-Mont. and House Speaker Carl Albert, D-Okla.

In foreign affairs the country was at peace, but the administration had to plunge into the labyrinths of relations with the Soviet Union and China and wrestle with attempts to achieve peace in the Middle East.

Carter did not hesitate to get to work on these difficult problems, early proposing an economic stimulus package and an energy program. It soon became clear, however, that major roadblocks stood in the way of enacting significant legislation, especially in the energy area.

The lack of consensus on crucial issues, both in Congress and among the public, was one problem. Another was the continued rivalry between the legislative and executive branches, with congressional leaders accusing the new administration of ineptness and lack of leadership and the executive pointing to Congress' inherent inability to lead.

The partial deadlock reflected the malaise of a country that seemed to be ending its era of predominance in the world and continued economic expansion at home. How the country would cope with the new era remained unclear at the close of 1978.

The House installed Thomas P. O'Neill Jr., D-Mass., as Speaker. In a sharp contest for House majority leader, moderate representative Jim Wright of Texas won out. In the Senate, Democratic whip Robert C. Byrd of West Virginia was chosen unanimously as the new majority leader. Republicans also had a leadership contest for Senate minority leader, with Sen. Howard H. Baker Jr., R-Tenn., the victor.

In January 1978 President Carter presented Congress with his major tax cut and reform program. After working on taxes most of the year, Congress gave final approval Oct. 15 to an $18.7 billion tax cut for 1979 that included a substantial reduction in the tax on capital gains. The bill provided individual income tax reductions that were designed to offset Social Security and inflation-induced tax increases for 1979. In addition, it provided about 4.3 million taxpayers—mostly in the middle- and upper-income ranges—with generous capital gains tax reductions. For businesses, the bill included a reduction in corporate income tax rates and expanded investment tax credits.

In April 1977 Carter introduced his energy policy. For most of 1978 the measure was bogged down in the conference committee trying to resolve differences over the natural gas pricing section. Finally, on Oct. 15, 1978, Congress cleared the bill and sent it to the president.

In the summer of 1977 a political scandal hit the Carter administration that damaged the president's popularity. Questions were raised in the press about the propriety of a number of transactions that Bert Lance, Carter's director of the Office of Management and Budget, had engaged in during his banking career. The Lance matter preoccupied the White House until Lance's resignation in September 1977.

The Carter administration in 1977 laid the groundwork for two treaties with Panama, which were ratified by the Senate in April 1978. One would turn over the Panama Canal to Panama by the year 2000; the second guaranteed the United States' right to defend the canal after that date.

Carter's greatest foreign policy triumph came in September 1978 when he met at Camp David with Egyptian president Anwar Sadat and Israeli prime minister Menachem Begin to hammer out the outlines of a Middle East peace. The success of that effort gave Carter a major boost in prestige and in the polls. And it laid the groundwork for a possible solution to the 30-year-old Middle East conflict.

President Carter had one more big foreign policy surprise for 1978. In a joint communiqué issued Dec. 15, the United States and the People's Republic of China announced that they would formally recognize each other by Jan. 1, 1979, and would exchange ambassadors and establish embassies March 1. This announcement ended another longstanding dispute: the 38-year refusal of the United States to recognize the Communists as the rulers of China.

## The 1978 Midterm Elections

Republicans in the 1978 midterm campaign were curiously unable to capitalize on their own carefully developed issues in what ought to have been their kind of year.

Without a Republican president to have to defend, GOP congressional candidates were free to run against every branch of the federal government, a traffic that brought them enormous gains the last time they tried it, in 1966. Besides, the rise of tax resentment gave them a drum to beat, and they pounded on it in virtually every contested congressional district in the country.

Humiliated by their failure to gain any House or Senate seats at all in 1976, Republicans redesigned their strategy for the 1978 campaign. In the House they abandoned their attempts to defeat many of the Democrats first elected in 1974, switching to place their emphasis on older incumbents weak in constituent service and name identification. In both the House and Senate they involved themselves in primaries to see that promising candidates won.

But Republican leaders made one other decision that did not work as well as they had hoped: they chose to base congressional campaigns throughout the country on a plan, proposed by Rep. Jack F. Kemp of New York and Sen. William V. Roth Jr. of Delaware, to cut federal income taxes by one-third. It was difficult to find a Republican nominee in any contested state or district who did not talk about Kemp-Roth.

The Republican approach allowed Democratic opponents to seize the popular side of the issue by charging that a Kemp-Roth tax cut was inflationary. Democrats insisted that spending cuts were the proper course, co-opting normal Republican rhetoric.

## Results of the 1978 Elections

The 1978 elections produced a Republican gain of three seats in the Senate, along with the second largest freshman Senate class in the history of popular elections. The new Senate lineup for the 96th Congress was 59 Democrats and 41 Republicans. The Democratic total included Harry F. Byrd Jr. of Virginia, elected as an Independent. While the GOP increase was not overwhelming, it was slightly greater than what GOP officials themselves expected a year before.

The GOP newcomers included Nancy Landon Kassebaum of Kansas, the first woman elected to the Senate without being preceded in Congress by her husband, and Thad Cochran, the first Republican senator elected in Mississippi since 1875. The only black in the Senate during the 95th Congress, Edward W. Brooke of Massachusetts, was defeated.

The large freshman classes of 1976 and 1978 differed markedly from their counterparts of the previous generation. The new freshman classes represented no distinct national trends. The 1976 class of 18 was composed of eight Republicans and 10 Democrats, and the 1978 newcomers included 11 Republicans and nine Democrats. The large Senate turnover in the 1970s meant that nearly half the members—48—were in their first terms as of January 1979.

The most notable conservative gains in the Senate occurred in Iowa, where Republican Roger Jepsen unseated incumbent Dick Clark, and in New Hampshire, where incumbent Democrat Thomas J. McIntyre lost to Gordon Humphrey.

The Democratic class of 1972 turned out to be somewhat more vulnerable than the Republican group. Democrats lost Clark, William D. Hathaway of Maine and Floyd K. Haskell of Colorado. In addition to their defeats, the seat of retiring Democratic senator James Abourezk of South Dakota was upturned by the Republicans.

Freshmen Democrats included Howell Heflin and Donald Stewart (both of Alabama), David Pryor (Arkansas),

Paul E. Tsongas (Massachusetts), Carl Levin (Michigan), Max Baucus (Montana), J. James Exon (Nebraska), Bill Bradley (New Jersey) and David L. Boren (Oklahoma). Republican newcomers were William L. Armstrong (Colorado), William S. Cohen (Maine), Rudy Boschwitz and David Durenberger (Minnesota), Larry Pressler (South Dakota), John Warner (Virginia) and Alan K. Simpson (Wyoming).

In the House, Republicans made modest inroads on the lopsided Democratic majority, making a net gain of 11 seats. But Democrats remained in firm control, winning 277 seats to 158 for the GOP. With a record 58 open seats in the House, Republicans hoped to make their biggest gains in the 39 open districts held by Democrats. But that strategy brought only a net gain of two, as Republicans captured eight Democratic-held open seats but lost six of their 19 vacant seats to the Democrats.

Campaigning against incumbents, usually a harder task, proved surprisingly successful for the GOP, as 14 Democratic House members were defeated, compared to five Republicans. It was the largest number of Democratic defeats since 1966, when 39 House Democrats, many of them brought in during the 1964 presidential landslide, lost their jobs.

In gubernatorial politics Republicans moved a step closer to respectability, increasing the number of statehouses under their control from 12 to 18. William Clements's upset election in Texas, Richard L. Thornburgh's come-from-behind triumph in Pennsylvania, and James A. Rhodes's narrow survival in Ohio guaranteed that the GOP would enter the 1980 election year with governors in five of the ten "megastates." That news diluted the Republican disappointment at failing to oust Democratic governor Hugh L. Carey in New York or even to come close against incumbent Democrat Edmund G. Brown in California.

# 1979-81:
# The 96th Congress

The first session of the 96th Congress passed into history as a contradiction. Members came to Washington in 1979 spurred by a nationwide anti-government mood. Legislators, even some of the more liberal ones, talked bravely of the need to limit federal spending. Contrary to the rhetoric, which continued throughout the year, that session of Congress voted for massive new spending efforts and laid the groundwork for significant new federal involvement in the lives of American businesses and citizens.

The most massive expansion of the federal role was in the package of energy legislation, which was the focus of congressional debate most of the year. It called for spending billions of dollars on synthetic fuels development and imposing a major federal presence in the energy industry. It also was a year when advocates of more defense spending finally recouped from the travails of the Vietnam era and won a pledge of extra billions for the military from a president who initially opposed such increases.

Support for the energy package was grounded in troubled U.S. relations with oil-exporting nations and a continuing upward spiral in the cost of imported oil. Those trends were exacerbated by the crumbling of relations between the United States and Iran after militant Iranians seized the U.S. Embassy in Tehran and held 53 Americans hostage for the return of that nation's deposed shah, Mohammed Reza Pahlavi.

Advocates of higher defense spending, using the Iranian hostage situation as an example, argued more vigorously than ever before that America's strength and influence in the world were declining and that U.S. military strength was falling far behind that of the Soviet Union.

But if Congress acted with determination on energy and some other issues, it acted virtually not at all on the economic troubles of the nation. Faced with double-digit inflation and the threatened onset of a recession, Congress—much like the president—did not seem to know what to do. It appeared both were marking time until 1980 to decide whether federal action would help or worsen America's economic problems.

Congress showed little interest in social, consumer and environmental legislation. The realization was growing that the federal budget was not open-ended and that government spending decisions required some distasteful choices. Nevertheless, members approved Carter's request to create a separate Department of Education.

In 1980, facing an aggressive and unified Republican Party and worried by its own reputation for big spending, the Democratic-controlled Congress began the election year concentrating on trimming programs in order to balance the federal budget. A recession combined with spiraling inflation soon dashed the Democrats' balanced-budget hopes. But these new economic woes also did nothing to encourage the Democrats to resume pushing for some of their favorite programs. In addition, because of escalating campaign pressures, Democratic leaders delayed until after the election consideration of the budget and a number of other key bills.

By year's end, however, the Democrats found their scheme had backfired. Instead of rewarding them for their restraint, the elections had deprived them of their control of the White House and Senate and put them in a substantially weaker position in the House in 1981.

## The 1980 Campaigns

President Carter won enough delegates at his party's primaries and caucuses to win the Democratic presidential nomination. But he faced significant opposition at the convention from Sen. Edward M. Kennedy of Massachusetts. Carter led Kennedy throughout the primary season, but as the convention neared, the momentum seemed to be with Kennedy. Although Carter continued to win more caucus delegates, Kennedy won five of the last eight primaries, which kept him in contention.

At the same time, the president's position in the popularity polls dropped, and Carter found himself in the midst of an embarrassing controversy over his brother Billy's connection with the Libyan government.

Alarmed by Carter's apparently diminishing reelection prospects, several party leaders grew concerned that a Carter defeat in November would drag down dozens of state and local candidates across the country. They called for an "open convention" that could nominate a compromise candidate. And they teamed up with Senator Kennedy to urge defeat of a proposed convention rule that would bind all delegates to vote on the first ballot for the candidate under whose banner they were elected.

When the convention opened, Carter could count 1,981.1 delegates pledged to him—315 more than he needed for the nomination. Kennedy had 1,225.8 delegates, and the only chance he had to gain the nomination was to defeat the rule. There were 122.1 uncommitted delegates and two for other candidates.

In the days before the convention opening Kennedy strategists claimed that there were continuing defections from the Carter camp. On Sunday they said they were within 50 to 100 votes of the majority needed to overturn the rule binding the delegates. But the Kennedy predictions and hopes proved to be exaggerated. The final tally on the rule showed 1,936.418 delegates favoring the binding rule and 1,390.580 opposing it. Passage of the rule ensured Carter's renomination. Shortly after the vote, Kennedy ended his nine-month challenge to the president by announcing that his name would not be placed in nomination on Aug. 13.

But Kennedy did not withdraw from the platform debate. The bitterly contested party platform pitted Carter against Kennedy and a coalition of special interest groups. The final document was filled with so many concessions to the Kennedy forces that it won only a halfhearted endorsement from the president.

Kennedy capped his platform victories with an Aug. 12 appearance before the delegates in which he presented a stunning speech to a tumultuous ovation. His speech created a sense of enormous energy within the hall and left the feeling that a significant political event had occurred.

By the following day Carter began to reassert control over the convention. In a statement issued just hours after the platform debate ended, the president refused to accept—as diplomatically as possible—many of the platform revisions. In his carefully worded statement, Carter did not flatly reject any of Kennedy's amendments, but he did not embrace them either. Carter concluded his statement with the unity refrain that had become the hallmark of every White House comment on the platform since the drafting process began: "The differences within our party on this platform are small in comparison with the differences between the Republican and Democratic party platforms."

Carter won his party's presidential nomination on the first ballot, and his vice president, Walter F. Mondale, easily won renomination. Kennedy pledged his support and even made a brief appearance on the platform with Carter and Mondale as the convention drew to a close. But it was uncertain whether the appeals for unity had succeeded.

On the Republican side Ronald Reagan had carefully cultivated an image as the presumed GOP front-runner for 1980 from the day Gerald Ford was defeated by Carter in 1976. During the primaries Reagan lost only four of the state preference primaries he entered. In states that chose their delegates in caucuses, Reagan was even more impressive, winning just under 400 of the 478 delegates picked by caucuses. But it was in the early primaries that Reagan was able to pare the field from a half-dozen major candidates to just two.

In South Carolina on March 8 Reagan knocked former Texas governor John B. Connally out of the race. Ten days later he deflated John B. Anderson's surging campaign with a victory in the representative's home state of Illinois. A similar result two weeks later in Wisconsin forced Anderson out of the GOP contest and into an unsuccessful Independent bid for the White House.

After four quick defeats Senate minority leader Howard H. Baker Jr. of Tennessee dropped out. Neither Rep. Philip M. Crane of Illinois nor Sen. Robert Dole of Kansas had ever caught the voters' attention. And on March 15 former president Gerald Ford put to rest growing speculation that he might jump into the race in an effort to stop Reagan. By April the GOP contest was reduced to former Texas representative George Bush's frantic efforts to catch Reagan in a few major states. It was too little, too late.

Having outdistanced all the competition, Reagan easily won his party's 1980 nomination at the Republican National Convention in Detroit. Reagan won on the first ballot, receiving 1,939 of the 1,994 delegate votes. His nomination was then made unanimous.

The unusual flap over the selection of the vice presidential nominee provided the only suspense at the convention. Rumors circulated that Ford was being tapped for the second spot. Ford himself had encouraged that speculation, although he declined to spell out his conditions. It became clear he wanted responsibilities that would have made him, in effect, co-president with Reagan. Late on July 16 the Reagan-Ford arrangement fell apart, and the two men agreed that it would be better for Ford to campaign for the GOP ticket than to be a member of it. The speculation prompted Reagan to make an unusual visit to the convention hall at 12:15 a.m. on July 17 to to announce his choice of George Bush as his running mate.

The American hostage crisis was injected into the campaign in the eleventh hour when Iranian leaders miscalculated that Carter would accept their demands in return for release of the hostages before election day. Although Carter tried to keep the negotiations—which reached a peak during the weekend before Nov. 4—out of the campaign, the publicity given them so close to the election worked against the president.

But what hurt Carter the most, in the opinion of many analysts, was his inability to improve the state of the economy. Throughout the fall campaign Reagan blamed Carter for almost tripling the inflation rate he had inherited from the Ford administration. During 1980 the rate averaged about 13 percent.

No one publicly forecast the rout that developed election night. Reagan's sweep was nationwide. In most of the states that were expected to be close or to go for Carter, Reagan won, frequently by comfortable margins. In states Reagan was expected to carry, he won overwhelmingly.

Reagan easily carried every region of the country, including the keystones of Carter's triumph four years before—the industrial Northeast and the president's native South.

## Results of the 1980 Elections

The Republican victory did not stop with the presidency. The GOP rode the crest of a breathtaking sweep to take control of the Senate for the first time in a quarter-century. Although the Democrats retained their majority in the House, the national shift to the political right combined with a variety of scandals, complacency by some incumbents and unusually strong Reagan coattails cost the Democrats a net loss of 33 seats in the House. That made the Republicans 26 seats shy of controlling the House, although conservative Democrats were expected to give the GOP an ideological edge on many issues.

The 12 Senate seats won by Republicans represented the largest net gain in the Senate for any party since 1958, when the Democrats took control over 15 new seats. The new lineup was 53 Republicans and 47 Democrats. The 1980 GOP Senate victory was the first since 1952 and ended the longest one-party dominance of the Senate in American history.

In addition to their increases the Republicans held on to the 10 seats that were up in 1980. That included holding three open seats in Pennsylvania, Oklahoma and North Dakota and the New York seat of Republican senator Jacob K. Javits, who was defeated for renomination in the primary but ran for reelection on the Liberal Party ticket.

Democrats had 24 seats before the election and lost half of them. Not only would the Senate be more Republican; it would be noticeably more conservative. Several pillars of Democratic liberalism went down to defeat, including George McGovern of South Dakota, Warren G. Magnuson of Washington and John C. Culver of Iowa.

To replace the Democrats, Republicans elected a freshman Senate class made up largely of dedicated conservatives. Representatives Charles E. Grassley of Iowa, Steven D. Symms of Idaho, James Abdnor of South Dakota and Robert W. Kasten Jr. of Wisconsin had compiled distinctively conservative records in the House. John P. East of North Carolina, an expert in conservative political thought, was expected to carry out his beliefs in the Senate.

But there was a contingent of Republican moderates that could leaven some of the conservative impulses. Warren Rudman of New Hampshire, Arlen Specter of Pennsylvania and Slade Gorton of Washington all were from the moderate wing of their party.

Among the losing Democrats were four of the six prime targets of the National Conservative Political Action Committee, which prepared hard-hitting ads attacking the records of liberal senators. The targeted senators were Birch Bayh of Indiana, Culver of Iowa, McGovern of South Dakota, Thomas F. Eagleton of Missouri, Frank Church of Idaho and Alan Cranston of California. Bayh, Culver, McGovern and Church went down to defeat.

In the House the lineup going into the election was 273 Democrats to 159 Republicans. There also were three vacancies that had been held by Democrats. After the November vote, the new lineup was 243 Democrats to 192 Republicans. The Democratic total included one Independent.

The Republican net gain of 33 seats was the largest increase for the GOP since 1966. Most of the GOP gains came at the expense of incumbents. In all, 31 of the 392 incumbents running for reelection were turned out. Of those, 27 were Democrats who lost to Republicans. Only three incumbent Republicans were defeated.

There were 74 new faces in the new House, three fewer than in 1978. Republican freshmen had the edge with 52 seats, compared to 22 for the Democrats. Four new women—all Republicans—were elected, bringing the total number of women in the House to 19. There were four black freshmen, for a total of 17 black voting members. All were Democrats.

Republicans increased their hold on governorships by four states, bringing their nationwide total to 23. Democrats still maintained a lead, with 27 governors' chairs. The Republican additions came in states west of the Mississippi River: Arkansas, Missouri, North Dakota and Washington.

The Republican gain continued the party's gradual comeback on the gubernatorial level. After 1968, when the party won 31 governorships compared with the Democrats' 19, GOP gubernatorial fortunes slid to a low of 12 in 1977. The party began to make gains again in 1978, boosting its total by six. In 1979 the GOP added another governor in Louisiana.

Despite the party's success in gubernatorial races, Republicans advanced only negligibly in state legislatures, which were to redraw political boundaries in post-1980 census redistricting.

# 1981-83:
# The 97th Congress

Dominated by Republicans for the first time in two and a half decades and guided by a forceful and popular president, Congress took bold steps in 1981 toward reducing the federal government's scope. Following the wishes of President Reagan, the 97th Congress slashed government spending, cut taxes for individuals and business and slimmed down federal regulatory activities.

The 1980 elections not only swept a conservative Republican into the White House but also floated the GOP into its first Senate majority since January 1955. The change in control meant that committee leadership shifted to the Republicans and that the Democrats were relegated to minority leadership. The new Senate majority leader was Howard H. Baker Jr. of Tennessee.

In the House the Democrats, under the leadership of Thomas P. O'Neill Jr. of Massachusetts, were still in the majority, though by a slimmer margin (243-192) than they enjoyed in the previous Congress. And the conservative leanings of many of their numbers made the Democratic leadership's grasp on House proceedings tentative at times.

When Reagan entered office in January 1981, he laid out what appeared to some to be contradictory goals for his presidency. To revitalize the economy and strengthen the nation, he would cut federal spending yet increase spending for defense, reduce taxes yet balance the budget. Many traditional Republicans in Congress were uneasy with this "supply-side" economic approach. But the GOP leaders in both houses proved to be effective and loyal lieutenants for their president.

Congress enacted $35.2 billion in fiscal 1982 program reductions, cut nearly $4 billion more from appropriations, approved a cut in individual and business taxes totaling $749 billion over a five-year period and added about $18 billion to the fiscal 1982 defense budget drafted by President Carter the year before. But the federal deficit for the year appeared to be heading over the $100 billion mark, and the economy was in recession. In the process of getting his program enacted, Reagan exhausted his winning coalition, stretched congressional procedures out of shape and bruised sensitive legislative egos.

Almost all the sweeping budget cuts Congress approved were made in one package, the budget "reconciliation" bill. The use of the reconciliation method in such a massive way was criticized by some members as an abuse of the budget process. The budget bill touched on virtually every federal activity except defense. Included in it were a multitude of changes in existing law, including provisions to tighten eligibility for public assistance, cut funds for subsidized housing programs, reduce school lunch subsidies and cut Medicaid payments to the states.

In September, when Reagan proposed a second package of $13 billion in further spending cuts and $3 billion in unspecified revenue increases for 1982, the president's coalition began to crumble. Even members who had worked hard for Reagan's first round of cuts had no stomach for a second in a single year. Moderate House Republicans threatened to desert him unless he shielded their pet programs. Conservative Democrats threatened to bail out over the growing deficit, and the Reagan team was split over the question of tax increases.

The president maintained symbolic pressure on Congress to make additional spending cuts, even bringing the government to a halt for a day in late November by vetoing a temporary funding resolution. But Congress was unwilling to make the cuts he demanded. The appropriations process ground to a halt, and the government limped through the end of the year on a series of temporary funding resolutions.

On defense, Congress granted Reagan's request for significant spending increases. The $200 billion fiscal 1982 defense appropriation was the largest peacetime appropriations bill ever approved.

Congress grew increasingly independent of the White House in 1982. The legislators adhered to President Reagan's general course of restraining domestic programs while increasing military spending, but they rejected many of the president's specific proposals. They substantially rewrote Reagan's fiscal 1983 budget and persuaded the president to support a large tax increase only a year after passing his three-year tax cut plan.

While modifying or rejecting many of Reagan's requests, Congress did not originate much of its own legislation in 1982. Faced with soaring federal deficits, members spent a lot of their time defending existing programs from budget cuts rather than trying to create new ones.

## The 1982 Midterm Elections

The 1982 midterm elections produced major change in the House but left the Senate comparatively untouched. A combination of redistricting and recession produced a huge crop of 81 House freshmen, 57 of them Democrats. In the previous 30 years only three other elections had brought in that many new Democrats.

Redistricting played a major role in 1982. This was the election in which reapportionment, the rise of the Sun Belt and the decline of the Frost Belt were supposed to catch up with the Democrats, setting in motion a decade of conservative and Republican advance of power in the House. But it did not work out that way.

The Sun Belt proved the Republicans' greatest disappointment. The nationwide shift in population away from the industrial North gave Southern and Western states 17 new districts, and the GOP at one time hoped to take at least a dozen of them. But Democratic legislative cartography and unfriendly federal court action got in the way, and in the end Democrats won 10 of the 17.

## Results of the 1982 Elections

The only thing remarkable about the 1982 Senate results was the sheer absence of change. Not only did the party ratio remain the same—54 Republicans and 46 Democrats—but 95 of the 100 senators returned to Washington. The class of five newcomers was the smallest in the 68-year history of popular Senate elections.

That stability was itself a dramatic reversal of recent election trends. During the previous decade a Senate seat had been one of the most difficult offices in U.S. politics to hold. While reelection rates for House incumbents regularly had run above 85 percent, senators struggled against well-financed challengers and effective special interest groups.

The Senate outcome was neither the "ratifying" election that Republicans had hoped for after their sweep of 1980 nor the "correcting" election that Democrats had wanted. But there were favorable results for both parties. Republicans kept their beachhead on Capitol Hill, ensuring that Ronald Reagan would be the first Republican president since Herbert Hoover to have a GOP Senate majority throughout his four-year term.

Democrats broke even in an election that could have relegated them to minority status in the Senate for a long time. Of the 33 seats that were contested in 1982, the Democrats were defending 19. They ended up winning 60.6 percent of the races.

In the House, Democrats scored a 26-seat gain, as voters expressed antipathy toward President Reagan's economic program but stopped short of repudiating it altogether. The

outcome revealed an unusual degree of voter frustration with a party only two years into national power.

Democrats won 269 seats to 166 seats for the GOP, giving the Democrats a 103-seat advantage. Going into the election, Democrats held 241 seats and Republicans 192, with vacancies in two districts formerly occupied by Democrats. Twenty-six Republican incumbents and three sitting Democrats were beaten, nearly a mirror image of the 1980 election, in which the GOP lost three incumbents and unseated 28 Democratic members.

Hurt by losses in the economically distressed Midwest, Republicans saw their hold on the nation's governorships dwindle to 16 in the Nov. 2 elections. The Democrats controlled statehouses in 34 states. The GOP's net loss of seven statehouses—the party dropped nine and picked up two—ended a comeback in the party's gubernatorial fortunes. Republicans had been posting gains since 1977, when they hit a low point of 12 governors' chairs.

Of the Republican governors' seats that switched to the Democrats, five were in the Midwest, where the recession had been most acute, hitting both manufacturing and farming. Michigan, Minnesota, Nebraska, Ohio and Wisconsin opted for Democrats. Republican incumbents were retiring in all these states except Nebraska, where Gov. Charles Thone was turned out.

Republicans also encountered a setback in their progress in the South. They held four of the region's 13 governorships in 1982; in 1983 they had just two. Only Tennessee's Lamar Alexander won reelection.

In addition, Democrats took over GOP statehouses in Alaska and Nevada. Republicans assumed power in California, where George Deukmejian edged out Democrat Tom Bradley, and in New Hampshire, where GOP challenger John H. Sununu unseated Democratic incumbent Hugh Gallen. Each party had six open seats at stake. Democrats held all theirs except for California. Republicans managed to retain only Iowa.

Democrats also turned the tables on the GOP in state legislative elections, regaining most of the chambers taken by the Republicans in the previous two elections and ending a six-year decline in the number of legislatures under Democratic control.

# 1983-85: The 98th Congress

Congress and President Reagan generally kept to their own turf in 1983, each going about business with little involvement from the other side. Unlike the first two years of the Reagan administration, when the president essentially wrote the economic script, Congress conducted its 1983 debate on deficits without Reagan's overt participation. And while Congress tried to assert itself on foreign policy, Reagan consistently called the global shots.

There were important bipartisan agreements in 1983 on Social Security, jobs legislation, the War Powers Resolution and fiscal 1984 appropriations bills. But these were rare commodities in a year in which political motivations ranked above policy considerations.

The prime example of this dilemma was the way Congress and Reagan reacted to massive federal deficits. No matter how many experts said soaring deficits hurt the economy, few people were willing to take the politically risky steps needed to cure the problem. Reagan made a calculated decision to stay out of the deficit debate, thereby ducking any responsibility for tax increases his advisers viewed as a

1984 election liability. Anti-deficit rhetoric was a constant refrain among legislators, but Congress took little decisive action on the issue.

Standing behind Reagan, House Speaker Thomas P. O'Neill Jr., D-Mass., in September helped push through a measure allowing the president to keep U.S. troops in Lebanon for up to eighteen months. In backing Reagan on Lebanon, Congress for the first time invoked major parts of the 1973 War Powers Resolution. On Oct. 23, 241 U.S. Marines, sailors and soldiers and 58 French paratroopers were killed by a terrorist truck bomb in Beirut. Subsequent efforts to revise or revoke the measure keeping troops in Lebanon failed in both houses. Under congressional pressure, Reagan announced in February 1984 that he had ordered the troop withdrawal.

Congress reluctantly continued to back Reagan's policy in Nicaragua. The House twice voted to force Reagan to stop backing rightist forces that were fighting to overthrow that country's leftist government. When the Senate refused to go along, a compromise was reached limiting aid to the rebels and requiring Reagan to seek explicit approval from Congress for additional aid.

Reagan won widespread approval in both chambers for the Oct. 25 invasion of the Caribbean island of Grenada. The president said the invasion was necessary to protect some one thousand Americans, mostly medical students, from civil strife that erupted following the murder of Marxist prime minister Maurice Bishop.

Reagan was victorious in most of his defense fights with Congress. He won the go-ahead for production of the MX missile, although the House came within a handful of votes of killing funding for the project.

On domestic issues Reagan met many disappointments on Capitol Hill in 1984. The president could not persuade Congress to approve his social agenda, which featured constitutional amendments to ban abortion and allow school prayer. Nor did Congress adopt his plan to give tuition tax credits to parents who sent their children to private schools, or his enterprise zone system to provide tax relief to businesses that created jobs in depressed areas.

One of the biggest problems remained the massive federal deficit. Although Congress took actions designed to reduce the deficit by $149 billion over three years, the tax increases and spending cuts were viewed as a mere "down payment" on a larger remedy. While legislators spent much of 1984 talking about the evils of the swelling federal deficit, they took only a first step toward a cure. Instead, many members figured they would deal with the problem in 1985, after the November elections.

## The 1984 Campaigns

The focus in the early months of the presidential election was not on Reagan but on the Democratic candidates seeking their party's nomination. Sen. Alan Cranston of California was the first to toss his hat in the ring formally, announcing his candidacy Feb. 2, 1983. But Walter Mondale had informally started his campaign shortly after he and President Jimmy Carter lost to Reagan and George Bush in 1980.

Mondale was never particularly popular with the voters. His public personality and speaking style were bland, his traditional "New Deal" Democratic message seemed stale and, to many, ineffective, and his identification as a candidate of the special interests led voters to look closely and often approvingly at Mondale's competitors.

Before the primaries began, Mondale's main opponent seemed to be John Glenn, senator from Ohio and former astronaut. But the first delegate selection event of the season, the Iowa precinct caucuses of Feb. 20, was disastrous for Glenn as well as for two other conservative Democrats in the race, South Carolina senator Ernest F. Hollings and former Florida governor Reubin Askew. Together these three drew less than 10 percent of the vote. In New Hampshire a week later the results for Glenn, Hollings and Askew were just as discouraging. Hollings and Askew withdrew from the race.

Other challenges came from Colorado senator Gary Hart and from George McGovern, the former South Dakota senator whose losing 1972 presidential campaign Hart had managed. Glenn and McGovern withdrew from the race after Super Tuesday, leaving in contention Mondale, Hart and the Rev. Jesse Jackson, the first black to pursue seriously the presidential nomination of any major political party.

Hart's momentum was blunted almost as quickly as it began. In the week after Super Tuesday, he ran behind Mondale in six of seven delegate selection events. Then Mondale got a much-needed boost by winning the New York and Pennsylvania primaries. His chance to eliminate Hart evaporated when Hart won Ohio and Indiana. Mondale continued to lead in the number of delegates committed to him, and with his win in New Jersey June 5 he had enough delegates to win the nomination. But his campaign ended on the same lackluster note that had characterized most of the last four months; the same day Mondale claimed the nomination, Hart won three other primaries including California's.

Despite the difficult, sometimes bitter, primary season campaign, Democrats mustered a display of party unity at their convention and made a historic vice presidential choice. The Democratic National Convention picked Mondale to be the party standard bearer against President Reagan. As in much of his drive for the nomination, Mondale was almost overshadowed again, this time by the attention generated by his selection of New York representative Geraldine A. Ferraro to be his running mate. Ferraro was the first woman ever chosen for the national ticket by a major party.

President Reagan enjoyed the smoothest road to renomination that any presidential candidate could have. Brimming with confidence that President Reagan and Vice President Bush would be "the winning team" in November, a jubilant Republican Party held its convention in Dallas Aug. 20-23. With the ticket's renomination certain beforehand, the convention was more a celebration for GOP activists than a business meeting. Criticisms from the party's shrinking band of moderates, worried by the strongly conservative tone of the platform, did little to dispel the optimistic mood of delegates, who looked forward with confidence to Reagan's easy reelection victory.

Highlights of the fall campaign were the two presidential debates. The first, held Oct. 7, was focused on domestic issues. Mondale made a strong showing, which lessened his negative image. Equally important was the perception that Reagan turned in a poor performance; the 73-year-old president seemed tired and disorganized, leading journalists and Democrats to suggest that age was catching up with Reagan.

The second debate, on Oct. 21, focusing on foreign affairs, was a draw in the opinion of most analysts. The debate was not a significant boost to Mondale's campaign, and it allowed Reagan to ease concerns about his age and competence raised by his performance during the first debate. The vice presidential candidates also held a nationally televised debate, on Oct. 11. Most analysts viewed it as a draw or gave a slight edge to Bush.

Almost every thrust Mondale made was effectively parried by his Republican opponents. Mondale's efforts to draw attention to the massive budget deficits run up during Reagan's first term by promising a tax increase did not stand a chance against Reagan's promise not to raise taxes. Similarly Mondale's attempts to paint Reagan as a man who favored the rich over the poor, the majority over the minority, did not overcome charges that Mondale was a tool of the special interests.

In the end perhaps no Democrat could have defeated Ronald Reagan in 1984. For one thing most voters thought they were better off than they had been four years earlier. (Reagan first asked that question during his 1980 run against Carter and Mondale.) Perhaps more important, voters seemed to respond to Reagan's upbeat attitude and his promise of continued peace and prosperity.

### Results of the 1984 Elections

There was never much doubt that Ronald Reagan, one of the most popular presidents in American history, would win reelection in 1984. And it would be hard to imagine a vote more decisive than the balloting that gave him his victory. Winning all but one state, he drew 59 percent of the popular vote, and he won a record 525 electoral votes.

Despite the size of Reagan's victory, its meaning remained unclear. The vote clearly exposed the Democrats' limited appeal in presidential elections. On the other hand, Democrats held their own in other elections. In the Senate, rather than gaining as most presidents do, Reagan lost two seats, reducing the Republican majority to 53-47. In the House of Representatives the president's party gained 14 seats, far short of the historical average for landslides. The GOP gained one governor for a lineup of 16 Republicans and 34 Democrats. Only in the state legislatures did the Republican Party make gains that could be considered significant.

Neither the Republicans nor the Democrats came away with quite what they wanted from the 1984 struggle for control of the Senate. Democrats had hoped to regain the majority they lost in 1980, when Republicans took control of the Senate for the first time since the 1954 elections. Republicans hoped that President Reagan's march to reelection would bring about a modest reprise of 1980, making the GOP hold on the Senate more secure.

But in this election Reagan was no trailblazer. Democrats retained 13 of the 14 seats they were defending, and a trio of Democratic House members captured Republican seats: Illinois representative Paul Simon edged out Sen. Charles H. Percy; Iowa representative Tom Harkin defeated Sen. Roger W. Jepsen; and Tennessee representative Albert Gore Jr. took the seat being vacated by Senate majority leader Howard H. Baker Jr. Countering the good news for the Democrats was an unexpected outcome in Kentucky: the defeat of Sen. Walter "Dee" Huddleston at the hands of Mitch McConnell.

Thus Democrats won a net gain of two Senate seats, shifting the party ratio to 53 Republicans and 47 Democrats. That standing was an improvement over the preelection ratio of 55-45 but a comedown from the Democrats' 1983 prediction that the party could recapture Senate control by picking up a number of Republican seats Democrats regarded as shaky.

As it turned out Democrats failed to win most of the GOP seats in the "at risk" category. The biggest Democratic disappointment came in North Carolina, where GOP incum-

bent Jesse Helms narrowly won his bitter battle with Democratic governor James B. Hunt Jr. It was the most expensive Senate contest ever, with the campaigns spending a total of about $22 million.

In four other key states where Democrats had hoped to pull upsets, Republicans prevailed easily: Mississippi senator Thad Cochran won against former governor William Winter; Sen. Gordon J. Humphrey won a second term in New Hampshire; Texas representative Phil Gramm, who switched parties in 1983, replaced retiring GOP senator John Tower; and Sen. Rudy Boschwitz took 58 percent in Minnesota, encountering no problems with Mondale's coattails because the Democratic presidential nominee barely carried his home state.

For the second time in a little over a decade, Republicans watched with disappointment as their presidential standard bearer swept triumphantly across the nation followed by a threadbare retinue of new U.S. House members. The Nov. 6 elections revealed considerable hesitation nationwide over an all-out endorsement of Republican policies, as voters in district after district stopped short of backing GOP challengers who campaigned on their loyalty to Ronald Reagan. After several closely contested battles were decided, Republicans had gained 14 seats, falling well short of making up the 26 seats they lost in the 1982 midterm elections. One seat, still undecided at year's end, eventually remained Democratic.

Not counting the undecided seat, Democrats retained control of the House with 252 members to the GOP's 182. Going into the election, Democrats held 266 seats and Republicans 167, with vacancies in a New Jersey district previously held by a Republican and in a Kentucky district held by a Democrat. Those seats stayed in their respective parties' hands and were filled for the remainder of the term in special elections. As a result of the election there were 43 House freshmen in 1985, a small class, due mostly to the relatively low number of open seats in 1984.

The gubernatorial elections did little to dent the Democratic Party's 2-1 advantage in governorships. Republicans notched victories in North Carolina, Rhode Island, Utah and West Virginia, where the statehouses were left vacant by departing Democratic incumbents. But the Democrats captured three seats, toppling Republican incumbents in North Dakota and Washington and picking up the seat left open by retiring GOP governor Richard A. Snelling in Vermont.

Republicans thus scored a net gain of one seat, boosting the total governorships under their control from 15 to 16 and reducing the number of states in the Democratic column from 35 to 34. The GOP's showing represented an improvement over 1982, when the party suffered a net loss of seven seats. Republicans still remained a long way, however, from capturing a majority of governorships, a feat they had last accomplished in 1969.

# 1985-87: The 99th Congress

The 99th Congress compiled an extraordinary record. It revised the tax code more dramatically than at any time since World War II, rewrote immigration law, approved the most far-reaching environmental bills since the 1970s, boosted student aid, reversed President Reagan's policy toward South Africa and joined him in openly seeking to overthrow Nicaragua's leftist government.

Congress seized the legislative initiative from the White House in 1985 and dominated the Capitol Hill agenda to a degree unmatched since President Reagan took office in 1981. Although Reagan was able to rescue his top domestic priority—tax-overhaul legislation—with a last-minute personal lobbying campaign, the close call was a testament to the altered relationship between the White House and Capitol Hill.

On other issues ranging from deficit reduction to federal farm spending, from South Africa sanctions to Middle East arms sales, Congress called the shots, in stark contrast to the opening year of Reagan's first term.

Lawmakers made a historic year-end decision: passage of the Gramm-Rudman-Hollings legislation, which mandated paring of the federal deficit over the next five years until the budget was balanced in fiscal 1991. Although Congress embraced the budget reduction plan—offered by Republican senators Phil Gramm of Texas and Warren B. Rudman of New Hampshire and Democratic senator Ernest F. Hollings of South Carolina—as the best hope for future deficit control, many who shaped the measure were skeptical about its chances for working.

Deficit reduction had been the top priority of Senate majority leader Bob Dole, R-Kan., when the 99th Congress opened, but the expected deficit bequeathed to the next Congress remained about $180 billion.

In the two most important elections of 1985, moderation seemed to be the winning theme. Democrats retained the governorship in Virginia with Gerald L. Baliles, who mimicked the moderate philosophy of outgoing Democratic governor Charles S. Robb. Similarly, New Jersey Republican governor Thomas H. Kean thrived at the polls by positioning himself as more moderate than his party's national image. Because neither of the gubernatorial elections produced a partisan shift, the nationwide party lineup of governors remained at 34 Democrats and 16 Republicans—unchanged from 1984.

## The 1986 Midterm Elections

The 1986 Senate campaigns deserve special notice for what they said about the state of electioneering in the latter half of the 1980s. Most spectacularly they laid to rest a theory that took hold in 1980—that the GOP's superior financial resources give it an infallible ability to win close contests. The notion gained widespread currency in 1982, when the GOP's high-tech campaign techniques and last-minute infusions of money saved several endangered Republican candidates. That year the GOP won five of the six contests in which the winner took 52 percent or less of the vote.

But in 1986 nine of the 11 races won by 52 percent or less went to Democrats. That achievement came in spite of daunting obstacles: the National Republican Senatorial Committee's nearly 8-1 funding advantage over its Democratic counterpart, a $10 million nationwide GOP get-out-the-vote effort, and an army of consultants, pollsters, media advisers and GOP field staff at the disposal of Republican candidates.

The difference lay in what each side did with the resources at its disposal. In many contests Democrats latched onto issues—of substance and of personality—that by election day were helping them frame the terms of the debate. Even more important, while the GOP was spending much of its money on television advertising and on a technology-driven voter mobilization effort, Democrats built on their strength at the grass roots. They developed extensive local organizations and, especially in the South, reawakened old party apparatuses and alliances.

In a year when there were so many close contests, the Republicans' lack of organizational depth hurt them, particularly in states where Democrats latched onto local issues that seemed more compelling to voters than national Republican pleas to keep the Senate in GOP hands.

The most striking examples of the Democrats' ability to outcampaign their opponents came in the South. All Democrats there used a variation on a single theme: that they were home-grown state patriots, while their opponents were national Republicans with little interest in local affairs. And all used their state's traditional Democratic base to surmount better-financed Republican efforts.

## Results of the 1986 Elections

Democrats on Nov. 4, 1986, regained control of the Senate, which they had lost to the GOP in 1980. Six Republicans who won their seats that year were defeated in their bids for reelection, as Democrats captured nine GOP seats and lost only one of their own to take a 55-45 Senate majority. The results also gave Democrats the largest class of freshman senators since 1958. Of the 13 new senators, 11 were Democrats.

The party's most significant set of victories came in the South, where Democrats won six of seven Senate contests. Their gains elsewhere were scattered across the map. Farm unrest in the Midwest cost two GOP members of the class of 1980 their seats. In Washington State controversy over the possible situating of a high-level nuclear waste site in Hanford helped Brock Adams unseat Republican Slade Gorton.

The Democrats' other gains came in Maryland, where Rep. Barbara A. Mikulski easily won the seat of retiring GOP Sen. Charles McC. Mathias Jr., and in Nevada, where Rep. Harry Reid defeated former representative Jim Santini for the right to succeed retiring GOP senator Paul Laxalt.

The sole Republican pickup was in Missouri. There, former governor Christopher S. "Kit" Bond won the seat held by retiring Democratic veteran Thomas F. Eagleton.

Not every potentially close election broke the Democrats' way. In Oklahoma and Pennsylvania, Democratic representatives James R. Jones and Bob Edgar tried to turn local economic troubles to their advantage. Neither, however, could arouse the core Democratic constituency in the western half of their states. Oklahoma representative Don Nickles and Pennsylvania Republican Arlen Specter both won handily. And in Idaho, Democratic governor John V. Evans lost to conservative Republican Steven D. Symms.

In North Carolina, Democrat Terry Sanford stressed his longstanding ties to the state. At the same time, he painted incumbent James T. Broyhill as a captive of the Washington establishment. In Alabama, Rep. Richard C. Shelby attacked Republican senator Jeremiah Denton for being more interested in his personal agenda of "family" and social issues than in helping Alabama's economy.

Democratic representative John B. Breaux overcame an early lead by GOP representative W. Henson Moore to hold on to the Louisiana seat of retiring Democratic senator Russell B. Long. Breaux hammered away at Moore as a representative of GOP policies that were hurting Louisiana's farmers and its oil and gas industry.

In Georgia, Rep. Wyche Fowler Jr. ran an almost picture-perfect campaign against Republican incumbent Mack Mattingly. Fowler carried just under two-thirds of the state's 159 counties.

Florida's Democratic governor Bob Graham, a popular moderate, put Paula Hawkins on the defensive by portraying the first-term senator as a lightweight with a narrow focus. Hawkins won only 45 percent of the vote, the worst showing of any Senate incumbent.

Superior organization proved to be the key element in Democratic representative Timothy E. Wirth's victory over GOP representative Ken Kramer for the Senate seat left vacant by retiring Colorado Democrat Gary Hart. In California, where media ads played a crucial role, Democratic senator Alan Cranston ran a masterful campaign that kept Rep. Ed Zschau's legislative record in the spotlight for much of the campaign and prevented the Republicans from focusing on Cranston's performance.

House Republicans lost only five seats in 1986, giving the Democrats a 258-177 edge for the 100th Congress. It was an extraordinarily good election for incumbents of both parties. The five Republican incumbents who went down to defeat were Mike Strang of Colorado; Webb Franklin of Mississippi; Fred J. Eckert of New York; and Bill Cobey and Bill Hendon, both of North Carolina. The Democrats suffered only one incumbent casualty: Robert A. Young of Missouri. The number of incumbents defeated was the lowest in postwar history.

The freshman House class of 1986 included 23 Republicans and 27 Democrats. That was larger than the 43-member freshman class of 1984 but much smaller than the 74-member GOP-dominated class of 1980 and the Democrat-heavy, 80-member contingent elected in 1982.

The Republican Party made a strong showing in gubernatorial contests in 1986, winning a net gain of eight governorships. The Democrats, who entered the election holding 34 of the 50 governorships, saw their advantage drop to 26-24. The GOP count was the largest since 1970, when the party last held a majority of the governorships.

Republicans unseated Democratic incumbents in Texas and Wisconsin and won nine open seats that had been held by Democrats, including upset wins in Alabama and Arizona and a solid victory in Florida. Those victories were offset by the loss of three open Republican seats: in Oregon, Pennsylvania and Tennessee.

The base of the Republican success was a small core of popular incumbents: California's George Deukmejian, Rhode Island's Edward DiPrete and New Hampshire's John H. Sununu. The farm crisis that helped oust at least two Republican senators did not hurt most of the party's gubernatorial nominees. Iowa incumbent Terry E. Branstad won, as did three GOP candidates for open seats: Mike Hayden in Kansas, Kay A. Orr in Nebraska and George S. Michelson in South Dakota. Republicans also picked up the governorship in Maine.

Democratic ineptness aided the Republicans in several states, particularly in Alabama, where Guy Hunt became the state's first Republican governor since Reconstruction. In Illinois, incumbent GOP governor James R. Thompson was considered vulnerable to a challenge from Adlai E. Stevenson III, until two associates of Lyndon H. LaRouche Jr. won Democratic primaries for state office, causing Stevenson to renounce his own nomination and run as an Independent. A three-way race in Arizona helped elect conservative Republican Evan Mecham to succeed Democratic governor Bruce Babbitt in Arizona.

Despite the GOP's poor showing in Senate elections in the South, the party made its greatest gubernatorial gains in that region. In addition to picking up Texas and Alabama, the GOP elected Tampa mayor Bob Martinez in Florida, former governor and senator Henry L. Bellmon in Oklahoma and Carroll A. Campbell Jr. in South Carolina.

Democrats claimed three of the four seats being given up by Republican incumbents. Their largest catch was Pennsylvania, where Bob Casey defeated Lt. Gov. William W. Scranton III.

Republicans, however, were disappointed in their efforts to capture state legislatures. Nationwide, Democrats improved their lead in the number of legislative seats they controlled by 179 and won control of the legislatures in 28 states, two more than they dominated before the election. Republicans controlled both chambers in 10 legislatures, down from 11 before the election. Legislative control was split between the two parties in 11 states. (Nebraska has a nonpartisan, unicameral legislature.)

# 1987-89:
# The 100th Congress

The 100th Congress, by its number, had a historic resonance. It convened in the year that the United States was celebrating the bicentennial of its Constitution and the government of checks and balances created by that Constitution.

Fittingly enough, members commemorated the separation of powers that lay at the heart of the Constitution by challenging the president over the Iran-contra affair and by checking his attempt to reshape the judiciary through the appointment of a controversial justice to a pivotal Supreme Court vacancy. The budget deficit engendered partisan wrangling within Congress and between Congress and the president for much of 1987. After the Oct. 19, 1987, stock market crash, however, Congress and Reagan reached accord on a two-year deficit-reduction package.

For the first time since 1981 Democrats were in control of both chambers. Senate Democrats returned to power with a 55-45 margin; Robert C. Byrd of West Virginia was restored to his former position as majority leader. House Democrats, who increased their already formidable edge to 258-177, named Majority Leader Jim Wright of Texas to succeed Speaker Thomas P. O'Neill Jr. of Massachusetts, who had retired in 1986. Wright was unopposed.

Two issues consumed as much if not more congressional attention than the perennial budget battles. The Iran-contra affair rarely left the front pages from February 1987, when a White House commission said the president had all but lost control of his national security apparatus, to November, when the Senate and House select committees investigating the scandal published their report. Continual revelations about the White House plan to sell arms to Iran in exchange for U.S. hostages in the Middle East and the subsequent diversion of profits from the arms sale to the contra guerrillas in Nicaragua severely damaged Reagan's public standing.

Almost as soon as the Iran-contra hearings concluded, Reagan's nomination to fill a Supreme Court vacancy created an equally clamorous controversy. Reagan nominated Robert H. Bork, a federal appeals court judge who had gained notoriety when, as solicitor general in 1973, he fired Watergate special prosecutor Archibald Cox. After a bitter fight, Bork was rejected. Reagan's second nominee, Douglas H. Ginsburg, was forced to withdraw his nomination after he admitted that he had smoked marijuana when he was a law student and law professor. Reagan's third nominee, Anthony M. Kennedy, was confirmed unanimously in February 1988.

Despite these divisive battles and other flare-ups between the Republican White House and the Democratic Congress, the two sides managed to reconcile their differences on a number of major issues, including measures to bail out the Farm Credit System and the Federal Savings and Loan Insurance Corporation. For all its productivity, however, the 100th Congress left for its successor a pile of unfinished business, with the deficit-ridden federal budget teetering at the top.

## The 1988 Campaigns

Vice President George Bush's nomination for the presidency was never in any real jeopardy. His candidacy, though, generated little enthusiasm, which encouraged several Republicans to enter the race. Two contenders, former Delaware governor Pierre S. du Pont IV and former secretary of state Alexander M. Haig Jr., left the race early.

The Iowa caucuses gave the Bush forces a momentary scare when their candidate came in third behind Sen. Bob Dole of Kansas and television evangelist Pat Robertson. A week later Bush trounced Dole in New Hampshire and then went on to sweep 16 states on Super Tuesday, shutting Dole out of the March 8 events altogether. New York representative Jack F. Kemp, who had hoped to win the backing of the party's conservative wing, did not fare well in the early primaries and decided to leave the race after Super Tuesday.

Bush confirmed his standing with Republican voters on March 15, decisively winning Illinois. Dole left the race two weeks later. On April 26 Bush won enough Pennsylvania delegates to clinch the Republican nomination.

On the Democratic side eight candidates entered the contest: former Arizona governor Bruce Babbitt; Delaware senator Joseph R. Biden Jr.; Gov. Michael Dukakis of Massachusetts; Rep. Richard A. Gephardt of Missouri; Sen. Albert Gore Jr. of Tennessee; former senator Gary Hart of Colorado; Jesse Jackson; and Sen. Paul Simon of Illinois. Dukakis did not emerge as the clear front-runner until well into the primary schedule.

By mid-March Jackson had accumulated more primary votes than any other Democrat and only four fewer delegates than Dukakis. Then came Wisconsin, where Dukakis beat Jackson by more than 200,000 votes. Dukakis followed his Wisconsin victory with a decisive win in New York. Dukakis went on to win all the remaining primaries except in the District of Columbia, which Jackson took. Even then, Dukakis was not assured of enough delegates until the last round of voting on June 7.

After years of internal warfare the Democrats staged a remarkable show of unity at their convention in Atlanta. The prospects for party peace were not at all guaranteed as the party gathered for its July 18-21 conclave. In the weeks before the convention Dukakis had two main tasks: to select a running mate and to find a way to involve Jackson in the fall campaign.

On July 12 Dukakis announced that he had chosen Texas senator Lloyd Bentsen to be his running mate. The decision angered Jackson supporters, who noted that Bentsen was both Southern and conservative and who believed that Jackson and his message had been slighted. Jackson then seemed to have scaled back his implicit demands that the vice presidential nomination be offered to him. At the same time Dukakis seemed to find ways to demonstrate his respect for Jackson without pandering to him. Both men seemed close to accommodation on platforms and rules issues.

Jackson's willingness to compromise on the platform contributed greatly to the bonhomie of Atlanta, signaling a victory of pragmatism over idealism. As a result the rest of the convention was tension-free, providing the backdrop for a Hollywood-style finale. Jackson himself kicked off the unity collaboration in an electrifying speech that unfurled his famous call for social justice and offered strong words of praise for Dukakis.

With the conclusion of Jackson's speech, his virtual domination of the convention gave way to the business at hand. On July 20 Democratic delegates nominated Dukakis, who won 2,876.25 votes to Jackson's 1,218.5. Jackson conceded by telephone, and the convention then ratified Dukakis's nomination by acclamation.

Running behind Michael Dukakis in the public opinion polls, George Bush came to the Republican National Convention in New Orleans in August with one main task: to convince delegates and the viewing public that he was not the "wimp" pictured by political cartoonists. His choice of Sen. Dan Quayle of Indiana as his running mate, however, heightened many of the doubts he had sought to dispel.

To maintain some suspense, Bush had not been expected to name his choice for vice president until the last day of the convention. But at a welcoming ceremony on Aug. 16, he announced his selection. Concern about Quayle's youth and government inexperience quickly surfaced. A major controversy erupted when reporters questioned Quayle about whether he had used family influence to get into the Indiana National Guard in 1969 to avoid service in the Vietnam War.

While controversy swirled around Quayle's selection, the convention business proceeded as if nothing unusual were happening. With no fights over the platform or party rules (both were approved without debate), the Republicans could concentrate on positioning themselves for the fall campaign.

Although Democrats began the fall campaign with high hopes for November, the campaign turned out to be a downhill slide for Dukakis. Dukakis left the Democratic convention as much as 17 points ahead of Bush in some polls. That lead evaporated under a withering Republican attack that began at the GOP convention. Despite continuing reservations among voters about the Quayle nomination, Bush surged ahead in the polls at the end of August. He maintained that advantage throughout the fall, emphasizing at every opportunity that Dukakis was a liberal out of step with the mainstream. Many scored Bush for his tactics, but few argued with their effectiveness.

Bush's ability to keep Dukakis on the defensive was reflected in the public opinion polls. A week before the election, they gave Bush as much as a 12-point lead.

## Results of the 1988 Elections

George Bush was elected the nation's 41st president on Nov. 8, winning 54 percent of the popular vote. Bush's victory confirmed that, absent economic crisis or White House scandal, the burden of proof was on the Democrats to convince voters that their party could be trusted with the executive branch of the federal government.

Bush was the first candidate since John F. Kennedy to win the White House while his party lost seats in the House. And unlike Kennedy's, Bush's victory margin was substantial in a number of states. His inability to carry others into office may have been partly due to his message, which was essentially a call to "stay the course."

In reviewing the results of the 1988 Senate elections, both parties had cause for rue and relief. But it was the Republicans who felt the keener disappointment. Democrats won 19 of the 33 races, maintaining the 55-45 majority they had seized in the 1986 elections. They successfully defended 15 of their 18 seats and took over Republican seats in Connecticut, Virginia, Nebraska and Nevada.

GOP Senate leader Bob Dole conceded on election night that reclaiming the Senate had not been realistic in 1988. And the party could be pleased at capturing three historically Democratic seats as well as holding 11 of its own 15. Of the four the GOP lost, the only surprise came in Connecticut, where incumbent Lowell P. Weicker Jr. was edged out by Joseph I. Lieberman.

The GOP had all but conceded the other three seats to the Democrats a year before the election. In Virginia former governor Charles S. Robb succeeded Republican Paul S. Trible Jr., who retired after a single term. David K. Karnes of Nebraska lost to former Democratic governor Robert Kerry, and Chic Hecht of Nevada lost to sitting Democratic governor Richard H. Bryan.

The only Democratic incumbent the Republicans defeated was John Melcher of Montana. Conrad Burns became the state's first Republican senator elected in 42 years. The other two new Republican seats in the Senate were won by House minority whip Trent Lott of Mississippi and Rep. Connie Mack of Florida. The latest emblems of the GOP's new day in the Old South, they replaced retiring Democrats John C. Stennis and Lawton Chiles.

An important measure of a party's performance in any election year is its score in contests where no incumbent is running. In this category the GOP won four of six. The party held on to retiring Robert T. Stafford's seat in Vermont, where at-large representative James M. Jeffords had no trouble moving in. And former GOP senator Slade Gorton, whom the voters had turned out two years before, was elected to succeed retiring Republican senator Daniel J. Evans. Mack and Lott picked up the other two open seats.

The two Democrats winning open seats were Robb and Herbert Kohl of Wisconsin. Kohl succeeded Democrat William Proxmire, who retired.

In the House of Representatives election day was cause for celebration for more than 98 percent of the members seeking reelection. Only six of 408 incumbents on the ballot lost, four Republicans and two Democrats. The Democrats picked up a net of two seats, putting the partisan lineup in the House at 260 Democrats and 175 Republicans.

The most prominent member to fall was Fernand J. St Germain of Rhode Island, who was soundly rejected after being dogged by questions about his ethical conduct. And in Georgia the Democrats had little trouble knocking off Republican representative Pat Swindall, who was under indictment for allegedly lying to a grand jury about a money-laundering scheme.

Democratic representative Bill Chappell Jr. lost his Florida district after being battered by public questions about his links to a defense-procurement scandal. Democratic representative Roy Dyson of Maryland, also plagued by unfavorable stories about his links to the procurement scandal and his conduct in office, narrowly eked out a victory over a challenger he was expected to trounce.

Many victories in 1988 depended on more than political skills, personality and partisan appeal. The powers of incumbency—free mailing, press attention and fund-raising advantages—played a significant role in the election.

If the advantage of incumbency helped to explain why Republicans were having trouble reducing the Democratic advantages in the House, it did little to explain why they made no headway in the battle for open seats. In all, only three of the 27 open seats changed partisan hands, with the Democrats winning two formerly GOP seats and the Republicans winning one seat held by the Democrats.

The 1988 results were unlikely to encourage challengers mulling the 1990 election. The 98 percent reelection rate from 1986 may well have played a role in discouraging competition in 1988, one of the quietest election years in recent memory.

There were 12 gubernatorial races on Nov. 8. Of the nine governors seeking reelection, eight won, all by stressing their managerial skill. The only incumbent to fail, West Virginia Republican Arch A. Moore Jr., was ousted because voters had lost confidence in his ability to steer the state's struggling economy toward better times. Democrat Gaston Caperton defeated Moore.

Two other GOP governors were as embattled as Moore—Edward DiPrete in Rhode Island and Norman H. Bangerter in Utah—but both eked out victories over stiff Democratic competition.

Those narrow GOP victories deflated the Democrats' high expectations of gubernatorial gains in 1988. Democrats were defending only four seats, compared with the GOP's eight. In addition, the three Democratic incumbents seeking reelection seemed solid, while Republicans looked to be struggling in at least four states. But on Nov. 8 the Democrats scored a net gain of just one governorship, bringing to 28 their number of chief executives. The GOP held 22 governorships.

While Democrats may have been disappointed in the results of the gubernatorial elections, Republican hopes for taking eventual control of Congress suffered a little-noticed but substantial setback when voters across the nation cast ballots for state legislative seats. In those seats would sit, by the early 1990s, the men and women who would redefine the 50 states' congressional districts. Most of them, it appeared, would be Democrats.

## The Post-Cold War Era

When the history of the early 1990s is written, the signal event will surely be the collapse of Soviet communism and the dissolution of the Union of Soviet Socialist Republics. The world watched as, one by one, the countries of the Warsaw Pact broke away from the Soviet Union to turn toward democracy and market economies and then as the Soviet Union itself broke apart. Seemingly overnight, the superpower rivalry that had dominated U.S. defense and foreign policy for nearly half a century was over.

For many Americans, however, these astounding events were overshadowed by economic recession. Faced with slow economic growth and high levels of unemployment, more and more people began to fear that they and their children would never be able to realize the American dream of a continually improving standard of living.

Those fears were to make Republican George Bush a one-term president. Bush had entered the White House on the popularity of his predecessor, Ronald Reagan, and saw his own public approval ratings soar to record heights after the successful U.S.-led military action against Iraq in 1991. But Bush was never able to persuade voters that he had a credible plan for rejuvenating the economy or addressing other domestic problems, including a failing health insurance system and the huge budget deficits caused in part by the Reagan-Bush economic policies.

The Democratic-controlled Congress gave the president little quarter, although the two did cooperate to enact a far-reaching rewrite of the Clean Air Act. Other major achievements of the 101st and 102nd Congresses included measures making public and work places accessible to Americans with disabilities and a restructuring of the thrift industry. But severe image problems overshadowed these achievements. More often than not, the Democratic Congress clashed with the Republican White House, with legislative gridlock the result. This perceived ineptitude combined with numerous scandals to drive congressional approval ratings to record lows.

The military victory in Iraq was the crowning moment of George Bush's presidency. But the euphoria was fleeting. Almost as soon as the war had ended, Democrats succeeded in turning the nation's attention to the economy's miserable performance.

When Bush assumed office, the economy was still in what would become the longest peacetime expansion. Unemployment stood at 5.3 percent, and the inflation rate was 4.2 percent. But the expansion slowed during the first quarter of 1989, and the economy slid into recession.

The single action that may have dealt the biggest blow to Bush's political fortunes occurred in 1990 when Bush broke his 1988 campaign promise not to raise taxes. Concerned that a hemorrhaging deficit could severely damage the economy and his own re-election chances in 1992, Bush sought the help of Democrats to work out a bipartisan package deal that was expected to reduce the deficit by $500 million over the next five years.

# 1989-91:
# The 101st Congress

Despite the momentous events that rocked the world and nation in 1989-91, Congress' focus was on internal politics. Congress was consigned to a role that was, if not peripheral, at most reactive. Moreover, the 1988 elections had not given either the new Republican president, George Bush, or the Democratic-controlled Congress any clear mandate, and neither party had a compelling agenda of its own.

For much of the two years, congressional attention was focused inward, on events surrounding the resignations of House Speaker Jim Wright, D-Texas—the first time in history a Speaker had quit midterm—and House Majority Whip Tony Coelho, D-Calif. Questions about their personal ethics forced both men out of office. Thomas S. Foley of Washington was elected to succeed Wright as Speaker.

Ethics problems also surfaced for five senators who had intervened with federal regulators in behalf of an ailing savings and loan institution. The senators became known as the Keating Five, after the thrift's owner, Charles H. Keating Jr.

In the Senate, Democrat George J. Mitchell of Maine was serving his first years as majority leader, where he cautiously proceeded to impose order on the legislative schedule and to find consensus among Democrats. Most senators said Mitchell lived up to his promise to have an open, consultative leadership style. Relations with Republicans were easier than they had been under his predecessor, Robert C. Byrd, D-W.Va.

In Virginia in 1989, the state that billed itself as the "cradle of the Confederacy," Democratic Lt. Gov. L. Douglas Wilder became the nation's first elected black governor.

## Results of the 1990 Elections

War and recession hovered ominously over the 1990 campaign, but neither figured prominently in its outcome.

Instead, the election campaigns looked more like a series of hard-fought city council contests, shaped largely by personalities, local issues and a pronounced absence of clear-cut national themes.

While frustrated voters talked about "throwing the bums out," on Nov. 6 they returned incumbents to Washington en masse. Only one of the 32 Senate incumbents seeking re-election lost, while only 15 of the 406 House members who ran in the general election were defeated.

Altogether, the Republicans lost one Senate seat and eight House seats, weakening the administration's hand. Bush had come to depend upon a strategy of governing by veto in dealing with the heavily Democratic Congress. (As it turned out, a Bush veto was not overridden until the final days of the 102nd Congress.)

Colorado in 1990 became the first state to impose term limits on federal officeholders. (California, Colorado and Oklahoma voters also adopted ballot initiatives capping the service of state legislators.) But the broad anti-incumbent sentiment expressed toward Congress in pre-election polls did not materialize at the ballot box. (*Term limits, box, pp. 624-625*)

Only one Senate incumbent, Republican Rudy Boschwitz of Minnesota, was defeated. In the House, 96 percent of the incumbents seeking re-election were returned. Total turnover, including retirements, amounted to just 10 percent.

Despite winning more House seats (267) in 1990 than in any other election since the recession-year contest of 1982, the Democrats' share of the total, nationwide congressional vote was their lowest for any midterm election since 1966. In 1990 Democratic candidates drew just 52.9 percent of all House votes. By comparison, when Democrats captured 269 seats in 1982, their share of the nationwide congressional vote was 55.2 percent, more than 2 percentage points higher than in 1990.

The statehouses proved to be the real workshop of democracy in 1990. Anti-incumbent sentiment overtook sitting Republican governors in four states and Democratic governors in two. Eight other statehouses also changed hands, with four going to Republicans, three to Democrats, and one (Alaska) to the Alaska Independence Party. All told, 14 governorships switched from one party to another and more incumbent governors were toppled than in any other year since 1970.

The GOP picked up Arizona's governorship in February 1991, when Republican candidate Fife Symington won a runoff election. And it gained another statehouse in March 1991 when Louisiana Gov. Buddy Roemer, elected as a Democrat in 1987, switched parties. That left the lineup at 27 Democrats, 21 Republicans and two independents.

Six of 23 gubernatorial incumbents who sought re-election lost their jobs. Two of the losses—Democrats James J. Blanchard of Michigan and Rudy Perpich of Minnesota—came as surprises.

In Connecticut, former GOP senator Lowell P. Weicker Jr. won the seat vacated by Democrat William A. O'Neill. Weicker, a maverick liberal Republican who lost a 1988 Senate re-election bid, chose to run on his own ticket instead of competing for the GOP nomination.

Alaska voters were similarly unfettered by convention, electing former Republican governor Walter J. Hickel. Hickel had thrown the race into disarray by jumping in on the Alaska Independence Party ticket only six weeks before the election. Republicans had nominated state senator Arliss

Sturgulewski, but some were uncomfortable with her abortion rights stance, and even her running mate abandoned the ticket to run with Hickel.

# 1991-93:
# The 102nd Congress

Hobbled by partisanship and purse strings, the 102nd Congress produced one of the shortest lists of legislative accomplishments in recent memory. Congress and the president enacted some notable measures, including the first overhaul of energy regulations in a decade, new regulation of the cable television industry and aid to the former Soviet republics. But the number of achievements paled in comparison with the number of bills that were considered but never enacted.

The 102nd Congress had hardly begun when its signal event arrived on Capitol Hill. After three days of somber but passionate debate, Congress on Jan. 12, 1991, gave President Bush authorization to go to war against Iraq. The vote represented the first time since Dec. 8, 1941, that Congress had exercised its constitutional authority to declare war.

Less than two months later, a triumphant Bush ascended the dais in the House of Representatives to tell the assembled Congress—and the nation—"Aggression is defeated; the war is over."

The end of the shooting war abroad, however, marked the beginning of a shouting war at home, as lawmakers turned their attention from the victory overseas to the sagging economy and other domestic concerns. But the budget deal that the White House and Congress wrote in 1990, combined with partisan politics in 1991, made significant progress on domestic issues nearly impossible. The Republican president used his veto, real and threatened, to stall Democratic measures he did not like, such as civil rights and extended unemployment benefits. Compromises were forged only after Bush's standing in the public opinion polls began to fall.

Once the war was successfully concluded, Operation Desert Storm receded from pre-eminence on the national agenda with startling speed. By late August, in what was likely to be a far more momentous development, the Soviet Union was falling apart.

While the war debate was Congress' finest hour in 1991, considerable competition existed for its low point. Two leading contenders were the confirmation hearings of Clarence Thomas to be an associate justice of the Supreme Court and the revelation that House members routinely wrote checks on the House bank without having the funds to cover them.

Thomas, a federal court of appeals judge, had been named to succeed Justice Thurgood Marshall, who was retiring. Thomas' conservative credentials had already made his confirmation as the second black to sit on the Court a subject of great controversy, but the hearings turned into a national soap opera in October after law school professor Anita F. Hill alleged that Thomas had sexually harassed her, and lurid details poured out of the hearing room. Thomas was confirmed, but the Senate's handling of the situation left women outraged and led many senators to call the confirmation process flawed.

The two-year Keating Five investigation also came to a conclusion in 1991. The Senate Ethics Committee reprimanded Alan Cranston, D-Calif., and it criticized in writing the four other senators—Democrats Dennis DeConcini of Arizona, John Glenn of Ohio, and Donald W. Riegle Jr. of Michigan, and Republican John McCain of Arizona—for their poor judgment in acting in behalf of Charles Keating, who owned a savings and loan that went bankrupt at a $2 billion cost to federal taxpayers.

Perhaps nothing symbolized the gridlock in Washington so much as the debate over urban aid in the wake of the Los Angeles riots in April 1992—the worst incident of domestic violence in 20 years. Congress and President Bush could not agree either on the amount and kind of aid or on how that aid should be funded. Democrats had to settle for $500 million in aid, a third of what they had proposed.

Congress' internal strife complicated matters. Along with the members' bank overdrafts problem, House leaders had to deal with a scandal at the House Post Office involving allegations that legislators had converted public funds into cash and that patronage employees sold drugs at the federal facility. Several employees pleaded guilty to various charges and a federal grand jury subpoenaed expense account records of three House members, including Ways and Means Chairman Dan Rostenkowski of Illinois.

## The 1992 Campaigns

A year before the 1992 presidential campaign began, President Bush seemed poised for one of the smoothest re-elections in White House history. After he led the nation to victory in the brief Persian Gulf War, the president's popularity soared. Yet when he formally launched his candidacy in Washington on Feb. 12, 1992, Bush faced the prospect of spirited competition not only in the fall from the Democrats but also in the Republican primaries.

In the intervening 11 months, the economy had gone into what even the president called a "free fall." So, too, had Bush's popularity. The president had dropped from a peak of 89 percent approval in the Gallup Poll in March 1991 to 44 percent in February 1992. Not much that the White House did before or during the campaign helped revitalize either the economy or the president's political standing.

On the Democratic side, the nomination of Arkansas Gov. Bill Clinton seemed the most likely outcome as the campaign got under way. His campaign was well-positioned on all major fronts—organization, message development, fund raising and endorsements. Clinton's early primary wins put him far ahead of the other Democratic contenders, but continuing doubts about Clinton's character raised questions about the governor's electability.

In addition to Clinton, just four other Democrats actively sought the nomination as the primary season began: former Massachusetts senator Paul E. Tsongas, former California governor Edmund G. "Jerry" Brown, and senators Tom Harkin of Iowa and Bob Kerrey of Nebraska. None of the four had much following beyond their own region, and all of them were long shots for the nomination. Brown, however, ran an innovative campaign, placing a $100 limit on contributions, which could be pledged by dialing a toll-free 800 number.

On the eve of the New Hampshire primary in February, renewed controversies surfaced about Clinton's draft status during the Vietnam War and allegations of marital infidelity. Calls went out for new candidates to enter the race. Some prominent Democrats considered but then dropped the idea because the nominating system seriously handicapped any late entry into the race.

As a result, voters in most states did not have a wide choice. In only five primaries could Democrats choose from a full field of active candidates. Clinton, Brown and Tsongas were the active candidates in just 10 other primaries. As

# Term Limits for Members of Congress . . .

In a backlash against career politicians, voters in 14 states on Nov. 3, 1992, approved initiatives to limit the length of service of their House members and senators. A 15th state, Colorado, had adopted a term-limit measure in 1990. Altogether, 181 House and Senate members entered the 103rd Congress (1993-95) with term limits.

All 15 states limited Senate service to 12 years. For Arizona, Arkansas, California, Michigan, Montana, Oregon, Washington and Wyoming, House tenure was capped at six years; Florida, Missouri, Nebraska and Ohio, eight years; and Colorado, North Dakota, and South Dakota, 12 years.

In most cases, support was overwhelming. Nearly 21 million Americans supported term limits, a 200-year-old concept revitalized by voters disgusted by congressional scandal and discontented with entrenched incumbents.

The legality of such limits under the Constitution had not been tested, however, and scholars disagreed sharply about whether enforced turnover would make Congress better or worse. Proponents said term limits would bring in fresh ideas and give lawmakers more leeway to do what is right for the country, rather than "play it safe" and do whatever it takes to get re-elected. Opponents argued that limits could force out some valued legislators simply because they had been in office a certain length of time.

One of the strongest voices for term limits was that of columnist and television commentator George F. Will, a former Senate aide who insisted that "I harbor no hostility toward government in general or Congress in particular." In a 1992 book, *Restoration: Congress, Term Limits and the Recovery of Deliberative Democracy,* Will said:

> I favor term limits not as a punitive measure but as a way of strengthening Congress as a countervailing power in a government in which the executive branch has become swollen and disproportionate, and the judiciary has become more intrusive than is healthy for our society.

## Constitutional Question

Many legal scholars say the only way that congressional term limits can be imposed is through an amendment to the Constitution, as was done with the two-term limit for presidents.

In the 1969 case *Powell v. McCormack,* the Supreme Court ruled 7-1 that the House had improperly denied Adam Clayton Powell Jr., D-N.Y., his seat. The justices maintained that Congress could not add to the Constitution's three qualifications for a House member (25 years of age, seven years of citizenship and residency in the state to be represented). (Senators must be at least 30, have nine years of citizenship and also be a resident of the state represented.)

Other scholars see term limits as a more complicated question because courts have upheld state eligibility restrictions such as prohibiting convicted felons from holding office. All agree that the current Supreme Court is more conservative than the 1969 one Chief Justice Earl Warren headed and that it may be more amenable to states' rights arguments.

House members serve two-year terms and all come up for election in even-numbered years. Senators serve six years and one-third of the Senate is elected every two years. Re-election rates in 1992 for incumbents who ran were 93.1 percent in the House, 85.7 percent in the Senate.

Term limits were considered at the Constitutional Convention in 1787 but they were considered too minor to be part of the remarkably brief Constitution, which established the U.S. government framework in broad terms. Article I, Section 4 left it to the state legislatures to determine the "Times, Places and Manner of holding" congressional elections, but it empowered Congress to "make or alter such Regulations."

States control their own elections and the legality of term limitations for governors has not been in dispute. As of 1994 more than half the states had such limitations. *(Gubernatorial Elections, p. 633)*

Mark Tushnet, a professor at Georgetown Law School, said he believes that state-mandated term limits for members of Congress are unconstitutional, but that it is impossible to predict how the Supreme Court would decide. "It's not something [justices] had to deal with at the lower courts," he said.

The constitutional argument could be made moot, of course, by a constitutional amendment. In the early 1990s efforts were under way on several fronts to push Congress into considering one. In 1992 Bill McCollum, R-Fla., led an unsuccessful effort to force House floor consideration of a proposed constitutional amendment that would limit Senate and House members to 12 years.

Two outside groups also sought pledges of support for a term-limit amendment. One group, Americans to Limit Congressional Terms, was led by former representative Jim Coyne, R-Pa., who served one term from 1981 to 1983. Coyne said he had watched the members elected with him transform from outsiders to entrenched incumbents. "People who I knew when I was there 10 years ago who came in as anti-politicians have all become one," he said.

Coyne pointed to the state pressure in the early 20th century to provide for the direct election of U.S. senators as an example of what a grass-roots movement can do. More than a dozen states decided to hold popular elections for Senate seats before the 17th Amendment was ratified as part of the Constitution in 1913.

The push for term limits "sends terror into the hearts of the political establishment," said Paul Jacob, campaign director of the other group, U.S. Term Limits.

---

Harkin, Kerrey and then Tsongas dropped out, Clinton's main competition in the last two dozen primaries came from Brown.

Although he lost in New Hampshire, Clinton became the first Democrat to win primary victories in each of the 10 largest states. He scored more primary victories (32) than any other Democratic candidate ever did. And his nearly 10.5 million primary votes were more than any previous candidate, Democrat or Republican, had ever won in the history of the presidential primaries.

Bush's nomination for a second term was never in jeopardy, despite his sagging popularity. His only real

# ... Gaining Support but Untested in Court

## 1994 District Court Ruling

Opponents of congressional term limits won the first round of their campaign in the courts on Feb. 10, 1994, when U.S. District Court Judge William L. Dwyer ruled in Seattle that state-mandated limits are unconstitutional.

House Speaker Thomas S. Foley, D-Wash., a plaintiff in the case, hailed the ruling as a vindication of his own view. Foley's position as Speaker was a factor in the surprise defeat of a term limits ballot initiative in his state in 1991. Washington voters feared a loss of power in Congress if the limitation passed, forcing Foley to retire. In 1992, however, the state's voters approved a similar measure that set limits (three terms for House members, two for senators) that were not retroactive. They began taking effect in 1993.

In his decision, Judge Dwyer cited the landmark *Powell* as prohibiting a state or even Congress from adding to the age, citizenship and residency requirements of the Constitution. He also wrote that the limits violated two amendments—the First (by constraining members' freedom of association) and the 14th (by imposing undue restrictions on ballot access for one "disfavored group of candidates"). "A state may not diminish its voters' constitutional freedom of choice by making would-be candidates for Congress ineligible on the basis of incumbency," Dwyer wrote.

In June 1994 the Court moved to end the speculation about how it would rule on term limits. It agreed to review an Arkansas Supreme Court decision that such limits cannot apply to members of Congress. The cases to be reviewed together were *U.S. Term Limits v. Thornton* and *Bryant v. Hill.*

## No Third Terms

The highest federal officeholder, the president, is limited to two terms by the 22nd Amendment, ratified in 1951. The amendment fixed in law the precedent set by George Washington when he declined a third term for personal reasons and adopted on philosophical grounds by the third president, Thomas Jefferson, who had argued for a term limit in the Constitution for presidents.

The amendment was intended to prevent a repetition of Franklin Delano Roosevelt's break with Jefferson's credo in winning third and fourth terms. FDR served longer than any other president, 12 years and 39 days, until his death on April 12, 1945, during his fourth term. His successor, Harry S. Truman, was exempt from the limitation, but he declined to seek a second full term in 1952. Republicans pushed for the no-third-term amendment to prevent another FDR situation, but, ironically, through 1992 it had affected only GOP presidents. No Democratic president since FDR had been elected more than once.

## How Long Is Too Long?

The high turnover in the 435-member House—110 new members elected in 1992, close to the postwar high of 118 in 1948—did not seem to be diminishing the fervor of limit advocates. "The insanity that is driving term limits does not understand that kind of reason," said Rep. Mike Synar, D-Okla.

Foley said one of the proponents' premises—that incumbents serve too long—is false. He said about two-thirds of the House membership had changed since 1980. Half of the Senate's membership had changed in the same period.

Jacob, from U.S. Term Limits, said that did not disprove the need for statutory limits. Congressional redistricting and the House bank scandal were the main reasons for 1992's high voluntary turnover (67 House members did not seek re-election), he said. "The only way an incumbent gets in trouble these days is if he gets his hand caught in the till."

Before the election, political scientist Thomas E. Mann of the Brookings Institution predicted the success of term limits. "Wherever it reaches the ballot," he said, "it will pass.... It's a visceral crying out against the system." Not until federal and state governments regain the confidence of the electorate will support for term limits begin to ebb, he added.

## States Where Adopted

Following are the states that adopted term limits for members of Congress in 1990 (Colorado) or 1992 (the remaining 14 states) and the limitations imposed:

| State | Term Limit (in Years) | | Percentage Voting for Passage |
| | Senate | House | |
| --- | --- | --- | --- |
| Arizona | 12 | 6 | 74.2 |
| Arkansas | 12 | 6 | 59.9 |
| California | 12 | 6 | 63.6 |
| Colorado | 12 | 12 | 70.7 |
| Florida | 12 | 8 | 76.8 |
| Michigan | 12 | 6 | 58.8 |
| Missouri | 12 | 8 | 74.0 |
| Montana | 12 | 6 | 66.9 |
| Nebraska | 12 | 8 | 68.2 |
| North Dakota | 12 | 12 | 55.5 |
| Ohio | 12 | 8 | 66.2 |
| Oregon | 12 | 6 | 69.5 |
| South Dakota | 12 | 12 | 63.5 |
| Washington | 12 | 6 | 52.4 |
| Wyoming | 12 | 6 | 77.2 |
| **Average** | | | 66.1 |

Source: U.S. Term Limits.

challenge came from the party's conservative wing, which had been suspicious of Bush since at least 1980 when he ran for the nomination against Ronald Reagan, the conservatives' hero. Seizing what he saw as an opportunity, conservative commentator Patrick J. Buchanan, a former speechwriter for President Richard Nixon and one-time communications director for the Reagan White House, entered the race.

Although he collected fewer than 100 delegates, Buchanan got in his licks. Bush won every primary, but he wound up with less than three-fourths of the Republican primary ballots, a far lower share than the last three elected

Republican presidents (Reagan, Nixon and Dwight D. Eisenhower) received on their road to re-election.

Former Louisiana state representative David Duke also ran a limited campaign for the presidency. But the former Ku Klux Klan member won little support among Republicans and ended his campaign on April 22.

After the conventions, Bush continued to try to focus voter attention on Clinton's character. But Clinton began the final phase of the campaign as the front runner, and nothing Bush did ever dislodged the Democrat from that position. By the time of the presidential debates in mid-October, the political community had reached virtually unanimous agreement that without a major news development or a Clinton misstep Bush was likely to lose his bid for a second term.

## Results of the 1992 Elections

A majority of American voters listened to Democratic presidential candidate Bill Clinton's call for change in 1992 and turned President George Bush out of office after only one term. Clinton, the governor of Arkansas, carried 32 states and the District of Columbia, won 370 of 538 electoral votes and outscored Bush by 5 percentage points—43 percent to 38 percent.

Clinton's was the most sweeping triumph for any Democrat since President Lyndon B. Johnson in 1964 and the best showing for any Democratic challenger since Franklin D. Roosevelt ousted Republican Herbert Hoover from the White House in 1932. In placing Clinton, 46, and Sen. Al Gore of Tennessee, 44, at the head of the government, Americans for the first time elected a president and vice president both born after World War II.

The widespread desire for a change in government also benefited independent candidate Ross Perot, the Texas billionaire who spoke bluntly of the need to reduce the federal budget deficit. Perot won 19 percent of the popular vote, the largest vote total for an independent candidate in presidential election history and the biggest vote share since 1912, when Theodore Roosevelt ran under the Progressive Party banner.

Change also reached Congress, where voters added record numbers of women, blacks and Hispanics. The new Senate would be the most diverse in history, with the addition of four women, including the first black woman ever elected to the body. A fourth of the House members in 1993 would be freshmen, a result of retirements and redistricting as well as voter rejection of incumbents.

Overall, however, the partisan lineup in Congress was virtually the same, with the Democrats firmly in control of both chambers. The lineup in the Senate remained at 57 Democrats and 43 Republicans. At the beginning of the 103rd Congress, the House had 258 Democrats, 176 Republicans and one independent. The Republicans had gained 10 seats.

Anti-incumbency and "Year of the Woman" themes may have worked well in some Senate and House elections, but they had little effect in the 12 gubernatorial races in 1992. Voters seemed more concerned about economics and ethics issues. The four incumbent governors running for re-election—all Democrats—were returned to office. And a former Democratic governor won back his job after an eight-year absence. The three women running for governor in Montana, New Hampshire and Rhode Island all lost. Women held the governorships in Kansas, Oregon and Texas.

Altogether, Democrats won three seats formerly held by Republicans, while the GOP picked up one seat held by a Democrat, for a net gain of two seats for the Democrats. That gave the Democrats a total of 30 governorships; the Republicans held 18. Two governors were independents.

Voters in 14 states in 1992 approved limits on the number of terms their representatives and senators in Congress could serve.

# The Historical Significance of Southern Primaries

Because of the overwhelming dominance of the Democratic Party in the South during the first half of the 20th century, the party's primaries became, in effect, the region's significant elections. The 11 states comprising the South — all members of the Civil War Confederacy — are Alabama, Arkansas, Florida, Georgia, Louisiana, Mississippi, North Carolina, South Carolina, Tennessee, Texas and Virginia.

In his classic study *Southern Politics in State and Nation,* V. O. Key Jr. concluded, "In fact, the Democratic primary is no nominating method at all. The primary is the election. . . ." That was in 1949, shortly before Republicans began seriously challenging Democrats for hegemony in the region.

But Key's observation holds true for the 20th century up through the time of his study and for much of the period since, depending on the particular state and election involved. Of the 114 gubernatorial elections held in the 11 former Confederate states in the period 1919-48, the Democratic nominee won 113 times. The exception was Tennessee's election of a Republican governor in the Harding presidential landslide of 1920. In the same period, the Democratic nominee won 131 of 132 elections to the Senate in these 11 states, the only exception being a special election in Arkansas in 1937 when the Democratic nominee lost to an independent Democrat.

Republican Party growth since 1948 has been steady though uneven. The first popularly elected Republican U.S. senator from the South, John G. Tower of Texas, won a special election in 1961. Thereafter, Republicans won their first Senate seats in South Carolina (1966), Tennessee (1966), Florida (1968), North Carolina and Virginia (1972), Mississippi (1978), and Alabama and Georgia (1980). Likewise, Republicans picked up governorships slowly after 1949, their first victories in the South coming in Arkansas and Florida in 1966.

But even in 1994 Republicans were a minority in the South, on the state level. They were outnumbered eight to three in governorships, 12 to 10 in Senate seats and 77 to 48 in U.S. House seats. Thus, the Democratic primaries continued to be the deciding election in most Southern states.

While the Democratic share of House seats in the South has been dropping, from 71.3 percent in 1978 to 61.6 percent in 1992, the Republicans' gain in the region has been more than offset by Democratic inroads in former GOP strongholds, notably the Northeast and Midwest. *(The Democratic House: A Life of Its Own, box, p. 920)*

On the presidential level, the inroads on Democratic strength have gone much deeper, with Republican presidential nominee Richard Nixon carrying all 11 states of the Old South with at least 65 percent of the vote in 1972. In 1984 and 1988 Ronald Reagan and George Bush did almost as well, carrying every Southern state with at least 58 percent (Reagan) or 54 percent (Bush) of the vote. But in 1992 with three Southerners competing, the GOP's Bush of Texas lost four Southern states to Democrat Bill Clinton. Independent Ross Perot of Texas won no states in the South or elsewhere. Clinton's only majority in the South (53 percent) was won in his own state of Arkansas.

## Runoff Primaries

The South along with the rest of the nation instituted primaries during the first two decades of the 20th century. By 1920 all 11 Southern states were choosing their Democratic gubernatorial and senatorial nominees through the primary process.

But because the primaries were, for all practical purposes, the deciding election, many legislators began to doubt the effectiveness of a system that frequently allowed a candidate in a multi-candidate race to win a plurality of the popular vote — and thus the Democratic nomination that ensured election — even though he received only a small percentage of the total primary vote.

So, most Southern states adopted the runoff primary — a second election following the first primary, usually by two to four weeks — that matched only the top two contenders from the first primary. The runoff system was adopted in Alabama in 1931, Arkansas in 1939, Florida in 1929, Georgia

---

## Sources

Heard, Alexander, and Donald S. Strong. *Southern Primaries and Elections, 1920-1949.* 1950. Reprint. Salem, N.H.: Ayers, 1970.

Key, V. O. Jr. *Southern Politics in State and Nation.* New York: Alfred A. Knopf, 1949.

Secretaries of state and state handbooks of the 11 Southern states.

in 1917 (with the county unit system, *see p. 629*), Louisiana in 1922, Mississippi in 1902, North Carolina in 1915, South Carolina in 1915 and Texas in 1918. (Arkansas had adopted the runoff in 1933, abandoned it in 1935, then reinstituted it in 1939.) Virginia adopted the runoff in 1969 but repealed it in 1971.

After 1969 Tennessee remained the only Southern state to nominate by plurality. In that state's 1974 gubernatorial race, Ray Blanton won the Democratic nomination with only 22.7 percent of the vote in a field of 12 candidates. Blanton went on to win the governorship in November.

Runoffs are not always obligatory. In most states, if the second-place finisher in the primary does not want a runoff, the first-place candidate is then the winner without a runoff. In the North Carolina Democratic gubernatorial primary of 1968, for example, front-runner Robert W. Scott narrowly missed winning a majority of the vote in the first primary, winding up with 48.1 percent. However, the second-place candidate, J. Melville Broughton Jr., who received 33.4 percent, declined a runoff. None was held and Scott automatically became the Democratic nominee.

## Jackson's Anti-runoff Campaign

Jesse L. Jackson, contender for the 1984 Democratic presidential nomination, mounted an attack against the runoff feature in the spring of that year. Jackson hoped to persuade the 10 other Southern states to join Tennessee in avoiding the runoff.

Jackson argued that runoffs injured black candidates' chances of victory because in the second election whites, who comprised the majority of registered voters, usually voted on the basis of race.

Jackson carried his plea to the Democratic National Convention, which defeated his move to abolish runoffs, 2,500.8 to 1,253.2. Supporters argued that runoffs prevented the election of fringe candidates when more qualified candidates split the vote in hotly contested primaries. In addition, conservative Southerners opposed having a national convention decide their own state election procedures.

## Preferential Primaries

Three Southern states — Alabama, Florida and Louisiana — tried to avoid the effort and expense of runoff elections by experimenting with a preferential system of primary voting. All three later switched to the runoff system — Alabama after the election of 1930, Florida after the election of 1928 and Louisiana (whose system was similar to Alabama's) after the election of 1920. Louisiana modified its system yet again in 1975, this time to a two-step process: an initial non-partisan primary followed by a general election runoff between the two top finishers.

Under the preferential system a voter, instead of simply marking an X opposite one candidate's name, writes the digits 1 *or* 2, beside the names of two candidates. This indicates the "preference" order the voter gives each of the candidates, the number one indicating his first choice, the number two his second choice. To determine the winner, without a runoff, second-choice votes are added to the first-choice votes and the candidate with the highest combined total wins.

**Alabama.** Under the Alabama system, each voter expressed a first and second choice. If no candidate received a majority of the first choices, all but the two leaders were eliminated. All second choices expressed for the two leaders

were then added to their first-choice totals, the candidate with the highest combined total winning.

In the Democratic primary for U.S. senator on May 13, 1920, for a special four-year term to fill a vacancy, the candidates were J. Thomas Heflin and three persons whose first names are not available: White, O'Neal and Rushton. Heflin, with 49,554 first-choice votes, led the field but received only 37.9 percent of the total. White ran second with 34,854 first-choice votes, or 26.6 percent; O'Neal had 33,174 first-choice votes, or 25.4 percent, and Rushton was last with 13,232 first-choice votes, or 10.1 percent. Thus, in many Southern states a runoff would have been necessary. But instead of a runoff all second-choice votes cast for the two leaders — Heflin and White — were added to their first-choice ballots. A total of 11,062 second-choice votes were cast for Heflin by voters whose first choice had gone to one of the other three candidates. Added to his first-choice vote of 49,554, this gave Heflin a grand total of 60,016 votes. White received 12,699 second-choice votes — more than Heflin — but the second-choice votes were not enough to raise his grand total above Heflin's. White thus wound up with a grand total of 47,553 votes, and Heflin was the winner.

**Florida.** The Florida system of preference voting differed somewhat from the Alabama system. In Florida, as in Alabama, each voter expressed a first and second choice. Also as in Alabama, if no candidate received a majority of first choices, all candidates but the two highest first-choice candidates were eliminated. To determine the winner, the second choices expressed for the two highest *on the ballots of eliminated candidates only* were added to the first-choice totals. (In Alabama, the second choices for the two leaders expressed on ballots for *all* candidates, including the two leaders, were added to the first-choice totals.)

For example, in the Florida Democratic gubernatorial election of 1924 there were five candidates. John W. Martin received 55,715 first-choice votes, to lead the field. His closest rival, Sidney J. Catts, received 43,230 votes. But a third major contender, Frank E. Jennings, received 37,962 first-choice votes, depriving either Martin or Catts of a majority. In addition, two other candidates also received first-choice votes — Worth W. Trammell with 8,381 and Charles H. Spencer with 1,408. The percentages stood Martin 38.0, Catts 29.5, Jennings 25.9, Trammell 5.7 and Spencer 0.9 percent.

To determine the winner, the second-choice votes cast for Martin (17,339) and Catts (6,067) by voters who had cast first-choice votes for Jennings, Trammell and Spencer were added to Martin's and Catts' first-choice totals. The result was Martin 73,054 and Catts 49,297, a clear win for Martin.

The preference system, however, did not prove useful. Apparently it was too confusing for voters, most of whom did not bother to cast second-choice votes. In the Alabama election discussed above, for example, there were 130,814 first-choice votes, but only 34,768 second-choice votes.

**Louisiana.** Not satisfied with either the partisan runoff or the preferential primary, Louisiana adopted a law in 1975 that allowed its voters to participate in an initial open primary followed by a runoff general election between the two top finishers. In the primary, all candidates of all parties were to be on the ballot, but party designations were optional and at the individual candidate's discretion. A candidate receiving more than 50 percent of the primary vote would be unopposed in the general election. If no candidate received more than 50 percent of the vote, the two candidates receiving the greatest number of votes — regardless of party — would oppose each other in the runoff general election.

Thus, in 1975, when the governor was chosen under this new system, six candidates, all Democrats, entered the initial open primary held on Nov. 1. There were no Republican, independent or minor party candidates. Gov. Edwin W. Edwards, D, received 62.4 percent of the vote, and only his name appeared on the Dec. 13 general election ballot. (Louisiana by 1978 dispensed with the runoff general election if the primary winner received more than 50 percent of the vote.) If Edwards had placed first with less than 50 percent of the vote, the runoff general election would have been between him and the second-place finisher, even though the other candidate was also a Democrat. In 1978 the law went into effect for House and Senate races.

## Georgia: County Unit System

Another variant of the primary system was Georgia's county unit system. Each county in the state was apportioned a certain number of unit votes. The candidate who received the largest number of popular votes in the county was awarded all the county's unit votes, even if he won only a plurality and not a majority. A candidate had to have a majority of the state's county unit votes to win the primary; otherwise a runoff became necessary. The runoff also was held on the basis of the county unit system.

For example, as of 1946, there were 410 county unit votes. The eight most populous counties had six unit votes each, the next 30 most populous counties had four each, and the remaining 121 counties had two each. The system was weighted toward rural and sparsely populated areas, because every county, no matter how small, had at least two unit votes.

The county unit system sometimes produced winners who received less than a majority of popular votes. Political scientist Key found that in two of 16 gubernatorial races between 1915 and 1948 the winner of a majority of county units received less than a majority of the popular votes. In a third case, that of 1946, the winner of the county unit vote, Eugene Talmadge, actually received fewer popular votes than his chief opponent, James V. Carmichael. The popular vote stood: Carmichael, 313,389 (45.3 percent); Talmadge, 297,245 (43.0 percent); E. D. Rivers, 69,489 (10.0 percent); and Hoke O'Kelly, 11,758 (1.7 percent). But the county unit totals were: Talmadge, 244 (59.5 percent); Carmichael, 144 (35.1 percent); Rivers, 22 (5.4 percent); and O'Kelly, 0 (0.0 percent).

Talmadge's victory was attributable to the rural orientation of the county unit system. His popularity in farm areas gave him an almost clean sweep of the small counties, allowing him to amass more county unit votes than Carmichael, whose strength was centered in the underrepresented urban areas. However, Talmadge died shortly after the November election, precipitating a crisis in Georgia's gubernatorial succession.

The county unit system fell before the Supreme Court's "one-person, one-vote" doctrine. In the 1963 case, *Gray v. Sanders,* the court declared the Georgia county unit system unconstitutional because of the disparity in representation between the urban and rural areas.

## Special Elections

As in other states, special elections in the South are held to fill vacancies for Senate seats or governorships when they occur. However, vacancies sometimes happen at times inconvenient for going through the lengthy runoff primary

### Preference and Runoff Primaries

| State | Preferential Primary | Runoff Primary Adopted |
|---|---|---|
| Alabama | Until 1931 | 1931 |
| Arkansas | — | 1939 [1] |
| Florida | Until 1929 | 1929 |
| Georgia | — | 1917 [2] |
| Louisiana [3] | Until 1922 | 1922 |
| Mississippi | — | 1902 |
| North Carolina | — | 1915 |
| South Carolina | — | 1915 |
| Tennessee [4] | — | — |
| Texas | — | 1918 |
| Virginia [5] | — | — |

1. Arkansas adopted the runoff in 1933, abandoned it in 1935 and reinstituted it in 1939.
2. Runoff held under county unit system; see text this page.
3. Louisiana used the runoff "for a time prior to 1916," according to political scientist V. O. Key, Jr.; in 1975 Louisiana adopted an initial non-partisan primary followed by a general election runoff.
4. Tennessee has never used the preferential or runoff primary. Candidates are nominated by winning a plurality; see text, p. 628.
5. Virginia adopted the runoff primary in 1969 and repealed it in 1971.

Sources: Heard, Alexander, and Donald S. Strong, *Southern Primaries and Elections* (1950 Reprint, Salem, N.H.: Ayers, 1970). Key, V. O. Jr. *Southern Politics in State and Nation* (New York: Alfred A. Knopf, 1949); Virginia secretary of state.

process prior to the special election. Either the filing deadline for the primaries has passed, or the vacancy occurs in a year when there is no regular primary scheduled. In such cases, the Democratic state committee sometimes selects the party nominee without holding a primary.

This process has led to unexpected results. In Arkansas in 1937, for example, a special election was held on Oct. 19 for the five years remaining in the term of Democratic senator Joseph T. Robinson, who had died in office. The Democratic state committee chose Gov. Carl E. Bailey as the party's official nominee. But Rep. John E. Miller of the 2nd District promptly jumped into the race as an independent Democrat, complaining that Democratic voters had not been given a choice of who their nominee should be. The result was a Miller victory, with 60.5 percent of the vote.

In an even more sensational case, this time in a regular election, the Democratic Party leadership in South Carolina found its wishes thwarted in 1954 when it nominated Edgar A. Brown following the death of Sen. Burnet R. Maybank, who had won renomination in the June Democratic primary. Former governor Strom Thurmond, feeling aggrieved that he had been deprived of a chance for the Senate nomination, entered the November election as a write-in candidate. With the backing of the outgoing governor, James F. Byrnes, Thurmond won the race overwhelmingly, 143,444 to 83,525 — making him the only senator ever elected on a write-in vote.

## Texas' Runoff Special Elections

To avoid the pitfalls sometimes encountered when candidates are chosen without a primary, Texas adopted a unique method of holding special elections for U.S. House and Senate seats. (Governors are not elected by special election. Instead, the lieutenant governor automatically becomes governor when a vacancy occurs.) All candidates, no matter which party they belong to, compete in a free-for-all first election. If no one receives a majority, a second election is held between the top two candidates, regardless of party. Thus, the second election could occur between two Democrats, between two Republicans, or between a Democrat and a Republican or even between third-party candidates. The system was used in the 1961 special Senate contest to fill the vacancy caused when Democratic senator Lyndon B. Johnson resigned to become vice president. In the first contest, there were 73 candidates competing, with Republican John G. Tower and Democrat William Blakley finishing first and second. The second election resulted in a Tower victory, 448,217 to 437,874. The same system prevails for Texas' special U.S. House elections.

# White Primaries

Closely connected with the history of Southern Democratic primaries is the issue of race. In many Southern states, blacks were long barred from participation in the Democratic primary, either on a statewide basis or in various counties. To exclude blacks from the primaries, the Democratic Party was designated as a private association or club. The practice was defended as constitutional because the 15th Amendment, ratified in 1870, prohibited only *states,* not private associations, from denying the right to vote to persons on account of race or color. However, in 1944 the Supreme Court, in the case of *Smith v. Allwright,* declared the white primary unconstitutional, holding that it was an integral part of the election machinery for choosing state and federal officials.

**Poll Tax.** Another device used in limiting both black and white voters was the poll tax, which required the payment of a fee before voting. The amount of the poll tax ranged from one to two dollars, but in Alabama, Mississippi, Virginia and Georgia before 1945 the tax was cumulative. Thus, a new voter in Georgia could face up to $47 in fees. Various regulations as to the time and manner of payment of the tax also substantially reduced the number of voters. In Mississippi, for example, a person wanting to vote in the Democratic primary (usually held in August) had to pay his poll tax on or before the first day of the two preceding Februarys — long before most voters had even begun to think about the election.

The poll tax was barred in federal elections by ratification of the 24th Amendment in January 1964. The amendment simply stated that the "right of citizens of the United States to vote in any primary or other election ... shall not be denied or abridged by the United States or any other State by reason of failure to pay any poll tax or other tax."

**Literacy Tests.** The literacy test was another method used to limit the Southern franchise to whites. Voters were required to read and/or write correctly — usually a section of the state or federal Constitution. Sometimes, voters who could not pass the test could have the materials read to them, to see if they could "understand" or "interpret" it correctly. This provision allowed local voting officials, inevitably whites, to judge whether voters passed the tests; it usually resulted in whites passing and blacks failing.

However, in his study of Southern politics, Key concluded that informal pressures — including economic reprisals and other sanctions — were more important in limiting the black franchise than were the official suffrage limitations.

By the 1970s most formal bars to voting in the South, and many informal ones, had been lifted, either by constitutional amendment, federal laws, state action or protest movements.

# Gubernatorial Elections

# Gubernatorial Elections

Governors were not popular during the period of the American Revolution. To the revolutionists, the British-appointed governors were symbols of the mother country's control and tyranny.

Before the Revolutionary War, colonial assemblies were able to assert their control over appropriations and thus became the champions of colonial rights against the governors. Thus, when forming their own state constitutions, the newly freed Americans tended to look with suspicion on the office of governor and gave most of the power to the legislative bodies.

For these reasons, early American governors found themselves hemmed in by restrictions. Among such restrictions were both the length of the term of office and the method of election.

To this day, the 50 state governors are among the most restricted of the officials elected under the United States' federal system of government. Presidents have been limited to two terms since 1951 by constitutional amendment but states only recently have begun trying to limit the length of service of their members of Congress. As of 1994, 15 states had approved such limits for senators and representatives. *(Term limits, box, p. 624)*

By contrast, more than half the states limit their governors to two consecutive terms or less. Almost all, however, had abandoned the original one- or two-year terms in favor of four-year terms that required fewer elections and permitted more stability in the nation's statehouses.

## Length of Terms

As of 1789 all four New England states — Connecticut, Massachusetts, New Hampshire and Rhode Island (Vermont was admitted in 1791 and Maine in 1820) — held gubernatorial elections every year. Some of the Middle Atlantic states favored somewhat longer terms; New York and Pennsylvania had three-year terms for their governors, although New Jersey instituted a one-year term. The Border and Southern states had a mix: Maryland and North Carolina governors served a one-year term, South Carolina had a two-year term, and Delaware, Virginia and Georgia had three-year terms. No state had a four-year term.

Over the years states have changed the length of gubernatorial terms. With some occasional back and forth movement, the general trend has been toward longer terms. New York, for example, has changed the term of office of its governor four times. Beginning in 1777 with a three-year term, the state switched to a two-year term in 1820, back to a three-year term in 1876, back to a two-year term in 1894, and to a four-year term beginning in 1938.

Maryland provides another example of a state that has changed its gubernatorial term several times. Beginning with one year in 1776, the state extended the term to three years in 1838, then to four years in 1851. Regular gubernatorial elections were held every second odd year from then through 1923, when the state had one three-year term so that future elections would be held in even-numbered years, beginning in 1926. Thus, the state held gubernatorial elections in 1919, 1923 and 1926 and then every four years after that.

The trend toward longer gubernatorial terms shows up clearly in a comparison of the length of terms in 1900 and 1994. Of the 45 states in the Union in 1900, 22, almost half, had two-year terms. One (New Jersey) had a three-year term, while Rhode Island and Massachusetts were the only states left with one-year terms. The remaining 20 states had four-year gubernatorial terms. *(Length of terms, box, p. 634)*

By mid-1994, 43 of those same states had four-year terms, and the five states admitted to the Union after 1900 — Oklahoma (1907), Arizona and New Mexico (1912), Alaska and Hawaii (1959) — also had four-year gubernatorial terms. This left only two states with two-year terms: New Hampshire and Vermont.

Arkansas, one of the last holdouts, voted in 1984 to switch to a four-year term, effective in 1986. Rhode Island voters in 1992 approved a constitutional change to a four-term beginning in 1995.

## Sources

*The Book of the States, 1992-1993,* vol. 29. Lexington, Ky.: Council of State Governments, 1992.

Lipson, Leslie, *The American Governor from Figurehead to Leader.* 1939. Reprint. Westport, Conn.: Greenwood Press, 1969.

Offices of secretaries of state of Connecticut, Georgia, Hawaii, Maine, Massachusetts, New Hampshire, Rhode Island, Vermont, Washington and West Virginia.

## Length of Governor Terms

| State | 1900 | 1994 | Year of Change to Longer Term |
|-------|------|------|-------------------------------|
| Alabama | 2 | 4 | 1902 |
| Alaska [1] | — | 4 | — |
| Arizona [1] | — | 4 | 1970 |
| Arkansas | 2 | 4 | 1986 |
| California | 4 | 4 | — |
| Colorado | 2 | 4 | 1958 |
| Connecticut | 2 | 4 | 1950 |
| Delaware | 4 | 4 | — |
| Florida | 4 | 4 | — |
| Georgia | 2 | 4 | 1942 |
| Hawaii [1] | — | 4 | — |
| Idaho | 2 | 4 | 1946 |
| Illinois | 4 | 4 | — |
| Indiana | 4 | 4 | — |
| Iowa | 2 | 4 | 1974 |
| Kansas | 2 | 4 | 1974 |
| Kentucky | 4 | 4 | — |
| Louisiana | 4 | 4 | — |
| Maine | 2 | 4 | 1958 |
| Maryland | 4 | 4 | — |
| Massachusetts [2] | 1 | 4 | 1920, 1966 |
| Michigan | 2 | 4 | 1966 |
| Minnesota | 2 | 4 | 1962 |
| Mississippi | 4 | 4 | — |
| Missouri | 4 | 4 | — |
| Montana | 4 | 4 | — |
| Nebraska | 2 | 4 | 1966 |
| Nevada | 4 | 4 | — |
| New Hampshire | 2 | 2 | — |
| New Jersey | 3 | 4 | 1949 |
| New Mexico [1] | — | 4 | 1970 |
| New York | 2 | 4 | 1938 |
| North Carolina | 4 | 4 | — |
| North Dakota | 2 | 4 | 1964 |
| Ohio | 2 | 4 | 1958 |
| Oklahoma [1] | — | 4 | — |
| Oregon | 4 | 4 | — |
| Pennsylvania | 4 | 4 | — |
| Rhode Island [3] | 1 | 2 | 1912, 1994 |
| South Carolina | 2 | 4 | 1926 |
| South Dakota | 2 | 4 | 1974 |
| Tennessee | 2 | 4 | 1954 |
| Texas | 2 | 4 | 1974 |
| Utah | 4 | 4 | — |
| Vermont | 2 | 2 | — |
| Virginia | 4 | 4 | — |
| Washington | 4 | 4 | — |
| West Virginia | 4 | 4 | — |
| Wisconsin | 2 | 4 | 1970 |
| Wyoming | 4 | 4 | — |

1. Oklahoma was admitted to the Union in 1907, Arizona and New Mexico in 1912, and Alaska and Hawaii in 1959. Oklahoma, Alaska and Hawaii have always had four-year gubernatorial terms; Arizona began with a two-year term and switched to four years in 1970. New Mexico (1912) began with a four-year term, changed to two years in 1916, and back to four years in 1970.

2. Massachusetts switched from a one- to a two-year term in 1920 and to a four-year term in 1966.

3. Rhode Island switched from a one- to a two-year term in 1912 and to a four-year term effective in 1995.

Source: *The Book of the States, 1992-1993*, vol. 29 (Lexington, Ky.: The Council of State Governments, 1992); *Congressional Quarterly Weekly Report*.

## Trend to Isolation

Along with the change to longer terms for governors came another trend — away from holding gubernatorial elections in presidential election years. Except for North Dakota, every state in the 20th century that switched to four-year gubernatorial terms scheduled its elections in non-presidential years. Moreover, Florida, which held its quadrennial gubernatorial elections in presidential years, changed to non-presidential years in 1966. To make the switch, the state shortened to two years the term of the governor elected in 1964, then resumed the four-year term in 1966. Thus, Florida held gubernatorial elections in 1960, 1964, 1966, 1970 and 1974.

Illinois made a similar switch in 1976-78, leaving nine states — Delaware, Indiana, Missouri, Montana, North Carolina, North Dakota, Utah, Washington and West Virginia — holding quadrennial gubernatorial elections at the same time as the presidential election. New Hampshire and Vermont still had two-year terms, so every other gubernatorial election in these two states occurred in a presidential year.

Arkansas and Rhode Island, the two most recent converts to four-year terms, chose to select their governors in non-presidential election years, beginning in 1986 for Arkansas and 1994 for Rhode Island.

## Methods of Election

Yet another way in which Americans of the early federal period restricted their governors was by the method of election. In 1789, only in New York and the four New England states did the people directly choose their governors by popular vote. In the remaining eight states, governors were chosen by the state legislatures, thus enhancing the power of the legislatures in their dealing with the governors. But several factors — including the democratic trend to elect public officials directly, the increasing trust in the office of governor and the need for a stronger and more independent chief executive — led to the gradual introduction of popular votes in all the states.

By the 1860s the remaining eight original states all had switched to popular ballots. Pennsylvania was first, in 1790, and was followed by Delaware in 1792, Georgia in 1824, North Carolina in 1835, Maryland in 1838, New Jersey in 1844, Virginia in 1851 and South Carolina in 1865, after the Civil War.

All the states admitted to the Union after the original 13, with one exception, made provision from the very beginning for popular election of their governors. The exception was Louisiana, which from its admission in 1812 until a change in the state constitution in 1845 had a unique system of gubernatorial elections. The people participated by voting in a first-step popular election. In a second step, the legislature was to select the governor from the two candidates receiving the highest popular vote.

Because of the domination of the Democratic Party in the South for many years after the Civil War, the Democratic primary was more important than the general election in the selection of governors and other officials in some Southern states. Victory in the party's primary often was tantamount to election, with the winner unopposed or facing token Republican opposition in the November election. *(The Historical Significance of Southern Primaries, p. 627)*

Although the so-called Solid South has become more of a two-party region in recent decades, the South continues to produce some anomalies in the election of governors. Louisiana, for example, holds an open primary for governor late in every fourth odd-numbered year. Candidates from all parties run on the same ballot. Any candidate who receives a majority is elected. If no candidate receives 50 percent, a runoff is held between the two top finishers.

## Number of Terms

Another limitation placed on governors is a restriction on the number of terms they are allowed to serve. In the early years at least three states had such limitations: governors of Maryland were eligible to serve three consecutive one-year terms and then were required to retire for at least one year; Pennsylvania allowed its governors three consecutive three-year terms and then forced retirement for at least one term; and in New Jersey, according to the constitution of 1844, a governor could serve only one three-year term before retiring for at least one term.

In 1994, 30 states had a limitation on the number of consecutive terms their governors could serve. Of these 30, two — Kentucky and Virginia — limited the governor to one term only. The remaining 28 states allowed their governors to seek re-election once but required that they step down after two terms for an interim of at least one term. Three states — Delaware, Missouri and North Carolina — imposed an absolute two-term limit. That is, a governor could serve only two terms, however spaced, in his lifetime. The remaining 20 states imposed no limits on the number of consecutive terms a governor could serve. *(Table on right.)*

## Majority Vote Requirement

One peculiarity of gubernatorial voting that has almost disappeared from the American political scene is the requirement that the winning gubernatorial candidate receive a majority of the popular vote. Otherwise, the choice devolves upon the state legislature or upon a runoff between the two highest candidates.

All six New England states had such a provision in their state constitutions at one time. New Hampshire, Vermont, Massachusetts and Connecticut had the provision when they entered the Union between 1788 and 1791. Rhode Island required a majority election but did not adopt a provision for legislative election until 1842; Maine adopted a majority provision when it split off from Massachusetts to form a separate state in 1820. Elsewhere, Georgia put the majority provision in its constitution when it switched from legislative to popular election of governors in 1825; Mississippi put it in its 1890 constitution; and Arizona adopted a runoff in 1990.

The purpose of the majority provision appears to have been to safeguard against a candidate's winning with a small fraction of the popular vote in a multiple field. In most of New England, the provision was part of the early state constitutions, formed largely in the 1780s, before the development of the two-party system.

The prospect of multiple-candidate fields diminished with the coming of the two-party system. Nevertheless, each of these states had occasion to use the provision at least once. Sometimes, in an extremely close election, minor party candidates received enough of a vote to keep the winner from getting a majority of the total vote. And at other times strong third-party movements or disintegration of the old party structure resulted in the election's being thrown into the state legislature.

## Limitations on Governor Terms

In most states with limits of one or two consecutive terms, governors may serve again after a one-term hiatus. Thus in a state with a one-term limitation, the governor must retire at the end of the first term. After a one-term interim, he or she may serve again.

| State | Maximum Number of Consecutive Terms (as of 1994) |
|---|---|
| Alabama | 2 |
| Alaska | 2 |
| Arizona | No limit |
| Arkansas | No limit |
| California | 2 |
| Colorado | 2 |
| Connecticut | No limit |
| Delaware [1] | 2 |
| Florida | 2 |
| Georgia | 2 |
| Hawaii | 2 |
| Idaho | No limit |
| Illinois | No limit |
| Indiana | 2 |
| Iowa | No limit |
| Kansas | 2 |
| Kentucky | 1 |
| Louisiana | 2 |
| Maine | 2 |
| Maryland | 2 |
| Massachusetts | No limit |
| Michigan | No limit |
| Minnesota | No limit |
| Mississippi | 2 |
| Missouri [1] | 2 |
| Montana | No limit |
| Nebraska | 2 |
| Nevada | 2 |
| New Hampshire | No limit |
| New Jersey | 2 |
| New Mexico | 2 |
| New York | No limit |
| North Carolina [1] | 2 |
| North Dakota | No limit |
| Ohio | 2 |
| Oklahoma | 2 |
| Oregon [2] | 2 |
| Pennsylvania | 2 |
| Rhode Island | No limit |
| South Carolina | 2 |
| South Dakota | 2 |
| Tennessee | 2 |
| Texas | No limit |
| Utah | No limit |
| Vermont | No limit |
| Virginia | 1 |
| Washington | No limit |
| West Virginia | 2 |
| Wisconsin | No limit |
| Wyoming | No limit |

*1. Delaware, Missouri and North Carolina have absolute two-term limits. That is, no person may serve more than two gubernatorial terms in his or her lifetime.*

*2. Oregon prohibits a person from serving more than eight years in any 12-year period.*

Source: *The Book of the States, 1992-1993*, vol. 29. Lexington, Ky.: The Council of State Governments, 1992.

# Party Lineup of Governors

The figures below show the number of governorships held by the two parties after each election since 1950.

| Year | Democrat | Republican | Independent |
|------|----------|------------|-------------|
| 1950 | 23 | 25 | 0 |
| 1952 | 18 | 30 | 0 |
| 1954 | 27 | 21 | 0 |
| 1956 | 29 | 19 | 0 |
| 1958 | 35 | 14 | 0 |
| 1960 | 34 | 16 | 0 |
| 1962 | 34 | 16 | 0 |
| 1964 | 33 | 17 | 0 |
| 1966 | 25 | 25 | 0 |
| 1968 | 19 | 31 | 0 |
| 1970 | 29 | 21 | 0 |
| 1972 | 31 | 19 | 0 |
| 1974 | 36 | 13 | 1 |
| 1976 | 37 | 12 | 1 |
| 1978 | 32 | 18 | 0 |
| 1980 | 26 | 24 | 0 |
| 1982 | 34 | 16 | 0 |
| 1984 | 34 | 16 | 0 |
| 1986 | 26 | 24 | 0 |
| 1988 | 28 | 22 | 0 |
| 1990 | 27 | 21 | 2 |
| 1992 | 30 | 18 | 2 |

SOURCE: Republican National Committee; *Congressional Quarterly Weekly Report.*

Five of the nine states that originally had a majority requirement have repeated it. Georgia maintains it but instead of legislative election, now provides for a runoff between the top two contenders three weeks after the general election. Mississippi's majority vote provision has never been used because the Democratic Party nominee always had received a majority (until 1991, when the Republican winner secured a majority).

Following are the states that had the majority vote provision for governor (except Mississippi), the years in which the choice devolved on the legislature because of it, and the year, if any, in which the requirement was repealed or changed:

**Arizona.** Arizona adopted and used a runoff provision in 1990 following impeachment of a governor elected with less than a majority.

**Connecticut.** No gubernatorial candidate received a majority of the popular vote, thus throwing the election into the legislature, in the following years subsequent to 1824: 1833, 1834, 1842, 1844, 1846, 1849, 1850, 1851, 1854, 1855, 1856, 1878, 1884, 1886, 1888 and 1890. Following the election of 1890, the legislature was unable to choose a new governor, so the outgoing governor, Morgan G. Bulkeley, R, continued to serve through the entire new term (1891-93). The provision was repealed in 1901. The years prior to 1824 in which the provision was used, if any, were unavailable from the Connecticut secretary of state's office.

**Georgia.** Although the majority vote requirement was initiated in 1825, when Georgia first elected its governor by popular vote, it was not used until the 20th century. In 1966, with an emerging Republican Party, a controversial Demo-

cratic nominee and an independent Democrat all affecting the gubernatorial race, no candidate received a majority. The legislature chose Democrat Lester Maddox. It was the controversy surrounding this experience that led to the change from legislative choice to a runoff between the top two contenders. Earlier, in 1946, the Georgia legislature also attempted to choose the governor, under unusual circumstances not covered by the majority vote requirement. The governor-elect, Eugene Talmadge, D, died before taking office. When it met, the legislature chose Talmadge's son, Herman E. Talmadge, as the new governor. Herman Talmadge was eligible for consideration on the basis that he received enough write-in votes in the general election to make him the second-place candidate. But the state Supreme Court voided the legislature's choice and declared that the lieutenant governor-elect, Melvin E. Thompson, D, should be governor. The runoff provision was first used in the 1992 election for U.S. senator.

**Maine.** Maine entered statehood in 1820 with a majority vote provision for governor but repealed it in 1880. During this 60-year span, the legislature was called on to choose the governor nine times, in 1840, 1846, 1848, 1852, 1853, 1854, 1855, 1878 and 1879.

**Massachusetts.** Like the other New England states, Massachusetts originally had a requirement for majority voting in gubernatorial elections. However, after the legislature was forced to choose the governor for six straight elections from 1848 to 1853, Massachusetts repealed the provision in 1855. The years in which it was used were 1785, 1833, 1842, 1843, 1845, 1848, 1849, 1850, 1851, 1852 and 1853.

**New Hampshire.** New Hampshire's mandated majority vote for governor was in force from 1784 through 1912, when it was repealed. The outcome of the following gubernatorial elections was determined by the legislature: 1785, 1787, 1789, 1790, 1812, 1824, 1846, 1851, 1856, 1863, 1871, 1874, 1875, 1886, 1888, 1890, 1906 and 1912.

**Rhode Island.** Under the constitution of 1842, Rhode Island required a majority to win the gubernatorial election. Under this mandate, the legislature chose the governor in the years 1846, 1875, 1876, 1880, 1889, 1890 and 1891. Because of a disagreement between the two houses of the state legislature, the ballots for governor were not counted in 1893, and Gov. D. Russell Brown, R, continued in office for another term of one year. The provision for majority voting then was repealed.

Before 1842 there was also a requirement for a popular majority, but the legislature was not allowed to choose a new governor if no candidate achieved a majority. Three times — in 1806, 1832 and 1839 — there was no majority in a gubernatorial election, with a different outcome each time. In 1806 the lieutenant governor-elect served as acting governor for the term. In 1832 the legislature mandated a new election, but still no majority choice was reached; three more elections were held, all without a majority being achieved, so the same state officers were continued until the next regular election. And in 1839, when neither the gubernatorial nor lieutenant governor's race yielded a winner by majority, the senior state senator acted as governor for the term.

**Vermont.** Vermont's provision for majority gubernatorial election resulted in the legislature's picking the governor 20 times: 1789, 1797, 1813, 1814, 1830, 1831, 1832, 1834, 1841, 1843, 1845, 1846, 1847, 1848, 1849, 1852, 1853, 1902, 1912 and 1986. On another occasion, 1835, the legislature failed to choose a new governor because of a deadlock and the lieutenant governor-elect served as governor for the term. The Vermont provision remains in force.

# Governors of the States, 1789-1994

# Sources: Governors of the States, 1789-1994

This section (pages 639-663) contains a listing of state governors through May 1994. Arranged alphabetically by state, the lists provide the name, political affiliation and dates of service of each state's governors in chronological order.

The following sources were used for the names, party affiliations and dates of service for governors.

● *Governors of the States 1900-1974*. Lexington, Ky.: Council of State Governments, 1974. Compiled by Samuel R. Solomon.

● *The Book of Governors*. Los Angeles: Washington Typographers, 1935. Compiled by William W. Hunt.

● Kallenbach, Joseph E., and Jessamine S. Kallenbach. *American State Governors, 1776-1976*. 3 vols. Dobbs Ferry, N.Y.: Oceana Publishing, 1977.

● Scammon, Richard M., and Alice V. McGillivray. *America Votes 20*. Washington, D.C.: Congressional Quarterly, 1993.

● State manuals published by the state governments.

● State governors' offices.

● Gubernatorial election returns provided by the Inter-University Consortium for Political and Social Research (ICPSR), appearing on pages 667 to 716.

● *The Encyclopedia Americana*. 30 vols. Danbury, Conn.: Grolier Education, 1982.

## Names, Party Affiliation and Dates of Service

For the 20th century, *The Governors of the States 1900-1974* was the primary source for the names of governors and dates of service. The party designations appearing in the ICPSR election returns were used to assign party affiliation. Where the ICPSR returns indicated two or more party designations, only the major party is listed. *(For a list of party abbreviations, see p. 1352; for other references to individual governors, see General Index, p. 1503.)*

For the 18th and 19th centuries, state manuals and Hunt's *The Book of Governors* were used for names and dates of service. Hunt provides the names of state governors and dates of service — in some cases complete dates (month, day and year), in other cases only month and year and in still other cases only the dates of gubernatorial elections. Congressional Quarterly has used the most precise dates available from Hunt and state manuals.

Because political parties did not exist formally in the early years of the Republic, classification of governors by party during this period can be difficult or misleading *("Pre-Convention Politics," p. 7; "Historical Profiles of American Political Parties," p. 259)*. In cases where party affiliation was not appropriate or could not be determined, no party designation appears. After 1824, the starting date for the ICPSR gubernatorial election returns, the ICPSR data were used where they provided information on party affiliation. State manuals and *The Encyclopedia Americana*, which gives governors' party affiliation for some states, were also consulted.

## Footnotes

Footnotes, based on information from the above sources, have been used to indicate the following circumstances:

● Deaths, resignations or removals from office and succession of lieutenant governors or other officials to governorships.

● Circumstances surrounding disputed elections.

For details on the 20th-century trend toward longer gubernatorial terms and limitations on the number of consecutive terms, as well as unusual gubernatorial election procedures in some states, see "Gubernatorial Elections," pages 633 to 636.

# Governors of the States, 1789-1994

## ALABAMA

(Became a state Dec. 14, 1819)

| Governors | Dates of Service | |
|---|---|---|
| William W. Bibb (D-R) | Nov. 9, 1819 | July 15, 1820 |
| Thomas Bibb (D-R) | July 15, 1820 | Nov. 9, 1821 |
| Israel Pickens (D-R) | Nov. 9, 1821 | Nov. 25, 1825 |
| John Murphy (JAC D) | Nov. 25, 1825 | Nov. 25, 1829 |
| Gabriel Moore (JAC D) | Nov. 25, 1829 | March 3, 1831 |
| Samuel B. Moore (D) | March 3, 1832 | Nov. 26, 1831 |
| John Gayle (D) | Nov. 26, 1831 | Nov. 21, 1835 |
| Clement C. Clay (D) | Nov. 21, 1835 | July 17, 1837 |
| Hugh McVay (D) | July 17, 1837 | Nov. 21, 1837 |
| Arthur P. Bagby (D) | Nov. 21, 1837 | Nov. 22, 1841 |
| Benjamin Fitzpatrick (D) | Nov. 22, 1841 | Dec. 10, 1845 |
| Joshua L. Martin (I) | Dec. 10, 1845 | Dec. 16, 1847 |
| Reuben Chapman (D) | Dec. 16, 1847 | Dec. 17, 1849 |
| Henry W. Collier (D) | Dec. 17, 1849 | Dec. 20, 1853 |
| John A. Winston (D) | Dec. 20, 1853 | Dec. 1, 1857 |
| Andrew B. Moore (D) | Dec. 1, 1857 | Dec. 2, 1861 |
| John Gill Shorter (D) | Dec. 2, 1861 | Dec. 1, 1863 |
| Thomas H. Watts (W) | Dec. 1, 1863 | May 1865 |
| Lewis E. Parsons[1] | June 21, 1865 | Dec. 20, 1865 |
| Robert M. Patton (W) | Dec. 20, 1865 | July 14, 1868 |
| William Hugh Smith (R) | July 14, 1868 | Nov. 26, 1870 |
| Robert B. Lindsay (D) | Nov. 26, 1870 | Nov. 17, 1872 |
| David P. Lewis (R) | Nov. 17, 1872 | Nov. 24, 1874 |
| George S. Houston (D) | Nov. 24, 1874 | Nov. 28, 1878 |
| Rufus W. Cobb (D) | Nov. 28, 1878 | Dec. 1, 1882 |
| Edward A. O'Neal (D) | Dec. 1, 1882 | Dec. 1, 1886 |
| Thomas Seay (D) | Dec. 1, 1886 | Dec. 1, 1890 |
| Thomas G. Jones (D) | Dec. 1, 1890 | Dec. 1, 1894 |
| William C. Oates (D) | Dec. 1, 1894 | Dec. 1, 1896 |
| Joseph F. Johnston (D) | Dec. 1, 1896 | Dec. 1, 1900 |
| William D. Jelks (D)[2] | Dec. 1, 1900 | Dec. 26, 1900 |
| William J. Samford (D)[3] | Dec. 26, 1900 | June 11, 1901 |
| William D. Jelks (D)[4] | June 11, 1901 | April 25, 1904 |
| Russell M. Cunningham (D)[5] | April 25, 1904 | March 5, 1905 |
| William D. Jelks (D) | March 5, 1905 | Jan. 14, 1907 |
| Braxton B. Comer (D) | Jan. 14, 1907 | Jan. 17, 1911 |
| Emmet O'Neal (D) | Jan. 17, 1911 | Jan. 18, 1915 |
| Charles Henderson (D) | Jan. 18, 1915 | Jan. 20, 1919 |
| Thomas E. Kilby (D) | Jan. 20, 1919 | Jan. 15, 1923 |
| William W. Brandon (D) | Jan. 15, 1923 | Jan. 17, 1927 |
| Bibb Graves (D) | Jan. 17, 1927 | Jan. 19, 1931 |
| Benjamin M. Miller (D) | Jan. 19, 1931 | Jan. 14, 1935 |
| Bibb Graves (D) | Jan. 14, 1935 | Jan. 17, 1939 |
| Frank M. Dixon (D) | Jan. 17, 1939 | Jan. 19, 1943 |
| Chauncey M. Sparks (D) | Jan. 19, 1943 | Jan. 20, 1947 |
| James E. Folsom (D) | Jan. 20, 1947 | Jan. 15, 1951 |
| Gordon Persons (D) | Jan. 15, 1951 | Jan. 17, 1955 |
| James E. Folsom (D) | Jan. 17, 1955 | Jan. 19, 1959 |
| John M. Patterson (D) | Jan. 19, 1959 | Jan. 14, 1963 |
| George C. Wallace (D) | Jan. 14, 1963 | Jan. 16, 1967 |
| Lurleen B. Wallace (D)[6] | Jan. 16, 1967 | May 7, 1968 |
| Albert P. Brewer (D)[7] | May 7, 1968 | Jan. 18, 1971 |
| George C. Wallace (D) | Jan. 18, 1971 | Jan. 15, 1979 |
| Forrest (Fob) James (D) | Jan. 15, 1979 | Jan. 17, 1983 |
| George C. Wallace (D) | Jan. 17, 1983 | Jan. 19, 1987 |
| Guy Hunt (R)[8] | Jan. 19, 1987 | April 22, 1993 |
| James E. Folsom Jr. (D)[9] | April 22, 1993 | |

**Alabama**
1. Provisional governor, appointed by president.
2. Jelks, as president of the state Senate, took office as acting governor due to the illness of governor-elect Samford.
3. Died June 11, 1901.
4. As president of the state Senate, Jelks became governor on Samford's death. Subsequently re-elected in 1902.
5. As lieutenant governor, he became acting governor due to the illness of Jelks.
6. Died May 7, 1968.
7. As lieutenant governor, he succeeded to office.
8. Removed from office upon conviction of misusing campaign funds.
9. As lieutenant governor, he succeeded to office.

## ALASKA

(Became a state Jan. 3, 1959)

| Governors | Dates of Service | |
|---|---|---|
| William A. Egan (D) | Jan. 3, 1959 | Dec. 5, 1966 |
| Walter J. Hickel (R)[1] | Dec. 5, 1966 | Jan. 29, 1969 |
| Keith H. Miller (R)[2] | Jan. 29, 1969 | Dec. 5, 1970 |
| William A. Egan (D) | Dec. 5, 1970 | Dec. 2, 1974 |
| Jay S. Hammond (R) | Dec. 2, 1974 | Dec. 6, 1982 |
| Bill Sheffield (D) | Dec. 6, 1982 | Dec. 1, 1986 |
| Steve C. Cowper (D) | Dec. 1, 1986 | Dec. 3, 1990 |
| Walter J. Hickel (ALI) | Dec. 3, 1990 | |

**Alaska**
1. Resigned Jan. 29, 1969.
2. As secretary of state, he succeeded to office.

## ARIZONA

(Became a state Feb. 14, 1912)

| Governors | Dates of Service | |
|---|---|---|
| George W. P. Hunt (D) | Feb. 14, 1912 | Jan. 1, 1917 |
| Thomas E. Campbell (R)[1] | Jan. 1, 1917 | Dec. 25, 1917 |
| George W. P. Hunt (D)[2] | Dec. 25, 1917 | Jan. 6, 1919 |
| Thomas E. Campbell (R) | Jan. 6, 1919 | Jan. 1, 1923 |
| George W. P. Hunt (D) | Jan. 1, 1923 | Jan. 7, 1929 |
| John C. Phillips (R) | Jan. 7, 1929 | Jan. 5, 1931 |
| George W. P. Hunt (D) | Jan. 5, 1931 | Jan. 2, 1933 |
| Benjamin B. Moeur (D) | Jan. 2, 1933 | Jan. 4, 1937 |
| Rawghile C. Stanford (D) | Jan. 4, 1937 | Jan. 2, 1939 |
| Robert T. Jones (D) | Jan. 2, 1939 | Jan. 6, 1941 |
| Sidney P. Osborn (D)[3] | Jan. 6, 1941 | May 25, 1948 |
| Dan E. Garvey (D)[4] | May 25, 1948 | Jan. 1, 1951 |
| J. Howard Pyle (R) | Jan. 1, 1951 | Jan. 3, 1955 |
| Ernest W. McFarland (D) | Jan. 3, 1955 | Jan. 5, 1959 |
| Paul J. Fannin (R) | Jan. 5, 1959 | Jan. 4, 1965 |
| Sam Goddard (D) | Jan. 4, 1965 | Jan. 2, 1967 |

| | | | | | |
|---|---|---|---|---|---|
| Jack Williams (R) | Jan. 2, 1967 | Jan. 6, 1975 | Dale Bumpers (D)[16] | Jan. 12, 1971 | Jan. 3, 1975 |
| Raul Castro (D)[5] | Jan. 6, 1975 | Oct. 20, 1977 | Bob Riley (D)[17] | Jan. 3, 1975 | Jan. 14, 1975 |
| Wesley Bolin (D)[6] | Oct. 20, 1977 | March 4, 1978 | David Pryor (D)[18] | Jan. 14, 1975 | Jan. 3, 1979 |
| Bruce Babbitt (D)[7] | March 4, 1978 | Jan. 5, 1987 | Joe Purcell (D)[19] | Jan. 3, 1979 | Jan. 9, 1979 |
| Evan Mecham (R)[8] | Jan. 5, 1987 | April 4, 1988 | Bill Clinton (D) | Jan. 9, 1979 | Jan. 19, 1981 |
| Rose Mofford (D)[9] | April 5, 1988 | March 6, 1991 | Frank D. White (R) | Jan. 19, 1981 | Jan. 11, 1983 |
| Fife Symington (R) | March 6, 1991 | | Bill Clinton (D)[20] | Jan. 11, 1983 | Dec. 12, 1992 |
| | | | Jim Guy Tucker (D)[21] | Dec. 12, 1992 | |

**Arizona**

1. Campbell was initially declared the winner, but the election was contested. After an extended recount, Hunt was declared the winner by 43 votes.
2. Hunt served out the remainder of the term following his successful challenge to Campbell's election.
3. Died May 25, 1948.
4. As secretary of state, he succeeded to office. Subsequently elected.
5. Resigned Oct. 20, 1977, to become ambassador to Argentina.
6. As secretary of state, he succeeded to office. Died March 4, 1978.
7. As attorney general, he succeeded to office. Subsequently elected.
8. Impeached; removed from office April 4, 1988.
9. As secretary of state, she succeeded to office.

**Arkansas**

1. Resigned April 29, 1844.
2. As president of the state Senate, he succeeded to office.
3. Resigned Jan. 10, 1849.
4. As president of the state Senate, he succeeded to office.
5. Acting governor.
6. Resigned March 17, 1871.
7. Succeeded to office.
8. Resigned Feb. 11, 1907.
9. Acting governor.
10. Elected president of the state Senate, he then succeeded to office as governor.
11. Resigned March 10, 1913.
12. As president of the state Senate, he succeeded to office.
13. As president of the state Senate, he succeeded to office.
14. Resigned March 4, 1928.
15. As lieutenant governor, he succeeded to office. Subsequently elected.
16. Resigned Jan. 3, 1975.
17. As lieutenant governor, he succeeded to office.
18. Resigned Jan. 3, 1979.
19. As lieutenant governor, he succeeded to office.
20. Resigned Dec. 12, 1992, having been elected president of the United States.
21. As lieutenant governor, he succeeded to office.

# ARKANSAS

(Became a state June 15, 1836)

| Governors | Dates of Service | |
|---|---|---|
| James S. Conway (D) | Sept. 13, 1836 | Nov. 4, 1840 |
| Archibald Yell (D)[1] | Nov. 4, 1840 | April 29, 1844 |
| Samuel Adams (D)[2] | April 24, 1844 | Nov. 5, 1844 |
| Thomas S. Drew (D)[3] | Nov. 5, 1844 | Jan. 10, 1849 |
| Richard C. Byrd (D)[4] | Jan. 11, 1849 | April 19, 1849 |
| John S. Roane (D) | April 19, 1849 | Nov. 15, 1852 |
| Elias N. Conway (D) | Nov. 15, 1852 | Nov. 16, 1860 |
| Henry M. Rector (ID) | Nov. 16, 1860 | Nov. 4, 1862 |
| Thomas Fletcher[5] | Nov. 4, 1862 | Nov. 15, 1862 |
| Harris Flannigan (D) | Nov. 15, 1862 | April 18, 1864 |
| Isaac Murphy (UN) | April 18, 1864 | July 2, 1868 |
| Powell Clayton (R)[6] | July 2, 1868 | March 17, 1871 |
| Ozra A. Hadley (R)[7] | March 17, 1871 | Jan. 6, 1873 |
| Elisha Baxter (R) | Jan. 6, 1873 | Nov. 12, 1874 |
| A. H. Garland (D) | Nov. 12, 1874 | Jan. 11, 1877 |
| William R. Miller (D) | Jan. 11, 1877 | Jan. 13, 1881 |
| Thomas J. Churchill (D) | Jan. 13, 1881 | Jan. 13, 1883 |
| James H. Berry (D) | Jan. 13, 1883 | Jan. 17, 1885 |
| Simon P. Hughes (D) | Jan. 17, 1885 | Jan. 17, 1889 |
| James P. Eagle (D) | Jan. 17, 1889 | Jan. 10, 1893 |
| William M. Fishback (D) | Jan. 10, 1893 | Jan. 18, 1895 |
| James P. Clarke (D) | Jan. 18, 1895 | Jan. 12, 1897 |
| Daniel Webster Jones (D) | Jan. 12, 1897 | Jan. 8, 1901 |
| Jeff Davis (D) | Jan. 8, 1901 | Jan. 8, 1907 |
| John S. Little (D)[8] | Jan. 8, 1907 | Feb. 11, 1907 |
| John I. Moore (D)[9] | Feb. 11, 1907 | May 11, 1907 |
| Xenophon O. Pindall (D)[10] | May 14, 1907 | Jan. 11, 1909 |
| George W. Donaghey (D) | Jan. 11, 1909 | Jan. 15, 1913 |
| Joseph T. Robinson (D)[11] | Jan. 15, 1913 | March 10, 1913 |
| William K. Oldham (D)[12] | March 10, 1913 | March 13, 1913 |
| Junius M. Futrell (D)[13] | March 13, 1913 | July 23, 1913 |
| George W. Hays (D) | July 23, 1913 | Jan. 9, 1917 |
| Charles H. Brough (D) | Jan. 9, 1917 | Jan. 11, 1921 |
| Thomas C. McRae (D) | Jan. 11, 1921 | Jan. 13, 1925 |
| Thomas J. Terrall (D) | Jan. 13, 1925 | Jan. 11, 1927 |
| John E. Martineau (D)[14] | Jan. 11, 1927 | March 4, 1928 |
| Harvey Parnell (D)[15] | March 4, 1928 | Jan. 10, 1933 |
| Junius M. Futrell (D) | Jan. 10, 1933 | Jan. 12, 1937 |
| Carl E. Bailey (D) | Jan. 12, 1937 | Jan. 14, 1941 |
| Homer M. Adkins (D) | Jan. 14, 1941 | Jan. 9, 1945 |
| Benjamin T. Laney (D) | Jan. 9, 1945 | Jan. 11, 1949 |
| Sidney S. McMath (D) | Jan. 11, 1949 | Jan. 13, 1953 |
| Frances A. Cherry (D) | Jan. 13, 1953 | Jan. 11, 1955 |
| Orval E. Faubus (D) | Jan. 11, 1955 | Jan. 10, 1967 |
| Winthrop Rockefeller (R) | Jan. 10, 1967 | Jan. 12, 1971 |

# CALIFORNIA

(Became a state Sept. 9, 1850)

| Governors | Dates of Service | |
|---|---|---|
| Peter H. Burnett (ID)[1] | Dec. 20, 1849 | Jan. 9, 1851 |
| John McDougal (ID)[2] | Jan. 9, 1851 | Jan. 8, 1852 |
| John Bigler (D) | Jan. 8, 1852 | Jan. 9, 1856 |
| J. Neely Johnson (AM) | Jan. 9, 1856 | Jan. 8, 1858 |
| John B. Weller (D) | Jan. 8, 1858 | Jan. 9, 1860 |
| Milton S. Latham (D)[3] | Jan. 9, 1860 | Jan. 14, 1860 |
| John G. Downey (D)[4] | Jan. 14, 1860 | Jan. 10, 1862 |
| Leland Stanford (R) | Jan. 10, 1862 | Dec. 10, 1863 |
| Frederick F. Low (UN R) | Dec. 10, 1863 | Dec. 5, 1867 |
| Henry H. Haight (D) | Dec. 5, 1867 | Dec. 8, 1871 |
| Newton Booth (R)[5] | Dec. 8, 1871 | Feb. 27, 1875 |
| Romualdo Pacheco (R)[6] | Feb. 27, 1875 | Dec. 9, 1875 |
| William Irwin (D) | Dec. 9, 1875 | Jan. 8, 1880 |
| George C. Perkins (R) | Jan. 8, 1880 | Jan. 10, 1883 |
| George Stoneman (D) | Jan. 10, 1883 | Jan. 8, 1887 |
| Washington Bartlett (D)[7] | Jan. 8, 1887 | Sept. 13, 1887 |
| Robert W. Waterman (R)[8] | Sept. 13, 1887 | Jan. 8, 1891 |
| Henry H. Markham (R) | Jan. 8, 1891 | Jan. 11, 1895 |
| James H. Budd (D) | Jan. 11, 1895 | Jan. 3, 1899 |
| Henry T. Gage (R & UL) | Jan. 3, 1899 | Jan. 6, 1903 |
| George C. Pardee (R) | Jan. 6, 1903 | Jan. 8, 1907 |
| James N. Gillett (R) | Jan. 8, 1907 | Jan. 3, 1911 |
| Hiram W. Johnson (R, PROG)[9] | Jan. 3, 1911 | March 15, 1917 |
| William D. Stephens (RP & PROG)[10] | March 15, 1917 | Jan. 9, 1923 |
| Friend William Richardson (R) | Jan. 9, 1923 | Jan. 4, 1927 |
| Clement C. Young (R) | Jan. 4, 1927 | Jan. 6, 1931 |
| James Rolph Jr. (R)[11] | Jan. 6, 1931 | June 2, 1934 |
| Frank F. Merriam (R)[12] | June 2, 1934 | Jan. 2, 1939 |
| Culbert L. Olson (D) | Jan. 2, 1939 | Jan. 4, 1943 |
| Earl Warren (R)[13] | Jan. 4, 1943 | Oct. 5, 1953 |
| Goodwin J. Knight (R)[14] | Oct. 5, 1953 | Jan. 5, 1959 |
| Edmund G. Brown (D) | Jan. 5, 1959 | Jan. 2, 1967 |

| | | |
|---|---|---|
| Ronald Reagan (R) | Jan. 1, 1967 | Jan. 6, 1975 |
| Edmund G. Brown Jr. (D) | Jan. 6, 1975 | Jan. 3, 1983 |
| George Deukmejian (R) | Jan. 3, 1983 | Jan. 7, 1991 |
| Pete Wilson (R) | Jan. 7, 1991 | |

**California**

*1. Resigned Jan. 9, 1851.*
*2. As lieutenant governor, he succeeded to office.*
*3. Resigned Jan. 14, 1860.*
*4. As lieutenant governor, he succeeded to office.*
*5. Resigned Feb. 27, 1875.*
*6. As lieutenant governor, he succeeded to office.*
*7. Died Sept. 13, 1887.*
*8. As lieutenant governor, he succeeded to office.*
*9. Elected as Republican in 1910. Elected as Progressive in 1914. Resigned March 15, 1917.*
*10. As lieutenant governor, he succeeded to office. Subsequently elected.*
*11. Died June 2, 1934.*
*12. As lieutenant governor, he succeeded to office. Subsequently elected.*
*13. Resigned Oct. 5, 1953.*
*14. As lieutenant governor, he succeeded to office. Subsequently elected.*

# COLORADO

(Became a state Aug. 1, 1876)

| Governors | Dates of Service | |
|---|---|---|
| John L. Routt (R) | Nov. 3, 1876 | Jan. 14, 1879 |
| Frederick W. Pitkin (R) | Jan. 14, 1879 | Jan. 9, 1883 |
| James B. Grant (D) | Jan. 9, 1883 | Jan. 13, 1885 |
| Benjamin H. Eaton (R) | Jan. 13, 1885 | Jan. 11, 1887 |
| Alva Adams (D) | Jan. 11, 1887 | Jan. 10, 1889 |
| Job A. Cooper (R) | Jan. 10, 1889 | Jan. 13, 1891 |
| John L. Routt (R) | Jan. 13, 1891 | Jan. 10, 1893 |
| Davis H. Waite (POP & SL D) | Jan. 10, 1893 | Jan. 8, 1895 |
| Albert W. McIntire (R) | Jan. 8, 1895 | Jan. 12, 1897 |
| Alva Adams (D) | Jan. 12, 1897 | Jan. 10, 1899 |
| Charles S. Thomas (FUS) | Jan. 10, 1899 | Jan. 8, 1901 |
| James B. Orman (FUS) | Jan. 8, 1901 | Jan. 13, 1903 |
| James H. Peabody (R)[1] | Jan. 13, 1903 | Jan. 10, 1905 |
| Alva Adams (D)[1] | Jan. 10, 1905 | March 16, 1905 |
| James H. Peabody (R) | March 16, 1905 | March 17, 1905 |
| Jesse F. McDonald (R)[2] | March 17, 1905 | Jan. 8, 1907 |
| Henry A. Buchtel (R) | Jan. 8, 1907 | Jan. 12, 1909 |
| John F. Shafroth (D) | Jan. 12, 1909 | Jan. 14, 1913 |
| Elias M. Ammons (D) | Jan. 14, 1913 | Jan. 12, 1915 |
| George A. Carlson (R) | Jan. 12, 1915 | Jan. 9, 1917 |
| Julius C. Gunter (D) | Jan. 9, 1917 | Jan. 14, 1919 |
| Oliver H. Shoup (R) | Jan. 14, 1919 | Jan. 9, 1923 |
| William E. Sweet (D) | Jan. 9, 1923 | Jan. 13, 1925 |
| Clarence J. Morley (R) | Jan. 13, 1925 | Jan. 11, 1927 |
| William H. Adams (D) | Jan. 11, 1927 | Jan. 10, 1933 |
| Edwin C. Johnson (D)[3] | Jan. 10, 1933 | Jan. 3, 1937 |
| Ray H. Talbot (D)[4] | Jan. 3, 1937 | Jan. 12, 1937 |
| Teller Ammons (D) | Jan. 12, 1937 | Jan. 10, 1939 |
| Ralph L. Carr (R) | Jan. 10, 1939 | Jan. 12, 1943 |
| John C. Vivian (R) | Jan. 12, 1943 | Jan. 14, 1947 |
| William L. Knous (D)[5] | Jan. 14, 1947 | April 15, 1950 |
| Walter W. Johnson (D)[6] | April 15, 1950 | Jan. 9, 1951 |
| Dan Thornton (R) | Jan. 9, 1951 | Jan. 11, 1955 |
| Edwin C. Johnson (D) | Jan. 11, 1955 | Jan. 8, 1957 |
| Stephen L. R. McNichols (D) | Jan. 8, 1957 | Jan. 8, 1963 |
| John A. Love (R)[7] | Jan. 8, 1963 | July 16, 1973 |
| John D. Vanderhoof (R)[8] | July 16, 1973 | Jan. 14, 1975 |
| Richard D. Lamm (D) | Jan. 14, 1975 | Jan 13, 1987 |
| Roy Romer (D) | Jan. 13, 1987 | |

**Colorado**

*1. The 1904 election between Alva Adams (D) and James H. Peabody (R) caused a dispute surrounding charges of fraud which had to be settled by the Legislature. Both contenders were asked to withdraw. Adams served as governor for 66 days and Peabody for one day.*

---

*2. As lieutenant governor, he succeeded to office.*
*3. Resigned Jan. 3, 1937.*
*4. As lieutenant governor, he succeeded to office.*
*5. Resigned April 15, 1950.*
*6. As lieutenant governor, he succeeded to office.*
*7. Resigned July 16, 1973.*
*8. As lieutenant governor, he succeeded to office.*

# CONNECTICUT

(Ratified the Constitution Jan. 9, 1788)

| Governors | Dates of Service | |
|---|---|---|
| Samuel Huntington[1] | May 11, 1786 | Jan. 5, 1796 |
| Oliver Wolcott (FED)[2] | Jan. 5, 1796 | Dec. 1, 1797 |
| Jonathan Trumbull (FED)[3] | Dec. 1, 1797 | Aug. 7, 1809 |
| John Treadwell (FED) | Aug. 7, 1809 | May 9, 1811 |
| Roger Griswold (FED)[4] | May 9, 1811 | Oct. 25, 1812 |
| John Cotton Smith (FED) | Oct. 25, 1812 | May 8, 1817 |
| Oliver Wolcott Jr. (D-R) | May 8, 1817 | May 2, 1827 |
| Gideon Tomlinson (D-R, NR)[5] | May 2, 1827 | March 1831 |
| John S. Peters (NR) | March 1831 | May 4, 1833 |
| Henry W. Edwards (D) | May 4, 1833 | May 7, 1834 |
| Samuel A. Foote (NR) | May 7, 1834 | May 6, 1835 |
| Henry W. Edwards (D) | May 6, 1835 | May 2, 1838 |
| William W. Ellsworth (W) | May 2, 1838 | May 4, 1842 |
| Chauncey F. Cleveland (D) | May 4, 1842 | May 1844 |
| Roger S. Baldwin (W) | May 1844 | May 6, 1846 |
| Isaac Toucey (D) | May 6, 1846 | May 5, 1847 |
| Clark Bissell (W) | May 5, 1847 | May 2, 1849 |
| Joseph Trumbull (W) | May 2, 1849 | May 4, 1850 |
| Thomas H. Seymour (D)[6] | May 4, 1850 | Oct. 13, 1853 |
| Charles H. Pond (D)[7] | Oct. 13, 1853 | May 1854 |
| Henry Dutton (W) | May 3, 1854 | May 1855 |
| William T. Minor (AM) | May 3, 1855 | May 6, 1857 |
| Alexander H. Holley (R) | May 6, 1857 | May 5, 1858 |
| William A. Buckingham (R) | May 5, 1858 | May 2, 1866 |
| Joseph R. Hawley (R) | May 2, 1866 | May 1, 1867 |
| James E. English (D) | May 1, 1867 | May 5, 1869 |
| Marshall Jewell (R) | May 5, 1869 | May 4, 1870 |
| James E. English (D) | May 4, 1870 | May 1871 |
| Marshall Jewell (R) | May 16, 1871 | May 7, 1873 |
| Charles R. Ingersoll (D) | May 7, 1873 | Jan. 3, 1877 |
| Richard D. Hubbard (D) | Jan. 3, 1877 | Jan. 9, 1879 |
| Charles B. Andrews (R) | Jan. 9, 1879 | Jan. 5, 1881 |
| Hobart B. Bigelow (R) | Jan. 5, 1881 | Jan. 3, 1883 |
| Thomas M. Waller (D) | Jan. 3, 1883 | Jan. 8, 1885 |
| Henry B. Harrison (R) | Jan. 8, 1885 | Jan. 7, 1887 |
| Phineas C. Lounsbury (R) | Jan. 7, 1887 | Jan. 10, 1889 |
| Morgan G. Bulkeley (R)[8] | Jan. 10, 1889 | Jan. 4, 1893 |
| Luzon B. Morris (D) | Jan. 4, 1893 | Jan. 9, 1895 |
| O. Vincent Coffin (R) | Jan. 9, 1895 | Jan. 6, 1897 |
| Lorrin A. Cooke (R) | Jan. 6, 1897 | Jan. 4, 1899 |
| George E. Lounsbury (R) | Jan. 4, 1899 | Jan. 9, 1901 |
| George P. McLean (R) | Jan. 9, 1901 | Jan. 7, 1903 |
| Abiram Chamberlain (R) | Jan. 7, 1903 | Jan. 4, 1905 |
| Henry Roberts (R) | Jan. 4, 1905 | Jan. 9, 1907 |
| Rollin S. Woodruff (R) | Jan. 9, 1907 | Jan. 6, 1909 |
| George L. Lilley (R)[9] | Jan. 6, 1909 | April 21, 1909 |
| Frank B. Weeks (R)[10] | April 21, 1909 | Jan. 4, 1911 |
| Simeon E. Baldwin (D) | Jan. 4, 1911 | Jan. 6, 1915 |
| Marcus H. Holcomb (R) | Jan. 6, 1915 | Jan. 5, 1921 |
| Everett J. Lake (R) | Jan. 5, 1921 | Jan. 3, 1923 |
| Charles A. Templeton (R) | Jan. 3, 1923 | Jan. 7, 1925 |
| Hiram Bingham (R)[11] | Jan. 7, 1925 | Jan. 8, 1925 |
| John H. Trumbull (R)[12] | Jan. 8, 1925 | Jan. 7, 1931 |
| Wilbur L. Cross (D) | Jan. 7, 1931 | Jan. 4, 1939 |
| Raymond E. Baldwin (R) | Jan. 4, 1939 | Jan. 8, 1941 |
| Robert A. Hurley (D) | Jan. 8, 1941 | Jan. 6, 1943 |
| Raymond E. Baldwin (R)[13] | Jan. 6, 1943 | Dec. 27, 1946 |

| | | |
|---|---|---|
| Wilbert Snow (D)[14] | Dec. 27, 1946 | Jan. 8, 1947 |
| James L. McConaughy (R)[15] | Jan. 8, 1947 | March 7, 1948 |
| James C. Shannon (R)[16] | March 7, 1948 | Jan. 5, 1949 |
| Chester Bowles (D) | Jan. 5, 1949 | Jan. 3, 1951 |
| John D. Lodge (R) | Jan. 3, 1951 | Jan. 5, 1955 |
| Abraham Ribicoff (D)[17] | Jan. 5, 1955 | Jan. 21, 1961 |
| John Dempsey (D)[18] | Jan. 21, 1961 | Jan. 6, 1971 |
| Thomas J. Meskill (R) | Jan. 6, 1971 | Jan. 8, 1975 |
| Ella T. Grasso (D)[19] | Jan. 8, 1975 | Dec. 31, 1980 |
| William A. O'Neill (D)[20] | Dec. 31, 1980 | Jan. 9, 1991 |
| Lowell P. Weicker Jr. (I) | Jan. 9, 1991 | |

**Connecticut**

1. Died Jan. 5, 1796.
2. Died Dec. 1, 1797.
3. Died Aug. 7, 1809.
4. Died Oct. 25, 1812.
5. Resigned in 1831 to become U.S. senator.
6. Resigned Oct. 13, 1853.
7. As lieutenant governor, he succeeded to office.
8. The 1890 election was disputed, with Democrats claiming that Luzon Morris had won a majority of the popular vote and been elected governor, and Republicans claiming that he had not and demanding an election by the legislature. Since control of the legislature was divided, the two houses could not agree on what to do, so Bulkeley remained in office for the term.
9. Died April 21, 1909.
10. As lieutenant governor, he succeeded to office.
11. Resigned Jan. 8, 1925.
12. As lieutenant governor, he succeeded to office. Subsequently elected.
13. Resigned Dec. 27, 1946.
14. As lieutenant governor, he succeeded to office.
15. Died March 7, 1948.
16. As lieutenant governor, he succeeded to office.
17. Resigned Jan. 21, 1961.
18. As lieutenant governor, he succeeded to office. Subsequently elected.
19. Resigned Dec. 31, 1980.
20. As lieutenant governor, he succeeded to office. Subsequently elected.

# DELAWARE

(Ratified the Constitution Dec. 7, 1787)

| Governors | Dates of Service | |
|---|---|---|
| Joshua Clayton (FED)[1] | June 2, 1789 | Jan. 13, 1796 |
| Gunning Bedford Sr. (FED)[2] | Jan. 13, 1796 | Sept. 28, 1797 |
| Daniel Rogers (FED)[3] | Sept. 28, 1797 | Jan. 9, 1799 |
| Richard Bassett (FED)[4] | Jan. 1799 | March 1801 |
| James Sykes (FED)[5] | March 1801 | Jan. 1802 |
| David Hall (D-R) | Jan. 1802 | Jan. 1805 |
| Nathaniel Mitchell (FED) | Jan. 1805 | Jan. 1808 |
| George Truitt (FED) | Jan. 1808 | Jan. 1811 |
| Joseph Haslet (D-R) | Jan. 1811 | Jan. 1814 |
| Daniel Rodney (FED) | Jan. 1814 | Jan. 1817 |
| John Clark (FED) | Jan. 1817 | Jan. 1820 |
| Henry Molleston[6] | | |
| Jacob Stout (FED)[7] | Jan. 1820 | Jan. 1821 |
| John Collins (D-R)[8] | Jan. 1821 | April 1822 |
| Caleb Rodney (D-R)[9] | April 1822 | Jan. 1823 |
| Joseph Haslet (D-R)[10] | Jan. 1823 | June 20, 1823 |
| Charles Thomas (D-R)[11] | June 20, 1823 | Jan. 1824 |
| Samuel Paynter (FED) | Jan. 1824 | Jan. 1827 |
| Charles Polk (FED) | Jan. 1827 | Jan. 1830 |
| David Hazzard (D) | Jan. 1830 | Jan. 1833 |
| Caleb P. Bennett (D)[12] | Jan. 1833 | April 9, 1836 |
| Charles Polk[13] | April 9, 1836 | Jan. 1837 |
| Cornelius P. Comegys (W) | Jan. 1837 | Jan. 1841 |
| William B. Cooper (W) | Jan. 1841 | Jan. 1845 |
| Thomas Stockton (W)[14] | Jan. 1845 | March 2, 1846 |
| Joseph Maull (W)[15] | March 2, 1846 | May 1, 1846 |
| William Temple (W)[16] | May 1, 1846 | Jan. 1847 |
| William Tharp (D) | Jan. 1847 | Jan. 1851 |
| William H. Ross (D) | Jan. 1851 | Jan. 1855 |

| | | |
|---|---|---|
| Peter F. Causey (AM) | Jan. 1855 | Jan. 1859 |
| William Burton (D) | Jan. 1859 | Jan. 1863 |
| William Cannon (UN)[17] | Jan. 1863 | March 1, 1865 |
| Gove Saulsbury (D)[18] | March 1, 1865 | Jan. 1871 |
| James Ponder (D) | Jan. 1871 | Jan. 1875 |
| John P. Cochran (D) | Jan. 1875 | Jan. 1879 |
| John W. Hall (D) | Jan. 1879 | Jan. 1883 |
| Charles C. Stockley (D) | Jan. 1883 | Jan. 1887 |
| Benjamin T. Biggs (D) | Jan. 1887 | Jan. 1891 |
| Robert J. Reynolds (D) | Jan. 1891 | Jan. 1895 |
| Joshua H. Marvel (R)[19] | Jan. 1895 | April 8, 1895 |
| William T. Watson (D)[20] | April 8, 1895 | Jan. 19, 1897 |
| Ebe W. Tunnell (D) | Jan. 19, 1897 | Jan. 15, 1901 |
| John Hunn (R) | Jan. 15, 1901 | Jan. 17, 1905 |
| Preston Lea (R) | Jan. 17, 1905 | Jan. 19, 1909 |
| Simeon S. Pennewill (R) | Jan. 19, 1909 | Jan. 21, 1913 |
| Charles R. Miller (R) | Jan. 21, 1913 | Jan. 17, 1917 |
| John G. Townsend Jr. (R) | Jan. 17, 1917 | Jan. 18, 1921 |
| William D. Denney (R) | Jan. 18, 1921 | Jan. 20, 1925 |
| Robert P. Robinson (R) | Jan. 20, 1925 | Jan. 15, 1929 |
| C. Douglass Buck (R) | Jan. 15, 1929 | Jan. 19, 1937 |
| Richard C. McMullen (D) | Jan. 19, 1937 | Jan. 21, 1941 |
| Walter W. Bacon (R) | Jan. 21, 1941 | Jan. 18, 1949 |
| Elbert N. Carvel (D) | Jan. 18, 1949 | Jan. 20, 1953 |
| J. Caleb Boggs (R)[21] | Jan. 20, 1953 | Dec. 30, 1960 |
| David P. Buckson (R)[22] | Dec. 30, 1960 | Jan. 17, 1961 |
| Elbert N. Carvel (D) | Jan. 17, 1961 | Jan. 19, 1965 |
| Charles L. Terry Jr. (D) | Jan. 19, 1965 | Jan. 21, 1969 |
| Russell W. Peterson (R) | Jan. 21, 1969 | Jan. 16, 1973 |
| Sherman W. Tribbitt (D) | Jan. 16, 1973 | Jan. 18, 1977 |
| Pierre duPont (R) | Jan. 18, 1977 | Jan. 15, 1985 |
| Michael N. Castle (R)[23] | Jan. 15, 1985 | Dec. 31, 1992 |
| Dale E. Wolf (R)[24] | Jan. 1, 1993 | Jan. 19, 1993 |
| Thomas R. Carper(D) | Jan. 19, 1993 | |

**Delaware**

1. Joshua Clayton was president of Delaware from 1789 to 1793 and governor from 1793 to 1796.
2. Died Sept. 28, 1797.
3. Acting governor.
4. Resigned in March 1801.
5. Acting governor.
6. Died before taking office.
7. Acting governor.
8. Died in April 1822.
9. Acting governor.
10. Died June 20, 1823.
11. Acting governor.
12. Died April 9, 1836.
13. Acting governor.
14. Died March 2, 1846.
15. Acting governor. Died May 1, 1846.
16. Acting governor.
17. Died March 1, 1865.
18. Acting governor. Subsequently elected.
19. Died April 8, 1895.
20. Acting governor.
21. Resigned Dec. 30, 1960.
22. As lieutenant governor, he succeeded to office.
23. Resigned Dec. 31, 1992, having been elected to the U.S. House.
24. As lieutenant governor, he succeeded to office.

# FLORIDA

(Became a state March 3, 1845)

| Governors | Dates of Service | |
|---|---|---|
| William D. Moseley (D) | June 25, 1845 | Oct. 1, 1849 |
| Thomas Brown (W) | Oct. 1, 1849 | Oct. 3, 1853 |
| James E. Broome (D) | Oct. 3, 1853 | Oct. 5, 1857 |
| Madison S. Perry (D) | Oct. 5, 1857 | Oct. 7, 1861 |
| John Milton (D)[1] | Oct. 7, 1861 | April 1, 1865 |

| | | |
|---|---|---|
| William Marvin[2] | July 13, 1865 | Dec. 20, 1865 |
| David S. Walker (C) | Dec. 20, 1865 | July 9, 1868 |
| Harrison Reed (R) | July 9, 1868 | Jan. 7, 1873 |
| Ossian B. Hart (R)[3] | Jan. 7, 1873 | March 18, 1874 |
| Marcellus L. Stearns (R)[4] | March 18, 1874 | Jan. 2, 1877 |
| George F. Drew (D) | Jan. 2, 1877 | Jan. 4, 1881 |
| William D. Bloxham (D) | Jan. 4, 1881 | Jan. 6, 1885 |
| Edward A. Perry (D) | Jan. 6, 1885 | Jan. 8, 1889 |
| Francis P. Fleming (D) | Jan. 8, 1889 | Jan. 3, 1893 |
| Henry L. Mitchell (D) | Jan. 3, 1893 | Jan. 5, 1897 |
| William D. Bloxham (D) | Jan. 5, 1897 | Jan. 8, 1901 |
| William S. Jennings (D) | Jan. 8, 1901 | Jan. 3, 1905 |
| Napoleon B. Broward (D) | Jan. 3, 1905 | Jan. 5, 1909 |
| Albert W. Gilchrist (D) | Jan. 5, 1909 | Jan. 7, 1913 |
| Park Trammell (D) | Jan. 7, 1913 | Jan. 2, 1917 |
| Sidney J. Catts (IP) | Jan. 2, 1917 | Jan. 4, 1921 |
| Cary A. Hardee (D) | Jan. 4, 1921 | Jan. 6, 1925 |
| John W. Martin (D) | Jan. 6, 1925 | Jan. 8, 1929 |
| Doyle E. Carlton (D) | Jan. 8, 1929 | Jan. 3, 1933 |
| David Sholtz (D) | Jan. 3, 1933 | Jan. 5, 1937 |
| Frederick P. Cone (D) | Jan. 5, 1937 | Jan. 7, 1941 |
| Spessard L. Holland (D) | Jan. 7, 1941 | Jan. 2, 1945 |
| Millard F. Caldwell (D) | Jan. 2, 1945 | Jan. 4, 1949 |
| Fuller Warren (D) | Jan. 4, 1949 | Jan. 6, 1953 |
| Daniel T. McCarty (D)[5] | Jan. 6, 1953 | Sept. 28, 1953 |
| Charley E. Johns (D)[6] | Sept. 18, 1953 | Jan. 4, 1955 |
| LeRoy Collins (D)[7] | Jan. 4, 1955 | Jan. 3, 1961 |
| Farris Bryant (D) | Jan. 3, 1961 | Jan. 5, 1965 |
| Haydon Burns (D) | Jan. 5, 1965 | Jan. 3, 1967 |
| Claude R. Kirk Jr. (R) | Jan. 3, 1967 | Jan. 5, 1971 |
| Reubin Askew (D) | Jan. 5, 1971 | Jan. 2, 1979 |
| Robert Graham (D)[8] | Jan. 2, 1979 | Jan. 3, 1987 |
| John W. Mixon (D)[9] | Jan. 3, 1987 | Jan. 6, 1987 |
| Bob Martinez (R) | Jan. 6, 1987 | Jan. 8, 1991 |
| Lawton Chiles (D) | Jan. 8, 1991 | |

**Florida**

*1. Died April 1, 1865.*

*2. Acting governor, appointed by president.*

*3. Died March 18, 1874.*

*4. As lieutenant governor, he succeeded to office.*

*5. Died Sept. 28, 1953.*

*6. As president of the state Senate, he succeeded to office for the remainder of the first half of McCarty's term.*

*7. Elected in a special election to serve the last two years of McCarty's term. Subsequently re-elected.*

*8. Resigned Jan. 3, 1987, having been elected to the U.S. Senate.*

*9. As lieutenant governor, he succeeded to office.*

# GEORGIA

(Ratified the Constitution Jan. 2, 1788)

| Governors | Dates of Service | |
|---|---|---|
| George Handley | Jan. 26, 1788 | Jan. 7, 1789 |
| George Walton (D-R) | Jan. 7, 1789 | Nov. 9, 1789 |
| Edward Telfair (D-R) | Nov. 9, 1789 | Nov. 7, 1793 |
| George Mathews (D-R) | Nov. 7, 1793 | Jan. 15, 1796 |
| Jared Irwin (D-R) | Jan. 15, 1796 | Jan. 12, 1798 |
| James Jackson (D-R) | Jan. 12, 1798 | March 3, 1801 |
| David Emanuel (D-R) | March 3, 1801 | Nov. 7, 1801 |
| Josiah Tattnall Jr. (D-R) | Nov. 7, 1801 | Nov. 4, 1802 |
| John Milledge (D-R) | Nov. 4, 1802 | Sept. 23, 1806 |
| Jared Irwin (D-R) | Sept. 23, 1806 | Nov. 10, 1809 |
| David B. Mitchell (D-R) | Nov. 10, 1809 | Nov. 5, 1813 |
| Peter Early (D-R) | Nov. 5, 1813 | Nov. 10, 1815 |
| David B. Mitchell (D-R) | Nov. 10, 1815 | March 4, 1817 |
| William Rabun (D-R) | March 4, 1817 | Oct. 24, 1819 |
| Matthew Talbot (D-R) | Oct. 24, 1819 | Nov. 5, 1819 |
| John Clark (D-R) | Nov. 5, 1819 | Nov. 7, 1823 |
| George M. Troup (D-R) | Nov. 7, 1823 | Nov. 7, 1827 |

| | | |
|---|---|---|
| John Forsyth (D-R) | Nov. 7, 1827 | Nov. 4, 1829 |
| George R. Gilmer (D) | Nov. 4, 1829 | Nov. 9, 1831 |
| Wilson Lumpkin (UN D) | Nov. 9, 1831 | Nov. 4, 1835 |
| William Schley (D) | Nov. 4, 1835 | Nov. 8, 1837 |
| George R. Gilmer (W) | Nov. 8, 1837 | Nov. 6, 1839 |
| Charles J. McDonald (D) | Nov. 6, 1839 | Nov. 8, 1843 |
| George W. Crawford (W) | Nov. 8, 1843 | Nov. 3, 1847 |
| George W. Towns (D) | Nov. 3, 1847 | Nov. 5, 1851 |
| Howell Cobb (UN D) | Nov. 5, 1851 | Nov. 9, 1853 |
| Herschel V. Johnson (D) | Nov. 9, 1853 | Nov. 6, 1857 |
| Joseph E. Brown (D) | Nov. 6, 1857 | June 17, 1865 |
| James Johnson (D) | June 17, 1865 | Dec. 14, 1865 |
| Charles J. Jenkins (D) | Dec. 14, 1865 | Jan. 13, 1868 |
| Gen. Thomas H. Ruger[1] | Jan. 13, 1868 | July 4, 1868 |
| Rufus Brown Bullock (R)[2] | July 4, 1868 | Oct. 23, 1871 |
| Benjamin Conley (R)[3] | Oct. 30, 1871 | Jan. 12, 1872 |
| James M. Smith (LR) | Jan. 12, 1872 | Jan. 12, 1877 |
| Alfred Holt Colquitt (D) | Jan. 12, 1877 | Nov. 4, 1882 |
| Alexander H. Stephens (D)[4] | Nov. 4, 1882 | March 4, 1883 |
| James H. Boynton (D)[5] | March 5, 1883 | May 10, 1883 |
| Henry D. McDaniel (D) | May 10, 1883 | Nov. 9, 1886 |
| John B. Gordon (D) | Nov. 9, 1886 | Nov. 8, 1890 |
| William J. Northen (D) | Nov. 8, 1890 | Oct. 27, 1894 |
| William Y. Atkinson (D) | Oct. 27, 1894 | Oct. 29, 1898 |
| Allen D. Candler (D) | Oct. 29, 1898 | Oct. 25, 1902 |
| Joseph M. Terrell (D) | Oct. 25, 1902 | June 29, 1907 |
| Hoke Smith (D) | June 29, 1907 | June 26, 1909 |
| Joseph M. Brown (D) | June 26, 1909 | July 1, 1911 |
| Hoke Smith (D)[6] | July 1, 1911 | Nov. 16, 1911 |
| John M. Slaton (D)[7] | Nov. 16, 1911 | Jan. 25, 1912 |
| Joseph M. Brown (D) | Jan. 25, 1912 | June 28, 1913 |
| John M. Slaton (D) | June 28, 1913 | June 26, 1915 |
| Nathaniel E. Harris (D) | June 26, 1915 | June 30, 1917 |
| Hugh M. Dorsey (D) | June 30, 1917 | June 25, 1921 |
| Thomas W. Hardwick (D) | June 25, 1921 | June 30, 1923 |
| Clifford M. Walker (D) | June 30, 1923 | June 25, 1927 |
| Lamartine G. Hardman (D) | June 25, 1927 | June 27, 1931 |
| Richard B. Russell (D)[8] | June 27, 1931 | Jan. 10, 1933 |
| Eugene Talmadge (D) | Jan. 10, 1933 | Jan. 12, 1937 |
| Eurith D. Rivers (D) | Jan. 12, 1937 | Jan. 14, 1941 |
| Eugene Talmadge (D) | Jan. 14, 1941 | Jan. 12, 1943 |
| Ellis G. Arnall (D) | Jan. 12, 1943 | Jan. 14, 1947 |
| Eugene Talmadge (D)[9] | | |
| Herman E. Talmadge (D)[10] | Jan. 14, 1947 | March 18, 1947 |
| Melvin E. Thompson (D) | March 18, 1947 | Nov. 17, 1948 |
| Herman E. Talmadge (D) | Nov. 17, 1948 | Jan. 11, 1955 |
| S. Marvin Griffin (D) | Jan. 11, 1955 | Jan. 13, 1959 |
| S. Ernest Vandiver Jr. (D) | Jan. 13, 1959 | Jan. 15, 1963 |
| Carl Edward Sanders (D) | Jan. 15, 1963 | Jan. 10, 1967 |
| Lester G. Maddox (D)[11] | Jan. 10, 1967 | Jan. 12, 1971 |
| Jimmy Carter (D) | Jan. 12, 1971 | Jan. 14, 1975 |
| George Busbee (D) | Jan. 14, 1975 | Jan. 11, 1983 |
| Joe Frank Harris (D) | Jan. 11, 1983 | Jan. 14, 1991 |
| Zell Miller (D) | Jan. 14, 1991 | |

**Georgia**

*1. Military governor.*

*2. Resigned Oct. 23, 1871.*

*3. As president of the state Senate, he succeeded to office.*

*4. Died March 4, 1883.*

*5. As president of the state Senate, he succeeded to office.*

*6. Resigned Nov. 16, 1911.*

*7. As president of the state Senate, he succeeded to office.*

*8. Resigned Jan. 10, 1933.*

*9. Died Dec. 21, 1946, before his inauguration.*

*10. Eugene Talmadge's death led to a famous controversy that lasted several months, during which three different men claimed office as governor. The Talmadge-dominated Legislature elected Herman Talmadge, Eugene's son, to serve out his term, but this action was disputed by outgoing governor Ellis Arnall and Lieutenant Governor-elect Melvin E. Thompson. Herman Talmadge seized the governor's mansion by force, but was thrown out after 67 days in office by the Georgia Supreme Court, which ruled his election by the Legislature unconstitutional. Thompson then assumed office as governor until 1948, when a special election was held. He lost the Democratic*

## Georgia (continued)

*nomination to Talmadge, who then won the special election for the remaining two years of the term. Talmadge was re-elected in 1950.*

*11. Republican candidate Howard Callaway led in the popular vote, but failed to win a majority because of write-in votes cast for former governor Ellis Arnall, who had lost the Democratic primary to Lester Maddox. The Legislature elected Maddox as governor.*

# HAWAII

(Became a state Aug. 21, 1959)

| Governors | Dates of Service | |
|---|---|---|
| William F. Quinn (R) | Aug. 21, 1959 | Dec. 3, 1962 |
| John A. Burns (D) | Dec. 3, 1962 | Dec. 2, 1974 |
| George R. Ariyoshi (D) | Dec. 2, 1974 | Dec. 1, 1986 |
| John Waihee (D) | Dec. 1, 1986 | |

# IDAHO

(Became a state July 3, 1890)

| Governors | Dates of Service | |
|---|---|---|
| George L. Shoup (R)[1] | Oct. 1, 1890 | Dec. 1890 |
| N. B. Willey (R)[2] | Dec. 19, 1890 | Jan. 1, 1893 |
| William J. McConnell (R) | Jan. 1893 | Jan. 4, 1897 |
| Frank Steunenberg (D) | Jan. 4, 1897 | Jan. 7, 1901 |
| Frank W. Hunt (D-FUS) | Jan. 7, 1901 | Jan. 5, 1903 |
| John T. Morrison (R) | Jan. 5, 1903 | Jan. 2, 1905 |
| Frank R. Gooding (R) | Jan. 2, 1905 | Jan. 4, 1909 |
| James H. Brady (R) | Jan. 4, 1909 | Jan. 2, 1911 |
| James H. Hawley (D) | Jan. 2, 1911 | Jan. 6, 1913 |
| John M. Haines (R) | Jan. 6, 1913 | Jan. 4, 1915 |
| Moses Alexander (D) | Jan. 4, 1915 | Jan. 6, 1919 |
| David W. Davis (R) | Jan. 6, 1919 | Jan. 1, 1923 |
| Charles C. Moore (R) | Jan. 1, 1923 | Jan. 3, 1927 |
| H. Clarence Baldridge (R) | Jan. 3, 1927 | Jan. 5, 1931 |
| C. Ben Ross (D) | Jan. 5, 1931 | Jan. 4, 1937 |
| Barzilla W. Clark (D) | Jan. 4, 1937 | Jan. 2, 1939 |
| Clarence A. Bottolfsen (R) | Jan. 2, 1939 | Jan. 6, 1941 |
| Chase A. Clark (D) | Jan. 6, 1941 | Jan. 4, 1943 |
| Clarence A. Bottolfsen (R) | Jan. 4, 1943 | Jan. 1, 1945 |
| Charles C. Gossett (D)[3] | Jan. 1, 1945 | Nov. 17, 1945 |
| Arnold Williams (D)[4] | Nov. 17, 1945 | Jan. 6, 1947 |
| Charles A. Robins (R) | Jan. 6, 1947 | Jan. 1, 1951 |
| Len B. Jordan (R) | Jan. 1, 1951 | Jan. 3, 1955 |
| Robert E. Smylie (R) | Jan. 3, 1955 | Jan. 2, 1967 |
| Don Samuelson (R) | Jan. 2, 1967 | Jan. 4, 1971 |
| Cecil D. Andrus (D)[5] | Jan. 4, 1971 | Jan. 24, 1977 |
| John V. Evans (D)[6] | Jan. 24, 1977 | Jan. 5, 1987 |
| Cecil D. Andrus (D) | Jan. 5, 1987 | |

### Idaho

1. Resigned in December 1890.
2. As lieutenant governor, he succeeded to office.
3. Resigned Nov. 17, 1945.
4. As lieutenant governor, he succeeded to office.
5. Resigned Jan. 24, 1977.
6. As lieutenant governor, he succeeded to office. Subsequently elected.

# ILLINOIS

(Became a state Dec. 3, 1818)

| Governors | Dates of Service | |
|---|---|---|
| Shadrach Bond (D-R) | Oct. 6, 1818 | Dec. 5, 1822 |
| Edward Coles (D-R) | Dec. 5, 1822 | Dec. 6, 1826 |
| Ninian Edwards (NR) | Dec. 6, 1826 | Dec. 6, 1830 |
| John Reynolds (NR)[1] | Dec. 6, 1830 | Nov. 17, 1834 |
| William L. D. Ewing[2] | Nov. 17, 1834 | Dec. 3, 1834 |
| Joseph Duncan (W) | Dec. 3, 1834 | Dec. 7, 1838 |
| Thomas Carlin (D) | Dec. 7, 1838 | Dec. 8, 1842 |
| Thomas Ford (D) | Dec. 8, 1842 | Dec. 9, 1846 |
| Augustus C. French (D) | Dec. 9, 1846 | Jan. 10, 1853 |
| Joel A. Matteson (D) | Jan. 10, 1853 | Jan. 12, 1857 |
| William H. Bissell (R)[3] | Jan. 12, 1857 | March 18, 1860 |
| John Wood (R)[4] | March 21, 1860 | Jan. 14, 1861 |
| Richard Yates (R) | Jan. 14, 1861 | Jan. 16, 1865 |
| Richard J. Oglesby (R) | Jan. 16, 1865 | Jan. 11, 1869 |
| John M. Palmer (R) | Jan. 11, 1869 | Jan. 13, 1873 |
| Richard J. Oglesby (R)[5] | Jan. 13, 1873 | Jan. 23, 1873 |
| John L. Beveridge (R)[6] | Jan. 23, 1873 | Jan. 8, 1877 |
| Shelby M. Cullom (R)[7] | Jan. 8, 1877 | Feb. 8, 1883 |
| John M. Hamilton (R)[8] | Feb. 16, 1883 | Jan. 30, 1885 |
| Richard J. Oglesby (R) | Jan. 30, 1885 | Jan. 14, 1889 |
| Joseph W. Fifer (R) | Jan. 14, 1889 | Jan. 10, 1893 |
| John P. Altgeld (D) | Jan. 10, 1893 | Jan. 11, 1897 |
| John R. Tanner (R) | Jan. 11, 1897 | Jan. 14, 1901 |
| Richard Yates (R) | Jan. 14, 1901 | Jan. 9, 1905 |
| Charles S. Deneen (R) | Jan. 9, 1905 | Feb. 3, 1913 |
| Edward F. Dunne (D) | Feb. 3, 1913 | Jan. 8, 1917 |
| Frank O. Lowden (R) | Jan. 8, 1917 | Jan. 10, 1921 |
| Len Small (R) | Jan. 10, 1921 | Jan. 14, 1929 |
| Louis L. Emmerson (R) | Jan. 14, 1929 | Jan. 9, 1933 |
| Henry Horner (D)[9] | Jan. 9, 1933 | Oct. 6, 1940 |
| John H. Stelle (D)[10] | Oct. 6, 1940 | Jan. 13, 1941 |
| Dwight H. Green (R) | Jan. 13, 1941 | Jan. 10, 1949 |
| Adlai E. Stevenson (D) | Jan. 10, 1949 | Jan. 12, 1953 |
| William G. Stratton (R) | Jan. 12, 1953 | Jan. 9, 1961 |
| Otto Kerner (D)[11] | Jan. 9, 1961 | May 22, 1968 |
| Samuel H. Shapiro (D)[12] | May 22, 1968 | Jan. 13, 1969 |
| Richard B. Ogilvie (R) | Jan. 13, 1969 | Jan. 8, 1973 |
| Daniel Walker (D) | Jan. 8, 1973 | Jan. 10, 1977 |
| James R. Thompson (R) | Jan. 10, 1977 | Jan. 14, 1991 |
| Jim Edgar (R) | Jan. 14, 1991 | |

### Illinois

1. Resigned Nov. 17, 1834.
2. Ewing was acting lieutenant governor and succeeded to office as governor following Reynolds' resignation.
3. Died March 18, 1860.
4. As lieutenant governor, he succeeded to office.
5. Resigned Jan. 23, 1873.
6. As lieutenant governor, he succeeded to office.
7. Resigned Feb. 8, 1883.
8. As lieutenant governor, he succeeded to office.
9. Died Oct. 6, 1940.
10. As lieutenant governor, he succeeded to office.
11. Resigned May 22, 1968.
12. As lieutenant governor, he succeeded to office.

# INDIANA

(Became a state Dec. 11, 1816)

| Governors | Dates of Service | |
|---|---|---|
| Jonathan Jennings (D-R)[1] | Nov. 7, 1816 | Sept. 12, 1822 |
| Ratliff Boon (D-R)[2] | Sept. 12, 1822 | Dec. 4, 1822 |
| William Hendricks (D-R)[3] | Dec. 5, 1822 | Feb. 12, 1825 |
| James B. Ray (CLAY R)[4] | Feb. 12, 1825 | Dec. 7, 1831 |
| Noah Noble (NR, W) | Dec. 7, 1831 | Dec. 6, 1837 |
| David Wallace (W) | Dec. 6, 1837 | Dec. 9, 1840 |
| Samuel Bigger (W) | Dec. 9, 1840 | Dec. 6, 1843 |
| James Whitcomb (D)[5] | Dec. 6, 1843 | Dec. 27, 1848 |
| Paris C. Dunning (D)[6] | Dec. 27, 1848 | Dec. 5, 1849 |
| Joseph A. Wright (D) | Dec. 5, 1849 | Jan. 12, 1857 |
| Ashbel P. Willard (D)[7] | Jan. 12, 1857 | Oct. 4, 1860 |
| Abraham A. Hammond (D)[8] | Oct. 4, 1860 | Jan. 14, 1861 |

| | | |
|---|---|---|
| Henry S. Lane (R)[9] | Jan. 14, 1861 | Jan. 16, 1861 |
| Oliver P. Morton (R)[10] | Jan. 16, 1861 | Jan. 23, 1867 |
| Conrad Baker (R)[11] | Jan. 24, 1867 | Jan. 13, 1873 |
| Thomas A. Hendricks (D) | Jan. 13, 1873 | Jan. 8, 1877 |
| James D. Williams (D)[12] | Jan. 8, 1877 | Nov. 20, 1880 |
| Isaac P. Gray (D)[13] | Nov. 20, 1880 | Jan. 10, 1881 |
| Albert G. Porter (R) | Jan. 10, 1881 | Jan. 12, 1885 |
| Isaac P. Gray (D) | Jan. 12, 1885 | Jan. 14, 1889 |
| Alvin P. Hovey (R)[14] | Jan. 14, 1889 | Nov. 21, 1891 |
| Ira Joy Chase (R)[15] | Nov. 21, 1891 | Jan. 9, 1893 |
| Claude Matthews (D) | Jan. 1893 | Jan. 11, 1897 |
| James A. Mount (R) | Jan. 11, 1897 | Jan. 14, 1901 |
| Winfield T. Durbin (R) | Jan. 14, 1901 | Jan. 9, 1905 |
| J. Frank Hanly (R) | Jan. 9, 1905 | Jan. 11, 1909 |
| Thomas H. Marshall (D) | Jan. 11, 1909 | Jan. 13, 1913 |
| Samuel M. Ralston (D) | Jan. 13, 1913 | Jan. 8, 1917 |
| James Putnam Goodrich (R) | Jan. 8, 1917 | Jan. 10, 1921 |
| Warren T. McCray (R)[16] | Jan. 10, 1921 | April 30, 1924 |
| Emmett F. Branch (R)[17] | April 30, 1924 | Jan. 12, 1925 |
| Edward Jackson (R) | Jan. 12, 1925 | Jan. 14, 1929 |
| Harry G. Leslie (R) | Jan. 14, 1929 | Jan. 9, 1933 |
| Paul V. McNutt (D) | Jan. 9, 1933 | Jan. 11, 1937 |
| M. Clifford Townsend (D) | Jan. 11, 1937 | Jan. 13, 1941 |
| Henry F. Schricker (D) | Jan. 13, 1941 | Jan. 8, 1945 |
| Ralph F. Gates (R) | Jan. 8, 1945 | Jan. 10, 1949 |
| Henry F. Schricker (D) | Jan. 10, 1949 | Jan. 12, 1953 |
| George N. Craig (R) | Jan. 12, 1953 | Jan. 14, 1957 |
| Harold W. Handley (R) | Jan. 14, 1957 | Jan. 9, 1961 |
| Matthew E. Welsh (D) | Jan. 9, 1961 | Jan. 11, 1965 |
| Roger D. Branigin (D) | Jan. 11, 1965 | Jan. 13, 1969 |
| Edgar D. Whitcomb (R) | Jan. 13, 1969 | Jan. 8, 1973 |
| Otis R. Bowen (R) | Jan. 8, 1973 | Jan. 12, 1981 |
| Robert D. Orr (R) | Jan. 12, 1981 | Jan. 9, 1989 |
| Evan Bayh (D) | Jan. 9, 1989 | |

**Indiana**

1. *Resigned Sept. 12, 1822.*
2. *Acting governor.*
3. *Resigned Feb. 12, 1825.*
4. *Acting governor. Subsequently elected.*
5. *Resigned Dec. 27, 1848.*
6. *Acting governor.*
7. *Died Oct. 4, 1860.*
8. *Acting governor.*
9. *Resigned Jan. 16, 1861.*
10. *Acting governor. Subsequently elected. Resigned in 1867.*
11. *Acting governor. Subsequently elected.*
12. *Died Nov. 20, 1880.*
13. *Acting governor.*
14. *Died Nov. 21, 1891.*
15. *Acting governor.*
16. *Resigned April 30, 1924.*
17. *As lieutenant governor, he succeeded to office.*

# IOWA

(Became a state Dec. 28, 1846)

| Governors | Dates of Service | |
|---|---|---|
| Ansel Briggs (D) | Dec. 3, 1846 | Dec. 4, 1850 |
| Stephen P. Hempstead (D) | Dec. 4, 1850 | Dec. 9, 1854 |
| James W. Grimes (R) | Dec. 9, 1854 | Jan. 13, 1858 |
| Ralph P. Lowe (R) | Jan. 13, 1858 | Jan. 11, 1860 |
| Samuel J. Kirkwood (R) | Jan. 11, 1860 | Jan. 14, 1864 |
| William M. Stone (UN R) | Jan. 14, 1864 | Jan. 16, 1868 |
| Samuel Merrill (R) | Jan. 16, 1868 | Jan. 11, 1872 |
| Cyrus C. Carpenter (R) | Jan. 11, 1872 | Jan. 13, 1876 |
| Samuel J. Kirkwood (R)[1] | Jan. 13, 1876 | Feb. 1, 1877 |
| Joshua G. Newbold (R)[2] | Feb. 1, 1877 | Jan. 17, 1878 |
| John H. Gear (R) | Jan. 17, 1878 | Jan. 12, 1882 |
| Buren R. Sherman (R) | Jan. 12, 1882 | Jan. 14, 1886 |

| | | |
|---|---|---|
| William Larrabee (R) | Jan. 14, 1886 | Feb. 26, 1890 |
| Horace Boies (D) | Feb. 27, 1890 | Jan. 11, 1894 |
| Frank D. Jackson (R) | Jan. 11, 1894 | Jan. 16, 1896 |
| Francis M. Drake (R) | Jan. 16, 1896 | Jan. 13, 1898 |
| Leslie M. Shaw (R) | Jan. 13, 1898 | Jan. 16, 1902 |
| Albert B. Cummins (R)[3] | Jan. 16, 1902 | Nov. 24, 1908 |
| Warren Garst (R)[4] | Nov. 24, 1908 | Jan. 14, 1909 |
| Beryl F. Carroll (R) | Jan. 14, 1909 | Jan. 16, 1913 |
| George W. Clarke (R) | Jan. 16, 1913 | Jan. 11, 1917 |
| William L. Harding (R) | Jan. 11, 1917 | Jan. 13, 1921 |
| Nathan E. Kendall (R) | Jan. 13, 1921 | Jan. 15, 1925 |
| John Hammill (R) | Jan. 15, 1925 | Jan. 15, 1931 |
| Daniel W. Turner (R) | Jan. 15, 1931 | Jan. 12, 1933 |
| Clyde L. Herring (D) | Jan. 12, 1933 | Jan. 14, 1937 |
| Nelson G. Kraschel (D) | Jan. 14, 1937 | Jan. 12, 1939 |
| George A. Wilson (R) | Jan. 12, 1939 | Jan. 14, 1943 |
| Bourke B. Hickenlooper (R) | Jan. 14, 1943 | Jan. 11, 1945 |
| Robert D. Blue (R) | Jan. 11, 1945 | Jan. 13, 1949 |
| William S. Beardsley (R)[5] | Jan. 13, 1949 | Nov. 21, 1954 |
| Leo Elthon (R)[6] | Nov. 22, 1954 | Jan. 13, 1955 |
| Leo Arthur Hoegh (R) | Jan. 13, 1955 | Jan. 17, 1957 |
| Herschel C. Loveless (D) | Jan. 17, 1957 | Jan. 12, 1961 |
| Norman A. Erbe (R) | Jan. 12, 1961 | Jan. 17, 1963 |
| Harold E. Hughes (D)[7] | Jan. 17, 1963 | Jan. 1, 1969 |
| Robert D. Fulton (D)[8] | Jan. 1, 1969 | Jan. 16, 1969 |
| Robert D. Ray (R) | Jan. 16, 1969 | Jan. 14, 1983 |
| Terry E. Branstad (R) | Jan. 14, 1983 | |

**Iowa**

1. *Resigned Feb. 1, 1877.*
2. *As lieutenant governor, he succeeded to office.*
3. *Resigned Nov. 24, 1908.*
4. *As lieutenant governor, he succeeded to office.*
5. *Died Nov. 21, 1954.*
6. *As lieutenant governor, he succeeded to office.*
7. *Resigned Jan. 1, 1969.*
8. *As lieutenant governor, he succeeded to office.*

# KANSAS

(Became a state Jan. 29, 1861)

| Governors | Dates of Service | |
|---|---|---|
| Charles Robinson (R) | Feb. 9, 1861 | Jan. 12, 1863 |
| Thomas Carney (R) | Jan. 12, 1863 | Jan. 9, 1865 |
| Samuel J. Crawford (R)[1] | Jan. 9, 1865 | Nov. 4, 1868 |
| Nehemiah Green (R)[2] | Nov. 4, 1868 | Jan. 11, 1869 |
| James Madison Harvey (R) | Jan. 11, 1869 | Jan. 13, 1873 |
| Thomas A. Osborn (R) | Jan. 13, 1873 | Jan. 18, 1877 |
| George T. Anthony (R) | Jan. 18, 1877 | Jan. 13, 1879 |
| John P. St. John (R) | Jan. 13, 1879 | Jan. 8, 1883 |
| George Washington Glick (D) | Jan. 8, 1883 | Jan. 13, 1885 |
| John A. Martin (R) | Jan. 13, 1885 | Jan. 14, 1889 |
| Lyman U. Humphrey (R) | Jan. 14, 1889 | Jan. 9, 1893 |
| Lorenzo D. Lewelling (POP) | Jan. 9, 1893 | Jan. 14, 1895 |
| Edmund N. Morrill (R) | Jan. 14, 1895 | Jan. 11, 1897 |
| John W. Leedy (D-PP) | Jan. 11, 1897 | Jan. 9, 1899 |
| William E. Stanley (R) | Jan. 9, 1899 | Jan. 12, 1903 |
| Willis J. Bailey (R) | Jan. 12, 1903 | Jan. 9, 1905 |
| Edward W. Hoch (R) | Jan. 9, 1905 | Jan. 11, 1909 |
| Walter R. Stubbs (R) | Jan. 11, 1909 | Jan. 13, 1913 |
| George H. Hodges (D) | Jan. 13, 1913 | Jan. 11, 1915 |
| Arthur Capper (R) | Jan. 11, 1915 | Jan. 13, 1919 |
| Henry J. Allen (R) | Jan. 13, 1919 | Jan. 8, 1923 |
| Jonathan McM. Davis (D) | Jan. 8, 1923 | Jan. 12, 1925 |
| Ben S. Paulen (R) | Jan. 12, 1925 | Jan. 14, 1929 |
| Clyde M. Reed (R) | Jan. 14, 1929 | Jan. 12, 1931 |
| Harry W. Woodring (D) | Jan. 12, 1931 | Jan. 9, 1933 |
| Alfred M. Landon (R) | Jan. 9, 1933 | Jan. 11, 1937 |
| Walter A. Huxman (D) | Jan. 11, 1937 | Jan. 9, 1939 |

| | | |
|---|---|---|
| Payne H. Ratner (R) | Jan. 9, 1939 | Jan. 11, 1943 |
| Andrew F. Schoeppel (R) | Jan. 11, 1943 | Jan. 13, 1947 |
| Frank Carlson (R)[3] | Jan. 13, 1947 | Nov. 28, 1950 |
| Frank L. Hagaman (R)[4] | Nov. 28, 1950 | Jan. 8, 1951 |
| Edward F. Arn (R) | Jan. 8, 1951 | Jan. 10, 1955 |
| Frederick L. Hall (R)[5] | Jan. 10, 1955 | Jan. 3, 1957 |
| John McCuish (R)[6] | Jan. 3, 1957 | Jan. 14, 1957 |
| George Docking (D) | Jan. 14, 1957 | Jan. 9, 1961 |
| John Anderson Jr. (R) | Jan. 9, 1961 | Jan. 11, 1965 |
| William H. Avery (R) | Jan. 11, 1965 | Jan. 9, 1967 |
| Robert B. Docking (D) | Jan. 9, 1967 | Jan. 13, 1975 |
| Robert F. Bennett (R) | Jan. 13, 1975 | Jan. 8, 1979 |
| John Carlin (D) | Jan. 8, 1979 | Jan. 12, 1987 |
| Mike Hayden (R) | Jan. 12, 1987 | Jan 14, 1991 |
| Joan Finney (D) | Jan. 14, 1991 | |

### Kansas

1. Resigned Nov. 4, 1868.
2. Succeeded to office.
3. Resigned Nov. 28, 1950.
4. As lieutenant governor, he succeeded to office.
5. Resigned Jan. 3, 1957.
6. As lieutenant governor, he succeeded to office.

# KENTUCKY

(Became a state June 1, 1792)

| Governors | Dates of Service | |
|---|---|---|
| Isaac Shelby (D-R) | June 4, 1792 | June 7, 1796 |
| James Garrard (D-R) | June 7, 1796 | June 1, 1804 |
| Christopher Greenup (D-R) | June 1, 1804 | June 1, 1808 |
| Charles Scott (D-R) | June 1, 1808 | June 1, 1812 |
| Isaac Shelby (D-R) | June 1, 1812 | June 1, 1816 |
| George Madison (D-R)[1] | June 1, 1816 | Oct. 21, 1816 |
| Gabriel Slaughter (D-R)[2] | Oct. 21, 1816 | June 1, 1820 |
| John Adair (D-R) | June 1, 1820 | June 1, 1824 |
| Joseph Desha (D-R) | June 1, 1824 | June 1, 1828 |
| Thomas Metcalfe (NR) | June 1, 1828 | June 1, 1832 |
| John Breathitt (D)[3] | June 1, 1832 | Feb. 22, 1834 |
| James Morehead (NR)[4] | Feb. 22, 1834 | June 1, 1836 |
| James Clark (W)[5] | June 1, 1836 | Oct. 5, 1839 |
| Charles A. Wickliffe (W)[6] | Oct. 5, 1839 | June 1, 1840 |
| Robert P. Letcher (W) | June 1, 1840 | June 1, 1844 |
| William Owsley (W) | June 1, 1844 | June 1, 1848 |
| John J. Crittenden (W)[7] | June 1, 1848 | July 31, 1850 |
| John L. Helm (W)[8] | July 31, 1850 | Sept. 2, 1851 |
| Lazarus W. Powell (D) | Sept. 1851 | Sept. 2, 1855 |
| Charles S. Morehead (AM) | Sept. 1855 | Sept. 1859 |
| Beriah Magoffin (D)[9] | Sept. 1859 | Aug. 18, 1862 |
| James F. Robinson (UN)[10] | Aug. 18, 1862 | Sept. 1863 |
| Thomas E. Bramlette (UN) | Sept. 1863 | Sept. 1867 |
| John L. Helm (D)[11] | Sept. 3, 1867 | Sept. 13, 1867 |
| John W. Stevenson (D)[12] | Sept. 13, 1867 | March 4, 1871 |
| Preston H. Leslie (D)[13] | March 4, 1871 | Sept. 1875 |
| James B. McCreary (D) | Sept. 1875 | Sept. 1879 |
| Luke P. Blackburn (D) | Sept. 1879 | Sept. 1883 |
| J. Procter Knott (D) | Sept. 1883 | Sept. 1887 |
| Simon B. Buckner (D) | Sept. 1887 | Sept. 1891 |
| John Y. Brown (D) | Sept. 1891 | Dec. 1895 |
| William O. Bradley (R) | Dec. 1895 | Dec. 12, 1899 |
| William S. Taylor (R)[14] | Dec. 12, 1899 | Jan. 31, 1900 |
| William Goebel (D)[15] | Jan. 31, 1900 | Feb. 3, 1900 |
| John C. W. Beckham (D)[16] | Feb. 3, 1900 | Dec. 10, 1907 |
| August E. Willson (R) | Dec. 10, 1907 | Dec. 12, 1911 |
| James B. McCreary (D) | Dec. 12, 1911 | Dec. 7, 1915 |
| Augustus O. Stanley (D)[17] | Dec. 7, 1915 | May 19, 1919 |
| James D. Black (D)[18] | May 19, 1919 | Dec. 9, 1919 |
| Edwin P. Morrow (R) | Dec. 9, 1919 | Dec. 11, 1923 |
| William J. Fields (D) | Dec. 11, 1923 | Dec. 13, 1927 |

| | | |
|---|---|---|
| Flem D. Sampson (R) | Dec. 13, 1927 | Dec. 8, 1931 |
| Ruby Lafoon (D) | Dec. 8, 1931 | Dec. 10, 1935 |
| Albert B. (Happy) Chandler (D)[19] | Dec. 10, 1935 | Oct. 9, 1939 |
| Keen Johnson (D)[20] | Oct. 9, 1939 | Dec. 7, 1943 |
| Simeon S. Willis (R) | Dec. 7, 1943 | Dec. 9, 1947 |
| Earle C. Clements (D)[21] | Dec. 9, 1947 | Nov. 27, 1950 |
| Lawrence W. Wetherby (D)[22] | Nov. 27, 1950 | Dec. 13, 1955 |
| Albert B. (Happy) Chandler (D) | Dec. 13, 1955 | Dec. 9, 1959 |
| Bert T. Combs (D) | Dec. 9, 1959 | Dec. 10, 1963 |
| Edward T. Breathitt (D) | Dec. 10, 1963 | Dec. 12, 1967 |
| Louie B. Nunn (R) | Dec. 12, 1967 | Dec. 7, 1971 |
| Wendell H. Ford (D)[23] | Dec. 7, 1971 | Dec. 28, 1974 |
| Julian Carroll (D)[24] | Dec. 28, 1974 | Dec. 11, 1979 |
| John Y. Brown Jr. (D) | Dec. 11, 1979 | Dec. 13, 1983 |
| Martha Layne Collins (D) | Dec. 13, 1983 | Dec. 8, 1987 |
| Wallace G. Wilkinson (D) | Dec. 8, 1987 | Dec. 10, 1991 |
| Brereton C. Jones (D) | Dec. 10, 1991 | |

### Kentucky

1. Died Oct. 21, 1816.
2. As lieutenant governor, he succeeded to office.
3. Died Feb. 22, 1834.
4. As lieutenant governor, he succeeded to office.
5. Died Oct. 5, 1839.
6. As lieutenant governor, he succeeded to office.
7. Resigned July 31, 1850.
8. As lieutenant governor, he succeeded to office.
9. Resigned Aug. 18, 1862.
10. As president of the state Senate, he succeeded to office.
11. Died Sept. 13, 1867.
12. As lieutenant governor, he succeeded to office. Subsequently elected. Resigned March 4, 1871.
13. As president of the state Senate, he succeeded to office. Subsequently elected.
14. Taylor was removed by the Legislature following an election challenge by his Democratic opponent, William Goebel.
15. Successfully challenged the election of William S. Taylor. Died Feb. 3, 1900.
16. As lieutenant governor, he succeeded to office. Subsequently elected.
17. Resigned May 19, 1919.
18. As lieutenant governor, he succeeded to office.
19. Resigned Oct. 9, 1939.
20. As lieutenant governor, he succeeded to office. Subsequently elected.
21. Resigned Nov. 27, 1950.
22. As lieutenant governor, he succeeded to office. Subsequently elected.
23. Resigned Dec. 28, 1974.
24. As lieutenant governor, he succeeded to office. Subsequently elected.

# LOUISIANA

(Became a state April 30, 1812)

| Governors | Dates of Service | |
|---|---|---|
| William C. C. Claiborne | July 30, 1812 | Dec. 16, 1816 |
| Jacques Philippe Villere | Dec. 17, 1816 | Dec. 17, 1820 |
| Thomas B. Robertson[1] | Dec. 18, 1820 | Nov. 15, 1824 |
| Henry S. Thibodeaux[2] | Nov. 15, 1824 | Dec. 13, 1824 |
| Henry S. Johnson (AM FAC) | Dec. 13, 1824 | Dec. 15, 1828 |
| Pierre Derbigny (NR)[3] | Dec. 15, 1828 | Oct. 6, 1829 |
| Armand Beauvais[4] | Oct. 6, 1829 | Jan. 14, 1830 |
| Jacques Dupre | Jan. 14, 1830 | Jan. 31, 1831 |
| Andre B. Roman (NR) | Jan. 31, 1831 | Feb. 4, 1835 |
| Edward E. White (W) | Feb. 4, 1835 | Feb. 4, 1839 |
| Andre B. Roman (W) | Feb. 4, 1839 | Jan. 30, 1843 |
| Alexander Mouton (D) | Jan. 30, 1843 | Feb. 11, 1846 |
| Isaac Johnson (D) | Feb. 12, 1846 | Jan. 27, 1850 |
| Joseph M. Walker (D) | Jan. 28, 1850 | Jan. 17, 1853 |
| Paul O. Hebert (D) | Jan. 18, 1853 | Jan. 21, 1856 |
| Robert C. Wickliffe (D) | Jan. 22, 1856 | Jan. 22, 1860 |
| Thomas O. Moore (D) | Jan. 23, 1860 | Jan. 25, 1864 |
| George F. Shepley[5] | July 2, 1862 | March 4, 1864 |

| | | |
|---|---|---|
| Henry W. Allen[6] | Jan. 25, 1864 | June 2, 1865 |
| Michael Hahn[7] | March 4, 1864 | March 4, 1865 |
| James M. Wells (D)[8] | March 4, 1865 | June 3, 1867 |
| Benjamin F. Flanders[9] | June 3, 1867 | Jan. 8, 1868 |
| Joshua Baker[10] | Jan. 8, 1868 | June 27, 1868 |
| Henry C. Warmoth (R) | June 27, 1868 | Dec. 9, 1872 |
| Pinckney B. S. Pinchback[11] | Dec. 9, 1872 | Jan. 13, 1873 |
| William P. Kellogg (R)[12] | Jan. 13, 1873 | Jan. 5, 1877 |
| Francis T. Nicholls (D)[13] | Jan. 8, 1877 | Jan. 13, 1880 |
| Louis A. Wiltz (D)[14] | Jan. 14, 1880 | Oct. 16, 1881 |
| Samuel D. McEnery (D)[15] | Oct. 16, 1881 | May 20, 1888 |
| Francis T. Nicholls (D) | May 21, 1888 | May 10, 1892 |
| Murphy J. Foster (A-LOT D, D) | May 10, 1892 | May 8, 1900 |
| William W. Heard (D) | May 8, 1900 | May 10, 1904 |
| Newton C. Blanchard (D) | May 10, 1904 | May 12, 1908 |
| Jared Y. Sanders (D) | May 12, 1908 | May 14, 1912 |
| Luther E. Hall (D) | May 14, 1912 | May 9, 1916 |
| Ruffin G. Pleasant (D) | May 9, 1916 | May 11, 1920 |
| John M Parker (D) | May 11, 1920 | May 13, 1924 |
| Henry L. Fuqua (D)[16] | May 13, 1924 | Oct. 11, 1926 |
| Oramel H. Simpson(D)[17] | Oct. 11, 1926 | May 21, 1928 |
| Huey P. Long Jr. (D)[18] | May 21, 1928 | Jan. 25, 1932 |
| Alvin O. King (D)[19] | Jan. 25, 1932 | May 10, 1932 |
| Oscar K. Allen (D)[20] | May 10, 1932 | Jan. 28, 1936 |
| James A. Noe (D)[21] | Jan. 28, 1936 | May 12, 1936 |
| Richard W. Leche (D)[22] | May 12, 1936 | June 26, 1939 |
| Earl K. Long (D)[23] | June 26, 1939 | May 14, 1940 |
| Sam H. Jones (D) | May 14, 1940 | May 9, 1944 |
| James H. Davis (D) | May 9, 1944 | May 11, 1948 |
| Earl K. Long (D) | May 11, 1948 | May 13, 1952 |
| Robert F. Kennon (D) | May 13, 1952 | May 8, 1956 |
| Earl K. Long (D) | May 8, 1956 | May 10, 1960 |
| James H. Davis (D) | May 10, 1960 | May 12, 1964 |
| John J. McKeithen (D) | May 12, 1964 | May 9, 1972 |
| Edwin W. Edwards (D) | May 9, 1972 | March 10, 1980 |
| David C. Treen (R) | March 10, 1980 | March 12, 1984 |
| Edwin W. Edwards (D) | March 12, 1984 | March 14, 1988 |
| Charles Roemer (D, R)[24] | March 14, 1988 | Jan. 8, 1992 |
| Edwin W. Edwards (D) | Jan. 8, 1992 | |

**Louisiana**

1. *Resigned Nov. 15, 1824.*
2. *As president of the state Senate, he succeeded to office.*
3. *Died Oct. 1, 1829.*
4. *As president of the state Senate, he succeeded to office.*
5. *Military governor within Union lines.*
6. *Last elected Confederate governor.*
7. *Elected within Union lines. Resigned March 4, 1865.*
8. *As lieutenant governor, he succeeded to office. Subsequently elected. Removed June 3, 1867.*
9. *Under military authority.*
10. *Under military authority.*
11. *Acting governor.*
12. *The 1872 gubernatorial election in Louisiana set off a bitter dispute between Republicans backing Kellogg and Democrats supporting his opponent, John McEnery. Each side organized its own boards to canvass the vote, resulting in two separate sets of election returns, one showing Kellogg the winner, the other McEnery. To add to the confusion, two rival legislatures assumed office, each claiming legitimacy, and Kellogg and McEnery were both inaugurated as governor by their respective factions. President Ulysses S. Grant (R) finally stepped in and recognized Kellogg as the legitimate governor on May 22, 1873.*
13. *The 1876 election set off a dispute similar to that of 1872. Nicholls, the Democrat, and Packard, the Republican, each had election returns showing him the winner. There were also two legislatures, each controlled by a different party. Nicholls set up a de facto state government and was recognized by federal authorities.*
14. *Died in October 1881.*
15. *As lieutenant governor, he succeeded to office. Subsequently elected.*
16. *Died Oct. 11, 1926.*
17. *As lieutenant governor, he succeeded to office.*
18. *Resigned Jan. 25, 1932.*
19. *As lieutenant governor, he succeeded to office.*
20. *Died Jan. 28, 1936.*

21. *As lieutenant governor, he succeeded to office.*
22. *Resigned June 26, 1939.*
23. *As lieutenant governor, he succeeded to office.*
24. *Elected in 1987 as a Democrat. Became a Republican in March 1991.*

# MAINE

(Became a state March 15, 1820)

| Governors | Dates of Service | |
|---|---|---|
| William King (D-R)[1] | May 31, 1820 | May 28, 1821 |
| William D. Williamson (D-R)[2] | May 29, 1821 | Dec. 25, 1821 |
| Benjamin Ames (D-R)[3] | Dec. 25, 1821 | Jan. 2, 1821 |
| Daniel Rose (D-R)[4] | Jan. 2, 1822 | Jan. 4, 1822 |
| Albion K. Parris (D-R) | Jan. 5, 1822 | Jan. 3, 1827 |
| Enoch Lincoln (D-R)[5] | Jan. 3, 1827 | Oct. 8, 1829 |
| Nathan Cutler (D)[6] | Oct. 12, 1829 | Feb. 5, 1830 |
| Joshua Hall (D)[7] | Feb. 5, 1830 | Feb. 10, 1830 |
| Jonathan G. Hunton (NR) | Feb. 10, 1830 | Jan. 5, 1831 |
| Samuel E. Smith (JAC D) | Jan. 5, 1831 | Jan. 1, 1834 |
| Robert P. Dunlap (D) | Jan. 1, 1834 | Jan. 3, 1838 |
| Edward Kent (W) | Jan. 3, 1838 | Jan. 2, 1839 |
| John Fairfield (D) | Jan. 2, 1839 | Jan. 6, 1841 |
| Richard H. Vose[8] | Jan. 12, 1841 | Jan. 13, 1841 |
| Edward Kent (W) | Jan. 13, 1841 | Jan. 5, 1842 |
| John Fairfield (D)[9] | Jan. 5, 1842 | March 7, 1843 |
| Edward Kavanagh (D)[10] | March 7, 1843 | Jan. 1, 1844 |
| David Dunn (D) | Jan. 2, 1844 | Jan. 3, 1844 |
| John W. Dana (D) | Jan. 3, 1844 | Jan. 5, 1844 |
| Hugh J. Anderson (D) | Jan. 5, 1844 | May 12, 1847 |
| John W. Dana (D) | May 13, 1847 | May 8, 1850 |
| John Hubbard (D) | May 9, 1850 | Jan. 5, 1853 |
| William G. Crosby (W) | Jan. 5, 1853 | Jan. 3, 1855 |
| Anson P. Morrill (R) | Jan. 3, 1855 | Jan. 2, 1856 |
| Samuel Wells (D) | Jan. 2, 1856 | Jan. 8, 1857 |
| Hannibal Hamlin (R)[11] | Jan. 8, 1857 | Feb. 25, 1857 |
| Joseph H. Williams (R)[12] | Feb. 26, 1857 | Jan. 8, 1858 |
| Lot M. Morrill (R) | Jan. 8, 1858 | Jan. 2, 1861 |
| Israel Washburn Jr. (R) | Jan. 2, 1861 | Jan. 7, 1863 |
| Abner Coburn (R) | Jan. 7, 1863 | Jan. 6, 1864 |
| Samuel Cony (UN R) | Jan. 6, 1864 | Jan. 2, 1867 |
| Joshua L. Chamberlain (R) | Jan. 2, 1867 | Jan. 4, 1871 |
| Sidney Perham (R) | Jan. 4, 1871 | Jan. 7, 1874 |
| Nelson Dingley Jr. (R) | Jan. 7, 1874 | Jan. 5, 1876 |
| Selden Connor (R) | Jan. 5, 1876 | Jan. 8, 1879 |
| Alonzo Garcelon (D) | Jan. 8, 1879 | Jan. 1880 |
| Daniel F. Davis (R) | Jan. 17, 1880 | Jan. 1881 |
| Harris M. Plaisted (D) | Jan. 13, 1881 | Jan. 3, 1883 |
| Frederick Robie (R) | Jan. 3, 1883 | Jan. 5, 1887 |
| Joseph R. Bodwell (R)[13] | Jan. 5, 1887 | Dec. 15, 1887 |
| Sebastian S. Marble (R)[14] | Dec. 16, 1887 | Jan. 2, 1889 |
| Edwin C. Burleigh (R) | Jan. 2, 1889 | Jan. 4, 1893 |
| Henry B. Cleaves (R) | Jan. 4, 1893 | Jan. 6, 1897 |
| Llewellyn Powers (R) | Jan. 6, 1897 | Jan. 2, 1901 |
| John F. Hill (R) | Jan. 2, 1901 | Jan. 4, 1905 |
| William T. Cobb (R) | Jan. 4, 1905 | Jan. 6, 1909 |
| Bert M. Fernald (R) | Jan. 6, 1909 | Jan. 4, 1911 |
| Frederick W. Plaisted (D) | Jan. 4, 1911 | Jan. 1, 1913 |
| William T. Haines (R) | Jan. 1, 1913 | Jan. 6, 1915 |
| Oakley C. Curtis (D) | Jan. 6, 1915 | Jan. 3, 1917 |
| Carl E. Milliken (R) | Jan. 3, 1917 | Jan. 5, 1921 |
| Frederic H. Parkhurst (R)[15] | Jan. 5, 1921 | Jan. 31, 1921 |
| Percival P. Baxter (R)[16] | Jan. 31, 1921 | Jan. 8, 1925 |
| Ralph O. Brewster (R) | Jan. 8, 1925 | Jan. 2, 1929 |
| William T. Gardiner (R) | Jan. 2, 1929 | Jan. 4, 1933 |
| Louis J. Brann (D) | Jan. 4, 1933 | Jan. 6, 1937 |
| Lewis O. Barrows (R) | Jan. 6, 1937 | Jan. 1, 1941 |
| Sumner Sewall (R) | Jan. 1, 1941 | Jan. 3, 1945 |
| Horace A. Hildreth (R) | Jan. 3, 1945 | Jan. 5, 1949 |
| Frederick G. Payne (R)[17] | Jan. 5, 1949 | Dec. 25, 1952 |

| | | |
|---|---|---|
| Burton M. Cross (R)[18] | Dec. 26, 1952 | Jan. 5, 1955 |
| Edmund S. Muskie (D)[19] | Jan. 5, 1955 | Jan. 3, 1959 |
| Robert N. Haskell (R)[20] | Jan. 3, 1959 | Jan. 8, 1959 |
| Clinton A. Clauson (D)[21] | Jan. 8, 1959 | Dec. 30, 1959 |
| John H. Reed (R)[22] | Dec. 30, 1959 | Jan. 5, 1967 |
| Kenneth M. Curtis (D) | Jan. 5, 1967 | Jan. 1, 1975 |
| James B. Longley (I) | Jan. 2, 1975 | Jan. 3, 1979 |
| Joseph E. Brennan (D) | Jan. 3, 1979 | Jan. 7, 1987 |
| John R. McKernan Jr. (R) | Jan. 7, 1987 | |

**Maine**

1. *Resigned May 28, 1821.*
2. *Acting governor. Resigned Dec. 25, 1821.*
3. *Acting governor.*
4. *Acting governor.*
5. *Died Oct. 8, 1829.*
6. *Acting governor.*
7. *Acting governor.*
8. *As president of the state Senate, acted as governor while an inconclusive popular election result was being resolved in the Legislature.*
9. *Resigned March 7, 1843.*
10. *Acting governor.*
11. *Resigned Feb. 25, 1857.*
12. *Acting governor.*
13. *Died Dec. 15, 1887.*
14. *Acting governor.*
15. *Died Jan. 31, 1921.*
16. *As president of the state Senate, he succeeded to office. Subsequently elected.*
17. *Resigned Dec. 25, 1952.*
18. *As president of the state Senate, he succeeded to office. Had previously been elected for a two-year term beginning January 1953.*
19. *Resigned Jan. 3, 1959.*
20. *As president of the state Senate, he succeeded to office.*
21. *Died Dec. 30, 1959.*
22. *As president of the state Senate, he succeeded to office. Subsequently elected in a special election for the remainder of Clauson's term. Re-elected in 1962.*

# MARYLAND

(Ratified the Constitution April 28, 1788)

| Governors | Dates of Service | |
|---|---|---|
| John Eager Howard (FED) | Nov. 24, 1788 | Nov. 14, 1791 |
| George Plater (FED)[1] | Nov. 14, 1791 | Feb. 10, 1792 |
| James Brice (FED)[2] | Feb. 13, 1792 | April 5, 1792 |
| Thomas Sim Lee (FED) | April 5, 1792 | Nov. 14, 1794 |
| John H. Stone (FED) | Nov. 14, 1794 | Nov. 17, 1797 |
| John Henry (FED) | Nov. 17, 1797 | Nov. 14, 1798 |
| Benjamin Ogle (FED) | Nov. 14, 1798 | Nov. 10, 1801 |
| John Francis Mercer (D-R) | Nov. 10, 1801 | Nov. 15, 1803 |
| Robert Bowie (D-R) | Nov. 15, 1803 | Nov. 10, 1806 |
| Robert Wright (D-R)[3] | Nov. 12, 1806 | May 6, 1809 |
| James Butcher (D-R)[4] | May 6, 1809 | June 9, 1809 |
| Edward Lloyd (D-R) | June 9, 1809 | Nov. 16, 1811 |
| Robert Bowie (D-R) | Nov. 16, 1811 | Nov. 25, 1812 |
| Levin Winder (FED) | Nov. 25, 1812 | Jan. 2, 1816 |
| Charles Ridgely (FED) | Jan. 2, 1816 | Jan. 8, 1819 |
| Charles Goldsborough (FED) | Jan. 8, 1819 | Dec. 20, 1819 |
| Samuel Sprigg (D-R) | Dec. 20, 1819 | Dec. 16, 1822 |
| Samuel Stevens Jr. (D-R) | Dec. 16, 1822 | Jan. 9, 1826 |
| Joseph Kent (D-R) | Jan. 9, 1826 | Jan. 15, 1829 |
| Daniel Martin (A-JAC D) | Jan. 15, 1829 | Jan. 15, 1830 |
| Thomas King Carroll (D) | Jan. 15, 1830 | Jan. 13, 1831 |
| Daniel Martin (A-JAC D)[5] | Jan. 13, 1831 | July 11, 1831 |
| George Howard (A-JAC D)[6] | July 11, 1831 | Jan. 17, 1833 |
| James Thomas (A-JAC D) | Jan. 17, 1833 | Jan. 14, 1836 |
| Thomas W. Veazey (W) | Jan. 14, 1836 | Jan. 7, 1839 |
| William Grason (D) | Jan. 7, 1839 | Jan. 3, 1842 |
| Francis Thomas (D) | Jan. 3, 1842 | Jan. 6, 1845 |
| Thomas G. Pratt (W) | Jan. 6, 1845 | Jan. 3, 1848 |

| | | |
|---|---|---|
| Philip Francis Thomas (D) | Jan. 3, 1848 | Jan. 6, 1851 |
| Enoch L. Lowe (D) | Jan. 6, 1851 | Jan. 11, 1854 |
| Thomas W. Ligon (D) | Jan. 11, 1854 | Jan. 13, 1858 |
| Thomas H. Hicks (AM) | Jan. 13, 1858 | Jan. 8, 1862 |
| Augustus W. Bradford (UN R) | Jan. 8, 1862 | Jan. 10, 1866 |
| Thomas Swann (UN R) | Jan. 10, 1866 | Jan. 13, 1869 |
| Oden Bowie (D) | Jan. 13, 1869 | Jan. 10, 1872 |
| William P. Whyte (D)[7] | Jan. 10, 1872 | March 4, 1874 |
| James B. Groome (D)[8] | March 4, 1874 | Jan. 12, 1876 |
| John Lee Carroll (D) | Jan. 12, 1876 | Jan. 14, 1880 |
| William T. Hamilton (D) | Jan. 14, 1880 | Jan. 9, 1884 |
| Robert M. McLane (D)[9] | Jan. 9, 1884 | March 27, 1885 |
| Henry Lloyd (D)[10] | March 27, 1885 | Jan. 11, 1888 |
| Elihu E. Jackson (D) | Jan. 11, 1888 | Jan. 13, 1892 |
| Frank Brown (D) | Jan. 13, 1892 | Jan. 8, 1896 |
| Lloyd Lowndes (R) | Jan. 8, 1896 | Jan. 10, 1900 |
| John W. Smith (D) | Jan. 10, 1900 | Jan. 13, 1904 |
| Edwin Warfield (D) | Jan. 1, 1904 | Jan. 8, 1908 |
| Austin L. Crothers (D) | Jan. 8, 1908 | Jan. 10, 1912 |
| Phillips L. Goldsborough (R) | Jan. 10, 1912 | Jan. 12, 1916 |
| Emerson C. Harrington (D) | Jan. 12, 1916 | Jan. 14, 1920 |
| Albert C. Ritchie (D) | Jan. 14, 1920 | Jan. 9, 1935 |
| Harry W. Nice (R) | Jan. 9, 1935 | Jan. 11, 1939 |
| Herbert R. O'Conor (D)[11] | Jan. 11, 1939 | Jan. 3, 1947 |
| William P. Lane Jr. (D)[12] | Jan. 3, 1947 | Jan. 10, 1951 |
| Theodore R. McKeldin (R) | Jan. 10, 1951 | Jan. 14, 1959 |
| J. Millard Tawes (D) | Jan. 14, 1959 | Jan. 25, 1967 |
| Spiro T. Agnew (R)[13] | Jan. 25, 1967 | Jan. 7, 1969 |
| Marvin Mandel (D)[14] | Jan. 7, 1969 | Jan. 15, 1979 |
| Blair Lee (D)[15] | Oct. 7, 1977 | Jan. 15, 1979 |
| Harry Hughes (D) | Jan. 17, 1979 | Jan 20, 1987 |
| William D. Schaefer (D) | Jan. 21, 1987 | |

**Maryland**

1. *Died Feb. 10, 1792.*
2. *Acting governor.*
3. *Resigned May 6, 1809.*
4. *Acting governor.*
5. *Died July 11, 1831.*
6. *Acting governor. Subsequently elected by the Legislature.*
7. *Resigned March 4, 1874.*
8. *Acting governor. Subsequently elected by the Legislature.*
9. *Resigned March 27, 1885.*
10. *Acting governor. Subsequently elected by the Legislature.*
11. *Resigned Jan. 3, 1947.*
12. *Elected by the Legislature to complete the remaining five days of O'Conor's term. Had previously been elected for a four-year term beginning January 8, 1947.*
13. *Resigned Jan. 7, 1969.*
14. *Elected by the Legislature to complete Agnew's term. Subsequently re-elected in 1970 and 1974. Suspended from office Oct. 7, 1977 - Jan. 15, 1979.*
15. *As lieutenant governor, served as acting governor.*

# MASSACHUSETTS

(Ratified the Constitution Feb. 6, 1788)

| Governors | Dates of Service | |
|---|---|---|
| John Hancock | May 30, 1787 | Oct. 8, 1793 |
| Samuel Adams | Oct. 8, 1793 | June 2, 1797 |
| Increase Sumner (FED) | June 2, 1797 | June 7, 1799 |
| Moses Gill (FED)[1] | June 7, 1799 | May 20, 1800 |
| Caleb Strong (FED) | May 30, 1800 | May 29, 1807 |
| James Sullivan (D-R) | May 29, 1807 | Dec. 10, 1808 |
| Levi Lincoln (D-R)[2] | Dec. 10, 1808 | May 1, 1809 |
| Christopher Gore (FED) | May 1809 | June 1810 |
| Elbridge Gerry (D-R) | June 1810 | June 1812 |
| Caleb Strong (FED) | June 1812 | May 30, 1816 |
| John Brooks (FED) | May 30, 1816 | May 31, 1823 |
| William Eustis (D-R) | May 31, 1823 | Feb. 6, 1825 |
| Marcus Morton (D-R)[3] | Feb. 6, 1825 | May 26, 1825 |

| | | |
|---|---|---|
| Levi Lincoln (AR, NR)[4] | May 26, 1825 | Jan. 9, 1834 |
| John Davis (NR, W) | Jan. 9, 1834 | March 1, 1835 |
| Samuel T. Armstrong (W)[5] | March 1, 1835 | Jan. 13, 1836 |
| Edward Everett (W) | Jan. 13, 1836 | Jan. 18, 1840 |
| Marcus Morton (D) | Jan. 18, 1840 | Jan. 7, 1841 |
| John Davis (W) | Jan. 7, 1841 | Jan. 17, 1843 |
| Marcus Morton (D) | Jan. 17, 1843 | Jan. 1844 |
| George N. Briggs (W) | Jan. 1844 | Jan. 11, 1851 |
| George S. Boutwell (D) | Jan. 11, 1851 | Jan. 14, 1853 |
| John H. Clifford (W) | Jan. 14, 1853 | Jan. 12, 1854 |
| Emory Washburn (W) | Jan. 12, 1854 | Jan. 4, 1855 |
| Henry J. Gardner (AM) | Jan. 4, 1855 | Jan. 7, 1858 |
| Nathaniel P. Banks (R) | Jan. 7, 1858 | Jan. 3, 1861 |
| John A. Andrew (R) | Jan. 3, 1861 | Jan. 4, 1866 |
| Alexander H. Bullock (UN) | Jan. 4, 1866 | Jan. 7, 1869 |
| William Claflin (R) | Jan. 7, 1869 | Jan. 4, 1872 |
| William B. Washburn (R)[6] | Jan. 4, 1872 | April 29, 1874 |
| Thomas Talbot (R)[7] | April 29, 1874 | Jan. 7, 1875 |
| William Gaston (D) | Jan. 7, 1875 | Jan. 6, 1876 |
| Alexander H. Rice (R) | Jan. 6, 1876 | Jan. 2, 1879 |
| Thomas Talbot (R) | Jan. 2, 1879 | Jan. 8, 1880 |
| John Davis Long (R) | Jan. 8, 1880 | Jan. 4, 1883 |
| Benjamin F. Butler (D) | Jan. 4, 1883 | Jan. 3, 1884 |
| George D. Robinson (R) | Jan. 3, 1884 | Jan. 6, 1887 |
| Oliver Ames (R) | Jan. 6, 1887 | Jan. 7, 1890 |
| John Q. A. Brackett (R) | Jan. 7, 1890 | Jan. 8, 1891 |
| William E. Russell (D) | Jan. 8, 1891 | Jan. 4, 1894 |
| Frederic T. Greenhalge (R)[8] | Jan. 4, 1894 | March 5, 1896 |
| Roger Wolcott (R)[9] | March 5, 1896 | Jan. 4, 1900 |
| Winthrop M. Crane (R) | Jan. 4, 1900 | Jan. 8, 1903 |
| John L. Bates (R) | Jan. 8, 1903 | Jan. 5, 1905 |
| William L. Douglas (D) | Jan. 5, 1905 | Jan. 4, 1906 |
| Curtis Guild Jr. (R) | Jan. 4, 1906 | Jan. 7, 1909 |
| Eban Sumner Draper (R) | Jan. 7, 1909 | Jan. 5, 1911 |
| Eugene N. Foss (D) | Jan. 5, 1911 | Jan. 8, 1914 |
| David I. Walsh (D) | Jan. 8, 1914 | Jan. 6, 1916 |
| Samuel W. McCall (R) | Jan. 6, 1916 | Jan. 2, 1919 |
| Calvin Coolidge (R) | Jan. 2, 1919 | Jan. 6, 1921 |
| Channing H. Cox (R) | Jan. 6, 1921 | Jan. 8, 1925 |
| Alvan T. Fuller (R) | Jan. 8, 1925 | Jan. 3, 1929 |
| Frank G. Allen (R) | Jan. 3, 1929 | Jan. 8, 1931 |
| Joseph B. Ely (D) | Jan. 8, 1931 | Jan. 3, 1935 |
| James M. Curley (D) | Jan. 3, 1935 | Jan. 7, 1937 |
| Charles F. Hurley (D) | Jan. 7, 1937 | Jan. 5, 1939 |
| Leverett Saltonstall (R) | Jan. 5, 1939 | Jan. 3, 1945 |
| Maurice J. Tobin (D) | Jan. 3, 1945 | Jan. 2, 1947 |
| Robert F. Bradford (R) | Jan. 2, 1947 | Jan. 6, 1949 |
| Paul A. Dever (D) | Jan. 6, 1949 | Jan. 8, 1953 |
| Christian A. Herter (R) | Jan. 8, 1953 | Jan. 3, 1957 |
| Foster J. Furcolo (D) | Jan. 3, 1957 | Jan. 5, 1961 |
| John A. Volpe (R) | Jan. 5, 1961 | Jan. 3, 1963 |
| Endicott Peabody (D) | Jan. 3, 1963 | Jan. 7, 1965 |
| John A. Volpe (R)[10] | Jan. 7, 1965 | Jan. 22, 1969 |
| Francis W. Sargent (R)[11] | Jan. 22, 1969 | Jan. 2, 1975 |
| Michael S. Dukakis (D) | Jan. 2, 1975 | Jan. 4, 1979 |
| Edward J. King (D) | Jan. 4, 1979 | Jan. 6, 1983 |
| Michael S. Dukakis (D) | Jan. 6, 1983 | Jan. 3, 1991 |
| William F. Weld (R) | Jan. 3, 1991 | |

**Massachusetts**

1. *Acting governor.*
2. *Acting governor.*
3. *Acting governor.*
4. *ICPSR data shows that there were two elections for governor in Massachusetts in 1831 and returns for both have been provided. The winner both times was incumbent Levi Lincoln. An explanation was obtained from Albert Bushnell Hart's* Commonwealth of Massachusetts, *vol. 4 (New York: States History Company, 1930), p. 82. Massachusetts had a one-year term for its governors during this period. Apparently the state decided in 1831 to move its gubernatorial election from April to November to coincide with presidential elections in 1832 and succeeding years. As a consequence, Lincoln was required to run twice within the same year to make the adjustment.*

5. *Acting governor.*
6. *Resigned May 1, 1874.*
7. *Acting governor.*
8. *Died March 5, 1896.*
9. *As lieutenant governor, he succeeded to office. Subsequently elected.*
10. *Resigned Jan. 22, 1969.*
11. *As lieutenant governor, he succeeded to office. Subsequently elected.*

# MICHIGAN

(Became a state Jan. 26, 1837)

| Governors | Dates of Service | |
|---|---|---|
| Stevens T. Mason (D) | Nov. 3, 1835 | Jan. 7, 1840 |
| Edward Mundy (D)[1] | April 3, 1838 | June 12, 1838 |
| William Woodbridge (W)[2] | Jan. 7, 1840 | Feb. 23, 1841 |
| James W. Gordon (W)[3] | Feb. 23, 1841 | Jan. 3, 1842 |
| John S. Barry (D) | Jan. 3, 1842 | Jan. 5, 1846 |
| Alpheus Felch (D)[4] | Jan. 5, 1846 | March 3, 1847 |
| William L. Greenly (D)[5] | March 3, 1847 | Jan. 3, 1848 |
| Epaphroditus Ransom (D) | Jan. 3, 1848 | Jan. 7, 1850 |
| John S. Barry (D) | Jan. 7, 1850 | Jan. 1, 1851 |
| Robert McClelland (D)[6] | Jan. 1, 1851 | March 7, 1853 |
| Andrew Parsons (D)[7] | March 7, 1853 | Jan. 3, 1855 |
| Kinsley S. Bingham (R) | Jan. 3, 1855 | Jan. 5, 1859 |
| Moses Wisner (R) | Jan. 5, 1859 | Jan. 2, 1861 |
| Austin Blair (R) | Jan. 2, 1861 | Jan. 4, 1865 |
| Henry H. Crapo (UN R) | Jan. 4, 1865 | Jan. 6, 1869 |
| Henry P. Baldwin (R) | Jan. 6, 1869 | Jan. 1, 1873 |
| John J. Bagley (R) | Jan. 1, 1873 | Jan. 3, 1877 |
| Charles M. Croswell (R) | Jan. 3, 1877 | Jan. 1, 1881 |
| David H. Jerome (R) | Jan. 1, 1881 | Jan. 1, 1883 |
| Josiah W. Begole (D) | Jan. 1, 1883 | Jan. 1, 1885 |
| Russell A. Alger (R) | Jan. 1, 1885 | Jan. 1, 1887 |
| Cyrus G. Luce (R) | Jan. 1, 1887 | Jan. 1, 1891 |
| Edward B. Winans (D) | Jan. 1, 1891 | Jan. 1, 1893 |
| John T. Rich (R) | Jan. 1, 1893 | Jan. 1, 1897 |
| Hazen S. Pingree (R) | Jan. 1, 1897 | Jan. 1, 1901 |
| Aaron T. Bliss (R) | Jan. 1, 1901 | Jan. 1, 1905 |
| Fred M. Warner (R) | Jan. 1, 1905 | Jan. 1, 1911 |
| Chase S. Osborn (R) | Jan. 1, 1911 | Jan. 1, 1913 |
| Woodbridge N. Ferris (D) | Jan. 1, 1913 | Jan. 1, 1917 |
| Albert E. Sleeper (R) | Jan. 1, 1917 | Jan. 1, 1921 |
| Alexander J. Groesbeck (R) | Jan. 1, 1921 | Jan. 1, 1927 |
| Fred W. Green (R) | Jan. 1, 1927 | Jan. 1, 1931 |
| Wilber M. Brucker (R) | Jan. 1, 1931 | Jan. 1, 1933 |
| William A. Comstock (D) | Jan. 1, 1933 | Jan. 1, 1935 |
| Frank D. Fitzgerald (R) | Jan. 1, 1935 | Jan. 1, 1937 |
| Frank Murphy (D) | Jan. 1, 1937 | Jan. 1, 1939 |
| Frank D. Fitzgerald (R)[8] | Jan. 1, 1939 | March 16, 1939 |
| Luren D. Dickinson (R)[9] | March 16, 1939 | Jan. 1, 1941 |
| Murray D. Van Wagoner (D) | Jan. 1, 1941 | Jan. 1, 1943 |
| Harry F. Kelly (R) | Jan. 1, 1943 | Jan. 1, 1947 |
| Kim Sigler (R) | Jan. 1, 1947 | Jan. 1, 1949 |
| G. Mennen Williams (D) | Jan. 1, 1949 | Jan. 1, 1961 |
| John B. Swainson (D) | Jan. 1, 1961 | Jan. 1, 1963 |
| George W. Romney (R)[10] | Jan. 1, 1963 | Jan. 22, 1969 |
| William G. Milliken (R)[11] | Jan. 22, 1969 | Jan. 1, 1983 |
| James J. Blanchard (D) | Jan. 1, 1983 | Jan. 1, 1991 |
| John Engler (R) | Jan. 1, 1991 | |

**Michigan**

1. *Lieutenant governor, serving as acting governor for several months in 1838.*
2. *Resigned Feb. 23, 1841.*
3. *As lieutenant governor, he succeeded to office.*
4. *Resigned March 3, 1847.*
5. *As lieutenant governor, he succeeded to office.*
6. *Resigned March 7, 1853.*
7. *As lieutenant governor, he succeeded to office.*
8. *Died March 16, 1939.*

**Michigan (continued)**
9. *As lieutenant governor, he succeeded to office.*
10. *Resigned Jan. 22, 1969.*
11. *As lieutenant governor, he succeeded to office. Subsequently elected.*

# MINNESOTA

(Became a state May 11, 1858)

| Governors | Dates of Service | |
| --- | --- | --- |
| Henry H. Sibley (D) | May 24, 1858 | Jan. 2, 1860 |
| Alexander Ramsey (R)[1] | Jan. 2, 1860 | July 10, 1863 |
| Henry A. Swift (R)[2] | July 10, 1863 | Jan. 11, 1864 |
| Stephen Miller (UN) | Jan. 11, 1864 | Jan. 8, 1866 |
| William R. Marshall (R) | Jan. 8, 1866 | Jan. 9, 1870 |
| Horace Austin (R) | Jan. 9, 1870 | Jan. 7, 1874 |
| Cushman K. Davis (R) | Jan. 7, 1874 | Jan. 7, 1876 |
| John S. Pillsbury (R) | Jan. 7, 1876 | Jan. 10, 1882 |
| Lucius F. Hubbard (R) | Jan. 10, 1882 | Jan. 5, 1887 |
| Andrew R. McGill (R) | Jan. 5, 1887 | Jan. 9, 1889 |
| William R. Merriam (R) | Jan. 9, 1889 | Jan. 4, 1893 |
| Knute Nelson (R) | Jan. 4, 1893 | Jan. 31, 1895 |
| David M. Clough (R) | Jan. 31, 1895 | Jan. 2, 1899 |
| John Lind (D & POP) | Jan. 2, 1899 | Jan. 7, 1901 |
| Samuel R. Van Sant (R) | Jan. 7, 1901 | Jan. 4, 1905 |
| John A. Johnson (D)[3] | Jan. 4, 1905 | Sept. 21, 1909 |
| Adolph O. Eberhart (R)[4] | Sept. 21, 1909 | Jan. 5, 1915 |
| Winfield S. Hammond (D)[5] | Jan. 5, 1915 | Dec. 30, 1915 |
| Joseph A. A. Burnquist (R)[6] | Dec. 30, 1915 | Jan. 5, 1921 |
| Jacob A. O. Preus (R) | Jan. 5, 1921 | Jan. 6, 1925 |
| Theodore Christianson (R) | Jan. 6, 1925 | Jan. 6, 1931 |
| Floyd B. Olson (F-LAB)[7] | Jan. 6, 1931 | Aug. 22, 1936 |
| Hjalmar Petersen (F-LAB)[8] | Aug. 22, 1936 | Jan. 4, 1937 |
| Elmer A. Benson (F-LAB) | Jan. 4, 1937 | Jan. 2, 1939 |
| Harold E. Stassen (R)[9] | Jan. 2, 1939 | April 27, 1943 |
| Edward J. Thye (R)[10] | April 27, 1943 | Jan. 8, 1947 |
| Luther W. Youngdahl (R)[11] | Jan. 8, 1947 | Sept. 27, 1951 |
| C. Elmer Anderson (R)[12] | Sept. 27, 1951 | Jan. 5, 1955 |
| Orville L. Freeman (DFL) | Jan. 5, 1955 | Jan. 2, 1961 |
| Elmer L. Andersen (R)[13] | Jan. 2, 1961 | March 25, 1963 |
| Karl F. Rolvaag (DFL)[14] | March 25, 1963 | Jan. 2, 1967 |
| Harold LeVander (R) | Jan. 2, 1967 | Jan. 4, 1971 |
| Wendell R. Anderson (DFL)[15] | Jan. 4, 1971 | Dec. 29, 1976 |
| Rudy Perpich (DFL)[16] | Dec. 29, 1976 | Jan. 1, 1979 |
| Albert H. Quie (I-R) | Jan. 1, 1979 | Jan. 3, 1983 |
| Rudy Perpich (DFL) | Jan. 3, 1983 | Jan. 7, 1991 |
| Arne Carlson (I-R) | Jan. 7, 1991 | |

**Minnesota**
1. *Resigned July 10, 1863.*
2. *As lieutenant governor, he succeeded to office.*
3. *Died Sept. 21, 1909.*
4. *As lieutenant governor, he succeeded to office. Subsequently elected.*
5. *Died Dec. 30, 1915.*
6. *As lieutenant governor, he succeeded to office. Subsequently elected.*
7. *Died Aug. 22, 1936.*
8. *As lieutenant governor, he succeeded to office.*
9. *Resigned April 27, 1943.*
10. *As lieutenant governor, he succeeded to office. Subsequently elected.*
11. *Resigned Sept. 27, 1951.*
12. *As lieutenant governor, he succeeded to office. Subsequently elected.*
13. *The 1962 election between incumbent Governor Andersen (R) and Lieutenant Governor Karl Rolvaag (DFL) was disputed. Andersen served for almost three months of the term before the Minnesota Supreme Court ruled that Rolvaag had won by 91 votes.*
14. *Served the remainder of the four-year term after the removal of Governor Andersen.*
15. *Resigned Dec. 29, 1976, having been appointed to the Senate.*
16. *As lieutenant governor, he succeeded to office.*

# MISSISSIPPI

(Became a state Dec. 10, 1817)

| Governors | Dates of Service | |
| --- | --- | --- |
| David Holmes (D-R) | Dec. 10, 1817 | Jan. 5, 1820 |
| George Poindexter (D-R) | Jan. 5, 1820 | Jan. 7, 1822 |
| Walter Leake (D-R)[1] | Jan. 7, 1822 | Nov. 17, 1825 |
| Gerard C. Brandon (D-R)[2] | Nov. 17, 1825 | Jan. 7, 1826 |
| David Holmes (D-R)[3] | Jan. 7, 1826 | July 25, 1826 |
| Gerard C. Brandon (D)[4] | July 25, 1826 | Jan. 9, 1832 |
| Abram M. Scott (NR)[5] | Jan. 9, 1832 | June 12, 1833 |
| Charles Lynch (NR)[6] | June 12, 1833 | Nov. 20, 1833 |
| Hiram G. Runnels (D)[7] | Nov. 20, 1833 | Nov. 20, 1835 |
| John A. Quitman (W)[8] | Dec. 3, 1835 | Jan. 7, 1836 |
| Charles Lynch (W) | Jan. 7, 1836 | Jan. 8, 1838 |
| Alexander G. McNutt (D) | Jan. 8, 1838 | Jan. 10, 1842 |
| Tilgham M. Tucker (D) | Jan. 10, 1842 | Jan. 10, 1844 |
| Albert G. Brown (D) | Jan. 10, 1844 | Jan. 10, 1848 |
| Joseph M. Matthews (D) | Jan. 10, 1848 | Jan. 10, 1850 |
| John A. Quitman (D)[9] | Jan. 10, 1850 | Feb. 3, 1851 |
| John I. Guion (D)[10] | Feb. 3, 1851 | Nov. 4, 1851 |
| James Whitfield (D)[11] | Nov. 24, 1851 | Jan. 10, 1852 |
| Henry S. Foote (UN)[12] | Jan. 10, 1852 | Jan. 5, 1854 |
| John J. Pettus (D)[13] | Jan. 5, 1854 | Jan. 10, 1854 |
| John J. McRae (D) | Jan. 10, 1854 | Nov. 16, 1857 |
| William McWillie (D) | Nov. 16, 1857 | Nov. 21, 1859 |
| John J. Pettus (D) | Nov. 21, 1859 | Nov. 16, 1863 |
| Charles Clark (D)[14] | Nov. 16, 1863 | May 22, 1865 |
| William L. Sharkey | June 13, 1865 | Oct. 16, 1865 |
| Benjamin G. Humphreys[15] | Oct. 16, 1865 | June 15, 1868 |
| Adelbert Ames | June 15, 1868 | March 10, 1870 |
| James L. Alcorn (R)[16] | March 10, 1870 | Nov. 30, 1871 |
| Ridgley C. Powers (R)[17] | Nov. 30, 1871 | Jan. 4, 1874 |
| Adelbert Ames (R)[18] | Jan. 4, 1874 | March 29, 1876 |
| John M. Stone (D)[19] | March 29, 1876 | Jan. 29, 1882 |
| Robert Lowry (D) | Jan. 29, 1882 | Jan. 13, 1890 |
| John M. Stone (D) | Jan. 13, 1890 | Jan. 20, 1896 |
| Anselm J. McLaurin (D) | Jan. 20, 1896 | Jan. 16, 1900 |
| Andrew H. Longino (D) | Jan. 16, 1900 | Jan. 19, 1904 |
| James Kimble Vardaman (D) | Jan. 19, 1904 | Jan. 21, 1908 |
| Edmond Favor Noel (D) | Jan. 21, 1908 | Jan. 16, 1912 |
| Earl LeRoy Brewer (D) | Jan. 16, 1912 | Jan. 18, 1916 |
| Theodore Gilmore Bilbo (D) | Jan. 18, 1916 | Jan. 20, 1920 |
| Lee Maurice Russell (D) | Jan. 20, 1920 | Jan. 22, 1924 |
| Henry Lewis Whitfield (D)[20] | Jan. 22, 1924 | March 18, 1927 |
| Dennis Murphree (D)[21] | March 18, 1927 | Jan. 17, 1928 |
| Theodore Gilmore Bilbo (D) | Jan. 17, 1928 | Jan. 19, 1932 |
| Martin Sennett Conner (D) | Jan. 19, 1932 | Jan. 21, 1936 |
| Hugh L. White (D) | Jan. 21, 1936 | Jan. 16, 1940 |
| Paul B. Johnson (D)[22] | Jan. 16, 1940 | Dec. 26, 1943 |
| Dennis Murphree (D)[23] | Dec. 26, 1943 | Jan. 18, 1944 |
| Thomas L. Bailey (D)[24] | Jan. 18, 1944 | Nov. 2, 1946 |
| Fielding L. Wright (D)[25] | Nov. 2, 1946 | Jan. 22, 1952 |
| Hugh L. White (D) | Jan. 22, 1952 | Jan. 17, 1956 |
| J. P. Coleman (D) | Jan. 17, 1956 | Jan. 19, 1960 |
| Ross R. Barnett (D) | Jan. 19, 1960 | Jan. 21, 1964 |
| Paul B. Johnson Jr. (D) | Jan. 21, 1964 | Jan. 16, 1968 |
| John Bell Williams (D) | Jan. 16, 1968 | Jan. 18, 1972 |
| William Lowe Waller (D) | Jan. 18, 1972 | Jan. 20, 1976 |
| Cliff Finch (D) | Jan. 20, 1976 | Jan. 22, 1980 |
| William Winter (D) | Jan. 22, 1980 | Jan. 10, 1984 |
| Bill Allain (D) | Jan. 10, 1984 | Jan. 12, 1988 |
| Ray Mabus (D) | Jan. 12, 1988 | Jan. 14, 1992 |
| Kirk Fordice (R) | Jan. 14, 1992 | |

**Mississippi**
1. *Died Nov. 17, 1825.*
2. *As lieutenant governor, he succeeded to office.*
3. *Resigned July 25, 1826.*
4. *As lieutenant governor, he succeeded to office. Subsequently elected.*

5. *Died June 12, 1833.*
6. *As president of the state Senate, he succeeded to office.*
7. *Resigned Nov. 20, 1835.*
8. *As president of the state Senate, he succeeded to office.*
9. *Resigned Feb. 3, 1851.*
10. *As president of the state Senate, he succeeded to office.*
11. *As president of the state Senate, he succeeded to office.*
12. *Resigned Jan. 5, 1854.*
13. *As president of the state Senate, he succeeded to office.*
14. *Removed from office May 22, 1865.*
15. *Removed from office June 15, 1868.*
16. *Resigned Nov. 30, 1871.*
17. *As lieutenant governor, he succeeded to office.*
18. *Resigned March 29, 1876.*
19. *As president of the state Senate, he succeeded to office. Subsequently elected*
20. *Died March 18, 1927.*
21. *As lieutenant governor, he succeeded to office.*
22. *Died Dec. 26, 1943.*
23. *As lieutenant governor, he succeeded to office.*
24. *Died Nov. 2, 1946.*
25. *As lieutenant governor, he succeeded to office. Subsequently elected.*

# MISSOURI

(Became a state Aug. 10, 1821)

| Governors | Dates of Service | |
|---|---|---|
| Alexander McNair (D-R) | Aug. 10, 1821 | Nov. 15, 1824 |
| Frederick Bates (AR)[1] | Nov. 15, 1824 | Aug. 4, 1825 |
| Abraham J. Williams (D-R)[2] | Aug. 4, 1825 | Jan. 20, 1826 |
| John Miller (JAC D) | Jan. 20, 1826 | Nov. 14, 1832 |
| Daniel Dunklin (D) | Nov. 14, 1832 | Sept. 13, 1836 |
| Lilburn W. Boggs (D) | Sept. 13, 1836 | Nov. 16, 1840 |
| Thomas Reynolds (D)[3] | Nov. 16, 1840 | Feb. 9, 1844 |
| Meredith M. Marmaduke (D)[4] | Feb. 9, 1844 | Nov. 20, 1844 |
| John C. Edwards (D) | Nov. 20, 1844 | Dec. 27, 1848 |
| Austin A. King (D) | Dec. 27, 1848 | Jan. 3, 1853 |
| Sterling Price (D) | Jan. 3, 1853 | Jan. 5, 1857 |
| Trusten Polk (D)[5] | Jan. 5, 1857 | Feb. 27, 1857 |
| Hancock Lee Jackson (D)[6] | Feb. 27, 1857 | Oct. 22, 1857 |
| Robert Marcellus Stewart (D) | Oct. 22, 1857 | Jan. 3, 1861 |
| Claiborne Fox Jackson (D)[7] | Jan. 31, 1861 | July 30, 1861 |
| Hamilton R. Gamble (UN)[8] | July 31, 1861 | Jan. 31, 1864 |
| Willard Preble Hall (UN)[9] | Jan. 31, 1864 | Jan. 2, 1865 |
| Thomas C. Fletcher (UN R) | Jan. 2, 1865 | Jan. 12, 1869 |
| Joseph W. McClurg (R) | Jan. 12, 1869 | Jan. 9, 1871 |
| Benjamin G. Brown (R) | Jan. 9, 1871 | Jan. 8, 1873 |
| Silas Woodson (D) | Jan. 8, 1873 | Jan. 12, 1875 |
| Charles Henry Hardin (D) | Jan. 12, 1875 | Jan. 8, 1877 |
| John S. Phelps (D) | Jan. 8, 1877 | Jan. 10, 1881 |
| Thomas T. Crittenden (D) | Jan. 10, 1881 | Jan. 12, 1885 |
| John S. Marmaduke (D)[10] | Jan. 12, 1885 | Dec. 28, 1887 |
| Albert P. Morehouse (D)[11] | Dec. 28, 1887 | Jan. 14, 1889 |
| David R. Francis (D) | Jan. 14, 1889 | Jan. 9, 1893 |
| William J. Stone (D) | Jan. 9, 1893 | Jan. 11, 1897 |
| Lawrence Vest Stephens (D) | Jan. 11, 1897 | Jan. 14, 1901 |
| Alexander M. Dockery (D) | Jan. 14, 1901 | Jan. 9, 1905 |
| Joseph W. Folk (D) | Jan. 9, 1905 | Jan. 11, 1909 |
| Herbert S. Hadley (R) | Jan. 11, 1909 | Jan. 13, 1913 |
| Elliot W. Major (D) | Jan. 13, 1913 | Jan. 8, 1917 |
| Frederick D. Gardner (D) | Jan. 8, 1917 | Jan. 10, 1921 |
| Arthur M. Hyde (R) | Jan. 10, 1921 | Jan. 12, 1925 |
| Samuel A. Baker (R) | Jan. 12, 1925 | Jan. 14, 1929 |
| Henry S. Caulfield (R) | Jan. 14, 1929 | Jan. 9, 1933 |
| Guy B. Park (D) | Jan. 9, 1933 | Jan. 11, 1937 |
| Lloyd C. Stark (D) | Jan. 11, 1937 | Jan. 13, 1941 |
| Forrest C. Donnell (R) | Jan. 13, 1941 | Jan. 8, 1945 |
| Phil M. Donnelly (D) | Jan. 8, 1945 | Jan. 10, 1949 |
| Forrest Smith (D) | Jan. 10, 1949 | Jan. 12, 1953 |
| Phil M. Donnelly (D) | Jan. 12, 1953 | Jan. 14, 1957 |
| James T. Blair Jr. (D) | Jan. 14, 1957 | Jan. 9, 1961 |
| John M. Dalton (D) | Jan. 9, 1961 | Jan. 11, 1965 |
| Warren E. Hearnes (D) | Jan. 11, 1965 | Jan. 8, 1973 |
| Christopher S. Bond (R) | Jan. 8, 1973 | Jan. 10, 1977 |
| Joseph P. Teasdale (D) | Jan. 10, 1977 | Jan. 12, 1981 |
| Christopher S. Bond (R) | Jan. 12, 1981 | Jan. 14, 1985 |
| John Ashcroft (R) | Jan. 14, 1985 | Jan. 11, 1993 |
| Mel Carnahan (D) | Jan. 11, 1993 | |

**Missouri**
1. *Died Aug. 4, 1825.*
2. *Acting governor.*
3. *Died in 1844.*
4. *Acting governor.*
5. *Resigned Feb. 27, 1857.*
6. *Acting governor.*
7. *Removed from office in 1861 by convention.*
8. *Appointed governor by convention. Died Jan. 31, 1864.*
9. *Acting governor.*
10. *Died Dec. 28, 1887.*
11. *Acting governor.*

# MONTANA

(Became a state Nov. 8, 1889)

| Governors | Dates of Service | |
|---|---|---|
| Joseph K. Toole (D) | Nov. 8, 1889 | Jan. 1, 1893 |
| John E. Rickards (R) | Jan. 2, 1893 | Jan. 3, 1897 |
| Robert B. Smith (PP & D) | Jan. 4, 1897 | Jan. 7, 1901 |
| Joseph K. Toole (D)[1] | Jan. 7, 1901 | April 1, 1908 |
| Edwin L. Norris (D)[2] | April 1, 1908 | Jan. 5, 1913 |
| Samuel V. Stewart (D) | Jan. 6, 1913 | Jan. 2, 1921 |
| Joseph M. Dixon (R) | Jan. 3, 1921 | Jan. 4, 1925 |
| John E. Erickson (D)[3] | Jan. 4, 1925 | March 13, 1933 |
| Frank H. Cooney (D)[4] | March 13, 1933 | Dec. 15, 1935 |
| William E. Holt (D)[5] | Dec. 16, 1935 | Jan. 4, 1937 |
| Roy E. Ayers (D) | Jan. 4, 1937 | Jan. 6, 1942 |
| Samuel C. Ford (R) | Jan. 6, 1941 | Jan. 3, 1949 |
| John W. Bonner (D) | Jan. 3, 1949 | Jan. 4, 1953 |
| J. Hugo Aronson (R) | Jan. 4, 1953 | Jan. 4, 1961 |
| Donald G. Nutter (R)[6] | Jan. 4, 1961 | Jan. 25, 1962 |
| Tim M. Babcock (R)[7] | Jan. 26, 1962 | Jan. 6, 1969 |
| Forrest H. Anderson (D) | Jan. 6, 1969 | Jan. 1, 1973 |
| Thomas L. Judge (D) | Jan. 1, 1973 | Jan. 5, 1981 |
| Ted Schwinden (D) | Jan. 5, 1981 | Jan. 2, 1989 |
| Stan Stephens (R) | Jan. 2, 1989 | Jan. 4, 1993 |
| Marc Racicot (R) | Jan. 4, 1993 | |

**Montana**
1. *Resigned April 1, 1908.*
2. *As lieutenant governor, he succeeded to office. Subsequently elected.*
3. *Resigned March 13, 1933.*
4. *As lieutenant governor, he succeeded to office. Died Dec. 15, 1935.*
5. *As president of the state Senate, he succeeded to office.*
6. *Died Jan. 25, 1962.*
7. *As lieutenant governor, he succeeded to office. Subsequently elected.*

# NEBRASKA

(Became a state March 1, 1867)

| Governors | Dates of Service | |
|---|---|---|
| David Butler (R)[1] | March 27, 1867 | June 2, 1871 |
| William H. James (R)[2] | June 2, 1871 | Jan. 13, 1873 |
| Robert W. Furnas (R) | Jan. 13, 1873 | Jan. 1875 |
| Silas Garber (R) | Jan. 1875 | Jan. 1879 |
| Albinus Nance (R) | Jan. 1879 | Jan. 1883 |
| James W. Dawes (R) | Jan. 1883 | Jan. 15, 1887 |
| John M. Thayer (R) | Jan. 15, 1887 | Jan. 15, 1891 |

| | | |
|---|---|---|
| James E. Boyd (D)[3] | Jan. 15, 1891 | May 5, 1891 |
| John M. Thayer (R)[4] | May 5, 1891 | Feb. 8, 1892 |
| James E. Boyd (D)[5] | Feb. 8, 1892 | Jan. 1893 |
| Lorenzo Crounse (R) | Jan. 1893 | Jan. 1895 |
| Silas A. Holcomb (D & PPI) | Jan. 1895 | Jan. 5, 1899 |
| William A. Poynter (FUS)[6] | Jan. 5, 1899 | Jan. 3, 1901 |
| Charles H. Dietrich (R)[7] | Jan. 3, 1901 | May 1, 1901 |
| Ezra P. Savage (R)[8] | May 1, 1901 | Jan. 8, 1903 |
| John H. Mickey (R) | Jan. 8, 1903 | Jan. 3, 1907 |
| George L. Sheldon (R) | Jan. 3, 1907 | Jan. 7, 1909 |
| Ashton C. Shallenberger (D) | Jan. 7, 1909 | Jan. 5, 1911 |
| Chester H. Aldrich (R) | Jan. 5, 1911 | Jan. 9, 1913 |
| John H. Morehead (D) | Jan. 9, 1913 | Jan. 4, 1917 |
| Keith Neville (D) | Jan. 4, 1917 | Jan. 9, 1919 |
| Samuel R. McKelvie (R) | Jan. 9, 1919 | Jan. 3, 1923 |
| Charles W. Bryan (D) | Jan. 4, 1923 | Jan. 8, 1925 |
| Adam McMullen (R) | Jan. 8, 1925 | Jan. 3, 1929 |
| Arthur J. Weaver (R) | Jan. 3, 1929 | Jan. 8, 1931 |
| Charles W. Bryan (D) | Jan. 8, 1931 | Jan. 3, 1935 |
| Robert L. Cochran (D) | Jan. 3, 1935 | Jan. 9, 1941 |
| Dwight P. Griswold (R) | Jan. 9, 1941 | Jan. 9, 1947 |
| Val Peterson (R) | Jan. 9, 1947 | Jan. 8, 1953 |
| Robert Berkey Crosby (R) | Jan. 8, 1953 | Jan. 6, 1955 |
| Victor E. Anderson (R) | Jan. 6, 1955 | Jan. 8, 1959 |
| Ralph G. Brooks (D)[9] | Jan. 8, 1959 | Sept. 9, 1960 |
| Dwight W. Burney (R)[10] | Sept. 9, 1960 | Jan. 5, 1961 |
| Frank B. Morrison (D) | Jan. 5, 1961 | Jan. 5, 1967 |
| Norbert T. Tiemann (R) | Jan. 5, 1967 | Jan. 7, 1971 |
| J. James Exon (D) | Jan. 7, 1971 | Jan. 3, 1979 |
| Charles Thone (R) | Jan. 4, 1979 | Jan. 6, 1983 |
| Bob Kerrey (D) | Jan. 6, 1983 | Jan. 9, 1987 |
| Kay A. Orr (R) | Jan. 9, 1987 | Jan. 9, 1991 |
| Ben Nelson (D) | Jan. 9, 1991 | |

**Nebraska**

1. *Impeached. Removed from office June 2, 1871.*
2. *As lieutenant governor, he succeeded to office.*
3. *The election of Boyd was challenged by Governor Thayer on the grounds that Boyd had been born in Ireland and was not an American citizen, and was thus ineligible to be governor. Boyd was removed by the Nebraska Supreme Court May 5, 1891.*
4. *Following the removal of Boyd, Thayer returned to office.*
5. *U.S. Supreme Court declared that Boyd was a citizen, and he returned to office Feb. 18, 1892, and served out the remainder of his term.*
6. *Fusion composed of Democrats and Populists.*
7. *Resigned May 1, 1901.*
8. *As lieutenant governor, he succeeded to office.*
9. *Died Sept. 9, 1960.*
10. *As lieutenant governor, he succeeded to office.*

# NEVADA

(Became a state Oct. 31, 1864)

| Governors | Dates of Service | |
|---|---|---|
| H. G. Blasdel (UN R) | Dec. 5, 1864 | Jan. 2, 1871 |
| L. R. Bradley (D) | Jan. 3, 1871 | Jan. 6, 1879 |
| John H. Kinkead (R) | Jan. 7, 1879 | Jan. 1, 1883 |
| Jewett W. Adams (D) | Jan. 2, 1883 | Jan. 3, 1887 |
| C. C. Stevenson (R)[1] | Jan. 4, 1887 | Sept. 2, 1890 |
| Frank Bell (R)[2] | Sept. 21, 1890 | Jan. 5, 1891 |
| R. K. Colcord (R) | Jan. 6, 1891 | Jan. 7, 1895 |
| John S. Jones (D SIL)[3] | Jan. 8, 1895 | April 10, 1896 |
| Reinhold Sadler (SIL R)[4] | April 10, 1896 | Jan. 1, 1903 |
| John Sparks (D & SILVER)[5] | Jan. 1, 1903 | May 22, 1908 |
| Denver S. Dickerson (D)[6] | May 22, 1908 | Jan. 2, 1911 |
| Tasker L. Oddie (R) | Jan. 2, 1911 | Jan. 4, 1915 |
| Emmet D. Boyle (D) | Jan. 4, 1915 | Jan. 1, 1923 |
| James G. Scrugham (D) | Jan. 1, 1923 | Jan. 3, 1927 |
| Frederick B. Balzar (R)[7] | Jan. 3, 1927 | March 21, 1934 |
| Morley I. Griswold (R)[8] | March 21, 1934 | Jan. 7, 1935 |

| | | |
|---|---|---|
| Richard Kirman Sr. (D) | Jan. 7, 1935 | Jan. 2, 1939 |
| Edward P. Carville (D)[9] | Jan. 2, 1939 | July 24, 1945 |
| Vail M. Pittman (D)[10] | July 24, 1945 | Jan. 1, 1951 |
| Charles H. Russell (R) | Jan. 1, 1951 | Jan. 5, 1959 |
| Grant Sawyer (D) | Jan. 5, 1959 | Jan. 2, 1967 |
| Paul D. Laxalt (R) | Jan. 2, 1967 | Jan. 4, 1971 |
| Mike O'Callaghan (D) | Jan. 4, 1971 | Jan. 1, 1979 |
| Robert F. List (R) | Jan. 1, 1979 | Jan. 3, 1983 |
| Richard H. Bryan (D)[11] | Jan. 3, 1983 | Jan. 3, 1989 |
| Bob J. Miller (D)[12] | Jan. 3, 1989 | |

**Nevada**

1. *Left office due to disability, Sept. 1, 1890. Died Sept. 21, 1890.*
2. *As lieutenant governor, he succeeded to office.*
3. *Died April 10, 1896.*
4. *As lieutenant governor, he succeeded to office. Subsequently elected.*
5. *Died May 22, 1908.*
6. *As lieutenant governor, he succeeded to office.*
7. *Died March 21, 1934.*
8. *As lieutenant governor, he succeeded to office.*
9. *Resigned July 24, 1945.*
10. *As lieutenant governor, he succeeded to office. Subsequently elected.*
11. *Resigned Jan. 3, 1989, having been elected to the U.S. Senate.*
12. *As lieutenant governor, he succeeded to office. Subsequently elected.*

# NEW HAMPSHIRE

(Ratified the Constitution June 21, 1788)

| Governors | Dates of Service | |
|---|---|---|
| John Sullivan (FED) | June 6, 1789 | June 5, 1790 |
| Josiah Bartlett (D-R) | June 5, 1790 | June 5, 1794 |
| Joseph T. Gilman (FED) | June 5, 1794 | June 6, 1805 |
| John Langdon (D-R) | June 6, 1805 | June 8, 1809 |
| Jeremiah Smith (FED) | June 8, 1809 | June 7, 1810 |
| John Langdon (D-R) | June 7, 1810 | June 5, 1812 |
| William Plumer (D-R) | June 5, 1812 | June 3, 1813 |
| John T. Gilman (FED) | June 13, 1813 | June 6, 1816 |
| William Plumer (D-R) | June 6, 1816 | June 3, 1819 |
| Samuel Bell (D-R) | June 3, 1819 | June 5, 1823 |
| Levi Woodbury (D-R) | June 5, 1823 | June 2, 1824 |
| David L. Morrill (D-R) | June 3, 1824 | June 7, 1827 |
| Benjamin Pierce (D-R) | June 7, 1827 | June 5, 1828 |
| John Bell (NR) | June 5, 1828 | June 4, 1829 |
| Benjamin Pierce (JAC D) | June 4, 1829 | June 3, 1830 |
| Matthew Harvey (JAC D)[1] | June 3, 1830 | Feb. 28, 1831 |
| Joseph M. Harper (D)[2] | Feb. 28, 1831 | June 2, 1831 |
| Samuel Dinsmoor (JAC D) | June 2, 1831 | June 5, 1834 |
| William Badger (D) | June 5, 1834 | June 2, 1836 |
| Isaac Hill (D) | June 2, 1836 | June 5, 1839 |
| John Page (D) | June 5, 1839 | June 2, 1842 |
| Henry Hubbard (D) | June 2, 1842 | June 6, 1844 |
| John H. Steele (D) | June 6, 1844 | June 4, 1846 |
| Anthony Colby (W) | June 4, 1846 | June 3, 1847 |
| Jared W. Williams (D) | June 3, 1847 | June 7, 1849 |
| Samuel Dinsmoor (D) | June 7, 1849 | June 3, 1852 |
| Noah Martin (D) | June 3, 1852 | June 8, 1854 |
| Nathaniel B. Baker (D) | June 8, 1854 | June 7, 1855 |
| Ralph Metcalf (AM) | June 7, 1855 | June 4, 1857 |
| William Haile (R) | June 4, 1857 | June 2, 1859 |
| Ichabod Goodwin (R) | June 2, 1859 | June 6, 1861 |
| Nathaniel S. Berry (R) | June 6, 1861 | June 3, 1863 |
| Joseph A. Gilmore (R) | June 3, 1863 | June 8, 1865 |
| Frederick Smyth (UN) | June 8, 1865 | June 6, 1867 |
| Walter Harriman (R) | June 6, 1867 | June 2, 1869 |
| Onslow Stearns (R) | June 3, 1869 | June 8, 1871 |
| James A. Weston (D) | June 14, 1871 | June 6, 1872 |
| Ezekiel A. Straw (R) | June 6, 1872 | June 3, 1874 |
| James A. Weston (D) | June 3, 1874 | June 10, 1875 |
| Person C. Cheney (R) | June 10, 1875 | June 6, 1877 |
| Benjamin F. Prescott (R) | June 7, 1877 | June 5, 1879 |

| | | |
|---|---|---|
| Natt Head (R) | June 5, 1879 | June 2, 1881 |
| Charles H. Bell (R) | June 2, 1881 | June 7, 1883 |
| Samuel W. Hale (R) | June 7, 1883 | June 4, 1885 |
| Moody Currier (R) | June 4, 1885 | June 2, 1887 |
| Charles H. Sawyer (R) | June 2, 1887 | June 6, 1889 |
| David H. Goodell (R) | June 6, 1889 | Jan. 8, 1891 |
| Hiram A. Tuttle (R) | Jan. 8, 1891 | Jan. 5, 1893 |
| John B. Smith (R) | Jan. 5, 1893 | Jan. 3, 1895 |
| Charles A. Busiel (R) | Jan. 3, 1895 | Jan. 7, 1897 |
| George A. Ramsdell (R) | Jan. 7, 1897 | Jan. 5, 1899 |
| Frank W. Rollins (R) | Jan. 5, 1899 | Jan. 3, 1901 |
| Chester B. Jordan (R) | Jan. 3, 1901 | Jan. 1, 1903 |
| Nahum J. Batcheler (R) | Jan. 1, 1903 | Jan. 5, 1905 |
| John McLane (R) | Jan. 5, 1905 | Jan. 3, 1907 |
| Charles M. Floyd (R) | Jan. 3, 1907 | Jan. 7, 1909 |
| Henry B. Quinby (R) | Jan. 7, 1909 | Jan. 5, 1911 |
| Robert P. Bass (R) | Jan. 5, 1911 | Jan. 2, 1913 |
| Samuel D. Felker (D) | Jan. 2, 1913 | Jan. 7, 1915 |
| Rolland H. Spaulding (R) | Jan. 7, 1915 | Jan. 3, 1917 |
| Henry Wilder Keyes (R)[3] | Jan. 3, 1917 | Jan. 2, 1919 |
| John H. Bartlett (R) | Jan. 2, 1919 | Jan. 6, 1921 |
| Albert O. Brown (R) | Jan. 6, 1921 | Jan. 4, 1923 |
| Fred H. Brown (D) | Jan. 4, 1923 | Jan. 1, 1925 |
| John G. Winant (R) | Jan. 1, 1925 | Jan. 6, 1927 |
| Huntley N. Spaulding (R) | Jan. 6, 1927 | Jan. 3, 1929 |
| Charles W. Tobey (R) | Jan. 3, 1929 | Jan. 1, 1931 |
| John G. Winant (R) | Jan. 1, 1931 | Jan. 3, 1935 |
| H. Styles Bridges (R) | Jan. 3, 1935 | Jan. 7, 1937 |
| Francis P. Murphy (R) | Jan. 7, 1937 | Jan. 2, 1941 |
| Robert O. Blood (R) | Jan. 2, 1941 | Jan. 4, 1945 |
| Charles M. Dale (R) | Jan. 4, 1945 | Jan. 6, 1949 |
| Sherman Adams (R) | Jan. 6, 1949 | Jan. 1, 1953 |
| Hugh Gregg (R) | Jan. 1, 1953 | Jan. 6, 1955 |
| Lane Dwinell (R) | Jan. 6, 1955 | Jan. 1, 1959 |
| Wesley Powell (R) | Jan. 1, 1959 | Jan. 3, 1963 |
| John W. King (D) | Jan. 3, 1963 | Jan. 2, 1969 |
| Walter Peterson (R) | Jan. 2, 1969 | Jan. 4, 1973 |
| Meldrim Thomson Jr. (R) | Jan. 4, 1973 | Jan. 4, 1979 |
| Hugh J. Gallen (D)[4] | Jan. 4, 1979 | Nov. 11, 1982 |
| Robert B. Monier (D)[5] | Nov. 11, 1982 | Nov. 30, 1982 |
| William M. Gardner (D)[6] | Nov. 30, 1982 | Dec. 1, 1982 |
| Vesta M. Roy (D)[7] | Dec. 1, 1982 | Jan. 6, 1983 |
| John H. Sununu (R) | Jan. 6, 1983 | Jan. 4, 1989 |
| Judd Gregg (R) | Jan. 4, 1989 | Jan. 7, 1993 |
| Steve Merrill (R) | Jan. 7, 1993 | |

**New Hampshire**
1. Resigned Feb. 28, 1831.
2. Acting governor in 1831.
3. Keyes was disqualified at the end of his term by illness and Jesse M. Barton, president of the state Senate, became acting governor.
4. Hospitalized Nov. 20, 1982. Died Dec. 29, 1982.
5. As president of the state Senate, served as acting governor until the Legislature dissolved on Nov. 30, 1982.
6. As secretary of state, served as acting governor until new members of the Legislature were sworn in.
7. As new president of the state Senate, served as acting governor.

# NEW JERSEY

(Ratified the Constitution Dec. 18, 1787)

| Governors | Dates of Service | |
|---|---|---|
| William Livingston (FED)[1] | Aug. 27, 1776 | July 25, 1790 |
| Elisha Lawrence (FED)[2] | July 25, 1790 | Oct. 30, 1790 |
| William Paterson (FED)[3] | Oct. 30, 1790 | March 4, 1793 |
| Thomas Henderson (FED) | March 30, 1793 | June 3, 1793 |
| Richard Howell (FED) | June 3, 1793 | Oct. 31, 1801 |
| Joseph Bloomfield (D-R) | Oct. 31, 1801 | Oct. 28, 1802 |
| John Lambert (D-R)[4] | Nov. 15, 1802 | Oct. 29, 1803 |
| Joseph Bloomfield (D-R) | Oct. 29, 1803 | Oct. 29, 1812 |

| | | |
|---|---|---|
| Aaron Ogden (FED) | Oct. 29, 1812 | Oct. 29, 1813 |
| William S. Pennington (D-R)[5] | Oct. 29, 1813 | June 19, 1815 |
| William Kennedy (D-R)[6] | June 19, 1815 | Oct. 25, 1815 |
| Mahlon Dickerson (D-R)[7] | Oct. 26, 1815 | Feb. 1, 1817 |
| Isaac H. Williamson (FED) | Feb. 6, 1817 | Oct. 30, 1829 |
| Peter D. Vroom (D) | Nov. 6, 1829 | Oct. 26, 1832 |
| Samuel L. Southard (W) | Oct. 26, 1832 | Feb. 1833 |
| Elias P. Seeley (W) | Feb. 27, 1833 | Oct. 23, 1833 |
| Peter D. Vroom (D) | Oct. 25, 1833 | Oct. 28, 1836 |
| Philemon Dickerson (D) | Nov. 3, 1836 | Oct. 27, 1837 |
| William Pennington (W) | Oct. 27, 1837 | Oct. 27, 1843 |
| Daniel Haines (D) | Oct. 27, 1843 | Jan. 21, 1845 |
| Charles C. Stratton (W) | Jan. 21, 1845 | Jan. 18, 1848 |
| Daniel Haines (D) | Jan. 18, 1848 | Jan. 20, 1851 |
| George F. Fort (D) | Jan. 21, 1851 | Jan. 17, 1854 |
| Rodman M. Price (D) | Jan. 17, 1854 | Jan. 20, 1857 |
| William A. Newell (FUS) | Jan. 20, 1857 | Jan. 17, 1860 |
| Charles S. Olden (R) | Jan. 17, 1860 | Jan. 20, 1863 |
| Joel Parker (D) | Jan. 20, 1863 | Jan. 16, 1866 |
| Marcus L. Ward (UN) | Jan. 16, 1866 | Jan. 19, 1869 |
| Theodore F. Randolph (D) | Jan. 19, 1869 | Jan. 16, 1872 |
| Joel Parker (D) | Jan. 16, 1872 | Jan. 19, 1875 |
| Joseph D. Bedle (D) | Jan. 19, 1875 | Jan. 15, 1878 |
| George B. McClellan (D) | Jan. 15, 1878 | Jan. 18, 1881 |
| George C. Ludlow (D) | Jan. 18, 1881 | Jan. 15, 1884 |
| Leon Abbett (D) | Jan. 15, 1884 | Jan. 18, 1887 |
| Robert S. Green (D) | Jan. 18, 1887 | Jan. 21, 1890 |
| Leon Abbett (D) | Jan. 21, 1890 | Jan. 17, 1893 |
| George T. Werts (D) | Jan. 17, 1893 | Jan. 21, 1896 |
| John W. Griggs (R)[8] | Jan. 21, 1896 | Jan. 31, 1898 |
| Foster M. Voorhees (R)[9] | Feb. 1, 1898 | Oct. 18, 1898 |
| David O. Watkins (R)[10] | Oct. 18, 1898 | Jan. 17, 1899 |
| Foster M. Voorhees (R) | Jan. 17, 1899 | Jan. 21, 1902 |
| Franklin Murphy (R) | Jan. 21, 1902 | Jan. 17, 1905 |
| Edward C. Stokes (R) | Jan. 17, 1905 | Jan. 21, 1908 |
| John F. Fort (R) | Jan. 21, 1908 | Jan. 17, 1911 |
| Woodrow Wilson (D)[11] | Jan. 17, 1911 | March 1, 1913 |
| James F. Fielder (D)[12] | March 1, 1913 | Oct. 28, 1913 |
| Leon R. Taylor (D)[13] | Oct. 28, 1913 | Jan. 20, 1914 |
| James F. Fielder (D) | Jan. 20, 1914 | Jan. 15, 1917 |
| Walter E. Edge (R)[14] | Jan. 15, 1917 | May 16, 1919 |
| William N. Runyon (R)[15] | May 16, 1919 | Jan. 13, 1920 |
| Clarence E. Case (R)[16] | Jan. 13, 1920 | Jan. 20, 1920 |
| Edward I. Edwards (D) | Jan. 20, 1920 | Jan. 15, 1923 |
| George S. Silzer (D) | Jan. 15, 1923 | Jan. 19, 1926 |
| Arthur Harry Moore (D) | Jan. 19, 1926 | Jan. 15, 1929 |
| Morgan F. Larson (R) | Jan. 15, 1929 | Jan. 19, 1932 |
| Arthur Harry Moore (D)[17] | Jan. 19, 1932 | Jan. 3, 1935 |
| Clifford R. Powell (R)[18] | Jan. 3, 1935 | Jan. 8, 1935 |
| Horace G. Prall (R)[19] | Jan. 8, 1935 | Jan. 15, 1935 |
| Harold G. Hoffman (R) | Jan. 15, 1935 | Jan. 18, 1938 |
| Arthur Harry Moore (D) | Jan. 18, 1938 | Jan. 21, 1941 |
| Charles Edison (D) | Jan. 21, 1941 | Jan. 18, 1944 |
| Walter E. Edge (R) | Jan. 18, 1944 | Jan. 21, 1947 |
| Alfred E. Driscoll (R) | Jan. 21, 1947 | Jan. 19, 1954 |
| Robert B. Meyner (D) | Jan. 19, 1954 | Jan. 16, 1962 |
| Richard J. Hughes (D) | Jan. 16, 1962 | Jan. 20, 1970 |
| William T. Cahill (R) | Jan. 20, 1970 | Jan. 15, 1974 |
| Brendan T. Byrne (D) | Jan. 15, 1974 | Jan. 19, 1982 |
| Thomas H. Kean (R) | Jan. 19, 1982 | Jan. 16, 1990 |
| James J. Florio (D) | Jan. 16, 1990 | Jan. 18, 1994 |
| Christine Todd Whitman (R) | Jan. 18, 1994 | |

**New Jersey**
1. Died in office.
2. As vice president of the Legislative Council, he succeeded to office.
3. Resigned March 4, 1793.
4. Acting governor.
5. Resigned June 19, 1815.
6. As vice president of the Legislative Council, he succeeded to office.
7. Resigned Feb. 1, 1817.
8. Resigned Jan. 31, 1898.
9. Acting governor.

**New Jersey (continued)**
*10. Acting governor.*
*11. Resigned March 1, 1913, having been elected president of the United States.*
*12. As president of the state Senate, he succeeded to office. Resigned Oct. 28, 1913.*
*13. Acting governor.*
*14. Resigned May 16, 1919.*
*15. As president of the state Senate, he succeeded to office. Service ended Jan. 13, 1920.*
*16. Acting governor.*
*17. Resigned Jan. 3, 1935.*
*18. As president of the state Senate, he succeeded to office. Service ended Jan. 8, 1935.*
*19. Acting governor.*

# NEW MEXICO

(Became a state Jan. 6, 1912)

| Governors | Dates of Service | |
| --- | --- | --- |
| William C. McDonald (D) | Jan. 6, 1912 | Jan. 1, 1917 |
| Ezequiel C. de Baca (D)[1] | Jan. 1, 1917 | Feb. 18, 1917 |
| Washington E. Lindsey (R)[2] | Feb. 19, 1917 | Jan. 1, 1919 |
| Octaviano A. Larrazolo (R) | Jan. 1, 1919 | Jan. 1, 1921 |
| Merritt C. Mechem (R) | Jan. 1, 1921 | Jan. 1, 1923 |
| James F. Hinkle (D) | Jan. 1, 1923 | Jan. 1, 1925 |
| Arthur T. Hannett (D) | Jan. 1, 1925 | Jan. 1, 1927 |
| Richard C. Dillon (R) | Jan. 1, 1927 | Jan. 1, 1931 |
| Arthur Seligman (D)[3] | Jan. 1, 1931 | Sept. 25, 1933 |
| Andrew W. Hockenhull (D)[4] | Sept. 25, 1933 | Jan. 1, 1935 |
| Clyde Tingley (D) | Jan. 1, 1935 | Jan. 1, 1939 |
| John E. Miles (D) | Jan. 1, 1939 | Jan. 1, 1943 |
| John J. Dempsey (D) | Jan. 1, 1943 | Jan. 1, 1947 |
| Thomas J. Mabry (D) | Jan. 1, 1947 | Jan. 1, 1951 |
| Edwin L. Mechem (R) | Jan. 1, 1951 | Jan. 1, 1955 |
| John F. Simms (D) | Jan. 1, 1955 | Jan. 1, 1957 |
| Edwin L. Mechem (R) | Jan. 1, 1957 | Jan. 1, 1959 |
| John Burroughs (D) | Jan. 1, 1959 | Jan. 1, 1961 |
| Edwin L. Mechem (R)[5] | Jan. 1, 1961 | Nov. 30, 1962 |
| Tom Bolack (R)[6] | Nov. 30, 1962 | Jan. 1, 1963 |
| Jack M. Campbell (D) | Jan. 1, 1963 | Jan. 1, 1967 |
| David F. Cargo (R) | Jan. 1, 1967 | Jan. 1, 1971 |
| Bruce King (D) | Jan. 1, 1971 | Jan. 1, 1975 |
| Jerry Apodaca (D) | Jan. 1, 1975 | Jan. 1, 1979 |
| Bruce King (D) | Jan. 1, 1979 | Jan. 1, 1983 |
| Toney Anaya (D) | Jan. 1, 1983 | Jan. 1, 1987 |
| Garrey E. Carruthers (R) | Jan. 1, 1987 | Jan. 1, 1991 |
| Bruce King (D) | Jan. 1, 1991 | |

**New Mexico**
*1. Died Feb. 18, 1917.*
*2. As lieutenant governor, he succeeded to office.*
*3. Died Sept. 25, 1933.*
*4. As lieutenant governor, he succeeded to office.*
*5. Resigned Nov. 30, 1962.*
*6. As lieutenant governor, he succeeded to office.*

# NEW YORK

(Ratified the Constitution July 26, 1788)

| Governors | Dates of Service | |
| --- | --- | --- |
| George Clinton (D-R) | July 9, 1777 | July 1, 1795 |
| John Jay (FED) | July 1, 1795 | July 1, 1801 |
| George Clinton (D-R) | July 1, 1801 | July 1, 1804 |
| Morgan Lewis (D-R) | July 1, 1804 | July 1, 1807 |
| Daniel D. Tompkins (D-R)[1] | July 1, 1807 | Feb. 24, 1817 |
| John Tayler (D-R)[2] | Feb. 24, 1817 | July 1, 1817 |
| De Witt Clinton (D-R) | July 1, 1817 | Jan. 1, 1823 |
| Joseph C. Yates (D-R) | Jan. 1, 1823 | Jan. 1, 1825 |
| De Witt Clinton (CLINT R)[3] | Jan. 1, 1825 | Feb. 11, 1828 |
| Nathaniel Pitcher (D-R)[4] | Feb. 11, 1828 | Jan. 1, 1829 |
| Martin Van Buren (JAC D)[5] | Jan. 1, 1829 | March 12, 1829 |
| Enos T. Throop (JAC D)[6] | March 12, 1829 | Jan. 1, 1833 |
| William L. Marcy (D) | Jan. 1, 1833 | Jan. 1, 1839 |
| William H. Seward (W) | Jan. 1, 1839 | Jan. 1, 1843 |
| William C. Bouck (D) | Jan. 1, 1843 | Jan. 1, 1845 |
| Silas Wright (D) | Jan. 1, 1845 | Jan. 1, 1847 |
| John Young (W) | Jan. 1, 1847 | Jan. 1, 1849 |
| Hamilton Fish (W) | Jan. 1, 1849 | Jan. 1, 1851 |
| Washington Hunt (W-A-RENT) | Jan. 1, 1851 | Jan. 1, 1853 |
| Horatio Seymour (D) | Jan. 1, 1853 | Jan. 1, 1855 |
| Myron H. Clark (FUS R) | Jan. 1, 1855 | Jan. 1, 1857 |
| John A. King (R) | Jan. 1, 1857 | Jan. 1, 1859 |
| Edwin D. Morgan (R) | Jan. 1, 1859 | Jan. 1, 1863 |
| Horatio Seymour (D) | Jan. 1, 1863 | Jan. 1, 1865 |
| Reuben E. Fenton (UN) | Jan. 1, 1865 | Jan. 1, 1869 |
| John T. Hoffman (D) | Jan. 1, 1869 | Jan. 1, 1873 |
| John A. Dix (R) | Jan. 1, 1873 | Jan. 1, 1875 |
| Samuel J. Tilden (D) | Jan. 1, 1875 | Jan. 1, 1877 |
| Lucius Robinson (D)[7] | Jan. 1, 1877 | Jan. 1, 1880 |
| Alonzo B. Cornell (R) | Jan. 1, 1880 | Jan. 1, 1883 |
| Grover Cleveland (D)[8] | Jan. 1, 1883 | Jan. 6, 1885 |
| David B. Hill (D)[9] | Jan. 6, 1885 | Jan. 1, 1892 |
| Roswell P. Flower (D) | Jan. 1, 1892 | Jan. 1, 1895 |
| Levi P. Morton (R)[10] | Jan. 1, 1895 | Jan. 1, 1897 |
| Frank S. Black (R) | Jan. 1, 1897 | Jan. 1, 1899 |
| Theodore Roosevelt (R) | Jan. 1, 1899 | Jan. 1, 1901 |
| Benjamin B. Odell Jr. (R) | Jan. 1, 1901 | Jan. 1, 1905 |
| Frank W. Higgins (R) | Jan. 1, 1905 | Jan. 1, 1907 |
| Charles Evans Hughes (R)[11] | Jan. 1, 1907 | Oct. 6, 1910 |
| Horace White (R)[12] | Oct. 6, 1910 | Jan. 1, 1911 |
| John A. Dix (D) | Jan. 1, 1911 | Jan. 1, 1913 |
| William Sulzer (D)[13] | Jan. 1, 1913 | Oct. 17, 1913 |
| Martin H. Glynn (D)[14] | Oct. 17, 1913 | Jan. 1, 1915 |
| Charles S. Whitman (R) | Jan. 1, 1915 | Jan. 1, 1919 |
| Alfred E. Smith (D) | Jan. 1, 1919 | Jan. 1, 1921 |
| Nathan L. Miller (R) | Jan. 1, 1921 | Jan. 1, 1923 |
| Alfred E. Smith (D) | Jan. 1, 1923 | Jan. 1, 1929 |
| Franklin D. Roosevelt (D) | Jan. 1, 1929 | Jan. 1, 1933 |
| Herbert H. Lehman (D)[15] | Jan. 1, 1933 | Dec. 3, 1942 |
| Charles Poletti (D)[16] | Dec. 3, 1942 | Jan. 1, 1943 |
| Thomas E. Dewey (R) | Jan. 1, 1943 | Jan. 1, 1955 |
| W. Averell Harriman (D) | Jan. 1, 1955 | Jan. 1, 1959 |
| Nelson A. Rockefeller (R)[17] | Jan. 1, 1959 | Dec. 18, 1973 |
| Malcolm Wilson (R)[18] | Dec. 18, 1973 | Jan. 1, 1975 |
| Hugh Carey (D) | Jan. 1, 1975 | Jan. 1, 1983 |
| Mario M. Cuomo (D) | Jan. 1, 1983 | |

**New York**
*1. Resigned Feb. 24, 1817, having been elected vice president of the United States.*
*2. As lieutenant governor, he succeeded to office.*
*3. Died Feb. 11, 1828.*
*4. As lieutenant governor, he succeeded to office.*
*5. Resigned March 12, 1829.*
*6. As lieutenant governor, he succeeded to office. Subsequently elected.*
*7. Term of office changed from two years to three years.*
*8. Resigned Jan. 6, 1885, having been elected president of the United States.*
*9. As lieutenant governor, he succeeded to office. Subsequently elected.*
*10. Term of office changed from three years to two years.*
*11. Resigned Oct. 6, 1910.*
*12. As lieutenant governor, he succeeded to office.*
*13. Impeached; removed from office Oct. 17, 1913.*
*14. As lieutenant governor, he succeeded to office.*
*15. First governor elected to a four-year term (in 1938). Resigned Dec. 3, 1942.*
*16. As lieutenant governor, he succeeded to office.*
*17. Resigned Dec. 18, 1973.*
*18. As lieutenant governor, he succeeded to office.*

# NORTH CAROLINA

(Ratified the Constitution Nov. 21, 1789)

| Governors | Dates of Service | |
|---|---|---|
| Samuel Johnston | Dec. 20, 1787 | Dec. 17, 1789 |
| Alexander Martin (FED) | Dec. 17, 1789 | Dec. 14, 1792 |
| Richard D. Spaight (D-R) | Dec. 14, 1792 | Nov. 19, 1795 |
| Samuel Ashe (D-R) | Nov. 19, 1795 | Dec. 7, 1798 |
| William R. Davie (FED) | Dec. 7, 1798 | Nov. 23, 1799 |
| Benjamin Williams (D-R) | Nov. 23, 1799 | Dec. 6, 1802 |
| James Turner (D-R) | Dec. 6, 1802 | Dec. 10, 1805 |
| Nathaniel Alexander (D-R) | Dec. 10, 1805 | Dec. 1, 1807 |
| Benjamin Wiliams (D-R) | Dec. 1, 1807 | Dec. 12, 1808 |
| David Stone (D-R) | Dec. 12, 1808 | Dec. 5, 1810 |
| Benjamin Smith (D-R) | Dec. 5, 1810 | Dec. 9, 1811 |
| William Hawkins (D-R) | Dec. 9, 1811 | Nov. 29, 1814 |
| William Miller (D-R) | Dec. 7, 1814 | Dec. 3, 1817 |
| John Branch (D-R) | Dec. 6, 1817 | Dec. 7, 1820 |
| Jesse Franklin (D-R) | Dec. 7, 1820 | Dec. 7, 1821 |
| Gabriel Holmes (D-R) | Dec. 7, 1821 | Dec. 7, 1824 |
| Hutchins G. Burton (D-R) | Dec. 7, 1824 | Dec. 8, 1827 |
| James Iredell (D-R) | Dec. 8, 1827 | Dec. 12, 1828 |
| John Owen (D) | Dec. 12, 1828 | Dec. 18, 1830 |
| Montfort Stokes (D) | Dec. 18, 1830 | Dec. 6, 1832 |
| David L. Swain (D) | Dec. 6, 1832 | Dec. 10, 1835 |
| Richard D. Spaight Jr. (D) | Dec. 10, 1835 | Dec. 31, 1836 |
| Edward B. Dudley (W) | Dec. 31, 1836 | Jan. 1, 1841 |
| John M. Morehead (W) | Jan. 1, 1841 | Jan. 1, 1845 |
| William A. Graham (W) | Jan. 1, 1845 | Jan. 1, 1849 |
| Charles Manly (W) | Jan. 1, 1849 | Jan. 1, 1851 |
| David S. Reid (D)[1] | Jan. 1, 1851 | Dec. 6, 1854 |
| Warren Winslow (D)[2] | Dec. 6, 1854 | Jan. 1, 1855 |
| Thomas Bragg (D) | Jan. 1, 1855 | Jan. 1, 1859 |
| John W. Ellis (D)[3] | Jan. 1, 1859 | July 7, 1861 |
| Henry T. Clark (D)[4] | July 7, 1861 | Sept. 8, 1862 |
| Zebulon B. Vance (C)[5] | Sept. 8, 1862 | May 29, 1865 |
| William W. Holden[6] | May 29, 1865 | Dec. 15, 1865 |
| Jonathan Worth (C)[7] | Dec. 15, 1865 | July 1, 1868 |
| William W. Holden (R)[8] | July 1, 1868 | Dec. 15, 1870 |
| Tod R. Caldwell (R)[9] | Dec. 15, 1870 | July 11, 1874 |
| Curtis H. Brogden (R)[10] | July 11, 1874 | Jan. 1, 1877 |
| Zebulon B. Vance (D)[11] | Jan. 1, 1877 | Feb. 5, 1879 |
| Thomas J. Jarvis (D)[12] | Feb. 5, 1879 | Jan. 21, 1885 |
| Alfred M. Scales (D) | Jan. 21, 1885 | Jan. 17, 1889 |
| Daniel G. Fowle (D)[13] | Jan. 17, 1889 | April 8, 1891 |
| Thomas M. Holt (D)[14] | April 8, 1891 | Jan. 18, 1893 |
| Elias Carr (D) | Jan. 18, 1893 | Jan. 12, 1897 |
| Daniel L. Russell (D) | Jan. 12, 1897 | Jan. 15, 1901 |
| Charles B. Aycock (D) | Jan. 15, 1901 | Jan. 11, 1905 |
| R. B. Glenn (D) | Jan. 11, 1905 | Jan. 12, 1909 |
| W. W. Kitchin (D) | Jan. 12, 1909 | Jan. 15, 1913 |
| Locke Craig (D) | Jan. 15, 1913 | Jan. 11, 1917 |
| Thomas W. Bickett (D) | Jan. 11, 1917 | Jan. 12, 1921 |
| Carmeron Morrison (D) | Jan. 12, 1921 | Jan. 14, 1925 |
| Angus Wilton McLean (D) | Jan. 14, 1925 | Jan. 11, 1929 |
| O. Max Gardner (D) | Jan. 11, 1929 | Jan. 5, 1933 |
| John C. B. Ehringhaus (D) | Jan. 5, 1933 | Jan. 7, 1937 |
| Clyde R. Hoey (D) | Jan. 7, 1937 | Jan. 9, 1941 |
| J. Melville Broughton (D) | Jan. 9, 1941 | Jan. 4, 1945 |
| R. Gregg Cherry (D) | Jan. 4, 1945 | Jan. 6, 1949 |
| W. Kerr Scott (D) | Jan. 6, 1949 | Jan. 8, 1953 |
| William B. Umstead (D)[15] | Jan. 8, 1953 | Nov. 7, 1954 |
| Luther H. Hodges (D)[16] | Nov. 7, 1954 | Jan. 5, 1961 |
| Terry Sanford (D) | Jan. 5, 1961 | Jan. 8, 1965 |
| Dan K. Moore (D) | Jan. 8, 1965 | Jan. 3, 1969 |
| Robert W. Scott (D) | Jan. 3, 1969 | Jan. 5, 1973 |
| James E. Holshouser Jr. (R) | Jan. 5, 1973 | Jan. 8, 1977 |
| James B. Hunt Jr. (D) | Jan. 8, 1977 | Jan. 5, 1985 |
| James G. Martin (R) | Jan. 5, 1985 | Jan. 9, 1993 |
| James B. Hunt Jr. (D) | Jan. 9, 1993 | |

**North Carolina**
1. Resigned Dec. 6, 1854.
2. Acting governor.
3. Died July 7, 1861.
4. Acting governor.
5. Removed from office. Last Confederate governor.
6. Provisional governor appointed by President Johnson.
7. Removed July 1, 1868.
8. Impeached. Removed from office Dec. 15, 1870.
9. As lieutenant governor, he succeeded to office. Subsequently elected. Died July 11, 1874.
10. As lieutenant governor, he succeeded to office.
11. Resigned Feb. 5, 1879.
12. As lieutenant governor, he succeeded to office. Subsequently elected.
13. Died April 8, 1891.
14. As lieutenant governor, he succeeded to office.
15. Died Nov. 7, 1954.
16. As lieutenant governor, he succeeded to office. Subsequently elected.

# NORTH DAKOTA

(Became a state Nov. 2, 1889)

| Governors | Dates of Service | |
|---|---|---|
| John Miller (R) | Nov. 4, 1889 | Jan. 6, 1891 |
| Andrew H. Burke (R) | Jan. 7, 1891 | Jan. 4, 1893 |
| Eli C. D. Shortridge (FUS) | Jan. 4, 1893 | Jan. 7, 1895 |
| Roger Allin (R) | Jan. 7, 1895 | Jan. 5, 1897 |
| Frank A. Briggs (R)[1] | Jan. 5, 1897 | Aug. 9, 1898 |
| Joseph M. Devine (R)[2] | Aug. 9, 1898 | Jan. 3, 1899 |
| Frederick B. Fancher (R) | Jan. 3, 1899 | Jan. 10, 1901 |
| Frank White (R) | Jan. 10, 1901 | Jan. 4, 1905 |
| Elmore Y. Sarles (R) | Jan. 5, 1905 | Jan. 9, 1907 |
| John Burke (D) | Jan. 9, 1907 | Jan. 8, 1913 |
| Louis B. Hanna (R) | Jan. 8, 1913 | Jan. 3, 1917 |
| Lynn J. Frazier (R)[3] | Jan. 3, 1917 | Nov. 23, 1921 |
| Ragnvald A. Nestos (R)[4] | Nov. 23, 1921 | Jan. 5, 1925 |
| Arthur G. Sorlie (R)[5] | Jan. 7, 1925 | Aug. 28, 1928 |
| Walter J. Maddock (R)[6] | Aug. 28, 1928 | Jan. 9, 1929 |
| George F. Shafer (R) | Jan. 9, 1929 | Dec. 31, 1932 |
| William Langer (R)[7] | Dec. 31, 1932 | July 17, 1934 |
| Ole H. Olson (R)[8] | July 17, 1934 | Jan. 7, 1935 |
| Thomas H. Moodie (D)[9] | Jan. 7, 1935 | Feb. 2, 1935 |
| Walter Welford (R)[10] | Feb. 2, 1935 | Jan. 6, 1937 |
| William Langer (I) | Jan. 6, 1937 | Jan. 5, 1939 |
| John Moses (D) | Jan. 5, 1939 | Jan. 4, 1945 |
| Fred G. Aandahl (R) | Jan. 4, 1945 | Jan. 3, 1951 |
| C. Norman Brunsdale (R) | Jan. 3, 1951 | Jan. 9, 1957 |
| John E. Davis (R) | Jan. 9, 1957 | Jan. 4, 1961 |
| William L. Guy (D) | Jan. 4, 1961 | Jan. 2, 1973 |
| Arthur A. Link (D) | Jan. 2, 1973 | Jan. 7, 1981 |
| Allen I. Olson (R)[11] | Jan. 7, 1981 | Jan. 8, 1985 |
| George Sinner (D)[11] | Jan. 8, 1985 | Jan. 5, 1993 |
| Edward T. Schafer (R) | Jan. 5, 1993 | |

**North Dakota**
1. Died in 1898.
2. As lieutenant governor, he succeeded to office.
3. Recalled in election of Oct. 28, 1921; removed Nov. 23, 1921.
4. Elected in recall election of 1921, which removed Governor Frazier. Subsequently elected for a full two-year term.
5. Died Aug. 28, 1928.
6. As lieutenant governor, he succeeded to office.
7. Removed by North Dakota Supreme Court July 17, 1934.
8. As lieutenant governor, he succeeded to office.
9. Disqualified by North Dakota Supreme Court Feb. 2, 1935.
10. As lieutenant governor, he succeeded to office.
11. Although Olson relinquished his office on Jan. 5 and Sinner assumed it Jan. 8, the North Dakota Supreme Court held that Sinner's term began Jan. 1.

# OHIO

(Became a state March 1, 1803)

| Governors | Dates of Service | |
|---|---|---|
| Edward Tiffin (D-R)[1] | March 3, 1803 | March 4, 1807 |
| Thomas Kirker (D-R)[2] | March 4, 1807 | Dec. 12, 1808 |
| Samuel Huntington (D-R) | Dec. 12, 1808 | Dec. 8, 1810 |
| Return Jonathan Meigs (D-R)[3] | Dec. 8, 1810 | March 24, 1814 |
| Othneil Looker (D-R)[4] | March 24, 1814 | Dec. 8, 1814 |
| Thomas Worthington (D-R) | Dec. 8, 1814 | Dec. 14, 1818 |
| Ethan Allen Brown (D-R)[5] | Dec. 14, 1818 | Jan. 4, 1822 |
| Allen Trimble (D-R)[6] | Jan. 4, 1822 | Dec. 28, 1822 |
| Jeremiah Morrow (JAC D) | Dec. 28, 1822 | Dec. 19, 1826 |
| Allen Trimble (NR) | Dec. 19, 1826 | Dec. 18, 1830 |
| Duncan McArthur (NR) | Dec. 18, 1830 | Dec. 7, 1832 |
| Robert Lucas (D) | Dec. 7, 1832 | Dec. 12, 1836 |
| Joseph Vance (W) | Dec. 12, 1836 | Dec. 13, 1838 |
| Wilson Shannon (D) | Dec. 13, 1838 | Dec. 16, 1840 |
| Thomas Corwin (W) | Dec. 16, 1840 | Dec. 14, 1842 |
| Wilson Shannon (D)[7] | Dec. 14, 1842 | April 15, 1844 |
| Thomas W. Bartley (D)[8] | April 15, 1844 | Dec. 3, 1844 |
| Mordecai Bartley (W) | Dec. 3, 1844 | Dec. 12, 1846 |
| William Bebb (W) | Dec. 12, 1846 | Jan. 22, 1849 |
| Seabury Ford (W)[9] | Jan. 22, 1849 | Dec. 12, 1850 |
| Reuben Wood (D)[10] | Dec. 12, 1850 | July 13, 1853 |
| William Medill (D)[11] | July 13, 1853 | Jan. 14, 1856 |
| Salmon P. Chase (R) | Jan. 14, 1856 | Jan. 9, 1860 |
| William Dennison Jr. (R) | Jan. 9, 1860 | Jan. 13, 1862 |
| David Tod (UN) | Jan. 13, 1862 | Jan. 11, 1864 |
| John Brough (UN)[12] | Jan. 11, 1864 | Aug. 29, 1865 |
| Charles Anderson (UN)[13] | Aug. 29, 1865 | Jan. 8, 1866 |
| Jacob D. Cox (UN) | Jan. 8, 1866 | Jan. 13, 1868 |
| Rutherford B. Hayes (R) | Jan. 13, 1868 | Jan. 8, 1872 |
| Edward F. Noyes (R) | Jan. 8, 1872 | Jan. 12, 1874 |
| William Allen (D) | Jan. 12, 1874 | Jan. 10, 1876 |
| Rutherford B. Hayes (R)[14] | Jan. 10, 1876 | March 2, 1877 |
| Thomas L. Young (R)[15] | March 2, 1877 | Jan. 14, 1878 |
| Richard M. Bishop (D) | Jan. 14, 1878 | Jan. 12, 1880 |
| Charles Foster (R) | Jan. 12, 1880 | Jan. 14, 1884 |
| George Hoadly (D) | Jan. 14, 1884 | Jan. 11, 1886 |
| Joseph B. Foraker (R) | Jan. 11, 1886 | Jan. 13, 1890 |
| James E. Campbell (D) | Jan. 13, 1890 | Jan. 11, 1892 |
| William McKinley Jr. (R) | Jan. 11, 1892 | Jan. 13, 1896 |
| Asa S. Bushnell (R) | Jan. 13, 1896 | Jan. 8, 1900 |
| George K. Nash (R) | Jan. 8, 1900 | Jan. 11, 1904 |
| Myron T. Herrick (R) | Jan. 11, 1904 | Jan. 8, 1906 |
| John M. Pattison (D)[16] | Jan. 8, 1906 | June 18, 1906 |
| Andrew L. Harris (R)[17] | June 18, 1906 | Jan. 11, 1909 |
| Judson Harmon (D) | Jan. 11, 1909 | Jan. 13, 1913 |
| James M. Cox (D) | Jan. 13, 1913 | Jan. 11, 1915 |
| Frank B. Willis (R) | Jan. 11, 1915 | Jan. 8, 1917 |
| James M. Cox (D) | Jan. 8, 1917 | Jan. 10, 1921 |
| Harry L. Davis (R) | Jan. 10, 1921 | Jan. 8, 1923 |
| Alvin Victor Donahey (D) | Jan. 8, 1923 | Jan. 14, 1929 |
| Myers Y. Cooper (R) | Jan. 14, 1929 | Jan. 12, 1931 |
| George White (D) | Jan. 12, 1931 | Jan. 14, 1935 |
| Martin L. Davey (D) | Jan. 14, 1935 | Jan. 9, 1939 |
| John W. Bricker (R) | Jan. 9, 1939 | Jan. 8, 1945 |
| Frank J. Lausche (D) | Jan. 8, 1945 | Jan. 13, 1947 |
| Thomas J. Herbert (R) | Jan. 13, 1947 | Jan. 10, 1949 |
| Frank J. Lausche (D)[18] | Jan. 10, 1949 | Jan. 3, 1957 |
| John W. Brown (R)[19] | Jan. 3, 1957 | Jan. 14, 1957 |
| C. William O'Neill (R) | Jan. 14, 1957 | Jan. 12, 1959 |
| Michael V. DiSalle (D) | Jan. 12, 1959 | Jan. 14, 1963 |
| James A. Rhodes (R) | Jan. 14, 1963 | Jan. 11, 1971 |
| John J. Gilligan (D) | Jan. 11, 1971 | Jan. 13, 1975 |
| James A. Rhodes (R) | Jan. 13, 1975 | Jan. 10, 1983 |
| Richard F. Celeste (D) | Jan. 10, 1983 | Jan. 14, 1991 |
| George V. Voinovich (R) | Jan. 14, 1991 | |

**Ohio**

1. Resigned March 4, 1807.
2. As Speaker of the state Senate, he succeeded to office.
3. Resigned March 24, 1814.
4. As Speaker of the state Senate, he succeeded to office.
5. Resigned Jan. 4, 1822.
6. As Speaker of the state Senate, he succeeded to office.
7. Resigned April 15, 1844.
8. As Speaker of the state Senate, he succeeded to office.
9. The election of 1848 was disputed, and Ford's election was delayed until Jan. 22, 1849.
10. Resigned July 13, 1853.
11. As lieutenant governor, he succeeded to office. Subsequently elected.
12. Died Aug. 29, 1865.
13. As lieutenant governor, he succeeded to office.
14. Resigned March 2, 1877, having been elected president of the United States.
15. As lieutenant governor, he succeeded to office.
16. Died June 18, 1906.
17. As lieutenant governor, he succeeded to office.
18. Resigned Jan. 3, 1957.
19. As lieutenant governor, he succeeded to office.

# OKLAHOMA

(Became a state Nov. 16, 1907)

| Governors | Dates of Service | |
|---|---|---|
| Charles N. Haskell (D) | Nov. 16, 1907 | Jan. 9, 1911 |
| Lee Cruce (D) | Jan. 9, 1911 | Jan. 11, 1915 |
| Robert L. Williams (D) | Jan. 11, 1915 | Jan. 13, 1919 |
| James B. A. Robertson (D) | Jan. 13, 1919 | Jan. 8, 1923 |
| John C. Walton (D)[1] | Jan. 8, 1923 | Nov. 19, 1923 |
| Martin E. Trapp (D)[2] | Nov. 19, 1923 | Jan. 10, 1927 |
| Henry S. Johnston (D)[3] | Jan. 10, 1927 | March 20, 1929 |
| William J. Holloway (D)[4] | March 20, 1929 | Jan. 12, 1931 |
| William H. Murray (D) | Jan. 12, 1931 | Jan. 14, 1935 |
| Ernest W. Marland (D) | Jan. 14, 1935 | Jan. 9, 1939 |
| Leon C. Phillips (D) | Jan. 9, 1939 | Jan. 11, 1943 |
| Robert S. Kerr (D) | Jan. 11, 1943 | Jan. 13, 1947 |
| Roy J. Turner (D) | Jan. 13, 1947 | Jan. 8, 1951 |
| Johnston Murray (D) | Jan. 8, 1951 | Jan. 10, 1955 |
| Raymond D. Gary (D) | Jan. 10, 1955 | Jan. 12, 1959 |
| J. Howard Edmondson (D)[5] | Jan. 12, 1959 | Jan. 6, 1963 |
| George P. Nigh (D)[6] | Jan. 6, 1963 | Jan. 14, 1963 |
| Henry L. Bellmon (R) | Jan. 14, 1963 | Jan. 9, 1967 |
| Dewey F. Bartlett (R) | Jan. 9, 1967 | Jan. 11, 1971 |
| David Hall (D) | Jan. 11, 1971 | Jan. 13, 1975 |
| David L. Boren (D) | Jan. 13, 1975 | Jan. 3, 1979 |
| George Nigh (D) | Jan. 3, 1979 | Jan. 12, 1987 |
| Henry L. Bellmon (R) | Jan. 12, 1987 | Jan. 14, 1991 |
| David Walters (D) | Jan. 14, 1991 | |

**Oklahoma**

1. Impeached; removed from office, Nov. 19, 1923.
2. As lieutenant governor, he succeeded to office.
3. Impeached; removed from office, March 20, 1929.
4. As lieutenant governor, he succeeded to office.
5. Resigned Jan. 6, 1963.
6. As lieutenant governor, he succeeded to office.

# OREGON

(Became a state Feb. 14, 1859)

| Governors | Dates of Service | |
|---|---|---|
| John Whiteaker (D) | March 3, 1859 | Sept. 10, 1862 |
| A. C. Gibbs (UN R) | Sept. 10, 1862 | Sept. 12, 1866 |
| George L. Woods (R) | Sept. 12, 1866 | Sept. 14, 1870 |
| La Fayette Grover (D)[1] | Sept. 14, 1870 | Feb. 1, 1877 |

| | | |
|---|---|---|
| Stephen F. Chadwick (D)[2] | Feb. 1, 1877 | Sept. 11, 1878 |
| William Wallace Thayer (D) | Sept. 11, 1878 | Sept. 13, 1882 |
| Zenas F. Moody (R) | Sept. 13, 1882 | Jan. 12, 1887 |
| Sylvester Pennoyer (D) | Jan. 12, 1887 | Jan. 14, 1895 |
| William P. Lord (R) | Jan. 14, 1895 | Jan. 9, 1899 |
| Theodore T. Geer (R) | Jan. 9, 1899 | Jan. 14, 1903 |
| George E. Chamberlain (D)[3] | Jan. 14, 1903 | March 1, 1909 |
| Frank W. Benson (R)[4] | March 1, 1909 | June 17, 1910 |
| Jay Bowerman (R)[5] | June 17, 1910 | Jan. 10, 1911 |
| Oswald West (D) | Jan. 10, 1911 | Jan. 12, 1915 |
| James Withycombe (R)[6] | Jan. 12, 1915 | March 3, 1919 |
| Ben W. Olcott (R)[7] | March 3, 1919 | Jan. 8, 1923 |
| Walter M. Pierce (D) | Jan. 8, 1923 | Jan. 10, 1927 |
| Isaac L. Patterson (R)[8] | Jan. 10, 1927 | Dec. 21, 1929 |
| A. W. Norblad (R)[9] | Dec. 22, 1929 | Jan. 12, 1931 |
| Julius L. Meier (I) | Jan. 12, 1931 | Jan. 14, 1935 |
| Charles H. Martin (D) | Jan. 14, 1935 | Jan. 9, 1939 |
| Charles A. Sprague (R) | Jan. 9, 1939 | Jan. 11, 1943 |
| Earl Snell (R)[10] | Jan. 11, 1943 | Oct. 28, 1947 |
| John H. Hall (R)[11] | Oct. 30, 1947 | Jan. 10, 1949 |
| Douglas McKay (R)[12] | Jan. 10, 1949 | Dec. 27, 1952 |
| Paul L. Patterson (R)[13] | Dec. 27, 1952 | Jan. 31, 1956 |
| Elmo Smith (R)[14] | Feb. 1, 1956 | Jan. 14, 1957 |
| Robert D. Holmes (D)[15] | Jan. 14, 1957 | Jan. 12, 1959 |
| Mark O. Hatfield (R) | Jan. 12, 1959 | Jan. 9, 1967 |
| Tom McCall (R) | Jan. 9, 1967 | Jan. 13, 1975 |
| Robert W. Straub (D) | Jan. 13, 1975 | Jan. 8, 1979 |
| Victor Atiyeh (R) | Jan. 8, 1979 | Jan. 12, 1987 |
| Neil Goldschmidt (D) | Jan. 12, 1987 | Jan. 14, 1991 |
| Barbara Roberts (D) | Jan. 14, 1991 | |

**Oregon**
*1. Resigned Feb. 1, 1877.*
*2. As secretary of state, he succeeded to office.*
*3. Resigned March 1, 1909.*
*4. As secretary of state, he succeeded to office. Resigned June 17, 1910.*
*5. As president of the state Senate, he succeeded to office.*
*6. Died March 3, 1919.*
*7. As secretary of state, he succeeded to office.*
*8. Died Dec. 21, 1929.*
*9. As president of the state Senate, he succeeded to office.*
*10. Died Oct. 28, 1947.*
*11. As speaker of the House, he succeeded to office for the remainder of the first two years of Snell's term.*
*12. Elected for the last two years of Snell's term in a special election. Subsequently re-elected. Resigned Dec. 27, 1952.*
*13. As president of the state senate, he succeeded to office. Subsequently elected. Died Jan. 31, 1956.*
*14. As president of the state Senate, he succeeded to office for the remainder of the first two years of Patterson's term.*
*15. Elected in a special election for the last two years of Patterson's term.*

# PENNSYLVANIA

(Ratified the Constitution Dec. 12, 1787)

| **Governors** | **Dates of Service** | |
|---|---|---|
| Peter Mulhenberg | Oct. 31, 1787 | Oct. 14, 1788 |
| David Redick | Oct. 14, 1788 | Nov. 5, 1788 |
| George Ross | Nov. 5, 1788 | Dec. 21, 1790 |
| Thomas Mifflin | Dec. 21, 1790 | Dec. 17, 1799 |
| Thomas McKean (D-R) | Dec. 17, 1799 | Dec. 20, 1808 |
| Simon Snyder (D-R) | Dec. 20, 1808 | Dec. 16, 1817 |
| William Findlay (D-R) | Dec. 16, 1817 | Dec. 19, 1820 |
| Joseph Hiester (D-R) | Dec. 19, 1820 | Dec. 16, 1823 |
| John A. Shulze (JAC D) | Dec. 16, 1823 | Dec. 15, 1829 |
| George Wolfe (JAC D) | Dec. 15, 1829 | Dec. 15, 1835 |
| Joseph Ritner (D) | Dec. 15, 1835 | Jan. 15, 1839 |
| David R. Porter (D) | Jan. 15, 1839 | Jan. 21, 1845 |
| Francis R. Shunk (D)[1] | Jan. 21, 1845 | July 9, 1848 |
| William F. Johnston (W)[2] | July 26, 1848 | Jan. 20, 1852 |
| William Bigler (D) | Jan. 20, 1852 | Jan. 16, 1855 |

| | | |
|---|---|---|
| James Pollock (W) | Jan. 16, 1855 | Jan. 19, 1858 |
| William F. Packer (D) | Jan. 19, 1858 | Jan. 15, 1861 |
| Andrew G. Curtin (R) | Jan. 15, 1861 | Jan. 15, 1867 |
| John W. Geary (R) | Jan. 15, 1867 | Jan. 21, 1873 |
| John F. Hartranft (R) | Jan. 21, 1873 | Jan. 18, 1879 |
| Henry M. Hoyt (R) | Jan. 21, 1879 | Jan. 16, 1883 |
| Robert E. Pattison (D) | Jan. 16, 1883 | Jan. 18, 1887 |
| James A. Beaver (R) | Jan. 18, 1887 | Jan. 20, 1891 |
| Robert E. Pattison (D) | Jan. 20, 1891 | Jan. 15, 1895 |
| Daniel H. Hastings (R) | Jan. 15, 1895 | Jan. 17, 1899 |
| William A. Stone (R) | Jan. 17, 1899 | Jan. 20, 1903 |
| Samuel W. Pennypacker (R) | Jan. 20, 1903 | Jan. 15, 1907 |
| Edwin S. Stuart (R) | Jan. 15, 1907 | Jan. 17, 1911 |
| John K. Tener (R) | Jan. 17, 1911 | Jan. 19, 1915 |
| Martin G. Brumbaugh (R) | Jan. 19, 1915 | Jan. 21, 1919 |
| William C. Sproul (R) | Jan. 21, 1919 | Jan. 16, 1923 |
| Gifford Pinchot (R) | Jan. 16, 1923 | Jan. 18, 1927 |
| John S. Fisher (R) | Jan. 18, 1927 | Jan. 20, 1931 |
| Gifford Pinchot (R, PROG) | Jan. 20, 1931 | Jan. 15, 1935 |
| George H. Earle (D) | Jan. 15, 1935 | Jan. 17, 1939 |
| Arthur H. James (R) | Jan. 17, 1939 | Jan. 19,1943 |
| Edward Martin (R)[3] | Jan. 19, 1943 | Jan. 2, 1947 |
| John C. Bell Jr. (R)[4] | Jan. 2, 1947 | Jan. 21, 1947 |
| James H. Duff (R) | Jan. 21, 1947 | Jan. 16, 1951 |
| John S. Fine (R) | Jan. 16, 1951 | Jan. 18, 1955 |
| George M. Leader (D) | Jan. 18, 1955 | Jan. 20, 1959 |
| David L. Lawrence (D) | Jan. 20, 1959 | Jan. 15, 1963 |
| William W. Scranton (R) | Jan. 15, 1963 | Jan. 17, 1967 |
| Raymond P. Shafer (R) | Jan. 17, 1967 | Jan. 19, 1971 |
| Milton J. Shapp (D) | Jan. 19, 1971 | Jan. 16, 1979 |
| Richard L. Thornburgh (R) | Jan. 16, 1979 | Jan. 20, 1987 |
| Robert P. Casey (D) | Jan. 20, 1987 | |

**Pennsylvania**
*1. Resigned July 9, 1848.*
*2. Interregnum from July 9 to July 26, 1848. Johnston became acting governor. Subsequently elected.*
*3. Resigned Jan. 2, 1947.*
*4. As lieutenant governor, he succeeded to office.*

# RHODE ISLAND

(Ratified the Constitution May 29, 1790)

| **Governors** | **Dates of Service** | |
|---|---|---|
| Arthur Fenner (D-R)[1] | May 5, 1790 | Oct. 15, 1805 |
| Henry Smith (D-R)[2] | Oct. 15, 1805 | May 7, 1806 |
| Isaac Wilbur (D-R)[3] | May 7, 1806 | May 6, 1807 |
| James Fenner | May 6, 1807 | May 1, 1811 |
| William Jones (FED) | May 1, 1811 | May 7, 1817 |
| Nehemiah R. Knight (D-R)[4] | May 7, 1817 | Jan. 9, 1821 |
| Edward Wilcox (D-R)[5] | Jan. 9, 1821 | May 2, 1821 |
| William C. Gibbs (D-R) | May 2, 1821 | May 5, 1824 |
| James Fenner (D-R) | May 5, 1824 | May 4, 1831 |
| Lemuel H. Arnold (D)[6] | May 4, 1831 | May 1, 1833 |
| John Brown Francis (D) | May 1, 1833 | May 2, 1838 |
| William Sprague (W) | May 2, 1838 | May 1, 1839 |
| Samuel Ward King (W)[7] | May 2, 1839 | May 2, 1843 |
| James Fenner (L & O W) | May 2, 1843 | May 6, 1845 |
| Charles Jackson (LIBER W) | May 6, 1845 | May 6, 1846 |
| Byron Diman (L & O W) | May 6, 1846 | May 4, 1847 |
| Elisha Harris (W) | May 4, 1847 | May 1, 1849 |
| Henry B. Anthony (W) | May 1, 1849 | May 6, 1851 |
| Philip Allen (D)[8] | May 6, 1851 | July 20, 1853 |
| Francis M. Dimond (D)[9] | July 20, 1853 | May 2, 1854 |
| William W. Hoppin (W, R) | May 2, 1854 | May 26, 1857 |
| Elisha Dyer (R) | May 26, 1857 | May 31, 1859 |
| Thomas G. Turner | May 31, 1859 | May 29, 1860 |
| William Sprague (FUS, UN)[10] | May 29, 1860 | March 3, 1863 |
| William C. Cozzens[11] | March 3, 1863 | May 26, 1863 |

| | | |
|---|---|---|
| James Y. Smith (UN R) | May 26, 1863 | May 29, 1866 |
| Ambrose E. Burnside (R) | May 29, 1866 | May 25, 1869 |
| Seth Padelford (R) | May 25, 1869 | May 27, 1873 |
| Henry Howard (R) | May 27, 1873 | May 25, 1875 |
| Henry Lippitt (R) | May 25, 1875 | May 29, 1877 |
| Charles Van Zandt (R & TEMP) | May 29, 1877 | May 25, 1880 |
| Alfred H. Littlefield (R) | May 25, 1880 | May 29, 1883 |
| Augustus O. Bourn (R) | May 29, 1883 | May 26, 1885 |
| George P. Wetmore (R) | May 26, 1885 | May 31, 1887 |
| John W. Davis (D) | May 31, 1887 | May 29, 1888 |
| Royal C. Taft (R) | May 29, 1888 | May 28, 1889 |
| Herbert W. Ladd (R) | May 28, 1889 | May 27, 1890 |
| John W. Davis (D) | May 27, 1890 | May 26, 1891 |
| Herbert W. Ladd (R) | May 26, 1891 | May 31, 1892 |
| D. Russell Brown (R)[12] | May 31, 1892 | May 29, 1895 |
| Charles W. Lippitt (R) | May 29, 1895 | May 25, 1897 |
| Elisha Dyer (R) | May 25, 1897 | May 29, 1900 |
| William Gregory (R)[13] | May 29, 1900 | Dec. 16, 1901 |
| Charles D. Kimball (R)[14] | Dec. 16, 1901 | Jan. 6, 1903 |
| Lucius F. C. Garvin (D) | Jan. 6, 1903 | Jan. 3, 1905 |
| George H. Utter (R) | Jan. 3, 1905 | Jan. 1, 1907 |
| James H. Higgins (D) | Jan. 1, 1907 | Jan. 5, 1909 |
| Aram J. Pothier (R) | Jan. 5, 1909 | Jan. 5, 1915 |
| R. Livingston Beeckman (R) | Jan. 5, 1915 | Jan. 4, 1921 |
| Emery J. San Souci (R) | Jan. 4, 1921 | Jan. 2, 1923 |
| William S. Flynn (D) | Jan. 2, 1923 | Jan. 6, 1925 |
| Aram J. Pothier (R)[15] | Jan. 6, 1925 | Feb. 4, 1928 |
| Norman S. Case (R)[16] | Feb. 4, 1928 | Jan. 3, 1933 |
| Theodore F. Green (D) | Jan. 3, 1933 | Jan. 5, 1937 |
| Robert E. Quinn (D) | Jan. 5, 1937 | Jan. 3, 1939 |
| William H. Vanderbilt (R) | Jan. 3, 1939 | Jan. 7, 1941 |
| J. Howard McGrath (D)[17] | Jan. 7, 1941 | Oct. 6, 1945 |
| John O. Pastore (D)[18] | Oct. 6, 1945 | Dec. 19, 1950 |
| John S. McKiernan (D)[19] | Dec. 19, 1950 | Jan. 2, 1951 |
| Dennis J. Roberts (D) | Jan. 2, 1951 | Jan. 6, 1959 |
| Christopher Del Sesto (R) | Jan. 6, 1959 | Jan. 3, 1961 |
| John A. Notte Jr. (D) | Jan. 3, 1961 | Jan. 1, 1963 |
| John H. Chafee (R) | Jan. 1, 1963 | Jan. 7, 1969 |
| Frank Licht (D) | Jan. 7, 1969 | Jan. 2, 1973 |
| Philip W. Noel (D) | Jan. 2, 1973 | Jan. 4, 1977 |
| Joseph J. Garrahy (D) | Jan. 4, 1977 | Jan. 1, 1985 |
| Edward D. DiPrete (R) | Jan. 1, 1985 | Jan. 1, 1991 |
| Bruce Sundlun (D) | Jan. 1, 1991 | |

**Rhode Island**

*1. Died Oct. 15, 1805.*

*2. Smith, as first senator, served as governor.*

*3. No governor was elected in 1806. Wilbur, the lieutenant governor, served as acting governor.*

*4. Resigned Jan. 9, 1821.*

*5. As lieutenant governor, he succeeded to office.*

*6. In the 1832 election, no candidate for governor received the majority of the total vote cast which was required for election. Elections were held four more times — on May 16, July 18, August 28 and Nov. 21 — each one resulting without choice. Arnold was continued in office until 1833. (The returns for this election, p. 524, show only the first election.)*

*7. No governor was elected in 1839, no candidate having received a majority of the vote. In addition, no lieutenant governor was elected. King, as first senator, became acting governor for the term. Subsequently re-elected three times.*

*8. Resigned July 20, 1853.*

*9. As lieutenant governor, he succeeded to office.*

*10. Resigned March 3, 1863.*

*11. As president of the state Senate, he succeeded to office.*

*12. No candidate received a majority of the vote in the election of 1893, and under the law the Legislature was required to elect the governor. However, because of a dispute between the two houses no choice was made. Governor Brown continued in office for the term. He was re-elected in 1894. The controversy over the election resulted in repeal of the majority-vote requirement in 1893.*

*13. Died Dec. 16, 1901.*

*14. As lieutenant governor, he succeeded to office.*

*15. Died Feb. 4, 1928.*

*16. As lieutenant governor, he succeeded to office. Subsequently elected.*

*17. Resigned Oct. 6, 1945.*

*18. As lieutenant governor, he succeeded to office. Subsequently elected. Resigned Dec. 19, 1950.*

*19. As lieutenant governor, he succeeded to office.*

# SOUTH CAROLINA

(Ratified the Constitution May 23, 1788)

| Governors | Dates of Service | |
|---|---|---|
| Charles Pinckney | Jan. 26, 1789 | Dec. 5, 1792 |
| William Moultrie (FED) | Dec. 5, 1792 | Dec. 1794 |
| Arnoldus Vander Horst (FED) | Dec. 1794 | Dec. 1796 |
| Charles Pinckney (D-R) | Dec. 1796 | Dec. 6, 1798 |
| Edward Rutledge (FED)[1] | Dec. 18, 1798 | Jan. 23, 1800 |
| John Drayton (D-R)[2] | Jan. 23, 1800 | Dec. 1802 |
| James B. Richardson (D-R) | Dec. 1802 | Dec. 1804 |
| Paul Hamilton (D-R) | Dec. 1804 | Dec. 1806 |
| Charles Pinckney (D-R) | Dec. 1806 | Dec. 10, 1808 |
| John Drayton (D-R) | Dec. 10, 1808 | Dec. 1810 |
| Henry Middleton (D-R) | Dec. 10, 1810 | Dec. 1812 |
| Joseph Alston (D-R) | Dec. 1812 | Dec. 1814 |
| David R. Williams (D-R) | Dec. 1814 | Dec. 1816 |
| Andrew Pickens (D-R) | Dec. 1816 | Dec. 1818 |
| John Geddes (D-R) | Dec. 1818 | Dec. 1820 |
| Thomas Bennett (D-R) | Dec. 1820 | Dec. 1822 |
| John Lyde Wilson (D-R) | Dec. 1822 | Dec. 1824 |
| Richard I. Manning (D-R) | Dec. 1824 | Dec. 1826 |
| John Taylor (D-R) | Dec. 1826 | Dec. 1828 |
| Stephen D. Miller (D) | Dec. 1828 | Dec. 1830 |
| James Hamilton Jr. (D) | Dec. 1830 | Dec. 13, 1832 |
| Robert Y. Hayne (D) | Dec. 13, 1832 | Dec. 11, 1834 |
| George McDuffie (D) | Dec. 11, 1834 | Dec. 1836 |
| Pierce M. Butler (D) | Dec. 1836 | Dec. 10, 1838 |
| Patrick Noble (D)[3] | Dec. 10, 1838 | April 7, 1840 |
| B. K. Henagan (D)[4] | April 7, 1840 | Dec. 10, 1840 |
| John P. Richardson (D) | Dec. 10, 1840 | Dec. 1842 |
| James H. Hammond (D) | Dec. 1842 | Dec. 1844 |
| William Aiken (D) | Dec. 1844 | Dec. 1846 |
| David Johnson (D) | Dec. 1846 | Dec. 1848 |
| Whitmarsh B. Seabrook (D) | Dec. 1848 | Dec. 1850 |
| John Hugh Means (D) | Dec. 16, 1850 | Dec. 1852 |
| John Laurence Manning (D) | Dec. 1852 | Dec. 1854 |
| James H. Adams (D) | Dec. 1854 | Dec. 1856 |
| Robert F. W. Alston (D) | Dec. 1856 | Dec. 1858 |
| William H. Gist (D) | Dec. 1858 | Dec. 1860 |
| Francis W. Pickens (D) | Dec. 1860 | Dec. 1862 |
| Milledge L. Bonham (D) | Dec. 1862 | Dec. 1864 |
| Andrew G. Magrath (D)[5] | Dec. 20, 1864 | May 25, 1865 |
| Benjamin F. Perry[6] | June 30, 1865 | Nov. 29, 1865 |
| James L. Orr (C)[7] | Nov. 29, 1865 | July 6, 1868 |
| Robert K. Scott (R) | July 9, 1868 | Dec. 7, 1872 |
| Franklin J. Moses Jr. (R) | Dec. 7, 1872 | Dec. 1, 1874 |
| Daniel H. Chamberlain (R)[8] | Dec. 1, 1874 | April 10, 1877 |
| Wade Hampton (D)[9] | Dec. 14, 1876 | Feb. 26, 1879 |
| William D. Simpson (D)[10] | Feb. 26, 1879 | Sept. 1, 1880 |
| Thomas B. Jeter (D)[11] | Sept. 1, 1880 | Nov. 30, 1880 |
| Johnson Hagood (D) | Nov. 30, 1880 | Dec. 1882 |
| Hugh Smith Thompson (D)[12] | Dec. 1882 | July 10, 1886 |
| John C. Sheppard (D)[13] | July 10, 1886 | Nov. 30, 1886 |
| John P. Richardson (D) | Nov. 30, 1886 | Dec. 4, 1890 |
| Benjamin Ryan Tillman (D) | Dec. 4, 1890 | Dec. 1894 |
| John Gary Evans (D) | Dec. 4, 1894 | Jan. 18, 1897 |
| William H. Ellerbe (D)[14] | Jan. 18, 1897 | June 2, 1899 |
| Miles B. McSweeney (D)[15] | June 2, 1899 | Jan. 20, 1903 |
| Duncan C. Heyward (D) | Jan. 20, 1903 | Jan. 15, 1907 |
| Martin F. Ansel (D) | Jan. 15, 1907 | Jan. 17, 1911 |
| Coleman L. Blease (D)[16] | Jan. 17, 1911 | Jan. 14, 1915 |
| Charles A. Smith (D)[17] | Jan. 14, 1915 | Jan. 19, 1915 |
| Richard I. Manning (D) | Jan. 19, 1915 | Jan. 21, 1919 |

| | | |
|---|---|---|
| Robert A. Cooper (D)[18] | Jan. 21, 1919 | May 20, 1922 |
| Wilson G. Harvey (D)[19] | May 20, 1922 | Jan. 16, 1923 |
| Thomas G. McLeod (D) | Jan. 16, 1923 | Jan. 18, 1927 |
| John G. Richards (D) | Jan. 18, 1927 | Jan. 20, 1931 |
| Ibra C. Blackwood (D) | Jan. 20, 1931 | Jan. 15, 1935 |
| Olin D. Johnston (D) | Jan. 15, 1935 | Jan. 17, 1939 |
| Burnet R. Maybank (D)[20] | Jan. 17, 1939 | Nov. 4, 1941 |
| Joseph E. Harley (D)[21] | Nov. 4, 1941 | Feb. 27, 1942 |
| Richard M. Jeffries (D)[22] | March 2, 1942 | Jan. 19, 1943 |
| Olin D. Johnston (D)[23] | Jan. 19, 1943 | Jan. 2, 1945 |
| Ransome J. Williams (D)[24] | Jan. 2, 1945 | Jan. 21, 1947 |
| J. Strom Thurmond (D) | Jan. 21, 1947 | Jan. 16, 1951 |
| James F. Byrnes (D) | Jan. 16, 1951 | Jan. 18, 1955 |
| George Bell<br>  Timmerman Jr. (D) | Jan. 18, 1955 | Jan. 20, 1959 |
| Ernest F. Hollings (D) | Jan. 20, 1959 | Jan. 15, 1963 |
| Donald S. Russell (D)[25] | Jan. 15, 1963 | April 22, 1965 |
| Robert E. McNair (D)[26] | April 22, 1965 | Jan. 19, 1971 |
| John C. West (D) | Jan. 19, 1971 | Jan. 21, 1975 |
| James Edwards (R) | Jan. 21, 1975 | Jan. 10, 1979 |
| Richard Riley (D) | Jan. 10, 1979 | Jan. 14, 1987 |
| Carroll Campbell (R) | Jan. 14, 1987 | |

**South Carolina**
1. Died Jan. 23, 1800.
2. As lieutenant governor, he succeeded to office. Subsequently elected.
3. Died April 7, 1840.
4. As lieutenant governor, he succeeded to office.
5. Last Confederate governor. Removed by federal authorities.
6. Provisional governor appointed by President Johnson.
7. Deposed by act of Congress.
8. There was a dispute between two factions in the House of Representatives over the elections and seating of eight of its members following the 1876 election. The pro-Chamberlain (R) faction declared Chamberlain to have been re-elected and he was re-inaugurated on December 7. The pro-Hampton (D) faction also organized as the House of Representatives and on December 14 declared Hampton to have been elected. He was inaugurated on the same day. For a time there were two rival state governments. In several cases arising later, raising the question of Hampton's authority to act as governor, the Supreme Court of the state declared him to be the lawfully elected chief executive of the state. Chamberlain dropped his claim to the office on April 10, 1877, following the withdrawal of federal troops from the state in March 1877 by President Hayes.
9. Resigned Feb. 26, 1879.
10. As lieutenant governor, he succeeded to office. Resigned in September 1880.
11. As president of the state Senate, he succeeded to office.
12. Resigned July 10, 1886.
13. As lieutenant governor, he succeeded to office.
14. Died June 2, 1899.
15. As lieutenant governor, he succeeded to office. Subsequently elected.
16. Resigned Jan. 14, 1915.
17. As lieutenant governor, he succeeded to office.
18. Resigned May 20, 1922.
19. As lieutenant governor, he succeeded to office.
20. Resigned Nov. 4, 1941.
21. As lieutenant governor, he succeeded to office. Died Feb. 27, 1942.
22. As president of the state Senate, he succeeded to office.
23. Resigned Jan. 2, 1945.
24. As lieutenant governor, he succeeded to office.
25. Resigned April 22, 1965.
26. As lieutenant governor, he succeeded to office. Subsequently elected.

# SOUTH DAKOTA

(Became a state Nov. 2, 1889)

| Governors | Dates of Service | |
|---|---|---|
| Arthur C. Melette (R) | Nov. 2, 1889 | Jan. 1893 |
| Charles H. Sheldon (R) | Jan. 1893 | Jan. 1, 1897 |
| Andrew E. Lee (PP, FUS) | Jan. 1, 1897 | Jan. 8, 1901 |
| Charles N. Herreid (R) | Jan. 8, 1901 | Jan. 3, 1905 |
| Samuel H. Elrod (R) | Jan. 3, 1905 | Jan. 8, 1907 |
| Coe I. Crawford (R) | Jan. 8, 1907 | Jan. 5, 1909 |

| | | |
|---|---|---|
| Robert S. Vessey (R) | Jan. 5, 1909 | Jan. 7, 1913 |
| Frank M. Byrne (R) | Jan. 7, 1913 | Jan. 2, 1917 |
| Peter Norbeck (R) | Jan. 2, 1917 | Jan. 4, 1921 |
| William H. McMaster (R) | Jan. 4, 1921 | Jan. 6, 1925 |
| Carl Gunderson (R) | Jan. 6, 1925 | Jan. 4, 1927 |
| William J. Bulow (D) | Jan. 4, 1927 | Jan. 6, 1931 |
| Warren E. Green (R) | Jan. 6, 1931 | Jan. 3, 1933 |
| Tom Berry (D) | Jan. 3, 1933 | Jan. 5, 1937 |
| Leslie Jensen (R) | Jan. 5, 1937 | Jan. 3, 1939 |
| Harlan J. Bushfield (R) | Jan. 3, 1939 | Jan. 5, 1943 |
| Merrell Q. Sharpe (R) | Jan. 5, 1943 | Jan. 7, 1947 |
| George T. Mickelson (R) | Jan. 7, 1947 | Jan. 2, 1951 |
| Sigurd Anderson (R) | Jan. 2, 1951 | Jan. 4, 1955 |
| Joe Foss (R) | Jan. 4, 1955 | Jan. 6, 1959 |
| Ralph E. Herseth (D) | Jan. 6, 1959 | Jan. 3, 1961 |
| Archie M. Gubbrud (R) | Jan. 3, 1961 | Jan. 5, 1965 |
| Nils A. Boe (R) | Jan. 5, 1965 | Jan. 7, 1969 |
| Frank L. Farrar (R) | Jan. 7, 1969 | Jan. 5, 1971 |
| Richard F. Kneip (D)[1] | Jan. 5, 1971 | July 24, 1978 |
| Harvey L. Wollman (D)[2] | July 24, 1978 | Jan. 1, 1979 |
| William J. Janklow (R) | Jan. 1, 1979 | Jan. 6, 1987 |
| George S. Mickelson (R)[3] | Jan. 6, 1987 | April 19, 1993 |
| Walter D. Miller (R)[4] | April 20, 1993 | |

**South Dakota**
1. Resigned July 24, 1978.
2. As lieutenant governor, he succeeded to office.
3. Died April 19, 1993.
4. As lieutenant governor, he succeeded to office.

# TENNESSEE

(Became a state June 1, 1796)

| Governors | Dates of Service | |
|---|---|---|
| John Sevier (D-R) | March 30, 1796 | Sept. 23, 1801 |
| Archibald Roane (D-R) | Sept. 23, 1801 | Sept. 23, 1803 |
| John Sevier (D-R) | Sept. 23, 1803 | Sept. 20, 1809 |
| Willie Blount (D-R) | Sept. 20, 1809 | Sept. 27, 1815 |
| Joseph McMinn (D-R) | Sept. 27, 1815 | Oct. 1, 1821 |
| William Carroll (D-R) | Oct. 1, 1821 | Oct. 1, 1827 |
| Sam Houston (D-R)[1] | Oct. 1, 1827 | April 16, 1829 |
| William Hall (D-R)[2] | April 16, 1829 | Oct. 1, 1829 |
| William Carroll (D) | Oct. 1, 1829 | Oct. 12, 1835 |
| Newton Cannon (W) | Oct. 12, 1835 | Oct. 14, 1839 |
| James K. Polk (D) | Oct. 14, 1839 | Oct. 15, 1841 |
| James C. Jones (W) | Oct. 15, 1841 | Oct. 14, 1845 |
| Aaron V. Brown (D) | Oct. 14, 1845 | Oct. 17, 1847 |
| Neill S. Brown (W) | Oct. 17, 1847 | Oct. 16, 1849 |
| William Trousdale (D) | Oct. 16, 1849 | Oct. 16, 1851 |
| William B. Campbell (W) | Oct. 16, 1851 | Oct. 17, 1853 |
| Andrew Johnson (D) | Oct. 17, 1853 | Nov. 3, 1857 |
| Isham G. Harris (D) | Nov. 3, 1857 | March 12, 1862 |
| Andrew Johnson[3] | March 12, 1862 | March 4, 1865 |
| William G. Brownlow (W, R)[4] | April 5, 1865 | Oct. 1867 |
| DeWitt Clinton Senter (CR)[5] | Oct. 11, 1867 | Oct. 10, 1871 |
| John C. Brown (D, LR) | Oct. 10, 1871 | Jan. 18, 1875 |
| James D. Porter Jr. (D) | Jan. 18, 1875 | Feb. 16, 1879 |
| Albert S. Marks (D) | Feb. 16, 1879 | Jan. 17, 1881 |
| Alvin Hawkins (R) | Jan. 17, 1881 | Jan. 15, 1883 |
| William B. Bate<br>  (LOWTAX D, D) | Jan. 15, 1883 | Jan. 17, 1887 |
| Robert L. Taylor (D) | Jan. 17, 1887 | Jan. 19, 1891 |
| John P. Buchanan (D) | Jan. 19, 1891 | Jan. 16, 1893 |
| Peter Turney (D)[6] | Jan. 16, 1893 | Jan. 21, 1897 |
| Robert L. Taylor (D) | Jan. 21, 1897 | Jan. 16, 1899 |
| Benton McMillin (D) | Jan. 16, 1899 | Jan. 19, 1903 |
| James B. Frazier (D)[7] | Jan. 19, 1903 | March 21, 1905 |
| John I. Cox (D)[8] | March 21, 1905 | Jan. 17, 1907 |
| Malcolm R. Patterson (D) | Jan. 17, 1907 | Jan. 26, 1911 |

| | | |
|---|---|---|
| Ben W. Hooper (R) | Jan. 26, 1911 | Jan. 17, 1915 |
| Thomas C. Rye (D) | Jan. 17, 1915 | Jan. 15, 1919 |
| Albert H. Roberts (D) | Jan. 15, 1919 | Jan. 15, 1921 |
| Alfred A. Taylor (R) | Jan. 15, 1921 | Jan. 16, 1923 |
| Austin Peay (D)[9] | Jan. 16, 1923 | Oct. 2, 1927 |
| Henry H. Horton (D)[10] | Oct. 3, 1927 | Jan. 17, 1933 |
| Hill McAlister (D) | Jan. 17, 1933 | Jan. 15, 1937 |
| Gordon Browning (D) | Jan. 15, 1937 | Jan. 16, 1939 |
| Prentice Cooper (D) | Jan. 16, 1939 | Jan. 16, 1945 |
| James N. McCord (D) | Jan. 16, 1945 | Jan. 17, 1949 |
| Gordon Browning (D) | Jan. 17, 1949 | Jan. 15, 1953 |
| Frank G. Clement (D) | Jan. 15, 1953 | Jan. 19, 1959 |
| Buford Ellington (D) | Jan. 19, 1959 | Jan. 15, 1963 |
| Frank G. Clement (D) | Jan. 15, 1963 | Jan. 16, 1967 |
| Buford Ellington (D) | Jan. 16, 1967 | Jan. 16, 1971 |
| Winfield Dunn (R) | Jan. 16, 1971 | Jan. 18, 1975 |
| Ray Blanton (D) | Jan. 18, 1975 | Jan. 17, 1979 |
| Lamar Alexander (R) | Jan. 17, 1979 | Jan. 17, 1987 |
| Ned R. McWherter (D) | Jan. 17, 1987 | |

**Tennessee**

1. Resigned April 16, 1829.
2. As Speaker of the state Senate, he succeeded to office.
3. Appointed military governor by President Lincoln.
4. Resigned in October 1867.
5. As Speaker of the state Senate, he succeeded to office. Subsequently elected.
6. Governor Turney ran for re-election in 1894, but his Republican opponent, H. Clay Evans, appeared to have won a narrow victory. There were allegations of fraud, however, resulting in a recount of the votes by the Legislature. The Legislature's count made Turney the winner, and he took office for a second term.
7. Resigned March 21, 1905.
8. As Speaker of the state Senate, he succeeded to office.
9. Died Oct. 2, 1927.
10. As Speaker of the state Senate, he succeeded to office. Subsequently elected.

| | | |
|---|---|---|
| Pat M. Neff (D) | Jan. 18, 1921 | Jan. 20, 1925 |
| Miriam A. Ferguson (D) | Jan. 20, 1925 | Jan. 18, 1927 |
| Dan Moody (D) | Jan. 18, 1927 | Jan. 20, 1931 |
| Ross M. Sterling (D) | Jan. 20, 1931 | Jan. 17, 1933 |
| Miriam A. Ferguson (D) | Jan. 17, 1933 | Jan. 15, 1935 |
| James V. Allred (D) | Jan. 15, 1935 | Jan. 17, 1939 |
| W. Lee O'Daniel (D)[13] | Jan. 17, 1939 | Aug. 4, 1941 |
| Coke R. Stevenson (D)[14] | Aug. 4, 1941 | Jan. 21, 1947 |
| Beauford H. Jester (D)[15] | Jan. 21, 1947 | July 11, 1949 |
| Allan Shivers (D)[16] | July 11, 1949 | Jan. 15, 1957 |
| Price Daniel (D) | Jan. 15, 1957 | Jan. 15, 1963 |
| John B. Connally (D) | Jan. 15, 1963 | Jan. 21, 1969 |
| Preston Smith (D) | Jan. 21, 1969 | Jan. 16, 1973 |
| Dolph Briscoe (D) | Jan. 16, 1973 | Jan. 16, 1979 |
| William P. Clements (R) | Jan. 16, 1979 | Jan. 18, 1983 |
| Mark White (D) | Jan. 18, 1983 | Jan. 20, 1987 |
| William P. Clements (R) | Jan. 20, 1987 | Jan. 15, 1991 |
| Ann W. Richards (D) | Jan. 15, 1991 | |

**Texas**

1. Resigned Nov. 23, 1853.
2. As lieutenant governor, he succeeded to office.
3. Resigned March 16, 1861.
4. As lieutenant governor, he succeeded to office.
5. Resigned Nov. 5, 1863.
6. Administration terminated June 17, 1865, due to fall of the Confederacy.
7. Provisional governor appointed by the president.
8. Appointed under martial law. Vacated office Sept. 30, 1869. Governorship is considered to have remained vacant until inauguration of Edmund J. Davis.
9. Resigned Dec. 1, 1876.
10. As lieutenant governor, he succeeded to office.
11. Impeached. Removed from office August 25, 1917.
12. As lieutenant governor, he succeeded to office. Subsequently elected.
13. Resigned Aug. 4, 1941.
14. As lieutenant governor, he succeeded to office. Subsequently elected.
15. Died July 11, 1949.
16. As lieutenant governor, he succeeded to office. Subsequently elected.

# TEXAS

(Became a state Dec. 29, 1845)

| Governors | Dates of Service | |
|---|---|---|
| Anson Jones (D) | Dec. 9, 1844 | Feb. 19, 1846 |
| J. Pinckney Henderson (D) | Feb. 19, 1846 | Dec. 21, 1847 |
| George T. Wood (D) | Dec. 21, 1847 | Dec. 21, 1849 |
| P. Hansbrough Bell (D)[1] | Dec. 21, 1849 | Nov. 23, 1853 |
| J. W. Henderson (D)[2] | Nov. 23, 1853 | Dec. 21, 1853 |
| Elisha M. Pease (D) | Dec. 21, 1853 | Dec. 21, 1857 |
| Hardin R. Runnels (D) | Dec. 21, 1857 | Dec. 21, 1859 |
| Sam Houston (ID)[3] | Dec. 21, 1859 | March 16, 1861 |
| Edward Clark (D)[4] | March 16, 1861 | Nov. 7, 1861 |
| Francis R. Lubbock[5] | Nov. 7, 1861 | Nov. 5, 1863 |
| Pendleton Murrah[6] | Nov. 5, 1863 | June 17, 1865 |
| Andrew J. Hamilton[7] | June 17, 1865 | Aug. 9, 1866 |
| J. W. Throckmorton (C) | Aug. 9, 1866 | Aug. 8, 1867 |
| Elisha M. Pease[8] | Aug. 8, 1867 | Sept. 30, 1869 |
| Edmund J. Davis (R) | Jan. 8, 1870 | Jan. 15, 1874 |
| Richard Coke (D)[9] | Jan. 15, 1874 | Dec. 1, 1876 |
| Richard B. Hubbard (D)[10] | Dec. 1, 1876 | Jan. 21, 1879 |
| Oran M. Roberts (D) | Jan. 21, 1879 | Jan. 16, 1883 |
| John Ireland (D) | Jan. 16, 1883 | Jan. 18, 1887 |
| Lawrence S. Ross (D) | Jan. 18, 1887 | Jan. 20, 1891 |
| James S. Hogg (D) | Jan. 20, 1891 | Jan. 15, 1895 |
| Charles A. Culberson (D) | Jan. 15, 1895 | Jan. 17, 1899 |
| Joseph D. Sayers (D) | Jan. 17, 1899 | Jan. 20, 1903 |
| Samuel W. T. Lanham (D) | Jan. 20, 1903 | Jan. 15, 1907 |
| Thomas M. Campbell (D) | Jan. 15, 1907 | Jan. 17, 1911 |
| Oscar B. Colquitt (D) | Jan. 17, 1911 | Jan. 19, 1915 |
| James E. Ferguson (D)[11] | Jan. 19, 1915 | Aug. 25, 1917 |
| William P. Hobby (D)[12] | Aug. 25, 1917 | Jan. 18, 1921 |

# UTAH

(Became a state Jan. 4, 1896)

| Governors | Dates of Service | |
|---|---|---|
| Heber Manning Wells (R) | Jan. 6, 1896 | Jan. 2, 1905 |
| John C. Cutler (R) | Jan. 2, 1905 | Jan. 4, 1909 |
| William Spry (R) | Jan. 4, 1909 | Jan. 1, 1917 |
| Simon Bamberger (D) | Jan. 1, 1917 | Jan. 3, 1921 |
| Charles R. Mabey (R) | Jan. 3, 1921 | Jan. 5, 1925 |
| George H. Dern (D) | Jan. 5, 1925 | Jan. 2, 1933 |
| Henry H. Blood (D) | Jan. 2, 1933 | Jan. 6, 1941 |
| Herbert B. Maw (D) | Jan. 6, 1941 | Jan. 3, 1949 |
| J. Bracken Lee (R) | Jan. 3, 1949 | Jan. 7, 1957 |
| George Dewey Clyde (R) | Jan. 7, 1957 | Jan. 4, 1965 |
| Calvin L. Rampton (D) | Jan. 4, 1965 | Jan. 3, 1977 |
| Scott M. Matheson (D) | Jan. 3, 1977 | Jan. 7, 1985 |
| Norman H. Bangerter (R) | Jan. 7, 1985 | Jan. 3, 1993 |
| Mike Leavitt (R) | Jan. 3, 1993 | |

# VERMONT

(Became a state March 4, 1791)

| Governors | Dates of Service | |
|---|---|---|
| Thomas Chittenden[1] | March 4, 1791 | Aug. 25, 1797 |
| Paul Brigham[2] | Aug. 25, 1797 | Oct. 16, 1797 |
| Isaac Tichenor (FED) | Oct. 16, 1797 | Oct. 9, 1807 |
| Israel Smith (D-R) | Oct. 9, 1807 | Oct. 14, 1808 |
| Isaac Tichenor (FED) | Oct. 14, 1808 | Oct. 14, 1809 |

| | | |
|---|---|---|
| Jonas Galusha (D-R) | Oct. 14, 1809 | Oct. 23, 1813 |
| Martin Chittenden (FED) | Oct. 23, 1813 | Oct. 14, 1815 |
| Jonas Galusha (D-R) | Oct. 14, 1815 | Oct. 13, 1820 |
| Richard Skinner (D-R) | Oct. 13, 1820 | Oct. 10, 1823 |
| Cornelius P. Van Ness (D-R) | Oct. 13, 1823 | Oct. 13, 1826 |
| Ezra Butler (D-R) | Oct. 13, 1826 | Oct. 10, 1828 |
| Samuel C. Crafts (NR) | Oct. 10, 1828 | Oct. 18, 1831 |
| William A. Palmer (A-MAS) | Oct. 18, 1831 | Nov. 2, 1835 |
| Silas H. Jennison (W)[3] | Nov. 2, 1835 | Oct. 15, 1841 |
| Charles Paine (W) | Oct. 15, 1841 | Oct. 13, 1843 |
| John Mattocks (W) | Oct. 13, 1843 | Oct. 11, 1844 |
| William Slade (W) | Oct. 11, 1844 | Oct. 9, 1846 |
| Horace Eaton (W) | Oct. 9, 1846 | Oct. 1848 |
| Carlos Coolidge (W) | Oct. 1848 | Oct. 11, 1850 |
| Charles K. Williams (W) | Oct. 11, 1850 | Oct. 1852 |
| Erastus Fairbanks (W) | Oct. 1852 | Oct. 1853 |
| John S. Robinson (D) | Oct. 1853 | Oct. 13, 1854 |
| Stephen Royce (W, R) | Oct. 13, 1854 | Oct. 10, 1856 |
| Ryland Fletcher (R) | Oct. 10, 1856 | Oct. 10, 1858 |
| Hiland Hall (R) | Oct. 10, 1858 | Oct. 12, 1860 |
| Erastus Fairbanks (R) | Oct. 12, 1860 | Oct. 11, 1861 |
| Frederick Holbrook (R) | Oct. 11, 1861 | Oct. 9, 1863 |
| John Gregory Smith (R) | Oct. 9, 1863 | Oct. 13, 1865 |
| Paul Dillingham (R) | Oct. 13, 1865 | Oct. 13, 1867 |
| John B. Page (R) | Oct. 13, 1867 | Oct. 15, 1869 |
| Peter T. Washburn (R)[4] | Oct. 15, 1869 | Feb. 7, 1870 |
| George W. Hendee (R)[5] | Feb. 7, 1870 | Oct. 6, 1870 |
| John W. Stewart (R) | Oct. 6, 1870 | Oct. 3, 1872 |
| Julius Converse (R) | Oct. 3, 1872 | Oct. 8, 1874 |
| Asahel Peck (R) | Oct. 8, 1874 | Oct. 5, 1876 |
| Horace Fairbanks (R) | Oct. 5, 1876 | Oct. 3, 1878 |
| Redfield Proctor (R) | Oct. 3, 1878 | Oct. 7, 1880 |
| Roswell Farnham (R) | Oct. 7, 1880 | Oct. 5, 1882 |
| John L. Barstow (R) | Oct. 5, 1882 | Oct. 2, 1884 |
| Samuel E. Pingree (R) | Oct. 2, 1884 | Oct. 7, 1886 |
| Ebenezer J. Ormsbee (R) | Oct. 7, 1886 | Oct. 4, 1888 |
| William P. Dillingham (R) | Oct. 4, 1888 | Oct. 2, 1890 |
| Carroll S. Page (R) | Oct. 2, 1890 | Oct. 6, 1892 |
| Levi K. Fuller (R) | Oct. 6, 1892 | Oct. 4, 1894 |
| Urban A. Woodbury (R) | Oct. 4, 1894 | Oct. 8, 1896 |
| Josiah Grout (R) | Oct. 8, 1896 | Oct. 6, 1898 |
| Edward C. Smith (R) | Oct. 6, 1898 | Oct. 4, 1900 |
| William W. Stickney (R) | Oct. 4, 1900 | Oct. 3, 1902 |
| John G. McCullough (R) | Oct. 3, 1902 | Oct. 6, 1904 |
| Charles J. Bell (R) | Oct. 6, 1904 | Oct. 4, 1906 |
| Fletcher D. Proctor (R) | Oct. 4, 1906 | Oct. 8, 1908 |
| George H. Prouty (R) | Oct. 8, 1908 | Oct. 5, 1910 |
| John A. Mead (R) | Oct. 5, 1910 | Oct. 3, 1912 |
| Allen M. Fletcher (R) | Oct. 3, 1912 | Jan. 7, 1915 |
| Charles W. Gates (R) | Jan. 7, 1915 | Jan. 4, 1917 |
| Horace F. Graham (R) | Jan. 4, 1917 | Jan. 9, 1919 |
| Percival W. Clement (R) | Jan. 9, 1919 | Jan. 6, 1921 |
| James Hartness (R) | Jan. 6, 1921 | Jan. 4, 1923 |
| Redfield Proctor (R) | Jan. 4, 1923 | Jan. 8, 1925 |
| Franklin S. Billings (R) | Jan. 8, 1925 | Jan. 6, 1927 |
| John E. Weeks (R) | Jan. 6, 1927 | Jan. 8, 1931 |
| Stanley C. Wilson (R) | Jan. 8, 1931 | Jan. 10, 1935 |
| Charles M. Smith (R) | Jan. 10, 1935 | Jan. 7, 1937 |
| George D. Aiken (R) | Jan. 7, 1937 | Jan. 9, 1941 |
| William H. Wills (R) | Jan. 9, 1941 | Jan. 4, 1945 |
| Mortimer R. Proctor (R) | Jan. 4, 1945 | Jan. 9, 1947 |
| Ernest W. Gibson (R)[6] | Jan. 9, 1947 | Jan. 16, 1950 |
| Harold J. Arthur (R)[7] | Jan. 16, 1950 | Jan. 4, 1951 |
| Lee E. Emerson (R) | Jan. 4, 1951 | Jan. 6, 1955 |
| Joseph B. Johnson (R) | Jan. 6, 1955 | Jan. 8, 1959 |
| Robert T. Stafford (R) | Jan. 8, 1959 | Jan. 5, 1961 |
| Frank Ray Keyser Jr. (R) | Jan. 5, 1961 | Jan. 10, 1963 |
| Philip H. Hoff (D) | Jan. 10, 1963 | Jan. 9, 1969 |
| Deane C. Davis (R) | Jan. 9, 1969 | Jan. 4, 1973 |
| Thomas P. Salmon (D) | Jan. 4, 1973 | Jan. 6, 1977 |
| Richard A. Snelling (R) | Jan. 6, 1977 | Jan. 10, 1985 |
| Madeleine M. Kunin (D) | Jan. 10, 1985 | Jan. 10, 1991 |
| Richard A. Snelling (R)[8] | Jan. 10, 1991 | Aug. 14, 1991 |
| Howard Dean (D)[9] | Aug. 14, 1991 | |

**Vermont**
1. *Died Aug. 25, 1797.*
2. *As lieutenant governor, he succeeded to office.*
3. *No candidate received a majority of the vote and the Legislature failed to elect a governor in 1835. Silas H. Jennison, the lieutenant governor, served as governor for the term and was subsequently elected.*
4. *Died Feb. 7, 1870.*
5. *As lieutenant governor, he succeeded to office.*
6. *Resigned Jan. 16, 1950.*
7. *As lieutenant governor, he succeeded to office.*
8. *Died Aug. 14, 1991.*
9. *As lieutenant governor, he succeeded to office. Subsequently elected.*

# VIRGINIA

(Ratified the Constitution June 25, 1788)

| Governors | Dates of Service | |
|---|---|---|
| Beverley Randolph | Dec. 3, 1788 | Dec. 1, 1791 |
| Henry Lee | Dec. 1, 1791 | Dec. 1, 1794 |
| Robert Brooke | Dec. 1, 1794 | Dec. 1, 1796 |
| James Wood (D-R) | Dec. 1, 1796 | Dec. 1, 1799 |
| James Monroe (D-R) | Dec. 1, 1799 | Dec. 1, 1802 |
| John Page (D-R) | Dec. 1, 1802 | Dec. 1, 1805 |
| William H. Cabell (D-R) | Dec. 7, 1805 | Dec. 1, 1808 |
| John Tyler Sr. (D-R) | Dec. 1, 1808 | Jan. 1811 |
| James Monroe (D-R)[1] | Jan. 16, 1811 | April 5, 1811 |
| George William Smith (D-R)[2] | April 6, 1811 | Dec. 26, 1811 |
| Peyton Randolph (D-R)[3] | Dec. 27, 1811 | Jan. 3, 1812 |
| James Barbour(D-R) | Jan. 3, 1812 | Dec. 1, 1814 |
| Wilson Carey Nicholas (D-R) | Dec. 1, 1814 | Dec. 1, 1816 |
| James P. Preston (D-R) | Dec. 1, 1816 | Dec. 1, 1819 |
| Thomas M. Randolph (D-R) | Dec. 1, 1819 | Dec. 1, 1822 |
| James Pleasants (D-R) | Dec. 1, 1822 | Dec. 1825 |
| John Tyler Jr. (D-R) | Dec. 10, 1825 | March 4, 1827 |
| William B. Giles (D) | March 4, 1827 | March 4, 1830 |
| John Floyd (D) | March 4, 1830 | March 31, 1834 |
| Littleton W. Tazewell (D)[4] | March 31, 1834 | April 30, 1836 |
| Wyndham Robertson (D)[5] | April 30, 1836 | March 31, 1837 |
| David Campbell (D) | March 31, 1837 | March 31, 1840 |
| Thomas W. Gilmer (W)[6] | March 31, 1840 | March 1841 |
| John Mercer Patton (W)[7] | March 18, 1841 | March 31, 1841 |
| John Rutherford (W)[8] | March 31, 1841 | March 31, 1842 |
| John M. Gregory (W)[9] | March 31, 1842 | Jan. 1, 1843 |
| James McDowell (W) | Jan. 1, 1843 | Jan. 1, 1846 |
| William Smith (D) | Jan. 1, 1846 | Jan. 1, 1849 |
| John B. Floyd (D) | Jan. 1, 1849 | Jan. 16, 1852 |
| Joseph Johnson (D) | Jan. 16, 1852 | Dec. 31, 1855 |
| Henry A. Wise (D) | Jan. 1, 1856 | Dec. 31, 1859 |
| John Letcher (D) | Jan. 1, 1860 | Dec. 31, 1863 |
| William Smith (D)[10] | Jan. 1, 1864 | April 1865 |
| Francis H. Peirpoint[11] | June 20, 1861 | April 4, 1868 |
| Henry H. Wells[12] | April 4, 1868 | Sept. 21, 1869 |
| Gilbert C. Walker (C)[13] | Sept. 21, 1869 | Jan. 1, 1874 |
| James Lawson Kemper (D) | Jan. 1, 1874 | Jan. 1, 1878 |
| Frederick W. M. Holliday (D) | Jan. 1, 1878 | Jan. 1, 1882 |
| William E. Cameron (READJ) | Jan. 1, 1882 | Jan. 1, 1886 |
| Fitzhugh Lee (D) | Jan. 1, 1886 | Jan. 1, 1890 |
| Philip W. McKinney (D) | Jan. 1, 1890 | Jan. 1, 1894 |
| Charles T. O'Ferrall (D) | Jan. 1, 1894 | Jan. 1, 1898 |
| James Hoge Tyler (D) | Jan. 1, 1898 | Jan. 1, 1902 |
| Andrew J. Montague (D) | Jan. 1, 1902 | Feb. 1, 1906 |
| Claude A. Swanson (D) | Feb. 1, 1906 | Feb. 1, 1910 |
| William H. Mann (D) | Feb. 1, 1910 | Feb. 1, 1914 |
| Henry C. Stuart (D) | Feb. 1, 1914 | Feb. 1, 1918 |
| Westmoreland Davis (D) | Feb. 1, 1918 | Feb. 1, 1922 |
| E. Lee Trinkle (D) | Feb. 1, 1922 | Feb. 1, 1926 |
| Harry F. Byrd (D) | Feb. 1, 1926 | Jan. 15, 1930 |

| | | |
|---|---|---|
| John G. Pollard (D) | Jan. 15, 1930 | Jan. 17, 1934 |
| George C. Peery (D) | Jan. 17, 1934 | Jan. 19, 1938 |
| James H. Price (D) | Jan. 19, 1938 | Jan. 21, 1942 |
| Colgate W. Darden Jr. (D) | Jan. 21, 1942 | Jan. 16, 1946 |
| William M. Tuck (D) | Jan. 16, 1946 | Jan. 18, 1950 |
| John S. Battle (D) | Jan. 18, 1950 | Jan. 20, 1954 |
| Thomas B. Stanley (D) | Jan. 20, 1954 | Jan. 11, 1958 |
| James Lindsay Almond Jr. (D) | Jan. 11, 1958 | Jan. 13, 1962 |
| Albertis S. Harrison Jr. (D) | Jan. 13, 1962 | Jan. 15, 1966 |
| Mills E. Godwin Jr. (D) | Jan. 16, 1966 | Jan. 17, 1970 |
| Linwood Holton (R) | Jan. 17, 1970 | Jan. 12, 1974 |
| Mills E. Godwin Jr. (R) | Jan. 12, 1974 | Jan. 14, 1978 |
| John Dalton (R) | Jan. 14, 1978 | Jan. 16, 1982 |
| Charles S. Robb (D) | Jan. 16, 1982 | Jan. 18, 1986 |
| Gerald L. Baliles (D) | Jan. 18, 1986 | Jan. 14, 1990 |
| L. Douglas Wilder (D) | Jan. 14, 1990 | Jan. 15, 1994 |
| George F. Allen (R) | Jan. 15, 1994 | |

**Virginia**

1. *Resigned April 5, 1811.*
2. *As senior member of the Council of State, became acting governor. Died Dec. 1811.*
3. *As senior member of the Council of State, became acting governor.*
4. *Resigned April 30, 1836.*
5. *As senior member of the Council of State, became acting governor.*
6. *Resigned in March 1841.*
7. *As senior member of the Council of State, became acting governor. Following Gilmer's resignation, the Legislature did not elect a new governor for 21 months. Patton, Rutherford and Gregory took turns as acting governor.*
8. *As senior member of the Council of State, became acting governor.*
9. *As senior member of the Council of State, became acting governor.*
10. *Last Confederate governor.*
11. *Became Union governor June 20, 1861. Appointed provisional governor May 9, 1865.*
12. *Provisional governor.*
13. *Provisional governor from September 1869 to Jan. 1, 1870. Elected to four-year term beginning Jan. 1, 1870.*

# WASHINGTON

(Became a state Nov. 11, 1889)

| Governors | Dates of Service | |
|---|---|---|
| Elisha P. Ferry (R) | Nov. 11, 1889 | Jan. 9, 1893 |
| John H. McGraw (R) | Jan. 9, 1893 | Jan. 11, 1897 |
| John R. Rogers (PP, D)[1] | Jan. 11, 1897 | Dec. 26, 1901 |
| Henry McBride (R)[2] | Dec. 26, 1901 | Jan. 9, 1905 |
| Albert E. Mead (R) | Jan. 9, 1905 | Jan. 27, 1909 |
| Samuel G. Cosgrove (R)[3] | Jan. 27, 1909 | March 28, 1909 |
| Marion E. Hay (R)[4] | March 29, 1909 | Jan. 11, 1913 |
| Ernest Lister (D)[5] | Jan. 11, 1913 | June 14, 1919 |
| Louis F. Hart (R)[6] | June 14, 1919 | Jan. 12, 1925 |
| Roland H. Hartley (R) | Jan. 12, 1925 | Jan. 9, 1933 |
| Clarence D. Martin (D) | Jan. 9, 1933 | Jan. 13, 1941 |
| Arthur B. Langlie (R) | Jan. 13, 1941 | Jan. 8, 1945 |
| Monrad C. Wallgren (D) | Jan. 8, 1945 | Jan. 10, 1949 |
| Arthur B. Langlie (R) | Jan. 10, 1949 | Jan. 14, 1957 |
| Albert D. Rosellini (D) | Jan. 14, 1957 | Jan. 11, 1965 |
| Daniel J. Evans (R) | Jan. 11, 1965 | Jan. 12, 1977 |
| Dixy Lee Ray (D) | Jan. 12, 1977 | Jan. 14, 1981 |
| John D. Spellman (R) | Jan. 14, 1981 | Jan. 16, 1985 |
| Booth Gardner (D) | Jan. 16, 1985 | Jan. 13, 1993 |
| Mike Lowry (D) | Jan. 13, 1993 | |

**Washington**

1. *Elected as a Populist in 1896. Elected as a Democrat in 1900. Died Dec. 26, 1901.*
2. *As lieutenant governor, he succeeded to office.*
3. *Died March 28, 1909.*
4. *As lieutenant governor, he succeeded to office.*

5. *Died June 14, 1919.*
6. *As lieutenant governor, he succeeded to office. Subsequently elected.*

# WEST VIRGINIA

(Became a state June 19, 1863)

| Governors | Dates of Service | |
|---|---|---|
| Arthur I. Boreman (UN R, R)[1] | June 20, 1863 | Feb. 26, 1869 |
| Daniel D. T. Farnsworth (R)[2] | Feb. 27, 1869 | March 3, 1869 |
| William E. Stevenson (R) | March 4, 1869 | March 3, 1871 |
| John Jeremiah Jacob (D, I) | March 4, 1871 | March 3, 1877 |
| Henry Mason Mathews (D) | March 4, 1877 | March 3, 1881 |
| Jacob B. Jackson (D) | March 4, 1881 | March 3, 1885 |
| Emanuel Willis Wilson (D)[3] | March 4, 1885 | Feb. 5, 1890 |
| Aretas Brooks Fleming (D)[4] | Feb. 6, 1890 | March 3, 1893 |
| William A. MacCorkle (D) | March 4, 1893 | March 3, 1897 |
| George W. Atkinson (R) | March 4, 1897 | March 4, 1901 |
| Albert B. White (R) | March 4, 1901 | March 4, 1905 |
| William M. O. Dawson (R) | March 4, 1905 | March 4, 1909 |
| William E. Glasscock (R) | March 4, 1909 | March 4, 1913 |
| Henry D. Hatfield (R) | March 4, 1913 | March 4, 1917 |
| John J. Cornwell (D) | March 4, 1917 | March 4, 1921 |
| Ephraim F. Morgan (R) | March 4, 1921 | March 4, 1925 |
| Howard M. Gore (R) | March 4, 1925 | March 4, 1929 |
| William G. Conley (R) | March 4, 1929 | March 4, 1933 |
| Herman G. Kump (D) | March 4, 1933 | Jan. 18, 1937 |
| Homer A. Holt (D) | Jan. 18, 1937 | Jan. 13, 1941 |
| Matthew M. Neely (D) | Jan. 13, 1941 | Jan. 15, 1945 |
| Clarence W. Meadows (D) | Jan. 15, 1945 | Jan. 17, 1949 |
| Okey L. Patteson (D) | Jan. 17, 1949 | Jan. 19, 1953 |
| William C. Marland (D) | Jan. 19, 1953 | Jan. 14, 1957 |
| Cecil H. Underwood (R) | Jan. 14, 1957 | Jan. 16, 1961 |
| William W. Barron (D) | Jan. 16, 1961 | Jan. 18, 1965 |
| Hulett C. Smith (D) | Jan. 18, 1965 | Jan. 13, 1969 |
| Arch A. Moore Jr. (R) | Jan. 13, 1969 | Jan. 17, 1977 |
| John D. Rockefeller (D) | Jan. 17, 1977 | Jan. 14, 1985 |
| Arch A. Moore Jr. (R) | Jan. 14, 1985 | Jan. 16, 1989 |
| Gaston Caperton (D) | Jan. 16, 1989 | |

**West Virginia**

1. *Resigned Feb. 26, 1869.*
2. *As president of the state Senate, he succeeded to office.*
3. *Wilson continued in office for almost one year beyond the expiration of his term pending a settlement of the disputed election of 1888.*
4. *The 1888 election between Democrat Aretas Brooks Fleming and Republican Nathan Goff was very close, and the final outcome was in dispute. After almost one year of investigation, the West Virginia Legislature declared Fleming the winner, and he took office Feb. 6, 1890.*

# WISCONSIN

(Became a state May 29, 1848)

| Governors | Dates of Service | |
|---|---|---|
| Nelson Dewey (D) | June 7, 1848 | Jan. 5, 1852 |
| Leonard J. Farwell (W) | Jan. 5, 1852 | Jan. 2, 1854 |
| William A. Barstow (D)[1] | Jan. 2, 1854 | March 21, 1856 |
| Arthur MacArthur (D)[2] | March 21, 1856 | March 25, 1856 |
| Coles Bashford (R)[3] | March 25, 1856 | |
| Alexander W. Randall (R) | Jan. 4, 1858 | Jan. 6, 1862 |
| Louis P. Harvey (R)[4] | Jan. 6, 1862 | April 19, 1862 |
| Edward Salomon (R)[5] | April 19, 1862 | Jan. 4, 1864 |
| James T. Lewis (R) | Jan. 4, 1864 | Jan. 1, 1866 |
| Lucius Fairchild (R) | Jan. 1, 1866 | Jan. 1, 1872 |
| Cadwallader C. Washburn (R) | Jan. 1, 1872 | Jan. 5, 1874 |
| William R. Taylor (D) | Jan. 5, 1874 | Jan. 3, 1876 |
| Harrison Ludington (R) | Jan. 3, 1876 | Jan. 7, 1878 |

| | | |
|---|---|---|
| William E. Smith (R) | Jan. 7, 1878 | Jan. 2, 1882 |
| Jeremiah M. Rusk (R) | Jan. 2, 1882 | Jan. 7, 1889 |
| William D. Hoard (R) | Jan. 7, 1889 | Jan. 5, 1891 |
| George W. Peck (D) | Jan. 5, 1891 | Jan. 7, 1895 |
| William H. Upham (R) | Jan. 7, 1895 | Jan. 4, 1897 |
| Edward Scofield (R) | Jan. 4, 1897 | Jan. 7, 1901 |
| Robert M. La Follette (R)[6] | Jan. 7, 1901 | Jan. 1, 1906 |
| James O. Davidson (R)[7] | Jan. 1, 1906 | Jan. 2, 1911 |
| Francis E. McGovern (R) | Jan. 2, 1911 | Jan. 4, 1915 |
| Emanuel L. Philipp (R) | Jan. 4, 1915 | Jan. 3, 1921 |
| John J. Blaine (R) | Jan. 3, 1921 | Jan. 3, 1927 |
| Fred R. Zimmerman (R) | Jan. 3, 1927 | Jan. 7, 1929 |
| Walter J. Kohler Sr. (R) | Jan. 7, 1929 | Jan. 5, 1931 |
| Philip F. La Follette (R) | Jan. 5, 1931 | Jan. 2, 1933 |
| Albert G. Schmedeman (D) | Jan. 2, 1933 | Jan. 7, 1935 |
| Philip F. La Follette (PROG) | Jan. 7, 1935 | Jan. 2, 1939 |
| Julius P. Heil (R) | Jan. 2, 1939 | Jan. 4, 1943 |
| Orland S. Loomis (PROG)[8] | | |
| Walter S. Goodland (R)[9] | Jan. 4, 1943 | March 12, 1947 |
| Oscar Rennebohm (R)[10] | March 12, 1947 | Jan. 1, 1951 |
| Walter J. Kohler Jr. (R) | Jan. 1, 1951 | Jan. 7, 1957 |
| Vernon W. Thomson (R) | Jan. 7, 1957 | Jan. 5, 1959 |
| Gaylord A. Nelson (D) | Jan. 5, 1959 | Jan. 7, 1963 |
| John W. Reynolds (D) | Jan. 7, 1963 | Jan. 4, 1965 |
| Warren P. Knowles (R) | Jan. 4, 1965 | Jan. 4, 1971 |
| Patrick J. Lucey (D)[11] | Jan. 4, 1971 | July 7, 1977 |
| M. J. Schreiber (D)[12] | July 7, 1977 | Jan. 1, 1979 |
| Lee S. Dreyfus (R) | Jan. 1, 1979 | Jan. 3, 1983 |
| Anthony S. Earl (D) | Jan. 3, 1983 | Jan. 5, 1987 |
| Tommy G. Thompson (R) | Jan. 5, 1987 | |

**Wisconsin**

*1. Barstow's election to a second term in 1855 was disputed by his opponent, Coles Bashford, who charged fraud. Barstow took office, but resigned while the case was pending in court. The office was awarded to Bashford several days later.*

*2. Acting governor.*

*3. Successfully contested the election of William Augustus Barstow and served out the remainder of the term.*

*4. Died April 19, 1862.*

*5. Acting governor.*

*6. Resigned Jan. 1, 1906.*

*7. As lieutenant governor, he succeeded to office. Subsequently elected.*

*8. Elected in 1942 for a two-year term, but died Dec. 7, 1942, before inauguration.*

*9. As lieutenant governor, he succeeded to office. Subsequently elected. Died March 12, 1947.*

*10. As lieutenant governor, he succeeded to office. Subsequently elected.*

*11. Resigned July 7, 1977.*

*12. As lieutenant governor, he succeeded to office.*

# WYOMING

(Became a state July 10, 1890)

| Governors | Dates of Service | |
|---|---|---|
| Francis E. Warren (R)[1] | Oct. 11, 1890 | Nov. 24, 1890 |
| Amos W. Barber (R)[2] | Nov. 24, 1890 | Jan. 2, 1893 |

| | | |
|---|---|---|
| John E. Osborne (D)[3] | Jan. 2, 1893 | Jan. 7, 1895 |
| William A. Richards (R) | Jan. 7, 1895 | Jan. 2, 1899 |
| DeForest Richards (R)[4] | Jan. 2, 1899 | April 28, 1903 |
| Fenimore C. Chatterton (R)[5] | April 28, 1903 | Jan. 2, 1905 |
| Bryant B. Brooks (R)[6] | Jan. 2, 1905 | Jan. 2, 1911 |
| Joseph M. Carey (D) | Jan. 2, 1911 | Jan. 4, 1915 |
| John B. Kendrick (D)[7] | Jan. 4, 1915 | Feb. 26, 1917 |
| Frank L. Houx (D)[8] | Feb. 26, 1917 | Jan. 6, 1919 |
| Robert D. Carey (R) | Jan. 6, 1919 | Jan. 1, 1923 |
| William B. Ross (D)[9] | Jan. 1, 1923 | Oct. 2, 1924 |
| Frank E. Lucas (R)[10] | Oct. 2, 1924 | Jan. 5, 1925 |
| Nellie T. Ross (D)[11] | Jan. 5, 1925 | Jan. 3, 1927 |
| Frank C. Emerson (R)[12] | Jan. 3, 1927 | Feb. 18, 1931 |
| Alonzo M. Clark (R)[13] | Feb. 18, 1931 | Jan. 2, 1933 |
| Leslie A. Miller (D)[14] | Jan. 2, 1933 | Jan. 2, 1939 |
| Nels H. Smith (R) | Jan. 2, 1939 | Jan. 4, 1943 |
| Lester C. Hunt (D)[15] | Jan. 4, 1943 | Jan. 3, 1949 |
| Arthur G. Crane (R)[16] | Jan. 3, 1949 | Jan. 1, 1951 |
| Frank A. Barrett (R)[17] | Jan. 1, 1951 | Jan. 3, 1953 |
| Clifford Joy Rogers (R)[18] | Jan. 3, 1953 | Jan. 3, 1955 |
| Milward L. Simpson (R) | Jan. 3, 1955 | Jan. 5, 1959 |
| John J. Hickey (D)[19] | Jan. 5, 1959 | Jan. 2, 1961 |
| Jack R. Gage (D)[20] | Jan. 2, 1961 | Jan. 6, 1963 |
| Clifford P. Hansen (R) | Jan. 7, 1963 | Jan. 2, 1967 |
| Stanley K. Hathaway (R) | Jan. 2, 1967 | Jan. 6, 1975 |
| Ed Herschler (D) | Jan. 6, 1975 | Jan. 5, 1987 |
| Michael J. Sullivan (D) | Jan. 5, 1987 | |

**Wyoming**

*1. Resigned Nov. 24, 1890.*

*2. As secretary of state, he succeeded to office for the remainder of the first half of Gov. Warren's term.*

*3. Elected in a special election for the second half of Warren's term.*

*4. Died April 28, 1903.*

*5. As secretary of state, he succeeded to office for the remainder of the first half of Richards' term.*

*6. Elected in a special election for second half of Richards' term. Subsequently re-elected.*

*7. Resigned Feb. 26, 1917.*

*8. As secretary of state, he succeeded to office.*

*9. Died Oct. 2, 1924.*

*10. As secretary of state, he succeeded to office for the remainder of the first half of Ross' term.*

*11. Elected in a special election for the second half of Ross' (her husband's) term.*

*12. Died Feb. 18, 1931.*

*13. As secretary of state, he succeeded to office for the remainder of the first half of Gov. Emerson's term.*

*14. Elected in a special election for the second half of Emerson's term. Subsequently re-elected.*

*15. Resigned Jan. 3, 1949.*

*16. As secretary of state, he succeeded to office.*

*17. Resigned Jan. 3, 1953.*

*18. As secretary of state, he succeeded to office.*

*19. Resigned Jan. 2, 1961.*

*20. As secretary of state, he succeeded to office.*

# Gubernatorial Popular
# Vote Returns, 1787-1993

# Sources for Gubernatorial Returns

The gubernatorial popular election returns presented in this section *(pp. 667-716)* for the years 1787 through 1823 were obtained from *American State Governors, 1776-1976,* by Joseph E. Kallenbach and Jessamine S. Kallenbach (Dobbs Ferry, N.Y.: Oceana Publishing, 1977). Those for 1824 through 1973 were obtained from the Inter-University Consortium for Political and Social Research (ICPSR) at the University of Michigan. Major sources for returns since 1973 were Congressional Quarterly, which obtained them from the state secretaries of state, and the *America Votes* series, compiled biennially by Richard M. Scammon and Alice V. McGillivray of the Elections Research Center, Washington, D.C., and published by Congressional Quarterly.

The symbol # next to returns before 1974 indicates that Congressional Quarterly obtained the returns from a source other than Kallenbach or the ICPSR. A complete list of other sources used appears on page 716. A "Gubernatorial Candidates Index" is located on pages 1368-1380.

While complete source annotations for the ICPSR collection are too extensive to publish here, information on the sources for returns from specific elections can be obtained through the ICPSR. *(ICPSR collection, box, p. x.)*

## Presentation of Returns

The gubernatorial returns are arranged alphabetically by state and in chronological order of election within each state listing. The candidate receiving the greatest number of popular votes is listed first with his or her vote total and percentage of the total vote cast, followed in descending order of votes received by all other candidates receiving *at least 5 percent* of the total vote cast.

Special elections to fill vacancies are designated in the returns.

## Vote Totals and Percentages

The ICPSR collection includes all candidates receiving popular votes. In the *Guide to U.S. Elections, Third Edition,* only gubernatorial candidates receiving *at least 5 percent of the total vote* for that election are included. For example, the ICPSR data collection for the 1908 Illinois gubernatorial election shows that 1,154,612 votes were cast, with Republican Charles S. Deneen receiving 550,076 votes (47.64 percent), Democrat Adlai E. Stevenson receiving 526,912 votes (45.64 percent) and four other candidates receiving the remaining 77,624 votes (6.72 percent). These four candidates do not appear on page 677 of this book because none of them received 5 percent or more of the vote.

The percentages used in this section were calculated to two decimal places on the basis of the total number of votes cast in the election and rounded to one place. Thus, on page 677, for the 1908 Illinois election, Deneen's percentage of the total vote is listed as 47.6 percent and Stevenson's as 45.6 percent. The percentages are rounded to one decimal place and do not add to 100 percent because of the scattered votes for the other four candidates.

## Names and Party Designations

Names are listed as they were recorded in the official returns or other source documentation. In some instances, particularly in the 19th century, candidate names in the ICPSR file are incomplete. First names were the most commonly missing elements in the original sources consulted by the scholars and archivists who gathered the ICPSR returns. Congressional Quarterly has added full names when they could be determined and has corrected obvious misspellings.

In the ICPSR returns, the distinct — and in many cases, *multiple* — party designations appearing in the original sources are preserved. In many cases party labels represent combinations of multi-party support received by individual candidates. If, for example, on the ballot and official returns more than one party name was listed next to a candidate's name, then the party designation appearing in the election returns for that candidate will be a unique abbreviation for that combination of parties. *(For a list of party abbreviations, see p. 1352.)*

In the special case of a candidate's name listed separately on the original ballot under more than one party — where returns were reported *separately* for each party — Congressional Quarterly has summed the votes recorded under the several parties and that figure appears as the candidate's total vote. Whenever separate party totals have been summed, a *comma* separates the abbreviations of the parties contributing the largest and second largest share of the total vote.

Most cases of this special situation occurred in New York and Pennsylvania during this century. For example, in the original ICPSR returns for New York's 1946 gubernatorial election, James M. Mead received 1,532,161 votes as Democratic Party candidate, 428,903 votes as American Labor Party candidate and 177,418 votes as Liberal Party candidate for a total of 2,138,482 votes.

In organizing the ICPSR data for publication, Congressional Quarterly has summed all votes Mead received from these three parties. Thus, on page 698 only Mead's total vote of 2,138,482 appears.

Congressional Quarterly has also included party abbreviations for the two parties that contributed the most votes to Mead's total — separated by a comma. Thus, immediately following his name appear the abbreviations — D, AM LAB — indicating that Mead was a candidate of at least two parties and that the greatest number of votes he received was as a Democrat.

# Gubernatorial Popular Vote Returns, 1787-1993

## ALABAMA

(Became a state Dec. 14, 1819)

| | Candidates | Votes | % |
|---|---|---|---|
| 1819 | William Wyatt Bibb (D-R) | 8,342 | 53.9 |
| | M. D. Williams | 7,140 | 46.1 |
| 1821 | Israel Pickens (D-R) | 9,616 | 57.4 |
| | Dr. Henry Chambers | 7,129 | 42.6 |
| 1823 | Israel Pickens (D-R) | 10,534 | 56.7 |
| | Dr. Henry Chambers | 8,035 | 43.3 |
| 1825 | John Murphy (JAC D) | 12,184 | 100.0 |
| 1827 | John Murphy (JAC D) | 8,334 | 99.2 |
| 1829 | Gabriel Moore (JAC D) | 10,956 | 100.0 |
| 1831 | John Gayle (D) | 15,309 | 55.5 |
| | Nicholas Davis (NR) | 8,923 | 32.4 |
| | Samuel B. Moore | 3,354 | 12.2 |
| 1833 | John Gayle (D) | 9,750 | 100.0 |
| 1835 | Clement Comer Clay (D) | 25,491 | 64.8 |
| | Enoch Parsons (SR W) | 13,760 | 35.0 |
| 1837 | Arthur P. Bagby (D) | 23,902 | 53.7 |
| | Samuel W. Oliver (A-VB D) | 20,605 | 46.3 |
| 1839 | Arthur P. Bagby (D) | 22,681 | 89.9 |
| | Arthur F. Hopkins (W) | 2,532 | 10.0 |
| 1841 | Benjamin Fitzpatrick (D) | 31,808 | 58.3 |
| | James W. McClung (IW) | 22,777 | 41.7 |
| 1843 | Benjamin Fitzpatrick (D) | ✔ | |
| 1845 | Joshua L. Martin (I) | 29,261 | 52.1 |
| | Nathaniel Terry (D) | 25,473 | 45.3 |
| 1847 | Reuben Chapman (D) | 35,880 | 55.7 |
| | Nicholas Davis (W) | 28,565 | 44.3 |
| 1849 | Henry Watkins Collier (D) | 37,221 | 98.1 |
| 1851 | Henry Watkins Collier (D) | 38,517 | 85.5 |
| | James Shields (W) | 5,760 | 12.8 |
| 1853 | John A. Winston (D) | 30,862 | 65.0 |
| | Earnest (W) | 9,499 | 20.0 |
| | Nicks (UN D) | 7,096 | 15.0 |
| 1855 | John A. Winston (D) | 43,936 | 57.2 |
| | Shortridge (AM) | 31,864 | 41.5 |
| 1857 | Andrew B. Moore (D) | 41,871 | 94.5 |
| 1859 | Andrew B. Moore (D) | 47,293 | 72.4 |
| | William F. Samford (SO RTS D) | 18,070 | 27.7 |
| 1861 | John Gill Shorter (D) | 38,221 | 57.5 |
| | Thomas Hill Watts (W) | 28,117 | 42.3 |
| 1863 | Thomas Hill Watts (W) | 28,201 | 71.7 |
| | John Gill Shorter (D) | 9,664 | 24.6 |
| 1865 | Robert Miller Patton (W) | 20,611 | 45.2 |
| | Michael J. Bulger (D) | 16,380 | 35.9 |
| | William R. Smith (UN) | 8,557 | 18.8 |
| 1868 | William Hugh Smith (R) | 62,067 | 100.0 |
| 1870 | Robert B. Lindsay (D) | 77,723 | 50.5 |
| | William Hugh Smith (R) | 76,282 | 49.5 |
| 1872 | David P. Lewis (R) | 89,868 | 52.5 |
| | Hendon (LR) | 81,371 | 47.5 |
| 1874 | George S. Houston (D) | 107,118 | 53.3 |
| | David P. Lewis (R) | 93,928 | 46.7 |

| | Candidates | Votes | % |
|---|---|---|---|
| 1876 | George S. Houston (D) | 96,401 | 63.4 |
| | Woodruff (R) | 55,682 | 36.6 |
| 1878 | Rufus W. Cobb (D) | 88,255 | 100.0 |
| 1880 | Rufus W. Cobb (D) | 134,905 | 76.1 |
| | Pickens (G) | 42,363 | 23.9 |
| 1882 | Edward A. O'Neal (D) | 102,617 | 68.7 |
| | J. L. Sheffield (R) | 46,742 | 31.3 |
| 1884 | Edward A. O'Neal (D) | 143,229 | 99.7 |
| 1886 | Thomas Seay (D) | 145,095 | 79.4 |
| | Arthur Bingham (R) | 36,793 | 20.1 |

## Explanation of Symbols

In the returns for gubernatorial elections, *symbols* are used to denote special circumstances. Where no symbol is used, the candidate who received the most votes won the election on the basis of the popular vote and served as governor. The following is a key to the symbols used:

✔ Elected and served as governor, but the number of votes and the percentage of the total received were not available.

† Elected governor by the state legislature because no candidate received a majority of the popular vote as required by state law at the time of the election. *(See p. 635 for an explanation of the election of governors by state legislatures.)*

\* Symbol used for two types of situations: (1) the candidate who won the election did not serve as governor because he died before assuming office; (2) none of the candidates running qualified to become governor on the basis of the election returns or action by the state legislature. *(For an explanation of a specific case, consult the appropriate state listed in the section, "Governors of the States, 1787-1994," pp. 639-663.)*

‡ Disputed election. The symbol is used in a variety of circumstances such as an election dispute resulting in the unseating of a governor after he assumed office or resulting in rival governors each claiming to have been legitimately elected. *(For an explanation of a specific case, consult the appropriate state listed in the selection, "Governors of the States, 1787-1994," pp. 639-663.)*

# Information was obtained from a source other than Congressional Quarterly's basic sources for this volume. *(For a list of the other sources used, see p. 716.)*

| | Candidates | Votes | % |
|---|---|---|---|
| 1888 | Thomas Seay (D) | 155,973 | 77.6 |
| | W. T. Ewing (R) | 44,707 | 22.2 |
| 1890 | Thomas G. Jones (D) | 139,912 | 76.1 |
| | Benjamin M. Long (R) | 42,391 | 23.1 |
| 1892 | Thomas G. Jones (D) | 126,955 | 52.2 |
| | R. F. Kolb (ID) | 115,732 | 47.5 |
| 1894 | W. C. Oates (D) | 110,875 | 57.1 |
| | R. F. Kolb (POP) | 83,292 | 42.9 |
| 1896 | Joseph F. Johnston (D) | 128,549 | 59.0 |
| | Albert T. Goodwyn (POP) | 89,290 | 41.0 |
| 1898 | Joseph F. Johnston (D) | 110,551 | 67.0 |
| | Gilbert B. Dean (POP) | 50,052 | 30.3 |
| 1900 | William J. Samford (D) | 115,167 | 71.0 |
| | John A. Steele (R) | 28,305 | 17.5 |
| | G. B. Crowe (POP) | 17,444 | 10.8 |
| 1902 | William D. Jelks (D) | 67,748 | 73.7 |
| | John A. W. Smith (R) | 24,150 | 26.3 |
| 1906 | B. B. Comer (D) | 61,223 | 85.5 |
| | Asa E. Stratton (R) | 9,981 | 13.9 |
| 1910 | Emmet O'Neal (D) | 77,694 | 78.7 |
| | Joseph O. Thompson (R) | 19,210 | 19.5 |
| 1914 | Charles Henderson (D) | 61,307 | 78.7 |
| | John B. Shields (R) | 11,773 | 15.1 |
| 1918 | Thomas E. Kilby (D) | 54,746 | 80.2 |
| | Smith | 13,497 | 19.8 |
| 1922 | William W. Brandon (D) | 113,605 | 77.6 |
| | O. D. Street (R) | 31,175 | 21.3 |
| 1926 | Bibb Graves (D) | 93,432 | 81.2 |
| | J. A. Bingham (R) | 21,605 | 18.8 |
| 1930 | B. M. Miller (D) | 155,034 | 61.8 |
| | Hugh A. Locke (I) | 95,745 | 38.2 |
| 1934 | Bibb Graves (D) | 155,197 | 86.9 |
| | Edmund H. Dryer (R) | 22,621 | 12.7 |
| 1938 | Frank Dixon (D) | 115,761 | 87.4 |
| | W. A. Clardy (R) | 16,513 | 12.5 |
| 1942 | Chauncey Sparks (D) | 69,048 | 89.0 |
| | Hugh McEniry (R) | 8,167 | 10.5 |
| 1946 | James E. Folsom (D) | 174,959 | 88.7 |
| | Lyman Ward (R) | 22,362 | 11.3 |
| 1950 | Gordon Persons (D) | 155,414 | 91.1 |
| | John S. Crowder (R) | 15,177 | 8.9 |
| 1954 | James E. Folsom (D) | 244,401 | 73.4 |
| | Tom Abernethy (R) | 88,688 | 26.6 |
| 1958 | John Patterson (D) | 239,633 | 88.4 |
| | William L. Longshore Jr. (R) | 30,415 | 11.2 |
| 1962 | George C. Wallace (D) | 303,987 | 96.3 |
| 1966 | Lurleen B. Wallace (D) | 537,505 | 63.4 |
| | James Martin (R) | 262,943 | 31.0 |
| | C. R. Robinson (I) | 47,653 | 5.6 |
| 1970 | George C. Wallace (D) | 637,046 | 74.5 |
| | John Logan Cashin (NDPA) | 125,491 | 14.7 |
| | A. C. Shelton (I) | 75,679 | 8.9 |
| 1974 | George C. Wallace (D) | 497,574 | 83.2 |
| | Elvin McCary (R) | 88,381 | 14.8 |
| 1978 | Forrest H. James (D) | 551,886 | 72.6 |
| | Guy Hunt (R) | 196,963 | 25.9 |
| 1982 | George C. Wallace (D) | 650,538 | 57.6 |
| | Emory Folmar (R) | 440,815 | 39.1 |
| 1986 | Guy Hunt (R) | 696,203 | 56.4 |
| | Bill Baxley (D) | 537,163 | 43.5 |
| 1990 | Guy Hunt (R) | 633,520 | 52.1 |
| | Paul Hubbert (D) | 582,106 | 47.9 |

# ALASKA

(Became a state Jan. 3, 1959)

| | Candidates | Votes | % |
|---|---|---|---|
| 1958 | William A. Egan (D) | 29,189 | 59.6 |
| | John Butrovich Jr. (R) | 19,299 | 39.4 |
| 1962 | William A. Egan (D) | 29,627 | 52.3 |
| | Mike Stepovich (R) | 27,054 | 47.7 |
| 1966 | Walter J. Hickel (R) | 33,145 | 50.0 |
| | William A. Egan (D) | 32,065 | 48.4 |
| 1970 | William A. Egan (D) | 42,309 | 52.4 |
| | Keith H. Miller (R) | 37,264 | 46.1 |
| 1974 | Jay S. Hammond (R) | 45,840 | 47.7 |
| | William A. Egan (D) | 45,553 | 47.4 |
| | Joseph E. Vogler (ALI) | 4,770 | 5.0 |
| 1978 | Jay S. Hammond (R) | 49,580 | 39.1 |
| | Walter J. Hickel (WRITE-IN) | 33,555 | 26.4 |
| | Chancy Croft (D) | 25,656 | 20.2 |
| | Tom Kelly (I) | 15,656 | 12.3 |
| 1982 | Bill Sheffield (D) | 89,918 | 46.1 |
| | Tom Fink (R) | 72,291 | 37.1 |
| | Richard L. Randolph (LIBERT) | 29,067 | 14.9 |
| 1986 | Steve C. Cowper (D) | 84,943 | 47.3 |
| | Arliss Sturgulewski (R) | 76,515 | 42.6 |
| | Joe Vogler (ALI) | 10,013 | 5.6 |
| 1990 | Walter J. Hickel (ALI) | 75,721 | 38.9 |
| | Tony Knowles (D) | 60,201 | 30.9 |
| | Arliss Sturgulewski (R) | 50,991 | 26.2 |

# ARIZONA

(Became a state Feb. 14, 1912)

| | Candidates | Votes | % |
|---|---|---|---|
| 1911 | George W. P. Hunt (D) | 11,123 | 51.5 |
| | Edward W. Wells (R) | 9,166 | 42.4 |
| | P. W. Gallentine (SOC) | 1,247 | 5.8 |
| 1914 | George W. P. Hunt (D) | 25,226 | 49.5 |
| | Ralph H. Cameron (R) | 17,602 | 34.5 |
| | George U. Young (PROG) | 5,206 | 10.2 |
| | J. R. Barnette (SOC) | 2,973 | 5.8 |
| 1916 | Thomas E. Campbell (R) | 27,976‡ | 48.0 |
| | George W. P. Hunt (D) | 27,946 | 47.9 |
| 1918 | Thomas E. Campbell (R) | 25,927 | 49.9 |
| | Fred T. Colter (D) | 25,588 | 49.3 |
| 1920 | Thomas E. Campbell (R) | 37,060 | 54.2 |
| | Mit Simms (D) | 31,385 | 45.9 |
| 1922 | George W. P. Hunt (D) | 37,310 | 54.9 |
| | Thomas E. Campbell (R) | 30,599 | 45.1 |
| 1924 | George W. P. Hunt (D) | 38,372 | 50.5 |
| | Dwight B. Heard (R) | 37,571 | 49.5 |
| 1926 | George W. P. Hunt (D) | 39,979 | 50.3 |
| | E. S. Clark (R) | 39,580 | 49.8 |
| 1928 | John C. Phillips (R) | 47,829 | 51.7 |
| | George W. P. Hunt (D) | 44,553 | 48.2 |
| 1930 | George W. P. Hunt (D) | 48,875 | 51.4 |
| | John C. Phillips (R) | 46,231 | 48.6 |
| 1932 | B. B. Moeur (D) | 75,314 | 63.2 |
| | J. C. Kinney (R) | 42,202 | 35.4 |
| 1934 | B. B. Moeur (D) | 61,355 | 59.7 |
| | Thomas Maddock (R) | 39,242 | 38.2 |
| 1936 | R. C. Stanford (D) | 87,678 | 70.7 |
| | Thomas E. Campbell (R) | 36,114 | 29.1 |
| 1938 | R. T. Jones (D) | 80,350 | 68.6 |
| | Jerrie W. Lee (R) | 32,022 | 27.3 |
| 1940 | Sidney P. Osborn (D) | 97,606 | 65.5 |
| | Jerrie W. Lee (R) | 50,358 | 33.8 |

| | Candidates | Votes | % |
|------|------------|-------|---|
| 1942 | Sidney P. Osborn (D) | 63,484 | 72.5 |
| | Jerrie W. Lee (R) | 23,562 | 26.9 |
| 1944 | Sidney P. Osborn (D) | 100,220 | 77.9 |
| | Jerrie W. Lee (R) | 27,261 | 21.2 |
| 1946 | Sidney P. Osborn (D) | 73,595 | 60.1 |
| | Bruce D. Brockett (R) | 48,867 | 39.9 |
| 1948 | Dan E. Garvey (D) | 104,008 | 59.2 |
| | Bruce D. Brockett (R) | 70,419 | 40.1 |
| 1950 | Howard Pyle (R) | 99,109 | 50.8 |
| | Ana Frohmiller (D) | 96,118 | 49.2 |
| 1952 | Howard Pyle (R) | 156,592 | 60.2 |
| | Joe C. Haldiman (D) | 103,693 | 39.8 |
| 1954 | Ernest W. McFarland (D) | 128,104 | 52.5 |
| | Howard Pyle (R) | 115,866 | 47.5 |
| 1956 | Ernest W. McFarland (D) | 171,848 | 59.6 |
| | Horace B. Griffen (R) | 116,744 | 40.5 |
| 1958 | Paul Fannin (R) | 160,136 | 55.1 |
| | Robert Morrison (D) | 130,329 | 44.9 |
| 1960 | Paul Fannin (R) | 235,502 | 59.3 |
| | Lee Ackerman (D) | 161,605 | 40.7 |
| 1962 | Paul Fannin (R) | 200,578 | 54.8 |
| | Sam Goddard (D) | 165,263 | 45.2 |
| 1964 | Sam Goddard (D) | 252,098 | 53.2 |
| | Richard Kleindienst (R) | 221,404 | 46.8 |
| 1966 | Jack Williams (R) | 203,438 | 53.8 |
| | Sam Goddard (D) | 174,904 | 46.2 |
| 1968 | Jack Williams (R) | 279,923 | 57.8 |
| | Sam Goddard (D) | 204,075 | 42.2 |
| 1970 | Jack Williams (R) | 209,356 | 50.9 |
| | Raul H. Castro (D) | 202,053 | 49.1 |
| 1974 | Raul H. Castro (D) | 278,375 | 50.4 |
| | Russell Williams (R) | 273,674 | 49.6 |
| 1978 | Bruce Babbitt (D) | 282,605 | 52.5 |
| | Evan Mecham (R) | 241,093 | 44.8 |
| 1982 | Bruce Babbitt (D) | 453,795 | 62.5 |
| | Leo Corbet (R) | 235,877 | 32.5 |
| | Sam Steiger (LIBERT) | 36,649 | 5.0 |
| 1986 | Evan Mecham (R) | 343,913 | 39.7 |
| | Carolyn Warner (D) | 298,986 | 34.5 |
| | Bill Schulz (I) | 224,085 | 25.8 |
| 1990 | Fife Symington (R) | 523,984 | 49.6 |
| | Terry Goddard (D) | 519,691 | 49.2 |

Runoff Election

| | | | |
|------|------------|-------|---|
| 1991 | Fife Symington (R) | 492,569 | 52.4 |
| | Terry Goddard (D) | 448,168 | 47.6 |

# ARKANSAS

(Became a state June 15, 1836)

| | Candidates | Votes | % |
|------|------------|-------|---|
| 1836 | James S. Conway (D) | 5,338 | 62.2 |
| | Absalom Fowler (W) | 3,222 | 37.5 |
| 1840 | Archibald Yell (D) | ✔ | |
| 1844 | Thomas S. Drew (D) | 8,859 | 47.6 |
| | Gibson (W) | 7,244 | 38.9 |
| | Byrd (I) | 2,507 | 13.5 |
| 1849 | John S. Roane (D) | 3,290 | 50.5 |
| | Wilson (W) | 3,228 | 49.5 |
| 1852 | Elias N. Conway (D) | 15,932 | 55.2 |
| | Smith (W) | 12,955 | 44.9 |
| 1856 | Elias N. Conway (D) | 28,159 | 64.6 |
| | Yell (AM) | 15,436 | 35.4 |
| 1860 | Henry M. Rector (ID) | 31,578 | 52.5 |
| | R. H. Johnson (D) | 28,622 | 47.5 |

| | Candidates | Votes | % |
|------|------------|-------|---|
| 1872 | Elisha Baxter (R) | 41,808 | 51.8 |
| | Joseph Brooks (D) | 38,909 | 48.2 |
| 1874 | A. H. Garland (D) | 76,552 | 100.0 |
| 1876 | William R. Miller (D) | 69,775 | 65.6 |
| | Bishop (R) | 36,272 | 34.1 |
| 1878 | William R. Miller (D) | 88,726 | 100.0 |
| 1880 | Thomas J. Churchill (D) | 84,185 | 72.8 |
| | Parks (G) | 31,424 | 27.2 |
| 1882 | James H. Berry (D) | 87,669 | 59.6 |
| | W. D. Slack (R) | 49,372 | 33.5 |
| | R. K. Garland (G) | 10,142 | 6.9 |
| 1884 | Simon P. Hughes (D) | 100,875 | 64.6 |
| | Thomas Boles (R) | 55,388 | 35.5 |
| 1886 | Simon P. Hughes (D) | 90,650 | 55.3 |
| | S. Gregg (R) | 54,063 | 33.0 |
| | C. E. Cunningham (AG WHEEL) | 19,169 | 11.7 |
| 1888 | James P. Eagle (D) | 99,229 | 54.1 |
| | C. M. Norwood (LAB) | 84,273 | 45.9 |
| 1890 | James P. Eagle (D) | 106,267 | 55.5 |
| | N. B. Fizer (R) | 85,181 | 44.5 |
| 1892 | W. M. Fishback (D) | 90,115 | 57.7 |
| | W. G. Whipple (R) | 33,634 | 21.5 |
| | J. P. Carnahan (POP) | 31,116 | 19.9 |
| 1894 | J. P. Clarke (D) | 74,809 | 59.1 |
| | H. L. Remmel (R) | 26,085 | 20.6 |
| | D. E. Barker (POP) | 24,181 | 19.1 |
| 1896 | Daniel Webster Jones (D) | 91,114 | 64.3 |
| | H. L. Remmel (R) | 35,837 | 25.3 |
| | A. W. Files (POP) | 13,980 | 9.9 |
| 1898 | Daniel Webster Jones (D) | 75,354 | 67.4 |
| | H. F. Auten (R) | 27,524 | 24.6 |
| | W. S. Morgan (POP) | 8,332 | 7.5 |
| 1900 | Jefferson Davis (D) | 88,636 | 66.7 |
| | H. L. Remmel (R) | 40,701 | 30.6 |
| 1902 | Jefferson Davis (D) | 77,354 | 64.6 |
| | Harry H. Meyers (R) | 29,251 | 24.4 |
| | Charles D. Greaves (POP) | 8,345 | 7.0 |
| 1904 | Jefferson Davis (D) | 90,263 | 61.0 |
| | Harry H. Myers (R) | 53,898 | 36.4 |
| 1906 | John S. Little (D) | 105,586 | 69.1 |
| | John I. Worthington (R) | 41,689 | 27.3 |
| 1908 | George W. Donaghey (D) | 110,418 | 68.1 |
| | John I. Worthington (R) | 44,863 | 27.7 |
| 1910 | George W. Donaghey (D) | 101,612 | 67.4 |
| | Andrew I. Roland (R) | 39,870 | 26.5 |
| | Dan Hogan (SOC) | 9,196 | 6.1 |
| 1912 | Joseph T. Robinson (D) | 109,825 | 64.7 |
| | Andrew I. Roland (R) | 46,440 | 27.4 |
| | G. E. Mikel (SOC) | 13,384 | 7.9 |

Special Election

| | | | |
|------|------------|-------|---|
| 1913 | George W. Hays (D) | 53,655 | 64.3 |
| | Harry H. Meyers (R) | 17,040 | 20.4 |
| | George W. Murphy (PROG) | 8,431 | 10.1 |
| | J. Emil Webber (SOC) | 4,378 | 5.2 |

| | | | |
|------|------------|-------|---|
| 1914 | George W. Hays (D) | 94,143 | 69.5 |
| | Audrey L. Kinney (R) | 30,947 | 22.8 |
| | Dan Hogan (SOC) | 10,434 | 7.7 |
| 1916 | Charles H. Brough (D) | 122,041 | 69.5 |
| | Wallace Townsend (R) | 43,963 | 25.0 |
| | William Davis (SOC) | 9,730 | 5.5 |
| 1918 | Charles H. Brough (D) | 68,192 | 93.4 |
| | Clay Fulks (SOC) | 4,792 | 6.6 |
| 1920 | Thomas C. McRae (D) | 123,637 | 65.0 |
| | Wallace Townsend (R) | 46,350 | 24.4 |
| | J. H. Blount (NEG I) | 15,627 | 8.2 |
| 1922 | Thomas C. McRae (D) | 99,987 | 78.1 |
| | John W. Grabiel (R) | 28,055 | 21.9 |

| | Candidates | Votes | % |
|---|---|---|---|
| 1924 | Thomas J. Terral (D) | 99,598 | 79.8 |
| | John W. Grabiel (R) | 25,152 | 20.2 |
| 1926 | John E. Martineau (D) | 116,735 | 76.5 |
| | M. D. Bowers (R) | 35,969 | 23.6 |
| 1928 | Harvey J. Parnell (D) | 151,743 | 77.3 |
| | M. D. Bowers (R) | 44,545 | 22.7 |
| 1930 | Harvey J. Parnell (D) | 112,847 | 81.2 |
| | J. O. Livesay (R) | 26,162 | 18.8 |
| 1932 | Julius M. Futrell (D) | 200,096 | 90.4 |
| | J. O. Livesay (R) | 19,717 | 8.9 |
| 1934 | Julius M. Futrell (D) | 123,918 | 89.2 |
| | C. C. Ledbetter (R) | 13,083 | 9.4 |
| 1936 | Carl E. Bailey (D) | 155,152 | 84.9 |
| | Osro Cobb (R) | 26,875 | 14.7 |
| 1938 | Carl E. Bailey (D) | 118,696 | 86.3 |
| | Charles S. Cole (I) | 12,077 | 8.8 |
| 1940 | Homer M. Adkins (D) | 184,578 | 91.4 |
| | H. C. Stump (R) | 16,600 | 8.2 |
| 1942 | Homer M. Adkins (D) | 98,871 | 100.0 |
| 1944 | Ben Laney (D) | 186,401 | 86.0 |
| | H. C. Stump (R) | 30,442 | 14.0 |
| 1946 | Ben Laney (D) | 128,029 | 84.1 |
| | W. T. Mills (R) | 24,133 | 15.9 |
| 1948 | Sidney S. McMath (D) | 217,771 | 89.2 |
| | C. R. Black (R) | 26,500 | 10.9 |
| 1950 | Sidney S. McMath (D) | 266,778 | 84.1 |
| | Jefferson W. Speck (R) | 50,303 | 15.9 |
| 1952 | Francis Cherry (D) | 342,292 | 87.4 |
| | Jefferson W. Speck (R) | 49,292 | 12.6 |
| 1954 | Orval E. Faubus (D) | 208,121 | 62.1 |
| | Pratt C. Remmel (R) | 127,004 | 37.9 |
| 1956 | Orval E. Faubus (D) | 321,797 | 80.7 |
| | Roy Mitchell (R) | 77,215 | 19.4 |
| 1958 | Orval E. Faubus (D) | 236,598 | 82.5 |
| | George W. Johnson (R) | 50,288 | 17.5 |
| 1960 | Orval E. Faubus (D) | 292,064 | 69.2 |
| | Henry M. Britt (R) | 129,921 | 30.8 |
| 1962 | Orval E. Faubus (D) | 225,743 | 73.3 |
| | Willis Ricketts (R) | 82,349 | 26.7 |
| 1964 | Orval E. Faubus (D) | 337,489 | 57.0 |
| | Winthrop Rockefeller (R) | 254,561 | 43.0 |
| 1966 | Winthrop Rockefeller (R) | 306,324 | 54.4 |
| | James Johnson (D) | 257,203 | 45.6 |
| 1968 | Winthrop Rockefeller (R) | 322,782 | 52.4 |
| | Marion Crank (D) | 292,813 | 47.6 |
| 1970 | Dale Bumpers (D) | 375,648 | 61.7 |
| | Winthrop Rockefeller (R) | 197,418 | 32.4 |
| | Walter L. Carruth (AM) | 36,132 | 5.9 |
| 1972 | Dale Bumpers (D) | 488,892 | 75.4 |
| | Len E. Blaylock (R) | 159,177 | 24.6 |
| 1974 | David H. Pryor (D) | 358,018 | 65.6 |
| | Ken Coon (R) | 187,872 | 34.4 |
| 1976 | David H. Pryor (D) | 605,083 | 83.2 |
| | Leon Griffith (R) | 121,716 | 16.7 |
| 1978 | Bill Clinton (D) | 335,101 | 63.4 |
| | A. Lynn Lowe (R) | 193,746 | 36.6 |
| 1980 | Frank D. White (R) | 435,684 | 51.9 |
| | Bill Clinton (D) | 403,241 | 48.1 |
| 1982 | Bill Clinton (D) | 431,855 | 54.7 |
| | Frank D. White (R) | 357,496 | 45.3 |
| 1984 | Bill Clinton (D) | 554,561 | 62.6 |
| | Woody Freeman (R) | 331,987 | 37.4 |
| 1986 | Bill Clinton (D) | 439,851 | 63.9 |
| | Frank White (R) | 248,415 | 36.1 |

| | Candidates | Votes | % |
|---|---|---|---|
| 1990 | Bill Clinton (D) | 400,386 | 57.5 |
| | Sheffield Nelson (R) | 295,925 | 42.5 |

# CALIFORNIA

(Became a state Sept. 9, 1850)

| | Candidates | Votes | % |
|---|---|---|---|
| 1849 | P. H. Burnett (ID) | 6,783 | 47.4 |
| | W. S. Sherwood | 3,220 | 22.7 |
| | J. A. Sutter | 2,201 | 15.5 |
| | J. W. Geary | 1,358 | 9.6 |
| 1851 | John Bigler (D) | 23,175 | 50.5 |
| | P. B. Reading (W) | 22,732 | 49.5 |
| 1853 | John Bigler (D) | 38,940 | 51.0 |
| | William Walde (W) | 37,454 | 49.0 |
| 1855 | J. N. Johnson (AM) | 51,157 | 52.5 |
| | John Bigler (D) | 46,225 | 47.5 |
| 1857 | J. B. Weller (D) | 53,122 | 56.7 |
| | Edward Stanly (R) | 21,040 | 22.5 |
| | G. W. Bowie (AM) | 19,481 | 20.8 |
| 1859 | M. S. Latham (D) | 61,352 | 59.7 |
| | John Currey (A-LEC D) | 31,298 | 30.5 |
| | Leland Stanford (R) | 10,110 | 9.8 |
| 1861 | Leland Stanford (R) | 56,036 | 46.8 |
| | J. R. McConnell (SEC D) | 32,751 | 27.4 |
| | John Conness (UN D) | 30,944 | 25.8 |
| 1863 | Frederick F. Low (UN R) | 64,283 | 59.0 |
| | J. G. Downey (D) | 44,622 | 41.0 |
| 1867 | H. H. Haight (D) | 49,895 | 54.0 |
| | George C. Gurham (R) | 40,359 | 43.7 |
| 1871 | Newton Booth (R) | 62,581 | 52.1 |
| | H. H. Haight (D) | 57,520 | 47.9 |
| 1875 | William Irwin (D) | 61,509 | 50.0 |
| | T. G. Phelps (R) | 31,322 | 25.5 |
| | John Bidwell (I) | 29,752 | 24.2 |
| 1879 | George C. Perkins (R) | 67,965 | 42.4 |
| | Hugh J. Glenn (D) | 47,667 | 29.8 |
| | William F. White (WMP/L) | 44,482 | 27.8 |
| 1882 | George Stoneman (D) | 90,694 | 55.1 |
| | Morris M. Estee (R) | 67,175 | 40.8 |
| 1886 | Washington Bartlett (D) | 84,965 | 43.4 |
| | John F. Swift (R) | 84,316 | 43.1 |
| | C. C. O'Donnell (I) | 12,227 | 6.3 |
| 1890 | H. H. Markham (R) | 125,129 | 49.6 |
| | E. B. Pond (D) | 117,184 | 46.4 |
| 1894 | James H. Budd (D) | 111,944 | 39.3 |
| | Morris M. Estee (R) | 110,738 | 38.9 |
| | J. V. Webster (PP) | 51,304 | 18.0 |
| 1898 | Henry T. Gage (R & UL) | 148,354 | 51.7 |
| | James G. Maguire (D & POP) | 129,261 | 45.0 |
| 1902 | George C. Pardee (R) | 146,332 | 48.1 |
| | Franklin K. Lane (D) | 143,783 | 47.2 |
| 1906 | James N. Gillett (R) | 125,887 | 40.4 |
| | Theodore A. Bell (D) | 117,590 | 37.7 |
| | W. H. Langdon (I LEAGUE) | 45,008 | 14.4 |
| | Austin Lewis (SOC) | 16,036 | 5.1 |
| 1910 | Hiram W. Johnson (R) | 177,191 | 45.9 |
| | Theodore A. Bell (D) | 154,835 | 40.1 |
| | J. Stitt Wilson (SOC) | 47,819 | 12.4 |
| 1914 | Hiram W. Johnson (PROG) | 460,495 | 49.7 |
| | John D. Fredericks (R) | 271,990 | 29.4 |
| | J. B. Curtin (D) | 116,121 | 12.5 |
| | Noble A. Richardson (SOC) | 50,716 | 5.5 |
| 1918 | William D. Stephens (R P&PROG) | 387,547 | 56.3 |
| | Theodore A. Bell (D) | 251,189 | 36.5 |
| 1922 | Friend William Richardson (R) | 576,445 | 59.7 |
| | Thomas Lee Woolwine (D) | 347,530 | 36.0 |

| | Candidates | Votes | % |
|---|---|---|---|
| 1926 | C. C. Young (R) | 814,815 | 71.2 |
| | Justus S. Wardell (D) | 282,451 | 24.7 |
| 1930 | James Rolph Jr. (R) | 999,393 | 72.2 |
| | Milton K. Young (D) | 333,973 | 24.1 |
| 1934 | Frank F. Merriam (R) | 1,138,620 | 48.9 |
| | Upton Sinclair (D) | 879,537 | 37.8 |
| | Raymond L. Haight (C PROG) | 302,519 | 13.0 |
| 1938 | Culbert L. Olson (D) | 1,391,734 | 52.5 |
| | Frank F. Merriam (R) | 1,171,019 | 44.2 |
| 1942 | Earl Warren (R) | 1,275,237 | 57.1 |
| | Culbert L. Olson (D) | 932,995 | 41.8 |
| 1946 | Earl Warren (R-D) | 2,344,542 | 91.6 |
| | Henry R. Schmidt (P) | 180,579 | 7.1 |
| 1950 | Earl Warren (R) | 2,461,754 | 64.9 |
| | James Roosevelt (D) | 1,333,856 | 35.1 |
| 1954 | Goodwin J. Knight (R) | 2,290,519 | 56.8 |
| | Richard Perrin Graves (D) | 1,739,368 | 43.2 |
| 1958 | Edmund G. Brown (D) | 3,140,076 | 59.8 |
| | William F. Knowland (R) | 2,110,911 | 40.2 |
| 1962 | Edmund G. Brown (D) | 3,037,109 | 51.9 |
| | Richard M. Nixon (R) | 2,740,351 | 46.8 |
| 1966 | Ronald Reagan (R) | 3,742,913 | 57.6 |
| | Edmund G. Brown (D) | 2,749,174 | 42.3 |
| 1970 | Ronald Reagan (R) | 3,439,664 | 52.8 |
| | Jess Unruh (D) | 2,938,607 | 45.1 |
| 1974 | Edmund G. Brown Jr. (D) | 3,131,648 | 50.1 |
| | Houston I. Flournoy (R) | 2,952,954 | 47.3 |
| 1978 | Edmund G. Brown Jr. (D) | 3,878,812 | 56.0 |
| | Evelle J. Younger (R) | 2,526,534 | 36.5 |
| | Ed Clark (I) | 377,960 | 5.5 |
| 1982 | George Deukmejian (R) | 3,881,014 | 49.3 |
| | Tom Bradley (D) | 3,787,669 | 48.1 |
| 1986 | George Deukmejian (R) | 4,506,601 | 60.5 |
| | Tom Bradley (D) | 2,781,714 | 37.4 |
| 1990 | Pete Wilson (R) | 3,791,904 | 49.2 |
| | Dianne Feinstein (D) | 3,525,197 | 45.8 |

# COLORADO

(Became a state Aug. 1, 1876)

| | Candidates | Votes | % |
|---|---|---|---|
| 1876 | John L. Routt (R) | 14,154 | 51.5 |
| | Hughes (D) | 13,316 | 48.5 |
| 1878 | Frederick W. Pitkin (R) | 14,308 | 50.0 |
| | W. A. H. Loveland (D) | 11,535 | 40.3 |
| | R. G. Buckingham (G) | 2,783 | 9.7 |
| 1880 | Frederick W. Pitkin (R) | 28,465 | 53.3 |
| | John S. Hough (D) | 23,547 | 44.1 |
| 1882 | James B. Grant (D) | 31,375 | 51.1 |
| | E. L. Campbell (R) | 28,820 | 46.9 |
| 1884 | Benjamin H. Eaton (R) | 33,845 | 50.7 |
| | Alva Adams (D) | 30,743 | 46.1 |
| 1886 | Alva Adams (D) | 29,234 | 49.7 |
| | William H. Meyer (R) | 26,816 | 45.6 |
| 1888 | Job A. Cooper (R) | 49,490 | 53.8 |
| | T. M. Patterson (D) | 39,197 | 42.6 |
| 1890 | John L. Routt (R) | 41,827 | 50.1 |
| | Caldwell Yeaman (D) | 35,359 | 42.4 |
| | John G. Coy (F ALNC) | 5,199 | 6.2 |
| 1892 | Davis H. Waite (POP & SL D) | 43,342 | 46.7 |
| | Joseph C. Helm (R) | 38,806 | 41.8 |
| | Joseph H. Maupin (D) | 8,944 | 9.6 |
| 1894 | Albert W. McIntire (R) | 93,502 | 52.0 |
| | Davis H. Waite (POP) | 73,894 | 41.1 |
| 1896 | Alva Adams (D) | 87,387 | 46.2 |
| | M. S. Bailey (N SILVER) | 71,808 | 38.0 |
| | G. H. Allen (R) | 23,945 | 12.7 |

| | Candidates | Votes | % |
|---|---|---|---|
| 1898 | Charles S. Thomas (FUS) | 93,966 | 62.8 |
| | Henry R. Wolcott (R) | 51,051 | 34.1 |
| 1900 | James B. Orman (FUS) | 118,647 | 53.8 |
| | Frank C. Goudy (R) | 96,027 | 43.5 |
| 1902 | James H. Peabody (R) | 87,684 | 46.9 |
| | E. C. Stimson (D) | 80,727 | 43.2 |
| 1904 | Alva Adams (D) | 123,092‡ | 50.6 |
| | James H. Peabody (R) | 113,754 | 46.8 |
| 1906 | Henry A. Buchtel (R) | 92,602 | 45.6 |
| | Alva Adams (D) | 74,416 | 36.6 |
| | Ben B. Lindsey (I) | 18,014 | 8.9 |
| | William D. Haywood (SOC) | 16,015 | 7.9 |
| 1908 | John F. Shafroth (D) | 130,141 | 49.4 |
| | Jesse F. McDonald (R) | 118,953 | 15.2 |
| 1910 | John F. Shafroth (D) | 114,676 | 54.0 |
| | John B. Stephen (R) | 97,691 | 46.0 |
| 1912 | Elias M. Ammons (D) | 114,044 | 42.9 |
| | Edward P. Costigan (PROG-BMR) | 66,132 | 24.9 |
| | C. C. Parks (R) | 63,061 | 23.7 |
| | Charles A. Ashelstrom (SOC) | 16,189 | 6.1 |
| 1914 | George A. Carlson (R) | 129,096 | 48.7 |
| | T. M. Patterson (D) | 90,640 | 34.2 |
| | Edward P. Costigan (PROG) | 32,920 | 12.4 |
| 1916 | Julius C. Gunter (D) | 151,912 | 53.3 |
| | George A. Carlson (R) | 117,723 | 41.3 |
| 1918 | Oliver H. Shoup (R) | 112,693 | 51.1 |
| | Tynan (D) | 102,397 | 46.5 |
| 1920 | Oliver H. Shoup (R) | 174,488 | 59.6 |
| | James M. Collins (D) | 108,738 | 37.1 |
| 1922 | William E. Sweet (D) | 138,098 | 49.6 |
| | Benjamin Griffith (R) | 134,353 | 48.3 |
| 1924 | Clarence J. Morley (R) | 178,078 | 51.9 |
| | William E. Sweet (D) | 151,041 | 44.0 |
| 1926 | William H. Adams (D) | 183,342 | 59.8 |
| | Oliver H. Shoup (R) | 116,756 | 38.1 |
| 1928 | William H. Adams (D) | 240,160 | 61.9 |
| | William L. Boatright (R) | 144,067 | 37.1 |
| 1930 | William H. Adams (D) | 197,067 | 60.4 |
| | Robert F. Rockwell (R) | 124,164 | 38.1 |
| 1932 | Edwin C. Johnson (D) | 257,188 | 57.2 |
| | James D. Parriott (R) | 183,258 | 40.8 |
| 1934 | Edwin C. Johnson (D) | 237,026 | 58.1 |
| | Nate C. Warren (R) | 162,791 | 39.9 |
| 1936 | Teller Ammons (D) | 263,311 | 54.6 |
| | Charles M. Armstrong (R) | 210,614 | 43.7 |
| 1938 | Ralph L. Carr (R) | 255,159 | 55.8 |
| | Teller Ammons (D) | 199,562 | 43.7 |
| 1940 | Ralph L. Carr (R) | 296,671 | 54.4 |
| | George E. Saunders (D) | 245,292 | 45.0 |
| 1942 | John C. Vivian (R) | 193,501 | 56.2 |
| | Homer F. Bedford (D) | 149,402 | 43.4 |
| 1944 | John C. Vivian (R) | 259,862 | 52.4 |
| | Roy Best (D) | 236,086 | 47.6 |
| 1946 | William Lee Knous (D) | 174,604 | 52.1 |
| | Leon E. Lavington (R) | 160,483 | 47.9 |
| 1948 | William Lee Knous (D) | 332,752 | 66.3 |
| | David A. Hamil (R) | 168,928 | 33.7 |
| 1950 | Dan Thornton (R) | 236,472 | 52.4 |
| | Walter W. Johnson (D) | 212,976 | 47.2 |
| 1952 | Dan Thornton (R) | 349,924 | 57.1 |
| | John W. Metzger (D) | 260,044 | 42.4 |
| 1954 | Edwin C. Johnson (D) | 262,205 | 53.6 |
| | Donald G. Brotzman (R) | 227,335 | 46.4 |
| 1956 | Stephen L. R. McNichols (D) | 331,283 | 51.3 |
| | Donald G. Brotzman (R) | 313,950 | 48.7 |
| 1958 | Stephen L. R. McNichols (D) | 321,165 | 58.4 |
| | Palmer L. Burch (R) | 228,643 | 41.6 |
| 1962 | John A. Love (R) | 349,342 | 56.7 |
| | Stephen L. R. McNichols (D) | 262,890 | 42.6 |
| 1966 | John A. Love (R) | 356,730 | 54.0 |
| | Robert L. Knous (D) | 287,132 | 43.5 |

| | Candidates | Votes | % |
|---|---|---|---|
| 1970 | John A. Love (R) | 350,690 | 52.5 |
| | Mark Hogan (D) | 302,432 | 45.2 |
| 1974 | Richard D. Lamm (D) | 441,408 | 53.2 |
| | John D. Vanderhoof (R) | 378,698 | 45.7 |
| 1978 | Richard D. Lamm (D) | 483,985 | 58.7 |
| | Ted Strickland (R) | 317,292 | 38.5 |
| 1982 | Richard D. Lamm (D) | 627,960 | 65.7 |
| | John D. Fuhr (R) | 302,740 | 31.7 |
| 1986 | Roy Romer (D) | 616,325 | 58.2 |
| | Ted Strickland (R) | 434,420 | 41.0 |
| 1990 | Roy Romer (D) | 626,032 | 61.9 |
| | John Andrews (R) | 358,403 | 35.4 |

# CONNECTICUT

(Ratified the Constitution Jan. 9, 1788)

| | Candidates | Votes | % |
|---|---|---|---|
| 1787-1795 | Samuel Huntington | ✔ | |
| 1796 | Oliver Wolcott Sr. | 3,805† | 48.8 |
| | Jonathan Trumbull II | 1,187 | 15.2 |
| | Jonathan Ingersoll | 937 | 12.0 |
| | Oliver Ellsworth | 629 | 8.1 |
| | Richard Law | 485 | 6.2 |
| 1797 | Oliver Wolcott Sr. | ✔ | |
| 1798-1800 | Jonathan Trumbull II | ✔ | |
| 1801 | Jonathan Trumbull II | 11,156 | 83.8 |
| | Richard Law | 1,056 | 7.9 |
| 1802 | Jonathan Trumbull II (FED) | 11,398 | 69.9 |
| | Ephraim Kirby (D-R) | 4,523 | 27.7 |
| 1803 | Jonathan Trumbull II (FED) | 14,375 | 64.0 |
| | Ephraim Kirby (D-R) | 7,848 | 35.0 |
| 1804 | Jonathan Trumbull II (FED) | 11,108 | 61.8 |
| | William Hart (D-R) | 6,871 | 38.2 |
| 1805 | Jonathan Trumbull II (FED) | 12,700 | 61.9 |
| | William Hart (D-R) | 7,810 | 38.1 |
| 1806 | Jonathan Trumbull II (FED) | 13,413 | 58.6 |
| | William Hart (D-R) | 9,460 | 41.4 |
| 1807 | Jonathan Trumbull II (FED) | 11,959 | 60.0 |
| | William Hart (D-R) | 7,971 | 40.0 |
| 1808 | Jonathan Trumbull II (FED) | 12,146 | 61.6 |
| | William Hart (D-R) | 7,566 | 38.4 |
| 1809 | Jonathan Trumbull II (FED) | 14,650 | 64.2 |
| | Asa Spalding (D-R) | 8,159 | 35.8 |
| 1810 | John Treadwell (FED) | 10,265† | 49.5 |
| | Asa Spalding (D-R) | 7,185 | 34.6 |
| | Roger Griswold (FED) | 3,110 | 15.0 |
| 1811 | Roger Griswold (FED) | ✔ | |
| | John Treadwell (FED) | | |
| 1812 | Roger Griswold (FED) | 11,721 | 86.1 |
| | Elijah Boardman (D-R) | 1,487 | 10.9 |
| 1813 | John C. Smith (FED) | 11,893 | 59.1 |
| | Elijah Boardman (D-R) | 7,201 | 35.8 |
| 1814 | John C. Smith (FED) | 9,415 | 72.9 |
| | Elijah Boardman (D-R) | 2,619 | 20.3 |
| 1815 | John C. Smith (FED) | 8,176 | 59.3 |
| | Elijah Boardman (D-R) | 4,876 | 35.3 |
| 1816 | John C. Smith (FED) | 11,386 | 52.3 |
| | Oliver Wolcott Jr. (AM, TOL[1]) | 10,170 | 46.7 |
| 1817 | Oliver Wolcott Jr. (TOL[1], REF) | 13,655 | 50.6 |
| | John C. Smith (FED) | 13,119 | 48.6 |
| 1818 | Oliver Wolcott Jr. (CONST, REF) | 16,432 | 87.0 |
| 1819 | Oliver Wolcott Jr. (TOL[1], REF) | 22,539 | 86.8 |
| 1820 | Oliver Wolcott Jr. (D-R) | 15,738 | 78.4 |
| 1821 | Oliver Wolcott Jr. (D-R) | 10,064 | 86.6 |
| 1822 | Oliver Wolcott Jr. (D-R) | 8,568 | 85.5 |
| 1823 | Oliver Wolcott Jr. (D-R) | 9,090 | 88.9 |

| | Candidates | Votes | % |
|---|---|---|---|
| 1824 | Oliver Wolcott Jr. (D-R) | 6,637 | 92.1 |
| | Timothy Pitkin (OPP R) | 466 | 6.5 |
| 1825 | Oliver Wolcott Jr. (D-R) | 7,147 | 70.1 |
| | David Daggett (FED) | 1,342 | 13.2 |
| | Nathan Smith (OPP R) | 863 | 8.5 |
| | Timothy Pitkin (OPP R) | 525 | 5.2 |
| 1826 | Oliver Wolcott Jr. (D-R) | 6,780 | 57.8 |
| | David Daggett (FED) | 4,340 | 37.0 |
| 1827 | Gideon Tomlinson (OLD R) | 7,681 | 57.7 |
| | Oliver Wolcott (OPP R) | 5,295 | 39.8 |
| 1828 | Gideon Tomlinson (NR) | 9,297 | 97.3 |
| 1829 | Gideon Tomlinson (NR) | 9,612 | 95.8 |
| 1830 | Gideon Tomlinson (NR) | 12,988 | 95.6 |
| 1831 | John S. Peters (NR) | 12,819 | 65.4 |
| | Zalmon Storrs (A-MASC) | 4,778 | 24.4 |
| 1832 | John S. Peters (NR) | 11,971 | 70.3 |
| | Calvin Willey (D) | 4,463 | 26.2 |
| 1833 | John S. Peters (NR) | 9,212 | 42.3 |
| | Henry W. Edwards (D) | 9,030† | 41.5 |
| | Zalmon Storrs (A-MASC) | 3,250 | 14.9 |
| 1834 | Samuel A. Foot (NR) | 18,411† | 49.8 |
| | Henry W. Edwards (D) | 15,834 | 42.9 |
| | Zalmon Storrs (A-MASC) | 2,398 | 6.5 |
| 1835 | Henry W. Edwards (D) | 22,129 | 51.5 |
| | Samuel A. Foot (W) | 20,335 | 47.3 |
| 1836 | Henry W. Edwards (D) | 20,360 | 53.6 |
| | Gideon Tomlinson (W) | 17,393 | 45.8 |
| 1837 | Henry W. Edwards (D) | 23,805 | 52.5 |
| | William W. Ellsworth (W) | 21,508 | 47.5 |
| 1838 | William W. Ellsworth (W) | 27,115 | 54.1 |
| | S. P. Beers (D) | 21,489 | 42.9 |
| 1839 | William W. Ellsworth (W) | 26,581 | 51.4 |
| | Niles (D) | 24,047 | 46.5 |
| 1840 | William W. Ellsworth (W) | 30,360 | 54.0 |
| | Niles (D) | 25,782 | 45.8 |
| 1841 | William W. Ellsworth (W) | 26,078 | 56.0 |
| | Nicoll (D) | 20,458 | 44.0 |
| 1842 | Chauncey F. Cleveland (D) | 25,564† | 49.9 |
| | William W. Ellsworth (W) | 23,700 | 46.2 |
| 1843 | Chauncey F. Cleveland (D) | 27,416 | 50.1 |
| | Roger S. Baldwin (W) | 25,401 | 46.4 |
| 1844 | Roger S. Baldwin (W) | 30,093† | 49.4 |
| | Chauncey F. Cleveland (D) | 28,846 | 47.3 |
| 1845 | Roger S. Baldwin (W) | 29,508 | 51.0 |
| | Isaac Toucey (D) | 26,258 | 45.3 |
| 1846 | Clark Bissell (W) | 27,822 | 48.6 |
| | Isaac Toucey (D) | 27,203† | 47.5 |
| 1847 | Clark Bissell (W) | 30,137 | 50.5 |
| | Whittlesey (D) | 27,402 | 45.9 |
| 1848 | Clark Bissell (W) | 30,717 | 50.4 |
| | George S. Catlin (D) | 28,525 | 46.8 |
| 1849 | Joseph Trumbull (W) | 27,300† | 48.8 |
| | Thomas H. Seymour (D) | 25,106 | 44.9 |
| | Niles (F SOIL) | 3,520 | 6.3 |
| 1850 | Thomas H. Seymour (D) | 29,022† | 48.3 |
| | Foster (W) | 28,209 | 46.9 |
| 1851 | Thomas H. Seymour (D) | 30,077† | 49.0 |
| | Foster (W) | 28,756 | 46.9 |
| 1852 | Thomas H. Seymour (D) | 31,624 | 50.4 |
| | Kendrick (W) | 28,241 | 45.0 |
| 1853 | Thomas H. Seymour (D) | 30,814 | 51.0 |
| | Dutton (W) | 20,671 | 34.2 |
| | Gillette (F SOIL) | 8,926 | 14.8 |
| 1854 | Ingham (D) | 28,538 | 48.6 |
| | Henry Dutton (W) | 19,465† | 33.2 |
| | Chapman (TEMP) | 10,672 | 18.2 |
| 1855 | William T. Minor (AM) | 28,080† | 43.5 |
| | Ingham (D) | 27,291 | 42.3 |
| | Henry Dutton (W) | 9,162 | 14.2 |
| 1856 | Ingham (D) | 32,704 | 49.0 |
| | William T. Minor (AM) | 26,008† | 39.0 |
| | Wells (R) | 6,740 | 10.1 |

| | Candidates | Votes | % |
|---|---|---|---|
| 1857 | Alexander H. Holley (R) | 31,709 | *50.4* |
| | Ingham (D) | 31,156 | *49.5* |
| 1858 | William A. Buckingham (R) | 36,298 | *51.8* |
| | Pratt (D) | 33,549 | *47.8* |
| 1859 | William A. Buckingham (R) | 40,247 | *51.1* |
| | Pratt (D) | 38,369 | *48.7* |
| 1860 | William A. Buckingham (R) | 44,458 | *50.3* |
| | Seymour (D) | 43,920 | *49.7* |
| 1861 | William A. Buckingham (R) | 43,012 | *51.2* |
| | Loomis (D) | 40,926 | *48.8* |
| 1862 | William A. Buckingham (R) | 39,782 | *56.5* |
| | Loomis (D) | 30,634 | *43.5* |
| 1863 | William A. Buckingham (R) | 41,032 | *51.6* |
| | Thomas H. Seymour (D) | 38,395 | *18.3* |
| 1864 | William A. Buckingham (UN R) | 39,820 | *53.8* |
| | Origen S. Seymour (D) | 34,162 | *46.2* |
| 1865 | William A. Buckingham (UN R) | 42,374 | *57.5* |
| | Origen S. Seymour (D) | 31,339 | *42.5* |
| 1866 | Joseph R. Hawley (R) | 43,974 | *50.3* |
| | James E. English (D) | 43,433 | *49.7* |
| 1867 | James E. English (D) | 47,565 | *50.5* |
| | Joseph R. Hawley (R) | 46,578 | *49.5* |
| 1868 | James E. English (D) | 50,541 | *50.9* |
| | Marshall Jewell (R) | 48,777 | *49.1* |
| 1869 | Marshall Jewell (R) | 45,493 | *50.2* |
| | James E. English (D) | 45,082 | *49.8* |
| 1870 | James E. English (D) | 44,128 | *50.5* |
| | Marshall Jewell (R) | 43,285 | *49.5* |
| 1871 | Marshall Jewell (R) | 47,473 | *50.1* |
| | James E. English (D) | 47,370 | *49.9* |
| 1872 | Marshall Jewell (R) | 46,563 | *50.0* |
| | Richard D. Hubbard (D) | 44,562 | *47.9* |
| 1873 | Charles R. Ingersoll (D) | 45,060 | *51.9* |
| | Haven (R) | 39,245 | *45.2* |
| 1874 | Charles R. Ingersoll (D) | 46,755 | *53.9* |
| | Harrison (R) | 39,973 | *46.1* |
| 1875 | Charles R. Ingersoll (D) | 53,752 | *53.2* |
| | Greene (R) | 44,272 | *43.9* |
| 1876 | Richard D. Hubbard (D) | 61,934 | *50.8* |
| | Robinson (R) | 58,514 | *48.0* |
| 1878 | Charles B. Andrews (R) | 48,867† | *46.7* |
| | Richard D. Hubbard (D) | 46,385 | *44.3* |
| | Atwater (N) | 8,314 | *7.9* |
| 1880 | Hobart B. Bigelow (R) | 67,070 | *50.5* |
| | James E. English (D) | 64,293 | *48.4* |
| 1882 | Thomas M. Waller (D) | 59,014 | *51.0* |
| | Morgan G. Bulkeley (R) | 54,853 | *47.4* |
| 1884 | Thomas M. Waller (D) | 67,910 | *49.3* |
| | Henry B. Harrison (R) | 66,274† | *48.1* |
| 1886 | Cleveland (D) | 58,818 | *47.7* |
| | Phineas C. Lounsbury (R) | 56,920† | *46.2* |
| 1888 | Luzon B. Morris (D) | 75,074 | *48.9* |
| | Morgan G. Bulkeley (R) | 73,659† | *47.9* |
| 1890 | Luzon B. Morris (D) | 67,658* | *50.0* |
| | S. E. Merwin (R) | 63,975 | *47.3* |
| 1892 | Luzon B. Morris (D) | 82,787 | *50.3* |
| | S. E. Merwin (R) | 76,745 | *46.6* |
| 1894 | O. Vincent Coffin (R) | 83,975 | *54.2* |
| | Cady (D) | 66,287 | *42.8* |
| 1896 | Lorrin A. Cooke (R) | 108,807 | *62.5* |
| | Sargent (D) | 56,524 | *32.5* |
| 1898 | George E. Lounsbury (R) | 81,015 | *54.2* |
| | Morgan (D) | 64,227 | *42.9* |
| 1900 | George P. McLean (R) | 95,822 | *53.0* |
| | S. L. Bronson (D) | 81,421 | *45.1* |
| 1902 | Abiram Chamberlain (R) | 85,338 | *53.4* |
| | Melbert B. Cary (D) | 69,330 | *43.4* |
| 1904 | Henry Roberts (R) | 104,736 | *54.9* |
| | A. Heaton Robertson (D) | 79,164 | *41.5* |
| 1906 | Rollin S. Woodruff (R) | 88,384 | *54.8* |
| | Charles Thayer (D) | 67,776 | *42.1* |

| | Candidates | Votes | % |
|---|---|---|---|
| 1908 | George L. Lilley (R) | 98,179 | *51.9* |
| | A. Heaton Robertson (D) | 82,260 | *43.5* |
| 1910 | Simeon E. Baldwin (D) | 77,243 | *46.5* |
| | Goodwin (R) | 73,528 | *44.3* |
| | Hunter (SOC) | 12,179 | *7.3* |
| 1912 | Simeon E. Baldwin (D) | 78,264 | *41.1* |
| | Studley (R) | 67,531 | *35.5* |
| | Smith (PROG) | 31,020 | *16.3* |
| | Beardsley (SOC) | 10,236 | *5.4* |
| 1914 | Marcus H. Holcomb (R) | 91,262 | *50.4* |
| | Lyman Tingier (D) | 73,888 | *40.8* |
| 1916 | Marcus H. Holcomb (R) | 109,293 | *51.1* |
| | Morris Beardsley (D) | 96,787 | *45.3* |
| 1918 | Marcus H. Holcomb (R) | 84,891 | *50.7* |
| | Thomas Spellacy (D) | 76,773 | *45.9* |
| 1920 | Everett J. Lake (R) | 230,792 | *63.0* |
| | Rollin U. Tyler (D) | 119,912 | *32.8* |
| 1922 | Charles A. Templeton (R) | 170,231 | *52.4* |
| | David Fitzgerald (D) | 148,641 | *45.7* |
| 1924 | Hiram Bingham (R) | 246,336 | *66.2* |
| | Charles Morris (D) | 118,676 | *31.9* |
| 1926 | John H. Trumbull (R) | 192,425 | *63.6* |
| | Charles Morris (D) | 107,045 | *35.4* |
| 1928 | John H. Trumbull (R) | 296,216 | *53.6* |
| | Charles Morris (D) | 252,209 | *45.6* |
| 1930 | Wilbur L. Cross (D) | 215,072 | *49.9* |
| | E. E. Rogers (R) | 209,607 | *48.6* |
| 1932 | Wilbur L. Cross (D) | 288,347 | *49.0* |
| | John H. Trumbull (R) | 277,503 | *47.1* |
| 1934 | Wilbur L. Cross (D) | 257,996 | *46.7* |
| | Hugh Meade Alcorn (R) | 249,397 | *45.2* |
| | Jasper McLevy (SOC) | 38,438 | *7.0* |
| 1936 | Wilbur L. Cross (D) | 372,953# | *55.3* |
| | Arthur M. Brown (R) | 277,190# | *41.1* |
| 1938 | Raymond E. Baldwin (R, UN) | 230,237 | *36.4* |
| | Wilbur L. Cross (D) | 227,549 | *36.0* |
| | Jasper McLevy (SOC) | 166,253 | *26.3* |
| 1940 | Robert A. Hurley (D) | 388,361 | *49.5* |
| | Raymond E. Baldwin (R, UN) | 374,581 | *47.8* |
| 1942 | Raymond E. Baldwin (R) | 281,362 | *48.9* |
| | Robert A. Hurley (D) | 255,166 | *44.4* |
| | Jasper McLevy (SOC) | 34,537 | *6.0* |
| 1944 | Raymond E. Baldwin (R) | 418,289 | *50.5* |
| | Robert A. Hurley (D) | 392,417 | *47.4* |
| 1946 | James L. McConaughy (R) | 371,852 | *54.4* |
| | Wilbert Snow (D) | 276,335 | *40.4* |
| 1948 | Chester Bowles (D) | 431,746 | *49.3* |
| | James C. Shannon (R) | 429,071 | *49.0* |
| 1950 | John D. Lodge (R) | 436,418 | *49.7* |
| | Chester Bowles (D) | 419,404 | *47.7* |
| 1954 | Abraham A. Ribicoff (D) | 463,643 | *49.5* |
| | John D. Lodge (R) | 460,528 | *49.2* |
| 1958 | Abraham A. Ribicoff (D) | 607,012 | *62.3* |
| | Fred R. Zeller (R) | 360,644 | *37.0* |
| 1962 | John N. Dempsey (D) | 549,027 | *53.2* |
| | John Alsop (R) | 482,852 | *46.8* |
| 1966 | John N. Dempsey (D) | 561,599 | *55.7* |
| | E. Clayton Gengras (R) | 446,536 | *44.3* |
| 1970 | Thomas J. Meskill (R) | 582,160 | *53.8* |
| | Emilio Q. Daddario (D) | 500,561 | *46.2* |
| 1974 | Ella T. Grasso (D) | 643,490 | *58.4* |
| | Robert H. Steele (R) | 440,169 | *39.9* |
| 1978 | Ella T. Grasso (D) | 613,109 | *59.1* |
| | Ronald A. Sarasin (R) | 422,316 | *40.7* |
| 1982 | William A. O'Neill (D) | 578,264 | *53.3* |
| | Lewis B. Rome (R) | 497,773 | *45.9* |
| 1986 | William A. O'Neill (D) | 575,638 | *57.9* |
| | Julie D. Belaga (R) | 408,489 | *41.1* |

| 1990 | Candidates | Votes | % |
|---|---|---|---|
| | Lowell P. Weicker Jr. (ACP) | 460,576 | 40.4 |
| | John G. Rowland (R) | 427,840 | 37.5 |
| | Bruce A. Morrison (D) | 236,641 | 20.7 |

**Connecticut**
1. *Toleration Party.*

# DELAWARE

(Ratified the Constitution Dec. 7, 1787)

| | Candidates | Votes | % |
|---|---|---|---|
| 1792 [1] | Joshua Clayton | 2,209 | 48.3 |
| | Thomas Montgomery | 1,902 | 41.6 |
| | George Mitchell | 458 | 10.0 |
| 1795 | Gunning Bedford Jr. | 2,352 | 52.3 |
| | Archibald Alexander | 2,142 | 47.7 |
| 1798 | Richard Bassett (FED) | 2,490 | 52.5 |
| | David Hall (D-R) | 2,068 | 43.6 |
| 1801 | David Hall (D-R) | 3,475 | 50.1 |
| | Nathanael Mitchell (FED) | 3,457 | 49.9 |
| 1804 | Nathanael Mitchell (FED) | 4,391 | 52.0 |
| | Joseph Hazlett (D-R) | 4,050 | 48.0 |
| 1807 | George Truitt (FED) | 3,309 | 51.9 |
| | Joseph Hazlett (D-R) | 3,062 | 48.1 |
| 1810 | Joseph Hazlett (D-R) | 3,664 | 50.5 |
| | Daniel Rodney (FED) | 3,593 | 49.5 |
| 1813 | Daniel Rodney (FED) | 4,643 | 55.2 |
| | James Riddle (D-R) | 3,768 | 44.8 |
| 1816 | John Clarke (FED) | 3,998 | 53.2 |
| | Mansen Bull (D-R) | 3,517 | 46.8 |
| 1819 | Henry Molleston (FED) | 3,823* | 54.6 |
| | Mansen Bull (D-R) | 3,185 | 45.4 |
| 1820 | John Collins (D-R) | 3,965 | 53.1 |
| | Jesse Green (FED) | 3,500 | 46.9 |
| 1822 | Joseph Hazlett (D-R) | 3,784 | 50.1 |
| | James Booth (FED) | 3,762 | 49.9 |
| 1823 | Samuel Paynter (FED) | 4,348 | 51.8 |
| | Daniel Hazzard (D-R) | 4,051 | 48.2 |
| 1826 | Charles Polk (FED) | 4,344# | 50.6 |
| | David Hazzard (D-R) | 4,238# | 49.4 |
| 1829 | David Hazzard (AM D-R) | ✔ # | |
| | A. Thompson (JAC D) # | | |
| 1832 | Caleb P. Bennett (D) | 4,220 | 50.3 |
| | Arnold Naudain (NR) | 4,166 | 49.7 |
| 1836 | Cornelius P. Comegys (W) | 4,693 | 52.3 |
| | Nehemiah Clark (D) | 4,276 | 47.7 |
| 1840 | William B. Cooper (W) | 5,855 | 53.8 |
| | Warren Jefferson (D) | 5,024 | 46.2 |
| 1844 | Thomas Stockton (W) | 6,140 | 50.2 |
| | William Tharp (D) | 6,095 | 49.8 |
| 1846 | William Tharp (D) | 6,148 | 50.6 |
| | Peter F. Causey (W) | 6,012 | 49.4 |
| 1850 | William H. Ross (D) | 6,001 | 48.3 |
| | Peter F. Causey (W) | 5,978 | 48.1 |
| 1854 | Peter F. Causey (AM) | 6,941 | 52.6 |
| | Barton (D) | 6,244 | 47.4 |
| 1858 | William Burton (D) | 7,758 | 50.7 |
| | Buckmaster | 7,554 | 49.3 |
| 1862 | William Cannon (UN) | 8,155 | 50.3 |
| | Jefferson (D) | 8,044 | 49.7 |
| 1866 | Gove Saulsbury (D) | 9,810 | 53.3 |
| | James Riddle (R) | 8,598 | 46.7 |
| 1870 | James Ponder (D) | 11,464 | 55.7 |
| | Thomas B. Coursey (R) | 9,130 | 44.3 |
| 1874 | John P. Cochran (D) | 12,488 | 52.6 |
| | Jump (R) | 11,259 | 47.4 |

| | Candidates | Votes | % |
|---|---|---|---|
| 1878 | John W. Hall (D) | 10,730 | 79.1 |
| | Stewart (NG) | 2,835 | 20.9 |
| 1882 | Charles C. Stockley (D) | 16,558 | 53.1 |
| | Curry (R) | 14,620 | 46.9 |
| 1886 | Benjamin T. Biggs (D) | 13,942 | 63.6 |
| | Hoffecker (TEMP REF) | 7,835 | 35.8 |
| 1890 | Robert J. Reynolds (D) | 17,801 | 50.4 |
| | Richardson (R) | 17,258 | 48.9 |
| 1894 | Joshua H. Marvel (R) | 19,880 | 50.8 |
| | Ebe W. Tunnell (D) | 18,659 | 47.7 |
| 1896 | Ebe W. Tunnell (D) | 15,507 | 44.2 |
| | John H. Hoffecker (R) | 11,014 | 31.4 |
| | John C. Higgins (A-AK R) | 7,154 | 20.4 |
| 1900 | John Hunn (R) | 22,421 | 53.6 |
| | Peter J. Ford (D) | 18,808 | 44.9 |
| 1904 | Preston Lea (R) | 22,532 | 51.4 |
| | Caleb S. Pennewill (D) | 19,780 | 45.1 |
| 1908 | Simeon S. Pennewill (R) | 24,905 | 52.0 |
| | Rowland G. Paynter (D) | 22,794 | 47.6 |
| 1912 | Charles R. Miller (R & PROG) | 22,745 | 47.0 |
| | Thomas M. Monaghan (D) | 21,460 | 44.3 |
| | George B. Hynson (PROG) | 3,019 | 6.2 |
| 1916 | John G. Townsend Jr. (R) | 26,664 | 52.1 |
| | James H. Hughes (D) | 24,053 | 47.0 |
| 1920 | William E. Denney (R) | 51,895 | 55.2 |
| | Andrew J. Lynch (D) | 41,038 | 43.7 |
| 1924 | Robert P. Robinson (R) | 53,046 | 59.6 |
| | Joseph Bancroft (D) | 34,830 | 39.2 |
| 1928 | C. Douglass Buck (R) | 63,716 | 61.2 |
| | Charles M. Wharton (D) | 40,346 | 38.8 |
| 1932 | Clayton Douglass Buck (R) | 60,903 | 54.2 |
| | L. Layton (D) | 50,401 | 44.9 |
| 1936 | Richard C. McMullen (D) | 65,437 | 51.6 |
| | Harry L. Cannon (R) | 52,782 | 41.6 |
| | Isaac Dolphus Short (IR) | 8,400 | 6.6 |
| 1940 | Walter W. Bacon (R) | 70,629 | 52.4 |
| | Josiah Marvel Jr. (D) | 61,237 | 45.4 |
| 1944 | Walter W. Bacon (R) | 63,829 | 50.5 |
| | Isaac J. MacCollum (D) | 62,156 | 49.2 |
| 1948 | Elbert N. Carvel (D) | 75,339 | 53.7 |
| | Hyland P. George (R) | 64,996 | 46.3 |
| 1952 | J. Caleb Boggs (R) | 88,977 | 52.1 |
| | Elbert N. Carvel (D) | 81,772 | 47.9 |
| 1956 | J. Caleb Boggs (R) | 91,965 | 52.0 |
| | J. H. Tyler McConnell (D) | 85,047 | 48.1 |
| 1960 | Elbert N. Carvel (D) | 100,792 | 51.7 |
| | John W. Rollins (R) | 94,043 | 48.3 |
| 1964 | Charles L. Terry Jr. (D) | 102,797 | 51.4 |
| | David P. Buckson (R) | 97,374 | 48.7 |
| 1968 | Russell W. Peterson (R) | 104,474 | 50.5 |
| | Charles L. Terry Jr. (D) | 102,360 | 49.5 |
| 1972 | Sherman W. Tribbitt (D) | 117,274 | 51.3 |
| | Russell W. Peterson (R) | 109,583 | 47.9 |
| 1976 | Pierre duPont (R) | 130,531 | 56.9 |
| | Sherman W. Tribbitt (D) | 97,480 | 42.5 |
| 1980 | Pierre duPont (R) | 159,004 | 70.6 |
| | William J. Gordy (D) | 64,217 | 28.5 |
| 1984 | Michael N. Castle (R) | 132,250 | 55.5 |
| | William T. Quillen (D) | 108,315 | 44.5 |
| 1988 | Michael N. Castle (R) | 169,733 | 70.7 |
| | Jacob Kreshtool (D) | 70,236 | 29.3 |
| 1992 | Thomas R. Carper (D) | 179,365 | 64.7 |
| | B. Gary Scott (R) | 90,725 | 32.7 |

**Delaware**
1. *Before 1792 governor chosen by legislature.*

# FLORIDA

(Became a state March 3, 1845)

| | Candidates | Votes | % |
|---|---|---|---|
| 1845 | William D. Moseley (D) | 3,292 | 55.1 |
| | R. K. McCall (W) | 2,679 | 44.9 |
| 1848 | Thomas S. Brown (W) | 4,147 | 53.3 |
| | W. Bailey (D) | 3,636 | 46.7 |
| 1852 | James E. Broome (D) | 4,628 | 51.6 |
| | George T. Ward (W) | 4,336 | 48.4 |
| 1856 | Madison S. Perry (D) | 6,208 | 51.3 |
| | David S. Walker (AM) | 5,894 | 48.7 |
| 1860 | John Milton (D) | 6,937 | 57.1 |
| | Edward Hopkins (CST U) | 5,215 | 42.9 |
| 1865 | David S. Walker (D) | 5,873# | 100.0 |
| 1868 | Harrison Reed (R) | 14,421# | 59.1 |
| | George W. Scott (D) | 7,731# | 31.7 |
| | Samuel Walker (RAD R) | 2,251# | 9.2 |
| 1872 | Ossian B. Hart (R) | 17,603 | 52.4 |
| | William D. Bloxham (LR) | 16,004 | 47.6 |
| 1876 | George F. Drew (D) | 24,613 | 50.5 |
| | Marcellus L. Stearns (R) | 24,116 | 49.5 |
| 1880 | William D. Bloxham (D) | 28,372 | 54.9 |
| | Simon B. Conover (R) | 23,307 | 45.1 |
| 1884 | Edward A. Perry (D) | 32,096 | 53.5 |
| | Pope (R) | 27,865 | 46.5 |
| 1888 | Francis P. Fleming (D) | 40,195 | 60.4 |
| | V. J. Shipman (R) | 26,385 | 39.6 |
| 1892 | Henry L. Mitchell (D) | 32,064 | 78.7 |
| | Alonzo P. Baskin (FLA PP) | 8,379 | 20.6 |
| 1896 | William D. Bloxham (D) | 27,171 | 66.6 |
| | E. R. Gunby (R) | 8,290 | 20.3 |
| | W. A. Wicks (POP) | 5,370 | 13.2 |
| 1900 | William S. Jennings (D) | 29,251 | 82.0 |
| | M. B. MacFarlane (R) | 6,438 | 18.0 |
| 1904 | Napoleon B. Broward (D) | 28,971 | 79.2 |
| | M. B. MacFarlane (R) | 6,357 | 17.4 |
| 1908 | Albert W. Gilchrist (D) | 33,036 | 78.8 |
| | John M. Cheney (R) | 6,453 | 15.4 |
| | A. J. Pettigrew (SOC) | 2,427 | 5.8 |
| 1912 | Park Trammell (D) | 38,377 | 80.2 |
| | Thomas W. Cox (SOC) | 3,467 | 7.2 |
| | William R. O'Neal (R) | 2,646 | 5.5 |
| 1916 | Sidney J. Catts (IP) | 39,546# | 47.7 |
| | W. V. Knott (D) | 30,343 | 36.6 |
| | George W. Allen (R) | 10,333 | 12.5 |
| 1920 | Cary A. Hardee (D) | 103,407 | 77.9 |
| | George E. Gay (R) | 23,788 | 17.9 |
| 1924 | John W. Martin (D) | 84,181 | 82.8 |
| | W. O'Neal | 17,499 | 17.2 |
| 1928 | Doyle E. Carlton (D) | 148,455 | 61.0 |
| | W. J. Howey (R) | 95,018 | 39.0 |
| 1932 | David Sholtz (D) | 186,270 | 66.6 |
| | W. J. Howey (R) | 93,323 | 33.4 |
| 1936 | Fred P. Cone (D) | 253,638 | 80.9 |
| | E. E. Callaway (R) | 59,832 | 19.1 |
| 1940 | Spessard L. Holland (D) | 334,152 | 100.0 |
| 1944 | Millard F. Caldwell (D) | 361,077 | 78.9 |
| | Bert Lee Acker (R) | 96,321 | 21.1 |
| 1948 | Fuller Warren (D) | 381,459 | 83.4 |
| | Bert Lee Acker (R) | 76,153 | 16.6 |
| 1952 | Daniel T. McCarty (D) | 624,463 | 74.8 |
| | Harry S. Swan (R) | 210,009 | 25.2 |

Special Election

| | | | |
|---|---|---|---|
| 1954 | Leroy Collins (D) | 287,769 | 80.5 |
| | J. Tom Watson (R) | 69,852 | 19.5 |

| | Candidates | Votes | % |
|---|---|---|---|
| 1956 | Leroy Collins (D) | 747,753 | 73.7 |
| | William A. Washburn Jr. (R) | 266,980 | 26.3 |
| 1960 | Farris Bryant (D) | 849,407 | 59.9 |
| | George C. Petersen (R) | 569,936 | 40.2 |
| 1964 | Haydon Burns (D) | 933,554 | 56.1 |
| | Charles R. Holley (R) | 686,297 | 41.3 |
| 1966 | Claude R. Kirk Jr. (R) | 821,190 | 55.1 |
| | Robert King High (D) | 668,233 | 44.9 |
| 1970 | Reubin Askew (D) | 984,305 | 56.8 |
| | Claude R. Kirk Jr. (R) | 746,243 | 43.0 |
| 1974 | Reubin Askew (D) | 1,118,954 | 61.2 |
| | Jerry Thomas (R) | 709,438 | 38.8 |
| 1978 | Robert Graham (D) | 1,406,580 | 55.6 |
| | Jack M. Eckerd (R) | 1,123,888 | 44.4 |
| 1982 | Robert Graham (D) | 1,739,553 | 64.7 |
| | L. A. Bafalis (R) | 949,013 | 35.3 |
| 1986 | Bob Martinez (R) | 1,847,525 | 54.6 |
| | Steve Pajcic (D) | 1,538,620 | 45.4 |
| 1990 | Lawton Chiles (D) | 1,995,206 | 56.5 |
| | Bob Martinez (R) | 1,535,068 | 43.5 |

# GEORGIA

(Ratified the Constitution Jan. 2, 1788)

| | Candidates | Votes | % |
|---|---|---|---|
| 1825 [1] | George M. Troup | 20,545 | 50.9 |
| | John Clark | 19,857 | 49.2 |
| 1827 | John Forsyth | 23,174 | 70.6 |
| 1829 | George R. Gilmer | 27,398 | 71.5 |
| | Joel Crawford | 10,946 | 28.6 |
| 1831 | Wilson Lumpkin | 27,224 | 51.7 |
| | George R. Gilmer | 25,468 | 48.3 |
| 1833 | Wilson Lumpkin | 30,868 | 51.4 |
| | Joel Crawford | 29,186 | 48.6 |
| 1835 | William Schley (D) | 31,190 | 52.3 |
| | Dougherty (W) | 28,497 | 47.7 |
| 1837 | George R. Gilmer (W) | ✔ | |
| | William Schley (D) | | |
| 1839 | Charles James McDonald (D) | 34,668 | 51.5 |
| | Dougherty (W) | 32,715 | 48.6 |
| 1841 | Charles James McDonald (D) | 38,514 | 52.7 |
| | William C. Dawson (W) | 34,511 | 47.3 |
| 1843 | George Walker Crawford (W) | 38,711 | 52.3 |
| | Mark A. Cooper (D) | 35,273 | 47.7 |
| 1845 | George Walker Crawford (W) | 41,523 | 51.1 |
| | McAllister (D) | 39,753 | 48.9 |
| 1847 | George Washington Towns (D) | 43,219 | 50.8 |
| | Clinch (W) | 41,941 | 49.3 |
| 1849 | George Washington Towns (D) | 46,634 | 51.8 |
| | Hill (W) | 43,349 | 48.2 |
| 1851 | Howell Cobb (UN) | 57,414 | 59.7 |
| | McDonald (SOR W) | 38,824 | 40.3 |
| 1853 | Hershel Vespasian Johnson (D) | 47,638 | 50.3 |
| | Jenkins (W) | 47,128 | 49.7 |
| 1855 | Hershel Vespasian Johnson (D) | 54,136 | 52.1 |
| | Andrews (AM) | 43,358 | 41.8 |
| | Overby (TEMP) | 6,333 | 6.1 |
| 1857 | Joseph Emerson Brown (D) | 57,631 | 55.1 |
| | Hill (AM) | 46,889 | 44.9 |
| 1859 | Joseph Emerson Brown (D) | 63,806 | 60.2 |
| | Akin (OPP) | 42,195 | 39.8 |
| 1868 | Rufus B. Bullock (R) | 83,107 | 52.1 |
| | Gordon (D) | 76,539 | 47.9 |
| 1872 | James Milton Smith (LR) | 104,539 | 69.2 |
| | Walker (R) | 46,475 | 30.8 |
| 1876 | Alfred Holt Colquitt (D) | 110,624 | 76.2 |
| | Norcross (R) | 34,492 | 23.8 |

| | Candidates | Votes | % |
|---|---|---|---|
| 1880 | Alfred Holt Colquitt (D) | 117,803 | 64.9 |
| | Norwood (ID) | 63,631 | 35.1 |
| 1882 | Alexander H. Stephens (D) | 107,649 | 70.6 |
| | Gartrell (ID) | 44,893 | 29.4 |
| 1884 | Henry D. McDaniel (D) | ✔ | |
| 1886 | John B. Gordon (D) | 101,159 | 99.2 |
| 1888 | John B. Gordon (D) | 121,999 | 100.0 |
| 1890 | William J. Northen (D) | 105,365 | 100.0 |
| 1892 | William J. Northen (D) | 136,543 | 66.7 |
| | Peck (PP) | 68,093 | 33.3 |
| 1894 | William Y. Atkinson (D) | 121,249 | 55.6 |
| | J. K. Hines (POP) | 96,990 | 44.4 |
| 1896 | William Y. Atkinson (D) | 123,206 | 58.9 |
| | Seaborn Wright (POP) | 85,981 | 41.1 |
| 1898 | Allen D. Candler (D) | 118,028 | 69.8 |
| | Hogan (POP) | 51,191 | 30.3 |
| 1900 | Allen D. Candler (D) | 92,729 | 78.6 |
| | George W. Trayler (POP) | 25,285 | 21.4 |
| 1902 | Joseph M. Terrell (D) | 81,548 | 93.6 |
| | Hines (POP) | 5,566 | 6.4 |
| 1904 | Joseph M. Terrell (D) | 67,523 | 100.0 |
| 1906 | Hoke Smith (D) | 94,223 | 99.9 |
| 1908 | Joseph M. Brown (D) | 112,292 | 90.5 |
| | Yancy Carter (I) | 11,746 | 9.5 |
| 1910 | Hoke Smith (D) | ✔ | |
| | Joseph M. Brown | | |
| 1912 | John M. Slaton (D) | ✔ | |
| 1914 | Nathaniel E. Harris (D) | ✔ | |
| 1916 | Hugh M. Dorsey (D) | ✔ | |
| 1918 | Hugh M. Dorsey (D) | 59,536 | 100.0 |
| 1920 | Thomas W. Hardwick (D) | ✔ | |
| 1922 | Clifford M. Walker (D) | 75,000 | 100.0 |
| 1924 | Clifford M. Walker (D) | 152,367 | 100.0 |
| 1926 | Lamartine G. Hardman (D) | 47,300 | 100.0 |
| 1928 | Lamartine G. Hardman (D) | ✔ | |
| 1930 | Richard B. Russell (D) | ✔ | |
| 1932 | Eugene Talmadge (D) | 240,242 | 100.0 |
| 1934 | Eugene Talmadge (D) | 53,101 | 100.0 |
| 1936 | Eurith D. Rivers (D) | 263,140 | 99.7 |
| 1938 | Eurith D. Rivers (D) | 66,863 | 94.3 |
| 1940 | Eugene Talmadge (D, ID) | 286,277 | 99.6 |
| 1942 | Ellis Arnall (D) | 62,220 | 96.3 |
| 1946 | Eugene Talmadge (D) | 144,067* | 99.1 |

Special Election

| | | | |
|---|---|---|---|
| 1948 | Herman E. Talmadge (D) | 354,712 | 97.5 |

| | | | |
|---|---|---|---|
| 1950 | Herman E. Talmadge (D) | 230,771 | 98.4 |
| 1954 | S. Marvin Griffin (D) | 331,899 | 100.0 |
| 1958 | S. Ernest Vandiver (D) | 168,414 | 100.0 |
| 1962 | Carl E. Sanders (D) | 311,524 | 100.0 |
| 1966 | Howard H. Callaway (R) | 453,665 | 47.8 |
| | Lester Maddox (D) | 450,626† | 47.4 |
| 1970 | Jimmy Carter (D) | 620,419 | 59.3 |
| | Hal Suit (R) | 424,983 | 40.6 |
| 1974 | George Busbee (D) | 646,777 | 69.1 |
| | Ronnie Thompson (R) | 289,113 | 30.9 |
| 1978 | George Busbee (D) | 534,572 | 80.6 |
| | Rodney M. Cook (R) | 128,139 | 19.3 |
| 1982 | Joe Frank Harris (D) | 734,090 | 62.8 |
| | Robert H. Bell (R) | 434,496 | 37.2 |
| 1986 | Joe Frank Harris (D) | 828,465 | 70.5 |
| | Guy Davis (R) | 346,512 | 29.5 |
| 1990 | Zell Miller (D) | 766,662 | 52.9 |
| | Johnny Isakson (R) | 645,625 | 44.5 |

**Georgia**
  1. *Before 1825 governor chosen by legislature.*

# HAWAII

(Became a state Aug. 21, 1959)

| | Candidates | Votes | % |
|---|---|---|---|
| 1959 | William F. Quinn (R) | 86,213 | 51.1 |
| | John A. Burns (D) | 82,074 | 48.7 |
| 1962 | John A. Burns (D) | 114,308 | 58.3 |
| | William F. Quinn (R) | 81,707 | 41.7 |
| 1966 | John A. Burns (D) | 108,840 | 51.1 |
| | Randolph Crossley (R) | 104,324 | 48.9 |
| 1970 | John A. Burns (D) | 137,812 | 57.7 |
| | Sam King (R) | 101,249 | 42.4 |
| 1974 | George R. Ariyoshi (D) | 136,262 | 54.6 |
| | Randolph Crossley (R) | 113,388 | 45.4 |
| 1978 | George R. Ariyoshi (D) | 153,394 | 54.5 |
| | John Leopold (R) | 124,610 | 44.3 |
| 1982 | George R. Ariyoshi (D) | 141,043 | 45.2 |
| | Frank F. Fasi (ID) | 89,303 | 28.6 |
| | D. G. Anderson (R) | 81,507 | 26.1 |
| 1986 | John Waihee (D) | 173,655 | 52.0 |
| | D. G. "Andy" Anderson (R) | 160,460 | 48.0 |
| 1990 | John Waihee (D) | 203,491 | 59.8 |
| | Fred Hemmings (R) | 131,310 | 38.6 |

# IDAHO

(Became a state July 3, 1890)

| | Candidates | Votes | % |
|---|---|---|---|
| 1890 | G. L. Shoup (R) | 10,262 | 56.4 |
| | Wilson (D) | 7,948 | 43.7 |
| 1892 | William J. McConnell (R) | 8,178 | 40.7 |
| | John M. Burke (D) | 6,769 | 33.7 |
| | Abraham J. Crook (PP) | 4,865 | 24.2 |
| 1894 | William J. McConnell (R) | 10,208 | 41.5 |
| | James W. Ballantine (PP) | 7,121 | 29.0 |
| | Edward A. Stevenson (D) | 7,057 | 28.7 |
| 1896 | Frank Steunenberg (PP-D-S-R) | 22,096 | 76.8 |
| | David H. Budlong (R) | 6,441 | 22.4 |
| 1898 | Frank Steunenberg (FUS) | 19,407 | 48.8 |
| | A. B. Moss (R) | 13,794 | 34.7 |
| | J. H. Anderson (PP) | 5,371 | 13.5 |
| 1900 | Frank W. Hunt (D-FUS) | 28,628 | 52.0 |
| | D. W. Standrod (R) | 26,468 | 48.0 |
| 1902 | John T. Morrison (R) | 31,874 | 52.9 |
| | Frank W. Hunt (D) | 26,021 | 43.2 |
| 1904 | Frank R. Gooding (R) | 41,877 | 58.7 |
| | Henry Heitfeld (D) | 24,252 | 34.0 |
| | Theodore B. Shaw (SOC) | 4,000 | 5.6 |
| 1906 | Frank R. Gooding (R) | 38,386 | 52.2 |
| | Charles O. Stockslager (D) | 29,496 | 40.1 |
| | Thomas F. Kelley (SOC) | 4,650 | 6.3 |
| 1908 | James H. Brady (R) | 47,864 | 49.6 |
| | Moses Alexander (D) | 40,145 | 41.6 |
| | Ernest Untermann (SOC) | 6,155 | 6.4 |
| 1910 | James H. Hawley (D) | 40,856 | 47.4 |
| | James H. Brady (R) | 39,961 | 46.4 |
| | S. W. Motley (SOC) | 5,342 | 6.2 |
| 1912 | John M. Haines (R) | 35,074 | 33.2 |
| | James H. Hawley (D) | 33,992 | 32.2 |
| | G. H. Martin (PROG) | 24,325 | 23.1 |
| | L. A. Coblentz (SOC) | 11,094 | 10.5 |
| 1914 | Moses Alexander (D) | 47,618 | 44.1 |
| | John M. Haines (R) | 40,349 | 37.4 |
| | Hugh E. McElroy (EP) | 10,583 | 9.8 |
| | L. A. Coblentz (SOC) | 7,967 | 7.4 |

| | Candidates | Votes | % |
|---|---|---|---|
| 1916 | Moses Alexander (D) | 63,877 | 47.5 |
| | David W. Davis (R) | 63,305 | 47.1 |
| | Annie E. Triplow (SOC) | 7,321 | 5.4 |
| 1918 | David W. Davis (R) | 57,626 | 60.0 |
| | H. F. Samuels (D) | 38,499 | 40.1 |
| 1920 | David W. Davis (R) | 75,748 | 53.0 |
| | Ted A. Walters (D) | 38,509 | 26.9 |
| | Sherman D. Fairchild (I) | 28,752 | 20.1 |
| 1922 | Charles C. Moore (R) | 50,538 | 39.5 |
| | H. F. Samuels (PROG) | 40,516 | 31.7 |
| | M. Alexander (D) | 36,810 | 28.8 |
| 1924 | Charles C. Moore (R) | 65,408 | 43.9 |
| | H. F. Samuels (PROG) | 58,163 | 39.0 |
| | A. L. Freehafer (D) | 25,081 | 16.8 |
| 1926 | H. C. Baldridge (R) | 61,575 | 51.1 |
| | W. Scott Hall (PROG) | 34,208 | 28.4 |
| | Asher B. Wilson (D) | 24,837 | 20.6 |
| 1928 | H. C. Baldridge (R) | 87,681 | 57.8 |
| | C. Ben Ross (D) | 63,046 | 41.6 |
| 1930 | C. Ben Ross (D) | 73,896 | 56.0 |
| | John McMurray (R) | 58,002 | 44.0 |
| 1932 | C. Ben Ross (D) | 116,663 | 61.7 |
| | Defenbach (R) | 68,863 | 36.4 |
| 1934 | C. Ben Ross (D) | 93,313 | 54.6 |
| | Frank L. Stephan (R) | 75,659 | 44.3 |
| 1936 | Barzilla W. Clark (D) | 115,098 | 57.2 |
| | Frank L. Stephan (R) | 83,430 | 41.5 |
| 1938 | C. A. Bottolfsen (R) | 106,268 | 57.3 |
| | C. Ben Ross (D) | 77,697 | 41.9 |
| 1940 | Chase A. Clark (D) | 120,420 | 50.5 |
| | C. A. Bottolfsen (R) | 118,117 | 49.5 |
| 1942 | C. A. Bottolfsen (R) | 72,260 | 50.2 |
| | Chase A. Clark (D) | 71,826 | 49.9 |
| 1944 | Charles C. Gossett (D) | 109,527 | 52.6 |
| | W. H. Detweiler (R) | 98,532 | 47.4 |
| 1946 | Charles A. Robins (R) | 102,233 | 56.4 |
| | Arnold Williams (D) | 79,131 | 43.6 |
| 1950 | Len B. Jordan (R) | 107,642 | 52.6 |
| | Calvin E. Wright (D) | 97,150 | 47.4 |
| 1954 | Robert E. Smylie (R) | 124,038 | 54.2 |
| | Clark Hamilton (D) | 104,647 | 45.8 |
| 1958 | Robert E. Smylie (R) | 121,810 | 51.0 |
| | A. M. Derr (D) | 117,236 | 49.0 |
| 1962 | Robert E. Smylie (R) | 139,578 | 54.6 |
| | Vernon K. Smith (D) | 115,876 | 45.4 |
| 1966 | Don Samuelson (R) | 104,586 | 41.4 |
| | Cecil D. Andrus (D) | 93,744 | 37.1 |
| | Perry Swisher (I) | 30,913 | 12.2 |
| | Philip W. Jungert (I) | 23,139 | 9.2 |
| 1970 | Cecil D. Andrus (D) | 128,004 | 52.2 |
| | Don Samuelson (R) | 117,108 | 47.8 |
| 1974 | Cecil D. Andrus (D) | 184,142 | 70.9 |
| | Jack M. Murphy (R) | 68,731 | 26.5 |
| 1978 | John V. Evans (D) | 169,540 | 58.8 |
| | Allan Larsen (R) | 114,149 | 39.6 |
| 1982 | John V. Evans (D) | 165,365 | 50.6 |
| | Philip Batt (R) | 161,157 | 49.4 |
| 1986 | Cecil D. Andrus (D) | 193,429 | 49.9 |
| | David H. Leroy (R) | 189,794 | 49.0 |
| 1990 | Cecil D. Andrus (D) | 218,673 | 68.2 |
| | Roger Fairchild (R) | 101,937 | 31.8 |

# ILLINOIS

(Became a state Dec. 3, 1818)

| | Candidates | Votes | % |
|---|---|---|---|
| 1818 | Shadrach Bond | 3,427 | |

| | Candidates | Votes | % |
|---|---|---|---|
| 1822 | Edward Coles | 2,854 | 33.2 |
| | Joseph B. Phillips | 2,687 | 31.2 |
| | Thomas C. Browne | 2,443 | 28.4 |
| | James B. Moore | 622 | 7.2 |
| 1826 | Ninian Edwards (NR) | 6,280 | 49.4 |
| | Thomas Sloo Jr. (JAC D) | 5,833 | 45.9 |
| 1830 | John Reynolds (NR) | 12,837 | 59.0 |
| | William Kinney (JAC D) | 8,938 | 41.1 |
| 1834 | Joseph Duncan (W) | 17,340 | 52.9 |
| | William Kinney (D) | 10,224 | 31.2 |
| | Robert H. McLaughlin | 4,315 | 13.2 |
| 1838 | Thomas Carlin (D) | 30,668 | 50.8 |
| | Cyrus Edwards (W) | 29,722 | 49.2 |
| 1842 | Thomas Ford (D) | 46,502 | 53.8 |
| | Joseph Duncan (W) | 39,030 | 45.2 |
| 1846 | Augustus C. French (D) | 58,660 | 58.2 |
| | Thomas M. Kilpatrick (W) | 37,033 | 36.7 |
| | Richard Eels (LIB) | 5,154 | 5.1 |
| 1848 | Augustus C. French (D) | 67,828 | 86.8 |
| | W. S. D. Morison | 5,659 | 7.2 |
| | Charles V. Dyer | 4,692 | 6.0 |
| 1852 | Joel A. Matteson (D) | 80,789 | 52.4 |
| | E. B. Webb (W) | 64,408 | 41.8 |
| | D. A. Knowlton (F SOIL) | 9,024 | 5.9 |
| 1856 | William H. Bissell (R) | 111,466 | 47.0 |
| | William A. Richardson (D) | 106,769 | 45.0 |
| | Buckner S. Morris (AM) | 19,078 | 8.0 |
| 1860 | Richard Yates (R) | 172,218 | 51.2 |
| | James C. Allen (D) | 159,293 | 47.3 |
| 1864 | Richard J. Oglesby (UN R) | 190,376 | 54.5 |
| | James C. Robinson (D) | 158,711 | 45.5 |
| 1868 | John M. Palmer (R) | 250,467 | 55.5 |
| | John R. Eden (D) | 200,813 | 44.5 |
| 1872 | Richard J. Oglesby (R) | 237,777 | 54.4 |
| | Gust Koener (LR) | 197,083 | 45.1 |
| 1876 | Shelby M. Cullom (R) | 279,263 | 50.6 |
| | Lewis Steward (D & G) | 272,495 | 49.4 |
| 1880 | Shelby M. Cullom (R) | 314,565 | 50.4 |
| | Lyman Trumbull (D) | 277,562 | 44.5 |
| 1884 | Richard J. Oglesby (R) | 334,234 | 49.6 |
| | Carter H. Harrison (D) | 319,645 | 47.5 |
| 1888 | Joseph W. Fifer (R) | 367,856 | 49.2 |
| | John M. Palmer (D) | 355,313 | 47.5 |
| 1892 | John P. Altgeld (D) | 425,498 | 48.7 |
| | Joseph W. Fifer (R) | 402,666 | 46.1 |
| 1896 | John R. Tanner (R) | 587,637 | 54.1 |
| | John P. Altgeld (R) | 474,256 | 43.7 |
| 1900 | Richard Yates (R) | 580,200 | 51.5 |
| | Samuel Alschuler (D) | 518,966 | 46.1 |
| 1904 | Charles S. Deneen (R) | 634,029 | 59.1 |
| | Lawrence B. Stringer (D) | 334,880 | 31.2 |
| | John Collins (SOC) | 59,062 | 5.5 |
| 1908 | Charles S. Deneen (R) | 550,076 | 47.6 |
| | Adlai E. Stevenson (D) | 526,912 | 45.6 |
| 1912 | Edward F. Dunne (D) | 443,120 | 38.1 |
| | Charles S. Deneen (R) | 318,469 | 27.4 |
| | Frank H. Funk (PROG) | 303,401 | 26.1 |
| | John C. Kennedy (SOC) | 78,679 | 6.8 |
| 1916 | Frank O. Lowden (R) | 696,535 | 52.7 |
| | Edward F. Dunne (D) | 556,654 | 42.1 |
| 1920 | Len Small (R) | 1,243,148 | 58.9 |
| | James Hamilton Lewis (D) | 731,541 | 34.6 |
| 1924 | Len Small (R) | 1,366,436 | 56.7 |
| | Norman L. Jones (D) | 1,021,408 | 42.4 |
| 1928 | Louis L. Emmerson (R) | 1,709,818 | 56.8 |
| | Floyd E. Thompson (D) | 1,284,897 | 42.7 |
| 1932 | Henry Horner (D) | 1,930,330 | 57.6 |
| | Len Small (R) | 1,364,043 | 40.7 |
| 1936 | Henry Horner (D) | 2,067,861 | 53.1 |
| | C. Wayland Brooks (R) | 1,682,674 | 43.2 |
| 1940 | Dwight H. Green (R) | 2,197,778 | 52.9 |
| | Harry B. Hershey (D) | 1,940,833 | 46.7 |

| | Candidates | Votes | % |
|---|---|---|---|
| 1944 | Dwight H. Green (R) | 2,013,270 | 50.8 |
| | Thomas J. Courtney (D) | 1,940,999 | 48.9 |
| 1948 | Adlai E. Stevenson (D) | 2,250,074 | 57.1 |
| | Dwight H. Green (R) | 1,678,007 | 42.6 |
| 1952 | William G. Stratton (R) | 2,317,363 | 52.5 |
| | Sherwood Dixon (D) | 2,089,721 | 47.3 |
| 1956 | William G. Stratton (R) | 2,171,786 | 50.3 |
| | Richard B. Austin (D) | 2,134,909 | 49.5 |
| 1960 | Otto Kerner (D) | 2,594,731 | 55.5 |
| | William G. Stratton (R) | 2,070,479 | 44.3 |
| 1964 | Otto Kerner (D) | 2,418,394 | 51.9 |
| | Charles H. Percy (R) | 2,239,095 | 48.1 |
| 1968 | Richard B. Ogilvie (R) | 2,307,295 | 51.2 |
| | Samuel H. Shapiro (D) | 2,179,501 | 48.4 |
| 1972 | Daniel Walker (D) | 2,371,303 | 50.7 |
| | Richard B. Ogilvie (R) | 2,293,809 | 49.0 |
| 1976 | James R. Thompson (R) | 3,000,395 | 64.7 |
| | Michael J. Howlett (D) | 1,610,258 | 34.7 |
| 1978 | James R. Thompson (R) | 1,859,684 | 59.0 |
| | Michael Bakalis (D) | 1,263,134 | 40.1 |
| 1982 | James R. Thompson (R) | 1,816,101 | 49.4 |
| | Adlai E. Stevenson III (D) | 1,811,027 | 49.3 |
| 1986 | James R. Thompson (R) | 1,655,945 | 52.7 |
| | Adlai E. Stevenson III (IS) | 1,256,725 | 40.0 |
| | "Democrat" (no candidate) | 208,841 | 6.6 |
| 1990 | Jim Edgar (R) | 1,653,126 | 50.7 |
| | Neil F. Hartigan (D) | 1,569,217 | 48.2 |

# INDIANA

(Became a state Dec. 11, 1816)

| | Candidates | Votes | % |
|---|---|---|---|
| 1816 | Jonathan Jennings | 5,211 | 57.0 |
| | Thomas Posey | 3,934 | 43.0 |
| 1819 | Jonathan Jennings | 9,168 | 81.4 |
| | Christopher Harrison | 2,088 | 18.6 |
| 1822 | William Hendricks | Unopposed | |
| 1825 | James Brown Ray (CLAY R) | 13,852 | 53.2 |
| | Isaac Blackford (NR) | 12,165 | 46.8 |
| 1828 | James Brown Ray (CLAY R) | 15,131 | 39.5 |
| | Israel T. Canby (JAC D) | 12,251 | 32.0 |
| | Harbin H. Moore (NR) | 10,898 | 28.5 |
| 1831 | Noah Noble (NR) | 23,518 | 45.6 |
| | James G. Read (JAC D) | 21,002 | 40.7 |
| | Milton Stapp (I) | 6,984 | 13.5 |
| 1834 | Noah Noble (W) | 36,797 | 57.4 |
| | James G. Read (D) | 27,276 | 42.6 |
| 1837 | David Wallace (W) | 46,067 | 55.5 |
| | John Dumont (W) | 36,915 | 44.5 |
| 1840 | Samuel Bigger (W) | 62,970 | 53.7 |
| | Tilghman A. Howard (D) | 54,297 | 46.3 |
| 1843 | James Whitcomb (D) | 60,930 | 50.2 |
| | Samuel Bigger (W) | 58,809 | 48.4 |
| 1846 | James Whitcomb (D) | 64,104 | 50.7 |
| | Joseph G. Marshall (W) | 60,138 | 47.5 |
| 1849 | Joseph A. Wright (D) | 76,996 | 52.3 |
| | John A. Matson (W) | 67,218 | 45.6 |
| 1852 | Joseph A. Wright (D) | 92,959 | 54.7 |
| | Nicholas McCarty (W) | 73,647 | 43.3 |
| 1856 | Ashbel P. Willard (D) | 117,981 | 51.3 |
| | Oliver P. Morton (R) | 112,039 | 48.7 |
| 1860 | Henry S. Lane (R) | 136,725 | 51.9 |
| | Thomas Andrews Hendricks (D) | 126,968 | 48.2 |
| 1864 | Oliver P. Morton (R) | 152,275 | 53.7 |
| | Joseph E. McDonald (D) | 131,200 | 46.3 |

| | Candidates | Votes | % |
|---|---|---|---|
| 1868 | Conrad Baker (R) | 171,523 | 50.1 |
| | Thomas Andrews Hendricks (D) | 170,602 | 49.9 |
| 1872 | Thomas Andrews Hendricks (D) | 189,424 | 50.1 |
| | Thomas McClelland Browne (R) | 188,276 | 49.8 |
| 1876 | James Douglas Williams (D) | 213,164 | 49.1 |
| | Benjamin Harrison (R) | 208,080 | 47.9 |
| 1880 | Albert Gallatin Porter (R) | 231,405 | 49.2 |
| | Franklin Landers (D) | 224,452 | 47.7 |
| 1884 | Isaac P. Gray (D) | 245,130 | 49.5 |
| | William H. Calkins (R) | 237,748 | 48.0 |
| 1888 | Alvin P. Hovey (R) | 263,194 | 49.0 |
| | Courtland C. Matson (D) | 260,994 | 48.6 |
| 1892 | Claude Matthews (D) | 260,601 | 47.5 |
| | Ira J. Chase (R) | 253,625 | 46.2 |
| 1896 | James A. Mount (R) | 320,936 | 50.9 |
| | Benjamin F. Shively (D) | 294,855 | 46.8 |
| 1900 | Winfield T. Durbin (R) | 331,531 | 50.5 |
| | John W. Kern (D) | 306,368 | 46.7 |
| 1904 | J. Frank Hanly (R) | 359,362 | 53.5 |
| | John W. Kern (D) | 274,998 | 41.0 |
| 1908 | Thomas R. Marshall (D) | 348,843 | 49.0 |
| | James E. Watson (R) | 334,040 | 46.9 |
| 1912 | Samuel M. Ralston (D) | 275,357 | 43.0 |
| | Albert J. Beveridge (PROG) | 166,654 | 26.0 |
| | Winfield T. Durbin (R) | 141,684 | 22.1 |
| | Stephen N. Reynolds (SOC) | 35,464 | 5.5 |
| 1916 | James P. Goodrich (R) | 337,831 | 47.8 |
| | John A. M. Adair (D) | 325,060 | 46.0 |
| 1920 | Warren T. McCray (R) | 683,253 | 54.6 |
| | Carleton B. McCulloch (D) | 515,253 | 41.2 |
| 1924 | Ed Jackson (R) | 654,184 | 52.9 |
| | Carleton B. McCulloch (D) | 572,303 | 46.3 |
| 1928 | Harry G. Leslie (R) | 728,203 | 51.3 |
| | Frank C. Dailey (D) | 683,545 | 48.1 |
| 1932 | Paul V. McNutt (D) | 862,127 | 55.0 |
| | Raymond S. Springer (R) | 669,797 | 42.8 |
| 1936 | Maurice Clifford Townsend (D) | 908,494 | 55.4 |
| | Raymond S. Springer (R) | 727,526 | 44.3 |
| 1940 | Henry F. Schricker (D) | 889,620 | 49.9 |
| | Glenn R. Hillis (R) | 885,657 | 49.7 |
| 1944 | Ralph F. Gates (R) | 849,346 | 51.0 |
| | Samuel D. Jackson (D) | 802,765 | 48.2 |
| 1948 | Henry F. Schricker (D) | 884,995 | 53.6 |
| | Hobart Creighton (R) | 745,892 | 45.1 |
| 1952 | George N. Craig (R) | 1,075,685 | 55.7 |
| | John A. Watkins (D) | 841,984 | 43.6 |
| 1956 | Harold W. Handley (R) | 1,086,868 | 55.6 |
| | Ralph Tucker (D) | 859,393 | 44.0 |
| 1960 | Matthew E. Welsh (D) | 1,072,717 | 50.4 |
| | Crawford F. Parker (R) | 1,049,540 | 49.3 |
| 1964 | Roger D. Branigin (D) | 1,164,763 | 56.2 |
| | Richard O. Ristine (R) | 901,342 | 43.5 |
| 1968 | Edgar D. Whitcomb (R) | 1,080,271 | 52.7 |
| | Robert L. Rock (D) | 965,816 | 47.1 |
| 1972 | Otis R. Bowen (R) | 1,203,903 | 56.8 |
| | Matthew E. Welsh (D) | 900,489 | 42.5 |
| 1976 | Otis R. Bowen (R) | 1,236,555 | 56.8 |
| | Larry A. Conrad (D) | 927,243 | 42.6 |
| 1980 | Robert D. Orr (R) | 1,257,383 | 57.7 |
| | John A. Hillenbrand (D) | 913,116 | 41.9 |
| 1984 | Robert D. Orr (R) | 1,146,497 | 52.2 |
| | W. Wayne Townsend (D) | 1,036,832 | 47.2 |
| 1988 | Evan Bayh (D) | 1,138,574 | 53.2 |
| | John M. Mutz (R) | 1,002,207 | 46.8 |
| 1992 | Evan Bayh (D) | 1,382,151 | 62.0 |
| | Linley E. Pearson (R) | 822,533 | 36.9 |

# IOWA

(Became a state Dec. 28, 1846)

| | Candidates | Votes | % |
|---|---|---|---|
| 1846 | Ansel Briggs (ER) | 7,626 | 50.8 |
| | Thomas McKnight (W) | 7,379 | 49.2 |
| 1850 | Stephen Hempstead (D) | 13,486 | 52.9 |
| | James L. Thompson (W) | 11,403 | 44.8 |
| 1854 | James W. Grimes (R) | 23,325 | 52.4 |
| | Curtis Bates (NEB) | 21,202 | 47.6 |
| 1857 | Ralph P. Lowe (R) | 38,498 | 50.9 |
| | Ben M. Samuels (D) | 36,088 | 47.7 |
| 1859 | Samuel J. Kirkwood (R) | 56,502 | 51.4 |
| | A. C. Dodge (D) | 53,332 | 48.6 |
| 1861 | Samuel J. Kirkwood (R) | 60,303 | 55.5 |
| | William H. Merritt (D) | 43,245 | 39.8 |
| 1863 | William M. Stone (UN) | 86,118 | 60.5 |
| | James M. Tuttle (D) | 56,169 | 39.5 |
| 1865 | William M. Stone (UN R) | 70,461 | 56.4 |
| | Thomas H. Benton (D) | 54,090 | 43.3 |
| 1867 | Samuel Merrill (R) | 90,204 | 58.9 |
| | Charles Mason (D) | 62,966 | 41.1 |
| 1869 | Samuel Merrill (R) | 97,243 | 62.9 |
| | George Gillaspie (D) | 57,287 | 37.1 |
| 1871 | Cyrus Clay Carpenter (R) | 109,328 | 61.6 |
| | J. C. Knapp (D) | 68,199 | 38.4 |
| 1873 | Cyrus Clay Carpenter (R) | 105,132 | 56.0 |
| | J. G. Vale (A-MONOP) | 82,556 | 44.0 |
| 1875 | Samuel Jordan Kirkwood (R) | 124,855 | 57.0 |
| | Shepherd Leffler (D) | 93,270 | 42.6 |
| 1877 | John Henry Gear (R) | 121,316 | 49.4 |
| | John P. Irish (D) | 79,304 | 32.3 |
| | Daniel P. Stubbs (G) | 34,316 | 14.0 |
| 1879 | John Henry Gear (R) | 157,408 | 53.9 |
| | Henry H. Trimble (D) | 85,364 | 29.3 |
| | Daniel Campbell (G) | 45,674 | 15.7 |
| 1881 | Buren R. Sherman (R) | 133,328 | 56.7 |
| | L. G. Kinne (D) | 73,344 | 31.2 |
| | D. M. Clark (G) | 28,112 | 12.0 |
| 1883 | Buren R. Sherman (R) | 164,095 | 50.1 |
| | L. G. Kinne (D) | 140,012 | 42.8 |
| | James B. Weaver (G) | 23,089 | 7.1 |
| 1885 | William Larrabee (R) | 175,605 | 50.8 |
| | Charles Whiting (D) | 168,584 | 48.7 |
| 1887 | William Larrabee (R) | 169,596 | 50.1 |
| | T. J. Anderson (D) | 153,706 | 45.4 |
| 1889 | Horace Boies (D) | 180,106 | 49.9 |
| | Joseph Hutchinson (R) | 173,450 | 48.1 |
| 1891 | Horace Boies (D) | 207,594 | 49.4 |
| | Herman C. Wheeler (R) | 199,381 | 47.5 |
| 1893 | Frank D. Jackson (R) | 206,821 | 49.7 |
| | Horace Boies (D) | 174,656 | 42.0 |
| | J. M. Joseph (PP) | 23,980 | 5.8 |
| 1895 | Francis M. Drake (R) | 208,708 | 52.0 |
| | W. I. Babb (D) | 149,428 | 37.2 |
| | S. B. Crane (PP) | 32,189 | 8.0 |
| 1897 | Leslie M. Shaw (R) | 224,729 | 51.3 |
| | Fred E. White (D) | 194,853 | 44.5 |
| 1899 | Leslie M. Shaw (R) | 239,464 | 55.3 |
| | Fred E. White (D) | 183,301 | 42.3 |
| 1901 | Albert B. Cummins (R) | 226,902 | 58.1 |
| | T. J. Phillips (D) | 143,783 | 36.8 |
| 1903 | Albert B. Cummins (R) | 238,804 | 57.1 |
| | J. B. Sullivan (D) | 159,725 | 38.2 |
| 1906 | Albert B. Cummins (R) | 216,995 | 50.2 |
| | Claude R. Porter (D) | 196,123 | 45.4 |
| 1908 | Beryl F. Carroll (R) | 256,980 | 54.6 |
| | Fred E. White (D) | 196,929 | 41.8 |
| 1910 | Beryl F. Carroll (R) | 205,678 | 49.8 |
| | Claude R. Porter (D) | 187,353 | 45.4 |
| 1912 | George W. Clarke (R) | 184,150 | 39.9 |
| | Edward G. Dunn (D) | 182,449 | 39.6 |
| | John L. Stevens (PROG) | 71,879 | 15.6 |
| 1914 | George W. Clarke (R) | 207,881 | 49.3 |
| | John T. Hamilton (D) | 181,036 | 42.9 |
| 1916 | William L. Harding (R) | 313,586 | 61.0 |
| | E. T. Meredith (D) | 186,832 | 36.4 |
| 1918 | William L. Harding (R) | 192,662 | 50.6 |
| | Claude R. Porter (D) | 178,815 | 46.9 |
| 1920 | Nathan E. Kendall (R) | 513,118 | 58.7 |
| | Clyde L. Herring (D) | 338,108 | 38.7 |
| 1922 | Nathan E. Kendall (R) | 419,648 | 70.5 |
| | J. R. Files (D) | 175,252 | 29.5 |
| 1924 | John Hammill (R) | 604,624 | 72.7 |
| | J. C. Murtagh (D) | 226,850 | 27.3 |
| 1926 | John Hammill (R) | 377,330 | 71.3 |
| | Alex R. Miller (D) | 150,374 | 28.4 |
| 1928 | John Hammill (R) | 591,720 | 62.8 |
| | L. W. Housel (D) | 350,722 | 37.2 |
| 1930 | Dan W. Turner (R) | 364,036 | 65.7 |
| | Fred P. Hageman (D) | 186,039 | 33.6 |
| 1932 | Clyde L. Herring (D) | 508,573 | 52.8 |
| | Dan W. Turner (R) | 455,145 | 47.2 |
| 1934 | Clyde L. Herring (D) | 468,921 | 54.3 |
| | Dan W. Turner (R) | 394,634 | 45.7 |
| 1936 | Nelson G. Kraschel (D) | 524,178 | 48.7 |
| | George Wilson (R) | 521,747 | 48.4 |
| 1938 | George Wilson (R) | 447,061 | 52.7 |
| | Nelson G. Kraschel (D) | 387,779 | 45.7 |
| 1940 | George Wilson (R) | 620,480 | 52.7 |
| | John Valentine (D) | 553,941 | 47.1 |
| 1942 | Bourke B. Hickenlooper (R) | 438,547 | 62.8 |
| | Nelson G. Kraschel (D) | 258,310 | 37.0 |
| 1944 | Robert D. Blue (R) | 561,827 | 56.0 |
| | R. F. Mitchell (D) | 437,684 | 43.6 |
| 1946 | Robert D. Blue (R) | 362,592 | 57.4 |
| | Frank Miles (D) | 266,190 | 42.1 |
| 1948 | William Beardsley (R) | 553,900 | 55.7 |
| | Carroll O. Switzer (D) | 434,432 | 43.7 |
| 1950 | William Beardsley (R) | 506,642 | 59.1 |
| | Lester S. Gillette (D) | 347,176 | 40.5 |
| 1952 | William Beardsley (R) | 638,388 | 51.9 |
| | Herschel C. Loveless (D) | 587,671 | 47.8 |
| 1954 | Leo A. Hoegh (R) | 435,944 | 51.4 |
| | Clyde E. Herring (D) | 410,255 | 48.4 |
| 1956 | Herschel C. Loveless (D) | 616,852 | 51.2 |
| | Leo A. Hoegh (R) | 587,383 | 48.8 |
| 1958 | Herschel C. Loveless (D) | 465,024 | 54.1 |
| | William G. Murray (R) | 394,071 | 45.9 |
| 1960 | Norman A. Erbe (R) | 645,026 | 52.1 |
| | E. J. McManus (D) | 592,063 | 47.9 |
| 1962 | Harold E. Hughes (D) | 430,899 | 52.6 |
| | Norman A. Erbe (R) | 388,955 | 47.4 |
| 1964 | Harold E. Hughes (D) | 794,610 | 68.1 |
| | Evan Hultman (R) | 365,131 | 31.3 |
| 1966 | Harold E. Hughes (D) | 494,259 | 55.3 |
| | William G. Murray (R) | 394,518 | 44.2 |
| 1968 | Robert D. Ray (R) | 614,328 | 54.1 |
| | Paul Franzenburg (D) | 521,216 | 45.9 |
| 1970 | Robert D. Ray (R) | 403,394 | 51.0 |
| | Robert D. Fulton (D) | 368,911 | 46.6 |
| 1972 | Robert D. Ray (R) | 707,177 | 58.4 |
| | Paul Franzenburg (D) | 487,282 | 40.3 |
| 1974 | Robert D. Ray (R) | 534,518 | 58.1 |
| | James F. Schaben (D) | 377,553 | 41.0 |
| 1978 | Robert D. Ray (R) | 491,713 | 58.3 |
| | Jerome D. Fitzgerald (D) | 345,519 | 41.0 |
| 1982 | Terry E. Branstad (R) | 548,313 | 52.8 |
| | Roxanne Conlin (D) | 483,291 | 46.5 |
| 1986 | Terry E. Branstad (R) | 472,712 | 51.9 |
| | Lowell L. Junkins (D) | 436,987 | 48.0 |

| | Candidates | Votes | % |
|---|---|---|---|
| 1990 | Terry E. Branstad (R) | 591,852 | 60.6 |
| | Donald D. Avenson (D) | 379,372 | 38.9 |

# KANSAS

(Became a state Jan. 29, 1861)

| | Candidates | Votes | % |
|---|---|---|---|
| 1862 | Thomas Carney (R) | 9,990 | 64.7 |
| | W. R. Wagstaff (UN R) | 5,456 | 35.3 |
| 1864 | Samuel J. Crawford (R) | 12,711 | 60.7 |
| | Solon O. Thacher (R-UNION) | 8,244 | 39.3 |
| 1866 | Samuel J. Crawford (R) | 19,370 | 70.4 |
| | J. L. McDowell (N UNION) | 8,151 | 29.6 |
| 1868 | James M. Harvey (R) | 29,795 | 68.2 |
| | George W. Glick (D) | 13,881 | 31.8 |
| 1870 | James M. Harvey (R) | 40,667 | 66.4 |
| | Isaac Sharp (D) | 20,496 | 33.5 |
| 1872 | Thomas A. Osborn (R) | 66,715 | 65.8 |
| | Thaddeus H. Walker (LR) | 34,698 | 34.2 |
| 1874 | Thomas A. Osborn (R) | 48,794 | 56.4 |
| | James C. Cusey (D) | 35,301 | 40.8 |
| 1876 | George T. Anthony (R) | 69,176 | 56.8 |
| | John Martin (D) | 46,201 | 37.9 |
| 1878 | John P. St. John (R) | 74,020 | 53.5 |
| | John R. Goodin (D) | 37,208 | 26.9 |
| | D. P. Mitchell (G) | 27,057 | 19.6 |
| 1880 | John P. St. John (R) | 115,144 | 57.9 |
| | Edmund G. Ross (D) | 63,557 | 32.0 |
| | H. P. Vrooman (G LAB) | 19,481 | 9.8 |
| 1882 | George W. Glick (D) | 83,232 | 46.4 |
| | John P. St. John (R) | 75,158 | 41.9 |
| | Charles Robinson (G LAB) | 20,933 | 11.7 |
| 1884 | John A. Martin (R) | 146,777 | 55.3 |
| | George W. Glick (D) | 108,284 | 40.8 |
| 1886 | John A. Martin (R) | 149,715 | 54.7 |
| | Thomas Moonlight (D) | 115,667 | 42.3 |
| 1888 | L. U. Humphrey (R) | 180,841 | 54.7 |
| | John Martin (D) | 107,582 | 32.5 |
| | P. P. Elder (UN LAB) | 35,847 | 10.8 |
| 1890 | L. U. Humphrey (R) | 115,024 | 39.1 |
| | J. F. Willits (ALNC D) | 106,945 | 36.3 |
| | Charles Robinson (D & RESUB) | 71,357 | 24.2 |
| 1892 | L. D. Lewelling (POP) | 162,507 | 50.0 |
| | Abram W. Smith (R) | 158,075 | 48.7 |
| 1894 | E. N. Morrill (R) | 148,700 | 49.5 |
| | L. D. Lewelling (D-PP) | 118,329 | 39.4 |
| | David Overmyer (STAL D) | 27,709 | 9.2 |
| 1896 | John W. Leedy (D-PP) | 167,941 | 50.5 |
| | E. N. Morrill (R) | 160,507 | 48.3 |
| 1898 | W. E. Stanley (R) | 149,312 | 51.8 |
| | John W. Leedy (D-PP) | 134,158 | 46.6 |
| 1900 | W. E. Stanley (R) | 181,897 | 51.9 |
| | John W. Breidenthal (D-PP) | 164,793 | 47.0 |
| 1902 | W. J. Bailey (R) | 159,242 | 55.5 |
| | W. H. Craddock (D) | 117,148 | 40.8 |
| 1904 | Edward W. Hoch (R) | 186,731 | 57.9 |
| | David M. Dale (D) | 116,991 | 36.3 |
| 1906 | Edward W. Hoch (R) | 152,147 | 48.2 |
| | William A. Harris (D) | 150,024 | 47.6 |
| 1908 | W. R. Stubbs (R) | 196,692 | 52.5 |
| | Jeremiah D. Botkin (D) | 162,385 | 43.3 |
| 1910 | W. R. Stubbs (R) | 162,181 | 49.8 |
| | George H. Hodges (D) | 146,014 | 44.8 |
| 1912 | George H. Hodges (D) | 167,437 | 46.6 |
| | Arthur Capper (R) | 167,408 | 46.5 |
| | George W. Kleihege (SOC) | 24,767 | 6.9 |

| | Candidates | Votes | % |
|---|---|---|---|
| 1914 | Arthur Capper (R) | 209,543 | 39.7 |
| | George H. Hodges (D) | 161,696 | 30.6 |
| | Henry J. Allen (PROG) | 84,060 | 15.9 |
| | J. B. Billard (I) | 47,201 | 8.9 |
| 1916 | Arthur Capper (R) | 353,169 | 60.8 |
| | W. C. Lansdon (D) | 192,037 | 33.1 |
| 1918 | Henry J. Allen (R) | 287,957 | 66.4 |
| | W. C. Lansdon (D) | 133,054 | 30.7 |
| 1920 | Henry J. Allen (R) | 319,914 | 58.4 |
| | Jonathan M. Davis (D) | 214,940 | 39.3 |
| 1922 | Jonathan M. Davis (D) | 271,058 | 50.9 |
| | W. Y. Morgan (R) | 252,602 | 47.4 |
| 1924 | Ben S. Paulen (R) | 323,402 | 49.0 |
| | Jonathan M. Davis (D) | 182,861 | 27.7 |
| | William Allen White (I) | 149,811 | 22.7 |
| 1926 | Ben S. Paulen (R) | 321,540 | 63.3 |
| | Jonathan M. Davis (D) | 179,308 | 35.3 |
| 1928 | Clyde M. Reed (R) | 433,395 | 65.6 |
| | Chauncey B. Little (D) | 219,327 | 33.2 |
| 1930 | Harry H. Woodring (D) | 217,171 | 35.0 |
| | Frank Haucke (R) | 216,920 | 34.9 |
| | John R. Brinkley (I) | 183,278 | 29.5 |
| 1932 | Alfred M. Landon (R) | 278,581 | 34.8 |
| | Harry H. Woodring (D) | 272,944 | 34.1 |
| | John R. Brinkley (I) | 244,607 | 30.6 |
| 1934 | Alfred M. Landon (R) | 422,030 | 53.5 |
| | Omar B. Ketchum (D) | 359,877 | 45.6 |
| 1936 | Walter A. Huxman (D) | 433,319 | 51.1 |
| | Will G. West (R) | 411,446 | 48.5 |
| 1938 | Payne Ratner (R) | 393,989 | 52.1 |
| | Walter A. Huxman (D) | 341,271 | 45.1 |
| 1940 | Payne Ratner (R) | 425,928 | 49.6 |
| | William H. Burke (D) | 425,498 | 49.6 |
| 1942 | Andrew F. Schoeppel (R) | 287,895 | 56.7 |
| | William H. Burke (D) | 212,071 | 41.8 |
| 1944 | Andrew F. Schoeppel (R) | 463,110 | 65.7 |
| | Robert S. Lemon (D) | 231,410 | 32.8 |
| 1946 | Frank Carlson (R) | 309,064 | 53.5 |
| | Harry H. Woodring (D) | 254,283 | 44.0 |
| 1948 | Frank Carlson (R) | 433,396 | 57.0 |
| | Randolph Carpenter (D) | 307,485 | 40.4 |
| 1950 | Edward F. Arn (R) | 333,001 | 53.8 |
| | Kenneth T. Anderson (D) | 275,494 | 44.5 |
| 1952 | Edward F. Arn (R) | 491,338 | 56.3 |
| | Charles Rooney (D) | 363,482 | 41.7 |
| 1954 | Fred Hall (R) | 329,868 | 53.0 |
| | George Docking (D) | 286,218 | 46.0 |
| 1956 | George Docking (D) | 479,701 | 55.5 |
| | Warren W. Shaw (R) | 364,340 | 42.1 |
| 1958 | George Docking (D) | 415,506 | 56.5 |
| | Clyde M. Reed (R) | 313,036 | 42.5 |
| 1960 | John Anderson Jr. (R) | 511,534 | 55.5 |
| | George Docking (D) | 402,261 | 43.6 |
| 1962 | John Anderson Jr. (R) | 341,257 | 53.4 |
| | Dale E. Saffels (D) | 291,285 | 45.6 |
| 1964 | William H. Avery (R) | 432,667 | 50.9 |
| | Harry G. Wiles (D) | 400,264 | 47.1 |
| 1966 | Robert Docking (D) | 380,030 | 54.8 |
| | William H. Avery (R) | 304,325 | 43.9 |
| 1968 | Robert Docking (D) | 447,269 | 51.9 |
| | Rick Harman (R) | 410,673 | 47.6 |
| 1970 | Robert Docking (D) | 404,611 | 54.3 |
| | Kent Frizzell (R) | 333,227 | 44.7 |
| 1972 | Robert Docking (D) | 571,256 | 62.0 |
| | Morris Kay (R) | 341,440 | 37.1 |
| 1974 | Robert F. Bennett (R) | 387,792 | 49.5 |
| | Vern Miller (D) | 384,115 | 49.0 |
| 1978 | John Carlin (D) | 363,835 | 49.4 |
| | Robert F. Bennett (R) | 348,015 | 47.3 |
| 1982 | John Carlin (D) | 405,772 | 53.2 |
| | Sam Hardage (R) | 339,356 | 44.5 |

| | Candidates | Votes | % |
|---|---|---|---|
| 1986 | Mike Hayden (R) | 436,267 | 51.9 |
| | Tom Docking (D) | 404,338 | 48.1 |
| 1990 | Joan Finney (D) | 380,609 | 48.6 |
| | Mike Hayden (R) | 333,589 | 42.6 |
| | Christina Campbell-Cline (I) | 69,127 | 8.8 |

# KENTUCKY

(Became a state June 1, 1792)

| | Candidates | Votes | % |
|---|---|---|---|
| 1800[1] | James Garrard | 8,390 | 39.4 |
| | Christopher Greenup | 6,745 | 31.7 |
| | Benjamin Logan | 3,995 | 18.8 |
| | Thomas Todd | 2,166 | 10.2 |
| 1804 | Christopher Greenup | 25,917 | |
| 1808 | Charles Scott | 22,050 | 61.3 |
| | John Allen | 8,430 | 23.4 |
| | Green Clay | 5,516 | 15.3 |
| 1812 | Isaac Shelby | 30,362 | 70.9 |
| | Gabriel Slaughter | 12,464 | 29.1 |
| 1816 | George Madison | Unopposed | |
| 1820 | John Adair | 20,493 | 32.8 |
| | William Logan | 19,947 | 32.0 |
| | Joseph Desha | 12,419 | 19.9 |
| | Anthony Butler | 9,567 | 15.3 |
| 1824 | Joseph Desha | 38,463 | 59.5 |
| | Christopher Tompkins | 22,300 | 34.5 |
| | William Russell | 3,899 | 6.0 |
| 1828 | Thomas Metcalfe (NR) | 38,940 | 50.5 |
| | William T. Barry (D) | 38,231 | 49.5 |
| 1832 | John Breathitt (D) | 40,780 | 50.9 |
| | Buck (NR) | 39,269 | 49.1 |
| 1836 | James Clark (W) | 38,591 | 55.8 |
| | M. Flournoy (D) | 30,576 | 44.2 |
| 1840 | Robert P. Letcher (W) | 54,892 | 58.4 |
| | French (D) | 39,160 | 41.6 |
| 1844 | William Owsley (W) | 59,792 | 52.1 |
| | Butler (D) | 55,089 | 48.0 |
| 1848 | John J. Crittenden (W) | 64,982 | 53.4 |
| | Lazarus W. Powell (D) | 56,675 | 46.6 |
| 1851 | Lazarus W. Powell (D) | 54,821 | 48.8 |
| | Archibald Dixon (W) | 54,023 | 48.1 |
| 1855 | Charles S. Morehead (AM) | 69,870 | 51.6 |
| | Clark (D) | 65,570 | 48.4 |
| 1859 | Beriah Magoffin (D) | 76,631 | 53.2 |
| | Joshua F. Bell (OPP) | 67,504 | 46.8 |
| 1863 | Thomas E. Branlette (UN) | 68,422 | 79.6 |
| | Charles A. Wickliffe (D) | 17,503 | 20.4 |
| 1867 | John Larue Helm (D) | 90,216 | 65.7 |
| | Sidney M. Barnes (R) | 33,939 | 24.7 |
| | William B. Kinkead (C) | 13,167 | 9.6 |

Special Election

| | | | |
|---|---|---|---|
| 1868 | John W. Stevenson (D) | 115,520 | 81.3 |
| | R. Tarvin Baker (R) | 26,610 | 18.7 |

| | | | |
|---|---|---|---|
| 1871 | Preston H. Leslie (D) | 126,445 | 58.6 |
| | George M. Thomas (R) | 89,298 | 41.4 |
| 1875 | James B. McCreary (D) | 126,976 | 58.3 |
| | John M. Harlan (R) | 90,795 | 41.7 |
| 1879 | Luke P. Blackburn (D) | 125,399 | 55.4 |
| | Walter Evans (R) | 81,881 | 36.2 |
| | C. W. Cook (G) | 18,954 | 8.4 |
| 1883 | J. Procter Knott (D) | 133,615 | 60.0 |
| | Thomas Z. Morrow (R) | 89,181 | 40.0 |

| | Candidates | Votes | % |
|---|---|---|---|
| 1887 | Simon B. Buckner (D) | 143,466 | 50.7 |
| | William O. Bradley (R) | 126,754 | 44.8 |
| 1891 | John Young Brown (D) | 144,168 | 49.9 |
| | Andrew T. Wood (R) | 116,087 | 40.1 |
| | S. B. Erwin (POP) | 25,631 | 8.9 |
| 1895 | William O. Bradley (R) | 172,436 | 48.3 |
| | Hardin (D) | 163,524 | 45.8 |
| 1899 | William S. Taylor (R) | 193,727‡ | 48.1 |
| | William Goebel (D) | 191,331 | 47.5 |

Special Election

| | | | |
|---|---|---|---|
| 1900 | John C. W. Beckham (D) | 233,197 | 49.9 |
| | John W. Yerkes (R) | 229,468 | 49.1 |

| | | | |
|---|---|---|---|
| 1903 | John C. W. Beckham (D) | 229,014 | 52.1 |
| | Belknap (R) | 202,862 | 46.2 |
| 1907 | August E. Willson (R) | 214,478 | 51.2 |
| | Hager (D) | 196,428 | 46.9 |
| 1911 | James B. McCreary (D) | 226,549 | 53.7 |
| | E. C. Orear (R) | 195,672 | 46.3 |
| 1915 | Augustus Owsley Stanley (D) | 219,991 | 49.1 |
| | Edwin P. Morrow (R) | 219,520 | 49.0 |
| 1919 | Edwin P. Morrow (R) | 254,472 | 53.8 |
| | J. D. Black (D) | 214,134 | 45.3 |
| 1923 | William J. Fields (D) | 356,045 | 53.3 |
| | Charles I. Dawson (R) | 306,277 | 45.8 |
| 1927 | Flem D. Sampson (R) | 399,698 | 52.1 |
| | John C. W. Beckham (D) | 367,576 | 47.9 |
| 1931 | Ruby Lafoon (D) | 438,513 | 54.3 |
| | William B. Harrison (R) | 366,982 | 45.4 |
| 1935 | Albert B. (Happy) Chandler (D) | 556,262 | 54.5 |
| | King Swope (R) | 461,104 | 45.1 |
| 1939 | Keen Johnson (D) | 460,834 | 56.5 |
| | King Swope (R) | 354,704 | 43.5 |
| 1943 | Simeon S. Willis (R) | 279,144 | 50.5 |
| | J. Lyter Donaldson (D) | 270,525 | 48.9 |
| 1947 | Earle C. Clements (D) | 387,795 | 57.2 |
| | Eldon S. Dummit (R) | 287,756 | 42.5 |
| 1951 | Lawrence W. Wetherby (D) | 346,345 | 54.6 |
| | Eugene Siler (R) | 288,014 | 45.4 |
| 1955 | Albert B. (Happy) Chandler (D) | 451,647 | 58.0 |
| | Edwin R. Denney (R) | 322,671 | 41.5 |
| 1959 | Bert T. Combs (D) | 516,549 | 60.6 |
| | John M. Robsion (R) | 336,456 | 39.4 |
| 1963 | Edward T. Breathitt (D) | 449,551 | 50.7 |
| | Louie B. Nunn (R) | 436,496 | 49.3 |
| 1967 | Louie B. Nunn (R) | 454,123 | 51.2 |
| | Henry Ward (D) | 425,674 | 48.0 |
| 1971 | Wendell H. Ford (D) | 470,720 | 50.6 |
| | Tom Emberton (R) | 412,653 | 44.3 |
| 1975 | Julian Carroll (D) | 470,159 | 62.8 |
| | Robert E. Gable (R) | 277,998 | 37.2 |
| 1979 | John Y. Brown Jr. (D) | 558,088 | 59.4 |
| | Louie B. Nunn (R) | 381,278 | 40.6 |
| 1983 | Martha Layne Collins (D) | 561,674 | 54.6 |
| | Jim Bunning (R) | 454,650 | 44.2 |
| 1987 | Wallace G. Wilkinson (D) | 504,367 | 64.9 |
| | John Harper (R) | 273,035 | 35.1 |
| 1991 | Brereton Jones (D) | 540,468 | 64.7 |
| | Larry J. Hopkins (R) | 294,452 | 35.3 |

**Kentucky**

1. Governors were chosen by a specially elected body of electors in 1792 and 1796.

# LOUISIANA

(Became a state April 30, 1812)

| | Candidates | Votes | % |
|---|---|---|---|
| 1812 [1] | W. C. C. Claiborne (AM FAC)[2] | 2,757 | 71.2 |
| | Jacques Villeré (CREOLE) | 946 | 24.4 |
| 1816 [1] | Jacques Villeré (CREOLE) | 2,314 | 51.9 |
| | Joshua Lewis (AM FAC)[2] | 2,145 | 48.1 |
| 1820 [1] | Thomas B. Robertson (AM FAC)[2] | 1,903 | 40.1 |
| | Pierre Derbigny (CREOLE) | 1,187 | 25.0 |
| | A. L. Duncan (AM FAC)[2] | 1,031 | 21.7 |
| | Jean Noel Destrehan (CREOLE) | 627 | 13.2 |
| 1824 [1] | Henry Johnson (AM FAC)[2] | 2,649 | 44.9 |
| | Jacques Villeré (CREOLE) | 1,773 | 30.0 |
| | Bernard Marigny (CREOLE) | 1,484 | 25.1 |
| 1828 [1] | Pierre Derbigny (NR) | 3,253 | 44.2 |
| | Thomas Butler (JAC D) | 1,629 | 22.1 |
| | Bernard Marigny (JAC D) | 1,291 | 17.5 |
| | Philemon Thomas (NR) | 1,194 | 16.2 |
| 1831 [1] | Andre B. Roman (NR) | 3,630 | 43.6 |
| | W. S. Hamilton (JAC D) | 2,730 | 32.8 |
| | Arnaud Beauvais (NR) | 1,502 | 18.1 |
| | David Randall (JAC D) | 456 | 5.5 |
| 1834 [1] | Edward D. White (W) | 6,018 | 57.6 |
| | Dawson (D) | 4,438 | 42.4 |
| 1838 [1] | Andre B. Roman (W) | 7,588 | 52.8 |
| | Prieur (D) | 6,776 | 47.2 |
| 1842 [1] | Alexander Mouton (D) | 9,716 | 54.2 |
| | Henry Johnson (W) | 8,204 | 45.8 |
| 1846 | Isaac Johnson (D) | 13,353 | 53.2 |
| | Debuys (W) | 11,101 | 44.2 |
| 1849 | Joseph Walker (D) | 18,459 | 51.5 |
| | Declouet (W) | 17,407 | 48.5 |
| 1852 | Paul O. Hebert (D) | 17,529 | 53.0 |
| | Louis Bordelon (W) | 15,532 | 47.0 |
| 1855 | Robert C. Wickliffe (D) | 22,382 | 53.6 |
| | Derbigny (AM) | 19,417 | 46.5 |
| 1859 | Thomas O. Moore (D) | 25,434 | 62.0 |
| | Wells (OPP) | 15,587 | 38.0 |
| 1864 | Henry W. Allen | 7,497 | 87.5 |
| | Stafford | 807 | 9.4 |
| 1865 | James Madison Wells (D) | 22,532 | 78.2 |
| | Henry W. Allen | 6,297 | 21.8 |
| 1868 | Henry C. Warmoth (R) | 64,271 | 62.8 |
| | James G. Taliaferro (D) | 38,118 | 37.2 |
| 1872 | William Pitt Kellogg (R) | 72,890‡ | 57.4 |
| | John McEnery (D) | 54,079 | 42.6 |
| 1876 | Francis T. Nicholls (D) | 84,487‡ | 52.5 |
| | Stephen B. Packard (R) | 76,476 | 47.5 |
| 1879 | Louis A. Wiltz (D) | 73,623 | 64.6 |
| | Taylor Beattie (R) | 40,415 | 35.4 |
| 1884 | Samuel D. McEnery (D) | 88,780 | 67.1 |
| | John A. Stevenson (R) | 43,502 | 32.9 |
| 1888 | Francis T. Nicholls (D) | 136,747 | 72.5 |
| | Henry C. Warmoth (R) | 51,993 | 27.6 |
| 1892 | Murphy J. Foster (A-LOT D) | 79,407 | 44.5 |
| | Samuel D. McEnery (D) | 47,046 | 26.4 |
| | A. H. Leonard (R) | 29,648 | 16.6 |
| | John E. Breaux (IR) | 12,409 | 7.0 |
| | R. H. Tannehill (POP) | 9,792 | 5.5 |
| 1896 | Murphy J. Foster (D) | 116,116 | 56.9 |
| | John N. Pharr (R POP FU) | 87,698 | 43.0 |
| 1900 | William Wright Heard (D) | 60,206 | 78.3 |
| | Don Caffery Jr. (R FUS, PP) | 14,215 | 18.5 |
| 1904 | Newton C. Blanchard (D) | 47,745 | 89.0 |
| | W. J. Behan (R) | 5,877 | 11.0 |
| 1908 | Jared Y. Sanders (D) | 60,066 | 87.1 |
| | Henry N. Pharr (R) | 7,617 | 11.1 |
| 1912 | Luther E. Hall (D) | 50,581 | 89.5 |
| | H. S. Suthon (R) | 4,961 | 8.8 |

| | Candidates | Votes | % |
|---|---|---|---|
| 1916 | Ruffin G. Pleasant (D) | 80,807 | 62.5 |
| | John M. Parker (PROG) | 48,085 | 37.2 |
| 1920 | John M. Parker (D) | 53,792# | 97.6 |
| 1924 | Henry L. Fuqua (D) | 66,203 | 97.9 |
| 1928 | Huey P. Long (D) | 92,941 | 96.1 |
| 1932 | Oscar K. Allen (D) | 110,193 | 100.0 |
| 1936 | Richard W. Leche (D) | 131,999 | 100.0 |
| 1940 | Sam H. Jones (D) | 225,841 | 99.4 |
| 1944 | Jimmie H. Davis (D) | 51,604 | 100.0 |
| 1948 | Earl K. Long (D) | 76,566 | 100.0 |
| 1952 | Robert F. Kennon (D) | 118,723 | 96.0 |
| 1956 | Earl K. Long (D) | 172,291 | 100.0 |
| 1960 | Jimmie H. Davis (D) | 407,907 | 80.5 |
| | F. C. Grevemberg (R) | 86,135 | 17.0 |
| 1964 | John J. McKeithen (D) | 469,589 | 60.7 |
| | Charlton H. Lyons Sr. (R) | 297,753 | 38.5 |
| 1968 | John J. McKeithen (D) | 372,762 | 100.0 |
| 1972 | Edwin W. Edwards (D) | 641,146 | 57.2 |
| | David C. Treen (R) | 480,424 | 42.8 |
| 1975 | Edwin W. Edwards (D) | 430,095 | 100.0 |
| 1979 | David C. Treen (R) | 690,691 | 50.3 |
| | Louis Lambert (D) | 681,134 | 49.7 |
| 1983 | Edwin W. Edwards (D) | 1,008,282 | 62.4 |
| | David C. Treen (R) | 586,643 | 36.3 |
| 1991 [3] | Edwin W. Edwards (D) | 1,057,031 | 61.2 |
| | David Duke (R) | 671,009 | 38.8 |

**Louisiana**

*1. Until 1845 the governor was elected by joint vote of the two houses of the legislature, which could choose one of the two who received the most popular votes. In all nine elections under this system the candidate receiving a popular plurality was subsequently chosen by the legislature. Thereafter elections were determined by a plurality of the popular vote.*

*2. Until 1828, contests were essentially between candidates supported by the "American" and "Creole" factions of the Jeffersonian Republican party.*

*3. The 1987 election was decided in the all-party primary unique to Louisiana. The candidate who finished second withdrew. See p. 739.*

# MAINE

(Became a state March 15, 1820)

| | Candidates | Votes | % |
|---|---|---|---|
| 1820 | William King (D-R) | 21,083 | 95.3 |
| 1821 | Albion K. Parris (D-R) | 12,887 | 52.8 |
| | Ezekiel Whitman (FED) | 6,811 | 27.9 |
| | Joshua Wingate Jr. (D-R) | 3,879 | 15.9 |
| 1822 | Albion K. Parris (D-R) | 15,476 | 69.8 |
| | Ezekiel Whitman (FED) | 5,795 | 26.1 |
| 1823 | Albion K. Parris (D-R) | 18,550 | 95.6 |
| 1824 | Albion K. Parris (D-R) | 19,759 | 96.8 |
| 1825 | Albion K. Parris (D-R) | 14,206 | 93.1 |
| 1826 | Enoch Lincoln (D-R) | 20,689 | 98.2 |
| 1827 | Enoch Lincoln (D-R) | 19,969 | 97.6 |
| 1828 | Enoch Lincoln (D-R) | 25,755 | 91.6 |
| 1829 | Jonathan G. Hunton (NR) | 23,315 | 50.1 |
| | Smith (JAC D) | 22,991 | 49.4 |
| 1830 | Samuel E. Smith (JAC D) | 30,215 | 51.1 |
| | Jonathan G. Hunton (NR) | 28,639 | 48.5 |
| 1831 | Samuel E. Smith (D) | 28,292 | 56.3 |
| | Daniel Goodenow (NR) | 21,821 | 43.5 |
| 1832 | Samuel E. Smith (D) | 31,987 | 52.8 |
| | Daniel Goodenow (NR) | 27,651 | 45.6 |
| 1833 | Robert P. Dunlap (D) | 25,731 | 52.1 |
| | Daniel Goodenow (W) | 18,112 | 36.7 |
| | Samuel E. Smith (DISS D) | 3,024 | 6.1 |
| 1834 | Robert P. Dunlap (D) | 38,133 | 52.1 |
| | Peleg Sprague (W) | 33,912 | 46.3 |
| 1835 | Robert P. Dunlap (D) | 27,733 | 61.4 |
| | William King (W) | 16,860 | 37.3 |

| | Candidates | Votes | % |
|---|---|---|---|
| 1836 | Robert P. Dunlap (D) | 31,837 | *58.2* |
| | Edward Kent (W) | 22,703 | *41.5* |
| 1837 | Edward Kent (W) | 34,358 | *50.1* |
| | Gorham Parks (D) | 33,879 | *49.4* |
| 1838 | John Fairfield (D) | 46,216 | *51.6* |
| | Edward Kent (W) | 42,897 | *47.9* |
| 1839 | John Fairfield (D) | 40,768 | *53.8* |
| | Edward Kent (W) | 34,749 | *45.9* |
| 1840 | Edward Kent (W) | 45,574† | *50.0* |
| | John Fairfield (D) | 45,507 | *49.9* |
| 1841 | John Fairfield (D) | 47,354 | *55.0* |
| | Edward Kent (W) | 36,780 | *42.7* |
| 1842 | John Fairfield (D) | 40,855 | *56.9* |
| | Edward Robinson (W) | 26,745 | *37.3* |
| | James Appleton | 4,080 | *5.7* |
| 1843 | Hugh J. Anderson (D) | 27,631 | *55.4* |
| | Edward Robinson (W) | 17,244 | *34.6* |
| | James Appleton (LIB & SC) | 4,962 | *10.0* |
| 1844 | Hugh J. Anderson (D) | 40,540 | *51.1* |
| | Edward Robinson (W) | 33,342 | *42.0* |
| | James Appleton (LIB & SC) | 5,527 | *7.0* |
| 1845 | Hugh J. Anderson (D) | 31,353 | *50.7* |
| | Freeman H. Morse (W) | 24,880 | *40.2* |
| 1846 | John W. Dana (D) | 33,805† | *46.9* |
| | David Bronson (W) | 28,986 | *40.2* |
| | Samuel Fessenden (LIB & SC) | 9,343 | *13.0* |
| 1847 | John W. Dana (D) | 33,461 | *51.3* |
| | David Bronson (W) | 24,304 | *37.2* |
| | Samuel Fessenden (LIB & SC) | 7,517 | *11.5* |
| 1848 | John W. Dana (D) | 37,310† | *47.0* |
| | Elijah L. Hamlin (W) | 30,026 | *37.9* |
| | Samuel Fessenden (F SOIL) | 11,978 | *15.1* |
| 1849 | John Hubbard (D) | 37,534 | *50.9* |
| | Elijah L. Hamlin (W) | 28,260 | *38.3* |
| | George F. Talbot (FS & SC) | 8,025 | *10.9* |
| 1850 | John Hubbard (D) | 41,220 | *51.0* |
| | William G. Crosby (W) | 32,308 | *40.0* |
| | George F. Talbot (F SOIL) | 7,271 | *9.0* |
| 1852 | John Hubbard (D) | 41,616† | *44.3* |
| | William G. Crosby (W) | 29,129 | *31.0* |
| | Anson G. Chandler (A-MAINE) | 21,589 | *23.0* |
| 1853 | Albert Pillsbury (D) | 36,127 | *43.3* |
| | William G. Crosby (W) | 27,259† | *32.7* |
| | Anson P. Morrill (WILDCAT) | 11,012 | *13.2* |
| | Ezekiel Holmes (FS & SC) | 9,039 | *10.8* |
| 1854 | Anson P. Morrill (R) | 44,817† | *49.5* |
| | Albion K. Parris (D) | 28,285 | *31.2* |
| | Isaac Reed (W) | 14,014 | *15.5* |
| 1855 | Anson P. Morrill (R) | 51,488 | *46.6* |
| | Samuel Wells (D) | 48,367† | *43.8* |
| | Isaac Reed (W) | 10,645 | *9.6* |
| 1856 | Hannibal Hamlin (R) | 69,444 | *57.4* |
| | Samuel Wells (D) | 44,912 | *37.1* |
| | George F. Patten (W) | 6,664 | *5.5* |
| 1857 | Lot M. Morrill (R) | 54,283 | *56.0* |
| | Manassah H. Smith (D) | 42,647 | *44.0* |
| 1858 | Lot M. Morrill (R) | 60,599 | *53.5* |
| | Manassah H. Smith (D) | 52,697 | *46.5* |
| 1859 | Lot M. Morrill (R) | 57,215 | *55.8* |
| | Manassah H. Smith (D) | 45,407 | *44.3* |
| 1860 | Israel Washburn Jr. (R) | 70,014 | *56.5* |
| | E. K. Smart (D) | 52,167 | *42.1* |
| 1861 | Israel Washburn Jr. (R) | 57,475 | *58.7* |
| | C. D. Jameson (D) | 21,119 | *21.6* |
| | John W. Dana (OPP D) | 19,363 | *19.8* |
| 1862 | Abner Coburn (R) | 46,689 | *53.3* |
| | Bion Bradbury (D) | 33,645 | *38.4* |
| | C. D. Jameson (D) | 7,302 | *8.3* |
| 1863 | Samuel Cony (UN R) | 67,916 | *57.4* |
| | Bion Bradbury (D) | 50,366 | *42.6* |
| 1864 | Samuel Cony (UN R) | 65,583 | *58.6* |
| | Joseph Howard (D) | 46,403 | *41.4* |

| | Candidates | Votes | % |
|---|---|---|---|
| 1865 | Samuel Cony (UN R) | 54,430 | *63.3* |
| | Joseph Howard (D) | 31,609 | *36.7* |
| 1866 | Joshua L. Chamberlain (R) | 69,626 | *62.4* |
| | Eben F. Pillsbury (D) | 41,939 | *37.6* |
| 1867 | Joshua L. Chamberlain (R) | 57,713 | *55.6* |
| | Eben F. Pillsbury (D) | 45,990 | *44.3* |
| 1868 | Joshua L. Chamberlain (R) | 75,523 | *57.3* |
| | Eben F. Pillsbury (D) | 56,207 | *42.7* |
| 1869 | Joshua L. Chamberlain (R) | 50,784 | *53.3* |
| | Franklin Smith (D) | 39,428 | *41.4* |
| | N. G. Hichborn (TEMP) | 5,028 | *5.3* |
| 1870 | Sidney Perham (R) | 54,019 | *54.1* |
| | Charles W. Roberts (D) | 45,732 | *45.8* |
| 1871 | Sidney Perham (R) | 58,285 | *55.1* |
| | Charles P. Kimball (D) | 47,538 | *44.9* |
| 1872 | Sidney Perham (R) | 71,883 | *56.5* |
| | Charles P. Kimball (D) | 55,343 | *43.5* |
| 1873 | Nelson Dingley Jr. (R) | 45,239 | *55.9* |
| | Joseph Titcomb (D) | 32,924 | *40.7* |
| 1874 | Nelson Dingley Jr. (R) | 50,865 | *53.4* |
| | Joseph Titcomb (D) | 41,898 | *44.0* |
| 1875 | Selden Connor (R) | 57,782 | *51.7* |
| | Charles W. Roberts (D) | 53,837 | *48.2* |
| 1876 | Selden Connor (R) | 75,867 | *55.5* |
| | John C. Talbot (D) | 60,423 | *44.2* |
| 1877 | Selden Connor (R) | 53,584 | *52.5* |
| | Joseph H. Williams (D) | 42,311 | *41.5* |
| | Henry C. Munson (G) | 5,291 | *5.2* |
| 1878 | Selden Connor (R) | 56,559 | *44.8* |
| | Joseph L. Smith (G) | 41,371 | *32.8* |
| | Alonzo Garcelon (D) | 28,218† | *22.4* |
| 1879 | Daniel F. Davis (R) | 68,527† | *49.5* |
| | Joseph L. Smith (NG) | 47,987 | *34.7* |
| | Alonzo Garcelon (D) | 21,525 | *15.6* |
| 1880 | Harris M. Plaisted (D & G) | 73,713 | *49.9* |
| | Daniel F. Davis (R) | 73,544 | *49.8* |
| 1882 | Frederick Robie (R) | 72,461 | *52.4* |
| | Harris M. Plaisted (FUS) | 63,921 | *46.2* |
| 1884 | Frederick Robie (R) | 78,699 | *55.4* |
| | John B. Redman (D) | 58,983 | *41.5* |
| 1886 | Joseph R. Bodwell (R) | 68,850 | *53.7* |
| | Clark S. Edwards (D) | 55,289 | *43.1* |
| 1888 | Edwin C. Burleigh (R) | 79,401 | *54.6* |
| | William L. Putnam (D) | 61,348 | *42.2* |
| 1890 | Edwin C. Burleigh (R) | 64,264 | *56.4* |
| | William P. Thompson (D) | 45,370 | *39.8* |
| 1892 | Henry B. Cleaves (R) | 67,900 | *52.1* |
| | Charles F. Johnson (D) | 55,392 | *42.5* |
| 1894 | Henry B. Cleaves (R) | 69,322 | *64.3* |
| | Charles F. Johnson (D) | 30,405 | *28.2* |
| 1896 | Llewellyn Powers (R) | 82,596 | *66.9* |
| | M. P. Frank (D) | 34,350 | *27.8* |
| 1898 | Llewellyn Powers (R) | 53,900 | *62.9* |
| | Samuel L. Lord (D) | 28,485 | *33.2* |
| 1900 | John F. Hill (R) | 73,470 | *62.3* |
| | Samuel L. Lord (D) | 40,086 | *34.0* |
| 1902 | John F. Hill (R) | 65,354 | *59.5* |
| | Samuel W. Gould (D) | 38,107 | *34.7* |
| 1904 | William T. Cobb (R) | 76,962 | *58.5* |
| | C. W. Davis (D) | 50,146 | *38.1* |
| 1906 | William T. Cobb (R) | 69,427 | *52.0* |
| | C. W. Davis (D) | 61,363 | *46.0* |
| 1908 | Bert M. Fernald (R) | 73,537 | *51.6* |
| | Obadiah Gardner (D) | 66,282 | *46.5* |
| 1910 | Frederick W. Plaisted (D) | 73,304 | *52.0* |
| | Bert M. Fernald (R) | 64,644 | *45.9* |
| 1912 | William T. Haines (R) | 70,931 | *50.0* |
| | Frederick W. Plaisted (D) | 67,702 | *47.7* |
| 1914 | Oakley C. Curtis (D) | 62,076 | *43.8* |
| | William T. Haines (R) | 58,887 | *41.6* |
| | H. P. Gardner (PROG) | 18,226 | *12.9* |

**683**

| | Candidates | Votes | % |
|---|---|---|---|
| 1916 | Carl E. Milliken (R) | 81,760 | *54.0* |
| | Oakley C. Curtis (D) | 67,930 | *44.9* |
| 1918 | Carl E. Milliken (R) | 63,607 | *52.3* |
| | Bertrand G. McIntire (D) | 58,062 | *47.7* |
| 1920 | Frederick H. Parkhurst (R) | 135,393 | *65.9* |
| | Bertrand G. McIntire (D) | 70,047 | *34.1* |
| 1922 | Percival P. Baxter (R) | 103,713 | *58.0* |
| | William R. Pattangall (D) | 75,226 | *42.0* |
| 1924 | Ralph O. Brewster (R) | 145,281 | *57.2* |
| | William R. Pattangall (D) | 108,626 | *42.8* |
| 1926 | Ralph O. Brewster (R) | 100,776 | *55.5* |
| | Ernest L. McLean (D) | 80,748 | *44.5* |
| 1928 | William Tudor Gardiner (R) | 148,053 | *69.3* |
| | Edward C. Moran Jr. (D) | 65,572 | *30.7* |
| 1930 | William Tudor Gardiner (R) | 82,310 | *55.1* |
| | Edward C. Moran Jr. (D) | 67,172 | *44.9* |
| 1932 | Louis J. Brann (D) | 121,158 | *50.3* |
| | Burleigh Martin (R) | 118,800 | *49.3* |
| 1934 | Louis J. Brann (D) | 156,917 | *54.0* |
| | Alfred K. Ames (R) | 133,414 | *45.9* |
| 1936 | Lewis O. Barrows (R) | 173,716 | *56.0* |
| | F. Harold Dubord (D) | 130,466 | *42.1* |
| 1938 | Lewis O. Barrows (R) | 157,206 | *52.9* |
| | Louis J. Brann (D) | 139,745 | *47.0* |
| 1940 | Sumner Sewall (R) | 162,719 | *63.8* |
| | Fulton J. Redman (D) | 92,053 | *36.1* |
| 1942 | Sumner Sewall (R) | 118,047 | *66.8* |
| | George W. Lane Jr. (D) | 58,558 | *33.2* |
| 1944 | Horace A. Hildreth (R) | 131,849 | *70.3* |
| | Paul J. Jullien (D) | 55,781 | *29.7* |
| 1946 | Horace A. Hildreth (R) | 110,327 | *61.3* |
| | F. Davis Clark (D) | 69,624 | *38.7* |
| 1948 | Frederick G. Payne (R) | 145,956 | *65.6* |
| | Louis B. Lausier (D) | 76,544 | *34.4* |
| 1950 | Frederick G. Payne (R) | 145,823 | *60.5* |
| | Earle S. Grant (D) | 94,304 | *39.1* |
| 1952 | Burton M. Cross (R) | 128,532 | *52.1* |
| | James C. Oliver (D) | 82,538 | *33.4* |
| | Neil Bishop (IR) | 35,732 | *14.5* |
| 1954 | Edmund S. Muskie (D) | 135,673 | *54.5* |
| | Burton M. Cross (R) | 113,298 | *45.5* |
| 1956 | Edmund S. Muskie (D) | 180,254 | *59.2* |
| | W. A. Trafton Jr. (R) | 124,395 | *40.8* |
| 1958 | Clinton A. Clauson (D) | 145,673 | *52.0* |
| | Horace A. Hildreth (R) | 134,572 | *48.0* |

Special Election

| | | | |
|---|---|---|---|
| 1960 | John H. Reed (R) | 219,768 | *52.7* |
| | Frank M. Coffin (D) | 197,447 | *47.3* |

| | | | |
|---|---|---|---|
| 1962 | John H. Reed (R) | 146,604 | *50.1* |
| | Maynard C. Dolloff (D) | 146,121 | *49.9* |
| 1966 | Kenneth M. Curtis (D) | 172,036 | *53.1* |
| | John H. Reed (R) | 151,802 | *46.9* |
| 1970 | Kenneth M. Curtis (D) | 163,138 | *50.1* |
| | James S. Erwin (R) | 162,248 | *49.9* |
| 1974 | James B. Longley (I) | 142,464 | *39.1* |
| | George J. Mitchell (D) | 132,219 | *36.3* |
| | James S. Erwin (R) | 84,176 | *23.1* |
| 1978 | Joseph E. Brennan (D) | 176,493 | *47.7* |
| | Linwood E. Palmer (R) | 126,862 | *34.3* |
| | Herman C. Frankland (I) | 65,889 | *17.8* |
| 1982 | Joseph E. Brennan (D) | 281,066 | *61.1* |
| | Charles R. Cragin (R) | 172,949 | *37.6* |
| 1986 | John R. McKernan Jr. (R) | 170,312 | *39.9* |
| | James Tierney (D) | 128,744 | *30.1* |
| | Sherry E. Huber (I) | 64,317 | *15.1* |
| | John E. Menario (I) | 63,474 | *14.9* |

| | Candidates | Votes | % |
|---|---|---|---|
| 1990 | John R. McKernan Jr. (R) | 243,766 | *46.7* |
| | Joseph E. Brennan (D) | 230,038 | *44.0* |
| | Andrew Adam (Unenrolled) | 48,377 | *9.3* |

# MARYLAND

(Ratified the Constitution April 28, 1788)

| | Candidates | Votes | % |
|---|---|---|---|
| 1838 [1] | William Grayson (D) | 27,722 | *50.3* |
| | John L. Steele (W) | 27,409 | *49.7* |
| 1841 | Francis Thomas (D) | 28,959 | *50.6* |
| | Johnson (W) | 28,320 | *49.4* |
| 1844 | Thomas G. Pratt (W) | 35,040 | *50.4* |
| | Carroll (D) | 34,495 | *49.6* |
| 1847 | Philip Francis Thomas (D) | 34,368 | *50.5* |
| | Goldsborough (W) | 33,730 | *49.5* |
| 1850 | Enoch L. Lowe (D) | 36,340 | *51.0* |
| | Clark (W) | 34,858 | *49.0* |
| 1853 | Thomas Watkins Ligon (D) | 39,087 | *52.8* |
| | Richard J. Bowie (W) | 34,939 | *47.2* |
| 1857 | Thomas Holliday Hicks (AM) | 47,141 | *54.9* |
| | John C. Groome (D) | 38,681 | *45.1* |
| 1861 | Augustus W. Bradford (UN R) | 57,498 | *68.8* |
| | Howard (PEACE D) | 26,086 | *31.2* |
| 1864 | Thomas Swann (UN R) | 40,579 | *55.9* |
| | E. F. Chambers | 32,068 | *44.1* |
| 1867 | Oden Bowie (D) | 63,694 | *74.3* |
| | Hugh L. Bond (R) | 22,050 | *25.7* |
| 1871 | William P. Whyte (D) | 73,959 | *55.7* |
| | Jacob Tome (R) | 58,824 | *44.3* |
| 1875 | John Lee Carroll (D) | 85,447 | *54.1* |
| | Harris (R) | 72,544 | *45.9* |
| 1879 | William T. Hamilton (D) | 90,731 | *56.9* |
| | Garey (R) | 68,619 | *43.1* |
| 1883 | Robert M. McLane (D) | 92,694 | *53.5* |
| | Holton (R) | 80,712 | *46.6* |
| 1887 | Elihu E. Jackson (D) | 99,038 | *52.1* |
| | Brooks (R) | 86,622 | *45.6* |
| 1891 | Frank Brown (D) | 108,539 | *56.5* |
| | Vannort (R) | 78,388 | *40.8* |
| 1895 | Lloyd Lowndes (R) | 124,936 | *52.0* |
| | John E. Hurst (D) | 106,169 | *44.2* |
| 1899 | John Walter Smith (D) | 128,409 | *51.1* |
| | Lloyd Lowndes (R) | 116,286 | *46.3* |
| 1903 | Edwin Warfield (D) | 108,548 | *52.0* |
| | S. A. Williams (R) | 95,923 | *46.0* |
| 1907 | Austin L. Crothers (D) | 102,051 | *50.7* |
| | Gaither (R) | 94,302 | *46.8* |
| 1911 | Phillips Lee Goldsborough (R) | 106,392 | *49.3* |
| | Arthur Pue Gorman (D) | 103,395 | *47.9* |
| 1915 | Emerson C. Harrington (D) | 119,317 | *49.6* |
| | Ovington E. Weller (R) | 116,136 | *48.2* |
| 1919 | Albert C. Ritchie (D) | 112,240 | *49.1* |
| | Harry W. Nice (R) | 112,075 | *49.0* |
| 1923 | Albert C. Ritchie (D) | 177,871 | *56.0* |
| | Alexander Armstrong (R) | 137,471 | *43.3* |
| 1926 | Albert C. Ritchie (D) | 207,435 | *57.9* |
| | Addison E. Mullikin (R) | 148,145 | *41.4* |
| 1930 | Albert C. Ritchie (D) | 283,639 | *56.0* |
| | William F. Broening (R) | 216,864 | *42.8* |
| 1934 | Harry W. Nice (R) | 253,813 | *49.5* |
| | Albert C. Ritchie (D) | 247,664 | *48.3* |
| 1938 | Herbert R. O'Conor (D) | 308,372 | *54.6* |
| | Harry W. Nice (R) | 242,095 | *42.9* |
| 1942 | Herbert R. O'Conor (D) | 198,486 | *52.6* |
| | Theodore R. McKeldin (R) | 179,206 | *47.5* |

| | Candidates | Votes | % |
|---|---|---|---|
| 1946 | William Preston Lane Jr. (D) | 268,084 | *54.7* |
| | Theodore R. McKeldin (R) | 221,752 | *45.3* |
| 1950 | Theodore R. McKeldin (R) | 369,807 | *57.3* |
| | William Preston Lane Jr. (D) | 275,824 | *42.7* |
| 1954 | Theodore R. McKeldin (R) | 381,451 | *54.5* |
| | Harry Clifton Byrd (D) | 319,033 | *45.5* |
| 1958 | J. Millard Tawes (D) | 485,061 | *63.6* |
| | James Patrick Devereux (R) | 278,173 | *36.5* |
| 1962 | J. Millard Tawes (D) | 428,071 | *55.6* |
| | Frank Small Jr. (R) | 341,271 | *44.4* |
| 1966 | Spiro T. Agnew (R) | 455,318 | *49.5* |
| | George P. Mahoney (D) | 373,543 | *40.6* |
| | Hyman A. Pressman (I) | 90,899 | *9.9* |
| 1970 | Marvin Mandel (D) | 639,579 | *65.7* |
| | C. Stanley Blair (R) | 314,336 | *32.3* |
| 1974 | Marvin Mandel (D) | 602,648 | *63.5* |
| | Louise Gore (R) | 346,449 | *36.5* |
| 1978 | Harry Hughes (D) | 718,328 | *71.0* |
| | J. Glenn Beall Jr. (R) | 293,635 | *29.0* |
| 1982 | Harry Hughes (D) | 705,910 | *62.0* |
| | Robert A. Pascal (R) | 432,826 | *38.0* |
| 1986 | William D. Schaefer (D) | 907,301 | *82.4* |
| | Thomas J. Mooney (R) | 194,187 | *17.6* |
| 1990 | William D. Schaefer (D) | 664,015 | *59.8* |
| | William S. Shepard (R) | 446,980 | *40.2* |

**Maryland**
*1. Before 1838 governor chosen by General Assembly.*

# MASSACHUSETTS

(Ratified the Constitution Feb. 6, 1788)

| | Candidates | Votes | % |
|---|---|---|---|
| 1788 | John Hancock | 17,841 | *80.5* |
| 1789 | John Hancock | 17,264 | *80.7* |
| 1790 | John Hancock | 14,283 | *86.5* |
| 1791 | John Hancock | 15,996 | *93.9* |
| 1792 | John Hancock | 14,628 | *86.6* |
| 1793 | John Hancock | 16,428 | *89.9* |
| 1794 | Samuel Adams | 14,425 | *61.5* |
| 1795 | Samuel Adams | 15,976 | *90.2* |
| 1796 [1] | Samuel Adams | 15,195 | *57.4* |
| | Increase Sumner (FED) | 11,298 | *42.6* |
| 1797 [1] | Increase Sumner (FED) | 14,540 | *56.7* |
| | James Sullivan (D-R) | 11,118 | *43.3* |
| 1798 [1] | Increase Sumner (FED) | 18,245 | *75.2* |
| | James Sullivan (D-R) | 6,014 | *24.8* |
| 1799 | Increase Sumner (FED) | 24,073 | *72.9* |
| 1800 | Caleb Strong (FED) | 19,630 | *50.3* |
| | Elbridge Gerry (D-R) | 17,019 | *43.6* |
| 1801 | Caleb Strong (FED) | 25,452 | *55.3* |
| | Elbridge Gerry (D-R) | 20,184 | *43.9* |
| 1802 | Caleb Strong (FED) | 29,983 | *60.5* |
| | Elbridge Gerry (D-R) | 19,443 | *43.9* |
| 1803 | Caleb Strong (FED) | 29,199 | *67.3* |
| | Elbridge Gerry (D-R) | 13,910 | *32.3* |
| 1804 | Caleb Strong (FED) | 30,011 | *55.1* |
| | James Sullivan (D-R) | 23,996 | *44.0* |
| 1805 | Caleb Strong (FED) | 35,204 | *51.0* |
| | James Sullivan (D-R) | 33,518 | *48.6* |
| 1806 | Caleb Strong (FED) | 37,740 | *50.2* |
| | James Sullivan (D-R) | 37,109 | *49.4* |
| 1807 | James Sullivan (D-R) | 41,954 | *51.5* |
| | Caleb Strong (FED) | 39,224 | *48.1* |
| 1808 | James Sullivan (D-R) | 41,193 | *50.8* |
| | Christopher Gore (FED) | 39,643 | *48.9* |

| | Candidates | Votes | % |
|---|---|---|---|
| 1809 | Christopher Gore (FED) | 47,916 | *51.3* |
| | Levi Lincoln I (D-R) | 45,118 | *48.3* |
| 1810 | Elbridge Gerry (D-R) | 46,541 | *51.2* |
| | Christopher Gore (FED) | 44,079 | *48.5* |
| 1811 | Elbridge Gerry (D-R) | 43,328 | *51.6* |
| | Christopher Gore (FED) | 40,142 | *47.8* |
| 1812 | Caleb Strong (FED) | 52,696 | *50.6* |
| | Elbridge Gerry (D-R) | 51,326 | *49.3* |
| 1813 | Caleb Strong (FED) | 56,754 | *56.6* |
| | Joseph B. Varnum (D-R) | 42,789 | *42.7* |
| 1814 | Caleb Strong (FED) | 56,374 | *55.0* |
| | Lemuel Dexter (D-R) | 45,953 | *44.8* |
| 1815 | Caleb Strong (FED) | 50,921 | *53.6* |
| | Lemuel Dexter (D-R) | 43,938 | *46.2* |
| 1816 | John Brooks (FED) | 49,527 | *51.1* |
| | Lemuel Dexter (D-R) | 47,321 | *48.8* |
| 1817 | John Brooks (FED) | 46,160 | *54.6* |
| | Henry Dearborn (D-R) | 38,129 | *45.1* |
| 1818 | John Brooks (FED) | 39,538 | *55.7* |
| | Benjamin W. Crowninshield (D-R) | 30,041 | *42.4* |
| 1819 | John Brooks (FED) | 42,875 | *53.7* |
| | Benjamin W. Crowninshield (D-R) | 35,277 | *44.2* |
| 1820 | John Brooks (FED) | 31,072 | *58.3* |
| | William Eustis (D-R) | 21,927 | *41.1* |
| 1821 | John Brooks (FED) | 28,608 | *58.3* |
| | William Eustis (D-R) | 20,268 | *41.3* |
| 1822 | John Brooks (FED) | 28,487 | *57.1* |
| | William Eustis (D-R) | 21,177 | *42.5* |
| 1823 | William Eustis (D-R) | 34,402 | *52.7* |
| | Harrison G. Otis (FED) | 30,171 | *46.2* |
| 1824 | William Eustis (D-R) | 38,650 | *52.9* |
| | Samuel Lathrop (FED) | 34,210 | *46.8* |
| 1825 | Levi Lincoln (R-FF) | 35,221 | *94.1* |
| 1826 | Levi Lincoln (AR) | 27,884 | *68.0* |
| | Samuel Hubbard (FED) | 9,044 | *22.1* |
| | James Lloyd (FED) | 2,212 | *5.4* |
| 1827 | Levi Lincoln (AR) | 29,029 | *74.2* |
| | William C. Jarvis (FB R) | 7,130 | *18.2* |
| 1828 | Levi Lincoln (AR) | 27,981 | *81.5* |
| | Marcus Morton (JAC R) | 4,423 | *12.9* |
| 1829 | Levi Lincoln (NR) | 25,217 | *71.6* |
| | Marcus Morton (JAC R) | 6,864 | *19.5* |
| 1830 | Levi Lincoln (NR) | 30,908 | *65.5* |
| | Marcus Morton (JAC R) | 14,440 | *30.6* |
| 1831 | Levi Lincoln (NR) | 31,875 | *65.2* |
| | Marcus Morton (JAC R) | 12,694 | *26.0* |
| 1831 | Levi Lincoln (NR) | 28,804 | *53.9* |
| | Samuel Lathrop (A-MAS) | 13,357 | *25.0* |
| | Marcus Morton (D) | 10,975 | *20.6* |
| 1832 | Levi Lincoln (NR) | 33,946 | *52.9* |
| | Marcus Morton (D) | 15,197 | *23.7* |
| | Samuel Lathrop (A-MAS) | 14,755 | *23.0* |
| 1833 | John Davis (NR) | 25,149† | *40.3* |
| | John Quincy Adams (A-MAS) | 18,274 | *29.3* |
| | Marcus Morton (D) | 15,493 | *24.8* |
| | Samuel L. Allen (WM) | 3,459 | *5.5* |
| 1834 | John Davis (W) | 43,757 | *58.1* |
| | Marcus Morton (D) | 18,683 | *24.8* |
| | John Bailey (A-MAS) | 10,160 | *13.5* |
| 1835 | Edward Everett (W) | 37,555 | *57.9* |
| | Marcus Morton (D) | 25,227 | *38.9* |
| 1836 | Edward Everett (W) | 42,160 | *53.8* |
| | Marcus Morton (D) | 35,992 | *45.9* |
| 1837 | Edward Everett (W) | 50,565 | *60.3* |
| | Marcus Morton (D) | 32,987 | *39.4* |
| 1838 | Edward Everett (W) | 51,642 | *55.0* |
| | Marcus Morton (D) | 41,795 | *44.5* |
| 1839 | Marcus Morton (D) | 51,034 | *50.0* |
| | Edward Everett (W) | 50,725 | *49.7* |
| 1840 | John Davis (W) | 70,884 | *55.7* |
| | Marcus Morton (D) | 55,169 | *43.3* |

| | Candidates | Votes | % |
|---|---|---|---|
| 1841 | John Davis (W) | 55,974 | 50.4 |
| | Marcus Morton (D) | 51,367 | 46.3 |
| 1842 | Marcus Morton (D) | 56,491† | 47.9 |
| | John Davis (W) | 54,939 | 46.6 |
| | Samuel E. Sewall (LIB) | 6,382 | 5.4 |
| 1843 | George N. Briggs (W) | 57,899† | 47.7 |
| | Marcus Morton (D) | 54,242 | 44.7 |
| | Samuel E. Sewall (LIB) | 8,903 | 7.3 |
| 1844 | George N. Briggs (W) | 69,570 | 51.8 |
| | George Bancroft (D) | 54,714 | 40.8 |
| | Samuel E. Sewall (LIB) | 9,734 | 7.3 |
| 1845 | George N. Briggs (W) | 51,638† | 48.8 |
| | Isaac Davis (D) | 37,427 | 35.3 |
| | Samuel E. Sewall (LIB) | 8,316 | 7.9 |
| | Henry Shaw (AM R) | 8,089 | 7.6 |
| 1846 | George N. Briggs (W) | 54,813 | 53.8 |
| | Isaac Davis (D) | 33,199 | 32.6 |
| | Samuel E. Sewall (LIB) | 9,997 | 9.8 |
| 1847 | George N. Briggs (W) | 53,742 | 51.0 |
| | Caleb Cushing (D) | 39,398 | 37.4 |
| | Samuel E. Sewall (LIB) | 9,157 | 8.7 |
| 1848 | George N. Briggs (W) | 61,640† | 49.7 |
| | Stephen C. Phillips (F SOIL) | 36,011 | 29.0 |
| | Caleb Cushing (D) | 25,323 | 20.4 |
| 1849 | George N. Briggs (W) | 54,009† | 49.3 |
| | George S. Boutwell (D) | 30,040 | 27.4 |
| | Stephen C. Phillips (F SOIL) | 25,247 | 23.1 |
| 1850 | George N. Briggs (W) | 56,778 | 46.8 |
| | George S. Boutwell (D) | 36,023† | 29.7 |
| | Stephen C. Phillips (F SOIL) | 27,636 | 22.8 |
| 1851 | Robert C. Winthrop (W) | 64,279 | 46.9 |
| | George S. Boutwell (D) | 43,889† | 32.0 |
| | John G. Palfrey (F SOIL) | 28,560 | 20.9 |
| 1852 | John H. Clifford (W) | 62,233† | 45.0 |
| | Henry W. Bishop (D) | 38,763 | 28.0 |
| | Horace Mann (F SOIL) | 36,740 | 26.5 |
| 1853 | Emory Washburn (W) | 59,224† | 45.9 |
| | Henry W. Bishop (D) | 35,086 | 27.2 |
| | Henry Wilson (F SOIL) | 29,020 | 22.5 |
| 1854 | Henry J. Gardner (AM) | 81,503 | 62.6 |
| | Emory Washburn (W) | 27,279 | 20.9 |
| | Henry W. Bishop (D) | 13,742 | 10.6 |
| 1855 | Henry J. Gardner (AM) | 51,497 | 37.7 |
| | Julius Rockwell (R) | 36,715 | 26.9 |
| | Erasmus D. Beach (D) | 34,728 | 25.5 |
| | Samuel H. Walley (W) | 13,296 | 9.7 |
| 1856 | Henry J. Gardner (FREM AM) | 92,467 | 58.9 |
| | Erasmus D. Beach (D) | 40,077 | 25.5 |
| | George W. Gordon (FILL AM) | 10,385 | 6.6 |
| 1857 | Nathaniel P. Banks (R) | 60,797 | 46.6 |
| | Henry J. Gardner (AM) | 37,596 | 28.8 |
| | Erasmus D. Beach (D) | 31,760 | 24.3 |
| 1858 | Nathaniel P. Banks (R) | 68,700 | 57.6 |
| | Erasmus D. Beach (D) | 38,298 | 32.1 |
| | Amos A. Lawrence (AM) | 12,084 | 10.1 |
| 1859 | Nathaniel P. Banks (R) | 58,780 | 54.0 |
| | Benjamin F. Butler (D) | 35,334 | 32.5 |
| | George N. Briggs (AM) | 14,365 | 13.2 |
| 1860 | John A. Andrew (R) | 104,527 | 61.6 |
| | Erasmus D. Beach (D) | 35,191 | 20.8 |
| | Amos A. Lawrence (CST U) | 23,816 | 14.0 |
| 1861 | John A. Andrew (R) | 65,261 | 67.1 |
| | Isaac Davis (D) | 31,266 | 32.1 |
| 1862 | John A. Andrew (R) | 79,835 | 59.5 |
| | Charles Devens Jr. (PP) | 54,167 | 40.4 |
| 1863 | John A. Andrew (UN R) | 70,483 | 70.7 |
| | Henry W. Paine (D) | 29,207 | 29.3 |
| 1864 | John A. Andrew (UN) | 125,281 | 71.8 |
| | Henry W. Paine (D) | 49,190 | 28.2 |
| 1865 | Alexander H. Bullock (UN) | 69,912 | 76.6 |
| | Darius N. Couch (D) | 21,245 | 23.3 |

| | Candidates | Votes | % |
|---|---|---|---|
| 1866 | Alexander H. Bullock (R) | 91,980 | 77.5 |
| | Theodore H. Sweetser (D) | 26,671 | 22.5 |
| 1867 | Alexander H. Bullock (R) | 98,306 | 58.3 |
| | John Quincy Adams (D) | 70,360 | 41.7 |
| 1868 | William Claflin (R) | 132,121 | 67.6 |
| | John Quincy Adams (D) | 63,266 | 32.4 |
| 1869 | William Claflin (R) | 74,106 | 53.5 |
| | John Quincy Adams (D) | 50,735 | 36.6 |
| | Edwin M. Chamberlain (LAB REF) | 13,567 | 9.8 |
| 1870 | William Claflin (R) | 79,549 | 53.0 |
| | John Quincy Adams (D) | 48,680 | 32.3 |
| | Wendell Phillips (LAB REF & P) | 21,946 | 14.6 |
| 1871 | William B. Washburn (R) | 75,129 | 54.9 |
| | John Quincy Adams (D) | 47,725 | 34.9 |
| | Edwin M. Chamberlain (LAB REF) | 6,848 | 5.0 |
| 1872 | William B. Washburn (R) | 133,900 | 69.1 |
| | Francis W. Bird (LR) | 59,626 | 30.8 |
| 1873 | William B. Washburn (R) | 72,183 | 54.6 |
| | William Gaston (D) | 59,360 | 44.9 |
| 1874 | William Gaston (D) | 96,376 | 51.8 |
| | Thomas Talbot (R) | 89,344 | 48.0 |
| 1875 | Alexander H. Rice (R) | 83,639 | 48.3 |
| | William Gaston (D) | 78,333 | 45.2 |
| | John I. Baker (TEMP) | 9,124 | 5.3 |
| 1876 | Alexander H. Rice (R) | 137,665 | 53.6 |
| | Charles Francis Adams (D) | 106,850 | 41.6 |
| 1877 | Alexander H. Rice (R) | 91,255 | 49.5 |
| | William Gaston (D) | 73,185 | 39.7 |
| | Robert C. Pitman (P) | 16,354 | 8.9 |
| 1878 | Thomas Talbot (R) | 134,725 | 52.6 |
| | Benjamin F. Butler (BUT D & R) | 109,435 | 42.7 |
| 1879 | John D. Long (R) | 122,751 | 50.4 |
| | Benjamin F. Butler (BUT D & R) | 109,149 | 44.8 |
| 1880 | John D. Long (R) | 164,926 | 58.4 |
| | Charles P. Thompson (D) | 111,410 | 39.5 |
| 1881 | John D. Long (R) | 96,609 | 61.2 |
| | Charles P. Thompson (D) | 54,586 | 34.6 |
| 1882 | Benjamin F. Butler (D-NG LAB) | 133,946 | 52.3 |
| | Robert R. Bishop (R) | 119,997 | 46.8 |
| 1883 | George D. Robinson (R) | 160,092 | 51.3 |
| | Benjamin F. Butler (D & G) | 150,228 | 48.1 |
| 1884 | George D. Robinson (R) | 159,345 | 52.4 |
| | William C. Endicott (D) | 111,829 | 36.8 |
| | Matthew J. McCafferty (G) | 24,363 | 8.0 |
| 1885 | George D. Robinson (R) | 112,243 | 53.5 |
| | Frederick O. Prince (D) | 90,346 | 43.1 |
| 1886 | Oliver Ames (R) | 122,346 | 50.2 |
| | John F. Andrew (D) | 112,883 | 46.3 |
| 1887 | Oliver Ames (R) | 136,000 | 51.1 |
| | Henry B. Lovering (D) | 118,394 | 44.5 |
| 1888 | Oliver Ames (R) | 180,849 | 52.7 |
| | William E. Russell (D) | 152,780 | 44.5 |
| 1889 | John Q. A. Brackett (R) | 127,357 | 48.4 |
| | William E. Russell (D) | 120,582 | 45.8 |
| | John Blackmer (P) | 15,108 | 5.7 |
| 1890 | William E. Russell (D) | 140,507 | 49.2 |
| | John Q. A. Brackett (R) | 131,454 | 46.0 |
| 1891 | William E. Russell (D) | 157,982 | 49.1 |
| | Charles H. Allen (R) | 151,515 | 47.1 |
| 1892 | William E. Russell (D) | 186,377 | 49.0 |
| | William H. Haile (R) | 183,843 | 48.4 |
| 1893 | Frederic T. Greenhalge (R) | 192,613 | 52.8 |
| | John E. Russell (D) | 156,916 | 43.0 |
| 1894 | Frederic T. Greenhalge (R) | 189,307 | 56.5 |
| | John E. Russell (D) | 123,930 | 37.0 |
| 1895 | Frederic T. Greenhalge (R) | 186,280 | 56.8 |
| | George Fred Williams (D) | 121,599 | 37.1 |
| 1896 | Roger Wolcott (R) | 258,204 | 67.1 |
| | George Fred Williams (D, BRYAN D) | 103,662 | 27.0 |
| 1897 | Roger Wolcott (R) | 165,095 | 61.2 |
| | George Fred Williams (D) | 79,552 | 29.5 |
| | William Everett (DN) | 13,879 | 5.1 |

| | Candidates | Votes | % |
|---|---|---|---|
| 1898 | Roger Wolcott (R) | 191,146 | 60.2 |
| | Alexander B. Bruce (D) | 107,960 | 34.0 |
| 1899 | Winthrop Murray Crane (R) | 168,902 | 56.5 |
| | Robert Treat Paine (D) | 103,802 | 34.7 |
| 1900 | Winthrop Murray Crane (R) | 228,054 | 59.1 |
| | Robert Treat Paine (D) | 130,078 | 33.7 |
| 1901 | Winthrop Murray Crane (R) | 185,809 | 57.3 |
| | Josiah Quincy (D) | 114,362 | 35.2 |
| 1902 | John L. Bates (R) | 196,276 | 49.2 |
| | William A. Gaston (D) | 159,156 | 39.9 |
| | John C. Chase (SOC) | 33,629 | 8.4 |
| 1903 | John L. Bates (R) | 199,684 | 50.4 |
| | William A. Gaston (D) | 163,700 | 41.3 |
| | John C. Chase (SOC) | 25,251 | 6.4 |
| 1904 | William L. Douglas (D) | 234,670 | 52.1 |
| | John L. Bates (R) | 198,681 | 44.1 |
| 1905 | Curtis Guild Jr. (R) | 197,469 | 50.5 |
| | Charles W. Bartlett (D) | 174,911 | 44.7 |
| 1906 | Curtis Guild Jr. (R) | 222,528 | 52.0 |
| | John B. Moran (D, I LEAGUE) | 192,295 | 44.9 |
| 1907 | Curtis Guild Jr. (R) | 188,068 | 50.3 |
| | Henry M. Whitney (D, D CIT) | 84,379 | 22.6 |
| | Thomas L. Hisgen (I LEAGUE) | 75,499 | 20.2 |
| 1908 | Eben S. Draper (R) | 228,318 | 51.6 |
| | James H. Vahey (D) | 168,162 | 38.0 |
| | William N. Osgood (I LEAGUE) | 23,101 | 5.2 |
| 1909 | Eben S. Draper (R) | 190,186 | 48.6 |
| | James H. Vahey (D) | 182,252 | 46.6 |
| 1910 | Eugene N. Foss (D, D & PROG) | 229,352 | 52.0 |
| | Eben S. Draper (R) | 194,173 | 44.1 |
| 1911 | Eugene N. Foss (D, D & PROG) | 214,897 | 48.8 |
| | Louis A. Frothingham (R) | 206,795 | 47.0 |
| 1912 | Eugene N. Foss (D) | 193,184 | 40.6 |
| | Joseph Walker (R) | 143,597 | 30.2 |
| | Charles S. Bird (PROG) | 122,602 | 25.8 |
| 1913 | David I. Walsh (D) | 183,267 | 39.8 |
| | Charles S. Bird (PROG) | 127,755 | 27.7 |
| | Augustus P. Gardner (R) | 116,705 | 25.3 |
| 1914 | David I. Walsh (D) | 210,442 | 45.9 |
| | Samuel W. McCall (R) | 198,627 | 43.4 |
| | Joseph Walker (PROG) | 32,145 | 7.0 |
| 1915 | Samuel W. McCall (R) | 235,863 | 47.0 |
| | David I. Walsh (D) | 229,550 | 45.7 |
| 1916 | Samuel W. McCall (R) | 276,123 | 52.5 |
| | Frederick W. Mansfield (D) | 229,883 | 43.7 |
| 1917 | Samuel W. McCall (R) | 226,145 | 58.3 |
| | Frederick W. Mansfield (D) | 135,676 | 35.0 |
| 1918 | Calvin Coolidge (R) | 214,863 | 50.9 |
| | Richard H. Long (D) | 197,828 | 46.8 |
| 1919 | Calvin Coolidge (R) | 317,774 | 60.9 |
| | Richard H. Long (D) | 192,673 | 37.0 |
| 1920 | Channing H. Cox (R) | 643,869 | 67.0 |
| | John J. Walsh (D) | 290,350 | 30.2 |
| 1922 | Channing H. Cox (R) | 464,873 | 52.2 |
| | John F. Fitzgerald (D) | 404,192 | 45.4 |
| 1924 | Alvan T. Fuller (R) | 650,817 | 56.0 |
| | James M. Curley (D) | 490,010 | 42.2 |
| 1926 | Alvan T. Fuller (R) | 595,006 | 58.8 |
| | William A. Gaston (D) | 407,389 | 40.3 |
| 1928 | Frank G. Allen (R) | 769,372 | 50.1 |
| | Charles H. Cole (D) | 750,137 | 48.8 |
| 1930 | Joseph B. Ely (D) | 606,902 | 49.5 |
| | Frank G. Allen (R) | 590,238 | 48.2 |
| 1932 | Joseph B. Ely (D) | 825,479 | 52.8 |
| | William Sterling Youngman (R) | 704,576 | 45.0 |
| 1934 | James M. Curley (D) | 736,463 | 49.7 |
| | Gaspar G. Bacon (R) | 627,413 | 42.3 |
| | Frank A. Goodwin (E TAX) | 94,141 | 6.4 |
| 1936 | Charles F. Hurley (D) | 867,743 | 47.6 |
| | John W. Haigis (R) | 839,740 | 46.1 |
| 1938 | Leverett Saltonstall (R) | 941,465 | 53.3 |
| | James M. Curley (D) | 793,884 | 45.0 |

| | Candidates | Votes | % |
|---|---|---|---|
| 1940 | Leverett Saltonstall (R) | 999,223 | 49.7 |
| | Paul A. Dever (D) | 993,635 | 49.5 |
| 1942 | Leverett Saltonstall (R) | 758,402 | 54.1 |
| | Roger L. Putnam (D) | 630,265 | 45.0 |
| 1944 | Maurice J. Tobin (D) | 1,048,284 | 53.6 |
| | Horace T. Cahill (R) | 897,708 | 45.9 |
| 1946 | Robert F. Bradford (R) | 911,152 | 54.1 |
| | Maurice J. Tobin (D) | 762,743 | 45.3 |
| 1948 | Paul A. Dever (D) | 1,239,247 | 59.0 |
| | Robert F. Bradford (R) | 849,895 | 40.5 |
| 1950 | Paul A. Dever (D) | 1,074,570 | 56.3 |
| | Arthur W. Coolidge (R) | 824,069 | 43.1 |
| 1952 | Christian A. Herter (R) | 1,175,955 | 49.9 |
| | Paul A. Dever (D) | 1,161,499 | 49.3 |
| 1954 | Christian A. Herter (R) | 985,339 | 51.8 |
| | Robert F. Murphy (D) | 910,087 | 47.8 |
| 1956 | Foster Furcolo (D) | 1,234,618 | 52.8 |
| | Sumner G. Whittier (R) | 1,096,759 | 46.9 |
| 1958 | Foster Furcolo (D) | 1,067,020 | 56.2 |
| | Charles Gibbons (R) | 818,463 | 43.1 |
| 1960 | John A. Volpe (R) | 1,269,295 | 52.5 |
| | Joseph D. Ward (D) | 1,130,810 | 46.8 |
| 1962 | Endicott Peabody (D) | 1,053,322 | 49.9 |
| | John A. Volpe (R) | 1,047,891 | 49.7 |
| 1964 | John A. Volpe (R) | 1,176,462 | 50.3 |
| | Francis X. Bellotti (D) | 1,153,416 | 49.3 |
| 1966 | John A. Volpe (R) | 1,277,358 | 62.6 |
| | Edward J. McCormack (D) | 752,720 | 36.9 |
| 1970 | Francis W. Sargent (R) | 1,058,623 | 56.7 |
| | Kevin H. White (D) | 799,269 | 42.8 |
| 1974 | Michael S. Dukakis (D) | 992,284 | 53.5 |
| | Francis W. Sargent (R) | 784,353 | 42.3 |
| 1978 | Edward J. King (D) | 1,030,294 | 52.5 |
| | Francis W. Hatch (R) | 926,072 | 47.2 |
| 1982 | Michael S. Dukakis (D) | 1,219,109 | 59.5 |
| | John W. Sears (R) | 749,679 | 36.6 |
| 1986 | Michael S. Dukakis (D) | 1,157,786 | 68.7 |
| | George Kariotis (R) | 525,364 | 31.2 |
| 1990 | William F. Weld (R) | 1,175,817 | 50.2 |
| | John Silber (D) | 1,099,878 | 46.9 |

**Massachusetts**

1. Totals for losing candidates in these elections include some votes for other candidates.

# MICHIGAN

(Became a state Jan. 26, 1837)

| | Candidates | Votes | % |
|---|---|---|---|
| 1835 | Stevens T. Mason (D) | 7,385 | 89.2 |
| | John Biddle (W) | 815 | 9.8 |
| 1837 | Stevens T. Mason (D) | 15,318 | 50.2 |
| | Charles C. Trowbridge (W) | 14,884 | 48.8 |
| 1839 | William Woodbridge (W) | 19,069 | 51.9 |
| | E. Farnsworth (D) | 17,710 | 48.2 |
| 1841 | John S. Barry (D) | 21,001 | 55.8 |
| | Philo C. Fuller (W) | 15,449 | 41.1 |
| 1843 | John S. Barry (D) | 21,394 | 54.6 |
| | Zind Pilcher (W) | 15,024 | 38.3 |
| | James G. Birney (LIB) | 2,736 | 7.0 |
| 1845 | Alpheus Felch (D) | 20,123 | 50.8 |
| | Stephen Vickery (W) | 16,322 | 41.2 |
| | James G. Birney (LIB) | 3,048 | 7.7 |
| 1847 | Epaphroditus Ransom (D) | 24,639 | 53.2 |
| | James M. Edmunds (W) | 18,990 | 41.0 |
| | Chester Gurney (LIB) | 2,585 | 5.6 |

| | Candidates | Votes | % | | Candidates | Votes | % |
|---|---|---|---|---|---|---|---|
| 1849 | John S. Barry (D) | 27,845 | 54.0 | 1912 | Woodbridge N. Ferris (D) | 194,017 | 35.4 |
| | Flavius Littlejohn (W FS) | 23,561 | 45.7 | | Amos S. Musselman (R) | 169,963 | 31.0 |
| 1851 | Robert McClelland (D) | 23,827 | 58.3 | | Lucius W. Watkins (N PROG) | 152,909 | 27.9 |
| | Townsend E. Gidley (W FS) | 16,901 | 41.3 | 1914 | Woodbridge N. Ferris (D) | 212,063 | 48.2 |
| 1852 | Robert McClelland (D) | 42,791 | 51.4 | | Chase S. Osborn (R) | 176,254 | 40.0 |
| | Zacharaiah Chandler (W) | 34,662 | 41.6 | | Henry R. Pattengill (N PROG) | 36,747 | 8.3 |
| | Isaac P. Christiancy (F SOIL) | 5,880 | 7.1 | 1916 | Albert E. Sleeper (R) | 363,724 | 55.8 |
| 1854 | Kinsley S. Bingham (R) | 43,652 | 53.0 | | Edwin F. Sweet (D) | 264,440 | 40.6 |
| | Barry (NEB D) | 38,676 | 47.0 | 1918 | Albert E. Sleeper (R) | 266,738 | 61.4 |
| 1856 | Kinsley S. Bingham (R) | 71,402 | 56.9 | | John W. Bailey (D) | 158,142 | 36.4 |
| | Felch (D) | 54,085 | 43.1 | 1920 | Alexander J. Groesbeck (R) | 703,180 | 66.4 |
| 1858 | Moses Wisner (R) | 65,201 | 53.8 | | Woodbridge N. Ferris (D) | 310,566 | 29.3 |
| | Stuart (D) | 56,060 | 46.2 | 1922 | Alexander J. Groesbeck (R) | 356,933 | 61.2 |
| 1860 | Austin Blair (R) | 87,780 | 56.7 | | Alva M. Cummins (D) | 218,252 | 37.4 |
| | Barry (D) | 67,053 | 43.3 | 1924 | Alexander J. Groesbeck (R) | 799,225 | 68.8 |
| 1862 | Austin Blair (R) | 68,716 | 52.5 | | Edward Frensdorf (D) | 343,577 | 29.6 |
| | Stout (D) | 62,102 | 47.5 | 1926 | Fred W. Green (R) | 399,564 | 63.4 |
| 1864 | Henry H. Crapo (UN R) | 91,353 | 55.2 | | William A. Comstock (D) | 227,155 | 36.0 |
| | William H. Fenton (D) | 74,293 | 44.9 | 1928 | Fred W. Green (R) | 961,179 | 69.9 |
| 1866 | Henry H. Crapo (R) | 97,112 | 58.6 | | William A. Comstock (D) | 404,546 | 29.4 |
| | Williams (D) | 68,650 | 41.4 | 1930 | Wilber M. Brucker (R) | 483,990 | 56.9 |
| 1868 | Henry P. Baldwin (R) | 128,042 | 56.8 | | William A. Comstock (D) | 357,664 | 42.0 |
| | John Moore (D) | 97,290 | 43.2 | 1932 | William A. Comstock (D) | 887,672 | 54.9 |
| 1870 | Henry P. Baldwin (R) | 100,176 | 53.8 | | Wilber M. Brucker (R) | 696,935 | 43.1 |
| | Charles C. Comstock (D) | 83,391 | 44.8 | 1934 | Frank D. Fitzgerald (R) | 659,743 | 52.4 |
| 1872 | John J. Bagley (R) | 137,602 | 63.0 | | Arthur J. Lacy (D) | 577,044 | 45.8 |
| | Blair (L) | 80,958 | 37.0 | 1936 | Frank Murphy (D) | 892,774 | 51.0 |
| 1874 | John J. Bagley (R) | 111,519 | 50.5 | | Frank D. Fitzgerald (R) | 843,855 | 48.2 |
| | Henry Chamberlain (D) | 105,550 | 47.8 | 1938 | Frank D. Fitzgerald (R) | 847,245 | 52.8 |
| 1876 | Charles M. Croswell (R) | 165,926 | 52.3 | | Frank Murphy (D) | 753,752 | 47.0 |
| | Webber (D) | 142,493 | 44.9 | 1940 | Murray D. Van Wagoner (D) | 1,077,065 | 53.1 |
| 1878 | Charles M. Croswell (R) | 126,280 | 45.4 | | Luren D. Dickinson (R) | 945,784 | 46.6 |
| | Barnes (D) | 78,503 | 28.2 | 1942 | Harry F. Kelly (R) | 645,335 | 52.6 |
| | Smith (NG) | 73,313 | 26.4 | | Murray D. Van Wagoner (D) | 573,314 | 46.7 |
| 1880 | David H. Jerome (R) | 178,944 | 51.3 | 1944 | Harry F. Kelly (R) | 1,208,859 | 54.7 |
| | Holloway (D) | 137,671 | 39.4 | | Edward J. Fry (D) | 989,307 | 44.8 |
| | Woodman (G) | 31,085 | 8.9 | 1946 | Kim Sigler (R) | 1,003,878 | 60.3 |
| 1882 | Josiah W. Begole (D & G) | 154,269 | 49.5 | | Murray D. Van Wagoner (D) | 644,540 | 38.7 |
| | David H. Jerome (R) | 149,697 | 48.0 | 1948 | G. Mennen Williams (D) | 1,128,664 | 53.4 |
| 1884 | Russell A. Alger (R) | 190,840 | 47.7 | | Kim Sigler (R) | 964,810 | 45.7 |
| | Josiah W. Begole (D & G) | 186,884 | 46.7 | 1950 | G. Mennen Williams (D) | 935,152 | 49.8 |
| | David Preston (P) | 22,307 | 5.6 | | Harry F. Kelly (R) | 933,998 | 49.7 |
| 1886 | Cyrus G. Luce (R) | 181,474 | 47.7 | 1952 | G. Mennen Williams (D) | 1,431,893 | 50.0 |
| | George L. Yaple (D) | 174,042 | 45.7 | | Fred M. Alger Jr. (R) | 1,423,275 | 49.7 |
| | Samuel Dickie (P) | 25,179 | 6.6 | 1954 | G. Mennen Williams (D) | 1,216,308 | 55.6 |
| 1888 | Cyrus G. Luce (R) | 233,595 | 49.2 | | Donald S. Leonard (R) | 963,300 | 44.1 |
| | Wellington R. Burt (D) | 216,450 | 45.6 | 1956 | G. Mennen Williams (D) | 1,666,689 | 54.7 |
| 1890 | Edward B. Winans (D) | 183,725 | 46.2 | | Albert E. Cobo (R) | 1,376,376 | 45.1 |
| | James M. Turner (R) | 172,205 | 43.3 | 1958 | G. Mennen Williams (D) | 1,225,533 | 53.0 |
| | Azariah S. Partridge (P) | 28,681 | 7.2 | | Paul D. Bagwell (R) | 1,078,089 | 46.6 |
| 1892 | John T. Rich (R) | 221,228 | 47.2 | 1960 | John B. Swainson (D) | 1,643,634 | 50.5 |
| | Allen B. Morse (D) | 205,138 | 43.8 | | Paul D. Bagwell (R) | 1,602,022 | 49.2 |
| 1894 | John T. Rich (R) | 237,215 | 56.9 | 1962 | George Romney (R) | 1,420,086 | 51.4 |
| | Spencer O. Fisher (D) | 130,823 | 31.4 | | John B. Swainson (D) | 1,339,513 | 48.5 |
| | Alva W. Nichols (PP) | 30,008 | 7.2 | 1964 | George Romney (R) | 1,764,355 | 55.9 |
| 1896 | Hazen S. Pingree (R) | 304,431 | 55.6 | | Neil Staebler (D) | 1,381,442 | 43.7 |
| | Charles R. Sligh (D & POP) | 225,200 | 41.1 | 1966 | George Romney (R) | 1,490,430 | 60.5 |
| 1898 | Hazen S. Pingree (R) | 243,239 | 57.8 | | Zolton A. Ferency (D) | 963,383 | 39.1 |
| | Justin R. Whiting (DPUS) | 168,142 | 39.9 | 1970 | William G. Milliken (R) | 1,338,711 | 50.4 |
| 1900 | Aaron T. Bliss (R) | 305,612 | 55.8 | | Sander Levin (D) | 1,294,600 | 48.7 |
| | William C. Maybury (D) | 226,208 | 41.3 | 1974 | William G. Milliken (R) | 1,356,865 | 51.1 |
| 1902 | Aaron T. Bliss (R) | 211,261 | 52.5 | | Sander Levin (D) | 1,242,247 | 46.8 |
| | Lorenzo T. Durand (D) | 174,077 | 43.3 | 1978 | William G. Milliken (R) | 1,628,485 | 56.8 |
| 1904 | Fred M. Warner (R) | 283,799 | 54.1 | | William Fitzgerald (D) | 1,237,256 | 43.2 |
| | Woodbridge N. Ferris (D) | 223,571 | 42.6 | 1982 | James J. Blanchard (D) | 1,561,291 | 51.4 |
| 1906 | Fred M. Warner (R) | 227,567 | 60.9 | | Richard H. Headlee (R) | 1,369,582 | 45.1 |
| | Charles H. Kimmerle (D) | 130,018 | 34.8 | 1986 | James J. Blanchard (D) | 1,632,138 | 68.1 |
| 1908 | Fred M. Warner (R) | 262,141 | 48.4 | | William Lucas (R) | 753,647 | 31.4 |
| | Lawton T. Hemans (D) | 252,611 | 46.6 | 1990 | John Engler (R) | 1,276,134 | 49.8 |
| 1910 | Chase S. Osborn (R) | 202,803 | 52.9 | | James J. Blanchard (D) | 1,258,539 | 49.1 |
| | Lawton T. Hemans (D) | 159,770 | 41.6 | | | | |

# MINNESOTA

(Became a state May 11, 1858)

| | Candidates | Votes | % |
|---|---|---|---|
| 1857 | Henry H. Sibley (D) | 17,790 | 50.3 |
| | Alexander Ramsey (R) | 17,550 | 49.7 |
| 1859 | Alexander Ramsey (R) | 21,335 | 54.8 |
| | George L. Becker (D) | 17,583 | 45.2 |
| 1861 | Alexander Ramsey (R) | 16,274# | 60.9 |
| | E. O. Hamlin (D) | 10,448# | 39.1 |
| 1863 | Stephen Miller (UN) | 19,628 | 60.6 |
| | Henry T. Wells (D) | 12,739 | 39.4 |
| 1865 | William R. Marshall (R) | 17,308 | 55.6 |
| | II. M. Rice (D) | 13,847 | 44.5 |
| 1867 | William R. Marshall (R) | 34,874 | 54.2 |
| | Charles E. Flandrau (D) | 29,511 | 45.8 |
| 1869 | Horace Austin (R) | 27,599 | 50.4 |
| | George L. Otis (D) | 25,390 | 46.4 |
| 1871 | Horace Austin (R) | 46,669 | 59.9 |
| | Winthrop Young (D) | 31,212 | 40.1 |
| 1873 | Cushman K. Davis (R) | 40,741# | 52.9 |
| | Ara Barton (IR & D) | 35,245# | 45.8 |
| 1875 | John S. Pillsbury (R) | 45,073# | 53.6 |
| | David L. Buell (D) | 35,275# | 41.9 |
| 1877 | John S. Pillsbury (R) | 57,071# | 57.9 |
| | W. L. Banning (D) | 39,147# | 39.7 |
| 1879 | John S. Pillsbury (R) | 57,522 | 54.0 |
| | Edmund Rice (D) | 41,844 | 39.3 |
| 1881 | Lucius F. Hubbard (R) | 65,025 | 63.6 |
| | R. W. Johnson (D) | 37,168 | 36.4 |
| 1883 | Lucius F. Hubbard (R) | 72,462 | 55.4 |
| | A. Bierman (D) | 58,245 | 44.6 |
| 1886 | A. R. McGill (R) | 106,966 | 48.5 |
| | A. A. Ames (D) | 104,483 | 47.4 |
| 1888 | William R. Merriam (R) | 134,355 | 51.3 |
| | Eugene M. Wilson (D) | 110,251 | 42.1 |
| | Hugh Harrison (P) | 17,150 | 6.6 |
| 1890 | William R. Merriam (R) | 88,111 | 36.6 |
| | Thomas Wilson (D) | 85,844 | 35.6 |
| | Sidney M. Owen (ALNC) | 58,513 | 24.3 |
| 1892 | Knute Nelson (R) | 109,220 | 42.7 |
| | Daniel W. Lawler (D) | 94,600 | 37.0 |
| | Ignatius Donnelly (PP) | 39,860 | 15.6 |
| 1894 | Knute Nelson (R) | 147,943 | 49.9 |
| | Sidney M. Owen (PP) | 87,898 | 29.7 |
| | George L. Becker (D) | 53,583 | 18.1 |
| 1896 | David M. Clough (R) | 165,906 | 49.2 |
| | John Lind (PP & D) | 162,254 | 48.1 |
| 1898 | John Lind (D & POP) | 131,980 | 52.3 |
| | William H. Eustis (R) | 111,796 | 44.3 |
| 1900 | Samuel R. Van Sant (R) | 152,905 | 48.7 |
| | John Lind (PP & D) | 150,651 | 48.0 |
| 1902 | Samuel R. Van Sant (R) | 155,849 | 57.5 |
| | Leonard A. Rosing (D) | 99,362 | 36.7 |
| 1904 | John A. Johnson (D) | 147,992 | 48.7 |
| | Robert C. Dunn (R) | 140,130 | 46.1 |
| 1906 | John A. Johnson (D) | 168,480 | 60.9 |
| | A. L. Cole (R) | 96,162 | 34.8 |
| 1908 | John A. Johnson (D) | 175,036 | 52.2 |
| | Jacob F. Jacobson (R) | 147,034 | 43.8 |
| 1910 | Adolph O. Eberhart (R) | 164,185 | 55.7 |
| | James Gray (D) | 103,779 | 35.2 |
| 1912 | Adolph O. Eberhart (R) | 129,688 | 40.7 |
| | Peter M. Ringdal (D) | 99,659 | 31.3 |
| | P. V. Collins (PROG) | 33,455 | 10.5 |
| | E. E. Lobeck (P) | 29,876 | 9.4 |
| | David Morgan (PUB OWN) | 25,769 | 8.1 |
| 1914 | Winfield S. Hammond (D) | 156,304 | 45.5 |
| | William E. Lee (R) | 143,730 | 41.9 |
| | W. G. Calderwood (P) | 18,582 | 5.4 |
| | Tom J. Lewis (SOC) | 17,325 | 5.1 |

| | Candidates | Votes | % |
|---|---|---|---|
| 1916 | Joseph A. A. Burnquist (R) | 245,841 | 62.9 |
| | Thomas P. Dwyer (D) | 93,112 | 23.8 |
| | J. O. Bentall (SOC) | 26,306 | 6.7 |
| | Thomas J. Anderson (P) | 19,884 | 5.1 |
| 1918 | Joseph A. A. Burnquist (R) | 166,615 | 45.1 |
| | David H. Evans (F-LAB) | 111,966 | 30.3 |
| | Fred E. Wheaton (D) | 76,838 | 20.8 |
| 1920 | Jacob A. O. Preus (R) | 415,805 | 53.1 |
| | Henrik Shipstead (I) | 281,406 | 35.9 |
| | L. C. Hodgson (D) | 81,291 | 10.4 |
| 1922 | Jacob A. O. Preus (R) | 309,756 | 45.2 |
| | Magnus Johnson (F-LAB) | 295,479 | 43.1 |
| | Edward Indrehus (D) | 79,903 | 11.7 |
| 1924 | Theodore Christianson (R) | 406,692 | 48.7 |
| | Floyd B. Olson (F-LAB) | 366,029 | 43.8 |
| | Carlos Avery (D) | 49,353 | 5.9 |
| 1926 | Theodore Christianson (R) | 395,779 | 56.5 |
| | Magnus Johnson (F-LAB) | 266,845 | 38.1 |
| | Alfred Jaques (D) | 38,008 | 5.4 |
| 1928 | Theodore Christianson (R) | 549,857 | 55.0 |
| | Ernest Lundeen (F-LAB) | 227,193 | 22.7 |
| | Andrew Nelson (D) | 213,734 | 21.4 |
| 1930 | Floyd B. Olson (F-LAB) | 472,354 | 59.3 |
| | Ray P. Chase (R) | 289,528 | 36.4 |
| 1932 | Floyd B. Olson (F-LAB) | 522,438 | 50.6 |
| | Earle Brown (R) | 334,081 | 32.3 |
| | John E. Regan (D) | 169,859 | 16.4 |
| 1934 | Floyd B. Olson (F-LAB) | 468,812 | 44.6 |
| | Martin A. Nelson (R) | 396,359 | 37.7 |
| | John E. Regan (D) | 176,928 | 16.8 |
| 1936 | Elmer A. Benson (F-LAB) | 680,342 | 60.7 |
| | Martin A. Nelson (R) | 431,841 | 38.6 |
| 1938 | Harold E. Stassen (R) | 678,839 | 59.9 |
| | Elmer A. Benson (F-LAB) | 387,263 | 34.2 |
| | Thomas Gallagher (D) | 65,875 | 5.8 |
| 1940 | Harold E. Stassen (R) | 654,686 | 52.1 |
| | Hjalmar Petersen (F-LAB) | 459,609 | 36.5 |
| | Ed Murphy (D) | 140,021 | 11.1 |
| 1942 | Harold E. Stassen (R) | 409,800 | 51.6 |
| | Hjalmar Petersen (F-LAB) | 299,917 | 37.8 |
| | John D. Sullivan (D) | 75,151 | 9.5 |
| 1944 | Edward J. Thye (R) | 701,185 | 61.1 |
| | Byron G. Allen (DFL) | 440,132 | 38.3 |
| 1946 | Luther W. Youngdahl (R) | 519,067 | 59.0 |
| | Harold H. Barker (DFL) | 349,565 | 39.7 |
| 1948 | Luther W. Youngdahl (R) | 643,572 | 53.2 |
| | Charles L. Halsted (DFL) | 545,746 | 45.1 |
| 1950 | Luther W. Youngdahl (R) | 635,800 | 60.8 |
| | Harry H. Peterson (DFL) | 400,637 | 38.3 |
| 1952 | C. Elmer Anderson (R) | 785,125 | 55.3 |
| | Orville L. Freeman (DFL) | 624,480 | 44.0 |
| 1954 | Orville L. Freeman (DFL) | 607,099 | 52.7 |
| | C. Elmer Anderson (R) | 538,865 | 46.8 |
| 1956 | Orville L. Freeman (DFL) | 731,180 | 51.4 |
| | Ancher Nelsen (R) | 685,196 | 48.2 |
| 1958 | Orville L. Freeman (DFL) | 658,326 | 56.8 |
| | George Mackinnon (R) | 490,731 | 42.3 |
| 1960 | Elmer L. Andersen (R) | 783,813 | 50.6 |
| | Orville L. Freeman (DFL) | 760,934 | 49.1 |
| 1962 | Karl F. Rolvaag (DFL) | 619,842‡ | 49.7 |
| | Elmer L. Andersen (R) | 619,751 | 49.7 |
| 1966 | Harold Levander (R) | 680,593 | 52.6 |
| | Karl F. Rolvaag (DFL) | 607,943 | 46.9 |
| 1970 | Wendell R. Anderson (DFL) | 737,921 | 54.3 |
| | Douglas M. Head (R) | 621,780 | 45.7 |
| 1974 | Wendell R. Anderson (DFL) | 786,787 | 62.8 |
| | John W. Johnson (R) | 367,722 | 29.3 |
| 1978 | Albert H. Quie (I-R) | 830,019 | 52.3 |
| | Rudy Perpich (DFL) | 718,244 | 45.3 |
| 1982 | Rudy Perpich (DFL) | 1,049,104 | 58.6 |
| | Wheelock Whitney (I-R) | 715,796 | 40.0 |

| | Candidates | Votes | % |
|---|---|---|---|
| 1986 | Rudy Perpich (DFL) | 790,138 | *55.8* |
| | Cal R. Ludeman (I-R) | 606,755 | *42.9* |
| 1990 | Arne Carlson (I-R) | 895,988 | *49.6* |
| | Rudy Perpich (DFL) | 836,218 | *46.3* |

# MISSISSIPPI

(Became a state Dec. 10, 1817)

| | Candidates | Votes | % |
|---|---|---|---|
| 1817 | David Holmes | 4,108 | |
| 1819 | George Poindexter | 2,721 | *61.5* |
| | Thomas Hinds | 1,702 | *38.5* |
| 1821 | Walter Leake | 4,730 | *78.8* |
| | Charles B. Green | 1,269 | *21.2* |
| 1823 | Walter Leake | 4,730 | *51.3* |
| | David Dickson | 2,511 | *27.2* |
| | William Lattimore | 1,986 | *21.5* |
| 1825 | David Holmes (OLD R) | 7,850 | *84.0* |
| | Cowles Mead (OLD R) | 1,499 | *16.0* |
| 1827 | Gerard C. Brandon | 5,482 | *51.0* |
| | Daniel Williams | 3,392 | *31.6* |
| | Beverly R. Grayson | 1,866 | *17.4* |
| 1829 | Gerard C. Brandon (JAC D) | 6,052 | *64.6* |
| | George W. Winchester (NR) | 3,310 | *35.4* |
| 1831 | Abram M. Scott (NR) | 3,953 | *30.5* |
| | Hiram G. Runnels (JAC D) | 3,711 | *28.6* |
| | Charles Lynch (JAC D) | 2,902 | *22.4* |
| | Wiley Harris (JAC D) | 1,899 | *14.7* |
| 1833 | Hiram G. Runnels (D) | 6,614 | *52.9* |
| | Abram M. Scott (W) | 5,900 | *47.2* |
| 1835 | Charles Lynch (W) | 9,877 | *51.1* |
| | Hiram G. Runnels (D) | 9,451 | *48.9* |
| 1837 | Alexander G. McNutt (D) | 12,823 | *46.4* |
| | Morgan | 9,861 | *35.7* |
| | Grimball (W) | 4,951 | *17.9* |
| 1839 | Alexander G. McNutt (D) | 18,880 | *54.3* |
| | Edward Turner (W) | 15,886 | *45.7* |
| 1841 | Tilgham M. Tucker (D) | 19,059 | *53.2* |
| | D. O. Shattuck (W) | 16,783 | *46.8* |
| 1843 | Albert G. Brown (A-RPT D) | 21,115 | *52.9* |
| | Clayton (W) | 17,442 | *43.7* |
| 1845 | Albert G. Brown (D) | 27,669 | *64.8* |
| | Coopwood (W) | 15,029 | *35.2* |
| 1849 | John A. Quitman (D) | 33,117 | *59.0* |
| | Lea (W) | 22,996 | *40.9* |
| 1851 | Henry S. Foote (UN) | 27,836 | *51.4* |
| | Jefferson Davis (SO RTS) | 26,301 | *48.6* |
| 1853 | John J. McCrae (D) | 30,460 | *54.0* |
| | Rogers (W) | 25,967 | *46.0* |
| 1855 | John J. McCrae (D) | 32,669 | *54.2* |
| | C. D. Fontaine (AM) | 27,578 | *45.8* |
| 1857 | William McWillie (D) | 27,376 | *66.0* |
| | William Yerger (AM) | 14,085 | *34.0* |
| 1859 | John J. Pettus (D) | 34,559 | *76.8* |
| | H. W. Walter (OPP) | 10,408 | *23.1* |
| 1861 | John J. Pettus (D) | 29,959 | *86.9* |
| | Jacob Thompson | 3,556 | *10.3* |
| 1863 | Charles Clark | 16,050 | *69.8* |
| | A. M. West | 4,914 | *21.4* |
| | Reuben Davis | 2,021 | *8.8* |
| 1865 | Benjamin G. Humphreys (SEC W) | 19,037 | *42.2* |
| | E. S. Fisher (UN) | 15,557 | *34.5* |
| | W. S. Patton | 10,519 | *23.3* |
| 1868 | Benjamin G. Humphreys (D) | 62,321 | *52.6* |
| | Beriah B. Eggleston (R) | 56,072 | *47.4* |
| 1869 | James L. Alcorn (R) | 76,186 | *66.7* |
| | Louis Dent (C) | 38,097 | *33.3* |

| | Candidates | Votes | % |
|---|---|---|---|
| 1873 | Adelbert Ames (R) | 73,324 | *58.1* |
| | James L. Alcorn (I) | 52,857 | *41.9* |
| 1877 | John M. Stone (D) | 96,376 | *98.8* |
| 1881 | Robert Lowry (D) | 76,805 | *59.6* |
| | King (G & R) | 51,994 | *40.4* |
| 1885 | Robert Lowry (D) | 88,783 | *100.0* |
| 1889 | John M. Stone (D) | 84,929 | *100.0* |
| 1895 | Anselm J. McLaurin (D) | 46,870 | *72.1* |
| | Frank Burkitt (PP) | 18,167 | *27.9* |
| 1899 | Andrew H. Longino (D) | 42,273 | *87.4* |
| | R. K. Prewitt (POP) | 6,097 | *12.6* |
| 1903 | James K. Vardaman (D) | 32,191 | *100.0* |
| 1907 | Edmund F. Noel (D) | 29,528 | *100.0* |
| 1911 | Earl Brewer (D) | 40,471 | *95.2* |
| 1915 | Theodore G. Bilbo (D) | 50,541 | *92.6* |
| | J. T. Lester (SOC) | 4,046 | *7.4* |
| 1919 | Lee M. Russell (D) | 39,239 | *96.9* |
| 1923 | Henry L. Whitfield (D) | 29,138 | *100.0* |
| 1927 | Theodore G. Bilbo (D) | 31,717 | *100.0* |
| 1931 | Martin S. Conner (D) | 45,942 | *100.0* |
| 1935 | Hugh L. White (D) | 45,881 | *100.0* |
| 1939 | Paul B. Johnson (D) | 61,614 | *100.0* |
| 1943 | Thomas L. Bailey (D) | 50,488 | *100.0* |
| 1947 | Fielding L. Wright (D) | 161,993 | *97.5* |
| 1951 | Hugh L. White (D) | 43,422 | *100.0* |
| 1955 | J. P. Coleman (D) | 40,707 | *100.0* |
| 1959 | Ross R. Barnett (D) | 57,671 | *100.0* |
| 1963 | Paul B. Johnson Jr. (D) | 225,456 | *61.9* |
| | Rubel L. Phillips (R) | 138,605 | *38.1* |
| 1967 | John Bell Williams (D) | 315,318 | *70.3* |
| | Rubel L. Phillips (R) | 133,379 | *29.7* |
| 1971 | William L. Waller (D) | 601,222 | *77.0* |
| | James Charles Evers (I) | 172,762 | *22.1* |
| 1975 | Cliff Finch (D) | 369,568 | *52.2* |
| | Gil Carmichael (R) | 319,632 | *45.1* |
| 1979 | William F. Winter (D) | 413,620 | *61.1* |
| | Gil Carmichael (R) | 263,702 | *38.9* |
| 1983 | Bill Allain (D) | 409,209# | *55.1* |
| | Leon Bramlett (R) | 288,764# | *38.9* |
| 1987 | Ray Mabus (D) | 387,346 | *53.8* |
| | Jack Reed (R) | 332,985 | *46.3* |
| 1991 | Kirk Fordice (R) | 361,500 | *50.8* |
| | Ray Mabus (D) | 338,435 | *47.6* |

# MISSOURI

(Became a state Aug. 10, 1821)

| | Candidates | Votes | % |
|---|---|---|---|
| 1820 | Alexander McNair (D-R) | 6,576 | *72.0* |
| | William Clark (D-R) | 2,556 | *28.0* |
| 1824 | Frederick Bates (AR) | 6,165 | *57.1* |
| | William H. Ashley (CLAY R) | 4,636 | *42.9* |
| 1825 | John Miller (JAC D) | 2,801 | *47.9* |
| | Carr (JAC D) | 1,622 | *27.8* |
| | Todd (NR) | 1,423 | *24.3* |
| 1828 | John Miller | 11,043 | *100.0* |
| 1832 | Daniel Dunklin (D) | 9,141 | *50.9* |
| | John Bull (A-JAC) | 8,132 | *45.2* |
| 1836 | Lilburn W. Boggs (D) | 14,315 | *52.3* |
| | Ashley (I) | 13,055 | *47.7* |
| 1840 | Thomas Reynolds (D) | 29,656 | *57.2* |
| | Clark (W) | 22,205 | *42.8* |
| 1844 | John Cummins Edwards (D) | 36,978 | *54.1* |
| | Allen (W) | 31,357 | *45.9* |

| | Candidates | Votes | % |
|---|---|---|---|
| 1848 | Austin A. King (D) | 48,921 | *59.0* |
| | James S. Rollins (W) | 33,942 | *41.0* |
| 1852 | Sterling Price (D) | 46,494 | *58.7* |
| | James Winston (W) | 32,706 | *41.3* |
| 1856 | Trusten Polk (D) | 47,066 | *40.8* |
| | R. C. Ewing (AM) | 40,620 | *35.2* |
| | Thomas Hart Benton (BENTON D) | 27,615 | *24.0* |

Special Election

| | | | |
|---|---|---|---|
| 1857 | R. M. Stewart (D) | 47,975 | *50.2* |
| | J. S. Rollins (AM & EMANC) | 47,619 | *49.8* |

| | | | |
|---|---|---|---|
| 1860 | Claiborne Fox Jackson (D) | 74,239 | *47.0* |
| | Sample Orr (OPP) | 66,400 | *42.0* |
| | Hancock Jackson (SOC) | 11,362 | *7.2* |
| 1864 | Thomas C. Fletcher (UN R) | 73,600 | *70.3* |
| | Thomas L. Price (D) | 31,064 | *29.7* |
| 1868 | Joseph W. McClurg (R) | 82,090 | *56.7* |
| | John S. Phelps (D) | 62,778 | *43.3* |
| 1870 | Benjamin Gratz Brown (D) | 104,374 | *62.3* |
| | Joseph W. McClurg (R) | 63,235 | *37.7* |
| 1872 | Silas Woodson (D & L) | 156,767 | *56.3* |
| | John B. Henderson (R) | 121,889 | *43.7* |
| 1874 | Charles H. Hardin (D) | 149,566 | *57.2* |
| | William Gentry (R) | 112,104 | *42.8* |
| 1876 | John S. Phelps (D) | 199,583 | *57.0* |
| | Gustavus A. Finkelnburg (R) | 147,684 | *42.2* |
| 1880 | Thomas Theodore Crittenden (D) | 207,670 | *52.2* |
| | Dyer (R) | 153,636 | *38.6* |
| | Brown (G) | 36,340 | *9.1* |
| 1884 | John Sappington Marmaduke (D) | 218,885 | *50.1* |
| | Nicholas Ford (G & R) | 207,939 | *47.5* |
| 1888 | David Rowland Francis (D) | 255,764 | *49.4* |
| | E. E. Kimball (R) | 242,531 | *46.8* |
| 1892 | William Joel Stone (D) | 265,044 | *49.0* |
| | William Warner (R) | 235,383 | *43.5* |
| | L. Leonard (PP) | 37,262 | *6.9* |
| 1896 | Lawrence Vest Stephens (D) | 351,062 | *52.9* |
| | Robert E. Lewis (R) | 307,729 | *46.4* |
| 1900 | Alexander Monroe Dockery (D) | 350,045 | *51.2* |
| | Flory (R) | 317,905 | *46.5* |
| 1904 | Joseph Wingate Folk (D) | 326,652 | *50.7* |
| | Cyrus P. Walbridge (R) | 296,552 | *46.1* |
| 1908 | Herbert Spencer Hadley (R) | 355,932 | *49.7* |
| | Cowherd (D) | 340,053 | *47.5* |
| 1912 | Elliott Woolfolk Major (D) | 337,019 | *48.2* |
| | John C. McKinley (R) | 217,819 | *31.2* |
| | Albert D. Nortoni (PROG) | 109,146 | *15.6* |
| 1916 | Frederick Dozier Gardner (D) | 382,355 | *48.7* |
| | Lamm (R) | 380,092 | *48.4* |
| 1920 | Arthur Mastick Hyde (R) | 722,020 | *54.3* |
| | Atkinson (D) | 580,726 | *43.6* |
| 1924 | Samuel Aaron Baker (R) | 640,135 | *49.4* |
| | A. T. Nelson (D) | 634,263 | *48.9* |
| 1928 | Henry Stewart Caulfield (R) | 784,311 | *51.6* |
| | Francis M. Wilson (D) | 731,783 | *48.2* |
| 1932 | Guy Brasfield Park (D) | 968,551 | *60.2* |
| | Edward H. Winter (R) | 629,428 | *39.1* |
| 1936 | Lloyd Crow Stark (D) | 1,037,133 | *57.1* |
| | Jesse W. Barrett (R) | 772,934 | *42.5* |
| 1940 | Forrest C. Donnell (R) | 911,530 | *50.1* |
| | Larry McDaniel (D) | 907,917 | *49.9* |
| 1944 | Phil M. Donnelly (D) | 793,490 | *50.9* |
| | Jean Paul Bradshaw (R) | 762,908 | *49.0* |
| 1948 | Forrest Smith (D) | 893,092 | *57.0* |
| | Murray E. Thompson (R) | 670,064 | *42.8* |
| 1952 | Phil M. Donnelly (D) | 983,169 | *52.6* |
| | Howard Elliott (R) | 886,270 | *47.4* |
| 1956 | James T. Blair Jr. (D) | 941,528 | *52.1* |
| | Lon Hocker (R) | 866,810 | *47.9* |

| | Candidates | Votes | % |
|---|---|---|---|
| 1960 | John M. Dalton (D) | 1,095,195 | *58.0* |
| | Edward G. Farmer (R) | 792,131 | *42.0* |
| 1964 | Warren E. Hearnes (D) | 1,110,651 | *62.1* |
| | Ethan A. H. Shepley (R) | 678,949 | *37.9* |
| 1968 | Warren E. Hearnes (D) | 1,063,495 | *60.7* |
| | Lawrence K. Roos (R) | 688,300 | *39.3* |
| 1972 | Christopher S. Bond (R) | 1,029,451 | *55.2* |
| | Edward L. Dowd (D) | 832,751 | *44.6* |
| 1976 | Joseph P. Teasdale (D) | 971,184 | *50.2* |
| | Christopher S. Bond (R) | 958,110 | *49.6* |
| 1980 | Christopher S. Bond (R) | 1,098,950 | *52.6* |
| | Joseph P. Teasdale (D) | 981,884 | *47.0* |
| 1984 | John Ashcroft (R) | 1,194,506 | *56.7* |
| | Kenneth J. Rothman (D) | 913,700 | *43.3* |
| 1988 | John Ashcroft (R) | 1,339,531 | *64.2* |
| | Betty Hearnes (D) | 724,919 | *34.8* |
| 1992 | Mel Carnahan (D) | 1,375,425 | *58.7* |
| | William L. Webster (R) | 968,574 | *41.3* |

# MONTANA

(Became a state Nov. 8, 1889)

| | Candidates | Votes | % |
|---|---|---|---|
| 1889 | Joseph K. Toole (D) | 19,735 | *51.0* |
| | Thomas C. Power (R) | 18,991 | *49.0* |
| 1892 | John E. Rickards (R) | 18,187 | *41.2* |
| | Timothy E. Collins (D) | 17,650 | *40.0* |
| | William Kennedy (PP) | 7,794 | *17.6* |
| 1896 | Robert B. Smith (PP & D) | 36,688 | *71.0* |
| | Alexander C. Botkin (R-SIL R) | 14,993 | *29.0* |
| 1900 | Joseph K. Toole (D) | 31,419 | *49.3* |
| | David S. Folsom (R) | 22,691 | *35.6* |
| | Thomas S. Hogan (ID) | 9,188 | *14.4* |
| 1904 | Joseph K. Toole (D-LAB-PP) | 35,377 | *53.8* |
| | William Lindsay (R) | 26,957 | *41.0* |
| | Malcolm A. O'Malley (SOC) | 3,431 | *5.2* |
| 1908 | Edwin L. Norris (D) | 32,282 | *47.3* |
| | Edward Donlan (R) | 30,792 | *45.2* |
| | Harry Hazelton (SOC) | 5,112 | *7.5* |
| 1912 | Samuel V. Stewart (D) | 25,371 | *31.7* |
| | Harry L. Wilson (R) | 22,950 | *28.7* |
| | Frank J. Edwards (PROG) | 18,881 | *23.6* |
| | Lewis J. Duncan (SOC) | 12,766 | *16.0* |
| 1916 | Samuel V. Stewart (D) | 85,683 | *49.4* |
| | Frank J. Edwards (R) | 76,556 | *44.1* |
| | Lewis J. Duncan (SOC) | 11,342 | *6.5* |
| 1920 | Joseph M. Dixon (R) | 111,113 | *59.7* |
| | Burton K. Wheeler (D) | 74,875 | *40.3* |
| 1924 | John E. Erickson (D) | 88,801 | *51.0* |
| | Joseph M. Dixon (R) | 74,126 | *42.6* |
| | Frank J. Edwards (F-LAB) | 10,576 | *6.1* |
| 1928 | John E. Erickson (D) | 114,256 | *58.7* |
| | Wellington D. Rankin (R) | 79,777 | *41.0* |
| 1932 | John E. Erickson (D) | 104,949 | *48.5* |
| | Frank A. Hazelbaker (R) | 101,105 | *46.7* |
| 1936 | Roy E. Ayers (D) | 115,310 | *51.0* |
| | Frank A. Hazelbaker (R) | 108,854 | *48.1* |
| 1940 | Samuel C. Ford (R) | 124,435 | *50.7* |
| | Roy E. Ayers (D) | 119,453 | *48.6* |
| 1944 | Samuel C. Ford (R) | 116,461 | *56.4* |
| | Leif Erickson (D) | 89,224 | *43.2* |
| 1948 | John W. Bonner (D) | 124,267 | *55.7* |
| | Samuel C. Ford (R) | 97,792 | *43.9* |
| 1952 | John Hugo Aronson (R) | 134,423 | *51.0* |
| | John W. Bonner (D) | 129,369 | *49.0* |
| 1956 | John Hugo Aronson (R) | 138,878 | *51.4* |
| | Arnold H. Olsen (D) | 131,488 | *48.6* |

| | Candidates | Votes | % |
|---|---|---|---|
| 1960 | Donald G. Nutter (R) | 154,230 | 55.1 |
| | Paul Cannon (D) | 125,651 | 44.9 |
| 1964 | Tim Babcock (R) | 144,113 | 51.3 |
| | Roland Renne (D) | 136,862 | 48.7 |
| 1968 | Forrest H. Anderson (D) | 150,481 | 54.1 |
| | Tim Babcock (R) | 116,432 | 41.9 |
| 1972 | Thomas L. Judge (D) | 172,523 | 54.1 |
| | Ed Smith (R) | 146,231 | 45.9 |
| 1976 | Thomas L. Judge (D) | 195,420 | 61.7 |
| | Robert Woodahl (R) | 115,848 | 36.6 |
| 1980 | Ted Schwinden (D) | 199,574 | 55.4 |
| | Jack Ramirez (R) | 160,892 | 44.6 |
| 1984 | Ted Schwinden (D) | 266,578 | 70.3 |
| | Pat M. Goodover (R) | 100,070 | 26.4 |
| 1988 | Stan Stephens (R) | 190,604 | 51.9 |
| | Thomas L. Judge (D) | 169,313 | 46.1 |
| 1992 | Marc Racicot (R) | 209,401 | 51.3 |
| | Dorothy Bradley (D) | 198,421 | 48.7 |

# NEBRASKA

(Became a state March 1, 1867)

| | Candidates | Votes | % |
|---|---|---|---|
| 1866 | David Butler (R) | 4,083 | 50.4 |
| | J. S. Morton (D) | 4,001 | 49.4 |
| 1868 | David Butler (R) | 8,576 | 57.5 |
| | T. R. Porter (D) | 6,349 | 42.5 |
| 1870 | David Butler (R) | 11,126 | 56.3 |
| | J. H. Croxton (D) | 8,648 | 43.7 |
| 1872 | Robert W. Furnas (R) | 16,543 | 59.6 |
| | H. C. Lett (D) | 11,227 | 40.4 |
| 1874 | Silas Garber (R) | 21,548 | 59.9 |
| | Albert Tuxbury (D) | 8,946 | 24.9 |
| | J. F. Gardner (PP I) | 4,159 | 11.6 |
| 1876 | Silas Garber (R) | 31,947 | 61.2 |
| | Paren England (D) | 17,219 | 33.0 |
| | J. F. Gardner (G) | 3,022 | 5.8 |
| 1878 | Albinus Nance (R) | 29,269 | 56.1 |
| | W. H. Webster (D) | 13,471 | 25.8 |
| | Levi G. Todd (G) | 9,484 | 18.2 |
| 1880 | Albinus Nance (R) | 55,237 | 63.2 |
| | T. W. Tipton (D) | 28,167 | 32.3 |
| 1882 | James W. Dawes (R) | 43,495 | 48.8 |
| | J. S. Morton (D) | 28,562 | 32.1 |
| | E. P. Ingersoll (G) | 16,991 | 19.1 |
| 1884 | James W. Dawes (R) | 72,835 | 54.5 |
| | J. S. Morton (D) | 57,634 | 43.2 |
| 1886 | John M. Thayer (R) | 76,456 | 55.2 |
| | J. E. North (D) | 52,456 | 37.9 |
| | H. W. Hardy (P) | 8,198 | 5.9 |
| 1888 | John M. Thayer (R) | 103,982 | 51.3 |
| | J. A. McShane (D) | 85,420 | 42.1 |
| 1890 | James E. Boyd (D) | 71,331‡ | 33.3 |
| | J. H. Powers (PP I) | 70,187 | 32.8 |
| | L. D. Richards (R) | 68,878 | 32.2 |
| 1892 | Lorenzo Crounse (R) | 78,426 | 39.7 |
| | Charles Henry Van Wyck (PP I) | 68,617 | 34.8 |
| | J. S. Morton (D) | 44,195 | 22.4 |
| 1894 | Silas A. Holcomb (D & PPI) | 97,825 | 48.0 |
| | T. J. Majors (R) | 94,613 | 46.4 |
| 1896 | Silas A. Holcomb (D & PPI) | 116,415 | 53.5 |
| | J. H. McColl (R) | 94,724 | 43.5 |
| 1898 | William A. Poynter (FUS) | 95,703 | 50.2 |
| | M. L. Hayward (R) | 92,982 | 48.8 |
| 1900 | Charles H. Dietrich (R) | 113,879 | 48.9 |
| | William A. Poynter (FUS) | 113,018 | 48.5 |

| | Candidates | Votes | % |
|---|---|---|---|
| 1902 | John H. Mickey (R) | 96,471 | 49.7 |
| | William H. Thompson (FUS) | 91,116 | 46.9 |
| 1904 | John H. Mickey (R) | 111,711 | 49.7 |
| | George W. Berge (FUS) | 102,568 | 45.6 |
| 1906 | George L. Sheldon (R) | 97,858 | 51.3 |
| | Ashton Shallenberger (D & PPI) | 84,885 | 44.5 |
| 1908 | Ashton Shallenberger (D & PPI) | 132,960 | 49.9 |
| | George L. Sheldon (R) | 125,967 | 47.3 |
| 1910 | Chester H. Aldrich (R) | 123,070 | 51.9 |
| | James C. Dahlman (D) | 107,760 | 45.5 |
| 1912 | John H. Morehead (D & PPI) | 123,997 | 49.3 |
| | Chester H. Aldrich (R & PROG) | 114,075 | 45.3 |
| 1914 | John H. Morehead (D & PPI) | 120,201 | 50.4 |
| | R. B. Howell (R) | 101,229 | 42.4 |
| 1916 | Keith Neville (D & PPI) | 143,564 | 49.3 |
| | Abraham L. Sutton (R & PROG) | 136,811 | 47.0 |
| 1918 | Samuel R. McKelvie (R) | 121,188 | 54.5 |
| | Keith Neville (D) | 97,886 | 44.0 |
| 1920 | Samuel R. McKelvie (R) | 152,863 | 40.4 |
| | John H. Morehead (D) | 130,433 | 34.5 |
| | Arthur G. Wray (NON PL) | 88,905 | 23.5 |
| 1922 | Charles W. Bryan (D) | 214,070 | 54.6 |
| | Charles H. Randall (R) | 164,435 | 42.0 |
| 1924 | Adam McMullen (R) | 229,067 | 51.1 |
| | J. N. Norton (D) | 183,709 | 41.0 |
| | Dan Butler (PROG) | 35,594 | 7.9 |
| 1926 | Adam McMullen (R) | 206,120 | 49.8 |
| | Charles W. Bryan (D) | 202,688 | 49.0 |
| 1928 | Arthur J. Weaver (R) | 308,262 | 57.0 |
| | Charles W. Bryan (D) | 230,640 | 42.6 |
| 1930 | Charles W. Bryan (D) | 222,161 | 50.8 |
| | Arthur J. Weaver (R) | 215,615 | 49.3 |
| 1932 | Charles W. Bryan (D) | 296,117 | 52.5 |
| | Dwight Griswold (R) | 260,888 | 46.3 |
| 1934 | Robert L. Cochran (D) | 284,095 | 50.8 |
| | Dwight Griswold (R) | 266,707 | 47.7 |
| 1936 | Robert L. Cochran (D) | 333,412 | 55.9 |
| | Dwight Griswold (R) | 257,279 | 43.1 |
| 1938 | Robert L. Cochran (D) | 218,787 | 44.0 |
| | Charles J. Warner (R) | 201,898 | 40.6 |
| | Charles W. Bryan | 76,258 | 15.4 |
| 1940 | Dwight Griswold (R) | 365,638 | 60.9 |
| | Terry Carpenter (D) | 235,167 | 39.1 |
| 1942 | Dwight Griswold (R) | 283,271 | 74.8 |
| | Charles W. Bryan (D) | 95,231 | 25.2 |
| 1944 | Dwight Griswold (R) | 410,136 | 76.1 |
| | George W. Olsen (D) | 128,760 | 23.9 |
| 1946 | Val Peterson (R) | 249,468 | 65.5 |
| | Frank Sorrell (D) | 131,367 | 34.5 |
| 1948 | Val Peterson (R) | 286,119 | 60.1 |
| | Frank Sorrell (D) | 190,214 | 39.9 |
| 1950 | Val Peterson (R) | 247,089 | 54.9 |
| | Walter R. Raecke (D) | 202,638 | 45.1 |
| 1952 | Robert B. Crosby (R) | 365,409 | 61.4 |
| | Walter R. Raecke (D) | 229,400 | 38.6 |
| 1954 | Victor E. Anderson (R) | 250,080 | 60.3 |
| | William Ritchie (D) | 164,753 | 39.7 |
| 1956 | Victor E. Anderson (R) | 308,285 | 54.3 |
| | Frank Sorrell (D) | 228,048 | 40.2 |
| | George L. Morris | 31,583 | 5.6 |
| 1958 | Ralph G. Brooks (D) | 211,345 | 50.2 |
| | Victor E. Anderson (R) | 209,705 | 49.8 |
| 1960 | Frank B. Morrison (D) | 311,344 | 52.0 |
| | John R. Cooper (R) | 287,302 | 48.0 |
| 1962 | Frank B. Morrison (D) | 242,669 | 52.2 |
| | Fred A. Seaton (R) | 221,884 | 47.8 |
| 1964 | Frank B. Morrison (D) | 347,026 | 60.0 |
| | Dwight W. Burney (R) | 231,029 | 40.0 |
| 1966 | Norbert T. Tiemann (R) | 299,245 | 61.5 |
| | Philip C. Sorensen (D) | 186,985 | 38.5 |
| 1970 | J. James Exon (D) | 248,552 | 53.8 |
| | Norbert T. Tiemann (R) | 201,994 | 43.8 |

| | Candidates | Votes | % |
|---|---|---|---|
| 1974 | J. James Exon (D) | 267,012 | *59.2* |
| | Richard D. Marvel (R) | 159,780 | *35.4* |
| | Ernest W. Chambers (I) | 24,320 | *5.4* |
| 1978 | Charles Thone (R) | 275,473 | *55.9* |
| | Gerald T. Whelan (D) | 216,754 | *44.0* |
| 1982 | Robert Kerrey (D) | 277,436 | *50.6* |
| | Charles Thone (R) | 270,203 | *49.3* |
| 1986 | Kay A. Orr (R) | 298,325 | *52.9* |
| | Helen Boosalis (D) | 265,156 | *47.0* |
| 1990 | Ben Nelson (D) | 292,771 | *49.9* |
| | Kay A. Orr (R) | 288,741 | *49.2* |

# NEVADA

(Became a state Oct. 31, 1864)

| | Candidates | Votes | % |
|---|---|---|---|
| 1864 | Henry G. Blasdel (UN R) | 9,834 | *60.0* |
| | David E. Buell (D) | 6,555 | *40.0* |
| 1866 | Henry G. Blasdel (R) | 5,125 | *55.5* |
| | John D. Winters (D) | 4,105 | *44.5* |
| 1870 | L. R. Bradley (D) | 7,200 | *53.9* |
| | F. A. Tritte (R) | 6,147 | *46.1* |
| 1874 | L. R. Bradley (D) | 10,339 | *57.1* |
| | Hazlett (R) | 7,754 | *42.9* |
| 1878 | John H. Kinkead (R) | 9,678 | *51.4* |
| | L. R. Bradley (D) | 9,151 | *48.6* |
| 1882 | Jewett W. Adams (D) | 7,770 | *54.3* |
| | Enoch Strother (R) | 6,535 | *45.7* |
| 1886 | C. C. Stevenson (R) | 6,463 | *52.4* |
| | Jewett W. Adams (D) | 5,869 | *47.6* |
| 1890 | R. K. Colcord (R) | 6,601 | *53.3* |
| | Thomas Winters (D) | 5,791 | *46.7* |
| 1894 | J. S. Jones (D SIL) | 5,223 | *49.9* |
| | A. C. Cleveland (R) | 3,861 | *36.9* |
| | G. E. Peckham (POP) | 711 | *6.8* |
| | Theodore Winters (D) | 678 | *6.5* |
| 1898 | Reinhold Sadler (SIL R) | 3,570 | *35.7* |
| | William McMillan (R) | 3,548 | *35.5* |
| | George Russell (D) | 2,057 | *20.6* |
| | J. B. McCullough (PP) | 833 | *8.3* |
| 1902 | John Sparks (D & SILVER) | 6,540 | *57.8* |
| | A. C. Cleveland (R) | 4,778 | *42.2* |
| 1906 | John Sparks (D & SILVER) | 8,686 | *58.5* |
| | James F. Mitchell (R) | 5,336 | *36.0* |
| | Thomas B. Casey (SOC) | 815 | *5.5* |
| 1910 | Tasker L. Oddie (R) | 10,435 | *50.6* |
| | D. S. Dickerson (D) | 8,798 | *42.7* |
| | Henry F. Gegax (SOC) | 1,393 | *6.8* |
| 1914 | Emmet D. Boyle (D) | 9,623 | *44.7* |
| | Tasker L. Oddie (R) | 8,537 | *39.6* |
| | W. A. Morgan (SOC) | 3,391 | *15.7* |
| 1918 | Emmet D. Boyle (D) | 12,875 | *52.1* |
| | Tasker L. Oddie (R) | 11,845 | *47.9* |
| 1922 | James G. Scrugham (D) | 15,437 | *53.9* |
| | John H. Miller (R) | 13,215 | *46.1* |
| 1926 | Fred B. Balzar (R) | 16,374 | *53.0* |
| | James G. Scrugham (D) | 14,521 | *47.0* |
| 1930 | Fred B. Balzar (R) | 18,442 | *53.3* |
| | C. L. Richards (D) | 16,192 | *46.8* |
| 1934 | Richard Kirman Sr. (D) | 23,088 | *53.9* |
| | Morley Griswold (R) | 14,778 | *34.5* |
| | L. C. Branson (I) | 4,940 | *11.5* |
| 1938 | Edward P. Carville (D) | 28,528 | *61.9* |
| | John A. Fulton (R) | 17,586 | *38.1* |
| 1942 | Edward P. Carville (D) | 24,505 | *60.3* |
| | A. V. Tallman (R) | 16,164 | *39.8* |

| | Candidates | Votes | % |
|---|---|---|---|
| 1946 | Vail Pittman (D) | 28,655 | *57.4* |
| | Melvin E. Jepson (R) | 21,247 | *42.6* |
| 1950 | Charles H. Russell (R) | 35,609 | *57.6* |
| | Vail Pittman (D) | 26,164 | *42.4* |
| 1954 | Charles H. Russell (R) | 41,665 | *53.1* |
| | Vail Pittman (D) | 36,797 | *46.9* |
| 1958 | Grant Sawyer (D) | 50,864 | *59.9* |
| | Charles H. Russell (R) | 34,025 | *40.1* |
| 1962 | Grant Sawyer (D) | 64,784 | *66.8* |
| | Oran K. Gragson (R) | 32,145 | *33.2* |
| 1966 | Paul Laxalt (R) | 71,807 | *52.2* |
| | Grant Sawyer (D) | 65,870 | *47.8* |
| 1970 | Mike O'Callaghan (D) | 70,697 | *48.1* |
| | Ed Fike (R) | 64,400 | *43.8* |
| 1974 | Mike O'Callaghan (D) | 114,114 | *67.4* |
| | Shirley Crumpler (R) | 28,959 | *17.1* |
| | James Ray Houston (IA) | 26,285 | *15.5* |
| 1978 | Robert F. List (R) | 108,097 | *56.2* |
| | Robert E. Rose (D) | 76,361 | *39.7* |
| 1982 | Richard H. Bryan (D) | 128,132 | *53.4* |
| | Robert F. List (R) | 100,104 | *41.8* |
| 1986 | Richard H. Bryan (D) | 187,268 | *71.9* |
| | Patty Cafferata (R) | 65,081 | *25.0* |
| 1990 | Bob J. Miller (D) | 207,878 | *64.8* |
| | Jim Gallaway (R) | 95,789 | *29.9* |

# NEW HAMPSHIRE

(Ratified the Constitution June 21, 1788)

| | Candidates | Votes | % |
|---|---|---|---|
| 1788 | John Langdon | 4,421 | *50.0* |
| | John Sullivan | 3,664 | *41.5* |
| 1789 | John Sullivan | 3,657† | *42.9* |
| | John Pickering | 3,488 | *40.9* |
| | Josiah Bartlett | 968 | *11.3* |
| 1790 | John Pickering | 3,189 | *41.0* |
| | Joshua Wentworth | 2,369 | *30.4* |
| | Josiah Bartlett | 1,676† | *21.5* |
| 1791 | Josiah Bartlett | 8,679 | *96.8* |
| 1792 | Josiah Bartlett | 8,092 | *96.5* |
| 1793 | Josiah Bartlett | 7,388 | *75.0* |
| | John Langdon | 1,306 | *13.3* |
| | John T. Gilman | 708 | *7.2* |
| 1794 | John T. Gilman | 7,629 | *72.9* |
| 1795 | John T. Gilman | 9,340 | *98.9* |
| 1796 | John T. Gilman (FED) | 7,809 | *72.5* |
| 1797 | John T. Gilman (FED) | 9,625 | *88.9* |
| 1798 | John T. Gilman (FED) | 9,397 | *77.3* |
| | Oliver Peabody (D-R) | 1,189 | *9.8* |
| | Timothy Walker | 734 | *6.0* |
| 1799 | John T. Gilman (FED) | 10,138 | *86.4* |
| 1800 | John T. Gilman (FED) | 10,362 | *61.8* |
| | Timothy Walker (D-R) | 6,039 | *36.0* |
| 1801 | John T. Gilman (FED) | 10,898 | *65.5* |
| | Timothy Walker (D-R) | 5,249 | *31.5* |
| 1802 | John T. Gilman (FED) | 10,377 | *54.1* |
| | John Langdon (D-R) | 8,753 | *45.7* |
| 1803 | John T. Gilman (FED) | 12,263 | *57.5* |
| | John Langdon (D-R) | 9,011 | *42.3* |
| 1804 | John T. Gilman (FED) | 12,246 | *50.4* |
| | John Langdon (D-R) | 12,009 | *49.5* |
| 1805 | John Langdon (D-R) | 16,097 | *56.6* |
| | John T. Gilman (FED) | 12,287 | *43.2* |
| 1806 | John Langdon (D-R) | 15,277 | *74.3* |
| | Timothy Farrar (FED) | 1,720 | *8.4* |
| | John T. Gilman (FED) | 1,553 | *7.5* |
| 1807 | John Langdon (D-R) | 13,912 | *82.5* |

| | Candidates | Votes | % | | Candidates | Votes | % |
|---|---|---|---|---|---|---|---|
| 1808 | John Langdon (D-R) | 12,641 | 79.5 | 1844 | John H. Steele (D) | 26,155 | 53.6 |
| | John T. Gilman (FED) | 1,261 | 7.9 | | Anthony Colby (W) | 14,794 | 30.3 |
| 1809 | Jeremiah Smith (FED) | 15,610 | 50.4 | | Daniel Hoit (AB) | 5,737 | 11.8 |
| | John Langdon (D-R) | 15,241 | 49.2 | 1845 | John H. Steele (D) | 23,298 | 51.3 |
| 1810 | John Langdon (D-R) | 16,325 | 51.7 | | Anthony Colby (FEDL) | 15,591 | 34.4 |
| | Jeremiah Smith (FED) | 15,166 | 48.0 | | Daniel Hoit (AB) | 5,464 | 12.0 |
| 1811 | John Langdon (D-R) | 17,554 | 54.7 | 1846 | Jared W. Williams (D) | 26,914 | 48.6 |
| | Jeremiah Smith (FED) | 14,477 | 45.1 | | Anthony Colby (W) | 17,704† | 32.0 |
| 1812 | John T. Gilman (FED) | 15,613 | 48.8 | | Nathaniel S. Berry (AB) | 10,406 | 18.8 |
| | William Plumer (D-R) | 15,492† | 48.4 | 1847 | Jared W. Williams (D) | 30,806 | 50.9 |
| 1813 | John T. Gilman (FED) | 18,107 | 50.7 | | Anthony Colby (W) | 21,109 | 34.9 |
| | William Plumer (D-R) | 17,410 | 48.7 | | Nathaniel S. Berry (AB) | 8,531 | 14.1 |
| 1814 | John T. Gilman (FED) | 19,695 | 51.1 | 1848 | Jared W. Williams (D) | 32,193 | 52.4 |
| | William Plumer (D-R) | 18,794 | 48.7 | | Nathaniel S. Berry (W FS) | 28,819 | 46.9 |
| 1815 | John T. Gilman (FED) | 18,357 | 50.7 | 1849 | Samuel Dinsmoor Jr. (D) | 30,107 | 53.6 |
| | William Plumer (D-R) | 17,799 | 49.2 | | Levi Chamberlain (W) | 18,764 | 33.4 |
| 1816 | William Plumer (D-R) | 20,338 | 53.0 | | Nathaniel S. Berry (FS & SC) | 7,162 | 12.8 |
| | James Sheafe (FED) | 17,994 | 46.9 | 1850 | Samuel Dinsmoor Jr. (D) | 30,683 | 55.1 |
| 1817 | William Plumer (D-R) | 19,088 | 54.0 | | Levi Chamberlain (W) | 18,387 | 33.0 |
| | James Sheafe (FED) | 12,029 | 34.0 | | Nathaniel S. Berry (F SOIL) | 6,556 | 11.8 |
| | Jeremiah Mason (FED) | 3,607 | 10.2 | 1851 | Samuel Dinsmoor Jr. (D) | 27,350† | 47.1 |
| 1818 | William Plumer (D-R) | 18,674 | 59.3 | | Thomas E. Sawyer (W) | 18,407 | 31.7 |
| | Jeremiah Mason (FED) | 6,850 | 21.8 | | John Atwood (F SOIL) | 12,159 | 20.9 |
| | William Hale (FED) | 5,019 | 16.0 | 1852 | Noah Martin (D) | 30,747 | 51.0 |
| 1819 | Samuel Bell (D-R) | 13,761 | 56.7 | | Thomas E. Sawyer (W) | 19,850 | 32.9 |
| | William Hale (D-R) | 8,660 | 35.7 | | John Atwood (F SOIL) | 9,483 | 15.7 |
| 1820 | Samuel Bell (D-R) | 22,212 | 89.7 | 1853 | Noah Martin (D) | 30,924 | 54.7 |
| 1821 | Samuel Bell (D-R) | 22,582 | 92.4 | | James Bell (W) | 17,580 | 31.1 |
| 1822 | Samuel Bell (D-R) | 22,934 | 95.6 | | John H. White (F SOIL) | 7,997 | 14.1 |
| 1823 | Levi Woodbury (D-R) | 16,985 | 56.7 | 1854 | Nathaniel B. Baker (D) | 29,788 | 51.3 |
| | Samuel Dinsmoor Sr. (D-R) | 12,718 | 42.5 | | James Bell (W) | 17,028 | 29.4 |
| 1824 | David L. Morrill | 14,429† | 49.7 | | Jared Perkins (F SOIL) | 11,081 | 19.1 |
| | Levi Woodbury | 11,274 | 38.9 | 1855 | Ralph Metcalf (AM) | 32,783 | 50.7 |
| | Jeremiah Smith | 2,868 | 9.9 | | Nathaniel B. Baker (D) | 27,055 | 41.8 |
| 1825 | David L. Morrill | ✔ | | | James Bell (W) | 3,436 | 5.3 |
| 1826 | David L. Morrill | 17,528 | 58.8 | 1856 | Ralph Metcalf (AM) | 32,119† | 48.2 |
| | Benjamin Pierce | 12,287 | 41.2 | | John S. Wells (D) | 32,031 | 48.0 |
| 1827 | Benjamin Pierce | ✔ | | 1857 | William Haile (R) | 34,214 | 51.9 |
| | David L. Morrill | | | | John S. Wells (D) | 31,209 | 47.4 |
| 1828 | John Bell (NR) | 21,784 | 52.7 | 1858 | William Haile (R) | 36,308 | 53.4 |
| | Benjamin Pierce (JAC D) | 19,562 | 47.3 | | Asa P. Cate (D) | 31,597 | 46.5 |
| 1829 | Benjamin Pierce (JAC D) | 21,601 | 53.6 | 1859 | Ichabod Goodwin (R) | 36,296 | 52.5 |
| | John Bell (NR) | 18,708 | 46.4 | | Asa P. Cate (D) | 32,802 | 47.5 |
| 1830 | Matthew Harvey (JAC D) | 22,502 | 54.9 | 1860 | Ichabod Goodwin (R) | 38,031 | 53.1 |
| | Upham (NR) | 18,490 | 45.1 | | Asa P. Cate (D) | 33,543 | 46.9 |
| 1831 | Samuel Dinsmoor (JAC D) | 23,503 | 55.6 | 1861 | Nathaniel S. Berry (R) | 35,467 | 52.9 |
| | Ichabod Bartlett (NR) | 18,681 | 44.2 | | Stark (D) | 31,452 | 46.9 |
| 1832 | Samuel Dinsmoor (D) | 24,175 | 62.3 | 1862 | Nathaniel S. Berry (R) | 32,150 | 51.5 |
| | Ichabod Bartlett | 14,604 | 37.7 | | Stark (D) | 28,566 | 45.8 |
| 1833 | Samuel Dinsmoor (D) | 28,270 | 84.5 | 1863 | Eastman (D) | 32,833 | 49.6 |
| 1834 | William Badger (D) | ✔ | | | Joseph A. Gilmore (R) | 29,035† | 43.8 |
| 1835 | William Badger (D) | 23,709 | 63.4 | | Harriman (UN) | 4,372 | 6.6 |
| | Joseph Healy | 13,707 | 36.6 | 1864 | Joseph A. Gilmore (UN) | 37,006 | 54.2 |
| 1836 | Isaac Hill (D) | ✔ | | | Edward W. Harrington (D) | 31,340 | 45.9 |
| 1837 | Isaac Hill (D) | ✔ | | 1865 | Frederick Smyth (UN) | 34,145 | 54.9 |
| 1838 | Isaac Hill (D) | 28,741 | 52.7 | | Edward W. Harrington (D) | 28,017 | 45.0 |
| | J. Wilson Jr. (W) | 25,565 | 46.9 | 1866 | Frederick Smyth (R) | 35,137 | 53.5 |
| 1839 | John Page (D) | 30,466 | 55.9 | | John G. Sinclair (D) | 30,481 | 46.4 |
| | J. Wilson Jr. (W) | 23,925 | 43.9 | 1867 | Walter Harriman (R) | 35,809 | 52.2 |
| 1840 | John Page (D) | 29,469 | 58.1 | | John G. Sinclair (D) | 32,663 | 47.6 |
| | Enos Stevens (W) | 20,700 | 40.8 | 1868 | Walter Harriman (R) | 39,785 | 51.6 |
| 1841 | John Page (D) | 29,453 | 56.7 | | John G. Sinclair (D) | 37,262 | 48.3 |
| | Enos Stevens (W) | 21,178 | 40.8 | 1869 | Onslow Stearns (R) | 35,777 | 52.8 |
| 1842 | Henry Hubbard (D) | 26,830 | 55.8 | | John Bedell (D) | 32,004 | 47.2 |
| | Enos Stevens (W) | 12,364 | 25.7 | 1870 | Onslow Stearns (R) | 34,912 | 51.0 |
| | John H. White (ID) | 5,994 | 12.5 | | John Bedell (D) | 25,023 | 36.6 |
| | Daniel Hoit (AB) | 2,756 | 5.7 | 1871 | James A. Weston (D) | 34,700† | 49.8 |
| 1843 | Henry Hubbard (D) | 23,052 | 51.7 | | James Pike (R) | 33,892 | 48.6 |
| | Anthony Colby (W) | 12,561 | 28.2 | 1872 | Ezekiel A. Straw (R) | 38,751 | 50.8 |
| | John H. White (C) | 5,497 | 12.3 | | James A. Weston (D) | 36,584 | 47.9 |
| | Daniel Hoit (AB) | 3,416 | 7.7 | 1873 | Ezekiel A. Straw (R) | 34,023 | 50.2 |
| | | | | | James A. Weston (D) | 32,016 | 47.2 |

| | Candidates | Votes | % |
|---|---|---|---|
| 1874 | James A. Weston (D) | 35,608† | 49.6 |
| | Luther McCutchins (R) | 34,143 | 47.5 |
| 1875 | Person C. Cheney (R) | 39,293† | 49.6 |
| | Hiram R. Roberts (D) | 39,121 | 49.4 |
| 1876 | Person C. Cheney (R) | 41,761 | 52.0 |
| | Marcy (D) | 38,133 | 47.5 |
| 1877 | Benjamin F. Prescott (R) | 40,757 | 52.3 |
| | Marcy (D) | 36,726 | 47.2 |
| 1878 | Benjamin F. Prescott (R) | 39,372 | 50.6 |
| | McKean (D) | 37,860 | 48.7 |
| 1879 | Natt Head (R) | 38,175 | 50.3 |
| | McKean (D) | 31,135 | 41.0 |
| | W. S. Brown (N) | 6,507 | 8.6 |
| 1880 | Charles H. Bell (R) | 44,434 | 51.6 |
| | Frank Jones (D) | 40,815 | 47.4 |
| 1882 | Samuel W. Hale (R) | 38,399 | 50.4 |
| | M. V. B. Edgerly (D) | 36,879 | 48.4 |
| 1884 | Moody Currier (R) | 42,514 | 50.3 |
| | Hill (D) | 39,637 | 46.9 |
| 1886 | Charles H. Sawyer (R) | 37,819† | 48.9 |
| | Cogswell (D) | 37,334 | 48.2 |
| 1888 | David H. Goodell (R) | 44,809† | 49.5 |
| | Charles H. Amsden (D) | 44,217 | 48.8 |
| 1890 | Hiram A. Tuttle (R) | 42,479† | 49.3 |
| | Charles H. Amsden (D) | 42,386 | 49.2 |
| 1892 | John B. Smith (R) | 43,676 | 50.2 |
| | Luther F. McKinney (D) | 41,501 | 47.7 |
| 1894 | Charles A. Busiel (R) | 46,491 | 56.0 |
| | Henry O. Kent (D) | 33,959 | 40.9 |
| 1896 | George A. Ramsdell (R) | 48,387 | 61.4 |
| | Henry O. Kent (D) | 28,333 | 36.0 |
| 1898 | Frank W. Rollins (R) | 44,730 | 54.2 |
| | Charles F. Stone (D) | 35,653 | 43.2 |
| 1900 | Chester B. Jordan (R) | 53,891 | 59.4 |
| | Frederick E. Potter (D) | 34,956 | 38.5 |
| 1902 | Nahum J. Bachelder (R) | 42,115 | 53.2 |
| | Henry F. Hollis (D) | 33,844 | 42.8 |
| 1904 | John McLane (R) | 51,171 | 57.8 |
| | Henry F. Hollis (D) | 35,437 | 40.1 |
| 1906 | Charles M. Floyd (R) | 40,581† | 49.8 |
| | Nathan C. Jameson (D) | 37,672 | 46.2 |
| 1908 | Henry B. Quinby (R) | 44,630 | 50.4 |
| | Clarence E. Carr (D) | 41,386 | 46.7 |
| 1910 | Robert P. Bass (R) | 44,908 | 53.4 |
| | Clarence E. Carr (D) | 37,737 | 44.8 |
| 1912 | Samuel D. Felker (D) | 34,203† | 41.1 |
| | Franklin Worcester (R) | 32,504 | 39.0 |
| | Winston Churchill (PROG) | 14,401 | 17.3 |
| 1914 | Rolland H. Spaulding (R) | 46,413 | 55.2 |
| | Albert W. Noone (D) | 33,674 | 40.0 |
| 1916 | Henry W. Keyes (R) | 45,851 | 53.2 |
| | John C. Hutchins (D) | 38,853 | 45.1 |
| 1918 | John H. Bartlett (R) | 38,228 | 54.1 |
| | Martin (D) | 32,383 | 45.9 |
| 1920 | Albert O. Brown (R) | 93,273 | 59.6 |
| | Charles E. Tilton (D) | 62,174 | 39.7 |
| 1922 | Fred H. Brown (D) | 70,160 | 53.3 |
| | Windsor H. Goodnow (R) | 61,526 | 46.7 |
| 1924 | John G. Winant (R) | 88,650 | 53.9 |
| | Fred H. Brown (D) | 75,691 | 46.1 |
| 1926 | Huntley N. Spaulding (R) | 77,394 | 59.7 |
| | Eaton D. Sargent (D) | 52,236 | 40.3 |
| 1928 | Charles W. Tobey (R) | 108,431 | 57.5 |
| | Eaton D. Sargent (D) | 79,798 | 42.3 |
| 1930 | John G. Winant (R) | 75,518 | 58.0 |
| | Albert W. Noone (D) | 54,441 | 41.8 |
| 1932 | John G. Winant (R) | 106,777 | 54.2 |
| | Henri Ledoux (D) | 89,487 | 45.4 |
| 1934 | H. Styles Bridges (R) | 89,481 | 50.6 |
| | John L. Sullivan (D) | 87,019 | 49.2 |
| 1936 | Francis P. Murphy (R) | 118,178 | 56.6 |
| | Amos Blandin (D) | 89,011 | 42.6 |

| | Candidates | Votes | % |
|---|---|---|---|
| 1938 | Francis P. Murphy (R) | 107,841 | 57.1 |
| | John L. Sullivan (D) | 80,847 | 42.8 |
| 1940 | Robert O. Blood (R) | 112,386 | 50.7 |
| | F. Clyde Keefe (D) | 109,093 | 49.3 |
| 1942 | Robert O. Blood (R) | 83,766 | 52.2 |
| | William J. Neal (D) | 76,782 | 47.8 |
| 1944 | Charles M. Dale (R) | 115,799 | 53.1 |
| | James J. Powers (D) | 102,232 | 46.9 |
| 1946 | Charles M. Dale (R) | 103,204 | 63.1 |
| | F. Clyde Keefe (D) | 60,247 | 36.9 |
| 1948 | Sherman Adams (R) | 116,212 | 52.2 |
| | Herbert W. Hill (D) | 105,207 | 47.3 |
| 1950 | Sherman Adams (R) | 108,907 | 57.0 |
| | Robert P. Bingham (D) | 82,258 | 43.0 |
| 1952 | Hugh Gregg (R) | 167,791 | 63.2 |
| | William H. Craig (D) | 97,924 | 36.9 |
| 1954 | Lane Dwinell (R) | 107,287 | 55.1 |
| | John Shaw (D) | 87,344 | 44.9 |
| 1956 | Lane Dwinell (R) | 141,578 | 54.7 |
| | John Shaw (D) | 117,117 | 45.3 |
| 1958 | Wesley Powell (R) | 106,790 | 51.7 |
| | Bernard L. Boutin (D) | 99,955 | 48.4 |
| 1960 | Wesley Powell (R) | 161,123 | 55.5 |
| | Bernard L. Boutin (D) | 129,404 | 44.5 |
| 1962 | John W. King (D) | 135,481 | 58.9 |
| | John Pillsbury (R) | 94,567 | 41.1 |
| 1964 | John W. King (D) | 190,863 | 66.8 |
| | John Pillsbury (R) | 94,824 | 33.2 |
| 1966 | John W. King (D) | 125,882 | 53.9 |
| | Hugh Gregg (R) | 107,259 | 45.9 |
| 1968 | Walter Peterson (R) | 149,902 | 52.5 |
| | Emile R. Bussiere (D) | 135,378 | 47.4 |
| 1970 | Walter Peterson (R) | 102,298 | 46.0 |
| | Roger J. Crowley Jr. (D) | 98,098 | 44.1 |
| | Meldrim Thomson Jr. (AM) | 22,033 | 9.9 |
| 1972 | Meldrim Thomson Jr. (R) | 133,702 | 41.4 |
| | Roger J. Crowley Jr. (D) | 126,107 | 39.0 |
| | Malcolm McLane (I) | 63,199 | 19.6 |
| 1974 | Meldrim Thomson Jr. (R) | 115,933 | 51.1 |
| | Richard W. Leonard (D) | 110,591 | 48.8 |
| 1976 | Meldrim Thomson Jr. (R) | 197,589 | 57.7 |
| | Harry V. Spanos (D) | 145,015 | 42.3 |
| 1978 | Hugh J. Gallen (D) | 133,133 | 49.4 |
| | Meldrim Thomson Jr. (R) | 122,464 | 45.4 |
| 1980 | Hugh J. Gallen (D) | 226,436 | 59.0 |
| | Meldrim Thomson Jr. (R) | 156,178 | 40.7 |
| 1982 | John H. Sununu (R) | 145,389 | 51.4 |
| | Hugh J. Gallen (D) | 132,317 | 46.8 |
| 1984 | John H. Sununu (R) | 256,571 | 66.8 |
| | Chris Spirou (D) | 127,156 | 33.1 |
| 1986 | John H. Sununu (R) | 134,824 | 53.7 |
| | Paul McEachern (D) | 116,142 | 46.3 |
| 1988 | Judd Gregg (R) | 267,064 | 60.4 |
| | Paul McEachern (D) | 172,543 | 39.1 |
| 1990 | Judd Gregg (R) | 177,611 | 60.2 |
| | J. Joseph Grandmaison (D) | 101,886 | 34.6 |
| 1992 | Steve Merrill (R) | 289,170 | 56.0 |
| | Deborah ("Arnie") Arnesen (D) | 206,232 | 40.0 |

# NEW JERSEY

(Ratified the Constitution Dec. 18, 1787)

| | Candidates | Votes | % |
|---|---|---|---|
| 1844 [1] | Charles C. Stratton (W) | 37,949 | 50.9 |
| | Thompson (D) | 36,591 | 49.1 |
| 1847 | Daniel Haines (D) | 34,765 | 51.9 |
| | William Wright (W) | 32,251 | 48.1 |

| | Candidates | Votes | % |
|---|---|---|---|
| 1850 | George F. Fort (D) | 39,723 | 53.8 |
| | Runk (W) | 34,054 | 46.2 |
| 1853 | Rodman M. Price (D) | 38,312 | 52.6 |
| | Haywood (W) | 34,530 | 47.4 |
| 1856 | William A. Newell (FUS) | 50,803 | 51.3 |
| | Alexander (D) | 48,246 | 48.7 |
| 1859 | Charles S. Olden (R) | 53,315 | 50.8 |
| | Wright (D) | 51,714 | 49.2 |
| 1862 | Joel Parker (D) | 61,307 | 56.8 |
| | Marcus L. Ward (UN) | 46,710 | 43.2 |
| 1865 | Marcus L. Ward (UN) | 67,525 | 51.1 |
| | Runvon (D) | 64,706 | 48.9 |
| 1868 | Theodore F. Randolph (D) | 83,955 | 51.4 |
| | John I. Blair (R) | 79,333 | 48.6 |
| 1871 | Joel Parker (D) | 82,362 | 51.9 |
| | Cornelius Walsh (R) | 76,383 | 48.1 |
| 1874 | Joseph D. Bedle (D) | 97,283 | 53.7 |
| | Halsey (R) | 84,050 | 46.4 |
| 1877 | George B. McClellan (D) | 97,837 | 51.7 |
| | Newell (R) | 85,094 | 44.9 |
| 1880 | George C. Ludlow (D) | 121,666 | 49.5 |
| | Potts (R) | 121,015 | 49.3 |
| 1883 | Leon Abbett (D) | 103,856 | 49.9 |
| | Dixon (R) | 97,047 | 46.7 |
| 1886 | Robert S. Green (D) | 109,939 | 47.4 |
| | Howey (R) | 101,919 | 44.0 |
| | Fisk (P) | 19,808 | 8.6 |
| 1889 | Leon Abbett (D) | 138,245 | 51.4 |
| | Grubb (R) | 123,992 | 46.1 |
| 1892 | George T. Werts (D) | 167,257 | 49.7 |
| | John Kean Jr. (R) | 159,632 | 47.4 |
| 1895 | John W. Griggs (R) | 162,900 | 52.3 |
| | McGill (D) | 136,000 | 43.6 |
| 1898 | Foster M. Voorhees (R) | 164,051 | 48.9 |
| | Elvin W. Crane (D & CD) | 158,552 | 47.3 |
| 1901 | Franklin Murphy (R) | 183,814 | 50.9 |
| | James M. Seymour (D) | 166,681 | 46.1 |
| 1904 | Edward C. Stokes (R) | 231,363 | 53.5 |
| | Black (D) | 179,719 | 41.6 |
| 1907 | John Franklin Fort (R) | 194,313 | 49.3 |
| | Katzenbach (D) | 186,300 | 47.3 |
| 1910 | Woodrow Wilson (D) | 233,682 | 53.9 |
| | Vivian M. Lewis (R) | 184,626 | 42.6 |
| 1913 | James F. Fielder (D) | 173,148 | 46.1 |
| | Edward C. Stokes (R) | 140,298 | 37.4 |
| | Everett Colby (PROG) | 41,132 | 11.0 |
| 1916 | Walter E. Edge (R) | 247,343 | 55.4 |
| | Wittpenn (D) | 177,696 | 39.8 |
| 1919 | Edward I. Edwards (D) | 217,486 | 49.2 |
| | Newton A. K. Bugbee (R) | 202,976 | 45.9 |
| 1922 | George S. Silzer (D) | 427,206 | 52.2 |
| | Runyon (R) | 383,312 | 46.8 |
| 1925 | Arthur Harry Moore (D) | 471,549 | 51.9 |
| | Arthur Whitney (R) | 433,121 | 47.6 |
| 1928 | Morgan F. Larson (R) | 824,005 | 54.9 |
| | William L. Dill (D) | 671,728 | 44.7 |
| 1931 | Arthur Harry Moore (D) | 735,504 | 57.8 |
| | David Baird Jr. (R) | 505,451 | 39.7 |
| 1934 | Harold G. Hoffman (R) | 686,530 | 49.9 |
| | William L. Dill (D) | 674,096 | 49.0 |
| 1937 | Arthur Harry Moore (D) | 746,033 | 50.8 |
| | Lester H. Clee (R) | 700,767 | 47.8 |
| 1940 | Charles Edison (D) | 984,407 | 51.4 |
| | Robert C. Hendrickson (R) | 920,512 | 48.0 |
| 1943 | Walter E. Edge (R) | 634,364 | 55.2 |
| | Vincent J. Murphy (D) | 506,604 | 44.1 |
| 1946 | Alfred E. Driscoll (R) | 807,378 | 57.1 |
| | Lewis G. Hansen (D) | 585,960 | 41.4 |
| 1949 | Alfred E. Driscoll (R) | 885,882 | 51.5 |
| | Elmer H. Wene (D) | 810,022 | 47.1 |
| 1953 | Robert B. Meyner (D) | 962,710 | 53.2 |
| | Paul L. Troast (R) | 809,068 | 44.7 |

| | Candidates | Votes | % |
|---|---|---|---|
| 1957 | Robert B. Meyner (D) | 1,101,130 | 54.6 |
| | Malcolm S. Forbes (R) | 897,321 | 44.5 |
| 1961 | Richard J. Hughes (D) | 1,084,194 | 50.4 |
| | James P. Mitchell (R) | 1,049,274 | 48.7 |
| 1965 | Richard J. Hughes (D) | 1,279,568 | 57.4 |
| | Wayne Dumont Jr. (R) | 915,996 | 41.1 |
| 1969 | William T. Cahill (R) | 1,411,905 | 59.7 |
| | Robert B. Meyner (D) | 911,003 | 38.5 |
| 1973 | Brendan T. Byrne (D) | 1,397,613 | 66.4 |
| | Charles W. Sandman Jr. (R) | 676,235 | 32.1 |
| 1977 | Brendan T. Byrne (D) | 1,184,564 | 55.7 |
| | Raymond H. Bateman (R) | 888,880 | 41.8 |
| 1981 | Thomas H. Kean (R) | 1,145,999 | 49.5 |
| | James J. Florio (D) | 1,144,202 | 49.4 |
| 1985 | Thomas H. Kean (R) | 1,372,631 | 70.3 |
| | Peter Shapiro (D) | 578,402 | 29.7 |
| 1989 | James J. Florio (D) | 1,379,937 | 61.2 |
| | Jim Courter (R) | 838,553 | 37.2 |
| 1993 | Christine Todd Whitman (R) | 1,236,124 | 49.3 |
| | James J. Florio (D) | 1,210,031 | 48.3 |

**New Jersey**
1. Before 1844 governor chosen by legislature.

# NEW MEXICO

(Became a state Jan. 6, 1912)

| | Candidates | Votes | % |
|---|---|---|---|
| 1911 | W. C. McDonald (D) | 31,036 | 51.0 |
| | Holm O. Bursum (R) | 28,019 | 46.1 |
| 1916 | Ezequiel C. deBaca (D) | 32,875 | 49.4 |
| | Holm O. Bursum (R) | 31,552 | 47.4 |
| 1918 | Octaviano A. Larrazolo (R) | 23,752 | 50.5 |
| | Felix Garcia (D) | 22,433 | 47.7 |
| 1920 | Merritt C. Mechem (R) | 54,426 | 51.3 |
| | Richard H. Hanna (D) | 50,755 | 47.8 |
| 1922 | James F. Hinkle (D) | 60,317 | 54.6 |
| | C. L. Hill (R) | 49,363 | 44.7 |
| 1924 | Arthur T. Hannett (D) | 56,183 | 48.8 |
| | Manuel B. Otero (R) | 55,984 | 48.6 |
| 1926 | Richard C. Dillon (R) | 56,294 | 51.6 |
| | Arthur T. Hannett (D) | 52,523 | 48.2 |
| 1928 | Richard C. Dillon (R) | 65,967 | 55.6 |
| | Robert C. Dow (D) | 52,550 | 44.3 |
| 1930 | Arthur Seligman (D) | 62,789 | 53.2 |
| | Clarence M. Botts (R) | 55,026 | 46.6 |
| 1932 | Arthur Seligman (D) | 83,612 | 54.8 |
| | Richard C. Dillon (R) | 67,406 | 44.2 |
| 1934 | Clyde Tingley (D) | 78,390 | 51.9 |
| | Jaffa Miller (R) | 71,899 | 47.6 |
| 1936 | Clyde Tingley (D) | 97,090 | 57.2 |
| | Jaffa Miller (R) | 72,539 | 42.8 |
| 1938 | John E. Miles (D) | 82,344 | 52.2 |
| | Albert K. Mitchell (R) | 75,017 | 47.6 |
| 1940 | John E. Miles (D) | 103,035 | 55.6 |
| | Maurice Miera (R) | 82,306 | 44.4 |
| 1942 | John J. Dempsey (D) | 59,258 | 54.6 |
| | Joseph F. Tondre (R) | 49,380 | 45.5 |
| 1944 | John J. Dempsey (D) | 76,443 | 51.8 |
| | Carroll G. Gunderson (R) | 71,113 | 48.2 |
| 1946 | Thomas J. Mabry (D) | 70,055 | 52.8 |
| | Edward L. Safford (R) | 62,575 | 47.2 |
| 1948 | Thomas J. Mabry (D) | 103,969 | 54.7 |
| | Manuel Lujan (R) | 86,023 | 45.3 |
| 1950 | Edwin L. Mechem (R) | 96,846 | 53.7 |
| | John E. Miles (D) | 83,359 | 46.3 |

| | Candidates | Votes | % |
|---|---|---|---|
| 1952 | Edwin L. Mechem (R) | 129,116 | 53.8 |
| | Everett Grantham (D) | 111,034 | 46.2 |
| 1954 | John F. Simms Jr. (D) | 110,583 | 57.0 |
| | Alvin Stockton (R) | 83,373 | 43.0 |
| 1956 | Edwin L. Mechem (R) | 131,488 | 52.2 |
| | John F. Simms Jr. (D) | 120,263 | 47.8 |
| 1958 | John Burroughs (D) | 103,481 | 50.5 |
| | Edwin L. Mechem (R) | 101,567 | 49.5 |
| 1960 | Edwin L. Mechem (R) | 153,765 | 50.3 |
| | John Burroughs (D) | 151,777 | 49.7 |
| 1962 | Jack M. Campbell (D) | 130,933 | 53.0 |
| | Edwin L. Mechem (R) | 116,184 | 47.0 |
| 1964 | Jack M. Campbell (D) | 191,497 | 60.2 |
| | Merle H. Tucker (R) | 126,540 | 39.8 |
| 1966 | David F. Cargo (R) | 134,625 | 51.7 |
| | T. E. Lusk (D) | 125,587 | 48.3 |
| 1968 | David F. Cargo (R) | 160,140 | 50.5 |
| | Fabian Chavez Jr. (D) | 157,230 | 49.5 |
| 1970 | Bruce King (D) | 148,835 | 51.3 |
| | Pete V. Domenici (R) | 134,640 | 46.4 |
| 1974 | Jerry Apodaca (D) | 164,172 | 49.9 |
| | Joseph R. Skeen (R) | 160,430 | 48.8 |
| 1978 | Bruce King (D) | 174,631 | 50.5 |
| | Joseph R. Skeen (R) | 170,848 | 49.4 |
| 1982 | Toney Anaya (D) | 215,840 | 53.0 |
| | John B. Irick (R) | 191,626 | 47.0 |
| 1986 | Garrey E. Carruthers (R) | 209,455 | 53.0 |
| | Ray B. Powell (D) | 185,378 | 47.0 |
| 1990 | Bruce King (D) | 224,564 | 54.6 |
| | Frank M. Bond (R) | 185,692 | 45.2 |

# NEW YORK

(Ratified the Constitution July 26, 1788)

| | Candidates | Votes | % |
|---|---|---|---|
| 1789 | George Clinton | 6,391 | 51.7 |
| | Robert Yates | 5,962 | 48.3 |
| 1792 | George Clinton (ANTI-FED)[1] | 8,440 | 50.3 |
| | John Jay (FED) | 8,332 | 49.7 |
| 1795 | John Jay (FED) | 13,481 | 53.1 |
| | Robert Yates (ANTI-FED)[1] | 11,892 | 46.9 |
| 1798 | John Jay (FED) | 16,012 | 54.0 |
| | Robert R. Livingston (ANTI-FED)[1] | 13,632 | 46.0 |
| 1801 | George Clinton (D-R) | 24,808 | 54.3 |
| | Stephen Van Rensselaer (FED) | 20,843 | 45.7 |
| 1804 | Morgan Lewis (FED) | 30,829 | 58.2 |
| | Aaron Burr (D-R) | 22,139 | 41.8 |
| 1807 | Daniel Tompkins (D-R) | 35,074 | 53.1 |
| | Morgan Lewis (ANTI-CLINT)[2] | 30,989 | 46.9 |
| 1810 | Daniel Tompkins (D-R) | 43,094 | 54.2 |
| | Jonas Platt (ANTI-CLINT)[2] | 36,484 | 45.8 |
| 1813 | Daniel Tompkins (D-R) | 43,324 | 52.2 |
| | Stephen Van Rensselaer (FED) | 39,718 | 47.8 |
| 1816 | Daniel Tompkins (D-R) | 45,412 | 54.0 |
| | Rufus King (FED) | 38,647 | 46.0 |

Special Election

| | | | |
|---|---|---|---|
| 1817 | De Witt Clinton (D-R) | 43,310 | 96.7 |

| | | | |
|---|---|---|---|
| 1820 | De Witt Clinton (CLINT R) | 47,447 | 50.8 |
| | Daniel Tompkins (ANTI-CL R)[3] | 45,990 | 49.2 |
| 1822 | Joseph C. Yates (D-R) | 128,493 | 97.8 |
| 1824 | De Witt Clinton (CLINT R) | 103,684 | 54.1 |
| | Samuel Young (VB R) | 88,037 | 45.9 |
| 1826 | De Witt Clinton (CLINT R) | 99,808 | 51.0 |
| | William B. Rochester (VB R) | 96,080 | 49.1 |

| | Candidates | Votes | % |
|---|---|---|---|
| 1828 | Martin Van Buren (JAC D) | 136,795 | 49.5 |
| | Smith Thompson (NR) | 106,415 | 38.5 |
| | Solomon Southwick (A-MAS) | 33,335 | 12.1 |
| 1830 | Enos T. Throop (JAC D) | 128,947 | 51.7 |
| | Francis Granger (NR) | 120,667 | 48.3 |
| 1832 | William L. Marcy (JAC D) | 166,410 | 51.5 |
| | Francis Granger (NR) | 156,672 | 48.5 |
| 1834 | William L. Marcy (D) | 181,900 | 51.8 |
| | William H. Seward (W) | 169,008 | 48.2 |
| 1836 | William L. Marcy (D) | 166,218 | 54.9 |
| | Jesse Buel (W) | 136,653 | 45.1 |
| 1838 | William H. Seward (W) | 192,882 | 51.4 |
| | William L. Marcy (D) | 182,461 | 48.6 |
| 1840 | Wiliam H. Seward (W) | 222,011 | 50.3 |
| | William C. Bouck (D) | 216,726 | 49.1 |
| 1842 | William C. Bouck (D) | 208,062 | 51.8 |
| | Luther Bradish (W) | 186,089 | 46.4 |
| 1844 | Silas Wright (D) | 241,087 | 49.5 |
| | Millard Fillmore (W) | 231,060 | 47.4 |
| 1846 | John Young (W) | 197,627 | 50.7 |
| | Silas Wright (D) | 192,361 | 49.3 |
| 1848 | Hamilton Fish (W) | 218,280 | 47.9 |
| | John Dix (F SOIL) | 123,360 | 27.1 |
| | Reuben Walworth (D) | 114,457 | 25.1 |
| 1850 | Washington Hunt (W-A-RENT) | 214,614 | 49.6 |
| | Horatio Seymour (D) | 214,352 | 49.6 |
| 1852 | Horatio Seymour (D) | 264,121 | 50.3 |
| | Washington Hunt (W) | 241,525 | 46.0 |
| 1854 | Myron H. Clark (FUS R) | 156,804 | 33.4 |
| | Horatio Seymour (SOFT D) | 156,495 | 33.3 |
| | Daniel Ullman (AM) | 122,282 | 26.1 |
| | Greene C. Bronson (HARD D) | 33,850 | 7.2 |
| 1856 | John A. King (R) | 264,400 | 44.5 |
| | Amasa J. Parker (D) | 198,616 | 33.4 |
| | Erastus Brooks (AM) | 130,870 | 22.0 |
| 1858 | Edwin D. Morgan (R) | 247,868 | 45.5 |
| | Amasa J. Parker (D) | 230,329 | 42.3 |
| | Lorenzo Burrows (AM) | 61,137 | 11.2 |
| 1860 | Edwin D. Morgan (R) | 358,002 | 53.2 |
| | William Kelly (DOUG D) | 294,803 | 43.8 |
| 1862 | Horatio Seymour (D) | 306,649 | 50.9 |
| | James S. Wadsworth (UN) | 295,897 | 49.1 |
| 1864 | Reuben E. Fenton (UN) | 369,557 | 50.6 |
| | Horatio Seymour (D) | 361,264 | 49.4 |
| 1866 | Reuben E. Fenton (UN) | 366,315 | 50.9 |
| | John T. Hoffman (D) | 352,526 | 49.0 |
| 1868 | John T. Hoffman (D) | 439,301 | 51.6 |
| | John A. Griswold (R) | 411,355 | 48.4 |
| 1870 | John T. Hoffman (D) | 399,552 | 51.9 |
| | Stewart L. Woodford (R) | 366,436 | 47.6 |
| 1872 | John A. Dix (R) | 445,801 | 53.2 |
| | Francis Kernan (LR) | 392,350 | 46.8 |
| 1874 | Samuel J. Tilden (D) | 416,391 | 52.4 |
| | John A. Dix (R) | 366,074 | 46.1 |
| 1876 | Lucius Robinson (D) | 519,832 | 51.3 |
| | Edwin D. Morgan (R) | 489,371 | 48.3 |
| 1879 | Alonzo B. Cornell (R) | 418,567 | 46.7 |
| | Lucius Robinson (D) | 375,790 | 41.9 |
| | John Kelly (TAM D) | 77,566 | 8.7 |
| 1882 | Grover Cleveland (D) | 535,318 | 58.5 |
| | Charles J. Folger (R) | 341,464 | 37.3 |
| 1885 | David B. Hill (D) | 501,456 | 48.9 |
| | Ira Davenport (R) | 490,331 | 47.9 |
| 1888 | David B. Hill (D) | 650,464 | 49.4 |
| | Warner Miller (R) | 631,303 | 48.0 |
| 1891 | Roswell P. Flower (D) | 582,893 | 50.1 |
| | Jacob Sloat Fassett (R) | 534,956 | 46.0 |
| 1894 | Levi P. Morton (R) | 673,818 | 53.1 |
| | David B. Hill (D) | 517,710 | 40.8 |
| 1896 | Frank S. Black (R) | 774,253 | 55.3 |
| | Wilbur E. Porter (D) | 561,361 | 40.1 |

| | Candidates | Votes | % |
|---|---|---|---|
| 1898 | Theodore Roosevelt (R) | 661,707 | 49.0 |
| | Augustus Van Wyck (D) | 643,921 | 47.7 |
| 1900 | Benjamin B. Odell Jr. (R) | 804,859 | 52.0 |
| | John B. Stanchfield (D) | 693,733 | 44.8 |
| 1902 | Benjamin B. Odell Jr. (R) | 665,150 | 48.1 |
| | Bird S. Coler (D) | 655,398 | 47.4 |
| 1904 | Frank W. Higgins (R) | 813,264 | 50.3 |
| | D. Cady Herrick (D) | 732,704 | 45.3 |
| 1906 | Charles Evans Hughes (R) | 749,002 | 50.5 |
| | William R. Hearst (D, I LEAGUE) | 691,105 | 46.6 |
| 1908 | Charles Evans Hughes (R) | 804,651 | 49.1 |
| | Lewis Stuyvesant Chanler (D) | 735,189 | 44.8 |
| 1910 | John A. Dix (D) | 689,700 | 48.0 |
| | Henry L. Stimson (R) | 622,299 | 43.3 |
| 1912 | William Sulzer (D) | 649,559 | 41.5 |
| | Job E. Hedges (R) | 444,105 | 28.3 |
| | Oscar S. Straus (IL & NPR) | 393,183 | 25.1 |
| 1914 | Charles S. Whitman (R) | 686,701 | 47.7 |
| | Martin H. Glynn (D, I LEAGUE) | 541,269 | 37.5 |
| | William Sulzer (AM, P) | 126,270 | 8.8 |
| 1916 | Charles S. Whitman (R, N PROG) | 850,020 | 52.6 |
| | Samuel Seabury (D) | 686,862 | 42.5 |
| 1918 | Alfred E. Smith (D) | 1,009,936 | 47.4 |
| | Charles S. Whitman (R, P) | 995,094 | 46.6 |
| | Charles W. Ervin (SOC) | 121,705 | 5.7 |
| 1920 | Nathan L. Miller (R) | 1,335,878 | 46.6 |
| | Alfred E. Smith (D) | 1,261,812 | 44.0 |
| | Joseph D. Cannon (SOC) | 159,804 | 5.6 |
| 1922 | Alfred E. Smith (D) | 1,397,657 | 55.2 |
| | Nathan L. Miller (R) | 1,011,725 | 40.0 |
| 1924 | Alfred E. Smith (D) | 1,627,111 | 50.0 |
| | Theodore Roosevelt Jr. (R) | 1,518,552 | 46.6 |
| 1926 | Alfred E. Smith (D) | 1,523,813 | 52.3 |
| | Ogden L. Mills (R) | 1,276,137 | 43.8 |
| 1928 | Franklin D. Roosevelt (D) | 2,130,238 | 49.0 |
| | Albert Ottinger (R) | 2,104,630 | 48.4 |
| 1930 | Franklin D. Roosevelt (D) | 1,770,342 | 56.1 |
| | Charles H. Tuttle (R) | 1,045,231 | 33.1 |
| | Robert P. Carroll (LAW PRES) | 191,666 | 6.1 |
| 1932 | Herbert H. Lehman (D) | 2,659,597 | 56.7 |
| | William J. Donovan (R) | 1,812,002 | 38.6 |
| 1934 | Herbert H. Lehman (D) | 2,201,727 | 57.8 |
| | Robert Moses (R) | 1,393,744 | 36.6 |
| 1936 | Herbert H. Lehman (D, AM LAB) | 2,970,595 | 53.5 |
| | William F. Bleakley (R) | 2,450,105 | 44.1 |
| 1938 | Herbert H. Lehman (D, AM LAB) | 2,391,331 | 50.4 |
| | Thomas E. Dewey (R, I PROG) | 2,326,892 | 49.0 |
| 1942 | Thomas E. Dewey (R) | 2,148,546 | 52.1 |
| | John J. Bennett Jr. (D) | 1,501,039 | 36.4 |
| | Dean Alfange (AM LAB) | 403,626 | 9.8 |
| 1946 | Thomas E. Dewey (R) | 2,825,633 | 56.9 |
| | James M. Mead (D, AM LAB) | 2,138,482 | 43.1 |
| 1950 | Thomas E. Dewey (R) | 2,819,523 | 53.1 |
| | Walter A. Lynch (D, L) | 2,246,855 | 42.3 |
| 1954 | Averell Harriman (D, L) | 2,560,738 | 49.6 |
| | Irving M. Ives (R) | 2,549,613 | 49.4 |
| 1958 | Nelson A. Rockefeller (R) | 3,126,929 | 54.7 |
| | Averell Harriman (D, L) | 2,553,895# | 44.7 |
| 1962 | Nelson A. Rockefeller (R) | 3,081,587 | 53.1 |
| | Robert M. Morgenthau (D, L) | 2,552,418 | 44.0 |
| 1966 | Nelson A. Rockefeller (R) | 2,690,626 | 44.6 |
| | Frank O'Connor (D) | 2,298,363 | 38.1 |
| | Paul L. Adams (C) | 510,023 | 8.5 |
| | Franklin Roosevelt Jr. (L) | 507,234 | 8.4 |
| 1970 | Nelson A. Rockefeller (R, CSI) | 3,151,432 | 52.4 |
| | Arthur J. Goldberg (D, L) | 2,421,426 | 40.3 |
| | Paul L. Adams (C) | 422,514 | 7.0 |
| 1974 | Hugh L. Carey (D, L) | 3,028,503 | 57.2 |
| | Malcolm Wilson (R, C) | 2,219,667 | 41.9 |
| 1978 | Hugh L. Carey (D, L) | 2,429,272 | 50.9 |
| | Perry B. Duryea (R, C) | 2,156,404 | 45.2 |

| | Candidates | Votes | % |
|---|---|---|---|
| 1982 | Mario M. Cuomo (D, L) | 2,675,213 | 50.9 |
| | Lew Lehrman (R, C) | 2,494,827 | 47.5 |
| 1986 | Mario M. Cuomo (D, L) | 2,775,229 | 64.6 |
| | Andrew P. O'Rourke (R, C) | 1,363,810 | 31.8 |
| 1990 | Mario M. Cuomo (D, L) | 2,157,087 | 53.2 |
| | Pierre A. Rinfret (R) | 865,948 | 21.3 |
| | Herbert I. London (C) | 827,614 | 20.4 |

**New York**
1. Anti-Federalist Party
2. Anti-Clinton Party
3. Anti-Clinton Republican Party

# NORTH CAROLINA

(Ratified the Constitution Nov. 21, 1789)

| | Candidates | Votes | % |
|---|---|---|---|
| 1836 [1] | Edward B. Dudley (W) | 33,993 | 53.2 |
| | Richard D. Spaight (D) | 29,950 | 46.8 |
| 1838 | Edward B. Dudley (W) | 38,119 | 64.2 |
| | John Branch (D) | 21,155 | 35.6 |
| 1840 | John M. Morehead (W) | 44,514 | 55.0 |
| | Romulus M. Saunders (D) | 36,428 | 45.0 |
| 1842 | John M. Morehead (W) | 39,596 | 53.1 |
| | Louis D. Henry (D) | 35,024 | 46.9 |
| 1844 | William A. Graham (W) | 42,586 | 51.9 |
| | Michael Hoke (D) | 39,433 | 48.1 |
| 1846 | William A. Graham (W) | 43,486 | 55.0 |
| | James B. Shepard (D) | 35,627 | 45.0 |
| 1848 | Charles Manly (W) | 42,536 | 50.5 |
| | David S. Reid (D) | 41,682 | 49.5 |
| 1850 | David S. Reid (D) | 45,058 | 51.6 |
| | Charles Manly (W) | 42,341 | 48.5 |
| 1852 | David S. Reid (D) | 48,484 | 53.0 |
| | John Kerr (W) | 42,993 | 47.0 |
| 1854 | Thomas Bragg (D) | 48,705 | 51.1 |
| | Alfred Dockery (W) | 46,644 | 48.9 |
| 1856 | Thomas Bragg (D) | 57,698 | 56.2 |
| | John A. Gilmer (AM) | 44,970 | 43.8 |
| 1858 | John W. Ellis (D) | 56,429 | 58.5 |
| | Duncan K. McCrae (DISTRIB) | 40,036 | 41.5 |
| 1860 | John W. Ellis (D) | 59,396 | 52.7 |
| | John Pool (W) | 53,303 | 47.3 |
| 1862 | Zebulon B. Vance | 55,282 | 72.7 |
| | William J. Johnston | 20,813 | 27.4 |
| 1864 | Zebulon B. Vance | 58,070 | 80.0 |
| | William W. Holden | 14,491 | 20.0 |
| 1865 | Jonathan Worth | 32,539 | 55.7 |
| | William W. Holden | 25,809 | 44.2 |
| 1866 | Jonathan Worth (C) | 34,250 | 75.9 |
| | Alfred Dockery (NC R) | 10,759 | 23.8 |
| 1868 | William W. Holden (R) | 92,235 | 55.5 |
| | Thomas S. Ashe (C) | 73,600 | 44.3 |
| 1872 | Tod R. Caldwell (R) | 98,630 | 50.5 |
| | Augustus S. Merrimon (D) | 96,731 | 49.5 |
| 1876 | Zebulon B. Vance (D) | 123,265 | 52.8 |
| | Thomas Settle (R) | 110,061 | 47.2 |
| 1880 | Thomas J. Jarvis (D) | 121,837 | 51.3 |
| | Ralph P. Buxton (R) | 115,559 | 48.7 |
| 1884 | Alfred M. Scales (D) | 143,249 | 53.8 |
| | Tyre York (R) | 122,795 | 46.1 |
| 1888 | Daniel G. Fowle (D) | 148,405 | 52.0 |
| | Oliver H. Dockery (R) | 134,035 | 46.9 |
| 1892 | Elias Carr (D) | 135,327 | 48.3 |
| | David M. Furches (R) | 94,681 | 33.8 |
| | Wyatt P. Exum (PP) | 47,747 | 17.0 |

| | Candidates | Votes | % |
|---|---|---|---|
| 1896 | Daniel L. Russell (R) | 154,025 | 46.5 |
| | Cyrus B. Watson (D) | 145,286 | 43.9 |
| | William A. Guthrie (PP) | 30,943 | 9.4 |
| 1900 | Charles B. Aycock (D) | 186,650 | 59.6 |
| | Spencer B. Adams (R) | 126,296 | 40.3 |
| 1904 | R. B. Glenn (D) | 128,761 | 61.7 |
| | C. J. Harris (R) | 79,505 | 38.1 |
| 1908 | W. W. Kitchin (D) | 145,102 | 57.3 |
| | J. E. Cox (R) | 107,760 | 42.6 |
| 1912 | Locke Craig (D) | 149,972 | 61.4 |
| | Iredell Meares (PROG) | 49,925 | 20.4 |
| | Thomas Settle (R) | 43,627 | 17.9 |
| 1916 | Thomas W. Bickett (D) | 167,664 | 58.1 |
| | Frank A. Linney (R) | 120,157 | 41.7 |
| 1920 | Cameron Morrison (D) | 308,151 | 57.2 |
| | John J. Parker (R) | 230,193 | 42.8 |
| 1924 | Angus Wilton McLean (D) | 294,441 | 61.3 |
| | I. M. Meekins (R) | 185,578 | 38.7 |
| 1928 | O. Max Gardner (D) | 362,009 | 55.6 |
| | H. F. Seawell (R) | 289,415 | 44.4 |
| 1932 | J. C. B. Ehringhaus (D) | 497,708 | 70.1 |
| | Clifford Frazier (R) | 212,561 | 29.9 |
| 1936 | Clyde R. Hoey (D) | 542,139 | 66.7 |
| | Gilliam Grissom (R) | 270,943 | 33.3 |
| 1940 | J. Melville Broughton (D) | 608,744 | 75.7 |
| | Robert H. McNeill (R) | 195,402 | 24.3 |
| 1944 | R. Gregg Cherry (D) | 528,995 | 69.6 |
| | Frank C. Patton (R) | 230,968 | 30.4 |
| 1948 | W. Kerr Scott (D) | 570,995 | 73.2 |
| | George M. Pritchard (R) | 206,166 | 26.4 |
| 1952 | William B. Umstead (D) | 796,306 | 67.5 |
| | H. F. Seawell Jr. (R) | 383,329 | 32.5 |
| 1956 | Luther H. Hodges (D) | 760,480 | 67.0 |
| | Kyle Hayes (R) | 375,379 | 33.1 |
| 1960 | Terry Sanford (D) | 735,248 | 54.5 |
| | Robert L. Gavin (R) | 613,975 | 45.5 |
| 1964 | Dan K. Moore (D) | 790,343 | 56.6 |
| | Robert L. Gavin (R) | 606,165 | 43.4 |
| 1968 | Robert W. Scott (D) | 821,232 | 52.7 |
| | James C. Gardner (R) | 737,075 | 47.3 |
| 1972 | James C. Holshouser Jr. (R) | 767,470 | 51.0 |
| | Hargrove Bowles Jr. (D) | 729,104 | 48.5 |
| 1976 | James B. Hunt Jr. (D) | 1,081,293 | 65.0 |
| | David T. Flaherty (R) | 564,102 | 33.9 |
| 1980 | James B. Hunt Jr. (D) | 1,143,145 | 61.9 |
| | Beverly Lake (R) | 691,449 | 37.4 |
| 1984 | James G. Martin (R) | 1,208,167 | 54.3 |
| | Rufus Edmisten (D) | 1,011,209 | 45.4 |
| 1988 | James G. Martin (R) | 1,222,338 | 56.1 |
| | Robert B. Jordan III (D) | 957,687 | 43.9 |
| 1992 | James B. Hunt Jr. (D) | 1,368,246 | 52.7 |
| | Jim Gardner (R) | 1,121,955 | 43.2 |

**North Carolina**
1. Before 1836 governor chosen by General Assembly.

# NORTH DAKOTA

(Became a state Nov. 2, 1889)

| | Candidates | Votes | % |
|---|---|---|---|
| 1889 | John Miller (R) | 25,365 | 66.6 |
| | William Roach (D) | 12,733 | 33.4 |
| 1890 | Andrew H. Burke (R) | 19,053 | 52.2 |
| | William Roach (D) | 12,604 | 34.6 |
| | Muir (I) | 4,821 | 13.2 |
| 1892 | Eli C. D. Shortridge (FUS) | 18,943 | 52.4 |
| | Andrew H. Burke (R) | 17,203 | 47.6 |

| | Candidates | Votes | % |
|---|---|---|---|
| 1894 | Roger Allin (R) | 23,723 | 55.8 |
| | Wallace (POP) | 9,354 | 22.0 |
| | Kinter (D) | 8,188 | 19.2 |
| 1896 | Frank A. Briggs (R) | 25,918 | 55.6 |
| | R. B. Richardson (FUS) | 20,690 | 44.4 |
| 1898 | Frederick B. Fancher (R) | 27,308 | 58.4 |
| | Holmes (FUS) | 19,496 | 41.7 |
| 1900 | Frank White (R) | 34,052 | 59.2 |
| | M. A. Wipperman (D & I) | 22,275 | 38.7 |
| 1902 | Frank White (R) | 31,613 | 62.7 |
| | Cronan (D) | 17,576 | 34.9 |
| 1904 | Elmore Y. Sarles (R) | 48,026 | 70.7 |
| | M. F. Hegge (D) | 16,744 | 24.7 |
| 1906 | John Burke (D) | 34,424 | 53.2 |
| | Elmore Y. Sarles (R) | 29,309 | 45.3 |
| 1908 | John Burke (D) | 49,398 | 51.1 |
| | C. A. Johnson (R) | 46,849 | 48.4 |
| 1910 | John Burke (D) | 47,005 | 50.0 |
| | C. A. Johnson (R) | 44,555 | 47.4 |
| 1912 | Louis B. Hanna (R) | 39,811 | 45.5 |
| | F. O. Hellstrom (D) | 31,544 | 36.0 |
| | W. D. Sweet (PROG) | 9,406 | 10.7 |
| | A. E. Bowen Jr. (SOC) | 6,835 | 7.8 |
| 1914 | Louis B. Hanna (R) | 44,279 | 49.6 |
| | F. O. Hellstrom (D) | 34,746 | 38.9 |
| | J. A. Williams (SOC) | 6,019 | 6.7 |
| 1916 | Lynn J. Frazier (R) | 87,665 | 79.2 |
| | D. H. McArthur (D) | 20,351 | 18.4 |
| 1918 | Lynn J. Frazier (R & NP) | 54,517 | 59.7 |
| | S. J. Doyle (D & I) | 36,733 | 40.3 |
| 1920 | Lynn J. Frazier (R & NP) | 117,018 | 51.0 |
| | J. F. T. O'Connor (D & I) | 112,488 | 49.0 |

**Special Election**

| | | | |
|---|---|---|---|
| 1921 | Ragnvald A. Nestos (IR) | 111,434 | 50.9 |
| | Lynn J. Frazier (R & NP) | 107,332 | 49.1 |

| | | | |
|---|---|---|---|
| 1922 | Ragnvald A. Nestos (R) | 110,321 | 57.7 |
| | William Lemke (NON PART) | 81,048 | 42.4 |
| 1924 | Arthur G. Sorlie (R) | 101,170 | 53.9 |
| | Halvor L. Halvorson (D) | 86,414 | 46.1 |
| 1926 | Arthur G. Sorlie (R) | 131,003 | 81.7 |
| | D. M. Holmes (D) | 24,287 | 15.2 |
| 1928 | George F. Shafer (R) | 131,193 | 56.5 |
| | Walter Maddock (D) | 100,205 | 43.2 |
| 1930 | George F. Shafer (R) | 133,264 | 73.6 |
| | Pierce Blewett (D) | 41,988 | 23.2 |
| 1932 | William Langer (R) | 134,231 | 54.8 |
| | Herbert C. Depuy (D) | 110,263 | 45.0 |
| 1934 | Thomas H. Moodie (D) | 145,433 | 53.0 |
| | Lydia Langer (R) | 127,954 | 46.6 |
| 1936 | William Langer (I) | 98,750 | 35.8 |
| | Walter Welford (R) | 95,697 | 34.7 |
| | John Moses (D) | 80,726 | 29.3 |
| 1938 | John Moses (D) | 138,270 | 52.5 |
| | John N. Hagan (R) | 125,246 | 47.5 |
| 1940 | John Moses (D) | 173,278 | 63.1 |
| | Jack A. Patterson (R) | 101,287 | 36.9 |
| 1942 | John Moses (D) | 101,390 | 57.6 |
| | Oscar W. Hagen (R) | 74,577 | 42.4 |
| 1944 | Fred G. Aandahl (R) | 107,863 | 52.0 |
| | William T. Depuy (D) | 59,961 | 28.9 |
| | Alvin C. Strutz (IR) | 38,997 | 18.8 |
| 1946 | Fred G. Aandahl (R) | 116,672 | 68.9 |
| | Quentin Burdick (D) | 52,719 | 31.1 |
| 1948 | Fred G. Aandahl (R) | 131,764 | 61.3 |
| | Howard Henry (D) | 80,655 | 37.5 |
| 1950 | Norman Brunsdale (R) | 121,822 | 66.3 |
| | Clyde G. Byerly (D) | 61,950 | 33.7 |

| | Candidates | Votes | % |
|---|---|---|---|
| 1952 | Norman Brunsdale (R) | 199,944 | 78.7 |
| | Ole S. Johnson (D) | 53,990 | 21.3 |
| 1954 | Norman Brunsdale (R) | 124,253 | 64.2 |
| | Cornelius Bymers (D) | 69,248 | 35.8 |
| 1956 | John E. Davis (R) | 147,566 | 58.5 |
| | Wallace E. Warner (D) | 104,869 | 41.5 |
| 1958 | John E. Davis (R) | 111,836 | 53.1 |
| | John F. Lord (D) | 98,763 | 46.9 |
| 1960 | William L. Guy (D) | 136,148 | 49.4 |
| | C. P. Dahl (R) | 122,486 | 44.5 |
| | Herschel Lashkowitz (I) | 16,741 | 6.1 |
| 1962 | William L. Guy (D) | 115,258 | 50.4 |
| | Mark Andrews (R) | 113,251 | 49.6 |
| 1964 | William L. Guy (D) | 146,414 | 55.7 |
| | Don Halcrow (R) | 116,247 | 44.3 |
| 1968 | William L. Guy (D) | 135,955 | 54.8 |
| | Robert P. McCarney (R) | 108,382 | 43.7 |
| 1972 | Arthur A. Link (D) | 143,899 | 51.0 |
| | Richard Larsen (R) | 138,032 | 49.0 |
| 1976 | Arthur A. Link (D) | 153,309 | 51.6 |
| | Richard Elkin (R) | 138,321 | 46.5 |
| 1980 | Allen I. Olson (R) | 162,230 | 53.6 |
| | Arthur A. Link (D) | 140,391 | 46.4 |
| 1984 | George Sinner (D) | 173,922 | 55.3 |
| | Allen I. Olson (R) | 140,460 | 44.7 |
| 1988 | George Sinner (D) | 179,094 | 59.9 |
| | Leon Mallberg (R) | 119,986 | 40.1 |
| 1992 | Edward T. Schafer (R) | 176,398 | 57.9 |
| | Nicholas Spaeth (D) | 123,845 | 40.6 |

# OHIO

(Became a state March 1, 1803)

| | Candidates | Votes | % |
|---|---|---|---|
| 1803 | Edward Tiffin (D-R) | 4,564 | |
| 1805 | Edward Tiffin (D-R) | 4,783 | |
| 1807 [1] | Return J. Meigs Jr. (D-R) | 5,550 | 53.8 |
| | Nathanael Massie (D-R) | 4,757 | 46.2 |
| 1808 | Samuel Huntington (D-R) | 7,293 | 44.8 |
| | Thomas Worthington (D-R) | 5,601 | 34.4 |
| | Thomas Kirker (D-R) | 3,397 | 20.9 |
| 1810 | Return J. Meigs Jr. (D-R) | 9,924 | 56.2 |
| | Thomas Worthington (D-R) | 7,731 | 43.8 |
| 1812 | Return J. Meigs Jr. (FED) | 11,859 | 60.0 |
| | Thomas Scott (D-R) | 7,903 | 40.0 |
| 1814 | Thomas Worthington (D-R) | 15,879 | 72.0 |
| | Othniel Looker (FED) | 6,171 | 28.0 |
| 1816 | Thomas Worthington (D-R) | 22,931 | 74.4 |
| | James Dunlap (D-R) | 6,295 | 20.4 |
| | Ethan A. Brown (FED) | 1,607 | 5.2 |
| 1818 | Ethan A. Brown (D-R) | 30,194 | 78.9 |
| | James Dunlap (D-R) | 8,075 | 21.1 |
| 1820 | Ethan A. Brown (D-R) | 34,836 | 71.3 |
| | Jeremiah Morrow (D-R) | 9,426 | 19.3 |
| | William H. Harrison (D-R) | 4,348 | 8.9 |
| 1822 | Jeremiah Morrow (D-R) | 26,059 | 43.4 |
| | Allen Trimble (FED) | 22,889 | 38.1 |
| | William W. Irwin (D-R) | 11,060 | 18.4 |
| 1824 | Jeremiah Morrow (JAC D) | 38,328 | 51.0 |
| | Allen Trimble (NR) | 36,869 | 49.0 |
| 1826 | Allen Trimble (NR) | 70,475 | 84.2 |
| | Alex Campbell | 4,765 | 5.7 |
| | Benjamin Tappan | 4,209 | 5.0 |
| 1828 | Allen Trimble (NR) | 53,971 | 51.4 |
| | John W. Campbell (JAC D) | 51,004 | 48.5 |
| 1830 | Duncan McArthur (NR) | 49,677 | 50.1 |
| | Robert Lucas (JAC D) | 49,186 | 49.6 |

| | Candidates | Votes | % |
|---|---|---|---|
| 1832 | Robert Lucas (D) | 71,038 | 52.9 |
| | Darius Lyman (NR) | 63,213 | 47.1 |
| 1834 | Robert Lucas (D) | 70,738 | 51.2 |
| | James Findlay (W) | 67,414 | 48.8 |
| 1836 | Joseph Vance (W) | 92,204 | 51.6 |
| | Eli Baldwin (D) | 86,158 | 48.3 |
| 1838 | Wilson Shannon (D) | 107,884 | 51.4 |
| | Joseph Vance (W) | 102,146 | 48.6 |
| 1840 | Thomas Corwin (W) | 145,444 | 52.9 |
| | Wilson Shannon (D) | 129,312 | 47.1 |
| 1842 | Wilson Shannon (D) | 119,774 | 49.3 |
| | Thomas Corwin (W) | 117,902 | 48.6 |
| 1844 | Mordecai Bartley (W) | 146,333 | 48.7 |
| | David Tod (D) | 145,062 | 48.3 |
| 1846 | William Bebb (W) | 118,857 | 48.3 |
| | David Tod (D) | 116,554 | 47.3 |
| 1848 | Seabury Ford (W) | 148,766‡ | 49.9 |
| | John B. Weller (D) | 148,452 | 49.8 |
| 1850 | Reuben Wood (D) | 133,093 | 49.7 |
| | William Johnston (W) | 121,105 | 45.2 |
| | Edward Smith (F SOIL) | 13,747 | 5.1 |
| 1851 | Reuben Wood (D) | 145,656 | 51.6 |
| | Samuel F. Vinton (W) | 119,550 | 42.4 |
| | Samuel Lewis (F SOIL) | 16,910 | 6.0 |
| 1853 | William Medill (D) | 147,663 | 52.1 |
| | Nelson Barrere (W) | 85,843 | 30.3 |
| | Samuel Lewis (F SOIL) | 49,846 | 17.6 |
| 1855 | Salmon P. Chase (R) | 146,720 | 48.6 |
| | William Medill (D) | 131,019 | 43.4 |
| | Allen Trimble (W) | 24,276 | 8.0 |
| 1857 | Salmon P. Chase (R) | 160,685 | 48.6 |
| | H. B. Payne (D) | 159,294 | 48.2 |
| 1859 | William Dennison Jr. (R) | 184,502 | 51.9 |
| | Rufus P. Ranney (D) | 171,266 | 48.1 |
| 1861 | David Tod (UN) | 206,997 | 57.7 |
| | Hugh J. Jewett (D) | 151,774 | 42.3 |
| 1863 | John Brough (UN) | 288,856 | 60.6 |
| | C. L. Vallandigham (D) | 187,728 | 39.4 |
| 1865 | Jacob D. Cox (UN) | 223,642 | 53.5 |
| | George W. Morgan (D) | 193,791 | 46.4 |
| 1867 | Rutherford B. Hayes (R) | 243,811 | 50.3 |
| | A. G. Thurman (D) | 240,622 | 49.7 |
| 1869 | Rutherford B. Hayes (R) | 236,092 | 50.7 |
| | George H. Pendleton (D) | 228,703 | 49.1 |
| 1871 | Edward F. Noyes (R) | 238,273 | 51.8 |
| | George W. McCook (D) | 218,105 | 47.4 |
| 1873 | William Allen (D) | 214,654 | 47.8 |
| | Edward F. Noyes (R) | 213,837 | 47.6 |
| 1875 | Rutherford B. Hayes (R) | 297,817 | 50.3 |
| | William Allen (D) | 292,279 | 49.3 |
| 1877 | Richard M. Bishop (D) | 271,642 | 48.9 |
| | William H. West (R) | 249,105 | 44.9 |
| 1879 | Charles Foster (R) | 336,321 | 50.3 |
| | Thomas Ewing (D) | 319,132 | 47.7 |
| 1881 | Charles Foster (R) | 312,785 | 50.1 |
| | John W. Bookwalter (D) | 288,426 | 46.2 |
| 1883 | George Hoadly (D) | 359,693 | 50.1 |
| | Joseph B. Foraker (R) | 347,164 | 48.3 |
| 1885 | Joseph B. Foraker (R) | 359,281 | 49.1 |
| | George Hoadly (D) | 341,830 | 46.8 |
| 1887 | Joseph B. Foraker (R) | 356,534 | 47.9 |
| | Thomas E. Powell (D) | 333,205 | 44.8 |
| 1889 | James E. Campbell (D) | 379,423 | 48.9 |
| | Joseph B. Foraker (R) | 368,551 | 47.5 |
| 1891 | William McKinley Jr. (R) | 386,739 | 48.6 |
| | James E. Campbell (D) | 365,228 | 45.9 |
| 1893 | William McKinley Jr. (R) | 433,342 | 52.6 |
| | Lawrence T. Neal (D) | 352,347 | 42.8 |
| 1895 | Asa S. Bushnell (R) | 427,141 | 51.0 |
| | James E. Campbell (D) | 334,519 | 40.0 |
| | Jacob S. Coxey (PP) | 52,625 | 6.3 |

| | Candidates | Votes | % |
|---|---|---|---|
| 1897 | Asa S. Bushnell (R) | 429,915 | 50.3 |
| | Horace L. Chapman (D) | 401,750 | 47.0 |
| 1899 | George K. Nash (R) | 417,199 | 45.9 |
| | John R. McLean (D) | 368,176 | 40.5 |
| | Samuel M. Jones (NON PART) | 106,721 | 11.8 |
| 1901 | George K. Nash (R) | 436,092 | 52.7 |
| | James Kilbourne (D) | 368,525 | 44.5 |
| 1903 | Myron T. Herrick (R) | 475,560 | 54.9 |
| | Tom L. Johnson (D) | 361,748 | 41.8 |
| 1905 | John M. Pattison (D) | 473,264 | 50.5 |
| | Myron T. Herrick (R) | 430,617 | 46.0 |
| 1908 | Judson Harmon (D) | 552,569 | 49.2 |
| | Andrew L. Harris (R) | 533,197 | 47.5 |
| 1910 | Judson Harmon (D) | 477,077 | 51.6 |
| | Warren G. Harding (R) | 376,700 | 40.8 |
| | Tom Clifford (SOC) | 60,637 | 6.6 |
| 1912 | James M. Cox (D) | 439,023 | 42.4 |
| | Robert B. Brown (R) | 272,500 | 26.3 |
| | Arthur L. Garford (PROG) | 217,903 | 21.0 |
| | C. E. Ruthenberg (SOC) | 87,709 | 8.5 |
| 1914 | Frank B. Willis (R) | 523,074 | 46.3 |
| | James M. Cox (D) | 493,804 | 43.7 |
| | James R. Garfield (PROG) | 60,904 | 5.4 |
| 1916 | James M. Cox (D) | 568,218 | 48.4 |
| | Frank B. Willis (R) | 561,602 | 47.8 |
| 1918 | James M. Cox (D) | 486,403 | 50.6 |
| | Frank B. Willis (R) | 474,559 | 49.4 |
| 1920 | Harry L. Davis (R) | 1,039,835 | 51.9 |
| | Vic Donahey (D) | 918,962 | 45.9 |
| 1922 | Vic Donahey (D) | 821,948 | 50.5 |
| | Carmi A. Thompson (R) | 804,200 | 49.4 |
| 1924 | Vic Donahey (D) | 1,065,981 | 54.0 |
| | Harry L. Davis (R) | 888,139 | 45.0 |
| 1926 | Vic Donahey (D) | 707,733 | 50.5 |
| | Myers Y. Cooper (R) | 685,897 | 49.0 |
| 1928 | Myers Y. Cooper (R) | 1,355,517 | 54.8 |
| | Martin L. Davey (D) | 1,106,739 | 44.7 |
| 1930 | George White (D) | 1,033,168 | 52.8 |
| | Myers Y. Cooper (R) | 923,538 | 47.2 |
| 1932 | George White (D) | 1,356,518 | 52.8 |
| | David S. Ingalls (R) | 1,151,933 | 44.9 |
| 1934 | Martin L. Davey (D) | 1,118,257 | 51.1 |
| | Clarence J. Brown (R) | 1,052,851 | 48.1 |
| 1936 | Martin L. Davey (D) | 1,539,461 | 52.0 |
| | John W. Bricker (R) | 1,412,773 | 47.7 |
| 1938 | John W. Bricker (R) | 1,265,548 | 52.5 |
| | Charles Sawyer (D) | 1,147,323 | 47.6 |
| 1940 | John W. Bricker (R) | 1,824,863 | 55.6 |
| | Martin L. Davey (D) | 1,460,396 | 44.5 |
| 1942 | John W. Bricker (R) | 1,086,937 | 60.5 |
| | John McSweeney (D) | 709,599 | 39.5 |
| 1944 | Frank J. Lausche (D) | 1,603,809 | 51.8 |
| | James Garfield Stewart (R) | 1,491,450 | 48.2 |
| 1946 | Thomas J. Herbert (R) | 1,166,550 | 50.6 |
| | Frank J. Lausche (D) | 1,125,997 | 48.9 |
| 1948 | Frank J. Lausche (D) | 1,619,775 | 53.7 |
| | Thomas J. Herbert (R) | 1,398,514 | 46.3 |
| 1950 | Frank J. Lausche (D) | 1,522,249 | 52.6 |
| | Don H. Ebright (R) | 1,370,570 | 47.4 |
| 1952 | Frank J. Lausche (D) | 2,015,110 | 55.9 |
| | Charles P. Taft (R) | 1,590,058 | 44.1 |
| 1954 | Frank J. Lausche (D) | 1,405,262 | 54.1 |
| | James A. Rhodes (R) | 1,192,528 | 45.9 |
| 1956 | C. William O'Neill (R) | 1,984,988 | 56.0 |
| | Michael V. DiSalle (D) | 1,557,103 | 44.0 |
| 1958 | Michael V. DiSalle (D) | 1,869,260 | 56.9 |
| | C. William O'Neill (R) | 1,414,874 | 43.1 |
| 1962 | James A. Rhodes (R) | 1,836,432 | 58.9 |
| | Michael V. DiSalle (D) | 1,280,521 | 41.1 |
| 1966 | James A. Rhodes (R) | 1,795,277 | 62.2 |
| | Frazier Reams Jr. (D) | 1,092,054 | 37.8 |

| | Candidates | Votes | % |
|---|---|---|---|
| 1970 | John J. Gilligan (D) | 1,725,560 | 54.2 |
| | Roger Cloud (R) | 1,382,659 | 43.4 |
| 1974 | James A. Rhodes (R) | 1,493,679 | 48.6 |
| | John J. Gilligan (D) | 1,482,191 | 48.2 |
| 1978 | James A. Rhodes (R) | 1,402,167 | 49.3 |
| | Richard F. Celeste (D) | 1,354,631 | 47.6 |
| 1982 | Richard F. Celeste (D) | 1,981,882 | 59.0 |
| | Clarence Brown Jr. (R) | 1,303,962 | 38.8 |
| 1986 | Richard F. Celeste (D) | 1,858,372 | 60.6 |
| | James A. Rhodes (R) | 1,207,264 | 39.4 |
| 1990 | George V. Voinovich (R) | 1,928,103 | 55.7 |
| | Anthony J. Celebrezze Jr. (D) | 1,539,416 | 44.3 |

**Ohio**

1. *The election was challenged by Massie. The legislature eventually declared Meigs ineligible and arranged for a new election in 1808. Pending the outcome of that election, Speaker of the Senate Thomas Kirker was acting governor.*

# OKLAHOMA

(Became a state Nov. 16, 1907)

| | Candidates | Votes | % |
|---|---|---|---|
| 1907 | Charles N. Haskell (D) | 137,633 | 53.4 |
| | Frank Frantz (R) | 110,296 | 42.8 |
| 1910 | Lee Cruce (D) | 119,873 | 48.6 |
| | J. W. McNeal (R) | 99,319 | 40.2 |
| | J. T. Crumbie (SOC) | 24,457 | 9.9 |
| 1914 | Robert L. Williams (D) | 100,596 | 39.7 |
| | John Fields (R) | 95,909 | 37.8 |
| | Fred W. Holt (SOC) | 52,704 | 20.8 |
| 1918 | James B. A. Robertson (D) | 104,132 | 53.5 |
| | Horace G. McKeever (R) | 82,905 | 42.6 |
| 1922 | John C. Walton (D) | 280,207 | 54.5 |
| | John Fields (R) | 230,469 | 44.8 |
| 1926 | Henry S. Johnston (D) | 213,162 | 54.9 |
| | Omer K. Benedict (R) | 171,710 | 44.2 |
| 1930 | William H. Murray (D) | 301,921 | 59.1 |
| | Ira A. Hill (R) | 208,575 | 40.8 |
| 1934 | E. W. Marland (D) | 365,992 | 58.2 |
| | William B. Pine (R) | 243,936 | 38.8 |
| 1938 | Leon C. Phillips (D) | 355,740 | 70.0 |
| | Ross Rizley (R) | 148,861 | 29.3 |
| 1942 | Robert S. Kerr (D) | 196,565 | 51.9 |
| | William J. Otjen (R) | 180,454 | 47.6 |
| 1946 | Roy J. Turner (D) | 259,491 | 52.5 |
| | Olney F. Flynn (R) | 227,426 | 46.0 |
| 1950 | Johnston Murray (D) | 329,308 | 51.1 |
| | Jo O. Ferguson (R) | 313,205 | 48.6 |
| 1954 | Raymond Gary (D) | 357,386 | 58.7 |
| | Reuben K. Sparks (R) | 251,808 | 41.3 |
| 1958 | J. Howard Edmondson (D) | 399,504 | 74.1 |
| | Phil Ferguson (R) | 107,495 | 20.0 |
| | D. A. Jelly Boyce (I) | 31,840 | 5.9 |
| 1962 | Henry L. Bellmon (R) | 392,316 | 55.3 |
| | W. P. Atkinson (D) | 315,357 | 44.4 |
| 1966 | Dewey F. Bartlett (R) | 377,078 | 55.7 |
| | Preston J. Moore (D) | 296,328 | 43.8 |
| 1970 | David Hall (D) | 338,338 | 48.4 |
| | Dewey F. Bartlett (R) | 336,157 | 48.1 |
| 1974 | David L. Boren (D) | 514,389 | 63.9 |
| | James M. Inhofe (R) | 290,459 | 36.1 |
| 1978 | George Nigh (D) | 402,240 | 51.7 |
| | Ron Shotts (R) | 367,055 | 47.2 |
| 1982 | George Nigh (D) | 548,159 | 62.1 |
| | Tom Daxon (R) | 332,207 | 37.6 |

| | Candidates | Votes | % |
|---|---|---|---|
| 1986 | Henry L. Bellmon (R) | 431,762 | 47.5 |
| | David Walters (D) | 405,295 | 44.5 |
| | Jerry Brown (I) | 60,115 | 6.6 |
| 1990 | David Walters (D) | 523,196 | 57.4 |
| | Bill Price (R) | 297,584 | 32.7 |
| | Thomas D. Ledgerwood II (I) | 90,534 | 9.9 |

# OREGON

(Became a state Feb. 14, 1859)

| | Candidates | Votes | % |
|---|---|---|---|
| 1858 | John Whiteaker (D) | 5,134 | 54.7 |
| | E. M. Barnum (OPP) | 4,213 | 44.9 |
| 1862 | A. C. Gibbs (UN R) | 7,039 | 67.1 |
| | John F. Miller (D) | 3,450 | 32.9 |
| 1866 | George L. Woods (R) | 10,316 | 50.7 |
| | James K. Kelly (D) | 10,039 | 49.3 |
| 1870 | La Fayette Grover (D) | 11,726 | 51.4 |
| | Joel Palmer (R) | 11,095 | 48.6 |
| 1874 | La Fayette Grover (D) | 9,713 | 38.2 |
| | J. C. Tolman (R) | 9,163 | 36.1 |
| | Thomas F. Campbell (I) | 6,532 | 25.7 |
| 1878 | William Wallace Thayer (D) | 15,689 | 47.9 |
| | C. C. Beekman (R) | 15,610 | 47.7 |
| 1882 | Zenas F. Moody (R) | 21,481 | 51.8 |
| | Smith (D) | 20,029 | 48.3 |
| 1886 | Sylvester Pennoyer (D) | 27,901 | 50.9 |
| | T. R. Cornelius (R) | 24,199 | 44.1 |
| 1890 | Sylvester Pennoyer (D) | 38,920 | 53.6 |
| | D. P. Thompson (R) | 33,765 | 46.5 |
| 1894 | William P. Lord (R) | 41,139 | 47.2 |
| | Nathan Pierce (PP) | 26,125 | 30.0 |
| | William Galloway (D) | 17,865 | 20.5 |
| 1898 | Theodore Thurston Geer (R) | 45,094 | 53.2 |
| | W. R. King (D-PP) | 34,542 | 40.8 |
| 1902 | George E. Chamberlain (D) | 41,857 | 46.2 |
| | W. J. Furnish (R) | 41,611 | 45.9 |
| 1906 | George E. Chamberlain (D) | 46,002 | 47.6 |
| | James Withycombe (R) | 43,508 | 45.0 |
| | C. W. Barzee (SOC) | 4,468 | 5.0 |
| 1910 | Oswald West (D) | 54,853 | 46.6 |
| | Jay Bowerman (R) | 48,751 | 41.4 |
| | W. S. Richards (SOC) | 8,040 | 6.8 |
| | A. E. Eaton (P) | 6,046 | 5.1 |
| 1914 | James Withycombe (R) | 121,037 | 48.8 |
| | C. J. Smith (D) | 94,594 | 38.1 |
| | W. J. Smith (SOC) | 14,284 | 5.8 |
| 1918 | James Withycombe (R) | 81,067 | 53.0 |
| | Walter M. Pierce (D) | 65,440 | 42.8 |
| 1922 | Walter M. Pierce (D) | 133,392 | 57.4 |
| | Ben W. Olcott (R) | 99,164 | 42.6 |
| 1926 | I. L. Patterson (R) | 120,073 | 53.1 |
| | Walter M. Pierce (D) | 93,470 | 41.4 |
| | H. H. Stallard (I) | 12,402 | 5.5 |
| 1930 | Julius L. Meier (I) | 135,608 | 54.5 |
| | Ed F. Bailey (D) | 62,434 | 25.1 |
| | Phil Metschan (R) | 46,840 | 18.8 |
| 1934 | Charles H. Martin (D) | 116,677 | 38.6 |
| | Peter Zimmerman (I) | 95,519 | 31.6 |
| | Joe E. Dunne (R) | 86,923 | 28.7 |
| 1938 | Charles A. Sprague (R) | 214,062 | 57.4 |
| | Henry L. Hess (D) | 158,744 | 42.6 |
| 1942 | Earl Snell (R) | 220,188 | 77.9 |
| | Lew Wallace (D) | 62,561 | 22.1 |
| 1946 | Earl Snell (R) | 237,681 | 69.1 |
| | Carl C. Donaugh (D) | 106,474 | 30.9 |

| | Candidates | Votes | % |
|---|---|---|---|
| Special Election | | | |
| 1948 | Douglas McKay (R) | 271,295 | 53.2 |
| | Lew Wallace (D) | 226,949 | 44.5 |
| 1950 | Douglas McKay (R) | 334,160 | 66.1 |
| | Austin F. Flegal (D) | 171,750 | 34.0 |
| 1954 | Paul Patterson (R) | 322,522 | 56.9 |
| | Joseph K. Carson Jr. (D) | 244,179 | 43.1 |
| Special Election | | | |
| 1956 | Robert D. Holmes (D) | 369,439 | 50.5 |
| | Elmo Smith (R) | 361,840 | 49.5 |
| 1958 | Mark O. Hatfield (R) | 331,900 | 55.3 |
| | Robert D. Holmes (D) | 267,934 | 44.7 |
| 1962 | Mark O. Hatfield (R) | 345,497 | 54.2 |
| | Robert Y. Thornton (D) | 265,359 | 41.6 |
| 1966 | Tom McCall (R) | 377,346 | 55.3 |
| | Robert W. Straub (D) | 305,008 | 44.7 |
| 1970 | Tom McCall (R) | 369,964 | 55.6 |
| | Robert W. Straub (D) | 293,892 | 44.2 |
| 1974 | Robert W. Straub (D) | 444,812 | 57.7 |
| | Victor Atiyeh (R) | 324,751 | 42.1 |
| 1978 | Victor Atiyeh (R) | 498,452 | 54.9 |
| | Robert W. Straub (D) | 409,411 | 44.9 |
| 1982 | Victor Atiyeh (R) | 639,841 | 61.4 |
| | Ted Kulongoski (D) | 374,316 | 35.9 |
| 1986 | Neil Goldschmidt (D) | 549,456 | 51.9 |
| | Norma Paulus (R) | 506,986 | 47.8 |
| 1990 | Barbara Roberts (D) | 508,749 | 45.7 |
| | Dave Frohnmayer (R) | 444,646 | 40.0 |
| | Al Mobley (I) | 144,062 | 12.9 |

# PENNSYLVANIA

(Ratified the Constitution Dec. 12, 1787)

| | Candidates | Votes | % |
|---|---|---|---|
| 1790 | Thomas Mifflin | 27,725 | 90.8 |
| | Arthur St. Clair (FED) | 2,802 | 9.2 |
| 1793 | Thomas Mifflin (D-R) | 18,590 | 63.5 |
| | Frederick A. Muhlenberg (FED) | 10,706 | 36.5 |
| 1796 | Thomas Mifflin (D-R) | 30,020 | 96.7 |
| 1799 | Thomas McKean (D-R) | 38,036 | 53.8 |
| | James Ross (FED) | 32,641 | 46.2 |
| 1802 | Thomas McKean (D-R) | 47,849 | 73.6 |
| | James Ross (FED) | 17,037 | 26.2 |
| 1805 | Thomas McKean (I D-R)[1] | 43,644 | 52.9 |
| | Simon Snyder (D-R) | 38,833 | 47.1 |
| 1808 | Simon Snyder (D-R) | 67,975 | 60.9 |
| | James Ross (FED) | 39,575 | 35.5 |
| 1811 | Simon Snyder (D-R) | 52,319 | 90.8 |
| | William Tilghman (FED) | 3,609 | 6.3 |
| 1814 | Simon Snyder (D-R) | 51,009 | 62.6 |
| | Isaac Wayne (FED) | 29,566 | 36.3 |
| 1817 | William Findlay (D-R) | 66,331 | 52.8 |
| | Joseph Hiester (D-R/FED) | 59,272 | 47.2 |
| 1820 | Joseph Hiester (D-R) | 67,905 | 50.6 |
| | William Findlay (D-R) | 66,300 | 49.4 |
| 1823 | John Andrew Schulze (D-R) | 89,928 | 58.3 |
| | Andrew Gregg (FED) | 64,211 | 41.7 |
| 1826 | John Andrew Schulze (JAC D) | 72,710 | 96.9 |
| 1829 | George Wolf (JAC D) | 78,138 | 60.1 |
| | Joseph Ritner (A-MAS) | 51,776 | 39.9 |
| 1832 | George Wolf (D) | 91,385 | 50.9 |
| | Joseph Ritner (A-MAS) | 88,115 | 49.1 |

| | Candidates | Votes | % |
|---|---|---|---|
| 1835 | Joseph Ritner (D) | 94,023 | *46.9* |
| | George Wolf (W) | 65,804 | *32.8* |
| | Henry Muhlenburgh | 40,586 | *20.3* |
| 1838 | David R. Porter (D) | 127,821 | *51.1* |
| | Joseph Ritner (A-MASC) | 122,325 | *48.9* |
| 1841 | David R. Porter (D) | 136,504 | *54.4* |
| | John Banks (W) | 113,453 | *45.3* |
| 1844 | Francis R. Shunk (D) | 160,322 | *50.3* |
| | Joseph Markle (W) | 156,041 | *48.9* |
| 1847 | Francis R. Shunk (D) | 146,081 | *50.8* |
| | James Irwin (W) | 128,148 | *44.6* |
| 1848 | William F. Johnston (W) | 168,522 | *50.0* |
| | Morris Longstreth (D) | 168,225 | *50.0* |
| 1851 | William Bigler (D) | 186,499 | *50.9* |
| | William F. Johnston (W) | 178,034 | *48.6* |
| 1854 | James Pollock (W) | 203,822 | *54.6* |
| | William Bigler (D) | 166,991 | *44.8* |
| 1857 | William F. Packer (D) | 188,836 | *52.0* |
| | David Wilmot (R) | 146,139 | *40.2* |
| | Isaac Hazlehurst (AM) | 28,168 | *7.8* |
| 1860 | Andrew G. Curtin (R) | 262,403 | *53.3* |
| | Henry D. Foster (D) | 230,269 | *46.7* |
| 1863 | Andrew G. Curtin (R) | 269,496 | *51.5* |
| | George W. Woodward (D) | 254,171 | *48.5* |
| 1866 | John White Geary (R) | 307,274 | *51.4* |
| | Hiester Clymer (D) | 290,096 | *48.6* |
| 1869 | John White Geary (R) | 290,552 | *50.4* |
| | Asa Packer (D) | 285,956 | *49.6* |
| 1872 | John Frederick Hartranft (R) | 353,387 | *52.6* |
| | Charles B. Buckalew (D) | 317,823 | *47.3* |
| 1875 | John Frederick Hartranft (R) | 304,175 | *49.9* |
| | Cyrus L. Pershing (D) | 292,136 | *47.9* |
| 1878 | Henry Martyn Hoyt (R) | 319,567 | *45.5* |
| | Andrew H. Dill (D) | 297,060 | *42.3* |
| | Samuel R. Mason (G) | 81,758 | *11.6* |
| 1882 | Robert E. Pattison (D) | 355,791 | *47.8* |
| | James A. Beaver (R) | 315,589 | *42.4* |
| | John Stewart (IR) | 43,743 | *5.9* |
| 1886 | James A. Beaver (R) | 412,285 | *50.3* |
| | Chauncey F. Black (D) | 369,634 | *45.1* |
| 1890 | Robert E. Pattison (D) | 464,209 | *50.0* |
| | George W. Delamater (R) | 447,655 | *48.2* |
| 1894 | Daniel H. Hastings (R) | 574,801 | *60.3* |
| | William M. Singerly (D) | 333,404 | *35.0* |
| 1898 | William A. Stone (R) | 476,206 | *49.0* |
| | George A. Jenks (D) | 358,300 | *36.9* |
| | Silas C. Swallow (P, HG) | 132,931 | *13.7* |
| 1902 | Samuel W. Pennypacker (R) | 592,867 | *54.2* |
| | Robert E. Pattison (D) | 436,451 | *39.9* |
| 1906 | Edwin S. Stuart (R) | 506,418 | *50.3* |
| | Lewis Emery Jr. (D, LINCOLN) | 458,064 | *45.5* |
| 1910 | John K. Tener (R) | 412,658 | *41.3* |
| | William H. Berry (KEY) | 382,127 | *38.3* |
| | Webster Grim (D) | 129,395 | *13.0* |
| | John W. Slayton (SOC) | 53,055 | *5.3* |
| 1914 | Martin G. Brumbaugh (R, KEY) | 588,705 | *53.0* |
| | Vance C. McCormick (D, WASH) | 453,880 | *40.8* |
| 1918 | William Sproul (R, WASH) | 552,537 | *61.1* |
| | Eugene C. Bonniwell (D, F PLAY) | 305,315 | *33.7* |
| 1922 | Gifford Pinchot (R) | 831,696 | *56.8* |
| | John A. McSparran (D) | 581,625 | *39.7* |
| 1926 | John S. Fisher (R) | 1,102,823 | *73.3* |
| | Eugene C. Bonniwell (D, LAB) | 365,280 | *24.3* |
| 1930 | Gifford Pinchot (R, P) | 1,068,874 | *50.8* |
| | John M. Hemphill (D, L) | 1,010,204 | *47.7* |
| 1934 | George H. Earle (D) | 1,476,377 | *50.0* |
| | William A. Schnader (R) | 1,410,138 | *47.8* |
| 1938 | Arthur H. James (R) | 2,036,345 | *53.4* |
| | Charles Jones (D, ROYAL OAK) | 1,756,280 | *46.1* |
| 1942 | Edward Martin (R) | 1,367,531 | *53.7* |
| | F. Clair Ross (D) | 1,149,897 | *45.1* |

| | Candidates | Votes | % |
|---|---|---|---|
| 1946 | James H. Duff (R) | 1,828,462 | *58.5* |
| | John S. Rice (D) | 1,270,947 | *40.7* |
| 1950 | John S. Fine (R) | 1,796,119 | *50.7* |
| | Richardson Dilworth (D) | 1,710,355 | *48.3* |
| 1954 | George M. Leader (D) | 1,996,266 | *53.7* |
| | Lloyd H. Wood (R) | 1,717,070 | *46.2* |
| 1958 | David L. Lawrence (D) | 2,024,852 | *50.8* |
| | Arthur T. McGonigle (R) | 1,948,769 | *48.9* |
| 1962 | William W. Scranton (R) | 2,424,918 | *55.4* |
| | Richardson Dilworth (D) | 1,938,627 | *44.3* |
| 1966 | Raymond P. Shafer (R) | 2,110,349 | *52.1* |
| | Milton Shapp (D) | 1,868,719 | *46.1* |
| 1970 | Milton Shapp (D) | 2,043,029 | *55.2* |
| | Raymond J. Broderick (R) | 1,542,854 | *41.7* |
| 1974 | Milton Shapp (D) | 1,878,252 | *53.8* |
| | Andrew L. Lewis Jr. (R) | 1,578,917 | *45.2* |
| 1978 | Richard L. Thornburgh (R) | 1,966,042 | *52.5* |
| | Peter Flaherty (D) | 1,737,888 | *46.4* |
| 1982 | Richard L. Thornburgh (R) | 1,872,784 | *50.8* |
| | Allen E. Ertel (D) | 1,772,353 | *48.1* |
| 1986 | Robert P. Casey (D) | 1,717,484 | *50.7* |
| | William W. Scranton (R) | 1,638,268 | *48.3* |
| 1990 | Robert P. Casey (D) | 2,065,244 | *67.7* |
| | Barbara Hafer (R) | 987,516 | *32.3* |

**Pennsylvania**
*1. Independent Democratic-Republican.*

# RHODE ISLAND

(Ratified the Constitution May 29, 1790)

| | Candidates | Votes | % |
|---|---|---|---|
| 1790-1796 | Arthur Fenner | ✔ | |
| 1797 | Arthur Fenner | 1,204 | |
| 1798-1800 | Arthur Fenner | ✔ | |
| 1801 | Arthur Fenner | 3,756 | |
| 1802 | Arthur Fenner | 3,802 | *66.3* |
| | William Greene | 1,934 | *33.7* |
| 1803-1805 | Arthur Fenner | ✔ | |
| 1806 | Richard Jackson Jr. | 1,662* | *43.1* |
| | Henry Smith | 1,097 | *28.4* |
| | Peleg Arnold | 1,094 | *28.3* |
| 1807 | James Fenner | 2,564 | *65.9* |
| | Seth Wheaton | 1,268 | *32.6* |
| 1808-1810 | James Fenner | ✔ | |
| 1811 | William Jones (FED) | 3,885 | *51.1* |
| | James Fenner | 3,651 | *48.1* |
| 1812 | William Jones (FED) | 4,122 | *51.5* |
| | James Fenner | 3,874 | *48.4* |
| 1813 | William Jones | 3,350 | |
| 1814 | William Jones | 2,713 | *76.6* |
| 1815 | William Jones (FED) | 3,372 | *56.6* |
| | Peleg Arnold (D-R) | 2,588 | *43.4* |
| 1816 | William Jones (FED) | 3,591 | *52.4* |
| | Nehemiah R. Knight (D-R) | 3,259 | *47.6* |
| 1817 | Nehemiah R. Knight (D-R) | 3,949 | *50.4* |
| | William Jones (FED) | 3,878 | *49.5* |
| 1818 | Nehemiah R. Knight (D-R) | 4,509 | *53.7* |
| | Elisha R. Potter (FED) | 3,893 | *46.3* |
| 1819 | Nehemiah R. Knight | 2,664 | |
| 1820 | Nehemiah R. Knight | 1,981 | *100.0* |
| 1821 | William C. Gibbs (D-R) | 3,801 | *57.6* |
| | Samuel W. Bridgham | 2,801[1] | |
| 1822 | William C. Gibbs | 2,092 | *100.0* |
| 1823 | William C. Gibbs | 1,647 | *100.0* |
| 1824 | James Fenner | 2,146 | *78.3* |
| | Wheeler Martin | 594 | *21.7* |

**703**

| | Candidates | Votes | % |
|---|---|---|---|
| 1825 | James Fenner | 1,731 | 100.0 |
| 1826 | James Fenner | ✔ | |
| 1827 | James Fenner | 2,421 | 100.0 |
| 1828 | James Fenner | 4,233 | 100.0 |
| 1829 | James Fenner | 3,584 | 100.0 |
| 1830 | James Fenner | 2,793 | 63.1 |
| | Asa Messer | 1,455 | 32.9 |
| 1831 | Lemuel H. Arnold | 3,780 | 56.8 |
| | James Fenner | 2,877 | 43.2 |
| 1832 | Lemuel H. Arnold | 2,711* | 48.5 |
| | James Fenner | 2,283 | 40.8 |
| | William Sprague | 592 | 10.6 |
| 1833 | John Brown Francis | 4,025 | 55.0 |
| | Lemuel H. Arnold | 3,292 | 45.0 |
| 1834 | John Brown Francis | 3,676 | 51.0 |
| | Nehemiah R. Knight | 3,520 | 48.9 |
| 1835 | John Brown Francis | 3,880 | 50.7 |
| | Nehemiah R. Knight | 3,774 | 49.3 |
| 1836 | John Brown Francis | 4,020 | 56.2 |
| | Tristam Burges | 2,984 | 41.7 |
| 1837 | John Brown Francis | 2,716 | 73.1 |
| | William Peckham | 946 | 25.5 |
| 1838 | William Sprague | 3,984 | 52.5 |
| | John Brown Francis | 3,504 | 46.2 |
| 1839 | William Sprague | 2,948* | 47.4 |
| | Nathaniel Bullock | 2,771 | 44.6 |
| | Tristam Burges | 457 | 7.4 |
| 1840 | Samuel Ward King (W) | 4,797 | 58.4 |
| | Thomas F. Carpenter | 3,418 | 41.6 |
| 1841 | Samuel Ward King (W) | 2,648 | 97.7 |
| 1842 | Samuel Ward King (W) | 4,866 | 67.9 |
| | Thomas F. Carpenter | 2,291 | 32.0 |
| 1843 | James Fenner (L & O W) | 9,140 | 55.3 |
| | Thomas F. Carpenter (D) | 7,393 | 44.7 |
| 1844 | James Fenner (LAW ORD) | 5,560 | 96.4 |
| 1845 | Charles Jackson (LIBER W) | 7,900 | 50.4 |
| | James Fenner (L & O W) | 7,699 | 49.2 |
| 1846 | Byron Diman (L & O W) | 7,477† | 49.8 |
| | Charles Jackson (D & LIBN) | 7,391 | 49.2 |
| 1847 | Elisha Harris (W) | 6,300 | 55.3 |
| | Olney Ballou (D) | 4,350 | 38.2 |
| 1848 | Elisha Harris (W) | 5,695 | 58.0 |
| | Adnah Sackett (D) | 3,683 | 37.5 |
| 1849 | Henry B. Anthony (W) | 5,081 | 59.0 |
| | Adnah Sackett (D) | 2,964 | 34.4 |
| | Edward Harris (F SOIL) | 458 | 5.3 |
| 1850 | Henry B. Anthony (W) | 3,629 | 80.2 |
| | Edward Harris (F SOIL) | 761 | 16.8 |
| 1851 | Philip Allen (D) | 6,958 | 52.6 |
| | Josiah Chapin (W) | 6,071 | 45.9 |
| 1852 | Philip Allen (D) | 9,184 | 51.2 |
| | Elisha Harris (W) | 8,746 | 48.8 |
| 1853 | Philip Allen (D) | 10,371 | 54.2 |
| | William W. Hoppin (W) | 8,228 | 43.0 |
| 1854 | William W. Hoppin (W) | 9,112 | 58.4 |
| | Francis M. Dimond (D) | 6,484 | 41.6 |
| 1855 | William W. Hoppin (W & AM) | 10,466 | 81.5 |
| | Americus V. Potter (D) | 2,306 | 18.0 |
| 1856 | William W. Hoppin (AM & R) | 10,035 | 58.3 |
| | Americus V. Potter (D) | 7,158 | 41.6 |
| 1857 | Elisha Dyer (R) | 9,621 | 65.3 |
| | Americus V. Potter (D) | 5,123 | 34.8 |
| 1858 | Elisha Dyer (R) | 7,934 | 69.0 |
| | Elisha R. Potter (D) | 3,572 | 31.0 |
| 1859 | Thomas G. Turner (R) | 8,904 | 71.3 |
| | Elisha R. Potter (D) | 3,567 | 28.6 |
| 1860 | William Sprague (FUS) | 12,295 | 52.8 |
| | Seth Padelford (R) | 10,835 | 46.6 |
| 1861 | William Sprague (UN) | 11,844 | 53.7 |
| | James Y. Smith (R) | 10,200 | 46.3 |
| 1862 | William Sprague (UN) | 11,195 | 99.5 |
| 1863 | James Y. Smith (R) | 10,828 | 58.0 |
| | William C. Cozzens (D & CST) | 7,537 | 40.4 |
| 1864 | James Y. Smith (UN R) | 8,840 | 50.4 |
| | George H. Browne (D) | 7,302 | 41.7 |
| | Amos C. Barstow (CONST) | 1,339 | 7.6 |
| 1865 | James Y. Smith (UN R) | 10,061 | 93.0 |
| 1866 | Ambrose E. Burnside (R) | 8,197 | 73.3 |
| | Lymon Pierce (D) | 2,816 | 25.2 |
| 1867 | Ambrose E. Burnside (R) | 7,372 | 69.9 |
| | Lymon Pierce (D) | 3,178 | 30.1 |
| 1868 | Ambrose E. Burnside (R) | 10,038 | 63.7 |
| | Lymon Pierce (D) | 5,731 | 36.3 |
| 1869 | Seth Padelford (R) | 7,370 | 68.5 |
| | Lymon Pierce (D) | 3,390 | 31.5 |
| 1870 | Seth Padelford (R) | 10,493 | 62.5 |
| | Lymon Pierce (D) | 6,295 | 37.5 |
| 1871 | Seth Padelford (R) | 8,838 | 62.2 |
| | Thomas Steere (D) | 5,367 | 37.8 |
| 1872 | Seth Padelford (R) | 9,455 | 53.6 |
| | Olney Arnold (D) | 8,193 | 46.4 |
| 1873 | Henry Howard (R) | 9,656 | 71.8 |
| | Benjamin G. Chace (D) | 3,786 | 28.2 |
| 1874 | Henry Howard (R) | 12,335 | 87.5 |
| | Lymon Pierce (D) | 1,589 | 11.3 |
| 1875 | Rowland Hazard (I) | 8,724 | 39.2 |
| | Henry Lippitt (R) | 8,368† | 37.6 |
| | Charles R. Cutler (D) | 5,166 | 23.2 |
| 1876 | Henry Lippitt (R) | 8,689† | 45.6 |
| | Albert C. Howard (P) | 6,733 | 35.4 |
| | William B. Beach (D) | 3,599 | 18.9 |
| 1877 | Charles C. Van Zandt (R & TEMP) | 12,455 | 50.9 |
| | Jerothmul B. Barnaby (D) | 11,783 | 48.2 |
| 1878 | Charles C. Van Zandt (R & TEMP) | 11,454 | 58.1 |
| | Isaac Lawrence (D) | 7,639 | 38.8 |
| 1879 | Charles C. Van Zandt (R & TEMP) | 9,717 | 62.1 |
| | Thomas W. Segar (D) | 5,506 | 35.2 |
| 1880 | Alfred H. Littlefield (R) | 10,224† | 44.8 |
| | Horace A. Kimball (D) | 7,440 | 32.6 |
| | Albert C. Howard (IR & P) | 5,047 | 22.1 |
| 1881 | Alfred H. Littlefield (R) | 10,849 | 67.0 |
| | Horace A. Kimball (D) | 4,756 | 29.4 |
| 1882 | Alfred H. Littlefield (R) | 10,056 | 64.8 |
| | Horace A. Kimball (D) | 5,311 | 34.2 |
| 1883 | Augustus O. Bourn (R) | 13,078 | 54.5 |
| | William Sprague (D) | 10,201 | 42.5 |
| 1884 | Augustus O. Bourn (R) | 15,936 | 62.4 |
| | Thomas W. Segar (D) | 9,592 | 37.6 |
| 1885 | George Peabody Wetmore (R) | 12,563 | 56.0 |
| | Ziba O. Slocum (D) | 8,674 | 38.6 |
| | George H. Slade (P) | 1,206 | 5.4 |
| 1886 | George Peabody Wetmore (R) | 14,340 | 53.4 |
| | Amasa Sprague (D) | 9,994 | 37.0 |
| | George H. Slade (P) | 2,585 | 9.6 |
| 1887 | John W. Davis (D) | 18,095 | 51.5 |
| | George Peabody Wetmore (R) | 15,111 | 43.0 |
| | Thomas H. Peabody (P) | 1,895 | 5.4 |
| 1888 | Royal C. Taft (R) | 20,744 | 52.3 |
| | John W. Davis (D) | 17,556 | 44.3 |
| 1889 | John W. Davis (D) | 21,289 | 49.4 |
| | Herbert W. Ladd (R) | 16,870† | 39.1 |
| | James H. Chace (LAW ENF) | 3,596 | 8.3 |
| 1890 | John W. Davis (D) | 20,548† | 48.8 |
| | Herbert W. Ladd (R) | 18,988 | 45.1 |
| 1891 | John W. Davis (D) | 22,249 | 49.0 |
| | Herbert W. Ladd (R) | 20,995† | 46.2 |
| 1892 | D. Russell Brown (R) | 27,461 | 50.2 |
| | William T. C. Wardwell (D) | 25,433 | 46.5 |
| 1893 | David S. Baker (D) | 22,015* | 46.7 |
| | D. Russell Brown (R) | 21,830 | 46.3 |
| | Metcalf (P) | 3,265 | 6.9 |
| 1894 | D. Russell Brown (R) | 29,157 | 53.2 |
| | David S. Baker Jr. (D) | 22,650 | 41.3 |

| | Candidates | Votes | % |
|------|------------|-------|---|
| 1895 | Charles Warren Lippitt (R) | 25,098 | *56.9* |
| | George L. Littlefield (D) | 14,289 | *32.4* |
| | Smith Quimby (P) | 2,624 | *6.0* |
| 1896 | Charles Warren Lippitt (R) | 28,472 | *56.4* |
| | George L. Littlefield (D) | 17,061 | *33.8* |
| | Thomas H. Peabody (P) | 2,950 | *5.8* |
| 1897 | Elisha Dyer (R) | 24,309 | *58.1* |
| | Daniel T. Church (D) | 13,675 | *32.7* |
| | Thomas H. Peabody (P) | 2,096 | *5.0* |
| 1898 | Elisha Dyer (R) | 24,743 | *57.7* |
| | Daniel T. Church (D) | 13,224 | *30.9* |
| | James P. Reid (SOC LAB) | 2,877 | *6.7* |
| 1899 | Elisha Dyer (R) | 24,308 | *56.4* |
| | George W. Greene (D) | 14,602 | *33.9* |
| | Thomas F. Herrick (SOC LAB) | 2,941 | *6.8* |
| 1900 | William Gregory (R) | 26,043 | *54.3* |
| | Nathan W. Littlefield (D) | 17,184 | *35.9* |
| | James P. Reid (SOC LAB) | 2,858 | *6.0* |
| 1901 | William Gregory (R) | 25,575 | *53.6* |
| | Lucius F. C. Garvin (D) | 19,038 | *39.9* |
| 1902 | Lucius F. C. Garvin (D) | 32,279 | *54.0* |
| | Charles Dean Kimball (R) | 24,541 | *41.0* |
| 1903 | Lucius F. C. Garvin (D) | 30,578 | *49.3* |
| | Samuel Pomeroy Colt (R) | 29,275 | *47.2* |
| 1904 | George H. Utter (R) | 33,821 | *48.9* |
| | Lucius F. C. Garvin (D) | 32,965 | *47.7* |
| 1905 | George H. Utter (R) | 31,311 | *53.3* |
| | Lucius F. C. Garvin (D) | 25,816 | *44.0* |
| 1906 | James H. Higgins (D) | 33,195 | *49.9* |
| | George H. Utter (R) | 31,877 | *47.9* |
| 1907 | James H. Higgins (D) | 33,300 | *50.4* |
| | Frederick H. Jackson (R) | 31,005 | *46.9* |
| 1908 | Aram J. Pothier (R) | 38,676 | *52.6* |
| | Olney Arnold (D) | 31,406 | *42.7* |
| 1909 | Aram J. Pothier (R) | 37,107 | *57.0* |
| | Olney Arnold (D) | 25,338 | *38.9* |
| 1910 | Aram J. Pothier (R) | 33,540 | *49.6* |
| | Lewis A. Waterman (D) | 32,400 | *47.9* |
| 1911 | Aram J. Pothier (R) | 37,969 | *53.4* |
| | Lewis A. Waterman (D) | 30,575 | *43.0* |
| 1912 | Aram J. Pothier (R) | 34,133 | *43.7* |
| | Theodore Francis Green (D) | 32,725 | *41.9* |
| | Albert H. Humes (PROG) | 8,457 | *10.8* |
| 1914 | R. Livingston Beeckman (R) | 41,996 | *53.8* |
| | Patrick H. Quinn (D) | 32,182 | *41.3* |
| 1916 | R. Livingston Beeckman (R) | 49,524 | *55.9* |
| | Addison P. Munroe (D) | 36,158 | *40.8* |
| 1918 | R. Livingston Beeckman (R) | 42,682 | *53.1* |
| | Alberic A. Archambault (D) | 36,031 | *44.8* |
| 1920 | Emery J. San Souci (R) | 109,138 | *64.6* |
| | Edward M. Sullivan (D) | 55,963 | *33.2* |
| 1922 | William S. Flynn (D) | 81,935 | *51.7* |
| | Harold J. Gross (R) | 74,724 | *47.2* |
| 1924 | Aram J. Pothier (R) | 122,749 | *58.6* |
| | Felix A. Toupin (D) | 85,942 | *41.0* |
| 1926 | Aram J. Pothier (R) | 89,574 | *53.9* |
| | Joseph H. Gainer (D) | 75,882 | *45.7* |
| 1928 | Norman S. Case (R) | 121,748 | *51.6* |
| | Alberic A. Archambault (D) | 113,594 | *48.1* |
| 1930 | Norman S. Case (R) | 112,070 | *50.5* |
| | Theodore Francis Green (D) | 108,558 | *48.9* |
| 1932 | Theodore Francis Green (D) | 146,474 | *55.2* |
| | Norman S. Case (R) | 115,438 | *43.5* |
| 1934 | Theodore Francis Green (D) | 140,258 | *56.6* |
| | Luke H. Callan (R) | 105,139 | *42.4* |
| 1936 | Robert E. Quinn (D) | 160,776 | *53.7* |
| | Charles P. Sisson (R) | 137,369 | *45.9* |
| 1938 | William H. Vanderbilt (R) | 167,003 | *53.7* |
| | Robert E. Quinn (D) | 129,603 | *41.6* |
| 1940 | J. Howard McGrath (D) | 177,937 | *55.8* |
| | William H. Vanderbilt (R) | 140,480 | *44.1* |

| | Candidates | Votes | % |
|------|------------|-------|---|
| 1942 | J. Howard McGrath (D) | 139,407 | *58.5* |
| | James O. McManus (R) | 98,741 | *41.5* |
| 1944 | J. Howard McGrath (D) | 179,010 | *60.7* |
| | Norman D. Macleod (R) | 116,158 | *39.4* |
| 1946 | John O. Pastore (D) | 148,885 | *54.1* |
| | John G. Murphy (R) | 126,456 | *45.9* |
| 1948 | John O. Pastore (D) | 198,056 | *61.2* |
| | Albert P. Ruerat (R) | 124,441 | *38.4* |
| 1950 | Dennis J. Roberts (D) | 176,125 | *59.3* |
| | Eugene J. Lachapelle (R) | 120,683 | *40.7* |
| 1952 | Dennis J. Roberts (D) | 215,587 | *52.6* |
| | Raoul Archambault Jr. (R) | 194,102 | *47.4* |
| 1954 | Dennis J. Roberts (D) | 189,595 | *57.7* |
| | Dean J. Lewis (R) | 137,131 | *41.7* |
| 1956 | Dennis J. Roberts (D) | 192,315 | *50.1* |
| | Christopher Del Sesto (R) | 191,604 | *49.9* |
| 1958 | Christopher Del Sesto (R) | 176,505 | *50.9* |
| | Dennis J. Roberts (D) | 170,275 | *49.1* |
| 1960 | John A. Notte Jr. (D) | 227,318 | *56.6* |
| | Christopher Del Sesto (R) | 174,044 | *43.4* |
| 1962 | John H. Chafee (R) | 163,952 | *50.1* |
| | John A. Notte Jr. (D) | 163,554 | *49.9* |
| 1964 | John H. Chafee (R) | 239,501 | *61.2* |
| | Edward P. Gallogly (D) | 152,165 | *38.9* |
| 1966 | John H. Chafee (R) | 210,202 | *63.3* |
| | Horace E. Hobbs (D) | 121,862 | *36.7* |
| 1968 | Frank Licht (D) | 195,766 | *51.0* |
| | John H. Chafee (R) | 187,958 | *49.0* |
| 1970 | Frank Licht (D) | 173,420 | *50.1* |
| | Herbert F. DeSimone (R) | 171,549 | *49.5* |
| 1972 | Philip W. Noel (D) | 216,953 | *52.6* |
| | Herbert F. DeSimone (R) | 194,315 | *47.1* |
| 1974 | Philip W. Noel (D) | 252,436 | *78.5* |
| | James W. Nugent (R) | 69,224 | *21.5* |
| 1976 | J. Joseph Garrahy (D) | 218,561 | *54.8* |
| | James L. Taft (R) | 178,254 | *44.7* |
| 1978 | J. Joseph Garrahy (D) | 197,386 | *62.8* |
| | Lincoln Almond (R) | 96,596 | *30.7* |
| | Joseph A. Doorley Jr. (I) | 20,381 | *6.5* |
| 1980 | J. Joseph Garrahy (D) | 299,174 | *73.7* |
| | Vincent A. Cianci (R) | 106,729 | *26.3* |
| 1982 | J. Joseph Garrahy (D) | 247,208 | *73.3* |
| | Vincent Mazullo (R) | 79,602 | *23.6* |
| 1984 | Edward D. DiPrete (R) | 245,059 | *60.0* |
| | Anthony J. Solomon (D) | 163,311 | *40.0* |
| 1986 | Edward D. DiPrete (R) | 208,822 | *64.7* |
| | Bruce Sundlun (D) | 104,508 | *32.4* |
| 1988 | Edward D. DiPrete (R) | 203,550 | *50.8* |
| | Bruce Sundlun (D) | 196,936 | *49.2* |
| 1990 | Bruce Sundlun (D) | 264,411 | *74.2* |
| | Edward D. DiPrete (R) | 92,177 | *25.8* |

**Rhode Island**
   1. *Includes votes for other candidates.*

# SOUTH CAROLINA

(Ratified the Constitution May 23, 1788)

| | Candidates | Votes | % |
|------|------------|-------|---|
| 1865 [1] | James L. Orr | 9,771 | *51.8* |
| | Wade Hampton | 9,109 | *48.3* |
| 1868 | Robert K. Scott (R) | 69,693 | *75.0* |
| | W. D. Porter | 23,087 | *24.8* |
| 1870 | Robert K. Scott (R) | 85,071 | *62.3* |
| | R. B. Carpenter (D) | 51,537 | *37.7* |
| 1872 | Franklin J. Moses Jr. (R) | 69,838 | *65.4* |
| | Reuben Tomlinson (ID) | 36,553 | *34.2* |

**705**

| | Candidates | Votes | % |
|---|---|---|---|
| 1874 | Daniel H. Chamberlain (R) | 80,403 | 53.9 |
| | John T. Green (I REF D) | 68,818 | 46.1 |
| 1876 | Wade Hampton (D) | 92,261 | 50.3 |
| | Daniel H. Chamberlain (R) | 91,127 | 49.7 |
| 1878 | Wade Hampton (D) | 119,550 | 99.8 |
| 1880 | Johnson Hagood (D) | 117,432 | 96.4 |
| 1882 | Hugh S. Thompson (D) | 67,158 | 79.5 |
| | McLane (G) | 17,319 | 20.5 |
| 1884 | Hugh S. Thompson (D) | 67,895 | 100.0 |
| 1886 | John P. Richardson (D) | 33,114 | 100.0 |
| 1888 | John P. Richardson (D) | 58,730 | 100.0 |
| 1890 | Benjamin Ryan Tillman (D) | 59,159 | 79.8 |
| | A. C. Haskell (ID) | 14,828 | 20.0 |
| 1892 | Benjamin Ryan Tillman (D) | 56,673 | 99.9 |
| 1894 | John Gary Evans (D) | 39,507 | 69.6 |
| | Sampson Pope (POP) | 17,278 | 30.4 |
| 1896 | William H. Ellerbe (D) | 59,424 | 89.1 |
| | Sampson Pope (LW R) | 4,432 | 6.7 |
| 1898 | William H. Ellerbe (D) | 28,225 | 100.0 |
| 1900 | Miles B. McSweeney (D) | 46,457 | 100.0 |
| 1902 | Duncan C. Heyward (D) | 31,817 | 100.0 |
| 1904 | Duncan C. Heyward (D) | 51,917 | 100.0 |
| 1906 | Martin F. Ansel (D) | 30,251 | 99.9 |
| 1908 | Martin F. Ansel (D) | 61,060 | 100.0 |
| 1910 | Coleman L. Blease (D) | 30,739 | 99.8 |
| 1912 | Coleman L. Blease (D) | 44,122 | 99.5 |
| 1914 | Richard I. Manning (D) | 34,600 | 99.8 |
| 1916 | Richard I. Manning (D) | 60,396 | 97.9 |
| 1918 | Robert A. Cooper (D) | 25,267 | 100.0 |
| 1920 | Robert A. Cooper (D) | 58,050 | 100.0 |
| 1922 | Thomas G. McLeod (D) | 34,065 | 100.0 |
| 1924 | Thomas G. McLeod (D) | 53,545 | 100.0 |
| 1926 | John G. Richards (D) | 16,589 | 100.0 |
| 1930 | Ibra C. Blackwood (D) | 17,790 | 100.0 |
| 1934 | Olin D. Johnston (D) | 23,177 | 100.0 |
| 1938 | Burnet R. Maybank (D) | 49,009 | 99.4 |
| 1942 | Olin D. Johnston (D) | 23,859 | 100.0 |
| 1946 | J. Strom Thurmond (D) | 26,520 | 100.0 |
| 1950 | James F. Byrnes (D) | 50,633 | 100.0 |
| 1954 | George Bell Timmerman Jr. (D) | 214,204 | 100.0 |
| 1958 | Ernest F. Hollings (D) | 77,714 | 100.0 |
| 1962 | Donald Russell (D) | 253,704 | 100.0 |
| 1966 | Robert E. McNair (D) | 255,854 | 58.2 |
| | Joseph O. Rogers Jr. (R) | 184,088 | 41.8 |
| 1970 | John C. West (D) | 250,551 | 51.7 |
| | Albert Watson (R) | 221,233 | 45.6 |
| 1974 | James B. Edwards (R) | 266,109 | 50.9 |
| | W. J. Bryan Dorn (D) | 248,938 | 47.6 |
| 1978 | Richard W. Riley (D) | 384,898 | 61.4 |
| | Edward L. Young (R) | 236,946 | 37.8 |
| 1982 | Richard W. Riley (D) | 468,819 | 69.8 |
| | W. D. Workman (R) | 202,806 | 30.2 |
| 1986 | Carroll Campbell (R) | 384,565 | 51.0 |
| | Mike Daniel (D) | 361,325 | 47.9 |
| 1990 | Carroll Campbell (R) | 528,831 | 69.5 |
| | Theo Mitchell (D) | 212,034 | 27.9 |

**South Carolina**
1. Before 1865 governor chosen by legislature.

# SOUTH DAKOTA

(Became a state Nov. 2, 1889)

| | Candidates | Votes | % |
|---|---|---|---|
| 1889 | Arthur C. Mellette (R) | 53,964 | 69.3 |
| | P. F. McClure (D) | 23,840 | 30.6 |

| | Candidates | Votes | % |
|---|---|---|---|
| 1890 | Arthur C. Mellette (R) | 34,487 | 44.5 |
| | H. L. Loucks (I) | 24,591 | 31.7 |
| | Maris Taylor (D) | 18,484 | 23.8 |
| 1892 | Charles H. Sheldon (R) | 33,214 | 47.2 |
| | A. L. Vanosdel (I) | 22,323 | 31.7 |
| | Peter Couchman (D) | 14,872 | 21.1 |
| 1894 | Charles H. Sheldon (R) | 40,402 | 52.0 |
| | Isaac Howe (I) | 27,568 | 35.5 |
| | James A. Ward (D) | 8,756 | 11.3 |
| 1896 | Andrew E. Lee (PP) | 41,177 | 49.8 |
| | A. O. Ringsrud (R) | 40,869 | 49.4 |
| 1898 | Andrew E. Lee (FUS) | 37,319 | 49.6 |
| | Kirk G. Phillips (R) | 36,980 | 49.2 |
| 1900 | Charles N. Herreid (R) | 53,788 | 56.3 |
| | Burre H. Lien (FUS) | 40,091 | 42.0 |
| 1902 | Charles N. Herreid (R) | 48,195 | 64.7 |
| | John W. Martin (D) | 21,396 | 28.7 |
| 1904 | Samuel H. Elrod (R) | 68,561 | 68.3 |
| | Louis N. Crill (D) | 24,772 | 24.7 |
| 1906 | Coe I. Crawford (R) | 48,709 | 65.3 |
| | John A. Stransky (D) | 19,923 | 26.7 |
| 1908 | Robert S. Vessey (R) | 62,989 | 55.3 |
| | Andrew E. Lee (D) | 44,876 | 39.4 |
| 1910 | Robert S. Vessey (R) | 61,744 | 58.4 |
| | Chauncey L. Wood (D) | 37,983 | 35.9 |
| 1912 | Frank M. Byrne (R) | 57,161 | 48.5 |
| | Edwin S. Johnson (D) | 53,850 | 45.7 |
| 1914 | Frank M. Byrne (R) | 49,138 | 50.1 |
| | J. W. McCarter (D) | 34,542 | 35.2 |
| | R. O. Richards (I) | 9,725 | 9.9 |
| 1916 | Peter Norbeck (R) | 72,789 | 56.6 |
| | Rinehart (D) | 50,545 | 39.3 |
| 1918 | Peter Norbeck (R) | 51,175 | 53.2 |
| | Mark P. Bates (NON PART) | 25,118 | 26.1 |
| | James B. Bird (D) | 17,858 | 18.6 |
| 1920 | William H. McMaster (R) | 103,592 | 56.3 |
| | Mark P. Bates (NON PART) | 48,426 | 26.3 |
| | W. W. Howes (D) | 31,870 | 17.3 |
| 1922 | William H. McMaster (R) | 78,984 | 45.0 |
| | Louis N. Crill (D) | 50,409 | 28.7 |
| | Lorraine Daly (NON PART) | 46,033 | 26.2 |
| 1924 | Carl Gunderson (R) | 109,914 | 53.9 |
| | William J. Bulow (D) | 46,613 | 22.9 |
| | A. L. Putnam (F-LAB) | 27,027 | 13.3 |
| | R. O. Richards (I) | 20,359 | 10.0 |
| 1926 | William J. Bulow (D) | 87,076 | 47.4 |
| | Carl Gunderson (R) | 74,101 | 40.3 |
| | Tom Ayres (F-LAB) | 11,958 | 6.5 |
| | John E. Hipple (I) | 10,637 | 5.8 |
| 1928 | William J. Bulow (D) | 136,016 | 52.5 |
| | Buell F. Jones (R) | 121,643 | 46.9 |
| 1930 | Warren E. Green (R) | 107,643 | 53.0 |
| | D. A. McCullough (D) | 93,954 | 46.2 |
| 1932 | Tom Berry (D) | 158,058 | 55.6 |
| | Warren E. Green (R) | 120,473 | 42.4 |
| 1934 | Tom Berry (D) | 172,228 | 58.6 |
| | William C. Allen (R) | 119,477 | 40.7 |
| 1936 | Leslie Jensen (R) | 151,659 | 51.6 |
| | Tom Berry (D) | 142,255 | 48.4 |
| 1938 | Harlan J. Bushfield (R) | 149,362 | 54.0 |
| | Oscar Fosheim (D) | 127,485 | 46.1 |
| 1940 | Harlan J. Bushfield (R) | 167,686 | 55.1 |
| | Lewis W. Bicknell (D) | 136,428 | 44.9 |
| 1942 | Merrell Q. Sharpe (R) | 109,786 | 61.5 |
| | Lewis B. Bicknell (D) | 68,706 | 38.5 |
| 1944 | Merrell Q. Sharpe (R) | 148,646 | 65.5 |
| | Lynn Fellows (D) | 78,276 | 34.5 |
| 1946 | George T. Mickelson (R) | 108,998 | 67.2 |
| | Richard Haeder (D) | 53,294 | 32.8 |
| 1948 | George T. Mickelson (R) | 149,883 | 61.1 |
| | Harold J. Volz (D) | 95,489 | 38.9 |

| | Candidates | Votes | % |
|------|------------|-------|---|
| 1950 | Sigurd Anderson (R) | 154,254 | 60.9 |
| | Joe Robbie (D) | 99,062 | 39.1 |
| 1952 | Sigurd Anderson (R) | 203,102 | 70.2 |
| | Sherman A. Iverson (D) | 86,412 | 29.9 |
| 1954 | Joe Foss (R) | 133,878 | 56.7 |
| | Ed C. Martin (D) | 102,377 | 43.3 |
| 1956 | Joe Foss (R) | 158,819 | 54.4 |
| | Ralph Herseth (D) | 133,198 | 45.6 |
| 1958 | Ralph Herseth (D) | 132,761 | 51.4 |
| | Phil Saunders (R) | 125,520 | 48.6 |
| 1960 | Archie M. Gubbrud (R) | 154,530 | 50.7 |
| | Ralph Herseth (D) | 150,095 | 49.3 |
| 1962 | Archie M. Gubbrud (R) | 143,682 | 56.1 |
| | Ralph Herseth (D) | 112,438 | 43.9 |
| 1964 | Nils A. Boe (R) | 150,151 | 51.7 |
| | John F. Lindley (D) | 140,419 | 48.3 |
| 1966 | Nils A. Boe (R) | 131,710 | 57.7 |
| | Robert Chamberlin (D) | 96,504 | 42.3 |
| 1968 | Frank L. Farrar (R) | 159,646 | 57.7 |
| | Robert Chamberlin (D) | 117,260 | 42.4 |
| 1970 | Richard F. Kneip (D) | 131,616 | 54.9 |
| | Frank L. Farrar (R) | 108,347 | 45.2 |
| 1972 | Richard F. Kneip (D) | 185,012 | 60.0 |
| | Carveth Thompson (R) | 123,165 | 40.0 |
| 1974 | Richard F. Kneip (D) | 149,151 | 53.6 |
| | John E. Olson (R) | 129,077 | 46.4 |
| 1978 | William J. Janklow (R) | 147,116 | 56.6 |
| | Roger McKellips (D) | 112,679 | 43.4 |
| 1982 | William J. Janklow (R) | 197,426 | 70.9 |
| | Michael J. O'Connor (D) | 81,136 | 29.1 |
| 1986 | George S. Mickelson (R) | 152,543 | 51.8 |
| | R. Lars Herseth (D) | 141,898 | 48.2 |
| 1990 | George S. Mickelson (R) | 151,198 | 58.9 |
| | Bob L. Samuelson (D) | 105,525 | 41.1 |

# TENNESSEE

(Became a state June 1, 1796)

| | Candidates | Votes | % |
|---------|------------|-------|---|
| 1796 [1] | John Sevier | ✔ | |
| 1797 | John Sevier | ✔ | |
| 1799 [2] | John Sevier | 5,295 | 99.7 |
| 1801 | Archibald Roane | 8,438 | 99.9 |
| 1803 | John Sevier | 6,786 | 58.0 |
| | Archibald Roane | 4,923 | 42.0 |
| 1805 [2] | John Sevier | 10,293 | 63.7 |
| | Archibald Roane | 5,855 | 36.3 |
| 1807 | John Sevier | ✔ | |
| | William Cocke | | |
| 1809 | Willie Blount | ✔ | |
| | William Cocke | | |
| 1811 | Willie Blount | ✔ | |
| 1813 | Willie Blount | 21,510 | |
| 1815 [2] | Joseph McMinn | 14,873 | 42.8 |
| | Robert Weakley | 7,209 | 20.7 |
| | Jesse Wharton | 6,038 | 17.4 |
| | Robert C. Foster | 3,809 | 11.0 |
| | Thomas Johnson | 2,826 | 8.1 |
| 1817 | Joseph McMinn | 27,802 | 64.3 |
| | Robert C. Foster | 15,450 | 35.7 |
| 1819 | Joseph McMinn | 35,244 | |
| | Enoch Parsons | | |
| 1821 | William Carroll | 42,210 | 79.0 |
| | Edward Ward | 11,200 | 21.0 |
| 1823 | William Carroll | 32,597 | |
| 1825 | William Carroll | 14,807 | 99.8 |

| | Candidates | Votes | % |
|------|------------|-------|---|
| 1827 | Samuel Houston | 40,017 | 54.7 |
| | Newton Cannon | 31,244 | 42.7 |
| 1829 | William Carroll | 59,875 | 99.8 |
| 1831 | William Carroll (D) | 64,834 | 97.3 |
| 1833 | William Carroll (D) | 53,224 | 97.8 |
| 1835 | Newton Cannon (W) | 41,862 | 50.4 |
| | William Carroll | 33,180 | 40.0 |
| | Humphries | 7,999 | 9.6 |
| 1837 | Newton Cannon (W) | 53,385 | 60.9 |
| | Armstrong (D) | 34,312 | 39.1 |
| 1839 | James K. Polk (D) | 53,714 | 51.0 |
| | Newton Cannon (W) | 51,624 | 49.0 |
| 1841 | James C. Jones (W) | 53,829 | 51.5 |
| | James K. Polk (D) | 50,705 | 48.5 |
| 1843 | James C. Jones (W) | 52,584 | 51.3 |
| | James K. Polk (D) | 49,944 | 48.7 |
| 1845 | Aaron V. Brown (D) | 58,277 | 50.6 |
| | Foster (W) | 56,805 | 49.4 |
| 1847 | Neill S. Brown (W) | 61,450 | 50.4 |
| | Aaron V. Brown (D) | 60,454 | 49.6 |
| 1849 | William Trousdale (D) | 61,740 | 50.6 |
| | Neill S. Brown (W) | 60,340 | 49.4 |
| 1851 | William B. Campbell (W) | 63,423 | 50.7 |
| | William Trousdale (D) | 61,648 | 49.3 |
| 1853 | Andrew Johnson (D) | 63,413 | 50.9 |
| | Henry (W) | 61,163 | 49.1 |
| 1855 | Andrew Johnson (D) | 67,499 | 50.8 |
| | Gentry (AM) | 65,332 | 49.2 |
| 1857 | Isham G. Harris (D) | 71,539 | 54.4 |
| | Hatton (AM) | 59,867 | 45.6 |
| 1859 | Isham G. Harris (D) | 76,226 | 52.8 |
| | Netherland (OPP) | 68,218 | 47.2 |
| 1863 | Robert L. Caruthers | 7,050 | 98.4 |
| 1865 | William G. Brownlow (W, R) | 22,814 | 99.9 |
| 1867 | William G. Brownlow (R) | 74,484 | 76.9 |
| | Emerson Etheridge (C) | 22,440 | 23.2 |
| 1869 | De Witt Clinton Senter (CR) | 120,333 | 68.6 |
| | William B. Stokes (RAD R) | 55,036 | 31.4 |
| 1870 | John C. Brown (D) | 76,666 | 65.0 |
| | W. H. Wisener (R) | 41,278 | 35.0 |
| 1872 | John C. Brown (LR) | 97,689 | 53.7 |
| | Freeman (R) | 84,100 | 46.3 |
| 1874 | James D. Porter Jr. (D) | 103,061 | 64.9 |
| | Horace Maynard (R) | 55,836 | 35.1 |
| 1876 | James D. Porter Jr. (D) | 123,740 | 58.8 |
| | Thomas (I) | 73,695 | 35.0 |
| 1878 | Albert S. Marks (D) | 89,097 | 60.3 |
| | E. M. Wight (R) | 43,175 | 29.2 |
| | R. M. Edwards (G) | 15,470 | 10.5 |
| 1880 | Alvin Hawkins (R) | 103,966 | 42.6 |
| | Wright (STC D) | 79,081 | 32.4 |
| | Wilson (LOWTAX D) | 57,568 | 23.6 |
| 1882 | William B. Bate (LOWTAX D) | 120,091 | 52.9 |
| | Alvin Hawkins (R) | 93,182 | 41.0 |
| 1884 | William B. Bate (D) | 132,201 | 51.3 |
| | Reid (R) | 125,276 | 48.7 |
| 1886 | Robert L. Taylor (D) | 126,491 | 53.5 |
| | Alfred A. Taylor (R) | 109,842 | 46.5 |
| 1888 | Robert L. Taylor (D) | 156,799 | 51.8 |
| | Samuel W. Hawkins (R) | 139,014 | 45.9 |
| 1890 | John P. Buchanan (D) | 113,536 | 56.6 |
| | Baxter (R) | 76,071 | 37.9 |
| | Kelly (P) | 11,011 | 5.5 |
| 1892 | Peter Turney (D) | 126,248 | 47.9 |
| | George W. Winsted (R) | 100,599 | 38.1 |
| | John P. Buchanan (PP) | 31,515 | 12.0 |
| 1894 | H. Clay Evans (R) | 105,164‡ | 45.2 |
| | Peter Turney (D) | 104,350 | 44.9 |
| | Mills (POP) | 23,129 | 9.9 |
| 1896 | Robert L. Taylor (D) | 156,227 | 48.8 |
| | G. N. Tillman (R) | 149,374 | 46.6 |

|      | Candidates | Votes | % |
|------|------------|------:|---:|
| 1898 | Benton McMillin (D) | 105,640 | *57.9* |
|      | Fowler (R) | 72,611 | *39.8* |
| 1900 | Benton McMillin (D) | 145,708 | *53.9* |
|      | John E. McCall (R) | 119,831 | *44.3* |
| 1902 | James B. Frazier (D) | 98,951 | *61.8* |
|      | Campbell (R) | 59,002 | *36.8* |
| 1904 | James B. Frazier (D) | 131,503 | *55.7* |
|      | Littleton (R) | 103,409 | *43.8* |
| 1906 | Malcolm R. Patterson (D) | 111,876 | *54.4* |
|      | Evans (R) | 92,804 | *45.2* |
| 1908 | Malcolm R. Patterson (D) | 133,176 | *53.7* |
|      | G. N. Tillman (R) | 113,269 | *45.7* |
| 1910 | Ben W. Hooper (R) | 133,076 | *51.9* |
|      | Robert L. Taylor (D) | 121,694 | *47.5* |
| 1912 | Ben W. Hooper (R) | 124,641 | *50.2* |
|      | Benton McMillin (D) | 116,610 | *46.9* |
| 1914 | Tom C. Rye (D) | 137,636 | *53.6* |
|      | Ben W. Hooper (R) | 117,717 | *45.8* |
| 1916 | Tom C. Rye (D) | 146,759 | *55.0* |
|      | John W. Overall (R) | 117,819 | *44.2* |
| 1918 | Albert H. Roberts (D) | 98,628 | *62.4* |
|      | H. B. Lindsay (R) | 59,518 | *37.6* |
| 1920 | Alfred A. Taylor (R) | 229,133 | *54.9* |
|      | Albert H. Roberts (D) | 185,890 | *44.6* |
| 1922 | Austin Peay (D) | 141,012 | *57.9* |
|      | Alfred A. Taylor (R) | 102,586 | *42.1* |
| 1924 | Austin Peay (D) | 162,002 | *57.2* |
|      | T. F. Peck (R) | 121,228 | *42.8* |
| 1926 | Austin Peay (D) | 84,979 | *64.7* |
|      | Walter White (R) | 46,238 | *35.2* |
| 1928 | Henry H. Horton (D) | 195,546 | *61.1* |
|      | Raleigh Hopkins (R) | 124,733 | *39.0* |
| 1930 | Henry H. Horton (D) | 153,341 | *63.8* |
|      | C. Arthur Bruce (R) | 85,558 | *35.6* |
| 1932 | Hill McAlister (D) | 169,075 | *42.8* |
|      | John E. McCall (R) | 117,797 | *29.8* |
|      | Lewis S. Pope (I) | 106,990 | *27.1* |
| 1934 | Hill McAlister (D) | 198,743 | *61.8* |
|      | Lewis S. Pope (FUS) | 122,965 | *38.2* |
| 1936 | Gordon Browning (D) | 332,523 | *80.4* |
|      | P. H. Thach (R) | 77,392 | *18.7* |
| 1938 | Prentice Cooper (D) | 210,567 | *71.7* |
|      | Howard H. Baker (R) | 83,031 | *28.3* |
| 1940 | Prentice Cooper (D) | 323,466 | *72.1* |
|      | C. Arthur Bruce (R) | 125,245 | *27.9* |
| 1942 | Prentice Cooper (D) | 120,148 | *70.2* |
|      | C. N. Frazier (R) | 51,120 | *29.9* |
| 1944 | James N. McCord (D) | 275,746 | *62.5* |
|      | J. W. Kilgo (R) | 158,742 | *36.0* |
| 1946 | James N. McCord (D) | 149,937 | *65.3* |
|      | W. O. Lowe (R) | 73,222 | *31.9* |
| 1948 | Gordon Browning (D) | 363,903 | *66.9* |
|      | Roy Acuff (R) | 179,957 | *33.1* |
| 1950 | Gordon Browning (D) | 184,437 | *78.1* |
|      | John R. Neal (R) | 51,757 | *21.9* |
| 1952 | Frank G. Clement (D) | 640,290 | *79.4* |
|      | R. Beecher Witt (R) | 166,377 | *20.6* |
| 1954 | Frank G. Clement (D) | 281,291 | *87.2* |
|      | John R. Neal (I) | 39,574 | *12.3* |
| 1958 | Buford Ellington (D) | 248,874 | *57.5* |
|      | James N. McCord (I) | 136,406 | *31.5* |
|      | Thomas P. Wall (R) | 35,938 | *8.3* |
| 1962 | Frank G. Clement (D) | 315,648 | *50.9* |
|      | William R. Anderson (I) | 203,765 | *32.8* |
|      | Hubert D. Patty (R) | 99,884 | *16.1* |
| 1966 | Buford Ellington (D) | 532,998 | *81.2* |
|      | H. L. Crowder (I) | 64,602 | *9.8* |
|      | Charles Moffett (I) | 50,221 | *7.7* |
| 1970 | Winfield Dunn (R) | 575,777 | *52.0* |
|      | John J. Hooker Jr. (D) | 509,521 | *46.0* |
| 1974 | Ray Blanton (D) | 576,833 | *55.4* |
|      | Lamar Alexander (R) | 455,467 | *43.8* |

|      | Candidates | Votes | % |
|------|------------|------:|---:|
| 1978 | Lamar Alexander (R) | 661,959 | *55.6* |
|      | Jake Butcher (D) | 523,495 | *44.0* |
| 1982 | Lamar Alexander (R) | 737,963 | *59.6* |
|      | Randy Tyree (D) | 500,937 | *40.4* |
| 1986 | Ned R. McWherter (D) | 656,602 | *54.3* |
|      | Winfield Dunn (R) | 553,449 | *45.7* |
| 1990 | Ned R. McWherter (D) | 480,885 | *60.8* |
|      | Dwight Henry (R) | 289,348 | *36.6* |

**Tennessee**

1. *Until the 1830s contests were essentially on a personal popularity basis among members of the Democratic-Republican Party.*

2. *Returns are incomplete.*

# TEXAS

(Became a state Dec. 29, 1845)

|      | Candidates | Votes | % |
|------|------------|------:|---:|
| 1845 | J. Pinckney Henderson | 7,853# | *82.0* |
|      | James B. Miller | 1,673# | *17.5* |
| 1847 | George T. Wood (D) | 6,801 | *53.5* |
|      | J. B. Miller (D) | 4,022 | *31.6* |
|      | N. H. Darnell | 1,285 | *10.1* |
| 1849 | P. Hansbrough Bell (D) | 10,226 | *48.0* |
|      | George T. Wood | 8,430 | *39.6* |
|      | John T. Mills | 2,632 | *12.4* |
| 1851 | P. Hansbrough Bell | 12,484 | *47.0* |
|      | M. T. Johnson | 5,029 | *18.9* |
|      | J. A. Green | 3,941 | *14.8* |
|      | B. H. Epperson | 2,868 | *10.8* |
|      | J. J. Chambers | 2,148 | *8.1* |
| 1853 | Elisha M. Pease (D) | 13,099 | *36.2* |
|      | W. B. Ochiltree (W) | 9,180 | *25.4* |
|      | G. T. Wood (D) | 5,983 | *16.5* |
|      | L. D. Evans (D) | 4,679 | *12.9* |
|      | T. J. Chambers (D) | 2,449 | *6.8* |
| 1855 | Elisha M. Pease (D) | 20,136 | *58.4* |
|      | D. C. Dickson (KN) | 13,081 | *37.9* |
| 1857 | Hardin R. Runnels (D) | 32,552 | *57.9* |
|      | Sam Houston (AM) | 23,628 | *42.1* |
| 1859 | Sam Houston (ID) | 36,227 | *56.8* |
|      | Hardin R. Runnels (D) | 27,500 | *43.2* |
| 1861 | Francis R. Lubbock | 21,860 | *38.1* |
|      | Edward Clark | 21,675 | *37.8* |
|      | T. J. Chambers | 13,759 | *24.0* |
| 1863 | Pendleton Murrah | 17,486 | *56.6* |
|      | T. J. Chambers | 12,254 | *39.7* |
| 1865 | J. W. Throckmorton (C) | 49,277 | *80.3* |
|      | Elisha M. Pease (R) | 12,068 | *19.7* |
| 1866 | J. W. Throckmorton (C) | 48,631 | *80.1* |
|      | Elisha M. Pease (R) | 12,051 | *19.9* |
| 1869 | Edmund J. Davis (R) | 39,838 | *50.2* |
|      | A. J. Hamilton (D) | 39,046 | *49.2* |
| 1873 | Richard Coke (D) | 98,906 | *66.0* |
|      | Edmund J. Davis (R) | 51,049 | *34.0* |
| 1875 | Richard Coke (D) | 149,974 | *75.0* |
|      | William Chambers (R) | 49,994 | *25.0* |
| 1878 | Oran M. Roberts (D) | 158,960 | *67.1* |
|      | William H. Hamman (NG) | 55,004 | *23.2* |
|      | A. B. Norton (R) | 22,941 | *9.7* |
| 1880 | Oran M. Roberts (D) | 165,949 | *62.9* |
|      | E. J. Davis (R) | 64,372 | *24.4* |
|      | W. H. Hamman (G) | 33,699 | *12.8* |
| 1882 | John Ireland (D) | 150,811 | *58.0* |
|      | George W. Jones (R-G-FUS) | 108,988 | *41.9* |

| | Candidates | Votes | % |
|------|-----------|-------|---|
| 1884 | John Ireland (D) | 210,691 | 63.2 |
| | George W. Jones (R) | 98,031 | 29.4 |
| | A. B. Norton (G) | 23,464 | 7.0 |
| 1886 | Lawrence S. Ross (D) | 229,806 | 73.0 |
| | A. M. Cochran (R) | 66,456 | 21.1 |
| | E. L. Dahoney (P) | 18,556 | 5.9 |
| 1888 | Lawrence S. Ross (D) | 249,361 | 70.8 |
| | Marion Martin (P & F ALNC) | 102,807 | 29.2 |
| 1890 | James S. Hogg (D) | 261,998 | 76.7 |
| | Webster Flanagan (R) | 76,932 | 22.5 |
| 1892 | James S. Hogg (D) | 190,386 | 43.7 |
| | George Clark (R) | 133,434 | 30.7 |
| | Thomas L. Nugent (POP) | 108,483 | 24.9 |
| 1894 | Charles A. Culberson (D) | 207,171 | 48.9 |
| | Thomas L. Nugent (POP) | 151,595 | 35.8 |
| | W. K. Makemson (R) | 54,525 | 12.9 |
| 1896 | Charles A. Culberson (D) | 298,568 | 55.3 |
| | Jerome C. Kearby (POP) | 238,688 | 44.2 |
| 1898 | Joseph D. Sayers (D) | 291,548 | 71.2 |
| | Barnett Gibbs (POP) | 114,865 | 28.1 |
| 1900 | Joseph D. Sayers (D) | 303,548 | 67.6 |
| | R. E. Hannay (R) | 112,864 | 25.1 |
| | T. J. McMinn (POP) | 26,579 | 5.9 |
| 1902 | Samuel W. T. Lanham (D) | 269,076 | 74.9 |
| | George W. Burkett (R) | 65,706 | 18.3 |
| 1904 | Samuel W. T. Lanham (D) | 204,961 | 73.6 |
| | J. G. Lowden (R) | 56,499 | 20.3 |
| 1906 | Thomas M. Campbell (D) | 149,263 | 81.2 |
| | C. A. Gray (R) | 23,779 | 12.9 |
| 1908 | Thomas M. Campbell (D) | 220,996 | 72.9 |
| | John N. Simpson (R) | 73,309 | 24.2 |
| 1910 | Oscar B. Colquitt (D) | 174,578 | 79.8 |
| | J. O. Terrell (R) | 26,176 | 12.0 |
| | Reddin Andrews (SOC) | 11,536 | 5.3 |
| 1912 | Oscar B. Colquitt (D) | 233,073 | 77.8 |
| | Reddin Andrews (SOC) | 25,238 | 8.4 |
| | C. W. Johnson (R) | 22,914 | 7.6 |
| | Ed C. Lasater (PROG) | 15,754 | 5.3 |
| 1914 | James E. Ferguson (D) | 176,601 | 82.0 |
| | E. R. Meitzen (SOC) | 24,977 | 11.6 |
| | John W. Philip (R) | 11,405 | 5.3 |
| 1916 | James E. Ferguson (D) | 297,177 | 80.5 |
| | R. B. Creager (R) | 49,117 | 13.3 |
| | E. R. Meitzen (SOC) | 19,278 | 5.2 |
| 1918 | William P. Hobby (D) | 148,982 | 84.0 |
| | Charles A. Boynton (R) | 26,713 | 15.1 |
| 1920 | Pat M. Neff (D) | 290,672 | 60.2 |
| | J. G. Culbertson (R) | 90,102 | 18.7 |
| | T. H. McGregor (AM) | 69,380 | 14.4 |
| | H. Capers (B & T R) | 26,128 | 5.4 |
| 1922 | Pat M. Neff (D) | 332,676 | 81.9 |
| | W. H. Atwell (R) | 73,569 | 18.1 |
| 1924 | Miriam A. Ferguson (D) | 422,563 | 58.9 |
| | George C. Butte (R) | 294,920 | 41.1 |
| 1926 | Dan Moody (D) | 233,002 | 87.5 |
| | H. H. Haines (R) | 32,434 | 12.2 |
| 1928 | Dan Moody (D) | 582,897 | 82.4 |
| | W. H. Holmes (R) | 123,337 | 17.4 |
| 1930 | Ross Sterling (D) | 253,732 | 80.0 |
| | W. E. Talbot (R) | 62,334 | 19.7 |
| 1932 | Miriam A. Ferguson (D) | 521,395 | 61.6 |
| | Orville Bullington (R) | 322,589 | 38.1 |
| 1934 | James V. Allred (D) | 428,755 | 96.4 |
| 1936 | James V. Allred (D) | 780,442 | 92.9 |
| | C. O. Harris (R) | 58,744 | 7.0 |
| 1938 | W. Lee O'Daniel (D) | 358,943 | 96.8 |
| 1940 | W. Lee O'Daniel (D) | 1,040,358 | 94.7 |
| | G. C. Hopkins (R) | 57,971 | 5.3 |
| 1942 | Coke R. Stevenson (D) | 280,735 | 96.8 |
| 1944 | Coke R. Stevenson (D) | 1,006,778 | 90.9 |
| | B. J. Peasley (R) | 101,110 | 9.1 |

| | Candidates | Votes | % |
|------|-----------|-------|---|
| 1946 | Beauford H. Jester (D) | 345,507 | 91.2 |
| | Eugene Nolte Jr. (R) | 33,277 | 8.8 |
| 1948 | Beauford H. Jester (D) | 1,024,160 | 84.7 |
| | Alvin H. Lane (R) | 177,399 | 14.7 |
| 1950 | Allan Shivers (D) | 367,345 | 90.2 |
| | Ralph W. Currie (R) | 39,793 | 9.8 |
| 1952 | Allan Shivers (D, R) | 1,853,863 | 99.9 |
| 1954 | Allan Shivers (D) | 569,533 | 89.4 |
| | Tod R. Adams (R) | 66,154 | 10.4 |
| 1956 | Price Daniel (D) | 1,433,051 | 78.4 |
| | William R. Bryant (R) | 271,088 | 14.8 |
| | W. Lee O'Daniel (write-in) | 122,103 | 6.7 |
| 1958 | Price Daniel (D) | 695,035 | 88.1 |
| | Edwin S. Mayer (R) | 94,098 | 11.9 |
| 1960 | Price Daniel (D) | 1,637,755 | 72.8 |
| | William M. Steger (R) | 612,963 | 27.2 |
| 1962 | John B. Connally (D) | 847,036 | 54.0 |
| | Jack Cox (R) | 715,025 | 45.6 |
| 1964 | John B. Connally (D) | 1,877,793 | 73.8 |
| | Jack Crichton (R) | 661,675 | 26.0 |
| 1966 | John B. Connally (D) | 1,037,517 | 72.8 |
| | T. E. Kennerly (R) | 368,025 | 25.8 |
| 1968 | Preston Smith (D) | 1,662,019 | 57.0 |
| | Paul Eggers (R) | 1,254,333 | 43.0 |
| 1970 | Preston Smith (D) | 1,197,726 | 53.6 |
| | Paul Eggers (R) | 1,037,723 | 46.4 |
| 1972 | Dolph Briscoe (D) | 1,633,493 | 47.9 |
| | Hank C. Grover (R) | 1,533,986 | 45.0 |
| | Ramsey Muniz (LRU) | 214,118 | 6.3 |
| 1974 | Dolph Briscoe (D) | 1,016,334 | 61.4 |
| | Jim Granberry (R) | 514,725 | 31.1 |
| | Ramsey Muniz (LRU) | 93,295 | 5.6 |
| 1978 | William P. Clements (R) | 1,183,839 | 50.0 |
| | John Hill (D) | 1,166,979 | 49.2 |
| 1982 | Mark White (D) | 1,697,870 | 53.2 |
| | William P. Clements (R) | 1,465,937 | 45.9 |
| 1986 | William P. Clements (R) | 1,813,779 | 52.7 |
| | Mark White (D) | 1,584,515 | 46.1 |
| 1990 | Ann W. Richards (D) | 1,925,670 | 49.5 |
| | Clayton Williams (R) | 1,826,431 | 46.9 |

# UTAH

(Became a state Jan. 4, 1896)

| | Candidates | Votes | % |
|------|-----------|-------|---|
| 1896 | Heber M. Wells (R) | 20,833 | 50.3 |
| | J. T. Caine (D) | 18,519 | 44.7 |
| 1900 | Heber M. Wells (R) | 47,600 | 51.7 |
| | James H. Moyle (D) | 44,447 | 48.3 |
| 1904 | John C. Cutler (R) | 50,837 | 50.0 |
| | James H. Moyle (D) | 38,047 | 37.4 |
| | William M. Ferry (AM) | 7,959 | 7.8 |
| 1908 | William Spry (R) | 52,913 | 47.5 |
| | Jesse William Knight (D) | 43,266 | 38.8 |
| | James A. Street (AM) | 11,404 | 10.2 |
| 1912 | William Spry (R) | 42,552 | 38.2 |
| | John F. Tolton (D) | 36,076 | 32.4 |
| | Nephi L. Morris (PROG) | 23,590 | 21.2 |
| | Homer P. Burt (SOC) | 8,797 | 7.9 |
| 1916 | Simon Bamberger (D) | 78,298 | 55.0 |
| | Nephi L. Morris (R) | 59,522 | 41.8 |
| 1920 | Charles R. Mabey (R) | 83,518 | 58.2 |
| | T. N. Taylor (D) | 54,913 | 38.3 |
| 1924 | George H. Dern (D) | 81,308 | 53.0 |
| | Charles R. Mabey (R) | 72,127 | 47.0 |
| 1928 | George H. Dern (D) | 102,953 | 58.5 |
| | William H. Wattis (R) | 72,306 | 41.1 |

| | Candidates | Votes | % |
|---|---|---|---|
| 1932 | Henry H. Blood (D) | 116,031 | 56.4 |
| | William W. Seegmiller (R) | 85,913 | 41.8 |
| 1936 | Henry H. Blood (D) | 109,656 | 51.0 |
| | Ray E. Dillman (R) | 80,118 | 37.2 |
| | Harman W. Peery | 24,754 | 11.5 |
| 1940 | Herbert B. Maw (D) | 128,519 | 52.1 |
| | Don B. Colton (R) | 117,713 | 47.7 |
| 1944 | Herbert B. Maw (D) | 123,907 | 50.2 |
| | J. Bracken Lee (R) | 122,851 | 49.8 |
| 1948 | J. Bracken Lee (R) | 151,253 | 55.0 |
| | Herbert B. Maw (D) | 123,814 | 45.0 |
| 1952 | J. Bracken Lee (R) | 180,516 | 55.1 |
| | Earl J. Glade (D) | 147,188 | 44.9 |
| 1956 | George Dewey Clyde (R) | 127,164 | 38.2 |
| | L. C. Romney (D) | 111,297 | 33.4 |
| | J. Bracken Lee (I) | 94,428 | 28.4 |
| 1960 | George Dewey Clyde (R) | 195,634 | 52.7 |
| | William A. Barlocker (D) | 175,855 | 47.3 |
| 1964 | Calvin L. Rampton (D) | 226,956 | 57.0 |
| | Mitchell Melich (R) | 171,300 | 43.0 |
| 1968 | Calvin L. Rampton (D) | 289,283 | 68.7 |
| | Carl W. Buehner (R) | 131,729 | 31.3 |
| 1972 | Calvin L. Rampton (D) | 331,998 | 69.7 |
| | Nicholas L. Strike (R) | 144,449 | 30.3 |
| 1976 | Scott M. Matheson (D) | 280,706 | 52.0 |
| | Vernon B. Romney (R) | 248,027 | 46.0 |
| 1980 | Scott M. Matheson (D) | 330,974 | 55.2 |
| | Bob Wright (R) | 266,578 | 44.4 |
| 1984 | Norman H. Bangerter (R) | 351,792 | 55.9 |
| | Wayne Owens (D) | 275,669 | 43.8 |
| 1988 | Norman H. Bangerter (R) | 260,462 | 40.1 |
| | Ted Wilson (D) | 249,321 | 38.4 |
| | Merrill Cook (I) | 136,651 | 21.0 |
| 1992 | Mike Leavitt (R) | 321,713 | 42.2 |
| | Merrill Cook (IP) | 255,753 | 33.5 |
| | Stewart Hanson (D) | 177,181 | 23.2 |

# VERMONT

(Became a state March 4, 1791)

| | Candidates | Votes | % |
|---|---|---|---|
| 1791 | Thomas Chittenden | ✔ | |
| 1792 | Thomas Chittenden | ✔ | |
| 1793 | Thomas Chittenden | 3,184 | 51.7 |
| | Isaac Tichenor | 2,712 | 44.1 |
| 1794 | Thomas Chittenden | 2,643 | 52.1 |
| | Isaac Tichenor | 2,000 | 39.4 |
| 1795 | Thomas Chittenden | 4,260 | 60.7 |
| | Isaac Tichenor | 2,038 | 29.1 |
| 1796 | Thomas Chittenden | ✔ | |
| 1797 | Isaac Tichenor (FED) | † | |
| 1798 | Isaac Tichenor (FED) | 6,211 | 66.4 |
| | Moses Robinson (D-R) | 2,805 | 30.0 |
| 1799 | Isaac Tichenor (FED) | ✔ | |
| 1800 | Isaac Tichenor (FED) | 6,444 | 64.0 |
| | Israel Smith (D-R) | 3,239 | 32.2 |
| 1801 | Isaac Tichenor (FED) | ✔ | |
| 1802 | Isaac Tichenor (FED) | 7,823 | 60.5 |
| | Israel Smith (D-R) | 5,085 | 39.3 |
| 1803 | Isaac Tichenor (FED) | ✔ | |
| 1804 | Isaac Tichenor (FED) | 8,075 | 56.6 |
| | Jonathan Robinson (D-R) | 6,184 | 43.4 |
| 1805 | Isaac Tichenor (FED) | 8,682 | 60.9 |
| | Jonathan Robinson (D-R) | 5,056 | 35.5 |
| 1806 | Isaac Tichenor (FED) | 8,551 | 54.1 |
| | Israel Smith (D-R) | 6,930 | 43.9 |

| | Candidates | Votes | % |
|---|---|---|---|
| 1807 | Israel Smith (D-R) | 9,983 | 53.2 |
| | Isaac Tichenor (FED) | 8,571 | 45.7 |
| 1808 | Isaac Tichenor (FED) | 13,634 | 50.8 |
| | Israel Smith (D-R) | 12,775 | 47.6 |
| 1809 | Jonas Galusha (D-R) | 14,583 | 51.1 |
| | Isaac Tichenor (FED) | 13,467 | 47.2 |
| 1810 | Jonas Galusha (D-R) | 13,810 | 57.3 |
| | Isaac Tichenor (FED) | 9,912 | 41.2 |
| 1811 | Jonas Galusha (D-R) | 13,828 | 54.0 |
| | Martin Chittenden (FED) | 11,214 | 43.8 |
| 1812 | Jonas Galusha (D-R) | 19,158 | 53.6 |
| | Martin Chittenden (FED) | 15,950 | 44.6 |
| 1813 | Jonas Galusha (D-R) | 16,828 | 49.5 |
| | Martin Chittenden (FED) | 16,532† | 48.7 |
| 1814 | Martin Chittenden (FED) | 17,466† | 49.4 |
| | Jonas Galusha (D-R) | 17,411 | 49.3 |
| 1815 | Jonas Galusha (D-R) | 18,055 | 52.1 |
| | Martin Chittenden (FED) | 16,032 | 46.3 |
| 1816 | Jonas Galusha (D-R) | 17,262 | 55.2 |
| | Samuel Strong (FED) | 13,888 | 44.4 |
| 1817 | Jonas Galusha (D-R) | 13,756 | 64.3 |
| | Isaac Tichenor (FED) | 7,430 | 34.7 |
| 1818 | Jonas Galusha (D-R) | 15,243 | 95.3 |
| 1819 | Jonas Galusha (D-R) | 12,268 | 81.5 |
| | William C. Bradley (D-R) | 1,035 | 6.9 |
| 1820 | Richard Skinner (D-R) | 13,152 | 93.4 |
| 1821 | Richard Skinner (D-R) | 12,434 | 98.7 |
| 1822 | Richard Skinner (D-R) | ✔ | |
| 1823 | Cornelius P. Van Ness (D-R) | 11,479 | 85.6 |
| | Dudley Chase | 1,088 | 8.1 |
| 1824 | Cornelius P. Van Ness (D-R) | 13,428 | 85.8 |
| | Joel Doolittle | 1,882 | 12.0 |
| 1825 | Cornelius P. Van Ness (D-R) | 12,229 | 98.4 |
| 1826 | Ezra Butler (D-R) | 8,966 | 63.3 |
| | Joel Doolittle | 3,157 | 22.3 |
| 1827 | Ezra Butler (D-R) | 13,699 | 85.2 |
| | Joel Doolittle | 1,951 | 12.1 |
| 1828 | Samuel C. Crafts (NR) | 16,285 | 91.8 |
| | Joel Doolittle | 933 | 5.3 |
| 1829 | Samuel C. Crafts (NR) | 14,325# | 55.7 |
| | Heman Allen (A-MASC) | 7,376# | 28.7 |
| | Joel Doolittle (JAC) | 3,973# | 15.4 |
| 1830 | Samuel C. Crafts (OPP)† | 13,476# | 43.9 |
| | William A. Palmer (A-MAS) | 10,923# | 35.6 |
| | Ezra Meech (JAC) | 6,285# | 20.5 |
| 1831 | William A. Palmer (A-MAS)† | 15,258# | 44.0 |
| | Heman Allen (NR) | 12,990# | 37.5 |
| | Ezra Meech (JAC) | 6,158# | 17.8 |
| 1832 | William A. Palmer (A-MAS)† | 17,318† | 42.2 |
| | Samuel C. Crafts (NR) | 15,499 | 37.7 |
| | Ezra Meech (D) | 8,210 | 20.0 |
| 1833 | William A. Palmer (A-MAS) | 20,565 | 52.9 |
| | Ezra Meech (FUS) | 15,683 | 40.3 |
| 1834 | William A. Palmer (A-MAS) | 17,131† | 45.4 |
| | William C. Bradley (D) | 10,385 | 27.5 |
| | Horatio Seymour (W) | 10,159 | 26.9 |
| 1835 | William A. Palmer (A-MAS) | 16,210* | 46.4 |
| | William C. Bradley (D) | 13,254 | 37.9 |
| | Charles Paine (W) | 5,435 | 15.6 |
| 1836 | Silas H. Jennison (W & A-MASC) | 20,371 | 55.8 |
| | William C. Bradley (D) | 16,134 | 44.2 |
| 1837 | Silas H. Jennison (W) | 22,257 | 55.7 |
| | William C. Bradley (D) | 17,722 | 44.3 |
| 1838 | Silas H. Jennison (W) | 22,169 | 56.0 |
| | William C. Bradley (D) | 17,416 | 44.0 |
| 1839 | Silas H. Jennison (W) | 24,621 | 52.5 |
| | Nathan Smilie (D) | 22,256 | 47.5 |
| 1840 | Silas H. Jennison (W) | 33,653 | 59.4 |
| | Paul Dillingham Jr. (D) | 23,000 | 40.6 |
| 1841 | Charles Paine (W) | 23,582† | 48.5 |
| | Nathan Smilie (D) | 21,693 | 44.6 |
| | Titus Hutchinson (LIB) | 3,091 | 6.4 |

| | Candidates | Votes | % | | Candidates | Votes | % |
|---|---|---|---|---|---|---|---|
| 1842 | Charles Paine (W) | 27,167 | 50.9 | 1872 | Julius Converse (R) | 41,946 | 71.6 |
| | Nathan Smilie (D) | 24,130 | 45.2 | | A. B. Gardner (LR) | 16,613 | 28.4 |
| 1843 | John Mattocks (W) | 24,465† | 48.7 | 1874 | Asahel Peck (R) | 33,582 | 71.7 |
| | Daniel Kellogg (D) | 21,982 | 43.8 | | W. H. H. Bingham (D) | 13,257 | 28.3 |
| | Charles K. Williams (LIB) | 3,766 | 7.5 | 1876 | Horace Fairbanks (R) | 44,723 | 68.0 |
| 1844 | William Slade (W) | 28,265 | 51.5 | | W. H. H. Bingham (D) | 20,988 | 31.9 |
| | Daniel Kellogg (D) | 20,930 | 38.2 | 1878 | Redfield Proctor (R) | 37,312 | 64.3 |
| | William R. Shafter (LIB) | 5,618 | 10.2 | | W. H. H. Bingham (D) | 17,274 | 29.8 |
| 1845 | William Slade (W) | 22,770† | 47.2 | 1880 | Roswell Farnham (R) | 47,848 | 67.7 |
| | Daniel Kellogg (D) | 18,591 | 38.5 | | Edward J. Phelps (D) | 21,245 | 30.1 |
| | William R. Shafter (LIB) | 6,534 | 13.5 | 1882 | John L. Barstow (R) | 35,839 | 69.1 |
| 1846 | Horace Eaton (W) | 23,638† | 48.5 | | George E. Eaton (D) | 14,466 | 27.9 |
| | John Smith (D) | 17,877 | 36.7 | 1884 | Samuel E. Pingree (R) | 42,524 | 67.3 |
| | Lawrence Brainerd (F SOIL) | 7,118 | 14.6 | | Lyman W. Redington (D) | 19,820 | 31.4 |
| 1847 | Horace Eaton (W) | 22,455† | 46.7 | 1886 | Ebenezer J. Ormsbee (R) | 37,709 | 66.0 |
| | Paul Dillingham Jr. (D) | 18,661 | 38.8 | | Stephen C. Shurtleff (D) | 17,187 | 30.1 |
| | Lawrence Brainerd (F SOIL) | 6,926 | 14.4 | 1888 | William P. Dillingham (R) | 48,522 | 69.9 |
| 1848 | Carlos Coolidge (W) | 22,132† | 43.7 | | Stephen C. Shurtleff (D) | 19,527 | 28.1 |
| | Oscar L. Shafter (F SOIL D) | 15,018 | 29.6 | 1890 | Carroll S. Page (R) | 33,462 | 62.1 |
| | Paul Dillingham (CASS D) | 13,477 | 26.6 | | Herbert F. Brigham (D) | 19,299 | 35.8 |
| 1849 | Carlos Coolidge (W) | 26,443† | 49.6 | 1892 | Levi K. Fuller (R) | 38,918 | 65.2 |
| | Horatio Needham (F SOIL D) | 23,492 | 44.1 | | B. B. Smalley (D) | 19,216 | 32.2 |
| | Jonas Clark (D) | 3,357 | 6.3 | 1894 | Urban A. Woodbury (R) | 42,663 | 73.6 |
| 1850 | Charles K. Williams (W) | 24,809 | 51.3 | | George W. Smith (D) | 14,142 | 24.4 |
| | Lucius B. Peck (F SOIL D) | 19,189 | 39.6 | 1896 | Josiah Grout (R) | 53,426 | 76.4 |
| | John Roberts (HUNKER D) | 4,379 | 9.1 | | J. Henry Jackson (D) | 14,855 | 21.3 |
| 1851 | Charles K. Williams (W) | 22,864 | 51.0 | 1898 | Edward C. Smith (R) | 38,555 | 71.0 |
| | Timothy B. Redfield (F SOIL) | 15,121 | 33.7 | | Thomas W. Moloney (D) | 14,686 | 27.0 |
| | John S. Robinson (HUNKER D) | 6,790 | 15.2 | 1900 | William W. Stickney (R) | 48,441 | 72.2 |
| 1852 | Erastus Fairbanks (W) | 23,795† | 49.3 | | John H. Center (D) | 17,129 | 25.5 |
| | John S. Robinson (D) | 15,001 | 31.1 | 1902 | John G. McCullough (R) | 31,864† | 45.6 |
| | Lawrence Brainerd (F SOIL) | 9,445 | 19.6 | | Percival W. Clement (H LIC) | 28,201 | 40.3 |
| 1853 | Erastus Fairbanks (W) | 21,118 | 44.1 | | Felix W. McGettrick (D) | 7,364 | 10.5 |
| | John S. Robinson (D) | 18,287† | 38.2 | 1904 | Charles J. Bell (R) | 48,115 | 72.2 |
| | Lawrence Brainerd (F SOIL) | 8,370 | 17.5 | | Eli H. Porter (D) | 16,556 | 24.9 |
| 1854 | Stephen Royce (W) | 27,811 | 62.4 | 1906 | Fletcher D. Proctor (R) | 42,332 | 60.1 |
| | Merritt Clark (D) | 15,130 | 33.9 | | Percival W. Clement (ID) | 26,912 | 38.2 |
| 1855 | Stephen Royce (R) | 25,699# | 59.0 | 1908 | George H. Prouty (R) | 45,598 | 70.8 |
| | Merritt Clark (D) | 12,800# | 29.4 | | James E. Burke (D) | 15,953 | 24.8 |
| | James M. Slade (AM) | 3,631# | 8.3 | 1910 | John A. Mead (R) | 35,263 | 64.2 |
| 1856 | Ryland Fletcher (R) | 34,757 | 74.3 | | Charles D. Watson (D) | 17,425 | 31.7 |
| | Henry Keyes (D) | 11,747 | 25.1 | 1912 | Allen M. Fletcher (R) | 26,237† | 40.5 |
| 1857 | Ryland Fletcher (R) | 27,065 | 67.1 | | Harland B. Howe (D) | 20,001 | 30.9 |
| | Henry Keyes (D) | 12,984 | 32.2 | | Frazer Metzger (PROG) | 15,629 | 24.1 |
| 1858 | Hiland Hall (R) | 29,460 | 68.5 | 1914 | Charles W. Gates (R) | 36,972 | 59.5 |
| | Henry Keyes (D) | 13,538 | 31.5 | | Harland B. Howe (D) | 16,191 | 26.1 |
| 1859 | Hiland Hall (R) | 31,367 | 68.4 | | Walter J. Aldrich (PROG) | 6,929 | 11.2 |
| | John G. Saxe (D) | 14,499 | 31.6 | 1916 | Horace F. Graham (R) | 43,265 | 71.1 |
| 1860 | Erastus Fairbanks (R) | 34,260 | 71.0 | | William B. Mayo (D) | 15,789 | 26.0 |
| | John G. Saxe (DOUG D) | 11,890 | 24.6 | 1918 | Percival W. Clement (R) | 28,358 | 67.2 |
| 1861 | Frederick Holbrook (UN R) | 33,155 | 78.8 | | William B. Mayo (D, P) | 13,859 | 32.8 |
| | Andrew Tracy (UN D) | 5,722 | 13.6 | 1920 | James Hartness (R, P) | 67,674 | 78.0 |
| | B. H. Smalley (BRECK D) | 3,190 | 7.6 | | Fred C. Martin (D) | 18,917 | 21.8 |
| 1862 | Frederick Holbrook (R) | 30,032 | 88.5 | 1922 | Redfield Proctor (R, P) | 51,104 | 74.8 |
| | B. H. Smalley (D) | 3,724 | 11.0 | | J. Holmes Jackson (D) | 17,059 | 25.0 |
| 1863 | John Gregory Smith (R) | 29,613 | 71.2 | 1924 | Franklin S. Billings (R) | 75,510 | 79.3 |
| | Timothy P. Redfield (D) | 11,962 | 22.8 | | Fred C. Martin (D) | 18,263 | 19.2 |
| 1864 | John Gregory Smith (UN) | 31,260 | 71.8 | 1926 | John E. Weeks (R) | 44,564 | 60.9 |
| | Timothy P. Redfield (D) | 12,283 | 28.2 | | Herbert C. Comings (D, P) | 28,651 | 39.1 |
| 1865 | Paul Dillingham (R) | 27,586 | 75.7 | 1928 | John E. Weeks (R) | 94,974 | 73.5 |
| | Charles N. Davenport (D) | 8,857 | 24.3 | | Harry C. Shurtleff (D) | 33,563 | 26.0 |
| 1866 | Paul Dillingham (R) | 34,117 | 75.1 | 1930 | Stanley C. Wilson (R) | 52,836 | 71.0 |
| | Charles N. Davenport (D) | 11,292 | 24.9 | | Park H. Pollard (D) | 21,540 | 28.9 |
| 1867 | John B. Page (R) | 31,694 | 73.3 | 1932 | Stanley C. Wilson (R) | 81,656 | 61.7 |
| | John L. Edwards (D) | 11,510 | 26.6 | | James P. Leamy (D) | 49,247 | 37.2 |
| 1868 | John B. Page (R) | 42,615 | 73.6 | 1934 | Charles M. Smith (R) | 73,620 | 57.3 |
| | John L. Edwards (D) | 15,289 | 26.4 | | James P. Leamy (D) | 54,159 | 42.1 |
| 1869 | Peter T. Washburn (R) | 31,834 | 73.5 | 1936 | George D. Aiken (R) | 83,602 | 60.9 |
| | Homer W. Heaton (D) | 11,455 | 26.5 | | Alfred H. Heininger (D) | 53,218 | 38.8 |
| 1870 | John W. Stewart (R) | 33,367 | 73.5 | 1938 | George D. Aiken (R) | 75,098 | 66.8 |
| | Homer W. Heaton (D) | 12,058 | 26.5 | | Fred C. Martin (D) | 37,404 | 33.3 |

| | Candidates | Votes | % |
|---|---|---|---|
| 1940 | William H. Wills (R) | 87,346 | *64.0* |
| | John McGrath (D) | 49,068 | *36.0* |
| 1942 | William H. Wills (R) | 44,804 | *77.9* |
| | Park H. Pollard (D) | 12,708 | *22.1* |
| 1944 | Mortimer R. Proctor (R) | 78,907 | *65.9* |
| | Ernest H. Bailey (D) | 40,835 | *34.1* |
| 1946 | Ernest W. Gibson (R) | 57,849 | *80.3* |
| | Berthold C. Coburn (D) | 14,096 | *19.6* |
| 1948 | Ernest W. Gibson (R) | 86,394 | *71.9* |
| | Charles F. Ryan (D) | 33,588 | *28.0* |
| 1950 | Lee E. Emerson (R) | 64,915 | *74.5* |
| | J. Edward Moran (D) | 22,227 | *25.5* |
| 1952 | Lee E. Emerson (R) | 78,338 | *51.9* |
| | Robert W. Larrow (D) | 60,051 | *39.8* |
| | Henry W. Vail (IR) | 12,447 | *8.3* |
| 1954 | Joseph B. Johnson (R) | 59,778 | *52.3* |
| | E. Frank Branon (D) | 54,554 | *47.7* |
| 1956 | Joseph B. Johnson (R) | 88,379 | *57.5* |
| | E. Frank Branon (D) | 65,420 | *42.5* |
| 1958 | Robert T. Stafford (R) | 62,222 | *50.3* |
| | Bernard J. Leddy (D) | 61,503 | *49.7* |
| 1960 | F. Ray Keyser Jr. (R) | 92,861 | *56.4* |
| | Russell F. Niquette (D) | 71,755 | *43.6* |
| 1962 | Philip H. Hoff (D, I) | 61,383 | *50.6* |
| | F. Ray Keyser Jr. (R) | 60,035 | *49.4* |
| 1964 | Philip H. Hoff (D) | 106,611 | *64.9* |
| | Ralph A. Foote (R, I) | 57,576 | *35.1* |
| 1966 | Philip H. Hoff (D) | 78,669 | *57.7* |
| | Richard A. Snelling (R) | 57,577 | *42.3* |
| 1968 | Deane C. Davis (R) | 89,387 | *55.5* |
| | John J. Daley (D) | 71,656 | *44.5* |
| 1970 | Deane C. Davis (R) | 87,458 | *57.0* |
| | Leo O'Brien Jr. (D) | 66,028 | *43.0* |
| 1972 | Thomas P. Salmon (D, I VT) | 104,533 | *55.2* |
| | Luther F. Hackett (R) | 82,491 | *43.6* |
| 1974 | Thomas P. Salmon (D, I VT) | 79,842 | *56.6* |
| | Walter L. Kennedy (R) | 53,672 | *38.0* |
| | Martha Abbott (LU) | 7,629 | *5.4* |
| 1976 | Richard A. Snelling (R) | 99,268 | *53.4* |
| | Stella B. Hackel (D) | 75,262 | *40.5* |
| | Bernard J. Sanders (LU) | 11,317 | *6.1* |
| 1978 | Richard A. Snelling (R) | 78,181 | *62.8* |
| | Edwin C. Granai (D) | 42,482 | *34.1* |
| 1980 | Richard A. Snelling (R) | 123,229 | *58.6* |
| | J. Jerome Diamond (D) | 77,363 | *36.8* |
| 1982 | Richard A. Snelling (R) | 93,111 | *55.0* |
| | Madeleine M. Kunin (D) | 74,394 | *44.0* |
| 1984 | Madeleine M. Kunin (D) | 116,938 | *50.0* |
| | John J. Easton (R) | 113,264 | *48.5* |
| 1986 | Madeleine M. Kunin [1] (D) | 92,379 | *47.0* |
| | Peter Smith (R) | 75,162 | *38.2* |
| | Bernard Sanders (I) | 28,430 | *14.5* |
| 1988 | Madeleine M. Kunin (D) | 134,438 | *55.4* |
| | Michael Bernhardt (R) | 105,191 | *43.3* |
| 1990 | Richard A. Snelling (R) | 109,540 | *51.8* |
| | Peter Welch (D) | 97,321 | *46.0* |
| 1992 | Howard Dean (D) | 213,523 | *74.7* |
| | John McClaughry (R) | 65,837 | *23.0* |

**Vermont**

1. *Since no candidate won a clear majority of the total vote cast for governor, the election passed to the state legislature. Sitting in joint assembly in January 1987, the legislature elected Kunin with 139 votes to 39 for Smith and 1 for Sanders.*

# VIRGINIA

(Ratified the Constitution June 25, 1788)

| | Candidates | Votes | % |
|---|---|---|---|
| 1851 [1] | Joseph Johnson (D) | 67,074 | *53.0* |
| | Summers (W) | 59,476 | *47.0* |
| 1855 | Henry A. Wise (D) | 83,224 | *53.2* |
| | Flournoy (AM) | 73,244 | *46.8* |
| 1859 | John Letcher (D) | 77,112 | *51.9* |
| | Goggin (OPP) | 71,543 | *48.1* |
| 1861 | John Letcher | ✔ | |
| 1863 | William Smith | ✔ | |
| | Munford | | |
| | Flournoy | | |
| 1869 | Gilbert C. Walker (C) | 119,535 | *54.2* |
| | H. H. Wells (RAD) | 101,204 | *45.9* |
| 1873 | James L. Kemper (D) | 119,672 | *56.2* |
| | Robert W. Hughes (R) | 93,413 | *43.8* |
| 1877 | Frederick W. M. Holliday (D) | 101,873 | *95.9* |
| 1881 | William E. Cameron (READJ) | 113,464 | *53.0* |
| | John W. Daniel (D) | 100,757 | *47.0* |
| 1885 | Fitzhugh Lee (D) | 152,547 | *52.8* |
| | John S. Wise (R) | 136,508 | *47.2* |
| 1889 | Philip W. McKinney (D) | 163,180 | *57.2* |
| | William Mahone (R) | 121,240 | *42.5* |
| 1893 | Charles T. O'Ferrall (D) | 128,144 | *59.7* |
| | Edmund R. Cocke (POP) | 79,653 | *37.1* |
| 1897 | James Hoge Tyler (D) | 110,253 | *64.6* |
| | Patrick H. McCaull (R) | 56,739 | *33.2* |
| 1901 | A. J. Montague (D) | 116,691 | *58.2* |
| | J. Hampton Hoge (R) | 81,366 | *40.6* |
| 1905 | Claude A. Swanson (D) | 84,235 | *64.5* |
| | Lunsford L. Lewis (R) | 45,815 | *35.1* |
| 1909 | William Hodges Mann (D) | 70,759 | *63.4* |
| | William P. Kent (R) | 40,357 | *36.1* |
| 1913 | Henry C. Stuart (D) | 66,518 | *91.9* |
| | C. Campbell (SOC) | 3,789 | *5.2* |
| 1917 | Westmoreland Davis (D) | 64,226 | *71.5* |
| | T. J. Muncy (R) | 24,957 | *27.8* |
| 1921 | Elbert Lee Trinkle (D) | 139,416 | *66.2* |
| | Henry W. Anderson (R) | 65,833 | *31.2* |
| 1925 | Harry F. Byrd (D) | 107,378 | *74.1* |
| | S. Harris Hoge (R) | 37,592 | *25.9* |
| 1929 | John Garland Pollard (D) | 169,329 | *62.8* |
| | William Moseley Brown (R) | 99,650 | *36.9* |
| 1933 | George C. Peery (D) | 122,820 | *73.7* |
| | Fred W. McWane (R) | 40,377 | *24.2* |
| 1937 | James H. Price (D) | 124,145 | *82.8* |
| | J. Powell Royall | 23,670 | *15.8* |
| 1941 | Colgate W. Darden Jr. (D) | 98,680 | *80.6* |
| | Muse | 21,896 | *17.9* |
| 1945 | William M. Tuck (D) | 112,355 | *66.6* |
| | S. Lloyd Landreth | 52,386 | *31.0* |
| 1949 | John S. Battle (D) | 184,772 | *70.4* |
| | Walter Johnson (R) | 71,991 | *27.4* |
| 1953 | Thomas B. Stanley (D) | 226,998 | *54.8* |
| | Ted Dalton (R) | 183,328 | *44.3* |
| 1957 | J. Lindsay Almond Jr. (D) | 326,921 | *63.2* |
| | Ted Dalton (R) | 188,628 | *36.4* |
| 1961 | Albertis S. Harrison Jr. (D) | 251,861 | *63.8* |
| | H. Clyde Pearson (R) | 142,567 | *36.1* |
| 1965 | Mills E. Godwin Jr. (D) | 269,526 | *47.9* |
| | Linwood Holton (R) | 212,207 | *37.7* |
| | William J. Story Jr. (C) | 75,307 | *13.4* |
| 1969 | Linwood Holton (R) | 480,869 | *52.5* |
| | William C. Battle (D) | 415,695 | *45.4* |
| 1973 | Mills E. Godwin Jr. (R) | 525,075 | *50.7* |
| | Henry Howell (I) | 510,103 | *49.3* |
| 1977 | John Dalton (R) | 699,302 | *55.9* |
| | Henry Howell (D) | 541,319 | *43.3* |

| | Candidates | Votes | % |
|---|---|---|---|
| 1981 | Charles S. Robb (D) | 760,357 | 53.5 |
| | J. Marshall Coleman (R) | 659,398 | 46.4 |
| 1985 | Gerald L. Baliles (D) | 741,438 | 55.2 |
| | Wyatt B. Durrette (R) | 601,652 | 44.8 |
| 1989 | L. Douglas Wilder (D) | 896,936 | 50.1 |
| | J. Marshall Coleman (R) | 890,195 | 49.8 |
| 1993 | George F. Allen (R) | 1,045,319 | 58.3 |
| | Mary Sue Terry (D) | 733,527 | 40.9 |

**Virginia**
1. Before 1851 governor was elected by General Assembly.

# WASHINGTON

(Became a state Nov. 11, 1889)

| | Candidates | Votes | % |
|---|---|---|---|
| 1889 | Elisha P. Ferry (R) | 33,711 | 57.7 |
| | Eugene Scruple (D) | 24,732 | 42.3 |
| 1892 | John H. McGraw (R) | 33,281 | 37.0 |
| | Henry J. Snively (D) | 28,959 | 32.2 |
| | C. W. Young (PP) | 23,750 | 26.4 |
| 1896 | John R. Rogers (PP) | 50,849 | 55.6 |
| | P. C. Sullivan (R) | 38,154 | 41.7 |
| 1900 | John R. Rogers (D) | 52,048 | 48.9 |
| | J. M. Frink (R) | 49,860 | 46.8 |
| 1904 | Albert E. Mead (R) | 74,278 | 51.3 |
| | George Turner (D) | 59,119 | 40.9 |
| | D. Burgess (SOC) | 7,421 | 5.1 |
| 1908 | Samuel G. Cosgrove (R) | 110,190 | 62.6 |
| | John Pattison (D) | 58,126 | 33.0 |
| 1912 | Ernest Lister (D) | 97,251 | 30.6 |
| | M. E. Hay (R) | 96,629 | 30.4 |
| | Robert T. Hodge (PROG) | 77,731 | 24.4 |
| | Anna A. Maley (SOC) | 37,155 | 11.7 |
| 1916 | Ernest Lister (D) | 181,745 | 48.1 |
| | Henry McBride (R) | 167,809 | 44.4 |
| | L. E. Katterfeld (SOC) | 21,117 | 5.6 |
| 1920 | Louis F. Hart (R) | 210,662 | 52.7 |
| | Robert Bridges (F-LAB) | 121,371 | 30.4 |
| | W. W. Black (D) | 66,079 | 16.5 |
| 1924 | Roland H. Hartley (R) | 220,162 | 56.4 |
| | Ben F. Hill (D) | 126,447 | 32.4 |
| | J. R. Oman (F-LAB) | 40,073 | 10.3 |
| 1928 | Roland H. Hartley (R) | 281,991 | 56.2 |
| | Scott Bullitt (D) | 214,334 | 42.7 |
| 1932 | Clarence D. Martin (D) | 352,215 | 57.3 |
| | John A. Gellatly (R) | 207,497 | 33.8 |
| | L. C. Hicks (LIB) | 41,710 | 6.8 |
| 1936 | Clarence D. Martin (D) | 466,550 | 69.4 |
| | Roland H. Hartley (R) | 189,141 | 28.1 |
| 1940 | Arthur B. Langlie (R) | 392,522 | 50.2 |
| | C. C. Dill (D) | 386,706 | 49.5 |
| 1944 | Monrad C. Wallgren (D) | 428,834 | 51.5 |
| | Arthur B. Langlie (R) | 400,604 | 48.1 |
| 1948 | Arthur B. Langlie (R) | 445,958 | 50.5 |
| | Monrad C. Wallgren (D) | 417,035 | 47.2 |
| 1952 | Arthur B. Langlie (R) | 567,822 | 52.7 |
| | Hugh B. Mitchell (D) | 510,675 | 47.4 |
| 1956 | Albert D. Rosellini (D) | 616,773 | 54.6 |
| | Emmett T. Anderson (R) | 508,041 | 45.0 |
| 1960 | Albert D. Rosellini (D) | 611,987 | 50.3 |
| | Lloyd Andrews (R) | 594,122 | 48.9 |
| 1964 | Daniel J. Evans (R) | 697,256 | 55.8 |
| | Albert D. Rosellini (D) | 548,692 | 43.9 |
| 1968 | Daniel J. Evans (R) | 692,378 | 54.7 |
| | John J. O'Connell (D) | 560,262 | 44.3 |

| | Candidates | Votes | % |
|---|---|---|---|
| 1972 | Daniel J. Evans (R) | 747,825 | 50.8 |
| | Albert D. Rosellini (D) | 630,613 | 42.8 |
| | Vick Gould (TPCT) | 86,843 | 5.9 |
| 1976 | Dixy Lee Ray (D) | 821,797 | 53.1 |
| | John D. Spellman (R) | 687,039 | 44.4 |
| 1980 | John D. Spellman (R) | 981,083 | 56.7 |
| | James A. McDermott (D) | 749,813 | 43.3 |
| 1984 | Booth Gardner (D) | 1,006,993 | 53.3 |
| | John D. Spellman (R) | 881,994 | 46.7 |
| 1988 | Booth Gardner (D) | 1,166,448 | 62.2 |
| | Bob Williams (R) | 708,481 | 37.8 |
| 1992 | Mike Lowry (D) | 1,184,315 | 52.2 |
| | Ken Eikenberry (R) | 1,086,216 | 47.8 |

# WEST VIRGINIA

(Became a state June 19, 1863)

| | Candidates | Votes | % |
|---|---|---|---|
| 1863 | Arthur I. Boreman (UN R) | 25,797 | 100.0 |
| 1864 | Arthur I. Boreman (UN R) | 19,353 | 100.0 |
| 1866 | Arthur I. Boreman (R) | 23,802 | 58.1 |
| | Benjamin H. Smith (D) | 17,158 | 41.9 |
| 1868 | William E. Stevenson (R) | 26,935 | 54.6 |
| | James M. Camden (D) | 22,358 | 45.4 |
| 1870 | John J. Jacob (D) | 29,097 | 51.9 |
| | William E. Stevenson (R) | 26,924 | 48.1 |
| 1872 | John J. Jacob (I) | 42,888 | 51.6 |
| | Johnson N. Camden (D) | 40,305 | 48.5 |
| 1876 | Henry M. Mathews (D) | 56,206 | 56.2 |
| | Nathan Goff (R) | 43,477 | 43.5 |
| 1880 | Jacob B. Jackson (D) | 60,991 | 51.3 |
| | George C. Sturgiss (R) | 44,855 | 37.7 |
| | N. B. French (G) | 13,027 | 11.0 |
| 1884 | E. Willis Wilson (D) | 71,408 | 52.0 |
| | Edwin Maxwell (R) | 66,059 | 48.1 |
| 1888 | Nathan Goff (R) | 78,904‡ | 50.0 |
| | A. Brooks Fleming (D) | 78,798 | 50.0 |
| 1892 | William A. MacCorkle (D) | 84,585 | 49.4 |
| | Thomas E. Davis (R) | 80,658 | 47.1 |
| 1896 | George W. Atkinson (R) | 105,588 | 52.4 |
| | Cornelius C. Watts (D) | 93,558 | 46.4 |
| 1900 | A. B. White (R) | 118,798 | 53.8 |
| | John H. Holt (D) | 100,233 | 45.4 |
| 1904 | William M. O. Dawson (R) | 121,540 | 50.8 |
| | John J. Cornwell (D) | 112,538 | 47.0 |
| 1908 | William E. Glasscock (R) | 130,807 | 50.7 |
| | Bennett (D) | 118,909 | 46.1 |
| 1912 | H. D. Hatfield (R) | 128,062 | 47.7 |
| | W. R. Thompson (D) | 119,292 | 44.5 |
| | Walter B. Hilton (SOC) | 15,048 | 5.6 |
| 1916 | John J. Cornwell (D) | 143,324 | 49.5 |
| | Robinson (R) | 140,558 | 48.6 |
| 1920 | Ephraim F. Morgan (R) | 242,237 | 47.3 |
| | Arthur B. Koontz (D) | 185,662 | 36.3 |
| | S. B. Montgomery (NON PART) | 81,330 | 15.9 |
| 1924 | Howard M. Gore (R) | 302,987 | 53.0 |
| | Jake Fisher (D) | 261,846 | 45.8 |
| 1928 | William G. Conley (R) | 345,729 | 53.7 |
| | J. Alfred Taylor (D) | 296,821 | 46.1 |
| 1932 | Herman G. Kump (D) | 402,316 | 53.8 |
| | T. C. Townsend (R) | 342,660 | 45.8 |
| 1936 | Homer A. Holt (D) | 492,333 | 59.2 |
| | Summers H. Sharp (R) | 339,890 | 40.8 |
| 1940 | Matthew M. Neely (D) | 496,028 | 56.4 |
| | Daniel Boone Dawson (R) | 383,698 | 43.6 |
| 1944 | Clarence W. Meadows (D) | 395,122 | 54.4 |
| | Daniel Boone Dawson (R) | 330,649 | 45.6 |

| | Candidates | Votes | % |
|---|---|---|---|
| 1948 | Okey L. Patteson (D) | 438,752 | 57.1 |
| | Herbert S. Boreman (R) | 329,309 | 42.9 |
| 1952 | William C. Marland (D) | 454,898 | 51.5 |
| | Rush D. Holt (R) | 427,629 | 48.5 |
| 1956 | Cecil H. Underwood (R) | 440,502 | 53.9 |
| | Robert H. Mollohan (D) | 377,121 | 46.1 |
| 1960 | W. W. Barron (D) | 446,755 | 54.0 |
| | Harold E. Neely (R) | 380,665 | 46.0 |
| 1964 | Hulett Smith (D) | 433,023 | 54.9 |
| | Cecil H. Underwood (R) | 355,559 | 45.1 |
| 1968 | Arch A. Moore Jr. (R) | 378,315 | 50.9 |
| | James M. Sprouse (D) | 365,530 | 49.1 |
| 1972 | Arch A. Moore Jr. (R) | 423,817 | 54.7 |
| | John D. Rockefeller IV (D) | 350,462 | 45.3 |
| 1976 | John D. Rockefeller IV (D) | 495,661 | 66.2 |
| | Cecil H. Underwood (R) | 253,420 | 33.8 |
| 1980 | John D. Rockefeller IV (D) | 401,863 | 54.1 |
| | Arch A. Moore Jr. (R) | 337,240 | 45.4 |
| 1984 | Arch A. Moore Jr. (R) | 394,937 | 53.3 |
| | Clyde M. See Jr. (D) | 346,565 | 46.7 |
| 1988 | Gaston Caperton (D) | 382,421 | 58.9 |
| | Arch A. Moore Jr. (R) | 267,172 | 41.1 |
| 1992 | Gaston Caperton (D) | 368,302 | 56.0 |
| | Cleve Benedict (R) | 240,390 | 36.6 |
| | Charlotte Jean Pritt (WRITE-IN) | 48,501 | 7.4 |

# WISCONSIN

(Became a state May 29, 1848)

| | Candidates | Votes | % |
|---|---|---|---|
| 1848 | Nelson Dewey (D) | 19,875 | 57.6 |
| | Tweedy (W) | 14,621 | 42.4 |
| 1849 | Nelson Dewey (D) | 16,701 | 52.6 |
| | Collins (W) | 11,317 | 35.6 |
| | Chase (F SOIL) | 3,761 | 11.8 |
| 1851 | Leonard J. Farwell (W) | 22,319 | 50.6 |
| | Upham (D) | 21,812 | 49.4 |
| 1853 | William Augustus Barstow (D) | 30,455 | 54.7 |
| | Holton (W) | 21,886 | 39.3 |
| | Baird (W) | 3,318 | 6.0 |
| 1855 | William Augustus Barstow (D) | 36,387‡ | 50.1 |
| | Coles Bashford (R) | 36,197 | 49.9 |
| 1857 | Alexander W. Randall (R) | 44,693 | 50.3 |
| | Cross (D) | 44,239 | 49.7 |
| 1859 | Alexander W. Randall (R) | 63,466 | 51.6 |
| | Harrison C. Hobart (D) | 59,525 | 48.4 |
| 1861 | Louis P. Harvey (R) | 53,777 | 54.2 |
| | Ferguson (D) | 45,456 | 45.8 |
| 1863 | James T. Lewis (R) | 78,470 | 58.8 |
| | Henry L. Palmer (D) | 55,049 | 41.2 |
| 1865 | Lucius Fairchild (R) | 58,332 | 54.7 |
| | Harrison C. Hobart (D) | 48,330 | 45.3 |
| 1867 | Lucius Fairchild (R) | 73,637 | 51.7 |
| | John J. Tallmadge (D) | 68,873 | 48.3 |
| 1869 | Lucius Fairchild (R) | 69,502 | 53.2 |
| | Charles D. Robinson (D) | 61,239 | 46.8 |
| 1871 | Cadwallader C. Washburn (R) | 78,301 | 53.2 |
| | James R. Doolittle (D) | 68,920 | 46.8 |
| 1873 | William R. Taylor (D) | 81,599 | 55.2 |
| | Cadwallader C. Washburn (R) | 66,224 | 44.8 |
| 1875 | Harrison Ludington (R) | 85,165 | 50.2 |
| | William R. Taylor (D) | 84,374 | 49.8 |
| 1877 | William E. Smith (R) | 78,750 | 44.9 |
| | Mallory (D) | 70,486 | 40.2 |
| | Edward P. Allis (G) | 26,116 | 14.9 |

| | Candidates | Votes | % |
|---|---|---|---|
| 1879 | William E. Smith (R) | 100,537 | 53.2 |
| | Jenkins (D) | 75,030 | 39.7 |
| | May (G) | 12,996 | 6.9 |
| 1881 | Jeremiah M. Rusk (R) | 81,754 | 47.6 |
| | Nicholas D. Fratt (D) | 69,797 | 40.6 |
| | Theodore D. Kanouse (P) | 13,225 | 7.7 |
| 1884 | Jeremiah M. Rusk (R) | 163,210 | 51.0 |
| | Nicholas D. Fratt (D) | 143,943 | 45.0 |
| 1886 | Jeremiah M. Rusk (R) | 133,247 | 46.5 |
| | Gilbert M. Woodward (D) | 114,525 | 40.0 |
| | John Cochrane (LAB) | 21,467 | 7.5 |
| | John M. Olin (P) | 17,089 | 6.0 |
| 1888 | William D. Hoard (R) | 175,696 | 49.5 |
| | James Morgan (D) | 155,423 | 43.8 |
| 1890 | George W. Peck (D) | 160,388 | 51.9 |
| | William D. Hoard (R) | 132,074 | 42.7 |
| 1892 | George W. Peck (D) | 178,135 | 47.9 |
| | John C. Spooner (R) | 170,538 | 45.9 |
| 1894 | William H. Upham (R) | 196,151 | 52.3 |
| | George W. Peck (D) | 142,250 | 37.9 |
| | D. Frank Powell (PP) | 25,604 | 6.8 |
| 1896 | Edward Scofield (R) | 264,981 | 59.7 |
| | Willis C. Silverthorn (D) | 169,257 | 38.1 |
| 1898 | Edward Scofield (R) | 173,137 | 52.6 |
| | Hiram Wilson Sawyer (D) | 135,353 | 41.1 |
| 1900 | Robert M. La Follette (R) | 264,419 | 59.8 |
| | Louis G. Bomrich (D) | 160,674 | 36.4 |
| 1902 | Robert M. La Follette (R) | 193,407 | 52.9 |
| | David S. Rose (D) | 145,820 | 39.9 |
| 1904 | Robert M. La Follette (R) | 227,253 | 50.6 |
| | George W. Peck (D) | 176,301 | 39.2 |
| | Arnold (SOCIAL D) | 24,857 | 5.5 |
| 1906 | James O. Davidson (R) | 183,526 | 57.4 |
| | John A. Aylward (D) | 103,114 | 32.3 |
| | Winfield R. Gaylord (SOCIAL D) | 24,435 | 7.6 |
| 1908 | James O. Davidson (R) | 242,963 | 54.0 |
| | John A. Aylward (D) | 165,977 | 36.9 |
| | Harvey D. Brown (SOCIAL D) | 28,583 | 6.4 |
| 1910 | Francis E. McGovern (R) | 161,559 | 50.6 |
| | Schmitz (D) | 110,446 | 34.6 |
| | Jacobs (SOCIAL D) | 39,539 | 12.4 |
| 1912 | Francis E. McGovern (R) | 179,317 | 45.6 |
| | John C. Karel (D) | 167,298 | 42.5 |
| | Carl D. Thompson (SOCIAL D) | 34,385 | 8.7 |
| 1914 | Emanuel L. Philipp (R) | 140,835 | 43.3 |
| | John C. Karel (D) | 119,567 | 36.7 |
| | John J. Blaine (I) | 32,543 | 10.0 |
| | Oscar Ameringer (SOCIAL D) | 25,940 | 8.0 |
| 1916 | Emanuel L. Philipp (R) | 227,896 | 52.7 |
| | Burt Williams (D) | 164,633 | 38.1 |
| | Rae Weaver (SOC) | 30,813 | 7.1 |
| 1918 | Emanuel L. Philipp (R) | 155,799 | 47.0 |
| | Moehlenpah (D) | 112,576 | 34.0 |
| | Seidel (SOC) | 57,532 | 17.4 |
| 1920 | John J. Blaine (R) | 366,247 | 53.0 |
| | McCoy (D) | 247,746 | 35.8 |
| | Coleman (SOC) | 71,103 | 10.3 |
| 1922 | John J. Blaine (R) | 367,929 | 76.4 |
| | Arthur A. Bentley (ID) | 51,061 | 10.6 |
| | Louis A. Arnold (SOC) | 39,570 | 8.2 |
| 1924 | John J. Blaine (R) | 412,255 | 51.8 |
| | Martin L. Lueck (D) | 317,550 | 39.9 |
| | William F. Quick (SOC) | 45,268 | 5.7 |
| 1926 | Fred R. Zimmerman (R) | 350,927 | 63.5 |
| | Charles B. Perry (I) | 76,507 | 13.8 |
| | Virgil H. Cady (I) | 72,627 | 13.1 |
| | Herman O. Kent (SOC) | 40,293 | 7.3 |
| 1928 | Walter J. Kohler Sr. (R) | 547,738 | 55.4 |
| | Albert G. Schmedeman (D) | 394,368 | 39.9 |
| 1930 | Philip F. La Follette (R) | 392,958 | 64.8 |
| | Hammersley (D) | 170,020 | 28.0 |

| | Candidates | Votes | % |
|---|---|---|---|
| 1932 | Albert G. Schmedeman (D) | 590,114 | *52.5* |
| | Walter J. Kohler Sr. (R) | 470,805 | *41.9* |
| | Metcalfe (SOC) | 56,965 | *5.1* |
| 1934 | Philip F. La Follette (PROG) | 373,083 | *39.1* |
| | Albert G. Schmedeman (D) | 359,467 | *37.7* |
| | Greene (R) | 172,980 | *18.1* |
| 1936 | Philip F. La Follette (PROG) | 573,724 | *46.4* |
| | Alexander Wiley (R) | 363,973 | *29.4* |
| | William L. Lueck (D) | 268,530 | *21.7* |
| 1938 | Julius P. Heil (R) | 543,675 | *55.4* |
| | Philip F. La Follette (PROG) | 353,381 | *36.0* |
| | Bolens (D) | 78,446 | *8.0* |
| 1940 | Julius P. Heil (R) | 558,678 | *40.7* |
| | Orland S. Loomis (PROG) | 546,436 | *39.0* |
| | McGovern (D) | 264,985 | *19.3* |
| 1942 | Orland S. Loomis (PROG) | 397,664* | *49.7* |
| | Julius P. Heil (R) | 291,945 | *36.5* |
| | Sullivan (D) | 98,153 | *12.3* |
| 1944 | Walter S. Goodland (R) | 697,740 | *52.8* |
| | Daniel W. Hoan (D) | 536,357 | *40.6* |
| | Benz (PROG) | 76,028 | *5.8* |
| 1946 | Walter S. Goodland (R) | 621,970 | *59.8* |
| | Daniel W. Hoan (D) | 406,499 | *39.1* |
| 1948 | Oscar Rennebohm (R) | 684,839 | *54.1* |
| | Carl W. Thompson (D) | 558,497 | *44.1* |
| 1950 | Walter J. Kohler Jr. (R) | 605,649 | *53.2* |
| | Carl W. Thompson (D) | 525,319 | *46.2* |
| 1952 | Walter J. Kohler Jr. (R) | 1,009,171 | *62.5* |
| | William Proxmire (D) | 601,844 | *37.3* |
| 1954 | Walter J. Kohler Jr. (R) | 596,158 | *51.5* |
| | William Proxmire (D) | 560,747 | *48.4* |
| 1956 | Vernon W. Thomson (R) | 808,273 | *51.9* |
| | William Proxmire (D) | 749,421 | *48.1* |
| 1958 | Gaylord A. Nelson (D) | 644,296 | *53.6* |
| | Vernon W. Thomson (R) | 556,391 | *46.3* |
| 1960 | Gaylord A. Nelson (D) | 890,868 | *51.6* |
| | Philip G. Kuehn (R) | 837,123 | *48.4* |
| 1962 | John W. Reynolds (D) | 637,491 | *50.4* |
| | Philip G. Kuehn (R) | 625,536 | *49.4* |
| 1964 | Warren P. Knowles (R) | 856,779 | *50.6* |
| | John W. Reynolds (D) | 837,901 | *49.4* |
| 1966 | Warren P. Knowles (R) | 626,041 | *53.5* |
| | Patrick J. Lucey (D) | 539,258 | *46.1* |
| 1968 | Warren P. Knowles (R) | 893,463 | *52.9* |
| | Bronson C. La Follette (D) | 791,100 | *46.8* |
| 1970 | Patrick J. Lucey (D) | 728,403 | *54.2* |
| | Jack B. Olson (R) | 602,617 | *44.9* |
| 1974 | Patrick J. Lucey (D) | 628,639 | *53.2* |
| | William D. Dyke (R) | 497,195 | *42.1* |
| 1978 | Lee S. Dreyfus (R) | 816,056 | *54.4* |
| | Martin J. Schreiber (D) | 673,813 | *44.9* |
| 1982 | Anthony S. Earl (D) | 896,812 | *56.7* |
| | Terry J. Kohler (R) | 662,838 | *41.9* |
| 1986 | Tommy G. Thompson (R) | 805,090 | *52.7* |
| | Anthony S. Earl(D) | 705,578 | *46.2* |
| 1990 | Tommy G. Thompson (R) | 802,321 | *58.2* |
| | Thomas Loftus (D) | 576,280 | *41.8* |

# WYOMING

(Became a state July 10, 1890)

| | Candidates | Votes | % |
|---|---|---|---|
| 1890 | Francis E. Warren (R) | 8,879 | *55.4* |
| | George W. Baxter (D) | 7,153 | *44.6* |

| | Candidates | Votes | % |
|---|---|---|---|
| | Special Election | | |
| 1892 | John E. Osborne (D) | 9,290 | *53.8* |
| | Edward Ivinson (R) | 7,509 | *43.5* |
| 1894 | William A. Richards (R) | 10,149 | *52.6* |
| | William H. Holliday (D) | 6,965 | *36.1* |
| | Lewis C. Tidball (POP) | 2,176 | *11.3* |
| 1898 | DeForest Richards (R) | 10,383 | *52.4* |
| | Horace C. Alger (D) | 8,989 | *45.4* |
| 1902 | DeForest Richards (R) | 14,483 | *57.8* |
| | George T. Beck (D) | 10,017 | *40.0* |
| | Special Election | | |
| 1904 | Bryant B. Brooks (R) | 17,765 | *57.5* |
| | John E. Osborne (D) | 12,137 | *39.3* |
| 1906 | Bryant B. Brooks (R) | 16,317 | *60.2* |
| | Stephen A. D. Keister (D) | 9,444 | *34.8* |
| 1910 | Joseph M. Carey (D) | 21,086 | *55.6* |
| | W. E. Mullen (R) | 15,235 | *40.2* |
| 1914 | John B. Kendrick (D) | 22,387 | *51.6* |
| | Hilliard S. Ridgely (R) | 19,174 | *44.2* |
| 1918 | Robert D. Carey (R) | 23,825 | *56.1* |
| | Frank L. Houx (D) | 18,640 | *43.9* |
| 1922 | William B. Ross (D) | 31,110 | *50.6* |
| | John W. Hay (R) | 30,387 | *49.4* |
| | Special Election | | |
| 1924 | Nellie T. Ross (D) | 43,323 | *55.1* |
| | E. J. Sullivan (R) | 35,275 | *44.9* |
| 1926 | Frank C. Emerson (R) | 35,651 | *50.9* |
| | Nellie T. Ross (D) | 34,286 | *49.0* |
| 1930 | Frank C. Emerson (R) | 38,058 | *50.6* |
| | Leslie A. Miller (D) | 37,188 | *49.4* |
| | Special Election | | |
| 1932 | Leslie A. Miller (D) | 48,130 | *50.9* |
| | Harry R. Weston (R) | 44,692 | *47.2* |
| 1934 | Leslie A. Miller (D) | 54,305 | *57.9* |
| | A. M. Clark (R) | 38,792 | *41.4* |
| 1938 | Nels H. Smith (R) | 57,288 | *59.8* |
| | Leslie A. Miller (D) | 38,501 | *40.2* |
| 1942 | Lester C. Hunt (D) | 39,599 | *51.3* |
| | Nels H. Smith (R) | 37,568 | *48.7* |
| 1946 | Lester C. Hunt (D) | 43,020 | *52.9* |
| | Earl Wright (R) | 38,333 | *47.1* |
| 1950 | Frank A. Barrett (R) | 54,441 | *56.2* |
| | John J. McIntyre (D) | 42,518 | *43.9* |
| 1954 | Milward L. Simpson (R) | 56,275 | *50.5* |
| | William Jack (D) | 55,163 | *49.5* |
| 1958 | J. J. Hickey (D) | 55,070 | *48.9* |
| | Milward L. Simpson (R) | 52,488 | *46.6* |
| 1962 | Clifford P. Hansen (R) | 64,970 | *54.5* |
| | Jack R. Gage (D) | 54,298 | *45.5* |
| 1966 | Stanley K. Hathaway (R) | 65,624 | *54.3* |
| | Ernest Wilkerson (D) | 55,249 | *45.7* |
| 1970 | Stanley K. Hathaway (R) | 74,249 | *62.8* |
| | John J. Rooney (D) | 44,008 | *37.2* |
| 1974 | Ed Herschler (D) | 71,741 | *55.9* |
| | Dick Jones (R) | 56,645 | *44.1* |
| 1978 | Ed Herschler (D) | 69,972 | *50.9* |
| | John C. Ostlund (R) | 67,595 | *49.1* |
| 1982 | Ed Herschler (D) | 106,427 | *63.1* |
| | Warren A. Morton (R) | 62,128 | *36.9* |

| | Candidates | Votes | % | | Candidates | Votes | % |
|---|---|---|---|---|---|---|---|
| 1986 | Michael J. Sullivan (D) | 88,879 | *54.0* | 1990 | Michael J. Sullivan (D) | 104,638 | *65.4* |
| | Pete Simpson (R) | 75,841 | *46.0* | | Mary Mead (R) | 55,471 | *34.6* |

# Governor Returns: Other Sources

In the preceding pages (667-715), the symbol # is used to denote returns taken from a source other than Congressional Quarterly's principal sources of historical gubernatorial popular election returns: the Inter-University Consortium for Political and Social Research (ICPSR) for 1824-1974 returns; Joseph E. Kallenbach and Jessamine S. Kallenbach, *American State Governors, 1776-1976,* vol. 1, Dobbs Ferry, N.Y.: Oceana Publications, 1977, for pre-1824 returns; and the biennial series *America Votes* by Richard M. Scammon and Alice V. McGillivray, Washington, D.C.: Congressional Quarterly for elections since 1975. This page lists the source for elections where the symbol # appears. *(For a description of the ICPSR collection, see pp. x, 666.)*

**Delaware**
1928: Secretary of State of Delaware.

**Florida**
1868: Morris, Allen. *The Florida Handbook 1975-76.* Tallahassee, Fla.: Peninsular Publishing, 1975; 532.

**Florida**
1916: *Governors of the States 1900-1974.* Lexington, Ky.: Council of State Governments; 16.

**Louisiana**
1920: Secretary of State of Louisiana.

**Minnesota**
1861, 1873, 1875, 1877: *The Minnesota Legislative Manual 1973-1974.* St. Paul, Minn.: State of Minnesota; 507-508.

**Mississippi**
1983: Secretary of State of Mississippi.

**New York**
1958: Scammon, Richard M. *America Votes 3.* Pittsburgh: University of Pittsburgh, 1959; 272.

**Texas**
1845: Kallenbach, Joseph E., and Jessamine S. Kallenbach. *American State Governors, 1776-1976.* vol. 1, Dobbs Ferry, N.Y.: Oceana Publications, 1977; 572.

**Vermont**
1829, 1830, 1831, 1855: *Vermont State Manual and Legislative Directory;* 314-315.

# Gubernatorial Primary Returns, 1919-93

# Sources: Gubernatorial Primary Returns

In previous editions of the *Guide to U.S. Elections,* Southern gubernatorial primary returns (for Alabama, Arkansas, Florida, Georgia, Louisiana, Mississippi, North Carolina, South Carolina, Tennessee, Texas and Virginia) were placed in a separate section. For the *Guide to U.S. Elections, Third Edition,* Gubernatorial primary returns for all 50 states are presented in this section (pages 719-773). For all non-Southern states, primary returns go back to 1956; for the 11 Southern states, primary returns go back to 1919 where available.

The major source for primary election returns for all non-Southern states was the *America Votes* series, compiled biennially by Richard M. Scammon and Alice V. McGillivray of the Elections Research Center, Washington, D.C., and published by Congressional Quarterly. Other sources were the returns obtained by Congressional Quarterly after each federal and gubernatorial election from the state secretaries of state. In cases of discrepancies, the *Guide to U.S. Elections, Third Edition,* accepted the *America Votes* figure. The first year for which *America Votes* reported primary returns, 1956, was chosen as the starting point because gubernatorial primary votes for earlier years are not readily available.

For the 11 Southern states that were members of the Civil War Confederacy (Alabama, Arkansas, Florida, Georgia, Louisiana, Mississippi, North Carolina, South Carolina, Tennessee, Texas and Virginia), the primary election returns presented for the years 1919 through 1973 were obtained, except where indicted by a footnote, from the Inter-University Consortium for Political and Social Research (ICPSR) at the University of Michigan. Major sources for returns since 1973 were Congressional Quarterly, which obtained them from the state secretaries of state and Scammon and McGillivray's *America Votes* series.

The vast majority of Southern primaries during the period of 1919 to 1973 were held to nominate candidates of the dominant Democratic Party. In many cases, the winner of the Democratic primary went into the general election facing no Republican opponent.

## Compilation of ICPSR Data File

Statewide candidate totals for Southern primary elections for governor were prepared by the ICPSR staff from several sources. Election returns for the years prior to 1949 were obtained from *Southern Primaries and Elections* (University, Ala.: University of Alabama Press, 1950), edited by Alexander Heard and Donald S. Strong. It should be noted that, although they transcribed their data from official returns, Professors Heard and Strong found that many of the returns contained errors and discrepancies between the sum of county totals and the state total, or returns published as final in newspapers and secretary of state reports. No attempt was made by Heard and Strong to correct these discrepancies because the source of the error could not be determined.

For the period from 1949 to 1973, candidate totals were acquired from two sources. The first was a collection of Southern primary electoral statistics prepared from official returns by Hugh Davis Graham, chairman, division of social sciences, University of Maryland (Baltimore County), and Numan V. Bartley, department of history, University of Georgia (Athens). In addition, reference was made to official returns supplied to ICPSR by the various secretaries of state in conjunction with the ICPSR effort to maintain its continuing collection of election materials. The returns obtained from Bartley and Graham, and the secretary of state offices, were compared with published reports of the election outcomes (notably state manuals and the *America Votes* series) to verify the completeness and accuracy of the returns.

## Presentation of Returns

The gubernatorial primary returns are arranged alphabetically by state and in chronological order of election within each state listing.

Candidates are listed in descending order, with the candidate receiving the greatest number of popular votes listed first. Percentage of the total vote is listed for each candidate who received *at least 5 percent* of the total vote cast.

Primaries for special elections to fill vacancies and runoff primaries are designated in the returns. For Southern states prior to 1974, Republican primary results have been included, whenever available.

## Names, Vote Totals and Percentages

The names of gubernatorial primary candidates are listed as they appeared in the source materials. In a few cases, first names are not known.

For pre-1976 Southern primary elections included in this section, the ICPSR computed statewide vote totals for each candidate. (County-level returns are available from the ICPSR.) *(ICPSR collection, box, p. x.)*

Percentages of the total vote were calculated on the basis of each candidate's proportion of the *total number of votes cast* for all candidates. Percentages have been calculated to two decimal places and rounded to one place. Due to rounding and the scattered votes of minor candidates, percentages in individual primary races may not add up to 100.

If no vote is shown for a candidate but the percentage of total vote is listed as 100 percent, in most cases the candidates in question ran unopposed and state election officials either did not bother to put the candidate's name on the ballot or simply did not make an effort to record the total number of votes.

When gubernatorial primary elections were held under a preferential voting system and the use of second choice votes was required to determine a winner, the symbol ✔ appears next to the winner's name. *(Explanation of preferential voting, p. 628.)*

Where no primary is indicated for a year in which a state elected a governor, it generally means that party conventions chose the nominees. Notes at the end of a state's listing explain other unusual circumstances.

# Gubernatorial Primary
# Returns, 1919-93

## ALABAMA

| Candidates | Votes | % |
|---|---|---|
| **1922** **Democratic Primary** | | |
| William W. Brandon (D) | 163,217 | 78.7 |
| Bibb Graves (D) | 44,151 | 21.3 |
| **1926** **Democratic Primary** | | |
| Bibb Graves (D) | 61,493✔ | 27.6 |
| McDowell (D) | 59,699 | 26.8 |
| Carmichael (D) | 54,072 | 24.3 |
| Patterson (D) | 47,411 | 21.3 |
| **Democratic Second Choice** | | |
| Bibb Graves (D) | 21,978 | 31.0 |
| Patterson (D) | 20,893 | 29.5 |
| Carmichael (D) | 20,061 | 28.3 |
| McDowell (D) | 7,943 | 11.2 |
| **1930** **Democratic Primary** | | |
| B. M. Miller (D) | 77,066✔ | 39.2 |
| W. C. Davis (D) | 70,966 | 36.1 |
| W. Finnell (D) | 19,320 | 9.8 |
| Charles C. McCall (D) | 19,004 | 9.7 |
| **Democratic Second Choice** | | |
| W. C. Davis (D) | 10,673 | 25.8 |
| B. M. Miller (D) | 9,994 | 24.2 |
| W. Finnell (D) | 9,867 | 23.9 |
| Charles C. McCall (D) | 6,467 | 15.7 |
| J. A. Carnley (D) | 2,819 | 6.8 |
| **1934** **Democratic Primary** | | |
| Bibb Graves (D) | 132,462 | 43.4 |
| Frank M. Dixon (D) | 97,508 | 32.0 |
| Leon McCord (D) | 75,208 | 24.6 |
| **Democratic Runoff** | | |
| Bibb Graves (D) | 157,140 | 53.7 |
| Frank M. Dixon (D) | 135,309 | 46.3 |
| **1938** **Democratic Primary** | | |
| Frank M. Dixon (D) | 152,860 | 48.6 |
| Chauncey Sparks (D)[1] | 74,554 | 23.7 |
| R. J. Goode (D) | 70,287 | 22.4 |

| Candidates | Votes | % |
|---|---|---|
| **1942** **Democratic Primary** | | |
| Chauncey Sparks (D) | 145,798 | 52.2 |
| James E. Folsom (D) | 73,306 | 26.2 |
| Chris J. Sherlock (D) | 53,448 | 19.1 |
| **1946** **Democratic Primary** | | |
| James E. Folsom (D) | 104,152 | 28.5 |
| Handy Ellis (D) | 88,459 | 24.2 |
| Joe N. Poole (D) | 70,925 | 19.4 |
| Elbert Boozer (D) | 58,134 | 15.9 |
| Gordon Persons (D) | 43,843 | 12.0 |
| **Democratic Runoff** | | |
| James E. Folsom (D) | 205,168 | 58.7 |
| Handy Ellis (D) | 144,126 | 41.3 |
| **1950** **Democratic Primary** | | |
| Gordon Persons (D) | 137,055 | 34.1 |
| Philip J. Hamm (D)[2] | 56,395 | 14.0 |
| Elbert Boozer (D) | 48,021 | 11.9 |
| J. Bruce Henderson (D) | 38,867 | 9.7 |
| Chauncey Sparks (D) | 27,404 | 6.8 |
| Eugene (Bull) Connor (D) | 20,629 | 5.1 |
| Robert K. (Buster) Bell (D) | 20,171 | 5.0 |
| **1954** **Democratic Primary** | | |
| James E. Folsom (D) | 305,384 | 51.4 |
| Jimmy Faulkner (D) | 151,925 | 25.6 |
| Jim Allen (D) | 61,530 | 10.4 |
| J. Bruce Henderson (D) | 47,969 | 8.1 |
| **1958** **Democratic Primary** | | |
| John Patterson (D) | 196,859 | 31.8 |
| George C. Wallace (D) | 162,435 | 26.3 |
| Jimmy Faulkner (D) | 91,512 | 14.8 |
| A. W. Todd (D) | 59,240 | 9.6 |
| Laurie C. Battle (D) | 38,955 | 6.3 |
| **Democratic Runoff** | | |
| John Patterson (D) | 315,353 | 55.7 |
| George C. Wallace (D) | 250,451 | 44.3 |
| **1962** **Democratic Primary** | | |
| George C. Wallace (D) | 207,062 | 32.5 |
| Ryan deGraffenried (D) | 160,704 | 25.2 |
| James E. Folsom (D) | 159,640 | 25.1 |
| Macdonald Gallion (D) | 80,374 | 12.6 |

| | Candidates | Votes | % |
|---|---|---|---|
| | **Democratic Runoff** | | |
| | George C. Wallace (D) | 340,730 | *55.9* |
| | Ryan deGraffenried (D) | 269,122 | *44.1* |
| 1966 | **Democratic Primary** | | |
| | Lurleen B. Wallace (D) | 480,841 | *54.1* |
| | Richmond M. Flowers (D) | 172,386 | *19.4* |
| | Carl Elliott (D) | 71,972 | *8.1* |
| | Bob Gilchrist (D) | 49,502 | *5.6* |
| 1970 | **Democratic Primary** | | |
| | Albert Brewer (D) | 428,146 | *42.0* |
| | George C. Wallace (D) | 416,443 | *40.8* |
| | Charles Woods (D) | 149,887 | *14.7* |
| | **Democratic Runoff** | | |
| | George C. Wallace (D) | 559,832 | *51.6* |
| | Albert Brewer (D) | 525,951 | *48.4* |
| 1974 | **Republican Primary** | | |
| | Elvin McCary (R) | | *100.0* |
| | **Democratic Primary** | | |
| | George C. Wallace (D) | 536,235 | *64.7* |
| | Gene McLain (D) | 249,695 | *30.1* |
| 1978 | **Republican Primary** | | |
| | Guy Hunt (R) | 21,499 | *83.2* |
| | Bert Hayes (R) | 2,817 | *10.9* |
| | Julian Elgin (R) | 1,534 | *5.9* |
| | **Democratic Primary** | | |
| | Forrest H. James (D) | 256,196 | *28.5* |
| | Bill Baxley (D) | 210,089 | *23.3* |
| | Albert Brewer (D) | 193,479 | *21.5* |
| | Sid McDonald (D) | 143,930 | *16.0* |
| | Jere Beasley (D) | 77,202 | *8.6* |
| | **Democratic Runoff** | | |
| | Forrest H. James (D) | 515,520 | *55.2* |
| | Bill Baxley (D) | 418,932 | *44.8* |
| 1982 | **Republican Primary** | | |
| | Emory Folmar (R) | | *100.0* |
| | **Democratic Primary** | | |
| | George C. Wallace (D) | 425,469 | *42.5* |
| | George McMillan (D) | 296,262 | *29.6* |
| | Joe C. McCorquodale (D) | 250,614 | *25.1* |
| | **Democratic Runoff** | | |
| | George C. Wallace (D) | 512,203 | *51.2* |
| | George McMillan (D) | 488,444 | *48.8* |
| 1986 | **Republican Primary** | | |
| | Guy Hunt (R) | 20,823 | *71.3* |
| | Doug Carter (R) | 8,371 | *28.7* |

| | Candidates | Votes | % |
|---|---|---|---|
| | **Democratic Primary** | | |
| | Bill Baxley (D) | 345,985 | *36.8* |
| | Charles Graddick (D) | 275,714 | *29.3* |
| | Forrest H. James (D) | 195,844 | *20.8* |
| | George McMillan (D) | 117,258 | *12.5* |
| | **Democratic Runoff** [3] | | |
| | Charles Graddick (D) | 470,051 | *50.5* |
| | Bill Baxley (D) | 461,295 | *49.5* |
| 1990 | **Republican Primary** | | |
| | Guy Hunt (R) | 119,877 | *95.8* |
| | **Democratic Primary** | | |
| | Paul R. Hubbert (D) | 233,808 | *31.5* |
| | Don Siegelman (D) | 184,635 | *24.9* |
| | Forrest H. James (D) | 160,121 | *21.6* |
| | Ronnie G. Flippo (D) | 128,105 | *17.3* |
| | **Democratic Runoff** | | |
| | Paul R. Hubbert (D) | 309,609 | *53.6* |
| | Don Siegelman (D) | 267,588 | *46.4* |

**Alabama**

*1. Sparks withdrew from the race May 11, 1938, declining a runoff with Dixon, who became the Democratic nominee.*

*2. Hamm withdrew May 12, 1950, declining a runoff with Persons, who became the Democratic nominee.*

*3. After the Democratic runoff primary a subcommittee of Alabama's Democratic party declared Baxley the nominee, deciding that voters who voted in the Republican primary had crossed over and voted in the Democratic runoff primary for Graddick, against party rules. This decision was contested through the courts, but the Democratic party decision was upheld.*

# ALASKA [1]

| | Candidates | Votes | % |
|---|---|---|---|
| 1958 | **Republican Primary** | | |
| | John Butrovich (R) | | *100.0* |
| | **Democratic Primary** | | |
| | William A. Egan (D) | 22,735 | *61.1* |
| | Victor Rivers (D) | 8,845 | *23.7* |
| | J. G. Williams (D) | 5,656 | *15.2* |
| 1962 | **Republican Primary** | | |
| | Mike Stepovich (R) | 6,415 | *38.1* |
| | Howard W. Pollock (R) | 5,247 | *31.2* |
| | John B. Coghill (R) | 2,295 | *13.6* |
| | Verne O. Martin (R) | 1,504 | *8.9* |
| | Milo H. Fritz (R) | 1,371 | *8.1* |
| | **Democratic Primary** | | |
| | William A. Egan (D) | 13,698 | *62.3* |
| | George H. Byer (D) | 5,275 | *24.0* |
| | Warren A. Taylor (D) | 2,386 | *10.8* |

| | Candidates | Votes | % |
|---|---|---|---|
| **1966** | **Republican Primary** | | |
| | Walter J. Hickel (R) | 10,580 | *55.3* |
| | Bruce Kendall (R) | 4,511 | *23.6* |
| | Mike Stepovich (R) | 4,039 | *21.1* |
| | **Democratic Primary** | | |
| | William A. Egan (D) | 19,801 | *61.0* |
| | Wendell P. Kay (D) | 12,660 | *39.0* |
| **1970** | **Republican Primary** | | |
| | Keith Miller (R) | 19,153 | *53.4* |
| | Howard W. Pollock (R) | 10,091 | *46.5* |
| | **Democratic Primary** | | |
| | William A. Egan (D) | 23,973 | *67.5* |
| | Larry Carr (D) | 11,350 | *31.9* |
| **1974** | **Republican Primary** | | |
| | Jay S. Hammond (R) | 28,602 | *47.2* |
| | Walter J. Hickel (R) | 20,728 | *34.2* |
| | Keith Miller (R) | 10,864 | *17.9* |
| | **Democratic Primary** | | |
| | William A. Egan (D) | 20,356 | *91.0* |
| **1978 [2]** | **Republican Primary** | | |
| | Jay S. Hammond (R) | 31,896 | *39.1* |
| | Walter J. Hickel (R) | 31,798 | *38.9* |
| | Tom Fink (R) | 17,487 | *21.4* |
| | **Democratic Primary** | | |
| | Chancy Croft (D) | 8,911 | *36.1* |
| | Edward A. Merdes (D) | 8,639 | *35.0* |
| | Jalmar M. Kerttula (D) | 7,125 | *28.9* |
| **1982** | **Republican Primary** | | |
| | Tom Fink (R) | 41,911 | *51.3* |
| | Terry Miller (R) | 36,594 | *44.8* |
| | **Democratic Primary** | | |
| | Bill Sheffield (D) | 21,940 | *39.7* |
| | Steve Cowper (D) | 21,680 | *39.2* |
| | H. A. Boucher (D) | 8,584 | *15.5* |
| **1986** | **Republican Primary** | | |
| | Arliss Sturgulewski (R) | 25,740 | *30.6* |
| | Walter J. Hickel (R) | 23,733 | *28.3* |
| | Richard Randolph (R) | 18,164 | *21.6* |
| | Joe L. Hayes (R) | 7,989 | *9.5* |
| | Bob Richards (R) | 4,973 | *5.9* |
| | **Democratic Primary** | | |
| | Steve Cowper (D) | 36,233 | *54.5* |
| | Bill Sheffield (D) | 29,935 | *45.0* |
| | **Alaskan Independence Primary** | | |
| | Joe Vogler | | *100.0* |

| | Candidates | Votes | % |
|---|---|---|---|
| | **Libertarian Primary** | | |
| | Mary O'Brannon (LIBERT) | 205 | *53.5* |
| | Ed Hoch (LIBERT) | 178 | *46.5* |
| **1990** | **Republican Primary [3]** | | |
| | Arliss Sturgulewski (R) | 26,906 | *36.4* |
| | James O. Campbell (R) | 23,442 | *31.7* |
| | Rick Halford (R) | 22,466 | *30.4* |
| | **Democratic Primary** | | |
| | Tony Knowles (D) | 36,019 | *56.1* |
| | Stephen McAlpine (D) | 27,656 | *43.0* |
| | **Alaskan Independence Primary** | | |
| | John Lindauer (ALI) [4] | 3,505 | *87.7* |
| | William DeRushe (ALI) | 492 | *12.3* |

**Alaska**

*1. In Alaska's so-called "jungle" primaries, all candidates for an office appeared together on the same ballot with their parties designated. Nominations went to the Republican and Democrat receiving the most votes for the office. Percentages were calculated here as if candidates had run in separate party primaries.*

*2. There were recounts of the votes received by the two top finishers in both primaries. In the Republican recount, Hammond's vote was 31,921 (50.0 percent) and Hickel's was 31,823 (49.9 percent). In the Democratic recount, Croft's vote was 8,910 (50.7 percent) and Merdes' was 8,655 (49.3 percent).*

*3. The Republican primary ballot was a single-ballot and only registered Republican, Non-Partisan, and Undeclared voters could participate in the primary. All other parties ran on a multiparty ballot and the primary was open to all registered voters except Republicans.*

*4. Lindauer withdrew after the primary and Walter J. Hickel was substituted by the party committee.*

# ARIZONA

| | Candidates | Votes | % |
|---|---|---|---|
| **1956** | **Republican Primary** | | |
| | Horace B. Griffen (R) | 20,471 | *46.0* |
| | O. D. Miller (R) | 17,858 | *40.1* |
| | Fred Trump (R) | 6,199 | *13.9* |
| | **Democratic Primary** | | |
| | Ernest W. McFarland (D) | | *100.0* |
| **1958** | **Republican Primary** | | |
| | Paul Fannin (R) | | *100.0* |
| | **Democratic Primary** | | |
| | Robert Morrison (D) | 77,931 | *50.4* |
| | Dick Searles (D) | 58,699 | *37.9* |
| | Marvin L. Burton (D) | 18,122 | *11.7* |
| **1960** | **Republican Primary** | | |
| | Paul Fannin (R) | | *100.0* |
| | **Democratic Primary** | | |
| | Lee Ackerman (D) | | *100.0* |

| | Candidates | Votes | % |
|---|---|---|---|
| 1962 | **Republican Primary** | | |
| | Paul Fannin (R) | | 100.0 |
| | **Democratic Primary** | | |
| | Sam Goddard (D) | 91,661 | 59.8 |
| | Joe Haldiman (D) | 41,645 | 27.2 |
| | J. M. Morris (D) | 19,850 | 13.0 |
| 1964 | **Republican Primary** | | |
| | Richard Kleindienst (R) | 64,310 | 62.8 |
| | Evan Mecham (R) | 38,131 | 37.2 |
| | **Democratic Primary** | | |
| | Sam Goddard (D) | 114,377 | 60.0 |
| | Art Brock (D) | 57,067 | 30.0 |
| | J. M. Morris (D) | 11,303 | 5.9 |
| 1966 | **Republican Primary** | | |
| | John R. Williams (R) | 37,409 | 44.3 |
| | John Haugh (R) | 25,905 | 30.6 |
| | Robert W. Pickrell (R) | 21,192 | 25.1 |
| | **Democratic Primary** | | |
| | Sam Goddard (D) | 63,180 | 45.5 |
| | Norman Green (D) | 53,921 | 38.9 |
| | Andrew J. Gilbert (D) | 23,637 | 17.0 |
| 1968 | **Republican Primary** | | |
| | John R. Williams (R) | | 100.0 |
| | **Democratic Primary** | | |
| | Sam Goddard (D) | 112,948 | 73.4 |
| | Currin V. Shields (D) | 30,337 | 19.7 |
| | Jack DeVault (D) | 10,613 | 6.9 |
| 1970 | **Republican Primary** | | |
| | John R. Williams (R) | | 100.0 |
| | **Democratic Primary** | | |
| | Raul H. Castro (D) | 63,294 | 52.0 |
| | Jack Ross (D) | 30,921 | 25.4 |
| | George Nader (D) | 27,534 | 22.6 |
| 1974 | **Republican Primary** | | |
| | Russell Williams (R) | 53,132 | 35.6 |
| | Evan Mecham (R) | 30,266 | 20.3 |
| | William C. Jacquin (R) | 27,138 | 18.2 |
| | John R. Driggs (R) | 23,519 | 15.7 |
| | Milton H. Graham (R) | 15,315 | 10.2 |
| | **Democratic Primary** | | |
| | Raul H. Castro (D) | 115,268 | 67.2 |
| | Jack Ross (D) | 31,250 | 18.2 |
| | David R. Moss (D) | 19,143 | 11.2 |
| 1978 | **Republican Primary** | | |
| | Evan Mecham (R) | 50,713 | 44.1 |
| | Jack Londen (R) | 40,116 | 34.9 |

| | Candidates | Votes | % |
|---|---|---|---|
| | **Democratic Primary** | | |
| | Bruce Babbitt (D) | 108,548 | 76.8 |
| | David R. Moss (D) | 32,785 | 23.2 |
| | **Libertarian Primary** | | |
| | V. Gene Lewter (LIBERT) | | 100.0 |
| | **Socialist Worker Primary** | | |
| | Jessica Sampson (SOC WORK) | | 100.0 |
| 1982 | **Republican Primary** | | |
| | Leo Corbet (R) | 108,766 | 61.7 |
| | Evan Mecham (R) | 67,456 | 38.3 |
| | **Democratic Primary** | | |
| | Bruce Babbitt (D) | 142,559 | 85.8 |
| | Steve Jancek (D) [1] | 23,492 | 14.1 |
| | **Libertarian Primary** | | |
| | Sam Stelger (LIBERT) | | 100.0 |
| 1986 | **Republican Primary** | | |
| | Evan Mecham (R) | 121,614 | 53.7 |
| | Burton S. Barr (R) | 104,682 | 46.3 |
| | **Democratic Primary** | | |
| | Carolyn Warner (D) | 106,687 | 50.6 |
| | Tony Mason (D) | 92,413 | 43.9 |
| | Dave Moss (D) | 11,588 | 5.5 |
| 1990 | **Republican Primary** | | |
| | Fife Symington (R) | 163,010 | 43.8 |
| | Evan Mecham (R) | 91,136 | 24.5 |
| | Fred Koory (R) | 61,487 | 16.5 |
| | Sam Steiger (R) | 49,019 | 13.2 |
| | **Democratic Primary** | | |
| | Terry Goddard (D) | 212,579 | 84.0 |
| | Dave Moss (D) | 40,478 | 16.0 |

**Arizona**
1. Jancek died before the primary, but his name remained on the ballot.

# ARKANSAS

| | Candidates | Votes | % |
|---|---|---|---|
| | | | |
| 1920 | **Democratic Primary** | | |
| | Thomas C. McRae (D) | 41,907 | 26.9 |
| | Smead Powell (D) | 32,263 | 20.7 |
| | Thomas J. Terral (D) | 29,303 | 18.8 |
| | J. C. Floyd (D) | 21,596 | 13.9 |
| | G. R. Haynie (D) | 16,747 | 10.8 |

| | Candidates | Votes | % |
|---|---|---|---|
| 1922 | **Democratic Primary** | | |
| | Thomas C. McRae (D) | 127,728 | 70.5 |
| | E. P. Toney (D) | 53,572 | 29.6 |
| 1924 | **Democratic Primary** | | |
| | Thomas J. Terral (D) | 54,533 | 26.3 |
| | Lee Cazort (D) | 43,466 | 21.0 |
| | John E. Martineau (D) | 35,438 | 17.1 |
| | Jim G. Ferguson (D) | 27,155 | 13.1 |
| | Hamp Williams (D) | 23,785 | 11.5 |
| | Jacob R. Willson (D) | 22,626 | 10.9 |
| 1926 | **Democratic Primary** | | |
| | John E. Martineau (D) | 117,232 | 53.5 |
| | Thomas J. Terral (D) | 101,981 | 46.5 |
| 1928 | **Democratic Primary** | | |
| | Harvey J. Parnell (D) | 94,207 | 41.7 |
| | Brooks Hays (D) | 57,497 | 25.4 |
| | Thomas J. Terral (D) | 34,476 | 15.2 |
| | J. Carrol Cone (D) | 31,786 | 14.1 |
| 1930 | **Democratic Primary** | | |
| | Harvey J. Parnell (D) | 133,870 | 54.2 |
| | Brooks Hays (D) | 88,541 | 35.8 |
| | J. C. Sheffield (D) | 20,133 | 8.2 |
| 1932 | **Democratic Primary** | | |
| | J. Marion Futrell (D) | 124,239 | 44.0 |
| | Thomas J. Terral (D) | 59,066 | 21.0 |
| | A. B. Priddy (D) | 37,134 | 13.2 |
| | D. H. Blackwood (D) | 33,147 | 11.8 |
| 1934 | **Democratic Primary** | | |
| | J. Marion Futrell (D) | 167,917 | 65.9 |
| | Howard Reed (D) | 86,894 | 34.1 |
| 1936 | **Democratic Primary** | | |
| | Carl E. Bailey (D) | 76,014 | 32.0 |
| | Ed F. McDonald (D) | 72,075 | 30.3 |
| | R. A. Cook (D) | 60,768 | 25.6 |
| | Thomas J. Terral (D) | 23,663 | 10.0 |
| 1938 | **Democratic Primary** | | |
| | Carl E. Bailey (D) | 146,472 | 51.5 |
| | R. A. Cook (D) | 131,791 | 46.3 |
| 1940 | **Democratic Primary** | | |
| | Homer M. Adkins (D) | 142,247 | 56.2 |
| | Carl E. Bailey (D) | 110,613 | 43.7 |
| 1942 | **Democratic Primary** | | |
| | Homer M. Adkins (D) | 120,811 | 71.8 |
| | Fred Keller (D) | 44,304 | 26.3 |
| 1944 | **Democratic Primary** | | |
| | Ben Laney (D) | 70,965 | 38.6 |
| | J. Bryan Sims (D) [1] | 63,454 | 34.5 |
| | David L. Terry (D) | 49,685 | 27.0 |

| | Candidates | Votes | % |
|---|---|---|---|
| 1946 | **Democratic Primary** | | |
| | Ben Laney (D) | 125,444 | 64.6 |
| | J. M. Malone (D) | 63,601 | 32.8 |
| 1948 | **Democratic Primary** | | |
| | Sidney S. McMath (D) | 87,829 | 34.1 |
| | Jack Holt (D) | 60,313 | 23.4 |
| | James McKrell (D) | 57,030 | 22.1 |
| | Horace Thompson (D) | 48,674 | 18.9 |
| | **Democratic Runoff** | | |
| | Sidney S. McMath (D) | 157,137 | 51.7 |
| | Jack Holt (D) | 146,880 | 48.3 |
| 1950 | **Democratic Primary** | | |
| | Sidney S. McMath (D) | 209,559 | 64.0 |
| | Ben T. Laney (D) | 112,651 | 34.4 |
| 1952 | **Democratic Primary** | | |
| | Sidney S. McMath (D) | 100,858 | 30.7 |
| | Francis Cherry (D) | 91,195 | 27.7 |
| | Tackett (D) | 63,827 | 19.4 |
| | Jack Holt (D) | 45,233 | 13.8 |
| | Murry (D) | 27,937 | 8.5 |
| | **Democratic Runoff** | | |
| | Francis Cherry (D) | 237,448 | 63.1 |
| | Sidney S. McMath (D) | 139,052 | 36.9 |
| 1954 | **Democratic Primary** | | |
| | Francis Cherry (D) | 154,879 | 47.7 |
| | Orval E. Faubus (D) | 109,614 | 33.8 |
| | Guy Jones (D) | 41,249 | 12.7 |
| | McMillan (D) | 18,857 | 5.8 |
| | **Democratic Runoff** | | |
| | Orval E. Faubus (D) | 191,328 | 50.9 |
| | Francis Cherry (D) | 184,509 | 49.1 |
| 1956 | **Democratic Primary** | | |
| | Orval E. Faubus (D) | 180,760 | 58.1 |
| | James Johnson (D) | 83,856 | 26.9 |
| | Jim Snoddy (D) | 43,630 | 14.0 |
| 1958 | **Republican Primary** | | |
| | George W. Johnson (R) | 3,147 | 72.7 |
| | Donald D. Layne (R) | 1,273 | 28.8 |
| | **Democratic Primary** | | |
| | Orval E. Faubus (D) | 264,346 | 68.9 |
| | Chris Finkbeiner (D) | 60,173 | 15.7 |
| | Lee Ward (D) | 59,385 | 15.5 |
| 1960 | **Republican Primary** | | |
| | Henry M. Britt (R) | | 100.0 |

**723**

| Candidates | Votes | % |
|---|---|---|
| **Democratic Primary** | | |
| Orval E. Faubus (D) | 238,997 | *58.8* |
| Joe C. Hardin (D) | 66,499 | *16.4* |
| Bruce Bennett (D) | 58,400 | *14.4* |
| H. E. Williams (D) | 33,374 | *8.2* |

**1962**

| **Republican Primary** | | |
|---|---|---|
| Willis Ricketts (R) | | *100.0* |

| **Democratic Primary** | | |
|---|---|---|
| Orval E. Faubus (D) | 208,996 | *51.6* |
| Sidney S. McMath (D) | 83,473 | *20.6* |
| Dale Alford (D) | 82,815 | *20.4* |
| Vernon H. Whitten (D) | 22,377 | *5.5* |

**1964**

| **Republican Primary** | | |
|---|---|---|
| Winthrop Rockefeller (R) | | *100.0* |

| **Democratic Primary** | | |
|---|---|---|
| Orval E. Faubus (D) | 239,890 | *65.7* |
| Ervin Odell Dorsey (D) | 69,638 | *19.1* |
| Joe Hubbard (D) | 39,199 | *10.7* |

**1966**

| **Republican Primary** | | |
|---|---|---|
| Winthrop Rockefeller (R) | 19,646 | *98.5* |

| **Democratic Primary** | | |
|---|---|---|
| James Johnson (D) | 105,607 | *25.1* |
| Frank Holt (D) | 92,711 | *22.1* |
| Brooks Hays (D) | 64,814 | *15.4* |
| Dale Alford (D) | 53,531 | *12.7* |
| Sam Boyce (D) | 49,744 | *11.8* |
| Raymond Rebsamen (D) | 35,607 | *8.5* |

| **Democratic Runoff** | | |
|---|---|---|
| James Johnson (D) | 210,543 | *51.9* |
| Frank Holt (D) | 195,442 | *48.1* |

**1968**

| **Republican Primary** | | |
|---|---|---|
| Winthrop Rockefeller (R) | 27,913 | *95.5* |

| **Democratic Primary** | | |
|---|---|---|
| Marion Crank (D) | 106,092 | *25.6* |
| Virginia Johnson (D) | 86,038 | *20.7* |
| Ted Boswell (D) | 85,629 | *20.6* |
| Bruce Bennett (D) | 65,095 | *15.7* |
| Frank Whitbeck (D) | 61,758 | *14.9* |

| **Democratic Runoff** | | |
|---|---|---|
| Marion Crank (D) | 215,087 | *63.3* |
| Virginia Johnson (D) | 124,880 | *36.7* |

**1970**

| **Republican Primary** | | |
|---|---|---|
| Winthrop Rockefeller (R) | 58,197 | *96.8* |

| Candidates | Votes | % |
|---|---|---|
| **Democratic Primary** | | |
| Orval E. Faubus (D) | 156,578 | *36.4* |
| Dale Bumpers (D) | 86,156 | *20.0* |
| Joe Purcell (D) | 81,566 | *18.9* |
| Hayes C. McClerkin (D) | 45,011 | *10.5* |
| Bill Wells (D) | 32,543 | *7.6* |

| **Democratic Runoff** | | |
|---|---|---|
| Dale Bumpers (D) | 259,780 | *58.7* |
| Orval E. Faubus (D) | 182,732 | *41.3* |

**1972**

| **Republican Primary** | | |
|---|---|---|
| Len E. Blaylock (R) | | *100.0* |

| **Democratic Primary** | | |
|---|---|---|
| Dale Bumpers (D) | 330,088 | *66.7* |
| Q. Byrum Hurst (D) | 81,239 | *16.4* |
| Mack Harbour (D) | 55,172 | *11.2* |

**1974**

| **Republican Primary** | | |
|---|---|---|
| Ken Coon (R) | 3,698 | *81.9* |
| Joseph Weston (R) | 815 | *18.1* |

| **Democratic Primary** | | |
|---|---|---|
| David Pryor (D) | 297,673 | *51.0* |
| Orval E. Faubus (D) | 193,105 | *33.1* |
| Bob Riley (D) | 92,612 | *15.9* |

**1976**

| **Republican Primary** | | |
|---|---|---|
| Leon Griffith (R) | 13,044 | *57.2* |
| Joseph Weston (R) | 9,753 | *42.8* |

| **Democratic Primary** | | |
|---|---|---|
| David Pryor (D) | 312,865 | *59.5* |
| Jim Lindsey (D) | 171,031 | *32.5* |
| Frank Lady (D) | 36,832 | *7.0* |

**1978**

| **Republican Primary** | | |
|---|---|---|
| A. Lynn Lowe (R) | | *100.0* |

| **Democratic Primary** | | |
|---|---|---|
| Bill Clinton (D) | 341,118 | *59.7* |
| Joe D. Woodward (D) | 123,674 | *21.6* |
| Frank Lady (D) | 76,026 | *13.1* |

**1980**

| **Republican Primary** | | |
|---|---|---|
| Frank D. White (R) | 5,867 | *71.8* |
| Marshall Chrisman (R) | 2,310 | *28.2* |

| **Democratic Primary** | | |
|---|---|---|
| Bill Clinton (D) | 306,735 | *68.9* |
| Monroe A. Schwarzlose (D) | 138,660 | *31.1* |

**1982**

| **Republican Primary** | | |
|---|---|---|
| Frank D. White (R) | 11,111 | *83.2* |
| Marshall Chrisman (R) | 1,410 | *10.6* |
| Connie Voll (R) | 826 | *6.2* |

| Candidates | Votes | % |
|---|---|---|
| **Democratic Primary** | | |
| Bill Clinton (D) | 236,961 | *41.8* |
| Joe Purcell (D) | 166,066 | *29.3* |
| Jim Guy Tucker (D) | 129,362 | *22.8* |
| **Democratic Runoff** | | |
| Bill Clinton (D) | 239,209 | *53.7* |
| Joe Purcell (D) | 206,358 | *46.3* |

**1984**

| Candidates | Votes | % |
|---|---|---|
| **Republican Primary** | | |
| Woody Freeman (R) | 13,030 | *68.4* |
| Erwin Davis (R) | 6,010 | *31.2* |
| **Democratic Primary** | | |
| Bill Clinton (D) | 317,577 | *64.4* |
| Lonnie Turner (D) | 119,266 | *24.2* |
| Kermit Moss (D) | 31,727 | *6.4* |

**1986**

| Candidates | Votes | % |
|---|---|---|
| **Republican Primary** | | |
| Frank D. White (R) | 13,831 | *61.9* |
| Wayne Lanier (R) | 4,576 | *20.5* |
| Maurice Britt (R) | 3,116 | *13.9* |
| **Democratic Primary** | | |
| Bill Clinton (D) | 315,397 | *60.6* |
| Orval E. Faubus (D) | 174,402 | *33.5* |
| Dean Goldsby (D) | 30,829 | *5.9* |

**1990**

| Candidates | Votes | % |
|---|---|---|
| **Republican Primary** | | |
| Sheffield Nelson (R) | 47,246 | *54.3* |
| Tommy F. Robinson (R) | 39,731 | *45.7* |
| **Democratic Primary** | | |
| Bill Clinton (D) | 269,329 | *54.8* |
| Tom McRae (D) | 190,887 | *38.9* |

**Arkansas**
1. *Sims withdrew from a runoff, and Laney became the Democratic nominee.*

# CALIFORNIA

| | Candidates | Votes | % |
|---|---|---|---|
| **1958** | **Republican Primary** | | |
| | William F. Knowland (R) | 1,290,106 | *77.5* |
| | Edmund G. Brown (D) | 374,879 | *22.5* |
| | **Democratic Primary** | | |
| | Edmund G. Brown (D) | 1,890,622 | *82.6* |
| | William F. Knowland (R) | 313,385 | *13.7* |
| **1962** | **Republican Primary** | | |
| | Richard M. Nixon (R) | 1,285,151 | *65.4* |
| | Joseph C. Shell (R) | 656,542 | *33.4* |

| | Candidates | Votes | % |
|---|---|---|---|
| | **Democratic Primary** | | |
| | Edmund G. Brown (D) | 1,739,792 | *81.4* |
| | **Prohibition Primary** | | |
| | Robert L. Wyckoff | | *100.0* |
| **1966** | **Republican Primary** | | |
| | Ronald Reagan (R) | 1,417,623 | *64.7* |
| | George Christopher (R) | 675,683 | *30.8* |
| | **Democratic Primary** | | |
| | Edmund G. Brown (D) | 1,355,262 | *51.9* |
| | Samuel W. Yorty (D) | 981,088 | *37.6* |
| **1970** | **Republican Primary** | | |
| | Ronald Reagan (R) | | *100.0* |
| | **Democratic Primary** | | |
| | Jess Unruh (D) | 1,602,690 | *64.0* |
| | Samuel W. Yorty (D) | 659,494 | *26.3* |
| | **American Independent Primary** | | |
| | William K. Shearer (AMI) | 14,069 | *61.4* |
| | Keith H. Greene (AMI) | 8,827 | *38.5* |
| | **Peace and Freedom Primary** | | |
| | Ricardo Romo (PFP) | 6,214 | *63.5* |
| | Warren A. Nielsen (PFP) | 3,569 | *36.5* |
| **1974** | **Republican Primary** | | |
| | Houston I. Flournoy (R) | 1,164,015 | *63.0* |
| | Ed Reinecke (R) | 556,259 | *30.1* |
| | **Democratic Primary** | | |
| | Edmund G. Brown Jr. (D) | 1,085,752 | *37.7* |
| | Joseph L. Alioto (D) | 544,007 | *18.9* |
| | Robert Moretti (D) | 478,469 | *16.6* |
| | William M. Roth (D) | 293,686 | *10.2* |
| | Jerome R. Waldie (D) | 227,489 | *7.9* |
| | **American Independent Primary** | | |
| | Edmon V. Kaiser (AMI) | | *100.0* |
| | **Peace and Freedom Primary** | | |
| | Elizabeth Keathley (PFP) | 2,111 | *28.1* |
| | Lester H. Higby (PFP) | 1,855 | *24.7* |
| | C. T. Weber (PFP) | 1,822 | *24.2* |
| | Trudy Saposhnek (PFP) | 1,417 | *18.8* |
| **1978** | **Republican Primary** | | |
| | Evelle J. Younger (R) | 1,008,087 | *40.0* |
| | Ed Davis (R) | 738,741 | *29.3* |
| | Ken Maddy (R) | 484,583 | *19.2* |
| | Pete Wilson (R) | 230,146 | *9.1* |
| | **Democratic Primary** | | |
| | Edmund G. Brown Jr. (D) | 2,567,067 | *77.5* |

**725**

| Candidates<br>**American Independent Primary** | Votes | % |
|---|---|---|
| Theresa F. Dietrich (AMI) | 12,278 | 57.4 |
| Laszlo Kecskemethy (AMI) | 9,112 | 42.6 |
| **Peace and Freedom Primary** | | |
| Marilyn Seals (PFP) | | 100.0 |

### 1982

| **Republican Primary** | | |
|---|---|---|
| George Deukmejian (R) | 1,165,266 | 51.1 |
| Mike Curb (R) | 1,020,935 | 44.8 |
| **Democratic Primary** | | |
| Tom Bradley (D) | 1,726,985 | 61.1 |
| John Garamendi (D) | 712,161 | 25.2 |
| **American Independent Primary** | | |
| James C. Griffin (AMI) | | 100.0 |
| **Peace and Freedom Primary** | | |
| Elizabeth Martinez (PFP) | 4,353 | 55.1 |
| Jan B. Tucker (PFP) | 3,552 | 44.9 |
| **Libertarian Primary** | | |
| Dan P. Dougherty (LIBERT) | | 100.0 |

### 1986

| **Republican Primary** | | |
|---|---|---|
| George Deukmejian (R) | 1,927,288 | 93.6 |
| William H. R. Clark (R) | 132,125 | 6.4 |
| **Democratic Primary** | | |
| Tom Bradley (D) | 1,768,042 | 81.5 |
| Hugh G. Bagley (D) | 141,217 | 6.5 |
| Charles Pineda (D) | 109,001 | 5.0 |
| **American Independent Primary** | | |
| Gary V. Miller (AMI) | | 100.0 |
| **Peace and Freedom Primary** | | |
| Maria E. Munoz (PFP) | 3,508 | 69.8 |
| Cheryl Zuur (PFP) | 1,519 | 30.2 |
| **Libertarian Primary** | | |
| Joseph Fuhrig (LIBERT) | | 100.0 |

### 1990

| **Republican Primary** | | |
|---|---|---|
| Pete Wilson (R) | 1,856,613 | 87.5 |
| David M. Williams (R) | 107,397 | 5.1 |
| **Democratic Primary** | | |
| Dianne Feinstein (D) | 1,361,361 | 52.3 |
| John Van de Kamp (D) | 1,067,899 | 41.0 |
| **American Independent Primary** | | |
| Jerome McCready (AMI) | 8,921 | 54.1 |
| Chuck Morsa (AMI) | 7,563 | 45.9 |

| Candidates<br>**Libertarian Primary** | Votes | % |
|---|---|---|
| Dennis Thompson (LIBERT) | | 100.0 |
| **Peace and Freedom Primary** | | |
| Maria E. Munoz (PFP) | 3,461 | 56.7 |
| Merle Woo (PFP) | 2,647 | 43.3 |

# COLORADO

| Candidates | Votes | % |
|---|---|---|

### 1956

| **Republican Primary** | | |
|---|---|---|
| Donald G. Brotzman (R) | | 100.0 |
| **Democratic Primary** | | |
| Stephen McNichols (D) | | 100.0 |

### 1958

| **Republican Primary** | | |
|---|---|---|
| Palmer L. Burch (R) | | 100.0 |
| **Democratic Primary** | | |
| Stephen McNichols (D) | | 100.0 |

### 1962

| **Republican Primary** | | |
|---|---|---|
| John A. Love (R) | 66,027 | 59.6 |
| David A. Hamil (R) | 44,693 | 40.4 |
| **Democratic Primary** | | |
| Stephen McNichols (D) | | 100.0 |

### 1966

| **Republican Primary** | | |
|---|---|---|
| John A. Love (R) | | 100.0 |
| **Democratic Primary** | | |
| Robert L. Knous (D) | | 100.0 |

### 1970

| **Republican Primary** | | |
|---|---|---|
| John A. Love (R) | | 100.0 |
| **Democratic Primary** | | |
| Mark Hogan (D) | | 100.0 |

### 1974

| **Republican Primary** | | |
|---|---|---|
| John D. Vanderhoof (R) | 94,334 | 60.5 |
| Robert W. Daniels (R) | 61,691 | 39.5 |
| **Democratic Primary** | | |
| Richard D. Lamm (D) | 120,452 | 58.7 |
| Thomas Farley (D) | 84,796 | 41.3 |

### 1978

| **Republican Primary** | | |
|---|---|---|
| Ted Strickland (R) | 87,248 | 59.0 |
| Richard Plock (R) | 60,597 | 41.0 |

| Candidates<br>Democratic Primary | Votes | % |
|---|---|---|
| Richard D. Lamm (D) | | 100.0 |

**1982** | **Republican Primary** | | |
| John D. Fuhr (R) | | 100.0 |

| **Democratic Primary** | | |
| Richard D. Lamm (D) | | 100.0 |

**1986** | **Republican Primary** | | |
| Ted Strickland (R) | 66,796 | 35.6 |
| Steve Schuck (R) | 64,245 | 34.2 |
| Bob Kirscht (R) | 56,779 | 30.2 |

| **Democratic Primary** | | |
| Roy Romer (D) | | 100.0 |

**1990** | **Republican Primary** | | |
| John Andrews (R) | | 100.0 |

| **Democratic Primary** | | |
| Roy Romer (D) | | 100.0 |

# CONNECTICUT [1]

| | Candidates | Votes | % |
|---|---|---|---|
| 1970 | **Republican Primary** | | |
| | Thomas J. Meskill (R) | 93,419 | 71.4 |
| | Wallace Barnes (R) | 37,383 | 28.6 |
| 1978 | **Democratic Primary** | | |
| | Ella T. Grasso (D) | 137,904 | 67.3 |
| | Robert K. Killian (D) | 66,924 | 32.7 |
| 1986 | **Republican Primary** | | |
| | Julie D. Belaga (R) | 39,074 | 41.3 |
| | Richard C. Bozzuto (R) | 33,852 | 35.8 |
| | Gerald Labriola (R) | 21,610 | 22.9 |
| 1990 | **Democratic Primary** | | |
| | Bruce A. Morrison (D) | 84,771 | 64.7 |
| | William J. Cibes (D) | 46,294 | 35.3 |

**Connecticut**

1. In Connecticut, party conventions nominated candidates subject to a system of ''challenge'' primaries that allowed defeated candidates to petition for a popular vote if they received at least 20 percent of the convention vote. Returns are given here for challenge primaries held for the governorship nomination between 1956 and 1990.

# DELAWARE [1]

| | Candidates | Votes | % |
|---|---|---|---|
| 1972 | **Republican Primary** | | |
| | Russell W. Peterson (R) | 23,929 | 54.3 |
| | David P. Buckson (R) | 20,138 | 45.7 |
| 1980 | **Republican Primary** | | |
| | Pierre S. (Pete) du Pont IV (R) | | 100.0 |
| | **Democratic Primary** | | |
| | William J. Gordy (D) | | 100.0 |
| 1984 | **Republican Primary** | | |
| | Michael N. Castle (R) | | 100.0 |
| | **Democratic Primary** | | |
| | William T. Quillen (D) | 20,473 | 59.1 |
| | Sherman W. Tribbitt (D) | 14,185 | 40.9 |
| 1988 | **Republican Primary** | | |
| | Michael N. Castle (R) | | 100.0 |
| | **Democratic Primary** | | |
| | Jacob Kreshtool (D) | | 100.0 |
| 1992 | **Republican Primary** | | |
| | B. Gary Scott (R) | 23,994 | 81.8 |
| | Wilfred Plomis (R) | 5,346 | 18.2 |
| | **Democratic Primary** | | |
| | Thomas R. Carper (D) | 36,600 | 89.2 |
| | Daniel D. Rappa (D) | 4,434 | 10.8 |

**Delaware**

1. From 1972 through 1992 Delaware used a system of ''challenge'' primaries, in which a candidate for statewide office who received at least 35 percent of the convention vote could challenge the endorsed candidate in a primary.

# FLORIDA

| | Candidates | Votes | % |
|---|---|---|---|
| 1920 | **Democratic Primary** | | |
| | Cary E. Hardee (D) | 52,591 | 59.5 |
| | V. C. Swearingen (D) | 30,240 | 34.2 |
| | Lincoln Hulley (D) | 5,591 | 6.3 |
| | **Democratic Second Choice** | | |
| | Cary A. Hardee (D) | 1,559 | 51.7 |
| | V. C. Swearingen (D) | 1,459 | 48.3 |

| | Candidates | Votes | % |
|---|---|---|---|
| 1924 | **Democratic Primary** | | |
| | John W. Martin (D) | 55,715✔ | 38.0 |
| | Sidney J. Catts (D) | 43,230 | 29.5 |
| | Frank E. Jennings (D) | 37,962 | 25.9 |
| | Worth W. Trammell (D) | 8,381 | 5.7 |
| | **Democratic Second Choice** | | |
| | John W. Martin (D) | 17,339 | 74.1 |
| | Sidney J. Catts (D) | 6,067 | 25.9 |
| 1928 | **Democratic Primary** | | |
| | Doyle E. Carlton (D) | 77,569✔ | 30.4 |
| | Sidney J. Catts (D) | 68,984 | 27.1 |
| | Fons A. Hathaway (D) | 67,849 | 26.6 |
| | John S. Taylor (D) | 37,304 | 14.6 |
| | **Democratic Second Choice** | | |
| | Doyle E. Carlton (D) | 28,471 | 75.9 |
| | Sidney J. Catts (D) | 9,066 | 24.2 |
| 1932 | **Democratic Primary** | | |
| | John W. Martin (D) | 66,940 | 24.2 |
| | David Sholtz (D) | 55,406 | 20.0 |
| | Cary A. Hardee (D) | 50,427 | 18.2 |
| | Stafford Caldwell (D) | 44,938 | 16.2 |
| | Charles M. Durrance (D) | 36,291 | 13.1 |
| | **Democratic Runoff** | | |
| | David Sholtz (D) | 173,540 | 62.8 |
| | John W. Martin (D) | 102,805 | 37.2 |
| 1936 | **Democratic Primary** | | |
| | Raleigh Pettaway (D) | 51,705 | 15.7 |
| | Fred P. Cone (D) | 46,842 | 14.3 |
| | William C. Hodges (D) | 46,471 | 14.1 |
| | Jerry W. Carter (D) | 35,578 | 10.8 |
| | B. F. Paty (D) | 34,153 | 10.4 |
| | Dan Chappell (D) | 29,494 | 9.0 |
| | Grady Burton (D) | 24,985 | 7.6 |
| | Peter Thomasello Jr. (D) | 22,355 | 6.8 |
| | Stafford Caldwell (D) | 19,789 | 6.0 |
| | **Democratic Runoff** | | |
| | Fred P. Cone (D) | 184,540 | 58.8 |
| | Raleigh Pettaway (D) | 129,150 | 41.2 |
| 1940 | **Democratic Primary** | | |
| | Spessard L. Holland (D) | 118,962 | 24.7 |
| | Francis P. Whitehair (D) | 95,431 | 19.8 |
| | Fuller Warren (D) | 83,316 | 17.3 |
| | B. F. Paty (D) | 75,608 | 15.7 |
| | W. B. Fraser (D) | 36,855 | 7.7 |
| | James Barbee (D) | 33,699 | 7.0 |
| | **Democratic Runoff** | | |
| | Spessard L. Holland (D) | 272,718 | 57.0 |
| | Francis P. Whitehair (D) | 206,158 | 43.1 |
| 1944 | **Republican Primary** | | |
| | Bert L. Acker (R) | 5,954 | 61.3 |
| | Edward T. Keenan (R) | 3,766 | 38.7 |

| | Candidates | Votes | % |
|---|---|---|---|
| | **Democratic Primary** | | |
| | Millard F. Caldwell (D) | 116,111 | 28.6 |
| | Robert A. (Lex) Green (D) | 113,300 | 27.9 |
| | E. R. Graham (D) | 91,174 | 22.5 |
| | F. D. Upchurch (D) | 30,524 | 7.5 |
| | Raymond Sheldon (D) | 27,940 | 6.9 |
| | J. Edwin Baker (D) | 27,028 | 6.6 |
| | **Democratic Runoff** | | |
| | Millard F. Caldwell (D) | 215,485 | 55.3 |
| | Robert A. (Lex) Green (D) | 174,100 | 44.7 |
| 1948 | **Republican Primary** | | |
| | Bert L. Acker (R) | 10,807 | 64.0 |
| | John L. Cogdill (R) | 6,079 | 36.0 |
| | **Democratic Primary** | | |
| | Fuller Warren (D) | 183,326 | 32.7 |
| | Daniel T. McCarty (D) | 161,788 | 28.9 |
| | Colin English (D) | 85,158 | 15.2 |
| | W. A. Shands (D) | 62,358 | 11.1 |
| | J. Tom Watson (D) | 51,505 | 9.2 |
| | **Democratic Runoff** | | |
| | Fuller Warren (D) | 299,641 | 52.0 |
| | Daniel T. McCarty (D) | 276,425 | 48.0 |
| 1952 | **Republican Primary** [1] | | |
| | Harry S. Swan (R) | 11,148 | 43.0 |
| | Bert L. Acker (R) | 9,728 | 37.5 |
| | Elmore F. Kitzmiller (R) | 5,050 | 19.5 |
| | **Republican Runoff** | | |
| | Harry S. Swan (R) | 10,217 | 63.0 |
| | Bert L. Acker (R) | 5,995 | 37.0 |
| | **Democratic Primary** | | |
| | Daniel T. McCarty (D) | 316,427 | 48.9 |
| | Brailey Odham (D) | 232,565 | 31.5 |
| | Alto Adams (D) | 126,426 | 17.1 |
| | **Democratic Runoff** | | |
| | Daniel T. McCarty (D) | 384,200 | 53.3 |
| | Brailey Odham (D) | 336,716 | 46.7 |
| 1954 [1] | **Republican Special Primary** | | |
| | J. Tom Watson (R) | 24,429 | 68.0 |
| | Charles E. Compton (R) | 11,552 | 32.0 |
| | **Democratic Special Primary** | | |
| | Charley E. Johns (D) | 255,787 | 38.4 |
| | Leroy Collins (D) | 222,791 | 33.4 |
| | Brailey Odham (D) | 187,782 | 28.2 |
| | **Democratic Special Runoff** | | |
| | Leroy Collins (D) | 380,323 | 54.8 |
| | Charley E. Johns (D) | 314,198 | 45.2 |

| | Candidates | Votes | % |
|---|---|---|---|
| 1956 | **Republican Primary** | | |
| | W. A. Washburn Jr. (R) | | *100.0* |
| | **Democratic Primary** | | |
| | Leroy Collins (D) | 434,274 | *51.7* |
| | Sumter L. Lowery (D) | 179,019 | *21.3* |
| | Farris Bryant (D) | 110,469 | *13.2* |
| | Fuller Warren (D) | 107,990 | *12.9* |
| 1960 | **Republican Primary** | | |
| | George C. Peterson (R) | 65,202 | *72.7* |
| | Emerson H. Rupert (R) | 24,484 | *27.3* |
| | **Democratic Primary** | | |
| | Farris Bryant (D) | 193,507 | *20.7* |
| | Doyle E. Carlton Jr. (D) | 186,228 | *19.9* |
| | Haydon Burns (D) | 166,352 | *17.8* |
| | John M. McCarty (D) | 144,750 | *15.5* |
| | Fred Dickinson (D) | 115,520 | *12.3* |
| | Thomas E. David (D) | 80,057 | *8.5* |
| | **Democratic Runoff** | | |
| | Farris Bryant (D) | 512,757 | *55.2* |
| | Doyle E. Carlton Jr. (D) | 416,052 | *44.8* |
| 1964 | **Republican Primary** | | |
| | Charles R. Holley (R) | 70,573 | *53.9* |
| | H. B. Foster (R) | 33,563 | *25.6* |
| | Ken Folks (R) | 26,815 | *20.5* |
| | **Democratic Primary** | | |
| | Haydon Burns (D) | 312,453 | *27.5* |
| | Robert King High (D) | 207,280 | *18.3* |
| | Scott Kelly (D) | 205,078 | *18.1* |
| | Fred Dickinson (D) | 184,865 | *16.3* |
| | John E. Mathews (D) | 140,210 | *12.3* |
| | Frederick B. Karl (D) | 85,953 | *7.6* |
| | **Democratic Runoff** | | |
| | Haydon Burns (D) | 648,093 | *58.2* |
| | Robert King High (D) | 465,547 | *41.8* |
| 1966 | **Republican Primary** | | |
| | Claude R. Kirk Jr. (R) | 100,838 | *80.8* |
| | Richard B. Muldrew (R) | 23,953 | *19.2* |
| | **Democratic Primary** | | |
| | Haydon Burns (D) | 372,451 | *35.4* |
| | Robert King High (D) | 338,281 | *32.1* |
| | Scott Kelly (D) | 331,580 | *31.5* |
| | **Democratic Runoff** | | |
| | Robert King High (D) | 596,471 | *53.9* |
| | Haydon Burns (D) | 509,271 | *46.1* |
| 1970 | **Republican Primary** | | |
| | Claude R. Kirk Jr. (R) | 172,888 | *48.1* |
| | Jack M. Eckerd (R) | 137,731 | *38.4* |
| | L. A. (Skip) Bafalis (R) | 48,378 | *13.5* |

| | Candidates | Votes | % |
|---|---|---|---|
| | **Republican Runoff** | | |
| | Claude R. Kirk Jr. (R) | 199,943 | *56.8* |
| | Jack M. Eckerd (R) | 152,327 | *43.2* |
| | **Democratic Primary** | | |
| | Earl Faircloth (D) | 227,413 | *30.0* |
| | Reubin Askew (D) | 206,333 | *27.2* |
| | John E. Matthews (D) | 186,053 | *24.5* |
| | Chuck Hall (D) | 139,384 | *18.4* |
| | **Democratic Runoff** | | |
| | Reubin Askew (D) | 447,025 | *57.7* |
| | Earl Faircloth (D) | 328,038 | *42.3* |
| 1974 | **Republican Primary** | | |
| | Jerry Thomas (R) | | *100.0* |
| | **Democratic Primary** | | |
| | Reubin Askew (D) | 597,137 | *68.8* |
| | Ben Hill Griffin (D) | 137,008 | *16.3* |
| | Tom Adams (D) | 85,557 | *10.2* |
| 1978 | **Republican Primary** | | |
| | Jack M. Eckerd (R) | 244,394 | *63.8* |
| | Louis Frey (R) | 138,437 | *36.2* |
| | **Democratic Primary** | | |
| | Robert L. Shevin (D) | 364,732 | *35.2* |
| | Bob Graham (D) | 261,972 | *25.2* |
| | Hans G. Tanzler (D) | 124,706 | *12.0* |
| | Jim Williams (D) | 124,427 | *12.0* |
| | Bruce A. Smathers (D) | 85,298 | *8.2* |
| | Claude R. Kirk Jr. (D) | 62,534 | *6.0* |
| | **Democratic Runoff** | | |
| | Bob Graham (D) | 482,535 | *53.5* |
| | Robert L. Shevin (D) | 418,636 | *46.5* |
| 1982 | **Republican Primary** | | |
| | L. A. (Skip) Bafalis (R) | 325,108 | *86.4* |
| | Vernon Davids (R) | 51,340 | *13.6* |
| | **Democratic Primary** | | |
| | Bob Graham (D) | 839,320 | *84.5* |
| | Fred Kuhn (D) | 93,078 | *9.4* |
| | Robert P. Kunst (D) | 61,136 | *6.2* |
| 1986 | **Republican Primary** | | |
| | Bob Martinez (R) | 244,499 | *44.1* |
| | Louis Frey (R) | 138,017 | *24.9* |
| | Tom Gallagher (R) | 127,709 | *23.0* |
| | Chester Clem (R) | 44,438 | *8.0* |
| | **Republican Runoff** | | |
| | Bob Martinez (R) | 259,333 | *66.3* |
| | Louis Frey (R) | 131,652 | *33.7* |

| Candidates | Votes | % |
|---|---|---|
| **Democratic Primary** | | |
| Steve Pajcic (D) | 361,359 | 35.9 |
| Jim Smith (D) | 310,479 | 30.8 |
| Harry Johnston (D) | 258,038 | 25.6 |
| Mark K. Goldstein (D) | 54,077 | 5.4 |
| **Democratic Runoff** | | |
| Steve Pajcic (D) | 429,427 | 50.6 |
| Jim Smith (D) | 418,614 | 49.4 |

**1990**

| Candidates | Votes | % |
|---|---|---|
| **Republican Primary** | | |
| Bob Martinez (R) | 460,718 | 69.0 |
| Marlene Howard (R) | 132,565 | 19.8 |
| John Davis (R) | 34,720 | 5.2 |
| **Democratic Primary** | | |
| Lawton Chiles (D) | 746,325 | 69.5 |
| Bill Nelson (D) | 327,731 | 30.5 |

**Florida**

1. Returns from *Florida Handbook, 1975-76,* p. 534.

# GEORGIA

| Candidates | Votes | % |
|---|---|---|

**1920**

| **Democratic Primary** | | |
|---|---|---|
| Thomas W. Hardwick (D) | 99,210 | 42.9 |
| Clifford M. Walker (D) | 90,738 | 39.2 |
| John N. Holder (D) | 37,957 | 16.4 |
| **Democratic Runoff** [1] | | |
| Thomas W. Hardwick (D) | 84,257 | 55.3 |
| Clifford M. Walker (D) | 68,234 | 44.8 |

**1922**

| **Democratic Primary** | | |
|---|---|---|
| Clifford M. Walker (D) | 123,784 | 58.1 |
| Thomas W. Hardwick (D) | 86,389 | 40.6 |

**1924**

| **Democratic Primary** | | |
|---|---|---|
| Clifford M. Walker (D) | | 100.0 |

**1926**

| **Democratic Primary** | | |
|---|---|---|
| John N. Holder (D) | 71,976 | 37.3 |
| Lamartine G. Hardman (D) | 67,708 | 35.1 |
| George H. Carswell (D) | 32,484 | 16.8 |
| J. O. Wood (D) | 20,857 | 10.8 |
| **Democratic Runoff** [1] | | |
| Lamartine G. Hardman (D) | 80,868 | 57.3 |
| John N. Holder (D) | 60,197 | 42.7 |

**1928**

| **Democratic Primary** | | |
|---|---|---|
| Lamartine G. Hardman (D) | 137,430 | 58.5 |
| Eurith D. Rivers (D) | 97,339 | 41.5 |

**1930**

| Candidates | Votes | % |
|---|---|---|
| **Democratic Primary** | | |
| Richard B. Russell (D) | 56,177 | 27.3 |
| George H. Carswell (D) | 51,851 | 25.2 |
| Eurith D. Rivers (D) | 47,121 | 22.9 |
| John N. Holder (D) | 44,318 | 21.5 |
| **Democratic Runoff** [1] | | |
| Richard B. Russell (D) | 99,505 | 67.9 |
| George H. Carswell (D) | 47,157 | 32.2 |

**1932**

| **Democratic Primary** | | |
|---|---|---|
| Eugene Talmadge (D) | 116,381 | 42.0 |
| Abit Nix (D) | 78,588 | 28.4 |
| Thomas W. Hardwick (D) | 35,252 | 12.7 |
| John N. Holder (D) | 19,697 | 7.1 |

**1934**

| **Democratic Primary** | | |
|---|---|---|
| Eugene Talmadge (D) | 178,409 | 66.0 |
| Claude Pittman (D) | 87,049 | 32.2 |

**1936**

| **Democratic Primary** | | |
|---|---|---|
| Eurith D. Rivers (D) | 233,503 | 60.0 |
| Charles D. Redwine (D) | 123,095 | 31.6 |
| Blanton Fortson (D) | 32,715 | 8.4 |

**1938**

| **Democratic Primary** | | |
|---|---|---|
| Eurith D. Rivers (D) | 160,459 | 51.1 |
| Hugh Howell (D) | 134,121 | 42.7 |
| J. J. Mangham (D) | 19,537 | 6.2 |

**1940**

| **Democratic Primary** | | |
|---|---|---|
| Eugene Talmadge (D) | 183,133 | 51.6 |
| Columbus Roberts (D) | 127,653 | 36.0 |
| Abit Nix (D) | 44,282 | 12.5 |

**1942**

| **Democratic Primary** | | |
|---|---|---|
| Ellis Arnall (D) | 174,757 | 57.7 |
| Eugene Talmadge (D) | 128,394 | 42.4 |

**1946**

| **Democratic Primary** | | |
|---|---|---|
| J. V. Carmichael (D) | 313,389 | 45.3 |
| Eugene Talmadge (D) [2] | 297,245 | 43.0 |
| Eurith D. Rivers (D) | 69,489 | 10.0 |

**1948**

| **Democratic Special Primary** | | |
|---|---|---|
| Herman E. Talmadge (D) | 357,865 | 51.8 |
| M. E. Thompson (D) | 312,035 | 45.1 |

**1950**

| **Democratic Primary** | | |
|---|---|---|
| Herman E. Talmadge (D) | 287,637 | 49.3 |
| M. E. Thompson (D) | 279,137 | 47.9 |

**1954**

| **Democratic Primary** | | |
|---|---|---|
| S. Marvin Griffin (D) | 234,690 | 36.3 |
| M. E. Thompson (D) | 162,007 | 25.1 |
| Tom Linder (D) | 87,204 | 13.5 |
| Fred Hand (D) | 78,125 | 12.1 |
| Charlie Gowen (D) | 73,809 | 11.4 |

| 1958 | Candidates **Democratic Primary** | Votes | % |
|---|---|---|---|
| | S. Ernest Vandiver (D) | 499,477 | 80.5 |
| | William T. Bodenhamer (D) | 87,830 | 14.2 |
| | Lee Roy Abernathy (D) | 33,099 | 5.3 |
| 1962 | **Democratic Primary** | | |
| | Carl E. Sanders (D) | 494,978 | 58.1 |
| | S. Marvin Griffin (D) | 332,746 | 39.0 |
| 1966 | **Democratic Primary** | | |
| | Ellis Arnall (D) | 231,480 | 29.4 |
| | Lester Maddox (D) | 185,672 | 23.6 |
| | Jimmy Carter (D) | 164,562 | 20.9 |
| | James H. Gray (D) | 152,973 | 19.4 |
| | Garland T. Byrd (D) | 39,994 | 5.1 |
| | **Democratic Runoff** | | |
| | Lester Maddox (D) | 443,055 | 54.3 |
| | Ellis Arnall (D) | 373,004 | 45.7 |
| 1970 | **Republican Primary** | | |
| | Hal Suit (R) | 62,868 | 58.5 |
| | James L. Bentley (R) | 40,251 | 37.4 |
| | **Democratic Primary** | | |
| | Jimmy Carter (D) | 388,280 | 48.6 |
| | Carl E. Sanders (D) | 301,659 | 37.8 |
| | C. B. King (D) | 70,424 | 8.8 |
| | **Democratic Runoff** | | |
| | Jimmy Carter (D) | 506,462 | 59.4 |
| | Carl E. Sanders (D) | 345,906 | 40.6 |
| 1974 | **Republican Primary** | | |
| | Ronnie Thompson (R) | 19,691 | 41.0 |
| | Harold Dye (R) | 10,912 | 22.7 |
| | George Lankford (R) | 8,618 | 17.9 |
| | Harry Geisinger (R) | 6,078 | 12.7 |
| | W. M. (Bill) Coolidge (R) | 2,723 | 5.7 |
| | **Republican Runoff** | | |
| | Ronnie Thompson (R) | 22,211 | 50.6 |
| | Harold Dye (R) | 21,669 | 49.4 |
| | **Democratic Primary** | | |
| | Lester Maddox (D) | 310,384 | 36.3 |
| | George Busbee (D) | 177,997 | 20.8 |
| | Bert Lance (D) | 147,026 | 17.2 |
| | David H. Gambrell (D) | 66,000 | 7.7 |
| | George T. Smith (D) | 43,196 | 5.1 |
| | **Democratic Runoff** | | |
| | George Busbee (D) | 551,106 | 59.9 |
| | Lester Maddox (D) | 369,608 | 40.1 |
| 1978 | **Republican Primary** | | |
| | Rodney M. Cook (R) | 23,231 | 87.3 |
| | Bud Herrin (R) | 3,374 | 12.7 |

| | Candidates **Democratic Primary** | Votes | % |
|---|---|---|---|
| | George Busbee (D) | 503,875 | 72.4 |
| | Roscoe Emory Dean (D) | 111,901 | 16.1 |
| | J. B. Stoner (D) | 37,654 | 5.4 |
| 1982 | **Republican Primary** | | |
| | Bob Bell (R) | 36,347 | 59.2 |
| | Ben Blackburn (R) | 25,063 | 40.8 |
| | **Democratic Primary** | | |
| | Bo Ginn (D) | 316,019 | 35.1 |
| | Joe Frank Harris (D) | 223,445 | 24.8 |
| | Norman Underwood (D) | 147,536 | 16.4 |
| | Jack Watson (D) | 114,533 | 12.7 |
| | Billy Lovett (D) | 62,341 | 6.9 |
| | **Democratic Runoff** | | |
| | Joe Frank Harris (D) | 500,765 | 55.0 |
| | Bo Ginn (D) | 410,259 | 45.0 |
| 1986 | **Republican Primary** | | |
| | Guy Davis (R) | | 100.0 |
| | **Democratic Primary** | | |
| | Joe Frank Harris (D) | 521,704 | 85.3 |
| | Kenneth B. Quarterman (D) | 89,759 | 14.7 |
| 1990 | **Republican Primary** | | |
| | Johnny Isakson (R) | 87,795 | 74.3 |
| | Bob Wood (R) | 14,496 | 12.3 |
| | Greeley Ellis (R) | 13,062 | 11.1 |
| | **Democratic Primary** | | |
| | Zell Miller (D) | 434,405 | 41.3 |
| | Andrew Young (D) | 303,159 | 28.8 |
| | Roy E. Barnes (D) | 219,136 | 20.8 |
| | Lauren McDonald (D) | 64,212 | 6.1 |
| | **Democratic Run-Off** | | |
| | Zell Miller (D) | 591,166 | 61.8 |
| | Andrew Young (D) | 364,861 | 38.2 |

**Georgia**

1. In the Georgia primaries for the Democratic nomination for governor in 1920, 1926, 1930 and 1948, no candidate received a majority of the county unit votes. Thus, runoffs were necessary in each case between the two candidates who received the most county unit votes; these also happened to be the candidates who had the most popular votes.

In the runoffs, the candidate who achieved a county unit majority was the winner, regardless of whether he had a popular vote majority; but the county unit winner also finished first in the popular vote in each case. (For an explanation of the Georgia county unit system, see p. 629.)

2. Under Georgia's county unit system, Talmadge actually won the primary easily even though he finished in second place in the popular vote. He received 244 county unit votes, 59.5 percent, to Carmichael's 144 votes, 35.1 percent. (Explanation of county unit system, p. 629)

Talmadge later won the general election but died before his term was to begin, precipitating a famous crisis in Georgia's gubernatorial succession. (Footnote, p. 643)

# HAWAII

| Candidates | Votes | % |
|---|---|---|
| **1959** | | |
| **Republican Primary** | | |
| William F. Quinn (R) | | 100.0 |
| **Democratic Primary** | | |
| John A. Burns (D) | 69,152 | 89.8 |
| E. D. Hitchcock (D) | 7,828 | 10.2 |
| **Commonwealth Primary** | | |
| David Kihei (CP) | 65 | 64.4 |
| Epifanio Taok (CP) | 36 | 35.6 |
| **1962** | | |
| **Republican Primary** | | |
| William F. Quinn (R) | 44,205 | 57.1 |
| James K. Kealoha (R) | 33,272 | 49.9 |
| **Democratic Primary** | | |
| John A. Burns (D) | 71,540 | 90.2 |
| Hyman Greenstein (D) | 7,781 | 9.8 |
| **1966** | | |
| **Republican Primary** | | |
| Randolph Crossley (R) | 35,311 | 98.1 |
| **Democratic Primary** | | |
| John A. Burns (D) | 86,825 | 79.5 |
| G. J. Fontes (D) | 22,401 | 20.5 |
| **1970** | | |
| **Republican Primary** | | |
| Samuel P. King (R) | 20,605 | 49.3 |
| Hebden Porteus (R) | 17,880 | 42.8 |
| David Watumull (R) | 3,318 | 7.9 |
| **Democratic Primary** | | |
| John A. Burns (D) | 82,441 | 53.2 |
| Thomas P. Gill (D) | 69,209 | 44.7 |
| **1974** | | |
| **Republican Primary** | | |
| Randolph Crossley (R) | 25,425 | 82.5 |
| Joseph K. Hao (R) | 5,405 | 17.5 |
| **Democratic Primary** | | |
| George R. Ariyoshi (D) | 71,319 | 36.2 |
| Frank F. Fasi (D) | 62,023 | 31.5 |
| Thomas P. Gill (D) | 59,280 | 30.1 |
| **1978** | | |
| **Republican Primary** | | |
| John Leopold (R) | 20,524 | 91.6 |
| **Democratic Primary** | | |
| George R. Ariyoshi (D) | 130,527 | 50.3 |
| Frank F. Fasi (D) | 126,903 | 48.9 |
| **Aloha Democrat Primary** | | |
| John Moore (A-D) | | 100.0 |

| Candidates | Votes | % |
|---|---|---|
| **Libertarian Primary** | | |
| Gregory Reeser (LIBERT) | | 100.0 |
| **Non-partisan Primary** | | |
| Alema Leota (NON-PART) | 236 | 58.9 |
| Frank Pore (NON-PART) | 165 | 41.1 |
| **1982** | | |
| **Republican Primary** | | |
| D. G. Anderson (R) | 11,997 | 96.8 |
| **Democratic Primary** | | |
| George R. Ariyoshi (D) | 128,993 | 53.9 |
| Jean King (D) | 106,935 | 44.7 |
| **Independent Democratic Primary** | | |
| Frank F. Fasi (ID) | | 100.0 |
| **Non-partisan Primary** | | |
| BraDa Ji Price (NON-PART) [1] | | 100.0 |
| **1986** | | |
| **Republican Primary** | | |
| D. G. Anderson (R) | 38,790 | 94.6 |
| **Democratic Primary** | | |
| John Waihee (D) | 105,579 | 45.6 |
| Cecil Heftel (D) | 83,939 | 36.2 |
| Patsy T. Mink (D) | 37,998 | 16.4 |
| **1990** | | |
| **Republican Primary** | | |
| Fred Hemmings (R) | 38,827 | 90.1 |
| **Democratic Primary** | | |
| John Waihee (D) | 179,383 | 88.5 |
| **Libertarian Primary** | | |
| Triaka-Don Smith (LIBERT) | | 100.0 |

Hawaii
1. Price withdrew and no substitution was made.

# IDAHO

| Candidates | Votes | % |
|---|---|---|
| **1958** | | |
| **Republican Primary** | | |
| Robert E. Smylie (R) | | 100.0 |
| **Democratic Primary** | | |
| A. M. Derr (D) | 25,599 | 34.5 |
| H. Max Hanson (D) | 25,477 | 34.3 |
| John Glasby (D) | 21,207 | 28.6 |

| 1962 | Candidates<br>**Republican Primary** | Votes | % |
|---|---|---|---|
| | Robert E. Smylie (R) | 37,761 | 57.2 |
| | Elvin A. Lindquist (R) | 16,565 | 25.1 |
| | George L. Crookham (R) | 11,669 | 17.7 |
| | **Democratic Primary** | | |
| | Vernon K. Smith (D) | 35,574 | 43.1 |
| | Charles Herndon (D) | 18,072 | 21.9 |
| | John G. Walters (D) | 13,186 | 16.0 |
| | Howard D. Hechtner (D) | 7,952 | 9.6 |
| | Conley Ward (D) | 5,427 | 6.6 |
| 1966 | **Republican Primary** | | |
| | Don Samuelson (R) | 52,891 | 61.0 |
| | Robert E. Smylie (R) | 33,753 | 39.0 |
| | **Democratic Primary** | | |
| | Charles Herndon (D) [1] | 28,926 | 40.7 |
| | Cecil D. Andrus (D) | 27,649 | 39.0 |
| | William J. Dee (D) | 14,409 | 20.3 |
| 1970 | **Republican Primary** | | |
| | Don Samuelson (R) | 46,719 | 58.4 |
| | Dick Smith (R) | 33,339 | 41.6 |
| | **Democratic Primary** | | |
| | Cecil D. Andrus (D) | 29,036 | 46.0 |
| | Vernon Ravenscroft (D) | 23,369 | 37.1 |
| | Lloyd Walker (D) | 10,664 | 16.9 |
| 1974 | **Republican Primary** | | |
| | Jack M. Murphy (R) | | 100.0 |
| | **Democratic Primary** | | |
| | Cecil D. Andrus (D) | | 100.0 |
| 1978 | **Republican Primary** | | |
| | Allan Larsen (R) | 33,778 | 28.7 |
| | Vernon Ravenscroft (D) | 32,455 | 27.6 |
| | C. L. Otter (R) | 30,523 | 26.0 |
| | Larry Jackson (R) | 13,510 | 11.5 |
| | **Democratic Primary** | | |
| | John V. Evans (D) | | 100.0 |
| | **American Primary** | | |
| | Wayne L. Loveless (AM) | | 100.0 |
| 1982 | **Republican Primary** | | |
| | Phillip Batt (R) | 63,622 | 63.9 |
| | Ralph Olmstead (R) | 35,932 | 36.1 |
| | **Democratic Primary** | | |
| | John V. Evans (D) | | 100.0 |
| 1986 | **Republican Primary** | | |
| | David H. Leroy (R) | | 100.0 |

| 1990 | Candidates<br>**Democratic Primary** | Votes | % |
|---|---|---|---|
| | Cecil D. Andrus (D) | | 100.0 |
| | **Republican Primary** | | |
| | Roger Fairchild (R) | 37,728 | 37.1 |
| | Rachel S. Gilbert (R) | 33,483 | 32.9 |
| | Milton E. Erhart (R) | 30,514 | 30.0 |
| | **Democratic Primary** | | |
| | Cecil D. Andrus (D) | | 100.0 |

**Idaho**

1. Herndon died after the primary and the Democratic state central committee substituted Andrus as the nominee.

# ILLINOIS

| 1956 | Candidates<br>**Republican Primary** | Votes | % |
|---|---|---|---|
| | William G. Stratton (R) | 556,909 | 69.8 |
| | Warren E. Wright (R) | 187,645 | 23.5 |
| | **Democratic Primary** | | |
| | Herbert C. Paschen (D) [1] | 475,813 | 57.8 |
| | Morris B. Sachs (D) | 347,458 | 42.2 |
| 1960 | **Republican Primary** | | |
| | William G. Stratton (R) | 499,365 | 59.1 |
| | Hayes Robertson (R) | 345,340 | 40.9 |
| | **Democratic Primary** | | |
| | Otto Kerner (D) | 649,253 | 60.9 |
| | Joseph D. Lohman (D) | 232,345 | 21.8 |
| | Stephen A. Mitchell (D) | 184,651 | 17.3 |
| 1964 | **Republican Primary** | | |
| | Charles H. Percy (R) | 626,111 | 60.3 |
| | William J. Scott (R) | 388,903 | 37.4 |
| | **Democratic Primary** | | |
| | Otto Kerner (D) | | 100.0 |
| 1968 | **Republican Primary** | | |
| | Richard B. Ogilvie (R) | 335,727 | 47.5 |
| | John H. Altofer (R) | 288,904 | 40.9 |
| | William G. Stratton (R) | 50,041 | 7.1 |
| | **Democratic Primary** | | |
| | Samuel H. Shapiro (D) | | 100.0 |
| 1972 | **Republican Primary** | | |
| | Richard B. Ogilvie (R) | 442,323 | 75.5 |
| | John Mathis (D) | 143,053 | 24.4 |

**733**

## INDIANA

| Candidates | Votes | % |
|---|---|---|
| **Democratic Primary** | | |
| Daniel Walker (D) | 735,193 | *51.4* |
| Paul Simon (D) | 694,900 | *48.6* |

**1976** **Republican Primary**

| Candidates | Votes | % |
|---|---|---|
| James R. Thompson (R) | 625,457 | *86.4* |
| Richard H. Cooper (R) | 97,937 | *13.5* |

**Democratic Primary**

| Candidates | Votes | % |
|---|---|---|
| Michael J. Howlett (D) | 811,721 | *53.8* |
| Daniel Walker (D) | 696,380 | *46.2* |

**1978** **Republican Primary**

| Candidates | Votes | % |
|---|---|---|
| James R. Thompson (R) | | *100.0* |

**Democratic Primary**

| Candidates | Votes | % |
|---|---|---|
| Michael Bakalis (D) | 601,045 | *82.8* |
| W. Dakin Williams (D) | 124,406 | *17.2* |

**1982** **Republican Primary**

| Candidates | Votes | % |
|---|---|---|
| James R. Thompson (R) | 507,893 | *83.7* |
| John E. Roche (R) | 54,858 | *9.0* |
| V. A. Kelley (R) | 43,627 | *7.2* |

**Democratic Primary**

| Candidates | Votes | % |
|---|---|---|
| Adlai E. Stevenson III (D) | | *100.0* |

**1986** **Republican Primary**

| Candidates | Votes | % |
|---|---|---|
| James R. Thompson (R) | 452,685 | *90.9* |
| Peter Bowen (R) | 45,236 | *9.1* |

**Democratic Primary**

| Candidates | Votes | % |
|---|---|---|
| Adlai E. Stevenson III (D) [2] | 735,249 | *92.9* |
| Larry Burgess (D) | 55,930 | *7.1* |

**1990** **Republican Primary**

| Candidates | Votes | % |
|---|---|---|
| Jim Edgar (R) | 482,441 | *62.8* |
| Steven Baer (R) | 256,889 | *33.5* |

**Democratic Primary**

| Candidates | Votes | % |
|---|---|---|
| Neil F. Hartigan (D) | | *100.0* |

**Illinois**

1. *Paschen withdrew after the primary and the Democratic state committee substituted Richard B. Austin as the party's nominee.*

2. *Stevenson withdrew after the primary on the ground that the nominated candidate for lieutenant governor was a known supporter of Lyndon LaRouche, whose views were so different from Stevenson's as to make a joint candidacy impossible. No replacement candidate was named by the Democratic party. A new party, Illinois Solidarity, was formed with Stevenson as its gubernatorial candidate.*

## INDIANA

| | Candidates | Votes | % |
|---|---|---|---|
| **1976** [1] | **Republican Primary** | | |
| | Otis R. Bowen (R) | | *100.0* |

**Democratic Primary**

| Candidates | Votes | % |
|---|---|---|
| Larry A. Conrad (D) | 358,421 | *64.5* |
| Jack L. New (D) | 105,965 | *19.1* |
| Robert J. Fair (D) | 91,606 | *16.5* |

**1980** **Republican Primary**

| Candidates | Votes | % |
|---|---|---|
| Robert D. Orr (R) | | *100.0* |

**Democratic Primary**

| Candidates | Votes | % |
|---|---|---|
| John A. Hillenbrand (D) | 284,182 | *52.4* |
| W. Wayne Townsend (D) | 257,779 | *47.6* |

**1984** **Republican Primary**

| Candidates | Votes | % |
|---|---|---|
| Robert D. Orr (R) | 319,889 | *71.6* |
| John Snyder (R) | 126,778 | *28.4* |

**Democratic Primary**

| Candidates | Votes | % |
|---|---|---|
| W. Wayne Townsend (D) | 347,948 | *56.9* |
| Virginia Dill McCarty (D) | 219,806 | *35.9* |
| Donald W. Mantooth (D) | 43,507 | *7.1* |

**1988** **Republican Primary**

| Candidates | Votes | % |
|---|---|---|
| John M. Mutz (R) | | *100.0* |

**Democratic Primary**

| Candidates | Votes | % |
|---|---|---|
| Evan Bayh (D) | 493,198 | *83.1* |
| Stephen J. Daily (D) | 66,242 | *11.2* |
| Frank L. O'Bannon (D) | 34,360 | *5.8* |

**1992** **Republican Primary**

| Candidates | Votes | % |
|---|---|---|
| Linley E. Pearson (R) | 223,373 | *48.9* |
| H. Dean Evans (R) | 153,089 | *33.5* |
| John A. Johnson (R) | 80,784 | *17.7* |

**Democratic Primary**

| Candidates | Votes | % |
|---|---|---|
| Evan Bayh (D) | 390,938 | *100.0* |

**Indiana**

1. *Until 1976 all nominations for statewide office in Indiana were made by state party conventions.*

## IOWA

| | Candidates | Votes | % |
|---|---|---|---|
| **1956** | **Republican Primary** | | |
| | Leo A. Hoegh (R) | | *100.0* |

| | Candidates | Votes | % |
|---|---|---|---|
| | **Democratic Primary** | | |
| | Herschel C. Loveless (D) | 77,206 | *70.0* |
| | Lawrence E. Plummer (D) | 33,103 | *30.0* |
| **1958** | **Republican Primary** | | |
| | William G. Murray (R) | 112,496 | *56.6* |
| | W. H. Nicholas (R) | 86,154 | *43.4* |
| | **Democratic Primary** | | |
| | Herschel C. Loveless (D) | | *100.0* |
| **1960** | **Republican Primary** | | |
| | Norman A. Erbe (R) | 81,869 | *36.3* |
| | Jack Schroeder (R) | 75,599 | *33.5* |
| | W. H. Nicholas (R) | 68,037 | *30.2* |
| | **Democratic Primary** | | |
| | E. J. McManus (D) | 74,990 | *61.7* |
| | Harold E. Hughes (D) | 46,542 | *38.3* |
| **1962** | **Republican Primary** | | |
| | Norman A. Erbe (R) | 134,010 | *67.7* |
| | W. H. Nicholas (R) | 63,966 | *32.3* |
| | **Democratic Primary** | | |
| | Harold E. Hughes (D) | 66,624 | *78.9* |
| | Lewis E. Lint (D) | 17,770 | *21.1* |
| **1964** | **Republican Primary** | | |
| | Evan Hultman (R) | | *100.0* |
| | **Democratic Primary** | | |
| | Harold E. Hughes (D) | | *100.0* |
| **1966** | **Republican Primary** | | |
| | William G. Murray (R) | 87,371 | *50.5* |
| | Robert K. Beck (R) | 85,733 | *49.5* |
| | **Democratic Primary** | | |
| | Harold E. Hughes (D) | | *100.0* |
| **1968** | **Republican Primary** | | |
| | Robert Ray (R) | 108,744 | *43.2* |
| | Donald E. Johnson (R) | 77,715 | *30.8* |
| | Robert K. Beck (R) | 65,439 | *26.0* |
| | **Democratic Primary** | | |
| | Paul Franzenburg | | *100.0* |
| **1970** | **Republican Primary** | | |
| | Robert Ray (R) | | *100.0* |
| | **Democratic Primary** | | |
| | Robert Fulton (D) | 48,459 | *46.7* |
| | William Gannon (D) | 46,524 | *44.8* |
| | Robert L. Nereim (D) | 8,796 | *8.5* |

| | Candidates | Votes | % |
|---|---|---|---|
| **1972** | **Republican Primary** | | |
| | Robert Ray (R) | | *100.0* |
| | **Democratic Primary** | | |
| | Paul Franzenburg (D) | 85,807 | *57.5* |
| | John Tapscott (D) | 63,284 | *42.4* |
| | **American Independent Primary** | | |
| | Robert D. Dilley (AMI) | | *100.0* |
| **1974** | **Republican Primary** | | |
| | Robert Ray (R) | | *100.0* |
| | **Democratic Primary** | | |
| | James F. Schaben (D) | 59,840 | *44.8* |
| | William Gannon (D) | 52,420 | *39.3* |
| | Clark Rasmussen (D) | 21,240 | *15.9* |
| **1978** | **Republican Primary** | | |
| | Robert Ray (R) | 136,517 | *87.5* |
| | Donovan D. Nelson (R) | 19,486 | *12.5* |
| | **Democratic Primary** | | |
| | Jerome D. Fitzgerald (D) | 58,039 | *55.5* |
| | Tom Whitney (D) | 37,132 | *35.5* |
| | Warren D. Strait (D) | 9,443 | *9.0* |
| **1982** | **Republican Primary** | | |
| | Terry Branstad (R) | | *100.0* |
| | **Democratic Primary** | | |
| | Roxanne Conlin (D) | 94,481 | *48.2* |
| | Jerome D. Fitzgerald (D) | 61,340 | *31.3* |
| | Edward L. Campbell (D) | 40,233 | *20.5* |
| **1986** | **Republican Primary** | | |
| | Terry E. Branstad (R) | | *100.0* |
| | **Democratic Primary** | | |
| | Lowell L. Junkins (D) | 70,605 | *52.6* |
| | Bob Anderson (D) | 44,550 | *33.2* |
| | George R. Kinley (D) | 15,473 | *11.5* |
| **1990** | **Republican Primary** | | |
| | Terry E. Branstad (R) | | *100.0* |
| | **Democratic Primary** | | |
| | Donald D. Avenson (D) | 79,022 | *39.5* |
| | Tom Miller (D) | 63,364 | *31.6* |
| | John Chrystal (D) | 52,170 | *26.0* |

**735**

# KANSAS

| | Candidates | Votes | % |
|---|---|---|---|
| **1956** | **Republican Primary** | | |
| | Warren W. Shaw (R) | 156,476 | *52.7* |
| | Fred Hall (R) | 123,398 | *41.5* |
| | **Democratic Primary** | | |
| | George Docking (D) | 76,544 | *50.3* |
| | Harry H. Woodring (D) | 75,548 | *49.7* |
| **1958** | **Republican Primary** | | |
| | Clyde M. Reed (R) | 142,247 | *72.6* |
| | Fred Hall (R) | 35,632 | *18.2* |
| | **Democratic Primary** | | |
| | George Docking (D) | | *100.0* |
| **1960** | **Republican Primary** | | |
| | John Anderson (R) | 128,081 | *48.7* |
| | McDill Boyd (R) | 116,725 | *44.4* |
| | William H. Addington (R) | 18,169 | *6.9* |
| | **Democratic Primary** | | |
| | George Docking (D) | | *100.0* |
| **1962** | **Republican Primary** | | |
| | John Anderson (R) | 164,888 | *84.1* |
| | Harvey F. Crouch (R) | 31,221 | *15.9* |
| | **Democratic Primary** | | |
| | Dale E. Saffels (D) | 69,728 | *59.7* |
| | George Hart (D) | 47,055 | *40.3* |
| **1964** | **Republican Primary** | | |
| | William H. Avery (R) | 85,746 | *30.4* |
| | McDill Boyd (R) | 75,451 | *26.7* |
| | Paul R. Wunsch (R) | 71,601 | *25.4* |
| | William M. Ferguson (R) | 36,622 | *13.0* |
| | **Democratic Primary** | | |
| | Harry G. Wiles (D) | 50,590 | *32.4* |
| | Jules V. Doty (D) | 37,305 | *23.9* |
| | George Hart (D) | 30,973 | *19.8* |
| | Joseph W. Henkle (D) | 21,304 | *13.6* |
| | J. Donald Coffin (D) | 9,140 | *5.9* |
| **1966** | **Republican Primary** | | |
| | William H. Avery (R) | 144,842 | *75.1* |
| | Dell Crozier (R) | 48,051 | *24.9* |
| | **Democratic Primary** | | |
| | Robert Docking (D) | 96,414 | *85.5* |
| | George Hart (D) | 16,385 | *14.5* |
| **1968** | **Republican Primary** | | |
| | Rick Harman (R) | 133,454 | *48.9* |
| | John Crutcher (R) | 128,635 | *47.1* |

| | Candidates | Votes | % |
|---|---|---|---|
| | **Democratic Primary** | | |
| | Robert Docking (D) | | *100.0* |
| **1970** | **Republican Primary** | | |
| | Kent Frizzell (R) | 141,298 | *60.5* |
| | Rick Harman (R) | 78,086 | *33.4* |
| | **Democratic Primary** | | |
| | Robert Docking (D) | | *100.0* |
| **1972** | **Republican Primary** | | |
| | Morris Kay (R) | 138,815 | *46.6* |
| | John Anderson (R) | 88,088 | *29.6* |
| | Ray E. Frisbie (R) | 46,125 | *15.5* |
| | Reynolds Shultz (R) | 24,911 | *8.4* |
| | **Democratic Primary** | | |
| | Robert Docking (D) | | *100.0* |
| **1974** | **Republican Primary** | | |
| | Robert F. Bennett (R) | 67,347 | *32.4* |
| | Donald O. Concannon (R) | 66,817 | *32.1* |
| | Forrest J. Robinson (R) | 56,440 | *27.2* |
| | Robert W. Clack (R) | 17,333 | *8.3* |
| | **Democratic Primary** | | |
| | Vern Miller (D) | | *100.0* |
| **1978** | **Republican Primary** | | |
| | Robert F. Bennett (R) | 142,239 | *69.2* |
| | Robert R. Sanders (R) | 40,542 | *19.7* |
| | Harold Knight (R) | 22,671 | *11.1* |
| | **Democratic Primary** | | |
| | John Carlin (D) | 71,366 | *55.2* |
| | Bert Chaney (D) | 34,132 | *26.4* |
| | Harry G. Wiles (D) | 23,762 | *18.4* |
| **1982** | **Republican Primary** | | |
| | Sam Hardage (R) | 86,692 | *36.8* |
| | Dave Owen (R) | 79,770 | *33.8* |
| | Wendell Lady (R) | 61,419 | *26.0* |
| | **Democratic Primary** | | |
| | John Carlin (D) | 103,780 | *78.9* |
| | Jimmy D. Montgomery (D) | 27,785 | *21.1* |
| **1986** | **Republican Primary** | | |
| | Mike Hayden (R) | 99,669 | *36.1* |
| | Larry Jones (R) | 85,989 | *31.1* |
| | Jack H. Brier (R) | 37,410 | *13.6* |
| | Gene Bicknell (R) | 25,733 | *9.3* |
| | Richard J. Peckham (R) | 18,876 | *6.8* |
| | **Democratic Primary** | | |
| | Thomas R. Docking (D) | | *100.0* |

| 1990 | Candidates<br>**Republican Primary** | Votes | % |
|---|---|---|---|
| | Mike Hayden (R) | 138,467 | *44.7* |
| | Nestor Weigand (R) | 130,816 | *42.3* |
| | Richard Peckham (R) | 29,033 | *9.4* |
| | **Democratic Primary** | | |
| | Joan Finney (D) | 81,250 | *47.2* |
| | John Carlin (D) | 79,406 | *46.1* |
| | Fred Phelps (D) | 11,572 | *6.7* |

# KENTUCKY

| | Candidates | Votes | % |
|---|---|---|---|
| 1959 | **Republican Primary** | | |
| | John M. Robsion (R) | 63,130 | *86.3* |
| | Thurman J. Hamlin (R) | 6,019 | *8.2* |
| | Granville Thomas (R) | 3,991 | *5.5* |
| | **Democratic Primary** | | |
| | Bert T. Combs (D) | 292,462 | *53.0* |
| | Harry Lee Waterfield (D) | 259,461 | *45.6* |
| 1963 | **Republican Primary** | | |
| | Louie B. Nunn (R) | 77,455 | *88.5* |
| | J. N. R. Cecil (R) | 10,039 | *11.5* |
| | **Democratic Primary** | | |
| | Edward T. Breathitt (D) | 318,858 | *53.8* |
| | Albert B. Chandler (D) | 256,451 | *43.2* |
| 1967 | **Republican Primary** | | |
| | Louie B. Nunn (R) | 90,216 | *50.4* |
| | Marlow W. Cook (R) | 86,397 | *48.3* |
| | **Democratic Primary** | | |
| | Henry Ward (D) | 207,797 | *52.4* |
| | Albert B. Chandler (D) | 111,782 | *28.2* |
| | Harry Lee Waterfield (D) | 42,583 | *10.7* |
| 1971 | **Republican Primary** | | |
| | Thomas Emberton (R) | 84,863 | *84.1* |
| | Ried Martin (R) | 6,379 | *6.3* |
| | Thurman J. Hamlin (R) | 5,469 | *5.4* |
| | **Democratic Primary** | | |
| | Wendell H. Ford (D) | 237,815 | *53.0* |
| | Bert T. Combs (D) | 195,678 | *43.6* |
| 1975 | **Republican Primary** | | |
| | Robert E. Gable (R) | 38,113 | *51.3* |
| | Elmer Begley (R) | 16,885 | *22.7* |
| | T. William Klein (R) | 10,844 | *14.6* |
| | Granville Thomas (R) | 8,426 | *11.3* |

| | Candidates<br>**Democratic Primary** | Votes | % |
|---|---|---|---|
| | Julian Carroll (D) | 263,965 | *66.3* |
| | Todd Hollenbach (D) | 113,285 | *28.5* |
| 1979 | **Republican Primary** | | |
| | Louie B. Nunn (R) | 106,006 | *79.6* |
| | Ray B. White (R) | 18,514 | *13.9* |
| | **Democratic Primary** | | |
| | John Y. Brown, Jr. (D) | 165,158 | *29.1* |
| | Harvey Sloane (D) | 139,713 | *24.6* |
| | Terry McBrayer (D) | 131,530 | *23.2* |
| | Carroll Hubbard (D) | 68,577 | *12.1* |
| | Thelma L. Stovall (D) | 47,633 | *8.4* |
| 1983 | **Republican Primary** | | |
| | Jim Bunning (R) | 72,808 | *74.4* |
| | Lester Burns (R) | 7,340 | *7.5* |
| | Donald Wiggins (R) | 5,464 | *5.6* |
| | Elizabeth Wickham (R) | 5,174 | *5.3* |
| | **Democratic Primary** | | |
| | Martha Layne Collins (D) | 223,692 | *34.0* |
| | Harvey Sloane (D) | 219,160 | *33.3* |
| | Grady Strumbo (D) | 199,795 | *30.3* |
| 1987 | **Republican Primary** | | |
| | John Harper (R) | 37,432 | *41.4* |
| | Joseph E. Johnson (R) | 22,396 | *24.8* |
| | Leonard W. Beasley (R) | 21,067 | *23.3* |
| | Thurman J. Hamlin (R) | 9,475 | *10.5* |
| | **Democratic Primary** | | |
| | Wallace G. Wilkinson (D) | 221,138 | *34.9* |
| | John Y. Brown, Jr. (D) | 163,204 | *25.8* |
| | Steven L. Beshear (D) | 114,439 | *18.1* |
| | Grady Stumbo (D) | 84,613 | *13.4* |
| | Julian Carroll (D) | 42,137 | *6.6* |
| 1991 | **Republican Primary** | | |
| | Larry J. Hopkins (R) | 81,526 | *50.6* |
| | Lawrence E. Forgy (R) | 79,581 | *49.4* |
| | **Democratic Primary** | | |
| | Brereton C. Jones (D) | 184,703 | *37.5* |
| | Scott Baesler (D) | 149,352 | *30.4* |
| | Floyd G. Poore (D) | 132,060 | *26.8* |
| | Gatewood Galbraith (D) | 25,834 | *5.3* |

# LOUISIANA

| | Candidates | Votes | % |
|---|---|---|---|
| 1920 | **Democratic Primary** | | |
| | John M. Parker (D) | 77,868 | *54.2* |
| | Frank P. Stubbs (D) | 65,685 | *45.8* |

**737**

| 1924 | Candidates | Votes | % |
|---|---|---|---|
| | **Democratic Primary** | | |
| | Hewitt Bouanchaud (D) | 84,162 | 35.1 |
| | Henry L. Fuqua (D) | 81,382 | 34.0 |
| | Huey P. Long (D) | 73,985 | 30.9 |
| | **Democratic Runoff** | | |
| | Henry L. Fuqua (D) | 125,880 | 57.8 |
| | Hewitt Bouanchaud (D) | 92,006 | 42.2 |
| 1928 | **Democratic Primary** | | |
| | Huey P. Long (D) | 126,842 | 43.9 |
| | Riley J. Wilson (D)[1] | 81,747 | 28.3 |
| | O. H. Simpson (D) | 80,326 | 27.8 |
| 1932 | **Democratic Primary** | | |
| | Oscar K. Allen (D) | 214,699 | 56.5 |
| | Dudley J. LeBlanc (D) | 110,048 | 29.0 |
| | George Seth Guion (D) | 53,756 | 14.2 |
| 1936 | **Democratic Primary** | | |
| | Richard W. Leche (D) | 362,502 | 67.1 |
| | Cleveland Dear (D) | 176,150 | 32.6 |
| 1940 | **Democratic Primary** | | |
| | Earl K. Long (D) | 226,385 | 40.9 |
| | Sam H. Jones (D) | 154,936 | 28.0 |
| | J. A. Noe (D) | 116,564 | 21.1 |
| | James H. Morrison (D) | 48,243 | 8.7 |
| | **Democratic Runoff** | | |
| | Sam H. Jones (D) | 284,437 | 51.7 |
| | Earl K. Long (D) | 265,403 | 48.3 |
| 1944 | **Democratic Primary** | | |
| | Jimmie H. Davis (D) | 167,434 | 34.9 |
| | Lewis L. Morgan (D) | 131,682 | 27.5 |
| | James H. Morrison (D) | 76,081 | 15.9 |
| | Dudley J. LeBlanc (D) | 40,392 | 8.4 |
| | Sam S. Caldwell (D) | 34,335 | 7.2 |
| | **Democratic Runoff** | | |
| | Jimmie H. Davis (D) | 251,228 | 53.6 |
| | Lewis L. Morgan (D) | 217,915 | 46.5 |
| 1948 | **Democratic Primary** | | |
| | Earl K. Long (D) | 267,253 | 41.5 |
| | Sam H. Jones (D) | 147,329 | 22.9 |
| | Robert F. Kennon (D) | 127,569 | 19.8 |
| | James H. Morrison (D) | 101,754 | 15.8 |
| | **Democratic Runoff** | | |
| | Earl K. Long (D) | 432,528 | 65.9 |
| | Sam H. Jones (D) | 223,971 | 34.1 |
| 1952 | **Democratic Primary** | | |
| | Carlos G. Spaht (D) | 173,987 | 22.8 |
| | Robert F. Kennon (D) | 163,434 | 21.5 |
| | Hale Boggs (D) | 142,542 | 18.7 |
| | James M. McLemore (D) | 116,405 | 15.3 |

| | Candidates | Votes | % |
|---|---|---|---|
| | William J. Dodd (D) | 90,925 | 11.9 |
| | Dudley J. LeBlanc (D) | 62,906 | 8.3 |
| | **Democratic Runoff** | | |
| | Robert F. Kennon (D) | 482,302 | 61.4 |
| | Carlos G. Spaht (D) | 302,743 | 38.6 |
| 1956 | **Democratic Primary** | | |
| | Earl K. Long (D) | 421,681 | 51.4 |
| | deLesseps S. Morrison (D) | 191,576 | 23.4 |
| | Frederick T. Preaus (D) | 95,955 | 11.7 |
| | Francis C. Grevemberg (D) | 62,309 | 7.6 |
| | James M. McLemore (D) | 48,188 | 5.9 |
| 1959[2] | **Republican Primary** | | |
| | F. C. Grevemberg (R) | | 100.0 |
| | **Democratic Primary** | | |
| | deLesseps S. Morrison (D) | 278,956 | 33.1 |
| | Jimmie H. Davis (D) | 213,551 | 25.3 |
| | William M. Rainach (D) | 143,095 | 17.0 |
| | James A. Noe (D) | 97,654 | 11.6 |
| | William J. Dodd (D) | 85,436 | 10.1 |
| | **Democratic Runoff** | | |
| | Jimmie H. Davis (R) | 487,681 | 54.1 |
| | deLesseps S. Morrison (D) | 414,110 | 45.9 |
| 1963[3] | **Republican Primary** | | |
| | Charlton H. Lyons Sr. (R) | | 100.0 |
| | **Democratic Primary** | | |
| | deLesseps S. Morrison (D) | 299,702 | 33.1 |
| | John J. McKeithen (D) | 157,304 | 17.4 |
| | Gillis W. Long (D) | 137,778 | 15.2 |
| | Robert F. Kennon (D) | 127,870 | 14.1 |
| | Shelby M. Jackson (D) | 103,949 | 11.5 |
| | **Democratic Runoff** | | |
| | John J. McKeithen (D) | 492,905 | 52.2 |
| | deLesseps S. Morrison (D) | 451,161 | 47.8 |
| 1967 | **Democratic Primary** | | |
| | John J. McKeithen (D) | 836,304 | 80.6 |
| | John R. Rarick (D) | 179,846 | 17.3 |
| 1971 | **Republican Primary** | | |
| | David C. Treen (R) | 9,732 | 92.1 |
| | Robert Ross (R) | 839 | 7.9 |
| | **Democratic Primary** | | |
| | Edwin W. Edwards (D) | 276,397 | 23.5 |
| | J. Bennett Johnston (D) | 208,830 | 17.8 |
| | Gillis W. Long (D) | 164,276 | 14.0 |
| | Jimmie H. Davis (D) | 138,756 | 11.8 |
| | John G. Schwegmann (D) | 92,072 | 7.8 |
| | A. A. Aycock (D) | 88,465 | 7.5 |
| | Samuel Bell (D) | 72,486 | 6.2 |
| | Speedy O. Long (D) | 61,359 | 5.2 |

| Candidates | Votes | % |
|---|---|---|
| **Democratic Runoff** | | |
| Edwin W. Edwards (D) | 584,262 | *50.2* |
| J. Bennett Johnston (D) | 579,774 | *49.8* |

1975 [4] **Open Primary**

| Candidates | Votes | % |
|---|---|---|
| Edwin W. Edwards (D) | 750,107 | *62.3* |
| Robert C. Jones (D) | 292,220 | *24.3* |
| Wade O. Martin (D) | 146,368 | *12.2* |

1979 [5] **Open Primary**

| Candidates | Votes | % |
|---|---|---|
| David C. Treen (R) | 297,674 | *21.0* |
| Louis Lambert (D) | 283,266 | *20.7* |
| James E. Fitzmorris (D) | 280,760 | *20.6* |
| Paul Hardy (D) | 227,026 | *16.6* |
| E. L. Henry (D) | 135,769 | *9.9* |
| Edgar G. Mouton (D) | 124,333 | *9.1* |

1987 **Open Primary**

| Candidates | Votes | % |
|---|---|---|
| Charles Roemer (D) | 516,078 | *33.1* |
| Edwin W. Edwards (D) [6] | 437,801 | *28.0* |
| Bob Livingston (R) | 287,780 | *18.5* |
| W. J. Tauzin (D) | 154,079 | *9.9* |
| James H. Brown (D) | 138,223 | *8.8* |

1991 **Open Primary**

| Candidates | Votes | % |
|---|---|---|
| Edwin W. Edwards (D) | 523,195 | *33.8* |
| David E. Duke (R) | 491,342 | *31.7* |
| Charles Roemer (R) | 410,690 | *26.5* |
| Clyde C. Holloway (R) | 82,683 | *5.3* |

**Louisiana**

*1. Wilson declined a runoff with Long, who became the Democratic nominee.*

*2. The Democratic and Republican primaries were held Dec. 5, 1959; the Democratic runoff was held Jan. 9, 1960.*

*3. The Democratic and Republican primaries were held Dec. 7, 1963; the Democratic runoff was held Jan. 11, 1964.*

*4. In 1975 Louisiana eliminated the partisan primary for governor and instituted an open primary with candidates from all parties running on the same ballot. Any candidate who received a majority appeared in the general election unopposed. If no candidate received 50 percent, a runoff was held between the two top finishers.*

*5. In 1979 there was a court-ordered recount of the votes for the top three candidates. Results were as follows: Treen: 297,469 votes, 34.6%; Lambert: 282,708, 32.8%; and Fitzmorris: 280,412, 32.6%.*

*6. Edwards withdrew and no runoff election was held in November.*

# MAINE

| Candidates | Votes | % |
|---|---|---|
| 1956 **Republican Primary** | | |
| Willis A Trafton (R) | 42,901 | *51.0* |
| Philip F. Chapman (R) | 24,787 | *29.4* |
| Alexander A. LaFleur (R) | 16,479 | *19.6* |
| **Democratic Primary** | | |
| Edmund S. Muskie (D) | | *100.0* |
| 1958 **Republican Primary** | | |
| Horace A. Hildreth (R) | 63,424 | *62.0* |
| Philip F. Chapman (R) | 38,865 | *38.0* |

| Candidates | Votes | % |
|---|---|---|
| **Democratic Primary** | | |
| Clinton A. Clauson (D) | 20,736 | *51.8* |
| Maynard C. Dolloff (D) | 19,301 | *48.2* |
| 1960 **Republican Primary** | | |
| John H. Reed (R) | | *100.0* |
| **Democratic Primary** | | |
| Frank M. Coffin (D) | | *100.0* |
| 1962 **Republican Primary** | | |
| John H. Reed (R) | | *100.0* |
| **Democratic Primary** | | |
| Maynard C. Dolloff (D) | 18,234 | *50.3* |
| Richard J. Dubord (D) | 18,007 | *49.7* |
| 1966 **Republican Primary** | | |
| John H. Reed (R) | 55,924 | *59.7* |
| James S. Erwin (R) | 37,765 | *40.3* |
| **Democratic Primary** | | |
| Kenneth M. Curtis (D) | 30,879 | *55.6* |
| Carlton D. Reed (D) | 13,839 | *24.9* |
| Dana W. Childs (D) | 10,793 | *19.4* |
| 1970 **Republican Primary** | | |
| James S. Erwin (R) | 72,760 | *89.1* |
| Calvin F. Grass (R) | 8,898 | *10.9* |
| **Democratic Primary** | | |
| Kenneth M. Curtis (D) | 33,052 | *63.2* |
| Plato Truman (D) | 19,266 | *36.8* |
| 1974 **Republican Primary** | | |
| James S. Erwin (R) | 38,044 | *39.3* |
| Harrison L. Richardson (R) | 36,693 | *37.9* |
| Wakine G. Tanous (R) | 18,786 | *19.4* |
| **Democratic Primary** | | |
| George J. Mitchell (D) | 33,312 | *37.5* |
| Joseph E. Brennan (D) | 23,443 | *26.4* |
| Peter S. Kelley (D) | 21,358 | *24.1* |
| Lloyd P. LaFountain (D) | 7,954 | *9.0* |
| 1978 **Republican Primary** | | |
| Linwood E. Palmer (R) | 35,976 | *48.7* |
| Charles L. Cragin (R) | 28,244 | *38.3* |
| Jerrold B. Speers (R) | 9,603 | *13.0* |
| **Democratic Primary** | | |
| Joseph E. Brennan (D) | 38,361 | *52.0* |
| Philip L. Merrill (D) | 26,803 | *36.3* |
| Richard J. Carey (D) | 8,588 | *11.6* |

| | Candidates | Votes | % |
|---|---|---|---|
| **1982** | **Republican Primary** | | |
| | Charles L. Cragin (R) | 32,235 | *38.0* |
| | Sherry F. Huber (R) | 27,739 | *32.7* |
| | Richard H. Pierce (R) | 24,820 | *29.3* |
| | **Democratic Primary** | | |
| | Joseph E. Brennan (D) | 56,990 | *76.8* |
| | Georgette B. Berube (D) | 17,219 | *23.2* |
| **1986** | **Republican Primary** | | |
| | John R. McKernan (R) | 79,393 | *68.4* |
| | Porter D. Leighton (R) | 36,705 | *31.6* |
| | **Democratic Primary** | | |
| | James Tierney (D) | 44,087 | *37.2* |
| | Severin M. Beliveau (D) | 27,991 | *23.6* |
| | G. William Diamond (D) | 24,693 | *20.8* |
| | David E. Redmond (D) | 17,598 | *14.9* |
| **1990** | **Republican Primary** | | |
| | John R. McKernan (R) | | *100.0* |
| | **Democratic Primary** | | |
| | Joseph E. Brennan (D) | | *100.0* |

# MARYLAND

| | Candidates | Votes | % |
|---|---|---|---|
| **1958** | **Republican Primary** | | |
| | James Devereux (R) | | *100.0* |
| | **Democratic Primary** | | |
| | J. Millard Tawes (D) | 261,594 | *82.0* |
| | Bruce S. Campbell (D) | 24,953 | *7.8* |
| | Morgan L. Amaimo (D) | 16,459 | *5.2* |
| | Joseph A. Phillips (D) | 15,836 | *5.0* |
| **1962** | **Republican Primary** | | |
| | Frank Small (R) | 71,791 | *77.8* |
| | Karla Balentine (R) | 11,504 | *12.5* |
| | Joseph L. Pavlock (R) | 8,972 | *9.7* |
| | **Democratic Primary** | | |
| | J. Millard Tawes (D) | 178,792 | *40.4* |
| | George P. Mahoney (D) | 125,966 | *28.5* |
| | David Hume (D) | 118,295 | *26.7* |
| **1966** | **Republican Primary** | | |
| | Spiro T. Agnew (R) | 98,531 | *83.2* |
| | Andrew J. Groszer (R) | 9,987 | *8.4* |
| | **Democratic Primary** | | |
| | George P. Mahoney (D) | 148,446 | *30.2* |
| | Carlton R. Sickles (D) | 146,507 | *29.8* |

| | Candidates | Votes | % |
|---|---|---|---|
| | Thomas B. Finan (D) | 134,216 | *27.3* |
| | Clarence W. Miles (D) | 42,304 | *8.6* |
| **1970** | **Republican Primary** | | |
| | C. Stanley Blair (R) | 101,541 | *81.5* |
| | Peter James (R) | 15,790 | *12.8* |
| | John C. Webb (R) | 7,194 | *5.7* |
| | **Democratic Primary** | | |
| | Marvin Mandel (D) | 414,160 | *89.1* |
| **1974** | **Republican Primary** | | |
| | Louise Gore (R) | 57,626 | *53.6* |
| | Lawrence J. Hogan (R) | 49,887 | *46.4* |
| | **Democratic Primary** | | |
| | Marvin Mandel (D) | 254,509 | *65.7* |
| | Wilson K. Barnes (D) | 96,902 | *25.0* |
| **1978** | **Republican Primary** | | |
| | J. Glenn Beall Jr. (R) | 76,011 | *57.7* |
| | Carlton Beall (R) | 30,119 | *22.8* |
| | Louise Gore (R) | 20,690 | *15.7* |
| | **Democratic Primary** | | |
| | Harry R. Hughes (D) | 213,457 | *37.2* |
| | Blair Lee (D) | 194,236 | *33.9* |
| | Theodore G. Venetoulis (D) | 140,486 | *24.5* |
| **1982** | **Republican Primary** | | |
| | Robert A. Pascal (R) | 113,425 | *84.3* |
| | Ross Z. Pierpont (R) | 21,165 | *15.7* |
| | **Democratic Primary** | | |
| | Harry R. Hughes (D) | 393,244 | *59.8* |
| | Harry J. McGuirk (D) | 129,049 | *26.3* |
| | Harry W. Kelley (D) | 61,271 | *12.5* |
| **1986** | **Republican Primary** | | |
| | Thomas J. Mooney (R) | | *100.0* |
| | **Democratic Primary** | | |
| | William D. Schaefer (D) | 395,170 | *61.7* |
| | Stephen H. Sachs (D) | 224,755 | *35.1* |
| **1990** | **Republican Primary** | | |
| | William S. Shepard (R) | 66,966 | *52.7* |
| | Ross Z. Pierpont (R) | 60,065 | *47.3* |
| | **Democratic Primary** | | |
| | William D. Schaefer (D) | 358,534 | *78.1* |
| | Frederick M. Griisser (D) | 100,816 | *21.9* |

# MASSACHUSETTS

| Candidates | Votes | % |
|---|---|---|
| **1956** **Republican Primary** | | |
| Sumner G. Whittier (R) | | 100.0 |
| **Democratic Primary** | | |
| Foster Furcolo (D) | 358,051 | 73.1 |
| Thomas H. Buckley (D) | 131,496 | 26.9 |
| **1958 [1]** **Republican Primary** | | |
| Charles Gibbons (R) | 158,944 | 84.3 |
| George Fingold (R) | 23,031 | 12.2 |
| **Democratic Primary** | | |
| Foster Furcolo (D) | | 100.0 |
| **1960** **Republican Primary** | | |
| John A. Volpe (R) | | 100.0 |
| **Democratic Primary** | | |
| Joseph D. Ward (D) | 180,848 | 30.2 |
| Endicott Peabody (D) | 152,762 | 25.5 |
| Francis E. Kelly (D) | 98,107 | 16.4 |
| Robert F. Murphy (D) | 76,577 | 12.8 |
| John F. Kennedy (D) [2] | 52,972 | 8.8 |
| **1962** **Republican Primary** | | |
| John A. Volpe (R) | | 100.0 |
| **Democratic Primary** | | |
| Endicott Peabody (D) | 596,553 | 80.0 |
| Clement A. Riley (D) | 149,499 | 20.0 |
| **1964** **Republican Primary** | | |
| John A. Volpe (R) | | 100.0 |
| **Democratic Primary** | | |
| Francis X. Bellotti (D) | 363,675 | 49.6 |
| Endicott Peabody (D) | 336,780 | 45.9 |
| **1966** **Republican Primary** | | |
| John A. Volpe (R) | | 100.0 |
| **Democratic Primary** | | |
| Edward J. McCormack (D) | 343,381 | 55.1 |
| Kenneth P. O'Donnell (D) | 279,541 | 44.9 |
| **1970** **Republican Primary** | | |
| Francis W. Sargent (R) | | 100.0 |
| **Democratic Primary** | | |
| Kevin H. White (D) | 231,605 | 34.3 |
| Maurice A. Donahue (D) | 218,665 | 32.4 |
| Francis X. Bellotti (D) | 164,313 | 24.4 |
| Kenneth P. O'Donnell (D) | 59,970 | 8.9 |

| Candidates | Votes | % |
|---|---|---|
| **1974** **Republican Primary** | | |
| Francis W. Sargent (R) | 124,250 | 63.3 |
| Carroll P. Sheehan (R) | 71,936 | 36.7 |
| **Democratic Primary** | | |
| Michael S. Dukakis (D) | 444,590 | 57.7 |
| Robert H. Quinn (D) | 326,385 | 42.3 |
| **1978** **Republican Primary** | | |
| Francis W. Hatch (R) | 141,070 | 56.0 |
| Edward F. King (R) | 110,932 | 44.0 |
| **Democratic Primary** | | |
| Edward J. King (D) | 442,174 | 51.1 |
| Michael S. Dukakis (D) | 365,417 | 42.2 |
| Barbara Ackermann (D) | 58,220 | 6.7 |
| **1982** **Republican Primary** | | |
| John W. Sears (R) | 90,617 | 50.7 |
| John R. Lakian (R) | 46,675 | 26.1 |
| Andrew H. Card (R) | 40,899 | 22.9 |
| **Democratic Primary** | | |
| Michael S. Dukakis (D) | 631,911 | 53.5 |
| Edward J. King (D) | 549,335 | 46.5 |
| **1986** **Republican Primary** | | |
| Gregory S. Hyatt (R) [3] | 31,021 | 48.2 |
| Royall H. Switzler (R) | 20,802 | 32.3 |
| George Kariotis (R) | 11,787 | 18.3 |
| **Democratic Primary** | | |
| Michael S. Dukakis (D) | | 100.0 |
| **1990** **Republican Primary** | | |
| William F. Weld (R) | 270,455 | 60.5 |
| Steven D. Pierce (R) | 176,184 | 39.4 |
| **Democratic Primary** | | |
| John Silber (D) | 562,222 | 53.4 |
| Francis X. Bellotti (D) | 459,128 | 43.6 |

**Massachusetts**

1. *Fingold died a few days before the primary. Charles Gibbons, supported by the Republican state committee, polled 158,944 sticker and write-in votes, followed by 23,031 for Fingold, whose name remained on the ballot, and 6,535 other write-ins.*

2. *John F. Kennedy of Canton, Mass.; not to be confused with Sen. John F. Kennedy, D-Mass., then a candidate for president.*

3. *Hyatt withdrew after the primary, and Kariotis was substituted by the Republican state central committee.*

# MICHIGAN

| Candidates | Votes | % |
|---|---|---|
| **1956** **Republican Primary** | | |
| Albert E. Cobo (R) | 348,652 | 69.0 |
| Donald S. Leonard (R) | 156,822 | 31.0 |

| | Candidates | Votes | % |
|---|---|---|---|
| | **Democratic Primary** | | |
| | G. Mennen Williams (D) | | *100.0* |
| **1958** | **Republican Primary** | | |
| | Paul D. Bagwell (R) | | *100.0* |
| | **Democratic Primary** | | |
| | G. Mennen Williams (D) | 385,864 | *85.5* |
| | W. L. Johnson (D) | 65,614 | *14.5* |
| **1960** | **Republican Primary** | | |
| | Paul D. Bagwell (R) | | *100.0* |
| | **Democratic Primary** | | |
| | John B. Swainson (D) | 274,743 | *50.8* |
| | James M. Hare (D) | 205,086 | *37.9* |
| | Edward Connor (D) | 60,895 | *11.3* |
| **1962** | **Republican Primary** | | |
| | George W. Romney (R) | | *100.0* |
| | **Democratic Primary** | | |
| | John B. Swainson (D) | | *100.0* |
| **1964** | **Republican Primary** | | |
| | George W. Romney (R) | 583,356 | *87.9* |
| | George N. Higgins (R) | 80,608 | *12.1* |
| | **Democratic Primary** | | |
| | Neil Staebler (D) | | *100.0* |
| **1966** | **Republican Primary** | | |
| | George W. Romney (R) | | *100.0* |
| | **Democratic Primary** | | |
| | Zoltan A. Ferency (D) | | *100.0* |
| **1970** | **Republican Primary** | | |
| | William G. Milliken (R) | 416,491 | *77.8* |
| | James C. Turner (R) | 119,140 | *22.2* |
| | **Democratic Primary** | | |
| | Sander Levin (D) | 304,343 | *54.1* |
| | Zolton A. Ferency (D) | 167,442 | *29.8* |
| | George N. Parris (D) | 49,559 | *8.8* |
| | George F. Montgomery (D) | 41,218 | *7.3* |
| | **American Independent Primary** | | |
| | James L. McCormick (WRITE IN) | | |
| **1974** | **Republican Primary** | | |
| | William G. Milliken (R) | | *100.0* |
| | **Democratic Primary** | | |
| | Sander M. Levin (D) | 445,273 | *61.3* |
| | Jerome P. Cavanagh (D) | 199,361 | *27.4* |
| | James E. Wells (D) | 81,844 | *11.3* |

| | Candidates | Votes | % |
|---|---|---|---|
| **1978** | **Republican Primary** | | |
| | William G. Milliken (R) | | *100.0* |
| | **Democratic Primary** | | |
| | William Fitzgerald (D) | 240,641 | *39.8* |
| | Zolton A. Ferency (D) | 151,062 | *25.0* |
| | Patrick McCullough (D) | 108,742 | *18.0* |
| | William Ralls (D) | 104,364 | *17.2* |
| **1982** | **Republican Primary** | | |
| | Richard H. Headlee (R) | 220,378 | *34.4* |
| | James H. Brickley (R) | 194,429 | *30.3* |
| | L. Brooks Patterson (R) | 180,065 | *28.1* |
| | Jack Welborn (R) | 46,505 | *7.2* |
| | **Democratic Primary** | | |
| | James J. Blanchard (D) | 406,941 | *50.2* |
| | William Fitzgerald (D) | 138,453 | *17.1* |
| | David A. Plawecki (D) | 95,805 | *11.8* |
| | Zolton A. Ferency (D) | 85,088 | *10.5* |
| | Edward C. Pierce (D) | 44,894 | *5.5* |
| **1986** | **Republican Primary** | | |
| | William Lucas (R) | 259,153 | *44.5* |
| | Dick Chrysler (R) | 198,174 | *34.0* |
| | Colleen Engler (R) | 63,927 | *11.0* |
| | Dan Murphy (R) | 61,073 | *10.5* |
| | **Democratic Primary** | | |
| | James J. Blanchard (D) | 428,125 | *93.7* |
| | Henry Wilson (D) | 28,940 | *6.3* |
| **1990** | **Republican Primary** | | |
| | John Engler (R) | 409,747 | *86.6* |
| | John Lauve (R) | 63,457 | *13.4* |
| | **Democratic Primary** | | |
| | James J. Blanchard (D) | | *100.0* |

# MINNESOTA [1]

| | Candidates | Votes | % |
|---|---|---|---|
| **1956** | **Republican Primary** | | |
| | Ancher Nelsen (R) | 283,844 | *94.4* |
| | **Democratic Primary** | | |
| | Orville L. Freeman (DFL) | 269,740 | *89.5* |
| **1958** | **Republican Primary** | | |
| | George MacKinnon (R) | 202,833 | *85.3* |
| | Glenn B. Brown (R) | 34,878 | *14.7* |
| | **Democratic Primary** | | |
| | Orville L. Freeman (DFL) | 331,822 | *87.6* |
| | Harold Strom (DFL) | 47,041 | *12.4* |

| | Candidates | Votes | % |
|---|---|---|---|
| 1960 | **Republican Primary** | | |
| | Elmer L. Andersen (R) | | *100.0* |
| | **Democratic Primary** | | |
| | Orville L. Freeman (DFL) | 264,571 | *88.8* |
| | Belmont Tudisco (DFL) | 33,452 | *11.2* |
| 1962 | **Republican Primary** | | |
| | Elmer L. Andersen (R) | | *100.0* |
| | **Democratic Primary** | | |
| | Karl F. Rolvaag (DFL) | 271,818 | *92.5* |
| | Belmont Tudisco (DFL) | 22,042 | *7.5* |
| 1966 | **Republican Primary** | | |
| | Harold LeVander (R) | 276,403 | *97.9* |
| | **Democratic Primary** | | |
| | Karl F. Rolvaag (DFL) | 336,656 | *66.3* |
| | A. M. Keith (DFL) | 157,661 | *31.0* |
| 1970 | **Republican Primary** | | |
| | Douglas M. Head (R) | 210,621 | *87.5* |
| | John C. Peterson (R) | 19,737 | *8.2* |
| | **Democratic Primary** | | |
| | Wendell R. Anderson (DFL) | | *100.0* |
| 1974 | **Republican Primary** | | |
| | John W. Johnson (R) | | *100.0* |
| | **Democratic Primary** | | |
| | Wendell R. Anderson (DFL) | 254,671 | *78.2* |
| | Thomas E. McDonald (DFL) | 70,871 | *21.8* |
| 1978 | **Republican Primary** | | |
| | Albert H. Quie (I-R) | 174,799 | *83.6* |
| | Robert W. Johnson (I-R) | 34,406 | *16.4* |
| | **Democratic Primary** | | |
| | Rudy Perpich (DFL) | 390,069 | *80.0* |
| | Alice Tripp (DFL) | 97,247 | *20.0* |
| | **American Primary** | | |
| | Richard Pedersen (AM) | | *100.0* |
| 1982 | **Republican Primary** | | |
| | Wheelock Whitney (I-R) | 185,801 | *60.1* |
| | Lou Wangberg (I-R) | 105,696 | *34.2* |
| | Harold E. Stassen (I-R) | 17,795 | *5.7* |
| | **Democratic Primary** | | |
| | Rudy Perpich (DFL) | 275,920 | *51.2* |
| | Warren Spannaus (DFL) | 248,218 | *46.1* |

| | Candidates | Votes | % |
|---|---|---|---|
| 1986 | **Republican Primary** | | |
| | Cal R. Ludeman (I-R) | 147,674 | *76.9* |
| | James H. Lindau (I-R) | 30,768 | *16.0* |
| | **Democratic Primary** | | |
| | Rudy Perpich (DFL) | 293,426 | *57.5* |
| | George Latimer (DFL) | 207,198 | *40.6* |
| 1990 | **Republican Primary** | | |
| | Jon Grunseth (I-R) [2] | 169,451 | *49.4* |
| | Arne Carlson (I-R) | 108,440 | *31.6* |
| | Doug Kelley (I-R) | 57,872 | *16.9* |
| | **Democratic Primary** | | |
| | Rudy Perpich (DFL) | 218,410 | *55.5* |
| | Mike Hatch (DFL) | 166,183 | *42.2* |

**Minnesota**

*1. In Minnesota, the Democratic Party is known as the Democratic-Farmer-Labor Party (DFL) and the Republican Party is known as the Independent Republican Party (I-R).*

*2. Grunseth withdrew after the primary and Carlson was substituted by the state party committee.*

# MISSISSIPPI

| | Candidates | Votes | % |
|---|---|---|---|
| 1919 | **Democratic Primary** | | |
| | Lee M. Russell (D) | 48,348 | *32.6* |
| | Oscar Johnston (D) | 39,206 | *26.4* |
| | A. H. Longino (D) | 30,831 | *20.8* |
| | Ross A. Collins (D) | 30,026 | *20.2* |
| | **Democratic Runoff** | | |
| | Lee M. Russell (D) | 77,427 | *52.7* |
| | Oscar Johnston (D) | 69,565 | *47.3* |
| 1923 | **Democratic Primary** | | |
| | Henry L. Whitfield (D) | 85,328 | *33.6* |
| | Theodore G. Bilbo (D) | 65,105 | *25.6* |
| | Martin S. Conner (D) | 48,739 | *19.2* |
| | L. C. Franklin (D) | 37,245 | *14.7* |
| | Percey Bell (D) | 17,724 | *7.0* |
| | **Democratic Runoff** | | |
| | Henry L. Whitfield (D) | 134,715 | *53.3* |
| | Theodore G. Bilbo (D) | 118,143 | *46.7* |
| 1927 | **Democratic Primary** | | |
| | Theodore G. Bilbo (D) | 135,065 | *46.9* |
| | Dennis Murphree (D) | 71,836 | *25.0* |
| | Martin S. Conner (D) | 57,402 | *19.9* |
| | A. C. Anderson (D) | 23,528 | *8.2* |
| | **Democratic Runoff** | | |
| | Theodore G. Bilbo (D) | 153,669 | *52.8* |
| | Dennis Murphree (D) | 137,130 | *47.2* |

| | Candidates | Votes | % |
|---|---|---|---|
| **1931** | **Democratic Primary** | | |
| | Hugh L. White (D) | 108,022 | *34.5* |
| | Martin S. Conner (D) | 92,089 | *29.4* |
| | Paul B. Johnson (D) | 58,668 | *18.7* |
| | Mitchell (D) | 54,202 | *17.3* |
| | **Democratic Runoff** | | |
| | Martin S. Conner (D) | 170,690 | *54.1* |
| | Hugh L. White (D) | 144,918 | *45.9* |
| **1935** | **Democratic Primary** | | |
| | Paul B. Johnson (D) | 111,523 | *31.5* |
| | Hugh L. White (D) | 110,825 | *31.3* |
| | Dennis Murphree (D) | 92,997 | *26.2* |
| | Franklin (D) | 34,700 | *9.8* |
| | **Democratic Runoff** | | |
| | Hugh L. White (D) | 182,771 | *51.7* |
| | Paul B. Johnson (D) | 170,705 | *48.3* |
| **1939** | **Democratic Primary** | | |
| | Paul B. Johnson (D) | 103,099 | *33.5* |
| | Martin S. Conner (D) | 79,305 | *25.8* |
| | Thomas L. Bailey (D) | 58,987 | *19.2* |
| | Franklin (D) | 31,845 | *10.4* |
| | Snider (D) | 24,244 | *7.9* |
| | **Democratic Runoff** | | |
| | Paul B. Johnson (D) | 163,620 | *54.7* |
| | Martin S. Conner (D) | 135,724 | *45.3* |
| **1943** | **Democratic Primary** | | |
| | Martin S. Conner (D) | 110,917 | *38.8* |
| | Thomas L. Bailey (D) | 68,963 | *24.1* |
| | Dennis Murphree (D) | 68,510 | *24.0* |
| | Franklin (D) | 37,240 | *13.0* |
| | **Democratic Runoff** | | |
| | Thomas L. Bailey (D) | 143,153 | *53.2* |
| | Martin S. Conner (D) | 125,882 | *46.8* |
| **1947** | **Democratic Primary** | | |
| | Fielding L. Wright (D) | 202,014 | *55.3* |
| | Paul B. Johnson Jr. (D) | 112,123 | *30.7* |
| | Jesse M. Byrd (D) | 37,997 | *10.4* |
| **1951** | **Democratic Primary** | | |
| | Hugh L. White (D) | 94,820 | *23.3* |
| | Paul B. Johnson Jr. (D) | 86,150 | *21.1* |
| | Sam Lumpkin (D) | 84,451 | *20.7* |
| | Ross R. Barnett (D) | 81,674 | *20.0* |
| | Mary D. Cain (D) | 24,756 | *6.1* |
| | Jesse M. Byrd (D) | 22,783 | *5.6* |
| | **Democratic Runoff** | | |
| | Hugh L. White (D) | 201,222 | *51.2* |
| | Paul B. Johnson Jr. (D) | 191,966 | *48.8* |

| | Candidates | Votes | % |
|---|---|---|---|
| **1955** | **Democratic Primary** | | |
| | Paul B. Johnson Jr. (D) | 122,423 | *28.1* |
| | James P. Coleman (D) | 104,140 | *23.9* |
| | Fielding L. Wright (D) | 94,410 | *21.6* |
| | Ross R. Barnett (D) | 92,785 | *21.3* |
| | Mary D. Cain (D) | 22,469 | *5.2* |
| | **Democratic Runoff** | | |
| | James P. Coleman (D) | 233,237 | *55.6* |
| | Paul B. Johnson Jr. (D) | 185,924 | *44.4* |
| **1959** | **Democratic Primary** | | |
| | Ross R. Barnett (D) | 155,508 | *35.3* |
| | Carroll Gartin (D) | 151,043 | *34.3* |
| | Charles L. Sullivan (D) | 131,792 | *29.9* |
| | **Democratic Runoff** | | |
| | Ross R. Barnett (D) | 230,557 | *54.3* |
| | Carroll Gartin (D) | 193,706 | *45.7* |
| **1963** | **Republican Primary** | | |
| | Rubel L. Phillips (R) | | *100.0* |
| | **Democratic Primary** | | |
| | Paul B. Johnson Jr. (D) | 182,540 | *38.5* |
| | James P. Coleman (D) | 156,296 | *33.0* |
| | Charles L. Sullivan (D) | 132,321 | *27.9* |
| | **Democratic Runoff** | | |
| | Paul B. Johnson Jr. (D) | 261,493 | *57.3* |
| | James P. Coleman (D) | 194,958 | *42.7* |
| **1967** | **Republican Primary** | | |
| | Rubel L. Phillips (R) | | *100.0* |
| | **Democratic Primary** | | |
| | William Winter (D) | 222,001 | *32.5* |
| | John Bell Williams (D) | 197,778 | *28.9* |
| | James E. (Jimmy) Swan (D) | 124,361 | *18.2* |
| | Ross R. Barnett (D) | 76,053 | *11.1* |
| | William L. Waller (D) | 60,090 | *8.8* |
| | **Democratic Runoff** | | |
| | John Bell Williams (D) | 371,815 | *54.5* |
| | William Winter (D) | 310,527 | *45.5* |
| **1971** | **Democratic Primary** | | |
| | Charles L. Sullivan (D) | 288,219 | *37.8* |
| | William L. Waller (D) | 227,424 | *29.8* |
| | James E. (Jimmy) Swan (D) | 128,946 | *16.9* |
| | Roy C. Adams (D) | 45,445 | *6.0* |
| | Ed Pittman (D) | 38,170 | *5.0* |
| | **Democratic Runoff** | | |
| | William L. Waller (D) | 389,952 | *54.2* |
| | Charles L. Sullivan (D) | 329,236 | *45.8* |

| Candidates | Votes | % |
|---|---|---|
| **Democratic Primary** 1975 | | |
| | | |
| William Winter (D) | 286,652 | *36.3* |
| Cliff Finch (D) | 253,829 | *32.1* |
| Maurice Dantin (D) | 179,472 | *22.7* |
| John Arthur Eaves (D) | 50,606 | *6.4* |
| | | |
| **Democratic Runoff** | | |
| | | |
| Cliff Finch (D) | 442,865 | *57.7* |
| William Winter (D) | 324,749 | *42.3* |
| | | |
| **Republican Primary** 1979 | | |
| | | |
| Gil Carmichael (R) | 17,216 | *53.1* |
| Leon Bramlett (R) | 15,236 | *46.9* |
| | | |
| **Democratic Primary** | | |
| | | |
| Evelyn Gandy (D) | 224,746 | *30.5* |
| William Winter (D) | 183,944 | *25.0* |
| John A. Eaves (D) | 143,411 | *19.5* |
| Jim Herring (D) | 135,812 | *18.4* |
| | | |
| **Democratic Runoff** | | |
| | | |
| William Winter (D) | 386,174 | *56.6* |
| Evelyn Gandy (D) | 295,835 | *43.4* |
| | | |
| **Republican Primary** 1983 | | |
| | | |
| Leon Bramlett (R) | | *100.0* |
| | | |
| **Democratic Primary** | | |
| | | |
| Evelyn Gandy (D) | 316,304 | *38.2* |
| William A. Allain (D) | 293,348 | *35.4* |
| Mike P. Sturdivant (D) | 172,526 | *21.0* |
| | | |
| **Democratic Runoff** | | |
| | | |
| William A. Allain (D) | 405,348 | *52.4* |
| Evelyn Gandy (D) | 367,953 | *47.5* |
| | | |
| **Republican Primary** 1987 | | |
| | | |
| Jack Reed (R) | 14,798 | *78.5* |
| Doug Lemon (R) | 4,057 | *21.5* |
| | | |
| **Democratic Primary** | | |
| | | |
| Ray Mabus (D) | 304,559 | *35.7* |
| Mike P. Sturdivant (D) | 131,180 | *16.2* |
| William L. Waller (D) | 105,056 | *13.0* |
| John A. Eaves (D) | 98,517 | *12.2* |
| Maurice Dantin (D) | 83,603 | *10.3* |
| Ed Pittman (D) | 73,667 | *9.1* |
| | | |
| **Democratic Runoff** | | |
| | | |
| Ray Mabus (D) | 428,883 | *64.3* |
| Mike P. Sturdivant (D) | 238,039 | *35.7* |
| | | |
| **Republican Primary** 1991 | | |
| | | |
| Kirk Fordice (R) | 28,411 | *44.7* |
| Pete Johnson (R) | 27,561 | *43.4* |
| Bobby Clanton (R) | 7,589 | *11.9* |

| Candidates | Votes | % |
|---|---|---|
| **Republican Runoff** | | |
| | | |
| Kirk Fordice (R) | 31,753 | *60.6* |
| Pete Johnson (R) | 20,622 | *39.4* |
| | | |
| **Democratic Primary** | | |
| | | |
| Ray Mabus (D) | 368,679 | *50.7* |
| Wayne Dowdy (D) | 299,172 | *41.2* |
| George Blair (D) | 58,614 | *8.1* |

# MISSOURI

| Candidates | Votes | % |
|---|---|---|
| **Republican Primary** 1956 | | |
| | | |
| Lon Hocker (R) | 136,388 | *66.9* |
| Joseph M. Whealen (R) | 53,811 | *26.4* |
| Winford Sidebotham (R) | 13,710 | *6.7* |
| | | |
| **Democratic Primary** | | |
| | | |
| James T. Blair (D) | 387,330 | *88.1* |
| Charles A. Lee (D) | 34,107 | *7.7* |
| | | |
| **Republican Primary** 1960 | | |
| | | |
| Edward G. Farmer (R) | 107,637 | *54.1* |
| William B. Ewald (R) | 57,953 | *29.1* |
| Harry C. Timmerman (R) | 33,388 | *16.8* |
| | | |
| **Democratic Primary** | | |
| | | |
| John M. Dalton (D) | 466,984 | *86.4* |
| | | |
| **Republican Primary** 1964 | | |
| | | |
| Ethan Shepley (R) | 161,327 | *75.7* |
| Harry C. Timmerman (R) | 17,510 | *8.2* |
| William B. Ewald (R) | 17,170 | *8.1* |
| Joseph M. Badgett (R) | 17,156 | *8.0* |
| | | |
| **Democratic Primary** | | |
| | | |
| Warren E. Hearnes (D) | 334,708 | *51.9* |
| Hilary A. Bush (D) | 283,640 | *44.0* |
| | | |
| **Republican Primary** 1968 | | |
| | | |
| Lawrence K. Roos (R) | 170,428 | *76.4* |
| Harry C. Timmerman (R) | 41,549 | *18.6* |
| Harvey F. Euge (R) | 10,994 | *5.0* |
| | | |
| **Democratic Primary** | | |
| | | |
| Warren E. Hearnes (D) | 497,056 | *85.5* |
| Robert B. Curtis (D) | 42,971 | *7.4* |
| Milton Morris (D) | 41,506 | *7.1* |
| | | |
| **Republican Primary** 1972 | | |
| | | |
| Christopher S. (Kit) Bond (R) | 265,467 | *75.1* |
| Gene McNary (R) | 56,652 | *16.0* |
| R. J. King (R) | 21,422 | *6.1* |

**745**

# MONTANA

| Candidates<br>Democratic Primary | Votes | % |
|---|---|---|
| Edward L. Dowd (D) | 265,011 | 40.8 |
| William S. Morris (D) | 152,055 | 23.4 |
| Joseph P. Teasdale (D) | 135,965 | 20.9 |
| Earl R. Blackwell (D) | 72,212 | 11.1 |

| Non-partisan Primary | Votes | % |
|---|---|---|
| Paul J. Leonard (NON-PART) | 606 | 55.4 |
| Charles S. Miller (NON-PART) | 487 | 44.6 |

**1976**

| Republican Primary | Votes | % |
|---|---|---|
| Christopher S. (Kit) Bond (R) | 286,377 | 92.0 |
| Harvey F. Euge (R) | 24,975 | 8.0 |

| Democratic Primary | Votes | % |
|---|---|---|
| Joseph P. Teasdale (D) | 419,656 | 48.6 |
| William Cason (D) | 340,208 | 39.4 |

**1980**

| Republican Primary | Votes | % |
|---|---|---|
| Christopher S. (Kit) Bond (R) | 223,678 | 63.5 |
| William Phelps (R) | 122,867 | 34.9 |

| Democratic Primary | Votes | % |
|---|---|---|
| Joseph P. Teasdale (D) | 359,263 | 54.0 |
| James I. Spainhower (D) | 294,917 | 44.3 |

**1984**

| Republican Primary | Votes | % |
|---|---|---|
| John Ashcroft (R) | 245,308 | 67.4 |
| Gene McNary (R) | 115,516 | 31.8 |

| Democratic Primary | Votes | % |
|---|---|---|
| Kenneth J. Rothman (D) | 288,543 | 56.0 |
| Mel Carnahan (D) | 104,368 | 20.3 |
| Norman L. Merrell (D) | 97,973 | 19.0 |

**1988**

| Republican Primary | Votes | % |
|---|---|---|
| John Ashcroft (R) | | 100.0 |

| Democratic Primary | Votes | % |
|---|---|---|
| Betty C. Hearnes (D) | 375,564 | 81.5 |
| Lavoy Reed (D) | 85,409 | 18.5 |

**1992**

| Republican Primary | Votes | % |
|---|---|---|
| William L. Webster (R) | 183,968 | 43.8 |
| Roy D. Blunt (R) | 163,719 | 39.0 |
| Wendell Bailey (R) | 63,481 | 15.1 |

| Democratic Primary | Votes | % |
|---|---|---|
| Mel Carnahan (D) | 388,098 | 55.4 |
| Vince Schoemehl (D) | 235,652 | 33.6 |
| Sharon Rogers (D) | 35,104 | 5.0 |

| | Candidates | Votes | % |
|---|---|---|---|
| **1956** | **Republican Primary** | | |
| | J. Hugo Aronson (R) | | 100.0 |
| | **Democratic Primary** | | |
| | Arnold H. Olsen (D) | 55,269 | 44.9 |
| | John W. Bonner (D) | 51,306 | 41.7 |
| | Danny O'Neill (D) | 14,777 | 12.0 |
| **1960** | **Republican Primary** | | |
| | Donald G. Nutter (R) | 33,099 | 50.4 |
| | Wesley A. D'Ewart (R) | 32,538 | 49.6 |
| | **Democratic Primary** | | |
| | Paul Cannon (D) | 44,690 | 34.9 |
| | Jack Toole (D) | 40,537 | 31.6 |
| | Mike Kuchera (D) | 33,216 | 25.9 |
| | Willard E. Fraser (D) | 6,505 | 5.1 |
| **1964** | **Republican Primary** | | |
| | Tim M. Babcock (R) | | 100.0 |
| | **Democratic Primary** | | |
| | Roland Renne (D) | 71,967 | 55.9 |
| | Mike Kuchera (D) | 56,710 | 44.1 |
| **1968** | **Republican Primary** | | |
| | Tim M. Babcock (R) | 50,369 | 55.1 |
| | Ted James (R) | 36,664 | 40.1 |
| | **Democratic Primary** | | |
| | Forrest H. Anderson (D) | 39,057 | 38.3 |
| | Eugene H. Mahoney (D) | 35,562 | 34.9 |
| | LeRoy Anderson (D) | 16,476 | 16.2 |
| | Willard E. Fraser (D) | 8,525 | 8.3 |
| **1972** | **Republican Primary** | | |
| | Ed Smith (R) | 39,552 | 40.6 |
| | Frank Dunkle (R) | 37,375 | 38.4 |
| | Tom A. Selstad (R) | 18,046 | 18.5 |
| | **Democratic Primary** | | |
| | Thomas L. Judge (D) | 75,917 | 59.9 |
| | Dick Dzivi (D) | 38,639 | 30.5 |
| **1976** | **Republican Primary** | | |
| | Robert Woodahl (R) | 47,629 | 56.7 |
| | John K. McDonald (R) | 36,420 | 43.3 |
| | **Democratic Primary** | | |
| | Thomas L. Judge (D) | | 100.0 |

| Candidates | Votes | % |
|---|---|---|
| **1980** | | |
| **Republican Primary** | | |
| Jack Ramirez (R) | 48,926 | 68.4 |
| Al Bishop (R) | 14,522 | 20.3 |
| Florence Haegen (R) | 8,118 | 11.3 |
| **Democratic Primary** | | |
| Ted Schwinden (D) | 69,051 | 50.6 |
| Thomas L. Judge (D) | 57,946 | 42.5 |
| **1984** | | |
| **Republican Primary** | | |
| Pat M. Goodover (R) | 56,199 | 100.0 |
| **Democratic Primary** | | |
| Ted Schwinden (D) | 80,633 | 81.4 |
| Robert Carlson Kelleher (D) | 18,423 | 18.6 |
| **1988** | | |
| **Republican Primary** | | |
| Stan Stephens (R) | 44,022 | 50.1 |
| Cal Winslow (R) | 37,875 | 43.1 |
| Jim Waltermire (R) [1] | 6,024 | 6.9 |
| **Democratic Primary** | | |
| Thomas L. Judge (D) | 46,412 | 39.3 |
| Frank Morrison (D) | 32,124 | 27.2 |
| Mike Greely (D) | 26,827 | 22.7 |
| Ted Neuman (D) | 7,297 | 6.2 |
| **1992** | | |
| **Republican Primary** | | |
| Marc Racicot (R) | 68,013 | 68.7 |
| Andrea Bennett (R) | 31,038 | 31.3 |
| **Democratic Primary** | | |
| Dorothy Bradley (D) | 54,453 | 41.2 |
| Mike McGrath (D) | 44,323 | 33.5 |
| Frank Morrison (D) | 23,883 | 18.1 |

**Montana**
1. Waltermire died two months before the primary.

# NEBRASKA

| Candidates | Votes | % |
|---|---|---|
| **1956** | | |
| **Republican Primary** | | |
| Victor E. Anderson (R) | 86,168 | 82.6 |
| Edwin L. Hart (R) | 18,202 | 17.4 |
| **Democratic Primary** | | |
| Frank Sorrell (D) | 43,301 | 69.9 |
| Ted Baum (D) | 18,667 | 30.1 |
| **1958** | | |
| **Republican Primary** | | |
| Victor E. Anderson (R) | 90,150 | 76.4 |
| Louis H. Hector (R) | 27,768 | 23.5 |

| Candidates | Votes | % |
|---|---|---|
| **Democratic Primary** | | |
| Ralph G. Brooks (D) | 37,816 | 54.8 |
| Edward A. Dosek (D) | 31,221 | 45.2 |
| **1960** | | |
| **Republican Primary** | | |
| John R. Cooper (R) | 61,286 | 37.7 |
| Hazel Abel (R) | 39,109 | 24.1 |
| Terry Carpenter (R) | 25,659 | 15.8 |
| Dwain Williams (R) | 23,545 | 14.5 |
| Del Lienemann (R) | 9,390 | 5.8 |
| **Democratic Primary** | | |
| Frank B. Morrison (D) | 51,335 | 48.0 |
| Robert Conrad (D) | 44,486 | 41.6 |
| Charles A. Bates (D) | 5,477 | 5.1 |
| **1962** | | |
| **Republican Primary** | | |
| Fred A. Seaton (R) | 130,816 | 85.3 |
| George A. Clarke (R) | 17,368 | 11.3 |
| **Democratic Primary** | | |
| Frank B. Morrison (D) | 78,817 | 76.6 |
| Mrs. Ralph G. Brooks (D) | 15,565 | 15.1 |
| Tony Mangiamelli (D) | 8,464 | 8.3 |
| **1964** | | |
| **Republican Primary** | | |
| Dwight W. Burney (R) | 82,256 | 58.8 |
| Jack Romans (R) | 44,102 | 31.5 |
| **Democratic Primary** | | |
| Frank B. Morrison (D) | 83,362 | 88.8 |
| Charles A. Bates (D) | 6,543 | 7.0 |
| **1966** | | |
| **Republican Primary** | | |
| Norbert T. Tiemann (R) | 78,338 | 44.0 |
| Val Peterson (R) | 63,589 | 35.7 |
| Bruce Hagemeister (R) | 22,574 | 12.7 |
| Henry E. Kuhlmann (R) | 12,052 | 6.8 |
| **Democratic Primary** | | |
| Philip C. Sorensen (D) | 65,051 | 56.8 |
| J. W. Burbach (D) | 35,439 | 30.9 |
| Henry E. Ley (D) | 13,819 | 12.1 |
| **1970** | | |
| **Republican Primary** | | |
| Norbert T. Tiemann (R) | 97,616 | 50.5 |
| Clifton B. Batchelder (R) | 89,355 | 46.2 |
| **Democratic Primary** | | |
| J. James Exon (D) | 54,783 | 44.6 |
| J. W. Burbach (D) | 51,760 | 42.2 |
| Richard R. Larsen (D) | 15,602 | 12.7 |
| **1974** | | |
| **Republican Primary** | | |
| Richard D. Marvel (R) | | 100.0 |
| **Democratic Primary** | | |
| J. James Exon (D) | 125,690 | 87.4 |
| Richard D. Schmitz (D) | 17,889 | 12.4 |

| | Candidates | Votes | % |
|---|---|---|---|
| 1978 | **Republican Primary** | | |
| | Charles Thone (R) | 89,378 | 45.3 |
| | Robert A. Phares (R) | 48,402 | 24.5 |
| | Stanley R. Juelfs (R) | 43,828 | 22.2 |
| | Vance D. Rogers (R) | 14,076 | 7.1 |
| | **Democratic Primary** | | |
| | Gerald T. Whelan (D) | 104,178 | 79.4 |
| | Robert V. Hansen (D) | 26,509 | 20.2 |
| 1982 | **Republican Primary** | | |
| | Charles Thone (R) | 115,750 | 62.5 |
| | Stan DeBoer (R) | 55,983 | 30.2 |
| | Barton E. Chandler (R) | 13,086 | 7.1 |
| | **Democratic Primary** | | |
| | Bob Kerrey (D) | 87,913 | 71.0 |
| | George Burrows (D) | 35,426 | 28.6 |
| 1986 | **Republican Primary** | | |
| | Kay Orr (R) | 75,914 | 39.4 |
| | Kermit Brashear (R) | 60,308 | 31.3 |
| | Nancy Hoch (R) | 42,649 | 22.1 |
| | **Democratic Primary** | | |
| | Helen Boosalis (D) | 63,833 | 44.0 |
| | David A. Domina (D) | 37,975 | 26.2 |
| | Chris Beutler (D) | 31,605 | 21.8 |
| 1990 | **Republican Primary** | | |
| | Kay Orr (R) | 130,045 | 68.1 |
| | Mort Sullivan (R) | 59,048 | 30.9 |
| | **Democratic Primary** [1] | | |
| | Ben Nelson (D) | 44,721 | 26.8 |
| | Bill Hoppner (D) | 44,679 | 26.7 |
| | Mike Boyle (D) | 41,227 | 24.7 |
| | Bill Harris (D) | 31,527 | 18.9 |

**Nebraska**
1. The figures for Nelson and Hoppner are for the re-count.

# NEVADA

| | Candidates | Votes | % |
|---|---|---|---|
| 1958 | **Republican Primary** | | |
| | Charles H. Russell (R) | | 100.0 |
| | **Democratic Primary** | | |
| | Grant Sawyer (D) | 20,711 | 46.3 |
| | Harvey Dickerson (D) | 13,372 | 29.9 |
| | George E. Franklin (D) | 10,175 | 22.7 |
| 1962 | **Republican Primary** | | |
| | Oran K. Gragson (R) | 16,538 | 64.3 |
| | H. M. Greenspun (R) | 9,176 | 35.7 |

| | Candidates | Votes | % |
|---|---|---|---|
| | **Democratic Primary** | | |
| | Grant Sawyer (D) | 40,168 | 81.4 |
| | Gene Austin (D) | 5,017 | 10.2 |
| 1966 | **Republican Primary** | | |
| | Paul Laxalt (R) | 32,768 | 94.7 |
| | John P. Screen (R) | 1,834 | 5.3 |
| | **Democratic Primary** | | |
| | Grant Sawyer (D) | 40,982 | 58.6 |
| | Edward G. Marshall (D) | 13,858 | 19.8 |
| | Charles E. Springer (D) | 13,270 | 19.0 |
| 1970 | **Republican Primary** | | |
| | Ed Fike (R) | 31,931 | 88.2 |
| | Margie Dyer (R) | 4,281 | 11.8 |
| | **Democratic Primary** | | |
| | Mike O'Callaghan (D) | 41,185 | 68.8 |
| | Hank Thornley (D) | 16,107 | 26.9 |
| 1974 | **Republican Primary** | | |
| | Shirley Crumpler (R) | 17,076 | 49.4 |
| | William Bickerstaff (R) | 13,632 | 39.5 |
| | Gilbert D. Buck (R) | 2,405 | 7.0 |
| | **Democratic Primary** | | |
| | Mike O'Callaghan (D) | 69,089 | 90.8 |
| 1978 | **Republican Primary** | | |
| | Robert F. List (R) | 39,997 | 82.4 |
| | William C. Allen (R) | 3,038 | 6.3 |
| | "None of these candidates" [1] | 3,570 | 7.3 |
| | **Democratic Primary** | | |
| | Robert E. Rose (D) | 41,672 | 48.1 |
| | John Foley (D) | 20,186 | 23.3 |
| | Jack Schofield (D) | 18,414 | 21.3 |
| 1982 | **Republican Primary** | | |
| | Robert F. List (R) | 39,319 | 57.0 |
| | Mike Moody (R) | 13,849 | 20.1 |
| | "None of these candidates" [1] | 13,252 | 19.2 |
| | **Democratic Primary** | | |
| | Richard H. Bryan (D) | 55,261 | 51.1 |
| | Myron E. Leavitt (D) | 34,783 | 32.1 |
| | Stan Colton (D) | 10,830 | 10.0 |
| 1986 | **Republican Primary** | | |
| | Patty Cafferata (R) | 31,430 | 46.1 |
| | Jim Stone (R) | 12,296 | 18.0 |
| | Marcia J. Wines (R) | 5,599 | 8.2 |
| | "None of these candidates" [1] | 15,116 | 22.2 |
| | **Democratic Primary** | | |
| | Richard H. Bryan (D) | 71,920 | 79.9 |
| | Herb Tobman (D) | 13,776 | 15.3 |

| | Candidates | Votes | % |
|---|---|---|---|
| 1990 | **Republican Primary** | | |
| | Jim Gallaway (R) | 37,467 | 49.3 |
| | "None of these candidates" [1] | 16,565 | 21.8 |
| | Charlie Brown (R) | 16,067 | 21.1 |
| | **Democratic Primary** | | |
| | Robert J. Miller (D) | 71,537 | 81.0 |
| | "None of these candidates" [1] | 7,394 | 8.4 |

**Nevada**
1. Nevada provided space on the ballot for a vote against the candidates listed.

# NEW HAMPSHIRE

| | Candidates | Votes | % |
|---|---|---|---|
| 1956 | **Republican Primary** | | |
| | Lane Dwinell (R) | 38,734 | 53.1 |
| | Wesley Powell (R) | 33,408 | 45.8 |
| | **Democratic Primary** | | |
| | John Shaw (D) | | 100.0 |
| 1958 | **Republican Primary** | | |
| | Wesley Powell (R) | 39,761 | 47.5 |
| | Hugh Gregg (R) | 39,365 | 47.1 |
| | **Democratic Primary** | | |
| | Bernard L. Boutin (D) | 16,646 | 47.0 |
| | John Shaw (D) | 12,783 | 36.1 |
| | Alfred J. Champagne (D) | 4,586 | 13.0 |
| 1960 | **Republican Primary** | | |
| | Wesley Powell (R) | 49,119 | 49.9 |
| | Hugh Gregg (R) | 48,108 | 48.8 |
| | **Democratic Primary** | | |
| | Bernard L. Boutin (D) | 31,650 | 77.6 |
| | John Shaw (D) | 7,151 | 17.5 |
| 1962 | **Republican Primary** | | |
| | John Pillsbury (R) | 55,784 | 56.4 |
| | Wesley Powell (R) | 42,005 | 42.4 |
| | **Democratic Primary** | | |
| | John W. King (D) | 27,933 | 93.2 |
| | Elmer E. Bussey (D) | 2,039 | 6.8 |
| 1964 | **Republican Primary** | | |
| | John Pillsbury (R) | 32,200 | 51.4 |
| | Wesley Powell (R) | 21,764 | 34.7 |
| | John W. King (WRITE IN) | 3,608 | 5.8 |
| | John C. Mongan (R) | 3,532 | 5.6 |

| | Candidates | Votes | % |
|---|---|---|---|
| | **Democratic Primary** | | |
| | John W. King (D) | | 100.0 |
| 1966 | **Republican Primary** | | |
| | Hugh Gregg (R) | 33,946 | 44.9 |
| | James J. Barry (R) | 20,791 | 27.5 |
| | Alexander M. Taft (R) | 14,845 | 19.6 |
| | **Democratic Primary** | | |
| | John W. King (D) | | 100.0 |
| 1968 | **Republican Primary** | | |
| | Walter R. Peterson (R) | 29,262 | 34.1 |
| | Wesley Powell (R) | 26,498 | 30.9 |
| | Meldrim Thomson (R) | 25,275 | 29.5 |
| | **Democratic Primary** | | |
| | Emile R. Bussiere (D) | 12,021 | 32.7 |
| | Henry P. Sullivan (D) | 10,895 | 29.6 |
| | Vincent P. Dunn (D) | 10,412 | 28.3 |
| 1970 | **Republican Primary** | | |
| | Walter R. Peterson (R) | 43,667 | 50.9 |
| | Meldrim Thomson Jr. (R) | 41,392 | 48.2 |
| | **Democratic Primary** | | |
| | Roger J. Crowley (D) | 17,089 | 47.5 |
| | Charles F. Whittemore (D) | 13,354 | 37.1 |
| | Dennis J. Sullivan (D) | 4,747 | 13.2 |
| 1972 | **Republican Primary** | | |
| | Meldrim Thomson Jr. (R) | 43,611 | 47.9 |
| | Walter R. Peterson (R) | 41,252 | 45.3 |
| | **Democratic Primary** | | |
| | Roger J. Crowley (D) | 29,326 | 61.4 |
| | Robert E. Raiche (D) | 16,216 | 33.9 |
| 1974 | **Republican Primary** | | |
| | Meldrim Thomson Jr. (R) | 47,244 | 54.9 |
| | David L. Nixon (R) | 37,286 | 43.3 |
| | **Democratic Primary** | | |
| | Richard W. Leonard (D) | 16,503 | 37.8 |
| | Harry V. Spanos (D) | 14,149 | 32.4 |
| | Hugh Gallen (D) | 13,030 | 29.8 |
| 1976 | **Republican Primary** | | |
| | Meldrim Thomson Jr. (R) | 52,968 | 64.6 |
| | Gerald J. Zeiller (R) | 26,728 | 32.6 |
| | **Democratic Primary** | | |
| | Harry V. Spanos (D) | 21,589 | 41.3 |
| | James A. Connor (D) | 15,758 | 30.2 |
| | Hugh Gallen (D) | 13,629 | 26.1 |

| 1978 | Candidates | Votes | % |
|------|-----------|-------|---|
| | **Republican Primary** | | |
| | Meldrim Thomson Jr. (R) | 45,069 | *59.7* |
| | Wesley Powell (R) | 28,286 | *37.4* |
| | **Democratic Primary** | | |
| | Hugh Gallen (D) | 26,217 | *73.0* |
| | Delbert F. Downing (D) | 9,688 | *27.0* |
| 1980 | **Republican Primary** | | |
| | Meldrim Thomson Jr. (R) | 55,554 | *56.4* |
| | Louis C. D'Allesandro (R) | 40,060 | *40.7* |
| | **Democratic Primary** | | |
| | Hugh Gallen (D) | 37,786 | *81.3* |
| | Thomas B. Wingate (D) | 8,689 | *18.7* |
| 1982 | **Republican Primary** | | |
| | John H. Sununu (R) | 26,617 | *31.9* |
| | Robert B. Monier (R) | 24,823 | *29.7* |
| | Louis C. D'Allesandro (R) | 24,163 | *29.0* |
| | **Democratic Primary** | | |
| | Hugh Gallen (D) | | *100.0* |
| 1984 | **Republican Primary** | | |
| | John H. Sununu (R) | 52,737 | *84.1* |
| | James F. Fallon (R) | 8,994 | *14.3* |
| | **Democratic Primary** | | |
| | Chris Spirou (D) | 22,835 | *49.5* |
| | Paul McEachern (D) | 18,460 | *40.0* |
| | Robert L. Dupay (D) | 4,060 | *8.8* |
| 1986 | **Republican Primary** | | |
| | John H. Sununu (R) | 44,906 | *77.3* |
| | Roger L. Easton (R) | 12,702 | *21.9* |
| | **Democratic Primary** | | |
| | Paul McEachern (D) | 19,731 | *54.6* |
| | Paul M. Gagnon (D) | 9,790 | *27.1* |
| | Bruce Anderson (D) | 5,816 | *16.1* |
| 1988 | **Republican Primary** | | |
| | Judd Gregg (R) | 65,777 | *79.0* |
| | Robert F. Shaw (R) | 15,133 | *18.2* |
| | **Democratic Primary** | | |
| | Paul McEachern (D) | | *100.0* |
| 1990 | **Republican Primary** | | |
| | Judd Gregg (R) | 67,934 | *80.8* |
| | Robert A. Bonser (R) | 15,207 | *18.1* |
| | **Democratic Primary** | | |
| | J. Joseph Grandmaison (D) | 22,246 | *45.7* |
| | Robert F. Preston (D) | 21,653 | *44.5* |
| | Paul Blacketor (D) | 3,923 | *8.1* |

| 1992 | Candidates | Votes | % |
|------|-----------|-------|---|
| | **Republican Primary** | | |
| | Steve Merrill (R) | 60,809 | *52.7* |
| | Edward C. du Pont (R) | 25,530 | *22.1* |
| | Elizabeth Hager (R) | 24,433 | *21.2* |
| | **Democratic Primary** | | |
| | Deborah A. Arnesen (D) | 41,770 | *47.7* |
| | Norman E. D'Amours (D) | 23,919 | *27.3* |
| | Ned Helms (D) | 19,792 | *22.6* |

# NEW JERSEY

| 1957 | Candidates | Votes | % |
|------|-----------|-------|---|
| | **Republican Primary** | | |
| | Malcolm S. Forbes (R) | 216,677 | *63.7* |
| | Wayne Dumont (R) | 123,350 | *36.3* |
| | **Democratic Primary** | | |
| | Robert B. Meyner (D) | | *100.0* |
| 1961 | **Republican Primary** | | |
| | James P. Mitchell (R) | 202,188 | *43.7* |
| | Walter H. Jones (R) | 160,553 | *34.7* |
| | Wayne Dumont (R) | 95,761 | *20.7* |
| | **Democratic Primary** | | |
| | Richard J. Hughes (D) | 222,789 | *84.2* |
| | Weldon R. Sheets (D) | 21,285 | *8.0* |
| | Eugene E. Demarest (D) | 20,487 | *7.7* |
| 1965 | **Republican Primary** | | |
| | Wayne Dumont (R) | 167,402 | *50.3* |
| | Charles W. Sandman (R) | 154,491 | *46.5* |
| | **Democratic Primary** | | |
| | Richard J. Hughes (D) | 236,518 | *90.9* |
| | William J. Clark (D) | 23,722 | *9.1* |
| 1969 | **Republican Primary** | | |
| | William T. Cahill (R) | 158,980 | *39.3* |
| | Charles W. Sandman (R) | 144,877 | *35.8* |
| | Harry L. Sears (R) | 46,778 | *11.6* |
| | Francis X. McDermott (R) | 35,503 | *8.8* |
| | **Democratic Primary** | | |
| | Robert B. Meyner (D) | 173,801 | *44.8* |
| | William F. Kelly (D) | 87,888 | *22.6* |
| | Henry Hellstoski (D) | 60,483 | *15.6* |
| | D. Louis Tonti (D) | 34,810 | *9.0* |
| | Ned J. Parsekian (D) | 24,908 | *6.4* |
| 1973 | **Republican Primary** | | |
| | Charles W. Sandman (R) | 209,657 | *57.5* |
| | William T. Cahill (R) | 148,034 | *40.6* |

| Candidates | Votes | % |
|---|---|---|
| **Democratic Primary** | | |
| Brendan T. Byrne (D) | 193,120 | *45.3* |
| Ann Klein (D) | 116,705 | *27.4* |
| Ralph C. DeRose (D) | 95,085 | *22.3* |

**1977**

| Candidates | Votes | % |
|---|---|---|
| **Republican Primary** | | |
| Raymond H. Bateman (R) | 196,592 | *54.7* |
| Thomas H. Kean (R) | 129,982 | *36.2* |
| C. Robert Sarcone (R) | 20,861 | *5.8* |
| **Democratic Primary** | | |
| Brendan T. Byrne (D) | 175,448 | *30.3* |
| Robert A. Roe (D) | 134,116 | *23.2* |
| Ralph C. DeRose (D) | 99,948 | *17.3* |
| James J. Florio (D) | 87,743 | *15.1* |
| Joseph A. Hoffman (D) | 58,835 | *10.2* |

**1981**

| Candidates | Votes | % |
|---|---|---|
| **Republican Primary** | | |
| Thomas H. Kean (R) | 122,512 | *30.7* |
| Lawrence F. Kramer (R) | 83,565 | *21.0* |
| Joseph Sullivan (R) | 67,651 | *17.0* |
| Jim Wallwork (R) | 61,816 | *15.5* |
| Barry T. Parker (R) | 26,040 | *6.5* |
| **Democratic Primary** | | |
| James J. Florio (D) | 164,179 | *25.9* |
| Robert A. Roe (D) | 98,660 | *15.6* |
| Kenneth A. Gibson (D) | 95,212 | *15.0* |
| Joseph P. Merlino (D) | 70,910 | *11.2* |
| John J. Degnan (D) | 65,844 | *10.4* |
| Thomas F. X. Smith (D) | 57,479 | *9.1* |

**1985**

| Candidates | Votes | % |
|---|---|---|
| **Republican Primary** | | |
| Thomas H. Kean (R) | | *100.0* |
| **Democratic Primary** | | |
| Peter Shapiro (D) | 101,243 | *31.0* |
| John F. Russo (D) | 86,827 | *26.6* |
| Kenneth A. Gibson (D) | 85,293 | *26.1* |
| Stephen B. Wiley (D) | 27,914 | *8.6* |
| Robert J. Del Tufo (D) | 19,742 | *6.0* |

**1989**

| Candidates | Votes | % |
|---|---|---|
| **Republican Primary** | | |
| James A. Courter (R) | 112,326 | *29.0* |
| Cary Edwards (R) | 85,313 | *22.0* |
| Chuck Hardwick (R) | 82,392 | *21.3* |
| Bill Gormley (R) | 66,430 | *17.2* |
| Gerald Cardinale (R) | 32,250 | *8.3* |
| **Democratic Primary** | | |
| James J. Florio (D) | 251,979 | *68.2* |
| Barbara Boggs Sigmund (D) | 61,033 | *16.5* |
| Alan J. Karcher (D) | 56,311 | *15.2* |

**1993**

| Candidates | Votes | % |
|---|---|---|
| **Republican Primary** | | |
| Christine Todd Whitman (R) | 159,765 | *40.0* |
| Cary Edwards (R) | 131.578 | *32.9* |
| Bill Wallwork (R) | 96,034 | *24.0* |
| **Democratic Primary** | | |
| James J. Florio (D) | | *100.0* |

# NEW MEXICO

| Candidates | Votes | % |
|---|---|---|
| **1956** | | |
| **Republican Primary** | | |
| Edwin L. Mechem (R) | | *100.0* |
| **Democratic Primary** | | |
| John F. Simms (D) | 46,722 | *48.3* |
| Ingram B. Pickett (D) | 43,937 | *45.4* |
| Robert F. Stephens (D) | 6,067 | *6.3* |
| **1958** | | |
| **Republican Primary** | | |
| Edwin L. Mechem (R) | | *100.0* |
| **Democratic Primary** | | |
| John Burroughs (D) | 46,344 | *43.8* |
| Joseph A. Bursey (D) | 33,623 | *31.7* |
| Ingram B. Pickett (D) | 18,150 | *17.1* |
| Robert C. Dow (D) | 5,569 | *5.2* |
| **1960** | | |
| **Republican Primary** | | |
| Edwin L. Mechem (R) | 29,486 | *76.0* |
| Paul W. Robinson (R) | 9,331 | *24.0* |
| **Democratic Primary** | | |
| John Burroughs (D) | 66,541 | *53.7* |
| Joseph A. Bursey (D) | 48,841 | *39.4* |
| Thomas E. Holland (D) | 8,413 | *6.8* |
| **1962** | | |
| **Republican Primary** | | |
| Edwin L. Mechem (R) | | *100.0* |
| **Democratic Primary** | | |
| Jack M. Campbell (D) | 47,873 | *38.7* |
| Ed V. Mead (D) | 44,385 | *35.9* |
| Leo T. Murphy (D) | 28,755 | *23.3* |
| **1964** | | |
| **Republican Primary** | | |
| Merle H. Tucker (R) | | *100.0* |
| **Democratic Primary** | | |
| Jack M. Campbell (D) | | *100.0* |
| **1966** | | |
| **Republican Primary** | | |
| David F. Cargo (R) | 17,836 | *51.8* |
| Clifford J. Hawley (R) | 16,588 | *48.2* |
| **Democratic Primary** | | |
| Thomas E. Lusk (D) | 85,211 | *59.9* |
| John Burroughs (D) | 57,143 | *40.1* |
| **1968** | | |
| **Republican Primary** | | |
| David F. Cargo (R) | 28,014 | *54.9* |
| Clifford J. Hawley (R) | 23,052 | *45.1* |

**751**

| Candidates | Votes | % |
|---|---|---|
| **Democratic Primary** | | |
| Fabian Chavez (D) | 41,348 | 30.9 |
| Bruce King (D) | 24,658 | 18.4 |
| Calvin Horn (D) | 24,376 | 18.2 |
| Mack Easley (D) | 21,436 | 16.0 |
| Bobby M. Mayfield (D) | 19,528 | 14.6 |

**1970**

| **Republican Primary** | Votes | % |
|---|---|---|
| Pete V. Domenici (R) | 25,881 | 46.0 |
| Stephen C. Helbing (R) | 13,265 | 23.6 |
| Edward M. Hartman (R) | 5,309 | 9.4 |
| Tom Clear (R) | 5,262 | 9.3 |
| Junio Lopez (R) | 4,272 | 7.6 |

| **Democratic Primary** | Votes | % |
|---|---|---|
| Bruce King (D) | 62,718 | 48.9 |
| Jack Daniels (D) | 47,523 | 37.1 |
| Alexander F. Sceresse (D) | 17,918 | 14.0 |

**1974**

| **Republican Primary** | Votes | % |
|---|---|---|
| Joe Skeen (R) | 28,227 | 55.4 |
| John P. Eastham (R) | 15,003 | 29.5 |
| James L. Hughes (R) | 4,758 | 9.3 |
| Walter E. Bruce (R) | 2,913 | 5.7 |

| **Democratic Primary** | Votes | % |
|---|---|---|
| Jerry Apodaca (D) | 45,447 | 30.6 |
| Tibo J. Chavez (D) | 35,090 | 23.6 |
| Odis Echols (D) | 25,760 | 17.3 |
| Bobby M. Mayfield (D) | 22,806 | 15.3 |
| Drew Cloud (D) | 12,707 | 8.6 |

**1978**

| **Republican Primary** | Votes | % |
|---|---|---|
| Joe Skeen (R) | 38,638 | 81.2 |
| Philip R. Grant (R) | 8,966 | 18.8 |

| **Democratic Primary** | Votes | % |
|---|---|---|
| Bruce King (D) | 92,432 | 61.3 |
| Robert E. Ferguson (D) | 58,334 | 38.7 |

**1982**

| **Republican Primary** | Votes | % |
|---|---|---|
| John B. Irick (R) | 35,789 | 54.5 |
| William A. Sego (R) | 27,220 | 41.5 |

| **Democratic Primary** | Votes | % |
|---|---|---|
| Toney Anaya (D) | 101,077 | 56.9 |
| Aubrey L. Dunn (D) | 60,866 | 34.3 |
| Fabian Chavez (D) | 11,874 | 6.7 |

**1986**

| **Republican Primary** | Votes | % |
|---|---|---|
| Garrey E. Carruthers (R) | 27,671 | 31.1 |
| Joseph H. Mercer (R) | 23,560 | 26.4 |
| Colin R. McMillan (R) | 19,807 | 22.2 |
| Frank M. Bond (R) | 10,619 | 11.9 |
| Paul F. Becht (R) | 6,566 | 7.4 |

| **Democratic Primary** | Votes | % |
|---|---|---|
| Ray B. Pohwell (D) | | 100.0 |

**1990**

| Candidates | Votes | % |
|---|---|---|
| **Republican Primary** | | |
| Frank M. Bond (R) | 44,928 | 55.5 |
| Les Houston (R) | 27,073 | 33.4 |
| James A. Caudell (R) | 4,681 | 5.8 |
| Harry F. Kinney (R) | 4,289 | 5.3 |

| **Democratic Primary** | Votes | % |
|---|---|---|
| Bruce King (D) | 95,884 | 52.9 |
| Paul Bardacke (D) | 70,169 | 38.7 |

# NEW YORK

| Candidates | Votes | % |
|---|---|---|
| **1970** [1] **Republican Primary** | | |
| Nelson A. Rockefeller (R) | | 100.0 |

| **Democratic Primary** | Votes | % |
|---|---|---|
| Arthur J. Goldberg (D) | 493,295 | 52.2 |
| Howard J. Samuels (D) | 451,703 | 47.8 |

| **Conservative Primary** | Votes | % |
|---|---|---|
| Paul L. Adams (C) | | 100.0 |

| **Liberal Primary** | Votes | % |
|---|---|---|
| Arthur J. Goldberg (L) | | 100.0 |

| **1974** **Republican Primary** | Votes | % |
|---|---|---|
| Malcolm Wilson (R) | | 100.0 |

| **Democratic Primary** | Votes | % |
|---|---|---|
| Hugh L. Carey (D) | 600,283 | 60.8 |
| Howard J. Samuels (D) | 387,369 | 39.2 |

| **Conservative Primary** | Votes | % |
|---|---|---|
| Malcolm Wilson (C) | | 100.0 |

| **Liberal Primary** | Votes | % |
|---|---|---|
| Edward Morrison (L) [2] | | 100.0 |

| **1978** **Republican Primary** | Votes | % |
|---|---|---|
| Perry B. Duryea (R) | | 100.0 |

| **Democratic Primary** | Votes | % |
|---|---|---|
| Hugh L. Carey (D) | 376,457 | 52.0 |
| Mary Anne Krupsak (D) | 244,252 | 33.7 |
| Jeremiah B. Bloom (D) | 103,479 | 14.3 |

| **Conservative Primary** | Votes | % |
|---|---|---|
| Perry B. Duryea (C) | | 100.0 |

| **Liberal Primary** | Votes | % |
|---|---|---|
| Hugh L. Carey (L) | | 100.0 |

# NORTH CAROLINA

| 1982 | Candidates<br>**Republican Primary** | Votes | % |
|------|------------|-------|---|
| | Lew Lehrman (R) | 464,231 | *80.6* |
| | Paul J. Curran (R) | 111,814 | *19.4* |
| | **Democratic Primary** | | |
| | Mario M. Cuomo (D) | 678,900 | *52.3* |
| | Edward I. Koch (D) | 618,356 | *47.7* |
| | **Conservative Primary** | | |
| | Low Lohrman (R) | | *100.0* |
| | **Liberal Primary** | | |
| | Mario M. Cuomo (L) | | *100.0* |
| | **Right to Life Primary** | | |
| | Robert J. Bohner (RTL) | | *100.0* |
| 1986 | **Republican Primary** | | |
| | Andrew P. O'Rouke (R) | | *100.0* |
| | **Democratic Primary** | | |
| | Mario M. Cuomo (D) | | *100.0* |
| | **Conservative Primary** | | |
| | Andrew P. O'Rouke (C) | | *100.0* |
| | **Liberal Primary** | | |
| | Mario M. Cuomo (L) | | *100.0* |
| | **Right to Life Primary** | | |
| | Denis E. Dillon (RTL) | | *100.0* |
| 1990 | **Republican Primary** | | |
| | Pierre A. Rinfret (R) | | *100.0* |
| | **Democratic Primary** | | |
| | Mario M. Cuomo (D) | | *100.0* |
| | **Conservative Primary** | | |
| | Herbert I. London (C) | | *100.0* |
| | **Liberal Primary** | | |
| | Mario M. Cuomo (L) | | *100.0* |
| | **Right to Life Primary** | | |
| | Louis P. Wein (RTL) | | *100.0* |

**New York**

*1. Until 1970, candidates for state office in New York were nominated by state party conventions or central committees.*

*2. Morrison withdrew after the primary and the Liberal state committee substituted Hugh L. Carey as the party's nominee.*

| | Candidates | Votes | % |
|------|------------|-------|---|
| 1920 | **Democratic Primary** | | |
| | Cameron Morrison (D) | 49,070 | *38.3* |
| | O. Max Gardner (D) | 48,983 | *38.2* |
| | R. N. Page (D) | 30,180 | *23.5* |
| | **Democratic Runoff** | | |
| | Cameron Morrison (D) | 70,332 | *53.5* |
| | O. Max Gardner (D) | 61,073 | *46.5* |
| 1924 | **Democratic Primary** | | |
| | Angus Wilton McLean (D) | 151,197 | *64.4* |
| | Josiah W. Bailey (D) | 83,573 | *35.6* |
| 1928 | **Democratic Primary** | | |
| | O. Max Gardner (D) | | *100.0* |
| 1932 | **Democratic Primary** | | |
| | J. C. B. Ehringhaus (D) | 162,498 | *42.8* |
| | R. T. Fountain (D) | 115,127 | *30.3* |
| | Allen J. Maxwell (D) | 102,032 | *26.9* |
| | **Democratic Runoff** | | |
| | J. C. B. Ehringhaus (D) | 182,005 | *51.9* |
| | R. T. Fountain (D) | 168,971 | *48.1* |
| 1936 | **Democratic Primary** | | |
| | Clyde R. Hoey (D) | 193,972 | *37.5* |
| | Ralph McDonald (D) | 189,504 | *36.7* |
| | A. H. Graham (D) | 126,782 | *24.5* |
| | **Democratic Runoff** | | |
| | Clyde R. Hoey (D) | 266,354 | *55.4* |
| | Ralph McDonald (D) | 214,414 | *44.6* |
| 1940 | **Republican Primary** | | |
| | Robert H. McNeill (R) | 13,190 | *47.3* |
| | Pritchard (R) | 11,847 | *42.7* |
| | Hoffman (R) | 2,773 | *10.0* |
| | **Democratic Primary** | | |
| | J. Melville Broughton (D) | 147,386 | *31.4* |
| | W. P. Horton (D) [1] | 105,916 | *22.6* |
| | A. J. Maxwell (D) | 102,095 | *21.8* |
| | Lee Gravely (D) | 63,030 | *13.4* |
| | Thomas E. Cooper (D) | 33,176 | *7.1* |
| 1944 | **Democratic Primary** | | |
| | R. Gregg Cherry (D) | 185,027 | *57.5* |
| | Ralph McDonald (D) | 134,661 | *41.9* |
| 1948 | **Democratic Primary** | | |
| | Charles M. Johnson (D) | 170,141 | *40.2* |
| | W. Kerr Scott (D) | 161,293 | *38.1* |
| | R. Mayne Albright (D) | 76,281 | *18.0* |

| | Candidates | Votes | % |
|---|---|---|---|
| | **Democratic Runoff** | | |
| | W. Kerr Scott (D) | 217,620 | *54.4* |
| | Charles M. Johnson (D) | 182,684 | *45.6* |
| **1952** | **Democratic Primary** | | |
| | William B. Ulmstead (D) | 294,170 | *52.1* |
| | Hubert E. Olive (D) | 265,675 | *47.1* |
| **1956** | **Republican Primary** | | |
| | Kyle Hayes (R) | | *100.0* |
| | **Democratic Primary** | | |
| | Luther H. Hodges (D) | 401,082 | *86.0* |
| | Tom Sawyer (D) | 29,248 | *6.3* |
| | Harry P. Stokely (D) | 24,416 | *5.2* |
| **1960** | **Republican Primary** | | |
| | Robert L. Gavin (R) | | *100.0* |
| | **Democratic Primary** | | |
| | Terry Sanford (D) | 269,463 | *41.3* |
| | I. Beverly Lake (D) | 181,692 | *27.8* |
| | Malcolm B. Seawell (D) | 101,148 | *15.5* |
| | John D. Larkins (D) | 100,757 | *15.4* |
| | **Democratic Runoff** | | |
| | Terry Sanford (D) | 352,133 | *56.1* |
| | I. Beverly Lake (D) | 275,905 | *43.9* |
| **1964** | **Republican Primary** | | |
| | Robert L. Gavin (R) | 53,145 | *83.3* |
| | Charles W. Strong (R) | 8,652 | *13.6* |
| | **Democratic Primary** | | |
| | Richardson Preyer (D) | 281,430 | *36.6* |
| | Dan K. Moore (D) | 257,872 | *33.5* |
| | I. Beverly Lake (D) | 217,172 | *28.2* |
| | **Democratic Runoff** | | |
| | Dan K. Moore (D) | 480,431 | *62.1* |
| | Richardson Preyer (D) | 293,863 | *38.0* |
| **1968** | **Republican Primary** | | |
| | James C. Gardner (R) | 113,584 | *72.7* |
| | John L. Stikley (R) | 42,483 | *27.3* |
| | **Democratic Primary** | | |
| | Robert W. Scott (D) | 337,368 | *48.1* |
| | J. Melville Broughton Jr. (D)[2] | 233,924 | *33.4* |
| | Reginald A. Hawkins (D) | 129,808 | *18.5* |
| **1972** | **Republican Primary** | | |
| | James C. Gardner (R) | 84,906 | *49.8* |
| | James E. Holshouser Jr. (R) | 83,637 | *49.0* |
| | **Republican Runoff** | | |
| | James E. Holshouser Jr. (R) | 69,916 | *50.6* |
| | James C. Gardner (R) | 68,134 | *49.4* |

| | Candidates | Votes | % |
|---|---|---|---|
| | **Democratic Primary** | | |
| | Hargrove (Skipper) Bowles Jr. (D) | 367,433 | *45.5* |
| | H. P. (Pat) Taylor (D) | 304,910 | *37.7* |
| | Reginald A. Hawkins (D) | 65,950 | *8.2* |
| | Wilbur Hobby (D) | 58,990 | *7.3* |
| | **Democratic Runoff** | | |
| | Hargrove (Skipper) Bowles Jr. (D) | 336,034 | *54.3* |
| | H. P. (Pat) Taylor (D) | 282,345 | *45.7* |
| **1976** | **Republican Primary** | | |
| | David T. Flaherty (R) | 57,663 | *49.8* |
| | Coy C. Privette (R) | 37,573 | *32.4* |
| | J. F. Alexander (R) | 16,149 | *13.9* |
| | **Republican Runoff** | | |
| | David T. Flaherty (R) | 45,661 | *60.5* |
| | Coy C. Privette (R) | 29,810 | *39.5* |
| | **Democratic Primary** | | |
| | James B. Hunt Jr. (D) | 362,102 | *53.4* |
| | Edward M. O'Herron (D) | 157,815 | *23.2* |
| | George Wood (D) | 121,673 | *17.9* |
| **1980** | **Republican Primary** | | |
| | I. Beverly Lake Jr. (R) | 119,255 | *80.8* |
| | C. J. Carstens (R) | 28,354 | *19.2* |
| | **Democratic Primary** | | |
| | James B. Hunt Jr. (D) | 524,844 | *69.6* |
| | Robert W. Scott (D) | 217,289 | *28.8* |
| **1984** | **Republican Primary** | | |
| | James G. Martin (R) | 128,714 | *91.7* |
| | Ruby T. Hooper (R) | 11,640 | *8.3* |
| | **Democratic Primary** | | |
| | Rufus Edmisten (D) | 295,051 | *30.9* |
| | H. Edward Knox (D) | 249,286 | *26.1* |
| | D. M. Faircloth (D) | 153,210 | *16.0* |
| | Thomas O. Gilmore (D) | 82,299 | *8.6* |
| | James C. Green (D) | 80,775 | *8.4* |
| | John Ingram (D) | 75,248 | *7.9* |
| | **Democratic Runoff** | | |
| | Rufus Edmisten (D) | 352,351 | *51.9* |
| | H. Edward Knox (D) | 326,278 | *48.1* |
| **1988** | **Republican Primary** | | |
| | James G. Martin (R) | | *100.0* |
| | **Democratic Primary** | | |
| | Robert B. Jordan (D) | 403,145 | *79.7* |
| | Billy Martin (D) | 60,770 | *12.0* |
| **1992** | **Republican Primary** | | |
| | James C. Gardner (R) | 215,528 | *82.0* |
| | Ruby T. Hooper (R) | 26,179 | *10.0* |
| | Gary M. Dunn (R) | 21,256 | *8.1* |

| Candidates<br>Democratic Primary | Votes | % |
|---|---|---|
| James B. Hunt Jr. (D) | 459,300 | 65.5 |
| Lacy H. Thornburg (D) | 188,806 | 26.9 |

**North Carolina**

1. Horton declined a runoff with Broughton, who became the Democratic nominee.

2. J. Melville Broughton Jr. declined a runoff with Scott, who became the Democratic nominee.

# NORTH DAKOTA

| | Candidates | Votes | % |
|---|---|---|---|
| 1956 | **Republican Primary** | | |
| | John E. Davis (R) | 55,149 | 53.3 |
| | Ray Schnell (R) | 48,296 | 46.7 |
| | **Democratic Primary** | | |
| | Wallace E. Warner (D) | | 100.0 |
| 1958 | **Republican Primary** | | |
| | John E. Davis (R) | | 100.0 |
| | **Democratic Primary** | | |
| | John F. Lord (D) | 26,447 | 55.4 |
| | Art Ford (D) | 21,271 | 44.6 |
| 1960 | **Republican Primary** | | |
| | C. P. Dahl (R) | 86,900 | 77.6 |
| | Orris G. Nordhougen (R) | 25,132 | 22.4 |
| | **Democratic Primary** | | |
| | William L. Guy (D) | | 100.0 |
| 1962 | **Republican Primary** | | |
| | Mark Andrews (R) | | 100.0 |
| | **Democratic Primary** | | |
| | William L. Guy (D) | | 100.0 |
| 1964 | **Republican Primary** | | |
| | Donald M. Halcrow (R) | 43,089 | 55.0 |
| | Robert P. McCarney (R) | 35,269 | 45.0 |
| | **Democratic Primary** | | |
| | William L. Guy (D) | | 100.0 |
| 1968 | **Republican Primary** | | |
| | Robert P. McCarney (R) | 47,324 | 52.5 |
| | Edward W. Doherty (R) | 42,845 | 47.5 |
| | **Democratic Primary** | | |
| | William L. Guy (D) | | 100.0 |

| | Candidates | Votes | % |
|---|---|---|---|
| 1972 | **Republican Primary** | | |
| | Richard Larsen (R) | 66,045 | 67.8 |
| | Robert P. McCarney (R) | 31,377 | 32.2 |
| | **Democratic Primary** | | |
| | Arthur A. Link (D) | 29,979 | 93.1 |
| | Edward P. Burns (D) | 2,231 | 6.9 |
| 1976 | **Republican Primary** | | |
| | Richard Elkin (R) | 54,427 | 81.9 |
| | Herb Geving (R) | 12,013 | 18.1 |
| | **Democratic Primary** | | |
| | Arthur A. Link (D) | | 100.0 |
| | **American Primary** | | |
| | Martin Vaaler (AM) | | 100.0 |
| 1980 | **Republican Primary** | | |
| | Allen I. Olson (R) | 60,016 | 75.7 |
| | Orville W. Hagen (R) | 19,306 | 24.3 |
| | **Democratic Primary** | | |
| | Arthur A. Link (D) | | 100.0 |
| 1984 | **Republican Primary** | | |
| | Allen I. Olson (R) | 41,191 | 100.0 |
| | **Democratic Primary** | | |
| | George A. Sinner (D) | 36,461 | 87.6 |
| | Anna Belle Bourgois (D) | 5,180 | 12.4 |
| 1988 | **Republican Primary** | | |
| | Leon L. Mallberg (R) | | 100.0 |
| | **Democratic Primary** | | |
| | George A. Sinner (D) | | 100.0 |
| 1992 | **Republican Primary** | | |
| | Edward T. Schafer (R) | 47,300 | 100.0 |
| | **Democratic Primary** | | |
| | Nicholas Spaeth (D) | 50,607 | 65.1 |
| | Bill Heigaard (D) | 27,161 | 34.9 |

# OHIO

| | Candidates | Votes | % |
|---|---|---|---|
| 1956 | **Republican Primary** | | |
| | C. William O'Neill (R) | 425,947 | 72.5 |
| | John W. Brown (R) | 161,826 | 27.5 |

| Candidates Democratic Primary | Votes | % |
|---|---|---|
| Michael V. DiSalle (D) | 279,831 | 57.4 |
| John E. Sweeney (D) | 106,071 | 21.8 |
| Robert W. Reider (D) | 41,224 | 8.5 |
| Frank X. Kryzan (D) | 37,290 | 7.6 |

**1958** **Republican Primary**

| | Votes | % |
|---|---|---|
| C. William O'Neill (R) | 346,660 | 63.6 |
| Charles P. Taft (R) | 198,173 | 36.4 |

**Democratic Primary**

| | Votes | % |
|---|---|---|
| Michael V. DiSalle (D) | 242,830 | 37.7 |
| Anthony J. Celebrezze (D) | 140,453 | 21.8 |
| Albert S. Porter (D) | 108,498 | 16.8 |
| Robert N. Gorman (D) | 57,694 | 9.0 |
| M. E. Sensenbrenner (D) | 52,350 | 8.1 |
| Clingan Jackson (D) | 35,175 | 5.5 |

**1962** **Republican Primary**

| | Votes | % |
|---|---|---|
| James A. Rhodes (R) | 520,868 | 89.6 |
| William L. White (R) | 59,916 | 10.3 |

**Democratic Primary**

| | Votes | % |
|---|---|---|
| Michael V. DiSalle (D) | 331,463 | 50.3 |
| Mark McElroy (D) | 299,207 | 45.4 |

**1966** **Republican Primary**

| | Votes | % |
|---|---|---|
| James A. Rhodes (R) | 577,827 | 88.7 |
| William L. White (R) | 73,428 | 11.3 |

**Democratic Primary**

| | Votes | % |
|---|---|---|
| Frazier Reams Jr. (D) | 326,419 | 58.5 |
| Harry H. McIlwain (D) | 231,406 | 41.5 |

**1970** **Republican Primary**

| | Votes | % |
|---|---|---|
| Roger Cloud (R) | 468,369 | 50.5 |
| Donald E. Lukens (R) | 283,257 | 30.5 |
| Paul W. Brown (R) | 164,672 | 17.7 |

**Democratic Primary**

| | Votes | % |
|---|---|---|
| John J. Gilligan (D) | 547,675 | 59.7 |
| Robert E. Sweeney (D) | 216,195 | 23.6 |
| Mark McElroy (D) | 153,702 | 16.7 |

**American Independent Primary**

| | Votes | % |
|---|---|---|
| Edwin G. Lawton (AMI) | 3,463 | 64.9 |
| Robert W. Annable (AMI) | 1,870 | 35.1 |

**1974** **Republican Primary**

| | Votes | % |
|---|---|---|
| James A. Rhodes (R) | 385,669 | 62.8 |
| Charles E. Fry (R) | 183,899 | 29.9 |
| Bert Dawson (R) | 44,938 | 7.3 |

**Democratic Primary**

| | Votes | % |
|---|---|---|
| John J. Gilligan (D) | 713,488 | 70.6 |
| James D. Nolan (D) | 297,244 | 29.4 |

**1978** 

| Candidates Republican Primary | Votes | % |
|---|---|---|
| James A. Rhodes (R) | 393,632 | 67.7 |
| Charles F. Kurfess (R) | 187,544 | 32.3 |

**Democratic Primary**

| | Votes | % |
|---|---|---|
| Richard F. Celeste (D) | 491,524 | 84.6 |
| Dale Reusch (D) | 88,314 | 15.2 |

**1982** **Republican Primary**

| | Votes | % |
|---|---|---|
| Clarence Brown Jr. (R) | 347,176 | 51.5 |
| Seth Taft (R) | 153,806 | 22.8 |
| Thomas A. Van Meter (R) | 136,761 | 20.3 |
| Robert W. Teater (R) | 35,821 | 5.3 |

**Democratic Primary**

| | Votes | % |
|---|---|---|
| Richard F. Celeste (D) | 436,887 | 42.4 |
| William J. Brown (D) | 383,007 | 37.2 |
| Jerry Springer (D) | 210,524 | 20.4 |

**Libertarian Primary**

| | Votes | % |
|---|---|---|
| Phyllis Goetz (LIBERT) | | 100.0 |

**1986** **Republican Primary**

| | Votes | % |
|---|---|---|
| James A. Rhodes (R) | 352,261 | 48.2 |
| Paul E. Gillmor (R) | 281,737 | 38.5 |
| Paul E. Pfeifer (R) | 96,948 | 13.3 |

**Democratic Primary**

| | Votes | % |
|---|---|---|
| Richard F. Celeste (D) | | 100.0 |

**1990** **Republican Primary**

| | Votes | % |
|---|---|---|
| George Voinovich (R) | | 100.0 |

**Democratic Primary**

| | Votes | % |
|---|---|---|
| Anthony J. Celebrezze (D) | 683,932 | 83.9 |
| Michael H. Lord (D) | 131,564 | 16.1 |

# OKLAHOMA

**1958**

| Candidates Republican Primary | Votes | % |
|---|---|---|
| Phil Ferguson (R) | 31,602 | 51.4 |
| Clarence E. Barnes (R) | 21,075 | 34.3 |
| Carmon C. Harris (R) | 5,941 | 9.7 |

**Democratic Primary**

| | Votes | % |
|---|---|---|
| J. Howard Edmondson (D) | 108,358 | 21.1 |
| W. P. Atkinson (D) | 107,616 | 20.9 |
| George Miskovsky (D) | 87,766 | 17.1 |
| William O. Coe (D) | 72,763 | 14.2 |
| Bill Doenges (D) | 57,990 | 11.3 |
| Jim A. Rinehart (D) | 39,279 | 7.6 |

| Candidates | Votes | % |
|---|---|---|
| **Democratic Runoff** | | |
| J. Howard Edmondson (D) | 363,742 | *69.6* |
| W. P. Atkinson (D) | 158,780 | *30.4* |

### 1962

**Republican Primary**

| Candidates | Votes | % |
|---|---|---|
| Henry L. Bellmon (R) | 56,560 | *91.4* |
| Leslie C. Skoien (R) | 5,313 | *8.6* |

**Democratic Primary**

| Candidates | Votes | % |
|---|---|---|
| Raymond Gary (D) | 176,525 | *33.0* |
| W. P. Atkinson (D) | 91,182 | *17.1* |
| Preston J. Moore (D) | 85,248 | *16.0* |
| George Nigh (D) | 84,404 | *15.8* |
| Fred R. Harris (D) | 78,476 | *14.7* |

**Democratic Runoff**

| Candidates | Votes | % |
|---|---|---|
| W. P. Atkinson (D) | 231,994 | *50.0* |
| Raymond Gary (D) | 231,545 | *49.9* |

### 1966

**Republican Primary**

| Candidates | Votes | % |
|---|---|---|
| Dewey F. Bartlett (R) | 46,053 | *49.0* |
| John N. H. Camp (R) | 45,185 | *48.1* |

**Democratic Primary**

| Candidates | Votes | % |
|---|---|---|
| Raymond Gary (D) | 160,825 | *31.6* |
| Preston J. Moore (D) | 104,081 | *20.4* |
| David Hall (D) | 94,309 | *18.5* |
| Cleeta J. Rogers (D) | 71,248 | *14.0* |
| Charles Nesbitt (D) | 26,546 | *5.2* |

**Republican Runoff**

| Candidates | Votes | % |
|---|---|---|
| Dewey F. Bartlett (R) | 46,916 | *55.2* |
| John N. H. Camp (R) | 38,043 | *44.8* |

**Democratic Runoff**

| Candidates | Votes | % |
|---|---|---|
| Preston J. Moore (D) | 228,625 | *53.7* |
| Raymond Gary (D) | 196,835 | *46.3* |

### 1970

**Republican Primary**

| Candidates | Votes | % |
|---|---|---|
| Dewey F. Bartlett (R) | | *100.0* |

**Democratic Primary**

| Candidates | Votes | % |
|---|---|---|
| David Hall (D) | 198,976 | *49.5* |
| Bryce Baggett (D) | 96,069 | *23.9* |
| Joe Cannon (D) | 56,842 | *14.1* |
| Wilburn Cartwright (D) | 50,396 | *12.5* |

**Democratic Runoff**

| Candidates | Votes | % |
|---|---|---|
| David Hall (D) | 179,902 | *57.5* |
| Bryce Baggett (D) | 132,952 | *42.5* |

### 1974

**Republican Primary**

| Candidates | Votes | % |
|---|---|---|
| James M. Inhofe (R) | 88,594 | *58.8* |
| Denzil D. Garrison (R) | 62,188 | *41.2* |

**Democratic Primary**

| Candidates | Votes | % |
|---|---|---|
| Clem R. McSpadden (D) | 238,534 | *37.7* |
| David L. Boren (D) | 225,321 | *35.6* |
| David Hall (D) | 169,290 | *26.7* |

| Candidates | Votes | % |
|---|---|---|
| **Democratic Runoff** | | |
| David L. Boren (D) | 286,171 | *53.5* |
| Clem R. McSpadden (D) | 248,623 | *46.5* |

### 1978

**Republican Primary**

| Candidates | Votes | % |
|---|---|---|
| Ron Shotts (R) | 82,895 | *76.8* |
| Jerry L. Mash (R) | 13,145 | *12.2* |
| Jim Head (R) | 11,826 | *11.0* |

**Democratic Primary**

| Candidates | Votes | % |
|---|---|---|
| George Nigh (D) | 276,910 | *49.9* |
| Larry Derryberry (D) | 208,055 | *37.5* |
| Bob Funston (D) | 69,475 | *12.5* |

**Democratic Runoff**

| Candidates | Votes | % |
|---|---|---|
| George Nigh (D) | 269,681 | *57.7* |
| Larry Derryberry (D) | 197,457 | *42.3* |

### 1982

**Republican Primary**

| Candidates | Votes | % |
|---|---|---|
| Tom Daxon (R) | 73,677 | *64.7* |
| Neal A. McCaleb (R) | 35,379 | *31.1* |

**Democratic Primary**

| Candidates | Votes | % |
|---|---|---|
| George Nigh (D) | 379,301 | *82.6* |
| Howard L. Bell (D) | 79,735 | *17.4* |

### 1986

**Republican Primary**

| Candidates | Votes | % |
|---|---|---|
| Henry L. Bellmon (R) | 111,665 | *70.3* |
| Mike Fair (R) | 33,266 | *20.9* |

**Democratic Primary**

| Candidates | Votes | % |
|---|---|---|
| David Walters (D) | 238,165 | *46.0* |
| Mike Turpen (D) | 207,357 | *40.0* |
| Leslie Fisher (D) | 33,639 | *6.5* |

**Democratic Runoff**

| Candidates | Votes | % |
|---|---|---|
| David Walters (D) | 235,373 | *50.4* |
| Mike Turpen (D) | 231,390 | *49.6* |

### 1990

**Republican Primary**

| Candidates | Votes | % |
|---|---|---|
| Vince Orza (R) | 75,992 | *40.1* |
| Bill Price (R) | 51,355 | *27.1* |
| Burns Hargis (R) | 33,641 | *17.8* |
| Jerry Brown (R) | 25,670 | *13.5* |

**Republican Runoff**

| Candidates | Votes | % |
|---|---|---|
| Bill Price (R) | 94,682 | *50.8* |
| Vince Orza (R) | 91,599 | *49.2* |

**Democratic Primary**

| Candidates | Votes | % |
|---|---|---|
| Wes Watkins (D) | 175,568 | *32.3* |
| David Walters (D) | 171,730 | *31.6* |
| Steve Lewis (D) | 160,455 | *29.5* |

**Democratic Runoff**

| Candidates | Votes | % |
|---|---|---|
| David Walters (D) | 243,252 | *50.7* |
| Wes Watkins (D) | 236,597 | *49.3* |

**757**

# OREGON

| Candidates | Votes | % |
|---|---|---|
| **1956** **Republican Primary** | | |
| Elmo E. Smith (R) | 225,748 | *91.0* |
| Earl L. Dickson (R) | 22,306 | *9.0* |
| **Democratic Primary** | | |
| Robert D. Holmes (D) | 112,307 | *50.8* |
| Lew Wallace (D) | 108,822 | *49.2* |
| **1958** **Republican Primary** | | |
| Mark O. Hatfield (R) | 106,687 | *47.9* |
| Sig Unander (R) | 65,180 | *29.2* |
| Warren Gill (R) | 40,489 | *18.2* |
| **Democratic Primary** | | |
| Robert D. Holmes (D) | 129,491 | *62.0* |
| Lew Wallace (D) | 59,992 | *28.7* |
| Wiley W. Smith (D) | 18,484 | *8.8* |
| **1962** **Republican Primary** | | |
| Mark O. Hatfield (R) | 174,811 | *82.2* |
| George Altvater (R) | 37,306 | *17.5* |
| **Democratic Primary** | | |
| Robert Y. Thornton (D) | 149,000 | *66.2* |
| Walter J. Pearson (D) | 62,331 | *27.7* |
| **1966** **Republican Primary** | | |
| Tom McCall (R) | 215,959 | *91.4* |
| John L. Reynolds (R) | 20,286 | *8.6* |
| **Democratic Primary** | | |
| Robert W. Straub (D) | 182,697 | *72.5* |
| Ben Musa (D) | 41,610 | *16.5* |
| Emmet T. Rogers (D) | 17,618 | *7.0* |
| **1970** **Republican Primary** | | |
| Tom McCall (R) | 183,298 | *74.4* |
| Robert H. Wampler (R) | 38,322 | *15.6* |
| Andrew R. Gigler (R) | 24,797 | *10.1* |
| **Democratic Primary** | | |
| Robert W. Straub (D) | 182,683 | *65.9* |
| Art Pearl (D) | 33,716 | *12.2* |
| Gracie Hansen (D) | 20,329 | *7.3* |
| Al Holdiman (D) | 18,180 | *6.6* |
| **1974** **Republican Primary** | | |
| Victor G. Atiyeh (R) | 144,454 | *60.7* |
| Clay Myers (R) | 79,003 | *33.2* |
| **Democratic Primary** | | |
| Robert W. Straub (D) | 107,205 | *33.6* |
| Betty Roberts (D) | 98,654 | *30.9* |
| Jim Redden (D) | 88,795 | *27.8* |

| | Candidates | Votes | % |
|---|---|---|---|
| **1978** | **Republican Primary** | | |
| | Victor G. Atiyeh (R) | 115,593 | *46.4* |
| | Tom McCall (R) | 83,568 | *33.5* |
| | Roger Martin (R) | 42,644 | *17.1* |
| | **Democratic Primary** | | |
| | Robert W. Straub (D) | 144,761 | *51.0* |
| | Marvin J. Hollingsworth (D) | 52,901 | *18.7* |
| | Emily Ashworth (D) | 49,201 | *17.3* |
| **1982** | **Republican Primary** | | |
| | Victor G. Atiyeh (R) | 208,333 | *82.4* |
| | Clif Everett (R) | 17,741 | *7.0* |
| | Walter Huss (R) | 16,892 | *6.7* |
| | **Democratic Primary** | | |
| | Ted Kulongoski (D) | 186,580 | *59.5* |
| | Don Clark (D) | 60,850 | *19.4* |
| | Jerry Rust (D) | 22,962 | *7.3* |
| **1986** | **Republican Primary** | | |
| | Norma Paulus (R) | 219,505 | *77.0* |
| | Betty Freauf (R) | 36,384 | *12.8* |
| | **Democratic Primary** | | |
| | Neil Goldschmidt (D) | 214,148 | *67.4* |
| | Edward N. Fadeley (D) | 81,300 | *25.6* |
| **1990** | **Republican Primary** | | |
| | Dave Frohnmayer (R) | 227,867 | *79.1* |
| | John K. Lim (R) | 32,397 | *11.2* |
| | **Democratic Primary** | | |
| | Barbara Roberts (D) | | *100.0* |

# PENNSYLVANIA

| | Candidates | Votes | % |
|---|---|---|---|
| **1958** | **Republican Primary** | | |
| | A. T. McGonigle (R) | 578,286 | *53.3* |
| | Harold E. Stassen (R) | 344,043 | *31.7* |
| | William S. Livengood (R) | 138,284 | *12.7* |
| | **Democratic Primary** | | |
| | David Lawrence (D) | 730,229 | *74.4* |
| | Roy E. Furman (D) | 194,464 | *19.8* |
| | Edward P. Lavelle (D) | 56,188 | *5.7* |
| **1962** | **Republican Primary** | | |
| | William W. Scranton (R) | 743,785 | *78.0* |
| | J. Collins McSparran (R) | 209,041 | *21.9* |

| Candidates | Votes | % |
|---|---|---|
| **Democratic Primary** | | |
| Richardson Dilworth (D) | 651,096 | *72.9* |
| Harvey F. Johnston (D) | 143,243 | *16.0* |
| Charles J. Schmitt (D) | 96,899 | *10.9* |

**1966**

| **Republican Primary** | | |
|---|---|---|
| Raymond P. Shafer (R) | 835,768 | *78.0* |
| Harold E. Stassen (R) | 172,150 | *16.1* |
| George J. Brett (R) | 63,366 | *5.9* |

| **Democratic Primary** | | |
|---|---|---|
| Milton Shapp (D) | 543,057 | *48.6* |
| Robert P. Casey (D) | 493,886 | *44.2* |
| Erwin L. Murray (D) | 80,803 | *7.2* |

**1970**

| **Republican Primary** | | |
|---|---|---|
| Raymond Broderick (R) | | *100.0* |

| **Democratic Primary** | | |
|---|---|---|
| Milton Shapp (D) | 519,161 | *49.1* |
| Robert P. Casey (D) | 480,944 | *45.5* |

| **American Independent Primary** | | |
|---|---|---|
| Francis T. McGeever (AMI) | | *100.0* |

| **Constitutional Primary** | | |
|---|---|---|
| Andrew J. Watson (CST) | | *100.0* |

**1974**

| **Republican Primary** | | |
|---|---|---|
| Andrew L. Lewis (R) | 534,637 | *76.9* |
| Alvin J. Jacobson (R) | 97,072 | *14.0* |
| Leonard M. Strunk (R) | 63,868 | *9.2* |

| **Democratic Primary** | | |
|---|---|---|
| Milton Shapp (D) | 729,201 | *70.4* |
| Martin P. Mullen (D) | 199,613 | *19.3* |
| Harvey F. Johnston (D) | 106,474 | *10.3* |

| **Constitutional Primary** | | |
|---|---|---|
| Stephen Depue (CST) | 1,006 | *52.8* |
| Norah M. Cope (CST) | 898 | *47.2* |

**1978**

| **Republican Primary** | | |
|---|---|---|
| Richard L. Thornburgh (R) | 325,376 | *32.6* |
| Arlen Specter (R) | 206,802 | *20.7* |
| Bob Butera (R) | 190,653 | *19.1* |
| David W. Marston (R) | 161,813 | *16.2* |
| Henry Hager (R) | 57,119 | *5.7* |

| **Democratic Primary** | | |
|---|---|---|
| Peter Flaherty (D) | 574,889 | *44.9* |
| Robert P. Casey (D) | 445,146 | *34.7* |
| Ernest P. Kline (D) | 223,811 | *17.5* |

**1982**

| **Republican Primary** | | |
|---|---|---|
| Richard L. Thornburgh (R) | | *100.0* |

| Candidates | Votes | % |
|---|---|---|
| **Democratic Primary** | | |
| Allen E. Ertel (D) | 436,251 | *57.6* |
| Steve Douglas (D) | 143,762 | *19.0* |
| Earl S. McDowell (D) | 116,880 | *15.4* |
| Eugene Knox (D) | 59,925 | *7.9* |

**1986**

| **Republican Primary** | | |
|---|---|---|
| William W. Scranton (R) | | *100.0* |

| **Democratic Primary** | | |
|---|---|---|
| Robert Casey (D) | 549,376 | *56.4* |
| Edward G. Rendell (D) | 385,539 | *39.6* |

**1990**

| **Republican Primary** | | |
|---|---|---|
| Barbara Hafer (R) | 321,026 | *54.4* |
| Marguerite A. Luksik (R) | 268,773 | *45.6* |

| **Democratic Primary** | | |
|---|---|---|
| Robert Casey (D) | 636,594 | *77.5* |
| Philip J. Berg (D) | 184,365 | *22.5* |

# RHODE ISLAND

| Candidates | Votes | % |
|---|---|---|
| **Republican Primary** | | |

**1956**

| Christopher Del Sesto (R) | | *100.0* |
|---|---|---|

| **Democratic Primary** | | |
|---|---|---|
| Dennis J. Roberts (D) | | *100.0* |

**1958**

| **Republican Primary** | | |
|---|---|---|
| Christopher Del Sesto (R) | | *100.0* |

| **Democratic Primary** | | |
|---|---|---|
| Dennis J. Roberts (D) | 53,121 | *56.1* |
| Armand H. Coté (D) | 41,536 | *43.9* |

**1960**

| **Republican Primary** | | |
|---|---|---|
| Christopher Del Sesto (R) | | *100.0* |

| **Democratic Primary** | | |
|---|---|---|
| John A. Notte (D) | 73,607 | *56.3* |
| Armand H. Coté (D) | 57,200 | *43.7* |

**1962**

| **Republican Primary** | | |
|---|---|---|
| John H. Chafee (R) | 17,756 | *62.5* |
| Louis Jackvony (R) | 10,459 | *36.8* |

| **Democratic Primary** | | |
|---|---|---|
| John A. Notte (D) | 49,204 | *53.1* |
| Kevin Coleman (D) | 41,658 | *45.0* |

**1964**

| **Republican Primary** | | |
|---|---|---|
| John H. Chafee (R) | | *100.0* |

| Candidates | Votes | % |
|---|---|---|
| **Democratic Primary** | | |
| Edward P. Gallogly (D) | 55,282 | *56.7* |
| Alexander R. Walsh (D) | 25,457 | *26.1* |
| John L. Rego (D) | 16,715 | *17.2* |

**1966** **Republican Primary**

| Candidates | Votes | % |
|---|---|---|
| John H. Chafee (R) | | *100.0* |

**Democratic Primary**

| | | |
|---|---|---|
| Horace E. Hobbs (D) | | *100.0* |

**1968** **Republican Primary**

| | | |
|---|---|---|
| John H. Chafee (R) | | *100.0* |

**Democratic Primary**

| | | |
|---|---|---|
| Frank Licht (D) | | *100.0* |

**1970** **Republican Primary**

| | | |
|---|---|---|
| Herbert F. DeSimone (R) | 11,826 | *96.0* |

**Democratic Primary**

| | | |
|---|---|---|
| Frank Licht (D) | | *100.0* |

**1972** **Republican Primary**

| | | |
|---|---|---|
| Herbert F. DeSimone (R) | | *100.0* |

**Democratic Primary**

| | | |
|---|---|---|
| Philip W. Noel (D) | | *100.0* |

**1974** **Republican Primary**

| | | |
|---|---|---|
| James W. Nugent (R) | | *100.0* |

**Democratic Primary**

| | | |
|---|---|---|
| Philip W. Noel (D) | | *100.0* |

**1976** **Republican Primary**

| | | |
|---|---|---|
| James L. Taft (R) | | *100.0* |

**Democratic Primary**

| | | |
|---|---|---|
| J. Joseph Garrahy (D) | 113,625 | *82.4* |
| Giovani Folcarelli (D) | 24,314 | *17.6* |

**1978** **Republican Primary**

| | | |
|---|---|---|
| Lincoln Almond (R) | | *100.0* |

**Democratic Primary**

| | | |
|---|---|---|
| J. Joseph Garrahy (D) | | *100.0* |

**1982** **Republican Primary**

| | | |
|---|---|---|
| Vincent Marzullo (R) | | *100.0* |

**Democratic Primary**

| | | |
|---|---|---|
| J. Joseph Garrahy (D) | | *100.0* |

**1984**

| Candidates | Votes | % |
|---|---|---|
| **Republican Primary** | | |
| Edward D. DiPrete (R) | 245,059 | *100.0* |
| **Democratic Primary** | | |
| Anthony J. Solomon (D) | 73,090 | *57.9* |
| Joseph W. Walsh (D) | 53,041 | *42.0* |

**1986** **Republican Primary**

| | | |
|---|---|---|
| Edward D. DiPrete (R) | | *100.0* |

**Democratic Primary**

| | | |
|---|---|---|
| Bruce G. Sundlun (D) | 43,120 | *75.3* |
| Steve White (D) | 14,124 | *24.7* |

**1988** **Republican Primary**

| | | |
|---|---|---|
| Edward D. DiPrete (R) | | *100.0* |

**Democratic Primary**

| | | |
|---|---|---|
| Bruce G. Sundlun (D) | 68,065 | *90.3* |
| Peter Van Daam (D) | 7,328 | *9.7* |

**1990** **Republican Primary**

| | | |
|---|---|---|
| Edward D. DiPrete (R) | 7,644 | *70.8* |
| Steve White (R) | 3,157 | *29.2* |

**Democratic Primary**

| | | |
|---|---|---|
| Bruce G. Sundlun (D) | 68,021 | *40.5* |
| Francis X. Flaherty (D) | 53,821 | *32.1* |
| Joseph R. Paolino (D) | 46,074 | *27.4* |

**1992** **Republican Primary**

| | | |
|---|---|---|
| Elizabeth Ann Leonard (R) | 7,534 | *52.1* |
| J. Michael Levesque (R) | 6,926 | *47.9* |

**Democratic Primary**

| | | |
|---|---|---|
| Bruce G. Sundlun (D) | 78,735 | *52.2* |
| Francis X. Flaherty (D) | 72,011 | *47.8* |

# SOUTH CAROLINA

| Candidates | Votes | % |
|---|---|---|
| **1920** **Democratic Primary** | | |
| Robert A. Cooper (D) | | *100.0* |
| **1922** **Democratic Primary** | | |
| Coleman L. Blease (D) | 77,798 | *44.8* |
| Thomas G. McLeod (D) | 65,768 | *37.9* |
| George K. Laney (D) | 23,164 | *13.4* |
| **Democratic Runoff** | | |
| Thomas G. McLeod (D) | 100,114 | *53.8* |
| Coleman L. Blease (D) | 85,834 | *46.2* |

| | Candidates | Votes | % |
|---|---|---|---|
| 1924 [1] | **Democratic Primary** | | |
| | Thomas G. McLeod (D) | 107,356 | *61.2* |
| | J. T. Duncan (D) | 68,155 | *38.8* |
| 1926 | **Democratic Primary** | | |
| | John G. Richards (D) | 44,806 | *25.8* |
| | Ibra C. Blackwood (D) | 34,870 | *20.1* |
| | Edmund B. Jackson (D) | 33,804 | *19.5* |
| | Carroll D. Nance (D) | 16,970 | *9.8* |
| | George K. Laney (D) | 13,386 | *7.7* |
| | Thomas H. Peeples (D) | 10,636 | *6.1* |
| | D. A. G. Ouzts (D) | 10,570 | *6.1* |
| | **Democratic Runoff** | | |
| | John G. Richards (D) | 95,007 | *58.2* |
| | Ibra C. Blackwood (D) | 68,224 | *41.8* |
| 1930 | **Democratic Primary** | | |
| | Olin D. Johnston (D) | 58,653 | *24.9* |
| | Ibra C. Blackwood (D) | 43,859 | *18.6* |
| | Lever (D) | 39,477 | *16.8* |
| | Williams (D) | 36,488 | *15.5* |
| | Keith (D) | 28,780 | *12.2* |
| | Herbert (D) | 17,102 | *7.3* |
| | **Democratic Runoff** | | |
| | Ibra C. Blackwood (D) | 118,721 | *50.2* |
| | Olin D. Johnston (D) | 117,752 | *49.8* |
| 1934 | **Democratic Primary** | | |
| | Olin D. Johnston (D) | 104,799 | *35.2* |
| | Coleman L. Blease (D) | 85,795 | *28.9* |
| | Wyndham Manning (D) | 55,767 | *18.8* |
| | Pearce (D) | 36,328 | *12.2* |
| | **Democratic Runoff** | | |
| | Olin D. Johnston (D) | 157,673 | *56.2* |
| | Coleman L. Blease (D) | 122,876 | *43.8* |
| 1938 | **Democratic Primary** | | |
| | Burnet R. Maybank (D) | 177,900 | *44.9* |
| | Wyndham Manning (D) | 74,356 | *18.8* |
| | Coleman L. Blease (D) | 60,823 | *15.4* |
| | Bennett (D) | 47,882 | *12.1* |
| | Adams (D) | 26,376 | *6.7* |
| | **Democratic Runoff** | | |
| | Burnet R. Maybank (D) | 163,947 | *52.3* |
| | Wyndham Manning (D) | 149,368 | *47.7* |
| 1942 | **Democratic Primary** | | |
| | Olin D. Johnston (D) | 121,465 | *51.8* |
| | Wyndham Manning (D) | 113,014 | *48.2* |
| 1946 | **Democratic Primary** | | |
| | Strom Thurmond (D) | 96,691 | *33.4* |
| | James C. McLeod (D) | 83,464 | *28.9* |
| | Williams (D) | 35,813 | *12.4* |
| | Taylor (D) | 22,447 | *7.8* |
| | O'Neal (D) | 16,574 | *5.7* |
| | Long (D) | 16,503 | *5.7* |

| | Candidates | Votes | % |
|---|---|---|---|
| | **Democratic Runoff** | | |
| | Strom Thurmond (D) | 144,420 | *57.0* |
| | James C. McLeod (D) | 109,169 | *43.1* |
| 1950 | **Democratic Primary** | | |
| | James F. Byrnes (D) | 248,069 | *71.6* |
| | Bates (D) | 63,143 | *18.2* |
| | Pope (D) | 29,622 | *8.6* |
| 1954 | **Democratic Primary** | | |
| | George Bell Timmerman Jr. (D) | 185,541 | *61.3* |
| | Bates (D) | 116,942 | *38.7* |
| 1958 | **Democratic Primary** | | |
| | Ernest F. Hollings (D) | 158,159 | *41.9* |
| | Donald S. Russell (D) | 132,099 | *35.0* |
| | William C. Johnston (D) | 86,981 | *23.1* |
| | **Democratic Runoff** | | |
| | Ernest F. Hollings (D) | 190,691 | *56.8* |
| | Donald S. Russell (D) | 145,162 | *43.2* |
| 1962 | **Democratic Primary** | | |
| | Donald S. Russell (D) | 199,619 | *60.8* |
| | Burnet R. Maybank (D) | 103,015 | *31.4* |
| | A. W. Bethea (D) | 17,251 | *5.3* |
| 1966 | **Democratic Primary** | | |
| | Robert E. McNair (D) | | *100.0* |
| 1970 | **Democratic Primary** | | |
| | John C. West (D) | | *100.0* |
| 1974 | **Republican Primary** | | |
| | James B. Edwards (R) | 20,177 | *57.7* |
| | William C. Westmoreland (R) | 14,777 | *42.3* |
| | **Democratic Primary** | | |
| | Charles D. Ravenel (D) | 107,345 | *33.6* |
| | William Jennings Bryan Dorn (D) | 105,734 | *33.1* |
| | Earle E. Morris Jr. (D) | 80,292 | *25.2* |
| | **Democratic Runoff** | | |
| | Charles D. Ravenel (D) [2] | 186,985 | *54.8* |
| | William Jennings Bryan Dorn (D) | 154,187 | *45.2* |
| 1978 | **Republican Primary** | | |
| | Edward L. Young (R) | 12,172 | *51.4* |
| | Raymond Finch (R) | 11,499 | *48.6* |
| | **Democratic Primary** | | |
| | W. Brantley Harvey (D) | 142,785 | *37.5* |
| | Richard Riley (D) | 125,185 | *32.9* |
| | William Jennings Bryan Dorn (D) | 112,793 | *29.6* |
| | **Democratic Runoff** | | |
| | Richard Riley (D) | 180,882 | *53.3* |
| | W. Brantley Harvey (D) | 158,665 | *46.7* |

| | Candidates | Votes | % |
|---|---|---|---|
| 1982 | **Republican Primary** | | |
| | W. D. Workman (R) | 17,128 | *81.8* |
| | Roddy T. Martin (R) | 3,816 | *18.2* |
| | **Democratic Primary** | | |
| | Richard Riley (D) | | *100.0* |
| 1986 | **Republican Primary** | | |
| | Carroll Campbell (R) | | *100.0* |
| | **Democratic Primary** [3] | | |
| | Mike Daniel (D) | 156,077 | *47.4* |
| | Phil Lader (D) | 86,136 | *26.1* |
| | Frank Eppes (D) | 59,125 | *17.9* |
| | Hugh Leatherman (D) | 28,158 | *8.5* |
| 1990 | **Republican Primary** | | |
| | Carroll Campbell (R) | | *100.0* |
| | **Democratic Primary** | | |
| | Theo Mitchell (D) | 116,471 | *60.1* |
| | Ernie Passailaigue (D) | 77,429 | *39.9* |

**South Carolina**

1. The New York Times *of Aug. 28, 1924, provided the returns given for McLeod and Duncan. Gov. McLeod was renominated and subsequently reelected to a second term.*

2. *Charles D. Ravenel was ruled ineligible by the state Supreme Court because he did not meet the state's residency requirement for gubernatorial candidates. At a special state party convention, Dorn was designated to replace Ravenel as the Democratic candidate.*

3. *Neither Lader nor the other two candidates requested a runoff primary, and Daniel was declared the nominee.*

# SOUTH DAKOTA

| | Candidates | Votes | % |
|---|---|---|---|
| 1956 | **Republican Primary** | | |
| | Joe J. Foss (R) | | *100.0* |
| | **Democratic Primary** | | |
| | Ralph Herseth (D) | | *100.0* |
| 1958 | **Republican Primary** | | |
| | Phil Saunders (R) | 49,746 | *61.6* |
| | L. R. Houck (R) | 21,621 | *26.8* |
| | Charles Lacey (R) | 9,384 | *11.6* |
| | **Democratic Primary** | | |
| | Ralph Herseth (D) | | *100.0* |
| 1960 | **Republican Primary** | | |
| | Archie M. Gubbrud (R) | | *100.0* |
| | **Democratic Primary** | | |
| | Ralph Herseth (D) | | *100.0* |

| | Candidates | Votes | % |
|---|---|---|---|
| 1962 | **Republican Primary** | | |
| | Archie M. Gubbrud (R) | | *100.0* |
| | **Democratic Primary** | | |
| | Ralph Herseth (D) | | *100.0* |
| 1964 | **Republican Primary** | | |
| | Nils A. Boe (R) | 50,335 | *53.5* |
| | Sigurd Anderson (R) | 43,809 | *46.5* |
| | **Democratic Primary** | | |
| | John F. Lindley (D) | 27,071 | *65.8* |
| | Merton B. Tice (D) | 14,051 | *34.2* |
| 1966 | **Republican Primary** | | |
| | Nils A. Boe (R) | | *100.0* |
| | **Democratic Primary** | | |
| | Robert Chamberlin (D) | | *100.0* |
| 1968 | **Republican Primary** | | |
| | Frank Farrar (R) | | *100.0* |
| | **Democratic Primary** | | |
| | Robert Chamberlin (D) | | *100.0* |
| 1970 | **Republican Primary** | | |
| | Frank Farrar (R) | 48,520 | *58.2* |
| | Frank E. Henderson (R) | 34,893 | *41.8* |
| | **Democratic Primary** | | |
| | Richard F. Kneip (D) | | *100.0* |
| 1972 | **Republican Primary** | | |
| | Carveth Thompson (R) | 65,538 | *72.4* |
| | Simon W. Chance (R) | 24,975 | *27.6* |
| | **Democratic Primary** | | |
| | Richard K. Kneip (D) | | *100.0* |
| 1974 | **Republican Primary** | | |
| | John E. Olson (R) | 49,973 | *55.6* |
| | Ronald F. Williamson (R) | 25,509 | *28.4* |
| | Oscar W. Hagen (R) | 14,444 | *16.1* |
| | **Democratic Primary** | | |
| | Richard F. Kneip (D) | 45,932 | *66.2* |
| | Bill Dougherty (D) | 23,467 | *33.8* |
| 1978 | **Republican Primary** | | |
| | William J. Janklow (R) | 46,423 | *50.9* |
| | LeRoy G. Hoffman (R) | 30,026 | *32.9* |
| | Clint Roberts (R) | 14,774 | *16.2* |

| Candidates Democratic Primary | Votes | % |
|---|---|---|
| Roger McKellips (D) | 34,160 | *49.1* |
| Harvey Wollman (D) | 32,690 | *47.0* |

**1982** Republican Primary

| | | |
|---|---|---|
| William J. Janklow (R) | | *100.0* |

**Democratic Primary**

| | | |
|---|---|---|
| Michael J. O'Connor (D) | 24,101 | *58.8* |
| Elvern R. Varilek (D) | 16,916 | *41.2* |

**1986** Republican Primary

| | | |
|---|---|---|
| George S. Mickelson (R) | 40,979 | *35.3* |
| Clint Roberts (R) | 37,250 | *32.1* |
| Lowell Hansen (R) | 21,884 | *18.8* |
| Alice Kundert (R) | 15,985 | *13.8* |

**Democratic Primary**

| | | |
|---|---|---|
| R. Lars Herseth (D) | 30,801 | *42.8* |
| Richard F. Kneip (D) | 27,811 | *38.7* |
| Kenneth D. Stofferahn (D) | 13,332 | *18.5* |

**1990** Republican Primary

| | | |
|---|---|---|
| George S. Mickelson (R) | | *100.0* |

**Democratic Primary**

| | | |
|---|---|---|
| Bob L. Samuelson (D) | | *100.0* |

# TENNESSEE

| Candidates | Votes | % |
|---|---|---|
| **1920** Democratic Primary | | |
| Albert H. Roberts (D) | 67,886 | *59.6* |
| W. R. Crabtree (D) | 44,853 | *39.4* |
| **1922** Democratic Primary | | |
| Austin Peay (D) | 63,940 | *39.2* |
| Benton McMillin (D) | 59,922 | *36.8* |
| Harvey Hannah (D) | 24,062 | *14.8* |
| L. E. Gwinn (D) | 15,137 | *9.3* |
| **1924** Democratic Primary | | |
| Austin Peay (D) | 125,031 | *79.0* |
| John R. Neal (D) | 33,199 | *21.0* |
| **1926** Democratic Primary | | |
| Austin Peay (D) | 96,545 | *51.6* |
| Hill McAlister (D) | 88,488 | *47.3* |
| **1928** Democratic Primary | | |
| Henry H. Horton (D) | 97,333 | *44.7* |
| Hill McAlister (D) | 92,017 | *42.3* |
| Lewis S. Pope (D) | 27,779 | *12.8* |

| | Candidates Democratic Primary | Votes | % |
|---|---|---|---|
| **1930** | Henry H. Horton (D) | 144,990 | *58.9* |
| | L. E. Gwinn (D) | 101,285 | *41.1* |
| **1932** | **Democratic Primary** | | |
| | Hill McAlister (D) | 116,020 | *40.9* |
| | Lewis S. Pope (D) | 106,450 | *37.5* |
| | M. R. Patterson (D) | 58,915 | *20.8* |
| **1934** | **Democratic Primary** | | |
| | Hill McAlister (D) | 191,460 | *58.3* |
| | Lewis S. Pope (D) | 137,253 | *41.8* |
| **1936** | **Democratic Primary** | | |
| | Gordon Browning (D) | 243,463 | *68.0* |
| | Burgin E. Dossett (D) | 109,170 | *30.5* |
| **1938** | **Democratic Primary** | | |
| | Prentice Cooper (D) | 237,853 | *59.5* |
| | Gordon Browning (D) | 158,854 | *39.7* |
| **1940** | **Democratic Primary** | | |
| | Prentice Cooper (D) | 240,427 | *83.6* |
| | Dempster (D) | 44,122 | *15.3* |
| **1942** | **Democratic Primary** | | |
| | Prentice Cooper (D) | 171,259 | *57.6* |
| | J. Ridley Mitchell (D) | 124,037 | *41.7* |
| **1944** | **Republican Primary** | | |
| | John W. Kilgo (R) | 33,979 | *63.9* |
| | W. O. Lowe (R) | 13,425 | *25.2* |
| | H. C. Lowery (R) | 3,681 | *6.9* |
| | **Democratic Primary** | | |
| | James N. McCord (D) | 132,466 | *87.4* |
| | John R. Neal (D) | 11,659 | *7.7* |
| **1946** | **Republican Primary** | | |
| | W. O. Lowe (R) | 33,269 | *100.0* |
| | **Democratic Primary** | | |
| | James N. McCord (D) | 187,119 | *59.8* |
| | Gordon Browning (D) | 120,535 | *38.5* |
| **1948** | **Republican Primary** | | |
| | Roy Acuff (R) | 90,140 | *80.6* |
| | Robert M. McMurry (R) | 21,765 | *19.5* |
| | **Democratic Primary** | | |
| | Gordon Browning (D) | 240,676 | *55.8* |
| | James N. McCord (D) | 183,948 | *42.6* |
| **1950** | **Democratic Primary** | | |
| | Gordon Browning (D) | 267,855 | *55.7* |
| | Clifford R. Allen (D) | 208,634 | *43.4* |

| | Candidates | Votes | % |
|---|---|---|---|
| 1952 | **Democratic Primary** | | |
| | Frank G. Clement (D) | 302,491 | *46.7* |
| | Gordon Browning (D) | 245,166 | *37.9* |
| | Clifford R. Allen (D) | 75,269 | *11.6* |
| 1954 | **Democratic Primary** | | |
| | Frank G. Clement (D) | 481,808 | *68.2* |
| | Gordon Browning (D) | 195,156 | *27.6* |
| 1958 | **Republican Primary** | | |
| | Robert L. Peters (R) | 18,323 | *59.3* |
| | Hansell Proffitt (R) | 12,565 | *40.7* |
| | **Democratic Primary** | | |
| | Buford Ellington (D) | 213,415 | *31.1* |
| | Andrew T. Taylor (D) | 204,629 | *29.9* |
| | Edmund Orgill (D) | 204,382 | *29.8* |
| | Clifford R. Allen (D) | 56,854 | *8.3* |
| 1962 | **Republican Primary** | | |
| | Hubert D. Patty | | *100.0* |
| | **Democratic Primary** | | |
| | Frank G. Clement (D) | 309,333 | *42.5* |
| | P. R. Olgiati (D) | 211,812 | *29.1* |
| | William W. Farris (D) | 202,813 | *27.9* |
| 1966 | **Democratic Primary** | | |
| | Buford Ellington (D) | 413,950 | *53.5* |
| | John J. Hooker (D) | 360,105 | *46.5* |
| 1970 | **Republican Primary** | | |
| | Winfield Dunn (R) | 81,475 | *33.2* |
| | Maxey Jarman (R) | 70,420 | *28.7* |
| | William Jenkins (R) | 50,910 | *20.8* |
| | Claude Robertson (R) | 40,547 | *16.5* |
| | **Democratic Primary** | | |
| | John J. Hooker (D) | 261,580 | *44.3* |
| | Stanley Snodgrass (D) | 193,199 | *32.7* |
| | Robert L. Taylor (D) | 90,009 | *15.3* |
| 1974 | **Republican Primary** | | |
| | Lamar Alexander (R) | 120,773 | *48.5* |
| | Nat Winston (R) | 90,980 | *36.5* |
| | Dortch Oldham (R) | 35,683 | *14.3* |
| | **Democratic Primary** | | |
| | Ray Blanton (D) | 148,062 | *22.7* |
| | Jake Butcher (D) | 131,412 | *20.2* |
| | Tom Wiseman (D) | 89,061 | *13.7* |
| | Hudley Crockett (D) | 86,852 | *13.2* |
| | Franklin Haney (D) | 84,155 | *12.9* |
| | Stanley Snodgrass (D) | 40,211 | *6.2* |
| 1978 | **Republican Primary** | | |
| | Lamar Alexander (R) | 230,922 | *86.0* |
| | Harold Sterling (R) | 34,037 | *12.7* |

| | Candidates | Votes | % |
|---|---|---|---|
| | **Democratic Primary** | | |
| | Jake Butcher (D) | 320,329 | *40.9* |
| | Bob Clement (D) | 288,577 | *36.9* |
| | Richard Fulton (D) | 122,101 | *15.6* |
| | Roger Murray (D) | 40,871 | *5.2* |
| 1982 | **Republican Primary** | | |
| | Lamar Alexander (R) | | *100.0* |
| | **Democratic Primary** | | |
| | Randy Tyree (D) | 318,205 | *50.0* |
| | Anna Belle Clement O'Brien (D) | 254,500 | *40.0* |
| 1986 | **Republican Primary** | | |
| | Winfield Dunn (R) | 222,458 | *94.2* |
| | **Democratic Primary** | | |
| | Ned McWherter (D) | 314,449 | *42.5* |
| | Jane Eskind (D) | 225,551 | *30.5* |
| | Richard Fulton (D) | 190,016 | *25.7* |
| 1990 | **Republican Primary** | | |
| | Dwight Henry (R) | 92,100 | *53.5* |
| | Charles R. Moffett (R) | 26,363 | *15.3* |
| | Terry A. Williams (R) | 18,153 | *10.6* |
| | Carroll Turner (R) | 16,293 | *9.5* |
| | Hubert D. Patty (R) | 10,097 | *5.9* |
| | Robert O. Watson (R) | 8,893 | *5.2* |
| | **Democratic Primary** | | |
| | Ned McWherter (D) | | *100.0* |

# TEXAS

| | Candidates | Votes | % |
|---|---|---|---|
| 1920 | **Democratic Primary** | | |
| | Joseph W. Bailey (D) | 152,340 | *33.9* |
| | Pat M. Neff (D) | 149,818 | *33.3* |
| | Robert E. Thomason (D) | 99,002 | *22.0* |
| | Ben F. Looney (D) | 48,640 | *10.8* |
| | **Democratic Runoff** | | |
| | Pat M. Neff (D) | 264,075 | *58.8* |
| | Joseph W. Bailey (D) | 184,702 | *41.2* |
| 1922 | **Democratic Primary** | | |
| | Pat M. Neff (D) | 318,000 | *53.9* |
| | Fred S. Rogers (D) | 195,941 | *33.2* |
| | Harry T. Warner (D) | 57,617 | *9.8* |
| 1924 | **Democratic Primary** | | |
| | F. D. Robertson (D) | 193,508 | *27.5* |
| | Miriam A. Ferguson (D) | 146,424 | *20.8* |
| | Lynch Davidson (D) | 141,208 | *20.1* |
| | T. W. Davidson (D) | 125,011 | *17.8* |

| Candidates | Votes | % |
|---|---|---|
| **Democratic Runoff** | | |
| Miriam A. Ferguson (D) | 413,751 | *56.7* |
| F. D. Robertson (D) | 316,019 | *43.3* |

**1926   Republican Primary**

| | | |
|---|---|---|
| H. H. Haines (R) | 11,215 | *73.4* |
| E. P. Scott (R) | 4,074 | *26.7* |

**Democratic Primary**

| | | |
|---|---|---|
| Dan Moody (D) | 400,732 | *49.9* |
| Miram A. Ferguson (D) | 283,482 | *34.5* |
| Lynch Davidson (D) | 122,449 | *14.9* |

**Democratic Runoff**

| | | |
|---|---|---|
| Dan Moody (D) | 495,723 | *64.7* |
| Miriam A. Ferguson (D) | 270,595 | *35.3* |

**1928   Democratic Primary**

| | | |
|---|---|---|
| Dan Moody (D) | 442,080 | *59.9* |
| Louis J. Wardlaw (D) | 245,508 | *33.3* |

**1930   Republican Primary**

| | | |
|---|---|---|
| George C. Butte (R) | 5,001 | *51.2* |
| H. E. Exum (R) | 2,773 | *28.4* |
| John F. Grant (R) | 1,800 | *18.4* |

**Democratic Primary**

| | | |
|---|---|---|
| Miriam A. Ferguson (D) | 242,959 | *29.2* |
| Ross S. Sterling (D) | 170,754 | *20.5* |
| Clint C. Small (D) | 138,934 | *16.7* |
| T. B. Love (D) | 87,068 | *10.5* |
| James Young (D) | 73,385 | *8.8* |
| Barry Miller (D) | 54,652 | *6.6* |
| E. B. Mayfield (D) | 54,459 | *6.5* |

**Democratic Runoff**

| | | |
|---|---|---|
| Ross S. Sterling (D) | 473,371 | *55.2* |
| Miriam A. Ferguson (D) | 384,402 | *44.8* |

**1932   Democratic Primary**

| | | |
|---|---|---|
| Miriam A. Ferguson (D) | 402,238 | *41.8* |
| Ross S. Sterling (D) | 296,383 | *30.8* |
| Tom F. Hunter (D) | 220,391 | *22.9* |

**Democratic Runoff**

| | | |
|---|---|---|
| Miriam A. Ferguson (D) | 477,644 | *50.2* |
| Ross S. Sterling (D) | 473,846 | *49.8* |

**1934   Republican Primary**

| | | |
|---|---|---|
| D. E. Waggoner (R) | 13,043 | *100.0* |

**Democratic Primary**

| | | |
|---|---|---|
| James V. Allred (D) | 298,903 | *29.9* |
| Tom F. Hunter (D) | 243,254 | *24.3* |
| C. C. McDonald (D) | 207,200 | *20.7* |
| Clint C. Small (D) | 125,324 | *12.5* |
| Edgar E. Witt (D) | 62,476 | *6.2* |
| Maury Hughes (D) | 58,815 | *5.9* |

| Candidates | Votes | % |
|---|---|---|
| **Democratic Runoff** | | |
| James V. Allred (D) | 499,343 | *52.1* |
| Tom F. Hunter (D) | 459,106 | *47.9* |

**1936   Democratic Primary**

| | | |
|---|---|---|
| James V. Allred (D) | 553,219 | *52.5* |
| Tom F. Hunter (D) | 239,460 | *22.7* |
| F. W. Fischer (D) | 145,877 | *13.9* |
| Roy Sanderford (D) | 81,170 | *7.7* |

**1938   Democratic Primary**

| | | |
|---|---|---|
| W. Lee O'Daniel (D) | 573,166 | *51.4* |
| Ernest O. Thompson (D) | 231,630 | *20.8* |
| William McCraw (D) | 152,278 | *13.7* |
| Tom F. Hunter (D) | 117,634 | *10.6* |

**1940   Democratic Primary**

| | | |
|---|---|---|
| W. Lee O'Daniel (D) | 645,646 | *54.3* |
| Ernest O. Thompson (D) | 256,923 | *21.6* |
| Harry Hines (D) | 119,121 | *10.0* |
| Miriam A. Ferguson (D) | 100,578 | *8.5* |
| Jerry Sadler (D) | 61,396 | *5.2* |

**1942   Democratic Primary**

| | | |
|---|---|---|
| Coke R. Stevenson (D) | 651,218 | *68.5* |
| Hal H. Collins (D) | 272,469 | *28.6* |

**1944   Democratic Primary**

| | | |
|---|---|---|
| Coke R. Stevenson (D) | 696,586 | *84.6* |
| Minnie F. Cunningham (D) | 48,039 | *5.8* |

**1946   Democratic Primary**

| | | |
|---|---|---|
| Beauford H. Jester (D) | 443,804 | *38.2* |
| Homer P. Rainey (D) | 291,282 | *25.0* |
| Grover Sellers (D) | 162,431 | *14.0* |
| Jerry Sadler (D) | 103,120 | *8.9* |
| John Lee Smith (D) | 102,941 | *8.9* |

**Democratic Runoff**

| | | |
|---|---|---|
| Beauford H. Jester (D) | 701,018 | *66.3* |
| Homer P. Rainey (D) | 355,654 | *33.7* |

**1948   Democratic Primary**

| | | |
|---|---|---|
| Beauford H. Jester (D) | 642,025 | *53.1* |
| Roger Q. Evans (D) | 279,602 | *23.1* |
| Caso March (D) | 187,658 | *15.5* |

**1950   Democratic Primary**

| | | |
|---|---|---|
| Allan Shivers (D) | 829,730 | *76.4* |
| Caso March (D) | 195,997 | *18.0* |

**1952   Democratic Primary**

| | | |
|---|---|---|
| Allan Shivers (D) | 833,861 | *61.5* |
| Ralph Yarborough (D) | 488,345 | *36.0* |

**1954   Democratic Primary**

| | | |
|---|---|---|
| Allan Shivers (D) | 668,913 | *49.5* |
| Ralph Yarborough (D) | 645,994 | *47.8* |

| Candidates | Votes | % |
|---|---|---|
| **Democratic Runoff** | | |
| Allan Shivers (D) | 775,088 | *53.2* |
| Ralph Yarborough (D) | 683,132 | *46.9* |

**1956** **Democratic Primary**

| Candidates | Votes | % |
|---|---|---|
| Price Daniel (D) | 628,914 | *39.9* |
| Ralph Yarborough (D) | 463,416 | *29.4* |
| W. Lee O'Daniel (D) | 347,757 | *22.1* |
| J. Evetts Haley (D) | 88,772 | *5.6* |

**Democratic Runoff**

| Candidates | Votes | % |
|---|---|---|
| Price Daniel (D) | 698,001 | *50.1* |
| Ralph Yarborough (D) | 694,830 | *49.9* |

**1958** **Republican Primary**

| Candidates | Votes | % |
|---|---|---|
| Edwin S. Mayer (R) | | *100.0* |

**Democratic Primary**

| Candidates | Votes | % |
|---|---|---|
| Price Daniel (D) | 799,107 | *60.7* |
| Henry B. Gonzalez (D) | 245,969 | *18.7* |
| W. Lee O'Daniel (D) | 238,767 | *18.1* |

**1960** **Democratic Primary**

| Candidates | Votes | % |
|---|---|---|
| Price Daniel (D) | 908,992 | *59.5* |
| Jack Cox (D) | 619,834 | *40.5* |

**1962** **Republican Primary**

| Candidates | Votes | % |
|---|---|---|
| Jack Cox (R) | 99,138 | *86.0* |
| Roy Whittenbury (R) | 16,112 | *14.0* |

**Democratic Primary**

| Candidates | Votes | % |
|---|---|---|
| John B. Connally (D) | 431,498 | *29.8* |
| Don Yarborough (D) | 317,986 | *22.0* |
| Price Daniel (D) | 248,524 | *17.2* |
| Will Wilson (D) | 171,617 | *11.9* |
| Marshall Formby (D) | 139,094 | *9.6* |
| Edwin A. Walker (D) | 138,387 | *9.6* |

**Democratic Runoff**

| Candidates | Votes | % |
|---|---|---|
| John B. Connally (D) | 565,174 | *51.2* |
| Don Yarborough (D) | 538,924 | *48.8* |

**1964** **Republican Primary**

| Candidates | Votes | % |
|---|---|---|
| Jack Crichton (R) | | *100.0* |

**Democratic Primary**

| Candidates | Votes | % |
|---|---|---|
| John B. Connally (D) | 1,125,884 | *69.1* |
| Don Yarborough (D) | 471,411 | *28.9* |

**1966** **Republican Primary**

| Candidates | Votes | % |
|---|---|---|
| T. E. Kennerly (R) | | *100.0* |

**Democratic Primary**

| Candidates | Votes | % |
|---|---|---|
| John B. Connally (D) | 932,641 | *74.3* |
| Stanley C. Woods (D) | 291,651 | *23.2* |

**1968** 

| Candidates | Votes | % |
|---|---|---|
| **Republican Primary** | | |
| Paul W. Eggers (R) | 65,501 | *62.5* |
| John R. Trice (R) | 28,849 | *27.5* |
| Wallace Sisk (R) | 10,415 | *10.0* |

**Democratic Primary**

| Candidates | Votes | % |
|---|---|---|
| Don Yarborough (D) | 419,003 | *23.9* |
| Preston Smith (D) | 389,564 | *22.3* |
| Waggoner Carr (D) | 257,535 | *14.7* |
| Dolph Briscoe (D) | 225,686 | *12.9* |
| Eugene Locke (D) | 218,118 | *12.5* |
| John Hill (D) | 154,908 | *8.9* |

**Democratic Runoff**

| Candidates | Votes | % |
|---|---|---|
| Preston Smith (D) | 767,490 | *55.3* |
| Don Yarborough (D) | 621,226 | *44.7* |

**1970** **Republican Primary**

| Candidates | Votes | % |
|---|---|---|
| Paul W. Eggers (R) | 101,875 | *93.4* |
| Roger Martin (R) | 7,146 | *6.6* |

**Democratic Primary**

| Candidates | Votes | % |
|---|---|---|
| Preston Smith (D) | | *100.0* |

**1972** **Republican Primary**

| Candidates | Votes | % |
|---|---|---|
| Henry C. Grover (R) | 37,118 | *32.6* |
| Albert B. Fay (R) | 24,329 | *21.3* |
| David Reagan (R) | 20,119 | *17.6* |
| Tom McElroy (R) | 19,559 | *17.2* |
| John Hall (R) | 4,864 | *7.0* |

**Republican Runoff**

| Candidates | Votes | % |
|---|---|---|
| Henry C. Grover (R) | 37,842 | *66.4* |
| Albert B. Fay (R) | 19,166 | *33.6* |

**Democratic Primary**

| Candidates | Votes | % |
|---|---|---|
| Dolph Briscoe (D) | 963,397 | *43.9* |
| Frances Farenthold (D) | 612,051 | *27.9* |
| Ben Barnes (D) | 392,356 | *17.9* |
| Preston Smith (D) | 190,709 | *8.7* |

**Democratic Runoff**

| Candidates | Votes | % |
|---|---|---|
| Dolph Briscoe (D) | 1,100,601 | *55.3* |
| Frances Farenthold (D) | 889,544 | *44.7* |

**1974** **Republican Primary**

| Candidates | Votes | % |
|---|---|---|
| Jim Granberry (R) | 53,617 | *77.6* |
| Odell McBrayer (R) | 15,484 | *22.4* |

**Democratic Primary**

| Candidates | Votes | % |
|---|---|---|
| Dolph Briscoe (D) | 1,025,632 | *67.4* |
| Frances Farenthold (D) | 437,287 | *28.7* |

**1978** **Republican Primary**

| Candidates | Votes | % |
|---|---|---|
| William P. Clements (R) | 115,345 | *72.8* |
| Ray Hutchison (R) | 38,268 | *24.2* |

| Candidates | Votes | % |
|---|---|---|
| **Democratic Primary** | | |
| John Hill (D) | 932,338 | 51.4 |
| Dolph Briscoe (D) | 753,305 | 41.6 |
| Preston Smith (D) | 92,088 | 5.1 |

**1982**    **Republican Primary**

| Candidates | Votes | % |
|---|---|---|
| William P. Clements (R) | 246,120 | 92.6 |
| Lowell D. Embs (R) | 19,731 | 7.4 |
| **Democratic Primary** | | |
| Mark White (D) | 592,210 | 44.9 |
| Buddy Temple [1] (D) | 402,567 | 30.5 |
| Bob Armstrong (D) | 261,940 | 19.9 |

**1986**    **Republican Primary**

| Candidates | Votes | % |
|---|---|---|
| William P. Clements (R) | 318,808 | 58.5 |
| Tom Loeffler (R) | 117,673 | 21.6 |
| Kent Hance (R) | 108,238 | 19.8 |
| **Democratic Primary** | | |
| Mark White (D) | 589,536 | 53.8 |
| Andrew C. Briscoe (D) | 248,850 | 22.7 |
| A. Don Crowder (D) | 120,999 | 11.0 |
| Bobby Locke (D) | 58,936 | 5.4 |

**1990**    **Republican Primary**

| Candidates | Votes | % |
|---|---|---|
| Clayton Williams (R) | 520,014 | 60.8 |
| Kent Hance (R) | 132,142 | 15.5 |
| Tom Luce (R) | 115,835 | 13.5 |
| Jack Rains (R) | 82,461 | 9.6 |
| **Democratic Primary** | | |
| Ann Richards (D) | 580,191 | 39.0 |
| Jim Mattox (D) | 546,103 | 36.7 |
| Mark White (D) | 286,161 | 19.2 |
| **Democratic Runoff** | | |
| Ann Richards (D) | 640,995 | 57.1 |
| Jim Mattox (D) | 481,739 | 42.9 |

**Texas**
1. Temple withdrew and no runoff was held.

# UTAH

| Candidates | Votes | % |
|---|---|---|
| **1956**   **Republican Primary** | | |
| George D. Clyde (R) | 62,811 | 53.5 |
| J. Bracken Lee (R) | 54,544 | 46.5 |
| **Democratic Primary** | | |
| L. C. Romney (D) | 40,908 | 52.0 |
| John S. Boyden (D) | 37,798 | 48.0 |
| **1960**   **Republican Primary** | | |
| George D. Clyde (R) | 50,592 | 57.8 |
| Lamont B. Gundersen (R) | 37,002 | 42.2 |

| Candidates | Votes | % |
|---|---|---|
| **Democratic Primary** | | |
| W. A. Barlocker (D) | 74,424 | 70.6 |
| Ira A. Huggins (D) | 31,045 | 29.4 |

**1964**    **Republican Primary**

| Candidates | Votes | % |
|---|---|---|
| Mitchell Melich (R) | 63,108 | 53.0 |
| D. James Cannon (R) | 55,938 | 47.0 |
| **Democratic Primary** | | |
| Calvin L. Rampton (D) | 57,848 | 62.7 |
| Ernest Howard Dean (D) | 34,470 | 37.3 |

**1968**    **Republican Primary**

| Candidates | Votes | % |
|---|---|---|
| Carl W. Buehner (R) | 93,635 | 70.1 |
| Lamar A. Rawlings (R) | 39,907 | 29.9 |
| **Democratic Primary** | | |
| Calvin L. Rampton (D) | | 100.0 |

**1972**    **Republican Primary**

| Candidates | Votes | % |
|---|---|---|
| Nicholas L. Strike (R) | | 100.0 |
| **Democratic Primary** | | |
| Calvin L. Rampton (D) | | 100.0 |

**1976**    **Republican Primary**

| Candidates | Votes | % |
|---|---|---|
| Vernon B. Romney (R) | 87,251 | 53.4 |
| Dixie L. Leavitt (R) | 76,139 | 46.6 |
| **Democratic Primary** | | |
| Scott M. Matheson (D) | 50,505 | 59.0 |
| John P. Creer (D) | 35,154 | 41.0 |

**1984**    **Republican Primary**

| Candidates | Votes | % |
|---|---|---|
| Norman H. Bangerter (R) | 94,347 | 56.4 |
| Dan Marriott (R) | 72,940 | 43.6 |
| **Democratic Primary** | | |
| Wayne Owens (D) | 51,302 | 62.0 |
| Kem C. Gardner (D) | 31,421 | 38.0 |

**1992**    **Republican Primary**

| Candidates | Votes | % |
|---|---|---|
| Mike Leavitt (R) | 143,514 | 56.0 |
| Richard M. Eyre (R) | 112,881 | 44.0 |
| **Democratic Primary** | | |
| Stewart Hanson (D) | 64,084 | 56.8 |
| Patrick Shea (D) | 48,758 | 43.2 |

# VERMONT

| Candidates | Votes | % |
|---|---|---|
| **1956**   **Republican Primary** | | |
| Joseph B. Johnson (R) | | 100.0 |

| | Candidates | Votes | % |
|---|---|---|---|
| | **Democratic Primary** | | |
| | E. Frank Branon (D) | | *100.0* |
| **1958** | **Republican Primary** | | |
| | Robert T. Stafford (R) | | *100.0* |
| | **Democratic Primary** | | |
| | Bernard J. Leddy (D) | | *100.0* |
| **1960** | **Republican Primary** | | |
| | F. Ray Keyser (R) | 17,491 | *29.6* |
| | Robert S. Babcock (R) | 16,762 | *28.4* |
| | A. Luke Crispe (R) | 14,874 | *25.2* |
| | W. A. Simpson (R) | 9,916 | *16.8* |
| | **Democratic Primary** | | |
| | Russell F. Niquette (D) | | *100.0* |
| **1962** | **Republican Primary** | | |
| | F. Ray Keyser (R) | | *100.0* |
| | **Democratic Primary** | | |
| | Philip H. Hoff (D) | | *100.0* |
| **1964** | **Republican Primary** | | |
| | Ralph A. Foote (R) | 19,121 | *42.8* |
| | Robert S. Babcock (R) | 16,225 | *36.3* |
| | Roger MacBride (R) | 9,265 | *20.7* |
| | **Democratic Primary** | | |
| | Philip H. Hoff (D) | | *100.0* |
| **1966** | **Republican Primary** | | |
| | Richard A. Snelling (R) | 22,069 | *59.0* |
| | Thomas L. Hayes (R) | 15,286 | *40.9* |
| | **Democratic Primary** | | |
| | Philip H. Hoff (D) | | *100.0* |
| **1968** | **Republican Primary** | | |
| | Deane C. Davis (R) | 36,719 | *62.7* |
| | James L. Oakes (R) | 21,791 | *37.2* |
| | **Democratic Primary** | | |
| | John J. Daley (D) | | *100.0* |
| **1970** | **Republican Primary** | | |
| | Deane C. Davis (R) | 31,549 | *79.3* |
| | Thomas L. Hayes (R) | 8,048 | *20.2* |
| | **Democratic Primary** | | |
| | Leo O'Brien (D) | 18,058 | *54.7* |
| | John J. Daley (D) | 14,795 | *44.8* |

| | Candidates | Votes | % |
|---|---|---|---|
| **1972** | **Republican Primary** | | |
| | Luther F. Hackett (R) | 33,323 | *54.4* |
| | James M. Jeffords (R) | 27,902 | *45.5* |
| | **Democratic Primary** | | |
| | Thomas P. Salmon (D) | | *100.0* |
| **1974** | **Republican Primary** | | |
| | Walter L. Kennedy (R) | 23,738 | *55.5* |
| | Harry R. Montague (R) | 13,901 | *32.5* |
| | T. James Lannon (R) | 4,667 | *10.9* |
| | **Democratic Primary** | | |
| | Thomas P. Salmon (D) | 18,498 | *83.6* |
| | John F. Reilly (D) | 3,537 | *16.0* |
| **1976** | **Republican Primary** | | |
| | Richard Snelling (R) | 24,279 | *70.8* |
| | William G. Craig (R) | 9,429 | *27.5* |
| | **Democratic Primary** | | |
| | Stella B. Hackel (D) | 18,522 | *44.0* |
| | Brian D. Burns (D) | 14,725 | *34.9* |
| | Robert O'Brien (D) | 8,809 | *20.9* |
| | **Liberty Union Primary** | | |
| | Bernard Sanders (LU) | | *100.0* |
| **1978** | **Republican Primary** | | |
| | Richard A. Snelling (R) | | *100.0* |
| | **Democratic Primary** | | |
| | Edwin C. Granai (D) | 8,572 | *64.6* |
| | Bernard G. O'Shea (D) | 4,570 | *34.4* |
| | **Liberty Union Primary** | | |
| | Earl S. Gardner (LU) | | *100.0* |
| **1980** | **Republican Primary** | | |
| | Richard A. Snelling (R) | 38,228 | *85.0* |
| | Clifford Thompson (R) | 3,432 | *7.6* |
| | Kirk E. Faryniasz (R) | 2,273 | *5.0* |
| | **Democratic Primary** | | |
| | M. Jerome Diamond (D) | 15,738 | *50.3* |
| | Timothy J. O'Connor (D) | 14,857 | *47.5* |
| **1982** | **Republican Primary** | | |
| | Richard A. Snelling (R) | | *100.0* |
| | **Democratic Primary** | | |
| | Madeleine M. Kunin (D) | 16,002 | *90.7* |
| | Clifford Thompson (D) | 1,433 | *8.1* |

| Candidates | Votes | % |
|---|---|---|
| **Liberty Union Primary** | | |
| Richard F. Gottlieb (LU) | | 100.0 |

**1984**

| | Votes | % |
|---|---|---|
| **Republican Primary** | | |
| John J. Easton (R) | 30,436 | 61.3 |
| Hilton Wick (R) | 19,170 | 38.2 |
| **Democratic Primary** | | |
| Madeleine M. Kunin (D) | 17,138 | 100.0 |
| **Liberty Union Primary** | | |
| Richard F. Gottlieb (LU) | | 100.0 |

**1986**

| | Votes | % |
|---|---|---|
| **Republican Primary** | | |
| Peter Smith (R) | | 100.0 |
| **Democratic Primary** | | |
| Madeleine M. Kunin (D) | | 100.0 |
| **Liberty Union Primary** | | |
| Richard F. Gottlieb (LU) | | 100.0 |

**1988**

| | Votes | % |
|---|---|---|
| **Republican Primary** | | |
| Michael Bernhardt (R) | | 100.0 |
| **Democratic Primary** | | |
| Madeleine M. Kunin (D) | | 100.0 |
| **Liberty Union Primary** | | |
| Richard F. Gottlieb (LU) | | 100.0 |

**1990**

| | Votes | % |
|---|---|---|
| **Republican Primary** | | |
| Richard A. Snelling (R) | 38,881 | 86.7 |
| Richard F. Gottlieb (R) | 5,503 | 12.3 |
| **Democratic Primary** | | |
| Peter Welch (D) | 14,656 | 86.6 |
| William Gwin (D) | 1,719 | 10.2 |
| **Libertarian Primary** | | |
| David Atkinson (LIBERT) | | 100.0 |

**1992**

| | Votes | % |
|---|---|---|
| **Republican Primary** | | |
| John McClaughry (R) | 28,026 | 92.5 |
| **Democratic Primary** | | |
| Howard B. Dean (D) | 25,504 | 98.5 |
| **Liberty Union Primary** | | |
| Richard F. Gottlieb (LU) | | 100.0 |

# VIRGINIA [1]

| Candidates | Votes | % |
|---|---|---|
| **1921 Democratic Primary** | | |
| Elbert Lee Trinkle (D) | 86,812 | 57.5 |
| Henry St. George Tucker (D) | 64,286 | 42.6 |
| **1925 Democratic Primary** | | |
| Harry F. Byrd (D) | 107,317 | 61.4 |
| G. Walter Mapp (D) | 67,579 | 38.6 |
| **1929 Democratic Primary** | | |
| John Garland Pollard (D) | 104,310 | 75.5 |
| G. Walter Mapp (D) | 29,386 | 21.3 |
| **1933 Democratic Primary** | | |
| George C. Peery (D) | 116,837 | 61.6 |
| J. T. Deal (D) | 40,268 | 21.2 |
| W. Worth Smith (D) | 32,518 | 17.2 |
| **1937 Democratic Primary** | | |
| James H. Price (D) | 166,319 | 86.1 |
| Vivian L. Page (D) | 26,955 | 14.0 |
| **1941 Democratic Primary** | | |
| Colgate W. Darden Jr. (D) | 105,655 | 76.6 |
| Vivian L. Page (D) | 19,526 | 14.2 |
| Hudson Cary (D) | 12,793 | 9.3 |
| **1945 Democratic Primary** | | |
| William M. Tuck (D) | 97,304 | 70.1 |
| Moss A. Plunkett (D) | 41,484 | 29.9 |
| **1949 Democratic Primary** | | |
| John S. Battle (D) | 135,426 | 42.8 |
| Francis P. Miller (D) | 111,697 | 35.3 |
| Horace H. Edwards (D) | 47,435 | 15.0 |
| Remmie L. Arnold (D) | 22,054 | 7.0 |
| **1953 Democratic Primary** | | |
| Thomas B. Stanley (D) | 150,499 | 65.9 |
| Charles R. Fenwick (D) | 77,715 | 34.1 |
| **1957 Democratic Primary** | | |
| J. Lindsay Almond Jr. (D) | 119,307 | 79.5 |
| Howard H. Carwile (D) | 30,794 | 20.5 |
| **1961 Democratic Primary** | | |
| Albertis S. Harrison Jr. (D) | 199,519 | 56.7 |
| A. E. S. Stephens (D) | 152,639 | 43.3 |
| **1965 Democratic Primary** | | |
| Mills E. Godwin Jr. (D) | | 100.0 |
| **1969 Democratic Primary** | | |
| William C. Battle (D) | 158,956 | 38.9 |
| Henry Howell (D) | 154,617 | 37.8 |
| Fred G. Pollard (D) | 95,057 | 23.3 |

| | Candidates<br>Democratic Runoff | Votes | % |
|---|---|---|---|
| | William C. Battle (D) | 226,108 | *52.5* |
| | Henry Howell (D) | 207,505 | *47.9* |
| **1977** | **Democratic Primary** | | |
| | Henry Howell (D) | 253,373 | *51.4* |
| | Andrew P. Miller (D) | 239,735 | *48.6* |
| **1989** | **Republican Primary** | | |
| | J. Marshall Coleman (R) | 147,941 | 36.8 |
| | Paul S. Trible (R) | 141,120 | 35.1 |
| | Stanford E. Parris (R) | 112,826 | 28.1 |

**Virginia**

1. After 1977, candidates were chosen by convention rather than through primaries, except for the Republican nomination in 1989.

# WASHINGTON [1]

| | Candidates | Votes | % |
|---|---|---|---|
| **1956** | **Republican Primary** | | |
| | Emmett T. Anderson (R) | 192,500 | *59.6* |
| | Don Eastvold (R) | 99,020 | *30.7* |
| | **Democratic Primary** | | |
| | Albert D. Rosellini (D) | 236,291 | *55.7* |
| | Earl S. Coe (D) | 140,882 | *33.2* |
| | Roderick Lindsay (D) | 39,072 | *9.2* |
| **1960** | **Republican Primary** | | |
| | Lloyd J. Andrews (R) | 263,897 | *64.6* |
| | Newman Clark (R) | 144,440 | *35.4* |
| | **Democratic Primary** | | |
| | Albert D. Rosellini (D) | 244,579 | *82.2* |
| | John Patric (D) | 28,970 | *9.7* |
| | Bruce M. Sigman (D) | 24,031 | *8.1* |
| **1964** | **Republican Primary** | | |
| | Daniel J. Evans (R) | 323,152 | *59.9* |
| | Richard G. Christensen (R) | 213,217 | *39.5* |
| | **Democratic Primary** | | |
| | Albert D. Rosellini (D) | 243,220 | *84.9* |
| | Jessop McDonnell (D) | 17,262 | *6.0* |
| **1968** | **Republican Primary** | | |
| | Daniel J. Evans (R) | 305,897 | *89.4* |
| | **Democratic Primary** | | |
| | John J. O'Connell (D) | 182,969 | *50.5* |
| | Martin J. Durkan (D) | 162,382 | *44.8* |
| **1972** | **Republican Primary** | | |
| | Daniel J. Evans (R) | 224,953 | *67.9* |
| | Perry B. Woodall (R) | 100,372 | *30.3* |

| | Candidates<br>Democratic Primary | Votes | % |
|---|---|---|---|
| | Albert D. Rosellini (D) | 276,121 | *47.5* |
| | Martin J. Durkan (D) | 195,931 | *33.7* |
| | James A. McDermott (D) | 99,155 | *17.1* |
| **1976** | **Republican Primary** | | |
| | John Spellman (R) | 185,439 | *60.5* |
| | Harley Hoppe (R) | 111,957 | *36.5* |
| | **Democratic Primary** | | |
| | Dixy Lee Ray (D) | 205,232 | *37.6* |
| | Wes Uhlman (D) | 198,336 | *36.4* |
| | Marvin Durning (D) | 136,290 | *25.0* |
| **1980** | **Republican Primary** | | |
| | John Spellman (R) | 162,426 | *40.6* |
| | Duane Berentson (R) | 154,724 | *38.7* |
| | Bruce Chapman (R) | 70,875 | *17.7* |
| | **Democratic Primary** | | |
| | James A. McDermott (D) | 321,256 | *56.4* |
| | Dixy Lee Ray (D) | 234,252 | *41.1* |
| **1984** | **Republican Primary** | | |
| | John Spellman (R) | 239,463 | *95.5* |
| | **Democratic Primary** | | |
| | Booth Gardner (D) | 421,087 | *64.4* |
| | Jim McDermott (D) | 209,435 | *32.0* |
| **1988** | **Republican Primary** | | |
| | Bob Williams (R) | 187,797 | *56.4* |
| | Norm Maleng (R) | 139,274 | *41.4* |
| | **Democratic Primary** | | |
| | Booth Gardner (D) | 539,243 | *90.6* |
| | Jeanne Dixon (D) | 31,917 | *5.4* |
| **1992** | **Republican Primary** | | |
| | Ken Eikenberry (R) | 258,553 | *39.1* |
| | Sid Morrison (R) | 250,418 | *37.9* |
| | Dan McDonald (R) | 144,050 | *21.8* |
| | **Democratic Primary** | | |
| | Mike Lowry (D) | 337,783 | *70.1* |
| | Joe King (D) | 96,480 | *20.0* |
| | Sally McQuown (D) | 31,175 | *6.5* |

**Washington**

1. In Washington's so-called "jungle" primaries, all candidates for an office appeared together on the same ballot with their parties designated. Nominations went to the Republican and Democrat receiving the most votes for the office. Independents and minor party candidates gained a place on the general election ballot by obtaining at least 1 percent of the total vote cast in the primary. Percentages were calculated here as if candidates had run in separate party primaries.

# WEST VIRGINIA

| Candidates | Votes | % |
|---|---|---|
| **1956** **Republican Primary** | | |
| Cecil H. Underwood (R) | 98,344 | *50.5* |
| John T. Copenhaver (R) | 91,088 | *46.8* |
| **Democratic Primary** | | |
| Robert H. Mollohan (D) | 148,557 | *42.6* |
| Milton J. Ferguson (D) | 95,869 | *27.5* |
| J. Howard Myers (D) | 75,606 | *21.7* |
| Joe F. Burdett (D) | 24,913 | *7.1* |
| **1960** **Republican Primary** | | |
| Harold E. Neely (R) | 102,618 | *55.3* |
| Chapman Revercomb (R) | 83,028 | *44.7* |
| **Democratic Primary** | | |
| W. W. Barron (D) | 187,501 | *51.0* |
| Hulett C. Smith (D) | 140,079 | *38.1* |
| Orel J. Skeen (D) | 39,907 | *10.9* |
| **1964** **Republican Primary** | | |
| Cecil H. Underwood (R) | 152,573 | *89.7* |
| Harry H. Cupp (R) | 11,325 | *6.7* |
| **Democratic Primary** | | |
| Hulett C. Smith (D) | 186,273 | *53.3* |
| Bonn Brown (D) | 85,527 | *24.4* |
| Julius W. Singleton (D) | 47,845 | *13.7* |
| Harold G. Cutright (D) | 30,119 | *8.6* |
| **1968** **Republican Primary** | | |
| Arch A. Moore Jr. (R) | 106,299 | *57.0* |
| Cecil H. Underwood (R) | 76,659 | *41.1* |
| **Democratic Primary** | | |
| James M. Sprouse (D) | 123,181 | *37.6* |
| C. Donald Robertson (D) | 118,637 | *36.2* |
| Paul J. Kaufman (D) | 72,917 | *22.3* |
| **1972** **Republican Primary** | | |
| Arch A. Moore Jr. (R) | | *100.0* |
| **Democratic Primary** | | |
| John D. (Jay) Rockefeller IV (D) | 262,613 | *72.2* |
| Lee M. Kenna (D) | 63,514 | *17.5* |
| Robert Myers (D) | 37,616 | *10.3* |
| **1976** **Republican Primary** | | |
| Cecil H. Underwood (R) | 97,671 | *64.4* |
| Ralph D. Albertazzie (R) | 44,393 | *29.3* |
| **Democratic Primary** | | |
| John D. (Jay) Rockefeller IV (D) | 206,732 | *49.7* |
| James M. Sprouse (D) | 118,707 | *28.5* |
| Ken Hechler (D) | 52,791 | *12.7* |
| John G. Hutchinson (D) | 26,222 | *6.3* |

| | Candidates | Votes | % |
|---|---|---|---|
| **1980** | **Republican Primary** | | |
| | Arch A. Moore Jr. (R) | | *100.0* |
| | **Democratic Primary** | | |
| | John D. (Jay) Rockefeller IV (D) | 250,550 | *78.0* |
| | H. John Rogers (D) | 70,452 | *21.9* |
| **1984** | **Republican Primary** | | |
| | Arch A. Moore Jr. (R) | 135,887 | *100.0* |
| | **Democratic Primary** | | |
| | Clyde M. See (D) | 148,049 | *39.8* |
| | Warren R. McGraw (D) | 104,138 | *28.0* |
| | Chauncey H. Browning (D) | 101,712 | *27.4* |
| **1988** | **Republican Primary** | | |
| | Arch A. Moore Jr. (R) | 78,495 | *53.2* |
| | John R. Raese (R) | 68,973 | *46.8* |
| | **Democratic Primary** | | |
| | Gaston Caperton (D) | 132,435 | *38.0* |
| | Clyde M. See (D) | 94,364 | *27.0* |
| | Mario J. Palumbo (D) | 51,722 | *14.8* |
| | Gus R. Douglass (D) | 48,748 | *14.0* |
| **1992** | **Republican Primary** | | |
| | Cleveland K. Benedict (R) | 104,169 | *86.4* |
| | Vernon Criss (R) | 16,350 | *13.6* |
| | **Democratic Primary** | | |
| | Gaston Caperton (D) | 142,261 | *42.7* |
| | Charlotte Pritt (D) | 115,498 | *34.7* |
| | Mario J. Palumbo (D) | 66,984 | *20.1* |

# WISCONSIN

| | Candidates | Votes | % |
|---|---|---|---|
| **1956** | **Republican Primary** | | |
| | Vernon W. Thomson (R) | | *100.0* |
| | **Democratic Primary** | | |
| | William Proxmire (D) | | *100.0* |
| **1958** | **Republican Primary** | | |
| | Vernon W. Thomson (R) | | *100.0* |
| | **Democratic Primary** | | |
| | Gaylord Nelson (D) | | *100.0* |
| **1960** | **Republican Primary** | | |
| | Philip G. Kuehn (R) | | *100.0* |
| | **Democratic Primary** | | |
| | Gaylord Nelson (D) | | *100.0* |

**771**

| | Candidates | Votes | % |
|---|---|---|---|
| 1962 | **Republican Primary** | | |
| | Philip G. Kuehn (R) | 250,539 | 53.8 |
| | Wilbur N. Renk (R) | 199,616 | 42.9 |
| | **Democratic Primary** | | |
| | John W. Reynolds (D) | | 100.0 |
| 1964 | **Republican Primary** | | |
| | Warren P. Knowles (R) | 246,760 | 71.9 |
| | Milo G. Knutson (R) | 96,421 | 28.1 |
| | **Democratic Primary** | | |
| | John W. Reynolds (D) | 241,170 | 70.3 |
| | Dominic H. Frinzi (D) | 102,066 | 29.7 |
| 1966 | **Republican Primary** | | |
| | Warren P. Knowles (R) | | 100.0 |
| | **Democratic Primary** | | |
| | Patrick J. Lucey (D) | 128,359 | 45.2 |
| | David Carley (D) | 95,803 | 33.7 |
| | Dominic H. Frinzi (D) | 44,344 | 15.6 |
| | Abe L. Swed (D) | 15,362 | 5.4 |
| 1968 | **Republican Primary** | | |
| | Warren P. Knowles (R) | | 100.0 |
| | **Democratic Primary** | | |
| | Bronson C. LaFollette (D) | 173,458 | 84.4 |
| | Floyd L. Wille (D) | 31,778 | 15.5 |
| 1970 | **Republican Primary** | | |
| | Jack B. Olson (R) | 203,434 | 91.4 |
| | Roman R. Blenski (R) | 19,061 | 8.6 |
| | **Democratic Primary** | | |
| | Patrick J. Lucey (D) | 177,584 | 60.6 |
| | Donald O. Peterson (D) | 105,849 | 36.1 |
| | **American Primary** | | |
| | Leo J. McDonald (AM) | | 100.0 |
| 1974 | **Republican Primary** | | |
| | William D. Dyke (R) | | 100.0 |
| | **Democratic Primary** | | |
| | Patrick J. Lucey (D) | 259,001 | 78.2 |
| | Edmond E. Hou-Seye (D) | 72,113 | 21.8 |
| | **American Primary** | | |
| | William H. Upham (AM) | | 100.0 |
| 1978 | **Republican Primary** | | |
| | Lee Sherman Dreyfus (R) | 197,279 | 57.9 |
| | Bob Kasten (R) | 143,361 | 42.1 |

| | Candidates | Votes | % |
|---|---|---|---|
| | **Democratic Primary** | | |
| | Martin J. Schreiber (D) | 217,572 | 60.4 |
| | David Carley (D) | 132,901 | 36.9 |
| | **Conservative Primary** | | |
| | Eugene R. Zimmerman (C) | | 100.0 |
| 1982 | **Republican Primary** | | |
| | Terry J. Kohler (R) | 227,844 | 68.2 |
| | Lowell B. Jackson (R) | 106,413 | 31.8 |
| | **Democratic Primary** | | |
| | Anthony S. Earl (D) | 268,857 | 45.9 |
| | Martin J. Schreiber (D) | 245,952 | 42.0 |
| | James B. Wood (D) | 71,282 | 12.2 |
| | **Libertarian Primary** | | |
| | Larry Smiley (LIBERT) | | 100.0 |
| | **Constitution Primary** | | |
| | James P. Wickstrom (CONST) | | 100.0 |
| | **Socialist Workers Primary** | | |
| | Peter Seidman (SOC WORK) | | 100.0 |
| 1986 | **Republican Primary** | | |
| | Tommy G. Thompson (R) | 156,875 | 52.1 |
| | Jonathan B. Barry (R) | 67,114 | 22.3 |
| | George Watts (R) | 58,424 | 19.4 |
| | Albert L. Wiley (R) | 15,233 | 5.1 |
| | **Democratic Primary** | | |
| | Anthony S. Earl (D) | 215,183 | 80.2 |
| | Edmond Hou-Seye (D) | 52,784 | 19.7 |
| | **Labor-Farm Primary** | | |
| | Kathryn A. Christensen (LAB F) | | 100.0 |
| 1990 | **Republican Primary** | | |
| | Tommy G. Thompson (R) | 201,467 | 92.5 |
| | Bennett A. Masel (R) | 11,230 | 5.2 |
| | **Democratic Primary** | | |
| | Thomas Loftus (D) | | 100.0 |

# WYOMING

| | Candidates | Votes | % |
|---|---|---|---|
| 1958 | **Republican Primary** | | |
| | Milward L. Simpson (R) | 28,749 | 77.6 |
| | Stanley Edwards (R) | 8,294 | 22.4 |

| | Candidates | Votes | % |
|---|---|---|---|
| | **Democratic Primary** | | |
| | J. J. Hickey (D) | | *100.0* |
| 1962 | **Republican Primary** | | |
| | Clifford P. Hansen (R) | 28,494 | *57.0* |
| | Charles M. Crowell (R) | 16,906 | *33.8* |
| | R. E. Cheever (R) | 4,575 | *9.1* |
| | **Democratic Primary** | | |
| | Jack R. Gage (D) | 21,051 | *55.5* |
| | William Jack (D) | 16,875 | *44.5* |
| 1966 | **Republican Primary** | | |
| | Stan Hathaway (R) | 26,110 | *55.2* |
| | Joe Burke (R) | 19,815 | *41.9* |
| | **Democratic Primary** | | |
| | Ernest Wilkerson (D) | 13,145 | *31.1* |
| | Bill Nation (D) | 9,834 | *23.2* |
| | Jack R. Gage (D) | 8,661 | *20.5* |
| | Raymond B. Whitaker (D) | 6,238 | *14.7* |
| | Howard L. Burke (D) | 4,426 | *10.5* |
| 1970 | **Republican Primary** | | |
| | Stan Hathaway (R) | | *100.0* |
| | **Democratic Primary** | | |
| | John J. Rooney (D) | | *100.0* |
| 1974 | **Republican Primary** | | |
| | Dick Jones (R) | 15,502 | *26.5* |
| | Malcolm Wallop (R) | 14,688 | *25.1* |
| | Roy Peck (R) | 14,217 | *24.3* |
| | Clarence Brimmer (R) | 14,014 | *24.0* |
| | **Democratic Primary** | | |
| | Ed Herschler (D) | 19,997 | *46.6* |
| | Harry E. Leimback (D) | 15,255 | *35.5* |
| | John J. Rooney (D) | 7,674 | *17.9* |

| | Candidates | Votes | % |
|---|---|---|---|
| 1978 | **Republican Primary** | | |
| | John C. Ostlund (R) | 40,251 | *58.9* |
| | Gus Fleischli (R) | 24,824 | *36.4* |
| | **Democratic Primary** | | |
| | Ed Herschler (D) | 28,406 | *65.3* |
| | Margaret McKinstry (D) | 15,111 | *34.7* |
| 1982 | **Republican Primary** | | |
| | Warren A. Morton (R) | 52,536 | *74.3* |
| | Rex G. Welty (R) | 9,106 | *12.9* |
| | Carl A. Johnson (R) | 9,025 | *12.8* |
| | **Democratic Primary** | | |
| | Ed Herschler (D) | 44,396 | *85.2* |
| | Pat McGuire (D) | 7,720 | *14.8* |
| 1986 | **Republican Primary** | | |
| | Peter Simpson (R) | 25,948 | *27.6* |
| | Bill Budd (R) | 25,495 | *27.1* |
| | Fred Schroeder (R) | 15,013 | *16.0* |
| | Russ Donley (R) | 12,979 | *13.8* |
| | David R. Nicholas (R) | 11,092 | *11.8* |
| | **Democratic Primary** | | |
| | Mike Sullivan (D) | 29,266 | *70.9* |
| | Pat McGuire (D) | 5,406 | *13.1* |
| | Keith B. Goodenough (D) | 4,039 | *9.8* |
| | Al Hamburg (D) | 2,554 | *6.2* |
| 1990 | **Republican Primary** | | |
| | Mary Mead (R) | 51,160 | *67.3* |
| | Nyla Murphy (R) | 24,916 | *32.7* |
| | **Democratic Primary** | | |
| | Mike Sullivan (D) | 38,447 | *88.4* |
| | Ron Clingman (D) | 5,026 | *11.6* |

# Senate Elections

# Senate Elections

The creation of the United States Senate was a result of the so-called "great compromise" at the Constitutional Convention in 1787. The small states wanted equal representation in Congress, fearing domination by the larger states under a population formula. The larger states, however, naturally wished for a legislature based on population, where their strength would prevail.

In compromising this dispute, delegates simply split the basis for representation between the two houses — population for the House of Representatives, equal representation by state for the Senate. By the terms of the compromise, each state was entitled to two senators. In a sense, they were conceived to be ambassadors from the states, representing the sovereign interests of the states to the federal government.

## Election by State Legislatures

To elect these "ambassadors," the Founders chose the state legislatures instead of the people themselves. The argument was that legislatures would be able to give more sober and reflective thought than the people at large to the kind of persons needed to represent the states' interests to the federal government. The delegates also thought the state legislatures and thus the states would take a greater interest in the fledgling national government if they were involved in its operations this way. Furthermore, the state legislatures had chosen the members of the Continental Congress (the Congress under the Articles of Confederation), as well as the members of the Constitutional Convention itself, so the procedure was familiar to the delegates.

In choosing the state legislatures as the instruments of election for senators, the Constitutional Convention considered and abandoned several alternatives. Some delegates had suggested that the senators be elected by the House or appointed by the president from a list of nominees selected by the state legislatures. These ideas were discarded as making the Senate too dependent on another part of the federal government. Also turned down was a scheme for a system of electors, similar to presidential electors, to choose the senators in each state. And popular election was rejected as being too radical and inconvenient.

So deeply entrenched was the ambassadorial aspect of a senator's duty that state legislatures sometimes took it upon themselves to instruct senators on how to vote. This occa-

sionally raised severe problems of conscience among senators and resulted in several resignations.

For example, in 1836 future president John Tyler was serving as a U.S. senator from Virginia. That year the Virginia legislature instructed him to vote for a resolution to expunge the Senate censure of President Andrew Jackson for his removal of the federal deposits from the Bank of the United States. Tyler, who had voted for the censure resolution, resigned from the Senate rather than comply.

In another instance, Sen. Hugh L. White of Tennessee, a Whig, resigned from the Senate in 1840 after being instructed by his state legislature to vote for the subtreasury bill, an economic measure supported by the Democratic Van Buren administration.

Another problem for the Founders was the length of the senatorial term. The framers of the Constitution tried to balance two principles: the belief that relatively frequent elections were necessary to promote good behavior and the need for steadiness and continuity in government.

Delegates proposed terms of three, four, five, six, seven and nine years. They finally settled on six-year staggered

## Sources

Haynes, George H. *The Election of Senators.* New York: Henry Holt, 1906.

———. *The Senate of the United States, Its History and Practice.* Boston: Houghton Mifflin, 1938.

Hupman, Richard D. *Senate Election, Expulsion and Censure Cases from 1793 to 1972.* Compiled by the Senate library under the direction of Francis R. Valeo, secretary of the Senate. Washington, D.C.: Government Printing Office, 1972.

Riddick, Floyd M., Senate parliamentarian. *The Term of a Senator, When Does It Begin and End? Constitution, Laws and Precedents Pertaining to the Term of a Senator.* Prepared under the direction of Emery L. Frazier, secretary of the Senate. Washington, D.C.: Government Printing Office, 1966.

U.S. Senate. Committee on Rules and Administration. *Senate Manual.* 103rd Cong., 1st sess., 1994.

terms, with one-third of the members coming up for election every two years. *(Classification of senators, terms, p. 780)*

# Changing Election Procedures

At first each state made its own arrangements for its state legislature to elect the senators. Many states required an election by the two chambers of the legislature sitting separately.

That is, each chamber had to vote for the same candidate for him to be elected. Other states, however, provided for election by a joint ballot of the two chambers sitting together.

However, the Constitution specifically authorized Congress to regulate senatorial elections if it so chose. Article I, Section 4, Paragraph 1 states, "The times, places and manner of holding elections for Senators and Representatives shall be prescribed in each state by the legislature thereof; but the Congress may at any time by law make or alter such regulations, except as to the places of chusing Senators." *(Constitutional provisions for election to the Senate, Appendix, p. 1346)*

## 1866 Act of Congress

In 1866 Congress decided to exercise its authority. Procedures in some states, particularly those requiring concurrent majorities in both houses of the state legislature for election to the Senate, had resulted in numerous delays and vacancies.

The new federal law set up the following procedure: The first ballot for senator was to be taken by the two chambers of each state legislature voting separately. If no candidate received a majority of the vote in both houses, then the two chambers were to meet and ballot jointly until a majority choice emerged.

Also included in the 1866 law were provisions for roll-call votes in the state legislatures (secret ballots had been taken in several states) and for a definite timetable. The law directed that the first vote take place on the second Tuesday after the meeting and organization of the legislature, followed by a minimum of a single ballot on every legislative day thereafter until election of a senator resulted.

But the new uniform system did not have the desired effect. The requirement for a majority vote continued the frequency of deadlock. In fact one of the worst deadlocks in senatorial election history happened under the 1866 federal law.

The case occurred in Delaware at the end of the 19th century. In 1899, with the legislature divided between two factions of the Republican Party and the Democrats in the minority, no majority selection could be made for the senatorial term beginning March 4, 1899. So bitter was the Republican factional dispute that neither side would support a candidate acceptable to the other; nor would the Democrats play kingmaker by siding with one or the other Republican group. The dispute continued throughout the life of the 56th Congress (1899-1901), leaving a seat unfilled.

Furthermore, the term of Delaware's other Senate seat ended in 1901, necessitating another election. The same pattern continued, with the legislature unable to fill either seat, leaving Delaware totally unrepresented in the Senate from March 4, 1901, until March 1, 1903, when two senators were finally elected in the closing days of the 57th Congress (1901-03). The deadlock was broken when the two Republican factions split the state's two seats between them.

## Abuses of Election by Legislatures

Besides the frequent deadlocks, critics pointed to what they saw as other faults in the system. They charged that the party caucuses in the state legislatures, as well as individual members, were subject to intense and unethical lobbying practices by supporters of various senatorial candidates. The relatively small size of the electing body and the high stakes involved — a seat in the Senate — often tempted the use of questionable methods in conducting the elections.

Allegations that such methods were used involved the Senate itself in election disputes. The Constitution makes Congress the judge of its own members. Article I, Section 5, Paragraph 1 states, "Each House shall be the judge of the elections, returns and qualifications of its own members. . . ."

One of the most sensational cases concerned the election of William Lorimer, R-Ill. Lorimer won on the 99th ballot taken by the Illinois legislature in 1909. A year after he had taken his seat, the Senate cleared Lorimer of charges that he had won election by bribery. But the revelation of new evidence prompted another investigation, and in 1912 the Senate voted that Lorimer's election was invalid and that he was not entitled to his seat.

Critics had still another grievance against the legislative method of choosing senators. They contended that elections to the state legislatures were often overshadowed by senatorial contests. Thus when voters went to the polls to choose their state legislators, they sometimes would be urged to disregard state and local issues and vote for a legislator who promised to support a certain candidate for the U.S. Senate. This, the critics said, led to neglect of state government and issues. Moreover, drawn-out Senate contests tended to hold up the consideration of state business.

# Demands for Popular Elections

But the main criticism of legislative elections was that they distorted or even blocked the will of the people. Throughout the 19th century, the movement toward popular election had taken away from the legislatures the right to elect government and presidential electors in states that had such provisions. Now attention focused on the Senate.

Five times around the turn of the century the House passed constitutional amendments to provide for Senate elections by popular vote — in the 52nd Congress on Jan. 16, 1893; in the 53rd Congress on July 21, 1894; in the 55th Congress on May 11, 1898; in the 56th Congress on April 13, 1900, and in the 57th Congress on Feb. 13, 1902. But each time the Senate refused to act.

Frustrated in their desire for direct popular elections, reformers began implementing various formulas for preselecting Senate candidates, attempting to reduce the legislative balloting to something approaching a mere formality. In some cases party conventions endorsed nominees for the Senate, allowing the voters at least to know who the members of the legislature were likely to support. Southern states early in the century adopted the party primary to choose Senate nominees. However, legislators never could be legally bound to support anyone because the Constitution gave them the unfettered power of electing to the Senate whomever they chose.

Oregon took the lead in instituting non-binding popular elections. Under a 1901 law, voters expressed their choice for senator in popular ballots. While the election results had no

# Senate Appointments and Special Elections

Governors were given specific authority in the Constitution to make temporary appointments to the Senate. Article I, Section 3, Paragraph 2 states: "If vacancies happen by resignation, or otherwise, during the recess of the legislature of any state, the executive thereof may make temporary appointments until the next meeting of the legislature, which shall then fill such vacancies."

The principle was established as early as 1794 that a vacancy created solely because a state legislature had failed to elect a new senator could not be filled by appointment, because the vacancy had not occurred "during the recess of the legislature."

For example, the term of Sen. Matthew Quay, R-Pa. (1887-99, 1901-04) expired March 3, 1899. The legislature was in session but had not re-elected him. Nor did it elect anyone before adjourning that April 20. Thereupon, the governor appointed Quay to the vacancy; but the Senate did not allow Quay to take the seat, because the vacancy had occurred during the meeting of the legislature. In 1901 the legislature elected Quay for the remainder of the term.

On the other hand, if a senator's term expired and the legislature was *not* in session, a governor was able to make an appointment — but only until the legislature either elected a successor or adjourned without electing one. For example, on March 3, 1809, the term of Sen. Samuel Smith, D-R-Md. (1803-15, 1822-33) expired. The legislature was not then in session and had not elected a successor. Therefore the governor appointed Smith to fill the vacancy until the next meeting of the legislature, which was scheduled for June 5, 1809. The Senate ruled that he was entitled to the seat. During the subsequent meeting of the state legislature that year, Smith was elected to a full term.

Whatever the condition under which an appointment had been made, it was to last only through the next state legislative session. Even if a legislature failed to elect a new senator, the appointed senator's service was to expire with the adjournment of the state legislature.

This principle was confirmed in the case of Sen. Samuel Phelps, Whig-Vt. (1839-51, 1853-54). Phelps was appointed in January 1853 to a vacancy caused by the death of Sen. William Upham, Whig-Vt. (1843-53), whose term was to run through March 3, 1855. As the legislature was in recess, Phelps continued to serve until the expiration of the 32nd Congress on March 3, 1853, and also during a special session of the 33rd Congress in March and April 1853. The Vermont legislature met during October and December without electing a senator to fill the unexpired term. Phelps then showed up for the regular session of the 33rd Congress in December, but the Senate in March 1854 decided he was not entitled to retain his seat, because the legislature had met and adjourned without electing a new senator.

## 17th Amendment and Special Elections

The adoption of the 17th Amendment in 1913, providing for popular election of senators, altered the provision for gubernatorial appointment of senators to fill vacancies. The amendment provided that, in case of a vacancy, "the executive authority of such state shall issue writs of election to fill such vacancies: *Provided*, that the legislature of any state may empower the executive thereof to make temporary appointments until the people fill the vacancies by election as the legislature may direct." Under this provision, state legislatures allowed governors to make temporary appointments until the vacancy could be filled by a special election. Special elections — elections held to fill unexpired terms — were usually held in November of an even-numbered year. Some states, however, provided for special elections to be held within just a few months after the vacancy occurred.

Before ratification of the 17th Amendment the term of an appointee generally ended when a successor was elected to fill the unexpired term or at the end of the six-year term, whichever occurred first. After the ratification of the 17th Amendment but before ratification of the 20th Amendment in 1933, senators who were elected to fill lengthy unexpired terms usually could take office immediately, displacing an appointee. If an appointee was serving near the close of a six-year term, most states would hold simultaneous elections to fill both the six-year term and the four-month "lame-duck" term. Sometimes different persons would be elected to each term.

To eliminate the lame-duck sessions that ran from December of an even-numbered year through March 3 of the next year, the 20th Amendment changed the March 3 beginning date of the terms for Congress and the president to Jan. 3. After the so-called lame-duck amendment took effect, senators elected to fill vacancies in terms that had several years to run would take office immediately, as before, but, if a vacancy occurred near the end of a six-year term, an appointee would often serve until the Jan. 3 expiration date, eliminating the necessity for a special election.

Some states, however, have held elections in November for the remaining two months of a term. Georgia voters in 1972, for example, found on the ballot two Senate elections, one for a six-year term and one for a two-month term to fill the unexpired term of Sen. Richard B. Russell, D (1933-71), who died in office.

## Dates of Service

Title II, Section 36 of the U.S. Code sets the dates on which senators appointed or elected to fill unexpired terms formally begin service and go on the payroll. The service of an appointee commences the day of appointment and continues until a successor is elected and qualified. If the Senate is in sine die adjournment when a new senator is elected to succeed an appointee, he will take office and begin receiving his salary on the day after the election.

If the Senate is in session when a new senator is elected to succeed an appointee, the new senator may take office when he presents himself before the Senate to take the oath; the appointee may continue in office until this occurs or the Senate adjourns sine die, whichever happens first. The term of the newly elected senator would then begin at sine die adjournment.

legal force, the law required that the popular returns be formally announced to the state legislature before it elected a senator.

At first the law did not work — the winner of the informal popular vote in 1902 was not chosen senator by the legislature. But the reformers increased their pressure, demanding that candidates for the legislature sign a pledge to vote for the winner of the popular vote. By 1908 the plan was successful. The Republican legislature elected to the Senate Democrat George Chamberlain, the winner of the popular contest. Several other states — including Colorado, Kansas, Minnesota, Montana, Nevada and Oklahoma — adopted the Oregon method.

### The 17th Amendment

Despite these palliatives, pressures continued to mount for a switch to straight popular elections. Frustrated at the failure of the Senate to act, proponents of change began pushing for a convention to propose this and perhaps other amendments to the Constitution. (Article V of the Constitution provides two methods of proposing amendments — either passage by two-thirds of both houses of Congress or through the calling of a special convention if requested by the legislatures of two-thirds of the states. In either case any amendment proposed by Congress or by a special convention must be ratified by three-fourths of the states.)

Conservatives began to fear a convention more than they did popular election of senators. There was no precedent for an amending convention and conservatives worried that it might be dominated by liberals and progressives who would propose numerous amendments and change the very nature of the government. Consequently, their opposition to popular election of senators diminished.

At the same time progressives of both parties made strong gains in the midterm elections of 1910. Some successful Senate candidates had made pledges to work for adoption of a constitutional amendment providing for popular election. In this atmosphere the Senate debated and finally passed the amendment on June 12, 1911, by a vote of 64-24. The House concurred in the Senate version on May 13, 1912, by a vote of 238-39. Ratification of the 17th Amendment was completed by the requisite number of states on April 8, 1913, and was proclaimed a part of the Constitution by Secretary of State William Jennings Bryan on May 31, 1913.

The first popularly elected senator was chosen in a special election in November 1913. He was Sen. Blair Lee, D-Md. (1914-17), elected for the remaining three years of the unexpired term of Sen. Isidor Rayner, D (1905-12), who had died in office.

There was no wholesale changeover in membership when the 17th Amendment became effective. In fact every one of the 23 senators elected by state legislatures for their previous terms, and running for re-election to full terms in November 1914, was successful. Seven had retired or died, and two had been defeated for renomination.

The changeover in method of electing senators ended the frequent legislative stalemates in choosing members of the Senate. Otherwise many things remained the same. There were still election disputes, including charges of corruption, as well as miscounting of votes.

### Election Disputes

Election disputes continued to occupy the Senate. A bitter contest for a New Hampshire Senate seat in 1974 between Republican representative Louis C. Wyman and Democrat John A. Durkin wound up in the Senate after a seesaw battle between New Hampshire authorities over who had won. The state Ballot Law Commission had finally awarded the victory to Wyman by two votes, but Durkin took his case to the Senate. After wrestling with the problem for seven months, the Senate gave up and declared the seat vacant. A new election was held Sept. 16, 1975, which Durkin won decisively.

## Senate's Three Classes

The Senate is divided into three classes or groups of members. A member's class depends on the year in which he or she is elected. Article I, Section 3, Paragraph 2 of the Constitution, relating to the classification of senators in the first and succeeding Congresses, provides that "Immediately after they shall be assembled in consequence of the first election, they shall be divided as equally as may be into three classes. The seats of the Senators of the first class shall be vacated at the expiration of the second year, of the second class at the expiration of the fourth year and of the third class at the expiration of the sixth year, so that one-third may be chosen every second year...."

Thus senators belonging to class one began their regular terms in the years 1789, 1791, 1797, 1803, etc., continuing through the present day to 1977, 1983, 1989 and coming up for re-election in 1994. Senators belonging to class two began their regular terms in 1789, 1793, 1799, 1805, etc., continuing through to the present day in 1973, 1979, 1985, 1991 and were to be up for election in 1996. And senators belonging to class three began their regular terms in 1789, 1795, 1801, 1807, etc., continuing through the present day to 1975, 1981, 1987, 1993 and coming up for re-election in 1998.

## Sessions and Terms

In the fall of 1788, the expiring Continental Congress established a schedule for the incoming government under the new Constitution. The Congress decided that the new government was to commence on the first Wednesday in March 1789 — March 4. Even though the House did not achieve a quorum until April 1 and the Senate April 6, and President Washington was not inaugurated until April 30, Senate, House and presidential terms were still considered to have begun March 4. The term of the first Congress continued through March 3, 1791. Because congressional and presidential terms were fixed at exactly two, four and six years, March 4 became the official date of transition from one administration to another every four years and from one Congress to another every two years.

### 'Long' and 'Short' Sessions

The Constitution did not mandate a regular congressional session to begin March 4. Instead, Article I, Section 4, Paragraph 2 called for at least one congressional session every year, to convene on the first Monday in December unless Congress by law set a different day. Consequently, except when called by the president for special sessions, or when Congress itself set a different day, Congress convened in regular session each December, until the passage of the 20th Amendment in 1933.

The December date resulted in a long and short session. The first (long) session would meet in December of an odd-numbered year and continue into the next year, usually adjourning some time the next summer. The second (short) session began in December of an even-numbered year and continued through March 3 of the next year, when its term ran out. It also became customary for the Senate to meet in brief special session on March 4 or March 5, especially in years when a new president was inaugurated, to act on presidential nominations.

To illustrate with an example of a typical Congress, the 29th (1845-47): President James K. Polk, D, was inaugurated on March 4, 1845. The Senate met in special session from March 4 to March 20 to confirm Polk's Cabinet and other appointments. Then the first regular session convened Dec. 1, 1845, working until Aug. 10, 1846, when it adjourned. The second, a short session, lasted from Dec. 7, 1846, through March 3, 1847.

Since it was not clear whether terms of members of Congress ended at midnight March 3 or noon March 4, the custom evolved of extending the legislative day of March 3, in odd-numbered years, to noon March 4.

## The 20th Amendment

The political consequence of the short session was to encourage filibusters and other delaying tactics by members determined to block legislation that would die upon the automatic adjournment of Congress on March 3. Moreover, the Congresses that met in short session always included a substantial number of "lame-duck" members who had been defeated at the polls, yet were able quite often to determine the legislative outcome of the session.

Dissatisfaction with the short session began to mount after 1900. During the Wilson administration (1913-21), each of four such sessions ended with a Senate filibuster and the loss of important bills including several funding bills. Sen. George W. Norris, R-Neb. (1913-43), became the leading advocate of a constitutional amendment to abolish the short session by starting the terms of Congress and the president in January instead of March. The Senate approved the Norris amendment five times during the 1920s, only to see it blocked in the House each time. It was finally approved by both chambers in 1932 and became the 20th Amendment upon ratification by the 36th state in 1933.

The amendment provided that the terms of senators and representatives would begin and end at noon on the third day of January of the year following the election. However, according to the *Senate Manual* (1989 edition, p. 769), "In view of the impracticality of dealing with split days, ... it has been the long established practice for payment of salaries, computation of allowances and recording of service to credit a Member for the full day of the third of January he takes office and consider his term as ended at the close of business on the second of January six years later." Congressional Quarterly has retained this convention in the list of senators in this volume, with dates of service shown as beginning on Jan. 3 and ending on Jan. 2.

The 20th Amendment also established noon Jan. 20 as the day on which the president and vice president take office. It provided also that Congress should meet annually on Jan. 3 "unless they shall by law appoint a different day." The second session of the 73rd Congress was the first to convene on the new date, Jan. 3, 1934. Franklin D. Roosevelt was the first president and John N. Garner the first vice president to be inaugurated on Jan. 20, at the start of their second terms in 1937.

The amendment was intended to permit Congress to extend its first session for as long as necessary and to complete the work of its second session before the next election, thereby obviating legislation by a lame-duck body.

# United States Senators, 1789-1994

# Sources: U.S. Senators, 1789-1994

This section (pages 785 to 811) contains a listing of United States senators who served from March 4, 1789, through May 1994 — from the 1st Congress to the second session of the 103rd Congress. Arranged alphabetically by state, the lists provide the name, political affiliation and dates of service of each senator in chronological order within each class. *(Explanation of Senate classes, p. 780)*

The primary source for the names, classes and dates of service of senators is the *Senate Manual* (U.S. Government Printing Office, Washington, D.C., 1994). Congressional Quarterly obtained additional information in certain cases from the *Biographical Directory of the United States Congress, 1774-1989* (U.S. Government Printing Office, Washington, D.C., 1989). State secretaries of state were the source for information after 1989. Footnotes were derived from all sources.

## Party Affiliation

Determinations of senators' party affiliations were based on three sources. From 1913, when the 197th Amendment established popular election of senators, to 1972 party designations were taken from the Inter-University Consortium for Political and Social Research (ICPSR) popular vote returns (pages 815 to 846). However, if a senator was elected in any one election with the support of more than one political party, only the major party is indicated in the listing. For example, Sen. Robert F. Kennedy of New York, who in 1964 was the nominee of both the Democratic and Liberal parties, appears as a Democrat (D).

Also from 1913 on, whenever senators switched parties during their period of service, each party is listed even if the senator was not formally elected as a nominee of the new party. For example, Sen. Wayne Morse of Oregon (1945-69) is listed as a Republican, Independent and Democrat (R,I,D). He was elected twice as a Republican in 1944 and 1950, left that party in 1952 and called himself an Independent until 1955, and then became a Democrat. He was re-elected as a Democrat in 1956 and 1962. *(For a list of party abbreviations, see page 1352; for other references to individual senators, see "General Index," p. 1503.)*

For the period before popular election of senators (1789-1913), party affiliations were taken from the *Biographical Directory of the United States Congress, 1774-*

*1989* and the *Dictionary of American Biography* (20 volumes, Charles Scribner's Sons, New York, 1928-58). Because political parties did not formally exist in the early years of the Republic, classification of senators by party during this period can be difficult or misleading. *(See Pre-Convention Politics, p. 7; Historical Profiles of American Political Parties, p. 259.)* In cases where party affiliation was not appropriate or could not be determined, no party designation appears.

Except where otherwise noted, senators were elected to office by state legislatures or, after ratification of the 17th Amendment in 1913, by popular vote.

Footnotes have been used to indicate the following circumstances:

● The appointment of a senator by the govenor of his state to fill an unexpired term. In such cases the service of an appointee ended at the expiration of the six-year term, or when a new senator was elected, or after the recess of the state legislature. *(For explanation of terms of appointees, see p. 779.)* In many cases, the appointee was elected to the Senate while serving there by appointment. In these cases, the footnote states that the senator was appointed and "subsequently elected."

● The death or resignation of a senator before the expiration of the term for which he was elected or appointed. In a number of instances, retiring or defeated senators resigned shortly before the start of a new congressional session. This enabled the succeeding senator to take office early by appointment, thereby giving him seniority over other newly elected senators. The practice has become less common due to changes in seniority rules. Resignations are footnoted but subsequent appointments are not. However, the dates of service shown in the main listing account for the complete period served.

● The expulsion of a senator by the Senate, and certain cases of disputed elections. Information on these was obtained from *Senate Election, Expulsion and Censure Cases* (S Doc 92-7), a publication prepared in 1972 by the Senate Rules and Administration Committee.

● A change in political party affiliation by a senator, if it could be determined that the senator was elected or appointed as a member of one political party but was subsequently re-elected as a nominee of a different party.

# United States Senators, 1789-1994

**Note:** In the footnotes, "elected" indicates election by the state legislature prior to ratification of the 17th Amendment, April 8, 1913.

## ALABAMA

(Became a state Dec. 14, 1819)

### Class 2

| Senators | Dates of Service | |
|---|---|---|
| William R. King (D-R, D)[1] | Dec. 14, 1819 | April 15, 1844 |
| Dixon H. Lewis (D)[2] | April 22, 1844 | Oct. 25, 1848 |
| Benjamin Fitzpatrick (D)[3] | Nov. 25, 1848 | Nov. 30, 1849 |
| Jeremiah Clemens (D) | Nov. 30, 1849 | March 3, 1853 |
| Clement Claiborne Clay Jr. (D)[4] | March 4, 1853 | March 14, 1861 |
| Willard Warner (R) | July 25, 1868 | March 3, 1871 |
| George Goldthwaite (D)[5] | March 4, 1871 | March 3, 1877 |
| John T. Morgan (D)[6] | March 4, 1877 | June 11, 1907 |
| John H. Bankhead (D)[7] | June 18, 1907 | March 1, 1920 |
| Braxton B. Comer (D)[8] | March 5, 1920 | Nov. 2, 1920 |
| J. Thomas Heflin (D) | Nov. 2, 1920 | March 3, 1931 |
| John H. Bankhead II (D)[9] | March 4, 1931 | June 12, 1946 |
| George R. Swift (D)[10] | June 15, 1946 | Nov. 5, 1946 |
| John Sparkman (D) | Nov. 6, 1946 | Jan. 2, 1979 |
| Howell Heflin (D) | Jan. 3, 1979 | |

### Class 3

| Senators | Dates of Service | |
|---|---|---|
| John W. Walker (D-R)[11] | Dec. 14, 1819 | Dec. 12, 1822 |
| William Kelly (D-R) | Dec. 12, 1822 | March 3, 1825 |
| Henry H. Chambers (D-R)[12] | March 4, 1825 | Jan. 25, 1826 |
| Israel Pickens (D-R)[13] | Feb. 17, 1826 | Nov. 27, 1826 |
| John McKinley (D-R, D) | Nov. 27, 1826 | March 3, 1831 |
| Gabriel Moore (D) | March 4, 1831 | March 3, 1837 |
| John McKinley (D)[14] | March 4, 1837 | April 22, 1837 |
| Clement Comer Clay (D)[15] | June 19, 1837 | Nov. 15, 1841 |
| Arthur P. Bagby (D)[16] | Nov. 24, 1841 | June 16, 1848 |
| William R. King (D)[17] | July 1, 1848 | Dec. 20, 1852 |
| Benjamin Fitzpatrick (D)[18] | Jan. 14, 1853 | Jan. 21, 1861 |
| George E. Spencer (R) | July 25, 1868 | March 3, 1879 |
| George S. Houston (D)[19] | March 4, 1879 | Dec. 31, 1879 |
| Luke Pryor (D)[20] | Jan. 7, 1880 | Nov. 23, 1880 |
| James L. Pugh (D) | Nov. 24, 1880 | March 3, 1897 |
| Edmund W. Pettus (D)[21] | March 4, 1897 | July 27, 1907 |
| Joseph F. Johnston (D)[22] | Aug. 6, 1907 | Aug. 8, 1913 |
| Francis S. White (D) | May 11, 1914 | March 3, 1915 |
| Oscar W. Underwood (D) | March 4, 1915 | March 3, 1927 |
| Hugo Black (D)[23] | March 4, 1927 | Aug. 19, 1937 |
| Dixie Bibb Graves (D)[24] | Aug. 20, 1937 | Jan. 10, 1938 |
| Lister Hill (D)[25] | Jan. 11, 1938 | Jan. 2, 1969 |
| James B. Allen (D)[26] | Jan. 3, 1969 | June 1, 1978 |
| Maryon Pittman Allen (D)[27] | June 8, 1978 | Nov. 7, 1978 |
| Donald W. Stewart (D)[28] | Nov. 8, 1978 | Jan. 1, 1981 |
| Jeremiah Denton (R) | Jan. 2, 1981 | Jan. 2, 1987 |
| Richard C. Shelby (D) | Jan. 3, 1987 | |

**Alabama**
 1. Resigned April 15, 1844.
 2. Appointed by governor to fill vacancy. Subsequently elected. Died Oct. 25, 1848.
 3. Appointed by governor to fill vacancy.

 4. Seat declared vacant March 14, 1861. Vacancy lasted until July 25, 1868, because of Civil War.
 5. Not sworn in until Jan. 15, 1872, because of protest.
 6. Died June 11, 1907.
 7. Appointed by governor to fill vacancy. Subsequently elected. Died March 1, 1920.
 8. Appointed by governor to fill vacancy.
 9. Died June 12, 1946.
 10. Appointed by governor to fill vacancy. Resigned Nov. 5, 1946.
 11. Resigned Dec. 12, 1822.
 12. Died Jan. 25, 1826.
 13. Appointed by governor to fill vacancy.
 14. Resigned April 22, 1837.
 15. Resigned Nov. 15, 1841.
 16. Resigned June 16, 1848.
 17. Appointed by governor to fill vacancy. Subsequently elected. Resigned Dec. 20, 1852.
 18. Appointed by governor to fill vacancy. Subsequently elected. Withdrew from Senate Jan. 21, 1861, because of Civil War. Seat remained vacant until July 25, 1868.
 19. Died Dec. 31, 1879.
 20. Appointed by governor to fill vacancy.
 21. Died July 27, 1907.
 22. Died Aug. 8, 1913.
 23. Resigned Aug. 19, 1937.
 24. Appointed by governor to fill vacancy. Resigned Jan. 10, 1938.
 25. Appointed by governor to fill vacancy. Subsequently elected.
 26. Died June 1, 1978.
 27. Appointed by governor to fill vacancy.
 28. Resigned Jan. 1, 1981.

## ALASKA

(Became a state Jan. 3, 1959)

### Class 2

| Senators | Dates of Service | |
|---|---|---|
| E. L. Bartlett (D)[1] | Jan. 3, 1959 | Dec. 11, 1968 |
| Ted Stevens (R)[2] | Dec. 24, 1968 | |

### Class 3

| Senators | Dates of Service | |
|---|---|---|
| Ernest Gruening (D) | Jan. 3, 1959 | Jan. 2, 1969 |
| Mike Gravel (D) | Jan. 3, 1969 | Jan. 2, 1981 |
| Frank H. Murkowski (R) | Jan. 3, 1981 | |

**Alaska**
 1. Died Dec. 11, 1968.
 2. Appointed by governor to fill vacancy. Subsequently elected.

## ARIZONA

(Became a state Feb. 14, 1912)

### Class 1

| Senators | Dates of Service | |
|---|---|---|
| Henry Fountain Ashurst (D) | March 27, 1912 | Jan. 2, 1941 |

| | | |
|---|---|---|
| Ernest W. McFarland (D) | Jan. 3, 1941 | Jan. 2, 1953 |
| Barry Goldwater (R) | Jan. 3, 1953 | Jan. 2, 1965 |
| Paul J. Fannin (R) | Jan. 3, 1965 | Jan. 2, 1977 |
| Dennis DeConcini (D) | Jan. 3, 1977 | |

### Class 3

| | | |
|---|---|---|
| Marcus A. Smith (D) | March 27, 1912 | March 3, 1921 |
| Ralph H. Cameron (R) | March 4, 1921 | March 3, 1927 |
| Carl Hayden (D) | March 4, 1927 | Jan. 2, 1969 |
| Barry Goldwater (R) | Jan. 3, 1969 | Jan. 2, 1987 |
| John McCain (R) | Jan. 3, 1987 | |

# ARKANSAS

(Became a state June 15, 1836)

## Class 2

| Senators | Dates of Service | |
|---|---|---|
| William S. Fulton (D)[1] | Sept. 18, 1836 | Aug. 15, 1844 |
| Chester Ashley (D)[2] | Nov. 8, 1844 | April 29, 1848 |
| William K. Sebastian (D)[3] | May 12, 1848 | July 11, 1861 |
| Alexander McDonald (R) | June 23, 1868 | March 3, 1871 |
| Powell Clayton (R) | March 14, 1871 | March 3, 1877 |
| Augustus H. Garland (D)[4] | March 4, 1877 | March 6, 1885 |
| James H. Berry (D) | March 20, 1885 | March 3, 1907 |
| Jeff Davis (D)[5] | March 4, 1907 | Jan. 3, 1913 |
| John N. Heiskell (D)[6] | Jan. 6, 1913 | Jan. 29, 1913 |
| William M. Kavanaugh (D) | Jan. 29, 1913 | March 3, 1913 |
| Joseph T. Robinson (D)[7] | March 10, 1913 | July 14, 1937 |
| John E. Miller (D)[8] | Nov. 15, 1937 | March 31, 1941 |
| Lloyd Spencer (D)[9] | April 1, 1941 | Jan. 2, 1943 |
| John L. McClellan (D)[10] | Jan. 3, 1943 | Nov. 28, 1977 |
| Kaneaster Hodges Jr. (D)[11] | Dec. 10, 1977 | Jan. 2, 1979 |
| David Pryor (D) | Jan. 3, 1979 | |

## Class 3

| | | |
|---|---|---|
| Ambrose H. Sevier (D)[12] | Sept. 18, 1836 | March 15, 1848 |
| Solon Borland (D)[13] | March 30, 1848 | April 3, 1853 |
| Robert W. Johnson (D)[14] | July 6, 1853 | March 3, 1861 |
| Charles B. Mitchel (D)[15] | March 4, 1861 | July 11, 1861 |
| Benjamin F. Rice (R) | June 23, 1868 | March 3, 1873 |
| Stephen W. Dorsey (R) | March 4, 1873 | March 3, 1879 |
| James D. Walker (D) | March 4, 1879 | March 3, 1885 |
| James K. Jones (D) | March 4, 1885 | March 3, 1903 |
| James P. Clarke (D)[16] | March 4, 1903 | Oct. 1, 1916 |
| William F. Kirby (D) | Nov. 8, 1916 | March 2, 1921 |
| Thaddeus H. Caraway (D)[17] | March 4, 1921 | Nov. 6, 1931 |
| Hattie W. Caraway (D)[18] | Nov. 13, 1931 | Jan. 2, 1945 |
| J. William Fulbright (D)[19] | Jan. 3, 1945 | Dec. 31, 1974 |
| Dale Bumpers (D) | Jan. 3, 1975 | |

**Arkansas**
1. *Died Aug. 15, 1844.*
2. *Died April 29, 1848.*
3. *Appointed by governor to fill vacancy. Subsequently elected. Expelled July 11, 1861. Seat remained vacant until June 23, 1868, because of Civil War.*
4. *Resigned March 6, 1885.*
5. *Died Jan. 3, 1913.*
6. *Appointed by governor to fill vacancy.*
7. *Died July 14, 1937.*
8. *Resigned March 31, 1941.*
9. *Appointed by governor to fill vacancy.*
10. *Died Nov. 28, 1977.*
11. *Appointed by governor to fill vacancy.*
12. *Resigned March 15, 1948.*
13. *Appointed by governor to fill vacancy. Subsequently elected. Resigned April 3, 1853.*

14. *Appointed by governor to fill vacancy. Subsequently elected.*
15. *Expelled July 11, 1861. Vacancy until June 23, 1868, because of Civil War.*
16. *Died Oct. 1, 1916.*
17. *Died Nov. 6, 1931.*
18. *Appointed by governor to fill vacancy. Subsequently elected.*
19. *Resigned Dec. 31, 1974.*

# CALIFORNIA

(Became a state Sept. 9, 1850)

## Class 1

| Senators | Dates of Service | |
|---|---|---|
| John C. Frémont (D) | Sept. 9, 1850 | March 3, 1851 |
| John B. Weller (D) | Jan. 30, 1852 | March 3, 1857 |
| David C. Broderick (D)[1] | March 4, 1857 | Sept. 16, 1859 |
| Henry P. Haun (D)[2] | Nov. 3, 1859 | March 4, 1860 |
| Milton S. Latham (D) | March 5, 1860 | March 3, 1863 |
| John Conness (UN R) | March 4, 1863 | March 3, 1869 |
| Eugene Casserly (D)[3] | March 4, 1869 | Nov. 29, 1873 |
| John S. Hager (A-MON D) | Dec. 23, 1873 | March 3, 1875 |
| Newton Booth (A-MONOPT) | March 4, 1875 | March 3, 1881 |
| John F. Miller (R)[4] | March 4, 1881 | March 8, 1886 |
| George Hearst (D)[5] | March 23, 1886 | Aug. 4, 1886 |
| Abram P. Williams (R) | Aug. 4, 1886 | March 3, 1887 |
| George Hearst (D)[6] | March 4, 1887 | Feb. 28, 1891 |
| Charles N. Felton (R) | March 19, 1891 | March 3, 1893 |
| Stephen M. White (D) | March 4, 1893 | March 3, 1899 |
| Thomas R. Bard (R) | Feb. 7, 1900 | March 3, 1905 |
| Frank P. Flint (R) | March 4, 1905 | March 3, 1911 |
| John D. Works (R) | March 4, 1911 | March 3, 1917 |
| Hiram W. Johnson (R)[7] | April 2, 1917 | Aug. 6, 1945 |
| William F. Knowland (R)[8] | Aug. 26, 1945 | Jan. 2, 1959 |
| Clair Engle (D)[9] | Jan. 3, 1959 | July 30, 1964 |
| Pierre Salinger (D)[10] | Aug. 4, 1964 | Dec. 31, 1964 |
| George Murphy (R)[11] | Jan. 1, 1965 | Jan. 2, 1971 |
| John V. Tunney (D)[12] | Jan. 2, 1971 | Jan. 1, 1977 |
| S. I. Hayakawa (R) | Jan. 2, 1977 | Jan. 2, 1983 |
| Pete Wilson (R)[13] | Jan. 3, 1983 | Jan. 7, 1991 |
| John Seymour (R)[14] | Jan. 10, 1991 | Nov. 3, 1992 |
| Dianne Feinstein (D) | Nov. 4, 1992 | |

## Class 3

| | | |
|---|---|---|
| William M. Gwin (D) | Sept. 9, 1850 | March 3, 1855 |
| William M. Gwin (D)[15] | Jan. 13, 1857 | March 3, 1861 |
| James A. McDougall (D) | March 4, 1861 | March 3, 1867 |
| Cornelius Cole (R) | March 4, 1867 | March 3, 1873 |
| Aaron A. Sargent (R) | March 4, 1873 | March 3, 1879 |
| James T. Farley (D) | March 4, 1879 | March 3, 1885 |
| Leland Stanford (R)[16] | March 4, 1885 | June 21, 1893 |
| George C. Perkins (R)[17] | July 26, 1893 | March 3, 1915 |
| James D. Phelan (D) | March 4, 1915 | March 3, 1921 |
| Samuel M. Shortridge (R) | March 4, 1921 | March 3, 1933 |
| William Gibbs McAdoo (D)[18] | March 4, 1933 | Nov. 8, 1938 |
| Thomas M. Storke (D)[19] | Nov. 9, 1938 | Jan. 2, 1939 |
| Sheridan Downey (D)[20] | Jan. 3, 1939 | Nov. 30, 1950 |
| Richard M. Nixon (R)[21] | Dec. 4, 1950 | Jan. 1, 1953 |
| Thomas H. Kuchel (R)[22] | Jan. 2, 1953 | Jan. 2, 1969 |
| Alan Cranston (D) | Jan. 3, 1969 | Jan. 2, 1993 |
| Barbara Boxer (D) | Jan. 3, 1993 | |

**California**
1. *Died Sept. 16, 1859.*
2. *Appointed by governor to fill vacancy.*
3. *Resigned Nov. 29, 1873.*
4. *Died March 8, 1886.*
5. *Appointed by governor to fill vacancy.*
6. *Died Feb. 28, 1891.*

7. Died Aug. 6, 1945.
8. Appointed by governor to fill vacancy. Subsequently elected.
9. Died July 30, 1964.
10. Appointed by governor to fill vacancy. Resigned Dec. 31, 1964.
11. Resigned Jan. 2, 1971.
12. Resigned Jan. 1, 1977.
13. Resigned Jan. 7, 1991, having been elected governor.
14. Appointed by governor to fill vacancy until special election in 1992. Resigned Nov. 3, 1992.
15. Vacancy from March 4, 1855, to Jan. 12, 1857, because of failure of legislature to elect.
16. Died June 21, 1893.
17. Appointed by governor to fill vacancy. Subsequently elected.
18. Resigned Nov. 8, 1938.
19. Appointed by governor to fill vacancy.
20. Resigned Nov. 30, 1950.
21. Resigned Jan. 1, 1953, having been elected U.S. vice president.
22. Appointed by governor to fill vacancy. Subsequently elected.

# COLORADO

(Became a state Aug. 1, 1876)

## Class 2

| Senators | Dates of Service | |
| --- | --- | --- |
| Henry M. Teller (R)[1] | Nov. 15, 1876 | April 17, 1882 |
| George M. Chilcott (R)[2] | April 17, 1882 | Jan. 27, 1883 |
| Horace A. W. Tabor (R) | Jan. 27, 1883 | March 3, 1883 |
| Thomas M. Bowen (R) | March 4, 1883 | March 3, 1889 |
| Edward O. Wolcott (R) | March 4, 1889 | March 3, 1901 |
| Thomas M. Patterson (D) | March 4, 1901 | March 3, 1907 |
| Simon Guggenheim (R) | March 4, 1907 | March 3, 1913 |
| John F. Shafroth (D) | March 4, 1913 | March 3, 1919 |
| Lawrence C. Phipps (R) | March 4, 1919 | March 3, 1931 |
| Edward P. Costigan (D) | March 4, 1931 | Jan. 2, 1937 |
| Edwin C. Johnson (D) | Jan. 3, 1937 | Jan. 2, 1955 |
| Gordon Allott (R) | Jan. 3, 1955 | Jan. 2, 1973 |
| Floyd K. Haskell (D) | Jan. 3, 1973 | Jan. 2, 1979 |
| William L. Armstrong (R) | Jan. 3, 1979 | Jan. 2, 1991 |
| Hank Brown (R) | Jan. 3, 1991 | |

## Class 3

| Senators | Dates of Service | |
| --- | --- | --- |
| Jerome B. Chaffee (R) | Nov. 15, 1876 | March 3, 1879 |
| Nathaniel P. Hill (R) | March 4, 1879 | March 3, 1885 |
| Henry M. Teller (R, I SIL R, D)[3] | March 4, 1885 | March 3, 1909 |
| Charles J. Hughes Jr. (D)[4] | March 4, 1909 | Jan. 11, 1911 |
| Charles S. Thomas (D) | Jan. 15, 1913 | March 3, 1921 |
| Samuel D. Nicholson (R)[5] | March 4, 1921 | March 24, 1923 |
| Alva B. Adams (D)[6] | May 17, 1923 | Nov. 30, 1924 |
| Rice W. Means (R) | Dec. 1, 1924 | March 3, 1927 |
| Charles W. Waterman (R)[7] | March 4, 1927 | Aug. 27, 1932 |
| Walter Walker (D)[8] | Sept. 26, 1932 | Dec. 6, 1932 |
| Karl C. Schuyler (R) | Dec. 7, 1932 | March 3, 1933 |
| Alva B. Adams (D)[9] | March 4, 1933 | Dec. 1, 1941 |
| Eugene D. Millikin (R)[10] | Dec. 20, 1941 | Jan. 2, 1957 |
| John A. Carroll (D) | Jan. 3, 1957 | Jan. 2, 1963 |
| Peter H. Dominick (R) | Jan. 3, 1963 | Jan. 2, 1975 |
| Gary Hart (D) | Jan. 3, 1975 | Jan. 2, 1987 |
| Timothy E. Wirth (D) | Jan. 3, 1987 | Jan. 2, 1993 |
| Ben Nighthorse Campbell (D) | Jan. 3, 1993 | |

**Colorado**
1. Resigned April 17, 1882.
2. Appointed by governor to fill vacancy.
3. Elected as a Republican in 1885 and 1891, an Independent Silver Republican in 1897 and a Democrat in 1903.
4. Died Jan. 11, 1911. Vacancy until Jan. 15, 1913, because of failure of legislature to elect.
5. Died March 24, 1923.
6. Appointed by governor to fill vacancy.

7. Died Aug. 27, 1932.
8. Appointed by governor to fill vacancy.
9. Died Dec. 1, 1941.
10. Appointed by governor to fill vacancy. Subsequently elected.

# CONNECTICUT

(Ratified the Constitution Jan. 9, 1788)

## Class 1

| Senators | Dates of Service | |
| --- | --- | --- |
| Oliver Ellsworth (FED)[1] | March 4, 1789 | March 8, 1796 |
| James Hillhouse (FED)[2] | May 12, 1796 | June 10, 1810 |
| Samuel W. Dana (FED) | May 10, 1810 | March 3, 1821 |
| Elijah Boardman (D-R)[3] | March 4, 1821 | Aug. 18, 1823 |
| Henry W. Edwards (D-R)[4] | Oct. 8, 1823 | March 3, 1827 |
| Samuel A. Foote (D-R) | March 4, 1827 | March 3, 1833 |
| Nathan Smith (W)[5] | March 4, 1833 | Dec. 6, 1835 |
| John M. Niles (D)[6] | Dec. 14, 1835 | March 3, 1839 |
| Thaddeus Betts (W)[7] | March 4, 1839 | April 7, 1840 |
| Jabez W. Huntington (W)[8] | May 4, 1840 | Nov. 2, 1847 |
| Roger S. Baldwin (W)[9] | Nov. 11, 1847 | March 3, 1851 |
| Isaac Toucey (D)[10] | May 12, 1852 | March 3, 1857 |
| James Dixon (R) | March 4, 1857 | March 3, 1869 |
| William A. Buckingham (R)[11] | March 4, 1869 | Feb. 5, 1875 |
| William W. Eaton (D)[12] | Feb. 5, 1875 | March 3, 1881 |
| Joseph R. Hawley (R) | March 4, 1881 | March 3, 1905 |
| Morgan G. Bulkeley (R) | March 4, 1905 | March 3, 1911 |
| George P. McLean (R) | March 4, 1911 | March 3, 1929 |
| Frederic C. Walcott (R) | March 4, 1929 | Jan. 2, 1935 |
| Francis Maloney (D)[13] | Jan. 3, 1935 | Jan. 16, 1945 |
| Thomas C. Hart (R)[14] | Feb. 15, 1945 | Nov. 5, 1946 |
| Raymond E. Baldwin (R)[15] | Dec. 27, 1946 | Dec. 17, 1949 |
| William Benton (D)[16] | Dec. 17, 1949 | Jan. 2, 1953 |
| William A. Purtell (R) | Jan. 3, 1953 | Jan. 2, 1959 |
| Thomas J. Dodd (D) | Jan. 3, 1959 | Jan. 2, 1971 |
| Lowell P. Weicker Jr. (R) | Jan. 3, 1971 | Jan. 2, 1989 |
| Joseph I. Lieberman (D) | Jan. 3, 1989 | |

## Class 3

| Senators | Dates of Service | |
| --- | --- | --- |
| William S. Johnson[17] | March 4, 1789 | March 4, 1791 |
| Roger Sherman[18] | June 13, 1791 | July 23, 1793 |
| Stephen M. Mitchell | Dec. 2, 1793 | March 3, 1795 |
| Jonathan Trumbull[19] | March 4, 1795 | June 10, 1796 |
| Uriah Tracy (FED)[20] | Oct. 13, 1796 | July 19, 1807 |
| Chauncey Goodrich (FED)[21] | Oct. 25, 1807 | May 1813 |
| David Daggett (FED) | May 13, 1813 | March 3, 1819 |
| James Lanman (D-R) | March 4, 1819 | March 3, 1825 |
| Calvin Willey (D-R) | May 4, 1825 | March 3, 1831 |
| Gideon Tomlinson (D) | March 4, 1831 | March 3, 1837 |
| Perry Smith (D) | March 4, 1837 | March 3, 1843 |
| John M. Niles (D) | March 4, 1843 | March 3, 1849 |
| Truman Smith (W)[22] | March 4, 1849 | May 24, 1854 |
| Francis Gillette (F SOIL W) | May 25, 1854 | March 3, 1855 |
| Lafayette S. Foster (R) | March 4, 1855 | March 3, 1867 |
| Orris S. Ferry (R)[23] | March 4, 1867 | Nov. 21, 1875 |
| James E. English (D)[24] | Nov. 27, 1875 | May 17, 1876 |
| William H. Barnum (D) | May 17, 1876 | March 3, 1879 |
| Orville H. Platt (R)[25] | March 4, 1879 | April 21, 1905 |
| Frank B. Brandegee (R)[26] | May 10, 1905 | Oct. 14, 1924 |
| Hiram Bingham (R) | Dec. 17, 1924 | March 3, 1933 |
| Augustine Lonergan (D) | March 4, 1933 | Jan. 2, 1939 |
| John A. Danaher (R) | Jan. 3, 1939 | Jan. 2, 1945 |
| Brien McMahon (D)[27] | Jan. 3, 1945 | July 28, 1952 |
| William A. Purtell (R)[28] | Aug. 29, 1952 | Nov. 4, 1952 |
| Prescott Bush (R) | Nov. 5, 1952 | Jan. 2, 1963 |
| Abraham Ribicoff (D) | Jan. 3, 1963 | Jan. 2, 1981 |
| Christopher J. Dodd (D) | Jan. 3, 1981 | |

**Connecticut**
1. *Resigned March 8, 1796.*
2. *Resigned June 10, 1810.*
3. *Died Aug. 18, 1823.*
4. *Appointed by governor to fill vacancy. Subsequently elected.*
5. *Died Dec. 6, 1835.*
6. *Appointed by governor to fill vacancy. Subsequently elected.*
7. *Died April 7, 1840.*
8. *Died Nov. 2, 1847.*
9. *Appointed by governor to fill vacancy. Subsequently elected.*
10. *Vacant from March 4, 1851, to May 11, 1852, because of failure of governor to appoint.*
11. *Died Feb. 5, 1875.*
12. *Appointed by governor to fill vacancy. Subsequently elected.*
13. *Died Jan. 16, 1945.*
14. *Appointed by governor to fill vacancy.*
15. *Resigned Dec. 17, 1949.*
16. *Appointed by governor to fill vacancy. Subsequently elected.*
17. *Resigned March 4, 1791.*
18. *Died July 23, 1793.*
19. *Resigned June 10, 1796.*
20. *Died July 19, 1807.*
21. *Resigned.*
22. *Resigned May 24, 1854.*
23. *Died Nov. 21, 1875.*
24. *Appointed by governor to fill vacancy.*
25. *Died April 21, 1905.*
26. *Died Oct. 14, 1924.*
27. *Died July 28, 1952.*
28. *Appointed by governor to fill vacancy.*

# DELAWARE

(Ratified the Constitution Dec. 7, 1787)

## Class 1

| Senators | Dates of Service | |
|---|---|---|
| George Read (FED)[1] | March 4, 1789 | Sept. 18, 1793 |
| Henry Latimer (FED)[2] | Feb. 7, 1795 | Feb. 28, 1801 |
| Samuel White (FED)[3] | Feb. 28, 1801 | Nov. 4, 1809 |
| Outerbridge Horsey (FED) | Jan. 12, 1810 | March 3, 1821 |
| Caesar A. Rodney (D-R)[4] | Jan. 10, 1822 | Jan. 29, 1823 |
| Thomas Clayton (FED) | Jan. 8, 1824 | March 3, 1827 |
| Louis McLane (D-R)[5] | March 4, 1827 | April 16, 1829 |
| Arnold Naudain (NR)[6] | Jan. 7, 1830 | June 16, 1836 |
| Richard H. Bayard (W)[7] | June 17, 1836 | Sept. 19, 1839 |
| Richard H. Bayard (W) | Jan. 12, 1841 | March 3, 1845 |
| John M. Clayton (W)[8] | March 4, 1845 | Feb. 23, 1849 |
| John Wales (W) | Feb. 23, 1849 | March 3, 1851 |
| James A. Bayard Jr. (W, D)[9] | March 4, 1851 | Jan. 29, 1864 |
| George Read Riddle (D)[10] | Jan. 29, 1864 | March 29, 1867 |
| James A. Bayard Jr. (D)[11] | April 5, 1867 | March 3, 1869 |
| Thomas F. Bayard Sr. (D)[12] | March 4, 1869 | March 6, 1885 |
| George Gray (D) | March 18, 1885 | March 3, 1899 |
| L. Heisler Ball (R)[13] | March 2, 1903 | March 3, 1905 |
| Henry A. du Pont (R)[14] | June 13, 1906 | March 3, 1917 |
| Josiah O. Wolcott (D)[15] | March 4, 1917 | July 2, 1921 |
| T. Coleman du Pont (R)[16] | July 7, 1921 | Nov. 6, 1922 |
| Thomas F. Bayard Jr. (D) | Nov. 7, 1922 | March 3, 1929 |
| John G. Townsend Jr. (R) | March 4, 1929 | Jan. 2, 1941 |
| James M. Tunnell (D) | Jan. 3, 1941 | Jan. 2, 1947 |
| John J. Williams (R)[17] | Jan. 3, 1947 | Dec. 31, 1970 |
| William V. Roth Jr. (R) | Jan. 1, 1971 | |

## Class 2

| | | |
|---|---|---|
| Richard Bassett (FED) | March 4, 1789 | March 3, 1793 |
| John Vining (FED)[18] | March 4, 1793 | Jan. 19, 1798 |
| Joshua Clayton (FED)[19] | Jan. 19, 1798 | Aug. 11, 1798 |
| William Hill Wells (FED)[20] | Jan. 17, 1799 | Nov. 6, 1804 |
| James A. Bayard Sr. (FED)[21] | Nov. 13, 1804 | March 3, 1813 |
| William Hill Wells (FED) | May 28, 1813 | March 3, 1817 |

| | | |
|---|---|---|
| Nicholas Van Dyke (FED)[22] | March 4, 1817 | May 21, 1826 |
| Daniel Rodney (FED)[23] | Nov. 8, 1826 | Jan. 12, 1827 |
| Henry M. Ridgeley | Jan. 12, 1827 | March 3, 1829 |
| John M. Clayton (NR, W)[24] | March 4, 1829 | Dec. 29, 1836 |
| Thomas Clayton (W) | Jan. 9, 1837 | March 3, 1847 |
| Presley Spruance (W) | March 4, 1847 | March 3, 1853 |
| John M. Clayton (W)[25] | March 4, 1853 | Nov. 9, 1856 |
| Joseph P. Comegys (W)[26] | Nov. 19, 1856 | Jan. 14, 1857 |
| Martin W. Bates (D) | Jan. 14, 1857 | March 3, 1859 |
| Willard Saulsbury Sr. (D) | March 4, 1859 | March 3, 1871 |
| Eli Saulsbury (D) | March 4, 1871 | March 3, 1889 |
| Anthony Higgins (R) | March 4, 1889 | March 3, 1895 |
| Richard R. Kenney (D)[27] | Jan. 19, 1897 | March 3, 1901 |
| James F. Allee (R)[28] | March 2, 1903 | March 3, 1907 |
| Harry A. Richardson (R) | March 4, 1907 | March 3, 1913 |
| Willard Saulsbury Jr. (D) | March 4, 1913 | March 3, 1919 |
| L. Heisler Ball (R) | March 4, 1919 | March 3, 1925 |
| T. Coleman du Pont (R)[29] | March 4, 1925 | Dec. 9, 1928 |
| Daniel O. Hastings (R)[30] | Dec. 10, 1928 | Jan. 2, 1937 |
| James H. Hughes (D) | Jan. 3, 1937 | Jan. 2, 1943 |
| C. Douglass Buck (R) | Jan. 3, 1943 | Jan. 2, 1949 |
| J. Allen Frear Jr. (D) | Jan. 3, 1949 | Jan. 2, 1961 |
| J. Caleb Boggs (R) | Jan. 3, 1961 | Jan. 2, 1973 |
| Joseph R. Biden Jr. (D) | Jan. 3, 1973 | |

**Delaware**
1. *Resigned Sept. 18, 1793.*
2. *Resigned Feb. 28, 1801.*
3. *Appointed by governor to fill vacancy. Subsequently elected. Died Nov. 4, 1809.*
4. *Resigned Jan. 29, 1823.*
5. *Resigned April 16, 1829.*
6. *Resigned June 16, 1836.*
7. *Resigned Sept. 19, 1839. Vacant until Jan. 12, 1841.*
8. *Resigned Feb. 23, 1849.*
9. *Resigned Jan. 29, 1864.*
10. *Died March 29, 1867.*
11. *Appointed by governor to fill vacancy. Subsequently elected.*
12. *Resigned March 6, 1885.*
13. *Vacant until March 2, 1903, because of failure of legislature to elect.*
14. *Vacant until June 13, 1906, because of failure of legislature to elect.*
15. *Resigned July 2, 1921.*
16. *Appointed by governor to fill vacancy.*
17. *Resigned Dec. 31, 1970.*
18. *Resigned Jan. 19, 1798.*
19. *Died Aug. 11, 1798.*
20. *Resigned Nov. 6, 1804.*
21. *Resigned March 3, 1813.*
22. *Died May 21, 1826.*
23. *Appointed by governor to fill vacancy.*
24. *Resigned Dec. 29, 1836.*
25. *Died Nov. 9, 1856.*
26. *Appointed by governor to fill vacancy.*
27. *Vacancy until Jan. 19, 1897, because of failure of legislature to elect.*
28. *Vacancy until March 2, 1903, because of failure of legislature to elect.*
29. *Resigned Dec. 9, 1928.*
30. *Appointed by governor to fill vacancy. Subsequently elected.*

# FLORIDA

(Became a state March 3, 1845)

## Class 1

| Senators | Dates of Service | |
|---|---|---|
| David Levy Yulee (D) | July 1, 1845 | March 3, 1851 |
| Stephen R. Mallory (D)[1] | March 4, 1851 | March 14, 1861 |
| Adonijah S. Welch (R) | July 2, 1868 | March 3, 1869 |
| Abijah Gilbert (R) | March 4, 1869 | March 3, 1875 |
| Charles W. Jones (D) | March 4, 1875 | March 3, 1887 |
| Samuel Pasco (D)[2] | May 19, 1887 | April 18, 1899 |
| James P. Taliaferro (D)[3] | April 19, 1899 | March 3, 1911 |
| Nathan P. Bryan (D)[4] | March 4, 1911 | March 3, 1917 |

| Park Trammell (D)[5] | March 4, 1917 | May 8, 1936 |
| Scott M. Loftin (D)[6] | May 26, 1936 | Nov. 3, 1936 |
| Charles O. Andrews (D)[7] | Nov. 4, 1936 | Sept. 18, 1946 |
| Spessard L. Holland (D)[8] | Sept. 25, 1946 | Jan. 2, 1971 |
| Lawton Chiles (D) | Jan. 3, 1971 | Jan. 2, 1989 |
| Connie Mack (R) | Jan. 3, 1989 | |

### Class 3

| James D. Westcott Jr. (D) | July 1, 1845 | March 3, 1849 |
| Jackson Morton (W) | March 4, 1849 | March 3, 1855 |
| David Levy Yulee (D)[9] | March 4, 1855 | Jan. 21, 1861 |
| Thomas W. Osborn (R) | June 30, 1868 | March 3, 1873 |
| Simon B. Conover (R) | March 4, 1873 | March 3, 1879 |
| Wilkinson Call (D) | March 4, 1879 | March 3, 1897 |
| Stephen R. Mallory (D)[10] | May 24, 1897 | Dec. 23, 1907 |
| William J. Bryan (D)[11] | Dec. 26, 1907 | March 22, 1908 |
| William H. Milton (D)[12] | March 27, 1908 | March 3, 1909 |
| Duncan U. Fletcher (D)[13] | March 4, 1909 | June 17, 1936 |
| William L. Hill (D)[14] | July 1, 1936 | Nov. 3, 1936 |
| Claude Pepper (D) | Nov. 4, 1936 | Jan. 2, 1951 |
| George A. Smathers (D) | Jan. 3, 1951 | Jan. 2, 1969 |
| Edward J. Gurney (R)[15] | Jan. 3, 1969 | Dec. 31, 1974 |
| Richard Stone (D)[16] | Jan. 2, 1975 | Dec. 31, 1980 |
| Paula Hawkins (R) | Jan. 1, 1981 | Jan. 2, 1987 |
| Bob Graham (D) | Jan. 3, 1987 | |

**Florida**

*1. Seat declared vacant March 14, 1861. Vacancy lasted until July 2, 1868, because of Civil War.*
*2. Pasco served continuously through this period, twice by appointment of the governor and twice by election.*
*3. Taliaferro served twice by election and once by appointment during his term of office.*
*4. Appointed by governor to fill vacancy. Subsequently elected.*
*5. Died May 8, 1936.*
*6. Appointed by governor to fill vacancy.*
*7. Died Sept. 18, 1946.*
*8. Appointed by governor to fill vacancy. Subsequently elected.*
*9. Retired from the Senate Jan. 21, 1861, because of Civil War. Seat remained vacant until June 30, 1868.*
*10. Mallory served twice by election and once by appointment during his term of office. Died Dec. 23, 1907.*
*11. Appointed by governor to fill vacancy. Died March 22, 1908.*
*12. Appointed by governor to fill vacancy.*
*13. Appointed by governor to fill vacancy. Subsequently elected. Died June 17, 1936.*
*14. Appointed by governor to fill vacancy.*
*15. Resigned Dec. 31, 1974.*
*16. Resigned Dec. 31, 1980.*

# GEORGIA

(Ratified the Constitution Jan. 2, 1788)

### Class 2

| Senators | Dates of Service | |
| --- | --- | --- |
| William Few (D-R) | March 4, 1789 | March 3, 1793 |
| James Jackson (D-R)[1] | March 4, 1793 | 1795 |
| George Walton[2] | Nov. 16, 1795 | Feb. 20, 1796 |
| Josiah Tatnall | Feb. 20, 1796 | March 3, 1799 |
| Abraham Baldwin (D-R)[3] | March 4, 1799 | March 4, 1807 |
| George Jones[4] | Aug. 27, 1807 | Nov. 7, 1807 |
| William H. Crawford (D-R)[5] | Nov. 7, 1807 | March 23, 1813 |
| William B. Bulloch (D-R)[6] | April 8, 1813 | Nov. 6, 1813 |
| William Wyatt Bibb (D-R)[7] | Nov. 6, 1813 | Nov. 9, 1816 |
| George M. Troup (D-R)[8] | Nov. 13, 1816 | Sept. 23, 1818 |
| John Forsyth (D-R)[9] | Nov. 23, 1818 | Feb. 17, 1819 |
| Freeman Walker (D-R)[10] | Nov. 6, 1819 | Aug. 8, 1821 |
| Nicholas Ware (D-R)[11] | Nov. 10, 1821 | Sept. 7, 1824 |
| Thomas W. Cobb (D-R)[12] | Nov. 4, 1824 | 1828 |

| Oliver H. Prince (D-R) | Nov. 7, 1828 | March 3, 1829 |
| George M. Troup (D-R)[13] | March 4, 1829 | March 2, 1833 |
| John Pendleton King (D)[14] | Nov. 21, 1833 | Nov. 1, 1837 |
| Wilson Lumpkin (D) | Nov. 22, 1837 | March 3, 1841 |
| John M. Berrien (W)[15] | March 4, 1841 | May 1845 |
| John M. Berrien (W) | Nov. 14, 1845 | March 3, 1847 |
| John M. Berrien (W)[16] | Nov. 13, 1847 | May 28, 1852 |
| Robert M. Charlton[17] | May 31, 1852 | March 3, 1853 |
| Robert Toombs (D)[18] | March 4, 1853 | March 14, 1861 |
| Homer V. M. Miller (D) | Feb. 24, 1871 | March 3, 1871 |
| Thomas M. Norwood (D) | Nov. 14, 1871 | March 3, 1877 |
| Benjamin H. Hill (D)[19] | March 4, 1877 | Aug. 16, 1882 |
| Pope Barrow (D) | Nov. 15, 1882 | March 3, 1883 |
| Alfred H. Colquitt (D)[20] | March 4, 1883 | March 26, 1894 |
| Patrick Walsh (D)[21] | April 2, 1894 | March 3, 1895 |
| Augustus O. Bacon (D)[22] | March 4, 1895 | Feb. 14, 1914 |
| William S. West (D)[23] | March 2, 1914 | Nov. 3, 1914 |
| Thomas W. Hardwick (D) | Nov. 4, 1914 | March 3, 1919 |
| William J. Harris (D)[24] | March 4, 1919 | April 18, 1932 |
| John S. Cohen (D)[25] | April 25, 1932 | Jan. 11, 1933 |
| Richard B. Russell (D)[26] | Jan. 12, 1933 | Jan. 21, 1971 |
| David H. Gambrell (D)[27] | Feb. 1, 1971 | Nov. 7, 1972 |
| Sam Nunn (D) | Nov. 8, 1972 | |

### Class 3

| James Gunn | March 4, 1789 | March 3, 1801 |
| James Jackson (D-R)[28] | March 4, 1801 | March 19, 1806 |
| John Milledge (D-R)[29] | June 19, 1806 | Nov. 14, 1809 |
| Charles Tait (D-R) | Nov. 27, 1809 | March 3, 1819 |
| John Elliott (D-R) | March 4, 1819 | March 3, 1825 |
| John M. Berrien (D-R)[30] | March 4, 1825 | March 9, 1829 |
| John Forsyth (D)[31] | Nov. 9, 1829 | June 27, 1834 |
| Alfred Cuthbert (D) | Jan. 12, 1835 | March 3, 1843 |
| Walter T. Colquitt (D)[32] | March 4, 1843 | February 1848 |
| Herschel V. Johnson (D)[33] | Feb. 4, 1848 | March 3, 1849 |
| William C. Dawson (W) | March 4, 1849 | March 3, 1855 |
| Alfred Iverson (D)[34] | March 4, 1855 | Jan. 28, 1861 |
| Joshua Hill (UN R) | Feb. 1, 1871 | March 3, 1873 |
| John B. Gordon (D)[35] | March 4, 1873 | May 26, 1880 |
| Joseph E. Brown (D)[36] | May 26, 1880 | March 3, 1891 |
| John B. Gordon (D) | March 4, 1891 | March 3, 1897 |
| Alexander S. Clay (D)[37] | March 4, 1897 | Nov. 13, 1910 |
| Joseph M. Terrell (D)[38] | Nov. 17, 1910 | July 14, 1911 |
| Hoke Smith (D) | Dec. 4, 1911 | March 3, 1921 |
| Thomas E. Watson (D)[39] | March 4, 1921 | Sept. 26, 1922 |
| Rebecca L. Felton (D)[40] | Oct. 3, 1922 | Nov. 21, 1922 |
| Walter F. George (D) | Nov. 22, 1922 | Jan. 2, 1957 |
| Herman E. Talmadge (D) | Jan. 3, 1957 | Jan. 2, 1981 |
| Mack Mattingly (R) | Jan. 3, 1981 | Jan. 2, 1987 |
| Wyche Fowler (D) | Jan. 3, 1987 | Jan. 2, 1993 |
| Paul Coverdell (R) | Jan. 3, 1993 | |

**Georgia**

*1. Resigned.*
*2. Appointed by governor to fill vacancy.*
*3. Died March 4, 1807.*
*4. Appointed by governor to fill vacancy.*
*5. Resigned March 23, 1813.*
*6. Appointed by governor to fill vacancy.*
*7. Resigned Nov. 9, 1816.*
*8. Resigned Sept. 23, 1818.*
*9. Resigned Feb. 17, 1819.*
*10. Resigned Aug. 8, 1821.*
*11. Died Sept. 7, 1824.*
*12. Resigned.*
*13. Resigned March 2, 1833.*
*14. Resigned Nov. 1, 1837.*
*15. Resigned in May 1845. Seat vacant until Nov. 14, 1845, because of failure of legislature to elect.*
*16. Vacant from March 4, 1847, to Nov. 13, 1847, because of failure of legislature to elect. Resigned May 28, 1952.*
*17. Appointed by governor to fill vacancy.*

**Georgia (continued)**

18. Seat declared vacant March 14, 1861. Remained vacant until Feb. 24, 1871, because of Civil War.
19. Died Aug. 16, 1882.
20. Died March 26, 1894.
21. Appointed by governor to fill vacancy. Subsequently elected.
22. Bacon was elected three times and appointed twice during his term of service. Died Feb. 14, 1914.
23. Appointed by governor to fill vacancy.
24. Died April 18, 1932.
25. Appointed by governor to fill vacancy.
26. Died Jan. 21, 1971.
27. Appointed by governor to fill vacancy.
28. Died March 19, 1806.
29. Resigned Nov. 14, 1809.
30. Resigned March 9, 1829.
31. Resigned June 27, 1834.
32. Resigned in February 1848.
33. Appointed by governor to fill vacancy.
34. Retired from Senate Jan. 28, 1861. Vacancy until Feb. 1, 1871, because of Civil War.
35. Resigned May 26, 1880.
36. Appointed by governor to fill vacancy. Subsequently elected.
37. Died Nov. 13, 1910.
38. Appointed by governor to fill vacancy. Resigned July 14, 1911.
39. Died Sept. 26, 1922.
40. Appointed by governor to fill vacancy.

# HAWAII

(Became a state Aug. 21, 1959)

### Class 1

| Senators | Dates of Service | |
|---|---|---|
| Hiram L. Fong (R) | Aug. 21, 1959 | Jan. 2, 1977 |
| Spark M. Matsunaga (D)[1] | Jan. 3, 1977 | April 15, 1990 |
| Daniel K. Akaka (D)[2] | May 16, 1990 | |

### Class 3

| | | |
|---|---|---|
| Oren E. Long (D) | Aug. 21, 1959 | Jan. 2, 1963 |
| Daniel K. Inouye (D) | Jan. 3, 1963 | |

**Hawaii**

1. Died April 15, 1990.
2. Appointed by governor to fill vacancy. Subsequently elected.

# IDAHO

(Became a state July 3, 1890)

### Class 2

| Senators | Dates of Service | |
|---|---|---|
| George L. Shoup (R) | Dec. 18, 1890 | March 3, 1901 |
| Fred T. Dubois (D) | March 4, 1901 | March 3, 1907 |
| William E. Borah (R)[1] | March 4, 1907 | Jan. 19, 1940 |
| John Thomas (R)[2] | Jan. 27, 1940 | Nov. 10, 1945 |
| Charles C. Gossett (D)[3] | Nov. 17, 1945 | Nov. 5, 1946 |
| Henry C. Dworshak (R) | Nov. 6, 1946 | Jan. 2, 1949 |
| Bert H. Miller (D)[4] | Jan. 3, 1949 | Oct. 8, 1949 |
| Henry C. Dworshak (R)[5] | Oct. 14, 1949 | July 23, 1962 |
| Len B. Jordan (R)[6] | Aug. 6, 1962 | Jan. 2, 1973 |
| James A. McClure (R) | Jan. 3, 1973 | Jan. 2, 1991 |
| Larry Craig (R) | Jan. 3, 1991 | |

### Class 3

| | | |
|---|---|---|
| William J. McConnell (R) | Dec. 18, 1890 | March 3, 1891 |
| Fred T. Dubois (R) | March 4, 1891 | March 3, 1897 |

| | | |
|---|---|---|
| Henry Heitfeld (POP) | March 4, 1897 | March 3, 1903 |
| Weldon B. Heyburn (R)[7] | March 4, 1903 | Oct. 17, 1912 |
| Kirtland I. Perky (D)[8] | Nov. 18, 1912 | Feb. 5, 1913 |
| James H. Brady (R)[9] | Feb. 6, 1913 | Jan. 13, 1918 |
| John F. Nugent (D)[10] | Jan. 22, 1918 | Jan. 14, 1921 |
| Frank R. Gooding (R)[11] | Jan. 15, 1921 | June 24, 1928 |
| John Thomas (R)[12] | June 30, 1928 | March 3, 1933 |
| James P. Pope (D) | March 4, 1933 | Jan. 2, 1939 |
| D. Worth Clark (D) | Jan. 3, 1939 | Jan. 2, 1945 |
| Glen H. Taylor (D) | Jan. 3, 1945 | Jan. 2, 1951 |
| Herman Welker (R) | Jan. 3, 1951 | Jan. 2, 1957 |
| Frank Church (D) | Jan. 3, 1957 | Jan. 2, 1981 |
| Steven D. Symms (R) | Jan. 3, 1981 | Jan. 2, 1993 |
| Dirk Kempthorne (R) | Jan. 3, 1993 | |

**Idaho**

1. Died Jan. 19, 1940.
2. Appointed by governor to fill vacancy. Subsequently elected. Died Nov. 10, 1945.
3. Appointed by governor to fill vacancy.
4. Died Oct. 8, 1949.
5. Appointed by governor to fill vacancy. Subsequently elected. Died July 23, 1962.
6. Appointed by governor to fill vacancy. Subsequently elected.
7. Died Oct. 17, 1912.
8. Appointed by governor to fill vacancy.
9. Died Jan. 13, 1918.
10. Appointed by governor to fill vacancy. Subsequently elected. Resigned Jan. 14, 1921.
11. Appointed by governor to fill vacancy. Subsequently elected. Died June 24, 1928.
12. Appointed by governor to fill vacancy. Subsequently elected.

# ILLINOIS

(Became a state Dec. 3, 1818)

### Class 2

| Senators | Dates of Service | |
|---|---|---|
| Jesse B. Thomas (D-R) | Dec. 3, 1818 | March 3, 1829 |
| John McLean (D)[1] | March 4, 1829 | Oct. 14, 1830 |
| David J. Baker (D)[2] | Nov. 12, 1830 | Dec. 11, 1830 |
| John M. Robinson (D) | Dec. 11, 1830 | March 3, 1841 |
| Samuel McRoberts (D)[3] | March 4, 1841 | March 27, 1843 |
| James Semple (D)[4] | Aug. 16, 1843 | March 3, 1847 |
| Stephen A. Douglas (D)[5] | March 4, 1847 | June 3, 1861 |
| Orville H. Browning (R)[6] | June 26, 1861 | Jan. 12, 1863 |
| William A. Richardson (D) | Jan. 12, 1863 | March 3, 1865 |
| Richard Yates (R) | March 4, 1865 | March 3, 1871 |
| John A. Logan (R) | March 4, 1871 | March 3, 1877 |
| David Davis (I) | March 4, 1877 | March 3, 1883 |
| Shelby M. Cullom (R) | March 4, 1883 | March 3, 1913 |
| James Hamilton Lewis (D) | March 26, 1913 | March 3, 1919 |
| Medill McCormick (R)[7] | March 4, 1919 | Feb. 25, 1925 |
| Charles S. Deneen (R)[8] | Feb. 26, 1925 | March 3, 1931 |
| James Hamilton Lewis (D)[9] | March 4, 1931 | April 9, 1939 |
| James M. Slattery (D)[10] | April 14, 1939 | Nov. 21, 1940 |
| C. Wayland Brooks (R) | Nov. 22, 1940 | Jan. 2, 1949 |
| Paul H. Douglas (D) | Jan. 3, 1949 | Jan. 2, 1967 |
| Charles H. Percy (R) | Jan. 3, 1967 | Jan. 2, 1985 |
| Paul Simon (D) | Jan. 3, 1985 | |

### Class 3

| | | |
|---|---|---|
| Ninian Edwards (D-R)[11] | Dec. 3, 1818 | March 4, 1824 |
| John McLean (D-R) | Nov. 23, 1824 | March 3, 1825 |
| Elias K. Kane (D)[12] | March 4, 1825 | Dec. 11, 1835 |
| William Lee D. Ewing (D) | Dec. 30, 1835 | March 3, 1837 |
| Richard M. Young (D) | March 4, 1837 | March 3, 1843 |
| Sidney Breese (D) | March 4, 1843 | March 3, 1849 |

| James Shields (D) | March 4, 1849 | March 15, 1849 |
| James Shields (D)[13] | Dec. 3, 1849 | March 3, 1855 |
| Lyman Trumbull (R) | March 4, 1855 | March 3, 1873 |
| Richard J. Oglesby (R) | March 4, 1873 | March 3, 1879 |
| John A. Logan (R)[14] | March 4, 1879 | Dec. 26, 1886 |
| Charles B. Farwell (R) | Jan. 19, 1887 | March 3, 1891 |
| John McAuley Palmer (D) | March 4, 1891 | March 3, 1897 |
| William E. Mason (R) | March 4, 1897 | March 3, 1903 |
| Albert J. Hopkins (R) | March 4, 1903 | March 3, 1909 |
| William Lorimer (R)[15] | June 18, 1909 | July 13, 1912 |
| Lawrence Y. Sherman (R) | March 26, 1913 | March 3, 1921 |
| William B. McKinley (R)[16] | March 4, 1921 | Dec. 7, 1926 |
| Frank L. Smith (R)[17] | | |
| Otis F. Glenn (R) | Dec. 3, 1928 | March 3, 1933 |
| William H. Dietrich (D) | March 4, 1933 | Jan. 2, 1939 |
| Scott W. Lucas (D) | Jan. 3, 1939 | Jan. 2, 1951 |
| Everett McKinley Dirksen (R)[18] | Jan. 3, 1951 | Sept. 7, 1969 |
| Ralph Tyler Smith (R)[19] | Sept. 17, 1969 | Nov. 16, 1970 |
| Adlai E. Stevenson III (D) | Nov. 17, 1970 | Jan. 2, 1981 |
| Alan J. Dixon (D) | Jan. 3, 1981 | Jan. 2, 1993 |
| Carol Moseley Braun (D) | Jan. 3, 1993 | |

**Illinois**

1. *Died Oct. 14, 1830.*
2. *Appointed by governor to fill vacancy.*
3. *Died March 27, 1843.*
4. *Appointed by governor to fill vacancy. Subsequently elected.*
5. *Died June 3, 1861.*
6. *Appointed by governor to fill vacancy.*
7. *Died Feb. 25, 1925.*
8. *Appointed by governor to fill vacancy. Subsequently elected.*
9. *Died April 9, 1939.*
10. *Appointed by governor to fill vacancy.*
11. *Resigned March 4, 1824.*
12. *Died Dec. 11, 1835.*
13. *Shields was seated but his election was declared void by the Senate March 15, 1849, because he had not been a citizen of the United States for the requisite number of years prior to his election. Subsequently elected to fill the vacancy and, having in the interim met the constitutional requirement, took his seat Dec. 3, 1849.*
14. *Died Dec. 26, 1886.*
15. *Lorimer was accused of bribery and other corrupt practices in securing his election to the Senate. After lengthy investigation, the Senate voted on July 13, 1912, to declare his election invalid.*
16. *Died Dec. 7, 1926.*
17. *Smith was appointed by the governor Dec. 6, 1926, to fill the remaining three months of McKinley's term. He had previously been elected for a full six-year term. He was not permitted to take the oath for either term. The Committee on Privileges and Elections recommended on Jan. 17, 1928, that Smith not be allowed to take his seat because of fraud and corruption during the campaign. The Senate adopted this resolution Jan. 19, 1928, and the seat was declared vacant. According to the Biographical Directory, Smith "resigned Feb. 9, 1928," but since the seat was already vacant, this action was apparently meaningless.*
18. *Died Sept. 7, 1969.*
19. *Appointed by governor to fill vacancy.*

# INDIANA

(Became a state Dec. 11, 1816)

## Class 1

| Senators | Dates of Service | |
| --- | --- | --- |
| James Noble (D-R)[1] | Dec. 11, 1816 | Feb. 26, 1831 |
| Robert Hanna (W)[2] | Aug. 19, 1831 | Jan. 3, 1832 |
| John Tipton (D) | Jan. 4, 1832 | March 3, 1839 |
| Albert S. White (W) | March 4, 1839 | March 3, 1845 |
| Jesse D. Bright (D)[3] | March 4, 1845 | Feb. 5, 1862 |
| Joseph A. Wright (D)[4] | Feb. 24, 1862 | Jan. 14, 1863 |
| David Turpie (D) | Jan. 14, 1863 | March 3, 1863 |
| Thomas A. Hendricks (D) | March 4, 1863 | March 3, 1869 |
| Daniel D. Pratt (R) | March 4, 1869 | March 3, 1875 |

| Joseph E. McDonald (D) | March 4, 1875 | March 3, 1881 |
| Benjamin Harrison (R) | March 4, 1881 | March 3, 1887 |
| David Turpie (D) | March 4, 1887 | March 3, 1899 |
| Albert J. Beveridge (R) | March 4, 1899 | March 3, 1911 |
| John W. Kern (D) | March 4, 1911 | March 3, 1917 |
| Harry S. New (R) | March 4, 1917 | March 3, 1923 |
| Samuel M. Ralston (D)[5] | March 4, 1923 | Oct. 14, 1925 |
| Arthur R. Robinson (R)[6] | Oct. 20, 1925 | Jan. 2, 1935 |
| Sherman Minton (D) | Jan. 3, 1935 | Jan. 2, 1941 |
| Raymond E. Willis (R) | Jan. 3, 1941 | Jan. 2, 1947 |
| William E. Jenner (R) | Jan. 3, 1947 | Jan. 2, 1959 |
| Vance Hartke (D) | Jan. 3, 1959 | Jan. 2, 1977 |
| Richard G. Lugar (R) | Jan. 3, 1977 | |

## Class 3

| Waller Taylor (D-R) | Dec. 11, 1816 | March 3, 1825 |
| William Hendricks (D) | March 4, 1825 | March 3, 1837 |
| Oliver H. Smith (W) | March 4, 1837 | March 3, 1843 |
| Edward A. Hannegan (D) | March 4, 1843 | March 3, 1849 |
| James Whitcomb (D)[7] | March 4, 1849 | Oct. 4, 1852 |
| Charles W. Cathcart (D)[8] | Nov. 23, 1852 | Jan. 11, 1853 |
| John Petit (D) | Jan. 11, 1853 | March 3, 1855 |
| Graham N. Fitch (D)[9] | Feb. 4, 1857 | March 3, 1861 |
| Henry S. Lane (R) | March 4, 1861 | March 3, 1867 |
| Oliver H. P. T. Morton (R)[10] | March 4, 1867 | Nov. 1, 1877 |
| Daniel W. Voorhees (D)[11] | Nov. 6, 1877 | March 3, 1897 |
| Charles W. Fairbanks (R)[12] | March 4, 1897 | March 3, 1905 |
| James A. Hemenway (R) | March 4, 1905 | March 3, 1909 |
| Benjamin F. Shively (D)[13] | March 4, 1909 | March 14, 1916 |
| Thomas Taggart (D)[14] | March 20, 1916 | Nov. 7, 1916 |
| James E. Watson (D) | Nov. 8, 1916 | March 3, 1933 |
| Frederick Van Nuys (D)[15] | March 4, 1933 | Jan. 25, 1944 |
| Samuel D. Jackson (D)[16] | Jan. 28, 1944 | Nov. 13, 1944 |
| William E. Jenner (R) | Nov. 14, 1944 | Jan. 2, 1945 |
| Homer E. Capehart (R) | Jan. 3, 1945 | Jan. 2, 1963 |
| Birch Bayh (D) | Jan. 3, 1963 | Jan. 2, 1981 |
| Dan Quayle (R)[17] | Jan. 3, 1981 | Jan. 2, 1989 |
| Daniel R. Coats (R)[18] | Jan. 3, 1989 | |

**Indiana**

1. *Died Feb. 26, 1831.*
2. *Appointed by governor to fill vacancy.*
3. *Expelled Feb. 5, 1862, for writing a letter to Jefferson Davis addressing him as "President of the Confederate States." (Biographical Directory, p. 637).*
4. *Appointed by governor to fill vacancy.*
5. *Died Oct. 14, 1925.*
6. *Appointed by governor to fill vacancy. Subsequently elected.*
7. *Died Oct. 4, 1852.*
8. *Appointed by governor to fill vacancy.*
9. *Vacancy from March 4, 1855, to Feb. 4, 1857.*
10. *Died Nov. 1, 1877.*
11. *Appointed by governor to fill vacancy. Subsequently elected.*
12. *Resigned March 3, 1905.*
13. *Died March 14, 1916.*
14. *Appointed by governor to fill vacancy.*
15. *Died Jan. 25, 1944.*
16. *Appointed by governor to fill vacancy.*
17. *Resigned Jan. 3, 1989, having been elected vice president of the United States.*
18. *Appointed by governor to fill vacancy. Subsequently elected.*

# IOWA

(Became a state Dec. 28, 1846)

## Class 2

| Senators | Dates of Service | |
| --- | --- | --- |
| George W. Jones (D) | Dec. 7, 1848 | March 3, 1859 |
| James W. Grimes (R)[1] | March 4, 1859 | Dec. 6, 1869 |

| | | |
|---|---|---|
| James B. Howell (R) | Jan. 18, 1870 | March 3, 1871 |
| George G. Wright (R) | March 4, 1871 | March 3, 1877 |
| Samuel J. Kirkwood (R)[2] | March 4, 1877 | March 7, 1881 |
| James W. McDill (R)[3] | March 8, 1881 | March 3, 1883 |
| James F. Wilson (R) | March 4, 1883 | March 3, 1895 |
| John H. Gear (R)[4] | March 4, 1895 | July 14, 1900 |
| Jonathan P. Dolliver (R)[5] | Aug. 22, 1900 | Oct. 15, 1910 |
| Lafayette Young (R)[6] | Nov. 12, 1910 | April 11, 1911 |
| William S. Kenyon (R)[7] | April 12, 1911 | Feb. 24, 1922 |
| Charles A. Rawson (R)[8] | Feb. 24, 1922 | Dec. 1, 1922 |
| Smith W. Brookhart (R)[9] | Dec. 2, 1922 | April 12, 1926 |
| Daniel F. Steck (D)[10] | April 12,1926 | March 3, 1931 |
| L. J. Dickinson (R) | March 4, 1931 | Jan. 2, 1937 |
| Clyde L. Herring (D) | Jan. 19, 1937 | Jan. 2, 1943 |
| George A. Wilson (R) | Jan. 14, 1943 | Jan. 2, 1949 |
| Guy M. Gillette (D) | Jan. 3, 1949 | Jan. 2, 1955 |
| Thomas E. Martin (R) | Jan. 3, 1955 | Jan. 2, 1961 |
| Jack Miller (R) | Jan. 3, 1961 | Jan. 2, 1973 |
| Dick Clark (D) | Jan. 3, 1973 | Jan. 2, 1979 |
| Roger W. Jepsen (R) | Jan. 3, 1979 | Jan. 2, 1985 |
| Tom Harkin (D) | Jan. 3, 1985 | |

### Class 3

| | | |
|---|---|---|
| Augustus C. Dodge (D)[11] | Dec. 7, 1848 | Feb. 22, 1855 |
| James Harlan (R)[12] | March 4, 1855 | Jan. 12, 1857 |
| James Harlan (R)[13] | Jan. 29, 1857 | May 15, 1865 |
| Samuel J. Kirkwood (R) | Jan. 13, 1866 | March 3, 1867 |
| James Harlan (R) | March 4, 1867 | March 3, 1873 |
| William B. Allison (R)[14] | March 4, 1873 | Aug. 4, 1908 |
| Albert B. Cummins (R)[15] | Nov. 24, 1908 | July 30, 1926 |
| David W. Stewart (R)[16] | Aug. 7, 1926 | March 3, 1927 |
| Smith W. Brookhart (R) | March 4, 1927 | March 3, 1933 |
| Richard Louis Murphy (D)[17] | March 4, 1933 | July 16, 1936 |
| Guy M. Gillette (D) | Nov. 4, 1936 | Jan. 2, 1945 |
| Bourke B. Hickenlooper (R) | Jan. 3, 1945 | Jan. 2, 1969 |
| Harold E. Hughes (D) | Jan. 3, 1969 | Jan. 2, 1975 |
| John C. Culver (D) | Jan. 3, 1975 | Jan. 2, 1981 |
| Charles E. Grassley (R) | Jan. 3, 1981 | |

**Iowa**
*1. Resigned Dec. 6, 1869.*
*2. Resigned March 7, 1881.*
*3. Appointed by governor to fill vacancy. Subsequently elected.*
*4. Died July 14, 1900.*
*5. Appointed by governor to fill vacancy. Subsequently elected. Died Oct. 15, 1910.*
*6. Appointed by governor to fill vacancy.*
*7. Resigned Feb. 24, 1922.*
*8. Appointed by governor to fill vacancy.*
*9. Elected to fill vacancy in term expiring March 3, 1925. Presented credentials for term expiring March 3, 1931, and was seated. Steck challenged Brookhart's right to the seat, alleging that ballots cast for Steck had either been rejected or counted for Brookhart, and that illegal votes had been cast for Brookhart. The Senate voted to unseat Brookhart and award the seat to Steck, who took the oath April 12, 1926, and served for the remainder of the term.*
*10. Successfully contested the election of Smith W. Brookhart.*
*11. Resigned Feb. 22, 1855.*
*12. Harlan was elected by the legislature for the term beginning March 4, 1855, and took his seat. The Senate voted Jan. 12, 1857, to deny him a seat, following protests that the legislature that elected him had not been properly constituted.*
*13. Elected to fill the vacancy caused by the Senate's having declared the seat vacant, and took his seat Jan. 29, 1857. Resigned May 15, 1865.*
*14. Died Aug. 4, 1908.*
*15. Died July 30, 1926.*
*16. Appointed by governor to fill vacancy. Subsequently elected.*
*17. Died July 16, 1936.*

# KANSAS

(Became a state Jan. 29, 1861)

### Class 2

| Senators | Dates of Service | |
|---|---|---|
| James H. Lane (R)[1] | April 4, 1861 | July 11, 1866 |
| Edmund G. Ross (R)[2] | July 19, 1866 | March 3, 1871 |
| Alexander Caldwell (R)[3] | March 4, 1871 | March 24, 1873 |
| Robert Crozier (R)[4] | Nov. 24, 1873 | Feb. 2, 1874 |
| James M. Harvey (R) | Feb. 2, 1874 | March 3, 1877 |
| Preston B. Plumb (R)[5] | March 4, 1877 | Dec. 20, 1891 |
| Bishop W. Perkins (R)[6] | Jan. 1, 1892 | March 3, 1893 |
| John Martin (D) | March 4, 1893 | March 3, 1895 |
| Lucien Baker (R) | March 4, 1895 | March 3, 1901 |
| Joseph R. Burton (R)[7] | March 4, 1901 | June 4, 1906 |
| Alfred W. Benson (R)[8] | June 11, 1906 | Jan. 23, 1907 |
| Charles Curtis (R) | Jan. 23, 1907 | March 3, 1913 |
| William H. Thompson (D) | March 4, 1913 | March 3, 1919 |
| Arthur Capper (R) | March 4, 1919 | Jan. 2, 1949 |
| Andrew F. Schoeppel (R)[9] | Jan. 3, 1949 | Jan. 21, 1962 |
| James B. Pearson (R)[10] | Jan. 31, 1962 | Dec. 23, 1978 |
| Nancy Landon Kassebaum (R) | Dec. 23, 1978 | |

### Class 3

| | | |
|---|---|---|
| Samuel C. Pomeroy (R) | April 4, 1861 | March 3, 1873 |
| John J. Ingalls (R) | March 4, 1873 | March 3, 1891 |
| William A. Peffer (POP) | March 4, 1891 | March 3, 1897 |
| William A. Harris (D) | March 4, 1897 | March 3, 1903 |
| Chester I. Long (R) | March 4, 1903 | March 3, 1909 |
| Joseph L. Bristow (R) | March 4, 1909 | March 3, 1915 |
| Charles Curtis (R)[11] | March 4, 1915 | March 3, 1929 |
| Henry J. Allen (R)[12] | April 1, 1929 | Nov. 30, 1930 |
| George McGill (D) | Dec. 1, 1930 | Jan. 2, 1939 |
| Clyde M. Reed (R)[13] | Jan. 3, 1939 | Nov. 8, 1949 |
| Harry Darby (R)[14] | Dec. 2, 1949 | Nov. 28, 1950 |
| Frank Carlson (R) | Nov. 29, 1950 | Jan. 2, 1969 |
| Robert Dole (R) | Jan. 3, 1969 | |

**Kansas**
*1. Died July 11, 1866.*
*2. Appointed by governor to fill vacancy. Subsequently elected.*
*3. Resigned March 24, 1873.*
*4. Appointed by governor to fill vacancy.*
*5. Died Dec. 20, 1891.*
*6. Appointed by governor to fill vacancy.*
*7. Resigned June 4, 1906.*
*8. Appointed by governor to fill vacancy.*
*9. Died Jan. 21, 1962.*
*10. Appointed by governor to fill vacancy. Subsequently elected. Resigned Dec. 23, 1978.*
*11. Resigned March 3, 1929.*
*12. Appointed by governor to fill vacancy.*
*13. Died Nov. 8, 1949.*
*14. Appointed by governor to fill vacancy.*

# KENTUCKY

(Became a state June 1, 1792)

### Class 2

| Senators | Dates of Service | |
|---|---|---|
| John Brown (D-R) | June 18, 1792 | March 3, 1805 |
| Buckner Thruston (D-R)[1] | March 4, 1805 | Dec. 18, 1809 |
| Henry Clay (D-R) | Jan. 4, 1810 | March 3, 1811 |
| George M. Bibb (D-R)[2] | March 4, 1811 | Aug. 23, 1814 |
| George Walker (D-R)[3] | Aug. 30, 1814 | Dec. 16, 1814 |

| | | |
|---|---|---|
| William T. Barry (D-R)[4] | Dec. 16, 1814 | May 1, 1816 |
| Martin D. Hardin (D-R)[5] | Nov. 13, 1816 | March 3, 1817 |
| John J. Crittenden (D-R)[6] | March 4, 1817 | March 3, 1819 |
| Richard M. Johnson (D-R) | Dec. 10, 1819 | March 3, 1829 |
| George M. Bibb (D-R) | March 4, 1829 | March 3, 1835 |
| John J. Crittenden (W) | March 4, 1835 | March 3, 1841 |
| James T. Morehead (W) | March 4, 1841 | March 3, 1847 |
| Joseph R. Underwood (W) | March 4, 1847 | March 3, 1853 |
| John B. Thompson (W) | March 4, 1853 | March 3, 1859 |
| Lazarus W. Powell (D) | March 4, 1859 | March 3, 1865 |
| James Guthrie (D)[7] | March 4, 1865 | Feb. 7, 1868 |
| Thomas C. McCreery (D) | Feb. 19, 1868 | March 3, 1871 |
| John W. Stevenson (D) | March 4, 1871 | March 3, 1877 |
| James D. Bock (D)[8] | March 4, 1877 | May 3, 1890 |
| John G. Carlisle (D)[9] | May 17, 1890 | Feb. 4, 1893 |
| William Lindsay (D) | Feb. 15, 1893 | March 3, 1901 |
| Joseph C. S. Blackburn (D) | March 4, 1901 | March 3, 1907 |
| Thomas H. Paynter (D) | March 4, 1907 | March 3, 1913 |
| Ollie M. James (D)[10] | March 4, 1913 | Aug. 28, 1918 |
| George B. Martin (D)[11] | Sept. 7, 1918 | March 3, 1919 |
| A. Owsley Stanley (D) | March 4, 1919 | March 3, 1925 |
| Fred M. Sackett (R)[12] | March 4, 1925 | Jan. 9, 1930 |
| John M. Robsion (R)[13] | Jan. 9, 1930 | Nov. 30, 1930 |
| Ben M. Williamson (D) | Dec. 1, 1930 | March 3, 1931 |
| Marvel M. Logan (D)[14] | March 4, 1931 | Oct. 3, 1939 |
| Albert B. Chandler (D)[15] | Oct. 10, 1939 | Nov. 1, 1945 |
| William A. Stanfill (R)[16] | Nov. 19, 1945 | Nov. 5, 1946 |
| John Sherman Cooper (R) | Nov. 6, 1946 | Jan. 2, 1949 |
| Virgil Chapman (D)[17] | Jan. 3, 1949 | March 8, 1951 |
| Thomas R. Underwood (D)[18] | March 19, 1951 | Nov. 4, 1952 |
| John Sherman Cooper (R) | Nov. 5, 1952 | Jan. 2, 1955 |
| Alben W. Barkley (D)[19] | Jan. 3, 1955 | April 30, 1956 |
| Robert Humphreys (D)[20] | June 21, 1956 | Nov. 6, 1956 |
| John Sherman Cooper (R) | Nov. 7, 1956 | Jan. 2, 1973 |
| Walter D. Huddleston (D) | Jan. 3, 1973 | Jan. 2, 1985 |
| Mitchell McConnell (R) | Jan. 3, 1985 | |

## Class 3

| | | |
|---|---|---|
| John Edwards (D-R) | June 18, 1792 | March 3, 1795 |
| Humphrey Marshall (FED) | March 4, 1795 | March 3, 1801 |
| John Breckinridge (D-R)[21] | March 4, 1801 | Aug. 7, 1805 |
| John Adair (D-R)[22] | Nov. 8, 1805 | Nov. 18, 1806 |
| Henry Clay (D-R) | Dec. 29, 1806 | March 3, 1807 |
| John Pope (D-R) | March 4, 1807 | March 3, 1813 |
| Jesse Bledsoe (D-R)[23] | March 4, 1813 | Dec. 24, 1814 |
| Isham Talbot (D-R) | Jan. 5, 1815 | March 3, 1819 |
| William Logan (D-R)[24] | March 4, 1819 | May 28, 1820 |
| Isham Talbot (D-R) | Oct. 19, 1820 | March 3, 1825 |
| John Rowan (D-R) | March 4, 1825 | March 3, 1831 |
| Henry Clay (NR, W)[25] | Nov. 10, 1831 | March 31, 1842 |
| John J. Crittenden (W)[26] | March 31, 1842 | June 12, 1848 |
| Thomas Metcalfe[27] | June 23, 1848 | March 3, 1849 |
| Henry Clay (W)[28] | March 4, 1849 | June 29, 1852 |
| David Meriwether (D)[29] | July 6, 1852 | Sept. 1, 1852 |
| Archibald Dixon (W) | Sept. 1, 1852 | March 3, 1855 |
| John J. Crittenden (W) | March 4, 1855 | March 3, 1861 |
| John C. Breckinridge (D)[30] | March 4, 1861 | Dec. 4, 1861 |
| Garrett Davis (D)[31] | Dec. 10, 1861 | Sept. 22, 1872 |
| Willis B. Machen (D)[32] | Sept. 27, 1872 | March 3, 1873 |
| Thomas C. McCreery (D) | March 4, 1873 | March 3, 1879 |
| John Stuart Williams (D) | March 4, 1879 | March 3, 1885 |
| Joseph C. S. Blackburn (D) | March 4, 1885 | March 3, 1897 |
| William J. Deboe (R) | March 4, 1897 | March 3, 1903 |
| James B. McCreary (D) | March 4, 1903 | March 3, 1909 |
| William O. Bradley (R)[33] | March 4, 1909 | May 23, 1914 |
| Johnson N. Camden Jr. (D)[34] | June 16, 1914 | March 3, 1915 |
| John C. W. Beckham (D) | March 4, 1915 | March 3, 1921 |
| Richard P. Ernst (R) | March 4, 1921 | March 3, 1927 |
| Alben W. Barkley (D)[35] | March 4, 1927 | Jan. 19, 1949 |
| Garrett L. Withers (D)[36] | Jan. 20, 1949 | Nov. 26, 1950 |
| Earle C. Clements (D) | Nov. 27, 1950 | Jan. 2, 1957 |

| | | |
|---|---|---|
| Thruston B. Morton (R)[37] | Jan. 3, 1957 | Dec. 16, 1968 |
| Marlow W. Cook (R)[38] | Dec. 17, 1968 | Dec. 27, 1974 |
| Wendell H. Ford (D) | Dec. 28, 1974 | |

**Kentucky**
1. Resigned Dec. 18, 1809.
2. Resigned Aug. 23, 1814.
3. Appointed by governor to fill vacancy.
4. Resigned May 1, 1816.
5. Appointed by governor to fill vacancy. Subsequently elected.
6. Resigned March 3, 1819.
7. Resigned Feb. 7, 1868.
8. Died May 3, 1890.
9. Resigned Feb. 4, 1893.
10. Died Aug. 28, 1918.
11. Appointed by governor to fill vacancy.
12. Resigned Jan. 9, 1930.
13. Appointed by governor to fill vacancy.
14. Died Oct. 3, 1939.
15. Appointed by governor to fill vacancy. Subsequently elected. Resigned Nov. 1, 1945.
16. Appointed by governor to fill vacancy.
17. Died March 8, 1951.
18. Appointed by governor to fill vacancy.
19. Died April 30, 1956.
20. Appointed by governor to fill vacancy.
21. Resigned Aug. 7, 1805.
22. Resigned Nov. 18, 1806.
23. Resigned Dec. 24, 1814.
24. Resigned May 28, 1820.
25. Resigned March 31, 1842.
26. Resigned June 12, 1848.
27. Appointed by governor to fill vacancy. Subsequently elected.
28. Died June 29, 1852.
29. Appointed by governor to fill vacancy.
30. Expelled Dec. 4, 1861.
31. Died Sept. 22, 1872.
32. Appointed by governor to fill vacancy. Subsequently elected.
33. Died May 23, 1914.
34. Appointed by governor to fill vacancy. Subsequently elected.
35. Resigned Jan. 19, 1949, to become vice president of the United States.
36. Appointed by governor to fill vacancy.
37. Resigned Dec. 16, 1968.
38. Resigned Dec. 27, 1974.

# LOUISIANA

(Became a state April 30, 1812)

### Class 2

| Senators | Dates of Service | |
|---|---|---|
| John N. Destrehan (D-R)[1] | | |
| Thomas Posey (D-R)[2] | Oct. 8, 1812 | Feb. 4, 1813 |
| James Brown (D-R) | Feb. 5, 1813 | March 3, 1817 |
| William C. C. Claiborne (D-R)[3] | March 4, 1817 | Nov. 23, 1817 |
| Henry Johnson (D-R)[4] | Jan. 12, 1818 | May 27, 1824 |
| Dominique Bouligny (D-R) | Nov. 19, 1824 | March 3, 1829 |
| Edward Livingston (D)[5] | March 4, 1829 | May 24, 1831 |
| George A. Waggaman (NR) | Nov. 15, 1831 | March 3, 1835 |
| Robert C. Nicholas (D) | Jan. 13, 1836 | March 3, 1841 |
| Alexander Barrow (W)[6] | March 4, 1841 | Dec. 29, 1846 |
| Pierre Soulé (D) | Jan. 21, 1847 | March 3, 1847 |
| Solomon W. Downs (D) | March 4, 1847 | March 3, 1853 |
| Judah P. Benjamin (W, D)[7] | March 4, 1853 | March 14, 1861 |
| John S. Harris (R) | July 17, 1868 | March 3, 1871 |
| J. Rodman West (R) | March 4, 1871 | March 3, 1877 |
| William P. Kellogg (R) | March 4, 1877 | March 3, 1883 |
| Randall L. Gibson (D)[8] | March 4, 1883 | Dec. 15, 1892 |
| Donelson Caffery (D)[9] | Dec. 31, 1892 | March 3, 1901 |
| Murphy J. Foster (D) | March 4, 1901 | March 3, 1913 |
| Joseph E. Ransdell (D) | March 4, 1913 | March 3, 1931 |
| Huey P. Long (D)[10] | Jan. 25, 1932 | Sept. 10, 1935 |
| Rose McConnell Long (D)[11] | Jan. 31, 1936 | Jan. 2, 1937 |

| | | |
|---|---|---|
| Allen J. Ellender (D)[12] | Jan. 3, 1937 | July 27, 1972 |
| Elaine S. Edwards (D)[13] | Aug. 1, 1972 | Nov. 13, 1972 |
| J. Bennett Johnston (D) | Nov. 14, 1972 | |

### Class 3

| | | |
|---|---|---|
| Allan B. Magruder (D-R) | Sept. 3, 1812 | March 3, 1813 |
| Eligius Fromentin (D-R) | March 4, 1813 | March 3, 1819 |
| James Brown (D-R)[14] | March 4, 1819 | Dec. 10, 1823 |
| Josiah S. Johnston (D-R)[15] | Jan. 15, 1824 | May 19, 1833 |
| Alexander Porter (W)[16] | Dec. 19, 1833 | Jan. 5, 1837 |
| Alexander Mouton (D)[17] | Jan. 12, 1837 | March 1, 1842 |
| Charles M. Conrad (W) | April 14, 1842 | March 3, 1843 |
| Henry Johnson (W)[18] | Feb. 12, 1844 | March 3, 1849 |
| Pierre Soulé (D)[19] | March 4, 1849 | April 11, 1853 |
| John Slidell (D)[20] | April 28, 1853 | Feb. 4, 1861 |
| William P. Kellogg (R)[21] | July 17, 1868 | Nov. 1, 1872 |
| James B. Eustis (D) | Jan. 12, 1876 | March 3, 1879 |
| Benjamin F. Jonas (D) | March 4, 1879 | March 3, 1885 |
| James B. Eustis (D) | March 4, 1885 | March 3, 1891 |
| Edward D. White (D)[22] | March 4, 1891 | March 12, 1894 |
| Newton C. Blanchard (D)[23] | March 12, 1894 | March 3, 1897 |
| Samuel D. McEnery (D)[24] | March 4, 1897 | June 28, 1910 |
| John R. Thornton (D) | Dec. 7, 1910 | March 3, 1915 |
| Robert F. Broussard (D)[25] | March 4, 1915 | April 12, 1918 |
| Walter Guion (D)[26] | April 22, 1918 | Nov. 5, 1918 |
| Edward J. Gay (D) | Nov. 6, 1918 | March 3, 1921 |
| Edwin S. Broussard (D) | March 4, 1921 | March 3, 1933 |
| John H. Overton (D)[27] | March 4, 1933 | May 14, 1948 |
| William C. Feazel (D)[28] | May 18, 1948 | Dec. 30, 1948 |
| Russell B. Long (D) | Dec. 31, 1948 | Jan. 2, 1987 |
| John B. Breaux (D) | Jan. 3, 1987 | |

**Louisiana**
1. *Elected Sept. 3, 1812, but did not take oath. Resigned Oct. 1, 1812.*
2. *Appointed by governor to fill vacancy.*
3. *Died Nov. 23, 1817.*
4. *Resigned May 27, 1824.*
5. *Resigned May 24, 1831.*
6. *Died Dec. 29, 1846.*
7. *Seat declared vacant March 14, 1861. Vacancy until July 17, 1868, because of Civil War.*
8. *Died Dec. 15, 1892.*
9. *Appointed by governor to fill vacancy. Subsequently elected.*
10. *Elected Nov. 4, 1930, but did not take oath until Jan. 25, 1932. Governor during interim. Died Sept. 10, 1935.*
11. *Appointed by governor to fill vacancy. Subsequently elected.*
12. *Died July 27, 1972.*
13. *Appointed by governor to fill vacancy. Resigned Nov. 13, 1972.*
14. *Resigned Dec. 10, 1823.*
15. *Died May 19, 1833.*
16. *Resigned Jan. 5, 1837.*
17. *Resigned March 1, 1842.*
18. *Vacancy from March 4, 1843, to Feb. 12, 1844.*
19. *Resigned April 11, 1853.*
20. *Retired Feb. 4, 1861. Vacancy until July 17, 1868, because of Civil War.*
21. *Resigned Nov. 1, 1872. Vacancy from Nov. 1, 1872, until Jan. 12, 1876.*
22. *Resigned March 12, 1894.*
23. *Appointed by governor to fill vacancy. Subsequently elected.*
24. *Died June 28, 1910.*
25. *Died April 12, 1918.*
26. *Appointed by governor to fill vacancy.*
27. *Died May 14, 1948.*
28. *Appointed by governor to fill vacancy.*

# MAINE

(Became a state March 15, 1820)

### Class 1

| Senators | Dates of Service | |
|---|---|---|
| John Holmes (D-R) | June 13, 1820 | March 3, 1827 |

| | | |
|---|---|---|
| Albion K. Parris (D-R)[1] | March 4, 1827 | Aug. 26, 1828 |
| John Holmes (NR) | Jan. 15, 1829 | March 3, 1833 |
| Ether Shepley (D)[2] | March 4, 1833 | March 3, 1836 |
| Judah Dana (D)[3] | Dec. 7, 1836 | Feb. 22, 1837 |
| Reuel Williams (D)[4] | Feb. 22, 1837 | Feb. 15, 1843 |
| John Fairfield (D)[5] | March 3, 1843 | Dec. 24, 1847 |
| Wyman B. S. Moor (D)[6] | Jan. 5, 1848 | May 26, 1848 |
| Hannibal Hamlin (D)[7] | June 8, 1848 | Jan. 7, 1857 |
| Amos Nourse | Jan. 16, 1857 | March 3, 1857 |
| Hannibal Hamlin (R)[8] | March 4, 1857 | Jan. 17, 1861 |
| Lot Myrick Morrill (R) | Jan. 17, 1861 | March 3, 1869 |
| Hannibal Hamlin (R) | March 4, 1869 | March 3, 1881 |
| Eugene Hale (R) | March 4, 1881 | March 3, 1911 |
| Charles F. Johnson (D) | March 4, 1911 | March 3, 1917 |
| Frederick Hale (R) | March 4, 1917 | Jan. 2, 1941 |
| Ralph O. Brewster (R) | Jan. 3, 1941 | Jan. 2, 1953 |
| Frederick G. Payne (R) | Jan. 3, 1953 | Jan. 2, 1959 |
| Edmund S. Muskie (D)[9] | Jan. 3, 1959 | May 7, 1980 |
| George J. Mitchell (D)[10] | May 17, 1980 | |

### Class 2

| | | |
|---|---|---|
| John Chandler (D-R) | June 14, 1820 | March 3, 1829 |
| Peleg Sprague (NR)[11] | March 4, 1829 | Jan. 1, 1835 |
| John Ruggles (D) | Jan. 20, 1835 | March 3, 1841 |
| George Evans (W) | March 4, 1841 | March 3, 1847 |
| James W. Bradbury (D) | March 4, 1847 | March 3, 1853 |
| William P. Fessenden (R)[12] | Feb. 10, 1854 | July 1, 1864 |
| Nathan A. Farwell (R)[13] | Oct. 27, 1864 | March 3, 1865 |
| William P. Fessenden (R)[14] | March 4, 1865 | Sept. 9, 1869 |
| Lot Myrick Morrill (R)[15] | Oct. 30, 1869 | July 7, 1876 |
| James G. Blaine (R)[16] | July 10, 1876 | March 5, 1881 |
| William P. Frye (R)[17] | March 18, 1881 | Aug. 8, 1911 |
| Obadiah Gardner (D)[18] | Sept. 23, 1911 | March 3, 1913 |
| Edwin C. Burleigh (R)[19] | March 4, 1913 | June 16, 1916 |
| Bert M. Fernald (R)[20] | Sept. 12, 1916 | Aug. 23, 1926 |
| Arthur R. Gould (R) | Nov. 30, 1926 | March 3, 1931 |
| Wallace H. White Jr. (R) | March 4, 1931 | Jan. 2, 1949 |
| Margaret Chase Smith (R) | Jan. 3, 1949 | Jan. 2, 1973 |
| William D. Hathaway (D) | Jan. 3, 1973 | Jan. 2, 1979 |
| William S. Cohen (R) | Jan. 3, 1979 | |

**Maine**
1. *Resigned Aug. 26, 1828.*
2. *Resigned March 3, 1836.*
3. *Appointed by governor to fill vacancy.*
4. *Resigned Feb. 15, 1843.*
5. *Died Dec. 24, 1847.*
6. *Appointed by governor to fill vacancy.*
7. *Resigned Jan. 7, 1857.*
8. *Resigned Jan. 17, 1861, to become vice president of the United States.*
9. *Resigned May 7, 1980, having been confirmed secretary of state.*
10. *Appointed by governor to fill vacancy. Subsequently elected.*
11. *Resigned Jan. 1, 1835.*
12. *Resigned July 1, 1864.*
13. *Appointed by governor to fill vacancy. Subsequently elected.*
14. *Died Sept. 9, 1869.*
15. *Appointed by governor to fill vacancy. Subsequently elected. Resigned July 7, 1876.*
16. *Appointed by governor to fill vacancy. Subsequently elected. Resigned March 5, 1881.*
17. *Died Aug. 8, 1911.*
18. *Appointed by governor to fill vacancy. Subsequently elected.*
19. *Died June 16, 1916.*
20. *Died Aug. 23, 1926.*

# MARYLAND

(Ratified the Constitution April 28, 1788)

## Class 1

| Senators | Dates of Service | |
|---|---|---|
| Charles Carroll (FED)[1] | March 4, 1789 | Nov. 30, 1792 |
| Richard Potts (FED)[2] | Jan. 10, 1793 | Oct. 24, 1796 |
| John E. Howard (FED) | Nov. 30, 1796 | March 3, 1803 |
| Samuel Smith (D-R)[3] | March 4, 1803 | March 3, 1815 |
| Robert G. Harper[4] | Jan. 29, 1816 | Dec. 6, 1816 |
| Alexander C. Hanson(FED)[5] | Dec. 20, 1816 | April 23, 1819 |
| William Pinkney (D-R)[6] | Dec. 21, 1819 | Feb. 25, 1822 |
| Samuel Smith (D-R) | Dec. 17, 1822 | March 3, 1833 |
| Joseph Kent (NR)[7] | March 4, 1833 | Nov. 24, 1837 |
| William D. Merrick (W) | Jan. 4, 1838 | March 3, 1845 |
| Reverdy Johnson (W)[8] | March 4, 1845 | March 7, 1849 |
| David Stewart (W)[9] | Dec. 6, 1849 | Jan. 12, 1850 |
| Thomas G. Pratt (W) | Jan. 12, 1850 | March 3, 1857 |
| Anthony Kennedy (UN) | March 4, 1857 | March 3, 1863 |
| Reverdy Johnson (D)[10] | March 4, 1863 | July 10, 1868 |
| William Pinkney Whyte (D)[11] | July 13, 1868 | March 3, 1869 |
| William T. Hamilton (D) | March 4, 1869 | March 3, 1875 |
| William Pinkney Whyte (D) | March 4, 1875 | March 3, 1881 |
| Arthur P. Gorman (D) | March 4, 1881 | March 3, 1899 |
| Louis E. McComas (R) | March 4, 1899 | March 3, 1905 |
| Isidor Rayner (D)[12] | March 4, 1905 | Nov. 25, 1912 |
| William P. Jackson (R)[13] | Nov. 29, 1912 | Jan. 28, 1914 |
| Blair Lee (D) | Jan. 29, 1914 | March 3, 1917 |
| Joseph I. France (R) | March 4, 1917 | March 3, 1923 |
| William Cabell Bruce (D) | March 4, 1923 | March 3, 1929 |
| Phillips Lee Goldsborough (R) | March 4, 1929 | Jan. 2, 1935 |
| George W. Radcliffe (D) | Jan. 3, 1935 | Jan. 2, 1947 |
| Herbert R. O'Conor (D) | Jan. 3, 1947 | Jan. 2, 1953 |
| J. Glenn Beall (R) | Jan. 3, 1953 | Jan. 2, 1965 |
| Joseph D. Tydings (D) | Jan. 3, 1965 | Jan. 2, 1971 |
| J. Glenn Beall Jr. (R) | Jan. 3, 1971 | Jan. 2, 1977 |
| Paul S. Sarbanes (D) | Jan. 3, 1977 | |

## Class 3

| Senators | Dates of Service | |
|---|---|---|
| John Henry (D-R)[14] | March 4, 1789 | Dec. 10, 1797 |
| James Lloyd (D-R)[15] | Dec. 11, 1797 | Dec. 1, 1800 |
| William Hindman (FED)[16] | Dec. 12, 1800 | Nov. 19, 1801 |
| Robert Wright (D-R)[17] | Nov. 19, 1801 | Nov. 12, 1806 |
| Philip Reed (D-R) | Nov. 25, 1806 | March 3, 1813 |
| Robert H. Goldsborough (FED) | May 21, 1813 | March 3, 1819 |
| Edward Lloyd (D-R)[18] | Dec. 21, 1819 | Jan. 14, 1826 |
| Ezekiel F. Chambers (W)[19] | Jan. 24, 1826 | Dec. 20, 1834 |
| Robert H. Goldsborough (W)[20] | Jan. 13, 1835 | Oct. 5, 1836 |
| John S. Spence (W)[21] | Dec. 31, 1836 | Oct. 24, 1840 |
| John Leeds Kerr (W) | Jan. 5, 1841 | March 3, 1843 |
| James A. Pearce (W, D)[22] | March 4, 1843 | Dec. 20, 1862 |
| Thomas H. Hicks (R)[23] | Dec. 29, 1862 | Feb. 14, 1865 |
| John A. J. Creswell (R) | March 9, 1865 | March 3, 1867 |
| George Vickers (D)[24] | March 7, 1868 | March 3, 1873 |
| George R. Dennis (D) | March 4, 1873 | March 3, 1879 |
| James B. Groome (D) | March 4, 1879 | March 3, 1885 |
| Ephraim King Wilson (D)[25] | March 4, 1885 | Feb. 24, 1891 |
| Charles H. Gibson (D)[26] | Nov. 19, 1891 | March 3, 1897 |
| George L. Wellington (R) | March 4, 1897 | March 3, 1903 |
| Arthur P. Gorman (D)[27] | March 4, 1903 | June 4, 1906 |
| William Pinkney Whyte (D)[28] | June 8, 1906 | March 17, 1908 |
| John Walter Smith (D) | March 25, 1908 | March 3, 1921 |
| Ovington E. Weller (R) | March 4, 1921 | March 3, 1927 |
| Millard E. Tydings (D) | March 4, 1927 | Jan. 2, 1951 |
| John Marshall Butler (R) | Jan. 3, 1951 | Jan. 2, 1963 |
| Daniel B. Brewster (D) | Jan. 3, 1963 | Jan. 2, 1969 |
| Charles Mathias Jr. (R) | Jan. 3, 1969 | Jan. 2, 1987 |
| Barbara A. Mikulski (D) | Jan. 3, 1987 | |

Maryland
  1. Resigned Nov. 30, 1792.
  2. Resigned Oct. 24, 1796.
  3. Served continuously during this period, twice by election, once by appointment of the governor.
  4. Resigned Dec. 6, 1816.
  5. Died April 23, 1819.
  6. Died Feb. 25, 1822.
  7. Died Nov. 24, 1837.
  8. Resigned March 7, 1849.
  9. Appointed by governor to fill vacancy.
  10. Resigned July 10, 1868.
  11. Appointed by governor to fill vacancy.
  12. Died Nov. 25, 1912.
  13. Appointed by governor to fill vacancy.
  14. Resigned Dec. 10, 1797.
  15. Resigned Dec. 1, 1800.
  16. Served first by election and subsequently by appointment of the governor during this period.
  17. Resigned Nov. 12, 1806.
  18. Resigned Jan. 14, 1826.
  19. Resigned Dec. 20, 1834.
  20. Died Oct. 5, 1836.
  21. Died Oct. 24, 1840.
  22. Died Dec. 20, 1862.
  23. Appointed by governor to fill vacancy. Subsequently elected. Died Feb. 14, 1865.
  24. Vacancy from March 4, 1867, to March 7, 1868.
  25. Died Feb. 24, 1891.
  26. Appointed by governor to fill vacancy. Subsequently elected.
  27. Died June 4, 1906.
  28. Appointed by governor to fill vacancy. Subsequently elected. Died March 17, 1908.

# MASSACHUSETTS

(Ratified the Constitution Feb. 6, 1788)

## Class 1

| Senators | Dates of Service | |
|---|---|---|
| Tristram Dalton (FED) | March 4, 1789 | March 3, 1791 |
| George Cabot (FED)[1] | March 4, 1791 | June 9, 1796 |
| Benjamin Goodhue (FED)[2] | June 11, 1796 | Nov. 8, 1800 |
| Jonathan Mason (FED) | Nov. 14, 1800 | March 3, 1803 |
| John Quincy Adams (FED, D-R)[3] | March 4, 1803 | June 8, 1808 |
| James Lloyd (FED)[4] | June 9, 1808 | May 1, 1813 |
| Christopher Gore (FED)[5] | May 5, 1813 | May 30, 1816 |
| Eli P. Ashmun (FED)[6] | June 12, 1816 | May 10, 1818 |
| Prentiss Mellen (FED)[7] | June 5, 1818 | May 15, 1820 |
| Elijah H. Mills (FED) | June 12, 1820 | March 3, 1827 |
| Daniel Webster (D-R, NR, W)[8] | May 30, 1827 | Feb. 22, 1841 |
| Rufus Choate (W) | Feb. 23, 1841 | March 3, 1845 |
| Daniel Webster (W)[9] | March 4, 1845 | July 22, 1850 |
| Robert C. Winthrop (W)[10] | July 30, 1850 | Feb. 1, 1851 |
| Robert Rantoul (D) | Feb. 1, 1851 | March 3, 1851 |
| Charles Sumner (F SOIL, R)[11] | March 4, 1851 | March 11, 1874 |
| William B. Washburn (R) | April 17, 1874 | March 3, 1875 |
| Henry L. Dawes (R) | March 4, 1875 | March 3, 1893 |
| Henry Cabot Lodge (R)[12] | March 4, 1893 | Nov. 9, 1924 |
| William M. Butler (R)[13] | Nov. 13, 1924 | Dec. 5, 1926 |
| David I. Walsh (D) | Dec. 6, 1926 | Jan. 2, 1947 |
| Henry Cabot Lodge Jr. (R) | Jan. 3, 1947 | Jan. 2, 1953 |
| John F. Kennedy (D)[14] | Jan. 3, 1953 | Dec. 22, 1960 |
| Benjamin A. Smith II (D)[15] | Dec. 27, 1960 | Nov. 6, 1962 |
| Edward M. Kennedy (D) | Nov. 7, 1962 | |

## Class 2

| Senators | Dates of Service | |
|---|---|---|
| Caleb Strong (FED)[16] | March 4, 1789 | June 1, 1796 |
| Theodore Sedgwick (FED) | June 11, 1796 | March 3, 1799 |
| Samuel Dexter (FED)[17] | March 4, 1799 | May 30, 1800 |
| Dwight Foster (FED)[18] | June 6, 1800 | March 3, 1803 |

| | | |
|---|---|---|
| Timothy Pickering (FED) | March 4, 1803 | March 3, 1811 |
| Joseph B. Varnum (D-R) | June 8, 1811 | March 3, 1817 |
| Harrison Gray Otis (FED)[19] | March 4, 1817 | May 30, 1822 |
| James Lloyd (FED)[20] | June 5, 1822 | May 23, 1826 |
| Nathaniel Silsbee (D-R, NR) | May 31, 1826 | March 3, 1835 |
| John Davis (W)[21] | March 4, 1835 | Jan. 5, 1841 |
| Isaac C. Bates (W)[22] | Jan. 13, 1841 | March 16, 1845 |
| John Davis (W) | March 24, 1845 | March 3, 1853 |
| Edward Everett (W)[23] | March 4, 1853 | June 1, 1854 |
| Julius Rockwell[24] | June 3, 1854 | Jan. 31, 1855 |
| Henry Wilson (R)[25] | Jan. 31, 1855 | March 3, 1873 |
| George S. Boutwell (R) | March 12, 1873 | March 3, 1877 |
| George F. Hoar (R)[26] | March 4, 1877 | Sept. 30, 1904 |
| Winthrop Murray Crane (R)[27] | Oct. 12, 1904 | March 3, 1913 |
| John W. Weeks (R) | March 4, 1913 | March 3, 1919 |
| David I. Walsh (D) | March 4, 1919 | March 3, 1925 |
| Frederick H. Gillett (R) | March 4, 1925 | March 3, 1931 |
| Marcus A. Coolidge (D) | March 4, 1931 | March 3, 1937 |
| Henry Cabot Lodge Jr. (R)[28] | Jan. 3, 1937 | Feb. 3, 1944 |
| Sinclair Weeks (R)[29] | Feb. 8, 1944 | Dec. 19, 1944 |
| Leverett Saltonstall (R) | Jan. 10, 1945 | Jan. 2, 1967 |
| Edward W. Brooke (R) | Jan. 3, 1967 | Jan. 2, 1979 |
| Paul E. Tsongas (D)[30] | Jan. 3, 1979 | Jan. 2, 1985 |
| John F. Kerry (D) | Jan. 3, 1985 | |

**Massachusetts**
1. *Resigned June 9, 1796.*
2. *Resigned Nov. 8, 1800.*
3. *Resigned June 8, 1808.*
4. *Resigned May 1, 1813.*
5. *Appointed by governor to fill vacancy. Subsequently elected. Resigned May 30, 1816.*
6. *Resigned May 10, 1818.*
7. *Resigned May 15, 1820.*
8. *Resigned Feb. 22, 1841.*
9. *Resigned July 22, 1850.*
10. *Appointed by governor to fill vacancy.*
11. *Died March 11, 1874.*
12. *Died Nov. 9, 1924.*
13. *Appointed by governor to fill vacancy.*
14. *Resigned Dec. 22, 1960, having been elected president of the United States.*
15. *Appointed by governor to fill vacancy.*
16. *Resigned June 1, 1796.*
17. *Resigned May 30, 1800.*
18. *Resigned March 3, 1803.*
19. *Resigned May 30, 1822.*
20. *Resigned May 23, 1826.*
21. *Resigned Jan. 5, 1841.*
22. *Died March 16, 1845.*
23. *Resigned June 1, 1854.*
24. *Appointed by governor to fill vacancy.*
25. *Resigned March 3, 1873.*
26. *Died Sept. 30, 1904.*
27. *Appointed by governor to fill vacancy. Subsequently elected.*
28. *Resigned Feb. 3, 1944.*
29. *Appointed by governor to fill vacancy.*
30. *Resigned Jan. 2, 1985.*

| | | |
|---|---|---|
| Zachariah Chandler (R)[4] | Feb. 19, 1879 | Nov. 1, 1879 |
| Henry P. Baldwin (R)[5] | Nov. 17, 1879 | March 3, 1881 |
| Omar D. Conger (R) | March 4, 1881 | March 3, 1887 |
| Francis B. Stockbridge (R)[6] | March 4, 1887 | April 30, 1894 |
| John Patton Jr. (R)[7] | May 5, 1894 | Jan. 14, 1895 |
| Julius C. Burrows (R) | Jan. 23, 1895 | March 3, 1911 |
| Charles E. Townsend (R) | March 4, 1911 | March 3, 1923 |
| Woodbridge N. Ferris (D)[8] | March 4, 1923 | March 23, 1928 |
| Arthur H. Vandenberg (R)[9] | March 31, 1928 | April 18, 1951 |
| Blair Moody (D)[10] | April 22, 1951 | Nov. 4, 1952 |
| Charles E. Potter (R) | Nov. 5, 1952 | Jan. 2, 1959 |
| Philip A. Hart (D)[11] | Jan. 3, 1959 | Dec. 26, 1976 |
| Donald W. Riegle Jr. (D) | Dec. 30, 1976 | |

## Class 2

| | | |
|---|---|---|
| John Norvell (D) | Jan. 26, 1837 | March 3, 1841 |
| William Woodbridge (W) | March 4, 1841 | March 3, 1847 |
| Alpheus Felch (D) | March 4, 1847 | March 3, 1853 |
| Charles E. Stuart (D) | March 4, 1853 | March 3, 1859 |
| Kinsley S. Bingham (R)[12] | March 4, 1859 | Oct. 5, 1861 |
| Jacob M. Howard (R) | Jan. 4, 1862 | March 3, 1871 |
| Thomas W. Ferry (R) | March 4, 1871 | March 3, 1883 |
| Thomas W. Palmer (R) | March 4, 1883 | March 3, 1889 |
| James McMillan (R)[13] | March 4, 1889 | Aug. 10, 1902 |
| Russell A. Alger (R)[14] | Sept. 27, 1902 | Jan. 24, 1907 |
| William Alden Smith (R) | Feb. 6, 1907 | March 3, 1919 |
| Truman H. Newberry (R)[15] | March 4, 1919 | Nov. 18, 1922 |
| James Couzens (R)[16] | Nov. 29, 1922 | Oct. 22, 1936 |
| Prentiss M. Brown (D) | Nov. 19, 1936 | Jan. 2, 1943 |
| Homer Ferguson (R) | Jan. 3, 1943 | Jan. 2, 1955 |
| Patrick V. McNamara (D)[17] | Jan. 3, 1955 | April 30, 1966 |
| Robert P. Griffin (R)[18] | May 11, 1966 | Jan. 2, 1979 |
| Carl Levin (D) | Jan. 3, 1979 | |

**Michigan**
1. *Resigned May 29, 1848.*
2. *Appointed by governor to fill vacancy.*
3. *Resigned Feb. 10, 1879.*
4. *Died Nov. 1, 1879.*
5. *Appointed by governor to fill vacancy. Subsequently elected.*
6. *Died April 30, 1894.*
7. *Appointed by governor to fill vacancy.*
8. *Died March 23, 1928.*
9. *Appointed by governor to fill vacancy. Subsequently elected. Died April 18, 1951.*
10. *Appointed by governor to fill vacancy.*
11. *Died Dec. 26, 1976.*
12. *Died Oct. 5, 1861.*
13. *Died Aug. 10, 1902.*
14. *Appointed by governor to fill vacancy. Subsequently elected. Died Jan. 24, 1907.*
15. *Resigned Nov. 18, 1922.*
16. *Appointed by governor to fill vacancy. Subsequently elected. Died Oct. 22, 1936.*
17. *Died April 30, 1966.*
18. *Appointed by governor to fill vacancy. Subsequently elected.*

# MICHIGAN

(Became a state Jan. 26, 1837)

## Class 1

| Senators | Dates of Service | |
|---|---|---|
| Lucius Lyon (D) | Jan. 26, 1837 | March 3, 1839 |
| Augustus S. Porter (W) | Jan. 20, 1840 | March 3, 1845 |
| Lewis Cass (D)[1] | March 4, 1845 | May 29, 1848 |
| Thomas Fitzgerald (D)[2] | June 8, 1848 | March 3, 1849 |
| Lewis Cass (D) | March 4, 1849 | March 3, 1857 |
| Zachariah Chandler (R) | March 4, 1857 | March 3, 1875 |
| Isaac P. Christiancy (R)[3] | March 4, 1875 | Feb. 10, 1879 |

# MINNESOTA

(Became a state May 11, 1858)

## Class 1

| Senators | Dates of Service | |
|---|---|---|
| Henry M. Rice (D) | May 11, 1858 | March 3, 1863 |
| Alexander Ramsey (R) | March 4, 1863 | March 3, 1875 |
| Samuel J. R. McMillan (R) | March 4, 1875 | March 3, 1887 |
| Cushman K. Davis (R)[1] | March 4, 1887 | Nov. 27, 1900 |
| Charles A. Towne (D)[2] | Dec. 5, 1900 | Jan. 23, 1901 |
| Moses E. Clapp (R) | Jan. 23, 1901 | March 3, 1917 |

| | | |
|---|---|---|
| Frank B. Kellogg (R) | March 4, 1917 | March 3, 1923 |
| Henrik Shipstead (F-LAB, R)[3] | March 4, 1923 | Jan. 2, 1947 |
| Edward J. Thye (R) | Jan. 3, 1947 | Jan. 2, 1959 |
| Eugene J. McCarthy (DFL) | Jan. 3, 1959 | Jan. 2, 1971 |
| Hubert H. Humphrey (DFL)[4] | Jan. 3, 1971 | Jan. 13, 1978 |
| Muriel Humphrey (DFL)[5] | Jan. 25, 1978 | Nov. 7, 1978 |
| Dave Durenberger (I-R) | Nov. 8, 1978 | |

### Class 2

| | | |
|---|---|---|
| James Shields (D) | May 11, 1858 | March 3, 1859 |
| Morton S. Wilkinson (R) | March 4, 1859 | March 3, 1865 |
| Daniel S. Norton (R)[6] | March 4, 1865 | July 13, 1870 |
| William Windom (R)[7] | July 15, 1870 | Jan. 22, 1871 |
| Ozora P. Stearns (R) | Jan. 18, 1871 | March 3, 1871 |
| William Windom (R)[8] | March 4, 1871 | March 4, 1881 |
| A. J. Edgerton (R)[9] | March 12, 1881 | Oct. 26, 1881 |
| William Windom (R) | Oct. 27, 1881 | March 3, 1883 |
| Dwight M. Sabin (R) | March 4, 1883 | March 3, 1889 |
| William D. Washburn (R) | March 4, 1889 | March 3, 1895 |
| Knute Nelson (R)[10] | March 4, 1895 | April 28, 1923 |
| Magnus Johnson (F-LAB) | July 16, 1923 | March 3, 1925 |
| Thomas D. Schall (R)[11] | March 4, 1925 | Dec. 22, 1935 |
| Elmer A. Benson (F-LAB)[12] | Dec. 27, 1935 | Nov. 3, 1936 |
| Guy V. Howard (R) | Nov. 4, 1936 | Jan. 2, 1937 |
| Ernest Lundeen (F-LAB)[13] | Jan. 3, 1937 | Aug. 31, 1940 |
| Joseph H. Ball (R)[14] | Oct. 14, 1940 | Nov. 17, 1942 |
| Arthur E. Nelson (R) | Nov. 18, 1942 | Jan. 2, 1843 |
| Joseph H. Ball (R) | Jan. 3, 1943 | Jan. 2, 1949 |
| Hubert H. Humphrey (DFL)[15] | Jan. 3, 1949 | Dec. 29, 1964 |
| Walter F. Mondale (DFL)[16] | Dec. 30, 1964 | Dec. 30, 1976 |
| Wendell R. Anderson (DFL)[17] | Dec. 30, 1976 | Dec. 29, 1978 |
| Rudy Boschwitz (I-R) | Dec. 30, 1978 | Jan. 2, 1991 |
| Paul Wellstone (DFL) | Jan. 3, 1991 | |

#### Minnesota
1. Died Nov. 27, 1900.
2. Appointed by governor to fill vacancy.
3. Elected as a Farmer-Laborite in 1922, 1928 and 1934, as a Republican in 1940.
4. Died Jan. 13, 1978.
5. Appointed by governor to fill vacancy.
6. Died July 13, 1870.
7. Appointed by governor to fill vacancy.
8. Resigned March 4, 1881.
9. Appointed by governor to fill vacancy.
10. Died April 28, 1923.
11. Died Dec. 22, 1935.
12. Appointed by governor to fill vacancy.
13. Died Aug. 31, 1940.
14. Appointed by governor to fill vacancy.
15. Resigned Dec. 29, 1964, having been elected vice president of the United States.
16. Appointed by governor to fill vacancy. Subsequently elected. Resigned Dec. 30, 1976, having been elected vice president of the United States.
17. Appointed by governor to fill vacancy. Resigned Dec. 29, 1978.

# MISSISSIPPI

(Became a state Dec. 10, 1817)

### Class 1

| Senators | Dates of Service | |
|---|---|---|
| Walter Leake (D-R)[1] | Dec. 10, 1817 | May 15, 1820 |
| David Holmes (D-R)[2] | Aug. 30, 1820 | Sept. 25, 1825 |
| Powhatan Ellis (D-R)[3] | Sept. 28, 1825 | Jan. 28, 1826 |
| Thomas B. Reed (D-R) | Jan. 28, 1826 | March 3, 1827 |
| Powhatan Ellis (D-R)[4] | March 4, 1827 | July 10, 1832 |
| John Black (D, W)[5] | Nov. 12, 1832 | Jan. 22, 1838 |
| James F. Trotter (D)[6] | Jan. 22, 1838 | July 10, 1838 |

| | | |
|---|---|---|
| Thomas Hickman Williams (D)[7] | Nov. 12, 1838 | March 3, 1839 |
| John Henderson (W) | March 4, 1839 | March 3, 1845 |
| Jesse Speight (D)[8] | March 4, 1845 | May 1, 1847 |
| Jefferson Davis (D)[9] | Aug. 10, 1847 | Sept. 23, 1851 |
| John J. McRae (D)[10] | Dec. 1, 1851 | March 17, 1852 |
| Stephen Adams (D) | March 17, 1852 | March 3, 1857 |
| Jefferson Davis (D)[11] | March 4, 1857 | March 14, 1861 |
| Adelbert Ames (R)[12] | April 1, 1870 | Jan. 10, 1874 |
| Henry R. Pease (R) | Feb. 3, 1874 | March 3, 1875 |
| Blanche K. Bruce (R) | March 4, 1875 | March 3, 1881 |
| James Z. George (D)[13] | March 4, 1881 | Aug. 14, 1897 |
| Hernando D. Money (D)[14] | Oct. 8, 1897 | March 3, 1911 |
| John Sharp Williams (D) | March 4, 1911 | March 3, 1923 |
| Hubert D. Stephens (D) | March 4, 1923 | Jan. 2, 1935 |
| Theodore G. Bilbo (D)[15] | Jan. 3, 1935 | Jan. 2, 1947 |
| John C. Stennis (D) | Nov. 5, 1947 | Jan. 2, 1989 |
| Trent Lott (R) | Jan. 3, 1989 | |

### Class 2

| | | |
|---|---|---|
| Thomas Hill Williams (D-R) | Dec. 10, 1817 | March 3, 1829 |
| Thomas B. Reed (D)[16] | March 4, 1829 | Nov. 26, 1829 |
| Robert H. Adams (D)[17] | Jan. 6, 1830 | July 2, 1830 |
| George Poindexter (D)[18] | Oct. 15, 1830 | March 3, 1835 |
| Robert J. Walker (D)[19] | March 4, 1835 | March 5, 1845 |
| Joseph W. Chalmers (D)[20] | Nov. 3, 1845 | March 3, 1847 |
| Henry Stuart Foote (W)[21] | March 4, 1847 | Jan. 8, 1852 |
| Walker Brooke (W) | Feb. 18, 1852 | March 3, 1853 |
| Albert G. Brown (D)[22] | March 4, 1853 | March 14, 1861 |
| Hiram R. Revels (R) | Feb. 25, 1870 | March 3, 1871 |
| James L. Alcorn (R)[23] | Dec. 4, 1871 | March 3, 1877 |
| Lucius Q. C. Lamar (D)[24] | March 4, 1877 | March 6, 1885 |
| Edward C. Walthall (D)[25] | March 9, 1885 | Jan. 24, 1894 |
| Anselm J. McLaurin (D) | Feb. 7, 1894 | March 3, 1895 |
| Edward C. Walthall (D)[26] | March 4, 1895 | April 21, 1898 |
| William V. Sullivan (D)[27] | May 31, 1898 | March 3, 1901 |
| Anselm J. McLaurin (D)[28] | March 4, 1901 | Dec. 22, 1909 |
| James Gordon (D)[29] | Dec. 27, 1909 | Feb. 22, 1910 |
| Le Roy Percy (D) | Feb. 23, 1910 | March 3, 1913 |
| James K. Vardaman (D) | March 4, 1913 | March 3, 1919 |
| Pat Harrison (D)[30] | March 4, 1919 | June 22, 1941 |
| James O. Eastland (D)[31] | June 30, 1941 | Sept. 28, 1941 |
| Wall Doxey (D) | Sept. 29, 1941 | Jan. 2, 1943 |
| James O. Eastland (D)[32] | Jan. 3, 1943 | Dec. 27, 1978 |
| Thad Cochran (R) | Dec. 27, 1978 | |

#### Mississippi
1. Resigned May 15, 1820.
2. Appointed by governor to fill vacancy. Subsequently elected. Resigned Sept. 25, 1825.
3. Appointed by governor to fill vacancy.
4. Resigned July 10, 1832.
5. Appointed by governor to fill vacancy. Subsequently elected. Resigned Jan. 22, 1838.
6. Resigned July 10, 1838.
7. Appointed by governor to fill vacancy. Subsequently elected.
8. Died May 1, 1847.
9. Appointed by governor to fill vacancy. Subsequently elected. Resigned Sept. 23, 1851.
10. Appointed by governor to fill vacancy.
11. Seat declared vacant March 14, 1861. Vacancy until April 1, 1870, because of Civil War.
12. Resigned Jan. 10, 1874.
13. Died Aug. 14, 1897.
14. Appointed by governor to fill vacancy. Subsequently elected.
15. Elected for term beginning Jan. 3, 1947, but was never sworn in. Died Aug. 21, 1947.
16. Died Nov. 26, 1829.
17. Died July 2, 1830.
18. Appointed by governor to fill vacancy. Subsequently elected.
19. Resigned March 5, 1845.
20. Appointed by governor to fill vacancy. Subsequently elected.
21. Resigned Jan. 8, 1852.
22. Seat declared vacant March 14, 1861. Vacancy until Feb. 25, 1870, because of Civil War.

**Mississippi (continued)**

*23. Elected Jan. 18, 1870. Took oath Dec. 4, 1871. Governor during interim.*
*24. Resigned March 6, 1885.*
*25. Appointed by governor to fill vacancy. Subsequently elected. Resigned Jan. 24, 1894.*
*26. Died April 21, 1898.*
*27. Appointed by governor to fill vacancy. Subsequently elected.*
*28. Died Dec. 22, 1909.*
*29. Appointed by governor to fill vacancy.*
*30. Died June 22, 1941.*
*31. Appointed by governor to fill vacancy.*
*32. Resigned Dec. 27, 1978.*

# MISSOURI

(Became a state Aug. 10, 1821)

## Class 1

| Senators | Dates of Service | |
|---|---|---|
| Thomas H. Benton (D-R, D) | Aug. 10, 1821 | March 3, 1851 |
| Henry S. Geyer (D) | March 4, 1851 | March 3, 1857 |
| Trusten Polk (D)[1] | March 4, 1857 | Jan. 10, 1862 |
| John B. Henderson (D)[2] | Jan. 17, 1862 | March 3, 1869 |
| Carl Schurz (R) | March 4, 1869 | March 3, 1875 |
| Francis M. Cockrell (D) | March 4, 1875 | March 3, 1905 |
| William Warner (R) | March 18, 1905 | March 3, 1911 |
| James A. Reed (D) | March 4, 1911 | March 3, 1929 |
| Roscoe C. Patterson (R) | March 4, 1929 | Jan. 2, 1935 |
| Harry S Truman (D)[3] | Jan. 3, 1935 | Jan. 18, 1945 |
| Frank P. Briggs (D)[4] | Jan. 18, 1945 | Jan. 2, 1947 |
| James P. Kem (R) | Jan. 3, 1947 | Jan. 2, 1953 |
| Stuart Symington (D)[5] | Jan. 3, 1953 | Dec. 27, 1976 |
| John C. Danforth (R) | Dec. 27, 1976 | |

## Class 3

| Senators | Dates of Service | |
|---|---|---|
| David Barton (D-R) | Aug. 10, 1821 | March 3, 1831 |
| Alexander Buckner (D)[6] | March 4, 1831 | June 6, 1833 |
| Lewis F. Linn (D)[7] | Oct. 25, 1833 | Oct. 3, 1843 |
| David R. Atchison (D)[8] | Oct. 14, 1843 | March 3, 1855 |
| James S. Green (D) | Jan. 12, 1857 | March 3, 1861 |
| Waldo P. Johnson (D)[9] | March 17, 1861 | Jan. 10, 1862 |
| Robert Wilson (UN)[10] | Jan. 17, 1862 | Nov. 13, 1863 |
| B. Gratz Brown (D) | Nov. 13, 1863 | March 3, 1867 |
| Charles D. Drake (R)[11] | March 4, 1867 | Dec. 19, 1870 |
| Daniel T. Jewett (R)[12] | Dec. 19, 1870 | Jan. 20, 1871 |
| Francis P. Blair (D) | Jan. 20, 1871 | March 3, 1873 |
| Lewis V. Bogy (D)[13] | March 4, 1873 | Sept. 20, 1877 |
| David H. Armstrong (D)[14] | Sept. 29, 1877 | Jan. 26, 1879 |
| James Shields (D) | Jan. 27, 1879 | March 3, 1879 |
| George G. Vest (D) | March 4, 1879 | March 3, 1903 |
| William J. Stone (D)[15] | March 4, 1903 | April 14, 1918 |
| Xenophon P. Wilfley (D)[16] | April 30, 1918 | Nov. 5, 1918 |
| Selden P. Spencer (R)[17] | Nov. 6, 1918 | May 16, 1925 |
| George H. Williams (R)[18] | May 25, 1925 | Dec. 5, 1926 |
| Harry B. Hawes (D)[19] | Dec. 6, 1926 | Feb. 3,1933 |
| Bennett Champ Clark (D) | Feb. 3, 1933 | Jan. 2, 1945 |
| Forrest C. Donnell (R) | Jan. 3, 1945 | Jan. 2, 1951 |
| Thomas C. Hennings Jr. (D)[20] | Jan. 3, 1951 | Sept. 13, 1960 |
| Edward V. Long (D)[21] | Sept. 23, 1960 | Dec. 27, 1968 |
| Thomas F. Eagleton (D) | Dec. 28, 1968 | Jan. 2, 1987 |
| Christopher S. Bond (R) | Jan. 3, 1987 | |

**Missouri**

*1. Expelled Jan. 10, 1862.*
*2. Appointed by governor to fill vacancy. Subsequently elected.*
*3. Resigned Jan. 18, 1945, having been elected vice president of the United States.*
*4. Appointed by governor to fill vacancy.*
*5. Resigned Dec. 27, 1976.*
*6. Died June 6, 1833.*

*7. Appointed by governor to fill vacancy. Subsequently elected. Died Oct. 3, 1843.*
*8. Appointed by governor to fill vacancy. Subsequently elected.*
*9. Expelled Jan. 10, 1862.*
*10. Appointed by governor to fill vacancy.*
*11. Resigned Dec. 19, 1870.*
*12. Appointed by governor to fill vacancy.*
*13. Died Sept. 20, 1877.*
*14. Appointed by governor to fill vacancy.*
*15. Died April 14, 1918.*
*16. Appointed by governor to fill vacancy.*
*17. Died May 16, 1925.*
*18. Appointed by governor to fill vacancy.*
*19. Resigned Feb. 3, 1933.*
*20. Died Sept. 13, 1960.*
*21. Appointed by governor to fill vacancy. Subsequently elected. Resigned Dec. 27, 1968.*

# MONTANA

(Became a state Nov. 8, 1889)

## Class 1

| Senators | Dates of Service | |
|---|---|---|
| Wilbur F. Sanders (R) | Jan. 1, 1890 | March 3, 1893 |
| Lee Mantle (R)[1] | Jan. 16, 1895 | March 3, 1899 |
| William A. Clark (D)[2] | March 4, 1899 | May 15, 1900 |
| Paris Gibson (D) | March 7, 1901 | March 3, 1905 |
| Thomas H. Carter (R) | March 4, 1905 | March 3, 1911 |
| Henry L. Myers (D) | March 4, 1911 | March 3, 1923 |
| Burton K. Wheeler (D) | March 4, 1923 | Jan. 2, 1947 |
| Zales N. Ecton (R) | Jan. 3, 1947 | Jan. 2, 1953 |
| Mike Mansfield (D) | Jan. 3, 1953 | Jan. 2, 1977 |
| John Melcher (D) | Jan. 3, 1977 | Jan. 2, 1989 |
| Conrad Burns (R) | Jan. 3, 1989 | |

## Class 2

| Senators | Dates of Service | |
|---|---|---|
| Thomas C. Power (R) | Jan. 2, 1890 | March 3, 1895 |
| Thomas H. Carter (R) | March 4, 1895 | March 3, 1901 |
| William A. Clark (D) | March 4, 1901 | March 3, 1907 |
| Joseph M. Dixon (R) | March 4, 1907 | March 3, 1913 |
| Thomas J. Walsh (D)[3] | March 4, 1913 | March 2, 1933 |
| John E. Erickson (D)[4] | March 13, 1933 | Nov. 6, 1934 |
| James E. Murray (D) | Nov. 7, 1934 | Jan. 2, 1961 |
| Lee Metcalf (D)[5] | Jan. 3, 1961 | Jan. 12, 1978 |
| Paul G. Hatfield (D)[6] | Jan. 22, 1978 | Dec. 14, 1978 |
| Max Baucus (D) | Dec. 15, 1978 | |

**Montana**

*1. Vacancy from March 4, 1893, to Jan. 16, 1895, because of failure of legislature to elect.*
*2. Resigned May 15, 1900.*
*3. Died March 2, 1933.*
*4. Appointed by governor to fill vacancy.*
*5. Died Jan. 12, 1978.*
*6. Appointed by governor to fill vacancy. Resigned Dec. 14, 1978.*

# NEBRASKA

(Became a state March 1, 1867)

## Class 1

| Senators | Dates of Service | |
|---|---|---|
| Thomas W. Tipton (R) | March 1, 1867 | March 3, 1875 |
| Algernon S. Paddock (R) | March 4, 1875 | March 3, 1881 |
| Charles H. Van Wyck (R) | March 4, 1881 | March 3, 1887 |
| Algernon S. Paddock (R) | March 4, 1887 | March 3, 1893 |
| William V. Allen (POP) | March 4, 1893 | March 3, 1899 |
| Monroe L. Hayward (R)[1] | March 8, 1899 | Dec. 5, 1899 |

| | | |
|---|---|---|
| William V. Allen (POP)[2] | Dec. 13, 1899 | March 28, 1901 |
| Charles H. Dietrich (R) | March 28, 1901 | March 3, 1905 |
| Elmer J. Burkett (R) | March 4, 1905 | March 3, 1911 |
| Gilbert M. Hitchcock (D) | March 4, 1911 | March 3, 1923 |
| Robert B. Howell (R)[3] | March 4, 1923 | March 11, 1933 |
| William H. Thompson (D)[4] | May 24, 1933 | Nov. 6, 1934 |
| Richard C. Hunter (D) | Nov. 7, 1934 | Jan. 2, 1935 |
| Edward R. Burke (D) | Jan. 3, 1935 | Jan. 2, 1941 |
| Hugh Butler (R)[5] | Jan. 3, 1941 | July 1, 1954 |
| Sam W. Reynolds (R)[6] | July 3, 1954 | Nov. 7, 1954 |
| Roman L. Hruska (R)[7] | Nov. 8, 1954 | Dec. 27, 1976 |
| Edward Zorinsky (D)[8] | Dec. 28, 1976 | March 6, 1987 |
| David Karnes (R)[9] | March 13, 1987 | Jan. 2, 1989 |
| Bob Kerrey (D) | Jan. 3, 1989 | |

### Class 2

| | | |
|---|---|---|
| John M. Thayer (R) | March 1, 1867 | March 3, 1871 |
| Phineas W. Hitchcock (R) | March 4, 1871 | March 3, 1877 |
| Alvin Saunders (R) | March 4, 1877 | March 3, 1883 |
| Charles F. Manderson (R) | March 4, 1883 | March 3, 1895 |
| John M. Thurston (R) | March 4, 1895 | March 3, 1901 |
| Joseph H. Millard (R) | March 28, 1901 | March 3, 1907 |
| Norris Brown (R) | March 4, 1907 | March 3, 1913 |
| George W. Norris (R, I)[10] | March 4, 1913 | Jan. 2, 1943 |
| Kenneth S. Wherry (R)[11] | Jan. 3, 1943 | Nov. 29, 1951 |
| Fred A. Seaton (R)[12] | Dec. 10, 1951 | Nov. 4, 1952 |
| Dwight Griswold (R)[13] | Nov. 5, 1952 | Apr. 12, 1954 |
| Eva Bowring (R)[14] | April 16, 1954 | Nov. 7, 1954 |
| Hazel H. Abel (R)[15] | Nov. 8, 1954 | Dec. 31, 1954 |
| Carl T. Curtis (R) | Jan. 1, 1955 | Jan. 2, 1979 |
| J. James Exon (D) | Jan. 3, 1979 | |

**Nebraska**
1. *Died Dec. 5, 1899.*
2. *Appointed by governor to fill vacancy.*
3. *Died March 11, 1933.*
4. *Appointed by governor to fill vacancy.*
5. *Died July 1, 1954.*
6. *Appointed by governor to fill vacancy.*
7. *Resigned Dec. 27, 1976.*
8. *Died March 6, 1987.*
9. *Appointed by governor to fill vacancy.*
10. *Norris elected as Republican in 1912, 1918, 1924 and 1930. Elected as Independent in 1936.*
11. *Died Nov. 29, 1951.*
12. *Appointed by governor to fill vacancy.*
13. *Died April 12, 1954.*
14. *Appointed by governor to fill vacancy.*
15. *Resigned Dec. 31, 1954.*

# NEVADA

(Became a state Oct. 31, 1864)

### Class 1

| Senators | Dates of Service | |
|---|---|---|
| William M. Stewart (R) | Dec. 15, 1864 | March 3, 1875 |
| William Sharon (R) | March 4, 1875 | March 3, 1881 |
| James G. Fair (D) | March 4, 1881 | March 3, 1887 |
| William M. Stewart (R) | March 4, 1887 | March 3, 1905 |
| George S. Nixon (R)[1] | March 4, 1905 | June 5, 1912 |
| William A. Massey (R)[2] | July 1, 1912 | Jan. 29, 1913 |
| Key Pittman (D)[3] | Jan. 29, 1913 | Nov. 10, 1940 |
| Berkeley L. Bunker (D)[4] | Nov. 27, 1940 | Dec. 6, 1942 |
| James G. Scrugham (D)[5] | Dec. 7, 1942 | June 23, 1945 |
| E. P. Carville (D)[6] | July 25, 1945 | Jan. 2, 1947 |
| George W. Malone (R) | Jan. 3, 1947 | Jan. 2, 1959 |
| Howard W. Cannon (D) | Jan. 3, 1959 | Jan. 2, 1983 |
| Chic Hecht (R) | Jan. 3, 1983 | Jan. 2, 1989 |

| | | |
|---|---|---|
| Richard H. Bryan (D) | Jan. 3, 1989 | |

### Class 3

| | | |
|---|---|---|
| James W. Nye (R) | Dec. 16, 1864 | March 3, 1873 |
| John P. Jones (R) | March 4, 1873 | March 3, 1903 |
| Francis G. Newlands (D)[7] | March 4, 1903 | Dec. 24, 1917 |
| Charles B. Henderson (D)[8] | Jan. 12, 1918 | March 3, 1921 |
| Tasker L. Oddie (R) | March 4, 1921 | March 3, 1933 |
| Patrick A. McCarran (D)[9] | March 4, 1933 | Sept. 28, 1954 |
| Ernest S. Brown (R)[10] | Oct. 1, 1954 | Dec. 1, 1954 |
| Alan Bible (D)[11] | Dec. 2, 1954 | Dec. 17, 1974 |
| Paul Laxalt (R) | Dec. 18, 1974 | Jan. 2, 1987 |
| Harry Reid (D) | Jan. 3, 1987 | |

**Nevada**
1. *Died June 5, 1912.*
2. *Appointed by governor to fill vacancy.*
3. *Died Nov. 10, 1940.*
4. *Appointed by governor to fill vacancy.*
5. *Died June 23, 1945.*
6. *Appointed by governor to fill vacancy.*
7. *Died Dec. 24, 1917.*
8. *Appointed by governor to fill vacancy. Subsequently elected.*
9. *Died Sept. 28, 1954.*
10. *Appointed by governor to fill vacancy.*
11. *Resigned Dec. 17, 1974.*

# NEW HAMPSHIRE

(Ratified the Constitution June 21, 1788)

### Class 2

| Senators | Dates of Service | |
|---|---|---|
| Paine Wingate (FED) | March 4, 1789 | March 3, 1793 |
| Samuel Livermore[1] | March 4, 1793 | June 12, 1801 |
| Simeon Olcott (FED) | June 17, 1801 | March 3, 1805 |
| Nicholas Gilman (D-R)[2] | March 4, 1805 | May 2, 1814 |
| Thomas W. Thompson | June 24, 1814 | March 3, 1817 |
| David L. Morrill (D-R) | March 4, 1817 | March 3, 1823 |
| Samuel Bell (D-R, NR, W) | March 4, 1823 | March 3, 1835 |
| Henry Hubbard (D) | March 4, 1835 | March 3, 1841 |
| Levi Woodbury (D)[3] | March 4, 1841 | Nov. 20, 1845 |
| Benning W. Jenness (D)[4] | Dec. 1, 1845 | June 13, 1846 |
| Joseph Cilley (D) | June 13, 1846 | March 3, 1847 |
| John P. Hale (D) | March 4, 1847 | March 3, 1853 |
| Charles G. Atherton (D)[5] | March 4, 1853 | Nov. 15, 1853 |
| Jared W. Williams[6] | Nov. 29, 1853 | Aug. 3, 1854 |
| John P. Hale (R) | July 30, 1855 | March 3, 1865 |
| Aaron H. Cragin (R) | March 4, 1865 | March 3, 1877 |
| Edward H. Rollins (R) | March 4, 1877 | March 3, 1883 |
| Austin F. Pike (R)[7] | March 4, 1883 | Oct. 8, 1886 |
| Person C. Cheney (R)[8] | Nov. 24, 1886 | June 14, 1887 |
| William E. Chandler (R) | June 14, 1887 | March 3, 1889 |
| Gilman Marston (R)[9] | March 4, 1889 | June 18, 1889 |
| William E. Chandler (R) | June 19, 1889 | March 3, 1901 |
| Henry E. Burnham (R) | March 4, 1901 | March 3, 1913 |
| Henry F. Hollis (D) | March 13, 1913 | March 3, 1919 |
| Henry W. Keyes (R) | March 4, 1919 | Jan. 2, 1937 |
| Styles Bridges (R)[10] | Jan. 3, 1937 | Nov. 26, 1961 |
| Maurice J. Murphy Jr. (R)[11] | Dec. 7, 1961 | Nov. 6, 1962 |
| Thomas J. McIntyre (D) | Nov. 7, 1962 | Jan. 2, 1979 |
| Gordon J. Humphrey (R)[12] | Jan. 3, 1979 | Dec. 4, 1990 |
| Robert F. Smith (R) | Dec. 7, 1990 | |

### Class 3

| | | |
|---|---|---|
| John Langdon (D-R) | March 4, 1789 | March 3, 1801 |
| James Sheafe (FED)[13] | March 4, 1801 | June 14, 1802 |
| William Plumer (FED) | June 17, 1802 | March 3, 1807 |

| | | |
|---|---|---|
| Nahum Parker[14] | March 4, 1807 | June 1, 1810 |
| Charles Cutts (FED)[15] | June 21, 1810 | June 10, 1813 |
| Jeremiah Mason (FED)[16] | June 10, 1813 | June 16, 1817 |
| Clement Storer | June 27, 1817 | March 3, 1819 |
| John F. Parrott (D-R) | March 4, 1819 | March 3, 1825 |
| Levi Woodbury (D-R) | June 16, 1825 | March 3, 1831 |
| Isaac Hill (D)[17] | March 4, 1831 | May 30, 1836 |
| John Page (D) | June 8, 1836 | March 3, 1837 |
| Franklin Pierce (D)[18] | March 4, 1837 | Feb. 28, 1842 |
| Leonard Wilcox (D)[19] | March 1, 1842 | March 3, 1843 |
| Charles G. Atherton (D) | March 4, 1843 | March 3, 1849 |
| Moses Norris Jr. (D)[20] | March 4, 1849 | Jan. 11, 1855 |
| John S. Wells [21] | Jan. 16, 1855 | March 3, 1855 |
| James Bell (R)[22] | July 30, 1855 | May 26, 1857 |
| Daniel Clark (R)[23] | June 27, 1857 | July 27, 1866 |
| George G. Fogg (R)[24] | Aug. 31, 1866 | March 3, 1867 |
| James E. Patterson (R) | March 4, 1867 | March 3, 1873 |
| Bainbridge Wadleigh (R) | March 4, 1873 | March 3, 1879 |
| Charles H. Bell (R)[25] | March 13, 1879 | June 16, 1879 |
| Henry W. Blair (R)[26] | June 17, 1879 | March 3, 1891 |
| Jacob H. Gallinger (R)[27] | March 4, 1891 | Aug. 17, 1918 |
| Irving W. Drew (R)[28] | Sept. 2, 1918 | Nov. 5, 1918 |
| George H. Moses (R) | Nov. 6, 1918 | March 3, 1933 |
| Fred H. Brown (D) | March 4, 1933 | Jan. 2, 1939 |
| Charles W. Tobey (R)[29] | Jan. 3, 1939 | July 24, 1953 |
| Robert W. Upton (R)[30] | Aug. 14, 1953 | Nov. 7, 1954 |
| Norris Cotton (R)[31] | Nov. 8, 1954 | Dec. 31, 1974 |
| Louis C. Wyman (R)[32] | Jan. 1, 1975 | Jan. 2, 1975 |
| Norris Cotton (R)[33] | Aug. 8, 1975 | Sept. 18, 1975 |
| John A. Durkin (D)[34] | Sept. 18, 1975 | Dec. 29, 1980 |
| Warren B. Rudman (R) | Dec. 29, 1980 | Jan. 2, 1993 |
| Judd Gregg (R) | Jan. 3, 1993 | |

**New Hampshire**

1. Resigned June 12, 1801.
2. Died May 2, 1814.
3. Resigned Nov. 20, 1845.
4. Appointed by governor to fill vacancy.
5. Died Nov. 15, 1853.
6. Appointed by governor to fill vacancy. Senate resolution of Aug. 3, 1854, declared that representation under the appointment had expired. Vacancy from Aug. 4, 1854, to July 29, 1855.
7. Died Oct. 8, 1886.
8. Appointed by governor to fill vacancy.
9. Appointed by governor to fill vacancy.
10. Died Nov. 26, 1961.
11. Appointed by governor to fill vacancy.
12. Resigned Dec. 4, 1990.
13. Resigned June 14, 1802.
14. Resigned June 1, 1810.
15. Elected, subsequently appointed by governor to fill vacancy.
16. Resigned June 16, 1817.
17. Resigned May 30, 1836.
18. Resigned Feb. 28, 1842.
19. Appointed by governor to fill vacancy. Subsequently elected.
20. Died Jan. 11, 1855.
21. Appointed by governor to fill vacancy.
22. Died May 26, 1857.
23. Resigned July 27, 1866.
24. Appointed by governor to fill vacancy.
25. Appointed by governor to fill vacancy.
26. Served continuously during this period; twice by election, once by appointment of the governor.
27. Died Aug. 17, 1918.
28. Appointed by governor to fill vacancy.
29. Died July 24, 1953.
30. Appointed by governor to fill vacancy.
31. Resigned Dec. 31, 1974.
32. Appointed by governor to fill vacancy. Wyman and John A. Durkin (D) both claimed to have been elected to the seat for a six-year term beginning Jan. 3, 1975. Neither was seated. After unsuccessfully attempting for seven months to determine the winner, the Senate July 30, 1975, voted to declare the seat vacant effective Aug. 8, 1975.
33. Appointed by governor to fill vacancy.
34. Won special election Sept. 16, 1975. Resigned Dec. 29, 1980.

# NEW JERSEY

(Ratified the Constitution Dec. 18, 1787)

## Class 1

| Senators | Dates of Service | |
|---|---|---|
| Jonathan Elmer (FED) | March 4, 1789 | March 3, 1791 |
| John Rutherfurd (FED)[1] | March 4, 1791 | Nov. 26, 1798 |
| Franklin Davenport[2] | Dec. 5, 1798 | March 3, 1799 |
| James Schureman[3] | March 4, 1799 | Feb. 16, 1801 |
| Aaron Ogden (FED) | Feb. 28, 1801 | March 3, 1803 |
| John Condit (D-R)[4] | Sept. 1, 1803 | March 3, 1809 |
| John Lambert | March 4, 1809 | March 3, 1815 |
| James J. Wilson (D-R)[5] | March 4, 1815 | Jan. 8, 1821 |
| Samuel L. Southard (D-R)[6] | Jan. 26, 1821 | March 3, 1823 |
| Joseph McIlvaine (D-R)[7] | Nov. 12, 1823 | Aug. 19, 1826 |
| Ephraim Bateman (D-R)[8] | Nov. 10, 1826 | Jan. 12, 1829 |
| Mahlon Dickerson (D) | Jan. 30, 1829 | March 3, 1833 |
| Samuel L. Southard (NR, W)[9] | March 4, 1833 | June 26, 1842 |
| William L. Dayton (W)[10] | July 2, 1842 | March 3, 1851 |
| Robert F. Stockton (D)[11] | March 4, 1851 | Jan. 10, 1853 |
| John R. Thomson (D)[12] | March 4, 1853 | Sept. 12, 1862 |
| Richard S. Field (R)[13] | Nov. 21, 1862 | Jan. 14, 1863 |
| James W. Wall (D) | Jan. 14, 1863 | March 3, 1863 |
| William Wright (D)[14] | March 4, 1863 | Nov. 1, 1866 |
| Frederick T. Frelinghuysen (R)[15] | Nov. 12, 1866 | March 3, 1869 |
| John P. Stockton (D) | March 4, 1869 | March 3, 1875 |
| Theodore F. Randolph (D) | March 4, 1875 | March 3, 1881 |
| William J. Sewell (R) | March 4, 1881 | March 3, 1887 |
| Rufus Blodgett (D) | March 4, 1887 | March 3, 1893 |
| James Smith Jr. (D) | March 4, 1893 | March 3, 1899 |
| John Kean (R) | March 4, 1899 | March 3, 1911 |
| James E. Martine (D) | March 4, 1911 | March 3, 1917 |
| Joseph S. Frelinghuysen (R) | March 4, 1917 | March 3, 1923 |
| Edward I. Edwards (D) | March 4, 1923 | March 3, 1929 |
| Hamilton F. Kean (R) | March 4, 1929 | Jan. 2, 1935 |
| A. Harry Moore (D)[16] | Jan. 3, 1935 | Jan. 18, 1938 |
| John Milton (D)[17] | Jan. 18, 1938 | Nov. 8, 1938 |
| W. Warren Barbour (R)[18] | Nov. 9, 1938 | Nov. 22, 1943 |
| Arthur Walsh (D)[19] | Nov. 26, 1943 | Dec. 6, 1944 |
| H. Alexander Smith (R) | Dec. 7, 1944 | Jan. 2, 1959 |
| Harrison A. Williams Jr. (D)[20] | Jan. 3, 1959 | March 11, 1982 |
| Nicholas F. Brady (R)[21] | April 12, 1982 | Dec. 26, 1982 |
| Frank R. Lautenberg (D) | Dec. 27, 1982 | |

## Class 2

| | | |
|---|---|---|
| William Paterson (FED)[22] | March 4, 1789 | Nov. 13, 1790 |
| Philemon Dickinson | Nov. 23, 1790 | March 3, 1793 |
| Frederick Frelinghuysen (FED)[23] | March 4, 1793 | Nov. 12, 1796 |
| Richard Stockton (FED) | Nov. 12, 1796 | March 3, 1799 |
| Jonathan Dayton | March 4, 1799 | March 3, 1805 |
| Aaron Kitchell[24] | March 4, 1805 | March 12, 1809 |
| John Condit (D-R)[25] | March 21, 1809 | March 3, 1817 |
| Mahlon Dickerson (D-R)[26] | March 4, 1817 | Jan. 30, 1829 |
| Theodore Frelinghuysen (NR) | March 4, 1829 | March 3, 1835 |
| Garret D. Wall (D) | March 4, 1835 | March 3, 1841 |
| Jacob W. Miller (W) | March 4, 1841 | March 3, 1853 |
| William Wright (D) | March 4, 1853 | March 3, 1859 |
| John C. Ten Eyck (R) | March 4, 1859 | March 3, 1865 |
| John P. Stockton (D)[27] | March 4, 1865 | March 27, 1866 |
| Alexander G. Cattell (R) | Sept. 19, 1866 | March 3, 1871 |
| Frederick T. Frelinghuysen (R) | March 4, 1871 | March 3, 1877 |
| John R. McPherson (D) | March 4, 1877 | March 3, 1895 |
| William J. Sewell (R)[28] | March 4, 1895 | Dec. 27, 1901 |
| John F. Dryden (R) | Jan. 29, 1902 | March 3, 1907 |
| Frank O. Briggs (R) | March 4, 1907 | March 3, 1913 |
| Wililam Hughes (D)[29] | March 4, 1913 | Jan. 30, 1918 |
| David Baird (R)[30] | Feb. 23, 1918 | March 3, 1919 |

| | | |
|---|---|---|
| Walter E. Edge (R)[31] | March 4, 1919 | Nov. 21, 1929 |
| David Baird Jr. (R)[32] | Nov. 30, 1929 | Dec. 2, 1930 |
| Dwight W. Morrow (R)[33] | Dec. 3, 1930 | Oct. 5, 1931 |
| W. Warren Barbour (R)[34] | Dec. 1, 1931 | Jan. 2, 1937 |
| William H. Smathers (D) | April 15, 1937 | Jan. 2, 1943 |
| Albert W. Hawkes (R) | Jan. 3, 1943 | Jan. 2, 1949 |
| Robert C. Hendrickson (R) | Jan. 3, 1949 | Jan. 2, 1955 |
| Clifford P. Case (R) | Jan. 3, 1955 | Jan. 2, 1979 |
| Bill Bradley (D) | Jan. 3, 1979 | |

**New Jersey**
1. Resigned Nov. 26, 1798.
2. Appointed by governor to fill vacancy.
3. Resigned Feb. 16, 1801.
4. Appointed by governor to fill vacancy. Subsequently elected.
5. Resigned Jan. 8, 1821.
6. Appointed by governor to fill vacancy. Subsequently elected. Resigned March 3, 1823.
7. Died Aug. 19, 1826.
8. Resigned Jan. 12, 1829.
9. Died June 26, 1842.
10. Appointed by governor to fill vacancy. Subsequently elected.
11. Resigned Jan. 10, 1853.
12. Died Sept. 12, 1862.
13. Appointed by governor to fill vacancy.
14. Died Nov. 1, 1866.
15. Appointed by governor to fill vacancy. Subsequently elected.
16. Resigned Jan. 18, 1938.
17. Appointed by governor to fill vacancy.
18. Died Nov. 22, 1943.
19. Appointed by governor to fill vacancy.
20. Resigned March 11, 1982.
21. Appointed by governor to fill vacancy. Resigned Dec. 26, 1982.
22. Resigned Nov. 13, 1790.
23. Resigned Nov. 12, 1796.
24. Resigned March 12, 1809.
25. Appointed by governor to fill vacancy. Subsequently elected.
26. Resigned Jan. 30, 1829.
27. Seat declared vacant March 27, 1866.
28. Died Dec. 27, 1901.
29. Died Jan. 30, 1918.
30. Appointed by governor to fill vacancy. Subsequently elected.
31. Resigned Nov. 21, 1929.
32. Appointed by governor to fill vacancy.
33. Died Oct. 5, 1931.
34. Appointed by governor to fill vacancy. Subsequently elected.

# NEW MEXICO

(Became a state Jan. 6, 1912)

## Class 1

| Senators | Dates of Service | |
|---|---|---|
| Thomas B. Catron (R) | March 27, 1912 | March 3, 1917 |
| Andrieus A. Jones (D)[1] | March 4, 1917 | Dec. 20, 1927 |
| Bronson Cutting (R)[2] | Dec. 29, 1927 | Dec. 6, 1928 |
| Octaviano A. Larrazolo (R) | Dec. 7, 1928 | March 3, 1929 |
| Bronson Cutting (R)[3] | March 4, 1929 | May 6, 1935 |
| Dennis Chavez (D)[4] | May 11, 1935 | Nov. 18, 1962 |
| Edwin L. Mechem (R)[5] | Nov. 30, 1962 | Nov. 3, 1964 |
| Joseph M. Montoya (D) | Nov. 4, 1964 | Jan. 2, 1977 |
| Harrison (Jack) Schmitt (R) | Jan. 3, 1977 | Jan. 2, 1983 |
| Jeff Bingaman (D) | Jan. 3, 1983 | |

## Class 2

| | | |
|---|---|---|
| Albert B. Fall (R)[6] | March 27, 1912 | March 4, 1921 |
| Holm O. Bursum (R)[7] | March 11, 1921 | March 3, 1925 |
| Sam G. Bratton (D)[8] | March 4, 1925 | June 24, 1933 |
| Carl A. Hatch (D)[9] | Oct. 10, 1933 | Jan. 2, 1949 |
| Clinton P. Anderson (D) | Jan. 3, 1949 | Jan. 2, 1973 |
| Pete V. Domenici (R) | Jan. 3, 1973 | |

**New Mexico**
1. Died Dec. 20, 1927.
2. Appointed by governor to fill vacancy.
3. Died May 6, 1935.
4. Appointed by governor to fill vacancy. Subsequently elected. Died Nov. 18, 1962.
5. Appointed by governor to fill vacancy.
6. Resigned March 4, 1921.
7. Appointed by governor to fill vacancy. Subsequently elected.
8. Resigned June 24, 1933.
9. Appointed by governor to fill vacancy. Subsequently elected.

# NEW YORK

(Ratified the Constitution July 26, 1788)

## Class 1

| Senators | Dates of Service | |
|---|---|---|
| Philip Schuyler (FED) | July 15, 1789 | March 3, 1791 |
| Aaron Burr (D-R) | March 4, 1791 | March 3, 1797 |
| Philip Schuyler (FED)[1] | March 4, 1797 | Jan. 3, 1798 |
| John S. Hobart (FED)[2] | Jan. 11, 1798 | April 16, 1798 |
| William North (FED)[3] | May 5, 1798 | Aug. 17, 1798 |
| James Watson (FED)[4] | Aug. 17, 1798 | March 19, 1800 |
| Gouverneur Morris (FED) | April 3, 1800 | March 3, 1803 |
| Theodorus Bailey (D-R)[5] | March 4, 1803 | Jan. 16, 1804 |
| John Armstrong (D-R)[6] | Feb. 4, 1804 | June 30, 1804 |
| Samuel L. Mitchill (D-R) | Nov. 9, 1804 | March 3, 1809 |
| Obadiah German (D-R) | March 4, 1809 | March 3, 1815 |
| Nathan Sanford (D-R) | March 4, 1815 | March 3, 1821 |
| Martin Van Buren (D-R)[7] | March 4, 1821 | Dec. 20, 1828 |
| Charles E. Dudley (D) | Jan. 15, 1829 | March 3, 1833 |
| Nathaniel P. Tallmadge (D)[8] | March 4, 1833 | June 17, 1844 |
| Daniel S. Dickinson (D)[9] | Nov. 30, 1844 | March 3, 1851 |
| Hamilton Fish (W) | March 4, 1851 | March 3, 1857 |
| Preston King (R) | March 4, 1857 | March 3, 1863 |
| Edwin D. Morgan (R) | March 4, 1863 | March 3, 1869 |
| Reuben E. Fenton (R) | March 4, 1869 | March 3, 1875 |
| Francis Kernan (D) | March 4, 1875 | March 3, 1881 |
| Thomas C. Platt (R)[10] | March 4, 1881 | May 16, 1881 |
| Warner Miller (R) | July 16, 1881 | March 3, 1887 |
| Frank Hiscock (R) | March 4, 1887 | March 3, 1893 |
| Edward Murphy Jr. (D) | March 4, 1893 | March 3, 1899 |
| Chauncey M. Depew (R) | March 4, 1899 | March 3, 1911 |
| James A. O'Gorman (D) | March 31, 1911 | March 3, 1917 |
| William M. Calder (R) | March 4, 1917 | March 3, 1923 |
| Royal S. Copeland (D)[11] | March 4, 1923 | June 17, 1938 |
| James M. Mead (D) | Dec. 3, 1938 | Jan. 2, 1947 |
| Irving M. Ives (R) | Jan. 3, 1947 | Jan. 2, 1959 |
| Kenneth B. Keating (R) | Jan. 3, 1959 | Jan. 2, 1965 |
| Robert F. Kennedy (D)[12] | Jan. 3, 1965 | June 6, 1968 |
| Charles E. Goodell (R)[13] | Sept. 10, 1968 | Jan. 2, 1971 |
| James L. Buckley (C-R) | Jan. 3, 1971 | Jan. 2, 1977 |
| Daniel Patrick Moynihan (D) | Jan. 3, 1977 | |

## Class 3

| | | |
|---|---|---|
| Rufus King (FED)[14] | July 16, 1789 | May 23, 1796 |
| John Laurance (FED)[15] | Nov. 9, 1796 | Aug. 1800 |
| John Armstrong (D-R)[16] | Nov. 6, 1800 | Feb. 5, 1802 |
| De Witt Clinton (D-R)[17] | Feb. 9, 1802 | Nov. 4, 1803 |
| John Armstrong (D-R)[18] | Nov. 10, 1803 | Feb. 4, 1804 |
| John Smith (D-R) | Feb. 4, 1804 | March 3, 1813 |
| Rufus King (FED) | March 4, 1813 | March 3, 1825 |
| Nathan Sanford (D-R) | Jan. 14, 1826 | March 3, 1831 |
| William L. Marcy (D)[19] | March 4, 1831 | Jan. 1, 1833 |
| Silas Wright Jr. (D)[20] | Jan. 4, 1833 | Nov. 26, 1844 |
| Henry A. Foster (D)[21] | Nov. 30, 1844 | Jan. 18, 1845 |
| John A. Dix (D) | Jan. 18, 1845 | March 3, 1849 |
| William H. Seward (W) | March 4, 1849 | March 3, 1861 |

| | | |
|---|---|---|
| Ira Harris (R) | March 4, 1861 | March 3, 1867 |
| Roscoe Conkling (R)[22] | March 4, 1867 | May 16, 1881 |
| Elbridge G. Lapham (R) | July 22, 1881 | March 3, 1885 |
| William M. Evarts (R) | March 4, 1885 | March 3, 1891 |
| David B. Hill (D) | Jan. 7, 1892 | March 3, 1897 |
| Thomas C. Platt (R) | March 4, 1897 | March 3, 1909 |
| Elihu Root (R) | March 4, 1909 | March 3, 1915 |
| James W. Wadsworth Jr. (R) | March 4, 1915 | March 3, 1927 |
| Robert F. Wagner (D)[23] | March 4, 1927 | June 28, 1949 |
| John Foster Dulles (R)[24] | July 7, 1949 | Nov. 8, 1949 |
| Herbert H. Lehman (D) | Nov. 9, 1949 | Jan. 2, 1957 |
| Jacob K. Javits (R) | Jan. 9, 1957 | Jan. 2, 1981 |
| Alfonse M. D'Amato (R) | Jan. 3, 1981 | |

**New York**
1. *Resigned Jan. 3, 1798.*
2. *Resigned April 16, 1798.*
3. *Appointed by governor to fill vacancy.*
4. *Resigned March 19, 1800.*
5. *Resigned Jan. 16, 1804.*
6. *Resigned June 30, 1804.*
7. *Resigned Dec. 20, 1828.*
8. *Resigned June 17, 1844.*
9. *Appointed by governor to fill vacancy. Subsequently elected.*
10. *Resigned May 16, 1881.*
11. *Died June 17, 1938.*
12. *Died June 6, 1968.*
13. *Appointed by governor to fill vacancy.*
14. *Resigned May 23, 1796.*
15. *Resigned in August 1800.*
16. *Resigned Feb. 5, 1802.*
17. *Resigned Nov. 4, 1803.*
18. *Appointed by governor to fill vacancy.*
19. *Resigned Jan. 1, 1833.*
20. *Resigned Nov. 26, 1844.*
21. *Appointed by governor to fill vacancy.*
22. *Resigned May 16, 1881.*
23. *Resigned June 28, 1949.*
24. *Appointed by governor to fill vacancy.*

# NORTH CAROLINA

(Ratified the Constitution Nov. 21, 1789)

### Class 2

| **Senators** | **Dates of Service** | |
|---|---|---|
| Samuel Johnston (FED) | Nov. 27, 1789 | March 3, 1793 |
| Alexander Martin (D-R) | March 4, 1793 | March 3, 1799 |
| Jesse Franklin (D-R) | March 4, 1799 | March 3, 1805 |
| James Turner (D-R)[1] | March 4, 1805 | Nov. 21, 1816 |
| Montfort Stokes (D-R) | Dec. 4, 1816 | March 3, 1823 |
| John Branch (D-R)[2] | March 4, 1823 | March 9, 1829 |
| Bedford Brown (D)[3] | Dec. 9, 1829 | Nov. 11, 1840 |
| Willie P. Mangum (W) | Nov. 25, 1840 | March 3, 1853 |
| David S. Reid (D)[4] | Dec. 6, 1854 | March 3, 1859 |
| Thomas Bragg (D)[5] | March 4, 1859 | July 11, 1861 |
| Joseph C. Abbott (R) | July 17, 1868 | March 3, 1871 |
| Matt W. Ransom (D) | Jan. 30, 1872 | March 3, 1895 |
| Marion Butler (POP) | March 4, 1895 | March 3, 1901 |
| Furnifold M. Simmons (D) | March 4, 1901 | March 3, 1931 |
| Josiah W. Bailey (D)[6] | March 4, 1931 | Dec. 15, 1946 |
| William B. Umstead (D)[7] | Dec. 18, 1946 | Dec. 30, 1948 |
| J. Melville Broughton (D)[8] | Dec. 31, 1948 | March 6, 1949 |
| Frank P. Graham (D)[9] | March 29, 1949 | Nov. 26, 1950 |
| Willis Smith (D)[10] | Nov. 27, 1950 | June 23, 1953 |
| Alton A. Lennon (D)[11] | July 10, 1953 | Nov. 28, 1954 |
| W. Kerr Scott (D)[12] | Nov. 29, 1954 | April 16, 1958 |
| B. Everett Jordan (D)[13] | April 19, 1958 | Jan. 2, 1973 |
| Jesse Helms (R) | Jan. 3, 1973 | |

### Class 3

| | | |
|---|---|---|
| Benjamin Hawkins (FED) | Nov. 27, 1789 | March 3, 1795 |
| Timothy Bloodworth (D-R) | March 4, 1795 | March 3, 1801 |
| David Stone (D-R)[14] | March 4, 1801 | Feb. 17, 1807 |
| Jesse Franklin (D-R) | March 4, 1807 | March 3, 1813 |
| David Stone (D-R)[15] | March 4, 1813 | Dec. 24, 1814 |
| Francis Locke (D-R)[16] | | |
| Nathaniel Macon (D-R)[17] | Dec. 5, 1815 | Nov. 14, 1828 |
| James Iredell (D-R) | Dec. 15, 1828 | March 3, 1831 |
| Willie P. Mangum (D)[18] | March 4, 1831 | Nov. 26, 1836 |
| Robert Strange (D)[19] | Dec. 5, 1836 | Nov. 16, 1840 |
| William A. Graham (W) | Nov. 25, 1840 | March 3, 1843 |
| William H. Haywood Jr. (D)[20] | March 4, 1843 | July 25, 1846 |
| George E. Badger (W) | Nov. 25, 1846 | March 3, 1855 |
| Asa Biggs (D)[21] | March 4, 1855 | May 5, 1858 |
| Thomas L. Clingman (D)[22] | May 6, 1858 | July 11, 1861 |
| John Pool (R) | July 17, 1868 | March 3, 1873 |
| Augustus S. Merrimon (D) | March 4, 1873 | March 3, 1879 |
| Zebulon B. Vance (D)[23] | March 4, 1879 | April 14, 1894 |
| Thomas J. Jarvis (D)[24] | April 19, 1894 | Jan. 23, 1895 |
| Jeter C. Pritchard (R) | Jan. 23, 1895 | March 3, 1903 |
| Lee S. Overman (D)[25] | March 4, 1903 | Dec. 12, 1930 |
| Cameron Morrison (D)[26] | Dec. 13, 1930 | Dec. 4, 1932 |
| Robert R. Reynolds (D) | Dec. 5, 1932 | Jan. 2, 1945 |
| Clyde R. Hoey (D)[27] | Jan. 3, 1945 | May 12, 1954 |
| Sam J. Ervin Jr. (D)[28] | June 5, 1954 | Dec. 31, 1974 |
| Robert Morgan (D) | Jan. 3, 1975 | Jan. 2, 1981 |
| John P. East (R)[29] | Jan. 3, 1981 | June 29, 1986 |
| James T. Broyhill (R)[30] | July 14, 1986 | Nov. 4, 1986 |
| Terry Sanford (D)[31] | Nov. 5, 1986 | Jan. 2, 1993 |
| Lauch Faircloth (R) | Jan. 3, 1993 | |

**North Carolina**
1. *Resigned Nov. 21, 1816.*
2. *Resigned March 9, 1829.*
3. *Resigned Nov. 11, 1840.*
4. *Vacancy from March 4, 1853, to Dec. 6, 1854.*
5. *Expelled July 11, 1861. Vacancy until July 17, 1868, because of Civil War.*
6. *Died Dec. 15, 1946.*
7. *Appointed by governor to fill vacancy.*
8. *Died March 6, 1949.*
9. *Appointed by governor to fill vacancy.*
10. *Died June 23, 1953.*
11. *Appointed by governor to fill vacancy.*
12. *Died April 16, 1958.*
13. *Appointed by governor to fill vacancy. Subsequently elected.*
14. *Approximate date of resignation, Feb. 17, 1807.*
15. *Resigned Dec. 24, 1814.*
16. *Elected in 1814 but never seated. Did not qualify. Resigned Dec. 5, 1815.*
17. *Resigned Nov. 14, 1828.*
18. *Resigned Nov. 26, 1836.*
19. *Resigned Nov. 16, 1840.*
20. *Resigned July 25, 1846.*
21. *Resigned May 5, 1858.*
22. *Appointed by governor to fill vacancy. Subsequently elected. Expelled July 11, 1861. Vacancy until July 17, 1868, because of Civil War.*
23. *Died April 14, 1894.*
24. *Appointed by governor to fill vacancy.*
25. *Died Dec. 12, 1930.*
26. *Appointed by governor to fill vacancy.*
27. *Died May 12, 1954.*
28. *Appointed by governor to fill vacancy. Subsequently elected. Resigned Dec. 31, 1974.*
29. *Died June 29, 1986.*
30. *Appointed by governor to fill vacancy.*
31. *Officially sworn in on Dec. 10, 1986.*

# NORTH DAKOTA

(Became a state Nov. 2, 1889)

### Class 1

| Senators | Dates of Service | |
|---|---|---|
| Lyman R. Casey (R) | Nov. 25, 1889 | March 3, 1893 |
| William N. Roach (D) | March 4, 1893 | March 3, 1899 |
| Porter J. McCumber (R) | March 4, 1899 | March 3, 1923 |
| Lynn J. Frazier (R) | March 4, 1923 | Jan. 2, 1941 |
| William Langer (R)[1] | Jan. 3, 1941 | Nov. 8, 1959 |
| C. Norman Brunsdale (R)[2] | Nov. 19, 1959 | Aug. 7, 1960 |
| Quentin N. Burdick (D)[3] | Aug. 8, 1960 | Sept. 8, 1992 |
| Jocelyn B. Burdick (D)[4] | Sept. 12, 1982 | Dec. 4, 1992 |
| Kent Conrad (D)[5] | Dec. 5, 1992 | |

### Class 3

| | | |
|---|---|---|
| Gilbert A. Pierce (R) | Nov. 21, 1889 | March 3, 1891 |
| Henry C. Hansbrough (R) | March 4, 1891 | March 3, 1909 |
| Martin N. Johnson (R)[6] | March 4, 1909 | Oct. 21, 1909 |
| Fountain L. Thompson (D)[7] | Nov. 10, 1909 | Jan. 31, 1910 |
| William E. Purcell (D)[8] | Feb. 1, 1910 | Feb. 1, 1911 |
| Asle J. Gronna (R) | Feb. 2, 1911 | March 3, 1921 |
| Edwin F. Ladd (R)[9] | March 4, 1921 | June 22, 1925 |
| Gerald P. Nye (R)[10] | Nov. 14, 1925 | Jan. 2, 1945 |
| John Moses (D)[11] | Jan. 3, 1945 | March 3, 1945 |
| Milton R. Young (R)[12] | March 12, 1945 | Jan. 2, 1981 |
| Mark Andrews (R) | Jan. 3, 1981 | Jan. 6, 1987 |
| Kent Conrad (D)[13] | Jan. 6, 1987 | Dec. 4, 1992 |
| Byron L. Dorgan (D) | Dec. 14, 1992 | |

**North Dakota**
*1. Died Nov. 8, 1959.*
*2. Appointed by governor to fill vacancy.*
*3. Died Sept. 8, 1992.*
*4. Appointed by governor to fill vacancy.*
*5. Elected in special election to fill remaining two years of term.*
*6. Died Oct. 21, 1909.*
*7. Appointed by governor to fill vacancy. Resigned Jan. 31, 1910.*
*8. Appointed by governor to fill vacancy.*
*9. Died June 22, 1925.*
*10. Appointed by governor to fill vacancy. Subsequently elected.*
*11. Died March 3, 1945.*
*12. Appointed by governor to fill vacancy. Subsequently elected.*
*13. Resigned Dec. 4, 1992.*

# OHIO

(Became a state March 1, 1803)

### Class 1

| Senators | Dates of Service | |
|---|---|---|
| John Smith (D-R)[1] | April 1, 1803 | April 25, 1808 |
| Return J. Meigs Jr. (D-R)[2] | Dec. 12, 1808 | May 10, 1810 |
| Thomas Worthington (D-R)[3] | Dec. 15, 1810 | Dec. 1, 1814 |
| Joseph Kerr (D-R) | Dec. 10, 1814 | March 3, 1815 |
| Benjamin Ruggles (D-R) | March 4, 1815 | March 3, 1833 |
| Thomas Morris (D) | March 4, 1833 | March 3, 1839 |
| Benjamin Tappan (D) | March 4, 1839 | March 3, 1845 |
| Thomas Corwin (W)[4] | March 4, 1845 | July 20, 1850 |
| Thomas Ewing (W)[5] | July 20, 1850 | March 3, 1851 |
| Benjamin F. Wade (W, R) | March 15, 1851 | March 3, 1869 |
| Allen G. Thurman (D) | March 4, 1869 | March 3, 1881 |
| John Sherman (R)[6] | March 4, 1881 | March 5, 1897 |
| Marcus A. Hanna (R)[7] | March 5, 1897 | Feb. 15, 1904 |
| Charles W. F. Dick (R) | March 2, 1904 | March 3, 1911 |

| | | |
|---|---|---|
| Atlee Pomerene (D) | March 4, 1911 | March 3, 1923 |
| Simeon D. Fess (R) | March 4, 1923 | Jan. 2, 1935 |
| Vic Donahey (D) | Jan. 3, 1935 | Jan. 2, 1941 |
| Harold H. Burton (R)[8] | Jan. 3, 1941 | Sept. 30, 1945 |
| James W. Huffman (D)[9] | Oct. 8, 1945 | Nov. 5, 1946 |
| Kingsley A. Taft (R) | Nov. 6, 1946 | Jan. 2, 1947 |
| John W. Bricker (R) | Jan. 3, 1947 | Jan. 2, 1959 |
| Stephen M. Young (D) | Jan. 3, 1959 | Jan. 2, 1971 |
| Robert Taft Jr. (R)[10] | Jan. 3, 1971 | Dec. 28, 1976 |
| Howard M. Metzenbaum (D) | Dec. 29, 1976 | |

### Class 3

| | | |
|---|---|---|
| Thomas Worthington (D-R) | April 1, 1803 | March 3, 1807 |
| Edward Tiffin (D-R)[11] | March 4, 1807 | March 3, 1809 |
| Stanley Griswold (D-R)[12] | May 18, 1809 | Dec. 11, 1809 |
| Alexander Campbell (D-R) | Dec. 11, 1809 | March 3, 1813 |
| Jeremiah Morrow (D-R) | March 4, 1813 | March 3, 1819 |
| William A. Trimble (D-R)[13] | March 4, 1819 | Dec. 13, 1821 |
| Ethan Allen Brown (D-R) | Jan. 3, 1822 | March 3, 1825 |
| William H. Harrison (D-R)[14] | March 4, 1825 | May 20, 1828 |
| Jacob Burnet | Dec. 10, 1828 | March 3, 1831 |
| Thomas Ewing (NR, W) | March 4, 1831 | March 3, 1837 |
| William Allen (D) | March 4, 1837 | March 3, 1849 |
| Salmon P. Chase (F SOIL D) | March 4, 1849 | March 3, 1855 |
| George E. Pugh (D) | March 4, 1855 | March 3, 1861 |
| Salmon P. Chase (R)[15] | March 4, 1861 | March 6, 1861 |
| John Sherman (R)[16] | March 21, 1861 | March 8, 1877 |
| Stanley Matthews (R) | March 21, 1877 | March 3, 1879 |
| George H. Pendleton (D) | March 4, 1879 | March 3, 1885 |
| Henry B. Payne (D) | March 4, 1885 | March 3, 1891 |
| Calvin S. Brice (D) | March 4, 1891 | March 3, 1897 |
| Joseph B. Foraker (R) | March 4, 1897 | March 3, 1909 |
| Theodore E. Burton (R) | March 4, 1909 | March 3, 1915 |
| Warren G. Harding (R)[17] | March 4, 1915 | Jan. 13, 1921 |
| Frank B. Willis (R)[18] | Jan. 14, 1921 | March 30, 1928 |
| Cyrus Locher (D)[19] | April 4, 1928 | Dec. 14, 1928 |
| Theodore E. Burton (R)[20] | Dec. 15, 1928 | Oct. 28, 1929 |
| Roscoe C. McCulloch (R)[21] | Nov. 5, 1929 | Nov. 30, 1930 |
| Robert J. Bulkley (D) | Dec. 1, 1930 | Jan. 2, 1939 |
| Robert A. Taft (R)[22] | Jan. 3, 1939 | July 31, 1953 |
| Thomas A. Burke (D)[23] | Nov. 10, 1953 | Dec. 2, 1954 |
| George H. Bender (R) | Dec. 16, 1954 | Jan. 2, 1957 |
| Frank J. Lausche (D) | Jan. 3, 1957 | Jan. 2, 1969 |
| William B. Saxbe (R)[24] | Jan. 3, 1969 | Jan. 4, 1974 |
| Howard M. Metzenbaum (D)[25] | Jan. 4, 1974 | Dec. 23, 1974 |
| John Glenn (D) | Dec. 24, 1974 | |

**Ohio**
*1. Resigned April 25, 1808.*
*2. Resigned May 10, 1810.*
*3. Resigned Dec. 1, 1814.*
*4. Resigned July 20, 1850.*
*5. Appointed by governor to fill vacancy.*
*6. Resigned March 5, 1897.*
*7. Appointed by governor to fill vacancy. Subsequently elected. Died Feb. 15, 1904.*
*8. Resigned Sept. 30, 1945.*
*9. Appointed by governor to fill vacancy.*
*10. Resigned Dec. 28, 1976.*
*11. Resigned March 3, 1809.*
*12. Appointed by governor to fill vacancy.*
*13. Died Dec. 13, 1821.*
*14. Resigned May 20, 1828.*
*15. Resigned March 6, 1861.*
*16. Resigned March 8, 1877.*
*17. Resigned Jan. 13, 1921, to become president of the United States.*
*18. Died March 30, 1928.*
*19. Appointed by governor to fill vacancy.*
*20. Died Oct. 28, 1929.*
*21. Appointed by governor to fill vacancy.*
*22. Died July 31, 1953.*
*23. Appointed by governor to fill vacancy.*
*24. Resigned Jan. 4, 1974.*
*25. Appointed by governor to fill vacancy. Resigned Dec. 23, 1974.*

# OKLAHOMA

(Became a state Nov. 16, 1907)

### Class 2

| Senators | Dates of Service | |
|---|---|---|
| Robert L. Owen (D) | Dec. 11, 1907 | March 3, 1925 |
| William B. Pine (R) | March 4, 1925 | March 3, 1931 |
| Thomas P. Gore (D) | March 4, 1931 | Jan. 2, 1937 |
| Josh Lee (D) | Jan. 3, 1937 | Jan. 2, 1943 |
| Edward H. Moore (R) | Jan. 3, 1943 | Jan. 2, 1949 |
| Robert S. Kerr (D)[1] | Jan. 3, 1949 | Jan. 1, 1963 |
| J. Howard Edmondson (D)[2] | Jan. 7, 1963 | Nov. 3, 1964 |
| Fred R. Harris (D) | Nov. 4, 1964 | Jan. 2, 1973 |
| Dewey F. Bartlett (R) | Jan. 3, 1973 | Jan. 2, 1979 |
| David L. Boren (D) | Jan. 3, 1979 | |

### Class 3

| | | |
|---|---|---|
| Thomas P. Gore (D) | Dec. 11, 1907 | March 3, 1921 |
| John W. Harreld (R) | March 4, 1921 | March 3, 1927 |
| Elmer Thomas (D) | March 4, 1927 | Jan. 2, 1951 |
| A. S. Mike Monroney (D) | Jan. 3, 1951 | Jan. 2, 1969 |
| Henry Bellmon (R) | Jan. 3, 1969 | Jan. 2, 1981 |
| Don Nickles (R) | Jan. 3, 1981 | |

**Oklahoma**
1. Died Jan. 1, 1963.
2. Appointed by governor to fill vacancy.

# OREGON

(Became a state Feb. 14, 1859)

### Class 2

| Senators | Dates of Service | |
|---|---|---|
| Delazon Smith (D) | Feb. 14, 1859 | March 3, 1859 |
| Edward D. Baker (R)[1] | Oct. 2, 1860 | Oct. 21, 1861 |
| Benjamin Stark (D)[2] | Oct. 29, 1861 | Sept. 12, 1862 |
| Benjamin F. Harding (R) | Sept. 12, 1862 | March 3, 1865 |
| George H. Williams (R) | March 4, 1865 | March 3, 1871 |
| James K. Kelly (D) | March 4, 1871 | March 3, 1877 |
| La Fayette Grover (D) | March 4, 1877 | March 3, 1883 |
| Joseph N. Dolph (R) | March 4, 1883 | March 3, 1895 |
| George W. McBride (R) | March 4, 1895 | March 3, 1901 |
| John H. Mitchell (R)[3] | March 4, 1901 | Dec. 8, 1905 |
| John M. Gearin (D)[4] | Dec. 13, 1905 | Jan. 23, 1907 |
| Frederick W. Mulkey (R) | Jan. 23, 1907 | March 3, 1907 |
| Jonathan Bourne Jr. (R) | March 4, 1907 | March 3, 1913 |
| Harry Lane (D)[5] | March 4, 1913 | May 23, 1917 |
| Charles L. McNary (R)[6] | May 29, 1917 | Nov. 5, 1918 |
| Frederick W. Mulkey (R)[7] | Nov. 6, 1918 | Dec. 17, 1918 |
| Charles L. McNary (R)[8] | Dec. 18, 1918 | Feb. 25, 1944 |
| Guy Cordon (R)[9] | March 4, 1944 | Jan. 2, 1955 |
| Richard L. Neuberger (D)[10] | Jan. 3, 1955 | March 9, 1960 |
| Hall S. Lusk (D)[11] | March 16, 1960 | Nov. 8, 1960 |
| Maurine B. Neuberger (D) | Nov. 9, 1960 | Jan. 2, 1967 |
| Mark O. Hatfield (R) | Jan. 10, 1967 | |

### Class 3

| | | |
|---|---|---|
| Joseph Lane (D) | Feb. 14, 1859 | March 3, 1861 |
| James W. Nesmith (D) | March 4, 1861 | March 3, 1867 |
| Henry W. Corbett (R) | March 4, 1867 | March 3, 1873 |
| John H. Mitchell (R) | March 4, 1873 | March 3, 1879 |
| James H. Slater (D) | March 4, 1879 | March 3, 1885 |
| John H. Mitchell (R) | Nov. 18, 1885 | March 3, 1897 |

| Joseph Simon (R)[12] | Oct. 8, 1898 | March 3, 1903 |
|---|---|---|
| Charles W. Fulton (R) | March 4, 1903 | March 3, 1909 |
| George E. Chamberlain (D) | March 4, 1909 | March 3, 1921 |
| Robert N. Stanfield (R) | March 4, 1921 | March 3, 1927 |
| Frederick Steiwer (R)[13] | March 4, 1927 | Jan. 31, 1938 |
| Alfred Evan Reames (D)[14] | Feb. 1, 1938 | Nov. 8, 1938 |
| Alexander G. Barry (R) | Nov. 9, 1938 | Jan. 2, 1939 |
| Rufus C. Holman (R) | Jan. 3, 1939 | Jan. 2, 1945 |
| Wayne L. Morse (R, I, D)[15] | Jan. 3, 1945 | Jan. 2, 1969 |
| Bob Packwood (R) | Jan. 3, 1969 | |

**Oregon**
1. Vacancy from March 4, 1859, to Oct. 2, 1860. Died Oct. 21, 1861.
2. Appointed by governor to fill vacancy.
3. Died Dec. 8, 1905.
4. Appointed by governor to fill vacancy.
5. Died May 23, 1917.
6. Appointed by governor to fill vacancy.
7. Resigned Dec. 17, 1918.
8. Appointed by governor to fill vacancy. Subsequently elected. Died Feb. 25, 1944.
9. Appointed by governor to fill vacancy. Subsequently elected.
10. Died March 9, 1960.
11. Appointed by governor to fill vacancy.
12. Vacancy from March 4, 1897, to Oct. 7, 1898, because of failure of legislature to elect.
13. Resigned Jan. 31, 1938.
14. Appointed by governor to fill vacancy.
15. Elected as a Republican in 1944 and 1950, as a Democrat in 1956 and 1962. Morse was also an Independent from Oct. 24, 1952, to Feb. 17, 1955.

# PENNSYLVANIA

(Ratified the Constitution Dec. 12, 1787)

### Class 1

| Senators | Dates of Service | |
|---|---|---|
| William Maclay (D-R)[1] | March 4, 1789 | March 3, 1791 |
| Albert Gallatin (D-R)[2] | Feb. 28, 1793 | Feb. 28, 1794 |
| James Ross (FED) | April 1, 1794 | March 3, 1803 |
| Samuel Maclay (D-R)[3] | March 4, 1803 | Jan. 4, 1809 |
| Michael Leib (D-R)[4] | Jan. 9, 1809 | Feb. 14, 1814 |
| Jonathan Roberts (D-R) | Feb. 24, 1814 | March 3, 1821 |
| William Findlay (D-R) | Dec. 10, 1821 | March 3, 1827 |
| Isaac D. Barnard[5] | March 4, 1827 | Dec. 6, 1831 |
| George M. Dallas (D) | Dec. 13, 1831 | March 3, 1833 |
| Samuel McKean (D) | Dec. 7, 1833 | March 3, 1839 |
| Daniel Sturgeon (D) | Jan. 14, 1840 | March 3, 1851 |
| Richard Brodhead (D) | March 4, 1851 | March 3, 1857 |
| Simon Cameron (R)[6] | March 4, 1857 | March 4, 1861 |
| David Wilmot (R) | March 14, 1861 | March 3, 1863 |
| Charles R. Buckalew (D) | March 4, 1863 | March 3, 1869 |
| John Scott (R) | March 4, 1869 | March 3, 1875 |
| William A. Wallace (D) | March 4, 1875 | March 3, 1881 |
| John I. Mitchell (R) | March 4, 1881 | March 3, 1887 |
| Matthew S. Quay (R)[7] | March 4, 1887 | March 3, 1899 |
| Matthew S. Quay (R)[8] | Jan. 17, 1901 | May 28, 1904 |
| Philander C. Knox (R)[9] | June 10, 1904 | March 4, 1909 |
| George T. Oliver (R) | March 17, 1909 | March 3, 1917 |
| Philander C. Knox (R)[10] | March 4, 1917 | Oct. 12, 1921 |
| William E. Crow (R)[11] | Oct. 24, 1921 | Aug. 2, 1822 |
| David A. Reed (R)[12] | Aug. 8, 1922 | Jan. 2, 1935 |
| Joseph F. Guffey (D) | Jan. 3, 1935 | Jan. 2, 1947 |
| Edward Martin (R) | Jan. 3, 1947 | Jan. 2, 1959 |
| Hugh Scott (R) | Jan. 3, 1959 | Jan. 2, 1977 |
| John Heinz (R)[13] | Jan. 3, 1977 | April 4, 1991 |
| Harris Wofford (D)[14] | May 9, 1991 | |

## Class 3

| | | |
|---|---|---|
| Robert Morris (FED) | March 4, 1789 | March 3, 1795 |
| William Bingham (FED) | March 4, 1795 | March 3, 1801 |
| John P. G. Muhlenberg (D-R)[15] | March 4, 1801 | June 30, 1801 |
| George Logan (D-R)[16] | July 13, 1801 | March 3, 1807 |
| Andrew Gregg (D-R) | March 4, 1807 | March 3, 1813 |
| Abner Lacock (D-R) | March 4, 1813 | March 3, 1819 |
| Walter Lowrie (D-R) | March 4, 1819 | March 3, 1825 |
| William Marks (D-R) | March 4, 1825 | March 3, 1831 |
| William Wilkins (D & A-MAS)[17] | March 4, 1831 | June 30, 1834 |
| James Buchanan (D)[18] | Dec. 6, 1834 | March 5, 1845 |
| Simon Cameron (D) | March 13, 1845 | March 3, 1849 |
| James Cooper (W) | March 4, 1849 | March 3, 1855 |
| William Bigler (D) | Jan. 14, 1856 | March 3, 1861 |
| Edgar Cowan (R) | March 4, 1861 | March 3, 1867 |
| Simon Cameron (R)[19] | March 4, 1867 | March 3, 1877 |
| J. Donald Cameron (R) | March 20, 1877 | March 3, 1897 |
| Boies Penrose (R)[20] | March 4, 1897 | Dec. 31, 1921 |
| George Wharton Pepper (R)[21] | Jan. 9, 1922 | March 3, 1927 |
| William S. Vare (R)[22] | | |
| Joseph R. Grundy (R)[23] | Dec. 11, 1929 | Dec. 1, 1930 |
| James J. Davis (R) | Dec. 2, 1930 | Jan. 2, 1945 |
| Francis J. Myers (D) | Jan. 3, 1945 | Jan. 2, 1951 |
| James H. Duff (R) | Jan. 16, 1951 | Jan. 2, 1957 |
| Joseph S. Clark (D) | Jan. 3, 1957 | Jan. 2, 1969 |
| Richard S. Schweiker (R) | Jan. 3, 1969 | Jan. 2, 1981 |
| Arlen Specter (R) | Jan. 3, 1981 | |

**Pennsylvania**

*1. Vacancy from March 4, 1791, to Feb. 28, 1793, because of failure of legislature to elect.*

*2. Senate resolution of Feb. 28, 1794, declared that Gallatin had not been a citizen for the nine years required by the Constitution for Senate membership.*

*3. Resigned Jan. 4, 1809.*

*4. Resigned Feb. 14, 1814.*

*5. Resigned Dec. 6, 1831.*

*6. Resigned March 4, 1861.*

*7. Quay was elected for two six-year terms, his second term expiring March 3, 1899. The legislature adjourned without electing a senator for the new term beginning March 4, 1899. Quay was appointed by the governor to fill the vacancy on April 21, 1899. When the Senate convened, he presented his credentials Dec. 25, 1899, but was not permitted to take his seat. On April 24, 1900, the seat was declared vacant. Quay was elected to fill the vacancy and took his seat Jan. 17, 1901.*

*8. Died May 28, 1904.*

*9. Appointed by governor to fill vacancy. Subsequently elected. Resigned March 4, 1909.*

*10. Died Oct. 12, 1921.*

*11. Appointed by governor to fill vacancy. Died Aug. 2, 1922.*

*12. Appointed by governor to fill vacancy. Subsequently elected.*

*13. Died April 4, 1991.*

*14. Appointed by governor to fill vacancy. Subsequently elected.*

*15. Resigned June 30, 1801.*

*16. Appointed by governor to fill vacancy. Subsequently elected.*

*17. Resigned June 30, 1834.*

*18. Resigned March 5, 1845.*

*19. Resigned March 3, 1877.*

*20. Died Dec. 31, 1921.*

*21. Appointed by governor to fill vacancy. Subsequently elected.*

*22. Credentials as senator-elect were presented and referred to the Committee on Privileges and Elections. Meanwhile Vare was not permitted to take his seat and on Dec. 6, 1929, was declared not entitled to a seat.*

*23. Appointed by governor to fill vacancy.*

# RHODE ISLAND

(Ratified the Constitution May 29, 1790)

## Class 1

| Senators | Dates of Service | |
|---|---|---|
| Theodore Foster (LAW ORD) | June 7, 1790 | March 3, 1803 |
| Samuel J. Potter[1] | March 4, 1803 | Oct. 14, 1804 |
| Benjamin Howland (D-R) | Oct. 29, 1804 | March 3, 1809 |
| Francis Malbone[2] | March 4, 1809 | June 4, 1809 |
| Christopher G. Champlin[3] | June 26, 1809 | Oct. 2, 1811 |
| William Hunter (FED) | Oct. 28, 1811 | March 3, 1821 |
| James De Wolf (D-R)[4] | March 4, 1821 | Oct. 31, 1825 |
| Asher Robbins (D-R, NR, W) | Oct. 31, 1825 | March 3, 1839 |
| Nathan F. Dixon (W)[5] | March 4, 1839 | Jan. 29, 1842 |
| William Sprague (W)[6] | Feb. 5, 1842 | Jan. 17, 1844 |
| John B. Francis (LAW ORD) | Jan. 25, 1844 | March 3, 1845 |
| Albert C. Greene (W) | March 4, 1845 | March 3, 1851 |
| Charles T. James (D) | March 4, 1851 | March 3, 1857 |
| James F. Simmons (R)[7] | March 4, 1857 | Aug. 15, 1862 |
| Samuel G. Arnold (R) | Sept. 5, 1862 | March 3, 1863 |
| Wiliam Sprague (R)[8] | March 4, 1863 | March 3, 1875 |
| Ambrose E. Burnside (R)[9] | March 4, 1875 | Sept. 13, 1881 |
| Nelson W. Aldrich (R) | Oct. 5, 1881 | March 3, 1911 |
| Henry F. Lippitt (R) | March 4, 1911 | March 3, 1917 |
| Peter G. Gerry (D) | March 4, 1917 | March 3, 1929 |
| Felix Hebert (R) | March 4, 1929 | Jan. 2, 1935 |
| Peter G. Gerry (D) | Jan. 3, 1935 | Jan. 2, 1947 |
| J. Howard McGrath (D)[10] | Jan. 3, 1947 | Aug. 23, 1949 |
| Edward L. Leahy (D)[11] | Aug. 24, 1949 | Dec. 18, 1950 |
| John O. Pastore (D)[12] | Dec. 19, 1950 | Dec. 28, 1976 |
| John H. Chafee (R) | Dec. 29, 1976 | |

## Class 2

| | | |
|---|---|---|
| Joseph Stanton Jr. (D-R) | June 7, 1790 | March 3, 1793 |
| William Bradford [13] | March 4, 1793 | October 1797 |
| Ray Greene (FED)[14] | Nov. 13, 1797 | March 5, 1801 |
| Christopher Ellery (D-R) | May 6, 1801 | March 3, 1805 |
| James Fenner (D-R)[15] | March 4, 1805 | September 1807 |
| Elisha Mathewson (D-R) | Oct. 26, 1807 | March 3, 1811 |
| Jeremiah B. Howell (FED) | March 4, 1811 | March 3, 1817 |
| James Burrill Jr. (D-R)[16] | March 4, 1817 | Dec. 25, 1820 |
| Nehemiah R. Knight (D-R, D) | Jan. 9, 1821 | March 3, 1841 |
| James F. Simmons (W) | March 4, 1841 | March 3, 1847 |
| John H. Clarke (W) | March 4, 1847 | March 3, 1853 |
| Philip Allen (D) | July 20, 1853 | March 3, 1859 |
| Henry B. Anthony (R)[17] | March 4, 1859 | Sept. 2, 1884 |
| William P. Sheffield (R)[18] | Nov. 19, 1884 | Jan. 20, 1885 |
| Jonathan Chace (R)[19] | Jan. 20, 1885 | April 9, 1889 |
| Nathan F. Dixon III (R) | April 10, 1889 | March 3, 1895 |
| George Peabody Wetmore (R) | March 4, 1895 | March 3, 1907 |
| George Peabody Wetmore (R)[20] | Jan. 22, 1908 | March 3, 1913 |
| LeBaron B. Colt (R)[21] | March 4, 1913 | Aug. 18, 1924 |
| Jesse H. Metcalf (R) | Nov. 5, 1924 | Jan. 2, 1937 |
| Theodore F. Green (D) | Jan. 3, 1937 | Jan. 2, 1961 |
| Claiborne Pell (D) | Jan. 3, 1961 | |

**Rhode Island**

*1. Died Oct. 14, 1804.*

*2. Died June 4, 1809.*

*3. Resigned Oct. 2, 1811.*

*4. Resigned Oct. 31, 1825.*

*5. Died Jan. 29, 1842.*

*6. Resigned Jan. 17, 1844.*

*7. Resigned Aug. 15, 1862.*

*8. Nephew of William Sprague, listed above with footnote 6.*

*9. Died Sept. 13, 1881.*

*10. Resigned Aug. 23, 1949.*

11. *Appointed by governor to fill vacancy.*
12. *Resigned Dec. 28, 1976.*
13. *Resigned in October 1797.*
14. *Resigned March 5, 1801.*
15. *Resigned in September 1807.*
16. *Died Dec. 25, 1820.*
17. *Died Sept. 2, 1884.*
18. *Appointed by governor to fill vacancy.*
19. *Resigned April 9, 1889.*
20. *Vacant March 4, 1907 to Jan. 22, 1908, because of failure of legislature to elect.*
21. *Died Aug. 18, 1924.*

# SOUTH CAROLINA

(Ratified the Constitution May 23, 1788)

## Class 2

| Senators | Dates of Service | |
|---|---|---|
| Pierce Butler (D-R)[1] | March 4, 1789 | Oct. 25, 1796 |
| John Hunter (FED)[2] | Dec. 8, 1796 | Nov. 26, 1798 |
| Charles Pinckney (D-R)[3] | Dec. 6, 1798 | 1801 |
| Thomas Sumter (D-R)[4] | Dec. 15, 1801 | Dec. 16, 1810 |
| John Taylor (D-R)[5] | Dec. 31, 1810 | November 1816 |
| William Smith (D-R) | Dec. 4, 1816 | March 3, 1823 |
| Robert Y. Hayne (D-R)[6] | March 4, 1823 | Dec. 13, 1832 |
| John C. Calhoun (D)[7] | Dec. 29, 1832 | March 3, 1843 |
| Daniel Elliott Huger (D)[8] | March 4, 1843 | March 3, 1845 |
| John C. Calhoun (D)[9] | Nov. 26, 1845 | March 31, 1850 |
| Franklin H. Elmore (D)[10] | April 11, 1850 | May 29, 1850 |
| Robert W. Barnwell (D)[11] | June 4, 1850 | Dec. 18, 1850 |
| R. Barnwell Rhett (D)[12] | Dec. 18, 1850 | May 7, 1852 |
| William F. DeSaussure (D)[13] | May 10, 1852 | March 3, 1853 |
| Josiah J. Evans (D)[14] | March 4, 1853 | May 6, 1858 |
| Arthur P. Hayne (D)[15] | May 11, 1858 | Dec. 2, 1858 |
| James Chestnut Jr. (D)[16] | Dec. 3, 1858 | July 11, 1861 |
| Thomas J. Robertson (R) | July 15, 1868 | March 3, 1877 |
| Matthew C. Butler (D) | March 4, 1877 | March 3, 1895 |
| Benjamin R. Tillman (D)[17] | March 4, 1895 | July 3, 1918 |
| Christie Bénet (D)[18] | July 6, 1918 | Nov. 5, 1918 |
| William P. Pollock (D) | Nov. 6, 1918 | March 3, 1919 |
| Nathaniel B. Dial (D) | March 4, 1919 | March 3, 1925 |
| Coleman L. Blease (D) | March 4, 1925 | March 3, 1931 |
| James F. Byrnes (D)[19] | March 4, 1931 | July 8, 1941 |
| Alva M. Lumpkin (D)[20] | July 17, 1941 | Aug. 1, 1941 |
| Roger C. Peace (D)[21] | Aug. 5, 1941 | Nov. 4, 1941 |
| Burnet R. Maybank (D)[22] | Nov. 5, 1941 | Sept. 1, 1954 |
| Charles E. Daniel (D)[23] | Sept. 6, 1954 | Dec. 23, 1954 |
| Strom Thurmond (D)[24] | Dec. 24, 1954 | April 4, 1956 |
| Thomas A. Wofford (D)[25] | April 5, 1956 | Nov. 6, 1956 |
| Strom Thurmond (D, R)[26] | Nov. 7, 1956 | |

## Class 3

| | | |
|---|---|---|
| Ralph Izard (FED) | March 4, 1789 | March 3, 1795 |
| Jacob Read (FED) | March 4, 1795 | March 3, 1801 |
| John E. Colhoun (D-R)[27] | March 4, 1801 | Oct. 26, 1802 |
| Pierce Butler (D-R)[28] | Nov. 4, 1802 | Nov. 21, 1804 |
| John Gaillard (D-R)[29] | Dec. 6, 1804 | Feb. 26, 1826 |
| William Harper (D-R)[30] | March 8, 1826 | Nov. 29, 1826 |
| William Smith (D-R) | Nov. 29, 1826 | March 3, 1831 |
| Stephen D. Miller (D)[31] | March 4, 1831 | March 2, 1833 |
| William C. Preston (D)[32] | Nov. 26, 1833 | Nov. 29, 1842 |
| George McDuffie (D)[33] | Dec. 2, 1842 | Aug. 17, 1846 |
| Andrew P. Butler (D)[34] | Dec. 4, 1846 | May 25, 1857 |
| James H. Hammond (D)[35] | Dec. 7, 1857 | Nov. 11, 1860 |
| Frederick A. Sawyer (R) | July 16, 1868 | March 3, 1873 |
| John J. Patterson (R) | March 4, 1873 | March 3, 1879 |
| Wade Hampton (D) | March 4, 1879 | March 3, 1891 |
| John L. M. Irby (D) | March 4, 1891 | March 3, 1897 |

| | | |
|---|---|---|
| Joseph H. Earle (D)[36] | March 4, 1897 | May 20, 1897 |
| John L. McLaurin (D)[37] | May 27, 1897 | March 3, 1903 |
| Asbury C. Latimer (D)[38] | March 4, 1903 | Feb. 20, 1908 |
| Frank B. Gary (D) | March 6, 1908 | March 3, 1909 |
| Ellison D. Smith (D)[39] | March 4, 1909 | Nov. 17, 1944 |
| Wilton E. Hall (D)[40] | Nov. 20, 1944 | Jan. 2, 1945 |
| Olin D. Johnston (D)[41] | Jan. 3, 1945 | April 18, 1965 |
| Donald Russell (D)[42] | April 22, 1965 | Nov. 8, 1966 |
| Ernest F. Hollings (D) | Nov. 9, 1966 | |

**South Carolina**
1. *Resigned Oct. 25, 1796.*
2. *Resigned Nov. 26, 1798.*
3. *Resigned in 1801.*
4. *Resigned Dec. 16, 1810.*
5. *Resigned in November 1816.*
6. *Resigned Dec. 13, 1832.*
7. *Resigned March 3, 1843.*
8. *Resigned March 3, 1845. Seat vacant until Nov. 26, 1845.*
9. *Died March 31, 1850.*
10. *Appointed by governor to fill vacancy. Died May 29, 1850.*
11. *Appointed by governor to fill vacancy.*
12. *Resigned May 7, 1852.*
13. *Appointed by governor to fill vacancy. Subsequently elected.*
14. *Died May 6, 1858.*
15. *Appointed by governor to fill vacancy.*
16. *Expelled July 11, 1861. Vacancy until July 15, 1868, because of Civil War.*
17. *Died July 3, 1918.*
18. *Appointed by governor to fill vacancy.*
19. *Resigned July 8, 1941.*
20. *Appointed by governor to fill vacancy. Died Aug. 1, 1941.*
21. *Appointed by governor to fill vacancy.*
22. *Died Sept. 1, 1954.*
23. *Appointed by governor to fill vacancy. Resigned Dec. 23, 1954.*
24. *Resigned April 4, 1956.*
25. *Appointed by governor to fill vacancy.*
26. *Became a Republican on Sept. 16, 1964.*
27. *Died Oct. 26, 1802.*
28. *Resigned Nov. 21, 1804.*
29. *Died Feb. 26, 1826.*
30. *Appointed by governor to fill vacancy.*
31. *Resigned March 2, 1833.*
32. *Resigned Nov. 29, 1842.*
33. *Resigned Aug. 17, 1846.*
34. *Died May 25, 1857.*
35. *Did not attend sessions of the Senate after Nov. 11, 1860. Vacancy until July 16, 1868, because of Civil War.*
36. *Died May 20, 1897.*
37. *Appointed by governor to fill vacancy. Subsequently elected.*
38. *Died Feb. 20, 1908.*
39. *Died Nov. 17, 1944.*
40. *Appointed by governor to fill vacancy.*
41. *Died April 18, 1965.*
42. *Appointed by governor to fill vacancy.*

# SOUTH DAKOTA

(Became a state Nov. 2, 1889)

## Class 2

| Senators | Dates of Service | |
|---|---|---|
| Richard F. Pettigrew (R) | Nov. 2, 1889 | March 3, 1901 |
| Robert J. Gamble (R) | March 4, 1901 | March 3, 1913 |
| Thomas Sterling (R) | March 4, 1913 | March 3, 1925 |
| William H. McMaster (R) | March 4, 1925 | March 3, 1931 |
| William J. Bulow (D) | March 4, 1931 | Jan. 2, 1943 |
| Harlan J. Bushfield (R)[1] | Jan. 3, 1943 | Sept. 27, 1948 |
| Vera C. Bushfield (R)[2] | Oct. 6, 1948 | Dec. 26, 1948 |
| Karl E. Mundt (R) | Dec. 31, 1948 | Jan. 2, 1973 |
| James Abourezk (D) | Jan. 3, 1973 | Jan. 2, 1979 |
| Larry Pressler (R) | Jan. 3, 1979 | |

## Class 3

| Senator | | |
|---|---|---|
| Gideon C. Moody (R) | Nov. 2, 1889 | March 3, 1891 |
| James H. Kyle (I)[3] | March 4, 1891 | July 1, 1901 |
| Alfred B. Kittredge (R)[4] | July 11, 1901 | March 3, 1909 |
| Coe I. Crawford (R) | March 4, 1909 | March 3, 1915 |
| Edwin S. Johnson (D) | March 4, 1915 | March 3, 1921 |
| Peter Norbeck (R)[5] | March 4, 1921 | Dec. 20, 1936 |
| Herbert E. Hitchcock (D)[6] | Dec. 29, 1936 | Nov. 8, 1938 |
| Gladys Pyle (R) | Nov. 9, 1938 | Jan. 2, 1939 |
| J. Chandler Gurney (R) | Jan. 3, 1939 | Jan. 2, 1951 |
| Francis Case (R)[7] | Jan. 3, 1951 | June 22, 1962 |
| Joe H. Bottum (R)[8] | July 9, 1962 | Jan. 2, 1963 |
| George McGovern (D) | Jan. 3, 1963 | Jan. 2, 1981 |
| James Abdnor (R) | Jan. 3, 1981 | Jan. 2, 1987 |
| Thomas A. Daschle (D) | Jan. 3, 1987 | |

**South Dakota**
1. Died Sept. 27, 1948.
2. Appointed by governor to fill vacancy. Resigned Dec. 26, 1948.
3. Died July 1, 1901.
4. Appointed by governor to fill vacancy. Subsequently elected.
5. Died Dec. 20, 1936.
6. Appointed by governor to fill vacancy.
7. Died June 22, 1962.
8. Appointed by governor to fill vacancy.

# TENNESSEE

(Became a state June 1, 1796)

## Class 1

| Senators | Dates of Service | |
|---|---|---|
| William Cocke (D-R) | Aug. 2, 1796 | March 3, 1797 |
| William Cocke (D-R)[1] | April 22, 1797 | Sept. 26, 1797 |
| Andrew Jackson (D-R)[2] | Sept. 26, 1797 | April 1798 |
| Daniel Smith (D-R)[3] | Oct. 6, 1798 | Dec. 12, 1798 |
| Joseph Anderson (D-R)[4] | March 4, 1799 | March 3, 1815 |
| George W. Campbell (D-R)[5] | Oct. 10, 1815 | April 20, 1818 |
| John H. Eaton (D-R)[6] | Sept. 5, 1818 | March 9, 1829 |
| Felix Grundy (D)[7] | Oct. 19, 1829 | July 4, 1838 |
| Ephraim H. Foster (W)[8] | Sept. 17, 1838 | March 3, 1839 |
| Felix Grundy (D)[9] | Dec. 14, 1839 | Dec. 19, 1840 |
| Alfred O. P. Nicholson (D)[10] | Dec. 25, 1840 | Feb. 7, 1942 |
| Ephraim H. Foster (W) | Oct. 17, 1843 | March 3, 1845 |
| Hopkins L. Turney (W) | March 4, 1845 | March 3, 1851 |
| James C. Jones (W) | March 4, 1851 | March 3, 1857 |
| Andrew Johnson (D)[11] | Oct. 8, 1857 | March 4, 1862 |
| David T. Patterson (D) | July 28, 1866 | March 3, 1869 |
| William G. Brownlow (R) | March 4, 1869 | March 3, 1875 |
| Andrew Johnson (D)[12] | March 4, 1875 | July 31, 1875 |
| David M. Key (D)[13] | Aug. 18, 1875 | Jan. 19, 1877 |
| James E. Bailey (D) | Jan. 19, 1877 | March 3, 1881 |
| Howell E. Jackson (D)[14] | March 4, 1881 | April 14, 1886 |
| W. C. Whitthorne (D)[15] | April 16, 1886 | March 3, 1887 |
| William B. Bate (D)[16] | March 4, 1887 | March 9, 1905 |
| James B. Frazier (D) | March 21, 1905 | March 3, 1911 |
| Luke Lea (D) | March 4, 1911 | March 3, 1917 |
| Kenneth D. McKellar (D) | March 4, 1917 | Jan. 2, 1953 |
| Albert Gore (D) | Jan. 3, 1953 | Jan. 2, 1971 |
| Bill Brock (R) | Jan. 3, 1971 | Jan. 2, 1977 |
| Jim Sasser (D) | Jan. 3, 1977 | |

## Class 2

| | | |
|---|---|---|
| William Blount (D-R)[17] | Aug. 2, 1796 | July 8, 1797 |
| Joseph Anderson (D-R) | Sept. 26, 1797 | March 3, 1799 |
| William Cocke (D-R) | March 4, 1799 | March 3, 1805 |
| Daniel Smith (D-R)[18] | March 4, 1805 | March 31, 1809 |

| | | |
|---|---|---|
| Jenkin Whiteside (D-R)[19] | April 11, 1809 | Oct. 8, 1811 |
| George W. Campbell (D-R)[20] | Oct. 8, 1811 | Feb. 11, 1814 |
| Jesse Wharton (D-R)[21] | March 17, 1814 | Oct. 10, 1815 |
| John Williams (D-R)[22] | Oct. 10, 1815 | March 3, 1823 |
| Andrew Jackson (D-R)[23] | March 4, 1823 | Oct. 14, 1825 |
| Hugh Lawson White (D-R, D) | Oct. 28, 1825 | March 3, 1835 |
| Hugh Lawson White (D)[24] | Oct. 6, 1835 | Jan. 13, 1840 |
| Alexander Anderson (D) | Jan. 27, 1840 | March 4, 1841 |
| Spencer Jarnagin (W)[25] | Oct. 17, 1843 | March 3, 1847 |
| John Bell (W) | Nov. 22, 1847 | March 3, 1853 |
| John Bell (W) | Oct. 29, 1853 | March 3, 1859 |
| Alfred O. P. Nicholson (D)[26] | March 4, 1859 | July 11, 1861 |
| Joseph S. Fowler (UN R) | July 25, 1866 | March 3, 1871 |
| Henry Cooper (D) | March 4, 1871 | March 3, 1877 |
| Isham G. Harris (D)[27] | March 4, 1877 | July 8, 1897 |
| Thomas B. Turley (D)[28] | July 20, 1897 | March 3, 1901 |
| Edward W. Carmack (D) | March 4, 1901 | March 3, 1907 |
| Robert L. Taylor (D)[29] | March 4, 1907 | March 31, 1912 |
| Newell Sanders (R)[30] | April 8, 1912 | Jan. 24, 1913 |
| William R. Webb (D) | Jan. 24, 1913 | March 3, 1913 |
| John K. Shields (D) | March 4, 1913 | March 3, 1925 |
| Lawrence D. Tyson (D)[31] | March 4, 1925 | Aug. 24, 1929 |
| William E. Brock (D)[32] | Sept. 2, 1929 | March 3, 1931 |
| Cordell Hull (D)[33] | March 4, 1931 | March 3, 1933 |
| Nathan L. Bachman (D)[34] | March 4, 1933 | April 23, 1937 |
| George L. Berry (D)[35] | May 6, 1937 | Nov. 8, 1938 |
| Tom Stewart (D) | Jan. 16, 1939 | Jan. 2, 1949 |
| Estes Kefauver (D)[36] | Jan. 3, 1949 | Aug. 10, 1963 |
| Herbert S. Walters (D)[37] | Aug. 20, 1963 | Nov. 3, 1964 |
| Ross Bass (D) | Nov. 4, 1964 | Jan. 2, 1967 |
| Howard H. Baker Jr. (R) | Jan. 3, 1967 | Jan. 2, 1985 |
| Albert Gore Jr. (D)[38] | Jan. 3, 1985 | Jan. 1, 1993 |
| Harlan Mathews (D)[39] | Jan. 2, 1993 | |

**Tennessee**
1. Appointed by governor to fill vacancy.
2. Resigned in April 1798.
3. Appointed by governor to fill vacancy.
4. Served twice through election and once by appointment of the governor during this period.
5. Resigned April 20, 1818.
6. Appointed by governor to fill vacancy. Resigned March 9, 1829.
7. Resigned July 4, 1838.
8. Appointed by governor to fill vacancy. Subsequently elected for term beginning March 4, 1839, but resigned March 3, 1839. Vacancy until Dec. 14, 1839.
9. Died Dec. 19, 1840.
10. Appointed by governor to fill vacancy.
11. Resigned March 4, 1862. Vacancy until July 28, 1866, because of Civil War.
12. Died July 31, 1875.
13. Appointed by governor to fill vacancy.
14. Resigned April 14, 1886.
15. Appointed by governor to fill vacancy.
16. Died March 9, 1905.
17. Expelled July 8, 1797.
18. Resigned March 31, 1809.
19. Resigned Oct. 8, 1811.
20. Resigned Feb. 11, 1814.
21. Appointed by governor to fill vacancy.
22. Williams served twice by election and once by appointment of the governor during this period.
23. Resigned Oct. 14, 1825.
24. White's seat was vacant between March 4, 1835, and Oct. 5, 1835. Resigned Jan. 13, 1840.
25. Vacancy from March 4, 1841, to Oct. 17, 1843.
26. Expelled July 11, 1861. Vacant until July 25, 1866, because of Civil War.
27. Died July 8, 1897.
28. Appointed by governor to fill vacancy. Subsequently elected.
29. Died March 31, 1912.
30. Appointed by governor to fill vacancy.
31. Died Aug. 24, 1929.
32. Appointed by governor to fill vacancy. Subsequently elected.
33. Resigned March 3, 1933.
34. Appointed by governor to fill vacancy. Subsequently elected. Died April 23, 1937.

35. *Appointed by governor to fill vacancy.*
36. *Died Aug. 10, 1963.*
37. *Appointed by governor to fill vacancy.*
38. *Resigned Jan. 1, 1993, having been elected vice president of the United States.*
39. *Appointed by governor to fill vacancy.*

# TEXAS

(Became a state Dec. 29, 1845)

## Class 1

| Senators | Dates of Service | |
|---|---|---|
| Thomas J. Rusk (D)[1] | Feb. 21, 1846 | July 29, 1857 |
| J. P. Henderson (D)[2] | Nov. 9, 1857 | June 4, 1858 |
| Matthias Ward (D)[3] | Sept. 27, 1858 | Dec. 5, 1859 |
| Louis T. Wigfall (D)[4] | Dec. 5, 1859 | July 11, 1861 |
| J. W. Flanagan (R) | March 31, 1870 | March 3, 1875 |
| Samuel B. Maxey (D) | March 4, 1875 | March 3, 1887 |
| John H. Reagan (D)[5] | March 4, 1887 | June 10, 1891 |
| Horace Chilton (D)[6] | June 10, 1891 | March 22, 1892 |
| Roger Q. Mills (D) | March 23, 1892 | March 3, 1899 |
| Charles A. Culberson (D) | March 4, 1899 | March 3, 1923 |
| Earle B. Mayfield (D) | March 4, 1923 | March 3, 1929 |
| Tom Connally (D) | March 4, 1929 | Jan. 2, 1953 |
| Price Daniel (D)[7] | Jan. 3, 1953 | Jan. 14, 1957 |
| William A. Blakley (D)[8] | Jan. 15, 1957 | April 28, 1957 |
| Ralph Yarborough (D) | April 29, 1957 | Jan. 2, 1971 |
| Lloyd Bentsen (D)[9] | Jan. 3, 1971 | Jan. 20, 1993 |
| Bob Krueger (D)[10] | Jan. 21, 1993 | June 13, 1993 |
| Kay Bailey Hutchison (R)[11] | June 14, 1993 | |

## Class 2

| Senators | Dates of Service | |
|---|---|---|
| Sam Houston (D) | Feb. 21, 1846 | March 3, 1859 |
| John Hemphill (D)[12] | March 4, 1859 | July 11, 1861 |
| Morgan C. Hamilton (R) | March 31, 1870 | March 3, 1877 |
| Richard Coke (D) | March 4, 1877 | March 3, 1895 |
| Horace Chilton (D) | March 4, 1895 | March 3, 1901 |
| Joseph W. Bailey (D)[13] | March 4, 1901 | Jan. 3, 1913 |
| Rienzi M. Johnston (D)[14] | Jan. 4, 1913 | Jan. 29, 1913 |
| Morris Sheppard (D)[15] | Jan. 29, 1913 | April 9, 1941 |
| Andrew Jackson Houston (D)[16] | April 21, 1941 | June 26, 1941 |
| W. Lee O'Daniel (D) | Aug. 4, 1941 | Jan. 2, 1949 |
| Lyndon B. Johnson (D)[17] | Jan. 3, 1949 | Jan. 3, 1961 |
| William A. Blakley (D)[18] | Jan. 3, 1961 | June 14, 1961 |
| John Tower (R) | June 15, 1961 | Jan. 2, 1985 |
| Phil Gramm (R) | Jan. 3, 1985 | |

**Texas**

1. *Died July 29, 1857.*
2. *Died June 4, 1858.*
3. *Appointed by governor to fill vacancy.*
4. *Expelled July 11, 1861. Vacant until March 31, 1870, because of Civil War.*
5. *Resigned June 10, 1891.*
6. *Appointed by governor to fill vacancy.*
7. *Resigned Jan. 14, 1957.*
8. *Appointed by governor to fill vacancy.*
9. *Resigned Jan. 20, 1993, having been appointed secretary of the treasury.*
10. *Appointed by governor to fill vacancy.*
11. *Elected in special election.*
12. *Expelled July 11, 1861. Vacant until March 31, 1870, because of Civil War.*
13. *Resigned Jan. 3, 1913.*
14. *Appointed by governor to fill vacancy.*
15. *Died April 9, 1941.*
16. *Appointed by governor to fill vacancy. Died June 26, 1941.*
17. *Resigned Jan. 3, 1961, immediately after taking oath of office, having been elected vice president of the United States.*
18. *Appointed by governor to fill vacancy.*

# UTAH

(Became a state Jan. 4, 1896)

## Class 1

| Senators | Dates of Service | |
|---|---|---|
| Frank J. Cannon (R) | Jan. 22, 1896 | March 3, 1899 |
| Thomas Kearns (R)[1] | Jan. 23, 1901 | March 3, 1905 |
| George Sutherland (R) | March 4, 1905 | March 3, 1917 |
| William H. King (D) | March 4, 1917 | Jan. 2, 1941 |
| Abe Murdock (D) | Jan. 3, 1941 | Jan. 2, 1947 |
| Arthur V. Watkins (R) | Jan. 3, 1947 | Jan. 2, 1959 |
| Frank E. Moss (D) | Jan. 3, 1959 | Jan. 2, 1977 |
| Orrin G. Hatch (R) | Jan. 3, 1977 | |

## Class 3

| Senators | Dates of Service | |
|---|---|---|
| Arthur Brown (R) | Jan. 22, 1896 | March 3, 1897 |
| Joseph L. Rawlins (D) | March 4, 1897 | March 3, 1903 |
| Reed Smoot (R) | March 4, 1903 | March 3, 1933 |
| Elbert D. Thomas (D) | March 4, 1933 | Jan. 2, 1951 |
| Wallace F. Bennett (R)[2] | Jan. 3, 1951 | Dec. 20, 1974 |
| Jake Garn (R) | Dec. 21, 1974 | Jan. 2, 1993 |
| Robert F. Bennett (R) | Jan. 3, 1993 | |

**Utah**

1. *Vacancy from March 4, 1899, to Jan. 22, 1901, because of failure of Legislature to elect.*
2. *Resigned Dec. 20, 1974.*

# VERMONT

(Became a state March 4, 1791)

## Class 1

| Senators | Dates of Service | |
|---|---|---|
| Moses Robinson (D-R)[1] | Oct. 17, 1791 | Oct. 15, 1796 |
| Isaac Tichenor (FED)[2] | Oct. 18, 1796 | Oct. 17, 1797 |
| Nathaniel Chipman (FED) | Oct. 17, 1797 | March 3, 1803 |
| Israel Smith (D-R)[3] | March 4, 1803 | Oct. 1, 1807 |
| Jonathan Robinson | Oct. 10, 1807 | March 3, 1815 |
| Isaac Tichenor (FED) | March 4, 1815 | March 3, 1821 |
| Horatio Seymour (D-R) | March 4, 1821 | March 3, 1833 |
| Benjamin Swift (D-R) | March 4, 1833 | March 3, 1839 |
| Samuel S. Phelps (W) | March 4, 1839 | March 3, 1851 |
| Solomon Foot (W, R)[4] | March 4, 1851 | March 28, 1866 |
| George F. Edmunds (R)[5] | April 3, 1866 | Nov. 1, 1891 |
| Redfield Proctor (R)[6] | Nov. 2, 1891 | March 4, 1908 |
| John W. Stewart (R)[7] | March 24, 1908 | Oct. 20, 1908 |
| Carroll S. Page (R) | Oct. 21, 1908 | March 3, 1923 |
| Frank L. Greene (R)[8] | March 4, 1923 | Dec. 17, 1930 |
| Frank C. Partridge (R)[9] | Dec. 23, 1930 | March 31, 1931 |
| Warren R. Austin (R)[10] | April 1, 1931 | Aug. 2, 1946 |
| Ralph E. Flanders (R)[11] | Nov. 1, 1946 | Jan. 2, 1959 |
| Winston L. Prouty (R)[12] | Jan. 3, 1959 | Sept. 10, 1971 |
| Robert T. Stafford (R)[13] | Sept. 16, 1971 | Jan 2, 1989 |
| James M. Jeffords (R) | Jan. 3, 1989 | |

## Class 3

| Senators | Dates of Service | |
|---|---|---|
| Stephen R. Bradley (D-R) | Oct. 17, 1791 | March 3, 1795 |
| Elijah Paine (FED)[14] | March 4, 1795 | Sept. 1, 1801 |
| Stephen R. Bradley (D-R) | Oct. 15, 1801 | March 3, 1813 |
| Dudley Chase (D-R)[15] | March 4, 1813 | Nov. 3, 1817 |
| James Fisk (D-R)[16] | Nov. 4, 1817 | Jan. 8, 1818 |
| William A. Palmer (D-R) | Oct. 20, 1818 | March 3, 1825 |
| Dudley Chase (D-R) | March 4, 1825 | March 3, 1831 |

| | | |
|---|---|---|
| Samuel Prentiss (W)[17] | March 4, 1831 | April 11, 1842 |
| Samuel C. Crafts (W)[18] | Apr. 23, 1842 | March 3, 1843 |
| William Upham (W)[19] | March 4, 1843 | Jan. 14, 1853 |
| Samuel S. Phelps (W)[20] | Jan. 17, 1853 | March 16, 1854 |
| Lawrence Brainerd | Oct. 14, 1854 | March 3, 1855 |
| Jacob Collamer (R)[21] | March 4, 1855 | Nov. 9, 1865 |
| Luke P. Poland (R)[22] | Nov. 21, 1865 | March 3, 1867 |
| Justin S. Morrill (R)[23] | March 4, 1867 | Dec. 28, 1898 |
| Jonathan Ross (R)[24] | Jan. 11, 1899 | Oct. 17, 1900 |
| William P. Dillingham (R)[25] | Oct. 18, 1900 | July 12, 1923 |
| Porter H. Dale (R)[26] | Nov. 6, 1923 | Oct. 6, 1933 |
| Ernest W. Gibson (R)[27] | Nov. 21, 1933 | June 20, 1940 |
| Ernest W. Gibson Jr. (R)[28] | June 24, 1940 | Jan. 2, 1941 |
| George D. Aiken (R) | Jan. 10, 1941 | Jan. 2, 1975 |
| Patrick J. Leahy (D) | Jan. 3, 1975 | |

**Vermont**
*1. Resigned Oct. 15, 1796.*
*2. Resigned Oct. 17, 1797.*
*3. Resigned Oct. 1, 1807.*
*4. Died March 28, 1866.*
*5. Appointed by governor to fill vacancy. Subsequently elected. Resigned Nov. 1, 1891.*
*6. Appointed by governor to fill vacancy. Subsequently elected. Died March 4, 1908.*
*7. Appointed by governor to fill vacancy.*
*8. Died Dec. 17, 1930.*
*9. Appointed by governor to fill vacancy.*
*10. Resigned Aug. 2, 1946.*
*11. Appointed by governor to fill vacancy. Subsequently elected.*
*12. Died Sept. 10, 1971.*
*13. Appointed by governor to fill vacancy. Subsequently elected.*
*14. Resigned Sept. 1, 1801.*
*15. Resigned Nov. 3, 1817.*
*16. Resigned Jan. 8, 1818.*
*17. Resigned April 11, 1842.*
*18. Appointed by governor to fill vacancy. Subsequently elected.*
*19. Died Jan. 14, 1853.*
*20. Appointed by governor to fill vacancy. By resolution of March 16, 1854, the Senate declared that he was not entitled to retain his seat. Seat remained vacant until Oct. 14, 1854.*
*21. Died Nov. 9, 1865.*
*22. Appointed by governor to fill vacancy. Subsequently elected.*
*23. Died Dec. 28, 1898.*
*24. Appointed by governor to fill vacancy.*
*25. Died July 12, 1923.*
*26. Died Oct. 6, 1933.*
*27. Appointed by governor to fill vacancy. Subsequently elected. Died June 20, 1940.*
*28. Appointed by governor to fill vacancy.*

# VIRGINIA

(Ratified the Constitution June 25, 1788)

## Class 1

| Senators | Dates of Service | |
|---|---|---|
| William Grayson (A-FED)[1] | March 4, 1789 | March 12, 1790 |
| John Walker[2] | March 31, 1790 | Nov. 9, 1790 |
| James Monroe (D-R)[3] | Nov. 9, 1790 | Nov. 18, 1794 |
| Stevens T. Mason (D-R)[4] | Nov. 18, 1794 | May 10, 1803 |
| John Taylor (D-R)[5] | June 4, 1803 | Dec. 7, 1803 |
| Abraham B. Venable (D-R)[6] | Dec. 7, 1803 | June 7, 1804 |
| William B. Giles (D-R)[7] | Aug. 11, 1804 | Dec. 4, 1804 |
| Andrew Moore (D-R) | Dec. 4, 1804 | March 3, 1809 |
| Richard Brent (D-R)[8] | March 4, 1809 | Dec. 30, 1814 |
| James C. Barbour (D-R)[9] | Jan. 2, 1815 | March 27, 1825 |
| John Randolph (D-R) | Dec. 9, 1825 | March 3, 1827 |
| John Tyler (D-R, D)[10] | March 4, 1827 | Feb. 29, 1836 |
| William C. Rives (D)[11] | March 4, 1836 | March 3, 1839 |
| William C. Rives (W) | Jan. 18, 1841 | March 3, 1845 |
| Isaac S. Pennybacker (D)[12] | Dec. 3, 1845 | Jan. 12, 1847 |

| | | |
|---|---|---|
| James M. Mason (D)[13] | Jan. 21, 1847 | July 11, 1861 |
| Waitman T. Willey (R)[14] | July 13, 1861 | March 3, 1863 |
| Lemuel J. Bowden (R)[15] | March 4, 1863 | Jan. 2, 1864 |
| John F. Lewis (R) | Jan. 27, 1870 | March 3, 1875 |
| Robert W. Withers (C) | March 4, 1875 | March 3, 1881 |
| William Mahone (R) | March 4, 1881 | March 3, 1887 |
| John W. Daniel (D)[16] | March 4, 1887 | June 29, 1910 |
| Claude A. Swanson (D)[17] | Aug. 1, 1910 | March 3, 1933 |
| Harry Flood Byrd (D)[18] | March 4, 1933 | Nov. 10, 1965 |
| Harry F. Byrd Jr. (D, I)[19] | Nov. 12, 1965 | Jan. 2, 1983 |
| Paul S. Trible Jr. (R) | Jan. 3, 1983 | Jan. 2, 1989 |
| Charles S. Robb (D) | Jan. 3, 1989 | |

### Class 2

| | | |
|---|---|---|
| Richard Henry Lee (A-FED)[20] | March 4, 1789 | Oct. 8, 1792 |
| John Taylor (D-R)[21] | Oct. 18, 1792 | May 11, 1794 |
| Henry Tazewell (D-R)[22] | Nov. 18, 1794 | Jan. 24, 1799 |
| Wilson C. Nicholas (D-R)[23] | Dec. 5, 1799 | May 22, 1804 |
| Andrew Moore (D-R)[24] | Aug. 11, 1804 | Dec. 4, 1804 |
| William B. Giles (D-R)[25] | Dec. 4, 1804 | March 3, 1815 |
| Armistead T. Mason (D-R) | Jan. 3, 1816 | March 3, 1817 |
| John W. Eppes (D-R)[26] | March 4, 1817 | Dec. 4, 1819 |
| James Pleasants (D-R)[27] | Dec. 10, 1819 | Dec. 15, 1822 |
| John Taylor (D-R)[28] | Dec. 18, 1822 | Aug. 20, 1824 |
| Littleton W. Tazewell (D-R, D)[29] | Dec. 7, 1824 | July 16, 1832 |
| William C. Rives (D)[30] | Dec. 10, 1832 | Feb. 22, 1834 |
| Benjamin W. Leigh (D)[31] | Feb. 26, 1834 | July 4, 1836 |
| Richard E. Parker (D)[32] | Dec. 12, 1836 | March 13, 1837 |
| William H. Roane (D) | March 14, 1837 | March 3, 1841 |
| William S. Archer (W) | March 4, 1841 | March 3, 1847 |
| Robert M. T. Hunter (D)[33] | March 4, 1847 | July 11, 1861 |
| John S. Carlile (UN)[34] | July 13, 1861 | March 3, 1865 |
| John W. Johnston (C)[35] | Jan. 28, 1870 | March 3, 1883 |
| H. H. Riddleberger (R) | March 4, 1883 | March 3, 1889 |
| John S. Barbour Jr. (D)[36] | March 4, 1889 | May 14, 1892 |
| Eppa Hunton (D)[37] | May 28, 1892 | March 3, 1895 |
| Thomas S. Martin (D)[38] | March 4, 1895 | Nov. 12, 1919 |
| Carter Glass (D)[39] | Feb. 2, 1920 | May 28, 1946 |
| Thomas G. Burch (D)[40] | May 31, 1946 | Nov. 5, 1946 |
| A. Willis Robertson (D)[41] | Nov. 6, 1946 | Dec. 30, 1966 |
| William B. Spong Jr. (D) | Dec. 31, 1966 | Jan. 2, 1973 |
| William Lloyd Scott (R)[42] | Jan. 3, 1973 | Jan. 1, 1979 |
| John W. Warner (R) | Jan. 2, 1979 | |

**Virginia**
*1. Died March 12, 1790.*
*2. Appointed by governor to fill vacancy.*
*3. Resigned Nov. 18, 1794.*
*4. Died May 10, 1803.*
*5. Appointed by governor to fill vacancy.*
*6. Resigned June 7, 1804.*
*7. Appointed by governor to fill vacancy.*
*8. Died Dec. 30, 1814.*
*9. Resigned March 27, 1825.*
*10. Resigned Feb. 29, 1836.*
*11. The seat was vacant between the expiration of Rives' first term March 3, 1839, and his re-election and subsequent service beginning Jan. 18, 1841.*
*12. Died Jan. 12, 1847.*
*13. Expelled July 11, 1861. Vacant until July 13, 1861.*
*14. Willey was elected by a "rump" state legislature which supported the Union and represented territory which was later to become West Virginia.*
*15. Died Jan. 2, 1864. Bowden, like Willey, his predecessor, was elected to represent Virginia by a "rump" state legislature which supported the Union. After his death, the seat remained vacant until Jan. 27, 1870, because of the Civil War.*
*16. Died June 29, 1910.*
*17. Appointed by governor to fill vacancy. Subsequently elected. Resigned March 3, 1933.*
*18. Appointed by governor to fill vacancy. Subsequently elected. Resigned Nov. 10, 1965.*
*19. Appointed by governor to fill vacancy. Subsequently elected as a Democrat in 1966, as an Independent in 1970.*
*20. Resigned Oct. 8, 1792.*
*21. Resigned May 11, 1794.*

**Virginia (continued)**
22. Died Jan. 24, 1799.
23. Resigned May 22, 1804.
24. Appointed by governor to fill vacancy.
25. Resigned March 3, 1815.
26. Resigned Dec. 4, 1819.
27. Resigned Dec. 15, 1822.
28. Died Aug. 20, 1824.
29. Resigned July 16, 1832.
30. Resigned Feb. 22, 1834.
31. Resigned July 4, 1836.
32. Resigned March 13, 1837.
33. Expelled July 11, 1861. Vacant until July 13, 1861.
34. Carlile was elected by a "rump" state legislature which supported the Union and represented territory which was later to become West Virginia. After the expiration of his term, the seat remained vacant until Jan. 28, 1870, because of Civil War.
35. The seat was vacant between the expiration of Johnston's first term March 3, 1871, and his re-election and subsequent seating March 15, 1871.
36. Died May 14, 1892.
37. Appointed by governor to fill vacancy. Subsequently elected.
38. Died Nov. 12, 1919.
39. Appointed by governor to fill vacancy. Subsequently elected. Died May 28, 1946.
40. Appointed by governor to fill vacancy.
41. Resigned Dec. 30, 1966.
42. Resigned Jan. 1, 1979.

# WASHINGTON

(Became a state Nov. 11, 1889)

## Class 1

| Senators | Dates of Service | |
|---|---|---|
| John B. Allen (R) | Nov. 20, 1889 | March 3, 1893 |
| John L. Wilson (R)[1] | Feb. 1, 1895 | March 3, 1899 |
| Addison G. Foster (R) | March 4, 1899 | March 3, 1905 |
| Samuel H. Piles (R) | March 4, 1905 | March 3, 1911 |
| Miles Poindexter (R) | March 4, 1911 | March 3, 1923 |
| Clarence C. Dill (D) | March 4, 1923 | Jan. 2, 1935 |
| L. B. Schwellenbach (D)[2] | Jan. 3, 1935 | Dec. 16, 1940 |
| Mon C. Wallgren (D)[3] | Dec. 19, 1940 | Jan. 10, 1945 |
| Hugh B. Mitchell (D)[4] | Jan. 10, 1945 | Dec. 25, 1946 |
| Harry P. Cain (R) | Dec. 26, 1946 | Jan. 2, 1953 |
| Henry M. Jackson (D)[5] | Jan. 3, 1953 | Sept. 1, 1983 |
| Daniel J. Evans (R)[6] | Sept. 12, 1983 | Jan. 2, 1989 |
| Slade Gorton (R) | Jan. 3, 1989 | |

## Class 3

| Senators | Dates of Service | |
|---|---|---|
| Watson C. Squire (R) | Nov. 20, 1889 | March 3, 1897 |
| George Turner (D) | March 4, 1897 | March 3, 1903 |
| Levi Ankeny (R) | March 4, 1903 | March 3, 1909 |
| Wesley L. Jones (R)[7] | March 4, 1909 | Nov. 19, 1932 |
| Elijah S. Grammer (R)[8] | Nov. 22, 1932 | March 3, 1933 |
| Homer T. Bone (D)[9] | March 4, 1933 | Nov. 13, 1944 |
| Warren G. Magnuson (D) | Dec. 14, 1944 | Jan. 2, 1981 |
| Slade Gorton (R) | Jan. 3, 1981 | Jan. 2, 1987 |
| Brock Adams (D) | Jan. 3, 1987 | Jan. 2, 1993 |
| Patty Murray (D) | Jan. 3, 1993 | |

**Washington**
1. Vacancy from March 4, 1893, to Feb. 1, 1895, because of failure of legislature to elect. John B. Allen was appointed by governor March 10, 1893, to fill vacancy, but by Senate resolution of Aug. 28, 1893, was declared not entitled to a seat.
2. Resigned Dec. 16, 1940.
3. Resigned Jan. 10, 1945.
4. Appointed by governor to fill vacancy. Resigned Dec. 25, 1946.
5. Died Sept. 1, 1983.
6. Appointed by governor to fill vacancy. Subsequently elected.
7. Died Nov. 19, 1932.
8. Appointed by governor to fill vacancy.
9. Resigned Nov. 13, 1944.

# WEST VIRGINIA

(Became a state June 19, 1863)

## Class 1

| Senators | Dates of Service | |
|---|---|---|
| Peter G. Van Winkle (R) | Aug. 4, 1863 | March 3, 1869 |
| Arthur I. Boreman (R) | March 4, 1869 | March 3, 1875 |
| Allen T. Caperton (D)[1] | March 4, 1875 | July 26, 1876 |
| Samuel Price[2] | Aug. 26, 1876 | Jan. 26, 1877 |
| Frank Hereford (D) | Jan. 26, 1877 | March 3, 1881 |
| Johnson N. Camden (D) | March 4, 1881 | March 3, 1887 |
| Charles J. Faulkner (D) | March 4, 1887 | March 3, 1899 |
| Nathan B. Scott (R) | March 4, 1899 | March 3, 1911 |
| William E. Chilton (D) | March 4, 1911 | March 3, 1917 |
| Howard Sutherland (R) | March 4, 1917 | March 3, 1923 |
| Matthew M. Neely (D) | March 4, 1923 | March 3, 1929 |
| Henry D. Hatfield (R) | March 4, 1929 | Jan. 2, 1935 |
| Rush D. Holt (D)[3] | June 21, 1935 | Jan. 2, 1941 |
| Harley M. Kilgore (D)[4] | Jan. 3, 1941 | Feb. 28, 1956 |
| William R. Laird III (D)[5] | March 13, 1956 | Nov. 6, 1956 |
| Chapman Revercomb (R) | Nov. 7, 1956 | Jan. 2, 1959 |
| Robert C. Byrd (D) | Jan. 3, 1959 | |

## Class 2

| Senators | Dates of Service | |
|---|---|---|
| Waitman T. Willey (R) | Aug. 4, 1863 | March 3, 1871 |
| Henry G. Davis (D) | March 4, 1871 | March 3, 1883 |
| John E. Kenna (D)[6] | March 4, 1883 | Jan. 11, 1893 |
| Johnson N. Camden (D) | Jan. 25, 1893 | March 3, 1895 |
| Stephen B. Elkins (R)[7] | March 4, 1895 | Jan. 4, 1911 |
| Davis Elkins (R)[8] | Jan. 9, 1911 | Jan. 31, 1911 |
| Clarence W. Watson (D) | Feb. 1, 1911 | March 3, 1913 |
| Nathan Goff (R) | March 4, 1913 | March 3, 1919 |
| Davis Elkins (R) | March 4, 1919 | March 3, 1925 |
| Guy D. Goff (R) | March 4, 1925 | March 3, 1931 |
| Matthew M. Neely (D)[9] | March 4, 1931 | Jan. 12, 1941 |
| Joseph Rosier (D)[10] | Jan. 13, 1941 | Nov. 17, 1942 |
| Hugh Ike Shott (R) | Nov. 18, 1942 | Jan. 2, 1943 |
| Chapman Revercomb (R) | Jan. 3, 1943 | Jan. 2, 1949 |
| Matthew M. Neely (D)[11] | Jan. 3, 1949 | Jan. 18, 1958 |
| John D. Hoblitzell Jr. (R)[12] | Jan. 25, 1958 | Nov. 4, 1958 |
| Jennings Randolph (D) | Nov. 5, 1958 | Jan. 2, 1985 |
| John D. Rockefeller (D) | Jan. 15, 1985 | |

**West Virginia**
1. Died July 26, 1876.
2. Appointed by governor to fill vacancy.
3. Elected Nov. 6, 1934, to a six-year term, but did not reach the age of 30—required by the Constitution for service in the Senate—until June 19, 1935. Took his seat June 21, 1935.
4. Died Feb. 28, 1956.
5. Appointed by governor to fill vacancy.
6. Died Jan. 11, 1893.
7. Died Jan. 4, 1911.
8. Appointed by governor to fill vacancy.
9. Resigned Jan. 12, 1941.
10. Appointed by governor to fill vacancy.
11. Died Jan. 18, 1958.
12. Appointed by governor to fill vacancy.

# WISCONSIN

(Became a state May 29, 1848)

## Class 1

| Senators | Dates of Service | |
|---|---|---|
| Henry Dodge (D) | June 8, 1848 | March 3, 1857 |

| | | |
|---|---|---|
| James R. Doolittle (R) | March 4, 1857 | March 3, 1869 |
| Matthew H. Carpenter (R) | March 4, 1869 | March 3, 1875 |
| Angus Cameron (R) | March 4, 1875 | March 3, 1881 |
| Philetus Sawyer (R) | March 4, 1881 | March 3, 1893 |
| John L. Mitchell (D) | March 4, 1893 | March 3, 1899 |
| Joseph V. Quarles (R) | March 4, 1899 | March 3, 1905 |
| Robert M. La Follette (R)[1] | Jan. 4, 1906 | June 18, 1925 |
| R. M. La Follette Jr. (R, PROG)[2] | Sept. 30, 1925 | Jan. 2, 1947 |
| Joseph R. McCarthy (R)[3] | Jan. 3, 1947 | May 2, 1957 |
| William Proxmire (D) | Aug. 28, 1957 | Jan. 2, 1989 |
| Herbert H. Kohl (D) | Jan. 3, 1989 | |

## Class 3

| | | |
|---|---|---|
| Isaac P. Walker (D) | June 8, 1848 | March 3, 1855 |
| Charles Durkee (R) | March 4, 1855 | March 3, 1861 |
| Timothy O. Howe (R) | March 4, 1861 | March 3, 1879 |
| Matthew H. Carpenter (R)[4] | March 4, 1879 | Feb. 24, 1881 |
| Angus Cameron (R) | March 10, 1881 | March 3, 1885 |
| John Coit Spooner (R) | March 4, 1885 | March 3, 1891 |
| William F. Vilas (D) | March 4, 1891 | March 3, 1897 |
| John Coit Spooner (R)[5] | March 4, 1897 | May 1, 1907 |
| Isaac Stephenson (R) | May 17, 1907 | March 3, 1915 |
| Paul O. Husting (D)[6] | March 4, 1915 | Oct. 21, 1917 |
| Irvine L. Lenroot (R) | April 18, 1918 | March 3, 1927 |
| John J. Blaine (R) | March 4, 1927 | March 3, 1933 |
| F. Ryan Duffy (D) | March 4, 1933 | Jan. 2, 1939 |
| Alexander Wiley (R) | Jan. 3, 1939 | Jan. 2, 1963 |
| Gaylord Nelson (D) | Jan. 8, 1963 | Jan. 2, 1981 |
| Bob Kasten (R) | Jan. 3, 1981 | Jan. 2, 1993 |
| Russell D. Feingold (D) | Jan. 3, 1993 | |

**Wisconsin**

1. Elected Jan. 25, 1905. Took oath Jan. 4, 1906. Governor during interim. Died June 18, 1925. Vacancy from June 19 to Sept. 29, 1925.
2. Elected as a Republican in 1925 and 1928, as a Progressive in 1934 and 1940.
3. Died May 2, 1957.
4. Died Feb. 24, 1881.
5. Resigned effective May 1, 1907.
6. Died Oct. 21, 1917. Seat vacant until April 18, 1918.

# WYOMING

(Became a state July 10, 1890)

## Class 1

| Senators | Dates of Service | |
|---|---|---|
| Francis E. Warren (R) | Nov. 18, 1890 | March 3, 1893 |
| Clarence D. Clark (R)[1] | Jan. 23, 1895 | March 3, 1917 |
| John B. Kendrick (D)[2] | March 4, 1917 | Nov. 3, 1933 |
| Joseph C. O'Mahoney (D)[3] | Jan. 1, 1934 | Jan. 2, 1953 |
| Frank A. Barrett (R) | Jan. 3, 1953 | Jan. 2, 1959 |
| Gale W. McGee (D) | Jan. 3, 1959 | Jan. 2, 1977 |
| Malcolm Wallop (R) | Jan. 3, 1977 | |

## Class 2

| | | |
|---|---|---|
| Joseph M. Carey (R) | Nov. 15, 1890 | March 3, 1895 |
| Francis E. Warren (R)[4] | March 4, 1895 | Nov. 24, 1929 |
| Patrick J. Sullivan (R)[5] | Dec. 5, 1929 | Nov. 30, 1930 |
| Robert D. Carey (R) | Dec. 1, 1930 | Jan. 2, 1937 |
| Harry H. Schwartz (D) | Jan. 3, 1937 | Jan. 2, 1943 |
| E. V. Robertson (R) | Jan. 3, 1943 | Jan. 2, 1949 |
| Lester C. Hunt (D)[6] | Jan. 3, 1949 | June 19, 1954 |
| Edward D. Crippa (R)[7] | June 24, 1954 | Nov. 28, 1954 |
| Joseph C. O'Mahoney (D) | Nov. 29, 1954 | Jan. 2, 1961 |
| John Joseph Hickey (D)[8] | Jan. 3, 1961 | Nov. 6, 1962 |
| Milward L. Simpson (R) | Nov. 7, 1962 | Jan. 2, 1967 |
| Clifford P. Hansen (R)[9] | Jan. 3, 1967 | Dec. 31, 1978 |
| Alan K. Simpson (R) | Jan. 1, 1979 | |

**Wyoming**

1. Vacancy from March 4, 1893, to Jan. 23, 1895, because of failure of legislature to elect.
2. Died Nov. 3, 1933. Vacancy from Nov. 4, 1933, to Jan. 1, 1934.
3. Appointed by governor to fill vacancy. Subsequently elected.
4. Died Nov. 24, 1929.
5. Appointed by governor to fill vacancy.
6. Died June 19, 1954.
7. Appointed by governor to fill vacancy.
8. Keith Thomson (R), who had been elected Nov. 8, 1960, to a full six-year term beginning Jan. 3, 1961, died Dec. 9, 1960. Hickey, the incumbent governor, resigned and was appointed by his successor to fill the vacancy.
9. Resigned Dec. 31, 1978.

# Senate Popular Vote Returns, 1913-93

# Sources for Senate Popular Returns

The Senate popular election returns presented in this section *(pp. 815-846)* for the years 1913 through 1973 were obtained from the Inter-University Consortium for Political and Social Research (ICPSR) at the University of Michigan. For Senate elections after 1974, returns were obtained from Richard M. Scammon and Alice V. McGillivray, *America Votes*, vols. 11-20 (Washington, D.C.: Congressional Quarterly, 1975-1993). Returns for the 1975 special election in New Hampshire were obtained form the New Hampshire secretary of state.

The symbol # next to returns before 1974 indicates that Congressional Quarterly obtained the returns from a source other than the ICPSR. A complete set of other sources used appears on page 847. A "Senate Candidates Index" is located on pages 1388-1394.

While the complete source annotations for the ICPSR collection are too extensive to publish here, information on the sources for specific election returns can be obtained through the ICPSR. *(ICPSR collection, box, p. x)*

## Presentation of Returns

The Senate returns are arranged alphabetically by state and in chronological order by class of senator within each state listing. *(For an explanation of Senate classes, see p. 780.)* The candidates receiving the greatest number of popular votes is listed first with his or her vote total and percentage of the total vote cast, followed in descending order of votes received by all other candidates who received *at least 5 percent* of the total vote cast.

Special elections to fill vacancies are designated in the returns. *(For an explanation of special elections, see p. 779)*

When a state *simultaneously* held a special election to fill the remaining few months of an unexpired term and a general election for the next full six-year term, the special election is listed *after* the general election. For example, see page 817 where the 1946 California general and special election returns appear.

Where a state had a special election and a general election for the same class in the same year, but not simultaneously, the elections appear in the order they occurred. For example, see page 826 where the 1936 Louisiana special election, held in April, precedes the general election, held in November.

## Vote Totals and Percentages

The ICPSR collection includes all candidates receiving popular votes. In the *Guide to U.S. Elections, Third Edition,* only Senate candidates receiving *at least 5 percent of the total vote* for that election are included. For example, the ICPSR data collection for the 1944 New York senatorial election, 6,209,317 votes were cast, with Robert F. Wagner receiving 3,294,576 votes (53.05 percent), Thomas J. Curran receiving 2,899,497 votes (46.69 percent) and a third candidate, Eric Haas, receiving the remaining 15,244 votes (0.25 percent).

The returns for the 1944 New York Senate election appear on page 834. Returns for Haas are not listed because he received less than 5 percent of the total vote. The percentage listed for Wagner is 53.1 and for Curran is 46.7. The procedure used throughout this section was to calculate percentages to two decimal places on the basis of the total number of votes cast in the election and round each percentage to one decimal place. Due to rounding and scattered votes for other candidates, percentages do not add to 100 percent.

## Party Designations

In the ICPSR returns, the distinct — and in many cases, *multiple* — party designations appearing in the original sources are preserved. In many cases party labels represent combinations of multi-party support received by individual candidates. If, for example, on the ballot and official returns more than one party name was listed next to a candidate's name, then the party designation appearing in the election returns for that candidate will be a unique abbreviation for that combination of parties. *(For a list of party abbreviations, see p. 1352.)*

In the special case of a candidate's name listed separately on the original ballot under more than one party — where returns were reported *separately* for each party — Congressional Quarterly has summed the votes recorded under the several parties and that figure appears as the candidate's total vote. Whenever separate party totals have been summed, a *comma* separates the abbreviations of the parties contributing the largest and second largest share of the total vote.

Most cases of this special situation occurred in New York and Pennsylvania during this century. For example, in the 1944 New York election cited above, Wagner's total vote of 3,294,576 was comprised of 2,485,735 as the Democratic Party nominee, 483,785 votes as American Labor Party candidate and 325,056 votes as Liberal Party nominee. On page 834, only Wagner's total vote of 3,294,576 appears.

Congressional Quarterly has also included party abbreviations for the two parties that contributed the most votes to Wagner's total — separated by a comma. Thus, immediately following his name appear the abbreviations — D, AM LAB — indicating that Wagner was a candidate of at least two parties and that the greatest number of votes he received was as a Democrat.

# Senate Popular Vote Returns, 1913-93

**Note:** Prior to ratification of the 17th Amendment, April 8, 1913, a number of states conducted non-binding popular polls for Senate candidates, designed to guide the state legislatures in choosing between candidates. The Inter-University Consortium for Political and Social Research obtained some of the returns for these polls, and they are published in the following list. *(Explanation of non-binding elections, p. 778)*

## ALABAMA

| Candidates | Votes | % |
|---|---|---|
| **Class 2** | | |
| **1918** John H. Bankhead (D) | 54,880 | 100.0 |
| Special Election | | |
| **1920** J. Thomas Heflin (D) | 161,531 | 71.4 |
| C. P. Lunsford (R) | 62,020 | 27.4 |
| **1924** J. Thomas Heflin (D) | 120,017 | 75.2 |
| F. H. Lathrop (R) | 39,623 | 24.8 |
| **1930** John H. Bankhead II (D) | 150,985 | 59.7 |
| J. Thomas Heflin (I) | 101,862 | 40.3 |
| **1936** John H. Bankhead II (D) | 239,632 | 87.0 |
| H. E. Berkstresser (R) | 33,698 | 12.2 |
| **1942** John H. Bankhead II (D) | 69,212 | 100.0 |
| Special Election | | |
| **1946** John Sparkman (D) | 163,217 | 100.0 |
| **1948** John Sparkman (D) | 185,534 | 84.0 |
| Paul G. Parsons (R) | 35,341 | 16.0 |
| **1954** John Sparkman (D) | 259,348 | 82.5 |
| J. Foy Guin Jr. (R) | 55,110 | 17.5 |
| **1960** John Sparkman (D) | 389,196 | 70.2 |
| Julian Elgin (R) | 164,868 | 29.8 |
| **1966** John Sparkman (D) | 482,138 | 60.1 |
| John Grenier (R) | 313,018 | 39.0 |
| **1972** John Sparkman (D) | 654,491 | 62.3 |
| Winton M. Blount (R) | 347,523 | 33.1 |
| **1978** Howell Heflin (D) | 547,054 | 94.0 |
| Jerome B. Couch (P) | 34,951 | 6.0 |
| **1984** Howell Heflin (D) | 860,535 | 62.8 |
| Albert Lee Smith Jr. (R) | 498,508 | 36.3 |
| **1990** Howell Heflin (D) | 717,814 | 60.6 |
| Bill Cabaniss (R) | 467,190 | 39.4 |
| **Class 3** | | |
| **1914** Oscar W. Underwood (D) | 63,338 | 78.1 |
| Alex C. Birch (R) | 12,320 | 15.2 |
| A. P. Longshore (PROG) | 4,263 | 5.3 |

| Candidates | Votes | % |
|---|---|---|
| Special Election | | |
| **1914** Frank S. White (D) | 102,326 | 99.9 |
| **1920** Oscar W. Underwood (D) | 155,664 | 68.0 |
| L. H. Reynolds (R) | 71,334 | 31.2 |
| **1926** Hugo L. Black (D) | 91,843 | 80.9 |
| E. H. Dryer (R) | 21,722 | 19.1 |
| **1932** Hugo L. Black (D) | 209,614 | 86.3 |
| J. Theodore Johnson (R) | 33,425 | 13.8 |
| Special Election | | |
| **1938** Lister Hill (D) | | |
| **1938** Lister Hill (D) | 113,413# | 86.4 |
| J. M. Pennington (R) | 17,885# | 13.6 |
| **1944** Lister Hill (D) | 202,604 | 81.8 |
| John A. Posey (R) | 41,983 | 17.0 |
| **1950** Lister Hill (D) | 125,534 | 76.5 |
| John G. Crommelin Jr. (I) | 38,477 | 23.5 |

## Explanation of Symbols

In the returns for Senate elections *symbols* are used to denote special circumstances. In cases where no symbol is used, the candidate who received the most votes won the election to the Senate.

The following is a key to the symbols used:

✔ Elected to the Senate, but the number of votes and the percentage of the total vote received by the winner are not available.

\* The symbol is used in two kinds of situations: (1) When the winner of the election died before the term of office was to begin; (2) When the apparent winner was not permitted to take office. *(For an explanation of specific cases, consult the appropriate state in the list of senators, pp. 785-811).*

\# Information was obtained from a source other than the Inter-University Consortium for Political and Social Research. *(For a listing of other sources, see p. 847)*

| | Candidates | Votes | % |
|---|---|---|---|
| 1956 | Lister Hill (D) | 330,182 | *100.0* |
| 1962 | Lister Hill (D) | 201,937 | *50.9* |
| | James D. Martin (R) | 195,134 | *49.1* |
| 1968 | Jim Allen (D) | 638,774 | *70.0* |
| | Perry Hooper (R) | 201,227 | *22.1* |
| | Robert Schwenn (NDPA) | 72,699 | *8.0* |
| 1974 | Jim Allen (D) | 501,541 | *95.8* |

### Special Election

| | | | |
|---|---|---|---|
| 1978 | Donald W. Stewart (D) | 401,852 | *54.9* |
| | James D. Martin (R) | 316,170 | *43.2* |
| 1980 | Jeremiah Denton (R) | 650,362 | *50.2* |
| | James E. Folsom Jr. (D) | 610,175 | *47.1* |
| 1986 | Richard C. Shelby (D) | 609,360 | *50.3* |
| | Jeremiah Denton (R) | 602,537 | *49.7* |
| 1992 | Richard C. Shelby (D) | 1,022,698 | *64.9* |
| | Richard Sellers (R) | 522,015 | *33.1* |

# ALASKA

| | Candidates | Votes | % |
|---|---|---|---|
| | **Class 2** | | |
| 1958 | E. L. Bartlett (D) | 40,939 | *83.8* |
| | R. E. Robertson (R) | 7,299 | *15.0* |
| 1960 | E. L. Bartlett (D) | 38,041 | *63.4* |
| | Lee L. McKinley (R) | 21,937 | *36.6* |
| 1966 | E. L. Bartlett (D) | 49,289 | *75.5* |
| | Lee L. McKinley (R) | 15,961 | *24.5* |

### Special Election

| | | | |
|---|---|---|---|
| 1970 | Ted Stevens (R) | 47,908 | *59.6* |
| | Wendell P. Kay (D) | 32,456 | *40.4* |
| 1972 | Ted Stevens (R) | 74,216 | *77.3* |
| | Gene Guess (D) | 21,791 | *22.7* |
| 1978 | Ted Stevens (R) | 92,783 | *75.6* |
| | Donald W. Hobbs (D) | 29,574 | *24.1* |
| 1984 | Ted Stevens (R) | 146,919 | *71.2* |
| | John E. Havelock (D) | 58,804 | *28.5* |
| 1990 | Ted Stevens (R) | 125,806 | *66.2* |
| | Michael Beasley (D) | 61,152 | *32.2* |

| | **Class 3** | | |
|---|---|---|---|
| 1958 | Ernest Gruening (D) | 26,063 | *52.6* |
| | Mike Stepovich (R) | 23,462 | *47.4* |
| 1962 | Ernest Gruening (D) | 33,827 | *58.1* |
| | Ted Stevens (R) | 24,354 | *41.9* |
| 1968 | Mike Gravel (D) | 36,527 | *45.1* |
| | Elmer Rasmuson (R) | 30,286 | *37.4* |
| | Ernest Gruening (I) | 14,118 | *17.4* |
| 1974 | Mike Gravel (D) | 54,361 | *58.3* |
| | C. R. Lewis (R) | 38,914 | *41.7* |
| 1980 | Frank H. Murkowski (R) | 84,159 | *53.7* |
| | Clark S. Gruening (D) | 72,007 | *45.9* |

| | Candidates | Votes | % |
|---|---|---|---|
| 1986 | Frank H. Murkowski (R) | 97,674 | *54.0* |
| | Glenn Olds (D) | 79,727 | *44.1* |
| 1992 | Frank H. Murkowski (R) | 127,163 | *53.0* |
| | Tony Smith (D) | 92,065 | *38.4* |
| | Mary E. Jordan (GREEN) | 20,019 | *8.4* |

# ARIZONA

| | Candidates | Votes | % |
|---|---|---|---|
| | **Class 1** | | |
| 1916 | Henry F. Ashurst (D) | 29,882 | *55.4* |
| | Joseph H. Kibbey (R) | 21,261 | *39.4* |
| | W. S. Bradford (SOC) | 2,827 | *5.2* |
| 1922 | Henry F. Ashurst (D) | 39,722 | *65.0* |
| | James H. McClintock (R) | 21,358 | *35.0* |
| 1928 | Henry F. Ashurst (D) | 47,013 | *54.3* |
| | Ralph H. Cameron (R) | 39,651 | *45.8* |
| 1934 | Henry F. Ashurst (D) | 67,648 | *72.0* |
| | J. E. Thompson (R) | 24,075 | *25.6* |
| 1940 | Ernest W. McFarland (D) | 101,495 | *71.6* |
| | I. A. Jennings (R) | 39,657 | *28.0* |
| 1946 | Ernest W. McFarland (D) | 80,415 | *69.2* |
| | Ward S. Powers (R) | 35,022 | *30.1* |
| 1952 | Barry Goldwater (R) | 132,063 | *51.3* |
| | Ernest W. McFarland (D) | 125,338 | *48.7* |
| 1958 | Barry Goldwater (R) | 164,593 | *56.1* |
| | Ernest W. McFarland (D) | 129,030 | *43.9* |
| 1964 | Paul Fannin (R) | 241,084 | *51.4* |
| | Roy Elson (D) | 227,704 | *48.6* |
| 1970 | Paul Fannin (R) | 228,284 | *56.0* |
| | Sam Grossman (D) | 179,512 | *44.0* |
| 1976 | Dennis DeConcini (D) | 400,334 | *54.0* |
| | Sam Steiger (R) | 321,236 | *43.3* |
| 1982 | Dennis DeConcini (D) | 411,970 | *56.9* |
| | Pete Dunn (R) | 291,749 | *40.3* |
| 1988 | Dennis DeConcini (D) | 660,403 | *56.7* |
| | Keith DeGreen (R) | 478,060 | *41.1* |

| | **Class 3** | | |
|---|---|---|---|
| 1914 | Marcus A. Smith (D) | 25,800 | *53.2* |
| | J. L. Hubbell (R) | 9,182 | *19.0* |
| | Eugene W. Chafin (IP) | 7,293 | *15.1* |
| | Bert Davis (SOC) | 3,582 | *7.4* |
| | J. Bernard Nelson (PROG) | 2,606 | *5.4* |
| 1920 | Ralph H. Cameron (R) | 35,893 | *55.2* |
| | Marcus A. Smith (D) | 29,169 | *44.8* |
| 1926 | Carl Hayden (D) | 44,591 | *58.3* |
| | Ralph H. Cameron (R) | 31,845 | *41.7* |
| 1932 | Carl Hayden (D) | 74,310 | *66.7* |
| | Ralph H. Cameron (R) | 35,737 | *32.1* |
| 1938 | Carl Hayden (D) | 82,714 | *76.5* |
| | B. H. Clingan (R) | 25,378 | *23.5* |
| 1944 | Carl Hayden (D) | 90,335 | *69.4* |
| | Fred W. Fickett (R) | 39,891 | *30.6* |
| 1950 | Carl Hayden (D) | 116,246 | *62.8* |
| | Bruce Brockett (R) | 68,846 | *37.2* |
| 1956 | Carl Hayden (D) | 170,816 | *61.4* |
| | Ross F. Jones (R) | 107,447 | *38.6* |
| 1962 | Carl Hayden (D) | 199,217 | *54.9* |
| | Evan Mecham (R) | 163,388 | *45.1* |

| | Candidates | Votes | % |
|---|---|---|---|
| 1968 | Barry Goldwater (R) | 274,607 | 57.2 |
| | Roy Elson (D) | 205,338 | 42.8 |
| 1974 | Barry Goldwater (R) | 320,396 | 58.3 |
| | Jonathan Marshall (D) | 229,523 | 41.7 |
| 1980 | Barry M. Goldwater (R) | 432,371 | 49.5 |
| | Bill Schulz (D) | 422,972 | 48.4 |
| 1986 | John McCain (R) | 521,850 | 60.5 |
| | Richard Kimball (D) | 340,965 | 39.5 |
| 1992 | John McCain (R) | 771,395 | 55.8 |
| | Claire Sargent (D) | 436,321 | 31.6 |
| | Evan Mecham (I) | 145,361 | 10.5 |

# ARKANSAS

| | Candidates | Votes | % |
|---|---|---|---|

### Class 2

| 1918 | Joseph T. Robinson (D) | 78,386 | 100.0 |
|---|---|---|---|
| 1924 | Joseph T. Robinson (D) | 100,408# | 73.5 |
| | Charles F. Cole (R) | 36,163# | 26.5 |
| 1930 | Joseph T. Robinson (D) | 141,806 | 100.0 |
| 1936 | Joseph T. Robinson (D) | 155,075 | 81.8 |
| | G. C. Ledbetter (R) | 30,997 | 16.4 |

Special Election

| 1937 | John E. Miller (I) | 66,990 | 60.7 |
|---|---|---|---|
| | Carl E. Bailey (D) | 43,406 | 39.3 |

| 1942 | John L. McClellan (D) | 99,126 | 100.0 |
|---|---|---|---|
| 1948 | John L. McClellan (D) | 216,401 | 93.3 |
| | R. Walter Tucker (I) | 15,521 | 6.7 |
| 1954 | John L. McClellan (D) | 291,058 | 100.0 |
| 1960 | John L. McClellan (D) | ✔ | |
| 1966 | John L. McClellan (D) | ✔ | |
| 1972 | John L. McClellan (D) | 386,398 | 60.8 |
| | Wayne H. Babbitt (R) | 248,238 | 39.1 |
| 1978 | David H. Pryor (D) | 399,916 | 76.6 |
| | Tom Kelly (R) | 84,722 | 16.2 |
| | John G. Black (I) | 37,488 | 7.2 |
| 1984 | David Pryor (D) | 502,341 | 57.3 |
| | Ed Bethune (R) | 373,615 | 42.7 |
| 1990 | David Pryor (D) | 493,910 | 99.8 |

### Class 3

| 1914 | James P. Clarke (D) | 33,449# | 74.9 |
|---|---|---|---|
| | Meyers (R) | 11,222# | 25.1 |

Special Election

| 1916 | William F. Kirby (D) | 110,293 | 69.3 |
|---|---|---|---|
| | H. L. Remmel (R) | 48,922 | 30.7 |

| 1920 | Thaddeus H. Caraway (D) | 126,577 | 65.9 |
|---|---|---|---|
| | Charles F. Cole (R) | 65,381 | 34.1 |
| 1926 | Thaddeus H. Caraway (D) | 28,064 | 82.8 |
| | R. A. Jones (R) | 5,848 | 17.2 |

| | Candidates | Votes | % |
|---|---|---|---|
| Special Election | | | |

| 1932 | Hattie W. Caraway (D) | 31,133# | 91.6 |
|---|---|---|---|
| | Rex Floyd (I) | 1,752# | 5.2 |

| 1932 | Hattie W. Caraway (D) | 183,795 | 89.5 |
|---|---|---|---|
| | John W. White (R) | 21,597 | 10.5 |
| 1938 | Hattie W. Caraway (D) | 122,871 | 89.6 |
| | C. D. Atkinson (R) | 14,240 | 10.4 |
| 1944 | J. William Fulbright (D) | 182,529 | 85.1 |
| | Victor M. Wade (R) | 31,942 | 14.9 |
| 1950 | J. William Fulbright (D) | 302,582 | 100.0 |
| 1956 | J. William Fulbright (D) | 331,679 | 83.0 |
| | Ben C. Henley (R) | 68,016 | 17.0 |
| 1962 | J. William Fulbright (D) | 214,867 | 68.7 |
| | Kenneth Jones (R) | 98,013 | 31.3 |
| 1968 | J. William Fulbright (D) | 349,965 | 59.2 |
| | Charles Bernard (R) | 241,739 | 40.9 |
| 1974 | Dale Bumpers (D) | 461,056 | 84.9 |
| | John Harris Jones (R) | 82,026 | 15.1 |
| 1980 | Dale Bumpers (D) | 477,905 | 59.1 |
| | Bill Clark (R) | 330,576 | 40.9 |
| 1986 | Dale Bumpers (D) | 433,092 | 62.3 |
| | Asa Hutchinson (R) | 262,300 | 37.7 |
| 1992 | Dale Bumpers (D) | 553,635 | 60.2 |
| | Mike Huckabee (R) | 366,373 | 39.8 |

# CALIFORNIA

| | Candidates | Votes | % |
|---|---|---|---|

### Class 1

| 1916 | Hiram W. Johnson (R & PROG) | 574,667 | 61.1 |
|---|---|---|---|
| | George S. Patton (D) | 277,852 | 29.5 |
| | Walter Thomas Mills (SOC) | 49,341 | 5.2 |
| 1922 | Hiram W. Johnson (R) | 564,422 | 62.2 |
| | William J. Pearson (D) | 215,748 | 23.8 |
| | H. Clay Needham (P) | 70,748 | 7.8 |
| | Upton Sinclair (SOC) | 56,982 | 6.3 |
| 1928 | Hiram W. Johnson (R) | 1,148,397 | 74.1 |
| | Minor Moore (D) | 282,411 | 18.2 |
| | Charles H. Randall (P) | 92,106 | 5.9 |
| 1934 | Hiram W. Johnson (R-D-PR-C) | 1,946,572 | 94.5 |
| | George R. Kirkpatrick (SOC) | 108,748 | 5.3 |
| 1940 | Hiram W. Johnson (R-D-PROG) | 2,238,899 | 82.5 |
| | Fred Dyster (P) | 366,044 | 13.5 |
| 1946 | William F. Knowland (R) | 1,428,067 | 54.1 |
| | Will Rogers Jr. (D) | 1,167,161 | 44.2 |

Special Election

| 1946 | William F. Knowland (R) | 425,273 | 74.3 |
|---|---|---|---|
| | Will Rogers Jr. (D) | 90,723 | 15.9 |

| 1952 | William F. Knowland (R-D) | 3,982,448 | 87.7 |
|---|---|---|---|
| | Reuben W. Borough (I PROG) | 542,270 | 11.9 |

**817**

| | Candidates | Votes | % |
|---|---|---|---|
| 1958 | Clair Engle (D) | 2,927,693 | *57.0* |
| | Goodwin J. Knight (R) | 2,204,337 | *42.9* |
| 1964 | George Murphy (R) | 3,628,555 | *51.5* |
| | Pierre Salinger (D) | 3,411,912 | *48.5* |
| 1970 | John V. Tunney (D) | 3,496,558 | *53.9* |
| | George Murphy (R) | 2,877,617 | *44.3* |
| 1976 | S. I. Hayakawa (R) | 3,748,973 | *50.2* |
| | John V. Tunney (D) | 3,502,862 | *46.9* |
| 1982 | Pete Wilson (R) | 4,022,565 | *51.5* |
| | Edmund G. Brown Jr. (D) | 3,494,968 | *44.8* |
| 1988 | Pete Wilson (R) | 5,143,409 | *52.8* |
| | Leo T. McCarthy (D) | 4,287,253 | *44.0* |

**Special Election**

| | | | |
|---|---|---|---|
| 1992 | Dianne Feinstein (D) | 5,853,651 | *54.3* |
| | John Seymour (R) | 4,093,501 | *38.0* |

### Class 3

| | | | |
|---|---|---|---|
| 1914 | James D. Phelan (D) | 279,896 | *31.6* |
| | Francis J. Heney (PROG) | 255,232 | *28.8* |
| | Joseph R. Knowland (R) | 254,159 | *28.7* |
| | Ernest Untermann (SOC) | 56,805 | *6.4* |
| 1920 | Samuel M. Shortridge (R) | 447,835 | *49.0* |
| | James D. Phelan (D) | 371,580 | *40.7* |
| | James S. Edwards (P) | 57,768 | *6.3* |
| 1926 | Samuel M. Shortridge (R) | 670,128 | *63.1* |
| | John B. Elliott (D) | 391,599 | *36.9* |
| 1932 | William Gibbs McAdoo (D) | 943,164 | *43.4* |
| | Tallant Tubbs (R) | 669,676 | *30.8* |
| | Robert P. Shuler (P) | 560,088 | *25.8* |
| 1938 | Sheridan Downey (D-PRO-TN) | 1,372,314 | *54.4* |
| | Philip Bancroft (R) | 1,126,240 | *44.7* |
| 1944 | Sheridan Downey (D) | 1,728,155 | *52.3* |
| | Frederick F. Houser (R) | 1,576,553 | *47.7* |
| 1950 | Richard M. Nixon (R) | 2,183,454 | *59.2* |
| | Helen Gahagan Douglas (D) | 1,502,507 | *40.8* |

**Special Election**

| | | | |
|---|---|---|---|
| 1954 | Thomas H. Kuchel (R) | 2,090,836 | *53.2* |
| | Samuel William Yorty (D) | 1,788,071 | *45.5* |
| 1956 | Thomas H. Kuchel (R) | 2,892,918 | *54.0* |
| | Richard Richards (D) | 2,445,816 | *45.6* |
| 1962 | Thomas H. Kuchel (R) | 3,180,483 | *56.3* |
| | Richard Richards (D) | 2,452,839 | *43.4* |
| 1968 | Alan Cranston (D) | 3,680,352 | *51.8* |
| | Max Rafferty (R) | 3,329,148 | *46.9* |
| 1974 | Alan Cranston (D) | 3,693,160 | *60.5* |
| | H. L. (Bill) Richardson (R) | 2,210,267 | *36.2* |
| 1980 | Alan Cranston (D) | 4,705,399 | *56.5* |
| | Paul Gann (R) | 3,093,426 | *37.1* |
| 1986 | Alan Cranston (D) | 3,646,672 | *49.3* |
| | Ed Zschau (R) | 3,541,804 | *47.9* |
| 1992 | Barbara Boxer (D) | 5,173,467 | *47.9* |
| | Bruce Herschensohn (R) | 4,644,182 | *43.0* |

# COLORADO

| | Candidates | Votes | % |
|---|---|---|---|
| | **Class 2** | | |
| 1912 | John F. Shafroth (D) | 118,260 | *47.3* |
| | Clyde C. Dawson (R) | 66,949 | *26.8* |
| | Frank D. Catlin (PROG-BMR) | 58,649 | *23.5* |
| 1918 | Lawrence C. Phipps (R) | 107,726 | *49.5* |
| | John F. Shafroth (D) | 104,347 | *47.9* |
| 1924 | Lawrence C. Phipps (R) | 159,698 | *50.2* |
| | Alva B. Adams (D) | 139,660 | *43.9* |
| | Morton Alexander (F-LAB) | 16,039 | *5.0* |
| 1930 | Edward P. Costigan (D) | 180,028 | *55.9* |
| | George H. Shaw (R) | 137,487 | *42.7* |
| 1936 | Edwin C. Johnson (D) | 299,376 | *63.5* |
| | Raymond L. Sauter (R) | 166,308 | *35.3* |
| 1942 | Edwin C. Johnson (D) | 174,612 | *50.2* |
| | Ralph L. Carr (R) | 170,970 | *49.2* |
| 1948 | Edwin C. Johnson (D) | 340,719 | *66.8* |
| | Will F. Nicholson (R) | 165,069 | *32.4* |
| 1954 | Gordon Allott (R) | 248,502 | *51.3* |
| | John A. Carroll (D) | 235,686 | *48.7* |
| 1960 | Gordon Allott (R) | 389,428 | *53.5* |
| | Robert L. Knous (D) | 334,854 | *46.0* |
| 1966 | Gordon Allott (R) | 368,307 | *58.0* |
| | Roy Romer (D) | 266,198 | *41.9* |
| 1972 | Floyd K. Haskell (D) | 457,545 | *49.4* |
| | Gordon Allott (R) | 447,957 | *48.4* |
| 1978 | William L. Armstrong (R) | 480,596 | *58.7* |
| | Floyd K. Haskell (D) | 330,247 | *40.3* |
| 1984 | Nancy Dick (D) | 449,327 | *34.6* |
| | William L. Armstrong (R) | 833,821 | *64.2* |
| 1990 | Hank Brown (R) | 569,048 | *55.7* |
| | Josie Heath (D) | 425,746 | *41.7* |

### Class 3

**Special Election**

| | | | |
|---|---|---|---|
| 1912 | Charles S. Thomas (D) | 111,633 | *44.9* |
| | Charles W. Waterman (R) | 66,627 | *26.8* |
| | I. N. Stevens (PROG-BMR) | 64,405 | *25.9* |
| 1914 | Charles S. Thomas (D) | 102,037 | *40.3* |
| | Hubert Work (R) | 98,728 | *39.0* |
| | Benjamin Griffith (PROG) | 27,072 | *10.7* |
| | J. C. Griffiths (SOC) | 13,943 | *5.5* |
| 1920 | Samuel D. Nicholson (R) | 156,577 | *54.5* |
| | Tully Scot (D) | 112,890 | *39.3* |

**Special Election**

| | | | |
|---|---|---|---|
| 1924 | Rice W. Means (R) | 159,353 | *50.2* |
| | Morrison Shafroth (D) | 138,714 | *43.7* |
| | Charles T. Philp (F-LAB) | 17,542 | *5.5* |
| 1926 | Charles W. Waterman (R) | 149,585 | *50.3* |
| | William E. Sweet (D) | 138,113 | *46.4* |
| 1932 | Alva B. Adams (D) | 226,516 | *51.9* |
| | Karl C. Schuyler (R) | 198,519 | *45.5* |

**Special Election**

| | | | |
|---|---|---|---|
| 1932 | Karl C. Schuyler (R) | 207,540 | *48.8* |
| | Walter Walker (D) | 206,475 | *48.5* |
| 1938 | Alva B. Adams (D) | 262,806 | *58.2* |
| | Archibald A. Lee (R) | 181,297 | *40.2* |

| | Candidates | Votes | % |
|---|---|---|---|
| **Special Election** | | | |
| 1942 | Eugene D. Millikin (R) | 191,517 | 56.1 |
| | James A. Marsh (D) | 143,817 | 42.1 |
| 1944 | Eugene D. Millikin (R) | 277,410# | 56.1 |
| | Barney L. Whatley (D) | 214,335# | 43.0 |
| 1950 | Eugene D. Millikin (R) | 239,734 | 53.3 |
| | John A. Carroll (D) | 210,442 | 46.8 |
| 1956 | John A. Carroll (D) | 319,872 | 50.2 |
| | Dan Thornton (R) | 317,102 | 49.8 |
| 1962 | Peter H. Dominick (R) | 328,655 | 53.6 |
| | John A. Carroll (D) | 279,586 | 45.6 |
| 1968 | Peter H. Dominick (R) | 459,952 | 58.6 |
| | Stephen L. R. McNichols (D) | 325,584 | 41.5 |
| 1974 | Gary Hart (D) | 471,691 | 57.2 |
| | Peter H. Dominick (R) | 325,508 | 39.5 |
| 1980 | Gary Hart (D) | 590,501 | 50.3 |
| | Mary E. Buchanan (R) | 571,295 | 48.7 |
| 1986 | Timothy E. Wirth (D) | 529,449 | 49.9 |
| | Ken Kramer (R) | 512,994 | 48.4 |
| 1992 | Ben Nighthorse Campbell (D) | 803,725 | 51.8 |
| | Terry Considine (R) | 662,893 | 42.7 |

# CONNECTICUT

| | Candidates | Votes | % |
|---|---|---|---|
| **Class 1** | | | |
| 1916 | George P. McLean (R) | 107,020 | 50.2 |
| | Homer Cummings (D) | 98,649 | 46.2 |
| 1922 | George P. McLean (R) | 169,524 | 52.3 |
| | Thomas J. Spellacy (D) | 147,276 | 45.5 |
| 1928 | Frederic C. Walcott (R) | 296,958 | 53.9 |
| | Augustine Lonergan (D) | 251,429 | 45.6 |
| 1934 | Francis T. Maloney (D) | 265,552 | 51.8 |
| | Frederic C. Walcott (R) | 247,623 | 48.3 |
| 1940 | Francis T. Maloney (D) | 416,740 | 53.2 |
| | Paul L. Cornell (R, UN) | 358,313 | 45.7 |
| 1946 | Raymond E. Baldwin (R) | 381,328 | 56.1 |
| | Joseph M. Tone (D) | 276,424 | 40.7 |

**Special Election**

| 1946 | Raymond E. Baldwin (R) | 378,707 | 55.8 |
|---|---|---|---|
| | Wilbur L. Cross (D) | 278,188 | 41.0 |

**Special Election**

| 1950 | William Benton (D) | 431,413 | 49.2 |
|---|---|---|---|
| | Prescott S. Bush (R) | 430,311 | 49.1 |

| 1952 | William A. Purtell (R) | 573,854 | 52.5 |
|---|---|---|---|
| | William Benton (D) | 485,066 | 44.4 |
| 1958 | Thomas J. Dodd (D) | 554,841 | 57.5 |
| | William A. Purtell (R) | 410,622 | 42.5 |
| 1964 | Thomas J. Dodd (D) | 781,008 | 64.6 |
| | John Lodge (R) | 426,939 | 35.3 |
| 1970 | Lowell P. Weicker Jr. (R) | 454,721 | 41.7 |
| | Joseph D. Duffey (D) | 368,111 | 33.8 |
| | Thomas J. Dodd (DODD I) | 266,497 | 24.5 |
| 1976 | Lowell P. Weicker Jr. (R) | 785,683 | 57.7 |
| | Gloria Schaffer (D) | 561,018 | 41.2 |
| 1982 | Lowell P. Weicker Jr. (R) | 545,987 | 50.4 |
| | Anthony T. Moffett (D) | 499,146 | 46.1 |

| | Candidates | Votes | % |
|---|---|---|---|
| 1988 | Joseph I. Lieberman (D) | 688,499 | 49.8 |
| | Lowell P. Weicker Jr. (R) | 678,454 | 49.0 |
| **Class 3** | | | |
| 1914 | Frank B. Brandegee (R) | 89,983 | 49.8 |
| | Simeon Baldwin (D) | 76,081 | 42.1 |
| 1920 | Frank B. Brandegee (R) | 216,792 | 59.4 |
| | Augustine Lonergan (D) | 131,824 | 36.1 |

**Special Election**

| 1924 | Hiram Bingham (R) | 112,400# | 60.4 |
|---|---|---|---|
| | Hamilton Holt (D) | 71,871# | 38.6 |

| 1926 | Hiram Bingham (R) | 191,401 | 63.3 |
|---|---|---|---|
| | Rollin U. Tyler (D) | 107,753 | 35.6 |
| 1932 | Augustine Lonergan (D) | 282,327 | 48.5 |
| | Hiram Bingham (R) | 278,061 | 47.7 |
| 1938 | John A. Danaher (R) | 270,413 | 42.9 |
| | Augustine Lonergan (D, UN) | 252,426 | 40.0 |
| | Bellani Trombley (SOC) | 99,282 | 15.8 |
| 1944 | Brien McMahon (D) | 430,716 | 52.0 |
| | John A. Danaher (R) | 391,748 | 47.3 |
| 1950 | Brien McMahon (D) | 453,646 | 51.7 |
| | Joseph E. Talbot (R) | 409,053 | 46.6 |

**Special Election**

| 1952 | Prescott S. Bush (R) | 559,465 | 51.2 |
|---|---|---|---|
| | Abraham A. Ribicoff (D) | 530,505 | 48.5 |

| 1956 | Prescott S. Bush (R) | 610,829 | 54.8 |
|---|---|---|---|
| | Thomas J. Dodd (D) | 479,460 | 43.1 |
| 1962 | Abraham A. Ribicoff (D) | 527,522 | 51.3 |
| | Horace Seely-Brown (R) | 501,694 | 48.8 |
| 1968 | Abraham A. Ribicoff (D) | 655,043 | 54.3 |
| | Edwin H. May (R) | 551,455 | 45.7 |
| 1974 | Abraham A. Ribicoff (D) | 690,820 | 63.7 |
| | James H. Brannen III (R) | 372,055 | 34.3 |
| 1980 | Christopher J. Dodd (D) | 763,969 | 56.3 |
| | James L. Buckley (R) | 581,884 | 42.9 |
| 1986 | Christopher J. Dodd (D) | 632,695 | 64.8 |
| | Roger W. Eddy (R) | 340,438 | 34.8 |
| 1992 | Christopher J. Dodd (D, ACP) | 882,569 | 58.8 |
| | Brook Johnson (R) | 572,036 | 38.1 |

# DELAWARE

| | Candidates | Votes | % |
|---|---|---|---|
| **Class 1** | | | |
| 1916 | Josiah O. Wolcott (D) | 25,434 | 49.7 |
| | Henry A. du Pont (R) | 22,925 | 44.8 |
| 1922 | Thomas F. Bayard (D) | 37,304 | 49.8 |
| | T. Coleman du Pont (R) | 36,979 | 49.4 |

**Special Election**

| 1922 | Thomas F. Bayard (D) | 36,954 | 49.7 |
|---|---|---|---|
| | T. Coleman du Pont (R) | 36,894 | 49.6 |

| 1928 | John G. Townsend Jr. (R) | 63,725 | 61.0 |
|---|---|---|---|
| | Thomas F. Bayard (D) | 40,828 | 39.1 |
| 1934 | John G. Townsend Jr. (R) | 52,829 | 53.3 |
| | Wilbur L. Adams (D) | 45,771 | 46.2 |
| 1940 | James M. Tunnell (D) | 68,294 | 50.6 |

| | Candidates | Votes | % |
|---|---|---|---|
| | John G. Townsend Jr. (R) | 63,799 | 47.3 |
| 1946 | John J. Williams (R) | 62,603 | 55.2 |
| | James M. Tunnell (D) | 50,910 | 44.9 |
| 1952 | John J. Williams (R) | 93,020 | 54.5 |
| | A. I. du Pont Bayard (D) | 77,685 | 45.5 |
| 1958 | John J. Williams (R) | 82,280 | 53.3 |
| | Elbert N. Carvel (D) | 72,152 | 46.7 |
| 1964 | John J. Williams (R) | 103,782 | 51.7 |
| | Elbert N. Carvel (D) | 96,850 | 48.3 |
| 1970 | William V. Roth Jr. (R) | 94,979 | 58.8 |
| | Jacob Zimmerman (D) | 64,740 | 40.1 |
| 1976 | William V. Roth Jr. (R) | 125,502 | 55.8 |
| | Thomas C. Maloney (D) | 98,055 | 43.6 |
| 1982 | William V. Roth Jr. (R) | 105,357 | 55.2 |
| | David N. Levinson (D) | 84,413 | 44.2 |
| 1988 | William V. Roth Jr. (R) | 151,115 | 62.1 |
| | S. B. Woo (D) | 92,378 | 37.9 |

### Class 2

| | | | |
|---|---|---|---|
| 1918 | Lewis Heisler Ball (R) | 21,519 | 51.2 |
| | Willard Saulsbury (D) | 20,113 | 47.8 |
| 1924 | T. Coleman du Pont (R) | 52,731 | 59.4 |
| | James M. Tunnell (D & PROG) | 36,085 | 40.6 |
| 1930 | Daniel O. Hastings (R) | 47,909 | 54.5 |
| | Thomas F. Bayard (D) | 39,881 | 45.4 |

Special Election

| | | | |
|---|---|---|---|
| 1930 | Daniel O. Hastings (R) | 47,665 | 54.8 |
| | Thomas F. Bayard (D) | 39,279 | 45.1 |
| 1936 | James H. Hughes (D) | 67,136 | 53.0 |
| | Daniel O. Hastings (R) | 52,460 | 41.4 |
| | Robert G. Houston (IR) | 6,897 | 5.4 |
| 1942 | Clayton Douglass Buck (R) | 46,210 | 54.2 |
| | E. Ennals Berl (D) | 38,322 | 44.9 |
| 1948 | J. Allen Frear Jr. (D) | 71,888 | 50.9 |
| | Clayton Douglass Buck (R) | 68,246 | 48.3 |
| 1954 | J. Allen Frear Jr. (D) | 82,511 | 56.9 |
| | Herbert B. Warburton (R) | 62,389 | 43.1 |
| 1960 | J. Caleb Boggs (R) | 98,874 | 50.7 |
| | J. Allen Frear Jr. (D) | 96,090 | 49.3 |
| 1966 | J. Caleb Boggs (R) | 97,268 | 59.1 |
| | James M. Tunnell Jr. (D) | 67,263 | 40.9 |
| 1972 | Joseph R. Biden Jr. (D) | 116,006 | 50.5 |
| | J. Caleb Boggs (R) | 112,844 | 49.1 |
| 1978 | Joseph R. Biden Jr. (D) | 93,930 | 58.0 |
| | James H. Baxter (R) | 66,479 | 41.0 |
| 1984 | Joseph R. Biden Jr. (D) | 147,831 | 60.1 |
| | John M. Burris (R) | 98,101 | 39.1 |
| 1990 | Joseph R. Biden Jr. (D) | 112,918 | 62.7 |
| | M. Jane Brady (R) | 64,554 | 35.8 |

# FLORIDA

| | Candidates | Votes | % |
|---|---|---|---|
| | **Class 1** | | |
| 1916 | Park Trammell (D) | 58,391 | 82.9 |
| | W. R. O'Neal (R) | 8,774 | 12.5 |

| | Candidates | Votes | % |
|---|---|---|---|
| 1922 | Park Trammell (D) | 45,707 | 88.0 |
| | W. C. Lawson (IR) | 6,074 | 11.7 |
| 1928 | Park Trammell (D) | 153,816 | 68.5 |
| | Barclay H. Warburton (R) | 70,633 | 31.5 |
| 1934 | Park Trammell (D) | 131,780 | 100.0 |

Special Election

| | | | |
|---|---|---|---|
| 1936 | Charles O. Andrews (D) | 241,528 | 80.9 |
| | Howard C. Babcock (R) | 57,016 | 19.1 |
| 1940 | Charles O. Andrews (D) | 323,216 | 100.0 |
| 1946 | Spessard L. Holland (D) | 156,232 | 78.7 |
| | J. Harry Schad (R) | 42,413 | 21.4 |
| 1952 | Spessard L. Holland (D) | 616,665 | 99.8 |
| 1958 | Spessard L. Holland (D) | 386,113 | 71.2 |
| | Leland Hyzer (R) | 155,956 | 28.8 |
| 1964 | Spessard L. Holland (D) | 997,585 | 63.9 |
| | Claude R. Kirk Jr. (R) | 562,212 | 36.0 |
| 1970 | Lawton Chiles (D) | 902,438 | 53.9 |
| | William C. Cramer (R) | 772,817 | 46.1 |
| 1976 | Lawton Chiles (D) | 1,799,518 | 63.0 |
| | John Grady (R) | 1,057,886 | 37.0 |
| 1982 | Lawton Chiles (D) | 1,637,667 | 61.7 |
| | Van B. Poole (R) | 1,015,330 | 38.3 |
| 1988 | Connie Mack (R) | 2,051,071 | 50.4 |
| | Buddy MacKay (D) | 2,016,553 | 49.6 |

### Class 3

| | | | |
|---|---|---|---|
| 1914 | Duncan U. Fletcher (D) | 22,761 | 99.5 |
| 1920 | Duncan U. Fletcher (D) | 98,966 | 74.3 |
| | John M. Cheney (R) | 27,914 | 21.0 |
| 1926 | Duncan U. Fletcher (D) | 51,054 | 77.9 |
| | John M. Lindsay (RDC) | 8,381 | 12.8 |
| | W. R. O'Neal (R) | 6,133 | 9.4 |
| 1932 | Duncan U. Fletcher (D) | 204,651 | 99.8 |

Special Election

| | | | |
|---|---|---|---|
| 1936 | Claude Pepper (D) | 246,050 | 100.0 |
| 1938 | Claude Pepper (D) | 145,757 | 82.5 |
| | Thomas E. Swanson (R) | 31,035 | 17.6 |
| 1944 | Claude Pepper (D) | 335,685 | 71.3 |
| | Miles H. Draper (R) | 135,258 | 28.7 |
| 1950 | George A. Smathers (D) | 238,987 | 76.2 |
| | John P. Booth (R) | 74,228 | 23.7 |
| 1956 | George A. Smathers (D) | 655,418 | 100.0 |
| 1962 | George A. Smathers (D) | 657,633 | 70.0 |
| | Emerson Rupert (R) | 281,381 | 30.0 |
| 1968 | Edward J. Gurney (R) | 1,131,499 | 55.9 |
| | Leroy Collins (D) | 892,637 | 44.1 |
| 1974 | Richard Stone (D) | 781,031 | 43.4 |
| | Jack Eckerd (R) | 736,674 | 40.9 |
| | John Grady (AM) | 282,659 | 15.7 |
| 1980 | Paula Hawkins (R) | 1,822,460 | 51.7 |
| | Bill Gunter (D) | 1,705,409 | 48.3 |
| 1986 | Bob Graham (D) | 1,877,231 | 54.7 |
| | Paula Hawkins (R) | 1,551,888 | 45.3 |
| 1992 | Bob Graham (D) | 3,244,299 | 65.4 |
| | Bill Grant (R) | 1,715,156 | 34.6 |

# GEORGIA

| Candidates | Votes | % |
|---|---|---|
| **Class 2** | | |
| **Special Election** | | |
| 1914  Thomas W. Hardwick (D) | 62,239 | 68.9 |
| Hutch (PROG) | 28,163 | 31.2 |
| 1918  William J. Harris (D) | 53,731 | 88.4 |
| Williams (R) | 7,078 | 11.6 |
| 1924  William J. Harris (D) | 155,497# | 100.0 |
| 1930  William J. Harris (D) | 55,606 | 100.0 |
| **Special Election** | | |
| 1932  Richard B. Russell (D) | 238,931 | 100.0 |
| 1936  Richard B. Russell (D) | 263,468 | 100.0 |
| 1942  Richard B. Russell (D) | 59,870 | 96.9 |
| 1948  Richard B. Russell (D) | 362,104 | 99.9 |
| 1954  Richard B. Russell (D) | 333,917 | 100.0 |
| 1960  Richard B. Russell (D) | 576,140 | 99.9 |
| 1966  Richard B. Russell (D) | 631,002 | 100.0 |
| 1972  Sam Nunn (D) | 635,970 | 54.0 |
| Fletcher Thompson (R) | 542,331 | 46.0 |
| **Special Election** | | |
| 1972  Sam Nunn (D) | 404,890 | 52.0 |
| Fletcher Thompson (R) | 362,501 | 46.5 |
| 1978  Sam Nunn (D) | 536,320 | 83.1 |
| John W. Stokes (R) | 108,808 | 16.9 |
| 1984  Sam Nunn (D) | 1,344,104 | 79.9 |
| Jon Michael Hicks (R) | 337,196 | 20.1 |
| 1990  Sam Nunn (D) | 1,033,439 | 100.0 |
| **Class 3** | | |
| 1914  Hoke Smith (D) | 61,489 | 68.4 |
| McClure (PROG) | 28,435 | 31.6 |
| 1920  Thomas Watson (D) | 124,630 | 94.9 |
| Harvey S. Edwards (I) | 6,700 | 5.1 |
| **Special Election** | | |
| 1922  Walter F. George (D) | 75,860 | 100.0 |
| 1926  Walter F. George (D) | 47,446 | 100.0 |
| 1932  Walter F. George (D) | 234,590 | 92.8 |
| James W. Arnold (R) | 18,151 | 7.2 |
| 1938  Walter F. George (D) | 66,897 | 95.1 |
| 1944  Walter F. George (D) | 272,541 | 100.0 |
| 1950  Walter F. George (D) | 261,290 | 100.0 |
| 1956  Herman E. Talmadge (D) | 541,094 | 100.0 |
| 1962  Herman E. Talmadge (D) | 306,250 | 100.0 |
| 1968  Herman E. Talmadge (D) | 885,103 | 77.5 |
| E. Earl Patton (R) | 256,796 | 22.5 |
| 1974  Herman E. Talmadge (D) | 627,376 | 71.7 |
| Jerry Johnson (R) | 246,866 | 28.2 |
| 1980  Mack Mattingly (R) | 803,686 | 50.9 |
| Herman E. Talmadge (D) | 776,143 | 49.1 |
| 1986  Wyche Fowler Jr. (D) | 623,707 | 50.9 |
| Mack Mattingly (R) | 601,241 | 49.1 |
| 1992 [1]  Wyche Fowler Jr. (D) | 1,108,416 | 49.2 |
| Paul Coverdell (R) | 1,073,282 | 47.7 |

| Candidates | Votes | % |
|---|---|---|
| **Runoff Election [1]** | | |
| 1992  Paul Coverdell (R) | 635,114 | 50.6 |
| Wyche Fowler Jr. (D) | 618,877 | 49.4 |

**Georgia**
1. Georgia law requires election by a majority of the popular vote and provides for a runoff between the two top finishers when neither gained a majority in the regular election.

# HAWAII

| Candidates | Votes | % |
|---|---|---|
| **Class 1** | | |
| 1959  Hiram L. Fong (R) | 87,161 | 52.9 |
| Frank F. Fasi (D) | 77,647 | 47.1 |
| 1964  Hiram L. Fong (R) | 110,747 | 53.0 |
| Thomas P. Gill (D) | 96,789 | 46.4 |
| 1970  Hiram L. Fong (R) | 124,163 | 51.6 |
| Cecil Heftel (D) | 116,597 | 48.4 |
| 1976  Spark M. Matsunaga (D) | 162,305 | 53.7 |
| William F. Quinn (R) | 122,724 | 40.6 |
| 1982  Spark M. Matsunaga (D) | 245,386 | 80.1 |
| Clarence J. Brown (R) | 52,071 | 17.0 |
| 1988  Spark M. Matsunaga (D) | 247,941 | 76.5 |
| Maria M. Hustace (R) | 66,987 | 20.7 |
| **Special Election** | | |
| 1990  Daniel K. Akaka (D) | 188,901 | 54.0 |
| Patricia Saiki (R) | 155,978 | 44.6 |
| **Class 3** | | |
| 1959  Oren E. Long (D) | 83,700 | 51.1 |
| Wilfred C. Tsukiyama (R) | 79,123 | 48.3 |
| 1962  Daniel K. Inouye (D) | 136,294 | 69.4 |
| Ben Dillingham (R) | 60,067 | 30.6 |
| 1968  Daniel K. Inouye (D) | 189,248 | 83.4 |
| Wayne C. Thiessen (R) | 34,008 | 15.0 |
| 1974  Daniel K. Inouye (D) | 207,454 | 82.9 |
| James D. Kimmel (PP) | 42,767 | 17.1 |
| 1980  Daniel K. Inouye (D) | 224,485 | 77.9 |
| Cooper Brown (R) | 53,068 | 18.4 |
| 1986  Daniel K. Inouye (D) | 241,887 | 73.6 |
| Frank Hutchinson (R) | 86,910 | 26.4 |
| 1992  Daniel K. Inouye (D) | 208,266 | 57.3 |
| Rick Reed (R) | 97,928 | 26.9 |
| Linda B. Martin (GREEN) | 49,921 | 13.7 |

# IDAHO

| Candidates | Votes | % |
|---|---|---|
| **Class 2** | | |
| 1918  William E. Borah (R) | 63,587 | 67.2 |
| Frank L. Moore (D) | 31,018 | 32.8 |
| 1924  William E. Borah (R) | 99,846 | 79.5 |
| Frank Martin (D) | 25,199 | 20.1 |
| 1930  William E. Borah (R) | 94,938 | 72.4 |
| Joseph M. Tyler (D) | 36,162 | 27.6 |

**821**

| | Candidates | Votes | % |
|---|---|---|---|
| 1936 | William E. Borah (R) | 128,723 | 63.4 |
| | C. Ben Ross (D) | 74,444 | 36.6 |

**Special Election**

| | | | |
|---|---|---|---|
| 1940 | John Thomas (R) | 124,535 | 53.0 |
| | Glen H. Taylor (D) | 110,664 | 47.1 |
| 1942 | John Thomas (R) | 73,353 | 51.5 |
| | Glen H. Taylor (D) | 68,989 | 48.5 |

**Special Election**

| | | | |
|---|---|---|---|
| 1946 | Henry C. Dworshak (R) | 105,523 | 58.6 |
| | George E. Donart (D) | 74,629 | 41.4 |
| 1948 | Bert C. Miller (D) | 107,000 | 50.0 |
| | Henry C. Dworshak (R) | 103,868 | 48.5 |

**Special Election**

| | | | |
|---|---|---|---|
| 1950 | Henry C. Dworshak (R) | 104,608 | 51.9 |
| | Claude J. Burtenshaw (D) | 97,092 | 48.1 |
| 1954 | Henry C. Dworshak (R) | 142,269 | 62.8 |
| | Glen H. Taylor (D) | 84,139 | 37.2 |
| 1960 | Henry C. Dworshak (R) | 152,648 | 52.3 |
| | R. F. (Bob) McLaughlin (D) | 139,448 | 47.7 |

**Special Election**

| | | | |
|---|---|---|---|
| 1962 | Len B. Jordan (R) | 131,279 | 51.0 |
| | Gracie Pfost (D) | 126,398 | 49.1 |
| 1966 | Len B. Jordan (R) | 139,819 | 55.4 |
| | Ralph R. Harding (D) | 112,637 | 44.6 |
| 1972 | James A. McClure (R) | 161,804 | 52.3 |
| | William E. (Bud) Davis (D) | 140,913 | 45.5 |
| 1978 | James A. McClure (R) | 194,412 | 68.4 |
| | Dwight Jensen (D) | 89,635 | 31.6 |
| 1984 | James A. McClure (R) | 293,193 | 72.2 |
| | Peter M. Busch (D) | 105,591 | 26.0 |
| 1990 | Larry E. Craig (R) | 193,641 | 61.3 |
| | Ron J. Twilegar (D) | 122,295 | 38.7 |

### Class 3

| | | | |
|---|---|---|---|
| 1914 | James H. Brady (R) | 47,486 | 43.9 |
| | James H. Hawley (D) | 41,266 | 38.1 |
| | Paul Clagstone (EP) | 10,321 | 9.5 |
| | C. W. Cooper (SOC) | 7,888 | 7.3 |

**Special Election**

| | | | |
|---|---|---|---|
| 1918 | John F. Nugent (D) | 48,467 | 50.5 |
| | Frank R. Gooding (R) | 47,497 | 49.5 |
| 1920 | Frank R. Gooding (R) | 75,985 | 54.1 |
| | John F. Nugent (D) | 64,513 | 45.9 |
| 1926 | Frank R. Gooding (R) | 56,847 | 45.4 |
| | H. F. Samuels (PROG) | 37,047 | 29.6 |
| | John F. Nugent (D) | 31,285 | 25.0 |

**Special Election**

| | | | |
|---|---|---|---|
| 1928 | John Thomas (R) | 90,922 | 62.6 |
| | Chase Clark (D) | 53,399 | 36.7 |
| 1932 | James Pope (D) | 103,020 | 55.7 |
| | John Thomas (R) | 78,225 | 42.3 |

| | Candidates | Votes | % |
|---|---|---|---|
| 1938 | D. Worth Clark (D) | 99,801 | 54.7 |
| | Donald A. Callahan (R) | 81,939 | 44.9 |
| 1944 | Glen H. Taylor (D) | 107,096 | 51.1 |
| | C. A. Bottolfsen (R) | 102,373 | 48.9 |
| 1950 | Herman Welker (R) | 124,237 | 61.7 |
| | D. Worth Clark (D) | 77,180 | 38.3 |
| 1956 | Frank Church (D) | 149,096 | 56.2 |
| | Herman Welker (R) | 102,781 | 38.7 |
| | Glen H. Taylor (WRITE IN) | 13,415 | 5.1 |
| 1962 | Frank Church (D) | 141,657 | 54.7 |
| | Jack Hawley (R) | 117,129 | 45.3 |
| 1968 | Frank Church (D) | 173,482 | 60.3 |
| | George V. Hansen (R) | 114,394 | 39.7 |
| 1974 | Frank Church (D) | 145,140 | 56.1 |
| | Robert L. Smith (R) | 109,072 | 42.1 |
| 1980 | Steven D. Symms (R) | 218,701 | 49.7 |
| | Frank Church (D) | 214,439 | 48.8 |
| 1986 | Steven D. Symms (R) | 196,958 | 51.6 |
| | John V. Evans (D) | 185,066 | 48.4 |
| 1992 | Dirk Kempthorne (R) | 270,468 | 56.5 |
| | Richard Stallings (D) | 208,036 | 43.5 |

# ILLINOIS

| | Candidates | Votes | % |
|---|---|---|---|

### Class 2

| | | | |
|---|---|---|---|
| 1918 | Medill McCormick (R) | 479,957 | 50.5 |
| | James Hamilton Lewis (D) | 426,943 | 44.9 |
| 1924 | Charles S. Deneen (R) | 1,449,180 | 63.5 |
| | Albert A. Sprague (D) | 806,702 | 35.4 |
| 1930 | James Hamilton Lewis (D) | 1,432,216 | 64.0 |
| | Ruth Hanna McCormick (R) | 687,469 | 30.7 |
| 1936 | James Hamilton Lewis (D) | 2,142,887 | 56.5 |
| | Otis F. Glenn (R) | 1,545,160 | 40.7 |

**Special Election**

| | | | |
|---|---|---|---|
| 1940 | C. Wayland Brooks (R) | 2,045,924 | 50.1 |
| | James M. Slattery (D) | 2,025,097 | 49.6 |
| 1942 | C. Wayland Brooks (R) | 1,582,887 | 53.2 |
| | Raymond S. McKeough (D) | 1,380,011 | 46.4 |
| 1948 | Paul H. Douglas (D) | 2,147,754 | 55.1 |
| | C. Wayland Brooks (R) | 1,740,026 | 44.6 |
| 1954 | Paul H. Douglas (D) | 1,804,338 | 53.6 |
| | Joseph T. Meek (R) | 1,563,683 | 46.4 |
| 1960 | Paul H. Douglas (D) | 2,530,943 | 54.6 |
| | Samuel W. Witwer (R) | 2,093,846 | 45.2 |
| 1966 | Charles H. Percy (R) | 2,100,449 | 55.0 |
| | Paul H. Douglas (D) | 1,678,147 | 43.9 |
| 1972 | Charles H. Percy (R) | 2,867,078 | 62.2 |
| | Roman Pucinski (D) | 1,721,031 | 37.4 |
| 1978 | Charles H. Percy (R) | 1,698,711 | 53.3 |
| | Alex Seith (D) | 1,448,187 | 45.5 |
| 1984 | Paul Simon (D) | 2,397,303 | 50.1 |
| | Charles H. Percy (R) | 2,308,039 | 48.2 |
| 1990 | Paul Simon (D) | 2,115,377 | 65.1 |
| | Lynn Martin (R) | 1,135,628 | 34.9 |

### Class 3

| | | | |
|---|---|---|---|
| 1914 | Lawrence Y. Sherman (R) | 390,661 | 38.5 |
| | Roger C. Sullivan (D) | 373,403 | 36.8 |
| | Raymond Robins (PROG) | 203,027 | 20.0 |
| 1920 | William B. McKinley (R) | 1,381,384 | 66.8 |
| | Peter A. Waller (D) | 554,372 | 26.8 |

| | Candidates | Votes | % |
|---|---|---|---|
| 1926 | Frank L. Smith (R) | 842,273* | 46.9 |
| | George E. Brennan (D) | 774,943 | 43.1 |
| | Hugh S. Magill (IR) | 156,245 | 8.7 |

Special Election

| | | | |
|---|---|---|---|
| 1928 | Otis F. Glenn (R) | 1,594,031 | 54.5 |
| | Anton J. Cermak (D) | 1,315,338 | 44.9 |

| | | | |
|---|---|---|---|
| 1932 | William H. Dieterich (D) | 1,670,466 | 52.2 |
| | Otis F. Glenn (R) | 1,471,841 | 46.0 |
| 1938 | Scott W. Lucas (D) | 1,638,162 | 51.3 |
| | Richard J. Lyons (R) | 1,542,574 | 48.3 |
| 1944 | Scott W. Lucas (D) | 2,059,023 | 52.6 |
| | Richard J. Lyons (R) | 1,841,793 | 47.1 |
| 1950 | Everett McKinley Dirksen (R) | 1,951,984 | 53.9 |
| | Scott W. Lucas (D) | 1,657,630 | 45.8 |
| 1956 | Everett McKinley Dirksen (R) | 2,307,352 | 54.1 |
| | Richard Stengel (D) | 1,949,883 | 45.7 |
| 1962 | Everett McKinley Dirksen (R) | 1,961,202 | 52.9 |
| | Sidney R. Yates (D) | 1,748,007 | 47.1 |
| 1968 | Everett McKinley Dirksen (R) | 2,358,947 | 53.0 |
| | William G. Clark (D) | 2,073,242 | 46.6 |

Special Election

| | | | |
|---|---|---|---|
| 1970 | Adlai E. Stevenson III (D) | 2,065,054 | 57.4 |
| | Ralph Tyler Smith (R) | 1,519,718 | 42.2 |

| | | | |
|---|---|---|---|
| 1974 | Adlai E. Stevenson III (D) | 1,811,496 | 62.2 |
| | George M. Burditt (R) | 1,084,884 | 37.2 |
| 1980 | Alan J. Dixon (D) | 2,565,302 | 56.0 |
| | David C. O'Neal (R) | 1,946,296 | 42.5 |
| 1986 | Alan J. Dixon (D) | 2,033,926 | 65.1 |
| | Judy Koehler (R) | 1,053,793 | 33.7 |
| 1992 | Carol Moseley-Braun (D) | 2,631,229 | 53.3 |
| | Richard S. Williamson (R) | 2,126,833 | 43.1 |

# INDIANA

| Candidates | Votes | % |
|---|---|---|
| **Class 1** | | |

| | | | |
|---|---|---|---|
| 1916 | Harry S. New (R) | 337,089 | 47.8 |
| | John W. Kern (D) | 325,588 | 46.1 |
| 1922 | Samuel M. Ralston (D) | 558,169 | 50.9 |
| | Albert J. Beveridge (R) | 524,558 | 47.8 |

Special Election

| | | | |
|---|---|---|---|
| 1926 | Arthur R. Robinson (R) | 519,401 | 50.6 |
| | Evans Woollen (D) | 496,540 | 48.4 |

| | | | |
|---|---|---|---|
| 1928 | Arthur R. Robinson (R) | 782,144 | 55.3 |
| | Albert Stump (D) | 623,996 | 44.1 |
| 1934 | Sherman Minton (D) | 758,801 | 51.5 |
| | Arthur R. Robinson (R) | 700,103 | 47.5 |
| 1940 | Raymond E. Willis (R) | 888,070 | 50.5 |
| | Sherman Minton (D) | 864,803 | 49.1 |
| 1946 | William E. Jenner (R) | 739,809 | 54.9 |
| | M. Clifford Townsend (D) | 584,288 | 43.4 |
| 1952 | William E. Jenner (R) | 1,020,605 | 52.4 |
| | Henry F. Schricker (D) | 911,169 | 46.8 |
| 1958 | R. Vance Hartke (D) | 973,636 | 56.5 |
| | Harold W. Handley (R) | 731,635 | 42.4 |
| 1964 | R. Vance Hartke (D) | 1,128,505 | 54.3 |

| | Candidates | Votes | % |
|---|---|---|---|
| | D. Russell Bontrager (R) | 941,519 | 45.3 |
| 1970 | R. Vance Hartke (D) | 870,990 | 50.1 |
| | Richard L. Roudebush (R) | 866,707 | 49.9 |
| 1976 | Richard G. Lugar (R) | 1,275,833 | 58.8 |
| | R. Vance Hartke (D) | 878,522 | 40.5 |
| 1982 | Richard G. Lugar (R) | 978,301 | 53.8 |
| | Floyd Fithian (D) | 828,400 | 45.6 |
| 1988 | Richard G. Lugar (R) | 1,430,525 | 68.1 |
| | Jack Wickes (D) | 668,778 | 31.9 |

**Class 3**

| | | | |
|---|---|---|---|
| 1914 | Benjamin F. Shively (D) | 272,249 | 42.1 |
| | Hugh Miller (R) | 226,766 | 35.1 |
| | Albert J. Beveridge (PROG) | 108,581 | 16.8 |

Special Election

| | | | |
|---|---|---|---|
| 1916 | James E. Watson (R) | 335,193 | 47.7 |
| | Thomas Taggart (D) | 325,607 | 46.3 |

| | | | |
|---|---|---|---|
| 1920 | James E. Watson (R) | 681,854 | 54.6 |
| | Thomas Taggart (D) | 514,191 | 41.2 |
| 1926 | James E. Watson (R) | 522,737 | 50.0 |
| | Albert Stump (D) | 511,454 | 49.0 |
| 1932 | Frederick Van Nuys (D) | 870,053 | 55.6 |
| | James E. Watson (R) | 661,750 | 42.3 |
| 1938 | Frederick Van Nuys (D) | 788,386 | 49.8 |
| | Raymond E. Willis (R) | 783,189 | 49.5 |

Special Election

| | | | |
|---|---|---|---|
| 1944 | William E. Jenner (R) | 857,250 | 52.1 |
| | Cornelius O'Brien (D) | 775,417 | 47.1 |

| | | | |
|---|---|---|---|
| 1944 | Homer E. Capehart (R) | 829,489 | 50.2 |
| | Henry F. Schricker (D) | 807,766 | 48.9 |
| 1950 | Homer E. Capehart (R) | 844,303 | 52.8 |
| | Alex M. Campbell (D) | 741,025 | 46.4 |
| 1956 | Homer E. Capehart (R) | 1,084,262 | 55.2 |
| | Claude R. Wickard (D) | 871,781 | 44.4 |
| 1962 | Birch Bayh (D) | 905,491 | 50.3 |
| | Homer E. Capehart (R) | 894,547 | 49.7 |
| 1968 | Birch Bayh (D) | 1,060,456 | 51.7 |
| | William D. Ruckelshaus (R) | 988,571 | 48.2 |
| 1974 | Birch Bayh (D) | 889,269 | 50.7 |
| | Richard G. Lugar (R) | 814,117 | 46.4 |
| 1980 | Dan Quayle (R) | 1,182,414 | 53.8 |
| | Birch Bayh (D) | 1,015,962 | 46.2 |
| 1986 | Dan Quayle (R) | 936,143 | 60.6 |
| | Jill Long (D) | 595,192 | 38.5 |

Special Election

| | | | |
|---|---|---|---|
| 1990 | Daniel R. Coats (R) | 806,048 | 53.6 |
| | Baron P. Hill (D) | 696,639 | 46.4 |

| | | | |
|---|---|---|---|
| 1992 | Daniel R. Coats (R) | 1,267,972 | 57.3 |
| | Joseph H. Hogsett (D) | 900,148 | 40.7 |

# IOWA

| Candidates | Votes | % |
|---|---|---|
| **Class 2** | | |

| | | | |
|---|---|---|---|
| 1918 | William S. Kenyon (R) | 230,264 | 65.4 |
| | Charles R. Keyes (D) | 121,830 | 34.6 |

| Candidates | Votes | % |
|---|---|---|
| Special Election | | |
| | | |
| 1922 Smith W. Brookhart (R) | 389,751 | 63.1 |
| Clyde L. Herring (D) | 227,833 | 36.9 |
| | | |
| 1924 [1] Smith W. Brookhart (R) | 447,594 | 50.0 |
| Daniel F. Steck (D) | 446,840 | 50.0 |
| 1930 Lester J. Dickinson (R) | 307,613 | 56.3 |
| Daniel F. Steck (D) | 235,186 | 43.0 |
| 1936 Clyde L. Herring (D) | 539,555 | 50.5 |
| Lester J. Dickinson (R) | 503,635 | 47.1 |
| 1942 George A. Wilson (R) | 410,333 | 58.0 |
| Clyde L. Herring (D) | 295,194 | 41.7 |
| 1948 Guy M. Gillette (D) | 578,226 | 57.8 |
| George A. Wilson (R) | 415,778 | 41.6 |
| 1954 Thomas E. Martin (R) | 442,409 | 52.2 |
| Guy M. Gillette (D) | 402,712 | 47.5 |
| 1960 Jack Miller (R) | 642,463 | 51.9 |
| Herschel C. Loveless (D) | 595,119 | 48.1 |
| 1966 Jack Miller (R) | 522,339 | 60.9 |
| E. B. Smith (D) | 324,114 | 37.8 |
| 1972 Dick Clark (D) | 662,637 | 55.1 |
| Jack Miller (R) | 530,525 | 44.1 |
| 1978 Roger W. Jepsen (R) | 421,598 | 51.1 |
| Dick Clark (D) | 395,066 | 47.9 |
| 1984 Tom Harkin (D) | 716,883 | 55.5 |
| Roger W. Jepsen (R) | 564,381 | 43.7 |
| 1990 Tom Harkin (D) | 535,975 | 54.5 |
| Tom Tauke (R) | 446,869 | 45.4 |

### Class 3

| | | | |
|---|---|---|---|
| 1914 | Albert B. Cummins (R) | 205,832 | 48.2 |
| | Connolly (D) | 167,251 | 39.2 |
| | Spurgeon (I) | 24,490 | 5.7 |
| 1920 | Albert B. Cummins (R) | 528,499 | 61.4 |
| | Claude R. Porter (D) | 322,015 | 37.4 |
| 1926 | Smith W. Brookhart (R) | 323,409 | 56.5 |
| | Claude R. Porter (D) | 247,869 | 43.3 |

Special Election

| | | | |
|---|---|---|---|
| 1926 | David W. Stewart (R) | 336,410 | 100.0 |

| | | | |
|---|---|---|---|
| 1932 | Richard Louis Murphy (D) | 538,422 | 54.9 |
| | Henry Field (R) | 399,929 | 40.8 |

Special Election

| | | | |
|---|---|---|---|
| 1936 | Guy M. Gillette (D) | 536,075 | 51.9 |
| | Berry F. Halden (R) | 481,521 | 46.6 |

| | | | |
|---|---|---|---|
| 1938 | Guy M. Gillette (D) | 413,788 | 49.7 |
| | Lester J. Dickinson (R) | 410,983 | 49.4 |
| 1944 | Bourke B. Hickenlooper (R) | 523,963 | 51.3 |
| | Guy M. Gillette (D) | 494,229 | 48.4 |
| 1950 | Bourke B. Hickenlooper (R) | 470,613 | 54.8 |
| | Albert J. Loveland (D) | 383,766 | 44.7 |
| 1956 | Bourke B. Hickenlooper (R) | 635,499 | 53.9 |
| | R. M. Evans (D) | 543,156 | 46.1 |
| 1962 | Bourke B. Hickenlooper (R) | 431,364 | 53.4 |
| | E. B. Smith (D) | 376,602 | 46.6 |
| 1968 | Harold E. Hughes (D) | 574,884 | 50.3 |
| | David M. Stanley (R) | 568,469 | 49.7 |
| 1974 | John C. Culver (D) | 462,947 | 52.0 |
| | David M. Stanley (R) | 420,546 | 47.3 |
| 1980 | Charles E. Grassley (R) | 683,014 | 53.5 |
| | John C. Culver (D) | 581,545 | 45.5 |
| 1986 | Charles E. Grassley (R) | 588,880 | 66.0 |
| | John P. Roehrick (D) | 299,406 | 33.6 |

| | | | |
|---|---|---|---|
| 1992 | Charles E. Grassley (R) | 899,761 | 69.6 |
| | Jean Lloyd-Jones (D) | 351,561 | 27.2 |

**Iowa**

1. Disputed election. See list of senators, Iowa, p. 792.

# KANSAS

| Candidates | Votes | % |
|---|---|---|
| **Class 2** | | |
| | | |
| 1912 William H. Thompson (D) | 172,601 | 49.3 |
| W. R. Stubbs (R) | 151,647 | 43.3 |
| Allan W. Ricker (SOC) | 25,610 | 7.3 |
| 1918 Arthur Capper (R) | 281,931 | 63.7 |
| William H. Thompson (D) | 149,300 | 33.7 |
| 1924 Arthur Capper (R) | 428,494 | 70.1 |
| James Malone (D) | 154,189 | 25.2 |
| 1930 Arthur Capper (R) | 364,548 | 61.1 |
| Jonathan M. Davis (D) | 232,161 | 38.9 |
| 1936 Arthur Capper (R) | 417,873 | 51.0 |
| Omar B. Ketchum (D) | 396,685 | 48.4 |
| 1942 Arthur Capper (R) | 284,059 | 57.1 |
| George McGill (D) | 200,437 | 40.3 |
| 1948 Andrew F. Schoeppel (R) | 393,412 | 54.9 |
| George McGill (D) | 305,987 | 42.7 |
| 1954 Andrew F. Schoeppel (R) | 348,144 | 56.3 |
| George McGill (D) | 258,575 | 41.8 |
| 1960 Andrew F. Schoeppel (R) | 485,499 | 54.6 |
| Frank Theis (D) | 388,895 | 43.8 |

Special Election

| | | | |
|---|---|---|---|
| 1962 | James B. Pearson (R) | 344,689 | 56.2 |
| | Paul L. Aylward (D) | 260,756 | 42.5 |

| | | | |
|---|---|---|---|
| 1966 | James B. Pearson (R) | 350,077 | 52.2 |
| | J. Floyd Breeding (D) | 303,223 | 45.2 |
| 1972 | James B. Pearson (R) | 622,591 | 71.4 |
| | Arch Tetzlaff (D) | 200,764 | 23.0 |
| 1978 | Nancy Landon Kassebaum (R) | 403,354 | 53.9 |
| | William R. Roy (D) | 317,602 | 42.4 |
| 1984 | Nancy Landon Kassebaum (R) | 757,402 | 76.0 |
| | James R. Maher (D) | 211,664 | 21.2 |
| 1990 | Nancy Landon Kassebaum (R) | 578,605 | 73.6 |
| | Dick Williams (D) | 207,491 | 26.4 |

### Class 3

| | | | |
|---|---|---|---|
| 1914 | Charles Curtis (R) | 180,823 | 35.5 |
| | George A. Neeley (D) | 176,929 | 34.8 |
| | Victor Murdock (PROG) | 116,755 | 22.9 |
| 1920 | Charles Curtis (R) | 327,072 | 64.0 |
| | George H. Hodges (D) | 170,443 | 33.4 |
| 1926 | Charles Curtis (R) | 308,222 | 63.6 |
| | Charles Stephens (D) | 168,446 | 34.7 |

Special Election

| | | | |
|---|---|---|---|
| 1930 | George McGill (D) | 288,889 | 50.0 |
| | Henry J. Allen (R) | 276,833 | 48.0 |

| | | | |
|---|---|---|---|
| 1932 | George McGill (D) | 328,992 | 45.7 |
| | Ben S. Paulen (R) | 302,809 | 42.0 |
| | George Alfred Brown (I) | 65,583 | 9.1 |
| 1938 | Clyde M. Reed (R) | 419,532 | 56.2 |
| | George McGill (D) | 326,774 | 43.8 |

| | Candidates | Votes | % |
|---|---|---|---|
| 1944 | Clyde M. Reed (R) | 387,090 | 57.8 |
| | Thurman Hill (D) | 272,053 | 40.7 |
| 1950 | Frank Carlson (R) | 335,880 | 54.3 |
| | Paul Aiken (D) | 271,365 | 43.8 |

Special Election

| | | | |
|---|---|---|---|
| 1950 | Frank Carlson (R) | 321,718 | 55.2 |
| | Paul Aiken (D) | 261,405 | 44.8 |
| 1956 | Frank Carlson (R) | 477,822 | 57.9 |
| | George Hart (D) | 333,939 | 40.5 |
| 1962 | Frank Carlson (H) | 388,500 | 62.4 |
| | K. L. Smith (D) | 223,630 | 35.9 |
| 1968 | Robert Dole (R) | 490,911 | 60.1 |
| | William I. Robinson (D) | 315,911 | 38.7 |
| 1974 | Robert Dole (R) | 403,983 | 50.9 |
| | William R. Roy (D) | 390,451 | 49.1 |
| 1980 | Robert Dole (R) | 598,686 | 63.8 |
| | John Simpson (D) | 340,271 | 36.2 |
| 1986 | Robert Dole (R) | 576,902 | 70.0 |
| | Guy MacDonald (D) | 246,664 | 30.0 |
| 1992 | Robert Dole (R) | 706,246 | 62.7 |
| | Gloria O'Dell (D) | 349,525 | 31.0 |

# KENTUCKY

| | Candidates | Votes | % |
|---|---|---|---|
| **Class 2** | | | |
| 1918 | Augustus Owsley Stanley (D) | 184,385 | 50.8 |
| | Ben L. Bruner (R) | 178,797 | 49.2 |
| 1924 | Frederic M. Sackett (R) | 406,123 | 51.6 |
| | Augustus Owsley Stanley (D) | 381,605 | 48.4 |
| 1930 | Marvel M. Logan (D) | 336,748 | 52.1 |
| | John M. Robsion (R) | 309,180 | 47.9 |
| 1936 | Marvel M. Logan (D) | 539,968 | 58.8 |
| | Robert M. Lucas (R) | 365,850 | 39.8 |

Special Election

| | | | |
|---|---|---|---|
| 1940 | Albert B. (Happy) Chandler (D) | 561,151 | 58.3 |
| | Walter B. Smith (R) | 401,812 | 41.7 |
| 1942 | Albert B. (Happy) Chandler (D) | 216,958 | 55.3 |
| | Richard J. Colbert (R) | 175,081 | 44.7 |

Special Election

| | | | |
|---|---|---|---|
| 1946 | John Sherman Cooper (R) | 327,652 | 53.3 |
| | John Young Brown (D) | 285,829 | 46.5 |
| 1948 | Virgil Chapman (D) | 408,256 | 51.4 |
| | John Sherman Cooper (R) | 383,776 | 48.3 |

Special Election

| | | | |
|---|---|---|---|
| 1952 | John Sherman Cooper (R) | 494,576 | 51.5 |
| | Thomas R. Underwood (D) | 465,652 | 48.5 |
| 1954 | Alben W. Barkley (D) | 434,109 | 54.5 |
| | John Sherman Cooper (R) | 362,948 | 45.5 |

Special Election

| | | | |
|---|---|---|---|
| 1956 | John Sherman Cooper (R) | 538,505 | 53.2 |
| | Lawrence W. Wetherby (D) | 473,140 | 46.8 |
| 1960 | John Sherman Cooper (R) | 644,087 | 59.2 |
| | Keen Johnson (D) | 444,290 | 40.8 |
| 1966 | John Sherman Cooper (R) | 483,805 | 64.5 |
| | John Young Brown (D) | 266,079 | 35.5 |
| 1972 | Walter D. Huddleston (D) | 528,550 | 50.9 |
| | Louie B. Nunn (R) | 494,337 | 47.6 |
| 1978 | Walter D. Huddleston (D) | 290,730 | 61.0 |
| | Louie Guenthner (R) | 175,766 | 36.9 |
| 1984 | Mitch McConnell (R) | 644,990 | 49.9 |
| | Walter D. Huddleston (D) | 639,721 | 49.5 |
| 1990 | Mitch McConnell (R) | 478,034 | 52.2 |
| | Harvey Sloane (D) | 437,976 | 47.8 |

## Class 3

| | | | |
|---|---|---|---|
| 1914 | John C. W. Beckham (D) | 175,999 | 51.8 |
| | Willson (R) | 144,758 | 42.6 |

Special Election

| | | | |
|---|---|---|---|
| 1914 | Johnson N. Camden Jr. (D) | 177,797 | 54.0 |
| | Bullitt (R) | 133,139 | 40.4 |
| 1920 | Richard P. Ernst (R) | 454,226 | 50.3 |
| | John C. W. Beckham (D) | 449,244 | 49.7 |
| 1926 | Alben W. Barkley (D) | 286,997 | 51.8 |
| | Richard P. Ernst (R) | 266,657 | 48.2 |
| 1932 | Alben W. Barkley (D) | 574,977 | 59.2 |
| | M. H. Thatcher (R) | 393,865 | 40.5 |
| 1938 | Alben W. Barkley (D) | 346,735 | 62.0 |
| | John P. Haswell (R) | 212,266 | 38.0 |
| 1944 | Alben W. Barkley (D) | 464,053 | 54.8 |
| | James Park (R) | 380,425 | 44.9 |
| 1950 | Earle C. Clements (D) | 334,249 | 54.2 |
| | Charles I. Dawson (R) | 278,368 | 45.1 |

Special Election

| | | | |
|---|---|---|---|
| 1950 | Earle C. Clements (D) | 317,320# | 54.4 |
| | Charles I. Dawson (R) | 265,994# | 45.6 |
| 1956 | Thruston B. Morton (R) | 506,903 | 50.4 |
| | Earle C. Clements (D) | 499,922 | 49.7 |
| 1962 | Thruston B. Morton (R) | 432,648 | 52.8 |
| | Wilson W. Wyatt (D) | 387,440 | 47.2 |
| 1968 | Marlow W. Cook (R) | 484,260 | 51.4 |
| | Katherine Peden (D) | 448,960 | 47.6 |
| 1974 | Wendell H. Ford (D) | 399,406 | 53.5 |
| | Marlow W. Cook (R) | 328,982 | 44.1 |
| 1980 | Wendell H. Ford (D) | 720,861 | 65.1 |
| | Mary Louise Foust (R) | 386,029 | 34.9 |
| 1986 | Wendell H. Ford (D) | 503,775 | 74.4 |
| | Jackson M. Andrews (R) | 173,330 | 25.6 |
| 1992 | Wendell H. Ford (D) | 836,888 | 62.9 |
| | David L. Williams (R) | 476,604 | 35.8 |

# LOUISIANA

| | Candidates | Votes | % |
|---|---|---|---|
| | **Class 2** | | |
| 1918 | Joseph E. Ransdell (D) | 44,224 | 100.0 |
| 1924 | Joseph E. Ransdell (D) | 94,939 | 100.0 |
| 1930 | Huey P. Long (D) | 130,536 | 100.0 |

**Special Election**

| 1936 | Rose McConnell Long (D) | 131,930# | 100.0 |
|---|---|---|---|

| 1936 | Allen J. Ellender (D) | 293,256 | 100.0 |
|---|---|---|---|
| 1942 | Allen J. Ellender (D) | 85,488 | 100.0 |
| 1948 | Allen J. Ellender (D) | 330,315 | 100.0 |
| 1954 | Allen J. Ellender (D) | 207,115 | 100.0 |
| 1960 | Allen J. Ellender (D) | 432,228 | 79.8 |
| | George W. Reese Jr. (R) | 109,698 | 20.2 |
| 1966 | Allen J. Ellender (D) | 437,695 | 100.0 |
| 1972 | J. Bennett Johnston (D) | 598,987 | 55.2 |
| | John J. McKeithen (I) | 250,161 | 23.1 |
| | Ben C. Toledano (R) | 206,846 | 19.1 |
| 1978 [1] | J. Bennett Johnston (D) | — | — |
| 1984 [1] | J. Bennett Johnston (D) | — | — |
| 1990 [1] | J. Bennett Johnston (D) | — | — |

**Class 3**

| 1914 | Robert F. Broussard (D) | ✔ | |
|---|---|---|---|

**Special Election**

| 1918 | Edward J. Gay (D) | 44,345 | 100.0 |
|---|---|---|---|

| 1920 | Edwin S. Broussard (D) | 94,944# | 100.0 |
|---|---|---|---|
| 1926 | Edwin S. Broussard (D) | 54,180 | 100.0 |
| 1932 | John H. Overton (D) | 249,189 | 100.0 |
| 1938 | John H. Overton (D) | 151,585 | 99.8 |
| 1944 | John H. Overton (D) | 286,365 | 100.0 |

**Special Election**

| 1948 | Russell B. Long (D) | 305,346 | 74.9 |
|---|---|---|---|
| | Clem S. Clarke (R) | 102,339 | 25.1 |

| 1950 | Russell B. Long (D) | 220,907 | 87.7 |
|---|---|---|---|
| | Charles S. Gerth (R) | 30,931 | 12.3 |
| 1956 | Russell B. Long (D) | 335,564 | 100.0 |
| 1962 | Russell B. Long (D) | 318,838 | 75.6 |
| | Taylor Walters O'Hearn (R) | 103,066 | 24.4 |
| 1968 | Russell B. Long (D) | 518,586 | 100.0 |
| 1974 | Russell B. Long (D) | 434,643 | 100.0 |
| 1980 [1] | Russell B. Long (D) | — | — |
| 1986 | John B. Breaux (D) | 723,586 | 52.8 |
| | W. Henson Moore (R) | 646,311 | 47.2 |
| 1992 [1] | John B. Breaux (D) | — | — |

**Louisiana**

1. *Dash (—) indicates candidate elected in primary. Since 1978, Louisiana has held an open-primary election with candidates from all parties running on the same ballot. Any candidate who receives a majority is elected; if no candidate receives 50 percent, there is a runoff election in November between the two top finishers.*

# MAINE

| | Candidates | Votes | % |
|---|---|---|---|
| | **Class 1** | | |
| 1916 | Frederick Hale (R) | 79,841 | 52.8 |
| | Charles Johnson (D) | 69,486 | 46.0 |
| 1922 | Frederick Hale (R) | 101,026 | 57.5 |
| | Oakley C. Curtis (D) | 74,659 | 42.5 |
| 1928 | Frederick Hale (R) | 145,501 | 69.6 |
| | Herbert E. Holmes (D) | 63,429 | 30.4 |
| 1934 | Frederick Hale (R) | 139,773 | 50.1 |
| | F. Harold Dubord (D) | 138,573 | 49.7 |
| 1940 | Ralph O. Brewster (R) | 150,149 | 58.6 |
| | Louis J. Brann (D) | 105,740 | 41.3 |
| 1946 | Ralph O. Brewster (R) | 111,215 | 63.6 |
| | Peter M. MacDonald (D) | 63,799 | 36.5 |
| 1952 | Frederick G. Payne (R) | 139,205 | 58.7 |
| | Roger P. Dube (D) | 82,665 | 34.9 |
| | Earl S. Grant (I) | 15,294# | 6.4 |
| 1958 | Edmund S. Muskie (D) | 172,842 | 60.8 |
| | Frederick G. Payne (R) | 111,522 | 39.2 |
| 1964 | Edmund S. Muskie (D) | 253,511 | 66.6 |
| | Clifford G. McIntire (R) | 127,040 | 33.4 |
| 1970 | Edmund S. Muskie (D) | 199,954 | 61.9 |
| | Neil S. Bishop (R) | 123,906 | 38.3 |
| 1976 | Edmund S. Muskie (D) | 292,704 | 60.2 |
| | Robert A. G. Monks (R) | 193,489 | 39.8 |
| 1982 | George J. Mitchell (D) | 279,819 | 60.9 |
| | David F. Emery (R) | 179,882 | 39.1 |
| 1988 | George J. Mitchell (D) | 452,590 | 81.2 |
| | Jasper S. Wyman (R) | 104,758 | 18.8 |

**Class 2**

**Special Election**

| 1916 | Bert M. Fernald (R) | 81,369 | 54.3 |
|---|---|---|---|
| | Kenneth Sills (D) | 68,201 | 45.5 |

| 1918 | Bert M. Fernald (R) | 66,858 | 55.6 |
|---|---|---|---|
| | Earl Newbert (D) | 53,460 | 44.4 |
| 1924 | Bert M. Fernald (R) | 148,783 | 60.4 |
| | Fulton J. Redman (D) | 97,428 | 39.6 |

**Special Election**

| 1926 | Arthur R. Gould (R) | 79,498 | 71.8 |
|---|---|---|---|
| | Fulton J. Redman (D) | 31,225 | 28.2 |

| 1930 | Wallace H. White Jr. (R) | 88,262 | 60.9 |
|---|---|---|---|
| | Frank H. Haskell (D) | 56,561 | 39.1 |
| 1936 | Wallace H. White Jr. (R) | 158,068 | 50.8 |
| | Louis J. Brann (D) | 153,420 | 49.3 |
| 1942 | Wallace H. White Jr. (R) | 111,520 | 66.7 |
| | Fulton J. Redman (D) | 55,754 | 33.3 |
| 1948 | Margaret Chase Smith (R) | 159,182 | 71.3 |
| | Adrian H. Scolten (D) | 64,074 | 28.7 |
| 1954 | Margaret Chase Smith (R) | 144,530 | 58.6 |
| | Paul A. Fullam (D) | 102,075 | 41.4 |
| 1960 | Margaret Chase Smith (R) | 256,890 | 61.7 |
| | Lucia M. Cormier (D) | 159,809 | 38.4 |
| 1966 | Margaret Chase Smith (R) | 188,291 | 59.0 |
| | Elmer H. Violette (D) | 131,136 | 41.1 |
| 1972 | William D. Hathaway (D) | 224,270 | 53.2 |
| | Margaret Chase Smith (R) | 197,040 | 46.8 |
| 1978 | William S. Cohen (R) | 212,294 | 56.6 |
| | William D. Hathaway (D) | 127,327 | 33.9 |
| | Hayes E. Gahagan (I) | 27,824 | 7.4 |
| 1984 | William S. Cohen (R) | 404,414 | 73.3 |
| | Elizabeth H. Mitchell (D) | 142,626 | 25.9 |

| | Candidates | Votes | % |
|---|---|---|---|
| 1990 | William S. Cohen (R) | 319,167 | 61.3 |
| | Neil Rolde (D) | 201,053 | 38.6 |

| | Candidates | Votes | % |
|---|---|---|---|
| | Edward T. Conroy (D) | 435,118 | 33.8 |
| 1986 | Barbara A. Mikulski (D) | 675,229 | 60.7 |
| | Linda Chavez (R) | 437,419 | 39.3 |
| 1992 | Barbara A. Mikulski (D) | 1,307,610 | 71.0 |
| | Alan L. Keyes (R) | 533,688 | 29.0 |

# MARYLAND

| | Candidates | Votes | % |
|---|---|---|---|

### Class 1

Special Election

| | | | |
|---|---|---|---|
| 1913 | Blair Lee (D) | 112,485# | 56.8 |
| | Thomas Parran (R) | 73,300# | 37.0 |

| | | | |
|---|---|---|---|
| 1916 | Joseph Irwin France (R) | 113,662 | 49.3 |
| | David J. Lewis (D) | 109,740 | 47.6 |
| 1922 | William Cabell Bruce (D) | 160,947 | 52.6 |
| | Joseph Irwin France (R) | 139,581 | 45.6 |
| 1928 | Phillips Lee Goldsborough (R) | 256,224 | 54.1 |
| | William Cabell Bruce (D) | 214,447 | 45.2 |
| 1934 | George L. Radcliffe (D) | 264,279 | 56.1 |
| | Joseph Irwin France (R) | 197,643 | 42.0 |
| 1940 | George L. Radcliffe (D) | 394,239# | 64.7 |
| | Harry W. Nice (R) | 203,912# | 33.5 |
| 1946 | Herbert R. O'Conor (D) | 237,232# | 50.2 |
| | David John Markey (R) | 235,000# | 49.8 |
| 1952 | J. Glenn Beall (R) | 449,823 | 52.5 |
| | George P. Mahoney (D) | 406,370 | 47.5 |
| 1958 | J. Glenn Beall (R) | 382,021 | 51.0 |
| | Thomas D'Alesandro Jr. (D) | 367,270 | 49.0 |
| 1964 | Joseph D. Tydings (D) | 678,649 | 62.8 |
| | J. Glenn Beall (R) | 402,393 | 37.2 |
| 1970 | J. Glenn Beall Jr. (R) | 484,960 | 50.7 |
| | Joseph D. Tydings (D) | 460,442 | 48.1 |
| 1976 | Paul S. Sarbanes (D) | 772,101 | 56.5 |
| | J. Glenn Beall Jr. (R) | 530,439 | 38.8 |
| 1982 | Paul S. Sarbanes (D) | 707,356 | 63.5 |
| | Lawrence J. Hogan (R) | 407,334 | 36.5 |
| 1988 | Paul S. Sarbanes (D) | 999,166 | 61.8 |
| | Alan L. Keyes (R) | 617,537 | 38.2 |

### Class 3

| | | | |
|---|---|---|---|
| 1914 | John Walter Smith (D) | 110,204 | 51.0 |
| | Edward C. Carrington Jr. (R) | 94,864 | 43.9 |
| 1920 | Ovington E. Weller (R) | 184,999 | 47.3 |
| | John Walter Smith (D) | 169,200 | 43.3 |
| | George D. Iverson Jr. (I) | 21,345 | 5.5 |
| 1926 | Millard E. Tydings (D) | 195,410 | 57.6 |
| | Ovington E. Weller (R) | 139,995 | 41.3 |
| 1932 | Millard E. Tydings (D) | 293,389 | 66.2 |
| | Wallace Williams (R) | 138,266 | 31.2 |
| 1938 | Millard E. Tydings (D) | 357,245 | 68.3 |
| | Oscar Leser (R) | 153,253 | 29.3 |
| 1944 | Millard E. Tydings (D) | 344,725 | 61.7 |
| | Blanchard Randall Jr. (R) | 213,705 | 38.3 |
| 1950 | John Marshall Butler (R) | 326,291 | 53.0 |
| | Millard E. Tydings (D) | 283,180 | 46.0 |
| 1956 | John Marshall Butler (R) | 473,059 | 53.0 |
| | George P. Mahoney (D) | 419,108 | 47.0 |
| 1962 | Daniel B. Brewster (D) | 439,723 | 62.0 |
| | Edward T. Miller (R) | 269,131 | 38.0 |
| 1968 | Charles McC. Mathias Jr. (R) | 541,893 | 47.8 |
| | Daniel B. Brewster (D) | 443,367 | 39.1 |
| | George P. Mahoney (I) | 148,467 | 13.1 |
| 1974 | Charles McC. Mathias Jr. (R) | 503,223 | 57.3 |
| | Barbara A. Mikulski (D) | 374,563 | 42.7 |
| 1980 | Charles McC. Mathias Jr. (R) | 850,970 | 66.2 |

# MASSACHUSETTS

| | Candidates | Votes | % |
|---|---|---|---|

### Class 1

| | | | |
|---|---|---|---|
| 1916 | Henry Cabot Lodge (R) | 267,177 | 51.7 |
| | John F. Fitzgerald (D) | 234,238 | 45.3 |
| 1922 | Henry Cabot Lodge (R) | 414,130 | 47.6 |
| | William A. Gaston (D) | 406,776 | 46.8 |

Special Election

| | | | |
|---|---|---|---|
| 1926 | David I. Walsh (D) | 525,303 | 52.0 |
| | William M. Butler (R) | 469,989 | 46.5 |

| | | | |
|---|---|---|---|
| 1928 | David I. Walsh (D) | 818,055 | 53.6 |
| | Benjamin Loring Young (R) | 693,563 | 45.5 |
| 1934 | David I. Walsh (D) | 852,776 | 59.4 |
| | Robert M. Washburn (R) | 536,692 | 37.4 |
| 1940 | David I. Walsh (D) | 1,088,838 | 55.6 |
| | Henry Parkman Jr. (R) | 838,122 | 42.8 |
| 1946 | Henry Cabot Lodge Jr. (R) | 989,736 | 59.6 |
| | David I. Walsh (D) | 660,200 | 39.7 |
| 1952 | John F. Kennedy (D) | 1,211,984 | 51.4 |
| | Henry Cabot Lodge Jr. (R) | 1,141,247 | 48.4 |
| 1958 | John F. Kennedy (D) | 1,362,926 | 73.2 |
| | Vincent J. Celeste (R) | 488,318 | 26.2 |

Special Election

| | | | |
|---|---|---|---|
| 1962 | Edward M. Kennedy (D) | 1,162,611 | 55.4 |
| | George C. Lodge (R) | 877,669 | 41.9 |

| | | | |
|---|---|---|---|
| 1964 | Edward M. Kennedy (D) | 1,716,907 | 74.3 |
| | Howard Whitmore Jr. (R) | 587,663 | 25.4 |
| 1970 | Edward M. Kennedy (D) | 1,202,856 | 62.1 |
| | Josiah A. Spaulding (R) | 715,978 | 37.0 |
| 1976 | Edward M. Kennedy (D) | 1,726,657 | 69.3 |
| | Michael Robertson (R) | 722,641 | 29.0 |
| 1982 | Edward M. Kennedy (D) | 1,247,084 | 60.8 |
| | Raymond Shamie (R) | 784,602 | 38.3 |
| 1988 | Edward M. Kennedy (D) | 1,693,344 | 65.0 |
| | Joseph D. Malone (R) | 884,267 | 33.9 |

### Class 2

| | | | |
|---|---|---|---|
| 1918 | David I. Walsh (D) | 207,478 | 49.7 |
| | John W. Weeks (R) | 188,287 | 45.1 |
| | Thomas W. Lawson (I) | 21,985 | 5.3 |
| 1924 | Frederick H. Gillett (R) | 566,188 | 50.3 |
| | David I. Walsh (D) | 547,600 | 48.6 |
| 1930 | Marcus A. Coolidge (D) | 651,939 | 54.0 |
| | William M. Butler (R) | 539,226 | 44.7 |
| 1936 | Henry Cabot Lodge Jr. (R) | 875,160 | 48.5 |
| | James M. Curley (D) | 739,751 | 41.0 |
| | Thomas C. O'Brien (UN) | 134,245 | 7.4 |
| 1942 | Henry Cabot Lodge Jr. (R) | 721,239 | 52.4 |
| | Joseph E. Casey (D) | 641,042 | 46.6 |

| Candidates | Votes | % |
|---|---|---|
| **Special Election** | | |
| 1944  Leverett Saltonstall (R) | 1,228,754 | 64.3 |
|       John H. Corcoran (D) | 667,086 | 34.9 |
| 1948  Leverett Saltonstall (R) | 1,088,475 | 53.0 |
|       John I. Fitzgerald (D) | 954,398 | 46.4 |
| 1954  Leverett Saltonstall (R) | 956,605 | 50.5 |
|       Foster Furcolo (D) | 927,899 | 49.0 |
| 1960  Leverett Saltonstall (R) | 1,358,556 | 56.2 |
|       Thomas J. O'Connor Jr. (D) | 1,050,725 | 43.5 |
| 1966  Edward W. Brooke (R) | 1,213,473 | 60.7 |
|       Endicott Peabody (D) | 774,761 | 38.7 |
| 1972  Edward W. Brooke (R) | 1,505,932 | 63.5 |
|       John J. Droney (D) | 823,278 | 34.7 |
| 1978  Paul E. Tsongas (D) | 1,093,283 | 55.1 |
|       Edward W. Brooke (R) | 890,584 | 44.8 |
| 1984  John F. Kerry (D) | 1,393,150 | 55.1 |
|       Raymond Shamie (R) | 1,136,913 | 44.9 |
| 1990  John F. Kerry (D) | 1,321,712 | 57.1 |
|       Jim Rappaport (R) | 992,917 | 42.9 |

# MICHIGAN

| Candidates | Votes | % |
|---|---|---|
| **Class 1** | | |
| 1916  Charles E. Townsend (R) | 364,657 | 56.3 |
|       Lawrence Price (D) | 257,954 | 39.9 |
| 1922  Woodbridge N. Ferris (D) | 294,932 | 50.6 |
|       Charles E. Townsend (R) | 281,843 | 48.4 |
| 1928  Arthur H. Vandenberg (R) | 977,893 | 71.8 |
|       John W. Bailey (D) | 376,592 | 27.7 |
| **Special Election** | | |
| 1928  Arthur H. Vandenberg (R) | 974,203 | 72.0 |
|       John W. Bailey (D) | 375,673 | 27.8 |
| 1934  Arthur H. Vandenberg (R) | 626,017 | 51.3 |
|       Frank A. Picard (D) | 573,574 | 47.0 |
| 1940  Arthur H. Vandenberg (R) | 1,053,104 | 52.7 |
|       Frank Fitzgerald (D) | 939,740 | 47.0 |
| 1946  Arthur H. Vandenberg (R) | 1,085,570 | 67.1 |
|       James H. Lee (D) | 517,923 | 32.0 |
| 1952  Charles E. Potter (R) | 1,428,352 | 50.6 |
|       Blair Moody (D) | 1,383,416 | 49.0 |
| **Special Election** | | |
| 1952  Charles E. Potter (R) | 1,417,032 | 51.2 |
|       Blair Moody (D) | 1,347,705 | 48.7 |
| 1958  Philip A. Hart (D) | 1,216,966 | 53.6 |
|       Charles E. Potter (R) | 1,046,963 | 46.1 |
| 1964  Philip A. Hart (D) | 1,996,912 | 64.4 |
|       Elly M. Peterson (R) | 1,096,272 | 35.3 |
| 1970  Philip A. Hart (D) | 1,744,672 | 66.8 |
|       Lenore Romney (R) | 858,438 | 32.9 |
| 1976  Donald W. Riegle Jr. (D) | 1,831,031 | 52.5 |
|       Marvin L. Esch (R) | 1,635,087 | 46.8 |
| 1982  Donald W. Riegle Jr. (D) | 1,728,793 | 57.7 |
|       Philip E. Ruppe (R) | 1,223,288 | 40.9 |
| 1988  Donald W. Riegle Jr. (D) | 2,116,865 | 60.4 |
|       Jim Dunn (R) | 1,348,219 | 38.5 |

| Candidates | Votes | % |
|---|---|---|
| **Class 2** | | |
| 1918  Truman H. Newberry (R) | 220,054 | 50.2 |
|       Henry Ford (D) | 212,487 | 48.5 |
| 1924  James Couzens (R) | 858,934 | 74.3 |
|       Mortimer E. Cooley (D) | 284,609 | 24.6 |
| **Special Election** | | |
| 1924  James Couzens (R) | 839,569 | 75.0 |
|       Mortimer E. Cooley (D) | 266,851 | 23.9 |
| 1930  James Couzens (R) | 634,577 | 78.2 |
|       Thomas A. E. Weadock (D) | 169,757 | 20.9 |
| 1936  Prentiss M. Brown (D) | 910,937 | 53.3 |
|       Wilber M. Brucker (R) | 714,602 | 41.8 |
| 1942  Homer Ferguson (R) | 589,652 | 49.6 |
|       Prentiss M. Brown (D) | 561,595 | 47.2 |
| 1948  Homer Ferguson (R) | 1,045,156 | 50.7 |
|       Frank E. Hook (D) | 1,000,329 | 48.5 |
| 1954  Patrick V. McNamara (D) | 1,088,550 | 50.8 |
|       Homer Ferguson (R) | 1,049,420 | 48.9 |
| 1960  Patrick V. McNamara (D) | 1,669,179 | 51.7 |
|       Alvin M. Bentley (R) | 1,548,873 | 48.0 |
| 1966  Robert P. Griffin (R) | 1,363,530 | 55.9 |
|       G. Mennen Williams (D) | 1,069,484 | 43.8 |
| **Special Election** | | |
| 1966  Robert P. Griffin (R) | 1,321,222 | 56.0 |
|       G. Mennen Williams (D) | 1,031,138 | 43.7 |
| 1972  Robert P. Griffin (R) | 1,781,065 | 52.3 |
|       Frank J. Kelley (D) | 1,577,178 | 46.3 |
| 1978  Carl Levin (D) | 1,484,193 | 52.1 |
|       Robert P. Griffin (R) | 1,362,165 | 47.9 |
| 1984  Carl Levin (D) | 1,915,831 | 51.8 |
|       Jack Lousma (R) | 1,745,302 | 47.2 |
| 1990  Carl Levin (D) | 1,471,753 | 57.5 |
|       Bill Schuette (R) | 1,055,695 | 41.2 |

# MINNESOTA

| Candidates | Votes | % |
|---|---|---|
| **Class 1** | | |
| 1916  Frank B. Kellogg (R) | 185,159 | 48.6 |
|       Daniel W. Lawler (D) | 117,541 | 30.8 |
|       W. G. Calderwood (P) | 78,425 | 20.6 |
| 1922  Henrik Shipstead (F-LAB) | 325,372 | 47.1 |
|       Frank B. Kellogg (R) | 241,833 | 35.0 |
|       Anna D. Olesen (D) | 123,624 | 17.9 |
| 1928  Henrik Shipstead (F-LAB) | 665,169 | 65.4 |
|       Arthur E. Nelson (R) | 342,992 | 33.7 |
| 1934  Henrik Shipstead (F-LAB) | 503,379 | 49.9 |
|       Einar Hoidale (D) | 294,757 | 29.2 |
|       N. J. Holmberg (R) | 200,083 | 19.8 |
| 1940  Henrik Shipstead (R) | 641,049 | 53.0 |
|       Elmer A. Benson (F-LAB) | 310,875 | 25.7 |
|       John E. Regan (D) | 248,658 | 20.6 |
| 1946  Edward J. Thye (R) | 517,775 | 58.9 |
|       Theodore Jorgenson (DFL) | 349,520 | 39.8 |
| 1952  Edward J. Thye (R) | 785,649 | 56.6 |
|       William E. Carlson (DFL) | 590,011 | 42.5 |
| 1958  Eugene J. McCarthy (DFL) | 608,847 | 52.9 |
|       Edward J. Thye (R) | 536,629 | 46.6 |
| 1964  Eugene J. McCarthy (DFL) | 931,363 | 60.3 |

| | | | |
|---|---|--:|--:|
| 1970 | Wheelock Whitney (R) | 605,933 | *39.3* |
| | Hubert H. Humphrey (DFL) | 788,256 | *57.8* |
| | Clark MacGregor (R) | 568,025 | *41.6* |
| 1976 | Hubert H. Humphrey (DFL) | 1,290,736 | *67.5* |
| | Gerald W. Brekke (R) | 478,611 | *25.0* |
| | Paul Helm (AM) | 125,612 | *6.6* |

Special Election

| | | | |
|---|---|--:|--:|
| 1978 | Dave Durenberger (I-R) | 957,908 | *61.4* |
| | Robert E. Short (DFL) | 538,675 | *34.5* |

| | | | |
|---|---|--:|--:|
| 1982 | Dave Durenberger (I-R) | 949,207 | *52.6* |
| | Mark Dayton (DFL) | 840,401 | *46.6* |
| 1988 | Dave Durenberger (I-R) | 1,176,210 | *56.2* |
| | Hubert H. Humphrey III (DFL) | 1,856,694 | *40.9* |

### Class 2

| | | | |
|---|---|--:|--:|
| 1912 | Knute Nelson (R) | 173,074 | *62.8* |
| | Daniel W. Lawler (D) | 102,691 | *37.2* |
| 1918 | Knute Nelson (R) | 206,687 | *60.1* |
| | W. G. Calderwood (N) | 137,294 | *39.9* |

Special Election

| | | | |
|---|---|--:|--:|
| 1923 | Magnus Johnson (F-LAB) | 290,165# | *57.5* |
| | J. A. O. Preus (R) | 195,319# | *38.7* |

| | | | |
|---|---|--:|--:|
| 1924 | Thomas D. Schall (R) | 388,594 | *46.5* |
| | Magnus Johnson (F-LAB) | 380,646 | *45.5* |
| | John J. Farrell (D) | 53,709 | *6.4* |
| 1930 | Thomas D. Schall (R) | 293,626 | *37.6* |
| | Einar Hoidale (D) | 282,018 | *36.1* |
| | Ernest Lundeen (F-LAB) | 178,671 | *22.9* |
| 1936 | Ernest Lundeen (F-LAB) | 663,363 | *62.2* |
| | Theodore Christianson (R) | 402,404 | *37.8* |

Special Election

| | | | |
|---|---|--:|--:|
| 1936 | Guy V. Howard (R) | 317,457 | *42.9* |
| | N. J. Holmberg (I) | 210,364 | *28.4* |
| | Andrew Olaf Devolt (I PROG) | 147,858 | *20.0* |
| | John G. Alexander (I) | 64,493 | *8.7* |

| | | | |
|---|---|--:|--:|
| 1942 | Joseph H. Ball (R) | 356,297 | *47.0* |
| | Elmer A. Benson (F-LAB) | 213,965 | *28.2* |
| | Martin A. Nelson (I PROG) | 109,231 | *14.4* |
| | Ed Murphy (D) | 78,959 | *10.4* |

Special Election

| | | | |
|---|---|--:|--:|
| 1942 | Arthur E. Nelson (R) | 372,240 | *56.1* |
| | Al Hansen (F-LAB) | 177,008 | *26.7* |
| | John E. O'Rourke (D) | 114,086 | *17.2* |

| | | | |
|---|---|--:|--:|
| 1948 | Hubert H. Humphrey (DFL) | 729,494 | *59.9* |
| | Joseph H. Ball (R) | 482,801 | *39.7* |
| 1954 | Hubert H. Humphrey (DFL) | 642,193 | *56.4* |
| | Val Bjornson (R) | 479,619 | *42.1* |
| 1960 | Hubert H. Humphrey (DFL) | 884,168 | *57.5* |
| | P. Kenneth Peterson (R) | 648,586 | *42.2* |
| 1966 | Walter F. Mondale (DFL) | 685,840 | *53.9* |
| | Robert A. Forsythe (R) | 574,868 | *45.2* |
| 1972 | Walter F. Mondale (DFL) | 981,320 | *56.7* |
| | Phil Hansen (R) | 742,121 | *42.9* |
| 1978 | Rudy Boschwitz (I-R) | 894,092 | *56.6* |
| | Wendell R. Anderson (DFL) | 638,375 | *40.4* |
| 1984 | Rudy Boschwitz (I-R) | 1,199,926 | *58.1* |
| | Joan Anderson Growe (DFL) | 852,844 | *41.3* |

| | | | |
|---|---|--:|--:|
| 1990 | Paul Wellstone (DFL) | 911,999 | *50.4* |
| | Rudy Boschwitz (I-R) | 864,375 | *47.8* |

# MISSISSIPPI

| Candidates | Votes | % |
|---|---|---|

### Class 1

| | | | |
|---|---|--:|--:|
| 1916 | John Sharp Williams (D) | 74,290 | *100.0* |
| 1922 | Hubert D. Stephens (D) | 63,636 | *93.2* |
| 1928 | Hubert D. Stephens (D) | 111,210 | *100.0* |
| 1934 | Theodore G. Bilbo (D) | 51,709 | *100.0* |
| 1940 | Theodore G. Bilbo (D) | 143,333 | *100.0* |
| 1946 | Theodore G. Bilbo (D) | 46,747* | *100.0* |

Special Election

| | | | |
|---|---|--:|--:|
| 1947 | John C. Stennis (D) | 52,068 | *26.9* |
| | William M. Colmer (D) | 45,725 | *23.6* |
| | Forrest B. Jackson (D) | 43,642 | *22.5* |
| | Paul B. Johnson Jr. (D) | 27,159 | *14.0* |
| | John E. Rankin (D) | 24,492 | *12.6* |

| | | | |
|---|---|--:|--:|
| 1952 | John C. Stennis (D) | 233,919 | *100.0* |
| 1958 | John C. Stennis (D) | 61,039 | *100.0* |
| 1964 | John C. Stennis (D) | 343,364 | *100.0* |
| 1970 | John C. Stennis (D) | 286,622 | *88.4* |
| | William R. Thompson (I) | 37,593 | *11.6* |
| 1976 | John C. Stennis (D) | 554,433 | *100.0* |
| 1982 | John C. Stennis (D) | 414,099 | *64.2* |
| | Haley Barbour (R) | 230,927 | *35.8* |
| 1988 | Trent Lott (R) | 510,380 | *53.9* |
| | Wayne Dowdy (D) | 436,339 | *46.1* |

### Class 2

| | | | |
|---|---|--:|--:|
| 1918 | Pat Harrison (D) | 30,055 | *95.0* |
| | Sumner W. Rose (S) | 1,569 | *5.0* |
| 1924 | Pat Harrison (D) | 97,257 | *100.0* |
| 1930 | Pat Harrison (D) | 33,953 | *100.0* |
| 1936 | Pat Harrison (D) | 140,570 | *100.0* |

Special Election

| | | | |
|---|---|--:|--:|
| 1941 | Wall Doxey (D) | 59,485 | *50.3* |
| | Ross Collins (D) | 58,809 | *49.7* |

| | | | |
|---|---|--:|--:|
| 1942 | James O. Eastland (D) | 51,355 | *100.0* |
| 1948 | James O. Eastland (D) | 151,478 | *100.0* |
| 1954 | James O. Eastland (D) | 100,848 | *95.6* |
| 1960 | James O. Eastland (D) | 244,341 | *91.8* |
| | Joe A. Moore (R) | 21,807 | *8.2* |
| 1966 | James O. Eastland (D) | 258,248 | *65.5* |
| | Prentiss Walker (R) | 105,652 | *26.8* |
| | Clifton R. Whitley (I) | 30,641 | *7.8* |
| 1972 | James O. Eastland (D) | 375,102 | *58.1* |
| | Gil Carmichael (R) | 249,779 | *38.7* |
| 1978 | Thad Cochran (R) | 263,089 | *45.1* |
| | Maurice Dantin (D) | 185,454 | *31.8* |
| | Charles Evers (I) | 133,646 | *22.9* |
| 1984 | Thad Cochran (R) | 580,314 | *60.9* |
| | William D. Winter (D) | 371,926 | *39.1* |
| 1990 | Thad Cochran (R) | 274,244 | *100.0* |

# MISSOURI

| | Candidates | Votes | % |
|---|---|---|---|
| | **Class 1** | | |
| 1916 | James A. Reed (D) | 396,166 | 50.6 |
| | Dickey (R) | 371,710 | 47.4 |
| 1922 | James A. Reed (D) | 506,267 | 51.9 |
| | R. R. Brewster (R) | 462,009 | 47.3 |
| 1928 | Roscoe C. Patterson (R) | 787,499 | 51.9 |
| | Charles M. Hay (D) | 726,322 | 47.9 |
| 1934 | Harry S Truman (D) | 787,110 | 59.5 |
| | Roscoe C. Patterson (R) | 524,954 | 39.7 |
| 1940 | Harry S Truman (D) | 930,775 | 51.2 |
| | Manvel H. Davis (R) | 886,376 | 48.7 |
| 1946 | James P. Kem (R) | 572,556 | 52.7 |
| | Frank Briggs (D) | 511,544 | 47.1 |
| 1952 | Stuart Symington (D) | 1,008,523 | 54.0 |
| | James P. Kem (R) | 858,170 | 45.9 |
| 1958 | Stuart Symington (D) | 780,083 | 66.5 |
| | Hazel Palmer (R) | 393,847 | 33.6 |
| 1964 | Stuart Symington (D) | 1,186,666 | 66.6 |
| | Jean Paul Bradshaw (R) | 596,377 | 33.5 |
| 1970 | Stuart Symington (D) | 655,431 | 51.1 |
| | John C. Danforth (R) | 617,903 | 48.2 |
| 1976 | John C. Danforth (R) | 1,090,067 | 56.9 |
| | Warren E. Hearnes (D) | 813,571 | 42.5 |
| 1982 | John C. Danforth (R) | 784,876 | 50.8 |
| | Harriett Woods (D) | 758,629 | 49.1 |
| 1988 | John C. Danforth (R) | 1,407,416 | 67.7 |
| | Jay Nixon (D) | 660,045 | 31.8 |
| | **Class 3** | | |
| 1914 | William J. Stone (D) | 311,616 | 50.4 |
| | Thomas J. Akins (R) | 257,054 | 41.6 |
| | Special Election | | |
| 1918 | Selden P. Spencer (R) | 302,680 | 52.4 |
| | Joseph Folk (D) | 267,397 | 46.3 |
| 1920 | Selden P. Spencer (R) | 711,161 | 53.7 |
| | Breckinridge Long (D) | 589,498 | 44.5 |
| 1926 | Harry B. Hawes (D) | 506,015 | 51.3 |
| | George H. Williams (R) | 470,654 | 47.7 |
| | Special Election | | |
| 1926 | Harry B. Hawes (D) | 509,439 | 51.9 |
| | George H. Williams (R) | 473,128 | 48.2 |
| 1932 | J. Bennett (Champ) Clark (D) | 1,017,046 | 63.2 |
| | Henry W. Kiel (R) | 577,184 | 35.9 |
| 1938 | J. Bennett (Champ) Clark (D) | 757,587 | 60.7 |
| | Henry S. Caulfield (R) | 488,687 | 39.2 |
| 1944 | Forrest C. Donnell (R) | 779,029 | 50.0 |
| | Roy McKittrick (D) | 777,229 | 49.9 |
| 1950 | Thomas C. Hennings Jr. (D) | 685,732 | 53.6 |
| | Forrest C. Donnell (R) | 593,139 | 46.4 |
| 1956 | Thomas C. Hennings Jr. (D) | 1,015,936 | 56.4 |
| | Herbert Douglas (R) | 785,048 | 43.6 |
| | Special Election | | |
| 1960 | Edward V. Long (D) | 999,656 | 53.2 |
| | Lon Hocker (R) | 880,576 | 46.8 |
| 1962 | Edward V. Long (D) | 666,929 | 54.6 |
| | Crosby Kemper (R) | 555,330 | 45.4 |

| | Candidates | Votes | % |
|---|---|---|---|
| 1968 | Thomas F. Eagleton (D) | 887,414 | 51.1 |
| | Thomas B. Curtis (R) | 850,544 | 48.9 |
| 1974 | Thomas F. Eagleton (D) | 735,433 | 60.1 |
| | Thomas B. Curtis (R) | 480,900 | 39.3 |
| 1980 | Thomas F. Eagleton (D) | 1,074,859 | 52.0 |
| | Gene McNary (R) | 985,399 | 47.7 |
| 1986 | Christopher S. Bond (R) | 777,612 | 52.6 |
| | Harriett Woods (D) | 699,624 | 47.4 |
| 1992 | Christopher S. Bond (R) | 1,221,901 | 51.9 |
| | Geri Rothman-Serot (D) | 1,057,967 | 44.9 |

# MONTANA

| | Candidates | Votes | % |
|---|---|---|---|
| | **Class 1** | | |
| 1916 | Henry L. Myers (D) | 85,585 | 51.1 |
| | Charles N. Pray (R) | 72,753 | 43.4 |
| | Henry Labeau (SOC) | 9,292 | 5.5 |
| 1922 | Burton K. Wheeler (D) | 88,205 | 55.4 |
| | Carl W. Riddick (R) | 69,464 | 43.6 |
| 1928 | Burton K. Wheeler (D) | 103,655 | 53.2 |
| | Joseph M. Dixon (R) | 91,185 | 46.8 |
| 1934 | Burton K. Wheeler (D) | 142,823 | 70.1 |
| | George M. Bourquin (R) | 58,519 | 28.7 |
| 1940 | Burton K. Wheeler (D) | 176,753 | 73.4 |
| | E. K. Cheadle (R) | 63,941 | 26.6 |
| 1946 | Zales N. Ecton (R) | 101,901 | 53.5 |
| | Leif Erickson (D) | 86,476 | 45.4 |
| 1952 | Mike Mansfield (D) | 133,109 | 50.8 |
| | Zales N. Ecton (R) | 127,360 | 48.6 |
| 1958 | Mike Mansfield (D) | 174,910 | 76.2 |
| | Lou W. Welch (R) | 54,573 | 23.8 |
| 1964 | Mike Mansfield (D) | 180,643 | 64.5 |
| | Alex Blewett (R) | 99,367 | 35.5 |
| 1970 | Mike Mansfield (D) | 150,060 | 60.5 |
| | Harold E. Wallace (R) | 97,809 | 39.5 |
| 1976 | John Melcher (D) | 206,232 | 64.2 |
| | Stanley C. Burger (R) | 115,213 | 35.8 |
| 1982 | John Melcher (D) | 174,861 | 54.5 |
| | Larry Williams (R) | 133,789 | 41.7 |
| 1988 | Conrad Burns (R) | 189,445 | 51.9 |
| | John Melcher (D) | 175,809 | 48.1 |
| | **Class 2** | | |
| 1912 | Thomas J. Walsh (D) | 28,421 | 41.2 |
| | Joseph M. Dixon (PROG) | 22,161 | 32.1 |
| | Henry C. Smith (R) | 18,450 | 26.7 |
| 1918 | Thomas J. Walsh (D) | 46,160 | 41.1 |
| | Oscar M. Lanstrum (R) | 40,229 | 35.8 |
| | Jeanette Rankin (N) | 26,013 | 23.1 |
| 1924 | Thomas J. Walsh (D) | 89,681 | 52.8 |
| | Frank B. Linderman (R) | 72,005 | 42.4 |
| 1930 | Thomas J. Walsh (D) | 106,274 | 60.3 |
| | Albert J. Galen (R) | 66,724 | 37.9 |
| | Special Election | | |
| 1934 | James E. Murray (D) | 116,965 | 59.6 |
| | Scott Leavitt (R) | 77,370 | 39.5 |
| 1936 | James E. Murray (D) | 121,769 | 55.0 |
| | T. O. Larson (R) | 60,038 | 27.1 |
| | Joseph P. Monaghan (I) | 39,655 | 17.9 |
| 1942 | James E. Murray (D) | 83,673 | 49.1 |
| | Wellington D. Rankin (R) | 82,461 | 48.4 |

| | Candidates | Votes | % |
|---|---|---|---|
| 1948 | James E. Murray (D) | 125,193 | *56.7* |
| | Tom J. Davis (R) | 94,458 | *42.7* |
| 1954 | James E. Murray (D) | 114,591 | *50.4* |
| | Wesley A. D'Ewart (R) | 112,863 | *49.6* |
| 1960 | Lee Metcalf (D) | 140,331 | *50.7* |
| | Orvin B. Fjare (R) | 136,281 | *49.3* |
| 1966 | Lee Metcalf (D) | 138,166 | *53.2* |
| | Tim Babcock (R) | 121,697 | *46.8* |
| 1972 | Lee Metcalf (D) | 163,609 | *52.0* |
| | Henry S. Hibbard (R) | 151,316 | *48.1* |
| 1978 | Max Baucus (D) | 160,353 | *55.7* |
| | Larry Williams (R) | 127,589 | *44.3* |
| 1984 | Max Baucus (D) | 215,704 | *56.9* |
| | Chuck Cozzens (R) | 154,308 | *40.7* |
| 1990 | Max Baucus (D) | 217,563 | *68.1* |
| | Allen C. Kolstad (R) | 93,836 | *29.4* |

# NEBRASKA

| | Candidates | Votes | % |
|---|---|---|---|
| | **Class 1** | | |
| 1916 | Gilbert M. Hitchcock (D & PRI) | 143,082 | *50.0* |
| | John L. Kennedy (R & PROG) | 131,359 | *45.9* |
| 1922 | Robert Beecher Howell (R) | 220,350 | *56.8* |
| | Gilbert M. Hitchcock (D) | 148,265 | *38.2* |
| 1928 | Robert Beecher Howell (R) | 324,014 | *61.3* |
| | Richard L. Metcalfe (D) | 204,737 | *38.7* |
| 1934 | Edward R. Burke (D) | 305,858 | *55.3* |
| | Robert G. Simmons (R) | 237,126 | *42.9* |

Special Election

| | | | |
|---|---|---|---|
| 1934 | Richard C. Hunter (D) | 281,421 | *56.5* |
| | J. H. Kemp (R) | 216,846 | *43.5* |
| 1940 | Hugh Butler (R) | 340,250 | *57.0* |
| | R. L. Cochran (D) | 247,659 | *41.5* |
| 1946 | Hugh Butler (R) | 271,208 | *70.8* |
| | John E. Mekota (D) | 111,751 | *29.2* |
| 1952 | Hugh Butler (R) | 408,971 | *69.1* |
| | Stanley D. Long (D) | 164,660 | *27.8* |

Special Election

| | | | |
|---|---|---|---|
| 1954 | Roman L. Hruska (R) | 250,341 | *60.9* |
| | James F. Green (D) | 160,881 | *39.1* |
| 1958 | Roman L. Hruska (R) | 232,227 | *55.6* |
| | Frank B. Morrison (D) | 185,152 | *44.4* |
| 1964 | Roman L. Hruska (R) | 345,772 | *61.4* |
| | Raymond W. Arndt (D) | 217,605 | *38.6* |
| 1970 | Roman L. Hruska (R) | 240,894 | *52.5* |
| | Frank B. Morrison (D) | 217,681 | *47.4* |
| 1976 | Edward Zorinsky (D) | 313,809 | *52.4* |
| | John Y. McCollister (R) | 284,284 | *47.5* |
| 1982 | Edward Zorinsky (D) | 363,350 | *66.6* |
| | Jim Keck (R) | 155,760 | *28.5* |
| 1988 | Bob Kerrey (D) | 378,717 | *56.7* |
| | David Karnes (R) | 278,250 | *41.7* |

| | **Class 2** | | |
|---|---|---|---|
| 1918 | George W. Norris (R) | 119,486 | *54.5* |
| | John H. Morehead (D) | 99,696 | *45.5* |
| 1924 | George W. Norris (R) | 274,640 | *62.4* |
| | J. J. Thomas (D & PROG) | 165,370 | *37.6* |

| | Candidates | Votes | % |
|---|---|---|---|
| 1930 | George W. Norris (R) | 247,118 | *56.8* |
| | Gilbert M. Hitchcock (D) | 172,795 | *39.7* |
| 1936 | George W. Norris (I) | 258,700 | *43.8* |
| | Robert G. Simmons (R) | 223,276 | *37.8* |
| | Terry Carpenter (D) | 108,391 | *18.4* |
| 1942 | Kenneth S. Wherry (R) | 186,207 | *49.0* |
| | George W. Norris (I) | 108,851 | *28.6* |
| | Foster May (D) | 83,763 | *22.0* |
| 1948 | Kenneth S. Wherry (R) | 267,575 | *56.7* |
| | Terry Carpenter (D) | 204,320 | *43.3* |

Special Election

| | | | |
|---|---|---|---|
| 1952 | Dwight Griswold (R) | 369,841 | *63.6* |
| | William Ritchie (D) | 211,898 | *36.4* |
| 1954 | Carl T. Curtis (R) | 255,695 | *61.1* |
| | Keith Neville (D) | 162,990 | *38.9* |

Special Election

| | | | |
|---|---|---|---|
| 1954 | Hazel H. Abel (R) | 233,589 | *57.8* |
| | William H. Meier (D) | 170,828 | *42.2* |
| 1960 | Carl T. Curtis (R) | 352,748 | *58.9* |
| | Robert B. Conrad (D) | 245,837 | *41.1* |
| 1966 | Carl T. Curtis (R) | 296,116 | *61.2* |
| | Frank B. Morrison (D) | 187,950 | *38.8* |
| 1972 | Carl T. Curtis (R) | 301,841 | *53.1* |
| | Terry Carpenter (D) | 265,922 | *46.8* |
| 1978 | J. James Exon (D) | 334,276 | *67.6* |
| | Donald Shasteen (R) | 159,806 | *32.3* |
| 1984 | J. James Exon (D) | 332,217 | *51.9* |
| | Nancy Hoch (R) | 307,147 | *48.0* |
| 1990 | J. James Exon (D) | 349,779 | *58.9* |
| | Hal Daub (R) | 243,013 | *40.9* |

# NEVADA

| | Candidates | Votes | % |
|---|---|---|---|
| | **Class 1** | | |
| 1910 | George S. Nixon (R) | 9,779 | *48.0* |
| | Key Pittman (D) | 8,624 | *42.4* |
| | Jud Harris (SOC) | 1,959 | *9.6* |

Special Election

| | | | |
|---|---|---|---|
| 1912 | Key Pittman (D) | 7,942 | *39.8* |
| | W. A. Massey (R) | 7,853 | *39.3* |
| | G. A. Steele (SOC) | 2,740 | *13.7* |
| | S. Summerfield (PROG) | 1,428 | *7.2* |
| 1916 | Key Pittman (D) | 12,765 | *38.8* |
| | Samuel Platt (R) | 10,618 | *32.3* |
| | A. Grant Miller (SOC) | 9,507 | *28.9* |
| 1922 | Key Pittman (D) | 18,201 | *62.8* |
| | Charles S. Chandler (R) | 10,770 | *37.2* |
| 1928 | Key Pittman (D) | 19,515 | *59.3* |
| | Samuel Platt (R) | 13,414 | *40.7* |
| 1934 | Key Pittman (D) | 27,581 | *64.5* |
| | George W. Malone (R) | 14,273 | *33.4* |
| 1940 | Key Pittman (D) | 31,351 | *60.5* |
| | Samuel Platt (R) | 20,488 | *39.5* |

## NEW HAMPSHIRE

| | Candidates | Votes | % |
|---|---|---|---|
| **Special Election** | | | |
| 1942 | J. G. Scrugham (D) | 23,805 | 58.7 |
| | Cecil W. Creel (R) | 16,735 | 41.3 |
| 1946 | George W. Malone (R) | 27,801 | 55.2 |
| | Berkeley L. Bunker (D) | 22,553 | 44.8 |
| 1952 | George W. Malone (R) | 41,906 | 51.7 |
| | Thomas B. Mechling (D) | 39,184 | 48.3 |
| 1958 | Howard W. Cannon (D) | 48,732 | 57.7 |
| | George W. Malone (R) | 35,760 | 42.3 |
| 1964 | Howard W. Cannon (D) | 67,336 | 50.0 |
| | Paul Laxalt (R) | 67,288 | 50.0 |
| 1970 | Howard W. Cannon (D) | 85,187 | 57.7 |
| | William J. Raggio (R) | 60,838 | 41.2 |
| 1976 | Howard W. Cannon (D) | 127,295 | 63.0 |
| | David Towell (R) | 63,471 | 31.4 |
| 1982 | Chic Hecht (R) | 120,377 | 50.1 |
| | Howard W. Cannon (D) | 114,720 | 47.7 |
| 1988 | Richard H. Bryan (D) | 175,548 | 50.2 |
| | Chic Hecht (R) | 161,336 | 46.1 |

### Class 3

| | Candidates | Votes | % |
|---|---|---|---|
| 1908 | Francis G. Newlands (D) | 12,473 | 53.4 |
| | P. L. Flanigan (R) | 8,972 | 38.4 |
| | T. C. Lutz (SOC) | 1,929 | 8.3 |
| 1914 | Francis G. Newlands (D) | 8,078 | 37.5 |
| | Samuel Platt (R) | 8,038 | 37.3 |
| | A. Grant Miller (SOC) | 5,451 | 25.3 |

**Special Election**

| | | | |
|---|---|---|---|
| 1918 | Charles B. Henderson (D) | 12,197 | 47.7 |
| | E. E. Roberts (R) | 8,053 | 31.5 |
| | Anne Martin (I) | 4,603 | 18.0 |
| 1920 | Tasker L. Oddie (R) | 11,550 | 42.1 |
| | Charles B. Henderson (D) | 10,402 | 37.9 |
| | Anne Martin (I) | 4,981 | 18.2 |
| 1926 | Tasker L. Oddie (R) | 17,430 | 55.8 |
| | Ray T. Baker (D) | 13,273 | 42.5 |
| 1932 | Patrick A. McCarran (D) | 21,398 | 52.1 |
| | Tasker L. Oddie (R) | 19,706 | 47.9 |
| 1938 | Patrick A. McCarran (D) | 27,406 | 59.0 |
| | Tasker L. Oddie (R) | 19,078 | 41.0 |
| 1944 | Patrick A. McCarran (D) | 30,595 | 58.4 |
| | George W. Malone (R) | 21,816 | 41.6 |
| 1950 | Patrick A. McCarran (D) | 35,829 | 58.0 |
| | George E. Marshall (R) | 25,933 | 42.0 |

**Special Election**

| | | | |
|---|---|---|---|
| 1954 | Alan Bible (D) | 45,043 | 58.1 |
| | Ernest S. Brown (R) | 32,470 | 41.9 |
| 1956 | Alan Bible (D) | 50,677 | 52.6 |
| | Cliff Young (R) | 45,712 | 47.4 |
| 1962 | Alan Bible (D) | 63,443 | 65.3 |
| | William B. Wright (R) | 33,749 | 34.7 |
| 1968 | Alan Bible (D) | 83,622 | 54.8 |
| | Ed Fike (R) | 69,068 | 45.2 |
| 1974 | Paul Laxalt (R) | 79,605 | 47.0 |
| | Harry Reid (D) | 78,981 | 46.6 |
| 1980 | Paul Laxalt (R) | 144,224 | 58.5 |
| | Mary Gojack (D) | 92,129 | 37.4 |
| 1986 | Harry Reid (D) | 130,955 | 50.0 |
| | Jim Santini (R) | 116,606 | 44.5 |
| 1992 | Harry Reid (D) | 253,150 | 51.0 |
| | Demar Dahl (R) | 199,413 | 40.2 |

## NEW HAMPSHIRE

| | Candidates | Votes | % |
|---|---|---|---|
| **Class 2** | | | |
| 1918 | Henry W. Keyes (R) | 37,787 | 53.6 |
| | Eugene E. Reed (D) | 32,763 | 46.4 |
| 1924 | Henry W. Keyes (R) | 94,432 | 59.8 |
| | George E. Farrand (D) | 63,596 | 40.2 |
| 1930 | Henry W. Keyes (R) | 72,225 | 57.9 |
| | Albert W. Noone (D) | 52,284 | 41.9 |
| 1936 | Styles Bridges (R) | 107,923 | 51.9 |
| | William N. Rogers (D) | 99,195 | 47.7 |
| 1942 | Styles Bridges (R) | 88,601 | 54.6 |
| | Francis P. Murphy (D) | 73,656 | 45.4 |
| 1948 | Styles Bridges (R) | 129,600 | 58.1 |
| | Alfred E. Fortin (D) | 91,760 | 41.2 |
| 1954 | Styles Bridges (R) | 117,150 | 60.2 |
| | Gerard L. Morin (D) | 77,386 | 39.8 |
| 1960 | Styles Bridges (R) | 173,521 | 60.4 |
| | Herbert W. Hill (D) | 114,024 | 39.7 |

**Special Election**

| | | | |
|---|---|---|---|
| 1962 | Thomas J. McIntyre (D) | 117,612 | 52.3 |
| | Perkins Bass (R) | 107,199 | 47.7 |
| 1966 | Thomas J. McIntyre (D) | 123,888 | 54.0 |
| | Harrison R. Thyng (R) | 105,241 | 45.9 |
| 1972 | Thomas J. McIntyre (D) | 184,495 | 56.9 |
| | Wesley Powell (R) | 139,852 | 43.1 |
| 1978 | Gordon J. Humphrey (R) | 133,745 | 50.7 |
| | Thomas J. McIntyre (D) | 127,945 | 48.5 |
| 1984 | Gordon J. Humphrey (R) | 225,828 | 58.7 |
| | Norman E. D'Amours (D) | 157,447 | 41.0 |
| 1990 | Robert C. Smith (R) | 189,792 | 65.1 |
| | John A. Durkin (D) | 91,299 | 31.3 |

### Class 3

| | | | |
|---|---|---|---|
| 1914 | Jacob H. Gallinger (R) | 42,113 | 51.7 |
| | Raymond B. Stevens (D) | 36,382 | 44.6 |

**Special Election**

| | | | |
|---|---|---|---|
| 1918 | George H. Moses (R) | 35,528 | 50.8 |
| | John B. Jameson (D) | 34,459 | 49.2 |
| 1920 | George H. Moses (R) | 90,173 | 57.7 |
| | Raymond B. Stevens (D) | 65,035 | 41.6 |
| 1926 | George H. Moses (R) | 79,279 | 62.3 |
| | Robert C. Murchie (D) | 47,935 | 37.7 |
| 1932 | Fred H. Brown (D) | 98,766 | 50.4 |
| | George H. Moses (R) | 96,649 | 49.3 |
| 1938 | Charles W. Tobey (R) | 100,633 | 54.2 |
| | Fred H. Brown (D) | 84,920 | 45.8 |
| 1944 | Charles W. Tobey (R) | 110,549 | 50.9 |
| | Joseph J. Betley (D) | 106,508 | 49.1 |
| 1950 | Charles W. Tobey (R) | 106,142 | 55.7 |
| | Emmet J. Kelley (D) | 72,473 | 38.0 |
| | Wesley Powell (I) | 11,958 | 6.3 |

**Special Election**

| | | | |
|---|---|---|---|
| 1954 | Norris Cotton (R) | 114,068 | 60.2 |
| | Stanley J. Betley (D) | 75,490 | 39.8 |
| 1956 | Norris Cotton (R) | 161,424 | 64.1 |
| | Laurence M. Pickett (D) | 90,519 | 35.9 |
| 1962 | Norris Cotton (R) | 134,035 | 59.7 |
| | Alfred Catalfo Jr. (D) | 90,444 | 40.3 |

| | Candidates | Votes | % |
|---|---|---|---|
| 1968 | Norris Cotton (R) | 170,163 | 59.3 |
| | John W. King (D) | 116,816 | 40.7 |
| 1974 [1] | Louis C. Wyman (R) | 110,926* | 49.7 |
| | John A. Durkin (D) | 110,924 | 49.7 |

**Special Election [1]**

| 1975 | John A. Durkin (D) | 140,778 | 53.6 |
|---|---|---|---|
| | Louis C. Wyman (R) | 113,007 | 43.1 |
| | Carmen C. Chimento (AM) | 8,787 | 3.3 |

| 1980 | Warren B. Rudman (R) | 195,563 | 52.1 |
|---|---|---|---|
| | John A. Durkin (D) | 179,455 | 47.8 |
| 1986 | Warren B. Rudman (R) | 154,090 | 62.9 |
| | Endicott Peabody (D) | 79,222 | 32.4 |
| 1992 | Judd Gregg (R) | 249,591 | 48.1 |
| | John Rauh (D) | 234,982 | 45.3 |

**New Hampshire**

1. Wyman's two-vote margin was challenged by Durkin. The Senate refused to seat either candidate. After seven months of fruitless efforts to decide a winner, the Senate voted July 30, 1975, to declare the seat vacant effective Aug. 8, 1975. In a special election Sept. 16, 1975, Durkin defeated Wyman.

# NEW JERSEY

| | Candidates | Votes | % |
|---|---|---|---|
| | **Class 1** | | |
| 1916 | Joseph S. Frelinghuysen (R) | 244,715 | 56.0 |
| | James Martine (D) | 170,019 | 38.9 |
| 1922 | Edward I. Edwards (D) | 451,832 | 54.9 |
| | Joseph S. Frelinghuysen (R) | 362,699 | 44.1 |
| 1928 | Hamilton F. Kean (R) | 841,752 | 57.9 |
| | Edward I. Edwards (D) | 608,623 | 41.8 |
| 1934 | A. Harry Moore (D) | 785,971 | 57.9 |
| | Hamilton F. Kean (R) | 554,483 | 40.9 |

**Special Election**

| 1938 | W. Warren Barbour (R) | 816,667 | 53.0 |
|---|---|---|---|
| | William H. J. Ely (D) | 704,159 | 45.7 |

| 1940 | W. Warren Barbour (R) | 1,029,331 | 55.1 |
|---|---|---|---|
| | James H. R. Cromwell (D) | 823,893 | 44.1 |

**Special Election**

| 1944 | H. Alexander Smith (R) | 939,987 | 50.4 |
|---|---|---|---|
| | Elmer H. Wene (D) | 910,096 | 48.8 |

| 1946 | H. Alexander Smith (R) | 799,808 | 58.5 |
|---|---|---|---|
| | George E. Brunner (D) | 548,458 | 40.1 |
| 1952 | H. Alexander Smith (R) | 1,286,782 | 55.5 |
| | Archibald S. Alexander (D) | 1,011,187 | 43.6 |
| 1958 | Harrison A. Williams Jr. (D) | 966,832 | 51.4 |
| | Robert Winthrop Kean (R) | 882,287 | 46.9 |
| 1964 | Harrison A. Williams Jr. (D) | 1,677,515 | 61.9 |
| | Bernard M. Shanley (R) | 1,011,280 | 37.3 |
| 1970 | Harrison A. Williams Jr. (D) | 1,157,074 | 54.0 |
| | Nelson G. Gross (R) | 903,026 | 42.2 |
| 1976 | Harrison A. Williams Jr. (D) | 1,681,140 | 60.7 |
| | David F. Norcross (R) | 1,054,508 | 38.0 |
| 1982 | Frank R. Lautenberg (D) | 1,117,549 | 50.9 |
| | Millicent Fenwick (R) | 1,047,626 | 47.8 |
| 1988 | Frank R. Lautenberg (D) | 1,599,905 | 53.5 |
| | Pete Dawkins (R) | 1,349,937 | 45.2 |

| | Candidates | Votes | % |
|---|---|---|---|
| | **Class 2** | | |
| 1918 | Walter E. Edge (R) | 179,022 | 50.3 |
| | George M. Lamonte (D) | 153,743 | 43.2 |

**Special Election**

| 1918 | David Baird (R) | 170,414 | 49.2 |
|---|---|---|---|
| | Charles O'Connor Hennessy (D) | 154,734 | 44.6 |

| 1924 | Walter E. Edge (R) | 608,020 | 61.8 |
|---|---|---|---|
| | Frederick W. Donnelly (D) | 331,034 | 33.7 |
| 1930 | Dwight W. Morrow (R) | 601,497 | 58.5 |
| | Alexander Simpson (D) | 401,007 | 39.0 |

**Special Elections**

| 1930 | Dwight W. Morrow (R) | 571,006 | 59.1 |
|---|---|---|---|
| | Thelma Parkinson (D) | 372,739 | 38.6 |
| 1932 | W. Warren Barbour (R) | 741,734 | 49.6 |
| | Percy H. Stewart (D) | 725,511 | 48.5 |

| 1936 | William H. Smathers (D) | 916,414 | 54.9 |
|---|---|---|---|
| | W. Warren Barbour (R) | 740,088 | 44.3 |
| 1942 | Albert W. Hawkes (R) | 648,855 | 53.1 |
| | William H. Smathers (D) | 559,851 | 45.8 |
| 1948 | Robert C. Hendrickson (R) | 934,720 | 50.0 |
| | Archibald S. Alexander (D) | 884,414 | 47.3 |
| 1954 | Clifford P. Case (R) | 861,528 | 48.7 |
| | Charles R. Howell (D) | 858,158 | 48.5 |
| 1960 | Clifford P. Case (R) | 1,483,832 | 55.7 |
| | Thorn Lord (D) | 1,151,385 | 43.2 |
| 1966 | Clifford P. Case (R) | 1,278,843 | 60.0 |
| | Warren W. Wilentz (D) | 788,021 | 37.0 |
| 1972 | Clifford P. Case (R) | 1,743,854 | 62.5 |
| | Paul J. Krebs (D) | 963,573 | 34.5 |
| 1978 | Bill Bradley (D) | 1,082,960 | 55.3 |
| | Jeffrey Bell (R) | 844,200 | 43.1 |
| 1984 | Bill Bradley (D) | 1,986,644 | 64.2 |
| | Mary V. Mochary (R) | 1,080,100 | 35.2 |
| 1990 | Bill Bradley (D) | 977,810 | 50.4 |
| | Christine Todd Whitman (R) | 918,874 | 47.4 |

# NEW MEXICO

| | Candidates | Votes | % |
|---|---|---|---|
| | **Class 1** | | |
| 1916 | Andrieus A. Jones (D) | 34,142 | 51.1 |
| | Frank A. Hubbell (R) | 30,622 | 45.8 |
| 1922 | Andrieus A. Jones (D) | 60,969 | 55.2 |
| | S. B. Davis Jr. (R) | 48,721 | 44.1 |
| 1928 | Bronson M. Cutting (R) | 68,070 | 57.7 |
| | Jethro S. Vaught (D) | 49,913 | 42.3 |

**Special Election**

| 1928 | Octaviano A. Larrazolo (R) | 64,623 | 55.7 |
|---|---|---|---|
| | Juan N. Vigil (D) | 51,495 | 44.4 |

| 1934 | Bronson M. Cutting (R) | 76,228 | 50.2 |
|---|---|---|---|
| | Dennis Chavez (D) | 74,944 | 49.4 |

| Candidates | Votes | % |
|---|---|---|
| **Special Election** | | |
| 1936 Dennis Chavez (D) | 94,585 | 55.7 |
| M. A. Otero Jr. (R) | 75,030 | 44.2 |
| 1940 Dennis Chavez (D) | 103,194 | 56.0 |
| Albert K. Mitchell (R) | 81,257 | 44.1 |
| 1946 Dennis Chavez (D) | 68,650 | 51.5 |
| Patrick J. Hurley (R) | 64,632 | 48.5 |
| 1952 Dennis Chavez (D) | 122,543 | 51.1 |
| Patrick J. Hurley (R) | 117,168 | 48.9 |
| 1958 Dennis Chavez (D) | 127,496 | 62.7 |
| Forrest S. Atchley (R) | 75,827 | 37.3 |
| 1964 Joseph M. Montoya (D) | 178,209 | 54.7 |
| Edwin L. Mechem (R) | 147,562 | 45.3 |
| 1970 Joseph M. Montoya (D) | 151,486 | 52.3 |
| Anderson Carter (R) | 135,004 | 46.6 |
| 1976 Harrison (Jack) Schmitt (R) | 234,681 | 56.8 |
| Joseph M. Montoya (D) | 176,382 | 42.7 |
| 1982 Jeff Bingaman (D) | 217,682 | 53.8 |
| Harrison (Jack) Schmitt (R) | 187,128 | 46.2 |
| 1988 Jeff Bingaman (D) | 321,983 | 63.3 |
| Bill Valentine (R) | 186,579 | 36.7 |

## Class 2

| Candidates | Votes | % |
|---|---|---|
| 1918 Albert B. Fall (R) | 24,322 | 51.4 |
| W. B. Walton (D) | 22,470 | 47.5 |
| **Special Election** | | |
| 1921 Holm O. Bursum (R) | 36,868 | 51.4 |
| R. H. Hanna (D) | 31,353 | 43.7 |
| 1924 Sam G. Bratton (D) | 57,355 | 49.9 |
| Holm O. Bursum (R) | 54,558 | 47.4 |
| 1930 Sam G. Bratton (D) | 69,356 | 58.6 |
| Herbert B. Holt (R) | 48,699 | 41.2 |
| **Special Election** | | |
| 1934 Carl A. Hatch (D) | 81,934 | 54.5 |
| Richard C. Dillon (R) | 67,577 | 45.0 |
| 1936 Carl A. Hatch (D) | 104,550 | 61.7 |
| Ernest W. Everly (R) | 64,817 | 38.3 |
| 1942 Carl A. Hatch (D) | 63,301 | 59.2 |
| J. Benson Newell (R) | 43,704 | 40.8 |
| 1948 Clinton P. Anderson (D) | 108,269 | 57.2 |
| Patrick J. Hurley (R) | 80,226 | 42.4 |
| 1954 Clinton P. Anderson (D) | 111,351 | 57.3 |
| Edwin L. Mechem (R) | 83,071 | 42.7 |
| 1960 Clinton P. Anderson (D) | 190,654 | 63.4 |
| William Colwes (R) | 109,897 | 36.6 |
| 1966 Clinton P. Anderson (D) | 137,205 | 53.1 |
| Anderson Carter (R) | 120,988 | 46.9 |
| 1972 Pete V. Domenici (R) | 204,253 | 54.0 |
| Jack Daniels (D) | 173,815 | 46.0 |
| 1978 Pete V. Domenici (R) | 183,442 | 53.4 |
| Toney Anaya (D) | 160,045 | 46.6 |
| 1984 Pete V. Domenici (R) | 361,371 | 71.9 |
| Judith A. Pratt (D) | 141,253 | 28.1 |
| 1990 Pete V. Domenici (R) | 296,712 | 72.9 |
| Tom R. Benavides (D) | 110,033 | 27.1 |

# NEW YORK

| Candidates | Votes | % |
|---|---|---|
| **Class 1** | | |
| 1916 William M. Calder (R) | 839,314 | 54.3 |
| William F. McCombs (D & AM) | 605,933 | 39.2 |
| 1922 Royal S. Copeland (D) | 1,276,667 | 52.6 |
| William M. Calder (R) | 995,421 | 41.0 |
| 1928 Royal S. Copeland (D) | 2,084,273 | 49.1 |
| Alanson B. Houghton (R) | 2,034,014 | 47.9 |
| 1934 Royal S. Copeland (D) | 2,046,377 | 55.3 |
| E. Harold Cluett (R) | 1,363,440 | 36.9 |
| Norman Thomas (SOC) | 194,952 | 5.3 |
| **Special Election** | | |
| 1938 James M. Mead (D, AM LAB) | 2,438,904 | 53.6 |
| Edward F. Corsi (R, I PROG) | 2,083,666 | 45.8 |
| 1940 James M. Mead (D, AM LAB) | 3,274,766 | 53.3 |
| Bruce Barton (R) | 2,868,852 | 46.7 |
| 1946 Irving M. Ives (R) | 2,559,365 | 52.6 |
| Herbert H. Lehman (D, AM LAB) | 2,308,112 | 47.4 |
| 1952 Irving M. Ives (R) | 3,853,934 | 55.2 |
| John Cashmore (D) | 2,521,736 | 36.1 |
| George S. Counts (L) | 489,775 | 7.0 |
| 1958 Kenneth B. Keating (R) | 2,842,942 | 50.8 |
| Frank S. Hogan (D, L) | 2,709,950 | 48.4 |
| 1964 Robert F. Kennedy (D, L) | 3,823,749 | 53.5 |
| Kenneth B. Keating (R) | 3,104,056 | 43.4 |
| 1970 James L. Buckley (C, I ALNC) | 2,288,190 | 38.8 |
| Richard L. Ottinger (D) | 2,171,232 | 36.8 |
| Charles E. Goodell (R, L) | 1,434,472 | 24.3 |
| 1976 Daniel Patrick Moynihan (D, L) | 3,422,594 | 54.2 |
| James L. Buckley (R, C) | 2,836,633 | 44.9 |
| 1982 Daniel Patrick Moynihan (D, L) | 3,232,146 | 65.1 |
| Florence M. Sullivan (R, C) | 1,696,766 | 34.2 |
| 1988 Daniel Patrick Moynihan (D, L) | 4,048,649 | 67.0 |
| Robert R. McMillan (R, C) | 1,875,784 | 31.1 |

## Class 3

| Candidates | Votes | % |
|---|---|---|
| 1914 James W. Wadsworth Jr. (R) | 639,112 | 47.0 |
| James W. Gerard (D, I LEAGUE) | 571,419 | 42.1 |
| 1920 James W. Wadsworth Jr. (R) | 1,434,393 | 52.4 |
| Harry C. Walker (D) | 901,310 | 32.9 |
| Jacob Panken (SOC) | 208,155 | 7.6 |
| Ella A. Boole (P) | 159,623 | 5.8 |
| 1926 Robert F. Wagner (D) | 1,321,463 | 46.5 |
| James W. Wadsworth Jr. (R) | 1,205,246 | 42.4 |
| F. W. Cristman (IR) | 231,906 | 8.2 |
| 1932 Robert F. Wagner (D) | 2,532,905 | 55.8 |
| George Z. Medalie (R) | 1,751,186 | 38.6 |
| 1938 Robert F. Wagner (D, AM LAB) | 2,497,029 | 54.5 |
| John Lord O'Brian (R, I PROG) | 2,058,615 | 45.0 |
| 1944 Robert F. Wagner (D, AM LAB) | 3,294,576 | 53.1 |
| Thomas J. Curran (R) | 2,899,497 | 46.7 |
| **Special Election** | | |
| 1949 Herbert H. Lehman (D, L) | 2,582,438 | 52.0 |
| John Foster Dulles (R) | 2,384,381 | 48.0 |
| 1950 Herbert H. Lehman (D, L) | 2,632,313 | 50.3 |
| Joe R. Hanley (R) | 2,367,353 | 45.3 |
| 1956 Jacob K. Javits (R) | 3,723,933 | 53.3 |
| Robert F. Wagner Jr. (D, L) | 3,265,159 | 46.7 |
| 1962 Jacob K. Javits (R) | 3,272,417 | 57.4 |
| James B. Donovan (D, L) | 2,289,323 | 40.1 |
| 1968 Jacob K. Javits (R, L) | 3,269,772 | 49.7 |

| | Candidates | Votes | % |
|---|---|---|---|
| | Paul O'Dwyer (D) | 2,150,695 | 32.7 |
| | James L. Buckley (C) | 1,139,402 | 17.3 |
| 1974 | Jacob K. Javits (R, L) | 2,340,188 | 45.3 |
| | Ramsey Clark (D) | 1,973,781 | 38.2 |
| | Barbara A. Keating (C) | 822,584 | 15.9 |
| 1980 | Alfonse M. D'Amato (R, C) | 2,699,652 | 44.9 |
| | Elizabeth Holtzman (D) | 2,618,661 | 43.5 |
| | Jacob K. Javits (L) | 664,544 | 11.0 |
| 1986 | Alfonse M. D'Amato (R, C) | 2,378,197 | 56.9 |
| | Mark Green (D) | 1,723,216 | 41.2 |
| 1992 | Alfonse M. D'Amato (R, C) | 3,166,994 | 49.0 |
| | Robert Abrams (D, L) | 3,086,200 | 47.8 |

# NORTH CAROLINA

| | Candidates | Votes | % |
|---|---|---|---|
| | **Class 2** | | |
| 1918 | Furnifold M. Simmons (D) | 143,519 | 60.5 |
| | John M. Morehead (R) | 93,707 | 39.5 |
| 1924 | Furnifold M. Simmons (D) | 295,344 | 61.6 |
| | A. A. Whitener (R) | 184,493 | 38.5 |
| 1930 | Josiah W. Bailey (D) | 324,293 | 60.6 |
| | George M. Pritchard (R) | 210,761 | 39.4 |
| 1936 | Josiah W. Bailey (D) | 564,088 | 70.8 |
| | Frank R. Patton (R) | 233,000 | 29.2 |
| 1942 | Josiah W. Bailey (D) | 230,427 | 65.9 |
| | Sam J. Morris (R) | 119,165 | 34.1 |
| 1948 | J. Melville Broughton (D) | 540,762 | 70.7 |
| | John A. Wilkinson (R) | 220,307 | 28.8 |

Special Election

| | | | |
|---|---|---|---|
| 1948 | J. Melville Broughton (D) | 534,917†† | 100.0 |

Special Election

| | | | |
|---|---|---|---|
| 1950 | Willis Smith (D) | 364,912 | 67.0 |
| | E. L. Gavin (R) | 177,753 | 32.6 |

| | | | |
|---|---|---|---|
| 1954 | W. Kerr Scott (D) | 408,312 | 65.9 |
| | Paul C. West (R) | 211,322 | 34.1 |

Special Election

| | | | |
|---|---|---|---|
| 1954 | W. Kerr Scott (D) | 402,268 | 100.0 |

Special Election

| | | | |
|---|---|---|---|
| 1958 | B. Everett Jordan (D) | 431,492 | 70.0 |
| | Richard C. Clarke Jr. (R) | 184,977 | 30.0 |

| | | | |
|---|---|---|---|
| 1960 | B. Everett Jordan (D) | 793,521 | 61.4 |
| | Kyle Hayes (R) | 497,964 | 38.6 |
| 1966 | B. Everett Jordan (D) | 501,440 | 55.6 |
| | John S. Shallcross (R) | 400,502 | 44.4 |
| 1972 | Jesse Helms (R) | 795,248 | 54.0 |
| | Nick Galifianakis (D) | 677,293 | 46.0 |
| 1978 | Jesse Helms (R) | 619,151 | 54.5 |
| | John Ingram (D) | 516,663 | 45.5 |
| 1984 | Jesse Helms (R) | 1,156,768 | 51.7 |
| | James B. Hunt, Jr. (D) | 1,070,488 | 47.8 |
| 1990 | Jesse Helms (R) | 1,087,331 | 52.5 |
| | Harvey B. Gantt (D) | 981,573 | 47.4 |

| | Candidates | Votes | % |
|---|---|---|---|
| | **Class 3** | | |
| | A. A. Whitener (R) | 87,101 | 41.7 |
| 1920 | Lee S. Overman (D) | 310,504 | 57.5 |
| | A. E. Holton (R) | 229,343 | 42.5 |
| 1926 | Lee S. Overman (D) | 218,934 | 60.5 |
| | Johnson J. Hayes (R) | 142,891 | 39.5 |
| 1932 | Robert R. Reynolds (D) | 476,048 | 68.3 |
| | Jake F. Newell (R) | 221,392 | 31.7 |
| 1938 | Robert R. Reynolds (D) | 316,685 | 63.8 |
| | Charles A. Jonas (R) | 179,461 | 36.2 |
| 1944 | Clyde R. Hoey (D) | 533,813 | 70.3 |
| | A. I. Ferree (R) | 226,037 | 29.8 |
| 1950 | Clyde R. Hoey (D) | 376,473 | 68.7 |
| | Halsey B. Leavitt (R) | 171,804 | 31.3 |

Special Election

| | | | |
|---|---|---|---|
| 1954 | Sam J. Ervin Jr. (D) | 410,574 | 100.0 |

| | | | |
|---|---|---|---|
| 1956 | Sam J. Ervin Jr. (D) | 731,353 | 66.6 |
| | Joel A. Johnson (R) | 367,475 | 33.4 |
| 1962 | Sam J. Ervin Jr. (D) | 491,520 | 60.5 |
| | Claude L. Greene Jr. (R) | 321,635 | 39.6 |
| 1968 | Sam J. Ervin Jr. (D) | 870,406 | 60.6 |
| | Robert Vance Somers (R) | 566,934 | 39.4 |
| 1974 | Robert B. Morgan (D) | 633,775 | 62.1 |
| | William E. Stevens (R) | 377,618 | 37.0 |
| 1980 | John P. East (R) | 898,064 | 50.0 |
| | Robert Morgan (D) | 887,653 | 49.4 |
| 1986 | Terry Sanford (D) | 823,662 | 51.8 |
| | James T. Broyhill (R) | 767,668 | 48.2 |
| 1992 | Lauch Faircloth (R) | 1,297,892 | 50.3 |
| | Terry Sanford (D) | 1,194,015 | 46.3 |

# NORTH DAKOTA

| | Candidates | Votes | % |
|---|---|---|---|
| | **Class 1** | | |
| 1916 | Porter J. McCumber (R) | 57,714 | 53.9 |
| | John Burke (D) | 40,988 | 38.2 |
| | E. R. Fry (SOC) | 8,472 | 7.9 |
| 1922 | Lynn J. Frazier (R & NP) | 101,312 | 52.3 |
| | J. F. T. O'Connor (D & I) | 92,464 | 47.7 |
| 1928 | Lynn J. Frazier (R) | 159,940 | 79.6 |
| | F. F. Burchard (D) | 38,856 | 19.4 |
| 1934 | Lynn J. Frazier (R) | 151,205 | 58.2 |
| | Henry Holt (D) | 104,477 | 40.2 |
| 1940 | William Langer (R) | 100,647 | 38.1 |
| | William Lemke (I) | 92,593 | 35.1 |
| | Charles V. Vogel (D) | 69,847 | 26.5 |
| 1946 | William Langer (R) | 88,210 | 53.3 |
| | Arthur E. Thompson (I) | 38,804 | 23.5 |
| | Abner B. Larson (D) | 38,368 | 23.2 |
| 1952 | William Langer (R) | 157,907 | 66.4 |
| | Harold A. Morrison (D) | 55,347 | 23.3 |
| | Fred G. Aandahl (I) | 24,741 | 10.4 |
| 1958 | William Langer (R) | 117,070 | 57.2 |
| | Raymond Vendsel (D) | 84,892 | 41.5 |

Special Election

| | | | |
|---|---|---|---|
| 1960 | Quentin N. Burdick (D) | 104,593 | 49.7 |
| | John E. Davis (R) | 103,475 | 49.2 |

| | | | |
|---|---|---|---|
| 1964 | Quentin N. Burdick (D) | 149,264 | 57.6 |

**835**

# OHIO

| | Candidates | Votes | % |
|---|---|---|---|
| 1970 | Thomas S. Kleppe (R) | 109,681 | 42.4 |
| | Quentin N. Burdick (D) | 134,519 | 61.3 |
| 1976 | Thomas S. Kleppe (R) | 82,996 | 37.8 |
| | Quentin N. Burdick (D) | 175,772 | 62.1 |
| 1982 | Richard Stroup (R) | 103,466 | 36.6 |
| | Quentin N. Burdick (D) | 164,873 | 62.8 |
| | Gene Knorr (R) | 89,304 | 34.0 |
| 1988 | Quentin N. Burdick (D) | 171,899 | 59.4 |
| | Earl Strinden (R) | 112,937 | 39.1 |

### Special Election

| | | | |
|---|---|---|---|
| 1992 | Kent Conrad (D) | 102,887 | 63.3 |
| | Jack Dalrymple (R) | 54,726 | 33.7 |

### Class 3

| | | | |
|---|---|---|---|
| 1914 | Asle J. Gronna (R) | 48,732 | 55.8 |
| | W. E. Purcell (D) | 29,640 | 34.0 |
| | W. H. Brown (SOC) | 6,231 | 7.1 |
| 1920 | Edwin F. Ladd (R & NP) | 130,614 | 59.8 |
| | H. H. Perry (D & I) | 87,765 | 40.2 |
| 1926 | Gerald P. Nye (R) | 107,921 | 69.6 |
| | Norris H. Nelson (I) | 18,951 | 12.2 |
| | F. F. Burchard (D) | 13,519 | 8.7 |
| | C. P. Stone (R) | 9,738 | 6.3 |

### Special Election

| | | | |
|---|---|---|---|
| 1926 | Gerald P. Nye (R) | 79,709 | 50.2 |
| | L. B. Hanna | 59,499 | 37.5 |
| | C. P. Stone | 19,586 | 12.3 |

| | | | |
|---|---|---|---|
| 1932 | Gerald P. Nye (R) | 172,796 | 72.3 |
| | P. W. Lanier (D) | 65,575 | 27.5 |
| 1938 | Gerald P. Nye (R) | 131,907 | 50.1 |
| | William Langer (I) | 112,007 | 42.6 |
| | J. J. Nygaard (D) | 19,244 | 7.3 |
| 1944 | John Moses (D) | 95,102 | 45.2 |
| | Gerald P. Nye (R) | 69,530 | 33.0 |
| | Lynn U. Stambaugh (IR) | 44,596 | 21.2 |

### Special Election

| | | | |
|---|---|---|---|
| 1946 | Milton R. Young (R) | 75,998 | 55.5 |
| | William Lanier (D) | 37,507 | 27.4 |
| | Gerald P. Nye (I) | 20,848 | 15.2 |

| | | | |
|---|---|---|---|
| 1950 | Milton R. Young (R) | 126,209 | 67.6 |
| | Harry O'Brien (D) | 60,507 | 32.4 |
| 1956 | Milton R. Young (R) | 155,305 | 63.6 |
| | Quentin N. Burdick (D) | 87,919 | 36.0 |
| 1962 | Milton R. Young (R) | 135,705 | 60.7 |
| | William Lanier (D) | 88,032 | 39.4 |
| 1968 | Milton R. Young (R) | 154,968 | 64.6 |
| | Herschel Lashkowitz (D) | 80,815 | 33.7 |
| 1974 | Milton R. Young (R) | 114,117 | 48.4 |
| | William L. Guy (D) | 113,931 | 48.3 |
| 1980 | Mark Andrews (R) | 210,347 | 70.3 |
| | Kent Johanneson (D) | 86,658 | 29.0 |
| 1986 | Kent Conrad (D) | 143,932 | 49.8 |
| | Mark Andrews (R) | 141,797 | 49.1 |
| 1992 | Byron L. Dorgan (D) | 179,347 | 59.0 |
| | Steve Sydness (R) | 118,162 | 38.9 |

## OHIO

| | Candidates | Votes | % |
|---|---|---|---|
| **Class 1** | | | |
| 1916 | Atlee Pomerene (D) | 571,488 | 49.3 |
| | Myron T. Herrick (R) | 535,391 | 46.2 |
| 1922 | Simeon D. Fess (R) | 794,149 | 50.9 |
| | Atlee Pomerene (D) | 744,558 | 47.7 |
| 1928 | Simeon D. Fess (R) | 1,412,805 | 60.7 |
| | Charles V. Truax (D) | 908,952 | 39.1 |
| 1934 | Vic Donahey (D) | 1,276,206 | 60.0 |
| | Simeon D. Fess (R) | 839,068 | 39.4 |
| 1940 | Harold H. Burton (R) | 1,602,567 | 52.4 |
| | John McSweeney (D) | 1,457,359 | 47.6 |
| 1946 | John W. Bricker (R) | 1,275,774 | 57.0 |
| | James W. Huffman (D) | 947,610 | 42.4 |

### Special Election

| | | | |
|---|---|---|---|
| 1946 | Kingsley A. Taft (R) | 1,193,942 | 56.2 |
| | Henry P. Webber (D) | 929,584 | 43.8 |

| | | | |
|---|---|---|---|
| 1952 | John W. Bricker (R) | 1,878,961 | 54.6 |
| | Michael V. DiSalle (D) | 1,563,330 | 45.4 |
| 1958 | Stephen M. Young (D) | 1,652,211 | 52.5 |
| | John W. Bricker (R) | 1,497,199 | 47.5 |
| 1964 | Stephen M. Young (D) | 1,923,608 | 50.2 |
| | Robert Taft Jr. (R) | 1,906,781 | 49.8 |
| 1970 | Robert Taft Jr. (R) | 1,565,682 | 49.7 |
| | Howard M. Metzenbaum (D) | 1,495,262 | 47.5 |
| 1976 | Howard M. Metzenbaum (D) | 1,941,113 | 49.5 |
| | Robert A. Taft Jr. (R) | 1,823,774 | 46.5 |
| 1982 | Howard M. Metzenbaum (D) | 1,923,767 | 56.7 |
| | Paul E. Pfeifer (R) | 1,396,790 | 41.1 |
| 1988 | Howard M. Metzenbaum (D) | 2,480,038 | 57.0 |
| | George V. Voinovich (R) | 1,872,716 | 43.0 |

### Class 3

| | | | |
|---|---|---|---|
| 1914 | Warren G. Harding (R) | 526,115 | 49.2 |
| | Timothy S. Hogan (D) | 423,742 | 39.6 |
| | Arthur L. Garford (PROG) | 67,509 | 6.3 |
| 1920 | Frank B. Willis (R) | 1,134,953 | 59.1 |
| | W. A. Julian (D) | 782,650 | 40.8 |
| 1926 | Frank B. Willis (R) | 711,359 | 53.2 |
| | Atlee Pomerene (D) | 623,221 | 46.6 |

### Special Election

| | | | |
|---|---|---|---|
| 1928 | Theodore E. Burton (R) | 1,429,534 | 62.4 |
| | Graham P. Hunt (D) | 856,807 | 37.4 |

### Special Election

| | | | |
|---|---|---|---|
| 1930 | Robert J. Bulkley (D) | 1,046,561# | 54.8 |
| | Roscoe C. McCulloch (R) | 863,944# | 45.2 |

| | | | |
|---|---|---|---|
| 1932 | Robert J. Bulkley (D) | 1,290,175 | 52.5 |
| | Gilbert Bettman (R) | 1,126,830 | 45.8 |
| 1938 | Robert A. Taft (R) | 1,257,412 | 53.6 |
| | Robert J. Bulkley (D) | 1,086,815 | 46.4 |
| 1944 | Robert A. Taft (R) | 1,500,809 | 50.3 |
| | William G. Pickrel (D) | 1,483,069 | 49.7 |
| 1950 | Robert A. Taft (R) | 1,645,643 | 57.5 |
| | Joseph T. Ferguson (D) | 1,214,459 | 42.5 |

| | Candidates | Votes | % |
|---|---|---|---|
| **Special Election** | | | |
| 1954 | George H. Bender (R) | 1,257,874 | 50.1 |
| | Thomas A. Burke (D) | 1,254,899 | 49.9 |
| 1956 | Frank J. Lausche (D) | 1,864,589 | 52.9 |
| | George H. Bender (R) | 1,660,910 | 47.1 |
| 1962 | Frank J. Lausche (D) | 1,843,813 | 61.6 |
| | John Marshall Briley (R) | 1,151,292 | 38.4 |
| 1968 | William B. Saxbe (R) | 1,928,964 | 51.5 |
| | John J. Gilligan (D) | 1,814,152 | 48.5 |
| 1974 | John Glenn (D) | 1,930,670 | 64.6 |
| | Ralph J. Perk (R) | 918,133 | 30.7 |
| 1980 | John Glenn (D) | 2,770,786 | 68.8 |
| | James E. Betts (R) | 1,137,695 | 28.2 |
| 1986 | John Glenn (D) | 1,949,208 | 62.5 |
| | Thomas N. Kindness (R) | 1,171,893 | 37.5 |
| 1992 | John Glenn (D) | 2,444,419 | 51.0 |
| | Mike DeWine (R) | 2,028,300 | 42.3 |
| | Martha K. Grevatt (I) | 321,234 | 6.7 |

## OKLAHOMA

| | Candidates | Votes | % |
|---|---|---|---|
| | **Class 2** | | |
| 1912 | Robert L. Owen (D) | 126,407 | 50.4 |
| | Dickerson (R) | 83,448 | 33.3 |
| 1918 | Robert L. Owen (D) | 105,050 | 55.4 |
| | Johnson (R) | 77,188 | 40.7 |
| 1924 | William B. Pine (R) | 341,720 | 61.6 |
| | John Calloway Walton (D) | 196,527 | 35.4 |
| 1930 | Thomas P. Gore (D) | 255,838 | 52.3 |
| | William B. Pine (R) | 232,589 | 47.5 |
| 1936 | Josh Lee (D) | 493,407 | 68.0 |
| | Herbert K. Hyde (R) | 229,004 | 31.6 |
| 1942 | Edward H. Moore (R) | 204,163 | 54.8 |
| | Josh Lee (D) | 166,653 | 44.8 |
| 1948 | Robert S. Kerr (D) | 441,654 | 62.3 |
| | Ross Rizley (R) | 265,169 | 37.4 |
| 1954 | Robert S. Kerr (D) | 335,127 | 55.8 |
| | Fred M. Mock (R) | 262,013 | 43.7 |
| 1960 | Robert S. Kerr (D) | 474,116 | 54.8 |
| | B. Hayden Crawford (R) | 385,646 | 44.6 |
| **Special Election** | | | |
| 1964 | Fred R. Harris (D) | 466,782 | 51.2 |
| | Bud Wilkinson (R) | 445,392 | 48.8 |
| 1966 | Fred R. Harris (D) | 343,157 | 53.7 |
| | Pat J. Patterson (R) | 295,585 | 46.3 |
| 1972 | Dewey F. Bartlett (R) | 516,934 | 51.4 |
| | Ed Edmondson (D) | 478,212 | 47.6 |
| 1978 | David L. Boren (D) | 493,953 | 65.5 |
| | Robert B. Kamm (R) | 247,857 | 32.9 |
| 1984 | David L. Boren (D) | 906,131 | 75.6 |
| | Will E. Crozier (R) | 280,638 | 23.4 |
| 1990 | David L. Boren (D) | 735,684 | 83.2 |
| | Stephen Jones (R) | 148,814 | 16.8 |
| | **Class 3** | | |
| 1914 | Thomas P. Gore (D) | 119,443 | 48.0 |
| | Burford (R) | 73,292 | 29.4 |
| | P. S. Nagle (SOC) | 52,259 | 21.0 |
| 1920 | John W. Harreld (R) | 247,721 | 50.6 |

| | Candidates | Votes | % |
|---|---|---|---|
| | Scott Ferris (D) | 218,371 | 44.6 |
| 1926 | Elmer Thomas (D) | 195,307 | 54.8 |
| | John W. Harreld (R) | 159,287 | 44.7 |
| 1932 | Elmer Thomas (D) | 426,130 | 65.6 |
| | Wirt Franklin (R) | 218,854 | 33.7 |
| 1938 | Elmer Thomas (D) | 307,936 | 65.4 |
| | Harry G. Glasser (R) | 159,734 | 33.9 |
| 1944 | Elmer Thomas (D) | 390,851 | 55.7 |
| | William J. Otjen (R) | 309,222 | 44.0 |
| 1950 | A. S. Mike Monroney (D) | 345,953 | 54.8 |
| | W. H. (Bill) Alexander (R) | 285,224 | 45.2 |
| 1956 | A. S. Mike Monroney (D) | 459,996 | 55.4 |
| | Douglas McKeever (R) | 371,146 | 44.7 |
| 1962 | A. S. Mike Monroney (D) | 353,890 | 53.2 |
| | B. Hayden Crawford (R) | 307,966 | 46.3 |
| 1968 | Henry Bellmon (R) | 470,120 | 51.7 |
| | A. S. Mike Monroney (D) | 419,658 | 46.2 |
| 1974 | Henry Bellmon (R) | 390,997 | 49.4 |
| | Ed Edmondson (D) | 387,162 | 48.9 |
| 1980 | Don Nickles (R) | 587,252 | 53.5 |
| | Andrew Coats (D) | 478,283 | 43.5 |
| 1986 | Don Nickles (R) | 493,436 | 55.2 |
| | James R. Jones (D) | 400,230 | 44.8 |
| 1992 | Don Nickles (R) | 757,876 | 58.5 |
| | Steve Lewis (D) | 494,350 | 38.2 |

## OREGON

| | Candidates | Votes | % |
|---|---|---|---|
| | **Class 2** | | |
| 1912 | Harry Lane (D) | 40,172 | 30.1 |
| | Ben Selling (R) | 38,453 | 28.8 |
| | Jonathan Bourne Jr. (POPU GOV) | 25,929 | 19.4 |
| | B. F. Ramp (SOC) | 11,093 | 8.3 |
| | A. E. Clark (PROG) | 11,083 | 8.3 |
| | B. Lee Paget (P) | 6,848 | 5.1 |
| 1918 | Charles L. McNary (R) | 82,360 | 54.2 |
| | Oswald West (D) | 64,303 | 42.3 |
| **Special Election** | | | |
| 1918 | Fred W. Mulkey (R) | 103,913 | 84.5 |
| | Martha E. Bean (SOC) | 19,014 | 15.5 |
| 1924 | Charles L. McNary (R) | 174,672 | 66.0 |
| | Milton A. Miller (D) | 65,340 | 24.7 |
| | F. E. Coulter (PROG) | 20,379 | 7.7 |
| 1930 | Charles L. McNary (R) | 137,231 | 58.1 |
| | Elton Watkins (D) | 66,028 | 27.9 |
| | L. A. Banks (I) | 17,488 | 7.4 |
| 1936 | Charles L. McNary (R) | 199,332 | 49.7 |
| | Willis Mahoney (D) | 193,822 | 48.3 |
| 1942 | Charles L. McNary (R) | 214,755 | 77.1 |
| | Walter W. Whitbeck (D) | 63,946 | 22.9 |
| **Special Election** | | | |
| 1944 | Guy Cordon (R) | 260,631 | 57.5 |
| | Willis Mahoney (D) | 192,305 | 42.5 |
| 1948 | Guy Cordon (R) | 299,295 | 60.0 |
| | Manley J. Wilson (D) | 199,275 | 40.0 |
| 1954 | Richard L. Neuberger (D) | 285,775 | 50.2 |
| | Guy Cordon (R) | 283,313 | 49.8 |
| 1960 | Maurine B. Neuberger (D) | 412,757 | 54.6 |

| Candidates | Votes | % |
|---|---|---|
| Elmo Smith (R) | 343,009 | 45.4 |

Special Election

| | Candidates | Votes | % |
|---|---|---|---|
| 1960 | Maurine B. Neuberger (D) | 422,024 | 55.0 |
| | Elmo Smith (R) | 345,464 | 45.0 |
| 1966 | Mark O. Hatfield (R) | 354,391 | 51.7 |
| | Robert B. Duncan (D) | 330,374 | 48.2 |
| 1972 | Mark O. Hatfield (R) | 494,671 | 53.7 |
| | Wayne Morse (D) | 425,036 | 46.2 |
| 1978 | Mark O. Hatfield (R) | 550,165 | 61.6 |
| | Vernon Cook (D) | 341,616 | 38.3 |
| 1984 | Mark O. Hatfield (R) | 808,152 | 66.5 |
| | Margie Hendricksen (D) | 406,122 | 33.4 |
| 1990 | Mark O. Hatfield (R) | 590,095 | 53.7 |
| | Harry Lonsdale (D) | 507,743 | 46.2 |

### Class 3

| | | | |
|---|---|---|---|
| 1908 | George E. Chamberlain (D) | 52,421 | 46.7 |
| | H. M. Cake (R) | 50,899 | 45.3 |
| 1914 | George E. Chamberlain (D) | 111,748 | 45.5 |
| | R. A. Booth (R) | 88,297 | 36.0 |
| | William Hanley (PROG) | 26,220 | 10.7 |
| 1920 | Robert N. Stanfield (R) | 116,696 | 50.7 |
| | George E. Chamberlain (D) | 100,124 | 43.5 |
| 1926 | Frederick Steiwer (R) | 89,007 | 39.8 |
| | Bert E. Haney (D) | 81,301 | 36.3 |
| | Robert N. Stanfield (I) | 50,246 | 22.5 |
| 1932 | Frederick Steiwer (R) | 186,210 | 52.7 |
| | Walter B. Gleason (D) | 137,237 | 38.9 |
| 1938 | Rufus C. Holman (R) | 203,120 | 54.9 |
| | Willis Mahoney (D) | 167,135 | 45.1 |

Special Election

| | | | |
|---|---|---|---|
| 1938 | Alexander G. Barry (R) | 180,815 | 54.2 |
| | Robert A. Miller (D) | 152,773 | 45.8 |
| 1944 | Wayne Morse (R) | 269,095 | 60.7 |
| | Edgar W. Smith (D) | 174,140 | 39.3 |
| 1950 | Wayne Morse (R) | 376,510 | 74.8 |
| | Howard Latourette (D) | 116,780 | 23.2 |
| 1956 | Wayne Morse (D) | 396,849 | 54.2 |
| | Douglas McKay (R) | 335,405 | 45.8 |
| 1962 | Wayne Morse (D) | 344,716 | 54.2 |
| | Sig Unander (R) | 291,587 | 45.8 |
| 1968 | Bob Packwood (R) | 408,825 | 50.2 |
| | Wayne Morse (D) | 405,380 | 49.8 |
| 1974 | Bob Packwood (R) | 420,984 | 54.9 |
| | Betty Roberts (D) | 338,591 | 44.2 |
| 1980 | Bob Packwood (R) | 594,290 | 52.1 |
| | Ted Kulongoski (D) | 501,963 | 44.0 |
| 1986 | Bob Packwood (R) | 656,317 | 63.0 |
| | Rick Bauman (D) | 375,735 | 36.0 |
| 1992 | Bob Packwood (R) | 717,455 | 52.1 |
| | Les AuCoin (D) | 639,851 | 46.5 |

# PENNSYLVANIA

| Candidates | Votes | % |
|---|---|---|

### Class 1

| | | | |
|---|---|---|---|
| 1916 | Philander C. Knox (R, RO PROG) | 680,447 | 56.3 |
| | Ellis L. Orvis (D) | 450,112 | 37.3 |
| 1922 | David A. Reed (R) | 802,146 | 56.0 |

| Candidates | Votes | % |
|---|---|---|
| Samuel E. Shull (D) | 423,583 | 29.6 |
| William J. Burke (PROG) | 127,180 | 8.9 |

Special Election

| | Candidates | Votes | % |
|---|---|---|---|
| 1922 | David A. Reed (R) | 860,483# | 86.1 |
| | Rachel C. Robinson (P) | 60,390# | 6.0 |
| | William J. VanEssen (SOC) | 55,703# | 5.6 |
| 1928 | David A. Reed (R) | 1,948,646 | 64.4 |
| | William N. McNair (D) | 1,029,055 | 34.0 |
| 1934 | Joseph F. Guffey (D) | 1,494,001 | 50.8 |
| | David A. Reed (R) | 1,366,877 | 46.5 |
| 1940 | Joseph F. Guffey (D) | 2,069,980 | 51.8 |
| | Jay Cooke (R) | 1,893,104 | 47.4 |
| 1946 | Edward Martin (R) | 1,853,458 | 59.3 |
| | Joseph F. Guffey (D) | 1,245,338 | 39.8 |
| 1952 | Edward Martin (R) | 2,331,034 | 51.6 |
| | Guy Kurtz Bard (D) | 2,168,546 | 48.0 |
| 1958 | Hugh Scott (R) | 2,042,586 | 51.2 |
| | George M. Leader (D) | 1,929,821 | 48.4 |
| 1964 | Hugh Scott (R) | 2,429,858 | 50.6 |
| | Genevieve Blatt (D) | 2,359,223 | 49.1 |
| 1970 | Hugh Scott (R) | 1,874,106 | 51.4 |
| | William G. Sesler (D) | 1,653,774 | 45.4 |
| 1976 | John Heinz (R) | 2,381,891 | 52.4 |
| | William J. Green III (R) | 2,126,977 | 46.8 |
| 1982 | John Heinz (R) | 2,136,418 | 59.3 |
| | Cyril H. Wecht (D) | 1,412,965 | 39.2 |
| 1988 | John Heinz (R) | 2,901,715 | 66.5 |
| | Joseph C. Vignola (D) | 1,416,764 | 32.4 |

Special Election

| | | | |
|---|---|---|---|
| 1991 | Harris Wofford (D) | 1,860,760 | 55.0 |
| | Dick Thornburgh (R) | 1,521,986 | 45.0 |

### Class 3

| | | | |
|---|---|---|---|
| 1914 | Boies Penrose (R, PERS LIB) | 519,801 | 46.8 |
| | Gifford Pinchot (WASH, B MOOSE) | 269,175 | 24.2 |
| | A. Mitchell Palmer (D) | 266,415 | 24.0 |
| 1920 | Boies Penrose (R) | 1,068,985 | 59.9 |
| | John A. Farrell (D) | 484,862 | 27.2 |
| | Leah Cobb Marion (P) | 132,610 | 7.4 |

Special Election

| | | | |
|---|---|---|---|
| 1922 | George Wharton Pepper (R) | 819,507 | 57.6 |
| | Fred B. Kerr (D) | 468,330 | 32.9 |
| 1926 | William S. Vare (R) | 822,187* | 54.6 |
| | William B. Wilson (D, LAB) | 648,680 | 43.1 |

Special Election

| | | | |
|---|---|---|---|
| 1930 | James J. Davis (R) | 1,462,186 | 71.5 |
| | Sedgwick Kistler (D) | 523,338 | 25.6 |
| 1932 | James J. Davis (R) | 1,371,844 | 49.3 |
| | Lawrence H. Rupp (D) | 1,200,767 | 43.2 |
| 1938 | James J. Davis (R) | 2,086,932 | 54.7 |
| | George H. Earle (D, ROYAL OAK) | 1,694,464 | 44.4 |
| 1944 | Francis J. Myers (D) | 1,864,735 | 50.0 |
| | James J. Davis (R) | 1,840,943 | 49.4 |
| 1950 | James H. Duff (R) | 1,820,400 | 51.3 |
| | Francis J. Myers (D) | 1,694,076 | 47.7 |
| 1956 | Joseph S. Clark (D) | 2,268,641 | 50.1 |
| | James H. Duff (R) | 2,250,671 | 49.7 |

| | Candidates | Votes | % |
|---|---|---|---|
| 1962 | Joseph S. Clark (D) | 2,238,383 | *51.1* |
| | James E. Van Zandt (R) | 2,134,649 | *48.7* |
| 1968 | Richard S. Schweiker (R) | 2,399,762 | *51.9* |
| | Joseph S. Clark (D) | 2,117,662 | *45.8* |
| 1974 | Richard S. Schweiker (R) | 1,843,317 | *53.0* |
| | Peter Flaherty (D) | 1,596,121 | *45.9* |
| 1980 | Arlen Specter (R) | 2,230,404 | *50.5* |
| | Peter Flaherty (D) | 2,122,391 | *48.0* |
| 1986 | Arlen Specter (R) | 1,906,537 | *56.4* |
| | Bob Edgar (D) | 1,448,219 | *42.9* |
| 1992 | Arlen Specter (R) | 2,358,125 | *49.1* |
| | Lynn Yeakel (D) | 2,224,966 | *46.3* |

## RHODE ISLAND

| | Candidates | Votes | % |
|---|---|---|---|

### Class 1

| | | Votes | % |
|---|---|---|---|
| 1916 | Peter G. Gerry (D) | 47,048 | *52.9* |
| | Henry Lippitt (R) | 39,211 | *44.1* |
| 1922 | Peter G. Gerry (D) | 82,889 | *52.2* |
| | R. Livingston Beeckman (R) | 68,930 | *43.4* |
| 1928 | Felix Hebert (R) | 119,228 | *50.6* |
| | Peter G. Gerry (D) | 116,234 | *49.3* |
| 1934 | Peter G. Gerry (D) | 140,700 | *57.1* |
| | Felix Hebert (R) | 105,545 | *42.9* |
| 1940 | Peter G. Gerry (D) | 173,847 | *55.2* |
| | James O. McManus (R) | 141,312 | *44.8* |
| 1946 | J. Howard McGrath (D) | 150,748 | *55.1* |
| | W. Gurnee Dyer (R) | 122,780 | *44.9* |

Special Election

| | | | |
|---|---|---|---|
| 1950 | John O. Pastore (D) | 184,520 | *61.6* |
| | Austin T. Levy (R) | 114,890 | *38.4* |

| | | | |
|---|---|---|---|
| 1952 | John O. Pastore (D) | 225,128 | *54.8* |
| | Bayard Ewing (R, CLEAN GV) | 185,850 | *45.2* |
| 1958 | John O. Pastore (D) | 222,166 | *64.5* |
| | Bayard Ewing (R) | 122,353 | *35.5* |
| 1964 | John O. Pastore (D) | 319,607 | *82.7* |
| | Ronald R. Lagueux (R) | 66,715 | *17.3* |
| 1970 | John O. Pastore (D) | 230,469 | *67.5* |
| | John McLaughlin (R) | 107,351 | *31.5* |
| 1976 | John H. Chafee (R) | 230,329 | *57.7* |
| | Richard P. Lorber (D) | 167,665 | *42.0* |
| 1982 | John H. Chafee (R) | 175,495 | *51.2* |
| | Julius C. Michaelson (D) | 167,283 | *48.8* |
| 1988 | John H. Chafee (R) | 217,273 | *54.6* |
| | Richard A. Licht (D) | 180,717 | *45.4* |

### Class 2

| | | | |
|---|---|---|---|
| 1918 | LeBaron B. Colt (R) | 42,055 | *51.8* |
| | George O'Shaunessy (D) | 37,573 | *46.2* |
| 1924 | Jesse H. Metcalf (R) | 120,815 | *57.6* |
| | William S. Flynn (D) | 87,620 | *41.8* |

Special Election

| | | | |
|---|---|---|---|
| 1924 | Jesse H. Metcalf (R) | 116,572 | *56.4* |
| | William S. Flynn (D) | 88,138 | *42.6* |

| | | | |
|---|---|---|---|
| 1930 | Jesse H. Metcalf (R) | 112,202 | *50.3* |
| | Peter G. Gerry (D) | 109,687 | *49.2* |
| 1936 | Theodore F. Green (D) | 149,157 | *48.6* |
| | Jesse H. Metcalf (R) | 136,174 | *44.4* |

| | Candidates | Votes | % |
|---|---|---|---|
| | Lapointe (UN) | 21,501 | *7.0* |
| 1942 | Theodore F. Green (D) | 138,239 | *58.0* |
| | Ira Lloyd Letts (R) | 100,236 | *42.0* |
| 1948 | Theodore F. Green (D) | 190,284 | *59.3* |
| | Thomas P. Hazard (R) | 130,668 | *40.7* |
| 1954 | Theodore F. Green (D) | 193,654 | *59.3* |
| | Walter I. Sundlun (R) | 132,970 | *40.7* |
| 1960 | Claiborne Pell (D) | 275,575 | *68.9* |
| | Raoul Archambault (R) | 124,408 | *31.1* |
| 1966 | Claiborne Pell (D) | 219,331 | *67.7* |
| | Ruth M. Briggs (R) | 104,838 | *32.3* |
| 1972 | Claiborne Pell (D) | 221,942 | *53.7* |
| | John H. Chafee (R) | 188,990 | *45.7* |
| 1978 | Claiborne Pell (D) | 229,557 | *75.1* |
| | James G. Reynolds (R) | 76,061 | *24.9* |
| 1984 | Claiborne Pell (D) | 286,780 | *72.6* |
| | Barbara Leonard (R) | 108,492 | *27.4* |
| 1990 | Claiborne Pell (D) | 225,105 | *61.8* |
| | Claudine Schneider (R) | 138,947 | *38.2* |

## SOUTH CAROLINA

| | Candidates | Votes | % |
|---|---|---|---|

### Class 2

| | | | |
|---|---|---|---|
| 1918 | Nathaniel B. Dial (D) | 25,792 | *100.0* |

Special Election

| | | | |
|---|---|---|---|
| 1918 | William P. Pollock (D) | ✔ | |

| | | | |
|---|---|---|---|
| 1924 | Coleman L. Blease (D) | 49,060 | *100.0* |
| 1930 | James F. Byrnes (D) | 16,213 | *100.0* |
| 1936 | James F. Byrnes (D) | 113,696 | *98.6* |

Special Election

| | | | |
|---|---|---|---|
| 1941 | Burnet R. Maybank (D) | ✔ | |

| | | | |
|---|---|---|---|
| 1942 | Burnet R. Maybank (D) | 23,356 | *100.0* |
| 1948 | Burnet R. Maybank (D) | 135,998 | *96.5* |
| 1954 | Strom Thurmond (WRITE IN) | 143,442 | *63.1* |
| | Edgar A. Brown (D) | 83,525 | *36.8* |

Special Election

| | | | |
|---|---|---|---|
| 1956 | Strom Thurmond (D) | 245,371 | *100.0* |

| | | | |
|---|---|---|---|
| 1960 | Strom Thurmond (D) | 330,164 | *100.0* |
| 1966 | Strom Thurmond (R) | 271,297 | *62.2* |
| | Bradley Morrah (D) | 164,955 | *37.8* |
| 1972 | Strom Thurmond (R) | 415,806 | *63.3* |
| | Eugene N. Zeigler (D) | 241,056 | *36.7* |
| 1978 | Strom Thurmond (R) | 351,733 | *55.6* |
| | Charles D. Ravenel (D) | 281,119 | *44.4* |
| 1984 | Strom Thurmond (R) | 644,815 | *66.8* |
| | Melvin Purvis Jr. (R) | 306,982 | *31.8* |
| 1990 | Strom Thurmond (R) | 482,032 | *64.2* |
| | Bob Cunningham (D) | 244,112 | *32.5* |

### Class 3

| | | | |
|---|---|---|---|
| 1914 | Ellison D. Smith (D) | 32,950 | *99.8* |
| 1920 | Ellison D. Smith (D) | 64,388 | *100.0* |
| 1926 | Ellison D. Smith (D) | 14,560 | *100.0* |
| 1932 | Ellison D. Smith (D) | 104,472 | *98.1* |
| 1938 | Ellison D. Smith (D) | 45,751 | *98.9* |

| | Candidates | Votes | % |
|---|---|---|---|
| 1944 | Olin D. Johnston (D) | 94,556 | 92.9 |
| 1950 | Olin D. Johnston (D) | 50,240 | 99.9 |
| 1956 | Olin D. Johnston (D) | 230,150 | 82.2 |
| | L. P. Crawford (R) | 49,695 | 17.8 |
| 1962 | Olin D. Johnston (D) | 178,712 | 57.2 |
| | W. D. Workman Jr. (R) | 133,930 | 42.8 |

**Special Election**

| | | | |
|---|---|---|---|
| 1966 | Ernest F. Hollings (D) | 223,790 | 51.4 |
| | Marshall Parker (R) | 212,032 | 48.7 |

| | | | |
|---|---|---|---|
| 1968 | Ernest F. Hollings (D) | 404,060 | 61.9 |
| | Marshall Parker (R) | 248,780 | 38.1 |
| 1974 | Ernest F. Hollings (D) | 356,126 | 69.5 |
| | Gwenyfred Bush (R) | 146,645 | 28.6 |
| 1980 | Ernest F. Hollings (D) | 612,554 | 70.4 |
| | Marshall T. Mays (R) | 257,946 | 29.6 |
| 1986 | Ernest F. Hollings (D) | 465,500 | 63.1 |
| | Henry D. McMaster (R) | 262,886 | 35.6 |
| 1992 | Ernest F. Hollings (D) | 591,030 | 50.1 |
| | Thomas F. Hartnett (R) | 554,175 | 46.9 |

# SOUTH DAKOTA

| | Candidates | Votes | % |
|---|---|---|---|

**Class 2**

| | | | |
|---|---|---|---|
| 1918 | Thomas Sterling (R) | 51,198 | 55.1 |
| | Rinehart (D) | 36,210 | 39.0 |
| | Rafferty (I) | 5,560 | 6.0 |
| 1924 | William H. McMaster (R) | 90,006 | 44.1 |
| | U. S. G. Cherry (D) | 63,548 | 31.2 |
| | Tom Ayres (F-LAB) | 21,136 | 10.4 |
| | George W. Egan (I) | 14,484 | 7.1 |
| 1930 | William J. Bulow (D) | 106,317 | 51.6 |
| | William H. McMaster (R) | 99,595 | 48.4 |
| 1936 | William J. Bulow (D) | 141,509 | 48.8 |
| | Chandler Gurney (R) | 135,461 | 46.8 |
| 1942 | Harlan J. Bushfield (R) | 106,704 | 58.7 |
| | Tom Berry (D) | 74,945 | 41.3 |
| 1948 | Karl E. Mundt (R) | 144,084 | 59.3 |
| | John A. Engel (D) | 98,749 | 40.7 |
| 1954 | Karl E. Mundt (R) | 135,071 | 57.3 |
| | Kenneth Holum (D) | 100,674 | 42.7 |
| 1960 | Karl E. Mundt (R) | 160,181 | 52.4 |
| | George McGovern (D) | 145,261 | 47.6 |
| 1966 | Karl E. Mundt (R) | 150,517 | 66.3 |
| | Donn H. Wright (D) | 76,563 | 33.7 |
| 1972 | James Abourezk (D) | 174,773 | 57.0 |
| | Robert W. Hirsch (R) | 131,613 | 42.9 |
| 1978 | Larry Pressler (R) | 170,832 | 66.8 |
| | Don Barnett (D) | 84,767 | 33.2 |
| 1984 | Larry Pressler (R) | 235,176 | 74.5 |
| | George V. Cunningham (D) | 80,537 | 25.5 |
| 1990 | Larry Pressler (R) | 135,682 | 52.4 |
| | Ted Muenster (D) | 116,727 | 45.1 |

**Class 3**

| | | | |
|---|---|---|---|
| 1914 | Edwin S. Johnson (D) | 47,668 | 48.1 |
| | Charles H. Burke (R) | 44,244 | 44.7 |
| 1920 | Peter Norbeck (R) | 92,267 | 50.1 |
| | Tom Ayres (NON PART) | 44,309 | 24.1 |
| | U. S. G. Cherry (D) | 36,833 | 20.0 |
| | R. O. Richards (I) | 10,032 | 5.5 |
| 1926 | Peter Norbeck (R) | 105,756 | 59.5 |

| | Candidates | Votes | % |
|---|---|---|---|
| | C. J. Gunderson (D) | 59,128 | 33.3 |
| | Howard Platt (F-LAB) | 12,797 | 7.2 |
| 1932 | Peter Norbeck (R) | 151,845 | 53.8 |
| | U. S. G. Cherry (D) | 125,731 | 44.6 |
| 1938 | Chandler Gurney (R) | 146,813 | 52.5 |
| | Tom Berry (D) | 133,064 | 47.5 |

**Special Election**

| | | | |
|---|---|---|---|
| 1938 | Gladys Pyle (R) | 155,292 | 58.1 |
| | John T. McCullen Sr. (D) | 112,177 | 41.9 |
| 1944 | Chandler Gurney (R) | 145,248 | 63.9 |
| | George M. Bradshaw (D) | 82,199 | 36.1 |
| 1950 | Francis Case (R) | 160,670 | 63.9 |
| | John A. Engel (D) | 90,692 | 36.1 |
| 1956 | Francis Case (R) | 147,621 | 50.8 |
| | Kenneth Holum (D) | 143,001 | 49.2 |
| 1962 | George McGovern (D) | 127,458 | 50.1 |
| | Joe Bottum (R) | 126,861 | 49.9 |
| 1968 | George McGovern (D) | 158,961 | 56.8 |
| | Archie Gubbrud (R) | 120,951 | 43.2 |
| 1974 | George McGovern (D) | 147,929 | 53.0 |
| | Leo K. Thorsness (R) | 130,955 | 47.0 |
| 1980 | James Abdnor (R) | 190,594 | 58.2 |
| | George McGovern (D) | 129,018 | 39.4 |
| 1986 | Thomas Daschle (D) | 152,657 | 51.6 |
| | James Abdnor (R) | 143,173 | 48.4 |
| 1992 | Thomas Daschle (D) | 217,095 | 64.9 |
| | Charlene Haar (R) | 108,733 | 32.5 |

# TENNESSEE

| | Candidates | Votes | % |
|---|---|---|---|

**Class 1**

| | | | |
|---|---|---|---|
| 1916 | Kenneth D. McKellar (D) | 143,718 | 54.4 |
| | Ben W. Hooper (R) | 118,174 | 44.8 |
| 1922 | Kenneth D. McKellar (D) | 151,523 | 68.0 |
| | Newell Sanders (R) | 71,199 | 32.0 |
| 1928 | Kenneth D. McKellar (D) | 175,431 | 59.3 |
| | J. A. Fowler (R) | 120,289 | 40.7 |
| 1934 | Kenneth D. McKellar (D) | 195,430 | 63.4 |
| | Ben W. Hooper (R) | 110,401 | 35.8 |
| 1940 | Kenneth D. McKellar (D) | 295,440 | 70.8 |
| | Howard Baker (R) | 121,790 | 29.2 |
| 1946 | Kenneth D. McKellar (D) | 145,654 | 66.6 |
| | W. B. Ladd (R) | 57,237 | 26.2 |
| | John R. Neal (I) | 11,516 | 5.3 |
| 1952 | Albert Gore (D) | 545,432 | 74.2 |
| | Hobart F. Atkins (R) | 153,479 | 20.9 |
| 1958 | Albert Gore (D) | 317,324 | 79.0 |
| | Hobart F. Atkins (R) | 76,371 | 19.0 |
| 1964 | Albert Gore (D) | 570,542 | 53.6 |
| | Dan H. Kuykendall (R) | 493,475 | 46.4 |
| 1970 | Bill Brock (R) | 562,645 | 51.3 |
| | Albert Gore (D) | 519,858 | 47.4 |
| 1976 | Jim Sasser (D) | 751,180 | 52.5 |
| | Bill Brock (R) | 673,231 | 47.0 |
| 1982 | Jim Sasser (D) | 780,113 | 61.9 |
| | Robin L. Beard (D) | 479,642 | 38.1 |
| 1988 | Jim Sasser (D) | 1,020,061 | 65.1 |
| | Bill Andersen (R) | 541,033 | 34.5 |

| | Candidates | Votes | % |
|---|---|---|---|
| | **Class 2** | | |
| 1918 | John K. Shields (D) | 98,605 | 62.2 |
| | H. Clay Evans (R) | 59,989 | 37.8 |
| 1924 | Lawrence D. Tyson (D) | 147,821 | 57.3 |
| | H. B. Lindsay (R) | 109,863 | 42.6 |
| 1930 | Cordell Hull (D) | 154,071 | 71.3 |
| | Paul E. Divine (R) | 58,550 | 27.1 |

**Special Election**

| 1930 | William E. Brock (D) | 144,021 | 74.4 |
|---|---|---|---|
| | F. Todd Meacham (R) | 49,634 | 25.6 |

**Special Election**

| 1934 | Nathan L. Bachman (D) | 200,249 | 80.1 |
|---|---|---|---|
| | John R. Neal (I) | 49,773 | 19.9 |
| 1936 | Nathan L. Bachman (D) | 273,298 | 76.4 |
| | Dwayne D. Maddox (R) | 67,238 | 18.8 |

**Special Election**

| 1938 | A. Tom Stewart (D) | 194,026 | 70.5 |
|---|---|---|---|
| | Harley G. Fowler (R) | 72,098 | 26.2 |
| 1942 | A. Tom Stewart (D) | 109,881 | 68.9 |
| | F. Todd Meacham (R) | 34,324 | 21.5 |
| | John R. Neal (I) | 15,317 | 9.6 |
| 1948 | Estes Kefauver (D) | 326,062 | 65.3 |
| | B. Carroll Reece (R) | 166,947 | 33.5 |
| 1954 | Estes Kefauver (D) | 249,121 | 70.0 |
| | Tom Wall (R) | 106,971 | 30.0 |
| 1960 | Estes Kefauver (D) | 594,460 | 71.8 |
| | A. Bradley Frazier (R) | 234,053 | 28.3 |

**Special Election**

| 1964 | Ross Bass (D) | 568,905 | 52.1 |
|---|---|---|---|
| | Howard H. Baker Jr. (R) | 517,330 | 47.4 |
| 1966 | Howard H. Baker Jr. (R) | 483,063 | 55.7 |
| | Frank G. Clement (D) | 383,843 | 44.3 |
| 1972 | Howard H. Baker Jr. (R) | 716,539 | 61.6 |
| | Ray Blanton (D) | 440,599 | 37.9 |
| 1978 | Howard H. Baker Jr. (R) | 642,644 | 55.5 |
| | Jane Eskind (D) | 466,228 | 40.3 |
| 1984 | Albert Gore Jr. (D) | 1,000,607 | 60.7 |
| | Victor Ashe (R) | 557,016 | 33.8 |
| | Ed McAteer (I) | 87,234 | 5.3 |
| 1990 | Albert Gore Jr. (D) | 530,898 | 67.7 |
| | William R. Hawkins (R) | 233,703 | 29.8 |

# TEXAS

| | Candidates | Votes | % |
|---|---|---|---|
| | **Class 1** | | |
| 1916 | Charles A. Culberson (D) | 303,035 | 81.3 |
| | Alex W. Atcheson (R) | 48,788 | 13.1 |
| 1922 | Earle B. Mayfield (D) | 261,063 | 66.6 |
| | George E. B. Peddy (R) | 130,731 | 33.4 |
| 1928 | Tom Connally (D) | 566,139 | 81.2 |
| | T.M. Kennerly (R) | 130,172 | 18.7 |
| 1934 | Tom Connally (D) | 437,254 | 96.7 |

| | Candidates | Votes | % |
|---|---|---|---|
| 1940 | Tom Connally (D) | 993,974 | 94.3 |
| | George I. Shannon (R) | 60,051 | 5.7 |
| 1946 | Tom Connally (D) | 336,931 | 88.5 |
| | Murray C. Sells (R) | 43,619 | 11.5 |
| 1952 | Price Daniel (D, R) | 1,894,671 | 100.0 |

**Special Election**

| 1957 | Ralph Yarborough (D) | 364,878 | 38.1 |
|---|---|---|---|
| | Martin Dies (D) | 290,869 | 30.4 |
| | Thad Hutcheson (R) | 219,591 | 22.9 |
| 1958 | Ralph Yarborough (D) | 587,030 | 74.6 |
| | Roy Whittenburg (R) | 185,926 | 23.6 |
| 1964 | Ralph Yarborough (D) | 1,463,958 | 56.2 |
| | George Bush (R) | 1,134,337 | 43.6 |
| 1970 | Lloyd Bentsen (D) | 1,193,814 | 53.5 |
| | George Bush (R) | 1,036,045 | 46.4 |
| 1976 | Lloyd Bentsen (D) | 2,199,956 | 56.8 |
| | Alan Steelman (R) | 1,636,370 | 42.2 |
| 1982 | Lloyd Bentsen (D) | 1,818,223 | 58.6 |
| | James M. Collins (R) | 1,256,759 | 40.5 |

**Special Primary [1]**

| 1993 | Kay Bailey Hutchison (R) | 593,338 | 29.0 |
|---|---|---|---|
| | Bob Krueger (D) | 593,239 | 29.0 |
| | Joe L. Barton (R) | 284,135 | 13.9 |
| | Jack Fields (R) | 277,560 | 13.6 |
| | Richard Fisher (D) | 165,564 | 8.1 |

**Special Runoff Election [1]**

| 1993 | Kay Bailey Hutchison (R) | 1,188,716 | 67.3 |
|---|---|---|---|
| | Bob Krueger (D) | 576,538 | 32.7 |

| | **Class 2** | | |
|---|---|---|---|
| 1918 | Morris Sheppard (D) | 155,178 | 86.7 |
| | J. Webs Flanagan (R) | 22,214 | 12.4 |
| 1924 | Morris Sheppard (D) | 592,057 | 85.4 |
| | T. M. Kennerly (R) | 101,252 | 14.6 |
| 1930 | Morris Sheppard (D) | 266,562 | 86.9 |
| | D. J. Haesly (R) | 39,053 | 12.7 |
| 1936 | Morris Sheppard (D) | 773,574 | 92.6 |
| | Carlos G. Watson (R) | 59,491 | 7.1 |

**Special Election**

| 1941 | W. Lee O'Daniel (D) | 175,590 | 30.5 |
|---|---|---|---|
| | Lyndon B. Johnson (D) | 174,284 | 30.3 |
| | Gerald C. Mann (D) | 140,807 | 24.5 |
| | Martin Dies (D) | 80,551 | 14.0 |
| 1942 | W. Lee O'Daniel (D) | 260,629 | 94.9 |
| 1948 | Lyndon B. Johnson (D) | 702,785 | 66.2 |
| | Jack Porter (R) | 349,665 | 32.9 |
| 1954 | Lyndon B. Johnson (D) | 539,319 | 84.7 |
| | Carlos G. Watson (R) | 94,131 | 14.8 |
| 1960 | Lyndon B. Johnson (D) | 1,306,605 | 58.0 |
| | John G. Tower (R) | 926,653 | 41.1 |

**Special Primary [1]**

| 1961 | John G. Tower (R) | 327,308# | 30.9 |
|---|---|---|---|
| | William A. Blakley (D) | 190,818# | 18.1 |
| | Jim Wright (D) | 171,328# | 16.2 |
| | Will Wilson (D) | 121,961# | 11.5 |

| | Candidates | Votes | % |
|---|---|---|---|
| | Maury Maverick Jr. (D) | 104,992# | 9.9 |
| | Henry B. Gonzalez (D) | 97,659# | 9.2 |

**Special Runoff Election [1]**

| | Candidates | Votes | % |
|---|---|---|---|
| 1961 | John G. Tower (R) | 448,217 | 50.6 |
| | William A. Blakley (D) | 437,874 | 49.4 |
| 1966 | John G. Tower (R) | 842,501 | 56.4 |
| | Waggoner Carr (D) | 643,855 | 43.1 |
| 1972 | John G. Tower (R) | 1,822,877 | 53.4 |
| | Barefoot Sanders (D) | 1,511,985 | 44.3 |
| 1978 | John G. Tower (R) | 1,151,376 | 49.8 |
| | Bob Krueger (D) | 1,139,149 | 49.3 |
| 1984 | Phil Gramm (R) | 3,111,348 | 58.5 |
| | Lloyd Doggett (D) | 2,202,557 | 41.4 |
| 1990 | Phil Gramm (R) | 2,302,357 | 60.2 |
| | Hugh Parmer (D) | 1,429,986 | 37.4 |

**Texas**

1. Under Texas law passed after the 1957 special election, candidates in special elections for the Senate would all run together in a primary with party affiliation. If none received a majority of the vote in the first primary, a runoff would be held between the top two contenders.

# UTAH

| | Candidates | Votes | % |
|---|---|---|---|
| | **Class 1** | | |
| 1916 | William H. King (D) | 81,057 | 56.9 |
| | George Sutherland (R) | 56,862 | 39.9 |
| 1922 | William H. King (D) | 58,749 | 48.6 |
| | Ernest Bamberger (R) | 58,188 | 48.2 |
| 1928 | William H. King (D) | 97,436 | 55.5 |
| | Ernest Bamberger (R) | 77,073 | 43.9 |
| 1934 | William H. King (D) | 95,931 | 53.1 |
| | Don B. Colton (R) | 82,154 | 45.4 |
| 1940 | Abe Murdock (D) | 155,499 | 62.9 |
| | Philo T. Farnsworth Jr. (R) | 91,931 | 37.2 |
| 1946 | Arthur V. Watkins (R) | 101,142 | 51.2 |
| | Abe Murdock (D) | 96,257 | 48.8 |
| 1952 | Arthur V. Watkins (R) | 177,435 | 54.3 |
| | Walter K. Granger (D) | 149,598 | 45.7 |
| 1958 | Frank E. Moss (D) | 112,827 | 38.7 |
| | Arthur V. Watkins (R) | 101,471 | 34.8 |
| | J. Bracken Lee (I) | 77,013 | 26.4 |
| 1964 | Frank E. Moss (D) | 227,822 | 57.3 |
| | Ernest L. Wilkinson (R) | 169,562 | 42.7 |
| 1970 | Frank E. Moss (D) | 210,207 | 56.2 |
| | Laurence J. Burton (R) | 159,004 | 42.5 |
| 1976 | Orrin G. Hatch (R) | 290,221 | 53.7 |
| | Moss E. Frank (D) | 241,948 | 44.8 |
| 1982 | Orrin G. Hatch (R) | 309,332 | 58.3 |
| | Ted Wilson (D) | 219,482 | 41.3 |
| 1988 | Orrin G. Hatch (R) | 430,089 | 67.1 |
| | Brian H. Moss (D) | 203,364 | 31.7 |
| | **Class 3** | | |
| 1914 | Reed Smoot (R) | 56,282 | 49.1 |
| | James H. Moyle (D & PROG) | 53,127 | 46.3 |
| 1920 | Reed Smoot (R) | 82,566 | 56.6 |
| | Milton H. Welling (D) | 56,280 | 38.6 |
| 1926 | Reed Smoot (R) | 88,101 | 61.5 |
| | Ashby Snow (D) | 53,809 | 37.6 |
| 1932 | Elbert D. Thomas (D) | 116,909 | 56.7 |

| | Candidates | Votes | % |
|---|---|---|---|
| | Reed Smoot (R) | 86,066 | 41.7 |
| 1938 | Elbert D. Thomas (D) | 102,353 | 55.8 |
| | Franklin S. Harris (R) | 81,071 | 44.2 |
| 1944 | Elbert D. Thomas (D) | 148,748 | 59.9 |
| | Adam S. Bennion (R) | 99,532 | 40.1 |
| 1950 | Wallace F. Bennett (R) | 142,427 | 53.9 |
| | Elbert D. Thomas (D) | 121,198 | 45.8 |
| 1956 | Wallace F. Bennett (R) | 178,261 | 54.0 |
| | Alonzo F. Hopkin (D) | 152,120 | 46.0 |
| 1962 | Wallace F. Bennett (R) | 166,755 | 52.4 |
| | David S. King (D) | 151,656 | 47.6 |
| 1968 | Wallace F. Bennett (R) | 225,075 | 53.7 |
| | Milton L. Weilenmann (D) | 192,168 | 45.8 |
| 1974 | Jake Garn (R) | 210,299 | 50.0 |
| | Wayne Owens (D) | 185,377 | 44.1 |
| 1980 | Jake Garn (R) | 437,675 | 73.6 |
| | Dan Berman (D) | 151,454 | 25.5 |
| 1986 | Jake Garn (R) | 314,608 | 72.3 |
| | Craig Oliver (D) | 115,523 | 26.6 |
| 1992 | Robert F. Bennett (R) | 420,069 | 55.4 |
| | Wayne Owens (D) | 301,228 | 39.7 |

# VERMONT

| | Candidates | Votes | % |
|---|---|---|---|
| | **Class 1** | | |
| 1916 | Carroll S. Page (R) | 47,362 | 74.2 |
| | Oscar C. Miller (D) | 14,956 | 23.4 |
| 1922 | Frank L. Greene (R) | 45,284 | 67.9 |
| | William B. Mayo (D) | 21,375 | 32.1 |
| 1928 | Frank L. Greene (R) | 93,136 | 71.6 |
| | Fred C. Martin (D) | 37,030 | 28.5 |

**Special Election**

| | Candidates | Votes | % |
|---|---|---|---|
| 1931 | Warren R. Austin (R) | 27,661# | 64.3 |
| | Stephen M. Driscoll (D) | 15,360# | 35.7 |
| 1934 | Warren R. Austin (R) | 67,146 | 51.0 |
| | Fred C. Martin (D) | 63,632 | 48.4 |
| 1940 | Warren R. Austin (R) | 93,283 | 66.5 |
| | Ona S. Searles (D) | 47,101 | 33.6 |
| 1946 | Ralph E. Flanders (R) | 54,729 | 74.6 |
| | Charles P. McDevitt (D) | 18,594 | 25.4 |
| 1952 | Ralph E. Flanders (R) | 111,406 | 72.3 |
| | Allan R. Johnston (D) | 42,630 | 27.7 |
| 1958 | Winston L. Prouty (R) | 64.900 | 52.2 |
| | Frederick J. Fayette (D) | 59,536 | 47.8 |
| 1964 | Winston L. Prouty (R, I) | 87,879 | 53.5 |
| | Frederick J. Fayette (D) | 76,457 | 46.5 |
| 1970 | Winston L. Prouty (R) | 91,198 | 58.9 |
| | Philip H. Hoff (D) | 62,271 | 40.2 |

**Special Election**

| | Candidates | Votes | % |
|---|---|---|---|
| 1972 | Robert T. Stafford (R) | 45,888# | 64.3 |
| | Randolph T. Major (D) | 23,842# | 33.4 |
| 1976 | Robert T. Stafford (R) | 94,481 | 50.0 |
| | Thomas P. Salmon (D) | 85,682 | 45.3 |
| 1982 | Robert T. Stafford (R) | 84,450 | 50.3 |
| | James A. Guest (D) | 79,340 | 47.2 |
| 1988 | James M. Jeffords (R) | 163,183 | 67.9 |
| | William Gray (D) | 71,460 | 29.8 |

| | Candidates | Votes | % |
|---|---|---|---|
| | **Class 3** | | |
| 1914 | William P. Dillingham (R) | 35,137 | 56.0 |
| | Charles A. Prouty (PROG D & P) | 26,776 | 42.7 |
| 1920 | William P. Dillingham (R) | 69,650 | 78.0 |
| | Howard E. Shaw (D) | 19,580 | 21.9 |

**Special Election**

| | | | |
|---|---|---|---|
| 1923 | Porter H. Dale (R) | 30,582 | 66.2 |
| | Park H. Pollard (D) | 15,621 | 33.8 |
| 1926 | Porter H. Dale (R, P) | 52,286 | 73.4 |
| | James E. Kennedy (D) | 18,878 | 26.5 |
| 1932 | Porter H. Dale (R) | 74,319 | 55.1 |
| | Fred C. Martin (D) | 60,453 | 44.9 |

**Special Election**

| | | | |
|---|---|---|---|
| 1934 | Ernest W. Gibson (R) | 28,436# | 58.2 |
| | Harry W. Witters (D) | 20,382# | 41.8 |

| | | | |
|---|---|---|---|
| 1938 | Ernest W. Gibson (R) | 73,990 | 65.7 |
| | John McGrath (D) | 38,673 | 34.3 |

**Special Election**

| | | | |
|---|---|---|---|
| 1940 | George D. Aiken (R) | 87,150 | 61.6 |
| | Herbert B. Comings (D) | 54,263 | 38.4 |

| | | | |
|---|---|---|---|
| 1944 | George D. Aiken (R) | 81,094 | 65.8 |
| | Harry W. Witters (D) | 42,136 | 34.2 |
| 1950 | George D. Aiken (R) | 69,543 | 78.0 |
| | James E. Bigelow (D) | 19,608 | 22.0 |
| 1956 | George D. Aiken (R) | 103,101 | 66.4 |
| | Bernard G. O'Shea (D) | 52,184 | 33.6 |
| 1962 | George D. Aiken (R) | 81,241 | 66.9 |
| | W. Robert Johnson (D) | 40,134 | 33.1 |
| 1968 | George D. Aiken (R, D) | 157,154 | 99.9 |
| 1974 | Patrick J. Leahy (D, I VT) | 70,629 | 49.5 |
| | Richard W. Mallary (R) | 66,223 | 46.4 |
| 1980 | Patrick J. Leahy (D) | 104,176 | 49.8 |
| | Stewart M. Ledbetter (R) | 101,421 | 48.5 |
| 1986 | Patrick J. Leahy (D) | 124,123 | 63.2 |
| | Richard A. Snelling (R) | 67,798 | 34.5 |
| 1992 | Patrick J. Leahy (D) | 154,762 | 54.2 |
| | James H. Douglas (R) | 123,854 | 43.3 |

# VIRGINIA

| | Candidates | Votes | % |
|---|---|---|---|
| | **Class 1** | | |
| 1916 | Claude A. Swanson (D) | 133,091 | 99.9 |
| 1922 | Claude A. Swanson (D) | 116,393 | 71.9 |
| | J. W. McGavock (R) | 42,903 | 26.5 |
| 1928 | Claude A. Swanson (D) | 275,425 | 99.8 |

**Special Election**

| | | | |
|---|---|---|---|
| 1933 | Harry F. Byrd (D) | 119,377 | 71.3 |
| | Henry A. Wise (R) | 44,648 | 26.7 |

| | | | |
|---|---|---|---|
| 1934 | Harry F. Byrd (D) | 109,963 | 76.0 |
| | Lawrence C. Page (R) | 30,289 | 20.9 |
| 1940 | Harry F. Byrd (D) | 274,260 | 93.3 |
| 1946 | Harry F. Byrd (D) | 163,960 | 64.9 |

| | Candidates | Votes | % |
|---|---|---|---|
| | Lester S. Parsons (R) | 77,005 | 30.5 |
| 1952 | Harry F. Byrd (D) | 398,677 | 73.4 |
| | H. M. Vise Sr. (ID) | 69,133 | 12.7 |
| | Clarke T. Robb (SOCIAL D) | 67,281 | 12.4 |
| 1958 | Harry F. Byrd (D) | 317,221 | 69.3 |
| | Louise Wensel (I) | 120,224 | 26.3 |
| 1964 | Harry F. Byrd (D) | 592,260 | 63.8 |
| | Richard A. May (R) | 176,624 | 19.0 |
| | James W. Respess (I) | 95,526 | 10.3 |

**Special Election**

| | | | |
|---|---|---|---|
| 1966 | Harry F. Byrd, Jr. (D) | 389,028 | 53.3 |
| | Lawrence M. Traylor (R) | 272,804 | 37.4 |
| | John W. Carter (C) | 57,692 | 7.9 |

| | | | |
|---|---|---|---|
| 1970 | Harry F. Byrd Jr. (I) | 506,623 | 53.5 |
| | George C. Rawlings Jr. (D) | 295,057 | 31.2 |
| | Ray Garland (R) | 145,031 | 15.3 |
| 1976 | Harry F. Byrd Jr. (I) | 890,778 | 57.2 |
| | Elmo R. Zumwalt (D) | 596,009 | 38.3 |
| 1982 | Paul S. Trible Jr. (R) | 724,571 | 51.2 |
| | Richard Davis (D) | 690,839 | 48.8 |
| 1988 | Charles S. Robb (D) | 1,474,086 | 71.2 |
| | Maurice A. Dawkins (R) | 593,652 | 28.7 |

| | Candidates | Votes | % |
|---|---|---|---|
| | **Class 2** | | |
| 1918 | Thomas S. Martin (D) | 40,403 | 99.7 |

**Special Election**

| | | | |
|---|---|---|---|
| 1920 | Carter Glass (D) | 184,646# | 91.3 |
| | J. R. Pollard (R) | 17,576# | 8.7 |

| | | | |
|---|---|---|---|
| 1924 | Carter Glass (D) | 151,498 | 73.1 |
| | Carroll Livingston Ricker (SOC) | 50,092 | 24.2 |
| 1930 | Carter Glass (D) | 112,002 | 76.7 |
| | J. Cloyd Byars (I) | 26,091 | 17.9 |
| | Joe C. Morgan (SOC) | 7,954 | 5.4 |
| 1936 | Carter Glass (D) | 244,518 | 91.7 |
| 1942 | Carter Glass (D) | 79,421 | 91.1 |
| | Lawrence S. Wilkes (SOC) | 5,690 | 6.5 |

**Special Election**

| | | | |
|---|---|---|---|
| 1946 | A. Willis Robertson (D) | 169,680 | 68.2 |
| | Robert H. Woods (R) | 72,253 | 29.0 |

| | | | |
|---|---|---|---|
| 1948 | A. Willis Robertson (D) | 253,865 | 65.6 |
| | Robert H. Woods (R) | 119,366 | 30.8 |
| 1954 | A. Willis Robertson (D) | 244,844 | 79.9 |
| | Charles William Lewis Jr. (ID) | 32,681 | 10.7 |
| | Clarke T. Robb (SOCIAL D) | 28,922 | 9.4 |
| 1960 | A. Willis Robertson (D) | 506,169 | 81.3 |
| | Stuart D. Baker (ID) | 88,718 | 14.2 |
| 1966 | William B. Spong Jr. (D) | 429,855 | 58.6 |
| | James P. Ould Jr. (R) | 245,681 | 33.5 |
| | F. Lee Hawthorne (C) | 58,251 | 7.9 |
| 1972 | William Lloyd Scott (R) | 718,337 | 51.5 |
| | William B. Spong Jr. (D) | 643,963 | 46.1 |
| 1978 | John W. Warner (R) | 613,232 | 50.2 |
| | Andrew P. Miller (D) | 608,511 | 49.8 |
| 1984 | John W. Warner (R) | 1,406,194 | 70.0 |
| | Edythe C. Harrison (D) | 601,142 | 29.9 |
| 1990 | John W. Warner (R) | 876,782 | 80.9 |
| | Nancy B. Spannaus (I) | 196,755 | 18.2 |

# WASHINGTON

| | Candidates | Votes | % |
|---|---|---|---|
| | **Class 1** | | |
| 1916 | Miles Poindexter (R) | 202,287 | *55.4* |
| | George Turner (D) | 135,339 | *37.1* |
| | Bruce Rogers (SOC) | 21,709 | *5.9* |
| 1922 | Clarence C. Dill (D) | 130,375 | *44.2* |
| | Miles Poindexter (R) | 126,556 | *43.0* |
| | James A. Duncan (F-LAB) | 35,352 | *12.0* |
| 1928 | Clarence C. Dill (D) | 261,524 | *53.4* |
| | Kenneth Mackintosh (R) | 227,415 | *46.5* |
| 1934 | Lewis B. Schwellenbach (D) | 302,606 | *60.9* |
| | Reno Odlin (R) | 168,994 | *34.0* |
| 1940 | Mon C. Wallgren (D) | 404,718 | *54.2* |
| | Stephen F. Chadwick (R) | 342,589 | *45.8* |
| 1946 | Harry P. Cain (R) | 358,847 | *54.3* |
| | Hugh B. Mitchell (D) | 298,683 | *45.2* |
| 1952 | Henry M. Jackson (D) | 595,288 | *56.2* |
| | Harry P. Cain (R) | 460,884 | *43.5* |
| 1958 | Henry M. Jackson (D) | 597,040 | *67.3* |
| | William B. Bantz (R) | 278,271 | *31.4* |
| 1964 | Henry M. Jackson (D) | 875,950 | *72.2* |
| | Lloyd J. Andrews (R) | 337,138 | *27.8* |
| 1970 | Henry M. Jackson (D) | 879,385 | *82.4* |
| | Charles W. Elicker (R) | 170,790 | *16.0* |
| 1976 | Henry M. Jackson (D) | 1,071,219 | *71.8* |
| | George M. Brown (R) | 361,546 | *24.2* |
| 1982 | Henry M. Jackson (D) | 943,655 | *69.0* |
| | Doug Jewett (R) | 332,273 | *24.3* |
| | King Lysen (I) | 72,297 | *5.3* |

**Special Election**

| | | | |
|---|---|---|---|
| 1983 | Daniel J. Evans (R) | 617,699 | *55.4* |
| | Mike Lowry (D) | 496,393 | *44.6* |
| 1988 | Slade Gorton (R) | 944,359 | *51.1* |
| | Mike Lowry (D) | 904,183 | *48.9* |

| | | | |
|---|---|---|---|
| | **Class 3** | | |
| 1914 | Wesley L. Jones (R) | 130,479 | *37.8* |
| | W. W. Black (D) | 91,733 | *26.6* |
| | Ole Hanson (PROG) | 83,282 | *24.1* |
| | Adam H. Barth (SOC) | 30,234 | *8.8* |
| 1920 | Wesley L. Jones (R) | 217,069 | *56.4* |
| | C. L. France (F-LAB) | 99,309 | *25.8* |
| | George F. Cotterill (D) | 68,488 | *17.8* |
| 1926 | Wesley L. Jones (R) | 164,130 | *51.3* |
| | A. Scott Bullitt (D) | 148,792 | *46.5* |
| 1932 | Homer T. Bone (D) | 365,949 | *60.6* |
| | Wesley L. Jones (R) | 197,450 | *32.7* |
| 1938 | Homer T. Bone (D) | 371,535 | *62.6* |
| | Ewing D. Colvin (R) | 220,204 | *37.1* |
| 1944 | Warren G. Magnuson (D) | 452,013 | *55.1* |
| | Harry P. Cain (R) | 364,356 | *44.4* |
| 1950 | Warren G. Magnuson (D) | 397,719 | *53.4* |
| | Walter Williams (R) | 342,464 | *46.0* |
| 1956 | Warren G. Magnuson (D) | 685,565 | *61.1* |
| | Arthur B. Langlie (R) | 436,652 | *38.9* |
| 1962 | Warren G. Magnuson (D) | 491,365 | *52.1* |
| | Richard G. Christensen (R) | 446,204 | *47.3* |
| 1968 | Warren G. Magnuson (D) | 796,183 | *64.4* |
| | Jack Metcalf (R) | 435,894 | *35.3* |
| 1974 | Warren G. Magnuson (D) | 611,811 | *60.7* |
| | Jack Metcalf (R) | 363,626 | *36.1* |
| 1980 | Slade Gorton (R) | 936,317 | *54.2* |
| | Warren G. Magnuson (D) | 792,052 | *45.8* |

| | Candidates | Votes | % |
|---|---|---|---|
| 1986 | Brock Adams (D) | 677,471 | *50.6* |
| | Slade Gorton (R) | 650,931 | *48.7* |
| 1992 | Patty Murray (D) | 1,197,973 | *54.0* |
| | Rod Chandler (R) | 1,020,829 | *46.0* |

# WEST VIRGINIA

| | Candidates | Votes | % |
|---|---|---|---|
| | **Class 1** | | |
| 1916 | Howard Sutherland (R) | 144,243 | *50.1* |
| | William E. Chilton (D) | 138,585 | *48.2* |
| 1922 | Matthew M. Neely (D) | 198,853 | *51.2* |
| | Howard Sutherland (R) | 185,046 | *47.6* |
| 1928 | Henry D. Hatfield (R) | 327,266 | *50.7* |
| | Matthew M. Neely (D) | 317,620 | *49.2* |
| 1934 | Rush D. Holt (D) | 349,882 | *55.1* |
| | Henry D. Hatfield (R) | 281,756 | *44.4* |
| 1940 | Harley M. Kilgore (D) | 492,413 | *56.3* |
| | Thomas Sweeney (R) | 381,806 | *43.7* |
| 1946 | Harley M. Kilgore (D) | 273,151 | *50.3* |
| | Thomas Sweeney (R) | 269,617 | *49.7* |
| 1952 | Harley M. Kilgore (D) | 470,019 | *53.6* |
| | Chapman Revercomb (R) | 406,554 | *46.4* |

**Special Election**

| | | | |
|---|---|---|---|
| 1956 | Chapman Revercomb (R) | 432,123 | *53.7* |
| | William C. Marland (D) | 373,051 | *46.3* |
| 1958 | Robert C. Byrd (D) | 381,745 | *59.2* |
| | Chapman Revercomb (R) | 263,172 | *40.8* |
| 1964 | Robert C. Byrd (D) | 515,015 | *67.7* |
| | Cooper P. Benedict (R) | 246,072 | *32.3* |
| 1970 | Robert C. Byrd (D) | 345,965 | *77.6* |
| | Elmer H. Dodson (R) | 99,658 | *22.4* |
| 1976 | Robert C. Byrd (D) | 566,423 | *99.9* |
| 1982 | Robert C. Byrd (D) | 387,170 | *68.5* |
| | Cleve K. Benedict (R) | 173,910 | *30.8* |
| 1988 | Robert C. Byrd (D) | 410,983 | *64.8* |
| | M. Jay Wolfe (R) | 223,564 | *35.2* |

| | | | |
|---|---|---|---|
| | **Class 2** | | |
| 1918 | David Elkins (R) | 115,216 | *53.5* |
| | Clarence W. Watson (D) | 97,715 | *45.4* |
| 1924 | Guy D. Goff (R) | 290,004 | *50.9* |
| | William E. Chilton (D) | 271,809 | *47.7* |
| 1930 | Matthew M. Neely (D) | 342,467 | *61.9* |
| | James Ellwood Jones (R) | 209,427 | *37.9* |
| 1936 | Matthew M. Neely (D) | 488,620 | *59.1* |
| | Hugh Ike Shott (R) | 338,363 | *40.9* |
| 1942 | Chapman Revercomb (R) | 256,816 | *55.4* |
| | Matthew M. Neely (D) | 207,045 | *44.6* |

**Special Election**

| | | | |
|---|---|---|---|
| 1942 | Hugh Ike Shott (R) | 227,469 | *52.3* |
| | Joseph Rosier (D) | 207,678 | *47.7* |
| 1948 | Matthew M. Neely (D) | 435,354 | *57.0* |
| | Chapman Revercomb (R) | 328,534 | *43.0* |
| 1954 | Matthew M. Neely (D) | 325,263 | *54.8* |
| | Thomas Sweeney (R) | 268,066 | *45.2* |

| | Candidates | Votes | % |
|---|---|---|---|
| **Special Election** | | | |
| 1958 | Jennings Randolph (D) | 374,167 | *59.3* |
| | John D. Hoblitzell Jr. (R) | 256,510 | *40.7* |
| 1960 | Jennings Randolph (D) | 458,355 | *55.3* |
| | Cecil H. Underwood (R) | 369,935 | *44.7* |
| 1966 | Jennings Randolph (D) | 292,325 | *59.5* |
| | Francis J. Love (R) | 198,891 | *40.5* |
| 1972 | Jennings Randolph (D) | 486,310 | *66.5* |
| | Louise Leonard (R) | 245,531 | *33.6* |
| 1978 | Jennings Randolph (D) | 249,034 | *50.5* |
| | Arch A. Moore Jr. (R) | 244,317 | *49.5* |
| 1984 | John D. (Jay) Rockefeller (D) | 374,233 | *51.8* |
| | John R. Raese (R) | 344,680 | *47.7* |
| 1990 | John D. Rockefeller IV (D) | 276,234 | *68.3* |
| | John Yoder (R) | 128,071 | *31.7* |

# WISCONSIN

| | Candidates | Votes | % |
|---|---|---|---|
| **Class 1** | | | |
| 1916 | Robert M. La Follette (R) | 251,303 | *60.5* |
| | William F. Wolfe (D) | 135,144 | *32.5* |
| | Richard Elsner (SOCIAL D) | 28,908 | *7.0* |
| 1922 | Robert M. La Follette (R) | 379,494 | *80.6* |
| | Jessie Jack Hooper (ID) | 78,029 | *16.6* |
| **Special Election** | | | |
| 1925 | Robert M. La Follette Jr. (R) | 237,719 | *67.5* |
| | Edward F. Dithmar (IR) | 91,318 | *25.9* |
| 1928 | Robert M. La Follette Jr. (R) | 635,376 | *85.6* |
| | William H. Markham (IR) | 81,302 | *11.0* |
| 1934 | Robert M. La Follette Jr. (PROG) | 440,513 | *47.8* |
| | John M. Callahan (D) | 223,438 | *24.2* |
| | John B. Chapple (R) | 210,569 | *22.8* |
| 1940 | Robert M. La Follette Jr. (PPOG) | 605,609 | *45.3* |
| | Fred H. Clausen (R) | 553,692 | *41.4* |
| | James E. Finnegan (D) | 176,688 | *13.2* |
| 1946 | Joseph R. McCarthy (R) | 620,430 | *61.3* |
| | Howard J. McMurray (D) | 378,772 | *37.4* |
| 1952 | Joseph R. McCarthy (R) | 870,444 | *54.2* |
| | Thomas E. Fairchild (D) | 731,402 | *45.6* |
| **Special Election** | | | |
| 1957 | William Proxmire (D) | 435,985 | *56.4* |
| | Walter J. Kohler Jr. (R) | 312,931 | *40.5* |
| 1958 | William Proxmire (D) | 682,440 | *57.1* |
| | Roland J. Steinle (R) | 510,398 | *42.7* |
| 1964 | William Proxmire (D) | 892,013 | *53.3* |
| | Wilbur N. Renk (R) | 780,116 | *46.6* |
| 1970 | William Proxmire (D) | 948,445 | *70.8* |
| | John E. Erickson (R) | 381,297 | *28.5* |
| 1976 | William Proxmire (D) | 1,396,970 | *72.2* |
| | Stanley York (R) | 521,902 | *27.0* |
| 1982 | William Proxmire (D) | 983,311 | *63.6* |
| | Scott McCallum (R) | 527,355 | *34.1* |
| 1988 | Herb Kohl (D) | 1,128,625 | *52.1* |
| | Susan Engeleiter (R) | 1,030,440 | *47.5* |

| | Candidates | Votes | % |
|---|---|---|---|
| **Class 3** | | | |
| 1914 | Paul O. Husting (D) | 134,925 | *43.8* |
| | Francis E. McGovern (R) | 133,969 | *43.5* |
| | Emil Seidel (SOCIAL D) | 29,774 | *9.7* |
| **Special Election** | | | |
| 1918 | Irvine L. Lenroot (R) | 163,980# | *38.7* |
| | John Davies (D) | 148,714# | *35.1* |
| | Victor L. Berger (SOC) | 110,487# | *26.1* |
| 1920 | Irvine L. Lenroot (R) | 281,576 | *41.6* |
| | James Thompson (I) | 235,029 | *34.7* |
| | Paul S. Reinsch (D) | 89,265 | *13.2* |
| | Frank J. Weber (SOC) | 66,172 | *9.8* |
| 1926 | John J. Blaine (R) | 300,759 | *55.0* |
| | Charles D. Rosa (I-PROG-R) | 111,122 | *20.3* |
| | Thomas M. Kearney (D) | 66,672 | *12.2* |
| | Leo Krzycki (SOC) | 31,317 | *5.7* |
| 1932 | F. Ryan Duffy (D) | 610,236 | *57.0* |
| | John B. Chapple (R) | 387,668 | *36.2* |
| | Emil Seidel (SOC) | 65,807 | *6.1* |
| 1938 | Alexander Wiley (R) | 446,770 | *47.7* |
| | Herman L. Ekern (PROG) | 249,209 | *26.6* |
| | F. Ryan Duffy (D) | 231,976 | *24.7* |
| 1944 | Alexander Wiley (R) | 634,513 | *50.5* |
| | Howard J. McMurray (D) | 537,144 | *42.8* |
| | Harry Sauthoff (PROG) | 73,089 | *5.8* |
| 1950 | Alexander Wiley (R) | 595,283 | *53.3* |
| | Thomas E. Fairchild (D) | 515,539 | *46.2* |
| 1956 | Alexander Wiley (R) | 892,473 | *58.6* |
| | Henry W. Maier (D) | 627,903 | *41.2* |
| 1962 | Gaylord Nelson (D) | 662,342 | *52.6* |
| | Alexander Wiley (R) | 594,846 | *47.2* |
| 1968 | Gaylord Nelson (D) | 1,020,931 | *61.7* |
| | Jerris Leonard (R) | 633,910 | *38.3* |
| 1974 | Gaylord Nelson (D) | 740,700 | *61.8* |
| | Thomas E. Petri (R) | 429,327 | *35.8* |
| 1980 | Bob Kasten (R) | 1,106,311 | *50.2* |
| | Gaylord Nelson (D) | 1,065,487 | *48.3* |
| 1986 | Bob Kasten (R) | 754,573 | *50.9* |
| | Ed Garvey (D) | 702,963 | *47.4* |
| 1992 | Russell D. Feingold (D) | 1,290,662 | *52.6* |
| | Bob Kasten (R) | 1,129,599 | *46.0* |

# WYOMING

| | Candidates | Votes | % |
|---|---|---|---|
| **Class 1** | | | |
| 1916 | John B. Kendrick (D) | 26,324 | *51.5* |
| | Clarence D. Clark (R) | 23,258 | *45.5* |
| 1922 | John B. Kendrick (D) | 35,734 | *57.3* |
| | F. W. Mondell (R) | 26,627 | *42.7* |
| 1928 | John B. Kendrick (D) | 43,032 | *53.5* |
| | Charles E. Winter (R) | 37,076 | *46.1* |
| 1934 | Joseph C. O'Mahoney (D) | 53,806 | *56.6* |
| | Vincent Carter (R) | 40,819 | *43.0* |
| **Special Election** | | | |
| 1934 | Joseph C. O'Mahoney (D) | 53,859 | *56.9* |
| | Vincent Carter (R) | 40,825 | *43.1* |
| 1940 | Joseph C. O'Mahoney (D) | 65,022 | *58.7* |
| | Milward L. Simpson (R) | 45,682 | *41.3* |

|      | Candidates | Votes | % |
|------|-----------|-------|---|
| 1946 | Joseph C. O'Mahoney (D) | 45,843 | *56.2* |
|      | Harry B. Henderson (R) | 35,714 | *43.8* |
| 1952 | Frank A. Barrett (R) | 67,176 | *51.6* |
|      | Joseph C. O'Mahoney (D) | 62,921 | *48.4* |
| 1958 | Gale McGee (D) | 58,035 | *50.8* |
|      | Frank A. Barrett (R) | 56,122 | *49.2* |
| 1964 | Gale McGee (D) | 76,485 | *54.0* |
|      | John S. Wold (R) | 65,185 | *46.0* |
| 1970 | Gale McGee (D) | 67,207 | *55.8* |
|      | John S. Wold (R) | 53,279 | *44.2* |
| 1976 | Malcolm Wallop (R) | 84,810 | *54.6* |
|      | Gale McGee (D) | 70,558 | *45.4* |
| 1982 | Malcolm Wallop (R) | 94,725 | *56.7* |
|      | Rodger McDaniel (D) | 72,466 | *43.3* |
| 1988 | Malcolm Wallop (R) | 91,143 | *50.4* |
|      | John Vinich (D) | 89,821 | *49.6* |

### Class 2

|      | Candidates | Votes | % |
|------|-----------|-------|---|
| 1918 | Francis E. Warren (R) | 23,975 | *57.8* |
|      | John E. Osborne (D) | 17,528 | *42.2* |
| 1924 | Francis E. Warren (R) | 41,293 | *55.2* |
|      | Robert R. Rose (D) | 33,536 | *44.8* |
| 1930 | Robert D. Carey (R) | 43,626 | *59.1* |
|      | Harry H. Schwartz (D) | 30,259 | *41.0* |

Special Election

|      |  |  |  |
|------|-----------|-------|---|
| 1930 | Robert D. Carey (R) | 42,726# | *58.8* |
|      | Harry H. Schwartz (D) | 29,904# | *41.2* |

|      |  |  |  |
|------|-----------|-------|---|
| 1936 | Harry H. Schwartz (D) | 53,919 | *53.8* |

|      | Candidates | Votes | % |
|------|-----------|-------|---|
|      | Robert D. Carey (R) | 45,483 | *45.4* |
| 1942 | Edward V. Robertson (R) | 41,486 | *54.6* |
|      | Harry H. Schwartz (D) | 34,503 | *45.4* |
| 1948 | Lester C. Hunt (D) | 57,953 | *57.1* |
|      | Edward V. Robertson (R) | 43,527 | *42.9* |
| 1954 | Joseph C. O'Mahoney (D) | 57,845 | *51.5* |
|      | William Henry Harrison (R) | 54,407 | *48.5* |

Special Election

|      |  |  |  |
|------|-----------|-------|---|
| 1954 | Joseph C. O'Mahoney (D) | 57,163 | *51.6* |
|      | William Henry Harrison (R) | 53,705 | *48.4* |
| 1960 | Keith Thomson (R) | 78,103* | *56.4* |
|      | Raymond B. Whitaker (D) | 60,447 | *43.6* |

Special Election

|      |  |  |  |
|------|-----------|-------|---|
| 1962 | Milward L. Simpson (R) | 69,043 | *57.8* |
|      | J. J. Hickey (D) | 50,329 | *42.2* |

|      |  |  |  |
|------|-----------|-------|---|
| 1966 | Clifford P. Hansen (R) | 63,548 | *51.8* |
|      | Teno Roncalio (D) | 59,141 | *48.2* |
| 1972 | Clifford P. Hansen (R) | 101,314 | *71.3* |
|      | Mike Vinich (D) | 40,753 | *28.7* |
| 1978 | Alan K. Simpson (R) | 82,908 | *62.2* |
|      | Raymond B. Whitaker (D) | 50,456 | *37.8* |
| 1984 | Alan K. Simpson (R) | 146,373 | *78.3* |
|      | Victor A. Ryan (D) | 40,525 | *21.7* |
| 1990 | Alan K. Simpson (R) | 100,784 | *63.9* |
|      | Kathy Helling (D) | 56,848 | *36.1* |

# Senate Returns: Other Sources

In the preceding pages of Senate popular election returns (815-846) the symbol # is used to denote 1913-75 returns taken from a source other than the election data provided by the Inter-University Consortium for Political and Social Research (ICPSR). This page lists the source for each of those returns.

The most frequently used alternative source was *Statistics of the Congressional Elections of ____*, published by the Clerk of the House of Representatives for every general election year since 1920.

**Alabama**

1938: *Statistics of the Congressional Election of Nov. 8. 1938.*

**Arkansas**

1924: *Statistics of the Congressional and Presidential Election of Nov. 4, 1924.*

1914:1916 *World Almanac*, published by the *New York World* newspaper.

1932 special election: Alexander Heard and Donald S. Strong, *Southern Primaries and Elections, 1920-1949.* p. 31.

**Colorado**

1944: *Statistics of the Congressional and Presidential Election of Nov. 7, 1944.*

**Connecticut**

1924 special election: *Statistics of the Congressional Election of Nov. 4, 1924.*

**Georgia**

1924: *Statistics of the Congressional and Presidential Election of Nov. 4, 1924.*

**Kentucky**

1950 special election: *Statistics of the Congressional Election of Nov. 7, 1950.*

**Louisiana**

1936 special election: Louisiana Secretary of State.

1920: *Statistics of the Congressional and Presidential Election of Nov. 2, 1920.*

**Maine**

1952: *Statistics of the Congressional and Presidential Election of Nov. 4, 1952.*

**Maryland**

1913 special election: Maryland Secretary of State.

1940: *Statistics of the Congressional and Presidential Election of Nov. 5, 1940.*

1946: *Statistics of the Congressional Election of Nov. 5, 1946.*

**Minnesota**

1923 special election: 1924 *World Almanac*, published by the *New York World* newspaper.

**North Carolina**

1948 special election: *Statistics of the Congressional and Presidential Election of Nov. 2, 1948.*

**Ohio**

1930 special election: *Statistics of the Congressional Election of Nov. 4, 1930.*

**Pennsylvania**

1922 special election: *Statistics of the Congressional Election of Nov. 7, 1922.*

**Texas**

1961 special primary: Richard M. Scammon (ed.), *America Votes 5*, (Pittsburgh, 1964), p. 401.

**Vermont**

1931 special election: Vermont Secretary of State.

1972 special election: Richard M. Scammon (ed.), *America Votes 10*, (Washington, 1973), p. 372.

1934 special election: Vermont Secretary of State.

**Virginia**

1920 special election: *Statistics of the Congressional and Presidential Election of Nov. 2, 1920.*

**Wisconsin**

1918 special election: Seward W. Livermore, *Politics is Adjourned: Woodrow Wilson and the War Congress.* (Middletown, Conn: Wesleyan University Press, 1966), p. 271.

**Wyoming**

1930 special election: *Statistics of the Congressional Election of Nov. 4, 1930.*

# Senate Primary Returns, 1920-93

# Sources: Senate Primary Returns

In previous editions of the *Guide to U.S. Elections,* Southern senatorial primary returns (for Alabama, Arkansas, Florida, Georgia, Louisiana, Mississippi, North Carolina, South Carolina, Tennessee, Texas and Virginia) were placed in a separate section. For the *Guide to U.S. Elections, Third Edition,* senatorial primary returns for all 50 states are presented in this section (pages 851-911). For all non-Southern states, primary returns go back to 1956; for the 11 Southern states, primary returns go back to 1920 where available.

The major source for primary election returns for all non-Southern states was the *America Votes* series, compiled biennially by Richard M. Scammon and Alice V. McGillivray of the Elections Research Center, Washington, D.C., and published by Congressional Quarterly. Other sources were the returns obtained by Congressional Quarterly after each federal and gubernatorial election from the state secretaries of state. In cases of discrepancies, the *Guide to U.S. Elections, Third Edition,* accepted the *America Votes* figure. The first year for which *America Votes* reported primary returns, 1956, was chosen as the starting point because gubernatorial primary votes for earlier years are not readily available.

For the 11 Southern states the primary election returns presented for the years 1920 through 1973 were obtained, except where indicted by a footnote, from the Inter-University Consortium for Political and Social Research (ICPSR) at the University of Michigan. Major sources for returns since 1973 were Congressional Quarterly, which obtained them from the state secretaries of state and Scammon and McGillivray's *America Votes* series.

The vast majority of Southern primaries during the period of 1920 to 1973 were held to nominate candidates of the dominant Democratic Party. In most cases, the winner of the Democratic primary went into the general election facing no Republican opponent and almost certain of victory.

## Compilation of ICPSR Data File

Statewide candidate totals for Southern primary elections for senator were prepared by the ICPSR staff from several sources. Election returns for the years prior to 1949 were obtained from *Southern Primaries and Elections* (University, Ala.: University of Alabama Press, 1950), edited by Alexander Heard and Donald S. Strong. It should be noted that, although they transcribed their data from official returns, Professors Heard and Strong found that many of the returns contained errors and discrepancies between the sum of county totals and the state total, or returns published as final in newspapers and secretary of state reports. No attempt was made by Heard and Strong to correct these discrepancies because the source of the error could not be determined.

For the period from 1949 to 1972, candidate totals were acquired from two sources. The first was a collection of Southern primary electoral statistics prepared from official returns by Hugh Davis Graham, chairman, division of social sciences, University of Maryland (Baltimore County), and Numan V. Bartley, department of history,

University of Georgia (Athens). In addition, reference was made to official returns supplied to ICPSR by the various secretaries of state in conjunction with the ICPSR effort to maintain its continuing collection of election materials. The returns obtained from Bartley and Graham, and the secretary of state offices, were compared with published reports of the election outcomes (notably state manuals and the *America Votes* series) to verify the completeness and accuracy of the returns.

## Presentation of Returns

The returns for Senate primaries are arranged alphabetically by state and in chronological order by class of senator within each state listing. *(For an explanation of Senate classes, see p. 780)* Candidates are listed in descending order, with the candidate receiving the greatest number of popular votes listed first. Percentage of the total vote is listed for each candidate who received *at least 5 percent* of the total vote cast.

Primaries for special elections to fill vacancies and runoff primaries are designated in the returns. For Southern states prior to 1974, Republican primary results have been included, whenever available.

## Names, Vote Totals and Percentages

The names of senatorial primary candidates are listed as they appeared in the source materials. In a few cases, first names are not known.

For pre-1976 primary elections included in this section, the ICPSR computed statewide vote totals for each candidate. (County-level returns are available from the ICPSR.) *(ICPSR collection, box, p. x)*

Percentages of the total vote were calculated on the basis of each candidate's proportion of the *total number of votes cast* for all candidates. Percentages have been calculated to two decimal places and rounded to one place. Due to rounding and the scattered votes of minor candidates, percentages in individual primary races may not add up to 100.

If no vote is shown for a candidate but the percentage of total vote is listed as 100 percent, in most cases the candidates in question ran unopposed and state election officials either did not bother to put the candidate's name on the ballot or simply did not make an effort to record the total number of votes.

When Senate primary elections were held under a preferential voting system and the use of second choice votes was required to determine a winner, the symbol ✔ appears next to the winner's name. *(Explanation of preferential voting, p. 628)*

There were a number of unusual cases in the history of Southern Senate primaries in which the nominee of one or both major parties was chosen by a party committee rather than in a primary. In these cases, the names of the nominees will appear in the primary returns along with a footnote indicating the particular circumstances.

Where no primary is indicated for a year in which a state elected a senator, it generally means that party conventions chose the nominees. Notes at the end of a state's listing explain other unusual circumstances.

# Senate Primary
# Returns, 1920-93

## ALABAMA

| Candidates | Votes | % |
|---|---|---|
| **Class 2** | | |

**1920**    **Democratic Special Primary**

| Candidates | Votes | % |
|---|---|---|
| J. Thomas Heflin (D) | 49,554✔ | 37.9 |
| White (D) | 34,854 | 26.6 |
| O'Neal (D) | 33,174 | 25.4 |
| Rushton (D) | 13,232 | 10.1 |

**Democratic Second Choice**

| Candidates | Votes | % |
|---|---|---|
| White (D) | 12,699 | 36.5 |
| J. Thomas Heflin (D) | 11,062 | 31.8 |
| Rushton (D) | 7,316 | 21.0 |
| O'Neal (D) | 3,691 | 10.6 |

**1924**    **Democratic Primary**

| | Votes | % |
|---|---|---|
| J. Thomas Heflin (D) | | 100.0 |

**1930**    **Democratic Primary**

| | Votes | % |
|---|---|---|
| John H. Bankhead II (D) | 102,462 | 63.9 |
| Fred I. Thompson (D) | 57,809 | 36.1 |

**1936**    **Democratic Primary**

| | Votes | % |
|---|---|---|
| John H. Bankhead II (D) | 178,500 | 81.1 |
| H. L. Anderson (D) | 41,673 | 18.9 |

**1942**    **Democratic Primary**

| | Votes | % |
|---|---|---|
| John H. Bankhead II (D) | | 100.0 |

**1946**    **Democratic Special Primary**

| | Votes | % |
|---|---|---|
| John Sparkman (D) | 85,049 | 50.1 |
| James A. Simpson (D) | 46,762 | 27.6 |
| Frank W. Boykin (D) | 35,982 | 21.2 |

**1948**    **Democratic Primary**

| | Votes | % |
|---|---|---|
| John Sparkman (D) | 235,464 | 75.7 |
| Philip J. Hamm (D) | 61,308 | 19.7 |

**1954**    **Democratic Primary**

| | Votes | % |
|---|---|---|
| John Sparkman (D) | 323,877 | 58.3 |
| Laurie C. Battle (D) | 208,166 | 37.4 |

**1960**    **Democratic Primary**

| | Votes | % |
|---|---|---|
| John Sparkman (D) | 335,722 | 83.1 |
| John G. Crommelin Jr. (D) | 51,571 | 12.8 |

| Candidates | Votes | % |
|---|---|---|

**1966**    **Democratic Primary**

| Candidates | Votes | % |
|---|---|---|
| John Sparkman (D) | 378,295 | 57.0 |
| Frank E. Dixon (D) | 133,139 | 20.1 |
| John G. Crommelin Jr. (D) | 114,622 | 17.3 |
| Mrs. Frank R. Stewart (D) | 37,889 | 5.7 |

**1972**    **Republican Primary**

| | Votes | % |
|---|---|---|
| Winton M. (Red) Blount (R) | 27,736 | 54.2 |
| James D. Martin (R) | 16,800 | 32.8 |
| Bert Nettles (R) | 5,765 | 11.3 |

**Democratic Primary**

| | Votes | % |
|---|---|---|
| John Sparkman (D) | 331,818 | 50.3 |
| Melba T. Allen (D) | 194,690 | 29.5 |
| Lambert C. Mims (D) | 87,461 | 13.3 |

**1978**    **Republican Primary**

| | Votes | % |
|---|---|---|
| James D. Martin (R) [1] | | 100.0 |

**Democratic Primary**

| | Votes | % |
|---|---|---|
| Howell Heflin (D) | 369,270 | 43.3 |
| Walter Flowers (D) | 236,894 | 27.8 |
| John Baker (D) | 191,110 | 22.4 |

**Democratic Runoff**

| | Votes | % |
|---|---|---|
| Howell Heflin (D) | 556,685 | 64.9 |
| Walter Flowers (D) | 300,654 | 35.1 |

**1984**    **Republican Primary**

| | Votes | % |
|---|---|---|
| Albert Lee Smith Jr. (R) | 27,304 | 61.8 |
| Doug Carter (R) | 8,067 | 18.3 |
| Joseph Keith (R) | 5,171 | 11.7 |
| Clint Wilkes (R) | 3,644 | 8.2 |

**Democratic Primary**

| | Votes | % |
|---|---|---|
| Howell Heflin (D) | 399,817 | 83.2 |
| Charles Wayne Borden (D) | 47,462 | 9.9 |
| Mrs. Frank Ross Stewart (D) | 33,114 | 6.9 |

**1990**    **Republican Primary**

| | Votes | % |
|---|---|---|
| Bill Cabaniss (R) | | 100.0 |

**Democratic Primary**

| | Votes | % |
|---|---|---|
| Howell Heflin (D) | 540,876 | 81.4 |
| Mrs. Frank Ross Stewart (D) | 123,508 | 18.6 |

| | Candidates | Votes | % | | Candidates | Votes | % |
|---|---|---|---|---|---|---|---|
| | **Class 3** | | | 1968 | **Democratic Primary** | | |
| 1920 | **Democratic Primary** | | | | James B. Allen (D) | 224,483 | *41.9* |
| | | | | | Armistead I. Selden (D) | 190,283 | *35.5* |
| | Oscar W. Underwood (D) | 66,916 | *50.3* | | Bob Smith (D) | 72,928 | *13.6* |
| | Musgrove (D) | 56,257 | *42.3* | | James E. Folsom (D) | 32,004 | *6.0* |
| | Weakley (D) | 9,766 | *7.4* | | | | |
| | | | | | **Democratic Runoff** | | |
| | **Democratic Second Choice** | | | | James B. Allen (D) | 196,511 | *50.5* |
| | | | | | Armistead I. Selden (D) | 192,448 | *49.5* |
| | Weakley (D) | 21,199 | *74.4* | | | | |
| | Musgrove (D) | 5,172 | *18.2* | 1974 | **Democratic Primary** | | |
| | Oscar W. Underwood (D) | 2,129 | *7.5* | | James B. Allen (D) | 572,584 | *82.8* |
| | | | | | John Taylor (D) | 118,848 | *17.2* |
| 1926 | **Democratic Primary** | | | | | | |
| | Hugo L. Black (D) | 71,916✔ | *33.4* | 1978 [2] | **Republican Special Primary** | | |
| | John H. Bankhead II (D) | 49,841 | *23.1* | | George Nichols (R) [3] | 15,637 | *72.5* |
| | Mayfield (D) | 34,326 | *15.9* | | Elvin McCary (R) | 5,941 | *27.5* |
| | Musgrove (D) | 30,454 | *14.1* | | | | |
| | Thomas E. Kilby (D) | 29,123 | *13.5* | | **Democratic Special Primary** | | |
| | | | | | Maryon Pittman Allen (D) | 334,758 | *44.6* |
| | **Democratic Second Choice** | | | | Donald W. Stewart (D) | 259,795 | *34.6* |
| | | | | | Ted Taylor (D) | 70,894 | *9.4* |
| | Mayfield (D) | 16,668 | *24.9* | | Dan Wiley (D) | 66,689 | *8.9* |
| | John H. Bankhead II (D) | 14,024 | *21.0* | | | | |
| | Hugo L. Black (D) | 12,961 | *19.4* | | **Democratic Special Runoff** | | |
| | Musgrove (D) | 12,598 | *18.9* | | Donald W. Stewart (D) | 502,346 | *57.2* |
| | Thomas E. Kilby (D) | 10,587 | *15.8* | | Maryon Pittman Allen (D) | 375,894 | *42.8* |
| | | | | | | | |
| 1932 | **Democratic Primary** | | | 1980 | **Republican Primary** | | |
| | Hugo L. Black (D) | 92,930 | *49.7* | | Jeremiah Denton (R) | 73,708 | *63.8* |
| | Thomas E. Kilby (D) | 57,875 | *30.9* | | Armistead Selden (R) | 41,825 | *36.2* |
| | John Morgan Burns (D) | 15,528 | *8.3* | | | | |
| | Charles C. McCall (D) | 11,376 | *6.1* | | **Democratic Primary** | | |
| | Henry L. Anderson (D) | 9,467 | *5.1* | | Donald W. Stewart (D) | 222,540 | *48.6* |
| | | | | | Jim Folsom Jr. (D) | 163,196 | *35.7* |
| | **Democratic Runoff** | | | | Finis St. John (D) | 51,260 | *11.2* |
| | Hugo L. Black (D) | 103,453 | *58.3* | | | | |
| | Thomas E. Kilby (D) | 74,039 | *41.7* | | **Democratic Runoff** | | |
| | | | | | Jim Folsom Jr. (D) | 204,486 | *50.6* |
| 1938 | **Democratic Special Primary** | | | | Donald W. Stewart (D) | 199,428 | *49.4* |
| | Lister Hill (D) | 90,601 | *61.8* | | | | |
| | J. Thomas Heflin (D) | 50,189 | *34.3* | 1986 | **Republican Primary** | | |
| | | | | | Jeremiah Denton (R) | 29,805 | *88.5* |
| 1938 | **Democratic Primary** | | | | Richard W. Vickers (R) | 3,854 | *11.5* |
| | Lister Hill (D) | | *100.0* | | | | |
| | | | | | **Democratic Primary** | | |
| 1944 | **Democratic Primary** | | | | Richard C. Shelby (D) | 420,155 | *51.3* |
| | Lister Hill (D) | 126,372 | *55.5* | | James B. Allen Jr. (D) | 284,206 | *34.7* |
| | James A. Simpson (D) | 101,176 | *44.5* | | Ted McLaughlin (D) | 70,784 | *8.6* |
| | | | | | | | |
| 1950 | **Democratic Primary** | | | 1992 | **Republican Primary** | | |
| | Lister Hill (D) | ✔ | | | Richard Sellers (R) | | *100.0* |
| | | | | | | | |
| 1956 | **Democratic Primary** | | | | **Democratic Primary** | | |
| | Lister Hill (D) | 247,519 | *68.2* | | Richard C. Shelby (D) | 304,957 | *61.5* |
| | John G. Crommelin Jr. (D) | 115,440 | *31.8* | | Chris McNair (D) | 136,836 | *27.6* |
| | | | | | Bob Miller (D) | 28,432 | *5.7* |
| 1962 | **Democratic Primary** | | | | Mrs. Frank Ross Stewart (D) | 25,956 | *5.2* |
| | Lister Hill (D) | 363,613 | *73.7* | | | | |
| | Donald G. Hallmark (D) | 72,855 | *14.8* | | | | |
| | John G. Crommelin Jr. (D) | 56,822 | *11.5* | | | | |

Alabama
1. *Martin withdrew after the primary to run for the short-term Senate seat. He was not replaced.*

2. *A special election was held in 1978 to fill the remaining two years of the term of Sen. James B. Allen (D), who died June 1, 1978.*

3. *Nichols withdrew after the primary and James D. Martin was substituted by the state committee.*

# ALASKA [1]

| Candidates | Votes | % |
|---|---|---|
| **Class 2** | | |
| **1958 [2] Republican Primary** | | |
| R E. Robertson (R) | | *100.0* |
| **Democratic Primary** | | |
| E. L. Bartlett (D) | | *100.0* |
| **1960 Republican Primary** | | |
| Lee L. McKinley (R) | 8,867 | *68.2* |
| Lawrence M. Brayton (R) | 4,131 | *31.8* |
| **Democratic Primary** | | |
| E. L. Bartlett (D) | | *100.0* |
| **1966 Republican Primary** | | |
| Lee L. McKinley (R) | 9,310 | *55.8* |
| Lawrence M. Brayton (R) | 5,492 | *32.9* |
| Maxine B. Whaley (R) | 1,866 | *11.2* |
| **Democratic Primary** | | |
| E. L. Bartlett (D) | 27,994 | *87.2* |
| T. J. Bichsel (D) | 1,864 | *5.8* |
| **1970 [3] Republican Special Primary** | | |
| Ted Stevens (R) | 39,062 | *96.7* |
| **Democratic Special Primary** | | |
| Wendell P. Kay (R) | 16,729 | *56.8* |
| Joe Josephson (R) | 12,730 | *43.2* |
| **1972 Republican Primary** | | |
| Ted Stevens (R) | | *100.0* |
| **Democratic Primary** | | |
| Gene Guess (D) | | *100.0* |
| **1978 Republican Primary** | | |
| Ted Stevens (R) | | *100.0* |
| **Democratic Primary** | | |
| Donald W. Hobbs (D) | 10,589 | *55.0* |
| Joe Sonneman (D) | 8,662 | *45.0* |

| | Candidates | Votes | % |
|---|---|---|---|
| **1984** | **Republican Primary** | | |
| | Ted Stevens (R) | 65,552 | *100.0* |
| | **Democratic Primary** | | |
| | John E. Havelock (D) | 19,074 | *65.5* |
| | Dave Carlson (D) | 4,620 | *15.9* |
| | Michael Beasley (D) | 2,443 | *8.4* |
| | Joe Tracanna (D) | 1,661 | *5.7* |
| **1990** | **Republican Primary** | | |
| | Ted Stevens (R) | 81,968 | *70.2* |
| | Robert M. Bird (R) | 34,824 | *29.8* |
| | **Democratic Primary** | | |
| | Michael Beasley (D) | 12,371 | *57.0* |
| | Tom Taggart (D) | 9,329 | *43.0* |
| | **Class 3** | | |
| **1958 [2]** | **Republican Primary** | | |
| | Mike Stepovich (R) | | *100.0* |
| | **Democratic Primary** | | |
| | Ernest Gruening (D) | | *100.0* |
| **1962** | **Republican Primary** | | |
| | Ted Stevens (R) | 11,000 | *72.5* |
| | Frank Cook (R) | 4,175 | *27.5* |
| | **Democratic Primary** | | |
| | Ernest Gruening (D) | 18,525 | *86.3* |
| | R. L. Veach (D) | 2,946 | *13.7* |
| **1968** | **Republican Primary** | | |
| | Elmer Rasmuson (R) | 10,320 | *53.1* |
| | Ted Stevens (R) | 9,111 | *46.9* |
| | **Democratic Primary** | | |
| | Mike Gravel (D) | 17,971 | *52.9* |
| | Ernest Gruening (D) | 16,015 | *47.1* |
| **1974** | **Republican Primary** | | |
| | C. R. Lewis (R) | 21,065 | *52.7* |
| | Terry Miller (R) | 16,336 | *40.8* |
| | Red Stevens (R) | 2,207 | *5.5* |
| | **Democratic Primary** | | |
| | Mike Gravel (D) | 22,834 | *54.3* |
| | Gene Guess (D) | 15,090 | *35.9* |
| | Richard J. Greuel (D) | 3,367 | *8.0* |
| **1980** | **Republican Primary** | | |
| | Frank H. Murkowski (R) | 16,292 | *59.0* |
| | Arthur R. Kennedy (R) | 5,527 | *20.0* |
| | Morris Thompson (R) | 3,635 | *13.2* |
| | **Democratic Primary** | | |
| | Clark S. Gruening (D) | 39,719 | *54.9* |
| | Mike Gravel (D) | 31,504 | *43.5* |

| | Candidates | Votes | % |
|---|---|---|---|
| 1986 | **Republican Primary** | | |
| | Frank H. Murkowski (R) | | 100.0 |
| | **Democratic Primary** | | |
| | Glenn Olds (D) | 36,995 | 75.0 |
| | Bill Barnes (D) | 4,871 | 9.9 |
| | Dave Carlson (D) | 4,211 | 8.5 |
| | **Libertarian Primary** | | |
| | Chuck House (LIBERT) | | 100.0 |
| 1992 [4] | **Republican Primary** | | |
| | Frank H. Murkowski (R) | 37,486 | 80.5 |
| | Jed Whittaker (R) | 9,065 | 19.5 |
| | **Democratic Primary** | | |
| | Tony Smith (D) | 33,162 | 48.8 |
| | William L. Hensley (D) | 29,586 | 43.5 |
| | **Green Primary** | | |
| | Mary E. Jodan (GREEN) | 5,989 | 100.0 |

**Alaska**

*1. In Alaska's so-called "jungle" primaries, all candidates for an office appeared together on the same ballot with their parties designated. Nominations went to the Republican and Democrat receiving the most votes for the office. Percentages were calculated here as if candidates had run in separate party primaries.*

*2. Alaska became a state Jan. 3, 1959. The first Senate elections for that state were for unspecified terms. The Senate later determined that Sen. Bartlett would serve two years (Class 2) and Sen. Gruening, four (Class 3).*

*3. A special election was held in 1970 to fill the remaining two years of the term of Sen. E. L. Bartlett (D), who died Dec. 11, 1968. The first two years of the vacancy were filled by appointee Ted Stevens (R).*

*4. In 1992 the Republican primary was a closed primary with only candidates from that party on the ballot. All other parties ran on a multi-party ballot with nominations going to the candidate with the highest vote in each party.*

# ARIZONA

| | Candidates | Votes | % |
|---|---|---|---|
| | **Class 1** | | |
| 1958 | **Republican Primary** | | |
| | Barry Goldwater (R) | | 100.0 |
| | **Democratic Primary** | | |
| | Ernest W. McFarland (D) | 111,429 | 72.5 |
| | Stephen W. Langmade (D) | 42,199 | 27.5 |
| 1964 | **Republican Primary** | | |
| | Paul Fannin (R) | | 100.0 |

| | Candidates | Votes | % |
|---|---|---|---|
| | **Democratic Primary** | | |
| | Roy L. Elson (D) | 76,697 | 41.4 |
| | Renz L. Jennings (D) | 64,331 | 34.7 |
| | Howard V. Peterson (D) | 22,424 | 12.1 |
| | George Gavin (D) | 10,291 | 5.6 |
| 1970 | **Republican Primary** | | |
| | Paul Fannin (R) | | 100.0 |
| | **Democratic Primary** | | |
| | Sam Grossman (D) | 78,006 | 65.2 |
| | John Kruglick (D) | 27,324 | 22.8 |
| | H. L. Kelly (D) | 14,238 | 11.9 |
| 1976 | **Republican Primary** | | |
| | Sam Steiger (R) | 102,843 | 52.5 |
| | John B. Conlan (R) | 93,033 | 47.5 |
| | **Democratic Primary** | | |
| | Dennis DeConcini (D) | 121,423 | 53.4 |
| | Carolyn Warner (D) | 71,612 | 31.5 |
| | Wade Church (D) | 34,266 | 15.1 |
| | **Libertarian Primary** | | |
| | Allan Norwitz (LIBERT) | | 100.0 |
| 1982 | **Republican Primary** | | |
| | Pete Dunn (R) | 97,391 | 55.1 |
| | Dean Sellers (R) | 79,375 | 44.9 |
| | **Democratic Primary** | | |
| | Dennis DeConcini (D) | 140,328 | 84.4 |
| | Caroline P. Killeen (D) | 25,909 | 15.6 |
| | **Libertarian Primary** | | |
| | Randall Clamons (LIBERT) | | 100.0 |
| 1988 | **Republican Primary** | | |
| | Keith DeGreen (R) | | 100.0 |
| | **Democratic Primary** | | |
| | Dennis DeConcini (D) | | 100.0 |

| | Candidates | Votes | % |
|---|---|---|---|
| | **Class 3** | | |
| 1956 | **Republican Primary** | | |
| | Ross F. Jones (R) | 31,246 | 79.3 |
| | Albert H. Mackenzie (R) | 8,147 | 20.7 |
| | **Democratic Primary** | | |
| | Carl Hayden (D) | 99,859 | 82.4 |
| | Robert E. Miller (D) | 21,370 | 17.6 |
| 1962 | **Republican Primary** | | |
| | Evan Mecham (R) | 40,300 | 59.0 |
| | Stephen Shadegg (R) | 27,965 | 41.0 |

| Candidates | Votes | % |
|---|---|---|
| **Democratic Primary** | | |
| Carl Hayden (D) | 117,688 | 76.5 |
| W. Lee McLane (D) | 36,158 | 23.5 |

**1968**

| Candidates | Votes | % |
|---|---|---|
| **Republican Primary** | | |
| Barry Goldwater (R) | | 100.0 |
| **Democratic Primary** | | |
| Roy L. Elson (D) | 95,231 | 62.8 |
| Bob Kennedy (D) | 41,397 | 27.3 |
| Dick Herbert (D) | 15,061 | 9.9 |

**1974**

| Candidates | Votes | % |
|---|---|---|
| **Republican Primary** | | |
| Barry Goldwater (R) | | 100.0 |
| **Democratic Primary** | | |
| Jonathan Marshall (D) | 79,225 | 53.6 |
| George Oglesby (D) | 36,262 | 24.5 |
| William M. Feighan (D) | 32,449 | 21.9 |

**1980**

| Candidates | Votes | % |
|---|---|---|
| **Republican Primary** | | |
| Barry Goldwater (R) | | 100.0 |
| **Democratic Primary** | | |
| Bill Schulz (D) | 97,520 | 55.4 |
| James F. McNulty Jr. (D) | 58,894 | 33.4 |
| Frank DePaoli (D) | 19,259 | 10.9 |
| **Libertarian Primary** | | |
| Fred Esser (LIBERT) | | 100.0 |

**1986**

| Candidates | Votes | % |
|---|---|---|
| **Republican Primary** | | |
| John McCain (R) | | 100.0 |
| **Democratic Primary** | | |
| Richard Kimball (D) | | 100.0 |

**1992**

| Candidates | Votes | % |
|---|---|---|
| **Republican Primary** | | |
| John McCain (R) | | 100.0 |
| **Democratic Primary** | | |
| Claire Sargent (D) | 124,174 | 56.8 |
| Truman Spangrud (D) | 94,326 | 43.2 |

# ARKANSAS

| Candidates | Votes | % |
|---|---|---|
| **Class 2** | | |

**1924**

| Candidates | Votes | % |
|---|---|---|
| **Democratic Primary** | | |
| Joseph T. Robinson (D) | | 100.0 |

**1930**

| Candidates | Votes | % |
|---|---|---|
| **Democratic Primary** | | |
| Joseph T. Robinson (D) | 167,167 | 76.6 |
| Tom W. Campbell (D) | 51,085 | 23.4 |

**1936**

| Candidates | Votes | % |
|---|---|---|
| **Democratic Primary** | | |
| Joseph T. Robinson (D) | 170,356 | 72.7 |
| Cleveland Holland (D) | 42,541 | 18.2 |
| J. Rosser Venable (D) | 21,352 | 9.1 |

**1937**

| Candidates | Votes | % |
|---|---|---|
| **Democratic Primary** | | |
| Carl E. Bailey (D) [1] | | |

**1942**

| Candidates | Votes | % |
|---|---|---|
| **Democratic Primary** | | |
| Jack Holt (D) | 54,185 | 32.1 |
| John L. McClellan (D) | 53,729 | 31.8 |
| Clyde Ellis (D) | 34,264 | 20.3 |
| David D. Terry (D) | 26,911 | 15.9 |
| **Democratic Runoff** | | |
| John L. McClellan (D) | 134,277 | 61.7 |
| Jack Holt (D) | 83,516 | 38.4 |

**1948**

| Candidates | Votes | % |
|---|---|---|
| **Democratic Primary** | | |
| John L. McClellan (D) | | 100.0 |

**1954**

| Candidates | Votes | % |
|---|---|---|
| **Democratic Primary** | | |
| John L. McClellan (D) | | 100.0 |

**1960**

| Candidates | Votes | % |
|---|---|---|
| **Democratic Primary** | | |
| John L. McClellan (D) | | 100.0 |

**1966**

| Candidates | Votes | % |
|---|---|---|
| **Democratic Primary** | | |
| John L. McClellan (D) | 310,526 | 77.2 |
| Foster Johnson (D) | 91,746 | 22.8 |

**1972**

| Candidates | Votes | % |
|---|---|---|
| **Republican Primary** | | |
| Wayne H. Babbitt (R) | | 100.0 |
| **Democratic Primary** | | |
| John L. McClellan (D) | 220,588 | 44.7 |
| David Pryor (D) | 204,058 | 41.4 |
| Ted Boswell (D) | 62,496 | 12.7 |
| **Democratic Runoff** | | |
| John L. McClellan (D) | 242,983 | 52.0 |
| David Pryor (D) | 224,262 | 48.0 |

**1978**

| Candidates | Votes | % |
|---|---|---|
| **Republican Primary** | | |
| Tom Kelly (R) | | 100.0 |
| **Democratic Primary** | | |
| David Pryor (D) | 198,039 | 34.3 |
| Jim Guy Tucker (D) | 187,568 | 32.5 |
| Ray Thornton (D) | 184,095 | 31.9 |

| | Candidates | Votes | % |
|---|---|---|---|
| | **Democratic Runoff** | | |
| | David Pryor (D) | 265,525 | *54.9* |
| | Jim Guy Tucker (D) | 218,026 | *45.1* |
| 1984 | **Republican Primary** | | |
| | Ed Bethune (R) | | *100.0* |
| | **Democratic Primary** | | |
| | David Pryor (D) | | *100.0* |
| 1990 | **Democratic Primary** | | |
| | David Pryor (D) | | *100.0* |

### Class 3

| | Candidates | Votes | % |
|---|---|---|---|
| 1920 | **Democratic Primary** | | |
| | Thaddeus H. Caraway (D) | 92,411 | *62.9* |
| | Charles F. Kirby (D) | 54,527 | *37.1* |
| 1926 | **Democratic Primary** | | |
| | Thaddeus H. Caraway (D) | | *100.0* |
| 1932 | **Democratic Primary** | | |
| | Hattie W. Caraway (D) | 127,702 | *44.7* |
| | O. L. Bodenhamer (D) | 63,858 | *22.4* |
| | Vincent M. Miles (D) | 30,423 | *10.7* |
| | Charles H. Brough (D) | 26,207 | *9.2* |
| | William F. Kirby (D) | 21,448 | *7.5* |
| 1938 | **Democratic Primary** | | |
| | Hattie W. Caraway (D) | 145,472 | *51.0* |
| | John L. McClellan (D) | 134,708 | *47.3* |
| 1944 | **Democratic Primary** | | |
| | J. William Fulbright (D) | 67,228 | *36.2* |
| | Homer M. Adkins (D) | 49,795 | *26.8* |
| | T. H. Barton (D) | 43,053 | *23.2* |
| | Hattie W. Caraway (D) | 24,881 | *13.4* |
| | **Democratic Runoff** | | |
| | J. William Fulbright (D) | 117,121 | *57.9* |
| | Homer M. Adkins (D) | 85,163 | *42.1* |
| 1950 | **Democratic Primary** | | |
| | J. William Fulbright (D) | 189,200 | *100.0* |
| 1956 | **Democratic Primary** | | |
| | J. William Fulbright (D) | | *100.0* |
| | **Republican Primary** | | |
| | Kenneth G. Jones (R) | | *100.0* |
| 1962 | **Democratic Primary** | | |
| | J. William Fulbright (D) | 253,751 | *66.1* |
| | Winston G. Chandler (D) | 129,987 | *33.9* |

| | Candidates | Votes | % |
|---|---|---|---|
| 1968 | **Republican Primary** | | |
| | Charles T. Bernard (R) | | *100.0* |
| | **Democratic Primary** | | |
| | J. William Fulbright (D) | 220,684 | *52.9* |
| | James Johnson (D) | 132,038 | *31.7* |
| | Bobby K. Hayes (D) | 52,906 | *12.7* |
| 1974 | **Republican Primary** | | |
| | John H. Jones (R) | | *100.0* |
| | **Democratic Primary** | | |
| | Dale Bumpers (D) | 380,748 | *65.0* |
| | J. William Fulbright (D) | 204,630 | *35.0* |
| 1980 | **Republican Primary** | | |
| | Bill Clark (R) | | *100.0* |
| | **Democratic Primary** | | |
| | Dale Bumpers (D) | | *100.0* |
| 1986 | **Republican Primary** | | |
| | Asa Hutchinson (R) | | *100.0* |
| | **Democratic Primary** | | |
| | Dale Bumpers (D) | | *100.0* |
| 1992 | **Republican Primary** | | |
| | Mike Huckabee (R) | 41,346 | *79.1* |
| | David Busby (R) | 10,892 | *20.9* |
| | **Democratic Primary** | | |
| | Dale Bumpers (D) | 322,458 | *64.5* |
| | Julia H. Jones (D) | 177,273 | *35.5* |

**Arkansas**

1. Robinson died July 14, 1937, a few months into his new six-year term. The state committee of the Democratic Party in Arkansas selected Gov. Carl E. Bailey as the Democratic nominee to run in an Oct. 19 special election; no Democratic primary was held. Bailey lost the special election to Rep. John E. Miller, a Democrat running as an Independent. (See p. 817)

# CALIFORNIA

| | Candidates | Votes | % |
|---|---|---|---|
| | **Class 1** | | |
| 1958 [1] | **Republican Primary** | | |
| | Goodwin J. Knight (R) | 790,939 | *49.1* |
| | George Christopher (R) | 558,245 | *34.7* |
| | Clair Engle (D) | 173,845 | *10.8* |
| | **Democratic Primary** | | |
| | Clair Engle (D) | 1,558,622 | *70.8* |
| | Goodwin J. Knight (R) | 385,170 | *17.5* |
| | George Christopher (R) | 221,783 | *10.1* |

| | Candidates | Votes | % |
|---|---|---|---|
| 1964 | **Republican Primary** | | |
| | George Murphy (R) | 1,121,591 | *54.1* |
| | Leland M. Kaiser (R) | 689,323 | *33.3* |
| | Fred Hall (R) | 261,036 | *12.6* |
| | **Democratic Primary** | | |
| | Pierre Salinger (D) | 1,177,517 | *44.3* |
| | Alan Cranston (D) | 1,037,748 | *39.0* |
| | George McLain (D) | 180,405 | *6.8* |
| 1970 | **Republican Primary** | | |
| | George Murphy (R) | 1,325,271 | *64.3* |
| | Norton Simon (R) | 670,702 | *32.5* |
| | **Democratic Primary** | | |
| | John V. Tunney (D) | 1,010,812 | *41.6* |
| | George E. Brown (D) | 812,463 | *33.4* |
| | Kenneth Hahn (D) | 417,970 | *17.2* |
| | **American Independent Primary** | | |
| | Charles C. Ripley (AMI) | 14,115 | *65.0* |
| | John Ortman (AMI) | 7,600 | *34.9* |
| | **Peace and Freedom Primary** | | |
| | Robert Scheer (PFP) | | *100.0* |
| 1976 | **Republican Primary** | | |
| | S. I. Hayakawa (R) | 886,743 | *38.2* |
| | Robert H. Finch (R) | 614,240 | *26.5* |
| | Alphonzo E. Bell (R) | 532,969 | *23.0* |
| | John L. Harmer (R) | 197,252 | *8.5* |
| | **Democratic Primary** | | |
| | John V. Tunney (D) | 1,774,879 | *53.8* |
| | Tom Hayden (D) | 1,210,637 | *36.7* |
| | **American Independent Primary** | | |
| | Jack McCoy (AMI) | | *100.0* |
| | **Peace and Freedom Primary** | | |
| | David Wald (PFP) | | *100.0* |
| 1982 | **Republican Primary** | | |
| | Pete Wilson (R) | 851,292 | *37.5* |
| | Paul N. McCloskey (R) | 577,267 | *25.5* |
| | Barry M. Goldwater Jr. (R) | 408,308 | *18.0* |
| | Robert K. Dornan (R) | 181,970 | *8.0* |
| | **Democratic Primary** | | |
| | Edmund G. Brown Jr. (D) | 1,392,660 | *50.7* |
| | Gore Vidal (D) | 415,366 | *15.1* |
| | Paul B. Carpenter (D) | 415,198 | *15.1* |
| | Daniel K. Whitehurst (D) | 167,574 | *6.1* |
| | **American Independent Primary** | | |
| | Theresa Dietrich (AMI) | | *100.0* |

| | Candidates | Votes | % |
|---|---|---|---|
| | **Peace and Freedom Primary** | | |
| | David Wald (PFP) | | *100.0* |
| | **Libertarian Primary** | | |
| | Joseph Fuhrig (LIBERT) | | *100.0* |
| 1988 | **Republican Primary** | | |
| | Pete Wilson (R) | | *100.0* |
| | **Democratic Primary** | | |
| | Leo T. McCarthy (D) | 2,367,067 | *81.7* |
| | John H. Abbott (D) | 220,331 | *7.6* |
| | Robert J. Banuelos (D) | 163,882 | *5.7* |
| | Charles Greene (D) | 146,307 | *5.0* |
| | **American Independent Primary** | | |
| | Merton D. Short (AMI) | | *100.0* |
| | **Libertarian Primary** | | |
| | Jack Dean (LIBERT) | | *100.0* |
| | **Peace and Freedom Primary** | | |
| | M. Elizabeth Munoz (PFP) | 3,701 | *58.5* |
| | Gloria Garcia (PFP) | 2,623 | *41.5* |
| 1992 [2] | **Republican Special Primary** | | |
| | John Seymour (R) | 1,216,096 | *51.2* |
| | William E. Dannemeyer (R) | 638,279 | *26.9* |
| | Jim Trinity (R) | 306,182 | *12.9* |
| | William B. Allen (R) | 216,177 | *9.1* |
| | **Democratic Special Primary** | | |
| | Dianne Feinstein (D) | 1,775,730 | *57.8* |
| | Gray Davis (D) | 1,009,761 | *32.8* |
| | **American Independent Special Primary** | | |
| | Paul Meeuwenberg (AMI) | | *100.0* |
| | **Libertarian Special Primary** | | |
| | Richard B. Boddie (LIBERT) | | *100.0* |
| | **Peace and Freedom Special Primary** | | |
| | Gerald Horne (PFP) | 5,681 | *64.0* |
| | Jamie Mangia (PFP) | 3,195 | *36.0* |

### Class 3

| | Candidates | Votes | % |
|---|---|---|---|
| 1956 [1] | **Republican Primary** | | |
| | Thomas H. Kuchel (R) | 1,332,074 | *90.4* |
| | **Democratic Primary** | | |
| | Richard Richards (D) | 1,004,336 | *53.4* |
| | Thomas H. Kuchel (R) | 494,066 | *26.2* |
| | Samuel W. Yorty (D) | 383,813 | *20.4* |

**857**

| Candidates<br>**Prohibition Party Primary** | Votes | % |
|---|---|---|
| Ray Gourley (P) | | *100.0* |

**1962**

| Candidates<br>**Republican Primary** | Votes | % |
|---|---|---|
| Thomas H. Kuchel (R) | 1,357,975 | *75.0* |
| Lloyd Wright (R) | 247,300 | *13.7* |
| Howard Jarvis (R) | 180,768 | *10.0* |

**Democratic Primary**

| | Votes | % |
|---|---|---|
| Richard Richards (D) | 1,674,563 | *82.6* |
| Gabriel Green (D) | 171,379 | *8.5* |
| J. F. Coleman (D) | 170,296 | *8.4* |

**1968**

**Republican Primary**

| | Votes | % |
|---|---|---|
| Max Rafferty (R) | 1,112,947 | *50.1* |
| Thomas H. Kuchel (R) | 1,043,315 | *46.9* |

**Democratic Primary**

| | Votes | % |
|---|---|---|
| Alan Cranston (D) | 1,681,825 | *59.0* |
| Anthony C. Beilenson (D) | 644,844 | *22.6* |
| Walter R. Buchanan (D) | 227,798 | *8.0* |
| William M. Bennett (D) | 207,720 | *7.3* |

**Peace and Freedom Primary**

| | Votes | % |
|---|---|---|
| Paul Jacobs (PFP) | | *100.0* |

**1974**

**Republican Primary**

| | Votes | % |
|---|---|---|
| H. L. (Bill) Richardson (R) | 1,061,986 | *64.6* |
| Earl W. Brian (R) | 273,636 | *16.7* |
| James E. Johnson (R) | 118,715 | *7.2* |
| William H. Reinholz (R) | 107,217 | *6.5* |

**Democratic Primary**

| | Votes | % |
|---|---|---|
| Alan Cranston (D) | 2,262,574 | *83.5* |
| Howard L. Gifford (D) | 318,080 | *11.7* |

**American Independent Primary**

| | Votes | % |
|---|---|---|
| Jack McCoy (AMI) | | *100.0* |

**Peace and Freedom Primary**

| | Votes | % |
|---|---|---|
| Gayle M. Justice (PFP) | | *100.0* |

**1980**

**Republican Primary**

| | Votes | % |
|---|---|---|
| Paul Gann (R) | 934,433 | *40.0* |
| Samuel W. Yorty (R) | 668,583 | *28.6* |
| John G. Schmitz (R) | 442,839 | *19.0* |

**Democratic Primary**

| | Votes | % |
|---|---|---|
| Alan Cranston (D) | 2,608,746 | *79.9* |
| Richard Morgan (D) | 350,394 | *10.7* |

**American Independent Primary**

| | Votes | % |
|---|---|---|
| James C. Griffin (AMI) | | *100.0* |

**Peace and Freedom Primary**

| | Votes | % |
|---|---|---|
| David Wald (PFP) | | *100.0* |

| Candidates<br>**Libertarian Primary** | Votes | % |
|---|---|---|
| David Bergland (LIBERT) | | *100.0* |

**1986**

**Republican Primary**

| | Votes | % |
|---|---|---|
| Ed Zschau (R) | 737,384 | *37.1* |
| Bruce Herschensohn (R) | 587,852 | *29.6* |
| Michael D. Antonovich (R) | 180,010 | *9.1* |
| Bobbi Fiedler (R) | 143,032 | *7.2* |
| Ed Davis (R) | 130,309 | *6.6* |

**Democratic Primary**

| | Votes | % |
|---|---|---|
| Alan Cranston (D) | 1,807,242 | *80.7* |
| Charles Greene (D) | 165,594 | *7.4* |
| John H. Abbott (D) | 124,218 | *5.5* |

**American Independent Primary**

| | Votes | % |
|---|---|---|
| Edward B. Vallen (AMI) | | *100.0* |

**Peace and Freedom Primary**

| | Votes | % |
|---|---|---|
| Paul Kangas (PFP) | 2,495 | *51.6* |
| Lenni Brenner (PFP) | 2,344 | *48.4* |

**Libertarian Primary**

| | Votes | % |
|---|---|---|
| Breck McKinley (LIBERT) | | *100.0* |

**1992**

**Republican Primary**

| | Votes | % |
|---|---|---|
| Bruce Herschensohn (R) | 956,146 | *38.2* |
| Tom Campbell (R) | 895,970 | *35.8* |
| Sonny Bono (R) | 417,848 | *16.7* |

**Democratic Primary**

| | Votes | % |
|---|---|---|
| Barbara Boxer (D) | 1,339,126 | *43.7* |
| Leo T. McCarthy (D) | 935,209 | *30.5* |
| Mel Levine (D) | 667,359 | *21.8* |

**American Independent Primary**

| | Votes | % |
|---|---|---|
| Jerome McCready (AMI) | | *100.0* |

**Libertarian Primary**

| | Votes | % |
|---|---|---|
| June R. Genis (LIBERT) | | *100.0* |

**Peace and Freedom Primary**

| | Votes | % |
|---|---|---|
| Genevieve Torres (PFP) | 5,492 | *60.3* |
| Shirley Lee (PFP) | 3,610 | *39.7* |

**California**

*1. California's cross-filing law permitted a candidate to enter both the Democratic and Republican primaries. The law was repealed after 1958.*

*2. A special election was held in 1992 to fill the remaining two years of the term of Sen. Pete Wilson (R), who resigned Jan. 7, 1991, after he was elected governor. The first two years of the vacancy were filled by appointee John Seymour (R).*

# COLORADO

| Candidates | Votes | % |
|---|---|---|

### Class 2

**1960**   **Republican Primary**

| Gordon Allott (R) | | 100.0 |

**Democratic Primary**

| Robert L. Knous (D) | | 100.0 |

**1966**   **Republican Primary**

| Gordon Allott (R) | | 100.0 |

**Democratic Primary**

| Roy Romer (D) | | 100.0 |

**1972**   **Republican Primary**

| Gordon Allott (R) | | 100.0 |

**Democratic Primary**

| Floyd K. Haskell (D) | 77,574 | 58.8 |
| Anthony F. Vollack (D) | 54,298 | 41.2 |

**1978**   **Republican Primary**

| William L. Armstrong (R) | 108,573 | 73.4 |
| Jack Swigert (R) | 39,247 | 26.6 |

**Democratic Primary**

| Floyd K. Haskell (D) | | 100.0 |

**1984**   **Republican Primary**

| William L. Armstrong (R) | 105,870 | 100.0 |

**Democratic Primary**

| Nancy Dick (D) | 78,248 | 51.0 |
| Carlos F. Lucero (D) | 75,277 | 49.0 |

**1990**   **Republican Primary**

| Hank Brown (R) | | 100.0 |

**Democratic Primary**

| Josie Heath (D) | 116,099 | 58.6 |
| Carlos F. Lucero (D) | 82,173 | 41.4 |

### Class 3

**1956**   **Republican Primary**

| Dan Thornton (R) | | 100.0 |

**Democratic Primary**

| John A. Carroll (D) | 62,688 | 50.8 |
| Charles Brannan (D) | 60,701 | 49.2 |

**1962**   **Republican Primary**

| Peter H. Dominick (R) | | 100.0 |

| Candidates | Votes | % |
|---|---|---|

**Democratic Primary**

| John A. Carroll (D) | | 100.0 |

**1968**   **Republican Primary**

| Peter H. Dominick (R) | | 100.0 |

**Democratic Primary**

| Stephen McNichols (D) | 92,250 | 58.5 |
| Kenneth Montfort (D) | 65,347 | 41.5 |

**1974**   **Republican Primary**

| Peter H. Dominick (R) | | 100.0 |

**Democratic Primary**

| Gary Hart (D) | 81,161 | 39.9 |
| Herrick S. Roth (D) | 66,819 | 32.9 |
| Martin P. Miller (D) | 55,339 | 27.2 |

**1980**   **Republican Primary**

| Mary E. Buchanan (R) | 65,803 | 30.8 |
| Howard W. Callaway (R) | 64,256 | 30.1 |
| Sam Zakhem (R) | 42,629 | 20.0 |
| John M. Cogswell (R) | 40,651 | 19.0 |

**Democratic Primary**

| Gary Hart (D) | | 100.0 |

**1986**   **Republican Primary**

| Ken Kramer (R) | | 100.0 |

**Democratic Primary**

| Timothy E. Wirth (D) | | 100.0 |

**1992**   **Republican Primary**

| Terry Considine (R) | 122,427 | 100.0 |

**Democratic Primary**

| Ben Nighthorse Campbell (D) | 117,634 | 45.5 |
| Richard D. Lamm (D) | 93,599 | 36.2 |
| Josie Heath (D) | 47,418 | 18.3 |

# CONNECTICUT [1]

| Candidates | Votes | % |
|---|---|---|

### Class 1

**1970**   **Republican Primary**

| Lowell P. Weicker Jr. (R) | 77,057 | 60.3 |
| John M. Lupton (R) | 50,657 | 39.7 |

| Candidates | Votes | % |
|---|---|---|
| **Democratic Primary** | | |
| Joseph D. Duffey (D) | 79,166 | 43.7 |
| Alphonsus J. Donahue (D) | 66,916 | 36.8 |
| Edward L. Marcus (D) | 35,715 | 19.7 |

### Class 3

**1980** — **Republican Primary**

| | Votes | % |
|---|---|---|
| James L. Buckley (R) | 64,962 | 56.5 |
| Richard C. Buzzuto (R) | 50,096 | 43.5 |

**1992** — **Republican Primary**

| | Votes | % |
|---|---|---|
| Brook Johnson (R) | 50,305 | 59.4 |
| Christopher Burnham (R) | 40,542 | 40.6 |

**Connecticut**

1. In Connecticut, party conventions nominated candidates subject to a system of "challenge" primaries that allowed defeated candidates to petition for a popular vote if they received at least 20 percent of the convention vote.

# DELAWARE

| Candidates | Votes | % |
|---|---|---|
| **Class 1** | | |

**1982** — **Republican Primary**

| | Votes | % |
|---|---|---|
| William V. Roth Jr. (R) | | 100.0 |

**Democratic Primary**

| | | |
|---|---|---|
| David N. Levinson (D) | | 100.0 |

**1988** — **Republican Primary**

| | | |
|---|---|---|
| William V. Roth Jr. (R) | | 100.0 |

**Democratic Primary [1]**

| | Votes | % |
|---|---|---|
| S. B. Woo (D) | 20,225 | 50.0 |
| Samuel S. Beard (D) | 20,154 | 50.0 |

### Class 2

**1978 [2]** — **Republican Primary**

| | Votes | % |
|---|---|---|
| James H. Baxter (R) | 12,107 | 53.7 |
| James E. Venema (R) | 10,422 | 46.3 |

**1984** — **Republican Primary**

| | | |
|---|---|---|
| John M. Burris (R) | | 100.0 |

**Democratic Primary**

| | | |
|---|---|---|
| Joseph R. Biden (D) | | 100.0 |

**1990** — **Republican Primary**

| | | |
|---|---|---|
| M. Jane Brady (R) | | 100.0 |

**Democratic Primary**

| | | |
|---|---|---|
| Joseph R. Biden (D) | | 100.0 |

**Delaware**

1. Data are given for the recount vote.

2. From 1972 through 1978 Delaware used a system of "challenge" primaries, in which a candidate for statewide office who received at least 35 percent of the convention vote could challenge the endorsed candidate in a primary. There was no Senate election in Delaware in 1980, the first year that the state used the direct primary system.

# FLORIDA

| Candidates | Votes | % |
|---|---|---|
| **Class 1** | | |

**1922** — **Democratic Primary**

| | Votes | % |
|---|---|---|
| Park Trammell (D) | 59,232 | 66.7 |
| Albert W. Gilchrist (D) | 29,527 | 33.3 |

**1928** — **Democratic Primary**

| | Votes | % |
|---|---|---|
| Park Trammell (D) | 138,534 | 58.0 |
| John W. Martin (D) | 100,454 | 42.0 |

**1934** — **Democratic Primary**

| | Votes | % |
|---|---|---|
| Park Trammell (D) | 81,321 | 38.0 |
| Claude Pepper (D) | 79,396 | 37.1 |
| Charles A. Mitchell (D) | 30,455 | 14.2 |
| James F. Sikes (D) | 14,558 | 6.8 |

**Democratic Runoff**

| | Votes | % |
|---|---|---|
| Park Trammell (D) | 103,028 | 51.0 |
| Claude Pepper (D) | 98,978 | 49.0 |

**1936** — **Democratic Special Primary**

| | Votes | % |
|---|---|---|
| Charles O. Andrews (D) | 67,387 | 51.9 |
| Doyle E. Carlton (D) | 62,530 | 48.1 |

**1940** — **Democratic Primary**

| | Votes | % |
|---|---|---|
| Charles O. Andrews (D) | 179,195 | 40.9 |
| Jerry W. Carter (D) | 80,869 | 18.5 |
| B. MacFadden (D) | 71,487 | 16.3 |
| Fred P. Cone (D) | 68,584 | 15.7 |
| Charles F. Coe (D) | 33,463 | 7.6 |

**Democratic Runoff**

| | Votes | % |
|---|---|---|
| Charles O. Andrews (D) | 312,293 | 69.4 |
| Jerry W. Carter (D) | 137,641 | 30.6 |

**1946** — **Democratic Primary**

| | Votes | % |
|---|---|---|
| Spessard L. Holland (D) | 204,352 | 60.7 |
| Robert A. (Lex) Green (D) | 109,040 | 32.4 |

**1952** — **Democratic Primary**

| | Votes | % |
|---|---|---|
| Spessard L. Holland (D) | 485,515 | 84.2 |
| William A. Gaston (D) | 91,011 | 15.8 |

**1958** — **Republican Primary**

| | | |
|---|---|---|
| Leland Hyzer (R) | | 100.0 |

| Candidates<br>**Democratic Primary** | Votes | % |
|---|---|---|
| Spessard L. Holland (D) | 408,084 | *55.9* |
| Claude Pepper (D) | 321,377 | *44.1* |

**1964**    **Republican Primary**

| Candidates | Votes | % |
|---|---|---|
| Claude R. Kirk Jr. (R) | | *100.0* |

**Democratic Primary**

| Candidates | Votes | % |
|---|---|---|
| Spessard L. Holland (D) | 676,014 | *70.0* |
| Brailey Odham (D) | 289,454 | *30.0* |

**1970**    **Republican Primary**

| Candidates | Votes | % |
|---|---|---|
| William C. Cramer (R) | 220,553 | *62.5* |
| G. Harrold Carswell (R) | 121,281 | *34.4* |

**Democratic Primary**

| Candidates | Votes | % |
|---|---|---|
| Farris Bryant (D) | 240,222 | *32.9* |
| Lawton Chiles (D) | 188,300 | *25.8* |
| Fred Schultz (D) | 175,745 | *24.1* |
| Al Hastings (D) | 91,948 | *12.6* |

**Democratic Runoff**

| Candidates | Votes | % |
|---|---|---|
| Lawton Chiles (D) | 474,420 | *65.7* |
| Farris Bryant (D) | 247,211 | *34.3* |

**1976**    **Republican Primary**

| Candidates | Votes | % |
|---|---|---|
| John Grady (R) | 164,644 | *54.5* |
| Walter Sims (R) | 74,684 | *24.7* |
| Helen S. Hansel (R) | 62,718 | *20.8* |

**Democratic Primary**

| Candidates | Votes | % |
|---|---|---|
| Lawton Chiles (D) | | *100.0* |

**1982**    **Republican Primary**

| Candidates | Votes | % |
|---|---|---|
| Van B. Poole | 154,158 | *41.6* |
| David H. Bludworth | 116,030 | *31.3* |
| George Snyder | 100,607 | *27.1* |

**Republican Runoff**

| Candidates | Votes | % |
|---|---|---|
| Van B. Poole | 131,638 | *58.1* |
| David H. Bludworth | 95,024 | *41.9* |

**Democratic Primary**

| Candidates | Votes | % |
|---|---|---|
| Lawton Chiles (D) | | *100.0* |

**1988**    **Republican Primary**

| Candidates | Votes | % |
|---|---|---|
| Connie Mack (R) | 405,296 | *61.8* |
| Robert W. Merkle (R) | 250,730 | *38.2* |

**Democratic Primary**

| Candidates | Votes | % |
|---|---|---|
| Bill Gunter (D) | 383,721 | *38.0* |
| Buddy McKay (D) | 263,946 | *26.1* |
| Dan Mica (D) | 179,524 | *17.8* |
| Patricia Prank (D) | 119,277 | *11.8* |
| Claude R. Kirk Jr. (D) | 51,387 | *5.0* |

| Candidates<br>**Democratic Runoff** | Votes | % |
|---|---|---|
| Buddy McKay (D) | 369,266 | *52.0* |
| Bill Gunter (D) | 340,918 | *48.0* |

## Class 3

**1920**    **Democratic Primary**

| Candidates | Votes | % |
|---|---|---|
| Duncan U. Fletcher (D) | 62,304 | *71.4* |
| Sidney J. Catts (D) | 25,007 | *28.6* |

**1926**    **Democratic Primary**

| Candidates | Votes | % |
|---|---|---|
| Duncan U. Fletcher (D) | 63,760 | *59.5* |
| Jerry W. Carter (D) | 39,143 | *36.5* |

**Democratic Second Choice**

| Candidates | Votes | % |
|---|---|---|
| Jerry W. Carter (D) | 932 | *53.4* |
| Duncan U. Fletcher (D) | 812 | *46.6* |

**1932**    **Democratic Primary**

| Candidates | Votes | % |
|---|---|---|
| Duncan U. Fletcher (D) | | *100.0* |

**1936**    **Democratic Special Primary**

| Candidates | Votes | % |
|---|---|---|
| Claude Pepper (D) | | *100.0* |

**1938**    **Democratic Primary**

| Candidates | Votes | % |
|---|---|---|
| Claude Pepper (D) | 242,350 | *58.4* |
| J. Mark Wilcox (D) | 110,675 | *26.7* |
| David Sholtz (D) | 52,785 | *12.7* |

**1944**    **Republican Primary**

| Candidates | Votes | % |
|---|---|---|
| Miles H. Draper (R) | 5,289 | *53.3* |
| H. K. Gibson (R) | 4,628 | *46.7* |

**Democratic Primary**

| Candidates | Votes | % |
|---|---|---|
| Claude Pepper (D) | 194,445 | *51.3* |
| J. Ollie Edmunds (D) | 127,158 | *33.5* |
| Millard B. Conklin (D) | 33,317 | *8.8* |

**1950**    **Democratic Primary**

| Candidates | Votes | % |
|---|---|---|
| George A. Smathers (D) | 387,215 | *54.8* |
| Claude Pepper (D) | 319,754 | *45.2* |

**1956**    **Democratic Primary**

| Candidates | Votes | % |
|---|---|---|
| George A. Smathers (D) | 614,663 | *87.5* |
| Erle Griffis (D) | 87,525 | *12.5* |

**1962**    **Republican Primary**

| Candidates | Votes | % |
|---|---|---|
| Emerson H. Rupert (R) | | *100.0* |

**Democratic Primary**

| Candidates | Votes | % |
|---|---|---|
| George A. Smathers (D) | 587,562 | *84.2* |
| Roger L. Davis (D) | 74,565 | *10.7* |
| Douglas Randolph Voorhees (D) | 35,832 | *5.1* |

**1968**    **Republican Primary**

| Candidates | Votes | % |
|---|---|---|
| Edward J. Gurney (R) | 169,805 | *80.0* |
| Herman W. Goldner (R) | 42,347 | *20.0* |

# GEORGIA

| Candidates | Votes | % |
|---|---|---|
| **Democratic Primary** | | |
| Leroy Collins (D) | 426,096 | *49.5* |
| Earl Faircloth (D) | 397,642 | *46.2* |
| **Democratic Runoff** | | |
| Leroy Collins (D) | 410,689 | *50.2* |
| Earl Faircloth (D) | 407,696 | *49.8* |

**1974**

| | Votes | % |
|---|---|---|
| **Republican Primary** | | |
| Jack M. Eckerd (R) | 186,897 | *67.5* |
| Paula Hawkins (R) | 90,049 | *32.5* |
| **Democratic Primary** | | |
| Bill Gunter (D) | 236,185 | *29.8* |
| Richard Stone (D) | 157,301 | *19.8* |
| Richard A. Pettigrew (D) | 146,728 | *18.5* |
| Mallory E. Horne (D) | 90,684 | *11.4* |
| Glenn W. Turner (D) | 51,326 | *6.5* |
| **Democratic Runoff** | | |
| Richard Stone (D) | 321,683 | *50.8* |
| Bill Gunter (D) | 311,044 | *49.2* |

**1980**

| | Votes | % |
|---|---|---|
| **Republican Primary** | | |
| Paula Hawkins (R) | 209,856 | *48.1* |
| Louis Frey (R) | 119,834 | *27.5* |
| Ander Crenshaw (R) | 54,767 | *12.6* |
| **Republican Runoff** | | |
| Paula Hawkins (R) | 293,600 | *61.6* |
| Louis Frey (R) | 182,911 | *38.4* |
| **Democratic Primary** | | |
| Richard Stone (D) | 355,287 | *32.1* |
| Bill Gunter (D) | 335,859 | *30.3* |
| Buddy MacKay (D) | 272,538 | *24.6* |
| Richard A. Pettigrew (D) | 108,154 | *9.8* |
| **Democratic Runoff** | | |
| Bill Gunter (D) | 594,676 | *51.8* |
| Richard Stone (D) | 554,268 | *48.2* |

**1986**

| | Votes | % |
|---|---|---|
| **Republican Primary** | | |
| Paula Hawkins (R) | 491,953 | *88.7* |
| Jon L. Shudlick (R) | 62,474 | *11.3* |
| **Democratic Primary** | | |
| Bob Graham (D) | 851,586 | *85.0* |
| Robert P. Kunst (D) | 149,797 | *15.0* |

**1992**

| | Votes | % |
|---|---|---|
| **Republican Primary** | | |
| Bill Grant (R) | 413,457 | *56.1* |
| Rob Quartel (R) | 196,524 | *26.7* |
| Hugh Brotherton (R) | 126,878 | *17.2* |
| **Democratic Primary** | | |
| Bob Graham (D) | 968,618 | *84.3* |
| Jim Mahorner (D) | 180,405 | *15.7* |

| | Candidates | Votes | % |
|---|---|---|---|
| | **Class 2** | | |
| **1924** | **Democratic Primary** | | |
| | William J. Harris (D) | 144,740 | *65.7* |
| | Thomas W. Hardwick (D) | 75,713 | *34.3* |
| **1930** | **Democratic Primary** | | |
| | William J. Harris (D) | 162,169 | *77.9* |
| | John M. Slaton (D) | 46,095 | *22.1* |
| **1932** | **Democratic Special Primary** | | |
| | Richard B. Russell (D) | 162,745 | *57.7* |
| | Charles R. Crisp (D) | 119,193 | *42.3* |
| **1936** | **Democratic Primary** | | |
| | Richard B. Russell (D) | 256,154 | *65.5* |
| | Eugene Talmadge (D) | 134,695 | *34.5* |
| **1942** | **Democratic Primary** | | |
| | Richard B. Russell (D) | 232,084 | *80.6* |
| | Will D. Upshaw (D) | 55,845 | *19.4* |
| **1948** | **Democratic Primary** | | |
| | Richard B. Russell (D) | 703,048 | *100.0* |
| **1954** | **Democratic Primary** | | |
| | Richard B. Russell (D) | 619,129 | *100.0* |
| **1960** | **Democratic Primary** | | |
| | Richard B. Russell (D) | 560,256 | *100.0* |
| **1966** | **Democratic Primary** | | |
| | Richard B. Russell (D) | 596,209 | *90.6* |
| | Harry L. Hyde (D) | 61,922 | *9.4* |
| **1972** [1] | **Republican Special Primary** | | |
| | Fletcher Thompson (R) | 70,859 | *100.0* |
| | **Republican Primary** | | |
| | Fletcher Thompson (R) | 71,464 | *91.1* |
| | **Democratic Special Primary** | | |
| | David H. Gambrell (D) | 258,216 | *34.3* |
| | Sam Nunn (D) | 170,689 | *22.7* |
| | S. Ernest Vandiver (D) | 151,908 | *20.2* |
| | Hosea Williams (D) | 45,613 | *6.1* |
| | J. B. Stoner (D) | 38,261 | *5.1* |
| | **Democratic Special Runoff** | | |
| | Sam Nunn (D) | 326,186 | *52.1* |
| | David H. Gambrell (D) | 299,919 | *47.9* |

| Candidates | Votes | % |
|---|---|---|
| **Democratic Primary** | | |
| David H. Gambrell (D) | 225,470 | *31.5* |
| Sam Nunn (D) | 166,035 | *23.2* |
| S. Ernest Vandiver (D) | 147,135 | *20.5* |
| Hosea Williams (D) | 46,153 | *6.4* |
| J. B. Stoner (D) | 40,675 | *5.7* |
| **Democratic Runoff** | | |
| Sam Nunn (D) | 334,670 | *54.2* |
| David H. Gambrell (D) | 283,414 | *45.9* |

**1978 Republican Primary**

| Candidates | Votes | % |
|---|---|---|
| John W. Stokes (R) | 14,443 | *58.5* |
| Dean Parkison (R) | 10,250 | *41.5* |
| **Democratic Primary** | | |
| Sam Nunn (D) | 525,703 | *80.0* |
| Jack Dorsey (D) | 71,223 | *10.8* |

**1984 Republican Primary**

| Candidates | Votes | % |
|---|---|---|
| Mike Hicks (R) | 27,547 | *41.1* |
| Kelly Stratton Brown (R) | 26,657 | *39.7* |
| J. W. Tibbs Jr. (R) | 12,849 | *19.2* |
| **Republican Runoff** | | |
| Mike Hicks (R) | 16,987 | *67.1* |
| J. W. Tibbs Jr. (R) | 8,336 | *32.9* |
| **Democratic Primary** | | |
| Sam Nunn (D) | 801,412 | *90.2* |
| Jim Boyd (D) | 86,973 | *9.8* |

**1990 Democratic Primary**

| Candidates | Votes | % |
|---|---|---|
| Sam Nunn (D) | | *100.0* |

## Class 3

**1920 Democratic Primary**

| Candidates | Votes | % |
|---|---|---|
| Thomas Watson (D) | 102,647 | *45.0* |
| Dorsey (D) | 68,220 | *29.9* |
| Smith (D) | 56,357 | *24.7* |

**1922 Democratic Special Primary**

| Candidates | Votes | % |
|---|---|---|
| Walter F. George (D) | 60,436 | *54.6* |
| Thomas W. Hardwick (D) | 36,328 | *32.9* |
| Wright (D) | 12,820 | *11.6* |

**1926 Democratic Primary**

| Candidates | Votes | % |
|---|---|---|
| Walter F. George (D) | 128,179 | *67.4* |
| Richard B. Russell (D) | 61,911 | *32.6* |

**1932 Democratic Primary**

| Candidates | Votes | % |
|---|---|---|
| Walter F. George (D) | | *100.0* |

**1938 Democratic Primary**

| Candidates | Votes | % |
|---|---|---|
| Walter F. George (D) | 141,235 | *44.0* |
| Eugene Talmadge (D) | 103,075 | *32.1* |
| L. S. Camp (D) | 76,778 | *23.9* |

**1944**

| Candidates | Votes | % |
|---|---|---|
| **Democratic Primary** | | |
| Walter F. George (D) | 211,081 | *86.0* |
| John W. Goolsby (D) | 34,465 | *14.0* |

**1950 Democratic Primary**

| Candidates | Votes | % |
|---|---|---|
| Walter F. George (D) | 470,156 | *82.5* |
| Alex McLennan (D) | 79,886 | *14.0* |

**1956 Democratic Primary**

| Candidates | Votes | % |
|---|---|---|
| Herman E. Talmadge (D) | 498,327 | *80.3* |
| M. E. Thompson (D) | 122,152 | *19.7* |

**1962 Democratic Primary**

| Candidates | Votes | % |
|---|---|---|
| Herman E. Talmadge (D) | 673,782 | *88.0* |
| Henry M. Henderson (D) | 91,664 | *12.0* |

**1968 Republican Primary**

| Candidates | Votes | % |
|---|---|---|
| E. Earl Patton (R) | 20,316 | *59.5* |
| Jack Sells (R) | 13,805 | *40.5* |
| **Democratic Primary** | | |
| Herman E. Talmadge (D) | 697,915 | *77.1* |
| Maynard H. Jackson Jr. (D) | 207,171 | *22.9* |

**1974 Republican Primary**

| Candidates | Votes | % |
|---|---|---|
| Jerry R. Johnson (R) | | *100.0* |
| **Democratic Primary** | | |
| Herman E. Talmadge (D) | 523,133 | *81.5* |
| Carlton Myers (D) | 119,011 | *18.5* |

**1980 Republican Primary**

| Candidates | Votes | % |
|---|---|---|
| Mack Mattingly (R) | 28,191 | *59.8* |
| E. J. Bagley (R) | 6,082 | *12.9* |
| Hulon M. Madeley (R) | 3,999 | *8.5* |
| Dean Parkison (R) | 3,219 | *6.8* |
| Nick M. Belluso (R) | 2,947 | *6.3* |
| J. W. Tibbs Jr. (R) | 2,700 | *5.7* |
| **Democratic Primary** | | |
| Herman E. Talmadge (D) | 432,215 | *42.0* |
| Zell Miller (D) | 247,766 | *24.1* |
| Norman Underwood (D) | 183,683 | *17.8* |
| Dawson Mathis (D) | 133,729 | *13.0* |
| **Democratic Runoff** | | |
| Herman E. Talmadge (D) | 559,615 | *58.6* |
| Zell Miller (D) | 395,773 | *41.4* |

**1986 Republican Primary**

| Candidates | Votes | % |
|---|---|---|
| Mack Mattingly (R) | 74,743 | *95.0* |
| **Democratic Primary** | | |
| Wyche Fowler (D) | 314,787 | *50.2* |
| Hamilton Jordan (D) | 196,307 | *31.3* |
| John D. Russell (D) | 100,881 | *16.1* |

|  | Candidates | Votes | % |
|---|---|---|---|
| 1992 | **Republican Primary** | | |
|  | Paul Coverdell (R) | 100,016 | *37.1* |
|  | Bob Barr (R) | 65,471 | *24.3* |
|  | John Knox (R) | 64,514 | *23.9* |
|  | Charles Tanksley (R) | 32,590 | *12.1* |
|  | **Republican Runoff** | | |
|  | Paul Coverdell (R) | 80,435 | *50.5* |
|  | Bob Barr (R) | 78,887 | *49.5* |
|  | **Democratic Primary** | | |
|  | Wyche Fowler (D) | 683,274 | *100.0* |

**Georgia**

1. *Two Senate primaries were held simultaneously in 1972, a special primary for the remainder of the term of Richard B. Russell (D), who died Jan. 21, 1971, and a regular primary for the full term beginning in January 1973. Gambrell, who was appointed to the Senate seat in 1971, led candidates in both primaries, but lost both primary runoffs to Nunn. Returns for the special primary from the Elections Research Center, Washington, D.C.*

# HAWAII

|  | Candidates | Votes | % |
|---|---|---|---|
|  | **Class 1** | | |
| 1959 [1] | **Republican Primary** | | |
|  | Hiram L. Fong (R) | | *100.0* |
|  | **Democratic Primary** | | |
|  | Frank F. Fasi (D) | 46,868 | *59.9* |
|  | William H. Heen (D) | 31,317 | *40.0* |
| 1964 | **Republican Primary** | | |
|  | Hiram L. Fong (R) | 31,770 | *95.2* |
|  | **Democratic Primary** | | |
|  | Thomas P. Gill (D) | 71,298 | *64.0* |
|  | Nadao Yoshinaga (D) | 37,253 | *33.4* |
| 1970 | **Republican Primary** | | |
|  | Hiram L. Fong (R) | | *100.0* |
|  | **Democratic Primary** | | |
|  | Cecil Heftel (D) | 78,934 | *62.4* |
|  | Tony N. Hodges (D) | 30,430 | *24.1* |
|  | Neil Abercrombie (D) | 17,058 | *13.5* |
| 1976 | **Republican Primary** | | |
|  | William F. Quinn (R) | 32,058 | *93.7* |
|  | Spencer J. Cabral (R) | 2,170 | *6.3* |
|  | **Democratic Primary** | | |
|  | Spark M. Matsunaga (D) | 105,731 | *51.0* |
|  | Patsy Mink (D) | 84,732 | *40.9* |

|  | Candidates | Votes | % |
|---|---|---|---|
|  | **Libertarian Primary** | | |
|  | Rockne Johnson (LIBERT) | | *100.0* |
|  | **Non-Partisan Primary** | | |
|  | James D. Kimmel (NON PART) | | *100.0* |
|  | **People's Primary** | | |
|  | Anthony N. Hodges (PP) | | *100.0* |
| 1982 | **Republican Primary** | | |
|  | Clarence J. Brown (R) | 6,142 | *65.2* |
|  | Arbis D. Shipley (R) | 3,279 | *34.8* |
|  | **Democratic Primary** | | |
|  | Spark M. Matsunaga (D) | | *100.0* |
|  | **Independent Democratic Primary** | | |
|  | E. F. Bernier-Nachtwey (ID) | | *100.0* |
| 1988 | **Republican Primary** | | |
|  | Maria M. Hustace (R) | 18,124 | *48.7* |
|  | Leonard Mednick (R) | 13,590 | *36.4* |
|  | Susanne Sydney (R) | 5,526 | *14.8* |
|  | **Democratic Primary** | | |
|  | Spark M. Matsunaga (D) | 180,853 | *86.9* |
|  | Robert Zimmerman (D) | 27,360 | *13.1* |
|  | **Libertarian Primary** | | |
|  | Ken Schoolland (LIBERT) | | *100.0* |
| 1990 [2] | **Republican Special Primary** | | |
|  | Patricia Saiki (R) | 39,847 | *85.8* |
|  | Richard I. C. Sutton (R) | 2,443 | *5.3* |
|  | **Democratic Special Primary** | | |
|  | Daniel K. Akaka (D) | 180,235 | *90.7* |
|  | Paul Snider (D) | 18,427 | *9.3* |
|  | **Libertarian Special Primary** | | |
|  | Ken Schoolland (LIBERT) | | *100.0* |
|  | **Class 3** | | |
| 1959 [1] | **Republican Primary** | | |
|  | Wilfred C. Tsukiyama (R) | | *100.0* |
|  | **Democratic Primary** | | |
|  | Oren E. Long (D) | 61,345 | *83.9* |
|  | Kenneth E. Young (D) | 9,036 | *12.3* |
|  | **Commonwealth Primary** | | |
|  | Eugene Ressencourt (CP) | | *100.0* |
| 1962 | **Republican Primary** | | |
|  | Ben F. Dillingham (R) | | *100.0* |

| Candidates | Votes | % |
|---|---|---|
| **Democratic Primary** | | |
| Daniel K. Inouye (D) | 80,707 | 93.6 |
| Frank Troy (D) | 5,476 | 6.3 |

**1968**

| **Republican Primary** | | |
|---|---|---|
| Wayne C. Thiessen (R) | | 100.0 |

| **Democratic Primary** | | |
|---|---|---|
| Daniel K. Inouye (D) | 111,135 | 87.5 |
| William Lampard (D) | 14,357 | 11.3 |

| **Peace and Freedom Primary** | | |
|---|---|---|
| Oliver Lee (PFP) | | 100.0 |

**1974**

| **Democratic Primary** | | |
|---|---|---|
| Daniel K. Inouye (D) | | 100.0 |

| **Peoples Primary** | | |
|---|---|---|
| James D. Kimmel (PP) | 61 | 64.9 |
| Floyd Nachtwey (PP) | 33 | 35.1 |

**1980**

| **Republican Primary** | | |
|---|---|---|
| Cooper Brown (R) | 3,219 | 39.0 |
| Lawrence I. Weisman (R) | 2,586 | 31.4 |
| Dan Dew (R) | 1,854 | 22.5 |
| E. F. Bernier-Nachtwey (R) | 584 | 7.1 |

| **Democratic Primary** | | |
|---|---|---|
| Daniel K. Inouye (D) | 198,468 | 87.5 |
| Kamuela Price (D) | 15,361 | 6.8 |
| John P. Fritz (D) | 12,929 | 5.7 |

| **Libertarian Primary** | | |
|---|---|---|
| H. E. Shasteen (LIBERT) | | 100.0 |

**1986**

| **Republican Primary** | | |
|---|---|---|
| Frank Hutchinson (R) | 20,375 | 67.7 |
| Marvin Franklin (R) | 9,714 | 32.3 |

| **Democratic Primary** | | |
|---|---|---|
| Daniel K. Inouye (D) | | 100.0 |

**1992**

| **Republican Primary** | | |
|---|---|---|
| Rick Reed (R) | 33,250 | 74.1 |
| Maria M. Hustace (R) | 9,348 | 20.8 |
| John James (R) | 2,250 | 5.0 |

| **Democratic Primary** | | |
|---|---|---|
| Daniel K. Inouye (D) | 141,273 | 76.1 |
| Wayne K. Nishiki (D) | 44,505 | 24.0 |

| **Green Primary** | | |
|---|---|---|
| Linda B. Martin (GREEN) | | 100.0 |

| Candidates | Votes | % |
|---|---|---|
| **Libertarian Primary** | | |
| Richard O. Rowland (LIBERT) | | 100.0 |

**Hawaii**

1. Hawaii became a state Aug. 21, 1959. The first Senate elections for that state were for unspecified terms. The Senate later determined that Sen. Fong would serve the long term (Class 1) and Sen. Long, the short term (Class 3).

2. A special election was held in 1990 to fill the remaining four years of the term of Sen. Spark Matsunaga (D), who died April 15, 1990.

# IDAHO

| Candidates | Votes | % |
|---|---|---|
| **Class 2** | | |

**1960**

| **Republican Primary** | | |
|---|---|---|
| Henry C. Dworshak (R) | | 100.0 |

| **Democratic Primary** | | |
|---|---|---|
| Gregg Potvin (D) | 16,524 | 23.7 |
| Bob McLaughlin (D) | 14,694 | 21.1 |
| Compton White (D) | 14,515 | 20.8 |
| A. W. Brunt (D) | 13,015 | 18.7 |
| Joseph R. Garry (D) | 10,899 | 15.6 |

| **Democratic Runoff** | | |
|---|---|---|
| R. F. (Bob) McLaughlin | 13,117 | 51.9 |
| Gregg Potvin | 12,174 | 48.1 |

**1966**

| **Republican Primary** | | |
|---|---|---|
| Len B. Jordan (R) | | 100.0 |

| **Democratic Primary** | | |
|---|---|---|
| Ralph R. Harding (D) | | 100.0 |

**1972**

| **Republican Primary** | | |
|---|---|---|
| James A. McClure (R) | 46,522 | 36.1 |
| George Hansen (R) | 35,412 | 27.4 |
| Glen Wegner (R) | 24,582 | 19.1 |
| Robert E. Smylie (R) | 22,497 | 17.4 |

| **Democratic Primary** | | |
|---|---|---|
| William E. (Bud) Davis (D) | 23,953 | 36.1 |
| W. Anthony Park (D) | 17,636 | 26.5 |
| Byron Johnson (D) | 15,526 | 23.4 |
| Rose Bowman (D) | 9,327 | 14.0 |

**1978**

| **Republican Primary** | | |
|---|---|---|
| James A. McClure (R) | | 100.0 |

| **Democratic Primary** | | |
|---|---|---|
| Dwight Jensen (D) | | 100.0 |

**1984**

| **Republican Primary** | | |
|---|---|---|
| James A. McClure (R) | 102,125 | 100.0 |

| Candidates | Votes | % |
|---|---|---|
| **Democratic Primary** | | |
| Peter M. Busch (D) | 27,871 | *62.0* |
| Louis A. Hatheway (D) | 17,065 | *38.0* |
| **1990**    **Republican Primary** | | |
| Larry Craig (R) | 65,830 | *59.0* |
| Jim Jones (R) | 45,733 | *41.0* |
| **Democratic Primary** | | |
| Ron J. Twilegar (D) | 30,154 | *64.5* |
| David C. Steed (D) | 16,587 | *35.5* |

### Class 3

| Candidates | Votes | % |
|---|---|---|
| **1956**    **Republican Primary** | | |
| Herman Welker (R) | 31,399 | *42.5* |
| William S. Holden (R) | 21,081 | *28.5* |
| Ray J. Davis (R) | 12,349 | *16.7* |
| John C. Sanborn (R) | 8,261 | *11.2* |
| **Democratic Primary** | | |
| Frank Church (D) | 27,942 | *37.7* |
| Glen H. Taylor (D) | 27,742 | *37.5* |
| Claude Burtenshaw (D) | 11,738 | *15.9* |
| Alvin McCormack (D) | 6,596 | *8.9* |
| **1962**    **Republican Primary** | | |
| Jack Hawley (R) | 38,210 | *60.2* |
| George Hansen (R) | 25,223 | *39.8* |
| **Democratic Primary** | | |
| Frank Church (D) | | *100.0* |
| **1968**    **Republican Primary** | | |
| George Hansen (R) | | *100.0* |
| **Democratic Primary** | | |
| Frank Church (D) | | *100.0* |
| **1974**    **Republican Primary** | | |
| Robert L. Smith (R) | 45,553 | *72.0* |
| Donald L. Winder (R) | 13,406 | *21.2* |
| Charles Bolstridge (R) | 4,331 | *6.8* |
| **Democratic Primary** | | |
| Frank Church (D) | 53,659 | *85.8* |
| Leon R. Olson (D) | 8,904 | *14.2* |
| **American Primary** | | |
| Jean L. Stoddard (AM) | | *100.0* |
| **1980**    **Republican Primary** | | |
| Steven D. Symms (R) | | *100.0* |
| **Democratic Primary** | | |
| Frank Church (D) | | *100.0* |

| Candidates | Votes | % |
|---|---|---|
| **Libertarian Primary** | | |
| Larry Fullmer (LIBERT) | | *100.0* |
| **1986**    **Republican Primary** | | |
| Steven D. Symms (R) | | *100.0* |
| **Democratic Primary** | | |
| John V. Evans (D) | | *100.0* |
| **1992**    **Republican Primary** | | |
| Dirk Kempthorne (R) | 67,001 | *57.4* |
| Rodney W. Beck (R) | 26,977 | *23.1* |
| Milton E. Erhart (R) | 22,682 | *19.4* |
| **Democratic Primary** | | |
| Richard Stallings (D) | 40,102 | *71.7* |
| Matt Schaffer (D) | 8,976 | *16.0* |
| David W. Shepherd (D) | 6,882 | *12.3* |

# ILLINOIS

| Candidates | Votes | % |
|---|---|---|
| **Class 2** | | |
| **1960**    **Republican Primary** | | |
| Samuel W. Witwer (R) | 249,849 | *31.5* |
| Warren E. Wright (R) | 226,449 | *28.6* |
| William H. Rentschler (R) | 202,600 | *25.6* |
| John W. Lewis (R) | 48,989 | *6.2* |
| **Democratic Primary** | | |
| Paul H. Douglas (D) | | *100.0* |
| **1966**    **Republican Primary** | | |
| Charles H. Percy (R) | 605,815 | *90.6* |
| Howard J. Doyle (R) | 38,636 | *5.8* |
| **Democratic Primary** | | |
| Paul H. Douglas (D) | | *100.0* |
| **1972**    **Republican Primary** | | |
| Charles H. Percy (R) | | *100.0* |
| **Democratic Primary** | | |
| Roman C. Pucinski (D) | 859,890 | *70.6* |
| W. Dakin Williams (D) | 357,744 | *29.4* |
| **1978**    **Republican Primary** | | |
| Charles H. Percy (R) | 401,409 | *84.2* |
| Lar Daly (R) | 74,739 | *15.7* |
| **Democratic Primary** | | |
| Alex Seith (D) | 483,196 | *69.5* |
| Anthony R. Martin-Trigona (D) | 212,105 | *30.5* |

| 1984 | Candidates<br>**Republican Primary** | Votes | % |
|---|---|---|---|
| | Charles H. Percy (R) | 387,865 | *59.3* |
| | Tom Corcoran (R) | 239,847 | *36.7* |
| | **Democratic Primary** | | |
| | Paul Simon (D) | 556,757 | *35.6* |
| | Roland W. Burris (D) | 360,182 | *23.0* |
| | Alex Seith (D) | 327,125 | *20.9* |
| | Philip J. Rock (D) | 303,397 | *19.4* |
| 1990 | **Republican Primary** | | |
| | Lynn Martin (R) | | *100.0* |
| | **Democratic Primary** | | |
| | Paul Simon (D) | | *100.0* |

### Class 3

| 1956 | **Republican Primary** | | |
|---|---|---|---|
| | Everett McKinley Dirksen (R) | | *100.0* |
| | **Democratic Primary** | | |
| | Richard Stengel (D) | | *100.0* |
| 1962 | **Republican Primary** | | |
| | Everett McKinley Dirksen (R) | 742,973 | *87.1* |
| | Harley D. Jones (R) | 109,574 | *12.8* |
| | **Democratic Primary** | | |
| | Sidney R. Yates (D) | 744,128 | *77.2* |
| | Lar Daly (D) | 219,169 | *22.7* |
| 1968 | **Republican Primary** | | |
| | Everett McKinley Dirksen (R) | 622,710 | *92.1* |
| | Roy C. Johnson (R) | 53,069 | *7.8* |
| | **Democratic Primary** | | |
| | William G. Clark (D) | | *100.0* |
| 1970 | **Republican Special Primary** | | |
| | Ralph Tyler Smith (R) | 414,489 | *58.9* |
| | William H. Rentschler (R) | 271,648 | *38.6* |
| | **Democratic Special Primary** | | |
| | Adlai E. Stevenson III (D) | | *100.0* |
| 1974 | **Republican Primary** | | |
| | George M. Burditt (R) | 432,796 | *84.7* |
| | Lar Daly (R) | 78,146 | *15.3* |
| | **Democratic Primary** | | |
| | Adlai E. Stevenson III (D) | 822,248 | *82.9* |
| | W. Dakin Williams (D) | 169,662 | *17.1* |
| 1980 | **Republican Primary** | | |
| | David C. O'Neal (R) | 424,634 | *41.5* |
| | William J. Scott (R) | 352,138 | *34.4* |
| | Richard E. Carver (R) | 245,668 | *24.1* |

| | Candidates<br>**Democratic Primary** | Votes | % |
|---|---|---|---|
| | Alan J. Dixon (D) | 671,746 | *66.9* |
| | Alex Seith (D) | 190,339 | *18.9* |
| | Robert A. Wallace (D) | 64,037 | *6.4* |
| 1986 | **Republican Primary** | | |
| | Judy Koehler (R) | 266,214 | *55.0* |
| | George A. Ranney (R) | 217,720 | *45.0* |
| | **Democratic Primary** | | |
| | Alan J. Dixon (D) | 720,571 | *84.8* |
| | Sheila Jones (D) | 129,474 | *15.2* |
| 1992 | **Republican Primary** | | |
| | Richard S. Williamson (R) | 608,079 | *100.0* |
| | **Democratic Primary** | | |
| | Carol Moseley-Braun (D) | 557,694 | *38.3* |
| | Alan J. Dixon (D) | 504,077 | *34.6* |
| | Albert F. Hofeld (D) | 394,497 | *27.1* |

# INDIANA

| | Candidates | Votes | % |
|---|---|---|---|

### Class 1

| 1976 [1] | **Republican Primary** | | |
|---|---|---|---|
| | Richard G. Lugar (R) | 393,064 | *65.5* |
| | Edgar D. Whitcomb (R) | 179,203 | *29.8* |
| | **Democratic Primary** | | |
| | R. Vance Hartke (D) | 304,076 | *53.1* |
| | Philip H. Hayes (D) | 268,790 | *46.9* |
| 1982 | **Republican Primary** | | |
| | Richard G. Lugar (R) | | *100.0* |
| | **Democratic Primary** | | |
| | Floyd Fithian (D) | 262,644 | *59.5* |
| | Michael Kendall (D) | 178,702 | *40.5* |
| 1988 | **Republican Primary** | | |
| | Richard G. Lugar (R) | | *100.0* |
| | **Democratic Primary** | | |
| | Jack Wickes (D) | | *100.0* |

### Class 3

| 1980 | **Republican Primary** | | |
|---|---|---|---|
| | Dan Quayle (R) | 397,273 | *77.1* |
| | Roger F. Marsh (R) | 118,273 | *22.9* |
| | **Democratic Primary** | | |
| | Birch Bayh (D) | | *100.0* |

| 1986 | Candidates<br>**Republican Primary** | Votes | % |
|---|---|---|---|
| | Dan Quayle (R) | | 100.0 |
| | **Democratic Primary** | | |
| | Jill Long (D) | 258,085 | 73.5 |
| | Georgia D. Irey (D) | 93,079 | 26.5 |
| 1990 [2] | **Republican Special Primary** | | |
| | Daniel R. Coats (R) | | 100.0 |
| | **Democratic Special Primary** | | |
| | Baron P. Hill (D) | | 100.0 |
| 1992 | **Republican Primary** | | |
| | Daniel R. Coats (R) | 389,119 | 100.0 |
| | **Democratic Primary** | | |
| | Joseph H. Hogsett (D) | 320,732 | 100.0 |

**Indiana**

1. Before 1976, when Indiana adopted a primary system, party conventions nominated candidates for statewide office.

2. A special election was held in 1990 to fill the remaining two years of the term of Sen. Dan Quayle (R), who resigned Jan. 3, 1989, after he was elected vice president. The first two years of the vacancy were filled by appointee Daniel R. Coats (R).

# IOWA

| | Candidates | Votes | % |
|---|---|---|---|
| | **Class 2** | | |
| 1960 [1] | **Republican Primary** | | |
| | Jack Miller (R) | 66,455 | 30.8 |
| | Dayton Countryman (R) | 62,500 | 29.0 |
| | Rollo Bergeson (R) | 31,559 | 14.6 |
| | Ken Stringer (R) | 29,927 | 13.9 |
| | Oliver J. Reeve (R) | 14,414 | 6.7 |
| | Ernest J. Seemann (R) | 10,931 | 5.1 |
| | **Democratic Primary** | | |
| | Herschel C. Loveless (D) | | 100.0 |
| 1966 | **Republican Primary** | | |
| | Jack Miller (R) | 141,141 | 83.9 |
| | Herbert H. Hoover (R) | 27,007 | 16.1 |
| | **Democratic Primary** | | |
| | E. B. Smith (D) | 39,870 | 50.1 |
| | Gary L. Cameron (D) | 22,650 | 28.5 |
| | Ernest J. Seeman (D) | 8,646 | 10.9 |
| | Robert L. Nereim (D) | 8,343 | 10.5 |
| 1972 | **Republican Primary** | | |
| | Jack Miller (R) | 170,590 | 84.4 |
| | Ralph Scott (R) | 31,607 | 15.6 |

| | Candidates<br>**Democratic Primary** | Votes | % |
|---|---|---|---|
| | Dick Clark (D) | | 100.0 |
| | **American Independent Primary** | | |
| | William A. Rocap (AMI) | | 100.0 |
| 1978 | **Republican Primary** | | |
| | Roger W. Jepsen (R) | 87,397 | 57.3 |
| | Maurie Van Nostrand (R) | 54,189 | 35.5 |
| | Joe Bertroche (R) | 10,860 | 7.1 |
| | **Democratic Primary** | | |
| | Dick Clark (D) | 87,880 | 80.5 |
| | Gerald Baker (D) | 13,132 | 12.0 |
| | Robert L. Nereim (D) | 8,176 | 7.5 |
| 1984 | **Republican Primary** | | |
| | Roger W. Jepsen (R) | 113,996 | 100.0 |
| | **Democratic Primary** | | |
| | Tom Harkin (D) | 106,005 | 100.0 |
| 1990 | **Republican Primary** | | |
| | Tom Tauke (R) | | 100.0 |
| | **Democratic Primary** | | |
| | Tom Harkin (D) | | 100.0 |
| | **Class 3** | | |
| 1956 | **Republican Primary** | | |
| | Bourke B. Hickenlooper (R) | 157,652 | 67.7 |
| | Dayton Countryman (R) | 75,264 | 32.3 |
| | **Democratic Primary** | | |
| | R. M. Evans (D) | 64,195 | 63.1 |
| | Lumund Wilcox (D) | 37,590 | 36.9 |
| 1962 | **Republican Primary** | | |
| | Bourke B. Hickenlooper (R) | 164,535 | 85.4 |
| | Herbert H. Hoover (R) | 28,095 | 14.6 |
| | **Democratic Primary** | | |
| | E. B. Smith (D) | | 100.0 |
| 1968 | **Republican Primary** | | |
| | David M. Stanley (R) | 143,854 | 58.7 |
| | James E. Bromwell (R) | 65,509 | 26.7 |
| | Dayton Countryman (R) | 22,049 | 9.0 |
| | William N. Plymat (R) | 13,485 | 5.5 |
| | **Democratic Primary** | | |
| | Harold E. Hughes (D) | 103,936 | 86.8 |
| | Robert L. Nereim (D) | 15,772 | 13.2 |

| 1974 | Candidates **Republican Primary** | Votes | % |
|------|-----------------------------------|-------|---|
| | David M. Stanley (R) | 87,464 | 66.9 |
| | George F. Milligan (R) | 43,206 | 33.1 |
| | **Democratic Primary** | | |
| | John C. Culver (D) | | 100.0 |
| 1980 | **Republican Primary** | | |
| | Charles E. Grassley (R) | 170,120 | 66.7 |
| | Tom Stoner (R) | 89,409 | 33.3 |
| | **Democratic Primary** | | |
| | John C. Culver (D) | | 100.0 |
| 1986 | **Republican Primary** | | |
| | Charles E. Grassley (R) | | 100.0 |
| | **Democratic Primary** | | |
| | John P. Roehrick (D) | 88,347 | 83.8 |
| | Juan Cortez (D) | 16,987 | 16.1 |
| 1992 | **Republican Primary** | | |
| | Charles E. Grassley (R) | 109,273 | 99.7 |
| | **Democratic Primary** | | |
| | Jean Lloyd-Jones (D) | 60,615 | 60.8 |
| | Rosanne Freeburg (D) | 38,774 | 38.9 |

**Iowa**

1. *Because no candidate in Iowa's 1960 Republican primary received the minimum percentage required for Senate nomination, a state convention was held, resulting in the nomination of Miller.*

# KANSAS

| | Candidates | Votes | % |
|------|-----------|-------|---|
| | **Class 2** | | |
| 1960 | **Republican Primary** | | |
| | Andrew F. Schoeppel (R) | 201,753 | 80.0 |
| | Henry P. Cleaver (R) | 50,507 | 20.0 |
| | **Democratic Primary** | | |
| | Frank Theis (D) | 88,194 | 59.1 |
| | Joseph W. Henkle (D) | 60,942 | 40.9 |
| 1962 [1] | **Republican Special Primary** | | |
| | James B. Pearson (R) | 124,854 | 62.3 |
| | Edward F. Arn (R) | 75,524 | 37.7 |
| | **Democratic Special Primary** | | |
| | Paul L. Aylward (D) | | 100.0 |

| 1966 | Candidates **Republican Primary** | Votes | % |
|------|-----------------------------------|-------|---|
| | James B. Pearson (R) | 101,523 | 50.3 |
| | R. F. Ellsworth (R) | 83,083 | 41.1 |
| | Ava A. Anderson (R) | 10,095 | 5.0 |
| | **Democratic Primary** | | |
| | J. Floyd Breeding (D) | 51,860 | 49.9 |
| | K. L. Smith (D) | 19,433 | 18.7 |
| | Harold S. Herd (D) | 16,963 | 16.3 |
| | Leigh Warner (D) | 15,625 | 15.0 |
| 1972 | **Republican Primary** | | |
| | James B. Pearson (R) | 229,908 | 82.2 |
| | Harlan D. House (R) | 49,825 | 17.8 |
| | **Democratic Primary** | | |
| | Arch O. Tezlaff (D) | | 100.0 |
| 1978 | **Republican Primary** | | |
| | Nancy Landon Kassebaum (R) | 67,324 | 30.6 |
| | Wayne Angell (R) | 54,161 | 24.6 |
| | Sam Hardage (R) | 30,248 | 13.7 |
| | Jan Meyers (R) | 20,933 | 9.5 |
| | Deryl K. Schuster (R) | 18,568 | 8.5 |
| | Norman E. Gaar (R) | 14,502 | 6.6 |
| | **Democratic Primary** | | |
| | William R. Roy (D) | 100,508 | 76.7 |
| | Dorothy K. White (D) | 13,865 | 10.6 |
| | James R. Maher (D) | 11,556 | 8.8 |
| 1984 | **Republican Primary** | | |
| | Nancy Landon Kassebaum (R) | 214,429 | 100.0 |
| | **Democratic Primary** | | |
| | James R. Maher (D) | 97,843 | 100.0 |
| 1990 | **Republican Primary** | | |
| | Nancy Landon Kassebaum (R) | 267,946 | 87.2 |
| | R. Gregory Walstrom (R) | 39,379 | 12.8 |
| | **Democratic Primary** | | |
| | William R. Roy (D) [2] | 86,174 | 56.9 |
| | Dick Williams (D) | 65,395 | 43.1 |
| | **Class 3** | | |
| 1956 | **Republican Primary** | | |
| | Frank Carlson (R) | 215,364 | 77.9 |
| | Walter I. Biddle (R) | 61,053 | 22.1 |
| | **Democratic Primary** | | |
| | George Hart (D) | 54,553 | 40.4 |
| | Paul L. Aylward (D) | 54,085 | 40.0 |
| | Fred Kilian (D) | 16,384 | 12.1 |
| | Marlyn Korf (D) | 10,176 | 7.5 |

| | Candidates | Votes | % |
|---|---|---|---|
| 1962 | **Republican Primary** | | |
| | Frank Carlson (R) | 167,498 | *86.9* |
| | Joe Corpstein (R) | 25,168 | *13.1* |
| | **Democratic Primary** | | |
| | K. L. Smith (D) | 65,876 | *62.5* |
| | Joseph J. Poizner (D) | 39,458 | *37.5* |
| 1968 | **Republican Primary** | | |
| | Robert Dole (R) | 190,782 | *68.5* |
| | William H. Avery (R) | 87,801 | *31.5* |
| | **Democratic Primary** | | |
| | William I. Robinson (D) | 56,242 | *40.9* |
| | James K. Logan (D) | 50,709 | *36.9* |
| | K. L. Smith (D) | 13,698 | *10.0* |
| 1974 | **Republican Primary** | | |
| | Robert Dole (R) | | *100.0* |
| | **Democratic Primary** | | |
| | William R. Roy (D) | 125,634 | *85.0* |
| | George Hart (D) | 22,109 | *15.0* |
| 1980 | **Republican Primary** | | |
| | Robert Dole (R) | 201,484 | *81.9* |
| | Jim H. Grainge (R) | 44,674 | *18.1* |
| | **Democratic Primary** | | |
| | John Simpson (D) | 52,004 | *35.8* |
| | James R. Maher (D) | 46,322 | *31.9* |
| | John A. Barnes (D) | 16,466 | *11.3* |
| | Ken North (D) | 14,218 | *9.8* |
| | Ed Phillips (D) | 8,838 | *6.1* |
| | Howard C. Lee (D) | 7,461 | *5.1* |
| 1986 | **Republican Primary** | | |
| | Robert Dole (R) | 228,301 | *84.4* |
| | Shirley J. A. Landis (R) | 42,237 | *15.6* |
| | **Democratic Primary** | | |
| | Guy MacDonald (D) | 31,942 | *27.7* |
| | Darrell T. Ringer (D) | 30,483 | *26.4* |
| | W. H. Addington (D) | 21,082 | *18.3* |
| | Lionel Kunst (D) | 18,795 | *16.3* |
| | Jim Oyler (D) | 13,201 | *11.4* |
| 1992 | **Republican Primary** | | |
| | Robert Dole (R) | 244,480 | *80.4* |
| | Richard W. Rodewald (R) | 59,589 | *19.6* |
| | **Democratic Primary** | | |
| | Gloria O'Dell (D) | 111,015 | *69.2* |
| | Fred Phelps (D) | 49,416 | *30.8* |

**Kansas**

1. A special election was held in 1962 to fill the remaining four years of the term of Sen. Andrew Schoeppel (R), who died Jan. 21, 1962.
2. Roy withdrew after the primary and Williams was substituted by the state party committee.

# KENTUCKY

| | Candidates | Votes | % |
|---|---|---|---|
| | **Class 2** | | |
| 1960 | **Republican Primary** | | |
| | John Sherman Cooper (R) | 50,896 | *96.3* |
| | **Democratic Primary** | | |
| | Keen Johnson (D) | 112,797 | *58.0* |
| | John Young Brown (D) | 75,897 | *39.0* |
| 1966 | **Republican Primary** | | |
| | John Sherman Cooper (R) | 65,023 | *92.8* |
| | **Democratic Primary** | | |
| | John Young Brown (D) | 71,759 | *75.6* |
| | Gaines P. Wilson (D) | 12,921 | *13.6* |
| | James Ward Lentz (D) | 5,399 | *5.7* |
| | J. N. R. Cecil (D) | 4,861 | *5.1* |
| 1972 | **Republican Primary** | | |
| | Louie B. Nunn (R) | 57,348 | *69.7* |
| | Robert E. Gable (R) | 18,107 | *22.0* |
| | **Democratic Primary** | | |
| | Walter D. Huddleston (D) | 106,144 | *71.6* |
| | Sandy Hockensmith (D) | 14,786 | *10.0* |
| | James E. Wallace (D) | 11,290 | *7.6* |
| | Willis V. Johnson (D) | 8,727 | *5.9* |
| 1978 | **Republican Primary** | | |
| | Louie Guenthner (R) | 14,218 | *47.2* |
| | Oline Carmical (R) | 9,346 | *31.0* |
| | Thurman J. Hamlin (R) | 6,550 | *21.8* |
| | **Democratic Primary** | | |
| | Walter D. Huddleston (D) | 89,333 | *75.6* |
| | Jack A. Watson (D) | 13,177 | *11.1* |
| | William J. Taylor (D) | 8,710 | *7.4* |
| | George W. Tolhurst (D) | 6,921 | *5.9* |
| 1984 | **Republican Primary** | | |
| | Mitchell McConnell (R) | 39,465 | *79.2* |
| | C. Roger Harker (R) | 3,798 | *7.6* |
| | T. William Klein (R) | 3,352 | *6.7* |
| | Thurman Hamlin (R) | 3,202 | *6.4* |
| | **Democratic Primary** | | |
| | Walter D. Huddleston (D) | | *100.0* |
| 1990 | **Republican Primary** | | |
| | Mitchell McConnell (R) | 64,063 | *88.5* |
| | Tommy Klein (R) | 8,310 | *11.5* |
| | **Democratic Primary** | | |
| | Harvey Sloane (D) | 183,789 | *59.3* |
| | John Brock (D) | 126,318 | *40.7* |

## Class 3

| Candidates | Votes | % |
|---|---|---|

**1956** [1]

**Republican Primary**

| Candidates | Votes | % |
|---|---|---|
| Thruston B. Morton (R) | 42,038 | 70.6 |
| Julian H. Golden (R) | 12,976 | 21.8 |
| Granville Thomas (R) | 4,495 | 7.6 |

**Democratic Primary**

| Earle C. Clements (D) | 218,353 | 60.8 |
|---|---|---|
| Joe B. Bates (D) | 136,533 | 38.0 |

**1962**    **Republican Primary**

| Thruston B. Morton (R) | 41,892 | 91.2 |
|---|---|---|
| Thurman J. Hamlin (R) | 4,048 | 8.8 |

**Democratic Primary**

| Wilson W. Wyatt (D) | 127,403 | 77.0 |
|---|---|---|
| Marion Vance (D) | 28,513 | 17.2 |
| James L. Delk (D) | 9,483 | 5.7 |

**1968**    **Republican Primary**

| Marlow W. Cook (R) | 73,171 | 62.0 |
|---|---|---|
| Eugene Siler (R) | 39,743 | 33.7 |

**Democratic Primary**

| Katherine Peden (D) | 86,317 | 43.8 |
|---|---|---|
| John Young Brown (D) | 51,509 | 26.2 |
| Foster Ockerman (D) | 25,602 | 13.0 |
| Ted Osborn (D) | 20,049 | 10.2 |

**1974**    **Republican Primary**

| Marlow W. Cook (R) | 35,904 | 87.6 |
|---|---|---|
| Thurman J. Hamlin (R) | 2,826 | 6.9 |
| T. William Klein (R) | 2,256 | 5.5 |

**Democratic Primary**

| Wendell H. Ford (D) | 136,458 | 84.8 |
|---|---|---|
| Harvey E. Brazin (D) | 24,436 | 15.2 |

**American Primary**

| William E. Parker (AM) | | 100.0 |
|---|---|---|

**1980**    **Republican Primary**

| Mary Louise Foust (R) | 25,717 | 42.0 |
|---|---|---|
| Granville Thomas (R) | 10,246 | 16.7 |
| Jackson M. Andrews (R) | 8,382 | 13.7 |
| T. William Klein (R) | 6,418 | 10.5 |
| Yale J. Lubkin (R) | 5,669 | 9.2 |
| DeSota Vaught (R) | 4,848 | 7.9 |

**Democratic Primary**

| Wendell H. Ford (D) | 188,047 | 87.0 |
|---|---|---|
| Flora T. Stuart (D) | 28,202 | 13.0 |

**1986**    **Republican Primary**

| Jackson M. Andrews (R) | 16,211 | 39.0 |
|---|---|---|
| Carl W. Brown (R) | 9,724 | 23.3 |
| Tommy Klein (R) | 8,595 | 20.6 |
| Thurman J. Hamlin (R) | 7,062 | 17.0 |

| Candidates | Votes | % |
|---|---|---|

**Democratic Primary**

| Wendell H. Ford (D) | | 100.0 |
|---|---|---|

**1992**    **Republican Primary**

| David L. Williams (R) | 49,880 | 60.9 |
|---|---|---|
| Philip Thompson (R) | 25,026 | 30.5 |
| Denny Ormerod (R) | 7,066 | 8.6 |

**Democratic Primary**

| Wendell H. Ford (D) | | 100.0 |
|---|---|---|

**Kentucky**

1. Candidates for the special election to fill the unexpired term of Sen. Alben W. Barkley (D), who died April 30, 1956, were nominated by the Democratic and Republican state committees, not by primaries. The 1956 Senate primary in Kentucky was for the Class 3 seat that was slated to be filled that year.

# LOUISIANA [1]

## Class 2

| Candidates | Votes | % |
|---|---|---|

**1924**    **Democratic Primary**

| Joseph E. Ransdell (D) | 104,312 | 54.9 |
|---|---|---|
| Lee E. Thomas (D) | 85,547 | 45.1 |

**1930**    **Democratic Primary**

| Huey P. Long (D) | 149,640 | 57.3 |
|---|---|---|
| Joseph E. Ransdell (D) | 111,451 | 42.7 |

**1936**    **Democratic Special Primary**

| Oscar K. Allen (D) [2] | 368,115 | 68.7 |
|---|---|---|
| Frank J. Looney (D) | 160,566 | 30.0 |

**1936**    **Democratic Primary**

| Allen J. Ellender (D) | 364,931 | 68.0 |
|---|---|---|
| John N. Sandlin (D) | 167,471 | 31.2 |

**1942**    **Democratic Primary**

| Allen J. Ellender (D) | 218,141 | 68.0 |
|---|---|---|
| E. A. Stephens (D) | 102,900 | 32.1 |

**1948**    **Democratic Primary**

| Allen J. Ellender (D) | 284,293 | 61.7 |
|---|---|---|
| James Domengeaux (D) | 119,459 | 25.9 |
| Charles S. Gerth (D) | 57,047 | 12.4 |

**1954**    **Democratic Primary**

| Allen J. Ellender (D) | 268,064 | 59.2 |
|---|---|---|
| Frank B. Ellis (D) | 162,775 | 35.9 |

**1960**    **Republican Primary**

| George W. Reese Jr. (R) | 726 | 72.3 |
|---|---|---|
| William Dane (R) | 278 | 27.7 |

| Candidates | Votes | % |
|---|---|---|
| **Democratic Primary** | | |
| Allen J. Ellender (D) | | *100.0* |

**1966**

| Candidates | Votes | % |
|---|---|---|
| **Democratic Primary** | | |
| Allen J. Ellender (D) | 494,519 | *74.2* |
| J. D. Deblieux (D) | 94,154 | *14.1* |
| Troyce E. Guice (D) | 78,137 | *11.7* |

**1972**

| Candidates | Votes | % |
|---|---|---|
| **Republican Primary** | | |
| C. M. McLean (R) [3] | | *100.0* |
| **Democratic Primary** | | |
| J. Bennett Johnston (D) | 623,078 | *79.4* |
| Frank Tunney Allen (D) | 88,198 | *11.2* |
| Allen J. Ellender (D) [4] | 73,088 | *9.3* |

**1978**

| Candidates | Votes | % |
|---|---|---|
| **Open Primary** | | |
| J. Bennett Johnston (D) | 498,773 | *59.4* |
| Louis (Woody) Jenkins (D) | 340,896 | *40.6* |

**1984**

| Candidates | Votes | % |
|---|---|---|
| **Open Primary** | | |
| J. Bennett Johnston (D) | 838,181 | *85.7* |
| Robert M. Ross (R) | 86,546 | *8.9* |
| Larry N. (Boo-ga-loo) Cooper (R) | 52,746 | *5.4* |

**1990**

| Candidates | Votes | % |
|---|---|---|
| **Open Primary** | | |
| J. Bennett Johnston (D) | 752,902 | *53.9* |
| David E. Duke (R) | 607,391 | *43.5* |

### Class 3

**1920**

| Candidates | Votes | % |
|---|---|---|
| **Democratic Primary** | | |
| Edwin S. Broussard (D) | 49,718 | *45.7* |
| Jared Y. Sanders (D) | 43,425 | *40.0* |
| D. Caffery (D) | 15,563 | *14.3* |
| **Democratic Second Choice** | | |
| D. Caffery (D) | 3,328 | *38.6* |
| Edwin S. Broussard (D) | 2,931 | *34.0* |
| Jared Y. Sanders (D) | 2,374 | *27.5* |

**1926**

| Candidates | Votes | % |
|---|---|---|
| **Democratic Primary** | | |
| Edwin S. Broussard (D) | 84,041 | *51.1* |
| Jared Y. Sanders (D) | 80,562 | *48.9* |

**1932**

| Candidates | Votes | % |
|---|---|---|
| **Democratic Primary** | | |
| John H. Overton (D) | 181,464 | *59.2* |
| Edwin S. Broussard (D) | 124,935 | *40.8* |

**1938**

| Candidates | Votes | % |
|---|---|---|
| **Democratic Primary** | | |
| John H. Overton (D) | | *100.0* |

**1944**

| Candidates | Votes | % |
|---|---|---|
| **Democratic Primary** | | |
| John H. Overton (D) | 151,886 | *61.6* |
| E. A. Stephens (D) | 68,408 | *27.8* |
| Griffin T. Hawkins (D) | 19,087 | *7.7* |

**1948**

| Candidates | Votes | % |
|---|---|---|
| **Democratic Special Primary** | | |
| Russell B. Long (D) | 264,143 | *51.0* |
| Robert F. Kennon (D) | 253,668 | *49.0* |

**1950**

| Candidates | Votes | % |
|---|---|---|
| **Democratic Primary** | | |
| Russell B. Long (D) | 359,330 | *68.5* |
| Malcolm E. LaFargue (D) | 156,918 | *29.9* |

**1956**

| Candidates | Votes | % |
|---|---|---|
| **Democratic Primary** | | |
| Russell B. Long (D) | | *100.0* |

**1962**

| Candidates | Votes | % |
|---|---|---|
| **Republican Primary** | | |
| Taylor W. O'Hearn (R) | | *100.0* |
| **Democratic Primary** | | |
| Russell B. Long (D) | 407,162 | *80.2* |
| Philemon A. Stamant (D) | 100,843 | *19.9* |

**1968**

| Candidates | Votes | % |
|---|---|---|
| **Republican Primary** | | |
| Richard H. Kilbourne (R) [5] | | *100.0* |
| **Democratic Primary** | | |
| Russell B. Long (D) | 494,467 | *87.0* |
| Maurice P. Blanche (D) | 73,791 | *13.0* |

**1974**

| Candidates | Votes | % |
|---|---|---|
| **Democratic Primary** | | |
| Russell B. Long (D) | 520,606 | *74.7* |
| Sherman A. Bernard (D) | 131,540 | *18.9* |
| Annie Smart (D) | 44,341 | *6.4* |

**1980**

| Candidates | Votes | % |
|---|---|---|
| **Open Primary** | | |
| Russell B. Long (D) | 484,770 | *57.6* |
| Louis (Woody) Jenkins (D) | 325,922 | *38.8* |

**1986**

| Candidates | Votes | % |
|---|---|---|
| **Open Primary** | | |
| W. Henson Moore (R) | 529,433 | *44.2* |
| John B. Breaux (D) | 447,328 | *37.3* |
| Samuel B. Nunez (D) | 73,505 | *6.1* |

**1992**

| Candidates | Votes | % |
|---|---|---|
| **Open Primary** | | |
| John B. Breaux (D) | 616,021 | *73.1* |
| John Khachturian (I) | 74,785 | *8.9* |
| Lyle Stockstill (R) | 69,986 | *8.3* |
| Nick J. Accardo (D) | 45,839 | *5.4* |

**Louisiana**

*1. In 1978 Louisiana eliminated the partisan primary for U.S. senator and instituted an open primary with candidates from all parties on the same ballot. Any candidate who receives a majority appears in the general election unopposed. If no candidate receives 50 percent of the vote, there is a runoff election, without regard to party affiliation, between the top two finishers.*

*2. Allen, the incumbent governor of Louisiana, died Jan. 28, 1936, just one week after winning the Democratic nomination for the Senate for the term ending Jan. 3, 1937. The Senate seat had been vacant since the assassination Sept. 10, 1935, of Sen. Huey P. Long, D (1932-35). The new governor appointed Long's widow, Rose McConnell Long, to the Senate seat and she took office Jan. 31, 1936. She was also designated the Democratic nominee to replace Allen in the April 20 special election, which she won without opposition.*

**Louisiana** *(continued)*

*3. McLean withdrew from the race after the primary. The Republican state central committee substituted Ben C. Toledano as the candidate for the general election.*

*4. Ellender died July 27, 1972, before the Aug. 19 primary in which he was a candidate for renomination to a seventh term. But Ellender's name remained on the ballot for the primary, which Johnston won without a runoff.*

*5. Kilbourne withdrew from the race after the primary. The Republicans did not choose any substitute candidate, thus allowing Long to run unopposed in the November election.*

# MAINE

| Candidates | Votes | % |
|---|---|---|
| **Class 1** | | |
| **1958** **Republican Primary** | | |
| Frederick G. Payne (R) | 82,448 | 83.6 |
| Herman D. Sahagian (R) | 16,133 | 16.4 |
| **Democratic Primary** | | |
| Edmund S. Muskie (D) | | 100.0 |
| **1964** **Republican Primary** | | |
| Clifford McIntire (R) | | 100.0 |
| **Democratic Primary** | | |
| Edmund S. Muskie (D) | | 100.0 |
| **1970** **Republican Primary** | | |
| Neil S. Bishop (R) | 45,216 | 59.8 |
| Abbott O. Greene (R) | 30,201 | 40.0 |
| **Democratic Primary** | | |
| Edmund S. Muskie (D) | | 100.0 |
| **1976** **Republican Primary** | | |
| Robert A. G. Monks (R) | 65,224 | 83.9 |
| Plato Truman (R) | 12,552 | 16.1 |
| **Democratic Primary** | | |
| Edmund S. Muskie (D) | | 100.0 |
| **1982** **Republican Primary** | | |
| David F. Emery (R) | | 100.0 |
| **Democratic Primary** | | |
| George J. Mitchell (D) | | 100.0 |
| **1988** **Republican Primary** | | |
| Jaspar S. Wyman (R) | | 100.0 |
| **Democratic Primary** | | |
| George J. Mitchell (D) | | 100.0 |

| Candidates | Votes | % |
|---|---|---|
| **Class 2** | | |
| **1960** **Republican Primary** | | |
| Margaret Chase Smith (R) | | 100.0 |
| **Democratic Primary** | | |
| Lucia M. Cormier (D) | | 100.0 |
| **1966** **Republican Primary** | | |
| Margaret Chase Smith (R) | | 100.0 |
| **Democratic Primary** | | |
| Elmer H. Violette (D) | 23,259 | 45.2 |
| Plato Truman (D) | 19,844 | 38.5 |
| Jack L. Smith (D) | 8,386 | 16.3 |
| **1972** **Republican Primary** | | |
| Margaret Chase Smith (R) | 76,964 | 66.7 |
| Robert A. G. Monks (R) | 38,345 | 33.3 |
| **Democratic Primary** | | |
| William D. Hathaway (D) | 61,921 | 90.8 |
| Jack L. Smith (D) | 6,263 | 9.2 |
| **1978** **Republican Primary** | | |
| William S. Cohen (R) | | 100.0 |
| **Democratic Primary** | | |
| William D. Hathaway (D) | | 100.0 |
| **1984** **Republican Primary** | | |
| William S. Cohen (R) | | 100.0 |
| **Democratic Primary** | | |
| Elizabeth H. Mitchell (D) | | 100.0 |
| **1990** **Republican Primary** | | |
| William S. Cohen (R) | | 100.0 |
| **Democratic Primary** | | |
| Neil Rolde (D) | | 100.0 |

# MARYLAND [1]

| Candidates | Votes | % |
|---|---|---|
| **Class 1** | | |
| **1958** **Republican Primary** | | |
| J. Glenn Beall (R) | 67,580 | 89.6 |
| Henry J. Laque (R) | 7,826 | 10.4 |

| Candidates | Votes | % | | Candidates | Votes | % |
|---|---|---|---|---|---|---|
| **Democratic Primary** | | | | **Class 3** | | |
| | | | | | | |
| Thomas D'Alesandro Jr. (D) | 125,408 | 34.7 | 1956 | **Republican Primary** | | |
| George P. Mahoney (D) | 119,796 | 33.2 | | | | |
| James Bruce (D) | 53,365 | 14.8 | | John Marshall Butler (R) | 58,642 | 86.6 |
| Clarence D. Long (D) | 47,290 | 13.1 | | Earl E. Knepper (R) | 5,376 | 7.9 |
| | | | | Henry J. Laque (R) | 3,696 | 5.5 |
| 1964 | **Republican Primary** | | | | | |
| | | | | **Democratic Primary** | | |
| J. Glenn Beall (R) | 68,930 | 59.8 | | | | |
| James P. Gleason (R) | 35,645 | 30.9 | | Millard E. Tydings [3] (D) | 142,238 | 47.5 |
| William A. Albaugh (R) | 8,352 | 7.2 | | George P. Mahoney (D) | 134,246 | 44.8 |
| | | | | | | |
| **Democratic Primary** | | | 1962 | **Republican Primary** | | |
| | | | | | | |
| Joseph D. Tydings (D) | 279,564 | 64.5 | | Edward T. Miller (R) | 43,437 | 48.1 |
| Louis L. Goldstein (D) | 155,086 | 26.6 | | James P. Gleason (R) | 34,523 | 38.3 |
| John J. Harbaugh (D) | 22,665 | 5.2 | | Harry L. Simms (R) | 7,689 | 8.5 |
| | | | | Henry J. Laque (R) | 4,565 | 5.1 |
| 1970 | **Republican Primary** | | | | | |
| | | | | **Democratic Primary** | | |
| J. Glenn Beall Jr. (R) | 99,687 | 83.5 | | | | |
| Harry L. Simms (R) | 9,927 | 8.3 | | Daniel B. Brewster (D) | 182,272 | 52.2 |
| Wainwright Dawson (R) | 9,786 | 8.2 | | Blair Lee (D) | 100,915 | 28.9 |
| | | | | Elbert M. Byrd (D) | 32,147 | 9.2 |
| **Democratic Primary** | | | | Herbert J. Hoover (D) | 19,719 | 5.6 |
| | | | | | | |
| Joseph D. Tydings (D) | 242,874 | 52.7 | 1968 | **Republican Primary** | | |
| George P. Mahoney (D) | 173,157 | 37.6 | | | | |
| Walter G. Finch (D) | 33,361 | 7.2 | | Charles McC. Mathias Jr. (R) | 66,777 | 80.0 |
| | | | | Harry L. Simms (R) | 11,927 | 14.3 |
| 1976 | **Republican Primary** | | | Paul F. Wattay (R) | 4,790 | 5.7 |
| | | | | | | |
| J. Glenn Beall Jr. (R) | | 100.0 | | **Democratic Primary** | | |
| | | | | | | |
| **Democratic Primary** | | | | Daniel B. Brewster (D) | 150,481 | 67.4 |
| | | | | Ross Z. Pierpont (D) | 38,555 | 17.3 |
| Paul S. Sarbanes (D) | 302,983 | 56.5 | | Walter G. Finch (D) | 19,829 | 8.9 |
| Joseph D. Tydings (D) | 191,875 | 35.8 | | Richard R. Howes (D) | 14,224 | 6.4 |
| | | | | | | |
| 1982 | **Republican Primary** | | 1974 | **Republican Primary** | | |
| | | | | | | |
| Lawrence J. Hogan (R) | 79,375 | 65.5 | | Charles McC. Mathias Jr. (R) | 79,823 | 75.8 |
| Donovan B. Finch (R) | 25,290 | 20.8 | | Ross Z. Pierpont (R) | 25,512 | 24.2 |
| William A. Albaugh (R) | 16,599 | 13.7 | | | | |
| | | | | **Democratic Primary** | | |
| **Democratic Primary** | | | | | | |
| | | | | Barbara A. Mikulski (D) | 132,658 | 40.9 |
| Paul S. Sarbanes (D) | 432,931 | 81.1 | | Bernard L. Talley (D) | 79,080 | 24.4 |
| | | | | Walter G. Finch (D) | 32,068 | 9.9 |
| 1988 | **Republican Primary** | | | Xavier A. Aragona (D) | 17,668 | 5.4 |
| | | | | | | |
| | | | 1980 | **Republican Primary** | | |
| Thomas L. Blair (R) [2] | 68,268 | 45.6 | | | | |
| James G. Bennett (R) | 19,720 | 13.2 | | Charles McC. Mathias Jr. (R) | 82,430 | 55.0 |
| Patrick L. McDonough (R) | 16,305 | 10.9 | | John M. Brennan (R) | 24,848 | 16.6 |
| E. Robert Zarwell (R) | 10,725 | 7.2 | | V. Dallas Merrell (R) | 23,073 | 15.4 |
| Albert Ceccone (R) | 9,601 | 6.4 | | Roscoe G. Bartlett (R) | 10,970 | 7.3 |
| John C. Webb (R) | 8,405 | 5.6 | | | | |
| Horace S. Rich (R) | 8,031 | 5.4 | | **Democratic Primary** | | |
| | | | | | | |
| **Democratic Primary** | | | | Edward T. Conroy (D) | 79,033 | 22.4 |
| | | | | Victor L. Crawford (D) | 52,803 | 15.0 |
| Paul S. Sarbanes (D) | 309,919 | 85.8 | | Robert L. Douglass (D) | 43,035 | 12.2 |
| B. Emerson Sweatt (D) | 25,932 | 7.2 | | Dennis C. McCoy (D) | 40,510 | 11.5 |
| A. Robert Kaufman (D) | 25,450 | 7.0 | | R. Spencer Oliver (D) | 35,407 | 10.4 |
| | | | | John A. Kennedy (D) | 20,255 | 5.7 |
| | | | | Frank J. Broschart (D) | 19,455 | 5.5 |

| 1986 | Candidates<br>**Republican Primary** | Votes | % |
|---|---|---|---|
| | Linda Chavez (R) | 100,888 | *73.1* |
| | Michael Schaefer (R) | 16,902 | *12.2* |
| | **Democratic Primary** | | |
| | Barbara A. Mikulski (D) | 307,876 | *49.5* |
| | Michael D. Barnes (D) | 195,086 | *31.4* |
| | Harry Hughes (D) | 88,908 | *14.3* |
| 1992 | **Republican Primary** | | |
| | Alan L. Keyes (R) | 95,831 | *45.9* |
| | Martha S. Klima (R) | 20,758 | *10.0* |
| | Joseph I. Cassilly (R) | 16,091 | *7.7* |
| | Ross Z. Pierpont (R) | 12,658 | *6.1* |
| | S. Rob Sobhani (R) | 12,423 | *6.0* |
| | **Democratic Primary** | | |
| | Barbara A. Mikulski (D) | 376,444 | *76.8* |
| | Thomas M. Wheatley (D) | 31,214 | *6.4* |
| | Walter Boyd (D) | 26,467 | *5.4* |

**Maryland**

1. *Until 1962 Maryland used a system of convention unit votes, with each county (and each of the six legislative districts into which Baltimore city was divided) being allocated as many unit votes as it had members of the state legislature, ranging from three to seven. These unit votes were automatically credited to the candidate carrying the county or legislative district.*

2. *Blair withdrew after the Republican primary. Alan L. Keyes was substituted by the party state central committee.*

3. *In 1956, because Tydings and Mahoney tied in unit votes at 76 each, Tydings won the nomination with the higher popular vote. But illness forced him to retire from the campaign and Mahoney was substituted by the party state committee.*

# MASSACHUSETTS

| | Candidates | Votes | % |
|---|---|---|---|
| | **Class 1** | | |
| 1958 | **Republican Primary** | | |
| | Vincent J. Celeste (R) | | *100.0* |
| | **Democratic Primary** | | |
| | John F. Kennedy (D) | | *100.0* |
| 1962 [1] | **Republican Special Primary** | | |
| | George C. Lodge (R) | 244,921 | *55.5* |
| | Laurence Curtis (R) | 196,444 | *44.5* |
| | **Democratic Special Primary** | | |
| | Edward M. Kennedy (D) | 559,303 | *72.9* |
| | Edward J. McCormack (D) | 247,403 | *27.1* |
| 1964 | **Republican Primary** | | |
| | Howard Whitmore (R) | | *100.0* |
| | **Democratic Primary** | | |
| | Edward M. Kennedy (D) | | *100.0* |

| | Candidates | Votes | % |
|---|---|---|---|
| 1970 | **Republican Primary** | | |
| | Josiah A. Spaulding (R) | 109,306 | *57.3* |
| | John J. McCarthy (R) | 81,356 | *42.7* |
| | **Democratic Primary** | | |
| | Edward M. Kennedy (D) | | *100.0* |
| 1976 | **Republican Primary** | | |
| | Michael Robertson (R) | | *100.0* |
| | **Democratic Primary** | | |
| | Edward M. Kennedy (D) | 534,725 | *73.9* |
| | Robert E. Dinsmore (D) | 117,496 | *16.2* |
| | Frederick C. Langone (D) | 59,315 | *8.2* |
| 1982 | **Republican Primary** | | |
| | Raymond Shamie (R) | | *100.0* |
| | **Democratic Primary** | | |
| | Edward M. Kennedy (D) | | *100.0* |
| 1988 | **Republican Primary** | | |
| | Joseph Malone (R) | | *100.0* |
| | **Democratic Primary** | | |
| | Edward M. Kennedy (D) | | *100.0* |
| | **Class 2** | | |
| 1960 | **Republican Primary** | | |
| | Leverett Saltonstall (R) | | *100.0* |
| | **Democratic Primary** | | |
| | Thomas J. O'Connor (D) | 270,081 | *48.3* |
| | Foster Furcolo (D) | 217,939 | *39.0* |
| | Edmund C. Buckley (D) | 70,744 | *12.7* |
| 1966 | **Republican Primary** | | |
| | Edward W. Brooke (R) | | *100.0* |
| | **Democratic Primary** | | |
| | Endicott Peabody (D) | 320,967 | *50.3* |
| | John F. Collins (D) | 265,016 | *41.6* |
| | Thomas B. Adams (D) | 51,435 | *8.1* |
| 1972 | **Republican Primary** | | |
| | Edward W. Brooke (R) | | *100.0* |
| | **Democratic Primary** | | |
| | John J. Droney (D) | 215,523 | *45.1* |
| | Gerald O'Leary (D) | 169,876 | *35.5* |
| | John P. Lynch (D) | 92,979 | *19.4* |
| 1978 | **Republican Primary** | | |
| | Edward W. Brooke (R) | 146,351 | *53.3* |
| | Avi Nelson (R) | 128,388 | *46.7* |

| Candidates | Votes | % |
|---|---|---|
| **Democratic Primary** | | |
| Paul E. Tsongas (D) | 296,915 | 35.6 |
| Paul Guzzi (D) | 258,960 | 31.0 |
| Kathleen Sullivan Alioto (D) | 161,036 | 19.3 |
| Howard Phillips (D) | 65,397 | 7.8 |
| Elaine Noble (D) | 52,464 | 6.3 |

**1984**

| **Republican Primary** | | |
|---|---|---|
| Raymond Shamie (R) | 173,851 | 62.4 |
| Elliot L. Richardson (R) | 104,761 | 37.6 |

| **Democratic Primary** | | |
|---|---|---|
| John F. Kerry (D) | 322,470 | 40.8 |
| James M. Shannon (D) | 297,941 | 37.7 |
| David M. Bartley (D) | 85,910 | 10.9 |
| Michael Joseph Connolly (D) | 82,999 | 10.5 |

**1990**

| **Republican Primary** | | |
|---|---|---|
| Jim Rappaport (R) | 265,093 | 66.2 |
| Daniel W. Daly (R) | 135,647 | 33.8 |

| **Democratic Primary** | | |
|---|---|---|
| John F. Kerry (D) | | 100.0 |

**Massachusetts**

1. A special election was held in 1962 to fill the remaining two years of the term of Sen. John F. Kennedy (D), who resigned Dec. 22, 1960, after he was elected president. The first two years of the vacancy were filled by appointee Benjamin A. Smith.

# MICHIGAN

| Candidates | Votes | % |
|---|---|---|

## Class 1

**1958**

| **Republican Primary** | | |
|---|---|---|
| Charles E. Potter (R) | | 100.0 |

| **Democratic Primary** | | |
|---|---|---|
| Philip A. Hart (D) | 297,767 | 80.2 |
| Homer Martin (D) | 73,334 | 19.8 |

**1964**

| **Republican Primary** | | |
|---|---|---|
| Elly M. Peterson (R) | 219,883 | 39.0 |
| James F. O'Neil (R) | 192,825 | 34.2 |
| Edward A. Meany (R) | 151,498 | 26.8 |

| **Democratic Primary** | | |
|---|---|---|
| Philip A. Hart (D) | | 100.0 |

**1970**

| **Republican Primary** | | |
|---|---|---|
| Lenore Romney (R) | 277,086 | 51.3 |
| Robert J. Huber (R) | 262,938 | 48.7 |

| **Democratic Primary** | | |
|---|---|---|
| Philip A. Hart (D) | | 100.0 |

**1976**

| Candidates | Votes | % |
|---|---|---|
| **Republican Primary** | | |
| Marvin L. Esch (R) | 209,250 | 44.2 |
| Thomas E. Brennan (R) | 129,917 | 27.5 |
| Robert J. Huber (R) | 82,092 | 17.3 |
| Deane Baker (R) | 51,852 | 11.0 |

| **Democratic Primary** | | |
|---|---|---|
| Donald W. Riegle Jr. (D) | 325,705 | 44.3 |
| Richard H. Austin (D) | 208,310 | 28.3 |
| James G. O'Hara (D) | 170,473 | 23.2 |

**1982**

| **Republican Primary** | | |
|---|---|---|
| Philip E. Ruppe (R) | 253,082 | 46.0 |
| William S. Ballenger (R) | 122,523 | 22.3 |
| Robert J. Huber (R) | 102,693 | 18.7 |
| Deane Baker (R) | 71,902 | 13.0 |

| **Democratic Primary** | | |
|---|---|---|
| Donald W. Riegle Jr. (D) | | 100.0 |

**1988**

| **Republican Primary** | | |
|---|---|---|
| Jim Dunn (R) | 245,275 | 61.1 |
| Robert J. Huber (R) | 155,984 | 38.9 |

| **Democratic Primary** | | |
|---|---|---|
| Donald W. Riegle (D) | | 100.0 |

## Class 2

**1960**

| **Republican Primary** | | |
|---|---|---|
| Alvin M. Bentley (R) | 344,043 | 72.0 |
| Donald S. Leonard (R) | 133,562 | 28.0 |

| **Democratic Primary** | | |
|---|---|---|
| Patrick V. McNamara (D) | | 100.0 |

**1966** [1]

| **Republican Special Primary** | | |
|---|---|---|
| Robert P. Griffin (R) | 356,700 | 100.0 |

| **Democratic Special Primary** | | |
|---|---|---|
| G. Mennen Williams (D) | 381,496 | 59.6 |
| Jerome P. Cavanagh (D) | 258,822 | 40.4 |

**1966**

| **Republican Primary** | | |
|---|---|---|
| Robert P. Griffin (R) | 387,892 | 100.0 |

| **Democratic Primary** | | |
|---|---|---|
| G. Mennen Williams (D) | 437,438 | 60.1 |
| Jerome P. Cavanagh (D) | 290,465 | 39.9 |

**1972**

| **Republican Primary** | | |
|---|---|---|
| Robert P. Griffin (R) | | 100.0 |

| **Democratic Primary** | | |
|---|---|---|
| Frank J. Kelley (D) | | 100.0 |

| | Candidates | Votes | % |
|---|---|---|---|
| **1978** | **Republican Primary** | | |
| | Robert P. Griffin (R) | 322,530 | *78.3* |
| | L. Brooks Patterson (R) | 89,383 | *21.7* |
| | **Democratic Primary** | | |
| | Carl Levin (D) | 226,584 | *38.9* |
| | Phil Power (D) | 115,117 | *19.8* |
| | Richard F. Vander Veen (D) | 89,257 | *15.3* |
| | Anthony Derezinski (D) | 53,696 | *9.2* |
| | John Otterbacher (D) | 50,860 | *8.7* |
| | Paul Rosenbaum (D) | 46,892 | *8.1* |
| **1984** | **Republican Primary** | | |
| | Jack Lousma (R) | 328,002 | *62.7* |
| | Jim Dunn (R) | 194,657 | *37.2* |
| | **Democratic Primary** | | |
| | Carl Levin (D) | 376,873 | *100.0* |
| **1990** | **Republican Primary** | | |
| | Bill Schuette (R) | 270,434 | *59.7* |
| | Clark Durant (R) | 182,592 | *40.3* |
| | **Democratic Primary** | | |
| | Carl Levin (D) | | *100.0* |

**Michigan**

1. *Robert P. Griffin (R) was appointed in May 1966 to fill the vacancy caused by the death of Sen. Patrick V. McNamara (D) on April 30. On Aug. 2 two Senate primaries were held simultaneously, a special primary for the remainder of McNamara's term and a regular primary for the full term beginning in January 1967. Griffin, who was unopposed for the Republican nomination, and G. Mennen Williams (D) won both primaries. In the November general election Griffin defeated Williams for both the short and the full terms. Returns for the special primary from the Elections Research Center, Washington, D.C.*

# MINNESOTA [1]

| | Candidates | Votes | % |
|---|---|---|---|
| | **Class 1** | | |
| **1958** | **Republican Primary** | | |
| | Edward J. Thye (R) | 202,241 | *91.0* |
| | E. C. Slettedahl (R) | 13,734 | *6.2* |
| | **Democratic Primary** | | |
| | Eugene J. McCarthy (DFL) | 279,796 | *75.7* |
| | Hjalmar Petersen (DFL) | 76,340 | *20.6* |
| **1964** | **Republican Primary** | | |
| | Wheelock Whitney (R) | | *100.0* |
| | **Democratic Primary** | | |
| | Eugene J. McCarthy (DFL) | 245,068 | *90.5* |
| | R. H. Underdahl (DFL) | 14,562 | *5.4* |

| | Candidates | Votes | % |
|---|---|---|---|
| **1970** | **Republican Primary** | | |
| | Clark MacGregor (R) | 220,353 | *93.3* |
| | John D. Baucom (R) | 15,797 | *6.7* |
| | **Democratic Primary** | | |
| | Hubert H. Humphrey (DFL) | 338,705 | *79.2* |
| | Earl D. Craig (DFL) | 88,709 | *20.8* |
| **1976** | **Republican Primary** | | |
| | Gerald W. Brokke (I-R) | 76,183 | *54.5* |
| | Richard Franson (I-R) | 32,115 | *23.0* |
| | John H. Glover (I-R) | 13,014 | *9.3* |
| | Roland Riemers (I-R) | 9,307 | *6.7* |
| | Bea Mooney (I-R) | 9,150 | *6.5* |
| | **Democratic Primary** | | |
| | Hubert H. Humphrey (DFL) | 317,632 | *91.3* |
| | Dick Bullock (DFL) | 30,262 | *8.7* |
| **1978** [2] | **Republican Special Primary** | | |
| | Dave Durenberger (I-R) | 139,187 | *67.3* |
| | Malcolm Moos (I-R) | 32,314 | *15.6* |
| | Ken Nordstrom (I-R) | 14,635 | *7.1* |
| | Will Lundquist (I-R) | 12,261 | *5.9* |
| | **Democratic Special Primary** | | |
| | Robert E. Short (DFL) | 257,269 | *48.0* |
| | Donald M. Fraser (DFL) | 253,818 | *47.4* |
| | **American Special Primary** | | |
| | Paul Helm (AM) | | *100.0* |
| **1982** | **Republican Primary** | | |
| | Dave Durenberger (I-R) | 287,651 | *93.4* |
| | Mary Jane Rachner (I-R) | 20,401 | *6.6* |
| | **Democratic Primary** | | |
| | Mark Dayton (DFL) | 359,014 | *69.1* |
| | Eugene J. McCarthy (DFL) | 125,229 | *24.1* |
| **1988** | **Republican Primary** | | |
| | Dave Durenberger (I-R) | 112,413 | *93.5* |
| | **Democratic Primary** | | |
| | Hubert H. Humphrey III (DFL) | 153,808 | *90.6* |
| | Kent S. Herschbach (DFL) | 15,994 | *9.4* |
| | **Class 2** | | |
| **1960** | **Republican Primary** | | |
| | P. K. Peterson (R) | 256,641 | *89.5* |
| | James Malcolm Williams (R) | 30,242 | *10.5* |

| Candidates | Votes | % |
|---|---|---|
| **Democratic Primary** | | |
| Hubert H. Humphrey (D) | | *100.0* |

**1966** **Republican Primary**

| | | |
|---|---|---|
| Robert A. Forsythe (R) | 211,282 | *81.2* |
| Henry A. Johnsen (R) | 48,941 | *18.8* |

**Democratic Primary**

| | | |
|---|---|---|
| Walter F. Mondale (DFL) | 410,841 | *91.0* |
| Ralph E. Franklin (DFL) | 40,785 | *9.0* |

**1972** **Republican Primary**

| | | |
|---|---|---|
| Philip Hansen (R) | | *100.0* |

**Democratic Primary**

| | | |
|---|---|---|
| Walter F. Mondale (DFL) | 230,679 | *89.9* |

**1978** **Republican Primary**

| | | |
|---|---|---|
| Rudy Boschwitz (I-R) | 185,393 | *86.8* |
| Harold E. Stassen (I-R) | 28,170 | *13.2* |

**Democratic Primary**

| | | |
|---|---|---|
| Wendell R. Anderson (DFL) | 286,209 | *56.9* |
| John S. Connolly (DFL) | 159,974 | *31.8* |

**American Primary**

| | | |
|---|---|---|
| Sal Carlone (AM) | | *100.0* |

**1984** **Republican Primary**

| | | |
|---|---|---|
| Rudy Boschwitz (I-R) | 162,555 | *96.6* |

**Democratic Primary**

| | | |
|---|---|---|
| Joan Anderson Growe (DFL) | 238,190 | *75.9* |
| Robert W. (Bob) Mattson (DFL) | 61,489 | *19.6* |

**1990** **Republican Primary**

| | | |
|---|---|---|
| Rudy Boschwitz (I-R) | 293,619 | *86.9* |
| John J. Zeleniak (I-R) | 44,202 | *13.1* |

**Democratic Primary**

| | | |
|---|---|---|
| Paul D. Wellstone (DFL) | 226,306 | *60.4* |
| James W. Nichols (DFL) | 129,302 | *34.5* |
| Gene Schenk (DFL) | 19,379 | *5.2* |

**Minnesota**

*1. In Minnesota, the Democratic Party is known as the Democratic-Farmer-Labor Party (DFL) and the Republican Party is known as the Independent Republican Party (I-R).*

*2. A special election was held to fill the unexpired term of Sen. Hubert H. Humphrey (DFL), who died Jan. 13, 1978.*

# MISSISSIPPI

| Candidates | Votes | % |
|---|---|---|
| **Class 1** | | |

**1922** **Democratic Primary**

| | | |
|---|---|---|
| James K. Vardaman (D) | 74,597 | *47.0* |
| Hubert D. Stephens (D) | 65,980 | *41.5* |
| Bell Kearney (D) | 18,303 | *11.5* |

**Democratic Runoff**

| | | |
|---|---|---|
| Hubert D. Stephens (D) | 95,351 | *52.3* |
| James K. Vardaman (D) | 86,853 | *47.7* |

**1928** **Democratic Primary**

| | | |
|---|---|---|
| Hubert D. Stephens (D) | 62,850 | *52.6* |
| T. Webber Wilson (D) | 56,641 | *47.4* |

**1934** **Democratic Primary**

| | | |
|---|---|---|
| Hubert D. Stephens (D) | 64,035 | *37.3* |
| Theodore G. Bilbo (D) | 63,752 | *37.2* |
| Ross A. Collins (D) | 42,209 | *24.6* |

**Democratic Runoff**

| | | |
|---|---|---|
| Theodore G. Bilbo (D) | 101,702 | *51.8* |
| Hubert D. Stephens (D) | 94,587 | *48.2* |

**1940** **Democratic Primary**

| | | |
|---|---|---|
| Theodore G. Bilbo (D) | 91,334 | *59.3* |
| Hugh L. White (D) | 62,641 | *40.7* |

**1946** **Democratic Primary**

| | | |
|---|---|---|
| Theodore G. Bilbo (D) | 97,820 | *51.0* |
| Ellis (D) | 58,005 | *30.2* |
| Ross A. Collins (D) | 18,875 | *9.8* |
| Levings (D) | 15,720 | *8.2* |

**1952** **Democratic Primary**

| | | |
|---|---|---|
| John C. Stennis (D) | 191,380 | *89.4* |
| William P. Davis (D) | 22,802 | *10.7* |

**1958** **Democratic Primary**

| | | |
|---|---|---|
| John C. Stennis (D) | | *100.0* |

**1964** **Democratic Primary**

| | | |
|---|---|---|
| John C. Stennis (D) | 173,764 | *97.4* |

**1970** **Democratic Primary**

| | | |
|---|---|---|
| John C. Stennis (D) | | *100.0* |

**1976** **Democratic Primary**

| | | |
|---|---|---|
| John C. Stennis (D) | 157,943 | *85.4* |
| E. Michael Marks (D) | 27,016 | *14.6* |

**1982** **Republican Primary**

| | | |
|---|---|---|
| Haley Barbour (R) | 30,636 | *74.2* |
| Bobby Richard (R) | 10,651 | *25.8* |

| Candidates | Votes | % |
|---|---|---|
| **Democratic Primary** | | |
| John C. Stennis (D) | 145,817 | *75.1* |
| Charles Pittman (D) | 33,651 | *17.3* |
| Colon Johnston (D) | 14,696 | *7.6* |

**1988** — **Republican Primary**

| Candidates | Votes | % |
|---|---|---|
| Trent Lott (R) | | *100.0* |

**Democratic Primary**

| Wayne Dowdy (D) | 189,954 | *53.4* |
| Dick Molpus (D) | 152,126 | *42.8* |

### Class 2

**1924** — **Democratic Primary**

| Pat Harrison (D) | 80,371 | *82.1* |
| Earl Brewer (D) | 17,496 | *17.9* |

**1930** — **Democratic Primary**

| Pat Harrison (D) | | *100.0* |

**1936** — **Democratic Primary**

| Pat Harrison (D) | 128,729 | *65.5* |
| M. S. Conner (D) | 65,296 | *33.2* |

**1942** — **Democratic Primary**

| James O. Eastland (D) | 50,112 | *37.6* |
| Wall Doxey (D) | 37,756 | *28.3* |
| Ross A. Collins (D) | 36,511 | *27.4* |
| Wall (D) | 8,077 | *6.1* |

**Democratic Runoff**

| James O. Eastland (D) | 74,747 | *56.8* |
| Wall Doxey (D) | 56,748 | *43.2* |

**1948** — **Democratic Primary**

| James O. Eastland (D) | | *100.0* |

**1954** — **Democratic Primary**

| James O. Eastland (D) | 136,836 | *62.0* |
| Carroll Gartin (D) | 83,761 | *38.0* |

**1960** — **Democratic Primary**

| James O. Eastland (D) | 136,735 | *94.2* |
| Ance Blakeney (D) | 8,397 | *5.8* |

**1966** — **Republican Primary**

| Prentiss Walker (R) | | *100.0* |

**Democratic Primary**

| James O. Eastland (D) | 240,171 | *83.1* |
| Clifton Whitley (D) | 34,323 | *11.9* |
| Charles P. Mosby (D) | 14,591 | *5.1* |

**1972** — **Republican Primary**

| Gil Carmichael (R) | 18,369 | *79.1* |
| James H. Meredith (R) | 4,859 | *20.9* |

---

| Candidates | Votes | % |
|---|---|---|
| **Democratic Primary** | | |
| James O. Eastland (D) | 203,847 | *70.2* |
| Taylor Webb (D) | 67,656 | *23.3* |
| Louis Fondren (D) | 18,753 | *6.5* |

**1978** — **Republican Primary**

| Thad Cochran (R) | 51,212 | *69.1* |
| Charles W. Pickering (R) | 22,949 | *30.9* |

**Democratic Primary**

| Maurice Dantin (D) | 102,968 | *27.2* |
| Cliff Finch (D) | 98,751 | *26.1* |
| Charles Sullivan (D) | 78,702 | *20.8* |
| William L. Waller (D) | 74,465 | *19.7* |

**Democratic Runoff**

| Maurice Dantin (D) | 235,904 | *65.3* |
| Cliff Finch (D) | 125,109 | *34.7* |

**1984** — **Republican Primary**

| Thad Cochran (R) | | *100.0* |

**Democratic Primary**

| William Winter (D) | 88,883 | *69.5* |
| W. W. Easley III (D) | 15,363 | *12.0* |
| William L. Gilbert (D) | 13,843 | *10.8* |
| Billy Taylor (D) | 9,786 | *7.6* |

**1990** — **Republican Primary**

| Thad Cochran (R) | | *100.0* |

# MISSOURI

| Candidates | Votes | % |
|---|---|---|
| **Class 1** | | |

**1958** — **Republican Primary**

| Hazel Palmer (R) | 61,481 | *44.6* |
| William M. Thomas (R) | 36,438 | *26.5* |
| Homer S. Cotton (R) | 27,023 | *19.6* |
| Hiram Grosby (R) | 12,818 | *9.3* |

**Democratic Primary**

| Stuart Symington (D) | 365,470 | *92.2* |
| Lawrence L. Hastings (D) | 19,954 | *5.0* |

**1964** — **Republican Primary**

| Jean P. Bradshaw (R) | 165,048 | *78.2* |
| Morris D. Duncan (R) | 46,030 | *21.8* |

**Democratic Primary**

| Stuart Symington (D) | 563,313 | *92.0* |
| William M. Thomas (D) | 35,509 | *5.8* |

| 1970 | **Candidates**<br>**Republican Primary** | **Votes** | **%** |
|---|---|---|---|
| | John C. Danforth (R) | 165,728 | *72.6* |
| | Doris M. Bass (R) | 45,049 | *19.7* |
| | Morris D. Duncan (R) | 17,670 | *7.7* |
| | **Democratic Primary** | | |
| | Stuart Symington (D) | 392,670 | *89.3* |
| | **American Primary** | | |
| | Gene Chapman (AM) | 684 | *47.1* |
| | Lawrence Petty (AM) | 400 | *27.5* |
| | Ralph A. DePugh (AM) | 368 | *25.4* |
| 1976 | **Republican Primary** | | |
| | John C. Danforth (R) | 284,025 | *93.5* |
| | Gregory Hansman (R) | 19,796 | *6.5* |
| | **Democratic Primary** | | |
| | Jerry Litton (D) [1] | 401,822 | *45.4* |
| | Warren E. Hearnes (D) | 233,544 | *26.4* |
| | James W. Symington (D) | 222,681 | *25.2* |
| 1982 | **Republican Primary** | | |
| | John C. Danforth (R) | 217,162 | *73.9* |
| | Mel Hancock (R) | 61,378 | *20.9* |
| | **Democratic Primary** | | |
| | Harriett Woods (D) | 263,259 | *44.8* |
| | Burleigh Arnold (D) | 140,446 | *23.9* |
| | Tom Ryan (D) | 75,599 | *12.9* |
| | Thomas E. Zych (D) | 35,876 | *6.1* |
| 1988 | **Republican Primary** | | |
| | John C. Danforth (R) | | *100.0* |
| | **Democratic Primary** | | |
| | Jeremiah W. Nixon (D) | | *100.0* |

## Class 3

| 1956 | **Republican Primary** | | |
|---|---|---|---|
| | Herbert Douglas (R) | 83,458 | *40.8* |
| | Albert E. Schoenbeck (R) | 78,747 | *38.5* |
| | William M. Thomas (R) | 28,924 | *14.1* |
| | William E. Van Taay (R) | 13,556 | *6.6* |
| | **Democratic Primary** | | |
| | Thomas C. Hennings Jr. (D) [2] | 389,986 | *95.9* |
| 1962 | **Republican Primary** | | |
| | Crosby Kemper (R) | 119,136 | *66.6* |
| | Duane Cox (R) | 23,606 | *13.2* |
| | Morris D. Duncan (R) | 15,109 | *8.5* |
| | William M. Thomas (R) | 14,131 | *7.9* |
| | **Democratic Primary** | | |
| | Edward V. Long (D) | 370,826 | *86.5* |
| | Lewis E. Morris (D) | 37,507 | *8.8* |

| 1968 | **Candidates**<br>**Republican Primary** | **Votes** | **%** |
|---|---|---|---|
| | Thomas B. Curtis (R) | 192,028 | *84.5* |
| | Morris D. Duncan (R) | 24,418 | *10.8* |
| | **Democratic Primary** | | |
| | Thomas F. Eagleton (D) | 224,017 | *36.6* |
| | Edward V. Long (D) | 198,901 | *32.5* |
| | True Davis (D) | 178,961 | *29.3* |
| 1974 | **Republican Primary** | | |
| | Thomas B. Curtis (R) | 136,447 | *81.9* |
| | Paul M. Robinett (R) | 16,882 | *10.1* |
| | Gregory Hansman (R) | 13,285 | *8.0* |
| | **Democratic Primary** | | |
| | Thomas F. Eagleton (D) | 420,681 | *87.5* |
| | Pat O'Brien (D) | 30,389 | *6.3* |
| | Lee C. Sutton (D) | 29,835 | *6.2* |
| 1980 | **Republican Primary** | | |
| | Gene McNary (R) | 197,060 | *61.5* |
| | David Doctorian (R) | 82,332 | *25.7* |
| | Morris D. Duncan (R) | 21,959 | *6.9* |
| | Gregory Hansman (R) | 18,893 | *5.9* |
| | **Democratic Primary** | | |
| | Thomas F. Eagleton (D) | 553,392 | *82.8* |
| | Lee C. Sutton (D) | 53,280 | *8.2* |
| | Herb Fillmore (D) | 38,677 | *6.0* |
| 1986 | **Republican Primary** | | |
| | Christopher Bond (R) | 239,961 | *88.9* |
| | **Democratic Primary** | | |
| | Harriett Woods (D) | 362,287 | *75.6* |
| | James J. Askew (D) | 44,292 | *9.2* |
| | Oren L. Staley (D) | 34,009 | *7.1* |
| 1992 | **Republican Primary** | | |
| | Christopher Bond (R) | 337,795 | *82.7* |
| | Wes Hummel (R) | 70,626 | *17.3* |
| | **Democratic Primary** | | |
| | Geri Rothman-Serot (D) | 224,984 | *35.6* |
| | Bill Peacock (D) | 67,723 | *10.7* |
| | Mert Bernstein (D) | 59,290 | *9.4* |
| | George D. Weber (D) | 57,254 | *9.1* |
| | Barbara M. Manson (D) | 50,091 | *7.9* |
| | Carol A. Coe (D) | 48,634 | *7.7* |
| | David Westfall (D) | 38,509 | *6.1* |

**Missouri**

1. Litton, the winner of the Democratic Senate primary on Aug. 3, 1976, died the same day and the Missouri Democratic central committee substituted Hearnes, the second-place finisher, as the party's nominee.

2. Candidates for the short-term Senate seat vacated by the death of Sen. Thomas C. Hennings Jr. (D) in September 1960 were nominated by the Democratic and Republican state committees of Missouri.

# MONTANA

| Candidates | Votes | % |
|---|---|---|
| **Class 1** | | |

## 1958 Republican Primary

| Candidates | Votes | % |
|---|---|---|
| Lou W. Welch (R) | 19,860 | 50.8 |
| Blanche Anderson (R) | 19,264 | 49.2 |

### Democratic Primary

| | | |
|---|---|---|
| Mike Mansfield (D) | 97,207 | 91.7 |

## 1964 Republican Primary

| | | |
|---|---|---|
| Alex Blewett (R) | 31,934 | 59.4 |
| Lyman Brewster (R) | 12,375 | 23.0 |
| Antoinette Rosell (R) | 9,480 | 17.6 |

### Democratic Primary

| | | |
|---|---|---|
| Mike Mansfield (D) | 109,904 | 85.5 |
| Joseph P. Monaghan (D) | 18,630 | 14.5 |

## 1970 Republican Primary

| | | |
|---|---|---|
| Harold E. Wallace (R) | | 100.0 |

### Democratic Primary

| | | |
|---|---|---|
| Mike Mansfield (D) | 68,146 | 77.2 |
| Tom McDonald (D) | 10,733 | 12.2 |
| John W. Lawlor (D) | 9,384 | 10.6 |

## 1976 Republican Primary

| | | |
|---|---|---|
| Stanley C. Burger (R) | 32,313 | 40.4 |
| Dave Drum (R) | 27,257 | 34.1 |
| John F. Tierney (R) | 15,129 | 18.9 |
| Larry L. Gilbert (R) | 5,258 | 6.6 |

### Democratic Primary

| | | |
|---|---|---|
| John Melcher (D) | 84,413 | 87.9 |
| Ray E. Gulick (D) | 11,593 | 12.1 |

## 1982 Republican Primary

| | | |
|---|---|---|
| Larry Williams (R) | 49,615 | 88.1 |
| Willie D. Morris (R) | 6,696 | 11.9 |

### Democratic Primary

| | | |
|---|---|---|
| John Melcher (D) | 83,539 | 68.3 |
| Michael A. Bond (D) | 33,565 | 27.4 |

## 1988 Republican Primary

| | | |
|---|---|---|
| Conrad Burns (R) | 63,330 | 84.7 |
| Tom Faranda (R) | 11,427 | 15.3 |

### Democratic Primary

| | | |
|---|---|---|
| John Melcher (D) | 88,457 | 74.5 |
| Robert C. Kelleher (D) | 30,212 | 25.5 |

| Candidates | Votes | % |
|---|---|---|
| **Class 2** | | |

## 1960 Republican Primary

| | | |
|---|---|---|
| Orvin B. Fjare (R) | 25,899 | 38.5 |
| Sumner Gerard (R) | 17,932 | 26.6 |
| Wayne Montgomery (R) | 13,527 | 20.1 |
| James H. Morrow (R) | 5,261 | 7.8 |

### Democratic Primary

| | | |
|---|---|---|
| Lee Metcalf (D) | 45,339 | 35.1 |
| John W. Bonner (D) | 33,246 | 25.8 |
| Le Roy Anderson (D) | 26,152 | 20.3 |
| John W. Mahan (D) | 24,208 | 18.8 |

## 1966 Republican Primary

| | | |
|---|---|---|
| Tim M. Babcock (R) | | 100.0 |

### Democratic Primary

| | | |
|---|---|---|
| Lee Metcalf (D) | | 100.0 |

## 1972 Republican Primary

| | | |
|---|---|---|
| Henry S. Hibbard (R) | 43,028 | 49.7 |
| Harold E. Wallace (R) | 26,463 | 30.6 |
| Norman C. Wheeler (R) | 13,826 | 16.0 |

### Democratic Primary

| | | |
|---|---|---|
| Lee Metcalf (D) | 106,491 | 86.4 |
| Jerome Peters (D) | 16,729 | 13.6 |

## 1978 Republican Primary

| | | |
|---|---|---|
| Larry Williams (R) | 35,479 | 61.6 |
| Bill Osborne (R) | 16,436 | 28.6 |
| Clancy Rich (R) | 5,622 | 9.8 |

### Democratic Primary

| | | |
|---|---|---|
| Max S. Baucus (D) | 87,085 | 65.3 |
| Paul Hatfield (D) | 25,789 | 19.3 |
| John Driscoll (D) | 18,184 | 13.6 |

## 1984 Republican Primary

| | | |
|---|---|---|
| Chuck Cozzens (R) | 33,661 | 50.7 |
| Ralph Bouma (R) | 17,900 | 27.0 |
| Aubyn Curtiss (R) | 14,729 | 22.2 |

### Democratic Primary

| | | |
|---|---|---|
| Max S. Baucus (D) | 80,726 | 79.4 |
| Bob Ripley (D) | 20,979 | 20.6 |

## 1990 Republican Primary

| | | |
|---|---|---|
| Allen C. Kolstad (R) | 38,097 | 43.6 |
| Bruce Vorhauer (R) | 30,837 | 35.3 |
| Bill Farrell (R) | 11,833 | 13.5 |
| John Domenech (R) | 6,654 | 7.6 |

### Democratic Primary

| | | |
|---|---|---|
| Max S. Baucus (D) | 81,687 | 82.8 |
| John Driscoll (D) | 12,622 | 12.8 |

# NEBRASKA

| Candidates | Votes | % |
|---|---|---|
| **Class 1** | | |

## Class 1

| Candidates | Votes | % |
|---|---|---|
| **1958** | **Republican Primary** | | |
| Roman L. Hruska (R) | | *100.0* |
| **Democratic Primary** | | |
| Frank B. Morrison (D) | 35,482 | *51.9* |
| Eugene O'Sullivan (D) | 26,436 | *38.6* |
| Mike F. Kracher (D) | 6,500 | *9.5* |
| **1964** | **Republican Primary** | | |
| Roman L. Hruska (R) | | *100.0* |
| **Democratic Primary** | | |
| Raymond W. Arndt (D) | | *100.0* |
| **1970** | **Republican Primary** | | |
| Roman L. Hruska (R) | 159,057 | *85.6* |
| Otis Glebe (R) | 26,627 | *14.3* |
| **Democratic Primary** | | |
| Frank B. Morrison (D) | 85,293 | *67.2* |
| Wallace C. Peterson (D) | 34,856 | *27.5* |
| David J. Thomas (D) | 6,610 | *5.2* |
| **1976** | **Republican Primary** | | |
| John Y. McCollister (R) | 150,732 | *78.3* |
| Richard F. Proud (R) | 41,519 | *21.6* |
| **Democratic Primary** | | |
| Edward Zorinsky (D) | 79,988 | *48.6* |
| Hess Dyas (D) | 77,384 | *47.0* |
| **1982** | **Republican Primary** | | |
| Jim Keck (R) | 104,550 | *66.0* |
| Ken Cameron (R) | 53,453 | *33.8* |
| **Democratic Primary** | | |
| Edward Zorinsky (D) | | *100.0* |
| **1988** | **Republican Primary** | | |
| David Karnes (R) | 117,439 | *54.8* |
| Harold J. Daub (R) | 96,436 | *45.0* |
| **Democratic Primary** | | |
| Bob Kerrey (D) | 156,498 | *91.4* |
| Ken L. Michaelis (D) | 14,248 | *8.3* |
| **New Alliance Primary** | | |
| Ernest Chambers (NA) | | *100.0* |

## Class 2

| Candidates | Votes | % |
|---|---|---|
| **1960** | **Republican Primary** | | |
| Carl T. Curtis (R) | | *100.0* |
| **Democratic Primary** | | |
| Ralph G. Brooks (D) [1] | 41,777 | *42.4* |
| Clair A. Callan (D) | 34,052 | *34.5* |
| Albert J. Baker (D) | 14,355 | *14.6* |
| Mike F. Kracher (D) | 8,424 | *8.5* |
| **1966** | **Republican Primary** | | |
| Carl T. Curtis (R) | | *100.0* |
| **Democratic Primary** | | |
| Frank B. Morrison (D) | 91,178 | *78.0* |
| Raymond W. Arndt (D) | 25,657 | *21.9* |
| **1972** | **Republican Primary** | | |
| Carl T. Curtis (R) | 141,213 | *74.0* |
| Ronald L. Blauvelt (R) | 30,138 | *15.8* |
| Christine M. Kneifl (R) | 10,941 | *5.7* |
| **Democratic Primary** | | |
| Terry Carpenter (D) | 52,779 | *29.0* |
| Wallace C. Peterson (D) | 49,569 | *27.2* |
| Wayne W. Ziebarth (D) | 42,181 | *23.1* |
| Donald Searcy (D) | 25,854 | *14.2* |
| **1978** | **Republican Primary** | | |
| Donald Shasteen (R) | 127,525 | *78.4* |
| Lenore R. Etchison (R) | 34,916 | *21.5* |
| **Democratic Primary** | | |
| J. James Exon (D) | | *100.0* |
| **1984** | **Republican Primary** | | |
| Nancy Hoch (R) | 61,009 | *40.5* |
| John W. DeCamp (R) | 24,730 | *16.4* |
| Richard N. Thompson (R) | 23,720 | *15.7* |
| Fred A. Lockwood (R) | 21,115 | *14.0* |
| Ken Cameron (R) | 16,123 | *10.7* |
| **Democratic Primary** | | |
| J. James Exon (D) | 135,242 | *100.0* |
| **1990** | **Republican Primary** | | |
| Harold J. Daub (R) | 178,232 | *91.3* |
| Otis Glebe (R) | 16,367 | *8.4* |
| **Democratic Primary** | | |
| J. James Exon (D) | | *100.0* |

**Nebraska**

*:. Brooks, winner of the Senate primary, died in September 1960 and the Nebraska Democratic state committee substituted Robert Conrad as the party's nominee. Conrad had been a candidate for the Democratic gubernatorial nomination.*

# NEVADA [1]

## Class 1

| Candidates | Votes | % |
|---|---|---|

### 1958 Republican Primary

| George W. Malone (R) | | 100.0 |

### Democratic Primary

| Howard W. Cannon (D) | 22,787 | 51.7 |
| Fred Anderson (D) | 21,319 | 48.3 |

### 1964 Republican Primary

| Paul Laxalt (R) | 25,220 | 90.3 |
| Wilford Owen Woodruff (R) | 1,433 | 5.1 |

### Democratic Primary

| Howard W. Cannon (D) | 36,320 | 59.6 |
| William A. Galt (D) | 12,054 | 19.8 |
| Harry Claiborne (D) | 10,807 | 17.7 |

### 1970 Republican Primary

| William J. Raggio (R) | 32,816 | 90.5 |
| Wilford O. Woodruff (R) | 3,456 | 9.5 |

### Democratic Primary

| Howard W. Cannon (D) | 54,320 | 89.3 |
| Walter D. Duesenberg (D) | 4,350 | 7.1 |

### 1976 Republican Primary

| David Towell (R) | 25,960 | 67.4 |
| S. M. Cavnar (R) | 5,964 | 15.5 |
| "None of these candidates" | 5,164 | 13.4 |

### Democratic Primary

| Howard W. Cannon (D) | 61,407 | 85.8 |
| "None of these candidates" | 4,817 | 6.7 |

### 1982 Republican Primary

| Chic Hecht (R) | 26,940 | 39.1 |
| Rick Fore (R) | 17,065 | 24.8 |
| Jack Kenney (R) | 12,191 | 17.7 |
| S. M. Cavnar (R) | 6,327 | 9.2 |
| "None of these candidates" | 5,411 | 7.8 |

### Democratic Primary

| Howard W. Cannon (D) | 54,288 | 49.7 |
| James Santini (D) | 49,735 | 45.5 |

### 1988 Republican Primary

| Chic Hecht (R) | 55,473 | 82.1 |
| Larry Scheffler (R) | 5,618 | 8.3 |
| "None of these candidates" | 6,460 | 9.6 |

### Democratic Primary

| Richard H. Bryan (D) | 62,278 | 79.5 |
| Patrick M. Fitzpatrick (D) | 4,721 | 6.0 |
| "None of these candidates" | 7,035 | 9.0 |

## Class 3

| Candidates | Votes | % |
|---|---|---|

### 1956 Republican Primary

| Clifton Young (R) | | 100.0 |

### Democratic Primary

| Alan Bible (D) | 26,784 | 68.2 |
| Mahlon Brown (D) | 8,043 | 20.5 |
| Harvey Dickerson (D) | 2,436 | 6.2 |
| Jay Sourwine (D) | 2,020 | 5.1 |

### 1962 Republican Primary

| William B. Wright (R) | 17,478 | 69.7 |
| Charles B. Grant (R) | 6,811 | 27.1 |

### Democratic Primary

| Alan Bible (D) | 38,556 | 76.2 |
| Jack Streeter (D) | 10,703 | 21.1 |

### 1968 Republican Primary

| Ed Fike (R) | 20,585 | 53.0 |
| William J. Raggio (R) | 17,634 | 45.4 |

### Democratic Primary

| Alan Bible (D) | | 100.0 |

### 1974 Republican Primary

| Paul Laxalt (R) | 33,660 | 81.3 |
| Jim Talbert (R) | 3,984 | 9.6 |
| S. M. Cavnar (R) | 3,752 | 9.1 |

### Democratic Primary

| Harry Reid (D) | 44,768 | 58.6 |
| Maya Miller (D) | 25,738 | 33.7 |
| Dan Miller (D) | 5,869 | 7.7 |

### 1980 Republican Primary

| Paul Laxalt (R) | 45,857 | 90.3 |
| Richard A. Glister (R) | 2,509 | 5.0 |

### Democratic Primary

| Mary Gojack (D) | | 100.0 |

### 1986 Republican Primary

| James Santini (R) | 55,947 | 80.3 |
| Richard Gilster (R) | 3,544 | 5.1 |
| "None of these candidates" | 8,214 | 11.8 |

### Democratic Primary

| Harry Reid (D) | 74,275 | 82.7 |
| Manny Beals (D) | 7,039 | 7.8 |
| "None of these candidates" | 8,486 | 9.4 |

### 1992 Republican Primary

| Demar Dahl (R) | 37,667 | 36.9 |
| Bob Gore (R) | 31,963 | 31.3 |
| "None of these candidates" | 13,523 | 13.2 |
| Andy Anderson (R) | 8,351 | 8.2 |

| Candidates Democratic Primary | Votes | % |
|---|---|---|
| Harry Reid (D) | 64,828 | *52.8* |
| Charles Wood (D) | 48,364 | *39.4* |

**Nevada**

1. *In Nevada, primary voters may vote for "None of these candidates." The "None of these candidates" vote is given here only where it amounted to 5 percent or more of the total.*

# NEW HAMPSHIRE

| Candidates | Votes | % |
|---|---|---|

## Class 2

### 1960 Republican Primary

| | | |
|---|---|---|
| Styles Bridges (R) | 87,629 | *92.9* |
| Albert Levitt (R) | 6,681 | *7.1* |

### Democratic Primary

| | | |
|---|---|---|
| Herbert W. Hill (D) | 16,198 | *40.2* |
| Alphonse Roy (D) | 13,782 | *34.3* |
| Frank L. Sullivan (D) | 10,266 | *25.5* |

### 1962 [1] Republican Special Primary

| | | |
|---|---|---|
| Perkins Bass (R) | 31,037 | *31.3* |
| Doloris Bridges (R) | 29,345 | *29.6* |
| Maurice J. Murphy (R) | 24,204 | *24.4* |
| Chester E. Merrow (R) | 14,417 | *14.6* |

### Democratic Special Primary

| | | |
|---|---|---|
| Thomas J. McIntyre (D) | | *100.0* |

### 1966 Republican Primary

| | | |
|---|---|---|
| Harrison R. Thyng (R) | 22,741 | *29.5* |
| Wesley Powell (R) | 18,145 | *23.5* |
| William R. Johnson (R) | 17,410 | *22.6* |
| Lane Dwinell (R) | 10,781 | *14.0* |
| Doloris Bridges (R) | 7,613 | *9.9* |

### Democratic Primary

| | | |
|---|---|---|
| Thomas J. McIntyre (D) | | *100.0* |

### 1972 Republican Primary

| | | |
|---|---|---|
| Wesley Powell (R) | 42,837 | *48.0* |
| Peter J. Booras (R) | 19,714 | *22.1* |
| David A. Brock (R) | 16,326 | *18.3* |
| Marshall W. Cobleigh (R) | 10,106 | *11.3* |

### Democratic Primary

| | | |
|---|---|---|
| Thomas J. McIntyre (D) | | *100.0* |

### 1978 Republican Primary

| | | |
|---|---|---|
| Gordon J. Humphrey (R) | 35,503 | *50.4* |
| James A. Masiello (R) | 18,371 | *26.1* |
| Alf E. Jacobson (R) | 13,619 | *19.4* |

| Candidates Democratic Primary | Votes | % |
|---|---|---|
| Thomas J. McIntyre (D) | 31,796 | *80.7* |
| Raymond J. Coughlan (D) | 7,605 | *19.3* |

### 1984 Republican Primary

| | | |
|---|---|---|
| Gordon J. Humphrey (R) | 57,763 | *99.1* |

### Democratic Primary

| | | |
|---|---|---|
| Norman E. D'Amours (D) | 42,371 | *99.3* |

### 1990 Republican Primary

| | | |
|---|---|---|
| Robert C. Smith (R) | 56,215 | *65.0* |
| Tom Christo (R) | 25,286 | *29.2* |

### Democratic Primary

| | | |
|---|---|---|
| John A. Durkin (D) | 20,222 | *41.4* |
| James W. Donchess (D) | 15,205 | *31.1* |
| John Rauh (D) | 12,935 | *26.5* |

## Class 3

### 1956 Republican Primary

| | | |
|---|---|---|
| Norris Cotton (R) | 61,673 | *89.5* |
| Joseph Moore (R) | 7,264 | *10.5* |

### Democratic Primary

| | | |
|---|---|---|
| Laurence M. Pickett (D) | | *100.0* |

### 1962 Republican Primary

| | | |
|---|---|---|
| Norris Cotton (R) | 87,445 | *94.4* |
| Norman LePage (R) | 5,167 | *5.6* |

### Democratic Primary

| | | |
|---|---|---|
| Alfred Catalfo (D) | | *100.0* |

### 1968 Republican Primary

| | | |
|---|---|---|
| Norris Cotton (R) | 78,058 | *92.4* |
| John C. Mongan (R) | 6,279 | *7.4* |

### Democratic Primary

| | | |
|---|---|---|
| John W. King (D) | | *100.0* |

### 1974 Republican Primary

| | | |
|---|---|---|
| Louis C. Wyman (R) | 66,749 | *83.0* |
| Leslie R. Babb (R) | 13,670 | *17.0* |

### Democratic Primary

| | | |
|---|---|---|
| John A. Durkin (D) | 22,258 | *50.0* |
| Laurence I. Radway (D) | 14,646 | *32.9* |
| Dennis J. Sullivan (D) | 6,330 | *14.2* |

### 1980 Republican Primary

| | | |
|---|---|---|
| Warren B. Rudman (R) | 20,206 | *20.3* |
| John H. Sununu (R) | 16,885 | *16.9* |
| Wesley Powell (R) | 14,861 | *14.9* |
| Edward B. Hager (R) | 9,821 | *9.9* |
| Lawrence J. Brady (R) | 9,426 | *9.5* |
| David H. Bradley (R) | 9,361 | *9.4* |

| Candidates | Votes | % |
|---|---|---|
| Anthony Campaigne (R) | 8,495 | *8.6* |
| George B. Roberts (R) | 7,397 | *7.4* |

**Democratic Primary**

| | | |
|---|---|---|
| John A. Durkin (D) | 36,933 | *79.6* |
| William F. Sullivan (D) | 9,486 | *20.4* |

**1986**    **Republican Primary**

| | | |
|---|---|---|
| Warren B. Rudman (R) | | *100.0* |

**Democratic Primary**

| | | |
|---|---|---|
| Endicott Peabody (D) | 20,568 | *61.2* |
| Robert L. Dupay (D) | 6,108 | *18.2* |
| Robert A. Patton (D) | 3,721 | *11.1* |
| Andrew D. Tempelman (D) | 2,601 | *7.8* |

**1992**    **Republican Primary**

| | | |
|---|---|---|
| Judd Gregg (R) | 57,141 | *49.8* |
| Harold Eckman (R) | 43,264 | *37.7* |
| Jean T. White (R) | 10,642 | *9.3* |

**Democratic Primary**

| | | |
|---|---|---|
| John Rauh (D) | 41,923 | *50.5* |
| Brenda J. Elias (D) | 15,943 | *19.2* |
| Terry Bennett (D) | 11,699 | *14.1* |
| Jeanne Stapleton (D) | 7,804 | *9.4* |

**New Hampshire**
1. A special election was held to fill the unexpired term of Sen. Styles Bridges (R), who died Nov. 26, 1961.

# NEW JERSEY

| Candidates | Votes | % |
|---|---|---|

## Class 1

**1958**    **Republican Primary**

| | | |
|---|---|---|
| Robert W. Kean (R) | 152,884 | *43.0* |
| Bernard M. Shanley (R) | 128,990 | *36.3* |
| Robert Morris (R) | 73,658 | *20.7* |

**Democratic Primary**

| | | |
|---|---|---|
| Harrison A. Williams Jr. (D) | 152,413 | *43.1* |
| John J. Grogan (D) | 139,605 | *39.5* |
| Joseph E. McLean (D) | 61,478 | *17.4* |

**1964**    **Republican Primary**

| | | |
|---|---|---|
| Bernard M. Shanley (R) | | *100.0* |

**Democratic Primary**

| | | |
|---|---|---|
| Harrison A. Williams Jr. (D) | | *100.0* |

**1970**    **Republican Primary**

| | | |
|---|---|---|
| Nelson G. Gross (R) | 150,662 | *65.4* |
| James A. Quaremba (R) | 43,547 | *18.9* |
| Joseph T. Gavin (R) | 36,208 | *15.7* |

| Candidates | Votes | % |
|---|---|---|

**Democratic Primary**

| | | |
|---|---|---|
| Harrison A. Williams Jr. (D) | 190,692 | *65.6* |
| Frank J. Guarini (D) | 100,045 | *34.4* |

**1976**    **Republican Primary**

| | | |
|---|---|---|
| David F. Norcross (R) | 196,457 | *68.3* |
| Martin E. Wendelken (R) | 45,472 | *15.8* |
| James E. Parker (R) | 27,672 | *9.6* |
| N. Leonard Smith (R) | 17,892 | *6.2* |

**Democratic Primary**

| | | |
|---|---|---|
| Harrison A. Williams Jr. (D) | 378,553 | *85.1* |
| Stephen J. Foley (D) | 66,178 | *14.9* |

**1982**    **Republican Primary**

| | | |
|---|---|---|
| Millicent Fenwick (R) | 193,683 | *54.3* |
| Jeffrey Bell (R) | 163,145 | *45.7* |

**Democratic Primary**

| | | |
|---|---|---|
| Frank R. Lautenberg (D) | 104,666 | *26.0* |
| Andrew Maguire (D) | 92,878 | *23.0* |
| Joseph A. LeFante (D) | 81,440 | *20.2* |
| Barbara B. Sigmund (D) | 45,708 | *11.3* |
| Howard Rosen (D) | 28,427 | *7.0* |

**1988**    **Republican Primary**

| | | |
|---|---|---|
| Peter M. Dawkins (R) | | *100.0* |

**Democratic Primary**

| | | |
|---|---|---|
| Frank R. Lautenberg (D) | 362,072 | *79.5* |
| Elnardo J. Webster (D) | 51,938 | *11.4* |
| Harold J. Young (D) | 41,303 | *9.1* |

## Class 2

**1960**    **Republican Primary**

| | | |
|---|---|---|
| Clifford P. Case (R) | 230,802 | *63.7* |
| Robert Morris (R) | 120,729 | *33.3* |

**Democratic Primary**

| | | |
|---|---|---|
| Thorn Lord (D) | 177,429 | *81.6* |
| Richard M. Glassner (D) | 40,134 | *18.4* |

**1966**    **Republican Primary**

| | | |
|---|---|---|
| Clifford P. Case (R) | | *100.0* |

**Democratic Primary**

| | | |
|---|---|---|
| Warren W. Wilentz (D) | 197,428 | *72.7* |
| David Frost (D) | 31,289 | *11.5* |
| John J. Winberry (D) | 19,745 | *7.3* |
| Clarence Coggins (D) | 16,775 | *6.2* |

**1972**    **Republican Primary**

| | | |
|---|---|---|
| Clifford P. Case (R) | 187,268 | *70.1* |
| James W. Ralph (R) | 79,776 | *29.9* |

**Democratic Primary**

| | | |
|---|---|---|
| Paul J. Krebs (D) | 135,000 | *43.2* |
| Daniel M. Gaby (D) | 86,213 | *27.6* |

| | Candidates | Votes | % |
|---|---|---|---|
| | Joseph T. Karcher (D) | 51,321 | 16.4 |
| | Henry Kielbasa (D) | 40,235 | 12.9 |
| **1978** | **Republican Primary** | | |
| | Jeffrey Bell (R) | 118,555 | 50.7 |
| | Clifford P. Case (R) | 115,082 | 49.3 |
| | **Democratic Primary** | | |
| | Bill Bradley (D) | 217,502 | 58.9 |
| | Richard C. Leone (D) | 97,667 | 26.4 |
| | Alexander J. Menza (D) | 32,386 | 8.8 |
| **1984** | **Republican Primary** | | |
| | Mary V. Mochary (R) | 111,851 | 61.4 |
| | Robert Morris (R) | 70,418 | 38.6 |
| | **Democratic Primary** | | |
| | Bill Bradley (D) | 404,301 | 92.9 |
| | Elliot Greenspan (D) | 30,680 | 7.0 |
| **1990** | **Republican Primary** | | |
| | Christine Todd Whitman (R) | | 100.0 |
| | **Democratic Primary** | | |
| | Bill Bradley (D) | 197,454 | 92.4 |
| | Daniel Z. Seyler (D) | 16,287 | 7.6 |

# NEW MEXICO

| | Candidates | Votes | % |
|---|---|---|---|
| | **Class 1** | | |
| **1958** | **Republican Primary** | | |
| | Forrest S. Atchley (R) | 10,384 | 51.3 |
| | Reginaldo Espinoza (R) | 9,861 | 48.7 |
| | **Democratic Primary** | | |
| | Dennis Chavez (D) | 68,689 | 65.7 |
| | E. S. Walker (D) | 35,927 | 34.3 |
| **1964** | **Republican Primary** | | |
| | Edwin L. Mechem (R) | | 100.0 |
| | **Democratic Primary** | | |
| | Joseph M. Montoya (D) | | 100.0 |
| **1970** | **Republican Primary** | | |
| | Anderson Carter (R) | 32,122 | 57.8 |
| | David F. Cargo (R) | 17,951 | 32.3 |
| | Harold G. Thompson (R) | 5,544 | 10.0 |
| | **Democratic Primary** | | |
| | Joseph M. Montoya (D) | 85,285 | 73.1 |
| | Richard B. Edwards (D) | 31,381 | 26.9 |

| | Candidates | Votes | % |
|---|---|---|---|
| **1976** | **Republican Primary** | | |
| | Harrison (Jack) Schmitt (R) | 34,074 | 71.7 |
| | Eugene W. Pierce (R) | 10,965 | 23.1 |
| | Arthur A. Lavine (R) | 2,481 | 5.2 |
| | **Democratic Primary** | | |
| | Joseph M. Montoya (D) | 96,063 | 66.3 |
| | Robert R. Sims (D) | 48,824 | 33.7 |
| **1982** | **Republican Primary** | | |
| | Harrison (Jack) Schmitt (R) | | 100.0 |
| | **Democratic Primary** | | |
| | Jeff Bingaman (D) | 91,780 | 54.4 |
| | Jerry Apodaca (D) | 66,598 | 39.4 |
| | Virginia R. Keehan (D) | 10,466 | 6.2 |
| **1988** | **Republican Primary** | | |
| | William Valentine (R) | 35,809 | 43.4 |
| | Rick Montoya (R) | 23,162 | 28.1 |
| | Corky Morris (R) | 16,539 | 20.1 |
| | Joseph J. Carraro (R) | 6,928 | 8.4 |
| | **Democratic Primary** | | |
| | Jeff Bingaman (D) | | 100.0 |
| | **Class 2** | | |
| **1960** | **Republican Primary** | | |
| | William F. Colwes (R) | 18,884 | 53.0 |
| | Joseph Rendon (R) | 11,866 | 33.3 |
| | Frederic W. Airy (R) | 4,859 | 13.6 |
| | **Democratic Primary** | | |
| | Clinton P. Anderson (D) | 98,037 | 81.3 |
| | James P. Speer (D) | 9,360 | 7.8 |
| | N. Tito Quintana (D) | 8,981 | 7.4 |
| **1966** | **Republican Primary** | | |
| | Anderson Carter (R) | | 100.0 |
| | **Democratic Primary** | | |
| | Clinton P. Anderson (D) | | 100.0 |
| **1972** | **Republican Primary** | | |
| | Pete V. Domenici (R) | 37,337 | 63.2 |
| | David F. Cargo (R) | 12,522 | 21.2 |
| | E. Lee Francis (R) | 4,583 | 7.8 |
| | **Democratic Primary** | | |
| | Jack Daniels (D) | 45,648 | 29.7 |
| | Robert A. Mondragon (D) | 29,603 | 19.3 |
| | David L. Norvell (D) | 24,917 | 16.2 |
| | Thomas G. Morris (D) | 22,849 | 14.9 |
| **1978** | **Republican Primary** | | |
| | Pete V. Domenici (R) | | 100.0 |

| Candidates<br>Democratic Primary | Votes | % |
|---|---|---|
| Toney Anaya (D) | | *100.0* |

**1984**

| Republican Primary | Votes | % |
|---|---|---|
| Pete V. Domenici (R) | 42,760 | *100.0* |

| Democratic Primary | Votes | % |
|---|---|---|
| Judith A. Pratt (D) | 67,722 | *45.5* |
| Nick Franklin (D) | 56,434 | *37.9* |
| Anselmo A. Chavez (D) | 24,694 | *16.6* |

**1990**

| Republican Primary | Votes | % |
|---|---|---|
| Pete V. Domenici (R) | | *100.0* |

| Democratic Primary | Votes | % |
|---|---|---|
| Tom R. Benavides (D) | | *100.0* |

# NEW YORK [1]

| Candidates | Votes | % |
|---|---|---|

## Class 1

**1970**

| Republican Primary | Votes | % |
|---|---|---|
| Charles E. Goodell (R) | | *100.0* |

| Democratic Primary | Votes | % |
|---|---|---|
| Richard L. Ottinger (D) | 366,789 | *39.6* |
| Paul O'Dwyer (D) | 302,438 | *32.7* |
| Theodore C. Sorensen (D) | 154,434 | *16.7* |
| Richard D. McCarthy (D) | 102,224 | *11.0* |

| Conservative Primary | Votes | % |
|---|---|---|
| James L. Buckley (C) | | *100.0* |

| Liberal Primary | Votes | % |
|---|---|---|
| Charles E. Goodell (L) | | *100.0* |

**1976**

| Republican Primary | Votes | % |
|---|---|---|
| James L. Buckley (R) | 242,527 | *70.5* |
| Peter A. Peyser (R) | 101,629 | *29.5* |

| Democratic Primary | Votes | % |
|---|---|---|
| Daniel Patrick Moynihan (D) | 333,697 | *36.4* |
| Bella S. Abzug (D) | 323,705 | *35.3* |
| Ramsey Clark (D) | 94,191 | *10.3* |
| Paul O'Dwyer (D) | 82,689 | *9.0* |
| Abraham J. Hirschfeld (D) | 82,331 | *9.0* |

| Conservative Primary | Votes | % |
|---|---|---|
| James L. Buckley (C) | | *100.0* |

| Liberal Primary | Votes | % |
|---|---|---|
| Henry S. Stern (L) [2] | | *100.0* |

**1982**

| Candidates<br>Republican Primary | Votes | % |
|---|---|---|
| Florence M. Sullivan (R) | 216,486 | *42.4* |
| Muriel Siebert (R) | 157,446 | *30.8* |
| Whitney N. Seymour (R) | 136,974 | *26.8* |

| Democratic Primary | Votes | % |
|---|---|---|
| Daniel Patrick Moynihan (D) | 922,059 | *85.1* |
| Melvin Klenetsky (D) | 161,012 | *14.9* |

| Conservative Primary | Votes | % |
|---|---|---|
| Florence M. Sullivan (C) | | *100.0* |

| Liberal Primary | Votes | % |
|---|---|---|
| Daniel Patrick Moynihan (L) | | *100.0* |

| Right to Life Primary | Votes | % |
|---|---|---|
| Florence M. Sullivan (RTL) | | *100.0* |

**1988**

| Republican Primary | Votes | % |
|---|---|---|
| Robert McMillan (R) | | *100.0* |

| Democratic Primary | Votes | % |
|---|---|---|
| Daniel Patrick Moynihan (D) | | *100.0* |

| Conservative Primary | Votes | % |
|---|---|---|
| Robert McMillan (R) | | *100.0* |

| Liberal Primary | Votes | % |
|---|---|---|
| Daniel Patrick Moynihan (L) | | *100.0* |

| Right to Life Primary | Votes | % |
|---|---|---|
| Adelle R. Nathanson (RTL) | | *100.0* |

## Class 3

**1968**

| Republican Primary | Votes | % |
|---|---|---|
| Jacob K. Javits (R) | | *100.0* |

| Democratic Primary | Votes | % |
|---|---|---|
| Paul O'Dwyer (D) | 275,877 | *36.1* |
| Eugene H. Nickerson (D) | 257,639 | *33.7* |
| Joseph Y. Resnick (D) | 229,893 | *30.1* |

| Conservative Primary | Votes | % |
|---|---|---|
| James L. Buckley (C) | | *100.0* |

| Liberal Primary | Votes | % |
|---|---|---|
| Jacob K. Javits (L) | 10,277 | *72.1* |
| Murray Baron (L) | 3,969 | *27.8* |

**1974**

| Republican Primary | Votes | % |
|---|---|---|
| Jacob K. Javits (R) | | *100.0* |

| Candidates | Votes | % |
|---|---|---|
| **Democratic Primary** | | |
| Ramsey Clark (D) | 414,327 | 48.0 |
| Lee Alexander (D) | 255,250 | 29.6 |
| Abraham J. Hirschfeld (D) | 194,076 | 22.5 |
| **Conservative Primary** | | |
| Barbara A. Keating (C) | | 100.0 |
| **Liberal Primary** | | |
| Jacob K. Javits (L) | | 100.0 |

**1980** **Republican Primary**

| Candidates | Votes | % |
|---|---|---|
| Alfonse M. D'Amato (R) | 323,468 | 55.7 |
| Jacob K. Javits (R) | 257,433 | 44.3 |
| **Democratic Primary** | | |
| Elizabeth Holtzman (D) | 378,567 | 40.7 |
| Bess Myerson (D) | 292,767 | 31.5 |
| John V. Lindsay (D) | 146,815 | 15.8 |
| John Santucci (D) | 111,129 | 12.0 |
| **Conservative Primary** | | |
| Alfonse M. D'Amato (C) | | 100.0 |
| **Liberal Primary** | | |
| Jacob K. Javits (R) | | 100.0 |
| **Right to Life Primary** | | |
| Alfonse M. D'Amato (RTL) | | 100.0 |

**1986** **Republican Primary**

| Candidates | Votes | % |
|---|---|---|
| Alfonse M. D'Amato (R) | | 100.0 |
| **Democratic Primary** | | |
| John S. Dyson (D) | | 100.0 |
| **Right to Life Primary** | | |
| Alfonse M. D'Amato (RTL) | | 100.0 |

**1992** **Republican Primary**

| Candidates | Votes | % |
|---|---|---|
| Alfonse M. D'Amato (R) | | 100.0 |
| **Democratic Primary** | | |
| Robert Abrams (D) | 426,904 | 37.0 |
| Geraldine A. Ferraro (D) | 415,650 | 36.0 |
| Al Sharpton (D) | 166,665 | 14.5 |
| Elizabeth Holtzman (D) | 144,026 | 12.5 |
| **Conservative Primary** | | |
| Alfonse M. D'Amato (C) | | 100.0 |
| **Liberal Primary** | | |
| Robert Abrams (L) | | 100.0 |
| **Right to Life Primary** | | |
| Alfonse M. D'Amato (RTL) | | 100.0 |

**New York**

1. *Until 1968, when New York adopted a primary system, party conventions or state central committees nominated candidates for statewide office.*

2. *Stern withdrew after the primary and the Liberal Party's state committee substituted Daniel Patrick Moynihan (D) as the Liberal nominee.*

# NORTH CAROLINA

| Candidates | Votes | % |
|---|---|---|
| **Class 2** | | |

**1924** **Democratic Primary**

| Candidates | Votes | % |
|---|---|---|
| Furnifold M. Simmons (D) | | 100.0 |

**1930** **Republican Primary**

| Candidates | Votes | % |
|---|---|---|
| George M. Pritchard (R) | 22,287 | 56.9 |
| G. E. Butler (R) | 9,098 | 23.2 |
| I. B. Tucker (R) | 6,277 | 16.0 |
| **Democratic Primary** | | |
| Josiah W. Bailey (D) | 200,242 | 60.2 |
| Furnifold M. Simmons (D) | 129,875 | 39.0 |

**1936** **Democratic Primary**

| Candidates | Votes | % |
|---|---|---|
| Josiah W. Bailey (D) | 247,365 | 52.5 |
| Richard T. Fountain (D) | 184,197 | 39.1 |
| W. H. Griffin (D) | 26,171 | 5.6 |

**1942** **Democratic Primary**

| Candidates | Votes | % |
|---|---|---|
| Josiah W. Bailey (D) | 211,038 | 65.8 |
| Richard T. Fountain (D) | 94,581 | 29.5 |

**1948** **Democratic Primary**

| Candidates | Votes | % |
|---|---|---|
| J. Melville Broughton (D) | 207,981 | 53.1 |
| William B. Umstead (D) | 183,865 | 46.9 |
| **Democratic Special Primary** | | |
| J. Melville Broughton (D) | 206,605 | 52.3 |
| William B. Umstead (D) | 188,420 | 47.7 |

**1950** **Democratic Special Primary**

| Candidates | Votes | % |
|---|---|---|
| Frank P. Graham (D) | 303,605 | 49.1 |
| Willis Smith (D) | 250,222 | 40.5 |
| Robert R. Reynolds (D) | 58,752 | 9.5 |
| **Democratic Special Runoff** | | |
| Willis Smith (D) | 281,114 | 51.8 |
| Frank P. Graham (D) | 261,789 | 48.2 |

**1954** **Democratic Primary**

| Candidates | Votes | % |
|---|---|---|
| W. Kerr Scott (D) | 312,053 | 50.8 |
| Alton Lennon (D) | 286,730 | 46.7 |
| **Democratic Special Primary** | | |
| W. Kerr Scott (D) | 274,674 | 49.4 |
| Alton Lennon (D) | 264,265 | 47.5 |

| | Candidates | Votes | % |
|---|---|---|---|
| 1958 | B. Everett Jordan (D) [1] | | |
| | Richard C. Clarke Jr. (R) | | |
| 1960 | **Republican Primary** | | |
| | Kyle Hayes (R) | | *100.0* |
| | **Democratic Primary** | | |
| | B. Everett Jordan (D) | 324,188 | *54.3* |
| | Addison Hewlett (D) | 217,899 | *36.5* |
| | Robert W. Gregory (D) | 31,463 | *5.3* |
| 1966 | **Republican Primary** | | |
| | John S. Shallcross (R) | | *100.0* |
| | **Democratic Primary** | | |
| | B. Everett Jordan (D) | 445,454 | *79.3* |
| | Hubert E. Seymour (D) | 116,548 | *20.7* |
| 1972 | **Republican Primary** | | |
| | Jesse Helms (R) | 92,496 | *60.1* |
| | James C. Johnson (R) | 45,303 | *29.5* |
| | William H. Booe (R) | 16,032 | *10.4* |
| | **Democratic Primary** | | |
| | Nick Galifianakis (D) | 377,993 | *49.3* |
| | B. Everett Jordan (D) | 340,391 | *44.4* |
| | **Democratic Runoff** | | |
| | Nick Galifianakis (D) | 333,558 | *55.5* |
| | B. Everett Jordan (D) | 267,997 | *44.6* |
| 1978 | **Republican Primary** | | |
| | Jesse Helms (R) | | *100.0* |
| | **Democratic Primary** | | |
| | Luther H. Hodges Jr. (D) | 260,868 | *40.1* |
| | John Ingram (D) | 170,715 | *26.2* |
| | Lawrence Davis (D) | 105,381 | *16.2* |
| | McNeill Smith (D) | 82,703 | *12.7* |
| | **Democratic Runoff** | | |
| | John Ingram (D) | 244,469 | *54.2* |
| | Luther H. Hodges Jr. (D) | 206,223 | *45.8* |
| 1984 | **Republican Primary** | | |
| | Jesse Helms (R) | 134,675 | *90.6* |
| | George Wimbish (R) | 13,899 | *9.4* |
| | **Democratic Primary** | | |
| | James B. Hunt Jr. (D) | 655,429 | *77.5* |
| | Thomas L. Allred (D) | 126,841 | *15.0* |
| | Harrill Jones (D) | 63,676 | *7.5* |
| 1990 | **Republican Primary** | | |
| | Jesse Helms (R) | 157,345 | *84.3* |
| | L. C. Nixon (R) | 15,355 | *8.2* |
| | George Wimbish (R) | 13,895 | *7.4* |

| | Candidates | Votes | % |
|---|---|---|---|
| | **Democratic Primary** | | |
| | Harvey B. Gantt (D) | 260,179 | *37.5* |
| | Mike Easley (D) | 209,934 | *30.3* |
| | John Ingram (D) | 120,990 | *17.4* |
| | R. P. Thomas (D) | 82,883 | *12.0* |
| | **Democratic Runoff** | | |
| | Harvey B. Gantt (D) | 273,567 | *56.9* |
| | Mike Easley (D) | 207,283 | *43.1* |

### Class 3

| | Candidates | Votes | % |
|---|---|---|---|
| 1920 | **Democratic Primary** | | |
| | Lee S. Overman (D) | 94,806 | *79.9* |
| | A. L. Brooks (D) | 23,869 | *20.1* |
| 1926 | **Democratic Primary** | | |
| | Lee S. Overman (D) | 140,260 | *60.4* |
| | Robert R. Reynolds (D) | 91,914 | *39.6* |
| 1932 | **Republican Primary** | | |
| | Jake F. Newell (R) | 29,906 | *86.5* |
| | G. W. DePriest (R) | 4,668 | *13.5* |
| | **Democratic Primary** | | |
| | Robert R. Reynolds (D) | 156,548 | *42.5* |
| | Cameron Morrison (D) | 143,179 | *38.9* |
| | Bowie (D) | 37,748 | *10.2* |
| | Grist (D) | 31,010 | *8.4* |
| | **Democratic Runoff** | | |
| | Robert R. Reynolds (D) | 227,864 | *65.4* |
| | Cameron Morrison (D) | 120,428 | *34.6* |
| 1938 | **Democratic Primary** | | |
| | Robert R. Reynolds (D) | 315,316 | *61.5* |
| | Frank Hancock (D) | 197,154 | *38.5* |
| 1944 | **Democratic Primary** | | |
| | Clyde R. Hoey (D) | 211,049 | *68.9* |
| | Cameron Morrison (D) | 80,154 | *26.2* |
| 1950 | **Democratic Primary** | | |
| | Clyde R. Hoey (D) | | *100.0* |
| 1954 | Sam J. Ervin Jr. (D) [2] | | |
| 1956 | **Republican Primary** | | |
| | Joel A. Johnson (R) | | *100.0* |
| | **Democratic Primary** | | |
| | Sam J. Ervin Jr. (D) | 360,967 | *84.6* |
| | Marshall C. Kurfees (D) | 65,512 | *15.4* |
| 1962 | **Republican Primary** | | |
| | Claude L. Greene Jr. (R) | 31,756 | *61.1* |
| | C. H. Babcock (R) | 20,246 | *38.9* |

| Candidates | Votes | % |
|---|---|---|
| **Democratic Primary** | | |
| Sam J. Ervin Jr. (D) | | *100.0* |

**1968**

| **Republican Primary** | | |
|---|---|---|
| Robert V. Somers (R) | 48,351 | *36.6* |
| J. L. Zimmerman (R) | 43,644 | *33.1* |
| Edwin W. Tenney (R) | 40,023 | *30.3* |

| **Republican Runoff** | | |
|---|---|---|
| Robert V. Somers (R) | 8,816 | *60.0* |
| J. L. Zimmerman (R) | 5,734 | *39.4* |

| **Democratic Primary** | | |
|---|---|---|
| Sam J. Ervin Jr. (D) | 499,392 | *78.3* |
| Charles A. Pratt (D) | 60,362 | *9.5* |
| John T. Gathings (D) | 48,357 | *7.6* |

**1974**

| **Republican Primary** | | |
|---|---|---|
| William E. Stevens (R) | 62,419 | *65.1* |
| Wood Hall Young (R) | 26,918 | *28.1* |
| B. E. (Bee) Sweatt (R) | 6,520 | *6.8* |

| **Democratic Primary** | | |
|---|---|---|
| Robert Morgan (D) | 294,986 | *50.4* |
| Nick Galifianakis (D) | 189,815 | *32.4* |
| Henry Hall Wilson (D) | 67,247 | *11.5* |

**1980**

| **Republican Primary** | | |
|---|---|---|
| John P. East (R) | | *100.0* |

| **Democratic Primary** | | |
|---|---|---|
| Robert Morgan (D) | | *100.0* |

**1986**

| **Republican Primary** | | |
|---|---|---|
| James T. Broyhill (R) | 139,570 | *66.5* |
| David B. Funderburk (R) | 63,593 | *30.3* |

| **Democratic Primary** | | |
|---|---|---|
| Terry Sanford (D) | 409,394 | *60.2* |
| John Ingram (D) | 111,557 | *16.4* |
| Fountain Odom (D) | 49,689 | *7.3* |
| William I. Belk (D) | 33,821 | *5.0* |

**1992**

| **Republican Primary** | | |
|---|---|---|
| Lauch Faircloth (R) | 129,159 | *47.7* |
| Sue Myrick (R) | 81,801 | *30.2* |
| Eugene Johnston (R) | 46,112 | *17.0* |
| Larry E. Harrington (R) | 13,496 | *5.0* |

| **Democratic Primary** | | |
|---|---|---|
| Terry Sanford (D) | | *100.0* |

**North Carolina**

1. Sen. W. Kerr Scott (D 1954-58) died April 16, 1958. Jordan was appointed to succeed him. Jordan and Clarke were designated by the state committee of their respective parties to run in the Nov. 4 special election for the remaining two years of Scott's term. Jordan won.

2. Sen. Clyde R. Hoey (D 1945-54) died May 12, 1954. Ervin was appointed to replace him and was also named by the Democratic state executive committee to run in a Nov. 2 special election for the remaining two years of the term.

# NORTH DAKOTA

| Candidates | Votes | % |
|---|---|---|
| **Class 1** | | |

**1958**

| **Republican Primary** | | |
|---|---|---|
| William Langer (R) [1] | 68,541 | *65.5* |
| Clyde Duffy (R) | 34,152 | *32.6* |

| **Democratic Primary** | | |
|---|---|---|
| Raymond Vendsel (D) | 30,775 | *65.8* |
| Anson Anderson (D) | 15,999 | *34.2* |

**1964**

| **Republican Primary** | | |
|---|---|---|
| Tom Kleppe (R) | | *100.0* |

| **Democratic Primary** | | |
|---|---|---|
| Quentin N. Burdick (D) | | *100.0* |

**1970**

| **Republican Primary** | | |
|---|---|---|
| Tom Kleppe (R) | | *100.0* |

| **Democratic Primary** | | |
|---|---|---|
| Quentin N. Burdick (D) | | *100.0* |

**1976**

| **Republican Primary** | | |
|---|---|---|
| Richard Stroup (R) | | *100.0* |

| **Democratic Primary** | | |
|---|---|---|
| Quentin N. Burdick (D) | | *100.0* |

| **American Primary** | | |
|---|---|---|
| Clarence Haggard (AM) | | *100.0* |

**1982**

| **Republican Primary** | | |
|---|---|---|
| Gene Knorr (R) | | *100.0* |

| **Democratic Primary** | | |
|---|---|---|
| Quentin N. Burdick (D) | | *100.0* |

**1988**

| **Republican Primary** | | |
|---|---|---|
| Earl Strinden (R) | | *100.0* |

| **Democratic Primary** | | |
|---|---|---|
| Quentin N. Burdick (D) [2] | | *100.0* |

| **Libertarian Primary** | | |
|---|---|---|
| Kenneth C. Gardner (LIBERT) | | *100.0* |

| **Class 3** | | |
|---|---|---|

**1956**

| **Republican Primary** | | |
|---|---|---|
| Milton R. Young (R) | 88,738 | *88.6* |
| Ray R. Lake (R) | 11,398 | *11.4* |

| Candidates Democratic Primary | Votes | % |
|---|---|---|
| Quentin N. Burdick (D) | | 100.0 |

**1962**

| Republican Primary | Votes | % |
|---|---|---|
| Milton R. Young (R) | 67,938 | 92.2 |
| Roger Vorachek (R) | 5,729 | 7.8 |

| Democratic Primary | Votes | % |
|---|---|---|
| William Lanier (D) | | 100.0 |

**1968**

| Republican Primary | Votes | % |
|---|---|---|
| Milton R. Young (R) | | 100.0 |

| Democratic Primary | Votes | % |
|---|---|---|
| Herschel Lashkowitz (D) | | 100.0 |

**1974**

| Republican Primary | Votes | % |
|---|---|---|
| Milton R. Young (R) | | 100.0 |

| Democratic Primary | Votes | % |
|---|---|---|
| William L. Guy (D) | 55,269 | 83.0 |
| Robert P. McCarney (D) | 11,286 | 17.0 |

**1980**

| Republican Primary | Votes | % |
|---|---|---|
| Mark Andrews (R) | | 100.0 |

| Democratic Primary | Votes | % |
|---|---|---|
| Kent Johanneson (D) | 30,789 | 77.4 |
| Michael P. Saba (D) | 9,013 | 22.6 |

**1986**

| Republican Primary | Votes | % |
|---|---|---|
| Mark Andrews (R) | | 100.0 |

| Democratic Primary | Votes | % |
|---|---|---|
| Kent Conrad (R) | | 100.0 |

**1992 [2]**

| Republican Primary | Votes | % |
|---|---|---|
| Steve Sydness (R) | 45,611 | 100.0 |

| Democratic Primary | Votes | % |
|---|---|---|
| Byron L. Dorgan (D) | 68,113 | 100.0 |

**North Dakota**

1. No primaries were held for the June 1960 special election in North Dakota to fill the vacancy caused by Langer's death. Nominees were selected by state conventions.

2. A special election was also held in 1992 to fill the remaining two years of the term of Sen. Quentin N. Burdick (D), who died Sept. 8, 1992. Both major-party candidates were nominated by the state party committees and no primaries were held.

# OHIO

| Candidates | Votes | % |
|---|---|---|
| **Class 1** | | |

**1958**

| Republican Primary | Votes | % |
|---|---|---|
| John W. Bricker (R) | | 100.0 |

| Democratic Primary | Votes | % |
|---|---|---|
| Stephen M. Young (D) | | 100.0 |

**1964**

| Republican Primary | Votes | % |
|---|---|---|
| Robert A. Taft Jr. (R) | 606,944 | 79.1 |
| Ted W. Brown (R) | 160,263 | 20.9 |

| Democratic Primary | Votes | % |
|---|---|---|
| Stephen M. Young (D) | 520,641 | 66.5 |
| John Glenn (D) | 206,956 | 26.4 |

**1970**

| Republican Primary | Votes | % |
|---|---|---|
| Robert A. Taft Jr. (R) | 472,202 | 50.3 |
| James A. Rhodes (R) | 466,932 | 49.7 |

| Democratic Primary | Votes | % |
|---|---|---|
| Howard M. Metzenbaum (D) | 430,469 | 46.3 |
| John Glenn (D) | 417,027 | 44.9 |
| Kenneth W. Clement (D) | 50,375 | 5.4 |

| American Independent Primary | Votes | % |
|---|---|---|
| Richard B. Kay (AMI) | | 100.0 |

**1976**

| Republican Primary | Votes | % |
|---|---|---|
| Robert A. Taft Jr. (R) | | 100.0 |

| Democratic Primary | Votes | % |
|---|---|---|
| Howard M. Metzenbaum (D) | 576,124 | 53.6 |
| James V. Stanton (D) | 400,552 | 37.3 |
| James D. Nolan (D) | 62,979 | 5.8 |

**1982**

| Republican Primary | Votes | % |
|---|---|---|
| Paul E. Pfeifer (R) | 364,579 | 60.0 |
| Walter E. Beckjord (R) | 180,198 | 29.7 |
| Bill Ress (WRITE IN) | 62,446 | 10.3 |

| Democratic Primary | Votes | % |
|---|---|---|
| Howard M. Metzenbaum (D) | 810,785 | 82.9 |
| Norbert G. Dennerll (D) | 167,778 | 17.1 |

| Libertarian Primary | Votes | % |
|---|---|---|
| Philip Herzing (LIBERT) | | 100.0 |

**1988**

| Republican Primary | Votes | % |
|---|---|---|
| George Voinovich (R) | | 100.0 |

| Democratic Primary | Votes | % |
|---|---|---|
| Howard Metzenbaum (D) | 1,070,934 | 83.6 |
| Ralph A. Applegate (D) | 210,508 | 16.4 |

# OKLAHOMA

| Candidates | Votes | % |
|---|---|---|
| **Class 3** | | |
| **1956 Republican Primary** | | |
| George H. Bender (R) | | *100.0* |
| **Democratic Primary** | | |
| Frank J. Lausche (D) | | *100.0* |
| **1962 Republican Primary** | | |
| John M. Briley (R) | 177,987 | *35.3* |
| Charles E. Fry (R) | 143,320 | *28.4* |
| John S. Ballard (R) | 132,924 | *26.3* |
| Ross Pepple (R) | 50,221 | *10.0* |
| **Democratic Primary** | | |
| Frank J. Lausche (D) | 437,902 | *74.0* |
| Albert T. Ball (D) | 90,609 | *15.3* |
| Raymond Warren Beringer (D) | 63,543 | *10.7* |
| **1968 Republican Primary** | | |
| William B. Saxbe (R) | 575,178 | *82.3* |
| William L. White (R) | 71,191 | *10.2* |
| Albert E. Payne (R) | 52,393 | *7.5* |
| **Democratic Primary** | | |
| John J. Gilligan (D) | 544,814 | *55.4* |
| Frank J. Lausche (D) | 438,588 | *44.6* |
| **1974 Republican Primary** | | |
| Ralph J. Perk (R) | 341,078 | *64.8* |
| Peter E. Voss (R) | 185,342 | *35.2* |
| **Democratic Primary** | | |
| John Glenn (D) | 571,871 | *54.4* |
| Howard M. Metzenbaum (D) | 480,123 | *45.6* |
| **1980 Republican Primary** | | |
| James E. Betts (R) | | *100.0* |
| **Democratic Primary** | | |
| John Glenn (D) | 934,230 | *85.9* |
| Frances A. Waterman (D) | 88,506 | *8.1* |
| Francis Hunstiger (D) | 64,270 | *5.9* |
| **1986 Republican Primary** | | |
| Thomas N. Kindness (R) | | *100.0* |
| **Democratic Primary** | | |
| John H. Glenn (D) | 678,171 | *87.6* |
| Don Scott (D) | 96,309 | *12.4* |
| **1992 Republican Primary** | | |
| Mike DeWine (R) | 583,805 | *70.3* |
| George H. Rhodes (R) | 246,625 | *29.7* |
| **Democratic Primary** | | |
| John H. Glenn (D) | 859,622 | *100.0* |

| Candidates | Votes | % |
|---|---|---|
| **Class 2** | | |
| **1960 Republican Primary** | | |
| B. Hayden Crawford (R) | 37,508 | *70.4* |
| Herbert K. Hyde (R) | 15,743 | *29.6* |
| **Democratic Primary** | | |
| Robert S. Kerr (D) | 300,061 | *77.6* |
| Thomas C. Dunn (D) | 65,139 | *16.8* |
| D. R. Condo (D) | 21,420 | *5.5* |
| **1964 [1] Republican Special Primary** | | |
| Bud Wilkinson (R) | 100,544 | *79.2* |
| Thomas J. Harris (R) | 19,170 | *15.1* |
| Forest W. Beall (R) | 7,211 | *5.7* |
| **Democratic Special Primary** | | |
| J. Howard Edmondson (D) | 215,455 | *36.4* |
| Fred R. Harris (D) | 190,868 | *32.3* |
| Raymond Gary (D) | 170,869 | *28.9* |
| **Democratic Special Runoff** | | |
| Fred R. Harris (D) | 277,362 | *60.9* |
| J. Howard Edmondson (D) | 178,051 | *39.1* |
| **1966 Republican Primary** | | |
| Pat J. Patterson (R) | 36,036 | *42.5* |
| Don Kinkaid (R) | 32,137 | *37.9* |
| Gustav K. Brandborg (R) | 16,617 | *19.6* |
| **Republican Runoff** | | |
| Pat J. Patterson (R) | 42,550 | *58.3* |
| Don Kinkaid (R) | 30,452 | *41.7* |
| **Democratic Primary** | | |
| Fred R. Harris (D) | 359,747 | *83.6* |
| W. R. Owens (D) | 41,580 | *9.7* |
| Billy E. Brown (D) | 29,184 | *6.8* |
| **1972 Republican Primary** | | |
| Dewey F. Bartlett (R) | 94,935 | *93.1* |
| C. W. Wood (R) | 7,029 | *6.9* |
| **Democratic Primary** | | |
| Ed Edmondson (D) | 249,729 | *56.3* |
| Charles Nesbitt (D) | 92,101 | *20.8* |
| Al Terrill (D) | 33,520 | *7.6* |
| Jed Johnson (D) | 28,795 | *6.5* |
| **1978 Republican Primary** | | |
| Robert B. Kamm (R) | | *100.0* |

| Candidates | Votes | % |
|---|---|---|
| **Democratic Primary** | | |
| David L. Boren (D) | 252,560 | *45.8* |
| Ed Edmondson (D) | 155,626 | *28.2* |
| Gene Stipe (D) | 114,423 | *20.8* |
| **Democratic Runoff** | | |
| David L. Boren (D) | 281,587 | *60.5* |
| Ed Edmondson (D) | 184,175 | *39.5* |

**1984**

| Candidates | Votes | % |
|---|---|---|
| **Republican Primary** | | |
| George L. Mothershed (R) | 46,933 | *39.3* |
| Will E. (Bill) Crozier (R) | 39,581 | *33.1* |
| Gar Graham (R) | 32,901 | *27.6* |
| **Democratic Primary** | | |
| David L. Boren (D) | 432,534 | *89.9* |
| Marshall Luse (D) | 48,761 | *10.1* |

**1990**

| Candidates | Votes | % |
|---|---|---|
| **Republican Primary** | | |
| Stephen Jones (R) | | *100.0* |
| **Democratic Primary** | | |
| David L. Boren (D) | 445,969 | *84.3* |
| Virginia Jenner (D) | 57,909 | *10.9* |

## Class 3

**1956**

| Candidates | Votes | % |
|---|---|---|
| **Republican Primary** | | |
| Douglas McKeever (R) | 24,447 | *55.5* |
| Paul V. Beck (R) | 7,666 | *17.4* |
| Ernest G. Albright (R) | 6,539 | *14.8* |
| Dan M. Madrano (R) | 5,379 | *12.2* |
| **Democratic Primary** | | |
| A. S. Mike Monroney (D) | 245,572 | *71.1* |
| H. O. Doenges (D) | 54,546 | *15.8* |
| Ora J. Fox (D) | 29,825 | *8.6* |

**1962**

| Candidates | Votes | % |
|---|---|---|
| **Republican Primary** | | |
| B. Hayden Crawford (R) | | *100.0* |
| **Democratic Primary** | | |
| A. S. Mike Monroney (D) | 335,922 | *74.3* |
| Wilson Wallace (D) | 64,996 | *14.4* |
| Billy E. Brown (D) | 26,440 | *5.8* |
| Woodrow W. Bussey (D) | 24,725 | *5.5* |

**1968**

| Candidates | Votes | % |
|---|---|---|
| **Republican Primary** | | |
| Henry Bellmon (R) | | *100.0* |
| **Democratic Primary** | | |
| A. S. Mike Monroney (D) | 281,697 | *76.3* |
| W. R. Owens (D) | 32,823 | *8.9* |
| Jesse L. Leeds (D) | 22,843 | *6.2* |
| Billy E. Brown (D) | 20,681 | *5.6* |
| **American Primary** | | |
| George Washington (AM) | 414 | *57.6* |
| Landis B. Hiniker (AM) | 305 | *42.4* |

**1974**

| Candidates | Votes | % |
|---|---|---|
| **Republican Primary** | | |
| Henry Bellmon (R) | 132,888 | *87.1* |
| Warner M. Hornbeck (R) | 19,733 | *12.9* |
| **Democratic Primary** | | |
| Ed Edmondson (D) | 288,665 | *48.7* |
| Charles Nesbitt (D) | 222,727 | *37.5* |
| Wilburn Cartwright (D) | 35,107 | *5.9* |
| **Democratic Runoff** | | |
| Ed Edmondson (D) | 306,178 | *58.7* |
| Charles Nesbitt (D) | 215,685 | *41.3* |

**1980**

| Candidates | Votes | % |
|---|---|---|
| **Republican Primary** | | |
| Don Nickles (R) | 47,879 | *34.7* |
| John Zink (R) | 45,914 | *33.3* |
| Ed Noble (R) | 39,839 | *28.9* |
| **Republican Runoff** | | |
| Don Nickles (R) | 81,697 | *65.6* |
| John Zink (R) | 42,818 | *34.4* |
| **Democratic Primary** | | |
| Robert S. Kerr Jr. (D) | 156,666 | *34.0* |
| Andrew Coats (D) | 154,762 | *33.6* |
| Gene Howard (D) | 55,503 | *12.1* |
| James E. Hamilton (D) | 49,369 | *10.7* |
| **Democratic Runoff** | | |
| Andrew Coats (D) | 209,952 | *53.0* |
| Robert S. Kerr Jr. (D) | 185,814 | *46.9* |
| **Libertarian Primary** | | |
| Robert Murphy (LIBERT) | | *100.0* |

**1986**

| Candidates | Votes | % |
|---|---|---|
| **Republican Primary** | | |
| Don Nickles (R) | | *100.0* |
| **Democratic Primary** | | |
| James R. Jones (R) | 324,907 | *67.4* |
| George Gentry (R) | 157,141 | *32.6* |

**1992**

| Candidates | Votes | % |
|---|---|---|
| **Republican Primary** | | |
| Don Nickles (R) | | *100.0* |
| **Democratic Primary** | | |
| Steve Lewis (D) | | *100.0* |

**Oklahoma**

*1. A special election was held in Oklahoma to fill the unexpired term of Sen. Robert S. Kerr (D), who died Jan. 1, 1963.*

# OREGON

| Candidates | Votes | % |
|---|---|---|
| **Class 2** | | |

**1960** [1] **Republican Special Primary**

| | | |
|---|---|---|
| Elmo E. Smith (R) | 201,024 | 85.5 |
| George Altvater (R) | 33,022 | 14.0 |

**Democratic Special Primary**

| | | |
|---|---|---|
| Maurine B. Neuberger (D) | 244,865 | 99.5 |

**1960** **Republican Primary**

| | | |
|---|---|---|
| Elmo E. Smith (R) | 179,575 | 76.5 |
| George Altvater (R) | 20,438 | 8.7 |
| R. F. Cook (R) | 19,443 | 8.3 |
| Thomas Killam (R) | 14,490 | 6.2 |

**Democratic Primary**

| | | |
|---|---|---|
| Maurine B. Neuberger (D) | 211,961 | 77.9 |
| Harry C. Fowler (D) | 28,032 | 10.3 |
| William B. Murphy (D) | 16,245 | 6.0 |

**1966** **Republican Primary**

| | | |
|---|---|---|
| Mark O. Hatfield (R) | 178,782 | 75.9 |
| Walter Huss (R) | 30,906 | 13.1 |
| James Bacaloff (R) | 19,699 | 8.4 |

**Democratic Primary**

| | | |
|---|---|---|
| Robert B. Duncan (D) | 161,189 | 62.2 |
| Howard Morgan (D) | 89,174 | 34.4 |

**1972** **Republican Primary**

| | | |
|---|---|---|
| Mark O. Hatfield (R) | 171,594 | 61.1 |
| Lynn Engdahl (R) | 63,859 | 22.8 |
| Kenneth A. Brown (R) | 30,826 | 11.0 |

**Democratic Primary**

| | | |
|---|---|---|
| Wayne L. Morse (D) | 173,147 | 43.7 |
| Robert B. Duncan (D) | 130,845 | 33.0 |
| Don Willner (D) | 74,060 | 18.7 |

**1978** **Republican Primary**

| | | |
|---|---|---|
| Mark O. Hatfield (R) | 159,617 | 65.7 |
| Bert W. Hawkins (R) | 43,350 | 17.8 |
| Robert D. Maxwell (R) | 24,294 | 10.0 |
| Richard L. Schnepel (R) | 15,628 | 6.4 |

**Democratic Primary**

| | | |
|---|---|---|
| Vernon Cook (D) | 151,754 | 58.3 |
| John Sweeney (D) | 41,599 | 16.0 |
| Jack A. Brown (D) | 35,211 | 13.5 |
| Steve Anderson (D) | 30,066 | 11.6 |

**1984** **Republican Primary**

| | | |
|---|---|---|
| Mark O. Hatfield (R) | 214,114 | 78.6 |
| John T. Schiess (R) | 26,848 | 9.9 |
| Sherry Reynolds (R) | 18,590 | 6.8 |

| Candidates | Votes | % |
|---|---|---|
| **Democratic Primary** | | |

| | | |
|---|---|---|
| Margie Hendriksen (D) | 249,142 | 75.8 |
| Sam Kahl (D) | 79,317 | 24.1 |

**1990** **Republican Primary**

| | | |
|---|---|---|
| Mark Hatfield (R) | 220,449 | 78.3 |
| Randy Prince (R) | 59,970 | 21.3 |

**Democratic Primary**

| | | |
|---|---|---|
| Harry Lonsdale (D) | 162,529 | 64.1 |
| Steve Anderson (D) | 34,305 | 13.5 |
| Neale S. Hyatt (D) | 20,684 | 8.2 |
| Brooks Washburne (D) | 13,766 | 5.4 |

| **Class 3** | | |
|---|---|---|

**1956** **Republican Primary**

| | | |
|---|---|---|
| Douglas McKay (R) | 123,281 | 49.5 |
| Phil Hitchcock (R) | 99,296 | 39.8 |
| Elmer Deetz (R) | 23,170 | 9.3 |

**Democratic Primary**

| | | |
|---|---|---|
| Wayne L. Morse (D) | 195,784 | 83.4 |
| Woody Smith (D) | 38,959 | 16.6 |

**1962** **Republican Primary**

| | | |
|---|---|---|
| Sig Ulander (R) | 106,821 | 50.1 |
| Edwin R. Durno (R) | 72,955 | 34.2 |
| Harold M. Livingston (R) | 16,880 | 7.9 |

**Democratic Primary**

| | | |
|---|---|---|
| Wayne L. Morse (D) | 183,385 | 79.8 |
| Charles E. Gilbert (D) | 46,171 | 20.1 |

**1968** **Republican Primary**

| | | |
|---|---|---|
| Bob Packwood (R) | 241,464 | 88.0 |
| John S. Boyd (R) | 32,807 | 12.0 |

**Democratic Primary**

| | | |
|---|---|---|
| Wayne L. Morse (D) | 185,091 | 49.0 |
| Robert B. Duncan (D) | 174,795 | 46.3 |

**1974** **Republican Primary**

| | | |
|---|---|---|
| Bob Packwood (R) | | 100.0 |

**Democratic Primary**

| | | |
|---|---|---|
| Wayne L. Morse (D) [2] | 155,729 | 49.0 |
| Jason Boe (D) | 125,055 | 39.3 |
| Robert T. Daly (D) | 21,881 | 6.9 |

**1980** **Republican Primary**

| | | |
|---|---|---|
| Bob Packwood (R) | 191,127 | 62.4 |
| Brenda Jose (R) | 45,973 | 15.0 |
| Kenneth A. Brown (R) | 23,599 | 7.7 |
| Rosalie Huss (R) | 22,929 | 7.5 |
| Willard D. Severn (R) | 22,281 | 7.3 |

| Candidates | Votes | % |
|---|---|---|
| **Democratic Primary** | | |
| Ted Kulongoski (D) | 161,153 | *47.7* |
| Charles O. Porter (D) | 69,649 | *20.6* |
| Jack Sumner (D) | 46,107 | *13.6* |
| John Sweeney (D) | 39,691 | *11.7* |
| Gene Arvidson (D) | 20,548 | *6.1* |

**1986** — **Republican Primary**

| Candidates | Votes | % |
|---|---|---|
| Bob Packwood (R) | 171,985 | *57.6* |
| Joe P. Lutz (R) | 126,315 | *42.3* |

**Democratic Primary**

| Candidates | Votes | % |
|---|---|---|
| James Weaver (D) [3] | 183,334 | *61.6* |
| Rod Monroe (D) | 44,553 | *15.0* |
| Rick Bauman (D) | 41,939 | *14.1* |
| Steve Anderson (D) | 26,130 | *8.8* |

**1992** — **Republican Primary**

| Candidates | Votes | % |
|---|---|---|
| Bob Packwood (R) | 176,939 | *59.1* |
| John DeZell (R) | 61,128 | *20.4* |
| Stephanie J. Salvey (R) | 27,088 | *9.0* |
| Randy Prince (R) | 20,358 | *6.8* |
| **Democratic Primary** | | |
| Les AuCoin (D) | 153,029 | *42.2* |
| Harry Lonsdale (D) | 152,699 | *42.1* |
| Joseph Wetzel (D) | 32,183 | *8.9* |
| Bob Bell (D) | 23,700 | *6.5* |

**Oregon**

1. *A special election to fill the unexpired term of Sen. Richard L. Neuberger (D), who died March 9, 1960, was held in conjunction with the election for the full term, beginning Jan. 3, 1961. His widow, Maurine B. Neuberger (D), and Elmo Smith (R), won both primaries and Maurine Neuberger went on to defeat Smith in the November general election for both the short and full terms. The short term had been filled until the election by Hall Lusk. Returns for the special primary from the Elections Research Center, Washington, D.C.*

2. *Sen. Morse died after winning the primary and the Democratic state central committee substituted Betty Roberts as the party's nominee.*

3. *Weaver withdrew after the Democratic primary. Bauman was substituted by the party state central committee.*

# PENNSYLVANIA

| Candidates | Votes | % |
|---|---|---|

## Class 1

**1958** — **Republican Primary**

| Candidates | Votes | % |
|---|---|---|
| Hugh Scott (R) | 766,102 | *74.0* |
| Weldon B. Heyburn (R) | 160,857 | *15.5* |
| Harrison A. Moyer (R) | 108,179 | *10.4* |

**Democratic Primary**

| Candidates | Votes | % |
|---|---|---|
| George M. Leader (D) | 724,645 | *74.2* |
| Clarence P. Bowers (D) | 252,468 | *25.8* |

**1964** — **Republican Primary**

| Candidates | Votes | % |
|---|---|---|
| Hugh Scott (R) | 869,774 | *88.9* |
| W. Henry McFarland (R) | 106,376 | *10.9* |

| Candidates | Votes | % |
|---|---|---|
| **Democratic Primary** | | |
| Genevieve Blatt (D) | 461,111 | *45.4* |
| Michael A. Musmanno (D) | 460,620 | *45.4* |
| David B. Roberts (D) | 93,311 | *9.2* |

**1970** — **Republican Primary**

| Candidates | Votes | % |
|---|---|---|
| Hugh Scott (R) | | *100.0* |

**Democratic Primary**

| Candidates | Votes | % |
|---|---|---|
| William G. Sesler (D) | 477,680 | *53.8* |
| Norval D. Reece (D) | 241,731 | *27.3* |
| Frank Mesaros (D) | 167,779 | *18.9* |

**American Independent Primary**

| Candidates | Votes | % |
|---|---|---|
| W. Henry McFarland (AMI) | | *100.0* |

**Constitution Primary**

| Candidates | Votes | % |
|---|---|---|
| Frank W. Gaydosh (CONST) | | *100.0* |

**1976** — **Republican Primary**

| Candidates | Votes | % |
|---|---|---|
| John Heinz (R) | 358,715 | *37.7* |
| Arlen Specter (R) | 332,513 | *35.0* |
| George R. Packard (R) | 160,379 | *16.9* |

**Democratic Primary**

| Candidates | Votes | % |
|---|---|---|
| William J. Green III (D) | 762,733 | *68.8* |
| Jeanette Reibman (D) | 345,264 | *31.1* |

**Constitution Primary**

| Candidates | Votes | % |
|---|---|---|
| Andrew J. Watson (CONST) | | *100.0* |

**1982** — **Republican Primary**

| Candidates | Votes | % |
|---|---|---|
| John Heinz (R) | | *100.0* |

**Democratic Primary**

| Candidates | Votes | % |
|---|---|---|
| Cyril H. Wecht (D) | 426,625 | *57.2* |
| John J. Logue (D) | 166,078 | *22.3* |
| Cyril E. Sagan (D) | 152,631 | *20.5* |

**1988** — **Republican Primary**

| Candidates | Votes | % |
|---|---|---|
| H. John Heinz (R) [1] | | *100.0* |

**Democratic Primary**

| Candidates | Votes | % |
|---|---|---|
| Joseph C. Vignola (D) | 492,153 | *45.4* |
| Susan S. Kefover (D) | 371,443 | *34.2* |
| Steve Douglas (D) | 145,614 | *13.4* |
| John J. Logue (D) | 76,020 | *7.0* |

## Class 3

**1956** — **Republican Primary**

| Candidates | Votes | % |
|---|---|---|
| James H. Duff (R) | 803,971 | *85.0* |
| Paul E. Sanger (R) | 141,820 | *15.0* |

**Democratic Primary**

| Candidates | Votes | % |
|---|---|---|
| Joseph S. Clark (D) | | *100.0* |

| 1962 | Candidates<br>**Republican Primary** | Votes | % |
|---|---|---|---|
| | James E. Van Zandt (R) | | 100.0 |
| | **Democratic Primary** | | |
| | Joseph S. Clark (D) | | 100.0 |
| 1968 | **Republican Primary** | | |
| | Richard S. Schweiker (R) | | 100.0 |
| | **Democratic Primary** | | |
| | Joseph S. Clark (D) | 460,380 | 53.3 |
| | John H. Dent (D) | 402,799 | 46.7 |
| 1974 | **Republican Primary** | | |
| | Richard S. Schweiker (R) | | 100.0 |
| | **Democratic Primary** | | |
| | Peter Flaherty (D) | 485,361 | 47.1 |
| | Herbert S. Denenberg (D) | 447,081 | 43.3 |
| | Frank Mesaros (D) | 64,070 | 6.2 |
| | **Constitution Primary** | | |
| | George W. Shankey (CONST) | | 100.0 |
| 1980 | **Republican Primary** | | |
| | Arlen Specter (R) | 419,372 | 36.4 |
| | Bud Haabestad (R) | 382,281 | 33.2 |
| | Edward L. Howard (R) | 148,200 | 12.9 |
| | **Democratic Primary** | | |
| | Peter Flaherty (D) | 771,119 | 53.2 |
| | Joseph Rhodes (D) | 179,107 | 12.4 |
| | Peter Liacouras (D) | 116,975 | 8.1 |
| | C. Delores Tucker (D) | 107,483 | 7.4 |
| | Ed Mezvinsky (D) | 100,841 | 7.0 |
| | Tom Anderson (D) | 89,656 | 6.2 |
| 1986 | **Republican Primary** | | |
| | Arlen Specter (R) | 434,623 | 76.2 |
| | Richard A. Stokes (R) | 135,673 | 23.8 |
| | **Democratic Primary** | | |
| | Robert W. Edgar (D) | 432,940 | 47.3 |
| | Don Bailey (D) | 408,460 | 44.7 |
| | George R. H. Elder (D) | 46,663 | 5.1 |
| 1992 | **Republican Primary** | | |
| | Arlen Specter (R) | 683,118 | 65.1 |
| | Stephen F. Freind (R) | 366,608 | 34.9 |
| | **Democratic Primary** | | |
| | Lynn Yeakel (D) | 556,372 | 44.8 |
| | Mark S. Singel (D) | 403,656 | 32.5 |
| | Bob Colville (D) | 172,845 | 13.9 |

1. Heinz died April 4, 1991. A special election was held in 1991 to fill the vacancy. Candidates were nominated by state party committees, therefore no primaries were held.

# RHODE ISLAND

| | Candidates | Votes | % |
|---|---|---|---|
| | **Class 1** | | |
| 1958 | **Republican Primary** | | |
| | Bayard Ewing (R) | | 100.0 |
| | **Democratic Primary** | | |
| | John O. Pastore (D) | | 100.0 |
| 1964 | **Republican Primary** | | |
| | Ronald R. Lagueux (R) | | 100.0 |
| | **Democratic Primary** | | |
| | John O. Pastore (D) | | 100.0 |
| 1970 | **Republican Primary** | | |
| | John McLaughlin (R) | | 100.0 |
| | **Democratic Primary** | | |
| | John O. Pastore (D) | 54,090 | 88.1 |
| | John Quattrocchi (D) | 7,332 | 11.9 |
| 1976 | **Republican Primary** | | |
| | John H. Chafee (R) | | 100.0 |
| | **Democratic Primary** | | |
| | Richard P. Lorber (D) | 60,118 | 37.8 |
| | Philip W. Noel (D) | 60,018 | 37.7 |
| | John P. Hawkins (D) | 25,456 | 16.0 |
| 1982 | **Republican Primary** | | |
| | John H. Chafee (R) | | 100.0 |
| | **Democratic Primary** | | |
| | Julius C. Michaelson (D) | 56,800 | 82.4 |
| | Helen E. Flynn (D) | 12,159 | 17.6 |
| 1988 | **Republican Primary** | | |
| | John H. Chafee (R) | | 100.0 |
| | **Democratic Primary** | | |
| | Richard A. Licht (D) | | 100.0 |
| | **Class 2** | | |
| 1960 | **Republican Primary** | | |
| | Raoul Archambault (R) | | 100.0 |
| | **Democratic Primary** | | |
| | Claiborne Pell (D) | 83,184 | 61.3 |
| | Dennis J. Roberts (D) | 44,924 | 33.1 |
| | Howard McGrath (D) | 7,535 | 5.6 |

| | Candidates | Votes | % |
|---|---|---|---|
| **1966** | **Republican Primary** | | |
| | Ruth M. Briggs (R) | 15,451 | *82.1* |
| | Charles H. Eden (R) | 3,363 | *17.9* |
| | **Democratic Primary** | | |
| | Claiborne Pell (D) | | *100.0* |
| **1972** | **Republican Primary** | | |
| | John H. Chafee (R) | | *100.0* |
| | **Democratic Primary** | | |
| | Claiborne Pell (D) | | *100.0* |
| **1978** | **Republican Primary** | | |
| | James G. Reynolds (R) | | *100.0* |
| | **Democratic Primary** | | |
| | Claiborne Pell (D) | 69,729 | *87.0* |
| | Raymond J. Greiner (D) | 6,076 | *7.6* |
| | Francis P. Kelley (D) | 4,330 | *5.4* |
| **1984** | **Republican Primary** | | |
| | Barbara Leonard (R) | 108,492 | *100.0* |
| | **Democratic Primary** | | |
| | Claiborne Pell (D) | 82,394 | *100.0* |
| **1990** | **Republican Primary** | | |
| | Claudine Schneider (R) | | *100.0* |
| | **Democratic Primary** | | |
| | Claiborne Pell (D) | | *100.0* |

# SOUTH CAROLINA

| | Candidates | Votes | % |
|---|---|---|---|
| | **Class 2** | | |
| **1924** | **Democratic Primary** | | |
| | Coleman L. Blease (D) | 83,738 | *41.8* |
| | James F. Byrnes (D) | 67,727 | *33.8* |
| | Nathan B. Dial (D) | 44,425 | *22.2* |
| | **Democratic Runoff** | | |
| | Coleman L. Blease (D) | 100,686 | *50.6* |
| | James F. Byrnes (D) | 98,465 | *49.4* |
| **1930** | **Democratic Primary** | | |
| | Coleman L. Blease (D) | 111,989 | *45.6* |
| | James F. Byrnes (D) | 94,242 | *38.4* |
| | Harris (D) | 39,512 | *16.1* |

| | Candidates | Votes | % |
|---|---|---|---|
| | **Democratic Runoff** | | |
| | James F. Byrnes (D) | 120,755 | *51.0* |
| | Coleman L. Blease (D) | 116,264 | *49.1* |
| **1936** | **Democratic Primary** | | |
| | James F. Byrnes (D) | 257,247 | *87.1* |
| | Stoney (D) | 25,672 | *8.7* |
| **1941** | **Democratic Special Primary** | | |
| | Burnet R. Maybank (D) | 59,017 | *47.4* |
| | Olin D. Johnston (D) | 40,296 | *32.4* |
| | Bryson (D) | 25,257 | *20.3* |
| | **Democratic Special Runoff** | | |
| | Burnet R. Maybank (D) | 92,100 | *56.6* |
| | Olin D. Johnston (D) | 70,687 | *43.4* |
| **1942** | **Democratic Primary** | | |
| | Burnet R. Maybank (D) | 120,731 | *51.4* |
| | Eugene Blease (D) | 114,241 | *48.6* |
| **1948** | **Democratic Primary** | | |
| | Burnet R. Maybank (D) | 172,611 | *51.6* |
| | William Jennings Bryan Dorn (D) | 83,068 | *24.9* |
| | Bennett (D) | 45,068 | *13.5* |
| | Johnstone (D) | 18,184 | *5.4* |
| **1954** | **Democratic Primary** | | |
| | Burnet R. Maybank (D) [1] | | *100.0* |
| **1956** | **Democratic Special Primary** | | |
| | Strom Thurmond (D) | | *100.0* |
| **1960** | **Democratic Primary** | | |
| | Strom Thurmond (D) | 273,795 | *89.5* |
| | R. B. Herbert (D) | 32,136 | *10.5* |
| **1966** | **Democratic Primary** | | |
| | Bradley Morrah (D) | 167,401 | *55.9* |
| | John B. Culbertson (D) | 131,870 | *44.1* |
| **1972** | **Democratic Primary** | | |
| | Eugene N. Ziegler (D) | 201,170 | *58.7* |
| | John B. Culbertson (D) | 141,757 | *41.3* |
| **1978** | **Republican Primary** | | |
| | Strom Thurmond (R) | | *100.0* |
| | **Democratic Primary** | | |
| | Charles D. Ravenel (D) | 205,348 | *55.9* |
| | John B. Culbertson (D) | 69,184 | *18.8* |
| | James T. Triplett (D) | 50,951 | *13.9* |
| | William T. McElveen (D) | 41,550 | *11.3* |
| **1984** | **Republican Primary** | | |
| | Strom Thurmond (R) | 44,662 | *94.3* |
| | R. H. Cunningham (R) | 2,693 | *5.7* |

| | Candidates<br>Democratic Primary | Votes | % |
|---|---|---|---|
| | Melvin Pervis Jr. (D) | 149,730 | *50.2* |
| | Cecil J. Williams (D) | 148,586 | *49.8* |
| 1990 | **Republican Primary** | | |
| | Strom Thurmond (R) | | *100.0* |
| | **Democratic Primary** | | |
| | Bob Cunningham (D) | | *100.0* |

## Class 3

| | | Votes | % |
|---|---|---|---|
| 1920 | **Democratic Primary** | | |
| | Ellison D. Smith (D) | 57,423 | *48.7* |
| | George Warren (D) | 36,272 | *30.8* |
| | W. P. Pollock (D) | 15,678 | *13.3* |
| | W. C. Irby (D) | 8,454 | *7.2* |
| | **Democratic Runoff** | | |
| | Ellison D. Smith (D) | 65,880 | *60.7* |
| | George Warren (D) | 42,735 | *39.3* |
| 1926 | **Democratic Primary** | | |
| | Ellison D. Smith (D) | 72,015 | *42.0* |
| | Edgar Brown (D) | 65,331 | *38.1* |
| | Nathan B. Dial (D) | 34,114 | *19.9* |
| | **Democratic Runoff** | | |
| | Ellison D. Smith (D) | 82,783 | *51.6* |
| | Edgar Brown (D) | 77,559 | *48.4* |
| 1932 | **Democratic Primary** | | |
| | Ellison D. Smith (D) | 100,270 | *37.0* |
| | Coleman L. Blease (D) | 81,297 | *30.0* |
| | Williams (D) | 48,084 | *17.7* |
| | Harris (D) | 41,748 | *15.4* |
| | **Democratic Runoff** | | |
| | Ellison D. Smith (D) | 150,468 | *56.7* |
| | Coleman L. Blease (D) | 114,840 | *43.3* |
| 1938 | **Democratic Primary** | | |
| | Ellison D. Smith (D) | 186,519 | *55.4* |
| | Olin D. Johnston (D) | 150,437 | *44.7* |
| 1944 | **Democratic Primary** | | |
| | Olin D. Johnston (D) | 138,440 | *55.2* |
| | Ellison D. Smith (D) | 88,045 | *35.1* |
| | Daniel (D) | 14,572 | *5.8* |
| 1950 | **Democratic Primary** | | |
| | Olin D. Johnston (D) | 186,180 | *54.0* |
| | Strom Thurmond (D) | 158,904 | *46.1* |
| 1956 | **Democratic Primary** | | |
| | Olin D. Johnston (D) | | *100.0* |

| | Candidates<br>Democratic Primary | Votes | % |
|---|---|---|---|
| 1962 | **Democratic Primary** | | |
| | Olin D. Johnston (D) | 210,918 | *65.7* |
| | Ernest F. Hollings (D) | 110,023 | *34.3* |
| 1966 | **Democratic Special Primary** | | |
| | Ernest F. Hollings (D) | 196,405 | *60.8* |
| | Donald S. Russell (D) | 126,595 | *39.2* |
| 1968 | **Democratic Primary** | | |
| | Ernest F. Hollings (D) | 307,561 | *78.3* |
| | John B. Culbertson (D) | 85,219 | *21.7* |
| 1974 | **Republican Primary** | | |
| | Gwenyfred Bush (R) | | *100.0* |
| | **Democratic Primary** | | |
| | Ernest F. Hollings (D) | | *100.0* |
| 1980 | **Republican Primary** | | |
| | Marshall T. Mays (R) | 14,075 | *42.6* |
| | Charles F. Rhodes (R) | 11,395 | *34.5* |
| | Robert K. Carley (R) | 7,575 | *22.9* |
| | **Republican Runoff** | | |
| | Marshall T. Mays (R) | 6,853 | *64.8* |
| | Charles F. Rhodes (R) | 3,717 | *35.2* |
| | **Democratic Primary** | | |
| | Ernest F. Hollings (D) | 266,796 | *81.2* |
| | Nettie D. Dickerson (D) | 34,720 | *10.6* |
| | William P. Kreml (D) | 27,049 | *8.2* |
| 1986 | **Republican Primary** | | |
| | Henry D. McMaster (R) | 27,695 | *53.4* |
| | Henry S. Jordan (R) | 24,164 | *46.6* |
| | **Democratic Primary** | | |
| | Ernest F. Hollings (D) | | *100.0* |
| 1992 | **Republican Primary** | | |
| | Thomas F. Hartnett (R) | 123,572 | *76.8* |
| | Charlie E. Thompson (R) | 37,352 | *23.2* |
| | **Democratic Primary** | | |
| | Ernest F. Hollings (D) | | *100.0* |

**South Carolina**

1. *Maybank had been renominated July 13, 1954, but died Sept. 1. Officials of the South Carolina Democratic Party, charged with replacing him on the ballot for the November general election, declined to order a new primary and selected state Sen. Edgar A. Brown as their candidate. He was defeated in the election by former governor Strom Thurmond (D 1947-51), who waged a successful write-in campaign.*

# SOUTH DAKOTA

| Candidates | Votes | % |
|---|---|---|
| **Class 2** | | |

**1960**

**Republican Primary**

| Karl E. Mundt (R) | | 100.0 |

**Democratic Primary**

| George McGovern (D) | | 100.0 |

**1966**   **Republican Primary**

| Karl E. Mundt (R) | 66,758 | 82.1 |
| Richard R. Murphy (R) | 14,593 | 17.9 |

**Democratic Primary**

| Donn H. Wright (D) | | 100.0 |

**1972**   **Republican Primary** [1]

| Robert W. Hirsch (R) | 27,322 | 27.4 |
| Gordon Mydland (R) | 22,297 | 22.3 |
| Chuck Lien (R) | 21,995 | 22.0 |
| Kenneth D. Stofferahn (R) | 16,615 | 16.6 |
| Tom Reardon (R) | 11,592 | 11.6 |

**Democratic Primary**

| James Abourezk (D) | 46,931 | 79.4 |
| George Blue (D) | 12,163 | 20.6 |

**1978**   **Republican Primary**

| Larry Pressler (R) | 66,893 | 73.9 |
| Ronald F. Williamson (R) | 23,646 | 26.1 |

**Democratic Primary**

| Don Barnett (D) | 37,319 | 55.1 |
| Kenneth D. Stofferahn (D) | 30,384 | 44.9 |

**1984**   **Republican Primary**

| Larry Pressler (R) | | 100.0 |

**Democratic Primary**

| George V. Cunningham (D) | 31,376 | 68.1 |
| Dean L. Sinclair (D) | 14,672 | 31.8 |

**1990**   **Republican Primary**

| Larry Pressler (R) | | 100.0 |

**Democratic Primary**

| Ted Muenster (D) | | 100.0 |

| **Class 3** | | |

**1956**   **Republican Primary**

| Francis Case (R) | | 100.0 |

| Candidates | Votes | % |
|---|---|---|
| **Democratic Primary** | | |

| Kenneth Holum (D) | 23,464 | 60.8 |
| Merton B. Tice (D) | 15,099 | 39.1 |

**1962**   **Republican Primary**

| Francis Case (R) [2] | 57,583 | 83.5 |
| A. C. Miller (R) | 11,414 | 16.5 |

**Democratic Primary**

| George McGovern (D) | | 100.0 |

**1968**   **Republican Primary**

| Archie M. Gubbrud (R) | | 100.0 |

**Democratic Primary**

| George McGovern (D) | | 100.0 |

**1974**   **Republican Primary**

| Leo K. Thorsness (R) | 49,716 | 52.3 |
| Al Schock (R) | 35,406 | 37.3 |
| Barbara B. Gunderson (R) | 9,852 | 10.4 |

**Democratic Primary**

| George McGovern (D) | | 100.0 |

**1980**   **Republican Primary**

| James Abdnor (R) | 68,196 | 72.9 |
| Dale Bell (R) | 25,314 | 27.1 |

**Democratic Primary**

| George McGovern (D) | 44,822 | 62.4 |
| Larry Schumaker (D) | 26,958 | 37.6 |

**1986**   **Republican Primary**

| James Abdnor (R) | 63,414 | 54.5 |
| William J. Janklow (R) | 52,924 | 45.5 |

**Democratic Primary**

| Thomas A. Daschle (D) | | 100.0 |

**1992**   **Republican Primary**

| Charlene Haar (R) | | 100.0 |

**Democratic Primary**

| Thomas A. Daschle (D) | | 100.0 |

**South Dakota**

1. *A state Republican convention was held June 26 because no one received the 35 percent required for nomination under the South Dakota primary law. Hirsch was nominated at this convention.*

2. *Case died shortly after winning the primary and the Republican state committee substituted Joe H. Bottum as the party's nominee.*

# TENNESSEE

| Candidates | Votes | % |
|---|---|---|

## Class 1

### 1922 **Democratic Primary**

| | | |
|---|---|---|
| Kenneth D. McKellar (D) | 102,692 | 64.0 |
| Fitzhugh (D) | 47,627 | 29.7 |
| Cooper (D) | 9,480 | 5.9 |

### 1928 **Democratic Primary**

| | | |
|---|---|---|
| Kenneth D. McKellar (D) | 120,298 | 63.3 |
| Finis Garrett (D) | 64,470 | 33.9 |

### 1934 **Democratic Primary**

| | | |
|---|---|---|
| Kenneth D. McKellar (D) | 212,226 | 84.0 |
| John R. Neal (D) | 40,463 | 16.0 |

### 1940 **Democratic Primary**

| | | |
|---|---|---|
| Kenneth D. McKellar (D) | 230,033 | 91.5 |
| John R. Neal (D) | 14,583 | 5.8 |

### 1946 **Republican Primary**

| | | |
|---|---|---|
| William B. Ladd (R) | 30,954 | 100.0 |

**Democratic Primary**

| | | |
|---|---|---|
| Kenneth D. McKellar (D) | 188,805 | 62.0 |
| Edward W. Carmack (D) | 107,363 | 35.2 |

### 1952 **Democratic Primary**

| | | |
|---|---|---|
| Albert Gore (D) | 334,957 | 56.5 |
| Kenneth D. McKellar (D) | 245,054 | 41.4 |

### 1958 **Republican Primary**

| | | |
|---|---|---|
| Hobart F. Atkins (R) | | 100.0 |

**Democratic Primary**

| | | |
|---|---|---|
| Albert Gore (D) | 375,439 | 59.0 |
| Prentice Cooper (D) | 253,191 | 39.8 |

### 1964 **Republican Primary**

| | | |
|---|---|---|
| Dan H. Kuykendall (R) | | 100.0 |

**Democratic Primary**

| | | |
|---|---|---|
| Albert Gore (D) | 401,163 | 84.7 |
| Sam J. Galloway (D) | 37,974 | 8.0 |

### 1970 **Republican Primary**

| | | |
|---|---|---|
| Bill Brock (R) | 176,703 | 74.9 |
| Tex Ritter (R) | 54,401 | 23.0 |

**Democratic Primary**

| | | |
|---|---|---|
| Albert Gore (D) | 269,770 | 51.0 |
| Hudley Crockett (D) | 238,767 | 45.2 |

### 1976 **Republican Primary**

| | | |
|---|---|---|
| Bill Brock (R) | | 100.0 |

| Candidates | Votes | % |
|---|---|---|
| **Democratic Primary** | | |

| | | |
|---|---|---|
| James R. Sasser (D) | 244,930 | 44.2 |
| John J. Hooker (D) | 171,716 | 31.0 |
| Harry Sadler (D) | 54,125 | 9.8 |
| David Bolin (D) | 44,056 | 8.0 |
| Lester Kefauver (D) | 29,864 | 5.4 |

### 1982 **Republican Primary**

| | | |
|---|---|---|
| Robin L. Beard (R) | 205,271 | 91.4 |
| William B. Thompson (R) | 19,277 | 8.6 |

**Democratic Primary**

| | | |
|---|---|---|
| James R. Sasser (D) | 511,059 | 88.9 |
| Charles G. Vick (D) | 13,488 | 11.1 |

### 1988 **Republican Primary**

| | | |
|---|---|---|
| Bill Anderson (R) | 115,341 | 72.9 |
| Alice W. Algood (R) | 34,413 | 21.8 |
| Hubert D. Patty (R) | 8,358 | 5.3 |

**Democratic Primary**

| | | |
|---|---|---|
| James R. Sasser (D) | | 100.0 |

## Class 2

### 1924 **Democratic Primary**

| | | |
|---|---|---|
| Lawrence D. Tyson (D) | 72,496 | 41.9 |
| John K. Shields (D) | 54,990 | 31.8 |
| Nathan L. Bachman (D) | 44,946 | 26.0 |

### 1930 **Democratic Primary**

| | | |
|---|---|---|
| Cordell Hull (D) | 140,802 | 62.9 |
| A. L. Todd (D) | 79,649 | 35.6 |

**Democratic Special Primary**

| | | |
|---|---|---|
| William E. Brock (D) | 113,492 | 70.7 |
| John R. Neal (D) | 47,110 | 29.3 |

### 1934 **Democratic Special Primary**

| | | |
|---|---|---|
| Nathan L. Bachman (D) | 166,293 | 57.9 |
| Gordon Browning (D) | 121,169 | 42.2 |

### 1936 **Democratic Primary**

| | | |
|---|---|---|
| Nathan L. Bachman (D) | 217,531 | 82.9 |
| John R. Neal (D) | 44,830 | 17.1 |

### 1938 **Democratic Special Primary**

| | | |
|---|---|---|
| A. Tom Stewart (D) | 174,940 | 49.3 |
| George Berry (D) | 101,966 | 28.7 |
| J. Ridley Mitchell (D) | 70,393 | 19.8 |

### 1942 **Democratic Primary**

| | | |
|---|---|---|
| A. Tom Stewart (D) | 136,415 | 51.9 |
| Edward W. Carmack (D) | 116,841 | 44.4 |

### 1948 **Republican Primary**

| | | |
|---|---|---|
| B. Carroll Reece (R) | 82,522 | 81.7 |
| Allen J. Strawbridge (R) | 18,526 | 18.3 |

| Candidates Democratic Primary | Votes | % |
|---|---|---|
| Estes Kefauver (D) | 171,791 | *42.4* |
| A. Tom Stewart (D) | 129,873 | *32.1* |
| John A. Mitchell (D) | 96,192 | *23.7* |

**1954 Democratic Primary**

| | | |
|---|---|---|
| Estes Kefauver (D) | 440,497 | *68.2* |
| Pat Sutton (D) | 186,363 | *28.9* |

**1960 Republican Primary**

| | | |
|---|---|---|
| A. Bradley Frazier (R) | 16,633 | *58.8* |
| Hansel Proffitt (R) | 11,667 | *41.2* |

**Democratic Primary**

| | | |
|---|---|---|
| Estes Kefauver (D) | 463,848 | *64.6* |
| Andrew T. Taylor (D) | 249,336 | *34.7* |

**1964[1] Republican Special Primary**

| | | |
|---|---|---|
| Howard H. Baker Jr. (R) | 93,301 | *85.0* |
| Charles Moffett (R) | 10,596 | *9.6* |
| Hubert D. Patty (R) | 5,947 | *5.4* |

**Democratic Special Primary**

| | | |
|---|---|---|
| Ross Bass (D) | 330,213 | *50.8* |
| Frank G. Clement (D) | 233,245 | *35.9* |
| M. M. Bullard (D) | 86,718 | *13.3* |

**1966 Republican Primary**

| | | |
|---|---|---|
| Howard H. Baker Jr. (R) | 112,617 | *75.7* |
| Kenneth Roberts (R) | 36,043 | *24.2* |

**Democratic Primary**

| | | |
|---|---|---|
| Frank G. Clement (D) | 384,322 | *51.2* |
| Ross Bass (D) | 366,079 | *48.8* |

**1972 Republican Primary**

| | | |
|---|---|---|
| Howard H. Baker Jr. (R) | 242,373 | *97.0* |

**Democratic Primary**

| | | |
|---|---|---|
| Ray Blanton (D) | 292,249 | *76.4* |
| Don Palmer (D) | 40,700 | *10.6* |

**1978 Republican Primary**

| | | |
|---|---|---|
| Howard H. Baker Jr. (R) | 205,680 | *83.4* |
| Harvey D. Howard (R) | 21,154 | *8.6* |

**Democratic Primary**

| | | |
|---|---|---|
| Jane Eskind (D) | 196,156 | *34.5* |
| Bill Bruce (D) | 170,795 | *30.1* |
| J. D. Lee (D) | 89,939 | *15.8* |
| James Boyd (D) | 48,458 | *8.5* |

**1984 Republican Primary**

| | | |
|---|---|---|
| Victor Ashe (R) | 145,774 | *86.5* |
| Jack McNeil (R) | 17,970 | *10.7* |

**Democratic Primary**

| | | |
|---|---|---|
| Albert Gore Jr. (D) | 345,527 | *100.0* |

**1990 Republican Primary**

| Candidates | Votes | % |
|---|---|---|
| William R. Hawkins (R) | 54,317 | *38.9* |
| Ralph Brown (R) | 53,873 | *38.5* |
| Patrick K. Hales (R) | 31,515 | *22.5* |

**Democratic Primary**

| | | |
|---|---|---|
| Albert Gore Jr. (D) | | *100.0* |

**Tennessee**

1. A special election was held in 1964 to fill the remaining two years of the term of Sen. Estes Kefauver (D), who died Aug. 10, 1963. The first year of the vacancy was filled by appointee Herbert S. Walker (D).

# TEXAS

| Candidates | Votes | % |
|---|---|---|

## Class 1

**1922 Democratic Primary**

| | | |
|---|---|---|
| Earle B. Mayfield (D) | 153,538 | *26.8* |
| James E. Ferguson (D) | 127,071 | *22.2* |
| Charles A. Culberson (D) | 99,635 | *17.4* |
| Cullen F. Thomas (D) | 88,026 | *15.4* |
| Clarence Ousley (D) | 62,451 | *10.9* |
| Robert L. Henry (D) | 41,567 | *7.3* |

**Democratic Runoff**

| | | |
|---|---|---|
| Earle B. Mayfield (D) | 273,308 | *54.4* |
| James E. Ferguson (D) | 228,701 | *45.6* |

**1928 Democratic Primary**

| | | |
|---|---|---|
| Earle B. Mayfield (D) | 200,246 | *29.7* |
| Tom Connally (D) | 178,091 | *26.4* |
| Alvin Owsley (D) | 131,755 | *19.5* |
| Thomas L. Blanton (D) | 126,758 | *18.8* |

**Democratic Runoff**

| | | |
|---|---|---|
| Tom Connally (D) | 320,071 | *55.4* |
| Earle B. Mayfield (D) | 257,747 | *44.6* |

**1934 Republican Primary**

| | | |
|---|---|---|
| U. S. Goen (R) | 1,148 | *100.0* |

**Democratic Primary**

| | | |
|---|---|---|
| Tom Connally (D) | 567,139 | *58.8* |
| J. W. Bailey (D) | 355,963 | *36.9* |

**1940 Democratic Primary**

| | | |
|---|---|---|
| Tom Connally (D) | 923,219 | *84.8* |
| Guy B. Fisher (D) | 98,125 | *9.0* |
| A. P. Belcher (D) | 66,962 | *6.2* |

**1946 Democratic Primary**

| | | |
|---|---|---|
| Tom Connally (D) | 823,818 | *75.4* |
| Floyd E. Ryan (D) | 85,292 | *7.8* |
| Cyclone Davis (D) | 74,252 | *6.8* |
| Terrell Sledge (D) | 66,947 | *6.1* |

| | Candidates | Votes | % |
|---|---|---|---|
| 1952 | **Democratic Primary** | | |
| | Price Daniel (D) | 940,770 | 72.6 |
| | Lindley Beckworth (D) | 285,842 | 22.0 |
| | E. W. Napier (D) | 70,132 | 5.4 |
| 1958 | **Republican Primary** | | |
| | Roy Whittenburg (R) | | 100.0 |
| | **Democratic Primary** | | |
| | Ralph Yarborough (D) | 761,511 | 58.7 |
| | William A. Blakley (D) | 535,418 | 41.3 |
| 1964 | **Republican Primary** | | |
| | George Bush (R) | 62,985 | 44.1 |
| | Jack Cox (R) | 45,561 | 31.9 |
| | Robert Morris (R) | 28,279 | 19.8 |
| | **Republican Runoff** | | |
| | George Bush (R) | 49,751 | 62.1 |
| | Jack Cox (R) | 30,333 | 37.9 |
| | **Democratic Primary** | | |
| | Ralph Yarborough (D) | 904,811 | 57.4 |
| | Gordon McLendon (D) | 672,573 | 42.6 |
| 1970 | **Republican Primary** | | |
| | George Bush (R) | 96,806 | 87.6 |
| | Robert Morris (R) | 13,654 | 12.4 |
| | **Democratic Primary** | | |
| | Lloyd Bentsen (D) | 816,641 | 53.0 |
| | Ralph Yarborough (D) | 724,122 | 47.0 |
| 1976 | **Republican Primary** | | |
| | Alan Steelman (R) | 251,252 | 70.5 |
| | Hugh Sweeney (R) | 64,404 | 18.1 |
| | Louis Leman (R) | 40,651 | 11.4 |
| | **Democratic Primary** | | |
| | Lloyd Bentsen (D) | 970,983 | 63.5 |
| | Phil Gramm (D) | 427,597 | 28.0 |
| | Hugh Wilson (D) | 10,715 | 7.2 |
| 1982 | **Republican Primary** | | |
| | James M. Collins (R) | 152,469 | 58.0 |
| | Walter H. Mengden (R) | 91,780 | 34.9 |
| | Don L. Richardson (R) | 18,616 | 7.1 |
| | **Democratic Primary** | | |
| | Lloyd Bentsen (D) | 987,153 | 78.1 |
| | Joe Sullivan (D) | 276,314 | 21.9 |
| 1988 | **Republican Primary** | | |
| | Wes Gilbreath (R) | 275,080 | 36.7 |
| | Beau Boulter (R) | 228,676 | 30.5 |
| | Milton E. Fox (R) | 138,031 | 18.4 |
| | Ned Snead (R) | 107,560 | 14.4 |

| | Candidates | Votes | % |
|---|---|---|---|
| | **Republican Runoff** | | |
| | Beau Boulter (R) | 111,134 | 60.2 |
| | Wes Gilbreath (R) | 73,573 | 40.0 |
| | **Democratic Primary** | | |
| | Lloyd Bentsen (D) | 1,365,736 | 84.8 |
| | Joe Sullivan (D) | 244,805 | 15.2 |

## Class 2

| | Candidates | Votes | % |
|---|---|---|---|
| 1924 | **Democratic Primary** | | |
| | Morris Sheppard (D) | 440,511 | 64.8 |
| | Fred W. Davis (D) | 159,663 | 23.5 |
| | John F. Maddox (D) | 80,070 | 11.8 |
| 1930 | **Republican Primary** | | |
| | Doran John Haesly (R) | 3,645 | 40.5 |
| | C. O. Harris (R) | 2,784 | 31.0 |
| | Harve H. Haines (R) | 2,568 | 28.5 |
| | **Democratic Primary** | | |
| | Morris Sheppard (D) | 526,293 | 71.1 |
| | Robert L. Henry (D) | 174,260 | 23.5 |
| | C. A. Mitchner (D) | 40,130 | 5.4 |
| 1936 | **Democratic Primary** | | |
| | Morris Sheppard (D) | 616,293 | 64.6 |
| | Joe H. Eagle (D) | 136,718 | 14.3 |
| | Guy B. Fisher (D) | 89,215 | 9.4 |
| 1942 | **Democratic Primary** | | |
| | W. Lee O'Daniel (D) | 475,541 | 48.3 |
| | James Allred (D) | 317,501 | 32.3 |
| | Moody (D) | 178,471 | 18.1 |
| | **Democratic Runoff** | | |
| | W. Lee O'Daniel (D) | 451,359 | 51.0 |
| | James Allred (D) | 433,203 | 49.0 |
| 1948 | **Democratic Primary** | | |
| | Coke R. Stevenson (D) | 477,077 | 39.7 |
| | Lyndon B. Johnson (D) | 405,617 | 33.7 |
| | George Peddy (D) | 237,195 | 19.7 |
| | **Democratic Runoff** | | |
| | Lyndon B. Johnson (D) | 494,191 | 50.0 |
| | Coke R. Stevenson (D) | 494,104 | 50.0 |
| 1954 | **Democratic Primary** | | |
| | Lyndon B. Johnson (D) | 883,264 | 71.4 |
| | Dudley T. Dougherty (D) | 354,188 | 28.6 |
| 1960 | **Democratic Primary** | | |
| | Lyndon B. Johnson (D) | | 100.0 |

| 1966 | Candidates<br>**Republican Primary** | Votes | % |
|---|---|---|---|
| | John Tower (R) | | *100.0* |
| | **Democratic Primary** | | |
| | Waggoner Carr (D) | 899,523 | *79.9* |
| | John R. Willoughby (D) | 226,598 | *20.1* |
| 1972 | **Republican Primary** | | |
| | John Tower (R) | | *100.0* |
| | **Democratic Primary** | | |
| | Ralph Yarborough (D) | 1,032,606 | *50.0* |
| | Barefoot Sanders (D) | 787,504 | *38.1* |
| | Hugh Wilson (D) | 125,460 | *6.1* |
| | **Democratic Runoff** | | |
| | Barefoot Sanders (D) | 1,008,499 | *52.1* |
| | Ralph Yarborough (D) | 928,132 | *47.9* |
| 1978 | **Republican Primary** | | |
| | John Tower (R) | | *100.0* |
| | **Democratic Primary** | | |
| | Robert Krueger (D) | 853,460 | *54.7* |
| | Joe Christie (D) | 707,738 | *45.3* |
| 1984 | **Republican Primary** | | |
| | Phil Gramm (R) | 246,716 | *73.2* |
| | Ron Paul (R) | 55,431 | *16.4* |
| | Rob Mosbacher (R) | 26,279 | *7.8* |
| | **Democratic Primary** | | |
| | Kent Hance (D) | 456,446 | *31.2* |
| | Lloyd Doggett (D) | 456,173 | *31.2* |
| | Robert Krueger (D) | 454,886 | *31.1* |
| | **Democratic Runoff** | | |
| | Lloyd Doggett (D) | 489,932 | *50.0* |
| | Kent Hance (D) | 489,834 | *50.0* |
| | **Democratic Runoff Recount** | | |
| | Lloyd Doggett (D) | 491,251 | *50.1* |
| | Kent Hance (D) | 489,906 | *50.0* |
| 1990 | **Republican Primary** | | |
| | Phil Gramm (R) | | *100.0* |
| | **Democratic Primary** | | |
| | Hugh Parmer (D) | 766,284 | *75.4* |
| | Harley Schlanger (D) | 249,445 | *24.6* |

# UTAH [1]

| | Candidates | Votes | % |
|---|---|---|---|
| | **Class 1** | | |
| 1958 | **Republican Primary** | | |
| | Arthur V. Watkins (R) | 39,593 | *68.1* |
| | Carvel Mattsson (R) | 18,563 | *31.9* |
| | **Democratic Primary** | | |
| | Frank E. Moss (D) | 35,862 | *59.2* |
| | Brigham E. Roberts (D) | 24,736 | *40.8* |
| 1964 | **Republican Primary** | | |
| | Ernest L. Wilkinson (R) | 61,167 | *50.7* |
| | Sherman P. Lloyd (R) | 59,398 | *49.3* |
| | **Democratic Primary** | | |
| | Frank E. Moss (D) | | *100.0* |
| 1970 | **Republican Primary** | | |
| | Laurence J. Burton (R) | | *100.0* |
| | **Democratic Primary** | | |
| | Frank E. Moss (D) | | *100.0* |
| 1976 | **Republican Primary** | | |
| | Orrin G. Hatch (R) | 104,490 | *64.6* |
| | Jack Carlson (R) | 57,249 | *35.4* |
| | **Democratic Primary** | | |
| | Frank E. Moss (D) | | *100.0* |
| | **Class 3** | | |
| 1956 | **Republican Primary** | | |
| | Wallace F. Bennett (R) | | *100.0* |
| | **Democratic Primary** | | |
| | Alonzo F. Hopkin (D) | 44,980 | *56.8* |
| | Herbert B. Maw (D) | 34,246 | *43.2* |
| 1962 | **Republican Primary** | | |
| | Wallace F. Bennett (R) | 70,519 | *59.2* |
| | J. Bracken Lee (R) | 48,606 | *40.8* |
| | **Democratic Primary** | | |
| | David S. King (D) | 55,965 | *77.4* |
| | Calvin L. Rampton (D) | 16,327 | *22.6* |
| 1968 | **Republican Primary** | | |
| | Wallace F. Bennett (R) | 81,945 | *60.9* |
| | Mark E. Anderson (R) | 52,689 | *39.1* |
| | **Democratic Primary** | | |
| | Milton Weilenmann (D) | 47,908 | *50.7* |
| | Phil L. Hansen (D) | 46,579 | *49.3* |

| | Candidates | Votes | % |
|---|---|---|---|
| 1974 | **Republican Primary** | | |
| | Jake Garn (R) | | 100.0 |
| | **Democratic Primary** | | |
| | Wayne Owens (D) | | 100.0 |
| | **American Primary** | | |
| | Bruce Bangerter (AM) | 2,254 | 50.9 |
| | Kenneth R. Larsen (AM) | 2,173 | 49.1 |
| 1980 | **Democratic Primary** | | |
| | Dan Berman (D) | 28,930 | 50.2 |
| | A. Stephen Dirks (D) | 28,643 | 49.7 |
| | **American Primary** | | |
| | George M. Batchelor (AM) | 675 | 54.5 |
| | Larry Topham (AM) | 563 | 45.5 |
| 1986 | **Democratic Primary** | | |
| | Craig Oliver (D) | 14,654 | 50.5 |
| | Terry Williams (D) | 14,379 | 49.5 |
| 1992 | **Republican Primary** | | |
| | Robert F. Bennett (R) | 135,514 | 51.4 |
| | Joe Cannon (R) | 128,125 | 48.6 |
| | **Democratic Primary** | | |
| | Wayne Owens (D) | 74,124 | 61.4 |
| | Doug Anderson (D) | 46,622 | 38.6 |

**Utah**

1. From 1980 to 1988, some Democratic and Republican candidates were nominated by convention.

# VERMONT

| | Candidates | Votes | % |
|---|---|---|---|
| | **Class 1** | | |
| 1958 | **Republican Primary** | | |
| | Winston L. Prouty (R) | 31,866 | 64.6 |
| | Lee E. Emerson (R) | 17,468 | 35.4 |
| | **Democratic Primary** | | |
| | Frederick J. Fayette (D) | | 100.0 |
| 1964 | **Republican Primary** | | |
| | Winston L. Prouty (R) | | 100.0 |
| | **Democratic Primary** | | |
| | Frederick J. Fayette (D) | 12,388 | 71.0 |
| | William H. Meyer (D) | 4,913 | 28.2 |
| 1970 | **Republican Primary** | | |
| | Winston L. Prouty (R) | | 100.0 |

| | Candidates | Votes | % |
|---|---|---|---|
| | **Democratic Primary** | | |
| | Philip H. Hoff (D) | 23,082 | 69.7 |
| | Fiore L. Bove (D) | 7,941 | 24.0 |
| | William H. Meyer (D) | 2,024 | 6.1 |
| 1972 [1] | **Republican Special Primary** | | |
| | Robert T. Stafford (R) | | 100.0 |
| | **Democratic Special Primary** | | |
| | Randolph T. Major (D) | | 100.0 |
| 1976 | **Republican Primary** | | |
| | Robert T. Stafford (R) | 24,338 | 68.7 |
| | John J. Welch (R) | 10,911 | 30.8 |
| | **Democratic Primary** | | |
| | Thomas P. Salmon (D) | 21,674 | 52.7 |
| | Scott Skinner (D) | 19,238 | 46.8 |
| | **Liberty Union Primary** | | |
| | Nancy Kaufman (LU) | 362 | 69.6 |
| | John Medeiros (LU) | 146 | 28.1 |
| 1982 | **Republican Primary** | | |
| | Robert T. Stafford (R) | 26,323 | 46.2 |
| | Stewart M. Ledbetter (R) | 19,743 | 34.7 |
| | John M. McClaughry (R) | 10,692 | 18.8 |
| | **Democratic Primary** | | |
| | James A. Guest (D) | 11,352 | 67.1 |
| | Thomas E. McGregor (D) | 3,749 | 22.1 |
| | Earl S. Gardner (D) | 1,281 | 7.6 |
| | **Citizens Primary** | | |
| | Ion Laskaris (CIT) | | 100.0 |
| | **Liberty Union Primary** | | |
| | Jerry Levy (LU) | | 100.0 |
| 1988 | **Republican Primary** | | |
| | James M. Jeffords (R) | 30,555 | 60.8 |
| | Mike Griffes (R) | 19,593 | 39.0 |
| | **Democratic Primary** | | |
| | William Gray (D) | | 100.0 |
| | **Liberty Union Primary** | | |
| | Jerry Levy (LU) | | 100.0 |
| | **Class 3** | | |
| 1956 | **Republican Primary** | | |
| | George D. Aiken (R) | | 100.0 |
| | **Democratic Primary** | | |
| | Bernard G. O'Shea (D) | | 100.0 |

| | Candidates | Votes | % |
|---|---|---|---|
| 1962 | **Republican Primary** | | |
| | George D. Aiken (R) | | 100.0 |
| | **Democratic Primary** | | |
| | W. Robert Johnson (D) | 5,718 | 54.7 |
| | William H. Meyer (D) | 4,741 | 45.3 |
| 1968 | **Republican Primary** | | |
| | George D. Aiken (R) | 42,248 | 72.8 |
| | William K. Tufts (R) | 15,786 | 27.2 |
| | **Democratic Primary** | | |
| | George D. Aiken (WRITE IN) | 1,354 | 61.8 |
| | Others (WRITE IN) | 438 | 20.0 |
| | Philip H. Hoff (WRITE IN) | 400 | 18.2 |
| 1974 | **Republican Primary** | | |
| | Richard W. Mallary (R) | 27,221 | 59.1 |
| | Charles R. Ross (R) | 16,479 | 35.8 |
| | **Democratic Primary** | | |
| | Patrick J. Leahy (D) | 19,801 | 83.9 |
| | Nathaniel Frothingham (D) | 3,703 | 15.7 |
| 1980 | **Republican Primary** | | |
| | Stewart M. Ledbetter (R) | 16,518 | 35.3 |
| | James E. Mullin (R) | 12,256 | 26.2 |
| | Tom Evslin (R) | 8,575 | 18.3 |
| | T. Garry Buckley (R) | 5,209 | 11.1 |
| | Robert Schuettinger (R) | 3,450 | 7.4 |
| | **Democratic Primary** | | |
| | Patrick J. Leahy (D) | | 100.0 |
| | **Liberty Union Primary** | | |
| | Earl S. Gardner (LU) | | 100.0 |
| 1986 | **Republican Primary** | | |
| | Richard A. Snelling (R) | 21,477 | 75.1 |
| | Anthony N. Doria (R) | 6,493 | 22.7 |
| | **Democratic Primary** | | |
| | Patrick J. Leahy (D) | | 100.0 |
| | **Liberty Union Primary** | | |
| | Jerry Levy (LU) | | 100.0 |
| 1992 | **Republican Primary** | | |
| | James H. Douglas (R) | 28,693 | 78.2 |
| | John L. Gropper (R) | 7,395 | 20.2 |
| | **Democratic Primary** | | |
| | Patrick J. Leahy (D) | 24,721 | 97.6 |

| Candidates | Votes | % |
|---|---|---|
| **Liberty Union Primary** | | |
| Jerry Levy (LU) | | 100.0 |

**Vermont**

1. *A special election was held in 1972 to fill the unexpired term of Sen. Winston L. Prouty (R), who died Sept. 10, 1971. Robert T. Stafford had been appointed to fill the vacancy on an interim basis.*

# VIRGINIA [1]

| | Candidates | Votes | % |
|---|---|---|---|
| | **Class 1** | | |
| 1922 | **Democratic Primary** | | |
| | Claude A. Swanson (D) | 102,045 | 73.0 |
| | Davis (D) | 37,671 | 27.0 |
| 1928 | **Democratic Primary** | | |
| | Claude A. Swanson (D) | ✔ | |
| 1933 | **Democratic Special Primary** | | |
| | Harry F. Byrd (D) | | 100.0 |
| 1934 | **Democratic Primary** | | |
| | Harry F. Byrd (D) | | 100.0 |
| 1940 | **Democratic Primary** | | |
| | Harry F. Byrd (D) | | 100.0 |
| 1946 | **Democratic Primary** | | |
| | Harry F. Byrd (D) | 141,923 | 63.5 |
| | Martin A. Hutchinson (D) | 81,605 | 36.5 |
| 1952 | **Democratic Primary** | | |
| | Harry F. Byrd (D) | 216,438 | 62.7 |
| | Francis Pickens Miller (D) | 128,869 | 37.3 |
| 1958 | **Democratic Primary** | | |
| | Harry F. Byrd (D) | | 100.0 |
| 1964 | **Democratic Primary** | | |
| | Harry F. Byrd (D) | | 100.0 |
| 1966 [2] | **Democratic Special Primary** | | |
| | Harry F. Byrd Jr. (D) | 221,221 | 51.0 |
| | Armistead L. Boothe (D) | 212,996 | 49.1 |
| 1970 | **Democratic Primary** [3] | | |
| | George C. Rawlings (D) | 58,874 | 45.7 |
| | Clive L. DuVal (D) | 58,174 | 45.1 |
| | Milton Colvin (D) | 11,911 | 9.2 |
| 1976 | **Democratic Primary** | | |
| | Elmo R. Zumwalt (D) | | 100.0 |

| Candidates | Votes | % |
|---|---|---|
| **Class 2** | | |
| **1920** **Democratic Special Primary** | | |
| Carter Glass (D) | | 100.0 |
| **1924** **Democratic Primary** | | |
| Carter Glass (D) | | 100.0 |
| **1930** **Democratic Primary** | | |
| Carter Glass (D) | | 100.0 |
| **1936** **Democratic Primary** | | |
| Carter Glass (D) | | 100.0 |
| **1942** **Democratic Primary** | | |
| Carter Glass (D) | | 100.0 |
| **1946** **Democratic Special Primary** | | |
| A. Willis Robertson (D) | ✔ | |
| **1948** **Democratic Primary** | | |
| A. Willis Robertson (D) | 80,340 | 70.3 |
| James P. Hart Jr. (D) | 33,928 | 29.7 |
| **1954** **Democratic Primary** | | |
| A. Willis Robertson (D) | | 100.0 |
| **1960** **Democratic Primary** | | |
| A. Willis Robertson (D) | | 100.0 |
| **1966** **Democratic Primary** | | |
| William B. Spong Jr. (D) | 216,885 | 50.1 |
| A. Willis Robertson (D) | 216,274 | 49.9 |
| **1972** **Democratic Primary** | | |
| William B. Spong Jr. (D) | | 100.0 |

**Virginia**
1. Following 1976, candidates were nominated by state party convention.
2. A special election was held in 1966 to fill the remaining four years of the term of Sen. Harry F. Byrd (D), who resigned Nov. 10, 1965. The first year of the vacancy was filled by Byrd's son, Harry F. Byrd Jr. (D), who went on to win the primary and election.
3. Rawlings became the Democratic nominee when DuVal did not request a runoff.

# WASHINGTON

| Candidates | Votes | % |
|---|---|---|
| **Class 1** | | |
| **1958** **Republican Primary** | | |
| William B. Bantz (R) | | 100.0 |

| Candidates | Votes | % |
|---|---|---|
| **Democratic Primary** | | |
| Henry M. Jackson (D) | 334,862 | 85.8 |
| Alice F. Bryant (D) | 55,200 | 14.1 |
| **1964** **Republican Primary** | | |
| Lloyd J. Andrews (R) | 216,616 | 81.2 |
| David J. Williams (R) | 37,450 | 14.0 |
| **Democratic Primary** | | |
| Henry M. Jackson (D) | 478,892 | 90.6 |
| Alice F. Bryant (D) | 29,052 | 5.5 |
| **1970** **Republican Primary** | | |
| Charles W. Elicker (R) | 33,262 | 37.1 |
| Howard S. Reed (R) | 22,293 | 24.9 |
| R. J. Odman (R) | 14,856 | 16.6 |
| William H. Davis (R) | 11,207 | 12.5 |
| Bill Patrick (R) | 7,976 | 8.9 |
| **Democratic Primary** | | |
| Henry M. Jackson (D) | 497,309 | 84.3 |
| Carl Maxey (D) | 79,201 | 13.4 |
| **1976** **Republican Primary** | | |
| George M. Brown (R) | 51,885 | 29.5 |
| Warren Hanson (R) | 43,905 | 25.0 |
| Harry C. Nielsen (R) | 28,030 | 15.9 |
| Wilbur R. Parkin (R) | 21,639 | 12.3 |
| William H. Davis (R) | 16,881 | 9.6 |
| Clarice L. R. Privette (R) | 13,526 | 7.7 |
| **Democratic Primary** | | |
| Henry M. Jackson (D) | 549,974 | 87.4 |
| Dennis Kelley (D) | 54,470 | 8.7 |
| **1982** **Republican Primary** | | |
| Doug Jewett (R) | 73,616 | 46.3 |
| Larry Penberthy (R) | 46,037 | 28.9 |
| Ken Talbott (R) | 15,581 | 9.8 |
| Patrick S. McGowan (R) | 13,054 | 8.2 |
| **Democratic Primary** | | |
| Henry M. Jackson (D) | 450,580 | 94.9 |
| **1983** [1] **Republican Special Primary** | | |
| Dan Evans (R) | 250,046 | 64.3 |
| Lloyd E. Cooney (R) | 133,799 | 34.4 |
| **Democratic Special Primary** | | |
| Mike Lowry (D) | 179,509 | 61.5 |
| Charles Royer (D) | 103,304 | 35.4 |
| **1988** **Republican Primary** | | |
| Slade Gorton (R) | 335,846 | 85.3 |
| Doug Smith (R) | 31,512 | 8.0 |
| William C. Goodloe (R) | 26,224 | 6.7 |

| Candidates<br>**Democratic Primary** | Votes | % |
|---|---|---|
| Mike Lowry (D) | 297,399 | *55.2* |
| Don Bonker (D) | 241,170 | *44.8* |

### Class 3

**1956**

| **Republican Primary** | Votes | % |
|---|---|---|
| Arthur B. Langlie (R) | | *100.0* |

| **Democratic Primary** | | |
|---|---|---|
| Warren G. Magnuson (D) | | *100.0* |

**1962**

| **Republican Primary** | | |
|---|---|---|
| Richard G. Christensen (R) | 178,616 | *82.1* |
| Ben Larson (R) | 38,759 | *17.8* |

| **Democratic Primary** | | |
|---|---|---|
| Warren G. Magnuson (D) | 280,981 | *93.7* |
| John Patric (D) | 18,849 | *6.3* |

**1968**

| **Republican Primary** | | |
|---|---|---|
| Jack Metcalf (R) | 210,981 | *73.6* |
| Harvey L. Cole (R) | 40,844 | *14.2* |
| Ralph O. Westlake (R) | 25,756 | *9.0* |

| **Democratic Primary** | | |
|---|---|---|
| Warren G. Magnuson (D) | 373,303 | *92.9* |
| Arthur DeWitt (D) | 28,683 | *7.1* |

**1974**

| **Republican Primary** | | |
|---|---|---|
| Jack Metcalf (R) | 103,616 | *61.0* |
| Jesse Chiang (R) | 31,193 | *18.4* |
| Donald C. Knutson (R) | 13,738 | *8.1* |
| June Riggs (R) | 8,491 | *5.0* |

| **Democratic Primary** | | |
|---|---|---|
| Warren G. Magnuson (D) | 288,038 | *92.5* |
| John Patric (D) | 23,438 | *7.5* |

**1980**

| **Republican Primary** | | |
|---|---|---|
| Slade Gorton (R) | 313,560 | *55.6* |
| Lloyd E. Cooney (R) | 229,178 | *40.7* |

| **Democratic Primary** | | |
|---|---|---|
| Warren G. Magnuson (D) | 348,471 | *92.4* |

**1986**

| **Republican Primary** | | |
|---|---|---|
| Slade Gorton (R) | 291,735 | *93.0* |

| **Democratic Primary** | | |
|---|---|---|
| Brock Adams (D) | 287,258 | *91.7* |

| **Socialist Workers Primary** | | |
|---|---|---|
| Jill Fein (SOC WORK) | | *100.0* |

**1992**

| Candidates<br>**Republican Primary** | Votes | % |
|---|---|---|
| Rod Chandler (R) | 228,083 | *42.1* |
| Leo K. Thorsness (R) | 185,498 | *34.2* |
| Tim Hill (R) | 128,232 | *23.7* |

| **Democratic Primary** | | |
|---|---|---|
| Patty Murray (D) | 318,455 | *56.7* |
| Don Bonker (D) | 208,321 | *37.1* |

**Washington**

*1. A special election was held to fill the five-year unexpired term of Sen. Henry M. Jackson (D), who died Sept. 1, 1983. Under Washington's so-called "jungle" primary, all 33 candidates appeared on the same Oct. 11 ballot with their party designations. The two highest vote getters, Dan Evans (R) and Mike Lowry (D), won ballot positions for the special election. Percentages are calculated here as if candidates had run in separate party primaries.*

# WEST VIRGINIA

| Candidates | Votes | % |
|---|---|---|

### Class 1

**1956** [1]

| **Republican Special Primary** | | |
|---|---|---|
| Chapman Revercomb (R) | 79,106 | *41.5* |
| Tom Sweeney (R) | 57,556 | *30.2* |
| Philip H. Hill (R) | 37,574 | *19.7* |
| A. J. Carey (R) | 11,268 | *5.9* |

| **Democratic Special Primary** | | |
|---|---|---|
| William C. Marland (D) | 118,159 | *37.2* |
| John G. Fox (D) | 104,869 | *33.1* |
| Byron B. Randolph (D) | 56,945 | *17.9* |
| Walter G. Crichton (D) | 26,972 | *8.5* |

**1958**

| **Republican Primary** | | |
|---|---|---|
| Chapman Revercomb (R) | | *100.0* |

| **Democratic Primary** | | |
|---|---|---|
| Robert C. Byrd (D) | 170,686 | *80.2* |
| Fleming N. Alderson (D) | 23,915 | *11.2* |
| Jack R. Delligatti (D) | 18,235 | *8.6* |

**1964**

| **Republican Primary** | | |
|---|---|---|
| Cooper P. Benedict (R) | | *100.0* |

| **Democratic Primary** | | |
|---|---|---|
| Robert C. Byrd (D) | 268,368 | *85.4* |
| William F. Champe (D) | 45,738 | *14.6* |

**1970** [2]

| **Democratic Primary** | | |
|---|---|---|
| Robert C. Byrd (D) | 195,725 | *89.0* |
| John J. McOwen (D) | 24,286 | *11.0* |

**1976** [2]

| **Democratic Primary** | | |
|---|---|---|
| Robert C. Byrd (D) | | *100.0* |

| 1982 | Candidates<br>Republican Primary | Votes | % |
|---|---|---|---|
| | Cleveland K. Benedict (R) | 73,638 | 80.9 |
| | James A. Washburn (R) | 9,877 | 10.8 |
| | Frederick A. Weiland (R) | 7,531 | 8.3 |
| | **Democratic Primary** | | |
| | Robert C. Byrd (D) | | 100.0 |
| 1988 | **Republican Primary** | | |
| | M. Jay Wolfe (R) | 81,286 | 70.3 |
| | Bernie Lumbert (R) | 34,273 | 29.7 |
| | **Democratic Primary** | | |
| | Robert C. Byrd (D) | 252,767 | 80.8 |
| | Bobbie E. Myers (D) | 60,186 | 19.2 |

### Class 2

| 1958 [3] | Republican Special Primary | | |
|---|---|---|---|
| | John D. Hoblitzell (R) | | 100.0 |
| | **Democratic Special Primary** | | |
| | Jennings Randolph (D) | 102,547 | 47.2 |
| | William C. Marland (D) | 77,901 | 35.8 |
| | Arnold M. Vickers (D) | 25,439 | 11.7 |
| | W. R. Wilson (D) | 11,540 | 5.3 |
| 1960 | **Republican Primary** | | |
| | Cecil H. Underwood (R) | | 100.0 |
| | **Democratic Primary** | | |
| | Jennings Randolph (R) | | 100.0 |
| 1966 | **Republican Primary** | | |
| | Francis J. Love (R) | 61,479 | 63.4 |
| | Harold G. Cutright (R) | 35,530 | 36.6 |
| | **Democratic Primary** | | |
| | Jennings Randolph (D) | | 100.0 |
| 1972 | **Republican Primary** | | |
| | Louise Leonard (R) | | 100.0 |
| | **Democratic Primary** | | |
| | Jennings Randolph (D) | | 100.0 |
| 1978 | **Republican Primary** | | |
| | Arch A. Moore Jr. (R) | 90,406 | 90.6 |
| | Donald G. Michels (R) | 9,414 | 9.4 |
| | **Democratic Primary** | | |
| | Jennings Randolph (D) | 181,480 | 80.5 |
| | Sharon Rogers (D) | 43,991 | 19.5 |

| 1984 | Candidates<br>Republican Primary | Votes | % |
|---|---|---|---|
| | John R. Raese (R) | 61,389 | 47.8 |
| | Samuel N. Kusic (R) | 44,820 | 34.9 |
| | J. Frank Deem (R) | 13,707 | 10.7 |
| | **Democratic Primary** | | |
| | John D. (Jay)<br> Rockefeller IV (D) | 240,559 | 66.3 |
| | Lacy Wright (D) | 51,591 | 14.2 |
| | Ken Auvil (D) | 41,408 | 11.4 |
| | Homer L. Harris (D) | 29,138 | 8.0 |
| 1990 | **Republican Primary** | | |
| | John Yoder (R) | | 100.0 |
| | **Democratic Primary** | | |
| | John D. (Jay) Rockefeller IV (D) | 200,161 | 84.7 |
| | Ken B. Thompson (D) | 21,669 | 9.2 |

**West Virginia**

1. A special election was held to fill the seat vacated by the death of Sen. Harley M. Kilgore (D) on Feb. 28, 1956.

2. No Republican candidates entered the 1970 and 1976 Senate primaries. After the primary date in 1970, the party designated Elmer H. Dodson as the Republican candidate. No Republican candidate was designated in 1976.

3. A special election was held to fill the seat of Sen. Matthew M. Neely (D), who died Jan. 18, 1958.

# WISCONSIN

| | Candidates | Votes | % |
|---|---|---|---|

### Class 1

| 1957 [1] | Republican Special Primary | | |
|---|---|---|---|
| | Walter J. Kohler (R) | 109,256 | 34.4 |
| | Glenn R. Davis (R) | 100,532 | 31.7 |
| | Alvin E. O'Konski (R) | 66,784 | 21.0 |
| | Warren P. Knowles (R) | 23,996 | 7.6 |
| | **Democratic Special Primary** | | |
| | William Proxmire (D) | 86,341 | 60.3 |
| | Clement J. Zablocki (D) | 56,817 | 39.7 |
| 1958 | **Republican Primary** | | |
| | Roland J. Steinle (R) | | 100.0 |
| | **Democratic Primary** | | |
| | William Proxmire (D) | 220,146 | 85.6 |
| | Harry Halloway (D) | 20,880 | 8.1 |
| | Arthur J. McGurn (D) | 16,014 | 6.2 |
| 1964 | **Republican Primary** | | |
| | Wilbur N. Renk (R) | | 100.0 |

| Candidates | Votes | % |
|---|---|---|
| **Democratic Primary** | | |
| William Proxmire (D) | 295,676 | *88.8* |
| Kenneth F. Klinkert (D) | 20,022 | *6.0* |
| Arlyn F. Wollenburg (D) | 17,333 | *5.2* |

**1970**

**Republican Primary**

| John E. Erickson (R) | | *100.0* |
|---|---|---|

**Democratic Primary**

| William Proxmire (D) | | *100.0* |
|---|---|---|

**American Primary**

| Edmond E. Hou-Seye (AM) | | *100.0* |
|---|---|---|

**1976**

**Republican Primary**

| Stanley York (R) | | *100.0* |
|---|---|---|

**Democratic Primary**

| William Proxmire (D) | | *100.0* |
|---|---|---|

**1982**

**Republican Primary**

| Scott McCallum (R) | 182,043 | *67.7* |
|---|---|---|
| Paul T. Brewer (R) | 86,728 | *32.3* |

**Democratic Primary**

| William Proxmire (D) | 467,214 | *86.1* |
|---|---|---|
| Marcel Dandeneau (D) | 75,258 | *13.9* |

**Libertarian Primary**

| George Liljenfeldt (LIBERT) | | *100.0* |
|---|---|---|

**Constitution Primary**

| Sanford G. Knapp (CONST) | | *100.0* |
|---|---|---|

**1988**

**Republican Primary**

| Susan Engeleiter (R) | 209,025 | *57.0* |
|---|---|---|
| Stephen B. King (R) | 148,601 | *40.5* |

**Democratic Primary**

| Herbert Kohl (D) | 249,226 | *46.8* |
|---|---|---|
| Anthony S. Earl (D) | 203,479 | *38.2* |
| Edward R. Garvey (D) | 55,225 | *10.4* |

### Class 3

**1956**

**Republican Primary**

| Alexander Wiley (R) | 221,042 | *48.9* |
|---|---|---|
| Glenn R. Davis (R) | 211,016 | *46.7* |

**Democratic Primary**

| Henry W. Maier (D) | 169,999 | *66.9* |
|---|---|---|
| Elliot N. Walstead (D) | 83,801 | *33.0* |

**1962**

**Republican Primary**

| Alexander Wiley (R) | 347,155 | *80.3* |
|---|---|---|
| Arlyn F. Wollenburg (R) | 85,044 | *19.7* |

| Candidates | Votes | % |
|---|---|---|
| **Democratic Primary** | | |
| Gaylord Nelson (D) | | *100.0* |

**1968**

**Republican Primary**

| Jerris Leonard (R) | 133,060 | *50.7* |
|---|---|---|
| Robert I. Johnson (R) | 73,344 | *28.0* |
| James J. Donohue (R) | 45,523 | *17.4* |

**Democratic Primary**

| Gaylord Nelson (D) | | *100.0* |
|---|---|---|

**1974**

**Republican Primary**

| Thomas E. Petri (R) | 130,523 | *85.2* |
|---|---|---|
| James A. Sigl (R) | 22,714 | *14.8* |

**Democratic Primary**

| Gaylord Nelson (D) | | *100.0* |
|---|---|---|

**American Primary**

| Gerald L. McFarren (AM) | | *100.0* |
|---|---|---|

**1980**

**Republican Primary**

| Robert W. Kasten (R) | 134,586 | *36.8* |
|---|---|---|
| Terry J. Kohler (R) | 106,270 | *29.0* |
| Douglass Cofrin (R) | 84,355 | *23.0* |
| Russell A. Olson (R) | 40,823 | *11.1* |

**Democratic Primary**

| Gaylord Nelson (D) | | *100.0* |
|---|---|---|

**Constitution Primary**

| James P. Wickstrom (CONST) | | *100.0* |
|---|---|---|

**Libertarian Primary**

| Bervin J. Larson (LIBERT) | | *100.0* |
|---|---|---|

**1986**

**Republican Primary**

| Robert W. Kasten (R) | | *100.0* |
|---|---|---|

**Democratic Primary**

| Edward R. Garvey (D) | 126,408 | *47.6* |
|---|---|---|
| Matthew J. Flynn (D) | 101,777 | *38.3* |
| Gary R. George (D) | 29,485 | *11.1* |

**1992**

**Republican Primary**

| Robert W. Kasten (R) | 197,488 | *80.5* |
|---|---|---|
| Roger W. Faulkner (R) | 47,804 | *19.5* |

**Democratic Primary**

| Russell D. Feingold (D) | 367,746 | *69.7* |
|---|---|---|
| Jim Moody (D) | 74,472 | *14.1* |
| Joseph W. Checota (D) | 71,570 | *13.6* |

**Wisconsin**
1. *A special election was held to fill the unexpired term of Sen. Joseph R. McCarthy (R), who died May 2, 1957.*

# WYOMING

| Candidates | Votes | % |
|---|---|---|
| **Class 1** | | |
| **1958 Republican Primary** | | |
| Frank A. Barrett (R) | | *100.0* |
| **Democratic Primary** | | |
| Gale McGee (D) | 22,098 | *59.5* |
| Hepburn T. Armstrong (D) | 15,024 | *40.5* |
| **1964 Republican Primary** | | |
| John S. Wold (R) | 23,278 | *52.0* |
| K. L. Sailors (R) | 21,522 | *48.0* |
| **Democratic Primary** | | |
| Gale McGee (D) | 39,140 | *89.6* |
| I. Wayne Kinney (D) | 4,535 | *10.4* |
| **1970 Republican Primary** | | |
| John S. Wold (R) | 40,276 | *88.0* |
| Arthur E. Linde (R) | 5,479 | *12.0* |
| **Democratic Primary** | | |
| Gale McGee (D) | 32,956 | *79.6* |
| D. P. Svilar (D) | 8,448 | *20.4* |
| **1976 Republican Primary** | | |
| Malcolm Wallop (R) | 41,445 | *76.6* |
| Nels T. Larson (R) | 6,965 | *12.9* |
| Doyle W. Henry (R) | 5,727 | *10.6* |
| **Democratic Primary** | | |
| Gale McGee (D) | | *100.0* |
| **1982 Republican Primary** | | |
| Malcolm Wallop (R) | 61,650 | *80.9* |
| Richard Redland (R) | 14,543 | *19.1* |
| **Democratic Primary** | | |
| Rodger McDaniel (D) | | *100.0* |
| **1988 Republican Primary** | | |
| Malcolm Wallop (R) | 55,752 | *83.2* |
| Nora M. Lewis (R) | 3,933 | *5.9* |
| I. W. Kinney (R) | 3,716 | *5.5* |
| **Democratic Primary** | | |
| John P. Vinich (D) | 23,214 | *47.2* |
| Pete Maxfield (D) | 14,613 | *29.7* |
| Lynn Simons (D) | 11,350 | *23.1* |

| Candidates | Votes | % |
|---|---|---|
| **Class 2** | | |
| **1960 Republican Primary** | | |
| E. Keith Thomson (R) | 31,596 | *69.1* |
| Frank A. Barrett (R) | 13,380 | *29.2* |
| **Democratic Primary** | | |
| Raymond B. Whitaker (D) | 18,031 | *44.1* |
| Velma Linford (D) | 13,792 | *33.8* |
| Carl A. Johnson (D) | 5,370 | *13.1* |
| Charles B. Chittim (D) | 3,653 | *8.9* |
| **1962 [1] Republican Special Primary** | | |
| Milward L. Simpson (R) | 30,124 | *59.6* |
| K. L. Sailors (R) | 20,383 | *40.4* |
| **Democratic Special Primary** | | |
| J. J. Hickey (D) | | *100.0* |
| **1966 Republican Primary** | | |
| Clifford P. Hansen (R) | 40,102 | *86.1* |
| I. Wayne Kinney (R) | 6,468 | *13.9* |
| **Democratic Primary** | | |
| Teno Roncalio (D) | | *100.0* |
| **1972 Republican Primary** | | |
| Clifford P. Hansen (R) | | *100.0* |
| **Democratic Primary** | | |
| Mike Vinich (D) | 16,148 | *52.5* |
| Doyle W. Henry (D) | 5,642 | *18.4* |
| Patrick E. Shanklin (D) | 4,665 | *15.2* |
| William E. Fritchell (D) | 4,281 | *13.9* |
| **1978 Republican Primary** | | |
| Alan K. Simpson (R) | 37,332 | *54.7* |
| Hugh Binford (R) | 20,768 | *30.4* |
| Gordon H. Barrows (R) | 8,494 | *12.4* |
| **Democratic Primary** | | |
| Raymond B. Whitaker (D) | 19,854 | *47.6* |
| Dean M. Larson (D) | 11,039 | *26.5* |
| Charles Carroll (D) | 10,797 | *25.9* |
| **1984 Republican Primary** | | |
| Alan K. Simpson (R) | 66,178 | *87.9* |
| Stephen Tarver (R) | 9,137 | *12.1* |
| **Democratic Primary** | | |
| Victor A. Ryan (D) | 17,608 | *45.3* |
| Al Hamburg (D) | 12,088 | *31.1* |
| Michael J. Dee (D) | 9,187 | *23.6* |
| **1990 Republican Primary** | | |
| Alan K. Simpson (R) | 69,142 | *84.4* |
| Nora M. Lewis (R) | 6,577 | *8.0* |
| Douglas W. Crook (R) | 6,201 | *7.6* |

| Candidates<br>Democratic Primary | Votes | % |
|---|---|---|
| Kathy Helling (D) | 12,103 | *35.1* |
| Howard O'Connor (D) | 7,196 | *20.9* |
| Al Hamburg (D) | 6,483 | *18.8* |
| Emmett Jones (D) | 4,455 | *12.9* |
| Dale Bulman (D) | 2,291 | *6.6* |
| Don C. Jolliffe (D) | 1,983 | *5.7* |

**Wyoming**

1. *A special election was held to fill the unexpired term of E. Keith Thomson (R), who died after winning the Senate seat in 1960. J. J. Hickey (D), the incumbent governor, resigned in January 1961 and his successor appointed him to the seat, where he served until after the special election was held, in November 1962.*

# House Elections

# House Elections

The authors of the Constitution of the United States recognized that the new government needed an executive to carry out the laws and a judiciary to resolve conflicts arising from them. But it was Congress, the lawmaking body, that the Founders designed to be the heart of the new Republic.

There was little question that the new Congress should be bicameral, in accordance with the practice of the English Parliament, which was followed by most of the colonial governments and 10 of the 13 states. As George Mason put it during the Constitutional Convention in 1787, the minds of Americans were settled on two points: "an attachment to republican government [and] an attachment to more than one branch in the Legislature."

But little agreement existed over how the members of each of the chambers should be chosen. The nationalists insisted that the new government rest on the consent of the people rather than the state legislatures. So they held it essential that at least "the first branch," or House, be elected popularly. The government "ought to possess . . . the mind or sense of the people at large," said one of the Framers, James Wilson of Pennsylvania. Those who were suspicious of a national government preferred election to the House by the state legislatures. "The people immediately should have as little to do" with electing the government as possible, said Roger Sherman, because "they want information and are constantly liable to be misled." Election by the legislatures was twice defeated, however, and popular election for the House agreed to with only one state dissenting.

There was little support for the view that the people also should elect the Senate. Nor did the delegates to the Constitutional Convention think that the House should choose members of the Senate from among persons nominated by the state legislatures. Election of the Senate by the state legislatures was agreed to with only two states dissenting.

For the sake of convenience, the Senate is often referred to as the "upper body" of Congress, and the House as the "lower body." But those terms are not used in the Constitution, and in fact the two chambers are equal in stature and legislative power. No bill can become law unless it is passed by both chambers in identical form and signed by the president.

Representatives naturally naturally resent having the House called the "lower body." Yet, from the earliest days of the Republic, the House has been generally regarded as somehow less prestigious than the Senate. The French scholar Alexis de Tocqueville wrote in the 1830s of being struck by "the vulgar demeanor" of the House as compared with the Senate, and the same impression still widely exists. But in the public mind today, neither chamber is held in very high esteem. *(Congressional Characteristics and Public Opinion, box, p. 917)*

## The People's Branch

The House of Representatives was to be the branch of government closest to the people. The members would be popularly elected; the terms of office would be two years so that the representatives would not lose touch with their homes; and the House would be a numerous branch, with members having relatively small constituencies.

The lower houses of the state legislatures served as models for the U.S. House. All the states had at least one chamber elected by popular vote. Ten states had two-house legislatures; Georgia, Pennsylvania and Vermont had popularly elected unicameral legislatures.

Article I, Section 2 of the Constitution set few requirements for election to the House: a representative had to be at least 25 years of age, have been a U.S. citizen for seven years and be an inhabitant of the state from which elected. *(Constitutional provisions for election to Congress, Appendix, p. 1346)*

The Constitution left the qualification of voters to the states, with one overriding principle: the qualifications could be no more restrictive than for the most numerous branch of each of the states' own legislatures. At first, property qualifications for voting were general. Five states required ownership of real estate, five mandated either real estate or other property and three required personal wealth or payment of public taxes. But the democratic trend of the early 19th century swept away most property qualifications, pro-

## Sources

Galloway, George B. *History of the House of Representatives.* 2nd ed. New York: Crowell, 1976.

Jones, Charles O. *Every Second Year.* Washington, D.C.: Brookings Institution, 1967.

ducing practically universal white male suffrage by the 1830s.

Over the years several changes in the Constitution also broadened the franchise. The 15th Amendment (1870) extended the franchise to newly freed slaves; the 19th Amendment (1920) granted the right of suffrage to women; the 23rd Amendment (1961) extended the presidential vote to the District of Columbia; the 24th Amendment (1964) abolished the poll tax; and the 26th Amendment (1971) lowered the voting age to 18 from 21. In 1965 Congress passed the Voting Rights Act to remove barriers several states and localities had erected to keep blacks and other minorities from voting.

## Two-Year Term

Many delegates to the Constitutional Convention preferred annual elections for the House, believing that the body should reflect the wishes of the people as closely as possible. James Madison, however, argued for a three-year term, to allow representatives to gain knowledge and experience in national affairs as well as the affairs of their own localities. The delegates compromised on two-year terms.

The two-year term has not been universally popular. From time to time proposals have been made to extend the term to four years. The movement to extend the House term to four years last gained momentum in 1966 after President Lyndon B. Johnson urged the extension in his State of the Union message Jan. 12. His proposal received more applause than any other part of his speech.

However, the proposed amendment never emerged from committee. Opponents criticized the proposal's provision that the four-year term coincide with the presidential term. This would create a House of "coattail riders," critics said, and end the minority party's traditional gains in non-presidential election years. This fear of diminishing the independence of the House appeared to be the principal factor that killed the proposal. *(Election Results, Congress and the Presidency, 1864-1992, table, p. 1344)*

## Size of the House

The size of the original House was written into Article I, Section 2 of the Constitution, along with directions to apportion the House according to population after the first census in 1790. Until the first census and apportionment, the 13 states were to have the following numbers of representatives: Connecticut, 5; Delaware, 1; Georgia, 3; Maryland, 6; Massachusetts, 8; New Hampshire, 3; New Jersey, 4; New York, 6; North Carolina, 5; Pennsylvania, 8; Rhode Island, 1; South Carolina, 5; Virginia, 10. This apportionment of seats — 65 in all — thus mandated by the Constitution remained in effect during the first and second Congresses (1789-93). (Seats allotted to North Carolina and Rhode Island were not filled until 1790, after those states had ratified the Constitution.)

By act of Congress (April 14, 1792), an apportionment measure provided for a ratio of one member for every 33,000 inhabitants and fixed the exact number of representatives to which each state was entitled. Congress enacted a new apportionment measure, including the mathematical formula to be used, every 10 years (except 1920) until a permanent law became effective in 1929. In 1911 Congress set the maximum size of the House at 435 members, where it has remained since the 1912. *(Reapportionment, p. 925)*

In an average-sized congressional district in the 1990s, the House member represented 572,500 persons.

## Majority Elections

Five New England states at one time or another had a requirement for majority victory in congressional elections. The requirement provided that, to win a seat in the U.S. House, a candidate had to achieve more than 50 percent of the popular vote. If no candidate gained such a majority, new elections were held until one contender succeeded.

The provision was last invoked in Maine in 1844, in New Hampshire in 1845, in Vermont in 1866, in Massachusetts in 1848 and in Rhode Island in 1892. Sometimes, multiple races were necessary because none of the candidates could achieve the required majority. In the 4th District of Massachusetts in 1848-49, for example, 12 successive elections were held to try to choose a representative. None of them was successful, and the district remained unrepresented in the House during the 31st Congress (1849-51).

## Multi-Member Districts

In the early days of the House several states had districts that elected more than one representative. For example, in 1824 Maryland's 5th District chose two representatives, while the remaining seven districts chose one each. And in Pennsylvania two districts (the 4th and 9th) elected three representatives each, and four districts (the 7th, 8th, 11th and 17th) chose two representatives each.

As late as 1838, New York still had as many as five multi-member districts — one (the 3rd) electing four members and four (the 8th, 17th, 22nd and 23rd) choosing two each. But the practice ended in 1842 when Congress enacted a law that "no one district may elect more than one Representative." The provision was a part of the reapportionment legislation following the census of 1840.

## Elections in Odd-Numbered Years

Another practice that has faded out over the years was general elections in odd-numbered years for the House. Prior to ratification of the 20th (lame-duck) Amendment in 1933, regular sessions of Congress began in December of odd-numbered years. There were, therefore, 11 months in the odd-numbered years to elect members before the beginning of the congressional session. For example, in 1841 the following states held general elections for representative for the 27th Congress, convening that year: Alabama, Connecticut, Illinois, Indiana, Kentucky, Maryland, Mississippi, New Hampshire, North Carolina, Rhode Island, Tennessee and Virginia.

The practice continued until late in the century. In 1875 four states still chose their representatives in regular odd-year elections: California, Connecticut, Mississippi and New Hampshire. But by 1880 all members of the House were being chosen in even-numbered years (except for special elections to fill vacancies). One major problem encountered by states choosing their representatives in odd-numbered years was the possibility of a special session of the new Congress being called before the states' elections were held. Depending on the date of the election, a state could be unrepresented in the House. For example, California elected its U.S. House delegation to the 40th Congress (1867-69) on Sept. 4, 1867, in plenty of time for the first regular session scheduled for Dec. 2. But the Congress already had met in two special sessions — March 4 to March 20 and July 3 to July 20 — without any representation from California.

# Congressional Characteristics and Public Opinion

From the early days of the Republic until the present, the American public has criticized the abilities, ethical standards and performance of members of Congress. Through the years the House has received more criticism than the Senate, perhaps because senators were not elected by popular vote until 1914.

An early but still familiar critique of Congress was written in the 1830s by Alexis de Tocqueville, the French aristocrat, scholar and astute observer of America. After he had seen both chambers in session, Tocqueville wrote the following in his famous book of observations, *Democracy in America*:

On entering the House of Representatives at Washington, one is struck by the vulgar demeanor of that great assembly. Often there is not a distinguished man in the whole number. Its members are almost all obscure individuals, whose names bring no associations to mind. They are mostly village lawyers, men in trade, or even persons belonging to the lower classes of society. In a country in which education is very general, it is said that the representatives of the people do not always know how to write correctly.

At a few yards' distance is the door of the Senate, which contains within a small space a large proportion of the celebrated men of America. Scarcely an individual is to be seen in it who has not had an active and illustrious career: the Senate is composed of eloquent advocates, distinguished generals, wise magistrates, and statesmen of note, whose arguments would do honor to the most remarkable parliamentary debates of Europe.

## Profile of 'Average' Member

A more modern — and charitable — description of the "average" member of Congress was presented in a popular textbook of the 1960s, *American Democracy*:

He is a little over 50, has served in Congress for a number of years, and has had previous political experience before coming to Congress, such as membership in his state legislature. He has a college degree, is a lawyer by profession, a war veteran, and, before coming to Congress, was a well-known and popular member of the community. He has been reasonably successful in business or the practice of law, although not so successful that he is sacrificing a huge income in giving up his private occupation for a public job. Congress is clearly not an accurate cross section of the American people but neither is it a community of intellectuals and technicians.

The description was accurate, even to the exclusive use of "he." Although the composition had changed some by the mid-1990s, most members of Congress were male, Caucasian and Christian, especially Protestant. Of the 535 members of Congress at the beginning of 1994, 55 were women, 40 were African American (including the non-voting delegate from the District of Columbia), 19 were Hispanic, and 8 were of Asian, Pacific Islander or Native American heritage. Among religious groups, Protestants have comprised nearly two-thirds of the membership of both houses in recent years, although Roman Catholic members have become more numerous than members belonging to any single Protestant denomination. Catholics took the lead from Methodists in 1965 and retained it 28 years later. At the beginning of 1994, there were 141 Catholics. More than two-thirds of the Protestant members were affiliated with four denominations: Methodists led with 67, followed by 61 Baptists, 53 Presbyterians and 51 Episcopalians. There were 41 Jewish members. The average age for senators was 58 while the average for representatives was 52.

It was likely that a senator was a former House member but rare that a representative had served earlier in the Senate. Only two former presidents served in Congress after their terms in the White House: John Quincy Adams and Andrew Johnson. *(Members of Congress Who Became President, box, page 590)*

Although by 1994 the legal profession long had been dominant among members, most other occupations — including banking, business, public service, education, journalism and farming — had been represented. The principal occupational groups underrepresented were the clergy and blue-collar workers. Scientists and physicians also had been underrepresented in Congress.

Although many members came from established professions, that did little to enhance their public image. Polls indicated that contemporary Americans retained a certain skepticism about the character of their politicians. A Gallup Poll taken in June 1979 found that only 19 percent of Americans approved of the way Congress was doing its job, while 61 percent disapproved. Another Gallup survey released nine months later showed that 78 percent of Americans believed that some members of Congress won election by using "unethical and illegal methods in their campaigns." In addition, four out of 10 persons surveyed believed that at least 20 percent of the members of Congress employed questionable methods to get elected. This poll was taken after disclosure of what came to be known as the Abscam affair, in which a few members were alleged to have taken bribes from undercover FBI agents posing as wealthy Arabs in return for political and legislative favors. Subsequent to the poll, one senator and six members of the House were convicted for their parts in the scandal.

More recent polls offered further evidence of the poor public image of politicians in the United States. Harris surveys found that the percentage of people with a positive view of the job done by Congress dropped from 47 percent in mid-1985 to 40 percent at the end of 1989. By October 1991, according to a *New York Times* poll, Congress' general approval rating was 27 percent. In a *Wall Street Journal*/NBC News poll released in April 1992, 71 percent thought Congress was contributing to the nation's problems.

# An Error Persists:
# The 1930 House Election

Did the Democrats capture the House of Representatives in 1930? The correct answer is "yes," but the election's unusual circumstances have led to some confusion about the actual outcome.

It is a classic case of how an error can sneak into a reference work, become accepted as fact and be repeated elsewhere because no one ever questioned it.

The error (repeated in Congressional Quarterly's *Guide to Congress*, 4th ed., p. 56) is the statement that the Republicans held the House in November 1930, despite the onset of the Great Depression, but lost control in a series of special elections during the ensuing 13 months before Congress finally convened in December 1931. That was before the 20th Amendment to the Constitution (the so-called lame-duck amendment), ratified in 1933, sharply curtailed the interval between election and taking office.

To set the record straight:

In November 1930, Republicans elected 218 representatives, but one was from a gangster-controlled district in Chicago. He was unseated by the House and replaced by his Democratic opponent, for a 217-217 tie. Also, the Democrats did gain one seat in a special election

when a Republican incumbent died in Texas. It was their only gain in a special election.

But immediately after the November 1930 general election a group of Farm Belt Republicans announced they would withhold their votes for Speaker Nicholas Longworth, R-Ohio, and permit the Democrats to organize the House — which they did. Thus the Democrats gained control of the House as a result of the general election long before the 72nd Congress finally convened 13 months later.

The dissidents' action against Longworth (who died shortly afterward) stemmed from GOP internal unrest. From the 1880s to the 1930s the Republicans, as the dominant party, were more divided than the Democrats in the House — usually over economic issues such as trusts, tariffs, farm relief, the gold standard and access to credit.

To verify election results and determine the party affiliations of certain representatives, editors of the *Guide to U.S. Elections*, 3rd ed., drew on the research in Kenneth C. Martis' *The Historical Atlas of Political Parties in the United States Congress*, New York: Mac-Millan, 1989.

## Southern Anomalies

Many of the anomalies in election of U.S. representatives occurred in the South. That region's experience with slavery, Civil War, Reconstruction and racial antagonisms created special problems for the regular electoral process.

Article I, Section 2 of the Constitution contained a formula for counting slaves for apportionment purposes: every five slaves would be counted as three persons. Thus, the total population of a state to be used in determining its congressional representation would be the free population plus three-fifths of the slave population.

After the Civil War and the emancipation of the slaves, blacks were fully counted for the purposes of apportionment. The 14th Amendment, required that apportionment be based on "the whole number of persons in each State...." On this basis, several Southern states tried to claim immediate additional representation on readmission to the Union. Tennessee, for example, chose an extra U.S. representative, electing him at large in 1868, and claimed that inasmuch as its slaves were now free the state had added to its apportionment population a sufficient number to give it nine instead of eight representatives. Virginia took similar action in 1869 and 1870; South Carolina did it in both 1868 and 1870. But the House declined to seat the additional representatives, declaring that states would have to await the regular reapportionment following the 1870 census for any changes in their representation.

Part of the 14th Amendment affected — or was intended to affect — Southern representation in the House. The second paragraph of the amendment states, "When the right to vote at any election for the choice of electors for President and Vice President of the United

States, Representatives in Congress, the executive and judicial officers of a State, or the members of the legislature thereof, is denied to any of the male inhabitants of such state, being twenty-one years of age, and citizens of the United States, or in any other way abridged, except for participation in rebellion, or other crime, the basis of representation [in the U.S. House] shall be reduced in the proportion which the number of such male citizens shall bear to the whole number of male citizens twenty-one years of age in such state."

Designed as a club to force the South to accept black voting participation, the provision was incorporated in the reapportionment legislation of 1872. According to the legislation, the number of representatives from any state interfering with the exercise of the right to vote was to be reduced in proportion to the number of inhabitants of voting age whose right to go to the polls was denied or abridged.

But the provision never was put into effect because of the difficulty of determining the exact number of persons whose right to vote was being abridged and also because of the decline of Northern enthusiasm for forcing Reconstruction policies on the South.

As an alternative to invoking the difficult 14th Amendment provision, Congress often considered election challenges filed against members from the South. When Republicans were in control of the House, several Democrats from the former Confederate states found themselves unseated, often on charges that black voting rights were abused in their districts.

During the 47th Congress (1881-83) five Democrats from former Confederate states were unseated; in the 51st Congress (1889-91), six; and in the 54th Congress (1895-97), seven.

# Special Elections

When a vacancy occurs in the House, the usual procedure is for the governor of the affected state to call a special election. Such elections may be held at any time throughout the year, and there are usually several during each two-year Congress.

At times there are delays in the calling of special elections. One of the longest periods in recent years when a congressional district went unrepresented occurred in 1959-60. On April 28, 1959, Rep. James G. Polk, D (1931-41, 1949-59), of the Ohio 6th District died. But not until November 1960 was there an election to replace him. It was held simultaneously with the general election, and the winner, Ward M. Miller, R, served only the two months remaining in the term. For the full term, both Republicans and Democrats nominated candidates different from those who ran for the short term.

In the days of the lame-duck sessions of Congress, elections for the remainder of a term quite often were held simultaneously with the general election, because the session following the election was an important working meeting that lasted until March 4.

However, since the passage of the 20th Amendment and the ending of most lame-duck sessions, elections for the remaining two months of a term have become less common. Miller, for example, never was sworn in because Congress was not in session during the period when he was waiting to serve as a representative.

Usually states are more prompt in holding special House elections than was Ohio in 1959-60. One of the most rapid instances of succession occurred in Texas' 10th District in 1963. Democratic representative Homer Thornberry (1949-63) submitted his resignation on Sept. 26, 1963, to take effect Dec. 20. On the strength of Thornberry's post-dated resignation, a special election was held in his district — the first election was held Nov. 9 and the runoff on Dec. 17. The winner, J. J. Pickle, D, was ready to take his seat as soon as Thornberry stepped down. He was sworn in the next day, Dec. 21, 1963.

# Disputed House Elections

Perhaps the most dramatic election dispute settled by the House in recent years was that of the Mississippi Five in 1965. The governor of Mississippi certified the election to the House in 1964 of four Democrats and one Republican. The Democrats were Thomas G. Abernethy, William M. Colmer, Jamie L. Whitten and John Bell Williams; the Republican was Prentiss Walker.

Their right to be seated was contested by a biracial group, the Mississippi Freedom Democratic Party, formed originally to challenge the seating of an all-white delegation from the state to the 1964 Democratic National Convention. This group, when unsuccessful in getting its candidates on the 1964 congressional election ballot, conducted a rump election in which Annie Devine, Virginia Gray and Fannie L. Hamer were the winners.

The three women, when they sought entrance to the House floor, were barred. However, Speaker John W. McCormack, D-Mass., asked the regular Mississippi representatives-elect to stand aside while the other members of the House were sworn in. William F. Ryan, D-N.Y., sponsor of the challenge, contended that the regular congressional election in Mississippi was invalid because blacks had been systematically prevented from voting. A resolution to seat the regular Mississippi delegation was adopted on Jan. 4, 1965, by a voice vote.

Later that year Congress enacted the Voting Rights Act of 1965, which contained strict sanctions against states that practiced discrimination against minority voters.

## McCloskey-McIntyre Contest

Three 1984 House races were so close that the losers contested the results. One race, in Indiana, led to four months of acrimony between Democrats and Republicans over what appeared to be the closest House contest in the 20th century. Debate on the race took up far more time than almost any other issue the House considered in 1985.

After the Nov. 6 election, incumbent Democrat Frank McCloskey appeared to have won reelection to his Indiana 8th District seat by 72 votes. But correction of an arithmetical error (ballots in two precincts were counted twice) gave Republican challenger Richard D. McIntyre an apparent 34-vote victory. On that basis, the Indiana secretary of state Dec. 14 certified McIntyre the winner.

But when Congress convened Jan. 3, 1985, the Democratic-controlled House refused to seat McIntyre, voting instead to declare the seat vacant pending an investigation of alleged irregularities in the election. Three times after that — in February, March and April — Republicans pushed the seating of McIntrye to a vote, losing each time while picking up no more than a handful of votes from the Democrats.

A recount completed Jan. 22 showed McIntyre's lead had increased to 418 votes, after more than 4,800 ballots were thrown out for technical reasons. But a House Administration Committee task force, with auditors from the General Accounting Office, conducted its own recount and, on a 2-1 partisan split, found McCloskey the winner by four votes. Republicans then tried to get a new election by declaring the seat vacant. Their attempt lost, 200-229. Nineteen Democrats joined 181 Republicans in voting for a new election.

The next day, before the House Administration Committee's recommendation to seat McCloskey came to a vote, Republicans moved to send the issue back to the panel with orders to count 32 controversial absentee ballots that the task force had decided, on a 2-1 vote, not to count. That motion was rejected, 183-246.

The House then approved the resolution 236-190, with 10 Democrats joining the Republicans in voting against it. GOP members walked out of the House chamber in protest, accusing Democrats of stealing the election.

The Supreme Court May 28 refused to get involved in the dispute. Without a dissenting vote, it denied Indiana permission to sue the House in the Supreme Court.

A U.S. district court judge in Washington, D.C., dismissing a suit brought by McIntyre against House Democrats and House officers, ruled March 1 that the House had the constitutional right to judge its own membership.

On Feb. 7, a federal district court in Indiana had dismissed a separate suit filed by McIntyre challenging recount procedures in two of the district's counties and ruled that the House alone was responsible for determining the validity of contested ballots.

## Other 1984 Contested Elections

Results in two other close House races also were contested, but those challenges, in Guam and Idaho, were unsuccessful. On July 24, the House agreed by voice vote to a resolution dismissing a challenge by Democrat

# The Democratic House: A Life of Its Own

In November 1930 the Democratic Party gained the House of Representatives from a Republican Party battered by the Great Depression. *(An Error Persists: The 1930 House Election, box, p. 918)*

Two years later Franklin D. Roosevelt unseated Herbert Hoover to capture the presidency, beginning two decades of Democratic domination interrupted only by a Republican victory in the 1946 House elections. In November 1952 the 20-year Democratic era ended when the Republicans elected Dwight D. Eisenhower as president and recaptured both houses of Congress.

At the time, both the beginning and end of the Democrats' hegemony were viewed as part of the natural swing of the political pendulum necessary to the healthy functioning of a democracy based on party responsibility. No one could have foreseen then, in 1930 or in 1952, that Democratic Party dominance of the House would develop a life of its own, separate from the ebb and flow of the party struggles elsewhere in American politics; and that the Democrats would control the House for 56 of the next 60 years.

## Watershed Year: 1956

Looking back from the 1990s, it can be seen that 1956 was the watershed year in the history of Democratic control of the House. In that year, President Eisenhower was re-elected in a landslide, but the Republicans failed to recapture the House. It was only the second time that had happened since popular voting for president began — and the first since 1848, when Zachary Taylor was elected president while his Whig Party lost control of the House to the Democrats. Taylor won even though the Whigs were beginning to disintegrate over the slavery issue. Political writers said that the results of 1848 and 1956 were flukes caused by war heroes whose support for president crossed party lines.

But American voters went on to elect a Republican president and a Democratic House five more times since 1956: in 1968, 1972, 1980, 1984 and 1988. They apparently preferred to have Republican presidents in charge of foreign and defense policies during the Cold War, and be in a position to hold taxes down, while at the same time they wanted Democratic representatives to create desirable domestic programs and perform services for constituents.

The table on the next few pages shows the results of congressional elections state by state since 1928, the last election of the Republican era that preceded the Great Depression. It goes through the 1930s, when the Democrats gained seats in four consecutive elections from 1930 through 1936; a long period of competitive equilibrium in the House (1938-58) between New Deal-Fair Deal national Democrats and a loose coalition of Republicans and Southern Democrats; and the more recent longer period of dominance by liberal-to-moderate national Democrats, marked by landslide victories in the congressional elections of 1958, 1964 and 1974 that echoed the earlier 1930-38 period.

## Offset to GOP Gains in South

The salient trend since the 1960s, as shown by the state-by-state results, is that of Republican gains in the South — which ceased to be solidly Democratic when the national Democratic Party committed itself to civil rights for blacks — being more than offset by Democratic gains in the Northeast and Midwest.

As recently as 1958 those two regions tended to be more Republican than the rest of the country, but starting in 1960, when the Democrats ran the first Catholic candidate for president, there has been a steady trend toward electing more Democrats there.

Paralleling this Republican decline has been the decline in the number of representatives from third parties. There has not been more than one "other" member of the House since 1946, when the last Wisconsin Progressive was re-elected as a Republican. Two years earlier in Minnesota, the Farmer-Labor Party had merged with the Democrats in that state.

---

Antonio Borja Won Pat, the former non-voting delegate from Guam, against Republican Ben Blaz. Won Pat, who had represented Guam in Congress since 1973, had lost the November 1984 election by about 350 votes. Won Pat had protested, among other things, that Blaz had not won an absolute majority of the votes cast, as required by law. On Oct. 2, the House threw out a challenge by former representative George Hansen, R-Idaho, against Democrat Richard H. Stallings. Hansen, who was convicted in 1984 of filing false financial disclosure forms, charged, among other things, vote fraud in his 170-vote loss to Stallings. The House dismissed the challenge by a 247-4 vote, with 169 members, mostly Republicans, voting "present."

# Results of House Elections, 1928-92

| | 1928 | 1930 | 1932 | 1934 | 1936 | 1938 | 1940 | 1942 | 1944 | 1946 | 1948 | 1950 | 1952 | 1954 | 1956 | 1958 | 1960 |
|---|---|---|---|---|---|---|---|---|---|---|---|---|---|---|---|---|---|
| **National Totals** | | | | | | | | | | | | | | | | | |
| Democrats | 165 | 217 | 313 | 322 | 334 | 262 | 268 | 222 | 242 | 188 | 263 | 235 | 213 | 232 | 234 | 283 | 263 |
| Republicans | 269 | 217 | 117 | 103 | 88 | 169 | 162 | 209 | 191 | 246 | 171 | 199 | 221 | 203 | 201 | 153 | 174 |
| **Alabama** | | | | | | | | | | | | | | | | | |
| Democrats | 10 | 10 | 9[1] | 9 | 9 | 9 | 9 | 9 | 9 | 9 | 9 | 9 | 9 | 9 | 9 | 9 | 9 |
| Republicans | 0 | 0 | 0 | 0 | 0 | 0 | 0 | 0 | 0 | 0 | 0 | 0 | 0 | 0 | 0 | 0 | 0 |
| **Alaska** | | | | | | | | | | | | | | | | | |
| Democrats | — | — | — | — | — | — | — | — | — | — | — | — | — | — | — | 1 | 1 |
| Republicans | — | — | — | — | — | — | — | — | — | — | — | — | — | — | — | 0 | 0 |
| **Arizona** | | | | | | | | | | | | | | | | | |
| Democrats | 1 | 1 | 1 | 1 | 1 | 1 | 1 | 2[2] | 2 | 2 | 2 | 2 | 1 | 1 | 1 | 1 | 1 |
| Republicans | 0 | 0 | 0 | 0 | 0 | 0 | 0 | 0 | 0 | 0 | 0 | 0 | 1 | 1 | 1 | 1 | 1 |
| **Arkansas** | | | | | | | | | | | | | | | | | |
| Democrats | 7 | 7 | 7 | 7 | 7 | 7 | 7 | 7 | 7 | 7 | 7 | 7 | 6[1] | 6 | 6 | 6 | 6 |
| Republicans | 0 | 0 | 0 | 0 | 0 | 0 | 0 | 0 | 0 | 0 | 0 | 0 | 0 | 0 | 0 | 0 | 0 |
| **California** | | | | | | | | | | | | | | | | | |
| Democrats | 1 | 1 | 11[2] | 13 | 15 | 12 | 11 | 12[2] | 16 | 9 | 10 | 10 | 11[2] | 11 | 13 | 16 | 16 |
| Republicans | 10 | 10 | 9 | 7 | 4 | 8 | 9 | 11 | 7 | 14 | 13 | 13 | 19 | 19 | 17 | 14 | 14 |
| **Colorado** | | | | | | | | | | | | | | | | | |
| Democrats | 1 | 1 | 4 | 4 | 4 | 4 | 2 | 1 | 0 | 1 | 3 | 2 | 2 | 2 | 2 | 3 | 2 |
| Republicans | 3 | 3 | 0 | 0 | 0 | 0 | 2 | 3 | 4 | 3 | 1 | 2 | 2 | 2 | 2 | 1 | 2 |
| **Connecticut** | | | | | | | | | | | | | | | | | |
| Democrats | 0 | 2 | 2[2] | 4 | 6 | 2 | 6 | 0 | 4 | 0 | 3 | 2 | 1 | 1 | 0 | 6 | 4 |
| Republicans | 5 | 3 | 4 | 2 | 0 | 4 | 0 | 6 | 2 | 6 | 3 | 4 | 5 | 5 | 6 | 0 | 2 |
| **Delaware** | | | | | | | | | | | | | | | | | |
| Democrats | 0 | 0 | 1 | 0 | 1 | 0 | 1 | 0 | 1 | 0 | 0 | 0 | 0 | 1 | 0 | 1 | 1 |
| Republicans | 1 | 1 | 0 | 1 | 0 | 1 | 0 | 1 | 0 | 1 | 1 | 0 | 1 | 0 | 0 | 0 | 0 |
| **Florida** | | | | | | | | | | | | | | | | | |
| Democrats | 4 | 4 | 5[2] | 5 | 5 | 5 | 5 | 6[2] | 6 | 6 | 6 | 6 | 8[2] | 7 | 7 | 7 | 7 |
| Republicans | 0 | 0 | 0 | 0 | 0 | 0 | 0 | 0 | 0 | 0 | 0 | 0 | 0 | 1 | 1 | 1 | 1 |
| **Georgia** | | | | | | | | | | | | | | | | | |
| Democrats | 12 | 12 | 10[1] | 10 | 10 | 10 | 10 | 10 | 10 | 10 | 10 | 10 | 10 | 10 | 10 | 10 | 10 |
| Republicans | 0 | 0 | 0 | 0 | 0 | 0 | 0 | 0 | 0 | 0 | 0 | 0 | 0 | 0 | 0 | 0 | 0 |
| **Hawaii** | | | | | | | | | | | | | | | | | |
| Democrats | — | — | — | — | — | — | — | — | — | — | — | — | — | — | — | — | 1 |
| Republicans | — | — | — | — | — | — | — | — | — | — | — | — | — | — | — | — | 0 |
| **Idaho** | | | | | | | | | | | | | | | | | |
| Democrats | 0 | 0 | 2 | 2 | 2 | 1 | 1 | 1 | 1 | 0 | 1 | 0 | 1 | 1 | 1 | 1 | 2 |
| Republicans | 2 | 2 | 0 | 0 | 0 | 1 | 1 | 1 | 1 | 2 | 1 | 2 | 1 | 1 | 1 | 1 | 0 |
| **Illinois** | | | | | | | | | | | | | | | | | |
| Democrats | 6 | 13[3] | 19 | 21 | 21 | 17 | 11 | 7[1] | 11 | 6 | 12 | 8 | 9[1] | 12 | 11 | 14 | 14 |
| Republicans | 21 | 14 | 8 | 6 | 6 | 10 | 16 | 19 | 15 | 20 | 14 | 18 | 16 | 13 | 14 | 11 | 11 |
| **Indiana** | | | | | | | | | | | | | | | | | |
| Democrats | 3 | 9 | 12[1] | 11 | 11 | 5 | 4 | 2[1] | 2 | 2 | 7 | 2 | 1 | 2 | 2 | 8 | 4[3] |
| Republicans | 10 | 4 | 0 | 1 | 1 | 7 | 8 | 9 | 9 | 9 | 4 | 9 | 10 | 9 | 9 | 3 | 7 |
| **Iowa** | | | | | | | | | | | | | | | | | |
| Democrats | 0 | 1 | 6[1] | 6 | 5 | 2 | 2 | 0[1] | 0 | 0 | 0 | 0 | 0 | 0 | 1 | 4 | 2 |
| Republicans | 11 | 10 | 3 | 3 | 4 | 7 | 7 | 8 | 8 | 8 | 8 | 8 | 8 | 8 | 7 | 4 | 6 |
| **Kansas** | | | | | | | | | | | | | | | | | |
| Democrats | 1 | 1 | 3[1] | 3 | 2 | 1 | 1 | 0[1] | 0 | 0 | 0 | 0 | 1 | 0 | 1 | 3 | 1 |
| Republicans | 7 | 7 | 4 | 4 | 5 | 6 | 6 | 6 | 6 | 6 | 6 | 6 | 5 | 6 | 5 | 3 | 5 |
| **Kentucky** | | | | | | | | | | | | | | | | | |
| Democrats | 2 | 9 | 9[1] | 8 | 8 | 8 | 8 | 8 | 8 | 6 | 7 | 7 | 6[1] | 6 | 6 | 7 | 7 |
| Republicans | 9 | 2 | 0 | 1 | 1 | 1 | 1 | 1 | 1 | 3 | 2 | 2 | 2 | 2 | 2 | 1 | 1 |
| **Louisiana** | | | | | | | | | | | | | | | | | |
| Democrats | 8 | 8 | 8 | 8 | 8 | 8 | 8 | 8 | 8 | 8 | 8 | 8 | 8 | 8 | 8 | 8 | 8 |
| Republicans | 0 | 0 | 0 | 0 | 0 | 0 | 0 | 0 | 0 | 0 | 0 | 0 | 0 | 0 | 0 | 0 | 0 |
| **Maine** | | | | | | | | | | | | | | | | | |
| Democrats | 0 | 0 | 2[1] | 2 | 0 | 0 | 0 | 0 | 0 | 0 | 0 | 0 | 0 | 0 | 1 | 2 | 0 |
| Republicans | 4 | 4 | 1 | 1 | 3 | 3 | 3 | 3 | 3 | 3 | 3 | 3 | 3 | 3 | 2 | 1 | 3 |
| **Maryland** | | | | | | | | | | | | | | | | | |
| Democrats | 4 | 6 | 6 | 6 | 6 | 6 | 6 | 4 | 5 | 4 | 4 | 3 | 3[2] | 4 | 4 | 7 | 6 |
| Republicans | 2 | 0 | 0 | 0 | 0 | 0 | 0 | 2 | 1 | 2 | 2 | 3 | 4 | 3 | 3 | 0 | 1 |
| **Massachusetts** | | | | | | | | | | | | | | | | | |
| Democrats | 3 | 4 | 5[1] | 7 | 5 | 5 | 6 | 4[1] | 4 | 5 | 4 | 6 | 6 | 7 | 7 | 8 | 8 |
| Republicans | 13 | 12 | 10 | 8 | 10 | 10 | 9 | 10 | 10 | 9 | 8 | 8 | 8 | 7 | 7 | 6 | 6 |
| **Michigan** | | | | | | | | | | | | | | | | | |
| Democrats | 0 | 0 | 10[2] | 6 | 8 | 5 | 6 | 5 | 6 | 3 | 5 | 5 | 5[2] | 7 | 6 | 7 | 7 |
| Republicans | 13 | 13 | 7 | 11 | 9 | 12 | 11 | 12 | 11 | 14 | 12 | 12 | 13 | 11 | 12 | 11 | 11 |
| **Minnesota** | | | | | | | | | | | | | | | | | |
| Democrats | 0 | 0 | 1[1] | 1 | 1 | 1 | 0 | 0 | 2 | 1 | 4 | 4 | 4 | 5 | 5 | 4 | 3 |
| Republicans | 9 | 9 | 3 | 5 | 3 | 7 | 8 | 8 | 7 | 8 | 5 | 5 | 5 | 4 | 4 | 5 | 6 |
| **Mississippi** | | | | | | | | | | | | | | | | | |
| Democrats | 8 | 8 | 7[1] | 7 | 7 | 7 | 7 | 7 | 7 | 7 | 7 | 7 | 6[1] | 6 | 6 | 6 | 6 |
| Republicans | 0 | 0 | 0 | 0 | 0 | 0 | 0 | 0 | 0 | 0 | 0 | 0 | 0 | 0 | 0 | 0 | 0 |
| **Missouri** | | | | | | | | | | | | | | | | | |
| Democrats | 6 | 12 | 13[1] | 12 | 12 | 12 | 10 | 5 | 7 | 4 | 12 | 10 | 7 | 9 | 10 | 10 | 9 |
| Republicans | 10 | 4 | 0 | 1 | 1 | 1 | 3 | 8 | 6 | 9 | 1 | 3 | 4 | 2 | 1 | 1 | 2 |

1. State lost seats due to reapportionment.
2. State gained seats due to reapportionment.
3. *Illinois 1930, New Hampshire 1936, Indiana 1960 and Indiana 1984: National and state totals reflect the final outcome of a contested election in which a Republican was first certified the winner, but the House decided to seat the Democrat.*

# Results of House Elections. . .

| | 1962 | 1964 | 1966 | 1968 | 1970 | 1972 | 1974 | 1976 | 1978 | 1980 | 1982 | 1984 | 1986 | 1988 | 1990 | 1992 |
|---|---|---|---|---|---|---|---|---|---|---|---|---|---|---|---|---|
| **National Totals** | | | | | | | | | | | | | | | | |
| Democrats | 259 | 295 | 248 | 243 | 255 | 243 | 291 | 292 | 277 | 243 | 269 | 253 | 258 | 260 | 267 | 258 |
| Republicans | 176 | 140 | 187 | 192 | 180 | 192 | 144 | 143 | 158 | 192 | 166 | 182 | 177 | 175 | 167 | 176 |
| **Alabama** | | | | | | | | | | | | | | | | |
| Democrats | 8[1] | 3 | 5 | 5 | 5 | 4[1] | 4 | 4 | 4 | 4 | 5 | 5 | 5 | 5 | 5 | 4 |
| Republicans | 0 | 5 | 3 | 3 | 3 | 3 | 3 | 3 | 3 | 3 | 2 | 2 | 2 | 2 | 2 | 3 |
| **Alaska** | | | | | | | | | | | | | | | | |
| Democrats | 1 | 1 | 0 | 0 | 1 | 1[4] | 0 | 0 | 0 | 0 | 0 | 0 | 0 | 0 | 0 | 0 |
| Republicans | 0 | 0 | 1 | 1 | 0 | 0 | 1 | 1 | 1 | 1 | 1 | 1 | 1 | 1 | 1 | 1 |
| **Arizona** | | | | | | | | | | | | | | | | |
| Democrats | 2[2] | 2 | 1 | 1 | 1 | 1[2] | 1 | 2 | 2 | 2 | 2[2] | 1 | 1 | 1 | 1 | 3[2] |
| Republicans | 1 | 1 | 2 | 2 | 2 | 3 | 3 | 2 | 2 | 2 | 3 | 4 | 4 | 4 | 4 | 3 |
| **Arkansas** | | | | | | | | | | | | | | | | |
| Democrats | 4[1] | 4 | 3 | 3 | 3 | 3 | 3 | 3 | 2 | 2 | 2 | 3 | 3 | 3 | 3 | 2 |
| Republicans | 0 | 0 | 1 | 1 | 1 | 1 | 1 | 1 | 2 | 2 | 2 | 1 | 1 | 1 | 1 | 2 |
| **California** | | | | | | | | | | | | | | | | |
| Democrats | 25[24] | 23 | 21 | 21 | 20 | 23[2] | 28 | 29 | 26 | 22 | 28[2] | 27 | 27 | 27 | 26 | 30[2] |
| Republicans | 13 | 15 | 17 | 17 | 18 | 20 | 15 | 14 | 17 | 21 | 17 | 18 | 18 | 18 | 19 | 22 |
| **Colorado** | | | | | | | | | | | | | | | | |
| Democrats | 2 | 4 | 3 | 3 | 2 | 2[2] | 3 | 3 | 3 | 3 | 3[2] | 2 | 3 | 3 | 3 | 2 |
| Republicans | 2 | 0 | 1 | 1 | 2 | 3 | 2 | 2 | 2 | 2 | 3 | 4 | 3 | 3 | 3 | 4 |
| **Connecticut** | | | | | | | | | | | | | | | | |
| Democrats | 5 | 6 | 5 | 4 | 3 | 3 | 4 | 4 | 5 | 4 | 4 | 3 | 3 | 3 | 3 | 3 |
| Republicans | 1 | 0 | 1 | 2 | 2 | 3 | 2 | 2 | 1 | 2 | 2 | 3 | 3 | 3 | 3 | 3 |
| **Delaware** | | | | | | | | | | | | | | | | |
| Democrats | 1 | 1 | 0 | 0 | 0 | 0 | 0 | 0 | 0 | 0 | 1 | 1 | 1 | 1 | 1 | 0 |
| Republicans | 0 | 0 | 1 | 1 | 1 | 1 | 1 | 1 | 1 | 1 | 0 | 0 | 0 | 0 | 0 | 1 |
| **Florida** | | | | | | | | | | | | | | | | |
| Democrats | 10[2] | 10 | 9 | 9 | 9 | 11[2] | 10 | 10 | 12 | 11 | 13[2] | 12 | 12 | 10 | 9 | 10[2] |
| Republicans | 2 | 2 | 3 | 3 | 3 | 4 | 5 | 5 | 3 | 4 | 6 | 7 | 7 | 9 | 10 | 13 |
| **Georgia** | | | | | | | | | | | | | | | | |
| Democrats | 10 | 9 | 8 | 8 | 8 | 9 | 10 | 10 | 9 | 9 | 9 | 8 | 8 | 9 | 9 | 7[2] |
| Republicans | 0 | 1 | 2 | 2 | 2 | 1 | 0 | 0 | 1 | 1 | 1 | 2 | 2 | 1 | 1 | 4 |
| **Hawaii** | | | | | | | | | | | | | | | | |
| Democrats | 2[2] | 2 | 2 | 2 | 2 | 2 | 2 | 2 | 2 | 2 | 2 | 2 | 1 | 1 | 2 | 2 |
| Republicans | 0 | 0 | 0 | 0 | 0 | 0 | 0 | 0 | 0 | 0 | 0 | 0 | 1 | 1 | 0 | 0 |
| **Idaho** | | | | | | | | | | | | | | | | |
| Democrats | 2 | 1 | 0 | 0 | 0 | 0 | 0 | 0 | 0 | 0 | 0 | 1 | 1 | 1 | 2 | 1 |
| Republicans | 0 | 1 | 2 | 2 | 2 | 2 | 2 | 2 | 2 | 2 | 2 | 1 | 1 | 1 | 0 | 1 |
| **Illinois** | | | | | | | | | | | | | | | | |
| Democrats | 12[1] | 13 | 12 | 12 | 12 | 10 | 13 | 12 | 11 | 10 | 12[1] | 13 | 13 | 14 | 15 | 12[1] |
| Republicans | 12 | 11 | 12 | 12 | 12 | 14 | 11 | 12 | 13 | 14 | 10 | 9 | 9 | 8 | 7 | 8 |
| **Indiana** | | | | | | | | | | | | | | | | |
| Democrats | 4 | 6 | 5 | 4 | 5 | 4 | 9 | 8 | 7 | 6 | 5[1] | 5[3] | 6 | 6 | 8 | 7 |
| Republicans | 7 | 5 | 6 | 7 | 6 | 7 | 2 | 3 | 4 | 5 | 5 | 5 | 4 | 4 | 2 | 3 |
| **Iowa** | | | | | | | | | | | | | | | | |
| Democrats | 1[1] | 6 | 2 | 2 | 2 | 3[1] | 5 | 4 | 3 | 3 | 3 | 2 | 2 | 2 | 2 | 1[1] |
| Republicans | 6 | 1 | 5 | 5 | 5 | 3 | 1 | 2 | 3 | 3 | 3 | 4 | 4 | 4 | 4 | 4 |
| **Kansas** | | | | | | | | | | | | | | | | |
| Democrats | 0[1] | 0 | 0 | 0 | 1 | 1 | 1 | 2 | 1 | 1 | 2 | 2 | 2 | 2 | 2 | 2[1] |
| Republicans | 5 | 5 | 5 | 5 | 4 | 4 | 4 | 3 | 4 | 4 | 3 | 3 | 3 | 3 | 3 | 2 |
| **Kentucky** | | | | | | | | | | | | | | | | |
| Democrats | 5[1] | 6 | 4 | 4 | 5 | 5 | 5 | 5 | 4 | 4 | 4 | 4 | 4 | 4 | 4 | 4[1] |
| Republicans | 2 | 1 | 3 | 3 | 2 | 2 | 2 | 2 | 3 | 3 | 3 | 3 | 3 | 3 | 3 | 2 |
| **Louisiana** | | | | | | | | | | | | | | | | |
| Democrats | 8 | 8 | 8 | 8 | 8 | 7[4] | 6[5] | 6 | 5 | 6 | 6 | 6 | 5 | 4 | 4 | 4[1] |
| Republicans | 0 | 0 | 0 | 0 | 0 | 1 | 2 | 2 | 3 | 2 | 2 | 2 | 3 | 4 | 4 | 3 |
| **Maine** | | | | | | | | | | | | | | | | |
| Democrats | 0[1] | 1 | 2 | 2 | 2 | 1 | 0 | 0 | 0 | 0 | 0 | 0 | 1 | 1 | 1 | 1 |
| Republicans | 2 | 1 | 0 | 0 | 0 | 1 | 2 | 2 | 2 | 2 | 2 | 2 | 1 | 1 | 1 | 1 |
| **Maryland** | | | | | | | | | | | | | | | | |
| Democrats | 6[2] | 6 | 5 | 4 | 5 | 4 | 5 | 5 | 6 | 7 | 7 | 6 | 6 | 6 | 5 | 4 |
| Republicans | 2 | 2 | 3 | 4 | 3 | 4 | 3 | 3 | 2 | 1 | 1 | 2 | 2 | 2 | 3 | 4 |
| **Massachusetts** | | | | | | | | | | | | | | | | |
| Democrats | 7[1] | 7 | 7 | 7 | 8 | 9[6] | 10 | 10 | 10 | 10 | 10[1] | 10 | 10 | 10 | 10 | 8[1] |
| Republicans | 5 | 5 | 5 | 5 | 4 | 3 | 2 | 2 | 2 | 2 | 1 | 1 | 1 | 1 | 1 | 2 |
| **Michigan** | | | | | | | | | | | | | | | | |
| Democrats | 8[2] | 12 | 7 | 7 | 7 | 7 | 12 | 11 | 13 | 12 | 12[1] | 11 | 11 | 11 | 11 | 10[1] |
| Republicans | 11 | 7 | 12 | 12 | 12 | 12 | 7 | 8 | 6 | 7 | 6 | 7 | 7 | 7 | 7 | 6 |
| **Minnesota** | | | | | | | | | | | | | | | | |
| Democrats | 4[1] | 4 | 3 | 3 | 4 | 4 | 5 | 5 | 4 | 3 | 5 | 5 | 5 | 5 | 6 | 6 |
| Republicans | 4 | 4 | 5 | 5 | 4 | 4 | 3 | 3 | 4 | 5 | 3 | 3 | 3 | 3 | 2 | 2 |
| **Mississippi** | | | | | | | | | | | | | | | | |
| Democrats | 5[1] | 4 | 5 | 5 | 5 | 3 | 3 | 3 | 3 | 3 | 3 | 3 | 4 | 4 | 5 | 5 |
| Republicans | 0 | 1 | 0 | 0 | 0 | 2 | 2 | 2 | 2 | 2 | 2 | 2 | 1 | 1 | 0 | 0 |
| **Missouri** | | | | | | | | | | | | | | | | |
| Democrats | 8[1] | 8 | 8 | 9 | 9 | 9 | 9 | 8 | 8 | 6 | 6[1] | 6 | 5 | 5 | 6 | 6 |
| Republicans | 2 | 2 | 2 | 1 | 1 | 1 | 1 | 2 | 2 | 4 | 3 | 3 | 4 | 4 | 3 | 3 |

4. California 1962, Alaska 1972 and Louisiana 1972: National and state totals reflect the re-election of a Democrat who died before the election but whose name remained on the ballot.

5. Louisiana 1974: National and state totals reflect the final outcome of a contested election in which no winner was declared, followed by a special election won by the Republican.

# ... 1928-92 (continued)

| | 1928 | 1930 | 1932 | 1934 | 1936 | 1938 | 1940 | 1942 | 1944 | 1946 | 1948 | 1950 | 1952 | 1954 | 1956 | 1958 | 1960 |
|---|---|---|---|---|---|---|---|---|---|---|---|---|---|---|---|---|---|
| **Montana** | | | | | | | | | | | | | | | | | |
| Democrats | 1 | 1 | 2 | 2 | 2 | 1 | 1 | 2 | 1 | 1 | 1 | 1 | 1 | 1 | 2 | 2 | 1 |
| Republicans | 1 | 1 | 0 | 0 | 0 | 1 | 1 | 0 | 1 | 1 | 1 | 1 | 1 | 1 | 0 | 0 | 1 |
| **Nebraska** | | | | | | | | | | | | | | | | | |
| Democrats | 2 | 4 | 5[1] | 4 | 4 | 2 | 2 | 0[1] | 0 | 0 | 1 | 0 | 0 | 0 | 0 | 2 | 0 |
| Republicans | 4 | 2 | 0 | 1 | 1 | 3 | 3 | 4 | 4 | 4 | 3 | 4 | 4 | 4 | 4 | 2 | 4 |
| **Nevada** | | | | | | | | | | | | | | | | | |
| Democrats | 0 | 0 | 1 | 1 | 1 | 1 | 1 | 1 | 1 | 0 | 1 | 1 | 0 | 0 | 1 | 1 | 1 |
| Republicans | 1 | 1 | 0 | 0 | 0 | 0 | 0 | 0 | 0 | 1 | 0 | 0 | 1 | 1 | 0 | 0 | 0 |
| **New Hampshire** | | | | | | | | | | | | | | | | | |
| Democrats | 0 | 0 | 1 | 1 | 1[3] | 0 | 0 | 0 | 0 | 0 | 0 | 0 | 0 | 0 | 0 | 0 | 0 |
| Republicans | 2 | 2 | 1 | 1 | 1 | 2 | 2 | 2 | 2 | 2 | 2 | 2 | 2 | 2 | 2 | 2 | 2 |
| **New Jersey** | | | | | | | | | | | | | | | | | |
| Democrats | 2 | 3 | 4[2] | 4 | 7 | 3 | 4 | 3 | 2 | 2 | 5 | 5 | 5 | 6 | 4 | 5 | 6 |
| Republicans | 10 | 9 | 10 | 10 | 7 | 11 | 10 | 11 | 12 | 12 | 9 | 9 | 9 | 8 | 10 | 9 | 8 |
| **New Mexico** | | | | | | | | | | | | | | | | | |
| Democrats | 0 | 1 | 1 | 1 | 1 | 1 | 1 | 2[2] | 2 | 2 | 2 | 2 | 2 | 2 | 2 | 2 | 2 |
| Republicans | 1 | 0 | 0 | 0 | 0 | 0 | 0 | 0 | 0 | 0 | 0 | 0 | 0 | 0 | 0 | 0 | 0 |
| **New York** | | | | | | | | | | | | | | | | | |
| Democrat | 23 | 23 | 29[2] | 29 | 29 | 25 | 25 | 23 | 22 | 16 | 24 | 23 | 16[1] | 17 | 17 | 19 | 22 |
| Republicans | 20 | 20 | 16 | 16 | 16 | 19 | 19 | 21 | 22 | 28 | 20 | 22 | 27 | 26 | 26 | 24 | 21 |
| **North Carolina** | | | | | | | | | | | | | | | | | |
| Democrats | 8 | 10 | 11[2] | 11 | 11 | 11 | 11 | 12[2] | 12 | 12 | 12 | 12 | 11 | 11 | 11 | 11 | 11 |
| Republicans | 2 | 0 | 0 | 0 | 0 | 0 | 0 | 0 | 0 | 0 | 0 | 0 | 1 | 1 | 1 | 1 | 1 |
| **North Dakota** | | | | | | | | | | | | | | | | | |
| Democrat | 0 | 0 | 0[1] | 0 | 0 | 0 | 0 | 0 | 0 | 0 | 0 | 0 | 0 | 0 | 0 | 1 | 0 |
| Republicans | 3 | 3 | 2 | 2 | 2 | 2 | 2 | 2 | 2 | 2 | 2 | 2 | 2 | 2 | 2 | 1 | 2 |
| **Ohio** | | | | | | | | | | | | | | | | | |
| Democrats | 3 | 9 | 18[2] | 18 | 22 | 9 | 12 | 3[1] | 6 | 4 | 12 | 7 | 6 | 6 | 6 | 9 | 7 |
| Republicans | 19 | 13 | 6 | 6 | 2 | 15 | 12 | 20 | 17 | 19 | 11 | 15 | 16 | 17 | 17 | 14 | 16 |
| **Oklahoma** | | | | | | | | | | | | | | | | | |
| Democrats | 5 | 7 | 9[2] | 9 | 9 | 9 | 8 | 7[1] | 6 | 6 | 8 | 6 | 5[1] | 5 | 5 | 5 | 5 |
| Republicans | 3 | 1 | 0 | 0 | 0 | 0 | 1 | 1 | 2 | 2 | 0 | 2 | 1 | 1 | 1 | 1 | 1 |
| **Oregon** | | | | | | | | | | | | | | | | | |
| Democrats | 0 | 1 | 2 | 1 | 2 | 1 | 1 | 0[2] | 0 | 0 | 0 | 0 | 0 | 1 | 3 | 3 | 2 |
| Republicans | 3 | 2 | 1 | 2 | 1 | 2 | 2 | 4 | 4 | 4 | 4 | 4 | 4 | 3 | 1 | 1 | 2 |
| **Pennsylvania** | | | | | | | | | | | | | | | | | |
| Democrats | 1 | 3 | 11[1] | 23 | 27 | 15 | 19 | 14[1] | 15 | 5 | 16 | 13 | 11[1] | 14 | 13 | 16 | 14 |
| Republicans | 35 | 33 | 23 | 11 | 7 | 9 | 15 | 19 | 18 | 28 | 19 | 20 | 19 | 16 | 17 | 14 | 16 |
| **Rhode Island** | | | | | | | | | | | | | | | | | |
| Democrats | 1 | 1 | 2[1] | 2 | 2 | 0 | 2 | 2 | 2 | 2 | 2 | 2 | 2 | 2 | 2 | 2 | 2 |
| Republicans | 2 | 2 | 0 | 0 | 0 | 2 | 0 | 0 | 0 | 0 | 0 | 0 | 0 | 0 | 0 | 0 | 0 |
| **South Carolina** | | | | | | | | | | | | | | | | | |
| Democrats | 7 | 7 | 6[1] | 6 | 6 | 6 | 6 | 6 | 6 | 6 | 6 | 6 | 6 | 6 | 6 | 6 | 6 |
| Republicans | 0 | 0 | 0 | 0 | 0 | 0 | 0 | 0 | 0 | 0 | 0 | 0 | 0 | 0 | 0 | 0 | 0 |
| **South Dakota** | | | | | | | | | | | | | | | | | |
| Democrats | 0 | 0 | 2[1] | 2 | 1 | 0 | 0 | 0 | 0 | 0 | 0 | 0 | 0 | 0 | 1 | 1 | 0 |
| Republicans | 3 | 3 | 0 | 0 | 1 | 2 | 2 | 2 | 2 | 2 | 2 | 2 | 2 | 2 | 1 | 1 | 2 |
| **Tennessee** | | | | | | | | | | | | | | | | | |
| Democrats | 8 | 8 | 7[1] | 7 | 7 | 7 | 7 | 8[2] | 8 | 8 | 8 | 8 | 7[1] | 7 | 7 | 7 | 7 |
| Republicans | 2 | 2 | 2 | 2 | 2 | 2 | 2 | 2 | 2 | 2 | 2 | 2 | 2 | 2 | 2 | 2 | 2 |
| **Texas** | | | | | | | | | | | | | | | | | |
| Democrats | 17 | 17 | 21[2] | 21 | 21 | 21 | 21 | 21 | 21 | 21 | 21 | 21 | 22[2] | 21 | 21 | 21 | 21 |
| Republicans | 1[7] | 1 | 0 | 0 | 0 | 0 | 0 | 0 | 0 | 0 | 0 | 0 | 0 | 1 | 1 | 1 | 1 |
| **Utah** | | | | | | | | | | | | | | | | | |
| Democrats | 0 | 0 | 2 | 2 | 2 | 2 | 2 | 2 | 2 | 1 | 2 | 2 | 0 | 0 | 0 | 1 | 2 |
| Republicans | 2 | 2 | 0 | 0 | 0 | 0 | 0 | 0 | 0 | 1 | 0 | 0 | 2 | 2 | 2 | 1 | 0 |
| **Vermont** | | | | | | | | | | | | | | | | | |
| Democrats | 0 | 0 | 0[1] | 0 | 0 | 0 | 0 | 0 | 0 | 0 | 0 | 0 | 0 | 0 | 0 | 1 | 0 |
| Republicans | 2 | 2 | 1 | 1 | 1 | 1 | 1 | 1 | 1 | 1 | 1 | 1 | 1 | 1 | 1 | 0 | 1 |
| **Virginia** | | | | | | | | | | | | | | | | | |
| Democrats | 8 | 9 | 9[1] | 9 | 9 | 9 | 9 | 9 | 9 | 9 | 9 | 9 | 7[2] | 8 | 8 | 8 | 8 |
| Republicans | 2 | 1 | 0 | 0 | 0 | 0 | 0 | 0 | 0 | 0 | 0 | 0 | 3 | 2 | 2 | 2 | 2 |
| **Washington** | | | | | | | | | | | | | | | | | |
| Democrats | 1 | 1 | 6[2] | 6 | 6 | 6 | 6 | 3 | 4 | 1 | 2 | 2 | 1[2] | 1 | 1 | 1 | 2 |
| Republicans | 4 | 4 | 0 | 0 | 0 | 0 | 0 | 3 | 2 | 5 | 4 | 4 | 6 | 6 | 6 | 6 | 5 |
| **West Virginia** | | | | | | | | | | | | | | | | | |
| Democrats | 1 | 2 | 6 | 6 | 6 | 5 | 6 | 3 | 5 | 2 | 6 | 6 | 5 | 6 | 4 | 5 | 5 |
| Republicans | 5 | 4 | 0 | 0 | 0 | 1 | 0 | 3 | 1 | 4 | 0 | 0 | 1 | 0 | 2 | 1 | 1 |
| **Wisconsin** | | | | | | | | | | | | | | | | | |
| Democrats | 0 | 1 | 5[1] | 3 | 3 | 0 | 1 | 3 | 2 | 0 | 2 | 1 | 1 | 3 | 3 | 5 | 4 |
| Republicans | 11 | 10 | 5 | 0 | 0 | 8 | 6 | 5 | 7 | 10 | 8 | 9 | 9 | 7 | 7 | 5 | 6 |
| **Wyoming** | | | | | | | | | | | | | | | | | |
| Democrats | 0 | 0 | 0 | 1 | 1 | 0 | 1 | 0 | 0 | 0 | 0 | 0 | 0 | 0 | 0 | 0 | 0 |
| Republicans | 1 | 1 | 1 | 0 | 0 | 1 | 0 | 1 | 1 | 1 | 1 | 1 | 1 | 1 | 1 | 1 | 1 |

6. Massachusetts 1972 and Pennsylvania 1980: National and state Democratic totals reflect the election of an Independent candidate who previously announced he would serve as a Democrats.

7. Texas 1928: National and state totals reflect the final outcome of a contested election in which a Democrats was at first certified the winner, but the House decided to seat the Republican.

# Results of House Elections, 1928-92 (continued)

| | 1962 | 1964 | 1966 | 1968 | 1970 | 1972 | 1974 | 1976 | 1978 | 1980 | 1982 | 1984 | 1986 | 1988 | 1990 | 1992 |
|---|---|---|---|---|---|---|---|---|---|---|---|---|---|---|---|---|
| **Montana** | | | | | | | | | | | | | | | | |
| Democrats | 1 | 1 | 1 | 1 | 1 | 1 | 2 | 1 | 1 | 1 | 1 | 1 | 1 | 1 | 1 | 1¹ |
| Republicans | 1 | 1 | 1 | 1 | 1 | 1 | 0 | 1 | 1 | 1 | 1 | 1 | 1 | 1 | 1 | 0 |
| **Nebraska** | | | | | | | | | | | | | | | | |
| Democrats | 0¹ | 1 | 0 | 0 | 0 | 0 | 0 | 1 | 1 | 0 | 0 | 0 | 0 | 1 | 1 | 1 |
| Republicans | 3 | 2 | 3 | 3 | 3 | 3 | 3 | 2 | 2 | 3 | 3 | 3 | 3 | 2 | 2 | 2 |
| **Nevada** | | | | | | | | | | | | | | | | |
| Democrats | 1 | 1 | 1 | 1 | 1 | 0 | 1 | 1 | 1 | 1 | 1² | 1 | 1 | 1 | 1 | 1 |
| Republicans | 0 | 0 | 0 | 0 | 0 | 1 | 0 | 0 | 0 | 0 | 1 | 1 | 1 | 1 | 1 | 1 |
| **New Hampshire** | | | | | | | | | | | | | | | | |
| Democrats | 0 | 1 | 0 | 0 | 0 | 0 | 1 | 1 | 1 | 1 | 1 | 0 | 0 | 0 | 1 | 1 |
| Republicans | 2 | 1 | 2 | 2 | 2 | 2 | 1 | 1 | 1 | 1 | 1 | 2 | 2 | 2 | 1 | 1 |
| **New Jersey** | | | | | | | | | | | | | | | | |
| Democrats | 7² | 11 | 9 | 9 | 9 | 8 | 12 | 11 | 10 | 8 | 9¹ | 8 | 8 | 8 | 8 | 7¹ |
| Republicans | 8 | 4 | 6 | 6 | 6 | 7 | 3 | 4 | 5 | 7 | 5 | 6 | 6 | 6 | 6 | 6 |
| **New Mexico** | | | | | | | | | | | | | | | | |
| Democrats | 2 | 2 | 2 | 0 | 1 | 1 | 1 | 1 | 1 | 0 | 1² | 1 | 1 | 1 | 1 | 1 |
| Republicans | 0 | 0 | 0 | 2 | 1 | 1 | 1 | 1 | 1 | 2 | 2 | 2 | 2 | 2 | 2 | 2 |
| **New York** | | | | | | | | | | | | | | | | |
| Democrats | 20¹ | 27 | 26 | 26 | 24 | 22¹ | 27 | 28 | 26 | 22 | 20¹ | 19 | 20 | 21 | 21 | 18¹ |
| Republicans | 21 | 14 | 15 | 15 | 17 | 17 | 12 | 11 | 13 | 17 | 14 | 15 | 14 | 13 | 13 | 13 |
| **North Carolina** | | | | | | | | | | | | | | | | |
| Democrats | 9¹ | 9 | 8 | 7 | 7 | 7 | 9 | 9 | 9 | 7 | 9 | 6 | 8 | 8 | 7 | 8² |
| Republicans | 2 | 2 | 3 | 4 | 4 | 4 | 2 | 2 | 2 | 4 | 2 | 5 | 3 | 3 | 4 | 4 |
| **North Dakota** | | | | | | | | | | | | | | | | |
| Democrats | 0 | 1 | 0 | 0 | 1 | 0¹ | 0 | 0 | 0 | 1 | 1 | 1 | 1 | 1 | 1 | 1 |
| Republicans | 2 | 1 | 2 | 2 | 1 | 1 | 1 | 1 | 1 | 0 | 0 | 0 | 0 | 0 | 0 | 0 |
| **Ohio** | | | | | | | | | | | | | | | | |
| Democrats | 6² | 10 | 5 | 6 | 7 | 7¹ | 8 | 10 | 10 | 11 | 10¹ | 11 | 11 | 11 | 11 | 10¹ |
| Republicans | 18 | 14 | 19 | 18 | 17 | 16 | 15 | 13 | 13 | 12 | 11 | 10 | 10 | 10 | 10 | 9 |
| **Oklahoma** | | | | | | | | | | | | | | | | |
| Democrats | 5 | 5 | 4 | 4 | 4 | 5 | 6 | 5 | 5 | 5 | 5 | 5 | 4 | 4 | 4 | 4 |
| Republicans | 1 | 1 | 2 | 2 | 2 | 1 | 0 | 1 | 1 | 1 | 1 | 1 | 2 | 2 | 2 | 2 |
| **Oregon** | | | | | | | | | | | | | | | | |
| Democrats | 3 | 3 | 2 | 2 | 2 | 2 | 4 | 4 | 4 | 3 | 3² | 3 | 3 | 3 | 4 | 4 |
| Republicans | 1 | 1 | 2 | 2 | 2 | 2 | 0 | 0 | 0 | 1 | 2 | 2 | 2 | 2 | 1 | 1 |
| **Pennsylvania** | | | | | | | | | | | | | | | | |
| Democrats | 13¹ | 15 | 14 | 14 | 14 | 13¹ | 14 | 17 | 15 | 13⁶ | 13¹ | 13 | 12 | 12 | 11 | 11¹ |
| Republicans | 14 | 12 | 13 | 13 | 13 | 12 | 11 | 8 | 10 | 12 | 10 | 10 | 11 | 11 | 12 | 10 |
| **Rhode Island** | | | | | | | | | | | | | | | | |
| Democrats | 2 | 2 | 2 | 2 | 2 | 2 | 2 | 2 | 2 | 1 | 1 | 1 | 1 | 0 | 1 | 1 |
| Republicans | 0 | 0 | 0 | 0 | 0 | 0 | 0 | 0 | 0 | 1 | 1 | 1 | 1 | 2 | 1 | 1 |
| **South Carolina** | | | | | | | | | | | | | | | | |
| Democrats | 6 | 6 | 5 | 5 | 5 | 4 | 5 | 5 | 4 | 2 | 3 | 3 | 4 | 4 | 4 | 3 |
| Republicans | 0 | 0 | 1 | 1 | 1 | 2 | 1 | 1 | 2 | 4 | 3 | 3 | 2 | 2 | 2 | 3 |
| **South Dakota** | | | | | | | | | | | | | | | | |
| Democrats | 0 | 0 | 0 | 0 | 2 | 1 | 0 | 0 | 1 | 1 | 1¹ | 1 | 1 | 1 | 1 | 1 |
| Republicans | 2 | 2 | 2 | 2 | 0 | 1 | 2 | 2 | 1 | 1 | 0 | 0 | 0 | 0 | 0 | 0 |
| **Tennessee** | | | | | | | | | | | | | | | | |
| Democrats | 6 | 6 | 5 | 5 | 5 | 3¹ | 5 | 5 | 5 | 5 | 6² | 6 | 6 | 6 | 6 | 6 |
| Republicans | 3 | 3 | 4 | 4 | 4 | 5 | 3 | 3 | 3 | 3 | 3 | 3 | 3 | 3 | 3 | 3 |
| **Texas** | | | | | | | | | | | | | | | | |
| Democrats | 21² | 23 | 21 | 20 | 20 | 20² | 21 | 22 | 20 | 19 | 22² | 17 | 17 | 19 | 19 | 21² |
| Republicans | 2 | 0 | 2 | 3 | 3 | 4 | 3 | 2 | 4 | 5 | 5 | 10 | 10 | 8 | 8 | 9 |
| **Utah** | | | | | | | | | | | | | | | | |
| Democrats | 0 | 1 | 0 | 0 | 1 | 2 | 2 | 1 | 1 | 0 | 0² | 0 | 1 | 1 | 2 | 2 |
| Republicans | 2 | 1 | 2 | 2 | 1 | 0 | 0 | 1 | 1 | 2 | 3 | 3 | 2 | 2 | 1 | 1 |
| **Vermont** | | | | | | | | | | | | | | | | |
| Democrats | 0 | 0 | 0 | 0 | 0 | 0 | 0 | 0 | 0 | 0 | 0 | 0 | 0 | 0 | 0 | 0 |
| Republicans | 1 | 1 | 1 | 1 | 1 | 1 | 1 | 1 | 1 | 1 | 1 | 1 | 1 | 1 | 0 | 0 |
| **Virginia** | | | | | | | | | | | | | | | | |
| Democrats | 8 | 8 | 6 | 5 | 4 | 3 | 5 | 4 | 4 | 1 | 4 | 4 | 5 | 5 | 6 | 7² |
| Republicans | 2 | 2 | 4 | 5 | 6 | 7 | 5 | 6 | 6 | 9 | 6 | 6 | 5 | 5 | 4 | 4 |
| **Washington** | | | | | | | | | | | | | | | | |
| Democrats | 1 | 5 | 5 | 5 | 6 | 6 | 6 | 6 | 6 | 5 | 5² | 5 | 5 | 5 | 5 | 8² |
| Republicans | 6 | 2 | 2 | 2 | 1 | 1 | 1 | 1 | 1 | 2 | 3 | 3 | 3 | 3 | 3 | 1 |
| **West Virginia** | | | | | | | | | | | | | | | | |
| Democrats | 4¹ | 4 | 4 | 5 | 5 | 4¹ | 4 | 4 | 4 | 2 | 4 | 4 | 4 | 4 | 4 | 3¹ |
| Republicans | 1 | 1 | 1 | 0 | 0 | 0 | 0 | 0 | 0 | 2 | 0 | 0 | 0 | 0 | 0 | 0 |
| **Wisconsin** | | | | | | | | | | | | | | | | |
| Democrats | 4 | 5 | 3 | 3 | 5 | 5¹ | 7 | 7 | 6 | 5 | 5 | 5 | 5 | 5 | 4 | 4 |
| Republicans | 6 | 5 | 7 | 7· | 5 | 4 | 2 | 2 | 3 | 4 | 4 | 4 | 4 | 4 | 5 | 5 |
| **Wyoming** | | | | | | | | | | | | | | | | |
| Democrats | 1 | 0 | 0 | 1 | 1 | 1 | 1 | 0 | 0 | 0 | 0 | 0 | 0 | 0 | 0 | 0 |
| Republicans | 1 | 0 | 1 | 1 | 0 | 0 | 0 | 0 | 1 | 1 | 1 | 1 | 1 | 1 | 1 | 1 |

*Note: The above totals do not include "other" representatives elected as independent or third party candidates. Those numbers are California: Progressive 1936 (1). (No formal party. The representative became a Democrat in 1938.) Minnesota: Farmer-Labor 1928 (1), 1930 (1), 1932 (5), 1934 (3), 1936 (5), 1938 (1), 1940 (1) and 1942 (1). (Merged with Democrats in 1944.) New York: American Labor 1938 through 1948 (1). (Party disbanded after 1954.) Ohio: Independent 1950 and 1952 (1). (Defeated by Democrat in 1954.) Wisconsin: Progressive 1934 (7), 1936 (7), 1938 (2), 1940 (3), 1942 (2) and 1944 (1). (Disbanded after 1944. The last Progressive became a Republican in 1946.) And Vermont: Independent 1990 and 1992 (1). National totals: 1928 (1), 1930 (1), 1932 (5), 1934 (10), 1936 (13), 1938 (4), 1940 (5), 1942 (4), 1944 (2), 1946 through 1952 (1), and 1990 and 1992 (1).*

# Reapportionment and Redistricting

Reapportionment, the redistribution of the 435 House seats among the states to reflect shifts in population, and redistricting, the redrawing of congressional district boundaries within the states, are among the most important processes in the U.S. political system. They help to determine whether the House will be dominated by Democrats or Republicans, liberals or conservatives, and whether racial or ethnic minorities receive fair representation.

Reapportionment and redistricting occur every 10 years on the basis of the decennial population census. States where populations grew quickly during the previous 10 years gain congressional seats, while those that lost population or grew much more slowly than the national average lose seats. The number of House members for the rest of the states remains the same.

The states that gain or lose seats must usually make extensive changes in their congressional maps. Even those states with stable delegations must make modifications that account for population shifts within their boundaries, in accordance with Supreme Court "one-person, one-vote" rulings.

In most states, the state legislatures are responsible for drawing up and enacting the new district map. The majority party in each state legislature is thus often in a position to draw a congressional district map that enhances the fortunes of its incumbents and candidates at the expense of the opposing party. "Some members may find their old district no longer recognizable, or their home located in someone else's district. Others will find the music has stopped and they are, quite literally, without a seat. Or they will find themselves thrown together in a single district with another incumbent — often from the same party," wrote one reporter. "The scramble to prevent or minimize such political problems involves some of the most brutal combat in American politics, for the power to draw district lines is the power not only to end one politician's career but often to enfranchise or disenfranchise a neighborhood, a city, a party, a social or economic group or even a race by concentrating or diluting their votes within a given district." [1]

Among the many unique features to emerge in the remarkable nation-creating endeavor of 1787 was a national legislative body whose membership was to be elected by the people and apportioned on the basis of population. In keeping with the nature of the Constitution, however, only fundamental rules and regulations were provided. The interpretation and implementation of the instructions contained in the document were left to future generations.

Within this flexible framework many questions soon arose. How large was the House of Representatives to be? What mathematical formula was to be used in calculating the distribution of seats among the various states? Were the representatives to be elected at large or by districts? If by districts, what standards should be used in fixing their boundaries? Congress and the courts have been wrestling with these questions for 200 years.

Until the mid-20th century such questions generally remained in the hands of the legislators. But with the population increasingly concentrated in urban areas, variations in populations among rural and urban districts in a single state grew more and more pronounced. Efforts to persuade Congress to address the issue of heavily populated but underrepresented areas proved unsuccessful. Legislators from rural areas were so intent on preventing power from slipping from their hands that they managed to block reapportionment of the House after the 1920 census.

Not long afterward litigants tried, repeatedly and unsuccessfully, to persuade the Supreme Court to order the states to revise congressional district boundaries in line with population shifts. A breakthrough finally occurred in 1964 in the case of *Wesberry v. Sanders,* when the Court declared that the Constitution required that "as nearly as practicable, one man's vote in a congressional election is to be worth as much as another's."

In the years that followed the Court repeatedly reaffirmed its one-person, one-vote requirement. Following the 1980 census several states adopted new maps that had districts of nearly equal population but that disregarded other traditional factors — such as the compactness of the district or the integrity of county and city lines. So long as they were equal in population, these partisan gerrymanders, designed to benefit one party at the expense of the other, seemed unassailable in the courts until 1986, when a slim majority of the Supreme Court held that political gerrymanders were subject to constitutional review by federal courts.

The Court, however, offered no opinion on what might constitute an impermissible political gerrymander. As Congress and the state legislatures prepared for the round of redistricting following the 1990 census, the one certainty appeared to be continued litigation on this and other redistricting issues.

## Early History

Modern legislative bodies are descended from the councils of feudal lords and gentry that medieval kings summoned for the purpose of raising revenues and armies. The councils represented only certain groups of people, such as the nobility, the clergy, the landed gentry and town merchants; the notion of equal representation for equal numbers of people or even for all groups of people had not yet begun to develop.

Beginning as little more than administrative and advisory arms of the throne, royal councils in time developed into lawmaking bodies and acquired powers that eventually eclipsed those of the monarchs they served. In England the king's council became Parliament, with the higher nobility and clergy making up the House of Lords and representatives of the gentry and merchants making up the House of Commons. The power struggle between king and council climaxed in the mid-1600s, when the king was executed and a "benevolent" dictatorship was set up under Oliver Cromwell. Although the monarchy was soon restored, by 1800 Parliament was clearly the more powerful branch of government.

The growth of the powers of Parliament, as well as the development of English ideas of representation during the 17th and 18th centuries, had a profound effect on the colonists in America. Representative assemblies were unifying forces behind the breakaway of the colonies from England and the establishment of the newly independent nation.

Colonists in America generally modeled their legislatures after England's, using both population and land units as bases for apportionment. Patterns of early representation varied. "Nowhere did representation bear any uniform relation to the number of electors. Here and there the factor of size had been crudely recognized," Robert Luce noted in his book *Legislative Principles*.[2]

The Continental Congress, with representation from every colony, proclaimed in the Declaration of Independence in 1776 that governments derive "their just powers from the consent of the governed" and that "the right of representation in the legislature" is an "inestimable right" of the people. The Constitutional Convention of 1787 included representatives from all the states. However, in neither of these bodies were the state delegations or voting powers proportional to population.

In New England the town was usually the basis for representation. In the Middle Atlantic region the county frequently was used. Virginia used the county with additional representation for specified cities. In many areas, towns and counties were fairly equal in population, and territorial representation afforded roughly equal representation for equal numbers of people. Delaware's three counties, for example, were of almost equal population and had the same representation in the legislature. But in Virginia the disparity was enormous (from 951 people in one county to 22,015 in another). Thomas Jefferson criticized the state's constitution on the ground that "among those who share the representation, the shares are unequal."[3]

## The Framers' Intentions

What, then, did the Framers of the Constitution have in mind about who would be represented in the House of Representatives and how?

The Constitution declares only that each state is to be allotted a certain number of representatives. It does not state specifically that congressional districts must be equal or nearly equal in population. Nor does it explicitly require that a state create districts at all. However, it seems clear that the first clause of Article I, Section 2, providing that House members should be chosen "by the people of the several states," indicates that the House of Representatives, in contrast to the Senate, was to represent people rather than states.

The third clause of Article I, Section 2, provided that congressional apportionment among the states must be according to population. "There is little point in giving the states congressmen 'according to their respective numbers' if the states do not redistribute the members of their delegations on the same principle," Andrew Hacker argued in his book *Congressional Districting*. "For representatives are not the property of the states, as are the senators, but rather belong to the people who happen to reside within the boundaries of those states. Thus, each citizen has a claim to be regarded as a political unit equal in value to his neighbors."[4]

Hacker also examined the Constitutional Convention, *The Federalist* papers (essays written by Alexander Hamilton, John Jay and James Madison in defense of the Constitution) and the state conventions ratifying the Constitution for evidence of the Framers' intentions with regard to representation. He found that the issue of unequal representation arose only once during debate in the Constitutional Convention. The occasion was Madison's defense of Article I, Section 4, of the proposed Constitution, giving Congress the power to override state regulations on "the times . . . and manner" of holding elections for members of Congress. Madison's argument related to the fact that many state legislatures of the time were badly malapportioned: "The inequality of the representation in the legislatures of particular states would produce a like inequality in their representation in the national legislature, as it was presumable that the counties having the power in the former case would secure it to themselves in the latter."[5]

The implication was that states would create congressional districts and that unequal districting was undesirable and should be prevented.

Madison made this interpretation even more clear in his contributions to *The Federalist* papers. Arguing in favor of the relatively small size of the projected House of Representatives, he wrote in No. 56: "Divide the largest state into ten or twelve districts and it will be found that there will be no peculiar local interests . . . which will not be within the knowledge of the Representative of the district."

In the same paper Madison said, "The Representatives of each state will not only bring with them a considerable knowledge of its laws, and a local knowledge of their respective districts, but will probably in all cases have been members, and may even at the very time be members, of the state legislature, where all the local information and interests of the state are assembled, and from whence they may easily be conveyed by a very few hands into the legislature of the United States." And, finally, in the *Federalist* No. 57 Madison stated that "each Representative of the United States will be elected by five or six thousand citizens." In making these arguments, Madison seems to have assumed that all or most representatives would be elected by districts rather than at large.[6]

In the states' ratifying conventions, the grant to Congress by Article I, Section 4, of ultimate jurisdiction over the "times, places and manner of holding elections" (except the places of choosing senators) held the attention of many delegates. There were differences over the merits of this section, but no justification of unequal districts was prominently used to attack the grant of power. Further evidence that individual districts were the intention of the Founding Fathers was given in the New York ratifying convention, when Alexander Hamilton said, "The natural and proper mode of holding elections will be to divide the state into districts in proportion to the number to be elected. This state will consequently be divided at first into six." [7]

From his study of the sources relating to the question of congressional districting, Hacker concluded,

> There is, then, a good deal of evidence that those who framed and ratified the Constitution intended that the House of Representatives have as its constituency a public in which the votes of all citizens were of equal weight.... The House of Representatives was designed to be a popular chamber, giving the same electoral power to all who had the vote. And the concern of Madison ... that districts be equal in size was an institutional step in the direction of securing this democratic principle.[8]

# Reapportionment: The Number of Seats

The Constitution made the first apportionment, which was to remain in effect until the first census was taken. No reliable figures on the population were available at the time. The Constitution's apportionment yielded a 65-member House. The seats were allotted among the 13 states as follows: New Hampshire, three; Massachusetts, eight; Rhode Island and Providence Plantations, one; Connecticut, five; New York, six; New Jersey, four; Pennsylvania, eight; Delaware, one; Maryland, six; Virginia, ten; North Carolina, five; South Carolina, five; and Georgia, three. This apportionment remained in effect during the First and Second Congresses (1789-93).

Apparently realizing that apportionment of the House was likely to become a major bone of contention, the First Congress submitted to the states a proposed constitutional amendment containing a formula to be used in future reapportionments. The amendment provided that following the taking of a decennial census one representative would be allotted for every 30,000 people until the House membership reached 100. Once that level was reached, there would be one representative for every 40,000 people until the House membership reached 200, when there would be one representative for every 50,000 people.

## First Apportionment by Congress

The states, however, refused to ratify the reapportionment-formula amendment, which forced Congress to enact apportionment legislation after the first census was taken in 1790. The first apportionment bill was sent to the president in March 1792. President George Washington sent the bill back to Congress without his signature — the first presidential veto.

The bill had incorporated the constitutional minimum of 30,000 as the size of each district. But the population of each state was not a simple multiple of 30,000; significant fractions were left over. For example, Vermont was found to be entitled to 2.851 representatives, New Jersey to 5.98 and Virginia to 21.018. A formula had to be found that would deal in the fairest possible manner with unavoidable variations from exact equality.

## Constitutional Provisions

**Article I, Section 2:** The House of Representatives shall be composed of Members chosen every second Year by the People of the several States, and the Electors in each State shall have the Qualifications requisite for Electors of the most numerous Branch of the State Legislature....

Representatives and direct Taxes shall be apportioned among the several States which may be included within this Union, according to their respective Numbers, which shall be determined by adding to the whole Number of free Persons, including those bound to Service for a Term of Years, and excluding Indians not taxed, three fifths of all other Persons. The actual Enumeration shall be made within three Years after the first Meeting of the Congress of the United States, and within every subsequent Term of ten Years, in such Manner as they shall by Law direct. The Number of Representatives shall not exceed one for every thirty thousand, but each State shall have at least one Representative....

**Article I, Section 4:** The Times, Places and Manner of holding Elections for Senators and Representatives, shall be prescribed in each State by the Legislature thereof; but the Congress may at any time by Law make or alter such Regulations, except as to the Place of Chusing Senators....

**Amendment XIV, Section 2 to Article I:** Representatives shall be apportioned among the several States according to their respective numbers, counting the whole number of persons in each State, excluding Indians not taxed. But when the right to vote at any election for the choice of electors for President and Vice President of the United States, Representatives in Congress, the Executive and Judicial officers of a State, or the members of the Legislature thereof, is denied to any of the male inhabitants of such State, being twenty-one years of age, and citizens of the United States, or in any way abridged, except for participation in rebellion, or other crime, the basis of representation therein shall be reduced in the proportion which the number of such male citizens shall bear to the whole number of male citizens twenty-one years of age in such State.

Accordingly, Congress proposed in the first apportionment bill to distribute the members on a fixed ratio of one representative for each 30,000 inhabitants, and give an additional member to each state with a fraction exceeding one-half. Washington's veto was based on the belief that eight states would receive more than one representative for each 30,000 people under this formula.

A motion to override the veto was unsuccessful. A new bill meeting the president's objections, approved in April 1792, provided for a ratio of one member for every 33,000 inhabitants and fixed the exact number of representatives to which each state was entitled. The total membership of the House was to be 105. In dividing the population of the various states by 33,000, all remainders were to be disregarded. Thomas Jefferson devised the solution, known as the method of rejected fractions.

## Jefferson's Method

Jefferson's method of reapportionment resulted in great inequalities among districts. A Vermont district would contain 42,766 inhabitants, a New Jersey district 35,911 and a Virginia district only 33,187. Jefferson's method emphasized what was considered to be the ideal size of a congressional district rather than what the size of the House ought to be.

The reapportionment act based on the census of 1800 continued the ratio of 33,000, which provided a House of 141 members. The third apportionment bill, enacted in 1811, fixed the ratio at 35,000, yielding a House of 181 members. Following the 1820 census Congress set the ratio at 40,000 inhabitants per district, which produced a House of 213 members. The act of May 22, 1832, fixed the ratio at 47,700, resulting in a House of 240 members.

Dissatisfaction with inequalities produced by the method of rejected fractions grew. Launching a vigorous attack against it, Daniel Webster urged adoption of a method that would assign an additional representative to each state with a large fraction. Webster outlined his reasoning in a report he submitted to Congress in 1832:

> The Constitution, therefore, must be understood not as enjoining an absolute relative equality — because that would be demanding an impossibility — but as requiring of Congress to make the apportionment of Representatives among the several states according to their respective numbers, *as near as may be.* That which cannot be done perfectly must be done in a manner as near perfection as can be.... In such a case approximation becomes a rule.[9]

Following the 1840 census Congress adopted a reapportionment method similar to that advocated by Webster. The method fixed a ratio of one representative for every 70,680 people. This figure was reached by deciding on a fixed size of the House in advance (223), dividing that figure into the total national "representative population," and using the result (70,680) as the fixed ratio. The population of each state was then divided by this ratio to find the number of its representatives and the states were assigned an additional representative for each fraction over one-half. Under this method the actual size of the House dropped. *(Congressional apportionment, table, p. 930)*

The modified reapportionment formula adopted by Congress in 1842 was more satisfactory than the previous method, but another change was made following the census of 1850. Proposed by Rep. Samuel F. Vinton of Ohio, the new system became known as the Vinton method.

## Vinton Apportionment Formula

Under the Vinton formula Congress first fixed the size of the House and then distributed the seats. The total qualifying population of the country was divided by the desired number of representatives, and the resulting number became the ratio of population to each representative. The population of each state was divided by this ratio, and each state received the number of representatives equal to the whole number in the quotient for that state. Then, to reach the required size of the House, additional representatives were assigned based on the remaining fractions, beginning with the state having the largest fraction. This procedure differed from the 1842 method only in the last step, which assigned one representative to every state having a fraction larger than one-half.

Proponents of the Vinton method pointed out that it had the distinct advantage of fixing the size of the House in advance and taking into account at least the largest fractions. The concern of the House turned from the ideal size of a congressional district to the ideal size of the House itself.

Under the 1842 reapportionment formula, the exact size of the House could not be fixed in advance. If every state with a fraction over one-half were given an additional representative, the House might wind up with a few more or a few less than the desired number. However, under the Vinton method, only states with the largest fractions were given additional House members and only up to the desired total size of the House.

## Vinton Apportionments

Six reapportionments were carried out under the Vinton method. The 1850 census act contained three provisions not included in any previous law. First, it required reapportionment not only after the census of 1850 but also after all the subsequent censuses; second, it purported to fix the size of the House permanently at 233 members; and third, it provided in advance for an automatic apportionment by the secretary of the interior under the method prescribed in the act.

Following the census of 1860 an automatic reapportionment was to be carried out by the Interior Department. However, because the size of the House was to remain at the 1850 level, some states faced loss of representation and others were to gain fewer seats than they expected. To avert that possibility, an act was approved in 1862 increasing the size of the House to 241 and giving an extra representative to eight states — Illinois, Iowa, Kentucky, Minnesota, Ohio, Pennsylvania, Rhode Island and Vermont.

Apportionment legislation following the 1870 census contained several new provisions. The act fixed the size of the House at 283, with the proviso that the number should be increased if new states were admitted. A supplemental act assigned one additional representative each to Alabama, Florida, Indiana, Louisiana, New Hampshire, New York, Pennsylvania, Tennessee and Vermont.

With the Reconstruction era at its height in the South, the reapportionment legislation of 1872 reflected the desire of Congress to enforce Section 2 of the new 14th Amendment. That section attempted to protect the right of blacks to vote by providing for reduction of representation in the House of a state that interfered with the exercise of that right. The number of representatives of such a state was to be reduced in proportion to the number of inhabitants of voting age whose right to go to the polls was denied or abridged. The reapportionment bill repeated the language of Section 2, but the provision never was put into effect because of the difficulty of determining the exact number of people whose right to vote was being abridged.

The reapportionment act of 1882 provided for a House of 325 members, with additional members for any new states admitted to the Union. No new apportionment provisions were added. The acts of 1891 and 1901 were routine as far as apportionment was concerned. The 1891 measure provided for a House of 356 members, and the 1901 statute increased the number to 386.

## Problems with Vinton Method

Despite the apparent advantages of the Vinton method, certain difficulties revealed themselves as the formula was applied. Zechariah Chafee Jr., of the Harvard Law School summarized these problems in an article in the *Harvard Law Review* in 1929. The method, he pointed out, suffered from what he called the "Alabama paradox." Under that aberration, an increase in the total size of the House might be accompanied by an actual loss of a seat by some states, even though there had been no corresponding change in population. This phenomenon first appeared in tables prepared for Congress in 1881, which gave Alabama eight members in a House of 299 but only seven members in a House of 300. It could even happen that the state that lost a seat was the one state that had expanded in population, while all the others had fewer people.

Chafee concluded from his study of the Vinton method:

> Thus, it is unsatisfactory to fix the ratio of population per Representative before seats are distributed. Either the size of the House comes out haphazard, or, if this be determined in advance, the absurdities of the "Alabama paradox" vitiate the apportionment. Under present conditions, it is essential to determine the size of the House in advance; the problem thereafter is to distribute the required number of seats among the several states as nearly as possible in proportion to their respective populations so that no state is treated unfairly in comparison with any other state.[10]

## Maximum Membership of House

In 1911 the membership of the House was fixed at 433. Provision was made for the addition of one representative each from Arizona and New Mexico, which were expected to become states in the near future. Thus, the size of the House reached 435, where it has remained with the exception of a brief period, 1959-63, when the admission of Alaska and Hawaii raised the total temporarily to 437.

Limiting the size of the House amounted to recognition that the body soon would expand to unmanageable proportions if Congress continued the practice of adding new seats every 10 years to match population gains without depriving any state of its existing representation. Agreement on a fixed number made the task of reapportionment all the more difficult when the population not only increased but became much more mobile. Population shifts brought Congress up hard against the politically painful necessity of taking seats away from slow-growing states to give the fast-growing states adequate representation.

A new mathematical calculation was adopted for the reapportionment following the 1910 census. Devised by W. F. Willcox of Cornell University, the new system established a priority list that assigned seats progressively, beginning with the first seat above the constitutional minimum of at least one seat for each state. When there were 48 states, this method was used to assign the forty-ninth member, the fiftieth member, and so on, until the agreed upon size of the House was reached. The method was called major fractions and was used after the censuses of 1910, 1930 and 1940. There was no reapportionment after the 1920 census.

## 1920s Struggle

The results of the 14th decennial census were announced in December 1920, just after the short session of the 66th Congress convened. The 1920 census showed that for the first time in history most Americans were urban residents. This came as a profound shock to people accustomed to emphasizing the nation's rural traditions and the virtues of life on farms and in small towns as Thomas Jefferson had. Jefferson once wrote:

> Those who labor in the earth are the chosen people of God, if ever He had a chosen people, whose breasts He had made His peculiar deposit for substantial and genuine virtue.... The mobs of great cities add just as much

to the support of pure government as sores do to the strength of the human body.... I think our governments will remain virtuous for many centuries as long as they are chiefly agricultural: and this shall be as long as there shall be vacant lands in any part of America. When they get piled up upon one another in large cities as in Europe, they will become corrupt as in Europe.[11]

As their power waned throughout the latter part of the nineteenth century and the early part of the twentieth, farmers clung to the Jeffersonian belief that somehow they were more pure and virtuous than the growing number of urban residents. When finally faced with the fact that they were in the minority, these country residents put up a strong rearguard action to prevent the inevitable shift of congressional districts to the cities. They succeeded in postponing reapportionment legislation for almost a decade.

Rural representatives insisted that, because the 1920 census was taken as of Jan. 1, the farm population had been undercounted. In support of this contention, they argued that many farm laborers were seasonally employed in the cities at that time of year. Furthermore, midwinter road conditions probably had prevented enumerators from visiting many farms, they said, and other farmers were said to have been uncounted because they were absent on winter vacation trips. The change of the census date to Jan. 1 in 1920 had been made to conform to recommendations of the U.S. Department of Agriculture, which had asserted that the census should be taken early in the year if an accurate statistical picture of farming conditions was to be obtained.

Another point raised by rural legislators was that large numbers of unnaturalized aliens were congregated in northern cities, with the result that these cities gained at the expense of constituencies made up mostly of citizens of the United States. Rep. Homer Hoch, R-Kan., submitted a table showing that in a House of 435 representatives, exclusion from the census count of people not naturalized would have altered the allocation of seats in 16 states. Southern and Western farming states would have retained the number of seats allocated to them in 1911 or would have gained, while Northern industrial states and California would have lost or at least would have gained fewer seats.

A constitutional amendment to exclude all aliens from the enumeration for purposes of reapportionment was proposed during the 70th Congress (1927-29) by Hoch, Sen. Arthur Capper, R-Kan., and others. But nothing further came of the proposals.

## Reapportionment Bills Opposed

The first bill to reapportion the House according to the 1920 census was drafted by the House Census Committee early in 1921. Proceeding on the principle that no state should have its representation reduced, the committee proposed to increase the total number of representatives from 435 to 483. But the House voted 267-76 to keep its membership at 435. The bill then was blocked by a Senate committee, where it died when the 66th Congress expired March 4, 1921.

Early in the 67th Congress, the House Census Committee again reported a bill, this time fixing the total membership at 460, an increase of 25. Two states — Maine and Massachusetts — would have lost one representative each and 16 states would have gained. On the House floor an unsuccessful attempt was made to fix the number at the existing 435, and the House sent the bill back to committee.

During the 68th Congress (1923-25), the House Census Committee failed to report any reapportionment bill. In April 1926, midway through the 69th Congress (1925-27), it

# Congressional Apportionment, 1789-1990

Year of Census[1]

| State | Constitution[2] (1789) | 1790 | 1800 | 1810 | 1820 | 1830 | 1840 | 1850 | 1860 | 1870 | 1880 | 1890 | 1900 | 1910 | 1930[3] | 1940 | 1950 | 1960 | 1970 | 1980 | 1990 |
|---|---|---|---|---|---|---|---|---|---|---|---|---|---|---|---|---|---|---|---|---|---|
| Ala. | | | | 1[4] | 3 | 5 | 7 | 7 | 6 | 8 | 8 | 9 | 9 | 10 | 9 | 9 | 9 | 8 | 7 | 7 | 7 |
| Alaska | | | | | | | | | | | | | | | | | 1[4] | 1 | 1 | 1 | 1 |
| Ariz. | | | | | | | | | | | | | | 1[4] | 1 | 2 | 2 | 3 | 4 | 5 | 6 |
| Ark. | | | | | | 1[4] | 1 | 2 | 3 | 4 | 5 | 6 | 7 | 7 | 7 | 7 | 6 | 4 | 4 | 4 | 4 |
| Calif. | | | | | | | 2[4] | 2 | 3 | 4 | 6 | 7 | 8 | 11 | 20 | 23 | 30 | 38 | 43 | 45 | 52 |
| Colo. | | | | | | | | | | 1[4] | 1 | 2 | 3 | 4 | 4 | 4 | 4 | 4 | 5 | 6 | 6 |
| Conn. | 5 | 7 | 7 | 7 | 6 | 6 | 4 | 4 | 4 | 4 | 4 | 4 | 5 | 5 | 6 | 6 | 6 | 6 | 6 | 6 | 6 |
| Del. | 1 | 1 | 1 | 2 | 1 | 1 | 1 | 1 | 1 | 1 | 1 | 1 | 1 | 1 | 1 | 1 | 1 | 1 | 1 | 1 | 1 |
| Fla. | | | | | | | 1[4] | 1 | 1 | 2 | 2 | 2 | 3 | 4 | 5 | 6 | 8 | 12 | 15 | 19 | 23 |
| Ga. | 3 | 2 | 4 | 6 | 7 | 9 | 8 | 8 | 7 | 9 | 10 | 11 | 11 | 12 | 10 | 10 | 10 | 10 | 10 | 10 | 11 |
| Hawaii | | | | | | | | | | | | | | | | | 1[4] | 2 | 2 | 2 | 2 |
| Idaho | | | | | | | | | | | 1[4] | 1 | 1 | 2 | 2 | 2 | 2 | 2 | 2 | 2 | 2 |
| Ill. | | | | 1[4] | 1 | 3 | 7 | 9 | 14 | 19 | 20 | 22 | 25 | 27 | 27 | 26 | 25 | 24 | 24 | 22 | 20 |
| Ind. | | | | 1[4] | 3 | 7 | 10 | 11 | 11 | 13 | 13 | 13 | 13 | 13 | 12 | 11 | 11 | 11 | 11 | 10 | 10 |
| Iowa | | | | | | | 2[4] | 2 | 6 | 9 | 11 | 11 | 11 | 11 | 9 | 8 | 8 | 7 | 6 | 6 | 5 |
| Kan. | | | | | | | | | 1 | 3 | 7 | 8 | 8 | 8 | 7 | 6 | 6 | 5 | 5 | 5 | 4 |
| Ky. | | 2 | 6 | 10 | 12 | 13 | 10 | 10 | 9 | 10 | 11 | 11 | 11 | 11 | 9 | 9 | 8 | 7 | 7 | 7 | 6 |
| La. | | | | 1[4] | 3 | 3 | 4 | 4 | 5 | 6 | 6 | 6 | 7 | 8 | 8 | 8 | 8 | 8 | 8 | 8 | 7 |
| Maine | | | | 7[4] | 7 | 8 | 7 | 6 | 5 | 5 | 4 | 4 | 4 | 4 | 3 | 3 | 3 | 2 | 2 | 2 | 2 |
| Md. | 6 | 8 | 9 | 9 | 9 | 8 | 6 | 6 | 5 | 6 | 6 | 6 | 6 | 6 | 6 | 6 | 7 | 8 | 8 | 8 | 8 |
| Mass. | 8 | 14 | 17 | 13[5] | 13 | 12 | 10 | 11 | 10 | 11 | 12 | 13 | 14 | 16 | 15 | 14 | 14 | 12 | 12 | 11 | 10 |
| Mich. | | | | | | 1[4] | 3 | 4 | 6 | 9 | 11 | 12 | 12 | 13 | 17 | 17 | 18 | 19 | 19 | 18 | 16 |
| Minn. | | | | | | | | 2[4] | 2 | 3 | 5 | 7 | 9 | 10 | 9 | 9 | 9 | 8 | 8 | 8 | 8 |
| Miss. | | | | 1[4] | 1 | 2 | 4 | 5 | 5 | 6 | 7 | 7 | 8 | 8 | 7 | 7 | 6 | 5 | 5 | 5 | 5 |
| Mo. | | | | | 1 | 2 | 5 | 7 | 9 | 13 | 14 | 15 | 16 | 16 | 13 | 13 | 11 | 10 | 10 | 9 | 9 |
| Mont. | | | | | | | | | | | 1[4] | 1 | 1 | 2 | 2 | 2 | 2 | 2 | 2 | 2 | 1 |
| Neb. | | | | | | | | | 1[4] | 1 | 3 | 6 | 6 | 6 | 5 | 4 | 4 | 3 | 3 | 3 | 3 |
| Nev. | | | | | | | | | 1[4] | 1 | 1 | 1 | 1 | 1 | 1 | 1 | 1 | 1 | 1 | 2 | 2 |
| N.H. | 3 | 4 | 5 | 6 | 6 | 5 | 4 | 3 | 3 | 3 | 2 | 2 | 2 | 2 | 2 | 2 | 2 | 2 | 2 | 2 | 2 |
| N.J. | 4 | 5 | 6 | 6 | 6 | 6 | 5 | 5 | 5 | 7 | 7 | 8 | 10 | 12 | 14 | 14 | 14 | 15 | 15 | 14 | 13 |
| N.M. | | | | | | | | | | | | | | 1[4] | 1 | 2 | 2 | 2 | 2 | 3 | 3 |
| N.Y. | 6 | 10 | 17 | 27 | 34 | 40 | 34 | 33 | 31 | 33 | 34 | 34 | 37 | 43 | 45 | 45 | 43 | 41 | 39 | 34 | 31 |
| N.C. | 5 | 10 | 12 | 13 | 13 | 13 | 9 | 8 | 7 | 8 | 9 | 9 | 10 | 10 | 11 | 12 | 12 | 11 | 11 | 11 | 12 |
| N.D. | | | | | | | | | | | 1[4] | 1 | 2 | 3 | 2 | 2 | 2 | 2 | 1 | 1 | 1 |
| Ohio | | | 1[4] | 6 | 14 | 19 | 21 | 21 | 19 | 20 | 21 | 21 | 21 | 22 | 24 | 23 | 23 | 24 | 23 | 21 | 19 |
| Okla. | | | | | | | | | | | | | 5[4] | 8 | 9 | 8 | 6 | 6 | 6 | 6 | 6 |
| Ore. | | | | | | | | 1[4] | 1 | 1 | 1 | 2 | 2 | 3 | 3 | 4 | 4 | 4 | 4 | 5 | 5 |
| Pa. | 8 | 13 | 18 | 23 | 26 | 28 | 24 | 25 | 24 | 27 | 28 | 30 | 32 | 36 | 34 | 33 | 30 | 27 | 25 | 23 | 21 |
| R.I. | 1 | 2 | 2 | 2 | 2 | 2 | 2 | 2 | 2 | 2 | 2 | 2 | 2 | 3 | 2 | 2 | 2 | 2 | 2 | 2 | 2 |
| S.C. | 5 | 6 | 8 | 9 | 9 | 9 | 7 | 6 | 4 | 5 | 7 | 7 | 7 | 7 | 6 | 6 | 6 | 6 | 6 | 6 | 6 |
| S.D. | | | | | | | | | | | 2[4] | 2 | 2 | 3 | 2 | 2 | 2 | 2 | 2 | 1 | 1 |
| Tenn. | | 1[4] | 3 | 6 | 9 | 13 | 11 | 10 | 8 | 10 | 10 | 10 | 10 | 10 | 9 | 10 | 9 | 9 | 8 | 9 | 9 |
| Texas | | | | | | | 2[4] | 2 | 4 | 6 | 11 | 13 | 16 | 18 | 21 | 21 | 22 | 23 | 24 | 27 | 30 |
| Utah | | | | | | | | | | | | 1[4] | 1 | 2 | 2 | 2 | 2 | 2 | 2 | 3 | 3 |
| Vt. | | 2 | 4 | 6 | 5 | 5 | 4 | 3 | 3 | 3 | 2 | 2 | 2 | 2 | 1 | 1 | 1 | 1 | 1 | 1 | 1 |
| Va. | 10 | 19 | 22 | 23 | 22 | 21 | 15 | 13 | 11 | 9 | 10 | 10 | 10 | 10 | 9 | 9 | 10 | 10 | 10 | 10 | 11 |
| Wash. | | | | | | | | | | | 1[4] | 2 | 3 | 5 | 6 | 6 | 7 | 7 | 7 | 8 | 9 |
| W.Va. | | | | | | | | | | 3 | 4 | 4 | 5 | 6 | 6 | 6 | 6 | 5 | 4 | 4 | 3 |
| Wis. | | | | | | | 2[4] | 3 | 6 | 8 | 9 | 10 | 11 | 11 | 10 | 10 | 10 | 10 | 9 | 9 | 9 |
| Wyo. | | | | | | | | | | | 1[4] | 1 | 1 | 1 | 1 | 1 | 1 | 1 | 1 | 1 | 1 |
| Total | 65 | 106 | 142 | 186 | 213 | 242 | 232 | 237 | 243 | 293 | 332 | 357 | 391 | 435 | 435 | 435 | 437[6] | 435 | 435 | 435 | 435 |

1. Apportionment effective with congressional election two years after census.
2. Original apportionment made in Constitution, pending first census.
3. No apportionment was made in 1920.
4. These figures are not based on any census, but indicate the provisional representation accorded newly admitted states by Congress, pending the next census.
5. Twenty members were assigned to Massachusetts, but seven of these were credited to Maine when that area became a state.
6. Normally 435, but temporarily increased two seats by Congress when Alaska and Hawaii became states.

Sources: *Biographical Directory of the United States Congress 1774-1989;* Bureau of the Census.

became apparent that the committee would not produce a reapportionment measure. A motion to discharge a reapportionment bill from the committee failed, however, and the matter once again put aside.

### Coolidge Intervention

President Calvin Coolidge, who previously had made no reference to reapportionment in his communications to Congress, announced in January 1927 that he favored passage of a new apportionment bill during the short session of the 69th Congress, which would end in less than two months. The House Census Committee refused to act. Its chairman, Rep. E. Hart Fenn, R-Conn., therefore moved in the House to suspend the rules and pass a bill he had introduced authorizing the secretary of commerce to reapportion the House immediately after the 1930 census. The motion was voted down 183-197.

The Fenn bill was rewritten early in the 70th Congress (1927-29) to give Congress itself a chance to act before the proposed reapportionment by the secretary of commerce should go into effect. The House passed an amended version of the Fenn bill in January 1929, and it was quickly reported by the Senate Commerce Committee. Repeated efforts to bring it up for floor action ahead of other bills failed. Its supporters gave up the fight when it became evident that senators from states slated to lose representation were ready to carry on a filibuster that would have blocked not only reapportionment but all other measures.

### Hoover Intervention

President Herbert Hoover listed provision for the 1930 census and reapportionment as "matters of emergency legislation" that should be acted upon in the special session of the 71st Congress, which was convened on April 15, 1929. In response to this urgent request, the Senate June 13 passed, 48-37, a combined census-reapportionment bill that had been approved by voice vote of the House two days earlier.

The 1929 law established a permanent system of reapportioning the 435 House seats following each census. It provided that immediately after the convening of the 71st Congress for its short session in December 1930, the president was to transmit to Congress a statement showing the population of each state together with an apportionment of representatives to each state based on the existing size of the House. Failing enactment of new apportionment legislation, that apportionment would go into effect without further action and would remain in effect for ensuing elections to the House of Representatives until another census had been taken and another reapportionment made.

Because two decades had passed between reapportionments, a greater shift than usual took place following the 1930 census. California's House delegation was almost doubled, rising from 11 to 20. Michigan gained four seats, Texas three, and New Jersey, New York and Ohio two each. Twenty-one states lost a total of 27 seats; Missouri lost three, and Georgia, Iowa, Kentucky and Pennsylvania each lost two.

To test the fairness of two allocation methods — the familiar major fractions and the new equal proportions system — the 1929 act required the president to report the distribution of seats by both methods. But, pending legislation to the contrary, the method of major fractions was to be used.

The two methods gave an identical distribution of seats based on 1930 census figures. However, in 1940 the two methods gave different results: under major fractions, Mich-

igan would gain a seat lost by Arkansas; under equal proportions, no change would occur in either state. The automatic reapportionment provisions of the 1929 act went into effect in January 1941. But the House Census Committee moved to reverse the result, favoring the method of equal proportions and the certain Democratic seat in Arkansas over a possible Republican gain if the seat were shifted to Michigan. The Democratic-controlled Congress went along, adopting equal proportions as the method to be used in reapportionment calculations after the 1950 and subsequent censuses, and making this action retroactive to January 1941 to save Arkansas its seat.

While politics doubtless played a part in the timing of the action taken in 1941, the method of equal proportions had come to be accepted as the best available: It had been worked out by Edward V. Huntington of Harvard in 1921. At the request of the Speaker of the House, all known methods of apportionment were considered in 1929 by the National Academy of Sciences Committee on Apportionment. The committee expressed its preference for equal proportions.

### Method of Equal Proportions

The method of equal proportions involves complicated mathematical calculations. In brief, each of the 50 states is initially assigned the one seat to which it is entitled by the Constitution. Then "priority numbers" for states to receive second seats, third seats and so on are calculated by dividing the state's population by the square root of $n(n-1)$, where "n" is the number of seats for that state. The priority numbers are then lined up in order and the seats given to the states with priority numbers until 435 are awarded.

The method is designed to make the proportional difference in the average district size in any two states as small as possible. After the 1981 reapportionment, for example, South Dakota's single district was the most populous, with 690,768 residents, while Montana's two districts, each with slightly fewer than 400,000 people, were the least populous. Under the 1990 apportionment, Montana lost a seat; its remaining district is the most populous, with 803,655 residents. With 455,975 people, Wyoming's single district is the least populous. The mean population per district nationwide is about 572,500.

### The 1990 Apportionment

Concern about the accuracy of the 1990 census, which is the basis for reapportionment and redistricting, led to calls for a statistical adjustment of the census count to compensate for a population undercount. An undercount was not a new problem. In 1980 the Census Bureau estimated that it counted about 99 percent of the white population but only about 94 percent of the blacks. In addition to determining the number of House seats each state has, the census is also the basis for distributing funding for many federal aid programs. Democrats, especially those representing inner-city districts where the undercount is comparatively high, have long argued for a statistical adjustment to compensate for undercounting. Several cities with large minority populations sought but failed to win adjustment of the 1980 census count.

Given the disappointing response to the census questionnaire and other problems encountered in conducting the 1990 census, many observers estimated that the undercount would be higher than the 1980 undercount. But the controversy over the 1990 count began even before the census was taken, when the Commerce Department, the parent agency to the Census Bureau, announced in 1987 that it would not

# Origins of the Gerrymander

The practice of "gerrymandering"—the excessive manipulation of the shape of a legislative district to benefit a certain incumbent or party — is probably as old as the Republic, but the name originated in 1812.

In that year the Massachusetts Legislature carved out of Essex County a district which historian John Fiske said had a "dragonlike contour." When the painter Gilbert Stuart saw the misshapen district, he penciled in a head, wings, and claws and exclaimed: "That will do for a salamander!" — to which editor Benjamin Russell replied: "Better say a Gerrymander" — after Elbridge Gerry, then governor of Massachusetts.

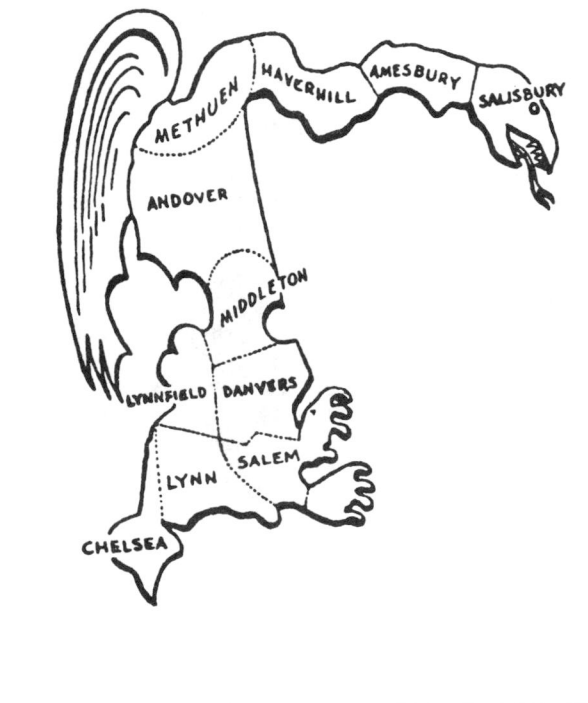

statistically adjust the 1990 data. That fueled charges that the Republican administration was undercounting a Democratic constituency. New York City, along with other cities, states and civil rights organizations, quickly brought a lawsuit to force the Census Bureau to make a statistical adjustment to account for people who were missed. But in April 1993 a federal judge in New York upheld the Commerce Department's decision not to adjust the head count.

## Redistricting: Drawing the Lines

Although the Constitution contained provisions for the apportionment of U.S. House seats among the states, it was silent about how the members should be elected. From the beginning most states divided their territory into geographic districts, permitting only one member of Congress to be elected from each district.

But some states allowed would-be House members to run at large, with voters able to cast as many votes as there

were seats to be filled. Still other states created what were known as multimember districts, in which a single geographic unit would elect two or more members of the House. At various times, some states used combinations of these methods. For example, a state might elect 10 representatives from 10 individual districts and two at large.

In the first few elections to the House, New Hampshire, Pennsylvania, New Jersey and Georgia elected their representatives at large, as did Rhode Island and Delaware, the two states with only a single representative. Districts were used in Massachusetts, New York, Maryland, Virginia and South Carolina. In Connecticut a preliminary election was held to nominate three times as many people as the number of representatives to be chosen at large in the subsequent election. In 1840, 22 of the 31 states elected their representatives by districts. New Hampshire, New Jersey, Georgia, Alabama, Mississippi and Missouri, with a combined representation of 33 House seats, elected their representatives at large. Three states, Arkansas, Delaware and Florida, had only one representative each.

Those states that used congressional districts quickly developed what came to be known as the gerrymander. The term refers to the practice of drawing district lines so as to maximize the advantage of a political party or interest group. The name originated from a salamander-shaped congressional district created by the Massachusetts legislature in 1812 when Elbridge Gerry was governor. *(Origins of the Gerrymander, box, this page)*

Constant efforts were made during the early 1800s to lay down national rules, by means of a constitutional amendment, for congressional districting. The first resolution proposing a mandatory division of each state into districts was introduced in Congress in 1800. In 1802 the legislatures of Vermont and North Carolina adopted resolutions in support of such action. From 1816 to 1826, 22 states adopted resolutions proposing the election of representatives by districts.

In Congress Sen. Mahlon Dickerson, R-N.J., proposed such an amendment regularly almost every year from 1817 to 1826. It was adopted by the Senate three times, in 1819, 1820 and 1822, but each time it failed to reach a vote in the House. Although the constitutional amendment was unsuccessful, a law passed in 1842 required contiguous single-member congressional districts. That law required representatives to be "elected by districts composed of contiguous territory equal in number to the representatives to which said state may be entitled, no one district electing more than one Representative."

The districting provisions of the 1842 act were not repeated in the legislation that followed the 1850 census. But in 1862 an act separate from the reapportionment act revived the provisions of the act of 1842 requiring districts to be composed of contiguous territory.

The 1872 reapportionment act again repeated the districting provisions and went even further by adding that districts should contain "as nearly as practicable an equal number of inhabitants." Similar provisions were included in the acts of 1881 and 1891. In the act of 1901, the words "compact territory" were added, and the clause then read "contiguous and compact territory and containing as nearly as practicable an equal number of inhabitants." This requirement appeared also in the legislation of 1911. The "contiguous and compact" provisions of the act subsequently lapsed, and Congress has never replaced them.

Several unsuccessful attempts were made to enforce redistricting provisions. Despite the districting requirements enacted in 1842, New Hampshire, Georgia, Mississippi and Missouri elected their representatives at large that autumn. When the new House convened for its first session, on December 4, 1843, objection was made to seating the representatives of the four states.

The House debated the matter in February 1844. With the Democratic party holding a majority of more than 60, and with 18 of the 21 challenged members being Democrats, the House decided to seat the members. However, by 1848 all four states had come around to electing their representatives by districts.

The next challenge a representative encountered over federal districting laws occurred in 1901. A charge was leveled that the existing Kentucky redistricting law did not comply with the reapportionment law of 1901; the charge aimed at preventing the seating of Rep. George G. Gilbert, D, of Kentucky's 8th District. The committee assigned to investigate the matter turned aside the challenge, asserting that the federal act was not binding on the states. The reasons given were practical and political:

> Your committee are therefore of opinion that a proper construction of the Constitution does not warrant the conclusion that by that instrument Congress is clothed with power to determine the boundaries of Congressional districts, or to revise the acts of a State Legislature in fixing such boundaries; and your committee is further of opinion that even if such power is to be implied from the language of the Constitution, it would be in the last degree unwise and intolerable that it should exercise it. To do so would be to put into the hands of Congress the ability to disfranchise, in effect, a large body of the electors. It would give Congress the power to apply to all the States, in favor of one party, a general system of gerrymandering. It is true that the same method is to a large degree resorted to by the several states, but the division of political power is so general and diverse that notwithstanding the inherent vice of the system of gerrymandering, some kind of equality of distribution results.[12]

In 1908 the Virginia legislature transferred Floyd County from the 5th District to the 6th District. As a result, the population of the 5th was reduced from 175,579 to 160,191 and that of the 6th was increased from 181,571 to 196,959. The average for the state was 185,418. The newly elected representative from the 5th District, Edward W. Saunders, D, was challenged by his opponent in the election on the ground that the Virginia law of 1908 was null and void because it did not conform with the federal reapportionment law of 1901, or with the constitution of Virginia. Had the district included the counties that were a part of it before enactment of the 1908 state legislation, Saunders's opponent would have had a majority of the votes.

The majority of the congressional investigating committee upheld the challenge and recommended that Saunders's opponent be seated. For the first time, it appeared that the districting legislation would be enforced, but the House did not take action on the committee's report and Saunders was seated.

# Court Action on Redistricting

After the long and desultory battle over reapportionment in the 1920s, those who were unhappy over the inaction of Congress and the state legislatures began taking their cases to court. At first, the protestors had no luck. But as the population disparities grew in both federal and state legislative districts and the Supreme Court began

to show a tendency to intervene, the objectors were more successful.

Finally, in a series of decisions beginning in 1962 with *Baker v. Carr* (369 U.S. 186) the Court exerted great influence over the redistricting process, ordering that congressional districts as well as state and local legislative districts be drawn so that their populations would be as nearly equal as possible.[13]

## Supreme Court's 1932 Decision

*Baker v. Carr* essentially reversed the direction the Court had taken in 1932. *Wood v. Broom* (287 U.S. 1) was a case challenging the constitutionality of a Mississippi redistricting law because it violated the standards of the 1911 federal redistricting act. The question was whether the federal act was still in effect. That law, which required that districts be separate, compact, contiguous and equally populated, had been neither specifically repealed nor reaffirmed in the 1929 reapportionment act.

Speaking for the Court, Chief Justice Charles Evans Hughes ruled that the 1911 act, in effect, had expired with the approval of the 1929 apportionment act and that the standards of the 1911 act therefore were no longer applicable. The Court reversed the decision of a lower federal court, which had permanently enjoined elections under the new Mississippi redistricting act.

That the Supreme Court upheld a state law that failed to provide for districts of equal population was almost less important than the minority opinion that the Court should not have heard the case. Justices Louis D. Brandeis, Harlan F. Stone, Owen J. Roberts and Benjamin N. Cardozo, while concurring in the majority opinion, said they would have dismissed the Wood suit for "want of equity." The "want-of-equity" phrase in this context suggested a policy of judicial self-limitation with respect to the entire question of judicial involvement in essentially "political" questions.

## 'Political Thicket'

Not until 1946, in *Colegrove v. Green* (328 U.S. 549), did the Court again rule in a significant case dealing with congressional redistricting. The case was brought by Kenneth Colegrove, a political science professor at Northwestern University, who alleged that congressional districts in Illinois, which varied between 112,116 and 914,053 in population, were so unequal that they violated the 14th Amendment's guarantee of equal protection of the laws. A seven-member Supreme Court divided 4-3 in dismissing the suit.

Justice Felix Frankfurter gave the opinion of the Court, speaking for himself and Justices Stanley F. Reed and Harold H. Burton. Frankfurter's opinion cited *Wood v. Broom* to indicate that Congress had deliberately removed the standard set by the 1911 act. He also said that he, Reed, and Burton agreed with the minority that the Court should have dismissed the case. The issue, Frankfurter said, was

> of a peculiarly political nature and therefore not meant for judicial interpretation.... The short of it is that the Constitution has conferred upon Congress exclusive authority to secure fair representation by the states in the popular House and has left to that House determination whether states have fulfilled their responsibility. If Congress failed in exercising its powers, whereby standards of fairness are offended, the remedy lies ultimately with the people.... To sustain this action would cut very deep into the very being of Congress. Courts ought not to enter this political thicket. The remedy for

unfairness in districting is to secure state legislatures that will apportion properly, or to invoke the ample powers of Congress.

Frankfurter also said that the Court could not affirmatively remap congressional districts and that elections at large would be politically undesirable.

In a dissenting opinion Justice Hugo L. Black, joined by Justices William O. Douglas and Frank Murphy, maintained that the district court did have jurisdiction over congressional redistricting. The three justices cited as evidence a section of the U.S. Code that allowed district courts to redress deprivations of constitutional rights occurring through action of the states. Black's opinion also rested on an earlier case in which the Court had indicated that federal constitutional questions, unless "frivolous," fall under the jurisdiction of the federal courts. Black asserted that the appellants had standing to sue and that the population disparities violated the equal protection clause of the 14th Amendment.

With the Court split 3-3 on whether the judiciary had or should exercise jurisdiction, Justice Wiley B. Rutledge cast the deciding vote in *Colegrove v. Green*. On the question of justiciability, Rutledge agreed with Black, Douglas and Murphy that the issue could be considered by the federal courts. Thus a majority of the Court participating in the *Colegrove* case felt that congressional redistricting cases were justiciable.

Yet on the question of granting relief in this specific instance, Rutledge agreed with Frankfurter, Reed and Burton that the case should be dismissed. He pointed out that four of the nine justices in *Wood v. Broom* had felt that dismissal should be for want of equity. Rutledge saw a "want-of-equity" situation in *Colegrove v. Green* as well. "I think the gravity of the constitutional questions raised [are] so great, together with the possibility of collision [with the political departments of the government], that the admonition [against avoidable constitutional decision] is appropriate to be followed here," Rutledge said. Jurisdiction, he thought, should be exercised "only in the most compelling circumstances." He thought that "the shortness of time remaining [before the forthcoming election] makes it doubtful whether action could or would be taken in time to secure for petitioners the effective relief they seek." Rutledge warned that congressional elections at large would deprive citizens of representation by districts, "which the prevailing policy of Congress demands." In the case of at-large elections, he said, "the cure sought may be worse than the disease." For all these reasons he concluded that the case was "one in which the Court may properly, and should, decline to exercise its jurisdiction."

## Changing Views

In the ensuing years, law professors, political scientists and other commentators increasingly criticized the *Colegrove* doctrine and grew impatient with the Supreme Court's reluctance to intervene in redistricting disputes. At the same time, the membership of the Court was changing, and the new members were more inclined toward judicial action on redistricting.

In the 1950s the Court decided two cases that laid some groundwork for its subsequent reapportionment decisions. The first was *Brown v. Board of Education* (347 U.S. 483, 1954), the historic school desegregation case, in which the Court decided that an individual citizen could assert a right to equal protection of the laws under the 14th Amendment,

contrary to the "separate but equal" doctrine of public facilities for white and black citizens. Six years later, in *Gomillion v. Lightfoot* (364 U.S. 339, 1960), the Court held that the Alabama legislature could not draw the city limits of Tuskegee so as to exclude nearly every black vote. In his opinion Justice Frankfurter drew a clear line between redistricting challenges based on the 14th Amendment, such as *Colegrove,* and challenges to discriminatory redistricting based on the 15th Amendment's voting rights protections, as in *Gomillion*. But Justice Charles E. Whittaker said that the equal protection clause was the proper constitutional basis for the decision. One commentator later remarked that *Gomillion* amounted to a "dragon" in the "political thicket" of *Colegrove*.

By 1962 only three members of the *Colegrove* Court remained: Justices Black and Douglas, dissenters in that case, and Justice Frankfurter, aging spokesman for restraint in the exercise of judicial power.

By then it was clear that malapportionment within the states no longer could be ignored. By 1960 not a single state legislative body existed in which there was not at least a 2-to-1 population disparity between the most and the least heavily populated districts. For example, the disparity was 242-1 in the Connecticut House, 223-1 in the Nevada Senate 141-1 in the Rhode Island Senate and 9-1 in the Georgia Senate. Studies of the effective vote of large and small counties in state legislatures between 1910 and 1960 showed that the effective vote of the most populous counties had slipped while their percentage of the national population had more than doubled. The most lightly populated counties, on the other hand, advanced from a position of slight overrepresentation to one of extreme overrepresentation, holding almost twice as many seats as they would be entitled to by population size alone. Predictably, the rural-dominated state legislatures resisted every move toward reapportioning state legislative districts to reflect new population patterns.

Population imbalance among congressional districts was substantially lopsided but by no means so gross. In Texas the 1960 census showed the most heavily populated district had four times as many inhabitants as the most lightly populated. Arizona, Maryland and Ohio each had at least one district with three times as many inhabitants as the least populated. In most cases rural areas benefited from the population imbalance in congressional districts. As a result of the postwar population movement out of central cities to the surrounding areas, the suburbs were the most underrepresented.

### Baker v. Carr

Against this background a group of Tennessee city dwellers successfully broke the longstanding precedent against federal court involvement in legislative apportionment problems. For more than half a century, since 1901, the Tennessee legislature had refused to reapportion itself, even though a decennial reapportionment based on population was specifically required by the state's constitution. In the meantime, Tennessee's population had grown and shifted dramatically to urban areas. By 1960 the House legislative districts ranged from 3,454 to 36,031 in population, while the Senate districts ranged from 39,727 to 108,094. Appeals by urban residents to the rural-controlled Tennessee legislature proved fruitless. A suit brought in the state courts to force reapportionment was rejected on grounds that the courts should stay out of legislative matters.

City dwellers then appealed to the federal courts, stating that they had no redress: the legislature had refused to act for more than half a century, the state courts had refused to intervene and Tennessee had no referendum or initiative laws. They charged that there was "a debasement of their votes by virtue of the incorrect, obsolete and unconstitutional apportionment" to such an extent that they were being deprived of their right to equal protection of the laws under the 14th Amendment.

The Supreme Court on March 26, 1962, handed down its historic decision in *Baker v. Carr,* ruling in favor of the Tennessee city dwellers by a 6-2 margin. In the majority opinion, Justice William J. Brennan, Jr., emphasized that the federal judiciary had the power to review the apportionment of state legislatures under the 14th Amendment's equal protection clause. "The mere fact that a suit seeks protection as a political right," Brennan wrote, "does not mean that it presents a political question" that the courts should avoid.

In a vigorous dissent, Justice Frankfurter said the majority decision constituted "a massive repudiation of the experience of our whole past" and was an assertion of "destructively novel judicial power." He contended that the lack of any clear basis for relief "catapults the lower courts" into a "mathematical quagmire." Frankfurter insisted that "there is not under our Constitution a judicial remedy for every political mischief." Appeal for relief, Frankfurter maintained, should not be made in the courts, but "to an informed civically militant electorate."

The Court had abandoned the view that malapportionment questions were outside its competence. But it stopped there and in *Baker v. Carr* did not address the merits of the challenge to the legislative districts.

## Gray v. Sanders

The one-person, one-vote rule was set out by the Court almost exactly one year after its decision in *Baker v. Carr.* But the case in which the announcement came did not involve congressional districts.

In *Gray v. Sanders* (372 U.S. 368, 1963) the Court found that Georgia's county-unit primary system for electing state officials — a system that weighted votes to give advantage to rural districts in statewide primary elections — denied voters equal protection of the laws. All votes in a statewide election must have equal weight, the Court held:

> How then can one person be given twice or 10 times the voting power of another person in a statewide election merely because he lives in a rural area or because he lives in the smallest rural county? Once the geographical unit for which a representative is to be chosen is designated, all who participate in the election are to have an equal vote — whatever their race, whatever their sex, whatever their occupation, whatever their income, and wherever their home may be in that geographical unit. This is required by the Equal Protection Clause of the Fourteenth Amendment. The concept of "we the people" under the Constitution visualizes no preferred class of voters but equality among those who meet the basic qualification. The idea that every voter is equal to every other voter in his State, when he casts his ballot in favor of one of several competing candidates, underlies many of our decisions. . . . The conception of political equality from the Declaration of Independence to Lincoln's Gettysburg Address, to the Fifteenth, Seventeenth, and Nineteenth Amendments can mean only one thing — one person, one vote.

## The Rule Applied

The Court's rulings in *Baker* and *Gray* concerned the equal weighting and counting of votes cast in state elections. In 1964, deciding the case of *Wesberry v. Sanders,* the Court applied the one-person, one-vote principle to congressional districts and set equality as the standard for congressional redistricting.

Shortly after the *Baker* decision was handed down, James P. Wesberry, Jr., an Atlanta resident and a member of the Georgia Senate, filed suit in federal court in Atlanta claiming that gross disparity in the population of Georgia's congressional districts violated 14th Amendment rights of equal protection of the laws. At the time, Georgia districts ranged in population from 272,154 in the rural 9th District in the northeastern part of the state to 823,860 in the 5th District in Atlanta and its suburbs. District lines had not been changed since 1931. The state's number of House seats remained the same in the interim, but Atlanta's district population — already high in 1931 compared with the others — had more than doubled in 30 years, making a 5th District vote worth about one-third that of a vote in the 9th District.

In June 1962 the three-judge federal court divided 2-1 in dismissing Wesberry's suit. The majority reasoned that the precedent of *Colegrove* still controlled in congressional district cases. The judges cautioned against federal judicial interference with Congress and against "depriving others of the right to vote" if the suit should result in at-large elections. They suggested that the Georgia legislature (under court order to reapportion itself) or the U.S. Congress might better provide relief. Wesberry then appealed to the Supreme Court.

On Feb. 17, 1964, the Supreme Court ruled in *Wesberry v. Sanders* (376 U.S. 1) that congressional districts must be substantially equal in population. The Court, which upheld Wesberry's challenge by a 6-3 decision, based its ruling on the history and wording of Article I, Section 2, of the Constitution, which states that representatives shall be apportioned among the states according to their respective numbers and be chosen by the people of the several states. This language, the Court stated, meant that "as nearly as is practicable, one man's vote in a congressional election is to be worth as much as another's."

The majority opinion, written by Justice Black and supported by Chief Justice Earl Warren and Justices Brennan, Douglas, Arthur J. Goldberg and Byron R. White, said: "While it may not be possible to draw congressional districts with mathematical precision, that is no excuse for ignoring our Constitution's plain objective of making equal representation for equal numbers of people the fundamental goal for the House of Representatives."

In a strongly worded dissent, Justice John M. Harlan asserted that the Constitution did not establish population as the only criterion of congressional districting but left the subject to the discretion of the states, subject only to the supervisory power of Congress. "The constitutional right which the Court creates is manufactured out of whole cloth," Harlan concluded.

The *Wesberry* opinion established no precise standards for districting beyond declaring that districts must be as nearly equal in population "as is practicable." In his dissent Harlan suggested that a disparity of more than 100,000 between a state's largest and smallest districts would "presumably" violate the equality standard enunciated by the majority. On that basis, Harlan estimated, the districts of 37

# Gerrymandering:
# The Shape of the House

Traditionally, there are two types of gerrymanders. One is the partisan gerrymander, where a single party draws the lines to its advantage. The other is the proincumbent (sometimes called the "bipartisan" or "sweetheart") gerrymander, where the lines are drawn to protect incumbents, with any gains or losses in the number of seats shared between the two parties. In states where control of the state government is divided, proincumbent gerrymanders are common.

In the eyes of some Republicans, either species of gerrymander was likely to ensure their continued minority status in the House. Democrats, who have controlled the House since 1955, countered that the GOP suffered from unattractive candidates, not gerrymandered districts. The 1990 reapportionment saw widespread examples of a third type of gerrymander: drawing lines to preserve or create minority districts.

Indeed, some academics maintain that the extent of gerrymandering and its impact on the composition of the House are exaggerated. "To a large extent," said Everett C. Ladd, the director of the Roper Center for Public Opinion at the University of Connecticut, "the population is voting without regard to party. So the precise location of the congressional district lines is not so important as it was in an earlier era."

Partisan gerrymanders do not always achieve their goals. Republican legislators in Indiana redrew their map in 1981 with the hope that it would turn the Democrats' congressional majority into a 7-3 GOP edge. Instead, by the end of the decade Democrats held a 7-3 advantage.

Given the extremely high incumbent reelection rates that have prevailed since the end of World War II, redistricting does increase the possibility of turnover, because most states must redraw their districts to accommodate population shifts within the state as well as the gain or loss of any seats. Typically, some members of the House of Representatives choose to retire rather than stand for election in redesigned districts. But with rare exceptions a proincumbent spin in much of the line drawing diminishes the prospects for dramatic partisan turnover.

Sweetheart gerrymandering rarely attracts much attention. But this method of mapping has a powerful effect on the House. "Districts get more Democratic for Democrats and more Republican for Republicans. Competition is minimized," said Bernard Grofman, a political scientist at the University of California at Irvine. "Because the majority of House seats are controlled by Democrats, proincumbent line drawing helps perpetuate the Democratic House majority."

---

states with 398 representatives would be unconstitutional, "leaving a constitutional House of 37 members now sitting."

Neither did the Court's decision make any reference to gerrymandering, since it discussed only the population, not the shape of districts. In a separate opinion handed down the same day as *Wesberry*, the Court dismissed a challenge to congressional districts in New York City, which had been brought by voters who charged that Manhattan's "silk-stocking" 17th District had been gerrymandered to exclude blacks and Puerto Ricans.

## Strict Equality

Five years elapsed between *Wesberry v. Sanders* and the Court's next application of constitutional standards to congressional districting. In 1967 the Court hinted at the strict stance it would adopt two years later. With two unsigned opinions, the Court sent back to Indiana and Missouri for revision those two states' congressional redistricting plans because they allowed variations of as much as 20 percent from the average district population.

Two years later Missouri's revised plan returned to the Court for full review. By a 6-3 vote, the Court rejected the plan. It was unacceptable, the Court held in *Kirkpatrick v. Preisler* (385 U.S. 450, 1969), because it allowed a variation of as much as 3.1 percent from perfectly equal population districts. Thus the Court made clear its stringent application of the one-person, one-vote rule to congressional districts.

There was no "fixed numerical or percentage population variance small enough to be considered *de minimis*

and to satisfy without question the 'as nearly as practicable' standard," Justice Brennan wrote for the Court in 1969. "Equal representation for equal numbers of people is a principle designed to prevent debasement of voting power and diminution of access to elected Representatives. Toleration of even small deviations detracts from these purposes."

The only permissible variances in population, the Court ruled, were those that were unavoidable despite the effort to achieve absolute equality or those that could be legally justified. The variances in Missouri could have been avoided, the Court said.

None of Missouri's arguments for the plan qualified as "legally acceptable" justifications. The Court rejected the argument that population variance was necessary to allow representation of distinct interest groups. It said that acceptance of such variances to produce districts with specific interests was "antithetical" to the basic purpose of equal representation.

Justice White dissented from the majority opinion, which he characterized as "an unduly rigid and unwarranted application of the Equal Protection Clause which will unnecessarily involve the courts in the abrasive task of drawing district lines." White added that some "acceptably small" population variance could be established. He indicated that considerations of existing political boundaries and geographical compactness could justify to him some variation from "absolute equality" of population.

Justice Harlan, joined by Justice Potter Stewart, dissented, saying that "whatever room remained under this Court's prior decisions for the free play of the political process in matters of reapportionment is now all but eliminated by today's Draconian judgments."

## Practical Results

As a result of the Court's decisions of the 1960s, nearly every state was forced to redraw its congressional district lines — sometimes more than once. By the end of the decade, 39 of the 45 states with more than one representative had made the necessary adjustments.

However, the effect of the one-person, one-vote standard on congressional districts did not bring about immediate population equality in districts. Most of the new districts were far from equal in population, because the only official population figures came from the 1960 census. Massive population shifts during the decade rendered most post-*Wesberry* efforts to achieve equality useless.

But redistricting based on the 1970 census resulted in districts that differed only slightly in population from the state average. Among House members elected in 1972, 385 of 435 represented districts that varied by less than 1 percent from the state average district population.

By contrast, only nine of the districts in the 88th Congress (elected in 1962) deviated less than 1 percent from the state average; 81 were between 1 and 5 percent; 87 from 5 to 10 percent; and in 236 districts the deviation was 10 percent or greater. Twenty-two House members were elected at large.

The Supreme Court made only one major ruling concerning congressional districts during the 1970s. In 1973 the Court declared the Texas congressional districts, as redrawn in 1971, unconstitutional because of excessive population variance among districts. The variance between the largest and smallest districts was 4.9872 percent. The Court returned the case to a three-judge federal panel, which adopted a new congressional district plan.

## Precise Equality

Following the 1980 census, several federal courts accepted or imposed redistricting maps that achieved population equality but were drawn for blatant partisan purposes. In Missouri a federal court accepted the Democrats' remap proposal over the Republican plan because its districts were more nearly equal in population. The Democratic map obtained population equality by dismantling a district in a part of the state where population was growing and preserving a district in inner-city St. Louis that had been losing population. The plan cost one Republican incumbent his seat.

In the 1990s most states came very close to precise population equality. For example, all 30 districts of Texas have exactly the same population: 566,217. To achieve such equality, however, the line for many districts in some states may cut through many small cities and towns, dividing their residents between two or three different districts.

Although maps such as these raised the question whether partisan gerrymandering was also a violation of an individual's voting rights, the Supreme Court in 1983 appeared to make it even more difficult to challenge a redistricting map on grounds other than population deviation. In a 5-4 decision, the Court ruled in *Karcher v. Daggett* (462 U.S. 725) that states must adhere as closely as possible to the one-person, one-vote standard and bear the burden of proving that deviations from precise population equality were made in pursuit of a legitimate goal. The decision overturned New Jersey's congressional map because the variation between the most populated and the least populated districts was 0.69 percent.

Brennan, who wrote the Court's opinion in *Baker* and *Kirkpatrick,* also wrote the opinion in *Karcher,* contending that population differences between districts "could have been avoided or significantly reduced with a good-faith effort to achieve population equality."

"Adopting any standard other than population equality, using the best census data available, would subtly erode the Constitution's ideal of equal representation," Brennan wrote. "In this case, appellants argue that a maximum deviation of approximately 0.7 percent should be considered *de minimis.* If we accept that argument, how are we to regard deviations of 0.8 percent, 0.95 percent, 1.0 percent or 1.1 percent? ... To accept the legitimacy of unjustified, though small population deviations in this case would mean to reject the basic premise of *Kirkpatrick* and *Wesberry.*"

Brennan said that "any number of consistently applied legislative policies might justify" some population variation. These included "making districts compact, respecting municipal boundaries, preserving the cores of prior districts, and avoiding contests between incumbent Representatives." However, he cautioned, the state must show "with some specificity that a particular objective required the specific deviations in its plan, rather than simply relying on general assertions."

In his dissent Justice White criticized the majority for its "unreasonable insistence on an unattainable perfection in the equalizing of congressional districts." He warned that the decision would invite "further litigation of virtually every congressional redistricting plan in the nation."

## Partisan Gerrymandering

In *Karcher* the Court did not address the underlying political issue in the New Jersey case, which was that its map had been drawn to serve Democratic interests. As a partisan gerrymander, the map had few peers, boasting some of the most oddly shaped districts in the country. One constituency, known as the "fishhook" by its detractors, twisted through central New Jersey's industrial landscape, picking up Democratic voters along the way. Another stretched from the suburbs of New York to the fringes of Trenton.

In separate dissents Justices Lewis F. Powell Jr., and John Paul Stevens broadly hinted that they were willing to hear constitutional challenges to instances of partisan gerrymandering. "A legislator cannot represent his constituents properly — nor can voters from a fragmented district exercise the ballot intelligently — when a voting district is nothing more than an artificial unit divorced from, and indeed often in conflict with, the various communities established in the State," wrote Powell.

The Court's opportunity to address that issue came in *Davis v. Bandemer* (478 U.S. 109). On June 30, 1986, the Court ruled that political gerrymanders are subject to constitutional review by federal courts, even if the disputed districts meet the one-person, one-vote test. The case arose from a challenge by Indiana Democrats who argued that the Republican-drawn map so heavily favored the Republican party that Democrats were denied appropriate representation. But the Court rejected the Democrats' challenge to the alleged gerrymander, saying that one election was insufficient to prove unconstitutional discrimination. Left unclear were what standards the Court would use to find a partisan gerrymander legally unacceptable.

National Republicans expressed delight with the *Bandemer* decision. The GOP had long held that Democratic control over most state legislatures had allowed them to draw congressional and legislative districts to their partisan advantage. In particular, Republicans expressed confidence that the *Bandemer* decision lay the groundwork for overturning California's congressional district map, created by Democratic Rep. Phillip Burton in the early 1980s.

Widely recognized as a classic example of a partisan gerrymander, the map featured a number of oddly shaped districts, drawn neither compactly nor with respect to community boundaries, but all with nearly equal populations. As one commentator described it, "Burton carefully stretched districts from one Democratic enclave to another — sometimes joining them with nothing but a bridge, a stretch of harbor, or a spit of land . . . — avoiding Republicans block for block and household for household." [14] Before the 1982 elections, Democrats held 22 congressional districts, Republicans 21. With the Burton map in place for the 1982 elections, Democrats held 28 seats, Republicans only 17.

Republican Rep. Robert E. Badham filed a lawsuit against the Burton plan in federal district court in 1983. In the wake of the *Bandemer* decision, that court held a hearing on *Badham v. Eu* but dismissed the Republican complaint by a 2-1 vote. The court in essence ruled that a party seeking to overturn a gerrymandered map must show a general pattern of exclusion from the political process, which the California Republican party, in control of the governorship, a Senate seat, and 40 percent of the House seats, could not do. The Republicans appealed to the Supreme Court, but the Court refused to become involved, voting 6-3 in 1989 to reaffirm the lower court's decision without comment.

## Minority Representation

One form of gerrymandering is expressly forbidden by law: redistricting for the purpose of racial discrimination. The Voting Rights Act of 1965, extended in 1970, 1975 and 1982, banned redistricting that diluted the voting strength of black communities. Other minorities, including Hispanics, Asian Americans, Native Americans and native Alaskans, subsequently were brought under the protection of the law.

In 1980 the Supreme Court for the first time narrowed the reach of the Voting Rights Act in the case of *Mobile v. Bolden,* a challenge to the at-large system of electing city commissioners used in Mobile, Alabama.[15] By a vote of 6-3, the Court ruled that proof of discriminatory intent by the commissioners was necessary before a violation could be found; the fact that no black had ever been elected under the challenged system was not proof enough.

The *Mobile* decision set off an immediate reaction on Capitol Hill. In extending the Voting Rights Act in 1982, Congress amended it to outlaw any practice that has the effect of discriminating against blacks or other minorities — regardless of the lawmakers' intent.

The Justice Department later adopted a similar "results test" for another part of the act (Section 5), which requires certain states and localities with a history of discrimination to have their electoral plans "precleared" by the department. In 1986 the Supreme Court applied this test in *Thornburg v. Gingles* (478 U.S. 30), ruling that six of North Carolina's multimember legislative districts impermissibly diluted black voting strength. Sharply departing from *Mobile,* the Court held that since very few blacks had been elected from these districts, the system must be in violation of the law.

The Court also used the *Thornburg* decision to develop three criteria that, if met, should lead to the creation of a minority legislative district: The minority group must be large and geographically compact enough to constitute a majority in a single-member electoral district, the group must be politically cohesive and the white majority must vote as a bloc to the degree that it usually can defeat candidates preferred by the minority. Thus, within a period of 10 years, the burden of proof was shifted from minorities, who had been required to show that lines were being drawn to dilute their voting strength, to lawmakers, who had to show that they had done all they could to maximize minority voting strength.

Another important ruling came in 1989, when a special three-judge federal panel ordered Arkansas to redraw its state legislative districts to create almost as many black majority districts as was mathematically possible. The *Jeffers v. Clinton* decision was left intact by the Supreme Court, which declined to hear the case.

Further, in 1990, a federal district judge ruled in *Garza v. County of Los Angeles* that the Los Angeles County Board of Supervisors had violated the Voting Rights Act by gerrymandering its districts to dilute the Hispanic vote. The judge ordered the creation of a majority-Hispanic district.

In the 1990s round of redistricting, for the first time, states operated under federal legal mandates to draw lines that maximized the number of "majority-minority" districts — constituencies where blacks and Hispanics made up a majority of the population. Redistricting experts also argued about how to draw lines in areas where the minority population was sizable but not large or compact enough to make up a majority in a new district. Some advocated "minority-influence" districts, which might be as much as 40 percent black or Hispanic, but others feared these districts could become polarized, with white representatives unconcerned about their minority constituents.

In the first lower court ruling on this matter, a three-judge panel in *Armour v. Ohio* ordered the pooling of blacks in the Youngstown area into a state House district whose population would be one-third black. The court said that minority voters then would have "the ability to elect the candidate of their choice" — though not necessarily a black candidate. In *Turner v. Arkansas,* a three-judge panel ruled against black and Republican plaintiffs who wanted Arkansas to create a 42 percent black minority-influence congressional district, maintaining that the criteria established in *Thornburg* required only the creation of majority-minority districts.

The Supreme Court on June 28, 1993, invited a new wave of lawsuits challenging the constitutionality of districts drawn to ensure the election of minorities. In a 5-4 ruling in *Shaw v. Reno,* the Court reinstated a suit by five white North Carolinians who contended that the state's congressional district map, which created in 1992 two sinuous majority-black districts, violated their 14th Amendment right to "equal protection under law." The Court, however, did not invalidate North Carolina's map or rule in favor of the plaintiffs' 14th Amendment complaint.

The ruling's implications extended well beyond the narrow action taken in *Shaw.* By calling into question the constitutionality of the amorphous computer-generated entities that wriggled through areas to collect a majority of minority voters, the Court gave legal standing to challenges to any congressional map with an oddly shaped majority-minority district that may not be defensible on grounds other than race, such as shared community interest or geographical compactness.

The decision triggered a debate among constitutional scholars, civil rights advocates and minority-group representatives over how effective majority-minority districts were in helping minorities attain equal representation. It also raised questions about the viability and constitutionality of the Voting Rights Act of 1965 and its 1982 amendments. More than anything, though, *Shaw* appeared to breed confusion over what, if any, new standards needed to be applied to a redistricting plan. For some, the case established a contradictory set of criteria for a state, subject to the Voting Rights Act, to win federal approval of a map. While the Justice Department or a federal court must approve the state's redistricting plans, *Shaw* raised the possibility that Justice Department insistence on creating the maximum number of minority districts may be challenged on constitutional grounds.

In her majority opinion, Justice Sandra Day O'Connor decried the creation of districts based solely on racial composition. She wrote, "[W]e believe that reapportionment is one area in which appearances do matter. A reapportionment plan that includes in one district individuals ... who may have little in common with one another but the color of their skin bears an uncomfortable resemblance to political apartheid." O'Connor's opinion was regarded as signaling dissatisfaction with the broad interpretation of the Voting Rights Act's mandate, as expressed in *Thornburg,* for states to create minority districts wherever possible.

A three-judge federal panel in Louisiana was the first to act on the *Shaw* decision. In the case of *Hays vs. Louisiana* the panel ruled in December 1993 that the district lines in place for the 1992 election were the product of unconstitutional racial gerrymandering. The main focus of the panel was the 4th District, which zigzagged across the state in order to create a black-minority district. In April 1994, the Louisiana legislature redrew the state's district lines in order to conform to the ruling. The new 4th District was more compact, with its black population reduced from 66 percent to 58 percent. The state of Louisiana appealed *Hays* to the Supreme Court. As of June 1994, the case was still pending.

# Congress and Redistricting

Congress considered several proposals in the post-World War II period to enact new legislation on redistricting. Only one of these efforts was successful — enactment of a measure barring at-large elections in states with more than one House seat.

In January 1951 President Harry S. Truman asked for a ban on gerrymandering, an end to at-large seats in states having more than one representative, and a sharp reduction in the huge differences in size among congressional districts within most states. On behalf of the administration, Emanuel Celler, D-N.Y., chairman of the House Judiciary Com-

mittee, introduced a bill reflecting these requests, but the committee took no action.

Celler regularly introduced his bill throughout the 1950s and early 1960s, but it made no headway until the Supreme Court handed down the *Wesberry* decision in 1964. The House passed a version of the Celler bill in 1965, largely to discourage the Supreme Court from imposing even more rigid criteria. The Senate, however, took no action and the measure died.

In 1967, after defeating a conference report that would have prevented the courts from ordering a state to redistrict or to hold at-large elections until after the 1970 census, Congress approved a measure to ban at-large elections in all states entitled to more than one representative. Exceptions were made for New Mexico and Hawaii, which had a tradition of electing their representatives at large. Both states, however, soon passed districting laws, New Mexico for the 1968 elections and Hawaii for 1970.

Bills to increase the size of the House to prevent states from losing seats as a result of population shifts have been introduced after most recent censuses, but Congress has given little consideration to any of them.

## Notes

1. Ronald D. Elving, "Redistricting: Drawing Power with a Map," *Editorial Research Reports,* February 15, 1991, 99.
2. Robert Luce, *Legislative Principles* (New York: Houghton Mifflin, 1930; New York: DaCapo Press, 1971), 342.
3. Thomas Jefferson, *The Portable Thomas Jefferson,* ed. Merrill D. Peterson, part 3, *Notes on the State of Virginia* (New York: Viking, 1965), 163.
4. Andrew Hacker, *Congressional Districting: The Issue of Equal Representation,* rev. ed. (Washington, D.C.: Brookings Institution, 1964), 6-7.
5. Max Farrand, ed., *The Records of the Federal Convention of 1787* (New Haven, Conn.: Yale University Press, 1911, 1966), vol. 2, 241.
6. *The Federalist Papers,* with an introduction by Clinton Rossiter (New York: New American Library, 1961), 347-348, 354.
7. Quoted in Laurence F. Schmeckebier, *Congressional Apportionment* (Washington, D.C.: Brookings Institution, 1941), 131.
8. Hacker, *Congressional Districting,* 14.
9. Quoted in Schmeckebier, *Congressional Apportionment,* 113.
10. Zechariah Chafee Jr., "Congressional Reapportionment," *Harvard Law Review* (1929): 1015-1047.
11. Jefferson, *Notes on the State of Virginia,* 217.
12. Quoted in Schmeckebier, *Congressional Apportionment,* 137.
13. The following summary is based on *Congressional Quarterly's Guide to the U.S. Supreme Court,* 2nd ed. (Washington, D.C.: Congressional Quarterly, 1990), 483-493.
14. Elving, "Redistricting," 107.
15. The discussion of minority representation is based on Rhodes Cook, "Map-Drawers Must Toe the Line in Upcoming Redistricting," *Congressional Quarterly Weekly Report,* September 1, 1990, 2786-2793.

# House Election Returns, 1824-1993

# Sources for House Popular Returns

The popular election returns for the House of Representatives presented in this section (pp. 943-1326) for the years 1824-1973 were obtained from the Inter-University Consortium for Political and Social Research (ICPSR) at the University of Michigan. Major sources for returns since 1973 were Congressional Quarterly, which obtained them from the state secretaries of state, and the *America Votes* series compiled biennially by Richard M. Scammon and Alice V. McGillivray of the Elections Research Center, Washington, D.C.

The symbol # next to returns before 1974 indicates that Congressional Quarterly obtained the returns from a source other than the ICPSR. A complete set of other sources used appears on page 1327. A "House Candidates Index" is located on pages 1402-1501.

While the complete source annotations for the ICPSR collection are too extensive to publish here, information on the sources for specific election returns can be obtained through the ICPSR. *(ICPSR collection, box, p. x)*

## Presentation of Returns

The House returns are arranged chronologically by year and alphabetically by state for each year. Within each state, single-member districts are listed first in numerical order. At-large seats appear at the end of the single-member districts with "AL" in the district identification column. Multi-member districts, in the few instances in which they appear in the 19th century, are listed in numerical order under the separate heading "Multi-Member Districts." *(For an explanation of multi-member districts, see p. 916.)*

Special election results appear after all general election returns for each state under a separate "Special Elections" heading. Returns for special off-year elections are listed at the end of the preceding year's general election returns.

## Names and Party Designations

Candidate names appear to the right of the district number, with the candidate receiving the highest number of votes listed first. Other candidates who received *at least 5 percent* of the total votes cast are listed in descending order. In multi-member districts or at-large districts electing more than one representative, candidates who received fewer than 100 votes were not listed.

In some instances, particularly in the 19th century, names in the ICPSR file are incomplete. First names were the element most commonly missing in the original sources consulted by the scholars and archivists who gathered the ICPSR returns. In cases where a vote total is known but there is no name at all, or the name obviously could not be identified, Congressional Quarterly has labeled the votes as being cast for an "Unidentified Candidate."

In the ICPSR returns, the distinct — and in many cases, *multiple* — party designations appearing in the original sources are preserved. In many cases party labels represent combinations of multi-party support received by individual candidates. If, for example, on the ballot and official returns more than one party name was listed next to a candidate's name, then the party designation appearing in the election returns for that candidate will be a unique abbreviation for that combination of parties. *(For a list of party abbreviations, see p. 1352.)*

In the special case of a candidate's name listed separately on the original ballot under more than one party — where returns were reported *separately* for each party — Congressional Quarterly has summed the votes recorded under the several parties and that figure appears as the candidate's total vote. Whenever separate party totals have been summed, a *comma* separates the abbreviations of the parties contributing the largest and second largest share of the total vote.

Most cases of this special situation occurred in New York and Pennsylvania during this century. For example, in the original ICPSR returns for the House election in New York's 10th District in 1938, Emanuel Celler received 31,645 votes as the Democratic Party candidate, 12,181 votes as the American Labor Party candidate and 55 votes as the City Fusion Party candidate, for a total of 43,881 votes. Congressional Quarterly summed all votes received by Celler from these three parties *(p. 1186)*.

Congressional Quarterly indicated the two parties that contributed the most votes to Celler's total — separated by a comma. Thus, immediately following his name appear the abbreviations (D, AM LAB), indicating that Celler was a candidate of two or more parties and that he received most votes as a Democrat.

## Vote Totals and Percentages

Each candidate's total vote and percentage of the total vote cast for all candidates appear in columns to the right of the candidate's name and party designation. Percentages have been calculated to two decimal places and rounded to one place. Due to rounding and the scattered votes of minor candidates, percentages in individual House races may not add up to 100.

Only candidates from single-member districts who received *at least 5 percent of the total vote* for that election are included. In multi-member districts or at-large districts electing more than one representative, candidates who received fewer than 100 votes were not listed.

If no vote total is shown for a candidate but the percentage listed is 100 percent, in most cases the candidate ran unopposed. State election officials either did not put the candidate's name on the ballot or simply did not make an effort to record the total number of votes.

No percentages of total vote have been computed for multi-member districts or at-large districts electing more than one representative. Candidates in these types of districts did not run against specific opponents, and in most cases the number of votes cast in any one contest could not be determined.

In some cases, percentages do not appear next to candidates in single-member districts because vote totals for all the candidates who ran in the district were not available even though the names of all candidates may appear. In such cases, the symbol ⊬ appears in the vote column of the winning candidate.

# House Popular Vote Returns, 1824-1985

## 1824 House Elections

### DELAWARE

| Candidates | Votes | % |
|---|---|---|
| AL Louis McLane (FED) | 3,387 | 51.7 |
| Arnold Naudain (OLD R) | 3,163 | 48.3 |

### GEORGIA

| | Votes | |
|---|---|---|
| AL Wiley Thompson | 10,543✔ | |
| John Forsyth | 10,219✔ | |
| Edward F. Tattnall | 10,043✔ | |
| Alfred Cuthbert | 9,950✔ | |
| George Cary | 9,672✔ | |
| James Meriwether | 9,491✔ | |
| Charles E. Haynes | 8,881✔ | |

**Special Election**

| | Votes | % |
|---|---|---|
| AL Richard H. Wilde | 5,002 | 61.0 |
| Lyman | 3,194 | 39.0 |

### ILLINOIS

| | Votes | % |
|---|---|---|
| AL Daniel P. Cook (NR) | 7,425 | 62.6 |
| Shadrack Bond | 4,409 | 37.2 |

### INDIANA

| | Votes | % |
|---|---|---|
| 1 Ratliff Boon (JAC D) | 4,281 | 42.1 |
| Jacob Call | 3,222 | 31.7 |
| Thomas H. Blake (NR) | 2,661 | 26.2 |
| 2 Jonathan Jennings (CLAY R) | 4,680 | 53.2 |
| Jeremiah Sullivan (NR) | 4,119 | 46.8 |
| 3 John Test (NR) | 3,434 | 47.1 |
| James Brown Ray (CLAY R) | 2,471 | 33.9 |
| Daniel J. Caswell | 1,388 | 19.0 |

**Special Election**

| | Votes | % |
|---|---|---|
| 1 Jacob Call (JAC D) | 2,155 | 50.4 |
| Thomas H. Blake (NR) | 2,087 | 48.8 |

### KENTUCKY

| | |
|---|---|
| 1 David Trimble (D) | ✔ |
| 2 Thomas Metcalfe (D) | ✔ |
| 3 Henry Clay | ✔ |
| 4 Robert P. Letcher (CD) | ✔ |
| 5 James Johnson (D) | ✔ |
| 6 Joseph Lecompte (D) | ✔ |
| 7 Thomas P. Moore (D) | ✔ |
| 8 Richard A. Buckner | ✔ |
| 9 Charles A. Wickliffe (D) | ✔ |
| 10 Francis Johnson (AD) | ✔ |
| 11 William S. Young (D) | ✔ |
| 12 Robert P. Henry (CLAY D) | ✔ |

### LOUISIANA

| | |
|---|---|
| 1 Edward Livingston (D) | ✔ |
| 2 Henry H. Gurley (W) | ✔ |
| 3 William L. Brent (W) | ✔ |

### MAINE

| | |
|---|---|
| 1 William Burleigh (AD) | ✔ |
| 2 John Anderson (JEFF D) | ✔ |
| 3 Ebenezer Herrick | ✔ |
| 4 Peleg Sprague | ✔ |
| 5 Enoch Lincoln | ✔ |
| 6 Jeremiah O'Brien (D) | ✔ |
| 7 David Kidder (W) | ✔ |

### MARYLAND

| Candidates | Votes | % |
|---|---|---|
| 1 Clement Dorsey | 1,824 | 55.3 |
| Raphael Neale | 1,476 | 44.7 |
| 2 Joseph Kent | 1,908 | 52.3 |
| John C. Weems | 1,741 | 47.7 |
| 3 George Peter | 1,602 | 52.5 |
| George C. Washington | 1,448 | 47.5 |

## Explanation of Symbols in House Returns

In the returns for House elections *symbols* are used to denote special circumstances. In cases where no symbol is used, the candidate who received the most votes won the election to the House. The following is a key to the symbols used:

✔ Elected to the House. The symbol is used to identify winning candidates in three types of situations: (1) When candidates ran for two or more at-large seats in states which chose all of their at-large representatives in a single election, or ran in a multi-member district; (2) when the vote total and percentage of one or more of the candidates are unavailable and (3) when a candidate who did not receive the highest vote total was seated by the House. *(Explanation of multi-member districts, see p. 916.)*

‡ The symbol is used when an election dispute resulted in the unseating of a representative *after* he was sworn in. *(For discussion of specific cases, consult the* Biographical Directory of the United States Congress, 1774-1989, *U.S. Government Printing Office, Washington, D.C., 1989; hereafter referred to as the* Biographical Directory.*)*

\* The symbol is used for three types of situations: (1) When a representative-elect died or declined his seat before the constitutionally set date for the beginning of his term—March 4 until 1935, and Jan. 3 thereafter; (2) when the House refused to seat any candidate claiming election to a seat and (3) when state law required a candidate to obtain a popular vote majority for election to the House, but the candidate receiving the most votes failed to receive a majority. *(For discussion of specific cases, consult the* Biographical Directory; *explanation of majority vote requirement, see p. 945.)*

# Information for 1824-1973 returns was obtained from a source other than the Inter-University Consortium for Political and Social Research. *(For a listing of other sources, see p. 1327.)*

**Footnotes.** Numbered footnotes are used to explain unusual situations, such as a series of elections in the same year in the same House district, anomalies resulting from reapportionment and special procedures for conducting House elections in certain states.

## MARYLAND

| | Candidates | Votes | % |
|---|---|---|---|
| 4 | Thomas Worthington | 4,321 | 55.3 |
| | John Lee | 3,491 | 44.7 |
| 6 | George Mitchell | 2,854 | 53.9 |
| | Phillip Reed | 2,439 | 46.1 |
| 7 | John Leeds Kerr | 1,950 | 50.3 |
| | Thomas Emory | 1,924 | 49.7 |
| 8 | Robert Martin | 3,088 | 51.9 |
| | John Spence | 2,858 | 48.1 |
| | **Multi-Member District** | | |
| 5 | Peter Little | 9,686✓ | |
| | John Barney | 5,515✓ | |
| | Isaac McKim | 5,346 | |

## MASSACHUSETTS

| | Candidates | Votes | % |
|---|---|---|---|
| 1 | Daniel Webster (AR) | 3,669 | 99.9 |
| 2 | Benjamin W. Crowninshield (AR) | 1,379 | 58.1 |
| | Frederick Howes | 760 | 32.0 |
| 3 | John Varnum | 1,736 | 50.2 |
| | John Merrill | 1,659 | 48.0 |
| 4 | Edward Everett | 1,906 | 57.2 |
| | Unidentified Candidate | 1,357 | 40.7 |
| 5 | John Locke (AR) | 1,524 | 60.6 |
| | Joseph G. Kendall | 423 | 16.8 |
| | Tomes | 186 | 7.4 |
| 6 | Samuel C. Allen (AR) | 1,726 | 55.7 |
| | George Grennell Jr | 1,335 | 43.1 |
| 7 | Henry W. Dwight (AR) | 1,742 | 54.8 |
| | Nathan Willis | 1,375 | 43.3 |
| 8 | Tom Lathrop (AR) | 1,874 | 58.2 |
| | James Fowler | 1,201 | 37.3 |
| 9 | John Bailey | 1,669 | 57.3 |
| | Sher Leland | 991 | 34.0 |
| 10 | Francis Baylies (JAC R) | 1,778 | 54.8 |
| | James L. Hodges | 1,363 | 42.0 |
| 11 | John Reed (AR) | 1,057 | 58.2 |
| | Barker Burnell | 460 | 25.3 |
| | Walter Folger | 297 | 16.4 |
| 12 | Aaron Hobart (AR) | 1,606 | 72.3 |
| | Ebenezer Gay | 320 | 14.4 |
| | William Baylies | 263 | 11.9 |
| 13 | John Davis (AR) | 1,262 | 51.2 |
| | James Libley | 1,195 | 48.5 |

## MISSOURI

| | Candidates | Votes | % |
|---|---|---|---|
| AL | John Scott (CLAY R) | 5,022 | 47.0 |
| | George F. Strother (JAC D) | 4,528 | 42.4 |
| | Robert Wash | 1,125 | 10.5 |

## NEW HAMPSHIRE [1]

| | Candidates | Votes | % |
|---|---|---|---|
| AL | Ichabod Bartlett | 11,603✓ | |
| | Thomas Whipple Jr. | 8,690✓ | |
| | James Miller | 6,923* | |
| | Nehemiah Eastman | 6,823 | |
| | Jonathan Harvey | 6,105✓ | |
| | Ezekiel Webster | 5,928 | |
| | Joseph Healy | 5,479 | |
| | Phinchas Handerson | 5,296 | |
| | Titus Brown | 5,222 | |
| | Atkinson | 4,670 | |
| | Livermore | 3,854 | |
| | (Scattering) | 801 | |
| | Evans | 672 | |

## NEW JERSEY

| | Candidates | Votes | % |
|---|---|---|---|
| AL | George Holcombe (D-R) | 17,706✓ | |
| | Samuel Swan (D-R) | 17,672✓ | |
| | Lewis Condict (D-R) | 17,668✓ | |
| | Daniel Garrison (D-R) | 17,595✓ | |
| | George Cassedy (D-R) | 17,550✓ | |
| | Ebenezer Tucker (D-R) | 17,022✓ | |

## NEW YORK

| | Candidates | Votes | % |
|---|---|---|---|
| 1 | Silas Wood | 2,140 | 60.5 |
| | James Lent | 1,398 | 39.5 |
| 2 | Joshua Sands | 1,683 | 53.1 |
| | John T. Bergen | 1,484 | 46.9 |
| 4 | Aaron Ward | 1,586 | 39.0 |
| | Jonathan Ward | 1,297 | 31.9 |
| | John Hunter | 1,188 | 29.2 |
| 5 | Bartow White | 3,596 | 52.8 |
| | Peter Livingston | 3,210 | 47.2 |
| 6 | John Hallock Jr | 2,103 | 47.2 |
| | Hector Craig | 1,978 | 44.4 |
| | Walter Case | 374 | 8.4 |
| 7 | Abraham Hasbrouck | 2,916 | 51.2 |
| | John Lounsberry | 2,781 | 48.8 |
| 8 | James Strong | 3,129 | 60.0 |
| | Robert Livingston | 2,089 | 40.0 |
| 9 | William McManus | 3,807 | 56.6 |
| | George R. Davis | 2,925 | 43.5 |
| 10 | Stephen Van Rensselaer | 3,850 | 100.0 |
| 11 | Henry Ashley | 3,531 | 58.4 |
| | William Heermance | 2,519 | 41.6 |
| 12 | William Deitz | 2,810 | 56.9 |
| | Constant Brown | 2,129 | 43.1 |
| 13 | William G. Angel | 3,379 | 52.2 |
| | William Campbell | 3,094 | 47.8 |
| 14 | Henry Storrs | 4,146 | 57.3 |
| | James Lynch | 3,094 | 42.7 |
| 15 | Michael Hoffman | 2,410 | 52.7 |
| | John Herkimer | 2,164 | 47.3 |
| 16 | Henry Markell | 3,114 | 54.9 |
| | William Dodge | 2,562 | 45.1 |
| 17 | John W. Taylor | 3,858 | 100.0 |
| 18 | Henry C. Martindale | 3,448 | 64.6 |
| | John Gale | 1,893 | 35.4 |
| 19 | Henry Ross | 3,209 | 52.3 |
| | William Hogan | 2,932 | 47.7 |
| 21 | Elias Whitmore | 3,128 | 50.4 |
| | Lot Clark | 3,073 | 49.6 |
| 22 | John Miller | 3,857 | 54.3 |
| | John Lynde | 3,243 | 45.7 |
| 23 | Luther Badger | 3,214 | 50.8 |
| | Elisha Litchfield | 3,116 | 49.2 |
| 24 | Charles Kellogg | 3,372 | 53.1 |
| | Rowland Day | 2,976 | 46.9 |
| 25 | Charles Humphrey | 3,144 | 51.2 |
| | David Woodcook | 2,999 | 48.8 |
| 27 | Moses Hayden | 4,456 | 59.5 |
| | Charles H. Carroll | 3,028 | 40.5 |
| 28 | Timothy Porter | 2,099 | 35.3 |
| | William Woods | 1,937 | 32.6 |
| | Daniel Cruger | 1,693 | 28.5 |
| 29 | Parmenio Adams | 4,035 | 57.6 |
| | Isaac Wilson | 2,969 | 42.4 |
| 30 | Daniel Garnsey | 2,387 | 35.4 |
| | William Hotchkiss | 2,235 | 33.1 |
| | John G. Camp | 2,127 | 31.5 |
| | **Multi-Member Districts** | | |
| 3 | Churchill C. Cambreleng | 5,650✓ | |
| | Gulian Verplanck | 4,863✓ | |
| | Jeromous Johnson | 4,588✓ | |
| | John Rathbone | 3,980 | |
| | Charles G. Haines | 3,855 | |
| | Peter Sharpe | 3,741 | |
| | Henry Wheaton | 750 | |
| 20 | Nicoll Fosdick | 5,676✓ | |
| | Egbert Ten Eyck | 5,484‡ | |
| | Daniel Hugunin Jr. | 5,128 | |
| | Horance Allen | 5,466 | |
| 26 | Dudley Marvin | 8,366✓ | |
| | Robert Rose | 4,899✓ | |
| | John Maynard | 4,438 | |
| | Aaron Remer | 2,732 | |

## OHIO [2]

| Candidates | Votes | % |
|---|---|---|
| David Jennings | ✓ | |
| Mordecai Bartley | ✓ | |
| William McLean | ✓ | |
| William Wilson | ✓ | |

| Candidates | Votes | % |
|---|---|---|
| Philemon Beecher (FED) | ✓ | |
| John C. Wright (AD) | ✓ | |
| John Sloane (W) | ✓ | |
| Elisha Whittlesey(W) | ✓ | |
| John Woods (W) | ✓ | |
| Samuel F. Vinton (W) | ✓ | |
| James Findlay (JAC D) | ✓ | |
| John W. Campbell (D) | ✓ | |
| John Thomson (D) | ✓ | |
| Joseph Vance (D) | ✓ | |

## PENNSYLVANIA

| | Candidates | Votes | % |
|---|---|---|---|
| 1 | John Wurts | ✓ | |
| 2 | Joseph Hemphill | ✓ | |
| 3 | Daniel H. Miller | ✓ | |
| 5 | Philip S. Markley | ✓ | |
| 6 | Robert Harris | ✓ | |
| | Christian Gleim | | |
| 10 | James S. Mitchell | ✓ | |
| 12 | John Mitchell | ✓ | |
| 13 | Alexander Thompson | ✓ | |
| 14 | Andrew Stewart | ✓ | |
| 15 | Joseph Lawrence | ✓ | |
| 16 | George Plumer | ✓ | |
| | John H. Wise | | |
| 18 | Patrick Farrelly | ✓ | |
| | **Multi-Member Districts** | | |
| 4 | James Buchanan | ✓ | |
| | Charles Miner | ✓ | |
| | Samuel Edwards | ✓ | |
| | William Anderson | | |
| | Isaac D. Barnard | | |
| | Samuel Houston | | |
| 7 | William Addams | ✓ | |
| | Henry Wilson | ✓ | |
| | George Keck | | |
| | Daniel Rose | | |
| 8 | George Wolf | ✓ | |
| | Samuel D. Ingham | ✓ | |
| 9 | Samuel McKean | ✓ | |
| | George Kremer | ✓ | |
| | Espy Van Horne | ✓ | |
| | William Cox Ellis | | |
| 11 | James Wilson | ✓ | |
| | John Findlay | ✓ | |
| 17 | James Allison Jr | ✓ | |
| | James S. Stevenson | ✓ | |

## SOUTH CAROLINA

| | Candidates | Votes | % |
|---|---|---|---|
| 1 | Joel R. Poinsett (D) | 1,474 | 58.4 |
| | Samuel Warren | 1,052 | 41.7 |
| 2 | James Hamilton Jr (SR FT) | | 100.0 |
| 3 | Thomas R. Mitchell | | 100.0 |
| 4 | Andrew R. Govan | | 100.0 |
| 5 | Starling Tucker | | 100.0 |
| 6 | George McDuffie (D) | ✓ | |
| 7 | Joseph Gist (D) | 3,398 | 54.8 |
| | J. McCreary | 1,869 | 30.2 |
| | F. W. Davie | 933 | 15.1 |
| 8 | John Wilson | ✓ | |
| 9 | John Carter | 1,882 | 46.3 |
| | Spann | 1,132 | 27.8 |
| | Levy | 1,055 | 25.9 |

## VERMONT

| | Candidates | Votes | % |
|---|---|---|---|
| 1 | William C. Bradley | ✓ | |
| 2 | Rollin C. Mallary | 3,284 | 95.6 |
| 3 | George E. Wales | ✓ | |
| 4 | Ezra Meech | 3,093 | 54.6 |
| | Benjamin Swift | 1,836 | 32.4 |
| | Stephen Royce | 404 | 7.1 |
| 5 | John Mattocks | 2,434 | 52.7 |
| | Daniel A. A. Buck | 2,099 | 45.4 |

*Footnotes, see p. 945.*

# 1825 House Elections

## ALABAMA

| Candidates | Votes | % |
|---|---|---|
| 1 Gabriel Moore (JAC D) | 5,098 | 71.1 |
| Clement Comer Clay (JAC D) | 2,070 | 28.9 |
| 2 Robert E. B. Baylor (JAC D) | 1,687 | 56.8 |
| John McKee | 972✓ | 31.7 |
| John D. Terrell (NR) | 342 | 11.5 |
| 3 George Owen (JAC D) | 543 | 100.0 |

## CONNECTICUT

| Candidates | Votes | |
|---|---|---|
| AL Gideon Tomlinson | 6,263✓ | |
| Elicha Phelps | 5,934✓ | |
| Ralph Ingersoll | 5,628✓ | |
| Orange Merwin | 5,518✓ | |
| Noyes Barber | 4,401✓ | |
| John Baldwin | 3,653✓ | |
| Daniel Burrows | 1,785 | |
| Elisha Tracy | 1,491 | |
| Timothy Pitkin | 1,293 | |
| Calvin Willey | 911 | |
| Samual Foot | 574 | |
| Dennis Kimberly | 415 | |
| Asa Barron | 407 | |
| George Learnid | 376 | |
| Samual Church | 305 | |
| Robert Fairchild | 220 | |
| Roger Sherman | 186 | |
| Lyman Law | 162 | |
| Calvin Goddard | 160 | |
| Thomas Williams | 149 | |

## MISSISSIPPI

| | Votes | % |
|---|---|---|
| AL Christopher Rankin (JAC D) | 5,671 | 99.1 |

## NEW HAMPSHIRE[1]

### Special Elections

| | Votes | % |
|---|---|---|
| AL Titus Brown | ✓ | |
| AL Joseph Healy | 13,600 | 56.4 |
| Ezekiel Webster | 10,523 | 43.6 |

## NORTH CAROLINA

| | Votes | % |
|---|---|---|
| 1 Lemuel Sawyer (OPP R) | 2,483 | 59.8 |
| Alfred M. Gatlin (OLD R) | 1,671 | 40.2 |

| Candidates | Votes | % |
|---|---|---|
| 2 Willis Alston (OPP R) | 1,321 | 42.1 |
| George Outlaw Sr (OLD R) | 978 | 31.2 |
| James Grant | 837 | 26.7 |
| 3 Richard Hines (OPP R) | 2,607 | 52.7 |
| Thomas H. Hall (OLD R) | 2,343 | 47.3 |
| 4 John H. Bryan (OPP R) | 2,488 | 51.0 |
| Richard D. Spaight (OLD R) | 2,392 | 49.0 |
| 5 Gabriel Holmes (OPP R) | 3,347 | 62.8 |
| Charles Hooks (OLD R) | 1,982 | 37.2 |
| 6 Weldon N. Edwards (OLD R) | | 100.0 |
| 7 Archibald McNeill (OLD R) | ✓ | |
| John Culpepper (OPP R) | | |
| 8 Willie P. Mangum (FED) | 2,301 | 50.6 |
| Josiah Crudup | 2,243 | 49.4 |
| 9 Romulus M. Saunders (LD R) | ✓ | |
| 10 John Long Jr | 3,252 | 52.9 |
| John Giles | 2,891 | 47.1 |
| 11 Henry W. Conner (OLD R) | ✓ | |
| T. Hunt (OPP R) | 86 | |
| 12 Samuel P. Carson (OPP R) | 2,081 | 35.2 |
| Robert B. Vance (OLD R) | 1,924 | 32.6 |
| James Graham (OLD R) | 1,903 | 32.2 |
| 13 Lewis Williams | ✓ | |

## RHODE ISLAND[2]

| | Votes | |
|---|---|---|
| AL Tristam Burges | 2,932✓ | |
| Dutee J. Pearce | 2,534 | |
| Job Durfee | 2,468 | |
| Samuel Eddy | 2,121 | |
| William Hunter | 364 | |

### Special Election

| | Votes | % |
|---|---|---|
| AL Dutee J. Pearce | 1,960 | 56.9 |
| Job Durfee | 1,482 | 43.0 |

## TENNESSEE

| | Votes | % |
|---|---|---|
| 1 John Blair | 3,613 | 51.9 |
| John Tipton | 3,348 | 48.1 |
| 2 John Cocke | 3,887 | 56.1 |
| Thomas Arnold | 3,044 | 43.9 |
| 3 James Standifer | 4,332 | 53.3 |
| James C. Mitchell | 3,793✓ | 46.7 |
| 4 Jacob C. Isacks | ✓ | |
| 6 James K. Polk | 3,659 | 35.3 |
| Andrew Erwin | 2,742 | 26.5 |
| Lunsford M. Bramlett | 2,347 | 22.7 |
| James Sanford | 1,508 | 14.6 |

| Candidates | Votes | % |
|---|---|---|
| 7 Samuel Houston | 5,684 | 84.8 |
| John Bruce | 1,014 | 15.1 |
| 8 John H. Marable | 2,177 | 38.7 |
| James B. Reynolds | 1,922 | 34.1 |
| Willie Blount | 1,533 | 27.2 |
| 9 Adam R. Alexander | 2,865 | 42.0 |
| David Crockett | 2,594 | 38.1 |
| James Ferrill | 912 | 13.4 |
| Thomas H. Persons | 447 | 6.6 |

## VIRGINIA

| | Votes | |
|---|---|---|
| 1 Thomas Newton Jr | ✓ | |
| 2 James Trezvant | ✓ | |
| Eppes | | |
| 3 William S. Archer | ✓ | |
| 4 Mark Alexander | ✓ | |
| 5 John Randolph | ✓ | |
| 6 Thomas Davenport | ✓ | |
| Urquehart | | |
| Lanier | | |
| Graves | | |
| 7 Nathaniel H. Claiborne | ✓ | |
| J. Leftwich | | |
| 8 Burwell Bassett | ✓ | |
| S. Jones | | |
| James | | |
| 9 Robert S. Garnett | ✓ | |
| Upshaw | | |
| 10 John Taliaferro | ✓ | |
| Hooe | | |
| 11 Andrew Stevenson | ✓ | |
| 12 William C. Rives | ✓ | |
| 13 Robert Taylor | ✓ | |
| 14 Charles F. Mercer | ✓ | |
| 15 William Armstrong | ✓ | |
| Colston | | |
| 16 William McCoy | ✓ | |
| Shetter | | |
| 17 John Floyd | ✓ | |
| 18 Benjamin Estill (AR) | ✓ | |
| Graham | | |
| Crockett | | |
| 19 William Smith | ✓ | |
| Lovell | | |
| 20 Alfred H. Powell | ✓ | |
| Smith | | |
| Steenberger | | |
| Kercheval | | |
| 21 Joseph Johnson | ✓ | |
| Doddridge | | |
| 22 John S. Barbour | ✓ | |
| Maxwell | | |

### 1824 Elections

*1. New Hampshire was entitled to six representatives in the House for the 19th Congress (1825-27). State law required that to be elected, a candidate had to receive a popular vote majority for any particular House seat. With candidates running at large, as they did in the 1824 election, the determination of what constituted a majority was calculated as follows:*

*First, the total vote was calculated by summing all votes cast for the House, yielding a figure of 72,066. This figure divided by six, the number of House seats to be filled, equals 12,011. In order to win, a candidate thus needed a majority of the 12,011 votes, that is, one half plus one additional vote. Dividing 12,011 by two equals 6,005.5, which was rounded up to whole votes to—6,006—the vote total needed for election.*

*Five candidates who were running—Bartlett, Whipple, Miller, Eastman and Harvey—received at least 6,006 votes and thus were elected. Miller did not serve in the House; thus an asterisk appears next to his vote total.*

*Since none of the other candidates qualified for the sixth seat, it remained vacant until a special election was held in 1825 between Webster and Healy, who finished sixth and seventh in 1824. (See 1825 New Hampshire, this page.)*

*2. No information available as to whether the Ohio representatives were elected by district or at large.*

### 1825 Elections

*1. Brown filed a vacancy left when James Miller was elected in 1824 but did not serve. Healy defeated Webster to fill the state's undecided sixth House seat, which no candidate had won in 1824 due to the majority vote requirement.*

*2. Rhode Island was entitled to two seats in the 19th Congress (1825-27), but state law required that a candidate receive a popular vote majority for election. Pearce failed to qualify in the general election but won the subsequent special election shown on this page. (Majority Vote Requirement, see box this page.)*

---

## Majority Vote Requirement

During part of the 19th century, five New England states—Maine, Massachusetts, New Hampshire, Rhode Island and Vermont—had state laws requiring that candidates win election to the House by a popular vote majority. The specific procedures varied among the five states. The majority vote requirement was last used in 1892 Rhode Island *(See p. 916).*

The footnote on this page for the 1824 New Hampshire section explains how the majority vote requirement worked in New Hampshire when two or more candidates running at-large could be elected. For the purpose of illustrating how the vote total required for election was determined, Congressional Quarterly has *included all election returns* provided by the ICPSR for this election.

In other at-large elections appearing in this section (pages 943 to 1292), candidates receiving fewer than 100 votes and scattered votes for unidentified candidates are *deleted.* Therefore, the calculation of the vote total needed for election in these five states, in cases where a majority was required, cannot be determined on the basis of the returns published in the *Guide to U.S. Elections, Third Edition.*

# 1826 House Elections

## DELAWARE

| | Candidates | Votes | % |
|---|---|---|---|
| AL | Louis McLane (FED) | 4,630* | 54.1 |
| | Arnold Naudain (OLD R) | 3,931 | 45.9 |

## GEORGIA

| | | Votes | % |
|---|---|---|---|
| 1 | Edward F. Tattnall | 1,623 | 100.0 |
| 2 | John Forsyth | 2,717 | 100.0 |
| 3 | Wiley Thompson | 3,042 | 60.3 |
| | Cleveland | 2,001 | 39.7 |
| 4 | Wilson Lumpkin | 4,070 | 50.3 |
| | Colquett | 4,026 | 49.7 |
| 5 | Charles E. Haynes | 2,369 | 78.7 |
| | Longstreet | 640 | 21.3 |
| 6 | Tomlinson Fort | 2,993 | 54.0 |
| | Cuthbert | 2,552 | 46.0 |
| 7 | John Floyd | 3,971 | 51.2 |
| | King | 3,786 | 48.8 |

## ILLINOIS

| | | Votes | % |
|---|---|---|---|
| AL | Joseph Duncan (JAC D) | 6,322 | 49.3 |
| | Daniel P. Cook (NR) | 5,669 | 44.2 |
| | James Tumey | 824 | 6.4 |

## INDIANA

| | | Votes | % |
|---|---|---|---|
| 1 | Thomas H. Blake (NR) | 5,223 | 43.0 |
| | Ratliff Boon (JAC D) | 5,202 | 42.8 |
| | Lawrence S. Shuler | 1,723 | 14.2 |
| 2 | Jonathan Jennings (CLAY R) | 7,913 | 99.5 |
| 3 | Oliver H. Smith (JAC D) | 6,015 | 54.9 |
| | John Test (NR) | 4,946 | 45.1 |

## KENTUCKY

### Special Elections

| | | Votes | % |
|---|---|---|---|
| 5 | Robert McHatton (JAC D) | 1,479 | 34.3 |
| | Alfred Sandford | 1,167 | 27.1 |
| | Nicholas D. Coleman | 992 | 23.0 |
| | William Brown | 677 | 15.7 |
| 12 | John F. Henry (NR) | 2,206 | 51.0 |
| | Chittenden Lyon (JAC D) | 2,119 | 49.0 |

## LOUISIANA

| | | | |
|---|---|---|---|
| 1 | Edward Livingston (D) | ✔ | |
| 2 | Henry H. Gurley (D) | ✔ | |
| 3 | William L. Brent (D) | ✔ | |

## MAINE

| | | Votes | % |
|---|---|---|---|
| 1 | William Burleigh (AD) | 2,140 | 60.5 |
| 2 | John Anderson (JEFF D) | 2,399 | 57.9 |
| 3 | Joseph F. Wingate (D) | 1,531 | 55.2 |
| 4 | Peleg Sprague (D) | 1,613 | 97.2 |
| 5 | James W. Ripley (D) | 1,504 | 52.7 |
| 6 | Jeremiah O'Brien (D) | 1,716 | 54.4 |
| 7 | Samuel Butman | ✔ | |
| | W. D. Williamson | | |

## MARYLAND

| | | Votes | % |
|---|---|---|---|
| 1 | Clement Dorsey | 1,580 | 91.1 |
| 2 | John C. Weems | 1,687 | 50.2 |
| | Regin Estep | 1,672 | 49.8 |
| 3 | George C. Washington | 2,100 | 53.6 |
| | George Peter | 1,815 | 46.4 |

| | Candidates | Votes | % |
|---|---|---|---|
| 4 | Michael C. Sprigg | 3,085 | 43.5 |
| | John Lee | 2,672 | 37.7 |
| | T. Kennedy | 671 | 9.5 |
| | S. Hughes | 668 | 9.4 |
| 6 | Levin Gale | 1,204 | 25.2 |
| | I. Demaulsby | 1,145 | 24.0 |
| | J. Williams | 1,008 | 21.1 |
| | William Colliller | 763 | 16.0 |
| | P. Reed | 551 | 11.5 |
| 7 | John L. Kerr | 1,890 | 52.9 |
| | P. B. Hopper | 1,680 | 47.1 |
| 8 | Ephraim K. Wilson | 3,514 | 97.7 |

### Multi-Member District

| | | Votes | |
|---|---|---|---|
| 5 | Peter Little | 7,017 | ✔ |
| | John Barney | 6,916 | ✔ |
| | John Kennedy | 3,997 | |

## MASSACHUSETTS

| | | Votes | % |
|---|---|---|---|
| 1 | Daniel Webster (AR) | 1,545 | 92.6 |
| 2 | Benjamin W. Crowninshield (AR) | 234 | 58.9 |
| | Stephen White | 39 | 9.8 |
| 3 | John Varnum | 1,773 | 61.0 |
| | Caleb Cushing | 916 | 31.5 |
| 4 | Edward Everett | 1,292 | 96.4 |
| 5 | John Locke (AR) | 886 | 55.2 |
| | Joseph Kendall | 539 | 33.6 |
| | Luther Lawrence | 140 | 8.7 |
| 6 | Samuel C. Allen (AR) | 1,227 | 57.6 |
| | George Grennell | 826 | 38.8 |
| 7 | Henry W. Dwight (AR) | 2,597 | 58.9 |
| | Nathan Willis | 1,082 | 24.5 |
| | Jon Allen | 561 | 12.7 |
| 8 | Isaac C. Bates | 1,833 | 60.8 |
| | Samuel C. Lathrop | 948 | 31.4 |
| | James Rowler | 220 | 7.3 |
| 9 | John Baily (AR) | 854 | 60.0 |
| | William Ellis | 331 | 23.2 |
| 10 | James L. Hodges | 1,551 | 56.1 |
| | Hercules Cushman | 717 | 25.9 |
| | Francis Bayleys (JACS R) | 429 | 15.5 |
| 11 | John Reed (AR) | 998 | 81.9 |
| | Walter Folger | 201 | 16.5 |
| 12 | Joseph Richardson | 1,188 | 58.9 |
| | Thomas L. Beats | 670 | 33.2 |
| 13 | John Davis (AR) | 1,316 | 90.1 |
| | Jonas Tibley | 110 | 7.5 |

## MISSOURI

| | | Votes | % |
|---|---|---|---|
| AL | Edward Bates (JAC D) | 6,636 | 61.5 |
| | Scott (NR) | 4,159 | 38.5 |

## NEW JERSEY

| | | Votes | |
|---|---|---|---|
| AL | George Holcombe (JAC&AR) | 24,538 | ✔ |
| | Lewis Condict (AR) | 15,615 | ✔ |
| | Samuel Swan (AR) | 14,701 | ✔ |
| | Isaac Pierson (AR) | 14,697 | ✔ |
| | Hedge Thompson (AR) | 14,479 | ✔ |
| | Ebenezer Tucker (AR) | 14,433 | ✔ |
| | Daniel Garrison (JAC R) | 10,166 | |
| | George Cassedy (JAC R) | 9,944 | |
| | Isaac G. Farlee (JAC R) | 9,752 | |
| | Benjamin B. Cooper (JAC R) | 9,512 | |
| | William Kennedy (JAC R) | 9,282 | |
| | James Parker | 637 | |
| | Ephraim Bateman | 297 | |
| | Peter D. Vroom | 136 | |
| | Caleb Newbold | 110 | |

## NEW YORK

| | Candidates | Votes | % |
|---|---|---|---|
| 1 | Silas Wood | 1,485 | 97.9 |
| 2 | John Wood | 1,335 | 54.7 |
| | John Smith | 1,104 | 45.3 |
| 4 | Aaron Ward | 2,566 | 59.6 |
| | John Haff | 1,738 | 40.4 |
| 5 | Thomas Oakley | 3,266 | 50.8 |
| | Edmund Pendleton | 3,159 | 49.2 |
| 6 | John Hallock Jr. | 2,393 | 56.8 |
| | Hector Craig | 1,817 | 43.2 |
| 7 | George Belden | 2,677 | 50.7 |
| | Lemuel Jenkins | 2,608 | 49.4 |
| 8 | James Strong | 2,984 | 59.9 |
| | Walter Patterson | 2,002 | 40.2 |
| 9 | John Dickinson | 3,339 | 51.9 |
| | James Hogeboom | 3,098 | 48.1 |
| 10 | Stephen Van Rensselaer | 3,006 | 100.0 |
| 11 | Selah Hobbie | 4,076 | 58.9 |
| | Isaac Burr | 2,847 | 41.1 |
| 12 | John De Graff | 3,309 | 100.0 |
| 13 | Samuel Chase | 2,618 | 50.9 |
| | George Morell | 2,389 | 46.4 |
| 14 | Henry Storrs | 4,174 | 69.8 |
| | Ezekiel Bacon | 1,808 | 30.2 |
| 15 | Michael Hoffman | 2,684 | 59.5 |
| | Daniel Van Horn | 1,829 | 40.5 |
| 16 | Henry Markell | 2,611 | 51.6 |
| | Aarron Haring | 2,445 | 48.4 |
| 17 | John W. Taylor | 2,910 | 57.5 |
| | Alphens Goodrich | 2,150 | 42.5 |
| 18 | Henry Martindale | 2,496 | 51.1 |
| | John Williard | 2,392 | 48.9 |
| 19 | Richard Keese | 3,328 | 52.4 |
| | Asa Hascall | 3,022 | 47.6 |
| 21 | John Clark | 3,354 | 52.6 |
| | Robert Monell | 3,024 | 47.4 |
| 22 | John G. Stower | 3,785 | 55.6 |
| | John Miller | 3,024 | 44.4 |
| 23 | Jonas Earll Jr | 3,420 | 51.8 |
| | Luther Badger | 3,178 | 48.2 |
| 24 | Nathaniel Garrow | 3,039 | 54.1 |
| | Elijah Miller | 2,575 | 45.9 |
| 25 | David Woodcook | 3,366 | 52.3 |
| | Charles Humphrey | 3,076 | 47.8 |
| 27 | Daniel Barnard | 4,299 | 52.3 |
| | Enos Pomeroy | 3,927 | 47.7 |
| 28 | John Magee | 3,300 | 40.8 |
| | Timothy Porter | 2,331 | 28.9 |
| | William Woods | 1,246 | 15.4 |
| | Phillip Church | 1,203 | 14.9 |
| 29 | David Evans | 3,843 | 54.2 |
| | Simeon Cumings | 3,251 | 45.8 |
| 30 | Daniel Garnsey | 4,801 | 55.1 |
| | Albert Tracy | 3,919 | 44.9 |

### Multi-Member Districts

| | | Votes | |
|---|---|---|---|
| 3 | Churchill C. Cambreleng | 9,108 | ✔ |
| | Gulian Verplanck | 5,705 | ✔ |
| | Jeromus Johnson | 5,376 | ✔ |
| | King | 3,814 | |
| | Vanwych | 3,631 | |
| 20 | Silas Wright | 6,579 | ✔ |
| | Rudolph Bunner | 6,558 | ✔ |
| | Nicolli Fosdick | 6,048 | |
| | Elisha Camp | 6,039 | |
| 26 | Dudley Marvin | 8,082 | ✔ |
| | John Maynard | 5,554 | ✔ |
| | Nathaniel Allen | 4,153 | |
| | John Knox | 2,631 | |

## OHIO

| | | Votes | % |
|---|---|---|---|
| 1 | James Findlay (JAC R) | 2,954 | 42.6 |
| | D. Morris (AR) | 2,443 | 35.2 |
| | T. Morris (JAC R) | 1,546 | 22.3 |
| 2 | John Woods (AR) | ✔ | |
| | T. R. Ross (JAC R) | | |

## OHIO

| | Candidates | Votes | % |
|---|---|---|---|
| 3 | William McLean (AR) | ✓ | |
| 4 | Joseph Vance (AR) | ✓ | |
| 5 | William Russell (JAC R) | 2,111 | 35.5 |
| | Collins (AR) | 1,444 | 24.3 |
| | Morris (AR) | 1,249 | 21.0 |
| | Shephard (AR) | 1,140 | 19.2 |
| 6 | William Creighton Jr (AR) | 3,652 | 63.5 |
| | John Thompson | 2,099 | 36.5 |
| 7 | Samuel F. Vinton (AR) | ✓ | |
| 8 | William Wilson (AR) | ✓ | |
| 9 | Philemon Beecher (AR) | 3,708 | 61.3 |
| | Mathews (JAC R) | 2,346 | 38.8 |
| 10 | John Davenport (AR) | ✓ | |
| 11 | John C. Wright (AR) | 2,344 | 35.5 |
| | Beebe (AR) | 2,136 | 32.4 |
| | John M. Goodenow (JAC R) | 2,116 | 32.1 |
| 12 | John Sloane (AR) | 3,417 | 50.7 |
| | John Tomson (JAC R) | 3,319 | 49.3 |
| 13 | Elisha Whittlesey (AR) | ✓ | |
| 14 | Mordecai Bartley (AR) | 2,500 | 59.7 |
| | Cooke | 1,688 | 40.3 |

### Special Election[1]

| | | | |
|---|---|---|---|
| | Thomas Shannon (D) | ✓ | |

## PENNSYLVANIA

| | | | |
|---|---|---|---|
| 1 | Joel Sutherland (JAC R) | ✓ | |
| | S. Breck (AR) | | |
| | W. Duane | | |
| 2 | John Sergeant (AR) | ✓ | |
| | Horn (JAC R) | | |
| | Thomas Kittera (UNP R) | | |
| 3 | Daniel H. Miller (JAC R) | ✓ | |
| | Harrison | | |

| | Candidates | Votes | % |
|---|---|---|---|
| 5 | John B. Sterigere | ✓ | |
| 6 | Innis Green | ✓ | |
| | John M. Forster | | |
| 10 | Adam King | ✓ | |
| 12 | John Mitchell | ✓ | |
| 13 | Chauncy Forward | ✓ | |
| 14 | Andrew Stewart | ✓ | |
| 15 | Joseph Lawrence | ✓ | |
| 16 | Richard Coulter (FED) | ✓ | |
| 18 | Stephan Barlow | ✓ | |

### Multi-Member Districts

| | | | |
|---|---|---|---|
| 4 | Charles Miner (FED) | ✓ | |
| | James Buchanan (FED) | ✓ | |
| | Samuel Anderson (FED) | ✓ | |
| 7 | Joseph Fry | ✓ | |
| | William Addams | ✓ | |
| 8 | Samuel D. Ingham | ✓ | |
| | George Wolf | ✓ | |
| 9 | Samuel McKean | ✓ | |
| | Espy Van Horne | ✓ | |
| | George Kremer | ✓ | |
| 11 | James Wilson | ✓ | |
| | William Ramsey | ✓ | |
| 17 | James S. Stevenson | ✓ | |
| | Robert Orr Jr. | ✓ | |

### Special Elections

| | | | |
|---|---|---|---|
| 2 | Thomas Kittera (FED) | ✓ | |
| | Horn (JAC R) | | |
| 13 | Chauncy Forward | ✓ | |
| | William Piper | | |
| 18 | Thomas H. Sill (FED) | 1,812 | 39.8 |
| | Barlow | 1,045 | 23.0 |
| | Hays | 937 | 20.6 |
| | Herrington | 760 | 16.7 |

## SOUTH CAROLINA

| | Candidates | Votes | % |
|---|---|---|---|
| 1 | William Drayton (UN D) | | 100.0 |
| 2 | James Hamilton Jr (SR FT) | | 100.0 |
| 3 | Thomas R. Mitchell | ✓ | |
| | Robert B. Campbell | | |
| 4 | William D. Martin (D) | ✓ | |
| | Andrew R. Govan | | |
| 5 | Starling Tucker | ✓ | |
| | Caldwell | | |
| 6 | George McDuffie (D) | ✓ | |
| 7 | William T. Nuckolls (D) | ✓ | |
| | Samuel McCreary | | |
| | James McKibbin | | |
| 8 | Warren R. Davis (SR D) | 2,478 | 50.3 |
| | John Wilson | 2,453 | 49.8 |
| 9 | John Carter | | 100.0 |

## VERMONT[2]

| | | | |
|---|---|---|---|
| 1 | Jonathan Hunt (NR) | ✓ | |
| 2 | Rollin C. Mallary | 3,050 | 98.3 |
| 3 | George E. Wales | 2,634 | 96.2 |
| 4 | Heman Allen | 2,631* | 46.5 |
| | Benjamin Swift | 2,546 | 45.0 |
| 5 | Daniel Azro Ashley Buck (D) | 4,400 | 73.0 |
| | James Bell (NR) | 1,542 | 25.6 |

## VIRGINIA

### Special Election

| | | | |
|---|---|---|---|
| 5 | George W. Crump (JAC R) | ✓ | |
| | Giles | | |

1. *No information available as to whether Shannon was elected in a district or at large.*

2. *In the 4th district, neither candidate received the majority of the vote required to win. In a later election, for which no returns are available, Swift was elected.*

---

# House Candidates Index

For an index of all House candidates listed in this section (pages 943-1326), see pages 1402-1501. Instructions for use of the House Candidates Index appear on page 1402.

---

# 1827 House Elections

## ALABAMA

| | Candidates | Votes | % |
|---|---|---|---|
| 1 | Gabriel Moore (JAC D) | 846 | 100.0 |
| 2 | John McKee | 1,140 | 69.5 |
| | Thomas W. Farrar | 500 | 30.5 |
| 3 | George Owen (JAC D) | | 100.0 |

## CONNECTICUT

| | Candidates | Votes | % |
|---|---|---|---|
| AL | Ralph Ingersoll | 7,838✔ | |
| | Elisha Phelps | 6,762✔ | |
| | David Plant | 4,890✔ | |
| | Orange Merwin | 4,472✔ | |
| | John Baldwin | 4,195✔ | |
| | Noyes Barber | 3,607✔ | |
| | Alexander Stewart | 2,690 | |
| | Ansel Sterling | 2,656 | |
| | Andrew Judson | 2,509 | |
| | Robert Fairchild | 2,451 | |
| | Timothy Pitkin | 1,304 | |
| | Lyman Law | 1,284 | |
| | Joseph Eaton | 1,211 | |
| | Noah Benedict | 948 | |
| | Gideon Tomlinson | 484 | |
| | Alexander Stewart | 474 | |
| | Roger Sherman | 448 | |
| | Nathan Pendleton | 416 | |
| | Thomas S. Williams | 351 | |

## DELAWARE

### Special Election

| | Candidates | Votes | % |
|---|---|---|---|
| AL | Kensey Johns Jr (FED) | 4,148 | 52.4 |
| | James A. Bayard (OLD R) | 3,753 | 47.4 |

## GEORGIA

### Special Elections

| | Candidates | Votes | % |
|---|---|---|---|
| AL | Richard H. Wilde | ✔ | |
| AL | George R. Gilmer | 21,008 | 63.5 |
| | Charlton | 12,094 | 36.5 |

## KENTUCKY

| | Candidates | Votes | % |
|---|---|---|---|
| 1 | Henry Daniel (JAC D) | 4,163 | 52.2 |
| | David Trimble (JAC D) | 3,811 | 47.8 |
| 2 | Thomas Metcalfe (JAC D) | 2,964 | 54.9 |
| | Conn | 2,436 | 45.1 |
| 3 | James Clark (JAC D) | 2,914 | 57.9 |
| | Taylor | 2,121 | 42.1 |
| 4 | Robert P. Letcher (W) | 3,637 | 53.3 |
| | Rodes | 3,182 | 46.7 |
| 5 | Robert L. McHatton (JAC D) | 3,307 | 52.5 |
| | Sandford | 2,988 | 47.5 |
| 6 | Joseph Lecompte (JAC D) | 3,546 | 50.9 |
| | Crittenden | 3,183 | 45.7 |
| 7 | Thomas P. Moore (JAC D) | 3,681 | 90.5 |
| | Thompson | 386 | 9.5 |
| 8 | Richard A. Buckner (A-JAC D) | 3,527 | 52.1 |
| | Owens | 3,247 | 47.9 |
| 9 | Charles A. Wickliffe (JAC D) | 3,856 | 66.1 |
| | White | 1,982 | 34.0 |
| 10 | Joel Yancey (JAC D) | 3,268 | 50.8 |
| | Johnson | 3,169 | 49.2 |

| | Candidates | Votes | % |
|---|---|---|---|
| 11 | William S. Young (JAC D) | 4,009 | 56.0 |
| | John Calhoun | 3,155 | 44.0 |
| 12 | Chittenden Lyon (JAC D) | 3,471 | 52.1 |
| | Henry (NR) | 2,070 | 31.1 |
| | New | 1,123 | 16.9 |

### Special Elections[1]

| | Candidates | Votes | % |
|---|---|---|---|
| 11 | John Calhoon | 2,290 * | |
| | Thomas Chilton | 1,685 | |
| 11 | Thomas Chilton | ✔ | |
| | John Calhoon | | |

## MAINE

### Special Election

| | Candidates | Votes | % |
|---|---|---|---|
| 1 | Rufus McIntire (JAC D) | 2,169 | 54.5 |
| | John Holmes | 1,814 | 45.5 |

## MISSISSIPPI

| | Candidates | Votes | % |
|---|---|---|---|
| AL | William Haile (JAC D) | 1,914 | 34.6 |
| | John Norton | 1,312 | 23.7 |
| | Beverly R. Grayson | 1,204 | 21.8 |
| | Adam Benjamin (NR) | 1,096 | 19.8 |

## NEW HAMPSHIRE

| | Candidates | Votes | % |
|---|---|---|---|
| AL | Ichabod Bartlett (OLD R) | 22,680✔ | |
| | Titus Brown (OLD R) | 22,354✔ | |
| | Joseph Healy (OLD R) | 21,515✔ | |
| | Jonathan Harvey (OLD R) | 20,873✔ | |
| | David Barker Jr (OLD R) | 14,456✔ | |
| | Thomas Whipple Jr (OLD R) | 12,189✔ | |
| | E. Web (AR) | | |
| | S. C. Web | | |
| | Eastman | | |
| | Cartland | | |

## NORTH CAROLINA

| | Candidates | Votes | % |
|---|---|---|---|
| 1 | Lemuel Sawyer (OLD R) | 2,943 | 65.1 |
| | William B. Shepard (OPP R) | 1,579 | 34.9 |
| 2 | Willis Alston | ✔ | |
| 3 | Thomas H. Hall (OPP R) | ✔ | |
| | Richard Hines (OLD R) | | |
| 4 | John H. Bryan | ✔ | |
| 5 | Gabriel Holmes | ✔ | |
| 6 | Daniel Turner | 1,116 | 28.5 |
| | Charles A. Hill | 1,049 | 26.8 |
| | Willis Boddie | 783 | 20.0 |
| | William M. Sneed | 620 | 15.8 |
| | Joseph H. Bryan | 345 | 8.8 |
| 7 | John Culpepper (AR) | 2,375 | 41.2 |
| | John A. Cameron | 1,990 | 34.5 |
| | John Gilchrist | 1,387 | 24.1 |
| 8 | Daniel L. Barringer (OLD R) | 2,398 | 53.3 |
| | Archibald D. Murphey (OPP R) | 2,102 | 46.7 |
| 9 | Augustine H. Shepperd (OLD R) | 4,304 | 64.6 |
| | Bedford Brown (OPP R) | 2,361 | 35.4 |
| 10 | John Long (AR) | ✔ | |
| | Asa Eubank | | |
| 11 | Henry W. Conner (OLD R) | 3,182 | 81.9 |
| | Samuel Henderson (OPP R) | 702 | 18.1 |
| 12 | Samuel P. Carson (OLD R) | 4,187 | 63.4 |
| | Robert B. Vance (OPP R) | 2,419 | 36.6 |

| | Candidates | Votes | % |
|---|---|---|---|
| 13 | Lewis Williams (AR) | ✔ | |
| | John Mushat | | |

## RHODE ISLAND

| | Candidates | Votes | % |
|---|---|---|---|
| AL | Tristam Burges (NR) | 2,230✔ | |
| | Dutee J. Pearce (NR) | 2,126✔ | |

## TENNESSEE

| | Candidates | Votes | % |
|---|---|---|---|
| 1 | John Blair | 4,216 | 55.8 |
| | John Tipton | 3,208 | 42.4 |
| 2 | Pryor Lea | 3,688 | 39.7 |
| | Thomas D. Arnold | 3,316 | 35.7 |
| | William B. Reese | 2,272 | 24.5 |
| 3 | James C. Mitchell | 5,732 | 55.7 |
| | James Standifer | 4,566 | 44.3 |
| 4 | Jacob C. Isacks | 6,823 | 100.0 |
| 5 | Robert Desha | 4,509 | 61.1 |
| | John Hall | 1,581 | 21.4 |
| | William Trousdale | 1,292 | 17.5 |
| 6 | James K. Polk | 6,351 | 56.6 |
| | Lunsford M. Bramlett | 4,878 | 43.4 |
| 7 | John Bell | 4,889 | 55.7 |
| | Felix Grundy | 3,887 | 44.3 |
| 8 | James B. Reynolds | 2,609 | 51.0 |
| | John H. Marable | 2,507✔ | 49.0 |
| 9 | David Crockett | 5,868 | 49.1 |
| | Adam R. Alexander | 3,646 | 30.5 |
| | William Arnold | 2,427 | 20.3 |

## VIRGINIA

| | Candidates | Votes | % |
|---|---|---|---|
| 1 | Thomas Newton Jr (AR) | ✔ | |
| | George Loyall | | |
| 2 | James Trezvant | ✔ | |
| 3 | William S. Archer | ✔ | |
| 4 | Mark Alexander | ✔ | |
| 5 | John Randolph | ✔ | |
| 6 | Thomas Davenport | ✔ | |
| 7 | Nathaniel H. Claiborne | ✔ | |
| | Campbell | | |
| 8 | Burwell Bassett | ✔ | |
| 9 | John Roane | ✔ | |
| 10 | John Taliaferro | ✔ | |
| 11 | Andrew Stevenson | ✔ | |
| 12 | William C. Rives | ✔ | |
| 13 | Philip P. Barbour (A-A) | ✔ | |
| 14 | Charles F. Mercer | ✔ | |
| | Thompson | | |
| 15 | William Armstrong | ✔ | |
| | Peter | | |
| 16 | William McCoy | ✔ | |
| 17 | John Floyd | ✔ | |
| 18 | Alexander Smyth | ✔ | |
| | Sharp | | |
| 19 | Lewis Maxwell | ✔ | |
| | Smith | | |
| | Lovell | | |
| 20 | Robert Allen | ✔ | |
| | Samuel Kercheval | | |
| | Alfred H. Powell | | |
| 21 | Isaac Leffler (AR) | ✔ | |
| | Haymond | | |
| | Johnson (JAC R) | | |
| 22 | John S. Barbour | ✔ | |
| | Hunton | | |

1. Rep. William S. Young died Sept. 20, 1827, and a special election was held to replace him in November of that year. In initial counting of the returns, Thomas Chilton led John Calhoon 2,704 votes to 2,679. But then returns from Hardin County were thrown out, with Chilton losing 1,019 votes and Calhoon losing only 389 votes, making Calhoon the winner. The returns minus Hardin County are listed in the ICPSR data above.

Calhoon then resigned, never having formally claimed the House seat, and both candidates then petitioned the governor to call a new election. A second special election was held Dec. 20-22, and was won by Chilton. No returns are available.

# 1828 House Elections

## DELAWARE

| Candidates | Votes | % |
|---|---|---|
| AL Kensey Johns Jr. (FED) | 4,769 | 52.2 |
| James A. Bayard (OLD R) | 4,347 | 47.5 |

## GEORGIA

| Candidates | Votes | % |
|---|---|---|
| AL George R. Gilmer | | * |
| Thomas F. Foster | | ✔ |
| Richard H. Wilde | | ✔ |
| Wilson Lumpkin | | ✔ |
| James M. Wayne | | ✔ |
| Charles E. Haynes | | ✔ |
| Wiley Thompson | | ✔ |

## ILLINOIS

| Candidates | Votes | % |
|---|---|---|
| AL Joseph Duncan (JAC D) | 10,447 | 62.9 |
| George Forquer (NR) | 6,158 | 37.1 |

## INDIANA

| | Candidates | Votes | % |
|---|---|---|---|
| 1 | Ratliff Boon (JAC D) | 7,272 | 52.2 |
| | Thomas H. Blake (NR) | 6,671 | 47.8 |
| 2 | Jonathan Jennings (CLAY R) | 7,659 | 73.3 |
| | John H. Thompson | 2,785 | 26.7 |
| 3 | John Test (NR) | 6,867 | 55.8 |
| | Jonathan McCarty (JAC D) | 5,433 | 44.2 |

## LOUISIANA

| | Candidates | Votes | % |
|---|---|---|---|
| 1 | Edward D. White | | ✔ |
| 2 | Henry H. Gurley | | ✔ |
| 3 | Walter H. Overton (D) | | ✔ |

## MAINE[1]

| | Candidates | Votes | % |
|---|---|---|---|
| 1 | Rufus McIntire (JAC D) | 2,981 | 66.0 |
| 2 | John Anderson (JEFF D) | 3,189 | 76.2 |
| 3 | Joseph F. Wingate (D) | 2,086 | 73.0 |
| 4 | Peleg Sprague | 2,086* | 94.4 |
| 5 | James W. Ripley (JAC R) | 2,394 | 56.9 |
| | Reuel Washburn (AR) | 1,813 | 43.1 |
| 6 | Jeremiah O'Brien (D) | 1,709* | 48.2 |
| | Hathaway | 1,119 | 31.5 |
| 7 | Samuel Butman | 3,336 | 62.0 |

## MASSACHUSETTS

| | Candidates | Votes | % |
|---|---|---|---|
| 1 | Benjamin Gorham | 3,234 | 78.3 |
| | William Ingalls | 819 | 19.8 |
| 2 | Benjamin W. Crowninshield (AR) | 1,326 | 54.0 |
| | Leverett Saltonstall | 631 | 25.7 |
| | Ezra Mudge | 284 | 11.6 |
| | Joseph S. Cabot (JACS R) | 186 | 7.6 |
| 3 | John Varnum | 1,663 | 72.6 |
| | George Savory | 379 | 16.6 |
| | Samuel Phillips | 149 | 6.5 |
| 4 | Edward Everett | 3,004 | 73.9 |
| | S. M. Parker | 470 | 11.6 |
| | S. Fiske | 465 | 11.4 |
| 5 | Joseph G. Kendall | 1,436 | 52.7 |
| | John Socke (AR) | 1,205 | 44.2 |
| 6 | George Grennell Jr | 2,023 | 69.7 |
| | Elihu Hoyt | 456 | 15.7 |
| | Samuel F. Dickinson | 277 | 9.5 |
| 7 | Henry W. Dwight (AR) | 2,237 | 53.0 |
| | George W. Briggs | 1,033 | 24.5 |
| | Nathan Willis (JACS R) | 922 | 21.8 |
| 8 | Isaac C. Bates (AR) | 2,133 | 87.7 |
| | John Mills | 192 | 7.9 |

| | Candidates | Votes | % |
|---|---|---|---|
| 9 | John Bailey (AR) | 2,047 | 77.4 |
| | William Ellis | 375 | 14.2 |
| | Ebenezer Seaver | 151 | 5.7 |
| 10 | James L. Hodges | 1,338 | 81.5 |
| | Francis Baylies | 129 | 7.9 |
| 11 | John Reed (AR) | 1,027 | 94.3 |
| 12 | Joseph Richardson | 1,114 | 50.4 |
| | Thomas P. Beal | 1,003 | 45.4 |
| 13 | John Davis (AR) | 2,293 | 89.6 |
| | Jonas Sibley (JACS R) | 184 | 7.2 |

## MISSISSIPPI

### Special Election

| | Candidates | Votes | % |
|---|---|---|---|
| AL | Thomas Hinds (JAC D) | 1,844 | 89.5 |

## MISSOURI

| | Candidates | Votes | % |
|---|---|---|---|
| AL | Spencer Pettis (JAC D) | 7,108 | 61.0 |
| | Edward Bates (NR) | 4,539 | 39.0 |

## NEW JERSEY

| | Candidates | Votes | % |
|---|---|---|---|
| AL | Lewis Condict (NR) | 23,783 | ✔ |
| | Richard M. Cooper (NR) | 23,737 | ✔ |
| | Isaac Pierson (NR) | 23,733 | ✔ |
| | Samuel Swan (NR) | 23,709 | ✔ |
| | James F. Randolph (NR) | 23,684 | ✔ |
| | Thomas H. Hughes (NR) | 23,604 | ✔ |
| | William N. Jeffers (JAC D) | 22,014 | |
| | James Parker (JAC D) | 22,003 | |
| | Peter D. Vroom Jr (JAC D) | 21,994 | |
| | John Clement (JAC D) | 21,949 | |
| | George Cassedy (JAC D) | 21,921 | |
| | Samuel Fowler (JAC D) | 21,902 | |

### Special Elections

| | Candidates | Votes | % |
|---|---|---|---|
| AL | Thomas Sinnickson (NR) | 23,425 | 51.8 |
| | James D. Westcott (JAC D) | 21,527 | 47.6 |
| AL | James F. Randolph (NR) | 23,388 | 51.7 |
| | James Parker (JAC D) | 21,752 | 48.1 |

## NEW YORK

| | Candidates | Votes | % |
|---|---|---|---|
| 1 | James Lent | 3,105 | 52.3 |
| | Silas Wood | 2,831 | 47.7 |
| 2 | Jacob Crocheron | 2,885 | 59.2 |
| | Peter Radcliff | 1,988 | 40.8 |
| 4 | Henry B. Cowles | 3,492 | 51.0 |
| | Tompkins | 3,352 | 49.0 |
| 5 | Abraham Bockee | 4,640 | 58.5 |
| | Pendleton | 3,293 | 41.5 |
| 6 | Hector Craig | 3,535 | 55.7 |
| | Wilkin | 2,816 | 44.3 |
| 7 | Charles G. De Witt | 4,203 | 61.9 |
| | Bevier | 1,857 | 27.4 |
| | Bogardus | 731 | 10.8 |
| 8 | James Strong | 3,592 | 50.9 |
| | James Vanderpoel | 3,459 | 49.1 |
| 9 | John Dickinson | 4,588 | 51.6 |
| | George Davis | 4,302 | 48.4 |
| 10 | Ambrose Spencer | 4,157 | 51.0 |
| | Charles Dudley | 3,889 | 47.7 |
| 11 | Perkins King | 5,342 | 61.6 |
| | Jacob Haight | 3,335 | 38.4 |
| 12 | Peter Borst | 3,637 | 57.5 |
| | Jacob Livingston | 2,688 | 42.5 |
| 13 | William Angel | 4,474 | 55.7 |
| | Erastus Crafts | 3,559 | 44.3 |
| 14 | Henry Storrs | 5,508 | 51.1 |
| | Greene C. Bronson | 5,274 | 48.9 |

| | Candidates | Votes | % |
|---|---|---|---|
| 15 | Michael Hoffman | 3,246 | 100.0 |
| 16 | Benedict Arnold | 4,064 | 52.9 |
| | William Dodge | 3,623 | 47.1 |
| 17 | John Taylor | 3,533 | 54.9 |
| | John Cramer | 2,900 | 45.1 |
| 18 | Henry Martindale | 3,902 | 58.0 |
| | John Willard | 2,823 | 42.0 |
| 19 | Isaac Finch | 4,682 | 51.8 |
| | William Hogan | 4,360 | 48.2 |
| 21 | Robert Monell | 4,720 | 63.6 |
| | Tilly Lynde | 2,704 | 36.4 |
| 22 | Thomas Beekman | 4,831 | 53.4 |
| | John Stower | 4,217 | 46.6 |
| 23 | Jonas Earll Jr | 4,068 | 44.9 |
| | Daniel Kellogg | 3,597 | 39.7 |
| | Parson Shippman | 1,402 | 15.5 |
| 24 | Gershom Powers | 4,098 | 61.6 |
| | Charles Kellogg | 1,651 | 24.8 |
| | Moses Dixon | 901 | 13.6 |
| 25 | Thomas Maxwell | 5,462 | 60.1 |
| | Daniel Woodcook | 3,623 | 39.9 |
| 27 | Timothy Childs | 6,520 | 54.6 |
| | Addison Gardiner | 4,294 | 36.0 |
| | Danial Barnard | 1,125 | 9.4 |
| 28 | John Magee | 5,390 | 55.2 |
| | Timothy Porter | 4,382 | 44.8 |
| 29 | Phinehas Tracy | 6,924 | 68.9 |
| | Herman Redfield | 3,123 | 31.1 |
| 30 | Ebenezer Norton | 5,226 | 45.0 |
| | John Birdsall | 2,820 | 24.3 |
| | John Camp | 2,003 | 17.3 |
| | Daniel Garnsey | 1,560 | 13.4 |

### Multi-Member Districts

| | Candidates | Votes | % |
|---|---|---|---|
| 3 | Campbell P. White | 18,070 | ✔ |
| | Gulian C. Verplanck | 14,138 | ✔ |
| | Churchill C. Cambreleng | 14,117 | ✔ |
| | Ogden | 11,204 | |
| | Taylor | 10,956 | |
| | Lord | 6,788 | |
| 20 | Joseph Hawkins | 9,060 | ✔ |
| | George Fisher | 8,939 | ‡ |
| | Silas Wright | 8,932 | |
| | Perley Keyes | 8,617 | |
| 26 | Robert Rose | 8,444 | ✔ |
| | Jehiel Halsey | 6,833 | ✔ |
| | Phineas Bates | 6,651 | |
| | Dudley Marvin | 5,138 | |
| | Isreal Richardson | 4,886 | |

## OHIO

| | Candidates | Votes | % |
|---|---|---|---|
| 1 | James Findlay (JAC R) | | ✔ |
| 2 | James Shields (JAC R) | | ✔ |
| | John Woods (AR) | | |
| 3 | Joseph H. Crane (AR) | | ✔ |
| 4 | Joseph Vance (AR) | | ✔ |
| 5 | William Russell (JAC R) | | ✔ |
| 6 | William Creighton Jr (AR) | | ✔ |
| 7 | Samuel F. Vinton (AR) | | ✔ |
| 8 | William Stanbery (JAC D) | | ✔ |
| 9 | William W. Irvin (JAC R) | | ✔ |
| | Philemon Beecher (AR) | | |
| 10 | William Kennon Sr (JAC R) | | ✔ |
| | John Davenport (AR) | | ✔ |
| 11 | John M. Goodenow (JAC R) | | ✔ |
| | John C. Wright (AR) | | |
| 12 | John Thomson (JAC R) | | ✔ |
| | John Sloane (AR) | | |
| 13 | Elisha Whittlesey (AR) | | ✔ |
| 14 | Mordecai Bartley (AR) | 2,632 | 50.0 |
| | Hunter | 1,432 | 27.2 |
| | Wood | 1,200 | 22.8 |

### Special Election

| | Candidates | Votes | % |
|---|---|---|---|
| 6 | Francis S. Muhlenberg (JAC R) | | ✔ |

1. In the 6th district, no candidate received the majority of the vote required to win. In a later election, for which no returns are available, Leonard Jarvis (D) was the winner.

## PENNSYLVANIA

| Candidates | Votes | % |
|---|---|---|
| 1 Joel B. Sutherland (JAC R) | ✔ | |
| Peter A. Browne (AR) | | |
| 2 Joseph Hemphill (JAC R) | ✔ | |
| John Sergeant (AR) | | |
| 3 Daniel H. Miller (JAC R) | ✔ | |
| Samuel Harvey (AR) | | |
| 5 John B. Sterigere (JAC R) | ✔ | |
| 6 Innis Green (JAC R) | ✔ | |
| Valentine Hummel | | |
| 10 Adam King (JAC R) | ✔ | |
| 12 John Scott (JAC R) | ✔ | |
| 13 Chauncey Forward (JAC R) | ✔ | |
| 14 Thomas Irwin (JAC R) | ✔ | |
| 15 William McCreery (JAC R) | ✔ | |
| 16 Richard Coulter (JAC R) | ✔ | |
| 18 Thomas H. Sill (AR) | ✔ | |

### Multi-Member Districts

| Candidates | Votes | % |
|---|---|---|
| 4 George C. Leiper (JAC R) | ✔ | |
| James Buchanan (JAC R) | ✔ | |
| Joshua Evans Jr. (JAC R) | ✔ | |
| Anderson | | |

| Candidates | Votes | % |
|---|---|---|
| Hiester | | |
| Haines | | |
| 7 Henry A. P. Muhlenburg (JAC R) | ✔ | |
| Joseph Fry Jr (JAC R) | ✔ | |
| Henry King | | |
| William Addams | | |
| 8 Samuel Ingham (JAC R) | ✔ | |
| George Wolf (JAC R) | ✔ | |
| 9 James Ford (JAC R) | ✔ | |
| Alem Marr (JAC R) | ✔ | |
| Philander Stephens (JAC R) | ✔ | |
| 11 William Ramsey (JAC R) | ✔ | |
| Thomas H. Crawford (JAC R) | ✔ | |
| 17 John Gilmore (JAC R) | ✔ | |
| William Wilkins | ✔ | |
| James S. Stevenson (JAC R) | | |
| Moore (AR) | | |

## SOUTH CAROLINA

| Candidates | Votes | % |
|---|---|---|
| 1 William Drayton (UN D) | | 100.0 |
| 2 Robert W. Barnwell (D) | | 100.0 |
| 3 John Campbell (SR W) | ✔ | |
| Thomas R. Mitchell | | |
| 4 William D. Martin (D) | | 100.0 |
| 5 Starling Tucker | ✔ | |
| 6 George McDuffie (D) | ✔ | |
| 7 William T. Nuckolls | ✔ | |
| 8 Warren R. Davis (SR D) | ✔ | |
| Cobb | | |
| 9 James Blair (UN D) | ✔ | |
| Richard I. Manning (D) | | |
| Spann | | |

## VERMONT[1]

| Candidates | Votes | % |
|---|---|---|
| 1 Jonathan Hunt (NR) | 3,028 | 86.2 |
| Daniel Kellogg | 327 | 9.3 |
| 2 Rollin Carolas Mallary | ✔ | |
| 3 Horace Everett (W) | ✔ | |
| 4 Benjamin Swift | 4,370 | 67.5 |
| Ezra Meech (D) | 1,936 | 29.9 |
| 5 Daniel Azro Ashley Buck (D) | 1,779* | 35.1 |
| William Cahoon (A-MASC) | 1,427 | 28.1 |
| Cushman (JAC) | 1,303 | 25.7 |
| James Bell (NR) | 564 | 11.1 |

1. *No candidate received the majority of the vote in the 5th district required for election. A series of special elections were held in an attempt to meet the requirement and fill the seat. In the eighth special election, William Cahoon was elected. No returns are available for these special elections.*

# 1829 House Elections

## ALABAMA

| | Candidates | Votes | % |
|---|---|---|---|
| 1 | Clement C. Clay (JAC D) | 4,309 | 52.1 |
| | Nicholas Davis (NR) | 3,960 | 47.9 |
| 2 | Robert E. B. Baylor (JAC D) | 3,845 | 54.5 |
| | Seth Barton | 1,879 | 26.6 |
| | Henry W. Ellis (JAC D) | 1,335 | 18.9 |
| 3 | Dixon Hall Lewis (SR D) | 4,227 | 44.1 |
| | Samuel Oliver | 2,908 | 30.3 |
| | Armstrong | 2,449 | 25.6 |

## CONNECTICUT

| | Candidates | Votes | |
|---|---|---|---|
| AL | Ralph Ingersoll | 8,281 | ✔ |
| | Noyes Barber | 7,552 | ✔ |
| | Ebenezer Young | 6,592 | ✔ |
| | Jabez Huntington | 6,285 | ✔ |
| | William Storrs | 5,671 | ✔ |
| | William Ellsworth | 5,588 | ✔ |
| | David Plant | 5,401 | |
| | John Niles | 3,189 | |
| | Andrew Judson | 3,052 | |
| | Orange Merwin | 3,009 | |
| | Elisha Phelps | 2,501 | |
| | John Trott | 2,278 | |
| | Hinman | 2,244 | |
| | Roger Sherman | 1,299 | |
| | Daniel Burrows | 1,256 | |
| | Joseph Eaton | 440 | |
| | Larrd Sherwood | 344 | |
| | Timothy Pitkin | 290 | |
| | Nathan Smith | 241 | |
| | Roger Huntington | 204 | |
| | Iriah Isham | 144 | |
| | Alex Stewart | 130 | |

## GEORGIA

**Special Election**

| | Candidates | Votes | % |
|---|---|---|---|
| AL | Henry G. Lamar | 20,706 | 57.5 |
| | Charlton | 15,296 | 42.5 |

## KENTUCKY

| | Candidates | Votes | % |
|---|---|---|---|
| 1 | Henry Daniel (JAC D) | ✔ | |
| | Harrison | | |
| 2 | Nicholas D. Coleman (JAC D) | 2,520 | 45.1 |
| | Adam Beatty (NR) | 2,519 | 45.1 |
| | George M. Bedinger (NR) | 461 | 8.3 |
| 3 | James Clark | 2,605 | 71.4 |
| | Matthews Flournoy | 1,045 | 28.6 |
| 4 | Robert P. Letcher (W) | ✔ | |
| 5 | Richard M. Johnson (JAC D) | 3,634 | 55.2 |
| | R. McHatton | 2,955 | 44.9 |
| 6 | Joseph Lecompte (JAC D) | 3,371 | 51.6 |
| | Thomas P. Wilson | 3,167 | 48.4 |
| 7 | John Kinkead (D) | 3,694 | 56.3 |
| | William B. Booker | 2,872 | 43.7 |
| 8 | Nathan Gaither (D) | 2,267 | 34.5 |
| | Martin Beatty | 2,168 | 33.0 |
| | William Owens | 988 | 15.0 |
| | Tunstal Quarles | 950 | 14.5 |
| 9 | Charles Wickliffe (D) | ✔ | |
| 10 | Joel Yancey (JAC D) | 3,235 | 50.8 |
| | Francis Johnson | 3,132 | 49.2 |
| 11 | Thomas Chilton | 4,185 | 64.7 |
| | James Crutcher | 2,282 | 35.3 |
| 12 | Chittenden Lyon | | 100.0 |

## MARYLAND

| | Candidates | Votes | % |
|---|---|---|---|
| 1 | Clement Dorsey | 1,316 | 88.0 |
| 2 | Benedict Semmes (D) | 1,947 | 54.2 |
| | John C. Weems | 1,625 | 45.2 |
| 3 | George C. Washington (W) | 3,116 | 100.0 |
| 4 | Michael C. Sprigg (D) | 4,190 | 56.0 |
| | William Price | 3,293 | 44.0 |
| 6 | George E. Mitchell | 2,591 | 53.5 |
| | James W. Williams | 2,253 | 46.5 |
| 7 | Richard Spencer (D) | 1,711 | 50.3 |
| | John Leeds Kerr (W) | 1,692 | 49.7 |
| 8 | Ephraim K. Wilson (D) | 4,374 | 98.0 |

**Multi-Member District**

| | Candidates | Votes | |
|---|---|---|---|
| 5 | Benjamin C. Howard (D) | 6,297 | ✔ |
| | Elias Brown (W) | 6,153 | ✔ |
| | P. Little | 4,745 | |
| | John Barney | 3,763 | |

## MISSISSIPPI

| | Candidates | Votes | % |
|---|---|---|---|
| AL | Thomas Hinds (JAC D) | 4,585 | 42.9 |
| | David Dickson (JAC D) | 2,425 | 22.7 |
| | A. L. Benjamin (NR) | 1,920 | 18.0 |
| | William Haile (JAC D) | 1,759 | 16.5 |

## NEW HAMPSHIRE

| | Candidates | |
|---|---|---|
| AL | John W. Weeks (JAC D) | ✔ |
| | Henry Hubbard (JAC D) | ✔ |
| | Thomas Chandler (JAC D) | ✔ |
| | Jonathan Harvey (JAC D) | ✔ |
| | John Brodhead (JAC D) | ✔ |
| | Joseph Hammons (JAC D) | ✔ |
| | Wallace (NR) | |
| | Boardman (NR) | |
| | Webster (NR) | |
| | Barker (NR) | |
| | Bell (NR) | |
| | Lord (NR) | |

## NORTH CAROLINA

| | Candidates | Votes | % |
|---|---|---|---|
| 1 | William B. Shepard (D-R) | 2,491 | 54.0 |
| | Lemuel Sawyer (OPP R) | 2,121 | 46.0 |
| 2 | Willis Alston | ✔ | |
| 3 | Thomas H. Hall (D-R) | | 100.0 |
| 4 | Jesse Speight (D-R) | 3,137 | 64.3 |
| | Thomas H. Daves (D-R) | 1,282 | 26.3 |
| | James Manney (OPP R) | 459 | 9.4 |
| 5 | Gabriel Holmes (D-R) | 2,551 | 52.2 |
| | Edward B. Dudley (D-R) | 2,333 | 47.8 |
| 6 | Robert Potter (D-R) | 2,661 | 83.9 |
| | Samuel Hillman (OPP R) | 396 | 12.5 |
| 7 | Edmund Deberry (AR) | 3,098 | 51.9 |
| | John A. Cameron (D-R) | 2,869 | 48.1 |
| 8 | Daniel L. Barringer (D-R) | 2,650 | 61.7 |
| | James A. Craig (D-R) | 1,590 | 37.0 |
| 9 | Augustine H. Shepard (D-R) | | 100.0 |
| 10 | John Giles (D-R) | 3,226* | 58.6 |
| | John Long (AR) | 2,281 | 41.4 |
| 11 | Henry W. Conner | ✔ | |
| 12 | Samuel P. Carson | ✔ | |
| 13 | Lewis Williams (NR) | ✔ | |
| | Samuel King (D-R) | | |

**Special Election**

| | Candidates | Votes | % |
|---|---|---|---|
| 10 | Abraham Rencher (NR) | 1,972 | 56.2 |
| | John Long (NR) | 1,538 | 43.8 |

## PENNSYLVANIA

**Special Election**

| | Candidates | Votes | % |
|---|---|---|---|
| 17 | Harmar Denny (A-MAS) | ✔ | |
| | James S. Stevenson (D) | | |

## RHODE ISLAND

| | Candidates | Votes | |
|---|---|---|---|
| AL | Dutee J. Pearce (NR) | 4,328 | ✔ |
| | Tristam Burges (NR) | 4,108 | ✔ |
| | Samuel Eddy (NR) | 1,251 | |
| | Job Durfee (NR) | 1,126 | |
| | Elisha R. Potter (NR) | 518 | |
| | John Dwolf Jr (NR) | 200 | |

## TENNESSEE

| | Candidates | Votes | % |
|---|---|---|---|
| 1 | John Blair | 3,899 | 67.2 |
| | John A. Rogers | 1,048 | 18.1 |
| | William Priestly | 856 | 14.8 |
| 2 | Pryor Lea | 4,813 | 51.7 |
| | Thomas D. Arnold | 4,496 | 48.3 |
| 3 | James Standifer | 8,383 | 82.3 |
| | John Lowry | 1,802 | 17.7 |
| 4 | Jacob C. Isacks | 3,869 | 100.0 |
| 5 | Robert Desha | 4,575 | 64.2 |
| | William Trousdale | 2,547 | 35.8 |
| 6 | James K. Polk | 9,963 | 100.0 |
| 7 | John Bell | 5,542 | 100.0 |
| 8 | Cave Johnson | 3,470 | 52.9 |
| | John H. Marable | 3,085 | 47.1 |
| 9 | David Crockett | 6,783 | 64.0 |
| | Adam R. Alexander | 3,643 | 34.4 |

## VIRGINIA

| | Candidates | |
|---|---|---|
| 1 | Thomas Newton Jr (NR) | ‡ |
| | George Loyall (JAC R) | |
| 2 | James Trezvant | ✔ |
| 3 | William S. Archer (JAC R) | ✔ |
| 4 | Mark Alexander | ✔ |
| 5 | Thomas T. Bouldin | ✔ |
| | Miller | |
| | George W. Crump | |
| 6 | Thomas Davenport | ✔ |
| 7 | Nathaniel H. Claiborne | ✔ |
| 8 | Richard Coke Jr | ✔ |
| | Burwell Bassett | |
| | Braxton | |
| 9 | John Roane | ✔ |
| 10 | John Taliaferro (NR) | ✔ |
| | Newton | |
| 11 | Andrew Stevenson (JAC R) | ✔ |
| 12 | William C. Rives (JAC R) | |
| 13 | Philip P. Barbour (JAC R) | ✔ |
| 14 | Charles F. Mercer | ✔ |
| | Gibson | |
| 15 | William Armstrong | ✔ |
| 16 | William McCoy | ✔ |
| 17 | Robert Craig | ✔ |
| | Miller | |
| 18 | Alexander Smyth | ✔ |
| 19 | Lewis Maxwell | ✔ |
| | Lovell | |
| | Smith | |
| 20 | Robert Allen | ✔ |
| | Kercheval | |
| 21 | Philip Doddridge | ✔ |
| | Johnson | |
| 22 | John S. Barbour | ✔ |

**Special Election**

| | Candidates | |
|---|---|---|
| 12 | William F. Gordon (JAC R) | ✔ |

# 1830 House Elections

## DELAWARE

| | Candidates | Votes | % |
|---|---|---|---|
| AL | John J. Milligan (NR) | 4,267 | 52.6 |
| | Henry M. Ridgely (JAC D) | 3,833 | 47.3 |

## GEORGIA

| | | Votes | |
|---|---|---|---|
| AL | Richard H. Wilde | 26,313✓ | |
| | Wilson Lumpkin | 25,896✓ | |
| | Daniel Newman | 24,459✓ | |
| | Henry G. Lamar | 22,422✓ | |
| | Thomas F. Foster | 21,443✓ | |
| | James M. Wayne | 21,210✓ | |
| | Wiley Thompson | 20,713✓ | |
| | Charles E. Haynes | 17,244 | |
| | T. U. T. Charlton | 15,049 | |
| | Roger L. Gamble | 14,263 | |
| | Seaton Grantland | 13,738 | |
| | Reuben C. Shorter | 5,150 | |

## LOUISIANA

| 1 | Edward D. White | ✓ |
|---|---|---|
| 2 | Philemon Thomas (D) | ✓ |
| 3 | Henry A. Bullard | ✓ |

## MAINE

| | | Votes | % |
|---|---|---|---|
| 1 | Rufus McIntire (JAC D) | ✓ | |
| 2 | John Anderson (JEFF D) | ✓ | |
| 3 | Edward Kavanagh (D) | 2,169 | 52.4 |
| | Moses Shaw (NR) | 1,712 | 41.4 |
| 4 | George Evans (NR) | ✓ | |
| 5 | Cornelius Holland (D) | ✓ | |
| 6 | Leonard Jarvis (D) | ✓ | |
| 7 | James Bates (D) | ✓ | |

## MASSACHUSETTS

| | | Votes | % |
|---|---|---|---|
| 1 | Nathan Appleton (NR) | 3,341 | 56.3 |
| | Henry Lee (A-TARIFF) | 2,475 | 41.7 |
| 2 | Rufus Choate (NR) | 1,740 | 59.1 |
| | Benjamin Crowninshield | 767 | 26.1 |
| | Cabot (JAC R) | 352 | 12.0 |
| 3 | Jeremiah Nelson (NR) | 2,952 | 62.3 |
| | Gayton S. Osgood (JACS R) | 1,695 | 35.8 |
| 4 | Edward Everett (NR) | 2,176 | 82.6 |
| | James Russell | 427 | 16.2 |
| 5 | Joseph Q. Kendall (NR) | 1,675 | 97.0 |
| 6 | George Grennell Jr (NR) | 1,515 | 72.4 |
| | Isaac Billings | 511 | 24.4 |
| 7 | George N. Briggs (NR) | 1,707 | 57.5 |
| | Nathan Willis (JACS R) | 825 | 27.8 |
| | Henry W. Dwight | 222 | 7.5 |
| 8 | Isaac C. Bates (NR) | 1,827 | 77.7 |
| | John Mills (JACS R) | 470 | 20.0 |
| 9 | Henry A. S. Dearborn (NR) | 1,872 | 55.0 |
| | Moses Thacher (A-MAS) | 1,088 | 32.0 |
| | Abel Cushing | 239 | 7.0 |
| 10 | James L. Hodges (NR) | 3,437 | 50.5 |
| | Micah H. Buggles (A-MASDNR) | 3,227 | 47.4 |
| 11 | John Reed (NR) | 949 | 94.3 |
| 12 | John Quincy Adams (NR) | 1,811 | 70.7 |
| | Arad Thompson | 378 | 14.8 |
| | William Baylies | 327 | 12.8 |
| 13 | John Davis (NR) | 2,014 | 72.7 |
| | Dan Thurber (JACS R) | 598 | 21.6 |
| | Unidentified Candidate (A-MAS&SC) | 160 | 5.8 |

## NEW JERSEY

| | | Votes | |
|---|---|---|---|
| AL | Lewis Condict (NR) | 15,268✓ | |
| | Thomas H. Hughes (NR) | 15,214✓ | |
| | Richard M. Cooper (NR) | 15,150✓ | |

| Candidates | Votes | % |
|---|---|---|
| Isaac Southard (NR) | 15,069✓ | |
| Silas Condit (NR) | 14,823✓ | |
| James F. Randolph (NR) | 14,513✓ | |
| Parker (D) | 14,361 | |
| Wurts (D) | 14,054 | |
| Mickle (D) | 14,011 | |
| Fowler (D) | 13,936 | |
| Travers (D) | 13,915 | |
| Jeffers (D) | 13,086 | |

## NEW YORK

| | Candidates | Votes | % |
|---|---|---|---|
| 1 | James Lent (JAC D) | 2,557 | 54.5 |
| | John King | 2,138 | 45.5 |
| 2 | John Bergen (JAC D) | 2,147 | 50.4 |
| | John Wyckoff | 2,116 | 49.6 |
| 4 | Aaron Ward (JAC D) | 2,998 | 53.6 |
| | John Hunter | 1,767 | 31.6 |
| | Jonathan Ferris | 830 | 14.8 |
| 5 | Edmund Pendleton (NR) | 3,463 | 52.3 |
| | Stoddard Judd | 3,161 | 47.7 |
| 6 | Samuel Wilkin (NR) | 2,498 | 50.9 |
| | Isaac Vanduzer | 2,414 | 49.1 |
| 7 | John Brodhead (JAC D) | 3,854 | 59.7 |
| | Thomas Lockwood | 2,602 | 40.3 |
| 8 | John King (JAC D) | 3,400 | 56.8 |
| | Robert Leroy Livingston | 2,586 | 43.2 |
| 9 | Job Pierson (JAC D) | 4,453 | 59.3 |
| | John Dickinson | 3,052 | 40.7 |
| 10 | Gerrit Lansing (JAC D) | 3,684 | 53.0 |
| | Ambrose Spencer | 3,274 | 47.1 |
| 11 | Erastus Root (JAC D) | 5,004 | 61.0 |
| | Isaac Ogden | 3,201 | 39.0 |
| 12 | Joseph Bouck (JAC D) | 3,509 | 64.9 |
| | Peter Mann | 1,898 | 35.1 |
| 13 | William Angel (JAC D) | 4,119 | 50.9 |
| | Horace Lathrop | 3,969 | 49.1 |
| 14 | Samuel Beardsley (JAC D) | 5,498 | 57.3 |
| | Simon Dexter | 3,850 | 40.1 |
| 15 | Michael Hoffman (JAC D) | 3,127 | 60.7 |
| | Hiram Nolton | 2,024 | 39.3 |
| 16 | Nathan Soule (JAC D) | 3,399 | 52.7 |
| | Daniel Cady | 3,049 | 47.3 |
| 17 | John Taylor (NR) | 2,597 | 42.0 |
| | Samuel Young | 2,350 | 38.0 |
| | David Garnsey | 1,238 | 20.0 |
| 18 | Nathaniel Pitcher (JAC D) | 3,294 | 52.5 |
| | Henry Martindale | 2,983 | 47.5 |
| 19 | William Hogan (JAC D) | 3,621 | 52.5 |
| | Luther Bradish | 1,843 | 26.7 |
| | Thomas Gilson | 1,434 | 20.8 |
| 21 | John Collier (NR) | 4,686 | 58.9 |
| | Abial Cook | 3,267 | 41.1 |
| 22 | Edward C. Reed (JAC D) | 4,531 | 51.7 |
| | Eleazer Edgcomb | 4,240 | 48.3 |
| 23 | Freeborn Jewett (JAC D) | 4,539 | 62.4 |
| | William Jerome | 2,739 | 37.6 |
| 24 | Ulysses Doubleday (JAC D) | 3,643 | 50.1 |
| | Josiah Hopkins | 3,399 | 46.8 |
| 25 | Gamaliel Barstow (NR) | 3,805 | 51.2 |
| | Charles Humphrey | 3,621 | 48.8 |
| 27 | Frederick Whittlesey (NR) | 7,410 | 65.8 |
| | Calvin Bryan | 3,846 | 34.2 |
| 28 | Grattan Wheeler (NR) | 5,950 | 54.5 |
| | John Magee | 4,961 | 45.5 |
| 29 | Phinehas Tracy (NR) | 6,802 | 68.9 |
| | Isaac Wilson | 3,071 | 31.1 |
| 30 | Bates Cooke (NR) | 6,997 | 66.7 |
| | Ebenezer Norton | 3,093 | 29.5 |

### Multi-Member Districts

| | Candidates | Votes | |
|---|---|---|---|
| 3 | Churchill G. Cambreleng (JAC D) | 10,974✓ | |
| | Campbell White (JAC D) | 10,801✓ | |
| | Gulian Verplanck (JAC D) | 10,791✓ | |
| | Abraham Lawrence | 7,614 | |
| | Thomas Smith | 7,420 | |
| | Adoniram Chandler | 7,331 | |
| | Thomas Hertell | 2,246 | |
| | John Frazce | 2,158 | |
| | Isaac Pierce | 2,126 | |
| 20 | Daniel Wardwell (JAC D) | 9,092✓ | |
| | Charles Dayan (JAC D) | 8,982✓ | |
| | Chester Buck | 6,172 | |
| | George Fisher | 6,044 | |
| 26 | John Dickson (NR) | 9,746✓ | |
| | William Babcock (NR) | 9,560✓ | |
| | Jarad Wilson | 7,361 | |
| | Jehiel Halsey | 7,281 | |

## OHIO

| | | Votes | % |
|---|---|---|---|
| 1 | James Findlay (JAC R) | ✓ | |
| | Benham (NR) | | |
| 2 | Thomas Corwin (NR) | ✓ | |
| | James Shields (JAC R) | | |
| 3 | Joseph H. Crane (NR) | ✓ | |
| 4 | Joseph Vance (NR) | ✓ | |
| 5 | William Russell (JAC R) | ✓ | |
| 6 | William Creighton Jr (NR) | ✓ | |
| 7 | Samuel F. Vinton (NR) | ✓ | |
| 8 | William Stanbery (NR) | ✓ | |
| | McLean | | |
| 9 | William W. Irvin (JAC R) | ✓ | |
| 10 | William Kennon Sr (NR) | ✓ | |
| 11 | Humphrey H. Leavitt (JAC R) | ✓ | |
| 12 | John Thomson (JAC R) | ✓ | |
| 13 | Elisha Whittlesey (NR) | 4,114 | 43.6 |
| | Sloane (A-MAS) | 3,383 | 35.9 |
| | Raven (JAC R) | 1,938 | 20.5 |
| 14 | Leonard Case (NR) | * | |

## PENNSYLVANIA

| 1 | Joel B. Sutherland (D) | ✓ |
|---|---|---|
| | Simpson (D) | |
| 2 | Henry Horn (JAC) | ✓ |
| | Coxe (NR) | |
| 3 | John G. Watmough (NR) | ✓ |
| | Daniel H. Miller (D) | |
| 5 | Joel K. Mann | ✓ |
| 6 | John C. Bucher | ✓ |
| | Valentine Hummel | |
| 10 | Adam King | ✓ |
| 12 | Robert Allison | ✓ |
| 13 | George Burd | ✓ |
| 14 | Andrew Stewart | ✓ |
| 15 | Thomas M. T. McKennan | ✓ |
| 16 | Richard Coulter | ✓ |
| 18 | John Banks | ✓ |

### Multi-Member Districts

| 4 | David Potts Jr | ✓ |
|---|---|---|
| | Joshua Evans Jr | ✓ |
| | William Hiester | ✓ |
| 7 | Henry King | ✓ |
| | Henry A. P. Muhlenburg | ✓ |
| 8 | Samuel A. Smith | ✓ |
| | Peter Ihrie Jr | ✓ |
| 9 | James Ford | ✓ |
| | Philander Stephens | ✓ |
| | Lewis Dewart | ✓ |
| 11 | Thomas H. Crawford | ✓ |
| | William Ramsey | ✓ |
| 17 | Harmar Denny | ✓ |
| | John Gilmore | ✓ |

## SOUTH CAROLINA

| Candidates | Votes | % |
|---|---|---|
| 1 William Drayton (UN D) | | 100.0 |
| 2 Robert W. Barnwell (D) | | 100.0 |
| 3 Thomas R. Mitchell | 2,200 | 53.8 |
| John Campbell (SR W) | 1,893 | 46.3 |
| 5 John K. Griffin (SR W) | ✔ | |
| B. Watts | | |
| 6 George McDuffie (D) | ✔ | |
| 7 William T. Nuckolls | ✔ | |

| Candidates | Votes | % |
|---|---|---|
| 8 Warren R. Davis (SR D) | ✔ | |
| 9 James Blair (D) | | 100.0 |

## VERMONT [1]

| Candidates | Votes | % |
|---|---|---|
| 1 Jonathan Hunt (NR) | 2,735 | 58.5 |
| Orsamus C. Merrill (D) | 1,483 | 31.7 |
| Samuel Elliott | 286 | 6.1 |

| Candidates | Votes | % |
|---|---|---|
| 2 Rollin C. Mallary | 3,750 | 84.8 |
| William Slade | 484 | 11.0 |
| 3 Horace Everett | 2,876 | 49.0 |
| Royal Ransom | 2,038 | 34.7 |
| Alden Patridge | 790 | 13.5 |
| 4 Bailey | 2,925* | 40.5 |
| Heman Allen | 2,613 | 36.2 |
| Galusha | 842 | 11.7 |
| 5 William Cahoon (A-MAS) | 4,128 | 52.6 |
| Israil P. Dana | 3,468 | 44.2 |

1. No candidate received a majority of the vote in the 4th district required for election. A series of special elections were held in an attempt to meet the requirement. Herman Allen was finally elected in the eighth special election. No returns are available for these special elections.

# 1831 House Elections

## ALABAMA

| Candidates | Votes | % |
|---|---|---|
| 1 Clement Comer Clay (D) | 2,770 | 100.0 |
| 2 Samuel W. Mardis (D) | 5,400 | 41.6 |
| Jesse Winston Garth (NR) | 4,611 | 35.5 |
| Robert E. B. Baylor (D) | 2,976 | 22.9 |
| 3 Dixon Hall Lewis (SR D) | 6,268 | 59.5 |
| John Murphy (D) | 4,270 | 40.5 |

## CONNECTICUT

| | Votes | % |
|---|---|---|
| AL Ebenezer Young (NR) | 15,889✔ | |
| Noyes Barber (NR) | 11,950✔ | |
| Ralph Ingersoll (NR) | 11,938✔ | |
| Jabez Huntington (NR) | 10,946✔ | |
| William Ellsworth (NR) | 10,931✔ | |
| William Storrs (NR) | 10,750✔ | |
| Simeon Miner (D) | 6,022 | |
| Isaac Touny (D) | 5,784 | |
| Elisha Haley (D) | 5,197 | |
| William Hollabird (D) | 4,010 | |
| Thaddeus Betts (D) | 3,242 | |

## ILLINOIS

| | Votes | % |
|---|---|---|
| AL Joseph Duncan (JAC D) | 13,052 | 54.0 |
| Sidney Breese | 4,659 | 19.3 |
| Edward Coles | 3,397 | 14.0 |
| Alexander P. Field | 1,844 | 7.6 |

## INDIANA

| | Votes | % |
|---|---|---|
| 1 Ratliff Boon (JAC D) | 11,280 | 50.9 |
| John Law (JAC D) | 10,868 | 49.1 |
| 2 John Carr (JAC D) | 4,854 | 32.8 |
| William W. Wick (NR) | 4,605 | 31.1 |
| James B. Ray (NR) | 1,732 | 11.7 |
| Jonathan Jennings (NR) | 1,680 | 11.3 |
| John H. Thompson (NR) | 1,486 | 10.0 |
| 3 Jonathan McCarty (JAC D) | 6,238 | 42.6 |
| Oliver H. Smith (JAC D) | 5,297 | 36.2 |
| John Test (NR) | 3,107 | 21.2 |

## KENTUCKY[1]

| | | |
|---|---|---|
| Chilton Allan (CLAY D) | ✔ | |
| Henry Daniel (JAC D) | ✔ | |
| Richard M. Johnson (JAC D) | ✔ | |
| Albert G. Hawes (JAC D) | ✔ | |
| Nathan Gaither (D) | ✔ | |
| Chittenden Lyon (D) | ✔ | |
| John Adair (D) | ✔ | |
| Charles A. Wickliffe (D) | ✔ | |
| Joseph Lecompte (D) | ✔ | |
| Robert P. Letcher (W) | ✔ | |
| Christopher Tompkins (W) | ✔ | |
| Thomas A. Marshall (W) | ✔ | |

## MARYLAND

| | Votes | % |
|---|---|---|
| 1 Daniel Jenifer (NR) | 1,717 | 59.0 |
| John J. Brooke | 1,194 | 41.0 |
| 2 Benedict J. Semmes (D) | 1,773 | 62.3 |
| Alexander Keech | 1,072 | 37.7 |
| 3 George C. Washington (W) | 3,145 | 100.0 |
| 4 Francis Thomas (D) | 4,452 | 53.5 |
| Michael C. Sprigg | 3,872 | 46.5 |
| 6 George E. Mitchell | 2,770 | 53.2 |
| James W. Williams | 2,438 | 46.8 |
| 7 John Leeds Kerr (W) | 1,794 | 50.5 |
| Richard Spencer (D) | 1,756 | 49.5 |
| 8 John S. Spence (D) | 3,150 | 92.5 |

### Multi-Member District

| Candidates | Votes | % |
|---|---|---|
| 5 Benjamin C. Howard (D) | 6,160✔ | |
| John T. H. Worthington (D) | 5,740✔ | |
| Ebenezer L. Finley | 4,973 | |
| Elias Brown (W) | 1,997 | |

## MISSISSIPPI

| | Votes | % |
|---|---|---|
| AL Franklin E. Plummer (JAC D) | 2,922 | 37.8 |
| David Dickson (JAC D) | 1,981 | 25.7 |
| John N. Norton | 979 | 12.7 |
| James C. Wilkins | 958 | 12.4 |
| William L. Sharkey (NR) | 744 | 9.6 |

## MISSOURI

| | Votes | % |
|---|---|---|
| AL Spencer D. Pettis (JAC D) | 8,302 | 63.5 |
| Barton (NR) | 4,775 | 36.5 |

### Special Election

| Candidates | Votes | % |
|---|---|---|
| AL William H. Ashley (D) | 4,897 | 50.3 |
| Wells (D) | 4,841 | 49.7 |

## NEW HAMPSHIRE

| | | |
|---|---|---|
| AL Joseph Hammons (JAC D) | ✔ | |
| Thomas Chandler (JAC D) | ✔ | |
| John W. Weeks (JAC D) | ✔ | |
| Henry Hubbard (JAC D) | ✔ | |
| John Brodhead (JAC D) | ✔ | |
| Joseph M. Harper (JAC D) | ✔ | |

## NORTH CAROLINA

| | Votes | % |
|---|---|---|
| 1 William B. Shepard (D-R) | 2,872 | 61.9 |
| John H. Wheeler (OPP R) | 1,768 | 38.1 |
| 2 John Branch | | 100.0 |
| 3 Thomas H. Hall (D-R) | 2,944 | 55.6 |
| Joseph R. Lloyd (OPP R) | 2,352 | 44.4 |

---

# Explanation of Symbols in House Returns

In the returns for House elections *symbols* are used to denote special circumstances. In cases where no symbol is used, the candidate who received the most votes won the election to the House. The following is a key to the symbols used:

✔ Elected to the House. The symbol is used to identify winning candidates in three types of situations: (1) When candidates ran for two or more at-large seats in states which chose all of their at-large representatives in a single election, or ran in a multi-member district; (2) when the vote total and percentage of one or more of the candidates are unavailable and (3) when a candidate who did not receive the highest vote total was seated by the House. *(Explanation of multi-member districts, see p. 916.)*

‡ The symbol is used when an election dispute resulted in the unseating of a representative *after* he was sworn in. *(For discussion of specific cases, consult the* Biographical Directory of the United States Congress, 1774-1989, *U.S. Government Printing Office, Washington, D.C., 1989; hereafter referred to as the* Biographical Directory.)

* The symbol is used for three types of situations: (1) When a representative-elect died or declined his seat before the constitutionally set date for the beginning of his term—March 4 until 1935, and Jan. 3 thereafter; (2) when the House refused to seat any candidate claiming election to a seat and (3) when state law required a candidate to obtain a popular vote majority for election to the House, but the candidate receiving the most votes failed to receive a majority. *(For discussion of specific cases, consult the* Biographical Directory; *explanation of majority vote requirement, see p. 945.)*

# Information for 1824-1973 returns was obtained from a source other than the Inter-University Consortium for Political and Social Research. *(For a listing of other sources, see p. 1327.)*

**Footnotes.** Numbered footnotes are used to explain unusual situations, such as a series of elections in the same year in the same House district, anomalies resulting from reapportionment and special procedures for conducting House elections in certain states.

*Footnote, see p. 955*

## NORTH CAROLINA

| | Candidates | Votes | % |
|---|---|---|---|
| 4 | Jesse Speight (D-R) | | 100.0 |
| 5 | James I. McKay | | 100.0 |
| 6 | Robert Potter (D-R) | | 100.0 |
| 7 | Lauchlin Bethune (D-R) | 3,086 | 50.3 |
| | Edmund Deberry (OPP R) | 3,049 | 49.7 |
| 8 | Daniel L. Barringer (D-R) | | 100.0 |
| 9 | Augustine H. Shepperd | | 100.0 |
| 10 | Abraham Rencher (OPP R) | | 100.0 |
| 11 | Henry W. Conner (D-R) | ✔ | |
| | Bartlett Shipp (OPP R) | | |
| 12 | Samuel P. Carson (D-R) | 4,422 | 76.5 |
| | Anthony Casey (OPP R) | 1,355 | 23.5 |
| 13 | Lewis Williams | | 100.0 |

### Special Election

| | Candidates | Votes | % |
|---|---|---|---|
| 6 | Micajah T. Hawkins (D-R) | 949 | 35.3 |
| | Mann (D-R) | 863 | 32.1 |
| | James Wyche (OPP R) | 533 | 19.8 |
| | Pope (OPP R) | 342 | 12.7 |

## PENNSYLVANIA

### Special Election

| | Candidates | Votes | % |
|---|---|---|---|
| 11 | Robert McCoy (WOLF D) | 2,459 | 44.4 |
| | Mahon (A-WOLF D) | 1,931 | 34.8 |
| | McSherry (A-MAS) | 1,154 | 20.8 |

## RHODE ISLAND

| | Candidates | Votes | % |
|---|---|---|---|
| AL | Tristam Burges (NR) | 2,931✔ | |
| | Dutee J. Pearce (NR) | 2,727✔ | |

1. *It is not known whether the Kentucky representatives were elected at large or in districts.*

## TENNESSEE

| | Candidates | Votes | % |
|---|---|---|---|
| 1 | John Blair (D) | 4,120 | 50.3 |
| | William B. Carter (W) | 4,076 | 49.7 |
| 2 | Thomas D. Arnold (W) | 4,935 | 51.2 |
| | Pryor Lea (D) | 4,702 | 48.8 |
| 3 | James Standifer (W) | 8,906 | 99.5 |
| 4 | Jacob C. Isacks | 3,538 | 45.0 |
| | John B. McCormick | 3,068 | 39.0 |
| | Hopkins L. Turney (D) | 1,256 | 16.0 |
| 5 | William Hall (D) | 4,040 | 50.7 |
| | Robert H. Burton | 3,928 | 49.3 |
| 6 | James K. Polk (D) | 6,993 | 99.4 |
| 7 | John Bell (W) | 6,934 | 100.0 |
| 8 | Cave Johnson (D) | 5,111 | 99.8 |
| 9 | William Fitzgerald (D) | 8,534 | 51.8 |
| | David Crockett (W) | 7,948 | 48.2 |

## VERMONT

### Special Election

| | Candidates | Votes | % |
|---|---|---|---|
| 2 | William Slade (A-MAS) | 4,614 | 49.0 |
| | Williams (NR) | 3,815 | 40.5 |
| | White (JAC) | 838 | 8.9 |

## VIRGINIA

| | Candidates | Votes | % |
|---|---|---|---|
| 1 | Thomas Newton Jr (NR) | ✔ | |
| | George Loyall (D) | | |
| 2 | John Y. Mason (D) | ✔ | |
| | Eppes | | |
| 3 | William S. Archer (D) | ✔ | |
| 4 | Mark Alexander | ✔ | |
| 5 | Thomas T. Bouldin | ✔ | |
| | George W. Crump | | |
| 6 | Thomas Davenport | ✔ | |
| 7 | Nathaniel H. Claiborne | ✔ | |
| 8 | Richard Coke Jr | ✔ | |
| | Braxton | | |
| 9 | John J. Roane | ✔ | |
| | Upshaw | | |
| | Bernard | | |
| 10 | Joseph W. Chinn (D) | ✔ | |
| | John Taliaferro (NR) | | |
| 11 | Andrew Stevenson (D) | ✔ | |
| 12 | William F. Gordon (D) | ✔ | |
| 13 | John M. Patton (D) | ✔ | |
| | Dade | | |
| 14 | Charles F. Mercer (NR) | ✔ | |
| | Gibson (D) | | |
| 15 | William Armstrong | ✔ | |
| | Lucas | | |
| 16 | William McCoy | ✔ | |
| | Stribling | | |
| 17 | Robert Craig | ✔ | |
| | Miller | | |
| 18 | Charles C. Johnson | ✔ | |
| | Joseph Draper | | |
| 19 | Lewis Maxwell (NR) | ✔ | |
| | Smith (NR) | | |
| | Reynolds | | |
| 20 | Robert Allen | ✔ | |
| | Mason | | |
| 21 | Philip Doddridge | ✔ | |
| 22 | John S. Barbour | ✔ | |
| | Wallace | | |

# 1832 House Elections

## DELAWARE

| | Candidates | Votes | % |
|---|---|---|---|
| AL | John J. Milligan (W) | 4,257 | 50.7 |
| | Martin W. Bates (D) | 4,142 | 49.3 |

## GEORGIA

| | | Votes |
|---|---|---|
| AL | James M. Wayne | 34,010✔ |
| | Richard H. Wilde | 29,813✔ |
| | George R. Gilmer | 26,061✔ |
| | Augustin S. Clayton | 25,854✔ |
| | Thomas F. Foster | 25,517✔ |
| | Roger L. Gamble | 24,278✔ |
| | Seaborn Jones | 22,640✔ |
| | William Schley | 22,376✔ |
| | John Coffee | 22,284✔ |
| | Haynes | 21,638 |
| | Owens | 21,362 |
| | Terrell | 21,361 |
| | Watson | 20,884 |
| | Branham | 20,535 |
| | Stewart | 20,006 |
| | Harris | 19,288 |
| | Newman | 16,278 |
| | Lamar | 16,136 |
| | Milton | 5,157 |

### Special Election

| | | Votes | % |
|---|---|---|---|
| AL | Augustin S. Clayton | 12,587 | 52.2 |
| | William Schley | 11,541 | 47.8 |

## ILLINOIS

| | Candidates | Votes | % |
|---|---|---|---|
| 1 | Charles Slade (D) | 2,470 | 31.3 |
| | Ninian Edwards (NR) | 2,078 | 26.3 |
| | Sidney Breese | 1,770 | 22.4 |
| | Charles Dunn | 1,020 | 12.9 |
| | Henry L. Webb | 551 | 7.0 |
| 2 | Zadoc Casey (D) | 3,208 | 46.0 |
| | William B. Archer (OPP D) | 2,168 | 31.1 |
| | Wickliff Kitchell | 1,593 | 22.9 |
| 3 | Joseph Duncan (D) | 8,234 | 76.8 |
| | Jonathan H. Pugh (OPP D) | 2,323 | 21.7 |

## LOUISIANA

| | | |
|---|---|---|
| 1 | Edward D. White (W) | ✔ |
| 2 | Philemon Thomas (D) | ✔ |
| 3 | Henry A. Bullard (W) | ✔ |

## MISSOURI[1]

| | | Votes | % |
|---|---|---|---|
| AL | William H. Ashley (A-BANK) | 9,498 | 51.8 |
| | Robert W. Wells (PRO-BANK) | 8,836 | 48.2 |

## NEW JERSEY

| | | Votes |
|---|---|---|
| AL | William N. Shinn (D) | 24,383✔ |
| | Ferdinand S. Schenck (D&A-MASC) | 24,288✔ |
| | Thomas Lee (D) | 24,265✔ |
| | James Parker (D) | 23,903✔ |
| | Philemon Dickerson (D&A-MASC) | 23,860✔ |
| | Samuel Fowler (D&A-MASC) | 23,808✔ |
| | Condict (NR-A-MAS) | 23,784 |
| | Wright (NR-A-MAS) | 23,779 |
| | Pennington (NR-A-MAS) | 23,770 |
| | Reeves (NR) | 23,325 |
| | Southard (NR) | 23,310 |
| | Budd (NR) | 23,257 |

## NEW YORK

| | Candidates | Votes | % |
|---|---|---|---|
| 1 | Abel Huntington (D) | 4,193 | 59.9 |
| | David Gardiner (NR) | 2,806 | 40.1 |
| 2 | Isaac Van Houten (D) | 3,007 | 57.5 |
| | John Gurnee (NR) | 2,224 | 42.5 |
| 4 | Aaron Ward (D) | 4,173 | 57.8 |
| | Henry B. Cowles (NR) | 3,051 | 42.2 |
| 5 | Abraham Bockee (D) | 4,728 | 52.7 |
| | Edmund Pendleton (NR) | 4,241 | 47.3 |
| 6 | John Brown (D) | 4,200 | 59.0 |
| | Samuel Wilkin (NR) | 2,923 | 41.0 |
| 7 | Charles Bodle (D) | 5,225 | 62.3 |
| | Thomas Lockwood (NR) | 3,167 | 37.7 |
| 9 | Job Pierson (D) | 4,849 | 53.5 |
| | John Dickinson (NR) | 4,213 | 46.5 |
| 10 | Gerrit Lansing (D) | 4,483 | 51.0 |
| | Ambrose Spencer (NR) | 4,302 | 49.0 |
| 11 | John Cramer (D) | 4,831 | 51.6 |
| | John Taylor (NR) | 4,531 | 48.4 |
| 12 | Henry Martindale (NR) | 3,037 | 44.5 |
| | John McIntyre (D) | 2,165 | 31.7 |
| | Samuel Stevens (NR) | 1,619 | 23.7 |
| 13 | Reuben Whallon (D) | 4,251 | 55.2 |
| | Thomas Gibson (NR) | 3,449 | 44.8 |
| 14 | Ranson Gillet (D) | 3,897 | 50.5 |
| | Luther Bradish (NR) | 3,817 | 49.5 |
| 15 | Charles McVean (D) | 4,554 | 56.2 |
| | Howland Fish (NR) | 3,546 | 43.8 |
| 16 | Abijah Mann Jr (D) | 4,964 | 59.6 |
| | Ela Collins (NR) | 3,362 | 40.4 |
| 18 | Daniel Wardwell (D) | 4,393 | 50.0 |
| | Daniel Lee (NR) | 4,387 | 50.0 |
| 19 | Sherman Page (D) | 4,914 | 54.9 |
| | John Morris (NR) | 4,039 | 45.1 |
| 20 | Noadiah Johnson (D) | 4,302 | 53.8 |
| | John Collier (NR) | 3,692 | 46.2 |
| 21 | Henry Mitchell (D) | 3,719 | 52.6 |
| | Tilly Lynde (NR) | 3,349 | 47.4 |
| 24 | Rowland Day (D) | 4,456 | 53.2 |
| | Laban Hoskins (NR) | 3,913 | 46.8 |
| 25 | Samuel Clark (D) | 4,899 | 52.4 |
| | Joseph Colt (NR) | 4,453 | 47.6 |
| 26 | John Dickson (NR) | 3,903 | 62.6 |
| | John Price (D) | 2,333 | 37.4 |
| 27 | Edward Howell (D) | 5,748 | 63.2 |
| | William Woods (NR) | 3,349 | 36.8 |
| 28 | Frederick Whittlesey (NR) | 4,828 | 58.9 |
| | Isaac Hills (D) | 3,374 | 41.1 |
| 29 | George Lay (NR) | 5,308 | 70.3 |
| | David Miller (D) | 2,248 | 29.8 |
| 30 | Philo Fuller (NR) | 5,248 | 57.8 |
| | James Faulkner (D) | 3,839 | 42.3 |
| 31 | Abner Hazeltine (NR) | 5,393 | 60.7 |
| | Alson Leavenworth (D) | 3,494 | 39.3 |
| 32 | Millard Fillmore (NR) | 4,184 | 69.6 |
| | Jonathan Hoyt (D) | 1,828 | 30.4 |
| 33 | Gideon Hard (NR) | 3,789 | 58.6 |
| | Franklin Butterfield (D) | 2,678 | 41.4 |

### Multi-Member Districts

| | | Votes | |
|---|---|---|---|
| 3 | Cornelius Lawrence (D) | 18,222✔ | |
| | Campbell White (D) | 18,171✔ | |
| | Dudley Selden (D) | 18,006✔ | |
| | Churchill C. Cambreleng (D) | 17,927✔ | |
| | David Ogden (NR) | 12,334 | |
| | Hubert Van Wagenen (NR) | 12,326 | |
| | Jonathan Thompson (NR) | 12,176 | |
| | George Talman (NR) | 12,158 | |
| 8 | John Adams (D) | 9,677✔ | |
| | Aaron Vanderpoel (D) | 9,565✔ | |
| | Jedediah Miller (NR) | 7,743 | |
| | John Martin (NR) | 7,642 | |
| 17 | Samuel Beardsley (D) | 9,121✔ | |
| | Joel Turrill (D) | 8,693✔ | |
| | Charles P. Kirkland (NR) | 8,487 | |
| | Peter Sken Smith (NR) | 8,220 | |
| 22 | Nicoll Halsey (D) | 8,329✔ | |
| | Samuel G. Hathaway (D) | 8,300✔ | |

| | Candidates | Votes | % |
|---|---|---|---|
| | Eleazer W. Edgecomb (NR) | 7,026 | |
| | Gamaliel H. Barstow (NR) | 7,009 | |
| 23 | William K. Fuller (D) | 8,934✔ | |
| | William Taylor (D) | 8,933✔ | |
| | Elijah Rhoades (NR) | 8,295 | |
| | James B. Eldredge (NR) | 8,279 | |

## OHIO

| | | Votes | % |
|---|---|---|---|
| 1 | Robert T. Lytle (D) | 4,458 | 53.7 |
| | Pendleton | 3,847 | 46.3 |
| 2 | Taylor Webster (D) | 3,635 | 57.6 |
| | Collins | 2,678 | 42.4 |
| 3 | Joseph H. Crane | 2,821 | 44.8 |
| | Helfenstein (D) | 2,588 | 41.1 |
| | Young | 893 | 14.2 |
| 4 | Thomas Corwin | 3,756 | 52.6 |
| | McLean (D) | 3,387 | 47.4 |
| 5 | Thomas L. Hamer (D) | 2,171 | 32.5 |
| | Fishback | 2,069 | 31.0 |
| | Morris (D) | 2,028 | 30.4 |
| | Russel | 403 | 6.0 |
| 6 | Samuel F. Vinton | 3,065 | 66.1 |
| | House (D) | 1,569 | 33.9 |
| 7 | William Allen (D) | 3,739 | 50.0 |
| | McArthur | 3,737 | 50.0 |
| 8 | Jeremiah McLene (D) | 3,769 | 45.6 |
| | Olds | 3,193 | 38.7 |
| | Parish | 1,296 | 15.7 |
| 9 | John Chaney (D) | 4,235 | 54.0 |
| | Irvin | 3,609 | 46.0 |
| 10 | Joseph Vance | 4,854 | 71.9 |
| | Shelby (D) | 1,866 | 27.6 |
| 11 | James M. Bell | 3,131 | 50.3 |
| | Shannon (D) | 3,091 | 49.7 |
| 12 | Robert Mitchell (D) | 4,002 | 52.7 |
| | Stanberry | 3,591 | 47.3 |
| 13 | David Spangler | 3,277 | 43.8 |
| | Colerick (D) | 2,170 | 29.0 |
| | Rigdon (D) | 2,038 | 27.2 |
| 14 | William Patterson (D) | 2,294 | 54.1 |
| | Cooke | 1,944 | 45.9 |
| 15 | Jonathan Sloane | 3,117 | 43.5 |
| | Wood (D) | 2,439 | 34.0 |
| | Humphrey | 1,614 | 22.5 |
| 16 | Elisha Whittlesey | 4,281 | 46.2 |
| | Rayen (D) | 2,980 | 32.2 |
| | Webb | 1,997 | 21.6 |
| 17 | John Thomson (D) | 2,856 | 55.5 |
| | Potter | 2,286 | 44.5 |
| 18 | Benjamin Jones (D) | 3,037 | 56.1 |
| | Quimby | 2,379 | 43.9 |
| 19 | Humphrey H. Leavitt (D) | 3,182 | 50.8 |
| | Stokely | 3,085 | 49.2 |

## PENNSYLVANIA

| | | Votes | % |
|---|---|---|---|
| 1 | Joel B. Sutherland (D) | 2,366 | 50.0 |
| | James Gowen (NR) | 1,916 | 40.5 |
| | Samuel B. Davis (UVD) | 451 | 9.5 |
| 3 | John G. Watnough (NR) | 4,041 | 56.3 |
| | J. R. Burden (D) | 2,268 | 31.6 |
| | Mahon M. Levis (UVD) | 869 | 12.1 |
| 5 | Joel K. Mann (D) | ✔ | |
| 6 | Robert Ramsey (D) | ✔ | |
| 7 | David D. Wagener (D) | ✔ | |
| 8 | Henry King (D) | ✔ | |
| 9 | Henry A. P. Muhlenburg (D) | ✔ | |
| 10 | William Clark (D) | ✔ | |
| 11 | Charles A. Barnitz (NR) | ✔ | |
| 12 | George Chambers (NR) | ✔ | |
| 13 | Jesse Miller (D) | ✔ | |
| 14 | Joseph Henderson (D) | ✔ | |
| 15 | Andrew Beaumont (D) | ✔ | |
| 16 | Joseph B. Anthony (D) | ✔ | |

*Footnote, see p. 957*

## PENNSYLVANIA

| Candidates | Votes | % |
|---|---|---|
| 17 John Laporte (D) | ✔ | |
| 18 George Burd (D) | ✔ | |
| 19 Richard Coulter (D) | ✔ | |
| 20 Andrew Stewart (NR) | ✔ | |
| 21 Thomas M. T. McKennan (NR) | ✔ | |
| 22 Harmar Denny (A-MAS) | ✔ | |
| 23 Samuel S. Harrison (D) | ✔ | |
| 24 John Banks (A-MAS) | ✔ | |
| 25 John Galbraith (D) | ✔ | |

| Candidates | Votes | % |
|---|---|---|
| **Multi-Member Districts** | | |
| 2 Horace Binney (NR) | 5,364 ✔ | |
| James Harper (NR) | 5,104 ✔ | |
| B. W. Richards (D) | 3,396 | |
| Henry Horn (D) | 3,191 | |
| 4 Edward Darlington (A-MAS) | ✔ | |
| William Hiester (A-MAS) | ✔ | |
| David Potts Jr (A-MAS) | ✔ | |

## VERMONT

| Candidates | Votes | % |
|---|---|---|
| 1 Hiland Hall (W) | ✔ | |
| 2 William Slade (W) | ✔ | |
| 3 Horace Everett (W) | ✔ | |
| 4 Heman Allen (W) | ✔ | |
| 5 Benjamin F. Deming (W) | ✔ | |

1. Missouri's House representation was raised from one seat to two after the 1830 reapportionment, but in the 1832 general election only one seat was filled. The second representative was elected in 1833. See Missouri 1833, p. 958.

# 1833 House Elections

## ALABAMA

| | Candidates | Votes | % |
|---|---|---|---|
| 1 | Clement C. Clay (D) | 1,310 | 100.0 |
| 2 | John McKinley (D) | 3,724 | 52.5 |
| | James Davis | 3,369 | 47.5 |
| 3 | Samuel W. Mardis (D) | 5,242 | 57.2 |
| | Elisha Young (NR) | 2,053 | 22.4 |
| | R. E. B. Baylor (D) | 1,867 | 20.4 |
| 4 | Dixon H. Lewis (SSR D) | | 100.0 |
| 5 | John Murphy (D) | ✔ | |
| | James Dellet (W) | | |

## CONNECTICUT

| | Candidates | Votes | |
|---|---|---|---|
| AL | Noyes Barber (NR) | 10,121 | ✔ |
| | William Ellsworth (NR) | 10,064 | ✔ |
| | Ebenezer Young (NR) | 10,045 | ✔ |
| | Jabez Huntington (NR) | 9,449 | ✔ |
| | Samuel Foot (NR) | 8,029 | ✔ |
| | Samuel Tweedy (NR) | 7,815 | ✔ |
| | Andrew Judson (D&A-MASC) | 7,469 | |
| | Epaphias Porter (D&A-MASC) | 7,376 | |
| | William Hollabird (D&A-MASC) | 7,229 | |
| | Samuel Simons (D&A-MASC) | 6,896 | |
| | Gideon Wells (D&A-MASC) | 6,842 | |
| | Labern Clarke (D&A-MASC) | 6,567 | |
| | Richard Hubbard | 2,143 | |
| | Alanson Hamlin | 2,021 | |
| | Luther Loomis | 446 | |
| | Zalman Wildman | 400 | |

## INDIANA

| | Candidates | Votes | % |
|---|---|---|---|
| 1 | Ratliff Boon (D) | 3,973 | 50.6 |
| | Dennis Pennington | 1,120 | 14.3 |
| | Robert M. Evans | 1,069 | 13.6 |
| | James R. E. Goodlet | 788 | 10.0 |
| | Seth M. Levenworth | 611 | 7.8 |
| 2 | John Ewing (W) | 1,921 | 20.9 |
| | John W. Davis (D) | 1,919 | 20.9 |
| | John Law | 1,668 | 18.2 |
| | George Boon | 1,459 | 15.9 |
| | William C. Linton | 1,183 | 12.9 |
| | Hugh L. Livingston | 1,022 | 11.1 |
| 3 | John Carr (D) | 4,530 | 58.2 |
| | Harbin H. Moore | 3,257 | 41.8 |
| 4 | Amos Lane (D) | 4,262 | 50.8 |
| | John Test (W) | 3,455 | 41.2 |
| | Enoch McCarty | 676 | 8.1 |
| 5 | Jonathan McCarty (W) | 4,590 | 51.8 |
| | Oliver H. Smith (D) | 4,268 | 48.2 |
| 6 | George L. Kinnard (D) | 5,412 | 52.8 |
| | William W. Wick | 4,818 | 47.0 |
| 7 | Edward A. Hannegan (D) | 4,794 | 54.0 |
| | Albert S. White (W) | 4,056 | 45.7 |

## KENTUCKY

| | Candidates | Votes | % |
|---|---|---|---|
| 1 | Chittenden Lyon | ✔ | |
| | Linn Boyd | | |
| 2 | Albert G. Hawes (D) | 2,998 | 50.8 |
| | Philip Thompson (OPP) | 2,902 | 49.2 |
| 3 | Christopher Tompkins (W) | 4,074 | 50.4 |
| | Elijah Hise (D) | 4,008 | 49.6 |
| 4 | Martin Beaty | ✔ | |
| | Nathan Gaither | | |
| | Elisha Smith | | |
| 5 | Thomas P. Moore (D) | 2,626* | 51.0 |
| | Robert P. Letcher (W) | 2,521 | 49.0 |
| 6 | Thomas Chilton | ✔ | |
| | James Allen | | |
| 7 | Benjamin Hardin (W) | 2,826 | 52.0 |
| | C. A. Rudd | 2,610 | 48.0 |
| 8 | Patrick H. Pope | ✔ | |
| | Henry Crittenden | | |

| | Candidates | Votes | % |
|---|---|---|---|
| 9 | James Love (D) | 2,445 | 41.3 |
| | John White (W) | 2,189 | 37.0 |
| | Smith | 1,050 | 17.7 |
| 10 | Chilton Allen | | 100.0 |
| 11 | Amos Davis | 2,990 ✔ | |
| | James Crawford | 2,372 | |
| | Henry Daniel | | |
| | Kenaz Farrow | | |
| 12 | Thomas A. Marshall (W) | 2,722 | 59.2 |
| | Adam Beatty | 1,874 | 40.8 |
| 13 | Richard M. Johnson (D) | 4,737 | 73.6 |
| | John P. Gaines (W) | 1,702 | 26.4 |

## MAINE

| | Candidates | Votes | % |
|---|---|---|---|
| 1 | Rufus McIntire (JAC D) | ✔ | |
| 2 | Francis O. J. Smith (D) | ✔ | |
| 3 | Edward Kavanagh (D) | ✔ | |
| 4 | George Evans (NR) | 3,542 | 52.1 |
| | White (D) | 2,693 | 39.6 |
| 5 | Moses Mason (D) | ✔ | |
| 6 | Joseph Hall (D) | ✔ | |
| 7 | Leonard Jarvis (D) | ✔ | |
| 8 | Gorham Parks (D) | ✔ | |

## MARYLAND

| | Candidates | Votes | % |
|---|---|---|---|
| 1 | Littleton P. Dennis (NR) | 3,213 | 51.7 |
| | Steuart (D) | 3,003 | 48.3 |
| 2 | Richard B. Carmichael (D) | 3,243 | 51.9 |
| | Hoffer (NR) | 3,004 | 48.1 |
| 3 | James Turner (NR) | 3,049 | 49.3 |
| | Sewell (D) | 1,570 | 25.4 |
| | Worthington | 1,563 | 25.3 |
| 4 | James P. Heath (NR) | 2,805 | 52.0 |
| | Howard (D) | 2,592 | 48.0 |
| 5 | Isaac McKim (D) | 3,181 | 53.3 |
| | Stewart (NR) | 2,792 | 46.7 |
| 6 | William Cost Johnson (NR) | 3,063 | 55.6 |
| | Dorsey (D) | 2,442 | 44.4 |
| 7 | Francis Thomas (D) | 4,012 | 54.0 |
| | Dixon (NR) | 3,421 | 46.0 |
| 8 | John T. Stoddert (D) | 2,360 | 51.3 |
| | Genifle (NR) | 2,244 | 48.7 |

## MASSACHUSETTS

| | Candidates | Votes | % |
|---|---|---|---|
| 1 | Benjamin Gorham (NR) | 2,304 | 56.1 |
| | Theodore Lyman (D) | 1,320 | 32.2 |
| | Amasa Walker (A-MAS) | 429 | 10.5 |
| 2 | Rufus Choate (NR) | 2,216 | 59.0 |
| | Joseph S. Cabot (D) | 1,204 | 32.1 |
| | William B. Breed | 324 | 8.6 |
| 3 | Gayton P. Osgood (D&A-MASC) | 3,279 | 51.4 |
| | Caleb Cushing (NR) | 2,895 | 45.4 |
| 4 | Edward Everett (NR) | 2,413 | 77.7 |
| | John Wade | 667 | 21.5 |
| 5 | John Davis (NR) | 2,848 | 85.9 |
| | John Spurry | 328 | 9.9 |
| 6 | George Grennell Jr (NR) | 2,521 | 71.6 |
| | William Whitaker | 599 | 17.0 |
| | Israel Billings | 309 | 8.8 |
| 7 | George N. Briggs (NR) | 2,705 | 64.4 |
| | Russell Brown | 1,273 | 30.3 |
| 8 | Isaac C. Bates (NR) | 2,168 | 72.6 |
| | William W. Thompson | 333 | 11.1 |
| | Samuel Lathrop (A-MAS) | 223 | 7.5 |
| 9 | William Jackson (A-MAS) | 2,869 | 50.9 |
| | Henry A. S. Dearborn (NR) | 1,841 | 32.7 |
| | Daniel Thurber (D) | 652 | 11.6 |
| 10 | William Baylies (NR) | 2,899 | 50.9 |
| | Micah H. Ruggles | 2,554 | 44.8 |
| 11 | John Reed (NR) | 1,442 | 96.9 |
| 12 | John Quincy Adams (A-MAS) | 2,592 | 75.5 |
| | Frederick Lincoln | 714 | 20.8 |

## MISSISSIPPI

| | Candidates | Votes | % |
|---|---|---|---|
| AL | Franklin E. Plummer (W) | 7,826 ✔ | |
| | Harry Cage (D) | 7,682 ✔ | |
| | John L. Guion (W) | 4,523 | |
| | Felix H. Walker | 2,243 | |
| | Nathan Bouldin | 1,223 | |

## MISSOURI[1]

| | Candidates | Votes | % |
|---|---|---|---|
| AL | John Bull (W) | 3,671 | 27.7 |
| | Strother (JAC D) | 3,630 | 27.4 |
| | Shannon (JAC D) | 3,430 | 25.9 |
| | Birch (I) | 2,130 | 16.1 |

## NEW HAMPSHIRE

| | Candidates | Votes | |
|---|---|---|---|
| AL | Henry Hubbard (D) | ✔ | |
| | Franklin Pierce (D) | ✔ | |
| | Robert Burns (D) | ✔ | |
| | Benning M. Bean (D) | ✔ | |
| | Joseph M. Harper (D) | ✔ | |
| | Azel Hatch (A-MAS) | | |
| | John Gould (A-MAS) | | |
| | D. C. Atkinson (A-MAS) | | |
| | John Harvey (A-MAS) | | |
| | Caleb Emery (A-MAS) | | |
| | Samuel E. Cones (NR) | | |
| | James Wilson Jr (NR) | | |
| | John Wingate (NR) | | |
| | Leonard Wilcox (NR) | | |
| | Anthony Colby (NR) | | |

## NORTH CAROLINA

| | Candidates | Votes | % |
|---|---|---|---|
| 1 | William B. Shepard (W) | | 100.0 |
| 2 | Jesse A. Bynum (W) | 2,198 | 59.8 |
| | Andrew Joyner | 1,476 | 40.2 |
| 3 | Thomas H. Hall | ✔ | |
| 4 | Jesse Speight (D) | | 100.0 |
| 5 | James I. McKay (D) | 2,570 | 55.6 |
| | Lewis Dishongh (W) | 2,056 | 44.4 |
| 6 | Micajah T. Hawkins (D) | 1,694 | 38.9 |
| | Robert P. Gilliam (W) | 1,472 | 33.8 |
| | William P. Williams | 1,189 | 27.3 |
| 7 | Edmund Deberry (W) | 3,268 | 50.3 |
| | Lauchlin Bethune (D) | 3,231 | 49.7 |
| 8 | Daniel L. Barringer (W) | 2,497 | 50.6 |
| | John G. A. Williamson (D) | 2,436 | 49.4 |
| 9 | Augustine H. Shepperd (D) | | 100.0 |
| 10 | Abraham Rencher (W) | | 100.0 |
| 11 | Henry W. Conner (D) | | 100.0 |
| 12 | James Graham (W) | 3,272 | 41.6 |
| | Samuel P. Carson (D) | 2,402 | 30.6 |
| | David Newland | 2,183 | 27.8 |
| 13 | Lewis Williams | | .0 |

## PENNSYLVANIA[2]

**Special Election**

| | Candidates | Votes | % |
|---|---|---|---|
| 1 | Joel B. Sutherland (D) | 2,835 | 57.0 |
| | John Sergeant | 2,139 | 43.0 |

## RHODE ISLAND[3]

| | Candidates | Votes | |
|---|---|---|---|
| AL | Tristam Burges (W) | 3,162 ✔ | |
| | Dutee J. Pearce (D) | 2,078 | |
| | Updike (W) | 1,913 | |
| | Sprague (D) | 1,499 | |
| | Cranston (W) | 376 | |
| | Greene (W) | 364 | |
| | Dixon (W) | 168 | |

**Special Election**

| | Candidates | Votes | % |
|---|---|---|---|
| AL | Dutee J. Pearce (D) | 2,152 | 55.2 |
| | Dixon (W) | 1,705 | 43.7 |

## SOUTH CAROLINA

| | Candidates | Votes | % |
|---|---|---|---|
| 1 | Henry L. Pinckney (D) | ✓ | |
| | A. M. S. Harris (UN) | | |
| | Joel R. Poinsett (UN) | | |
| 2 | William J. Grayson (W) | 1,282 | 79.2 |
| | Benjamin Allston (UN) | 335 | 20.7 |
| 3 | Thomas Singleton (SR) | 2,089 | 55.7 |
| | Thomas R. Mitchell (UN) | 1,665 | 44.4 |
| 4 | John M. Felder (D) | ✓ | |
| 5 | John K. Griffin (SR W) | ✓ | |
| 6 | George McDuffie (D) | 2,991 | 70.4 |
| | J. Pressley (UN) | 1,254 | 29.5 |
| 7 | William K. Clowney (SR) | 4,514 | 51.2 |
| | Thomas Williams (UN) | 4,309 | 48.8 |
| 8 | Warren R. Davis (SR D) | ✓ | |
| | Grisham (UN) | | |
| 9 | James Blair (D) | | 100.0 |

## TENNESSEE

| | Candidates | Votes | % |
|---|---|---|---|
| 1 | John Blair (D) | 3,236 | 42.4 |
| | William B. Carter (W) | 2,642 | 34.7 |
| | Thomas D. Arnold (W) | 1,747 | 22.9 |
| 2 | Samuel Bunch (W) | 4,319 | 70.4 |
| | John Cocke (D) | 1,815 | 29.6 |
| 3 | Luke Lea (UN D) | 3,558 | 46.7 |
| | Joseph Williams (W) | 2,145 | 28.1 |
| | John F. Gillespie | 1,921 | 25.2 |
| 4 | James Standifer (W) | 4,172 | 57.4 |
| | James Greene | 3,100 | 42.6 |
| 5 | John B. Forester | 3,862 | 55.9 |
| | Jacob C. Isaacs | 3,051 | 44.1 |

| | Candidates | Votes | % |
|---|---|---|---|
| 6 | Balie Peyton (W) | 4,710 | 74.4 |
| | Archibald W. Overton | 1,621 | 25.6 |
| 7 | John Bell (W) | 5,951 | 100.0 |
| 8 | David W. Dickinson (D) | 2,452 | 42.4 |
| | William Brady | 2,209 | 38.2 |
| | Abraham Maury (W) | 1,129 | 19.5 |
| 9 | James K. Polk (D) | 4,751 | 68.5 |
| | Thomas Porter | 1,512 | 21.8 |
| | T. F. Bradford | 671 | 9.7 |
| 10 | William M. Inge (D) | 5,013 | 61.8 |
| | James W. Combs | 1,593 | 19.6 |
| | Thomas D. Davenport | 1,508 | 18.6 |
| 11 | Cave Johnson (D) | 3,386 | 45.1 |
| | Richard Cheatham (W) | 2,468 | 32.9 |
| | John H. Marable | 1,651 | 22.0 |
| 12 | David Crockett (W) | 3,985 | 51.1 |
| | William Fitzgerald (D) | 3,812 | 48.9 |
| 13 | Christopher H. Williams (W) | 2,374 | 34.6 |
| | William C. Dunlap (D) | 2,364 ✓ | 34.5 |
| | Adam R. Alexander | 2,123 | 30.9 |

## VIRGINIA

| | Candidates | Votes | % |
|---|---|---|---|
| 1 | George Loyall (D) | 1,428 | 53.1 |
| | Miles King (NR) | 1,261 | 46.9 |
| 2 | John Y. Mason (D) | ✓ | |
| 3 | William S. Archer (D) | ✓ | |
| 4 | James H. Gholson (NR) | ✓ | |
| | George C. Dromgoole (D) | | |
| | Knox | | |
| | Goode | | |
| 5 | John Randolph (NR) | ✓ | |

| | Candidates | Votes | % |
|---|---|---|---|
| 6 | Thomas Davenport (NR) | ✓ | |
| | Cabell | | |
| 7 | Nathaniel H. Claiborne (D) | | |
| 8 | Henry A. Wise (D) | ✓ | |
| | Richard Coke Jr (NR) | | |
| 9 | William P. Taylor (NR) | ✓ | |
| | John J. Roane (D) | | |
| | Upshaw | | |
| 10 | Joseph W. Chinn (D) | ✓ | |
| | John Taliaferro (NR) | | |
| 11 | Andrew Stevenson (D) | ✓ | |
| | John Robertson (NR) | | |
| 12 | William F. Gordon (NR) | ✓ | |
| 13 | John M. Patton (D) | ✓ | |
| 14 | Charles F. Mercer (NR) | ✓ | |
| | Mason (D) | | |
| 15 | Edward Lucas (D) | ✓ | |
| | Archer | | |
| | Naylor | | |
| | A. Smith | | |
| 16 | James M. H. Beale (D) | ✓ | |
| | Meyerhoeffer | | |
| | Steele | | |
| 17 | Samuel McDowell Moore (NR) | ✓ | |
| | Craig (D) | | |
| 18 | John H. Fulton (D) | ✓ | |
| | Byars | | |
| 19 | William McComas (D) | ✓ | |
| | Smith | | |
| 20 | John J. Allen (NR) | ✓ | |
| | Maxwell | | |
| 21 | Edgar C. Wilson (NR) | ✓ | |
| | Morgan | | |

1. Missouri added a second representative after the 1830 census. See Missouri 1832, p. 956.

2. Joel B. Sutherland was elected from Pennsylvania's 1st district in 1832. He subsequently resigned to become an associate judge of the court of common pleas in Philadelphia, but then ran for and won back his House seat in an 1833 special election.

3. Rhode Island had two House seats for the 23rd Congress (1833-35). A majority of the vote was required for election. Dutee J. Pearce failed to qualify in the initial election, but was later elected over Dixon in a special election for which no returns are available.

# 1834 House Elections

## CONNECTICUT

### Special Election

| | Candidates | Votes | % |
|---|---|---|---|
| AL | Phineas Miner (W) | 17,007✔ | |
| | Ebenezer Jackson (W) | 16,920✔ | |
| | Joseph Trumbull (W) | 16,906✔ | |
| | Luther Loomis (D) | 16,696 | |
| | Lancelot Phelps (D) | 16,668 | |
| | Samuel Ingham (D) | 16,464 | |
| | Richard Hubbard (A-MASC) | 1,186 | |
| | Horace Cowles (A-MASC) | 1,150 | |
| | Sheldon Leavitt (A-MASC) | 1,104 | |
| | Samuel Ingram | 230 | |

## DELAWARE

| | Candidates | Votes | % |
|---|---|---|---|
| AL | John J. Milligan (W) | 4,779 | 50.8 |
| | Bayard (D) | 4,626 | 49.2 |

## GEORGIA

| | Candidates | Votes | % |
|---|---|---|---|
| AL | James M. Wayne (D) | 32,933* | |
| | William Schley (D) | 32,852✔ | |
| | Charles E. Haynes (D) | 32,609✔ | |
| | George W. B. Towns (D) | 32,603✔ | |
| | John Coffee (D) | 32,581✔ | |
| | George W. Owens (D) | 32,530✔ | |
| | James C. Terrell (D) | 32,493✔ | |
| | Seaton Grantland (D) | 32,445✔ | |
| | John W. A. Sanford (D) | 32,412✔ | |
| | Gilmer (W) | 28,417 | |
| | Wilde (W) | 28,294 | |
| | Foster (W) | 28,036 | |
| | Gamble (W) | 27,835 | |
| | Chappell (W) | 27,673 | |
| | Lamar (W) | 27,507 | |
| | Beall (W) | 27,500 | |
| | Newman (W) | 27,457 | |
| | Daniel (W) | 27,447 | |

## ILLINOIS

| | Candidates | Votes | % |
|---|---|---|---|
| 1 | John Reynolds (D) | 4,523 | 45.9 |
| | Adam W. Snider (D) | 3,723 | 37.8 |
| | Edward Humphrey | 1,603 | 16.3 |
| 2 | Zadoc Casey (D) | 5,647 | 58.3 |
| | William H. Davidson | 4,036 | 41.7 |
| 3 | William L. May (D) | 6,828 | 52.8 |
| | Benjamin Mills | 6,117 | 47.3 |

### Special Elections

| | Candidates | Votes | % |
|---|---|---|---|
| 1 | John Reynolds (D) | 1,721 | 48.0 |
| | Perrie Menard | 871 | 24.3 |
| | William Orr | 501 | 14.0 |
| | H. L. Webb | 490 | 13.7 |
| 3 | William May (D) | 2,705 | 72.7 |
| | Benjamin Mills | 956 | 25.7 |

## KENTUCKY

### Special Election

| | Candidates | Votes | % |
|---|---|---|---|
| 5 | Robert P. Letcher (W) | 3,731 | 51.9 |
| | Thomas P. Moore (D) | 3,461 | 48.1 |

## LOUISIANA

| | Candidates | Votes | % |
|---|---|---|---|
| 1 | Henry Johnson (W) | 2,417 | 55.9 |
| | Gayarre | 1,384 | 32.0 |
| | Nicholls | 523 | 12.1 |
| 2 | Eleazer W. Ripley (D) | 1,162 | 42.2 |
| | Chinn (W) | 900 | 32.7 |

| | Candidates | Votes | % |
|---|---|---|---|
| | J. M. Bradford | 434 | 15.8 |
| | Woodroof | 258 | 9.4 |
| 3 | Rice Garland (W) | 1,989 | 59.1 |
| | Walker | 1,378 | 40.9 |

## MAINE[1]

| | Candidates | Votes | % |
|---|---|---|---|
| 1 | Jeremiah Goodwin (D) | 3,685* | 43.9 |
| | Horace Porter (W) | 3,511 | 41.9 |
| | W. A. Hayes | 500 | 6.0 |
| | J. McDonald | 492 | 5.9 |
| 2 | Francis O. J. Smith (D) | 5,262 | 51.9 |
| | James C. Churchill (W) | 4,827 | 47.7 |
| 3 | Jeremiah Bailey (W) | 4,240 | 51.7 |
| | Edward Kavanagh (D) | 3,778 | 46.1 |
| 4 | George Evans (W) | 5,134 | 59.4 |
| | Amos Nourse (D) | 3,301 | 38.2 |
| 5 | Moses Mason Jr. (D) | 4,791 | 53.8 |
| | Oliver Herrick (W) | 3,736 | 41.9 |
| 6 | Joseph Hall (D) | 4,251 | 61.9 |
| | Webster Kelly (W) | 2,402 | 35.0 |
| 7 | Leonard Jarvis (D) | 3,742 | 50.7 |
| | Elijah Hamlin (W) | 3,417 | 46.3 |
| 8 | Gorham Parks (D) | 6,192 | 55.4 |
| | Edward Kent (W) | 4,831 | 43.3 |

## MASSACHUSETTS

| | Candidates | Votes | % |
|---|---|---|---|
| 1 | Abbott Lawrence (W) | 5,508 | 64.9 |
| | William Foster (D) | 2,528 | 29.8 |
| 2 | Stephen C. Phillips (W) | 4,230 | 59.9 |
| | Joseph S. Cabot (D) | 2,784 | 39.4 |
| 3 | Caleb Cushing (W) | 4,353 | 58.1 |
| | Gayton P. Osgood (D) | 2,683 | 35.8 |
| 4 | Samuel Hoar (W) | 2,153 | 54.5 |
| | Herman Lincoln | 871 | 22.1 |
| | James Russell | 646 | 16.4 |
| 5 | Levi Lincoln (W) | 4,777 | 74.1 |
| | Madison S. Fisher (D) | 1,653 | 25.6 |
| 6 | George Grennell Jr (W) | 3,434 | 65.5 |
| | Israel Billings (A-MAS) | 1,520 | 29.0 |
| 7 | George N. Briggs (W) | 4,229 | 59.1 |
| | Theodore Sedgwick (D) | 2,902 | 40.6 |
| 8 | William B. Calhoun (W) | 3,839 | 61.3 |
| | Oliver Warner (D) | 2,409 | 38.4 |
| 9 | William Jackson (A-MAS) | 3,003 | 67.5 |
| | Daniel Thurber (D) | 1,121 | 25.2 |
| 10 | Nathaniel B. Borden (D) | 4,306 | 53.5 |
| | William Baylis (W) | 3,697 | 45.9 |
| 11 | John Reed (A-MAS) | 2,352 | 79.1 |
| | William J. A. Bradford (D) | 607 | 20.4 |
| 12 | John Quincy Adams (A-MAS) | 3,234 | 86.8 |

### Special Elections

| | Candidates | Votes | % |
|---|---|---|---|
| 2 | Stephen C. Phillips (W) | 4,245 | 60.1 |
| | Joseph S. Cabot (D) | 2,778 | 39.3 |
| 5 | Levi Lincoln (W) | 4,226 | 77.3 |
| | Isaac Davis (D) | 1,113 | 20.4 |

## NEW JERSEY

| | Candidates | Votes | % |
|---|---|---|---|
| AL | William N. Shinn (D) | 27,413✔ | |
| | Philemon Dickerson (D) | 27,404✔ | |
| | Ferdinand S. Schenck (D) | 27,398✔ | |
| | Thomas Lee (D) | 27,396✔ | |
| | James Parker (D) | 27,390✔ | |
| | Samuel Fowler (D) | 27,358✔ | |
| | Condict (W) | 26,413 | |
| | Randolph (W) | 26,393 | |
| | Pennington (W) | 26,384 | |
| | Spencer (W) | 26,373 | |
| | Ogden (W) | 26,372 | |
| | Brick (W) | 26,339 | |

## NEW YORK

| | Candidates | Votes | % |
|---|---|---|---|
| 1 | Abel Huntingdon (D) | 4,442 | 58.5 |
| | Abraham T. Rose (W) | 3,152 | 41.5 |
| 2 | Samuel Barton (D) | 3,943 | 59.9 |
| | Billop B. Seaman (W) | 2,642 | 40.1 |
| 4 | Aaron Ward (D) | 4,527 | 57.9 |
| | Horace Bailey (W) | 3,290 | 42.1 |
| 5 | Abraham Rockee (D) | 4,948 | 55.2 |
| | Edmund H. Pendleton (W) | 4,022 | 44.8 |
| 6 | John W. Brown (D) | 4,337 | 55.7 |
| | Thomas McKissock (W) | 3,445 | 44.3 |
| 7 | Nicholas Sickles (D) | 5,676 | 62.6 |
| | Jacob H. Dewitt (W) | 3,393 | 37.4 |
| 9 | Hiram P. Hunt (W) | 4,985 | 50.1 |
| | Job Pierson (D) | 4,961 | 49.9 |
| 10 | Gerit Y. Lansing (D) | 4,944 | 52.2 |
| | Daniel D. Barnard (W) | 4,521 | 47.8 |
| 11 | John Cramer (D) | 5,160 | 50.9 |
| | Anson Brown (W) | 4,978 | 49.1 |
| 12 | David Russell (W) | 3,942 | 59.5 |
| | John McLean (D) | 2,681 | 40.5 |
| 13 | Henry H. Ross (W) | 4,296 | 50.3 |
| | Dudley Farlin (D) | 4,246 | 49.7 |
| 14 | Ransom H. Gillet (D) | 4,134 | 53.5 |
| | Joseph W. Smith (W) | 3,589 | 46.5 |
| 15 | Matthias J. Bovee (D) | 4,695 | 53.4 |
| | Peter J. Waggoner (W) | 4,104 | 46.6 |
| 16 | Abijah Mann Jr. (D) | 5,246 | 62.3 |
| | Elisha P. Hurlbut (W) | 3,175 | 37.7 |
| 18 | Daniel Wardwell (D) | 4,512 | 50.3 |
| | Jesse Smith (W) | 4,467 | 49.8 |
| 19 | Sherman Page (D) | 5,122 | 57.9 |
| | Don F. Herrick (W) | 3,719 | 42.1 |
| 20 | William Seymour (D) | 4,950 | 58.4 |
| | Erastus Root (W) | 3,532 | 41.6 |
| 21 | William Mason (D) | 3,930 | 54.2 |
| | Alvah Hunt (W) | 3,320 | 45.8 |
| 24 | U. F. Doubleday (D) | 4,759 | 55.0 |
| | Laban Hoskins (W) | 3,898 | 45.0 |
| 25 | Graham H. Chapin (D) | 5,183 | 52.0 |
| | John M. Holley (W) | 4,781 | 48.0 |
| 26 | Francis Granger (W) | 4,378 | 59.5 |
| | Oliver Phelps (D) | 2,986 | 40.6 |
| 27 | Joshua Lee (D) | 6,077 | 60.9 |
| | Aaron Remur (W) | 3,907 | 39.1 |
| 28 | Timothy Childs (W) | 5,076 | 54.9 |
| | Fletcher M. Haight (D) | 4,164 | 45.1 |
| 29 | George W. Lay (W) | 6,409 | 62.5 |
| | John B. Skinner (D) | 3,844 | 37.5 |
| 30 | Philo C. Fuller (W) | 5,928 | 56.0 |
| | James McCall (D) | 4,658 | 44.0 |
| 31 | Abner Hazeltine (W) | 6,250 | 55.8 |
| | Oliver Lee (D) | 4,946 | 44.2 |
| 32 | Thomas C. Love (W) | 4,783 | 66.0 |
| | George P. Barker (D) | 2,468 | 34.0 |
| 33 | Gideon Hard (W) | 4,156 | 51.9 |
| | Nathan Dayton (D) | 3,854 | 48.1 |

### Multi-Member Districts

| | Candidates | Votes | % |
|---|---|---|---|
| 3 | Churchill C. Cambreleng (D) | 19,019✔ | |
| | Campbell P. White (D) | 18,983✔ | |
| | John McKeon (D) | 18,871✔ | |
| | Ely Moore (D) | 18,552✔ | |
| | Ogden Hoffman (W) | 16,822 | |
| | G. C. Verplanck (W) | 16,807 | |
| | James G. King (W) | 16,642 | |
| | Dudley Selden (W) | 16,578 | |
| 8 | Aaron Vanderpoel (D) | 10,287✔ | |
| | Valentine Efner (D) | 10,210✔ | |
| | Killian Miller (W) | 8,166 | |
| | Benjamin Pond (W) | 8,153 | |
| 17 | Samuel Beardsley (D) | 9,597✔ | |
| | Joel Turrill (D) | 9,488✔ | |
| | Joshua A. Spencer (W) | 8,665 | |
| | Peter Sken Smith (W) | 8,546 | |
| 22 | Joseph Reynolds (D) | 8,870✔ | |
| | Stephen B. Leonard (D) | 8,859✔ | |
| | William A. Ely (W) | 7,644 | |

*Footnote, see p. 961*

## NEW YORK

| Candidates | Votes | % |
|---|---|---|
| John James Speed Jr (W) | 7,220 | |
| 23 William Taylor (D) | 9,466✔ | |
| William K. Fuller (D) | 9,461✔ | |
| Victory Birdseye (W) | 8,045 | |
| J. D. Ledyard (W) | 8,034 | |

## OHIO

| | Candidates | Votes | % |
|---|---|---|---|
| 1 | Bellamy Storer (W) | 4,327 | 50.6 |
| | Lytle (D) | 4,231 | 49.4 |
| 2 | Taylor Webster (D) | 3,328 | 52.6 |
| | McNutt (W) | 3,001 | 47.4 |
| 3 | Joseph H. Crane (W) | 4,165 | 52.4 |
| | Helfenstein (D) | 3,781 | 47.6 |
| 4 | Thomas Corwin (W) | 3,847 | 58.6 |
| | McDowell (D) | 2,723 | 41.5 |
| 5 | Thomas L. Hamer (D) | 3,479 | 68.7 |
| | Jones (W) | 1,586 | 31.3 |
| 6 | Samuel F. Vinton (W) | 3,825 | 62.6 |
| | Jolline (D) | 2,283 | 37.4 |
| 7 | William K. Bond (W) | 4,333 | 51.8 |
| | Allen (D) | 4,037 | 48.2 |
| 8 | Jeremiah McLene (D) | 3,919 | 51.1 |
| | Olds (W) | 3,751 | 48.9 |
| 9 | John Chaney (D) | 4,447 | 58.5 |
| | Irvin (W) | 3,158 | 41.5 |
| 10 | Samson Mason (W) | 4,382 | 66.2 |
| | Ellsbury (D) | 1,950 | 29.5 |
| 11 | William Kennon Sr (D) | 3,496 | 50.5 |
| | Bell (W) | 3,427 | 49.5 |
| 12 | Elias Howell (W) | 4,294 | 54.3 |
| | Mitchell (D) | 3,610 | 45.7 |
| 13 | David Spangler (W) | 3,410 | 56.3 |
| | Colerick (D) | 2,644 | 43.7 |
| 14 | William Patterson (D) | 4,731 | 52.7 |
| | Bartley (W) | 4,243 | 47.3 |
| 15 | Jonathan Sloane (W) | 5,453 | 51.6 |
| | Rice (D) | 5,116 | 48.4 |
| 16 | Elisha Whittlesey (W) | 5,616 | 60.2 |
| | Dart (D) | 3,721 | 39.9 |
| 17 | John Thompson (D) | 2,346 | 59.8 |
| | Richardson (W) | 1,327 | 33.8 |
| | McCraig (A-MASC) | 253 | 6.4 |
| 18 | Benjamin Jones (D) | 2,739 | 51.8 |
| | Quinby (W) | 2,548 | 48.2 |
| 19 | Daniel Kilgore (D) | 3,370 | 51.7 |
| | Stokely (W) | 3,143 | 48.3 |

## PENNSYLVANIA

| | Candidates | Votes | % |
|---|---|---|---|
| 1 | Joel B. Sutherland (D) | 3,782 | 61.7 |
| | Gowen (W) | 2,345 | 38.3 |
| 3 | Michael W. Ash (D) | 5,757 | 55.6 |
| | Watmough (W) | 4,598 | 44.4 |

| | Candidates | Votes | % |
|---|---|---|---|
| 5 | Jacob Fry Jr (D) | 3,766 | 55.3 |
| | Royer (W) | 3,047 | 44.7 |
| 6 | Mathias Morris (W) | 3,341 | 52.4 |
| | Chapman (D) | 3,040 | 47.6 |
| 7 | David D. Wagener (D) | 4,602 | 72.8 |
| | Brown (W) | 1,718 | 27.2 |
| 8 | Edward B. Hubley (D) | 3,648 | 59.6 |
| | Livingston (W) | 2,478 | 40.5 |
| 9 | Henry A. P. Muhlenburg (D) | 4,816 | 69.3 |
| | Kirbey (W) | 2,132 | 30.7 |
| 10 | William Clark (W) | 3,396 | 54.3 |
| | Bucher (D) | 2,859 | 45.7 |
| 11 | Henry Logan (D) | 3,218 | 55.1 |
| | Barnitz (W) | 2,619 | 44.9 |
| 12 | George Chambers (W) | 4,085 | 59.8 |
| | Heck (D) | 2,751 | 40.2 |
| 13 | Jesse Miller (D) | 3,906 | 51.4 |
| | Whitesides (W) | 3,696 | 48.6 |
| 14 | Joseph Henderson (D) | 4,239 | 52.5 |
| | Milliken (W) | 3,830 | 47.5 |
| 15 | Andrew Beaumont (D) | 3,902 | 56.1 |
| | Shoemaker (W) | 3,051 | 43.9 |
| 16 | Joseph B. Anthony (D) | 5,437 | 62.8 |
| | Packer (W) | 3,226 | 37.2 |
| 17 | John Laporte (D) | 4,264 | 56.8 |
| | Williston (W) | 3,239 | 43.2 |
| 18 | Job Mann (D) | 3,535 | 54.6 |
| | Ogle (W) | 2,938 | 45.4 |
| 19 | John Klingensmith Jr (D) | 4,359 | 59.7 |
| | Coulter (W) | 2,939 | 40.3 |
| 20 | Andrew Buchanan (D) | 3,428 | 59.0 |
| | Stewart (W) | 2,387 | 41.1 |
| 21 | Thomas M. T. McKennan (W) | 2,703 | 51.3 |
| | Ringland (D) | 2,569 | 48.7 |
| 22 | Harmar Denny (W) | 3,428 | 53.5 |
| | Snowden (D) | 2,976 | 46.5 |
| 23 | Samuel S. Harrison (D) | 3,845 | 69.8 |
| | Gilmore (W) | 1,664 | 30.2 |
| 24 | John Banks (W) | 2,748 | 52.2 |
| | Power (D) | 2,514 | 47.8 |
| 25 | John Galbraith (D) | 4,642 | 60.7 |
| | Sill (W) | 3,011 | 39.3 |

### Multi-Member Districts

| | Candidates | Votes | % |
|---|---|---|---|
| 2 | Joseph R. Ingersoll (W) | 5,589✔ | |
| | James Harper (W) | 5,560✔ | |
| | Linnard (D) | 3,710 | |
| | Horn (D) | 3,671 | |
| 4 | David Potts Jr (W) | 10,348✔ | |
| | William Heister (W) | 10,348✔ | |
| | Edward Darlington (W) | 10,329✔ | |
| | Archibald T. Dick (D) | 8,477 | |
| | Benjamin Champneys (D) | 8,472 | |
| | John Morgan (D) | 8,471 | |

## SOUTH CAROLINA

| | Candidates | Votes | % |
|---|---|---|---|
| 1 | Henry L. Pinckney (SR) | 1,680 | 52.8 |
| | Alfred Huger (UN) | 1,503 | 47.2 |
| 2 | William J. Grayson (SR) | ✔ | |
| | Unidentified Candidate (SSR & SC) | | |
| 3 | Robert B. Campbell (SR) | 2,242 | 53.2 |
| | James C. Postell (UN) | 1,948 | 46.3 |
| 4 | James H. Hammond (SR) | 4,025 | 100.0 |
| 5 | John K. Griffin (SR) | | 100.0 |
| 6 | Francis W. Pickens (SR) | 2,836 | 74.6 |
| | John S. Pressly (UN) | 968 | 25.5 |
| 7 | James Rogers (UN) | 4,213 | 51.1 |
| | William K. Clowney (SR) | 4,038 | 48.9 |
| 8 | Warren R. Davis (SR) | 2,925* | 50.6 |
| | Perry (UN) | 2,855 | 49.4 |
| 9 | Richard I. Manning (UN) | 1,392 | 64.5 |
| | Rees (SR) | 765 | 35.5 |

### Special Elections

| | Candidates | Votes | % |
|---|---|---|---|
| 3 | Robert B. Campbell (NULL) | ✔ | |
| | James C. Postell (UN) | | |
| 6 | Francis W. Pickens (SR) | ✔ | |
| | John S. Pressly (UN) | | |

## VERMONT

| | Candidates | Votes | % |
|---|---|---|---|
| 1 | Hiland Hall (W) | 3,395 | 50.7 |
| | Robinson (D) | 1,872 | 28.0 |
| 2 | William Slade (A-MAS) | 4,012 | 55.0 |
| | Jonas Clark (W) | 1,494 | 20.5 |
| | Robert Pierpont (W) | 1,491 | 20.5 |
| 3 | Horace Everett (W) | 3,717 | 44.6 |
| | Sam C. Loveland (A-MAS) | 2,774 | 33.3 |
| | Alden Partridge (D) | 1,768 | 21.2 |
| 4 | Heman Allen (W) | 2,574 | 51.2 |
| | Vanness (D) | 1,678 | 33.4 |
| | Smith | 778 | 15.5 |
| 5 | Henry F. Janes (A-MAS) | 3,641 | 51.5 |
| | Isaac Fletcher (D) | 3,398 | 48.1 |

## VIRGINIA

### Special Elections

| | Candidates | Votes | % |
|---|---|---|---|
| 5 | James W. Bouldin (D) | ✔ | |
| | Beverly Tucker (W) | | |
| 11 | John Robertson (W) | 689 | 67.6 |
| | Roane (D) | 331 | 32.5 |

*1. No candidate in Maine's 1st district received the majority vote required for election. At a later special election, Rufus McIntyre was elected. No returns are available for the special election.*

# 1835 House Elections

## ALABAMA

| | Candidates | Votes | % |
|---|---|---|---|
| 1 | Reuben Chapman (D) | 4,403 | 47.8 |
| | Clascock (D) | 2,993 | 32.5 |
| | Scott (D) | 1,819 | 19.7 |
| 2 | Joshua L. Martin (D) | ✓ | |
| | Davis | | |
| | Thatch | | |
| 3 | Joab Lawler (W) | 2,498 | 40.2 |
| | Shortridge (D) | 2,362 | 38.0 |
| | May | 1,356 | 21.8 |
| 4 | Dixon H. Lewis (SR D) | | 100.0 |
| 5 | Francis S. Lyon (W) | ✓ | |
| | Baylor (D) | | |
| | Bates | | |

## CONNECTICUT

| | | Votes | |
|---|---|---|---|
| AL | Samuel Ingham (D) | 21,286 ✓ | |
| | Isaac Toucey (D) | 21,262 ✓ | |
| | Zalmon Wildman (D) | 21,220 ✓ | |
| | Andrew T. Judson (D) | 21,160 ✓ | |
| | Lancelot Phelps (D) | 21,059 ✓ | |
| | Elisha Haley (D) | 21,019 ✓ | |
| | John Holley (W) | 19,170 | |
| | Noyes Barbor (W) | 18,931 | |
| | Ebenezer Young (W) | 18,888 | |
| | Samuel Tweedy (W) | 18,881 | |
| | Ebenezer Jackson (W) | 18,809 | |
| | Joseph Trumbull (W) | 18,649 | |
| | Horace Cowles | 353 | |
| | Sheldon Leavit | 328 | |
| | Elisha Stearns | 313 | |
| | Richard Hubbard | 313 | |
| | William Waterbury | 301 | |

## GEORGIA

### Special Election

| | | Votes | |
|---|---|---|---|
| AL | Thomas Glascock (D) | 30,540 ✓ | |
| | Jesse F. Cleveland (D) | 30,077 ✓ | |
| | Jabez Y. Jackson (D) | 30,072 ✓ | |
| | Hopkins Holsey (D) | 29,727 ✓ | |
| | Wilde (W) | 27,542 | |
| | Foster (W) | 27,525 | |
| | Gamble (W) | 27,266 | |
| | Beall (W) | 26,871 | |

## INDIANA

| | | Votes | % |
|---|---|---|---|
| 1 | Ratliff Boon (D) | 4,028 | 51.4 |
| | John G. Clendenin (W) | 3,815 | 48.6 |
| 2 | John W. Davis (D) | 5,499 | 55.3 |
| | John Ewing (W) | 4,440 | 44.7 |
| 3 | John Carr (D) | 5,048 | 56.1 |
| | Charles Dewey (W) | 3,954 | 43.9 |
| 4 | Amos Lane (D) | 4,769 | 50.4 |
| | George H. Dunn (W) | 4,687 | 49.6 |
| 5 | Jonathan McCarty (W) | 4,824 | 48.9 |
| | James Rariden (W) | 2,684 | 27.2 |
| | John Finley | 2,353 | 23.9 |
| 6 | George L. Kinnard (D) | 7,483 | 61.6 |
| | Jacob B. Lowe | 4,658 | 38.4 |
| 7 | Edward A. Hannegan (D) | 6,910 | 66.3 |
| | James Gregory (W) | 3,515 | 33.7 |

## KENTUCKY

| | | | |
|---|---|---|---|
| 1 | Linn Boyd (D) | ✓ | |
| 2 | Albert G. Hawes (JAC D) | | |
| 3 | Joseph R. Underwood (W) | | |

| | Candidates | Votes | % |
|---|---|---|---|
| 4 | Sherrod Williams (W) | ✓ | |
| 5 | James Harlan (W) | ✓ | |
| 6 | John Calhoon (W) | ✓ | |
| 7 | Benjamin Hardin (W) | ✓ | |
| 8 | William J. Graves (W) | ✓ | |
| 9 | John White (W) | ✓ | |
| 10 | Chilton Allan (CLAY D) | ✓ | |
| 11 | Richard French (D) | ✓ | |
| 12 | John Chambers (W) | ✓ | |
| 13 | Richard M. Johnson (JAC D) | ✓ | |

## MARYLAND

| | | Votes | % |
|---|---|---|---|
| 1 | John N. Steele (W) | 1,967 | 100.0 |
| 2 | James A. Pearce (W) | 3,386 | 50.2 |
| | Unidentified Candidate (D) | 3,363 | 49.8 |
| 3 | James Turner (W) | 2,866 | 51.1 |
| | Unidentified Candidate (D) | 2,748 | 49.0 |
| 5 | George C. Washington (W) | 1,058 | 100.0 |
| 6 | Francis Thomas (D) | 3,838 | 53.0 |
| | Unidentified Candidate (W) | 3,405 | 47.0 |
| 7 | Daniel Jenifer (W) | 1,919 | 58.7 |
| | Unidentified Candidate (D) | 1,352 | 41.3 |

### Multi-Member District

| | | Votes | |
|---|---|---|---|
| 4 | Benjamin C. Howard (D) | 6,738 ✓ | |
| | Isaac McKim (D) | 6,675 ✓ | |
| | Unidentified Candidate (W) | 6,205 | |
| | Unidentified Candidate (W) | 6,111 | |

## MICHIGAN [1]

*(Became a state Jan. 26, 1837)*

| | | Votes | % |
|---|---|---|---|
| AL | Issac Crary (D) | 7,019 | 94.9 |

## MISSISSIPPI

| | | Votes | |
|---|---|---|---|
| AL | David Dickson (D) | 9,387 ✓ | |
| | John F. H. Claiborne (D) | 8,836 ✓ | |
| | James C. Wilkins (W) | 7,445 | |
| | Benjamin W. Edwards (D) | 7,396 | |
| | Harry Vose | 224 | |

## MISSOURI

| | | Votes | |
|---|---|---|---|
| AL | William H. Ashley (I) | 12,825 ✓ | |
| | Albert G. Harrison (D) | 10,856 ✓ | |
| | Strother (D) | 10,677 | |
| | Birch (I) | 8,843 | |

## NEW HAMPSHIRE

| | | | |
|---|---|---|---|
| AL | Robert Burns (D) | ✓ | |
| | Samuel Cushman (D) | ✓ | |
| | Joseph Weeks (D) | ✓ | |
| | Franklin Pierce (D) | ✓ | |
| | Benning M. Bean (D) | ✓ | |
| | Samuel Hale | | |
| | Samuel W. Carr | | |
| | James Wilson Jr | | |
| | Anthony Colby | | |
| | Joseph Bell | | |

## NORTH CAROLINA

| | | Votes | % |
|---|---|---|---|
| 1 | William B. Shepard (W) | 2,534 | 85.5 |
| | Isaac Pipkin (D) | 429 | 14.5 |
| 2 | Jesse A. Bynum (D) | 2,228 | 52.9 |
| | William L. Long (W) | 1,986 | 47.1 |
| 3 | Ebenezer Pettigrew (W) | 3,072 | 54.9 |
| | Thomas H. Hall (D) | 2,529 | 45.2 |
| 4 | Jesse Speight (D) | 3,017 | 57.3 |
| | John McLeod (W) | 2,250 | 42.7 |

| | Candidates | Votes | % |
|---|---|---|---|
| 5 | James I. McKay (D) | 2,690 | 63.4 |
| | Lewis Dishongh (W) | 1,553 | 36.6 |
| 6 | Micajah T. Hawkins (D) | 2,540 | 62.5 |
| | Josiah Crudup (W) | 1,522 | 37.5 |
| 7 | Edmund Deberry (W) | 3,426 | 53.8 |
| | Lauchlin Bethune (D) | 2,940 | 46.2 |
| 8 | William Montgomery (D) | 2,695 | 50.4 |
| | Daniel L. Barringer (W) | 2,654 | 49.6 |
| 9 | Augustine H. Shepperd (W) | ✓ | |
| 10 | Abraham Rencher (SR W) | 3,078 | 51.4 |
| | Burton Craige (W) | 1,619 | 27.0 |
| | Richard M. Pearson (W) | 1,297 | 21.6 |
| 11 | Henry W. Conner (D) | 3,385 | 63.2 |
| | Bartlett Shipp (W) | 1,974 | 36.8 |
| 12 | James Graham (W) | 3,733 ‡ | 48.6 |
| | David Newland (W) | 3,726 | 48.5 |
| 13 | Lewls Wllliams (W) | ✓ | |

## RHODE ISLAND

| | | Votes | |
|---|---|---|---|
| AL | William Sprague (D) | 3,924 ✓ | |
| | Dutee J. Pearce (D) | 3,901 ✓ | |
| | Burges (W) | 3,776 | |
| | Cranston (W) | 3,659 | |
| | Ruyers | 101 | |

## TENNESSEE

| | | Votes | % |
|---|---|---|---|
| 1 | William B. Carter (W) | 3,696 | 48.6 |
| | Alexander Anderson (D) | 2,054 | 27.0 |
| | Thomas D. Arnold (W) | 1,863 | 24.5 |
| 2 | Samuel Bunch (W) | 4,370 | 68.3 |
| | David Adams (D) | 2,026 | 31.7 |
| 3 | Luke Lea (UN D) | 4,250 | 58.7 |
| | Joseph L. Williams (W) | 2,992 | 41.3 |
| 4 | James Standifer (W) | 4,383 | 60.1 |
| | William T. Senter (D) | 2,915 | 39.9 |
| 5 | John B. Forester (W) | 5,645 | 83.5 |
| | Peter Buram (D) | 1,112 | 16.5 |
| 6 | Balie Peyton (W) | 3,530 | 100.0 |
| 7 | John Bell (W) | 4,832 | 100.0 |
| 8 | Abram P. Maury (W) | 3,006 | 60.6 |
| | Robert Jetton (D) | 1,956 | 39.4 |
| 9 | James K. Polk (D) | 5,165 | 100.0 |
| 10 | Ebenezer J. Shields (W) | 3,217 | 40.5 |
| | Thomas Porter | 2,381 | 30.0 |
| | A. A. Kincannon | 2,344 | 29.5 |
| 11 | Cave Johnson (D) | 2,714 | 63.7 |
| | William Turner (W) | 1,549 | 36.3 |
| 12 | Adam Huntsman (D) | 4,652 | 51.4 |
| | David Crockett (W) | 4,400 | 48.6 |
| 13 | William C. Dunlap (D) | 4,903 | 63.9 |
| | C. H. Williams (W) | 2,770 | 36.1 |

## VIRGINIA

| | | Votes | % |
|---|---|---|---|
| 1 | George Loyall (D) | 1,625 | 52.5 |
| | Emmerson (W) | 1,471 | 47.5 |
| 2 | John Y. Mason (D) | 1,193 | 70.2 |
| | Urquehart (W) | 507 | 29.8 |
| 3 | John W. Jones (D) | 1,566 | 68.3 |
| | Archer (W) | 728 | 31.7 |
| 4 | George C. Droomgoole (D) | 1,365 | 55.7 |
| | Gholson (W) | 1,088 | 44.4 |
| 5 | James W. Bouldin (D) | 1,264 | 59.0 |
| | Bolling (W) | 879 | 41.0 |
| 6 | Walter Coles (D) | 1,728 | 54.1 |
| | Davenport (W) | 1,467 | 45.9 |
| 7 | Nathaniel H. Claiborne (W) | 1,680 | 51.3 |
| | Stuart (D) | 1,592 | 48.7 |
| 8 | Henry A. Wise (W) | 1,212 | 62.9 |
| | Coke (W) | 716 | 37.1 |
| 9 | John Roane Jr (D) | 1,150 | 50.3 |
| | Taylor (W) | 1,138 | 49.7 |

*1. Crary was elected to the House from Michigan in 1835 in anticipation that admission to the Union would follow soon thereafter. However, Michigan's admission was delayed until Jan. 26, 1837. Crary took his seat the next day. Thus, the 1835 election entitled him to serve just over one month (Jan. 27, 1837-March 3, 1837) in the 24th Congress (1835-37).*

## VIRGINIA

| Candidates | Votes | % |
|---|---|---|
| 10 John Taliaferro (W) | 869 | 50.5 |
| Chino (D) | 852 | 49.5 |
| 11 John Robertson (W) | 1,384 | 53.6 |
| Roane (D) | 1,199 | 46.4 |
| 12 James Garland (D) | 1,970 | 55.6 |
| Gordon (W) | 1,576 | 44.4 |
| 13 John M. Patton (D) | 406 | 100.0 |

| Candidates | Votes | % |
|---|---|---|
| 14 Charles F. Mercer (W) | 692 | 83.6 |
| Mason (D) | 136 | 16.4 |
| 15 Edward Lucas (D) | 1,971 | 51.6 |
| Cooke (W) | 1,849 | 48.4 |
| 16 James M. H. Beale (D) | 2,112 | 93.2 |
| Jones (W) | 154 | 6.8 |
| 17 Robert Craig (D) | 2,592 | 50.3 |
| Moore (W) | 2,564 | 49.7 |

| Candidates | Votes | % |
|---|---|---|
| 18 George W. Hopkins (D) | 2,518 | 64.3 |
| Fulton (W) | 1,399 | 35.7 |
| 19 William McComas (W) | 2,121 | 55.0 |
| Smith (D) | 1,733 | 45.0 |
| 20 Joseph Johnson (D) | 1,858 | 46.4 |
| Allen (W) | 1,809 | 45.1 |
| Maxwell | 342 | 8.5 |
| 21 William S. Morgan (D) | 2,311 | 57.5 |
| Wilson (W) | 1,710 | 42.5 |

# 1836 House Elections

## ARKANSAS

(Became a state June 15, 1836)

| Candidates | Votes | % |
|---|---|---|
| AL Archibald Yell (D) | 5,420 | 73.4 |
| William Cummins (W) | 1,967 | 26.6 |

### Special Election

| | | |
|---|---|---|
| AL Archibald Yell (VB D) | ✔ | |

## CONNECTICUT

### Special Election

| | | |
|---|---|---|
| AL Orrin Holt (D) | 17,367 | 51.4 |
| John Brockway (W) | 16,431 | 48.6 |

## DELAWARE

| | | |
|---|---|---|
| AL John J. Milligan (W) | 4,705 | 52.3 |
| Unidentified Candidate (D) | 4,297 | 47.7 |

## GEORGIA

| | | |
|---|---|---|
| AL Thomas Glascock (D) | 48,448 ✔ | |
| George W. B. Towns (D) | 29,600 ✔ | |
| Jesse F. Cleveland (D) | 29,580 ✔ | |
| Charles E. Haynes (D) | 29,490 ✔ | |
| Seaton Grantland (D) | 29,343 ✔ | |
| George W. Owens (D) | 29,316 ✔ | |
| Hopkins Holsey (D) | 29,227 ✔ | |
| Jabez Y. Jackson (D) | 29,227 ✔ | |
| William C. Dawson (W) | 29,003 ✔ | |
| Julius C. Alford (W) | 28,855 | |
| Colquette (D) | 28,677 | |
| Habersham (W) | 28,557 | |
| John Coffee (D) | 28,543 | |
| King (W) | 28,458 | |
| Nesbit (W) | 28,419 | |
| Black (W) | 28,407 | |
| Joseph Jackson (W) | 28,353 | |

### Special Election

| | | |
|---|---|---|
| AL William C. Dawson (W) | 24,239 | 53.0 |
| John W. A. Sanford (D) | 21,472 | 47.0 |

## ILLINOIS

| | | |
|---|---|---|
| 1 Adam W. Snyder (VB D) | 4,552 | 40.4 |
| John Reynolds (D) | 4,441 | 39.4 |
| William J. Gatewood | 2,270 | 20.2 |
| 2 Zadoc Casey (D) | 7,142 | 65.8 |
| Alexander P. Field | 3,568 | 32.9 |
| 3 William L. May (D) | 11,764 | 54.1 |
| John T. Stewart | 10,001 | 46.0 |

## LOUISIANA

| | | |
|---|---|---|
| 1 Henry Johnson (W) | ✔ | |
| 2 Eleazer W. Ripley (D) | * | |
| 3 Rice Garland (W) | ✔ | |

## MAINE [1]

| | | |
|---|---|---|
| 1 John Fairfield (D) | ✔ | |
| 2 Francis O. J. Smith (D) | 4,237 | 52.1 |
| James Brooks | 3,583 | 44.0 |
| 3 Jonathan Cilley (D) | 2,153 | 48.6 |
| Jeremiah Bailey (W) | 2,048 | 46.2 |
| 4 George Evans (W) | ✔ | |
| 5 Timothy J. Carter (D) | 4,165 | 59.9 |
| Oliver Herrick (W) | 2,397 | 34.5 |

| Candidates | Votes | % |
|---|---|---|
| 6 Alfred Marshall | 1,387* | 45.9 |
| Hugh J. Anderson (D) | 854 | 28.2 |
| Philip Morrill | 766 | 25.3 |
| 7 Joseph C. Noyes (W) | ✔ | |
| Timothy Pilsbury | 1,848 | |
| Frederic Hobbs | 1,544 | |
| Anson G. Chandler | 895 | |
| 8 Thomas Davee (D) | 3,498 | 58.1 |
| John S. Tenney (W) | 2,458 | 40.8 |

## MASSACHUSETTS

| | | |
|---|---|---|
| 1 Richard Fletcher (W) | 4,702 | 61.8 |
| Amasa Walker (D) | 2,895 | 38.0 |
| 2 Stephen C. Phillips (W) | 3,920 | 51.1 |
| Joseph S. Cabot (D) | 3,749 | 48.9 |
| 3 Caleb Cushing (W) | 3,949 | 57.2 |
| Gayton P. Osgood (D) | 2,916 | 42.2 |
| 4 William Parmenter (D) | 4,034 | 56.5 |
| Samuel Hoar (W) | 3,097 | 43.4 |
| 5 Levi Lincoln (W) | 4,697 | 65.5 |
| Jubal Harrington (D) | 2,443 | 34.1 |
| 6 George Grennell Jr (W) | 3,872 | 69.9 |
| Samuel C. Allen (D) | 1,645 | 29.7 |
| 7 George A. Briggs (W) | 3,567 | 54.5 |
| Theodore Sedgwick (D) | 2,961 | 45.2 |
| 8 William B. Calhoun (W) | 3,798 | 57.5 |
| George Bancroft (D) | 2,794 | 42.3 |
| 9 William S. Hastings (W) | 3,137 | 55.2 |
| Alexander H. Everett (D) | 2,495 | 43.9 |
| 10 Nathaniel B. Borden (D) | 3,093 | 68.7 |
| William Baylies (W) | 1,399 | 31.1 |
| 11 John Reed (W) | 2,628 | 55.8 |
| Henry Crocker (D) | 2,079 | 44.2 |
| 12 John Quincy Adams (W) | 3,125 | 82.6 |
| Solomon Lincoln (D) | 260 | 6.9 |
| John Thomas | 222 | 5.9 |

## MISSOURI

| | | |
|---|---|---|
| AL Albert G. Harrison (D) | 16,468 ✔ | |
| John Miller (D) | 15,129 ✔ | |
| Birch (WHITE D) | 10,007 | |
| Unidentified Candidate | 7,533 | |

## NEW JERSEY

| | | |
|---|---|---|
| AL Charles C. Stratton (W) | ✔ | |
| Thomas Jones Yorke (W) | ✔ | |
| John B. Aycrigg (W) | ✔ | |
| John P. B. Maxwell (W) | ✔ | |
| Joseph F. Randolph (W) | ✔ | |
| William Halstead (W) | ✔ | |

## NEW YORK

| | | |
|---|---|---|
| 1 Thomas Jackson (D) | 3,731 | 61.9 |
| Abraham Rose (W) | 2,297 | 38.1 |
| 2 Abraham Vanderveer (D) | 3,893 | 56.3 |
| John Dikeman (W) | 3,019 | 43.7 |
| 4 Gouverneur Kemble (D) | 2,738 | 45.9 |
| James Turk | 1,962 | 32.9 |
| Walker Todd | 1,265 | 21.2 |
| 5 Obadiah Titus (D) | 3,687 | 63.9 |
| Bartow White (W) | 2,082 | 36.1 |
| 6 Nathaniel Jones (D) | 3,479 | 60.3 |
| Samuel Eager | 2,289 | 39.7 |
| 7 John Brodhead (D) | 3,276 | 41.5 |
| Benjamin Bevier | 2,947 | 37.3 |
| Steveryn Bruyn | 1,669 | 21.2 |
| 9 Henry Vail (D) | 4,935 | 51.1 |
| Hiram Hunt (W) | 4,729 | 48.9 |

| Candidates | Votes | % |
|---|---|---|
| 10 Albert Gallup (D) | 4,882 | 52.9 |
| Jonathan Jenkins | 4,351 | 47.1 |
| 11 John De Graff (D) | 5,322 | 57.0 |
| John Taylor | 4,014 | 43.0 |
| 12 David Russell (W) | 3,543 | 57.4 |
| Orville Clark | 2,629 | 42.6 |
| 13 John Palmer (D) | 4,259 | 56.8 |
| Reuben Sandford | 3,240 | 43.2 |
| 14 James Spencer (D) | 3,843 | 54.5 |
| Asa Hascall (W) | 3,212 | 45.5 |
| 15 John Edwards (D) | 3,740 | 51.2 |
| Cornelius Patman | 3,571 | 48.8 |
| 16 Arphaxed Loomis (D) | 3,410 | 100.0 |
| 18 Isaac Bronson (D) | 4,669 | 56.1 |
| Elisha Camp | 3,653 | 43.9 |
| 19 John Prentiss (D) | 3,784 | 54.0 |
| Eben Morehouse | 3,229 | 46.0 |
| 20 Amasa Parker (D) | 4,501 | 100.0 |
| 21 John Clark (D) | 3,701 | 58.7 |
| Abial Cook | 2,602 | 41.3 |
| 24 William Noble (D) | 4,303 | 53.7 |
| Robert Muir | 3,715 | 46.3 |
| 25 Samuel Birdsall (D) | 4,915 | 53.9 |
| John Maynard (W) | 4,213 | 46.2 |
| 26 Mark Sibley (W) | 3,410 | 55.3 |
| Jared Willson | 2,754 | 44.7 |
| 27 John Andrews (D) | 5,219 | 59.3 |
| George Edwards | 3,576 | 40.7 |
| 28 Timothy Childs (W) | 4,693 | 53.6 |
| Horace Gay | 4,067 | 46.4 |
| 29 William Patterson (W) | 5,040 | 60.6 |
| William Mitchell | 3,279 | 39.4 |
| 30 Luther Peck (W) | 5,456 | 53.5 |
| James Faulkner | 4,741 | 46.5 |
| 31 Richard Marvin (W) | 5,372 | 52.9 |
| Oliver Lee (D) | 4,782 | 47.1 |
| 32 Millard Fillmore (W) | 4,475 | 61.4 |
| Thomas Sherwood | 2,810 | 38.6 |
| 33 Charles Mitchell (W) | 4,091 | 50.7 |
| Washington Hunt | 3,980 | 49.3 |

### Multi-Member Districts

| | | |
|---|---|---|
| 3 Edward Curtis (W) | 17,524 ✔ | |
| Ely Moore (D) | 16,673 ✔ | |
| Churchill Cambreleng (D) | 16,447 ✔ | |
| J. Ogden Hoffman (W) | 16,441 ✔ | |
| Gideon Lee (D) | 16,198 | |
| John McKeon (D) | 15,943 | |
| Ira Wheeler (W) | 15,920 | |
| Hubert Wagenen (W) | 14,703 | |
| James Monroe (W) | 3,144 | |
| Stephen Hasbrook | 1,334 | |
| 8 Zadock Pratt (D) | 9,085 ✔ | |
| Robert McClellan (D) | 8,156 ✔ | |
| Colba Reed | 6,309 | |
| Ambrose Jordan | 6,293 | |
| 17 Abraham Grant (D) | 8,249 ✔ | |
| Henry Foster (D) | 6,878 ✔ | |
| Joshua Spencer | 5,570 | |
| John Grant | 5,570 | |
| Israel Stoddard | 1,417 | |
| 22 Andrew Bruyn (D) | 8,151 ✔ | |
| Hiram Gray (D) | 7,779 ✔ | |
| Charles Cook | 7,244 | |
| Benjamin Ferris | 6,915 | |
| 23 William Taylor (D) | 7,665 ✔ | |
| Bennet Bicknell (D) | 7,635 ✔ | |
| B. Davis Noxon | 4,676 | |
| Eliphalet Jackson | 4,675 | |

## NORTH CAROLINA

### Special Election

| | | |
|---|---|---|
| 12 James Graham (W) | 4,791 | 60.1 |
| David Newland (W) | 3,177 | 39.9 |

## OHIO

| | Candidates | Votes | % |
|---|---|---|---|
| 1 | Alexander Duncan (D) | 4,734 | 52.2 |
| | Bellamy Storer (W) | 4,333 | 47.8 |
| 2 | Taylor Webster (D) | 3,891 | 52.5 |
| | Jesse Corwin (W) | 3,523 | 47.5 |
| 3 | Patrick G. Goode (W) | 6,300 | 55.7 |
| | James Brown (D) | 5,018 | 44.3 |
| 4 | Thomas Corwin (W) | 4,770 | 64.6 |
| | Samuel H. Hale (D) | 2,614 | 35.4 |
| 5 | Thomas L. Hamer (D) | 4,375 | 57.0 |
| | Owen T. Fishback (W) | 3,305 | 43.0 |
| 6 | Calvary Morris (W) | 3,780 | 50.4 |
| | Nahum Ward (D) | 3,703 | 49.3 |
| 7 | William Key Bond (W) | 4,844 | 52.4 |
| | William Allen (D) | 4,395 | 47.6 |
| 8 | Joseph Ridgway (W) | 6,499 | 56.9 |
| | Jeremiah M. Lene | 4,915 | 43.1 |
| 9 | John Chaney (D) | 5,838 | 60.7 |
| | Henry Stanberry (W) | 3,784 | 39.3 |
| 10 | Sampson Mason (W) | 6,907 | 67.8 |
| | John Shelby (D) | 3,267 | 32.1 |
| 11 | James Alexander Jr. (W) | 4,305 | 51.2 |
| | William Kennon Sr. (D) | 4,102 | 48.8 |
| 12 | Alex Harper (W) | 5,018 | 52.1 |
| | Jno Hamm (D) | 4,619 | 47.9 |
| 13 | Daniel P. Leadbetter (D) | 5,027 | 56.9 |
| | Abraham Shane (W) | 3,802 | 43.1 |
| 14 | William H. Hunter (D) | 6,422 | 52.7 |
| | Jabez Wright (W) | 5,766 | 47.3 |
| 15 | J. W. Allen (W) | 8,206 | 55.6 |
| | Harvey Rice (D) | 6,489 | 44.0 |
| 16 | Elisha Whittlesey (W) | 7,691 | 62.8 |
| | Ashbel Dart (D) | 4,550 | 37.2 |
| 17 | Andrew W. Loomis (D) | 3,382 | 50.2 |
| | George McCook (W) | 3,359 | 49.8 |
| 18 | Matthias Shepler (D) | 4,384 | 56.9 |
| | Samuel Quinby (W) | 3,325 | 43.1 |
| 19 | Daniel Kilgore (D) | 3,570 | 61.1 |
| | John B. Bayliss (W) | 2,274 | 38.9 |

## PENNSYLVANIA

| | Candidates | Votes | % |
|---|---|---|---|
| 1 | Lemuel Paynter (D) | 2,568 | 55.3 |
| | Unidentified Candidate (W) | 2,074 | 44.7 |
| 3 | Francis J. Harper (D) | 4,432 | 50.5 |
| | Unidentified Candidate (W) | 4,339 | 49.5 |

| | Candidates | Votes | % |
|---|---|---|---|
| 5 | Jacob Fry Jr (D) | 3,194 | 61.9 |
| | Unidentified Candidate (W) | 1,963 | 38.1 |
| 6 | Mathias Morris (W) | 3,260 | 51.4 |
| | Unidentified Candidate (D) | 3,085 | 48.6 |
| 7 | David D. Wagener (D) | ✔ | |
| | Unidentified Candidate (W) | | |
| 8 | Edward B. Hubley (D) | 2,881 | 54.3 |
| | Unidentified Candidate (W) | 2,430 | 45.8 |
| 9 | Henry A. P. Muhlenberg (D) | 4,276 | 57.5 |
| | Unidentified Candidate (W) | 3,160 | 42.5 |
| 10 | Luther Reily (D) | 2,885 | 50.8 |
| | Unidentified Candidate (W) | 2,795 | 49.2 |
| 11 | Henry Logan (D) | 3,366 | 58.2 |
| | Unidentified Candidate (W) | 2,414 | 41.8 |
| 12 | Daniel Sheffer (D) | 3,100 | 50.5 |
| | Unidentified Candidate (W) | 3,047 | 49.5 |
| 13 | Charles McClure (D) | 3,633 | 57.8 |
| | Unidentified Candidate (W) | 2,655 | 42.2 |
| 14 | William W. Potter (D) | 4,914 | 61.1 |
| | Unidentified Candidate (W) | 3,134 | 38.9 |
| 15 | Robert H. Hammond (D) | 2,881 | 52.1 |
| | Unidentified Candidate (W) | 2,646 | 47.9 |
| 16 | David Petrikin (D) | 4,275 | 58.6 |
| | Unidentified Candidate (W) | 3,026 | 41.5 |
| 17 | Samuel W. Morris (D) | 3,888 | 60.5 |
| | Unidentified Candidate (W) | 2,536 | 39.5 |
| 18 | Charles Ogle (W) | ✔ | |
| | Unidentified Candidate (D) | | |
| 19 | John Klingensmith Jr (D) | 3,694 | 58.0 |
| | Unidentified Candidate (W) | 2,674 | 42.0 |
| 20 | Andrew Buchanan (D) | 3,252 | 100.0 |
| 21 | Thomas M. T. McKennan (W) | 2,766 | 52.2 |
| | Unidentified Candidate (D) | 2,537 | 47.8 |
| 22 | Richard Biddle (W) | 3,155 | 51.4 |
| | Unidentified Candidate (D) | 2,984 | 48.6 |
| 23 | William Beatty (D) | ✔ | |
| | Unidentified Candidate (W) | | |
| 24 | Thomas Henry (W) | ✔ | |
| | Unidentified Candidate (D) | | |
| 25 | Arnold Plummer (D) | 4,281 | 54.4 |
| | Unidentified Candidate (W) | 3,582 | 45.6 |

**Multi-Member Districts**

| | Candidates | Votes | % |
|---|---|---|---|
| 2 | George W. Toland (W) | ✔ | |
| | John Sergeant (W) | 5,317✔ | |
| | Unidentified Candidate (D) | 3,072 | |

| | Candidates | Votes | % |
|---|---|---|---|
| | Unidentified Candidate (D) | | |
| 4 | David Potts Jr (W) | ✔ | |
| | Edward Davies (W) | ✔ | |
| | Edward Darlington (W) | 9,916✔ | |
| | Unidentified Candidate (D) | 8,561 | |
| | Unidentified Candidate (D) | | |
| | Unidentified Candidate (D) | | |

**Special Elections**

| | Candidates | Votes | % |
|---|---|---|---|
| 13 | James Black (D) | ✔ | |
| | Robert Elliot (A-MAS) | | |
| 24 | John James Pearson (W) | ✔ | |

## SOUTH CAROLINA

| | Candidates | Votes | % |
|---|---|---|---|
| 1 | Hugh S. Legare (UN D) | ✔ | |
| | Henry L. Pinckney (D) | | |
| 2 | Robert Barnwell Smith (D) | ✔ | |
| | William J. Grayson (SR W) | | |
| 3 | John Campbell (SR D) | ✔ | |
| | Thomas Smith | | |
| 4 | Franklin H. Elmore (SR D) | | 100.0 |
| 5 | John K. Griffin (SR W) | ✔ | |
| 6 | Francis W. Pickens (SSR NULL) | ✔ | |
| 7 | William K. Clowney (SR D) | ✔ | |
| | James Rogers (D) | | |
| 8 | Waddy Thompson Jr (W) | ✔ | |
| 9 | John P. Richardson (SR D) | ✔ | |
| | J. G. Bowman | | |

## VERMONT

| | Candidates | Votes | % |
|---|---|---|---|
| 1 | Hiland Hall (W) | 4,220 | 57.2 |
| | John S. Robinson | 3,023 | 41.0 |
| 2 | William Slade (W) | 3,918 | 64.5 |
| | Jonas Clark | 1,536 | 25.3 |
| | E. D. Barber | 481 | 7.9 |
| 3 | Horace Everett (W) | 3,747 | 47.1 |
| | Alden Partridge | 3,180 | 40.0 |
| | Martin Flint | 961 | 12.1 |
| 4 | Heman Allen (W) | 3,522 | 60.2 |
| | C. P. Vanness | 2,203 | 37.7 |
| 5 | Isaac Fletcher (D) | 3,765 | 52.8 |
| | Henry F. Janes (W) | 3,324 | 46.6 |

*1. In Maine's 6th district, no candidate received the required majority. A series of special elections were held in an attempt to meet the requirement. In the 5th special election, Anderson was elected. No returns are available for these special elections.*

# 1837 House Elections

## ALABAMA

| | Candidates | Votes | % |
|---|---|---|---|
| 1 | Reuben Chapman (D) | 7,599 | 81.4 |
| | Gabriel Moore (W) | 1,742 | 18.7 |
| 2 | Joshua L. Martin (D) | 2,496 | 46.2 |
| | David Greenhill Lyon (W) | 1,461 | 27.0 |
| | Stone | 1,446 | 26.8 |
| 3 | Joab Lawler (W) | 5,874 | 52.7 |
| | Henry W. Ellis (D) | 5,277 | 47.3 |
| 4 | Dixon H. Lewis (SR W) | | 100.0 |
| 5 | Francis Lyon (D) | 3,651 | 50.3 |
| | R. E. B. Baylor (NULL-NR) | 3,604 | 49.7 |

## CONNECTICUT

| | Candidates | Votes | % |
|---|---|---|---|
| 1 | Isaac Toucey (D) | 4,410 | 50.4 |
| | Joseph Trumbull (W) | 4,334 | 49.6 |
| 2 | Samuel Ingham (D) | 10,194 | 54.4 |
| | Henry Flagg (W) | 8,558 | 45.6 |
| 3 | Elisha Haley (D) | 2,367 | 51.2 |
| | Thomas Williams (W) | 2,252 | 48.8 |
| 4 | Thomas Whittlesey (D) | 3,604 | 52.7 |
| | Gideon Tomlinson (W) | 3,239 | 47.3 |
| 5 | Lancelot Phelps (D) | 3,493 | 50.7 |
| | Phineas Miner (W) | 3,391 | 49.3 |
| 6 | Orrin Holt (D) | 5,301 | 52.3 |
| | John Brockway (W) | 4,843 | 47.7 |

## GEORGIA

### Special Election

| | Candidates | Votes | % |
|---|---|---|---|
| AL | Julius C. Alford (W) | 17,754 | 53.4 |
| | Liddell (D) | 15,480 | 46.6 |

## INDIANA

| | Candidates | Votes | % |
|---|---|---|---|
| 1 | Ratliff Boon (D) | 4,534 | 50.4 |
| | John Pitcher (W) | 4,467 | 49.6 |
| 2 | John Ewing (W) | 5,820 | 54.4 |
| | John Law (D) | 4,887 | 45.6 |
| 3 | William Graham (W) | 5,717 | 56.6 |
| | John S. Simonson (D) | 4,390 | 43.4 |
| 4 | George H. Dunn (W) | 6,091 | 54.6 |
| | Amos Lane (D) | 5,057 | 45.4 |
| 5 | James Rariden (W) | 6,599 | 57.5 |
| | Johnathan McCarty (W) | 4,845 | 42.2 |
| 6 | William Herod (W) | 9,635 | 62.1 |
| | James B. Ray (D) | 5,888 | 37.9 |
| 7 | Albert S. White (W) | 10,937 | 74.2 |
| | Nathan Jackson (W) | 3,789 | 25.7 |

### Special Election

| | | Votes | % |
|---|---|---|---|
| 6 | William Herod (W) | 3,703 | 51.5 |
| | William W. Wick | 3,493 | 48.5 |

## KENTUCKY

| | Candidates | Votes | % |
|---|---|---|---|
| 1 | John L. Murray (D) | 2,921 | 39.7 |
| | Linn Boyd (D) | 2,547 | 34.6 |
| | Campbell (W) | 1,888 | 25.7 |
| 2 | Edward Rumsey (W) | 4,035 | 89.1 |
| | Jones (D) | 496 | 11.0 |
| 3 | Joseph R. Underwood (W) | 4,589 | 100.0 |
| 4 | Sherrod Williams (W) | 3,189 | 47.1 |
| | McHenry (D) | 1,819 | 26.9 |
| | Monroe (W) | 1,764 | 26.1 |
| 5 | James Harlan (W) | | 100.0 |
| 6 | John Calhoon (W) | 3,656 | 55.7 |
| | Vanmetre (D) | 2,902 | 44.2 |
| 7 | John Pope (I) | 3,248 | 54.4 |
| | Hardin (D) | 2,728 | 45.7 |
| 8 | William J. Graves (W) | 5,021 | 63.0 |
| | T. F. Marshall (W) | 2,950 | 37.0 |

| | Candidates | Votes | % |
|---|---|---|---|
| 9 | John White (W) | 3,700 | 60.0 |
| | Garrard (D) | 2,464 | 40.0 |
| 10 | Richard Hawes (W) | | 100.0 |
| 11 | Richard H. Menifee (W) | 4,084 | 51.5 |
| | French (D) | 3,850 | 48.5 |
| 12 | John Chambers (W) | 2,886 | 74.5 |
| | Leach (D) | 989 | 25.5 |
| 13 | William W. Southgate (W) | 4,457 | 50.7 |
| | Phelps (D) | 4,116 | 46.8 |

## MARYLAND

| | Candidates | Votes | % |
|---|---|---|---|
| 1 | John Dennis (W) | 2,076 | 59.6 |
| | Handy (W) | 1,409 | 40.4 |
| 2 | James A. Pearce (W) | 2,714 | 53.2 |
| | Evans (D) | 2,388 | 46.8 |
| 3 | John T. H. Worthington (D) | 2,413 | 53.2 |
| | Brown (W) | 2,126 | 46.8 |
| 5 | William Cost Johnson (I) | 1,292 | 52.8 |
| | Kimmell (W) | 1,153 | 47.2 |
| 6 | Francis Thomas (D) | 3,819 | 52.0 |
| | Merrick (W) | 3,523 | 48.0 |
| 7 | Daniel Jenifer (W) | | 100.0 |

### Multi-Member District

| | Candidates | Votes | % |
|---|---|---|---|
| 4 | Benjamin C. Howard (D) | 7,184 ✓ | |
| | Isaac McKim (D) | 7,141 ✓ | |
| | Kennedy (W) | 6,950 | |
| | Ridgely (W) | 6,873 | |

## MICHIGAN

| | Candidates | Votes | % |
|---|---|---|---|
| AL | Isaac Crary (D) | 11,451 | 52.6 |
| | Hezekiah Wells (W) | 10,329 | 47.4 |

## MISSISSIPPI

| | Candidates | Votes | % |
|---|---|---|---|
| AL | Sergeant S. Prentiss (W) | 13,688 ‡ | |
| | Thomas Word (W) | 12,374 ‡ | |
| | John F. H. Claiborne (D) | 6,206 | |
| | Samuel Gholson (D) | 5,881 | |

### Special Election

| | Candidates | Votes | % |
|---|---|---|---|
| AL | John F. H. Claiborne (D) | 11,198 ‡ | |
| | Samuel Gholson (D) | 9,971 ‡ | |
| | Prentiss (W) | 7,153 | |
| | Acee (W) | 6,632 | |

## NEW HAMPSHIRE

| | Candidates | Votes | % |
|---|---|---|---|
| AL | Charles G. Atherton (D) | ✓ | |
| | Jared W. Williams (D) | ✓ | |
| | James Farrington (D) | ✓ | |
| | Samuel Cushman (D) | ✓ | |
| | Joseph Weeks (D) | ✓ | |
| | Charles B. Goodrich | | |
| | Joseph Bell | | |
| | Richard Bradley | | |
| | Anthony Colby | | |
| | James Wilson Jr. | | |

## NORTH CAROLINA

| | Candidates | Votes | % |
|---|---|---|---|
| 1 | Samuel T. Sawyer (D) | 2,111 | 55.3 |
| | G. C. Moore (D) | 1,706 | 44.7 |
| 2 | Jesse Bynum (D) | ✓ | |
| | William L. Long (W) | | |
| 3 | Edward Stanly (W) | 2,842 | 56.6 |
| | Louis D. Wilson (D) | 2,176 | 43.4 |
| 4 | Charles Shepard (W) | 2,392 | 55.6 |
| | William D. Moseley (D) | 1,914 | 44.5 |
| 5 | James I. McKay (D) | 3,023 | 81.9 |
| | T. C. Miller (D) | 668 | 18.1 |

| | Candidates | Votes | % |
|---|---|---|---|
| 6 | Micajah T. Hawkins (D) | 1,949 | 54.1 |
| | Joseph Macklin (D) | 894 | 24.8 |
| | John L. Henderson (W) | 762 | 21.1 |
| 7 | Edmund Deberry (W) | 3,323 | 57.4 |
| | Lauchlin Bethune (D) | 2,465 | 42.6 |
| 8 | William Montgomery (D) | 2,591 | 51.9 |
| | William A. Graham (W) | 2,400 | 48.1 |
| 9 | Augustine H. Shepperd (W) | 3,359 | 50.9 |
| | John Hill (D) | 3,239 | 49.1 |
| 10 | Abraham Rencher (W) | 3,041 | 90.6 |
| | Micajah Cox (D) | 205 | 6.1 |
| 11 | Henry W. Conner (D) | | 100.0 |
| 12 | James Graham (W) | ✓ | |
| 13 | Lewis Williams (D) | ✓ | |
| | Samuel Patterson | | |

## PENNSYLVANIA

### Special Election

| | Candidates | Votes | % |
|---|---|---|---|
| 3 | Charles Naylor (W) | 2,356 | 56.0 |
| | Ingersoll (D) | 1,853 | 44.0 |

## RHODE ISLAND

| | Candidates | Votes | % |
|---|---|---|---|
| AL | Joseph L. Tillinghast (W) | 4,282 ✓ | |
| | Robert B. Cranston (W) | 4,221 ✓ | |
| | Dutee J. Pearce (D) | 3,261 | |
| | Howard (D) | 3,201 | |
| | Dorr (D) | 72 | |
| | King (CONST) | 25 | |

## TENNESSEE

| | Candidates | Votes | % |
|---|---|---|---|
| 1 | William B. Carter (W) | 3,994 | 51.5 |
| | Thomas D. Arnold (W) | 3,756 | 48.5 |
| 2 | Abraham McClellan (D) | 3,612 | 52.9 |
| | Samuel Bunch (W) | 2,357 | 34.5 |
| | Eliot (W) | 865 | 12.7 |
| 3 | Joseph L. Williams (W) | 6,812 | 72.0 |
| | R. M. Anderson (W) | 2,653 | 28.0 |
| 4 | James Standifer (W) | 5,110 | 66.4 |
| | Stone (D) | 2,581 | 33.6 |
| 5 | Hopkins L. Turney (D) | 3,437 | 49.9 |
| | Coxe (W) | 2,984 | 43.3 |
| | Peter Burum (D) | 466 | 6.8 |
| 6 | William B. Campbell (W) | 4,142 | 60.0 |
| | William C. Trousdale (D) | 2,760 | 40.0 |
| 7 | John Bell (W) | 4,639 | 100.0 |
| 8 | Abram P. Maury (W) | 3,043 | 55.3 |
| | William Crockett (D) | 2,458 | 44.7 |
| 9 | James K. Polk (D) | 4,245 | 100.0 |
| 10 | Ebenezer J. Shields (W) | 4,432 | 55.7 |
| | A. A. Kincannon (D) | 3,521 | 44.3 |
| 11 | Richard Cheatham (W) | 3,822 | 50.6 |
| | Cave Johnson (D) | 3,731 | 49.4 |
| 12 | John W. Crockett (W) | 8,456 | 85.7 |
| | A. M. Hughes (W) | 1,413 | 14.3 |
| 13 | Christopher H. Williams (W) | 5,360 | 60.7 |
| | William C. Dunlap (D) | 3,478 | 39.4 |

## VIRGINIA

| | Candidates | Votes | % |
|---|---|---|---|
| 1 | Francis Mallory (W) | ✓ | |
| | Joel Holleman (D) | | |
| 2 | Francis E. Rives (D) | ✓ | |
| | William B. Goodyear (D) | | |
| 3 | John W. Jones (D) | ✓ | |
| 4 | George C. Dromgoole (D) | ✓ | |
| 5 | James W. Bouldin (D) | ✓ | |
| 6 | Walter Coles (D) | ✓ | |
| | J. Kerr (W) | | |

## VIRGINIA

| Candidates | Votes | % |
|---|---|---|
| 7 Archibald Stuart (D) | ✔ | |
| Nathaniel H. Claiborne (W) | | |
| 8 Henry A. Wise (W) | ✔ | |
| 9 Robert M. T. Hunter (W) | ✔ | |
| Upshaw (D) | | |
| Harwood (D) | | |
| 10 John Talliaferro (W) | ✔ | |
| J. Gibson | | |

| Candidates | Votes | % |
|---|---|---|
| 11 John Robertson (W) | ✔ | |
| 12 James Garland (D) | ✔ | |
| 13 John M. Patton (D) | ✔ | |
| 14 Charles F. Mercer (W) | ✔ | |
| William T. T. Mason (D) | | |
| 15 James M. Mason (D) | ✔ | |
| J. B. D. Smith (W) | | |
| 16 Isaac S. Pennybacker (D) | ✔ | |
| David Steele (W) | | |

| Candidates | Votes | % |
|---|---|---|
| 17 Robert Craig (D) | ✔ | |
| E. Johnston (W) | | |
| 18 George W. Hopkins (D) | ✔ | |
| John N. Humes (D) | | |
| 19 Andrew Beirne (D) | ✔ | |
| Andrew Donnally (W) | | |
| 20 Joseph Johnson (D) | ✔ | |
| John J. Jackson (W) | | |
| 21 William S. Morgan (D) | ✔ | |

---

# House Candidates Index

For an index of all House candidates listed in this section (pages 943-1326), see pages 1402-1501. Instructions for use of the House Candidates Index appear on page 1402.

---

# 1838 House Elections

## ARKANSAS

| Candidates | Votes | % |
|---|---|---|
| AL Edward Cross (D) | 6,771 | 61.0 |
| Cummings (W) | 4,328 | 39.0 |

## DELAWARE

| | Votes | % |
|---|---|---|
| AL Thomas Robinson Jr (D) | 4,451 | 50.3 |
| John J. Milligan (W) | 4,399 | 49.7 |

## GEORGIA

| | | |
|---|---|---|
| AL William C. Dawson (SR W) | 33,278 | ✔ |
| Julius C. Alford (SR W) | 32,320 | ✔ |
| Walter T.Colquitt (SR W) | 32,299 | ✔ |
| Richard W. Habersham (SR W) | 32,282 | ✔ |
| Thomas Butler King (SR W) | 32,213 | ✔ |
| Lott Warren (SR W) | 31,887 | ✔ |
| Eugenius A. Nisbet (SR W) | 31,841 | ✔ |
| Edward J. Black (SR W) | 31,801 | ✔ |
| Mark A. Cooper (SR W) | 31,723 | ✔ |
| David C. Campbell (D) | 31,270 | |
| Alfred Iverson (D) | 31,238 | |
| Josiah S. Patterson (D) | 31,187 | |
| Graves (D) | 31,074 | |
| Robert W. Pooler (D) | 31,042 | |
| Junius Hillyer (D) | 30,967 | |
| Burney (D) | 30,932 | |
| McWhorter (D) | 30,796 | |
| Nelson (D) | 30,782 | |

## ILLINOIS

| | | Votes | % |
|---|---|---|---|
| 1 | John Reynolds (D) | 8,029 | 61.2 |
| | John Hogan (W) | 5,100 | 38.9 |
| 2 | Zadock Casey (D) | 8,367 | 94.3 |
| | Samuel McRoberts (W) | 501 | 5.6 |
| 3 | John T. Stuart (W) | 18,248 | 50.0 |
| | Stephen A. Douglas (D) | 18,213 | 49.9 |

## LOUISIANA

| | | Votes | % |
|---|---|---|---|
| 1 | Edward D. White (W) | 3,351 | 57.4 |
| | Slidell (D) | 2,486 | 42.6 |
| 2 | Thomas W. Chinn (W) | 1,790 | 55.7 |
| | Lawson (D) | 1,423 | 44.3 |
| 3 | Rice Garland (W) | | 100.0 |

## MAINE

| | | Votes | % |
|---|---|---|---|
| 1 | Nathan Clifford (D) | 5,568 | 54.8 |
| | Nathan D. Appleton (W) | 4,560 | 44.9 |
| 2 | Albert Smith (D) | 5,709 | 50.1 |
| | Ezekiel Whitman (W) | 5,623 | 49.3 |
| 3 | John D. McCrate (D) | 4,859 | 50.6 |
| | Benjamin Randall (W) | 4,652 ✔ | 48.5 |
| 4 | George Evans (W) | 7,143 | 60.9 |
| | John Hubbard (D) | 4,591 | 39.1 |
| 5 | Virgil D. Parris (D) | 6,765 | 57.4 |
| | Zadoc Long (W) | 4,999 | 42.4 |
| 6 | Hugh J. Anderson (D) | 5,727 | 60.9 |
| | William G. Crosby (W) | 3,519 | 37.4 |
| 7 | Joshua A. Lowell (D) | 5,033 | 51.8 |
| | Joseph C. Noyes (W) | 4,666 | 48.1 |
| 8 | Thomas Davee (D) | 7,839 | 51.9 |
| | John S. Tenney (W) | 7,042 | 46.6 |

### Special Elections

| | | Votes | % |
|---|---|---|---|
| 3 | Edward Robinson (W) | ✔ | |
| | John D. McCrate (D) | | |
| 5 | Virgil D. Parris (D) | 4,349 | 57.4 |
| | Zadoc Long (W) | 3,690 | 42.4 |

## MARYLAND

### Special Election

| | Candidates | Votes | % |
|---|---|---|---|
| 4 | John P. Kennedy (W) | 7,153 | 53.2 |
| | Marriott (D) | 6,291 | 46.8 |

## MASSACHUSETTS[1]

| | | Votes | % |
|---|---|---|---|
| 1 | Richard Fletcher (W) | 5,145* | 63.1 |
| | Bradford Sumner (D) | 2,952 | 36.2 |
| 2 | Leverett Saltonstall (W) | 3,734 | 59.1 |
| | Robert Rantoul Jr (D) | 2,031 | 32.1 |
| | Joseph S. Cabot (D) | 536 | 8.5 |
| 3 | Caleb Cushing (W) | 4,762 | 61.1 |
| | Gayton P. Osgood (D) | 2,730 | 35.0 |
| 4 | William Parmenter (D) | 4,972 | 50.1 |
| | Nathan Brooks (W) | 4,433 | 44.7 |
| 5 | Levi Lincoln (W) | 4,251 | 55.2 |
| | Isaac Davis (D) | 2,630 | 34.1 |
| | Charles Allen | 797 | 10.3 |
| 6 | James C. Alvord (W) | 4,440 | 61.8 |
| | Thomas Nims (D) | 2,054 | 28.6 |
| | Osmyn Baker (W) | 653 | 9.1 |
| 7 | George N. Briggs (W) | 4,328 | 54.5 |
| | Henry W. Bishop (D) | 3,601 | 45.3 |
| 8 | William B. Calhoun (W) | 4,363 | 59.4 |
| | William W. Thompson (D) | 2,957 | 40.3 |
| 9 | William S. Hastings (W) | 4,049 | 56.6 |
| | Alexander H. Everett (D) | 3,090 | 43.2 |
| 10 | Henry Williams (D) | 3,306 | 51.7 |
| | Nathaniel B. Borden (W) | 2,920 | 45.7 |
| 11 | John Reed (W) | 3,519 | 56.4 |
| | Henry Crocker (D) | 2,703 | 43.3 |
| 12 | John Quincy Adams (W) | 4,100 | 59.0 |
| | William M. Jackson (D) | 2,822 | 40.6 |

### Special Election

| | | Votes | % |
|---|---|---|---|
| 2 | Leverett Saltonstall (W) | 3,730 | 58.9 |
| | Robert Rantoul Jr (D) | 2,034 | 32.1 |
| | Joseph S. Cabot (D) | 542 | 8.6 |

## MICHIGAN

| | | Votes | % |
|---|---|---|---|
| AL | Isaac E. Crary (D) | 16,360 | 50.4 |
| | Hezekiah E. Wells (W) | 16,099 | 49.6 |

## MISSISSIPPI

### Special Election

| | | Votes | % |
|---|---|---|---|
| AL | Sergeant S. Prentiss (W) | 12,721 | ✔ |
| | Thomas Word (W) | 12,077 | ✔ |
| | J. F. H. Claiborne (D) | 11,767 | |
| | Reuben Davis (D) | 11,346 | |

## MISSOURI

| | | Votes | |
|---|---|---|---|
| AL | Albert G. Harrison (D) | 23,410 | ✔ |
| | John Miller (D) | 23,182 | ✔ |
| | Allen (W) | 17,191 | |
| | Wilson (W) | 16,706 | |

## NEW JERSEY

| | | Votes | |
|---|---|---|---|
| AL | Peter D. Vroom (D) | 28,492 | ✔ |
| | William R. Cooper (D) | 28,455 | ✔ |
| | Philemon Dickerson (D) | 28,453 | ✔ |
| | Daniel B. Ryall (D) | 28,441 | ✔ |
| | Joseph Kille (D) | 28,426 | ✔ |
| | Joseph Randolph (W) | 28,426 | ✔ |

| Candidates | Votes | % |
|---|---|---|
| Strat (W) | 28,395 | |
| Max (W) | 28,386 | |
| Hal (W) | 28,337 | |
| Yorke (W) | 28,321 | |
| Force (D) | 28,315 | |
| Aigg (W) | 28,295 | |

## NEW YORK

| | | Votes | % |
|---|---|---|---|
| 1 | Thomas Jackson (D) | 4,896 | 56.5 |
| | Nathaniel Miller (W) | 3,776 | 43.5 |
| 2 | James De la Montanya (D) | 4,405 | 55.2 |
| | John Gurnee (W) | 3,576 | 44.8 |
| 4 | Gouverneur Kemble (D) | 4,986 | 54.3 |
| | Joshua Brown (W) | 4,203 | 45.7 |
| 5 | Charles Johnston (W) | 5,262 | 53.1 |
| | Obadiah Titus (D) | 4,645 | 46.9 |
| 6 | Nathaniel Jones (D) | 4,184 | 51.3 |
| | Thomas McKissock (W) | 3,978 | 48.7 |
| 7 | Rufus Palen (D) | 5,453 | 54.2 |
| | Anthony Hasbrouck (W) | 4,615 | 45.8 |
| 9 | Hiram Hunt (W) | 5,483 | 52.8 |
| | Henry Vail (D) | 4,909 | 47.2 |
| 10 | Daniel Barnard (W) | 5,680 | 52.5 |
| | Albert Gallup (D) | 5,145 | 47.5 |
| 11 | Anson Brown (W) | 5,401 | 51.8 |
| | Nicholas Hill (D) | 5,028 | 48.2 |
| 12 | David Russell (W) | 4,346 | 61.9 |
| | John Williams (D) | 2,671 | 38.1 |
| 13 | Augustus Hand (D) | 4,480 | 50.3 |
| | Thomas Tomlinson (W) | 4,436 | 49.8 |
| 14 | John Fine (D) | 4,756 | 50.5 |
| | Henry Van Rensselaer (W) | 4,663 | 49.5 |
| 15 | Peter Wagner (W) | 4,491 | 50.3 |
| | David Sacia (D) | 4,441 | 49.7 |
| 16 | Andrew Doig (D) | 5,043 | 56.8 |
| | Seth Miller (W) | 3,835 | 43.2 |
| 18 | Thomas Chittenden (W) | 4,989 | 53.7 |
| | Issac Bronson (D) | 4,309 | 46.3 |
| 19 | John Prentiss (D) | 4,724 | 52.8 |
| | William Averill (W) | 4,216 | 47.2 |
| 20 | Judson Allen (D) | 5,072 | 54.2 |
| | Erastus Root (W) | 4,284 | 45.8 |
| 21 | John Clark (W) | 3,908 | 52.3 |
| | John Clapp (D) | 3,563 | 47.7 |
| 24 | Christopher Morgan (W) | 4,631 | 50.9 |
| | William Noble (D) | 4,464 | 49.1 |
| 25 | Theron Strong (D) | 5,824 | 50.7 |
| | John Holley (W) | 5,670 | 49.3 |
| 26 | Francis Granger (W) | 4,233 | 57.9 |
| | Jared Willson (D) | 3,083 | 42.1 |
| 27 | Meredith Mallory (D) | 5,438 | 51.2 |
| | Thomas Johnson (W) | 5,182 | 48.8 |
| 28 | Thomas Kempshall (W) | 5,476 | 56.9 |
| | Henry Selden (D) | 4,144 | 43.1 |
| 29 | Seth Gates (W) | 6,033 | 65.3 |
| | William Mitchell (D) | 3,202 | 34.7 |
| 30 | Luther Peck (W) | 6,521 | 57.8 |
| | Calvin Chamberlain (D) | 4,763 | 42.2 |
| 31 | Richard Marvin (W) | 7,053 | 57.6 |
| | Charles Williams (D) | 5,198 | 42.4 |
| 32 | Millard Fillmore (W) | 5,414 | 65.7 |
| | George Barker (D) | 2,831 | 34.3 |
| 33 | Charles Mitchell (W) | 4,690 | 55.0 |
| | Henry Curtis (D) | 3,840 | 45.0 |

### Multi-Member Districts

| | | Votes | |
|---|---|---|---|
| 3 | Ogden Hoffman (W) | 20,577 | ✔ |
| | Moses Grinnell (W) | 20,563 | ✔ |
| | Edward Curtis (W) | 20,458 | ✔ |
| | James Monroe (W) | 20,454 | ✔ |
| | John McKeon (D) | 19,227 | |
| | Isaac Varian (D) | 19,206 | |
| | Churchill Cambreleng (D) | 19,205 | |
| | Ely Moore (D) | 18,843 | |
| 8 | John Ely (D) | 9,668 | ✔ |
| | Aaron Vanderpoel (D) | 9,628 | ✔ |

*Footnote, see p. 969.*

## NEW YORK

| Candidates | Votes | % |
|---|---|---|
| Mitchell Sanford (W) | 9,499 | |
| Robert Dorlon (W) | 9,469 | |
| 17 David Brewster (D) | 9,395✓ | |
| John Floyd (D) | 9,286✓ | |
| Henry Fitzhugh (W) | 8,601 | |
| Charles Kirkland (W) | 8,362 | |
| 22 Amasa Dana (D) | 9,157✓ | |
| Stephen Leonard (D) | 9,152✓ | |
| William Ely (W) | 8,757 | |
| John Miller (W) | 8,725 | |
| 23 Nehemiah Earll (D) | 9,189✓ | |
| Edward Rogers (D) | 9,099✓ | |
| A. Lawrence Foster (W) | 9,056 | |
| Victory Birdseye (W) | 9,015 | |

## OHIO

| Candidates | Votes | % |
|---|---|---|
| 1 Alexander Duncan (D) | 4,572 | 51.0 |
| N. G. Pendleton (W) | 4,396 | 49.0 |
| 2 John B. Weller (D) | 4,877 | 54.9 |
| John Beers (W) | 4,010 | 45.1 |
| 3 Patrick G. Goode (W) | 7,589 | 50.7 |
| William Sawyer (D) | 7,368 | 49.3 |
| 4 Thomas Corwin (W) | 5,866 | 99.6 |
| 5 William Doan (D) | 4,543 | 56.6 |
| Daniel Fisher (W) | 3,479 | 43.4 |
| 6 Calvery Morris (W) | 5,321 | 55.1 |
| Joseph Morris (D) | 4,337 | 44.9 |
| 7 William K. Bond (W) | 4,834 | 50.9 |
| Allen Latham (D) | 4,658 | 49.1 |
| 8 Joseph Ridgway (W) | 6,916 | 51.4 |
| John McElvain (D) | 6,552 | 48.7 |
| 9 William Medill (D) | 6,791 | 64.6 |
| John M. Creed (W) | 3,729 | 35.5 |
| 10 Samson Mason (W) | 6,997 | 58.1 |
| Rowland Brown (D) | 5,040 | 41.9 |
| 11 Isaac Parrish (D) | 4,692 | 52.7 |
| James Alexander Jr (W) | 4,220 | 47.4 |
| 12 Jonathan Taylor (D) | 5,668 | 51.5 |
| Alexander Harper (W) | 5,347 | 48.5 |
| 13 Daniel P. Leadbetter (D) | 7,515 | 57.5 |
| James S. Irwin (W) | 5,555 | 42.5 |
| 14 George Sweeny (D) | 8,601 | 56.4 |
| Joseph M. Root (W) | 6,654 | 43.6 |
| 15 John W. Allen (W) | 8,800 | 53.8 |
| John W. Willey (D) | 7,558 | 46.2 |
| 16 Joshua R. Giddings (W) | 7,581 | 57.7 |
| Benjamin Bissell (D) | 5,556 | 42.3 |
| 17 John Hastings (D) | 4,952 | 53.2 |
| Charles D. Coffin (W) | 4,349 | 46.8 |

| Candidates | Votes | % |
|---|---|---|
| 18 David A. Starkweather (D) | 6,154 | 60.6 |
| Hiram B. Wellman (W) | 4,010 | 39.5 |
| 19 Henry Swearingen (D) | 4,036 | 52.9 |
| Samuel Stokely (W) | 3,589 | 47.1 |

## PENNSYLVANIA

| Candidates | Votes | % |
|---|---|---|
| 1 Lemuel Paynter (D) | 3,675 | 55.1 |
| J. B. Sutherland (W) | 2,994 | 44.9 |
| 3 Charles Naylor (W) | 6,670 | 53.1 |
| C. J. Ingersoll (D) | 5,894 | 46.9 |
| 5 Joseph Fornance (D) | 4,527 | 54.9 |
| Joseph Royer (W) | 3,723 | 45.1 |
| 6 John Davis (D) | 4,464 | 51.9 |
| Matthew Morris (W) | 4,138 | 48.1 |
| 7 David D. Wagener (D) | 6,189 | 62.8 |
| P. S. Michler (W) | 3,672 | 37.2 |
| 8 Peter Newhard (D) | 4,636 | 54.5 |
| W. C. Livingston (W) | 3,876 | 45.5 |
| 9 George M. Keim (D) | 7,030 | 68.6 |
| D. M. Bieber (W) | 3,212 | 31.4 |
| 10 William Simonton (W) | 5,000 | 58.7 |
| William Reily (D) | 3,514 | 41.3 |
| 11 James Gerry (D) | 4,197 | 56.6 |
| C. A. Barnitz (W) | 3,220 | 43.4 |
| 12 James Cooper (W) | 5,738 | 56.0 |
| Daniel Sheffer (D) | 4,503 | 44.0 |
| 13 William S. Ramsey (D) | 5,569 | 57.3 |
| Frederick Watts (W) | 4,145 | 42.7 |
| 14 William W. Potter (D) | 6,510 | 50.9 |
| William Irvin (W) | 6,288 | 49.1 |
| 15 Robert Hammond (D) | 5,156 | 56.7 |
| James Merrill (W) | 3,946 | 43.4 |
| 16 David Petrikin (D) | 6,225 | 53.5 |
| David Hurley (W) | 5,411 | 46.5 |
| 17 Samuel W. Morris (D) | 5,147 | 54.2 |
| William Willard (W) | 4,354 | 45.8 |
| 18 Charles Ogle (W) | 5,106 | 55.1 |
| Job Mann (D) | 4,158 | 44.9 |
| 19 Albert G. Marchand (D) | 5,800 | 60.5 |
| Joseph Markle (W) | 3,784 | 39.5 |
| 20 Enos Hook (D) | 4,498 | 63.0 |
| H. Oliphant (W) | 2,643 | 37.0 |
| 21 Isaac Leet (D) | 3,508 | 50.2 |
| Joseph Lawrence (W) | 3,487 | 49.9 |
| 22 Richard Biddle (W) | 6,090 | 58.1 |
| James Power (D) | 4,391 | 41.9 |
| 23 William Beatty (D) | 5,694 | 61.1 |
| George W. Smith (W) | 3,625 | 38.9 |
| 24 Thomas Henry (W) | 5,265 | 54.9 |
| James D. White (D) | 4,330 | 45.1 |

| Candidates | Votes | % |
|---|---|---|
| 25 John Galbraith (D) | 6,208 | 51.2 |
| David Dick (W) | 5,920 | 48.8 |

**Multi-Member Districts**

| Candidates | Votes | % |
|---|---|---|
| 2 George W. Toland | ✓ | |
| John Sergeant (W) | 7,132✓ | |
| J. R. Evans (D) | 3,152 | |
| J. Brasnears (D) | | |
| 4 John Edwards (W) | ✓ | |
| Francis James (W) | ✓ | |
| Edward Davies (W) | 15,192✓ | |
| R. Frazer (D) | 11,353 | |
| John Evans (D) | | |
| G. G. Leiper (D) | | |

**Special Election**

| Candidates | Votes | % |
|---|---|---|
| 9 George M. Keim (D) | 2,115 | 89.8 |

## SOUTH CAROLINA [2]

| Candidates | Votes | % |
|---|---|---|
| 1 Isaac E. Holmes (D) | 1,504 | 63.8 |
| Hugh S. Legare (UN D) | 854 | 36.2 |
| 2 R. Barnwell Rhett (D) | | 100.0 |
| 3 John Campbell (SR D) | 1,280 | 67.4 |
| Thomas Smith | 620 | 32.6 |
| 4 Franklin H. Elmore (SR D) | * | 100.0 |
| 5 John K. Griffin (SR W) | | 100.0 |
| 6 Francis W. Pickens (NULL) | | 100.0 |
| 7 James Rogers (D) | ✓ | |
| F. W. Davie | | |
| 8 Waddy Thompson Jr (W) | 3,339 | 58.9 |
| J. N. Witner | 2,327 | 41.1 |
| 9 John P. Richardson (SR D) | * | 100.0 |

## VERMONT

| Candidates | Votes | % |
|---|---|---|
| 1 Hiland Hall (W) | 5,211 | 53.9 |
| John Roberts (D) | 4,328 | 44.7 |
| 2 William Slade (W) | 4,752 | 68.9 |
| Charles Linsley (D) | 2,095 | 30.4 |
| 3 Horace Everett (W) | 5,183 | 56.8 |
| Alden Partridge (D) | 3,841 | 42.1 |
| 4 John Smith (D) | 4,375 | 49.0 |
| Heman Allen (W) | 4,085 | 45.8 |
| 5 Isaac Fletcher (D) | 4,996 | 52.2 |
| William Upham (W) | 4,515 | 47.2 |

## VIRGINIA

**Special Election**

| Candidates | Votes | % |
|---|---|---|
| 13 Linn Banks (D) | ✓ | |
| Daniel F. Slaughter (W) | | |

1. *Richard Fletcher of the 1st district never served in the 26th Congress (1839-41). In an 1839 special election, Abbott Lawrence was elected to succeed him. (See p. 970.)*

2. *Franklin H. Elmore of the 4th district and John P. Richardson of the 9th district did not serve in the 26th Congress (1839-41). Sampson Butler and Thomas Sumter were later elected to the seats in special elections for which returns are unavailable.*

# 1839 House Elections

## ALABAMA

| Candidates | Votes | % |
|---|---|---|
| 1 Reuben Chapman (D) | 7,384 | 100.0 |
| 2 David Hubbard (D) | 3,303 | 56.3 |
| Lyon (W) | 2,561 | 43.7 |
| 3 George W. Crabb (W) | 5,927 | 50.5 |
| Ellis (D) | 5,816 | 49.5 |
| 4 Dixon H. Lewis (SR W) | | 100.0 |
| 5 James Dellet (W) | 4,350 | 52.6 |
| Murphey (D) | 3,927 | 47.4 |

## CONNECTICUT

| Candidates | Votes | % |
|---|---|---|
| 1 Joseph Trumbull (W) | 5,180 | 53.2 |
| Isaac Toucey (D) | 4,108 | 42.2 |
| 2 William L. Storrs (W) | 10,525 | 51.5 |
| Samuel Ingham (D) | 9,924 | 48.5 |
| 3 Thomas Williams (W) | 3,066 | 50.7 |
| Codington Billings (D) | 2,978 | 49.3 |
| 4 Thomas B. Osborne (W) | 3,968 | 52.4 |
| Thomas Whittlesey (D) | 3,604 | 47.6 |
| 5 Truman Smith (W) | 3,988 | 53.5 |
| Charles Phelps (D) | 3,466 | 46.5 |
| 6 John Brockway (W) | 3,997 | 52.5 |
| Chauncey Cleveland (D) | 3,565 | 46.8 |

## INDIANA

| Candidates | Votes | % |
|---|---|---|
| 1 George H. Proffit (W) | 6,008 | 53.5 |
| Robert Dale Owen (D) | 5,229 | 46.5 |
| 2 John W. Davis (D) | 7,516 | 54.7 |
| John Ewing (W) | 6,217 | 45.3 |
| 3 John Carr (D) | 6,998 | 57.7 |
| William Graham (W) | 5,121 | 42.3 |
| 4 Thomas Smith (D) | 6,541 | 54.1 |
| George H. Dunn (W) | 5,542 | 45.9 |
| 5 James Rariden (W) | 6,257 | 40.2 |
| William Thompson (D) | 5,333 | 34.3 |
| Jonathan McCarty (W) | 3,961 | 25.5 |
| 6 William W. Wick (D) | 9,505 | 52.8 |
| William Herod (W) | 8,494 | 47.2 |
| 7 Tilghman A. Howard (D) | 9,929 | 55.3 |
| Thomas J. Evans (W) | 8,036 | 44.7 |

## KENTUCKY

| Candidates | Votes | % |
|---|---|---|
| 1 Linn Boyd (D) | ✔ | |
| 2 Phillip Triplett (W) | ✔ | |
| 3 Joseph R. Underwood (W) | ✔ | |
| 4 Sherrod Williams (W) | ✔ | |
| 5 Simeon H. Anderson (W) | ✔ | |
| 6 Willis Green (W) | ✔ | |
| 7 John Pope (D) | ✔ | |
| 8 William J. Graves (W) | ✔ | |
| 9 John White (W) | ✔ | |
| 10 Richard Hawes (W) | ✔ | |
| 11 Landaff W. Andrews (W) | ✔ | |
| 12 Garrett Davis (HC W) | ✔ | |
| 13 William O. Butler (D) | ✔ | |

## MARYLAND

| Candidates | Votes | % |
|---|---|---|
| 1 John Dennis (W) | 2,062 | 52.8 |
| Stewart (D) | 1,817 | 46.5 |
| 2 Philip F. Thomas (D) | 3,831 | 51.3 |
| Pearce (W) | 3,643 | 48.7 |
| 3 John T. H. Worthington (D) | 3,924 | 62.3 |
| Turner (I) | 2,378 | 37.7 |
| 5 William Cost Johnson (W) | 3,325 | 56.7 |
| Duvall (D) | 2,535 | 43.3 |
| 6 Francis Thomas (D) | 4,279 | 53.3 |
| Price (W) | 3,704 | 46.2 |
| 7 Daniel Jenifer (W) | 1,984 | 56.1 |
| Key (D) | 1,553 | 43.9 |
| **Multi-Member District** | | |
| 4 James Carroll (D) | 8,018✔ | |
| Soloman Hillen Jr (D) | 8,011✔ | |

| Candidates | Votes | % |
|---|---|---|
| Kennedy (W) | 7,634 | |
| Pitts (W) | 7,629 | |

## MASSACHUSETTS

### Special Elections

| Candidates | Votes | % |
|---|---|---|
| 1 Abbott Lawrence (W) | 4,963 | 57.4 |
| Bradford Sumner (D) | 3,665 | 42.4 |
| 6 Osmyn Baker (W) | 2,581 | 50.8 |
| Rodolphus Dickinson (D) | 2,020 | 39.8 |
| Israel Billings (AB-D) | 451 | 8.9 |

## MISSISSIPPI

| Candidates | Votes | % |
|---|---|---|
| AL Albert G. Brown (D) | 16,730✔ | |
| Jacob Thompson (D) | 16,501✔ | |
| A. L. Benjamin (W) | 14,094 | |
| Reuben Davis (W) | 13,808 | |

## NEW HAMPSHIRE

| Candidates | Votes | % |
|---|---|---|
| AL Ira A. Eastman (D) | ✔ | |
| Edmund Burke (D) | ✔ | |
| Tristram Shaw (D) | ✔ | |
| Charles G. Atherton (D) | ✔ | |
| Jared W. Williams (D) | ✔ | |
| P. Handerson (FED) | | |
| J. Smith (FED) | | |
| Joel Eastman (FED) | | |
| A. Colby (FED) | | |
| I. Bartlett (FED) | | |
| D. Hoit (FEDL AB) | | |
| P. P. Woodbury (FEDL AB) | | |
| J. M. Harper (FEDL AB) | | |
| Southworth (FEDL AB) | | |

## NORTH CAROLINA

| Candidates | Votes | % |
|---|---|---|
| 1 Kenneth Rayner (W) | 2,635 | 56.7 |
| Samuel T. Sawyer (D) | 2,009 | 43.3 |
| 2 Jesse A. Bynum (D) | ✔ | |
| William L. Long (W) | | |
| 3 Edward Stanly (W) | 3,098 | 54.8 |
| Thomas H. Hall (D) | 2,554 | 45.2 |
| 4 Charles Shepard (D) | 2,890 | 57.1 |
| Samuel J. Biddle (W) | 2,175 | 42.9 |
| 5 James I. McKay (D) | 2,360 | 87.9 |
| Frederick J. Hill (W) | 325 | 12.1 |
| 6 Micajah T. Hawkins (D) | 1,625 | 50.1 |
| Robert C. Hilliard (D) | 1,621 | 49.9 |
| 7 Edmund Deberry (W) | 3,649 | 57.0 |
| William A. Morris (D) | 2,753 | 43.0 |
| 8 William Montgomery (D) | 2,916 | 53.3 |
| G. W. Haywood (W) | 2,553 | 46.7 |
| 9 John Hill (D) | 3,743 | 50.3 |
| Augustine H. Shepperd (W) | 3,696 | 49.7 |
| 10 Charles Fisher (D) | 3,539 | 51.4 |
| Pleasant Henderson (W) | 3,348 | 48.6 |
| 11 Henry W. Conner (D) | 3,041 | 54.8 |
| Edney (W) | 2,504 | 45.2 |
| 12 James Graham (W) | ✔ | |
| 13 Lewis Williams (D) | 2,900 | 51.5 |
| Roderick Murchison (W) | 2,731 | 48.5 |

## PENNSYLVANIA

### Special Election

| Candidates | Votes | % |
|---|---|---|
| 14 George McCullough (D) | 4,094 | 50.9 |
| Irvin (W) | 3,956 | 49.1 |

## RHODE ISLAND

| Candidates | Votes | % |
|---|---|---|
| AL Joseph L. Tillinghast (W) | 4,050✔ | |
| Robert B. Cranston (W) | 3,912✔ | |

| Candidates | Votes | % |
|---|---|---|
| Thomas W. Dorr (D) | 3,660 | |
| Benjamin B. Thurston (D) | 3,595 | |

## TENNESSEE

| Candidates | Votes | % |
|---|---|---|
| 1 William B. Carter (W) | 4,787 | 59.0 |
| Joseph Powell (D) | 3,334 | 41.1 |
| 2 Abraham M. McClellan (D) | 3,363 | 65.3 |
| John A. McKenny (W) | 1,790 | 34.7 |
| 3 Joseph L. Williams (W) | 5,173 | 99.9 |
| 4 Julius W. Blackwell (D) | 4,448 | 61.3 |
| William Stone (W) | 2,806 | 38.7 |
| 5 Hopkins L. Turney (D) | 4,953 | 65.6 |
| Anthony Dibrell (W) | 2,603 | 34.5 |
| 6 William B. Campbell (W) | 5,126 | 60.5 |
| William Trousdale (D) | 3,350 | 39.5 |
| 7 John Bell (W) | 3,895 | 59.4 |
| Robert M. Burton (D) | 2,665 | 40.6 |
| 8 Meredith P. Gentry (W) | 3,245 | 54.2 |
| William G. Childress (D) | 2,744 | 45.8 |
| 9 Harvey M. Watterson (D) | 4,521 | 58.9 |
| Daniel L. Barenger (W) | 3,154 | 41.1 |
| 10 Aaron V. Brown (D) | 5,017 | 57.8 |
| Ebenezer Shields (W) | 3,668 | 42.2 |
| 11 Cave Johnson (D) | 4,289 | 57.9 |
| Richard Cheatham (W) | 3,117 | 42.1 |
| 12 John W. Crockett (W) | 5,155 | 58.1 |
| Stephen C. Pavatt (D) | 3,719 | 41.9 |
| 13 Christopher H. Williams (W) | 3,447 | 55.5 |
| William C. Dunlap (D) | 2,767 | 44.5 |

## VIRGINIA

| Candidates | Votes | % |
|---|---|---|
| 1 Joel Holleman (D) | 1,920 | 51.9 |
| Mallory (W) | 1,781 | 48.1 |
| 2 Francis E. Rives (D) | 1,334 | 57.6 |
| Pegram (W) | 982 | 42.4 |
| 3 John W. Jones (D) | 409 | 58.5 |
| Taylor (W) | 290 | 41.5 |
| 4 George C. Dromgoole (D) | 1,236 | 57.1 |
| Gholson (W) | 927 | 42.9 |
| 5 John Hill (W) | 835 | 54.1 |
| Wilson (D) | 708 | 45.9 |
| 6 Walter Coles (D) | 1,564 | 51.6 |
| Witcher (W) | 1,465 | 48.4 |
| 7 William L. Goggin (W) | 1,498 | 52.7 |
| Stuart (D) | 1,347 | 47.4 |
| 8 Henry A. Wise (W) | 858 | 88.4 |
| Shultice (D) | 113 | 11.6 |
| 9 Robert M. T. Hunter (W) | 1,203 | 52.0 |
| Scott (D) | 1,109 | 48.0 |
| 10 John Taliaferro (W) | 1,331 | 51.4 |
| Grayson (D) | 1,258 | 48.6 |
| 11 John M. Botts (W) | 1,459 | 53.8 |
| Selden (D) | 1,251 | 46.2 |
| 12 James Garland (W) | 1,638 | 66.3 |
| Gordon (D) | 831 | 33.7 |
| 13 Linn Banks (D) | 1,785 | 56.1 |
| Slaughter (W) | 1,396 | 43.9 |
| 14 Charles F. Mercer (W) | 1,355 | 59.3 |
| Mason (D) | 932 | 40.8 |
| 15 William Lucas (D) | 2,074 | 50.1 |
| Barton (W) | 2,070 | 50.0 |
| 16 Green B. Samuels (D) | 1,826 | 60.3 |
| Steele (W) | 1,201 | 39.7 |
| 17 Robert Craig (D) | 2,336 | 58.8 |
| Moore (W) | 1,635 | 41.2 |
| 18 George W. Hopkins (W) | 2,921 | 55.9 |
| George (D) | 2,308 | 44.1 |
| 19 Andrew Beirne (D) | 2,745 | 61.5 |
| Wethered (W) | 1,721 | 38.5 |
| 20 Joseph Johnson (D) | 2,370 | 47.2 |
| Camden (W) | 1,967 | 39.2 |
| Shinn (D) | 682 | 13.6 |
| 21 Lewis Steenrod (D) | 2,667 | 55.8 |
| Hammond (W) | 2,112 | 44.2 |

# 1840 House Elections

### ARKANSAS

| Candidates | Votes | % |
|---|---|---|
| AL Edward Cross (D) | 7,876 | 57.6 |
| Fowler (W) | 5,788 | 42.4 |

### DELAWARE

| | Votes | % |
|---|---|---|
| AL George B. Rodney (W) | 5,896 | 54.2 |
| Thomas Robinson Jr. (D) | 4,974 | 45.8 |

### GEORGIA

| | Votes | % |
|---|---|---|
| AL William C. Dawson (W) | 39,299✓ | |
| Richard W. Habersham (W) | 39,105✓ | |
| Eugenius A. Nisbet (W) | 39,098✓ | |
| Thomas F. Foster (W) | 39,004✓ | |
| Lott Warren (W) | 39,001✓ | |
| Julius C. Alford (W) | 38,980✓ | |
| Roger L. Gamble (W) | 38,924✓ | |
| Thomas Butler King (W) | 38,895✓ | |
| James A. Meriwether (W) | 38,840✓ | |
| Mark A. Cooper (D) | 35,922 | |
| Edward J. Black (D) | 35,783 | |
| Lumpkin (D) | 35,730 | |
| Campbell (D) | 35,678 | |
| Hillyer (D) | 35,660 | |
| Pooler (D) | 35,657 | |
| Patterson (D) | 35,615 | |
| Iverson (D) | 35,608 | |

#### Special Election

| | Votes | % |
|---|---|---|
| AL Hines Holt (W) | ✓ | # |

### INDIANA

#### Special Election

| | Votes | % |
|---|---|---|
| 7 Henry S. Lane (W) | 11,726 | 53.1 |
| Edward A. Hannegan (D) | 10,376 | 47.0 |

### LOUISIANA

| | Votes | % |
|---|---|---|
| 1 Edward D. White (W) | 3,802 | 68.4 |
| Leonard (D) | 1,757 | 31.6 |
| 2 John B. Dawson (D) | 1,933 | 50.2 |
| Morgan (W) | 1,920 | 49.8 |
| 3 John Moore (W) | 3,427 | 50.6 |
| Winn (D) | 3,353 | 49.5 |

### MAINE

| | Votes | % |
|---|---|---|
| 1 Nathan Clifford (D) | 5,428 | 54.6 |
| Daniel Goodenow (W) | 4,516 | 45.4 |
| 2 William Pitt Fessenden (W) | 5,794 | 50.5 |
| Albert Smith (D) | 5,659 | 49.3 |
| 3 Benjamin Randall (W) | 5,720 | 54.3 |
| Joseph Sewall (D) | 4,769 | 45.3 |
| 4 George Evans (W) | 7,430* | 62.5 |
| John Hubbard (D) | 4,450 | 37.4 |
| 5 Nathaniel S. Littlefield (D) | 2,144 | 47.0 |
| Zadoc Long (W) | 2,123 | 46.6 |
| 6 Alfred Marshall (D) | 5,805 | 58.9 |
| Stanford A. Kingsbury (W) | 3,965 | 40.2 |
| 7 Joshua A. Lowell (D) | 5,194 | 50.0 |
| Joseph C. Noyes (W) | 5,051 | 48.6 |
| 8 Elisha H. Allen (W) | 7,738 | 51.5 |
| Hannibal Hamlin (D) | 7,115 | 47.4 |

### MASSACHUSETTS

| | Votes | % |
|---|---|---|
| 1 Robert C. Winthrop (W) | 7,286 | 63.0 |
| Bradford Sumner (D) | 4,232 | 36.6 |
| 2 Leverett Saltonstall (W) | 6,153 | 58.4 |
| Robert Rantoul (D) | 4,276 | 40.6 |
| 3 Caleb Cushing (W) | 6,529 | 60.9 |
| Gayton P. Osgood (D) | 4,047 | 37.8 |

| Candidates | Votes | % |
|---|---|---|
| 4 William Parmenter (D) | 6,156 | 50.3 |
| Nathan Brooks (W) | 5,912 | 48.3 |
| 5 Levi Lincoln (W) | 7,069 | 62.4 |
| Isaac Davis (D) | 4,126 | 36.4 |
| 6 Osmyn Baker (W) | 6,167 | 62.6 |
| Rhodelphius Larkenson (D) | 3,537 | 35.9 |
| 7 George N. Briggs (W) | 5,447 | 54.1 |
| Henry W. Bishop (D) | 4,561 | 45.3 |
| 8 William B. Calhoun (W) | 5,701 | 56.0 |
| Chester W. Chapin (D) | 4,300 | 42.2 |
| 9 William S. Hastings (W) | 5,906 | 57.8 |
| Alexander H. Everett (D) | 4,197 | 41.1 |
| 10 Nathaniel B. Borden (W) | 4,320 | 52.4 |
| Henry Williams (D) | 3,730 | 45.2 |
| 11 Barker Burnell (W) | 5,120 | 59.5 |
| Henry Crocker (D) | 3,378 | 39.3 |
| 12 John Quincy Adams (W) | 5,948 | 54.2 |
| William M. Jackson (D) | 4,945 | 45.0 |

#### Special Election

| | Votes | % |
|---|---|---|
| 1 Robert C. Winthrop (W) | 7,280 | 62.9 |
| Bradford Sumner (D) | 4,239 | 36.7 |

### MICHIGAN

| | Votes | % |
|---|---|---|
| AL Jacob M. Howard (W) | 22,841 | 51.2 |
| Alpheus Felch (D) | 21,464 | 48.1 |

### MISSOURI

| | Votes | % |
|---|---|---|
| AL John Miller (D) | 29,594✓ | |
| John C. Edwards (D) | 29,382✓ | |
| Samuels (W) | 21,492 | |
| Sibley (W) | 21,331 | |

### NEW JERSEY

| | Votes | % |
|---|---|---|
| AL William Halsted (W) | 33,342✓ | |
| Joseph F. Randolph (W) | 33,321✓ | |
| John B. Aycrigg (W) | 33,315✓ | |
| John P. B. Maxwell (W) | 33,315✓ | |
| Charles C. Stratton (W) | 33,313✓ | |
| Thomas Jones Yorke (W) | 33,299✓ | |
| Peter D. Vroom (D) | 31,138 | |
| William R. Cooper (D) | 31,109 | |
| Joseph Kille (D) | 31,106 | |
| Kennedy (D) | 31,103 | |
| Philemon Dickerson (D) | 31,101 | |
| Daniel B. Ryall (D) | 31,098 | |

### NEW YORK

| | Votes | % |
|---|---|---|
| 1 Charles Floyd (D) | 6,069 | 55.4 |
| William Buffett (W) | 4,880 | 44.6 |
| 2 Joseph Egbert (D) | 5,620 | 54.0 |
| Lawrence Hillyer (W) | 4,780 | 46.0 |
| 4 Aaron Ward (D) | 5,949 | 54.6 |
| Nicholas Cruger (W) | 4,955 | 45.4 |
| 5 Richard Davis (D) | 5,164 | 51.1 |
| Charles Johnston (W) | 4,947 | 48.9 |
| 6 James Clinton (W) | 4,867 | 52.8 |
| Thomas McKissock (W) | 4,343 | 47.2 |
| 7 John Van Buren (D) | 6,007 | 50.3 |
| Benjamin Bevier (W) | 5,930 | 49.7 |
| 9 Hiram Hunt (W) | 5,732 | 51.0 |
| Samuel Fowler (D) | 5,466 | 48.7 |
| 10 Daniel Barnard (W) | 6,351 | 51.4 |
| James French (D) | 5,973 | 48.3 |
| 11 Archibald Linn (W) | 6,074 | 52.1 |
| John Cramer (D) | 5,579 | 47.8 |
| 12 Bernard Blair (W) | 4,996 | 61.7 |
| Orville Clark (D) | 3,061 | 37.8 |

| Candidates | Votes | % |
|---|---|---|
| 13 Thomas Tomlinson (W) | 5,906 | 53.6 |
| Augustus Hand (D) | 5,107 | 46.4 |
| 14 Henry Van B. Rensselaer (W) | 6,258 | 51.3 |
| Preston King (D) | 5,948 | 48.7 |
| 15 John Sanford (D) | 5,341 | 53.0 |
| Marcellus Weston (W) | 4,732 | 47.0 |
| 16 Andrew Doig (D) | 5,981 | 55.2 |
| Harvey Doolittle (W) | 4,774 | 44.1 |
| 18 Thomas Chittenden (W) | 6,212 | 51.9 |
| Alpheus Greene (D) | 5,750 | 48.1 |
| 19 Samuel Bowne (D) | 5,612 | 53.5 |
| David Hard (W) | 4,831 | 46.0 |
| 20 Samuel Gordon (D) | 5,976 | 52.4 |
| Herman Gold (W) | 5,434 | 47.6 |
| 21 John Clark (W) | 4,306 | 51.3 |
| John Tacy (D) | 4,085 | 48.7 |
| 24 Christopher Morgan (W) | 5,148 | 50.8 |
| Peter Yawger (D) | 4,935 | 48.7 |
| 25 John Maynard (W) | 6,749 | 50.6 |
| John Demott (D) | 6,551 | 49.2 |
| 26 Francis Granger (W) | 4,800 | 57.1 |
| Jared Willson (D) | 3,457 | 41.1 |
| 27 William Oliver (W) | 6,949 | 53.0 |
| Thomas Johnson (W) | 6,170 | 47.0 |
| 28 Timothy Childs (W) | 6,052 | 53.9 |
| Lyman Langworthy (D) | 5,092 | 45.4 |
| 29 Seth Gates (W) | 6,970 | 63.4 |
| John Skinner (D) | 3,881 | 35.3 |
| 30 John Young (W) | 7,974 | 56.7 |
| Leman Gibbs (D) | 6,096 | 43.3 |
| 31 Staley Clarke (W) | 8,909 | 60.2 |
| Benjamin Chamberlain (D) | 5,789 | 39.2 |
| 32 Millard Fillmore (W) | 6,682 | 63.9 |
| Leader Roberts (D) | 3,742 | 35.8 |
| 33 Alfred Babcock (W) | 5,524 | 55.4 |
| Silas Burroughs (D) | 4,309 | 43.2 |

#### Multi-Member Districts

| | Votes | % |
|---|---|---|
| 3 James Roosevelt (D) | 22,010✓ | |
| Charles Ferris (D) | 21,975✓ | |
| John McKeon (D) | 21,748✓ | |
| Fernando Wood (D) | 21,730✓ | |
| Moses Grinnell (W) | 20,996 | |
| James Monroe (W) | 20,862 | |
| Robert Smith (W) | 20,862 | |
| Prescott Hall (W) | 20,838 | |
| 8 Jacob Houck Jr. (D) | 11,210✓ | |
| Robert McClellan (D) | 11,194✓ | |
| Jededia Miller (D) | 10,143 | |
| Justus McKinstry (W) | 10,139 | |
| 17 David Brewster (D) | 11,837✓ | |
| John Floyd (D) | 11,775✓ | |
| Fortune White (W) | 11,364 | |
| Thomas Bond (W) | 11,328 | |
| Arba Blair (LIB) | 506 | |
| James Brown (LIB) | 505 | |
| 22 Samuel Partridge (D) | 10,374✓ | |
| Lewis Riggs (D) | 10,363✓ | |
| Ezra Sweet (W) | 10,245 | |
| James Dunn (W) | 10,243 | |
| 23 Victory Birdseye (W) | 10,854✓ | |
| A. Lawrence Foster (W) | 10,826✓ | |
| Nehemiah Earll (D) | 10,772 | |
| William Hough (D) | 10,747 | |
| John Pratt (LIB) | 274 | |
| Robert Furman (LIB) | 233 | |

### OHIO

| | Votes | % |
|---|---|---|
| 1 Nathaniel G. Pendleton (W) | 6,119 | 50.7 |
| Alexander Duncan (D) | 5,959 | 49.3 |
| 2 John B. Weller (D) | 5,730 | 50.3 |
| Lewis D. Campbell (W) | 5,661 | 49.7 |
| 3 Patrick G. Goode (W) | 10,438 | 50.4 |
| William Sawyer (D) | 10,275 | 49.6 |
| 4 Jeremiah Morrow (W) | 6,796 | 60.0 |
| Benjamin Baldwin (D) | 4,529 | 40.0 |

*Footnote, see p. 972.*

## OHIO

| | Candidates | Votes | % |
|---|---|---|---|
| 5 | William Doan (D) | 5,671 | 53.7 |
| | Thomas L. Shields (W) | 4,884 | 46.3 |
| 6 | Calvary Morris (W) | 8,724 | 55.8 |
| | George House (D) | 6,882 | 44.0 |
| 7 | William Russell (W) | 6,953 | 56.8 |
| | Allen Latham (D) | 5,287 | 43.2 |
| 8 | Joseph Ridgway (W) | 9,909 | 57.5 |
| | Henry N. Hedges Sr (D) | 7,326 | 42.5 |
| 9 | William Medill (D) | 8,218 | 57.1 |
| | George Sanderson (W) | 6,163 | 42.9 |
| 10 | Sampson Mason (W) | 10,055 | 61.4 |
| | Matthew Bonner (D) | 6,317 | 38.6 |
| 11 | Benjamin S. Cowan (W) | 5,791 | 53.0 |
| | Isaac Parrish (D) | 5,129 | 47.0 |
| 12 | Joshua Mathiot (W) | 7,540 | 53.7 |
| | Jonathan Taylor (D) | 6,497 | 46.3 |
| 13 | James Matthews (D) | 8,679 | 53.6 |
| | Henry B. Curtis (W) | 7,508 | 46.4 |
| 14 | George Sweeny (D) | 11,211 | 52.3 |
| | James Hedges (W) | 10,245 | 47.8 |
| 15 | Sherlock J. Andrews (W) | 11,874 | 57.8 |
| | David K. Carter (D) | 8,663 | 42.2 |
| 16 | Joshua R. Giddings (W) | 11,725 | 66.0 |
| | Thomas J. Main (D) | 6,033 | 34.0 |
| 17 | John Hastings (D) | 5,278 | 50.3 |
| | Charles D. Coffin (W) | 5,223 | 49.7 |
| 18 | Ezra Dean (D) | 6,508 | 54.7 |
| | Levi Cox (W) | 5,399 | 45.3 |
| 19 | Samuel Stokely (W) | 4,390 | 51.8 |
| | William C. McAuslen (D) | 4,092 | 48.2 |

## PENNSYLVANIA

| | Candidates | Votes | % |
|---|---|---|---|
| 1 | Charles Brown (D) | ✔ | |
| 3 | Charles J. Ingersoll (D) | ✔ | |
| 5 | Joseph Fornance (D) | 4,507 | 54.9 |
| | Unidentified Candidate (W) | 3,704 | 45.1 |
| 6 | Robert Ramsey (W) | 4,411 | 50.1 |
| | Unidentified Candidate (D) | 4,389 | 49.9 |
| 7 | John Westbrook (D) | 5,331 | 64.0 |
| | Unidentified Candidate (W) | 3,000 | 36.0 |
| 8 | Peter Newhard (D) | 4,299 | 55.7 |
| | Unidentified Candidate (W) | 3,415 | 44.3 |

| | Candidates | Votes | % |
|---|---|---|---|
| 9 | George M. Keim (D) | 4,033 | 100.0 |
| 10 | William Simonton (W) | 4,525 | 56.7 |
| | Unidentified Candidate (D) | 3,462 | 43.4 |
| 11 | James Gerry (D) | 3,711 | 53.3 |
| | Unidentified Candidate (D) | 3,248 | 46.7 |
| 12 | James Cooper (W) | 5,475 | 55.5 |
| | Unidentified Candidate (D) | 4,384 | 44.5 |
| 13 | William S. Ramsey (D) | 5,311* | 56.2 |
| | Unidentified Candidate (D) | 4,142 | 43.8 |
| 14 | James Irvin (W) | 6,762 | 51.6 |
| | Unidentified Candidate (D) | 6,336 | 48.4 |
| 15 | Benjamin A. Bidlack (D) | 6,040 | 60.4 |
| | Unidentified Candidate (W) | 3,959 | 39.6 |
| 16 | John Snyder (D) | 5,138 | 51.6 |
| | Unidentified Candidate (W) | 4,813 | 48.4 |
| 17 | Davis Dimock Jr (D) | 7,054 | 58.7 |
| | Unidentified Candidate (W) | 4,961 | 41.3 |
| 18 | Charles Ogle (W) | 5,449 | 56.7 |
| | Unidentified Candidate (D) | 4,160 | 43.3 |
| 19 | Albert G. Marchand (D) | 5,188 | 59.5 |
| | Unidentified Candidate (W) | 3,532 | 40.5 |
| 20 | Enos Hook (D) | 4,757 | 56.3 |
| | Unidentified Candidate (W) | 3,686 | 43.7 |
| 21 | Joseph Lawrence (W) | 4,045 | 52.2 |
| | Unidentified Candidate (D) | 3,712 | 47.9 |
| 22 | William W. Irwin (W) | 6,831 | 61.4 |
| | Unidentified Candidate (D) | 4,287 | 38.6 |
| 23 | William Jack (D) | 4,414 | 52.5 |
| | Unidentified Candidate (W) | 4,001 | 47.6 |
| 24 | Thomas Henry (W) | 5,372 | 56.6 |
| | Unidentified Candidate (D) | 4,120 | 43.4 |
| 25 | Arnold Plummer (D) | 7,906 | 51.0 |
| | Unidentified Candidate (W) | 7,600 | 49.0 |

### Multi-Member Districts

| | Candidates | Votes | % |
|---|---|---|---|
| 2 | George W. Toland (W) | ✔ | |
| | John Sergeant (W) | ✔ | |
| 4 | John Edwards (W) | ✔ | |
| | Francis James (W) | ✔ | |
| | Jeremiah Brown (W) | 15,779 ✔ | |
| | Unidentified Candidate (D) | | |
| | Unidentified Candidate (D) | | |
| | Unidentified Candidate (D) | | |

### Special Elections

| | Candidates | Votes | % |
|---|---|---|---|
| 13 | Charles McClure (D) | 3,452 | 94.7 |
| 22 | Henry M. Brackenridge (W) | 6,858 | 61.5 |
| | Wilkens (D) | 4,297 | 38.5 |

## SOUTH CAROLINA

| | | Votes | % |
|---|---|---|---|
| 1 | Isaac E. Holmes (D) | 1,413 | 86.9 |
| | Hugh S. Legare | 213 | 13.1 |
| 2 | R. Barnwell Rhett (D) | | 100.0 |
| 3 | John Campbell (SR D) | | 100.0 |
| 4 | Sampson H. Butler (D) | | 100.0 |
| 5 | Patrick C. Caldwell (D) | 2,040 | 39.3 |
| | James Irby (W) | 1,812 | 34.9 |
| | S. Barkley (D) | 1,340 | 25.8 |
| 6 | Francis W. Pickens (NULL D) | | 100.0 |
| 7 | James Rogers (D) | | 100.0 |
| 8 | William Butler (W) | 2,718 | 46.8 |
| | J. W. Norris (D) | 2,571 | 44.2 |
| | J. Powell (D) | 523 | 9.0 |
| 9 | Thomas D. Sumter (D) | ✔ | |
| | Evans (D) | | |

## VERMONT

| | | Votes | % |
|---|---|---|---|
| 1 | Hiland Hall (W) | 6,923 | 62.7 |
| | Daniel Kellogg (D) | 4,084 | 37.0 |
| 2 | William Slade (W) | 6,728 | 68.6 |
| | Charles Lindsley (D) | 3,034 | 30.9 |
| 3 | Horace Everett (W) | 6,729 | 59.1 |
| | Truman B. Ransom (D) | 4,497 | 39.5 |
| 4 | Augustus Young (W) | 6,148 | 55.9 |
| | John Smith (D) | 4,791 | 43.6 |
| 5 | John Mattocks (W) | 5,479 | 50.6 |
| | Isaac Fletcher (D) | 5,248 | 48.4 |

## VIRGINIA

### Special Election

| | | Votes | % |
|---|---|---|---|
| 14 | William M. McCarty (W) | 1,033 | 56.6 |
| | Cuthbert Powell (W) | 722 | 39.6 |

# 1841 House Elections

## ALABAMA

| Candidates | Votes | % |
|---|---|---|
| AL Reuben Chapman (D) | 23,376✔ | |
| Dixon H. Lewis (D) | 23,339✔ | |
| Benjamin Glover Shields (D) | 23,092✔ | |
| William Winter Payne (D) | 23,090✔ | |
| George Houston (D) | 23,036✔ | |
| George Crabb (W) | 17,828 | |
| Henry W. Hilliard (W) | 17,429 | |
| James Taylor Rather (W) | 17,290 | |
| John M. Lewis (D) | 17,271 | |
| J. Burke (W) | 16,656 | |
| William D. Dunn (W) | 627 | |

## CONNECTICUT

| Candidates | Votes | % |
|---|---|---|
| 1 Joseph Trumbull (W) | 5,142 | 57.1 |
| Thomas Seymour (D) | 3,867 | 42.9 |
| 2 William Boardman (W) | 6,225 | 54.3 |
| Charles Ingersoll (D) | 5,234 | 45.7 |
| 3 Thomas Williams (W) | 3,230 | 55.7 |
| Erastus Coit (D) | 2,565 | 44.3 |
| 4 Thomas Osborne (W) | 4,089 | 55.6 |
| William Pomeroy (D) | 3,269 | 44.4 |

| Candidates | Votes | % |
|---|---|---|
| 5 Truman Smith (W) | 3,993 | 55.9 |
| John Smith (D) | 3,157 | 44.2 |
| 6 John Brockway (W) | 4,121 | 57.3 |
| Chauncey Cleveland (D) | 3,076 | 42.7 |

## ILLINOIS

| | | |
|---|---|---|
| 1 John Reynolds (D) | 8,046 | 59.5 |
| Henry L. Webb (W) | 5,313 | 39.3 |
| 2 Zadoc Casey (W) | 7,121 | 50.6 |
| S. H. Anderson (D) | 6,949 | 49.4 |
| 3 John T. Stuart (W) | 21,726 | 52.0 |
| James H. Ralston (D) | 19,562 | 46.8 |

## INDIANA

| | | |
|---|---|---|
| 1 George H. Proffit (W) | 5,311 | 57.4 |
| James Lockhart (D) | 3,946 | 42.6 |
| 2 Richard W. Thompson (W) | 6,323 | 52.7 |
| John W. Davis (D) | 5,670 | 47.3 |
| 3 Joseph L. White (W) | 5,596 | 51.6 |
| John Carr (D) | 5,250 | 48.4 |

---

## Explanation of Symbols in House Returns

In the returns for House elections *symbols* are used to denote special circumstances. In cases where no symbol is used, the candidate who received the most votes won the election to the House. The following is a key to the symbols used:

✔ Elected to the House. The symbol is used to identify winning candidates in three types of situations: (1) When candidates ran for two or more at-large seats in states which chose all of their at-large representatives in a single election, or ran in a multi-member district; (2) when the vote total and percentage of one or more of the candidates are unavailable and (3) when a candidate who did not receive the highest vote total was seated by the House. *(Explanation of multi-member districts, see p. 916.)*

‡ The symbol is used when an election dispute resulted in the unseating of a representative *after* he was sworn in. *(For discussion of specific cases, consult the* Biographical Directory of the United States Congress, 1774-1989, *U.S. Government Printing Office, Washington, D.C., 1989; hereafter referred to as the* Biographical Directory.)

* The symbol is used for three types of situations: (1) When a representative-elect died or declined his seat before the constitutionally set date for the beginning of his term—March 4 until 1935, and Jan. 3 thereafter; (2) when the House refused to seat any candidate claiming election to a seat and (3) when state law required a candidate to obtain a popular vote majority for election to the House, but the candidate receiving the most votes failed to receive a majority. *(For discussion of specific cases, consult the Biographical Directory; explanation of majority vote requirement, see p. 945.)*

# Information for 1824-1973 returns was obtained from a source other than the Inter-University Consortium for Political and Social Research. *(For a listing of other sources, see p. 1327.)*

**Footnotes.** Numbered footnotes are used to explain unusual situations, such as a series of elections in the same year in the same House district, anomalies resulting from reapportionment and special procedures for conducting House elections in certain states.

---

| Candidates | Votes | % |
|---|---|---|
| 4 James H. Cravens (W) | 6,056 | 54.4 |
| Thomas Smith (D) | 5,026 | 45.2 |
| 5 Andrew Kennedy (D) | 5,664 | 39.8 |
| Jonathan McCarty (W) | 4,299 | 30.2 |
| Caleb B. Smith (W) | 4,048 | 28.5 |
| 6 David Wallace (W) | 8,206 | 53.9 |
| Nathan B. Palmer (D) | 7,009 | 46.1 |
| 7 Henry S. Lane (W) | 9,477 | 59.7 |
| John Bryce (D) | 6,392 | 40.3 |

## KENTUCKY

| | | |
|---|---|---|
| 1 Linn Boyd (D) | ✔ | |
| 2 Philip Triplett (W) | ✔ | |
| John H. McHenry (W) | | |
| 3 Joseph R. Underwood (W) | 3,924 | 72.7 |
| J. W. Irwin (W) | 1,477 | 27.4 |
| 4 Bryan Y. Owsley (W) | ✔ | |
| Martin Beatty (W) | | |
| Nathan Gaither (D) | | |
| 5 John B. Thompson (W) | 2,106 | 36.6 |
| Thomas P. Moore (D) | 1,939 | 33.7 |
| John Kinkead (W) | 1,704 | 29.6 |
| 6 Willis Green (W) | 2,640 | 38.2 |
| John L. Helm (W) | 2,298 | 33.2 |
| Hough | 1,978 | 28.6 |
| 7 John Pope (W) | 1,012 | 87.6 |
| Gray | 58 | 5.0 |
| 8 James C. Sprigg (W) | 2,576 | 66.4 |
| William H. Field (W) | 1,306 | 33.6 |
| 9 John White (W) | 1,424 | 100.0 |
| 10 Thomas F. Marshall (W) | ✔ | |
| L. B. Smith (W) | | |
| 11 Landaff W. Andrews (W) | ✔ | |
| J. C. Mason (D) | | |
| 12 Garret Davis (W) | | 100.0 |
| 13 William O. Butler (D) | 4,840 | 52.8 |
| W. W. Southgate (W) | 4,334 | 47.2 |

## MAINE

### Special Election

| | | |
|---|---|---|
| 4 David Bronson (W) | ✔ | |

## MARYLAND

| | | |
|---|---|---|
| 1 Isaac D. Jones (W) | 1,910 | 50.1 |
| Cottman (W) | 1,904 | 49.9 |
| 2 James Alfred Pearce (W) | 1,357 | 100.0 |
| 3 James W. Williams (D) | 2,563 | 68.4 |
| Orrick (D) | 1,187 | 31.7 |
| 5 William Cost Johnson (W) | 2,627 | 68.7 |
| Kimmell (W) | 1,195 | 31.3 |
| 6 John T. Mason (D) | 4,130 | 52.6 |
| Lynch (W) | 3,727 | 47.4 |
| 7 Augustus R. Sollers (W) | ✔ | |
| Somervell (I) | | |

### Multi-Member District

| | | |
|---|---|---|
| 4 Alexander Randall (W) | 7,783✔ | |
| John P. Kennedy (W) | 7,733✔ | |
| Murray (D) | 7,657 | |
| Gallagher (D) | 7,654 | |

## MASSACHUSETTS

### Special Election

| | | |
|---|---|---|
| 5 Charles Hudson (W) | 3,099 | 57.8 |
| Isaac Davis (D) | 1,782 | 33.2 |
| Cyrus B. Grovesnor | 333 | 6.2 |

## MISSISSIPPI

| | | |
|---|---|---|
| AL William L. Gwin (D) | 18,988✔ | |
| Jacob Thompson (D) | 18,956✔ | |

## MISSISSIPPI

| Candidates | Votes | % |
|---|---|---|
| Adam Benjamin (W) | 16,593 | |
| William Harley (W) | 16,333 | |

## NEW HAMPSHIRE

| | Candidates | Votes | % |
|---|---|---|---|
| AL | Charles G. Atherton (D) | ✔ | |
| | Edmund Burke (D) | ✔ | |
| | John R. Reding (D) | ✔ | |
| | Tristram Shaw (D) | 28,870✔ | |
| | Ira A. Eastman (D) | 20,833✔ | |

## NORTH CAROLINA

| | Candidates | Votes | % |
|---|---|---|---|
| 1 | Kenneth Rayner (W) | 1,593 | 93.5 |
| 2 | John R. J. Daniel (D) | ✔ | |
| | William W. Cherry (W) | | |
| 3 | Edward Stanly (W) | ✔ | |
| | H. I. Toole (D) | | |
| 4 | William H. Washington (W) | ✔ | |
| | Joshiah O. Watson (D) | | |
| 5 | James I. McKay (D) | 1,706 | 85.7 |
| | Baker (W) | 284 | 14.3 |
| 6 | Archibald H. Arrington (D) | 1,569 | 46.6 |
| | Micajah T. Hawkins (D) | 1,450 | 43.0 |
| | William Russell (D) | 351 | 10.4 |
| 7 | Edmund Deberry (W) | 2,769 | 70.8 |
| | Edward McCollum (D) | 1,145 | 29.3 |
| 8 | Romulus M. Saunders (D) | 2,576 | 55.2 |
| | James S. Smith (W) | 2,090 | 44.8 |
| 9 | Augustine H. Shepperd (W) | 3,689 | 52.6 |
| | David S. Reid (D) | 3,321 | 47.4 |
| 10 | Abraham Rencher (W) | ✔ | |
| | Charles Fisher (D) | | |
| | Jonathan Worth (W) | | |
| 11 | Greene W. Caldwell (D) | 3,063 | 57.2 |
| | Daniel M. Barringer (W) | 2,293 | 42.8 |
| 12 | James Graham (W) | 3,546 | 61.8 |
| | Thomas L. Clingman (W) | 2,188 | 38.2 |
| 13 | Lewis Williams (D) | 3,373 | 65.7 |
| | Roderick Murchison (W) | 1,760 | 34.3 |

## PENNSYLVANIA

**Special Elections**

| | Candidates | Votes | % |
|---|---|---|---|
| 2 | Joseph R. Ingersoll (W) | 5,822 | 55.4 |
| | Pettit (D) | 4,596 | 43.7 |
| 18 | Henry Black (W) | 3,220 | 68.1 |
| | Philson (D) | 1,507 | 31.9 |
| 20 | Henry W. Beeson (D) | 3,777 | 56.5 |
| | Andrew Stewart (W) | 2,914 | 43.6 |

## RHODE ISLAND

| | Candidates | Votes | % |
|---|---|---|---|
| AL | Robert B. Cranston (W) | 2,516✔ | |
| | Joseph L. Tillinghast (W) | 2,487✔ | |

## TENNESSEE

| | Candidates | Votes | % |
|---|---|---|---|
| 1 | Thomas D. Arnold (W) | 2,506 | 88.3 |
| | Robert J. McKinney | 157 | 5.5 |
| 2 | Abraham McClelland (D) | 3,484 | 53.0 |
| | William T. Senter (W) | 3,089 | 47.0 |
| 3 | Joseph L. Williams (W) | 1,022 | 99.4 |
| 4 | Thomas J. Campbell (W) | 3,757 | 49.4 |
| | Julius W. Blackwell (D) | 3,699 | 48.6 |
| 5 | Hopkins L. Turney (D) | 3,974 | 68.0 |
| | John Goodall (W) | 1,872 | 32.0 |
| 6 | William B. Campbell (W) | 2,207 | 89.1 |
| | Jesse Skein | 271 | 10.9 |
| 7 | Robert L. Caruthers (W) | 3,211 | 72.3 |
| | John Hall (D) | 1,231 | 27.7 |
| 8 | Meredith P. Gentry (W) | 2,813 | 70.1 |
| | Thomas Hogan (D) | 1,200 | 29.9 |
| 9 | Harvey M. Watterson (D) | 3,557 | 54.8 |
| | Terry H. Cahal (W) | 2,933 | 45.2 |
| 10 | Aaron V. Brown (D) | 3,448 | 83.7 |
| | Ebenezer J. Shields (W) | 670 | 16.3 |
| 11 | Cave Johnson (D) | 3,264 | 74.3 |
| | N. H. Allen (W) | 1,132 | 25.8 |
| 12 | Milton Brown (W) | 5,503 | 63.3 |
| | Stephen C. Davatt (D) | 3,195 | 36.7 |
| 13 | Christopher H. Williams (W) | 4,370 | 57.9 |
| | Levin H. Coe (D) | 3,178 | 42.1 |

## VIRGINIA

| | Candidates | Votes | % |
|---|---|---|---|
| 1 | Francis Mallory (W) | ✔ | |
| | Waltas | | |
| 3 | George B. Cary (D) | ✔ | |
| | Collier | | |
| 3 | John W. Jones (D) | ✔ | |
| | J. Leigh | | |
| 4 | William O. Goode (D) | ✔ | |
| | Baptist | | |
| | Marshall | | |
| 5 | Edmund W. Hubard (D) | ✔ | |
| | John Hill (W) | | |
| 6 | Walter Coles (D) | ✔ | |
| | Witcher (W) | | |
| 7 | William L. Goggin (W) | ✔ | |
| | Stuart (D) | | |
| 8 | Henry A. Wise (W) | ✔ | |
| 9 | Robert M. T. Hunter (I) | ✔ | |
| | Corbin (W) | | |
| | Braxton (D) | | |
| 10 | John Taliaferro (W) | ✔ | |
| | Grayson (D) | | |
| 11 | John M. Botts (W) | ✔ | |
| 12 | Thomas W. Gilmer (W) | ✔ | |
| | Garland | | |
| | Holladay | | |
| 13 | William Smith (D) | ‡ | |
| | Linn Banks (D) | | |
| 14 | Cuthbert Powell (W) | ✔ | |
| | Shreve | | |
| 15 | Richard W. Barton (W) | ✔ | |
| | William Lucas (D) | | |
| 16 | William A. Harris (D) | ✔ | |
| | Samuel C. Williams (D) | | |
| | M. H. Beale | | |
| | G. T. Barbee | | |
| 17 | Alexander H. H. Stuart (W) | ✔ | |
| | McDowell | | |
| 18 | George W. Hopkins (D) | ✔ | |
| | J. Watson (W) | | |
| 19 | George W. Summers (W) | ✔ | |
| | Ellis | | |
| | Caperton | | |
| 20 | Samuel L. Hayes (D) | ✔ | |
| | Augustine J. Smith (W) | | |
| 21 | Lewis Stennrod (D) | ✔ | |

# 1842 House Elections

## ARKANSAS

| Candidates | Votes | % |
|---|---|---|
| AL Edward Cross (D) | 9,413 | 57.4 |
| Cummins (W) | 5,315 | 32.4 |
| Evans (I) | 1,686 | 10.3 |

## DELAWARE

| | Votes | % |
|---|---|---|
| AL George B. Rodney (W) | 5,467 | 50.0 |
| Jones (D) | 5,458 | 50.0 |

## GEORGIA

| | Votes |
|---|---|
| AL Mark A. Cooper (D) | 35,451✓ |
| John B. Lamar (D) | 35,307✓ |
| Howell Cobb (D) | 35,217✓ |
| Edward J. Black (D) | 35,181✓ |
| William H. Stiles (D) | 35,176✓ |
| Hugh A. Haralson (D) | 35,162✓ |
| Joseph H. Lumpkin (D) | 35,159✓ |
| John Millen (D) | 35,026✓ |
| Richard W. Habersham (W) | 33,474 |
| Roger L. Gamble (W) | 33,249 |
| Augustus R. Wright (W) | 33,214 |
| Richard H. Wilde (W) | 32,997 |
| Absalom H. Chappell (W) | 32,980 |
| Agustus H. Kenan (W) | 32,827 |
| Thomas B. King (W) | 32,822 |
| Henry P. Smead (W) | 32,560 |

## LOUISIANA

| | |
|---|---|
| 1 John Slidell (SR D) | ✓ |
| 2 Alcee La Branche (D) | ✓ |
| 3 John B. Dawson (D) | ✓ |
| 4 Pierre E. J. B. Bossier (CALH D) | ✓ |

## MASSACHUSETTS

| | Votes | % |
|---|---|---|
| 1 Robert C. Winthrop (W) | 5,782 | 53.7 |
| William Washburn (D) | 4,473 | 41.5 |
| 2 Daniel P. King (W) | 3,711 | 50.6 |
| J. C. Stickney (D) | 2,854 | 38.9 |
| Moses P. Hanson | 660 | 9.0 |
| 3 Amos Abbott (W) | 3,932 | 50.4 |
| Gayton P. Osgood (D) | 3,064 | 39.3 |
| Gardner B. Perry | 708 | 9.1 |
| 4 William Parmenter (D) | 5,339 | 52.5 |
| Samuel Hoar (W) | 4,010 | 39.5 |
| Thomas W. Ward | 783 | 7.7 |
| 5 Charles Hudson (W) | 5,010 | 50.9 |
| David Henshaw (D) | 4,090 | 41.6 |
| Phineas Crandall | 682 | 6.9 |
| 6 Osmyn Baker (W) | 5,150 | 50.1 |
| Chester W. Chapin (D) | 4,127 | 40.2 |

| Candidates | Votes | % |
|---|---|---|
| Lucius Boltwood (LIB) | 971 | 9.5 |
| 7 Julius Rockwell (W) | 4,680 | 53.6 |
| Brown | 3,335 | 38.2 |
| Joel Hayden | 643 | 7.4 |
| 8 John Quincy Adams (W) | 5,996 | 51.8 |
| Ezra Wilkinson (D) | 5,418 | 46.8 |
| 9 Henry Williams (D) | 6,575 | 55.0 |
| Seth Sprague (W) | 4,510 | 37.7 |
| Hedges Read | 800 | 6.7 |
| 10 Barker Burnell (W) | 4,776 | 52.0 |
| Julius H. Shaw | 4,085 | 44.5 |

### Special Elections [1]

| | Votes | % |
|---|---|---|
| 1 Nathan Appleton (W) | 2,753 | 67.0 |
| William Washburn (D) | 1,232 | 30.0 |
| 1 Robert Winthrop (W) | 5,781 | 53.8 |
| William Washburn (D) | 4,468 | 41.6 |
| 9 William Jackson (W) | 2,775* | 48.3 |
| Ezra Wilkinson (D) | 2,773 | 48.2 |

## MISSOURI

| | |
|---|---|
| AL James H. Relfe (D) | ✓ |
| John Jameson (D) | ✓ |
| Gustavus M. Bower (D) | ✓ |
| James B. Bowlin (D) | ✓ |
| James M. Hughes (D) | ✓ |
| John P. Campbell | |

## NEW YORK

| | Votes | % |
|---|---|---|
| 1 Selah B. Strong (D) | 5,463 | 61.9 |
| King (W) | 3,354 | 38.0 |
| 2 Henry C. Murphy (D) | 4,563 | 51.6 |
| Silliman (W) | 4,214 | 47.7 |
| 3 J. Phillips Phoenix (W) | 5,084 | 54.9 |
| Nicoll (D) | 4,156 | 44.8 |
| 4 William B. Maclay (D) | 5,549 | 53.7 |
| Williams (W) | 4,777 | 46.2 |
| 5 Moses G. Leonard (D) | 5,282 | 54.6 |
| Scoles (W) | 4,389 | 45.4 |
| 6 Hamilton Fish (W) | 5,904 | 50.8 |
| McKeon (D) | 5,699 | 49.1 |
| 7 Joseph H. Anderson (D) | 4,811 | 58.3 |
| Cruger (W) | 3,435 | 41.7 |
| 8 Richard D. Davis (D) | 6,069 | 57.2 |
| Rankin (W) | 4,527 | 42.6 |
| 9 James G. Clinton (D) | 5,563 | 55.6 |
| Wheeler (W) | 4,439 | 44.4 |
| 10 Jeremiah Russell (D) | 7,376 | 57.6 |
| Elting (W) | 5,436 | 42.4 |
| 11 Zadock Pratt (D) | 6,967 | 54.6 |
| Palen (W) | 5,772 | 45.2 |

| Candidates | Votes | % |
|---|---|---|
| 12 David L. Seymour (D) | 5,419 | 50.0 |
| Stevenson (W) | 5,335 | 49.3 |
| 13 Daniel D. Barnard (W) | 6,317 | 51.0 |
| French (D) | 5,980 | 48.3 |
| 14 Charles Rogers (W) | 6,143 | 71.0 |
| Hunter (D) | 2,263 | 26.2 |
| 15 Lemuel Stetson (D) | 4,635 | 52.1 |
| McDonald (W) | 4,092 | 46.0 |
| 16 Chesselden Ellis (D) | 7,328 | 50.4 |
| Linn (W) | 7,110 | 48.9 |
| 17 Charles S. Benton (D) | 6,750 | 57.4 |
| Frey (W) | 4,870 | 41.4 |
| 18 Preston King (D) | 6,578 | 56.2 |
| Sherman (W) | 4,785 | 40.9 |
| 19 Orville Hungerford (D) | 5,579 | 52.3 |
| Merrick (W) | 4,810 | 45.1 |
| 20 Samuel Beardsley (D) | 6,404 | 50.5 |
| Kirkland (W) | 5,619 | 44.4 |
| Delong (LIB) | 647 | 5.1 |
| 21 Jeremiah Cary (D) | 8,085 | 57.4 |
| Tuckerman (W) | 5,893 | 41.8 |
| 22 Smith M. Purdy (D) | 8,560 | 52.4 |
| Hunt (W) | 7,597 | 46.5 |
| 23 Orville Robinson (D) | 7,819 | 50.9 |
| Duer (W) | 6,598 | 42.9 |
| Jackson (LIB) | 956 | 6.2 |
| 24 Horace Wheaton (D) | 6,558 | 51.1 |
| Granger (W) | 6,024 | 46.9 |
| 25 George Rathbun (D) | 7,177 | 50.0 |
| Morgan (W) | 6,686 | 46.6 |
| 26 Amasa Dana (D) | 7,796 | 53.0 |
| Woodwh (W) | 6,626 | 45.0 |
| 27 Byram Green (D) | 6,446 | 52.3 |
| Adams (W) | 5,611 | 45.5 |
| 28 Thomas J. Patterson (W) | 5,333 | 48.9 |
| Sampson (D) | 5,298 | 48.6 |
| 29 Charles H. Carroll (W) | 6,979 | 91.8 |
| Pitts (LIB) | 623 | 8.2 |
| 30 William S. Hubbell (D) | 7,692 | 51.9 |
| Sherman (W) | 6,847 | 46.2 |
| 31 Asher Tyler (W) | 7,521 | 56.0 |
| Tenbrk (D) | 5,667 | 42.2 |
| 32 William A. Moseley (W) | 4,826 | 51.9 |
| Vosbgh (D) | 4,113 | 44.2 |
| 33 Albert Smith (W) | 4,844 | 53.3 |
| Cooley (D) | 3,894 | 42.9 |
| 34 Washington Hunt (W) | 4,672 | 50.5 |
| Piper (D) | 4,347 | 47.0 |

## PENNSYLVANIA

### Special Elections

| | Votes | % |
|---|---|---|
| 17 Almon H. Read (D) | 4,479 | 60.1 |
| Kingsbury (W) | 2,605 | 34.9 |
| 18 Philson (D) | 2,711 | 50.0 |
| James M. Russell (W) | 2,634✓ | 48.6 |

*1. In the 9th district, William S. Hastings, who had been elected in 1840, died June 17, 1842. In the special election to succeed him for the remainder of the 27th Congress (1841-43), no candidate received the requisite majority. A series of special elections were held, all resulting without choice, so the seat remained vacant for the remainder of the term. No returns are available for these special elections.*

# 1843 House Elections

## ALABAMA

| | Candidates | Votes | % |
|---|---|---|---|
| 1 | James Dellet (W) | 4,843 | 50.7 |
| | Goldthwaite (D) | 4,708 | 49.3 |
| 2 | James E. Belser (D) | 3,960 | 52.2 |
| | Pettit (W) | 3,633 | 47.9 |
| 3 | Dixon H. Lewis (D) | 3,509 | 52.3 |
| | Lea (W) | 3,202 | 47.7 |
| 4 | William W. Payne (D) | 4,298 | 51.7 |
| | Young (D) | 4,021 | 48.3 |
| 5 | George S. Houston (D) | 2,518 | 50.3 |
| | Armstrong (D) | 2,488 | 49.7 |
| 6 | Reuben Chapman (D) | | 100.0 |
| 7 | Felix G. McConnell (D) | 4,456 | 52.4 |
| | Chilton (W) | 3,860 | 45.4 |

## CONNECTICUT

| | Candidates | Votes | % |
|---|---|---|---|
| 1 | Thomas H. Seymour (D) | 7,005 | 49.1 |
| | T. K. Brace (W) | 6,949 | 48.7 |
| 2 | John J. Stewart (D) | 6,577 | 48.9 |
| | S. D. Hubbard (W) | 6,500 | 48.3 |
| 3 | George S. Catlin (D) | 5,582 | 52.8 |
| | E. Eldredge (W) | 4,332 | 41.0 |
| | I. Wilson (LIB) | 534 | 5.1 |
| 4 | Samuel Simons (D) | 8,061 | 49.2 |
| | T. B. Osborne (W) | 7,948 | 48.5 |

## GEORGIA

### Special Election

| | Candidates | Votes | % |
|---|---|---|---|
| AL | Alexander H. Stephens (W) | 38,471✔ | |
| | Absalom H. Chappell (W) | 37,463✔ | |
| | James H. Stark (D) | 34,961 | |
| | Herschel V. Johnson (D) | 34,757 | |

## ILLINOIS

| | Candidates | Votes | % |
|---|---|---|---|
| 1 | Robert Smith (D) | 7,347 | 56.1 |
| | J. L. D. Morrison (W) | 5,568 | 42.5 |
| 2 | John McClernand (D) | 6,364 | 63.7 |
| | Zadock Casey (W) | 3,629 | 36.3 |
| 3 | Orlando B. Ficklin (D) | 6,425 | 53.8 |
| | Justin Hardin (W) | 5,528 | 46.3 |
| 4 | John Wentworth (D) | 7,552 | 51.5 |
| | Giles Spring (W) | 5,931 | 40.5 |
| | John H. Henderson (LIB) | 1,167 | 8.0 |
| 5 | Stephen A. Douglas (D) | 8,641 | 50.6 |
| | Orville H. Browning (W) | 8,180 | 47.9 |
| 6 | Joseph P. Hoge (D) | 7,796 | 51.0 |
| | Cyrus Walker (W) | 7,222 | 47.3 |
| 7 | John J. Hardin (W) | 6,230 | 52.9 |
| | James A. McDougall (D) | 5,357 | 45.4 |

## INDIANA

| | Candidates | Votes | % |
|---|---|---|---|
| 1 | Robert Dale Owen (D) | 6,679 | 52.2 |
| | John W. Payne (W) | 6,127 | 47.8 |
| 2 | Thomas J. Henley (D) | 7,020 | 53.6 |
| | Joseph L. White (W) | 6,070 | 46.4 |
| 3 | Thomas Smith (D) | 7,021 | 50.9 |
| | John A. Matson (W) | 6,766 | 49.1 |
| 4 | Caleb B. Smith (W) | 4,097 | 49.1 |
| | Charles H. Test | 3,442 | 41.3 |
| | Hiram P. Bennett | 749 | 9.0 |
| 5 | William J. Brown (D) | 7,399 | 54.0 |
| | David Wallace (W) | 6,314 | 46.0 |
| 6 | John W. Davis (D) | 7,167 | 53.6 |
| | George G. Dunn (W) | 6,205 | 46.4 |
| 7 | Joseph A. Wright (D) | 5,441 | 50.0 |
| | Edward W. McGaughey (W) | 5,438 | 50.0 |
| 8 | John Pettit (D) | 6,403 | 51.7 |
| | James R. M. Bryant (W) | 5,985 | 48.3 |

| | Candidates | Votes | % |
|---|---|---|---|
| 9 | Samuel C. Sample (W) | 5,693 | 50.8 |
| | Ebenezer M. Chamberlain (D) | 5,379 | 48.0 |
| 10 | Andrew Kennedy (D) | 5,358 | 51.2 |
| | Lewis G. Thompson (W) | 5,098 | 48.7 |

## KENTUCKY

| | Candidates | Votes | % |
|---|---|---|---|
| 1 | Linn Boyd (D) | 6,097 | 56.7 |
| | Barbour (W) | 4,649 | 43.3 |
| 2 | Willis Green (W) | 5,236 | 51.2 |
| | McCreary (D) | 4,984 | 48.8 |
| 3 | Henry Grider (W) | 4,434 | 51.6 |
| | Irwin (W) | 4,167 | 48.5 |
| 4 | George A. Caldwell (D) | 4,560 | 45.0 |
| | Owsley (W) | 4,066 | 40.1 |
| | Stone (W) | 1,507 | 14.9 |
| 5 | James W. Stone (D) | 4,872 | 44.7 |
| | Grigsby (W) | 3,701 | 33.9 |
| | John Pope (D) | 2,338 | 21.4 |
| 6 | John White (W) | 6,850 | 90.6 |
| | Daniel Garrard (D) | 709 | 9.4 |
| 7 | William P. Thomasson (W) | 4,900 | 46.5 |
| | Lecompte (D) | 4,497 | 42.6 |
| | Sprigg (W) | 1,152 | 10.9 |
| 8 | Garrett Davis (W) | 5,788 | 54.1 |
| | C. A. Wickliffe (D) | 4,916 | 45.9 |
| 9 | Richard French (D) | 5,481 | 51.9 |
| | L. W. Andrews (W) | 5,073 | 48.1 |
| 10 | John W. Tibbatts (D) | 6,507 | 51.8 |
| | Wall (W) | 6,064 | 48.2 |

## MAINE

| | Candidates | Votes | % |
|---|---|---|---|
| 1 | Joshua Herrick (D) | 4,421 | 50.6 |
| | Jonathan Tucker | 1,142 | 13.1 |
| | Burleigh Smart | 1,114 | 12.7 |
| | Nathan Clifford | 1,063 | 12.2 |
| 2 | Robert P. Dunlap (D) | 4,837 | 55.3 |
| | Josiah S. Little | 2,790 | 31.9 |
| | Samuel Fessenden | 956 | 10.9 |
| 3 | Luther Severance (W) | 3,799 | 53.3 |
| | Samuel Wells (D) | 2,700 | 37.9 |
| | Seth May (LIB) | 621 | 8.7 |
| 4 | Freeman H. Morse (W) | 3,546 | 50.2 |
| | Charles Andrews (D) | 2,701 | 38.3 |
| 5 | Benjamin White (D) | 6,167 | 51.2 |
| | William G. Crosby (W) | 4,558 | 37.8 |
| | James Bowen | 699 | 5.8 |
| 6 | Hannibal Hamlin (D) | 4,638 | 54.5 |
| | Elisha Allen | 2,673 | 31.4 |
| | David Shepherd | 1,182 | 13.9 |
| 7 | Shepard Cary (D) | 5,309 | 52.9 |
| | Thomas Robinson (W) | 4,505 | 44.9 |

## MARYLAND

| | Candidates | Votes | % |
|---|---|---|---|
| 1 | John M. S. Causin (W) | 3,776 | 57.9 |
| | Bowie (D) | 2,741 | 42.1 |
| 2 | Francis Brengle (W) | 6,116 | 51.8 |
| | J. T. Mason (D) | 5,694 | 48.2 |
| 3 | John Wethered (W) | 4,448 | 52.2 |
| | S. Brady (D) | 4,074 | 47.8 |
| 4 | John P. Kennedy (W) | 5,894 | 52.7 |
| | J. Legrand (D) | 5,299 | 47.3 |
| 5 | Jacob A. Preston (W) | 4,229 | 50.1 |
| | A. Constable (D) | 4,211 | 49.9 |
| 6 | Thomas Spence (W) | 2,197 | 91.1 |

## MASSACHUSETTS

### Special Election

| | Candidates | Votes | % |
|---|---|---|---|
| 10 | Joseph Grinnell (W) | 4,943 | 53.2 |
| | Sampson Perkins | 3,927 | 42.3 |

## MICHIGAN

| | Candidates | Votes | % |
|---|---|---|---|
| 1 | Robert McClelland (D) | 7,862 | 55.3 |
| | Jacob M. Howard (W) | 5,495 | 38.7 |
| | Arthur S. Porter (LIB) | 829 | 5.8 |
| 2 | Lucius Lyon (D) | 7,171 | 52.6 |
| | Joseph R. Williams (W) | 5,202 | 38.2 |
| | Rufus B. Bement (LIB) | 1,246 | 9.1 |
| 3 | James B. Hunt (D) | 6,209 | 56.4 |
| | Thomas J. Drake (W) | 4,007 | 36.4 |
| | William Caufield (LIB) | 749 | 6.8 |

## MISSISSIPPI

| | Candidates | Votes | % |
|---|---|---|---|
| AL | Jacob Thompson (A-RPT D) | 19,861✔ | |
| | William H. Hammett (A-RPT D) | 18,813✔ | |
| | Robert W. Roberts (A-RPT D) | 18,518✔ | |
| | Tilghman M. Tucker (A-RPT D) | 15,923✔ | |
| | Howard (REDEM D) | 15,468 | |
| | Dunbar (REDEM D) | 15,185 | |
| | Gilmer (REDEM D) | 14,744 | |
| | Kendall (REDEM D) | 14,124 | |

## NEW HAMPSHIRE

| Candidates | Votes | % |
|---|---|---|
| Edmund Burke (D) | ✔ | |
| John R. Reding (D) | ✔ | |
| Moses Norris Jr (D) | ✔ | |
| John P. Hale (D) | ✔ | |

## NEW JERSEY

| | Candidates | Votes | % |
|---|---|---|---|
| 1 | Lucius Q. C. Elmer (D) | 5,668 | 51.3 |
| | Unidentified Candidate (W) | 5,374 | 48.7 |
| 2 | George Sykes (D) | 7,573 | 52.0 |
| | Unidentified Candidate (W) | 6,995 | 48.0 |
| 3 | Isaac G. Farlee (D) | | 100.0 |
| 4 | Littleton Kirkpatrick (D) | 6,207 | 51.1 |
| | Unidentified Candidate (W) | 5,949 | 48.9 |
| 5 | William Wright (IRR W) | 5,313 | 52.7 |
| | Unidentified Candidate (W) | 4,773 | 47.3 |

## NORTH CAROLINA

| | Candidates | Votes | % |
|---|---|---|---|
| 1 | Thomas L. Clingman (W) | 3,817 | 56.9 |
| | James Graham (W) | 2,888 | 43.1 |
| 2 | Daniel M. Barringer (W) | 4,136 | 52.2 |
| | Burton Craige (D) | 3,788 | 47.8 |
| 3 | David S. Reid (D) | 4,195 | 52.3 |
| | Anderson Mitchell (W) | 3,827 | 47.7 |
| 4 | Edmund Deberry (W) | 2,042 | 52.5 |
| | George C. Mendenhall (W) | 1,850 | 47.5 |
| 5 | Romulus M. Saunders (D) | 3,142 | 51.2 |
| | Henry W. Miller (W) | 3,001 | 48.9 |
| 6 | James I. McKay (D) | 1,737 | 79.0 |
| | Leach (W) | 462 | 21.0 |
| 7 | John R. J. Daniel (D) | 3,644 | 51.1 |
| | Henry K. Nash (W) | 3,486 | 48.9 |
| 8 | Archibald H. Arrington (D) | 4,803 | 53.0 |
| | Edward Stanly (W) | 4,264 | 47.0 |
| 9 | Kenneth Rayner (W) | 3,719 | 56.4 |
| | Moore (D) | 2,879 | 43.6 |

## OHIO

| | Candidates | Votes | % |
|---|---|---|---|
| 1 | Alexander Duncan (D) | 6,058 | 52.3 |
| | Haines (I) | 5,044 | 43.6 |
| 2 | John B. Weller (D) | 5,563 | 50.7 |
| | Campbell (W) | 5,308 | 48.4 |
| 3 | Robert C. Schenck (W) | 7,870 | 56.9 |
| | Lowe (D) | 5,571 | 40.2 |
| 4 | Joseph Vance (W) | 7,510 | 61.1 |
| | Hunt (D) | 4,552 | 37.0 |

## OHIO

| Candidates | Votes | % |
|---|---|---|
| 5 Emery D. Potter (D) | 4,894 | 55.9 |
| Tilden (W) | 3,856 | 44.1 |
| 6 Henry St. John (D) | 4,367 | 99.0 |
| 7 Joseph J. McDowell (D) | 5,376 | 49.9 |
| Thompson (W) | 5,052 | 46.9 |
| 8 John I. Vanmeter (W) | 5,344 | 50.5 |
| Lucas (D) | 5,142 | 48.6 |
| 9 Elias Florence (W) | 5,429 | 52.7 |
| Medill (D) | 4,864 | 47.3 |
| 10 Heman Allen Moore (D) | 7,194 | 49.6 |
| Ridgway (W) | 6,939 | 47.9 |
| 11 Jacob Brinckerhoff (D) | 5,814 | 56.3 |
| Irwin (I) | 2,520 | 24.4 |
| Waldan (W) | 1,996 | 19.3 |
| 12 Samuel F. Vinton (W) | 4,133 | 54.3 |
| Cleveland (D) | 3,269 | 42.9 |
| 13 Perley B. Johnson (W) | 4,658 | 51.0 |
| Barker (D) | 4,410 | 48.3 |
| 14 Alexander Harper (W) | 5,196 | 54.7 |
| Jennings (D) | 4,002 | 42.1 |
| 15 Joseph Morris (D) | 5,321 | 50.9 |
| Cowen (W) | 4,617 | 44.2 |
| 16 James Mathews (D) | 4,427 | 55.7 |
| Douglass (W) | 3,524 | 44.3 |
| 17 William C. McCauslin (D) | 6,741 | 51.6 |
| Hanna (W) | 5,883 | 45.1 |
| 18 Ezra Dean (D) | 3,668 | 68.5 |
| Wellhouse (W) | 1,588 | 29.7 |
| 19 Daniel R. Tilden (W) | 6,712 | 47.9 |
| Luman (D) | 6,310 | 45.1 |
| Hall (LIB) | 986 | 7.0 |
| 20 Joshua R. Giddings (W) | 6,140 | 57.4 |
| Ranney (D) | 3,757 | 35.1 |
| Wade (LIB) | 797 | 7.5 |
| 21 Henry R. Brinckerhoff (D) | 5,949 | 49.0 |
| Hamlin (W) | 5,533 | 45.6 |
| Parish (LIB) | 650 | 5.4 |

## PENNSYLVANIA

| Candidates | Votes | % |
|---|---|---|
| 1 Edward Joy Morris (W) | 2,855 | 45.3 |
| McCully (D) | 2,379 | 37.7 |
| Croust (D) | 1,072 | 17.0 |
| 2 Joseph R. Ingersoll (W) | 5,414 | 63.2 |
| Neal (D) | 3,153 | 36.8 |
| 3 John T. Smith (D) | 3,997 | 55.8 |
| Sargent (W) | 3,162 | 44.2 |
| 4 Charles J. Ingersoll (D) | 3,316 | 55.5 |
| Conrad (W) | 2,664 | 44.6 |
| 5 Jacob S. Yost (D) | 4,845 | 54.6 |
| Huddleson (W) | 4,022 | 45.4 |
| 6 Michael H. Jenks (W) | 5,750 | 53.0 |
| Davis (D) | 5,101 | 47.0 |
| 7 Abraham R. McIlvaine (W) | 4,391 | 51.7 |
| Allison (D) | 4,106 | 48.3 |
| 8 Jeremiah Brown (W) | 4,898 | 47.0 |
| Martin (D) | 3,940 | 37.8 |
| Roberts (A-MAS) | 1,582 | 15.2 |
| 9 John Ritter (D) | 3,941 | 69.3 |
| Hehn (W) | 1,747 | 30.7 |
| 10 Richard Brodhead (D) | 5,049 | 100.0 |

| Candidates | Votes | % |
|---|---|---|
| 11 Benjamin A. Bidlack (D) | 5,007 | 64.8 |
| Willits (W) | 2,716 | 35.2 |
| 12 Almon H. Read (D) | 4,243 | 56.5 |
| Jones (W) | 3,266 | 43.5 |
| 13 Henry Frick (W) | 5,430 | 51.2 |
| Snyder (D) | 5,181 | 48.8 |
| 14 Alexander Ramsey (W) | 5,893 | 52.5 |
| Umberger (D) | 5,326 | 47.5 |
| 15 Henry Nes (W) | 4,016 | 54.1 |
| Small (D) | 3,413 | 45.9 |
| 16 James Black (D) | 5,617 | 52.0 |
| Miller (W) | 5,189 | 48.0 |
| 17 James Irvin (W) | 5,725 | 56.6 |
| McCulloh (D) | 4,389 | 43.4 |
| 18 Andrew Stewart (W) | 5,141 | 50.7 |
| Clevenger (D) | 5,004 | 49.3 |
| 19 Henry D. Foster (D) | 6,432 | 100.0 |
| 20 John Dickey (W) | 4,962 | 47.1 |
| Leet (D) | 4,903 | 46.5 |
| Lemoyne (LIB) | 681 | 6.5 |
| 21 William Wilkins (D) | 4,438 | 49.7 |
| Craig (W&A-MASC) | 2,237 | 25.0 |
| Breckenridge (W) | 1,884 | 21.1 |
| 22 Samuel Hays (D) | 5,044 | 85.0 |
| Doughty (A-MASC) | 892 | 15.0 |
| 23 Charles M. Reed (W) | 5,073 | 50.2 |
| Irvine (D) | 5,033 | 49.8 |
| 24 Joseph Buffington (W) | 5,079 | 55.4 |
| Lorain (D) | 4,082 | 44.6 |

## RHODE ISLAND

| Candidates | Votes | % |
|---|---|---|
| 1 Henry Y. Cranston (L & O W) | 4,078 | 61.3 |
| John H. Weeden (D) | 2,557 | 38.4 |
| 2 Elisha R. Potter (L & O W) | 2,917 | 61.2 |
| Wilmarth N. Aldrich (D) | 1,846 | 38.7 |

## SOUTH CAROLINA

| Candidates | Votes | % |
|---|---|---|
| 1 James A. Black (CALH D) | ✔ | |
| William K. Clowney (SR D) | | |
| 2 Richard F. Simpson (D) | ✔ | |
| William Butler (W) | | |
| Downs (D) | | |
| 3 Joseph A. Woodward (D) | ✔ | |
| Thomas D. Sumter (D) | | |
| 4 John Campbell (SR D) | ✔ | |
| 5 Armistead Burt (D) | 2,198 | 44.1 |
| Patrick C. Caldwell (SSR D) | 1,564 | 31.4 |
| Brooks | 1,225 | 24.6 |
| 6 Isaac E. Holmes (D) | ✔ | |
| James S. Rhett | | |
| 7 R. Barnwell Rhett (D) | 1,883 | 58.0 |
| S. Trotti | 1,363 | 42.0 |

## TENNESSEE

| Candidates | Votes | % |
|---|---|---|
| 1 Andrew Johnson (D) | 5,495 | 52.9 |
| Aikin (W) | 4,892 | 47.1 |
| 2 William T. Senter (W) | 6,310 | 59.6 |
| Wallace (D) | 4,280 | 40.4 |

| Candidates | Votes | % |
|---|---|---|
| 3 Julius W. Blackwell (D) | 5,793 | 50.4 |
| Campbell (W) | 5,700 | 49.6 |
| 4 Alvan Cullom (D) | 5,180 | 58.7 |
| Bransford (W) | 3,650 | 41.3 |
| 5 George M. Jones (D) | 5,111 | 63.5 |
| Long (W) | 2,943 | 36.5 |
| 6 Aaron V. Brown (D) | 5,259 | 52.3 |
| N. S. Brown (W) | 4,798 | 47.7 |
| 7 David W. Dickerson (W) | 6,137 | 100.0 |
| 8 Joseph H. Peyton (W) | 4,853 | 55.6 |
| Donnelson (D) | 3,874 | 44.4 |
| 9 Cave Johnson (D) | 4,904 | 51.2 |
| Henry (W) | 4,676 | 48.8 |
| 10 John B. Ashe (W) | 5,457 | 50.9 |
| Staunton (D) | 5,264 | 49.1 |
| 11 Milton Brown (W) | 5,852 | 61.1 |
| Pavatt (D) | 3,723 | 38.9 |

## VERMONT

| Candidates | Votes | % |
|---|---|---|
| 1 Solomon Foot (W) | 6,698 | 54.9 |
| C. B. Harrington (D) | 4,926 | 40.4 |
| 2 Jacob Collamer (W) | 5,825 | 48.9 |
| Truman B. Ransom (D) | 4,833 | 40.5 |
| Titus Hutchinson (LIB) | 1,003 | 8.4 |
| 3 George Perkins Marsh (W) | 6,254 | 53.5 |
| John Smith (D) | 4,595 | 39.3 |
| W. H. French (LIB) | 718 | 6.1 |
| 4 Paul Dillingham Jr (D) | 6,317 | 50.8 |
| George B. Chandler (W) | 4,957 | 39.8 |
| G. Putnam (LIB) | 797 | 6.4 |

## VIRGINIA

| Candidates | Votes | % |
|---|---|---|
| 1 Archibald Atkinson (D) | 1,789 | 50.2 |
| Langhorne (W) | 1,778 | 49.9 |
| 2 George C. Dromgoole (D) | 762 | 80.6 |
| 3 Walter Coles (D) | 2,017 | 51.4 |
| Gilmer (W) | 1,911 | 48.7 |
| 4 Edmund W. Hubard (D) | 2,164 | 51.5 |
| Toler (W) | 2,037 | 48.5 |
| 5 Thomas W. Gilmer (D) | 2,361 | 50.2 |
| Goggin (W) | 2,341 | 49.8 |
| 6 John W. Jones (D) | 2,368 | 50.4 |
| Botts (W) | 2,335 | 49.7 |
| 7 Henry A. Wise (D) | 1,470 | 57.1 |
| Carter (W) | 1,105 | 42.9 |
| 8 Willoughby Newton (W) | 1,008 | 55.2 |
| Hunter (D) | 818 | 44.8 |
| 9 Samuel Chilton (W) | 1,532 | 57.1 |
| Smith (D) | 1,149 | 42.9 |
| 10 William Lucas (D) | 2,698 | 56.2 |
| Faulkner (W) | 2,104 | 43.8 |
| 11 William Taylor (D) | 1,979 | 83.5 |
| Stuart (W) | 392 | 16.5 |
| 12 Augustus A. Chapman (D) | 2,552 | 64.5 |
| Watts (W) | 1,402 | 35.5 |
| 13 George W. Hopkins (D) | 761 | 57.7 |
| Fulton (W) | 558 | 42.3 |
| 14 George W. Summers (W) | 3,271 | 52.7 |
| Hays (D) | 2,942 | 47.4 |
| 15 Lewis Steenrod (D) | | 100.0 |

# 1844 House Elections

## ALABAMA

### Special Election

| Candidates | Votes | % |
|---|---|---|
| 3 William L. Yancey (D) | 2,197 | 50.7 |
| Daniel Watrous (W) | 2,137 | 49.3 |

## ARKANSAS

| | Votes | % |
|---|---|---|
| AL Archibald Yell (D) | 11,112 | 59.1 |
| Walker (W) | 7,576 | 40.3 |

## DELAWARE

| | Votes | % |
|---|---|---|
| AL John W. Houston (W) | 6,221 | 50.7 |
| Biddle (D) | 6,043 | 49.3 |

## GEORGIA

| | Votes | % |
|---|---|---|
| 1 Thomas Butler King (W) | 3,702 | 55.9 |
| Spalding (D) | 2,918 | 44.1 |
| 2 Seaborn Jones (D) | 6,460 | 51.1 |
| Crawford (W) | 6,182 | 48.9 |
| 3 Washington Poe (W) | 4,881* | 50.7 |
| Chappell (D) | 4,741 | 49.3 |
| 4 Hugh A. Haralson (D) | 5,771 | 52.5 |
| Floyd (W) | 5,214 | 47.5 |
| 5 John H. Lumpkin (D) | 7,720 | 61.2 |
| Miller (W) | 4,889 | 38.8 |
| 6 Howell Cobb (D) | 6,306 | 59.0 |
| Underwood (W) | 4,379 | 41.0 |
| 7 Alexander H. Stephens (W) | 4,199 | 57.1 |
| Janes (D) | 3,152 | 42.9 |
| 8 Robert Toombs (W) | 4,665 | 58.5 |
| Black (D) | 3,309 | 41.5 |

### Special Election

| | Votes | % |
|---|---|---|
| AL Duncan L. Clinch (W) | 33,506 | 53.4 |
| Sanford (D) | 29,206 | 46.6 |

## ILLINOIS

| | Votes | % |
|---|---|---|
| 1 Robert Smith (D) | 7,966 | 64.7 |
| John Reynolds (OPP D) | 4,146 | 33.7 |
| 2 John A. McClernand (D) | 7,968 | 99.0 |
| 3 Orlando B. Ficklin (D) | 7,786 | 57.6 |
| Usher F. Linder (W) | 5,311 | 39.3 |
| 4 John Wentworth (D) | 9,516 | 54.9 |
| Buckner S. Morris (W) | 5,910 | 34.1 |
| John H. Henderson (LIB) | 1,875 | 10.8 |
| 5 Stephen A. Douglas (D) | 9,799 | 53.9 |
| David M. Woodson (W) | 8,043 | 44.2 |
| 6 Joseph P. Hoge (D) | 8,752 | 52.0 |
| Martin P. Sweet (W) | 7,563 | 45.0 |
| 7 Edwin D. Baker (W) | 6,658 | 52.4 |
| John Calhoun (D) | 5,948 | 46.9 |

## LOUISIANA

| | | |
|---|---|---|
| 1 John Slidell (SR D) | ✔ | |
| 2 Bannon G. Thibodeaux (W) | ✔ | |
| 3 John H. Harmanson (D) | ✔ | |
| 4 Isaac E. Morse (D) | ✔ | |

## MAINE [1]

| | Votes | % |
|---|---|---|
| 1 William A. Hayes | 5,321* | 46.5 |
| George Scamman | 3,377 | 29.5 |
| Joshua Herrick | 2,061 | 18.0 |
| 2 Robert P. Dunlap (D) | ✔ | |
| 3 Luther Severance (W) | ✔ | |
| 4 John D. McCrate (D) | 7,464 | 52.8 |
| F. H. Morse | 5,948 | 42.1 |

---

| Candidates | Votes | % |
|---|---|---|
| 5 Cullen Sawtelle (D) | 6,377 | 53.2 |
| William G. Crosby | 4,625 | 38.6 |
| Drummond Farnsworth | 678 | 5.7 |
| 6 Hannibal Hamlin (D) | ✔ | |
| 7 Hezekiah Williams (D) | ✔ | |

## MASSACHUSETTS

| | Votes | % |
|---|---|---|
| 1 Robert C. Winthrop (W) | 8,455 | 62.7 |
| Benjamin F. Hallett | 4,461 | 33.1 |
| 2 Daniel P. King (W) | 4,986 | 57.6 |
| George Herod (D) | 2,770 | 32.0 |
| Henry B. Hanton | 886 | 10.2 |
| 3 Amos Abbott (W) | 6,315 | 52.1 |
| George S. Boutwell (D) | 4,770 | 39.4 |
| Abner L. Bailey | 1,001 | 8.3 |
| 4 Benjamin Thompson (W) | 5,269 | 51.7 |
| William Parmenter (D) | 4,405 | 43.2 |
| Thomas W. Ward | 516 | 5.1 |
| 5 Charles Hudson (W) | 5,463 | 55.8 |
| Isaac Davis (D) | 3,518 | 36.0 |
| Rudolphius B. Hubbard | 795 | 8.1 |
| 6 George Ashmun (W) | 7,467 | 51.7 |
| Chester W. Chapin (D) | 5,850 | 40.5 |
| Lucius Boltwood (LIB) | 1,014 | 7.0 |
| 7 Julius Rockwell (W) | 6,769 | 51.5 |
| Increase Sumner | 5,235 | 39.8 |
| Joel Hayden | 970 | 7.4 |
| 8 John Quincy Adams (W) | 8,089 | 56.6 |
| Isaac H. Wright | 5,340 | 37.4 |
| Appleton Howe | 733 | 5.1 |
| 9 Artemas Hale (W) | 4,881 | 50.5 |
| Foster Hooper | 3,599 | 37.2 |
| Laban M. Wheaton | 998 | 10.3 |
| 10 Joseph Grinnell (W) | 5,924 | 58.5 |
| Edward W. Greene | 3,772 | 37.3 |

## MICHIGAN

| | Votes | % |
|---|---|---|
| 1 Robert McClelland (D) | 10,132 | 51.2 |
| Edwin Lawrence (W) | 8,677 | 43.9 |
| 2 John J. Chipman (D) | 9,435 | 47.7 |
| Henry W. Taylor (W) | 8,967 | 45.4 |
| Edwin A. Atlee (LIB) | 1,240 | 6.3 |
| 3 James B. Hunt (D) | 8,331 | 51.3 |
| George W. Wisner (W) | 6,967 | 42.9 |
| William Caufield (LIB) | 934 | 5.8 |

## MISSOURI

| | Votes | % |
|---|---|---|
| AL John S. Phelps (D) | 36,023 ✔ | |
| James B. Bowlin (D) | 35,510 ✔ | |
| Sterling Price (D) | 35,128 ✔ | |
| James H. Relfe (D) | 35,007 ✔ | |
| Leonard H. Sims (W) | 29,225 ✔ | |
| Thomas B. Hudson (W) | 28,309 | |
| J. Thornton (W) | 27,685 | |
| Ratliff Boone (W) | 27,263 | |
| A. Jones (W) | 27,226 | |
| D. C. M. Parsons (D) | 19,123 | |

## NEW JERSEY

| | Votes | % |
|---|---|---|
| 1 James G. Hampton (W) | 7,440 | 54.7 |
| Elmer (D) | 6,153 | 45.3 |
| 2 Samuel G. Wright (W) | 6,910 | 51.5 |
| Sykes (D) | 6,503 | 48.5 |
| 3 John Runk (W) | 8,942 | 50.0 |
| Isaac G. Farlee (D) | 8,926 | 50.0 |
| 4 Joseph E. Edsall (D) | 8,779 | 60.0 |
| Robtsn (W) | 5,848 | 40.0 |
| 5 William Wright (W) | 9,996 | 100.0 |

## NEW YORK

| Candidates | Votes | % |
|---|---|---|
| 1 John W. Lawrence (D) | 6,132 | 55.4 |
| Cogswell (W) | 4,935 | 44.6 |
| 2 Henry I. Seaman (NAM) | 6,164 | 51.8 |
| Murphy (D) | 5,686 | 47.7 |
| 3 William S. Miller (NAM) | 6,613 | 54.7 |
| Nicoll (D) | 5,388 | 44.6 |
| 4 William B. Maclay (D) | 6,783 | 51.0 |
| Lawrence (NAM) | 6,428 | 48.4 |
| 5 Thomas M. Woodruff (NAM) | 6,214 | 49.7 |
| Leonard (D) | 6,009 | 48.1 |
| 6 William W. Campbell (NAM) | 7,856 | 48.8 |
| Moore (D) | 7,750 | 48.2 |
| 7 Joseph H. Anderson (D) | 6,098 | 55.8 |
| Barretto (W) | 4,807 | 44.0 |
| 8 William W. Woodworth (D) | 7,340 | 52.1 |
| Rankin (W) | 6,710 | 47.6 |
| 9 Archibald C. Niven (D) | 7,162 | 52.3 |
| Hasbrouck (W) | 6,474 | 47.3 |
| 10 Samuel Gordon (D) | 8,645 | 51.1 |
| Gould (W) | 8,121 | 48.0 |
| 11 John F. Collin (D) | 8,226 | 53.1 |
| Sanford (W) | 7,254 | 46.9 |
| 12 Richard P. Herrick (W) | 6,242 | 51.6 |
| Seymour (D) | 5,692 | 47.0 |
| 13 Bradford R. Wood (D) | 7,058 | 50.0 |
| Wheaton (W) | 6,967 | 49.3 |
| 14 Erastus D. Culver (W) | 7,512 | 56.6 |
| Bishop (D) | 5,297 | 39.9 |
| 15 Joseph Russell (D) | 5,441 | 50.4 |
| Moore (W) | 4,750 | 44.0 |
| Boardn (LIB) | 606 | 5.6 |
| 16 Hugh White (W) | 8,423 | 50.1 |
| Ellis (D) | 8,124 | 48.4 |
| 17 Charles S. Benton (D) | 7,691 | 54.7 |
| Alexander (W) | 5,706 | 40.6 |
| 18 Preston King (D) | 8,145 | 54.1 |
| Hopkins (W) | 6,295 | 41.8 |
| 19 Orville Hungerford (D) | 6,304 | 50.0 |
| Bradley (W) | 5,587 | 44.3 |
| Porter (LIB) | 717 | 5.7 |
| 20 Timothy Jenkins (D) | 7,617 | 48.2 |
| White (W) | 7,094 | 44.9 |
| Allen (LIB) | 1,086 | 6.9 |
| 21 Charles Goodyear (D) | 9,298 | 52.3 |
| Danforth (W) | 7,966 | 44.8 |
| 22 Stephen Strong (D) | 9,608 | 50.9 |
| Sweet (W) | 8,818 | 46.7 |
| 23 William J. Hough (D) | 8,128 | 45.6 |
| Ledyd (W) | 7,426 | 41.7 |
| Brown (LIB) | 2,268 | 12.7 |
| 24 Horace Wheaton (D) | 6,961 | 49.2 |
| Noxon (W) | 6,495 | 45.9 |
| 25 George Rathbun (D) | 7,511 | 48.3 |
| Richardson (W) | 7,130 | 45.8 |
| Stayles (LIB) | 921 | 5.9 |
| 26 Samuel S. Ellsworth (D) | 8,763 | 51.5 |
| Judd (W) | 7,662 | 45.0 |
| 27 John De Mott (D) | 6,581 | 48.4 |
| Holley (W) | 6,387 | 47.0 |
| 28 Elias B. Holmes (W) | 6,807 | 52.7 |
| Selden (D) | 5,722 | 44.3 |
| 29 Charles H. Carroll (W) | 8,310 | 53.9 |
| Wadsworth (D) | 6,465 | 42.0 |
| 30 Martin Grover (D) | 9,115 | 50.6 |
| Cady (W) | 8,893 | 49.4 |
| 31 Abner Lewis (W) | 8,299 | 59.9 |
| Campbell (D) | 3,446 | 24.9 |
| Allen (LIB) | 2,114 | 15.3 |
| 32 William A. Moseley (W) | 6,910 | 55.7 |
| Stevens (D) | 5,081 | 41.0 |
| 33 Albert Smith (W) | 6,366 | 56.3 |
| Chand (D) | 4,215 | 37.2 |
| McKay (LIB) | 736 | 6.5 |
| 34 Washington Hunt (W) | 5,733 | 51.0 |
| Piper (D) | 4,948 | 44.1 |

*Footnote, see p. 979.*

## OHIO

| | Candidates | Votes | % |
|---|---|---|---|
| 1 | James J. Faran (D) | 8,760 | 54.2 |
| | George P. Torrence (W) | 7,071 | 43.8 |
| 2 | Francis A. Cunningham (D) | 6,381 | 51.6 |
| | Lewis D. Campbell (W) | 5,881 | 47.5 |
| 3 | Robert C. Schenck (W) | 9,850 | 55.3 |
| | Edward A. King (D) | 7,428 | 41.7 |
| 4 | Joseph Vance (W) | 10,470 | 60.9 |
| | John H. Young (D) | 6,413 | 37.3 |
| 5 | William Sawyer (D) | 5,916 | 54.6 |
| | J. W. Riley (W) | 4,901 | 45.2 |
| 6 | Henry St. John (D) | 6,975 | 56.8 |
| | Abel Rawson (W) | 5,278 | 43.0 |
| 7 | Joseph J. McDowell (D) | 7,004 | 52.3 |
| | James H. Thompson (W) | 6,044 | 45.2 |
| 8 | Allen G. Thurman (D) | 7,039 | 50.6 |
| | John J. Vanmetre (W) | 6,707 | 48.2 |
| 9 | Augustus L. Perrill (D) | 6,475 | 52.5 |
| | Elias Florence (W) | 5,797 | 47.0 |
| 10 | Columbus Delano (W) | 9,297 | 49.3 |
| | Caleb J. McNulty (D) | 9,285 | 49.3 |
| 11 | Jacob Brinkerhoff (D) | 8,466 | 51.9 |
| | William McLaughlin (W) | 7,501 | 46.0 |
| 12 | Samuel F. Vinton (W) | 6,750 | 58.4 |
| | Elisha Morgan (D) | 3,753 | 32.5 |
| | Francis Cleveland (ID) | 738 | 6.4 |
| 13 | Isaac Parrish (D) | 5,825 | 50.3 |
| | Perley B. Johnson (W) | 5,620 | 48.5 |
| 14 | Alexander Harper (W) | 6,951 | 53.0 |
| | George W. Manypenny (D) | 5,814 | 44.3 |
| 15 | Joseph Morris (D) | 6,807 | 50.3 |
| | Joseph A. Ramage (W) | 6,207 | 45.9 |
| 16 | John D. Cummins (D) | 6,568 | 54.6 |
| | Christian Deardorff (W) | 5,465 | 45.4 |
| 17 | George Fries (D) | 7,699 | 50.0 |
| | Samuel Stokely (W) | 7,236 | 47.0 |
| 18 | David A. Starkweather (D) | 6,981 | 55.4 |
| | John Augustine (W) | 5,449 | 43.3 |
| 19 | Daniel R. Tilden (W) | 8,744 | 48.8 |
| | William Coolman (D) | 7,934 | 44.3 |

| | Candidates | Votes | % |
|---|---|---|---|
| | Lyman W. Hall (LIB) | 1,229 | 6.9 |
| 20 | Joshua R. Giddings (F SOIL W) | 10,048 | 60.3 |
| | Samuel Starkweather (D) | 5,287 | 31.7 |
| | Edward Wade (LIB) | 1,312 | 7.9 |
| 21 | Joseph M. Root (W) | 7,641 | 48.6 |
| | Richard Warner (D) | 7,140 | 45.4 |
| | Joel Tiffany (LIB) | 954 | 6.1 |

**Special Election**

| | Candidates | Votes | % |
|---|---|---|---|
| 10 | Alfred Parish Stone (D) | ✓ | # |
| | James R. Stanberry (W) | | |

## PENNSYLVANIA

| | Candidates | Votes |
|---|---|---|
| 1 | Lewis C. Levin (AM) | ✓ |
| 2 | Joseph R. Ingersoll (W) | ✓ |
| 3 | John H. Campbell (AM) | ✓ |
| 4 | Charles J. Ingersoll (D) | ✓ |
| 5 | Jacob S. Yost (D) | ✓ |
| 6 | Jacob Erdman (D) | ✓ |
| 7 | Abraham R. McIlvaine (W) | ✓ |
| 8 | John Strohm (W) | ✓ |
| 9 | John Ritter (D) | ✓ |
| 10 | Richard Brodhead Jr (D) | ✓ |
| 11 | Owen D. Leib (D) | ✓ |
| 12 | David Wilmot (D) | ✓ |
| 13 | James Pollock (W) | ✓ |
| 14 | Alexander Ramsey (W) | ✓ |
| 15 | Moses McLean (D) | ✓ |
| 16 | James Black (D) | ✓ |
| 17 | John Blanchard (W) | ✓ |
| 18 | Andrew Stewart (W) | ✓ |
| 19 | Henry D. Foster (D) | ✓ |
| 20 | John H. Ewing (W) | ✓ |
| 21 | Cornelius Darragh (W) | ✓ |
| 22 | William S. Garvin (D) | ✓ |
| 23 | James Thompson (D) | ✓ |
| 24 | Joseph Buffington (W) | ✓ |

| | Candidates | Votes | % |
|---|---|---|---|
| | **Special Elections** | | |
| 12 | George Fuller (D) | ✓ | |
| 13 | James Pollock (W) | ✓ | |
| 21 | Cornelius Darragh (W) | ✓ | |

## SOUTH CAROLINA

| | Candidates | Votes | % |
|---|---|---|---|
| 1 | James A. Black (CALH D) | | 100.0 |
| 2 | Richard F. Simpson (D) | 5,162 | 64.0 |
| | William Butler (W) | 2,902 | 36.0 |
| 3 | Joseph A. Woodward (D) | | 100.0 |
| 4 | Alexander D. Sims (D) | 2,706 | 52.5 |
| | John McQueen (D) | 2,448 | 47.5 |
| 5 | Armistead Burt (D) | | 100.0 |
| 6 | Isaac E. Holmes (D) | | 100.0 |
| 7 | R. Barnwell Rhett (D) | ✓ | |

## VERMONT

| | Candidates | Votes | % |
|---|---|---|---|
| 1 | Solomon Foot (W) | 7,696 | 56.7 |
| | Charles K. Field (D) | 4,681 | 34.5 |
| | Oscar L. Shafter (LIB) | 1,119 | 8.2 |
| 2 | Jacob Collamer (W) | 7,108 | 55.4 |
| | Levi B. Vilas (D) | 4,527 | 35.3 |
| | Titus Hutchinson (LIB) | 1,189 | 9.3 |
| 3 | George P. Marsh (W) | 6,331 | 56.9 |
| | John Smith (D) | 3,423 | 30.8 |
| | William H. French (LIB) | 1,357 | 12.2 |
| 4 | Paul Dillingham Jr. (D) | 6,551 | 47.9 |
| | George B. Chandler (W) | 5,696 | 41.7 |
| | George Putnam (LIB) | 1,369 | 10.0 |

## VIRGINIA

**Special Elections**

| | Candidates | Votes |
|---|---|---|
| 5 | William L. Goggin (W) | ✓ |
| 7 | Thomas H. Bayly (D) | ✓ |
| | Carter (W) | |

1. In Maine's 1st district, no candidate received the necessary majority. In a special election for which returns are unavailable, John F. Scamman (D) was chosen to fill the vacancy.

# 1845 House Elections

## ALABAMA

| | Candidates | Votes | % |
|---|---|---|---|
| 1 | Edmund S. Dargan (D) | 4,962 | 51.6 |
| | Dunn (W) | 4,649 | 48.4 |
| 2 | Henry W. Hilliard (W) | 5,386 | 50.6 |
| | Cochran (D) | 5,258 | 49.4 |
| 3 | William L. Yancey (D) | 4,987 | 100.0 |
| 4 | William W. Payne (D) | 4,935 | 63.7 |
| | Erwin (D) | 2,818 | 36.4 |
| 5 | George S. Houston (D) | 4,035 | 81.4 |
| | Nool (D) | 922 | 18.6 |
| 6 | Reuben Chapman (D) | | 100.0 |
| 7 | Felix G. McConnell (D) | 3,305 | 56.9 |
| | Rice (D) | 2,504 | 43.1 |

## CONNECTICUT

| | Candidates | Votes | % |
|---|---|---|---|
| 1 | James Dixon (W) | 7,612 | 50.9 |
| | Seymour (D) | 6,941 | 46.5 |
| 2 | Samuel Hubbard (W) | 7,266 | 54.2 |
| | Stewart (D) | 5,814 | 43.4 |
| 3 | John Rockwell (W) | 5,734 | 48.1 |
| | Catlin (D) | 5,391 | 45.3 |
| | Wilson (LIB) | 784 | 6.6 |
| 4 | Truman Smith (W) | 8,957 | 51.7 |
| | J. C. Smith (D) | 7,856 | 45.3 |

## FLORIDA

*(Became a state Mar. 3, 1845)*

| | Candidates | Votes | % |
|---|---|---|---|
| AL | Edward C. Cabell (W) | 2,523‡ | 50.5 |
| | William H. Brockenbrough (D) | 2,472 | 49.5 |

## INDIANA

| | Candidates | Votes | % |
|---|---|---|---|
| 1 | Robert Dale Owen (D) | 7,336 | 53.7 |
| | George P. R. Wilson (W) | 6,331 | 46.3 |
| 2 | Thomas J. Henley (D) | 7,219 | 53.1 |
| | Roger Martin (W) | 6,376 | 46.9 |
| 3 | Thomas Smith (D) | 7,246 | 51.1 |
| | Joseph C. Eggleston (W) | 6,706 | 47.3 |
| 4 | Caleb B. Smith (W) | 4,863 | 56.4 |
| | John Finley (D) | 3,201 | 37.2 |
| | Matthew R. Hull (LIB) | 553 | 6.4 |
| 5 | William W. Wick (D) | 7,459 | 54.8 |
| | James P. Foley (W) | 5,883 | 43.2 |
| 6 | John W. Davis (D) | 8,183 | 60.9 |
| | Eli P. Farmer (W) | 5,253 | 39.1 |
| 7 | Edward W. McGaughey (W) | 6,192 | 50.7 |
| | Joseph A. Wright (D) | 6,023 | 49.3 |
| 8 | John Pettit (D) | 6,260 | 51.6 |
| | Albert L. Holmes (W) | 5,771 | 47.6 |
| 9 | Charles W. Cathcart (D) | 6,231 | 50.0 |
| | Samuel C. Sample (W) | 5,959 | 47.8 |
| 10 | Andrew Kennedy (D) | 5,837 | 50.0 |
| | Lewis G. Thompson (W) | 5,482 | 47.0 |

## KENTUCKY

| | Candidates | Votes | % |
|---|---|---|---|
| 1 | Linn Boyd (D) | 6,377 | 97.1 |
| 2 | John H. McHenry (W) | 6,070 | 53.0 |
| | Thomas McCreery (D) | 5,385 | 47.0 |
| 3 | Henry Grider (W) | 5,511 | 56.0 |
| | S. A. Atchison (D) | 4,338 | 44.1 |
| 4 | Joshua F. Bell (W) | 6,044 | 50.3 |
| | G. A. Caldwell (D) | 5,965 | 49.7 |
| 5 | Bryan R. Young (W) | 6,126 | 51.1 |
| | James W. Stone (D) | 5,869 | 48.9 |

| | Candidates | Votes | % |
|---|---|---|---|
| 6 | John P. Martin (D) | 4,074 | 37.1 |
| | G. Adams (W) | 3,658 | 33.3 |
| | G. R. McKee (W) | 3,240 | 29.5 |
| 7 | William P. Thomasson (W) | 6,023 | 52.2 |
| | Elijah Nuttall (D) | 5,510 | 47.8 |
| 8 | Garret Davis (W) | 5,819 | 53.3 |
| | T. F. Marshall (D) | 5,109 | 46.8 |
| 9 | Andrew Trumbo (W) | 5,741 | 51.6 |
| | Richard French (D) | 5,381 | 48.4 |
| 10 | John W. Tibbatts (D) | 7,107 | 50.8 |
| | John P. Gaines (W) | 6,875 | 49.2 |

## MARYLAND

| | Candidates | Votes | % |
|---|---|---|---|
| 1 | John G. Chapman (W) | 4,238 | 52.2 |
| | Key (D) | 3,884 | 47.8 |
| 2 | Thomas J. Perry (D) | 6,789 | 52.7 |
| | Snively (W) | 6,095 | 47.3 |
| 3 | Thomas W. Ligon (D) | 5,924 | 54.1 |
| | Wethered (W) | 5,030 | 45.9 |
| 4 | William F. Giles (D) | 5,824 | 48.8 |
| | Kennedy (W) | 4,962 | 41.6 |
| | Duncan (AM) | 1,147 | 9.6 |
| 5 | Albert Constable (D) | 4,631 | 51.0 |
| | Wright (W) | 4,444 | 49.0 |
| 6 | Edward H. C. Long (W) | 3,735 | 51.1 |
| | Martin (D) | 3,577 | 48.9 |

## MISSISSIPPI

| | Candidates | Votes | % |
|---|---|---|---|
| AL | Jacob Thompson (D) | 27,423✔ | |
| | Jefferson Davis (D) | 27,193✔ | |
| | Stephen Adams (D) | 26,836✔ | |
| | Robert W. Roberts (D) | 26,059✔ | |
| | Tompkins (W) | 18,194 | |
| | Starke (W) | 17,452 | |
| | Brooke (W) | 17,094 | |

## NEW HAMPSHIRE [1]

| | Candidates | Votes | % |
|---|---|---|---|
| AL | Mace Moulton (D) | 24,068✔ | |
| | James H. Johnson (D) | 24,011✔ | |
| | Moses Norris Jr (D) | 23,765✔ | |
| | Woodbury (D) | 21,913 | |
| | Edwards (FEDL) | 14,692 | |
| | Nesmith (FEDL) | 14,690 | |
| | Goodwin (FEDL) | 14,562 | |
| | Sawyer (FEDL) | 13,833 | |
| | Hale | 7,053 | |
| | Porter (AB) | 5,272 | |
| | Moore (AB) | 4,968 | |
| | Perkins (AB) | 4,554 | |
| | Cilley (AB) | 4,503 | |

## NORTH CAROLINA

| | Candidates | Votes | % |
|---|---|---|---|
| 1 | James Graham (W) | 5,245 | 51.6 |
| | Thomas L. Clingman (W) | 4,918 | 48.4 |
| 2 | Daniel M. Barringer (W) | 5,368 | 50.1 |
| | Charles Fisher (D) | 5,342 | 49.9 |
| 3 | David S. Reid (D) | 5,133 | 54.0 |
| | Alexander B. McMillan (W) | 4,369 | 46.0 |
| 4 | Alfred Dockery (W) | 4,078 | 56.5 |
| | Jonathan Worth (W) | 3,135 | 43.5 |
| 5 | James C. Dobbin (D) | 5,242 | 61.8 |
| | John H. Haughton (W) | 3,236 | 38.2 |

| | Candidates | Votes | % |
|---|---|---|---|
| 6 | James I. McKay (D) | 5,169 | 66.3 |
| | Thomas D. Meares (W) | 2,633 | 33.8 |
| 7 | John R. J. Daniel (D) | 4,872 | 64.1 |
| | Robert C. Bond (W) | 2,729 | 35.9 |
| 8 | Henry S. Clarke (D) | 4,654 | 53.7 |
| | Richard S. Donnell (W) | 4,009 | 46.3 |
| 9 | Asa Biggs (D) | 3,695 | 51.0 |
| | David Outlaw (W) | 3,549 | 49.0 |

## RHODE ISLAND

| | Candidates | Votes | % |
|---|---|---|---|
| 1 | Henry Cranston (W) | 4,900 | 98.8 |
| 2 | Lemuel H. Arnold (LIBER W) | 3,202 | 51.1 |
| | Elisha R. Potter (L & O W) | 2,995 | 47.8 |

## TENNESSEE

| | Candidates | Votes | % |
|---|---|---|---|
| 1 | Andrew Johnson (D) | 6,068 | 56.3 |
| | William B. Brownlow (W) | 4,715 | 43.7 |
| 2 | William M. Cocke (W) | 4,884 | 45.0 |
| | George S. Gilbert (D) | 3,864 | 35.6 |
| | Lewis Reneau (IW) | 2,098 | 19.3 |
| 3 | John H. Crozier (W) | 6,179 | 51.4 |
| | Julius W. Blackwell (D) | 5,841 | 48.6 |
| 4 | Alvin Cullom (D) | 6,266 | 93.1 |
| | Isaac Clendenon | 467 | 6.9 |
| 5 | George W. Jones (D) | 6,528 | 100.0 |
| 6 | Barclay Martin (D) | 4,476 | 59.8 |
| | William D. Kindrick (W) | 3,009 | 40.2 |
| 7 | Meredith T. Gentry (W) | 5,849 | 67.9 |
| | Charles L. Nelson (D) | 2,760 | 32.1 |
| 8 | Edwin Hickman Ewing (W) | ✔ | # |
| | Joseph H. Peyton (W) | 5,204 | 55.3 |
| | William Trousdale (D) | 4,202 | 44.7 |
| 9 | Lucien B. Chase (D) | 4,281 | 57.6 |
| | John J. Mathewson (W) | 3,156 | 42.4 |
| 10 | Frederick P. Stanton (D) | 5,901 | 52.8 |
| | Phineas T. Scruggs (W) | 5,283 | 47.2 |
| 11 | Milton Brown (W) | 5,166 | 59.9 |
| | Nelson Hess (D) | 3,454 | 40.1 |

## VIRGINIA

| | Candidates | Votes | % |
|---|---|---|---|
| 1 | Archibald Atkinson (D) | | ✔ |
| | Whitfield | | |
| 2 | George C. Dromgoole (D) | | ✔ |
| 3 | William M. Tredway (D) | | ✔ |
| 4 | Edmund W. Hubard (D) | | ✔ |
| 5 | Shelton F. Leake (D) | | ✔ |
| | Irving | | |
| 6 | James A. Seddon (D) | | ✔ |
| | John M. Botts (W) | | |
| 7 | Thomas H. Bayly (D) | | ✔ |
| | Southall | | |
| 8 | Robert M. T. Hunter (D) | | ✔ |
| | Willoughby Newton (W) | | |
| 9 | John S. Pendleton (W) | | ✔ |
| | McCarty | | |
| 10 | Henry Bedinger (D) | | ✔ |
| | Lucas | | |
| 11 | William Taylor (D) | | ✔ |
| 12 | Augustus A. Chapman (D) | | ✔ |
| 13 | George W. Hopkins (D) | | ✔ |
| 14 | Joseph Johnson (D) | | ✔ |
| | Camden | | |
| 15 | William G. Brown (D) | | ✔ |
| | Allen | | |

1. *New Hampshire was entitled to four seats in the 29th Congress (1845-47), but only elected three representatives. Woodbury did not receive the necessary number of votes to be elected in the 1845 at-large election, and no winner was subsequently chosen in a special election. (See New Hampshire, 1846.) So the fourth seat remained vacant for the entire Congress. (Explanation of New Hampshire majority vote requirement, p. 945.)*

# 1846 House Elections

## ALABAMA

### Special Elections

| | Candidates | Votes | % |
|---|---|---|---|
| 3 | James L. F. Cottrell (D) | 3,299 | 50.2 |
| | Samuel S. Beeman (W) | 3,269 | 49.8 |
| 7 | Franklin W. Bowdon (D) | 2,704 | 45.2 |
| | Benjamin Goodman (W) | 1,979 | 33.1 |
| | T. A. Walker (D) | 1,303 | 21.8 |

## ARKANSAS

| | | Votes | % |
|---|---|---|---|
| AL | Robert W. Johnson (LOCOFOCO) | ✔ | |

### Special Election

| | | Votes | % |
|---|---|---|---|
| AL | Thomas W. Newton (W) | 1,753 | 28.6 |
| | Paschal | 1,722 | 28.1 |
| | Albert Rust (D) | 1,654 | 27.0 |
| | Noland (W) | 858 | 14.0 |

## DELAWARE

| | | Votes | % |
|---|---|---|---|
| AL | John W. Houston (W) | 6,154 | 50.6 |
| | Dillw (D) | 6,007 | 49.4 |

## FLORIDA

| | | Votes | % |
|---|---|---|---|
| AL | Edward C. Cabell (W) | ✔ | |

## GEORGIA

| | Candidates | Votes | % |
|---|---|---|---|
| 1 | Thomas Butler King (W) | 3,274 | 59.6 |
| | Cohen (D) | 2,220 | 40.4 |
| 2 | Alfred Iverson (D) | 5,599 | 51.8 |
| | Crawford (W) | 5,202 | 48.2 |
| 3 | John W. Jones (W) | 4,083 | 51.1 |
| | George W. B. Towns (D) | 3,904 | 48.9 |
| 4 | Hugh A. Haralson (D) | 4,908 | 50.8 |
| | Mosley (W) | 4,756 | 49.2 |
| 5 | John H. Lumpkin (D) | 5,349 | 79.4 |
| | Crook (W) | 1,263 | 18.8 |
| 6 | Howell Cobb (D) | 4,368 | 59.5 |
| | Cleveland (W) | 2,968 | 40.5 |
| 7 | Alexander H. Stephens (W) | 3,507 | 62.8 |
| | Turner (D) | 2,078 | 37.2 |
| 8 | Robert Toombs (W) | 3,560 | 65.0 |
| | Unidentified Candidate (D) | 1,917 | 35.0 |

### Special Election

| | | Votes | % |
|---|---|---|---|
| 3 | George W. B. Towns (D) | 4,026 | 51.6 |
| | Baber (W) | 3,773 | 48.4 |

## ILLINOIS

| | | Votes | % |
|---|---|---|---|
| 1 | Robert Smith (OPP D) | 7,068 | 58.1 |
| | Lyman Trumbull (D) | 5,019 | 41.3 |
| 2 | John A. McClernand (D) | 7,151 | 97.3 |
| 3 | Orlando B. Ficklin (D) | 6,707 | 57.1 |
| | Robert K. McLaughlin (I) | 5,014 | 42.7 |
| 4 | John Wentworth (D) | 12,115 | 55.8 |
| | John Kerr (W) | 6,079 | 28.0 |
| | Owen Lovejoy (LIB) | 3,531 | 16.3 |
| 5 | Stephen A. Douglas (D) | 9,629* | 57.0 |
| | Isaac VanderVenter (W) | 6,864 | 40.6 |
| 6 | Thomas J. Turner (D) | 8,843 | 48.4 |
| | James Knox (W) | 8,456 | 46.3 |
| | Wade Talcott (LIB) | 947 | 5.2 |
| 7 | Abraham Lincoln (W) | 6,340 | 55.5 |
| | Peter Cartwright (D) | 4,829 | 42.3 |

## IOWA[1]

(Became a state Dec. 28, 1846)

| | | Votes | % |
|---|---|---|---|
| | S. Clinton Hastings (D) | ✔ | |
| | Shepherd Leffler (D) | ✔ | |

1. *Information unavailable as to whether the Iowa elections were at large or by district.*
2. *Woodbury did not receive the required majority. (See New Hampshire, 1845, p. 980.)*

## MASSACHUSETTS

| | Candidates | Votes | % |
|---|---|---|---|
| 1 | Robert C. Winthrop (W) | 5,980 | 63.9 |
| | Peter F. Homer (D) | 1,688 | 18.1 |
| | Samuel G. Howe (LIB) | 1,334 | 14.3 |
| 2 | Daniel P. King (W) | 3,735 | 62.6 |
| | George W. Dike (D) | 1,621 | 27.2 |
| | Samuel Gall (LIB) | 427 | 7.2 |
| 3 | Amos Abbott (W) | 4,965 | 52.5 |
| | George S. Boutwell (D) | 3,098 | 32.7 |
| | Chauncey L. Knapp (LIB) | 1,108 | 11.7 |
| 4 | John G. Palfrey (W) | 4,513 | 50.6 |
| | Frederick Robinson (D) | 3,754 | 42.1 |
| | James G. Carter (LIB) | 544 | 6.1 |
| 5 | Charles Hudson (W) | 6,068 | 50.3 |
| | Walter A. Bryant (D) | 4,107 | 34.1 |
| | R. B. Hubbard (LIB) | 1,508 | 12.5 |
| 6 | George Ashmun (W) | 6,628 | 55.1 |
| | Stephen S. W. Taber (D) | 4,245 | 35.3 |
| | John Dickinson Jr (LIB) | 1,021 | 8.5 |
| 7 | Julius Rockwell (W) | 5,716 | 53.1 |
| | Heratio Byington (D) | 4,138 | 38.4 |
| | Jasper Bement (LIB) | 861 | 8.0 |
| 8 | John Quincy Adams (W) | 5,765 | 61.6 |
| | Isaac H. Wright (D) | 2,617 | 28.0 |
| | Appleton Howe (LIB) | 882 | 9.4 |
| 9 | Artemas Hale (W) | 4,937 | 50.1 |
| | Foster Hooper (D) | 3,718 | 37.7 |
| | Laban M. Wheaton (LIB) | 1,023 | 10.4 |
| 10 | Joseph Grinnell (W) | 3,806 | 62.8 |
| | Timothy G. Coffin (D) | 1,788 | 29.5 |

## MICHIGAN

| | | Votes | % |
|---|---|---|---|
| 1 | Robert McClelland (D) | 7,877 | 52.1 |
| | Edwin Lawrence (W) | 6,442 | 42.6 |
| | Charles H. Stewart (LIB) | 791 | 5.2 |
| 2 | Edward Bradley (D) | 9,517 | 49.1 |
| | James W. Gordon (W) | 8,681 | 44.8 |
| | Erastus Hussey (LIB) | 1,156 | 6.0 |
| 3 | Kinsley S. Bingham (D) | 6,529 | 48.9 |
| | George W. Wisner (W) | 5,811 | 43.5 |
| | William Caufield (LIB) | 981 | 7.4 |

## MISSOURI

| | | Votes | % |
|---|---|---|---|
| 1 | James B. Bowlin (D) | 7,466 | 52.2 |
| | Uriel Wright (W) | 5,268 | 36.8 |
| | William Milburn | 1,572 | 11.0 |
| 2 | John Jamison (D) | 8,156 | 80.3 |
| | Preston P. Brickey (W) | 1,814 | 17.9 |
| 3 | James S. Green (D) | 8,624 | 55.3 |
| | John G. Miller (W) | 6,981 | 44.7 |
| 4 | Willard P. Hall (D) | 8,884 | 65.0 |
| | James H. Birch (W) | 4,789 | 35.0 |
| 5 | John S. Phelps (D) | 7,195 | 53.1 |
| | John P. Campbell (W) | 6,348 | 46.9 |

### Special Election

| | | Votes | % |
|---|---|---|---|
| AL | William McDaniel (D) | 9,155 | 48.6 |
| | William M. Kincaid (W) | 8,610 | 45.7 |

## NEW HAMPSHIRE[2]

### Special Election

| | | Votes | % |
|---|---|---|---|
| AL | Woodbury (D) | 26,810* | 48.8 |
| | Goodwin (W) | 16,567 | 30.1 |
| | Hale (I) | 11,475 | 20.9 |

## NEW JERSEY

| | | Votes | % |
|---|---|---|---|
| 1 | James G. Hampton (W) | ✔ | |
| 2 | William A. Newell (W) | ✔ | |

| | Candidates | Votes | % |
|---|---|---|---|
| 3 | Joseph E. Edsall (D) | ✔ | |
| 4 | John Van Dyke (W) | ✔ | |
| 5 | Dudley S. Gregory (W) | ✔ | |

## NEW YORK

| | | Votes | % |
|---|---|---|---|
| 1 | Frederick Lord (D) | 4,045 | 54.7 |
| | Abraham Rose (W) | 3,353 | 45.3 |
| 2 | Henry Murphy (D) | 5,267 | 45.9 |
| | Gerret Van Wagenan (W) | 5,070 | 44.2 |
| | Honry Seaman (AM) | 771 | 6.7 |
| 3 | Henry Nicoll (D) | 4,609 | 48.6 |
| | Phillip Phoenix (W) | 4,560 | 48.1 |
| 4 | William Maclay (D) | 4,749 | 46.1 |
| | John Williams (W) | 4,057 | 39.4 |
| | William Picall (AM) | 865 | 8.4 |
| 5 | Frederick Tallmadge (W) | 4,205 | 42.1 |
| | David Broderick (D) | 3,809 | 38.2 |
| | David Wheeler (AM) | 1,493 | 15.0 |
| 6 | David S. Jackson (D) | 6,071‡ | 43.3 |
| | James Monroe (W) | 5,928 | 42.3 |
| | William Campbell (AM) | 1,841 | 13.1 |
| 7 | William Nelson (W) | 4,324 | 51.2 |
| | Edward Suffem (D) | 4,099 | 48.5 |
| 8 | Cornelius Warren (W) | 5,450 | 45.7 |
| | Henry Delamater (D) | 5,221 | 43.8 |
| | Charles Haight | 1,251 | 10.5 |
| 9 | Daniel St.John (W) | 6,158 | 56.3 |
| | John Monell (D) | 4,719 | 43.1 |
| 10 | Eliakim Sherrill (W) | 7,967 | 53.6 |
| | Jeremiah Russell (D) | 6,742 | 45.4 |
| 11 | Peter Sylvester (W) | 6,586 | 53.3 |
| | Silas Camp (D) | 5,770 | 46.7 |
| 12 | Gideon Reynold (W) | 5,509 | 52.8 |
| | Nicholas Masters (D) | 4,822 | 46.3 |
| 13 | John Slingerland (W-A-RENT) | 7,155 | 58.1 |
| | Bradford Wood (D) | 5,087 | 41.3 |
| 14 | Orlando Kellogg (W) | 9,449 | 67.7 |
| | Winslow Watson (D) | 4,020 | 28.8 |
| 15 | Sidney Lawrence (D) | 5,174 | 53.4 |
| | William McLean (W) | 4,181 | 43.2 |
| 16 | Hugh White (W) | 7,576 | 51.3 |
| | Lucio Smith (D) | 7,024 | 47.5 |
| 17 | George Petrie (ID) | 5,532 | 51.1 |
| | Abraham Van Alstine (D) | 4,717 | 43.6 |
| | John Underwood | 576 | 5.3 |
| 18 | William Collins (W) | 5,878 | 48.2 |
| | Francis Seger (D-HANKER) | 5,732 | 47.0 |
| 19 | Joseph Mullin (W) | 4,915 | 46.6 |
| | Orville Hungerford (D) | 4,871 | 46.2 |
| | Hugh Smith | 763 | 7.2 |
| 20 | Timothy Jenkins (D) | 6,018 | 47.6 |
| | Orsamus Matteson (W) | 5,693 | 45.0 |
| | James Delong | 940 | 7.4 |
| 21 | George Starkweather (D) | 7,209 | 50.1 |
| | Ebenezer Blakeley (W) | 6,889 | 47.9 |
| 22 | Ausburn Birdsall (D) | 7,904 | 51.7 |
| | Gideon Chase (BARN D) | 6,995 | 45.8 |
| 23 | William Duer (W) | 6,431 | 45.0 |
| | Avery Skinner (D) | 6,186 | 43.3 |
| | Cyrus Hawley | 1,597 | 11.2 |
| 24 | Daniel Gott (W) | 5,561 | 49.2 |
| | William Fuller (D) | 5,157 | 45.6 |
| | Charles Wheaton | 569 | 5.0 |
| 25 | Harmon Conger (W) | 6,253 | 47.7 |
| | William Shankland (D) | 6,036 | 46.1 |
| | John Boyd | 811 | 6.2 |
| 26 | William Lawrence (W) | 6,753 | 48.6 |
| | John Wisner (D) | 6,739 | 48.5 |
| 27 | John Holley (W) | 5,468 | 48.3 |
| | James Wilson (D) | 5,180 | 45.7 |
| | Levi Gaylord | 678 | 6.0 |
| 28 | Elias Holmes (W) | 6,131 | 54.0 |
| | Maltby Strong (IW) | 4,370 | 38.5 |
| | Samuel Porter | 855 | 7.5 |

## NEW YORK

| | Candidates | Votes | % |
|---|---|---|---|
| 29 | Robert Rose (W) | 7,539 | 55.9 |
| | Peter Mitchel (D) | 5,451 | 40.5 |
| 30 | David Rumsey Jr (W) | 7,034 | 51.8 |
| | Hugh Magee (D) | 6,126 | 45.1 |
| 31 | Dudley Marvin (W) | 7,022 | 63.8 |
| | Ebenezer Lester (D) | 3,279 | 29.8 |
| | Constant Allen | 711 | 6.5 |
| 32 | Nathan Hall (W) | 5,660 | 54.5 |
| | Hiram Barney (D) | 4,385 | 42.2 |
| 33 | Harvey Putnam (W) | 5,628 | 58.9 |
| | Junius Smith (D) | 3,151 | 33.0 |
| | Ferdinand McKay | 559 | 5.9 |
| 34 | Washington Hunt (W) | 4,992 | 51.3 |
| | Sanford Church (D) | 4,347 | 44.7 |

## OHIO

| | Candidates | Votes | % |
|---|---|---|---|
| 1 | James J. Faran (D) | 7,055 | 54.1 |
| | Thomas J. Straight (W) | 4,301 | 33.0 |
| | William Green | 1,143 | 8.8 |
| 2 | David Fisher (W) | 7,086 | 52.7 |
| | Elijah Vance (D) | 5,915 | 44.0 |
| 3 | Robert C. Schenck (W) | 8,863 | 55.4 |
| | F. A. Cunningham (D) | 6,681 | 41.7 |
| 4 | Richard S. Canby (W) | 7,822 | 57.5 |
| | William Kershner (D) | 5,226 | 38.4 |
| 5 | William Sawyer (D) | 5,483 | 53.3 |
| | Morrison R. Waite (W) | 4,764 | 46.3 |
| 6 | Rodolphus Dickinson (D) | 5,802 | 57.2 |
| | Eli Dresback (W) | 4,159 | 41.0 |
| 7 | Thomas L. Hamer (D) | 6,785* | 92.1 |
| | Alex Campbell | 384 | 5.2 |
| 8 | John L. Taylor (W) | 6,127 | 51.6 |
| | L. Byington (D) | 5,465 | 46.0 |
| 9 | Thomas O. Edwards (W) | 6,030 | 50.8 |
| | A. L. Perrill (D) | 5,779 | 48.7 |
| 10 | Daniel Duncan (W) | 7,539 | 49.2 |
| | Samuel Medary (D) | 7,239 | 47.3 |
| 11 | John K. Miller (D) | 7,645 | 57.8 |
| | W. McLaughlin (W) | 2,237 | 16.9 |
| | J. H. Godman (D) | 1,949 | 14.7 |
| | C. Delano (W) | 989 | 7.5 |
| 12 | Samuel F. Vinton (W) | 3,424 | 38.8 |
| | Flavius Case (D) | 3,245 | 36.8 |
| | C. Morris | 1,240 | 14.1 |
| | A. Cushing | 568 | 6.4 |

| | Candidates | Votes | % |
|---|---|---|---|
| 13 | Thomas Ritchey (D) | 5,032 | 48.8 |
| | P. B. Johnson (W) | 5,005 | 48.5 |
| 14 | Nathan Evans (W) | 5,529 | 52.0 |
| | W. W. Tracy (D) | 4,674 | 44.0 |
| 15 | William Kennon Jr (D) | 5,386 | 50.1 |
| | B. S. Cowan (W) | 4,988 | 46.4 |
| 16 | John D. Cummins (D) | 5,080 | 54.0 |
| | John Everhard (W) | 4,180 | 44.4 |
| 17 | George Fries (D) | 5,318 | 50.4 |
| | Van Brown (W) | 4,906 | 46.5 |
| 18 | Samuel Lahm (D) | 4,651 | 50.0 |
| | David A. Starkweather (W) | 4,530 | 48.7 |
| 19 | John Crowell (W) | 6,573 | 48.2 |
| | Rufus P. Ranney (D) | 6,041 | 44.3 |
| | John Hutchins (LIB) | 1,016 | 7.5 |
| 20 | Joshua R. Giddings (W) | 6,548 | 60.6 |
| | Zenas Blish (D) | 2,865 | 26.5 |
| | Edw. Wade (LIB) | 1,398 | 12.9 |
| 21 | Joseph M. Root (W) | 6,126 | 48.0 |
| | Josiah Harris (D) | 5,160 | 40.4 |
| | Joel Tiffany (LIB) | 1,471 | 11.5 |

## PENNSYLVANIA

| | Candidates | | |
|---|---|---|---|
| 1 | Lewis C. Levin (AM) | ✓ | |
| 2 | Joseph R. Ingersoll (W) | ✓ | |
| 3 | Charles Brown (D) | ✓ | |
| 4 | Charles J. Ingersoll (D) | ✓ | |
| 5 | John Freedly (W) | ✓ | |
| 6 | John W. Hornbeck (W) | ✓ | |
| 7 | Abraham R. McIlvaine (W) | ✓ | |
| 8 | John Strohm (W) | ✓ | |
| 9 | William Strong (D) | ✓ | |
| 10 | Richard Brodhead (D) | ✓ | |
| 11 | Chester P. Butler (W) | ✓ | |
| 12 | David Wilmot (D) | ✓ | |
| 13 | James Pollock (W) | ✓ | |
| 14 | George N. Eckert (W) | ✓ | |
| 15 | Henry Nes (W) | ✓ | |
| 16 | Jasper E. Brady (W) | ✓ | |
| 17 | John Blanchard (W) | ✓ | |
| 18 | Andrew Stewart (W) | ✓ | |
| 19 | Job Mann (D) | ✓ | |
| 20 | John Dickey (W) | ✓ | |
| 21 | Moses Hampton (W) | ✓ | |
| 22 | John W. Farrelly (W) | ✓ | |
| 23 | James Thompson (D) | ✓ | |
| 24 | Alexander Irvin (W) | ✓ | |

## SOUTH CAROLINA

| | Candidates | Votes | % |
|---|---|---|---|
| 1 | James A. Black (CALH D) | 4,364 | 61.2 |
| | L. P. Herndon | 1,665 | 23.4 |
| | G. A. Alston | 1,099 | 15.4 |
| 2 | Richard F. Simpson (D) | | 100.0 |
| 3 | Joseph A. Woodward (D) | ✓ | |
| 4 | Alexander D. Sims (D) | ✓ | |
| 5 | Armistead Burt (D) | | 100.0 |
| 6 | Isaac E. Holmes (D) | ✓ | |
| | D. J. Dowling | | |
| 7 | R. Barnwell Rhett (D) | | 100.0 |

## TEXAS

(Became a state Dec. 29, 1845)

| | | Votes | % |
|---|---|---|---|
| 1 | David Kaufman (D) | 589 | 98.7 |
| 2 | Timothy Pillsbury (CALH D) | 1,751 | 49.9 |
| | William E. Jones | 678 | 19.3 |
| | S. M. Williams | 621 | 17.7 |
| | R. E. B. Baylor | 458 | 13.0 |

### Special Elections

| | | Votes | % |
|---|---|---|---|
| 1 | David S. Kaufman (D) | 1,478 | 58.9 |
| | William R. Scurry | 532 | 21.2 |
| | William B. Ochiltree | 497 | 19.8 |
| 2 | Timothy Pillsbury (CALH D) | 1,276 | 30.0 |
| | Samuel M. Williams | 1,233 | 29.0 |
| | William G. Cooke | 954 | 22.5 |
| | N. Lewis | 423 | 10.0 |
| | Joseph C. Megginson | 253 | 6.0 |

## VERMONT

| | | Votes | % |
|---|---|---|---|
| 1 | William Henry (W) | 6,627 | 54.0 |
| | Bradley (D) | 3,071 | 25.0 |
| | Unidentified Candidate (LIB&SC) | 2,580 | 21.0 |
| 2 | Jacob Collamer (W) | 5,457 | 49.1 |
| | Hugh H. Henry (D) | 3,854 | 34.7 |
| | Titus Hutchinson (LIB) | 1,732 | 15.6 |
| 3 | George Perkins Marsh (W) | 5,644 | 53.9 |
| | Homer E. Hubbell (D) | 3,207 | 30.7 |
| | Norris Day (LIB) | 1,575 | 15.1 |
| 4 | Lucius B. Peck (D) | 5,594 | 44.1 |
| | George B. Chandler (W) | 5,059 | 39.9 |
| | Rowell (LIB) | 1,255 | 9.9 |

# 1847 House Elections

## ALABAMA

| | Candidates | Votes | % |
|---|---|---|---|
| 1 | John Gayle (W) | 5,050 | 52.9 |
| | John Taylor (D) | 4,490 | 47.1 |
| 2 | Henry W. Hilliard (W) | | 100.0 |
| 3 | Sampson W. Harris (D) | | 100.0 |
| 4 | Samuel W. Inge (D) | 4,528 | 51.0 |
| | W. M. Murphy (W) | 4,360 | 49.1 |
| 5 | George S. Houston (D) | 4,476 | 60.1 |
| | D. Hubbard (D) | 2,978 | 40.0 |
| 6 | Williamson R. W. Cobb (D) | 3,321 | 45.2 |
| | William Acklen (D) | 2,747 | 37.4 |
| | B. F. Pope (W) | 1,284 | 17.5 |
| 7 | Franklin W. Bowdon (D) | 5,419 | 52.3 |
| | S. F. Rice (D) | 4,024 | 38.9 |
| | Phillips | 793 | 7.7 |

## CONNECTICUT

| | Candidates | Votes | % |
|---|---|---|---|
| 1 | James Dixon (W) | 7,676 | 50.5 |
| | William Hammersley (D) | 7,167 | 47.1 |
| 2 | Samuel D. Hubbard (W) | 7,325 | 50.9 |
| | Samuel Ingham (D) | 6,669 | 46.4 |
| 3 | John A. Rockwell (W) | 6,112 | 49.5 |
| | Noyes Billings (D) | 5,578 | 45.2 |
| | Increase Wilson (LIB) | 653 | 5.3 |
| 4 | Truman Smith (W) | 9,082 | 52.0 |
| | George Taylor (D) | 7,980 | 45.7 |

## ILLINOIS

**Special Elections**

| | Candidates | Votes | % |
|---|---|---|---|
| 5 | William A. Richardson (D) | 11,423 | 77.5 |
| | Nathaniel G. Wilcox (W) | 3,312 | 22.5 |
| 7 | John Henry (W) | 2,411 | 56.8 |
| | Issur W. Crosby (D) | 1,289 | 30.3 |
| | Archibald Job (OPP D) | 293 | 6.9 |

## INDIANA

| | Candidates | Votes | % |
|---|---|---|---|
| 1 | Elisha Embree (W) | 7,446 | 51.4 |
| | Robert Dale Owen (D) | 7,054 | 48.7 |
| 2 | Thomas J. Henley (D) | 7,170 | 50.1 |
| | John S. Davis (W) | 7,130 | 49.9 |
| 3 | John L. Robinson (D) | 7,908 | 51.5 |
| | Pleasant A. Hackleman (W) | 7,422 | 48.3 |
| 4 | Caleb B. Smith (W) | 4,988 | 58.5 |
| | Charles H. Test | 3,540 | 41.5 |
| 5 | William W. Wick (D) | 7,087 | 50.4 |
| | Nicolas McCarty (W) | 6,799 | 48.4 |
| 6 | George G. Dunn (W) | 7,455 | 50.0 |
| | David M. Dobson (D) | 7,454 | 50.0 |
| 7 | Richard W. Thompson (W) | 6,402 | 50.7 |
| | Joseph A. Wright (D) | 6,224 | 49.3 |
| 8 | John Pettit (D) | 6,931 | 51.0 |
| | David Brier (W) | 6,511 | 47.9 |
| 9 | Charles W. Cathcart (D) | 7,555 | 51.0 |
| | Daniel D. Pratt (W) | 7,063 | 47.7 |
| 10 | William Rockhill (D) | 6,617 | 50.4 |
| | William G. Ewing (W) | 6,441 | 49.1 |

## IOWA

| | Candidates | Votes | % |
|---|---|---|---|
| 1 | William Thompson (D) | 5,530 | 52.6 |
| | Jesse B. Browne (W) | 4,986 | 47.4 |
| 2 | Shepherd Leffler (D) | 5,160 | 51.4 |
| | Thomas McKnight (W) | 4,873 | 48.6 |

## KENTUCKY

| | Candidates | Votes | % |
|---|---|---|---|
| 1 | Linn Boyd (D) | 7,421 | 63.9 |
| | Delaney (W) | 4,194 | 36.1 |
| 2 | Samuel O. Peyton (D) | 6,068 | 50.5 |
| | Waddill (W) | 5,958 | 49.5 |

| | Candidates | Votes | % |
|---|---|---|---|
| 3 | Beverly L. Clarke (D) | 5,291 | 51.1 |
| | Todd (W) | 5,065 | 48.9 |
| 4 | Aylett Buckner (W) | 6,177 | 51.6 |
| | James (D) | 5,791 | 48.4 |
| 5 | John B. Thompson (W) | 6,779 | 53.0 |
| | Wickliffe (D) | 6,019 | 47.0 |
| 6 | Green Adams (W) | 6,303 | 54.3 |
| | Price (W) | 5,307 | 45.7 |
| 7 | W. Garnett Duncan (W) | 6,760 | 51.1 |
| | David Meriwether (D) | 6,477 | 48.9 |
| 8 | Charles S. Morehead (W) | 4,348 | 41.3 |
| | S. F. J. Trabue (AM) | 3,143 | 29.9 |
| | A. K. Marshall (D) | 3,037 | 28.9 |
| 9 | Richard French (D) | 6,473 | 51.2 |
| | Cox (W) | 6,166 | 48.8 |
| 10 | John P. Gaines (W) | 7,496 | 50.4 |
| | L. B. Desha (D) | 7,372 | 49.6 |

## LOUISIANA

| | Candidates | Votes | % |
|---|---|---|---|
| 1 | Emile La Sere (D) | 2,813 | 63.6 |
| | Montegut (W) | 1,613 | 36.4 |
| 2 | Bannon G. Thibodeaux (W) | 4,280 | 55.1 |
| | Landry (D) | 3,489 | 44.9 |
| 3 | John H. Harmanson (D) | 4,118 | 54.8 |
| | Saunders (W) | 3,399 | 45.2 |
| 4 | Isaac E. Morse (D) | 4,138 | 53.9 |
| | Waddell (W) | 3,534 | 46.1 |

## MAINE

| | Candidates | Votes | % |
|---|---|---|---|
| 1 | David Hammons (D) | 5,430 | 53.6 |
| | Samuel Hopkins (W) | 3,521 | 34.7 |
| | Theodore Stevens Jr (LIB) | 1,101 | 10.9 |
| 2 | Asa W. H. Clapp (D) | 4,369 | 52.0 |
| | Josiah S. Little (W) | 3,023 | 36.0 |
| | Unidentified Candidate (LIB & SC) | 1,010 | 12.0 |
| 3 | Hiram Belcher (W) | 5,687 | 51.8 |
| | Cutter (D) | 3,487 | 31.7 |
| | Unidentified Candidate (LIB & SC) | 1,812 | 16.5 |
| 4 | Franklin Clark (D) | 5,266 | 49.2 |
| | Freeman H. Morse (W) | 4,657 | 43.5 |
| | Unidentified Candidate (LIB & SC) | 775 | 7.2 |
| 5 | Ephraim K. Smart (D) | 4,548 | 44.2 |
| | Levi Johnson (W) | 3,852 | 37.4 |
| | Unidentified Candidate (LIB & SC) | 1,892 | 18.4 |
| 6 | James S. Wiley (D) | 4,817 | 48.2 |
| | Sanford Kingsbury (W) | 3,615 | 36.2 |
| | Unidentified Candidate (LIB & SC) | 1,560 | 15.6 |
| 7 | Hezekiah Williams (D) | 5,033 | 52.0 |
| | Pike (W) | 3,740 | 38.6 |
| | Unidentified Candidate (LIB & SC) | 910 | 9.4 |

## MARYLAND

| | Candidates | Votes | % |
|---|---|---|---|
| 1 | John G. Chapman (W) | | 100.0 |
| 2 | J. Dixon Roman (W) | 7,136 | 51.1 |
| | Shriver (D) | 6,820 | 48.9 |
| 3 | Thomas W. Ligon (D) | 4,202 | 55.0 |
| | Unidentified Candidate (W) | 3,433 | 45.0 |
| 4 | Robert M. McLane (D) | 10,158 | 53.8 |
| | Kennedy (W) | 8,720 | 46.2 |
| 5 | Alexander Evans (W) | 4,909 | 52.5 |
| | Carmichael (D) | 4,444 | 47.5 |
| 6 | John W. Crisfield (W) | 4,497 | 54.5 |
| | Unidentified Candidate (D) | 3,760 | 45.5 |

## MICHIGAN

**Special Election**

| | Candidates | Votes | % |
|---|---|---|---|
| 2 | Charles E. Stuart (D) | 10,052 | 52.1 |
| | James W. Gordon (W) | 8,455 | 43.8 |

## MISSISSIPPI

| | Candidates | Votes | % |
|---|---|---|---|
| 1 | Jacob Thompson (D) | 7,191 | 54.4 |
| | Josselyn (ID) | 6,033 | 45.6 |
| 2 | Winfield S. Featherston (D) | 6,433 | 53.5 |
| | McClung (W) | 5,587 | 46.5 |
| 3 | Patrick W. Tompkins (W) | 6,939 | 52.1 |
| | Roberts (D) | 6,390 | 47.9 |
| 4 | Albert G. Brown (D) | ✓ | |
| | John A. Quitman | | |

## NEW HAMPSHIRE

| | Candidates | Votes | % |
|---|---|---|---|
| 1 | Amos Tuck (I) | 5,608 | 57.7 |
| | Jennes (LOCOFOCO) | 4,025 | 41.4 |
| 2 | Charles H. Peaslee (D) | 8,873 | 57.2 |
| | Unidentified Candidate | 4,275 | 27.6 |
| | Unidentified Candidate | 2,356 | 15.2 |
| 3 | James Wilson (W) | 5,926 | 51.2 |
| | Moulton (LOCOFOCO) | 5,086 | 44.0 |
| 4 | James H. Johnson (LOCOFOCO) | ✓ | |

## NORTH CAROLINA

| | Candidates | Votes | % |
|---|---|---|---|
| 1 | Thomas L. Clingman (W) | 4,550 | 57.1 |
| | John Gray Bynum (W) | 3,426 | 43.0 |
| 2 | Nathaniel Boyden (W) | 3,882 | 51.7 |
| | Joseph M. Bogle (IW) | 3,025 | 40.3 |
| | John N. Vogler (ID) | 606 | 8.1 |
| 3 | Daniel M. Barringer (W) | 3,412 | 81.2 |
| | Walter F. Leake (D) | 792 | 18.8 |
| 4 | Augustine H. Shepperd (W) | 4,022 | 60.4 |
| | Junius L. Clemmons (D) | 2,634 | 39.6 |
| 5 | Abraham W. Venable (D) | 4,588 | 50.9 |
| | John Kerr (W) | 4,435 | 49.2 |
| 6 | John R. J. Daniel (D) | 3,896 | 51.8 |
| | Archibald H. Arrington (ID) | 3,410 | 45.4 |
| 7 | James J. McKay (D) | 3,894 | 65.8 |
| | William R. Hall (W) | 1,827 | 30.9 |
| 8 | Richard S. Donnell (W) | 4,293 | 52.3 |
| | William K. Lane (D) | 3,924 | 47.8 |
| 9 | David Outlaw (W) | 3,795 | 55.3 |
| | Asa Biggs (D) | 3,071 | 44.7 |

## RHODE ISLAND[1]

| | Candidates | Votes | % |
|---|---|---|---|
| 1 | Robert B. Cranston (W) | 3,303 | 50.4 |
| | Fenner Brown (D) | 2,429 | 37.0 |
| 2 | Wilkins Updike (W) | 2,035* | 44.2 |
| | Benjamin B. Thurston (D) | 1,928 | 41.8 |
| | Lemuel H. Arnold (W) | 453 | 9.8 |

**Special Election**

| | Candidates | Votes | % |
|---|---|---|---|
| 2 | Benjamin B. Thurston (D) | 2,415 | 50.0 |
| | Wilkins Updike (W) | 2,350 | 48.6 |

## TENNESSEE

| | Candidates | Votes | % |
|---|---|---|---|
| 1 | Andrew Johnson (D) | 5,658 | 51.4 |
| | Oliver P. Temple (W) | 5,342 | 48.6 |
| 2 | William M. Cocke (W) | 7,277 | 61.0 |
| | Wayne W. Wallace (D) | 4,650 | 39.0 |
| 3 | John H. Crozier (W) | 6,945 | 51.8 |
| | Samuel S. Smith (D) | 6,474 | 48.3 |
| 4 | Hugh L. W. Hill (D) | 5,604 | 58.7 |
| | John L. Goodall (W) | 3,947 | 41.3 |
| 5 | George W. Jones (D) | 4,697 | 98.8 |

*1. In the 1847 general election, no candidate in the 2nd district received the required majority. In a special election for which returns are unavailable, Thurston was the winner.*

## TENNESSEE

| Candidates | Votes | % |
|---|---|---|
| 6 James H. Thomas (D) | 5,562 | 55.6 |
| Boling Gordan (W) | 4,443 | 44.4 |
| 7 Meredith P. Gentry (W) | 5,989 | 65.1 |
| R. G. Ellis (D) | 3,207 | 34.9 |
| 8 Washington Barrow (W) | 5,544 | 58.8 |
| John B. Pittman (D) | 3,887 | 41.2 |
| 9 Lucien B. Chase (D) | 4,898 | 53.8 |
| John T. Swayne (W) | 4,205 | 46.2 |
| 10 Frederick P. Stanton (D) | 5,564 | 50.1 |
| John W. Harris (W) | 5,539 | 49.9 |
| 11 William T. Haskell (W) | 6,380 | 57.2 |
| John Gardner (D) | 4,771 | 42.8 |

## VIRGINIA

| Candidates | Votes | % |
|---|---|---|
| 1 Archibald Atkinson (D) | 2,238 | 50.8 |
| Watts (W) | 2,166 | 49.2 |
| 2 George C. Dromgoole (D) | 1,641 | 50.2 |
| Bolling (W) | 1,625 | 49.8 |
| 3 Thomas S. Flournoy (W) | 650 | 50.0 |
| Treadway (D) | 649 | 50.0 |
| 4 Thomas S. Bocock (D) | 2,263 | 51.4 |
| Irving (W) | 2,138 | 48.6 |
| 5 William L. Goggin (W) | 2,980 | 50.9 |
| Leake (D) | 2,870 | 49.1 |
| 6 John M. Botts (W) | 2,959 | 54.5 |
| Leake (D) | 2,468 | 45.5 |
| 7 Thomas H. Bayly (D) | 1,107 | 56.1 |
| Jones (W) | 866 | 43.9 |
| 8 Richard L. T. Beale (D) | 2,016 | 51.0 |
| Newton (W) | 1,934 | 49.0 |
| 9 John S. Pendleton (W) | 2,861 | 58.3 |
| Hunter (D) | 2,045 | 41.7 |
| 10 Henry Bedinger (D) | 3,053 | 52.7 |
| Kennedy (W) | 2,746 | 47.4 |
| 11 James McDowell (D) | 2,995 | 58.4 |
| Gray (W) | 2,135 | 41.6 |
| 12 William B. Preston (W) | 3,583 | 52.4 |
| Chapman (D) | 3,257 | 47.6 |
| 13 Andrew S. Fulton (W) | 2,094 | 38.8 |
| McMullen (D) | 2,078 | 38.5 |
| Goodson | 1,230 | 22.8 |
| 14 Robert A. Thompson (D) | 3,290 | 50.4 |
| McComas (W) | 3,235 | 49.6 |
| 15 William G. Brown (D) | ✓ | |

### Special Election

| | | |
|---|---|---|
| 2 Richard K. Meade (D) | ✓ | |

# 1848 House Elections

## ARKANSAS

| Candidates | Votes | % |
|---|---|---|
| AL Robert W. Johnson (D) | 14,456 | 60.8 |
| Newton (W) | 9,328 | 39.2 |

## DELAWARE

| | Votes | % |
|---|---|---|
| AL John W. Houston (W) | 6,369 | 51.4 |
| Whiteley (D) | 6,026 | 48.6 |

## FLORIDA

| | Votes | % |
|---|---|---|
| AL Edward Cabell (W) | 4,382 | 53.5 |
| William P. Duval (D) | 3,805 | 46.5 |

## GEORGIA

| | Votes | % |
|---|---|---|
| 1 Thomas Butler King (W) | 3,549 | 57.0 |
| Joseph W. Jackson (D) | 2,680 | 43.0 |
| 2 Marshall J. Wellborn (D) | 6,625 | 50.3 |
| James S. Calhoun (W) | 6,538 | 49.7 |
| 3 Allen F. Owen (W) | 4,754 | 52.7 |
| John I. Carey (D) | 4,260 | 47.3 |
| 4 Hugh A. Haralson (D) | 5,532 | 50.9 |
| John A. Williamson (W) | 5,341 | 49.1 |
| 5 Thomas C. Hackett (D) | 8,767 | 59.8 |
| James M. Calhoun (W) | 5,904 | 40.2 |
| 6 Howell Cobb (D) | 5,891 | 57.7 |
| James W. Harris (W) | 4,314 | 42.3 |
| 7 Alexander H. Stephens (W) | 4,019 | 60.7 |
| Joseph (D) | 2,602 | 39.3 |
| 8 Robert Toombs (W) | 4,232 | 62.4 |
| Unindentified Candidate (D) | 2,551 | 37.6 |

## ILLINOIS

| | Votes | % |
|---|---|---|
| 1 William H. Bissell (D) | 9,892 | 97.1 |
| 2 John A. McClernand (D) | 6,537 | 65.0 |
| Samuel Marshall (W) | 3,514 | 34.9 |
| 3 Timothy R. Young (D) | 8,207 | 61.3 |
| George M. Hanson (W) | 5,151 | 38.5 |
| 4 John Wentworth (D) | 11,857 | 50.9 |
| J. Young Scammon (W) | 8,302 | 35.6 |
| Owen Lovejoy (F SOIL) | 3,138 | 13.5 |
| 5 William A. Richardson (D) | 11,463 | 95.9 |
| 6 Edward D. Baker (W) | 10,325 | 50.9 |
| Joseph B. Wells (D) | 9,292 | 45.8 |
| 7 Thomas L. Harris (D) | 7,201 | 49.8 |
| Stephen V. Logan (W) | 7,095 | 49.1 |

## IOWA

| | Votes | % |
|---|---|---|
| 1 William Thompson (D) | 6,477 | 50.3 |
| Daniel F. Miller (W) | 6,091 | 47.3 |
| 2 Shepherd Leffler (D) | 5,789 | 50.9 |
| Timothy Davis (W) | 5,398 | 47.5 |

## MAINE

| | Votes | % |
|---|---|---|
| 1 Elbridge Gerry (D) | 5,897 | 54.4 |
| John Jameson | 3,984 | 36.8 |
| David Gerry | 840 | 7.8 |
| 2 Nathaniel S. Littlefield (D) | 5,160 | 46.7 |
| Isaac Lincoln | 4,407 | 39.9 |
| Samuel Fessenden | 1,438 | 13.0 |
| 3 John Otis (W) | 5,274 | 44.2 |
| Moses Shelburne | 4,132 | 34.6 |
| Ezekiel Holmes | 2,526 | 21.2 |
| 4 Rufus K. Goodenow (W) | 6,582 | 48.6 |
| John D. McCrate | 5,607 | 41.4 |
| William H. Vinton | 977 | 7.2 |
| 5 Cullen Sawtelle (D) | 5,875 | 50.4 |
| Abner Coburn | 3,589 | 30.8 |

| | Votes | % |
|---|---|---|
| Cyrus Fletcher | 2,063 | 17.7 |
| 6 Charles Stetson (D) | 5,095 | 40.8 |
| Israel Washburn Jr | 4,492 | 36.0 |
| Jeremiah Curtis | 2,043 | 16.4 |
| Samuel Veazie | 849 | 6.8 |
| 7 Thomas J. D. Fuller (D) | 5,807 | 53.8 |
| George Downes | 4,269 | 39.6 |
| Tristram Redman | 661 | 6.1 |

## MASSACHUSETTS [1]

| | Votes | % |
|---|---|---|
| 1 Robert C. Winthrop (W) | 7,726 | 66.9 |
| Charles Sumner (F SOIL) | 2,336 | 20.2 |
| Benjamin F. Hallett (D) | 1,460 | 12.7 |
| 2 Daniel P. King (W) | 4,201 | 54.5 |
| Benjamin F. Newhall | 1,903 | 24.7 |
| Robert Rantoul Jr. (D) | 1,588 | 20.6 |
| 3 James H. Duncan (W) | 6,685 | 53.0 |
| Chauncey L. Knapp (F SOIL) | 3,038 | 24.1 |
| George S. Boutwell (D) | 2,868 | 22.8 |
| 4 Benjamin Thompson (W) | 3,852* | 42.6 |
| John G. Palfrey (F SOIL) | 3,038 | 33.6 |
| Richard Frothingham Jr. | 2,060 | 22.8 |
| 5 Charles Allen (F SOIL) | 5,847 | 58.7 |
| Charles Hudson (W) | 2,868 | 28.8 |
| Isaac Davis (D) | 1,217 | 12.2 |
| 6 George Ashmun (W) | 7,073 | 52.2 |
| Muling Guswold | 3,766 | 27.8 |
| Daniel W. | 2,677 | 19.8 |
| 7 Julius Rockwell (W) | 5,865 | 51.3 |
| Thomas F. Plunkett | 3,220 | 28.2 |
| Charles Sedgwick | 2,325 | 20.4 |
| 8 Horace Mann (W) | 11,087 | 83.9 |
| Bradford S. Wales | 2,027 | 15.3 |
| 9 Orin Fowler (F SOIL W) | 3,726 | 51.2 |
| Nathaniel Morton | 2,128 | 29.2 |
| Foster Hooper | 1,414 | 19.4 |
| 10 Joseph Grinnell (W) | 4,719 | 56.2 |
| A. H. Howland | 1,504 | 17.9 |
| Charles B. H. Fessenden | 1,199 | 14.3 |
| Simpson Hart | 673 | 8.0 |

### Special Election

| | Votes | % |
|---|---|---|
| 8 Horace Mann (W) | 4,357 | 58.3 |
| Edgar K. Mutaker | 1,952 | 26.1 |
| Appleton Howe | 944 | 12.6 |

## MICHIGAN

| | Votes | % |
|---|---|---|
| 1 Alexander W. Buel (D) | 10,015 | 46.7 |
| George C. Bates (W) | 8,747 | 40.8 |
| Caleb N. Ormsby (F SOIL) | 2,665 | 12.4 |
| 2 William Sprague (W FS) | 13,559 | 53.3 |
| Charles E. Stuart (D) | 11,881 | 46.7 |
| 3 Kinsley S. Bingham (D) | 9,348 | 49.1 |
| George H. Hazelton (W) | 7,802 | 40.9 |
| John M. Lamb (F SOIL) | 1,899 | 10.0 |

## MISSOURI

| | Votes | % |
|---|---|---|
| 1 James B. Bowlin (D) | 10,312 | 60.4 |
| Cook (W) | 6,776 | 39.7 |
| 2 William V. N. Bay (D) | 8,394 | 54.6 |
| Porter (W) | 6,968 | 45.4 |
| 3 James S. Green (D) | 9,754 | 56.8 |
| Wilson (W) | 7,417 | 43.2 |
| 4 Willard P. Hall (D) | 10,840 | 71.0 |
| Samuel (W) | 4,418 | 29.0 |
| 5 John S. Phelps (D) | 11,062 | 65.4 |
| Winston (W) | 5,848 | 34.6 |

## NEW JERSEY

| Candidates | Votes | % |
|---|---|---|
| 1 Andrew K. Hay (W) | 7,052 | 51.1 |
| Unidentified Candidate (D) | 6,043 | 43.8 |
| Unidentified Candidate (AM) | 718 | 5.2 |
| 2 William A. Newell (W) | 9,877 | 54.1 |
| Unidentified Candidate (D) | 8,382 | 45.9 |
| 3 Isaac Wildrick (D) | 9,215 | 76.8 |
| Unidentified Candidate (W) | 2,778 | 23.2 |
| 4 John Van Dyke (W) | 7,282 | 54.5 |
| Unidentified Candidate (D) | 6,023 | 45.1 |
| 5 James G. King (W) | 9,679 | 56.7 |
| Unidentified Candidate (D) | 6,716 | 39.3 |

## NEW YORK

| | Votes | % |
|---|---|---|
| 1 John A. King (W) | 4,397 | 47.9 |
| Jones (F SOIL) | 2,457 | 26.8 |
| Brown (D) | 2,332 | 25.4 |
| 2 David A. Bokee (W) | 8,168 | 54.2 |
| Mereac (D) | 5,812 | 38.6 |
| Crooke (F SOIL) | 1,087 | 7.2 |
| 3 J. Phillips Phoenix (W) | 5,601 | 55.0 |
| Hart (D) | 3,788 | 37.2 |
| Smith (F SOIL) | 793 | 7.8 |
| 4 Walter Underhill (W) | 5,649 | 49.0 |
| Maclay (D) | 3,904 | 33.9 |
| Hecker (F SOIL) | 1,035 | 9.0 |
| Foote (D) | 944 | 8.2 |
| 5 George Briggs (W) | 5,627 | 49.1 |
| Walsh (D) | 2,765 | 24.1 |
| Hasbrouck (D) | 1,602 | 14.0 |
| Spencer (F SOIL) | 1,476 | 12.9 |
| 6 James Brooks (W) | 9,709 | 51.7 |
| Law (D) | 6,976 | 37.2 |
| Field (F SOIL) | 2,042 | 10.9 |
| 7 William Nelson (W) | 4,948 | 50.3 |
| N. C. Blvt (D) | 3,133 | 31.9 |
| J. C. Blvt (F SOIL) | 1,754 | 17.8 |
| 8 Hansom Halloway (W) | 6,301 | 51.2 |
| Nun (D) | 4,333 | 35.2 |
| Bailey (F SOIL) | 1,681 | 13.7 |
| 9 Thomas McKissock (W) | 5,876 | 47.3 |
| Woodward (D) | 4,667 | 37.6 |
| Curtis (F SOIL) | 1,874 | 15.1 |
| 10 Herman D. Gould (W) | 6,267 | 40.0 |
| Edgerton (F SOIL) | 4,443 | 28.3 |
| Fitch (A-RENT) | 3,013 | 19.2 |
| Wheeler (D) | 1,953 | 12.5 |
| 11 Peter H. Silvester (W) | 6,621 | 47.4 |
| Olney (D) | 3,893 | 27.9 |
| Beekman (F SOIL) | 3,453 | 24.7 |
| 12 Gideon Reynolds (D&A-RENT) | 6,055 | 53.0 |
| Warren (W) | 5,362 | 47.0 |
| 13 John L. Schoolcraft (W) | 7,227 | 53.9 |
| Bouton (D) | 3,876 | 28.9 |
| Wood (F SOIL) | 2,315 | 17.3 |
| 14 George R. Andrews (W) | 7,088 | 57.0 |
| Culver (F SOIL) | 3,166 | 25.5 |
| Cutting (D) | 2,186 | 17.6 |
| 15 John R. Thurman (W) | 4,670 | 42.6 |
| Heding (D) | 3,455 | 31.5 |
| Lawrence (F SOIL) | 2,828 | 25.8 |
| 16 Hugh White (W) | 8,183 | 52.3 |
| Campbell (D) | 4,059 | 26.0 |
| Cowen (F SOIL) | 3,392 | 21.7 |
| 17 Henry P. Alexander (W) | 6,109 | 47.2 |
| Nellis (F SOIL) | 5,564 | 43.0 |
| Samons (D) | 1,264 | 9.8 |
| 18 Preston King (F SOIL) | 7,309 | 53.1 |
| Squire (D) | 5,133 | 37.3 |
| Dodge (D) | 1,325 | 9.6 |
| 19 Charles E. Clarke (W) | 4,636 | 39.7 |
| Ives (F SOIL) | 4,427 | 37.9 |
| Dann (D) | 2,624 | 22.5 |
| 20 Orsamus B. Matteson (W) | 6,094 | 42.4 |
| Mann (F SOIL) | 5,069 | 35.3 |

*1. In the 4th district, no candidate received the necessary majority. Twelve elections were held to try to fill the seat, but all of them resulted without choice. The seat was vacant for the entire 31st Congress (1849-51).*

## NEW YORK

| | Candidates | Votes | % |
|---|---|---|---|
| | Williams (D) | 3,214 | 22.4 |
| 21 | Hiram Walden (D) | 6,636 | 42.1 |
| | Smith (W) | 6,330 | 40.2 |
| | Hammond (F SOIL) | 2,787 | 17.7 |
| 22 | Henry Bennett (W) | 8,014 | 46.5 |
| | Mason (D) | 6,394 | 37.1 |
| | Smith (F SOIL) | 2,839 | 16.5 |
| 23 | William Duer (W) | 8,107 | 48.2 |
| | Nye (F SOIL) | 6,884 | 41.0 |
| | Crouse (D) | 1,640 | 9.8 |
| 24 | Daniel Gott (W) | 5,403 | 42.2 |
| | Sedgwick (F SOIL) | 4,906 | 38.3 |
| | Baldwin (D) | 2,498 | 19.5 |
| 25 | Harmon S. Conger (W) | 6,732 | 46.9 |
| | Ballard (F SOIL) | 5,747 | 40.1 |
| | Hyde (D) | 1,870 | 13.0 |
| 26 | William T. Jackson (W) | 6,444 | 40.4 |
| | Wisner (F SOIL) | 6,396 | 40.1 |
| | Hathaway (D) | 3,117 | 19.5 |
| 27 | William A. Sackett (W) | 5,845 | 45.2 |
| | Bascom (F SOIL) | 5,260 | 40.7 |
| | Bigelow (D) | 1,802 | 14.1 |
| 28 | Abraham M. Schermerhorn (W) | 6,611 | 52.0 |
| | Selden (F SOIL) | 4,746 | 37.3 |
| | Smith (D) | 1,367 | 10.7 |
| 29 | Robert L. Rose (W) | 7,816 | 53.4 |
| | Garlghse (F SOIL) | 4,659 | 31.8 |
| | Parburt (D) | 2,166 | 14.8 |
| 30 | David Rumsey Jr (W) | 7,282 | 45.0 |
| | Grover (F SOIL) | 5,938 | 36.7 |
| | Angel (D) | 2,982 | 18.4 |
| 31 | Elijah Risley (W) | 6,946 | 51.7 |
| | Chaffee (D) | 3,649 | 27.2 |
| | Colman (F SOIL) | 2,832 | 21.1 |
| 32 | Elbridge G. Spaulding (W) | 7,622 | 56.9 |
| | Clinton (D) | 3,408 | 25.4 |
| | Wadsworth (F SOIL) | 2,367 | 17.7 |
| 33 | Harvey Putnam (W) | 5,489 | 50.6 |
| | Smith (F SOIL) | 2,780 | 25.6 |
| | Willett (D) | 2,575 | 23.8 |
| 34 | Lorenzo Burrows (W) | 5,372 | 47.0 |
| | Davis (F SOIL) | 3,846 | 33.6 |
| | Burroughs (D) | 2,214 | 19.4 |

### Special Elections

| | Candidates | Votes | % |
|---|---|---|---|
| 6 | Horace Greeley (W) | 9,932 | 53.9 |
| | Bradhst | 6,826 | 37.0 |
| | Townsend | 1,681 | 9.1 |
| 27 | Blackmar (W) | 5,921 | 45.6 |
| | Smith (F SOIL) | 5,308 | 40.9 |
| | Foster (HUNKER) | 1,751 | 13.5 |

## OHIO

| | Candidates | Votes | % |
|---|---|---|---|
| 1 | David T. Disney (D) | 9,292 | 50.9 |
| | Thomas J. Strait (W) | 6,297 | 34.5 |
| | Samuel Lewis (F SOIL) | 2,158 | 11.8 |
| 2 | Lewis D. Campbell (F SOIL W) | 6,914 | 51.6 |
| | William H. Baldwin (D) | 6,479 | 48.4 |
| 3 | Robert C. Schenck (W) | 9,289 | 53.5 |
| | Joseph W. McCorkle (D) | 8,082 | 46.5 |
| 4 | Moses B. Corwin (W) | 8,761 | 54.7 |
| | John A. Corwin (D) | 6,215 | 38.8 |
| | William A. Rogers (F SOIL) | 1,030 | 6.4 |
| 5 | Emery D. Potter (D) | 7,029 | 62.2 |
| | John Fitch (W) | 4,240 | 37.5 |
| 6 | Rodolphus Dickinson (D) | 7,404 | 58.8 |
| | Cooper K. Watson (W) | 5,184 | 41.2 |

| | Candidates | Votes | % |
|---|---|---|---|
| 7 | Jonathan D. Morris (D) | 7,135 | 59.5 |
| | John Joliffe (W) | 3,583 | 29.9 |
| | Thomas Gatch (IW) | 1,278 | 10.7 |
| 8 | John L. Taylor (W) | 7,449 | 52.9 |
| | Francis Cleveland (D) | 6,624 | 47.1 |
| 9 | Edson B. Olds (D) | 6,984 | 50.3 |
| | Thomas O. Edwards (W) | 6,906 | 49.7 |
| 10 | Charles Sweetzer (D) | 8,454 | 49.5 |
| | Daniel Duncan (W) | 8,438 | 49.4 |
| 11 | John K. Miller (D) | 9,165 | 62.6 |
| | Jacob Brinkerhoff (W) | 5,462 | 37.3 |
| 12 | Samuel F. Vinton (W) | 5,799 | 53.3 |
| | Simeon W. Tucker (D) | 4,416 | 40.6 |
| | David Richmond (ID) | 670 | 6.2 |
| 13 | William A. Whittlesey (D) | 6,375 | 51.4 |
| | William P. Cutler (W) | 6,037 | 48.6 |
| 14 | Nathan Evans (W) | 6,606 | 53.1 |
| | Matthew Gaston (D) | 5,840 | 46.9 |
| 15 | William F. Hunter (W) | 6,711 | 51.4 |
| | William Kennon Jr. (D) | 6,338 | 48.5 |
| 16 | Moses Hoagland (D) | 6,104 | 54.0 |
| | Martin Welker (W) | 5,144 | 45.5 |
| 17 | Joseph Cable (D) | 6,987 | 50.2 |
| | James Mason (W) | 6,330 | 45.5 |
| 18 | David K. Carter (D) | 6,682 | 60.0 |
| | Samuel Hemphill (W) | 4,448 | 40.0 |
| 19 | John Crowell (W) | 9,561 | 56.0 |
| | Rufus P. Ranney (D) | 7,507 | 44.0 |
| 20 | Joshua R. Giddings (F SOIL W) | 5,879 | 62.7 |
| | Bushnell White (D) | 3,155 | 33.6 |
| 21 | Joseph M. Root (F SOIL W) | 8,434 | 57.8 |
| | E. M. Stone (D) | 6,077 | 41.6 |

## PENNSYLVANIA

| | Candidates | Votes | % |
|---|---|---|---|
| 1 | Lewis C. Levin (AM) | 4,897 | 52.2 |
| | Florence (D) | 4,228 | 45.1 |
| 2 | Joseph R. Chandler (W) | 6,656 | 63.2 |
| | Van Dyke (D) | 3,874 | 36.8 |
| 3 | Henry D. Moore (W) | 6,844 | 52.9 |
| | Hallowell (D) | 6,098 | 47.1 |
| 4 | John Robbins Jr (D) | 6,661 | 51.6 |
| | John S. Littell (W) | 6,251 | 48.4 |
| 5 | John Freedley (W) | 6,655 | 50.7 |
| | McKeever (D) | 6,474 | 49.3 |
| 6 | Thomas Ross (D) | 8,036 | 51.0 |
| | Taylor (W) | 7,716 | 49.0 |
| 7 | Jesse C. Dickey (W) | 5,786 | 52.9 |
| | Hemphill (D) | 5,160 | 47.1 |
| 8 | Thaddeus Stevens (W) | 9,565 | 63.6 |
| | Shaffer (D) | 5,464 | 36.4 |
| 9 | William Strong (D) | 8,451 | 67.8 |
| | Adams (W) | 4,014 | 32.2 |
| 10 | Milo M. Dimmick (D) | 7,764 | 63.6 |
| | Wheeler (W) | 4,444 | 36.4 |
| 11 | Chester P. Butler (W) | 5,032 | 42.4 |
| | Wright (D) | 4,902 | 41.3 |
| | Collings (ID) | 1,938 | 16.3 |
| 12 | David Wilmot (F SOIL D) | 8,619 | 60.2 |
| | Tracy (D) | 4,773 | 33.3 |
| | Brewster (CASS D) | 922 | 6.4 |
| 13 | Joseph Casey (D) | 6,817 | 51.0 |
| | Unidentified Candidate (D) | 6,555 | 49.0 |
| 14 | Charles W. Pitman (W) | 10,203 | 57.7 |
| | Dock (D) | 7,472 | 42.3 |
| 15 | Henry Nes (W) | 6,599 | 52.4 |
| | Joel B. Danner (D) | 5,989 | 47.6 |
| 16 | James X. McLanahan (D) | 8,725 | 53.9 |
| | Brady (W) | 7,472 | 46.1 |

| | Candidates | Votes | % |
|---|---|---|---|
| 17 | Samuel Calvin (W) | 8,712 | 50.2 |
| | Parker (D) | 8,648 | 49.8 |
| 18 | Andrew Jackson Ogle (W) | 6,902 | 50.9 |
| | Dawson (D) | 6,649 | 49.1 |
| 19 | Job Mann (D) | 9,110 | 58.7 |
| | Livergood (W) | 6,398 | 41.3 |
| 20 | Robert R. Reed (W) | 6,417 | 49.5 |
| | Hopkins (D) | 6,359 | 49.1 |
| 21 | Moses Hampton (W) | 7,666 | 50.8 |
| | Black (D) | 6,613 | 43.8 |
| 22 | John W. Howe (F SOIL) | 7,509 | 51.2 |
| | McFarland (D) | 7,161 | 48.8 |
| 23 | James Thompson (D) | 7,509 | 50.9 |
| | Campbell (W) | 7,026 | 47.6 |
| 24 | Alfred Gilmore (D) | 7,267 | 50.2 |
| | Smith (W) | 7,008 | 48.4 |

### Special Election

| | Candidates | Votes | % |
|---|---|---|---|
| 6 | Samuel A. Bridges (D) | 6,526 | 50.5 |
| | Lesher Trexler (W) | 6,393 | 49.5 |

## SOUTH CAROLINA[1]

| | Candidates | Votes | % |
|---|---|---|---|
| 1 | Daniel Wallace (W) | 3,369 | 39.8 |
| | Thompson | 3,044 | 35.9 |
| | Davie | 2,061 | 24.3 |
| 2 | James L. Orr (D) | ✔ | |
| | B. F. Perry (D) | | |
| 3 | Joseph A. Woodward (D) | ✔ | |
| | J. O'Hanlon | | |
| 4 | Alexander D. Sims (D) | * | |
| | John McQueen (D) | | |
| 5 | Armistead Burt (D) | 5,991 | 84.2 |
| | Heller | 1,121 | 15.8 |
| 6 | Isaac E. Holmes (TAYLOR D) | ✔ | |
| | Samuel G. Barker (CASS D) | | |
| | W. C. Clayton | | |
| 7 | William F. Colcock (D) | ✔ | |

### Special Election

| | Candidates | Votes | % |
|---|---|---|---|
| 1 | Daniel Wallace (W) | 2,139 | 36.9 |
| | Thompson | 2,134 | 36.8 |
| | Davis | 1,525 | 26.3 |

## VERMONT

| | Candidates | Votes | % |
|---|---|---|---|
| 1 | William P. Henry (W) | ✔ | |
| 2 | William Hebard (W) | ✔ | |
| 3 | George P. Marsh (W) | ✔ | |
| 4 | Lucius B. Peck (D) | ✔ | |

## WISCONSIN

(Became a state May 29, 1848)

| | Candidates | Votes | % |
|---|---|---|---|
| 1 | Charles Durkee (F SOIL) | 5,038 | 38.5 |
| | William P. Lynde (D) | 4,436 | 33.9 |
| | Finch (W) | 3,615 | 27.6 |
| 2 | Orsamus Cole (W) | 6,280 | 45.2 |
| | Smith (D) | 5,690 | 41.0 |
| | Crabb (F SOIL) | 1,916 | 13.8 |
| 3 | James Duane Doty (D) | 5,746 | 50.3 |
| | Howe (W) | 3,338 | 29.2 |
| | Judd (F SOIL) | 2,330 | 20.4 |

### Special Election[2]

| Candidates | Votes | % |
|---|---|---|
| Mason C. Darling (D) | ✔ | |
| William P. Lynde (D) | ✔ | |

1. *In the South Carolina 4th district, Sims was elected but died Jan. 16, 1848. McQueen was chosen to succeed him in a special election for which no returns are available.*

2. *This was the first House election held by Wisconsin after it achieved statehood. Information is unavailable as to whether the elections were at-large or by district.*

# 1849 House Elections

## ALABAMA

| | Candidates | Votes | % |
|---|---|---|---|
| 1 | William J. Alston (TAYLOR W) | 4,922 | 51.8 |
| | C. C. Sellers (SO RTS D) | 4,588 | 48.2 |
| 2 | Henry W. Hilliard (W) | 6,770 | 53.1 |
| | J. L. Pugh (IW) | 5,975 | 46.9 |
| 3 | Sampson W. Harris (D) | 5,511 | 52.6 |
| | John Hunter (W) | 4,962 | 47.4 |
| 4 | Samuel W. Inge (D) | 4,665 | 52.4 |
| | Joseph Baldwin (W) | 4,245 | 47.6 |
| 5 | David Hubbard (D) | 4,575 | 49.1 |
| | Wood (W) | 3,084 | 33.1 |
| | O'Neal (D) | 1,655 | 17.8 |
| 6 | Williamson R. W. Cobb (D) | 4,594 | 53.4 |
| | Jere Clemens (D) | 4,005 | 46.6 |
| 7 | Franklin W. Bowdon (D) | 6,002 | 55.1 |
| | Bradford (W) | 4,895 | 44.9 |

## CALIFORNIA

(Became a state Sept. 9, 1850)

| | Candidates | Votes | % |
|---|---|---|---|
| AL | George W. Wright (I) | 5,451✔ | |
| | Edward Gilbert (D) | 5,300✔ | |
| | R. M. Price | 4,040 | |
| | Lewis Dent | 2,129 | |
| | D. A. Morse | 2,066 | |
| | E. J. C. Kewen | 1,826 | |
| | William M. Shepard | 1,773 | |
| | W. E. Shannon | 1,327 | |
| | P. O. Halsted | 1,271 | |
| | L. W. Hastings | 215 | |

## CONNECTICUT

| | Candidates | Votes | % |
|---|---|---|---|
| 1 | Loren P. Waldo (D) | 7,444 | 50.4 |
| | Charles Chapman (W) | 7,327 | 49.6 |
| 2 | Walter Booth (D) | 6,672 | 50.1 |
| | James F. Babcock (W) | 6,532 | 49.0 |
| 3 | Chauncey F. Cleveland (D) | 6,140 | 50.6 |
| | John A. Rockwell (W) | 5,992 | 49.4 |
| 4 | Thomas B. Butler (W) | 8,172 | 51.6 |
| | Nathaniel H. Wildman (D) | 7,028 | 44.4 |

## INDIANA

| | Candidates | Votes | % |
|---|---|---|---|
| 1 | Nathaniel Albertson (D) | 8,271 | 52.1 |
| | Elisha Embree (W) | 7,598 | 47.9 |
| 2 | Cyrus L. Dunham (D) | 7,823 | 51.6 |
| | William McKee Dunn (W) | 7,338 | 48.4 |
| 3 | John L. Robinson (D) | 8,120 | 52.5 |
| | Joseph Robinson (W) | 7,348 | 47.5 |
| 4 | George W. Julian (F SOIL) | 4,737 | 50.8 |
| | Samuel W. Parker (W) | 4,583 | 49.1 |
| 5 | William J. Brown (D) | 8,762 | 54.7 |
| | William Herod (W) | 7,265 | 45.3 |
| 6 | Willis A. Gorman (D) | 8,466 | 54.1 |
| | John S. Watts (W) | 7,196 | 45.9 |
| 7 | Edward W. McGaughey (W) | 6,782 | 58.0 |
| | Grafton F. Cookerly | 4,909 | 42.0 |
| 8 | Joseph E. McDonald (D) | 7,432 | 51.2 |
| | Henry S. Lane (W) | 7,098 | 48.9 |
| 9 | Graham N. Fitch (D) | 8,800 | 50.8 |
| | Williamson Wright (W) | 8,519 | 49.2 |
| 10 | Andrew J. Harlan (D) | 7,366 | 52.1 |
| | David Kilgore (W) | 6,777 | 47.9 |

## KENTUCKY

| | Candidates | Votes | % |
|---|---|---|---|
| 1 | Linn Boyd (D) | 5,208 | 100.0 |
| 2 | James L. Johnson (W) | 8,031 | 67.4 |
| | Peyton (D) | 3,878 | 32.6 |
| 3 | Finis E. McLean (W) | 5,679 | 100.0 |
| 4 | George A. Caldwell (D) | 6,719 | 54.6 |
| | Buckner (W) | 5,579 | 45.4 |

| | Candidates | Votes | % |
|---|---|---|---|
| 5 | John B. Thompson (W) | 6,586 | 100.0 |
| 6 | Daniel Breck (W) | 6,353 | 54.7 |
| | Martin (D) | 5,271 | 45.4 |
| 7 | Humphrey Marshall (W) | 6,261 | 50.3 |
| | Lane (D) | 6,197 | 49.7 |
| 8 | Charles S. Morehead (W) | 5,195 | 52.7 |
| | Trabue (AM) | 4,665 | 47.3 |
| 9 | John C. Mason (D) | 6,882 | 52.8 |
| | Houston (W) | 6,164 | 47.3 |
| 10 | Richard H. Stanton (D) | 7,764 | 51.2 |
| | Gaines (W) | 7,400 | 48.8 |

## LOUISIANA

| | Candidates | Votes | % |
|---|---|---|---|
| 1 | Emile La Sere (D) | 3,295 | 56.3 |
| | Jackson (W) | 2,559 | 43.7 |
| 2 | Charles M. Conrad (W) | 5,092 | 52.4 |
| | Beatty (D) | 4,622 | 47.6 |
| 3 | John H. Harmanson (D) | 2,464 | 53.8 |
| | Stewart (W) | 2,117 | 46.2 |
| 4 | Isaac E. Morse (D) | 4,751 | 51.3 |
| | Ogden (W) | 4,516 | 48.7 |

## MARYLAND

| | Candidates | Votes | % |
|---|---|---|---|
| 1 | Richard J. Bowie (W) | 4,283 | 100.0 |
| 2 | William T. Hamilton (D) | 7,307 | 50.4 |
| | T. J. McKaig (W) | 7,191 | 49.6 |
| 3 | Edward Hammond (D) | 6,903 | 60.8 |
| | George W. Gray (W) | 4,456 | 39.2 |
| 4 | Robert M. McLane (D) | 7,277 | 53.5 |
| | John R. Kenly (W) | 6,326 | 46.5 |
| 5 | Alexander Evans (W) | 4,986 | 52.6 |
| | S. M. Magraw (D) | 4,487 | 47.4 |
| 6 | John Bozman Kerr (W) | 3,457 | 100.0 |

## MISSISSIPPI

| | Candidates | Votes | % |
|---|---|---|---|
| 1 | Jacob Thompson (D) | 9,109 | 57.3 |
| | Bradford (W) | 6,801 | 42.8 |
| 2 | Winfield S. Featherston (D) | 7,237 | 54.0 |
| | Harris (W) | 6,170 | 46.0 |
| 3 | William McWillie (D) | 7,406 | 52.0 |
| | Gray (W) | 6,834 | 48.0 |
| 4 | Albert G. Brown (D) | 7,980 | 67.6 |
| | Winans (W) | 3,820 | 32.4 |

## NEW HAMPSHIRE

| | Candidates | Votes | % |
|---|---|---|---|
| 1 | Amos Tuck (F SOIL) | 6,971 | 51.1 |
| | G. W. Kit (D) | 6,638 | 48.6 |
| 2 | Charles H. Peaslee (D) | 8,590 | 60.6 |
| | Eastman (F SOIL) | 3,673 | 25.9 |
| | Stewart | 1,914 | 13.5 |
| 3 | James Wilson (F SOIL) | 7,766 | 51.2 |
| | Vose (D) | 7,378 | 48.7 |
| 4 | Harry Hibbard (D) | 7,363 | 57.8 |
| | J. Kittredge (F SOIL) | 3,658 | 28.7 |
| | Unidentified Candidate | 1,712 | 13.5 |

## NORTH CAROLINA

| | Candidates | Votes | % |
|---|---|---|---|
| 1 | Thomas L. Clingman (W) | 7,231 | 86.3 |
| 2 | Joseph P. Caldwell (W) | 6,353 | 78.0 |
| | Montford S. Stokes (D) | 1,795 | 22.0 |
| 3 | Edmund Deberry (W) | 4,899 | 53.3 |
| | Green W. Caldwell (D) | 4,299 | 46.7 |
| 4 | Augustine H. Shepperd (W) | 4,405 | 58.4 |
| | Thomas W. Keene (D) | 3,138 | 41.6 |
| 5 | Abraham W. Venable (D) | 5,025 | 53.8 |
| | Henry K. Nash (W) | 4,315 | 46.2 |
| 6 | John R. J. Daniel (D) | 4,413 | 64.5 |
| | William J. Clarke (D) | 2,430 | 35.5 |

| | Candidates | Votes | % |
|---|---|---|---|
| 7 | William S. Ashe (D) | 5,128 | 64.6 |
| | David Reid (D) | 2,813 | 35.4 |
| 8 | Edward Stanly (W) | 4,987 | 50.2 |
| | William K. Lane (D) | 4,940 | 49.8 |
| 9 | David Outlaw (W) | 4,053 | 53.8 |
| | Thomas Person (D) | 3,477 | 46.2 |

## OHIO

### Special Election

| | Candidates | Votes | % |
|---|---|---|---|
| 6 | Amos E. Wood (D) | ✔ | |

## RHODE ISLAND[1]

| | Candidates | Votes | % |
|---|---|---|---|
| 1 | George G. King (W) | 3,005 | 67.3 |
| | Fenner Brown (D) | 1,250 | 28.0 |
| 2 | Benjamin B. Thurston (D) | 2,017* | 48.5 |
| | Sylvester G. Sherman (W) | 1,959 | 47.1 |

### Special Election

| | Candidates | Votes | % |
|---|---|---|---|
| 2 | Nathan F. Dixon (W) | 2,824 | 56.1 |
| | Benjamin B. Thurston (FS CLN) | 2,209 | 43.9 |

## TENNESSEE

| | Candidates | Votes | % |
|---|---|---|---|
| 1 | Andrew Johnson (D) | 6,068 | 54.5 |
| | Taylor (W) | 5,060 | 45.5 |
| 2 | Albert G. Watkins (W) | 7,125 | 58.9 |
| | Cocke (D) | 4,968 | 41.1 |
| 3 | Josiah M. Anderson (W) | 7,269 | 54.7 |
| | Lyon (D) | 6,018 | 45.3 |
| 4 | John H. Savage (D) | 4,713 | 79.2 |
| | Rogs (W) | 1,239 | 20.8 |
| 5 | George W. Jones (D) | 6,736 | 100.0 |
| 6 | James H. Thomas (D) | 6,135 | 56.1 |
| | Buchanan (W) | 4,802 | 43.9 |
| 7 | Meredith P. Gentry (W) | 5,766 | 100.0 |
| 8 | Andrew Ewing (D) | 4,894 | 50.4 |
| | Cullom (W) | 4,816 | 49.6 |
| 9 | Isham G. Harris (D) | 5,433 | 55.8 |
| | Morris (W) | 4,302 | 44.2 |
| 10 | Frederick P. Stanton (D) | 6,250 | 51.9 |
| | Harris (W) | 5,799 | 48.1 |
| 11 | Christopher H. Williams (W) | 8,944 | 100.0 |

## TEXAS

| | Candidates | Votes | % |
|---|---|---|---|
| 1 | David S. Kaufman (D) | 8,944 | 96.0 |
| 2 | Volney E. Howard (D) | 4,120 | 58.1 |
| | Williamson | 2,976 | 41.9 |

## VERMONT

### Special Election

| | Candidates | Votes | % |
|---|---|---|---|
| 3 | James Meacham (W) | 6,645 | 54.5 |
| | Peck (EVA) | 4,716 | 38.7 |
| | Harrington (OPP&SC) | 835 | 6.9 |

## VIRGINIA

| | Candidates | Votes | % |
|---|---|---|---|
| 1 | John S. Millson (D) | 2,736 | 51.7 |
| | Wats (W) | 2,559 | 48.3 |
| 2 | Richard K. Meade (D) | | 100.0 |
| 3 | Thomas H. Averett (D) | 2,113 | 50.8 |
| | Fly (W) | 2,048 | 49.2 |
| 4 | Thomas S. Bocock (D) | 2,694 | 53.0 |
| | Irving (W) | 2,388 | 47.0 |
| 5 | Paulus Powell (D) | 3,136 | 50.9 |
| | Goggin (W) | 3,029 | 49.1 |

1. *In the second district, no candidate received the required majority. In the subsequent special election shown on this page, Nathan F. Dixon defeated Thurston.*

## VIRGINIA

| Candidates | Votes | % |
|---|---|---|
| 6 James A. Seddon (D) | 2,844 | *53.6* |
| Botts (W) | 2,458 | *46.4* |
| 7 Thomas H. Bayly (D) | 1,653 | *64.8* |
| Mallory (W) | 900 | *35.3* |
| 8 Alexander R. Holladay (D) | 2,163 | *51.0* |
| Forbes (W) | 2,078 | *49.0* |
| 9 Jeremiah Morton (D) | 2,798 | *54.0* |
| Pendleton (W) | 2,381 | *46.0* |

| Candidates | Votes | % |
|---|---|---|
| 10 Richard Parker (D) | 3,429 | *55.2* |
| Far (W) | 2,787 | *44.8* |
| 11 James McDowell (D) | | *100.0* |
| 12 Henry A. Edmundson (D) | 2,540 | *54.0* |
| Anderson (W) | 2,161 | *46.0* |
| 13 Fayette McMullen (D) | 4,421 | *67.2* |
| George (W) | 2,155 | *32.8* |
| 14 James M. H. Beale (D) | 4,312 | *51.3* |
| McComas (W) | 4,094 | *48.7* |

| Candidates | Votes | % |
|---|---|---|
| 15 Alexander Newman (D) | 2,926 | *53.0* |
| Russell (W) | 2,598 | *47.0* |

**Special Election**

| Candidates | Votes | % |
|---|---|---|
| 15 Thomas S. Haymond (W) | 2,873 | *50.6* |
| Thompson (D) | 2,807 | *49.4* |

---

# House Candidates Index

For an index of all House candidates listed in this section (pages 943-1326), see pages 1402-1501. Instructions for use of the House Candidates Index appear on page 1402.

# 1850 House Elections

## DELAWARE

| Candidates | Votes | % |
|---|---|---|
| AL George Read Riddle (D) | 6,055 | 48.7 |
| Rodney (W) | 5,926 | 47.7 |

## FLORIDA

| Candidates | Votes | % |
|---|---|---|
| AL Edward C. Cabell (W) | 4,531 | 52.8 |
| John Beard (D) | 4,050 | 47.2 |

## ILLINOIS

| | Candidates | Votes | % |
|---|---|---|---|
| 1 | William H. Bissell (D) | 12,841 | 100.0 |
| 2 | Willis Allen (D) | 5,763 | 54.5 |
| | Thomas G. C. Davis (W) | 4,816 | 45.5 |
| 3 | Orlando B. Ficklin (D) | 7,429 | 56.3 |
| | E. G. Ryan (W) | 5,739 | 43.5 |
| 4 | Richard S. Molony (D) | 11,231 | 48.9 |
| | Churchill Coffing (W) | 10,587 | 46.1 |
| 5 | William A. Richardson (D) | 8,099 | 53.0 |
| | Orville H. Browning (W) | 7,197 | 47.1 |
| 6 | Thompson Campbell (D) | 8,181 | 50.7 |
| | Martin P. Sweet (W) | 7,857 | 48.7 |
| 7 | Richard Yates (W) | 7,008 | 52.8 |
| | Thomas L. Harris (D) | 6,254 | 47.1 |

## IOWA

| | Candidates | Votes | % |
|---|---|---|---|
| 1 | Bernhart Henn (D) | 7,437 | 50.5 |
| | George G. Wright (W) | 6,985 | 47.4 |
| 2 | Lincoln Clark (D) | 5,745 | 54.0 |
| | William H. Henderson (W) | 4,725 | 44.4 |

### Special Election

| | | Votes | % |
|---|---|---|---|
| 1 | Daniel F. Miller (W) | 5,463 | 51.3 |
| | William Thompson (D) | 4,801 | 45.1 |

## MAINE

| | Candidates | Votes | % |
|---|---|---|---|
| 1 | Moses MacDonald (D) | 5,173 | 49.6 |
| | N. D. Appleton (W) | 4,683 | 44.9 |
| | M. Sweat (F SOIL) | 530 | 5.1 |
| 2 | John Appleton (D) | 5,943 | 50.1 |
| | William Pitt Fessenden (W FS) | 5,903 | 49.8 |
| 3 | Robert Goodenow (W) | 4,831 | 44.7 |
| | Lot M. Merrill (D) | 4,700 | 43.5 |
| | Seth May (F SOIL) | 1,272 | 11.8 |
| 4 | Charles Andrews (D) | 6,718 | 49.6 |
| | Isaac Reed (W) | 6,652 | 49.1 |
| 5 | Ephraim K. Smart (D) | 5,911 | 52.5 |
| | Theophilus Cushing (W) | 5,295 | 47.0 |
| 6 | Israel Washburn Jr (W) | 5,412 | 46.3 |
| | Strickland (D) | 3,696 | 31.6 |
| | Stetson (D) | 2,554 | 21.8 |
| 7 | Thomas J. D. Fuller (D) | 4,814 | 47.0 |
| | James S. Pike (W) | 4,629 | 45.2 |
| | S. C. Foster (F SOIL) | 716 | 7.0 |

## MASSACHUSETTS

| | Candidates | Votes | % |
|---|---|---|---|
| 1 | William Appleton (W) | 5,839 | 65.6 |
| | John T. Heard | 1,855 | 20.9 |
| | Benjamin B. Mufsey (F SOIL) | 1,167 | 13.1 |
| 2 | Robert Rantoul Jr (D) | 7,183 | 51.4 |
| | Charles W. Upham (W) | 6,089 | 43.6 |
| 3 | James H. Duncan (W) | 4,250 | 56.8 |
| | Alpheus R. Brown | 1,764 | 23.6 |
| | Thomas W. Higginson (F SOIL) | 1,255 | 16.8 |
| 4 | Benjamin Thompson (W) | 6,380 | 47.6 |
| | John G. Palfrey (F SOIL) | 6,293 | 47.0 |
| | Richard Frothingham Jr. | 717 | 5.4 |
| 5 | Charles Allen (F SOIL) | 4,819 | 51.1 |
| | Ira M. Barton (W) | 2,620 | 27.8 |
| | I. S. C. Knowlton | 1,990 | 21.1 |
| 6 | George T. Davis (W) | 4,877 | 51.8 |
| | Chester W. Chapin | 3,031 | 32.2 |
| | Samuel Williston | 1,460 | 15.5 |
| 7 | John Z. Goodrich (W) | 4,623 | 52.8 |
| | Henry W. Bishop | 4,056 | 46.3 |
| 8 | Horace Mann (F SOIL) | 6,697 | 50.3 |
| | Samuel H. Walley (W) | 4,301 | 32.3 |
| | Edgar H. Whittaker | 2,262 | 17.0 |
| 9 | Orin Fowler (F SOIL W) | 6,345 | 66.1 |
| | Edward P. Little (D) | 2,795 | 29.1 |
| 10 | Zeno Scudder (W) | 2,179 | 55.3 |
| | Charles B. H. Fessenden | 907 | 23.0 |
| | Simpson Hart (F SOIL) | 429 | 10.9 |
| | Daniel Fisher | 239 | 6.1 |

### Special Election

| | | Votes | % |
|---|---|---|---|
| 1 | Samuel A. Elliott (W) | 2,355 | 74.9 |
| | Charles Sumner (F SOIL) | 473 | 15.0 |
| | John T. Heard | 297 | 9.4 |

## MICHIGAN

| | Candidates | Votes | % |
|---|---|---|---|
| 1 | Ebenezer J. Penniman (W FS) | 10,766 | 54.7 |
| | Alexander W. Buel (D) | 8,914 | 45.3 |
| 2 | Charles E. Stuart (D) | 11,929 | 50.8 |
| | Joseph R. Williams (W FS) | 11,517 | 49.0 |
| 3 | James L. Conger (W FS) | 8,646 | 50.5 |
| | Charles C. Hascall (D) | 8,427 | 49.2 |

## MISSOURI

| | Candidates | Votes | % |
|---|---|---|---|
| 1 | John F. Darby (W) | 7,145 | 39.6 |
| | Rozier (BENTON D) | 5,600 | 31.0 |
| | Bowlin (A-BEN D) | 5,317 | 29.4 |
| 2 | Gilchrist Porter (W) | 6,889 | 52.9 |
| | Henderson (D) | 5,878 | 45.1 |
| 3 | John G. Miller (W) | 6,578 | 42.3 |
| | Green (A-BEN D) | 6,554 | 42.2 |
| | J. Miller (BENTON D) | 2,411 | 15.5 |
| 4 | Willard P. Hall (A-BEN D) | 5,606 | 37.5 |
| | Bowman (W) | 5,505 | 36.9 |
| | Gardenhire (BENTON D) | 3,826 | 25.6 |
| 5 | John S. Phelps (BENTON D) | 8,473 | 52.4 |
| | Woodson (W) | 5,667 | 35.0 |
| | Shields (A-BEN D) | 2,035 | 12.6 |

## NEW JERSEY

| | Candidates | Votes | % |
|---|---|---|---|
| 1 | Nathan T. Stratton (D) | 6,475 | 52.7 |
| | Whitney (W) | 5,824 | 47.4 |
| 2 | Charles Skelton (D) | 9,259 | 52.6 |
| | Richards (W) | 8,358 | 47.4 |
| 3 | Isaac Wildrick (D) | 9,097 | 66.9 |
| | Edsall (W) | 4,498 | 33.1 |
| 4 | George H. Brown (W) | 6,470 | 50.9 |
| | Vail (D) | 6,251 | 49.1 |
| 5 | Rodman M. Price (D) | 8,286 | 50.3 |
| | Ryerson (W) | 8,149 | 49.5 |

## NEW YORK

| | Candidates | Votes | % |
|---|---|---|---|
| 1 | John G. Floyd (D) | 4,125 | 53.0 |
| | Rose (W) | 3,661 | 47.0 |
| 2 | Obadiah Bowne (W) | 7,728 | 52.3 |
| | Bogardus (D) | 6,428 | 43.5 |
| 3 | Emanuel B. Hart (D) | 3,679 | 48.4 |
| | Rodman (W) | 2,164 | 28.5 |
| | Bowen (W) | 1,755 | 23.1 |
| 4 | J. H. Hobart Haws (W) | 4,155 | 48.8 |
| | Marsh (D) | 3,824 | 44.9 |
| | McGrath (D) | 541 | 6.4 |
| 5 | George Briggs (W) | 4,444 | 51.9 |
| | Arculars (D) | 4,114 | 48.1 |
| 6 | James Brooks (W) | 8,357 | 54.6 |
| | Cochran (D) | 6,724 | 44.0 |
| 7 | Abraham P. Stevens (D) | 4,851 | 52.6 |
| | Gurnee (W) | 4,372 | 47.4 |
| 8 | Gilbert Dean (D) | 6,218 | 51.1 |
| | Cruger (W) | 5,942 | 48.9 |
| 9 | William Murray (D) | 5,810 | 51.1 |
| | McKissock (W) | 5,563 | 48.9 |
| 10 | Marius Schoonmaker (W) | 7,851 | 52.4 |
| | Allaben (D) | 7,135 | 47.6 |
| 11 | Josiah Sutherland (D) | 6,672 | 52.9 |
| | Cowles (W) | 5,940 | 47.1 |
| 12 | David L. Seymour (D) | 5,811 | 51.0 |
| | Sage (W) | 5,594 | 49.1 |
| 13 | John L. Schoolcraft (W) | 7,032 | 51.0 |
| | Corning (D) | 6,746 | 49.0 |
| 14 | John H. Boyd (W) | 6,286 | 58.7 |
| | Thompson (D) | 4,415 | 41.3 |
| 15 | Joseph Russell (D) | 5,506 | 50.8 |
| | Tabor (W) | 5,324 | 49.2 |
| 16 | John Wells (W) | 8,428 | 53.1 |
| | Marvin (D) | 7,460 | 47.0 |
| 17 | Alexander H. Buel (D) | 6,685 | 52.5 |
| | Alexander (W) | 6,047 | 47.5 |
| 18 | Preston King (D) | 7,101 | 59.2 |
| | Grant (W) | 4,893 | 40.8 |
| 19 | Willard Ives (D) | 5,477 | 52.0 |
| | Clarke (W) | 5,058 | 48.0 |
| 20 | Timothy Jenkins (D) | 7,828 | 50.4 |
| | Matteson (W) | 7,711 | 49.6 |
| 21 | William Snow (D) | 7,664 | 50.2 |
| | Chase (W) | 7,608 | 49.8 |
| 22 | Henry Bennett (W) | 9,170 | 53.0 |
| | Taylor (D) | 8,131 | 47.0 |
| 23 | Leander Babcock (D) | 8,423 | 54.1 |
| | Williams (W) | 7,136 | 45.9 |
| 24 | Daniel T. Jones (D) | 6,186 | 51.7 |
| | Smith (W) | 5,419 | 45.3 |
| 25 | Thomas Y. Howe Jr (D) | 7,037 | 50.1 |
| | Morgan (W) | 7,011 | 49.9 |
| 26 | Henry S. Walbridge (W) | 7,700 | 50.7 |
| | Halsey (D) | 7,497 | 49.3 |
| 27 | William A. Sackett (W) | 6,305 | 52.0 |
| | Smith (D) | 5,814 | 48.0 |
| 28 | Abraham M. Schermerhorn (W) | 6,036 | 51.8 |
| | Buchan (D) | 5,623 | 48.2 |
| 29 | Jerediah Horsford (W) | 7,727 | 57.9 |
| | Wadsworth (D) | 5,609 | 42.1 |
| 30 | Reuben Robie (D) | 8,368 | 52.6 |
| | Church (W) | 7,538 | 47.4 |
| 31 | Frederick S. Martin (W) | 7,210 | 52.4 |
| | Waite (D) | 6,549 | 47.6 |
| 32 | Soloman G. Haven (W) | 6,613 | 55.2 |
| | Stevens (D) | 5,365 | 44.8 |
| 33 | Augustus P. Hascall (W) | 5,715 | 60.7 |
| | Sprague (D) | 3,699 | 39.3 |
| 34 | Lorenzo Burrows (W) | 5,753 | 51.9 |
| | Piper (D) | 5,332 | 48.1 |

## OHIO

| | Candidates | Votes | % |
|---|---|---|---|
| 1 | David T. Disney (D) | 16,640 | 99.3 |
| 2 | Lewis D. Campbell (W) | 5,992 | 53.2 |
| | Elijah Vance (D) | 5,279 | 46.8 |
| 3 | Hiram Bell (W) | 8,014 | 53.1 |
| | George B. Holt (D) | 7,088 | 46.9 |
| 4 | Benjamin Stanton (W) | 8,110 | 60.0 |
| | John A. Corwin (D) | 5,181 | 38.3 |
| 5 | Alfred P. Edgerton (D) | 7,684 | 59.2 |
| | James W. Riley (W) | 5,281 | 40.7 |
| 6 | Frederick W. Green (D) | 7,224 | 91.8 |
| | John C. Spink | 609 | 7.7 |

## OHIO

| | Candidates | Votes | % |
|---|---|---|---|
| 7 | Nelson Barrere (W) | 5,515 | 51.4 |
| | Enoch M. Ellsberry (D) | 5,219 | 48.6 |
| 8 | John L. Taylor (W) | 5,850 | 51.9 |
| | Joseph McCormick (D) | 5,321 | 47.2 |
| 9 | Edson B. Olds (D) | 6,283 | 50.7 |
| | P. Van Trump (W) | 6,110 | 49.3 |
| 10 | Charles Sweetser (D) | 8,579 | 50.4 |
| | Samuel Galloway (W) | 8,442 | 49.6 |
| 11 | George H. Busby (D) | 7,615 | 58.6 |
| | Thomas H. Ford (W) | 5,037 | 38.8 |
| 12 | John Welch (W) | 5,261 | 54.9 |
| | Hiram G. Daniels (D) | 4,037 | 42.1 |
| 13 | James M. Gaylord (D) | 5,744 | 49.3 |
| | William E. Finck (W) | 5,698 | 48.9 |
| 14 | Alexander Harper (W) | 5,108 | 50.2 |
| | Thomas Maxfield (D) | 4,750 | 46.7 |
| 15 | William F. Hunter (W) | 5,751 | 51.1 |
| | Thomas L. Jewett (D) | 5,506 | 48.9 |
| 16 | John Johnson (W) | 5,458 | 51.4 |
| | Moses Hoagland (D) | 5,156 | 48.6 |
| 17 | Joseph Cable (D) | 6,685 | 55.8 |
| | Matthew Roberts (W) | 5,303 | 44.2 |
| 18 | David K. Carter (D) | 5,754 | 62.3 |
| | John Brown (W) | 3,477 | 37.7 |
| 19 | Eben Newton (W) | 8,277 | 56.5 |
| | Luther Day (D) | 6,382 | 43.5 |
| 20 | Joshua R. Giddings (F SOIL W) | 6,896 | 77.8 |
| | Irad Kelley | 1,716 | 19.4 |
| 21 | Norton S. Townshend (D) | 6,677 | 47.6 |
| | Samuel T. Worcester (W) | 6,230 | 44.4 |
| | Joseph Root (F SOIL) | 1,120 | 8.0 |

## PENNSYLVANIA

| | Candidates | Votes | % |
|---|---|---|---|
| 1 | Thomas B. Florence (D) | 5,352 | 52.9 |
| | Levin (AM) | 4,164 | 41.1 |
| | Savery (W) | 609 | 6.0 |
| 2 | Joseph R. Chandler (W) | 5,912 | 60.7 |
| | Martin (D) | 3,714 | 38.1 |
| 3 | Henry D. Moore (W) | 5,604 | 51.2 |
| | Lundy (D) | 5,333 | 48.8 |

| | Candidates | Votes | % |
|---|---|---|---|
| 4 | John Robbins Jr (D) | 6,173 | 57.6 |
| | Littell (W) | 4,554 | 42.5 |
| 5 | John McNair (D) | 5,925 | 53.3 |
| | Freedley (W) | 5,199 | 46.7 |
| 6 | Thomas Ross (D) | 7,568 | 50.8 |
| | Taylor (W) | 7,328 | 49.2 |
| 7 | John A. Morrison (D) | 4,671 | 50.4 |
| | Dickey (W) | 4,601 | 49.6 |
| 8 | Thaddeus Stevens (W) | 5,701 | 58.4 |
| | Unindentified Candidate (D) | 4,069 | 41.7 |
| 9 | J. Glancey Jones (D) | 5,377 | 52.6 |
| | Keim (W) | 4,847 | 47.4 |
| 10 | Milo M. Dimmick (D) | 6,400 | 54.6 |
| | Henry M. Fuller (W) | 6,216 | 50.2 |
| 11 | Wright (D) | 6,157 | 49.8 |
| 12 | Galusha A. Grow (D) | 6,880 | 54.6 |
| | Adams (W) | 5,730 | 45.4 |
| 13 | James Gamble (D) | 6,832 | 52.5 |
| | Armstrong (W) | 6,172 | 47.5 |
| 14 | Thomas M. Bibighaus (W) | 7,048 | 53.6 |
| | Boas (W) | 6,095 | 46.4 |
| 15 | William H. Kurtz (D) | 5,765 | 51.8 |
| | Smyser (W) | 5,372 | 48.2 |
| 16 | James X. McLanahan (D) | 7,276 | 52.0 |
| | Bard (W) | 6,705 | 48.0 |
| 17 | Andrew Parker (D) | 7,270 | 51.4 |
| | McCulloch (W) | 6,863 | 48.6 |
| 18 | John L. Dawson (D) | 6,404 | 51.1 |
| | Ogle (W) | 6,135 | 48.9 |
| 19 | Joseph H. Kuhns (W) | 5,745 | 42.4 |
| | Unindentified Candidate (D) | 4,688 | 34.6 |
| | McKinney (D) | 1,716 | 12.7 |
| | McDonald (D) | 1,391 | 10.3 |
| 20 | John Allison (W) | 5,596 | 50.5 |
| | Power (D) | 5,489 | 49.5 |
| 21 | Thomas M. Howe (W) | 5,406 | 51.6 |
| | Salisbery (D) | 4,247 | 40.5 |
| | Cullen (NAM) | 539 | 5.1 |
| 22 | John W. Howe (W) | 6,284 | 51.7 |
| | Shatk (D) | 5,882 | 48.4 |
| 23 | Carlton B. Curtis (D) | 6,522 | 50.4 |
| | Walker (W) | 6,416 | 49.6 |
| 24 | Alfred Gilmore (D) | 6,513 | 53.6 |
| | Taylor (W) | 5,644 | 46.4 |

**Special Election**

| | Candidates | Votes | % |
|---|---|---|---|
| 15 | Joel B. Danner (D) | 5,970 | 53.5 |
| | W. McIlwain (W) | 5,193 | 46.5 |

## SOUTH CAROLINA

| | Candidates | Votes | % |
|---|---|---|---|
| 1 | Daniel Wallace (W) | | 100.0 |
| 2 | James L. Orr (D) | | 100.0 |
| 3 | Joseph A. Woodward (D) | | 100.0 |
| 4 | John McQueen (D) | | 100.0 |
| 5 | Armistead Burt (D) | | 100.0 |
| 6 | William Aiken (D) | 1,928 | 59.2 |
| | Isaac E. Holmes (D) | 1,097 | 33.7 |
| | J. Smith Rhett | 232 | 7.1 |
| 7 | William F. Colcock (D) | | 100.0 |

## VERMONT

| | Candidates | Votes | % |
|---|---|---|---|
| 1 | A. L. Miner (W) | 4,369 | 37.5 |
| | A. P. Lyman (D) | 4,126 | 35.4 |
| | D. Roberts Jr (D) | 2,689 | 23.1 |
| 2 | William Hebard (W) | 5,652 | 55.2 |
| | Jefferson P. Kidder (D) | 4,384 | 42.8 |
| 3 | James Meacham (W) | 5,945 | 56.5 |
| | Beardsley (D) | 2,960 | 28.1 |
| | Harrington (OPP) | 1,521 | 14.5 |
| 4 | Thomas Bartlett Jr (D) | 7,009 | 54.9 |
| | B. N. Davis (W) | 5,014 | 39.2 |
| | Willard (OPP) | 640 | 5.0 |

## WISCONSIN

| | Candidates | Votes | % |
|---|---|---|---|
| 1 | Charles Durkee (F SOIL) | 7,512 | 57.4 |
| | Elme (D) | 5,574 | 42.6 |
| 2 | Ben C. Eastman (D) | 7,262 | 55.4 |
| | Cole (W) | 5,852 | 44.6 |
| 3 | James Duane Doty (F SOIL) | 11,159 | 67.5 |
| | Hobt (D) | 5,372 | 32.5 |

# 1851 House Elections

## ALABAMA

| | Candidates | Votes | % |
|---|---|---|---|
| 1 | John Bragg (SO RTS D) | 5,372 | 58.3 |
| | C. C. Langdon (UNT) | 3,849 | 41.7 |
| 2 | James Abercrombie (UN W) | 7,598 | 56.2 |
| | John Cochran (SEC) | 5,911 | 43.8 |
| 3 | Sampson W. Harris (SEC D) | 4,967 | 53.1 |
| | W. S. Mudd (UN W) | 4,385 | 46.9 |
| 4 | William R. Smith (UNT) | 4,173 | 50.4 |
| | John Erwin (SO RTS D) | 4,114 | 49.6 |
| 5 | George S. Houston (UN D) | ✔ | |
| | D. Hubbard (SEC D) | | |
| 6 | Williamson R. W. Cobb (UN D) | 3,708 | 74.0 |
| | Robert Murphy (SO RTS D) | 1,303 | 26.0 |
| 7 | Alexander White (UN W) | 5,744 | 51.7 |
| | S. F. Rice (SEC D) | 5,371 | 48.3 |

## ARKANSAS

| | Candidates | Votes | % |
|---|---|---|---|
| AL | Robert W. Johnson (D) | 11,970 | 57.4 |
| | Preston (W) | 8,877 | 42.6 |

## CALIFORNIA

| | Candidates | Votes | % |
|---|---|---|---|
| AL | Edward C. Marshall (D) | 24,469 ✔ | |
| | Joseph W. McCorkle (D) | 24,315 ✔ | |
| | E. J. C. Kewew (W) | 21,460 | |
| | B. J. Moore (W) | 20,224 | |

## CONNECTICUT

| | Candidates | Votes | % |
|---|---|---|---|
| 1 | Charles Chapman (W) | 7,805 | 48.8 |
| | Loren P. Waldo (D) | 7,759 | 48.5 |
| 2 | Colin M. Ingersoll (D) | 7,331 | 50.1 |
| | Babcock (W) | 6,786 | 46.3 |
| 3 | Chauncey F. Cleveland (D) | 6,261 | 51.0 |
| | Ames (W) | 5,810 | 47.3 |
| 4 | Origen S. Seymour (D) | 8,633 | 49.3 |
| | Butler (W) | 8,485 | 48.4 |

## GEORGIA

| | Candidates | Votes | % |
|---|---|---|---|
| 1 | Joseph W. Jackson (SOR W) | 4,279 | 51.6 |
| | Hopkins (UN) | 4,011 | 48.4 |
| 2 | James Johnson (UN) | 8,107 | 53.7 |
| | Bening (SOR W) | 6,985 | 46.3 |
| 3 | David J. Bailey (SOR W) | 6,011 | 50.7 |
| | Chappel (UN) | 5,853 | 49.3 |
| 4 | Charles Murphey (UN) | 7,750 | 58.1 |
| | Stell (SOR W) | 5,601 | 42.0 |
| 5 | Elijah W. Chastain (UN) | 13,882 | 65.0 |
| | Stiles (SOR W) | 7,481 | 35.0 |
| 6 | Junius Hillyer (UN) | 6,937 | 71.1 |
| | Jones (SOR W) | 2,819 | 28.9 |
| 7 | Alexander H. Stephens (UN) | 4,744 | 70.8 |
| | Lewis (SOR W) | 1,955 | 29.2 |
| 8 | Robert Toombs (UN) | 4,704 | 65.0 |
| | McMillan (SOR W) | 2,538 | 35.1 |

## INDIANA

| | Candidates | Votes | % |
|---|---|---|---|
| 1 | James Lockhart (D) | 8,173 | 51.0 |
| | Lemuel Debruler (W) | 7,855 | 49.0 |
| 2 | Cyrus L. Dunham (D) | 8,097 | 53.2 |
| | Roger Martin (W) | 7,125 | 46.8 |
| 3 | John L. Robinson (D) | 8,242 | 50.2 |
| | Johnson Watts (W) | 8,173 | 49.8 |
| 4 | Samuel W. Parker (W) | 5,102 | 52.9 |
| | George W. Julian (F SOIL) | 4,540 | 47.1 |
| 5 | Thomas A. Hendricks (D) | 9,062 | 62.1 |
| | William P. Rush (W) | 5,543 | 38.0 |
| 6 | Willis A. Gorman (D) | 9,474 | 66.9 |
| | Eli P. Farmer (W) | 4,693 | 33.1 |
| 7 | John G. Davis (D) | 6,076 | 51.1 |
| | Edward W. McGaughey (W) | 5,814 | 48.9 |

| | Candidates | Votes | % |
|---|---|---|---|
| 8 | Daniel Mace (D) | 7,552 | 50.8 |
| | David Brier (W) | 7,294 | 49.0 |
| 9 | Graham N. Fitch (D) | 9,356 | 50.6 |
| | Schuyler Colfax (W) | 9,118 | 49.4 |
| 10 | Samuel Brenton (W FS) | 8,776 | 50.9 |
| | James W. Borden (D) | 8,483 | 49.2 |

## KENTUCKY

| | Candidates | Votes | % |
|---|---|---|---|
| 1 | Linn Boyd (D) | 6,638 | 57.5 |
| | H. M. McCarty (W) | 3,446 | 29.9 |
| | Hiram McElroy | 1,460 | 12.7 |
| 2 | Benjamin E. Grey (W) | 5,751 | 63.5 |
| | Jeff Jennings | 3,301 | 36.5 |
| 3 | Presley U. Ewing (W) | 5,405 | 52.1 |
| | Beverly L. Clarke | 4,978 | 47.9 |
| 4 | William T. Ward (W) | 4,582 | 100.0 |
| 5 | James W. Stone (D) | 5,843 | 51.6 |
| | C. S. Hill | 5,480 | 48.4 |
| 6 | Addison White (W) | 5,846 | 56.6 |
| | Theodore T. Garrard | 4,130 | 40.0 |
| 7 | Humphrey Marshall (W) | 6,333 | 50.5 |
| | David Merriwether | 6,216 | 49.5 |
| 8 | John C. Breckinridge (D) | 5,671 | 52.5 |
| | Leslie Combs (W) | 5,141 | 47.6 |
| 9 | John C. Mason (D) | 5,929 | 72.1 |
| | Samuel Montgomery (W) | 2,236 | 27.2 |
| 10 | Richard Stanton (D) | 7,649 | 53.6 |
| | William C. Marshall (W) | 6,622 | 46.4 |

## LOUISIANA

| | Candidates | Votes | % |
|---|---|---|---|
| 1 | Louis St.Martin (D) | 3,199 | 53.7 |
| | Hagan (W) | 2,763 | 46.3 |
| 2 | J. Aristide Landry (W) | 5,933 | 56.9 |
| | Vanwinder (D) | 4,500 | 43.1 |
| 3 | Alexander G. Penn (D) | 4,740 | 56.9 |
| | Upton (W) | 3,590 | 43.1 |
| 4 | John Moore (W) | 5,852 | 52.9 |
| | Isaac E. Morse (D) | 5,214 | 47.1 |

## MARYLAND

| | Candidates | Votes | % |
|---|---|---|---|
| 1 | Richard J. Bowie (W) | ✔ | |
| | T. F. Bowie (IW) | | |
| 2 | William T. Hamilton (D) | 6,863 | 50.9 |
| | Roman (W) | 6,626 | 49.1 |
| 3 | Edward Hammond (D) | 5,434 | 64.7 |
| | Lynch (I) | 2,968 | 35.3 |
| 4 | Thomas Yates Walsh (W) | 6,683 | 50.9 |
| | William P. Whyte (D) | 6,453 | 49.1 |
| 5 | Alexander Evans (W) | 4,992 | 52.7 |
| | McCullough | 4,486 | 47.3 |
| 6 | Joseph S. Cottman (IW) | ✔ | |
| | Henry (W) | | |

## MISSISSIPPI

| | Candidates | Votes | % |
|---|---|---|---|
| 1 | Benjamin D. Nabers (UN) | 9,659 | 57.5 |
| | Thompson (SR) | 7,155 | 42.6 |
| 2 | John A. Wilcox (UN) | 6,927 | 52.8 |
| | Unidentified Candidate (SR) | 6,201 | 47.2 |
| 3 | John D. Freeman (UN) | 7,774 | 51.8 |
| | Unidentified Candidate (SR) | 7,241 | 48.2 |
| 4 | Albert G. Brown (SR) | 7,010 | 57.8 |
| | Dawson (UN) | 5,119 | 42.2 |

## NEW HAMPSHIRE

| | Candidates | Votes | % |
|---|---|---|---|
| 1 | Amos Tuck (W FS) | 7,691 | 51.3 |
| | Kittredge (D) | 7,304 | 48.7 |
| 2 | Charles H. Peaslee (D) | 7,170 | 55.0 |
| | Colby (W) | 3,803 | 29.2 |
| | Fowler (F SOIL) | 2,060 | 15.8 |

| | Candidates | Votes | % |
|---|---|---|---|
| 3 | Jared Perkins (W FS) | 8,682 | 52.9 |
| | Morrison (D) | 7,741 | 47.1 |
| 4 | Harry Hibbard (D) | 5,125 | 61.1 |
| | Kittredge (W) | 2,248 | 26.8 |
| | White (F SOIL) | 1,018 | 12.1 |

## NORTH CAROLINA

| | Candidates | Votes | % |
|---|---|---|---|
| 1 | Thomas L. Clingman (SEC W) | 6,600 | 70.1 |
| | Burgess S. Gaither (W) | 2,819 | 29.9 |
| 2 | Joseph P. Caldwell (W) | ✔ | |
| 3 | Alfred Dockery (W) | 5,344 | 55.6 |
| | Green W. Caldwell (D) | 4,260 | 44.4 |
| 4 | James T. Morehead (W) | 2,512 | 86.4 |
| 5 | Abraham W. Venable (SEC D) | 4,057 | 60.0 |
| | Calvin Graves (UN D) | 2,710 | 40.1 |
| 6 | John R. J. Daniel (SEC D) | 2,815 | 72.1 |
| | Henry W. Miller (W) | 928 | 23.8 |
| 7 | William S. Ashe (D) | ✔ | |
| 8 | Edward Stanly (W) | 5,236 | 51.3 |
| | Thomas Ruffin (SEC D) | 4,966 | 48.7 |
| 9 | David Outlaw (W) | 2,868 | 61.6 |
| | William F. Martin (D) | 1,759 | 37.8 |

## PENNSYLVANIA

### Special Election

| | Candidates | Votes | % |
|---|---|---|---|
| 11 | John Brisbin (D) | 3,625 | 52.5 |
| | Dana (W) | 3,283 | 47.5 |

## RHODE ISLAND

| | Candidates | Votes | % |
|---|---|---|---|
| 1 | George G. King (W) | 3,486 | 51.2 |
| | Welcome B. Sayles (D) | 3,270 | 48.0 |
| 2 | Benjamin B. Thurston (D) | 3,335 | 59.6 |
| | Charles Jackson (W) | 2,150 | 38.4 |

## TENNESSEE

| | Candidates | Votes | % |
|---|---|---|---|
| 1 | Andrew Johnson (D) | 6,538 | 57.4 |
| | Hayns (W) | 4,844 | 42.6 |
| 2 | Albert G. Watkins (W) | 9,592 | 81.9 |
| | Hurley (D) | 2,125 | 18.1 |
| 3 | William M. Churchwell (D) | 6,674 | 50.1 |
| | Anderson (W) | 6,658 | 49.9 |
| 4 | John H. Savage (D) | 5,816 | 57.2 |
| | Goodpasture (W) | 4,352 | 42.8 |
| 5 | George W. Jones (D) | 5,937 | 100.0 |
| 6 | William H. Polk (W) | 4,228 | 53.5 |
| | James H. Thomas (D) | 3,672 | 46.5 |
| 7 | Meredith P. Gentry (W) | 2,572 | 100.0 |
| 8 | William Cullom (W) | 5,196 | 55.6 |
| | South (D) | 4,145 | 44.4 |
| 9 | Isham G. Harris (D) | 3,654 | 56.2 |
| | Hornberger (W) | 2,852 | 43.8 |
| 10 | Frederick P. Stanton (D) | 6,495 | 51.8 |
| | Coleman (W) | 6,042 | 48.2 |
| 11 | Christopher H. Williams (W) | 10,693 | 100.0 |

## TEXAS

| | Candidates | Votes | % |
|---|---|---|---|
| 1 | Richardson Scurry (D) | 6,758 | 53.9 |
| | William B. Ochiltree (W) | 4,009 | 32.0 |
| | B. R. Wallace | 1,126 | 9.0 |
| 2 | Volney E. Howard (D) | 6,724 | 48.7 |
| | G. K. Lewis | 2,904 | 21.0 |
| | H. McLeod | 2,798 | 20.3 |
| | H. N. Patter | 1,200 | 8.7 |

## VIRGINIA

| | Candidates | Votes | % |
|---|---|---|---|
| 1 | John S. Millson (D) | 2,271 | 59.6 |
| | Cowper (W) | 1,541 | 40.4 |

## VIRGINIA

| | Candidates | Votes | % |
|---|---|---|---|
| 2 | Richard K. Meade (D) | | 100.0 |
| 3 | Thomas H. Averett (D) | 1,365 | 57.4 |
| | Flournoy (W) | 1,014 | 42.6 |
| 4 | Thomas S. Bocock (D) | 1,596 | 61.2 |
| | Bolling (W) | 1,014 | 38.9 |
| 5 | Paulus Powell (D) | 2,857 | 51.5 |
| | Goggin (W) | 2,695 | 48.5 |

| | Candidates | Votes | % |
|---|---|---|---|
| 6 | John S. Caskie (D) | 2,960 | 54.5 |
| | Botts (W) | 2,472 | 45.5 |
| 7 | Thomas H. Bayly (D) | | 100.0 |
| 8 | Alexander R. Holladay (D) | | 100.0 |
| 9 | James F. Strother (W) | 2,367 | 55.9 |
| | Mton (D) | 1,868 | 44.1 |
| 10 | Charles J. Faulkner (W) | 2,351 | 53.7 |
| | Bedinger (D) | 2,031 | 46.4 |

| | Candidates | Votes | % |
|---|---|---|---|
| 11 | John Letcher (D) | | 100.0 |
| 12 | Henry A. Edmundson (D) | | 100.0 |
| 13 | Fayette McMullen (D) | | 100.0 |
| 14 | James M. H. Beale (D) | 4,012 | 58.8 |
| | Smith (W) | 2,813 | 41.2 |
| 15 | George W. Thompson (D) | 4,251 | 52.5 |
| | Haymond (W) | 3,850 | 47.5 |

# 1852 House Elections

## ARKANSAS

| | Candidates | Votes | % |
|---|---|---|---|
| 1 | Alfred B. Greenwood (D) | 7,939 | 100.0 |
| 2 | Edward A. Warren (D) | 3,748 | 53.2 |
| | Unidentified Candidate (W) | 3,301 | 46.8 |

## CALIFORNIA

| | | Votes | % |
|---|---|---|---|
| AL | Milton S. Latham (D) | 39,881 ✓ | |
| | James A. McDougall (D) | 39,387 ✓ | |
| | P. L. Edwards (W) | 34,933 | |
| | G. B. Tingley (W) | 34,299 | |

## DELAWARE

| | | Votes | % |
|---|---|---|---|
| AL | George Read Riddle (D) | 6,692 | 50.2 |
| | John W. Houston (W) | 6,630 | 49.8 |

## FLORIDA

| | | Votes | % |
|---|---|---|---|
| AL | Augustus E. Maxwell (D) | 4,637 | 50.3 |
| | Cabell (W) | 4,587 | 49.7 |

## ILLINOIS

| | | Votes | % |
|---|---|---|---|
| 1 | Elihu B. Washburne (W) | 7,392 | 43.9 |
| | Thompson Campbell (D) | 7,106 | 42.2 |
| | Newman Campbell (F SOIL) | 2,245 | 13.3 |
| 2 | John Wentworth (D) | 7,538 | 46.7 |
| | Cyrus Aldrich (W) | 6,437 | 39.9 |
| | James H. Collins (F SOIL) | 2,149 | 13.3 |
| 3 | Jesse O. Norton (W) | 8,268 | 46.0 |
| | William Reddick (D) | 8,092 | 45.0 |
| | J. H. Bryant (F SOIL) | 1,603 | 8.9 |
| 4 | James Knox (W) | 9,871 | 47.4 |
| | Lewis W. Rop (D) | 9,684 | 46.5 |
| | L. W. Curtis (F SOIL) | 1,290 | 6.2 |
| 5 | William A. Richardson (D) | 9,018 | 51.6 |
| | O. H. Browning (W) | 8,397 | 48.1 |
| 6 | Richard Yates (W) | 10,105 | 51.1 |
| | John Calhoun (D) | 9,675 | 48.9 |
| 7 | James C. Allen (D) | 8,283 | 54.1 |
| | Charles H. Constable (W) | 7,005 | 45.8 |
| 8 | William H. Bissell (ID) | 5,937 | 39.8 |
| | Joseph Gillespie (W) | 4,683 | 31.4 |
| | T. B. Fouke (D) | 4,301 | 28.8 |
| 9 | Willis Allen (D) | 12,100 | 98.5 |

## INDIANA

| | | Votes | % |
|---|---|---|---|
| 1 | Smith Miller (D) | 9,007 | 59.0 |
| | Kea (W) | 6,252 | 41.0 |
| 2 | William H. English (D) | 8,654 | 55.0 |
| | Fergason (W) | 7,094 | 45.1 |
| 3 | Cyrus L. Dunham (D) | 8,911 | 52.8 |
| | Marshall (W) | 7,980 | 47.2 |
| 4 | James H. Lane (D) | 8,783 | 53.0 |
| | Farquhar (W) | 7,789 | 47.0 |
| 5 | Samuel W. Parker (W) | 7,181 | 53.9 |
| | Grose (W) | 6,153 | 46.2 |
| 6 | Thomas A. Hendricks (D) | 8,240 | 53.6 |
| | Bradley (W) | 7,135 | 46.4 |
| 7 | John G. Davis (D) | 8,607 | 56.3 |
| | Barbour (W) | 6,685 | 43.7 |
| 8 | Daniel Mace (D) | 8,740 | 54.4 |
| | Gregory (W) | 7,337 | 45.6 |
| 9 | Norman Eddy (D) | 8,038 | 53.7 |
| | Biddle (W) | 6,930 | 46.3 |
| 10 | Ebenezer M. Chamberlain (D) | 6,875 | 53.5 |
| | Brenton (W) | 5,966 | 46.5 |
| 11 | Andrew J. Harlan (D) | 7,779 | 54.1 |
| | Wallace (W) | 6,608 | 45.9 |

## IOWA

| | Candidates | Votes | % |
|---|---|---|---|
| 1 | Bernhart Henn (D) | 9,709 | 55.2 |
| | P. Veile (W) | 7,874 | 44.8 |
| 2 | John P. Cook (W) | 7,777 | 52.2 |
| | L. Clark (D) | 7,114 | 47.8 |

## KENTUCKY

### Special Election

| | | Votes | % |
|---|---|---|---|
| 7 | William Preston (W) | 6,560 | 57.5 |
| | Calvin Sanders (D) | 4,841 | 42.5 |

## MAINE

| | | Votes | % |
|---|---|---|---|
| 1 | Moses MacDonald (D) | 9,218 | 57.8 |
| | Appleton (W) | 5,333 | 33.4 |
| | Fessenden (F SOIL) | 1,358 | 8.5 |
| 2 | Samuel Mayall (D) | 9,917 | 52.6 |
| | Gilman (W) | 7,932 | 42.0 |
| 3 | E. Wilder Farley (W) | 5,255 | 36.4 |
| | Kimball (D) | 4,724 | 32.7 |
| | Smith (D) | 3,874 | 26.8 |
| 4 | Samuel P. Benson (W) | 8,708 | 54.4 |
| | Porter (D) | 5,433 | 33.9 |
| | May (F SOIL) | 1,580 | 9.9 |
| 5 | Israel Washburn Jr (W) | 8,227 | 51.1 |
| | Strickland (D) | 4,376 | 27.2 |
| | Waterhouse (D) | 3,444 | 21.4 |
| 6 | Thomas J. D. Fuller (D) | 6,283 | 52.6 |
| | Robinson (W) | 5,280 | 44.2 |

## MASSACHUSETTS

| | | Votes | % |
|---|---|---|---|
| 1 | Zeno Scudder (W) | 4,016 | 61.3 |
| | A. H. Howland | 2,368 | 36.2 |
| 2 | Samuel L. Crocker (W) | 3,599 | 45.8 |
| | Geishom Weston (F SOIL) | 3,455 | 44.0 |
| | M. Ide (D) | 738 | 9.4 |
| 3 | J. Wiley Edmands (W) | 3,416 | 48.5 |
| | Charles F. Adams (F SOIL) | 2,978 | 42.3 |
| | Arthur W. Austin (D) | 471 | 6.7 |
| 4 | Samuel H. Walley (W) | 4,290 | 60.5 |
| | Levi A. Dowley (D) | 1,745 | 24.6 |
| | Charles M. Ellis (F SOIL) | 1,028 | 14.5 |
| 5 | William Appleton (W) | 4,672 | 55.7 |
| | Adam W. Thasler Jr. (D) | 2,081 | 24.8 |
| | Anson Burlingame (F SOIL) | 1,550 | 18.5 |
| 6 | Charles W. Upham (W) | 4,265 | 46.6 |
| | George Hood (F SOIL) | 4,096 | 44.8 |
| | Nathaniel J. Lord | 532 | 5.8 |
| 7 | Nathaniel P. Banks (D) | 4,605 | 50.1 |
| | Luther V. Bell (W) | 4,300 | 46.8 |
| 8 | Tappan Wentworth (W) | 4,411 | 45.9 |
| | Henry Wilson (F SOIL) | 4,319 | 44.9 |
| | Benjamin F. Butler (D) | 481 | 5.0 |
| 9 | Alexander De Witt (F SOIL) | 4,039 | 41.3 |
| | Isaac Davis (D) | 2,925 | 29.9 |
| | Ira M. Barton (W) | 2,796 | 28.6 |
| 10 | Edward Dickinson (W) | 4,160 | 56.9 |
| | Samuel F. Cutler (D) | 1,625 | 22.2 |
| | Eustus Hopkins (F SOIL) | 1,507 | 20.6 |
| 11 | John Z. Goodrich (W) | 5,579 | 51.9 |
| | Whiting Griswold (D) | 4,842 | 45.1 |

### Special Elections

| | | Votes | % |
|---|---|---|---|
| 2 | Francis Fay (W) | 4,989 | 47.2 |
| | George Hood (F SOIL) | 4,821 | 45.6 |
| 4 | Lorenzo Labine (W) | 4,620 | 50.9 |
| | John A. Bolles (F SOIL) | 4,055 | 44.7 |
| 9 | Edward P. Little (D) | 3,711 | 50.4 |
| | Jacob H. Loud (W) | 3,595 | 48.8 |

## MICHIGAN

| | Candidates | Votes | % |
|---|---|---|---|
| 1 | David Stuart (D) | 10,127 | 50.4 |
| | William A. Howard (W) | 9,370 | 46.6 |
| 2 | David A. Noble (D) | 10,024 | 51.7 |
| | Joseph R. Williams (W FS) | 9,367 | 48.3 |
| 3 | Samuel Clark (D) | 10,765 | 49.2 |
| | Henry R. Williams (W) | 9,969 | 45.6 |
| 4 | Hestor L. Stevens (D) | 10,746 | 51.8 |
| | George Bradley (W) | 8,948 | 43.1 |
| | Ephraim Calkins (F SOIL) | 1,048 | 5.1 |

## MISSOURI[1]

| | | Votes | % |
|---|---|---|---|
| 1 | Thomas H. Benton (BENTON D) | 8,437 | 45.3 |
| | Car (W) | 7,595 | 40.7 |
| | Bogy (A-BEN D) | 2,615 | 14.0 |
| 2 | Alfred W. Lamb (D) | 7,007 | 53.0 |
| | Por (W) | 6,224 | 47.0 |
| 3 | John G. Miller (W) | 8,297 | 51.3 |
| | Green (D) | 7,869 | 48.7 |
| 4 | Mordecai Oliver (W) | 7,612 | 46.7 |
| | Unidentified Candidate (A-BEN D) | 4,452 | 27.3 |
| | King (BENTON D) | 4,243 | 26.0 |
| 5 | John S. Phelps (D) | 11,392 | 67.6 |
| | Price (W) | 5,458 | 32.4 |

## NEW JERSEY

| | | Votes | % |
|---|---|---|---|
| 1 | Nathan T. Stratton (D) | 7,185 | 51.3 |
| | Boyle (W) | 6,816 | 48.7 |
| 2 | Charles Skelton (D) | 10,229 | 52.6 |
| | Brown (W) | 9,238 | 47.5 |
| 3 | Samuel Lilly (D) | 10,193 | 55.1 |
| | Brown (W) | 8,315 | 44.9 |
| 4 | George Vail (D) | 9,247 | 59.6 |
| | Coursen (W) | 6,265 | 40.4 |
| 5 | Alexander C. M. Pennington (W) | 7,636 | 50.6 |
| | Price (D) | 7,469 | 49.5 |

## NEW YORK

| | | Votes | % |
|---|---|---|---|
| 1 | James Maurice (D) | 7,801 | 53.7 |
| | King (W) | 6,136 | 42.3 |
| 2 | Thomas W. Cumming (D) | 7,228 | 51.5 |
| | Sanford (W) | 6,789 | 48.4 |
| 3 | Hiram Walbridge (D) | 5,814 | 54.4 |
| | Bowen (W) | 4,797 | 44.9 |
| 4 | Mike Walsh (D) | 4,802 | 52.9 |
| | Hawes (W) | 2,564 | 28.2 |
| | Kly (W) | 1,712 | 18.9 |
| 5 | William M. Tweed (D) | 5,394 | 51.6 |
| | Hoxie (W) | 4,243 | 40.6 |
| | Mor (W) | 818 | 7.8 |
| 6 | John Wheeler (D) | 6,354 | 54.4 |
| | Varnum (W) | 5,243 | 44.9 |
| 7 | William A. Walker (D) | 5,801 | 52.1 |
| | Roberts (W) | 4,702 | 42.2 |
| 8 | Francis B. Cutting (D) | 4,414 | 56.5 |
| | Brooks (W) | 3,398 | 43.5 |
| 9 | Jared V. Peck (D) | 8,533 | 59.4 |
| | Clark (W) | 5,827 | 40.6 |
| 10 | William Murray (D) | 7,768 | 54.8 |
| | Farnham (W) | 6,407 | 45.2 |
| 11 | Theodore R. Westbrook (D) | 9,092 | 53.5 |
| | Smith (W) | 7,902 | 46.5 |
| 12 | Gilbert Dean (D) | 9,937 | 50.4 |
| | Cruger (W) | 9,798 | 49.7 |
| 13 | Russell Sage (W) | 6,583 | 51.0 |
| | Seyr (D) | 6,185 | 47.9 |
| 14 | Rufus W. Peckham (D) | 8,363 | 53.5 |
| | Egberts (W) | 7,190 | 46.0 |
| 15 | Charles Hughes (D) | 9,988 | 49.5 |
| | Northrup (W) | 9,693 | 48.0 |

1. Missouri's House representation rose from five seats to seven following the 1850 reapportionment, but elections to the two additional seats were not held in time for the regular 1852 election. Instead, they were held in 1853. See Missouri 1853, p. 995.

## NEW YORK

| Candidates | Votes | % |
|---|---|---|
| 16 George A. Simmons (W) | 7,093 | 50.9 |
| Ireland (D) | 6,852 | 49.1 |
| 17 Bishop Perkins (D) | 10,085 | 53.2 |
| Vanrenr (W) | 7,274 | 38.4 |
| Reddington (F SOIL) | 1,601 | 8.4 |
| 18 Peter Rowe (D) | 10,916 | 52.1 |
| Miller (W) | 10,057 | 48.0 |
| 19 George W. Chase (W) | 9,550 | 54.3 |
| Gordon (D) | 8,034 | 45.7 |
| 20 Orsamus B. Matteson (W) | 8,530 | 50.2 |
| Mouln (D) | 6,600 | 38.9 |
| Spen (W) | 1,542 | 9.1 |
| 21 Henry Bennett (W) | 9,876 | 49.9 |
| Smith (D) | 9,534 | 48.2 |
| 22 Gerrit Smith (ULTRA AB) | 8,049 | 40.5 |
| Hoh (D) | 6,206 | 31.2 |
| Tenck (W) | 5,620 | 28.3 |
| 23 Caleb Lyon (IW) | 8,937 | 53.1 |
| Mundy (D) | 7,891 | 46.9 |
| 24 Daniel T. Jones (D) | 6,605 | 46.6 |
| Gott (W) | 6,120 | 43.2 |
| Ray (F SOIL) | 1,458 | 10.3 |
| 25 Edwin B. Morgan (W) | 9,150 | 47.4 |
| How (D) | 8,996 | 46.6 |
| Cuyler (F SOIL) | 1,147 | 6.0 |
| 26 Andrew Oliver (D) | 8,546 | 49.2 |
| Woods (W) | 8,529 | 49.1 |
| 27 John J. Taylor (D) | 9,426 | 50.4 |
| Cook (W) | 8,410 | 45.0 |
| 28 George Hastings (D) | 10,681 | 53.7 |
| Irvine (W) | 9,225 | 46.3 |
| 29 Azariah Boody (W) | 7,290 | 50.2 |
| Field (D) | 6,578 | 45.3 |
| 30 Benjamin Pringle (W) | 9,386 | 48.7 |
| Sherman (D) | 8,903 | 46.2 |
| Landon (F SOIL) | 976 | 5.1 |
| 31 Thomas T. Flagler (W) | 5,858 | 46.0 |
| Woods (D) | 5,508 | 43.3 |
| Murphy (F SOIL) | 1,358 | 10.7 |
| 32 Solomon G. Haven (W) | 8,037 | 51.8 |
| Verk (D) | 7,054 | 45.4 |
| 33 Reuben E. Fenton (D) | 8,717 | 48.8 |
| Crooker (W) | 8,661 | 48.5 |

## OHIO

| Candidates | Votes | % |
|---|---|---|
| 1 David T. Disney (D) | 5,852 | 57.1 |
| Cassilly (W) | 4,317 | 42.1 |
| 2 John Scott Harrison (W) | 4,780 | 54.5 |
| Roll (D) | 3,849 | 43.9 |
| 3 Lewis D. Campbell (W) | 8,680 | 50.4 |
| Vallandigham (D) | 8,533 | 49.6 |
| 4 Matthias H. Nichols (D) | 7,648 | 53.8 |
| Plunkett (W) | 6,378 | 44.9 |
| 5 Alfred P. Edgerton (D) | 9,072 | 66.1 |
| Parker (W) | 4,561 | 33.2 |
| 6 Andrew Ellison (D) | 7,479 | 50.6 |
| Barrere (W) | 7,208 | 48.7 |
| 7 Aaron Harlan (W) | 7,580 | 54.7 |
| Telfair (D) | 5,018 | 36.2 |
| Nix (F SOIL) | 1,252 | 9.0 |
| 8 Moses B. Corwin (W) | 8,561 | 57.9 |
| Young (D) | 5,780 | 39.1 |

| Candidates | Votes | % |
|---|---|---|
| 9 Fred W. Green (D) | 8,198 | 74.1 |
| Goodman (W) | 2,095 | 18.9 |
| Sam (F SOIL) | 768 | 6.9 |
| 10 John L. Taylor (W) | 7,653 | 53.1 |
| Sherer (D) | 6,763 | 46.9 |
| 11 Thomas Ritchey (D) | 9,037 | 56.3 |
| Welch (W) | 6,681 | 41.7 |
| 12 Edson B. Olds (D) | 8,549 | 49.2 |
| Galloway (W) | 8,480 | 48.8 |
| 13 William D. Lindsley (D) | 6,739 | 44.4 |
| Saddler (W) | 6,035 | 39.8 |
| Jacob Brinkerhoff (F SOIL) | 2,390 | 15.8 |
| 14 Harvey H. Johnson (D) | 7,591 | 49.3 |
| Lockwood (W) | 4,763 | 31.0 |
| Norton S. Townshend (F SOIL) | 3,030 | 19.7 |
| 15 William R. Sapp (W) | 6,140 | 38.8 |
| William Winnell (D) | 6,109 | 38.6 |
| Rich (F SOIL) | 2,650 | 16.8 |
| Vance | 924 | 5.8 |
| 16 Edward Ball (W) | 7,161 | 52.3 |
| Gaylord (D) | 6,347 | 46.3 |
| 17 Wilson Shannon (D) | 7,142 | 54.1 |
| Hollister (W) | 6,054 | 45.9 |
| 18 George Bliss (D) | 6,140 | 46.7 |
| Lyman (W) | 5,307 | 40.3 |
| Earl (F SOIL) | 1,708 | 13.0 |
| 19 Edward Wade (F SOIL) | 5,274 | 40.5 |
| Case (W) | 4,046 | 31.0 |
| Wilson (D) | 3,715 | 28.5 |
| 20 Joshua R. Giddings (F SOIL) | 5,752 | 40.1 |
| Woods (D) | 4,427 | 30.8 |
| Newton (W) | 4,179 | 29.1 |
| 21 Andrew Stuart (D) | 7,423 | 47.8 |
| Brewer (W) | 6,885 | 44.3 |
| Lee (F SOIL) | 1,220 | 7.9 |

## PENNSYLVANIA

| Candidates | Votes | % |
|---|---|---|
| 1 Thomas B. Florence (D) | 4,937 | 44.5 |
| Price (W) | 3,200 | 28.9 |
| Levin (NAM) | 2,953 | 26.6 |
| 2 Joseph R. Chandler (W) | 6,594 | 62.4 |
| Ham (D) | 3,556 | 33.7 |
| 3 John Robbins Jr (D) | 5,857 | 51.5 |
| Sanderson (W) | 3,300 | 29.0 |
| Painter (NAM) | 2,206 | 19.4 |
| 4 William H. Witte (D) | 5,843 | 46.9 |
| Lambert (W) | 4,546 | 36.5 |
| Cornman (NAM) | 2,065 | 16.6 |
| 5 John McNair (D) | 7,168 | 50.9 |
| Hitner (W) | 6,336 | 45.0 |
| 6 William Everhart (W) | 7,641 | 54.2 |
| Mur (D) | 6,464 | 45.8 |
| 7 Samuel A. Bridges (D) | 8,339 | 52.7 |
| Taylor (W) | 7,486 | 47.3 |
| 8 Henry A. Muhlenberg (D) | 7,543 | 68.5 |
| Beiber (W) | 3,476 | 31.6 |
| 9 Isaac E. Heister (W) | 8,840 | 57.8 |
| Samp (D) | 6,456 | 42.2 |
| 10 Ner Middleswarth (W) | 7,921 | 55.8 |
| Seir (D) | 6,278 | 44.2 |
| 11 Christian M. Straub (D) | 5,729 | 51.5 |
| Krebs (W) | 5,388 | 48.5 |

| Candidates | Votes | % |
|---|---|---|
| 12 Hendrick B. Wright (D) | 7,523 | 50.6 |
| Fuller (W) | 7,350 | 49.4 |
| 13 Asa Packer (D) | 8,909 | 74.6 |
| Foster (W) | 3,035 | 25.4 |
| 14 Galusha A. Grow (D) | 8,062 | 94.2 |
| Horton (W) | 495 | 5.8 |
| 15 James Gamble (D) | 8,742 | 59.2 |
| Irwin (W) | 6,026 | 40.8 |
| 16 William H. Kurtz (D) | 9,513 | 56.6 |
| Biddle (W) | 7,306 | 43.4 |
| 17 Samuel L. Russell (W) | 9,216 | 51.0 |
| Danr (D) | 8,845 | 49.0 |
| 18 John McCulloch (W) | 7,847 | 56.2 |
| Shaffr (D) | 6,112 | 43.8 |
| 19 Augustus Drum (D) | 7,968 | 57.2 |
| Kuhns (W) | 5,959 | 42.8 |
| 20 John L. Dawson (D) | 9,791 | 56.8 |
| Gow (W) | 7,460 | 43.2 |
| 21 David Ritchie (W) | 4,939 | 52.2 |
| Shan (D) | 4,532 | 47.9 |
| 22 Thomas M. Howe (W) | 4,620 | 54.8 |
| Glbn (D) | 3,817 | 45.2 |
| 23 Michael C. Trout (D) | 5,369 | 45.6 |
| Alln (W) | 5,340 | 45.4 |
| Unidentified Candidate (F SOIL) | 1,056 | 9.0 |
| 24 Carlton B. Curtis (D) | 8,321 | 65.5 |
| Kerr (W) | 4,375 | 34.5 |
| 25 John Dick (W) | 6,057 | 54.8 |
| Cutr (D) | 4,049 | 36.6 |
| Unidentified Candidate (F SOIL) | 951 | 8.6 |

## VERMONT

| Candidates | Votes | % |
|---|---|---|
| 1 James Meacham (W) | 7,138 | 56.5 |
| Pierpoint (F SOIL) | 2,801 | 22.2 |
| Tucke (D) | 2,704 | 21.4 |
| 2 Andrew Tracy (W) | 9,319 | 52.2 |
| Daniel Kellogg (D) | 3,261 | 18.3 |
| Isaac Fletcher (F SOIL) | 2,928 | 16.4 |
| Hugh H. Henry (D) | 1,675 | 9.4 |
| 3 Alvah Sabin (W) | 5,706 | 48.3 |
| Heyward (D) | 3,803 | 32.2 |
| Kasson (F SOIL) | 2,294 | 19.4 |

## VIRGINIA

**Special Election**

| Candidates | Votes | % |
|---|---|---|
| 15 Sherrard Clemens (D) | ✔ | |

## WISCONSIN

| Candidates | Votes | % |
|---|---|---|
| 1 Daniel Wells Jr (D) | 8,342 | 46.5 |
| Dur (F SOIL) | 5,731 | 31.9 |
| Dur (W) | 3,870 | 21.6 |
| 2 Ben C. Eastman (D) | 10,893 | 53.9 |
| Abbott (W) | 7,816 | 38.7 |
| Enos (F SOIL) | 1,506 | 7.5 |
| 3 John B. Macy (D) | 14,596 | 55.6 |
| Shafter (W) | 9,513 | 36.2 |
| McKee (F SOIL) | 2,168 | 8.3 |

# 1853 House Elections

## ALABAMA

| | Candidates | Votes | % |
|---|---|---|---|
| 1 | Philip Phillips (SO RTS D) | 4,880 | 50.5 |
| | E. Lockwood (UN W) | 4,777 | 49.5 |
| 2 | James Abercrombie (UN W) | 7,474 | 56.1 |
| | D. Clopton (D) | 5,838 | 43.9 |
| 3 | Sampson W. Harris (SO RTS D) | 6,394 | 79.8 |
| | Moore (UN W) | 1,622 | 20.2 |
| 4 | William R. Smith (UN D) | 3,045 | 34.7 |
| | Sydenham Moore (SO RTS D) | 2,974 | 33.8 |
| | S. F. Hale (W) | 2,769 | 31.5 |
| 5 | George S. Houston (D) | 4,022 | 95.0 |
| 6 | Williamson R. W. Cobb (UN D) | 5,221 | 58.2 |
| | C. C. Clay Jr. (D) | 3,744 | 11.8 |
| 7 | James F. Dowdell (SO RTS D) | 6,098 | 65.6 |
| | T. G. Garrett (IUN W) | 3,200 | 34.4 |

## CONNECTICUT

| | Candidates | Votes | % |
|---|---|---|---|
| 1 | James T. Pratt (D) | 8,225 | 52.3 |
| | Charles Chapman (W) | 6,963 | 44.2 |
| 2 | Colin M. Ingersoll (D) | 8,551 | 53.1 |
| | Austin Baldwin (W) | 6,773 | 42.0 |
| 3 | Nathan Belcher (D) | 6,129 | 51.8 |
| | Daniel P. Tyler (W) | 3,906 | 33.0 |
| | Albert G. Stark (F SOIL) | 1,800 | 15.2 |
| 4 | Origen S. Seymour (D) | 8,700 | 54.2 |
| | William W. Welch (W) | 7,249 | 45.2 |

## GEORGIA

| | Candidates | Votes | % |
|---|---|---|---|
| 1 | James L. Seward (D) | 4,429 | 51.1 |
| | Barton (W) | 4,238 | 48.9 |
| 2 | Alfred H. Colquitt (D) | 6,795 | 52.1 |
| | Johnson (W) | 6,249 | 47.9 |
| 3 | David J. Bailey (D) | 5,232 | 50.0 |
| | Robert P. Trippe (W) | 5,227 | 50.0 |
| 4 | William B. W. Dent (D) | 6,701 | 51.3 |
| | Calhoun (W) | 6,368 | 48.7 |
| 5 | Elijah W. Chastain (D) | 8,118 | 50.8 |
| | Tumlin (D) | 7,866 | 49.2 |
| 6 | Junius Hillyer (D) | 5,439 | 64.8 |
| | Wofld (D) | 2,954 | 35.2 |
| 7 | David A. Reese (W) | 4,997 | 56.3 |
| | Saffold (D) | 3,883 | 43.7 |
| 8 | Alexander H. Stephens (W) | 5,634 | 69.7 |
| | Jones (D) | 2,444 | 30.3 |

## KENTUCKY

| | Candidates | Votes | % |
|---|---|---|---|
| 1 | Linn Boyd (D) | 7,585 | 57.6 |
| | Jefferson Brown (ID) | 5,590 | 42.4 |
| 2 | Ben E. Grey (W) | 7,076 | 52.5 |
| | W. J. Davie (D) | 6,408 | 47.5 |
| 3 | Presley Ewing (W) | 5,318 | 100.0 |
| 4 | James S. Crisman (D) | 5,657 | 50.2 |
| | Thomas E. Bramlette (W) | 5,622 | 49.8 |
| 5 | Clement S. Hill (W) | 6,126 | 50.5 |
| | James W. Stone (D) | 5,996 | 49.5 |
| 6 | John M. Elliott (D) | 6,257 | 53.8 |
| | Jeremiah S. Pierce (W) | 5,376 | 46.2 |
| 7 | William Preston (W) | 6,609 | 57.7 |
| | S. S. English (D) | 4,847 | 42.3 |
| 8 | John C. Breckinridge (D) | 6,532 | 52.1 |
| | Robert P. Letcher (W) | 6,006 | 47.9 |
| 9 | Leander M. Cox (AM) | 6,606 | 52.5 |
| | James M. Rice (D) | 5,974 | 47.5 |
| 10 | Richard H. Stanton (D) | 7,583 | 51.8 |
| | George B. Hodge (W) | 7,070 | 48.3 |

## LOUISIANA

| | Candidates | Votes | % |
|---|---|---|---|
| 1 | William Dunbar (D) | 4,550 | 62.8 |
| | Gayarre (W) | 2,691 | 37.2 |
| 2 | Theodore G. Hunt (W) | 6,558 | 54.6 |
| | Davis (D) | 5,445 | 45.4 |
| 3 | John Perkins Jr. (D) | 4,965 | 56.7 |
| | Pond (W) | 3,787 | 43.3 |
| 4 | Roland Jones (D) | 7,494 | 56.8 |
| | Smith (W) | 5,695 | 43.2 |

## MARYLAND

| | Candidates | Votes | % |
|---|---|---|---|
| 1 | John R. Franklin (W) | 5,815 | 53.1 |
| | Stevn (I) | 5,127 | 46.9 |
| 2 | Jacob Shower(I) | 7,246 | 53.4 |
| | Wethered (W) | 6,330 | 46.6 |
| 3 | Joshua Vansant (ID) | 5,876 | 53.7 |
| | Preston (W) | 5,061 | 46.3 |
| 4 | Henry May (ID) | 6,792 | 51.3 |
| | Walsh (W) | 6,440 | 48.7 |
| 5 | William T. Hamilton (ID) | 7,545 | 54.0 |
| | Thomas (W) | 6,429 | 46.0 |
| 6 | Augustus R. Sollers (W) | 3,815 | 61.0 |
| | Jenr (I) | 2,438 | 39.0 |

## MISSISSIPPI

| | Candidates | Votes | % |
|---|---|---|---|
| 1 | Daniel B. Wright (D) | 8,984 | 51.6 |
| | Nabers (W) | 8,414 | 48.4 |
| 2 | William T. S. Barry (D) | 7,039 | 50.7 |
| | Wilcox (W) | 6,837 | 49.3 |
| 3 | Otho R. Singleton (D) | 8,367 | 55.7 |
| | McLung (W) | 6,669 | 44.4 |
| 4 | Wiley P. Harris (D) | | 100.0 |
| AL | William Barksdale (D) | 29,702 | 54.1 |
| | Unidentified Candidate (W) | 25,183 | 45.9 |

## MISSOURI [1]

| | Candidates | Votes | % |
|---|---|---|---|
| 3 | James J. Lindley (W) | 6,828 | 50.6 |
| | Jackson (A-BEN D) | 6,674 | 49.4 |
| 7 | Samuel Caruthers (W) | 4,447 | 39.8 |
| | Jackson (BENTON D) | 2,542 | 22.8 |
| | English (A-BEN D) | 2,424 | 21.7 |
| | Rosier (BENTON D) | 1,750 | 15.7 |

## NEW HAMPSHIRE

| | Candidates | Votes | % |
|---|---|---|---|
| 1 | George W. Kittredge (D) | 10,168 | 53.2 |
| | Amos Tuck (W) | 8,962 | 46.9 |
| 2 | George W. Morrison (D) | 9,050 | 67.5 |
| | Hughes (W) | 4,353 | 32.5 |
| 3 | Harry Hibbard (D) | 9,635 | 56.1 |
| | Perkins (W) | 7,556 | 44.0 |

## NORTH CAROLINA

| | Candidates | Votes | % |
|---|---|---|---|
| 1 | Henry M. Shaw (D) | 4,833 | 50.5 |
| | David Outlaw (W) | 4,746 | 49.6 |
| 2 | Thomas Ruffin(D) | 5,812 | 68.7 |
| | W. C. Loftin (ID) | 2,653 | 31.3 |
| 3 | Wlliam S. Ashe (D) | 5,520 | 62.2 |
| | Walter F. Leake (LD D) | 3,351 | 37.8 |
| 4 | Sion H. Rogers (W) | 4,201 | 38.9 |
| | Abraham W. Venable (LD D) | 4,133 | 38.3 |
| | Augustus M. Lewis (A-LD D) | 2,454 | 22.8 |
| 5 | John Kerr (W) | 6,037 | 86.2 |
| | Abraham Rencher (ID) | 963 | 13.8 |
| 6 | Richard C. Puryear (W) | 6,173 | 51.6 |
| | George D. Boyd (D) | 5,788 | 48.4 |
| 7 | F. Burton Craige (D) | 5,965 | 51.4 |
| | James W. Osborne (W) | 5,649 | 48.6 |
| 8 | Thomas L. Clingman (D) | 7,606 | 59.3 |
| | Burgess S. Gaither (W) | 5,214 | 40.7 |

## RHODE ISLAND

| | Candidates | Votes | % |
|---|---|---|---|
| 1 | Thomas Davis (D) | 5,524 | 50.8 |
| | George G. King (W) | 4,942 | 45.5 |
| 2 | Benjamin B. Thurston (D) | 4,436 | 90.5 |
| | Elisha M. Aldrich (W) | 450 | 9.2 |

## SOUTH CAROLINA

| | Candidates | Votes | % |
|---|---|---|---|
| 1 | John McQueen (D) | | 100.0 |
| 2 | William Aiken (D) | | 100.0 |
| 3 | Laurence M. Keitt (D) | | 100.0 |
| 4 | Preston S. Brooks (SSR D) | 2,098 | 32.3 |
| | Sullivan | 1,497 | 23.0 |
| | Francis W. Pickens (NULL D) | 1,492 | 23.0 |
| | Marshall | 1,415 | 21.8 |
| 5 | James L. Orr (D) | | 100.0 |
| 6 | William W. Boyce (SSR D) | 2,549 | 51.0 |
| | Moses | 2,270 | 45.4 |

## TENNESSEE

| | Candidates | Votes | % |
|---|---|---|---|
| 1 | Brookins Campbell (D) | 5,525* | 37.1 |
| | Nathaniel G. Taylor (W) | 5,387 | 36.2 |
| | Albert G. Watkins (W) | 3,988 | 26.8 |
| 2 | William M. Churchwell (D) | 6,266 | 56.6 |
| | Maynard (W) | 4,797 | 43.4 |
| 3 | Samuel A. Smith (D) | 7,703 | 55.5 |
| | Van Dyke (W) | 6,180 | 44.5 |
| 4 | William Cullom (W) | 5,630 | 50.2 |
| | Gardner (D) | 5,593 | 49.8 |
| 5 | Charles Ready (W) | 6,143 | 57.3 |
| | Barry (D) | 4,577 | 42.7 |
| 6 | George W. Jones (D) | | 100.0 |
| 7 | Robert M. Bugg (W) | 6,421 | 52.3 |
| | Pavott (D) | 5,865 | 47.7 |
| 8 | Felix K. Zollicoffer (W) | 5,808 | 53.0 |
| | Allison (D) | 5,157 | 47.0 |
| 9 | Emerson Etheridge (W) | | 100.0 |
| 10 | Frederick P. Stanton (D) | 5,126 | 50.0 |
| | Yerger (W) | 5,120 | 50.0 |

## TEXAS

| | Candidates | Votes | % |
|---|---|---|---|
| 1 | George M. Smyth (D) | 12,126 | 98.8 |
| 2 | Peter H. Bell (D) | 5,918 | 41.4 |
| | William R. Scurry (D) | 2,963 | 20.7 |
| | G. K. Lewis (D) | 2,411 | 16.9 |
| | B. F. Carothers (W) | 2,126 | 14.9 |
| | F. M. Blake (D) | 869 | 6.1 |

## VIRGINIA

| | Candidates | Votes | % |
|---|---|---|---|
| 1 | Thomas H. Bayly (D) | | 100.0 |
| 2 | John S. Millson (D) | 3,206 | 56.7 |
| | Chambliss (W) | 2,071 | 36.6 |
| | Roberts (I) | 379 | 6.7 |
| 3 | John S. Caskie (D) | 4,333 | 54.9 |
| | Coleman (W) | 3,561 | 45.1 |
| 4 | William O. Goode (D) | | 100.0 |
| 5 | Thomas S. Bocock (D) | 4,304 | 51.7 |
| | Wootton (W) | 3,586 | 43.1 |
| | Arnett (I) | 428 | 5.2 |
| 6 | Paulus Powell (D) | 4,751 | 54.8 |
| | Mosely (W) | 3,912 | 45.2 |
| 7 | William Smith (D) | 4,223 | 51.8 |
| | Snowden (W) | 3,931 | 48.2 |
| 8 | Charles J. Faulkner (D) | 6,106 | 52.3 |
| | Boteler (W) | 5,560 | 47.7 |
| 9 | John Letcher (D) | | 100.0 |
| 10 | Zedekiah Kidwell (D) | | 100.0 |
| 11 | John F. Snodgrass (D) | 4,707 | 40.2 |
| | Lewis (W) | 4,497 | 38.4 |
| | Sterrett (W) | 2,506 | 21.4 |
| 12 | Henry A. Edmonson (D) | | 100.0 |
| 13 | Fayette McMullen (D) | | 100.0 |

1. Missouri elected two additional House members to raise its total to the seven seats allotted by the 1850 census. The state was redistricted from five seats to seven, with the new districts labeled "3" and "7". The 3rd congressional district of 1853 is not the same 3rd district that elected a representative in 1852. (See Missouri 1852, p. 993.)

# 1854 House Elections

## ARKANSAS

| | Candidates | Votes | % |
|---|---|---|---|
| 1 | Alfred B. Greenwood (D) | 15,374 | 97.3 |
| 2 | Albert Rust (D) | 8,893 | 67.0 |
| | E. G. Walker (W) | 4,371 | 32.9 |

## CALIFORNIA

| | | Votes | % |
|---|---|---|---|
| AL | James W. Denver (A-BROD D) | 36,819✔ | |
| | Philemon T. Herbert (A-BROD D) | 36,542✔ | |
| | G. W. Bowie (W) | 34,741 | |
| | Cal Benham (W) | 34,411 | |
| | J. Churchman (BROD D) | 10,006 | |
| | J. A. Mc Dougal (BROD D) | 9,968 | |
| | M. S. Latham (BROD D) | 1,843 | |

## DELAWARE

| | | Votes | % |
|---|---|---|---|
| AL | Elisha D. Cullen (AM) | 6,820 | 51.9 |
| | George Read Riddle (D) | 6,334 | 48.2 |

## FLORIDA

| | | Votes | % |
|---|---|---|---|
| AL | Augustus Maxwell (D) | 5,642 | 55.2 |
| | Thomas Brown (W) | 4,583 | 44.8 |

## ILLINOIS

| | | Votes | % |
|---|---|---|---|
| 1 | Elihu B. Washburne (R) | 8,372 | 69.3 |
| | William M. Jackon (D) | 2,776 | 23.0 |
| | E. P. Ferry (A-NEB D) | 927 | 7.7 |
| 2 | James H. Woodworth (R) | 6,927 | 53.1 |
| | Robert S. Blackwell (W) | 2,591 | 19.8 |
| | John B. Turner (D) | 2,544 | 19.5 |
| | Edward L. Mayo (A-NEB D) | 996 | 7.6 |
| 3 | Jesse O. Norton (R) | 10,474 | 62.8 |
| | John A. Drake (D) | 6,216 | 37.2 |
| 4 | James Knox (R) | 10,146 | 57.0 |
| | Unidentified Candidate (D) | 7,588 | 42.6 |
| 5 | William A. Richardson (D) | 8,935 | 52.4 |
| | Arch Williams (R) | 8,122 | 47.6 |
| 6 | Thomas L. Harris (D) | 10,090 | 50.5 |
| | Richard Gates (R) | 9,890 | 49.5 |
| 7 | James C. Allen (D) | 8,452‡ | 50.0 |
| | William B. Archer (R) | 8,451 | 50.0 |
| 8 | Lyman Trumbull (R) | 7,917* | 58.1 |
| | Philip B. Fouke (D) | 5,306 | 38.9 |
| 9 | Samuel S. Marshall (D) | 8,497 | 64.4 |
| | L. Jay S. Turney (R) | 2,911 | 22.0 |
| | Dewitt C. Barber | 1,276 | 9.7 |

## INDIANA

| | | Votes | % |
|---|---|---|---|
| 1 | Smith Miller (NEB D) | 9,864 | 52.2 |
| | Hall (R) | 9,051 | 47.9 |
| 2 | William H. English (NEB D) | 8,931 | 51.7 |
| | Shanter (R) | 8,345 | 48.3 |
| 3 | George G. Dunn (R) | 9,989 | 54.5 |
| | Dunm (NEB D) | 8,329 | 45.5 |
| 4 | William Cumback (R) | 9,061 | 51.9 |
| | Holn (NEB D) | 8,391 | 48.1 |
| 5 | David P. Holloway (R) | 9,419 | 64.3 |
| | Buckles (NEB D) | 5,242 | 35.8 |
| 6 | Lucien Barbour (R) | 9,824 | 51.4 |
| | Henkr (NEB D) | 9,286 | 48.6 |
| 7 | Harvey D. Scott (R) | 9,515 | 52.6 |
| | Davis (NEB D) | 8,580 | 47.4 |
| 8 | Daniel Mace (R) | 10,357 | 56.9 |
| | Davis (NEB D) | 7,838 | 43.1 |
| 9 | Schuyler Colfax (R) | 9,989 | 54.9 |
| | Eddy (NEB D) | 8,223 | 45.2 |
| 10 | Samuel Brenton (R) | 7,485 | 56.0 |
| | Chamln (NEB D) | 5,881 | 44.0 |

| | Candidates | Votes | % |
|---|---|---|---|
| 11 | John U. Pettit (R) | 9,389 | 56.6 |
| | Slack (NEB D) | 7,201 | 43.4 |

## IOWA

| | | Votes | % |
|---|---|---|---|
| 1 | Augustus Hall (D) | 11,213 | 50.3 |
| | R. L. B. Clark (R) | 11,042 | 49.5 |
| 2 | James Thorington (R) | 11,424 | 53.3 |
| | Stephen Hempstead (D) | 9,872 | 46.1 |

## KENTUCKY

### Special Election

| | | Votes | % |
|---|---|---|---|
| 3 | Francis M. Bristow (W) | 2,533 | 81.6 |
| | A. J. Harberson (D) | 572 | 18.4 |

## MAINE

| | | Votes | % |
|---|---|---|---|
| 1 | John M. Wood (R) | 9,227 | 59.8 |
| | Samuel Wells (D) | 6,196 | 40.2 |
| 2 | John J. Perry (R) | 10,007 | 57.8 |
| | William Kimball (D) | 7,313 | 42.2 |
| 3 | Ebenezer Knowlton (R) | 5,995 | 43.9 |
| | J. G. Dickerson (D) | 4,072 | 29.8 |
| | E. W. Farley (W) | 3,587 | 26.3 |
| 4 | Samuel P. Benson (R) | 11,610 | 77.0 |
| | George Rogers (D) | 3,467 | 23.0 |
| 5 | Israel Washburn Jr (R) | 10,224 | 63.0 |
| | Samuel H. Blake (D) | 6,010 | 37.0 |
| 6 | Thomas J. D. Fuller (D) | 4,713 | 42.4 |
| | J. A. Milliken (R) | 4,307 | 38.7 |
| | N. Smith Jr. (W) | 2,099 | 18.9 |

## MASSACHUSETTS

| | | Votes | % |
|---|---|---|---|
| 1 | Robert B. Hall (AM) | 5,353 | 63.3 |
| | Thomas D. Eliot (W) | 2,238 | 26.5 |
| | Abraham H. Howland | 812 | 9.6 |
| 2 | James Buffington (AM) | 8,074 | 68.2 |
| | Samuel L. Crocker (W) | 1,914 | 16.2 |
| | Charles R. Vickery | 1,064 | 9.0 |
| | Gersham B. Weston (F SOIL) | 774 | 6.5 |
| 3 | William S. Damrell (AM) | 8,668 | 74.4 |
| | Nathaniel F. Safford (W) | 1,933 | 16.6 |
| | Edward Avery | 624 | 5.4 |
| 4 | Linus B. Comins (AM) | 4,972 | 57.4 |
| | Samuel H. Walley (W) | 2,770 | 32.0 |
| | Samuel R. Spinney | 913 | 10.5 |
| 5 | Anson Burlingame (AM) | 5,967 | 61.5 |
| | William Appleton (W) | 3,109 | 32.1 |
| | William Parmenter (D) | 604 | 6.2 |
| 6 | Timothy Davis (AM) | 7,428 | 65.3 |
| | Charles W. Upham (W) | 3,231 | 28.4 |
| | Nathaniel J. Lord | 633 | 5.6 |
| 7 | Nathaniel P. Banks (AM) | 8,928 | 73.3 |
| | Luther V. Bell (W) | 2,481 | 20.4 |
| | Bowen Bualman | 724 | 5.9 |
| 8 | Chauncy L. Knapp (AM) | 7,004 | 62.7 |
| | Tappan Wentworth (W) | 3,556 | 31.8 |
| | Daniel Needham | 593 | 5.3 |
| 9 | Alexander De Witt (AM) | 8,797 | 77.0 |
| | Isaac Davis (D) | 1,526 | 13.4 |
| | Ira M. Barton (W) | 851 | 7.5 |
| 10 | Henry Morris (AM) | 7,723* | 64.6 |
| | Edward Dickinson (W) | 2,757 | 23.1 |
| | Stephen C. Bemis | 1,338 | 11.2 |
| 11 | Mark Trafton (AM) | 6,640 | 50.4 |
| | John L. Goodrich (W) | 3,998 | 30.4 |
| | Whiting Griswold | 2,505 | 19.0 |

### Special Election

| | | Votes | % |
|---|---|---|---|
| 1 | Thomas D. Eliot (W) | 4,059 | 51.5 |
| | Abraham Howland | 3,741 | 47.4 |

## MICHIGAN

| | Candidates | Votes | % |
|---|---|---|---|
| 1 | William A. Howard (R) | 9,877 | 53.1 |
| | David Stuart (D) | 8,723 | 46.9 |
| 2 | Henry Waldron (R) | 11,055 | 57.7 |
| | David A. Noble (D) | 8,113 | 42.3 |
| 3 | David S. Walbridge (R) | 12,865 | 55.8 |
| | Samuel Clark (D) | 10,178 | 44.1 |
| 4 | George W. Peck (D) | 11,233 | 53.2 |
| | Moses Wisner (R) | 9,863 | 46.7 |

## MISSOURI

| | | Votes | % |
|---|---|---|---|
| 1 | Luther M. Kennett (W) | 6,259 | 52.4 |
| | Benton (BENTON D) | 5,298 | 44.4 |
| 2 | Gilchrist Porter (W) | 8,119 | 54.1 |
| | Corneck | 6,877 | 45.9 |
| 3 | James J. Lindley (W) | 8,150 | 52.5 |
| | Fournoy (A-BEN D) | 7,386 | 47.5 |
| 4 | Mordecai Oliver (W) | 6,129 | 44.1 |
| | Leonard (A-BEN D) | 4,998 | 35.9 |
| | Lowe (BENTON D) | 2,787 | 20.0 |
| 5 | John G. Miller (W) | 6,372* | 46.2 |
| | Price (BENTON D) | 4,904 | 35.5 |
| | Hough (A-BEN D) | 2,530 | 18.3 |
| 6 | John S. Phelps (A-BEN D) | 8,342 | 51.1 |
| | Johnson (BENTON D) | 7,982 | 48.9 |
| 7 | Samuel Caruthers (W) | 8,045 | 58.9 |
| | Jones (BENTON D) | 5,625 | 41.2 |

## NEW JERSEY

| | | Votes | % |
|---|---|---|---|
| 1 | Isaiah D. Clawson (W) | 6,269 | 42.9 |
| | Mulford (NEB) | 4,383 | 30.0 |
| | Hazltn (TEMP) | 3,949 | 27.1 |
| 2 | George R. Robbins (W) | 10,539 | 57.6 |
| | Rue (NEB) | 7,769 | 42.4 |
| 3 | James Bishop (W) | 9,051 | 54.4 |
| | Lilly (NEB) | 7,603 | 45.7 |
| 4 | George Vail (NEB) | 7,281 | 51.7 |
| | Osborn (A-NEB) | 6,816 | 48.4 |
| 5 | Alexander C. M. Pennington (W) | 8,137 | 54.4 |
| | Darey (NEB) | 6,816 | 45.6 |

## NEW YORK

| | | Votes | % |
|---|---|---|---|
| 1 | William W. Valk (SOFTD&AM) | 3,753 | 28.1 |
| | Allen (HARD D) | 2,778 | 20.8 |
| | Vail (W) | 2,676 | 20.1 |
| | Lord (SOFT D) | 2,227 | 16.7 |
| | Disosway (TEMP) | 1,902 | 14.3 |
| 2 | James S. T. Stranahan (W) | 7,927 | 50.9 |
| | Taylor (HARD D) | 7,623 | 49.0 |
| 3 | Guy R. Pelton (W & AM) | 4,084 | 52.6 |
| | Clinton (HARD D) | 2,559 | 33.0 |
| | Miner (SOFT D) | 1,123 | 14.5 |
| 4 | John Kelly (SOFT D) | 3,068 | 36.0 |
| | Walsh (HARD D) | 3,047 | 35.7 |
| | Bryle (W & AM) | 1,594 | 18.7 |
| | Macomber (W) | 821 | 9.6 |
| 5 | Thomas R. Whitney (W & AM) | 3,321 | 30.9 |
| | Andrews (W) | 2,765 | 25.7 |
| | Hamilton (HARD D) | 2,718 | 25.3 |
| | Berry (SOFT D) | 1,954 | 18.2 |
| 6 | John Wheeler (HARDD&AM) | 5,101 | 46.3 |
| | Murphy (SOFT D) | 2,533 | 23.0 |
| | Marshal (SOFT D) | 2,256 | 20.5 |
| | Mead (I HARD D) | 1,128 | 10.2 |
| 7 | Thomas Child Jr (W & AM) | 6,557* | 56.3 |
| | Kennedy (SOFT D) | 5,094 | 43.7 |
| 8 | Abram Wakeman (W & AM) | 4,895 | 51.2 |
| | Curtis (HARD D) | 2,969 | 31.1 |
| | Fellows (SOFT D) | 1,699 | 17.8 |
| 9 | Bayard Clarke (W & AM) | 7,764 | 61.1 |
| | Branth (HARD D) | 2,540 | 20.0 |

## NEW YORK

| | Candidates | Votes | % |
|---|---|---|---|
| | Whiting (HARD D) | 2,038 | 16.0 |
| 10 | Ambrose S. Murray (W) | 5,209 | 44.0 |
| | Woodward (HARDD&AM) | 4,574 | 38.6 |
| | Strtn (SOFT D) | 2,053 | 17.4 |
| 11 | Rufus H. King (W) | 8,576 | 63.0 |
| | Strong (HARD D) | 5,042 | 37.0 |
| 12 | Killian Miller (W) | 8,376 | 51.1 |
| | McClellan (SOFTD&AM) | 5,540 | 33.8 |
| | Wilson (HARD D) | 2,486 | 15.2 |
| 13 | Russell Sage (W & AM) | 6,954 | 63.2 |
| | Clum (SOFT D) | 2,075 | 18.9 |
| | Cook (HARD D) | 1,971 | 17.9 |
| 14 | Samuel Dickson (W) | 4,638 | 32.2 |
| | Harct (SOFTD&AM) | 4,270 | 29.6 |
| | Pruyn (SOFT D) | 3,244 | 22.5 |
| | Hamilton | 2,255 | 15.7 |
| 15 | Edward Dodd (W) | 6,760 | 37.7 |
| | Clark (HARD D) | 6,358 | 35.4 |
| | Hughes (SOFT D) | 2,428 | 13.5 |
| | Andrews (TEMP) | 2,399 | 13.4 |
| 16 | George A. Simmons (W) | 5,533 | 48.7 |
| | Bailey (SOFTD&AM) | 3,062 | 26.9 |
| | Thomas (SOFT D) | 1,752 | 15.4 |
| | Flanders (HARD D) | 1,025 | 9.0 |
| 17 | Francis E. Spinner (SOFT D) | 7,618 | 46.5 |
| | Alexander (W) | 5,357 | 32.7 |
| | Benton (HARD D) | 3,414 | 20.8 |
| 18 | Thomas R. Horton (W) | 9,431 | 51.3 |
| | Jackson (HARD D) | 8,945 | 48.7 |
| 19 | Jonas A. Hughson (W) | 6,744 | 43.3 |
| | Palmer (SOFT D) | 6,444 | 41.3 |
| | Hawes (F SOIL) | 1,339 | 8.6 |
| | Sturges | 1,066 | 6.8 |
| 20 | Orsamus B. Matteson (W) | 6,492 | 38.2 |
| | Johnson (SOFT D) | 5,172 | 30.4 |
| | Huntington (W) | 4,759 | 28.0 |
| 21 | Henry Bennett (W) | 9,757 | 56.0 |
| | Tompkins (HARD D) | 5,579 | 32.0 |
| | Crocker (SOFT D) | 2,077 | 11.9 |
| 22 | Andrew Z. McCarty (W) | 5,535 | 32.2 |
| | Babcock (SOFT D) | 4,728 | 27.5 |
| | Case (F SOIL) | 3,652 | 21.2 |
| | Lewis (HARD D) | 3,281 | 19.1 |
| 23 | William A. Gilbert (W) | 6,251 | 46.4 |
| | Ives (SOFT D) | 5,645 | 41.9 |
| | Brown (HARD D) | 1,513 | 11.2 |
| 24 | Amos P. Granger (W) | 4,803 | 37.5 |
| | Alvord (SOFT D) | 4,109 | 32.1 |
| | Noxon (W & AM) | 3,409 | 26.6 |
| 25 | Edwin B. Morgan (W) | 7,684 | 48.4 |
| | Midton (SOFTD&AM) | 6,910 | 43.5 |
| | Aldrich (HARD D) | 1,296 | 8.2 |
| 26 | Andrew Oliver (SOFTD&AM) | 6,880 | 48.0 |
| | Seeley (W) | 5,304 | 37.0 |
| | Howell (HARD D) | 2,163 | 15.1 |
| 27 | John M. Parker (W) | 7,915 | 59.3 |
| | McDowell (SOFT D) | 3,467 | 26.0 |
| | Cushing (HARD D) | 1,964 | 14.7 |
| 28 | William H. Kelsey (W & AM) | 11,061 | 70.8 |
| | Hastings (SOFT D) | 4,450 | 28.5 |
| 29 | John Williams (SOFTD&AM) | 5,609 | 47.9 |
| | Carpenter (W) | 4,227 | 36.1 |
| | Sibley (HARD D) | 1,865 | 15.9 |
| 30 | Benjamin Pringle (W & AM) | 9,510 | 57.6 |
| | Laning (SOFT D) | 3,829 | 23.2 |
| | Belden (HARD D) | 2,483 | 15.0 |
| 31 | Thomas T. Flagler (W & AM) | 7,190 | 76.6 |
| | Baker (HARD D) | 1,231 | 13.1 |
| | Chase (F SOIL) | 962 | 10.3 |

| | Candidates | Votes | % |
|---|---|---|---|
| 32 | Solomon G. Haven (W & AM) | 9,075 | 62.8 |
| | Hatch (SOFT D) | 5,388 | 37.3 |
| 33 | Francis S. Edwards (W & AM) | 8,359 | 55.6 |
| | Fenton (SOFT D) | 6,442 | 42.8 |

## OHIO

| | | Votes | % |
|---|---|---|---|
| 1 | Timothy C. Day (R) | 7,716 | 63.5 |
| | George H. Pendleton (D) | 4,442 | 36.5 |
| 2 | John Scott Harrison (R) | 7,562 | 66.0 |
| | Groek (D) | 3,891 | 34.0 |
| 3 | Lewis D. Campbell (R) | 9,058 | 58.3 |
| | Valm (D) | 6,493 | 41.8 |
| 4 | Matthias H. Nicholas (R) | 10,307 | 70.2 |
| | Dorsey (D) | 4,377 | 29.8 |
| 5 | Richard Mott (R) | 8,253 | 61.6 |
| | Commaqer (D) | 5,141 | 38.4 |
| 6 | Jonas R. Emrie (R) | 9,990 | 65.0 |
| | Ellison (D) | 5,370 | 35.0 |
| 7 | Aaron Harlan (R) | 9,928 | 81.1 |
| | Hinkson (D) | 2,307 | 18.9 |
| 8 | Benjamin Stanton (R) | 11,000 | 76.7 |
| | Dial (D) | 3,350 | 23.3 |
| 9 | Cooper K. Watson (R) | 8,399 | 59.9 |
| | Plants (D) | 5,618 | 40.1 |
| 10 | Oscar F. Moore (R) | 8,865 | 65.3 |
| | Davis (D) | 4,706 | 34.7 |
| 11 | Valentine B. Horton (R) | 9,818 | 58.7 |
| | Smith (D) | 6,907 | 41.3 |
| 12 | Samuel Galloway (R) | 9,698 | 60.3 |
| | Olds (D) | 6,390 | 39.7 |
| 13 | John Sherman (R) | 8,617 | 59.8 |
| | Lindy (D) | 5,794 | 40.2 |
| 14 | Philemon Bliss (R) | 8,788 | 59.3 |
| | Johnson (D) | 6,041 | 40.7 |
| 15 | William Sapp (R) | 9,371 | 59.0 |
| | Dunbar (D) | 6,516 | 41.0 |
| 16 | Edward Ball (R) | 7,265 | 58.9 |
| | Galighr (D) | 5,072 | 41.1 |
| 17 | Charles J. Albright (R) | 8,332 | 58.1 |
| | Wire (D) | 6,017 | 41.9 |
| 18 | Benjamin F. Leiter (R) | 8,738 | 63.4 |
| | Spalding (D) | 5,053 | 36.6 |
| 19 | Edward Wade (R) | 7,699 | 71.4 |
| | Wilder (D) | 3,079 | 28.6 |
| 20 | Joshua R. Giddings (R) | 6,972 | 64.8 |
| | Lee (D) | 3,782 | 35.2 |
| 21 | John A. Bingham (R) | 9,860 | 65.3 |
| | Unidentified Candidate (D) | 5,238 | 34.7 |

## PENNSYLVANIA

| | | Votes | % |
|---|---|---|---|
| 1 | Thomas B. Florence (D) | 6,439 | 51.8 |
| | Morris (W) | 5,999 | 48.2 |
| 2 | Job R. Tyson (W) | 5,654 | 61.8 |
| | Haml (D) | 3,500 | 38.2 |
| 3 | William Millward (W) | 5,888 | 51.6 |
| | Landy (D) | 5,525 | 48.4 |
| 4 | Jacob Broom (NAM) | 6,747 | 53.0 |
| | Philps (D) | 5,993 | 47.0 |
| 5 | John Cadwalader (D) | 7,842 | 50.0 |
| | Jones (W) | 7,834 | 50.0 |
| 6 | John Hickman (D) | 8,733 | 59.0 |
| | Brooml (W) | 6,077 | 41.0 |
| 7 | Samuel C. Bradshaw (W) | 8,527 | 51.0 |
| | Samuel A. Bridges (D) | 8,182 | 49.0 |
| 8 | J. Glancy Jones (D) | 8,152 | 59.8 |
| | Myers (W) | 5,486 | 40.2 |

| | Candidates | Votes | % |
|---|---|---|---|
| 9 | Anthony E. Roberts (W) | 6,561 | 40.5 |
| | Hiester | 5,371 | 33.2 |
| | Leferre | 4,266 | 26.3 |
| 10 | John C. Kunkel (W) | 8,500 | 58.4 |
| | Bougtr (D) | 6,049 | 41.6 |
| 11 | James H. Campbell (W) | 5,384 | 51.5 |
| | Dewart (D) | 5,081 | 48.6 |
| 12 | Henry M. Fuller (W) | 9,115 | 56.3 |
| | Wright (D) | 7,087 | 43.7 |
| 13 | Asa Packer (D) | 9,136 | 58.7 |
| | Stewart (W) | 6,433 | 41.3 |
| 14 | Galusha A. Grow (F SOIL D) | | 100.0 |
| 15 | John J. Pierce (W) | 9,588 | 56.0 |
| | White (D) | 7,528 | 44.0 |
| 16 | Lemuel Todd (W) | 10,472 | 55.7 |
| | Booham (D) | 8,319 | 44.3 |
| 17 | David F. Robison (W) | 9,641 | 51.7 |
| | Reiliy (D) | 9,025 | 48.4 |
| 18 | John R. Edie (W) | 8,423 | 72.4 |
| | Cresswl (D) | 3,218 | 27.6 |
| 19 | John Covode (W) | 9,342 | 58.7 |
| | Drum (D) | 6,585 | 41.3 |
| 20 | Jonathan Knight (W) | 9,912 | 56.8 |
| | Montgomery (D) | 7,552 | 43.2 |
| 21 | David Ritchie (W) | 5,705 | 60.6 |
| | Shaler (D) | 3,714 | 39.4 |
| 22 | Samuel A. Purviance (W) | 5,926 | 60.7 |
| | Palmer (D) | 3,832 | 39.3 |
| 23 | John Allison (W) | 7,808 | 60.2 |
| | Trout (D) | 5,172 | 39.9 |
| 24 | David Barclay (D) | 10,415 | 74.7 |
| | Arthurs (W) | 3,527 | 25.3 |
| 25 | John Dick (W) | | 100.0 |

### Special Election

| | | Votes | % |
|---|---|---|---|
| 8 | J. Glancy Jones (D) | 5,078 | 60.0 |
| | Keim (W) | 3,382 | 40.0 |

## SOUTH CAROLINA

| | | Votes | % |
|---|---|---|---|
| 1 | John McQueen (D) | 5,154 | 67.4 |
| | Wilson | 2,488 | 32.6 |
| 2 | William Aiken (D) | | 100.0 |
| 3 | Laurence M. Keitt (D) | | 100.0 |
| 4 | Preston S. Brooks (SSR D) | 6,118 | 66.7 |
| | Garlington | 3,051 | 33.3 |
| 5 | James L. Orr (D) | | 100.0 |
| 6 | William W. Boyce (SSR D) | | 100.0 |

## VERMONT

| | | Votes | % |
|---|---|---|---|
| 1 | James Meacham (W) | 8,626 | 70.3 |
| | S. W. Jewett (D) | 3,464 | 28.3 |
| 2 | Justin S. Morrill (W) | 8,380 | 50.2 |
| | J. W. D. Parker (D) | 5,848 | 35.0 |
| | Oscar L. Shafter | 2,473 | 14.8 |
| 3 | Alvah Sabin (W) | 7,862 | 68.4 |
| | W. Heywood (D) | 3,608 | 31.4 |

## WISCONSIN

| | | Votes | % |
|---|---|---|---|
| 1 | Daniel Wells Jr (D) | 8,458 | 54.6 |
| | Spooner (R) | 7,026 | 45.4 |
| 2 | Cadwallader C. Washburn (R) | 11,936 | 60.2 |
| | Hoyt (D) | 7,894 | 39.8 |
| 3 | Charles Billinghurst (R) | 13,359 | 60.9 |
| | Macy (D) | 8,596 | 39.2 |

# 1855 House Elections

## ALABAMA

| | Candidates | Votes | % |
|---|---|---|---|
| 1 | Percy Walker (AM) | 5,656 | 52.4 |
| | James A. Stallworth (D) | 5,137 | 47.6 |
| 2 | Eli S. Shorter (A-KN D) | 6,718 | 55.0 |
| | J. C. Alford (D) | 5,490 | 45.0 |
| 3 | James F. Dowdell (D) | 6,327 | 52.2 |
| | T. H. Watts (AM) | 5,786 | 47.8 |
| 4 | William R. Smith (AM) | 4,984 | 61.1 |
| | Sydenham Moore (D) | 3,177 | 38.9 |
| 5 | George S. Houston (D) | 5,770 | 100.0 |
| 6 | Williamson R. W. Cobb (D) | 6,260 | 62.9 |
| | J. M. Adams (A-KN I) | 3,697 | 37.1 |
| 7 | Sampson W. Harris (D) | 6,990 | 57.3 |
| | W. B. Martin (A-KN ID) | 5,220 | 42.8 |

## CONNECTICUT

| | Candidates | Votes | % |
|---|---|---|---|
| 1 | Ezra Clark Jr (AM) | 8,519 | 52.0 |
| | Pratt (D) | 7,852 | 48.0 |
| 2 | John Woodruff (AM) | 9,876 | 55.5 |
| | Arld (D) | 7,918 | 44.5 |
| 3 | Sidney Dean (AM) | 8,055 | 67.5 |
| | White (D) | 3,877 | 32.5 |
| 4 | William W. Welch (AM) | 9,701 | 55.7 |
| | Noble (D) | 7,702 | 44.3 |

## GEORGIA

| | Candidates | Votes | % |
|---|---|---|---|
| 1 | James L. Seward (D) | 6,179 | 57.6 |
| | Varnadoe (AM) | 4,541 | 42.4 |
| 2 | Martin J. Crawford (D) | 7,746 | 52.0 |
| | Hawkins (AM) | 7,153 | 48.0 |
| 3 | Robert P. Trippe (AM) | 6,112 | 54.0 |
| | Smith (D) | 5,216 | 46.1 |
| 4 | Hiram Warner (D) | 6,883 | 50.3 |
| | Hill (AM) | 6,813 | 49.7 |
| 5 | John H. Lumpkin (D) | 11,290 | 58.6 |
| | Tumlin (AM) | 7,978 | 41.4 |
| 6 | Howell Cobb (D) | 9,203 | 63.8 |
| | Franklin (AM) | 5,227 | 36.2 |
| 7 | Nathaniel G. Foster (AM) | 4,792 | 51.1 |
| | Stephens (D) | 4,580 | 48.9 |
| 8 | Alexander H. Stephens (D) | 5,808 | 65.4 |
| | Lamar (AM) | 3,079 | 34.7 |

## KENTUCKY

| | Candidates | Votes | % |
|---|---|---|---|
| 1 | Henry C. Burnett (D) | 9,323 | 62.0 |
| | W. G. Hughes (AM) | 5,708 | 38.0 |
| 2 | John P. Campbell (AM) | 7,533 | 55.3 |
| | Samuel O. Peyton (D) | 6,092 | 44.7 |
| 3 | Warner L. Underwood (AM) | 7,362 | 56.9 |
| | James P. Bates (D) | 5,580 | 43.1 |
| 4 | Albert G. Talbott (D) | 6,586 | 50.1 |
| | F. T. Fox (AM) | 6,570 | 49.9 |
| 5 | Joshua H. Jewett (D) | 7,076 | 51.6 |
| | C. G. Wintersmith (AM) | 6,628 | 48.4 |
| 6 | John M. Elliott (D) | 7,685 | 54.8 |
| | George W. Dunlap (AM) | 6,340 | 45.2 |
| 7 | Humphrey Marshall (AM) | 6,932 | 61.3 |
| | William Preston (D) | 4,378 | 38.7 |
| 8 | Alexander Keith Marshall (AM) | 7,039 | 56.0 |
| | James O. Harrison (D) | 5,536 | 44.0 |
| 9 | Leander M. Cox (AM) | 8,085 | 55.1 |
| | R. H. Stanton (D) | 6,598 | 44.9 |
| 10 | Samuel F. Swope (AM) | 7,490 | 51.7 |
| | Henry C. Harris (D) | 6,991 | 48.3 |

## LOUISIANA

| | Candidates | Votes | % |
|---|---|---|---|
| 1 | George Eustis Jr (AM) | 2,588 | 53.4 |
| | Albert Fabre (D) | 2,258 | 46.6 |
| 2 | Miles Taylor (D) | 6,175 | 51.5 |
| | Hunt (AM) | 5,810 | 48.5 |
| 3 | Thomas G. Davidson (D) | 4,731 | 50.6 |
| | Pond (AM) | 4,616 | 49.4 |
| 4 | John M. Sandidge (D) | 8,942 | 58.1 |
| | Lewis (AM) | 6,461 | 42.0 |

## MARYLAND

| | Candidates | Votes | % |
|---|---|---|---|
| 1 | James A. Stewart (D) | 6,173 | 51.3 |
| | Dennis (AM) | 5,868 | 48.7 |
| 2 | James B. Ricaud (AM) | 8,479 | 56.6 |
| | Jacob Shower (D) | 6,506 | 43.4 |
| 3 | J. Morrison Harris (AM) | 6,538 | 50.2 |
| | Vansant (D) | 6,484 | 49.8 |
| 4 | H. Winter Davis (AM) | 7,988 | 51.6 |
| | May (D) | 7,493 | 48.4 |
| 5 | Henry W. Hoffman (AM) | 8,320 | 52.4 |
| | Hamiln (D) | 7,569 | 47.6 |
| 6 | Thomas F. Bowie (D) | 5,539 | 53.9 |
| | Watkins (AM) | 4,736 | 46.1 |

## MASSACHUSETTS

### Special Election

| | Candidates | Votes | % |
|---|---|---|---|
| 10 | Calvin C. Chaffee (AM) | 4,716 | 36.0 |
| | John W. Foster | 4,349 | 33.2 |
| | Haynes H. Chilson | 3,317 | 25.3 |
| | Edward Dickenson (W) | 725 | 5.5 |

## MISSISSIPPI

| | Candidates | Votes | % |
|---|---|---|---|
| 1 | Daniel B. Wright (D) | 6,547 | 56.4 |
| | J. H. R. Taylor (AM) | 5,055 | 43.6 |
| 2 | Hendley S. Bennett (D) | 4,229 | 51.9 |
| | L. E. Housten (AM) | 3,922 | 48.1 |
| 3 | William Barksdale (D) | 6,850 | 55.3 |
| | Joseph B. Cobb (AM) | 5,542 | 44.7 |
| 4 | William A. Lake (W) | 5,196 | 52.0 |
| | Otho R. Singleton (D) | 4,792 | 48.0 |
| 5 | John A. Quitman (D) | 5,887 | 58.5 |
| | Giles M. Hillyer (W) | 4,178 | 41.5 |

## NEW HAMPSHIRE

| | Candidates | Votes | % |
|---|---|---|---|
| 1 | James Pike (AM) | 12,806 | 56.9 |
| | Kittredge (D) | 9,697 | 43.1 |
| 2 | Mason W. Tappan (AM) | 12,202 | 59.3 |
| | Morrison (D) | 8,392 | 40.8 |
| 3 | Aaron H. Cragin (AM) | 11,715 | 59.1 |
| | Wheeler (D) | 8,099 | 40.9 |

## NORTH CAROLINA

| | Candidates | Votes | % |
|---|---|---|---|
| 1 | Robert T. Paine (AM) | 5,228 | 51.7 |
| | Henry M. Shaw (D) | 4,882 | 48.3 |
| 2 | Thomas Ruffin (D) | 6,739 | 66.1 |
| | Thomas J. Latham (AM) | 3,464 | 34.0 |
| 3 | Warren Winslow (D) | 5,929 | 54.9 |
| | David Reid (AM) | 4,863 | 45.1 |
| 4 | Lawrence O'B. Branch (D) | 6,794 | 61.7 |
| | James B. Shepard (AM) | 4,223 | 38.3 |
| 5 | Edwin G. Reade (AM) | 7,061 | 65.3 |
| | John Kerr (W) | 3,756 | 34.7 |

| | Candidates | Votes | % |
|---|---|---|---|
| 6 | Richard C. Puryear (AM) | 6,516 | 51.4 |
| | Alfred M. Scales (D) | 6,150 | 48.6 |
| 7 | F. Burton Craige (D) | 6,745 | 62.2 |
| | Samuel N. Stowe (AM) | 4,104 | 37.8 |
| 8 | Thomas L. Clingman (D) | 8,079 | 55.1 |
| | Leander B. Carmichael (AM) | 6,584 | 44.9 |

## RHODE ISLAND

| | | Votes | % |
|---|---|---|---|
| 1 | Nathaniel B. Durfee (AM) | 5,004 | 72.9 |
| | Thomas Davis (D) | 1,576 | 23.0 |
| 2 | Benjamin B. Thurston (AM) | 4,359 | 87.9 |

## TENNESSEE

| | | Votes | % |
|---|---|---|---|
| 1 | Albert G. Watkins (D) | 7,781 | 50.9 |
| | Taylor (AM) | 7,511 | 49.1 |
| 2 | William H. Sneed (AM) | 6,246 | 54.0 |
| | Cummins (D) | 5,327 | 46.0 |
| 3 | Samuel A. Smith (D) | 7,872 | 51.8 |
| | Anderson (AM) | 7,331 | 48.2 |
| 4 | John H. Savage (D) | 6,016 | 52.0 |
| | Cullom (D) | 5,563 | 48.0 |
| 5 | Charles Ready (AM) | 7,069 | 91.8 |
| | Keeble (D) | 632 | 8.2 |
| 6 | George W. Jones (D) | 8,476 | 65.6 |
| | Gordon (AM) | 4,445 | 34.4 |
| 7 | John V. Wright (D) | 7,927 | 57.2 |
| | Kendrick (AM) | 5,922 | 42.8 |
| 8 | Felix K. Zollicoffer (AM) | 6,958 | 58.9 |
| | Torbett (D) | 4,857 | 41.1 |
| 9 | Emerson Etheridge (AM) | 7,952 | 51.8 |
| | Freeman (D) | 7,394 | 48.2 |
| 10 | Thomas Rivers (AM) | 5,860 | 53.3 |
| | Currin (D) | 5,136 | 46.7 |

## TEXAS

| | | Votes | % |
|---|---|---|---|
| 1 | Peter H. Bell (D) | 10,342 | 50.1 |
| | Hancock (AM) | 10,311 | 49.9 |
| 2 | Lemuel D. Evans (AM) | 14,379 | 60.2 |
| | Ward (D) | 9,496 | 39.8 |

## VIRGINIA

| | | Votes | % |
|---|---|---|---|
| 1 | Thomas H. Bayly (D) | | 100.0 |
| 2 | John S. Millson (D) | 4,769 | 53.3 |
| | Watts (AM) | 4,180 | 46.7 |
| 3 | John S. Caskie (D) | 5,951 | 52.1 |
| | Scott (AM) | 5,466 | 47.9 |
| 4 | William O. Goode (D) | 1,163 | 63.8 |
| | Tazewell (AM) | 661 | 36.2 |
| 5 | Thomas S. Bocock (D) | 4,566 | 52.9 |
| | Claiborne (AM) | 4,073 | 47.2 |
| 6 | Paulus Powell (D) | 3,834 | 56.3 |
| | Ligon (AM) | 2,976 | 43.7 |
| 7 | William Smith (D) | | 100.0 |
| 8 | Charles J. Faulkner (D) | 7,158 | 50.7 |
| | Boteler (AM) | 6,959 | 49.3 |
| 9 | John Letcher (D) | | 100.0 |
| 10 | Zedekiah Kidwell (D) | 6,615 | 56.7 |
| | Pendleton (AM) | 5,059 | 43.3 |
| 11 | John S. Carlisle (AM) | 8,333 | 51.2 |
| | Lewis (D) | 7,942 | 48.8 |
| 12 | Henry A. Edmundson (D) | 7,492 | 54.0 |
| | Staples (AM) | 6,385 | 46.0 |
| 13 | Fayette McMullen (D) | 4,289 | 60.5 |
| | Trigg (AM) | 2,803 | 39.5 |

# 1856 House Elections

## ARKANSAS

| | | | |
|---|---|---|---|
| 1 | Alfred B. Greenwood (D) | 15,399 | 71.4 |
| | Thomason (AM) | 6,161 | 28.6 |
| 2 | Edward A. Warren (D) | 11,835 | 57.6 |
| | Fowler (AM) | 8,701 | 42.4 |

## CALIFORNIA

| | | | |
|---|---|---|---|
| AL | Joseph C. McKibbin (D) | 50,895✓ | |
| | Charles L. Scott (D) | 50,813✓ | |
| | B. C. Whitman (AM) | 36,078 | |
| | A. B. Dibble (AM) | 35,325 | |
| | L. P. Rankin (R) | 21,075 | |
| | J. D. Turner (R) | 21,164 | |

## DELAWARE

| | | | |
|---|---|---|---|
| AL | William G. Whiteley (D) | 8,111 | 56.1 |
| | Elisha D. Cullen (AM) | 6,360 | 44.0 |

## FLORIDA

| | | | |
|---|---|---|---|
| AL | George S. Hawkins (D) | 6,392 | 53.1 |
| | James M. Baker (AM) | 5,650 | 46.9 |

## ILLINOIS

| | | | |
|---|---|---|---|
| 1 | Elihu B. Washburne (R) | 18,070 | 72.6 |
| | Richard S. S. Malony (D) | 6,227 | 25.0 |
| 2 | John F. Farnsworth (R) | 21,518 | 67.2 |
| | John Van Nortwick (D) | 9,814 | 30.7 |
| 3 | Owen Lovejoy (R) | 19,068 | 59.4 |
| | Osgood (D) | 13,007 | 40.5 |
| 4 | William Kellogg (R) | 16,175 | 51.1 |
| | James W. Davison (D) | 14,474 | 45.7 |
| 5 | Isaac N. Morris (D) | 12,059 | 53.7 |
| | Jackson Grimshaw (R) | 10,294 | 45.8 |
| 6 | Thomas L. Harris (D) | 14,196 | 54.0 |
| | John Williams (R) | 12,077 | 46.0 |
| 7 | Aaron Shaw (D) | 12,994 | 56.8 |
| | Henry P. H. Bromwell (R) | 9,878 | 43.2 |
| 8 | Robert Smith (D) | 11,299 | 60.1 |
| | I. D. Lansing (R) | 7,512 | 39.9 |
| 9 | Samuel S. Marshall (D) | 15,968 | 81.5 |
| | Benjamin L. Wiley (R) | 3,419 | 17.4 |

### Special Elections

| | | | |
|---|---|---|---|
| 5 | Jacob C. Davis (D) | 12,212 | 52.6 |
| | Thomas C. Sharp (R) | 8,182 | 35.2 |
| | James B. Kyle | 2,826 | 12.2 |
| 7 | James C. Allen (D) | 13,081 | 56.3 |
| | William B. Archer (R) | 10,136 | 43.7 |
| 8 | I. L. D. Morrison (D) | 10,756 | 55.8 |
| | John Thomas (R) | 8,231 | 42.7 |

## INDIANA

| | | | |
|---|---|---|---|
| 1 | James Lockhart (D) | 12,747 | 61.5 |
| | Veach (R) | 7,977 | 38.5 |
| 2 | William H. English (D) | 10,577 | 57.2 |
| | Wilson (R) | 7,927 | 42.8 |
| 3 | James Hughes (D) | 10,629 | 53.8 |
| | Hendks (R) | 9,113 | 46.2 |
| 4 | James B. Foley (D) | 10,451 | 53.7 |
| | Cumback (R) | 8,998 | 46.3 |
| 5 | David Kilgore (R) | 11,132 | 60.8 |
| | Johnson (D) | 7,183 | 39.2 |
| 6 | James M. Gregg (D) | 11,787 | 52.1 |
| | Coburn (R) | 10,840 | 47.9 |
| 7 | John G. Davis (D) | 11,137 | 53.9 |
| | Usher (R) | 9,529 | 46.1 |

| | | | |
|---|---|---|---|
| 8 | James Wilson (R) | 11,302 | 50.5 |
| | Voorhees (D) | 11,072 | 49.5 |
| 9 | Schuyler Colfax (R) | 12,921 | 52.1 |
| | Stuart (D) | 11,890 | 47.9 |
| 10 | Samuel Brenton (R) | 10,699 | 51.7 |
| | Lowry (D) | 9,989 | 48.3 |
| 11 | John U. Pettit (R) | 11,235 | 51.8 |
| | Garver (D) | 10,443 | 48.2 |

## IOWA

| | | | |
|---|---|---|---|
| 1 | Samuel R. Curtis (R) | 18,065 | 50.2 |
| | Augustus Hall (D) | 17,110 | 47.5 |
| 2 | Timothy Davis (R) | 21,888 | 57.9 |
| | Shepherd Leffler (D) | 15,868 | 42.0 |

## MAINE

| | | | |
|---|---|---|---|
| 1 | John M. Wood (R) | 11,215 | 53.4 |
| | Little (COALIT) | 9,776 | 46.6 |
| 2 | Charles J. Gilman (R) | 12,953 | 57.3 |
| | Pillsbury (COALIT) | 9,670 | 42.7 |
| 3 | Nehemiah Abbott (R) | 10,562 | 56.1 |
| | Ingalls (COALIT) | 8,252 | 43.9 |
| 4 | Freeman H. Morse (R) | 13,750 | 65.0 |
| | Bronson (COALIT) | 7,378 | 35.0 |
| 5 | Israel Washburn Jr (R) | 12,517 | 60.1 |
| | Sanborn (COALIT) | 8,312 | 39.9 |
| 6 | Stephen C. Foster (R) | 8,503 | 52.9 |
| | Wiswell (COALIT) | 7,567 | 47.1 |

## MASSACHUSETTS

| | | | |
|---|---|---|---|
| 1 | Robert B. Hall (R) | 7,904 | 69.6 |
| | Moses Bates Jr (D) | 1,830 | 16.1 |
| | Daniel Fisher (AM) | 1,601 | 14.1 |
| 2 | James Buffington (R) | 11,658 | 72.4 |
| | Charles R. Vickery (D) | 3,314 | 20.6 |
| | Danius Dunbar (AM) | 1,132 | 7.0 |
| 3 | William L. Damrell (R) | 10,433 | 61.5 |
| | Arthur W. Austin (D) | 5,077 | 29.9 |
| | Alfred B. Ely (AM) | 1,435 | 8.5 |
| 4 | Linus B. Comins (R) | 5,188 | 45.8 |
| | Charles G. Greene (D) | 4,431 | 39.1 |
| | Benjamin F. Cooke (AM) | 1,678 | 14.8 |
| 5 | Anson Burlingame (AM) | 6,582 | 50.2 |
| | William Appleton (D & AM) | 6,513 | 49.7 |
| 6 | Timothy Davis (R) | 10,044 | 69.4 |
| | Ruth J. Lord (D) | 3,214 | 22.2 |
| | Benjamin Parley Poor (AM) | 1,121 | 7.7 |
| 7 | Nathaniel P. Banks (R) | 10,814 | 61.9 |
| | Isaac H. Wright (D) | 4,593 | 26.3 |
| | Isaac Storey (D) | 2,049 | 11.7 |
| 8 | Chauncey L. Knapp (R) | 9,616 | 67.4 |
| | Benjamin F. Butler (D) | 3,686 | 25.9 |
| | Abiel L. Lewis (AM) | 864 | 6.1 |
| 9 | Eli Thayer (R) | 8,920 | 53.7 |
| | Alex Dewitt (AM) | 4,414 | 26.6 |
| | Nathaniel Wood (D) | 2,987 | 18.0 |
| 10 | Calvin C. Chaffee (R) | 10,845 | 72.4 |
| | William C. Fowler (D & AM) | 4,081 | 27.2 |
| 11 | Henry L Dawes (R) | 6,709 | 43.8 |
| | Josiah D. Weston (D) | 4,398 | 28.7 |
| | Mark Trafton (AM) | 4,194 | 27.4 |

## MICHIGAN

| | | | |
|---|---|---|---|
| 1 | William A. Howard (R) | 13,658 | 51.6 |
| | George Lathrop (D) | 12,791 | 48.4 |
| 2 | Henry Waldron (R) | 16,467 | 62.1 |
| | John S. Barry (D) | 10,064 | 37.9 |
| 3 | David S. Walbridge (R) | 23,970 | 59.6 |
| | Flavius Littlejohn (D) | 16,268 | 40.4 |
| 4 | De Witt C. Leach (R) | 18,715 | 55.2 |
| | George W. Peck (D) | 15,186 | 44.8 |

## MISSOURI

| | | | |
|---|---|---|---|
| 1 | Francis P. Blair Jr (BENTON D) | 6,035 | 43.8 |
| | Kennett (AM) | 5,549 | 40.3 |
| | Reynolds (D) | 2,181 | 15.8 |
| 2 | Thomas L. Anderson (AM) | 8,876 | 52.1 |
| | Richmond (D) | 8,149 | 47.9 |
| 3 | James S. Green (D) | 10,126* | 55.3 |
| | Lindley (AM) | 8,172 | 44.7 |
| 4 | James Craig (D) | 8,742 | 56.8 |
| | Moss (AM) | 6,274 | 40.8 |
| 5 | Samuel H. Woodson (AM) | 6,006 | 41.6 |
| | Douglas (D) | 4,684 | 32.4 |
| | Price (BENTON D) | 3,755 | 26.0 |
| 6 | John S. Phelps (D) | 9,718 | 58.1 |
| | Emerson (AM) | 6,911 | 41.3 |
| 7 | Samuel Caruthers (D) | 8,291 | 52.7 |
| | Perryman (AM) | 4,883 | 31.0 |
| | Stevson (BENTON D) | 2,556 | 16.3 |

### Special Election

| | | | |
|---|---|---|---|
| 5 | Thomas P. Akers (AM) | 6,569 | 55.8 |
| | Jackson (D) | 5,211 | 44.2 |

## NEW JERSEY

| | | | |
|---|---|---|---|
| 1 | Isaiah D. Clawson (FUS) | 9,673 | 56.8 |
| | Hineline (D) | 7,351 | 43.2 |
| 2 | George R. Robbins (FUS) | 11,723 | 52.3 |
| | Wall (D) | 10,692 | 47.7 |
| 3 | Garnett B. Adrain (D) | 10,781 | 52.5 |
| | Bishop (FUS) | 9,768 | 47.5 |
| 4 | John Huyler (D) | 9,165 | 52.7 |
| | Osborne (R) | 5,876 | 33.8 |
| | Inglis (AM) | 2,355 | 13.5 |
| 5 | Jacob R. Wortendyke (D) | 9,099 | 42.9 |
| | Dodd (R) | 6,480 | 30.5 |
| | Betts (AM) | 5,638 | 26.6 |

## NEW YORK

| | | | |
|---|---|---|---|
| 1 | John A. Searing (D) | 8,960 | 44.1 |
| | Jennings (AM) | 5,892 | 29.0 |
| | Lord (R) | 5,449 | 26.8 |
| 2 | George Taylor (D) | 8,591 | 40.8 |
| | Stranhan (R) | 5,869 | 27.9 |
| | Wood (AM) | 5,476 | 26.0 |
| | McCue | 1,123 | 5.3 |
| 3 | Daniel E. Sickles (D) | 5,716 | 53.2 |
| | Duganne (AM) | 2,905 | 27.0 |
| | Guy R. Pelton (R) | 2,126 | 19.8 |
| 4 | John Kelly (D) | 8,319 | 72.0 |
| | Gould (AM) | 1,735 | 15.0 |
| | Ryckman (R) | 1,497 | 13.0 |
| 5 | William B. Maclay (D) | 5,863 | 41.6 |
| | Northp (AM) | 3,798 | 26.9 |
| | Andrews (R) | 3,274 | 23.2 |
| | Hamilton (ID) | 1,169 | 8.3 |
| 6 | John Cochrane (D) | 7,531 | 49.6 |
| | Stillman (R) | 3,991 | 26.3 |
| | Williams (AM) | 3,658 | 24.1 |
| 7 | Elijah Ward (D) | 6,531 | 41.0 |
| | Briggs (AM) | 4,461 | 28.0 |
| | Nye (R) | 4,100 | 25.7 |
| | Bulloc | 854 | 5.4 |
| 8 | Horace F. Clark (D) | 7,482 | 50.2 |
| | Abram Wakeman (R) | 3,760 | 25.3 |
| | Knapp (AM) | 3,651 | 24.5 |
| 9 | John B. Haskin (D) | 7,195 | 39.5 |
| | Strang (R) | 5,935 | 32.6 |
| | Cobb (AM) | 5,084 | 27.9 |
| 10 | Ambrose S. Murray (R) | 6,156 | 39.3 |
| | Fowler (D) | 5,581 | 35.6 |
| | Trotter (AM) | 3,936 | 25.1 |

## NEW YORK

| | Candidates | Votes | % |
|---|---|---|---|
| 11 | William F. Russell (D) | 6,878 | 38.9 |
| | Fream (AM) | 5,902 | 33.4 |
| | Brodhd (R) | 4,912 | 27.8 |
| 12 | John Thompson (R) | 9,247 | 45.5 |
| | Chamberlain (D) | 7,972 | 39.2 |
| | Teller (AM) | 3,116 | 15.3 |
| 13 | Abram B. Olin (R) | 5,206 | 37.0 |
| | Griswold (D) | 4,758 | 33.8 |
| | Fonda (AM) | 4,108 | 29.2 |
| 14 | Erastus Corning (D) | 8,296 | 46.0 |
| | Perry (AM) | 5,095 | 28.3 |
| | Van Dyck (R) | 4,631 | 25.7 |
| 15 | Edward Dodd (R) | 11,717 | 51.6 |
| | Cramer (AM) | 5,633 | 24.8 |
| | Gray (D) | 5,373 | 23.7 |
| 16 | George W. Palmer (R) | 6,799 | 44.5 |
| | Averill (D) | 4,363 | 28.5 |
| | Ross (AM) | 4,129 | 27.0 |
| 17 | Francis E. Spinner (R) | 14,722 | 70.7 |
| | Dodge (D & AM) | 6,115 | 29.4 |
| 18 | Clark B. Cochrane (R) | 9,719 | 44.6 |
| | Rossiter (D) | 6,123 | 28.1 |
| | Smith (AM) | 5,936 | 27.3 |
| 19 | Oliver A. Morse (R) | 10,724 | 54.7 |
| | Gregory (D & AM) | 8,881 | 45.3 |
| 20 | Orsamus B. Matteson (R) | 10,618 | 56.2 |
| | Johnson (D & AM) | 8,275 | 43.8 |
| 21 | Henry Bennett (R) | 13,357 | 62.0 |
| | Hyde (D & AM) | 8,192 | 38.0 |
| 22 | Henry C. Goodwin (R) | 14,380 | 65.0 |
| | Clark (D) | 6,080 | 27.5 |
| | Culver (AM) | 1,671 | 7.6 |
| 23 | Charles B. Hoard (R) | 11,149 | 64.6 |
| | Dorwin (D) | 6,070 | 35.2 |
| 24 | Amos P. Granger (R) | 9,748 | 61.0 |
| | Peck (D) | 4,525 | 28.3 |
| | Beach (AM) | 1,720 | 10.8 |
| 25 | Edwin B. Morgan (R) | 12,631 | 63.3 |
| | Richmond (D) | 3,685 | 18.5 |
| | Fosgt (AM) | 3,644 | 18.3 |
| 26 | Emory B. Pottle (R) | 9,368 | 53.0 |
| | Andrew Oliver (AM) | 4,411 | 25.0 |
| | Ogden (D) | 3,897 | 22.1 |
| 27 | John M. Parker (R) | 12,383 | 56.3 |
| | Hathaway (D) | 8,377 | 38.1 |
| | Lawr (AM) | 1,229 | 5.6 |
| 28 | William H. Kelsey (R) | 10,509 | 53.4 |
| | Hallett (AM) | 4,895 | 24.9 |
| | Angel (D) | 4,266 | 21.7 |
| 29 | Samuel G. Andrews (R) | 7,786 | 51.0 |
| | Paine (D) | 4,337 | 28.4 |
| | Clark (AM) | 3,156 | 20.7 |
| 30 | Judson W. Sherman (R) | 13,867 | 64.0 |
| | Richmond (D) | 5,032 | 23.2 |
| | Cooly (AM) | 2,758 | 12.7 |
| 31 | Silas M. Burroughs (R) | 6,885 | 51.7 |
| | Hunt (AM) | 4,694 | 35.3 |
| | Church (D) | 1,731 | 13.0 |
| 32 | Israel T. Hatch (D) | 7,399 | 37.2 |
| | Spaulding (R) | 6,923 | 34.8 |
| | Haven (AM) | 5,548 | 27.9 |
| 33 | Reuben E. Fenton (R) | 12,046 | 64.3 |
| | Allen (D) | 3,436 | 18.3 |
| | Edwds (AM) | 3,251 | 17.4 |

## OHIO

| | Candidates | Votes | % |
|---|---|---|---|
| 1 | George H. Pendleton (D) | 6,133 | 47.1 |
| | Taft (R) | 4,256 | 32.7 |
| | Tornce (AM) | 2,642 | 20.3 |
| 2 | William S. Groesbeck (D) | 5,738 | 43.1 |
| | Gurley (R) | 4,343 | 32.6 |
| | Harrison (AM) | 3,229 | 24.3 |
| 3 | Lewis D. Campbell (R) | 9,338‡ | 50.1 |
| | Clement I. Vallandigham (D) | 9,319 | 50.0 |
| 4 | Mathias H. Nichols (R) | 9,415 | 49.7 |
| | Dorsey (D) | 9,172 | 48.4 |
| 5 | Richard Mott (R) | 10,018 | 51.0 |
| | Edgerton (D) | 9,157 | 46.6 |
| 6 | Joseph R. Cockerill (D) | 8,603 | 48.7 |
| | Jonas R. Emrie (R) | 7,460 | 42.2 |
| | Trimbel (AM) | 1,598 | 9.1 |
| 7 | Aaron Harlan (R) | 9,027 | 59.7 |
| | Ward (D) | 5,076 | 33.6 |
| | Elsbury (AM) | 1,011 | 6.7 |
| 8 | Benjamin Stanton (R) | 9,756 | 56.7 |
| | Runkle (D) | 6,210 | 36.1 |
| | Glover (AM) | 1,239 | 7.2 |
| 9 | Lawrence W. Hall (D) | 9,561 | 49.7 |
| | Cooper K. Watson (R) | 9,382 | 48.7 |
| 10 | Joseph Miller (D) | 7,403 | 42.6 |
| | Hoffman (R) | 5,633 | 32.4 |
| | Oscar F. Moore (AM) | 4,326 | 24.9 |
| 11 | Valentine B. Horton (R) | 10,272 | 50.9 |
| | Medill (D) | 9,927 | 49.2 |
| 12 | Samuel S. Cox (D) | 8,938 | 48.7 |
| | Galloway (R) | 8,582 | 46.7 |
| 13 | John Sherman (R) | 9,926 | 58.4 |
| | Bramback (D) | 7,065 | 41.6 |
| 14 | Philemon Bliss (R) | 10,414 | 57.8 |
| | Firestone (D) | 7,617 | 42.2 |
| 15 | Joseph Burns (D) | 9,194 | 50.1 |
| | Sapp (R) | 9,143 | 49.9 |
| 16 | Cydnor B. Tompkins (R) | 7,248 | 48.0 |
| | Smith (D) | 6,462 | 42.8 |
| | Haynes (AM) | 1,382 | 9.2 |
| 17 | William Lawrence (D) | 8,085 | 47.8 |
| | Albright (R) | 6,805 | 40.3 |
| | Davenport (AM) | 2,013 | 11.9 |
| 18 | Benjamin F. Leiter (R) | 9,394 | 58.0 |
| | Lahm (D) | 6,799 | 42.0 |
| 19 | Edward Wade (R) | 9,431 | 67.9 |
| | Hilliard (D) | 4,467 | 32.1 |
| 20 | Joshua R. Giddings (R) | 9,567 | 66.6 |
| | Burchard (D) | 4,795 | 33.4 |
| 21 | John A. Bingham (R) | 9,444 | 57.7 |
| | Woods (D) | 6,933 | 42.3 |

## PENNSYLVANIA

| | Candidates | Votes | % |
|---|---|---|---|
| 1 | Thomas B. Florence (D) | 9,495 | 56.6 |
| | Knight (UN) | 7,275 | 43.4 |
| 2 | Edward Joy Morris (UN) | 6,411 | 51.6 |
| | Marsll (D) | 6,018 | 48.4 |
| 3 | James Landy (D) | 7,933 | 54.0 |
| | William Millward (UN) | 6,753 | 46.0 |
| 4 | Henry M. Phillips (D) | 9,279 | 50.7 |
| | Forst (D) | 6,560 | 35.9 |
| | William D. Kelley (R) | 2,457 | 13.4 |
| 5 | Owen Jones (D) | 9,674 | 54.9 |
| | Mulvany (UN) | 7,961 | 45.1 |
| 6 | John Hickman (D) | 8,024 | 48.9 |
| | Bowen (UN) | 7,851 | 47.9 |
| 7 | Henry Chapman (D) | 10,321 | 54.0 |
| | Bradshaw (R) | 8,789 | 46.0 |
| 8 | J. Glancy Jones (D) | 9,951 | 71.6 |
| | Yoder (UN) | 3,947 | 28.4 |
| 9 | Anthony E. Roberts (UN) | 10,001 | 54.6 |
| | Heister (D) | 8,320 | 45.4 |
| 10 | John C. Kunkel (UN) | 9,227 | 55.6 |
| | Eyer (D) | 7,360 | 44.4 |
| 11 | William L. Dewart (D) | 8,959 | 58.3 |
| | Campbell (UN) | 6,418 | 41.7 |
| 12 | John G. Montgomery (D) | 10,442 | 57.7 |
| | Smith (UN) | 7,657 | 42.3 |
| 13 | William H. Dimmick (D) | 11,235 | 68.9 |
| | E. S. Dimk (UN) | 5,065 | 31.1 |
| 14 | Galusha A. Grow (R) | 13,325 | 71.3 |
| | Sherwd (D) | 5,361 | 28.7 |
| 15 | Allison White (D) | 9,980 | 51.4 |
| | Irwin (R) | 9,450 | 48.6 |
| 16 | John A. Ahl (D) | 11,191 | 53.7 |
| | Todd (UN) | 9,670 | 46.4 |
| 17 | Wilson Reilly (D) | 10,224 | 51.3 |
| | Pumroy (UN) | 9,715 | 48.7 |
| 18 | John R. Edie (UN) | 8,792 | 50.8 |
| | Pershing (D) | 8,508 | 49.2 |
| 19 | John Covode (UN) | 10,409 | 54.4 |
| | McKinley (D) | 8,724 | 45.6 |
| 20 | William Montgomery (D) | 10,256 | 52.2 |
| | Knight (UN) | 9,411 | 47.9 |
| 21 | David Ritchie (R) | 7,674 | 54.6 |
| | McCans (D) | 5,944 | 42.3 |
| 22 | Samuel A. Purviance (R) | 6,840 | 57.1 |
| | Gibson (D) | 4,854 | 40.5 |
| 23 | William Stewart (UN) | 8,552 | 61.0 |
| | Cunningham (D) | 5,467 | 39.0 |
| 24 | James L. Gillis (D) | 9,785 | 51.8 |
| | Myers (UN) | 9,114 | 48.2 |
| 25 | John Dick (R) | 8,944 | 68.0 |
| | McFadn (D) | 4,215 | 32.0 |

## SOUTH CAROLINA [1]

| | Candidates | Votes | % |
|---|---|---|---|
| 1 | John McQueen (D) | | 100.0 |
| 2 | W. Porcher Miles (D) | 2,323 | 50.5 |
| | James Gadsden | 1,684 | 36.0 |
| | John Cunningham | 590 | 12.8 |
| 3 | Laurence M. Keitt (D) | | 100.0 |
| 4 | Preston S. Brooks (SSR D) * | | 100.0 |
| 5 | James L. Orr (D) | | 100.0 |
| 6 | William W. Boyce (SSR D) | | 100.0 |

### Special Elections

| | | Votes | % |
|---|---|---|---|
| 3 | Laurence M. Keitt (D) | ✔ | |
| 4 | Preston S. Brooks (SSR D) | 7,922 | 100.0 |

## VERMONT

| | Candidates | Votes | % |
|---|---|---|---|
| 1 | Eliakim Persons Walton (R) | 10,398 | 76.2 |
| | Needhm (D) | 3,242 | 23.8 |
| 2 | Justin S. Morrill (R) | 13,695 | 75.8 |
| | Chase (D) | 4,358 | 24.2 |
| 3 | Homer Elihu Royce (R) | 9,116 | 74.4 |
| | Bingm (D) | 3,134 | 25.6 |

## WISCONSIN

| | Candidates | Votes | % |
|---|---|---|---|
| 1 | John F. Potter (R) | 13,111 | 50.6 |
| | Hadley (D) | 12,814 | 49.4 |
| 2 | Cadwallader C. Washburn (R) | 26,004 | 61.6 |
| | Crawford (D) | 16,233 | 38.4 |
| 3 | Charles Billinghurst (R) | 25,808 | 52.2 |
| | Hobart (D) | 23,648 | 47.8 |

1. Preston S. Brooks of South Carolina's 4th district, who was serving in the 34th Congress (1855-57) following his election in 1854, resigned July 14, 1856. He was subsequently re-elected to the 34th Congress in a special election which appears on this page. He took his seat Aug. 1, 1856 and was re-elected in the general election later in 1856 to the 35th Congress (1857-59). He died Jan. 27, 1857, and thus did not serve in that Congress.

Laurence M. Keitt of the 3rd district was also serving in the 34th Congress when he resigned July 16, 1856. Subsequently re-elected to the 34th Congress in the special election shown on this page to fill the vacancy caused by his resignation, he returned to the House Aug. 6, 1856. Later that year he was re-elected to the 35th Congress in the general election.

# 1857 House Elections

## ALABAMA

| | Candidates | Votes | % |
|---|---|---|---|
| 1 | James A. Stallworth (D) | 7,058 | 62.0 |
| | J. McCaskill (AM) | 4,330 | 38.0 |
| 2 | Eli S. Shorter (D) | 7,417 | 62.5 |
| | B. Peterson (AM) | 4,454 | 37.5 |
| 3 | James F. Dowdell (D) | 6,505 | 50.3 |
| | T. J. Judge (SR W) | 6,419 | 49.7 |
| 4 | Sydenham Moore (D) | 6,432 | 56.5 |
| | W. R. Smith (D) | 4,952 | 43.5 |
| 5 | George S. Houston (D) | 4,853 | 55.1 |
| | D. Hubbard (SO RTS D) | 3,956 | 44.9 |
| 6 | Williamson R. W. Cobb (D) | 5,975 | 61.0 |
| | Henry Sanford (D) | 3,504 | 36.7 |
| 7 | Jabez L. M. Curry (D) | 8,311 | 98.5 |

## CONNECTICUT

| | Candidates | Votes | % |
|---|---|---|---|
| 1 | Ezra Clark Jr (R) | 8,410 | 51.3 |
| | Hubbard (D) | 7,973 | 48.7 |
| 2 | Samuel Arnold (D) | 9,403 | 51.4 |
| | Woodruff (R) | 8,906 | 48.6 |
| 3 | Sidney Dean (R) | 6,082 | 54.9 |
| | Hovey (D) | 5,006 | 45.2 |
| 4 | William D. Bishop (D) | 8,403 | 50.1 |
| | Ferry (R) | 8,387 | 50.0 |

## GEORGIA

| | Candidates | Votes | % |
|---|---|---|---|
| 1 | James L. Seward (D) | 5,870 | 51.2 |
| | Bartow (AM) | 5,093 | 44.4 |
| 2 | Martin J. Crawford (D) | 8,220 | 56.4 |
| | Elam (AM) | 6,365 | 43.6 |
| 3 | Robert P. Trippe (AM) | 5,803 | 51.7 |
| | Bailey (D) | 5,423 | 48.3 |
| 4 | Lucius J. Gartrell (D) | 8,008 | 53.6 |
| | Tidwell (AM) | 6,939 | 46.4 |
| 5 | Augustus R. Wright (D) | 9,669 | 63.0 |
| | Hooper (ID) | 5,690 | 37.1 |
| 6 | James Jackson (D) | 7,751 | 56.6 |
| | Simmons (ID) | 5,956 | 43.5 |
| 7 | Joshua Hill (AM) | 4,800 | 51.5 |
| | L. Stephens (D) | 4,525 | 48.5 |
| 8 | Alexander H. Stephens (D) | 5,151 | 55.7 |
| | Miller (AM) | 4,096 | 44.3 |

## KENTUCKY

| | Candidates | Votes | % |
|---|---|---|---|
| 1 | Henry C. Burnett (D) | 8,989 | 75.3 |
| | Owen Grimes (AM) | 2,945 | 24.7 |
| 2 | Samuel O. Peyton (D) | 7,212 | 53.9 |
| | James L. Johnson (AM) | 6,173 | 46.1 |
| 3 | Warner L. Underwood (AM) | 6,359 | 50.8 |
| | Joseph H. Lewis (D) | 6,156 | 49.2 |
| 4 | Albert G. Talbott (D) | 7,025 | 50.6 |
| | William C. Anderson (AM) | 6,861 | 49.4 |
| 5 | Joshua H. Jewett (D) | 7,377 | 59.6 |
| | Bryan R. Young (AM) | 4,996 | 40.4 |
| 6 | John M. Elliott (D) | 7,470 | 55.7 |
| | John A. Moore (AM) | 5,950 | 44.3 |
| 7 | Humphrey Marshall (AM) | 6,085 | 55.0 |
| | Thomas H. Holt (D) | 4,979 | 45.0 |
| 8 | James B. Clay (D) | 6,577 | 50.5 |
| | Roger W. Hanson (AM) | 6,451 | 49.5 |
| 9 | John C. Mason (D) | 8,148 | 52.0 |
| | Leander M. Cox (AM) | 7,534 | 48.0 |
| 10 | John W. Stevenson (D) | 8,748 | 67.3 |
| | William Rankin (AM) | 4,185 | 32.2 |

## LOUISIANA

| | Candidates | Votes | % |
|---|---|---|---|
| 1 | George Eustis Jr (AM) | 2,336 | 60.5 |
| | Villiers (D) | 1,528 | 39.5 |
| 2 | Miles Taylor (D) | 4,950 | 50.3 |
| | Burke (AM) | 4,892 | 49.7 |
| 3 | Thomas G. Davidson (D) | 4,270 | 54.9 |
| | Watrsn (AM) | 3,512 | 45.1 |
| 4 | John M. Sandidge (D) | 9,060 | 63.5 |
| | Sparks (AM) | 5,205 | 36.5 |

## MARYLAND

| | Candidates | Votes | % |
|---|---|---|---|
| 1 | James A. Stewart (D) | 6,339 | 50.7 |
| | Townsend (AM) | 6,163 | 49.3 |
| 2 | James B. Ricaud (AM) | 8,701 | 52.3 |
| | McHenry (D) | 7,935 | 47.7 |
| 3 | J. Morrison Harris (AM) | 8,761 | 61.6 |
| | William Pinkney Whyte (D) | 5,455 | 38.4 |
| 4 | H. Winter Davis (AM) | 10,515 | 72.6 |
| | Henry P. Brooks (D) | 3,979 | 27.5 |
| 5 | Jacob M. Kunkel (D) | 8,376 | 50.5 |
| | Hoffman (AM) | 8,208 | 49.5 |
| 6 | Thomas F. Bowie (D) | 5,735 | 56.3 |
| | Blackistone (AM) | 4,453 | 43.7 |

## MINNESOTA

(Became a state May 11, 1858)

| | Candidates | Votes | % |
|---|---|---|---|
| AL | William W. Phelps (D) | 18,218 | |
| | James M. Cavanaugh (D) | 18,064 | |
| | G. L. Becker (D) | 18,019 | |
| | C. Aldrich (R) | 16,955 | |
| | M. S. Wilkinson (R) | 16,938 | |
| | H. A. Swift (R) | 16,827 | |

## MISSISSIPPI

| | Candidates | Votes | % |
|---|---|---|---|
| 1 | Lucius Q. C. Lamar (D) | 3,705 | 61.8 |
| | James L. Alcorn (W) | 2,288 | 38.2 |
| 2 | Reuben Davis (D) | 5,026 | 59.4 |
| | Charles Clark (W) | 3,431 | 40.6 |
| 3 | William Barksdale (D) | 5,129 | 97.7 |
| 4 | Otho R. Singleton (D) | 5,940 | 54.3 |
| | William H. Lake (W) | 4,997 | 45.7 |
| 5 | John A. Quitman (D) | 4,017 | 98.1 |

## NEW HAMPSHIRE

| | Candidates | Votes | % |
|---|---|---|---|
| 1 | James Pike (R) | 12,242 | 52.2 |
| | Kittridge (D) | 11,206 | 47.8 |
| 2 | Mason W. Tappan (R) | 10,685 | 53.8 |
| | Morrison (D) | 9,180 | 46.2 |
| 3 | Aaron H. Cragin (R) | 10,983 | 52.7 |
| | Wheeler (D) | 9,841 | 47.3 |

## NORTH CAROLINA

| | Candidates | Votes | % |
|---|---|---|---|
| 1 | Henry M. Shaw (D) | 5,293 | 50.2 |
| | William N. H. Smith (AM) | 5,255 | 49.8 |
| 2 | Thomas Ruffin (D) | 5,940 | 90.6 |
| 3 | Warren Winslow (D) | 6,337 | 81.0 |
| | O. P. Meares (AM) | 1,488 | 19.0 |
| 4 | Lawrence O'B. Branch (D) | 7,375 | 87.0 |
| 5 | John A. Gilmer (AM) | 5,692 | 54.0 |
| | Stephen W. Williams (D) | 4,845 | 46.0 |
| 6 | Alfred M. Scales (D) | 7,679 | 52.5 |
| | Richard C. Puryear (AM) | 6,950 | 47.5 |
| 7 | F. Burton Craige (D) | 6,482 | 92.2 |
| 8 | Thomas L. Clingman (D) | 8,674 | 69.8 |

## PENNSYLVANIA

**Special Election**

| | Candidates | Votes | % |
|---|---|---|---|
| 12 | Paul Leidy (D) | 9,826 | 61.0 |
| | Smith Thompson (R) | 6,294 | 39.0 |

## RHODE ISLAND

| | Candidates | Votes | % |
|---|---|---|---|
| 1 | Nathaniel B. Durfee (R) | 5,442 | 73.3 |
| | Ambrose E. Burnside (D) | 1,961 | 26.4 |
| 2 | William D. Brayton (AM & R) | 3,933 | 54.4 |
| | Charles Jackson (D) | 3,209 | 44.4 |

## SOUTH CAROLINA

**Special Election**

| | Candidates | Votes | % |
|---|---|---|---|
| 4 | Milledge L. Bonham (SSR D) | 3,646 | 63.5 |
| | C. P. Sullivan | 2,093 | 36.5 |

## TENNESSEE

| | Candidates | Votes | % |
|---|---|---|---|
| 1 | Albert G. Watkins (D) | 7,647 | 50.6 |
| | Taylor (AM) | 7,471 | 49.4 |
| 2 | Horace Maynard (AM) | 5,565 | 50.9 |
| | Wallace (D) | 5,360 | 49.1 |
| 3 | Samuel A. Smith (D) | 7,662 | 53.0 |
| | Heiskell (AM) | 6,800 | 47.0 |
| 4 | John H. Savage (D) | 6,435 | 55.2 |
| | Pickett (AM) | 5,232 | 44.8 |
| 5 | Charles Ready (AM) | 6,151 | 51.3 |
| | Guild (D) | 5,851 | 48.8 |
| 6 | George W. Jones (D) | 8,516 | 100.0 |
| 7 | John V. Wright (D) | 8,620 | 83.8 |
| | McElrath (AM) | 1,665 | 16.2 |
| 8 | Felix K. Zollicoffer (AM) | 6,088 | 52.2 |
| | James M. Quarles (D) | 5,580 | 47.8 |
| 9 | John D. C. Atkins (D) | 8,603 | 50.4 |
| | Etheridge (AM) | 8,474 | 49.6 |
| 10 | William T. Avery (D) | 6,006 | 51.3 |
| | Stevens (AM) | 5,707 | 48.7 |

## TEXAS

| | Candidates | Votes | % |
|---|---|---|---|
| 1 | John H. Reagan (D) | 15,799 | 61.0 |
| | Evans (AM) | 10,085 | 39.0 |
| 2 | Guy M. Bryan (D) | 21,142 | 80.8 |
| | Howth (AM) | 5,013 | 19.2 |

## VIRGINIA

| | Candidates | Votes | % |
|---|---|---|---|
| 1 | Muscoe R. H. Garnett (D) | 1,881 | 60.5 |
| | Critcher (AM) | 1,226 | 39.5 |
| 2 | John S. Millson (D) | | 100.0 |
| 3 | John S. Caskie (D) | 5,148 | 63.7 |
| | Crane (AM) | 2,931 | 36.3 |
| 4 | William O. Goode (D) | 3,579 | 76.0 |
| | Collier (AM) | 1,132 | 24.0 |
| 5 | Thomas S. Bocock (D) | | 100.0 |
| 6 | Paulus Powell (D) | | 100.0 |
| 7 | William Smith (D) | 5,332 | 57.5 |
| | Snowdon (AM) | 3,941 | 42.5 |
| 8 | Charles J. Faulkner (D) | 6,631 | 59.5 |
| | Lucas (AM) | 4,516 | 40.5 |
| 9 | John Letcher (D) | | 100.0 |
| 10 | Sherrard Clemens (D) | 7,074 | 71.5 |
| | Dunngton (AM) | 2,821 | 28.5 |
| 11 | Albert G. Jenkins (D) | 7,758 | 53.8 |
| | Carlisle (AM) | 6,653 | 46.2 |
| 12 | Henry A. Edmundson (D) | | 100.0 |
| 13 | George W. Hopkins (D) | 5,318 | 50.3 |
| | Martin (AM) | 5,249 | 49.7 |

# 1858 House Elections

## ARKANSAS

| | Candidates | Votes | % |
|---|---|---|---|
| 1 | Thomas C. Hindman (D) | 19,146 | 87.0 |
| | W. M. Crosby (AM) | 2,864 | 13.0 |
| 2 | Albert Rust (D) | 16,302 | 70.3 |
| | Thomas S. Drew (ID) | 3,780 | 16.3 |
| | James A. Jones (AM) | 3,106 | 13.4 |

## CALIFORNIA[1]

| | Candidates | Votes | % |
|---|---|---|---|
| AL | Joseph C. McKibbin (A-LEC DR) | 32,102* | |
| | W. L. Dudley (A-LEC D) | 22,782* | |
| | L. L. Tracy (R) | 9,381 | |

## DELAWARE

| | Candidates | Votes | % |
|---|---|---|---|
| AL | William G. Whiteley (D) | 7,868 | 51.4 |
| | Morris | 7,452 | 48.6 |

## FLORIDA

| | Candidates | Votes | % |
|---|---|---|---|
| AL | George S. Hawkins (D) | 6,465 | 61.4 |
| | Westcott (ID) | 4,070 | 38.6 |

## ILLINOIS

| | Candidates | Votes | % |
|---|---|---|---|
| 1 | Elihu B. Washburne (R) | 15,811 | 69.8 |
| | Hiram Bright (D) | 6,457 | 28.5 |
| 2 | John F. Farnsworth (R) | 21,797 | 61.1 |
| | Thomas Dyer (D) | 13,198 | 37.0 |
| 3 | Owen Lovejoy (R) | 22,313 | 57.7 |
| | George W. Armstrong (D) | 14,988 | 38.8 |
| 4 | William Kellogg (R) | 19,487 | 52.8 |
| | James W. Davidson (D) | 16,860 | 45.7 |
| 5 | Isaac N. Morris (D) | 13,529 | 52.7 |
| | Jackson Grimshaw (R) | 11,648 | 45.4 |
| 6 | Thomas L. Harris (D) | 16,193* | 57.6 |
| | James N. Mathews (R) | 11,646 | 41.4 |
| 7 | James C. Robinson (D) | 13,588 | 53.5 |
| | Richard J. Oglesby (R) | 11,760 | 46.3 |
| 8 | Phillip B. Fouke (D) | 11,490 | 57.2 |
| | John Baker (R) | 8,410 | 41.8 |
| 9 | John A. Logan (D) | 15,878 | 84.2 |
| | David L. Phillips (R) | 2,796 | 14.8 |

## INDIANA

| | Candidates | Votes | % |
|---|---|---|---|
| 1 | William E. Niblack (D) | 10,329 | 53.6 |
| | Hovey (A-LEC D) | 8,946 | 46.4 |
| 2 | William H. English (D) | 9,293 | 55.6 |
| | Wilson (R) | 7,434 | 44.4 |
| 3 | William McKee Dunn (R) | 9,363 | 52.8 |
| | Hughes (D) | 8,385 | 47.2 |
| 4 | William S. Holman (D) | 9,425 | 54.5 |
| | Hackleman (R) | 7,856 | 45.5 |
| 5 | David Kilgore (R) | 9,383 | 61.3 |
| | Devlin (D) | 5,921 | 38.7 |
| 6 | Albert G. Porter (R) | 10,776 | 52.6 |
| | Rar (D) | 9,716 | 47.4 |
| 7 | John G. Davis (A-LEC D) | 10,893 | 59.0 |
| | Sect (D) | 7,584 | 41.1 |
| 8 | James Wilson (R) | 11,028 | 51.5 |
| | Blake (D) | 10,387 | 48.5 |
| 9 | Schuyler Colfax (R) | 14,541 | 53.6 |
| | Walker (D) | 12,610 | 46.4 |
| 10 | Charles Case (R) | 10,780 | 53.4 |
| | Dawson (D) | 9,417 | 46.6 |
| 11 | John U. Pettit (R) | 10,748 | 51.7 |
| | Coffroth (D) | 10,038 | 48.3 |

## IOWA

| | Candidates | Votes | % |
|---|---|---|---|
| 1 | Samuel R. Curtis (R) | 23,529 | 50.7 |
| | Henry H. Trimble (D) | 22,929 | 49.4 |
| 2 | William Vandever (R) | 25,503 | 52.8 |
| | William E. Leffingwell (D) | 22,764 | 47.2 |

## MAINE

| | Candidates | Votes | % |
|---|---|---|---|
| 1 | Daniel E. Somes (R) | 10,410 | 50.6 |
| | Drew (D) | 9,955 | 48.4 |
| 2 | John J. Perry (R) | 12,031 | 54.5 |
| | Hastings (D) | 10,032 | 45.5 |
| 3 | Ezra B. French (R) | 8,994 | 50.2 |
| | Johnson (D) | 8,931 | 49.8 |
| 4 | Freeman H. Morse (R) | 10,552 | 60.1 |
| | Gile (D) | 6,990 | 39.8 |
| 5 | Israel Washburn Jr (R) | 10,300 | 55.7 |
| | Wiley (D) | 8,184 | 44.3 |
| 6 | Stephen C. Foster (R) | 8,297 | 51.5 |
| | Bradbury (D) | 7,804 | 48.5 |

## MASSACHUSETTS

| | Candidates | Votes | % |
|---|---|---|---|
| 1 | Thomas D. Eliot (R) | 4,854 | 72.6 |
| | Moses Bates Jr. (D) | 1,709 | 25.6 |
| 2 | James Buffinton (R) | 7,385 | 71.4 |
| | John Wilson (D) | 2,941 | 28.5 |
| 3 | Charles F. Adams (R) | 6,524 | 54.9 |
| | Authur W. Austin (D) | 3,880 | 32.6 |
| | Moses G. Cobb (AM) | 1,462 | 12.3 |
| 4 | Alexander H. Rice (R) | 4,507 | 47.7 |
| | Samuel W. Waldron (D) | 3,511 | 37.2 |
| | Newell A. Thompson (AM) | 1,396 | 14.8 |
| 5 | Anson Burlingame (R) | 6,214 | 51.5 |
| | John F. Heard (D) | 5,823 | 48.2 |
| 6 | John B. Alley (R) | 5,587 | 52.0 |
| | Otis P. Lord (AM) | 3,017 | 28.1 |
| | George B. Loring (D) | 2,116 | 19.7 |
| 7 | Daniel W. Gooch (R) | 7,129 | 60.3 |
| | Charles A. Welch (D) | 3,868 | 32.7 |
| | Elihu C. Baker (AM) | 810 | 6.9 |
| 8 | Charles R. Train (R) | 6,196 | 58.9 |
| | Benjamin F. Butler (D) | 3,514 | 33.4 |
| | Josiah N. Temple (AM) | 576 | 5.5 |
| 9 | Eli Thayer (R) | 7,280 | 70.9 |
| | Nathaniel Wood (D) | 2,962 | 28.8 |
| 10 | Charles Delano (R) | 6,847 | 64.1 |
| | Charles Osgood (D) | 3,276 | 30.7 |
| 11 | Henry L. Dawes (R) | 7,631 | 60.8 |
| | Thomas F. Plunkett (D) | 4,911 | 39.1 |

### Special Election

| | Candidates | Votes | % |
|---|---|---|---|
| 7 | Daniel W. Gooch (R) | 4,168 | 61.5 |
| | George Ashborne | 2,162 | 31.9 |

## MICHIGAN

| | Candidates | Votes | % |
|---|---|---|---|
| 1 | George B. Cooper (D) | 13,123‡ | 50.1 |
| | William A. Howard (R) | 13,048 | 49.8 |
| 2 | Henry Waldron (R) | 14,655 | 59.1 |
| | Consider A. Stacy (D) | 10,138 | 40.9 |
| 3 | Francis W. Kellogg (R) | 21,952 | 55.7 |
| | Thomas B. Church (D) | 17,438 | 44.3 |
| 4 | De Witt C. Leach (R) | 16,193 | 51.7 |
| | Robert W. Davis (D) | 15,120 | 48.3 |

## MISSOURI

| | Candidates | Votes | % |
|---|---|---|---|
| 1 | John R. Barrett (D) | 7,057‡ | 36.5 |
| | Francis P. Blair Jr. (R) | 6,631 | 34.3 |
| | Buck (AM) | 5,668 | 29.3 |
| 2 | Thomas L. Anderson (ID) | 10,902 | 64.2 |
| | Hendern (D) | 6,089 | 35.8 |
| 3 | John B. Clark (D) | | .0 |
| 4 | James Craig (D) | 12,439 | 61.4 |
| | Adams | 7,824 | 38.6 |
| 5 | Samuel H. Woodson (AM) | 7,942 | 53.3 |
| | Reid (D) | 6,947 | 46.7 |
| 6 | John S. Phelps (D) | 13,424 | 62.5 |
| | Richardson | 8,050 | 37.5 |
| 7 | John W. Noell (D) | 10,404 | 64.2 |
| | Zeigler | 5,808 | 35.8 |

## NEW JERSEY

| | Candidates | Votes | % |
|---|---|---|---|
| 1 | John T. Nixon (R) | 8,393 | 48.0 |
| | Walker (D) | 5,342 | 30.6 |
| | Jones (AM) | 3,739 | 21.4 |
| 2 | John L. N. Stratton (R) | 11,471 | 56.7 |
| | Wall (D) | 8,767 | 43.3 |
| 3 | Garnett B. Adrain (R) | 9,713 | 51.2 |
| | Paterson (D) | 9,255 | 48.8 |
| 4 | Jetur R. Riggs (A-LEC D) | 8,837 | 52.0 |
| | Huyler (D) | 8,154 | 48.0 |
| 5 | William Pennington (R) | 11,641 | 53.8 |
| | Wortendyke (D) | 9,982 | 46.2 |

## NEW YORK

| | Candidates | Votes | % |
|---|---|---|---|
| 1 | Luther C. Carter (R AM) | 8,122 | 52.5 |
| | John A. Searing (D) | 7,339 | 47.5 |
| 2 | James Humphrey (R AM) | 6,475 | 36.8 |
| | Litchfield (ID) | 5,581 | 31.7 |
| | Taylor (D) | 4,578 | 26.0 |
| | Backhouse (AM) | 974 | 5.5 |
| 3 | Daniel E. Sickles (D) | 3,177 | 35.0 |
| | Amor J. Williamson (R AM) | 3,015 | 33.3 |
| | Walbe (ID) | 2,874 | 31.7 |
| 4 | Thomas J. Barr (ID) | 3,949 | 39.7 |
| | Stephens (D) | 2,671 | 26.8 |
| | Brennau (R) | 2,290 | 23.0 |
| | Farmer (D) | 710 | 7.1 |
| 5 | William B. Maclay (D) | 5,780 | 49.8 |
| | Hamilton (R AM) | 4,982 | 42.9 |
| | Dean (AM) | 821 | 7.1 |
| 6 | John Cochrane (D) | 7,336 | 57.1 |
| | McCurdy (R AM) | 5,520 | 42.9 |
| 7 | George Briggs (R AM) | 8,306 | 55.8 |
| | Ward (D) | 6,591 | 44.2 |
| 8 | Horace F. Clark (R AM) | 9,035 | 58.8 |
| | Herrick (D) | 6,338 | 41.2 |
| 9 | John B. Haskin (R AM) | 7,637 | 48.3 |
| | Kemble (D) | 7,624 | 48.2 |
| 10 | Charles H. Van Wyck (R) | 6,681 | 48.4 |
| | Niven (D) | 5,532 | 40.1 |
| | Friend (ID) | 1,587 | 11.5 |
| 11 | William S. Kenyon (R AM) | 8,166 | 50.3 |
| | Strong (D) | 8,067 | 49.7 |
| 12 | Charles L. Beale (R AM) | 10,750 | 56.2 |
| | McClellan (D) | 8,385 | 43.8 |
| 13 | Abram B. Olin (R AM) | 8,267 | 61.1 |
| | Seymour (D) | 5,254 | 38.9 |
| 14 | John H. Reynolds (R AM) | 9,571 | 52 |
| | Erastus Corning (D) | 8,371 | 46 |
| 15 | James B. McKean (R) | 11,428 | 53.8 |
| | Odell (D) | 9,808 | 46.2 |
| 16 | George W. Palmer (R) | 7,058 | 47.9 |
| | Waldo (D) | 6,079 | 41.3 |
| | Watson (AM) | 1,589 | 10.8 |
| 17 | Francis E. Spinner (R) | 12,582 | 68.7 |
| | Goodrich (D) | 5,737 | 31.3 |
| 18 | Clark B. Cochrane (R AM) | 10,581 | 53.2 |
| | Goodyear (D) | 9,320 | 46.8 |
| 19 | James H. Graham (R) | 9,981 | 55.1 |
| | Parker (D) | 8,142 | 44.9 |
| 20 | Roscoe Conkling (R) | 11,084 | 57.3 |
| | Root (D) | 8,251 | 42.7 |
| 21 | R. Holland Duell (R) | 10,951 | 57.3 |
| | Sands (D) | 8,147 | 42.7 |
| 22 | M. Lindley Lee (R) | 11,450 | 57.4 |
| | Asher Tyler (D) | 7,425 | 37.2 |
| | Perry (AM) | 1,065 | 5.3 |

*Footnote, see p. 1003.*

## NEW YORK

| | Candidates | Votes | % |
|---|---|---|---|
| 23 | Charles B. Hoard (R) | 9,162 | 56.1 |
| | Lyon (D) | 7,177 | 43.9 |
| 24 | Charles B. Sedgwick (R) | 8,478 | 55.1 |
| | Taylor (D) | 6,267 | 40.7 |
| 25 | Martin Butterfield (R) | 10,855 | 60.7 |
| | Griswold (D) | 5,389 | 30.2 |
| | Sisson (AM) | 1,631 | 9.1 |
| 26 | Emory B. Pottle (R) | 8,598 | 54.5 |
| | Ogden (D) | 7,173 | 45.5 |
| 27 | Alfred Wells (R) | 10,131 | 49.2 |
| | Arnot (D) | 9,788 | 47.5 |
| 28 | William Irvine (R) | 9,382 | 53.3 |
| | Bradley (D) | 6,568 | 37.3 |
| | Denston (AM) | 1,651 | 9.4 |
| 29 | Alfred Ely (R) | 7,276 | 52.8 |
| | Trimmer (D) | 5,114 | 37.1 |
| | Angle (AM) | 1,393 | 10.1 |
| 30 | Augustus Frank (R) | 9,917 | 56.6 |
| | Skinner (D) | 5,355 | 30.5 |
| | Black (AM) | 2,264 | 12.9 |
| 31 | Silas M. Burroughs (R) | 6,093 | 52.5 |
| | Trott (D) | 3,376 | 29.1 |
| | White (AM) | 2,132 | 18.4 |
| 32 | Elbridge G. Spaulding (R AM) | 12,427 | 62.2 |
| | Hatch (D) | 7,539 | 37.8 |
| 33 | Reuben E. Fenton (R) | 10,018 | 60.3 |
| | Jenks (D) | 4,711 | 28.4 |
| | Johnn (AM) | 1,886 | 11.4 |

## NORTH CAROLINA

### Special Election

| | Candidates | Votes | % |
|---|---|---|---|
| 8 | Zebulon B. Vance (AM) | 8,321 | 57.0 |
| | William W. Avery (D) | 6,272 | 43.0 |

## OHIO

| | Candidates | Votes | % |
|---|---|---|---|
| 1 | George H. Pendleton (D) | 7,131 | 51.2 |
| | Day (R) | 6,785 | 48.8 |
| 2 | John A. Gurley (R) | 8,054 | 52.6 |
| | Groesbeck (D) | 7,263 | 47.4 |
| 3 | Clement L. Vallandigham (D) | 9,903 | 50.5 |
| | Campbell (R) | 9,715 | 49.5 |
| 4 | William Allen (D) | 9,558 | 50.5 |
| | Nichols (R) | 9,371 | 49.5 |
| 5 | James M. Ashley (R) | 10,532 | 51.2 |
| | Mungen (D) | 9,986 | 48.5 |
| 6 | William Howard (D) | 7,792 | 51.6 |
| | Clark (R) | 6,922 | 45.8 |
| 7 | Thomas Corwin (R) | 8,866 | 63.9 |
| | Blair (D) | 5,020 | 36.2 |
| 8 | Benjamin Stanton (R) | 8,716 | 59.5 |
| | Hubbard (D) | 5,928 | 40.5 |
| 9 | John Carey (R) | 9,304 | 50.3 |
| | Hall (D) | 9,197 | 49.7 |
| 10 | Carey A. Trimble (R) | 10,592 | 55.1 |
| | Joseph Miller (D) | 8,643 | 44.9 |
| 11 | Charles D. Martin (D) | 9,723 | 50.7 |
| | Nelson H. Van Vorhes (R) | 9,446 | 49.3 |
| 12 | Samuel S. Cox (D) | 9,560 | 51.8 |
| | Case (R) | 8,913 | 48.3 |
| 13 | John Sherman (R) | 9,426 | 57.1 |
| | Patrick (D) | 7,095 | 43.0 |
| 14 | Cyrus Spink (R) | 9,438 | 56.3 |
| | Jeffries (D) | 7,318 | 43.7 |
| 15 | William Helmick (R) | 8,949 | 50.7 |
| | Burns (D) | 8,719 | 49.4 |
| 16 | Cydnor B. Tomkins (R) | 7,677 | 52.8 |
| | Money (D) | 6,855 | 47.2 |
| 17 | Thomas C. Theaker (R) | 7,311 | 50.3 |
| | Spriggs (D) | 7,219 | 49.7 |
| 18 | Sidney Edgerton (R) | 8,184 | 53.3 |
| | Ranney (D) | 7,162 | 46.7 |
| 19 | Edward Wade (R) | 8,557 | 65.1 |
| | Gray (D) | 4,597 | 35.0 |
| 20 | John Hutchins (R) | 8,321 | 62.8 |
| | Tod (D) | 4,541 | 34.3 |
| 21 | John A. Bingham (R) | 8,883 | 57.5 |
| | Mans (D) | 6,577 | 42.5 |

## OREGON

(Became a state Feb. 14, 1859)

| | Candidates | Votes | % |
|---|---|---|---|
| AL | La Fayette Grover (D) | 5,859 | 57.9 |
| | James K. Kelley (OPP) | 4,210 | 41.6 |

## PENNSYLVANIA

| | Candidates | Votes | % |
|---|---|---|---|
| 1 | Thomas B. Florence (D) | 6,823 | 43.3 |
| | Ryan (UN) | 6,492 | 41.2 |
| | Nebg (A-LEC D) | 2,442 | 15.5 |
| 2 | Edward Joy Morris (UN) | 5,653 | 58.4 |
| | Martin (D) | 4,030 | 41.6 |
| 3 | John P. Verree (UN) | 6,977 | 54.2 |
| | Landy (D) | 5,834 | 45.4 |
| 4 | William Millward (UN) | 9,749 | 59.3 |
| | Phillips (D) | 6,451 | 39.2 |
| 5 | John Wood (UN) | 9,701 | 57.4 |
| | Jones (D) | 7,209 | 42.6 |
| 6 | John Hickman (A-LEC D) | 6,786 | 40.8 |
| | Manley (D) | 5,185 | 31.2 |
| | Broomall (UN) | 4,676 | 28.1 |
| 7 | Henry C. Longnecker (UN) | 8,324 | 50.8 |
| | Roberts (D) | 8,076 | 49.2 |
| 8 | John Schwartz (UN) | 7,321 | 50.1 |
| | Jones (D) | 7,302 | 49.9 |
| 9 | Thaddeus Stevens (U) | 9,513 | 60.0 |
| | Hopkins (D) | 6,341 | 40.0 |
| 10 | John W. Killinger (UN) | 8,897 | 61.4 |
| | Weidle (D) | 5,589 | 38.6 |
| 11 | James H. Campbell (UN) | 7,153 | 47.2 |
| | Dewart (D) | 4,387 | 29.0 |
| | Cake (A-LEC D) | 3,614 | 23.9 |
| 12 | George W. Scranton (UN) | 10,023 | 61.8 |
| | McReynolds (D) | 6,186 | 38.2 |
| 13 | William H. Dimmick (D) | 8,009 | 55.0 |
| | Shoemaker (UN) | 6,566 | 45.1 |
| 14 | Galusha A. Grow (UN) | 11,165 | 76.9 |
| | Parkhurst (D) | 3,359 | 23.1 |
| 15 | James T. Hale (UN) | 9,238 | 55.7 |
| | Allison White (D) | 7,349 | 44.3 |
| 16 | Benjamin F. Junkin (UN) | 8,646 | 50.1 |
| | Fisher (D) | 8,600 | 49.9 |
| 17 | Edward McPherson (UN) | 9,348 | 50.7 |
| | Reilly (D) | 9,081 | 49.3 |
| 18 | Samuel S. Blair (UN) | 9,114 | 57.7 |
| | Pershing (D) | 6,679 | 42.3 |
| 19 | John Covode (UN) | 9,257 | 53.1 |
| | Foster (D) | 8,165 | 46.9 |
| 20 | William Montgomery (D) | 9,254 | 61.5 |
| | Knight (UN) | 5,798 | 38.5 |
| 21 | James K. Moorhead (UN) | 6,539 | 57.3 |
| | Burke (D) | 4,879 | 42.7 |
| 22 | Robert McKnight (UN) | 5,438 | 55.3 |
| | Williams (A-TAX) | 3,903 | 39.7 |
| | Birmingham (D) | 502 | 5.1 |
| 23 | William Stewart (UN) | 6,721 | 64.0 |
| | McGuffin (D) | 3,777 | 36.0 |
| 24 | Chapin Hall (UN) | 8,905 | 52.3 |
| | Gillis (D) | 8,111 | 47.7 |
| 25 | Elijah Babbitt (UN) | 6,360 | 60.7 |
| | Marshall (D) | 4,113 | 39.3 |

### Special Election

| | Candidates | Votes | % |
|---|---|---|---|
| 8 | William H. Keim (R) | 6,156 | 52.0 |
| | Wanner (D) | 5,687 | 48.0 |

## SOUTH CAROLINA

| | Candidates | Votes | % |
|---|---|---|---|
| 1 | John McQueen (D) | | 100.0 |
| 2 | William P. Miles (D) | | 100.0 |
| 3 | Lawrence M. Keitt (D) | | 100.0 |
| 4 | Milledge L. Bonham (SSR D) | | 100.0 |
| 5 | John D. Ashmore (D) | 7,198 | 59.4 |
| | Thomas O. P. Vernon | 4,926 | 40.6 |
| 6 | William W. Boyce (SSR D) | | 100.0 |

## VERMONT

| | Candidates | Votes | % |
|---|---|---|---|
| 1 | Eliakim P. Walton (R) | 9,615 | 72.9 |
| | Eastman (D) | 3,577 | 27.1 |
| 2 | Justin S. Morrill (R) | 11,576 | 70.7 |
| | Chase (D) | 4,806 | 29.3 |
| 3 | Homer E. Royce (R) | 7,418 | 69.3 |
| | Bingham (D) | 3,280 | 30.7 |

## WISCONSIN

| | Candidates | Votes | % |
|---|---|---|---|
| 1 | John F. Potter (R) | 14,428 | 56.4 |
| | Brown (D) | 11,171 | 43.6 |
| 2 | Cadwallader C. Washburn (R) | 23,917 | 54.3 |
| | Dunn (D) | 20,167 | 45.8 |
| 3 | Charles H. Larrabee (D) | 23,910 | 51.0 |
| | Billinghurst (R) | 23,011 | 49.0 |

1. The California Blue Book reports that the California election to the House of Representatives for the 36th Congress was in 1859, not 1858 as reported here by ICPSR. The vote according to the Blue Book was as follows:

| | | | |
|---|---|---|---|
| AL | John C. Burch (LEC D) | 57,665 | 28.4 |
| | Charles L. Scott (LEC D) | 56,998 | 28.1 |
| | Joseph C. McKibben (A-LEC D) | 43,474 | 21.4 |
| | Edward D. Baker (R) | 41,438 | 20.4 |

This corresponds to the Biographical Directory, which lists Burch and Scott as representing California in the House from 1859-61.

# 1859 House Elections

## ALABAMA

| | Candidates | Votes | % |
|---|---|---|---|
| 1 | James A. Stallworth (D) | 7,352 | 63.3 |
| | F. B. Shepard (SEC D) | 4,258 | 36.7 |
| 2 | James L. Pugh (D) | 2,643 | 81.1 |
| | J. E. Sappington (SO RTS) | 615 | 18.9 |
| 3 | David Clopton (D) | 6,879 | 50.8 |
| | T. J. Judge (SR W) | 6,666 | 49.2 |
| 4 | Sydenham Moore (D) | 1,648 | 96.9 |
| 5 | George S. Houston (D) | 5,964 | 58.1 |
| | W. A. Hewlett (D) | 4,298 | 41.9 |
| 6 | Williamson R. W. Cobb (D) | 5,731 | 55.0 |
| | Alex Snodgrass (D) | 2,112 | 20.3 |
| | Edwin Wallace | 1,885 | 18.1 |
| | H. R. Beaver | 695 | 6.7 |
| 7 | Jabez L. M. Curry (SO RTS D) | ✔ | |

## CONNECTICUT

| | | Votes | % |
|---|---|---|---|
| 1 | Dwight Loomis (R) | 9,940 | 49.6 |
| | Alvan P. Hyde (D) | 9,875 | 49.3 |
| 2 | John Woodruff (R) | 10,669 | 50.6 |
| | Samuel Arnold (D) | 10,347 | 49.0 |
| 3 | Alfred A. Burnham (R) | 7,586 | 51.7 |
| | Rufus L. Baker (D) | 6,883 | 47.0 |
| 4 | Orris S. Ferry (R) | 11,536 | 51.3 |
| | William D. Bishop (D) | 10,966 | 48.7 |

## GEORGIA

| | | Votes | % |
|---|---|---|---|
| 1 | Peter E. Love (D) | 7,253 | 65.1 |
| | McIntyre (OPP) | 3,881 | 34.9 |
| 2 | Martin J. Crawford (D) | 8,279 | 56.3 |
| | Douglas (OPP) | 6,437 | 43.7 |
| 3 | Thomas Hardman (OPP) | 5,636 | 50.7 |
| | Speer (D) | 5,483 | 49.3 |
| 4 | Lucius J. Gartrell (D) | 8,877 | 59.5 |
| | Wright (OPP) | 6,053 | 40.5 |
| 5 | John W. H. Underwood (D) | 12,339 | 85.1 |
| | Shackleford (OPP) | 2,162 | 14.9 |
| 6 | James Jackson (D) | 9,644 | 74.8 |
| | Lytle (OPP) | 3,251 | 25.2 |
| 7 | Joshua Hill (OPP) | 4,492 | 50.8 |
| | Harper (D) | 4,353 | 49.2 |
| 8 | John J. Jones (D) | 4,912 | 52.2 |
| | Wright (OPP) | 4,507 | 47.9 |

## ILLINOIS[1]

### Special Elections

| | | Votes | % |
|---|---|---|---|
| 6 | Charles D. Hodges (D) | 11,014 | 61.1 |
| | James C. Coukling | 6,951 | 38.6 |
| 6 | John A. McClernand (D) | 14,337 | 58.9 |
| | John M. Palmer | 10,001 | 41.1 |

## KENTUCKY

| | | Votes | % |
|---|---|---|---|
| 1 | Henry C. Burnett (D) | 11,540 | 83.7 |
| | William Morrow | 2,248 | 16.3 |
| 2 | Samuel O. Peyton (D) | 7,939 | 52.4 |
| | James S. Jackson (UNT) | 7,199 | 47.6 |
| 3 | Francis M. Bristow (D) | 7,164 | 56.2 |
| | W. W. Sale (D) | 5,575 | 43.8 |
| 4 | William C. Anderson (AM) | 7,204 | 50.0 |
| | James S. Chrisman (D) | 7,201 | 50.0 |
| 5 | John Young Brown (D) | 6,927 | 57.8 |
| | J. H. Jewett (ID) | 5,066 | 42.2 |
| 6 | Green Adams (AM) | 8,164 | 53.0 |
| | T. T. Garrard (D) | 7,231 | 47.0 |
| 7 | Robert Mallory (UN D) | 6,416 | 53.1 |
| | Thomas Holt (D) | 5,675 | 46.9 |
| 8 | William E. Simms (D) | 6,932 | 50.2 |
| | John M. Harlan | 6,865 | 49.8 |

| | Candidates | Votes | % |
|---|---|---|---|
| 9 | Laban T. Moore (N AM) | 8,505 | 50.8 |
| | James W. Moore (D) | 8,227 | 49.2 |
| 10 | John W. Stevenson (D) | 9,295 | 61.4 |
| | Thomas L. Jones | 5,839 | 38.6 |

## LOUISIANA

| | | Votes | % |
|---|---|---|---|
| 1 | John E. Bouligny (OPP) | 2,215 | 55.2 |
| | Lasere (D) | 1,796 | 44.8 |
| 2 | Miles Taylor (D) | 5,908 | 57.0 |
| | Nichols (OPP) | 4,459 | 43.0 |
| 3 | Thomas G. Davidson (D) | 6,288 | 89.7 |
| | Cannon (OPP) | 726 | 10.4 |
| 4 | John M. Landrum (D) | 8,823 | 73.3 |
| | Jones (OPP) | 3,220 | 26.7 |

## MARYLAND

| | | Votes | % |
|---|---|---|---|
| 1 | James A. Stewart (D) | 6,934 | 52.1 |
| | Cox (AM) | 6,384 | 47.9 |
| 2 | Edwin H. Webster (AM) | 9,237 | 52.0 |
| | McHenry (D) | 8,518 | 48.0 |
| 3 | J. Morrison Harris (AM) | 9,612 | 69.5 |
| | William P. Preston (D) | 4,224 | 30.5 |
| 4 | H. Winter Davis (AM) | 10,068 | 78.3 |
| | William G. Harrison (I) | 2,796 | 21.7 |
| 5 | Jacob M. Kunkel (D) | 8,852 | 50.4 |
| | Hoffman (AM) | 8,719 | 49.6 |
| 6 | George W. Hughes (D) | 6,337 | 54.2 |
| | Hagner (I) | 5,353 | 45.8 |

## MINNESOTA

| | | Votes | % |
|---|---|---|---|
| AL | Cyrus Aldrich (R) | 21,360 | ✔ |
| | William Windom (R) | 21,016 | ✔ |
| | James M. Cavanaugh (D) | 17,666 | |
| | Graham (D) | 17,514 | |

## MISSISSIPPI

| | | Votes | % |
|---|---|---|---|
| 1 | L. Q. C. Lamar (D) | 4,140 | 97.8 |
| 2 | Reuben Davis (D) | 7,555 | 96.3 |
| 3 | William Barksdale (D) | 6,699 | 100.0 |
| 4 | Otho R. Singleton (D) | 6,686 | 74.7 |
| | Frank Smith (UN D) | 2,262 | 25.3 |
| 5 | John L. McRae (D) | 4,567 | 89.8 |
| | G. W. Wilcox | 517 | 10.2 |

## NEW HAMPSHIRE

| | | Votes | % |
|---|---|---|---|
| 1 | Gilman Marston (R) | 12,839 | 51.5 |
| | Marcy (D) | 12,082 | 48.5 |
| 2 | Mason W. Tappan (R) | 11,288 | 52.5 |
| | George (D) | 10,228 | 47.5 |
| 3 | Thomas M. Edwards (R) | 11,717 | 52.4 |
| | Burns (D) | 10,639 | 47.6 |

## NORTH CAROLINA

| | | Votes | % |
|---|---|---|---|
| 1 | William N. H. Smith (OPP D) | 6,045 | 52.2 |
| | Henry M. Shaw (D) | 5,531 | 47.8 |
| 2 | Thomas Ruffin (D) | 4,382 | 90.2 |
| 3 | Warren Winslow (D) | 4,774 | 78.8 |
| | Malcom J. McDuffie (D & AM) | 1,284 | 21.2 |
| 4 | Lawrence O'B. Branch (D) | 5,764 | 70.2 |
| | Linn B. Sanders (OPP D) | 2,446 | 29.8 |
| 5 | John A. Gilmer (OPP D) | 6,361 | 58.1 |
| | Stephen E. Williams (D) | 4,512 | 41.2 |
| 6 | James M. Leach (OPP D) | 8,566 | 52.8 |
| | Alfred M. Scales (D) | 7,664 | 47.2 |
| 7 | F. Burton Craige (D) | 5,495 | 57.4 |
| | Samuel H. Walkup (OPP D) | 4,075 | 42.6 |
| 8 | Zebulon B. Vance (OPP D) | 8,026 | 55.9 |
| | David Coleman (D) | 6,331 | 44.1 |

## OREGON

| | Candidates | Votes | % |
|---|---|---|---|
| AL | Lansing Stout (D) | 5,646 | 50.1 |
| | David Logan (R) | 5,630 | 49.9 |

## RHODE ISLAND[2]

| | | Votes | % |
|---|---|---|---|
| 1 | Christopher Robinson (AM & R) | 3,797 | 49.0 |
| | Thomas Davis (R) | 2,422 | 31.2 |
| | Olney Arnold (D) | 1,532 | 19.8 |
| 2 | William D. Brayton (R) | 3,101 | 63.9 |
| | Alfred Anthony (D) | 1,746 | 36.0 |

### Special Election

| | | Votes | % |
|---|---|---|---|
| 1 | Christopher Robinson (AM & R) | 3,414 | 56.0 |
| | Thomas Davis (R) | 2,648 | 43.4 |

## TENNESSEE

| | | Votes | % |
|---|---|---|---|
| 1 | Thomas A. R. Nelson (OPP) | 7,931 | 50.3 |
| | Haynes (D) | 7,827 | 49.7 |
| 2 | Horace Maynard (OPP) | 6,476 | 56.8 |
| | Ramsay (D) | 4,930 | 43.2 |
| 3 | Reese B. Brabson (OPP) | 8,372 | 50.2 |
| | Smith (D) | 8,313 | 49.8 |
| 4 | William B. Stokes (OPP) | 6,633 | 51.9 |
| | Savage (D) | 6,160 | 48.2 |
| 5 | Robert H. Hatton (OPP) | 6,719 | 53.5 |
| | Charles Ready (I & D) | 5,844 | 46.5 |
| 6 | James H. Thomas (D) | 9,023 | 100.0 |
| 7 | John V. Wright (D) | 9,380 | 77.6 |
| | Gibbs (OPP) | 2,711 | 22.4 |
| 8 | James M. Quarles (OPP) | 6,994 | 52.9 |
| | Menees (D) | 6,236 | 47.1 |
| 9 | Emerson Etheridge (OPP) | 9,437 | 50.0 |
| | Atkins (D) | 9,430 | 50.0 |
| 10 | William T. Avery (D) | 5,954 | 50.3 |
| | Sneed (OPP) | 5,648 | 47.7 |

## TEXAS

| | | Votes | % |
|---|---|---|---|
| 1 | John H. Reagan (D) | 20,565 | 85.3 |
| | Ochiltree | 3,541 | 14.7 |
| 2 | Andrew J. Hamilton (ID) | 16,521 | 50.7 |
| | Waul (D) | 16,079 | 49.3 |

## VIRGINIA

| | | Votes | % |
|---|---|---|---|
| 1 | Muscoe H. R. Garnett (D) | | 100.0 |
| 2 | John S. Millson (D) | | 100.0 |
| 3 | Daniel C. De Jarnette (ID&OPP) | 5,581 | 50.5 |
| | Caskie (D) | 5,481 | 49.6 |
| 4 | William O. Goode (D) | 3,820 | 63.6 |
| | Flournoy (ID&OPP) | 2,185 | 36.4 |
| 5 | Thomas S. Bocock (D) | | 100.0 |
| 6 | Shelton F. Leake (ID) | 5,003 | 59.2 |
| | Powell (D) | 3,453 | 40.8 |
| 7 | William Smith (D) | 5,147 | 49.4 |
| | Thomas (OPP) | 4,845 | 46.5 |
| 8 | Alexander R. Boteler (OPP) | 6,616 | 50.6 |
| | Faulkner (D) | 6,449 | 49.4 |
| 9 | John T. Harris (ID) | 5,345 | 52.2 |
| | Skinner (D) | 4,900 | 47.8 |
| 10 | Sherrard Clemens (D) | | 100.0 |
| 11 | Albert G. Jenkins (D) | 9,038 | 55.6 |
| | Laidley (OPP) | 7,228 | 44.4 |
| 12 | Henry A. Edmundson (D) | | 100.0 |
| 13 | Elbert S. Martin (ID) | 6,382 | 53.4 |
| | Floyd (D) | 5,579 | 46.6 |

### Special Election

| | | Votes | % |
|---|---|---|---|
| 4 | Roger A. Pryor (D) | | ✔ |

*Footnotes, see p. 1006.*

# 1860 House Elections

## ARKANSAS

(Seceded May 8, 1861)

| Candidates | Votes | % |
|---|---|---|
| 1 Thomas C. Hindman (D) | 20,051* | 67.4 |
| Cypert (I) | 9,699 | 32.6 |
| 2 Gantt (I) | 16,569* | 56.0 |
| Mitchell (D) | 13,007 | 44.0 |

## DELAWARE

| | | |
|---|---|---|
| AL George P. Fisher (UN) | 7,732 | 48.4 |
| Briggs (SO D) | 7,475 | 46.8 |

## FLORIDA

(Seceded Jan. 11, 1861)

| | | |
|---|---|---|
| AL R. B. Hilton (D) | 7,722* | 59.9 |
| B. F. Allen (KST U) | 5,172 | 40.1 |

## ILLINOIS

| | | |
|---|---|---|
| 1 Elihu B. Washburne (R) | 21,436 | 70.6 |
| Theodore A. C. Beard (D) | 8,929 | 29.4 |
| 2 Isaac N. Arnold (R) | 30,834 | 64.4 |
| Augustus M. Herrington (D) | 16,950 | 35.4 |
| 3 Owen Lovejoy (R) | 29,600 | 59.9 |
| Robert N. Murray (D) | 18,843 | 38.2 |
| 4 William Kellogg (R) | 25,668 | 54.6 |
| Robert G. Ingersoll (D) | 21,297 | 45.3 |
| 5 William A. Richardson (D) | 16,946 | 53.5 |
| Bug Prentiss (R) | 14,684 | 46.4 |
| 6 John A. McClernand (D) | 21,206 | 56.6 |
| Henry Case (R) | 16,244 | 43.4 |
| 7 James C. Robinson (D) | 19,206 | 54.1 |
| James T. Cunningham (R) | 16,313 | 45.9 |
| 8 Philip B. Fouke (D) | 16,592 | 55.2 |
| Joseph Gillespie (R) | 13,315 | 44.3 |
| 9 John A. Logan (D) | 20,863 | 79.5 |
| Unidentified Candidate (R) | 5,207 | 19.9 |

## INDIANA

| | | |
|---|---|---|
| 1 John Law (D) | 13,476 | 55.7 |
| Debruler (R) | 10,731 | 44.3 |
| 2 James A. Cravens (D) | 10,811 | 51.3 |
| Davis (R) | 10,272 | 48.7 |
| 3 William McKee Dunn (R) | 11,545 | 54.5 |
| Daily (D) | 9,622 | 45.5 |
| 4 William S. Holman (D) | 10,299 | 50.7 |
| Yatar (R) | 10,007 | 49.3 |
| 5 George W. Julian (R) | 12,237 | 62.0 |
| Bickle (D) | 7,501 | 38.0 |
| 6 Albert G. Porter (R) | 13,029 | 52.3 |
| Walpole (D) | 11,887 | 47.7 |
| 7 Daniel W. Voorhees (D) | 12,535 | 52.1 |
| Nelson (R) | 11,516 | 47.9 |
| 8 Albert S. White (R) | 13,310 | 53.7 |
| Wilson (D) | 11,489 | 46.3 |
| 9 Schuyler Colfax (R) | 16,860 | 55.6 |
| Cathcart (D) | 13,458 | 44.4 |
| 10 William Mitchell (R) | 14,267 | 55.6 |
| Kenkle (D) | 11,378 | 44.4 |
| 11 John P. C. Shanks (R) | 13,885 | 54.1 |
| Steele (D) | 11,796 | 45.9 |

## IOWA

| | | |
|---|---|---|
| 1 Samuel R. Curtis (R) | 33,936 | 52.9 |
| C. C. Cole (D) | 30,240 | 47.1 |
| 2 William Vandever (R) | 36,805 | 57.5 |
| Ben M. Samuels (D) | 27,206 | 42.5 |

## MAINE

| Candidates | Votes | % |
|---|---|---|
| 1 John N. Goodwin (R) | 12,018 | 53.0 |
| Hayes (D) | 10,556 | 46.5 |
| 2 Charles W. Walton (R) | 12,806 | 55.6 |
| Record (D) | 10,192 | 44.3 |
| 3 Samuel C. Fessenden (R) | 10,065 | 52.5 |
| Johnson (D) | 9,090 | 47.4 |
| 4 Anson P. Morrill (R) | 12,666 | 61.6 |
| Fuller (D) | 7,262 | 35.3 |
| 5 John H. Rice (R) | 12,317 | 59.8 |
| Blake (D) | 7,965 | 38.7 |
| 6 Frederick A. Pike (R) | 9,451 | 53.9 |
| Bradbury (D) | 7,893 | 45.1 |

## MASSACHUSETTS

| | | |
|---|---|---|
| 1 Thomas D. Eliot (R) | 7,350 | 72.5 |
| Daniel Fisher | 1,061 | 10.5 |
| Moses Bates | 878 | 8.7 |
| F. C. Sandford | 845 | 8.3 |
| 2 James Buffinton (R) | 10,103 | 68.4 |
| Aaron Hobart | 4,409 | 29.9 |
| 3 Charles F. Adams (R) | 10,530 | 58.4 |
| Leverett Saltonstall | 7,449 | 41.3 |
| 4 Alexander H. Rice (R) | 7,292 | 52.3 |
| Erastus B. Bigelow | 6,645 | 47.6 |
| 5 William Appleton (R) | 8,014 | 50.8 |
| Anson Burlingame | 7,756 | 49.2 |
| 6 John B. Alley (R) | 9,644 | 63.1 |
| Otis P. Lord | 2,471 | 16.2 |
| Jefferson Knight | 2,200 | 14.4 |
| 7 Daniel W. Gooch (R) | 11,373 | 60.2 |
| Charles A. Welch | 6,730 | 35.6 |
| 8 Charles R. Train (R) | 9,272 | 64.6 |
| A. R. Brown | 2,390 | 16.6 |
| Winthrop E. Faulkner | 2,239 | 15.6 |
| 9 Goldsmith F. Bailey (R) | 9,745 | 54.6 |
| Eli Thayer (I) | 7,949 | 44.6 |
| 10 Charles Delano (R) | 10,021 | 75.1 |
| Josiah Allis | 2,528 | 18.9 |
| B. Leavitt | 744 | 5.6 |
| 11 Henry L. Dawes (R) | 10,409 | 67.6 |
| Norman T. Leonard | 4,396 | 28.5 |

## MICHIGAN

| | | |
|---|---|---|
| 1 Bradley F. Granger (R) | 16,997 | 52.5 |
| George V. N. Lathrop (D) | 15,216 | 47.0 |
| 2 Fernando C. Beaman (R) | 19,162 | 60.1 |
| Salathiel C. Coffenberry (D) | 12,700 | 39.8 |
| 3 Francis W. Kellogg (R) | 28,641 | 59.0 |
| Thomas B. Church (D) | 19,737 | 40.6 |
| 4 Rowland E. Trowbridge (R) | 23,650 | 55.3 |
| Edward Thompson (D) | 19,099 | 44.7 |

## MINNESOTA

| | | |
|---|---|---|
| AL Cyrus Aldrich (R) | 22,333✔ | |
| William Windom (R) | 22,165✔ | |
| James George (D) | 12,172 | |
| J. M. Gilman (D) | 12,168 | |
| A. J. Edgerton (SO D) | 787 | |
| J. W. Taylor (SO D) | 776 | |

## MISSOURI

| | | |
|---|---|---|
| 1 Francis P. Blair Jr. (R) | 11,453 | 44.1 |
| John H. Barret (D) | 9,967 | 38.4 |
| Todd (AM) | 4,542 | 17.5 |
| 2 James S. Rollins (OPP) | 11,161 | 50.6 |
| Henderson (D) | 10,908 | 49.4 |
| 3 John B. Clark (D) | 14,822 | 59.1 |
| Hawkins (OPP) | 10,276 | 40.9 |

| Candidates | Votes | % |
|---|---|---|
| 4 Elijah H. Norton (D) | 13,797 | 62.3 |
| Scott (OPP) | 8,350 | 37.7 |
| 5 John W. Reid (D) | 11,689 | 52.8 |
| Mitchell (OPP) | 10,432 | 47.2 |
| 6 John S. Phelps (D) | 11,363 | 55.0 |
| Rains (OPP) | 9,301 | 45.0 |
| 7 John W. Noell (D) | 11,191 | 73.6 |
| Perryman (OPP) | 4,007 | 26.4 |

### Special Election

| | | |
|---|---|---|
| 1 John R. Barret (D) | 12,682‡ | 50.3 |
| Francis P. Blair Jr (R) | 12,538 | 49.7 |

## NEW JERSEY

| | | |
|---|---|---|
| 1 John T. Nixon (R) | 10,843 | 52.7 |
| Leaming (D) | 9,737 | 47.3 |
| 2 John L. N. Stratton (R) | 13,582 | 52.8 |
| Green (D) | 12,154 | 47.2 |
| 3 William G. Steele (D) | 12,843 | 55.2 |
| Berthoud (R) | 10,438 | 44.8 |
| 4 George T. Cobb (D) | 10,789 | 52.6 |
| Edsall (R) | 9,711 | 47.4 |
| 5 Nehemiah Perry (D) | 16,200 | 50.6 |
| Pennington (R) | 15,802 | 49.4 |

## NEW YORK

| | | |
|---|---|---|
| 1 Edward H. Smith (FUS) | 11,882 | 52.8 |
| Carter (R) | 10,631 | 47.2 |
| 2 Moses F. Odell (FUS) | 13,322 | 55.1 |
| Humphrey (R) | 10,870 | 44.9 |
| 3 Benjamin Wood (D) | 5,892 | 52.8 |
| Williamson (R) | 4,585 | 41.1 |
| Savage (ID) | 675 | 6.1 |
| 4 James E. Kerrigan (ID) | 5,145 | 41.3 |
| Tuomy (D) | 3,989 | 32.0 |
| Commerford (R) | 3,324 | 26.7 |
| 5 William Wall (R) | 6,877 | 41.0 |
| Taylor (D) | 6,811 | 40.6 |
| Duffy (ID) | 3,085 | 18.4 |
| 6 Frederick A. Conkling (R) | 6,536 | 35.1 |
| Cochran (ID) | 6,360 | 34.2 |
| Chanler (D) | 5,724 | 30.7 |
| 7 Elijah Ward (D) | 10,814 | 56.2 |
| Dow (R) | 8,417 | 43.8 |
| 8 Isaac C. Delaplaine (D) | 13,576 | 59.0 |
| Abram Wakeman (R) | 9,417 | 41.0 |
| 9 Edward Haight (D) | 11,389 | 53.5 |
| Nelson (R) | 9,882 | 46.5 |
| 10 Charles H. Van Wyck (R) | 8,311 | 50.5 |
| St. John (ID) | 8,163 | 49.6 |
| 11 John B. Steele (D) | 9,938 | 50.4 |
| Sylvester (R) | 9,789 | 49.6 |
| 12 Stephen Baker (R) | 11,795 | 52.0 |
| Wager (D) | 10,514 | 46.3 |
| 13 Abram B. Olin (R) | 8,650 | 51.1 |
| McConihe (D) | 8,268 | 48.9 |
| 14 Erastus Corning (D) | 10,814 | 51.9 |
| Olcott (R) | 10,043 | 48.2 |
| 15 James B. McKean (R) | 14,924 | 58.8 |
| Davis (D) | 10,474 | 41.2 |
| 16 William A. Wheeler (R) | 10,571 | 58.7 |
| Hand (D) | 7,427 | 41.3 |
| 17 Socrates N. Sherman (R) | 16,134 | 68.4 |
| Foote (D) | 7,456 | 31.6 |
| 18 Chauncey Vibbard (D) | 12,019 | 50.9 |
| Mix (R) | 11,602 | 49.1 |
| 19 Richard Franchot (R) | 11,310 | 57.0 |
| Walworth (D) | 8,542 | 43.0 |
| 20 Roscoe Conkling (R) | 12,536 | 58.3 |
| Grove (D) | 8,973 | 41.7 |
| 21 R. Holland Duell (R) | 13,960 | 62.2 |
| Hitchcock (D) | 4,923 | 21.9 |
| Nelson (BRECK D) | 3,559 | 15.9 |

## NEW YORK

| | Candidates | Votes | % |
|---|---|---|---|
| 22 | William E. Lansing (R) | 15,253 | 63.7 |
| | Chapman (D) | 8,682 | 36.3 |
| 23 | Ambrose W. Clark (R) | 11,865 | 59.9 |
| | Starbuck (D) | 7,568 | 38.2 |
| 24 | Charles B. Sedgwick (R) | 11,175 | 60.4 |
| | Teft (D) | 6,088 | 32.9 |
| | Hay (BRECK D) | 1,233 | 6.7 |
| 25 | Theodore M. Pomeroy (R) | 14,437 | 64.5 |
| | Beardsley (D) | 7,961 | 35.5 |
| 26 | Jacob P. Chamberlain (R) | 11,581 | 58.3 |
| | Lewis (D) | 8,153 | 41.0 |
| 27 | Alexander S. Diven (R) | 13,482 | 57.2 |
| | Dowe (D) | 10,088 | 42.8 |
| 28 | Robert B. Van Valkenburg (R) | 13,167 | 60.8 |
| | Walker (D) | 8,507 | 39.3 |
| 29 | Alfred Ely (R) | 10,704 | 59.4 |
| | Reynolds (D) | 7,314 | 40.6 |
| 30 | Augustus Frank (R) | 15,342 | 67.5 |
| | Robinson (D) | 7,389 | 32.5 |
| 31 | Burt Van Horn (R) | 8,662 | 58.8 |
| | Ely (D) | 5,882 | 39.9 |
| 32 | Elbridge G. Spaulding (R) | 12,256 | 52.8 |
| | Haven (D) | 10,947 | 47.2 |
| 33 | Reuben E. Fenton (R) | 14,303 | 66.8 |
| | Lee (D) | 7,111 | 33.2 |

### Special Election

| | | Votes | % |
|---|---|---|---|
| 31 | Edwin R. Reynolds (R) | 8,759 | 59.4 |
| | Peck (D) | 5,801 | 39.4 |

## OHIO

| | | Votes | % |
|---|---|---|---|
| 1 | George H. Pendleton (D) | 7,485 | 48.9 |
| | Spencer (R) | 6,582 | 43.0 |
| | Jones | 1,250 | 8.2 |
| 2 | John A. Gurley (R) | 8,469 | 48.1 |
| | Long (D) | 7,586 | 43.1 |
| | Harrison | 1,555 | 8.8 |
| 3 | Clement L. Vallandigham (D) | 11,052 | 50.2 |
| | Craighead (R) | 10,918 | 49.6 |
| 4 | William Allen (D) | 11,756 | 51.7 |
| | Hart (R) | 10,968 | 48.3 |
| 5 | James M. Ashley (R) | 13,756 | 52.3 |
| | Steedman (D) | 12,552 | 47.7 |
| 6 | Chilton A. White (D) | 10,046 | 53.2 |
| | Murphy (R) | 8,828 | 46.8 |
| 7 | Thomas Corwin (R) | 10,693 | 70.0 |
| | Telfair (D) | 3,082 | 20.2 |
| | Stokes | 1,512 | 9.9 |
| 8 | Samuel Shellabarger (R) | 10,931 | 58.3 |
| | Harrison (D) | 7,831 | 41.7 |
| 9 | Warren P. Noble (D) | 12,650 | 51.1 |
| | Carey (R) | 12,096 | 48.9 |
| 10 | Carey A. Trimble (R) | 11,593 | 51.3 |
| | Hutchinson (D) | 11,025 | 48.7 |
| 11 | Valentine B. Horton (R) | 11,965 | 51.5 |
| | Martin (D) | 11,275 | 48.5 |

| | Candidates | Votes | % |
|---|---|---|---|
| 12 | Samuel S. Cox (D) | 11,014 | 52.1 |
| | Galloway | 10,131 | 47.9 |
| 13 | John Sherman (R) | 11,428 | 57.2 |
| | Burns (D) | 8,564 | 42.8 |
| 14 | Harrison G. O. Blake (R) | 12,040 | 57.1 |
| | Prentiss (D) | 9,053 | 42.9 |
| 15 | Robert H. Nugen (D) | 10,281 | 52.1 |
| | William Helmick (R) | 9,439 | 47.9 |
| 16 | William P. Cutler (R) | 8,560 | 50.2 |
| | Jewett (D) | 8,496 | 49.8 |
| 17 | James R. Morris (D) | 9,609 | 51.0 |
| | Thomas C. Theaker (R) | 8,510 | 45.2 |
| 18 | Sidney Edgerton (R) | 9,720 | 58.3 |
| | Starkweather (D) | 6,956 | 41.7 |
| 19 | Albert G. Riddle (R) | 11,927 | 69.1 |
| | Williams (D) | 5,343 | 30.9 |
| 20 | John Hutchins (R) | 10,840 | 72.0 |
| | Wilson (D) | 4,222 | 28.0 |
| 21 | John A. Bingham (R) | 9,170 | 61.2 |
| | Wells (D) | 5,053 | 33.7 |
| | Blakeley | 768 | 5.1 |

## OREGON

| | | Votes | % |
|---|---|---|---|
| AL | George K. Sheil (D) | 6,632 | 50.4 |
| | D. Logan (R) | 6,529 | 49.6 |

## PENNSYLVANIA

| | | Votes | % |
|---|---|---|---|
| 1 | John M. Butler (R) | 8,581 | 45.1 |
| | William E. Lehman (D) | 8,383 | 44.1 |
| | King (UN) | 2,057 | 10.8 |
| 2 | Edward Joy Morris (R) | 6,259 | 46.6 |
| | Brodhead (D) | 5,410 | 40.3 |
| | Fuller (UN) | 1,760 | 13.1 |
| 3 | John P. Verre (R) | 8,931 | 49.1 |
| | Kline (D) | 8,909 | 49.0 |
| 4 | William D. Kelley (R) | 11,568 | 49.3 |
| | Morgan (D) | 10,195 | 43.4 |
| | Robinson (UN) | 1,715 | 7.3 |
| 5 | William Morris Davis (R) | 10,020 | 50.8 |
| | Ingersoll (D) | 9,724 | 49.3 |
| 6 | John Hickman (R) | 10,140 | 56.8 |
| | Brinton (D) | 7,701 | 43.2 |
| 7 | Thomas B. Cooper (D) | 10,762 | 50.3 |
| | Longnecker (R) | 10,620 | 49.7 |
| 8 | Sydenham E. Ancona (D) | 9,993 | 58.4 |
| | Smith (R) | 7,111 | 41.6 |
| 9 | Thaddeus Stevens (R) | 12,964 | 96.5 |
| 10 | John W. Killinger (R) | 12,246 | 62.1 |
| | Worrell (D) | 7,488 | 37.9 |
| 11 | James H. Campbell (R) | 9,867 | 50.9 |
| | Hughes (D) | 9,518 | 49.1 |
| 12 | George W. Scranton (R) | 11,719 | 51.5 |
| | Randall (D) | 11,024 | 48.5 |
| 13 | Philip Johnson (D) | 12,208 | 57.3 |
| | Shoemaker (R) | 9,096 | 42.7 |
| 14 | Galusha A. Grow (R) | 14,922 | 71.4 |
| | Sherwood (D) | 5,984 | 28.6 |

| | Candidates | Votes | % |
|---|---|---|---|
| 15 | James T. Hale (R) | 11,907 | 53.8 |
| | Fleming (D) | 10,243 | 46.2 |
| 16 | Joseph Bailey (D) | 12,069 | 50.8 |
| | Junkin (R) | 11,712 | 49.3 |
| 17 | Edward McPherson (R) | 11,945 | 51.2 |
| | Schell (D) | 11,372 | 48.8 |
| 18 | Samuel S. Blair (R) | 11,185 | 57.6 |
| | McAllister (D) | 8,220 | 42.4 |
| 19 | John Covode (R) | 11,769 | 54.7 |
| | Phelps (D) | 9,761 | 45.3 |
| 20 | Jesse Lazear (D) | 10,607 | 52.9 |
| | Stewart (R) | 9,443 | 47.1 |
| 21 | James K. Morehead (R) | 10,507 | 61.3 |
| | Kerr (D) | 6,631 | 38.7 |
| 22 | Robert McKnight (R) | 7,978 | 72.8 |
| | Mitchell (D) | 2,979 | 27.2 |
| 23 | John W. Wallace (R) | 7,636 | 55.6 |
| | Holstein (D) | 6,102 | 44.4 |
| 24 | John D. Patton (R) | 11,745 | 52.6 |
| | Kerr (D) | 10,582 | 47.4 |
| 25 | Elijah Babbitt (R) | 10,705 | 65.9 |
| | Wilson (D) | 5,551 | 34.2 |

### Special Election

| | | Votes | % |
|---|---|---|---|
| 8 | Jacob K. McKenty (D) | 9,595 | 56.2 |
| | McKnight (R) | 7,482 | 43.8 |

## SOUTH CAROLINA [1]

(Seceded Dec. 20, 1860)

| | | | % |
|---|---|---|---|
| 1 | John McQueen (D) | | |
| | C. W. Miller | | |
| 2 | William P. Miles (D) | | 100.0 |
| 3 | George P. Elliott | | |
| | Lewis M. Ayer | | |
| 4 | Milledge L. Bonham (SSR D) | | 100.0 |
| 5 | John D. Ashmore (D) | | 100.0 |
| 6 | William W. Boyce (SSR D) | | 100.0 |

## VERMONT

| | | Votes | % |
|---|---|---|---|
| 1 | Eliakim Persons Walton (R) | 10,268 | 75.2 |
| | Wilcox (D) | 3,389 | 24.8 |
| 2 | Justin S. Morrill (R) | 12,555 | 79.2 |
| | Charles N. Davenport (D) | 3,295 | 20.8 |
| 3 | Portus Baxter (R) | 8,326 | 76.3 |
| | Chaffee (D) | 2,588 | 23.7 |

## WISCONSIN

| | | Votes | % |
|---|---|---|---|
| 1 | John F. Potter (R) | 16,197 | 54.5 |
| | Arnold (D) | 13,508 | 45.5 |
| 2 | Luther Hanchett (R) | 36,223 | 61.2 |
| | Reynolds (D) | 23,008 | 38.8 |
| 3 | A. Scott Sloan (R) | 34,002 | 54.0 |
| | Charles H. Larrabee (D) | 28,986 | 46.0 |

**1859 Elections**

1. Rep. Thomas L. Harris died Nov. 24, 1858, following his re-election to the 36th Congress (1859-61). In a special election in January 1859 to fill the remaining few months of Harris' term in the 35th Congress (1857-59), the winner was Charles D. Hodges. John A. McClernand was elected in November 1859 to the unexpired term in the 36th Congress.

2. In the 1st district, no candidate received the majority required by state law for election. In a later special election, Christopher Robinson was finally chosen.

**1860 Election**

1. South Carolina's six representatives withdrew from the House before the beginning of the 37th Congress (1861-63), and thus never assumed the seats they were elected to.

# 1861 House Elections

## ALABAMA

(Seceded Jan. 11, 1861)

## CALIFORNIA [1]

| Candidates | Votes | % |
|---|---|---|
| AL Timothy G. Phelps (R) | 51,651✔ | |
| Aaron A. Sargent (R) | 50,692✔ | |
| H. Edgerton (UN D) | 35,449 | |
| J. C. McKibben (UN D) | 35,401 | |
| D. O. Shattuck (SEC D) | 31,712 | |
| H. P. Barber (SEC D) | 31,591 | |
| AL Frederick F. Low | 39,059 | 45.6 |
| F Gunahl | 24,036 | 20.1 |
| J.R. Gitchell | 22,550 | 26.3 |

## CONNECTICUT

| | Candidates | Votes | % |
|---|---|---|---|
| 1 | Dwight Loomis (R) | 10,701 | 50.3 |
| | Hyde (D) | 10,563 | 49.7 |
| 2 | James E. English (D) | 12,490 | 52.3 |
| | Wdff (R) | 11,396 | 47.7 |
| 3 | Alfred A. Burnham (R) | 8,701 | 57.3 |
| | Baker (D) | 6,496 | 42.8 |
| 4 | George C. Woodruff (D) | 11,739 | 50.2 |
| | Ferry (R) | 11,668 | 49.9 |

## GEORGIA

(Seceded Jan. 28, 1861)

## ILLINOIS

### Special Election

| | | Votes | % |
|---|---|---|---|
| 6 | Anthony L. Knapp (D) | 8,283 | 98.0 |

## IOWA

### Special Election

| | Candidates | Votes | % |
|---|---|---|---|
| 1 | James F. Wilson (R) | 28,133 | 56.7 |
| | Juirus E. Neal (D) | 20,328 | 40.9 |

## KANSAS

(Became a state Jan. 29, 1861)

| | | | |
|---|---|---|---|
| AL | Martin F. Conway (R) | ✔ | |

## KENTUCKY

| | | Votes | % |
|---|---|---|---|
| 1 | Henry C. Burnett (SEC D) | 8,988 | 59.1 |
| | Lawrence S. Trimble (UN) | 6,225 | 40.9 |
| 2 | James S. Jackson (UN) | 9,281 | 73.4 |
| | John T. Bunch (SEC D) | 3,364 | 26.6 |
| 3 | Henry Grider (UN) | 10,392 | 77.0 |
| | Joseph H. Lewis (SEC D) | 3,113 | 23.1 |
| 4 | Aaron Harding (UN) | 10,339 | 80.7 |
| | Albert G. Talbott (SEC D) | 2,469 | 19.3 |
| 5 | Charles A. Wickliffe (UN) | 8,217 | 75.1 |
| | H. E. Read (SEC D) | 2,719 | 24.9 |
| 6 | George W. Dunlop (UN) | 8,101 | 97.3 |
| 7 | Robert Mallory (UN) | 11,035 | 79.4 |
| | Horatio W. Bruce (SEC D) | 2,862 | 20.6 |
| 8 | John J. Crittenden (UN) | 8,272 | 59.2 |
| | William E. Simms (SEC D) | 5,706 | 40.8 |
| 9 | William H. Wadsworth (UN) | 12,130 | 75.9 |
| | John L. Williams (SEC D) | 3,850 | 24.1 |
| 10 | John W. Menzies (UN) | 8,373 | 64.9 |
| | Overton P. Hogan (SEC D) | 3,774 | 29.3 |
| | Thomas L. Jones | 698 | 5.4 |

## LOUISIANA

(Seceded Jan. 26, 1861)

## MARYLAND

| | Candidates | Votes | % |
|---|---|---|---|
| 1 | John W. Crisfield (UN R) | 7,181 | 57.4 |
| | Hny (PEACE D) | 5,331 | 42.6 |
| 2 | Edwin H. Webster (UN R) | 7,251 | 98.3 |
| 3 | Cornelius L. L. Leary (UN R) | 6,702 | 52.0 |
| | Preston (PEACE D) | 6,200 | 48.1 |
| 4 | Henry May (PEACE D) | 8,424 | 57.6 |
| | Davis (UN R) | 6,214 | 42.5 |
| 5 | Francis Thomas (UN R) | 10,582 | 97.1 |
| 6 | Charles B. Calvert (UN R) | 4,467 | 50.9 |
| | Harris (PEACE D) | 4,305 | 49.1 |

## MISSISSIPPI

(Seceded Jan. 9, 1861)

## NEW HAMPSHIRE

| | | Votes | % |
|---|---|---|---|
| 1 | Gilman Marston (R) | 13,055 | 52.9 |
| | Marcy (D) | 11,642 | 47.1 |
| 2 | Edward H. Rollins (R) | 10,763 | 52.4 |
| | Bell (D) | 9,791 | 47.6 |
| 3 | Thomas M. Edwards (R) | 11,778 | 54.2 |
| | Burns (D) | 9,940 | 45.8 |

## NORTH CAROLINA

(Seceded May 21, 1861)

## RHODE ISLAND

| | | Votes | % |
|---|---|---|---|
| 1 | William P. Sheffield (UN) | 6,998 | 51.2 |
| | Robinson (R) | 6,656 | 48.7 |
| 2 | George H. Browne (UN) | 4,411 | 53.3 |
| | Brayton (R) | 3,856 | 46.6 |

## TENNESSEE

(Seceded June 8, 1861)

## TEXAS

(Seceded Feb. 1, 1861)

## VIRGINIA

(Seceded April 17, 1861)

---

*1. California had two seats in the House during the 36th Congress (1859-61), but following the reapportionment after the census of 1860 it would have been entitled to three in the 38th Congress (1863-65). Most states held House elections in even-numbered years, so those which were entitled to larger House representation would have had to wait until after the election of 1862 to claim it. But California held its regular House election in 1861, and tried to fill three seats.*

*Phelps and Sargent were elected to California's two regular seats. The Biographical Directory says that Frederick F. Low presented credentials and claimed a third seat Dec. 2, 1861, but the House May 6, 1862, declared him not entitled to a seat. Following passage of an act of June 2, 1862, granting California its third seat before it normally would have received it, he was admitted.*

*The ballot arrangement for California's 1861 House election was ambiguous. The ICPSR returns suggest that Low, Gunahl and Gitchell were probably listed in a separate column on the ballot as candidates in a separate at-large election for the prospective third seat, and Low's claim to the seat would be based on his having finished first among the three.*

*A second possibility is that all nine candidates for the House ran against each other in one at-large election. Low would have finished with the third highest number of votes in such a contest, and could conceivably have claimed the House seat on that basis.*

# 1862 House Elections

.

## DELAWARE

| | Candidates | Votes | % |
|---|---|---|---|
| AL | William Temple (D) | 8,051 | 50.1 |
| | George P. Fisher (UN) | 8,014 | 49.9 |

## ILLINOIS

| | Candidates | Votes | % |
|---|---|---|---|
| 1 | Isaac N. Arnold (R) | 10,025 | 54.5 |
| | Francis C. Sherman (D) | 8,387 | 45.6 |
| 2 | John F. Farnsworth (R) | 12,612 | 72.5 |
| | Neil Donnelly (D) | 4,785 | 27.5 |
| 3 | Elihu B. Washburne (R) | 10,496 | 60.7 |
| | Elias B. Stiles (D) | 6,785 | 39.3 |
| 4 | Charles M. Harris (D) | 11,626 | 57.2 |
| | Charles B. Lawrence (R) | 8,711 | 42.8 |
| 5 | Owen Lovejoy (R) | 11,683 | 50.1 |
| | Thomas J. Henderson (D) | 11,020 | 47.3 |
| 6 | Jesse O. Norton (R) | 10,604 | 55.7 |
| | F. Lyle Dickey (D) | 8,419 | 44.3 |
| 7 | John R. Eden (D) | 11,361 | 53.2 |
| | Elijah McCarty (R) | 10,004 | 46.8 |
| 8 | John T. Stuart (D) | 12,808 | 52.8 |
| | Leonard Swett (R) | 11,443 | 47.2 |
| 9 | Lewis W. Ross (D) | 13,391 | 99.1 |
| 10 | Anthony L. Knapp (D) | 14,259 | 64.8 |
| | Samuel W. Moulton (R) | 7,712 | 35.0 |
| 11 | James C. Robinson (D) | 13,644 | 71.2 |
| | Stephen G. Hicks (R) | 5,521 | 28.8 |
| 12 | William R. Morrison (D) | 10,999 | 61.6 |
| | Robert Smith (R) | 6,854 | 38.4 |
| 13 | William J. Allen (D) | 9,497 | 68.8 |
| | Milton Bartley (R) | 4,290 | 31.1 |
| AL | James C. Allen (D) | 136,257 | 53.2 |
| | Ebon C. Ingersoll (R) | 119,819 | 46.8 |

### Special Election

| | | | |
|---|---|---|---|
| 9 | William J. Allen (D) | 4,795 | 35.7 |
| | Irham W. Hayrin | 4,053 | 30.2 |
| | Samuel S. Marshall | 3,983 | 29.6 |

## INDIANA

| | | | |
|---|---|---|---|
| 1 | John Law (D) | 11,963 | 53.1 |
| | Johnson (UN R) | 10,583 | 46.9 |
| 2 | James A. Cravens (D) | 10,911 | 64.7 |
| | May (UN R) | 5,951 | 35.3 |
| 3 | Henry W. Harrington (D) | 11,524 | 53.4 |
| | William McKee Dunn (UN R) | 10,044 | 46.6 |
| 4 | William S. Holman (D) | 10,926 | 57.8 |
| | Gavin (UN R) | 7,992 | 42.3 |
| 5 | George W. Julian (UN R) | 9,272 | 55.6 |
| | Johnson (D) | 7,414 | 44.4 |
| 6 | Ebenezer Dumont (UN R) | 12,525 | 53.4 |
| | Contt (D) | 10,954 | 46.7 |
| 7 | Daniel W. Voorhees (D) | 12,457 | 55.5 |
| | Scott (UN R) | 9,976 | 44.5 |
| 8 | Godlove S. Orth (UN R) | 12,032 | 51.8 |
| | Pettit (D) | 11,181 | 48.2 |
| 9 | Schuyler Colfax (UN R) | 14,768 | 50.4 |
| | Turpie (D) | 14,546 | 49.6 |
| 10 | Joseph K. Edgerton (D) | 12,353 | 50.9 |
| | Mitchell (UN R) | 11,917 | 49.1 |
| 11 | James F. McDowell (D) | 13,142 | 51.8 |
| | Shanks (UN R) | 12,219 | 48.2 |

## IOWA

| | | | |
|---|---|---|---|
| 1 | James F. Wilson (R) | 12,705 | 54.8 |
| | Joseph K. Hornish (D) | 10,486 | 45.2 |
| 2 | Hiram Price (R) | 12,433 | 58.2 |
| | Edward H. Thayer (D) | 8,930 | 41.8 |
| 3 | William B. Allison (R) | 12,112 | 58.8 |
| | Dennis A. Mahoney (D) | 8,452 | 41.1 |

| | Candidates | Votes | % |
|---|---|---|---|
| 4 | Josiah B. Grinnell (R) | 12,900 | 52.8 |
| | Hugh M. Martin (D) | 11,529 | 47.2 |
| 5 | John A. Kasson (R) | 10,306 | 58.4 |
| | D. O. Finch (D) | 7,346 | 41.6 |
| 6 | Asahel W. Hubbard (R) | 5,386 | 66.2 |
| | John F. Duncombe (D) | 2,755 | 33.8 |

## KANSAS

| | | | |
|---|---|---|---|
| AL | A. Carter Wilder (R) | 9,671 | 63.3 |
| | Marcus J. Parrott (UN) | 4,666 | 30.6 |
| | William G. Mathias (D) | 930 | 6.1 |

## KENTUCKY

### Special Elections

| | | | |
|---|---|---|---|
| 1 | Samuel L. Casey (R) | 541 | 54.1 |
| | L. S. Trimble | 442 | 44.2 |
| 2 | George H. Yeaman (UN) | 2,242 | 55.7 |
| | Edward R. Weir | 1,756 | 43.6 |

## LOUISIANA[1]

### Special Elections

| | | | |
|---|---|---|---|
| 1 | Benjamin F. Flanders (UN) | 2,330 | 93.7 |
| | Bolgny (UN) | 157 | 6.3 |
| 2 | Michael Hahn (UN) | 2,581 | 57.8 |
| | Durell (UN) | 1,450 | 32.5 |
| | Barker (SEC) | 436 | 9.8 |

## MAINE

| | | | |
|---|---|---|---|
| 1 | Lorenzo D. M. Sweat (D) | 10,452 | 48.9 |
| | Goodwin (R) | 10,205 | 47.8 |
| 2 | Sidney Perham (R) | 9,976 | 56.7 |
| | Bates (D) | 7,519 | 42.7 |
| 3 | James G. Blaine (R) | 9,971 | 54.9 |
| | Gould (D) | 7,153 | 39.4 |
| 4 | John H. Rice (R) | 8,107 | 60.4 |
| | Boynton (D) | 3,806 | 28.4 |
| 5 | Frederick A. Pike (R) | 8,998 | 54.3 |
| | White (D) | 7,308 | 44.1 |

## MASSACHUSETTS

| | | | |
|---|---|---|---|
| 1 | Thomas D. Eliot (R) | 8,399 | 74.2 |
| | Daniel Fisher (PP) | 2,762 | 24.4 |
| 2 | Oakes Ames (R) | 9,271 | 61.1 |
| | William D. Swan (PP) | 5,907 | 38.9 |
| 3 | Alexander H. Rice (R) | 5,044 | 50.1 |
| | John Sleeper (PP) | 5,020 | 49.8 |
| 4 | Samuel Hooper (R) | 5,828 | 52.1 |
| | Josiah G. Abbott (PP) | 5,351 | 47.8 |
| 5 | John B. Alley (R) | 8,505 | 61.0 |
| | Benjamin Poole (PP) | 5,398 | 38.7 |
| 6 | Daniel W. Gooch (R) | 8,124 | 56.9 |
| | Oliver Hazzard Perry (PP) | 6,150 | 43.1 |
| 7 | George S. Boutwell (R) | 7,994 | 55.2 |
| | Benjamin F. Thomas (PP) | 6,496 | 44.8 |
| 8 | John D. Baldwin (R) | 10,128 | 66.2 |
| | Paul Whitin (PP) | 5,178 | 33.8 |
| 9 | William B. Washburne (R) | 14,311 | 99.2 |
| 10 | Henry L. Dawes (R) | 7,449 | 56.3 |
| | Chester W. Chapin (PP) | 5,785 | 43.7 |

## MICHIGAN

| | | | |
|---|---|---|---|
| 1 | Fernando C. Beaman (R) | 13,400 | 50.4 |
| | Ebenezer J. Penniman (R) | 13,210 | 49.6 |
| 2 | Charles Upson (R) | 14,148 | 55.4 |
| | John W. Turner (D) | 11,387 | 44.6 |

| | Candidates | Votes | % |
|---|---|---|---|
| 3 | John W. Longyear (R) | 12,317 | 51.7 |
| | Bradley F. Granger (D) | 11,488 | 48.3 |
| 4 | Francis W. Kellogg (R) | 10,013 | 57.8 |
| | Thomas B. Church (D) | 7,308 | 42.2 |
| 5 | Augustus C. Baldwin (D) | 10,697 | 50.6 |
| | Rowland E. Trowbridge (R) | 10,435 | 49.4 |
| 6 | John F. Driggs (R) | 8,188 | 53.7 |
| | John Moore (D) | 7,047 | 46.2 |

## MINNESOTA

| | | | |
|---|---|---|---|
| 1 | William Windom (R) | 8,663 | 57.4 |
| | A. G. Chatfield (D) | 6,423 | 42.6 |
| 2 | Ignatius Donnelly (R) | 7,091 | 58.6 |
| | W. J. Cullen (D) | 5,019 | 41.5 |

## MISSOURI

| | | | |
|---|---|---|---|
| 1 | Francis P. Blair Jr (R) | 4,743‡ | 40.0 |
| | Samuel Knox (EMANCIP) | 4,590 | 38.7 |
| | Bogy (D) | 2,536 | 21.4 |
| 2 | Henry T. Blow (EMANCIP) | 7,164 | 69.6 |
| | Allen (D) | 2,984 | 29.0 |
| 3 | John W. Noell (EMANCIP) | | ✔ |
| | John G. Scott (D) | | |
| | Lawson (I) | | |
| 4 | Sempronius H. Boyd (EMANCIP) | | ✔ |
| | Phelps (D) | | |
| 5 | Joseph W. McClurg (EMANCIP) | 4,930 | 53.2 |
| | Thomas L. Price (D) | 4,333 | 46.8 |
| 6 | Austin A. King (D) | 4,243 | 45.3 |
| | Birch (SEC) | 2,857 | 30.5 |
| | Samuel (ID) | 1,626 | 17.4 |
| | Bouton (EMANCIP) | 644 | 6.9 |
| 7 | Benjamin F. Loan (EMANCIP) | 6,580 | 48.4 |
| | John P. Bruce (D) | 4,554 | 33.5 |
| | Branch (I) | 2,465 | 18.1 |
| 8 | William A. Hall (D) | 6,244 | 53.0 |
| | Green (EMANCIP) | 5,534 | 47.0 |
| 9 | James S. Rollins (R) | 7,700 | 73.4 |
| | Krekel (EMANCIP) | 2,797 | 26.7 |

## NEW JERSEY

| | | | |
|---|---|---|---|
| 1 | John F. Starr (UN) | 9,491 | 51.4 |
| | Stratton (D) | 8,961 | 48.5 |
| 2 | George Middleton (D) | 12,182 | 52.9 |
| | Brown (UN) | 10,834 | 47.1 |
| 3 | William G. Steele (D) | 15,708 | 63.3 |
| | Brwnsn (UN) | 9,093 | 36.7 |
| 4 | Andrew J. Rogers (D) | 12,791 | 56.1 |
| | Linn (UN) | 10,024 | 43.9 |
| 5 | Nehemiah Perry (D) | 10,779 | 58.6 |
| | Bradley (UN) | 7,622 | 41.4 |

## NEW YORK

| | | | |
|---|---|---|---|
| 1 | Henry G. Stebbins (D) | 9,908 | 56.1 |
| | McCormick (UN) | 7,759 | 43.9 |
| 2 | Martin Kalbfleisch (D) | 10,586 | 66.3 |
| | Wall (UN) | 5,381 | 33.7 |
| 3 | Moses F. Odell (D) | 8,915 | 54.3 |
| | Humphrey (UN) | 7,506 | 45.7 |
| 4 | Benjamin Wood (D) | 7,828 | 63.3 |
| | Walbridge (UN) | 4,535 | 36.7 |
| 5 | Fernando Wood (D) | 8,176 | 70.1 |
| | Duffy (UN) | 3,488 | 29.9 |
| 6 | Elijah Ward (D) | 6,942 | 54.3 |
| | Conkling (UN) | 4,839 | 37.9 |
| | Blunt (I) | 996 | 7.8 |
| 7 | John W. Chanler (D) | 9,326 | 76.1 |
| | Burr (UN) | 2,937 | 24.0 |
| 8 | James Brooks (D) | 9,625 | 63.3 |
| | Cowdin (UN) | 5,570 | 36.7 |

1. Elected from areas under federal control.

## NEW YORK

| | Candidates | Votes | % |
|---|---|---|---|
| 9 | Anson Herrick (D) | 7,323 | 64.2 |
| | Murphy (UN) | 4,085 | 35.8 |
| 10 | William Radford (D) | 8,878 | 45.8 |
| | Haight (UN) | 7,921 | 40.9 |
| | Suffn (I) | 2,576 | 13.3 |
| 11 | Charles H. Winfield (D) | 9,326 | 55.2 |
| | Fullerton (UN) | 7,572 | 44.8 |
| 12 | Homer A. Nelson (D) | 10,712 | 53.0 |
| | Beale (UN) | 9,512 | 47.0 |
| 13 | John B. Steele (D) | 10,263 | 54.9 |
| | Cornell (UN) | 8,422 | 45.1 |
| 14 | Erastus Corning (D) | 15,715 | 59.6 |
| | Smith (UN) | 10,665 | 40.4 |
| 15 | John A. Griswold (D) | 12,226 | 52.8 |
| | Dodd (UN) | 10,939 | 47.2 |
| 16 | Orlando Kellogg (UN) | 7,654 | 52.3 |
| | Burhans (D) | 6,987 | 47.7 |
| 17 | Calvin T. Hulburd (UN) | 12,015 | 67.2 |
| | Judson (D) | 5,867 | 32.8 |
| 18 | James M. Marvin (UN) | 13,096 | 51.0 |
| | Blood (D) | 12,582 | 49.0 |
| 19 | Samuel F. Miller (UN) | 14,918 | 52.5 |
| | Parker (D) | 13,523 | 47.6 |
| 20 | Ambrose W. Clark (UN) | 14,826 | 57.3 |
| | Carryl (D) | 11,031 | 42.7 |
| 21 | Francis Kernan (D) | 9,943 | 50.3 |
| | Conkling (UN) | 9,845 | 49.8 |
| 22 | De Witt C. Littlejohn (UN) | 12,667 | 60.0 |
| | Titus (D) | 8,453 | 40.0 |
| 23 | Thomas T. Davis (UN) | 13,032 | 58.5 |
| | Strong (D) | 9,257 | 41.5 |
| 24 | Theodore M. Pomeroy (UN) | 13,834 | 55.3 |
| | Hadley (D) | 11,196 | 44.7 |
| 25 | Daniel Morris (UN) | 11,615 | 58.7 |
| | Lord (D) | 8,157 | 41.3 |
| 26 | Giles W. Hotchkiss (UN) | 13,889 | 58.7 |
| | Day (D) | 9,781 | 41.3 |
| 27 | Robert B. Van Valkenburg (UN) | 14,887 | 58.0 |
| | Hathawy (D) | 10,774 | 42.0 |
| 28 | Freeman Clarke (UN) | 11,193 | 53.2 |
| | Church (D) | 9,833 | 46.8 |
| 29 | Augustus Frank (UN) | 10,470 | 52.1 |
| | Hunt (D) | 9,627 | 47.9 |
| 30 | John Ganson (D) | 12,400 | 58.0 |
| | Spaulding (UN) | 8,985 | 42.0 |
| 31 | Reuben E. Fenton (UN) | 11,950 | 63.1 |
| | Caldwell (D) | 6,982 | 36.9 |

## OHIO

| | Candidates | Votes | % |
|---|---|---|---|
| 1 | George H. Pendleton (D) | 7,545 | 54.0 |
| | Groesbeck (UN R) | 6,418 | 46.0 |
| 2 | Alexander Long (D) | 7,212 | 50.5 |
| | Gurley (UN R) | 7,081 | 49.5 |
| 3 | Robert C. Schenck (UN R) | 13,027 | 52.5 |
| | Vallandigham (D) | 11,770 | 47.5 |
| 4 | John F. McKinney (D) | 10,218 | 52.0 |
| | West (UN R) | 9,435 | 48.0 |
| 5 | Francis C. Le Blond (D) | 10,561 | 63.0 |
| | Gatch (UN R) | 6,202 | 37.0 |
| 6 | Joseph W. White (D) | 10,087 | 52.0 |
| | Briggs (UN R) | 9,320 | 48.0 |
| 7 | Samuel S. Cox (D) | 10,372 | 50.7 |
| | Shellabarger (UN R) | 10,100 | 49.3 |
| 8 | William Johnston (D) | 9,012 | 51.1 |
| | Godman (UN R) | 8,642 | 49.0 |
| 9 | Warren P. Noble (D) | 11,765 | 52.8 |
| | Worcester (UN R) | 10,523 | 47.2 |
| 10 | James M. Ashley (UN R) | 6,908 | 38.6 |
| | Waite | 5,781 | 32.3 |
| | Phlpa | 5,232 | 29.2 |
| 11 | Wells A. Hutchins (D) | 8,605 | 56.2 |
| | Bundy (UN R) | 6,702 | 43.8 |
| 12 | William E. Finck (D) | 13,631 | 62.8 |
| | Trimble (UN R) | 8,087 | 37.2 |
| 13 | John O'Neill (D) | 12,763 | 56.8 |
| | Wright (UN R) | 9,699 | 43.2 |
| 14 | George Bliss (D) | 10,490 | 50.1 |
| | Welker (UN R) | 10,454 | 49.9 |
| 15 | James R. Morris (D) | 10,332 | 52.9 |
| | Cutler (UN R) | 9,183 | 47.1 |
| 16 | Chilton A. White (D) | 12,299 | 55.2 |
| | Bingham (UN R) | 9,999 | 44.8 |
| 17 | Ephraim R. Eckley (UN R) | 10,018 | 52.4 |
| | Belden (D) | 9,085 | 47.6 |
| 18 | Rufus P. Spalding (UN R) | 9,293 | 68.8 |
| | Paige (D) | 4,183 | 31.0 |
| 19 | James A. Garfield (UN R) | 13,288 | 66.3 |
| | Wood (D) | 6,763 | 33.7 |

## OREGON

| | Candidates | Votes | % |
|---|---|---|---|
| AL | John R. McBride (UN R) | 6,809 | 65.2 |
| | A. E. Wait (D) | 3,632 | 34.8 |

## PENNSYLVANIA

| | Candidates | Votes | % |
|---|---|---|---|
| 1 | Samuel J. Randall (D) | 7,720 | 55.2 |
| | Webb (UN) | 6,273 | 44.8 |
| 2 | Charles O'Neill (UN) | 8,614 | 58.7 |
| | Biddle (D) | 6,068 | 41.3 |
| 3 | Leonard Myers (UN) | 8,285 | 50.1 |
| | Kline (D) | 8,243 | 49.9 |
| 4 | William D. Kelley (UN) | 8,946 | 52.4 |
| | Nichn (D) | 8,118 | 47.6 |
| 5 | M. Russell Thayer (UN) | 9,605 | 50.2 |
| | Carrin (D) | 9,543 | 49.8 |
| 6 | John D. Stiles (D) | 11,316 | 58.3 |
| | Krause (UN) | 8,092 | 41.7 |
| 7 | John M. Broomall (UN) | 9,891 | 60.6 |
| | McCall (D) | 6,445 | 39.5 |
| 8 | Sydenham E. Ancona (D) | 10,022 | 67.2 |
| | Wanner (UN) | 4,898 | 32.8 |
| 9 | Thaddeus Stevens (UN) | 11,174 | 62.7 |
| | Steinn (D) | 6,650 | 37.3 |
| 10 | Myer Strouse (D) | 9,239 | 52.0 |
| | Campbell (UN) | 8,518 | 48.0 |
| 11 | Philip Johnson (D) | 11,676 | 81.8 |
| | Rouch (UN) | 2,592 | 18.2 |
| 12 | Charles Denison (D) | 11,408 | 54.2 |
| | Grow (UN) | 9,641 | 45.8 |
| 13 | Henry W. Tracy (UN) | 9,520 | 55.3 |
| | Clark (D) | 7,703 | 44.7 |
| 14 | William H. Miller (D) | 10,630 | 51.3 |
| | Patterson (UN) | 10,109 | 48.7 |
| 15 | Joseph Baily (UN) | 11,965 | 55.1 |
| | Glossbrenner (D) | 9,746 | 44.9 |
| 16 | Alexander H. Coffroth (D) | 10,963 | 51.3 |
| | Edward McPherson (UN) | 10,426 | 48.7 |
| 17 | Archibald McAllister (D) | 8,328 | 52.4 |
| | Blair (UN) | 7,556 | 47.6 |
| 18 | James T. Hale (D) | 9,272 | 49.4 |
| | Armstrong (UN) | 8,855 | 47.2 |
| 19 | Glenni W. Scofield (UN) | 9,954 | 51.3 |
| | Courtht (D) | 9,462 | 48.7 |
| 20 | Amos Myers (UN) | 12,440 | 51.7 |
| | Church (D) | 11,586 | 48.3 |
| 21 | John L. Dawson (D) | 10,234 | 50.6 |
| | Steward (UN) | 10,009 | 49.4 |
| 22 | James K. Moorhead (UN) | 8,037 | 58.6 |
| | Hamilton (D) | 5,678 | 41.4 |
| 23 | Thomas Williams (UN) | 8,989 | 54.1 |
| | Ziegler (D) | 7,635 | 45.9 |
| 24 | Jesse Lazear (D) | 9,984 | 51.1 |
| | Wallace (UN) | 9,547 | 48.9 |

## WISCONSIN

| | Candidates | Votes | % |
|---|---|---|---|
| 1 | James S. Brown (D) | 14,291 | 54.1 |
| | Potter (R) | 12,106 | 45.9 |
| 2 | Ithamar C. Sloan (R) | 13,105 | 54.4 |
| | Guppy (D) | 10,974 | 45.6 |
| 3 | Amasa Cobb (R) | 11,365 | 55.3 |
| | Simpson (R) | 9,184 | 44.7 |
| 4 | Charles A. Eldridge (D) | 15,343 | 61.5 |
| | Bragg (R) | 9,613 | 38.5 |
| 5 | Ezra Wheeler (D) | 11,021 | 52.4 |
| | Brown (R) | 10,005 | 47.6 |
| 6 | Luther Hanchett (R) | 9,276* | 57.5 |
| | Stoddard (D) | 6,774 | 42.0 |

# 1863 House Elections

## CALIFORNIA

| | Candidates | Votes | % |
|---|---|---|---|
| AL | Corneilus Cole (UN R) | 65,085✔ | |
| | Thomas B. Shannon (UN R) | 64,914✔ | |
| | William Higby (UN R) | 64,883✔ | |
| | J. B. Weller (D) | 43,567 | |
| | John Bigle (D) | 43,520 | |

## CONNECTICUT

| | Candidates | Votes | % |
|---|---|---|---|
| 1 | Henry C. Deming (R) | 10,493 | 50.8 |
| | Hyde (D) | 10,158 | 49.2 |
| 2 | James E. English (D) | 11,450 | 52.4 |
| | Warner (R) | 10,420 | 47.7 |
| 3 | Augustus Brandegee (UN R) | 8,878 | 58.2 |
| | Convse (D) | 6,381 | 41.8 |
| 4 | John H. Hubbard (R) | 11,248 | 50.8 |
| | Woodruff (D) | 10,892 | 49.2 |

## DELAWARE

**Special Election**

| | | Votes | % |
|---|---|---|---|
| AL | Nathaniel B. Smithers (UN) | 8,220 | 99.8 |

## KENTUCKY

| | | Votes | % |
|---|---|---|---|
| 1 | Lucien Anderson (UN) | 4,323 | 82.4 |
| | L. S. Trimble (D) | 711 | 13.6 |
| 2 | George H. Yeaman (UN) | 8,311 | 72.9 |
| | John H. McHenry Jr. (D) | 3,087 | 27.1 |
| 3 | Henry Grider (UN) | 8,654 | 87.0 |
| | Thomas C. Winfrey (D) | 1,293 | 13.0 |
| 4 | Aaron Harding (UN) | 10,435 | 80.6 |
| | William J. Heady (D) | 2,508 | 19.4 |

| | Candidates | Votes | % |
|---|---|---|---|
| 5 | Robert Mallory (UN) | 6,257 | 71.6 |
| | Nathaniel Wolfe (D) | 2,477 | 28.4 |
| 6 | Green Clay Smith (UN) | 6,936 | 61.9 |
| | J. W. Menzies (D) | 2,283 | 20.4 |
| | J. W. Leathers (D) | 1,970 | 17.6 |
| 7 | Brutus J. Clay (UN) | 4,711 | 50.4 |
| | J. T. Boyle (D) | 2,487 | 26.6 |
| | R. A. Buckner (D) | 2,143 | 22.9 |
| 8 | William H. Randall (UN) | 8,321 | 97.2 |
| 9 | William H. Wadsworth (UN) | 6,889 | 89.0 |
| | Thomas S. Brown (D) | 849 | 11.0 |

## MARYLAND

| | | Votes | % |
|---|---|---|---|
| 1 | John A. J. Creswell (UN R) | 6,743 | 55.2 |
| | Crisfield (D) | 5,482 | 44.8 |
| 2 | Edwin H. Webster (UN R) | 7,736 | 100.0 |
| 3 | Henry Winter Davis (UN R) | 6,200 | 99.7 |
| 4 | Francis Thomas (UN R) | 13,462 | 100.0 |
| 5 | Benjamin G. Harris (D) | 4,939 | 46.9 |
| | Holland (UN R) | 3,352 | 31.8 |
| | Calvert (KST U) | 2,237 | 21.3 |

## MISSOURI

**Special Election**

| | | Votes | % |
|---|---|---|---|
| 3 | John G. Scott (D) | 3,559 | 50.3 |
| | Lindsay (UN) | 3,070 | 43.4 |
| | Bogy (ID) | 444 | 6.3 |

## NEW HAMPSHIRE

| | | Votes | % |
|---|---|---|---|
| 1 | Daniel Marcy (D) | 12,059 | 50.2 |
| | Eastman (R) | 11,979 | 49.8 |

| | Candidates | Votes | % |
|---|---|---|---|
| 2 | Edward H. Rollins (R) | 10,365 | 50.9 |
| | George (D) | 9,999 | 49.1 |
| 3 | James W. Patterson (R) | 10,847 | 50.6 |
| | Burns (D) | 10,571 | 49.4 |

## RHODE ISLAND

| | | Votes | % |
|---|---|---|---|
| 1 | Thomas A. Jenckes (R) | 6,532 | 58.2 |
| | Bradley (D) | 4,616 | 41.1 |
| 2 | Nathan F. Dixon (R) | 4,077 | 56.4 |
| | Browne (D) | 3,121 | 43.2 |

## VERMONT

| | | Votes | % |
|---|---|---|---|
| 1 | Frederick E. Woodbridge (R) | 8,565 | 70.8 |
| | John A. S. White (D) | 3,486 | 28.8 |
| 2 | Justin S. Morrill (R) | 11,358 | 70.3 |
| | Charles N. Davenport (D) | 4,785 | 29.6 |
| 3 | Portus Baxter (R) | 7,234 | 71.0 |
| | Giles Harrington (D) | 2,673 | 26.2 |

## WEST VIRGINIA

(Became a state June 19, 1863)

| | | Votes | % |
|---|---|---|---|
| 1 | Jacob B. Blair (UN R) | 8,066 | 93.0 |
| | Dehass (UN R) | 605 | 7.0 |
| 2 | William G. Brown (UN R) | 3,576 | 57.9 |
| | Burdett (UN R) | 1,804 | 29.2 |
| | Zinn (UN R) | 800 | 12.9 |
| 3 | Kellian V. Whaley (UN R) | 2,746 | 55.7 |
| | Frost (UN R) | 2,184 | 44.3 |

---

# House Candidates Index

For an index of all House candidates listed in this section (pages 943-1326), see pages 1402-1501. Instructions for use of the House Candidates Index appear on page 1402.

---

# 1864 House Elections

## CALIFORNIA

| | Candidates | Votes | % |
|---|---|---|---|
| 1 | Donald C. McRuer (UN R) | 20,370 | 58.9 |
| | J. B. Crocker (D) | 14,191 | 41.1 |
| 2 | William Higby (UN R) | 23,414 | 61.6 |
| | J. W. Coffroth (D) | 14,581 | 38.4 |
| 3 | John Bidwell (UN R) | 18,255 | 56.1 |
| | Jack Temple (D) | 14,273 | 43.9 |

## DELAWARE

| | | Votes | % |
|---|---|---|---|
| AL | John A. Nicholson (D) | 8,762 | 51.5 |
| | Nathaniel B. Smithers (UN R) | 8,253 | 48.5 |

## ILLINOIS

| | | Votes | % |
|---|---|---|---|
| 1 | John Wentworth (UN R) | 18,557 | 56.5 |
| | Cyrus H. McCormick (D) | 14,277 | 43.5 |
| 2 | John F. Farnsworth (UN R) | 18,298 | 77.8 |
| | M. C. Johnson (D) | 5,237 | 22.3 |
| 3 | Elihu B. Washburne (UN R) | 15,711 | 67.9 |
| | Elius B. Stiles (D) | 7,421 | 32.1 |
| 4 | Abner C. Harding (UN R) | 13,569 | 51.6 |
| | Charles M. Harris (D) | 12,721 | 48.4 |
| 5 | Ebon C. Ingersoll (UN R) | 18,152 | 61.7 |
| | James S. Echels (D) | 11,287 | 38.3 |
| 6 | Burton C. Cook (UN R) | 15,598 | 61.0 |
| | Samuel K. Casey (D) | 9,980 | 39.0 |
| 7 | Henry P. H. Bromwell (UN R) | 15,373 | 56.1 |
| | John R. Eden (D) | 12,027 | 43.9 |
| 8 | Shelby M. Cullom (UN R) | 15,812 | 53.0 |
| | John T. Stuart (D) | 14,027 | 47.0 |
| 9 | Lewis W. Ross (D) | 15,296 | 55.6 |
| | Hugh Fullerton (UN R) | 12,239 | 44.5 |
| 10 | Anthony Thornton (UN R) | 16,902 | 58.1 |
| | N. M. Knapp (D) | 12,176 | 41.9 |
| 11 | Samuel S. Marshall (D) | 16,703 | 61.0 |
| | Ethelbert Callahan (UN R) | 10,696 | 39.0 |
| 12 | John Baker (UN R) | 11,817 | 50.2 |
| | William R. Morrison (D) | 11,741 | 49.8 |
| 13 | Andrew J. Kuykendall (UN R) | 11,762 | 52.1 |
| | William J. Allen (D) | 10,759 | 47.7 |
| AL | Samuel W. Moulton (UN R) | 190,216 | 54.5 |
| | J. C. Allen (D) | 158,781 | 45.5 |

### Special Election

| | | Votes | % |
|---|---|---|---|
| 5 | Ebon C. Ingersoll (R) | 12,986 | 62.8 |
| | H. M. Wead | 7,677 | 37.1 |

## INDIANA

| | | Votes | % |
|---|---|---|---|
| 1 | William E. Niblack (D) | 14,718 | 53.9 |
| | Cyrus M. Allen (UN R) | 12,616 | 46.2 |
| 2 | Michael C. Kerr (D) | 11,407 | 54.3 |
| | William W. Curry (UN R) | 9,614 | 45.7 |
| 3 | Ralph Hill (UN R) | 12,017 | 51.8 |
| | Henry W. Harrington (D) | 11,173 | 48.2 |
| 4 | John H. Farquhar (UN R) | 10,015 | 50.2 |
| | George Berry (D) | 9,949 | 49.8 |
| 5 | George W. Julian (UN R) | 13,529 | 68.7 |
| | James Brown (D) | 6,161 | 31.3 |
| 6 | Ebenezer Dumont (UN R) | 18,886 | 63.4 |
| | John Love (D) | 10,905 | 36.6 |
| 7 | Daniel W. Voorhees (D) | 12,880‡ | 51.2 |
| | Henry D. Washburn (UN R) | 12,296 | 48.8 |
| 8 | Godlove S. Orth (UN R) | 13,536 | 52.3 |
| | James F. Harney (D) | 12,349 | 47.7 |
| 9 | Schuyler Colfax (UN R) | 16,658 | 52.7 |
| | David Turpie (D) | 14,942 | 47.3 |
| 10 | Joseph D. Defrees (UN R) | 14,617 | 51.0 |
| | Joseph K. Edgerton (D) | 14,037 | 49.0 |
| 11 | Thomas F. Stillwell (UN R) | 15,623 | 53.9 |
| | James F. McDowell (D) | 13,383 | 46.1 |

## IOWA

| | Candidates | Votes | % |
|---|---|---|---|
| 1 | James F. Wilson (UN R) | 16,977 | 65.2 |
| | J. K. Hornish (D) | 9,078 | 34.8 |
| 2 | Hiram Price (UN R) | 16,571 | 65.3 |
| | George H. Parker (D) | 8,822 | 34.7 |
| 3 | William B. Allison (UN R) | 16,130 | 60.4 |
| | B. B. Richards (D) | 10,578 | 39.6 |
| 4 | Josiah B. Grinnell (UN R) | 17,169 | 61.5 |
| | Ira C. Mitchell (D) | 10,619 | 38.1 |
| 5 | John A. Kasson (UN R) | 13,640 | 65.8 |
| | M. D. McHenry (D) | 7,104 | 34.3 |
| 6 | Asahel W. Hubbard (UN R) | 8,455 | 72.8 |
| | Seander Chapman (D) | 3,162 | 27.2 |

## KANSAS

| | | Votes | % |
|---|---|---|---|
| AL | Sidney Clarke (R) | 10,820 | 52.7 |
| | A. L. Lee (R-UNION) | 9,708 | 47.3 |

## MAINE

| | | Votes | % |
|---|---|---|---|
| 1 | John Lynch (UN) | 15,096 | 54.6 |
| | Sweat (D) | 12,568 | 45.4 |
| 2 | Sidney Perham (UN) | 13,030 | 61.0 |
| | Andrews (D) | 8,344 | 39.0 |
| 3 | James G. Blaine (UN) | 14,055 | 59.3 |
| | Gould (D) | 9,647 | 40.7 |
| 4 | John H. Rice (UN) | 11,002 | 61.2 |
| | Madigan (D) | 6,983 | 38.8 |
| 5 | Frederick A. Pike (UN) | 12,538 | 58.2 |
| | White (D) | 9,016 | 41.8 |

## MARYLAND

| | | Votes | % |
|---|---|---|---|
| 1 | Hiram McCullough (D) | 9,677 | 60.5 |
| | J. A. J. Cresswell (UN R) | 6,307 | 39.5 |
| 2 | Edwin H. Webster (UN R) | 9,541 | 69.9 |
| | William Kimmell (D) | 4,102 | 30.1 |
| 3 | Charles E. Phelps (UN R) | 9,313 | 84.2 |
| | A. Lewis Knott (D) | 1,753 | 15.8 |
| 4 | Francis Thomas (UN R) | 11,898 | 61.2 |
| | Syester (D) | 7,551 | 38.8 |
| 5 | Benjamin G. Harris (D) | 8,839 | 72.3 |
| | John C. Holland (UN R) | 3,389 | 27.7 |

## MASSACHUSETTS

| | | Votes | % |
|---|---|---|---|
| 1 | Thomas D. Eliot (UNT) | 13,687 | 82.8 |
| | Sylvanus B. Phinney (D) | 2,850 | 17.2 |
| 2 | Oakes Ames (UNT) | 13,591 | 72.1 |
| | James McGuire (D) | 5,266 | 27.9 |
| 3 | Alexander H. Rice (UNT) | 9,711 | 62.3 |
| | John S. Sleeper (D) | 5,864 | 37.7 |
| 4 | Samuel Hooper (UNT) | 10,403 | 65.5 |
| | Josiah G. Abbott (D) | 5,485 | 34.5 |
| 5 | John B. Alley (UNT) | 13,086 | 75.8 |
| | Joseph B. Morss (D) | 4,158 | 24.1 |
| 6 | Daniel W. Gooch (UNT) | 13,082 | 71.7 |
| | Thomas J. Greenwood (D) | 5,174 | 28.3 |
| 7 | George S. Boutwell (UNT) | 12,087 | 69.0 |
| | Theodore H. Sweetser (D) | 5,433 | 31.0 |
| 8 | John D. Baldwin (UNT) | 12,955 | 74.8 |
| | George Hodges (D) | 4,377 | 25.3 |
| 9 | William B. Washburn (UNT) | 15,721 | 81.5 |
| | Nathaniel Wood (D) | 3,575 | 18.5 |
| 10 | Henry L. Dawes (UNT) | 11,600 | 64.7 |
| | Harry Arnold (D) | 6,315 | 35.2 |

## MICHIGAN

| | | Votes | % |
|---|---|---|---|
| 1 | Fernando C. Beaman (UN) | 17,908 | 53.4 |
| | David A. Noble (D) | 15,602 | 46.5 |
| 2 | Charles Upson (UN) | 19,151 | 60.4 |
| | Nathaniel A. Balch (D) | 12,538 | 39.6 |

| | Candidates | Votes | % |
|---|---|---|---|
| 3 | John W. Longyear (UN) | 15,432 | 54.7 |
| | David Johnson (D) | 12,758 | 45.3 |
| 4 | Thomas W. Ferry (UN) | 13,428 | 59.2 |
| | Frederick Hall (D) | 9,256 | 40.8 |
| 5 | Rowland E. Trowbridge (UN) | 12,651 | 51.5 |
| | Augustus C. Baldwin (D) | 11,937 | 48.5 |
| 6 | John F. Driggs (UN) | 12,784 | 53.4 |
| | William Willard (D) | 11,166 | 46.6 |

## MINNESOTA

| | | Votes | % |
|---|---|---|---|
| 1 | William Windom (UN R) | 13,965 | 60.6 |
| | Henry W. Lamberton (D) | 9,092 | 30.4 |
| 2 | Ignatius Donnelly (UN R) | 10,874 | 57.0 |
| | John M. Gilman (D) | 8,211 | 43.0 |

## MISSOURI

| | | Votes | % |
|---|---|---|---|
| 1 | John Hogan (D) | 6,026 | 43.2 |
| | Charles P. Johnson (RAD R) | 4,781 | 34.2 |
| | Samuel Knox (RAD R) | 3,157 | 22.6 |
| 2 | Henry T. Blow (RAD R) | 11,580 | 90.2 |
| | E. Stafford | 1,253 | 9.8 |
| 3 | Thomas E. Noell (RAD R) | 4,075 | 61.7 |
| | D. C. Tuttle (D) | 1,868 | 28.3 |
| | W. T. Leeper (I RAD R) | 659 | 10.0 |
| 4 | John R. Kelso (I RAD R) | 3,841 | 49.3 |
| | Sempronius H. Boyd (RAD R) | 3,548 | 45.6 |
| | M. J. Hubble (D) | 400 | 5.1 |
| 5 | Joseph W. McClurg (RAD R) | 6,976 | 72.4 |
| | Sample Orr (D) | 2,659 | 27.6 |
| 6 | Robert T. Van Horn (RAD R) | 3,498 | 47.2 |
| | Elijah H. Norton (D) | 3,226 | 43.5 |
| | Austin A. King (ID) | 695 | 9.4 |
| 7 | Benjamin F. Loan (RAD R) | 10,445 | 85.9 |
| | H. B. Branch | 1,674 | 13.8 |
| 8 | John F. Benjamin (RAD R) | 8,536 | 74.1 |
| | John M. Glover (C) | 2,978 | 25.9 |
| 9 | George W. Anderson (RAD R) | 5,329 | 51.8 |
| | Odon Guitar (D) | 4,950 | 48.2 |

## NEVADA

(Became a state Oct. 31, 1864)

| | | Votes | % |
|---|---|---|---|
| AL | Henry G. Worthington (UN R) | 9,776 | 59.9 |
| | A. C. Bradford (D) | 6,552 | 40.1 |

## NEW JERSEY

| | | Votes | % |
|---|---|---|---|
| 1 | John F. Starr (UN) | 12,091 | 54.4 |
| | Dickinson (D) | 10,126 | 45.6 |
| 2 | William A. Newell (UN) | 13,953 | 51.6 |
| | Middleton (D) | 13,091 | 48.4 |
| 3 | Charles Sitgreaves (D) | 16,942 | 58.4 |
| | Scranton (UN) | 12,080 | 41.6 |
| 4 | Andrew J. Rogers (D) | 14,059 | 53.6 |
| | Little (UN) | 12,173 | 46.4 |
| 5 | Edwin R. V. Wright (D) | 13,390 | 53.9 |
| | Wakeman (UN) | 11,448 | 46.1 |

## NEW YORK

| | | Votes | % |
|---|---|---|---|
| 1 | Stephen Taber (D) | 12,232 | 55.0 |
| | George V. Curtis (UN) | 10,023 | 45.0 |
| 2 | Teunis G. Bergen (D) | 13,630 | 60.7 |
| | Samuel T. Maddox (UN) | 8,829 | 39.3 |
| 3 | James Humphrey (UN) | 11,752 | 51.3 |
| | Thomas H. Faron (D) | 11,168 | 48.7 |
| 4 | Morgan Jones (TAM D) | 9,605 | 57.2 |
| | William Walsh (MOZART D) | 5,512 | 32.8 |
| | Carolan O. Bryant (UN) | 1,684 | 10.0 |
| 5 | Nelson Taylor (TAM D) | 9,272 | 53.1 |
| | William B. Maclay (MOZART D) | 4,286 | 24.5 |

## NEW YORK

| Candidates | Votes | % |
|---|---|---|
| Epes P. Ellery (UN) | 3,921 | 22.4 |
| 6 Henry J. Raymond (UN) | 7,315 | 42.4 |
| Elijah Ward (TAM D) | 6,929 | 40.2 |
| Eli P. Norton (MOZART D) | 1,647 | 9.6 |
| Rush C. Hawkins (IRR U) | 1,347 | 7.8 |
| 7 John Winthrop Chanler (UN) | 11,513 | 67.1 |
| William Boardman (D) | 5,638 | 32.9 |
| 8 James Brooks (D) | 8,583‡ | 39.8 |
| William E. Dodge (R) | 8,435 | 39.1 |
| Thomas J. Barr (TAM D) | 4,544 | 21.1 |
| 9 William A. Darling (UN) | 5,822 | 38.9 |
| Fernando Wood (MOZART D) | 4,749 | 31.7 |
| Anson Herrick (TAM D) | 4,397 | 29.4 |
| 10 William Radford (D) | 13,033 | 56.1 |
| Francis Larkin (UN) | 10,218 | 44.0 |
| 11 Charles H. Winfield (D) | 9,975 | 50.6 |
| Ambrose S. Murray (UN) | 9,736 | 49.4 |
| 12 John H. Ketcham (UN) | 12,229 | 51.4 |
| Homer A. Nelson (D) | 11,559 | 48.6 |
| 13 Edwin N. Hubbell (D) | 11,373 | 53.1 |
| Theodore B. Gates (UN) | 10,028 | 46.9 |
| 14 Charles Goodyear (D) | 17,497 | 57.5 |
| John H. Gardiner (UN) | 12,942 | 42.5 |
| 15 John A. Griswold (UN) | 15,251 | 54.1 |
| William A. Van Alstyne (D) | 12,928 | 45.9 |
| 16 Orlando Kellogg (UN) | 8,988 | 53.9 |
| Thomas S. Gray (D) | 7,675 | 46.1 |
| 17 Calvin T. Hulburd (UN) | 13,183 | 70.0 |
| William J. Averill (D) | 5,659 | 30.0 |
| 18 James M. Marvin (UN) | 14,453 | 51.6 |
| Alonzo C. Paige (D) | 13,572 | 48.4 |
| 19 Demas Hubbard Jr (UN) | 17,067 | 54.8 |
| Hezekiah Sturges (D) | 14,078 | 45.2 |
| 20 Addison H. Laflin (UN) | 16,441 | 56.4 |
| Frederick W. Hubbard (D) | 12,704 | 43.6 |
| 21 Roscoe Conkling (UN) | 11,966 | 52.5 |
| Francis Kernan (D) | 10,816 | 47.5 |
| 22 Sidney T. Holmes (UN) | 14,638 | 60.0 |
| Albertus Perry (D) | 9,781 | 40.1 |
| 23 Thomas T. Davis (UN) | 14,800 | 58.6 |
| William C. Ruger (D) | 10,464 | 41.4 |
| 24 Theodore M. Pomeroy (UN) | 16,027 | 57.5 |
| George W. Cuyler (D) | 11,832 | 42.5 |
| 25 Daniel Morris (UN) | 12,763 | 58.8 |
| Barzillai Slosson (D) | 8,962 | 41.3 |
| 26 Giles W. Hotchkiss (UN) | 15,543 | 59.0 |
| John Magee (D) | 10,806 | 41.0 |
| 27 Hamilton Ward (UN) | 16,945 | 60.3 |
| Andrew J. McNett (D) | 11,176 | 39.7 |
| 28 Roswell Hart (UN) | 13,081 | 52.5 |
| James L. Angle (D) | 11,841 | 47.5 |
| 29 Burt Van Horn (UN) | 12,671 | 57.1 |
| James M. Willett (D) | 9,533 | 42.9 |
| 30 James M. Humphrey (D) | 13,231 | 50.7 |
| Samuel J. Holley (UN) | 12,861 | 49.3 |
| 31 Henry Van Aernam (UN) | 13,996 | 65.5 |
| Jonas K. Button (D) | 7,374 | 34.5 |

### Special Election

| Candidates | Votes | % |
|---|---|---|
| 1 Dwight Townsend (D) | 11,828 | 55.0 |
| Henry G. Stebbins (UN) | 9,697 | 45.1 |

## OHIO

| Candidates | Votes | % |
|---|---|---|
| 1 Benjamin Eggleston (UN R) | 9,893 | 57.0 |
| George E. Pugh (D) | 7,464 | 43.0 |
| 2 Rutherford B. Hays (UN R) | 10,425 | 58.7 |
| J. C. Butler (D) | 7,327 | 41.3 |
| 3 Robert C. Schenck (UN R) | 14,371 | 55.3 |
| David A. Houk (D) | 11,605 | 44.7 |
| 4 William Lawrence (UN R) | 12,242 | 56.1 |
| John F. McKinney (D) | 9,578 | 43.9 |
| 5 Frank C. Le Blond (D) | 11,048 | 55.2 |
| Moses B. Walker (UN R) | 8,957 | 44.8 |
| 6 Reader W. Clarke (UN R) | 12,615 | 55.3 |
| Chilton A. White (D) | 10,183 | 44.7 |
| 7 Samuel Shellabarger (UN R) | 12,756 | 57.1 |
| Samuel S. Cox (D) | 9,587 | 42.9 |
| 8 James R. Hubbell (UN R) | 10,903 | 54.8 |
| William Johnston (D) | 8,983 | 45.2 |
| 9 Ralph P. Buckland (UN R) | 13,511 | 53.6 |
| Warren P. Noble (D) | 11,717 | 46.4 |
| 10 James M. Ashley (UN R) | 11,732 | 51.8 |
| Americus V. Rice (D) | 10,905 | 48.2 |
| 11 Hezekiah S. Bundy (UN R) | 11,581 | 59.8 |
| William A. Hutchins (D) | 7,793 | 40.2 |
| 12 William E. Finck (D) | 12,965 | 53.3 |
| Job E. Stevenson (UN R) | 11,349 | 46.7 |
| 13 Columbus Delano (UN R) | 11,876 | 50.5 |
| Charles Follet (D) | 11,651 | 49.5 |
| 14 Martin Welker (UN R) | 12,844 | 55.5 |
| George Bliss (D) | 10,313 | 44.5 |
| 15 Tobias A. Plants (UN R) | 12,847 | 57.3 |
| James M. Morris (D) | 9,564 | 42.7 |
| 16 John A. Bingham (UN R) | 12,377 | 52.7 |
| Joseph White (D) | 11,119 | 47.3 |
| 17 Ephraim R. Eckley (UN R) | 12,758 | 59.3 |
| J. H. Wallace (D) | 8,746 | 40.7 |
| 18 Rufus P. Spalding (UN R) | 14,472 | 68.5 |
| J. H. Wade (D) | 6,661 | 31.5 |
| 19 James A. Garfield (UN R) | 18,086 | 74.1 |
| Halsey H. Moses (D) | 6,315 | 25.9 |

## OREGON

| Candidates | Votes | % |
|---|---|---|
| AL James H. D. Henderson (UN R) | 8,759 | 59.4 |
| James K. Kelly (D) | 5,996 | 40.6 |

## PENNSYLVANIA

| Candidates | Votes | % |
|---|---|---|
| 1 Samuel J. Randall (D) | 9,764 | 55.8 |
| John M. Butler (UN R) | 7,742 | 44.2 |
| 2 Charles O'Neill (UN R) | 11,767 | 61.8 |
| William M. Reilly (D) | 7,290 | 38.3 |
| 3 Leonard Myers (UN R) | 11,467 | 53.4 |
| Charles Buckwalter (D) | 9,992 | 46.6 |
| 4 William D. Kelley (UN R) | 13,088 | 58.4 |
| Charles Northrop (D) | 9,344 | 41.7 |
| 5 M. Russell Thayer (UN R) | 11,007 | 50.6 |
| Henry P. Ross (D) | 10,729 | 49.4 |
| 6 Benjamin M. Boyer (D) | 12,847 | 57.1 |
| George Bullock (UN R) | 9,661 | 42.9 |
| 7 John M. Broomall (UN R) | 10,908 | 60.1 |
| John C. Beatty (D) | 7,231 | 39.9 |
| 8 Sydenham E. Ancona (D) | 12,076 | 66.9 |
| William M. Heister (UN R) | 5,971 | 33.1 |
| 9 Thaddeus Stevens (UN R) | 11,804 | 61.7 |
| Henry M. North (D) | 7,344 | 38.4 |
| 10 Myer Strouse (D) | 11,154 | 51.2 |
| Howell Fisher (UN R) | 10,629 | 48.8 |
| 11 Philip Johnson (D) | 13,007 | 67.1 |
| James L. Selfridge (UN R) | 6,384 | 32.9 |
| 12 Charles Dennison (D) | 10,573 | 51.3 |
| Winthrop W. Ketcham (UN R) | 10,058 | 48.8 |
| 13 Ulysses Mercur (UN R) | 9,727 | 52.7 |
| Victor E. Piollet (D) | 8,723 | 47.3 |
| 14 George F. Miller (UN R) | 11,619 | 51.2 |
| W. H. Miller (D) | 11,092 | 48.8 |
| 15 Adam J. Glossbrenner (D) | 13,382 | 55.9 |
| Joseph Baily (UN R) | 10,576 | 44.1 |
| 16 William H. Koontz (UN R) | 11,242‡ | 50.2 |
| Alexander H. Coffroth (D) | 11,174 | 49.9 |
| 17 Abraham A. Barker (UN R) | 9,225 | 51.4 |
| Robert L. Johnston (D) | 8,716 | 48.6 |
| 18 Stephen F. Wilson (UN R) | 11,533 | 51.9 |
| Theo Wright (D) | 10,681 | 48.1 |
| 19 Glenni W. Scofield (UN R) | 11,631 | 54.0 |
| William Bigler (D) | 9,914 | 46.0 |
| 20 Charles V. Culver (UN R) | 13,350 | 52.8 |
| William L. Corbett (D) | 11,942 | 47.2 |
| 21 John L. Dawson (D) | 10,855 | 50.3 |
| Smith Fuller (UN R) | 10,730 | 49.7 |
| 22 James K. Moorhead (UN R) | 11,233 | 61.6 |
| James H. Hopkins (D) | 7,013 | 38.4 |
| 23 Thomas Williams (UN R) | 11,682 | 59.0 |
| William J. Kountz (D) | 8,122 | 41.0 |
| 24 George V. Lawrence (UN R) | 11,727 | 53.7 |
| Jesse Lazear (D) | 10,112 | 46.3 |

## VERMONT

| Candidates | Votes | % |
|---|---|---|
| 1 Frederick E. Woodbridge (UN) | 9,133 | 71.5 |
| Samuel Wells (D) | 3,626 | 28.4 |
| 2 Justin S. Morrill (UN | 12,409 | 72.0 |
| Unidentified Candidate (D) | 4,793 | 27.8 |
| 3 Portus Baxter (UN) | 9,408 | 74.1 |
| Giles Harrington (D) | 3,281 | 25.9 |

## WEST VIRGINIA

| Candidates | Votes | % |
|---|---|---|
| 1 Chester D. Hubbard (UN R) | 7,198 | 62.5 |
| Samuel Crane | 4,315 | 37.5 |
| 2 George R. Latham (UN R) | 5,663 | 84.4 |
| William B. Zinn | 721 | 10.8 |
| 3 Kellian V. Whaley (UN R) | 2,446 | 66.8 |
| John M. Phelps | 1,216 | 33.2 |

## WISCONSIN

| Candidates | Votes | % |
|---|---|---|
| 1 Halbert E. Paine (R) | 13,716 | 50.9 |
| Cary (D) | 13,230 | 49.1 |
| 2 Ithamar C. Sloan (R) | 15,148 | 60.3 |
| Smith (D) | 9,969 | 39.7 |
| 3 Amasa Cobb (R) | 14,342 | 63.2 |
| Rodolf (D) | 8,354 | 36.8 |
| 4 Charles A. Eldridge (D) | 15,547 | 58.9 |
| Sloan (R) | 10,835 | 41.1 |
| 5 Philetus Sawyer (R) | 12,576 | 56.8 |
| Bouck (D) | 9,550 | 43.2 |
| 6 Walter D. McIndoe (R) | 12,962 | 65.5 |
| Reed (D) | 6,836 | 34.5 |

# 1865 House Elections

## ALABAMA [1]

| | Candidates | Votes | % |
|---|---|---|---|
| 1 | Charles C. Langdon | 2,628* | 60.2 |
| | Mathews | 918 | 21.0 |
| | Cleveland | 812 | 18.6 |
| 2 | George Freeman | 6,038* | 82.7 |
| | Benjamin Gardner | 1,249 | 17.1 |
| 3 | Cullen A. Battle | 3,914* | 44.5 |
| | George Reese | 2,031 | 23.1 |
| | Robert F. Ligon | 1,891 | 21.5 |
| | E. Hamill | 671 | 7.6 |
| 4 | J. Taylor | 5,619* | 69.6 |
| | C. W. Lee | 2,446 | 30.3 |
| 5 | Burwell Pope | 3,218 | 38.9 |
| | James Shield | 3,187 | 38.6 |
| | Morris | 1,620 | 19.6 |
| 6 | Thomas J. Foster | 3,511* | 45.1 |
| | Sheats | 1,992 | 25.6 |
| | Skinner | 1,471 | 18.9 |
| | Garth | 491 | 6.3 |

## CONNECTICUT

| | Candidates | Votes | % |
|---|---|---|---|
| 1 | Henry C. Deming (UN R) | 10,619 | 56.0 |
| | Mitchell (D) | 8,033 | 42.4 |
| 2 | Samuel L. Warner (UN R) | 11,236 | 54.1 |
| | Russell (D) | 9,521 | 45.9 |
| 3 | Augustus Brandegee (UNR) | 8,566 | 66.3 |
| | Allen (D) | 4,349 | 33.7 |
| 4 | John H. Hubbard (UN R) | 11,747 | 56.3 |
| | Taylor (D) | 9,112 | 43.7 |

## KENTUCKY

| | Candidates | Votes | % |
|---|---|---|---|
| 1 | Lawrence S. Trimble (C) | 5,749 | 61.9 |
| | C. D. Bradley (UN) | 3,542 | 38.1 |
| 2 | Burwell C. Ritter (C) | 6,974 | 54.7 |
| | George H. Yeaman (UN) | 5,786 | 45.3 |
| 3 | Henry Grider (C) | 6,528 | 57.3 |
| | J. H. Lowry (UN) | 4,871 | 42.7 |
| 4 | Aaron Harding (C) | 9,437 | 72.1 |
| | Marion C. Taylor (UN) | 3,652 | 27.9 |
| 5 | Lovell H. Rousseau (UN) | 5,751 | 54.1 |
| | Robert Mallory (C) | 4,704 | 44.3 |
| 6 | Green Clay Smith (UN) | 7,666 | 54.4 |
| | A. H. Ward (C) | 6,421 | 45.6 |
| 7 | George S. Shanklin (C) | 7,624 | 65.9 |
| | Speed S. Fry (UN) | 3,943 | 34.1 |
| 8 | William H. Randell (UN) | 10,634 | 73.6 |
| | T. T. Garrard (C) | 3,824 | 26.5 |
| 9 | Samuel McKee (UN) | 8,163 | 56.7 |
| | J. Smith Hurt (C) | 6,241 | 43.3 |

## MARYLAND

### Special Election

| | Candidates | Votes | % |
|---|---|---|---|
| 2 | John L. Thomas Jr (UN R) | 4,677 | 83.1 |
| | Kimmel (D) | 950 | 16.9 |

## MASSACHUSETTS

### Special Election

| | | Votes | % |
|---|---|---|---|
| 6 | Nathaniel P. Banks (UNT) | 8,128 | 80.4 |
| | Thomas Greenwood (D) | 1,938 | 19.2 |

## NEVADA

| | | Votes | % |
|---|---|---|---|
| AL | Delos R. Ashley (UN) | 3,691 | 62.5 |
| | H. K. Mitchell (D) | 2,215 | 37.5 |

## NEW HAMPSHIRE

| | | Votes | % |
|---|---|---|---|
| 1 | Gilman Marston (UN) | 12,906 | 55.9 |
| | Marcy (D) | 10,190 | 44.1 |
| 2 | Edward H. Rollins (UN) | 10,984 | 55.3 |
| | Clark (D) | 8,894 | 44.7 |
| 3 | James W. Patterson (UN) | 11,687 | 56.2 |
| | Bingham (D) | 9,099 | 43.8 |

## NEW YORK

### Special Election

| | | Votes | % |
|---|---|---|---|
| 16 | Robert S. Hale (UN) | 7,146 | 54.5 |
| | Halsey R. Wing (D) | 5,979 | 45.6 |

## NORTH CAROLINA [2]

| | | Votes | % |
|---|---|---|---|
| 1 | Jesse R. Stubbs | * | |
| 2 | Charles C. Clark (N UNION) | 4,479* | 93.1 |
| 3 | Thomas C. Fuller (N UNION) | 3,094* | 52.8 |
| | Alexander Little (N UNION) | 2,292 | 39.2 |
| | Thomas S. Ashe (N UNION) | 469 | 8.0 |
| 4 | Josiah Turner Jr. (N UNION) | 4,179* | 54.1 |
| | John P. H. Russ (N UNION) | 3,229 | 41.8 |
| 5 | Bedford Brown (N UNION) | 4,354* | 50.6 |
| | Lewis Hawes (N UNION) | 4,257 | 49.4 |
| 6 | Samuel H. Walkup (N UNION) | 3,455* | 41.4 |
| | James G. Ramsay (N UNION) | 3,397 | 40.7 |
| | William Sloan (N UNION) | 1,503 | 18.0 |
| 7 | Alexander H. Jones (N UNION) | * | |
| | Tod R. Caldwell (N UNION) | | |
| | Burgess S. Gaither (N UNION) | | |
| | J. R. Love (N UNION) | | |

## RHODE ISLAND

| | Candidates | Votes | % |
|---|---|---|---|
| 1 | Thomas A. Jenckes (R) | 5,683 | 99.1 |
| 2 | Nathan F. Dixon (R) | 2,384 | 64.9 |
| | Bradford (D) | 1,286 | 35.0 |

## TENNESSEE

### (Readmitted July 24, 1866)

| | | Votes | % |
|---|---|---|---|
| 1 | Nathaniel G. Taylor (UN) | 5,056 | 49.2 |
| | J. R. Miller (C) | 3,620 | 35.2 |
| | Randolph | 1,594 | 15.5 |
| 2 | Horace Maynard (UN) | 5,599 | 53.0 |
| | J. Λ. Coopor (C) | 2,001 | 19.7 |
| | Hank | 1,650 | 15.7 |
| | Boyd | 1,210 | 11.5 |
| 3 | William B. Stokes (UN) | 2,599 | 68.3 |
| | Asa Faulkner (C) | 1,024 | 26.9 |
| | Hood | 181 | 4.8 |
| 4 | Edmund Cooper (C) | 5,318 | 96.2 |
| 5 | William B. Campbell (C) | 1,311 | 86.3 |
| | S. J. Carter (UN) | 208 | 13.7 |
| 6 | Samuel M. Arnell (UN) | 1,547 | 74.8 |
| | Dorsey B. Thomas (C) | 521 | 25.2 |
| 7 | Isaac R. Hawkins (UN) | 2,068 | 62.7 |
| | Etheridge (C) | 704 | 21.4 |
| | Saunders | 525 | 15.9 |
| 8 | John W. Leftwich (C) | 1,368 | 44.9 |
| | John Bullock (UN) | 597 | 19.6 |
| | Sands | 589 | 19.3 |
| | Dunlap | 493 | 16.2 |

## VIRGINIA [3]

| | | Votes | % |
|---|---|---|---|
| 1 | Curtis | 978* | 37.8 |
| | Christian | 856 | 33.1 |
| | Doug | 756 | 29.2 |
| 2 | L. H. Chandler (UN) | 1,583* | 50.2 |
| | John S. Millson | 1,029 | 32.6 |
| | Kilby | 544 | 17.2 |
| 3 | B. Johnson Barbour | 4,944* | 79.4 |
| | Pendleton | 906 | 14.6 |
| | Martin Lipscomb | 334 | 5.4 |
| 4 | Robert Ridgway | 3,369* | 76.9 |
| | Alexander Fitzpatrick | 1,010 | 23.1 |
| 5 | Davis | 1,718* | 29.3 |
| | Stovall | 1,675 | 28.6 |
| | Mosby | 1,187 | 20.2 |
| | Withers | 958 | 16.3 |
| 6 | Alexander H. H. Stuart | 4,653* | 67.3 |
| | John F. Lewis | 2,194 | 31.7 |
| 7 | Robert Y. Conrad | 4,853* | 72.1 |
| | Lewis McKenzie | 1,722 | 25.6 |
| 8 | Hoge | 4,897* | 64.6 |
| | Miller | 1,259 | 16.6 |
| | Longley | 1,118 | 14.8 |

1. Alabama held elections for the House but none of the winners was seated. The state was not readmitted until July 13, 1868.

2. North Carolina held elections for the House but none of the winners was seated. The state was not readmitted until July 4, 1868.

3. Virginia held elections for the House but none of the winners was seated. The state was not readmitted until Jan. 26, 1870.

# 1866 House Elections

## ALABAMA[1]

### Special Election

| Candidates | Votes | % |
|---|---|---|
| 2 J. M. Wiley | | |
| J. L. Pugh | | |
| Bolling Hall | | |
| J. Clements | | |

## DELAWARE

| | Candidates | Votes | % |
|---|---|---|---|
| AL | John A. Nicholson (D) | 9,933 | 53.7 |
| | John L. McKim (R) | 8,553 | 46.3 |

## ILLINOIS

| | Candidates | Votes | % |
|---|---|---|---|
| 1 | Norman B. Judd (R) | 15,247 | 72.9 |
| | M. R. M. Wallace (D) | 5,667 | 27.1 |
| 2 | John F. Farnsworth (R) | 16,185 | 82.9 |
| | E. M. Haines (D) | 3,346 | 17.1 |
| 3 | Elihu B. Washburne (R) | 14,657 | 70.9 |
| | Thomas J. Turner (D) | 5,897 | 28.5 |
| 4 | Abner C. Harding (R) | 15,952 | 54.4 |
| | John S. Thompson (D) | 13,391 | 45.6 |
| 5 | Ebon C. Ingersoll (R) | 18,437 | 65.6 |
| | Silas Ramsey (D) | 9,665 | 34.4 |
| 6 | Burton C. Cook (R) | 15,015 | 66.0 |
| | S. H. Harris (D) | 7,721 | 34.0 |
| 7 | Henry P. H. Bromwell (R) | 17,410 | 56.7 |
| | Charles Black (D) | 13,272 | 43.3 |
| 8 | Shelby M. Cullom (R) | 18,623 | 56.2 |
| | Edwin S. Fowler (D) | 14,520 | 43.8 |
| 9 | Lewis W. Ross (D) | 15,496 | 51.3 |
| | Charles E. Lippencott (R) | 14,721 | 48.7 |
| 10 | Albert G. Burr (D) | 17,116 | 53.7 |
| | Henry Case (R) | 14,743 | 46.3 |
| 11 | Samuel S. Marshall (D) | 16,668 | 53.7 |
| | Edward Kitchell (R) | 14,378 | 46.3 |
| 12 | Jehu Baker (R) | 13,032 | 52.2 |
| | William R. Morrison (D) | 11,956 | 47.9 |
| 13 | Green B. Raum (R) | 13,459 | 51.1 |
| | William J. Allen (D) | 12,890 | 48.9 |
| AL | John A. Logan (R) | 203,045 | 57.9 |
| | T. Lyle Dickey (D) | 147,435 | 42.1 |

## INDIANA

| | Candidates | Votes | % |
|---|---|---|---|
| 1 | William E. Niblack (D) | 17,255 | 52.0 |
| | Debruler (R) | 15,905 | 48.0 |
| 2 | Michael C. Kerr (D) | 13,421 | 53.5 |
| | Gresham (R) | 11,678 | 46.5 |
| 3 | Morton C. Hunter (R) | 13,848 | 51.3 |
| | Harrgtn (D) | 13,158 | 48.7 |
| 4 | William S. Holman (D) | 11,921 | 51.9 |
| | Grover (R) | 11,052 | 48.1 |
| 5 | George W. Julian (R) | 13,416 | 65.1 |
| | Bundy (D) | 7,188 | 34.9 |
| 6 | John Coburn (R) | 16,719 | 54.0 |
| | Lord (D) | 14,245 | 46.0 |
| 7 | Henry D. Washburn (R) | 14,871 | 50.9 |
| | Claypl (D) | 14,358 | 49.1 |
| 8 | Godlove S. Orth (R) | 14,933 | 50.4 |
| | Purdue (D) | 14,728 | 49.7 |
| 9 | Schuyler Colfax (R) | 20,221 | 52.8 |
| | David Turpie (D) | 18,073 | 47.2 |
| 10 | William Williams (R) | 17,414 | 51.9 |
| | Lowry (D) | 16,142 | 48.1 |
| 11 | John P. C. Shanks (R) | 18,145 | 54.3 |
| | Snow (D) | 15,268 | 45.7 |

## IOWA

| | Candidates | Votes | % |
|---|---|---|---|
| 1 | James F. Wilson (R) | 16,388 | 60.9 |
| | Fitz Henry Warren (D) | 10,515 | 39.1 |
| 2 | Hiram Price (R) | 16,257 | 63.8 |
| | John P. Cook (D) | 9,220 | 36.2 |
| 3 | William B. Allison (R) | 15,472 | 58.7 |
| | Reuben Noble (D) | 10,470 | 39.7 |
| 4 | William Loughridge (R) | 18,529 | 59.8 |
| | Cyms H. Mackey (D) | 12,395 | 40.0 |
| 5 | Grenville M. Dodge (R) | 14,236 | 59.0 |
| | James M. Tuttle (D) | 9,897 | 41.0 |
| 6 | Asahel W. Hubbard (R) | 9,970 | 69.9 |
| | J. D. Thompson (D) | 3,938 | 27.6 |

## KANSAS

| | Candidates | Votes | % |
|---|---|---|---|
| AL | Sidney Clarke (R) | 19,200 | 70.0 |
| | C. W. Blair (N UNION) | 8,206 | 29.9 |

## KENTUCKY

### Special Elections

| | Candidates | Votes | % |
|---|---|---|---|
| 3 | Elijah Hise (D) | 6,493 | 74.3 |
| | P. B. Hawkins (UN) | 2,244 | 25.7 |
| 5 | Lovell H. Rousseau (R) | 2,494 | 99.0 |
| 6 | Andrew H. Ward (D) | 8,725 | 88.4 |
| | R. R. Carpenter (UN) | 1,068 | 10.8 |

## MAINE

| | Candidates | Votes | % |
|---|---|---|---|
| 1 | John Lynch (R) | 15,612 | 57.0 |
| | Sweat (D) | 11,753 | 42.9 |
| 2 | Sidney Perham (R) | 13,883 | 65.3 |
| | Morrill | 7,363 | 34.7 |
| 3 | James G. Blaine (R) | 14,909 | 63.8 |
| | Heath (D) | 8,338 | 35.7 |
| 4 | John A. Peters (R) | 11,911 | 64.4 |
| | Weston (D) | 6,565 | 35.5 |
| 5 | Frederick A. Pike (R) | 12,422 | 61.0 |
| | Crosby (D) | 7,773 | 38.1 |

## MARYLAND

| | Candidates | Votes | % |
|---|---|---|---|
| 1 | Hiram McCullough (D) | 11,729 | 74.2 |
| | George Russum (R) | 4,052 | 25.6 |
| 2 | Stevenson Archer (D) | 7,091 | 58.6 |
| | John Thomas (R) | 5,014 | 41.4 |
| 3 | Charles E. Phelps (D) | 5,545 | 54.8 |
| | J. J. Stewart (R) | 4,568 | 45.2 |
| 4 | Francis Thomas (R) | 10,252 | 52.6 |
| | William Omauleby (D) | 9,230 | 47.4 |
| 5 | Frederick Stone (D) | 8,708 | 81.1 |
| | William Albert (R) | 2,032 | 18.9 |

## MASSACHUSETTS

| | Candidates | Votes | % |
|---|---|---|---|
| 1 | Thomas D. Eliot (R) | 8,184 | 84.1 |
| | Mathias Ellias (D) | 1,539 | 15.8 |
| 2 | Oakes Ames (R) | 9,581 | 79.4 |
| | Unidentified Candidate (D) | 2,456 | 20.4 |
| 3 | Ginery Twichell (R) | 6,084 | 66.5 |
| | William Aspinwall (D) | 2,601 | 28.4 |
| | P. R. Guiney (WM) | 463 | 5.1 |
| 4 | Samuel Hooper (R) | 7,901 | 71.2 |
| | Joseph Wightman (D) | 3,187 | 28.7 |
| 5 | Benjamin F. Butler (R) | 9,021 | 75.6 |
| | William D. Northend (D) | 2,838 | 23.8 |
| 6 | Nathaniel P. Banks (R) | 10,075 | 74.7 |
| | F. O. Prince (D) | 3,366 | 24.9 |
| 7 | George S. Boutwell (R) | 9,847 | 77.3 |
| | Leverett Saltonstall (D) | 2,885 | 22.7 |
| 8 | John D. Baldwin (R) | 9,039 | 82.5 |
| | William A. Williams (D) | 1,901 | 17.4 |
| 9 | William B. Washburn (R) | 11,895 | 87.0 |
| | Levi Haywood (D) | 1,768 | 12.9 |
| 10 | Henry L. Dawes (R) | 8,125 | 65.7 |
| | Abijah W. Chapin (D) | 4,185 | 33.9 |

## MICHIGAN

| | Candidates | Votes | % |
|---|---|---|---|
| 1 | Fernando C. Beaman (R) | 17,319 | 56.3 |
| | Chipman (D) | 13,443 | 43.7 |
| 2 | Charles Upson (R) | 19,623 | 63.6 |
| | Severns (D) | 11,228 | 36.4 |
| 3 | Austin Blair (R) | 16,240 | 56.9 |
| | Granger (D) | 12,288 | 43.1 |
| 4 | Thomas W. Ferry (R) | 15,305 | 65.2 |
| | Hutchins (D) | 8,154 | 34.8 |
| 5 | Rowland E. Trowbridge (R) | 14,046 | 54.5 |
| | Bancroft (D) | 11,664 | 45.4 |
| 6 | John F. Driggs (R) | 14,476 | 57.8 |
| | Rose (D) | 10,570 | 42.2 |

## MINNESOTA

| | Candidates | Votes | % |
|---|---|---|---|
| 1 | William Windom (R) | 14,810 | 64.2 |
| | Jones (D) | 8,245 | 35.8 |
| 2 | Ignatius Donnelly (R) | 12,022 | 60.8 |
| | Colvill (D) | 7,754 | 39.2 |

## MISSOURI

| | Candidates | Votes | % |
|---|---|---|---|
| 1 | William A. Pile (R) | 6,728 | 50.8 |
| | John Hogan | 6,510 | 49.2 |
| 2 | Carman A. Newcomb (R) | 9,568 | 59.1 |
| | William V. N. Bay | 6,636 | 41.0 |
| 3 | Thomas E. Noell (RAD R) | ✔ | |
| | Albert Jackson | | |
| 4 | Joseph J. Gravely (R) | ✔ | |
| | John S. Waddill | | |
| 5 | Joseph W. McClurg (RAD R) | ✔ | |
| | Thomas L. Price | | |
| 6 | Robert T. Van Horn (R) | ✔ | |
| | James H. Birgh | | |
| | L. S. McCoy | | |
| 7 | Benjamin F. Loan (RAD R) | ✔ | |
| | George A. Hawley | | |
| 8 | John F. Benjamin (R) | ✔ | |
| | John M. Glover | | |
| 9 | George W. Anderson (RAD R) | ✔ | |
| | William F. Switzler (D) | | |

## NEBRASKA

(Became a state March 1, 1867)

| | Candidates | Votes | % |
|---|---|---|---|
| AL | John Taffe (UN R) | 4,621 | 53.0 |
| | A. S. Paddock (D) | 4,072 | 46.7 |

### Special Election

| | Candidates | Votes | % |
|---|---|---|---|
| AL | Turner M. Marquette (R) | 4,820 | 54.2 |
| | J. R. Brooke (D) | 4,072 | 45.8 |

## NEVADA

| | Candidates | Votes | % |
|---|---|---|---|
| AL | Delos R. Ashley (R) | 5,047 | 54.6 |
| | H. K. Mitchell (D) | 4,196 | 45.4 |

## NEW JERSEY

| | Candidates | Votes | % |
|---|---|---|---|
| 1 | William Moore (R) | 12,468 | 57.8 |
| | Slape (D) | 9,108 | 42.2 |
| 2 | Charles Haight (D) | 13,825 | 50.6 |
| | Newell (R) | 13,476 | 49.4 |
| 3 | Charles Sitgreaves (D) | 15,768 | 54.9 |
| | Davidson (R) | 12,955 | 45.1 |
| 4 | John Hill (R) | 13,861 | 50.5 |
| | Rogers (D) | 13,399 | 48.8 |
| 5 | George A. Halsey (R) | 12,782 | 51.9 |
| | Gilchrist (D) | 11,847 | 48.1 |

1. The winner of this election is unknown and was not seated by the House.

## NEW YORK

| | Candidates | Votes | % |
|---|---|---|---|
| 1 | Stephen Taber (D) | 10,458 | 52.8 |
| | William H. Gleason (R) | 9,362 | 47.2 |
| 2 | Demas Barnes (D) | 15,614 | 62.5 |
| | James A. Vanbrunt (R) | 8,985 | 36.0 |
| 3 | William E. Robinson (D) | 12,634 | 53.9 |
| | Simeon B. Chittenden (R) | 10,803 | 46.1 |
| 4 | John Fox (D) | 14,003 | 78.9 |
| | Horace Greeley (R) | 3,743 | 21.1 |
| 5 | John Morrissey (ID) | 9,162 | 51.0 |
| | Nelson Taylor (D) | 6,503 | 36.2 |
| | Eneas Elliott (R) | 2,293 | 12.8 |
| 6 | Thomas E. Stewart (C) | 9,452 | 55.2 |
| | Charles S. Spencer (R) | 6,955 | 40.6 |
| 7 | John W. Chanler (D) | 11,503 | 63.0 |
| | George F. Steinbrenner (R) | 6,743 | 37.0 |
| 8 | James Brooks (D) | 13,816 | 62.7 |
| | Legrand B. Cannon (R) | 8,210 | 37.2 |
| 9 | Fernando Wood (D) | 9,605 | 54.6 |
| | William A. Darling (R) | 7,995 | 45.4 |
| 10 | William H. Robertson (R) | 12,012 | 54.7 |
| | William Radford (D) | 9,957 | 45.3 |
| 11 | Charles H. Van Wyck (R) | 10,194 | 50.7 |
| | Isaac Anderson (D) | 9,933 | 49.4 |
| 12 | John H. Ketcham (R) | 12,535 | 53.6 |
| | Casper P. Collier (D) | 10,840 | 46.4 |
| 13 | Thomas Cornell (R) | 10,521 | 50.8 |
| | Joseph H. Tuthill (D) | 10,179 | 49.2 |
| 14 | John V. L. Pruyn (D) | 15,620 | 51.1 |
| | Joseph H. Ramsey (R) | 14,972 | 48.9 |
| 15 | John A. Griswold (R) | 15,689 | 60.2 |
| | Nathaniel B. Milliman (D) | 10,373 | 39.8 |
| 16 | Orange Ferris (R) | 9,341 | 55.8 |
| | George V. Hoyle (D) | 7,412 | 44.2 |
| 17 | Calvin T. Hulburd (R) | 13,449 | 72.4 |
| | Darius W. Lawrence (D) | 5,116 | 27.6 |
| 18 | James M. Marvin (R) | 15,496 | 55.7 |
| | Thomas R. Horton (D) | 12,342 | 44.3 |
| 19 | William C. Fields (R) | 17,277 | 55.9 |
| | Stephen C. Johnson (D) | 13,621 | 44.1 |
| 20 | Addison H. Laflin (R) | 16,498 | 58.4 |
| | Edward S. Lansing (D) | 11,734 | 41.6 |
| 21 | Roscoe Conkling (R) | 12,470* | 53.0 |
| | Palmer V. Kellogg (D) | 11,053 | 47.0 |
| 22 | John C. Churchill (R) | 14,461 | 62.1 |
| | Albertus Perry (D) | 8,827 | 37.9 |
| 23 | Dennis McCarthy (R) | 15,260 | 60.5 |
| | William C. Ruger (D) | 9,966 | 39.5 |
| 24 | Theodore M. Pomeroy (R) | 16,189 | 58.7 |
| | George Humphreys (D) | 11,404 | 41.3 |
| 25 | William H. Kelsey (R) | 12,637 | 60.3 |
| | Henry O. Chesebro (D) | 8,334 | 39.7 |
| 26 | William S. Lincoln (R) | 16,264 | 60.0 |
| | Henry McCormick (D) | 10,849 | 40.0 |
| 27 | Hamilton Ward (R) | 17,750 | 60.8 |
| | John G. Collins (D) | 11,435 | 39.2 |
| 28 | Lewis Selye (D) | 12,791 | 54.3 |
| | Roswell Hart (R) | 10,757 | 45.7 |
| 29 | Burt Van Horn (R) | 12,204 | 57.2 |
| | Harlow S. Comstock (D) | 9,131 | 42.8 |
| 30 | James M. Humphrey (D) | 13,402 | 52.6 |
| | Almon M. Clapp (R) | 12,085 | 47.4 |
| 31 | Henry Van Aernam (R) | 14,405 | 66.4 |
| | Hanson A. Risley (D) | 7,299 | 33.6 |

### Special Election

| | | Votes | % |
|---|---|---|---|
| 3 | John W. Hunter (D) | 12,774 | 54.4 |
| | Simeon B. Chittenden (R) | 10,715 | 45.6 |

## OHIO

| | Candidates | Votes | % |
|---|---|---|---|
| 1 | Benjamin Eggleston (UN R) | 10,422 | 52.3 |
| | George H. Pendleton (D) | 9,496 | 47.7 |
| 2 | Rutherford B. Hayes (UN R) | 11,549 | 56.2 |
| | Theodore Cook (D) | 8,991 | 43.8 |
| 3 | Robert C. Schenck (UN R) | 15,027 | 51.8 |
| | J. Durbin Ward (D) | 13,960 | 48.2 |
| 4 | William Lawrence (UN R) | 13,313 | 54.6 |
| | John F. McKinney (D) | 11,059 | 45.4 |
| 5 | William Mungen (D) | 13,524 | 55.4 |
| | Moses B. Walker (UN R) | 10,872 | 44.6 |
| 6 | Reader W. Clarke (UN R) | 13,846 | 53.0 |
| | William Howard (D) | 12,267 | 47.0 |
| 7 | Samuel Shellabarger (UN R) | 13,687 | 54.3 |
| | Thomas Miller (D) | 11,516 | 45.7 |
| 8 | Cornelius S. Hamilton (UN R) | 11,710 | 54.3 |
| | William P. Reid (D) | 9,858 | 45.7 |
| 9 | Ralph P. Buckland (UN R) | 15,231 | 52.2 |
| | T. P. Finefrock (D) | 13,944 | 47.8 |
| 10 | James M. Ashley (UN R) | 14,873 | 53.4 |
| | H. S. Commager (D) | 12,956 | 46.6 |
| 11 | John T. Wilson (UN R) | 12,783 | 56.2 |
| | Oscar F. Moore (D) | 9,945 | 43.8 |
| 12 | Philadelph Van Trump (D) | 14,546 | 56.2 |
| | Wells S. Jones (UN R) | 11,336 | 43.8 |
| 13 | George W. Morgan (D) | 13,228‡ | 50.5 |
| | Columbus Delano (UN R) | 12,957 | 49.5 |
| 14 | Martin Welker (UN R) | 13,494 | 53.4 |
| | J. B. Young (D) | 11,787 | 46.6 |
| 15 | Tobias A. Plants (UN R) | 12,816 | 54.4 |
| | M. D. Follett (D) | 10,752 | 45.6 |
| 16 | John A. Bingham (UN R) | 13,369 | 52.8 |
| | C. H. Mitchner (D) | 11,947 | 47.2 |
| 17 | Ephraim R. Eckley (UN R) | 13,917 | 60.0 |
| | Louis Schaefer (D) | 9,275 | 40.0 |
| 18 | Rufus P. Spalding (UN R) | 14,479 | 64.5 |
| | Oliver H. Payne (D) | 7,974 | 35.5 |
| 19 | James A. Garfield (UN R) | 18,362 | 71.3 |
| | D. C. Coolman (D) | 7,376 | 28.7 |

## OREGON

| | | Votes | % |
|---|---|---|---|
| AL | Rufus Mallory (R) | 10,362 | 51.4 |
| | James D. Fay (D) | 9,808 | 48.6 |

## PENNSYLVANIA

| | | Votes | % |
|---|---|---|---|
| 1 | Samuel J. Randall (D) | 12,192 | 61.2 |
| | Charles Gibbons (R) | 7,728 | 38.8 |
| 2 | Charles O'Neill (R) | 12,612 | 57.1 |
| | John Hulme (D) | 9,475 | 42.9 |
| 3 | Leonard Myers (R) | 12,520 | 52.1 |
| | C. Buckwalter (D) | 11,516 | 47.9 |
| 4 | William D. Kelley (R) | 14,551 | 54.6 |
| | John Welsh (D) | 12,126 | 45.5 |
| 5 | Caleb N. Taylor (R) | 12,259 | 51.0 |
| | H. P. Ross (D) | 11,800 | 49.0 |
| 6 | Benjamin M. Boyer (D) | 14,009 | 55.0 |
| | David Thomas (R) | 11,447 | 45.0 |
| 7 | John N. Broomall (R) | 12,011 | 58.5 |
| | N. Pratt (D) | 8,531 | 41.5 |
| 8 | J. Lawrence Getz (D) | 13,188 | 65.3 |
| | D. J. Lincoln (R) | 6,999 | 34.7 |
| 9 | Thaddeus Stevens (R) | 14,298 | 62.2 |
| | S. H. Reynolds (D) | 8,675 | 37.8 |

| | Candidates | Votes | % |
|---|---|---|---|
| 10 | Henry L. Cake (R) | 13,186 | 50.4 |
| | C. D. Gloninger (D) | 12,971 | 49.6 |
| 11 | Daniel M. Van Auken (D) | 15,907 | 63.4 |
| | William Lilly (R) | 9,195 | 36.6 |
| 12 | Charles Denison (D) | 15,280 | 53.5 |
| | James Archibald (R) | 13,274 | 46.5 |
| 13 | Ulysses Mercur (R) | 11,940 | 52.9 |
| | William Elwell (D) | 10,653 | 47.2 |
| 14 | George F. Miller (R) | 14,190 | 52.8 |
| | Bower (D) | 12,675 | 47.2 |
| 15 | Adam J. Glossbrenner (D) | 15,830 | 55.9 |
| | R. M. Henderson (R) | 12,489 | 44.1 |
| 16 | William H. Koontz (R) | 13,589 | 51.2 |
| | Sharpe (D) | 12,964 | 48.8 |
| 17 | Daniel J. Morrell (R) | 11,298 | 52.4 |
| | R. L. Johnston (D) | 10,249 | 47.6 |
| 18 | Stephen F. Wilson (R) | 14,734 | 53.7 |
| | Theo F. Wright (D) | 12,688 | 46.3 |
| 19 | Glenni W. Scofield (R) | 15,107 | 54.8 |
| | W. W. L. Scott (D) | 12,481 | 45.2 |
| 20 | Darwin A. Finney (R) | 17,106 | 52.9 |
| | A. B. McCalmont (D) | 15,225 | 47.1 |
| 21 | John Covode (R) | 13,023 | 50.7 |
| | Wier (D) | 12,669 | 49.3 |
| 22 | James K. Moorhead (R) | 12,720 | 56.9 |
| | J. B. Switzer (D) | 9,655 | 43.2 |
| 23 | Thomas Williams (R) | 14,197 | 58.6 |
| | B. G. Childs (D) | 10,012 | 41.4 |
| 24 | George V. Lawrence (R) | 13,391 | 53.1 |
| | W. Montgomery (D) | 11,853 | 47.0 |

## VERMONT [1]

| | | Votes | % |
|---|---|---|---|
| 1 | Frederick E. Woodbridge (R) | 10,568 | 77.5 |
| | Samuel Wells (D) | 3,036 | 22.3 |
| 2 | Luke P. Poland (R) | 10,844 | 72.2 |
| | Charles M. Chase (D) | 3,935 | 26.2 |
| 3 | Portus Baxter (R) | 7,329* | 46.8 |
| | Hogt (D) | 4,511 | 28.8 |
| | Brigham | 3,395 | 21.7 |

## WEST VIRGINIA

| | | Votes | % |
|---|---|---|---|
| 1 | Chester D. Hubbard (R) | 10,001 | 54.8 |
| | D. D. Johnson (D) | 8,239 | 45.2 |
| 2 | Bethuel M. Kitchen (R) | 8,296 | 61.5 |
| | E. W. Andrews (D) | 5,190 | 38.5 |
| 3 | Daniel Polsley (R) | 4,927 | 58.8 |
| | John H. Oley (D) | 3,456 | 41.2 |

## WISCONSIN

| | | Votes | % |
|---|---|---|---|
| 1 | Halbert E. Paine (R) | 14,678 | 58.8 |
| | Brown (D) | 10,298 | 41.2 |
| 2 | Benjamin F. Hopkins (R) | 14,129 | 61.5 |
| | Pease (D) | 8,833 | 38.5 |
| 3 | Amasa Cobb (R) | 13,006 | 63.0 |
| | Virgin (D) | 7,655 | 37.1 |
| 4 | Charles A. Eldridge (D) | 12,839 | 56.6 |
| | Hatch (R) | 9,855 | 43.4 |
| 5 | Philetus Sawyer (R) | 14,341 | 60.5 |
| | Martin (D) | 9,347 | 39.5 |
| 6 | Cadwallader C. Washburn (R) | 13,161 | 66.4 |
| | Park (D) | 6,648 | 33.6 |

1. No candidate received a majority of the vote in the 3rd district, which was required for election. Portus Baxter declined to enter a later special election held to determine a winner. Worthington C. Smith (R) was eventually elected; returns are unavailable. (Majority vote requirement, see p. 945.)

# 1867 House Elections

## CALIFORNIA

| | Candidates | Votes | % |
|---|---|---|---|
| 1 | Samuel B. Axtell (D) | 18,793 | 57.3 |
| | Timothy G. Phelps (R) | 13,989 | 42.7 |
| 2 | William Higby (R) | 16,053 | 52.1 |
| | J. W. Coffroth (D) | 14,786 | 48.0 |
| 3 | James A. Johnson (D) | 14,767 | 50.6 |
| | C. Hartson (R) | 14,394 | 49.4 |

## CONNECTICUT

| | | Votes | % |
|---|---|---|---|
| 1 | Richard D. Hubbard (D) | 11,994 | 51.1 |
| | Henry C. Deming (R) | 11,477 | 48.9 |
| 2 | Julius Hotchkiss (D) | 14,730 | 53.2 |
| | Cyrus Northrop (R) | 12,937 | 46.8 |
| 3 | Henry H. Starkweather (R) | 9,723 | 55.4 |
| | Earl Martin (D) | 7,827 | 44.6 |
| 4 | William H. Barnum (D) | 13,083 | 51.9 |
| | Phineas T. Barnum (R) | 12,103 | 48.0 |

## KENTUCKY

| | | Votes | % |
|---|---|---|---|
| 1 | Lawrence S. Trimble (D) | 9,787 | 84.6 |
| | George G. Symes (R) | 1,780 | 15.4 |
| 2 | John Y. Brown (D) | 8,922* | 69.2 |
| | Samuel E. Smith (R) | 2,816 | 21.8 |
| | B. C. Ritter (C) | 1,155 | 9.0 |
| 3 | Elijah Hise (D) | 7,740 | 86.6 |
| | George D. Blakey (R) | 1,201 | 13.4 |
| 4 | J. Proctor Knott (D) | 8,199 | 74.6 |
| | Marion C. Taylor (R) | 2,277 | 20.7 |
| 5 | Asa P. Grover (D) | 7,118 | 69.3 |
| | R. J. Jacob (C) | 2,417 | 23.5 |
| | William A. Bullitt (R) | 742 | 7.2 |
| 6 | Thomas L. Jones (D) | 9,488 | 72.4 |
| | W. L. Rankin (R) | 3,587 | 27.4 |

| | Candidates | Votes | % |
|---|---|---|---|
| 7 | James B. Beck (D) | 9,716 | 76.1 |
| | William Brown (R) | 1,664 | 13.0 |
| | Charles Hanson (C) | 1,388 | 10.9 |
| 8 | George M. Adams (D) | 7,609 | 51.2 |
| | Milton L. Rice (R) | 7,244 | 48.8 |
| 9 | John D. Young (D) | 9,042 | 51.8 |
| | Samuel McKee (R) | 7,563✔ | 43.3 |

### Special Election

| | | Votes | % |
|---|---|---|---|
| 3 | Jacob S. Golladay (D) | 6,619 | 76.2 |
| | J. R. Curd (C) | 1,175 | 13.5 |
| | W. T. Jackman (R) | 850 | 9.8 |

## MISSOURI

### Special Election

| | | | |
|---|---|---|---|
| 3 | James R. McCormick (D) | | ✔ |
| | James H. Chase (R) | | |

## NEW HAMPSHIRE

| | | Votes | % |
|---|---|---|---|
| 1 | Jacob H. Ela (R) | 13,243 | 51.9 |
| | Daniel Marcy (D) | 12,247 | 48.0 |
| 2 | Aaron F. Stevens (R) | 11,260 | 52.2 |
| | Edward W. Harrington (D) | 10,305 | 47.8 |
| 3 | Jacob Benton (R) | 11,294 | 52.2 |
| | Harry Bingham (D) | 10,246 | 47.3 |

## OHIO

### Special Election

| | | Votes | % |
|---|---|---|---|
| 2 | Samuel F. Cary (IR) | 10,390 | 52.1 |
| | Richard Smith (R) | 9,431 | 47.3 |

## PENNSYLVANIA

### Special Election

| | Candidates | Votes | % |
|---|---|---|---|
| 12 | George W. Woodward (D) | 12,623 | 51.1 |
| | W. W. Kotcham (R) | 12,078 | 48.9 |

## RHODE ISLAND

| | | Votes | % |
|---|---|---|---|
| 1 | Thomas A. Jenckes (R) | 4,311 | 97.7 |
| 2 | Nathan F. Dixon (R) | 2,669 | 64.2 |
| | Carder (D) | 1,480 | 35.6 |

## TENNESSEE

| | | Votes | % |
|---|---|---|---|
| 1 | Roderick R. Butler (R) | 12,472✔ | |
| | J. White (C) | 1,746 | |
| | Joseph Powell (R) | | |
| 2 | Horace Maynard (R) | 11,994 | 79.8 |
| | John Williams (C) | 3,039 | 20.2 |
| 3 | William B. Stokes (R) | 8,030 | 83.3 |
| | Eli G. Fleming (C) | 1,614 | 16.7 |
| 4 | James Mullins (R) | 9,448 | 74.6 |
| | Edward Cooper (C) | 3,221 | 25.4 |
| 5 | John Trimble (R) | 9,357✔ | |
| | Bailey Peyton (C) | 3,163 | |
| | D. H. Mason (IR) | | |
| 6 | Samuel M. Arnell (R) | 7,596 | 77.8 |
| | Dorsey B. Thomas (C) | 2,170 | 22.2 |
| 7 | Isaac R. Hawkins (R) | 5,000 | 83.6 |
| | W. P. Coldwell (C) | 981 | 16.4 |
| 8 | David A. Nunn (R) | 9,057 | 59.4 |
| | J. F. Leftwick (C) | 6,189 | 40.6 |

# 1868 House Elections

## ALABAMA[1]
### (Readmitted July 13, 1868)

| | Candidates | Votes | % |
|---|---|---|---|
| 1 | Francis W. Kellogg (R) | 16,094 | 100.0 |
| 2 | Charles W. Buckley (R) | 8,440 | 100.0 |
| 3 | Benjamin W. Norris (R) | 9,451 | 99.6 |
| 4 | Charles W. Pierce (R) | 19,593 | 99.8 |
| 5 | John B. Callis (R) | 3,569 | 54.0 |
| | J. W. Burke | 2,458 | 37.2 |
| | Whitley Thomas Ewing | 573 | 8.7 |
| 6 | Thomas Haughey | 2,678 | 44.1 |
| | McCauley | 1,440 | 23.7 |
| | Cramer | 1,021 | 16.8 |
| | Snelling (R) | 825 | 13.6 |

## ARKANSAS[2]
### (Readmitted June 22, 1868)

| | Candidates | Votes | % |
|---|---|---|---|
| 1 | Logan H. Roots (R) | 7,151 | 50.6 |
| | Charles S. Cameron (D) | 6,987 | 49.4 |
| 2 | Anthony A. C. Rogers (D) | 6,518 | 55.0 |
| | James T. Elliott (R) | 5,332 | 45.0 |
| 3 | Thomas Boles (R) | 9,547 | 62.9 |
| | L. B. Nash (D) | 5,630 | 37.1 |

## CALIFORNIA

| | Candidates | Votes | % |
|---|---|---|---|
| 1 | Samuel B. Axtell (D) | 23,632 | 54.1 |
| | F. M. Pixley (R) | 20,081 | 45.9 |
| 2 | Aaron A. Sargent (R) | 18,264 | 54.7 |
| | J. W. Coffroth (D) | 15,124 | 45.3 |
| 3 | James A. Johnson (D) | 15,792 | 50.4 |
| | C. Hartson (R) | 15,527 | 49.6 |

## DELAWARE

| | Candidates | Votes | % |
|---|---|---|---|
| AL | Benjamin T. Biggs (D) | 10,961 | 58.9 |
| | Torbert (R) | 7,636 | 41.1 |

## FLORIDA[3]
### (Readmitted June 25, 1868)

| | Candidates | Votes | % |
|---|---|---|---|
| AL | Charles M. Hamilton (R) | ✔ | |
| | Friend (D) | | |
| | Liberty Billings | | |

## GEORGIA[4]

| | Candidates | Votes | % |
|---|---|---|---|
| 1 | Joseph W. Clift (R) | 11,990 | 59.6 |
| | Fitch (D) | 8,141 | 40.4 |
| 2 | Nelson Tift (D) | 13,645 | 53.9 |
| | Richard H. Whitely (R) | 11,696 | 46.2 |
| 3 | William P. Edwards (R) | 12,806 | 52.5 |
| | Alexander (D) | 11,581 | 47.5 |
| 4 | Samuel F. Gove (R) | 11,078 | 50.4 |
| | Lochrane (D) | 10,917 | 49.6 |
| 5 | Charles H. Prince (R) | ✔ | |
| | Hilliard (D) | | |
| 6 | John H. Christy (D) | 8,340* | 51.3 |
| | John A. Wimpey (R) | 7,929 | 48.7 |
| 7 | Pierce M. B. Young (D) | 11,160 | 58.1 |
| | James Adkins (R) | 8,054 | 41.9 |

## ILLINOIS

| | Candidates | Votes | % |
|---|---|---|---|
| 1 | Norman B. Judd (R) | 27,414 | 58.8 |
| | M. R. M. Wallace (D) | 19,233 | 41.2 |
| 2 | John F. Farnsworth (R) | 20,725 | 76.7 |
| | A. M. Herrington (D) | 6,307 | 23.3 |
| 3 | Elihu B. Washburne (R) | 18,584 | 65.9 |
| | W. J. McKim (D) | 9,612 | 34.1 |
| 4 | John B. Hawley (R) | 17,269 | 52.6 |
| | James W. Singleton (D) | 15,547 | 47.4 |
| 5 | Ebon C. Ingersoll (R) | 20,991 | 60.2 |
| | John N. Niglas (D) | 13,686 | 39.2 |

## ILLINOIS

| | Candidates | Votes | % |
|---|---|---|---|
| 6 | Burton C. Cook (R) | 19,607 | 62.1 |
| | Oliver C. Gray (D) | 11,946 | 37.9 |
| 7 | Jesse H. Moore (R) | 22,321 | 56.5 |
| | Thomas Brewer (D) | 17,171 | 43.5 |
| 8 | Shelby M. Cullom (R) | 22,193 | 53.5 |
| | B. S. Edwards (D) | 19,309 | 46.5 |
| 9 | Thompson W. McNeely (D) | 17,877 | 53.9 |
| | Leonard F. Ross (R) | 15,279 | 46.1 |
| 10 | Albert G. Burr (D) | 21,420 | 55.2 |
| | Iona B. Turner (R) | 17,397 | 44.8 |
| 11 | Samuel S. Marshall (D) | 20,475 | 55.2 |
| | James S. Martin (D) | 16,642 | 44.8 |
| 12 | John B. Hays (R) | 14,080 | 52.9 |
| | William M. Snyder (D) | 13,338 | 47.1 |
| 13 | John M. Crebs (D) | 14,764 | 50.9 |
| | Green B. Raum (R) | 14,261 | 49.1 |
| AL | John A. Logan (R) | 249,422 | 55.5 |
| | William W. O'Brien (D) | 199,861 | 44.5 |

## INDIANA

| | Candidates | Votes | % |
|---|---|---|---|
| 1 | William E. Niblack (D) | 18,116 | 52.1 |
| | Veatch (R) | 16,631 | 47.9 |
| 2 | Michael C. Kerr (D) | 18,779 | 60.3 |
| | Gresham (R) | 12,343 | 39.7 |
| 3 | William S. Holman (D) | 15,665 | 51.3 |
| | Lamb (R) | 14,903 | 48.8 |
| 4 | George W. Julian (R) | 13,413 | 50.2 |
| | Reid (D) | 13,297 | 49.8 |
| 5 | John Coburn (R) | 15,715 | 51.7 |
| | Keightly (D) | 14,683 | 48.3 |
| 6 | Daniel W. Voorhees (D) | 16,582 | 50.2 |
| | Carter (R) | 16,455 | 49.8 |
| 7 | Godlove S. Orth (R) | 16,117 | 50.7 |
| | Mahlon D. Manson (D) | 15,660 | 49.3 |
| 8 | Daniel D. Pratt (R) | 17,227* | 53.5 |
| | Ross (D) | 14,946 | 46.5 |
| 9 | John P. C. Shanks (R) | 15,597 | 51.6 |
| | Lowry (D) | 14,656 | 48.4 |
| 10 | William Williams (R) | 16,551 | 53.8 |
| | Ellison (D) | 14,228 | 46.2 |
| 11 | Jasper Packard (R) | 15,489 | 52.1 |
| | Farrand (D) | 14,268 | 48.0 |

## IOWA

| | Candidates | Votes | % |
|---|---|---|---|
| 1 | George W. McCrary (R) | 17,718 | 58.2 |
| | T. W. Clagett (D) | 12,705 | 41.8 |
| 2 | William Smyth (R) | 18,753 | 58.6 |
| | William E. Leffingwell (D) | 13,227 | 41.4 |
| 3 | William B. Allison (R) | 20,119 | 58.5 |
| | William Mills (D) | 14,120 | 41.1 |
| 4 | William Loughridge (R) | 24,057 | 59.3 |
| | J. P. Irish (D) | 16,531 | 40.7 |
| 5 | Francis W. Palmer (R) | 20,409 | 60.4 |
| | P. Gad Bryan (D) | 13,402 | 39.6 |
| 6 | Charles Pomeroy (R) | 16,775 | 72.8 |
| | G. A. L. Roszell (D) | 6,257 | 27.2 |

## KANSAS

| | Candidates | Votes | % |
|---|---|---|---|
| AL | Sidney Clarke (R) | 29,324 | 67.7 |
| | C. W. Blair (D) | 13,969 | 32.3 |

## KENTUCKY

| | Candidates | Votes | % |
|---|---|---|---|
| 1 | Lawrence S. Trimble (D) | 13,608 | 87.0 |
| | Charles A. Marshall (R) | 1,731 | 11.1 |
| 2 | William N. Sweeney (D) | 12,786 | 78.3 |
| | Samuel W. Langley (R) | 3,538 | 21.7 |

## KENTUCKY

| | Candidates | Votes | % |
|---|---|---|---|
| 3 | Jacob S. Golladay (D) | 9,469 | 80.4 |
| | William E. Hobson (R) | 2,303 | 19.6 |
| 4 | J. Proctor Knott (D) | 13,166 | 87.9 |
| | William H. Hays (R) | 1,811 | 12.1 |
| 5 | Boyd Winchester (D) | 15,108 | 90.9 |
| | J. B. English (R) | 1,515 | 9.1 |
| 6 | Thomas L. Jones (D) | 14,082 | 69.7 |
| | O. W. Root (R) | 6,137 | 30.4 |
| 7 | James B. Beck (D) | 13,019 | 84.6 |
| | Charles Eginton (R) | 2,373 | 15.4 |
| 8 | George M. Adams (D) | 10,318 | 51.1 |
| | Sydney W. Barnes (R) | 9,861 | 40.9 |
| 9 | John M. Rice (D) | 10,510 | 61.2 |
| | J. L. Zeigler (R) | 6,652 | 38.8 |

## LOUISIANA[5]
### (Readmitted July 9, 1868)

| | Candidates | Votes | % |
|---|---|---|---|
| 1 | Louis St.Martin (D) | 12,377* | 85.1 |
| | J. Hale Sypher (R) | 2,175 | 15.0 |
| 2 | Caleb S. Hunt (D) | 14,829 | 44.8 |
| | Lionel A. Sheldon (R) | 9,695✔ | 29.3 |
| | J. W. Menard (R) | 8,615 | 26.0 |
| 3 | Adolphe Bailey (D) | 17,513 | 67.1 |
| | Chester B. Darrall (R) | 8,593✔ | 32.9 |
| 4 | Michael Ryan (D) | 13,352 | 64.4 |
| | Joseph P. Newsham (R) | 7,395✔ | 35.6 |
| 5 | G. W. McCranie (D) | 13,716* | 67.9 |
| | Frank Morey (R) | 3,423 | 16.9 |
| | P. J. Kennedy (R) | 3,076 | 15.2 |

## MAINE

| | Candidates | Votes | % |
|---|---|---|---|
| 1 | John Lynch (R) | 16,818 | 53.6 |
| | Charles A. Shaw (D) | 14,579 | 46.4 |
| 2 | Samuel P. Morrill (R) | 14,281 | 59.6 |
| | Alonzo Garcelon (D) | 9,653 | 40.3 |
| 3 | James G. Blaine (R) | 16,121 | 57.3 |
| | E. Wilder Farley (D) | 11,982 | 42.6 |
| 4 | John A. Peters (R) | 13,338 | 61.2 |
| | George W. Ladd (D) | 8,304 | 38.1 |
| 5 | Eugene Hale (R) | 14,363 | 55.2 |
| | Arno Wiswell (D) | 11,680 | 44.9 |

## MARYLAND

| | Candidates | Votes | % |
|---|---|---|---|
| 1 | Samuel Hambleton (D) | 12,703 | 73.4 |
| | Henry R. Torbert (R) | 4,606 | 26.6 |
| 2 | Stevenson Archer (D) | 12,671 | 68.6 |
| | John T. Ensor (R) | 5,796 | 31.4 |
| 3 | Thomas Swann (D) | 13,056 | 69.7 |
| | Adam E. King (R) | 5,667 | 30.3 |
| 4 | Patrick Hamill (D) | 12,289 | 51.3 |
| | Daniel E. Weisel (R) | 11,653 | 48.7 |
| 5 | Frederick Stone (D) | 9,924 | 82.0 |
| | William J. Albert (R) | 2,176 | 18.0 |

## MASSACHUSETTS

| | Candidates | Votes | % |
|---|---|---|---|
| 1 | James Buffinton (R) | 12,975 | 78.5 |
| | Philandor Cobb | 3,486 | 21.1 |
| 2 | Oakes Ames (R) | 14,498 | 71.8 |
| | Edward Arery (D) | 5,695 | 28.2 |
| 3 | Ginery Twichell (R) | 9,074 | 56.8 |
| | Edwin C. Bailey (D) | 6,892 | 43.1 |
| 4 | Samuel Hooper (R) | 11,328 | 56.9 |
| | Peter Harvey (D) | 8,592 | 43.1 |
| 5 | Benjamin F. Butler (R) | 13,109 | 65.5 |
| | Otis P. Lord (D) | 5,061 | 25.3 |
| | Richard A. Dana Jr (IR) | 1,811 | 9.1 |
| 6 | Nathaniel P. Banks (R) | 13,933 | 65.9 |
| | Frederick O. Prince (D) | 7,187 | 34.0 |

*Footnotes, see p. 1019.*

## MASSACHUSETTS

| | Candidates | Votes | % |
|---|---|---|---|
| 7 | George S. Boutwell (R) | 13,214 | 65.4 |
| | Leverett Saltonstall (D) | 6,995 | 34.6 |
| 8 | George F. Hoar (R) | 14,317 | 74.1 |
| | Henry H. Stevens (D) | 4,974 | 25.8 |
| 9 | William B. Washburn (R) | 16,985 | 82.9 |
| | Levi Heywood (D) | 1,814 | 8.9 |
| | Charles Heywood (D) | 1,691 | 8.3 |
| 10 | Henry L. Dawes (R) | 12,260 | 62.1 |
| | Abijah W. Chapin (D) | 7,490 | 37.9 |

## MICHIGAN

| | | Votes | % |
|---|---|---|---|
| 1 | Fernando C. Beaman (R) | 22,197 | 51.9 |
| | Merrill I. Mills (D) | 20,595 | 48.1 |
| 2 | William L. Stoughton (R) | 25,205 | 59.2 |
| | Henry Chamberlain (D) | 17,401 | 40.8 |
| 3 | Austin Blair (R) | 19,268 | 54.2 |
| | Isaac M. Crane (D) | 16,268 | 45.8 |
| 4 | Thomas W. Ferry (R) | 23,043 | 62.7 |
| | Lyman G. Mason (D) | 13,714 | 37.3 |
| 5 | Omar D. Conger (R) | 16,347 | 52.8 |
| | Byron G. Stout (D) | 14,622 | 47.2 |
| 6 | Randolph Strickland (R) | 20,118 | 54.6 |
| | William Newton (D) | 16,720 | 45.4 |

## MINNESOTA

| | | Votes | % |
|---|---|---|---|
| 1 | Morton S. Wilkinson (R) | 23,764 | 61.9 |
| | Batchelder (D) | 14,646 | 38.1 |
| 2 | Eugene M. Wilson (D) | 13,506 | 40.5 |
| | Ignatius Donnelly (OPP R) | 11,265 | 33.8 |
| | Andrews (R) | 8,598 | 25.8 |

## MISSISSIPPI[6]

(Readmitted Feb. 23, 1870)

| | | Votes | % |
|---|---|---|---|
| 1 | Townsend (D) | 11,029 | 65.5 |
| | Wofford (R) | 5,823 | 34.6 |
| 2 | Martin (D) | 11,504 | 65.5 |
| | Railsback (R) | 6,068 | 34.5 |
| 3 | Turner (D) | 11,681 | 53.4 |
| | Sullivan (R) | 10,181 | 46.6 |
| 4 | George C. McKee (R) | 20,444 | 56.9 |
| | Potter | 15,510 | 43.1 |
| 5 | Martin (D) | 12,686 | 51.6 |
| | Pierce (R) | 11,886 | 48.4 |

## MISSOURI

| | | Votes | % |
|---|---|---|---|
| 1 | Erastus Wells (D) | 9,734 | 50.5 |
| | William A. Pile (R) | 9,553 | 49.5 |
| 2 | Gustavus A. Finkelnburg (R) | 11,506 | 58.2 |
| | James J. Lindley (D) | 8,279 | 41.8 |
| 3 | James R. McCormick (D) | 5,153 | 54.9 |
| | John F. Bush (R) | 4,226 | 45.1 |
| 4 | Sempronius H. Boyd (R) | 8,919 | 58.5 |
| | Charles B. McAfee (D) | 4,949 | 32.5 |
| | John R. Kelso (R) | 1,384 | 9.1 |
| 5 | Samuel S. Burdett (R) | 11,187 | 58.5 |
| | John F. Phillips (D) | 7,941 | 41.5 |
| 6 | Robert T. Van Horn (R) | 5,427 | 54.3 |
| | James Shields (D) | 4,560 | 45.7 |
| 7 | Joel F. Asper (R) | 15,272 | 65.5 |
| | Mordecai Oliver (D) | 8,029 | 34.5 |
| 8 | John F. Benjamin (R) | 8,954 | 52.1 |
| | John F. Williams (D) | 8,248 | 48.0 |
| 9 | David P. Dyer (R) | 5,407 | 52.1 |
| | William F. Switzler (D) | 4,981 | 48.0 |

### Special Election

| | | Votes | % |
|---|---|---|---|
| 5 | John H. Stover (R) | 11,387 | 59.5 |
| | Ignatius Hazel (D) | 7,757 | 40.5 |

## NEBRASKA

| | Candidates | Votes | % |
|---|---|---|---|
| AL | John Taffe (R) | 8,715 | 58.5 |
| | Andrew J. Poppleton (D) | 6,192 | 41.5 |

## NEVADA

| | | Votes | % |
|---|---|---|---|
| AL | Thomas Fitch (R) | 6,230 | 53.8 |
| | William F. Anderson (D) | 5,349 | 46.2 |

## NEW JERSEY

| | | Votes | % |
|---|---|---|---|
| 1 | William Moore (R) | 15,214 | 56.9 |
| | Samuel J. Bayard (D) | 11,539 | 43.1 |
| 2 | Charles Haight (D) | 16,299 | 51.3 |
| | James F. Rusling (R) | 15,494 | 48.7 |
| 3 | John T. Bird (D) | 19,580 | 55.9 |
| | Amos Clark (R) | 15,456 | 44.1 |
| 4 | John Hill (R) | 16,468 | 50.1 |
| | Philip Rafferty (D) | 16,389 | 49.9 |
| 5 | Orestes Cleveland (D) | 19,110 | 53.1 |
| | George A. Halsey (R) | 16,862 | 46.9 |

## NEW YORK

| | | Votes | % |
|---|---|---|---|
| 1 | Henry A. Reeves (D) | 13,338 | 52.8 |
| | Alfred M. Wood (R) | 11,945 | 47.3 |
| 2 | John G. Schumacher (D) | 24,418 | 66.2 |
| | Henry S. Bellows (R) | 12,492 | 33.8 |
| 3 | Henry W. Slocum (D) | 16,598 | 54.7 |
| | Samuel Booth (R) | 13,734 | 45.3 |
| 4 | John Fox (D) | 20,074 | 83.3 |
| | Charles V. Lewis (R) | 4,024 | 16.7 |
| 5 | John Morrissey (D) | 16,064 | 69.4 |
| | James M. McCartin (R) | 4,494 | 19.4 |
| | George Francis Train (ID) | 2,583 | 11.2 |
| 6 | Samuel S. Cox (D) | 12,362 | 56.1 |
| | George Starr (R) | 9,682 | 43.9 |
| 7 | Hervey C. Calkin (D) | 18,485 | 75.5 |
| | Joseph C. Pinckney (R) | 5,987 | 24.5 |
| 8 | James Brooks (D) | 21,487 | 68.5 |
| | William Laimbeer (R) | 9,866 | 31.5 |
| 9 | Fernando Wood (D) | 14,648 | 57.5 |
| | Francis A. Thomas (R) | 9,087 | 35.6 |
| | John Savage (ID) | 1,759 | 6.9 |
| 10 | Clarkson N. Potter (D) | 16,533 | 56.6 |
| | David O. Bradley (R) | 12,700 | 43.4 |
| 11 | George W. Greene (D) | 11,620‡ | 50.7 |
| | Charles H. Van Wyck (R) | 11,298 | 49.3 |
| 12 | John H. Ketcham (R) | 13,568 | 50.8 |
| | Charles Wheaton (D) | 13,144 | 49.2 |
| 13 | John A. Griswold (D) | 12,201 | 51.1 |
| | Thomas Cornell (R) | 11,692 | 48.9 |
| 14 | Stephen L. Mayham (D) | 18,477 | 54.0 |
| | Joseph H. Ramsay (R) | 15,734 | 46.0 |
| 15 | Adolphus H. Tanner (R) | 17,054 | 53.8 |
| | Jason C. Osgood (D) | 14,641 | 46.2 |
| 16 | Orange Ferriss (R) | 10,428 | 55.9 |
| | Robert W. Livingston (D) | 8,218 | 44.1 |
| 17 | William A. Wheeler (R) | 15,262 | 70.8 |
| | William H. Wallace (D) | 6,284 | 29.2 |
| 18 | Stephen Sanford (R) | 16,611 | 53.4 |
| | John H. White (D) | 14,508 | 46.6 |
| 19 | Charles Knapp (R) | 17,949 | 55.2 |
| | Francis R. Gilbert (D) | 14,584 | 44.8 |
| 20 | Addison H. Laflin (R) | 16,856 | 55.5 |
| | Andrew Cornwall (D) | 13,508 | 44.5 |
| 21 | Alexander H. Bailey (R) | 12,543 | 52.7 |
| | J. Thomas Spriggs (D) | 11,240 | 47.3 |
| 22 | John C. Churchill (R) | 15,761 | 71.9 |
| | Charles Stebbins Jr (D) | 6,169 | 28.1 |
| 23 | Dennis McCarthy (R) | 16,470 | 59.0 |
| | William Porter (D) | 11,455 | 41.0 |
| 24 | George W. Cowles (R) | 17,234 | 57.5 |
| | Elmore P. Ross (D) | 12,743 | 42.5 |
| 25 | William H. Kelsey (R) | 13,418 | 58.3 |
| | Lester B. Faulkner (D) | 9,610 | 41.7 |

| | Candidates | Votes | % |
|---|---|---|---|
| 26 | Giles W. Hotchkiss (R) | 17,398 | 58.6 |
| | Alvin Devereaux (D) | 12,280 | 41.4 |
| 27 | Hamilton Ward (R) | 18,647 | 58.6 |
| | Curtiss C. Gardiner (D) | 13,180 | 41.4 |
| 28 | Noah Davis (R) | 15,389 | 54.8 |
| | John McConville (D) | 12,699 | 45.2 |
| 29 | John Fisher (R) | 13,432 | 56.6 |
| | James Jackson Jr (D) | 10,294 | 43.4 |
| 30 | David S. Bennett (R) | 16,004 | 52.8 |
| | Isaac A. Verplanck (D) | 14,293 | 47.2 |
| 31 | Porter Sheldon (R) | 15,416 | 64.6 |
| | John S. Beggs (D) | 8,433 | 35.4 |

## NORTH CAROLINA[7]

(Readmitted July 4, 1868)

| | | Votes | % |
|---|---|---|---|
| 1 | Clinton L. Cobb (R) | 15,474 | 56.5 |
| | David A. Barnes (C) | 11,893 | 43.5 |
| 2 | David Heaton (R) | 14,895 | 54.8 |
| | Thomas S. Kenan (D) | 12,293 | 45.2 |
| 3 | Oliver H. Dockery (R) | 15,314 | 53.4 |
| | A. A. McKoy (C) | 13,353 | 46.6 |
| 4 | John T. Deweese (R) | 14,796 | 52.2 |
| | Sion H. Rogers (C) | 13,556 | 47.8 |
| 5 | Israel G. Lash (R) | 14,525 | 56.6 |
| | Livingston Brown (C) | 11,123 | 43.4 |
| 6 | Francis E. Shober (C) | 12,192 | 52.3 |
| | Nathaniel Boyden (R) | 11,103 | 47.7 |
| 7 | Plato Durham (C) | 10,347 | 50.0 |
| | Alexander H. Jones (R) | 10,329✔ | 50.0 |

### Special Elections

| | | Votes | % |
|---|---|---|---|
| 1 | John R. French (R) | 14,664 | 58.5 |
| | Henry A. Gilliam (C) | 10,407 | 41.5 |
| 2 | David Heaton (R) | 14,693 | 56.8 |
| | Thomas S. Kenan (C) | 11,172 | 43.2 |
| 3 | Oliver H. Dockery (R) | 15,090 | 56.9 |
| | Thomas C. Fuller (C) | 11,444 | 43.1 |
| 4 | John T. Deweese (R) | 14,436 | 55.4 |
| | Samuel T. Williams (C) | 11,630 | 44.6 |
| 5 | Israel G. Lash (R) | 13,020 | 58.7 |
| | David F. Caldwell (C) | 9,141 | 41.2 |
| 6 | Nathaniel Boyden (R) | 11,477 | 52.8 |
| | Calvin I. Cowles (R) | 10,251 | 47.2 |
| 7 | Alexander H. Jones (R) | 10,049 | 54.2 |
| | Burgess S. Gaither (C) | 8,467 | 45.7 |

## OHIO

| | | Votes | % |
|---|---|---|---|
| 1 | Philip W. Strader (D) | 10,483 | 50.5 |
| | Benjamin Eggleston (R) | 10,272 | 49.5 |
| 2 | Job E. Stevenson (R) | 11,694 | 51.1 |
| | Samuel F. Cary (D) | 11,197 | 48.9 |
| 3 | Robert C. Schenck (R) | 16,293 | 50.7 |
| | C. L. Vallandigham (D) | 15,818 | 49.3 |
| 4 | William Lawrence (R) | 13,656 | 51.2 |
| | John S. Leedom (D) | 13,027 | 48.8 |
| 5 | William Mungen (D) | 15,435 | 59.3 |
| | Thomas E. Grissell (R) | 10,589 | 40.7 |
| 6 | John A. Smith (R) | 13,463 | 50.7 |
| | Nelson Barrere (D) | 13,120 | 49.4 |
| 7 | James J. Winans (R) | 13,978 | 50.2 |
| | John H. Thomas (D) | 13,873 | 49.8 |
| 8 | John Beatty (R) | 12,198 | 52.0 |
| | J. H. Benson (D) | 11,250 | 48.0 |
| 9 | Edward F. Dickinson (D) | 16,322 | 52.7 |
| | William H. Gibson (R) | 14,677 | 47.4 |
| 10 | Truman H. Hoag (D) | 15,507 | 51.5 |
| | James M. Ashley (R) | 14,595 | 48.5 |
| 11 | John T. Wilson (R) | 13,614 | 54.2 |
| | John Sands (D) | 11,503 | 45.8 |
| 12 | Philadelph Van Trump (D) | 16,287 | 58.9 |
| | Nelson J. Turney (R) | 11,374 | 41.1 |
| 13 | George W. Morgan (D) | 14,614 | 53.0 |
| | Charles Cooper (R) | 12,980 | 47.0 |

*Footnotes, see p. 1019.*

## OHIO

| | Candidates | Votes | % |
|---|---|---|---|
| 14 | Martin Welker (R) | 13,575 | 50.9 |
| | L. R. Critchfield (D) | 13,113 | 49.1 |
| 15 | Eliakim H. Moore (R) | 13,773 | 51.8 |
| | Martin D. Follett (D) | 12,817 | 48.2 |
| 16 | John A. Bingham (R) | 13,757 | 50.8 |
| | Josiah M. Estep (D) | 13,341 | 49.2 |
| 17 | Jacob A. Ambler (R) | 14,998 | 56.4 |
| | Daniel T. Lawson (D) | 11,602 | 43.6 |
| 18 | William H. Upson (R) | 18,359 | 60.5 |
| | Franklin T. Backus (D) | 11,980 | 39.5 |
| 19 | James A. Garfield (R) | 20,187 | 67.4 |
| | James McEwen | 9,759 | 32.6 |

### Special Election

| | | | |
|---|---|---|---|
| 8 | John Beatty (R) | 11,820 | 51.8 |
| | Burns | 10,985 | 48.2 |

## OREGON

| | | | |
|---|---|---|---|
| AL | Joseph S. Smith (D) | 11,754 | 52.7 |
| | David Logan (R) | 10,555 | 47.3 |

## PENNSYLVANIA

| | | | |
|---|---|---|---|
| 1 | Samuel J. Randall (D) | 14,745 | 63.7 |
| | Benjamin L. Berry (R) | 8,408 | 36.3 |
| 2 | Charles O'Neill (R) | 14,533 | 55.0 |
| | Thomas B. Florence (D) | 11,913 | 45.1 |
| 3 | John Moffet (D) | 13,856‡ | 50.2 |
| | Leonard Myers (R) | 13,729 | 49.8 |
| 4 | William D. Kelley (R) | 17,107 | 52.9 |
| | James B. Nicholson (D) | 15,248 | 47.1 |
| 5 | John R. Reading (D) | 13,199‡ | 50.1 |
| | Caleb N. Taylor (R) | 13,158 | 49.9 |
| 6 | John D. Stiles (D) | 15,247 | 54.8 |
| | John R. Breitenbach (R) | 12,568 | 45.2 |
| 7 | Washington Townsend (R) | 12,771 | 57.4 |
| | Robert C. Monaghan (D) | 9,481 | 42.6 |
| 8 | J. Lawrence Getz (D) | 13,738 | 64.8 |
| | Henry S. Eckert (R) | 7,472 | 35.2 |
| 9 | Oliver J. Dickey (R) | 14,993 | 63.4 |
| | Hiram B. Swarr (D) | 8,674 | 36.7 |
| 10 | Henry L. Cake (R) | 12,501 | 50.5 |
| | James J. Conner (D) | 12,276 | 49.6 |
| 11 | Daniel M. Van Auken (D) | 17,930 | 63.4 |
| | John Torrey (R) | 10,367 | 36.6 |
| 12 | George W. Woodward (D) | 16,687 | 52.8 |
| | Theodore Strong (R) | 14,898 | 47.2 |
| 13 | Ulysses Mercur (R) | 12,723 | 50.6 |
| | Victor E. Piolet (D) | 12,412 | 49.4 |
| 14 | John B. Packer (R) | 15,598 | 54.7 |
| | Joseph F. Knipe (D) | 12,902 | 45.3 |

| | Candidates | Votes | % |
|---|---|---|---|
| 15 | Richard J. Haldeman (D) | 15,818 | 55.8 |
| | Samuel Small (R) | 12,519 | 44.2 |
| 16 | John Cessna (R) | 13,653 | 50.3 |
| | Fran M. Kimmell (D) | 13,509 | 49.7 |
| 17 | Daniel J. Morrell (R) | 12,100 | 52.4 |
| | John P. Linton (D) | 11,006 | 47.6 |
| 18 | William H. Armstrong (R) | 16,760 | 53.2 |
| | Levi A. Mackey (D) | 14,732 | 46.8 |
| 19 | Glenni W. Scofield (R) | 16,903 | 54.1 |
| | Rasselas Brown (D) | 14,355 | 45.9 |
| 20 | Calvin W. Gilfillan (R) | 18,079 | 52.6 |
| | Robert M. Defrance (D) | 16,267 | 47.4 |
| 21 | Henry D. Foster (D) | 13,807 | 50.1 |
| | John Covode (R) | 13,766✔ | 49.9 |
| 22 | James S. Negley (R) | 15,175 | 58.7 |
| | Andrew Burt (D) | 10,696 | 41.3 |
| 23 | Darwin Phelps (R) | 16,095 | 59.3 |
| | Lewis Z. Mitchell (D) | 11,046 | 40.7 |
| 24 | Joseph B. Donley (R) | 13,860 | 52.1 |
| | David Crawford (D) | 12,737 | 47.9 |

### Special Elections

| | | | |
|---|---|---|---|
| 9 | Oliver J. Dickey (R) | 15,000 | 63.3 |
| | Robert Crane (D) | 8,689 | 36.7 |
| 20 | S. Newton Pettus (R) | 17,906 | 52.2 |
| | James B. Knox (D) | 16,390 | 47.8 |

## RHODE ISLAND

| | | | |
|---|---|---|---|
| 1 | Thomas A. Jenckes (R) | 7,995 | 66.4 |
| | Arnold (D) | 3,980 | 33.1 |
| 2 | Nathan F. Dixon (R) | 4,133 | 60.9 |
| | Waterhouse (D) | 2,640 | 38.9 |

## SOUTH CAROLINA[8]
(Readmitted July 9, 1868)

| | | | |
|---|---|---|---|
| 1 | B. Frank Whittemore (R) | 17,467 | 61.3 |
| | H. J. Covington (D) | 11,017 | 38.7 |
| 2 | Christopher C. Bowen (R) | 25,845 | 75.7 |
| | R. W. Seymour (D) | 8,296 | 24.3 |
| 3 | J. P. Reed (D) | 11,774 | 57.3 |
| | Solomon L. Hoge (R) | 8,766✔ | 42.7 |
| 4 | William D. Simpson (D) | 14,098 | 59.0 |
| | Alexander S. Wallace (R) | 9,807✔ | 41.0 |
| AL | J. P. M. Epping | 68,477* | 50.2 |
| | E. E. Dickson | 67,654 | 49.6 |

### Special Elections

| | | | |
|---|---|---|---|
| 1 | B. Frank Whittemore (R) | 17,512 | 74.2 |
| | J. N. Frierson (D) | 6,075 | 25.8 |
| 2 | Christopher C. Bowen (R) | 18,000 | 96.0 |
| | W. Brisbane (R) | 5,322 | 28.4 |
| 3 | M. Simeon Corley (R) | 15,681 | 71.0 |
| | S. McGowan (D) | 6,413 | 29.0 |

| | Candidates | Votes | % |
|---|---|---|---|
| 4 | James H. Goss (R) | 12,016 | 57.2 |
| | S. McAllilly (D) | 8,993 | 42.8 |

## TENNESSEE

| | | | |
|---|---|---|---|
| 1 | Roderick R. Butler (R) | 10,107 | 98.5 |
| 2 | Horace Maynard (R) | 10,403 | 79.5 |
| | C. Houk (I) | 2,681 | 20.5 |
| 3 | William B. Stokes (R) | 5,915 | 74.4 |
| | E. A. Garrett (I) | 2,037 | 25.6 |
| 4 | C. A. Sheafe (D) | 4,476 | 54.0 |
| | Lewis Tillman (R) | 3,810✔ | 46.0 |
| 5 | William F. Prosser (R) | 5,804 | 56.5 |
| | Joseph Motley (D) | 2,655 | 25.8 |
| | Samuel C. Mercer (I) | 1,817 | 17.7 |
| 6 | Samuel M. Arnell (R) | 5,143 | 70.6 |
| | John J. Buck (IR) | 2,141 | 29.4 |
| 7 | Isaac R. Hawkins (R) | 2,825 | 71.3 |
| | George R. Foote (D) | 1,136 | 28.7 |
| 8 | John W. Leftwich (D) | 6,533 | 40.6 |
| | William J. Smith (R) | 5,543✔ | 34.4 |
| | David A. Nunn (R) | 4,024 | 25.0 |

## VERMONT

| | | | |
|---|---|---|---|
| 1 | Charles W. Willard (R) | 13,999 | 76.1 |
| | John Cain (D) | 4,396 | 23.9 |
| 2 | Luke P. Poland (R) | 15,407 | 74.6 |
| | Charles M. Chase (D) | 5,252 | 25.4 |
| 3 | Worthington C. Smith (R) | 11,105 | 72.4 |
| | Waldo Brigham (D) | 4,237 | 27.6 |

## WEST VIRGINIA

| | | | |
|---|---|---|---|
| 1 | Issac H. Duval (R) | 11,569 | 51.9 |
| | H. S. Walker (D) | 10,729 | 48.1 |
| 2 | James C. McGrew (R) | 9,147 | 58.4 |
| | William G. Brown (D) | 6,517 | 41.6 |
| 3 | John S. Witcher (R) | 6,215 | 56.4 |
| | Charles P. J. Moore (D) | 4,806 | 43.6 |

## WISCONSIN

| | | | |
|---|---|---|---|
| 1 | Halbert E. Paine (R) | 17,513 | 50.6 |
| | Mitchell (D) | 17,084 | 49.4 |
| 2 | Benjamin F. Hopkins (R) | 18,333 | 59.2 |
| | Winans (D) | 12,659 | 40.9 |
| 3 | Amasa Cobb (R) | 17,903 | 61.6 |
| | Passmore (D) | 11,162 | 38.4 |
| 4 | Charles A. Eldridge (D) | 17,688 | 57.3 |
| | Frisby (R) | 13,205 | 42.7 |
| 5 | Philetus Sawyer (R) | 19,622 | 55.8 |
| | Vilas (D) | 15,534 | 44.2 |
| 6 | Cadwallader C. Washburn (R) | 21,236 | 64.9 |
| | Ellis (D) | 11,481 | 35.1 |

1. These were six special elections to fill Alabama's House seats for the remainder of the 40th Congress (1867-69).

2. These three elections were for a full two-year term in the 41st Congress (1869-71). Arkansas was readmitted to the Union and had three representatives for part of the 40th Congress (1867-69), but returns for their election were not available.

3. Florida was readmitted during the 40th Congress (1867-69) and Charles M. Hamilton served for the remainder of that Congress. He was then re-elected to a full term in the 41st Congress (1869-71). The Florida candidates shown on page 619 were running for the full term in the 41st Congress.

4. Figures represent returns in seven special elections held April 20, 1868. All winners listed, except John H. Christy in the 6th District, were seated July 25, 1868 to serve for the remainder of the 40th Congress (1867-69), even though Georgia had not been formally re-admitted to the Union.

On the convening of the 41st Congress in 1869, the six incumbent Georgia Representatives claimed their election of April 20, 1868 also entitled them to seats in the 41st Congress. The House rejected the claim and Georgia then elected representatives to the 41st Congress, but these returns are not available. According to Georgia secretary of state archives, William Wiseham Paine (D) served in the House from the 1st

District March 4, 1869, to March 3, 1871; Marion Bethune (R), 3rd District, served Jan. 16, 1871-March 3, 1871; and Stephen Alfestus Corker (D), 5th District, served Jan. 24, 1871-March 3, 1871. No returns on their elections are available. Georgia was readmitted to representation by act of July 15, 1870.

5. Louisiana was readmitted during the 40th Congress (1867-69) and elected several representatives, but these returns are unavailable. The five elections shown here are for a full two-year term in the 41st Congress (1869-71).

6. No representatives from Mississippi were seated from this election. Mississippi was not readmitted until Feb. 23, 1870.

7. The special elections were for unexpired terms in the 40th Congress (1867-69). The general elections were for full two-year terms in the 41st Congress (1869-71).

8. The "Special Elections" were to fill unexpired terms in the 40th Congress (1867-69), while the others were for full terms in the 41st Congress (1869-71). The at-large election in which J. P. M. Epping was the apparent winner was rejected by the House. According to the Biographical Directory, a number of southern states upon readmission claimed that since their slaves were emancipated, they were entitled to larger delegations in the House. Epping's election falls in this category. The claims were rejected by the House.

# 1869 House Elections

## ALABAMA

| | Candidates | Votes | % |
|---|---|---|---|
| 1 | Alfred E. Buck (R) | 14,191 | 54.0 |
| | W. D. Mann (D) | 12,080 | 46.0 |
| 2 | Charles W. Buckley (R) | 14,933 | 58.1 |
| | A. N. Worthy (D) | 10,786 | 41.9 |
| 3 | Robert S. Heflin (R) | 9,895 | 50.6 |
| | J. C. Parkinson (D) | 9,652 | 49.4 |
| 4 | Charles Hays (R) | 17,243 | 71.5 |
| | John B. Reed (D) | 4,881 | 20.2 |
| | C. W. Dunstan (I) | 2,010 | 8.3 |
| 5 | Peter M. Dox (D) | 6,047 | 55.1 |
| | W. J. Haralson (R) | 4,933 | 44.9 |
| 6 | William C. Sherrod (D) | 4,932 | 57.7 |
| | J. J. Hinds (R) | 2,836 | 33.2 |
| | Thomas Haughey (I) | 775 | 9.1 |

## CONNECTICUT

| | | Votes | % |
|---|---|---|---|
| 1 | Julius L. Strong (R) | 11,617 | 51.6 |
| | Dixon (D) | 10,881 | 48.4 |
| 2 | Stephen W. Kellogg (R) | 13,102 | 50.8 |
| | Babk (D) | 12,678 | 49.2 |
| 3 | Henry H. Starkweather (R) | 9,212 | 57.5 |
| | Conv (D) | 6,813 | 42.5 |
| 4 | William H. Barnum (D) | 13,075 | 52.3 |
| | William H. Beard (R) | 11,915 | 47.7 |

## ILLINOIS

### Special Election

| | | Votes | % |
|---|---|---|---|
| 3 | Horatio C. Burchard (R) | 6,213 | 76.1 |
| | John V. Eustace | 1,843 | 22.6 |

## MASSACHUSETTS

| | Candidates | Votes | % |
|---|---|---|---|
| | **Special Election** | | |
| 7 | George M. Brooks (R) | 8,809 | 67.3 |
| | Leverett Saltonstall (D) | 4,284 | 32.7 |

## MISSISSIPPI

| | | Votes | % |
|---|---|---|---|
| 1 | George E. Harris (R) | 10,215 | 61.5 |
| | Jefferson L. Wafford (C) | 6,389 | 38.5 |
| 2 | Joseph L. Morphis (R) | 9,089 | 62.9 |
| | William Kellogg (C) | 5,353 | 37.1 |
| 3 | Henry W. Barry (R) | 12,912 | 62.9 |
| | Schuyler B. Steers (C) | 7,630 | 37.1 |
| 4 | George C. McKee (R) | 25,082 | 71.9 |
| | Archie C. Fisk (C) | 9,811 | 28.1 |
| 5 | Legrand W. Perce (R) | 14,450 | 64.1 |
| | Loroy S. Brown (C) | 8,080 | 35.9 |

## NEW HAMPSHIRE

| | | Votes | % |
|---|---|---|---|
| 1 | Jacob H. Ela (R) | 13,138 | 53.6 |
| | E. A. Hibbard (D) | 11,376 | 46.4 |
| 2 | Aaron F. Stevens (R) | 11,513 | 53.9 |
| | Edward W. Harrington (D) | 9,866 | 46.2 |
| 3 | Jacob Benton (R) | 11,254 | 51.3 |
| | Hosea W. Parker (D) | 10,691 | 48.7 |

## TEXAS

### (Readmitted March 30, 1870)

| | | Votes | % |
|---|---|---|---|
| 1 | George W. Whitmore (R) | 8,456 | 52.0 |
| | James Armstrong (D) | 7,406 | 45.6 |

| | Candidates | Votes | % |
|---|---|---|---|
| 2 | John C. Conner (D) | 6,378 | 41.9 |
| | B. F. Grafton (R) | 4,355 | 28.6 |
| | J. F. Johnson (ID) | 3,540 | 23.2 |
| | R. H. Taylor (I) | 944 | 6.2 |
| 3 | William T. Clark (R) | 16,582 | 65.9 |
| | Jacob Elliot (D) | 8,564 | 34.0 |
| 4 | Edward Degener (R) | 9,312 | 47.7 |
| | J. L. Haynes (D) | 9,240 | 47.3 |

## VIRGINIA [1]

### (Readmitted Jan. 26, 1870)

| | | Votes | % |
|---|---|---|---|
| 1 | Richard S. Ayer (RAD) | 8,023 | 29.7 |
| | Joseph Segar (I) | 7,377 | 27.3 |
| | Norton (I) | 6,523 | 24.2 |
| | Lewis (C) | 5,056 | 18.7 |
| 2 | James H. Platt Jr (RAD) | 16,781 | 53.4 |
| | D. J. Godwin (C) | 11,255 | 35.8 |
| | Bayne (I) | 2,736 | 8.7 |
| 3 | Charles H. Porter (RAD) | 17,311 | 55.0 |
| | J. W. Hunnicut (C) | 13,101 | 41.6 |
| 4 | George W. Booker (C) | 13,101 | 48.0 |
| | George Tucker (RAD) | 9,568 | 35.0 |
| | Stowell (I) | 4,639 | 17.0 |
| 5 | Robert Ridgway (C) | 16,732 | 55.2 |
| | G. G. Curtis (RAD) | 13,571 | 44.8 |
| 6 | William Milnes Jr (C) | 12,123 | 56.8 |
| | John T. Harris (I) | 6,815 | 31.9 |
| | Phelps (RAD) | 2,425 | 11.4 |
| 7 | Lewis McKenzie (C) | 15,878 | 58.9 |
| | Charles Whittlesey (RAD) | 11,073 | 41.1 |
| 8 | James King Gibson (C) | 14,717 | 69.6 |
| | G. S. Smith (RAD) | 6,244 | 29.5 |
| AL | Joseph Segar (C) | 117,499* | 53.9 |
| | A. M. Crane (RAD) | 100,424 | 46.1 |

1. According to the Biographical Directory Virginia claimed an extra House seat and elected Joseph Segar at-large to fill it. The House rejected the claim.

# 1870 House Elections

## ALABAMA

| Candidates | Votes | % |
|---|---|---|
| 1 Benjamin S. Turner (R) | 18,226 | 57.5 |
| S. J. Cumming (D) | 13,466 | 42.5 |
| 2 Charles W. Buckley (R) | 19,647 | 55.4 |
| M. B. Welbourn (D) | 15,831 | 44.6 |
| 3 William A. Handley (D) | 12,710 | 57.1 |
| B. W. Norris (R) | 9,568 | 43.0 |
| 4 Charles Hays (R) | 18,373 | 52.6 |
| J. G. Harris (D) | 16,540 | 47.4 |
| 5 Peter M. Dox (D) | 10,689 | 70.3 |
| L. J. Standifee (R) | 4,523 | 29.7 |
| 6 Joseph H. Sloss (D) | 9,221 | 69.4 |
| B. O. Masterson (R) | 4,068 | 30.6 |

## ARKANSAS

| Candidates | Votes | % |
|---|---|---|
| 1 James M. Hanks (D) | 5,394 | 61.4 |
| Logan H. Roots (R) | 3,398 | 38.7 |
| 2 Oliver P. Snyder (R) | 8,956 | 59.1 |
| A. A. C. Rogers (D) | 6,211 | 41.0 |
| 3 John Edwards (D) | 6,874‡ | 53.7 |
| Thomas Boles (R) | 5,919 | 46.3 |

## DELAWARE

| Candidates | Votes | % |
|---|---|---|
| AL Benjamin T. Biggs (D) | 11,446 | 55.6 |
| Joshua T. Heald (R) | 9,150 | 44.4 |

## FLORIDA

| Candidates | Votes | % |
|---|---|---|
| AL Josiah T. Walls (R) | 12,439‡ | 51.3 |
| Silas L. Niblack (D) | 11,810 | 48.7 |

## GEORGIA

(Readmitted July 15, 1870)

| Candidates | Votes | % |
|---|---|---|
| 1 Archibald T. MacIntyre (D) | 15,581 | 56.9 |
| Virgil Hillyer (R) | 9,662 | 35.3 |
| A. A. Bradley (IR) | 2,142 | 7.8 |
| 2 Nelson Tift (D) | 14,969 | 51.5 |
| Richard H. Whiteley (R) | 14,088✓ | 48.5 |
| 3 John S. Bigby (R) | 14,212 | 52.9 |
| William F. Wright (D) | 12,649 | 47.1 |
| 4 Thomas J. Speer (R) | 11,211 | 51.1 |
| Winburn J. Lawton (D) | 10,725 | 48.9 |
| 5 Dudley M. DuBose (D) | 15,363 | 62.3 |
| Isham S. Fannin (R) | 9,302 | 37.7 |
| 6 William P. Price (D) | 10,358 | 68.6 |
| John A. Wimpey (R) | 3,911 | 25.9 |
| Weir Boyd (ID) | 823 | 5.5 |
| 7 Pierce M. B. Young (D) | 14,768 | 73.8 |
| George P. Burnett (R) | 5,257 | 26.3 |

## ILLINOIS

| Candidates | Votes | % |
|---|---|---|
| 1 Charles B. Farwell (R) | 20,342 | 57.5 |
| John Wentworth (D) | 15,025 | 42.4 |
| 2 John F. Farnsworth (R) | 8,396 | 48.6 |
| J. C. Stoughton (P) | 6,516 | 37.8 |
| Richard Bischop (D) | 2,349 | 13.6 |
| 3 Horatio C. Burchard (R) | 11,718 | 65.3 |
| Charles Betts (D) | 6,219 | 34.6 |
| 4 John B. Hawley (R) | 12,023 | 50.1 |
| P. L. Cable (D) | 11,982 | 49.9 |
| 5 Bradford N. Stevens (D) | 11,579 | 51.7 |
| E. C. Ingersoll (R) | 9,963 | 44.5 |
| 6 Burton C. Cook (R) | 10,452 | 56.5 |
| Julias Avery (D) | 7,839 | 42.4 |
| 7 Jesse H. Moore (R) | 14,089 | 51.2 |
| Andrew J. Hunter (D) | 13,418 | 48.8 |
| 8 James C. Robinson (D) | 13,702 | 50.1 |
| Jonathan Merriam (R) | 12,448 | 45.6 |
| 9 Thompson W. McNeely (D) | 12,691 | 55.2 |
| B. F. Westlake (R) | 10,297 | 44.8 |

| Candidates | Votes | % |
|---|---|---|
| 10 Edward Y. Rice (D) | 13,963 | 53.7 |
| J. W. Kitchell (R) | 12,028 | 46.3 |
| 11 Samuel S. Marshall (D) | 15,771 | 57.7 |
| William H. Robinson (R) | 11,546 | 42.3 |
| 12 John B. Hays (R) | 10,903 | 51.8 |
| William Hartzell (D) | 10,126 | 48.2 |
| 13 John M. Crebs (D) | 13,947 | 53.0 |
| Daniel W. Munn (R) | 12,366 | 47.0 |
| AL John A. Logan (R) | 168,801* | 53.2 |
| William B. Anerson (D) | 145,191 | 45.8 |

## INDIANA

| Candidates | Votes | % |
|---|---|---|
| 1 William E. Niblack (D) | 17,577 | 53.4 |
| Hy C. Gooding (R) | 15,327 | 46.6 |
| 2 Michael C. Kerr (D) | 16,950 | 60.4 |
| Carr (R) | 11,116 | 39.6 |
| 3 William S. Holman (D) | 15,396 | 54.3 |
| Pritchard (R) | 12,972 | 45.7 |
| 4 Jeremiah M. Wilson (R) | 12,561 | 50.0 |
| David S. Gooding (D) | 12,557 | 50.0 |
| 5 John Coburn (R) | 14,123 | 50.8 |
| Cottrell (D) | 13,707 | 49.3 |
| 6 Daniel W. Voorhees (D) | 17,268 | 52.2 |
| Dunn (R) | 15,843 | 47.9 |
| 7 Mahlon D. Manson (D) | 15,539 | 50.6 |
| L. Wallace (R) | 15,146 | 49.4 |
| 8 James F. Tyner (R) | 15,113 | 53.5 |
| J. T. Henderson (D) | 13,149 | 46.5 |
| 9 John P. C. Shanks (R) | 13,790 | 50.7 |
| Colerick (D) | 13,396 | 49.3 |
| 10 William Williams (R) | 14,130 | 60.8 |
| M. S. Hascall (IR) | 9,112 | 39.2 |
| 11 Jasper Packard (R) | 14,459 | 52.6 |
| S. I. Anthony (D) | 13,052 | 47.4 |

## IOWA

| Candidates | Votes | % |
|---|---|---|
| 1 George W. McCrary (R) | 13,327 | 57.2 |
| Edmund Jaeger (D) | 9,961 | 42.8 |
| 2 Aylett R. Cotton (R) | 13,586 | 59.3 |
| William E. Leffingwell (D) | 9,338 | 40.7 |
| 3 William G. Donnan (R) | 15,927 | 59.2 |
| John T. Stoneman (D) | 10,961 | 40.8 |
| 4 Madison M. Walden (R) | 19,005 | 56.0 |
| William T. Smith (D) | 14,883 | 43.9 |
| 5 Frank W. Palmer (R) | 19,798 | 61.2 |
| B. F. Montgomery (D) | 12,516 | 38.7 |
| 6 Jackson Orr (R) | 16,993 | 73.9 |
| C. C. Smettzer (D) | 5,977 | 26.0 |

### Special Election

| Candidates | Votes | % |
|---|---|---|
| 2 William P. Wolf (R) | 13,858 | 66.6 |
| J. M. Preston | 4,834 | 23.2 |
| R. M. Preston | 1,048 | 5.0 |

## KANSAS

| Candidates | Votes | % |
|---|---|---|
| AL David P. Lowe (R) | 40,368 | 65.8 |
| R. C. Foster (D) | 20,950 | 34.2 |

## KENTUCKY

| Candidates | Votes | % |
|---|---|---|
| 1 Edward Crossland (D) | 7,930 | 64.4 |
| N. R. Black (R) | 2,982 | 24.2 |
| W. C. Clark (ID) | 1,405 | 11.4 |
| 2 Henry D. McHenry (D) | 8,214 | 59.9 |
| Milton J. Roach (R) | 5,490 | 40.1 |
| 3 Joseph H. Lewis (D) | 7,314 | 56.4 |
| D. R. Carr (R) | 5,657 | 43.6 |
| 4 William B. Read (D) | 9,314 | 70.9 |
| James M. Fidler (R) | 3,831 | 29.1 |
| 5 Boyd Winchester (D) | 10,599 | 66.1 |
| James Speed (R) | 5,426 | 33.9 |

| Candidates | Votes | % |
|---|---|---|
| 6 William E. Arthur (D) | 9,213 | 66.7 |
| Thomas Wrightson (R) | 4,578 | 33.1 |
| 7 James B. Beck (D) | 14,312 | 56.7 |
| William Brown (R) | 10,916 | 43.3 |
| 8 George M. Adams (D) | 12,226 | 50.0 |
| Hugh F. Finley (R) | 12,208 | 50.0 |
| 9 John M. Rice (D) | 9,823 | 60.3 |
| George M. Thomas (R) | 6,463 | 39.7 |

### Special Election

| Candidates | Votes | % |
|---|---|---|
| 3 Joseph H. Lewis (D) | 9,847 | 65.1 |
| J. H. Lowry | 5,289 | 34.9 |

## LOUISIANA

| Candidates | Votes | % |
|---|---|---|
| 1 J. Hale Sypher (R) | 13,971 | 62.0 |
| A. W. Walker (D) | 8,579 | 38.0 |
| 2 Lionel A. Sheldon (R) | 17,512 | 69.6 |
| John A. Walsh (D) | 7,640 | 30.4 |
| 3 Chester B. Darrall (R) | 13,202 | 60.9 |
| Adolph Bailey (D) | 8,483 | 39.1 |
| 4 James McCleery (R) | 11,786 | 62.2 |
| Michael Ryan (D) | 7,171 | 37.8 |
| 5 Frank Morey (R) | 9,521 | 58.7 |
| J. D. Watkins (D) | 6,713 | 41.4 |

## MAINE

| Candidates | Votes | % |
|---|---|---|
| 1 John Lynch (R) | 12,571 | 53.2 |
| Haines (D) | 11,075 | 46.8 |
| 2 William P. Frye (R) | 10,245 | 56.3 |
| Black (D) | 7,924 | 43.6 |
| 3 James G. Blaine (R) | 11,590 | 55.0 |
| Farley (D) | 9,279 | 44.1 |
| 4 John A. Peters (R) | 9,962 | 57.6 |
| Emery (D) | 7,322 | 42.3 |
| 5 Eugene Hale (R) | 10,086 | 52.9 |
| Carlton (D) | 8,876 | 46.5 |

## MARYLAND

| Candidates | Votes | % |
|---|---|---|
| 1 Samuel Hambleton (D) | 17,314 | 56.5 |
| Henry R. Torbert (R) | 13,348 | 43.5 |
| 2 Stevenson Archer (D) | 14,622 | 64.5 |
| W. M. Marine (R) | 8,062 | 35.5 |
| 3 Thomas Swann (D) | 15,137 | 59.2 |
| Washington Booth (R) | 10,414 | 40.8 |
| 4 John Ritchie (D) | 14,304 | 53.4 |
| John E. Smith (R) | 12,486 | 46.6 |
| 5 William H. Merrick (D) | 15,231 | 53.1 |
| James A. Gary (R) | 13,440 | 46.9 |

## MASSACHUSETTS

| Candidates | Votes | % |
|---|---|---|
| 1 James Buffinton (R) | 8,281 | 64.3 |
| Robert Pitnam (I) | 2,667 | 20.7 |
| William W. Comstock (D) | 1,704 | 13.2 |
| 2 Oakes Ames (R) | 9,367 | 60.0 |
| Edward Avery (D) | 6,013 | 38.5 |
| 3 Ginery Twichell (R) | 6,233 | 50.7 |
| William Gaiton (D) | 5,640 | 45.9 |
| 4 Samuel Hooper (R) | 8,025 | 56.0 |
| Leopold Morse (D) | 5,605 | 39.1 |
| 5 Benjamin F. Butler (R) | 8,333 | 60.4 |
| William Endicott (D) | 4,297 | 31.1 |
| Unidentified Candidate (I) | 1,076 | 7.8 |
| 6 Nathaniel P. Banks (R) | 10,548 | 64.4 |
| John K. Tarbox (D) | 5,123 | 31.3 |
| 7 George M. Brooks (R) | 8,406 | 57.6 |
| Seth Adams (D) | 4,561 | 31.3 |
| J. Chillis Kimball (LAB REF) | 1,489 | 10.2 |
| 8 George F. Hoar (R) | 8,487 | 56.2 |
| Alvin Cook (D) | 4,282 | 28.4 |
| Moses Johnson (LAB REF) | 1,734 | 11.5 |

## MASSACHUSETTS

| | Candidates | Votes | % |
|---|---|---|---|
| 9 | William B. Washburn (R) | 10,903 | 70.4 |
| | Lysander B. Jaquith (D) | 4,185 | 27.0 |
| 10 | Henry L. Dawes (R) | 8,419 | 52.9 |
| | Reuben Noble (D) | 7,077 | 44.5 |

## MICHIGAN

| | | Votes | % |
|---|---|---|---|
| 1 | Henry Waldron (R) | 18,348 | 50.6 |
| | N. B. Eldridge (D) | 17,447 | 48.2 |
| 2 | William L. Stoughton (R) | 17,502 | 54.6 |
| | Henry Chamberlain (D) | 13,923 | 43.5 |
| 3 | Austin Blair (R) | 15,236 | 51.5 |
| | D. D. Hughes (D) | 13,768 | 46.6 |
| 4 | Thomas W. Ferry (R) | 16,854* | 60.8 |
| | Myron Rider (D) | 10,384 | 37.4 |
| 5 | Omar D. Conger (R) | 13,782 | 49.9 |
| | Byron G. Stout (D) | 13,593 | 49.2 |
| 6 | Jabez G. Sutherland (D) | 16,618 | 52.7 |
| | John F. Driggs (R) | 14,879 | 47.2 |

## MINNESOTA

| | | Votes | % |
|---|---|---|---|
| 1 | Mark H. Dunnell (R) | 19,606 | 56.8 |
| | Buck (D) | 14,904 | 43.2 |
| 2 | John T. Averill (R) | 17,133 | 54.2 |
| | Donnelly (D) | 14,491 | 45.8 |

## MISSISSIPPI

| | | Votes | % |
|---|---|---|---|
| 1 | George E. Harris (R) | ✔ | |
| 2 | Joseph L. Morphis (R) | ✔ | |
| 3 | Henry W. Barry (R) | ✔ | |
| 4 | George C. McKee (R) | ✔ | |
| 5 | Legrand W. Perce (R) | ✔ | |

## MISSOURI

| | | Votes | % |
|---|---|---|---|
| 1 | Erastus Wells (D) | 7,629 | 50.9 |
| | Charles Johnson (LR) | 5,444 | 36.3 |
| | Iron Z. Smith (RAD R) | 1,928 | 12.9 |
| 2 | Gustavus A. Finkelnburg (LR) | 12,708 | 90.3 |
| | A. Vanwormer (RAD R) | 1,359 | 9.7 |
| 3 | James R. McCormick (D) | 7,572 | 63.5 |
| | G. J. Vanallen (RAD R) | 2,331 | 19.6 |
| | William M. Nalle (LR) | 2,015 | 16.9 |
| 4 | Harrison E. Havens (RAD R) | 8,830 | 54.4 |
| | William E. Gilmore (LR) | 7,416 | 45.7 |
| 5 | Samuel S. Burdett (RAD R) | 10,790 | 47.1 |
| | George R. Smith (LR) | 9,066 | 39.6 |
| | Douglass Dale (D) | 3,062 | 13.4 |
| 6 | Abraham Comingo (D) | 12,511 | 58.9 |
| | George R. Smith (RAD R) | 8,718 | 41.1 |
| 7 | Isaac C. Parker (LR) | 13,713 | 56.1 |
| | John H. Ellis (D) | 10,723 | 43.9 |
| 8 | James G. Blair (LR) | 11,710 | 56.3 |
| | J. T. K. Hayward (RAD R) | 9,106 | 43.8 |
| 9 | Andrew King (D) | 10,393 | 59.7 |
| | David P. Dyer (LR) | 3,803 | 21.8 |
| | Edward Draper (RAD R) | 3,227 | 18.5 |

## NEBRASKA

| | | Votes | % |
|---|---|---|---|
| AL | John Taffe (R) | 12,375 | 60.8 |
| | George B. Lake (D) | 7,967 | 39.2 |

## NEVADA

| | | Votes | % |
|---|---|---|---|
| AL | Charles W. Kendall (D) | 6,821 | 52.5 |
| | Thomas Fitch (R) | 6,161 | 47.5 |

## NEW JERSEY

| | | Votes | % |
|---|---|---|---|
| 1 | John W. Hazleton (R) | 14,502 | 53.8 |
| | Benjamin F. Lee (D) | 12,469 | 46.2 |

| | Candidates | Votes | % |
|---|---|---|---|
| 2 | Samuel C. Forker (D) | 15,899 | 50.7 |
| | William A. Newell (R) | 15,452 | 49.3 |
| 3 | John T. Bird (D) | 18,007 | 55.7 |
| | Robert Rusling (R) | 14,323 | 44.3 |
| 4 | John Hill (R) | 18,057 | 54.1 |
| | Philip Rafferty (D) | 15,304 | 45.9 |
| 5 | George A. Halsey (R) | 18,092 | 54.2 |
| | Orestes Cleveland (D) | 14,694 | 44.0 |

## NEW YORK

| | | Votes | % |
|---|---|---|---|
| 1 | Dwight Townsend (D) | 12,632 | 52.4 |
| | Caleb C. Norvell (R) | 11,466 | 47.6 |
| 2 | Thomas Kinsella (D) | 20,704 | 62.4 |
| | Silas B. Dutcher (R) | 12,482 | 37.6 |
| 3 | Henry W. Slocum (D) | 13,799 | 53.8 |
| | Erastus D. Webster (R) | 8,623 | 33.6 |
| | R. M. Whiting Jr. (IR) | 3,248 | 12.7 |
| 4 | Robert B. Roosevelt (D) | 10,702 | 63.0 |
| | M. T. McMahon (R&YD) | 5,501 | 32.4 |
| 5 | William R. Roberts (D) | 14,556 | 86.0 |
| | James A. Briggs (R) | 2,215 | 13.1 |
| 6 | Samuel S. Cox (D) | 9,228 | 52.9 |
| | Greeley (R) | 8,203 | 47.1 |
| 7 | Smith Ely Jr (D) | 12,514 | 73.9 |
| | McAlpin (R) | 3,503 | 20.7 |
| | Willis (R) | 929 | 5.5 |
| 8 | James Brooks (D) | 12,845 | 52.6 |
| | George Wilkes (R) | 7,348 | 30.1 |
| | J. Wadsworth (YD) | 4,243 | 17.4 |
| 9 | Fernando Wood (D) | 15,630 | 64.8 |
| | W. S. Hillyer (YD&R) | 4,789 | 19.9 |
| | Morris Ellinger (R) | 3,708 | 15.4 |
| 10 | Clarkson N. Potter (D) | 14,249 | 57.2 |
| | James Westervelt (R) | 10,685 | 42.9 |
| 11 | Charles St.John (R) | 11,247 | 51.1 |
| | Sherman (D) | 10,747 | 48.9 |
| 12 | John H. Ketcham (R) | 14,432 | 55.1 |
| | Philip (D) | 11,748 | 44.9 |
| 13 | Joseph H. Tuthill (D) | 11,559 | 50.7 |
| | Lindsley (R) | 11,257 | 49.3 |
| 14 | Eli Perry (D) | 17,716 | 54.6 |
| | Harder (R) | 14,726 | 45.4 |
| 15 | Joseph M. Warren (D) | 17,793 | 60.4 |
| | J. Thomas Davis (R) | 11,659 | 39.6 |
| 16 | John Rogers (D) | 9,444 | 50.5 |
| | Andrew Williams (R) | 9,272 | 49.5 |
| 17 | William A. Wheeler (R) | 13,020 | 69.6 |
| | George Mott (D) | 5,699 | 30.4 |
| 18 | John M. Carroll (D) | 14,828 | 48.6 |
| | James M. Marvin (R) | 13,390 | 43.9 |
| | Samuel McKean (IR) | 2,286 | 7.5 |
| 19 | Elizur H. Prindle (R) | 16,752 | 53.8 |
| | Juliand (D) | 14,389 | 46.2 |
| 20 | Clinton L. Merriam (R) | 14,863 | 53.5 |
| | Andrew Cornwall (D) | 12,899 | 46.5 |
| 21 | Ellis H. Roberts (R) | 12,322 | 53.7 |
| | Weaver (D) | 10,606 | 46.3 |
| 22 | William E. Lansing (R) | 13,450 | 56.5 |
| | M. J. Shoecraft (D) | 9,780 | 41.1 |
| 23 | R. Holland Duell (R) | 12,954 | 55.1 |
| | Dennis McCarthy (IR & D) | 10,540 | 44.9 |
| 24 | John E. Seeley (R) | 15,276 | 55.7 |
| | Daniels (D) | 12,134 | 44.3 |
| 25 | William H. Lamport (R) | 12,115 | 56.4 |
| | Harlow L. Comstock (D) | 9,367 | 43.6 |
| 26 | Milo Goodrich (R) | 15,471 | 56.3 |
| | Apgar (D) | 12,029 | 43.7 |
| 27 | H. Boardman Smith (R) | 16,276 | 54.9 |
| | Lucius Robinson (D) | 13,352 | 45.1 |
| 28 | Freeman Clarke (R) | 13,844 | 55.3 |
| | J. H. White (D) | 11,187 | 44.7 |
| 29 | Seth Wakeman (R) | 12,134 | 57.3 |
| | James G. Shepard (D) | 9,039 | 42.7 |
| 30 | William Williams (D) | 15,018 | 51.0 |
| | Bass (R) | 14,415 | 49.0 |
| 31 | Walter L. Sessions (R) | 10,170 | 50.9 |
| | Murray (D) | 9,793 | 49.1 |

**Special Election**

| | | Votes | % |
|---|---|---|---|
| 28 | Charles H. Holmes (R) | ✔ | |
| | Alex P. Butts | | |

## NORTH CAROLINA

| | Candidates | Votes | % |
|---|---|---|---|
| 1 | Clinton L. Cobb (R) | 10,054 | 60.7 |
| | Timothy Morgan (IR) | 6,520 | 39.3 |
| 2 | Charles R. Thomas (R) | 15,099 | 55.0 |
| | Lott W. Humphrey (C) | 12,352 | 45.0 |
| 3 | Alfred M. Waddell (C) | 13,828 | 50.6 |
| | Oliver H. Dockery (R) | 13,477 | 49.4 |
| 4 | Sion H. Rogers (C) | 14,106 | 51.7 |
| | James Harris (R) | 13,201 | 48.3 |
| 5 | James M. Leach (C) | 12,541 | 52.6 |
| | William L. Scott (R) | 11,302 | 47.4 |
| 6 | Francis E. Shober (C) | 12,474 | 60.0 |
| | Frederick H. Sprague (R) | 8,324 | 40.0 |
| 7 | James C. Harper (C) | 10,967 | 56.7 |
| | Alexander H. Jones (R) | 8,373 | 43.3 |

**Special Elections [1]**

| | | Votes | % |
|---|---|---|---|
| 2 | Joseph Dixon (R) | 14,976 | 54.7 |
| | C. J. O'Hagan (C) | 12,396 | 45.3 |
| 4 | Robert B. Gilliam (C) | 14,014* | 50.8 |
| | Madison Hawkins (R) | 13,556 | 49.2 |
| 4 | John Manning Jr. (C) | 11,797 | 50.7 |
| | Joseph W. Holden (R) | 11,472 | 49.3 |

## OHIO

| | | Votes | % |
|---|---|---|---|
| 1 | Aaron F. Perry (R) | 8,039 | 52.4 |
| | Milton Sayler (D) | 7,294 | 47.6 |
| 2 | Job E. Stevenson (R) | 9,294 | 54.6 |
| | Samuel F. Cary (R) | 7,745 | 45.5 |
| 3 | Lewis D. Campbell (D) | 14,838 | 50.1 |
| | Robert C. Schenck (R) | 14,785 | 49.9 |
| 4 | John F. McKinney (D) | 11,966 | 50.2 |
| | W. B. McClung (R) | 11,741 | 49.3 |
| 5 | Charles L. Lamison (D) | 11,997 | 57.4 |
| | Clark (R) | 8,894 | 42.6 |
| 6 | John A. Smith (R) | 12,063 | 49.8 |
| | J. W. Denver (D) | 11,827 | 48.8 |
| 7 | Samuel Shellabarger (R) | 13,488 | 52.8 |
| | Hugh J. Jewett (D) | 12,060 | 47.2 |
| 8 | John Beatty (R) | 10,610 | 52.0 |
| | James R. Hubbell (D) | 9,450 | 46.3 |
| 9 | Charles Foster (R) | 13,274 | 51.2 |
| | Edward F. Dickinson (D) | 12,498 | 48.2 |
| 10 | Erasmus D. Peck (R) | 11,302 | 52.2 |
| | William F. Lockwood (D) | 10,242 | 47.3 |
| 11 | John T. Wilson (R) | 11,294 | 52.6 |
| | Ralph Leete (D) | 10,189 | 47.4 |
| 12 | Philadelph Van Trump (D) | 14,123 | 57.9 |
| | Charles E. Brown (R) | 10,265 | 42.1 |
| 13 | George W. Morgan (D) | 14,196 | 54.1 |
| | C. W. Potwin (R) | 12,047 | 45.9 |
| 14 | James Monroe (R) | 12,271 | 51.3 |
| | L. R. Critchfield (D) | 11,545 | 48.3 |
| 15 | William P. Sprague (R) | 11,263 | 51.3 |
| | John Cartwright (D) | 10,547 | 48.0 |
| 16 | John A. Bingham (R) | 12,435 | 51.0 |
| | Robert E. Chambers (D) | 11,958 | 49.0 |
| 17 | Jacob A. Ambler (R) | 11,685 | 55.1 |
| | John Ball (D) | 9,514 | 44.9 |
| 18 | William H. Upson (R) | 11,053 | 60.7 |
| | J. M. Coffinberry (D) | 6,695 | 36.8 |
| 19 | James A. Garfield (R) | 13,538 | 65.1 |
| | Howard (D) | 7,263 | 34.9 |

## OREGON

| | | Votes | % |
|---|---|---|---|
| AL | James H. Slater (D) | 11,588 | 50.8 |
| | Joseph G. Wilson (R) | 11,245 | 49.3 |

## PENNSYLVANIA

| | | Votes | % |
|---|---|---|---|
| 1 | Samuel J. Randall (D) | 10,853 | 61.8 |
| | Benjamin Huckell (R) | 6,705 | 38.2 |
| 2 | John V. Creely (D) | 11,059 | 52.2 |
| | Charles O'Neill (R) | 10,134 | 47.8 |
| 3 | Leonard Myers (R) | 9,778 | 53.6 |
| | John Moffet (D) | 8,453 | 46.4 |

1. Rep. John T. Deweese of the 4th district resigned Feb. 28, 1870. In the first special election held to fill the remainder of Deweese's term in the 41st Congress (1869-71), Robert B. Gilliam was elected, but he never claimed the seat. In a second special election, John Manning Jr. was elected and took his seat Dec. 7, 1870.

## PENNSYLVANIA

| Candidates | Votes | % |
|---|---|---|
| 4 William D. Kelley (R) | 14,324 | 55.2 |
| William B. Thomas (D) | 11,622 | 44.8 |
| 5 Alfred C. Harmer (R) | 11,561 | 50.4 |
| John R. Reading (D) | 11,401 | 49.7 |
| 6 Ephraim L. Acker (D) | 12,049 | 52.1 |
| John A. Oliver (R) | 11,072 | 47.9 |
| 7 Washington Townsend (R) | 10,408 | 55.8 |
| J. H. Askin (D) | 8,231 | 44.2 |
| 8 J. Lawrence Getz (D) | 10,411 | 67.4 |
| Nicholas Hunter (D) | 5,045 | 32.6 |
| 9 Oliver J. Dickey (R) | 9,722 | 56.7 |
| A. K. Witmer (D) | 7,411 | 43.3 |
| 10 John W. Killinger (R) | 11,326 | 51.4 |
| Cyrus D. Gloninger (D) | 10,697 | 48.6 |
| 11 John B. Storm (D) | 12,454 | 70.3 |
| William Davis (R) | 5,269 | 29.7 |
| 12 Lazarus D. Shoemaker (R) | 13,279 | 52.4 |
| J. B. McCollum (D) | 12,059 | 47.6 |
| 13 Ulysses Mercur (R) | 11,117 | 50.3 |
| Charles B. Brockway (D) | 10,993 | 49.7 |
| 14 John B. Packer (R) | 13,620 | 54.7 |
| E. G. Scott (D) | 11,266 | 45.3 |
| 15 Richard J. Haldeman (D) | 13,866 | 57.1 |
| William B. Rober (R) | 10,416 | 42.9 |
| 16 Benjamin F. Meyers (D) | 12,859 | 50.0 |
| John Cessna (R) | 12,844 | 50.0 |
| 17 R. Milton Speer (D) | 10,335 | 50.0 |
| Daniel J. Morrell (R) | 10,324 | 50.0 |
| 18 Henry Sherwood (D) | 13,205 | 50.1 |
| William H. Armstrong (R) | 13,178 | 50.0 |
| 19 Glenni W. Scofield (R) | 13,055 | 51.2 |
| Selden Marvin (D) | 12,451 | 48.8 |
| 20 Samuel Griffith (D) | 14,146 | 51.4 |
| Calvin W. Gilfillan (R) | 13,377 | 48.6 |
| 21 Henry D. Foster (D) | 12,399 | 51.5 |
| Andrew Stewart (R) | 11,669 | 48.5 |
| 22 James S. Negley (R) | 11,230 | 54.5 |
| James H. Hopkins (D) | 8,018 | 38.9 |
| Frew (IR) | 1,372 | 6.7 |
| 23 Ebenezer McJunkin (R) | 12,591 | 58.6 |
| William Sirwell (D) | 8,891 | 41.4 |
| 24 William McClelland (D) | 12,264 | 51.6 |
| Joseph B. Donley (R) | 11,505 | 48.4 |

## RHODE ISLAND

| Candidates | Votes | % |
|---|---|---|
| 1 Benjamin T. Eames (R) | 4,952 | 50.9 |
| Thomas A. Jenckes (R) | 1,977 | 20.3 |
| Van Slyck (D) | 1,402 | 14.4 |
| Davis (R) | 1,085 | 11.1 |

| Candidates | Votes | % |
|---|---|---|
| 2 James M. Pendleton (R) | 1,457 | 57.7 |
| Rodman (D) | 941 | 37.2 |

## SOUTH CAROLINA[1]

| Candidates | Votes | % |
|---|---|---|
| 1 Joseph H. Rainey (R) | 20,221 | 63.5 |
| C. W. Dudley (D) | 11,628 | 36.5 |
| 2 Robert C. De Large (IR) | 16,686‡ | 49.6 |
| Christopher C. Bowen (R) | 15,700 | 46.7 |
| 3 Robert B. Elliott (R) | 20,664 | 59.6 |
| John E. Bacon (D) | 13,994 | 40.4 |
| 4 Alexander S. Wallace (R) | 16,746 | 55.3 |
| Isaac G. McKissick (D) | 13,442 | 44.4 |
| AL J. P. M. Epping (R) | 71,803* | 50.0 |
| L. Wimbush (R) | 71,742 | 50.0 |

### Special Election

| Candidates | Votes | % |
|---|---|---|
| 1 Joseph H. Rainey (R) | 20,385 | 86.5 |
| C. W. Dudley (D) | 3,192 | 13.5 |

## TENNESSEE

| Candidates | Votes | % |
|---|---|---|
| 1 Roderick R. Butler (R) | 6,584 | 47.1 |
| James White (R) | 5,979 | 42.7 |
| N. G. Taylor (IR) | 1,432 | 10.2 |
| 2 Horace Maynard (R) | 8,351 | 51.7 |
| A. Blizard (D) | 7,819 | 48.4 |
| 3 Abraham E. Garrett (D) | 9,602 | 69.7 |
| William B. Stokes (R) | 4,168 | 30.3 |
| 4 John M. Bright (D) | 11,827 | 86.5 |
| James Mullins (R) | 1,843 | 13.5 |
| 5 Edward J. Golliday (D) | 7,991 | 59.6 |
| William F. Prosser (R) | 5,428 | 40.5 |
| 6 Washington C. Whitthorne (D) | 9,057 | 76.3 |
| T. J. Cypert (R) | 2,816 | 23.7 |
| 7 Robert P. Caldwell (D) | 8,227 | 81.7 |
| John Norman (R) | 1,848 | 18.3 |
| 8 William W. Vaughan (D) | 13,990 | 72.4 |
| W. J. Smith (R) | 5,346 | 27.7 |

## VERMONT

| Candidates | Votes | % |
|---|---|---|
| 1 Charles W. Willard (R) | 10,476 | 74.0 |
| John Cain (D) | 3,675 | 26.0 |
| 2 Luke P. Poland (R) | 10,479 | 76.6 |
| L. S. Partridge (D) | 3,206 | 23.4 |
| 3 Worthington C. Smith (R) | 9,116 | 75.0 |
| Henry Gillett (D) | 3,047 | 25.1 |

## VIRGINIA [2]

| Candidates | Votes | % |
|---|---|---|
| 1 John Critcher (C) | 10,252 | 46.3 |
| Walter W. Douglas (RAD) | 6,618 | 29.9 |
| Daniel M. Norton (RAD) | 5,293 | 23.9 |
| 2 James H. Platt Jr (RAD) | 15,880 | 59.2 |
| Robert B. Bolling (C) | 10,902 | 40.7 |
| 3 Charles H. Porter (RAD) | 13,555 | 56.0 |
| Albert Ordway (C) | 10,647 | 44.0 |
| 4 William H. H. Stowell (RAD) | 13,205 | 56.9 |
| William L. Owen (C) | 9,989 | 43.1 |
| 5 Richard T. W. Duke (C) | 12,596 | 52.4 |
| Alexander Rives (RAD) | 11,430 | 47.6 |
| 6 John T. Harris | 7,006 | 49.3 |
| Corbin M. Reynolds | 4,591 | 32.3 |
| C. Douglas Gray | 2,626 | 18.5 |
| 7 Elliott M. Braxton (C) | 12,719 | 53.1 |
| Lewis McKenzie (RAD) | 11,203 | 46.8 |
| 8 William Terry (C) | 9,916 | 56.9 |
| Fayette McMullen (I) | 4,017 | 23.0 |
| Robert W. Hughes (RAD) | 3,508 | 20.1 |
| AL Raleigh T. Daniel (C) | 78,437* | 99.6 |

### Special Election

| Candidates | Votes | % |
|---|---|---|
| 5 Richard T. W. Duke (C) | 12,469 | 52.3 |
| Alexander Rives (RAD) | 11,378 | 47.7 |

## WEST VIRGINIA

| Candidates | Votes | % |
|---|---|---|
| 1 John J. Davis (D) | 11,630 | 52.4 |
| Nathan Goff Jr (R) | 10,569 | 47.6 |
| 2 James C. McGrew (R) | 9,011 | 52.7 |
| O. P. Downey (D) | 8,098 | 47.3 |
| 3 Frank Hereford (D) | 8,732 | 54.9 |
| Witcher (R) | 7,189 | 45.2 |

## WISCONSIN

| Candidates | Votes | % |
|---|---|---|
| 1 Alexander Mitchell (D) | 16,558 | 57.5 |
| Lyon (R) | 12,250 | 42.5 |
| 2 Gerry W. Hazelton (R) | 11,467 | 54.5 |
| Cook (D) | 9,568 | 45.5 |
| 3 J. Allen Barber (R) | 11,503 | 58.5 |
| Strachan (D) | 8,157 | 41.5 |
| 4 Charles A. Eldridge (D) | 15,019 | 62.4 |
| Watrous (R) | 9,056 | 37.6 |
| 5 Philetus Sawyer (R) | 17,258 | 59.4 |
| Stringm (D) | 11,822 | 40.7 |
| 6 Jeremiah M. Rusk (R) | 15,042 | 61.3 |
| Meggett (D) | 9,514 | 38.7 |

# 1871 House Elections

## CALIFORNIA

| Candidates | Votes | % |
|---|---|---|
| 1 Sherman O. Houghton (R) | 25,971 | 51.6 |
| L. Archer (D) | 24,374 | 48.4 |
| 2 Aaron A. Sargent (R) | 18,065 | 54.0 |
| J. W. Coffroth (D) | 15,382 | 46.0 |
| 3 John M. Coghlan (R) | 18,503 | 51.7 |
| George Pearce (D) | 17,309 | 48.3 |

## CONNECTICUT

| Candidates | Votes | % |
|---|---|---|
| 1 Julius L. Strong (R) | 11,983 | 50.5 |
| Goodrich (D) | 11,736 | 49.5 |
| 2 Stephen W. Kellogg (R) | 13,784 | 50.0 |
| Kendrick (D) | 13,761 | 50.0 |
| 3 Henry H. Starkweather (R) | 8,937 | 54.5 |
| Stedman (D) | 7,472 | 45.5 |

| Candidates | Votes | % |
|---|---|---|
| 4 William H. Barnum (D) | 13,653 | 52.1 |
| Coffing (R) | 12,577 | 48.0 |

## ILLINOIS

### Special Elections

| Candidates | Votes | % |
|---|---|---|
| 6 Henry Snapp (R) | 9,112 | 57.2 |
| Lorenzo Leland (D) | 6,809 | 42.8 |
| AL John L. Beveridge (R) | 136,879 | 53.9 |
| L. L. Hayes (D) | 116,482 | 45.9 |

## NEW HAMPSHIRE

| Candidates | Votes | % |
|---|---|---|
| 1 Ellery A. Hibbard (D) | 12,444 | 50.3 |
| William B. Small (R) | 12,085 | 48.8 |

| Candidates | Votes | % |
|---|---|---|
| 2 Samuel N. Bell (D) | 11,484 | 51.5 |
| Aaron F. Stevens (R) | 10,635 | 47.7 |
| 3 Hosea W. Parker (D) | 11,170 | 49.5 |
| Simon W. Griffin (R) | 11,038 | 48.9 |

## TEXAS

| Candidates | Votes | % |
|---|---|---|
| 1 William S. Herndon (D) | 16,172 | 58.3 |
| G. W. Whitmore (R) | 11,572 | 41.7 |
| 2 John C. Connor (D) | 18,285 | 75.5 |
| A. M. Bryant (R) | 5,948 | 24.6 |
| 3 De Witt C. Giddings (D) | 23,374‡ | 53.4 |
| William T. Clark (R) | 20,406 | 46.6 |
| 4 John Hancock (D) | 17,010 | 57.4 |
| Edward Degener (R) | 12,636 | 42.6 |

1. South Carolina claimed an extra seat in the House and J. P. M. Epping was elected at-large to fill it. The House refused to seat him. (See South Carolina 1868, p. 1019.)

2. Virginia claimed an extra seat in the House, and Raleigh T. Daniel was elected at-large to fill it. The House refused to seat him. (See Virginia 1869, p. 1019.)

# 1872 House Elections

## ALABAMA

| | Candidates | Votes | % |
|---|---|---|---|
| 1 | Frederick G. Bromberg (LR) | 15,607 | 54.2 |
| | Benjamin S. Turner (R) | 13,174 | 45.8 |
| 2 | James T. Rapier (R) | 19,397 | 54.5 |
| | Oates (LR) | 16,221 | 45.5 |
| 3 | Charles Pelham (R) | 14,957 | 51.0 |
| | William A. Handley (LR) | 14,371 | 49.0 |
| 4 | Charles Hays (R) | 20,333 | 57.4 |
| | Smith (LR) | 15,121 | 42.7 |
| 5 | John H. Caldwell (LR) | 10,544 | 62.6 |
| | Campbell (R) | 6,293 | 37.4 |
| 6 | Joseph H. Sloss (LR) | 9,288 | 66.9 |
| | Parrish (R) | 4,593 | 33.1 |
| AL | Alexander White (R) | 89,480✔ | |
| | Charles C. Sheats (R) | 89,195✔ | |
| | Baker (D) | 81,311 | |
| | Jolly (D) | 81,171 | |

## ARKANSAS

| | | Votes | % |
|---|---|---|---|
| 1 | Lucien C. Gause (D) | 11,591 | 54.1 |
| | Asa Hodges (R) | 9,853✔ | 46.0 |
| 2 | Marcus L. Bell (D) | 13,758 | 52.8 |
| | Oliver P. Snyder (R) | 12,284✔ | 47.2 |
| 3 | Thomas M. Gunter (D) | 12,298‡ | 56.6 |
| | William W. Wilshire (R) | 9,431 | 43.4 |
| AL | William J. Hynes (B-T R) | 40,023 | 50.0 |
| | J. M. Bradley (MR) | 39,586 | 49.4 |

## CALIFORNIA

| | | Votes | % |
|---|---|---|---|
| 1 | Charles Clayton (R) | 11,938 | 52.2 |
| | William A. Piper (LR) | 10,883 | 47.6 |
| 2 | Horace Frank Page (R) | 13,803 | 51.5 |
| | Pasz Coggins (LR) | 12,816 | 47.8 |
| 3 | John K. Luttrell (LR) | 14,032 | 51.7 |
| | J. M. Coghlan (R) | 13,110 | 48.3 |
| 4 | Sherman O. Houghton (R) | 10,396 | 53.2 |
| | E. J. C. Kewen (LR) | 9,030 | 46.2 |

## CONNECTICUT

### Special Election

| | | Votes | % |
|---|---|---|---|
| 1 | Joseph R. Hawley (R) | 13,030 | 51.2 |
| | William W. Eaton (D) | 12,397 | 48.8 |

## DELAWARE

| | | Votes | % |
|---|---|---|---|
| AL | James R. Lofland (R) | 11,377 | 50.8 |
| | Wright (LR) | 11,015 | 49.2 |

## FLORIDA

| | | Votes | % |
|---|---|---|---|
| AL | William J. Purman (R) | 17,537✔ | |
| | Josiah T. Walls (R) | 17,503✔ | |
| | Silas L. Niblack (LR) | 15,881 | |
| | Charles W. Jones (LR) | 15,811 | |

## GEORGIA

| | | Votes | % |
|---|---|---|---|
| 1 | Morgan Rawls (LR) | 8,319‡ | 54.4 |
| | Andrew Sloan (R) | 6,979 | 45.6 |
| 2 | Richard H. Whiteley (R) | 9,616 | 50.2 |
| | G. J. Wright (LR) | 9,530 | 49.8 |
| 3 | Philip Cook (LR) | 6,147 | 57.8 |
| | Brown (R) | 4,490 | 42.2 |
| 4 | Henry R. Harris (LR) | 10,319 | 54.9 |
| | M. Bethune (R) | 8,466 | 45.1 |
| 5 | James C. Freeman (R) | 10,910 | 50.7 |
| | Glenn (LR) | 10,631 | 49.4 |
| 6 | James H. Blount (LR) | 9,993 | 61.7 |
| | Anderson (R) | 6,196 | 38.3 |

| | Candidates | Votes | % |
|---|---|---|---|
| 7 | Pierce M. B. Young (LR) | 8,067 | 64.5 |
| | Dever (R) | 4,443 | 35.5 |
| 8 | Ambrose R. Wright (LR) | 9,697* | 56.3 |
| | Clayton (R) | 6,230 | 36.2 |
| | D. M. Dubose | 1,293 | 7.5 |
| 9 | Hiram P. Bell (LR) | 7,437 | 63.2 |
| | Darrell (R) | 4,325 | 36.8 |

### Special Election

| | | Votes | % |
|---|---|---|---|
| 4 | Erasmus Williams Beck (D) | ✔ | # |

## ILLINOIS

| | | Votes | % |
|---|---|---|---|
| 1 | John B. Rice (R) | 12,870 | 64.0 |
| | Lusien B. Otis (LR) | 7,235 | 36.0 |
| 2 | Jasper D. Ward (R) | 12,182 | 57.9 |
| | Carter Henry Harrison (LR) | 8,873 | 42.1 |
| 3 | Charles B. Farwell (R) | 9,202 | 65.0 |
| | John Valcoulon Lemoyne (LR) | 4,962 | 35.0 |
| 4 | Stephen A. Hurlbut (R) | 15,532 | 75.2 |
| | Seymour G. Bronson (LR) | 5,134 | 24.8 |
| 5 | Horatio C. Burchard (R) | 14,036 | 65.1 |
| | James Dinsmoor (LR) | 7,538 | 34.9 |
| 6 | John B. Hawley (R) | 13,123 | 64.5 |
| | Calvin Truesdale (LR) | 7,216 | 35.5 |
| 7 | Franklin Corwin (R) | 12,404 | 59.9 |
| | G. D. A. Parks (LR) | 8,293 | 40.1 |
| 8 | Greenbury L. Fort (R) | 13,401 | 61.7 |
| | George O. Barnes (LR) | 8,304 | 38.3 |
| 9 | Granville Barrere (R) | 12,600 | 53.9 |
| | N. C. Worthington (LR) | 10,799 | 46.2 |
| 10 | William H. Ray (R) | 12,962 | 52.1 |
| | William H. Neece (LR) | 11,897 | 47.9 |
| 11 | Robert M. Knapp (LR) | 13,818 | 55.2 |
| | Asa C. Matthews (R) | 10,939 | 43.7 |
| 12 | James C. Robinson (LR) | 13,234 | 51.8 |
| | M. N. Chamberlin (R) | 12,311 | 48.2 |
| 13 | John McNulta (R) | 13,490 | 54.7 |
| | Clifton H. Moore (LR) | 10,850 | 44.0 |
| 14 | Joseph G. Cannon (R) | 15,161 | 57.1 |
| | William Nelson (LR) | 11,405 | 42.9 |
| 15 | John R. Eden (LR) | 14,653 | 54.4 |
| | George Hunt (R) | 12,298 | 45.6 |
| 16 | James S. Martin (R) | 12,266 | 50.5 |
| | Silas L. Bryan (LR) | 12,016 | 49.5 |
| 17 | William R. Morrison (LR) | 13,215 | 53.9 |
| | John B. Hay (R) | 11,316 | 46.1 |
| 18 | Isaac Clements (R) | 12,999 | 53.1 |
| | George W. Wall (LR) | 11,478 | 46.9 |
| 19 | Samuel S. Marshall (LR) | 13,297 | 54.1 |
| | Green B. Raum (R) | 11,282 | 45.9 |

## INDIANA

| | | Votes | % |
|---|---|---|---|
| 1 | William E. Niblack (LR) | 19,259 | 50.2 |
| | Heilman (R) | 19,127 | 49.8 |
| 2 | Simeon K. Wolfe (LR) | 19,336 | 58.6 |
| | Voyles (R) | 13,652 | 41.4 |
| 3 | William S. Holman (LR) | 16,367 | 52.1 |
| | Herod (R) | 15,039 | 47.9 |
| 4 | Jeremiah M. Wilson (R) | 14,499 | 50.7 |
| | Gooding (LR) | 14,119 | 49.3 |
| 5 | John Coburn (R) | 18,794 | 51.1 |
| | McNutt (LR) | 18,001 | 48.9 |
| 6 | Morton C. Hunter (R) | 18,792 | 50.9 |
| | Daniel Wolsey Voorhees (LR) | 18,135 | 49.1 |
| 7 | Thomas J. Cason (R) | 17,927 | 50.3 |
| | Mahlon Dickerson Manson (LR) | 17,730 | 49.7 |
| 8 | James M. Tyner (R) | 19,737 | 54.0 |
| | Whiteside (LR) | 16,798 | 46.0 |
| 9 | John E. Neff (LR) | 17,082 | 50.0 |
| | John Peter Cleaver Shanks (R) | 17,058✔ | 50.0 |
| 10 | Henry B. Sayler (R) | 17,334 | 53.4 |
| | Long (LR) | 15,149 | 46.6 |
| 11 | Jaspar Packard (R) | 16,813 | 51.5 |

| | Candidates | Votes | % |
|---|---|---|---|
| | Hendricks (LR) | 15,828 | 48.5 |
| AL | William Williams (R) | 188,762✔ | |
| | Godlove S. Orth (R) | 188,664✔ | |
| | Michael C. Kerr (LR) | 188,502 | |
| | John S. Williams (LR) | 188,227 | |

## IOWA

| | | Votes | % |
|---|---|---|---|
| 1 | George W. McCrary (R) | 15,149 | 58.0 |
| | James M. Shelby (D) | 10,961 | 42.0 |
| 2 | Aylett R. Cotton (R) | 12,521 | 50.4 |
| | William E. Leffingwell (D) | 12,346 | 49.7 |
| 3 | William G. Donnan (R) | 13,654 | 53.7 |
| | John T. Stoneman (D) | 11,774 | 46.3 |
| 4 | Henry O. Pratt (R) | 15,615 | 77.0 |
| | A. T. Lusch (D) | 4,574 | 22.6 |
| 5 | James Wilson (R) | 15,531 | 67.6 |
| | John P. Irish (D) | 7,434 | 32.4 |
| 6 | William Loughridge (R) | 14,638 | 55.4 |
| | H. H. Trimble (D) | 11,703 | 44.3 |
| 7 | John A. Kasson (R) | 14,909 | 65.9 |
| | Q. Palmer (D) | 7,702 | 34.1 |
| 8 | James W. McDill (R) | 12,675 | 64.4 |
| | W. W. Merritt (D) | 6,999 | 35.6 |
| 9 | Jackson Orr (R) | 12,402 | 66.8 |
| | John F. Duncomb (D) | 6,152 | 33.1 |

## KANSAS

| | | Votes | % |
|---|---|---|---|
| AL | David P. Lowe (R) | 67,400✔ | |
| | William A. Phillips (R) | 67,114✔ | |
| | Stephen A. Cobb (R) | 66,345✔ | |
| | Samuel A. Riggs (D) | 34,450 | |
| | R. B. Mitchell (D) | 33,985 | |
| | W. R. Laughlin (D) | 33,264 | |

## KENTUCKY

| | | Votes | % |
|---|---|---|---|
| 1 | Edward Crossland (D) | 10,276 | 64.0 |
| | J. H. Trabue (I) | 2,510 | 15.6 |
| | H. H. Houston | 1,796 | 11.2 |
| | John Martin | 1,473 | 9.2 |
| 2 | John Y. Brown (D) | 10,878 | 95.3 |
| 3 | Charles W. Milliken (D) | 8,796 | 64.3 |
| | Jacob S. Golladay | 4,853 | 35.5 |
| 4 | William B. Read (D) | 8,221 | 92.8 |
| | E. H. Hobson | 548 | 6.2 |
| 5 | Elisha D. Standiford (D) | 11,179 | 68.9 |
| | W. P. Boone | 5,053 | 31.1 |
| 6 | William E. Arthur (D) | 11,424 | 63.5 |
| | Harvey Myers | 6,564 | 36.5 |
| 7 | James B. Beck (D) | 13,978 | 68.9 |
| | S. F. J. Trabue | 6,322 | 31.1 |
| 8 | Milton J. Durham (D) | 10,736 | 51.6 |
| | W. O. Bradley (R) | 10,063 | 48.4 |
| 9 | George M. Adams (D) | 9,683 | 54.2 |
| | A. T. Woods (R) | 8,199 | 45.9 |
| 10 | John D. Young (D) | 9,075 | 50.5 |
| | J. M. Burns (R) | 8,885 | 49.5 |

## LOUISIANA

| | | Votes | % |
|---|---|---|---|
| 1 | J. Hale Sypher (R) | 12,300‡ | 50.2 |
| | Effingham Lawrence (LR) | 12,225 | 49.9 |
| 2 | Lionel A. Sheldon (R) | 17,068 | 52.5 |
| | Randall L. Gibson (LR) | 15,453 | 47.5 |
| 3 | Chester Bidwell Darrall (R) | 14,396 | 53.7 |
| | J. B. Price (LR) | 7,724 | 28.8 |
| | Elbert Gantt (LR) | 4,701 | 17.5 |
| 4 | Samuel Peters (R) | 13,787* | 64.0 |
| | E. C. Davidson (LR) | 7,752 | 36.0 |
| 5 | Frank Morey (R) | 14,060 | 62.1 |
| | G. W. McCraney (LR) | 8,597 | 37.9 |
| AL | George Augustus Sheridan (D) | 64,975 | 55.1 |
| | Pinckney B. S. Pinchback (R) | 53,011 | 44.9 |

## LOUISIANA

### Special Election

| Candidates | Votes | % |
|---|---|---|
| 4 Harry Lott (R) | 13,790 | 64.0 |
| Alexander Boarman (LR) | 7,768 | 36.0 |

## MAINE

| | | |
|---|---|---|
| 1 John H. Burleigh (R) | 15,485 | 53.8 |
| Clifford (D) | 13,216 | 45.9 |
| 2 William P. Frye (R) | 13,540 | 59.1 |
| Alonzo Garcelon (D) | 9,362 | 40.8 |
| 3 James G. Blaine (R) | 15,084 | 56.6 |
| Lang (D) | 11,566 | 43.4 |
| 4 Samuel Hersey (R) | 13,804 | 61.3 |
| Emery (D) | 8,706 | 38.7 |
| 5 Eugene Hale (R) | 14,181 | 55.7 |
| Frederick Augustus Pike (D) | 11,300 | 44.3 |

## MARYLAND

| | | |
|---|---|---|
| 1 Ephraim K. Wilson (LR) | 12,464 | 51.3 |
| Spence (R) | 11,826 | 48.7 |
| 2 Stevenson Archer (LR) | 10,591 | 50.7 |
| Hancock (R) | 10,303 | 49.3 |
| 3 William J. O'Brien (LR) | 9,670 | 53.7 |
| Turner (R) | 8,346 | 46.3 |
| 4 Thomas Swann (LR) | 12,148 | 52.7 |
| Griswold (R) | 10,886 | 47.3 |
| 5 William J. Albert (R) | 11,405 | 52.6 |
| Merrick (LR) | 10,300 | 47.5 |
| 6 Lloyd Lowndes Jr (R) | 14,258 | 53.2 |
| Ritchie (LR) | 12,545 | 46.8 |

## MASSACHUSETTS

| | | |
|---|---|---|
| 1 James Buffinton (R) | 12,448 | 82.6 |
| Joseph M. Day (LR) | 2,609 | 17.3 |
| 2 Benjamin W. Harris (R) | 13,752 | 73.0 |
| Edward Avery (LR) | 5,090 | 27.0 |
| 3 William Whiting (R) | 8,931 | 63.4 |
| Samuel C. Cobb (LR) | 5,139 | 36.5 |
| 4 Samuel Hooper (R) | 8,715 | 58.1 |
| Leopold Morse (LR) | 6,262 | 41.8 |
| 5 Daniel W. Gooch (R) | 12,472 | 60.8 |
| Nathaniel P. Banks (LR) | 8,039 | 39.2 |
| 6 Benjamin F. Butler (R) | 11,881 | 67.2 |
| Charles P. Thompson (LR) | 5,737 | 32.5 |
| 7 Ebenezer R. Hoar (R) | 11,742 | 64.9 |
| John K. Tarbox (LR) | 5,989 | 33.1 |
| 8 John M. S. Williams (R) | 11,929 | 67.2 |
| William W. Warren (LR) | 5,829 | 32.8 |
| 9 George F. Hoar (R) | 12,696 | 71.0 |
| George F. Verry (LR) | 5,012 | 28.0 |
| 10 Alvah Crocker (R) | 14,919 | 76.4 |
| D. W. Bond (LR) | 4,588 | 23.5 |
| 11 Henry L. Dawes (R) | 12,260 | 63.9 |
| John F. Arnold (LR) | 6,927 | 36.1 |

### Special Election

| | | |
|---|---|---|
| 7 Constantine C. Esty (R) | 13,583 | 71.4 |
| George Stevens | 5,274 | 27.7 |

## MICHIGAN

| | | |
|---|---|---|
| 1 Moses W. Field (R) | 11,703 | 53.8 |
| Bagg (D) | 9,843 | 45.3 |
| 2 Henry Waldron (R) | 17,427 | 62.4 |
| Mahan (D) | 10,522 | 37.6 |
| 3 George Willard (R) | 17,822 | 62.6 |
| Parkhurst (D) | 10,275 | 36.1 |
| 4 Julius C. Burrows (R) | 16,717 | 59.3 |
| Potter (D) | 11,451 | 40.6 |
| 5 Wilder Foster (R) | 17,353 | 66.5 |
| McReynolds (D) | 8,744 | 33.5 |
| 6 Josiah W. Begole (R) | 19,486 | 58.0 |
| Baldwin (D) | 13,994 | 41.6 |

| Candidates | Votes | % |
|---|---|---|
| 7 Omar D. Conger (R) | 12,037 | 60.5 |
| Richardson (D) | 7,790 | 39.2 |
| 8 Nathan B. Bradley (R) | 11,333 | 58.0 |
| Wisner (D) | 7,995 | 40.9 |
| 9 Jay A. Hubbell (R) | 11,951 | 68.3 |
| Ely (D) | 5,546 | 31.7 |

## MINNESOTA

| | | |
|---|---|---|
| 1 Mark H. Dunnell (R) | 20,806 | 65.6 |
| M. S. Wilkinson (D) | 10,901 | 34.4 |
| 2 Horace B. Strait (R) | 15,712 | 57.4 |
| C. C. Graham (D) | 11,668 | 42.6 |
| 3 John T. Averill (R) | 19,663 | 60.7 |
| G. L. Becker (D) | 12,712 | 39.3 |

## MISSISSIPPI

| | | |
|---|---|---|
| 1 Lucius Q. C. Lamar (LR) | 9,679 | 66.2 |
| Flournoy (R) | 4,954 | 33.9 |
| 2 Albert R. Howe (R) | 14,831 | 64.4 |
| Alcorn (LR) | 8,216 | 35.7 |
| 3 Henry W. Barry (R) | 15,047 | 70.0 |
| Bolding (LR) | 6,440 | 30.0 |
| 4 Jason R. Niles (R) | 15,795 | 69.7 |
| 5 George C. McKee (R) | 14,817 | 64.7 |
| Shelby (LR) | 8,073 | 35.3 |
| 6 John R. Lynch (R) | 15,101 | 64.0 |
| Cassidy (LR) | 8,509 | 36.0 |

## MISSOURI

| | | |
|---|---|---|
| 1 Edwin O. Stanard (R) | 5,271 | 50.7 |
| Grosvenor (R) | 5,129 | 49.3 |
| 2 Erastus Wells (LR) | 8,268 | 58.7 |
| Bryton (R) | 5,807 | 41.3 |
| 3 William H. Stone (LR) | 5,197 | 51.7 |
| Hilton (R) | 4,859 | 48.3 |
| 4 Robert A. Hatcher (LR) | 13,340 | 74.4 |
| Ward (R) | 4,594 | 25.6 |
| 5 Richard P. Bland (LR) | 9,974 | 53.1 |
| Seay (R) | 8,820 | 46.9 |
| 6 Harrison E. Havens (R) | 13,156 | 51.1 |
| McAffee (LR) | 12,578 | 48.9 |
| 7 Thomas T. Crittenden (LR) | 16,341 | 52.5 |
| Burdett (R) | 14,770 | 47.5 |
| 8 Abram Comingo (LR) | 13,235 | 64.4 |
| Twichell (R) | 7,317 | 35.6 |
| 9 Isaac C. Parker (R) | 12,136 | 50.2 |
| Pike (LR) | 12,053 | 49.8 |
| 10 Ira B. Hyde (R) | 13,953 | 53.1 |
| Mansur (LR) | 12,318 | 46.9 |
| 11 John B. Clark Jr. (LR) | 17,341 | 67.7 |
| Demotte (R) | 8,280 | 32.3 |
| 12 John M. Glover (LR) | 13,006 | 54.9 |
| Benjamin (R) | 10,672 | 45.1 |
| 13 Aylett H. Buckner (LR) | 16,249 | 67.8 |
| Flagg (R) | 7,710 | 32.2 |

## NEBRASKA

| | | |
|---|---|---|
| AL Lorenzo Crounse (R) | 17,124 | 62.2 |
| Warner (LR) | 10,412 | 37.8 |

## NEVADA

| | | |
|---|---|---|
| AL Charles W. Kendall (D) | 7,847 | 52.3 |
| C. C. Goodwin | 7,146 | 47.7 |

## NEW JERSEY

| | | |
|---|---|---|
| 1 John W. Hazleton (R) | 15,312 | 63.1 |
| Clute (D) | 8,948 | 36.9 |
| 2 Samuel A. Dobbins (R) | 14,192 | 54.6 |
| Forker (LR) | 11,787 | 45.4 |

| Candidates | Votes | % |
|---|---|---|
| 3 Amos Clark Jr (R) | 14,794 | 54.0 |
| Patterson (LR) | 12,618 | 46.0 |
| 4 Robert Hamilton (LR) | 13,458 | 55.0 |
| Potts (R) | 10,994 | 45.0 |
| 5 William W. Phelps (R) | 12,701 | 56.0 |
| Woodruff (LR) | 9,986 | 44.0 |
| 6 Marcus L. Ward (R) | 16,061 | 60.7 |
| Randall (LR) | 10,403 | 39.3 |
| 7 Isaac W. Scudder (R) | 10,377 | 53.3 |
| Taylor (LR) | 9,108 | 46.7 |

## NEW YORK

| | | |
|---|---|---|
| 1 Henry J. Scudder (R) | 13,877 | 54.1 |
| Covert (LR) | 11,797 | 46.0 |
| 2 John G. Schumaker (LR) | 13,345 | 58.7 |
| Perry (R) | 8,378 | 36.8 |
| 3 Stewart L. Woodford (R) | 15,177 | 56.9 |
| Goodrich (LR) | 11,506 | 43.1 |
| 4 Philip S. Crooke (R) | 11,012 | 51.9 |
| Colahan (LR) | 10,202 | 48.1 |
| 5 William R. Roberts (LR) | 20,281 | 79.1 |
| Matthew Stewart (R) | 5,356 | 20.9 |
| 6 James Brooks (LR) | 16,645 | 76.9 |
| Adolph G. Dunn (R) | 5,005 | 23.1 |
| 7 Thomas J. Creamer (LR) | 10,012 | 54.7 |
| Conrad Geib (R) | 8,279 | 45.3 |
| 8 John D. Lawson (R) | 13,305 | 58.6 |
| Charles P. Shaw (LR) | 9,395 | 41.4 |
| 9 David B. Mellish (R) | 7,841 | 37.8 |
| John Hardy (APOLLO) | 7,068 | 34.1 |
| Michael Connolly (LR) | 5,847 | 28.2 |
| 10 Fernando Wood (LR) | 10,526 | 52.2 |
| William A. Darling (R) | 9,641 | 47.8 |
| 11 Clarkson N. Potter (LR) | 15,204 | 51.7 |
| Flagg (R) | 14,179 | 48.3 |
| 12 Charles St.John (R) | 11,842 | 51.1 |
| Horton (LR) | 11,318 | 48.9 |
| 13 John O. Whitehouse (LR) | 14,859 | 51.6 |
| Ketchim (R) | 13,932 | 48.4 |
| 14 David M. De Witt (LR) | 12,031 | 50.0 |
| Maxwell (R) | 12,014 | 50.0 |
| 15 Eli Perry (LR) | 18,676 | 51.6 |
| Adams (R) | 17,538 | 48.4 |
| 16 James S. Smart (R) | 17,835 | 57.2 |
| Thayer (LR) | 13,352 | 42.8 |
| 17 Robert S. Hale (R) | 11,025 | 57.4 |
| Heaton (LR) | 8,174 | 42.6 |
| 18 William A. Wheeler (R) | 14,725 | 69.2 |
| Cantwell (LR) | 6,565 | 30.8 |
| 19 Henry H. Hathorn (R) | 17,762 | 54.6 |
| Judson (LR) | 14,756 | 45.4 |
| 20 David Wilbur (R) | 17,368 | 53.4 |
| Sturges (LR) | 15,171 | 46.6 |
| 21 Clinton L. Merriam (R) | 17,337 | 56.7 |
| Brockway (LR) | 13,220 | 43.3 |
| 22 Ellis H. Roberts (R) | 13,284 | 55.9 |
| Sherman (LR) | 10,481 | 44.1 |
| 23 William E. Lansing (R) | 15,410 | 58.7 |
| Foster (LR) | 10,841 | 41.3 |
| 24 R. Holland Duell (R) | 15,457 | 53.8 |
| Hiscock (LR) | 13,289 | 46.2 |
| 25 Clinton D. MacDougall (R) | 16,486 | 57.2 |
| Graves (LR) | 12,325 | 42.8 |
| 26 William H. Lamport (R) | 12,886 | 57.0 |
| White (LR) | 9,730 | 43.0 |
| 27 Thomas C. Platt (R) | 16,603 | 55.3 |
| Goodrich (LR) | 13,406 | 44.7 |
| 28 Horace Boardman Smith (R) | 18,738 | 56.8 |
| Hayt (LR) | 14,262 | 43.2 |
| 29 Freeman Clarke (R) | 16,342 | 56.7 |
| Gordon (LR) | 12,470 | 43.3 |
| 30 George G. Hoskins (R) | 13,233 | 58.0 |
| Southworth (LR) | 9,599 | 42.0 |
| 31 Lyman K. Bass (R) | 17,929 | 58.3 |
| Williams (LR) | 12,813 | 41.7 |
| 32 Walter L. Sessions (R) | 12,922 | 57.4 |
| Murray (LR) | 9,573 | 42.6 |
| AL Lyman Tremain (R) | 438,396 | 52.2 |
| Samuel S. Cox (LR) | 400,797 | 47.8 |

## NORTH CAROLINA

| | Candidates | Votes | % |
|---|---|---|---|
| 1 | Clinton L. Cobb (R) | 13,522 | 52.8 |
| | David M. Carter (D) | 12,101 | 47.2 |
| 2 | Charles R. Thomas (R) | 20,072 | 63.3 |
| | William H. Kitchen (D) | 11,627 | 36.7 |
| 3 | Alfred M. Waddell (D) | 14,286 | 52.7 |
| | Neil McKay (R) | 12,848 | 47.4 |
| 4 | William A. Smith (R) | 13,879 | 51.4 |
| | Sion H. Rogers (D) | 13,147 | 48.7 |
| 5 | James M. Leach (D) | 10,755 | 50.6 |
| | Thomas Settle (R) | 10,497 | 49.4 |
| 6 | Thomas S. Ashe (D) | 12,700 | 54.6 |
| | Oliver H. Dockery (R) | 10,561 | 45.4 |
| 7 | William M. Robbins (D) | 10,072 | 54.4 |
| | David M. Furches (R) | 8,459 | 45.7 |
| 8 | Robert B. Vance (D) | 11,038 | 55.5 |
| | William G. Candler (R) | 8,853 | 44.5 |

## OHIO

| | Candidates | Votes | % |
|---|---|---|---|
| 1 | Milton Sayler (D) | 12,474 | 58.4 |
| | Benjamin Eggleston (R) | 8,905 | 41.7 |
| 2 | Henry B. Banning (D) | 11,034 | 53.7 |
| | Rutherford B. Hayes (R) | 9,532 | 46.4 |
| 3 | John Q. Smith (R) | 14,929 | 52.1 |
| | John W. Sohn (D) | 13,700 | 47.8 |
| 4 | Lewis B. Gunckel (R) | 16,604 | 52.9 |
| | J. J. Winans (D) | 14,677 | 46.8 |
| 5 | Charles N. Lamison (D) | 15,530 | 60.3 |
| | Samuel Lybrand (R) | 10,224 | 39.7 |
| 6 | Isaac R. Sherwood (R) | 13,471 | 51.9 |
| | F. H. Hurd (D) | 12,406 | 47.8 |
| 7 | Lawrence T. Neal (D) | 13,379 | 52.5 |
| | John T. Wilson (R) | 12,106 | 47.5 |
| 8 | William Lawrence (R) | 14,748 | 57.8 |
| | J. J. Musson (D) | 10,705 | 41.9 |
| 9 | James W. Robinson (R) | 13,573 | 50.4 |
| | George W. Morgan (D) | 13,146 | 48.8 |
| 10 | Charles Foster (R) | 14,997 | 51.0 |
| | Rush R. Sloane (D) | 14,271 | 48.6 |
| 11 | Hezekiah S. Bundy (R) | 13,267 | 56.2 |
| | Samuel A. Nash (D) | 10,360 | 43.9 |
| 12 | Hugh J. Jewett (D) | 15,613 | 58.5 |
| | James Taylor (R) | 10,936 | 41.0 |
| 13 | Milton I. Southard (D) | 15,109 | 54.5 |
| | Lucius P. Marsh (R) | 12,638 | 45.6 |
| 14 | John Berry (D) | 13,668 | 57.8 |
| | Thomas E. Douglass (R) | 9,925 | 42.0 |
| 15 | William P. Sprague (R) | 12,987 | 51.9 |
| | Richard R. Hudson (D) | 11,996 | 47.9 |
| 16 | Lorenzo Danford (R) | 14,350 | 56.3 |
| | C. L. Poorman (D) | 11,052 | 43.4 |
| 17 | Laurin D. Woodworth (R) | 15,368 | 54.0 |
| | Richard Brown (D) | 13,106 | 46.0 |
| 18 | James Monroe (R) | 14,662 | 58.6 |
| | N. S. Townshend (D) | 10,298 | 41.2 |
| 19 | James A. Garfield (R) | 19,189 | 69.4 |
| | M. Sutliff (D) | 8,254 | 29.9 |
| 20 | Richard C. Parsons (R) | 13,101 | 55.4 |
| | Selah Chamberlain (D) | 10,377 | 43.9 |

## OREGON

| | Candidates | Votes | % |
|---|---|---|---|
| AL | Joseph G. Wilson (R) | 13,168 | 51.7 |
| | John Burnett (D) | 12,317 | 48.3 |

## PENNSYLVANIA

| | Candidates | Votes | % |
|---|---|---|---|
| 1 | Samuel J. Randall (LR) | 10,133 | 53.4 |
| | Houst (R) | 8,845 | 46.6 |
| 2 | Charles O'Neill (R) | 17,253 | 63.9 |
| | Morris (LR) | 9,728 | 36.1 |
| 3 | Leonard Meyers (R) | 15,429 | 59.4 |
| | Vogelbach (LR) | 10,530 | 40.6 |
| 4 | William D. Kelley (R) | 20,955 | 61.2 |
| | Mitchell (LR) | 13,301 | 38.8 |
| 5 | Alfred C. Harmer (R) | 14,743 | 55.1 |
| | Phillips (LR) | 12,040 | 45.0 |
| 6 | James S. Biery (R) | 13,906 | 55.0 |
| | Witte (LR) | 11,400 | 45.1 |

| | Candidates | Votes | % |
|---|---|---|---|
| 7 | Washington Townsend (R) | 14,011 | 61.4 |
| | Taylor (LR) | 8,819 | 38.6 |
| 8 | Heister Clymer (LR) | 13,854 | 64.0 |
| | Millhol (R) | 7,783 | 36.0 |
| 9 | A. Herr Smith (R) | 14,501 | 63.0 |
| | North (LR) | 8,526 | 37.0 |
| 10 | John W. Killinger (R) | 14,419 | 56.6 |
| | Rielly (LR) | 11,049 | 43.4 |
| 11 | John B. Storm (LR) | 16,808 | 61.4 |
| | Howell (R) | 10,569 | 38.6 |
| 12 | Lazarus D. Shoemaker (R) | 17,551 | 51.1 |
| | Woodward (LR) | 16,811 | 48.9 |
| 13 | James D. Strawbridge (R) | 13,079 | 51.7 |
| | Rhodes (LR) | 12,243 | 48.4 |
| 14 | John B. Packer (R) | 17,545 | 56.5 |
| | Rutherford (LR) | 13,486 | 43.5 |
| 15 | John A. Magee (LR) | 15,358 | 53.2 |
| | Sponsler (R) | 13,532 | 46.8 |
| 16 | John Cessna (R) | 14,383 | 52.4 |
| | Meyers (LR) | 13,067 | 47.6 |
| 17 | R. Milton Speer (LR) | 12,011 | 51.3 |
| | Barker (R) | 11,422 | 48.7 |
| 18 | Sobieski Ross (R) | 17,041 | 53.8 |
| | Henry Sherwood (LR) | 14,627 | 46.2 |
| 19 | Carlton B. Curtis (R) | 17,742 | 52.2 |
| | Kane (LR) | 16,238 | 47.8 |
| 20 | Hiram Richmond (R) | 20,704 | 52.6 |
| | Samuel Griffith (LR) | 18,627 | 47.4 |
| 21 | Alexander W. Taylor (R) | 13,980 | 51.3 |
| | Foster (LR) | 13,289 | 48.7 |
| 22 | James S. Negley (R) | 17,248 | 61.2 |
| | King (LR) | 10,930 | 38.8 |
| 23 | Ebenezer McJunkin (R) | 17,431 | 60.7 |
| | Johnston (LR) | 11,306 | 39.3 |
| 24 | William S. Moore (R) | 14,195 | 51.9 |
| | McClelland (LR) | 13,169 | 48.1 |
| AL | Glenni W. Scofield (R) | 358,013 | 53.3 |
| | E. B. Wright (LR) | 314,014 | 46.7 |
| AL | Charles Albright (R) | 360,546 | 53.7 |
| | Richard Vaux (LR) | 311,036 | 46.3 |
| AL | Lemuel Todd (R) | 357,743 | 53.3 |
| | J. H. Hopkins (LR) | 313,534 | 46.7 |

### Special Election

| | Candidates | Votes | % |
|---|---|---|---|
| 13 | Frank Charles Bunnell (R) | 6,000✔ | # |
| | Piolett (D) | 5,001 | # |

## SOUTH CAROLINA

| | Candidates | Votes | % |
|---|---|---|---|
| 1 | Joseph H. Rainey (R) | 19,765 | 100.0 |
| 2 | Alonzo J. Ransier (R) | 20,061 | 75.4 |
| | William Gurney (D) | 6,549 | 24.6 |
| 3 | Robert B. Elliott (R) | 21,627 | 92.8 |
| 4 | Alexander S. Wallace (R) | 14,590 | 53.1 |
| | B. F. Perry (D) | 12,879 | 46.9 |
| AL | Richard H. Cain (R) | 68,825 | 71.2 |
| | L. E. Johnson (ID) | 26,394 | 27.3 |

## TENNESSEE

| | Candidates | Votes | % |
|---|---|---|---|
| 1 | Roderick R. Butler (R) | 10,289 | 56.7 |
| | Carter (LR) | 7,849 | 43.3 |
| 2 | Jacob M. Thornburgh (R) | 10,015 | 55.7 |
| | Caldwell (LR) | 5,403 | 30.1 |
| | Garrett (I) | 2,563 | 14.3 |
| 3 | William Crutchfield (R) | 10,041 | 52.8 |
| | Key (LR) | 8,960 | 47.2 |
| 4 | John M. Bright (LR) | 12,585 | 69.8 |
| | Steele (R) | 5,442 | 30.2 |
| 5 | Horace H. Harrison (R) | 10,033 | 42.1 |
| | Gellad (LR) | 8,131 | 34.1 |
| | Brien (I) | 5,684 | 23.8 |
| 6 | Washington C. Whitthorne (LR) | 9,058 | 53.9 |
| | Gibbs (R) | 6,849 | 40.7 |
| | Morris (I) | 903 | 5.4 |
| 7 | John D. C. Atkins (LR) | 11,411 | 55.6 |
| | Murray (R) | 7,734 | 37.7 |
| | Travis (I) | 1,369 | 6.7 |
| 8 | David A. Nunn (R) | 7,580 | 37.9 |
| | Campbell (LR) | 5,967 | 29.8 |

| | Candidates | Votes | % |
|---|---|---|---|
| | Caldw (I) | 4,476 | 22.4 |
| | Beel (I) | 1,979 | 9.9 |
| 9 | Barbour Lewis (R) | 13,784 | 56.7 |
| | Haynes (LR) | 10,541 | 43.3 |
| AL | Horace Maynard (R) | 80,825 | 44.0 |
| | Benjamin F. Cheatham (LR) | 65,188 | 35.5 |
| | Andrew Johnson (I) | 37,900 | 20.6 |

## TEXAS

| | Candidates | Votes | % |
|---|---|---|---|
| 1 | William S. Herndon (D) | 13,417 | 57.1 |
| | R. K. Smith | 8,780 | 37.4 |
| | William Chambers | 1,261 | 5.4 |
| 2 | William P. McLean (D) | 15,924 | 73.9 |
| | F. W. Minor | 5,617 | 26.1 |
| 3 | De Witt C. Giddings (D) | 20,464 | 51.5 |
| | A. J. Evans | 19,287 | 48.5 |
| 4 | John Hancock (D) | 18,172 | 61.7 |
| | W. O. Hutchinson | 11,281 | 38.3 |
| AL | Asa H. Willie (D) | 69,085✔ | |
| | Roger Q. Mills (D) | 68,936✔ | |
| | Evans (R) | 47,096 | |
| | Norton (R) | 47,075 | |

## VERMONT

| | Candidates | Votes | % |
|---|---|---|---|
| 1 | Charles W. Willard (R) | 14,061 | 79.5 |
| | Heaton (LR) | 3,618 | 20.5 |
| 2 | Luke P. Poland (R) | 11,070 | 65.3 |
| | Steele (LR) | 2,929 | 17.3 |
| | J. M. Pierce (I) | 2,554 | 15.1 |
| 3 | George W. Hendee (R) | 11,473 | 78.3 |
| | Adams (LR) | 3,182 | 21.7 |

## VIRGINIA

| | Candidates | Votes | % |
|---|---|---|---|
| 1 | James B. Sener (R) | 10,685 | 50.9 |
| | E. M. Braxton (CD) | 10,312 | 49.1 |
| 2 | James H. Platt Jr (R) | 15,554 | 59.9 |
| | Baker R. Lee (CD) | 10,339 | 39.8 |
| 3 | J. Ambler Smith (R) | 13,082 | 51.1 |
| | George D. Wise (CD) | 12,514 | 48.9 |
| 4 | William H. H. Stowell (R) | 15,393 | 65.6 |
| | P. W. McKinney (CD) | 8,068 | 34.4 |
| 5 | Alexander M. Davis (R) | 9,175‡ | 50.5 |
| | Christopher Y. Thomas (CD) | 8,975 | 49.4 |
| 6 | Thomas Whitehead (CD) | 11,401 | 51.3 |
| | J. Foote Johnson (I) | 10,779 | 48.5 |
| 7 | John T. Harris (CD) | 10,894 | 61.8 |
| | C. T. O. Ferrall (I) | 6,738 | 38.2 |
| 8 | Eppa Hunton (CD) | 11,782 | 56.2 |
| | Edward Daniels (R) | 9,178 | 43.8 |
| 9 | Rees T. Bowen (CD) | 10,352 | 66.1 |
| | Robert W. Hughes (R) | 5,304 | 33.9 |

## WEST VIRGINIA

| | Candidates | Votes | % |
|---|---|---|---|
| 1 | Benjamin Wilson (D) | 8,054 | 52.4 |
| | John J. Davis (D) | 7,317✔ | 47.6 |
| 2 | John M. Hagans (R) | 3,441 | 82.3 |
| | Alexander R. Boteler (R) | 387 | 9.3 |
| | Ward Lamar | 255 | 6.1 |
| 3 | Frank Hereford (D) | 11,417 | 80.5 |
| | J. B. Walker (R) | 2,769 | 19.5 |

## WISCONSIN

| | Candidates | Votes | % |
|---|---|---|---|
| 1 | Charles G. Williams (R) | 15,666 | 62.6 |
| | Sloan (D) | 9,380 | 37.5 |
| 2 | Gerry W. Hazelton (R) | 13,408 | 53.2 |
| | Smith (D) | 11,784 | 46.8 |
| 3 | J. Allen Barber (R) | 13,745 | 58.2 |
| | Warden (D) | 9,880 | 41.8 |
| 4 | Alexander Mitchell (D) | 13,281 | 65.1 |
| | Winkler (R) | 7,120 | 34.9 |
| 5 | Charles A. Eldridge (D) | 15,587 | 55.5 |
| | Baetz (R) | 12,507 | 44.5 |

## WISCONSIN

| Candidates | Votes | % | Candidates | Votes | % | Candidates | Votes | % |
|---|---|---|---|---|---|---|---|---|
| 6 Philetus Sawyer (R) | 15,803 | 56.1 | 7 Jeremiah M. Rusk (R) | 16,183 | 65.4 | 8 Alexander S. McDill (R) | 10,711 | 59.7 |
| Lindsley (D) | 12,358 | 43.9 | Marston (D) | 8,547 | 34.6 | Carson (D) | 7,238 | 40.3 |

# 1873 House Elections

## CONNECTICUT

| | Votes | % |
|---|---|---|
| 1 Joseph R. Hawley (R) | 12,030 | 52.8 |
| Kendall (D) | 10,764 | 47.2 |
| 2 Stephen W. Kellogg (R) | 12,761 | 51.2 |
| English (D) | 12,173 | 48.8 |
| 3 Henry H. Starkweather (R) | 7,764 | 56.4 |
| Bill (D) | 6,000 | 43.6 |
| 4 William H. Barnum (D) | 12,561 | 53.8 |
| Miner (R) | 10,797 | 46.2 |

## LOUISIANA

| | | |
|---|---|---|
| 4 George Luke Smith (D) | ✔ # | |

## MICHIGAN

### Special Election

| | Votes | % |
|---|---|---|
| 5 William B. Williams (R) | 6,598 | 50.4 |
| Comstock (D) | 6,484 | 49.6 |

## NEW HAMPSHIRE

| | Votes | % |
|---|---|---|
| 1 William B. Small (R) | 12,103 | 49.8 |
| Hibbard (D) | 11,725 | 48.2 |
| 2 Austin F. Pike (R) | 10,780 | 49.3 |
| Bell (D) | 10,773 | 49.3 |
| 3 Hosea W. Parker (D) | 10,633 | 49.9 |
| Griffin (R) | 10,295 | 48.3 |

## OREGON

### Special Election

| | Votes | % |
|---|---|---|
| AL James W. Nesmith (D) | 8,194 | 57.2 |
| Smith (R) | 6,123 | 42.8 |

## RHODE ISLAND

| | Votes | % |
|---|---|---|
| 1 Benjamin T. Eames (R) | 8,977 | 74.0 |
| Thomas Davis (D) | 3,138 | 25.9 |
| 2 James M. Pendleton (R) | 4,310 | 63.2 |
| George H. Browne (D) | 2,505 | 36.8 |

# Explanation of Symbols in House Returns

In the returns for House elections *symbols* are used to denote special circumstances. In cases where no symbol is used, the candidate who received the most votes won the election to the House. The following is a key to the symbols used:

✔ Elected to the House. The symbol is used to identify winning candidates in three types of situations: (1) When candidates ran for two or more at-large seats in states which chose all of their at-large representatives in a single election, or ran in a multi-member district; (2) when the vote total and percentage of one or more of the candidates are unavailable and (3) when a candidate who did not receive the highest vote total was seated by the House. *(Explanation of multi-member districts, see p. 916.)*

‡ The symbol is used when an election dispute resulted in the unseating of a representative *after* he was sworn in. *(For discussion of specific cases, consult the* Biographical Directory of the United States Congress, 1774-1989, *U.S. Government Printing Office, Washington, D.C., 1989; hereafter referred to as the* Biographical Directory.*)*

* The symbol is used for three types of situations: (1) When a representative-elect died or declined his seat before the constitutionally set date for the beginning of his term—March 4 until 1935, and Jan. 3 thereafter; (2) when the House refused to seat any candidate claiming election to a seat and (3) when state law required a candidate to obtain a popular vote majority for election to the House, but the candidate receiving the most votes failed to receive a majority. *(For discussion of specific cases, consult the* Biographical Directory; *explanation of majority vote requirement, see p. 945.)*

# Information for 1824-1973 returns was obtained from a source other than the Inter-University Consortium for Political and Social Research. *(For a listing of other sources, see p. 1327.)*

**Footnotes.** Numbered footnotes are used to explain unusual situations, such as a series of elections in the same year in the same House district, anomalies resulting from reapportionment and special procedures for conducting House elections in certain states.

# 1874 House Elections

## ALABAMA

| Candidates | Votes | % |
|---|---|---|
| 1 Jeremiah Haralson (R) | 19,545 | 53.6 |
| Frederick G. Bromberg (D) | 16,953 | 46.5 |
| 2 Jeremiah N. Williams (D) | 20,180 | 51.3 |
| James T. Rapier (R) | 19,124 | 48.7 |
| 3 Taul Bradford (D) | 19,424 | 58.0 |
| Betts (R) | 14,076 | 42.0 |
| 4 Charles Hays (R) | 23,900 | 56.5 |
| Jones (D) | 18,378 | 43.5 |
| 5 John H. Caldwell (D) | 13,011 | 59.2 |
| Sheffield (R) | 8,969 | 40.8 |
| 6 Goldsmith W. Hewitt (D) | 15,048 | 62.1 |
| Joseph H. Sloss (R) | 9,172 | 37.9 |
| AL Burwell B. Lewis (D) | 106,023 | 54.1 |
| Hristopher C. Sheets (R) | 89,909 | 46.0 |
| AL William H. Forney (D) | 106,080 | 54.0 |
| Alexander White (R) | 89,909 | 46.0 |

## ARKANSAS

| Candidates | Votes | % |
|---|---|---|
| 1 Lucien C. Gause (C) | 9,211 | 64.0 |
| Rogers (R) | 5,183 | 36.0 |
| 2 William F. Slemmons (C) | 12,166 | 53.7 |
| Clayton (R) | 10,485 | 46.3 |
| 3 William W. Wilshire (C) | 11,733 | 65.0 |
| Hynes (R) | 6,328 | 35.0 |
| 4 Thomas M. Gunter (C) | 7,828 | 90.8 |
| Lander (R) | 791 | 9.2 |

## DELAWARE

| Candidates | Votes | % |
|---|---|---|
| AL James Williams (D) | 12,602 | 53.3 |
| James R. Lofland (R) | 11,024 | 46.7 |

## FLORIDA

| Candidates | Votes | % |
|---|---|---|
| 1 William J. Purman (R) | 10,052 | 51.7 |
| Henderson (D) | 9,377 | 48.3 |
| 2 Josiah T. Walls (R) | 8,557‡ | 51.1 |
| Jesse J. Finley (D) | 8,178 | 48.9 |

## GEORGIA

| Candidates | Votes | % |
|---|---|---|
| 1 Julian Hartridge (D) | 11,252 | 59.4 |
| Bryant (R) | 6,714 | 35.5 |
| John Wimberley (IR) | 974 | 5.1 |
| 2 William E. Smith (D) | 12,098 | 55.3 |
| Whiteley (R) | 9,789 | 44.7 |
| 3 Philip Cook (D) | 8,677 | 67.4 |
| Brown (R) | 4,199 | 32.6 |
| 4 Henry R. Harris (D) | 9,230 | 100.0 |
| 5 Milton A. Candler (D) | 12,450 | 66.5 |
| Mills (R) | 6,273 | 33.5 |
| 6 James H. Blount (D) | 10,007 | 78.4 |
| Gove (R) | 2,756 | 21.6 |
| 7 William H. Felton (I) | 7,587 | 49.6 |
| William H. Dabney (D) | 7,505 | 49.1 |
| 8 Alexander H. Stephens (D) | 6,822 | 99.8 |
| 9 Garnett McMillan (D) | 7,885* | 77.3 |
| O'Neal (R) | 2,318 | 22.7 |

## ILLINOIS

| Candidates | Votes | % |
|---|---|---|
| 1 Bernard G. Caulfield (D) | 10,211 | 51.0 |
| Sidney Smith (R) | 9,803 | 49.0 |
| 2 Carter H. Harrison (D) | 9,189 | 49.2 |
| Jasper D. Ward (R) | 9,181 | 49.1 |
| 3 Charles B. Farwell (R) | 8,177‡ | 50.1 |
| John V. Le Moyne (D) | 7,991 | 49.0 |
| 4 Stephen A. Hurlbut (R) | 9,326 | 53.3 |
| John F. Farnsworth (D) | 8,167 | 46.7 |
| 5 Horatio C. Burchard (R) | 9,232 | 56.8 |
| David J. Pinkney (D) | 7,008 | 43.1 |

| Candidates | Votes | % |
|---|---|---|
| 6 Thomas J. Henderson (R) | 9,390 | 59.8 |
| Isaac H. Elliott (D) | 6,299 | 40.1 |
| 7 Alexander Campbell (D) | 10,308 | 56.6 |
| Franklin Corwin (R) | 7,905 | 43.4 |
| 8 Greenbury L. Fort (R) | 8,753 | 53.9 |
| J. G. Bayne (D) | 7,463 | 45.9 |
| 9 Richard H. Whiting (R) | 9,755 | 50.7 |
| Leonard F. Ross (D) | 9,495 | 49.3 |
| 10 John C. Bagby (D) | 9,784 | 52.6 |
| Henderson Richey (R) | 8,824 | 47.4 |
| 11 Scott Wike (D) | 11,489 | 59.2 |
| David Beatty (R) | 7,429 | 38.3 |
| 12 William M. Springer (D) | 10,623 | 48.1 |
| Andrew Simpson (R) | 9,027 | 40.9 |
| J. B. Turner (IR) | 2,417 | 11.0 |
| 13 Adlai E. Stevenson (D) | 11,135 | 52.6 |
| John McNulta (R) | 9,903 | 46.8 |
| 14 Joseph G. Cannon (R) | 11,244 | 51.5 |
| James H. Pickrell (D) | 10,603 | 48.5 |
| 15 John R. Eden (D) | 12,084 | 52.8 |
| Jacob W. Wilkin (R) | 10,789 | 47.2 |
| 16 William A. J. Sparks (D) | 8,723 | 42.2 |
| James S. Martin (R) | 7,932 | 38.4 |
| Rolla B. Henry (IR) | 4,023 | 19.5 |
| 17 William R. Morrison (D) | 13,086 | 60.8 |
| John I. Rinaker (R) | 8,438 | 39.2 |
| 18 William Hartzell (D) | 10,866 | 53.9 |
| Isaac Clements (R) | 9,280 | 46.1 |
| 19 William B. Anderson (ID) | 8,293 | 38.9 |
| Samuel S. Marshall (D) | 7,556 | 35.4 |
| Green B. Rainn (R) | 5,486 | 25.7 |

## INDIANA

| Candidates | Votes | % |
|---|---|---|
| 1 Benoni S. Fuller (D) | 12,864 | 50.7 |
| Heilman (R) | 12,527 | 49.3 |
| 2 James Douglas Williams (D) | 17,404 | 64.6 |
| Ferguson (R) | 9,088 | 33.7 |
| 3 Michael C. Kerr (D) | 13,891 | 52.3 |
| Cravens (R) | 12,682 | 47.7 |
| 4 Jeptha D. New (D) | 13,683 | 52.5 |
| Robinson (R) | 12,378 | 47.5 |
| 5 William S. Holman (D) | 13,302 | 55.1 |
| Claypool (R) | 10,835 | 44.9 |
| 6 Milton Stapp Robinson (R) | 12,471 | 44.0 |
| Johnson (D) | 12,017 | 42.4 |
| A. V. Pendleton (I) | 3,888 | 13.7 |
| 7 Franklin Landers (D) | 16,977 | 50.9 |
| John Coburn (R) | 16,411 | 49.2 |
| 8 Morton C. Hunter (R) | 14,005 | 50.4 |
| Rice (D) | 13,798 | 49.6 |
| 9 Thomas J. Cason (R) | 13,188 | 42.3 |
| McClarg (D) | 12,754 | 40.9 |
| C. J. Bowles (I) | 5,259 | 16.9 |
| 10 William Summerville Haymond (D) | 15,088 | 51.1 |
| Calkins (R) | 14,423 | 48.9 |
| 11 James L. Evans (R) | 14,595 | 52.1 |
| Cox (D) | 13,426 | 47.9 |
| 12 Andrew H. Hamilton (D) | 14,318 | 53.2 |
| Taylor (R) | 12,623 | 46.9 |
| 13 John H. Baker (R) | 13,671 | 50.1 |
| Kelley (D) | 13,613 | 49.9 |

## IOWA

| Candidates | Votes | % |
|---|---|---|
| 1 George W. McCrary (R) | 11,384 | 54.5 |
| Leroy G. Palmer (A-MONOP) | 9,521 | 45.5 |
| 2 John Q. Tufts (R) | 10,779 | 51.6 |
| J. S. Sheean (A-MONOP) | 10,122 | 48.4 |
| 3 Lucien Lester Ainsworth (A-MONOP) | 11,066 | 50.1 |
| Charles F. Granger (R) | 11,007 | 49.8 |
| 4 Henry O. Pratt (R) | 10,725 | 60.4 |
| John Bowman (A-MONOP) | 6,975 | 39.3 |

| Candidates | Votes | % |
|---|---|---|
| 5 James Wilson (R) | 12,724 | 63.0 |
| James Wilkinson (A-MONOP) | 7,481 | 37.0 |
| 6 Ezekiel Silas Sampson (R) | 12,461 | 56.1 |
| E. N. Gates (A-MONOP) | 9,737 | 43.8 |
| 7 John A. Kasson (R) | 12,274 | 55.2 |
| John D. Whitman (A-MONOP) | 9,974 | 44.8 |
| 8 James W. McDill (R) | 10,808 | 57.1 |
| Anson Rood (A-MONOP) | 8,115 | 42.8 |
| 9 Samuel Addison Oliver (R) | 12,657 | 64.9 |
| C. E. Whiting (A-MONOP) | 6,825 | 35.0 |

## KANSAS

| Candidates | Votes | % |
|---|---|---|
| 1 William A. Phillips (R) | 20,087 | 60.2 |
| M. J. Parrott (D) | 11,223 | 33.6 |
| N. Green (G) | 2,074 | 6.2 |
| 2 John R. Goodin (I) | 14,965 | 51.2 |
| S. A. Cobb (R) | 14,240 | 48.7 |
| 3 William R. Brown (R) | 14,581 | 59.3 |
| J. K. Hudson (I) | 9,932 | 40.4 |

## KENTUCKY

| Candidates | Votes | % |
|---|---|---|
| 1 Andrew R. Boone (D) | 5,882 | 45.5 |
| Oscar Turner (ID) | 5,799 | 44.8 |
| T. J. Pickett (IR) | 1,255 | 9.7 |
| 2 John Y. Brown (D) | 7,381 | 61.3 |
| George Smith (I) | 3,864 | 32.1 |
| E. R. Weir (I) | 797 | 6.6 |
| 3 Charles W. Millikin (D) | 6,875 | 72.9 |
| Franklin Gorin (IR) | 2,086 | 22.1 |
| 4 J. Proctor Knott (D) | 8,182 | 64.0 |
| Clement S. Hill (I) | 4,601 | 36.0 |
| 5 Edward Y. Parsons (D) | 4,300 | 78.6 |
| John T. Gray (I) | 859 | 15.7 |
| L. O. Wood (I) | 313 | 5.7 |
| 6 Thomas L. Jones (D) | 7,268 | 48.9 |
| Charles Eginton (R) | 4,141 | 27.9 |
| O. P. Hogan (I) | 3,452 | 23.2 |
| 7 Joseph C. S. Blackburn (D) | 11,298 | 69.1 |
| Edward C. Marshall (I) | 5,045 | 30.9 |
| 8 Milton J. Durham (D) | 8,195 | 94.8 |
| J. L. McMurtry (R) | 438 | 5.1 |
| 9 John D. White (R) | 8,774 | 51.3 |
| Harrison Cockrell (D) | 8,145 | 47.6 |
| 10 John B. Clarke (D) | 9,324 | 58.9 |
| John Means (R) | 6,326 | 40.0 |

## LOUISIANA

| Candidates | Votes | % |
|---|---|---|
| 1 Randall L. Gibson (D) | | ✔ |
| 2 E. John Ellis (D) | | ✔ |
| 3 Chester B. Darrall (R) | | ✔ |
| J. A. Preux (D) | | |
| 4 William M. Levy (D) | | ✔ |
| 5 Frank Morey (R) | | † |
| William B. Spencer (D) | | |
| 6 Charles E. Nash (R) | | ✔ |

## MAINE

| Candidates | Votes | % |
|---|---|---|
| 1 John H. Burleigh (R) | 12,275 | 53.2 |
| Bradbury (D) | 10,805 | 46.8 |
| 2 William P. Frye (R) | 9,088 | 57.1 |
| Clark (D) | 6,673 | 41.9 |
| 3 James G. Blaine (R) | 11,494 | 56.8 |
| E. K. O'Brien (D) | 8,693 | 43.0 |
| 4 Samuel F. Hersey (R) | 9,648* | 58.8 |
| Boynton (D) | 6,705 | 40.9 |
| 5 Eugene Hale (R) | 10,695 | 56.9 |
| Spofford (D) | 8,116 | 43.1 |

## MARYLAND

| | Candidates | Votes | % |
|---|---|---|---|
| 1 | Philip F. Thomas (D) | 12,465 | 55.1 |
| | Golds (R) | 10,147 | 44.9 |
| 2 | Charles B. Roberts (D) | 10,682 | 56.5 |
| | Ensor (R) | 8,238 | 43.5 |
| 3 | William J. O'Brien (D) | 9,237 | 65.7 |
| | Suter (R) | 4,834 | 34.4 |
| 4 | Thomas Swann (D) | 10,244 | 60.1 |
| | Cox (R) | 6,810 | 39.9 |
| 5 | Eli J. Henkle (D) | 11,856 | 53.2 |
| | Hagner (R) | 10,452 | 46.9 |
| 6 | William Walsh (D) | 12,974 | 50.2 |
| | Lloyd Lowndes (R) | 12,896 | 49.9 |

## MASSACHUSETTS

| | Candidates | Votes | % |
|---|---|---|---|
| 1 | James Buffinton (R) | 9,927 | 68.8 |
| | Louis Laphani (D & L) | 4,171 | 28.9 |
| 2 | Benjamin W. Harris (R) | 9,651 | 59.0 |
| | Edward Avery (D & L) | 6,688 | 40.9 |
| 3 | Henry L. Pierce (R) | 8,011 | 61.9 |
| | Benjamin Dean (D & L) | 4,927 | 38.1 |
| 4 | Rufus S. Frost (R) | 6,721‡ | 50.6 |
| | Josiah G. Abbott (D & L) | 6,511 | 49.0 |
| 5 | Nathaniel P. Banks (D & L) | 13,438 | 64.8 |
| | Daniel W. Gooch (R) | 7,263 | 35.0 |
| 6 | Charles P. Thompson (D & L) | 8,716 | 52.9 |
| | Benjamin F. Butler (R) | 7,747 | 47.1 |
| 7 | John K. Tarbox (D & L) | 8,979 | 54.8 |
| | James C. Ayer (R) | 7,415 | 45.2 |
| 8 | William Wirt Warren (D & L) | 8,585 | 52.0 |
| | John M. S. Williams (R) | 7,861 | 47.6 |
| 9 | George F. Hoar (R) | 9,423 | 51.2 |
| | Eli Thayer (D & L) | 8,961 | 48.7 |
| 10 | Julius H. Seelye (D & L) | 7,773 | 41.8 |
| | Charles A. Stevens (R) | 7,353 | 39.5 |
| | Henry C. Hill | 3,474 | 18.7 |
| 11 | Chester W. Chapin (D & L) | 11,964 | 65.5 |
| | Henry Alexander Jr. (R) | 6,227 | 34.1 |

## MICHIGAN

| | Candidates | Votes | % |
|---|---|---|---|
| 1 | Alpheus S. Williams (D) | 10,848 | 54.8 |
| | Field (R) | 8,892 | 44.9 |
| 2 | Henry Waldron (R) | 14,611 | 52.8 |
| | Robison (D) | 13,075 | 47.2 |
| 3 | George Willard (R) | 13,372 | 50.5 |
| | Livermore (D) | 12,174 | 45.9 |
| 4 | Allen Potter (I) | 13,317 | 52.0 |
| | Burrows (R) | 12,278 | 48.0 |
| 5 | William B. Williams (R) | 13,370 | 51.5 |
| | Wilber (D) | 12,212 | 47.0 |
| 6 | George H. Durand (D) | 17,758 | 50.9 |
| | Begole (R) | 16,122 | 46.2 |
| 7 | Omar D. Conger (R) | 10,185 | 54.0 |
| | Goodrich (D) | 8,203 | 43.5 |
| 8 | Nathan B. Bradley (R) | 10,258 | 50.7 |
| | Lewis (D) | 9,979 | 49.3 |
| 9 | Jay A. Hubbell (R) | 12,877 | 78.8 |
| | Noble (D) | 3,460 | 21.2 |

## MINNESOTA

| | Candidates | Votes | % |
|---|---|---|---|
| 1 | Mark H. Dunnell (R) | 16,716 | 54.9 |
| | Waite (D) | 13,712 | 45.1 |
| 2 | Horace B. Strait (R) | 13,742 | 50.4 |
| | Cox (D) | 13,521 | 49.6 |
| 3 | William S. King (R) | 18,179 | 53.4 |
| | Wilson (D) | 15,861 | 46.6 |

## MISSOURI

| | Candidates | Votes | % |
|---|---|---|---|
| 1 | Edward C. Kehr (D) | 5,921 | 51.0 |
| | Stanard (R) | 5,693 | 49.0 |
| 2 | Erastus Wells (D) | 9,040 | 71.5 |
| | Fisher (R) | 3,597 | 28.5 |

| | Candidates | Votes | % |
|---|---|---|---|
| 3 | William H. Stone (D) | 7,145 | 56.7 |
| | Wingate | 5,466 | 43.3 |
| 4 | Robert A. Hatcher (D) | 19,087 | 100.0 |
| 5 | Richard P. Bland (D) | 11,350 | 56.0 |
| | Seay (R) | 8,929 | 44.0 |
| 6 | Charles H. Morgan (D) | 12,869 | 54.7 |
| | Thrasher (R) | 10,640 | 45.3 |
| 7 | John F. Philips (D) | 14,446 | 88.8 |
| | Lay (I) | 1,831 | 11.3 |
| 8 | Benjamin J. Franklin (D) | 11,546 | 63.9 |
| | Alexander (I) | 3,595 | 19.9 |
| | Powell (R) | 2,926 | 16.2 |
| 9 | David Rea (D) | 12,953 | 55.5 |
| | Thompson (R) | 10,395 | 44.5 |
| 10 | Rezin A. De Bolt (D) | 11,727 | 50.5 |
| | Hyde (I) | 11,510 | 49.5 |
| 11 | John B. Clark Jr. (D) | 19,344 | 100.0 |
| 12 | John M. Glover (D) | 12,206 | 57.9 |
| | Lipscomb (I) | 8,867 | 42.1 |
| 13 | Aylett H. Buckner (D) | 17,516 | 76.1 |
| | Krezel (R) | 5,491 | 23.9 |

## NEBRASKA

| | Candidates | Votes | % |
|---|---|---|---|
| AL | Lorenzo Crounse (R) | 22,532 | 62.7 |
| | James W. Savage (D) | 8,360 | 23.3 |
| | James W. Davis (I) | 4,074 | 11.3 |

## NEVADA

| | Candidates | Votes | % |
|---|---|---|---|
| AL | William Woodburn (R) | 9,317 | 52.1 |
| | Ellis (D) | 8,567 | 47.9 |

## NEW JERSEY

| | Candidates | Votes | % |
|---|---|---|---|
| 1 | Clement H. Sinnickson (R) | 14,209 | 52.2 |
| | Albtson (D) | 13,019 | 47.8 |
| 2 | Samuel A. Dobbins (R) | 13,977 | 51.8 |
| | Smith (D) | 13,011 | 48.2 |
| 3 | Miles Ross (D) | 15,682 | 53.5 |
| | Clark (R) | 13,629 | 46.5 |
| 4 | Robert Hamilton (D) | 14,585 | 59.5 |
| | Place (R) | 9,931 | 40.5 |
| 5 | Augustus W. Cutler (D) | 11,677 | 50.0 |
| | Phelps (R) | 11,670 | 50.0 |
| 6 | Frederick H. Teese (D) | 13,876 | 50.2 |
| | Marcus L. Ward (R) | 13,768 | 49.8 |
| 7 | Augustus A. Hardenbergh (D) | 13,189 | 61.5 |
| | Isaac W. Scudder (R) | 8,272 | 38.5 |

## NEW YORK

| | Candidates | Votes | % |
|---|---|---|---|
| 1 | Henry B. Metcalfe (D) | 12,184 | 52.6 |
| | French (R) | 11,002 | 47.5 |
| 2 | John G. Schumaker (D) | 15,123 | 69.5 |
| | Wood (R) | 6,652 | 30.6 |
| 3 | Simeon B. Chittenden (D) | 14,539 | 61.8 |
| | Ostrander (R) | 8,996 | 38.2 |
| 4 | Archibald M. Bliss (D) | 12,439 | 61.3 |
| | Bennett (R) | 7,862 | 38.7 |
| 5 | Edwin R. Meade (D) | 9,199 | 50.5 |
| | Hogan (R) | 9,024 | 49.5 |
| 6 | Samuel S. Cox (D) | 13,762 | 80.1 |
| | Campbell (R) | 3,428 | 19.9 |
| 7 | Smith Ely Jr. (D) | 7,689 | 54.5 |
| | Spencer (R) | 6,418 | 45.5 |
| 8 | Elijah Ward (D) | 10,113 | 52.3 |
| | Lawson (R) | 9,232 | 47.7 |
| 9 | Fernando Wood (D) | 8,763 | 50.6 |
| | Hardy (I) | 6,428 | 37.1 |
| | Robert S. Newton | 2,131 | 12.3 |
| 10 | Abram S. Hewitt (D) | 9,503 | 54.0 |
| | O'Brien (I) | 8,083 | 46.0 |
| 11 | Benjamin A. Willis (D) | 10,354 | 56.3 |
| | Bailey (I) | 8,036 | 43.7 |
| 12 | N. Holmes Odell (D) | 12,082 | 58.2 |
| | Wight (R) | 8,391 | 40.4 |

| | Candidates | Votes | % |
|---|---|---|---|
| 13 | John O. Whitehouse (D) | 16,181 | 57.2 |
| | Beale (R) | 11,344 | 40.1 |
| 14 | George M. Beebe (D) | 14,518 | 56.4 |
| | Everett (R) | 11,229 | 43.6 |
| 15 | John H. Bagley Jr. (D) | 16,205 | 56.1 |
| | Stebbins (R) | 12,700 | 43.9 |
| 16 | Charles H. Adams (R) | 12,626 | 44.1 |
| | Terrance J. Quinn (D) | 9,903 | 34.6 |
| | Eli Perry (D) | 6,108 | 21.3 |
| 17 | Martin I. Townsend (R) | 15,445 | 50.9 |
| | Hughes (D) | 14,931 | 49.2 |
| 18 | Andrew Williams (R) | 11,251 | 57.4 |
| | Waldo (D) | 8,336 | 42.6 |
| 19 | William A. Wheeler (R) | 12,323 | 68.9 |
| | Sawyer (D) | 5,553 | 31.1 |
| 20 | Henry H. Hathorn (R) | 15,933 | 51.2 |
| | Sanders (D) | 15,183 | 48.8 |
| 21 | Samuel F. Miller (R) | 15,574 | 51.9 |
| | Allaben (D) | 14,431 | 48.1 |
| 22 | George A. Bagley (R) | 14,391 | 52.1 |
| | Graves (D) | 13,255 | 48.0 |
| 23 | Scott Lord (D) | 11,922 | 52.3 |
| | Roberts (R) | 10,496 | 46.0 |
| 24 | William H. Baker (R) | 12,123 | 52.2 |
| | Warner (D) | 11,109 | 47.8 |
| 25 | Elias W. Leavenworth (R) | 14,949 | 57.3 |
| | Comstock (D) | 11,158 | 42.7 |
| 26 | Clinton D. MacDougall (R) | 13,433 | 53.1 |
| | Wilson (D) | 11,857 | 46.9 |
| 27 | Elbridge G. Lapham (R) | 10,814 | 49.7 |
| | Pierpont (D) | 9,770 | 44.9 |
| | S. B. Ayres (TEMP) | 1,163 | 5.4 |
| 28 | Thomas C. Platt (R) | 13,766 | 49.6 |
| | Jones (D) | 13,013 | 46.9 |
| 29 | Charles C. B. Walker (D) | 17,020 | 54.6 |
| | Hakes (R) | 14,148 | 45.4 |
| 30 | John M. Davy (R) | 12,770 | 49.2 |
| | Angle (D) | 12,522 | 48.2 |
| 31 | George B. Hoskins (R) | 11,323 | 54.7 |
| | Buck (D) | 9,398 | 45.4 |
| 32 | Lyman K. Bass (R) | 15,968 | 51.6 |
| | Nicholls (D) | 14,970 | 48.4 |
| 33 | Augustus F. Allen (D) | 12,302* | 54.1 |
| | Sessions (R) | 10,459 | 46.0 |

### Special Election

| | Candidates | Votes | % |
|---|---|---|---|
| 9 | Richard Schell (D) | 12,562 | 67.9 |
| | John Hardy (ID) | 5,947 | 32.1 |

## NORTH CAROLINA

| | Candidates | Votes | % |
|---|---|---|---|
| 1 | Jesse J. Yeats (D) | 14,071 | 52.8 |
| | Clinton L. Cobb (R) | 12,590 | 47.2 |
| 2 | John A. Hyman (R) | 18,176 | 62.0 |
| | George W. Blount (D) | 11,144 | 38.0 |
| 3 | Alfred M. Waddell (D) | 15,572 | 52.2 |
| | Neil McKay (D) | 14,285 | 47.8 |
| 4 | Joseph J. Davis (D) | 14,924 | 52.9 |
| | James H. Headen (R) | 13,312 | 47.2 |
| 5 | Alfred M. Scales (D) | 10,529 | 54.2 |
| | William F. Henderson (R) | 8,909 | 45.8 |
| 6 | Thomas S. Ashe (D) | 13,579 | 64.5 |
| | E. C. Davidson (I) | 7,469 | 35.5 |
| 7 | William M. Robbins (D) | 11,372 | 61.9 |
| | Columbus L. Cook (R) | 6,999 | 38.1 |
| 8 | Robert B. Vance (D) | 11,126 | 61.8 |
| | Plato Durham (IC) | 6,887 | 38.2 |

## OHIO

| | Candidates | Votes | % |
|---|---|---|---|
| 1 | Milton Sayler (D) | 11,566 | 61.5 |
| | John K. Green (R) | 7,250 | 38.5 |
| 2 | Henry B. Banning (D) | 10,852 | 53.8 |
| | Job E. Stevenson (R) | 9,317 | 46.2 |
| 3 | John S. Savage (D) | 12,972 | 52.3 |
| | John Q. Smith (R) | 11,810 | 47.6 |
| 4 | John A. McMahon (D) | 15,411 | 51.5 |
| | Lewis B. Gunckle (R) | 14,312 | 47.8 |

## OHIO

| Candidates | Votes | % |
|---|---|---|
| 5 Americus V. Rice (D) | 13,477 | 61.9 |
| Reynold K. Lytle (R) | 8,279 | 38.0 |
| 6 Frank H. Hurd (D) | 13,108 | 51.9 |
| Albert M. Pratt (R) | 11,271 | 44.6 |
| 7 Lawrence T. Neal (D) | 11,333 | 55.4 |
| Thomas W. Gordon (R) | 9,108 | 44.5 |
| 8 William Lawrence (R) | 10,756 | 48.6 |
| Joseph E. Pearson (D) | 10,378 | 46.9 |
| 9 E. F. Poppleton (D) | 11,627 | 48.7 |
| James W. Robinson (R) | 11,199 | 46.9 |
| 10 Charles Foster (R) | 13,778 | 49.8 |
| George E. Seney (D) | 13,619 | 49.2 |
| 11 John L. Vance (D) | 12,437 | 53.7 |
| H. S. Bundy (R) | 10,496 | 45.3 |
| 12 Ansel T. Walling (D) | 13,580 | 57.5 |
| David Taylor Jr. (R) | 9,667 | 40.9 |
| 13 Milton I. Southard (D) | 13,602 | 57.8 |
| John H. Barnhill (R) | 9,651 | 41.0 |
| 14 Jacob B. Cowan (D) | 12,394 | 62.0 |
| William W. Armstrong (R) | 7,214 | 36.1 |
| 15 Nelson H. Van Vorhes (R) | 11,655 | 51.4 |
| Wiley H. Oldham (D) | 10,656 | 47.0 |
| 16 Lorenzo Danford (R) | 12,097 | 52.6 |
| Henry Boyles (D) | 10,861 | 47.2 |
| 17 Laurin D. Woodworth (R) | 11,113 | 49.6 |
| David M. Wilson (D) | 10,837 | 48.4 |
| 18 James Monroe (R) | 12,229 | 54.5 |
| John K. McBride (D) | 10,095 | 45.0 |
| 19 James A. Garfield (R) | 12,591 | 55.6 |
| Daniel B. Woods (D) | 6,245 | 27.6 |
| R. H. Hurlburt (IR) | 3,427 | 15.1 |
| 20 Henry B. Payne (D) | 13,849 | 54.2 |
| Richard C. Parsons (R) | 11,330 | 44.3 |

**Special Election**

| Candidates | Votes | % |
|---|---|---|
| 12 William E. Finck (D) | 14,090 | 59.3 |
| David Taylor Jr. (R) | 9,301 | 39.2 |

## OREGON

| Candidates | Votes | % |
|---|---|---|
| AL George A. La Dow (D) | 9,642 | 38.1 |
| Richard Williams (R) | 9,340 | 36.9 |
| T. W. Davenport (I) | 6,350 | 25.1 |

## PENNSYLVANIA

| Candidates | Votes | % |
|---|---|---|
| 1 Chapman Freeman (R) | 9,637 | 48.2 |
| T. B. Florence (D) | 7,970 | 39.9 |
| David Branson (I) | 2,370 | 11.9 |
| 2 Charles O'Neill (R) | 11,692 | 54.8 |
| Benjamin Rush (D) | 9,660 | 45.2 |
| 3 Samuel J. Randall (D) | 9,703 | 57.8 |
| D. F. Houston (R) | 7,060 | 42.1 |
| 4 William D. Kelley (R) | 12,436 | 57.9 |
| W. V. McGrath (D) | 9,049 | 42.1 |
| 5 John Robbins (D) | 10,228 | 38.0 |
| A. C. Harmer (R) | 9,095 | 33.8 |
| L. Myers (IR) | 7,579 | 28.2 |
| 6 Washington Townsend (R) | 9,485 | 57.8 |
| J. S. Forwood (D) | 6,916 | 42.2 |
| 7 Allan Wood (R) | 12,630 | 52.5 |
| E. L. Acker (D) | 11,432 | 47.5 |
| 8 Heister Clymer (D) | 10,553 | 66.3 |
| Charles B. McNight (R) | 5,358 | 33.7 |
| 9 A. Herr Smith (R) | 10,505 | 62.8 |
| William Patton (D) | 6,220 | 37.2 |
| 10 William Mutchler (D) | 13,737 | 67.2 |
| S. V. B. Kachline (R) | 6,710 | 32.8 |
| 11 Francis D. Collins (D) | 12,986 | 69.0 |
| A. W. Butler (R) | 5,846 | 31.0 |
| 12 Winthrop W. Ketcham (R) | 7,932 | 52.5 |
| H. B. Wright (D) | 7,165 | 47.5 |
| 13 James B. Reilly (D) | 8,600 | 51.2 |
| Theodore Garrettson (R) | 8,056 | 48.0 |

| Candidates | Votes | % |
|---|---|---|
| 14 John B. Packer (R) | 12,528 | 56.4 |
| William M. Breslin (D) | 9,673 | 43.6 |
| 15 Joseph Powell (D) | 12,183 | 50.2 |
| B. Laporte (R) | 12,082 | 49.8 |
| 16 Sobieski Ross (R) | 10,660 | 53.3 |
| W. W. Early (D) | 9,331 | 46.7 |
| 17 John Reilly (D) | 11,727 | 52.6 |
| S. S. Blair (R) | 10,580 | 47.4 |
| 18 William S. Stenger (D) | 12,804 | 52.1 |
| Langhorne Wister (R) | 11,781 | 47.9 |
| 19 Levi Maish (D) | 14,534 | 58.7 |
| H. G. McNair (R) | 7,230 | 29.2 |
| William McConky (I) | 2,984 | 12.1 |
| 20 Levi A. Mackey (D) | 12,050 | 58.1 |
| C. T. Alexander (I) | 8,677 | 41.9 |
| 21 Jacob Turney (D) | 12,065 | 57.7 |
| Andrew Stewart (R) | 8,854 | 42.3 |
| 22 James H. Hopkins (D) | 10,091 | 55.8 |
| James S. Negley (R) | 7,777 | 43.0 |
| 23 Alexander G. Cochran (D) | 5,206 | 40.0 |
| Thomas M. Bayne (R) | 4,996 | 38.4 |
| S. A. Purviance (I) | 2,803 | 21.6 |
| 24 John W. Wallace (R) | 9,347 | 52.3 |
| George W. Miller (D) | 8,538 | 47.7 |
| 25 George A. Jenks (D) | 11,627 | 51.1 |
| Harry White (R) | 11,109 | 48.9 |
| 26 James Sheakley (D) | 12,810 | 50.1 |
| John G. White (R) | 12,737 | 49.9 |
| 27 Albert G. Egbert (D) | 10,393 | 50.0 |
| C. B. Curtis (R) | 10,381 | 50.0 |

## RHODE ISLAND

| Candidates | Votes | % |
|---|---|---|
| 1 Benjamin T. Eames (R) | 2,292 | 73.3 |
| Beach (D) | 824 | 26.4 |
| 2 Latimer W. Ballou (R) | 2,362 | 65.0 |
| Redman (D) | 1,235 | 34.0 |

## SOUTH CAROLINA

| Candidates | Votes | % |
|---|---|---|
| 1 Joseph H. Rainey (R) | 14,360 | 51.4 |
| Samuel Lee (I REF D) | 13,563 | 48.6 |
| 2 Edmund W. M. Mackey (I REF D) | 16,746‡ | 54.1 |
| Charles W. Buttz (R) | 14,204 | 45.9 |
| 3 Solomon L. Hoge (R) | 16,431 | 56.1 |
| Samuel McGowan (D) | 12,873 | 43.9 |
| 4 Alexander S. Wallace (R) | 16,452 | 53.2 |
| J. B. Kershaw (D) | 14,455 | 46.8 |
| 5 Robert Smalls (R) | 17,752 | 79.4 |
| J. P. M. Epping (I) | 4,461 | 20.0 |

**Special Election**

| Candidates | Votes | % |
|---|---|---|
| 3 Lewis Cass Carpenter (R) | 21,248 | 99.6 |

## TENNESSEE

| Candidates | Votes | % |
|---|---|---|
| 1 William McFarland (D) | 8,783 | 55.7 |
| Butler (R) | 6,995 | 44.3 |
| 2 Jacob M. Thornburgh (R) | 8,168 | 52.7 |
| Mabry (D) | 7,338 | 47.3 |
| 3 George G. Dibrell (D) | 9,559 | 65.7 |
| Nelson (D) | 4,597 | 31.6 |
| 4 John W. Head (D) | 10,430* | 100.0 |
| 5 John M. Bright (D) | 10,224 | 72.7 |
| Wisener (R) | 3,831 | 27.3 |
| 6 John F. House (D) | 11,992 | 62.4 |
| Harrison (R) | 7,227 | 37.6 |
| 7 Washington C. Whitthorne (D) | 9,672 | 78.2 |
| Gibbs (R) | 1,773 | 14.3 |
| G. W. Blackburn (IR) | 928 | 7.5 |
| 8 John D. C. Atkins (D) | 9,446 | 66.4 |
| Muse (R) | 4,789 | 33.6 |
| 9 William P. Caldwell (D) | 11,128 | 72.0 |
| Nunn (R) | 4,336 | 28.0 |
| 10 H. Casey Young (D) | 13,825 | 60.4 |
| Lewis (R) | 9,071 | 39.6 |

**Special Election**

| Candidates | Votes | % |
|---|---|---|
| 4 Samuel McClary Fite (CD) | ✓ | |

## TEXAS

| Candidates | Votes | % |
|---|---|---|
| 1 John H. Reagan (D) | 5,793 | 75.6 |
| William Chambers | 1,855 | 24.2 |
| 2 David B. Culberson (D) | 3,804 | 99.6 |
| 3 James W. Throckmorton (D) | 4,392 | 93.0 |
| J. M. Valentine | 262 | 5.5 |
| 4 Roger Q. Mills (D) | 9,395 | 72.2 |
| Pleasant M. Yell (R) | 3,615 | 27.8 |
| 5 John Hancock (D) | 3,526 | 97.3 |
| 6 Gustave Schleicher (D) | 5,082 | 69.3 |
| Jeremiah Galvan | 2,234 | 30.5 |

## VERMONT

| Candidates | Votes | % |
|---|---|---|
| 1 Charles H. Joyce (R) | 9,638 | 69.5 |
| Heaton (D) | 2,597 | 18.7 |
| Charles W. Willard | 1,635 | 11.8 |
| 2 Dudley C. Denison (IR) | 7,038 | 44.7 |
| Luke P. Poland (R) | 5,756 | 36.6 |
| C. W. Davenport (D) | 1,960 | 12.5 |
| 3 George W. Hendee (R) | 9,043 | 71.3 |
| Edwards (D) | 3,646 | 28.7 |

## VIRGINIA

| Candidates | Votes | % |
|---|---|---|
| 1 Beverly B. Douglas (D) | 10,783 | 50.7 |
| James B. Sinen (R) | 10,488 | 49.3 |
| 2 John Goode Jr. (D) | 13,521 | 49.4 |
| James H. Platt Jr. (R) | 13,390 | 49.0 |
| 3 Gilbert C. Walker (D) | 13,325 | 55.3 |
| Rush Bargess (R) | 10,710 | 44.5 |
| 4 William H. H. Stowell (R) | 14,583 | 63.9 |
| W. H. Mann (D) | 8,201 | 35.9 |
| 5 George C. Cabell (D) | 10,291 | 57.1 |
| C. Y. Thomas (R) | 7,723 | 42.9 |
| 6 John Randolph Tucker (D) | 10,708 | 65.2 |
| J. F. Johnson (R) | 5,707 | 34.8 |
| 7 John T. Harris (D) | 9,266 | 73.6 |
| John F. Lewis (R) | 3,214 | 25.5 |
| 8 Eppa Hunton (D) | 9,809 | 51.4 |
| James Barbour (R) | 9,291 | 48.6 |
| 9 William Terry (D) | 8,052 | 48.4 |
| Fayette McMullen (ID) | 6,760 | 40.6 |
| George W. Henderlite (R) | 1,821 | 11.0 |

## WEST VIRGINIA

| Candidates | Votes | % |
|---|---|---|
| 1 Benjamin Wilson (D) | 12,796 | 50.3 |
| Nathan Goff Jr. (R) | 12,631 | 49.7 |
| 2 Charles J. Faulkner (D) | 11,499 | 57.5 |
| Alexander R. Boteler (R) | 8,064 | 40.3 |
| 3 Frank Hereford (D) | 13,524 | 63.6 |
| John D. Witcher (R) | 7,745 | 36.4 |

## WISCONSIN

| Candidates | Votes | % |
|---|---|---|
| 1 Charles G. Williams (R) | 12,568 | 56.9 |
| Fratt (REF) | 9,532 | 43.1 |
| 2 Lucien B. Caswell (R) | 11,676 | 50.5 |
| Cook (REF) | 11,459 | 49.5 |
| 3 Henry S. Magoon (R) | 11,535 | 52.6 |
| Thompson (REF) | 10,400 | 47.4 |
| 4 William P. Lynde (REF) | 12,046 | 55.8 |
| Ludington (R) | 9,545 | 44.2 |
| 5 Samuel D. Burchard (REF) | 15,784 | 61.5 |
| Barber (R) | 9,889 | 38.5 |
| 6 Alanson M. Kimball (R) | 14,733 | 50.2 |
| Bouck (REF) | 14,641 | 49.8 |
| 7 Jeremiah M. Rusk (R) | 13,637 | 57.2 |
| Fulton (REF) | 10,196 | 42.8 |
| 8 George W. Cate (REF) | 9,546 | 50.0 |
| McDill (R) | 9,544 | 50.0 |

# 1875 House Elections

## CALIFORNIA

| | Candidates | Votes | % |
|---|---|---|---|
| 1 | William A. Piper (D) | 12,417 | 49.0 |
| | Iva P. Rankin (R) | 6,791 | 26.8 |
| | John F. Swift (I) | 6,103 | 24.1 |
| 2 | Horace F. Page (R) | 13,624 | 43.4 |
| | Hy Larkin (D) | 12,329 | 39.3 |
| | C. R. Tuttle (I) | 5,414 | 17.3 |
| 3 | John K. Luttrell (D) | 18,468 | 55.1 |
| | C. B. Denio (R) | 8,284 | 24.7 |
| | Charles F. Reed (I) | 6,761 | 20.2 |
| 4 | Peter D. Wigginton (D) | 15,649 | 48.7 |
| | S. O. Houghton (R) | 11,090 | 34.5 |
| | J. S. Thompson (I) | 5,413 | 16.8 |

## CONNECTICUT

| | Candidates | Votes | % |
|---|---|---|---|
| 1 | George M. Landers (D) | 13,434 | 50.5 |
| | Joseph R. Hawley (R) | 12,946 | 48.7 |
| 2 | James Phelps (D) | 15,440 | 51.6 |
| | Stephen Wright Kellogg (R) | 13,831 | 46.3 |
| 3 | Henry H. Starkweather (R) | 9,000 | 51.1 |
| | Foster (D) | 8,054 | 45.7 |
| 4 | William H. Barnum (D) | 14,273 | 53.8 |
| | Hubbard (R) | 11,648 | 43.9 |

## ILLINOIS

### Special Election

| | Candidates | Votes | % |
|---|---|---|---|
| 1 | Bernard G. Caulfield (D) | 3,461 | 80.7 |
| | Henry Vallettee | 454 | 10.6 |
| | William H. Eddy | 308 | 7.2 |

## MASSACHUSETTS

### Special Elections

| | Candidates | Votes | % |
|---|---|---|---|
| 1 | William W. Crapo (R) | 9,553 | 65.5 |
| | Charles G. Davis | 5,017 | 34.4 |
| 10 | Charles A. Stevens (R) | 2,850 | 43.7 |
| | Henry M. Burleigh | 2,369 | 36.3 |
| | Lafayette Mattby | 727 | 11.1 |
| | Levi Stockbridge | 562 | 8.6 |

## MISSISSIPPI

| | Candidates | Votes | % |
|---|---|---|---|
| 1 | Lucius Q. C. Lamar (D) | 19,233 | 100.0 |
| 2 | G. Wiley Wells (I) | 19,250 | 59.4 |
| | Howe (R) | 13,149 | 40.6 |
| 3 | Hernando D. Money (D) | 15,128 | 68.1 |
| | Powers (R) | 7,085 | 31.9 |
| 4 | Otho R. Singleton (D) | 19,890 | 66.6 |
| | Niles (R) | 9,987 | 33.4 |

| | Candidates | Votes | % |
|---|---|---|---|
| 5 | Charles E. Hooker (D) | 16,255 | 59.9 |
| | Hill (R) | 10,878 | 40.1 |
| 6 | John R. Lynch (R) | 13,746 | 50.5 |
| | Seal (D) | 13,460 | 49.5 |

## NEW HAMPSHIRE

| | Candidates | Votes | % |
|---|---|---|---|
| 1 | Frank Jones (D) | 13,967 | 50.0 |
| | Withhorn (R) | 13,631 | 48.8 |
| 2 | Samuel N. Bell (D) | 13,084 | 49.9 |
| | Pike (R) | 12,930 | 49.3 |
| 3 | Henry W. Blair (R) | 12,389 | 50.1 |
| | Kent (D) | 12,180 | 49.3 |

## NEW YORK

### Special Election

| | Candidates | Votes | % |
|---|---|---|---|
| 33 | Nelson I. Norton (R) | 10,770 | 53.9 |
| | Charles S. Cary | 9,139 | 45.7 |

## OREGON

### Special Election

| | Candidates | Votes | % |
|---|---|---|---|
| AL | La Fayette Lane (D) | 9,373 | 47.6 |
| | H. Warren (R) | 9,106 | 46.3 |

---

# House Candidates Index

For an index of all House candidates listed in this section (pages 943-1326), see pages 1402-1501. Instructions for use of the House Candidates Index appear on page 1402.

---

# 1876 House Elections

## ALABAMA

| | Candidates | Votes | % |
|---|---|---|---|
| 1 | James T. Jones (D) | 10,582 | 49.3 |
| | Bromberg (ID) | 8,771 | 40.8 |
| | Turner (R) | 2,132 | 9.9 |
| 2 | Hilary A. Herbert (D) | 11,435 | 54.9 |
| | Hall (R) | 9,393 | 45.1 |
| 3 | Jeremiah N. Williams (D) | 14,089 | 78.3 |
| | Betts (R) | 3,896 | 21.7 |
| 4 | Charles M. Shelley (D) | 9,655 | 37.8 |
| | Haralson (R) | 8,670 | 33.9 |
| | James T. Rapier (COLOR R) | 7,236 | 28.3 |
| 5 | Robert F. Ligon (R) | 13,107 | 64.8 |
| | Booth (D) | 7,120 | 35.2 |
| 6 | Goldsmith W. Hewitt (D) | 13,634 | 100.0 |
| 7 | William H. Forney (D) | 14,319 | 100.0 |
| 8 | William W. Garth (D) | 14,529 | 62.0 |
| | McClellan (ID) | 8,910 | 38.0 |

## ARKANSAS

| | Candidates | Votes | % |
|---|---|---|---|
| 1 | Lucien C. Gause (D) | 15,840 | 97.5 |
| 2 | William F. Slemons (D) | 15,566 | 52.4 |
| | Snyder (R) | 14,159 | 47.6 |
| 3 | Jordan E. Cravens (BOLT D) | 8,277 | 35.9 |
| | McClure (R) | 8,016 | 34.7 |
| | Stuart (D) | 5,927 | 25.7 |
| 4 | Thomas M. Gunter (D) | 12,355 | 74.7 |
| | Huckleberry (R) | 4,176 | 25.3 |

## CALIFORNIA

| | Candidates | Votes | % |
|---|---|---|---|
| 1 | Horace Davis (R) | 22,134 | 53.3 |
| | William A. Piper (D) | 19,363 | 46.7 |
| 2 | Horace F. Page (R) | 20,815 | 56.7 |
| | G. J. Carpenter (D) | 15,916 | 43.3 |
| 3 | John K. Luttrell (D) | 19,846 | 51.1 |
| | Joseph McKenney (R) | 18,990 | 48.9 |
| 4 | Romualdo Pacheco (R) | 19,104‡ | 50.0 |
| | Peter D. Wigginton (D) | 19,083 | 49.9 |

## COLORADO[1]

### (Became a state Aug. 1, 1876)

| | | Votes | % |
|---|---|---|---|
| AL | James B. Belford (LR) | 13,532‡ | 51.9 |
| | Thomas M. Patterson (D) | 12,541 | 48.1 |

### Special Election

| | | Votes | % |
|---|---|---|---|
| AL | James B. Belford (R) | 13,302 | 52.0 |
| | Thomas M. Patterson (D) | 12,267 | 48.0 |

## CONNECTICUT

| | | Votes | % |
|---|---|---|---|
| 1 | George M. Landers (D) | 15,529 | 50.0 |
| | Hawley (R) | 15,390 | 49.5 |
| 2 | James Phelps (D) | 19,500 | 53.4 |
| | Stephen Wright Kellogg (R) | 16,777 | 45.9 |
| 3 | John T. Wait (R) | 11,283 | 53.8 |
| | Waller (D) | 9,535 | 45.4 |
| 4 | Levi Warner (D) | 17,233 | 52.5 |
| | Robert Hubbard (R) | 15,501 | 47.2 |

### Special Election

| | | Votes | % |
|---|---|---|---|
| 4 | Levi Warner (D) | 17,250 | 52.7 |
| | Robert Hubbard (R) | 15,459 | 47.3 |

## DELAWARE

| | | Votes | % |
|---|---|---|---|
| AL | James Williams (D) | 13,169 | 55.4 |
| | Bird (R) | 10,592 | 44.6 |

## FLORIDA

| | Candidates | Votes | % |
|---|---|---|---|
| 1 | Robert H. M. Davidson (D) | 13,163 | 51.1 |
| | Purman (R) | 12,623 | 49.0 |
| 2 | Horatio Bisbee Jr. (R) | 11,470‡ | 50.0 |
| | Jesse J. Finley (D) | 11,453 | 50.0 |

## GEORGIA

| | | Votes | % |
|---|---|---|---|
| 1 | Julian Hartridge (D) | 11,465 | 65.9 |
| | Bayant (R) | 5,922 | 34.1 |
| 2 | William E. Smith (D) | 13,627 | 63.0 |
| | Whitley (R) | 8,015 | 37.0 |
| 3 | Philip Cook (D) | 10,684 | 71.4 |
| | Pierce (R) | 4,280 | 28.6 |
| 4 | Henry R. Harris (D) | 13,797 | 70.5 |
| | Hilliard (R) | 5,785 | 29.5 |
| 5 | Milton A. Candler (D) | 18,083 | 67.5 |
| | Markham (R) | 8,714 | 32.5 |
| 6 | James H. Blount (D) | 12,996 | 74.0 |
| | Gove (R) | 4,578 | 26.1 |
| 7 | William H. Felton (ID) | 13,269 | 55.1 |
| | Dabney (R) | 10,807 | 44.9 |
| 8 | Alexander H. Stephens (D) | 14,471 | 91.9 |
| | Tennelle (R) | 1,277 | 8.1 |
| 9 | Benjamin H. Hill (D) | 14,790* | 100.0 |

## ILLINOIS

| | | Votes | % |
|---|---|---|---|
| 1 | William Aldrich (R) | 16,578 | 53.2 |
| | John R. Hoxie (D) | 14,101 | 45.2 |
| 2 | Carter H. Harrison (D) | 14,732 | 50.9 |
| | George R. Davis (R) | 14,090 | 48.7 |
| 3 | Lorenzo Brentano (R) | 11,722 | 50.6 |
| | John V. Lemoyne (D) | 11,435 | 49.4 |
| 4 | William Lathrop (R) | 13,241 | 48.4 |
| | John F. Farnsworth (D) | 8,149 | 29.8 |
| | Stephen A. Hurlbut (IR) | 5,991 | 21.9 |
| 5 | Horatio C. Burchard (R) | 15,793 | 59.8 |
| | Pattison (D) | 10,600 | 40.2 |
| 6 | Thomas J. Henderson (R) | 15,560 | 60.6 |
| | Charles Dunham (D) | 9,821 | 38.3 |
| 7 | Philip C. Hayes (R) | 14,849 | 52.7 |
| | Alexander Campbell (D) | 13,313 | 47.3 |
| 8 | Greenbury L. Fort (R) | 15,011 | 55.1 |
| | George W. Parker (D) | 12,211 | 44.9 |
| 9 | Thomas A. Boyd (R) | 14,548 | 49.8 |
| | George A. Wilson (D) | 14,001 | 47.9 |
| 10 | Benjamin F. Marsh (R) | 14,252 | 51.1 |
| | J. H. Hungate (D) | 13,496 | 48.4 |
| 11 | Robert M. Knapp (D) | 17,949 | 58.7 |
| | Joseph Robbins (R) | 12,618 | 41.2 |
| 12 | William M. Springer (D) | 17,400 | 55.8 |
| | David L. Phillips (R) | 13,754 | 44.1 |
| 13 | Thomas F. Tipton (R) | 15,229 | 50.4 |
| | Adlai E. Stevenson (D) | 14,977 | 49.6 |
| 14 | Joseph G. Cannon (R) | 17,796 | 52.0 |
| | John C. Black (D) | 16,404 | 48.0 |
| 15 | John R. Eden (D) | 18,714 | 57.5 |
| | George D. Chape (R) | 13,765 | 42.3 |
| 16 | William A. J. Sparks (D) | 14,591 | 53.3 |
| | Edwin M. Ashcraft (R) | 12,763 | 46.7 |
| 17 | William R. Morrison (D) | 17,036 | 56.7 |
| | Henry S. Baker (R) | 13,029 | 43.3 |
| 18 | William Hartzell (D) | 14,691 | 50.0 |
| | Benjamin L. Wiley (R) | 14,671 | 50.0 |
| 19 | Richard W. Townshend (D) | 12,720 | 44.3 |
| | Edward Bonham (R) | 8,558 | 29.8 |
| | William B. Anderson (G) | 7,463 | 26.0 |

## INDIANA

| | | Votes | % |
|---|---|---|---|
| 1 | Benoni S. Fuller (D) | 14,727 | 50.6 |
| | C. A. Debruler (R) | 13,158 | 45.2 |
| 2 | Thomas R. Cobb (D) | 18,918 | 56.3 |
| | Loveless (R) | 13,735 | 40.9 |

| | Candidates | Votes | % |
|---|---|---|---|
| 3 | George A. Bicknell (D) | 17,225 | 57.4 |
| | Newsom (R) | 11,747 | 39.2 |
| 4 | Leonidas Sexton (R) | 14,902 | 49.9 |
| | Woolen (D) | 14,570 | 48.8 |
| 5 | Thomas M. Browne (R) | 15,578 | 52.5 |
| | Holman (D) | 14,069 | 47.5 |
| 6 | Milton Stapp Robinson (R) | 17,403 | 49.3 |
| | Chamber (D) | 17,118 | 48.5 |
| 7 | John Hanna (R) | 19,634 | 49.8 |
| | Franklin Landers (D) | 18,236 | 46.2 |
| 8 | Morton C. Hunter (R) | 14,265 | 44.4 |
| | McLean (D) | 13,155 | 41.0 |
| | Davis (G) | 4,704 | 14.6 |
| 9 | Michael D. White (R) | 16,990 | 50.0 |
| | Williams (D) | 13,564 | 39.9 |
| | Leroy Templeton (G) | 3,449 | 10.1 |
| 10 | William Henry Calkins (R) | 17,952 | 51.8 |
| | William Summerville Haymond (D) | 16,693 | 48.1 |
| 11 | James L. Evans (R) | 18,030 | 52.2 |
| | Armstrong (D) | 16,482 | 47.8 |
| 12 | Andrew H. Hamilton (D) | 18,842 | 58.5 |
| | Bonham (R) | 12,718 | 39.5 |
| 13 | John H. Baker (R) | 18,481 | 52.9 |
| | Kelley (D) | 16,273 | 46.6 |

### Special Elections

| | | Votes | % |
|---|---|---|---|
| 2 | Andrew Humphreys (D) | 18,724 | 55.7 |
| | W. F. Spicely (R) | 14,919 | 44.4 |
| 3 | Nathan Tracy Carr (D) | 17,214 | 59.4 |
| | Ara E. S. Long (R) | 11,782 | 40.6 |

## IOWA

| | | Votes | % |
|---|---|---|---|
| 1 | Joseph C. Stone (R) | 17,188 | 53.4 |
| | Wesley C. Hobbs (D) | 14,814 | 46.1 |
| 2 | Hiram Price (R) | 16,439 | 52.8 |
| | Jeremiah Henry Murphy (D) | 14,683 | 47.2 |
| 3 | Theodore W. Burdick (R) | 17,423 | 51.5 |
| | Jeffrey M. Griffith (D) | 16,100 | 47.6 |
| 4 | Nathaniel C. Deering (R) | 20,770 | 68.9 |
| | Cyrus Foreman (D) | 9,379 | 31.1 |
| 5 | Rush Clark (R) | 19,274 | 60.4 |
| | Nathan Worley (D) | 11,154 | 35.0 |
| 6 | Ezekiel Silas Sampson (R) | 18,768 | 54.7 |
| | H. B. Hendershott (D) | 14,719 | 42.9 |
| 7 | Henry J. B. Cummings (R) | 19,496 | 58.3 |
| | Samuel J. Gilpin (D) | 11,688 | 34.9 |
| | Andrew Hastie (G) | 2,160 | 6.5 |
| 8 | William F. Sapp (R) | 19,358 | 56.0 |
| | L. R. Bolter (D) | 15,236 | 44.0 |
| 9 | S. Addison Oliver (R) | 19,563 | 63.5 |
| | Samuel Rees (D) | 10,583 | 34.3 |

## KANSAS

| | | Votes | % |
|---|---|---|---|
| 1 | William A. Phillips (R) | 29,352 | 64.8 |
| | Thomas Fenlon (D) | 15,642 | 34.5 |
| 2 | Dudley C. Haskell (R) | 22,088 | 55.7 |
| | J. R. Goodin (IG) | 17,518 | 44.2 |
| 3 | Thomas Ryan (R) | 25,171 | 68.3 |
| | S. J. Crawford (IG) | 11,634 | 31.6 |

## KENTUCKY

| | | Votes | % |
|---|---|---|---|
| 1 | Andrew R. Boone (D) | 10,994 | 45.1 |
| | Oscar Turner (ID) | 7,540 | 30.9 |
| | H. H. Houston (R) | 5,835 | 23.9 |
| 2 | James A. McKenzie (D) | 17,557 | 65.2 |
| | J. Z. Moore (R) | 9,374 | 34.8 |
| 3 | John W. Caldwell (D) | 13,285 | 54.0 |
| | E. L. Mottley (R) | 10,590 | 43.1 |
| 4 | J. Proctor Knott (D) | 15,735 | 68.9 |
| | J. W. Lewis (R) | 7,053 | 30.9 |

1. The special election in Colorado in 1876 was held to elect a representative for the remainder of the 44th Congress (1875-77). The general election House race was for a full two-year term in the 45th Congress (1877-79).

1032

## KENTUCKY

| | Candidates | Votes | % |
|---|---|---|---|
| 5 | Albert S. Willis (D) | 15,046 | 73.0 |
| | Walter Evans (R) | 5,567 | 27.0 |
| 6 | John G. Carlisle (D) | 16,404 | 66.9 |
| | John J. Landrum (R) | 8,133 | 33.1 |
| 7 | Joseph C. S. Blackburn (D) | 18,884 | 62.5 |
| | T. O. Shackelford (R) | 11,348 | 37.5 |
| 8 | Milton J. Durham (D) | 15,484 | 55.0 |
| | W. O. Bradley (R) | 12,654 | 44.9 |
| 9 | Thomas Turner (D) | 13,103 | 50.8 |
| | Robert Boyd (R) | 12,710 | 49.2 |
| 10 | John B. Clarke (D) | 14,409 | 57.7 |
| | O. S. Deming (R) | 10,561 | 42.3 |

### Special Election

| | | | |
|---|---|---|---|
| 5 | Henry Watterson (D) | 11,567 | 94.5 |
| | William J. Heady | 677 | 5.5 |

## LOUISIANA

| | | | |
|---|---|---|---|
| 1 | Randall L. Gibson (D) | 14,876 | 55.4 |
| | William M. Burwell (R) | 11,978 | 44.6 |
| 2 | E. John Ellis (D) | 14,145 | 55.1 |
| | Henry C. Dibble (R) | 11,515 | 44.9 |
| 3 | Chester B. Darrall (D) | 15,782‡ | 51.8 |
| | Joseph H. Acklen (D) | 14,695 | 48.2 |
| 4 | Joseph B. Elam (D) | 12,136 | 51.3 |
| | George L. Smith (R) | 11,540 | 48.7 |
| 5 | John Edwards Leonard (R) | 14,423 | 52.6 |
| | William W. Farmer (D) | 13,016 | 47.4 |
| 6 | Edward W. Robertson (D) | 15,520 | 58.2 |
| | Charles E. Nash (R) | 11,147 | 41.8 |

## MAINE

| | | | |
|---|---|---|---|
| 1 | Thomas B. Reed (R) | 16,248 | 51.4 |
| | John M. Goodwin (D) | 15,156 | 47.9 |
| 2 | William P. Frye (R) | 13,681 | 55.7 |
| | S. Clifford Belcher (D) | 10,323 | 42.0 |
| 3 | Stephen D. Lindsey (R) | 15,741 | 55.2 |
| | E. K. O'Brien (D) | 12,788 | 44.8 |
| 4 | Llewellyn Powers (R) | 12,866 | 53.8 |
| | John P. Donworth (D) | 10,069 | 42.1 |
| 5 | Eugene Hale (R) | 15,089 | 55.1 |
| | William H. McClellan (D) | 12,278 | 44.8 |

### Special Election

| | | | |
|---|---|---|---|
| 3 | Edwin Flye (R) | 15,611 | 54.8 |
| | Isaac Reed (D) | 12,848 | 45.1 |

## MARYLAND

| | | | |
|---|---|---|---|
| 1 | Daniel M. Henry (D) | 15,287 | 56.2 |
| | Spence (R) | 11,905 | 43.8 |
| 2 | Charles B. Roberts (D) | 15,033 | 55.6 |
| | Morrison J. Harris (R) | 11,984 | 44.4 |
| 3 | William Kimmell (D) | 14,251 | 62.4 |
| | W. E. Goldsborough (R) | 8,592 | 37.6 |
| 4 | Thomas Swann (D) | 15,259 | 54.5 |
| | James H. Butler (R) | 12,728 | 45.5 |
| 5 | Eli J. Henkle (D) | 14,436 | 55.2 |
| | John Henry Sellman (R) | 11,705 | 44.8 |
| 6 | William Walsh (D) | 15,727 | 50.0 |
| | Louis McComas (R) | 15,713 | 50.0 |

## MASSACHUSETTS

| | | | |
|---|---|---|---|
| 1 | William W. Crapo (R) | 14,153 | 69.6 |
| | Day (D) | 6,179 | 30.4 |
| 2 | Benjamin W. Harris (R) | 15,550 | 61.4 |
| | Avery (D) | 9,757 | 38.5 |
| 3 | Walbridge A. Field (R) | 9,323‡ | 50.0 |
| | Benjamin Dean (D) | 9,315 | 50.0 |
| 4 | Leopold Morse (D) | 10,249 | 52.6 |
| | Frost (R) | 9,215 | 47.3 |
| 5 | Nathaniel P. Banks (R) | 13,325 | 51.9 |
| | Frothingham (D) | 12,317 | 47.9 |
| 6 | George B. Loring (R) | 12,319 | 52.4 |
| | Thompson (D) | 11,171 | 47.5 |
| 7 | Benjamin F. Butler (R) | 12,100 | 51.6 |
| | Tarbox (D) | 9,379 | 40.0 |
| | Hoar (IR) | 1,955 | 8.3 |
| 8 | William C. Claflin (R) | 14,245 | 53.2 |
| | Warren (D) | 12,497 | 46.7 |
| 9 | William W. Rice (R) | 13,890 | 57.5 |
| | Verry (D) | 10,248 | 42.4 |
| 10 | Amasa Norcross (R) | 15,779 | 63.9 |
| | Lamb (D) | 8,928 | 36.1 |
| 11 | George D. Robinson (R) | 11,922 | 54.0 |
| | Chapin (D) | 9,760 | 44.2 |

## MICHIGAN

| | | | |
|---|---|---|---|
| 1 | Alpheus S. Williams (D) | 14,471 | 50.5 |
| | Duffield (R) | 12,417 | 43.3 |
| | Ruehle (G) | 1,736 | 6.1 |
| 2 | Edwin Willits (R) | 19,211 | 52.0 |
| | Robison (D) | 17,024 | 46.1 |
| 3 | Jonas H. McGowan (R) | 19,878 | 51.8 |
| | Livermore (D) | 17,223 | 44.9 |
| 4 | Edwin W. Keightley (R) | 18,716 | 53.4 |
| | Chamberlain (D & G) | 11,330 | 46.6 |
| 5 | John W. Stone (R) | 21,908 | 54.1 |
| | Harris (D & G) | 18,546 | 45.8 |
| 6 | Mark S. Brewer (R) | 23,356 | 51.9 |
| | Durand (D) | 21,615 | 48.1 |
| 7 | Omar D. Conger (R) | 15,818 | 54.1 |
| | Chadwick (D) | 13,177 | 45.1 |
| 8 | Charles C. Ellsworth (R) | 16,098 | 50.5 |
| | Potter (D) | 15,760 | 49.5 |
| 9 | Jay A. Hubbell (R) | 18,224 | 59.0 |
| | Kilbourne (D & G) | 12,656 | 41.0 |

## MINNESOTA

| | | | |
|---|---|---|---|
| 1 | Mark H. Dunnell (R) | 26,010 | 61.8 |
| | Stacy (D) | 16,064 | 38.2 |
| 2 | Horace B. Strait (R) | 19,730 | 52.5 |
| | Wilder (D) | 14,990 | 39.9 |
| | Donnelly (G) | 2,879 | 7.7 |
| 3 | Jacob H. Stewart (R) | 22,823 | 52.4 |
| | McNair (D) | 20,717 | 47.6 |

## MISSISSIPPI

| | | | |
|---|---|---|---|
| 1 | Henry L. Muldrow (D) | 20,597 | 76.2 |
| | Lee (R) | 6,420 | 23.8 |
| 2 | Vannoy H. Manning (D) | 20,328 | 61.0 |
| | Watson (R) | 12,589 | 37.8 |
| 3 | Hernando D. Money (D) | 17,983 | 71.1 |
| | Chisholm (R) | 7,320 | 28.9 |
| 4 | Otho R. Singleton (D) | 19,130 | 80.8 |
| | Hancock (R) | 4,547 | 19.2 |
| 5 | Charles E. Hooker (D) | 19,858 | 69.7 |
| | Shaughnessey (R) | 8,646 | 30.3 |
| 6 | James R. Chalmers (D) | 15,788 | 56.0 |
| | John R. Lynch (R) | 12,386 | 44.0 |

## MISSOURI

| | | | |
|---|---|---|---|
| 1 | Anthony Ittner (R) | 7,043 | 50.7 |
| | E. C. Kerr (D) | 6,834 | 49.2 |
| 2 | Nathan Cole (R) | 7,316 | 41.3 |
| | E. Wells (D) | 7,026 | 39.7 |
| | A. W. Slayback (D) | 3,229 | 18.2 |
| 3 | Lyne S. Metcalfe (R) | 8,099 | 50.1 |
| | Richard G. Frost (D) | 8,080 | 49.9 |
| 4 | Robert A. Hatcher (D) | 21,390 | 79.0 |
| | L. Davis | 3,953 | 14.6 |
| | W. Ballentine | 1,738 | 6.4 |
| 5 | Richard P. Bland (D) | 14,599 | 56.1 |
| | J. Q. Thompson (R) | 11,414 | 43.9 |
| 6 | Charles H. Morgan (D) | 18,080 | 49.9 |
| | H. E. Havens (R) | 17,357 | 47.9 |
| 7 | Thomas T. Crittenden (D) | 18,700 | 54.9 |
| | J. H. Stover (R) | 15,353 | 45.1 |
| 8 | Benjamin J. Franklin (D) | 15,229 | 68.0 |
| | D. S. Twitchell (R) | 7,160 | 32.0 |
| 9 | David Rea (D) | 15,715 | 54.1 |
| | B. F. Loan (R) | 13,343 | 45.9 |
| 10 | Henry M. Pollard (R) | 16,582 | 51.0 |
| | R. A. Debolt (D) | 15,802 | 48.6 |
| 11 | John B. Clark Jr. (D) | 21,671 | 68.6 |
| | M. L. Demotte (R) | 9,915 | 31.4 |
| 12 | John M. Glover (D) | 16,154 | 57.1 |
| | Hayward (R) | 11,646 | 41.1 |
| 13 | Aylett H. Buckner (D) | 21,573 | 79.2 |
| | T. B. Robinson (R) | 4,715 | 17.3 |

## NEBRASKA

| | | | |
|---|---|---|---|
| AL | Frank Welch (R) | 30,900 | 59.7 |
| | Joseph Hollman (D) | 17,206 | 33.2 |
| | Marvin Warren (G) | 3,589 | 6.9 |

## NEVADA

| | | | |
|---|---|---|---|
| AL | Thomas Wren (R) | 10,241 | 52.3 |
| | Ellis (D) | 9,330 | 47.7 |

## NEW JERSEY

| | | | |
|---|---|---|---|
| 1 | Clement H. Sinnickson (R) | 17,362 | 52.9 |
| | Simrman (D) | 15,472 | 47.1 |
| 2 | John H. Pugh (R) | 16,015 | 50.8 |
| | Smith (D) | 15,485 | 49.2 |
| 3 | Miles Ross (D) | 18,525 | 54.7 |
| | Atherton (R) | 15,359 | 45.3 |
| 4 | Alvah A. Clark (D) | 17,351 | 59.3 |
| | Veghte (ID) | 11,900 | 40.7 |
| 5 | Augustus W. Cutler (D) | 15,034 | 53.9 |
| | Mills (R) | 12,882 | 46.2 |
| 6 | Thomas B. Peddie (R) | 17,565 | 51.5 |
| | Righter (D) | 16,041 | 47.0 |
| 7 | Augustus A. Hardenbergh (D) | 17,260 | 60.2 |
| | Stiastny (R) | 11,391 | 39.8 |

## NEW YORK

| | | | |
|---|---|---|---|
| 1 | James W. Covert (D) | 20,145 | 56.7 |
| | King (R) | 15,222 | 42.8 |
| 2 | William D. Veeder (D) | 13,406 | 60.2 |
| | Cavanagh (R) | 8,331 | 37.4 |
| 3 | Simeon B. Chittenden (R) | 18,110 | 50.2 |
| | Dakin (D) | 17,858 | 49.5 |
| 4 | Archibald M. Bliss (D) | 18,506 | 61.5 |
| | Spitzer (R) | 11,492 | 38.2 |
| 5 | Nicholas Muller (D) | 15,259 | 75.2 |
| | Kerrigan (I) | 4,755 | 23.4 |
| 6 | Samuel S. Cox (D) | 17,098 | 95.0 |
| 7 | Anthony Eickhoff (D) | 13,199 | 68.1 |
| | Groom (R) | 6,051 | 31.2 |
| 8 | Anson G. McCook (R) | 13,221 | 51.3 |
| | Ward (D) | 12,408 | 48.1 |
| 9 | Fernando Wood (D) | 14,280 | 62.1 |
| | Ducunha (D) | 8,217 | 35.8 |
| 10 | Abram S. Hewitt (D) | 17,136 | 69.6 |
| | Babcock (R) | 6,805 | 27.6 |
| 11 | Benjamin A. Willis (D) | 12,519 | 49.7 |
| | Morton (R) | 12,092 | 48.0 |
| 12 | Clarkson N. Potter (D) | 16,078 | 59.0 |
| | Brandreth (R) | 11,160 | 41.0 |
| 13 | John H. Ketcham (R) | 18,225 | 52.7 |
| | Davies (D) | 16,113 | 46.6 |
| 14 | George M. Beebe (D) | 17,732 | 54.7 |
| | Sweet (R) | 14,667 | 45.3 |
| 15 | Stephen L. Mayham (D) | 20,498 | 55.7 |
| | Tremper (R) | 16,267 | 44.2 |

## NEW YORK

| | Candidates | Votes | % |
|---|---|---|---|
| 16 | Terence J. Quinn (D) | 17,497 | 51.3 |
| | Harris (R) | 16,596 | 48.7 |
| 17 | Martin I. Townsend (R) | 19,689 | 53.0 |
| | Parmenter (D) | 17,448 | 47.0 |
| 18 | Andrew Williams (R) | 13,177 | 56.3 |
| | Platt (D) | 10,246 | 43.7 |
| 19 | Amaziah B. James (R) | 17,275 | 66.4 |
| | Magove (D) | 8,756 | 33.6 |
| 20 | John H. Starin (R) | 19,142 | 51.4 |
| | Decker (D) | 18,089 | 48.6 |
| 21 | Solomon Bundy (R) | 18,825 | 52.5 |
| | Matteson (D) | 17,056 | 47.5 |
| 22 | George A. Bagley (R) | 18,668 | 53.6 |
| | Smith (D) | 15,995 | 45.9 |
| 23 | William J. Bacon (R) | 13,779 | 51.3 |
| | Lord (D) | 13,069 | 48.7 |
| 24 | William H. Baker (R) | 16,555 | 57.3 |
| | Bond (D & P) | 11,798 | 40.8 |
| 25 | Frank Hiscock (R) | 18,425 | 57.1 |
| | Pratt (D) | 13,834 | 42.9 |
| 26 | John H. Camp (R) | 19,036 | 56.1 |
| | Vanauken (D) | 14,879 | 43.9 |
| 27 | Elbridge G. Lapham (R) | 14,726 | 55.3 |
| | Comstock (D) | 11,852 | 44.5 |
| 28 | Jeremiah W. Dwight (R) | 18,839 | 54.3 |
| | Jones (D) | 15,662 | 45.1 |
| 29 | John N. Hungerford (R) | 21,087 | 54.0 |
| | Loveridge (D) | 17,973 | 46.0 |
| 30 | E. Kirke Hart (D) | 17,797 | 50.7 |
| | Davy (R) | 17,138 | 48.8 |
| 31 | Charles B. Benedict (D) | 12,250 | 42.3 |
| | Hoskins (R) | 11,866 | 41.0 |
| | Thomas T. Flagler (IR) | 4,837 | 16.7 |
| 32 | Daniel N. Lockwood (D) | 20,125 | 50.5 |
| | Spaulding (R) | 19,716 | 49.4 |
| 33 | George W. Patterson (R) | 16,910 | 61.3 |
| | Unidentified Candidate (D) | 10,601 | 38.4 |

## NORTH CAROLINA

| | Candidates | Votes | % |
|---|---|---|---|
| 1 | Jesse J. Yeates (D) | 15,151 | 51.7 |
| | D. McDonald Lindsey (R) | 14,154 | 48.3 |
| 2 | Curtis H. Brogden (R) | 21,060 | 64.0 |
| | Wharton J. Green (D) | 11,874 | 36.1 |
| 3 | Alfred M. Waddell (D) | 17,515 | 52.5 |
| | William P. Canaday (R) | 15,826 | 47.5 |
| 4 | Joseph J. Davis (D) | 16,832 | 52.5 |
| | Isaac J. Young (R) | 15,229 | 47.5 |
| 5 | Alfred M. Scales (D) | 13,264 | 54.7 |
| | James E. Boyd (R) | 11,001 | 45.3 |
| 6 | Walter L. Steele (D) | 17,256 | 62.7 |
| | Allen Jordan (R) | 10,283 | 37.3 |
| 7 | William M. Robbins (D) | 13,724 | 59.2 |
| | Thomas J. Dula (R) | 9,467 | 40.8 |
| 8 | Robert B. Vance (D) | 15,868 | 67.9 |
| | Erastus P. Hampton (R) | 7,493 | 32.1 |

## OHIO

| | Candidates | Votes | % |
|---|---|---|---|
| 1 | Milton Sayler (D) | 14,144 | 51.2 |
| | Manning F. Force (R) | 13,474 | 48.8 |
| 2 | Henry B. Banning (D) | 14,133 | 50.1 |
| | Stanley Matthews (R) | 14,058 | 49.9 |
| 3 | Mills Gardner (R) | 16,594 | 50.8 |
| | John S. Savage (D) | 16,098 | 49.2 |
| 4 | John A. McMahon (D) | 18,557 | 50.0 |
| | John Howard (R) | 18,461 | 49.7 |
| 5 | Americus V. Rice (D) | 20,643 | 62.0 |
| | J. L. H. Long (R) | 12,645 | 38.0 |
| 6 | Jacob D. Cox (R) | 17,276 | 50.0 |
| | Frank H. Hurd (D) | 15,361 | 44.5 |
| | E. B. Hall (P) | 1,887 | 5.5 |
| 7 | Henry L. Dickey (D) | 14,859 | 52.3 |
| | A. L. Brown (R) | 13,518 | 47.6 |
| 8 | J. Warren Keifer (R) | 17,728 | 55.5 |
| | George Arthur (D) | 14,012 | 43.9 |
| 9 | John S. Jones (R) | 15,968 | 50.7 |
| | L. F. Poppleton (D) | 15,175 | 48.2 |

| | Candidates | Votes | % |
|---|---|---|---|
| 10 | Charles Foster (R) | 17,324 | 50.3 |
| | John H. Hudson (D) | 17,053 | 49.5 |
| 11 | Henry S. Neal (R) | 15,213 | 50.9 |
| | John L. Vance (D) | 14,639 | 49.0 |
| 12 | Thomas Ewing (D) | 19,628 | 57.2 |
| | George K. Nash (R) | 14,541 | 42.4 |
| 13 | Milton I. Southard (D) | 17,706 | 54.7 |
| | John H. Barnhill (R) | 14,642 | 45.2 |
| 14 | Ebenezer B. Finley (D) | 16,654 | 60.0 |
| | Peter S. Grosscut (R) | 11,067 | 39.9 |
| 15 | Nelson H. Van Vorhes (R) | 14,620 | 50.5 |
| | William W. Poston (D) | 14,113 | 48.8 |
| 16 | Lorenzo Danford (R) | 16,089 | 53.7 |
| | William Lawrence (D) | 13,837 | 46.2 |
| 17 | William McKinley Jr (R) | 16,489 | 50.2 |
| | Levi L. Lanborn (D) | 13,185 | 40.2 |
| | John B. Powell (G) | 2,446 | 7.5 |
| 18 | James Monroe (R) | 16,906 | 56.9 |
| | John J. Hall (D) | 12,772 | 43.0 |
| 19 | James A. Garfield (R) | 20,012 | 63.8 |
| | John S. Casement (D) | 11,352 | 36.2 |
| 20 | Amos Townsend (R) | 17,894 | 55.0 |
| | Henry B. Payne (D) | 14,516 | 44.6 |

## OREGON

| | Candidates | Votes | % |
|---|---|---|---|
| AL | Richard Williams (R) | 15,347 | 51.9 |
| | L. F. Lane (D) | 14,239 | 48.1 |

## PENNSYLVANIA

| | Candidates | Votes | % |
|---|---|---|---|
| 1 | Chapman Freeman (R) | 15,021 | 57.2 |
| | J. S. Thackray (D) | 11,231 | 42.8 |
| 2 | Charles O'Neill (R) | 15,198 | 56.1 |
| | C. H. Gibson (D) | 11,881 | 43.9 |
| 3 | Samuel J. Randall (D) | 11,651 | 56.3 |
| | Benjamin L. Berry (R) | 9,041 | 43.7 |
| 4 | William D. Kelley (R) | 18,820 | 60.2 |
| | J. T. School (D) | 12,432 | 39.8 |
| 5 | Alfred C. Harmer (R) | 17,973 | 55.0 |
| | Jacob Duvall (D) | 14,722 | 45.0 |
| 6 | William Ward (R) | 15,220 | 61.0 |
| | W. D. Hartman (D) | 9,717 | 39.0 |
| 7 | I. Newton Evans (R) | 15,765 | 52.5 |
| | Abel Rambo (D) | 14,247 | 47.5 |
| 8 | Hiester Clymer (D) | 15,239 | 65.6 |
| | H. D. Markley (R) | 6,213 | 26.7 |
| | C. Shearer (G) | 1,780 | 7.7 |
| 9 | A. Herr Smith (R) | 17,419 | 64.5 |
| | George Nauman (D) | 9,574 | 35.5 |
| 10 | Samuel A. Bridges (D) | 20,113 | 62.1 |
| | Howard J. Reeder (R) | 12,255 | 37.9 |
| 11 | Francis D. Collins (D) | 18,548 | 64.6 |
| | D. J. Waller (R) | 10,172 | 35.4 |
| 12 | Hendrick B. Wright (D) | 13,557 | 52.7 |
| | H. B. Payne (R) | 12,101 | 47.0 |
| 13 | James B. Reilly (D) | 10,107 | 50.2 |
| | J. S. Nutting (R) | 10,026 | 49.8 |
| 14 | John W. Killinger (R) | 16,453 | 53.6 |
| | W. B. Wilson (D) | 13,723 | 44.7 |
| 15 | Edward Overton Jr. (R) | 16,954 | 53.1 |
| | Joseph Powell (D) | 14,952 | 46.9 |
| 16 | John I. Mitchell (R) | 13,575 | 50.3 |
| | Henry White (D) | 12,097 | 44.8 |
| 17 | Jacob M. Campbell (R) | 14,668 | 50.9 |
| | John Reilly (D) | 14,148 | 49.1 |
| 18 | William S. Stenger (D) | 15,301 | 50.1 |
| | Thad M. Mahon (R) | 15,232 | 49.9 |
| 19 | Levi Maish (D) | 18,932 | 57.7 |
| | C. H. Bressler (R) | 13,898 | 42.3 |
| 20 | Levi A. Mackey (D) | 16,229 | 59.2 |
| | R. V. B. Lincoln (R) | 11,193 | 40.8 |
| 21 | Jacob Turney (D) | 16,962 | 57.1 |
| | Jacob Rush (R) | 12,763 | 42.9 |
| 22 | Russell Errett (R) | 14,551 | 53.0 |
| | James H. Hopkins (D) | 12,913 | 47.0 |
| 23 | Thomas M. Bayne (R) | 12,506 | 59.6 |
| | A. G. Cochrane (D) | 8,326 | 39.7 |
| 24 | William S. Shallenberger (R) | 13,151 | 55.0 |

| | Candidates | Votes | % |
|---|---|---|---|
| | R. B. McComb (D) | 10,648 | 44.5 |
| 25 | Harry White (R) | 15,156 | 53.1 |
| | George A. Jenks (D) | 13,397 | 46.9 |
| 26 | John M. Thompson (R) | 18,511 | 52.7 |
| | James Sheakley (D) | 16,486 | 46.9 |
| 27 | Lewis F. Watson (R) | 15,640 | 55.9 |
| | W. L. Scott (D) | 12,093 | 43.2 |

### Special Election

| | | | |
|---|---|---|---|
| 12 | W. H. Stanton (D) | 12,703 | 50.3 |
| | Edward Jones (R) | 12,417 | 49.1 |

## RHODE ISLAND

| | | | |
|---|---|---|---|
| 1 | Benjamin T. Eames (R) | 8,516 | 62.5 |
| | Brunsen (D) | 5,063 | 37.2 |
| 2 | Latimer W. Ballou (R) | 7,179 | 57.3 |
| | Page (D) | 5,295 | 42.3 |

## SOUTH CAROLINA

| | | | |
|---|---|---|---|
| 1 | Joseph H. Rainey (R) | 18,180 | 52.2 |
| | John S. Richardson (D) | 16,661 | 47.8 |
| 2 | Richard H. Cain (R) | 21,385 | 62.1 |
| | Michael P. O'Connor (D) | 13,028 | 37.9 |
| 3 | D. Wyatt Aiken (D) | 21,479 | 58.0 |
| | L. Cass Carpenter (R) | 15,553 | 42.0 |
| 4 | John H. Evins (R) | 21,875 | 57.7 |
| | A. S. Wallace (R) | 16,071 | 42.4 |
| 5 | Robert Smalls (R) | 19,954 | 51.9 |
| | G. D. Tilman (D) | 18,516 | 48.1 |

### Special Election

| | | | |
|---|---|---|---|
| 2 | Charles W. Buttz (R) | 21,378 | 62.1 |
| | Michael P. O'Connor (D) | 13,030 | 37.9 |

## TENNESSEE

| | | | |
|---|---|---|---|
| 1 | James H. Randolph (R) | 12,349 | 52.4 |
| | McFarland (D) | 11,215 | 47.6 |
| 2 | Jacob M. Thornburgh (R) | 14,328 | 59.9 |
| | Cullom (D) | 9,603 | 40.1 |
| 3 | George G. Dibrell (D) | 13,132 | 61.5 |
| | Drake (R) | 8,218 | 38.5 |
| 4 | Haywood Y. Riddle (D) | 11,957 | 70.6 |
| | Cox (R) | 3,545 | 20.9 |
| | Patton (R) | 1,437 | 8.5 |
| 5 | John M. Bright (D) | 15,094 | 74.0 |
| | Galbraith (R) | 5,309 | 26.0 |
| 6 | John F. House (D) | 15,719 | 63.6 |
| | Presser (R) | 8,987 | 36.4 |
| 7 | Washington C. Whitthorne (D) | 12,257 | 68.7 |
| | Cliffe (R) | 3,757 | 21.0 |
| | G. W. Blackburn (IR) | 1,841 | 10.3 |
| 8 | John D. C. Atkins (D) | 13,412 | 61.8 |
| | Hawkins (R) | 8,296 | 38.2 |
| 9 | William P. Caldwell (D) | 14,799 | 69.5 |
| | Folk (R) | 6,509 | 30.6 |
| 10 | H. Casey Young (D) | 13,014 | 51.8 |
| | Randolph (R) | 12,134 | 48.3 |

## TEXAS

| | | | |
|---|---|---|---|
| 1 | John H. Reagan (D) | 13,097 | 67.0 |
| | L. W. Cooper (R) | 6,415 | 32.8 |
| 2 | David B. Culberson (D) | 17,326 | 65.5 |
| | S. H. Russell (R) | 9,130 | 34.5 |
| 3 | James W. Throckmorton (D) | 24,138 | 91.4 |
| | J. C. Bigger (R) | 2,281 | 8.6 |
| 4 | Roger Q. Mills (D) | 20,975 | 73.2 |
| | J. P. Osterhaut (R) | 7,655 | 26.7 |
| 5 | De Witt C. Giddings (D) | 15,886 | 54.3 |
| | G. W. Jones (R) | 13,277 | 45.4 |
| 6 | Gustave Schleicher (D) | 12,242 | 81.2 |
| | James P. Newcomb (R) | 2,693 | 17.9 |

## VERMONT

| Candidates | Votes | % |
|---|---|---|
| 1 Charles H. Joyce (R) | 14,496 | 67.2 |
| Childs (D) | 7,057 | 32.7 |
| 2 Dudley C. Denison (R) | 13,630 | 70.0 |
| Dickey (D) | 5,739 | 29.5 |
| 3 George W. Hendee (R) | 11,974 | 68.5 |
| Edwards (D) | 5,367 | 30.7 |
| | | |
| 1 Beverly B. Douglas (D) | 14,228 | 56.5 |
| L. C. Boiston (R) | 10,940 | 43.5 |
| 2 John Goode Jr. (D) | 16,885 | 53.0 |
| Joseph Secar (R) | 14,989 | 47.0 |
| 3 Gilbert C. Walker (D) | 15,536 | 53.6 |
| Charles S. Mills (R) | 13,430 | 46.4 |
| 4 Joseph Jorgensen (R) | 13,896 | 51.9 |
| William E. Hunton Jr. (D) | 12,492 | 46.7 |

| Candidates | Votes | % |
|---|---|---|
| 5 George C. Cabell (D) | 15,146 | 60.6 |
| Daniel S. Lewis (R) | 9,842 | 39.4 |
| 6 John R. Tucker (D) | 16,425 | 59.6 |
| George H. Burch (R) | 11,127 | 40.4 |
| 7 John T. Harris (D) | 17,143 | 73.1 |
| Evenett W. Early (R) | 6,250 | 26.7 |
| 8 Eppa Hunton (D) | 16,660 | 62.1 |
| I. C. O'Neal (R) | 10,175 | 37.9 |
| 9 Auburn L. Pridemore (D) | 15,127 | 75.8 |
| George T. Egbert (R) | 4,791 | 24.0 |

### WEST VIRGINIA

| | Votes | % |
|---|---|---|
| 1 Benjamin Wilson (D) | 17,902 | 52.7 |
| G. F. Scott (R) | 16,067 | 47.3 |
| 2 Benjamin F. Martin (D) | 18,156 | 50.0 |
| Ward H. Lamon (R) | 14,283 | 44.0 |
| 3 John E. Kenna (D) | 20,292 | 61.5 |
| Benjamin J. Redmund (R) | 12,719 | 38.5 |

## WISCONSIN

| Candidates | Votes | % |
|---|---|---|
| 1 Charles G. Williams (R) | 18,206 | 59.3 |
| Winslow (D) | 12,478 | 40.6 |
| 2 Lucien B. Caswell (R) | 15,073 | 50.5 |
| Orton (D) | 14,745 | 49.4 |
| 3 George C. Hazelton (R) | 15,582 | 54.4 |
| Orton (D) | 13,034 | 45.5 |
| 4 William P. Lynde (D) | 17,653 | 59.6 |
| Smith (R) | 11,952 | 40.4 |
| 5 Edward S. Bragg (D) | 19,544 | 58.1 |
| Carter (R) | 14,031 | 41.7 |
| 6 Gabriel Bouck (D) | 20,623 | 53.6 |
| Kimball (R) | 17,847 | 46.4 |
| 7 Herman L. Humphrey (R) | 20,702 | 58.4 |
| Gage (D) | 13,220 | 37.3 |
| 8 Thaddeus C. Pound (R) | 14,838 | 51.7 |
| Cate (D) | 13,860 | 48.3 |

# 1877 House Elections

## GEORGIA

### Special Election

| | Votes | % |
|---|---|---|
| 9 Hiram P. Bell (D) | 5,173 | 49.1 |
| Speer (I) | 3,734 | 35.5 |
| Archer (R) | 1,619 | 15.4 |

## NEW HAMPSHIRE

| | Votes | % |
|---|---|---|
| 1 Frank Jones (D) | 13,925 | 49.8 |
| Marston (R) | 13,885 | 49.7 |
| 2 James F. Briggs (R) | 13,209 | 52.0 |
| Sulloway (D) | 12,111 | 47.7 |
| 3 Henry W. Blair (R) | 12,682 | 51.6 |
| Kent (D) | 11,832 | 48.1 |

## NEW YORK

### Special Election

| | Votes | % |
|---|---|---|
| 7 David Dudley Field (D) | 4,884 | 77.1 |
| Christian Goetz (R) | 1,435 | 22.7 |

# 1878 House Elections

## ALABAMA

| Candidates | Votes | % |
|---|---|---|
| 1 Thomas H. Herndon (D) | 6,577 | 69.1 |
| Bailey (G) | 2,941 | 30.9 |
| 2 Hilary A. Herbert (D) | 8,364 | 56.3 |
| N. Armstrong (G) | 6,505 | 43.8 |
| 3 William J. Samford (D) | 6,199 | 88.4 |
| Strange (ID) | 676 | 9.6 |
| 4 Charles M. Shelley (D) | 8,514 | 55.4 |
| Haralson (R) | 6,545 | 42.6 |
| 5 Thomas Williams (D) | 6,537 | 70.5 |
| Nunn (G) | 2,734 | 29.5 |
| 6 Burwell B. Lewis (D) | 7,652 | 70.5 |
| Smith (ID) | 3,201 | 29.5 |
| 7 William H. Forney (D) | 2,653 | 96.6 |
| 8 William M. Lowe (GD) | 10,373 | 55.6 |
| Garth (D) | 8,279 | 44.4 |

## ARKANSAS

| Candidates | Votes | % |
|---|---|---|
| 1 Poindexter Dunn (D) | 8,863 | 100.0 |
| 2 William F. Slemons (D) | 11,226 | 57.2 |
| Bradley (G) | 8,390 | 42.8 |
| 3 Jordan E. Cravens (D) | 7,202 | 51.2 |
| Rice (G) | 6,868 | 48.8 |
| 4 Thomas M. Gunter (D) | 5,361 | 59.8 |
| Cunningham (ID) | 2,639 | 29.4 |
| Smith (G) | 969 | 10.8 |

## COLORADO

| Candidates | Votes | % |
|---|---|---|
| AL James B. Belford (R) | 14,294 | 49.9 |
| Thomas M. Patterson (D) | 12,003 | 41.9 |
| Childs (G) | 2,329 | 8.1 |

## CONNECTICUT

| Candidates | Votes | % |
|---|---|---|
| 1 Joseph R. Hawley (R) | 14,187 | 52.2 |
| Landers (D) | 11,900 | 43.8 |
| 2 James Phelps (D) | 16,504 | 53.2 |
| Douglas (R) | 14,231 | 45.9 |
| 3 John T. Wait (R) | 9,236 | 53.8 |
| Carter (D) | 7,571 | 44.1 |
| 4 Frederick Miles (R) | 14,109 | 48.7 |
| Bruggerhoff (D) | 12,930 | 44.6 |
| Taylor (N) | 1,848 | 6.4 |

## DELAWARE

| Candidates | Votes | % |
|---|---|---|
| AL Edward L. Martin (D) | 10,576 | 78.1 |
| Jackson (NG) | 2,966 | 21.9 |

## FLORIDA

| Candidates | Votes | % |
|---|---|---|
| 1 Robert H. M. Davidson (D) | 11,527 | 58.1 |
| Conover (R) | 8,302 | 41.9 |
| 2 Noble A. Hull (D) | 9,648‡ | 50.1 |
| Horatio Bisbee Jr. (R) | 9,626 | 49.9 |

## GEORGIA

| Candidates | Votes | % |
|---|---|---|
| 1 John C. Nicholls (D) | 8,477 | 62.8 |
| Corker (G) | 5,031 | 37.2 |
| 2 William E. Smith (D) | 8,126 | 69.1 |
| Wade (R) | 3,643 | 31.0 |
| 3 Philip Cook (D) | 2,628 | 99.8 |
| 4 Henry Persons (ID) | 13,336 | 56.9 |
| Harris (D) | 10,101 | 43.1 |
| 5 Nathaniel J. Hammond (D) | 10,269 | 55.6 |
| Arnold (D) | 8,196 | 44.4 |
| 6 James H. Blount (D) | 3,192 | 99.4 |
| 7 William H. Felton (ID) | 14,315 | 52.5 |
| Lester (D) | 12,971 | 47.5 |
| 8 Alexander H. Stephens (D) | 3,673 | 98.6 |
| 9 Emory Speer (ID) | 10,897 | 50.3 |
| Billups (D) | 10,675 | 49.3 |

## ILLINOIS

| Candidates | Votes | % |
|---|---|---|
| 1 William Aldrich (R) | 12,165 | 51.8 |
| James R. Doolittle (D) | 7,136 | 30.4 |
| John McAscliff (SOC) | 2,322 | 9.9 |
| William V. Barr (NG) | 1,844 | 7.9 |
| 2 George R. Davis (R) | 10,347 | 49.6 |
| Miles Kehoe (D) | 6,111 | 29.3 |
| George A. Schilling (SOC) | 2,473 | 11.9 |
| James Felch (NG) | 1,600 | 7.7 |
| 3 Hiram Barber Jr. (R) | 9,574 | 53.1 |
| Lambert Tree (D) | 5,280 | 29.3 |
| Benjamin Sebley (I) | 2,306 | 12.8 |
| 4 John C. Sherwin (R) | 12,753 | 61.8 |
| Jonathan C. Staighton (D) | 4,438 | 21.5 |
| Augustus Adams (NG) | 3,448 | 16.7 |
| 5 Robert M. A. Hawk (R) | 11,042 | 53.4 |
| Mortimer D. Hathaway (D) | 4,823 | 23.3 |
| John M. King (NG) | 4,804 | 23.2 |
| 6 Thomas J. Henderson (R) | 10,964 | 52.5 |
| James W. Haney (NG) | 6,675 | 31.9 |
| Charles Dunham (D) | 3,257 | 15.6 |
| 7 Philip C. Hayes (R) | 10,712 | 46.5 |
| Alexander Campbell (NG) | 6,512 | 28.3 |
| W. S. Brooks (D) | 5,795 | 25.2 |
| 8 Greenbury L. Fort (R) | 11,271 | 49.7 |
| Chris C. Strawn (NG) | 6,575 | 29.0 |
| Thomas M. Shaw (D) | 4,822 | 21.3 |
| 9 Thomas A. Boyd (R) | 10,543 | 43.8 |
| George A. Wilson (D) | 9,802 | 40.7 |
| Aloxr H. Keighan (NG) | 3,749 | 15.6 |
| 10 Benjamin F. Marsh (R) | 11,814 | 44.5 |
| Delos P. Phelps (D) | 11,238 | 42.3 |
| Alson J. Streeter (NG) | 3,496 | 13.2 |
| 11 James W. Singleton (D) | 11,961 | 54.5 |
| James P. Dimmitt (R) | 6,956 | 31.7 |
| William H. Pogue (P) | 3,034 | 13.8 |
| 12 William M. Springer (D) | 12,542 | 47.7 |
| John Cook (D) | 9,146 | 34.8 |
| John Mathers (NG) | 4,611 | 17.5 |
| 13 Adlai E. Stevenson (D) | 13,870 | 53.2 |
| Thomas F. Tipton (R) | 12,058 | 46.3 |
| 14 Joseph G. Cannon (R) | 13,698 | 46.2 |
| Maldon Jones (D) | 11,527 | 38.8 |
| Jesse Harper (NG) | 4,451 | 15.0 |
| 15 Albert P. Forsythe (R) | 13,106 | 50.3 |
| Hiram B. Decias (D) | 12,942 | 49.7 |
| 16 William A. J. Sparks (D) | 11,493 | 48.7 |
| Basil B. Smith (R) | 9,946 | 42.2 |
| James Creed (NG) | 2,139 | 9.1 |
| 17 William R. Morrison (D) | 12,436 | 50.5 |
| John Baker (R) | 10,605 | 43.0 |
| William E. Moberly (NG) | 1,598 | 6.5 |
| 18 John R. Thomas (R) | 12,686 | 46.6 |
| N. J. Allen (D) | 12,074 | 44.4 |
| S. J. Davis (NG) | 2,454 | 9.0 |
| 19 Richard W. Townshend (R) | 12,603 | 53.3 |
| Robert Bell (D) | 8,190 | 34.6 |
| Seth F. Crews (NG) | 2,847 | 12.0 |

## INDIANA

| Candidates | Votes | % |
|---|---|---|
| 1 William Heilman (R) | 13,928 | 48.7 |
| Thomas E. Garvin (D) | 13,099 | 45.8 |
| Thomas F. Debruler (NG) | 1,595 | 5.6 |
| 2 Thomas R. Cobb (D) | 17,317 | 55.1 |
| Richard M. Welman (R) | 12,032 | 38.3 |
| William L. Green (NG) | 2,103 | 6.7 |
| 3 George A. Bicknell (D) | 15,074 | 57.9 |
| Ara E. S. Long (R) | 9,369 | 36.0 |
| John F. Willy (NG) | 1,588 | 6.1 |
| 4 Jeptha D. New (D) | 15,146 | 50.5 |
| Leonidas Sexton (R) | 14,655 | 48.9 |
| 5 Thomas M. Browne (R) | 13,776 | 50.1 |
| William S. Holman (D) | 12,936 | 47.0 |
| 6 William R. Myers (D) | 16,167 | 47.9 |
| William Grose (R) | 15,548 | 46.1 |
| Reuben A. Riley (NG) | 2,044 | 6.1 |
| 7 Gilbert De La Matyr (A-D-FUS) | 18,720 | 51.2 |
| John Hanna (R) | 17,881 | 48.9 |
| 8 Abraham J. Hostetler (D) | 13,164 | 40.9 |
| Morton C. Hunter (R) | 12,124 | 37.6 |
| Henry A. White (NG) | 6,929 | 21.5 |
| 9 Godlove S. Orth (R) | 15,608 | 43.7 |
| James McCabe (D) | 15,510 | 43.5 |
| Leroy Templeton (NG) | 4,571 | 12.8 |
| 10 William H. Calkins (R) | 15,365 | 45.2 |
| Morgan H. Weir (D) | 13,408 | 39.4 |
| John N. Skinner (NG) | 5,252 | 15.4 |
| 11 Calvin Cowgill (R) | 15,547 | 47.8 |
| David D. Dykeman (D) | 13,102 | 40.3 |
| David Moss (NG) | 3,866 | 11.9 |
| 12 Walpole G. Colerick (D) | 17,067 | 63.7 |
| John Studebaker (R & NG) | 9,712 | 36.3 |
| 13 John B. Baker (R) | 15,184 | 47.2 |
| John B. Stoll (D) | 13,523 | 42.0 |
| William C. Williams (NG) | 3,462 | 10.8 |

## IOWA

| Candidates | Votes | % |
|---|---|---|
| 1 Moses A. McCoid (R) | 12,705 | 48.6 |
| Wesley C. Hobbs (D) | 7,945 | 30.4 |
| A. H. Bereman (G) | 5,505 | 21.0 |
| 2 Hiram Price (R) | 13,337 | 49.9 |
| W. F. Brannan (D) | 9,509 | 35.5 |
| Jacob Geiger (G) | 3,960 | 14.8 |
| 3 Thomas Updegraff (R) | 12,723 | 43.9 |
| Fred O'Donnall (D) | 10,886 | 37.5 |
| S. T. Spangler (G) | 5,406 | 18.6 |
| 4 Nathaniel C. Deering (R) | 17,134 | 60.8 |
| L. H. Weller (G) | 5,742 | 20.4 |
| William V. Allen (D) | 5,293 | 18.8 |
| 5 Rush Clark (R) | 14,205 | 52.8 |
| George Carter (G) | 12,011 | 44.6 |
| 6 James Baird Weaver (D & G) | 16,366 | 53.3 |
| Ezekiel Silas Sampson (R) | 14,308 | 46.6 |
| 7 Edward Hooker Gillette (D & G) | 16,474 | 51.4 |
| Henry Johnson Brodhead Cummings (R) | 15,546 | 48.5 |
| 8 William F. Sapp (R) | 15,343 | 50.2 |
| George C. Hieks (G) | 7,760 | 25.4 |
| John H. Keatley (D) | 7,453 | 24.4 |
| 9 Cyrus C. Carpenter (R) | 16,489 | 54.7 |
| L. Q. Hoggatt (G & D) | 12,338 | 41.0 |

## KANSAS

| Candidates | Votes | % |
|---|---|---|
| 1 John A. Anderson (R) | 30,457 | 59.6 |
| J. R. McClure (D) | 14,919 | 29.2 |
| E. Gale (G) | 5,716 | 11.2 |
| 2 Dudley C. Haskell (R) | 19,029 | 45.0 |
| C. W. Blair (D) | 13,327 | 31.5 |
| P. P. Elder (G) | 9,962 | 23.5 |
| 3 Thomas Ryan (R) | 25,228 | 56.8 |
| F. Doster (G) | 11,055 | 24.9 |
| J. B. Fugate (D) | 8,109 | 18.3 |

## KENTUCKY

| Candidates | Votes | % |
|---|---|---|
| 1 Oscar Turner (ID) | 6,878 | 42.9 |
| L. S. Trimble (D) | 5,611 | 35.0 |
| E. W. Bagby (R) | 3,554 | 22.2 |

## KENTUCKY

| Candidates | Votes | % |
|---|---|---|
| 2 James A. McKenzie (D) | 8,328 | 61.2 |
| John W. Feighan (R) | 3,189 | 23.4 |
| Francis M. English (G) | 2,051 | 15.1 |
| 3 John W. Caldwell (D) | 9,354 | 46.3 |
| W. G. Hunter (R) | 8,502 | 42.1 |
| George Wright (G) | 2,339 | 11.6 |
| 4 J. Proctor Knott (D) | 8,969 | 64.5 |
| J. D. Belden (R) | 4,616 | 33.2 |
| 5 Albert Willis (D) | 9,115 | 40.5 |
| J. Watts Kearney (D) | 7,492 | 33.3 |
| Horace Scott (R) | 5,508 | 24.5 |
| 6 John G. Carlisle (D) | 5,901 | 75.6 |
| Joseph H. Hermes (I) | 1,877 | 24.1 |
| 7 Joseph C. S. Blackburn (D) | 8,632 | 69.7 |
| S. T. Drane (G) | 3,548 | 28.7 |
| 8 Philip B. Thompson Jr. (D) | 12,538 | 53.8 |
| George Denny (R) | 10,766 | 46.2 |
| 9 Thomas Turner (D) | 10,784 | 55.4 |
| John Dills | 8,392 | 43.2 |
| 10 Elijah C. Phister (D) | 7,293 | 65.2 |
| B. F. Bennett (R) | 2,645 | 23.7 |
| James Kilgore (G) | 1,224 | 11.0 |

## LOUISIANA

| | Votes | % |
|---|---|---|
| 1 Randall L. Gibson (D) | 12,419 | 63.6 |
| H. C. Castellanos (R) | 7,108 | 36.4 |
| 2 E. John Ellis (D) | 10,263 | 59.0 |
| E. N. Cullom (RG) | 6,076 | 34.9 |
| Michael Hahn (R) | 1,065 | 6.1 |
| 3 Joseph Hayes Acklen (D) | 10,309 | 48.8 |
| R. O. Hebert (R) | 7,163 | 33.9 |
| W. B. Merchant (ID) | 3,666 | 17.3 |
| 4 Joseph B. Elam (D) | 14,432 | 89.2 |
| J. M. Wells (R) | 1,756 | 10.9 |
| 5 J. Floyd King (D) | 17,261 | 77.9 |
| J. T. Ludling (R) | 4,905 | 22.1 |
| 6 Edward W. Robertson (D) | 13,977 | 66.1 |
| W. L. Larimore (I) | 7,155 | 33.9 |

## MAINE

| | Votes | % |
|---|---|---|
| 1 Thomas B. Reed (R) | 13,483 | 46.2 |
| Samuel J. Anderson (D) | 9,332 | 32.0 |
| Edward H. Gove (NG) | 6,348 | 21.8 |
| 2 William P. Frye (R) | 11,431 | 49.0 |
| Solon Chase (NG) | 8,472 | 36.3 |
| S. Clifford Belcher (D) | 3,407 | 14.6 |
| 3 Stephen D. Lindsey (R) | 11,384 | 44.4 |
| William Philbrick (NG) | 8,333 | 32.5 |
| Franklin Smith (D) | 5,895 | 23.0 |
| 4 George W. Ladd (NG) | 12,921 | 56.1 |
| Llewellyn Powers (R) | 10,095 | 43.8 |
| 5 Thompson H. Murch (NG) | 11,371 | 47.3 |
| Eugene Hale (R) | 10,251 | 42.7 |
| Joseph H. Martin (D) | 2,255 | 9.4 |

## MARYLAND

| | Votes | % |
|---|---|---|
| 1 Daniel M. Henry (D) | 11,419 | 52.5 |
| Graham (R) | 10,338 | 47.5 |
| 2 J. Fred. C. Talbott (D) | 9,826 | 66.9 |
| Milligan (ID) | 3,598 | 24.5 |
| McCombs (G) | 1,268 | 8.6 |
| 3 William Kimmel (D) | 11,676 | 70.4 |
| Thompson (LAB) | 4,908 | 29.6 |
| 4 Robert M. McLane (D) | 11,064 | 59.0 |
| Holland (R) | 6,671 | 35.6 |
| 5 Eli J. Henkle (D) | 11,558 | 54.4 |
| Crane (R) | 9,679 | 45.6 |
| 6 Milton G. Urner (R) | 14,148 | 53.2 |
| Peter (D) | 12,437 | 46.8 |

## MASSACHUSETTS

| | Votes | % |
|---|---|---|
| 1 William W. Crapo (R) | 12,575 | 62.2 |
| Ellis (D) | 7,383 | 36.5 |

| Candidates | Votes | % |
|---|---|---|
| 2 Benjamin W. Harris (R) | 14,579 | 58.4 |
| Dean (N) | 5,472 | 21.9 |
| Avery (D) | 4,374 | 17.5 |
| 3 Walbridge A. Field (R) | 10,919 | 50.5 |
| Dean (D) | 10,478 | 48.5 |
| 4 Leopold Morse (D) | 11,647 | 60.0 |
| Brimmer (R) | 7,654 | 39.4 |
| 5 Selwyn Z. Bowman (R) | 15,308 | 58.2 |
| Clark (D, N) | 10,918 | 41.5 |
| 6 George B. Loring (R) | 10,339 | 44.4 |
| E. Moody Boynton (N) | 10,226 | 43.9 |
| Carleton (D) | 2,658 | 11.4 |
| 7 William A. Russell (R) | 13,169 | 55.2 |
| Tarbox (D) | 7,700 | 32.3 |
| Stevens (N) | 2,831 | 11.9 |
| 8 William Claflin (R) | 14,300 | 54.3 |
| Bradford (D) | 11,758 | 44.7 |
| 9 William W. Rice (R) | 13,295 | 59.0 |
| Thayer (D) | 8,960 | 39.8 |
| 10 Amasa Norcross (R) | 13,051 | 55.5 |
| W. F. Whitney (N) | 6,839 | 29.1 |
| Grinnell (D) | 3,609 | 15.3 |
| 11 George D. Robinson (R) | 10,927 | 51.4 |
| Lathrop (BUT D&N) | 7,994 | 37.6 |
| Dunham (D) | 2,069 | 9.7 |

## MICHIGAN

| | Votes | % |
|---|---|---|
| 1 John S. Newberry (R) | 9,894 | 40.8 |
| Williams (D) | 8,567 | 35.3 |
| Heffron (NG) | 5,760 | 23.7 |
| 2 Edwin Willits (R) | 14,312 | 44.5 |
| Card (D) | 9,557 | 29.7 |
| Thomas (NG) | 7,742 | 24.1 |
| 3 Jonas H. McGowan (R) | 14,381 | 41.7 |
| Dawson (NG) | 12,347 | 35.8 |
| Upton (D) | 6,341 | 18.4 |
| 4 Julius C. Burrows (R) | 14,236 | 47.1 |
| Eldred (D) | 8,171 | 27.1 |
| Sherwood (NG) | 7,791 | 25.8 |
| 5 John W. Stone (R) | 15,983 | 45.8 |
| Comstock (NG) | 15,273 | 43.7 |
| Hoyt (D) | 3,468 | 9.9 |
| 6 Mark S. Brewer (R) | 18,459 | 45.1 |
| McCurdy (D) | 15,549 | 38.0 |
| Meade (NG) | 6,271 | 15.3 |
| 7 Omar D. Conger (R) | 11,939 | 47.4 |
| Mitchell (D) | 8,940 | 35.5 |
| Mallory (NG) | 4,316 | 17.1 |
| 8 Roswell G. Horr (R) | 11,993 | 39.7 |
| Thompson (D) | 9,571 | 31.7 |
| Hoyt (NG) | 8,500 | 28.2 |
| 9 Jay A. Hubbell (R) | 15,264 | 53.1 |
| Power (D) | 7,478 | 26.0 |
| Parmelee (NG) | 6,014 | 20.9 |

## MINNESOTA

| | Votes | % |
|---|---|---|
| 1 Mark H. Dunnell (R) | 18,613 | 59.2 |
| Meighen (D) | 12,845 | 40.8 |
| 2 Henry Poehler (D) | 14,467 | 51.3 |
| Strait (R) | 13,743 | 48.7 |
| 3 William D. Washburn (R) | 20,954 | 53.9 |
| Donnelly (D) | 17,938 | 46.1 |

## MISSISSIPPI

| | Votes | % |
|---|---|---|
| 1 Henry L. Muldrow (D) | 9,632 | 59.3 |
| Davis (G) | 6,533 | 40.3 |
| 2 Vannoy H. Manning (D) | 7,339 | 53.5 |
| Amacker (N) | 5,969 | 43.5 |
| 3 Hernando D. Money (D) | 4,028 | 99.7 |
| 4 Otho R. Singleton (D) | 4,650 | 99.6 |
| 5 Charles E. Hooker (D) | 4,816 | 87.5 |
| Deason (R) | 686 | 12.5 |
| 6 James R. Chalmers (D) | 6,663 | 82.7 |
| Castello (R) | 1,370 | 17.0 |

## MISSOURI

| Candidates | Votes | % |
|---|---|---|
| 1 Martin L. Clardy (D) | 9,437 | 48.3 |
| H. Ziegenhein (R) | 6,498 | 33.3 |
| E. Eshbaugh (G) | 2,476 | 12.7 |
| F. Westermeyer (SOC) | 1,110 | 5.7 |
| 2 Erastus Wells (D) | 7,669 | 42.7 |
| Nathan Cole (R) | 7,403 | 41.2 |
| John Hogan (G) | 2,391 | 13.3 |
| 3 Richard G. Frost (D) | 7,237 | 45.5 |
| L. S. Metcalf (R) | 5,319 | 33.4 |
| H. C. Vandillen (G) | 2,213 | 13.9 |
| Bartholomeus (SOC) | 1,140 | 7.2 |
| 4 Lowndes H. Davis (D) | 12,052 | 61.4 |
| Sol G. Kitchen (G) | 6,834 | 34.8 |
| 5 Richard P. Bland (D) | 11,291 | 56.6 |
| J. J. Ware (G) | 8,022 | 40.2 |
| 6 James R. Waddill (D) | 17,769 | 44.0 |
| C. G. Burton (R) | 11,622 | 28.8 |
| M. H. Ritchey (G) | 11,004 | 27.2 |
| 7 Alfred M. Lay (D) | 16,960 | 51.5 |
| James Boyd (G) | 8,810 | 26.8 |
| A. Underwood (R) | 7,170 | 21.8 |
| 8 Samuel L. Sawyer (D) | 9,727 | 49.0 |
| John T. Crisp (D) | 8,917 | 44.9 |
| L. G. Jeffers (G) | 1,227 | 6.2 |
| 9 Nicholas Ford (G) | 17,430 | 51.7 |
| David Rea (D) | 16,257 | 48.2 |
| 10 Gideon F. Rothwell (D) | 14,793 | 47.2 |
| H. M. Pollard (R) | 10,875 | 34.7 |
| E. J. Broaddus (G) | 5,682 | 18.1 |
| 11 John B. Clark Jr. (D) | 16,600 | 98.9 |
| 12 William H. Hatch (D) | 12,463 | 45.1 |
| John M. London (G) | 10,597 | 38.3 |
| Dan M. Draper (R) | 4,578 | 16.6 |
| 13 Aylett H. Buckner (D) | 15,591 | 59.2 |
| T. J. C. Fagg (G & R) | 8,575 | 32.6 |
| T. B. Robinson (R) | 2,164 | 8.2 |

## NEBRASKA

| | Votes | % |
|---|---|---|
| AL Edward K. Valentine (R) | 28,347 | 56.4 |
| J. W. Davis (D & G) | 21,722 | 43.3 |

### Special Election

| | Votes | % |
|---|---|---|
| AL Thomas J. Majors (R) | 28,211 | 57.3 |
| Alex Bear (D) | 21,015 | 42.7 |

## NEVADA

| | Votes | % |
|---|---|---|
| AL Rollin M. Daggett (R) | 9,727 | 51.8 |
| Deal (D) | 9,047 | 48.2 |

## NEW HAMPSHIRE

| | Votes | % |
|---|---|---|
| 1 Joshua G. Hall (R) | 13,510 | 50.3 |
| Norris (D) | 11,026 | 41.1 |
| Chesley (G) | 2,284 | 8.5 |
| 2 James F. Briggs (R) | 12,981 | 52.1 |
| A. W. Sulloway (D) | 9,860 | 39.5 |
| C. A. Sulloway (G) | 2,077 | 8.3 |
| 3 Evarts W. Farr (R) | 11,708 | 48.8 |
| Kent (D) | 10,663 | 44.5 |
| Johnson (G) | 1,496 | 6.2 |

## NEW JERSEY

| | Votes | % |
|---|---|---|
| 1 George M. Robeson (R) | 14,924 | 48.1 |
| Grosscup (G) | 9,879 | 31.9 |
| Stratton (D) | 6,215 | 20.0 |
| 2 Hezekiah B. Smith (D & G) | 14,610 | 50.6 |
| Pugh (R) | 13,699 | 47.4 |
| 3 Miles Ross (D) | 13,509 | 44.2 |
| Clark (R) | 13,176 | 43.1 |
| Hope (G) | 3,843 | 12.6 |
| 4 Alvah A. Clark (D) | 11,449 | 45.1 |
| Potts (R) | 9,852 | 38.8 |
| Larrison (G) | 4,111 | 16.2 |

## NEW JERSEY

| Candidates | Votes | % |
|---|---|---|
| 5 Charles H. Voorhis (R) | 10,893 | 44.9 |
| Demarest (D) | 10,089 | 41.6 |
| Potter (G) | 3,268 | 13.5 |
| 6 John L. Blake (R) | 14,771 | 49.7 |
| Allbright (D) | 12,832 | 43.2 |
| Bliss (G) | 2,106 | 7.1 |
| 7 Lewis A. Brigham (R) | 13,199 | 50.8 |
| Laverty (D) | 11,234 | 43.3 |
| Winant (G) | 1,424 | 5.5 |

## NEW YORK

| Candidates | Votes | % |
|---|---|---|
| 1 James W. Covert (D) | 13,809 | 50.8 |
| Otis (R) | 11,798 | 43.4 |
| Crooks (G) | 1,430 | 5.3 |
| 2 Daniel O'Reilly (R & ID) | 13,138 | 54.8 |
| Litchfield (D) | 9,881 | 41.2 |
| 3 Simeon B. Chittenden (R) | 16,667 | 58.2 |
| Huntley (D) | 10,017 | 35.0 |
| 4 Archibald M. Bliss (D) | 13,020 | 53.8 |
| Lyon (R) | 8,742 | 36.2 |
| 5 Nicholas Muller (TAM) | 9,466 | 52.3 |
| Bourke (A-TAM) | 8,327 | 46.0 |
| 6 Samuel S. Cox (G & TAM) | 10,908 | 62.4 |
| D'Vries (A-TAM) | 6,327 | 36.2 |
| 7 Edwin Einstein (R & A-TAM) | 7,617 | 48.3 |
| Eickhoff (TAM) | 7,162 | 45.4 |
| Jahelka (G) | 803 | 5.1 |
| 8 Anson G. McCook (R) | 12,854 | 60.4 |
| Jerome (TAM) | 7,512 | 35.3 |
| 9 Fernando Wood (TAM) | 7,277 | 36.7 |
| Hardy (A-TAM) | 6,480 | 32.7 |
| Berryman (R) | 5,726 | 28.9 |
| 10 James O'Brien (A-TAM) | 11,319 | 53.3 |
| Potter (TAM) | 9,046 | 42.6 |
| 11 Levi P. Morton (R) | 14,078 | 64.7 |
| Willis (D) | 7,060 | 32.4 |
| 12 Alexander Smith (R) | 11,338* | 49.5 |
| Cobb (D) | 9,083 | 39.7 |
| N. Smith (G) | 2,421 | 10.6 |
| 13 John H. Ketcham (R) | 18,240 | 62.6 |
| Baker (D) | 9,700 | 33.3 |
| 14 John W. Ferdon (R) | 11,861 | 44.4 |
| Beebe (D) | 11,323 | 42.4 |
| Voorhis (G) | 3,261 | 12.2 |
| 15 William Lounsbery (D) | 13,680 | 47.4 |
| Nichols (R) | 11,442 | 39.7 |
| Erkson (G) | 3,524 | 12.2 |
| 16 John M. Bailey (R) | 12,199 | 41.0 |
| Woods (D) | 12,004 | 40.4 |
| Hilton (G) | 5,455 | 18.3 |
| 17 Walter A. Wood (R) | 16,771 | 55.3 |
| Patterson (D) | 9,655 | 31.8 |
| Ferguson (G) | 3,878 | 12.8 |
| 18 John Hammond (R) | 10,650 | 54.8 |
| Ross (D) | 5,765 | 29.7 |
| McDonald (G) | 3,005 | 15.5 |
| 19 Amaziah B. James (R) | 12,133 | 70.5 |
| Hasbrouck (D) | 5,056 | 29.4 |
| 20 John H. Starin (R) | 17,738 | 56.7 |
| Thomson (D) | 10,880 | 34.8 |
| Wendell (G) | 2,588 | 8.3 |
| 21 David Wilber (R) | 15,377 | 48.1 |
| Scofield (D) | 10,180 | 31.8 |
| Cone (G) | 6,017 | 18.8 |
| 22 Warner Miller (R) | 14,855 | 51.4 |
| Brown (D) | 11,658 | 40.3 |
| Lewis (G) | 2,102 | 7.3 |
| 23 Cyrus D. Prescott (R) | 9,762 | 42.9 |
| Spriggs (D) | 8,730 | 38.4 |
| Mitchell (G) | 3,787 | 16.6 |
| 24 Joseph Mason (R) | 12,043 | 50.6 |
| Sebastian Duffy (G & D) | 11,307 | 47.5 |
| 25 Frank Hiscock (R) | 14,599 | 55.9 |
| Wieting (G & D) | 11,174 | 42.8 |
| 26 John H. Camp (R) | 14,355 | 53.0 |
| Walley (G) | 10,979 | 40.5 |
| Durston (D) | 1,638 | 6.1 |
| 27 Elbridge G. Lapham (R) | 12,270 | 54.4 |
| Pierpont (G & D) | 10,232 | 45.4 |
| 28 Jeremiah W. Dwight (R) | 15,569 | 53.9 |
| Howe (G) | 11,162 | 38.7 |
| Mudge (D) | 1,883 | 6.5 |
| 29 David P. Richardson (R) | 14,330 | 42.8 |
| Babcock (D) | 10,960 | 32.7 |
| Beaumont (G) | 8,174 | 24.4 |
| 30 John Van Voorhis (R) | 12,008 | 43.4 |
| Lamberton (D) | 10,367 | 37.5 |
| Brown (D) | 2,760 | 10.0 |
| Alphonso A. Hopkins (P) | 2,476 | 9.0 |
| 31 Richard Crowley (R) | 12,529 | 56.7 |
| Davis (D) | 8,713 | 39.5 |
| 32 Ray V. Pierce (R) | 18,998 | 52.3 |
| Lockwood (D) | 16,105 | 44.3 |
| 33 Henry Van Aernam (R) | 11,364 | 49.8 |
| Morris (D) | 6,732 | 29.5 |
| Vinton (G) | 4,689 | 20.6 |

### Special Election

| Candidates | Votes | % |
|---|---|---|
| 16 John M. Bailey (R) | 12,062 | 40.5 |
| Francis H. D. Woods (D) | 11,962 | 40.2 |
| Philip E. Marshall (G) | 5,549 | 18.7 |

## NORTH CAROLINA

| Candidates | Votes | % |
|---|---|---|
| 1 Joseph J. Martin (R) | 12,135‡ | 49.2 |
| Jesse J. Yeates (D) | 12,084 | 49.0 |
| 2 William H. Kitchin (D) | 10,704 | 42.9 |
| James E. O'Hara (IR) | 9,682 | 38.8 |
| James H. Harris (R) | 3,948 | 15.8 |
| 3 Daniel L. Russell (G & R) | 11,611 | 51.9 |
| Alfred M. Waddell (D) | 10,730 | 48.0 |
| 4 Joseph J. Davis (D) | 11,864 | 51.1 |
| Josiah Turner (IR) | 8,353 | 36.0 |
| Wiley D. Jones (R) | 2,911 | 12.5 |
| 5 Alfred M. Scales (D) | 10,326 | 57.3 |
| Albion W. Tourgee (R) | 7,680 | 42.6 |
| 6 Walter L. Steele (D) | 4,908 | 92.1 |
| 7 Robert F. Armfield (D) | 4,753 | 55.7 |
| John M. Brower (G & R) | 3,650 | 42.8 |
| 8 Robert B. Vance (D) | 2,894 | 96.8 |

## OHIO

| Candidates | Votes | % |
|---|---|---|
| 1 Benjamin Butterworth (R) | 12,756 | 50.5 |
| Milton Sayler (D) | 12,036 | 47.7 |
| 2 Thomas L. Young (R) | 12,914 | 50.9 |
| Leonard W. Goss (D) | 11,940 | 47.0 |
| 3 John A. McMahon (D) | 15,437 | 51.0 |
| Emanuel Schultz (R) | 14,352 | 47.5 |
| 4 J. Warren Keifer (R) | 15,895 | 56.6 |
| William V. Marquis (D) | 10,805 | 38.5 |
| 5 Benjamin Le Fevre (D) | 14,676 | 48.5 |
| Harrison Wilson (R) | 12,843 | 42.5 |
| Stephen Johnson (G) | 2,392 | 7.9 |
| 6 William D. Hill (D) | 16,110 | 52.4 |
| James L. Price (R) | 12,072 | 39.3 |
| William C. Holgate (G) | 2,544 | 8.3 |
| 7 Frank H. Hurd (D) | 13,182 | 40.7 |
| James B. Luckey (R) | 11,278 | 34.8 |
| Henry Kahlo (G) | 7,893 | 24.4 |
| 8 Ebenezer B. Finley (D) | 16,237 | 50.2 |
| Charles Foster (R) | 14,982 | 46.3 |
| 9 George L. Converse (D) | 17,786 | 48.9 |
| Lorenzo English (R) | 16,798 | 46.2 |
| 10 Thomas Ewing (D) | 12,679 | 50.4 |
| Valentine B. Horton (R) | 12,245 | 48.7 |
| 11 Henry L. Dickey (D) | 15,355 | 50.4 |
| W. W. McKnight (R) | 13,986 | 45.9 |
| 12 Henry S. Neal (R) | 14,566 | 52.0 |
| James Emmitt (D) | 12,490 | 44.6 |
| 13 Adoniram J. Warner (D) | 11,950 | 46.7 |
| Nelson H. Van Voorhees (R) | 11,827 | 46.2 |
| George E. Geddes (G) | 1,487 | 5.8 |
| 14 Gibson Atherton (D) | 14,350 | 49.7 |
| Isaac Morton (R) | 12,063 | 41.7 |
| Thomas J. McGinnis (G) | 2,491 | 8.6 |
| 15 George W. Geddes (D) | 15,597 | 54.3 |
| Goshorn A. Jones (R) | 11,029 | 38.4 |
| George W. Pepper (G) | 1,849 | 6.4 |
| 16 William McKinley Jr. (R) | 15,489 | 49.8 |
| Aquila Wiley (D) | 14,255 | 45.8 |
| 17 James Monroe (R) | 17,213 | 54.2 |
| Lewis Miller (D & G) | 14,575 | 45.9 |
| 18 Jonathan T. Updegraff (R) | 15,320 | 50.6 |
| Daniel T. Lawson (D) | 12,593 | 41.6 |
| George Smith (G) | 2,231 | 7.4 |
| 19 James A. Garfield (R) | 17,166 | 61.4 |
| John C. Hubbard (D) | 7,553 | 27.0 |
| Grandison. N. Tuttle (G) | 3,148 | 11.3 |
| 20 Amos Townsend (R) | 13,081 | 47.8 |
| Joseph M. Poe (D) | 7,271 | 26.6 |
| Gilbert O. Shove (P) | 4,934 | 18.0 |
| William H. Doan (G) | 2,085 | 7.6 |

## OREGON

| Candidates | Votes | % |
|---|---|---|
| AL John Whiteaker (D) | 16,744 | 49.9 |
| H. K. Hines (R) | 15,593 | 46.5 |

## PENNSYLVANIA

| Candidates | Votes | % |
|---|---|---|
| 1 Henry H. Bingham (R) | 13,751 | 56.5 |
| William McCandless (D) | 6,324 | 26.0 |
| Maxwell Stevenson (G) | 4,267 | 17.5 |
| 2 Charles O'Neill (R) | 14,063 | 59.5 |
| Charles H. Gibson (D) | 9,177 | 38.8 |
| 3 Samuel J. Randall (D) | 10,717 | 57.4 |
| John Shedden (RG) | 7,970 | 42.7 |
| 4 William D. Kelley (RG) | 17,786 | 60.3 |
| Charles H. Barnes (D) | 11,697 | 39.7 |
| 5 Alfred C. Harmer (R) | 16,784 | 55.8 |
| David E. Dallam (D) | 11,745 | 39.1 |
| U. S. Stephens (G) | 1,539 | 5.1 |
| 6 William Ward (R) | 13,041 | 57.8 |
| Bethel M. Custer (D) | 8,285 | 36.7 |
| 7 William Godshalk (R) | 15,092 | 51.3 |
| Oliver P. James (D) | 13,754 | 46.8 |
| 8 Hiester Clymer (D) | 12,419 | 58.6 |
| H. Maltzberger (R) | 6,428 | 30.4 |
| Daniel B. Yoder (G) | 2,330 | 11.0 |
| 9 A. Herr Smith (R) | 15,486 | 62.8 |
| W. R. Wilson (D) | 8,605 | 34.9 |
| 10 Reuben K. Bachman (D) | 16,678 | 58.7 |
| A. Brower Longaker (G) | 7,329 | 25.8 |
| George W. Whittaker (R) | 4,429 | 15.6 |
| 11 Robert Klotz (D) | 8,211 | 31.8 |
| Edwin Albright (R) | 8,116 | 31.4 |
| E. E. Orvis (G) | 5,193 | 20.1 |
| C. B. Brockway (D) | 4,339 | 16.8 |
| 12 Hendrick B. Wright (D & G) | 11,817 | 55.9 |
| Henry Roberts (R) | 9,124 | 43.2 |
| 13 John W. Ryon (D) | 7,320 | 36.3 |
| Charles N. Brumm (G) | 7,128 | 35.4 |
| Howell Fisher (R) | 5,698 | 28.3 |
| 14 John W. Killinger (R) | 13,660 | 46.1 |
| M. J. D. Withington (D) | 12,033 | 40.6 |
| D. S. Earley (G) | 3,962 | 13.4 |
| 15 Edward Overton Jr (R) | 13,160 | 49.2 |
| D. C. Dewitt (D) | 9,320 | 34.9 |
| William H. Dimmick (D) | 3,783 | 14.1 |
| 16 John I. Mitchell (R) | 11,133 | 41.0 |
| J. F. Davis (G) | 10,163 | 37.4 |
| R. B. Smith (D) | 5,849 | 21.6 |
| 17 Alexander H. Coffroth (D) | 12,472 | 46.3 |
| Jacob M. Campbell (R) | 12,167 | 45.2 |
| Samuel Adams (G) | 2,275 | 8.5 |
| 18 Horatio G. Fisher (R) | 14,878 | 49.1 |
| William S. Stenger (D) | 14,671 | 48.4 |
| 19 Frank E. Beltzhoover (D) | 17,819 | 57.5 |
| Thomas E. Cochran (R) | 12,321 | 39.8 |
| 20 Seth H. Yocum (G & R) | 13,454 | 50.1 |
| Andrew G. Curtin (D) | 13,381 | 49.9 |
| 21 Morgan R. Wise (D) | 12,880 | 49.5 |
| S. M. Bailey (R) | 9,330 | 35.8 |
| A. L. McFarlane (G) | 3,819 | 14.7 |
| 22 Russell Errett (R) | 9,099 | 38.0 |
| David Kirk (G) | 7,447 | 31.1 |
| James K. P. Duff (D) | 7,260 | 30.4 |

## PENNSYLVANIA

| Candidates | Votes | % |
|---|---|---|
| 23 Thomas M. Bayne (R) | 9,104 | 51.2 |
| C. F. Mckenna (D) | 5,621 | 31.6 |
| Samuel Watson (G) | 2,781 | 15.6 |
| 24 William S. Shallenberger (R) | 11,261 | 48.6 |
| R. W. Clendennin (D) | 10,025 | 43.2 |
| | 1,911 | 8.2 |
| 25 Harry White (R) | 10,715 | 37.6 |
| James M. Guffey (D) | 8,931 | 31.3 |
| James Mosgrove (G) | 8,874 | 31.1 |
| 26 Samuel B. Dick (R) | 14,010 | 41.7 |
| William C. Plummer (G) | 12,716 | 37.8 |
| John T. Bard (D) | 6,558 | 19.5 |
| 27 James H. Osmer (R) | 11,205 | 44.5 |
| George A. Allen (G) | 8,551 | 34.0 |
| Cyrus C. Camp (G) | 5,127 | 20.4 |

## RHODE ISLAND

| | | |
|---|---|---|
| 1 Nelson W. Aldrich (R) | 5,969 | 74.5 |
| Thomas Davis (D) | 1,332 | 16.6 |
| Lycurgus Sayles (G) | 625 | 7.8 |
| 2 Latimer W. Ballou (R) | 5,431 | 53.3 |
| Jerothmul B. Barnaby (D) | 4,438 | 43.6 |

## SOUTH CAROLINA

| | | |
|---|---|---|
| 1 John S. Richardson (D) | 22,707 | 61.7 |
| J. H. Rainey (R) | 14,096 | 38.3 |
| 2 Michael P. O'Connor (D) | 20,568 | 60.9 |
| E. W. M. Mackey (R) | 13,182 | 39.1 |
| 3 D. Wyatt Aiken (D) | 24,533 | 79.1 |
| J. F. Ensor (R) | 6,348 | 20.5 |
| 4 John H. Evins (D) | 22,702 | 96.8 |
| 5 George D. Tillman (D) | 26,409 | 71.2 |
| Robert Smalls (R) | 10,664 | 28.8 |

## TENNESSEE

| | | |
|---|---|---|
| 1 Robert L. Taylor (D) | 11,698 | 51.6 |
| Pettibone (R) | 10,960 | 48.4 |
| 2 Leonidas C. Houk (R) | 9,548 | 57.1 |
| Watkins (ID) | 7,167 | 42.9 |
| 3 George G. Dibrell (D) | 9,399 | 69.1 |
| Wheeler (R) | 4,205 | 30.9 |
| 4 Benton McMillin (D) | 7,966 | 65.0 |
| Golliday (ID) | 4,291 | 35.0 |
| 5 John M. Bright (D) | 8,385 | 65.4 |
| Lillard (D) | 2,594 | 20.2 |

| Candidates | Votes | % |
|---|---|---|
| Warder (R) | 965 | 7.5 |
| Isbell (G) | 876 | 6.8 |
| 6 John F. House (D) | 9,614 | 57.2 |
| Akers (G) | 4,666 | 27.8 |
| Prosser (R) | 2,403 | 14.3 |
| 7 Washington C. Whitthorne (D) | 6,581 | 43.2 |
| Moore (D) | 5,533 | 36.3 |
| Hughes (R) | 3,133 | 20.6 |
| 8 John D. C. Atkins (D) | 8,361 | 61.4 |
| Warren (G) | 5,257 | 38.6 |
| 9 Charles B. Simonton (D) | 7,998 | 63.7 |
| Black (G) | 4,564 | 36.3 |
| 10 H. Casey Young (D) | 5,522 | 54.8 |
| Randolph (R) | 3,199 | 31.7 |
| Keller (G) | 1,357 | 13.5 |

## TEXAS

| | | |
|---|---|---|
| 1 John H. Reagan (D) | 18,038 | 98.7 |
| 2 David B. Culberson (D) | 19,721 | 63.1 |
| O'Neill (G) | 9,617 | 30.8 |
| 3 Olin Wellborn (D) | 40,845 | 80.5 |
| Daggett (R) | 9,718 | 19.2 |
| 4 Roger Q. Mills (D) | 30,535 | 75.7 |
| Smith (R) | 9,039 | 22.4 |
| 5 George W. Jones (G & D) | 21,095 | 51.6 |
| Hancock (D) | 19,721 | 48.2 |
| 6 Gustave Schleicher (D) | 19,699* | 56.7 |
| Ireland (ID) | 15,050 | 43.3 |

## VERMONT

| | | |
|---|---|---|
| 1 Charles H. Joyce (R) | 12,599 | 68.1 |
| Randall (D) | 5,894 | 31.8 |
| 2 James M. Tyler (R) | 12,281 | 71.3 |
| Dickey (D) | 4,890 | 28.4 |
| 3 Bradley Barlow (N) | 8,367 | 60.4 |
| Grout (R) | 4,330 | 31.3 |
| Waterman (D) | 1,095 | 7.9 |

## VIRGINIA

| | | |
|---|---|---|
| 1 Richard Lee T. Beale (D) | 7,266 | 48.3 |
| George C. Round (R) | 5,474 | 36.4 |
| John Critcher (ID) | 2,296 | 15.3 |
| 2 John Goode Jr. (D) | 11,547 | 56.7 |
| John F. Dezendorf (R) | 8,808 | 43.3 |
| 3 Joseph E. Johnston (D) | 5,787 | 58.1 |
| William W. Newman (G) | 4,172 | 41.9 |

| Candidates | Votes | % |
|---|---|---|
| 4 Joseph Jorgensen (R) | 12,322 | 60.7 |
| William E. Hinton (D) | 7,976 | 39.3 |
| 5 George C. Cabell (D) | 8,545 | 66.7 |
| William A. Witcher (ID) | 4,267 | 33.3 |
| 6 John Randolph Tucker (D) | 7,893 | 63.4 |
| Camm Patteson (ID) | 4,520 | 36.3 |
| 7 John T. Harris (D) | 7,235 | 56.4 |
| John Paul (D) | 5,580 | 43.5 |
| 8 Eppa Hunton (D) | 5,772 | 77.9 |
| John R. Carton (ID) | 1,119 | 15.1 |
| James Cochran (I) | 506 | 6.8 |
| 9 James B. Richmond (D) | 5,120 | 33.7 |
| Fayette McMullens (ID) | 4,827 | 31.7 |
| Samuel H. Newberry (ID) | 4,640 | 30.5 |

## WEST VIRGINIA

| | | |
|---|---|---|
| 1 Benjamin Wilson (D) | 15,857 | 49.0 |
| J. R. Hubbard (R) | 12,448 | 38.4 |
| James Bassell (N) | 4,086 | 12.6 |
| 2 Benjamin F. Martin (D) | 15,421 | 56.6 |
| F. A. Burr (R) | 7,587 | 27.9 |
| J. H. Thompson (N) | 4,231 | 15.5 |
| 3 John E. Kenna (D) | 19,040 | 54.0 |
| Henry I. Walker (R) | 16,213 | 46.0 |

## WISCONSIN

| | | |
|---|---|---|
| 1 Charles G. Williams (R) | 14,629 | 59.5 |
| Parker (D) | 9,949 | 40.5 |
| 2 Lucien B. Caswell (R) | 12,607 | 51.5 |
| Davis (D) | 9,502 | 38.8 |
| Tenney (G) | 2,376 | 9.7 |
| 3 George C. Hazelton (R) | 11,695 | 50.2 |
| King (D) | 11,603 | 49.8 |
| 4 Peter V. Deuster (D) | 11,157 | 47.4 |
| Frisby (R) | 11,022 | 46.8 |
| Judd (G) | 1,351 | 5.7 |
| 5 Edward S. Bragg (D) | 12,392 | 46.2 |
| Smith (R) | 10,285 | 38.3 |
| Giddings (G) | 4,157 | 15.5 |
| 6 Gabriel Bouck (D) | 14,349 | 45.9 |
| Jones (R) | 11,748 | 37.6 |
| Steele (G) | 5,144 | 16.5 |
| 7 Herman L. Humphrey (R) | 15,256 | 54.2 |
| Parker (D) | 12,880 | 45.8 |
| 8 Thaddeus C. Pound (R) | 12,795 | 52.8 |
| Barrows (D) | 11,421 | 47.2 |

# 1879 House Elections

## CALIFORNIA

### Special Elections

| | | |
|---|---|---|
| 1 Horace Davis (R) | 20,074 | 48.4 |
| Clitus Barbour (WMP/L) | 18,448 | 44.5 |
| C. R. Sumner (D) | 2,940 | 7.1 |
| 2 Horace F. Page (R) | 19,386 | 51.9 |
| T. J. Clunie (D) | 12,847 | 34.4 |

| | | |
|---|---|---|
| H. P. Williams (WMP/L) | 5,139 | 13.8 |
| 3 Campbell P. Berry (D-WM) | 20,019 | 50.1 |
| Joseph McKennon (R) | 19,800 | 49.6 |
| 4 Romualdo Pacheco (R) | 15,391 | 40.5 |
| Wallace Leach (D) | 12,109 | 31.8 |
| J. J. Ayres (WMP/L) | 10,527 | 27.7 |

## NEW YORK

### Special Election

| | | |
|---|---|---|
| 12 Waldo Hutchins (D) | 13,543 | 56.9 |
| N. Smith (R) | 10,146 | 42.7 |

# 1880 House Elections

## ALABAMA

| | Candidates | Votes | % |
|---|---|---|---|
| 1 | Thomas H. Herndon (D) | 10,027 | 53.8 |
| | J. Gillett (R) | 5,595 | 30.0 |
| | F. H. Threatt (R) | 2,303 | 12.4 |
| 2 | Hilary A. Herbert (D) | 13,271 | 59.8 |
| | Strobach (R) | 8,884 | 40.0 |
| 3 | William C. Oates (D) | 10,614 | 64.3 |
| | A. A. Mabson (R) | 5,836 | 35.3 |
| 4 | Charles M. Shelley (D) | 9,301‡ | 52.7 |
| | James Q. Smith (R) | 6,650 | 37.7 |
| | Stevens (R) | 1,693 | 9.6 |
| 5 | Thomas Williams (D) | 11,219 | 100.0 |
| 6 | Goldsmith W. Hewitt (D) | 10,043 | 100.0 |
| 7 | William H. Forney (D) | 13,636 | 71.4 |
| | Arthur Bingham (R) | 5,468 | 28.6 |
| 8 | Joseph Wheeler (D) | 12,808‡ | 50.1 |
| | William M. Lowe (GD) | 12,765 | 49.9 |

**Special Election**

| | | | |
|---|---|---|---|
| 6 | Newton N. Clements | 9,973 | 100.0 |

## ARKANSAS

| | | | |
|---|---|---|---|
| 1 | Poindexter Dunn (D) | 15,753 | 60.2 |
| | Johnson (R) | 10,407 | 39.8 |
| 2 | James K. Jones (D) | 16,517 | 47.3 |
| | Williams (R) | 14,513 | 41.5 |
| | Garland (G) | 3,920 | 11.2 |
| 3 | Jordan E. Cravens (D) | 15,781 | 57.7 |
| | Boles (R) | 11,552 | 42.3 |
| 4 | Thomas M. Gunter (D) | 7,387 | 42.8 |
| | Peel (ID) | 5,731 | 33.2 |
| | Murphy (R) | 4,125 | 23.9 |

## CALIFORNIA

| | | | |
|---|---|---|---|
| 1 | William S. Rosecrans (D-WM) | 21,005 | 51.0 |
| | Horace Davis (R) | 19,496 | 47.3 |
| 2 | Horace F. Page (R) | 22,038 | 53.5 |
| | J. R. Glasscock (D-WM) | 18,859 | 45.8 |
| 3 | Campbell P. Berry (D) | 21,743 | 51.2 |
| | George A. Knight (R) | 20,494 | 48.2 |
| 4 | Romualdo Pacheco (R) | 17,768 | 45.8 |
| | W. A. Leach (D) | 17,577 | 45.3 |
| | J. F. Godfrey | 3,461 | 8.9 |

## COLORADO

| | | | |
|---|---|---|---|
| AL | James B. Belford (R) | 27,069 | 50.8 |
| | Robert S. Morrison (D) | 24,476 | 46.0 |

## CONNECTICUT

| | | | |
|---|---|---|---|
| 1 | John R. Buck (R) | 17,048 | 52.6 |
| | Beach (D) | 15,114 | 46.7 |
| 2 | James Phelps (D) | 21,632 | 51.7 |
| | Wallace (R) | 20,068 | 48.0 |
| 3 | John T. Wait (R) | 12,099 | 56.1 |
| | Sawyer (D) | 9,125 | 42.3 |
| 4 | Frederick Miles (R) | 18,168 | 50.4 |
| | Peet (D) | 17,634 | 48.9 |

## DELAWARE

| | | | |
|---|---|---|---|
| AL | Edward L. Martin (D) | 14,966 | 51.1 |
| | Houston (R) | 14,336 | 48.9 |

## FLORIDA

| | | | |
|---|---|---|---|
| 1 | Robert H. M. Davidson (D) | 14,971 | 57.5 |
| | Witherspoon (R) | 11,082 | 42.5 |

| | Candidates | Votes | % |
|---|---|---|---|
| 2 | Jesse J. Finley (D) | 13,105‡ | 52.3 |
| | Horatio Bisbee Jr. (R) | 11,953 | 47.7 |

## GEORGIA

| | | | |
|---|---|---|---|
| 1 | George R. Black (D) | 11,712 | 58.6 |
| | Collins (R) | 8,265 | 41.4 |
| 2 | Henry G. Turner (D) | 11,496 | 64.2 |
| | Brimberry (R) | 6,417 | 35.8 |
| 3 | Philip Cook (D) | 7,122 | 68.7 |
| | Parker (R) | 3,245 | 31.3 |
| 4 | Hugh Buchanan (D) | 9,998 | 58.1 |
| | Pou (ID) | 7,224 | 42.0 |
| 5 | Nathaniel J. Hammond (D) | 11,947 | 62.6 |
| | Clark (R) | 7,133 | 37.4 |
| 6 | James H. Blount (D) | 8,373 | 100.0 |
| 7 | Judson C. Clements (D) | 11,572 | 51.9 |
| | Felton (ID) | 10,727 | 48.1 |
| 8 | Alexander H. Stephens (D) | 11,341 | 99.9 |
| 9 | Emory Speer (ID) | 12,653 | 59.6 |
| | Bell (D) | 8,590 | 40.4 |

## ILLINOIS

| | | | |
|---|---|---|---|
| 1 | William Aldrich (R) | 22,307 | 53.8 |
| | John Mattocks (D) | 18,024 | 43.5 |
| 2 | George R. Davis (R) | 20,603 | 54.8 |
| | V. F. Farnsworth (D) | 16,014 | 42.6 |
| 3 | Charles B. Farwell (R) | 16,627 | 57.3 |
| | Perry H. Smith Jr (D) | 11,903 | 41.0 |
| 4 | John C. Sherwin (R) | 20,381 | 68.9 |
| | Norman C. Warner (D) | 8,055 | 27.2 |
| 5 | Robert M. A. Hawk (R) | 17,061 | 59.5 |
| | Larmon G. Johnson (D) | 7,468 | 26.0 |
| | John M. King (G) | 4,160 | 14.5 |
| 6 | Thomas J. Henderson (R) | 16,650 | 57.6 |
| | Bernard N. Trusdell (D) | 9,631 | 33.3 |
| | P. L. McKinney (G) | 2,637 | 9.1 |
| 7 | William Cullen (R) | 16,628 | 53.8 |
| | Daniel Evans (D) | 12,064 | 39.0 |
| | Royal E. Barber (G) | 2,204 | 7.1 |
| 8 | Lewis E. Payson (R) | 16,704 | 54.4 |
| | Robert R. Wallace (D) | 13,972 | 45.5 |
| 9 | John H. Lewis (R) | 14,658 | 46.5 |
| | John S. Lee (D) | 14,294 | 45.4 |
| | William H. Reynolds (G) | 2,548 | 8.1 |
| 10 | Benjamin F. Marsh (R) | 14,798 | 50.4 |
| | Robert Holloway (D) | 13,877 | 47.2 |
| 11 | James W. Singleton (D) | 17,842 | 55.6 |
| | William H. Edgar (R) | 12,490 | 38.9 |
| | A. B. Allen (G) | 1,765 | 5.5 |
| 12 | William M. Springer (D) | 17,376 | 51.6 |
| | Isaac L. Morrison (R) | 14,761 | 43.8 |
| 13 | Dietrich Smith (R) | 16,433 | 50.5 |
| | Adlai E. Stevenson (D) | 16,115 | 49.5 |
| 14 | Joseph G. Cannon (R) | 19,710 | 52.6 |
| | James R. Scott (D) | 17,734 | 47.4 |
| 15 | Samuel W. Moulton (D) | 19,364 | 53.5 |
| | Albert P. Forsythe (R) | 16,810 | 46.5 |
| 16 | William A. J. Sparks (D) | 15,392 | 50.2 |
| | P. E. Hosmer (R) | 13,921 | 45.4 |
| 17 | William R. Morrison (D) | 16,950 | 51.5 |
| | John B. Hay (R) | 15,986 | 48.5 |
| 18 | John R. Thomas (R) | 16,873 | 51.1 |
| | William Hartzell (D) | 15,146 | 45.9 |
| 19 | Richard W. Townsend (D) | 18,021 | 52.9 |
| | Charles W. Pavey (R) | 14,561 | 42.8 |

## INDIANA

| | | | |
|---|---|---|---|
| 1 | William Heilman (R) | 17,719 | 49.4 |
| | John Kleiner (D) | 17,420 | 48.6 |
| 2 | Thomas R. Cobb (D) | 18,443 | 54.3 |
| | Braden (R) | 14,676 | 43.2 |

| | Candidates | Votes | % |
|---|---|---|---|
| 3 | Strother M. Stockslager (D) | 18,800 | 55.2 |
| | Charles (R) | 14,493 | 42.6 |
| 4 | William S. Holman (D) | 17,388 | 52.0 |
| | J. O. Cravens (R) | 15,641 | 46.7 |
| 5 | Courtland C. Matson (D) | 17,411 | 49.5 |
| | Treat (R) | 16,496 | 46.9 |
| 6 | Thomas M. Browne (R) | 22,136 | 62.2 |
| | Miller (D) | 12,676 | 35.6 |
| 7 | Stanton J. Peelle (R) | 17,610 | 48.3 |
| | Byfield (D) | 16,736 | 45.9 |
| | Delamatyr (NG) | 2,135 | 5.9 |
| 8 | Robert B. F. Peirce (R) | 19,291 | 49.0 |
| | Hanna (D) | 16,995 | 43.1 |
| | Copner (NG) | 3,120 | 7.9 |
| 9 | Godlove S. Orth (R) | 18,287 | 49.6 |
| | William Ralph Myers (D) | 17,475 | 47.4 |
| 10 | Mark L. DeMotte (R) | 18,024 | 51.5 |
| | Skinner (D) | 17,006 | 48.5 |
| 11 | George Washington Steele (R) | 20,246 | 48.1 |
| | Slack (D) | 19,713 | 46.8 |
| | Studebaker (NG) | 2,168 | 5.2 |
| 12 | Walpole G. Colerick (D) | 17,800 | 51.1 |
| | Taylor (R) | 17,030 | 48.9 |
| 13 | William Henry Calkins (R) | 17,981 | 49.2 |
| | McDonald (D) | 16,817 | 46.0 |

## IOWA

| | | | |
|---|---|---|---|
| 1 | Moses A. McCoid (R) | 17,117 | 53.9 |
| | W. B. Culbertson (D) | 12,119 | 38.2 |
| | D. P. Stubbs (R) | 2,497 | 7.9 |
| 2 | Sewall S. Farwell (R) | 17,465 | 54.9 |
| | Roderick Rose (D) | 13,100 | 41.2 |
| 3 | Thomas Updegraff (R) | 17,359 | 51.8 |
| | William G. Stewart (D) | 13,969 | 41.7 |
| | M. H. Moore (G) | 2,193 | 6.5 |
| 4 | Nathaniel C. Deering (R) | 21,940 | 65.4 |
| | Joseph S. Root (D) | 8,731 | 26.0 |
| | M. B. Doolittle (G) | 2,191 | 6.5 |
| 5 | William G. Thompson (R) | 20,016 | 59.8 |
| | R. E. Austin (D) | 11,315 | 33.8 |
| | A. F. Palmer (G) | 2,114 | 6.3 |
| 6 | Marsena E. Cutts (R) | 18,017‡ | 50.1 |
| | John Calhoun Cook (D & G) | 17,911 | 49.8 |
| 7 | John A. Kasson (R) | 19,932 | 53.8 |
| | Edward Hooker Gillette (D & G) | 16,776 | 45.3 |
| 8 | William P. Hepburn (R) | 24,358 | 56.3 |
| | Robert Percival (D) | 12,984 | 30.0 |
| | H. C. Ayres (G) | 5,920 | 13.7 |
| 9 | Cyrus Clay Carpenter (R) | 25,533 | 63.4 |
| | P. M. Guthrie (D) | 12,267 | 30.5 |
| | Daniel Campbell (G) | 2,363 | 5.9 |

## KANSAS

| | | | |
|---|---|---|---|
| 1 | John A. Anderson (R) | 48,599 | 61.8 |
| | C. C. Burnes (D) | 22,727 | 28.9 |
| | John Davis (G) | 7,318 | 9.3 |
| 2 | Dudley C. Haskell (R) | 30,758 | 56.4 |
| | Louis F. Green (G) | 23,737 | 43.5 |
| 3 | Thomas Ryan (R) | 41,094 | 60.9 |
| | J. Wade McDonald (D) | 16,976 | 25.2 |
| | D. P. Mitchell (G LAB) | 9,396 | 13.9 |

## KENTUCKY

| | | | |
|---|---|---|---|
| 1 | Oscar Turner (D) | 11,448 | 53.6 |
| | R. B. Ratliff (R) | 6,318 | 29.6 |
| | W. W. Tice (D) | 3,572 | 16.7 |
| 2 | James A. McKenzie (D) | 14,694 | 52.0 |
| | John Feland (D) | 8,354 | 29.5 |
| | Charles W. Cook (G) | 5,233 | 18.5 |

## KENTUCKY

| Candidates | Votes | % |
|---|---|---|
| 3 John W. Caldwell (D) | 13,089 | 50.7 |
| M. T. Flippin (R) | 10,987 | 42.6 |
| George Wright (G) | 1,736 | 6.7 |
| 4 J. Proctor Knott (D) | 13,778 | 59.2 |
| William T. Thurmond (R) | 6,603 | 28.4 |
| L. E. Green (G) | 2,820 | 12.1 |
| 5 Albert S. Willis (D) | 11,934 | 48.5 |
| Thomas E. Burns (R) | 8,445 | 34.3 |
| Thomas Hays (G) | 3,794 | 15.4 |
| 6 John G. Carlisle (D) | 17,291 | 63.7 |
| Oliver H. Root (R) | 9,862 | 36.3 |
| 7 Joseph C. S. Blackburn (D) | 16,799 | 70.6 |
| Lycander Hord (R) | 5,692 | 23.9 |
| W. C. Goodloe (R) | 1,207 | 5.1 |
| 8 Philip B. Thompson Jr. (D) | 14,249 | 53.0 |
| Speed S. Fry (R) | 12,004 | 44.6 |
| 9 John D. White (R) | 15,317 | 53.5 |
| Thomas Turner (D) | 13,326 | 46.5 |
| 10 Elijah C. Phister (D) | 13,944 | 51.8 |
| George M. Thomas (R) | 12,955 | 48.1 |

## LOUISIANA

| Candidates | Votes | % |
|---|---|---|
| 1 Randall L. Gibson (D) | 10,526 | 66.6 |
| A. J. Ker (R) | 5,291 | 33.5 |
| 2 E. John Ellis (D) | 10,032 | 60.0 |
| Michael Hahn (R) | 6,701 | 40.1 |
| 3 Chester B. Darrall (R) | 13,371 | 63.2 |
| J. S. Billiu (D) | 7,794 | 36.8 |
| 4 Newton C. Blanchard (D) | 12,446 | 88.4 |
| A. C. Wells (R) | 1,638 | 11.6 |
| 5 J. Floyd King (D) | 15,305 | 82.2 |
| R. H. Lanier (R) | 3,318 | 17.8 |
| 6 Edward W. Robertson (D) | 9,941 | 64.9 |
| Alexander Smith (R) | 5,372 | 35.1 |

## MAINE

| Candidates | Votes | % |
|---|---|---|
| 1 Thomas B. Reed (R) | 16,920 | 49.8 |
| Samuel J. Anderson (D & G) | 16,803 | 49.4 |
| 2 William P. Frye (R) | 14,417 | 53.6 |
| Frank M. Fogg (D & G) | 12,343 | 45.9 |
| 3 Stephen D. Lindsey (R) | 15,131 | 50.5 |
| William Philbrick (D & G) | 14,824 | 49.5 |
| 4 George W. Ladd (D & G) | 14,047 | 51.5 |
| Charles A. Boutelle (R) | 13,194 | 48.4 |
| 5 Thompson H. Murch (D & G) | 14,942 | 51.6 |
| Seth L. Milliken (R) | 13,977 | 48.3 |

## MARYLAND

| Candidates | Votes | % |
|---|---|---|
| 1 George W. Covington (D) | 16,025 | 54.2 |
| Smith (R) | 13,532 | 45.8 |
| 2 J. Fred. C. Talbott (D) | 14,988 | 52.7 |
| Webster (R) | 13,472 | 47.3 |
| 3 Fetter S. Hoblitzell (D) | 13,629 | 57.7 |
| Horner (R) | 9,975 | 42.3 |
| 4 Robert M. McLane (D) | 15,702 | 53.7 |
| Maund (R) | 13,540 | 46.3 |
| 5 Andrew G. Chapman (D) | 14,448 | 53.3 |
| Wilmer (R) | 12,665 | 46.7 |
| 6 Milton G. Urner (R) | 17,129 | 50.5 |
| Schley (D) | 16,339 | 48.2 |

## MASSACHUSETTS

| Candidates | Votes | % |
|---|---|---|
| 1 William W. Crapo (R) | 16,384 | 69.7 |
| Davis (D) | 6,669 | 28.4 |
| 2 Benjamin W. Harris (R) | 17,047 | 62.8 |
| Dean (D) | 9,718 | 35.8 |
| 3 Ambrose A. Ranney (R) | 13,132 | 51.9 |
| Dearborn (D) | 12,073 | 47.7 |
| 4 Leopold Morse (D) | 10,616 | 49.4 |
| Hayes (R) | 10,501 | 48.9 |
| 5 Selwyn Z. Bowman (R) | 16,688 | 55.9 |
| Beebe (D) | 11,729 | 39.3 |

| Candidates | Votes | % |
|---|---|---|
| 6 Eben F. Stone (R) | 14,124 | 54.2 |
| Boynton (D) | 11,900 | 45.7 |
| 7 William A. Russell (R) | 14,982 | 58.8 |
| Aldrich (D) | 10,027 | 39.4 |
| 8 John W. Candler (R) | 16,644 | 58.2 |
| Russell (D) | 11,542 | 40.3 |
| 9 William W. Rice (R) | 14,935 | 61.5 |
| McCafferty (D) | 8,925 | 36.7 |
| 10 Amasa Norcross (R) | 15,608 | 62.8 |
| Ivord (D) | 8,627 | 34.7 |
| 11 George D. Robinson (R) | 14,235 | 58.3 |
| Woodworth (D) | 10,007 | 41.0 |

## MICHIGAN

| Candidates | Votes | % |
|---|---|---|
| 1 Henry W. Lord (R) | 15,962 | 49.9 |
| Maybury (D) | 15,388 | 48.1 |
| 2 Edwin Willits (R) | 18,945 | 50.7 |
| Waldby (D) | 16,596 | 44.4 |
| 3 Edward S. Lacey (R) | 21,267 | 52.9 |
| Pringle (D) | 9,739 | 24.2 |
| Hodge (G) | 8,959 | 22.3 |
| 4 Julius C. Burrows (R) | 19,096 | 53.4 |
| Powers (D) | 12,424 | 34.8 |
| Yaple (NG) | 4,193 | 11.7 |
| 5 George W. Webber (R) | 22,824 | 52.1 |
| Randall (D) | 11,435 | 26.1 |
| Blanchard (G) | 9,506 | 21.7 |
| 6 Oliver L. Spaulding (R) | 23,551 | 49.5 |
| Winans (D) | 18,235 | 38.3 |
| Begole (G) | 5,690 | 12.0 |
| 7 Omar D. Conger (R) | 17,490* | 53.5 |
| Black (D) | 13,806 | 42.2 |
| 8 Roswell G. Horr (R) | 21,224 | 48.3 |
| Tarsney (D) | 18,857 | 42.9 |
| Smith (G) | 3,829 | 8.7 |
| 9 Jay A. Hubbell (R) | 23,437 | 60.1 |
| Pratt (D) | 14,642 | 37.5 |

## MINNESOTA

| Candidates | Votes | % |
|---|---|---|
| 1 Mark H. Dunnell (R) | 22,392 | 51.1 |
| Wells (D) | 13,768 | 31.4 |
| Ward (IR) | 7,656 | 17.5 |
| 2 Horace B. Strait (R) | 24,508 | 56.7 |
| Poehler (D) | 18,707 | 43.3 |
| 3 William D. Washburn (R) | 36,428 | 60.5 |
| Sibley (D) | 23,804 | 39.5 |

## MISSISSIPPI

| Candidates | Votes | % |
|---|---|---|
| 1 Henry L. Muldrow (D) | 14,456 | 74.7 |
| Morphis (R) | 3,828 | 19.8 |
| Davidson (G) | 1,058 | 5.5 |
| 2 Vannoy H. Manning (D) | 15,255 | 52.9 |
| George M. Buchanan (R) | 9,996 | 34.7 |
| Harris (G) | 3,585 | 12.4 |
| 3 Hernando D. Money (D) | 11,722 | 80.7 |
| Gunn (G) | 2,790 | 19.2 |
| 4 Otho R. Singleton (D) | 13,749 | 76.7 |
| Drennan (R) | 4,177 | 23.3 |
| 5 Charles E. Hooker (D) | 11,771 | 63.5 |
| Deason (IR) | 5,618 | 30.3 |
| 6 James R. Chalmers (D) | 9,172‡ | 63.0 |
| John R. Lynch (R) | 5,393 | 37.0 |

## MISSOURI

| Candidates | Votes | % |
|---|---|---|
| 1 Martin L. Clardy (D) | 11,681 | 51.6 |
| Fletcher (R) | 10,892 | 48.2 |
| 2 Thomas Allen (D) | 12,458 | 55.4 |
| Rosenblatt (R) | 10,022 | 44.6 |
| 3 Richard G. Frost (D) | 9,487‡ | 49.8 |
| Gustavus Sessinghaus (R) | 9,290 | 48.8 |
| 4 Lowndes H. Davis (D) | 19,949 | 94.1 |
| Simpson (D) | 1,251 | 5.9 |
| 5 Richard P. Bland (D) | 12,977 | 54.5 |
| Palmer (GD) | 10,799 | 45.4 |

| Candidates | Votes | % |
|---|---|---|
| 6 Ira S. Hazeltine (G & R) | 22,787 | 50.1 |
| Waddill (D) | 22,680 | 49.8 |
| 7 Theron M. Rice (G & R) | 19,744 | 50.8 |
| Philips (D) | 19,146 | 49.2 |
| 8 Robert T. Van Horn (R) | 8,050 | 33.2 |
| Allen (D) | 7,656 | 31.6 |
| Crisp (D) | 7,459 | 30.8 |
| 9 Nicholas Ford (G & R) | 20,770 | 50.0 |
| Craig (D) | 20,768 | 50.0 |
| 10 Joseph H. Burrows (G & R) | 17,284 | 50.1 |
| Mansur (D) | 17,219 | 49.9 |
| 11 John B. Clark Jr. (D) | 17,021 | 69.7 |
| Heberling (GD) | 7,370 | 30.2 |
| 12 William H. Hatch (D) | 17,401 | 53.3 |
| London (G & R) | 15,236 | 46.7 |
| 13 Aylett H. Buckner (D) | 17,233 | 69.3 |
| Haley (GD) | 7,394 | 29.7 |

## NEBRASKA

| Candidates | Votes | % |
|---|---|---|
| AL Edward K. Valentine (R) | 52,648 | 62.5 |
| James E. North (D) | 23,634 | 28.1 |

## NEVADA

| Candidates | Votes | % |
|---|---|---|
| AL George W. Cassidy (D) | 9,815 | 53.4 |
| Daggett (R) | 8,578 | 46.6 |

## NEW HAMPSHIRE

| Candidates | Votes | % |
|---|---|---|
| 1 Joshua G. Hall (R) | 16,310 | 51.5 |
| Sanborn (D) | 15,047 | 47.5 |
| 2 James F. Briggs (R) | 14,480 | 52.4 |
| Sulloway (D) | 13,000 | 47.1 |
| 3 Evarts W. Farr (R) | 13,861* | 51.3 |
| Bingham (D) | 12,896 | 47.7 |

## NEW JERSEY

| Candidates | Votes | % |
|---|---|---|
| 1 George M. Robeson (R) | 19,807 | 53.6 |
| Carter (D) | 16,350 | 44.2 |
| 2 J. Hart Brewer (R) | 18,580 | 52.4 |
| Smith (D) | 16,536 | 46.6 |
| 3 Miles Ross (D) | 19,725 | 53.3 |
| Robbins (R) | 16,953 | 45.8 |
| 4 Henry S. Harris (D) | 17,043 | 56.1 |
| Kilpatrick (R) | 12,870 | 42.4 |
| 5 John Hill (R) | 16,766 | 52.0 |
| Cutler (D) | 15,165 | 47.0 |
| 6 Phineas Jones (R) | 20,424 | 52.5 |
| Balbach Jr (D) | 17,888 | 46.0 |
| 7 Augustus A. Hardenbergh (D) | 19,462 | 56.7 |
| Brigham (R) | 14,714 | 42.9 |

## NEW YORK

| Candidates | Votes | % |
|---|---|---|
| 1 Perry Belmont (D) | 20,805 | 53.1 |
| J. A. King (R) | 18,163 | 46.3 |
| 2 William E. Robinson (D) | 20,122 | 60.7 |
| Daniel O'Reilly (R) | 12,166 | 36.7 |
| 3 J. Hyatt Smith (D & G) | 22,085 | 51.3 |
| S. B. Chittenden (R) | 20,626 | 48.0 |
| 4 Archibald M. Bliss (D) | 20,030 | 56.9 |
| D. W. Talmage (R) | 14,614 | 41.5 |
| 5 Benjamin Wood (D) | 11,411 | 47.6 |
| N. Muller (ID) | 9,750 | 40.6 |
| C. L. Brockmeier (R) | 2,714 | 11.3 |
| 6 Samuel S. Cox (D) | 17,025 | 69.7 |
| Victor Heimberger (R) | 7,162 | 29.3 |
| 7 Philip Henry Dugro (D) | 11,723 | 49.5 |
| W. W. Astor (R) | 11,550 | 48.8 |
| 8 Anson G. McCook (R) | 17,392 | 57.9 |
| John G. Davis (D) | 12,468 | 41.5 |
| 9 Fernando Wood (D) | 10,842* | 38.0 |
| J. L. N. Hunt (R) | 9,313 | 32.6 |
| John Hardy | 8,251 | 28.9 |

## NEW YORK

| Candidates | Votes | % |
|---|---|---|
| 10 Abram S. Hewitt (D) | 19,961 | 65.3 |
| James Talcott (R) | 10,098 | 33.1 |
| 11 Levi P. Morton (R) | 18,232 | 54.7 |
| James W. Gerard (D) | 14,898 | 44.7 |
| 12 Waldo Hutchins (D) | 15,852 | 51.6 |
| Alex Taylor Jr. (R) | 14,803 | 48.2 |
| 13 John H. Ketcham (R) | 20,355 | 56.8 |
| Edward L. Gaul (D) | 15,312 | 42.7 |
| 14 Lewis Beach (D) | 16,664 | 49.8 |
| Charles T. Pierson (R) | 16,134 | 48.2 |
| 15 Thomas Cornell (R) | 18,845 | 50.7 |
| John S. Pindar (D) | 17,991 | 48.4 |
| 16 Michael N. Nolan (D) | 19,176 | 52.7 |
| S. O. Vanderpool (R) | 16,974 | 46.7 |
| 17 Walter A. Wood (R) | 21,902 | 80.8 |
| R. H. Ferguson (D) | 5,163 | 19.1 |
| 18 John Hammond (R) | 14,281 | 58.6 |
| T. H. Walker (D) | 9,360 | 38.4 |
| 19 Abraham X. Parker (R) | 17,569 | 66.7 |
| A. Andrus (D) | 8,385 | 31.8 |
| 20 George West (R) | 21,693 | 56.2 |
| N. H. Decker (D) | 16,490 | 42.8 |
| 21 Ferris Jacobs Jr. (R) | 19,078 | 51.7 |
| F. R. Gilbert (D) | 16,496 | 44.7 |
| 22 Warner Miller (R) | 19,792 | 55.3 |
| Dennis O'Brien (D) | 15,906 | 44.4 |
| 23 Cyrus D. Prescott (R) | 14,499 | 52.8 |
| R. E. Sutton (D) | 12,532 | 45.6 |
| 24 Joseph Mason (R) | 17,101 | 57.9 |
| Benjamin F. Lewis (D) | 11,510 | 39.0 |
| 25 Frank Hiscock (R) | 19,828 | 57.4 |
| William C. Ruger (D) | 14,634 | 42.4 |
| 26 John H. Camp (R) | 20,259 | 56.4 |
| P. H. Van Auken (D) | 14,555 | 40.5 |
| 27 Elbridge G. Lapham (R) | 15,673 | 55.2 |
| C. W. Bennett (D) | 12,263 | 43.2 |
| 28 Jeremiah W. Dwight (R) | 19,510 | 54.7 |
| F. Davis Jr. (D) | 15,082 | 42.3 |
| 29 David P. Richardson (R) | 21,211 | 52.4 |
| T. K. Beecher (GD) | 19,288 | 47.6 |
| 30 John Van Voorhis (R) | 21,481 | 55.4 |
| A. S. Warner (D) | 16,701 | 43.1 |
| 31 Richard Crowley (R) | 15,759 | 54.7 |
| R. S. Stevens (D) | 12,871 | 44.6 |
| 32 Jonathan Scoville (D) | 22,702 | 50.0 |
| M. P. Bush (R) | 22,329 | 49.2 |
| 33 Henry Van Aernam (R) | 17,429 | 58.5 |
| Van Campen (D) | 10,584 | 35.5 |

## NORTH CAROLINA

| Candidates | Votes | % |
|---|---|---|
| 1 Louis C. Latham (D) | 14,796 | 50.9 |
| Cyrus W. Grandy (R) | 14,290 | 49.1 |
| 2 Orlando Hubbs (R) | 19,259 | 57.2 |
| William H. Kitchin (D) | 14,305 | 42.5 |
| 3 John W. Shackelford (D) | 16,356 | 51.1 |
| William P. Canaday (R) | 15,017 | 46.9 |
| 4 William R. Cox (D) | 17,557 | 52.0 |
| Moses A. Bledsoe (R) | 16,241 | 48.1 |
| 5 Alfred M. Scales (D) | 13,634 | 52.8 |
| Thomas B. Keogh (R) | 11,623 | 45.0 |
| 6 Clement Dowd (D) | 16,401 | 57.0 |
| William R. Myers (R) | 12,366 | 43.0 |
| 7 Robert F. Armfield (D) | 13,331 | 53.9 |
| David M. Furches (R) | 11,383 | 46.1 |
| 8 Robert B. Vance (D) | 14,099 | 65.0 |
| Natt Atkinson (I) | 6,244 | 28.8 |
| Samuel L. Love (I) | 1,336 | 6.2 |

## OHIO

| Candidates | Votes | % |
|---|---|---|
| 1 Benjamin Butterworth (R) | 16,455 | 52.0 |
| Samuel F. Hunt (D) | 15,157 | 47.9 |
| 2 Thomas L. Young (R) | 17,385 | 51.5 |
| Henry B. Banning (D) | 16,381 | 48.5 |
| 3 Henry L. Morey (R) | 17,863 | 49.7 |
| Durbin Ward (D) | 17,835 | 49.6 |

| Candidates | Votes | % |
|---|---|---|
| 4 Emanuel Schultz (R) | 21,572 | 50.0 |
| John A. McMahon (D) | 21,244 | 49.3 |
| 5 Benjamin Le Fevre (D) | 23,598 | 60.1 |
| W. K. Boone (R) | 15,488 | 39.5 |
| 6 James M. Ritchie (R) | 19,773 | 49.4 |
| Frank H. Hurd (D) | 19,097 | 47.7 |
| 7 John P. Leedom (D) | 17,365 | 52.6 |
| Alphonso Hart (R) | 15,663 | 47.4 |
| 8 J. Warren Keifer (R) | 21,182 | 57.3 |
| Frank Chance (D) | 15,264 | 41.3 |
| 9 James S. Robinson (R) | 18,146 | 51.0 |
| Caleb H. Norris (D) | 17,007 | 47.8 |
| 10 John B. Rice (D) | 18,394 | 50.9 |
| Morgan D. Shaffer (D) | 17,026 | 47.1 |
| 11 Henry S. Neal (R) | 17,218 | 52.9 |
| William A. Hutchins (D) | 15,080 | 46.3 |
| 12 George L. Converse (D) | 21,673 | 54.4 |
| John Groce (D) | 17,484 | 43.9 |
| 13 Gibson Atherton (D) | 19,038 | 53.0 |
| Appleton B. Clarke (R) | 16,565 | 46.1 |
| 14 George W. Geddes (D) | 18,520 | 59.3 |
| S. Ellis Fink (R) | 12,653 | 40.5 |
| 15 Rufus R. Dawes (R) | 16,283 | 50.1 |
| A. J. Warner (D) | 15,781 | 48.5 |
| 16 Jonathan T. Updegraff (R) | 17,998 | 54.2 |
| James F. Charlesworth (D) | 15,150 | 45.7 |
| 17 William McKinley Jr. (R) | 20,221 | 53.5 |
| Leroy D. Thoman (D) | 16,650 | 44.1 |
| 18 Addison S. McClure (R) | 18,570 | 57.0 |
| David L. Wadsworth (D) | 13,474 | 41.4 |
| 19 Ezra B. Taylor (R) | 22,794 | 67.3 |
| Charles D. Adams (D) | 10,116 | 29.9 |
| 20 Amos Townsend (R) | 20,333 | 56.0 |
| John C. Hutchins (D) | 15,106 | 41.6 |

## OREGON

| Candidates | Votes | % |
|---|---|---|
| AL Melvin C. George (R) | 19,578 | 51.4 |
| John Whiteaker (D) | 18,181 | 47.8 |

## PENNSYLVANIA

| Candidates | Votes | % |
|---|---|---|
| 1 Henry H. Bingham (R) | 18,914 | 57.2 |
| George R. Snowden (D) | 14,178 | 42.8 |
| 2 Charles O'Neill (R) | 18,924 | 60.9 |
| A. S. Hartranft (D) | 12,122 | 39.0 |
| 3 Samuel J. Randall (D) | 13,639 | 57.8 |
| Benjamin L. Berry (R) | 9,912 | 42.0 |
| 4 William D. Kelley (R) | 25,968 | 61.2 |
| George Bull (D) | 16,487 | 38.8 |
| 5 Alfred C. Harmer (R) | 23,468 | 57.2 |
| John K. Folwell (D) | 17,332 | 42.3 |
| 6 William Ward (R) | 18,368 | 60.8 |
| R. J. Monaghan (D) | 11,847 | 39.2 |
| 7 William Godshalk (R) | 17,944 | 52.6 |
| John Slingluff (D) | 16,080 | 47.1 |
| 8 Daniel Ermentrout (D) | 16,049 | 63.1 |
| J. Howard Jacobs (R) | 9,152 | 36.0 |
| 9 A. Herr Smith (R) | 19,466 | 64.3 |
| J. L. Steinmetz (D) | 10,655 | 35.2 |
| 10 William Mutchler (D) | 21,464 | 61.3 |
| Hiram H. Fisher (R) | 13,326 | 38.1 |
| 11 Robert Klotz (D) | 19,812 | 62.3 |
| W. J. Scott (R) | 11,465 | 36.1 |
| 12 Joseph A. Scranton (R) | 13,455 | 47.1 |
| D. W. Connelly (D) | 10,948 | 38.3 |
| Hendk B. Wright (NG) | 4,174 | 14.6 |
| 13 Charles N. Brumm (G & R) | 12,038 | 52.2 |
| John W. Ryon (D) | 11,007 | 47.8 |
| 14 Samuel F. Barr (R) | 18,320 | 52.7 |
| Grant Weidman (D) | 15,771 | 45.4 |
| 15 Cornelius C. Jadwin (R) | 18,223 | 55.2 |
| Robert H. Packer (D) | 13,602 | 41.2 |
| 16 Robert J. C. Walker (R) | 17,850 | 50.8 |
| David Kirk (D & G) | 17,304 | 49.2 |
| 17 Jacob M. Campbell (R) | 17,300 | 51.6 |
| A. H. Coffroth (D) | 15,864 | 47.3 |
| 18 Horatio G. Fisher (R) | 16,847 | 51.1 |
| R. Milton Speer (D) | 16,130 | 48.9 |

| Candidates | Votes | % |
|---|---|---|
| 19 Frank E. Beltzhoover (D) | 20,858 | 57.5 |
| Charles J. Little (R) | 15,351 | 42.3 |
| 20 Andrew G. Curtin (D) | 17,461 | 54.7 |
| Thomas H. Murray (R) | 14,472 | 45.3 |
| 21 Morgan R. Wise (D) | 18,486 | 53.7 |
| James E. Sayers (R) | 11,879 | 34.5 |
| George W. K. Minor (NG) | 4,083 | 11.9 |
| 22 Russell Errett (R) | 18,241 | 53.3 |
| James H. Hopkins (D) | 14,084 | 41.1 |
| M. J. Sullivan (G) | 1,923 | 5.6 |
| 23 Thomas M. Bayne (R) | 15,641 | 63.2 |
| George T. Miller (D) | 8,278 | 33.5 |
| 24 William S. Shallenberger (R) | 15,567 | 56.6 |
| J. M. Clark (D) | 10,986 | 39.9 |
| 25 James Mosgrove (D & G) | 16,044 | 51.2 |
| Harry White (R) | 15,287 | 48.8 |
| 26 Samuel H. Miller (R) | 17,630 | 47.9 |
| James H. Caldwell (D) | 14,976 | 40.7 |
| W. C. Plummer (NG) | 3,895 | 10.6 |
| 27 Lewis F. Watson (R) | 15,740 | 52.0 |
| Alf Short (D & G) | 14,438 | 47.7 |

## RHODE ISLAND

| Candidates | Votes | % |
|---|---|---|
| 1 Nelson W. Aldrich (R) | 9,641 | 67.6 |
| Isaac Lawrence (D) | 4,446 | 31.2 |
| 2 Jonathan Chace (R) | 8,515 | 58.0 |
| Franklin Treat (D) | 6,031 | 41.1 |

## SOUTH CAROLINA

| Candidates | Votes | % |
|---|---|---|
| 1 John S. Richardson (D) | 20,142 | 63.3 |
| Samuel J. Lee (R) | 11,674 | 36.7 |
| 2 Michael P. O'Connor (D) | 17,569‡ | 58.8 |
| Edmund W. M. Mackey (R) | 12,297 | 41.2 |
| 3 D. Wyatt Aiken (D) | 27,863 | 74.1 |
| C. J. Stollbrand (R) | 9,758 | 25.9 |
| 4 John H. Evins (D) | 27,985 | 69.7 |
| A. Blythe (R) | 11,780 | 29.3 |
| 5 George D. Tillman (D) | 23,325‡ | 60.4 |
| Robert Smalls (R) | 15,287 | 39.6 |

## TENNESSEE

| Candidates | Votes | % |
|---|---|---|
| 1 Augustus H. Pettibone (R) | 15,117 | 52.5 |
| Taylor (D) | 13,693 | 47.5 |
| 2 Leonidas C. Houk (R) | 17,479 | 65.1 |
| Williams (D) | 9,380 | 34.9 |
| 3 George G. Dibrell (D) | 12,806 | 53.6 |
| Case (R) | 9,918 | 41.5 |
| 4 Benton McMillin (D) | 12,405 | 65.0 |
| Sanders (R) | 6,694 | 35.1 |
| 5 Richard Warner (LOWTAX D) | 7,777 | 36.3 |
| Bright (D) | 6,307 | 29.4 |
| Holman (R) | 5,077 | 23.7 |
| Tillman (G) | 2,263 | 10.6 |
| 6 John F. House (D) | 15,631 | 60.6 |
| McClain (R) | 9,389 | 36.4 |
| 7 Washington C. Whitthorne (D) | 11,118 | 58.0 |
| Hughes (R) | 8,056 | 42.0 |
| 8 John D. C. Atkins (D) | 10,999 | 46.6 |
| Hawkins (R) | 9,876 | 41.9 |
| Travis (D) | 2,723 | 11.5 |
| 9 Charles B. Simonton (D) | 12,150 | 52.8 |
| Shackleford (R) | 10,865 | 47.2 |
| 10 William R. Moore (R) | 11,844 | 50.7 |
| Young (D) | 10,998 | 47.1 |

## TEXAS

| Candidates | Votes | % |
|---|---|---|
| 1 John H. Reagan (D) | 21,227 | 77.7 |
| S. R. Withers (G) | 6,095 | 22.3 |
| 2 David B. Culberson (D) | 26,624 | 68.6 |
| H. F. O'Neal (G) | 12,194 | 31.4 |
| 3 Olin Wellborn (D) | 48,005 | 78.7 |
| J. C. Kirby (G) | 13,014 | 21.3 |

## TEXAS

| Candidates | Votes | % |
|---|---|---|
| 4 Roger Q. Mills (D) | 30,087 | 62.6 |
| J. T. Brady (G) | 17,977 | 37.4 |
| 5 George W. Jones (G) | 22,941 | 50.3 |
| Seth Shepard (D) | 22,708 | 49.7 |
| 6 Christopher C. Upson (D) | 27,521 | 97.3 |

## VERMONT

| Candidates | Votes | % |
|---|---|---|
| 1 Charles H. Joyce (R) | 15,645 | 68.6 |
| Randall (D) | 6,771 | 29.7 |
| 2 James M. Tyler (R) | 15,960 | 69.0 |
| Campbell (D) | 6,698 | 29.0 |
| 3 William W. Grout (R) | 12,253 | 61.9 |
| Curree (D) | 6,191 | 31.3 |
| Tarbell (G) | 1,256 | 6.4 |

## VIRGINIA

| Candidates | Votes | % |
|---|---|---|
| 1 George T. Garrison (D) | 11,595 | 48.2 |
| John W. Woltz (R) | 10,250 | 42.6 |
| John Critcher (READJ) | 2,217 | 9.2 |
| 2 John F. Dezendorf (R) | 14,775 | 52.6 |

| Candidates | Votes | % |
|---|---|---|
| John Goode (D) | 9,709 | 34.6 |
| B. W. Lacy (READJ) | 3,600 | 12.8 |
| 3 George D. Wise (D) | 10,931 | 55.9 |
| John S. Wise (READJ) | 8,566 | 43.8 |
| 4 Joseph Jorgensen (R) | 13,825 | 70.1 |
| Samuel F. Coleman (D) | 5,771 | 29.2 |
| 5 George C. Cabell (D) | 11,778 | 51.9 |
| John T. Stovall (READJ) | 10,919 | 48.1 |
| 6 John Randolph Tucker (D) | 13,646 | 59.5 |
| James A. Frazier (READJ) | 9,265 | 40.4 |
| 7 John Paul (READJ) | 10,665 | 49.3 |
| Henry C. Allen (D) | 9,938 | 45.9 |
| 8 John S. Barbour (D) | 15,546 | 56.6 |
| Sampson P. Bagley (R) | 9,170 | 33.4 |
| James H. Williams (READJ) | 2,732 | 10.0 |
| 9 Abram Fulkerson (READJ) | 8,096 | 40.7 |
| Connally F. Trigg (D) | 7,621 | 38.3 |
| G. G. Goodell (R) | 3,660 | 18.4 |

## WEST VIRGINIA

| Candidates | Votes | % |
|---|---|---|
| 1 Benjamin Wilson (D) | 18,460 | 46.6 |
| John H. Hutchinson (R) | 18,350 | 46.3 |
| James Bassil (G) | 2,515 | 6.3 |

| Candidates | Votes | % |
|---|---|---|
| 2 John B. Hogue (D) | 17,277 | 50.5 |
| J. T. Hoke (R) | 14,565 | 42.6 |
| D. Farnsworth (G) | 2,356 | 6.9 |
| 3 John E. Kenna (D) | 21,407 | 57.0 |
| H. I. Walker (R) | 16,097 | 42.9 |

## WISCONSIN

| Candidates | Votes | % |
|---|---|---|
| 1 Charles G. Williams (R) | 19,014 | 61.0 |
| Babbitt (D) | 11,782 | 37.8 |
| 2 Lucien B. Caswell (R) | 16,041 | 52.0 |
| Gregory (D) | 14,390 | 46.6 |
| 3 George C. Hazelton (R) | 16,236 | 55.6 |
| Cothren (D) | 12,941 | 44.3 |
| 4 Peter V. Deuster (D) | 17,574 | 53.7 |
| Sanger (R) | 15,018 | 45.9 |
| 5 Edward S. Bragg (D) | 16,984 | 51.6 |
| Colman (R) | 14,753 | 44.8 |
| 6 Richard W. Guenther (R) | 20,168 | 52.5 |
| Bouck (D) | 16,807 | 43.7 |
| 7 Herman L. Humphrey (R) | 23,179 | 64.7 |
| Froeman (D) | 10,994 | 30.7 |
| 8 Thaddeus C. Pound (R) | 19,256 | 56.8 |
| Silverthorn (D) | 14,590 | 43.1 |

# 1881 House Elections

## MAINE

### Special Election

| Candidates | Votes | % |
|---|---|---|
| 2 Nelson Dingley Jr. (R) | 10,961 | 65.3 |
| Gilbert (G) | 5,519 | 32.9 |

## MICHIGAN

### Special Election

| | Votes | % |
|---|---|---|
| 11 John T. Rich (R) | 15,279 | 55.7 |
| Cyrenius P. Black | 10,740 | 39.2 |

## NEW YORK

### Special Elections

| | Votes | % |
|---|---|---|
| 9 John Hardy (D) | 13,013 | 62.4 |
| Murphy (R) | 7,705 | 37.0 |
| 11 Roswell P. Flower (D) | 13,739 | 56.0 |
| Astor (R) | 10,626 | 43.3 |
| 22 Charles R. Skinner (R) | 16,222 | 54.8 |
| Lansing (D) | 13,065 | 44.1 |
| 27 James W. Wadsworth (R) | 12,086 | 54.2 |
| Faulkner (D) | 9,600 | 43.0 |

## RHODE ISLAND

### Special Election

| | Votes | % |
|---|---|---|
| 1 Henry J. Spooner (R) | 3,623 | 66.4 |
| Henry O. Sisson (D) | 1,103 | 20.2 |
| C. C. Van Zandt (R) | 709 | 13.0 |

# 1882 House Elections

## ALABAMA

| Candidates | Votes | % |
|---|---|---|
| 1 Thomas H. Herndon (D) | 9,609 | 57.4 |
| Smith (R) | 7,130 | 42.6 |
| 2 Hilary A. Herbert (D) | 12,823 | 58.4 |
| Rice (R) | 9,121 | 41.6 |
| 3 William C. Oates (D) | 11,238 | 87.9 |
| Millen (R) | 1,549 | 12.1 |
| 4 Charles M. Shelley (D) | 7,119‡ | 60.8 |
| George H. Craig (R) | 4,435 | 37.9 |
| 5 Thomas Williams (D) | 9,629 | 62.0 |
| McCoy (ID) | 5,880 | 37.9 |
| 6 Goldsmith W. Hewitt (D) | 6,402 | 72.7 |
| Carpenter (G) | 2,406 | 27.3 |
| 7 William H. Forney (D) | 7,750 | 80.7 |
| Bingham (R) | 1,859 | 19.4 |
| 8 Luke Pryor (D) | 12,155 | 51.6 |
| Shelby (ID) | 11,418 | 48.4 |

## ARKANSAS

| Candidates | Votes | % |
|---|---|---|
| 1 Poindexter Dunn (D) | 12,685 | 94.4 |
| J. B. Miles (R) | 719 | 5.4 |
| 2 James K. Jones (D) | 14,831 | 55.5 |
| J. A. Williams (R) | 11,525 | 43.1 |
| 3 John H. Rogers (D) | 10,522 | 57.3 |
| M. W. Benjamin (R) | 7,840 | 42.7 |
| 4 Samuel W. Peel (D) | 5,668 | 80.6 |
| Truman Niman (R) | 1,008 | 14.3 |
| AL Clifton R. Breckinridge (D) | 43,619 | 66.6 |
| C. E. Cunningham (G) | 21,422 | 32.7 |

## CALIFORNIA

| Candidates | Votes | % |
|---|---|---|
| 1 William S. Rosecrans (D) | 22,733 | 59.4 |
| Paul Neumann (R) | 14,847 | 38.8 |
| 2 James H. Budd (D) | 20,229 | 50.5 |
| H. F. Page (R) | 19,246 | 48.1 |
| 3 Barclay Henley (D) | 21,807 | 51.3 |
| J. J. DeHaven (R) | 19,470 | 45.8 |
| 4 Pleasant B. Tully (D) | 23,105 | 54.3 |
| George L. Woods (R) | 18,387 | 43.2 |
| AL John R. Glascock (D) | 87,259✔ | |
| Charles A. Sumner (D) | 87,233✔ | |
| W. W. Morrow (R) | 73,647 | |
| Henry Edgerton (R) | 73,454 | |
| J. B. Hotchkiss (P) | 2,776 | |
| J. Yarnell (P) | 2,722 | |
| Warren Chase (G) | 1,139 | |
| S. Maybell (G) | 1,090 | |

## COLORADO

| Candidates | Votes | % |
|---|---|---|
| AL James B. Belford (R) | 30,847 | 50.2 |
| S. S. Wallace (D) | 29,380 | 47.8 |

## CONNECTICUT

| Candidates | Votes | % |
|---|---|---|
| 1 William W. Eaton (D) | 14,740 | 50.7 |
| John R. Buck (R) | 14,047 | 48.3 |
| 2 Charles L. Mitchell (D) | 19,325 | 51.7 |
| Merwin (R) | 17,530 | 46.9 |
| 3 John T. Wait (R) | 9,882 | 53.4 |
| Penrose (D) | 8,227 | 44.5 |
| 4 Edward W. Seymour (D) | 15,703 | 51.8 |
| Coe (R) | 14,263 | 47.0 |

## DELAWARE

| Candidates | Votes | % |
|---|---|---|
| AL Charles B. Lore (D) | 16,563 | 53.0 |
| Washington Hastings (R) | 14,640 | 46.9 |

## FLORIDA

| Candidates | Votes | % |
|---|---|---|
| 1 Robert H. M. Davidson (D) | 11,244 | 51.5 |
| Skinner (R) | 7,017 | 32.2 |
| McKinnon | 3,553 | 16.3 |
| 2 Horatio Bisbee Jr. (R) | 13,122 | 50.6 |
| Finley (D) | 12,823 | 49.4 |

## GEORGIA

| Candidates | Votes | % |
|---|---|---|
| 1 John C. Nichols (D) | 6,055 | 60.9 |
| Atkins (R) | 3,884 | 39.1 |
| 2 Henry G. Turner (D) | 7,794 | 63.9 |
| Wessolowsky (R) | 4,406 | 36.1 |
| 3 Charles F. Crisp (D) | 4,121 | 92.6 |
| Harrall (R) | 329 | 7.4 |
| 4 Hugh Buchanan (D) | 5,583 | 78.5 |
| Pou (I) | 1,502 | 21.1 |
| 5 Nathaniel J. Hammond (D) | 10,788 | 65.2 |
| Buck (IR) | 5,756 | 34.8 |
| 6 James H. Blount (D) | 3,514 | 99.3 |
| 7 Judson C. Clements (D) | 12,408 | 53.6 |
| Felton (ID) | 10,746 | 46.4 |
| 8 Seaborn Reese (D) | 4,384 | 96.0 |
| 9 Allen D. Candler (D) | 14,521 | 54.9 |
| Speer (ID) | 11,915 | 45.1 |
| AL Thomas Hardeman (D) | 79,540 | 76.3 |
| Forsyth (R) | 24,645 | 23.7 |

### Special Election

| Candidates | Votes | % |
|---|---|---|
| 8 Seaborn Reese (D) | 4,282 | 100.0 |

## ILLINOIS

| Candidates | Votes | % |
|---|---|---|
| 1 Ransom W. Dunham (R) | 11,571 | 50.9 |
| John W. Downes (D) | 10,534 | 46.3 |
| 2 John F. Finerty (ID) | 9,360 | 56.2 |
| Henry F. Sheridan (D) | 6,939 | 41.6 |
| 3 George R. Davis (R) | 12,511 | 53.2 |
| William T. Black (A-MON D) | 10,274 | 43.7 |
| 4 George E. Adams (R) | 11,686 | 53.3 |
| Lamberd Tree (D) | 9,446 | 43.1 |
| 5 Reuben Ellwood (R) | 12,994 | 70.6 |
| William Price (D) | 5,127 | 27.9 |
| 6 Robert R. Hitt (R) | 12,726 | 57.1 |
| James S. Ticknor (D) | 9,045 | 40.6 |
| 7 Thomas J. Henderson (R) | 12,751 | 61.1 |
| Larmon G. Johnson (D) | 6,369 | 30.5 |
| M. B. Loyd (P) | 1,673 | 8.0 |
| 8 William Cullen (R) | 13,851 | 46.9 |
| Patrick C. Haley (D) | 13,673 | 46.3 |
| 9 Lewis E. Payson (R) | 12,619 | 52.4 |
| E. B. Buck (D) | 9,243 | 38.4 |
| O. W. Barnard (G) | 2,138 | 8.9 |
| 10 Nicholas E. Worthington (D) | 13,571 | 48.3 |
| John H. Lewis (R) | 13,180 | 46.9 |
| 11 William W. Neece (D) | 14,604 | 45.3 |
| Benjamin F. Marsh (R) | 13,975 | 43.3 |
| Richard Haney (P) | 3,671 | 11.4 |
| 12 James M. Riggs (D) | 15,316 | 49.0 |
| James W. Singleton (ID) | 11,782 | 37.7 |
| Philip N. Minier (P) | 4,130 | 13.2 |
| 13 William M. Springer (D) | 18,360 | 54.4 |
| Dietrich C. Smith (R) | 14,042 | 41.6 |
| 14 Jonathan H. Rowell (R) | 15,273 | 48.8 |
| Adlai E. Stevenson (D) | 14,598 | 46.7 |
| 15 Joseph G. Cannon (R) | 15,868 | 51.1 |
| Andrew J. Hunter (D) | 14,651 | 47.2 |
| 16 Aaron Shaw (D) | 14,557 | 50.7 |
| E. B. Green (R) | 13,689 | 47.7 |
| 17 Samuel W. Moulton (D) | 14,495 | 55.9 |
| William H. Barlow (R) | 10,068 | 38.8 |
| B. W. F. Corley (P) | 1,386 | 5.3 |
| 18 William R. Morrison (D) | 14,906 | 52.2 |
| W. C. Keuffner (R) | 12,561 | 44.0 |

| Candidates | Votes | % |
|---|---|---|
| 19 Richard W. Townshend (D) | 15,606 | 60.7 |
| George C. Ross (R) | 9,930 | 38.6 |
| 20 John R. Thomas (R) | 14,504 | 49.0 |
| William K. Murphy (D) | 14,113 | 47.6 |

### Special Election

| Candidates | Votes | % |
|---|---|---|
| 5 Robert R. Hitt (R) | 12,430 | 59.9 |
| Larmon G. Johnson (D) | 8,138 | 39.2 |

## INDIANA

| Candidates | Votes | % |
|---|---|---|
| 1 John Kleiner (D) | 18,048 | 51.6 |
| William Heilman (R) | 16,399 | 46.9 |
| 2 Thomas R. Cobb (D) | 16,339 | 55.1 |
| A. J. Hostetter (R) | 13,288 | 44.8 |
| 3 Strother M. Stockslager (D) | 17,122 | 56.2 |
| Will T. Walker (R) | 12,538 | 41.2 |
| 4 William S. Holman (D) | 16,640 | 55.4 |
| W. J. Johnson (R) | 13,146 | 43.8 |
| 5 Courtland C. Matson (D) | 16,851 | 55.9 |
| Wallingford (R) | 13,298 | 44.1 |
| 6 Thomas M. Browne (R) | 19,562 | 60.1 |
| J. L. Pender (D) | 12,249 | 37.6 |
| 7 Stanton J. Peelle (R)‡ | 17,451‡ | 49.4 |
| William Estin English (D) | 17,373 | 49.1 |
| 8 John Edward Lamb (D) | 18,110 | 47.9 |
| Robert Bruce Frasen Peirce (R) | 17,823 | 47.2 |
| 9 Thomas Bayless Ward (D) | 17,357 | 49.7 |
| Godlove S. Orth (R) | 16,481 | 47.2 |
| 10 Thomas J. Wood (D) | 17,237 | 49.5 |
| Mark Lindsey Demotte (R) | 16,223 | 46.6 |
| 11 George Washington Steele (R) | 19,863 | 48.6 |
| Dailey (D) | 19,530 | 47.8 |
| 12 Robert Lowry (D) | 16,986 | 54.4 |
| Glasgow (R) | 13,623 | 43.6 |
| 13 William Henry Calkins (R) | 17,478 | 47.9 |
| Winterbotham (D) | 17,087 | 46.8 |
| Shively (NG) | 1,942 | 5.3 |

### Special Election

| Candidates | Votes | % |
|---|---|---|
| 9 Charles T. Doxey (R) | ✔ | |

## IOWA

| Candidates | Votes | % |
|---|---|---|
| 1 Moses A. McCoid (R) | 13,549 | 48.1 |
| Benton J. Hall (D) | 13,311 | 47.3 |
| 2 Jeremiah Henry Murphy (D) | 15,760 | 54.6 |
| Sewell S. Farwell (R) | 12,561 | 43.5 |
| 3 David B. Henderson (R) | 12,907 | 50.4 |
| C. M. Durham (D) | 11,604 | 45.3 |
| 4 Luman Hamlin Weller (D) | 11,473 | 51.5 |
| Thomas Updegraff (R) | 10,762 | 48.3 |
| 5 James Wilson (R) | 11,791‡ | 47.5 |
| Benjamin Todd Frederick (D) | 11,768 | 47.4 |
| David Platner (G) | 1,253 | 5.1 |
| 6 Marsena E. Cutts (R) | 11,250 | 40.4 |
| James Baird Weaver (G) | 8,569 | 30.8 |
| C. H. Mackey (D) | 8,040 | 28.9 |
| 7 John A. Kasson (R) | 13,631 | 50.8 |
| T. C. Gilpin (D) | 7,068 | 26.3 |
| E. H. Gillette (G) | 6,131 | 22.9 |
| 8 William P. Hepburn (R) | 13,792 | 51.7 |
| D. M. Clark (G) | 7,344 | 27.5 |
| Lewis Bonnett (D) | 5,533 | 20.7 |
| 9 William H. M. Pusey (D) | 14,186 | 49.0 |
| Albert Raney Anderson (R) | 11,987 | 41.4 |
| J. B. Hatton (G) | 2,753 | 9.5 |
| 10 Adoniram J. Holmes (R) | 14,250 | 62.2 |
| John Cliggitt (D) | 6,853 | 29.9 |
| Josial Doane (G) | 1,799 | 7.9 |
| 11 Isaac S. Struble (R) | 15,315 | 58.0 |
| John P. Allison (D) | 9,867 | 37.3 |

## KANSAS

| Candidates | Votes | % |
|---|---|---|
| 1 John A. Anderson (R) | 41,251 | 68.3 |
| Charles H. Moody (G LAB) | 17,816 | 29.5 |
| 2 Dudley C. Haskell (R) | 23,601 | 48.7 |
| N. F. Acers (D) | 19,116 | 39.5 |
| Alfred Taylor (G LAB) | 5,710 | 11.8 |
| 3 Thomas Ryan (R) | 36,091 | 57.1 |
| John C. Cannon (D) | 17,729 | 28.1 |
| D. J. Cole (G LAB) | 9,356 | 14.8 |
| AL Samuel R. Peters (R) | 99,866✓ | |
| Edmund N. Morrill (R) | 98,649✓ | |
| Bishop W. Perkins (R) | 98,338✓ | |
| Lewis Hanback (R) | 97,354✓ | |
| Samuel N. Wood (D) | 83,433 | |
| O'Flanagan (D) | 59,872 | |
| Leland (D) | 50,079 | |
| Davis (G LAB) | 26,701 | |
| Phillips (D) | 25,644 | |
| Williams (G LAB) | 22,243 | |
| Bennett (G LAB) | 1,417 | |
| Cannon (G LAB) | 588 | |

## KENTUCKY

| Candidates | Votes | % |
|---|---|---|
| 1 Oscar Turner (ID) | 8,705 | 39.3 |
| John R. Grace (D) | 7,627 | 34.5 |
| Henry Houston (R) | 5,803 | 26.2 |
| 2 James F. Clay (D) | 5,747 | 70.7 |
| W. M. Fuqua (R) | 1,979 | 24.3 |
| 3 John E. Halsell (D) | 13,546 | 50.4 |
| W. G. Hunter (R) | 13,356 | 49.7 |
| 4 Thomas A. Robertson (D) | 5,878 | 74.8 |
| W. H. Parrish (R) | 1,974 | 25.1 |
| 5 Albert S. Willis (D) | 6,492 | 62.5 |
| Silas F. Miller (R) | 3,557 | 34.3 |
| 6 John G. Carlisle (D) | 4,990 | 98.2 |
| 7 Joseph C. S. Blackburn (D) | 11,789 | 63.8 |
| John W. Asbury (R) | 6,692 | 36.2 |
| 8 P. B. Thompson Jr. (D) | 11,202 | 52.0 |
| R. L. Ewell (R) | 10,338 | 48.0 |
| 9 William W. Culbertson (R) | 11,217 | 53.0 |
| Z. Smith Hurt (D) | 9,948 | 47.0 |
| 10 John D. White (R) | 14,240 | 52.5 |
| G. M. Adams (D) | 12,870 | 47.5 |
| 11 Frank L. Wolford (D) | 12,007 | 54.7 |
| D. R. Carr (R) | 9,934 | 45.3 |

## LOUISIANA

| Candidates | Votes | % |
|---|---|---|
| 1 Carleton Hunt (D) | 8,498 | 63.7 |
| A. C. Janin (R) | 4,852 | 36.3 |
| 2 E. John Ellis (D) | 7,701 | 58.4 |
| Morris Marks (IR) | 2,789 | 21.1 |
| Henry Demas (R) | 2,666 | 20.2 |
| 3 William Pitt Kellogg (R) | 7,453 | 45.7 |
| Joseph Hayes Acklen (D) | 5,564 | 34.1 |
| Taylor Beattie (IR) | 3,301 | 20.2 |
| 4 Newton C. Blanchard (D) | 5,765 | 99.8 |
| 5 J. Floyd King (D) | 13,295 | 76.9 |
| W. L. Mcmillen (R) | 3,986 | 23.1 |
| 6 Andrew S. Herron (D) | 8,004* | 66.9 |
| Louis Trager (R) | 3,965 | 33.1 |

## MAINE

| Candidates | Votes | % |
|---|---|---|
| AL Thomas B. Reed (R) | 72,811✓ | |
| Nelson Dingley Jr (R) | 72,494✓ | |
| Charles A. Boutelle (R) | 72,352✓ | |
| Seth Llewellyn Milliken (R) | 72,310✓ | |
| Daniel H. Thing (FUS) | 63,321 | |
| Joseph Dane (FUS) | 63,304 | |
| George W. Ladd (FUS) | 63,192 | |
| Thompson H. Murch (FUS) | 62,616 | |
| W. F. Eaton (G) | 1,319 | |
| B. D. Averill (G) | 1,290 | |
| B. K. Kalloch (G) | 1,260 | |
| Eben O. Gerry (G) | 1,241 | |
| James M. Stone (IR&P) | 583 | |

| Candidates | Votes | % |
|---|---|---|
| Henry Tallman (P) | 295 | |
| N. G. Axtell (P) | 293 | |
| Joseph E. Ladd (P) | 291 | |
| Charles E. Nash (IR) | 264 | |
| Daniel Stickney (IR) | 198 | |

## MARYLAND

| | Votes | % |
|---|---|---|
| 1 George W. Covington (D) | 13,170 | 52.8 |
| Millikin (R) | 11,788 | 47.2 |
| 2 J. Fred C. Talbott (D) | 12,728 | 52.2 |
| Blair (R) | 11,641 | 47.8 |
| 3 Fetter S. Hoblitzell (D) | 13,917 | 56.8 |
| Lang (R) | 9,029 | 36.8 |
| Kimmel (I) | 1,576 | 6.4 |
| 4 John V. L. Findlay (D) | 14,457 | 53.1 |
| Stockbridge (R) | 12,793 | 47.0 |
| 5 Hart B. Holton (R) | 13,550 | 53.0 |
| Chapman (D) | 12,011 | 47.0 |
| 6 Louis E. McComas (R) | 15,720 | 51.7 |
| Blair (D) | 14,440 | 47.5 |

## MASSACHUSETTS

| | Votes | % |
|---|---|---|
| 1 Robert T. Davis (R) | 11,475 | 66.0 |
| Nicholas Hathaway (D) | 5,581 | 32.1 |
| 2 John D. Long (R) | 12,915 | 53.9 |
| Edgar E. Dean (D) | 10,152 | 42.4 |
| 3 Ambrose A. Ranney (R) | 11,968 | 57.8 |
| Horatio E. Swasey (D) | 8,540 | 41.3 |
| 4 Patrick A. Collins (D) | 12,884 | 73.1 |
| Charles T. Gallagher (R) | 4,546 | 25.8 |
| 5 Leopold Morse (D) | 11,301 | 56.0 |
| Selwyn Z. Bowman (R) | 8,791 | 43.6 |
| 6 Henry B. Lovering (D & G) | 12,840 | 51.8 |
| Elisha S. Converse (R) | 11,960 | 48.2 |
| 7 Eben F. Stone (R) | 10,056 | 44.3 |
| Charles P. Thompson (D) | 8,764 | 38.6 |
| Eben Moody Boynton (G) | 3,825 | 16.9 |
| 8 William A. Russell (R) | 11,269 | 51.0 |
| Charles S. Lilley (D) | 10,743 | 48.6 |
| 9 Theodore Lyman (CSR&D) | 12,076 | 54.4 |
| John W. Candler (R) | 9,703 | 43.7 |
| 10 William W. Rice (R) | 11,846 | 55.5 |
| John Hopkins (D) | 9,404 | 44.1 |
| 11 William Whiting (R) | 14,485 | 64.2 |
| Edward J. Sawyer (D) | 7,600 | 33.7 |
| 12 George D. Robinson (R) | 11,294 | 53.3 |
| Reuben Noble (D) | 9,889 | 46.7 |

## MICHIGAN

| | Votes | % |
|---|---|---|
| 1 William C. Maybury (FUS) | 16,148 | 57.4 |
| Henry W. Lord (R) | 11,209 | 39.8 |
| 2 Nathaniel B. Eldredge (D) | 15,251 | 48.2 |
| John K. Boies (R) | 14,709 | 46.5 |
| 3 Edward S. Lacey (R) | 18,023 | 52.0 |
| Hiram C. Hodge (FUS) | 16,329 | 47.1 |
| 4 George L. Yaple (FUS) | 16,329 | 50.4 |
| Julius C. Burrows (R) | 16,077 | 49.6 |
| 5 Julius Houseman (FUS) | 16,725 | 49.5 |
| William O. Webster (R) | 16,609 | 49.2 |
| 6 Edwin B. Winans (FUS) | 18,516 | 49.8 |
| Oliver L. Spaulding (R) | 18,484 | 49.8 |
| 7 Ezra C. Carleton (FUS) | 11,540 | 50.6 |
| John T. Rich (R) | 11,252 | 49.4 |
| 8 Roswell G. Horr (R) | 14,872 | 50.7 |
| Charles J. Willet (FUS) | 13,918 | 47.5 |
| 9 Byron M. Cutcheon (R) | 13,529 | 55.4 |
| Stephen Bronson (FUS) | 10,897 | 44.6 |
| 10 Herschel H. Hatch (R) | 11,327 | 52.6 |
| Andrew C. Maxwell (FUS) | 7,749 | 36.0 |
| Jesse M. Miller | 2,434 | 11.3 |
| 11 Edward Breitung (R) | 11,428 | 68.5 |
| Peter White (FUS) | 4,840 | 29.0 |

## MINNESOTA

| Candidates | Votes | % |
|---|---|---|
| 1 Milo White (R) | 12,458 | 49.1 |
| A. Bierman (D) | 11,789 | 46.4 |
| 2 James B. Wakefield (R) | 17,187 | 63.6 |
| F. A. Bohrer (D) | 6,750 | 25.0 |
| J. A. Latimer (P) | 3,085 | 11.4 |
| 3 Horace B. Strait (R) | 16,583 | 68.2 |
| C. P. Adams (D) | 7,047 | 29.0 |
| 4 William D. Washburn (R) | 17,380 | 51.5 |
| A. A. Ames (D) | 14,820 | 43.9 |
| 5 Knute Nelson (IR) | 16,956 | 47.8 |
| C. F. Kindred (R) | 12,238 | 34.5 |
| E P. Barnum (D) | 6,248 | 17.6 |

## MISSISSIPPI

| | Votes | % |
|---|---|---|
| 1 Henry L. Muldrow (D) | 6,390 | 81.9 |
| Lyon (R) | 1,414 | 18.1 |
| 2 James R. Chalmers (I) | 9,729‡ | 52.3 |
| Vannoy H. Manning (D) | 8,749 | 47.0 |
| 3 Elza Jeffords (R) | 4,127 | 69.1 |
| Clarke (D) | 1,321 | 22.1 |
| Waddell | 521 | 8.7 |
| 4 Hernando D. Money (D) | 6,848 | 68.8 |
| Griffin (R) | 2,644 | 26.5 |
| 5 Otho R. Singleton (D) | 6,121 | 98.9 |
| 6 Henry S. Van Eaton (D) | 7,615 | 53.2 |
| Lynch (R) | 6,706 | 46.8 |
| 7 Ethelbert Barksdale (D) | 10,933 | 66.6 |
| Hill (R) | 5,478 | 33.4 |

## MISSOURI

| | Votes | % |
|---|---|---|
| 1 William H. Hatch (D) | 16,243 | 57.4 |
| Glover (ID) | 11,415 | 40.3 |
| 2 Armstead M. Alexander (D) | 19,033 | 57.7 |
| Dorsey (R) | 8,628 | 26.2 |
| Quayle (GD) | 5,302 | 16.1 |
| 3 Alexander M. Dockery (D) | 17,261 | 52.9 |
| Thomas (R) | 12,887 | 39.5 |
| Burrows (G & R) | 2,485 | 7.6 |
| 4 James N. Burnes (D) | 13,325 | 51.1 |
| Reed (R) | 10,571 | 40.5 |
| Sisson (GD) | 2,185 | 8.4 |
| 5 Alexander Graves (D) | 12,695 | 58.8 |
| Crisp (ID) | 8,672 | 40.1 |
| 6 John Cosgrove (D) | 17,149 | 60.2 |
| Alldridge (GD) | 11,349 | 39.8 |
| 7 Aylett H. Buckner (D) | 14,370 | 55.2 |
| Daudt (R) | 9,857 | 37.9 |
| McNair (GD) | 1,786 | 6.9 |
| 8 John J. O'Neill (D) | 6,446 | 47.7 |
| Sessinghaus (R) | 4,795 | 35.5 |
| Dailey (R) | 1,282 | 9.5 |
| Sullivan (GD) | 997 | 7.4 |
| 9 James O. Broadhead (D) | 6,860 | 48.7 |
| McLean (R) | 6,758 | 48.0 |
| 10 Martin L. Clardy (D) | 13,536 | 57.2 |
| Manistre (R) | 7,455 | 31.5 |
| Jackson (G & R) | 2,667 | 11.3 |
| 11 Richard P. Bland (D) | 14,259 | 54.9 |
| Wallace (R) | 10,530 | 40.5 |
| 12 Charles H. Morgan (D) | 14,768 | 53.9 |
| Terrell (R) | 9,061 | 33.1 |
| Spring (G) | 3,550 | 13.0 |
| 13 Robert W. Fyan (D) | 13,904 | 42.9 |
| Cloud (R) | 12,424 | 38.3 |
| Haseltine (G) | 6,122 | 18.9 |
| 14 Lowndes H. Davis (D) | 14,023 | 58.1 |
| Carroll (R) | 7,177 | 29.8 |
| Kitchen (G) | 2,920 | 12.1 |

### Special Election

| | Votes | % |
|---|---|---|
| 9 James O. Broadhead (D) | 6,591 | 49.4 |
| McLean (R) | 6,386 | 47.9 |

## NEBRASKA

| Candidates | Votes | % |
|---|---|---|
| 1 Archibald J. Weaver (R) | 17,022 | 50.9 |
| John I. Reddick (D) | 12,690 | 38.0 |
| W. S. Gilbert (A-MONOP) | 3,707 | 11.1 |
| 2 James Laird (R) | 12,983 | 49.8 |
| V. S. Moore (A-MONOP) | 10,012 | 38.4 |
| F. A. Harman (D) | 3,070 | 11.8 |
| 3 Edward K. Valentine (R) | 11,272 | 39.5 |
| W. H. Munger (D) | 9,932 | 34.8 |
| M. K. Turner (A-MONOP) | 7,342 | 25.7 |

## NEVADA

| Candidates | Votes | % |
|---|---|---|
| AL George W. Cassidy (D) | 7,720 | 54.4 |
| Powning (R) | 6,462 | 45.6 |

## NEW HAMPSHIRE

| Candidates | Votes | % |
|---|---|---|
| 1 Martin A. Haynes (R) | 19,378 | 54.4 |
| Chandler (D) | 15,920 | 44.7 |
| 2 Ossian Ray (R) | 21,294 | 52.2 |
| Hosley (D) | 19,139 | 46.9 |

## NEW JERSEY

| Candidates | Votes | % |
|---|---|---|
| 1 Thomas M. Ferrell (D) | 16,541 | 50.1 |
| Robeson (R) | 14,825 | 44.9 |
| 2 J. Hart Brewer (R) | 15,604 | 51.3 |
| Parker Jr. (D) | 14,535 | 47.8 |
| 3 John Kean Jr. (R) | 15,186 | 48.2 |
| Ross (D) | 12,891 | 40.9 |
| Urner (G) | 3,463 | 11.0 |
| 4 Benjamin F. Howey (R) | 11,567 | 49.2 |
| Harris (D, P) | 11,073 | 47.1 |
| 5 William W. Phelps (R) | 14,341 | 50.4 |
| Ryle (D) | 12,703 | 44.6 |
| 6 William H. F. Fiedler (D) | 17,200 | 53.2 |
| Blake (R) | 14,780 | 45.7 |
| 7 William McAdoo (D) | 15,147 | 56.6 |
| Collins (R) | 11,566 | 43.2 |

## NEW YORK

| Candidates | Votes | % |
|---|---|---|
| 1 Perry Belmont (D) | 18,688 | 77.6 |
| Townsend (ID) | 4,957 | 20.6 |
| 2 William E. Robinson (D) | 19,004 | 63.1 |
| Boody (R & ID) | 10,778 | 35.8 |
| 3 Darwin R. James (R) | 19,260 | 52.5 |
| Hester (D) | 16,882 | 46.0 |
| 4 Felix Campbell (D) | 18,282 | 61.5 |
| Godard (R) | 10,732 | 36.1 |
| 5 Nicholas Muller (D) | 16,148 | 86.7 |
| 6 Samuel S. Cox (D) | 16,624 | 74.6 |
| Quinn (R) | 5,307 | 23.8 |
| 7 William Dorsheimer (D) | 11,401 | 57.7 |
| Brodsky (R) | 6,787 | 34.4 |
| McCabe (L) | 1,562 | 7.9 |
| 8 John J. Adams (D) | 12,089 | 51.3 |
| Russell (R) | 10,904 | 46.3 |
| 9 John Hardy (D) | 16,191 | 69.2 |
| O'Beirne (R) | 7,217 | 30.8 |
| 10 Abram S. Hewitt (D) | 22,144 | 90.7 |
| 11 Orlando B. Potter (D) | 15,049 | 51.9 |
| Strong (R) | 13,947 | 48.1 |
| 12 Waldo Hutchins (D) | 15,663 | 63.7 |
| Long (R) | 8,938 | 36.3 |
| 13 John H. Ketcham (R) | 16,217 | 90.1 |
| Dorland (D) | 916 | 5.1 |
| 14 Lewis Beach (D) | 13,454 | 49.8 |
| Low (R) | 12,821 | 47.5 |
| 15 John H. Bagley Jr. (D) | 16,625 | 55.7 |
| Bray (R) | 13,168 | 44.1 |
| 16 Thomas J. Van Alstyne (D) | 17,797 | 57.0 |
| Van Heusen (R) | 11,404 | 36.5 |
| Lemon Thompson (LAB) | 2,010 | 6.4 |
| 17 Henry G. Burleigh (R) | 17,685 | 100.0 |

| Candidates | Votes | % |
|---|---|---|
| 18 Frederick A. Johnson (R) | 10,667 | 87.8 |
| Fassett (D) | 1,476 | 12.2 |
| 19 Abraham X. Parker (R) | 12,578 | 63.1 |
| Smith (D) | 7,365 | 36.9 |
| 20 Edward Wemple (D) | 17,831 | 50.0 |
| West (R) | 17,742 | 49.8 |
| 21 George W. Ray (R) | 15,188 | 48.0 |
| Babcock (D) | 14,742 | 46.6 |
| 22 Charles R. Skinner (R) | 15,236 | 52.2 |
| Davenport (D) | 13,967 | 47.8 |
| 23 John T. Spriggs (D) | 12,299 | 51.9 |
| Fox (R) | 10,623 | 44.8 |
| 24 Newton W. Nutting (R) | 11,516 | 52.0 |
| Rhodes (D) | 9,905 | 44.8 |
| 25 Frank Hiscock (R) | 14,563 | 48.7 |
| Davis (D) | 13,831 | 46.2 |
| 26 Sereno E. Payne (R) | 13,607 | 48.8 |
| Hammond (D) | 12,651 | 45.3 |
| 27 James W. Wadsworth (R) | 12,013 | 52.3 |
| Pierpont (D) | 10,931 | 47.6 |
| 28 Stephen C. Millard (R) | 15,087 | 51.8 |
| Davis Jr. (D) | 13,378 | 45.9 |
| 29 John Arnot Jr. (D) | 17,769 | 50.0 |
| Baxter (R) | 14,988 | 42.1 |
| Baldwin (P) | 2,081 | 5.9 |
| 30 Halbert S. Greenleaf (D) | 18,042 | 56.2 |
| Vanvoorhis (R) | 12,308 | 38.4 |
| 31 Robert S. Stevens (D) | 12,009 | 53.6 |
| Watson (R) | 9,379 | 41.8 |
| 32 William F. Rogers (D) | 20,531 | 49.5 |
| Moulton (R) | 19,804 | 47.7 |
| 33 Francis B. Brewer (R) | 12,123 | 51.4 |
| Lowry (D) | 9,591 | 40.7 |
| AL Henry Slocum (D) | 503,934 | 56.1 |
| Unidentified Candidate (R) | 394,232 | 43.9 |

## NORTH CAROLINA

| Candidates | Votes | % |
|---|---|---|
| 1 Walter F. Pool (L) | 14,213 | 51.0 |
| Louis C. Latham (D) | 13,628 | 48.9 |
| 2 James E. O'Hara (R) | 18,531 | 93.8 |
| Unidentified Candidate (D) | 1,226 | 6.2 |
| 3 Wharton J. Green (D) | 16,095 | 50.8 |
| William P. Canaday (L) | 15,595 | 49.2 |
| 4 William R. Cox (D) | 16,586 | 50.6 |
| Thomas P. Devereux (L) | 16,174 | 49.4 |
| 5 Alfred M. Scales (D) | 12,533 | 55.4 |
| John R. Winston (L) | 9,932 | 43.9 |
| 6 Clement Dowd (D) | 15,549 | 57.2 |
| William Johnston (L) | 11,648 | 42.8 |
| 7 Tyre York (L) | 11,415 | 48.6 |
| William M. Robbins (D) | 11,159 | 47.5 |
| 8 Robert B. Vance (D) | 13,000 | 56.4 |
| William M. Cooke Jr. (L) | 10,038 | 43.6 |
| AL Risden T. Bennett (D) | 111,763 | 50.1 |
| Oliver H. Dockery (L) | 111,320 | 49.9 |

## OHIO

| Candidates | Votes | % |
|---|---|---|
| 1 John F. Follett (D) | 14,540 | 51.4 |
| Benjamin Butterworth (R) | 13,721 | 48.5 |
| 2 Isaac M. Jordan (D) | 15,983 | 53.0 |
| Amor Smith (R) | 14,166 | 47.0 |
| 3 Robert M. Murray (D) | 16,106 | 49.6 |
| Emanuel Shultz (R) | 15,826 | 48.8 |
| 4 Benjamin Le Fevre (D) | 16,596 | 62.7 |
| Jacob S. Conklin (R) | 9,683 | 36.6 |
| 5 George E. Seney (D) | 16,619 | 59.0 |
| Lovell B. Harris (R) | 11,006 | 39.1 |
| 6 William D. Hill (D) | 16,201 | 49.7 |
| Joseph H. Brigham (R) | 15,480 | 47.5 |
| 7 Henry L. Morey (R) | 14,451‡ | 49.7 |
| James E. Campbell (D) | 14,410 | 49.6 |
| 8 J. Warren Keifer (R) | 14,397 | 50.2 |
| J. H. Young (D) | 13,171 | 45.9 |
| 9 James S. Robinson (R) | 15,864 | 48.8 |
| Thomas E. Powell (D) | 15,458 | 47.5 |
| 10 Frank H. Hurd (D) | 14,534 | 51.2 |
| Charles A. King (R) | 13,430 | 47.3 |

| Candidates | Votes | % |
|---|---|---|
| 11 John W. McCormick (R) | 15,228 | 53.3 |
| John P. Leedom (D) | 13,037 | 45.6 |
| 12 Alphonso Hart (R) | 16,898 | 48.9 |
| Lawrence T. Neal (D) | 16,888 | 48.9 |
| 13 George L. Converse (D) | 17,766 | 54.2 |
| H. C. Drinkle (R) | 14,092 | 43.0 |
| 14 George W. Geddes (D) | 14,277 | 51.2 |
| Rollin A. Horr (R) | 12,604 | 45.2 |
| 15 Adoniram J. Warner (D) | 13,739 | 50.4 |
| Rufus R. Dawes (R) | 13,048 | 47.9 |
| 16 Beriah Wilkins (D) | 19,743 | 57.3 |
| A. B. Clark (R) | 14,422 | 41.9 |
| 17 Jonathan T. Updegraff (R) | 14,165* | 50.4 |
| Ross J. Alexander (D) | 13,265 | 47.2 |
| 18 William McKinley Jr. (R) | 16,906‡ | 48.2 |
| Jonathan H. Wallace (D) | 16,898 | 48.2 |
| 19 Ezra B. Taylor (R) | 15,739 | 62.7 |
| David L. Rockwell (D) | 7,708 | 30.7 |
| 20 David R. Paige (D) | 14,090 | 47.9 |
| Addison S. McClure (R) | 13,980 | 47.6 |
| 21 Martin A. Foran (D) | 15,946 | 54.3 |
| Sylvester T. Everett (R) | 11,408 | 38.9 |
| William H. Doan (P) | 1,999 | 6.8 |

## OREGON

| Candidates | Votes | % |
|---|---|---|
| AL Melvin C. George (R) | 22,517 | 54.0 |
| W. D. Fenton (D) | 19,152 | 46.0 |

## PENNSYLVANIA

| Candidates | Votes | % |
|---|---|---|
| 1 Henry H. Bingham (R) | 15,709 | 55.7 |
| John Cadwalader (D) | 11,875 | 42.1 |
| 2 Charles O'Neill (R) | 14,984 | 56.7 |
| W. Wurt Dundas (D) | 11,440 | 43.3 |
| 3 Samuel J. Randall (D) | 11,688 | 61.6 |
| W. M. Maull (R) | 7,302 | 38.5 |
| 4 William D. Kelley (R) | 21,896 | 61.3 |
| C. M. Swaim (D) | 13,824 | 38.7 |
| 5 Alfred C. Harmer (R) | 19,049 | 53.2 |
| T. J. Martin (D&I) | 16,776 | 46.8 |
| 6 James B. Everhart (R) | 14,615 | 59.1 |
| J. Edward Clyde (D) | 9,810 | 39.7 |
| 7 I. Newton Evans (R) | 15,732 | 51.0 |
| W. W. H. Davis (D) | 15,102 | 49.0 |
| 8 Daniel Ermentrout (D) | 15,623 | 64.2 |
| Isaac McHose (R) | 8,466 | 34.8 |
| 9 A. Herr Smith (R) | 16,425 | 62.8 |
| William B. Given (D) | 9,740 | 37.2 |
| 10 William Mutchler (D) | 19,867 | 63.1 |
| James S. Biery (R) | 11,644 | 37.0 |
| 11 John B. Storm (D) | 17,810 | 64.5 |
| H. C. Smith (R) | 9,805 | 35.5 |
| 12 Daniel W. Connelly (D) | 11,811 | 47.9 |
| Joseph A. Scranton (R) | 10,822 | 43.9 |
| R. J. Flick (G LAB) | 2,016 | 8.2 |
| 13 Charles N. Brumm (G LAB R) | 10,773 | 51.5 |
| J. M. Wetherill (D) | 10,149 | 48.5 |
| 14 Samuel F. Barr (R) | 14,184 | 46.3 |
| Henry McCormick (D) | 14,039 | 45.9 |
| John McLeery (IR) | 1,870 | 6.1 |
| 15 George A. Post (D) | 11,555 | 42.1 |
| C. C. Jadwin (IR) | 9,101 | 33.1 |
| Edward Overton (R) | 5,675 | 20.7 |
| 16 William W. Brown (R) | 12,876 | 48.8 |
| H. W. Earley (D) | 11,747 | 44.5 |
| J. Stickel (G LAB) | 1,756 | 6.7 |
| 17 Jacob M. Campbell (R) | 14,961 | 49.2 |
| Alex H. Coffroth (D) | 14,410 | 47.4 |
| 18 Louis E. Atkinson (R) | 14,779 | 50.6 |
| F. M. Kimmell (D) | 14,049 | 48.1 |
| 19 William A. Duncan (D) | 16,780 | 54.8 |
| William McSherry (ID) | 13,603 | 44.4 |
| 20 Andrew G. Curtin (D) | 16,515 | 59.3 |
| Samuel H. Orwig (R) | 11,288 | 40.5 |
| 21 Charles E. Boyle (D) | 16,033 | 55.6 |
| Charles S. Seaton (G LAB R) | 12,709 | 44.1 |
| 22 James H. Hopkins (D) | 12,420 | 47.5 |
| Russell Errett (R) | 11,191 | 42.8 |
| James Campbell (G LAB) | 2,345 | 9.0 |

### PENNSYLVANIA

| | Candidates | Votes | % |
|---|---|---|---|
| 23 | Thomas M. Bayne (R) | 11,734 | 83.7 |
| | S. G. Barnes (G LAB) | 1,882 | 13.4 |
| 24 | George V. Lawrence (R) | 11,674 | 50.4 |
| | J. G. McConahy (D) | 10,888 | 47.0 |
| 25 | John D. Patton (D) | 13,990 | 51.9 |
| | Harry White (R) | 12,990 | 48.2 |
| 26 | Samuel H. Miller (R) | 14,098 | 47.9 |
| | J. H. Caldwell (D) | 13,365 | 45.4 |
| 27 | Samuel M. Brainerd (R) | 11,170 | 45.8 |
| | H. B. Plumer (D) | 10,247 | 42.0 |
| | W. T. Everson (G LAB&P) | 2,992 | 12.3 |
| AL | Mortimer Elliott (D) | 352,855 | 47.5 |
| | Marriott Brosius (R) | 323,255 | 43.5 |
| | William McMichael (IR) | 40,995 | 5.5 |

### RHODE ISLAND

| | | | |
|---|---|---|---|
| 1 | Henry J. Spooner (R) | 3,515 | 70.0 |
| | Oscar Lapham (D) | 1,491 | 29.7 |
| 2 | Jonathan Chace (R) | 3,349 | 64.6 |
| | Wheeler (D) | 1,831 | 35.3 |

### SOUTH CAROLINA

| | | | |
|---|---|---|---|
| 1 | Samuel Dibble (D) | 8,674 | 56.9 |
| | J. B. Campbell (IG&R) | 6,565 | 43.1 |
| 2 | George D. Tillman (D) | 11,388 | 67.8 |
| | E. M. Brayton (R) | 5,361 | 31.9 |
| 3 | D. Wyatt Aiken (D) | 9,245 | 84.7 |
| | T. H. Russell (G & R) | 1,677 | 15.4 |
| 4 | John H. Evins (D) | 11,662 | 71.8 |
| | D. R. Elkins (R) | 4,588 | 28.2 |
| 5 | John J. Hemphill (D) | 9,518 | 56.0 |
| | E. B. C. Cash (IG&R) | 7,471 | 44.0 |
| 6 | George W. Dargan (D) | 10,814 | 64.7 |
| | E. H. Deas (R) | 3,628 | 21.7 |
| | A. H. Bowen (G) | 2,263 | 13.6 |
| 7 | Edmund W. M. Mackey (R) | 18,469 | 64.8 |
| | Samuel Lee (IR) | 10,017 | 35.2 |

### TENNESSEE

| | | | |
|---|---|---|---|
| 1 | Augustus H. Pettibone (R) | 14,702 | 53.9 |
| | Taylor (D) | 12,571 | 46.1 |
| 2 | Leonidas C. Houck (R) | 14,535 | 62.2 |
| | Rule (IR) | 8,821 | 37.8 |
| 3 | George G. Dibrell (D) | 11,403 | 53.5 |
| | Trewhitt (R) | 9,698 | 45.5 |
| 4 | Benton McMillin (D) | 14,452 | 77.9 |
| | Stokes (R) | 4,106 | 22.1 |
| 5 | Richard Warner (D) | 10,911 | 54.4 |
| | Tillman (STC D) | 7,906 | 39.4 |
| | Duggan R) | 1,247 | 6.2 |
| 6 | Andrew J. Caldwell () | 15,951 | 61.9 |
| | Dillon (R) | 8,856 | 34.4 |

| Candidates | Votes | % |
|---|---|---|
| 7 John G. Ballentine (D) | 12,635 | 63.0 |
| Perkins (ID) | 7,432 | 37.0 |
| 8 John M. Taylor (D) | 10,995 | 51.8 |
| Hawkins (R) | 8,175 | 38.5 |
| Warren (G) | 1,479 | 7.0 |
| 9 Rice A. Pierce (D) | 12,812 | 61.1 |
| Lyle (R) | 7,885 | 37.6 |
| 10 H. Casey Young (D) | 10,696 | 51.1 |
| Smith (R) | 9,837 | 47.0 |

### TEXAS

| | | | |
|---|---|---|---|
| 1 | Charles Stewart (D) | 14,882 | 62.5 |
| | William Chambers (R) | 8,850 | 37.2 |
| 2 | John H. Reagan (D) | 12,035 | 82.6 |
| 3 | James H. Jones (D) | 14,045 | 57.9 |
| | S. H. Russell (R) | 9,492 | 39.1 |
| 4 | David B. Culberson (D) | 13,487 | 63.4 |
| | E. L. Dehoney (G) | 7,785 | 36.6 |
| 5 | James W. Throckmorton (D) | 16,163 | 72.0 |
| | J. N. Dixon (G) | 6,280 | 28.0 |
| 6 | Olin Wellborn (D) | 17,510 | 71.6 |
| | J. C. Kearby (G) | 6,949 | 28.4 |
| 7 | Thomas P. Ochiltree (I) | 12,457 | 55.8 |
| | George P. Finlay (D) | 9,851 | 44.1 |
| 8 | James F. Miller (D) | 12,297 | 59.0 |
| | R. Zapp (G) | 6,528 | 31.3 |
| | Joseph O'Connor (I) | 1,774 | 8.5 |
| 9 | Roger Q. Mills (D) | 14,730 | 63.9 |
| | J. D. Rankin (G) | 8,329 | 36.1 |
| 10 | John Hancock (D) | 16,098 | 62.2 |
| | E. J. Davis (R) | 9,783 | 37.8 |
| 11 | Samuel W. T. Lanham (D) | 10,493 | 51.0 |
| | J. W. Barnett (G) | 4,744 | 23.1 |
| | J. H. Davenport (ID) | 3,807 | 18.5 |
| | S. C. Buck (ID) | 1,532 | 7.4 |

### VERMONT

| | | | |
|---|---|---|---|
| 1 | John W. Stewart (R) | 15,638 | 69.3 |
| | Syman W. Redington (D) | 6,009 | 26.6 |
| 2 | Luke P. Poland (R) | 12,795 | 51.8 |
| | George S. Fletcher (D) | 6,363 | 25.8 |
| | Wilpam W. Grout (R) | 4,598 | 18.6 |

### VIRGINIA

| | | | |
|---|---|---|---|
| 1 | Robert M. Mayo (READJ) | 10,505‡ | 49.6 |
| | George T. Garrison (D) | 10,504 | 49.6 |
| 2 | Harry Libbey (READJ) | 13,226 | 49.7 |
| | Richard C. Marshall (D) | 10,282 | 38.6 |
| | John F. Dezendorf (R) | 3,114 | 11.7 |
| 3 | George D. Wise (D) | 10,736 | 57.1 |
| | John Ambler Smith (READJ) | 8,060 | 42.9 |

| Candidates | Votes | % |
|---|---|---|
| 4 Benjamin S. Hooper (READJ) | 14,764 | 75.5 |
| W. A. Reese (D) | 4,552 | 23.3 |
| 5 George C. Cabell (D) | 12,948 | 53.0 |
| William E. Sims (READJ) | 11,489 | 47.0 |
| 6 John Randolph Tucker (D) | 12,765 | 55.0 |
| J. Henry Rives (READJ) | 10,362 | 44.6 |
| 7 John Paul (READJ) | 12,146‡ | 50.2 |
| Charles T. O'Ferrall (D) | 11,941 | 49.4 |
| 8 John S. Barbour (D) | 14,256 | 60.6 |
| Richard R. Farr (READJ) | 9,034 | 38.4 |
| 9 Henry Bowen (READJ) | 10,073 | 57.7 |
| Abram Fulkerson (D) | 5,603 | 32.1 |
| Samuel H. Newberry (I) | 1,467 | 8.4 |
| AL John S. Wise (READJ) | 99,992 | 50.4 |
| John E. Massey (D) | 94,184 | 47.4 |

### WEST VIRGINIA

| | | | |
|---|---|---|---|
| 1 | Nathan Goff Jr. (R) | 14,154 | 52.2 |
| | John H. Good (D) | 12,335 | 45.5 |
| 2 | William L. Wilson (D) | 11,406 | 48.5 |
| | John W. Mason (R) | 11,396 | 48.5 |
| 3 | John E. Kenna (D) | 10,279* | 58.3 |
| | E. S. Buttrick (R) | 5,814 | 33.0 |
| | P. B. Reynolds (G) | 1,454 | 8.3 |
| 4 | Eustace Gibson (D) | 11,151 | 47.9 |
| | George Loomis (R) | 9,863 | 42.3 |
| | A. R. Barber (G) | 2,287 | 9.8 |

### WISCONSIN

| | | | |
|---|---|---|---|
| 1 | John Winans (D) | 12,307 | 46.6 |
| | C. G. Williams (R) | 11,853 | 44.9 |
| | C. M. Blackman (P) | 2,217 | 8.4 |
| 2 | Daniel H. Sumner (D) | 10,671 | 50.4 |
| | J. S. Rowell (R) | 8,870 | 41.9 |
| 3 | Burr W. Jones (D) | 13,035 | 46.0 |
| | G. C. Hazelton (R) | 7,924 | 28.0 |
| | E. W. Keyes (IR) | 3,791 | 13.4 |
| | S. D. Hastings (P) | 3,152 | 11.1 |
| 4 | Peter V. Deuster (D) | 9,688 | 48.6 |
| | F. C. Winckler (R) | 8,320 | 41.7 |
| | G. B. Goodwin (LAB) | 1,922 | 9.6 |
| 5 | Joseph Rankin (D) | 12,933 | 62.7 |
| | L. Howland (R) | 6,108 | 29.6 |
| 6 | Richard Guenther (R) | 10,303 | 44.1 |
| | A. Haben (D) | 9,265 | 39.7 |
| | T. D. Kanouse (P) | 3,275 | 14.0 |
| 7 | Gilbert M. Woodward (D) | 11,908 | 48.1 |
| | C. M. Butt (R) | 10,604 | 42.8 |
| | B. F. Parker (P) | 1,887 | 7.6 |
| 8 | William T. Price (R) | 14,059 | 55.4 |
| | W. F. Bailey (D) | 11,315 | 44.6 |
| 9 | Isaac Stephenson (R) | 12,774 | 47.4 |
| | G. L. Park (D) | 12,518 | 46.4 |
| | H. H. Woodmansec (P) | 1,460 | 5.4 |

# 1883 House Elections

### KANSAS

**Special Election**

| | | | |
|---|---|---|---|
| 2 | Edward H. Funston (R) | 24,116 | 57.4 |
| | S. A. Riggs (D) | 17,924 | 42.6 |

### LOUISIANA

**Special Election**

| | | | |
|---|---|---|---|
| 6 | Edward T. Lewis (D) | 6,366 | 91.8 |
| | Louis Trager (R) | 568 | 8.2 |

### OHIO[1]

**Special Election**

| | | | |
|---|---|---|---|
| 16 | Joseph D. Taylor (R) | 14,179 | 53.5 |
| | Ross J. Alexander (D) | 12,313 | 46.5 |
| 16 | Joseph D. Taylor (R) | 14,159 | 53.5 |
| | Ross J. Alexander (D) | 12,322 | 46.5 |

*1. The first special election in the 16th district was held in January 1883 to fill the remaining two months of the term in the 47th Congress (1881-83). The second special election was held in February 1883, to fill the House seat for a full term in the 48th Congress (1883-85). Both elections were necessitated by the death of Rep. Jonathan T. Updegraff Nov. 30, 1882, following his re-election to the 48th Congress.*

# 1884 House Elections

## ALABAMA

| | Candidates | Votes | % |
|---|---|---|---|
| 1 | James T. Jones (D) | 8,871 | 58.1 |
| | Thweatt (R) | 6,403 | 41.9 |
| 2 | Hilary A. Herbert (D) | 11,331 | 55.8 |
| | Whitehead (R) | 8,991 | 44.2 |
| 3 | William C. Oates (D) | 10,965 | 71.6 |
| | Mabson (R) | 4,349 | 28.4 |
| 4 | Alexander C. Davidson (D) | 14,225 | 63.7 |
| | Craig (R) | 6,749 | 30.2 |
| 5 | Thomas W. Sadler (D) | 10,775 | 98.0 |
| 6 | John M. Martin (D) | 10,132 | 99.3 |
| 7 | William H. Forney (D) | 14,187 | 63.3 |
| | Ewing (R) | 8,217 | 36.7 |
| 8 | Joseph Wheeler (D) | 12,912 | 52.8 |
| | Day (IR) | 11,559 | 47.2 |

## ARKANSAS

| | | Votes | % |
|---|---|---|---|
| 1 | Poindexter Dunn (D) | 15,002 | 61.7 |
| | Remmel (R) | 9,322 | 38.3 |
| 2 | Clifton R. Breckinridge (D) | 13,792 | 53.0 |
| | Rogers (R) | 12,229 | 47.0 |
| 3 | James K. Jones (D) | 16,193* | 54.1 |
| | Mitchell (R) | 13,722 | 45.9 |
| 4 | John H. Rogers (D) | 15,174 | 57.3 |
| | Sarber (R) | 11,307 | 42.7 |
| 5 | Samuel W. Peel (D) | 11,542 | 69.1 |
| | Keenor (R) | 5,158 | 30.9 |

## CALIFORNIA

| | | Votes | % |
|---|---|---|---|
| 1 | Barclay Henley (D) | 16,461 | 49.7 |
| | T. L. Carothers (R) | 16,316 | 49.3 |
| 2 | James A. Louttit (R) | 18,327 | 49.4 |
| | Charles A. Sumner (D) | 18,208 | 49.1 |
| 3 | Joseph McKenna (R) | 17,435 | 55.8 |
| | J. A. Glascock (D) | 13,197 | 42.3 |
| 4 | William W. Morrow (R) | 15,083 | 58.7 |
| | R. P. Hastings (D) | 10,422 | 40.6 |
| 5 | Charles N. Felton (R) | 17,014 | 51.6 |
| | F. J. Sullivan (D) | 15,676 | 47.6 |
| 6 | Henry H. Markham (R) | 17,397 | 49.1 |
| | A. F. Devalle (D) | 16,988 | 47.9 |

## COLORADO

| | | Votes | % |
|---|---|---|---|
| AL | George G. Symes (R) | 35,446 | 53.2 |
| | Charles S. Thomas (D) | 28,720 | 43.1 |

## CONNECTICUT

| | | Votes | % |
|---|---|---|---|
| 1 | John R. Buck (R) | 16,589 | 49.7 |
| | William W. Eaton (D) | 16,285 | 48.8 |
| 2 | Charles L. Mitchell (D) | 22,589 | 50.8 |
| | Allen (R) | 20,573 | 46.3 |
| 3 | John T. Wait (R) | 11,700 | 54.4 |
| | Johnson (D) | 9,258 | 43.1 |
| 4 | Edward W. Seymour (D) | 18,526 | 49.0 |
| | Coe (R) | 18,373 | 48.6 |

## DELAWARE

| | | Votes | % |
|---|---|---|---|
| AL | Charles B. Lore (D) | 17,054 | 56.7 |
| | Anthony Higgins (R) | 12,978 | 43.2 |

## FLORIDA

| | | Votes | % |
|---|---|---|---|
| 1 | Robert H. M. Davidson (D) | 14,619 | 55.1 |
| | Locke (R) | 11,893 | 44.9 |
| 2 | Charles Dougherty (D) | 17,248 | 51.8 |
| | Bisbee (R) | 15,857 | 47.6 |

## GEORGIA

| | Candidates | Votes | % |
|---|---|---|---|
| 1 | Thomas M. Norwood (D) | 10,857 | 64.4 |
| | Pleasant (R) | 6,012 | 35.6 |
| 2 | Henry G. Turner (R) | 7,828 | 100.0 |
| 3 | Charles F. Crisp (D) | 9,963 | 69.6 |
| | Bell (R) | 4,268 | 29.8 |
| 4 | Henry R. Harris (D) | 10,608 | 52.4 |
| | Henry Person (ID) | 5,473 | 27.0 |
| | Milner (R) | 4,156 | 20.5 |
| 5 | Nathaniel J. Hammond (D) | 9,008 | 63.7 |
| | Martin (R) | 5,130 | 36.3 |
| 6 | James H. Blount (R) | 7,922 | 100.0 |
| 7 | Judson C. Clements (D) | 10,496 | 71.1 |
| | Kirkwood (R) | 3,417 | 23.1 |
| 8 | Seaborn Reese (D) | 7,834 | 70.4 |
| | Martin (R) | 3,250 | 29.2 |
| 9 | Allen D. Candler (D) | 8,137 | 100.0 |
| 10 | George T. Barnes (D) | 9,166 | 86.2 |
| | Wright (R) | 1,277 | 12.0 |

## ILLINOIS

| | | Votes | % |
|---|---|---|---|
| 1 | Ransom W. Dunham (R) | 20,245 | 56.7 |
| | William M. Tilden (D) | 14,655 | 41.1 |
| 2 | Francis Lawler (D) | 13,954 | 54.7 |
| | John F. Finnerty (R&A-MONO) | 11,552 | 45.3 |
| 3 | James H. Ward (D) | 15,601 | 43.5 |
| | William E. Mason (R) | 10,806 | 30.1 |
| | Charles Fitz Simmons (R) | 8,928 | 24.9 |
| 4 | George E. Adams (R) | 18,333 | 53.8 |
| | John P. Altgeld (D) | 15,291 | 44.9 |
| 5 | Reuben Ellwood (R & P) | 20,500 | 68.4 |
| | Richard Bishop (D) | 9,424 | 31.5 |
| 6 | Robert R. Hitt (R) | 18,048 | 61.5 |
| | E. W. Blaisdell (D) | 10,891 | 37.1 |
| 7 | Thomas J. Henderson (R) | 15,498 | 57.6 |
| | James S. Eckels (D) | 10,689 | 39.7 |
| 8 | Ralph Plumb (R) | 18,707 | 51.8 |
| | Pat C. Haley (D) | 15,953 | 44.2 |
| 9 | Lewis E. Payson (R) | 16,481 | 53.4 |
| | James Kirk (D) | 13,716 | 44.5 |
| 10 | Nicholas E. Worthington (D) | 16,758 | 50.1 |
| | Julius S. Starr (R) | 16,582 | 49.6 |
| 11 | William H. Neece (A-MON D) | 18,291 | 50.1 |
| | Alexander P. Petrie (R) | 17,864 | 48.9 |
| 12 | James M. Riggs (D) | 22,046 | 57.7 |
| | Thomas G. Black (R) | 15,177 | 39.7 |
| 13 | William M. Springer (D) | 20,808 | 53.1 |
| | James M. Taylor (R) | 16,971 | 43.3 |
| 14 | Jonathan H. Rowell (R) | 18,052 | 51.4 |
| | C. C. Clark (D) | 15,673 | 44.6 |
| 15 | Joseph G. Cannon (R) | 17,852 | 50.2 |
| | John C. Black (D) | 17,360 | 48.8 |
| 16 | Silas Z. Landes (D) | 17,109 | 50.2 |
| | James McCartney (R) | 16,791 | 49.2 |
| 17 | John R. Eden (D) | 18,402 | 55.0 |
| | Howland J. Hamlin (G & R) | 14,576 | 43.5 |
| 18 | William R. Morrison (D) | 17,695 | 53.2 |
| | Thomas B. Needles (R) | 15,136 | 45.5 |
| 19 | Richard W. Townshend (D) | 18,296 | 56.7 |
| | Thomas S. Ridgway (R) | 13,615 | 42.2 |
| 20 | John R. Thomas (R) | 17,890 | 52.1 |
| | Fountain E. Albright (D) | 15,788 | 45.9 |

## INDIANA

| | | Votes | % |
|---|---|---|---|
| 1 | John J. Kleiner (D) | 19,930 | 51.5 |
| | William H. Gudgel (R) | 18,493 | 47.8 |
| 2 | Thomas R. Cobb (D) | 18,832 | 55.5 |
| | George H. Reiley (R) | 15,128 | 44.6 |
| 3 | Jonas G. Howard (D) | 19,550 | 56.3 |
| | James Keigwin (R) | 14,923 | 43.0 |
| 4 | William S. Holman (D) | 17,233 | 52.6 |
| | John O. Cravens (R) | 15,494 | 47.2 |

| | Candidates | Votes | % |
|---|---|---|---|
| 5 | Courtland C. Matson (D) | 17,951 | 51.3 |
| | George W. Grubbs (R) | 16,582 | 47.4 |
| 6 | Thomas M. Browne (R) | 22,115 | 61.1 |
| | Nelson G. Smith (D) | 13,625 | 37.7 |
| 7 | William D. Bynum (D) | 20,240 | 51.0 |
| | Stanton J. Peelle (R) | 18,995 | 47.9 |
| 8 | James C. Johnston (R) | 20,185 | 50.0 |
| | John Edward Lamb (D) | 20,035 | 49.6 |
| 9 | Thomas B. Ward (D) | 19,241 | 49.7 |
| | Charles T. Doxey (R) | 18,628 | 48.1 |
| 10 | William D. Owen (R) | 19,262 | 50.0 |
| | Thomas J. Wood (D) | 18,781 | 48.8 |
| 11 | George W. Steele (R) | 22,679 | 48.7 |
| | Meredith H. Kidd (D) | 22,625 | 48.6 |
| 12 | Robert Lowry (D) | 19,507 | 52.5 |
| | T. P. Keator (R) | 16,957 | 45.7 |
| 13 | George Ford (D) | 20,971 | 52.7 |
| | Henry Thayer (R) | 18,792 | 47.3 |

**Special Election**

| | | Votes | % |
|---|---|---|---|
| 13 | Benjamin Franklin Shively (N) | 20,964 | 52.8 |
| | John Reynolds (R) | 18,736 | 47.2 |

## IOWA

| | | Votes | % |
|---|---|---|---|
| 1 | Benton Jay Hall (D) | 16,734 | 50.0 |
| | John S. Woolson (R) | 16,661 | 49.7 |
| 2 | Jeremiah Henry Murphy (D) | 19,730 | 56.4 |
| | William T. Shaw (R) | 15,241 | 43.6 |
| 3 | David B. Henderson (R) | 16,431 | 52.1 |
| | John J. Linehan (D) | 15,105 | 47.9 |
| 4 | William Elijah Fuller (R) | 15,082 | 50.4 |
| | Luman Hamlin Weller (G & D) | 14,852 | 49.6 |
| 5 | Benjamin Todd Frederick (D) | 16,679 | 50.2 |
| | Milo P. Smith (R) | 16,541 | 49.7 |
| 6 | James Baird Weaver (G & D) | 16,684 | 50.1 |
| | Frank T. Campbell (R) | 16,617 | 49.9 |
| 7 | Edwin H. Conger (R) | 19,274 | 54.8 |
| | W. H. McHenry (D) | 15,924 | 45.2 |
| 8 | William P. Hepburn (R) | 17,671 | 53.6 |
| | S. R. Davis (D) | 15,294 | 46.4 |
| 9 | Joseph H. Lyman (R) | 19,071 | 50.7 |
| | William H. M. Pusey (D) | 18,509 | 49.2 |
| 10 | Adoniram J. Holmes (R) | 20,328 | 62.7 |
| | H. C. McCoy (D) | 12,117 | 37.3 |
| 11 | Isaac S. Struble (R) | 24,063 | 58.4 |
| | Thomas F. Barbee (D) | 17,107 | 41.6 |

**Special Election**

| | | Votes | % |
|---|---|---|---|
| 7 | Hiram Ypsilanti Smith (R) | 18,905 | 53.9 |
| | E. H. Kridler (D) | 16,151 | 46.1 |

## KANSAS

| | | Votes | % |
|---|---|---|---|
| 1 | Edmund N. Morrill (R) | 19,535 | 55.1 |
| | Thomas P. Fenlon (D) | 15,934 | 44.9 |
| 2 | Edward H. Funston (R) | 22,518 | 60.4 |
| | W. J. Nicholson (D) | 14,703 | 39.4 |
| 3 | Bishop W. Perkins (R) | 23,854 | 56.3 |
| | G. W. Gabriel (D) | 13,341 | 31.5 |
| | W. A. Tipton (G LAB) | 5,163 | 12.2 |
| 4 | Thomas Ryan (R) | 26,177 | 61.9 |
| | S. N. Wood (D) | 15,799 | 37.4 |
| 5 | John A. Anderson (R) | 22,548 | 64.1 |
| | A. A. Carnahan (D) | 10,866 | 30.9 |
| | M. D. Tenney (G LAB) | 1,784 | 5.1 |
| 6 | Lewis Hanback (R) | 14,776 | 59.5 |
| | L. C. Uhl (D) | 10,068 | 40.5 |
| 7 | Samuel R. Peters (R) | 25,740 | 61.0 |
| | H. M. Bickel (D) | 15,913 | 37.7 |

## KENTUCKY

| Candidates | Votes | % |
|---|---|---|
| 1 William J. Stone (D) | 10,503 | 41.8 |
| Oscar Turner (ID) | 7,440 | 29.6 |
| H. H. Houston (R) | 7,161 | 28.5 |
| 2 Polk Laffoon (D) | 12,472 | 56.8 |
| T. Z. Moore (R) | 9,485 | 43.2 |
| 3 John E. Halsell (D) | 12,833 | 55.3 |
| J. S. Golladay (R) | 10,376 | 44.7 |
| 4 Thomas A. Robertson (D) | 12,153 | 100.0 |
| 5 Albert S. Willis (D) | 12,152 | 59.0 |
| A. E. Wilson (R) | 8,373 | 40.7 |
| 6 John G. Carlisle (D) | 15,261 | 60.6 |
| J. J. Landrum (R) | 9,329 | 37.1 |
| 7 William C. P. Breckinridge (D) | 16,236 | 93.2 |
| D. W. Lindsey (R) | 1,173 | 6.7 |
| 8 James B. McCreary (D) | 14,924 | 53.9 |
| J. M. Sebastian (R) | 12,778 | 46.1 |
| 9 William H. Wadsworth (R) | 16,189 | 50.2 |
| Frank Powers (D) | 16,087 | 49.8 |
| 10 William P. Taulbee (D) | 14,266 | 53.7 |
| A. J. Auxier (R) | 12,308 | 46.3 |
| 11 Frank L. Wolford (D) | 10,748 | 52.0 |
| W. W. Jones (R) | 9,932 | 48.0 |

## LOUISIANA

| Candidates | Votes | % |
|---|---|---|
| 1 Louis St.Martin (D) | 5,685 | 41.9 |
| Carleton Hunt (ID) | 4,458 | 32.9 |
| J. A. Acklin (R) | 3,411 | 25.2 |
| 2 Michael Hahn (R) | 7,356 | 54.7 |
| W. T. Houston (D) | 6,103 | 45.4 |
| 3 Edward J. Gay (D) | 15,302 | 51.2 |
| William Pitt Kellogg (R) | 14,603 | 48.8 |
| 4 Newton C. Blanchard (D) | 12,269 | 89.9 |
| J. B. Slattery (R) | 1,377 | 10.1 |
| 5 J. Floyd King (D) | 11,692 | 59.1 |
| Charles J. Boatner (ID) | 5,513 | 27.9 |
| Frank Morey (R) | 2,565 | 13.0 |
| 6 Alfred B. Irion (D) | 9,927 | 61.6 |
| C. C. Swayzie (R) | 6,197 | 38.4 |

## MAINE

| Candidates | Votes | % |
|---|---|---|
| 1 Thomas B. Reed (R) | 17,594 | 51.0 |
| N. Cleaves (D) | 16,669 | 48.3 |
| 2 Nelson Dingley Jr. (R) | 20,795 | 55.1 |
| D. R. Hastings (D) | 15,006 | 39.8 |
| 3 Seth L. Milliken (R) | 20,083 | 57.9 |
| Daniel H. Thing (D) | 13,866 | 40.0 |
| 4 Charles A. Boutelle (R) | 19,643 | 56.1 |
| John F. Lynch (D) | 14,165 | 40.5 |

## MARYLAND

| Candidates | Votes | % |
|---|---|---|
| 1 Charles H. Gibson (D) | 16,726 | 53.3 |
| Russum (R) | 14,641 | 46.7 |
| 2 Frank T. Shaw (D) | 16,274 | 53.8 |
| Blair (R) | 14,003 | 46.3 |
| 3 William H. Cole (D) | 16,032 | 58.6 |
| Pentz (R) | 10,756 | 39.3 |
| 4 John V. L. Findlay (D) | 15,726 | 51.2 |
| Brown (R) | 14,324 | 46.7 |
| 5 Barnes Compton (D) | 15,612 | 51.6 |
| Holton (R) | 14,641 | 48.4 |
| 6 Louis E. McComas (R) | 17,995 | 52.3 |
| Nelson (D) | 16,379 | 47.6 |

## MASSACHUSETTS

| Candidates | Votes | % |
|---|---|---|
| 1 Robert T. Davis (R) | 14,080 | 66.5 |
| Weston Howland (D) | 5,307 | 25.1 |
| 2 John D. Long (R) | 15,039 | 53.0 |
| William Everett (D) | 9,734 | 34.3 |
| Edgar E. Dean (G) | 2,630 | 9.3 |
| 3 Ambrose A. Ranney (R) | 13,596 | 53.0 |
| Horatio Swasey (D) | 9,248 | 36.1 |
| Eleazer B. Loring (G) | 2,412 | 9.4 |

| Candidates | Votes | % |
|---|---|---|
| 4 Patrick A. Collins (D) | 13,664 | 64.8 |
| Joseph H. O'Neill (R) | 7,182 | 34.1 |
| 5 Edward D. Hayden (R) | 13,290 | 52.0 |
| Robert Trete Paine Jr. (D) | 11,018 | 43.1 |
| 6 Henry B. Lovering (D & G) | 15,146 | 49.6 |
| Henry Cabot Lodge (R) | 14,881 | 48.7 |
| 7 Eben F. Stone (R) | 12,475 | 47.8 |
| Richard S. Spofford (D) | 9,623 | 36.9 |
| John Baker (G) | 3,948 | 15.1 |
| 8 Charles H. Allen (R) | 12,643 | 53.6 |
| Charles S. Lilley (D) | 9,446 | 40.1 |
| 9 Frederick D. Ely (R) | 12,265 | 47.4 |
| Henry E. Fales (D) | 6,301 | 24.4 |
| Theodore Lyman (I) | 4,265 | 16.5 |
| Henry E. Lemon Jr. (G) | 2,429 | 9.4 |
| 10 William W. Rice (R) | 13,940 | 58.8 |
| James E. Esterbrook (D) | 6,556 | 27.6 |
| Unidentified Candidate (G) | 2,637 | 11.1 |
| 11 William Whiting (R) | 15,335 | 59.9 |
| David Hill (D) | 8,693 | 34.0 |
| 12 Francis W. Rockwell (R) | 13,012 | 51.7 |
| Jarvis N. Dunham (D) | 10,856 | 43.1 |

## MICHIGAN

| Candidates | Votes | % |
|---|---|---|
| 1 William C. Maybury (D) | 21,673 | 55.8 |
| John Atkinson (R) | 15,549 | 40.0 |
| 2 Nathaniel B. Eldredge (D & G) | 17,710 | 46.9 |
| Edward P. Allen (R) | 17,656 | 46.7 |
| Charles Mosher (P) | 2,420 | 6.4 |
| 3 James O'Donnell (R) | 20,438 | 48.5 |
| Henry F. Pennington (D & G) | 19,210 | 45.5 |
| Michael J. Fanning (P) | 2,531 | 6.0 |
| 4 Julius C. Burrows (R) | 18,564 | 48.8 |
| George L. Yaple (D & G) | 18,212 | 47.9 |
| 5 Charles C. Comstock (D & G) | 20,406 | 47.6 |
| John C. Fitzgerald (R) | 20,050 | 46.7 |
| Wilson C. Edsell (P) | 2,449 | 5.7 |
| 6 Edwin B. Winans (D & G) | 19,857 | 48.8 |
| James C. Willson (R) | 18,377 | 45.2 |
| Leander C. Smith (P) | 2,445 | 6.0 |
| 7 Ezra C. Carlton (D) | 14,535 | 50.2 |
| Edgar Weeks (R) | 12,316 | 42.5 |
| 8 Timothy E. Tarsney (D) | 19,446 | 50.6 |
| Roswell G. Horr (R) | 17,824 | 46.4 |
| 9 Byron M. Cutcheon (R) | 18,963 | 51.4 |
| Silas S. Fallas (D & G) | 16,207 | 44.0 |
| 10 Spencer O. Fisher (D & G) | 15,366 | 52.4 |
| Charles F. Gibson (R) | 13,081 | 44.6 |
| 11 Seth C. Moffatt (R) | 16,464 | 64.7 |
| John Powers (D) | 8,992 | 35.3 |

## MINNESOTA

| Candidates | Votes | % |
|---|---|---|
| 1 Milo White (R) | 16,604 | 53.3 |
| A. Bierman (D) | 13,961 | 44.8 |
| 2 James B. Wakefield (R) | 20,813 | 64.0 |
| J. J. Thornton (D) | 10,639 | 32.7 |
| 3 Horace B. Strait (R) | 16,456 | 51.3 |
| I. Donnelly (D) | 15,038 | 46.9 |
| 4 John B. Gilfillan (R) | 28,930 | 53.2 |
| O. C. Merriman (D) | 24,496 | 45.0 |
| 5 Knute Nelson (R) | 25,609 | 66.0 |
| L. L. Baxter (D) | 13,176 | 34.0 |

## MISSISSIPPI

| Candidates | Votes | % |
|---|---|---|
| 1 John M. Allen (D) | 11,862 | 81.7 |
| Chandler (R) | 2,657 | 18.3 |
| 2 James B. Morgan (D) | 13,963 | 57.5 |
| Chalmers (R) | 10,008 | 41.2 |
| 3 Thomas C. Catchings (D) | 9,783 | 69.5 |
| Pearce (R) | 4,297 | 30.5 |
| 4 Frederick G. Barry (D) | 13,200 | 69.8 |
| Frazee (R) | 5,723 | 30.2 |

| Candidates | Votes | % |
|---|---|---|
| 5 Otho R. Singleton (D) | 11,934 | 76.5 |
| Smith (R) | 3,665 | 23.5 |
| 6 Henry S. Van Eaton (D) | 10,190 | 60.8 |
| Lynch (R) | 6,570 | 39.2 |
| 7 Ethelbert Barksdale (D) | 10,946 | 66.6 |
| Yellowley (R) | 5,485 | 33.4 |

## MISSOURI

| Candidates | Votes | % |
|---|---|---|
| 1 William H. Hatch (D) | 18,932 | 54.3 |
| Gray (FUS) | 15,955 | 45.7 |
| 2 John B. Hale (D) | 20,204 | 56.2 |
| Norville (FUS) | 15,749 | 43.8 |
| 3 Alexander M. Dockery (D) | 19,129 | 53.4 |
| Harwood (R) | 15,854 | 44.2 |
| 4 James N. Burnes (D) | 16,397 | 55.5 |
| Kelly (FUS) | 13,141 | 44.5 |
| 5 William Warner (FUS) | 16,176 | 52.5 |
| Graves (D) | 14,651 | 47.5 |
| 6 John T. Heard (D) | 21,107 | 56.7 |
| Shirk (R) | 16,139 | 43.3 |
| 7 John E. Hutton (D) | 16,712 | 52.8 |
| Reynolds (FUS) | 14,946 | 47.2 |
| 8 John J. O'Neill (D) | 9,657 | 54.7 |
| Eccles (FUS) | 8,006 | 45.3 |
| 9 John M. Glover (D) | 9,830 | 54.7 |
| McLean (FU) | 8,133 | 45.3 |
| 10 Martin L. Clardy (D) | 15,329 | 52.8 |
| Morse (FUS) | 12,797 | 44.1 |
| 11 Richard P. Bland (D) | 16,959 | 54.3 |
| Dallmyer (FUS) | 14,288 | 45.7 |
| 12 William J. Stone (D) | 20,091 | 55.3 |
| Warden (FUS) | 16,222 | 44.7 |
| 13 William H. Wade (FUS) | 20,101 | 50.3 |
| Thomas (D) | 17,981 | 45.0 |
| 14 William Dawson (D) | 17,694 | 61.6 |
| Cramer (FUS) | 11,020 | 38.4 |

## NEBRASKA

| Candidates | Votes | % |
|---|---|---|
| 1 Archibald J. Weaver (R) | 22,644 | 50.0 |
| Charles H. Brown (D) | 21,669 | 47.8 |
| 2 James Laird (R) | 21,182 | 52.9 |
| J. H. Stickel (D) | 17,650 | 44.1 |
| 3 George W. E. Dorsey (R) | 25,685 | 54.7 |
| William Neville (D) | 20,671 | 44.1 |

## NEVADA

| Candidates | Votes | % |
|---|---|---|
| AL William Woodburn (R) | 6,797 | 53.1 |
| George W. Cassidy (D) | 6,002 | 46.9 |

## NEW HAMPSHIRE

| Candidates | Votes | % |
|---|---|---|
| 1 Martin A. Haynes (R) | 20,623 | 51.8 |
| McKinney (D) | 18,383 | 46.2 |
| 2 Jacob H. Gallinger (R) | 22,801 | 51.5 |
| George (D) | 20,426 | 46.1 |

## NEW JERSEY

| Candidates | Votes | % |
|---|---|---|
| 1 George Hires (R) | 19,745 | 50.0 |
| Ferrell (D) | 18,003 | 45.6 |
| 2 James Buchanan (R) | 19,144 | 51.5 |
| Gauntt (D) | 16,853 | 45.4 |
| 3 Robert S. Green (D) | 19,604 | 50.8 |
| John Kean Jr. (R) | 17,756 | 46.0 |
| 4 James N. Pidcock (D) | 15,225 | 51.3 |
| Howey (R) | 12,972 | 43.7 |
| 5 William W. Phelps (R) | 17,367 | 51.7 |
| Stevenson (D) | 15,126 | 45.0 |
| 6 Herman Lehlbach (R) | 21,162 | 49.4 |
| Fiedler (D) | 20,818 | 48.6 |
| 7 William McAdoo (D) | 21,985 | 56.7 |
| Brigham (R) | 16,654 | 43.0 |

## NEW YORK

| | Candidates | Votes | % |
|---|---|---|---|
| 1 | Perry Belmont (D) | 22,050 | 54.9 |
| | Platt (R) | 18,104 | 45.1 |
| 2 | Felix Campbell (D) | 17,503 | 58.5 |
| | Sheridan (R) | 11,771 | 39.4 |
| 3 | Darwin R. James (R) | 20,125 | 60.5 |
| | Smith (D) | 13,000 | 39.1 |
| 4 | Peter P. Mahoney (D) | 18,971 | 57.8 |
| | Mullholland (R) | 13,339 | 40.7 |
| 5 | Archibald M. Bliss (D) | 13,985 | 50.1 |
| | Worth (R) | 12,865 | 46.1 |
| 6 | Nicholas Muller (D) | 13,307 | 56.9 |
| | House (R) | 6,796 | 29.1 |
| | Fitzgerald (ID) | 2,863 | 12.2 |
| 7 | John J. Adams (D) | 15,864 | 65.3 |
| | Conkling (R) | 8,228 | 33.9 |
| 8 | Samuel S. Cox (TAM D) | 19,386 | 80.7 |
| | Hall (CO D) | 4,483 | 18.7 |
| 9 | Joseph Pulitzer (D) | 15,518 | 63.6 |
| | Thum (R) | 8,497 | 34.8 |
| 10 | Abram S. Hewitt (D) | 15,254 | 64.1 |
| | Biglin (R) | 8,392 | 35.3 |
| 11 | Truman A. Merriman (CO D) | 19,588 | 62.4 |
| | Hardy (TAM D) | 11,563 | 36.8 |
| 12 | Abraham Dowdney (D) | 18,380 | 61.3 |
| | Perley (R) | 11,354 | 37.8 |
| 13 | Egbert L. Viele (D) | 17,622 | 60.6 |
| | Smith (R) | 11,027 | 37.9 |
| 14 | William G. Stahlnecker (D) | 17,507 | 51.9 |
| | McAlpin (R) | 15,745 | 46.7 |
| 15 | Lewis Beach (D) | 17,728 | 51.7 |
| | Snow (R) | 15,794 | 46.0 |
| 16 | John H. Ketcham (R) | 18,942 | 54.1 |
| | Huntington (D) | 15,391 | 43.9 |
| 17 | James G. Lindsley (R) | 20,557 | 50.9 |
| | Bagley (D) | 18,671 | 46.2 |
| 18 | Henry G. Burleigh (R) | 20,732 | 88.0 |
| | McClellan (D) | 2,775 | 11.8 |
| 19 | John Swinburne (R) | 19,790 | 53.0 |
| | Van Alstyne (D) | 17,286 | 46.3 |
| 20 | George West (R) | 21,174 | 51.2 |
| | Wemple (D) | 19,467 | 47.0 |
| 21 | Frederick A. Johnson (R) | 19,049 | 58.6 |
| | Smith (D) | 13,462 | 41.4 |
| 22 | Abraham X. Parker (R) | 22,541 | 62.1 |
| | Hall (D) | 12,920 | 35.6 |
| 23 | John T. Spriggs (D) | 18,164 | 49.9 |
| | Cookingham (R) | 17,327 | 47.6 |
| 24 | John S. Pindar (D) | 17,884 | 50.5 |
| | Ramsey (R) | 16,772 | 47.4 |
| 25 | Frank Hiscock (R) | 21,148 | 56.4 |
| | W. Porter (D, P) | 16,326 | 43.5 |
| 26 | Stephen C. Millard (R) | 23,773 | 519 |
| | Remick (D) | 18,783 | 42.6 |
| 27 | Sereno E. Payne (R) | 26,446 | 57.1 |
| | Beardsley (D) | 17,798 | 38.4 |
| 28 | John Arnot Jr. (D-R) | 28,000 | 91.0 |
| | Beecher (G) | 2,044 | 6.6 |
| 29 | Ira Davenport (R) | 19,987 | 52.5 |
| | Pierpont (D) | 16,377 | 43.0 |
| 30 | Charles S. Baker (R) | 16,733 | 50.2 |
| | Greenleaf (D) | 15,496 | 46.5 |
| 31 | John G. Sawyer (R) | 17,529 | 51.4 |
| | Stevens (D) | 14,474 | 42.4 |
| | Richmond (P) | 1,869 | 5.5 |
| 32 | John M. Farquhar (R) | 17,469 | 50.0 |
| | Lockwood (D) | 17,302 | 49.5 |
| 33 | John B. Weber (R) | 14,545 | 49.1 |
| | Payne (D) | 13,957 | 47.2 |
| 34 | Walter L. Sessions (R) | 24,068 | 54.7 |
| | Smith (D) | 15,525 | 35.3 |
| | Sill (P) | 2,522 | 5.7 |

## NORTH CAROLINA

| | | | |
|---|---|---|---|
| 1 | Thomas G. Skinner (D) | 16,381 | 53.8 |
| | John B. Respess (R) | 14,093 | 46.3 |
| 2 | James E. O'Hara (R) | 22,309 | 58.7 |
| | Frederick A. Woodward (D) | 15,699 | 41.3 |
| 3 | Wharton J. Green (D) | 16,785 | 57.8 |
| | Curtis H. Brogden (R) | 12,156 | 41.9 |

| | Candidates | Votes | % |
|---|---|---|---|
| 4 | William R. Cox (D) | 18,930 | 58.5 |
| | Josiah Turner (R) | 13,448 | 41.5 |
| 5 | James W. Reid (D) | 15,047 | 54.6 |
| | Leonidas C. Edwards (R) | 12,522 | 45.4 |
| 6 | Risden T. Bennett (D) | 19,344 | 58.0 |
| | Oliver H. Dockery (R) | 14,010 | 42.0 |
| 7 | John S. Henderson (D) | 14,262 | 56.8 |
| | James G. Ramsey (R) | 10,851 | 43.2 |
| 8 | William H. H. Cowles (D) | 11,422 | 58.7 |
| | Leander L. Green (R) | 8,036 | 41.3 |
| 9 | Thomas D. Johnston (D) | 13,024 | 53.2 |
| | Hamilton G. Ewart (R) | 11,465 | 46.8 |

## OHIO

| | | | |
|---|---|---|---|
| 1 | Benjamin Butterworth (R) | 17,929 | 52.1 |
| | John F. Follett (D) | 16,320 | 47.4 |
| 2 | Charles E. Brown (R) | 19,718 | 52.8 |
| | Adam A. Kramer (D) | 17,513 | 46.9 |
| 3 | James E. Campbell (D) | 16,398 | 50.3 |
| | Henry L. Morey (R) | 15,986 | 49.0 |
| 4 | Charles M. Anderson (D) | 21,087 | 50.0 |
| | John F. Sinks (R) | 20,786 | 49.3 |
| 5 | Benjamin Le Fevre (D) | 21,968 | 56.3 |
| | William D. Davis (R) | 16,852 | 43.2 |
| 6 | William D. Hill (D) | 20,684 | 54.1 |
| | Hiram C. Glenn (R) | 17,154 | 44.9 |
| 7 | George E. Seney (D) | 20,615 | 54.5 |
| | Daniel Babst Jr. (R) | 16,609 | 43.9 |
| 8 | John Little (R) | 23,019 | 58.5 |
| | James W. Denver (D) | 15,381 | 39.1 |
| 9 | William C. Cooper (R) | 18,415 | 51.1 |
| | E. F. Poppleton (D) | 16,634 | 46.2 |
| 10 | Jacob Romeis (R) | 17,605 | 50.0 |
| | Frank H. Hurd (D) | 17,366 | 49.4 |
| 11 | William W. Ellsberry (D) | 15,251 | 50.7 |
| | Alphonzo Hart (R) | 14,841 | 49.3 |
| 12 | Albert C. Thompson (R) | 15,782 | 53.8 |
| | Leo Ebert (D) | 13,384 | 45.7 |
| 13 | Joseph H. Outhwaite (D) | 23,475 | 55.2 |
| | Allen Miller (R) | 18,607 | 43.8 |
| 14 | Charles H. Grosvenor (R) | 17,008 | 56.0 |
| | John L. Vance (D) | 11,281 | 37.2 |
| | Christopher Evans (G) | 1,689 | 5.6 |
| 15 | Beriah Wilkins (D) | 20,717 | 54.1 |
| | Elijah Little (R) | 17,421 | 45.5 |
| 16 | George W. Geddes (D) | 18,528 | 50.0 |
| | Henry C. Hedges (R) | 17,835 | 48.2 |
| 17 | Adoniram J. Warner (D) | 19,173 | 49.9 |
| | Joseph D. Taylor (R) | 18,957 | 49.3 |
| 18 | Isaac H. Taylor (R) | 22,459 | 56.3 |
| | Jonathan H. Wallace (D) | 16,309 | 40.9 |
| 19 | Ezra B. Taylor (R) | 27,039 | 65.0 |
| | Horace Alvord (D) | 13,053 | 31.4 |
| 20 | William McKinley Jr. (R) | 22,672 | 51.6 |
| | David R. Paige (D) | 20,643 | 47.0 |
| 21 | Martin A. Foran (D & G) | 19,154 | 51.4 |
| | Charles C. Burnett (R) | 17,884 | 48.0 |

## OREGON

| | | | |
|---|---|---|---|
| AL | Binger Herman (R) | 25,699 | 52.1 |
| | John Myers (D) | 23,652 | 47.9 |

## PENNSYLVANIA

| | | | |
|---|---|---|---|
| 1 | Henry H. Bingham (R) | 20,227 | 60.2 |
| | Tipton (D) | 13,403 | 39.9 |
| 2 | Charles O'Neill (R) | 18,336 | 60.5 |
| | Dotts (D) | 11,952 | 39.5 |
| 3 | Samuel J. Randall (D) | 12,340 | 57.7 |
| | Gumper (R) | 9,055 | 42.3 |
| 4 | William D. Kelley (R) | 27,421 | 63.3 |
| | Fahy (D) | 15,817 | 36.5 |
| 5 | Alfred C. Harmar (R) | 26,618 | 99.9 |
| 6 | James B. Everhart (R) | 18,593 | 60.5 |
| | Heckel (D) | 11,551 | 37.6 |

| | Candidates | Votes | % |
|---|---|---|---|
| 7 | I. Newton Evans (R) | 18,048 | 52.4 |
| | Ross (D) | 16,425 | 47.7 |
| 8 | Daniel Ermentrout (D) | 16,577 | 63.8 |
| | Richards (R) | 9,405 | 36.2 |
| 9 | John A. Hiestand (R) | 19,649 | 65.6 |
| | Haldeman (D) | 9,894 | 33.0 |
| 10 | William H. Sowden (D) | 20,797 | 59.2 |
| | Chidsey (R) | 14,349 | 40.8 |
| 11 | John B. Storm (D) | 19,394 | 60.4 |
| | Walter (R) | 12,622 | 39.3 |
| 12 | Joseph A. Scranton (R) | 17,016 | 51.3 |
| | Connoly (D) | 15,179 | 45.7 |
| 13 | Charles N. Brumm (R) | 12,875 | 52.4 |
| | Reilly (D) | 11,677 | 47.6 |
| 14 | Franklin Bound (R) | 20,767 | 57.7 |
| | Foster (D) | 15,256 | 42.4 |
| 15 | Frank C. Bunnell (R) | 17,006 | 54.4 |
| | Post (D) | 12,679 | 40.6 |
| 16 | William W. Brown (R) | 19,400 | 53.3 |
| | Kennedy (D) | 16,440 | 45.2 |
| 17 | Jacob M. Campbell (R) | 19,579 | 54.3 |
| | Enfield (D) | 16,005 | 44.4 |
| 18 | Louis E. Atkinson (R) | 18,367 | 54.6 |
| | Patterson (D) | 15,277 | 45.4 |
| 19 | William A. Duncan (D) | 20,356* | 55.9 |
| | Seitz (R) | 16,094 | 44.2 |
| 20 | Andrew G. Curtin (D) | 17,656 | 51.4 |
| | Patton (R) | 16,419 | 47.8 |
| 21 | Charles E. Boyle (D) | 19,506 | 52.8 |
| | Ray (R) | 17,006 | 46.0 |
| 22 | James S. Negley (R) | 20,136 | 56.7 |
| | Hopkins (D) | 15,113 | 42.5 |
| 23 | Thomas M. Bayne (R) | 15,854 | 64.9 |
| | Foster (D) | 8,073 | 33.0 |
| 24 | Oscar L. Jackson (R) | 16,436 | 57.0 |
| | Stockdale (D) | 11,538 | 40.0 |
| 25 | Alexander C. White (R) | 16,714 | 52.8 |
| | Reitz (D) | 14,929 | 47.2 |
| 26 | George W. Fleeger (R) | 17,290 | 47.0 |
| | McKinney (D) | 15,674 | 42.6 |
| | Roberts (IR) | 2,702 | 7.4 |
| 27 | William L. Scott (D) | 16,002 | 49.2 |
| | Mackey (R) | 15,340 | 47.1 |
| AL | Edwin S. Osborne (R) | 478,240 | 53.2 |
| | Davis (D) | 401,042 | 44.6 |

### Special Election

| | | | |
|---|---|---|---|
| 19 | John Augustus Swope (D) | ✔ | # |

## RHODE ISLAND

| | | | |
|---|---|---|---|
| 1 | Henry J. Spooner (R) | 10,140 | 60.0 |
| | Tiba O. Slocum (D) | 5,976 | 35.4 |
| 2 | William A. Pirce (R) | 7,752‡ | 50.1 |
| | Charles H. Page (D) | 5,995 | 38.7 |
| | Alfred B. Chadsey (P) | 1,501 | 9.7 |

## SOUTH CAROLINA

| | | | |
|---|---|---|---|
| 1 | Samuel Dibble (D) | 8,612 | 73.5 |
| | W. N. Taft (R) | 3,108 | 26.5 |
| 2 | George D. Tillman (D) | 11,419 | 85.6 |
| | E. J. Dickersin (R) | 1,920 | 14.4 |
| 3 | D. Wyatt Aiken (D) | 10,855 | 93.5 |
| | John R. Tolbert (R) | 752 | 6.5 |
| 4 | William H. Perry (D) | 13,008 | 100.0 |
| 5 | John J. Hemphill (D) | 9,861 | 77.4 |
| | C. C. Macey (R) | 2,881 | 22.6 |
| 6 | George W. Dargan (D) | 10,465 | 76.1 |
| | Edmund H. Deas (R) | 3,289 | 23.9 |
| 7 | Robert Smalls (R) | 8,419 | 64.8 |
| | William Elliott (D) | 4,584 | 35.3 |

### Special Election

| | | | |
|---|---|---|---|
| 4 | John Bratton (D) | 3,339✔ | # |

## TENNESSEE

| | | | |
|---|---|---|---|
| 1 | Augustus H. Pettibone (R) | 15,478 | 54.4 |
| | King (D) | 12,981 | 45.6 |
| 2 | Leonidas C. Houk (R) | 19,357 | 68.3 |
| | Ledgerwood (D) | 8,975 | 31.7 |

## TENNESSEE

| Candidates | Votes | % |
|---|---|---|
| 3 John R. Neal (D) | 14,284 | 51.2 |
| Evans (R) | 13,624 | 48.8 |
| 4 Benton McMillin (D) | 12,956 | 88.0 |
| Smith (R) | 1,771 | 12.0 |
| 5 James D. Richardson (D) | 13,285 | 58.5 |
| Warder (R) | 7,144 | 31.4 |
| Martin (ID) | 1,882 | 8.3 |
| 6 Andrew J. Caldwell (D) | 16,873 | 58.2 |
| Baker (R) | 12,124 | 41.8 |
| 7 John G. Ballentine (D) | 12,157 | 55.7 |
| Cliff (R) | 9,682 | 44.3 |
| 8 John M. Taylor (D) | 12,783 | 52.6 |
| Warren (R) | 11,529 | 47.4 |
| 9 Presley T. Glass (D) | 13,451 | 55.0 |
| Etheridge (R) | 11,019 | 45.0 |
| 10 Zachary Taylor (R) | 14,271 | 51.0 |
| Harris (D) | 13,713 | 49.0 |

## TEXAS

| Candidates | Votes | % |
|---|---|---|
| 1 Charles Stewart (D) | 24,150 | 99.9 |
| 2 John H. Reagan (D) | 16,840 | 67.1 |
| A. T. Monroe (R) | 8,276 | 33.0 |
| 3 James H. Jones (D) | 23,504 | 97.2 |
| 4 David B. Culberson (D) | 23,165 | 100.0 |
| 5 James W. Throckmorton (D) | 29,462 | 98.9 |
| 6 Olin Wellborn (D) | 27,804 | 85.5 |
| J. C. Bigger (R) | 4,721 | 14.5 |
| 7 William H. Crain (D) | 15,471 | 59.2 |
| R. B. Rentfro (R) | 9,586 | 36.7 |
| 8 James F. Miller (D) | 17,143 | 66.9 |
| W. P. Burns (R) | 8,473 | 33.1 |
| 9 Roger Q. Mills (D) | 22,333 | 71.2 |

| Candidates | Votes | % |
|---|---|---|
| J. P. Osterhout (R) | 9,049 | 28.8 |
| 10 Joseph D. Sayers (D) | 21,523 | 63.7 |
| J. B. Rector (IR) | 12,253 | 36.3 |
| 11 Samuel W. T. Lanham (D) | 29,738 | 99.4 |

## VERMONT

| Candidates | Votes | % |
|---|---|---|
| 1 John W. Stewart (R) | 18,899 | 73.5 |
| George H. Simmons (D) | 6,591 | 25.6 |
| 2 William W. Grout (R) | 20,026 | 69.6 |
| Martin H. Goddard (D) | 8,479 | 29.5 |

## VIRGINIA

| Candidates | Votes | % |
|---|---|---|
| 1 Thomas Croxton (D) | 14,136 | 51.0 |
| R. M. Mayo (R) | 13,579 | 49.0 |
| 2 Harry Libby (R) | 19,083 | 58.3 |
| R. C. Marshall (D) | 13,652 | 41.7 |
| 3 George D. Wise (D) | 15,741 | 52.4 |
| Robert T. Hubard (R) | 14,301 | 47.6 |
| 4 James D. Brady (R) | 11,408 | 40.5 |
| George E. Rives (D) | 10,326 | 36.6 |
| Joseph P. Evans | 6,451 | 22.9 |
| 5 George C. Cabell (D) | 13,588 | 55.0 |
| J. W. Hartwell (R) | 11,100 | 45.0 |
| 6 John W. Daniel (D) | 17,177 | 55.9 |
| R. P. W. Morris (R) | 13,526 | 44.1 |
| 7 Charles T. O'Ferrall (D) | 15,791 | 56.4 |
| J. B. Webb (R) | 12,221 | 43.6 |
| 8 John S. Barbour (D) | 15,792 | 55.6 |
| Duff Green (R) | 12,598 | 44.4 |
| 9 Connally F. Trigg (D) | 13,844 | 52.2 |
| Daniel F. Bailey (R) | 12,660 | 47.8 |

| Candidates | Votes | % |
|---|---|---|
| 10 John R. Tucker (D) | 15,059 | 52.1 |
| Jacob Yost (R) | 13,872 | 48.0 |

## WEST VIRGINIA

| Candidates | Votes | % |
|---|---|---|
| 1 Nathan Goff Jr. (R) | 17,462 | 50.3 |
| John Brannon (D) | 17,258 | 49.7 |
| 2 William L. Wilson (D) | 18,266 | 52.2 |
| Francis M. Reynolds (R) | 16,737 | 47.8 |
| 3 Charles P. Snyder (D) | 15,359 | 53.7 |
| James W. Davis (R) | 13,240 | 46.3 |
| 4 Eustace Gibson (D) | 16,598 | 50.2 |
| A. R. Barbee (G & R) | 16,445 | 49.8 |

## WISCONSIN

| Candidates | Votes | % |
|---|---|---|
| 1 Lucien B. Caswell (R) | 19,284 | 54.6 |
| Ernst Merton (D) | 14,590 | 41.3 |
| 2 Edward S. Bragg (D) | 16,865 | 55.4 |
| Samuel S. Barney (R) | 12,643 | 41.6 |
| 3 Robert M. LaFollette (R) | 17,433 | 48.1 |
| Burr W. Jones (D) | 16,942 | 46.7 |
| John M. Olin (P) | 1,885 | 5.2 |
| 4 Isaac W. Van Schaick (R) | 16,783 | 49.1 |
| P. V. Deuster (D) | 15,907 | 46.5 |
| 5 Joseph Rankin (D) | 17,851 | 59.3 |
| Charles Luling (R) | 11,610 | 38.5 |
| 6 Richard W. Guenther (R) | 16,425 | 49.9 |
| A. L. Smith (D) | 15,197 | 46.2 |
| 7 Ormsby B. Thomas (R) | 18,437 | 52.6 |
| G. M. Woodward (D) | 15,446 | 44.1 |
| 8 William T. Price (R & P) | 24,460 | 60.2 |
| L. R. Larson (D) | 16,183 | 39.8 |
| 9 Isaac Stephenson (R) | 23,414 | 53.5 |
| James Meehan (D) | 19,885 | 45.4 |

# 1885 House Elections

## ILLINOIS

### Special Election

| | Votes | % |
|---|---|---|
| 5 Albert J. Hopkins (R) | 8,977 | 73.3 |
| Richard Bishop (D) | 3,211 | 26.2 |

## NORTH CAROLINA

### Special Election

| | Votes | % |
|---|---|---|
| 5 James W. Reid (D) | 4,707 | 90.5 |
| Joseph S. Worth (R) | 356 | 6.8 |

## RHODE ISLAND

### Special Election

| | Votes | % |
|---|---|---|
| 2 Nathan F. Dixon (R) | 2,258 | 69.3 |
| Philip W. Hawkins (D) | 998 | 30.6 |

# 1886 House Elections

## ALABAMA

| | Candidates | Votes | % |
|---|---|---|---|
| 1 | James T. Jones (D) | 4,220 | 99.6 |
| 2 | Hilary A. Herbert (D) | 5,659 | 100.0 |
| 3 | William C. Oates (D) | 4,660 | 100.0 |
| 4 | Alexander C. Davidson (D) | 14,913 | 71.2 |
| | McDuffie (R) | 3,526 | 16.8 |
| | Turner (IR) | 2,519 | 12.0 |
| 5 | James E. Cobb (D) | 5,558 | 87.8 |
| | Edwards (R) | 775 | 12.2 |
| 6 | John H. Bankhead (D) | 7,968 | 64.6 |
| | Long (R) | 4,369 | 35.4 |
| 7 | William H. Forney (D) | 7,549 | 62.0 |
| | Hardie (R) | 4,608 | 37.8 |
| 8 | Joseph Wheeler (D) | 11,684 | 57.5 |
| | Jackson (R) | 8,639 | 42.5 |

## ARKANSAS

| | Candidates | Votes | % |
|---|---|---|---|
| 1 | Poindexter Dunn (D) | 6,092 | 100.0 |
| 2 | Clifton R. Breckinridge (D) | 8,612 | 54.4 |
| | D. D. Leach (R) | 4,380 | 27.7 |
| | R. B. Carllee (AG WHEEL) | 2,846 | 18.0 |
| 3 | Thomas C. McRae (D) | 8,909 | 57.8 |
| | J. C. Ray (R) | 4,169 | 27.0 |
| | L. H. Hitt (G) | 2,343 | 15.2 |
| 4 | John H. Rogers (D) | 8,314 | 62.1 |
| | Isom P. Langley (LAB) | 5,077 | 37.9 |
| 5 | Samuel W. Peel (D) | 4,746 | 100.0 |

## CALIFORNIA

| | Candidates | Votes | % |
|---|---|---|---|
| 1 | Thomas L. Thompson (D) | 16,499 | 50.0 |
| | C. A. Gartern (R) | 15,526 | 47.1 |
| 2 | Marion Biggs (D) | 17,667 | 49.8 |
| | J. C. Campbell (R) | 16,594 | 46.8 |
| 3 | Joseph McKenna (R) | 15,801 | 53.0 |
| | H. C. McPike (D) | 13,277 | 44.5 |
| 4 | William W. Morrow (R) | 11,413 | 48.4 |
| | F. McCoppin (D) | 9,854 | 41.8 |
| | C. A. Sumner (LAB) | 2,184 | 9.3 |
| 5 | Charles N. Felton (R) | 16,328 | 48.5 |
| | F. J. Sullivan (D) | 16,209 | 48.2 |
| 6 | William Vandever (R) | 18,259 | 47.3 |
| | Joe D. Lynch (D) | 18,204 | 47.1 |
| | W. H. Harris (P) | 2,159 | 5.6 |

## COLORADO

| | Candidates | Votes | % |
|---|---|---|---|
| AL | George G. Symes (R) | 27,732 | 47.6 |
| | Myron W. Reed (D) | 26,929 | 46.2 |
| | Joseph Murray (P) | 3,597 | 6.2 |

## CONNECTICUT

| | Candidates | Votes | % |
|---|---|---|---|
| 1 | Robert J. Vance (D) | 14,898 | 48.3 |
| | John R. Buck (R) | 14,552 | 47.2 |
| 2 | Carlos French (D) | 18,730 | 47.9 |
| | Lewis (R) | 17,402 | 44.5 |
| 3 | Charles A. Russell (R) | 9,366 | 48.9 |
| | Hyde (D) | 8,718 | 45.5 |
| | Rockwell (P) | 1,066 | 5.6 |
| 4 | Miles T. Granger (D) | 16,235 | 47.8 |
| | Miles (R) | 15,914 | 46.9 |

## DELAWARE

| | Candidates | Votes | % |
|---|---|---|---|
| AL | John B. Penington (D) | 13,837 | 62.2 |
| | Cooper (TEMP REF) | 8,393 | 37.8 |

## FLORIDA

| | Candidates | Votes | % |
|---|---|---|---|
| 1 | Robert H. M. Davidson (D) | 14,493 | 66.2 |
| | Pendleton (R) | 7,389 | 33.8 |
| 2 | Charles Dougherty (D) | 18,890 | 54.1 |
| | Greeley (R) | 15,764 | 45.2 |

## GEORGIA

| | Candidates | Votes | % |
|---|---|---|---|
| 1 | Thomas M. Norwood (D) | 2,061 | 99.2 |
| 2 | Henry G. Turner (D) | 2,411 | 99.7 |
| 3 | Charles F. Crisp (D) | 1,704 | 100.0 |
| 4 | Thomas W. Grimes (D) | 2,909 | 89.8 |
| | Carmical (I) | 330 | 10.2 |
| 5 | John D. Stewart (D) | 2,999 | 100.0 |
| 6 | James H. Blount (D) | 1,722 | 99.9 |
| 7 | Judson C. Clements (D) | 5,043 | 75.5 |
| | Felton (I) | 1,537 | 23.0 |
| 8 | Henry H. Carlton (D) | 2,322 | 97.7 |
| 9 | Allen D. Candler (D) | 2,355 | 98.9 |
| 10 | George T. Barnes (D) | 1,944 | 99.6 |

## ILLINOIS

| | Candidates | Votes | % |
|---|---|---|---|
| 1 | Ransom W. Dunham (R) | 12,321 | 46.9 |
| | Edgar Terhunr (D) | 7,258 | 27.6 |
| | Harvey Sheldon Jr. (UN LAB) | 6,358 | 24.2 |
| 2 | Frank Lawler (D) | 7,369 | 39.3 |
| | Daniel F. Gluson (UN LAB) | 7,353 | 39.3 |
| | Charles W. Woodman (R) | 3,976 | 21.2 |
| 3 | William E. Mason (R) | 13,721 | 66.2 |
| | B. W. Goodhur (UN LAB) | 6,352 | 30.7 |
| 4 | George E. Adams (R) | 12,147 | 48.1 |
| | J. B. Taylor (D) | 7,480 | 29.6 |
| | I. A. Hawkins (UN LAB) | 4,997 | 19.8 |
| 5 | Albert J. Hopkins (R) | 14,224 | 62.9 |
| | J. F. Glidden (D) | 6,258 | 27.7 |
| | Charles Wheaton (P) | 2,121 | 9.4 |
| 6 | Robert R. Hitt (R) | 13,106 | 55.5 |
| | James McNamara (D) | 8,650 | 36.6 |
| | Spencer Rising (P) | 1,878 | 8.0 |
| 7 | Thomas J. Henderson (R) | 12,586 | 58.2 |
| | Sherwood Dixon (D) | 7,731 | 35.8 |
| | David E. Holmes (P) | 1,296 | 6.0 |
| 8 | Ralph Plumb (R) | 16,827 | 52.1 |
| | Hiram H. Cady (D) | 13,893 | 43.0 |
| 9 | Lewis E. Payson (R) | 13,753 | 54.2 |
| | Mathews H. Peters (D) | 10,633 | 41.9 |
| 10 | Philip Sidney Post (R) | 15,186 | 48.7 |
| | Nicholas E. Worthington (D) | 15,157 | 48.6 |
| 11 | William A. Gest (R) | 16,733 | 48.8 |
| | William H. Neece (D & G) | 16,397 | 47.9 |
| 12 | George A. Anderson (D & G) | 18,718 | 57.5 |
| | Oruan Pierson (R) | 12,755 | 39.2 |
| 13 | William M. Springer (D) | 17,433 | 49.5 |
| | James A. Connelly (R) | 16,453 | 46.7 |
| | William W. Alder (P) | 1,786 | 6.0 |
| 14 | Jonathan H. Rowell (R) | 15,319 | 51.0 |
| | William Voorhees (D) | 12,917 | 43.0 |
| 15 | Joseph G. Cannon (R) | 16,739 | 50.9 |
| | D. H. Lindsey (D) | 15,314 | 46.6 |
| 16 | Silas Z. Landes (D) | 16,424 | 50.2 |
| | Charles Churchill (R) | 15,564 | 47.6 |
| 17 | Edward Lane (D) | 14,937 | 53.9 |
| | Robert McWilliams (R) * | 11,557 | 41.7 |
| 18 | Jehu Baker (R) | 15,396 | 50.8 |
| | William R. Morrison (D) | 14,234 | 46.9 |
| 19 | Richard W. Townshend (D) | 16,316 | 56.1 |
| | James S. Martin (R) | 11,972 | 41.2 |
| 20 | John R. Thomas (R) | 16,246 | 50.9 |
| | William Hartzell (D) | 15,074 | 47.3 |

## INDIANA

| | Candidates | Votes | % |
|---|---|---|---|
| 1 | Alvin P. Hovey (R) | 18,258 | 49.0 |
| | J. E. McCullough (D) | 16,901 | 45.4 |
| 2 | John H. O'Neal (D) | 16,075 | 51.8 |
| | M. S. Ragsdale (R) | 14,871 | 47.9 |
| 3 | Jonas G. Howard (D) | 12,458 | 46.4 |
| | James K. Marsh (ID) | 9,854 | 36.7 |
| | James Kugwin (IR) | 3,714 | 13.8 |
| 4 | William S. Holman (D) | 15,777 | 50.8 |
| | Thomas J. Lucas (R) | 14,989 | 48.3 |

| | Candidates | Votes | % |
|---|---|---|---|
| 5 | Courtland Cushing Matson (D) | 16,694 | 49.9 |
| | Ira J. Chase (R) | 16,162 | 48.3 |
| 6 | Thomas M. Browne (R) | 20,397 | 60.4 |
| | George S. Jones (D) | 12,253 | 36.3 |
| 7 | William D. Bynum (D) | 22,882 | 51.3 |
| | Addison C. Harris (R) | 21,108 | 47.3 |
| 8 | James T. Johnston (R) | 20,918 | 50.6 |
| | John Edward Lamb (D) | 19,816 | 47.9 |
| 9 | Joseph B. Cheadle (R) | 22,437 | 53.0 |
| | Benjamin F. Ham (D) | 19,021 | 44.9 |
| 10 | William D. Owen (R) | 18,114 | 52.1 |
| | Hiram D. Hattery (D) | 16,041 | 46.1 |
| 11 | George Washington Steele (R) | 19,649 | 48.9 |
| | James C. Branyan (D) | 19,241 | 47.9 |
| 12 | James B. White (R) | 17,900 | 51.8 |
| | Robert Lowry (D) | 15,416 | 44.6 |
| 13 | Benjamin Franklin Shively (D) | 19,105 | 50.5 |
| | Jasper Packard (R) | 18,087 | 47.8 |

## IOWA

| | Candidates | Votes | % |
|---|---|---|---|
| 1 | John Henry Gear (R) | 16,115 | 51.1 |
| | Benton Jay Hall (FUS) | 15,078 | 47.8 |
| 2 | Walter I. Hayes (FUS) | 15,309 | 48.0 |
| | Thomas J. O'Meara (LAB) | 8,602 | 27.0 |
| | Samuel Jordan Kirkwood (R) | 8,009 | 25.1 |
| 3 | David B. Henderson (R) | 18,201 | 54.4 |
| | W. H. Chamberlain (FUS) | 15,272 | 45.6 |
| 4 | William Elijah Fuller (R) | 17,062 | 53.0 |
| | Willard C. Earle (FUS) | 15,132 | 47.0 |
| 5 | Daniel Kerr (R) | 16,696 | 51.0 |
| | Benjamin Todd Frederick (FUS) | 15,963 | 48.8 |
| 6 | James Baird Weaver (FUS) | 16,572 | 50.9 |
| | John A. Donnell (R) | 15,954 | 49.0 |
| 7 | Edwin H. Conger (R) | 15,165 | 51.6 |
| | W. L. Carpenter (FUS) | 14,239 | 48.4 |
| 8 | Albert Raney Anderson (IR) | 17,970 | 53.2 |
| | William P. Hepburn (R) | 15,745 | 46.7 |
| 9 | Joseph Lyman (R) | 16,953 | 53.4 |
| | John H. Keatley (FUS) | 14,747 | 46.5 |
| 10 | Adoniram J. Holmes (R) | 16,767 | 56.6 |
| | George Wilmot (FUS) | 12,868 | 43.4 |
| 11 | Isaac S. Struble (R) | 15,356 | 58.4 |
| | E. C. Palmer (FUS) | 10,919 | 41.5 |

## KANSAS

| | Candidates | Votes | % |
|---|---|---|---|
| 1 | Edmund N. Morrill (R) | 17,347 | 55.3 |
| | E. Bierer (D) | 13,832 | 44.1 |
| 2 | Edward H. Funston (R) | 18,037 | 51.9 |
| | Charles Robinson (D) | 15,416 | 44.3 |
| 3 | Bishop W. Perkins (R) | 19,614 | 53.4 |
| | Frank Bacon (D) | 15,875 | 43.2 |
| 4 | Thomas Ryan (R) | 21,961 | 56.2 |
| | John Martin (D) | 15,706 | 40.2 |
| 5 | John A. Anderson (R) | 19,240 | 53.1 |
| | J. G. Lowe (D) | 12,751 | 35.2 |
| | A. S. Wilson (IR) | 3,856 | 10.6 |
| 6 | Erastus J. Turner (R) | 19,624 | 58.5 |
| | W. S. Gile (D) | 11,359 | 33.9 |
| | C. H. Moody (A-MONOP) | 2,098 | 6.3 |
| 7 | Samuel R. Peters (R) | 34,515 | 56.2 |
| | Thomas George (D) | 25,070 | 40.8 |

## KENTUCKY

| | Candidates | Votes | % |
|---|---|---|---|
| 1 | William J. Stone (D) | 9,730 | 53.4 |
| | Oscar Turner (ID) | 8,476 | 46.5 |
| 2 | Polk Laffoon (D) | 10,715 | 58.2 |
| | George W. Jolly (R) | 7,695 | 41.8 |
| 3 | W. Godfrey Hunter (R) | 13,379 | 51.8 |
| | John S. Rhea (D) | 12,372 | 47.9 |

## KENTUCKY

| Candidates | Votes | % |
|---|---|---|
| 4 Alexander B. Montgomery (D) | 9,892 | 56.6 |
| J. D. Belden (R) | 7,572 | 43.4 |
| 5 Asher G. Caruth (D) | 9,964 | 50.4 |
| A. E. Willson (R) | 9,824 | 49.7 |
| 6 John G. Carlisle (D) | 6,476 | 53.3 |
| George H. Thoebe (LAB) | 5,651 | 46.5 |
| 7 William C. P. Breckinridge (D) | 4,791 | 99.7 |
| 8 James B. McCreary (D) | 10,540 | 59.8 |
| Thomas Todd (R) | 7,077 | 40.2 |
| 9 George M. Thomas (R) | 13,693 | 50.3 |
| Garrett S. Wall (D) | 13,546 | 49.7 |
| 10 William P. Taulbee (D) | 11,940 | 51.6 |
| William L. Hurst (R) | 11,194 | 48.4 |
| 11 Hugh L. Finly (R) | 12,824 | 53.2 |
| W. H. Botts (D) | 11,278 | 46.8 |

## LOUISIANA

| | Votes | % |
|---|---|---|
| 1 Theodore S. Wilkinson (D) | 11,350 | 87.3 |
| William M. Burwell (R) | 1,649 | 12.7 |
| 2 Matthew D. Lagan (D) | 7,930 | 53.7 |
| A. Hero Jr. (R) | 6,537 | 44.3 |
| 3 Edward J. Gay (D) | 14,782 | 55.1 |
| Chester B. Darrall (R) | 11,692 | 43.6 |
| 4 Newton C. Blanchard (D) | 5,747 | 99.8 |
| 5 Cherubusco Newton (D) | 13,618 | 95.6 |
| 6 Edward W. Robertson (D) | 9,676 | 95.8 |

**Special Election**

| | Votes | % |
|---|---|---|
| 2 Nathaniel Dick Wallace (D) | ✔ | # |

## MAINE

| | Votes | % |
|---|---|---|
| 1 Thomas B. Reed (R) | 15,486 | 49.9 |
| W. H. Clifford (D) | 14,298 | 46.0 |
| 2 Nelson Dingley Jr. (R) | 18,137 | 53.3 |
| Alonzo Garcelon (D) | 11,920 | 35.1 |
| William T. Eustis (P-LAB) | 3,939 | 11.6 |
| 3 Seth Llewellyn Milliken (R) | 17,992 | 56.5 |
| Joseph E. Ladd (D) | 12,781 | 40.1 |
| 4 Charles A. Boutelle (R) | 17,372 | 54.6 |
| John F. Lynch (D) | 13,655 | 42.9 |

## MARYLAND

| | Votes | % |
|---|---|---|
| 1 Charles H. Gibson (D) | 12,791 | 49.3 |
| Hodson (R) | 11,640 | 44.8 |
| Melson (P) | 1,529 | 5.9 |
| 2 Frank T. Shaw (D) | 12,016 | 55.5 |
| Marine (R) | 8,362 | 38.6 |
| Zouck (P) | 1,283 | 5.9 |
| 3 Harry W. Rusk (D) | 13,634 | 72.3 |
| Bosse (LAB-R) | 3,300 | 17.5 |
| Glass (P) | 1,726 | 9.2 |
| 4 Isidor Rayner (D) | 14,750 | 62.6 |
| Findlay (I) | 7,220 | 30.6 |
| Weatherby (R) | 1,569 | 6.7 |
| 5 Barnes Compton (D) | 13,579 | 54.8 |
| Tuck (R) | 10,850 | 43.8 |
| 6 Louis E. McComas (R) | 16,851 | 49.7 |
| Baughman (D) | 16,438 | 48.5 |

## MASSACHUSETTS

| | Votes | % |
|---|---|---|
| 1 Robert T. Davis (R) | 9,416 | 58.6 |
| McLaughlin (D) | 5,768 | 35.9 |
| Hatfield (P) | 847 | 5.3 |
| 2 John D. Long (R) | 11,317 | 52.2 |
| Morse (D) | 9,495 | 43.8 |
| 3 Leopold Morse (D) | 11,199 | 53.7 |
| Ranney (R) | 9,438 | 45.3 |
| 4 Patrick A. Collins (D) | 11,201 | 73.4 |
| Cutler (R) | 3,829 | 25.1 |
| 5 Edward D. Hayden (R) | 11,364 | 57.3 |
| Randall (D) | 8,006 | 40.3 |
| 6 Henry Cabot Lodge (R) | 13,495 | 50.5 |
| Lovering (D) | 12,767 | 47.8 |
| 7 William Cogswell (R) | 9,863 | 46.9 |
| French (D) | 8,489 | 40.4 |

| Candidates | Votes | % |
|---|---|---|
| Spaulding (G & P) | 2,663 | 12.7 |
| 8 Charles H. Allen (R) | 10,216 | 50.2 |
| Donovan (D) | 9,684 | 47.6 |
| 9 Edward Burnett (D) | 10,354 | 48.7 |
| Ely (R) | 10,143 | 47.7 |
| 10 John E. Russell (D) | 9,728 | 49.7 |
| Rice (R) | 8,977 | 45.8 |
| 11 William Whiting (R) | 10,861 | 53.5 |
| Currier (D) | 8,098 | 39.9 |
| Watkins (P) | 1,320 | 6.5 |
| 12 Francis W. Rockwell (R) | 10,181 | 49.6 |
| Joyner (D) | 9,366 | 45.6 |

## MICHIGAN

| | Votes | % |
|---|---|---|
| 1 John Logan Chipman (D) | 17,367 | 51.0 |
| Henry A. Robinson (R) | 15,801 | 46.4 |
| 2 Edward P. Allen (R) | 16,518 | 47.9 |
| Lester H. Salsbury (D) | 15,486 | 45.0 |
| Alfred O. Crozier (P) | 2,448 | 7.1 |
| 3 James O'Donnell (R) | 20,215 | 51.4 |
| Patrick Hankerd (D) | 15,499 | 39.4 |
| Hiram D. Allen (P) | 3,594 | 9.1 |
| 4 Julius C. Burrows (R) | 18,257 | 50.7 |
| Harvey C. Sherwood (D) | 15,744 | 43.7 |
| Jesse S. Boyden (P) | 1,999 | 5.6 |
| 5 Melbourne H. Ford (D) | 18,567 | 46.7 |
| George W. McBride (R) | 18,120 | 45.6 |
| Edward L. Briggs (P) | 3,086 | 7.8 |
| 6 Mark S. Brewer (R) | 19,034 | 48.1 |
| John H. Fedewa (D) | 17,148 | 43.3 |
| Azariah S. Partridge (P) | 3,427 | 8.7 |
| 7 Justin R. Whiting (D) | 13,777 | 48.6 |
| John P. Sanborn (R) | 12,963 | 45.8 |
| William F. Clark (P) | 1,593 | 5.6 |
| 8 Timothy E. Tarsney (D) | 18,301 | 48.4 |
| Roswell G. Horr (R) | 17,615 | 46.5 |
| George W. Abbey (P) | 1,930 | 5.1 |
| 9 Byron M. Cutcheon (R) | 17,226 | 50.9 |
| Lyman G. Mason (D) | 14,198 | 42.0 |
| Lathrop S. Ellis (P) | 2,393 | 7.1 |
| 10 Spencer O. Fisher (D) | 15,047 | 53.3 |
| Henry M. Loud (R) | 12,900 | 45.7 |
| 11 Seth C. Moffatt (R) | 14,485 | 53.6 |
| John Power (D) | 12,242 | 45.3 |

## MINNESOTA

| | Votes | % |
|---|---|---|
| 1 Thomas Wilson (D) | 17,491 | 52.0 |
| John A. Lovely (R) | 14,663 | 3.6 |
| 2 John Lind (R) | 22,908 | 59.8 |
| A. H. Bullis (D&F ALNC) | 13,260 | 34.6 |
| George J. Day (P) | 2,114 | 5.5 |
| 3 John L. MacDonald (D) | 16,788 | 50.3 |
| B. B. Herbert (R) | 15,583 | 46.7 |
| 4 Edmund Rice (D) | 34,034 | 52.4 |
| J. B. Gilfillan (R) | 28,909 | 44.5 |
| 5 Knute Nelson (R) | 43,937 | 97.3 |

## MISSISSIPPI

| | Votes | % |
|---|---|---|
| 1 John M. Allen (D) | 3,140 | 99.2 |
| 2 James B. Morgan (D) | 7,857 | 62.1 |
| Chalmers (R) | 4,791 | 37.9 |
| 3 Thomas C. Catchings (D) | 4,518 | 65.5 |
| Simrall (R) | 2,382 | 34.5 |
| 4 Frederick G. Barry (D) | 2,964 | 96.1 |
| 5 Chapman L. Anderson (D) | 4,289 | 99.4 |
| 6 Thomas R. Stockdale (D) | 8,284 | 68.4 |
| Lynch (R) | 3,825 | 31.6 |
| 7 Charles E. Hooker (D) | 4,507 | 100.0 |

## MISSOURI

| | Votes | % |
|---|---|---|
| 1 William H. Hatch (D) | 17,323 | 54.5 |
| Harrison (R) | 14,455 | 45.5 |

| Candidates | Votes | % |
|---|---|---|
| 2 Charles H. Mansur (D) | 17,171 | 49.2 |
| Hale (ID) | 16,441 | 47.1 |
| 3 Alexander M. Dockery (D) | 19,689 | 56.0 |
| Harwood (R) | 15,327 | 43.6 |
| 4 James N. Burnes (D) | 14,051 | 53.2 |
| Dunn (R) | 11,964 | 45.3 |
| 5 William Warner (R) | 16,368 | 50.9 |
| Phillips (D) | 15,583 | 48.4 |
| 6 John T. Heard (D) | 21,558 | 53.6 |
| Guitar (R) | 18,678 | 46.4 |
| 7 John E. Hutton (D) | 15,212 | 53.7 |
| Martin (R) | 13,135 | 46.3 |
| 8 John J. O'Neill (D) | 8,166 | 47.8 |
| Cumings (R) | 6,802 | 39.8 |
| Wind (UN LAB) | 2,030 | 11.9 |
| 9 John M. Glover (D) | 7,202 | 44.3 |
| Nathan Frank (R) | 7,102 | 43.7 |
| Davisson (UN LAB) | 1,792 | 11.0 |
| 10 Martin L. Clardy (D) | 13,145 | 45.1 |
| Ledgerber (R) | 12,097 | 41.5 |
| Ratchford (UN LAB) | 3,927 | 13.5 |
| 11 Richard P. Bland (D) | 16,594 | 54.3 |
| Parker (R) | 13,996 | 45.8 |
| 12 William J. Stone (D) | 21,205 | 53.9 |
| Kimball (R) | 17,540 | 44.5 |
| 13 William H. Wade (R) | 14,631 | 51.8 |
| Cravens (D) | 12,674 | 44.9 |
| 14 James P. Walker (D) | 18,400 | 63.6 |
| Davidson (FUS) | 10,533 | 36.4 |

## NEBRASKA

| | Votes | % |
|---|---|---|
| 1 John A. McShane (D) | 23,396 | 54.9 |
| Church Howe (R) | 16,373 | 38.4 |
| George Bigelow (P) | 2,867 | 6.7 |
| 2 James Laird (R) | 21,373 | 51.5 |
| W. A. McKeighan (D) | 16,315 | 39.3 |
| C. S. Harrison (P) | 3,789 | 9.1 |
| 3 George W. E. Dorsey (R) | 28,681 | 55.2 |
| A. H. Webster (D) | 20,933 | 40.3 |

## NEVADA

| | Votes | % |
|---|---|---|
| AL William Woodburn (R) | 6,700 | 54.2 |
| J. H. Macmillan (D) | 5,670 | 45.8 |

## NEW HAMPSHIRE

| | Votes | % |
|---|---|---|
| 1 Luther F. McKinney (D) | 18,370 | 49.1 |
| Martin A. Haynes (R) | 18,165 | 48.5 |
| 2 Jacob H. Gallinger (R) | 19,715 | 49.8 |
| William W. Bailey (D) | 18,549 | 46.9 |

## NEW JERSEY

| | Votes | % |
|---|---|---|
| 1 George Hires (R) | 18,347 | 49.0 |
| Wescott (D) | 15,013 | 40.1 |
| Nicholson (P) | 4,072 | 10.9 |
| 2 James Buchanan (R) | 17,767 | 50.2 |
| Reed (D) | 15,065 | 42.6 |
| Brown (P) | 2,547 | 7.2 |
| 3 John Kean Jr. (R) | 15,567 | 46.5 |
| McMahon (D) | 14,930 | 44.6 |
| Parker (P) | 2,980 | 8.9 |
| 4 James N. Pidcock (D) | 11,686 | 44.9 |
| Vanblarcom (R) | 11,563 | 44.4 |
| Morrow (P) | 2,772 | 10.7 |
| 5 William W. Phelps (R) | 15,297 | 51.8 |
| Skinner (D) | 12,461 | 42.2 |
| Church (P) | 1,780 | 6.0 |
| 6 Herman Lehlbach (R) | 15,492 | 40.8 |
| Haynes (D) | 13,719 | 36.1 |
| Beckmeyer (LAB) | 6,331 | 16.7 |
| Anderson (P) | 2,429 | 6.4 |
| 7 William McAdoo (D) | 15,688 | 49.7 |
| Hammerschlag (R) | 11,435 | 36.2 |
| Kerr (ID) | 3,668 | 11.6 |

## NEW YORK

| Candidates | Votes | % |
|---|---|---|
| 1 Perry Belmont (D) | 16,286 | 50.0 |
| McCormick (R) | 15,360 | 47.1 |
| 2 Felix Campbell (D) | 16,679 | 70.8 |
| Donovan (R) | 5,580 | 23.7 |
| 3 Stephen V. White (R) | 12,740 | 48.6 |
| Bell (D) | 12,568 | 48.0 |
| 4 Peter P. Mahoney (D) | 13,879 | 53.6 |
| O'Connor (R) | 10,251 | 39.6 |
| 5 Archibald M. Bliss (D) | 11,583 | 50.1 |
| Waters (R) | 11,111 | 48.0 |
| 6 Amos J. Cummings (D) | 13,799 | 96.4 |
| 7 Lloyd S. Bryce (D) | 12,895 | 64.2 |
| Lawson (R) | 6,972 | 34.7 |
| 8 Timothy J. Campbell (D) | 12,179 | 50.4 |
| Grady (ID) | 11,799 | 48.8 |
| 9 Samuel S. Cox (D) | 13,754 | 62.3 |
| Wagener (R) | 8,259 | 37.4 |
| 10 Francis B. Spinola (D) | 10,847 | 50.7 |
| Rice (R) | 10,320 | 48.2 |
| 11 Truman A. Merriman (D) | 24,502 | 97.8 |
| 12 W. Bourke Cockran (D) | 15,886 | 59.3 |
| Pell (R) | 10,680 | 39.9 |
| 13 Ashbel P. Fitch (R) | 17,614 | 55.3 |
| Viele (D) | 13,939 | 43.8 |
| 14 William G. Stahlnecker (D) | 15,828 | 52.3 |
| Wood (R) | 13,392 | 44.3 |
| 15 Henry Bacon (D) | 13,488 | 48.7 |
| Stivers (R) | 13,027 | 47.0 |
| 16 John H. Ketcham (R) | 15,585 | 55.2 |
| Sackett (D) | 11,583 | 41.0 |
| 17 Stephen T. Hopkins (R) | 17,805 | 52.3 |
| Lounsbery (D) | 14,317 | 42.1 |
| Howie (P) | 1,872 | 5.5 |
| 18 Edward W. Greenman (D) | 17,082 | 49.8 |
| Burleigh (R) | 15,819 | 46.1 |
| 19 Nicholas T. Kane (D) | 16,552 | 47.8 |
| Swinburne (R) | 16,385 | 47.3 |
| 20 George West R) | 16,339 | 54.7 |
| Wick (D) | 10,035 | 33.6 |
| French (P) | 3,344 | 11.2 |
| 21 John H. Moffitt (R) | 15,376 | 68.4 |
| Winslow (D) | 6,049 | 26.9 |
| 22 Abraham X. Parker (R) | 14,450 | 57.5 |
| Corbin (D) | 9,120 | 36.3 |
| Huntington (P) | 1,523 | 6.1 |
| 23 James S. Sherman (R) | 15,914 | 49.2 |
| Spriggs (D) | 14,430 | 44.6 |
| Hendee (P) | 1,966 | 6.1 |
| 24 David Wilber (R) | 16,314 | 50.3 |
| Smith (D) | 14,549 | 44.9 |
| 25 Frank Hiscock (R) | 16,087* | 58.2 |
| Angel (D) | 11,498 | 41.6 |
| 26 Milton De Lano (R) | 19,155 | 55.3 |
| Downs (D) | 12,362 | 35.7 |
| Williams (P) | 3,086 | 8.9 |
| 27 Newton W. Nutting (R) | 21,465 | 60.7 |
| Beardsley (D) | 11,679 | 33.0 |
| 28 Thomas S. Flood (R) | 14,124 | 52.3 |
| McGuire (D) | 11,611 | 43.0 |
| 29 Ira Davenport (R) | 17,047 | 82.8 |
| Ladd (D) | 3,009 | 14.6 |
| 30 Charles S. Baker (R) | 13,170 | 53.2 |
| Bacon (D) | 10,509 | 42.5 |
| 31 John G. Sawyer (R) | 14,611 | 54.3 |
| Wadsworth (D) | 10,022 | 37.2 |
| Sparrow (P) | 2,286 | 8.5 |
| 32 John M. Farquhar (R) | 16,785 | 55.2 |
| Rogers (D) | 13,452 | 44.2 |
| 33 John B. Weber (R) | 12,215 | 49.3 |
| Spalding (D) | 11,082 | 44.7 |
| Smith (P) | 1,465 | 5.9 |
| 34 William G. Laidlaw (R) | 16,966 | 52.8 |
| Wood (D) | 9,305 | 28.9 |
| Huntington (P) | 5,505 | 17.1 |

## NORTH CAROLINA

| Candidates | Votes | % |
|---|---|---|
| 1 Louis C. Latham (D) | 13,390 | 54.6 |
| Lycurgus J. Barrett | 10,635 | 43.4 |
| 2 Furnifold M. Simmons (D) | 15,158 | 44.8 |
| James E. O'Hara (R) | 13,060 | 38.6 |
| Israel B. Abbott (IR) | 5,020 | 14.9 |
| 3 Charles W. McClammy (D) | 14,538 | 60.7 |
| F. D. Koonce (R) | 8,164 | 34.1 |
| 4 John Nichols (I) | 15,861 | 52.4 |
| John W. Graham (D) | 14,423 | 47.6 |
| 5 John M. Brower (R) | 13,282 | 49.7 |
| James W. Reid (D) | 11,702 | 43.8 |
| 6 Alfred Rowland (D) | 14,261 | 62.5 |
| Charles R. Jones (ID) | 7,659 | 33.6 |
| 7 John S. Henderson (D) | 10,565 | 78.6 |
| Joseph A. Blair | 1,473 | 11.0 |
| James E. Walker (P) | 1,401 | 10.4 |
| 8 William H. H. Cowles (D) | 9,997 | 65.2 |
| Leander L. Green (R) | 5,325 | 34.7 |
| 9 Thomas D. Johnston (D) | 11,754 | 54.2 |
| William H. Malone (ID) | 7,014 | 32.3 |
| Alexander H. Jones (R) | 2,934 | 13.5 |

## OHIO

| Candidates | Votes | % |
|---|---|---|
| 1 Benjamin Butterworth (R) | 15,522 | 53.4 |
| Samuel A. Miller (D) | 13,166 | 45.3 |
| 2 Charles E. Brown (R) | 17,009 | 52.3 |
| Hugh Shiels (D) | 15,210 | 46.8 |
| 3 Elihu S. Williams (R) | 17,235 | 47.1 |
| Robert M. Murray (D) | 16,102 | 44.0 |
| Jacob W. Nigh (LAB) | 2,132 | 5.8 |
| 4 Samuel S. Yoder (D) | 16,959 | 59.2 |
| Theodore W. Brotherton (R) | 10,753 | 37.5 |
| 5 George E. Seney (D) | 16,996 | 70.8 |
| David Harpster (R) | 5,023 | 20.9 |
| Rudolph Rock (P) | 1,629 | 6.8 |
| 6 Melvin M. Boothman (R) | 19,476 | 50.0 |
| William D. Hill (D) | 18,099 | 46.5 |
| 7 James E. Campbell (D) | 15,303 | 48.4 |
| John Little (R) | 15,301 | 48.4 |
| 8 Robert P. Kennedy (R) | 18,080 | 49.6 |
| Thomas R. McMillen (D) | 16,692 | 45.8 |
| 9 William C. Cooper (R) | 17,659 | 49.8 |
| John C. Levering (D) | 15,790 | 44.6 |
| William H. Elsom (P) | 1,900 | 5.4 |
| 10 Jacob Romeis (R) | 17,180 | 51.7 |
| Frank H. Hurd (D) | 15,592 | 46.9 |
| 11 Albert C. Thompson (R) | 17,550 | 55.3 |
| Irvin Dungan (D) | 13,202 | 41.6 |
| 12 Jacob J. Pugsley (R) | 18,283 | 49.6 |
| James W. Denver (D) | 17,025 | 46.2 |
| 13 Joseph H. Outhwaite (D) | 20,310 | 51.7 |
| William Shepard (R) | 17,730 | 45.1 |
| 14 Charles P. Wickham (R) | 13,835 | 49.1 |
| Thomas G. Bristor (D) | 12,764 | 45.3 |
| Corydon L. Tambling (P) | 1,576 | 5.6 |
| 15 Charles H. Grosvenor (R) | 15,794 | 51.0 |
| Adoniram J. Warner (D) | 14,324 | 46.3 |
| 16 Beriah Wilkins (D) | 20,258 | 53.3 |
| Caleb B. Downs (R) | 16,284 | 42.8 |
| 17 Joseph D. Taylor (R) | 17,623 | 52.4 |
| David C. Kennon (D) | 14,010 | 41.7 |
| James M. Monroe (P) | 1,948 | 5.8 |
| 18 William McKinley Jr (R) | 18,776 | 49.1 |
| Wallace H. Phelps (D) | 16,217 | 42.4 |
| 19 Ezra B. Taylor (R) | 17,707 | 63.2 |
| Thaddeus E. Hoyt (D) | 7,831 | 28.0 |
| Charles E. Holt (P) | 2,291 | 8.2 |
| 20 George W. Crouse (R) | 15,777 | 48.5 |
| William Dorsey (D) | 14,890 | 45.8 |
| John J. Ashenhurst (P) | 1,805 | 5.6 |
| 21 Martin A. Foran (D) | 14,899 | 51.2 |
| Amos Townsend (R) | 13,466 | 46.3 |

## OREGON

| Candidates | Votes | % |
|---|---|---|
| AL Binger Hermann (R) | 26,918 | 49.0 |
| N. L. Butler (D) | 25,221 | 46.0 |
| G. M. Miller (P) | 2,753 | 5.0 |

## PENNSYLVANIA

| Candidates | Votes | % |
|---|---|---|
| 1 Henry H. Bingham (R) | 18,225 | 60.0 |
| Ryan (D) | 11,826 | 38.9 |
| 2 Charles O'Neill (R) | 15,480 | 59.0 |
| Beasley (D) | 9,847 | 38.1 |
| 3 Samuel J. Randall (D) | 11,320 | 98.4 |
| 4 William D. Kelley (R) | 25,391 | 62.7 |
| Laverty (D) | 13,882 | 34.3 |
| 5 Alfred C. Harmer (R) | 23,464 | 57.4 |
| Smith (D) | 12,276 | 30.1 |
| Herwig (LAB) | 4,159 | 10.2 |
| 6 Smedley Darlington (R) | 11,841 | 41.4 |
| Dickinson (D) | 10,529 | 36.8 |
| Everhart (IR) | 4,966 | 17.4 |
| 7 Robert M. Yardley (R) | 17,079 | 52.0 |
| Satterthwaite (D) | 14,944 | 45.5 |
| 8 Daniel Ermentrout (D) | 13,978 | 59.6 |
| Stitzel (R) | 9,163 | 39.0 |
| 9 John A. Hiestand (R) | 18,683 | 65.7 |
| McGovern (D) | 9,049 | 31.8 |
| 10 William H. Sowden (D) | 21,370 | 96.8 |
| 11 Charles R. Buckalew (D) | 18,337 | 95.9 |
| 12 John Lynch (D) | 14,176 | 48.3 |
| Joseph A. Scranton (R) | 13,526 | 46.1 |
| Knapp (P) | 1,663 | 5.7 |
| 13 Charles N. Brumm (R) | 11,293 | 50.2 |
| Shepherd (D) | 10,519 | 46.8 |
| 14 Franklin Bound (R) | 17,116 | 51.9 |
| McDevitt (D) | 14,485 | 43.9 |
| 15 Frank C. Bunnell (R) | 16,113 | 56.3 |
| Piolett (D) | 10,453 | 36.5 |
| Dodson (P) | 2,041 | 7.1 |
| 16 Henry C. McCormick (R) | 17,393 | 55.3 |
| Keenan (D) | 12,567 | 40.0 |
| 17 Edward Scull (R) | 16,548 | 49.7 |
| Tate (D) | 15,649 | 47.0 |
| 18 Louis E. Atkinson (R) | 17,020 | 54.2 |
| Jacobs (D) | 13,773 | 43.9 |
| 19 Levi Maish (D) | 18,174 | 54.3 |
| Seitz (R) | 14,228 | 42.5 |
| 20 John Patton (R) | 16,566 | 48.8 |
| Hall (D) | 16,413 | 48.4 |
| 21 Welty McCullogh (R) | 15,381 | 45.2 |
| Donnelly (D) | 15,126 | 44.4 |
| Rafferty (D) | 2,581 | 7.6 |
| 22 John Dalzell (R) | 16,631 | 54.3 |
| Parkinson (D) | 12,626 | 41.2 |
| 23 Thomas M. Bayne (R) | 12,133 | 58.9 |
| Alcorn (D) | 7,094 | 34.4 |
| Rabe (P) | 1,385 | 6.7 |
| 24 Oscar L. Jackson (R) | 14,787 | 55.3 |
| Baird (D) | 10,347 | 38.7 |
| Irish (P) | 1,465 | 5.5 |
| 25 James T. Maffett (R) | 14,322 | 51.3 |
| St.Clair (D) | 12,700 | 45.5 |
| 26 Norman Hall (D) | 14,565 | 46.3 |
| Roberts (R) | 14,034 | 44.6 |
| Cunningham (P) | 2,288 | 7.3 |
| 27 William L. Scott (D) | 14,787 | 48.5 |
| Mackey (R) | 13,574 | 44.5 |
| Andrews (P) | 2,140 | 7.0 |
| AL Edwin S. Osborne (R) | 415,166 | 50.8 |
| Maxwell Stevenson (D) | 367,551 | 45.0 |

## RHODE ISLAND [1]

| Candidates | Votes | % |
|---|---|---|
| 1 Henry J. Spooner (R) | 3,457 | 52.9 |
| Oscar Lapham (D) | 2,337 | 35.7 |
| Howard (P) | 746 | 11.4 |
| 2 Charles S. Bradley (D) | 5,426* | 48.2 |
| Nathan F. Dixon (R) | 4,849 | 43.1 |
| Chace (P) | 852 | 7.6 |

## SOUTH CAROLINA

| Candidates | Votes | % |
|---|---|---|
| 1 Samuel Dibble (D) | 3,315 | 100.0 |
| 2 George D. Tillman (D) | 5,232 | 99.6 |
| 3 James C. Cothran (D) | 4,402 | 99.8 |

*1. No candidate in the 2nd district secured the majority needed to win in the general election. (Majority vote requirement. see p. 945.)*

## SOUTH CAROLINA

| Candidates | Votes | % |
|---|---|---|
| 4 William H. Perry (D) | 4,470 | 100.0 |
| 5 John J. Hemphill (D) | 4,696 | 99.9 |
| 6 George W. Dargan (D) | 4,361 | 98.7 |
| 7 William Elliott (D) | 6,493 | 52.1 |
| Robert Smalls (R) | 5,961 | 47.9 |

## TENNESSEE

| Candidates | Votes | % |
|---|---|---|
| | 16,393 | 60.0 |
| James White (D) | 10,953 | 40.1 |
| 2 Leonidas C. Houk (R) | 15,837 | 67.0 |
| S. G. Heiskell (D) | 7,780 | 32.9 |
| 3 John R. Neal (D) | 14,115 | 50.6 |
| John T. Wilder (R) | 13,768 | 49.4 |
| 4 Benton McMillin (D) | 12,441 | 61.5 |
| J. J. Turner (R) | 7,792 | 38.5 |
| 5 James D. Richardson (D) | 13,756 | 68.9 |
| S. D. Mathew (R) | 6,210 | 31.1 |
| 6 Joseph E. Washington (D) | 14,919 | 61.8 |
| John H. Nye (R) | 9,218 | 38.2 |
| 7 Washington C. Whitthorne (D) | 12,083 | 58.8 |
| G. W. Blackburn (R) | 8,459 | 41.2 |
| 8 Benjamin A. Enloe (D) | 13,059 | 53.5 |
| S. W. Hawkins (R) | 11,362 | 46.5 |
| 9 Presley T. Glass (D) | 14,272 | 59.0 |
| D. A. Nunn (R) | 9,934 | 41.0 |
| 10 James Phelan (D) | 11,979 | 60.0 |
| Zack Taylor (R) | 7,983 | 40.0 |

## TEXAS

| Candidates | Votes | % |
|---|---|---|
| 1 Charles Stewart (D) | 16,844 | 61.9 |
| H. D. Johnson (R) | 10,344 | 38.0 |
| 2 John H. Reagan (D) | 16,413* | 95.7 |
| 3 Constantine B. Kilgore (D) | 16,695 | 69.3 |
| W. E. Farmer (I) | 7,359 | 30.6 |
| 4 David B. Culberson (D) | 17,234 | 78.5 |
| James T. Fleming (I) | 4,701 | 21.4 |
| 5 Silas Hare (D) | 11,774 | 41.8 |
| G. B. Pickett (ID) | 8,315 | 29.5 |
| H. C. Mack (I) | 8,065 | 28.6 |

| Candidates | Votes | % |
|---|---|---|
| 6 Jo Abbott (D) | 19,185 | 59.9 |
| J. C. Kearby (I) | 11,756 | 36.7 |
| 7 William H. Crain (D) | 18,511 | 89.1 |
| J. L. Haynes (R) | 1,293 | 6.2 |
| 8 Littleton W. Moore (D) | 22,908 | 92.1 |
| W. O. Hutchinson (R) | 1,912 | 7.7 |
| 9 Roger Q. Mills (D) | 17,168 | 60.2 |
| J. D. Rankin (P-LAB) | 11,337 | 39.8 |
| 10 Joseph D. Sayers (D) | 26,809 | 78.1 |
| J. P. Newcomb (R) | 7,492 | 21.8 |
| 11 Samuel W. T. Lanham (D) | 21,980 | 74.0 |
| Unidentified Candidate (I) | 7,744 | 26.1 |

## VERMONT

| Candidates | Votes | % |
|---|---|---|
| 1 John W. Stewart (R) | 15,632 | 72.5 |
| Waldo Brigham (D) | 5,655 | 26.2 |
| 2 William W. Grout (R) | 18,685 | 69.4 |
| Harley E. Folsom (D) | 8,176 | 30.4 |

## VIRGINIA

| Candidates | Votes | % |
|---|---|---|
| 1 Thomas H. B. Browne (R) | 12,591 | 54.1 |
| Thomas Croxton (D) | 10,696 | 45.9 |
| 2 George E. Bowden (R) | 15,449 | 60.7 |
| Marshall Parks (D) | 9,993 | 39.3 |
| 3 George D. Wise (D) | 14,001 | 52.7 |
| Edmond Waddell Jr. (R) | 12,549 | 47.2 |
| 4 William E. Gaines (R) | 14,708 | 70.2 |
| Mann Page (D) | 6,233 | 29.8 |
| 5 John R. Brown (R) | 12,773 | 57.1 |
| George C. Cabell (D) | 9,614 | 42.9 |
| 6 Samuel I. Hopkins (LAB) | 9,470 | 50.9 |
| Samuel Griffin (D) | 9,020 | 48.4 |
| 7 Charles T. O'Ferrall (D) | 11,580 | 51.7 |
| John E. Roller (ID) | 10,816 | 48.3 |
| 8 William H. F. Lee (D) | 9,836 | 57.5 |
| W. C. Elam (R) | 7,274 | 42.5 |
| 9 Henry Bowen (R) | 13,826 | 57.6 |
| R. R. Henry (D) | 10,196 | 42.4 |

| Candidates | Votes | % |
|---|---|---|
| 10 Jacob Yost (R) | 12,975 | 53.4 |
| James Bumgardner Jr. (D) | 11,321 | 46.6 |

## WEST VIRGINIA

| Candidates | Votes | % |
|---|---|---|
| 1 Nathan Goff Jr. (R) | 17,559 | 50.8 |
| John Bannon (D) | 16,732 | 48.4 |
| 2 William L. Wilson (D) | 17,112 | 49.9 |
| W. H. H. Flick (R) | 17,022 | 49.6 |
| 3 Charles P. Snyder (D) | 14,906 | 50.6 |
| James H. Brown (R) | 14,011 | 47.6 |
| 4 Charles E. Hogg (D) | 16,434 | 50.3 |
| John H. Hutchinson (R) | 15,687 | 48.0 |

## WISCONSIN

| Candidates | Votes | % |
|---|---|---|
| 1 Lucien B. Caswell (R) | 13,739 | 46.9 |
| James R. Doolittle (D) | 13,166 | 44.9 |
| Edward G. Durand (P) | 2,404 | 8.2 |
| 2 Richard Guenther (R) | 15,366 | 55.7 |
| A. K. Delaney (D) | 11,138 | 40.4 |
| 3 Robert M. LaFollette (R) | 16,711 | 50.3 |
| Hugh J. Gallagher (D) | 13,201 | 39.8 |
| T. C. Richmond (P) | 3,258 | 9.8 |
| 4 Henry Smith (LAB) | 13,355 | 42.5 |
| Thomas H. Brown (R) | 9,645 | 30.7 |
| John Black (D) | 8,233 | 26.2 |
| 5 Thomas R. Hudd (D) | 15,716 | 60.6 |
| G. Keusterman (R) | 10,168 | 39.2 |
| 6 Charles B. Clark (R) | 15,983 | 54.6 |
| Andrew Haben (D) | 11,526 | 39.4 |
| E. D. Kanouse (P) | 1,761 | 6.0 |
| 7 Ormsby B. Thomas (R) | 16,720 | 54.2 |
| S. N. Dickenson (D) | 11,917 | 38.7 |
| S. B. Loomis (P) | 2,175 | 7.1 |
| 8 William T. Price (R) | 23,857* | 66.7 |
| James Bracklin (D) | 11,850 | 33.2 |
| 9 Isaac Stephenson (R) | 22,518 | 55.8 |
| John Ringle (D) | 17,763 | 44.0 |
| **Special Election** | | |
| 5 Thomas R. Hudd (D) | 9,633 | 62.2 |
| Charles Luling (R) | 5,852 | 37.8 |

# 1887 House Elections

## LOUISIANA

**Special Election**

| Candidates | Votes | % |
|---|---|---|
| 6 Samuel M. Robertson (D) | 6,706 | 72.5 |
| John Yoist (R) | 2,550 | 27.6 |

## MICHIGAN

**Special Election**

| Candidates | Votes | % |
|---|---|---|
| 11 Henry W. Seymour (R) | 11,014 | 49.7 |
| Bartley Breen (FUS) | 10,612 | 47.8 |

## NEW YORK

**Special Elections**

| Candidates | Votes | % |
|---|---|---|
| 19 Charles Tracey (D) | 17,796 | 49.9 |
| Bailey (R) | 16,187 | 45.4 |
| 25 James J. Belden (R) | 20,144 | 60.0 |
| Davis (D) | 11,608 | 34.6 |
| Sinclair (P) | 1,798 | 5.4 |

## RHODE ISLAND[1]

**Special Elections**

| Candidates | Votes | % |
|---|---|---|
| 2 Charles H. Page (D) | 5,790 | 49.3 |
| William A. Pirce (R) | 5,495 | 46.7 |

| Candidates | Votes | % |
|---|---|---|
| 2 Warren O. Arnold (R) | 8,086 | 51.8 |
| Charles S. Bradley (D) | 7,248 | 46.4 |

## WISCONSIN

**Special Elections**

| Candidates | Votes | % |
|---|---|---|
| 8 Hugh H. Price (R) | 12,238 | 69.9 |
| James Bardon (D) | 5,209 | 29.8 |
| 8 Nils P. Haugen (R) | 8,159 | 46.3 |
| Samuel C. Johnson (D) | 6,803 | 38.6 |
| Peter Truax (P) | 2,620 | 14.9 |

1. The first special election, won by Charles H. Page, was to fill a vacancy in the 49th Congress (1885-87.) A majority of the total vote was apparently not required to win this election. (Majority vote requirement, see p. 945.)

The second special, won by Warren O. Arnold, was for a full term in the 50th Congress (1887-89.) The seat had been left unfilled in the regular 1886 general election because no candidate had the requisite majority. (See Rhode Island 1886, p. 1054.)

---

## House Candidates Index

# 1888 House Elections

## ALABAMA

| | Candidates | Votes | % |
|---|---|---|---|
| 1 | Richard H. Clarke (D) | 11,594 | 62.0 |
| | Frank H. Threet (R) | 7,105 | 38.0 |
| 2 | Hilary A. Herbert (D) | 14,041 | 66.1 |
| | Buckley (R) | 7,204 | 33.9 |
| 3 | William C. Oates (D) | 13,287 | 82.3 |
| | Harvey (R) | 2,868 | 17.8 |
| 4 | Louis W. Turpin (D) | 18,778‡ | 77.0 |
| | John V. McDuffie (R) | 5,625 | 23.1 |
| 5 | James E. Cobb (D) | 12,597 | 64.7 |
| | Bingham (R) | 6,861 | 35.3 |
| 6 | John H. Bankhead (D) | 16,491 | 67.8 |
| | Hanlan (R) | 7,849 | 32.3 |
| 7 | William H. Forney (D) | 17,706 | 65.7 |
| | Hardy (R) | 8,265 | 30.7 |
| 8 | Joseph Wheeler (D) | 14,091 | 61.6 |
| | McClellan (R) | 8,770 | 38.4 |

## ARKANSAS

| | Candidates | Votes | % |
|---|---|---|---|
| 1 | William H. Cate (D) | 15,576‡ | 51.9 |
| | Lewis P. Featherston (IR) | 14,228 | 47.4 |
| 2 | Clifton R. Breckinridge (D) | 17,857‡ | 51.2 |
| | John M. Clayton (R) | 17,011 | 48.8 |
| 3 | Thomas C. McRae (D) | 20,046 | 59.7 |
| | J. A. Ansley (I) | 13,553 | 40.3 |
| 4 | John H. Rogers (D) | 20,448 | 57.7 |
| | I. McCracken (I) | 14,933 | 42.2 |
| 5 | Samuel W. Peel (D) | 15,649 | 68.9 |
| | E. P. Watson (I) | 5,000 | 22.0 |
| | John Gates (R) | 2,075 | 9.1 |

## CALIFORNIA

| | Candidates | Votes | % |
|---|---|---|---|
| 1 | John J. De Haven (R) | 19,345 | 49.9 |
| | T. L. Thompson (D) | 19,019 | 49.0 |
| 2 | Marion Biggs (D) | 19,064 | 50.7 |
| | John A. Eagon (R) | 17,541 | 46.6 |
| 3 | Joseph McKenna (R) | 19,912 | 56.0 |
| | Ben Morgan (D) | 14,633 | 41.2 |
| 4 | William W. Morrow (R) | 14,217 | 50.6 |
| | Robert Ferral (D) | 13,624 | 48.5 |
| 5 | Thomas J. Clunie (D) | 20,276 | 48.9 |
| | L. G. Phelps (R) | 20,225 | 48.8 |
| 6 | William Vandever (R) | 35,406 | 52.4 |
| | R. B. Terry (D) | 29,453 | 43.5 |

## COLORADO

| | Candidates | Votes | % |
|---|---|---|---|
| AL | Hosea Townsend (R) | 50,620 | 55.0 |
| | Thomas Macon (D) | 37,725 | 41.0 |

## CONNECTICUT

| | Candidates | Votes | % |
|---|---|---|---|
| 1 | William E. Simonds (R) | 18,255 | 49.7 |
| | Vance (D) | 17,442 | 47.5 |
| 2 | Washington F. Wilcox (D) | 24,959 | 49.6 |
| | Lines (R) | 24,161 | 48.0 |
| 3 | Charles A. Russell (R) | 11,710 | 49.8 |
| | Hall (D) | 10,962 | 46.6 |
| 4 | Frederick Miles (R) | 21,003 | 48.7 |
| | Seymour (D) | 20,977 | 48.7 |

## DELAWARE

| | Candidates | Votes | % |
|---|---|---|---|
| AL | John B. Penington (D) | 16,396 | 55.2 |
| | Charles H. Treat (R) | 12,935 | 43.5 |

## FLORIDA

| | Candidates | Votes | % |
|---|---|---|---|
| 1 | Robert H. M. Davidson (D) | 19,822 | 67.1 |
| | Benjamin (R) | 9,727 | 32.9 |
| 2 | Robert Bullock (D) | 19,512 | 52.8 |
| | Goodrich (R) | 17,417 | 47.2 |

## GEORGIA

| | Candidates | Votes | % |
|---|---|---|---|
| 1 | Rufus E. Lester (D) | 11,736 | 69.6 |
| | Floyd Snelson (R) | 5,116 | 30.4 |
| 2 | Henry G. Turner (D) | 11,000 | 100.0 |
| 3 | Charles F. Crisp (D) | 9,254 | 72.7 |
| | Peter O. Gibson (R) | 3,130 | 24.6 |
| 4 | Thomas W. Grimes (D) | 9,798 | 70.4 |
| | Marion Bethune (R) | 4,122 | 29.6 |
| 5 | John D. Stewart (D) | 10,971 | 68.6 |
| | George S. Thomas (R) | 5,032 | 31.4 |
| 6 | James H. Blount (D) | 8,931 | 100.0 |
| 7 | Judson C. Clements (D) | 9,051 | 74.8 |
| | Z. B. Hargraves (R) | 3,054 | 25.2 |
| 8 | Henry H. Carlton (D) | 7,348 | 76.7 |
| | E. T. Fleming (R) | 2,227 | 23.3 |
| 9 | Allen D. Candler (D) | 11,260 | 53.0 |
| | Thaddeus Pickett (I) | 9,975 | 47.0 |
| 10 | George T. Barnes (D) | 6,474 | 89.0 |
| | Judson W. Lyon (R) | 797 | 11.0 |

## ILLINOIS

| | Candidates | Votes | % |
|---|---|---|---|
| 1 | Abner Taylor (R) | 26,553 | 52.7 |
| | James F. Todd (D) | 22,697 | 45.1 |
| 2 | Frank Lawler (D) | 19,051 | 59.2 |
| | Daniel F. Gleason (R) | 12,969 | 40.3 |
| 3 | William E. Mason (R) | 23,671 | 50.8 |
| | Milton R. Freshwater (D) | 21,295 | 45.7 |
| 4 | George E. Adams (R) | 22,273 | 51.3 |
| | Jonathan B. Taylor (D) | 19,755 | 45.5 |
| 5 | Albert J. Hopkins (R) | 20,077 | 63.0 |
| | James Herrington (D) | 10,018 | 31.4 |
| | John M. Strong (P) | 1,765 | 5.5 |
| 6 | Robert R. Hitt (R) | 18,139 | 57.2 |
| | Rufus M. Cook (D) | 11,903 | 37.6 |
| | George Richardson (P) | 1,659 | 5.2 |
| 7 | Thomas J. Henderson (R) | 16,380 | 56.7 |
| | Owen G. Lovejoy (D) | 11,341 | 39.2 |
| 8 | Charles A. Hill (R) | 20,596 | 51.4 |
| | Lafayette W. Brewer (D) | 17,454 | 43.6 |
| 9 | Lewis E. Payson (R) | 16,871 | 51.5 |
| | Herman W. Snow (D) | 14,490 | 44.2 |
| 10 | Philip S. Post (R) | 18,824 | 52.6 |
| | Nicholas E. Worthington (D) | 16,166 | 45.2 |
| 11 | William H. Gest (R) | 19,657 | 51.3 |
| | William Prentiss (D) | 17,580 | 45.8 |
| 12 | Scott Wike (D) | 21,938 | 54.1 |
| | William H. Collins (R) | 16,628 | 41.0 |
| 13 | William M. Springer (D) | 21,364 | 51.4 |
| | Charles Kerr (R) | 18,450 | 44.4 |
| 14 | Jonathan H. Rowell (R) | 18,570 | 50.1 |
| | Ethelbert Stewart (D) | 16,740 | 45.2 |
| 15 | Joseph G. Cannon (R) | 19,897 | 51.8 |
| | Robert L. McKinlay (D) | 17,204 | 44.8 |
| 16 | George W. Fithian (D) | 17,742 | 49.6 |
| | Edwin Harlan (R) | 17,037 | 47.6 |
| 17 | Edward Lane (D) | 19,385 | 54.8 |
| | John J. Brown (R) | 14,775 | 41.7 |
| 18 | William S. Forman (D) | 16,167 | 47.7 |
| | Jehu Baker (R) | 16,151 | 47.7 |
| 19 | Richard W. Townshend (D) | 18,086 | 53.0 |
| | W. L. Crim (R) | 15,615 | 45.8 |
| 20 | George W. Smith (R) | 19,005 | 51.6 |
| | Thomas T. Robinson (D) | 17,186 | 46.6 |

## INDIANA

| | Candidates | Votes | % |
|---|---|---|---|
| 1 | William F. Parrett (D) | 20,647 | 49.3 |
| | Frank B. Posey (R) | 20,627 | 49.3 |
| 2 | John H. O'Neall (D) | 18,537 | 52.3 |
| | Thomas N. Braxton (R) | 16,653 | 47.0 |
| 3 | Jason B. Brown (D) | 18,274 | 54.0 |
| | Stephen D. Sayles (R) | 15,198 | 44.9 |
| 4 | William S. Holman (D) | 16,905 | 50.7 |
| | Manly D. Wilson (R) | 16,176 | 48.5 |
| 5 | George W. Cooper (D) | 18,206 | 49.6 |
| | Henry C. Duncan (R) | 17,506 | 47.7 |
| 6 | Thomas M. Browne (R) | 23,424 | 60.3 |
| | Douglas Morris (D) | 14,302 | 36.8 |
| 7 | William D. Bynum (D) | 27,227 | 50.9 |
| | Thomas E. Chandler (R) | 25,500 | 47.6 |
| 8 | Elijah V. Brookshire (D) | 23,153 | 49.0 |
| | James F. Johnston (R) | 23,084 | 48.8 |
| 9 | Joseph B. Cheadle (R) | 24,717 | 53.1 |
| | James McCabe (D) | 20,267 | 43.5 |
| 10 | William D. Owen (R) | 19,546 | 50.4 |
| | Valentine Zimmerman (D) | 18,390 | 47.5 |
| 11 | Augustus N. Martin (D) | 22,375 | 48.9 |
| | George W. Steele (R) | 21,900 | 47.8 |
| 12 | Charles A. O. McClellan (D) | 20,139 | 50.4 |
| | James B. White (R) | 18,828 | 47.1 |
| 13 | Benjamin F. Shively (D & LAB) | 21,561 | 49.4 |
| | William Hoynes (R) | 21,206 | 48.6 |

## IOWA

| | Candidates | Votes | % |
|---|---|---|---|
| 1 | John H. Gear (R) | 18,130 | 51.0 |
| | John J. Seerley (D) | 17,256 | 48.5 |
| 2 | Walter I. Hayes (D) | 20,874 | 56.8 |
| | Parker W. McManus (R&LAB) | 15,842 | 43.1 |
| 3 | David B. Henderson (R) | 21,457 | 56.0 |
| | B. B. Richards (D) | 16,872 | 44.0 |
| 4 | Joseph H. Sweney (R) | 18,852 | 52.4 |
| | L. S. Reque (D) | 16,630 | 46.2 |
| 5 | Daniel Kerr (R) | 19,453 | 52.5 |
| | J. H. Preston (D) | 16,937 | 45.7 |
| 6 | John F. Lacey (R) | 18,009 | 51.0 |
| | James B. Weaver (D & LAB) | 17,181 | 48.6 |
| 7 | Edwin H. Conger (R) | 18,424 | 55.8 |
| | A. E. Morrison (D) | 13,027 | 39.5 |
| 8 | James P. Flick (R) | 19,207 | 50.9 |
| | A. R. Anderson (D & LAB) | 18,212 | 48.2 |
| 9 | Joseph R. Reed (R) | 20,380 | 52.6 |
| | D. M. Harris (D) | 16,686 | 43.0 |
| 10 | Jonathan P. Dolliver (R) | 20,864 | 56.8 |
| | J. A. Yeoman (D) | 15,496 | 42.2 |
| 11 | Isaac S. Struble (R) | 21,472 | 57.1 |
| | M. A. Kilso (D) | 15,213 | 40.4 |

## KANSAS

| | Candidates | Votes | % |
|---|---|---|---|
| 1 | Edmund N. Morrill (R) | 20,879 | 56.3 |
| | E. K. Townsend (D) | 14,536 | 39.2 |
| 2 | Edward H. Funston (R) | 24,632 | 54.6 |
| | J.T. Burris (D) | 14,969 | 33.2 |
| | Delos Walker (UN LAB) | 5,517 | 12.2 |
| 3 | Bishop W. Perkins (R) | 23,315 | 50.4 |
| | W. H. Utley (UN LAB) | 11,775 | 25.5 |
| | J. A. Eaton (D) | 10,556 | 22.8 |
| 4 | Thomas Ryan (R) | 29,338 | 59.8 |
| | D. Overmeyer (D) | 14,323 | 29.2 |
| | John Heaton (UN LAB) | 4,350 | 8.9 |
| 5 | John A. Anderson (R) | 22,848 | 59.6 |
| | N. D. Toby (D) | 14,347 | 37.4 |
| 6 | Erastus J. Turner (R) | 23,428 | 57.4 |
| | S. W. McElroy (D) | 12,282 | 30.1 |
| | H. A. Hart (UN LAB) | 4,550 | 11.2 |
| 7 | Samuel R. Peters (R) | 37,935 | 53.2 |
| | C. S. Ebey (D) | 22,616 | 31.7 |
| | S. H. Snyder (UN LAB) | 9,489 | 13.3 |

## KENTUCKY

| | Candidates | Votes | % |
|---|---|---|---|
| 1 | William J. Stone (D) | 14,195 | 60.2 |
| | Edwin Earley (R) | 8,850 | 37.6 |

## KENTUCKY

| Candidates | Votes | % |
|---|---|---|
| 2 William T. Ellis (D) | 16,459 | 54.8 |
| George W. Jolly (R) | 13,006 | 43.3 |
| 3 Isaac H. Goodnight (D) | 17,365 | 52.4 |
| W. Godfrey Hunter (R) | 15,630 | 47.1 |
| 4 Alexander B. Montgomery (D) | 15,477 | 57.9 |
| C. M. Pendleton (R) | 11,019 | 41.3 |
| 5 Asher G. Caruth (D) | 16,588 | 54.9 |
| Augustus E. Willson (R) | 13,561 | 44.9 |
| 6 John G. Carlisle (D) | 18,907 | 58.7 |
| Robert Hamilton (R) | 12,887 | 40.0 |
| 7 William C. P. Breckinridge (D) | 18,920 | 57.5 |
| Armstead M. Swope (R) | 13,265 | 40.3 |
| 8 James B. McCreary (D) | 16,209 | 51.5 |
| R. L. Ewell (R) | 14,660 | 46.6 |
| 9 Thomas H. Paynter (D) | 18,664 | 40.0 |
| Drury J. Burchett (R) | 18,285 | 48.9 |
| 10 John H. Wilson (R) | 15,725 | 50.6 |
| B. F. Day (D) | 15,247 | 49.1 |
| 11 Hugh F. Finley (R) | 15,822 | 52.4 |
| F. L. Wolford (D) | 14,006 | 46.4 |

## LOUISIANA

| Candidates | Votes | % |
|---|---|---|
| 1 Theodore S. Wilkinson (D) | 8,979 | 64.5 |
| Charles B. Wilson (R) | 4,927 | 35.4 |
| 2 H. Dudley Coleman (R) | 9,121 | 50.5 |
| Benjamin C. Elliott (D) | 8,947 | 49.5 |
| 3 Edward J. Gay (D) | 18,854 | 74.8 |
| James R. Jolley (R) | 6,341 | 25.2 |
| 4 Newton C. Blanchard (D) | 16,302 | 94.4 |
| W. E. Maples (R) | 963 | 5.6 |
| 5 Charles J. Boatner (D) | 21,275 | 93.9 |
| Frank Morey (R) | 1,151 | 5.1 |
| 6 Samuel M. Robertson (D) | 12,078 | 73.7 |
| W. H. Harrison (R) | 4,314 | 26.3 |

## MAINE

| Candidates | Votes | % |
|---|---|---|
| 1 Thomas B. Reed (R) | 18,288 | 52.3 |
| William Emery (D) | 15,849 | 45.3 |
| 2 Nelson Dingley Jr. (R) | 21,075 | 55.2 |
| Charles E. Allen (D) | 15,614 | 40.9 |
| 3 Seth L. Milliken (R) | 20,558 | 58.0 |
| S. S. Brown (D) | 14,026 | 39.5 |
| 4 Charles A. Boutelle (R) | 19,823 | 54.6 |
| T. J. Stewart (D) | 15,481 | 42.7 |

## MARYLAND

| Candidates | Votes | % |
|---|---|---|
| 1 Charles H. Gibson (D) | 15,627 | 48.3 |
| Hodson (R) | 15,145 | 46.8 |
| 2 Herman Stump (D) | 18,470 | 51.2 |
| Lang (R) | 16,588 | 46.0 |
| 3 Harry W. Rusk (D) | 19,578 | 57.2 |
| Brinton (R) | 14,289 | 41.7 |
| 4 Henry Stockbridge Jr. (R) | 19,078 | 49.5 |
| Rayner (D) | 18,998 | 49.3 |
| 5 Barnes Compton (D) | 16,000‡ | 49.8 |
| Sydney E. Mudd (R) | 15,819 | 49.2 |
| 6 Louis E. McComas (R) | 19,056 | 51.6 |
| Douglas (D) | 17,422 | 47.2 |

## MASSACHUSETTS

| Candidates | Votes | % |
|---|---|---|
| 1 Charles S. Randall (R) | 14,588 | 60.8 |
| Cummings (D) | 5,103 | 21.3 |
| Delano (D) | 3,468 | 14.5 |
| 2 Elijah A. Morse (R) | 17,072 | 54.2 |
| Quincy (D) | 13,388 | 42.5 |
| 3 John F. Andrew (D) | 16,338 | 52.0 |
| Beard (R) | 14,780 | 47.0 |
| 4 Joseph H. O'Neil (D) | 14,749 | 68.0 |
| Morrison (R) | 6,718 | 31.0 |
| 5 Nathaniel P. Banks (R) | 14,929 | 51.8 |
| Higginson (D) | 13,465 | 46.7 |

| Candidates | Votes | % |
|---|---|---|
| 6 Henry Cabot Lodge (R) | 19,598 | 56.3 |
| Usher (D) | 14,304 | 41.1 |
| 7 William Cogswell (R) | 16,796 | 56.8 |
| Roads (D) | 12,224 | 41.3 |
| 8 Frederic T. Greenhalge (R) | 14,493 | 55.3 |
| Donovan (D) | 11,273 | 43.0 |
| 9 John W. Candler (R) | 15,714 | 52.2 |
| Burnett (D) | 13,678 | 45.4 |
| 10 Joseph H. Walker (R) | 13,965 | 52.0 |
| Sayles (D) | 12,050 | 44.9 |
| 11 Rodney Wallace (R) | 16,335 | 56.4 |
| Skinner (D) | 11,519 | 39.7 |
| 12 Francis W. Rockwell (R) | 14,853 | 52.1 |
| Ely (D) | 12,826 | 45.0 |

## MICHIGAN

| Candidates | Votes | % |
|---|---|---|
| 1 J. Logan Chipman (D) | 25,179 | 52.4 |
| Hibbard Baker (R) | 22,076 | 45.9 |
| 2 Edward P. Allen (R) | 19,660 | 49.3 |
| Willard Stearns (D & G) | 18,096 | 45.3 |
| Charles M. Fellows (P) | 2,010 | 5.0 |
| 3 James O'Donnell (R) | 24,097 | 53.5 |
| Eugene Pringle (D) | 17,495 | 38.9 |
| Almon G. Bruce (P) | 2,609 | 5.8 |
| 4 Julius C. Burrows (R) | 21,649 | 52.9 |
| Charles S. Maynard (D) | 17,464 | 42.7 |
| 5 Charles E. Belknap (R) | 26,309 | 50.4 |
| Melbourne H. Ford (D) | 23,642 | 45.3 |
| 6 Mark S. Brewer (R) | 21,271 | 47.6 |
| Orlando F. Barnes (D) | 20,904 | 46.8 |
| William W. Root (P) | 2,251 | 5.0 |
| 7 Justin R. Whiting (D) | 16,894 | 47.7 |
| William Hartsuff (R) | 16,488 | 46.6 |
| 8 Aaron T. Bliss (R) | 23,028 | 50.4 |
| Timothy E. Tarsney (D) | 20,943 | 45.9 |
| 9 Byron M. Cutcheon (R) | 23,025 | 52.2 |
| Hiram B. Hudson (D) | 18,651 | 42.2 |
| Lathrop S. Ellis (P) | 2,476 | 5.6 |
| 10 Frank W. Wheeler (R) | 18,959 | 48.3 |
| Spencer O. Fisher (D) | 18,844 | 48.0 |
| 11 Samuel M. Stephenson (R) | 20,336 | 52.8 |
| John Power (D) | 16,978 | 44.1 |

## MINNESOTA

| Candidates | Votes | % |
|---|---|---|
| 1 Mark H. Dunnell (R) | 18,829 | 50.4 |
| Thomas Wilson (D) | 16,985 | 45.4 |
| 2 John Lind (R) | 25,699 | 57.0 |
| M. S. Wilkinson (D) | 16,480 | 36.5 |
| D. W. Edwards (P) | 2,924 | 6.5 |
| 3 Darwin S. Hall (R) | 19,259 | 51.4 |
| J. L. Macdonald (D) | 16,391 | 43.7 |
| 4 Samuel P. Snider (R) | 44,329 | 53.8 |
| E. Rice (D) | 34,323 | 41.7 |
| 5 Solomon G. Comstock (R) | 31,350 | 52.7 |
| Charles Canning (D) | 23,833 | 40.1 |
| Z.D. Scott (P) | 4,254 | 7.2 |

## MISSISSIPPI

| Candidates | Votes | % |
|---|---|---|
| 1 John M. Allen (D) | 11,353 | 86.8 |
| Joseph M. Bynum (R) | 1,732 | 13.2 |
| 2 John B. Morgan (D) | 13,978 | 70.6 |
| James R. Chalmers (R) | 5,817 | 29.4 |
| 3 Thomas C. Catchings (D) | 11,624 | 71.6 |
| James Hill (R) | 4,614 | 28.4 |
| 4 Clarke Lewis (D) | 12,855 | 84.3 |
| Matthew K. Mister (R) | 2,396 | 15.7 |
| 5 Chapman L. Anderson (D) | 16,247 | 80.3 |
| F. M. B. Cook (R) | 3,993 | 19.7 |
| 6 Thomas R. Stockdale (D) | 10,580 | 70.3 |
| Leon C. Duchesne (R) | 4,464 | 29.7 |
| 7 Charles E. Hooker (D) | 11,977 | 77.0 |
| Henry Kernaghan (R) | 3,587 | 23.1 |

## MISSOURI

| Candidates | Votes | % |
|---|---|---|
| 1 William H. Hatch (D) | 20,049 | 52.9 |
| Brock (R) | 17,349 | 45.8 |

| Candidates | Votes | % |
|---|---|---|
| 2 Charles H. Mansur (D) | 21,608 | 53.8 |
| Eubanks (R) | 16,949 | 42.2 |
| 3 Alexander M. Dockery (D) | 20,414 | 53.4 |
| Love (R) | 16,743 | 43.8 |
| 4 James N. Burnes (D) | 16,866* | 52.5 |
| Hartwig (R) | 13,729 | 42.7 |
| 5 John C. Tarsney (D) | 22,635 | 52.5 |
| Bullene (R) | 20,499 | 47.5 |
| 6 John T. Heard (D) | 25,129 | 52.0 |
| Upton (R) | 21,249 | 44.0 |
| 7 Richard H. Norton (D) | 18,275 | 52.8 |
| Edwards (R) | 16,312 | 47.2 |
| 8 Frederick G. Niedringhaus (R) | 14,210 | 52.2 |
| O'Neill (D) | 12,394 | 45.5 |
| 9 Nathan Frank (R) | 13,762 | 54.7 |
| Castleman (D) | 11,312 | 45.0 |
| 10 William M. Kinsey (R) | 18,980 | 50.8 |
| Clardy (D) | 16,886 | 45.2 |
| 11 Richard P. Bland (D) | 18,095 | 50.4 |
| Musick (R) | 15,836 | 44.1 |
| Needham (UN LAB) | 1,954 | 5.5 |
| 12 William J. Stone (D) | 24,054 | 49.4 |
| Hannah (R) | 19,431 | 39.9 |
| Page (UN LAB) | 4,613 | 9.5 |
| 13 William H. Wade (R) | 16,480 | 48.4 |
| Matlock (D) | 13,601 | 40.0 |
| Alter (UN LAB) | 3,792 | 11.1 |
| 14 James P. Walker (D) | 19,878 | 58.4 |
| Whybark (R) | 14,139 | 41.6 |

### Special Election

| Candidates | Votes | % |
|---|---|---|
| 4 Charles F. Booher (D) | 12,750 | 52.3 |
| R. Posegate (R) | 11,632 | 47.7 |

## NEBRASKA

| Candidates | Votes | % |
|---|---|---|
| 1 William J. Connell (R) | 32,926 | 49.8 |
| J. Sterling Morton (D) | 29,519 | 44.7 |
| 2 James Laird (R) | 30,959 | 53.4 |
| W. G. Hastings (D) | 21,201 | 36.6 |
| George Scott (P) | 4,114 | 7.1 |
| 3 George W. E. Dorsey (R) | 42,188 | 54.2 |
| E. P. Weatherby (D) | 31,118 | 40.0 |

## NEVADA

| Candidates | Votes | % |
|---|---|---|
| AL Horace F. Bartine (R) | 6,921 | 54.9 |
| G. W. Cassidy (D) | 5,682 | 45.1 |

## NEW HAMPSHIRE

| Candidates | Votes | % |
|---|---|---|
| 1 Alonzo Nute (R) | 21,754 | 49.6 |
| McKinney (D) | 21,395 | 48.8 |
| 2 Orren C. Moore (R) | 23,517 | 50.2 |
| Mann (D) | 22,540 | 48.1 |

## NEW JERSEY

| Candidates | Votes | % |
|---|---|---|
| 1 Christopher A. Bergen (R) | 24,906 | 53.6 |
| Brindle (D) | 19,440 | 41.9 |
| 2 James Buchanan (R) | 22,407 | 52.4 |
| Beasley (D) | 19,104 | 44.6 |
| 3 Jacob A. Geissenhainer (D) | 22,961 | 51.7 |
| Kean (R) | 20,368 | 45.8 |
| 4 Samuel Fowler (D) | 12,190 | 39.4 |
| Voorhees (R) | 12,117 | 39.2 |
| Roe (ID) | 5,079 | 16.4 |
| 5 Charles D. Beckwith (R) | 20,277 | 50.2 |
| Hoagland (D) | 19,205 | 47.6 |
| 6 Herman Lehlbach (R) | 25,536 | 49.4 |
| Haynes (D) | 24,762 | 48.4 |
| 7 William McAdoo (D) | 26,498 | 56.1 |
| Collins (R) | 20,424 | 43.3 |

## NEW YORK

| Candidates | Votes | % |
|---|---|---|
| 1 James W. Covert (D) | 24,374 | 50.8 |
| Cromwell (R) | 22,711 | 47.3 |
| 2 Felix Campbell (D) | 23,497 | 56.3 |
| T. Seward (R) | 17,625 | 42.2 |
| 3 William C. Wallace (R) | 21,281 | 52.9 |
| Combs (D) | 18,410 | 45.7 |
| 4 John M. Clancy (D) | 20,987 | 59.1 |
| Robinson (R) | 14,060 | 39.6 |
| 5 Thomas F. Magner (D) | 18,613 | 52.2 |
| Hesse (R) | 16,469 | 46.2 |
| 6 Frank T. Fitzgerald (TAM D&UL) | 13,079 | 55.8 |
| Cavanagh (R) | 9,833 | 42.0 |
| 7 Edward J. Dunphy (TAM D) | 10,257 | 40.6 |
| Taintor (R) | 8,343 | 33.0 |
| Lloyd S. Bryce (CIT&CO D) | 6,482 | 25.7 |
| 8 John H. McCarthy (TAM D) | 14,827 | 52.3 |
| Campbell (CIT&CO D) | 9,778 | 34.5 |
| Schwartz (R) | 3,456 | 12.2 |
| 9 Samuel S. Cox (UN LAB&D) | 18,267 | 68.3 |
| McMackin (R) | 7,320 | 27.4 |
| 10 Francis B. Spinola (UN LAB&D) | 13,749 | 52.1 |
| Boyhan (R & UL) | 12,016 | 45.5 |
| 11 John Quinn (UN LAB&D) | 20,073 | 55.3 |
| Winch (R & UL) | 15,619 | 43.0 |
| 12 Roswell P. Flower (D&UN LAB) | 25,546 | 65.8 |
| Hildreth (R) | 12,273 | 31.6 |
| 13 Ashbel P. Fitch (D) | 28,580 | 58.9 |
| Hoyt (R) | 19,412 | 40.0 |
| 14 William G. Stahlnecker (UN LAB&D) | 22,485 | 53.7 |
| Wood (R) | 18,356 | 43.9 |
| 15 Moses D. Stivers (R) | 18,358 | 48.8 |
| Bacon (UN LAB&D) | 18,284 | 48.6 |
| 16 John H. Ketcham (R) | 18,912 | 74.6 |
| Downing (P) | 6,370 | 25.1 |
| 17 Charles J. Knapp (R) | 21,826 | 50.2 |
| Gilbert (D) | 20,217 | 46.5 |
| 18 John A. Quackenbush (R) | 23,639 | 53.4 |
| Sanford (D) | 19,717 | 44.6 |
| 19 Charles Tracey (D) | 21,294 | 52.3 |
| Dodge (R) | 18,988 | 46.6 |
| 20 John Sanford (R) | 23,966 | 52.2 |
| Westbrook (D) | 20,665 | 45.0 |
| 21 John H. Moffitt (R) | 21,361 | 95.2 |
| 22 Frederick Lansing (R) | 24,309 | 62.0 |
| Sawyer (D) | 13,582 | 34.7 |
| 23 James S. Sherman (R) | 20,119 | 50.8 |
| McMahon (D) | 18,387 | 46.4 |
| 24 David Wilber (R) | 18,502 | 50.2 |
| John S. Pindar (D) | 17,273 | 46.9 |
| 25 James J. Belden (R) | 24,672 | 78.0 |
| Vanderbilt (P) | 6,691 | 21.2 |
| 26 Milton De Lano (R) | 26,267 | 55.4 |
| Maloney (D) | 18,955 | 40.0 |
| 27 Newton W. Nutting (R) | 28,803 | 58.6 |
| Titus (D) | 18,327 | 37.3 |
| 28 Thomas S. Flood (R) | 16,822 | 50.3 |
| Tuttle (D) | 15,564 | 46.5 |
| 29 John Raines (R) | 21,794 | 53.6 |
| Dininny (D) | 16,969 | 41.7 |
| 30 Charles S. Baker (R) | 21,810 | 55.4 |
| Nash (D) | 16,106 | 40.9 |
| 31 John G. Sawyer (R) | 19,506 | 54.4 |
| Stevens (D) | 14,082 | 39.3 |
| Barnum (P) | 2,284 | 6.4 |
| 32 John M. Farquhar (R) | 22,468 | 51.6 |
| Mackey (D) | 20,859 | 47.9 |
| 33 John McC. Wiley (D) | 15,705 | 48.8 |
| Crowley (R) | 15,141 | 47.0 |
| 34 William G. Laidlaw (R) | 27,453 | 58.9 |
| Howe (D) | 15,523 | 33.3 |
| Corey (P) | 3,170 | 6.8 |

## NORTH CAROLINA

| Candidates | Votes | % |
|---|---|---|
| 1 Thomas G. Skinner (D) | 16,615 | 51.4 |
| Elihu A. White (R) | 15,457 | 47.8 |
| 2 Henry P. Cheatham (R) | 16,704 | 51.0 |
| Furnifold M. Simmons (D) | 16,051 | 49.0 |
| 3 Charles W. McClammy (D) | 16,809 | 56.7 |
| William Robinson (R) | 12,825 | 43.3 |
| 4 Benjamin H. Bunn (D) | 19,926 | 53.4 |
| John Nichols (R) | 17,368 | 46.6 |
| 5 John M. Brower (R) | 15,940 | 50.4 |
| James T. Morehead (D) | 15,265 | 48.2 |
| 6 Alfred Rowland (D) | 20,502 | 58.1 |
| Caleb P. Lockey (R) | 14,797 | 41.9 |
| 7 John S. Henderson (D) | 15,122 | 54.3 |
| William J. Ellis (R) | 12,125 | 43.5 |
| 8 William H. H. Cowles (D) | 13,139 | 56.7 |
| Edward W. Ward (R) | 10,031 | 43.3 |
| 9 Hamilton G. Ewart (R) | 15,433 | 50.9 |
| Thomas D. Johnston (D) | 14,915 | 49.2 |

## OHIO

| Candidates | Votes | % |
|---|---|---|
| 1 Benjamin Butterworth (R) | 19,336 | 51.9 |
| Otway J. Cosgrave (D) | 17,437 | 46.8 |
| 2 John A. Caldwell (R) | 21,627 | 51.0 |
| Clinton W. Gerard (D) | 20,031 | 47.2 |
| 3 Elihu S. Williams (R) | 20,912 | 49.2 |
| George W. Houk (D) | 20,497 | 48.2 |
| 4 Samuel S. Yoder (D) | 22,296 | 58.9 |
| Robert L. Mattingly (R) | 14,500 | 38.3 |
| 5 George E. Seney (D) | 22,075 | 56.1 |
| Wilson Vance (R) | 16,081 | 40.9 |
| 6 Melvin M. Boothman (R) | 22,434 | 48.4 |
| Gaylard M. Saltzgaber (D) | 22,339 | 48.2 |
| 7 Henry L. Morey (R) | 17,600 | 49.9 |
| John M. Pattison (D) | 16,742 | 47.5 |
| 8 Robert P. Kennedy (R) | 20,898 | 51.8 |
| Andrew R. Bolin (D) | 17,628 | 43.7 |
| 9 William C. Cooper (R) | 19,491 | 50.7 |
| John S. Braddock (D) | 17,267 | 44.9 |
| 10 William E. Haynes (D) | 19,637 | 50.7 |
| Jacob Romeis (R) | 18,496 | 47.8 |
| 11 Albert C. Thompson (R) | 20,802 | 55.6 |
| Joseph W. Shinn (D) | 15,817 | 42.3 |
| 12 Jacob J. Pugsley (R) | 20,133 | 49.6 |
| Lawrence T. Neal (D) | 19,453 | 47.9 |
| 13 Joseph H. Outhwaite (D) | 24,869 | 51.4 |
| John B. Neil (R) | 22,298 | 46.1 |
| 14 Charles P. Wickham (R) | 16,211 | 49.5 |
| David L. Wadsworth (D) | 15,254 | 46.6 |
| 15 Charles H. Grosvenor (R) | 17,591 | 51.9 |
| John P. Spriggs (D) | 15,284 | 45.1 |
| 16 James W. Owens (D) | 24,444 | 53.8 |
| Edwin L. Lybarger (R) | 19,819 | 43.6 |
| 17 Joseph D. Taylor (R) | 20,584 | 54.4 |
| William Lawrence Jr. (D) | 15,580 | 41.2 |
| 18 William McKinley Jr. (R) | 25,249 | 52.3 |
| George P. Ikert (D) | 21,160 | 43.8 |
| 19 Ezra B. Taylor (R) | 22,991 | 63.5 |
| Henry Apthorp (D) | 11,091 | 30.6 |
| William H. Dana (P) | 2,004 | 5.5 |
| 20 Martin L. Smyser (R) | 19,381 | 50.6 |
| Calvin P. Humphrey (D) | 17,283 | 45.1 |
| 21 Theodore E. Burton (R) | 20,086 | 49.8 |
| Tom L. Johnson (D) | 19,470 | 48.3 |

## OREGON

| Candidates | Votes | % |
|---|---|---|
| AL Binger Hermann (R) | 32,820 | 54.5 |
| John M. Gearin (D) | 25,413 | 42.2 |

## PENNSYLVANIA

| Candidates | Votes | % |
|---|---|---|
| 1 Henry H. Bingham (R) | 22,523 | 57.1 |
| Flanigan (D) | 16,838 | 42.7 |
| 2 Charles O'Neill (R) | 16,776 | 57.2 |
| Dougherty (D) | 12,368 | 42.2 |
| 3 Samuel J. Randall (D) | 17,642 | 99.4 |
| 4 William D. Kelley (R) | 32,841 | 58.1 |
| Ayers (D) | 23,202 | 41.1 |
| 5 Alfred C. Harmer (R) | 29,466 | 56.2 |
| Herwig (D) | 22,781 | 43.4 |
| 6 Smedley Darlington (R) | 19,299 | 58.1 |
| Greenwood (D) | 12,799 | 38.5 |
| 7 Robert M. Yardley (R) | 22,226 | 50.7 |
| Ross (D) | 21,215 | 48.4 |
| 8 William Mutchler (D) | 18,071 | 59.8 |
| Reeder (R) | 11,731 | 38.8 |
| 9 David B. Brunner (D) | 27,032 | 60.3 |
| Biery (R) | 17,373 | 38.8 |
| 10 Marriott Brosius (R) | 21,796 | 66.4 |
| Haldeman (D) | 10,622 | 32.4 |
| 11 Joseph A. Scranton (R) | 10,844 | 51.1 |
| Collins (D) | 9,158 | 43.2 |
| Lathrope (P) | 1,212 | 5.7 |
| 12 Edwin S. Osborne (R) | 16,117 | 51.3 |
| Lynch (D) | 14,618 | 46.5 |
| 13 James B. Reilly (D) | 13,258 | 51.0 |
| Brumm (RG) | 12,570 | 48.4 |
| 14 John W. Rife (R) | 20,206 | 58.3 |
| Bower (D) | 13,944 | 40.3 |
| 15 Myron B. Wright (R) | 18,833 | 56.8 |
| Ham (D) | 12,494 | 37.7 |
| Brown (P) | 1,810 | 5.5 |
| 16 Henry C. McCormick (R) | 19,204 | 54.2 |
| Steck (D & LAB) | 15,550 | 43.9 |
| 17 Charles R. Buckalew (D) | 14,012 | 54.5 |
| Robinson (R) | 11,356 | 44.2 |
| 18 Louis E. Atkinson (R) | 20,583 | 56.2 |
| McWilliams (D) | 15,867 | 43.3 |
| 19 Levi Maish (D) | 21,480 | 55.1 |
| Young (R) | 16,901 | 43.4 |
| 20 Edward Scull (R) | 21,739 | 54.3 |
| Greevy (D) | 17,458 | 43.6 |
| 21 Samuel A. Craig (R) | 24,151 | 54.0 |
| Donnelly (D) | 18,930 | 42.3 |
| 22 John Dalzell (R) | 21,970 | 62.0 |
| Parkinson (D) | 13,065 | 36.9 |
| 23 Thomas M. Bayne (R) | 13,999 | 66.8 |
| Langfitt (D) | 6,711 | 32.0 |
| 24 Joseph W. Ray (R) | 26,246 | 53.2 |
| Wampler (D) | 21,908 | 44.4 |
| 25 Charles C. Townsend (R) | 21,686 | 56.5 |
| Griffith (D) | 14,481 | 37.8 |
| 26 William C. Culbertson (R) | 16,924 | 52.5 |
| Burns (D) | 13,852 | 43.0 |
| 27 Lewis F. Watson (R) | 13,582 | 53.2 |
| Rankin (D) | 9,370 | 36.7 |
| Miller (P) | 1,670 | 6.5 |
| 28 James Kerr (D) | 17,588 | 53.5 |
| Rynder (R) | 14,899 | 45.3 |

## RHODE ISLAND

| Candidates | Votes | % |
|---|---|---|
| 1 Henry J. Spooner (R) | 11,092 | 53.3 |
| Oscar Lapham (D) | 9,002 | 43.3 |
| 2 Warren O. Arnold (R) | 10,940 | 55.9 |
| Baker (D) | 8,049 | 41.1 |

## SOUTH CAROLINA

| Candidates | Votes | % |
|---|---|---|
| 1 Samuel Dibble (D) | 8,540 | 86.7 |
| S. W. McKinlay (R) | 1,296 | 13.2 |
| 2 George D. Tillman (D) | 10,704 | 86.8 |
| Seymour E. Smith (R) | 1,405 | 11.4 |
| 3 James S. Cothran (D) | 8,758 | 99.8 |
| 4 William H. Perry (D) | 11,410 | 100.0 |
| 5 John J. Hemphill (D) | 9,559 | 99.7 |
| 6 George W. Dargan (D) | 8,586 | 95.7 |
| 7 William Elliott (D) | 8,358‡ | 54.2 |
| Thomas E. Miller (R) | 7,003 | 45.4 |

## TENNESSEE

| Candidates | Votes | % |
|---|---|---|
| 1 Alfred A. Taylor (R) | 19,465 | 59.9 |
| Wilcox (D) | 12,324 | 38.0 |
| 2 Leonidas C. Houk (R) | 23,368 | 68.8 |
| Heiskell (D) | 9,844 | 29.0 |

## TENNESSEE

| | Candidates | Votes | % |
|---|---|---|---|
| 3 | H. Clay Evans (R) | 18,641 | 50.0 |
| | Bates (D) | 18,353 | 49.2 |
| 4 | Benton McMillin (D) | 16,162 | 61.6 |
| | Wooten (R) | 10,068 | 38.4 |
| 5 | James D. Richardson (D) | 17,754 | 67.8 |
| | Shoffner (R) | 8,426 | 32.2 |
| 6 | Joseph E. Washington (D) | 18,956 | 57.2 |
| | Young (R) | 12,677 | 38.3 |
| 7 | Washington C. Whitthorne (D) | 14,362 | 57.8 |
| | Hagard (R) | 10,507 | 42.3 |
| 8 | Benjamin A. Enloe (D) | 14,385 | 54.7 |
| | Smith (R) | 11,905 | 45.3 |
| 9 | Rice A. Pierce (D) | 17,217 | 63.0 |
| | Brown (R) | 10,127 | 37.0 |
| 10 | James Phelan (D) | 20,149 | 63.2 |
| | Eaton (R) | 11,730 | 36.8 |

## TEXAS

| | Candidates | Votes | % |
|---|---|---|---|
| 1 | Charles Stewart (D) | 16,242 | 49.8 |
| | Lock McDaniel (R) | 12,003 | 36.8 |
| | Jack Davis (I) | 4,271 | 13.1 |
| 2 | William H. Martin (D) | 16,210 | 70.9 |
| | R. M. Humphries (UN LAB) | 6,656 | 29.1 |
| 3 | Constantine B. Kilgore (D) | 20,579 | 68.0 |
| | W. E. Farmer (LAB-R) | 9,697 | 32.0 |
| 4 | David B. Culberson (D) | 26,060 | 99.9 |
| 5 | Silas Hare (D) | 26,946 | 85.0 |
| | J. W. Thomas (R) | 4,468 | 14.1 |
| 6 | Jo O. Abbott (D) | 26,815 | 68.9 |
| | Sam Evans (LAB) | 12,126 | 31.1 |
| 7 | William H. Crain (D) | 15,610 | 56.4 |
| | Calvin J. Brewster (R) | 12,070 | 43.6 |
| 8 | Littleton W. Moore (D) | 21,022 | 69.3 |
| | T. C. Cook (R) | 8,460 | 27.9 |

| | Candidates | Votes | % |
|---|---|---|---|
| 9 | Roger Q. Mills (D) | 20,701 | 57.5 |
| | E. A. Jones (ID R&P) | 15,316 | 42.5 |
| 10 | Joseph D. Sayers (D) | 24,094 | 66.3 |
| | A. Belknap (R) | 12,251 | 33.7 |
| 11 | Samuel W. T. Lanham (D) | 28,535 | 85.9 |
| | D. M. Rumph (R) | 3,403 | 10.2 |

## VERMONT

| | | | |
|---|---|---|---|
| 1 | John W. Stewart (R) | 23,892 | 70.2 |
| | Ozro Meacham (D) | 9,746 | 28.6 |
| 2 | William W. Grout (R) | 24,219 | 70.8 |
| | George W. Smith (D) | 9,605 | 28.1 |

## VIRGINIA

| | | | |
|---|---|---|---|
| 1 | Thomas H. B. Browne (R) | 14,731 | 50.7 |
| | G. S. Kendall (D) | 14,317 | 49.3 |
| 2 | George E. Bowden (R) | 19,821 | 58.7 |
| | R. C. Marshall (D) | 13,726 | 40.6 |
| 3 | George D. Wise (D) | 15,608‡ | 50.4 |
| | Edmond Waddill Jr (R) | 15,347 | 49.6 |
| 4 | Edward C. Venable (D) | 13,298‡ | 45.6 |
| | John M. Langston (R) | 12,657 | 43.4 |
| | R. W. Arnold | 3,207 | 11.0 |
| 5 | Posey G. Lester (D) | 14,417 | 52.5 |
| | J. D. Blackwell (R) | 13,044 | 47.5 |
| 6 | Paul C. Edmunds (D) | 17,559 | 55.6 |
| | P. H. McCaull (R) | 13,822 | 43.8 |
| 7 | Charles T. O'Ferrall (D) | 16,443 | 54.3 |
| | J. E. Roller (R) | 13,623 | 45.0 |
| 8 | William H. F. Lee (D) | 15,414 | 51.8 |
| | Park Agnew (R) | 14,291 | 48.0 |
| 9 | John A. Buchanan (D) | 16,520 | 50.7 |
| | Henry Bowen (R) | 16,042 | 49.3 |
| 10 | Henry St.George Tucker (D) | 14,587 | 51.0 |
| | Jacob Yost (R) | 13,994 | 49.0 |

## WEST VIRGINIA

| | Candidates | Votes | % |
|---|---|---|---|
| 1 | John O. Pendleton (D) | 19,264‡ | 49.5 |
| | George W. Atkinson (R) | 19,242 | 49.5 |
| 2 | William L. Wilson (D) | 20,468 | 50.1 |
| | W. H. H. Flick (R) | 20,091 | 49.2 |
| 3 | John D. Alderson (D) | 15,474 | 50.8 |
| | James H. McGinnis (R) | 14,681 | 48.2 |
| 4 | James M. Jackson (D) | 19,837‡ | 49.7 |
| | Charles B. Smith (R) | 19,834 | 49.6 |

## WISCONSIN

| | | | |
|---|---|---|---|
| 1 | Lucien B. Caswell (R) | 19,311 | 53.4 |
| | Joseph B. Doe Jr (D) | 14,997 | 41.5 |
| | Stephen Faville (P) | 1,809 | 5.0 |
| 2 | Charles Barwig (D) | 16,813 | 53.2 |
| | E. C. McFetridge (R) | 13,859 | 43.8 |
| 3 | Robert M. LaFollette (R) | 19,052 | 50.0 |
| | John B. Parkinson (D) | 16,123 | 42.3 |
| | T. C. Richmond (P) | 2,654 | 7.0 |
| 4 | Isaac W. Van Schaick (R) | 22,212 | 50.8 |
| | Henry Smith (D & LAB) | 20,685 | 47.3 |
| 5 | George H. Brickner (D) | 17,051 | 55.2 |
| | Gustav Kustermann (R) | 12,825 | 41.5 |
| 6 | Charles B. Clark (R) | 17,977 | 52.5 |
| | Charles W. Felger (D) | 14,213 | 41.5 |
| 7 | Ormsby B. Thomas (R) | 19,918 | 53.5 |
| | Frank P. Coburn (D) | 15,433 | 41.5 |
| | J. H. Mosely (P) | 1,871 | 5.0 |
| 8 | Nils P. Haugen (R) | 26,909 | 57.0 |
| | S. C. Johnson (D & LAB) | 16,476 | 34.9 |
| | Charles Alexander (P) | 3,687 | 7.8 |
| 9 | Myron H. McCord (R) | 27,538 | 50.5 |
| | H. W. Early (D) | 24,775 | 45.4 |

# 1889 House Elections

## ILLINOIS

**Special Election**

| | Candidates | Votes | % |
|---|---|---|---|
| 19 | James R. Williams (D) | 14,858 | 54.6 |
| | Thomas S. Ridgway (R) | 10,462 | 38.4 |
| | John P. Stelle (F ALNC) | 1,645 | 6.0 |

## KANSAS

**Special Election**

| | | | |
|---|---|---|---|
| 4 | Harrison Kelley (R) | 10,506 | 85.3 |
| | John Heaston (D) | 1,530 | 12.4 |

## LOUISIANA

**Special Election**

| | | | |
|---|---|---|---|
| 3 | Edward J. Gay (D) | 18,856 | 74.8 |
| | Jolley (R) | 6,351 | 25.2 |

## MISSOURI

**Special Election**

| | Candidates | Votes | % |
|---|---|---|---|
| 4 | Robert P. C. Wilson (D) | 12,496 | 51.4 |
| | R. Posegate (R) | 11,812 | 48.6 |

## MONTANA

(Became a State Nov. 8, 1889)

| | | | |
|---|---|---|---|
| AL | Thomas H. Carter (R) | 19,915 | 51.9 |
| | Martin Maginnis (D) | 18,435 | 48.1 |

## NEBRASKA

**Special Election**

| | | | |
|---|---|---|---|
| 2 | Gilbert L. Laws (R) | 27,775 | 54.8 |
| | C. D. Casper (D) | 21,123 | 41.7 |

## NEW YORK

**Special Elections**

| | | | |
|---|---|---|---|
| 6 | Charles H. Turner (D) | 6,811 | 82.3 |
| | Collier (R) | 1,149 | 13.9 |
| 9 | Amos J. Cummings (D) | 15,508 | 99.7 |

| | Candidates | Votes | % |
|---|---|---|---|
| 27 | Sereno E. Payne (R) | 20,794 | 60.1 |
| | Hopkins (D) | 13,249 | 38.3 |

## NORTH DAKOTA

(Became a State Nov. 2, 1889)

| | | | |
|---|---|---|---|
| AL | Henry C. Hansbrough (R) | 26,077 | 68.5 |
| | Maratta (D) | 12,006 | 31.5 |

## SOUTH DAKOTA

(Became a State Nov. 2, 1889)

| | | |
|---|---|---|
| AL | Oscar S. Gifford (R) | 54,983✔ |
| | John A. Pickler (R) | 54,105✔ |
| | Linneus Q. Jeffries (D) | 23,229 |
| | S. M. Booth (D) | 22,541 |

## WASHINGTON

(Became a State Nov. 11, 1889)

| | | | |
|---|---|---|---|
| AL | John L. Wilson (R) | 34,039 | 58.1 |
| | Thomas C. Griffiths (D) | 24,492 | 41.8 |

# 1890 House Elections

## ALABAMA

| Candidates | Votes | % |
|---|---|---|
| 1 Richard Henry Clarke (D) | 10,071 | 69.9 |
| Frank H. Threatt (R) | 2,448 | 17.0 |
| A. J. Warner | 1,890 | 13.1 |
| 2 Hilary A. Herbert (D) | 10,611 | 79.8 |
| S. A. Pilley | 2,681 | 20.2 |
| 3 William C. Oates (D) | 10,268 | 91.7 |
| Treadwell | 930 | 8.3 |
| 4 Louis W. Turpin (D) | 9,595 | 52.1 |
| John V. McDuffie (R) | 4,931 | 26.8 |
| G. McCall | 3,899 | 21.2 |
| 5 James E. Cobb (D) | 5,548 | 99.8 |
| 6 John H. Bankhead (D) | 9,182 | 95.1 |
| 7 William H. Forney (D) | 10,054 | 59.2 |
| Butler | 6,060 | 35.7 |
| Logan | 862 | 5.1 |
| 8 Joseph Wheeler (D) | 16,821 | 58.2 |
| R. W. Austin | 12,076 | 41.8 |

## ARKANSAS

| Candidates | Votes | % |
|---|---|---|
| 1 William H. Cate (D | 15,437 | 51.0 |
| L. P. Featherston (POP) | 14,834 | 49.0 |
| 2 Clifton R. Breckinridge (D) | 20,816 | 51.1 |
| I. P. Langley (POP) | 19,941 | 48.9 |
| 3 Thomas C. McRae (D) | 13,111 | 96.6 |
| 4 William L. Terry (D) | 12,670 | 62.9 |
| E. M. Harrison (R) | 7,488 | 37.1 |
| 5 Samuel W. Peel (D) | 7,734 | 97.4 |

### Special Election

| | Votes | % |
|---|---|---|
| 2 Clifton R. Breckinridge (D) | 20,828 | 51.0 |
| Isom P. Langley (POP) | 20,017 | 49.0 |

## CALIFORNIA

| Candidates | Votes | % |
|---|---|---|
| 1 Thomas J. Geary (D) | 19,334 | 49.3 |
| J.A. Barham (R) | 19,117 | 48.7 |
| 2 Anthony Caminetti (D) | 18,644 | 49.0 |
| G. G. Blanchard (R) | 18,485 | 48.6 |
| 3 Joseph McKenna (R) | 20,834 | 55.0 |
| J. P. Irish (D) | 15,997 | 42.2 |
| 4 John P. Cutting (R) | 13,196 | 49.2 |
| Robert Ferral (D) | 12,091 | 45.1 |
| Thomas V. Cator (REF D) | 1,492 | 5.6 |
| 5 Eugene F. Loud (R) | 22,871 | 52.7 |
| T. J. Clunie (D) | 19,899 | 45.8 |
| 6 William W. Bowers (R) | 33,522 | 50.4 |
| W. J. Curtis (D) | 28,904 | 43.5 |

### Special Election

| | Votes | % |
|---|---|---|
| 1 Thomas J. Geary (D) | 15,750 | 49.6 |
| J. A. Barham (R) | 15,397 | 48.5 |

## COLORADO

| Candidates | Votes | % |
|---|---|---|
| AL Hosea Townsend (R) | 43,118 | 51.3 |
| T. J. O'Donnell (D) | 34,736 | 41.3 |
| J. D. Burr (I) | 5,207 | 12.0 |

## CONNECTICUT

| Candidates | Votes | % |
|---|---|---|
| 1 Lewis Sperry (D) | 16,195 | 49.8 |
| Simonds (R) | 15,503 | 47.7 |
| 2 Washington F. Wilcox (D) | 23,367 | 52.9 |
| Hubbard (R) | 19,836 | 44.9 |
| 3 Charles A. Russell (R) | 10,541 | 50.7 |
| Wells | 9,549 | 45.9 |
| 4 Robert E. De Forest (D) | 18,777 | 50.2 |
| Miles (R) | 17,821 | 47.7 |

## DELAWARE

| Candidates | Votes | % |
|---|---|---|
| AL John W. Causey (D) | 17,848 | 50.6 |
| Henry P. Carmon (R) | 17,150 | 48.7 |

## FLORIDA

| Candidates | Votes | % |
|---|---|---|
| 1 Stephen R. Mallory (D) | 11,731 | 77.7 |
| Reed (R) | 3,362 | 22.3 |
| 2 Robert Bullock (D) | 16,735 | 58.7 |
| Shipling (R) | 11,786 | 41.3 |

## GEORGIA

| Candidates | Votes | % |
|---|---|---|
| 1 Rufus G. Lester (D) | 10,905 | 77.7 |
| Michael G. Doyle (R) | 3,127 | 22.3 |
| 2 Henry G. Turner (D) | 7,361 | 88.6 |
| C. B. Matteson (R) | 948 | 11.4 |
| 3 Charles F. Crisp (D) | 8,038 | 86.6 |
| Peter O. Gibson (R) | 1,248 | 13.4 |
| 4 Charles L. Moses (D) | 9,609 | 73.7 |
| Walter L. Johnson (R) | 3,438 | 26.4 |
| 5 Leonidas F. Livingston (D) | 8,688 | 70.7 |
| Will Haight (R) | 3,608 | 29.3 |
| 6 James H. Blount (D) | 2,860 | 100.0 |
| 7 R. W. Everett (D) | 11,031 | 54.8 |
| W. H. Felton (D) | 8,460 | 42.0 |
| 8 Thomas G. Lawson (D) | 3,405 | 100.0 |
| 9 Thomas E. Winn (D) | 10,315 | 58.8 |
| T. Pickett (I) | 4,087 | 23.3 |
| S. A. Darnell (R) | 3,133 | 17.9 |
| 10 Thomas G. Watson (D) | 5,456 | 90.1 |
| Anthony E. Williams (R) | 597 | 9.9 |

## IDAHO

(Became a state July 3, 1890)

| Candidates | Votes | % |
|---|---|---|
| AL Willis Sweet (R) | 10,171 | 56.0 |
| Alex E. Mayhew (D) | 7,985 | 44.0 |

### Special Election

| | Votes | % |
|---|---|---|
| AL Willis Sweet (R) | 10,130 | 55.8 |
| Alex E. Mayhew (D) | 8,026 | 44.2 |

## ILLINOIS

| Candidates | Votes | % |
|---|---|---|
| 1 Abner Taylor (R) | 22,235 | 50.0 |
| William G. Ewing (D) | 21,796 | 49.0 |
| 2 Lawrence E. McGann (D) | 17,383 | 60.4 |
| John G. Schaar (R) | 10,633 | 36.9 |
| 3 Allan C. Durborow Jr. (D) | 21,069 | 53.7 |
| William E. Mason (R) | 17,933 | 45.7 |
| 4 Walter C. Newberry (D) | 19,835 | 50.1 |
| George E. Adams (R) | 19,173 | 48.4 |
| 5 Albert J. Hopkins (R) | 15,845 | 59.7 |
| Jacob Haish (D) | 9,664 | 36.4 |
| 6 Robert R. Hitt (R) | 14,028 | 50.9 |
| Andrew Ashton (D) | 13,517 | 49.1 |
| 7 Thomas J. Henderson (R) | 12,946 | 53.8 |
| John W. Blee (D) | 10,374 | 43.1 |
| 8 Lewis Steward (D) | 17,496 | 49.4 |
| Charles A. Hill (R) | 16,794 | 47.4 |
| 9 Herman W. Snow (D) | 15,427 | 50.1 |
| Lewis E. Payson (R) | 14,480 | 47.0 |
| 10 Philip S. Post (R) | 16,194 | 50.1 |
| George A. Wilson (D) | 15,576 | 48.2 |
| 11 Benjamin T. Cable (D) | 19,334 | 51.2 |
| William H. Gest (R) | 17,461 | 46.3 |
| 12 Scott Wike (D) | 20,805 | 58.1 |
| Milton McClure (R) | 13,336 | 37.2 |
| 13 William M. Springer (D) | 20,951 | 54.3 |
| Jesse Hanon (R) | 15,946 | 41.4 |
| 14 Owen Scott (D) | 16,670 | 49.5 |
| Jonathan H. Rowell (R) | 15,448 | 45.9 |

| Candidates | Votes | % |
|---|---|---|
| 15 Samuel T. Busey (D) | 19,010 | 49.7 |
| Joseph G. Cannon (R) | 18,428 | 48.2 |
| 16 George W. Fithian (D) | 16,473 | 50.3 |
| John D. Reeder (R) | 15,957 | 48.7 |
| 17 Edward Lane (D) | 16,700 | 51.7 |
| Fletcher H. Chapman (R) | 9,761 | 30.2 |
| Edward Roessler (F ALNC) | 4,845 | 15.0 |
| 18 William S. Forman (D) | 16,279 | 51.7 |
| Cicero J. Lindley (R) | 14,529 | 46.2 |
| 19 James R. Williams (D) | 17,410 | 56.4 |
| George W. Pillow (R) | 12,613 | 40.9 |
| 20 George H. Smith (R) | 17,580 | 49.5 |
| William S. Morris (D) | 16,273 | 45.9 |

## INDIANA

| Candidates | Votes | % |
|---|---|---|
| 1 William F. Parrett (D) | 17,730 | 50.4 |
| James S. Wright (R) | 16,875 | 48.0 |
| 2 John L. Bretz (D) | 14,697 | 43.6 |
| William N. Darnell (R) | 11,996 | 35.6 |
| Sampson Cox (PP) | 6,649 | 19.7 |
| 3 Jason B. Brown (D) | 16,369 | 56.2 |
| William J. Durham (R) | 12,430 | 42.7 |
| 4 William S. Holman (D) | 15,639 | 52.4 |
| John T. Rankin (R) | 13,867 | 46.4 |
| 5 George W. Cooper (D) | 17,070 | 51.5 |
| John G. Dunbar (R) | 15,355 | 46.3 |
| 6 Henry U. Johnson (R) | 18,786 | 57.3 |
| David S. Trowbridge (D) | 12,807 | 39.1 |
| 7 William D. Bynum (D) | 27,401 | 54.2 |
| John J. W. Billingsly (R) | 22,086 | 43.7 |
| 8 Elijah V. Brookshire (D) | 21,389 | 52.8 |
| James A. Mount (R) | 18,333 | 45.2 |
| 9 Daniel Waugh (R) | 20,752 | 50.2 |
| Leroy Templeton (D) | 19,453 | 47.1 |
| 10 David H. Patton (D) | 17,262 | 50.3 |
| William D. Owen (R) | 16,100 | 46.9 |
| 11 Augustus N. Martin (D) | 20,813 | 51.5 |
| Cyrus E. Bryant (R) | 18,000 | 44.5 |
| 12 Charles A. O. McClellan (D) | 17,970 | 54.7 |
| Jaques N. Babcock (R) | 13,920 | 42.4 |
| 13 Benjamin F. Shively (D) | 20,311 | 52.2 |
| H. B. Wilson (R) | 17,614 | 45.2 |

## IOWA

| Candidates | Votes | % |
|---|---|---|
| 1 John J. Seerley (D) | 17,459 | 51.4 |
| John H. Gier (R) | 16,388 | 48.2 |
| 2 Walter I. Hayes (D) | 20,748 | 63.8 |
| Bruce T. Seaman (R) | 11,740 | 36.1 |
| 3 David B. Henderson (R) | 19,689 | 50.2 |
| C. F. Couch (D) | 19,491 | 49.7 |
| 4 Walter H. Butler (D) | 17,972 | 52.7 |
| J. H. Swaney (R) | 16,023 | 47.0 |
| 5 John T. Hamilton (D) | 18,153 | 50.1 |
| George R. Struble (R) | 17,860 | 49.2 |
| 6 Frederick E. White (D) | 17,092 | 49.0 |
| John F. Lacey (R) | 16,572 | 47.5 |
| 7 John A. T. Hull (R) | 16,821 | 53.9 |
| H. C. Hargis (D) | 14,276 | 45.8 |
| 8 James P. Flick (R) | 19,003 | 49.6 |
| Allen R. Anderson (D) | 18,887 | 49.3 |
| 9 Thomas Bowman (D) | 18,685 | 50.1 |
| Joseph R. Reed (R) | 17,322 | 46.4 |
| 10 Jonathan P. Dolliver (R) | 18,395 | 51.7 |
| I. L. Woode (D) | 17,084 | 48.0 |
| 11 George D. Perkins (R) | 15,972 | 44.6 |
| John Pallison (D) | 15,065 | 42.1 |
| A. J. Westfall (PP) | 4,658 | 13.0 |

### Special Election

| | Votes | % |
|---|---|---|
| 7 Edward R. Hayes (R) | 16,702 | 54.1 |
| J. H. Barnett | 14,142 | 45.8 |

## KANSAS

| | Candidates | Votes | % |
|---|---|---|---|
| 1 | Case Broderick (R) | 14,630 | 41.7 |
| | Thomas Moonlight (D) | 13,250 | 37.7 |
| | L. C. Clark (ALNC D) | 7,176 | 20.4 |
| 2 | Edward H. Funston (R) | 17,713 | 43.9 |
| | A. F. Allen (ALNC D) | 12,273 | 30.4 |
| | J. B. Chapman (D) | 10,130 | 25.1 |
| 3 | Benjamin H. Clover (ALNC D) | 23,492 | 55.2 |
| | Bishop W. Perkins (R) | 19,061 | 44.8 |
| 4 | John G. Otis (ALNC D) | 24,993 | 55.6 |
| | Harrison Kelley (R) | 19,984 | 44.4 |
| 5 | John Davis (ALNC D) | 19,482 | 52.9 |
| | William A. Phillips (R) | 13,998 | 38.0 |
| | Park S. Warren (D) | 3,337 | 9.1 |
| 6 | William Baker (ALNC D) | 20,749 | 62.6 |
| | Webb McNall (R) | 12,105 | 36.5 |
| 7 | Jerry Simpson (ALNC D) | 32,603 | 56.4 |
| | James R. Hallowell (R) | 25,181 | 43.6 |

## KENTUCKY

| | | Votes | % |
|---|---|---|---|
| 1 | William J. Stone (D) | 9,749 | 66.9 |
| | E. F. Franks (R) | 3,743 | 25.7 |
| | William Curd (P) | 1,086 | 7.5 |
| 2 | William T. Ellis (D) | 13,983 | 56.9 |
| | H. R. Bourland (R&F ALNC) | 10,592 | 43.1 |
| 3 | Isaac H. Goodnight (D) | 11,649 | 61.1 |
| | Addison D. James (R) | 7,426 | 38.9 |
| 4 | Alexander B. Montgomery (D) | 11,036 | 61.2 |
| | G. W. Long (R) | 6,990 | 38.8 |
| 5 | Asher G. Caruth (D) | 14,395 | 60.8 |
| | St. John Boyle (R) | 9,291 | 39.2 |
| 6 | William W. Dickerson (D) | 11,310 | 62.3 |
| | Weden O'Neal (R) | 6,801 | 37.4 |
| 7 | William C. P. Breckinridge (D) | 7,146 | 92.9 |
| | Hiram Ford (P) | 442 | 5.7 |
| 8 | James B. McCreary (D) | 7,430 | 94.8 |
| | J. C. Gilliam (R) | 394 | 5.0 |
| 9 | Thomas H. Paynter (D) | 15,276 | 60.0 |
| | Alexander Bruce (R) | 10,053 | 39.5 |
| 10 | John W. Kendall (D) | 10,746 | 53.8 |
| | R. C. Hill (R) | 9,218 | 46.1 |
| 11 | John H. Wilson (R) | 9,612 | 60.5 |
| | E. J. Howard (D) | 5,964 | 37.5 |

### Special Election

| | | Votes | % |
|---|---|---|---|
| 6 | William W. Dickerson (D) | 8,412 | 63.7 |
| | Wesley M. Rardin (R) | 4,742 | 35.9 |

## LOUISIANA

| | | Votes | % |
|---|---|---|---|
| 1 | Adolph Meyer (D) | 10,824 | 63.2 |
| | H. C. Warmoth (R) | 6,155 | 36.0 |
| 2 | Matthew D. Lagan (D) | 10,948 | 61.6 |
| | H. D. Coleman (R) | 6,412 | 36.1 |
| 3 | Andrew Price (D) | 11,318 | 99.4 |
| 4 | Newton C. Blanchard (D) | 8,307 | 96.3 |
| 5 | Charles J. Boatner (D) | 11,793 | 92.7 |
| 6 | Samuel M. Robertson (D) | 6,611 | 99.9 |

## MAINE

| | | Votes | % |
|---|---|---|---|
| 1 | Thomas B. Reed (R) | 16,797 | 57.2 |
| | M. P. Frank (D) | 11,971 | 40.7 |
| 2 | Nelson Dingley Jr. (R) | 16,499 | 58.0 |
| | E. Allen (D) | 11,187 | 39.3 |
| 3 | Seth L. Milliken (R) | 14,477 | 54.5 |
| | Charles Baker (D) | 11,011 | 41.5 |
| 4 | Charles A. Boutelle (R) | 15,713 | 56.2 |
| | Josiah Crosby (D) | 11,144 | 39.9 |

## MARYLAND

| | | Votes | % |
|---|---|---|---|
| 1 | Henry Page (D) | 14,817 | 52.4 |
| | George M. Russum (R) | 12,437 | 44.0 |

| | Candidates | Votes | % |
|---|---|---|---|
| 2 | Herman Stump (D) | 17,740 | 57.1 |
| | John E. Wilson (R) | 12,130 | 39.0 |
| 3 | Harry Wells Rusk (D) | 16,914 | 59.1 |
| | Royal H. Pullman (R) | 11,273 | 39.4 |
| 4 | Isidor Rayner (D) | 18,740 | 59.7 |
| | Henry H. Goldsborough (R) | 12,106 | 38.6 |
| 5 | Barnes Compton (D) | 14,697 | 54.0 |
| | Sidney E. Mudd (R) | 12,479 | 45.8 |
| 6 | William M. McKaig (D) | 16,940 | 49.3 |
| | Louis E. McComas (R) | 16,775 | 48.8 |

## MASSACHUSETTS

| | | Votes | % |
|---|---|---|---|
| 1 | Charles S. Randall (R) | 8,728 | 53.8 |
| | Charles R. Codman (D) | 6,518 | 40.2 |
| | John D. Flint (P) | 984 | 6.1 |
| 2 | Elijah A. Morse (R) | 12,339 | 52.3 |
| | Bushrod Morse (D) | 10,489 | 44.4 |
| 3 | John F. Andrew (D) | 14,992 | 56.2 |
| | Edward L. Pierce (R) | 11,184 | 41.9 |
| 4 | Joseph H. O'Neil (D) | 11,780 | 72.4 |
| | Thomas Copeland (R) | 4,170 | 25.6 |
| 5 | Sherman Hoar (D) | 13,081 | 53.0 |
| | James A. Fox (R) | 10,807 | 43.8 |
| 6 | Henry Cabot Lodge (R) | 14,579 | 50.0 |
| | William Everett (D) | 13,539 | 46.4 |
| 7 | William Cogswell (R) | 12,496 | 51.5 |
| | Jonas H. French (D) | 10,910 | 45.0 |
| 8 | Moses T. Stevens (D) | 11,726 | 49.9 |
| | Frederic T. Greenhalge (R) | 11,272 | 47.9 |
| 9 | George Fred Williams (D) | 12,207 | 48.5 |
| | John W. Candler (R) | 12,076 | 48.0 |
| 10 | Joseph H. Walker (R) | 11,130 | 49.4 |
| | Charles B. Pratt (D) | 10,431 | 46.3 |
| 11 | Frederick S. Coolidge (D) | 9,304 | 40.0 |
| | Timothy G. Spaulding (R) | 9,145 | 39.3 |
| | Myron P. Walker (IR) | 3,533 | 15.2 |
| | Henry C. Smith (P) | 1,260 | 5.4 |
| 12 | John C. Crosby (D) | 12,106 | 49.0 |
| | Francis W. Rockwell (R) | 11,724 | 47.5 |

## MICHIGAN

| | | Votes | % |
|---|---|---|---|
| 1 | J. Logan Chipman (D) | 21,791 | 56.5 |
| | Hibbard Baker (R) | 15,861 | 41.1 |
| 2 | James S. Gorman (D) | 16,471 | 49.1 |
| | Edward P. Allen (R) | 14,568 | 43.4 |
| | Thomas F. Moore (P) | 2,522 | 7.5 |
| 3 | James O'Donnell (R) | 16,679 | 44.5 |
| | John W. Fletcher (D) | 14,216 | 37.9 |
| | Robert Fraser (P) | 3,423 | 9.1 |
| | Samuel Dickie (INDUST) | 3,187 | 8.5 |
| 4 | Julius C. Burrows (R) | 16,067 | 45.3 |
| | George L. Yaple (D) | 15,673 | 44.1 |
| | George F. Cunningham (P) | 2,843 | 8.0 |
| 5 | Melbourne Ford (D) | 22,451 | 49.6 |
| | Charles W. Watkins (R) | 20,153 | 44.5 |
| | Edward L. Briggs (P) | 2,587 | 5.7 |
| 6 | Byron G. Stout (D) | 17,140 | 44.5 |
| | William Ball (R) | 16,457 | 42.7 |
| | Jay Sessions (P) | 3,004 | 7.8 |
| | George W. Caswell (INDUST) | 1,940 | 5.0 |
| 7 | Justin R. Whiting (D) | 14,553 | 50.7 |
| | James S. Ayres (R) | 12,566 | 43.8 |
| 8 | Henry M. Youmans (D) | 17,230 | 47.2 |
| | Aaron T. Bliss (R) | 17,154 | 47.0 |
| | William M. Smith (P) | 2,106 | 5.8 |
| 9 | Harrison H. Wheeler (D) | 15,854 | 45.7 |
| | Byron M. Cutcheon (R) | 15,794 | 45.6 |
| | Oscar M. Brownson (P) | 2,778 | 8.0 |
| 10 | Thomas A. E. Weadock (D) | 16,721 | 50.6 |
| | Watts S. Humphrey (R) | 15,055 | 45.6 |
| 11 | Samuel M. Stephenson (R) | 16,667 | 50.4 |
| | John Semer (D) | 14,549 | 44.0 |
| | William H. Simmons (P) | 1,759 | 5.3 |

## MINNESOTA

| | Candidates | Votes | % |
|---|---|---|---|
| 1 | William H. Harries (D) | 17,198 | 53.6 |
| | Dunnell (R) | 14,875 | 46.4 |
| 2 | John Lind (R) | 20,789 | 49.2 |
| | Baker (ALNC D) | 20,306 | 48.1 |
| 3 | Osee M. Hall (D) | 17,639 | 50.5 |
| | D. S. Hall (R) | 13,106 | 37.5 |
| | Gamble (ALNC D) | 3,054 | 8.8 |
| 4 | James N. Castle (D) | 35,903 | 51.8 |
| | R. Snider (R) | 30,175 | 43.5 |
| 5 | Kittel Halvorson (ALNC D) | 21,514 | 37.7 |
| | Comstock (R) | 19,372 | 33.9 |
| | Whiteman (D) | 16,203 | 28.4 |

## MISSISSIPPI

| | | Votes | % |
|---|---|---|---|
| 1 | John M. Allen (D) | 3,501 | 100.0 |
| 2 | John C. Kyle (D) | 8,282 | 70.5 |
| | G. M. Buchanan (R) | 3,468 | 29.5 |
| 3 | Thomas C. Catchings (D) | 8,689 | 76.2 |
| | James Hill (R) | 2,717 | 23.8 |
| 4 | Clarke Lewis (D) | 6,753 | 81.1 |
| | W. D. Frazer (R) | 1,572 | 18.9 |
| 5 | Joseph H. Beeman (D) | 6,305 | 100.0 |
| 6 | Thomas R. Stockdale (D) | 9,340 | 71.3 |
| | H. C. Griffin (R) | 3,768 | 28.8 |
| 7 | Charles E. Hooker (D) | 6,284 | 75.6 |
| | J. M. Matthews (R) | 2,028 | 24.4 |

## MISSOURI

| | | Votes | % |
|---|---|---|---|
| 1 | William H. Hatch (D) | 20,234 | 56.7 |
| | Harrington (R) | 15,080 | 42.3 |
| 2 | Charles H. Mansur (D) | 20,527 | 57.2 |
| | Pettyjohn (R) | 13,147 | 36.7 |
| | Donovan (UN LAB) | 2,188 | 6.1 |
| 3 | Alexander M. Dockery (D) | 20,594 | 55.0 |
| | Kinney (R) | 13,139 | 35.1 |
| | Hillis (UN LAB) | 3,681 | 9.8 |
| 4 | Robert P. C. Wilson (D) | 15,753 | 51.4 |
| | Ford (R) | 12,444 | 40.6 |
| | Whipple (UN LAB) | 2,191 | 7.2 |
| 5 | John C. Tarsney (D) | 19,387 | 57.7 |
| | Twitchell (R) | 13,505 | 40.2 |
| 6 | John T. Heard (D) | 24,027 | 54.6 |
| | Redman (R) | 16,365 | 37.2 |
| | Alldredge (UN LAB) | 3,625 | 8.2 |
| 7 | Richard H. Norton (D) | 17,926 | 58.1 |
| | Barnett (R) | 12,946 | 41.9 |
| 8 | John J. O'Neill (D) | 11,621 | 54.9 |
| | Joy (R) | 9,563 | 45.1 |
| 9 | Seth W. Cobb (D) | 10,576 | 58.8 |
| | Prosser (R) | 6,962 | 38.7 |
| 10 | Samuel Byrns (D) | 16,744 | 52.5 |
| | Kinsey (R) | 15,095 | 47.3 |
| 11 | Richard P. Bland (D) | 18,991 | 56.1 |
| | Erwin (R) | 14,885 | 43.9 |
| 12 | David A. De Armond (D) | 21,556 | 48.2 |
| | Lewis (R) | 14,441 | 32.3 |
| | Wykoff (UN LAB) | 8,537 | 19.1 |
| 13 | Robert W. Fyan (D) | 16,488 | 49.9 |
| | Wade (R) | 13,728 | 41.6 |
| | Vertrees (UN LAB) | 2,803 | 8.5 |
| 14 | Marshall Arnold (D) | 19,312 | 59.7 |
| | Rogers (R) | 13,037 | 40.3 |

### Special Election

| | | Votes | % |
|---|---|---|---|
| 14 | Robert H. Whitelaw (D) | 19,329 | 60.8 |
| | Farnsworth (R) | 12,481 | 39.2 |

## MONTANA

| | | Votes | % |
|---|---|---|---|
| AL | William W. Dixon (D) | 15,411 | 49.6 |
| | Thomas H. Carter (R) | 15,128 | 48.7 |

## NEBRASKA

| | Candidates | Votes | % |
|---|---|---|---|
| 1 | William Jennings Bryan (D) | 32,376 | 44.5 |
| | W. J. Connell (R) | 25,663 | 35.3 |
| | Allen Root (I) | 13,066 | 18.0 |
| 2 | William A. McKeighan (I & D) | 36,104 | 61.1 |
| | N. V. Harlan (R) | 21,776 | 36.9 |
| 3 | Omer M. Kem (I) | 31,731 | 39.4 |
| | George W. E. Dorsey (R) | 25,440 | 31.6 |
| | W. H. Thompson (D) | 22,353 | 27.8 |

## NEVADA

| | Candidates | Votes | % |
|---|---|---|---|
| AL | Horace F. Bartine (R) | 6,610 | 53.4 |
| | George W. Cassidy (D) | 5,736 | 46.3 |

## NEW HAMPSHIRE

| | Candidates | Votes | % |
|---|---|---|---|
| 1 | Luther F. McKinney (D) | 21,432 | 50.7 |
| | David A. Taggart (R) | 20,296 | 48.0 |
| 2 | Warren F. Daniell (D) | 21,438 | 49.7 |
| | Orren C. Moore (R) | 21,079 | 48.8 |

## NEW JERSEY

| | Candidates | Votes | % |
|---|---|---|---|
| 1 | Christopher A. Bergen (R) | 19,082 | 50.9 |
| | Newell (D) | 16,372 | 43.7 |
| | Nicholson (P) | 2,007 | 5.4 |
| 2 | James Buchanan (R) | 17,515 | 50.0 |
| | Haven (D) | 16,352 | 46.6 |
| 3 | Jacob A. Geissenhainer (D) | 20,266 | 54.6 |
| | Clark Jr (R) | 15,748 | 42.4 |
| 4 | Samuel Fowler (D) | 13,459 | 56.5 |
| | Goodman (R) | 8,775 | 36.8 |
| | Schenk (P) | 1,583 | 6.7 |
| 5 | Cornelius A. Cadmus (D) | 16,815 | 50.4 |
| | Beckwith (R) | 15,459 | 46.4 |
| 6 | Thomas D. English (D) | 23,278 | 50.9 |
| | Condit (R) | 21,468 | 46.9 |
| 7 | Edward F. McDonald (D) | 21,875 | 56.0 |
| | McEwan Jr. (R) | 16,761 | 42.9 |

## NEW YORK

| | Candidates | Votes | % |
|---|---|---|---|
| 1 | James W. Covert (D) | 18,999 | 56.0 |
| | John Lewis Childs (R) | 14,085 | 41.5 |
| 2 | David A. Boody (D) | 21,609 | 57.7 |
| | James Gresham (R) | 15,028 | 40.1 |
| 3 | William J. Coombs (D) | 15,670 | 48.9 |
| | William . Wallace (R) | 15,652 | 48.8 |
| 4 | John M. Clancy (D) | 18,216 | 67.6 |
| | Andrew J. Perry (R) | 8,454 | 31.4 |
| 5 | Thomas F. Magner (D) | 16,470 | 58.4 |
| | John R. Smith (R) | 10,814 | 38.4 |
| 6 | John R. Fellows (D) | 10,170 | 57.2 |
| | Cornelius Donovan (R) | 5,574 | 31.3 |
| | Edwin L. Abbett (CO D) | 1,928 | 10.8 |
| 7 | Edward J. Dunphy (D) | 10,855 | 60.0 |
| | William Morgan (R) | 4,351 | 24.1 |
| | William T. Croasdale (CO D) | 2,787 | 15.4 |
| 8 | Timothy J. Campbell (D) | 15,958 | 77.9 |
| | Samuel Rinaldo (R) | 3,840 | 18.7 |
| 9 | Amos J. Cummings (D) | 14,252 | 71.8 |
| | John Weiss (R) | 4,462 | 22.5 |
| | Christian Ensminger (CO D) | 1,072 | 5.4 |
| 10 | Francis B. Spinola (D) | 13,884 | 70.5 |
| | Cortlandt S. Van Rensselaer (R) | 5,288 | 26.9 |
| 11 | John De Witt Warner (D) | 17,033 | 64.2 |
| | Charles A. Flammer (R) | 8,850 | 33.3 |
| 12 | Roswell P. Flower (D) | 19,160 | 69.4 |
| | Charles H. Blair (R) | 7,187 | 26.0 |
| 13 | Ashbel P. Fitch (D) | 28,268 | 68.9 |
| | Percy D. Adams (R) | 11,820 | 28.8 |
| 14 | William G. Stahlnecker (D) | 18,391 | 53.4 |
| | J. Thomas Stearns (R) | 12,211 | 35.5 |
| | Alexander Taylor Jr. | 2,561 | 7.4 |
| 15 | Henry Bacon (D) | 14,640 | 50.9 |
| | Clarence Lexow (R) | 13,061 | 45.4 |

| | Candidates | Votes | % |
|---|---|---|---|
| 16 | John H. Ketcham (R) | 13,474 | 75.3 |
| | William W. Smith (P) | 4,428 | 24.7 |
| 17 | Isaac N. Cox (D) | 15,439 | 53.5 |
| | Theodore C. Teale (R) | 13,429 | 46.5 |
| 18 | John A. Quackenbush (R) | 17,185 | 50.2 |
| | Michael F. Collins (D) | 15,939 | 46.6 |
| 19 | Charles Tracey (D) | 18,021 | 56.9 |
| | Angus McDuffie Shoemaker (R) | 12,942 | 40.9 |
| 20 | John Sanford (R) | 18,369 | 50.4 |
| | Alexander B. Baucus (D) | 16,788 | 46.1 |
| 21 | John M. Wever (R) | 13,314 | 55.6 |
| | Anthony J.B. Ross (D) | 9,820 | 41.0 |
| 22 | Leslie W. Russell (R) | 13,893 | 56.3 |
| | Smith T. Woolworth (D) | 9,116 | 36.9 |
| | Henry P. Forbes (P) | 1,679 | 6.8 |
| 23 | Henry W. Bentley (D) | 15,449 | 50.4 |
| | James S. Sherman (R) | 14,933 | 48.7 |
| 24 | George Van Horn (D) | 14,127 | 48.3 |
| | Frank B. Arnold (R) | 13,929 | 47.6 |
| 25 | James J. Belden (R) | 17,283 | 57.1 |
| | William Stitt (D) | 11,455 | 37.8 |
| | Andrew N. Vanderbilt (P) | 1,547 | 5.1 |
| 26 | George W. Ray (R) | 17,804 | 51.7 |
| | Thomas H. Beal (D) | 14,402 | 41.9 |
| | Mott C. Dixon (P) | 2,208 | 6.4 |
| 27 | Sereno E. Payne (R) | 17,970 | 50.6 |
| | Edwin K. Burnham (D) | 15,978 | 45.0 |
| 28 | Hosea H. Rockwell (D) | 12,440 | 47.9 |
| | Henry T. Noyes (R) | 12,351 | 47.6 |
| 29 | John Raines (R) | 14,722 | 49.7 |
| | Demerville Page (D) | 13,369 | 45.1 |
| | Daniel J. Chittenden (P) | 1,540 | 5.2 |
| 30 | Halbert S. Greenleaf (D) | 15,047 | 48.5 |
| | John Van Voorhis (R) | 14,796 | 47.7 |
| 31 | James W. Wadsworth (R) | 13,716 | 82.2 |
| | Alva Carpenter (P) | 2,275 | 13.6 |
| 32 | Daniel N. Lockwood (D) | 21,213 | 55.7 |
| | Benjamin H. Williams (R) | 16,240 | 42.6 |
| 33 | Thomas L. Bunting (D) | 12,585 | 51.6 |
| | George A. Davis (R) | 10,793 | 44.2 |
| 34 | Warren B. Hooker (R) | 15,843 | 54.7 |
| | Hiram Smith (D) | 10,117 | 35.0 |
| | Jesse D. Rogers (P) | 2,981 | 10.3 |

### Special Election

| | Candidates | Votes | % |
|---|---|---|---|
| 24 | John S. Pindar (D) | 14,030 | 48.1 |
| | Frank B. Arnold (R) | 13,916 | 47.7 |

## NORTH CAROLINA

| | Candidates | Votes | % |
|---|---|---|---|
| 1 | William A. B. Branch (D) | 16,436 | 56.3 |
| | Claude M. Bernard (R) | 12,683 | 43.4 |
| 2 | Henry P. Cheatham (R) | 16,942 | 51.7 |
| | James M. Mewboorne (D) | 15,713 | 47.9 |
| 3 | Benjamin F. Grady (D) | 17,348 | 67.0 |
| | George C. Scurlock (R) | 8,541 | 33.0 |
| 4 | Benjamin H. Bunn (D) | 18,995 | 59.8 |
| | Alexander McIver (R&F ALNC) | 12,417 | 39.1 |
| 5 | Archibald H. A. Williams (D) | 16,143 | 52.6 |
| | John M. Brower (R) | 14,204 | 46.2 |
| 6 | Sydenham B. Alexander (D) | 16,820 | 66.6 |
| | Richard M. Norment (R) | 8,424 | 33.4 |
| 7 | John S. Henderson (D) | 13,246 | 57.4 |
| | Pleasant C. Thomas (R) | 9,280 | 40.2 |
| 8 | William H. H. Cowles (D) | 8,586 | 53.7 |
| | Edward W. Faucette (R) | 7,256 | 45.4 |
| 9 | William T. Crawford (D) | 15,979 | 51.8 |
| | Hamilton G. Ewart (R) | 14,851 | 48.2 |

## NORTH DAKOTA

| | Candidates | Votes | % |
|---|---|---|---|
| AL | Martin N. Johnson (R) | 21,365 | 59.0 |
| | Benton (D) | 14,830 | 41.0 |

## OHIO

| | Candidates | Votes | % |
|---|---|---|---|
| 1 | Bellamy Storer (R) | 16,661 | 53.3 |
| | O. J. Cosgrave (D) | 14,373 | 46.0 |

| | Candidates | Votes | % |
|---|---|---|---|
| 2 | John A. Caldwell (R) | 22,021 | 59.9 |
| | Oliver Brown (D) | 14,291 | 38.9 |
| 3 | George W. Houk (D) | 21,270 | 51.5 |
| | H. L. Morey (R) | 18,639 | 45.1 |
| 4 | Martin K. Gantz (D) | 20,705 | 49.5 |
| | William P. Orr (R) | 19,295 | 46.2 |
| 5 | Fernando C. Layton (D) | 20,179 | 52.7 |
| | L. K. Stroup (R) | 15,973 | 41.7 |
| 6 | Dennis D. Donovan (D) | 18,741 | 51.0 |
| | J. H. Brigham (R) | 17,029 | 46.3 |
| 7 | William E. Haynes (D) | 18,126 | 52.4 |
| | J. M. Ashley (R) | 16,070 | 46.4 |
| 8 | Darius D. Hare (D) | 17,414 | 48.3 |
| | Charles Foster (R) | 17,220 | 47.7 |
| 9 | Joseph H. Outhwaite (D) | 18,550 | 51.8 |
| | T. B. Wilson (R) | 16,418 | 45.8 |
| 10 | Robert E. Doan (R) | 19,353 | 52.5 |
| | J. Q. Smith (D) | 15,569 | 42.2 |
| | R. Rathburn (P) | 1,954 | 5.3 |
| 11 | John M. Pattison (D) | 16,110 | 51.9 |
| | D. W. C. Loudon (R) | 13,157 | 42.4 |
| 12 | W. H. Enochs (R) | 16,851 | 61.1 |
| | Ezra V. Dean (D) | 9,814 | 35.6 |
| 13 | Irvine Dungan (D) | 16,225 | 50.7 |
| | William T. Lewis (R) | 14,759 | 46.1 |
| 14 | James W. Owens (D) | 19,193 | 53.2 |
| | Samuel Slade (R) | 15,773 | 43.8 |
| 15 | Michael D. Harter (D) | 19,832 | 52.5 |
| | G. L. Sackett (R) | 16,084 | 42.6 |
| 16 | John G. Warwick (D) | 20,059 | 49.3 |
| | William McKinley Jr. (R) | 19,757 | 48.6 |
| 17 | Albert J. Pearson (D) | 14,928 | 49.8 |
| | C. L. Poorman (R) | 14,224 | 47.5 |
| 18 | Joseph D. Taylor (R) | 16,993 | 56.0 |
| | H. H. McFadden (D) | 11,783 | 38.8 |
| | S. W. Wilkins (P) | 1,568 | 5.2 |
| 19 | Ezra B. Taylor (R) | 19,419 | 58.5 |
| | T. E. Hoyt (D) | 11,972 | 36.1 |
| | Richard Brown (P) | 1,753 | 5.3 |
| 20 | Vincent A. Taylor (R) | 22,672 | 58.1 |
| | H. L. Stewart (D) | 14,748 | 37.8 |
| 21 | Tom L. Johnson (D) | 17,646 | 54.6 |
| | T. E. Burton (R) | 14,256 | 44.1 |

## OREGON

| | Candidates | Votes | % |
|---|---|---|---|
| AL | Binger Herman (R) | 40,176 | 54.8 |
| | Robert A. Miller (D) | 30,263 | 41.3 |

## PENNSYLVANIA

| | Candidates | Votes | % |
|---|---|---|---|
| 1 | Henry H. Bingham (R) | 22,166 | 60.3 |
| | Edwin G. Flanagan (D) | 14,497 | 39.5 |
| 2 | Charles O'Neill (R) | 16,324 | 62.2 |
| | Edwin F. Lott (D) | 9,785 | 37.3 |
| 3 | William McAleer (D) | 13,121 | 56.6 |
| | Richard Vaux (ID) | 10,037 | 43.3 |
| 4 | John E. Reyburn (R) | 33,253 | 60.9 |
| | William M. Ayres (D) | 20,988 | 38.4 |
| 5 | Alfred C. Harmer (R) | 30,616 | 61.2 |
| | J. Henry Taylor (D) | 19,213 | 38.4 |
| 6 | John B. Robinson (R) | 17,447 | 55.0 |
| | Thomas W. Pierce (D) | 13,342 | 42.1 |
| 7 | Edwin Hallowell (D) | 20,810 | 49.5 |
| | Irving P. Wauger (R) | 20,623 | 49.1 |
| 8 | William Mutchler (D) | 17,424 | 62.3 |
| | George M. Davies (R) | 10,549 | 37.7 |
| 9 | David B. Brunner (D) | 26,627 | 62.8 |
| | Daniel H. Wingerd (R) | 15,434 | 36.4 |
| 10 | Marriott Brosius (R) | 19,126 | 66.4 |
| | D. F. Magee (D) | 9,358 | 32.5 |
| 11 | Lemuel Amerman (D) | 9,336 | 48.6 |
| | Joseph A. Scranton (R) | 9,033 | 47.0 |
| 12 | George W. Shonk (R) | 14,558 | 51.3 |
| | John B. Reynolds (D) | 13,074 | 46.0 |
| 13 | James B. Reilly (D) | 13,308 | 52.9 |
| | John T. Shoener (R) | 11,828 | 47.1 |
| 14 | John W. Rife (R) | 17,795 | 54.8 |
| | William L. Gorgas (D) | 14,308 | 44.0 |

## PENNSYLVANIA

| | Candidates | Votes | % |
|---|---|---|---|
| 15 | Myron B. Wright (R) | 16,076 | 51.8 |
| | Clar W. Canfield (D) | 13,854 | 44.7 |
| 16 | Albert C. Hopkins (R) | 15,824 | 48.5 |
| | Mortimer F. Elliott (D) | 15,773 | 48.3 |
| 17 | Simon P. Wolverton (D) | 15,178 | 60.2 |
| | W. C. Farnsworth (R) | 9,234 | 36.6 |
| 18 | Louis E. Atkinson (R) | 17,443 | 50.9 |
| | George W. Skinner (D) | 16,834 | 49.1 |
| 19 | Frank E. Beltzhoover (D) | 21,969 | 58.7 |
| | D. K. Trimmer (R) | 14,860 | 39.7 |
| 20 | Edward Scull (R) | 17,434 | 49.5 |
| | Thomas H. Greevy (D) | 16,908 | 48.0 |
| 21 | George F. Huff (R) | 21,212 | 51.8 |
| | Jacob Creps (D) | 19,714 | 48.2 |
| 22 | John Dalzell (R) | 21,464 | 60.9 |
| | William J. Brennan (D) | 13,559 | 38.4 |
| 23 | William A. Stone (R) | 13,904 | 66.8 |
| | Morrison Foster (D) | 6,788 | 32.6 |
| 24 | Andrew J. Stewart (R) | 21,708‡ | 49.0 |
| | Alexander K. Craig (D) | 21,585 | 48.7 |
| 25 | Eugene P. Gillespie (D) | 13,797 | 38.3 |
| | Thomas W. Phillips (R) | 10,636 | 29.5 |
| | Alex McDowell (R) | 10,531 | 29.2 |
| 26 | Matthew Griswold (R) | 13,779 | 49.8 |
| | A. L. Tilden (D) | 12,891 | 46.6 |
| 27 | Charles W. Stone (R) | 12,718 | 54.5 |
| | Robert W. Dunn (D) | 9,405 | 40.3 |
| | D. H. Boulton (P) | 1,212 | 5.2 |
| 28 | George F. Kribbs (D) | 17,636 | 56.4 |
| | Daniel C. Oyster (R) | 12,944 | 41.4 |

### Special Elections

| | | | |
|---|---|---|---|
| 3 | Richard Vaux (D) | 7,977 | 92.1 |
| 4 | John E. Reyburn (R) | 25,152 | 59.9 |
| | William M. Ayres (D) | 16,573 | 39.5 |
| 27 | Charles W. Stone (R) | 11,825 | 72.0 |
| | Robert W. Dunn (D) | 4,499 | 27.4 |

## RHODE ISLAND [1]

| | | | |
|---|---|---|---|
| 1 | Oscar Lapham (D) | 10,382 | 52.6 |
| | Henry J. Spooner (R) | 8,616 | 43.6 |
| 2 | Charles H. Page (D) | 8,341* | 47.8 |
| | Warren O. Arnold (R) | 8,325 | 47.7 |

## SOUTH CAROLINA

| | | | |
|---|---|---|---|
| 1 | William H. Brawley (D) | 7,249 | 84.2 |
| | William D. Crum (R) | 1,349 | 15.7 |
| 2 | George D. Tillman (D) | 9,996 | 85.6 |
| | S. E. Smith (R) | 1,671 | 14.3 |
| 3 | George Johnstone (D) | 8,942 | 91.4 |
| | John R. Tolbert (R) | 803 | 8.2 |
| 4 | George W. Shell (D) | 10,372 | 81.9 |
| | J. F. Ensor (R) | 2,258 | 17.8 |
| 5 | John J. Hemphill (D) | 9,432 | 87.1 |
| | G. G. Alexander (R) | 1,321 | 12.2 |
| 6 | Eli T. Stackhouse (D) | 9,022 | 78.8 |
| | Edmund H. Deas (R) | 2,352 | 20.5 |
| 7 | William Elliott (D) | 3,792 | 44.4 |
| | Thomas E. Miller (R) | 3,315 | 38.8 |
| | E. W. Brayton (IR) | 1,410 | 16.5 |

## SOUTH DAKOTA

| | | | |
|---|---|---|---|
| AL | John A. Pickler (R) | 34,856✔ | |
| | John R. Gamble (R) | 34,553✔ | |
| | F. A. Leavitt (I) | 24,907 | |

| Candidates | Votes | % |
|---|---|---|
| Fred Zipp (I) | 24,808 | |
| F. A. Clark (D) | 17,527 | |
| W. Y. Quigley (D) | 17,267 | |

## TENNESSEE

| | | | |
|---|---|---|---|
| 1 | Alfred A. Taylor (R) | 11,466 | 49.0 |
| | R. R. Butler (IR) | 10,717 | 45.8 |
| 2 | Leonidas C. Houk (R) | 12,765 | 60.1 |
| | J. C. J. Williams (D) | 7,378 | 34.8 |
| 3 | Henry C. Snodgrass (D) | 13,773 | 50.3 |
| | H. Clay Evans (R) | 13,250 | 48.4 |
| 4 | Benton McMillin (D) | 14,514 | 64.0 |
| | C. W. Garratt (R) | 7,630 | 33.7 |
| 5 | James D. Richardson (D) | 12,890 | 68.4 |
| | P. C. Smithson (R) | 4,340 | 23.0 |
| | H. R. Moore (P) | 1,474 | 7.8 |
| 6 | Joseph E. Washington (D) | 11,656 | 74.4 |
| | L. M. Watson (R) | 2,708 | 17.3 |
| | W. D. Turnley (P) | 1,302 | 8.3 |
| 7 | Nicholas N. Cox (D) | 10,362 | 60.7 |
| | A. M. Hughes Jr. (R) | 5,364 | 31.4 |
| | John Graham (P) | 1,289 | 7.6 |
| 8 | Benjamin A. Enloe (D) | 12,444 | 62.7 |
| | J. R. McKinney (R) | 4,469 | 22.5 |
| | George T. McCall (R) | 1,339 | 6.7 |
| | John T. Warren (P) | 1,070 | 5.4 |
| 9 | Rice A. Pierce (D) | 12,191 | 70.6 |
| | W. F. Poston (R) | 3,959 | 22.9 |
| | J. B. Cummings (P) | 1,109 | 6.4 |
| 10 | Josiah Patterson (D) | 9,108 | 74.5 |
| | L. B. Eaton (R) | 3,033 | 24.8 |

## TEXAS

| | | | |
|---|---|---|---|
| 1 | Charles Stewart (D) | 19,356 | 63.1 |
| | E.L. Angier (R) | 11,292 | 36.8 |
| 2 | John B. Long (D) | 12,973 | 99.6 |
| 3 | Constantine B. Kilgore (D) | 19,038 | 71.3 |
| | L. B. Fish (R) | 7,340 | 27.5 |
| 4 | David B. Culberson (D) | 17,290 | 74.8 |
| | J. C. Gibbons (R) | 5,279 | 22.8 |
| 5 | Joseph W. Bailey (D) | 26,791 | 81.9 |
| | A. W. Achison (R) | 4,252 | 13.0 |
| | W. R. Lamb (I) | 1,683 | 5.1 |
| 6 | Jo Abbott (D) | 29,982 | 85.7 |
| | Darter Isaac (R) | 4,430 | 12.7 |
| 7 | William H. Crain (D) | 18,550 | 67.2 |
| | J. V. Spohn (R) | 9,069 | 32.8 |
| 8 | Littleton W. Moore (D) | 20,739 | 71.2 |
| | William Greene (R) | 8,368 | 28.8 |
| 9 | Roger Q. Mills (D) | 21,847 | 79.6 |
| | D. W. Roberts (R) | 5,600 | 20.4 |
| 10 | Joseph D. Sayers (D) | 32,479 | 92.4 |
| | W. G. Robinson (R) | 2,537 | 7.2 |
| 11 | Samuel W. T. Lanham (D) | 38,348 | 97.8 |

## VERMONT

| | | | |
|---|---|---|---|
| 1 | H. Henry Powers (R) | 17,136 | 66.5 |
| | Thomas W. Moloney (D) | 8,605 | 33.4 |
| 2 | William W. Grout (R) | 18,092 | 66.8 |
| | Stephen C. Shurtleff (D) | 8,960 | 33.1 |

## VIRGINIA

| | | | |
|---|---|---|---|
| 1 | William A. Jones (D) | 14,613 | 54.3 |
| | I.H. Bayly Browne (R) | 12,150 | 45.2 |

| | Candidates | Votes | % |
|---|---|---|---|
| 2 | John W. Lawson (D) | 13,484 | 50.7 |
| | George E. Bowden (R) | 12,317 | 46.3 |
| 3 | George D. Wise (D) | 13,937 | 99.9 |
| 4 | James F. Epes (D) | 13,325 | 57.1 |
| | J. M. Langston (R) | 9,991 | 42.8 |
| 5 | Posey G. Lester (D) | 10,569 | 82.0 |
| | S. C. Adams (I) | 1,360 | 10.6 |
| | J. Ring (I) | 959 | 7.4 |
| 6 | Paul C. Edmunds (D) | 11,615 | 92.6 |
| | William J. Shelburne (P) | 901 | 7.2 |
| 7 | Charles T. O'Ferrall (D) | 10,167 | 89.0 |
| | I. M. Underwood (P) | 1,225 | 10.7 |
| 8 | William H. F. Lee (D) | 13,499 | 57.0 |
| | Frank Hume (ID) | 10,181 | 43.0 |
| 9 | John A. Buchanan (D) | 15,324 | 56.1 |
| | George T. Mills (R) | 11,977 | 43.9 |
| 10 | Henry St.George Tucker (D) | 9,721 | 94.6 |
| | A. J. Taylor (I) | 531 | 5.2 |

## WASHINGTON

| | | | |
|---|---|---|---|
| AL | John L. Wilson (R) | 29,133 | 56.0 |
| | Carroll (D) | 22,861 | 44.0 |

## WEST VIRGINIA

| | | | |
|---|---|---|---|
| 1 | John O. Pendleton (D) | 18,470 | 50.2 |
| | William P. Hubbard (R) | 17,831 | 48.5 |
| 2 | William L. Wilson (D) | 20,439 | 52.5 |
| | George Hourian (R) | 18,374 | 47.2 |
| 3 | John D. Alderson (D) | 20,433 | 56.1 |
| | Theophilus Gaines (R) | 15,778 | 43.3 |
| 4 | Jones Capehart (D) | 19,576 | 52.3 |
| | C.B. Smith (R) | 17,648 | 47.2 |

## WISCONSIN

| | | | |
|---|---|---|---|
| 1 | Clinton Babbitt (D) | 14,532 | 48.3 |
| | Cooper (R) | 14,209 | 47.3 |
| 2 | Charles Barwig (D) | 17,826 | 65.8 |
| | D. C. Van Brunt (R) | 9,266 | 34.2 |
| 3 | Allen R. Bushneil (D) | 16,432 | 49.2 |
| | Robert M. LaFollette (R) | 15,430 | 46.2 |
| 4 | John L. Mitchell (D) | 24,679 | 56.1 |
| | R.C. Spencer (R) | 17,605 | 40.0 |
| 5 | George H. Brickner (D) | 17,708 | 67.2 |
| | Blackstock (R) | 8,093 | 30.7 |
| 6 | Lucas M. Miller (D) | 15,573 | 51.7 |
| | Clark (R) | 13,409 | 44.5 |
| 7 | Frank P. Coburn (D) | 15,399 | 50.8 |
| | Thomas (R) | 13,397 | 44.2 |
| 8 | Nils P. Haugen (R) | 17,609 | 49.2 |
| | Bailey (D) | 15,261 | 42.7 |
| | Jones (P) | 2,911 | 8.1 |
| 9 | Thomas Lynch (D) | 24,491 | 54.4 |
| | Myron H. McCord (R) | 19,161 | 42.6 |

## WYOMING

(Became a state July 10, 1890)

| | | | |
|---|---|---|---|
| AL | Clarence D. Clark (R) | 9,087 | 58.2 |
| | George T. Beck (D) | 6,520 | 41.8 |

1. No candidate in the 2nd district received the majority of the vote required for election. (Majority vote requirement, p. 945.)

# 1891 House Elections

## MICHIGAN

### Special Election

| Candidates | Votes | % |
|---|---|---|
| 5 Charles E. Belknap (R) | 14,652 | 44.5 |
| John S. Lawrence (D) | 13,150 | 40.0 |
| Edward Hutchins (PP) | 3,687 | 11.2 |

## NEW YORK

### Special Elections

| | | |
|---|---|---|
| 2 Alfred C. Chapin (D) | 24,018 | 52.7 |
| Bristow (R) | 21,522 | 47.3 |
| 10 W. Bourke Cockran (TAM&NY D) | 13,234 | 63.5 |
| Townsend (R) | 7,160 | 34.4 |
| 12 Joseph J. Little (TAM&NY D) | 19,306 | 58.1 |
| McMichael (R) | 11,465 | 34.5 |
| 22 Newton M. Curtis (R) | 19,096 | 54.8 |
| Porter (D) | 14,423 | 41.4 |

## RHODE ISLAND [1]

### Special Election

| Candidates | Votes | % |
|---|---|---|
| 2 Charles H. Page (D) | 6,899 | 85.4 |
| Warren O. Arnold (R) | 721 | 8.9 |
| Tripp (P) | 461 | 5.7 |

## SOUTH DAKOTA

### Special Election

| | | |
|---|---|---|
| AL John L. Jolley (R) | 17,614 | 44.5 |
| Henry W. Smith (I) | 14,687 | 37.1 |
| James M. Wood (D) | 7,299 | 18.4 |

## TENNESSEE

### Special Election

| Candidates | Votes | % |
|---|---|---|
| 2 John C. Houk (R) | 14,095 | 63.7 |
| J. C. J. Williams (D) | 7,829 | 35.4 |

## VIRGINIA

### Special Election

| | | |
|---|---|---|
| 8 Elisha E. Meredith (R) | 8,891 | 67.8 |
| John Ambler Brooks | 4,218 | 32.2 |

1. *Since no candidate running for the House in Rhode Island's 2nd District in 1890 received the majority needed for election (see Rhode Island 1890, p. 1063), a special election in 1891 was ordered by the legislature. According to the Biographical Directory, incumbent Warren O. Arnold, who had run for re-election in 1890, but failed to win a majority, refused to participate actively in the special election. Without serious opposition, Charles H. Page won easily.*

# 1892 House Elections

## ALABAMA

| | Candidates | Votes | % |
|---|---|---|---|
| 1 | Richard H. Clarke (D) | 12,514 | 60.5 |
| | William Mason (K POP) | 7,156 | 34.6 |
| 2 | Jesse F. Stallings (D) | 16,781 | 58.6 |
| | Frank Baltzell (K POP) | 10,331 | 36.1 |
| | John D. Bibb (R) | 1,506 | 5.3 |
| 3 | William Oates (D) | 16,885 | 62.4 |
| | J. F. Tate (K POP) | 9,931 | 36.7 |
| 4 | Gaston A. Robbins (D) | 16,159 | 60.7 |
| | Adolphus P. Longshore (K POP) | 8,534 | 32.1 |
| | George H. Craig (R) | 1,848 | 6.9 |
| 5 | James E. Cobb (D) | 13,456 | 49.4 |
| | M. W. Whatley (K POP) | 11,468 | 42.1 |
| | John McDuffie (R) | 2,306 | 8.5 |
| 6 | John Bankhead (D) | 14,342 | 62.8 |
| | T. M. Barbour (K POP) | 6,453 | 28.2 |
| | Ignatius Green (R) | 2,054 | 9.0 |
| 7 | William H. Denson (D) | 10,911 | 54.3 |
| | William Wood (K POP) | 9,091 | 45.2 |
| 8 | Joseph Wheeler (D) | 15,607 | 52.4 |
| | R. W. Austin (POP) | 11,868 | 39.9 |
| | R. T. Blackwell (R) | 2,279 | 7.7 |
| 9 | L. W. Turpin (D) | 19,848 | 67.4 |
| | Joseph H. Parsons (POP) | 8,954 | 30.4 |

## ARKANSAS

| | | | |
|---|---|---|---|
| 1 | Philip D. McCulloch Jr. (D) | 16,680 | 63.6 |
| | Jacob Trieber (R) | 9,541 | 36.4 |
| 2 | Clifton R. Breckinridge (D) | 16,508 | 70.8 |
| | W. B. W. Heartsill (PP) | 6,808 | 29.2 |
| 3 | Thomas C. McRae (D) | 17,493 | 68.1 |
| | J. O. A. Bush (PP) | 8,197 | 31.9 |
| 4 | William L. Terry (D) | 13,630 | 69.7 |
| | T. M. C. Birmingham (PP) | 5,910 | 30.2 |
| 5 | Hugh A. Dinsmore (D) | 13,698 | 57.2 |
| | J. E. Bryan (PP) | 10,267 | 42.8 |
| 6 | Robert Neill (D) | 16,594 | 87.6 |
| | George Martin (I) | 1,926 | 10.2 |

## CALIFORNIA

| | | | |
|---|---|---|---|
| 1 | Thomas J. Geary (D) | 19,308 | 56.8 |
| | Edw. W. Davis (R) | 13,123 | 38.6 |
| 2 | Anthony Caminetti (D) | 20,741 | 53.2 |
| | John F. Davis (R) | 16,781 | 43.1 |
| 3 | Samuel G. Hilborn (R) | 13,163‡ | 43.2 |
| | Warren B. English (D) | 13,138 | 43.1 |
| | J. L. Lyon (PP) | 3,495 | 11.5 |
| 4 | James G. Maguire (D) | 14,997 | 49.2 |
| | C. O. Alexander (R) | 13,226 | 43.4 |
| | E. P. Burman (PP) | 1,980 | 6.5 |
| 5 | Eugene F. Loud (R) | 14,660 | 46.4 |
| | J. W. Ryland (D) | 13,694 | 43.3 |
| | J. J. Morrison (PP) | 2,484 | 7.9 |
| 6 | Marion Cannon (D, PP) | 20,680 | 56.3 |
| | Hervey Lindley (R) | 14,271 | 38.8 |
| 7 | William W. Bowers (R) | 15,856 | 41.6 |
| | Olin Welborn (D) | 14,869 | 39.0 |
| | Hiram Hamilton (PP) | 5,578 | 14.6 |

### Special Election

| | | | |
|---|---|---|---|
| 3 | Samuel G. Hilborn (R) | 16,911 | 47.3 |
| | Warren B. English (D) | 14,493 | 40.5 |
| | J. L. Lyon (PP) | 4,326 | 12.1 |

## COLORADO

| | | | |
|---|---|---|---|
| 1 | Lafayette Pence (D & POP) | 20,004 | 49.1 |
| | Earl B. Coe (R) | 17,609 | 43.2 |
| | John G. Taylor (D) | 2,240 | 5.5 |
| 2 | John C. Bell (D & POP) | 31,587 | 61.0 |
| | Henderson H. Eddy (R) | 19,572 | 37.8 |

## CONNECTICUT

| | Candidates | Votes | % |
|---|---|---|---|
| 1 | Lewis Sperry (D) | 19,068 | 49.0 |
| | Henry (R) | 18,506 | 47.5 |
| 2 | James P. Pigott (D) | 27,624 | 50.9 |
| | Kellogg (R) | 24,772 | 45.7 |
| 3 | Charles A. Russell (R) | 11,928 | 49.5 |
| | Thayer (D) | 11,277 | 46.8 |
| 4 | Robert E. DeForest (D) | 24,035 | 51.3 |
| | Frederick Miles (R) | 21,825 | 46.6 |

## DELAWARE

| | | | |
|---|---|---|---|
| AL | John W. Causey (D) | 18,554 | 49.9 |
| | Jonathan S. Willis (R) | 18,080 | 48.6 |

## FLORIDA

| | | | |
|---|---|---|---|
| 1 | Stephen R. Mallory (PP & D) | 16,114 | 99.2 |
| 2 | Charles M. Cooper (D) | 14,668 | 75.8 |
| | Austin S. Mann (PP) | 4,636 | 24.0 |

## GEORGIA

| | | | |
|---|---|---|---|
| 1 | Rufus E. Lester (D) | 12,337 | 62.6 |
| | Louis M. Pleasant (R) | 4,414 | 22.4 |
| | W. R. Kemp (PP) | 2,944 | 15.0 |
| 2 | Benjamin E. Russell (D) | 11,517 | 65.2 |
| | I. H. Hand (PP) | 6,060 | 34.3 |
| 3 | Charles F. Crisp (D) | 11,574 | 69.9 |
| | F. D. Wimberly (PP & R) | 4,982 | 30.1 |
| 4 | Charles L. Moses (D) | 12,779 | 64.1 |
| | J. H. Turner (PP & R) | 7,145 | 35.9 |
| 5 | Leonidas F. Livingston (D) | 9,732 | 60.2 |
| | Samuel Small (PP & R) | 6,447 | 39.9 |
| 6 | Thomas B. Cabaniss (D) | 11,628 | 64.6 |
| | C. F. Turner (PP & R) | 6,387 | 35.5 |
| 7 | John W. Maddox (D) | 13,572 | 65.9 |
| | John A. Sibley (PP & R) | 7,037 | 34.2 |
| 8 | Thomas G. Lawson (D) | 11,133 | 66.7 |
| | James B. Robins (PP & R) | 5,550 | 33.3 |
| 9 | Farish C. Tate (D) | 13,952 | 59.5 |
| | Thaddeus K. Pickett (PP & R) | 9,481 | 40.5 |
| 10 | James C. C. Black (D) | 17,772 | 59.0 |
| | Thomas E. Watson (PP & R) | 12,330 | 41.0 |
| 11 | Henry G. Turner (D) | 11,091 | 65.3 |
| | Lucius C. Mattox (PP & R) | 5,882 | 34.7 |

## IDAHO

| | | | |
|---|---|---|---|
| AL | Willis Sweet (R) | 8,549 | 44.1 |
| | Edward B. True (D) | 6,029 | 31.1 |
| | James Gunn (PP) | 4,567 | 23.6 |

## ILLINOIS

| | | | |
|---|---|---|---|
| 1 | J. Frank Aldrich (R) | 39,726 | 49.7 |
| | Edwin B. Smith (D) | 37,904 | 47.4 |
| 2 | Lawrence E. McGann (D) | 32,609 | 68.9 |
| | Edward D. Connor (R) | 14,168 | 29.9 |
| 3 | Allan C. Durborow Jr. (D) | 38,652 | 57.4 |
| | Thomas C. Macmillan (R) | 27,392 | 40.7 |
| 4 | Julius Goldzier (D) | 34,454 | 52.2 |
| | William Vocke (R) | 29,851 | 45.2 |
| 5 | Albert J. Hopkins (R) | 19,864 | 58.1 |
| | Samuel Alschuler (D) | 12,486 | 36.5 |
| | Henry Wood (P) | 1,861 | 5.4 |
| 6 | Robert R. Hitt (R) | 18,307 | 54.9 |
| | Henry D. Dennis (D) | 12,794 | 38.4 |
| 7 | Thomas J. Henderson (R) | 15,849 | 52.1 |
| | James E. McPherran (D) | 11,350 | 37.3 |
| | Horace M. Gilbert (PP) | 1,965 | 6.5 |
| 8 | Robert A. Childs (R) | 20,852 | 48.2 |
| | Lewis Steward (D) | 20,835 | 48.2 |

| | Candidates | Votes | % |
|---|---|---|---|
| 9 | Hamilton K. Wheeler (R) | 16,921 | 48.2 |
| | Herman W. Snow (D) | 16,403 | 46.7 |
| 10 | Philip Sidney Post (R) | 19,215 | 49.7 |
| | James W. Hunter (D) | 17,246 | 44.6 |
| 11 | Benjamin F. Marsh (R) | 19,652 | 48.0 |
| | Truman Plantz (D) | 18,594 | 45.4 |
| 12 | John J. McDannold (D) | 22,207 | 53.1 |
| | T. M. Rogers (R) | 15,940 | 38.1 |
| | William Hess (PP) | 2,489 | 6.0 |
| 13 | William M. Springer (D) | 22,954 | 52.1 |
| | Charles P. Kane (R) | 18,238 | 41.4 |
| 14 | Benjamin F. Funk (R) | 18,578 | 48.0 |
| | Owen Scott (D) | 18,264 | 47.2 |
| 15 | Joseph G. Cannon (R) | 20,596 | 49.6 |
| | Samuel T. Busey (D) | 19,098 | 46.0 |
| 16 | George W. Fithian (D) | 17,320 | 46.0 |
| | J. O. Burton (R) | 16,540 | 43.9 |
| | Thomas Ratcliff (PP) | 2,794 | 7.4 |
| 17 | Edward Lane (D) | 19,107 | 51.9 |
| | John N. Gwin (R) | 13,710 | 37.2 |
| | Presley G. Donaldson (PP) | 2,554 | 6.9 |
| 18 | William S. Forman (D) | 17,696 | 49.2 |
| | W. A. Northcott (R) | 16,552 | 46.0 |
| 19 | James R. Williams (D) | 18,411 | 49.8 |
| | Norman H. Moss (R) | 14,972 | 40.5 |
| | Joseph H. Crasno (PP) | 2,599 | 7.0 |
| 20 | George W. Smith (R) | 19,944 | 51.7 |
| | Benjamin W. Pope (D) | 17,446 | 45.2 |
| AL | John C. Black (D) | 425,336✔ | |
| | Andrew J. Hunter (D) | 423,868✔ | |
| | Richard Yates (R) | 399,321 | |
| | George S. Willits (R) | 399,096 | |
| | Frances E. Andrews (P) | 25,596 | |
| | James S. Felter (P) | 25,428 | |
| | Jesse Harper (PP) | 21,707 | |
| | Michael McDonough (PP) | 21,541 | |

## INDIANA

| | | | |
|---|---|---|---|
| 1 | Arthur H. Taylor (D) | 19,720 | 47.4 |
| | A. P. Twineham (R) | 19,266 | 46.3 |
| | Moses Smith (PP) | 2,110 | 5.1 |
| 2 | John L. Bretz (D) | 17,700 | 47.9 |
| | Ben L. Willoughby (R) | 15,731 | 42.6 |
| | Merrick W. Ackerty (PP) | 3,010 | 8.2 |
| 3 | Jason B. Brown (D) | 20,928 | 51.6 |
| | William W. Borden (R) | 17,957 | 44.3 |
| 4 | William S. Holman (D) | 19,008 | 52.5 |
| | Samuel M. Jones (R) | 15,927 | 44.0 |
| 5 | George W. Cooper (D) | 17,698 | 48.3 |
| | John Worrell (R) | 16,640 | 45.4 |
| 6 | Henry U. Johnson (R) | 20,444 | 56.7 |
| | Luther M. Mering (D) | 11,820 | 32.8 |
| | Nathan T. Butts (PP) | 2,581 | 7.2 |
| 7 | William D. Bynum (D) | 28,267 | 49.5 |
| | Charles L. Henry (R) | 26,951 | 47.2 |
| 8 | Elijah V. Brookshire (D) | 22,949 | 48.4 |
| | Winfield S. Carpenter (R) | 21,327 | 45.0 |
| 9 | Daniel Waugh (R) | 23,416 | 50.1 |
| | Eli W. Brown (D) | 19,291 | 41.3 |
| | George W. Swan (PP) | 2,517 | 5.4 |
| 10 | Thomas Hammond (D) | 18,298 | 46.1 |
| | William Johnston (R) | 18,256 | 46.0 |
| 11 | Augustus N. Martin (D) | 21,893 | 45.9 |
| | William T. Daley (R) | 21,060 | 44.1 |
| | Joshua Strange (PP) | 3,026 | 6.3 |
| 12 | William F. McNagny (D) | 19,991 | 50.0 |
| | Adolph J. You (R) | 16,926 | 42.3 |
| | Calvin Husselman (PP) | 2,027 | 5.1 |
| 13 | Charles G. Conn (D) | 21,627 | 50.4 |
| | James S. Dodge (R) | 19,687 | 45.9 |

## IOWA

| | | | |
|---|---|---|---|
| 1 | John H. Gear (R) | 18,416 | 49.4 |
| | John J. Surley (D) | 17,787 | 47.7 |

## IOWA

| | Candidates | Votes | % |
|---|---|---|---|
| 2 | Walter I. Hayes (D) | 23,129 | 58.9 |
| | John H. Munroe (R) | 15,357 | 39.1 |
| 3 | David B. Henderson (R) | 22,045 | 51.3 |
| | James H. Shields (D) | 20,586 | 47.9 |
| 4 | Thomas Updegraff (R) | 19,681 | 51.5 |
| | W. H. Butler (D) | 18,091 | 47.4 |
| 5 | Roberts G. Cousins (R) | 20,033 | 49.9 |
| | John T. Hamilton (D) | 18,935 | 47.2 |
| 6 | John F. Lacey (R) | 17,747 | 47.1 |
| | F. E. White (D) | 16,572 | 44.0 |
| | E. S. Owens (PP) | 2,889 | 7.7 |
| 7 | John A. T. Hull (R) | 19,963 | 54.0 |
| | Joseph A. Dyer (D) | 13,883 | 37.5 |
| | Ed A. Ott (PP) | 2,562 | 6.9 |
| 8 | William P. Hepburn (R) | 20,299 | 49.8 |
| | Thomas L. Maxwell (D) | 15,968 | 39.2 |
| | Walter S. Scott (PP) | 3,687 | 9.0 |
| 9 | Alva L. Hager (R) | 20,287 | 49.3 |
| | John E. F. McGee (D) | 17,809 | 43.3 |
| | F. W. Myers (PP) | 2,610 | 6.4 |
| 10 | Jonathan P. Dolliver (R) | 23,402 | 53.7 |
| | J. J. Ryan (D) | 18,458 | 42.4 |
| 11 | George D. Perkins (R) | 21,984 | 50.6 |
| | Daniel Campbell (D-PP) | 20,707 | 47.6 |

## KANSAS

| | Candidates | Votes | % |
|---|---|---|---|
| 1 | Case Broderick (R) | 19,401 | 54.5 |
| | Fred J. Close (PP) | 15,782 | 44.3 |
| 2 | Edward H. Funston (R) | 22,900‡ | 49.4 |
| | Horace L. Moore (D-PP) | 22,817 | 49.2 |
| 3 | Thomas J. Hudson (D-PP) | 23,998 | 52.2 |
| | L. U. Humphrey (R) | 21,594 | 47.0 |
| 4 | Charles Curtis (R) | 25,327 | 52.0 |
| | E. V. Wharton (D-PP) | 22,603 | 46.4 |
| 5 | John Davis (PP) | 20,162 | 50.3 |
| | Joseph R. Burton (R) | 18,842 | 47.0 |
| 6 | William Baker (PP) | 19,398 | 49.9 |
| | H. L. Pestana (R) | 17,887 | 46.0 |
| 7 | Jeremiah Simpson (D-PP) | 33,812 | 50.8 |
| | Chester I. Long (R) | 32,053 | 48.2 |
| AL | William A. Harris (PP & D) | 164,624 | 50.7 |
| | George T. Anthony (R) | 155,791 | 48.0 |

## KENTUCKY

| | Candidates | Votes | % |
|---|---|---|---|
| 1 | William J. Stone (D) | 15,295 | 53.0 |
| | W. J. Deboe (R) | 8,438 | 29.2 |
| | B. C. Key (POP) | 4,686 | 16.2 |
| 2 | William T. Ellis (D) | 15,053 | 47.4 |
| | J. T. Kimbly (R) | 9,781 | 30.8 |
| | Thomas S. Pettit (POP) | 6,903 | 21.8 |
| 3 | Isaac H. Goodnight (D) | 14,986 | 47.2 |
| | W. G. Hunter (R) | 14,056 | 44.2 |
| | C. W. Biggers (POP) | 2,742 | 8.6 |
| 4 | Alexander B. Montgomery (D) | 16,043 | 48.1 |
| | C. M. Barnett (R) | 11,385 | 34.1 |
| | M. R. Gardner (POP) | 5,954 | 17.8 |
| 5 | Asher G. Caruth (D) | 20,445 | 58.7 |
| | Augustus E. Willson (R) | 13,767 | 39.6 |
| 6 | Albert S. Berry (D) | 18,564 | 60.7 |
| | Weden O'Neal (R) | 10,731 | 35.1 |
| 7 | William C. P. Breckinridge (D) | 16,588 | 62.0 |
| | T. J. Hardin (R) | 9,433 | 35.3 |
| 8 | James B. McCreary (D) | 14,092 | 100.0 |
| 9 | Thomas H. Paynter (D) | 18,295 | 53.3 |
| | John P. McCartney (R) | 15,339 | 44.7 |
| 10 | Marcus C. Lisle (D) | 14,515 | 54.9 |
| | Charles W. Russell (R) | 11,943 | 45.1 |
| 11 | Silas R. Adams (R) | 17,087 | 59.5 |
| | James R. Hindman (D) | 10,483 | 36.5 |

### Special Election

| | | Votes | % |
|---|---|---|---|
| 10 | Joseph M. Kendall (D) | 5,846 | 91.2 |
| | C. F. Ward | 544 | 8.5 |

## LOUISIANA

| | Candidates | Votes | % |
|---|---|---|---|
| 1 | Adolph Meyer (D) | 10,878 | 69.2 |
| | James Wilkinson (ID) | 4,787 | 30.5 |
| 2 | Robert C. Davey (D) | 12,588 | 67.4 |
| | Morris Marks (POP & R) | 6,102 | 32.7 |
| 3 | Andrew Price (D) | 14,033 | 81.8 |
| | I. J. Willis (POP & R) | 3,123 | 18.2 |
| 4 | Newton C. Blanchard (D) | 16,432 | 76.1 |
| | T. J. Guice (POP & R) | 5,167 | 23.9 |
| 5 | Charles J. Boatner (D) | 19,371 | 72.3 |
| | R. P. Welch (POP & R) | 4,301 | 16.0 |
| | A. A. Gundy (ID) | 3,119 | 11.6 |
| 6 | Samuel M. Robertson (D) | 11,758 | 85.2 |
| | J. Kleinpeter (POP & R) | 2,043 | 14.8 |

## MAINE

| | | Votes | % |
|---|---|---|---|
| 1 | Thomas B. Reed (R) | 16,312 | 51.5 |
| | D. H. Ingraham (D) | 14,635 | 46.2 |
| 2 | Nelson Dingley Jr. (R) | 17,194 | 52.4 |
| | D. J. McGillicuddy (D) | 13,546 | 41.3 |
| 3 | Seth L. Milliken (R) | 15,582 | 50.3 |
| | W. P. Thompson (D) | 13,700 | 44.2 |
| 4 | Charles A. Boutelle (R) | 16,549 | 51.3 |
| | D. A. H. Powers (D) | 12,261 | 38.0 |
| | S. D. Leavitt (ID) | 1,616 | 5.0 |

## MARYLAND

| | | Votes | % |
|---|---|---|---|
| 1 | Robert F. Brattan (D) | 15,608 | 49.7 |
| | George M. Russum (R) | 13,714 | 43.6 |
| | D. Miles (P) | 1,778 | 5.7 |
| 2 | J. Fred C. Talbott (D) | 22,772 | 54.0 |
| | George Baker (R) | 17,926 | 42.5 |
| 3 | Harry Wells Rusk (D) | 19,806 | 58.4 |
| | Charles Herzog (R) | 13,679 | 40.3 |
| 4 | Isidor Rayner (D) | 21,455 | 58.4 |
| | Alburtus Spates (R) | 14,646 | 39.8 |
| 5 | Barnes Compton (D) | 15,391 | 52.3 |
| | Thomas Parrau (R) | 13,505 | 45.9 |
| 6 | William M. McKaig (D) | 18,899 | 49.8 |
| | George Willington (R) | 18,292 | 48.2 |

### Special Election

| | | Votes | % |
|---|---|---|---|
| 1 | John Brown (D) | 15,502 | 52.3 |
| | George M. Russum (R) | 13,787 | 46.5 |

## MASSACHUSETTS

| | | Votes | % |
|---|---|---|---|
| 1 | Ashley B. Wright (R) | 14,198 | 48.8 |
| | John C. Crosby (D) | 13,995 | 48.1 |
| 2 | Frederick H. Gillett (R) | 15,131 | 52.4 |
| | Edward Howard (D) | 12,718 | 44.1 |
| 3 | Joseph H. Walker (R) | 14,139 | 50.1 |
| | John R. Thayer (D) | 13,262 | 47.0 |
| 4 | Lewis D. Apsley (R) | 16,209 | 53.7 |
| | Frederic S. Coolidge (D) | 13,058 | 43.3 |
| 5 | Moses T. Stevens (D) | 14,423 | 52.3 |
| | William S. Knox (R) | 12,645 | 45.8 |
| 6 | William Cogswell (R) | 16,385 | 58.4 |
| | Henry B. Little (D) | 10,228 | 36.5 |
| 7 | Henry Cabot Lodge (R) | 17,002* | 52.7 |
| | William Everett (D) | 14,391 | 44.6 |
| 8 | Samuel W. McCall (R) | 15,671 | 51.6 |
| | John F. Andrew (D) | 14,679 | 48.4 |
| 9 | Joseph H. O'Neil (D) | 14,354 | 61.1 |
| | Benjamin C. Lane (R) | 8,622 | 36.7 |
| 10 | Michael J. McEttrick (D & CIT) | 9,507 | 33.4 |
| | Harrison H. Atwood (R) | 8,822 | 31.0 |
| | William S. McNary (D) | 7,591 | 26.7 |
| | Richard C. Humphreys (I) | 2,235 | 7.9 |
| 11 | William F. Draper (R) | 16,961 | 53.1 |
| | George Fred Williams (D) | 14,404 | 45.1 |
| 12 | Elijah A. Morse (R) | 17,316 | 56.0 |
| | Elbridge Cushman (D) | 12,673 | 41.0 |
| 13 | Charles S. Randall (R) | 13,945 | 60.7 |
| | Henry C. Thacher (D) | 9,006 | 39.2 |

## MICHIGAN

| | Candidates | Votes | % |
|---|---|---|---|
| 1 | John Logan Chipman (D) | 20,239 | 52.4 |
| | Frank J. Hecker (R) | 17,533 | 45.4 |
| 2 | James S. Gorman (D) | 22,007 | 47.0 |
| | James O'Donnell (R) | 21,443 | 45.8 |
| 3 | Julius C. Burrows (R) | 21,287 | 50.1 |
| | Daniel Strange (D) | 15,802 | 37.2 |
| | Leroy E. Lockwood (POP) | 2,898 | 6.8 |
| | Paul T. Butler (P) | 2,510 | 5.9 |
| 4 | Henry F. Thomas (R) | 21,352 | 49.1 |
| | George L. Yaple (D & POP) | 20,246 | 46.5 |
| 5 | Charles E. Belknap (R) | 20,139 | 47.8 |
| | George F. Richardson (D & POP) | 20,120✔ | 47.8 |
| 6 | David D. Aitken (R) | 21,046 | 46.5 |
| | Byron G. Stout (D) | 19,669 | 43.5 |
| | Arthur E. Cole (POP) | 2,289 | 5.1 |
| 7 | Justin R. Whiting (D) | 16,125 | 46.3 |
| | Philip L. Wixson (R) | 15,602 | 44.8 |
| | Alfred Pagett (POP) | 1,837 | 5.3 |
| 8 | William S. Linton (R) | 17,411 | 49.2 |
| | Henry M. Youmins (D & POP) | 15,886 | 44.9 |
| 9 | John W. Moon (R) | 13,969 | 47.0 |
| | Harrison H. Wheeler (D) | 13,053 | 43.9 |
| | Charles A. Sessions (P) | 1,673 | 5.6 |
| 10 | Thomas A. E. Weadock (D) | 14,858 | 47.7 |
| | James Van Kleeck (R) | 14,599 | 46.8 |
| 11 | John Avery (R) | 18,359 | 50.6 |
| | Woodbridge N. Ferris (D & POP) | 16,038 | 44.2 |
| | George R. Catton (P) | 1,886 | 5.2 |
| 12 | Samuel M. Stephenson (R) | 20,097 | 50.7 |
| | J. Maurice Finn (D & POP) | 16,674 | 42.1 |

## MINNESOTA

| | | Votes | % |
|---|---|---|---|
| 1 | James A. Tawney (R) | 18,146 | 49.0 |
| | William H. Harries (D) | 14,995 | 40.5 |
| | James I. Vermilya (PP) | 2,342 | 6.3 |
| 2 | James T. McCleary (R) | 18,207 | 48.4 |
| | Winfield S. Hammond (D) | 11,298 | 30.0 |
| | S. C. Long (PP) | 6,268 | 16.7 |
| 3 | Osee M. Hall (D) | 15,890 | 44.8 |
| | Joel P. Heatwole (R) | 14,727 | 41.5 |
| | Ferdinand Borchert (PP) | 3,464 | 9.8 |
| 4 | Andrew R. Kiefer (R) | 16,624 | 48.6 |
| | James N. Castle (D) | 13,435 | 39.2 |
| | James G. Dougherty (PP) | 2,213 | 6.5 |
| | David Morgan (P) | 1,963 | 5.7 |
| 5 | Loren Fletcher (R) | 18,463 | 46.1 |
| | James W. Lawrence (D) | 15,960 | 39.9 |
| | Thomas H. Lucas (PP) | 3,151 | 7.9 |
| | J. T. Caton (P) | 2,458 | 6.1 |
| 6 | Melvin R. Baldwin (D) | 17,317 | 43.4 |
| | Dolson B. Searle (R) | 16,941 | 42.4 |
| | A. C. Parsons (PP) | 3,973 | 10.0 |
| 7 | Haldor E. Boen (PP) | 12,614 | 35.6 |
| | Henry Feig (R) | 12,529 | 35.4 |
| | W. F. Kelso (D) | 7,526 | 21.3 |
| | L. F. Hampson (P) | 2,731 | 7.7 |

## MISSISSIPPI

| | | Votes | % |
|---|---|---|---|
| 1 | John M. Allen (D) | 5,605 | 79.8 |
| | James Burkitt (PP) | 1,272 | 18.1 |
| 2 | John C. Kyle (D) | 6,113 | 77.8 |
| | J. H. Simpson (PP) | 1,740 | 22.2 |
| 3 | Thomas C. Catchings (D) | 2,750 | 93.4 |
| | George W. Gayles (R) | 194 | 6.6 |
| 4 | Hernando D. Money (D) | 6,223 | 61.4 |
| | Frank Burkitt (PP) | 3,905 | 38.6 |
| 5 | John S. Williams (D) | 7,541 | 71.4 |
| | W. P. Ratliff (PP) | 3,028 | 28.7 |
| 6 | Thomas R. Stockdale (D) | 4,984 | 82.5 |
| | T. N. Jackson (PP) | 1,054 | 17.5 |
| 7 | Charles E. Hooker (D) | 4,984 | 72.4 |
| | S. W. Robinson (PP) | 1,695 | 24.6 |

## MISSOURI

| | Candidates | Votes | % |
|---|---|---|---|
| 1 | William H. Hatch (D) | 19,263 | 50.0 |
| | Cramer (R) | 15,919 | 41.3 |
| | Bronson (PP) | 3,316 | 8.6 |
| 2 | Uriel S. Hall (D) | 21,928 | 53.7 |
| | Burkholder (R) | 16,626 | 40.7 |
| | Jackson (PP) | 2,317 | 5.7 |
| 3 | Alexander M. Dockery (D) | 18,749 | 48.8 |
| | Birch (R) | 15,288 | 39.8 |
| | Reece (PP) | 4,365 | 11.4 |
| 4 | Daniel D. Burnes (D) | 15,859 | 46.7 |
| | Crowther (R) | 14,600 | 43.0 |
| | Wilcox (PP) | 3,221 | 9.5 |
| 5 | John C. Tarsney (D) | 19,407 | 55.0 |
| | Davis (R) | 14,240 | 40.4 |
| 6 | David A. De Armond (D) | 16,545 | 46.3 |
| | Cundiff (R) | 13,151 | 36.8 |
| | Donnohue (PP) | 5,587 | 15.6 |
| 7 | John T. Heard (D) | 21,549 | 48.7 |
| | Hastain (R) | 17,843 | 40.3 |
| | Pinkham (PP) | 4,847 | 11.0 |
| 8 | Richard P. Bland (D) | 18,927 | 53.3 |
| | Murphy (R) | 16,453 | 46.4 |
| 9 | James Beauchamp Clark (D) | 17,536 | 53.0 |
| | Morsey (R) | 14,944 | 45.2 |
| 10 | Richard Bartholdt (R) | 15,628 | 54.6 |
| | Kehr (D) | 12,465 | 43.5 |
| 11 | Charles F. Joy (R) | 14,969‡ | 49.5 |
| | John J. O'Neill (D) | 14,902 | 49.3 |
| 12 | Seth W. Cobb (D) | 12,813 | 52.0 |
| | Rodgers (R) | 11,481 | 46.6 |
| 13 | Robert W. Fyan (D) | 19,993 | 57.1 |
| | Whitledge (R) | 15,006 | 42.8 |
| 14 | Marshall Arnold (D) | 19,440 | 49.8 |
| | Clarke (R) | 15,737 | 40.3 |
| | Taber (PP) | 3,864 | 9.9 |
| 15 | Charles H. Morgan (D) | 17,489 | 44.2 |
| | Purdy (R) | 15,767 | 39.8 |
| | Withers (PP) | 5,815 | 14.7 |

## MONTANA

| | Candidates | Votes | % |
|---|---|---|---|
| AL | Charles S. Hartman (R) | 17,934 | 41.4 |
| | William W. Dixon (D) | 17,762 | 41.0 |
| | Caldwell Edwards (PP) | 7,027 | 16.2 |

## NEBRASKA

| | Candidates | Votes | % |
|---|---|---|---|
| 1 | William Jennings Bryan (D) | 13,784 | 44.9 |
| | Allen W. Field (R) | 13,644 | 44.4 |
| | Jerome Shamp (POP) | 2,409 | 7.9 |
| 2 | David H. Mercer (R) | 11,488 | 45.3 |
| | George W. Doane (D) | 10,388 | 40.9 |
| | Robert L. Wheeler (POP) | 3,152 | 12.4 |
| 3 | George Meiklejohn (R) | 13,635 | 39.2 |
| | George F. Keiper (D) | 10,630 | 30.6 |
| | W. A. Poynter (POP) | 9,636 | 27.7 |
| 4 | Eugene J. Hainer (R) | 15,648 | 41.8 |
| | William H. Dech (POP) | 11,486 | 30.7 |
| | Victor Vifquain (D) | 8,988 | 24.0 |
| 5 | William A. McKeighan (D & POP) | 17,490 | 53.7 |
| | W. E. Andrews (R) | 14,230 | 43.7 |
| 6 | Omer M. Kem (POP) | 16,328 | 46.1 |
| | James Whitehead (R) | 14,197 | 40.1 |
| | A. T. Gatewood (D) | 4,202 | 11.9 |

## NEVADA

| | Candidates | Votes | % |
|---|---|---|---|
| AL | Francis G. Newlands (POP SIL) | 7,171 | 72.5 |
| | William Woodburn (R) | 2,295 | 23.2 |

## NEW HAMPSHIRE

| | Candidates | Votes | % |
|---|---|---|---|
| 1 | Henry W. Blair (R) | 21,031 | 49.9 |
| | Charles F. Stone (D) | 20,412 | 48.4 |

| | Candidates | Votes | % |
|---|---|---|---|
| 2 | Henry M. Baker (R) | 21,425 | 49.3 |
| | Hosea W. Parker (D) | 20,996 | 48.3 |

## NEW JERSEY

| | Candidates | Votes | % |
|---|---|---|---|
| 1 | Henry C. Loudenslager (R) | 25,099 | 50.7 |
| | Porch (D) | 22,511 | 45.4 |
| 2 | John J. Gardner (R) | 22,716 | 50.7 |
| | Wetherill (D) | 20,592 | 45.9 |
| 3 | Jacob A. Geissenhainer (D) | 20,407 | 53.0 |
| | Hoffman (R) | 17,080 | 44.4 |
| 4 | Johnston Cornish (D) | 21,765 | 48.0 |
| | Howey (R) | 20,726 | 45.7 |
| | Johnston (P) | 2,307 | 5.1 |
| 5 | Cornelius A. Cadmus (D) | 20,693 | 50.7 |
| | Doherty (R) | 19,231 | 47.1 |
| 6 | Thomas D. English (D) | 21,651 | 51.0 |
| | Richard W. Parker (R) | 20,284 | 47.8 |
| 7 | George B. Fielder (D) | 22,416 | 49.9 |
| | Cole (R) | 19,585 | 43.6 |
| | Edward F. McDonald (D) | 2,368 | 5.3 |
| 8 | John T. Dunn (D) | 14,393 | 50.4 |
| | Chamberlin (R) | 13,470 | 47.1 |

## NEW YORK

| | Candidates | Votes | % |
|---|---|---|---|
| 1 | James W. Covert (D) | 21,550 | 52.1 |
| | John Lewis Childs (R) | 18,749 | 45.3 |
| 2 | John M. Clancy (D) | 20,697 | 59.1 |
| | William H. Grace (R) | 13,593 | 38.8 |
| 3 | Joseph C. Hendrix (D) | 21,607 | 55.9 |
| | Michael J. Dady (R) | 15,907 | 41.1 |
| 4 | William J. Coombs (D) | 22,818 | 58.5 |
| | Charles B. Hobbs (R) | 14,885 | 38.1 |
| 5 | John H. Graham (D) | 16,675 | 50.8 |
| | Charles G. Bennett (R) | 14,488 | 44.2 |
| 6 | Thomas F. Magner (D) | 17,151 | 56.1 |
| | John Greaney (R) | 12,131 | 39.7 |
| 7 | Franklin Bartlett (D) | 14,905 | 66.3 |
| | Samuel A. Brown (R) | 7,122 | 31.7 |
| 8 | Edward J. Dunphy (D) | 15,287 | 66.3 |
| | Austin E. Ford (R) | 7,132 | 30.9 |
| 9 | Timothy J. Campbell (D) | 16,897 | 66.2 |
| | John Phelan (R) | 7,175 | 28.1 |
| 10 | Daniel E. Sickles (D) | 18,452 | 58.0 |
| | Charles E. Coon (R) | 12,224 | 38.5 |
| 11 | Amos J. Cummings (D) | 16,780 | 63.0 |
| | Abraham H. Sarasohn (R) | 8,355 | 31.4 |
| 12 | William Bourke Cockran (D) | 16,575 | 65.6 |
| | Daniel Butterfield (D) | 7,766 | 30.7 |
| 13 | J. De Witt Warner (D) | 18,979 | 60.8 |
| | James J. Flick (R) | 11,181 | 35.8 |
| 14 | John R. Fellows (D) | 26,267 | 57.8 |
| | H. Charles Ullman (R) | 17,442 | 38.4 |
| 15 | Ashbel P. Fitch (D) | 27,741 | 61.2 |
| | Henry C. Robinson (R) | 15,872 | 35.0 |
| 16 | William Ryan (D) | 25,795 | 55.0 |
| | George A. Brandreth (R) | 19,312 | 41.2 |
| 17 | Francis Marvin (R) | 17,806 | 48.5 |
| | Henry Bacon (D) | 17,659 | 48.1 |
| 18 | Jacob Le Fever (R) | 21,034 | 49.3 |
| | Isaac N. Cox (D) | 20,114 | 47.1 |
| 19 | Charles D. Haines (D) | 20,757 | 50.7 |
| | John A. Quackenbush (R) | 19,104 | 46.6 |
| 20 | Charles Tracey (D) | 19,509 | 50.3 |
| | John G. Ward (R) | 17,883 | 44.7 |
| 21 | Simon J. Schermerhorn (D) | 24,508 | 49.5 |
| | Erastus F. Beadle (R) | 23,181 | 46.8 |
| 22 | Newton Martin Curtis (R) | 26,207 | 57.4 |
| | Warren Curtis (D) | 16,707 | 36.6 |
| 23 | John M. Wever (R) | 25,690 | 57.7 |
| | George S. Weed (D) | 16,947 | 38.1 |
| 24 | Charles A. Chickering (R) | 23,858 | 55.8 |
| | William A. Kelley (D) | 17,283 | 40.4 |
| 25 | James S. Sherman (R) | 20,443 | 49.7 |
| | Henry W. Bentley (D) | 19,299 | 46.9 |
| 26 | George W. Ray (R) | 28,979 | 85.9 |
| | George F. Hand (P) | 3,871 | 11.5 |

| | Candidates | Votes | % |
|---|---|---|---|
| 27 | James . Belden (R) | 25,737 | 55.5 |
| | Riley V. Miller (D) | 18,412 | 39.7 |
| 28 | Sereno E. Payne (R) | 28,723 | 55.3 |
| | Hull Greenfield (D) | 20,601 | 39.7 |
| 29 | Charles W. Gillet (R) | 21,443 | 50.4 |
| | Franz S. Wolf (D) | 17,646 | 41.5 |
| | Albert C. Hill (P) | 2,242 | 5.3 |
| 30 | James W. Wadsworth (R) | 24,205 | 51.2 |
| | John F. McDonald (D) | 19,679 | 41.6 |
| | Albert J. Rumsey (P) | 2,494 | 5.3 |
| 31 | John Van Voorhis (R) | 19,762 | 47.8 |
| | Donald McNaughton (D) | 19,255 | 46.6 |
| 32 | Daniel N. Lockwood (D) | 16,440 | 52.9 |
| | Rowland B. Mahany (R) | 12,966 | 41.8 |
| 33 | Charles Daniels (R) | 19,701 | 53.0 |
| | John S. Hertel (D) | 15,548 | 41.8 |
| 34 | Warren B. Hooker (R) | 24,951 | 55.0 |
| | Andrew J. McNett (D) | 15,098 | 33.3 |
| | Benjamin W. Taylor (P) | 2,905 | 6.4 |
| | F. Eugene Hammond (POP) | 2,395 | 5.3 |

## NORTH CAROLINA

| | Candidates | Votes | % |
|---|---|---|---|
| 1 | William A. B. Branch (D) | 14,263 | 55.1 |
| | Reddick Gatling (PP) | 11,579 | 44.7 |
| 2 | Frederick A. Woodard (D) | 13,925 | 44.4 |
| | Henry P. Cheatham (R) | 11,896 | 37.9 |
| | Edward A. Thorne (PP) | 5,457 | 17.4 |
| 3 | Benjamin F. Grady (D) | 12,457 | 45.0 |
| | Frank D. Koonce (PP) | 9,869 | 35.6 |
| | Asoph M. Clark (R) | 5,271 | 19.0 |
| 4 | Benjamin H. Bunn (D) | 14,630 | 48.4 |
| | William F. Strowd (PP) | 13,125 | 43.4 |
| | John H. Williamson (R) | 2,106 | 7.0 |
| 5 | Thomas Settle (R) | 14,148 | 43.3 |
| | Archibald H. A. Williams (D) | 13,746 | 42.1 |
| | William R. Lindsay (PP) | 4,358 | 13.3 |
| 6 | Sydenham B. Alexander (D) | 16,624 | 57.8 |
| | Atlas A. Maynard (PP) | 12,127 | 42.1 |
| 7 | John S. Henderson (D) | 14,303 | 49.2 |
| | Alfred E. Holton (R) | 9,136 | 31.4 |
| | Alonzo C. Shuford (PP) | 5,399 | 18.6 |
| 8 | William H. Bower (D) | 16,886 | 50.1 |
| | Joseph B. Wilcox (R) | 13,215 | 39.2 |
| | Robert L. Patton (PP) | 3,564 | 10.6 |
| 9 | William T. Crawford (D) | 16,010 | 50.9 |
| | Jeter C. Pritchard (R) | 14,560 | 46.3 |

## NORTH DAKOTA

| | Candidates | Votes | % |
|---|---|---|---|
| AL | Martin N. Johnson (R) | 17,715 | 49.0 |
| | O'Brien (D) | 11,021 | 30.5 |
| | Foss (I) | 7,439 | 20.6 |

## OHIO

| | Candidates | Votes | % |
|---|---|---|---|
| 1 | Bellamy Storer (R) | 19,269 | 50.6 |
| | Robert B. Bowler (D) | 18,014 | 47.3 |
| 2 | John A. Caldwell (R) | 22,240 | 51.5 |
| | Charles T. Greve (D) | 20,074 | 46.5 |
| 3 | George W. Houk (D) | 24,686 | 53.0 |
| | Charles C. Donley (R) | 20,370 | 43.7 |
| 4 | Fernando C. Layton (D) | 20,417 | 56.7 |
| | C. S. Mauk (R) | 12,823 | 35.6 |
| 5 | Dennis D. Donovan (D) | 19,873 | 53.4 |
| | George L. Griffeth (R) | 15,269 | 41.0 |
| 6 | George W. Hulick (R) | 21,341 | 51.4 |
| | John M. Pattison (D) | 18,091 | 43.6 |
| 7 | George W. Wilson (R) | 19,434 | 49.6 |
| | Martin K. Gantz (D) | 17,608 | 45.0 |
| 8 | Luther M. Strong (R) | 21,742 | 51.7 |
| | Fremont Arford (D) | 18,384 | 43.7 |
| 9 | Byron F. Ritchie (D) | 20,041 | 48.0 |
| | James Am Ashley (R) | 20,027 | 48.0 |
| 10 | William H. Enochs (R) | 19,847 | 55.2 |
| | Irvine Dungan (D) | 15,486 | 43.0 |
| 11 | Charles H. Grosvenor (R) | 19,905 | 51.4 |
| | Charles E. Peoples (D) | 17,254 | 44.6 |

## OHIO

| | Candidates | Votes | % |
|---|---|---|---|
| 12 | Joseph H. Outhwaite (D) | 20,298 | 52.6 |
| | Edward N. Huggins (R) | 17,045 | 44.2 |
| 13 | Darius D. Hare (D) | 24,186 | 54.8 |
| | Lewis W. Hull (R) | 17,937 | 40.7 |
| 14 | Michael D. Harter (D) | 22,285 | 49.8 |
| | Elizur G. Johnson (R) | 20,396 | 45.6 |
| 15 | Henry C. Van Voorhis (R) | 18,718 | 49.4 |
| | Milton Turner (D) | 17,550 | 46.4 |
| 16 | Albert J. Pearson (D) | 17,314 | 47.5 |
| | Christian L. Poorman (R) | 17,273 | 47.3 |
| 17 | James A. D. Richards (D) | 23,077 | 55.8 |
| | Arthur H. Walkey (R) | 16,723 | 40.5 |
| 18 | George B. Ikirt (D) | 22,600 | 48.2 |
| | Thomas R. Morgan Sr. (R) | 21,389 | 45.6 |
| 19 | Stephen A. Northway (R) | 23,870 | 55.2 |
| | A. H. Tidball (D) | 16,069 | 37.2 |
| | Bailey S. Dean (P) | 2,185 | 5.1 |
| 20 | William White (R) | 17,417 | 49.1 |
| | John S. Ellen (D) | 16,460 | 46.4 |
| 21 | Tom L. Johnson (D) | 17,389 | 53.4 |
| | Orlando J. Hodge (R) | 14,165 | 43.5 |

### Special Election

| | | Votes | % |
|---|---|---|---|
| 16 | Lewis P. Ohliger (D) | 20,220 | 52.5 |
| | George Adams (R) | 16,958 | 44.0 |

## OREGON

| | | Votes | % |
|---|---|---|---|
| 1 | Binger Hermann (R) | 18,929 | 46.5 |
| | R. M. Veatch (D) | 13,019 | 32.0 |
| | M. V. Rork (POP) | 7,518 | 18.5 |
| 2 | William R. Ellis (R) | 15,657 | 44.9 |
| | James H. Slater (D) | 12,120 | 34.7 |
| | John C. Luce (POP) | 5,940 | 17.0 |

## PENNSYLVANIA

| | | Votes | % |
|---|---|---|---|
| 1 | Henry H. Bingham (R) | 22,908 | 62.6 |
| | Edwin G. Flanigen (D) | 13,693 | 37.4 |
| 2 | Charles O'Neill (R) | 16,107 | 64.0 |
| | John J. Malony (D) | 9,056 | 36.0 |
| 3 | William McAleer (ID) | 15,516 | 73.8 |
| | William W. Ker (D) | 5,500 | 26.2 |
| 4 | John E. Reyburn (R) | 37,200 | 61.4 |
| | Elbridge E. Nock (D) | 22,950 | 37.9 |
| 5 | Alfred C. Harmer (R) | 32,638 | 60.4 |
| | Frederick A. Herwig (D) | 21,426 | 39.6 |
| 6 | John B. Robinson (R) | 19,129 | 55.3 |
| | Garrett C. Smedley (D) | 13,938 | 40.3 |
| 7 | Irving P. Wanger (R) | 21,985 | 49.5 |
| | Edwin Hallowell (D) | 21,805 | 49.0 |
| 8 | William Mutchler (D) | 17,837 | 60.6 |
| | Thomas C. Walton (R) | 11,593 | 39.4 |
| 9 | Constantine J. Erdman (D) | 28,175 | 62.1 |
| | H. A. Muhlenberg (R) | 17,217 | 37.9 |
| 10 | Marriott Brosius (R) | 20,052 | 64.7 |
| | John E. Malone (D) | 10,266 | 33.1 |
| 11 | Joseph A. Scranton (R) | 10,814 | 49.0 |
| | Lemuel Amerman (D) | 10,225 | 46.3 |
| 12 | William H. Hines (D) | 15,554 | 50.1 |
| | Charles D. Foster (R) | 14,092 | 45.4 |
| 13 | James B. Reilly (D) | 13,440 | 53.2 |
| | Charles W. Brumm (R) | 11,539 | 45.7 |
| 14 | Ephraim M. Woomer (R) | 19,058 | 56.0 |
| | William M. Breslin (D) | 13,993 | 41.1 |
| 15 | Myron B. Wright (R) | 17,241 | 55.1 |
| | Roger S. Searle (D) | 12,655 | 40.4 |
| 16 | Albert C. Hopkins (R) | 17,966 | 52.6 |
| | Frederick K. Wright (D) | 14,724 | 43.1 |
| 17 | Simon P. Wolverton (D) | 15,333 | 58.4 |
| | Chandlee Eves (R) | 10,030 | 38.2 |
| 18 | Thaddeus M. Mahon (R) | 19,247 | 54.1 |
| | William W. Trout (D) | 15,631 | 44.0 |
| 19 | Frank E. Beltzhoover (D) | 21,963 | 56.6 |
| | Nesbit S. Ross (R) | 16,198 | 41.7 |
| 20 | Josiah D. Hicks (R) | 22,601 | 56.0 |
| | Lucian D. Woodruff (D) | 17,420 | 43.2 |

| | Candidates | Votes | % |
|---|---|---|---|
| 21 | Daniel B. Heiner (R) | 23,942 | 52.6 |
| | John B. Keenan (D) | 20,245 | 44.5 |
| 22 | John Dalzell (R) | 22,674 | 58.3 |
| | James W. Breen (D) | 15,939 | 41.0 |
| 23 | William A. Stone (R) | 14,628 | 63.6 |
| | Frank C. Osburn (D) | 8,177 | 35.6 |
| 24 | William A. Sipe (D) | 25,224 | 48.2 |
| | Ernest F. Acheson (R) | 23,971 | 45.8 |
| 25 | Thomas W. Phillips (R) | 19,658 | 51.8 |
| | Eugene P. Gillespie (D) | 15,559 | 41.0 |
| | Judson W. Vandeventer (P) | 1,930 | 5.1 |
| 26 | Joseph C. Sibley (D) | 17,887 | 54.9 |
| | Theodore L. Flood (R) | 14,500 | 44.5 |
| 27 | Charles W. Stone (R) | 12,479 | 51.9 |
| | James D. Hancock (D) | 9,523 | 39.6 |
| | Charles Lott (P) | 1,486 | 6.2 |
| 28 | George F. Kribbs (D) | 17,285 | 54.3 |
| | Charles E. Andrews (R) | 13,284 | 41.7 |
| AL | William Lilly (R) | 512,557✔ | |
| | Alexander McDowell (R) | 511,433✔ | |
| | George A. Allen (D) | 448,714 | |
| | Thomas Polk Merritt (D) | 447,456 | |
| | Simeon B. Chase (P) | 23,677 | |
| | James T. McCrory (P) | 22,930 | |
| | S. P. Chase (PP) | 7,466 | |
| | G. W. Dawson (PP) | 7,313 | |
| | J. Mahlon Barnes (SOC LAB) | 674 | |
| | Thomas Grundy (SOC LAB) | 625 | |

### Special Election

| | | Votes | % |
|---|---|---|---|
| 24 | William A. Sipe (D) | 25,181 | 49.1 |
| | Andrew Stewart (R) | 24,635 | 48.1 |

## RHODE ISLAND[1]

| | | Votes | % |
|---|---|---|---|
| 1 | Melville Bull (R) | 13,645* | 49.3 |
| | Oscar Lapham (D) | 13,051 | 47.2 |
| 2 | Adin B. Capron (R) | 11,523* | 49.5 |
| | Charles H. Page (D) | 10,591 | 45.5 |

## SOUTH CAROLINA

| | | Votes | % |
|---|---|---|---|
| 1 | William H. Brawley (D) | 6,318 | 99.8 |
| 2 | W. Jasper Talbert (D) | 8,001 | 99.6 |
| 3 | Asbury C. Latimer (D) | 8,330 | 89.7 |
| | John R. Tolbert (R) | 787 | 8.5 |
| 4 | George W. Shell (D) | 10,401 | 85.7 |
| | Joshua A. T. Ensor (R) | 1,730 | 14.3 |
| 5 | Thomas J. Strait (D) | 8,791 | 80.7 |
| | E. Brooks Sligh (R) | 2,099 | 19.3 |
| 6 | John L. McLaurin (D) | 10,133 | 84.6 |
| | E. J. Sawyer (R) | 1,832 | 15.3 |
| 7 | George W. Murray (R) | 4,995 | 50.0 |
| | E. M. Moise (D) | 4,955 | 49.6 |

### Special Election

| | | Votes | % |
|---|---|---|---|
| 6 | John L. McLaurin (D) | 8,572 | 90.2 |
| | Sawyer (R) | 934 | 9.8 |

## SOUTH DAKOTA

| | | Votes | % |
|---|---|---|---|
| AL | John A. Pickler (R) | 33,769✔ | |
| | William V. Lucas (R) | 33,350✔ | |
| | J. E. Kelley (PP) | 25,444 | |
| | William Lardner (PP) | 24,539 | |
| | L. E. Whitcher (D) | 14,218 | |
| | Chauncey L. Wood (D) | 736 | |

## TENNESSEE

| | | Votes | % |
|---|---|---|---|
| 1 | Alfred A. Taylor (R) | 17,890 | 56.2 |
| | W. J. McSween (D) | 13,207 | 41.5 |
| 2 | John C. Houk (R) | 18,952 | 67.2 |
| | W. L. Welcker (D) | 7,815 | 27.7 |
| 3 | Henry C. Snodgrass (D) | 15,984 | 47.5 |
| | H. Clay Evans (R) | 15,035 | 44.6 |

| | Candidates | Votes | % |
|---|---|---|---|
| | Frank P. Dickey (POP) | 2,171 | 6.5 |
| 4 | Benton McMillin (D) | 14,010 | 55.5 |
| | W. D. Gold (R & ID) | 11,225 | 44.5 |
| 5 | James D. Richardson (D) | 13,709 | 61.1 |
| | Thomas J. Ogilivie (R) | 8,062 | 36.0 |
| 6 | Joseph E. Washington (D) | 15,645 | 62.0 |
| | John B. Allen (R) | 9,002 | 35.7 |
| 7 | Nicholas N. Cox (D) | 12,113 | 57.5 |
| | W. A. Witherspoon (POP) | 8,480 | 40.3 |
| 8 | Benjamin A. Enloe (D) | 13,038 | 50.2 |
| | P. H. Threasher (R) | 12,920 | 49.7 |
| 9 | James C. McDearmon (D) | 14,334 | 56.1 |
| | Rice A. Pearce (ID) | 10,883 | 42.6 |
| 10 | Josiah Patterson (D) | 12,164 | 71.8 |
| | T. V. Neal (R) | 4,785 | 28.2 |

## TEXAS

| | | Votes | % |
|---|---|---|---|
| 1 | Joseph C. Hutcheson (D) | 14,489 | 59.7 |
| | J. B. Stephenson (PP) | 6,081 | 25.1 |
| | Daniel Taylor (R) | 3,703 | 15.3 |
| 2 | Samuel B. Cooper (D) | 19,894 | 61.4 |
| | T. A. Wilson (PP) | 10,275 | 31.7 |
| 3 | Constantine B. Kilgore (D) | 16,335 | 57.3 |
| | J. M. Perdue (PP) | 12,177 | 42.7 |
| 4 | David B. Culberson (D) | 16,521 | 52.3 |
| | Pat B. Clark (PP) | 10,371 | 32.8 |
| | J. A. Hurley (R) | 4,709 | 14.9 |
| 5 | Joseph W. Bailey (D) | 24,983 | 66.2 |
| | R. B. Bell (LW R) | 8,170 | 21.7 |
| | John Grant (D) | 4,563 | 12.1 |
| 6 | Jo Abbott (D) | 24,913 | 59.3 |
| | J. C. Kearby (PP & R) | 17,078 | 40.6 |
| 7 | George C. Pendleton (D) | 19,937 | 56.1 |
| | I. N. Barber (PP) | 15,587 | 43.8 |
| 8 | Charles K. Bell (D) | 17,997 | 54.5 |
| | Evan Jones (PP) | 12,937 | 39.2 |
| | C. C. Drake (R) | 2,009 | 6.1 |
| 9 | Joseph D. Sayers (D) | 19,763 | 61.5 |
| | J. M. Horner (PP & R) | 12,384 | 38.5 |
| 10 | Walter Gresham (D) | 13,017 | 48.6 |
| | A. J. Rosenthal (R) | 9,452 | 35.3 |
| | E. O. Meitzn (PP) | 4,297 | 16.1 |
| 11 | William H. Crain (D) | 15,257 | 52.4 |
| | C. G. Brewster (R) | 8,075 | 27.7 |
| | Ben Terrell (PP) | 5,770 | 19.8 |
| 12 | Thomas M. Paschal (D) | 13,930 | 50.1 |
| | Henry Terrell (R) | 7,290 | 26.2 |
| | T. J. McMinn (PP) | 6,574 | 23.6 |
| 13 | Jeremiah V. Cockrell (D) | 21,922 | 65.5 |
| | W. J. Maltby (PP) | 9,825 | 29.4 |

### Special Election

| | | Votes | % |
|---|---|---|---|
| 9 | Edwin LeRoy Antony (D) | ✔ | # |

## VERMONT

| | | Votes | % |
|---|---|---|---|
| 1 | H. Henry Powers (R) | 19,427 | 65.9 |
| | Felix W. McGettrick (D) | 9,396 | 31.9 |
| 2 | William W. Grout (R) | 18,568 | 66.7 |
| | George W. Smith (D) | 8,649 | 31.1 |

## VIRGINIA

| | | Votes | % |
|---|---|---|---|
| 1 | William A. Jones (D) | 15,004 | 56.2 |
| | Orres A. Browne (R) | 11,543 | 43.2 |
| 2 | D. Gardiner Tyler (D) | 17,432 | 55.6 |
| | P. C. Garrigan (IR) | 8,594 | 27.4 |
| | John F. Deyendorf (R) | 3,870 | 12.3 |
| 3 | George D. Wise (D) | 18,595 | 63.9 |
| | Walter E. Grant (R) | 10,489 | 36.1 |
| 4 | James F. Epes (D) | 10,330 | 52.1 |
| | J. Thomas Goode (POP) | 9,462 | 47.8 |
| 5 | Claude A. Swanson (D) | 14,112 | 53.9 |
| | Benjamin T. Jones (POP) | 12,066 | 46.1 |
| 6 | Paul C. Edmunds (D) | 18,265 | 58.6 |
| | Thomas E. Cobbs (POP) | 12,924 | 41.4 |
| 7 | Charles T. O'Ferrall (D) | 18,558 | 64.0 |
| | J. R. C. Lewis (POP) | 10,441 | 36.0 |

1. In both congressional districts, no candidate received the majority of the votes necessary to win in the 1892 general election. (See Rhode Island 1893, p. 1069.)

## VIRGINIA

| Candidates | Votes | % |
|---|---|---|
| 8 Elisha E. Meredith (D) | 17,124 | 63.0 |
| B. B. Turner (POP) | 10,066 | 37.0 |
| 9 James W. Marshall (D) | 18,431 | 55.9 |
| Henry C. Wood (R) | 12,699 | 38.5 |
| George R. Cowan (POP) | 1,709 | 5.2 |
| 0 Henry St. George Tucker (D) | 17,779 | 57.7 |
| D. Mott Robertson (POP) | 13,027 | 42.3 |

## WASHINGTON

| | Votes | |
|---|---|---|
| L  William H. Doolittle (R) | 35,434✔ | |
| John L. Wilson (R) | 35,407✔ | |
| Thomas Carroll (D) | 30,659 | |
| James A. Munday (D) | 27,014 | |
| M. F. Knox (PP) | 20,083 | |
| J. C. Van Patton (PP) | 19,891 | |
| D. E. Newberry (P) | 2,412 | |
| A. C. Dickinson (P) | 2,357 | |

## WEST VIRGINIA

| Candidates | Votes | % |
|---|---|---|
| 1 John O. Pendleton (D) | 19,314 | 47.6 |
| B. B. Dovener (R) | 19,108 | 47.1 |
| 2 William L. Wilson (D) | 21,807 | 50.2 |
| J. Nelson Wisner (R) | 20,702 | 47.7 |
| 3 John D. Alderson (D) | 22,696 | 51.3 |
| Edgar P. Rucker (R) | 20,750 | 46.9 |
| 4 James Capehart (D) | 22,006 | 52.4 |
| Charles T. Caldwell (R) | 19,924 | 47.4 |

## WISCONSIN

| Candidates | Votes | % |
|---|---|---|
| 1 Henry Allen Cooper (R) | 20,222 | 52.3 |
| Babbitt (D) | 16,449 | 42.5 |
| Murdock (P) | 2,021 | 5.2 |
| 2 Charles Barwig (D) | 21,303 | 55.9 |
| L. B. Caswell (R) | 15,003 | 39.4 |
| 3 Joseph W. Babcock (R) | 19,506 | 50.4 |
| A. H. Krauskop (D) | 16,419 | 42.4 |
| 4 John L. Mitchell (D) | 19,616* | 50.2 |
| Theobald Otjen (R) | 18,294 | 46.8 |

| Candidates | Votes | % |
|---|---|---|
| 5 George H. Brickner (D) | 17,929 | 51.7 |
| Julius Wechselberg (R) | 15,960 | 46.0 |
| 6 Owen A. Wells (D) | 20,212 | 51.1 |
| Emil Baensch (R) | 17,847 | 45.1 |
| 7 George B. Shaw (R) | 15,344 | 48.5 |
| Frank P. Coburn (D) | 13,074 | 41.3 |
| Ole B. Oleson (P) | 1,635 | 5.2 |
| 8 Lyman E. Barnes (D) | 18,187 | 52.9 |
| H. A. Frambach (R) | 15,173 | 44.1 |
| 9 Thomas Lynch (D) | 19,608 | 52.2 |
| Myron H. McCord (R) | 16,519 | 44.0 |
| 10 Nils P. Haugen (R) | 17,674 | 50.6 |
| Daniel Bachanan Jr. (D) | 13,044 | 37.4 |
| Peter L. Scritsmier (PP) | 4,186 | 12.0 |

## WYOMING

| | Votes | % |
|---|---|---|
| AL  Henry A. Coffeen (D) | 8,855 | 51.3 |
| Clarence D. Clark (R) | 8,394 | 48.6 |

# 1893 House Elections

## MASSACHUSETTS

### Special Election

| | Votes | % |
|---|---|---|
| 7  William Everett (D) | 9,733 | 46.3 |
| William E. Barrett (R) | 9,699 | 46.1 |

## MICHIGAN

### Special Election

| | Votes | % |
|---|---|---|
| 1  Levi T. Griffin (D) | 18,854 | 50.3 |
| James H. Stone (R) | 17,587 | 46.9 |

## OHIO

### Special Election

| | | |
|---|---|---|
| 10  Hezekiah S. Bundy (R) | | ✔ |

## PENNSYLVANIA

### Special Elections

| | Votes | % |
|---|---|---|
| 2  Robert Adams Jr (R) | 10,487 | 97.0 |
| 8  Howard Mutchler (D) | 10,143 | 64.0 |
| Frank Reeder (R) | 5,663 | 35.8 |

## RHODE ISLAND[1]

### Special Elections

| | Votes | % |
|---|---|---|
| 1  Oscar Lapham (D) | 11,298 | 47.7 |
| Melville Bull (R) | 10,816 | 45.7 |
| 2  Charles H. Page (D) | 10,670 | 47.6 |
| Adin B. Capron (R) | 10,021 | 44.7 |
| Lewis (P) | 1,571 | 7.0 |

## WISCONSIN

### Special Election

| | Votes | % |
|---|---|---|
| 4  Peter J. Somers (D) | 13,567 | 51.3 |
| Theobald Otgen (R) | 12,125 | 45.8 |

1. No candidate in either congressional district had received a majority of the vote in the November 1892 general election for the House, so a special election was necessary in April 1893. Under the usual practice, the state kept holding elections until a majority was received, but in 1893 it was agreed that whoever received the most votes in the special election would be considered as elected, regardless of whether a majority was achieved. So Lapham and Page were elected and took their seats in the 53rd Congress (1893-95) even though neither won a majority and would not have qualified under the usual practices of Rhode Island law. The majority requirement — which caused problems in elections for other offices as well as the House — was repealed in a referendum in November 1893. (Majority vote requirement, see p 945.)

# 1894 House Elections

## ALABAMA

| Candidates | Votes | % |
|---|---|---|
| 1 Richard H. Clarke (D) | 6,314 | 76.9 |
| Sibley (POP) | 1,898 | 23.1 |
| 2 Jesse F. Stallings (D) | 9,728 | 64.6 |
| Gardner (POP) | 5,324 | 35.4 |
| 3 George P. Harrison (D) | 10,719 | 65.2 |
| Robinson (POP) | 5,713 | 34.8 |
| 4 Gaston A. Robbins (D) | 10,494‡ | 58.6 |
| William F. Aldrich (R) | 7,406 | 41.4 |
| 5 James E. Cobb (D) | 10,651‡ | 51.8 |
| Albert T. Goodwyn (POP) | 9,903 | 48.2 |
| 6 John H. Bankhead (D) | 5,721 | 55.8 |
| Sanford (POP) | 2,622 | 25.6 |
| Long (R) | 1,914 | 18.7 |
| 7 Milford W. Howard (POP) | 6,838 | 66.5 |
| William H. Denson (D) | 3,452 | 33.6 |
| 8 Joseph Wheeler (D) | 8,901 | 57.9 |
| Crandall (POP) | 6,474 | 42.1 |
| 9 Oscar W. Underwood (D) | 7,319‡ | 54.3 |
| Truman H. Aldrich (R) | 6,153 | 45.7 |

### Special Election

| | Votes | % |
|---|---|---|
| 3 George P. Harrison (D) | 10,822 | 65.3 |
| W. C. Robinson (POP) | 5,743 | 34.7 |

## ARKANSAS

| | Votes | % |
|---|---|---|
| 1 Philip D. McCulloch Jr. (D) | 6,025 | 31.8 |
| Russ Coffman (POP) | 1,299 | 17.6 |
| 2 John S. Little (D) | 5,097 | 94.5 |
| 3 Thomas C. McRae (D) | 6,193 | 97.1 |
| 4 William L. Terry (D) | 6,299 | 62.2 |
| P. Raleigh (R) | 2,260 | 22.3 |
| J. H. Cherry (POP) | 1,557 | 15.4 |
| 5 Hugh A. Dinsmore (D) | 7,531 | 56.8 |
| T. J. Hunt (R) | 4,976 | 37.5 |
| W. M. Peel (POP) | 759 | 5.7 |
| 6 Robert Neill (D) | 6,439 | 65.0 |
| H. H. Myers (R) | 3,153 | 31.8 |

## CALIFORNIA

| | Votes | % |
|---|---|---|
| 1 John A. Barham (R) | 15,101 | 41.1 |
| Thomas J. Geary (D) | 13,570 | 37.0 |
| Robert F. Grigsby (PP) | 7,246 | 19.7 |
| 2 Grove L. Johnson (R) | 19,302 | 43.0 |
| Anthony Caminetti (D) | 15,732 | 35.1 |
| Burdett Cornell (PP) | 8,946 | 20.0 |
| 3 Samuel G. Hilborn (R) | 15,795 | 45.5 |
| Warren B. English (D) | 13,103 | 37.8 |
| W. A. Vann (PP) | 5,162 | 14.9 |
| 4 James G. Maguire (D) | 14,748 | 48.3 |
| Thomas B. Shannon (R) | 9,785 | 32.0 |
| B. K. Collier (PP) | 5,627 | 18.4 |
| 5 Eugene F. Loud (R) | 13,379 | 35.9 |
| Joseph P. Kelly (D) | 8,384 | 22.5 |
| James T. Rogers (PP) | 7,820 | 21.0 |
| James Denman (I DEMOC) | 6,811 | 18.3 |
| 6 James McLachlan (R) | 18,746 | 44.3 |
| George S. Patton (D) | 11,693 | 27.6 |
| W. C. Bowman (PP) | 9,769 | 23.1 |
| J. E. McComas (P) | 2,120 | 5.0 |
| 7 William W. Bowers (R) | 18,434 | 42.9 |
| W. H. Alford (D) | 12,111 | 28.2 |
| J. L. Gilbert (PP) | 10,719 | 25.0 |

## COLORADO

| | Votes | % |
|---|---|---|
| 1 John F. Shafroth (R) | 47,710 | 55.3 |
| La Fayette Pence (POP) | 34,223 | 39.7 |
| 2 John C. Bell (POP & D) | 47,703 | 51.7 |
| T. M. Bowen (R) | 42,369 | 45.9 |

## CONNECTICUT

| Candidates | Votes | % |
|---|---|---|
| 1 E. Stevens Henry (R) | 20,322 | 55.4 |
| Lewis Sperry (D) | 15,115 | 41.2 |
| 2 Nehemiah D. Sperry (R) | 28,749 | 54.9 |
| Pigott (D) | 21,821 | 41.7 |
| 3 Charles A. Russell (R) | 12,095 | 55.5 |
| Beckwith (D) | 9,047 | 41.6 |
| 4 Ebenezer J. Hill (R) | 24,012 | 55.2 |
| Deforest (D) | 18,559 | 42.7 |

## DELAWARE

| | Votes | % |
|---|---|---|
| AL Jonathan S. Willis (R) | 19,699 | 50.7 |
| S. H. Bancroft Jr. (D) | 18,492 | 47.6 |

## FLORIDA

| | Votes | % |
|---|---|---|
| 1 Stephen M. Sparkman (D) | 12,397 | 85.1 |
| D. L. McKinnon (POP) | 2,135 | 14.7 |
| 2 Charles M. Cooper (D) | 9,229 | 79.6 |
| M. Atkinson (POP) | 2,334 | 20.1 |

## GEORGIA

| | Votes | % |
|---|---|---|
| 1 Rufus E. Lester (D) | 14,024 | 72.0 |
| J. F. Brown (PP) | 5,453 | 28.0 |
| 2 Benjamin E. Russell (D) | 10,073 | 62.4 |
| William E. Smith (PP) | 6,064 | 37.6 |
| 3 Charles F. Crisp (D) | 9,037 | 74.7 |
| Andrew White (PP) | 3,062 | 25.3 |
| 4 Charles L. Moses (D) | 10,293 | 57.4 |
| Carey Thornton (PP) | 7,637 | 42.6 |
| 5 Leonidas F. Livingston (D) | 7,781 | 59.7 |
| Robert Todd (PP) | 5,264 | 40.4 |
| 6 Charles L. Bartlett (D) | 11,671 | 65.5 |
| W. T. Whitaker (PP) | 6,147 | 34.5 |
| 7 John W. Maddox (D) | 11,500 | 54.4 |
| William H. Felton (PP) | 9,646 | 45.6 |
| 8 Thomas G. Lawson (D) | 11,066 | 59.5 |
| W. T. Carter (PP) | 7,527 | 40.5 |
| 9 Farish C. Tate (D) | 13,059 | 56.1 |
| J. N. Twitty (PP) | 10,201 | 43.9 |
| 10 James C. C. Black (D) | 20,942 | 60.8 |
| Thomas E. Watson (PP) | 13,498 | 39.2 |
| 11 Henry G. Turner (D) | 9,085 | 60.2 |
| W. S. Johnson (PP) | 6,015 | 39.8 |

## IDAHO

| | Votes | % |
|---|---|---|
| AL Edgar Wilson (R) | 10,383 | 43.4 |
| James Gunn (PP) | 7,547 | 31.5 |
| James M. Ballentine (D) | 5,834 | 24.4 |

## ILLINOIS

| | Votes | % |
|---|---|---|
| 1 J. Frank Aldrich (R) | 33,902 | 63.2 |
| Max Dembufsky (D) | 12,854 | 23.9 |
| Howard S. Taylor (POP) | 5,996 | 11.2 |
| 2 William Lorimer (R) | 21,194 | 45.6 |
| John J. Hanahan (D) | 16,852 | 36.2 |
| John Z. White (POP) | 8,484 | 18.2 |
| 3 Lawrence E. McGann (D) | 15,356‡ | 44.4 |
| Hugh R. Belknap (R) | 15,325 | 44.3 |
| John B. Clarke (POP) | 3,945 | 11.4 |
| 4 Charles W. Woodman (R) | 14,017 | 38.2 |
| Frank Lawler (I) | 10,638 | 29.0 |
| T. E. Ryan (D) | 8,801 | 24.0 |
| Patrick J. Miniter (POP) | 2,812 | 7.7 |
| 5 George E. White (R) | 18,732 | 49.5 |
| Edward T. Noonan (D) | 14,875 | 39.3 |
| Charles G. Dixon (POP) | 4,143 | 10.9 |
| 6 Edward D. Cooke (R) | 17,602 | 47.3 |
| Julius Goldzier (D) | 15,433 | 41.5 |

| Candidates | Votes | % |
|---|---|---|
| Louis W. Rogers (POP) | 4,159 | 11.2 |
| 7 George Edmund Foss (R) | 25,546 | 59.3 |
| Philip Jackson (D) | 11,450 | 26.6 |
| Henry D. Lloyd (POP) | 6,109 | 14.2 |
| 8 Albert J. Hopkins (R) | 22,631 | 66.0 |
| Lewis Steward (D) | 9,104 | 26.6 |
| 9 Robert R. Hitt (R) | 24,177 | 63.9 |
| David F. Thompson (D) | 11,301 | 29.9 |
| 10 Philip S. Post (R) | 22,949* | 63.7 |
| Jonas W. Olson (D) | 9,770 | 27.1 |
| William W. Mathews (POP) | 2,143 | 6.0 |
| 11 Walter Reeves (R) | 19,372 | 52.3 |
| Robert R. Gibbons (D) | 14,390 | 38.8 |
| William M. Hirschy (POP) | 2,216 | 6.0 |
| 12 Joseph G. Cannon (R) | 21,122 | 59.4 |
| Thomas F. Donovan (D) | 11,925 | 33.5 |
| 13 Vespasian Warner (R) | 20,896 | 57.8 |
| A. J. Barr (D) | 12,725 | 35.2 |
| 14 Joseph R. Graff (R) | 20,579 | 51.2 |
| George O. Barnes (D) | 17,224 | 42.8 |
| 15 Benjamin F. Marsh (R) | 20,550 | 48.4 |
| Truman Plantz (D) | 19,115 | 45.0 |
| 16 Finis E. Downing (D) | 17,816‡ | 46.5 |
| John I. Rinaker (R) | 17,776 | 46.4 |
| Peter D. Stout (POP) | 1,929 | 5.0 |
| 17 James A. Connolly (R) | 20,441 | 50.3 |
| William M. Springer (D) | 17,503 | 43.0 |
| 18 Frederick Remann (R) | 16,669 | 49.4 |
| Edward Lane (D) | 14,069 | 41.7 |
| Joseph S. Barnes (POP) | 2,020 | 6.0 |
| 19 Benson Wood (R) | 20,028 | 48.2 |
| George W. Fithian (D) | 18,758 | 45.1 |
| 20 Orlando Burrell (R) | 17,429 | 47.6 |
| James R. Williams (D) | 15,775 | 43.1 |
| Harvey G. Jones (POP) | 2,769 | 7.6 |
| 21 Everett J. Murphy (R) | 18,958 | 48.0 |
| John J. Higgins (D) | 17,159 | 43.4 |
| Henry C. McDill (POP) | 2,764 | 7.0 |
| 22 George W. Smith (R) | 18,180 | 57.4 |
| Francis M. Youngblood (D) | 10,585 | 33.4 |
| John J. Hall (POP) | 2,509 | 7.9 |

## INDIANA

| | Votes | % |
|---|---|---|
| 1 James A. Hemenway (R) | 20,535 | 47.8 |
| Arthur H. Taylor (D) | 18,245 | 42.5 |
| James A. Boyce (POP) | 3,820 | 8.9 |
| 2 Alexander M. Hardy (R) | 17,624 | 47.6 |
| John L. Bretz (D) | 15,896 | 42.9 |
| Elisha A. Riggins (POP) | 3,217 | 8.7 |
| 3 Robert J. Tracewell (R) | 19,709 | 49.0 |
| Strother M. Stockslager (D) | 19,153 | 47.6 |
| 4 James E. Watson (R) | 17,905 | 48.9 |
| William S. Holman (D) | 17,471 | 47.7 |
| 5 Jesse Overstreet (R) | 18,286 | 49.5 |
| George W. Cooper (D) | 16,416 | 44.4 |
| 6 Henry U. Johnson (R) | 22,724 | 63.1 |
| Nimrod R. Elliott (D) | 10,707 | 29.7 |
| 7 Charles L. Henry (R) | 29,900 | 51.1 |
| William D. Bynum (D) | 25,557 | 43.7 |
| 8 George W. Faris (R) | 23,238 | 48.0 |
| Elijah V. Brookshire (D) | 20,669 | 42.7 |
| Morton C. Rankin (POP) | 3,658 | 7.6 |
| 9 J. Frank Hanly (R) | 25,479 | 54.1 |
| A. G. Burkhart (D) | 20,237 | 43.0 |
| 10 Jethro A. Hatch (R) | 20,858 | 51.0 |
| Valentine Zimmerman (D) | 16,923 | 41.4 |
| Samuel M. Hathorn (POP) | 2,296 | 5.6 |
| 11 George W. Steele (R) | 25,008 | 50.1 |
| Augustus N. Martin (D) | 21,079 | 42.2 |
| 12 Jacob D. Leighty (R) | 19,658 | 49.9 |
| William F. McNagny (D) | 17,145 | 43.5 |
| Freeman Kelly (POP) | 2,195 | 5.6 |
| 13 Lemuel W. Royse (R) | 23,523 | 52.3 |
| Lewellyn Wanner (D) | 19,376 | 43.1 |

## IOWA

| Candidates | Votes | % |
|---|---|---|
| 1 Samuel M. Clark (R) | 17,583 | 51.9 |
| W. A. Buckworth (D) | 13,747 | 40.6 |
| J. O. Bube (PP) | 2,065 | 6.1 |
| 2 George M. Curtis (R) | 18,710 | 48.4 |
| Walter I. Hayes (D) | 18,274 | 47.2 |
| 3 David B. Henderson (R) | 22,892 | 57.1 |
| Stephen H. Bashor (D-PP) | 17,200 | 42.9 |
| 4 Thomas Updegraff (R) | 20,457 | 57.4 |
| James F. Babcock (D) | 13,267 | 37.2 |
| 5 Robert G. Cousins (R) | 21,261 | 55.2 |
| William P. Daniels (D) | 15,487 | 40.2 |
| 6 John F. Lacey (R) | 18,418 | 50.9 |
| W. H. Taylor (D) | 11,587 | 32.0 |
| Allen Clark (PP) | 5,663 | 15.7 |
| 7 John A. T. Hull (R) | 20,167 | 60.9 |
| J. R. Barcott (D-PP) | 12,942 | 39.1 |
| 8 William P. Hepburn (R) | 21,672 | 55.3 |
| Frank G. Stuart (D-PP) | 17,538 | 44.7 |
| 9 Alva L. Hager (R) | 21,874 | 53.3 |
| James B. Weaver (D-PP) | 18,817 | 45.8 |
| 10 Jonathan P. Dolliver (R) | 25,262 | 59.9 |
| J. C. Baker (D-PP) | 16,905 | 40.1 |
| 11 George D. Perkins (R) | 22,406 | 54.7 |
| Bernard Graiser (D) | 12,425 | 30.3 |
| J. L. Bartholomew (PP) | 5,265 | 12.8 |

## KANSAS

| Candidates | Votes | % |
|---|---|---|
| Case Broderick (R) | 19,202 | 54.2 |
| H. C. Solomon (FUS) | 15,844 | 44.7 |
| Orrin L. Miller (R) | 22,763 | 53.9 |
| F. A. Willard (PP) | 13,811 | 32.7 |
| H. L. Moore (D) | 4,780 | 11.3 |
| Snyder S. Kirkpatrick (R) | 20,631 | 49.3 |
| Jeremiah D. Botkin (PP) | 18,505 | 44.2 |
| William F. Sapp (D) | 2,695 | 6.4 |
| Charles Curtis (R) | 25,154 | 53.3 |
| S. M. Scott (PP) | 18,790 | 39.8 |
| Thomas J. O'Neil (D) | 2,546 | 5.4 |
| William A. Calderhead (R) | 18,428 | 49.1 |
| John Davis (PP) | 15,831 | 42.1 |
| C. W. Brandenburg (D) | 2,788 | 7.4 |
| William Baker (PP) | 16,585 | 45.7 |
| Abram H. Ellis (R) | 16,391 | 45.1 |
| Roscoe G. Heard (D) | 2,934 | 8.1 |
| Chester I. Long (R) | 27,444 | 50.9 |
| Jerry Simpson (D-PP) | 25,459 | 47.2 |
| Richard W. Blue (R) | 147,858 | 50.4 |
| W. A. Harris (PP) | 114,429 | 39.0 |
| Joseph G. Lowe (D) | 26,093 | 8.9 |

## KENTUCKY

| Candidates | Votes | % |
|---|---|---|
| John K. Hendrick (D) | 13,912 | 49.8 |
| Ben C. Keys (POP) | 10,794 | 38.7 |
| W. J. Chitwood (D) | 2,701 | 9.7 |
| John D. Clardy (D) | 13,363 | 46.8 |
| Elijah G. Sebree Jr. (R) | 10,381 | 36.3 |
| Henry Turner (POP) | 4,385 | 15.3 |
| W. Godfrey Hunter (R) | 16,545 | 49.7 |
| C. McElroy (D) | 15,644 | 47.0 |
| John W. Lewis (R) | 16,826 | 51.0 |
| Alexander B. Montgomery (D) | 15,636 | 47.4 |
| Walter Evans (R) | 20,592 | 55.6 |
| E. J. McDermott (D) | 16,462 | 44.4 |
| Albert S. Berry (D) | 14,008 | 52.1 |
| Thomas B. Mathews (R) | 11,968 | 44.5 |
| William C. Owens (D) | 13,677 | 48.7 |
| George Denny Jr. (R) | 13,576 | 48.4 |
| James B. McCreary (D) | 13,532 | 50.6 |
| Phil Roberts (R) | 12,155 | 45.4 |
| Samuel J. Pugh (R) | 19,058 | 50.2 |
| Rawleigh N. Hart (D) | 18,396 | 48.4 |
| Joseph M. Kendall (D) | 14,845‡ | 50.4 |
| Nathan T. Hopkins (R) | 14,592 | 49.6 |
| David G. Colson (R) | 14,628 | 47.7 |
| George E. Stone (D) | 10,932 | 35.6 |
| Silas Adams (IR) | 4,975 | 16.2 |

### Special Election

| Candidates | Votes | % |
|---|---|---|
| 10 William M. Beckner (D) | 14,231 | 52.3 |
| John L. Bosley (R) | 12,970 | 47.7 |

## LOUISIANA

| Candidates | Votes | % |
|---|---|---|
| 1 Adolph Meyer (D) | 13,405 | 65.5 |
| H. P. Kernochan (R) | 6,676 | 32.6 |
| 2 Charles F. Buck (D) | 14,864 | 66.8 |
| H. D. Coleman (R) | 7,211 | 32.4 |
| 3 Andrew Price (D) | 14,388 | 60.8 |
| Taylor Beattle (R) | 8,620 | 36.5 |
| 4 Henry W. Ogden (D) | 12,257 | 67.4 |
| B. W. Bailey (POP) | 5,932 | 32.6 |
| 5 Charles J. Boatner (D) | 14,755‡ | 76.4 |
| Alexis Benoit (POP) | 4,549 | 23.6 |
| 6 Samuel M. Robertson (D) | 7,981 | 78.2 |
| M. R. Wilson (POP) | 2,230 | 21.8 |

### Special Election

| Candidates | Votes | % |
|---|---|---|
| 4 Henry W. Ogden (D) | 8,261 | 71.2 |
| C. D. Hicks (POP & R) | 3,333 | 28.7 |

## MAINE

| Candidates | Votes | % |
|---|---|---|
| 1 Thomas B. Reed (R) | 17,086 | 63.5 |
| J. W. Deering (D) | 8,901 | 33.1 |
| 2 Nelson Dingley Jr. (R) | 18,097 | 63.7 |
| D. J. McGillicuddy (D) | 8,059 | 28.4 |
| Elb Y. Turner (PP) | 1,693 | 6.0 |
| 3 Seth L. Milliken (R) | 16,891 | 64.7 |
| M. R. Leighton (D) | 6,663 | 25.5 |
| G. C. Sheldon (PP) | 1,986 | 7.6 |
| 4 Charles A. Boutelle (R) | 17,383 | 65.5 |
| A. L. Simpson (D) | 6,879 | 25.9 |

## MARYLAND

| Candidates | Votes | % |
|---|---|---|
| 1 Joshua W. Miles (D) | 13,953 | 43.2 |
| A. L. Dryden (R) | 12,914 | 40.0 |
| B. P. Miles (P) | 2,728 | 8.4 |
| B. Morris (PP) | 2,728 | 8.4 |
| 2 William B. Baker (R) | 19,291 | 48.0 |
| J. F. Talbott (D) | 19,100 | 47.5 |
| 3 Harry W. Rusk (D) | 16,228 | 49.8 |
| William Booze (R) | 15,709 | 48.2 |
| 4 John K. Cowen (D) | 17,184 | 50.5 |
| Robert Smith (R) | 16,178 | 47.5 |
| 5 Charles E. Coffin (R) | 15,443 | 52.0 |
| John Rogers (D) | 13,421 | 45.2 |
| 6 George L. Wellington (R) | 19,709 | 52.1 |
| Frederick Williams (D) | 16,742 | 44.2 |

### Special Elections

| Candidates | Votes | % |
|---|---|---|
| 1 W. L. Henry (D) | 13,858 | 46.3 |
| Joseph Mallalieu (R) | 12,955 | 43.2 |
| James Anthony (P) | 2,763 | 9.2 |
| 5 Charles E. Coffin (R) | 15,492 | 52.0 |
| George Welles (D) | 13,495 | 45.3 |

## MASSACHUSETTS

| Candidates | Votes | % |
|---|---|---|
| 1 Ashley B. Wright (R) | 14,018 | 55.2 |
| Addison L. Green (D) | 9,961 | 39.2 |
| 2 Frederick H. Gillett (R) | 15,480 | 61.4 |
| Edward A. Hall (D) | 7,924 | 31.4 |
| 3 Joseph H. Walker (R) | 13,788 | 59.4 |
| Charles Haggerty (D) | 8,251 | 35.6 |
| 4 Lewis D. Apsley (R) | 16,992 | 64.8 |
| John J. Desmond (D) | 8,432 | 32.2 |
| 5 William S. Knox (R) | 14,372 | 51.7 |
| George W. Fifield (D) | 12,341 | 44.4 |
| 6 William Cogswell (R) | 16,206 | 68.3 |
| Henry B. Little (D) | 5,747 | 24.2 |
| Joseph K. Harris (PP) | 1,772 | 7.5 |
| 7 William E. Barrett (R) | 16,453 | 57.7 |
| Samuel K. Hamilton (D) | 9,601 | 33.7 |
| 8 Samuel W. McCall (R) | 15,188 | 61.5 |
| Charles A. Conant (R) | 8,747 | 35.4 |
| 9 John F. Fitzgerald (D) | 11,459 | 53.3 |
| Jesse M. Gove (R) | 9,545 | 44.4 |
| 10 Harrison H. Atwood (R) | 9,833 | 35.9 |
| Michael J. McEttrick (D & CIT) | 8,868 | 32.4 |
| William S. McNary (D) | 7,113 | 26.0 |
| 11 William F. Draper (R) | 16,905 | 62.0 |
| Bentley Wirt Warren (D) | 9,456 | 34.7 |
| 12 Elijah A. Morse (R) | 15,865 | 65.3 |
| William H. Jordan (D) | 6,359 | 26.2 |
| Elbridge Gerry Brown (PP) | 2,065 | 8.5 |
| 13 John Simpkins (R) | 13,497 | 61.1 |
| Robert Howard (D) | 8,548 | 38.7 |

## MICHIGAN

| Candidates | Votes | % |
|---|---|---|
| 1 John B. Corliss (R) | 18,605 | 55.0 |
| Levi T. Griffin (D) | 13,441 | 39.7 |
| 2 George Spalding (R) | 23,708 | 54.7 |
| Thomas E. Barkworth (PP & D) | 17,596 | 40.6 |
| 3 Julius Burrows (R) | 20,115* | 58.7 |
| Nathaniel H. Stewart (D) | 8,075 | 23.6 |
| Frederick Lackore (PP) | 3,888 | 11.3 |
| Lucian W. Underwood (P) | 2,217 | 6.5 |
| 4 Henry F. Thomas (R) | 21,722 | 58.8 |
| Leroy F. Weaver (D) | 9,874 | 26.7 |
| Sullivan Cook (PP) | 3,744 | 10.1 |
| 5 William Alden Smith (R) | 19,973 | 58.5 |
| Gideon L. Rutherford (D) | 10,405 | 30.5 |
| Josiah Tibbitts (PP) | 2,168 | 6.4 |
| 6 David D. Aitken (R) | 22,894 | 57.3 |
| Elliott R. Wilcox (D) | 13,831 | 34.6 |
| Thomas C. Williams (P) | 2,394 | 6.0 |
| 7 Horace G. Snover (R) | 18,172 | 54.6 |
| Ezra C. Carleton (D) | 12,334 | 37.1 |
| 8 William S. Linton (R) | 16,565 | 54.1 |
| Rowland Connor (D) | 10,118 | 33.0 |
| Emery L. Brewer (P) | 1,572 | 5.1 |
| Poe R. Crosby (PP) | 1,778 | 5.8 |
| 9 Roswell P. Bishop (R) | 15,761 | 58.4 |
| William T. Evans (D) | 7,142 | 26.5 |
| Norman B. Farnsworth (PP) | 2,768 | 10.3 |
| 10 Rousseau O. Crump (R) | 16,304 | 52.6 |
| Worthy L. Churchill (D) | 12,456 | 40.2 |
| Alexander Forsyth (PP) | 2,130 | 6.9 |
| 11 John Avery (R) | 19,575 | 62.2 |
| Hiram B. Hudson (D) | 6,503 | 20.7 |
| William T. Pitt (PP) | 3,660 | 11.6 |
| Austin Barber (P) | 1,728 | 5.5 |
| 12 Samuel M. Stephenson (R) | 20,935 | 64.0 |
| Rush Culver (D) | 8,714 | 27.0 |
| Andrew E. Anderson (PP) | 3,053 | 9.3 |

## MINNESOTA

| Candidates | Votes | % |
|---|---|---|
| 1 James A. Tawney (R) | 22,651 | 58.0 |
| John Moonan (D) | 10,479 | 26.8 |
| Thomas G. Meighen (PP) | 4,675 | 12.0 |
| 2 James T. McCleary (R) | 23,136 | 53.9 |
| L. C. Long (PP) | 10,362 | 24.2 |
| James H. Baker (D) | 7,912 | 18.5 |
| 3 Joel P. Heatwole (R) | 19,461 | 49.2 |
| Osee M. Hall (D) | 14,193 | 35.9 |
| J. M. Bowler (PP) | 4,988 | 12.6 |
| 4 Andrew R. Keifer (R) | 20,573 | 56.5 |
| Edw. J. Darragh (D) | 10,168 | 28.0 |
| Francis H. Clark (PP) | 5,055 | 13.9 |
| 5 Loren Fletcher (R) | 20,465 | 51.1 |
| Oliver T. Erickson (D) | 11,506 | 28.7 |
| Ernest F. Clark (PP) | 7,043 | 17.6 |
| 6 Charles A. Towne (R) | 25,487 | 53.3 |
| M. R. Baldwin (D) | 15,846 | 33.2 |
| Kittl Halvorsen (PP) | 6,475 | 13.5 |
| 7 Frank M. Eddy (R) | 18,200 | 43.5 |
| Haldor E. Boen (PP) | 17,408 | 41.6 |

## MINNESOTA

| Candidates | Votes | % |
|---|---|---|
| Thomas N. McLean (D) | 3,486 | 8.3 |
| Ole Kron (P) | 2,726 | 6.5 |

## MISSISSIPPI

| Candidates | Votes | % |
|---|---|---|
| 1 John M. Allen (D) | 3,177 | 76.3 |
| J. A. Brown (PP) | 985 | 23.7 |
| 2 John C. Kyle (D) | 3,845 | 75.3 |
| R. J. Lyle (PP) | 1,067 | 20.9 |
| 3 Thomas C. Catchings (D) | 1,696 | 87.1 |
| Thomas Monuh (P) | 207 | 10.6 |
| 4 Hernando D. Money (D) | 5,213 | 57.9 |
| J. H. Jamison (PP) | 3,751 | 41.7 |
| 5 John Sharp Williams (D) | 5,319 | 69.1 |
| W. P. Ratiff (POP) | 2,380 | 30.9 |
| 6 Walter McK. Denny (D) | 3,889 | 64.6 |
| A. C. Hathorn (POP) | 2,127 | 35.4 |
| 7 James G. Spencer (D) | 3,597 | 70.5 |
| A. M. Newman (PP) | 1,329 | 26.1 |

## MISSOURI

| Candidates | Votes | % |
|---|---|---|
| 1 Charles N. Clark (R) | 15,786 | 44.3 |
| Hatch (D) | 15,367 | 43.1 |
| London (PP) | 4,270 | 12.0 |
| 2 Uriel S. Hall (D) | 18,039 | 48.8 |
| Loomis (R) | 16,178 | 43.8 |
| Goodson (PP) | 2,761 | 7.5 |
| 3 Alexander M. Dockery (D) | 16,230 | 44.5 |
| Orton (R) | 15,890 | 43.6 |
| Penny (PP) | 4,053 | 11.1 |
| 4 George C. Crowther (R) | 15,695 | 47.8 |
| Ellison (D) | 14,034 | 42.7 |
| Missemer (PP) | 2,910 | 8.9 |
| 5 John C. Tarsney (D) | 16,538‡ | 47.3 |
| Robert T. Van Horn (R) | 5,798 | 45.2 |
| Crosby (PP) | 2,541 | 7.3 |
| 6 David A. De Armond (D) | 13,735 | 40.7 |
| Lewis (R) | 13,643 | 40.4 |
| Francisco (PP) | 6,391 | 18.9 |
| 7 John P. Tracey (R) | 17,775 | 45.5 |
| Heard (D) | 17,490 | 44.7 |
| Tippin (PP) | 3,567 | 9.1 |
| 8 Joel D. Hubbard (R) | 16,885 | 45.4 |
| Richard P. Bland (D) | 16,815 | 45.2 |
| Alldredge (PP) | 3,528 | 9.5 |
| 9 William M. Trelcar (R) | 15,082 | 49.2 |
| Clark (D) | 14,950 | 48.8 |
| 10 Richard Bartholdt (R) | 16,654 | 62.2 |
| Coppinger (D) | 8,887 | 33.2 |
| 11 Charles F. Joy (R) | 15,175 | 52.5 |
| Espenschled (D) | 12,893 | 44.6 |
| 12 Seth W. Cobb (D) | 10,095 | 53.4 |
| Sterrett (R) | 7,469 | 39.5 |
| Nelson (I) | 1,094 | 5.8 |
| 13 John H. Raney (R) | 16,849 | 51.3 |
| Fox (D) | 16,021 | 48.7 |
| 14 Norman A. Mozley (R) | 16,184 | 43.9 |
| Arnold (D) | 15,097 | 40.9 |
| Livingston (PP) | 5,591 | 15.2 |
| 15 Charles G. Burton (R) | 16,630 | 45.2 |
| Morgan (D) | 14,036 | 38.2 |
| Bigbee (PP) | 5,741 | 15.6 |

## MONTANA

| Candidates | Votes | % |
|---|---|---|
| AL Charles S. Hartman (R) | 23,140 | 47.0 |
| Robert B. Smith (PP) | 15,240 | 30.9 |
| Hal S. Corbett (D) | 10,369 | 21.1 |

## NEBRASKA

| Candidates | Votes | % |
|---|---|---|
| 1 Jesse B. Strode (R) | 18,185 | 56.8 |
| Austin H. Weir (D-POP I) | 12,730 | 39.8 |
| 2 David Mercer (R) | 12,946 | 50.8 |
| James E. Boyd (D) | 8,165 | 32.0 |
| D. Clem Deaver (POP I) | 4,007 | 15.7 |

| Candidates | Votes | % |
|---|---|---|
| 3 George D. Meiklejohn (R) | 16,531 | 45.2 |
| John M. Devine (POP I) | 11,138 | 30.5 |
| W. A. Hensley (D) | 8,018 | 21.9 |
| 4 Eugene J. Hainer (R) | 19,493 | 50.4 |
| William L. Stark (D-POP I) | 15,542 | 40.2 |
| Shannon S. Alley (D) | 2,763 | 7.1 |
| 5 William E. Andrews (R) | 16,270 | 48.9 |
| W. A. McKeighan (D-POP I) | 15,460 | 46.5 |
| 6 O. M. Kem (D-POP I) | 17,077 | 52.3 |
| Matt A. Daugherty (R) | 14,676 | 45.0 |

## NEVADA

| Candidates | Votes | % |
|---|---|---|
| AL Francis G. Newlands (D SIL) | 4,581 | 44.4 |
| Bartine (R) | 2,774 | 26.9 |
| J. C. Doughty (POP) | 2,751 | 26.7 |

## NEW HAMPSHIRE

| Candidates | Votes | % |
|---|---|---|
| 1 Cyrus A. Sulloway (R) | 22,730 | 56.3 |
| John B. Nash (D) | 16,507 | 40.9 |
| 2 Henry M. Baker (R) | 23,416 | 56.3 |
| Charles McDaniel (D) | 17,122 | 41.2 |

## NEW JERSEY

| Candidates | Votes | % |
|---|---|---|
| 1 Henry C. Loudenslager (R) | 24,462 | 61.0 |
| Ferrell (D) | 12,082 | 30.1 |
| 2 John J. Gardner (R) | 22,641 | 60.5 |
| Haines (D) | 12,900 | 34.5 |
| 3 Benjamin F. Howell (R) | 18,403 | 53.7 |
| Geisenhainer (D) | 14,427 | 42.1 |
| 4 Mahlon Pitney (R) | 16,116 | 49.0 |
| Cornish (D) | 14,709 | 44.7 |
| 5 James F. Stewart (R) | 16,441 | 54.9 |
| Demarest (D) | 10,469 | 34.9 |
| Ball (SOC LAB) | 2,511 | 8.4 |
| 6 Richard W. Parker (R) | 23,219 | 57.9 |
| English (D) | 14,746 | 36.8 |
| 7 Thomas McEwan Jr. (R) | 23,500 | 48.8 |
| Stevens (D) | 2,207 | 48.2 |
| 8 Charles N. Fowler (R) | 19,041 | 57.4 |
| Dunn (D) | 12,805 | 38.6 |

## NEW YORK

| Candidates | Votes | % |
|---|---|---|
| 1 Richard C. McCormick (R) | 20,864 | 56.9 |
| Joseph Fitch (D) | 14,961 | 40.8 |
| 2 Denis M. Hurley (R) | 14,507 | 45.1 |
| James O. Cleveland (D) | 13,194 | 41.0 |
| Daniel Bradley (D-REF) | 3,924 | 12.2 |
| 3 Francis H. Willis (R) | 18,568 | 49.8 |
| James A. Murtha Jr. (D) | 14,215 | 38.2 |
| Stephen Perry Sturges (D-REF) | 3,741 | 10.0 |
| 4 Israel T. Fischer (R) | 19,802 | 51.5 |
| William J. Coombs (D) | 17,514 | 45.6 |
| 5 Charles G. Bennett (R) | 19,372 | 58.8 |
| Anton Vigelius (D) | 11,885 | 36.1 |
| 6 James R. Howe (R) | 14,427 | 51.5 |
| Arthur Somers (D) | 12,525 | 44.7 |
| 7 Franklin Bartlett (D) | 9,138 | 47.0 |
| Austin E. Ford (R) | 7,676 | 39.5 |
| John Murphy (STATE D) | 2,159 | 11.1 |
| 8 James J. Walsh (D) | 9,466‡ | 50.3 |
| John M. Mitchell (R) | 9,099 | 48.3 |
| 9 Henry C. Miner (D) | 8,038 | 35.1 |
| Timothy J. Campbell (SOCIAL D) | 7,084 | 31.0 |
| John Simpson (R) | 5,214 | 22.8 |
| Daniel Deleon (SOC LAB) | 2,358 | 10.3 |
| 10 Andrew J. Campbell (R) | 13,845* | 46.5 |
| Daniel E. Sickles (D) | 12,982 | 43.6 |
| George Karsch (STATE D) | 2,331 | 7.8 |
| 11 William Sulzer (D) | 11,208 | 47.9 |
| Ferdinand Eidmann (R) | 10,524 | 45.0 |
| Francis H. Koenig (SOC WB) | 1,448 | 6.2 |

| Candidates | Votes | % |
|---|---|---|
| 12 George B. McClellan (D) | 10,933 | 47.4 |
| Robert A. Chesebrough (R) | 9,592 | 41.6 |
| George Walton Green (STATE D) | 2,042 | 8.9 |
| 13 Richard C. Shannon (R) | 13,555 | 46.3 |
| Amos J. Cummings (D) | 13,089 | 44.7 |
| Edward C. Baker (STATE D) | 1,943 | 6.6 |
| 14 Lemuel E. Quigg (R) | 24,332 | 55.4 |
| John Connelly (D) | 18,355 | 41.8 |
| 15 Philip B. Low (R) | 21,562 | 48.0 |
| Jacob A. Cantor (D) | 17,028 | 37.9 |
| Robert G. Monroe (STATE D) | 4,827 | 10.7 |
| 16 Benjamin L. Fairchild (R) | 24,853 | 54.1 |
| William Ryan (D) | 19,294 | 42.0 |
| 17 Benjamin B. Odell Jr. (R) | 19,327 | 57.5 |
| Eugene S. Ives (D) | 13,520 | 40.2 |
| 18 Jacob Le Fever (R) | 22,169 | 55.8 |
| William M. Ketcham (D) | 16,640 | 41.9 |
| 19 Frank S. Black (R) | 20,954 | 53.4 |
| Charles D. Haines (D) | 17,514 | 44.6 |
| 20 George N. Southwick (R) | 19,199 | 51.1 |
| Charles Tracey (D) | 17,549 | 46.7 |
| 21 David Forrest Wilber (R) | 24,472 | 53.1 |
| George Vanhorn (D) | 20,395 | 44.2 |
| 22 Newton M. Curtis (R) | 22,383 | 61.0 |
| Thomas R. Hossie (D) | 12,785 | 34.8 |
| 23 Wallace T. Foote Jr. (R) | 25,526 | 69.6 |
| Winslow C. Watson (D) | 11,143 | 30.3 |
| 24 Charles A. Chickering (R) | 23,320 | 61.3 |
| Washington T. Henderson (D) | 13,473 | 35. |
| 25 James S. Sherman (R) | 22,371 | 56. |
| John D. Henderson (D) | 16,130 | 40. |
| 26 George W. Ray (R) | 29,149 | 63. |
| Sherrill E. Smith (D) | 15,877 | 34. |
| 27 Theodore L. Poole (R) | 24,647 | 57. |
| Walter E. Northrup (D) | 16,307 | 37. |
| 28 Sereno E. Payne (R) | 29,528 | 61. |
| Eli McConnell (D) | 15,926 | 33. |
| 29 Charles W. Gillet (R) | 22,051 | 54. |
| George Henry Roberts (D) | 16,510 | 40. |
| 30 James S. Wadsworth (R) | 24,541 | 59. |
| Francis Murphy (D) | 13,950 | 34. |
| 31 Henry C. Brewster (R) | 21,488 | 55. |
| John D. Lynn (D) | 15,530 | 40. |
| 32 Rowland B. Mahany (R) | 15,548 | 51. |
| J. Cavin (D) | 13,893 | 45. |
| 33 Charles Daniels (R) | 23,595 | 65. |
| J. Morgenstein (D) | 11,095 | 30. |
| 34 Warren B. Hooker (R) | 25,964 | 64. |
| Staley N. Wood (D) | 10,674 | 26. |
| Andrew Yates Freeman (P) | 2,181 | 5. |

### Special Elections

| Candidates | Votes | % |
|---|---|---|
| 14 Lemuel E. Quigg (R) | 13,535 | 50 |
| Brown (D) | 12,586 | 46 |
| 15 Isidor Straus (D) | 15,364 | 55 |
| Sigrist (R) | 10,653 | 38 |

## NORTH CAROLINA

| Candidates | Votes | % |
|---|---|---|
| 1 Harry Skinner (PP) | 16,510 | 54 |
| William A. B. Branch (D) | 13,546 | 45 |
| 2 Frederick A. Woodard (D) | 14,721 | 50 |
| Henry P. Cheatham (R) | 9,413 | 31 |
| Howard F. Freeman | 5,314 | 18 |
| 3 John G. Shaw (D) | 10,699 | 39 |
| Cyrus Thompson (PP) | 9,705 | 35 |
| Oscar J. Spear (R) | 6,966 | 25 |
| 4 William F. Strowd (PP & R) | 18,667 | 56 |
| Charles M. Cooke (D) | 14,335 | 43 |
| 5 Thomas Settle (R) | 16,934 | 50 |
| Augustus W. Graham (D) | 14,046 | 42 |
| William Merritt | 2,104 | 6 |
| 6 James H. Lockhart (D) | 13,996‡ | 50 |
| Charles H. Martin (R) | 13,505 | 49 |
| 7 Alonzo C. Shuford (PP) | 15,383 | 5. |
| John S. Henderson (D) | 13,124 | 46 |
| 8 Romulus Z. Linney (PP & R) | 18,775 | 54 |
| William H. Bower (D) | 15,491 | 45 |

## NORTH CAROLINA

| | Candidates | Votes | % |
|---|---|---|---|
| 9 | Richmond Pearson (R) | 16,869 | 50.2 |
| | William T. Crawford (D) | 16,734 | 49.8 |

## NORTH DAKOTA

| | | Votes | % |
|---|---|---|---|
| AL | Martin N. Johnson (R) | 21,615 | 57.3 |
| | Muir (POP) | 15,660 | 41.5 |

## OHIO

| | Candidates | Votes | % |
|---|---|---|---|
| 1 | Charles P. Taft (R) | 19,315 | 61.0 |
| | Hiram D. Peck (D) | 10,378 | 32.8 |
| | Thomas John Donnelly (PP) | 1,679 | 5.3 |
| 2 | Jacob H. Bromwell (R) | 22,221 | 62.5 |
| | James B. Matson (D) | 10,667 | 30.0 |
| | Robert H. H. Wheeler (PP) | 2,456 | 6.9 |
| 3 | Paul J. Sorg (D) | 22,529 | 48.0 |
| | Andrew L. Harris (R) | 22,327 | 47.6 |
| 4 | Fernando C. Layton (D) | 15,388 | 47.2 |
| | William D. Davies (R) | 13,910 | 42.6 |
| | Joseph White (PP) | 2,323 | 7.1 |
| 5 | Francis B. De Witt (R) | 16,546 | 49.4 |
| | John S. Snook (D) | 14,899 | 44.5 |
| | Henry L. Goll (PP) | 2,015 | 6.0 |
| 6 | George W. Hulick (R) | 20,283 | 57.3 |
| | Joseph L. Stephens (D) | 12,505 | 35.3 |
| 7 | George W. Wilson (R) | 18,021 | 54.9 |
| | Charles E. Gain (D) | 11,731 | 35.8 |
| 8 | Luther M. Strong (R) | 21,730 | 58.5 |
| | Elijah T. Dunn (D) | 11,740 | 31.6 |
| | George Riddle (PP) | 2,045 | 5.5 |
| 9 | James Harding Southard (R) | 20,715 | 54.8 |
| | Byron F. Ritchie (D) | 14,109 | 37.3 |
| | George Candee (PP, P) | 2,964 | 7.8 |
| 10 | Lucien J. Fenton (R) | 19,768 | 62.5 |
| | John O. Yates (D) | 9,465 | 30.0 |
| 11 | Charles H. Grosvenor (R) | 20,731 | 56.9 |
| | Eli Reynolds Lash (D) | 11,601 | 31.8 |
| | William H. Crawford (PP) | 3,115 | 8.6 |
| 12 | David K. Watson (R) | 18,953 | 49.4 |
| | Joseph H. Outhwaite (D) | 17,362 | 45.3 |
| | George F. Ebner (PP) | 2,015 | 5.3 |
| 13 | Stephen R. Harris (R) | 19,131 | 46.0 |
| | Boston G. Young (D) | 18,453 | 44.4 |
| | Amos Kellar (PP) | 2,983 | 7.2 |
| 14 | Winfield S. Kerr (R) | 21,302 | 54.6 |
| | James C. Laser (D) | 14,262 | 36.6 |
| 15 | Henry C. Van Voorhis (R) | 19,291 | 56.7 |
| | Charles Richardson (D) | 12,010 | 35.3 |
| 16 | Lorenzo Danford (R) | 17,481 | 55.9 |
| | Albert O. Barnes (D) | 10,300 | 33.0 |
| | James Brettelle (PP) | 1,977 | 6.3 |
| 17 | Addison S. McClure (R) | 19,061 | 48.8 |
| | James A. D. Richards (D) | 17,403 | 44.5 |
| | William F. Loyd (PP) | 2,268 | 5.8 |
| 18 | Robert W. Tayler (R) | 20,803 | 49.0 |
| | Edward S. Raff (D) | 11,051 | 26.0 |
| | Jacob S. Coxey (PP) | 8,912 | 21.0 |
| 19 | Stephen A. Northway (R) | 22,361 | 62.9 |
| | Henry Apthorp (D) | 7,164 | 20.2 |
| | George A. Wise (PP) | 4,492 | 12.6 |
| 20 | Clifton B. Beach (R) | 17,327 | 59.1 |
| | H. B. Harrington (D) | 8,351 | 28.5 |
| | Luther S. Copper (PP) | 2,456 | 8.4 |
| 21 | Theodore E. Burton (R) | 17,968 | 53.4 |
| | Tom L. Johnson (D) | 13,260 | 39.4 |
| | George A. Groot (PP) | 1,805 | 5.4 |

### Special Election

| | | Votes | % |
|---|---|---|---|
| 2 | Jacob H. Bromwell (R) | 22,247 | 62.4 |
| | James B. Matson (D) | 10,709 | 30.1 |
| | William R. Fox (PP) | 2,448 | 6.9 |

## OREGON

| | | Votes | % |
|---|---|---|---|
| 1 | Binger Hermann (R) | 22,264 | 47.6 |
| | Charles Miller (POP) | 12,620 | 27.0 |

| | Candidates | Votes | % |
|---|---|---|---|
| | J. K. Weatherford (D) | 10,790 | 23.1 |
| 2 | William R. Ellis (R) | 18,875 | 47.9 |
| | Joseph Waldrop (POP) | 10,749 | 27.3 |
| | James H. Raley (D) | 9,013 | 22.9 |

## PENNSYLVANIA

| | | Votes | % |
|---|---|---|---|
| 1 | Henry H. Bingham (R) | 26,957 | 70.7 |
| | Denis J. Callaghan (D) | 10,995 | 28.8 |
| 2 | Robert Adams Jr. (R) | 17,550 | 75.7 |
| | Max Herzberg (D) | 5,488 | 23.7 |
| 3 | Frederick Halterman (R) | 13,443 | 65.8 |
| | Joseph P. McCullen (D) | 6,980 | 34.2 |
| 4 | John E. Reyburn (R) | 42,461 | 71.8 |
| | Gustav A. Muller (D) | 16,056 | 27.2 |
| 5 | Alfred C. Harmer (R) | 38,986 | 74.8 |
| | David Moffet (D) | 12,530 | 24.1 |
| 6 | John B. Robinson (R) | 20,717 | 64.7 |
| | Thomas E. Parke (D) | 9,803 | 30.6 |
| 7 | Irving P. Wanger (R) | 22,913 | 54.8 |
| | John Todd (D) | 18,087 | 43.3 |
| 8 | Joseph J. Hart (D) | 14,762 | 49.2 |
| | William S. Kirkpatrick (R) | 14,565 | 48.5 |
| 9 | Constantine J. Erdman (D) | 21,273 | 51.7 |
| | Jeremiah S. Trexler (R) | 19,325 | 47.0 |
| 10 | Marriott Brosius (R) | 19,266 | 70.9 |
| | John A. Coyle (D) | 7,181 | 26.4 |
| 11 | Joseph A. Scranton (R) | 14,104 | 51.1 |
| | Edward Merrifield (D) | 12,027 | 43.5 |
| 12 | John Leisenring (R) | 18,114 | 56.1 |
| | William H. Hines (D) | 12,644 | 39.2 |
| 13 | Charles N. Brumm (R) | 13,947 | 54.3 |
| | James B. Reilly (D) | 11,718 | 45.7 |
| 14 | Ephraim M. Woomer (R) | 19,139 | 64.1 |
| | William H. Minick (D) | 9,177 | 30.7 |
| 15 | Myron B. Wright (R) | 15,651* | 64.3 |
| | Rhamanthus M. Stocker (D) | 7,501 | 30.8 |
| 16 | Fred C. Leonard (R) | 16,791 | 53.8 |
| | James B. Benson (D) | 11,687 | 37.5 |
| | Andrew Sherwood (P) | 1,676 | 5.4 |
| 17 | Monroe H. Kulp (R) | 12,677 | 49.3 |
| | Charles R. Buckalew (D) | 11,783 | 45.8 |
| 18 | Thaddeus M. Mahon (R) | 19,597 | 61.1 |
| | D. G. Smith (D) | 12,456 | 38.9 |
| 19 | James A. Stable (R) | 21,138 | 52.1 |
| | Peter H. Strubinger (D) | 18,754 | 46.2 |
| 20 | Josiah D. Hicks (R) | 23,969 | 62.9 |
| | Thomas J. Burke (D) | 12,592 | 33.1 |
| 21 | Daniel B. Heiner (R) | 24,754 | 56.7 |
| | William M. Fairman (D) | 14,107 | 32.3 |
| 22 | John Dalzell (R) | 29,136 | 76.6 |
| | James A. Wakefield (D) | 7,430 | 19.5 |
| 23 | William A. Stone (R) | 13,731 | 77.6 |
| | James Semple (D) | 3,420 | 19.3 |
| 24 | Ernest F. Acheson (R) | 27,538 | 57.2 |
| | William A. Sipe (D) | 17,304 | 35.9 |
| 25 | Thomas W. Phillips (R) | 22,156 | 61.6 |
| | Joseph C. Vanderlin (D) | 10,435 | 29.0 |
| | William J. Kirker (PP) | 1,919 | 5.3 |
| 26 | Matthew Griswold (R) | 15,729 | 52.9 |
| | Joseph C. Sibley (D) | 13,265 | 44.6 |
| 27 | Charles W. Stone (R) | 11,717 | 61.1 |
| | John F. Parsons (D) | 4,845 | 25.2 |
| | S. P. McCalmont (P) | 1,724 | 9.0 |
| 28 | William C. Arnold (R) | 16,994 | 50.6 |
| | Aaron Williams (D) | 15,197 | 45.2 |
| AL | Galusha A. Grow (R, IR) | 571,124✓ | |
| | George F. Huff (R, IR) | 566,290✓ | |
| | Henry Meyer (D) | 328,677 | |
| | Thomas Collins (D) | 324,623 | |
| | Elisha Kent Kane (P) | 23,481 | |
| | Lewis G. Jordan (P) | 22,980 | |
| | Victor A. Lotier (PP) | 17,820 | |
| | B. F. Greenman (PP) | 17,299 | |
| | Ernest Kreft (SOC LAB) | 1,524 | |
| | Gottfried Metzler (SOC LAB) | 1,466 | |

### Special Election

| | | Votes | % |
|---|---|---|---|
| AL | Galusha A. Grow (R) | 485,804 | 60.4 |
| | James Denton Hancock (D) | 297,966 | 37.0 |

## RHODE ISLAND

| | Candidates | Votes | % |
|---|---|---|---|
| 1 | Melville Bull (R) | 11,422 | 57.2 |
| | Oscar Lapham (D) | 7,311 | 36.6 |
| 2 | Warren O. Arnold (R) | 11,259 | 59.8 |
| | Garvin (D) | 6,555 | 34.8 |

## SOUTH CAROLINA

| | | Votes | % |
|---|---|---|---|
| 1 | William Elliott (D) | 5,650‡ | 59.1 |
| | George W. Murray (R) | 3,913 | 40.9 |
| 2 | W. Jasper Talbert (D) | 5,942 | 99.5 |
| 3 | Asbury C. Latimer (D) | 5,778 | 81.3 |
| | Robert Moorman (R) | 985 | 13.9 |
| 4 | Stanyarne Wilson (D) | 8,425 | 75.1 |
| | L. D. Metton (R) | 2,771 | 24.7 |
| 5 | Thomas J. Straight (D) | 6,141 | 67.6 |
| | G. G. Alexander (R) | 1,545 | 17.0 |
| | W. R. Davie (ID) | 1,163 | 12.8 |
| 6 | John L. McLaurin (D) | 8,171 | 76.9 |
| | J. E. Wilson (R) | 2,452 | 23.1 |
| 7 | J. William Stokes (D) | 7,358‡ | 73.0 |
| | James B. Johnston (R) | 2,656 | 26.3 |

## SOUTH DAKOTA

| | | Votes | % |
|---|---|---|---|
| AL | Robert J. Gamble (R) | 40,683✓ | |
| | John A. Pickler (R) | 40,623✓ | |
| | John E. Kelley (I) | 27,379 | |
| | Freeman Knowles (I) | 27,348 | |
| | William A. Lynch (D) | 8,102 | |
| | Roger F. Connor (D) | 8,041 | |
| | George A. Ragan (P) | 872 | |
| | A. Jamieson (P) | 833 | |

## TENNESSEE

| | | Votes | % |
|---|---|---|---|
| 1 | William C. Anderson (R) | 18,017 | 61.7 |
| | Thad A. Cox (D) | 8,542 | 29.2 |
| | R. S. Cheves (P) | 2,662 | 9.1 |
| 2 | Henry R. Gibson (R) | 16,215 | 53.2 |
| | John C. Hauk (R-D) | 13,191 | 43.3 |
| 3 | Foster V. Brown (R) | 17,019 | 52.2 |
| | H. C. Snadgrass (D) | 13,947 | 42.7 |
| | F. B. Dickey (POP) | 1,669 | 5.1 |
| 4 | Benton McMillin (D) | 11,958 | 54.2 |
| | J. A. Denton (R) | 10,115 | 45.8 |
| 5 | James D. Richardson (D) | 11,440 | 53.7 |
| | W. W. Erwin (POP) | 9,543 | 44.8 |
| 6 | James E. Washington (D) | 11,234 | 54.0 |
| | Tip Gamble (R) | 4,798 | 23.1 |
| | T. N. Lewis (POP) | 4,783 | 23.0 |
| 7 | Nicholas N. Cox (D) | 9,098 | 52.6 |
| | H. F. Farris (R) | 6,366 | 36.8 |
| | J. K. P. Blackburn (POP) | 1,844 | 10.7 |
| 8 | John E. McCall (R) | 13,064 | 51.6 |
| | B. A. Enloe (D) | 12,243 | 48.4 |
| 9 | James C. McDearmon (D) | 10,634 | 57.1 |
| | Atwood Pierson (POP) | 7,983 | 42.9 |
| 10 | Josiah Patterson (D) | 6,654 | 66.1 |
| | J. N. Brown (R) | 1,955 | 19.4 |
| | R. J. Rawlings (POP) | 1,454 | 14.5 |

## TEXAS

| | | Votes | % |
|---|---|---|---|
| 1 | Joseph C. Hutcheson (D) | 14,920 | 55.0 |
| | J. J. Burroughs (POP) | 10,037 | 37.0 |
| | L. E. Dunn (R) | 2,164 | 8.0 |
| 2 | Samuel B. Cooper (D) | 23,323 | 59.3 |
| | B. A. Calhoun (POP) | 16,025 | 40.7 |
| 3 | Charles H. Yoakum (D) | 15,461 | 55.5 |
| | J. M. Perdue (POP) | 12,411 | 44.5 |
| 4 | David B. Culberson (D) | 15,872 | 49.2 |
| | J. H. Davis (POP) | 14,604 | 45.3 |
| | H. S. Sanderson (R) | 1,728 | 5.4 |
| 5 | Joseph W. Bailey (D) | 19,722 | 56.7 |
| | N. M. Browder (POP) | 13,540 | 38.9 |
| 6 | Jo Abbott (D) | 19,965 | 49.2 |
| | J. C. Kearby (POP) | 19,621 | 48.4 |

## TEXAS

| | Candidates | Votes | % |
|---|---|---|---|
| 7 | George C. Pendleton (D) | 18,822 | 52.4 |
| | I. N. Barber (POP) | 17,092 | 47.6 |
| 8 | Charles K. Bell (D) | 16,480 | 50.6 |
| | C. H. Jenkins (POP) | 16,104 | 49.4 |
| 9 | Joseph D. Sayers (D) | 18,460 | 52.7 |
| | W. O. Hutchison (POP) | 16,591 | 47.3 |
| 10 | Miles Crowley (D) | 12,177 | 39.4 |
| | A. J. Rosenthal (R) | 10,874 | 35.2 |
| | J. C. McBride (POP) | 7,847 | 25.4 |
| 11 | William H. Crain (D) | 17,946 | 52.7 |
| | V. Weldon (POP) | 16,089 | 47.3 |
| 12 | George H. Noonan (R) | 11,958 | 43.4 |
| | A. W. Houston (D) | 11,045 | 40.1 |
| | A. V. Gates (POP) | 4,545 | 16.5 |
| 13 | Jeremiah V. Cockrell (D) | 13,687 | 39.8 |
| | D. B. Gilliland (POP) | 13,321 | 38.8 |
| | J. M. Dean (ID) | 5,780 | 16.8 |

## VERMONT

| | | Votes | % |
|---|---|---|---|
| 1 | H. Henry Powers (R) | 21,546 | 75.5 |
| | Vernon A. Rutlard (D) | 6,987 | 24.5 |
| 2 | William W. Grout (R) | 20,337 | 75.2 |
| | George S. Fletcher (D) | 6,658 | 24.6 |

## VIRGINIA

| | | Votes | % |
|---|---|---|---|
| 1 | William A. Jones (D) | 11,598 | 60.1 |
| | James J. McDonald (R) | 6,944 | 36.0 |
| 2 | D. Gardiner Tyler (D) | 12,375 | 56.3 |
| | T. R. Borland (R) | 8,868 | 40.3 |
| 3 | Tazewell Ellett (D) | 11,745 | 63.3 |
| | J. W. Southward (R) | 4,653 | 25.1 |
| | James M. Gregory (POP) | 1,788 | 9.6 |
| 4 | William R. McKenney (D) | 8,773‡ | 48.1 |
| | Robert T. Thorp (R) | 7,909 | 43.3 |
| | J. Haskins Hobson (POP) | 1,107 | 6.1 |
| 5 | Claude A. Swanson (D) | 10,750 | 52.3 |
| | George W. Cornett (R) | 8,417 | 41.0 |
| | G. W. B. Hale (POP) | 1,121 | 5.5 |

| | Candidates | Votes | % |
|---|---|---|---|
| 6 | Peter J. Otey (D) | 10,602 | 47.1 |
| | John Hampton Hoge (R) | 8,288 | 36.9 |
| | O. C. Rucker (POP) | 3,550 | 15.8 |
| 7 | Smith S. Turner (D) | 11,041 | 52.1 |
| | Robert J. Walker (R) | 9,500 | 44.9 |
| 8 | Elisha E. Meredith (D) | 10,801 | 54.3 |
| | P. H. McCaull (R) | 8,450 | 42.5 |
| 9 | James Alexander Walker (R) | 14,287 | 51.2 |
| | H. S. K. Morison (D) | 13,332 | 47.8 |
| 10 | Henry St.George Tucker (D) | 12,422 | 50.3 |
| | J. Yost (R) | 11,530 | 46.7 |

### Special Election

| | | Votes | % |
|---|---|---|---|
| 7 | Smith S. Turner (D) | 7,882 | 65.0 |
| | E. D. Root | 4,189 | 34.5 |

## WASHINGTON

| | | Votes | % |
|---|---|---|---|
| AL | William H. Doolittle (R) | 35,981✔ | |
| | Samuel C. Hyde (R) | 35,075✔ | |
| | W. P. C. Adams (PP, SPP) | 26,285 | |
| | J. C. Van Patten (PP, SPP) | 25,643 | |
| | B. F. Heuston (D) | 14,602 | |
| | N. T. Caton (D) | 14,503 | |
| | W. W.Van Dusen (P) | 210 | |
| | B. F. Brown (P) | 203 | |
| | W. P. C. Adams (SPP) | 157 | |
| | Lawrence E. Doyle (I) | 110 | |

## WEST VIRGINIA

| | | Votes | % |
|---|---|---|---|
| 1 | Blackburn B. Dovener (R) | 21,821 | 53.4 |
| | John A. Howard (D) | 17,375 | 42.5 |
| 2 | Alston G. Dayton (R) | 23,444 | 51.8 |
| | William S. Wilson (D) | 21,397 | 47.3 |
| 3 | James H. Huling (R) | 23,457 | 53.5 |
| | John D. Alderson (D) | 19,538 | 44.5 |
| 4 | Warren Miller (R) | 20,795 | 52.0 |
| | Thomas H. Harvey (D) | 17,767 | 44.4 |

## WISCONSIN

| | Candidates | Votes | % |
|---|---|---|---|
| 1 | Henry Allen Cooper (R) | 21,972 | 56.7 |
| | Andrew Kull (D) | 12,334 | 31.8 |
| | Hamilton Utley (PP) | 2,828 | 7.3 |
| 2 | Edward Sauerhering (R) | 18,197 | 47.9 |
| | Charles Barwig (D) | 17,932 | 47.2 |
| 3 | Joseph W. Babcock (R) | 22,262 | 58.2 |
| | Cyrus M. Butt (D & POP) | 14,608 | 38.2 |
| 4 | Theobald Otjen (R) | 17,719 | 47.9 |
| | David S. Rose (D) | 12,214 | 33.0 |
| | Henry Smith (PP) | 7,092 | 19.2 |
| 5 | Samuel S. Barney (R) | 18,681 | 52.6 |
| | Henry Blank (D) | 13,057 | 36.7 |
| | Fred C. Runge (PP) | 3,794 | 10.7 |
| 6 | Samuel A. Cook (R) | 21,718 | 55.8 |
| | Owen A. Wells (D) | 14,919 | 38.3 |
| 7 | Michael Griffin (R) | 17,489 | 57.4 |
| | George W. Levis (D) | 9,996 | 32.8 |
| | Clements H. Van Worner (PP) | 1,626 | 5.3 |
| 8 | Edward S. Minor (R) | 19,902 | 54.2 |
| | Lyman E. Barnes (D) | 15,522 | 42.3 |
| 9 | Alexander Stewart (R) | 22,741 | 56.0 |
| | Thomas Lynch (D) | 14,910 | 36.7 |
| | John F. Miles (PP) | 2,187 | 5.4 |
| 10 | John J. Jenkins (R) | 19,836 | 57.9 |
| | E. C. Kennedy (D) | 9,054 | 26.4 |
| | William Munro (PP) | 3,855 | 11.3 |

### Special Election

| | | Votes | % |
|---|---|---|---|
| 7 | Michael Griffin (R) | 17,766 | 57.8 |
| | George W. Levis (D) | 9,992 | 32.5 |
| | Clement H. Van Worner (PP) | 1,619 | 5.3 |

## WYOMING

| | | Votes | % |
|---|---|---|---|
| AL | Frank W. Mondell (R) | 10,068 | 52.6 |
| | Henry A. Coffeen (D) | 6,152 | 32.2 |
| | Shakespeare E. Sealey (POP) | 2,906 | 15.2 |

# 1895 House Elections

### Special Elections

| | | Votes | % |
|---|---|---|---|
| 10 | George W. Prince (R) | 21,829 | 66.0 |
| | Fred K. Bastian (D) | 8,392 | 25.4 |
| | E. K. Kempster | 2,877 | 8.7 |
| 18 | William F. L. Hadley (R) | 15,291 | 51.8 |
| | Edward Lane (D) | 12,040 | 40.8 |

## MASSACHUSETTS

### Special Election

| | | Votes | % |
|---|---|---|---|
| 6 | William H. Moody (R) | 15,064 | 66.3 |
| | Harvey N. Shepard (D) | 5,819 | 25.6 |
| | Wilbert Ormand Dwinell (PP) | 1,299 | 5.7 |

## MICHIGAN

### Special Election

| | | Votes | % |
|---|---|---|---|
| 3 | Alfred Milnes (R) | 16,167 | 51.7 |
| | Albert M. Todd (DPOP PFS) | 14,851 | 47.5 |

## NEW YORK

### Special Election

| | | Votes | % |
|---|---|---|---|
| 10 | Amos J. Cummin (TAM) | 15,295 | 56.4 |
| | R. A. Greacen (R) | 10,223 | 37.7 |

## PENNSYLVANIA[1]

### Special Elections

| | | Votes | % |
|---|---|---|---|
| 15 | Edwin J. Jorden (R) | 13,445 | 64.1 |
| | Rhamanthus M. Stocker (D) | 6,690 | 31.9 |
| 15 | James H. Codding (R) | 14,356 | 66.0 |
| | Rhamanthus M. Stocker (D) | 6,575 | 30.2 |

1. *Edwin J. Jorden was elected to fill an unexpired term in the 53rd Congress (1893-95) following the death of incumbent Myron B. Wright. Wright had previously been reelected to the 54th Congress (1895-97). James H. Codding was elected to a full two-year term to replace Wright. (See Pennsylvania's 15th district for 1892 and 1894, pp. 1068, 1073.)*

# 1896 House Elections

## ALABAMA

| | Candidates | Votes | % |
|---|---|---|---|
| 1 | George W. Taylor (D SIL) | 11,890 | 70.5 |
| | Frank H. Threatt (R) | 4,281 | 25.4 |
| 2 | Jesse Stallings (D SIL) | 11,703 | 55.9 |
| | Thomas H. Clarke (D SM) | 5,361 | 25.6 |
| | John C. Fonville (POP) | 3,856 | 18.4 |
| 3 | Henry Clayton (D SIL) | 11,671 | 52.6 |
| | George S. Youngblood (D SM) | 5,754 | 25.9 |
| | Emmett C. Jackson (POP) | 759 | 21.5 |
| 4 | Thomas S. Plowman (D SIL) | 10,312‡ | 56.3 |
| | William F. Aldrich (POP & R) | 7,345 | 40.1 |
| 5 | Willis Brewer (D SIL) | 13,587 | 60.9 |
| | A. T. Goodwyn (POP & R) | 8,742 | 39.2 |
| 6 | John H. Bankhead (D) | 10,148 | 55.1 |
| | A. S. Van de Graaf (D SM) | 4,985 | 27.1 |
| | George S. Youngblood (POP) | 3,295 | 17.9 |
| 7 | Milford W. Howard (POP) | 6,168 | 35.8 |
| | William I. Bullock (D SIL) | 5,628 | 32.7 |
| | Curtis (R) | 4,982 | 28.9 |
| 8 | Joseph Wheeler (D) | 15,640 | 56.7 |
| | Oscar R. Hundley (R) | 11,630 | 42.1 |
| 9 | Oscar Underwood (D SIL) | 13,499 | 63.0 |
| | Grattan B. Crowe (POP) | 5,618 | 26.2 |
| | Lawson (D SM) | 2,316 | 10.8 |

## ARKANSAS

| | Candidates | Votes | % |
|---|---|---|---|
| 1 | Philip D. McCulloch Jr. (D) | 20,419 | 76.8 |
| | F. W. Tucker (R) | 6,178 | 23.2 |
| 2 | John S. Little (D) | 19,099 | 74.7 |
| | C. D. Greaves (R) | 6,483 | 25.3 |
| 3 | Thomas C. McRae (D) | 19,321 | 70.0 |
| | J. B. Freidheim (R) | 8,273 | 30.0 |
| 4 | William L. Terry (D) | 16,133 | 70.6 |
| | C. C. Waters (R) | 6,714 | 29.4 |
| 5 | Hugh A. Dinsmore (D) | 17,566 | 65.9 |
| | W. H. Neal (R) | 9,087 | 34.1 |
| 6 | Stephen Brundidge Jr. (D) | 17,106 | 77.4 |
| | B. F. Bodenhammer (R) | 5,010 | 22.7 |

## CALIFORNIA

| | Candidates | Votes | % |
|---|---|---|---|
| 1 | John A. Barham (R) | 17,826 | 49.7 |
| | Fletcher A. Cutler (D) | 16,328 | 45.5 |
| 2 | Marion De Vries (D&I POP) | 24,434 | 55.5 |
| | Grove L. Johnson (R) | 18,613 | 42.3 |
| 3 | Samuel G. Hilborn (R) | 19,778 | 54.0 |
| | Warren B. English (D-PP) | 16,119 | 44.0 |
| 4 | James G. Maguire (D-PP) | 19,074 | 61.0 |
| | Thomas B. O'Brien (R) | 10,940 | 35.0 |
| 5 | Eugene F. Loud (R) | 19,351 | 48.6 |
| | Joseph P. Kelly (D) | 10,494 | 26.4 |
| | A. B. Kinne (PP) | 8,825 | 22.2 |
| 6 | Charles A. Barlow (D-PP) | 24,157 | 48.9 |
| | James McLachlan (R) | 23,494 | 47.6 |
| 7 | Curtis H. Castle (D-PP) | 19,183 | 46.7 |
| | William W. Bowers (R) | 18,939 | 46.1 |
| | William H. Carlson (I) | 2,139 | 5.2 |

## COLORADO

| | Candidates | Votes | % |
|---|---|---|---|
| 1 | John F. Shafroth (FUS) | 67,821 | 84.9 |
| | T. E. McClelland (R) | 9,625 | 12.1 |
| 2 | John C. Bell (FUS) | 84,018 | 84.5 |
| | T. F. Hoffmire (R) | 14,385 | 14.5 |

## CONNECTICUT

| | Candidates | Votes | % |
|---|---|---|---|
| 1 | E. Stevens Henry (R) | 27,623 | 66.7 |
| | Tuttle (D) | 10,859 | 26.2 |
| | Hyde (ND) | 2,114 | 5.1 |
| 2 | Nehemiah D. Sperry (R) | 35,944 | 59.3 |
| | Fuller (D) | 22,317 | 36.8 |

| | Candidates | Votes | % |
|---|---|---|---|
| 3 | Charles A. Russell (R) | 15,269 | 64.0 |
| | Fanning (D) | 7,665 | 32.1 |
| 4 | Ebenezer J. Hill (R) | 30,658 | 63.3 |
| | Houlihan (D) | 15,723 | 32.5 |

## DELAWARE

| | Candidates | Votes | % |
|---|---|---|---|
| AL | Levin Irving Handy (D) | 15,407 | 44.0 |
| | Jonathan S. Willis (AK R) | 11,159 | 31.8 |
| | Robert G. Houston (HIG R) | 7,123 | 20.3 |

## FLORIDA

| | Candidates | Votes | % |
|---|---|---|---|
| 1 | Stephen M. Sparkman (D) | 14,822 | 77.5 |
| | E. K. Nichols (R) | 2,797 | 14.6 |
| | J. Asakiah Williams (POP) | 1,308 | 6.8 |
| 2 | Robert W. Davis (D) | 14,375 | 61.9 |
| | Joseph N. Stripling (R) | 6,633 | 28.6 |

## GEORGIA

| | Candidates | Votes | % |
|---|---|---|---|
| 1 | Rufus E. Lester (D) | 8,063 | 53.8 |
| | Joseph F. Doyle (R) | 4,095 | 27.3 |
| | George H. Miller (POP) | 2,826 | 18.9 |
| 2 | James M. Griggs (D) | 7,104 | 53.2 |
| | J. E. Peterson (R) | 3,780 | 28.3 |
| | John A. Sibley (POP) | 2,483 | 18.6 |
| 3 | Elijah B. Lewis (D) | 7,459 | 70.7 |
| | Seaborn S. Montgomery (POP) | 3,096 | 29.3 |
| 4 | William C. Adamson (D) | 8,519 | 65.2 |
| | A. H. Freeman (R) | 4,304 | 32.9 |
| 5 | Leonidas F. Livingston (D) | 9,258 | 58.0 |
| | J. C. Hendrix (R) | 6,715 | 42.0 |
| 6 | Charles L. Bartlett (D) | 8,236 | 63.7 |
| | A. A. Murphy (POP) | 4,696 | 36.3 |
| 7 | John W. Maddox (D) | 10,719 | 53.4 |
| | W. L. Massey (R) | 5,087 | 25.4 |
| | J. W. McGarrity (POP) | 4,256 | 21.2 |
| 8 | William M. Howard (D) | 9,088 | 61.6 |
| | G. L. Anderson (POP) | 2,962 | 20.1 |
| | W. Patrick Henry (R) | 2,701 | 18.3 |
| 9 | Farish C. Tate (D) | 11,037 | 54.2 |
| | H. P. Farrow (R) | 5,421 | 26.6 |
| | Thomas C. Winn (POP) | 3,926 | 19.3 |
| 10 | William H. Fleming (D) | 10,119 | 58.8 |
| | John T. West (POP) | 7,105 | 41.3 |
| 11 | William G. Brantley (D) | 9,141 | 60.3 |
| | Benjamin Milliken (POP) | 6,019 | 39.7 |

## IDAHO

| | Candidates | Votes | % |
|---|---|---|---|
| AL | James T. Gunn (POP & D) | 13,187 | 46.6 |
| | William E. Borah (SIL R) | 9,034 | 32.0 |
| | John T. Morrison (R) | 6,054 | 21.4 |

## ILLINOIS

| | Candidates | Votes | % |
|---|---|---|---|
| 1 | James R. Mann (R) | 51,582 | 67.6 |
| | James H. Teller (D) | 23,123 | 30.3 |
| 2 | William Lorimer (R) | 35,045 | 54.3 |
| | John Z. White (D & POP) | 28,309 | 43.9 |
| 3 | Hugh R. Belknap (R) | 22,075 | 50.0 |
| | Clarence S. Darrow (D&SILVER) | 21,485 | 48.7 |
| 4 | Daniel W. Mills (R) | 22,364 | 50.9 |
| | James McAndrews (D&SILVER) | 20,454 | 46.5 |
| 5 | George E. White (R) | 23,053 | 50.9 |
| | Edward T. Noonan (D & POP) | 19,975 | 44.1 |
| 6 | Edward D. Cooke (R) | 25,723 | 56.3 |
| | Joseph L. Martin (D & POP) | 19,144 | 41.9 |
| 7 | George Edmund Foss (R) | 41,510 | 65.1 |
| | Olaf E. Ray (D & POP) | 21,213 | 33.3 |

| | Candidates | Votes | % |
|---|---|---|---|
| 8 | Albert J. Hopkins (R) | 32,073 | 70.1 |
| | Simeon N. Hoover (D) | 12,861 | 28.1 |
| 9 | Robert R. Hitt (R) | 32,949 | 67.2 |
| | Charles O. Knudson (D) | 15,241 | 31.1 |
| 10 | George W. Prince (R) | 31,459 | 64.0 |
| | William M. Moore (D) | 15,741 | 32.0 |
| 11 | Walter Reeves (R) | 24,765 | 56.5 |
| | Charles M. Golden (D) | 18,514 | 42.2 |
| 12 | Joseph G. Cannon (R) | 28,566 | 59.9 |
| | George L. Vance (D & POP) | 18,613 | 39.1 |
| 13 | Vespasian Warner (R) | 27,324 | 58.2 |
| | Frank M. Palmer (D & POP) | 18,811 | 40.1 |
| 14 | Joseph V. Graff (R) | 25,144 | 50.9 |
| | Nicholas E. Worthington (D) | 23,413 | 47.4 |
| 15 | Benjamin F. Marsh (R) | 24,605 | 49.7 |
| | William H. Neece (D) | 24,296 | 49.1 |
| 16 | William H. Hinrichsen (D & POP) | 26,615 | 56.0 |
| | John I. Rinaker (R) | 20,472 | 43.1 |
| 17 | James A. Connolly (R) | 23,813 | 49.4 |
| | Benjamin F. Caldwell (D) | 23,714 | 49.2 |
| 18 | Thomas M. Jett (D) | 22,358 | 51.5 |
| | William F. L. Hadley (R) | 20,599 | 47.4 |
| 19 | Andrew J. Hunter (D & POP) | 23,960 | 50.0 |
| | Benson Wood (R) | 22,793 | 47.6 |
| 20 | James R. Campbell (D & POP) | 22,359 | 53.3 |
| | Orlando Burrel (R) | 19,508 | 46.5 |
| 21 | Jehu Baker (D) | 23,581 | 50.4 |
| | Everett J. Murphy (R) | 23,179 | 49.6 |
| 22 | George W. Smith (R) | 22,066 | 55.3 |
| | John J. Hale (D & POP) | 17,811 | 44.7 |

## INDIANA

| | Candidates | Votes | % |
|---|---|---|---|
| 1 | James A. Hemenway (R) | 21,807 | 49.6 |
| | Thomas Duncan (D) | 20,856 | 47.4 |
| 2 | Robert W. Miers (D) | 21,757 | 48.2 |
| | Alexander M. Hardy (R) | 20,759 | 46.0 |
| | Newel H. Motsinger (POP) | 2,625 | 5.8 |
| 3 | William J. Zenor (D) | 22,418 | 52.6 |
| | Robert J. Tracewell (R) | 19,984 | 46.9 |
| 4 | William S. Holman (D) | 23,594 | 50.8 |
| | Marcus R. Sulzer (R) | 22,769 | 49.0 |
| 5 | George W. Faris (R) | 25,290 | 50.4 |
| | John Clark Ridpath (D & POP) | 24,925 | 49.6 |
| 6 | Henry U. Johnson (R) | 24,083 | 52.4 |
| | Charles A. Robinson (D & POP) | 21,867 | 47.6 |
| 7 | Jesse Overstreet (R) | 29,075 | 53.8 |
| | Charles M. Cooper (D & POP) | 24,187 | 44.8 |
| 8 | Charles L. Henry (R) | 30,045 | 52.3 |
| | John R. Brunt (D & POP) | 27,413 | 47.7 |
| 9 | Charles B. Landis (R) | 23,616 | 50.3 |
| | Joseph B. Cheadle (D & POP) | 23,367 | 49.7 |
| 10 | Edgar D. Crumpacker (R) | 28,259 | 55.0 |
| | Martin L. Kruger (D & POP) | 23,120 | 45.0 |
| 11 | George W. Steele (R) | 27,853 | 53.5 |
| | Joseph H. Larimer (D) | 23,584 | 45.3 |
| 12 | James N. Robinson (D & POP) | 22,752 | 50.6 |
| | Jacob D. Leighty (R) | 22,196 | 49.4 |
| 13 | Lemuel W. Royse (R) | 25,514 | 51.6 |
| | Charles Kellison (D & POP) | 23,928 | 48.4 |

## IOWA

| | Candidates | Votes | % |
|---|---|---|---|
| 1 | Samuel M. Clark (R) | 21,944 | 53.7 |
| | Sabut M. Casey (D-PP) | 18,649 | 45.6 |
| 2 | George M. Curtis (R) | 23,202 | 52.8 |
| | Alfred Hurst (D) | 19,882 | 45.2 |
| 3 | David B. Henderson (R) | 29,654 | 60.7 |
| | George Stachl (D) | 19,231 | 39.3 |
| 4 | Thomas Updegraff (R) | 26,659 | 59.6 |
| | F. D. Bayless (D-PP) | 17,791 | 39.8 |
| 5 | Robert G. Cousins (R) | 26,133 | 57.7 |
| | John R. Caldwell (D-PP) | 18,765 | 41.5 |

## IOWA

| | Candidates | Votes | % |
|---|---|---|---|
| 6 | John F. Lacey (R) | 21,970 | 51.1 |
| | F. E. White (D-PP) | 20,769 | 48.3 |
| 7 | John A. T. Hull (R) | 25,578 | 56.9 |
| | Frank W. Evans (D-PP) | 19,352 | 43.1 |
| 8 | William P. Hepburn (R) | 24,783 | 50.9 |
| | W. H. Robb (D-PP) | 23,956 | 49.2 |
| 9 | Alva L. Hager (R) | 24,904 | 52.4 |
| | L. T. Genning (D-PP) | 22,522 | 47.4 |
| 10 | Jonathan P. Dolliver (R) | 33,523 | 59.4 |
| | John B. Romans (D-PP) | 22,555 | 40.0 |
| 11 | George D. Perkins (R) | 29,601 | 56.1 |
| | H. Vanwagener (D-PP) | 22,773 | 43.2 |

## KANSAS

| | Candidates | Votes | % |
|---|---|---|---|
| 1 | Case Broderick (R) | 22,115 | 53.1 |
| | H. E. Ballou (D-PP) | 19,513 | 46.9 |
| 2 | Mason S. Peters (D-PP) | 26,307 | 50.4 |
| | John P. Harris (R) | 25,919 | 49.6 |
| 3 | Edwin R. Ridgely (D-PP) | 27,034 | 54.2 |
| | S. S. Kirkpatrick (R) | 22,849 | 45.8 |
| 4 | Charles Curtis (R) | 26,643 | 50.7 |
| | John Madden (D-PP) | 25,889 | 49.3 |
| 5 | William D. Vincent (D-PP) | 19,735 | 50.8 |
| | W. A. Calderhead (R) | 19,101 | 49.2 |
| 6 | Nelson B. McCormick (PP) | 18,257 | 50.8 |
| | A. H. Ellis (R) | 16,106 | 44.9 |
| 7 | Jeremiah Simpson (D-PP) | 29,789 | 52.5 |
| | Chester I. Long (R) | 26,966 | 47.5 |
| AL | Jeremiah D. Botkin (PP & D) | 168,420 | 51.3 |
| | R. W. Blue (R) | 158,147 | 48.2 |

## KENTUCKY

| | Candidates | Votes | % |
|---|---|---|---|
| 1 | Charles K. Wheeler (D) | 14,808 | 37.4 |
| | G. P. Thomas (R) | 12,842 | 32.4 |
| | B. F. Keys (POP) | 11,991 | 30.3 |
| 2 | John D. Clardy (D) | 23,535 | 57.0 |
| | E. T. Franks (R) | 17,276 | 41.8 |
| 3 | John S. Rhea (D) | 19,670 | 49.6 |
| | W. G. Hunter (R) | 19,324 | 48.7 |
| 4 | David H. Smith (D) | 21,655 | 49.1 |
| | John W. Lewis (R) | 20,222 | 45.8 |
| 5 | Walter Evans (R) | 27,780 | 59.7 |
| | John Y. Brown (D) | 17,150 | 36.8 |
| 6 | Albert S. Berry (D) | 16,660 | 58.9 |
| | Richard P. Ernst (R) | 11,638 | 41.1 |
| 7 | Evan E. Settle (D) | 18,826 | 52.5 |
| | W. C. P. Breckinridge (R-GOLD D) | 17,019 | 47.5 |
| 8 | George M. Davison (R) | 18,110 | 53.7 |
| | John B. Thompson (D) | 15,629 | 46.3 |
| 9 | Samuel J. Pugh (R) | 22,014 | 50.5 |
| | W. Larue Thomas (D) | 21,591 | 49.5 |
| 10 | Thomas Y. Fitzpatrick (D) | 17,453 | 51.9 |
| | John W. Langley (R) | 16,196 | 48.1 |
| 11 | David G. Colson (R) | 22,391 | 56.2 |
| | James D. Black (D) | 12,878 | 32.3 |
| | J. D. White (I) | 4,547 | 11.4 |

## LOUISIANA

| | Candidates | Votes | % |
|---|---|---|---|
| 1 | Adolph Meyer (D) | 10,776 | 70.5 |
| | Armand Romain (IR) | 3,982 | 26.1 |
| 2 | Robert C. Davey (D) | 10,269 | 60.8 |
| | James Legendre (NR) | 5,235 | 31.0 |
| | Fred N. Wicker (R) | 1,344 | 8.0 |
| 3 | Robert F. Broussard (D) | 9,323 | 57.7 |
| | Taylor Beattle (NR) | 6,490 | 40.2 |
| 4 | Henry W. Ogden (D) | 10,775 | 66.7 |
| | B. W. Bailey (POP) | 4,726 | 29.3 |
| 5 | Samuel T. Baird (D) | 11,494 | 70.2 |
| | Alexis Benoit (POP) | 4,870 | 29.8 |
| 6 | Samuel M. Robertson (D) | 11,872 | 72.0 |
| | C. C. Duson (NR) | 3,686 | 22.4 |
| | William M. Thompson (POP) | 924 | 5.6 |

## MAINE

| | Candidates | Votes | % |
|---|---|---|---|
| 1 | Thomas B. Reed (R) | 19,329 | 66.9 |
| | E. W. Staples (D) | 8,790 | 30.4 |
| 2 | Nelson Dingley Jr. (R) | 22,418 | 69.2 |
| | A. Levensaler (D) | 8,424 | 26.0 |
| 3 | Seth L. Milliken (R) | 20,900 | 68.2 |
| | M. S. Holway (D) | 8,024 | 26.2 |
| 4 | Charles A. Boutelle (R) | 21,300 | 65.9 |
| | A. J. Chase (D) | 9,166 | 28.4 |

## MARYLAND

| | Candidates | Votes | % |
|---|---|---|---|
| 1 | Isaac A. Barber (R) | 17,969 | 48.5 |
| | John Miles (D SIL) | 17,389 | 46.9 |
| 2 | William B. Baker (R) | 28,530 | 53.6 |
| | George Jewett (D SIL) | 23,163 | 43.5 |
| 3 | William S. Booze (R) | 22,671 | 57.2 |
| | Thomas Weeks (D) | 15,977 | 40.3 |
| 4 | William W. McIntire (R) | 24,899 | 59.3 |
| | William Ogden (D) | 16,424 | 39.1 |
| 5 | Sydney E. Mudd (R) | 18,954 | 54.3 |
| | Robert Mass (D) | 15,442 | 44.3 |
| 6 | John McDonald (R) | 22,400 | 53.3 |
| | Blair Lee (D) | 18,837 | 44.8 |

## MASSACHUSETTS

| | Candidates | Votes | % |
|---|---|---|---|
| 1 | Ashley B. Wright (R) | 18,075 | 65.4 |
| | Patrick H. Sheehan (D) | 8,579 | 31.0 |
| 2 | Frederick H. Gillett (R) | 19,793 | 71.8 |
| | Thomas A. Fitzgibbon (D) | 7,778 | 28.2 |
| 3 | Joseph H. Walker (R) | 18,993 | 72.5 |
| | John O'Gara (D) | 7,185 | 27.4 |
| 4 | George W. Weymouth (R) | 20,062 | 69.3 |
| | I. Porter Morse (D) | 8,847 | 30.6 |
| 5 | William S. Knox (R) | 17,835 | 60.7 |
| | John H. Harrington (D) | 11,531 | 39.3 |
| 6 | William H. Moody (R) | 19,947 | 72.8 |
| | Eben Moody Boynton (D) | 7,460 | 27.2 |
| 7 | William E. Barrett (R) | 22,759 | 68.2 |
| | Philip J. Doherty (D) | 10,609 | 31.8 |
| 8 | Samuel W. McCall (R) | 22,054 | 74.4 |
| | Frederick H. Jackson (D) | 7,590 | 25.6 |
| 9 | John F. Fitzgerald (D) | 13,979 | 54.7 |
| | Walter Lincoln Sears (R) | 7,819 | 30.6 |
| | John A. Ryan (D SIL) | 3,238 | 12.7 |
| 10 | Samuel J. Barrows (R) | 17,147 | 50.4 |
| | Bordman Hall (D) | 14,259 | 41.9 |
| | William L. Chase (R CIT) | 2,612 | 7.7 |
| 11 | Charles F. Sprague (R) | 22,993 | 69.3 |
| | William H. Baker (D) | 10,154 | 30.6 |
| 12 | William C. Lovering (R) | 21,107 | 76.8 |
| | Elbridge Gerry Brown (PPL DR S) | 6,354 | 23.1 |
| 13 | John Simpkins (R) | 17,685 | 74.7 |
| | James Francis Morris (D) | 5,993 | 25.3 |

## MICHIGAN

| | Candidates | Votes | % |
|---|---|---|---|
| 1 | John B. Corliss (R) | 24,021 | 55.5 |
| | Edwin Henderson (DPUS) | 19,291 | 44.5 |
| 2 | George Spalding (R) | 26,557 | 50.5 |
| | Thomas E. Barkworth (DPUS) | 25,061 | 47.7 |
| 3 | Albert M. Todd (DPUS) | 24,466 | 49.4 |
| | Alfred Milnes (R) | 24,041 | 48.5 |
| 4 | Edward L. Hamilton (R) | 26,518 | 53.6 |
| | Roman I. Jarvis (DPUS) | 22,994 | 46.4 |
| 5 | William Alden Smith (R) | 26,819 | 54.8 |
| | George P. Hummer (DPUS) | 22,155 | 45.2 |
| 6 | Samuel W. Smith (R) | 26,889 | 53.4 |
| | Quincy A. Smith (DPUS) | 23,474 | 46.6 |
| 7 | Horace G. Snover (R) | 22,761 | 55.5 |
| | O'Brien J. Atkinson (DPUS) | 18,267 | 44.5 |
| 8 | Ferdinand Brucker (DPUS) | 20,992 | 51.0 |
| | William S. Linton (R) | 20,158 | 49.0 |
| 9 | Roswell P. Bishop (R) | 20,418 | 58.3 |
| | Armond F. Tibbitts (DPUS) | 14,243 | 40.6 |

| | Candidates | Votes | % |
|---|---|---|---|
| 10 | Rousseau O. Crump (R) | 19,535 | 52.7 |
| | Charles S. Hampton (DPUS) | 17,536 | 47.3 |
| 11 | William S. Mesick (R) | 24,368 | 54.9 |
| | Jonathan G. Ramsdell (DPUS) | 19,605 | 44.1 |
| 12 | Carlos D. Shelden (R) | 29,612 | 70.4 |
| | Henry W. Seymour (DPUS) | 12,479 | 29.7 |

## MINNESOTA

| | Candidates | Votes | % |
|---|---|---|---|
| 1 | James A. Tawney (R) | 27,920 | 60.7 |
| | P. Fitzpatrick (PP & ) | 17,219 | 37.4 |
| 2 | James T. McCleary (R) | 29,481 | 57.1 |
| | Frank A. Day (PP & D) | 21,142 | 40.9 |
| 3 | Joel P. Heatwole (R) | 24,483 | 55.9 |
| | H. J. Peck (PP & D) | 18,532 | 42.3 |
| 4 | Frederick C. Stevens (R) | 24,854 | 62.2 |
| | Francis H. Clark (PP & D) | 14,640 | 36.7 |
| 5 | Loren Fletcher (R) | 24,508 | 53.2 |
| | S. M. Owen (PP & D) | 21,521 | 46.8 |
| 6 | R. Page W. Morris (R) | 30,317 | 50.6 |
| | Charles A. Towne (PP & D) | 29,598 | 49.4 |
| 7 | Frank M. Eddy (R) | 26,003 | 50.9 |
| | Edwin E. Lommen (PP & D) | 23,932 | 46.8 |

## MISSISSIPPI

| | Candidates | Votes | % |
|---|---|---|---|
| 1 | John M. Allen (D) | 7,221 | 86.9 |
| | A. W. Kearley (POP) | 752 | 9.1 |
| 2 | William V. Sullivan (D) | 6,941 | 70.2 |
| | F. E. Ray (POP) | 1,472 | 14.9 |
| | W. D. Miller (GOLD D) | 779 | 7.9 |
| | M. A. Montgomery (R) | 692 | 7.0 |
| 3 | Thomas C. Catchings (D) | 3,069 | 75.8 |
| | J. R. Chalmers (F SIL R) | 532 | 13.1 |
| | C. J. Jones (R) | 369 | 9.1 |
| 4 | Andrew F. Fox (D) | 8,343 | 70.0 |
| | R. K. Prewitt (POP) | 3,086 | 25.9 |
| 5 | John Sharp Williams (D) | 10,475 | 80.1 |
| | W. H. Stinson (POP) | 2,248 | 17.2 |
| 6 | William F. Love (D) | 6,718 | 64.3 |
| | N. C. Hathorn (POP) | 2,683 | 25.7 |
| | H. C. Griffin (R) | 1,055 | 10.1 |
| 7 | Patrick Henry (D) | 7,327 | 84.7 |
| | G. M. Cain (POP) | 897 | 10.4 |

## MISSOURI

| | Candidates | Votes | % |
|---|---|---|---|
| 1 | Richard P. Giles (D) | 24,044* | 53.3 |
| | Clark (R) | 19,320 | 42.8 |
| 2 | Robert N. Bodine (D) | 25,862 | 55.7 |
| | Loomis (R) | 19,367 | 41.7 |
| 3 | Alexander M. Dockery (D) | 23,952 | 53.5 |
| | Orton (R) | 18,634 | 41.6 |
| 4 | Charles F. Cochran (D) | 21,512 | 54.7 |
| | Crowther (R) | 17,683 | 45.0 |
| 5 | William S. Cowherd (D) | 25,966 | 54.9 |
| | Neff (R) | 21,306 | 45.1 |
| 6 | David A. De Armond (D) | 22,524 | 53.5 |
| | Hamilton (R) | 16,722 | 39.7 |
| | Linton (PP) | 2,606 | 6.2 |
| 7 | James Cooney (D) | 27,846 | 53.5 |
| | Tracy (R) | 21,772 | 41.8 |
| 8 | Richard P. Bland (D) | 24,605 | 53.7 |
| | Hubbard (R) | 19,754 | 43.1 |
| 9 | James Beauchamp Clark (D) | 19,970 | 53.0 |
| | Treloar (R) | 17,475 | 46.4 |
| 10 | Richard Bartholdt (R) | 25,513 | 73.2 |
| | Lemp (D) | 9,060 | 26.0 |
| 11 | Charles F. Joy (R) | 28,341 | 53.3 |
| | Hunt (D-PP) | 24,676 | 46.4 |
| 12 | Charles E. Pearce (R) | 21,483 | 54.9 |
| | Kern (D) | 17,568 | 44.9 |
| 13 | Edward Robb (D) | 22,310 | 51.9 |
| | Steel (R) | 19,062 | 44.4 |
| 14 | Willard D. Vandiver (D) | 25,089 | 49.6 |
| | Snider (R) | 20,659 | 40.8 |
| | Livingston (PP) | 4,860 | 9.6 |

## MISSOURI

| Candidates | Votes | % |
|---|---|---|
| 5 Maecenas E. Benton (D) | 24,155 | 55.7 |
| Burton (R) | 17,010 | 39.2 |

## MONTANA

| | | |
|---|---|---|
| L Charles S. Hartman (SIL R) | 33,932 | 78.1 |
| O. F. Goddard (R) | 9,492 | 21.9 |

## NEBRASKA

| | | |
|---|---|---|
| 1 Jesse B. Strode (R) | 17,356 | 49.4 |
| Jefferson H. Broady (D-POP I) | 17,137 | 48.8 |
| 2 David H. Mercer (R) | 14,861 | 52.3 |
| Edward R. Duffie (D POP I) | 13,286 | 16.8 |
| 3 Samuel Maxwell (D-POP I) | 23,487 | 54.8 |
| R. L. Hammond (R) | 18,633 | 43.4 |
| 4 William L. Stark (D-POP I) | 20,515 | 50.5 |
| E. J. Hainer (R) | 18,844 | 46.4 |
| 5 Roderick D. Sutherland (D-POP I) | 18,332 | 52.8 |
| William E. Andrews (R) | 15,541 | 44.8 |
| 6 William L. Greene (D-POP I) | 19,378 | 55.7 |
| Addison E. Cady (R) | 14,841 | 42.7 |

## NEVADA

| | | |
|---|---|---|
| L Francis G. Newlands (D SIL) | 6,429 | 66.3 |
| James C. Doughty (PP) | 1,948 | 20.1 |
| M. J. Davis (R) | 1,319 | 13.6 |

## NEW HAMPSHIRE

| | | |
|---|---|---|
| 1 Cyrus A. Sulloway (R) | 25,661 | 63.0 |
| John B. Nash (D) | 13,928 | 34.2 |
| 2 Frank G. Clarke (R) | 26,689 | 64.3 |
| Daniel M. White (D) | 13,877 | 33.4 |

## NEW JERSEY

| | | |
|---|---|---|
| 1 Henry C. Loudenslager (R) | 33,659 | 64.2 |
| John T. Wright (D & N S) | 17,118 | 32.6 |
| 2 John J. Gardner (R) | 31,418 | 66.0 |
| Abraham E. Conrow (D & N S) | 13,969 | 29.3 |
| 3 Benjamin F. Howell (R) | 24,308 | 57.8 |
| John A. Wells (D) | 16,087 | 38.3 |
| 4 Mahlon Pitney (R & ND) | 20,494 | 52.5 |
| Augustus W. Cutler (D) | 17,517 | 44.8 |
| 5 James F. Stewart (R) | 23,845 | 59.9 |
| Addison Ely (D) | 13,667 | 34.3 |
| 6 Richard Wayne Parker (R) | 31,059 | 64.2 |
| Joseph A. Beecher (D) | 15,393 | 31.8 |
| 7 Thomas McEwan Jr. (R) | 30,557 | 51.8 |
| Alexander C. Young (D) | 26,080 | 44.2 |
| 8 Charles N. Fowler (R) | 25,131 | 61.7 |
| Freeman O. Willey (D) | 13,487 | 33.1 |

## NEW YORK

| | | |
|---|---|---|
| 1 Joseph M. Belford (R) | 27,191 | 59.4 |
| William D. Marvel (D) | 15,923 | 34.8 |
| 2 Denis M. Hurley (R) | 18,268 | 50.8 |
| John M. Clancy (D) | 15,901 | 44.2 |
| 3 Francis H. Wilson (R) | 23,813 | 56.3 |
| Charles F. Brandt (D) | 16,260 | 38.5 |
| 4 Israel F. Fischer (R) | 25,810 | 56.2 |
| Thomas F. Larkin (D) | 18,381 | 40.0 |
| 5 Charles G. Bennett (R) | 22,605 | 57.4 |
| Thomas S. Delaney (D) | 14,186 | 36.1 |
| 6 James R. Howe (R) | 15,314 | 49.1 |
| William Fickermann (D) | 14,287 | 45.8 |
| 7 John H. G. Vehslage (D) | 11,032 | 51.9 |
| Franklin Bartlett (R & ND) | 9,848 | 46.4 |
| 8 John Murray Mitchell (R & ND) | 10,488 | 52.6 |
| James J. Walsh (D) | 9,219 | 46.3 |
| 9 Thomas J. Bradley (D) | 11,002 | 46.3 |
| Timothy J. Campbell (R & ND) | 8,379 | 35.2 |
| Daniel Deleon (SOC LAB) | 4,371 | 18.4 |
| 10 Amos J. Cummings (D) | 17,446 | 53.3 |
| Clarence W. Meade (R) | 14,245 | 43.5 |
| 11 William Sulzer (D) | 12,195 | 48.8 |
| Ferdinand Eldmann (R) | 10,435 | 41.8 |
| Herman Miller (SOC LAB) | 2,011 | 8.1 |
| 12 George B. McClellan (D) | 12,815 | 50.9 |
| Charles A. Hess (R) | 11,038 | 43.9 |
| 13 Richard C. Shannon (R) | 15,413 | 48.0 |
| Thomas Smith (D) | 14,067 | 43.8 |
| 14 Lemuel E. Quigg (R) | 27,875 | 55.5 |
| John Quincy Adams (D) | 18,553 | 37.0 |
| 15 Philip B. Low (R & ND) | 29,602 | 54.5 |
| William H. Burke (D) | 22,520 | 41.5 |
| 16 William L. Ward (R) | 30,709 | 52.6 |
| Eugene B. Travis (D) | 23,456 | 40.2 |
| 17 Benjamin B. Odell Jr. (R) | 22,622 | 58.5 |
| David A. Morrison (D) | 15,500 | 40.1 |
| 18 John H. Ketcham (R) | 25,531 | 60.9 |
| Richard E. Connell (D) | 15,956 | 38.0 |
| 19 Aaron V. S. Cochrane (R) | 23,509 | 55.7 |
| George G. Miller (D) | 17,735 | 42.0 |
| 20 George N. Southwick (R) | 22,342 | 54.7 |
| Thomas F. Wilkinson (D) | 17,637 | 43.2 |
| 21 David Forrest Wilber (R) | 28,567 | 55.7 |
| John H. Bagley (D) | 22,267 | 43.4 |
| 22 Lucius N. Littauer (R) | 32,269 | 93.3 |
| 23 Wallace T. Foote Jr. (R) | 30,475 | 97.0 |
| 24 Charles A. Chickering (R) | 27,242 | 61.4 |
| Oscar M. Wood (D) | 16,248 | 36.6 |
| 25 James S. Sherman (R) | 26,996 | 60.8 |
| Cornelius Haley (D) | 16,512 | 37.2 |
| 26 George W. Ray (R) | 34,686 | 60.8 |
| Alexander D. Wales (D) | 20,383 | 35.7 |
| 27 James J. Belden (R) | 27,427 | 53.2 |
| Theodore L. Poole (D) | 22,657 | 44.0 |
| 28 Sereno E. Payne (R) | 33,628 | 62.4 |
| Robert L. Drummond (D) | 19,822 | 36.8 |
| 29 Charles W. Gillet (R) | 27,192 | 59.7 |
| Henry W. Bowes (D) | 17,994 | 39.5 |
| 30 James W. Wadsworth (R) | 28,478 | 57.3 |
| Frank P. Hulette (D) | 19,066 | 38.4 |
| 31 Henry C. Brewster (R) | 25,399 | 56.9 |
| William E. Ryan (D) | 17,109 | 38.3 |
| 32 Rowland B. Mahany (R) | 18,623 | 54.7 |
| Charles Rung (D) | 14,765 | 43.4 |
| 33 De Alva S. Alexander (R) | 27,573 | 63.0 |
| Harvey W. Richardson (D) | 14,636 | 33.4 |
| 34 Warren B. Hooker (R) | 30,696 | 86.0 |
| David F. Allen (POP & R) | 3,298 | 9.2 |

## NORTH CAROLINA

| | | |
|---|---|---|
| 1 Harry Skinner (POP & R) | 20,724 | 58.3 |
| Wilson H. Lucas (D) | 14,849 | 41.7 |
| 2 George H. White (R) | 19,332 | 51.6 |
| Frederick A. Woodard (D) | 15,378 | 41.1 |
| D. S. Moss (POP) | 2,738 | 7.3 |
| 3 John E. Fowler (POP & R) | 17,989 | 58.9 |
| Frank Thompson (D) | 12,536 | 41.1 |
| 4 William F. Strowd (POP) | 20,977 | 55.6 |
| Edward W. Pou (D) | 16,405 | 43.5 |
| 5 William W. Kitchin (D) | 19,082 | 49.9 |
| Thomas Settle (R) | 18,639 | 48.8 |
| 6 Charles H. Martin (POP & R) | 22,051 | 56.1 |
| James A. Lockhart (D) | 17,235 | 43.9 |
| 7 Alonzo C. Shuford (POP & R) | 17,669 | 55.3 |
| Samuel J. Pemberton (D) | 14,289 | 44.7 |
| 8 Romulus Z. Linney (POP & R) | 19,419 | 51.8 |
| Rufus A. Doughton (D) | 18,007 | 48.0 |
| 9 Richmond Pearson (POP & R) | 20,495 | 51.6 |
| Joseph S. Adams (D) | 19,189 | 48.3 |

## NORTH DAKOTA

| | | |
|---|---|---|
| AL Martin N. Johnson (R) | 25,233 | 54.0 |
| Burke (FUS) | 21,172 | 45.3 |

## OHIO

| Candidates | Votes | % |
|---|---|---|
| 1 William B. Shattuc (R) | 27,093 | 60.8 |
| Thomas J. Donnelly (D) | 17,466 | 39.2 |
| 2 Jacob H. Bromwell (R) | 30,075 | 59.0 |
| David S. Oliver (D) | 20,878 | 41.0 |
| 3 John L. Brenner (D) | 27,435 | 49.7 |
| Robert M. Nevin (R) | 27,334 | 49.5 |
| 4 George A. Marshall (D) | 25,688 | 59.5 |
| John P. MacLean (R) | 16,671 | 38.6 |
| 5 David Meekison (D) | 24,383 | 56.1 |
| Francis B. DeWitt (R) | 18,478 | 42.5 |
| 6 Seth W. Brown (R) | 25,360 | 53.9 |
| Harry P. Paxton (D) | 21,358 | 45.4 |
| 7 Walter L. Weaver (R) | 22,745 | 51.4 |
| Francis M. Hunt (D) | 21,171 | 47.8 |
| 8 Archibald Lybrand (R) | 26,211 | 53.8 |
| McEldin Dun (D) | 22,519 | 16.2 |
| 9 James H. Southard (R) | 29,603 | 53.5 |
| Stephen Brophy (D) | 25,698 | 46.5 |
| 10 Lucien J. Fenton (R) | 24,809 | 57.9 |
| T. S. Hogan (D) | 18,029 | 42.1 |
| 11 Charles H. Grosvenor (R) | 24,333 | 54.8 |
| William E. Finck Jr. (D) | 19,850 | 44.7 |
| 12 John J. Lentz (D) | 23,673 | 49.7 |
| David K. Watson (R) | 23,624 | 49.6 |
| 13 James A. Norton (D) | 28,878 | 54.4 |
| Stephen R. Harris (R) | 23,506 | 44.3 |
| 14 Winfield S. Kerr (R) | 26,850 | 52.0 |
| John B. Coffinberry (D) | 24,574 | 47.6 |
| 15 Henry Clay Van Voorhis (R) | 22,560 | 52.6 |
| James B. Tannehill (D) | 19,837 | 46.2 |
| 16 Lorenzo Danford (R) | 21,690 | 53.8 |
| Henry H. McFadden (D) | 18,635 | 46.2 |
| 17 John A. McDowell (D) | 26,109 | 54.7 |
| Addison S. McClure (R) | 21,169 | 44.3 |
| 18 Robert W. Tayler (R) | 29,814 | 54.2 |
| Isaac R. Sherwood (D) | 24,770 | 45.0 |
| 19 Stephen A. Northway (R) | 31,789 | 60.3 |
| William T. Sawyer (D) | 20,626 | 39.1 |
| 20 Clifton B. Beach (R) | 24,531 | 52.8 |
| A. T. Vantassel (D) | 21,384 | 46.0 |
| 21 Theodore E. Burton (R) | 25,527 | 55.2 |
| L. A. Russell (D) | 20,025 | 43.3 |

## OREGON

| | | |
|---|---|---|
| 1 Thomas H. Tongue (R) | 19,355 | 40.4 |
| W. S. Vanderburg (POP) | 19,292 | 40.3 |
| Jefferson Myers (D) | 7,914 | 16.5 |
| 2 William R. Ellis (R) | 12,617 | 30.4 |
| Martin Quinn (POP) | 12,239 | 29.5 |
| H. H. Northup (SM D) | 8,807 | 21.2 |
| A. S. Bennett (D) | 7,099 | 17.1 |

## PENNSYLVANIA

| | | |
|---|---|---|
| 1 Henry H. Bingham (R) | 32,466 | 69.7 |
| Horace E. James (D) | 13,962 | 30.0 |
| 2 Robert Adams Jr (R) | 22,205 | 78.0 |
| Fenton P. F. Mullins (D) | 6,100 | 21.4 |
| 3 William McAleer (D) | 11,655 | 49.7 |
| Frederick Halterman (R) | 9,556 | 40.7 |
| Samuel E. Hudson (F SIL) | 2,064 | 8.8 |
| 4 James Rankin Young (R) | 59,147 | 77.6 |
| Mark D. Cunningham (D) | 16,536 | 21.7 |
| 5 Alfred C. Harmer (R) | 47,953 | 76.1 |
| Frank D. Wright (D) | 14,484 | 23.0 |
| 6 Thomas S. Butler (BUT R) | 15,016 | 39.4 |
| John B. Robinson (ROB R) | 13,369 | 35.1 |
| William H. Berry (DN&FS) | 9,288 | 24.4 |
| 7 Irving P. Wanger (R) | 26,725 | 60.7 |
| Charles S. Van de Grift (D) | 16,740 | 38.1 |
| 8 William S. Kirkpatrick (R) | 17,072 | 50.5 |
| Laird H. Barber (D) | 16,743 | 49.5 |
| 9 Daniel Ermentrout (D) | 26,123 | 51.1 |
| Oliver Williams (R) | 23,022 | 45.0 |
| 10 Marriott Brosius (R) | 24,122 | 73.3 |
| Edward D. Reilly (D) | 8,252 | 25.1 |

## PENNSYLVANIA

| District | Candidates | Votes | % |
|---|---|---|---|
| 11 | William Connell (R) | 18,598 | 61.6 |
| | Edward Merrifield (D) | 10,741 | 35.6 |
| 12 | Morgan B. Williams (R) | 20,920 | 52.4 |
| | John M. Garman (D) | 17,976 | 45.0 |
| 13 | Charles N. Brumm (R) | 16,613 | 53.0 |
| | Watson F. Shepherd (D) | 14,512 | 46.3 |
| 14 | Marlin E. Olmsted (R) | 25,014 | 87.6 |
| | Abraham Mattis (PP) | 1,948 | 6.8 |
| 15 | James H. Codding (R) | 20,210 | 61.6 |
| | Charles Percival Shaw (D) | 11,444 | 34.9 |
| 16 | Horace B. Packer (R) | 21,543 | 56.2 |
| | Luther B. Seibert (D) | 15,152 | 39.5 |
| 17 | Monroe H. Kulp (R) | 15,195 | 50.1 |
| | Alphonsus Walsh (D) | 14,073 | 46.4 |
| 18 | Thaddeus M. Mahon (R) | 22,455 | 61.2 |
| | Willis F. Kearns (D) | 14,222 | 38.8 |
| 19 | George J. Benner (D) | 22,160 | 49.7 |
| | Frank E. Hollar (R) | 21,382 | 48.0 |
| 20 | Josiah D. Hicks (MCK SM) | 19,974 | 43.8 |
| | Robert C. McNamara (D) | 17,297 | 37.9 |
| | Joseph E. Thropp (PT) | 7,468 | 16.4 |
| 21 | Edward E. Robbins (R) | 32,149 | 59.9 |
| | Samuel S. Blyholder (D) | 19,464 | 36.3 |
| 22 | John Dalzell (R) | 28,860 | 69.0 |
| | John F. Miller (D) | 12,788 | 30.6 |
| 23 | William A. Stone (R) | 21,379 | 77.2 |
| | Morrison Foster (D) | 6,191 | 22.3 |
| 24 | Ernest F. Acheson (R) | 36,554 | 57.1 |
| | John Purman (D) | 26,538 | 41.5 |
| 25 | James J. Davidson (R) | 26,529* | 59.5 |
| | John G. McConahy (D) | 17,050 | 38.2 |
| 26 | John C. Sturtevant (R) | 18,840 | 50.4 |
| | Joseph C. Sibley (D) | 18,114 | 48.5 |
| 27 | Charles W. Stone (R) | 15,777 | 58.3 |
| | William J. Breene (D) | 10,058 | 37.2 |
| 28 | William C. Arnold (R) | 19,295 | 50.2 |
| | Jackson L. Spangler (D) | 18,090 | 47.1 |
| AL | Galusha A. Grow (R, MCK CIT) | 711,346✔ | |
| | Samuel A. Davenport (R, MCK CIT) | 708,633✔ | |
| | Jerome T. Ailman (D, PP) | 418,218 | |
| | DeWitt C. DeWitt (D, F SIL) | 413,802 | |
| | Abraham A. Barker (P) | 18,336 | |
| | George Alcorn (P) | 18,091 | |
| | John P. Correll (PP) | 7,482 | |
| | Hay Walker Jr. (JEFFS) | 7,255 | |
| | Benjamin C. Potts (JEFFS) | 7,237 | |
| | Emil Guwang (SOC LAB) | 1,455 | |
| | Fred W. Long (SOC LAB) | 1,432 | |
| | Henry S. Kent (N) | 671 | |
| | Isaac G. Pollard (N) | 663 | |

## RHODE ISLAND

| District | Candidates | Votes | % |
|---|---|---|---|
| 1 | Melville Bull (R) | 17,378 | 63.7 |
| | Brown (D) | 8,542 | 31.3 |
| 2 | Adin B. Capron (R) | 16,612 | 63.5 |
| | Garvin (D) | 8,088 | 30.9 |

## SOUTH CAROLINA

| District | Candidates | Votes | % |
|---|---|---|---|
| 1 | William Elliott (D) | 4,648 | 63.7 |
| | George W. Murray (LW R) | 2,478 | 34.0 |
| 2 | W. Jasper Talbert (D) | 7,999 | 92.4 |
| | B. P. Chatfield (R) | 635 | 7.3 |
| 3 | Asbury C. Latimer (D) | 9,746 | 92.0 |
| | A. C. Merrick (B&T R) | 659 | 6.2 |
| 4 | Stanyarne Wilson (D) | 11,230 | 92.2 |
| 5 | Thomas J. Strait (D) | 8,511 | 91.0 |
| | John F. Jones (R) | 838 | 9.0 |
| 6 | John L. McLaurin (D) | 9,731 | 87.7 |
| | J. E. Wilson (B&T R) | 878 | 7.9 |
| 7 | J. William Stokes (D) | 8,065 | 85.5 |
| | T. B. Johnson (B&T R) | 1,342 | 14.2 |

### Special Election

| District | Candidates | Votes | % |
|---|---|---|---|
| 7 | J. William Stokes (D) | 8,223 | 88.3 |
| | T. B. Johnson (B&T R) | 1,068 | 11.5 |

## SOUTH DAKOTA

| District | Candidates | Votes | % |
|---|---|---|---|
| AL | Freeman Knowles (PP) | 41,216✔ | |
| | John E. Kelley (PP) | 41,122✔ | |
| | Robert J. Gamble (R) | 40,943 | |
| | Coe I. Crawford (R) | 40,575 | |
| | K. Lewis (P) | 723 | |
| | M. H. Alexander (P) | 683 | |

## TENNESSEE

| District | Candidates | Votes | % |
|---|---|---|---|
| 1 | Walter P. Brownlow (R) | 25,075 | 62.4 |
| | L. L. Lawrence (D) | 13,956 | 34.7 |
| 2 | Henry R. Gibson (R) | 28,112 | 74.3 |
| | W. L. Ledgerwood (D) | 9,448 | 25.0 |
| 3 | John A. Moon (D) | 19,498 | 51.9 |
| | W. J. Clift (R) | 17,716 | 47.2 |
| 4 | Benton McMillin (D) | 18,070 | 59.6 |
| | C. H. Whitney (R) | 12,269 | 40.4 |
| 5 | James D. Richardson (D) | 16,089 | 58.6 |
| | Syd Houston (R) | 9,000 | 32.8 |
| | W. W. Erwin (POP) | 2,384 | 8.7 |
| 6 | John W. Gaines (D SIL) | 17,646 | 57.5 |
| | J. C. McReynold (GOLD D) | 12,135 | 39.5 |
| 7 | Nicholas N. Cox (D) | 15,434 | 55.2 |
| | A. M. Hughes Jr. (R) | 10,744 | 38.4 |
| | J. K. P. Blackburn (POP) | 1,794 | 6.4 |
| 8 | Thetus W. Sims (D) | 16,568 | 53.4 |
| | J. E. McCall (R) | 13,219 | 42.6 |
| 9 | Rice A. Pierce (D SIL) | 19,138 | 64.1 |
| | J. H. McDowell (POP) | 10,714 | 35.9 |
| 10 | Edward W. Carmack (D SIL) | 10,924 | 48.8 |
| | Josiah Patterson (GOLD D) | 10,556 | 47.1 |

## TEXAS

| District | Candidates | Votes | % |
|---|---|---|---|
| 1 | Thomas H. Ball (D) | 19,161 | 55.5 |
| | Joe H. Eagle (POP & R) | 15,189 | 44.0 |
| 2 | Samuel B. Cooper (D) | 25,158 | 57.0 |
| | B. A. Calhoun (POP) | 12,822 | 29.0 |
| | J. M. Claiborne (D) | 6,188 | 14.0 |
| 3 | Reese C. De Graffenreid (D) | 21,208 | 56.5 |
| | W. E. Farmer (POP) | 16,351 | 43.5 |
| 4 | John W. Cranford (D) | 20,187 | 54.0 |
| | J. H. Davis (POP) | 13,703 | 36.7 |
| | M. W. Johnson (R) | 3,468 | 9.3 |
| 5 | Joseph W. Bailey (D) | 28,416 | 61.2 |
| | W. D. Gordon (R) | 13,242 | 28.5 |
| | R. C. Foster (POP) | 4,747 | 10.2 |
| 6 | Robert E. Burke (D) | 33,144 | 56.8 |
| | Barnett Gibbs (POP) | 25,230 | 43.2 |
| 7 | Robert L. Henry (D) | 26,151 | 55.2 |
| | T. A. Pope (R) | 11,632 | 24.5 |
| | W. F. Douthitt (POP) | 9,634 | 20.3 |
| 8 | Samuel W. T. Lanham (D) | 20,935 | 53.4 |
| | C. H. Jenkins (POP) | 17,510 | 44.7 |
| 9 | Joseph D. Sayers (D) | 20,381 | 51.4 |
| | W. K. Makemson (R) | 11,495 | 29.0 |
| | Reddin Andrews (POP) | 6,787 | 17.1 |
| 10 | Robert B. Hawley (R) | 17,936 | 45.7 |
| | J. H. Shelburne (POP) | 15,757 | 40.2 |
| | Noah Allen (POP) | 5,476 | 14.0 |
| 11 | Rudolph Kleburg (D) | 19,059 | 45.6 |
| | H. Gras (R) | 18,449 | 44.1 |
| | J. M. Smith (POP) | 4,074 | 9.8 |
| 12 | James L. Slayden (D) | 14,744 | 46.0 |
| | G. H. Noonan (R) | 13,558 | 42.3 |
| | Taylor McRae (POP) | 3,730 | 11.6 |
| 13 | John H. Stephens (D) | 22,988 | 61.0 |
| | H. L. Bentley (R) | 14,219 | 37.8 |

## UTAH

(Became a state Jan. 4, 1896)

| District | Candidates | Votes | % |
|---|---|---|---|
| AL | William H. King (D) | 47,456 | 61.2 |
| | Holbrook (SIL R) | 27,813 | 35.9 |

### Special Election

| District | Candidates | Votes | % |
|---|---|---|---|
| AL | C. E. Allen (R) | 20,563 | 49.7 |
| | B. H. Roberts (D) | 19,666 | 47.5 |

## VERMONT

| District | Candidates | Votes | % |
|---|---|---|---|
| 1 | H. Henry Powers (R) | 26,145 | 76.4 |
| | Peter F. McManus (D) | 7,693 | 22.5 |
| 2 | William W. Grout (R) | 26,319 | 80.4 |
| | Henry E. Fitzgerald (D) | 6,202 | 18.9 |

## VIRGINIA

| District | Candidates | Votes | % |
|---|---|---|---|
| 1 | William A. Jones (D) | 15,525 | 58.4 |
| | Walter B. Tyler (R) | 10,752 | 40.5 |
| 2 | William A. Young (D) | 15,789‡ | 50.5 |
| | Richard A. Wise (R) | 13,390 | 42.8 |
| | W. M. Whaley (SM D) | 1,895 | 6.1 |
| 3 | John Lamb (D) | 16,634 | 55.5 |
| | L. L. Lewis (R) | 12,716 | 42.5 |
| 4 | Sydney P. Epes (D) | 12,894‡ | 54.4 |
| | Robert T. Thorp (R) | 10,273 | 43.4 |
| 5 | Claude A. Swanson (D) | 14,333 | 51.0 |
| | John R. Brown (R) | 13,782 | 49.0 |
| 6 | Peter J. Otey (D) | 17,187 | 57.0 |
| | Duval Radford (SM D) | 11,682 | 38.7 |
| 7 | James Hay (D) | 17,447 | 55.8 |
| | Robert J. Walker (R) | 13,250 | 42.4 |
| 8 | John F. Rixey (D) | 17,030 | 56.1 |
| | Patrick H. McCaull (R) | 13,114 | 43.2 |
| 9 | James Alexander Walker (R) | 20,024 | 52.7 |
| | Samuel Walker Williams (D) | 17,944 | 47.3 |
| 10 | Jacob Yost (R) | 16,095 | 49.8 |
| | Henry D. Flood (D) | 16,047 | 49.6 |

## WASHINGTON

| District | Candidates | Votes | % |
|---|---|---|---|
| AL | James Hamilton Lewis (PP) | 51,554✔ | |
| | William C. Jones (PP) | 51,158✔ | |
| | W. H. Doolittle (R) | 38,196 | |
| | S. C. Hyde (R) | 37,939 | |
| | C. A. Salyer (P) | 1,011 | |
| | Martin Olsen (P) | 887 | |
| | C. E. Mix (N) | 154 | |

## WEST VIRGINIA

| District | Candidates | Votes | % |
|---|---|---|---|
| 1 | Blackburn B. Dovener (R) | 25,232 | 53.5 |
| | W. W. Arnett (D) | 21,687 | 46.6 |
| 2 | Alston G. Dayton (R) | 25,500 | 52.3 |
| | William G. Brown (D) | 23,249 | 47.7 |
| 3 | Charles P. Dorr (R) | 29,277 | 52.9 |
| | E. W. Wilson (D) | 26,029 | 47.1 |
| 4 | Warren Miller (R) | 24,942 | 51.2 |
| | Walter Pendleton (D) | 23,774 | 48.8 |

## WISCONSIN

| District | Candidates | Votes | % |
|---|---|---|---|
| 1 | Henry Allen Cooper (R) | 28,235 | 64. |
| | Jeremiah L. Mahoney (D) | 14,723 | 33. |
| 2 | Edward Sauerherring (R) | 24,011 | 56.8 |
| | William H. Rogers (D) | 17,480 | 41. |
| 3 | Joseph W. Babcock (R) | 26,691 | 63. |
| | Alfred J. Davis (D) | 15,168 | 36.2 |
| 4 | Theobald Otjen (R) | 25,896 | 54. |
| | Robert Schilling (D) | 21,429 | 44. |
| 5 | Samuel S. Barney (R) | 26,613 | 61. |
| | George W. Winans (D) | 16,492 | 37. |
| 6 | James H. Davidson (R) | 26,649 | 57. |
| | William F. Gruenewald (D) | 18,944 | 41. |
| 7 | Michael Griffin (R) | 24,073 | 65. |
| | Caleb M. Hilliard (D) | 11,718 | 32. |
| 8 | Edward S. Minor (R) | 26,471 | 60. |
| | George W. Cate (D) | 16,845 | 38. |
| 9 | Alexander Stewart (R) | 30,438 | 63. |
| | William W. O'Keefe (D) | 17,705 | 36. |
| 10 | John J. Jenkins (R) | 28,149 | 65. |
| | Frederick H. Remington (D) | 14,823 | 34. |

## WYOMING

| District | Candidates | Votes | % |
|---|---|---|---|
| AL | John E. Osborne (D) | 10,310 | 49. |
| | F. W. Mondell (R) | 10,044 | 47. |

# 1897 House Elections

## ILLINOIS

### Special Election

| Candidates | Votes | % |
| --- | --- | --- |
| 6 Henry Sherman Boutell (R) | 10,211 | 51.4 |
| Vincent H. Perkins (D) | 9,349 | 47.0 |

## MAINE

### Special Election

| | | |
| --- | --- | --- |
| 3 E. C. Burleigh (R) | 9,699 | 73.9 |
| Frederick W. Plaisted (D) | 3,128 | 23.8 |

## MASSACHUSETTS

### Special Election

| Candidates | Votes | % |
| --- | --- | --- |
| 1 George P. Lawrence (R) | 11,889 | 58.6 |
| Roger P. Donoghue (D) | 7,573 | 37.3 |

## MISSOURI

### Special Election

| | | |
| --- | --- | --- |
| 1 James T. Lloyd (D) | 18,809 | 56.9 |
| Clark (R) | 13,158 | 39.8 |

## NEW YORK

### Special Election

| Candidates | Votes | % |
| --- | --- | --- |
| 3 Edmund H. Driggs (D) | 16,753 | 47.6 |
| William A. Prendergast (R) | 14,557 | 41.4 |
| Horatio C. King (ND) | 3,390 | 9.6 |

## PENNSYLVANIA

### Special Election

| | | |
| --- | --- | --- |
| 25 Joseph B. Showalter (R) | 12,221 | 66.2 |
| Salem Heilman (D) | 6,222 | 33.7 |

---

## House Candidates Index

For an index of all House candidates listed in this section (pages 943-1326), see pages 1402-1501. Instructions for use of the House Candidates Index appear on page 1402.

---

# 1898 House Elections

## ALABAMA

| | Candidates | Votes | % |
|---|---|---|---|
| 1 | George W. Taylor (D) | 5,886 | 84.7 |
| | Johnson (COLOR R) | 1,061 | 15.3 |
| 2 | Jesse Stallings (D) | 9,145 | 83.3 |
| | Simmons (R) | 1,620 | 14.8 |
| 3 | Henry Clayton (D) | 8,287 | 96.6 |
| 4 | Gaston A. Robbins (D) | 6,915‡ | 54.9 |
| | William F. Aldrich (R) | 5,685 | 45.1 |
| 5 | Willis Brewer (D) | 8,842 | 77.8 |
| | Smith (R) | 2,504 | 22.0 |
| 6 | John H. Bankhead (D) | 7,009 | 69.8 |
| | Daniel N. Cooper (R) | 2,942 | 29.3 |
| 7 | John L. Burnett (D) | 6,949 | 44.4 |
| | Oliver Day Street (R) | 5,032 | 32.2 |
| | Lathrop (R) | 3,592 | 23.0 |
| 8 | Joseph Wheeler (D) | 6,368 | 99.9 |
| 9 | Oscar W. Underwood (D) | 7,155 | 83.0 |
| | McEniry (R) | 1,051 | 12.2 |

## ARKANSAS

| | Candidates | Votes | % |
|---|---|---|---|
| 1 | Philip D. McCulloch (D) | 4,103 | 99.3 |
| 2 | John S. Little (D) | 3,615 | 99.8 |
| 3 | Thomas C. McRae (D) | 4,066 | 100.0 |
| 4 | William T. Terry (D) | 3,665 | 99.0 |
| 5 | Hugh A. Dinsmore (D) | 6,633 | 71.0 |
| | J. T. Hopper (R) | 2,706 | 29.0 |
| 6 | Stephen Brundidge Jr. (D) | 2,732 | 99.9 |

## CALIFORNIA

| | Candidates | Votes | % |
|---|---|---|---|
| 1 | John A. Barham (R) | 19,598 | 51.8 |
| | Emmet Seawell (D & POP) | 18,244 | 48.2 |
| 2 | Marion De Vries (D & POP) | 25,196 | 55.2 |
| | Frank D. Ryan (R) | 20,400 | 44.7 |
| 3 | Victor H. Metcalf (R) | 20,592 | 57.3 |
| | John Aubrey Jones (D & POP) | 14,051 | 39.1 |
| 4 | Julius Kahn (R) | 13,695 | 50.0 |
| | James H. Barry (D & POP) | 12,084 | 44.1 |
| 5 | Eugene F. Loud (R) | 20,254 | 51.8 |
| | William Craig (D & POP) | 17,352 | 44.3 |
| 6 | Russell J. Waters (R) | 24,050 | 52.6 |
| | Charles A. Barlow (D & POP) | 20,499 | 44.9 |
| 7 | James C. Needham (R) | 20,793 | 50.1 |
| | Curtis H. Castle (D & POP) | 20,680 | 49.8 |

## COLORADO

| | Candidates | Votes | % |
|---|---|---|---|
| 1 | John F. Shafroth (FUS) | 43,111 | 67.6 |
| | Charles Hartsell (R) | 18,580 | 29.1 |
| 2 | John C. Bell (FUS) | 52,372 | 64.9 |
| | B. Clark Wheeler (R) | 27,583 | 34.2 |

## CONNECTICUT

| | Candidates | Votes | % |
|---|---|---|---|
| 1 | E. Stevens Henry (R) | 18,818 | 55.5 |
| | Vance (D) | 13,520 | 39.9 |
| 2 | Nehemiah D. Sperry (R) | 27,004 | 51.9 |
| | Webb (D) | 23,556 | 45.2 |
| 3 | Charles A. Russell (R) | 12,218 | 58.1 |
| | Thayer (D) | 8,507 | 40.4 |
| 4 | Ebenezer J. Hill (R) | 23,707 | 56.1 |
| | Lyman (D) | 17,754 | 42.0 |

## DELAWARE

| | Candidates | Votes | % |
|---|---|---|---|
| AL | John H. Hoffecker (R) | 17,566 | 53.1 |
| | L. Irving Handy (D) | 15,053 | 45.5 |

## FLORIDA

| | Candidates | Votes | % |
|---|---|---|---|
| 1 | Robert W. Davis (D) | 12,150 | 71.8 |
| | H. L. Anderson (R) | 4,773 | 28.2 |
| 2 | Stephen M. Sparkman (D) | 13,506 | 84.1 |
| | E. R. Gunby (R) | 2,543 | 15.8 |

## GEORGIA

| | Candidates | Votes | % |
|---|---|---|---|
| 1 | Rufus E. Lester (D) | 5,344 | 86.0 |
| | John E. Myrick (R) | 873 | 14.0 |
| 2 | James M. Griggs (D) | 8,298 | 80.0 |
| | J. H. Smith (R) | 2,071 | 20.0 |
| 3 | Elijah B. Lewis (D) | 3,539 | 96.2 |
| 4 | William C. Adamson (D) | 3,218 | 99.1 |
| 5 | Leonidas F. Livingston (D) | 3,027 | 97.6 |
| 6 | Charles L. Bartlett (D) | 3,008 | 99.9 |
| 7 | John W. Maddox (D) | 5,296 | 80.7 |
| | A. B. Austin (POP) | 1,252 | 19.1 |
| 8 | William M. Howard (D) | 4,379 | 83.5 |
| | John A. Neese (POP) | 861 | 16.4 |
| 9 | Farish C. Tate (D) | 9,277 | 72.3 |
| | J. P. Brooke (POP) | 3,557 | 27.7 |
| 10 | William H. Fleming (D) | 2,290 | 97.6 |
| 11 | William G. Brantley (D) | 9,256 | 69.2 |
| | J. M. Wilkinson (R) | 4,112 | 30.8 |

## IDAHO

| | Candidates | Votes | % |
|---|---|---|---|
| AL | Edgar Wilson (SIL-R-D) | 17,694 | 45.3 |
| | Weldon B. Heyburn (R) | 13,056 | 33.4 |
| | James Gunn (PP) | 7,428 | 19.0 |

## ILLINOIS

| | Candidates | Votes | % |
|---|---|---|---|
| 1 | James R. Mann (R) | 37,506 | 63.2 |
| | Rollin B. Organ (D) | 20,424 | 34.4 |
| 2 | William Lorimer (R) | 27,151 | 52.1 |
| | C. Porter Johnson)D) | 23,354 | 44.8 |
| 3 | George P. Foster (D) | 18,463 | 53.3 |
| | Hugh R. Belknap (R) | 15,659 | 45.2 |
| 4 | Thomas Cusack (D) | 18,876 | 52.6 |
| | Daniel W. Mills (R) | 16,656 | 46.4 |
| 5 | Edward T. Noonan (D) | 19,186 | 53.3 |
| | George E. White (R) | 16,018 | 44.5 |
| 6 | Henry Sherman Boutell (R) | 18,283 | 50.7 |
| | Emil Hoechster (D) | 17,167 | 47.6 |
| 7 | George Edmund Foss (R) | 30,903 | 60.8 |
| | Frank O. Rogers (D) | 18,572 | 36.5 |
| 8 | Albert J. Hopkins (R) | 19,592 | 68.2 |
| | John W. Leonard (D) | 8,000 | 27.8 |
| 9 | Robert R. Hitt (R) | 22,165 | 64.9 |
| | William H. Wagner (D) | 11,020 | 32.3 |
| 10 | George W. Prince (R) | 24,469 | 66.1 |
| | Francis E. Andrews (D) | 12,042 | 32.5 |
| 11 | Walter Reeves (R) | 20,060 | 53.5 |
| | Maurice T. Moloney (D) | 16,564 | 44.1 |
| 12 | Joseph G. Cannon (R) | 21,484 | 59.1 |
| | John M. Thompson (D) | 14,178 | 39.0 |
| 13 | Vespasian Warner (R) | 20,635 | 56.6 |
| | Jerome G. Quisenbery (D) | 14,977 | 41.1 |
| 14 | Joseph V. Graff (R) | 21,417 | 51.6 |
| | Charles N. Barnes (D) | 19,431 | 46.8 |
| 15 | Benjamin F. Marsh (R) | 21,143 | 49.1 |
| | Joseph A. Roy (D) | 20,901 | 48.6 |
| 16 | William Elza Williams (D) | 21,682 | 54.6 |
| | James H. Danskin (R) | 17,021 | 42.9 |
| 17 | Ben F. Caldwell (D) | 23,293 | 51.9 |
| | Isaac R. Mills (R) | 21,053 | 46.9 |
| 18 | Thomas M. Jett (D) | 18,829 | 49.5 |
| | Benjamin F. Johnston (R) | 18,109 | 47.6 |
| 19 | Joseph B. Crowley (D) | 21,520 | 50.5 |
| | William W. Jacobs (R) | 20,006 | 47.0 |
| 20 | James R. Williams (D) | 18,321 | 51.5 |
| | Theodore G. Risley (R) | 16,307 | 45.9 |

## INDIANA

| | Candidates | Votes | % |
|---|---|---|---|
| 21 | William A. Rodenberg (R) | 20,461 | 49.1 |
| | Frederick J. Kern (D) | 19,956 | 47.9 |
| 22 | George W. Smith (R) | 17,200 | 54.5 |
| | A. B. Garrett (D) | 14,131 | 44.8 |
| 1 | James A. Hemenway (R) | 20,383 | 50.7 |
| | Thomas Duncan (D) | 19,337 | 48.1 |
| 2 | Robert W. Miers (D) | 20,245 | 50.3 |
| | William R. Gardiner (R) | 18,656 | 46.4 |
| 3 | William T. Zenor (D) | 21,111 | 55.2 |
| | Isaac F. Whiteside (R) | 16,791 | 43.9 |
| 4 | Francis M. Griffith (D) | 21,751 | 52.2 |
| | Charles W. Lee (R) | 19,733 | 47.3 |
| 5 | George W. Faris (R) | 22,557 | 49.4 |
| | Samuel R. Hamill (D) | 22,305 | 48.8 |
| 6 | James E. Watson (R) | 21,048 | 52.6 |
| | Charles A. Robinson (D) | 18,844 | 47.1 |
| 7 | Jesse Overstreet (R) | 25,868 | 51.8 |
| | Leon O. Bailey (D) | 23,269 | 46.6 |
| 8 | George W. Cromer (R) | 25,388 | 50.1 |
| | Orlando J. Lotz (D) | 24,021 | 47.4 |
| 9 | Charles B. Landis (R) | 22,447 | 50.2 |
| | Joseph B. Cheadle (D) | 21,357 | 47.7 |
| 10 | Edgar D. Crumpacker (R) | 24,656 | 55.0 |
| | John Ross (D) | 20,206 | 45.0 |
| 11 | George W. Steele (R) | 24,367 | 52.7 |
| | George W. Michael (D) | 20,281 | 43.9 |
| 12 | James M. Robinson (D) | 19,484 | 51.3 |
| | Christian B. Stevens (R) | 18,044 | 47.5 |
| 13 | Abraham L. Brick (R) | 23,368 | 51.4 |
| | Medary M. Hathaway (D) | 20,886 | 46.0 |

## IOWA

| | Candidates | Votes | % |
|---|---|---|---|
| 1 | Thomas Hedge (R) | 17,817 | 54.3 |
| | D. J. O'Connell (D) | 14,568 | 44.4 |
| 2 | Joseph R. Lane (R) | 18,790 | 50.6 |
| | John J. Ney (D) | 17,508 | 47.1 |
| 3 | David B. Henderson (R) | 22,512 | 59.1 |
| | John H. Howell (D) | 15,493 | 40.7 |
| 4 | Gilbert N. Haugen (R) | 21,468 | 59.8 |
| | T. T. Blaise (D) | 13,849 | 38.6 |
| 5 | Robert G. Cousins (R) | 21,335 | 55.9 |
| | L. J. Rowell (D) | 15,970 | 41.9 |
| 6 | John F. Lacey (R) | 19,738 | 50.9 |
| | James B. Weaver (D) | 18,267 | 47.1 |
| 7 | John A. T. Hull (R) | 19,913 | 59.3 |
| | Charles O. Holly (D) | 12,261 | 36.5 |
| 8 | William P. Hepburn (R) | 22,327 | 53.1 |
| | George L. Finn (D) | 18,503 | 44.0 |
| 9 | Smith McPherson (R) | 21,976 | 54.8 |
| | J. A. Lyons (D) | 17,484 | 43.6 |
| 10 | Jonathan P. Dolliver (R) | 25,180 | 57.6 |
| | Edwin Anderson (D) | 17,777 | 40.7 |
| 11 | Lot Thomas (R) | 22,400 | 56.6 |
| | Arthur S. Garretson (D) | 16,117 | 40.7 |

## KANSAS

| | Candidates | Votes | % |
|---|---|---|---|
| 1 | Charles Curtis (R) | 23,899 | 59.6 |
| | W. W. Price (D-PP) | 16,187 | 40.4 |
| 2 | Justin D. Bowersock (R) | 21,029 | 52.5 |
| | M. S. Peters (D-PP) | 19,024 | 47.5 |
| 3 | Edwin R. Ridgely (D-PP) | 21,739 | 51.4 |
| | S. S. Kirkpatrick (R) | 20,589 | 48.6 |
| 4 | James M. Miller (R) | 20,312 | 53.9 |
| | Henderson S. Martin (D-PP) | 17,410 | 46.2 |
| 5 | William A. Calderhead (R) | 18,991 | 53.5 |
| | W. D. Vincent (D-PP) | 16,508 | 46.5 |
| 6 | William A. Reeder (R) | 16,833 | 49.7 |
| | N. B. McCormick (PP) | 14,732 | 43.5 |
| | William G. Hoffer (D) | 2,334 | 6.9 |

## KANSAS

| Candidates | Votes | % |
|---|---|---|
| 7 Chester I. Long (R) | 26,622 | 51.7 |
| Jerry Simpson (D-PP) | 24,834 | 48.3 |
| L Willis J. Bailey (R) | 147,691 | 52.5 |
| J. D. Botkin (D-PP) | 130,801 | 46.5 |

## KENTUCKY

| | Votes | % |
|---|---|---|
| 1 Charles K. Wheeler (D) | 10,580 | 67.7 |
| G. W. Reeves (R) | 5,036 | 32.2 |
| 2 Henry D. Allen (D) | 8,939 | 57.3 |
| W. T. Fowler (R) | 4,463 | 28.6 |
| G. W. Jolly (I) | 1,641 | 10.5 |
| 3 John S. Rhea (D) | 14,771 | 54.9 |
| M. P. Creel (R) | 11,748 | 43.7 |
| 4 David H. Smith (D) | 16,696 | 55.3 |
| Charles Biford (R) | 12,826 | 42.5 |
| 5 Oscar Turner (D) | 14,770 | 49.6 |
| Walter Evans (R) | 14,202 | 47.7 |
| 6 Albert S. Berry (D) | 13,130 | 59.4 |
| W. M. Donson (R) | 8,962 | 40.6 |
| 7 Evan E. Settle (D) | 12,904 | 67.7 |
| T. J. Hardin (R) | 6,168 | 32.3 |
| 8 George G. Gilbert (D) | 13,047 | 50.8 |
| G. M. Davson (R) | 12,206 | 47.5 |
| 9 Samuel J. Pugh (R) | ✓ | |
| Mordecal Williams (D) | | |
| 10 Thomas Y. Fitzpatrick (D) | 13,456 | 54.1 |
| W. J. Seitz (R) | 11,402 | 45.9 |
| 11 Vincent Boreing (R) | 15,706 | 51.5 |
| J. D. White (IR) | 11,324 | 37.2 |
| H. H. Tye (D) | 3,319 | 10.9 |

## LOUISIANA

| | Votes | % |
|---|---|---|
| 1 Adolph Meyer (D) | 5,422 | 85.8 |
| C. W. Keeting (R) | 896 | 14.2 |
| 2 Robert C. Davey (D) | 6,802 | 86.6 |
| Frank N. Wicker (R) | 1,054 | 13.4 |
| 3 Robert F. Broussard (D) | 4,928 | 84.9 |
| Charles Fontelleu (R) | 874 | 15.1 |
| 4 Phanor Breazeale (D) | 4,524 | 75.3 |
| Hardy L. Brian (POP) | 1,476 | 24.6 |
| 5 Samuel T. Baird (D) | 3,558 | 74.0 |
| J. G. Taliaferro (R) | 1,096 | 22.8 |
| 6 Samuel M. Robertson (D) | 2,494 | 99.6 |

## MAINE

| | Votes | % |
|---|---|---|
| 1 Thomas B. Reed (R) | 14,598 | 59.8 |
| L. F. McKinney (D) | 9,072 | 37.2 |
| 2 Nelson Dingley Jr. (R) | 15,149* | 63.7 |
| John Scott (D) | 8,126 | 34.2 |
| 3 Edwin C. Burleigh (R) | 12,854 | 64.3 |
| F. W. Plaisted (D) | 6,634 | 33.2 |
| 4 Charles A. Boutelle (R) | 12,380 | 66.5 |
| A. J. Chase (D) | 5,534 | 29.7 |

### Special Election

| | Votes | % |
|---|---|---|
| 4 Amos L. Allen (R) | 12,337 | 61.6 |
| L. F. McKinney (D) | 7,705 | 38.4 |

## MARYLAND

| | Votes | % |
|---|---|---|
| 1 John W. Smith (D) | 16,748 | 47.9 |
| W. F. Jackson (R) | 15,823 | 45.3 |
| J. Swann (P) | 1,823 | 5.2 |
| 2 William B. Baker (R) | 20,806 | 48.4 |
| Richard Tippett (D) | 20,436 | 47.5 |
| 3 Frank C. Wachter (R) | 17,508 | 49.1 |
| J. Schwatka (D) | 17,386 | 48.8 |
| 4 James W. Denny (D) | 17,260 | 48.8 |
| William McIntire (R) | 16,664 | 47.1 |
| 5 Sydney E. Mudd (R) | 17,248 | 52.1 |
| J. S. Cummings (D) | 14,672 | 44.3 |
| 6 George Alexander Parre (R) | 18,878 | 54.8 |
| T. A. Poffenberger (D) | 14,372 | 41.8 |

## MASSACHUSETTS

| Candidates | Votes | % |
|---|---|---|
| 1 George P. Lawrence (R) | 14,315 | 58.0 |
| Charles P. Davis (D) | 8,760 | 35.5 |
| Edward A. Buckland (SOC LAB) | 1,602 | 6.5 |
| 2 Frederick H. Gillett (R) | 13,327 | 60.3 |
| Robert E. Bisbee (D) | 8,054 | 36.5 |
| 3 John R. Thayer (D) | 11,167 | 50.4 |
| Joseph H. Walker (R) | 11,008 | 49.6 |
| 4 George W. Weymouth (R) | 14,411 | 62.9 |
| I. Porter Morse (D) | 8,485 | 37.1 |
| 5 William S. Knox (R) | 14,737 | 51.8 |
| Joseph J. Flynn (D) | 13,716 | 48.2 |
| 6 William H. Moody (R) | 13,494 | 64.5 |
| E. Moody Boynton (D) | 6,035 | 28.9 |
| Albert L. Gillen (D SOCIAL) | 1,390 | 6.6 |
| 7 Ernest W. Roberts (R) | 16,559 | 55.8 |
| Walter L. Ramsdell (D) | 12,338 | 41.0 |
| 8 Samuel W. McCall (R) | 14,935 | 69.9 |
| George A. Perkins (D) | 5,846 | 27.4 |
| 9 John F. Fitzgerald (D) | 10,303 | 48.7 |
| Franz H. Krebs (R) | 5,450 | 25.8 |
| James A. Gallvan (DI) | 5,000 | 23.6 |
| 10 Henry F. Naphen (D) | 17,149 | 55.2 |
| Samuel J. Barrows (R) | 13,909 | 44.8 |
| 11 Charles F. Sprague (R) | 17,001 | 61.3 |
| William H. Baker (D) | 10,709 | 38.6 |
| 12 William C. Lovering (R) | 13,653 | 65.9 |
| Philip E. Brady (D) | 6,210 | 30.0 |
| 13 William S. Greene (R) | 13,463 | 68.6 |
| Charles T. Luce (D) | 4,868 | 24.8 |
| Thomas Stevenson (SOC LAB) | 1,287 | 6.6 |

## MICHIGAN

| | Votes | % |
|---|---|---|
| 1 John B. Corliss (R) | 16,659 | 51.2 |
| James H. Pound (DPUS) | 15,401 | 47.3 |
| 2 Henry C. Smith (R) | 21,912 | 51.2 |
| Orrin R. Pierce (DPUS) | 19,999 | 46.7 |
| 3 Washington Gardner (R) | 21,182 | 51.6 |
| Albert M. Todd (DPUS) | 19,864 | 48.4 |
| 4 Edward L. Hamilton (R) | 21,740 | 54.8 |
| Roman I. Jarvis (DPUS) | 17,146 | 43.2 |
| 5 William Alden Smith (R) | 22,021 | 56.8 |
| George R. Perry (DPUS) | 16,064 | 41.4 |
| 6 Samuel W. Smith (R) | 22,981 | 55.8 |
| Charles Fishbeck (DPUS) | 17,171 | 41.7 |
| 7 Edgar Weeks (R) | 18,623 | 58.6 |
| Fred E. Burton (DPUS) | 12,888 | 40.5 |
| 8 Joseph W. Fordney (R) | 16,798 | 52.7 |
| Ferdinand Brucker (DPUS) | 15,089 | 47.3 |
| 9 Roswell P. Bishop (R) | 15,687 | 61.3 |
| Chauncey J. Chaddock (DPUS) | 9,291 | 36.3 |
| 10 Rousseau O. Crump (R) | 16,482 | 55.3 |
| Robert J. Kelly (DPUS) | 13,230 | 44.4 |
| 11 William S. Mesick (R) | 18,545 | 59.9 |
| Alva W. Nichols (DPUS) | 11,799 | 38.1 |
| 12 Carlos D. Shelden (R) | 19,895 | 66.9 |
| Solomon S. Curry (DPUS) | 8,921 | 30.0 |

## MINNESOTA

| | Votes | % |
|---|---|---|
| 1 James A. Tawney (R) | 18,939 | 59.3 |
| White (PP & D) | 11,931 | 37.3 |
| 2 James T. McCleary (R) | 21,296 | 57.0 |
| Evans (PP & D) | 14,784 | 39.6 |
| 3 Joel P. Heatwole (R) | 19,271 | 56.9 |
| Hinds (PP & D) | 13,183 | 38.9 |
| 4 Frederick C. Stevens (R) | 15,952 | 54.1 |
| Willis (D) | 11,602 | 39.3 |
| 5 Loren Fletcher (R) | 18,736 | 55.4 |
| Caton (PP & D) | 2,896 | 38.1 |
| 6 R. Page W. Morris (R) | 22,194 | 50.1 |
| Towne (PP & D) | 21,731 | 49.0 |
| 7 Frank M. Eddy (R) | 20,409 | 52.6 |
| Ringdal (PP & D) | 16,715 | 43.1 |

## MISSISSIPPI

| Candidates | Votes | % |
|---|---|---|
| 1 John M. Allen (D) | 2,469 | 100.0 |
| 2 Thomas Spight (D) | 2,949 | 92.9 |
| C. M. Haynie (POP) | 167 | 5.3 |
| 3 Thomas C. Catchings (D) | 2,068 | 85.1 |
| C. T. Jones (COLOR R) | 363 | 14.9 |
| 4 Andrew F. Fox (D) | 3,431 | 77.1 |
| Raleigh Brewer (POP) | 1,020 | 22.9 |
| 5 John Sharp Williams (D) | 4,941 | 97.0 |
| 6 Frank A. McLain (D) | 3,276 | 53.7 |
| M. M. Evans (ID) | 1,390 | 22.8 |
| N. C. Hathorn (POP) | 998 | 16.4 |
| H. C. Turley (R) | 427 | 7.0 |
| 7 Patrick Henry (D) | 3,278 | 91.0 |

### Special Election

| | Votes | % |
|---|---|---|
| 2 Thomas Spight (D) | 2,722 | 46.6 |
| Z. M. Stephens | 2,461 | 42.2 |
| L. L. Pearson | 653 | 11.2 |

## MISSOURI

| | Votes | % |
|---|---|---|
| 1 James T. Lloyd (D) | 20,068 | 55.3 |
| Seaber (R) | 15,460 | 42.6 |
| 2 William W. Rucker (D) | 20,768 | 56.3 |
| Irwin (R) | 15,627 | 42.4 |
| 3 John Dougherty (D) | 19,560 | 53.1 |
| Goodrich (R) | 16,440 | 44.6 |
| 4 Charles F. Cochran (D) | 18,294 | 52.9 |
| Brewster (R) | 16,261 | 47.1 |
| 5 William S. Cowherd (D) | 20,487 | 53.6 |
| Welborn (R) | 17,144 | 44.8 |
| 6 David A. De Armond (D) | 16,645 | 52.0 |
| Jurden (R) | 13,595 | 42.4 |
| 7 James Cooney (D) | 22,586 | 55.2 |
| Robertson (R) | 17,642 | 43.1 |
| 8 Richard P. Bland (D) | 21,674 | 53.1 |
| Vosholl (R) | 18,831 | 46.2 |
| 9 James Beauchamp Clark (D) | 17,463 | 4.4 |
| Shackelford (R) | 14,449 | 45.0 |
| 10 Richard Bartholdt (R) | 19,850 | 59.3 |
| Gill (D) | 13,254 | 39.6 |
| 11 Charles F. Joy (R) | 21,315 | 52.3 |
| Noonan (D) | 18,657 | 45.7 |
| 12 Charles E. Pearce (R) | 15,300 | 52.6 |
| Kern (D) | 12,989 | 44.7 |
| 13 Edward Robb (D) | 20,601 | 52.0 |
| Reppy (R) | 18,314 | 46.2 |
| 14 Willard D. Vandiver (D) | 21,771 | 51.3 |
| Miley (R) | 18,650 | 43.9 |
| 15 Maecenas E. Benton (D) | 20,202 | 54.3 |
| Williams (R) | 16,918 | 45.5 |

## MONTANA

| | Votes | % |
|---|---|---|
| AL Albert J. Campbell (D) | 23,351 | 46.9 |
| Thomas C. Marshall (R) | 14,829 | 29.8 |
| Thomas S. Hogan (PP&SIL R) | 11,607 | 23.3 |

## NEBRASKA

| | Votes | % |
|---|---|---|
| 1 Elmer J. Burkett (R) | 16,960 | 53.9 |
| James Manahan (D & POP) | 14,466 | 46.0 |
| 2 David H. Mercer (R) | 11,951 | 52.0 |
| G. M. Hitchcock (D & POP) | 11,023 | 48.0 |
| 3 John S. Robinson (D & POP) | 18,722 | 51.9 |
| W. F. Norris (R) | 17,333 | 48.1 |
| 4 William L. Stark (D & POP) | 18,904 | 50.7 |
| E. H. Hinshaw (R) | 18,377 | 49.3 |
| 5 Roderick D. Sutherland (D & POP) | 16,354 | 51.4 |
| C. E. Adams (R) | 15,487 | 48.6 |
| 6 William L. Greene (D & POP) | 15,415 | 53.5 |
| Norris Brown (R) | 13,401 | 46.5 |

## NEVADA

| Candidates | Votes | % |
|---|---|---|
| AL Francis G. Newlands (D SIL) | 5,766 | 65.0 |
| Thomas Wren (PP) | 3,111 | 35.1 |

## NEW HAMPSHIRE

| | Candidates | Votes | % |
|---|---|---|---|
| 1 | Cyrus A. Sulloway (R) | 21,373 | 52.2 |
| | Edgar J. Knowlton (D) | 18,518 | 45.2 |
| 2 | Frank G. Clarke (R) | 22,395 | 55.5 |
| | Warren F. Daniell (D) | 17,266 | 42.8 |

## NEW JERSEY

| | Candidates | Votes | % |
|---|---|---|---|
| 1 | Henry C. Loudenslager (R) | 23,864 | 54.3 |
| | Samuel Iredell (D) | 18,102 | 41.2 |
| 2 | John J. Gardner (R) | 24,035 | 56.1 |
| | John F. Hall (D) | 17,367 | 40.5 |
| 3 | Benjamin F. Howell (R) | 19,412 | 49.8 |
| | Patrick Convery (D) | 18,683 | 48.0 |
| 4 | Joshua S. Salmon (D) | 17,866 | 51.5 |
| | John I. Blair Reiley (R) | 15,207 | 43.8 |
| 5 | James F. Stewart (R) | 18,367 | 50.6 |
| | Francis J. Marley (D) | 16,342 | 45.0 |
| 6 | Richard Wayne Parker (R) | 23,843 | 52.5 |
| | Henry G. Atwater (D) | 20,150 | 44.4 |
| 7 | William D. Daly (D) | 30,270 | 57.8 |
| | Zebina K. Pangborn (R) | 20,162 | 38.5 |
| 8 | Charles N. Fowler (R) | 20,230 | 54.1 |
| | Edward H. Snyder (D) | 15,878 | 42.4 |

## NEW YORK

| | Candidates | Votes | % |
|---|---|---|---|
| 1 | Townsend Scudder (D) | 22,893 | 49.8 |
| | Joseph M. Belford (R) | 22,483 | 48.9 |
| 2 | John J. Fitzgerald (D) | 18,431 | 55.6 |
| | Denis M. Hurley (R) | 14,323 | 43.2 |
| 3 | Edmund H. Driggs (D) | 20,995 | 50.7 |
| | William A. Prendergast (R) | 19,872 | 48.0 |
| 4 | Bertram T. Clayton (D) | 24,581 | 52.8 |
| | Israel T. Fischer (R) | 20,893 | 44.9 |
| 5 | Frank E. Wilson (D) | 19,579 | 51.4 |
| | Charles E. Bennett (R) | 16,669 | 43.8 |
| 6 | Mitchell May (D) | 16,215 | 55.4 |
| | Henry C. Fischer (R) | 11,899 | 40.6 |
| 7 | Nicholas Muller (D) | 14,122 | 66.5 |
| | Charles Wilmot Townsend (R) | 6,639 | 31.3 |
| 8 | Daniel J. Riordan (D) | 10,716 | 58.6 |
| | John Murray Mitchell (R) | 7,347 | 40.2 |
| 9 | Thomas J. Bradley (D) | 11,694 | 56.8 |
| | John Stiebling (R) | 6,447 | 31.3 |
| | Lucien Sanial (SOC LAB) | 2,396 | 11.7 |
| 10 | Amos J. Cummings (D) | 18,859 | 62.8 |
| | Elijah M. Fisher (R) | 10,620 | 35.4 |
| 11 | William Sulzer (D) | 14,364 | 62.8 |
| | William Volkel (R) | 6,178 | 27.0 |
| | Howard Balkam (SOC LAB) | 2,310 | 10.1 |
| 12 | George B. McClellan (D) | 15,108 | 64.5 |
| | Howard Conkling (R) | 7,710 | 32.9 |
| 13 | Jefferson M. Levy (D) | 17,985 | 59.8 |
| | James W. Perry (R) | 11,393 | 37.9 |
| 14 | William Astor Chanler (D) | 31,604 | 54.3 |
| | Lemuel E. Quigg (R) | 25,209 | 43.3 |
| 15 | Jacob Ruppert Jr. (D) | 31,292 | 57.8 |
| | Philip B. Low (R) | 20,848 | 38.5 |
| 16 | John Q. Underhill (D) | 32,578 | 54.6 |
| | James Irving Burns (R) | 26,130 | 43.8 |
| 17 | Arthur S. Tompkins (R) | 19,195 | 54.2 |
| | Samuel D. Roberson (D) | 15,564 | 43.9 |
| 18 | John H. Ketcham (R) | 23,276 | 55.1 |
| | Thomas E. Benedict (D) | 18,348 | 43.4 |
| 19 | Aaron V. S. Cochrane (R) | 19,593 | 49.1 |
| | John Henry Livingston (D) | 19,565 | 49.1 |
| 20 | Martin H. Glynn (D) | 20,026 | 50.1 |
| | George N. Southwick (R) | 19,475 | 48.7 |
| 21 | John K. Stewart (R) | 25,561 | 50.9 |
| | Stephen L. Mayham (D) | 23,347 | 46.5 |
| 22 | Lucius N. Littauer (R) | 27,083 | 61.3 |
| | Dennis B. Lucy (D) | 15,448 | 35.0 |

| | Candidates | Votes | % |
|---|---|---|---|
| 23 | Louis W. Emerson (R) | 25,662 | 96.3 |
| 24 | Charles A. Chickering (R) | 23,991 | 58.9 |
| | Eber T. Strickland (D) | 15,724 | 38.6 |
| 25 | James S. Sherman (R) | 22,368 | 52.8 |
| | Walter Ballou (D) | 19,160 | 45.2 |
| 26 | George W. Ray (R) | 30,007 | 58.6 |
| | Edward E. Pease (D) | 19,199 | 37.5 |
| 27 | Michael E. Driscoll (R) | 26,025 | 56.5 |
| | George H. Gilbert (D) | 14,207 | 30.9 |
| | Thomas Crimmins | 2,434 | 5.3 |
| | John McCarthy | 2,433 | 5.3 |
| 28 | Sereno E. Payne (R) | 29,536 | 59.4 |
| | John H. Young (D) | 18,831 | 37.9 |
| 29 | Charles W. Gillet (R) | 22,348 | 52.7 |
| | Albert L. Childs (D) | 18,311 | 43.2 |
| 30 | James W. Wadsworth (R) | 25,799 | 55.8 |
| | James T. Gordon (D) | 18,911 | 40.9 |
| 31 | James M. E. O'Grady (R) | 20,717 | 51.8 |
| | John R. Fanning (D) | 17,227 | 43.1 |
| 32 | William H. Ryan (D) | 15,546 | 49.5 |
| | Rowland B. Mahany | 14,858 | 47.4 |
| 33 | De Alva S. Alexander (R) | 22,924 | 55.8 |
| | Harvey W. Richardson (D) | 17,233 | 41.9 |
| 34 | Warren B. Hooker (R) | 25,856* | 62.8 |
| | William J. Sanbury (D) | 13,666 | 33.2 |

## NORTH CAROLINA

| | Candidates | Votes | % |
|---|---|---|---|
| 1 | John H. Small (D) | 19,732 | 51.8 |
| | Harry Skinner (POP & R) | 18,263 | 47.9 |
| 2 | George H. White (R) | 17,560 | 49.5 |
| | William E. Fountain (D) | 14,947 | 42.1 |
| | James B. Lloyd (POP) | 2,447 | 6.9 |
| 3 | Charles R. Thomas (D) | 16,008 | 50.3 |
| | John E. Fowler (POP & R) | 15,819 | 49.7 |
| 4 | John M. Atwater (POP & R) | 19,416 | 51.1 |
| | Joseph J. Jenkins (POP & R) | 18,577 | 48.9 |
| 5 | William W. Kitchin (D) | 20,869 | 52.9 |
| | Spencer B. Adams (POP & R) | 18,607 | 47.1 |
| 6 | John D. Bellamy (D) | 23,213 | 57.2 |
| | Oliver H. Dockery (POP & R) | 17,359 | 42.8 |
| 7 | Theodore F. Kluttz (D) | 20,733 | 58.5 |
| | Morrison H. Caldwell (POP) | 14,651 | 41.3 |
| 8 | Romulus Z. Linney (POP & R) | 17,414 | 51.7 |
| | Edward F. Lovell (D) | 16,137 | 47.9 |
| 9 | William T. Crawford (D) | 19,606‡ | 50.2 |
| | Richmond Pearson (POP) | 19,368 | 49.6 |

## NORTH DAKOTA

| | Candidates | Votes | % |
|---|---|---|---|
| AL | Burleigh F. Spalding (R) | 27,776 | 60.9 |
| | Creel (FUS) | 17,844 | 39.1 |

## OHIO

| | Candidates | Votes | % |
|---|---|---|---|
| 1 | William B. Shattuc (R) | 20,132 | 58.5 |
| | John F. Follett (D) | 13,980 | 40.6 |
| 2 | Jacob H. Bromwell (R) | 22,506 | 58.0 |
| | Charles L. Swain (D) | 15,998 | 41.3 |
| 3 | John L. Brenner (D) | 21,449 | 50.1 |
| | William J. White (R) | 21,327 | 49.9 |
| 4 | Robert B. Gordon (D) | 18,020 | 57.7 |
| | Philip Sheets (R) | 12,276 | 39.3 |
| 5 | David Meekison (D) | 19,264 | 54.1 |
| | Alfred N. Wilcox (R) | 15,612 | 43.9 |
| 6 | Seth W. Brown (R) | 19,896 | 54.0 |
| | Lewis H. Whiteman (D) | 16,206 | 44.0 |
| 7 | Walter L. Weaver (R) | 17,565 | 49.5 |
| | John L. Zimmerman (D) | 17,159 | 48.4 |
| 8 | Archibald Lybrand (R) | 21,560 | 51.6 |
| | Harvey Walter Doty (D) | 19,156 | 45.8 |
| 9 | James H. Southard (R) | 21,913 | 54.8 |
| | Samuel E. Niece (D) | 18,081 | 45.2 |
| 10 | Stephen Morgan (R) | 19,297 | 58.4 |
| | Alva Crabtree (D) | 13,769 | 41.6 |
| 11 | Charles H. Grosvenor (R) | 19,806 | 54.6 |
| | Charles E. Peoples (D) | 16,434 | 45.3 |

| | Candidates | Votes | % |
|---|---|---|---|
| 12 | John J. Lentz (D) | 21,232 | 50.2 |
| | Edward N. Huggins (R) | 20,530 | 48.6 |
| 13 | James A. Norton (D) | 21,410 | 54.1 |
| | Henry L. Wenner (R) | 17,606 | 44.5 |
| 14 | Winfield Kerr (R) | 22,464 | 54.0 |
| | Thomas A. Gruber (D) | 19,134 | 46.0 |
| 15 | Henry Clay Van Voorhis (R) | 19,404 | 54.0 |
| | Henry R. Stanbery (D) | 16,509 | 46.0 |
| 16 | Lorenzo Danford (R) | 16,263 | 54.9 |
| | Elliott D. Moore (D) | 13,377 | 45.1 |
| 17 | John A. McDowell (D) | 19,989 | 55.5 |
| | George E. Broome (R) | 16,016 | 44.5 |
| 18 | Robert W. Tayler (R) | 22,635 | 51.8 |
| | Charles C. Weybrecht (D) | 19,575 | 44.8 |
| 19 | Charles Dick (R) | 23,358 | 64.9 |
| | Isaac H. Phelps (D) | 12,612 | 35.1 |
| 20 | Fremont O. Phillips (R) | 16,894 | 56.5 |
| | William J. Hart (D) | 11,992 | 40.1 |
| 21 | Theodore E. Burton (R) | 17,599 | 59.2 |
| | Lemuel A. Russell (D) | 10,823 | 36.4 |

### Special Election

| | Candidates | Votes | % |
|---|---|---|---|
| 19 | Charles Dick (R) | 23,359 | 65.0 |
| | Unidentified Candidate (D) | 12,574 | 35.0 |

## OREGON

| | Candidates | Votes | % |
|---|---|---|---|
| 1 | Thomas H. Tongue (R) | 21,324 | 49.0 |
| | R. M. Veatch (FUS) | 19,287 | 44.3 |
| 2 | Malcolm A. Moody (R) | 21,291 | 54.2 |
| | C. M. Donaldson (FUS) | 14,634 | 37.2 |
| | H. E. Courtney (POP) | 2,273 | 5.8 |

## PENNSYLVANIA

| | Candidates | Votes | % |
|---|---|---|---|
| 1 | Henry H. Bingham (R) | 25,665 | 72.1 |
| | Michael Francis Doyle (D) | 8,213 | 23.1 |
| 2 | Robert Adams Jr. (R) | 19,547 | 83.5 |
| | Herman V. Hetzel (D) | 3,850 | 16.5 |
| 3 | William McAleer (R, D) | 18,321 | 98.3 |
| 4 | James Rankin Young (R) | 41,627 | 72.3 |
| | Gideon Sibley (D) | 12,250 | 21.4 |
| | Clinton C. Hancock (P) | 3,372 | 5.9 |
| 5 | Alfred C. Harmer (R) | 39,239 | 79.8 |
| | Frank D. Wright (D) | 9,942 | 20.2 |
| 6 | Thomas S. Butler (BC) | 15,169 | 53.7 |
| | John B. Robinson (ROBINSON, HG) | 6,537 | 23.6 |
| | William H. Berry (D, L) | 6,514 | 23.1 |
| 7 | Irving P. Wanger (R) | 21,567 | 53.1 |
| | Clinton Rorer (D) | 17,872 | 44.0 |
| 8 | Laird H. Barber (D) | 16,400 | 54.8 |
| | William S. Kirkpatrick (R) | 13,516 | 45.2 |
| 9 | Daniel Ermentrout (D) | 24,137 | 57.3 |
| | Jeremiah S. Parvin (R) | 16,613 | 39.4 |
| 10 | Marriott Brosius (R) | 17,482 | 67.9 |
| | A. J. Steinman (D) | 7,083 | 27.5 |
| 11 | William Connell (R) | 11,404 | 46.1 |
| | M. F. Sando (D) | 9,861 | 39.8 |
| | Freeman Leach (P, HG) | 3,164 | 12.8 |
| 12 | Stanley W. Davenport (D) | 17,220 | 49.9 |
| | Morgan B. Williams (R) | 15,772 | 45.7 |
| 13 | James W. Ryan (D) | 15,042 | 54.2 |
| | Charles N. Brumm (R) | 12,542 | 45.2 |
| 14 | Marlin E. Olmsted (R) | 19,352 | 60.8 |
| | Wilson W. Gray (D) | 9,926 | 31.2 |
| | Lee L. Grumbine (P) | 2,564 | 8.1 |
| 15 | Charles Frederick Wright (R) | 14,541 | 55.3 |
| | Archibald B. Gammell (D) | 9,331 | 35.5 |
| | Chauncey S. Russell (P) | 2,416 | 9.2 |
| 16 | Horace B. Packer (R) | 15,839 | 49.4 |
| | Jonathan F. Strieby (D) | 12,858 | 40.1 |
| | Lewis P. Thurston (P) | 3,378 | 10.5 |
| 17 | Rufus K. Polk (D) | 14,792 | 51.8 |
| | William Hartman Woodin (R) | 12,487 | 43.8 |
| 18 | Thaddeus M. Mahon (R) | 17,722 | 57.8 |
| | Robert McMeen (D) | 12,921 | 42.2 |

## PENNSYLVANIA

| Candidates | Votes | % |
|---|---|---|
| 9 Edward D. Ziegler (D) | 20,126 | 51.4 |
| Robert J. Lewis (R) | 19,016 | 48.6 |
| 20 Joseph E. Thropp (R) | 19,358 | 48.9 |
| James M. Walters (D) | 17,858 | 45.2 |
| John J. Irwin (P) | 2,091 | 5.3 |
| 21 Summers M. Jack (R) | 23,277 | 55.7 |
| Jacob R. Spiegel (D) | 16,191 | 38.7 |
| Thomas J. Baldridge (P) | 2,360 | 5.6 |
| 22 John Dalzell (R) | 25,693 | 66.6 |
| George W. Acklin (D) | 11,049 | 28.6 |
| 23 William H. Graham (R) | 14,008 | 68.1 |
| John H. Stevenson (D) | 5,608 | 27.3 |
| 24 Ernest F. Acheson (R) | 25,524 | 54.5 |
| Mark M. Cochran (D) | 21,290 | 45.5 |
| 25 Joseph B. Showalter (R) | 18,220 | 51.3 |
| M. L. Lockwood (D) | 15,271 | 43.0 |
| John A. Bailey (P) | 2,000 | 5.7 |
| 26 Athelston Gaston (D) | 13,516 | 47.8 |
| George H. Higgins (R) | 13,482 | 47.6 |
| 27 Joseph C. Sibley (D) | 14,138 | 52.1 |
| Charles W. Stone (R) | 11,757 | 43.3 |
| 28 James K. P. Hall (D) | 17,550 | 52.1 |
| William J. Arnold (R) | 14,209 | 42.2 |
| George W. Rheem (P) | 1,898 | 5.6 |
| AL Galusha A. Grow (R) | 532,890✔ | |
| Samuel A. Davenport (R) | 520,774✔ | |
| Jerry N. Weiler (D, PP) | 357,500 | |
| Franklin P. Iams (D) | 350,214 | |
| George H. Garber (P) | 48,600 | |
| Pennock E. Sharpless (P) | 47,543 | |
| John R. Root (SOC LAB) | 4,495 | |
| Donald L. Munro (SOC LAB) | 4,300 | |
| Dennis E. Johnston (PP) | 3,995 | |
| J. Acker Guss (L) | 839 | |
| Charles P. Shaw (L) | 837 | |

## RHODE ISLAND

| Candidates | Votes | % |
|---|---|---|
| 1 Melville Bull (R) | 12,081 | 60.4 |
| Hogan (D) | 6,392 | 31.9 |
| Theinert (SOC LAB) | 1,081 | 5.4 |
| 2 Adin B. Capron (R) | 9,095 | 52.0 |
| Garvin (D) | 6,435 | 36.8 |
| Dana (SOC LAB) | 1,473 | 8.4 |

## SOUTH CAROLINA

| Candidates | Votes | % |
|---|---|---|
| 1 William Elliott (D) | 3,030 | 66.5 |
| G. W. Murray (R) | 1,529 | 33.5 |
| 2 W. Jasper Talbert (D) | 4,013 | 97.0 |
| 3 Asbury C. Latimer (D) | 4,029 | 92.1 |
| R. R. Tolbert (R) | 332 | 7.6 |
| 4 Stanyarne Wilson (D) | 4,467 | 96.4 |
| 5 David L. Finley (D) | 4,230 | 100.0 |
| 6 James Norton (D) | 4,765 | 96.9 |
| 7 J. William Stokes (D) | 4,433 | 89.8 |
| James Weston (R) | 505 | 10.2 |

## SOUTH DAKOTA

| Candidates | Votes | % |
|---|---|---|
| Robert J. Gamble (R) | 38,780✔ | |
| Charles H. Burke (R) | 36,295✔ | |
| J. E. Kelley (FUS) | 32,314 | |
| F. Knowles (FUS) | 32,240 | |
| A. Jamieson (P) | 882 | |
| M. D. Alexander (P) | 849 | |

## TENNESSEE

| Candidates | Votes | % |
|---|---|---|
| Walter P. Brownlow (R) | 14,616 | 55.0 |
| Gouchenaur (D) | 11,732 | 44.1 |
| Henry R. Gibson (R) | 13,848 | 66.3 |
| Davis (D) | 6,904 | 33.1 |

| Candidates | Votes | % |
|---|---|---|
| 3 John A. Moon (D) | 13,347 | 58.9 |
| Cate (R) | 9,209 | 40.6 |
| 4 Charles E. Snodgrass (D) | 13,413 | 62.3 |
| Morgan (R) | 8,122 | 37.7 |
| 5 James D. Richardson (D) | 11,087 | 69.8 |
| Elliott (R) | 4,800 | 30.2 |
| 6 John W. Gaines (D) | 11,539 | 78.8 |
| Napier (R) | 2,088 | 14.3 |
| Gill (P) | 1,021 | 7.0 |
| 7 Nicholas N. Cox (D) | 9,590 | 70.3 |
| Cunningham (R) | 4,055 | 29.7 |
| 8 Thetus W. Sims (D) | 10,747 | 60.3 |
| Hinkle (R) | 6,549 | 36.8 |
| 9 Rice A. Pierce (D) | 9,860 | 76.8 |
| Reville (R) | 2,728 | 21.3 |
| 10 Edward W. Carmack (D) | 8,419 | 81.8 |
| Vernon (R) | 1,873 | 18.2 |

## TEXAS

| Candidates | Votes | % |
|---|---|---|
| 1 Thomas H. Ball (D) | 18,544 | 67.2 |
| O. A. Blackwell (R) | 5,276 | 19.1 |
| Joe Eagle (POP) | 3,764 | 13.6 |
| 2 Samuel B. Cooper (D) | 22,086 | 68.9 |
| T. J. Russell (POP) | 7,853 | 24.5 |
| J. A. McAyeal (R) | 2,021 | 6.3 |
| 3 Reese C. De Graffenreid (D) | 17,996 | 66.3 |
| H. D. Wood (POP) | 9,169 | 33.8 |
| 4 John L. Sheppard (D) | 18,190 | 63.6 |
| J. L. Whittle (POP) | 10,409 | 36.4 |
| 5 Joseph W. Bailey (D) | 16,978 | 74.1 |
| W. S. Holt (POP) | 4,345 | 19.0 |
| A. W. Acheson (R) | 1,487 | 6.5 |
| 6 Robert E. Burke (D) | 25,116 | 65.8 |
| T. B. Goren (POP) | 9,677 | 25.4 |
| A. J. Houston (R) | 3,375 | 8.8 |
| 7 Robert L. Henry (D) | 22,203 | 68.7 |
| A. W. Cunningham (POP) | 7,927 | 24.5 |
| Russell Kingsbury (R) | 2,197 | 6.8 |
| 8 Samuel W. T. Lanham (D) | 18,580 | 58.1 |
| W. J. Shands (POP) | 11,138 | 34.9 |
| Arthur Springer (R) | 2,239 | 7.0 |
| 9 Albert S. Burleson (D) | 20,378 | 61.7 |
| G. W. Jones (POP) | 12,628 | 38.3 |
| 10 Robert B. Hawley (R) | 17,759 | 48.0 |
| W. S. Robson (D) | 16,462 | 44.5 |
| J. W. Baird (POP) | 2,604 | 7.0 |
| 11 Rudolph Kleberg (D) | 18,319 | 55.5 |
| B. L. Crouch (R) | 14,687 | 44.5 |
| 12 James L. Slayden (D) | 16,363 | 56.1 |
| G. H. Nooran (R) | 10,472 | 35.9 |
| A. B. Surber | 2,114 | 7.3 |
| 13 John H. Stephens (D) | 25,000 | 73.5 |
| J. J. Eager (POP) | 8,995 | 26.5 |

## UTAH

| Candidates | Votes | % |
|---|---|---|
| AL Brigham H. Roberts (D) | 35,646* | 54.6 |
| Eldridge (R) | 29,603 | 45.4 |

## VERMONT

| Candidates | Votes | % |
|---|---|---|
| 1 H. Henry Powers (R) | 20,350 | 71.7 |
| Herbert F. Brigham (D) | 8,026 | 28.3 |
| 2 William W. Grout (R) | 17,728 | 74.6 |
| C. A. G. Jackson (D) | 5,967 | 25.1 |

## VIRGINIA

| Candidates | Votes | % |
|---|---|---|
| 1 William A. Jones (D) | 8,934 | 66.5 |
| Joseph A. Bristow (R) | 4,270 | 31.8 |
| 2 William A. Young (D) | 12,183‡ | 55.8 |
| Richard A. Wise (R) | 6,204 | 28.4 |

| Candidates | Votes | % |
|---|---|---|
| William S. Holland (IR) | 3,445 | 15.8 |
| 3 John Lamb (D) | 7,058 | 69.1 |
| Otis H. Russell (R) | 1,914 | 18.8 |
| Benjamin B. Weisiger (R) | 1,138 | 11.1 |
| 4 Sydney P. Epes (D) | 8,633 | 57.5 |
| R. T. Thorp (R) | 5,889 | 39.2 |
| 5 Claude A. Swanson (D) | 13,459 | 57.0 |
| E. Parr (R) | 9,858 | 41.8 |
| 6 Peter J. Otey (D) | 10,759 | 66.9 |
| Daniel Butler (R) | 2,535 | 15.8 |
| Charles A. Heermans (R) | 2,310 | 14.4 |
| 7 James Hay (D) | 9,841 | 77.1 |
| D. C. O'Flaherty (D SIL) | 2,931 | 23.0 |
| 8 John F. Rixey (D) | 6,469 | 88.6 |
| Edward Hughes (I) | 616 | 8.4 |
| 9 William F. Rhea (D) | 17,344 | 51.0 |
| James A. Walker (R) | 16,505 | 48.8 |
| 10 Julian M. Quarles (D) | 10,784 | 56.1 |
| Robert T. Hubard (R) | 8,377 | 43.6 |

## WASHINGTON

| Candidates | Votes | % |
|---|---|---|
| AL Wesley L. Jones (R) | 39,809✔ | |
| Francis W. Cushman (R) | 38,983✔ | |
| James Hamilton Lewis (PP) | 36,385 | |
| William C. Jones (PP) | 32,903 | |
| A. C. Dickenson (P) | 1,169 | |
| C. L. Haggard (P) | 1,037 | |
| M. A. Hamilton (SOC LAB) | 929 | |
| Walter Walker (SOC LAB) | 897 | |

## WEST VIRGINIA

| Candidates | Votes | % |
|---|---|---|
| 1 Blackburn B. Dovener (R) | 20,891 | 51.9 |
| J. V. Blair (D) | 19,031 | 47.3 |
| 2 Alston G. Dayton (R) | 23,364 | 50.3 |
| John T. McGraw (D) | 22,720 | 49.0 |
| 3 David Johnston (D) | 22,802 | 50.6 |
| William S. Edwards (R) | 22,037 | 48.9 |
| 4 Romeo H. Freer (R) | 21,727 | 50.8 |
| George I. Neal (D) | 20,896 | 48.8 |

## WISCONSIN

| Candidates | Votes | % |
|---|---|---|
| 1 Henry Allen Cooper (R) | 19,887 | 61.5 |
| Clinton Babbitt (D) | 11,447 | 35.4 |
| 2 Herman B. Dahle (R) | 16,892 | 50.4 |
| James E. Jones (D) | 15,768 | 47.0 |
| 3 Joseph W. Babcock (R) | 19,195 | 59.5 |
| Thomas L. Cleary (D) | 12,037 | 37.3 |
| 4 Theobald Otjen (R) | 15,903 | 47.3 |
| Joseph G. Donnelly (D) | 14,022 | 41.7 |
| Robert Schilling (PP) | 2,227 | 6.6 |
| 5 Samuel S. Barney (R) | 17,056 | 51.8 |
| Charles E. Armin (D) | 13,233 | 40.2 |
| 6 James H. Davidson (R) | 20,107 | 53.6 |
| Frank C. Stewart (D) | 1,680 | 44.5 |
| 7 John J. Esch (R) | 16,136 | 64.7 |
| John F. Doherty (D) | 8,128 | 32.6 |
| 8 Edward S. Minor (R) | 16,910 | 54.2 |
| Philip Sheridan (D) | 13,668 | 43.8 |
| 9 Alexander Stewart (R) | 20,825 | 58.1 |
| Wells M. Ruggles (D) | 14,373 | 401 |
| 10 John J. Jenkins (R) | 17,601 | 63.2 |
| John R. Mathews (D) | 8,435 | 30.3 |

## WYOMING

| Candidates | Votes | % |
|---|---|---|
| AL Frank W. Mondell (R) | 10,762 | 54.7 |
| Constantine P. Arnold (D) | 8,466 | 43.0 |

# 1899 House Elections

### MAINE
**Special Election**

| | Candidates | Votes | % |
|---|---|---|---|
| 2 | Charles E. Littlefield (R) | 11,624 | 81.0 |
| | John Scott (D) | 2,736 | 19.1 |

### NEBRASKA
**Special Election**

| | Candidates | Votes | % |
|---|---|---|---|
| 6 | William Neville (FUS) | 18,759 | 53.4 |
| | Moses P. Kinkaid (R) | 16,399 | 46.6 |

### OHIO
**Special Election**

| | Candidates | Votes | % |
|---|---|---|---|
| 16 | Joseph J. Gill (R) | 19,368 | 55.5 |
| | Lavosier Spence (D) | 15,302 | 43.8 |

### MISSOURI
**Special Election**

| | Candidates | Votes | % |
|---|---|---|---|
| 8 | Dorsey W. Shackleford (D) | 19,331 | 53.6 |
| | W. J. Vosholl (R) | 15,858 | 44.0 |

### NEW YORK
**Special Election**

| | Candidates | Votes | % |
|---|---|---|---|
| 34 | Edward B. Vreeland (R) | 21,773 | 63.7 |
| | S. E. Lewis (D) | 12,406 | 36.3 |

### PENNSYLVANIA
**Special Election**

| | Candidates | Votes | % |
|---|---|---|---|
| 9 | Henry D. Green (D) | 17,736 | 59.9 |
| | Jeremiah S. Parvin | 11,878 | 40.1 |

# 1900 House Elections

## ALABAMA

| | Candidates | Votes | % |
|---|---|---|---|
| 1 | George Taylor (D) | 9,804 | 82.7 |
| | John W. Schell (R) | 2,046 | 17.3 |
| 2 | Ariosto A. Wiley (D) | 12,496 | 98.3 |
| 3 | Henry Clayton (D) | 13,420 | 80.2 |
| | W. O. Mulkey (POP & R) | 3,179 | 19.0 |
| 4 | Sidney J. Bowie (D) | 10,733 | 97.3 |
| 5 | Charles W. Thompson (D) | 15,767 | 66.9 |
| | Andrew J. Milstead (R) | 7,782 | 33.0 |
| 6 | John Bankhead (D) | 8,073 | 65.7 |
| | Thomas B. Morton (R) | 4,218 | 34.3 |
| 7 | John L. Burnett (D) | 10,549 | 51.8 |
| | N. B. Spears (R) | 9,802 | 48.2 |
| 8 | William Richardson (D) | 13,193 | 59.7 |
| | A. N. Holland (R) | 8,900 | 40.3 |
| 9 | Oscar Underwood (D) | 10,591 | 99.9 |

### Special Election

| | | Votes | % |
|---|---|---|---|
| 8 | William Richardson (D) | 14,632 | 84.8 |
| | Cutler Smith (R) | 2,631 | 15.2 |

## ARKANSAS

| | Candidates | Votes | % |
|---|---|---|---|
| 1 | Philip D. McCulloch (D) | 17,066 | 72.4 |
| | T. O. Fitzpatrick (R) | 6,496 | 27.6 |
| 2 | John S. Little (D) | 13,792 | 67.9 |
| | E. H. Vance Jr. (R) | 6,522 | 32.1 |
| 3 | Thomas C. McRae (D) | 14,945 | 63.3 |
| | B. M. Foreman (R) | 8,664 | 36.7 |
| 4 | Charles C. Reid (D) | 12,336 | 65.3 |
| | Sam Davis (R) | 6,556 | 34.7 |
| 5 | Hugh A. Dinsmore (D) | 13,924 | 61.1 |
| | U. S. Bratton (R) | 8,885 | 39.0 |
| 6 | Stephen Brundidge Jr. (D) | 12,256 | 68.9 |
| | C. F. Cole (R) | 5,527 | 31.1 |

## CALIFORNIA

| | Candidates | Votes | % |
|---|---|---|---|
| 1 | Frank L. Coombs (R) | 21,227 | 55.3 |
| | James F. Farraher (D) | 16,270 | 42.4 |
| 2 | Samuel D. Woods (R) | 23,019 | 50.4 |
| | J. D. Sproul (D) | 21,851 | 47.9 |
| 3 | Victor H. Metcalf (R) | 22,109 | 58.3 |
| | Frank Freeman (D) | 14,408 | 38.0 |
| 4 | Julius Kahn (R) | 18,904 | 56.8 |
| | R. Porter Ashe (D) | 12,336 | 37.1 |
| 5 | Eugene F. Loud (R) | 21,651 | 54.4 |
| | J. H. Henry (D) | 16,781 | 42.1 |
| 6 | James McLachlan (R) | 27,081 | 51.8 |
| | William Graves (D) | 19,793 | 37.9 |
| | Unidentified Candidate (SOC LAB) | 3,674 | 7.0 |
| 7 | James Carson Needham (R) | 23,450 | 52.4 |
| | W. D. Crichton (D) | 18,981 | 42.4 |

### Special Election

| | | Votes | % |
|---|---|---|---|
| 2 | Samuel D. Woods (R) | 22,799 | 51.0 |
| | J. D. Sproul (D) | 21,917 | 49.0 |

## COLORADO

| | Candidates | Votes | % |
|---|---|---|---|
| 1 | John F. Shafroth (FUS) | 54,591 | 55.3 |
| | Robert W. Bonynge (R) | 41,518 | 42.1 |
| 2 | John C. Bell (FUS) | 66,361 | 56.0 |
| | Herschel M. Hogg (R) | 51,287 | 43.3 |

## CONNECTICUT

| | Candidates | Votes | % |
|---|---|---|---|
| 1 | E. Stevens Henry (R) | 25,048 | 58.2 |
| | Tuttle (D) | 16,836 | 39.1 |
| 2 | Nehemiah D. Sperry (R) | 33,205 | 52.9 |
| | Gildersleeve (D) | 28,349 | 45.2 |
| 3 | Charles A. Russell (R) | 14,727 | 60.4 |
| | Potter (D) | 9,284 | 38.1 |
| 4 | Ebenezer J. Hill (R) | 29,579 | 58.2 |
| | Lyman (D) | 20,520 | 40.3 |

## DELAWARE

| | Candidates | Votes | % |
|---|---|---|---|
| AL | Lewis Heisler Ball (R) | 22,353 | 53.1 |
| | Alexander M. Daly (D) | 19,157 | 45.5 |

### Special Election

| | | Votes | % |
|---|---|---|---|
| AL | Walter O. Hoffecker (R) | 22,389 | 53.5 |
| | Edward Fowler (D) | 19,012 | 45.4 |

## FLORIDA

| | Candidates | Votes | % |
|---|---|---|---|
| 1 | Stephen M. Sparkman (D) | 13,440 | 87.0 |
| | G. Brown Patterson (R) | 2,005 | 13.0 |
| 2 | Robert W. Davis (D) | 13,011 | 80.0 |
| | John M. Cheney (R) | 3,259 | 20.0 |

## GEORGIA

| | Candidates | Votes | % |
|---|---|---|---|
| 1 | Rufus E. Lester (D) | 7,272 | 64.0 |
| | W. R. Leaken (R) | 4,098 | 36.0 |
| 2 | James M. Griggs (D) | 7,299 | 99.7 |
| 3 | Elijah B. Lewis (D) | 6,119 | 99.9 |
| 4 | William C. Adamson (D) | 7,234 | 76.0 |
| | A. H. Freeman (R) | 2,238 | 23.5 |
| 5 | Leonidas F. Livingston (D) | 8,828 | 76.6 |
| | Charles I. Brannan (I) | 2,685 | 23.3 |
| 6 | Charles L. Bartlett (D) | 7,375 | 94.1 |
| | J. T. Dickey (POP) | 449 | 5.7 |
| 7 | John W. Maddox (D) | 9,113 | 62.0 |
| | S. J. McKnight (POP) | 4,574 | 31.1 |
| | J. J. Hamilton (R) | 1,006 | 6.9 |
| 8 | William M. Howard (D) | 6,952 | 92.0 |
| | S. P. Bond (POP) | 597 | 7.9 |
| 9 | Farish C. Tate (D) | 9,140 | 83.6 |
| | H. L. Peeples (POP) | 1,690 | 15.5 |
| 10 | William H. Fleming (D) | 5,585 | 92.2 |
| 11 | W. G. Brantley (D) | 8,587 | 66.8 |
| | W. H. Marston (R) | 4,263 | 33.2 |

## IDAHO

| | Candidates | Votes | % |
|---|---|---|---|
| AL | Thomas L. Glenn (POP & D) | 28,079 | 51.1 |
| | J. T. Morrison (R) | 26,860 | 48.9 |

## ILLINOIS

| | Candidates | Votes | % |
|---|---|---|---|
| 1 | James R. Mann (R) | 52,775 | 63.0 |
| | Leon Hornstein (D) | 28,858 | 34.5 |
| 2 | John J. Feely (D) | 34,946 | 50.1 |
| | William Lorimer (R) | 32,921 | 47.2 |
| 3 | George P. Foster (D) | 23,142 | 55.4 |
| | William E. O'Neill (R) | 17,920 | 42.9 |
| 4 | James McAndrews (D) | 24,435 | 54.4 |
| | Daniel W. Mills (R) | 19,346 | 43.1 |
| 5 | William F. Mahoney (D) | 23,648 | 53.8 |
| | Charles C. Carnahan (R) | 19,254 | 43.8 |
| 6 | Henry Sherman Boutell (R) | 22,655 | 49.5 |
| | Emil Hoechster (D) | 22,125 | 48.3 |
| 7 | George Edmund Foss (R) | 41,841 | 57.5 |
| | William Peacock (D) | 28,581 | 39.3 |
| 8 | Albert J. Hopkins (R) | 32,452 | 68.5 |
| | John W. Leonard (D) | 13,683 | 28.9 |
| 9 | Robert R. Hitt (R) | 32,616 | 65.7 |
| | Hiram A. Brooks (D) | 15,692 | 31.6 |
| 10 | George W. Prince (R) | 33,454 | 65.2 |
| | Lavergne B. DeForest (D) | 16,699 | 32.6 |
| 11 | Walter Reeves (R) | 25,367 | 56.1 |
| | Edgar P. Holley (D) | 18,835 | 41.6 |
| 12 | Joseph G. Cannon (R) | 30,633 | 60.2 |
| | C. M. Briggs (D) | 19,226 | 37.8 |
| 13 | Vespasian Warner (R) | 26,865 | 56.2 |
| | John Eddy (D) | 19,397 | 40.6 |
| 14 | Joseph V. Graff (R) | 25,169 | 49.5 |
| | Jesse Black Jr (D) | 24,775 | 48.7 |
| 15 | J. Ross Mickey (D) | 24,491 | 49.5 |
| | Benjamin F. Marsh (R) | 24,175 | 48.8 |
| 16 | Thomas J. Selby (D) | 25,795 | 55.7 |
| | Thomas Worthington (R) | 19,618 | 42.3 |
| 17 | Ben F. Caldwell (D) | 25,673 | 51.2 |
| | David Ross (R) | 23,648 | 47.2 |
| 18 | Thomas M. Jett (D) | 22,847 | 50.8 |
| | John Jacob Brenholt (R) | 21,245 | 47.2 |
| 19 | Joseph B. Crowley (D) | 24,536 | 50.7 |
| | Horace S. Clark (R) | 23,057 | 47.6 |
| 20 | James R. Williams (D) | 21,976 | 51.8 |
| | Alexander M. Funkhouser (R) | 19,716 | 46.4 |
| 21 | Frederick J. Kern (D) | 25,299 | 49.8 |
| | William A. Rodenberg (R) | 24,810 | 48.8 |
| 22 | George W. Smith (R) | 22,349 | 55.5 |
| | Lindorf O. Whitnel (D) | 17,528 | 43.6 |

## INDIANA

| | Candidates | Votes | % |
|---|---|---|---|
| 1 | James H. Hemenway (R) | 22,262 | 49.7 |
| | Alfred Dale Owen (D) | 22,060 | 49.3 |
| 2 | Robert W. Miers (D) | 24,420 | 51.8 |
| | Peter R. Wadsworth (R) | 21,799 | 46.3 |
| 3 | William T. Zenor (D) | 24,049 | 54.9 |
| | Hugh T. O'Conner (R) | 19,440 | 44.4 |
| 4 | Francis M. Griffith (D) | 24,249 | 51.2 |
| | Nathan Powell (R) | 22,641 | 47.8 |
| 5 | Elias S. Holliday (R) | 25,932 | 50.6 |
| | Frank A. Horner (D) | 24,244 | 47.3 |
| 6 | James E. Watson (R) | 24,203 | 52.0 |
| | David W. McKee (D) | 21,320 | 45.8 |
| 7 | Jesse Overstreet (R) | 31,021 | 52.4 |
| | Frank B. Burke (D) | 27,012 | 45.7 |
| 8 | George W. Cromer (R) | 31,949 | 51.7 |
| | Joseph T. Day (D) | 28,180 | 45.6 |
| 9 | Charles B. Landis (R) | 24,138 | 50.3 |
| | David F. Allen (D) | 22,621 | 47.1 |
| 10 | Edgar D. Crumpacker (R) | 29,537 | 55.5 |
| | John Ross (D) | 23,045 | 43.3 |
| 11 | George W. Steele (R) | 29,177 | 53.3 |
| | William J. Houck (D) | 23,688 | 43.2 |
| 12 | James M. Robinson (D) | 22,750 | 49.7 |
| | Robert B. Hanna (R) | 22,122 | 48.4 |
| 13 | Abraham L. Brick (R) | 26,592 | 51.1 |
| | Charles C. Bower (D) | 24,376 | 46.8 |

## IOWA

| | Candidates | Votes | % |
|---|---|---|---|
| 1 | Thomas Hedge (R) | 21,419 | 53.1 |
| | D. J. O'Connell (D) | 18,051 | 44.8 |
| 2 | John N. W. Rumple (R) | 23,202 | 50.4 |
| | Henry Vollmer (D) | 21,737 | 47.2 |
| 3 | David B. Henderson (R) | 30,181 | 61.4 |
| | Willis N. Birdsall (D) | 18,856 | 38.3 |
| 4 | Gilbert N. Haugen (R) | 27,659 | 61.2 |
| | John Foley (D) | 16,796 | 37.1 |
| 5 | Robert G. Cousins (R) | 27,124 | 59.5 |
| | Daniel Kerr (D) | 18,266 | 40.1 |
| 6 | John F. Lacey (R) | 22,956 | 53.2 |
| | A. C. Steck (D) | 19,812 | 45.9 |
| 7 | John A. T. Hull (R) | 28,508 | 61.6 |
| | George C. Crozier (D) | 16,365 | 35.4 |
| 8 | William P. Hepburn (R) | 26,798 | 54.7 |
| | V. R. McGinnis (D) | 21,347 | 43.6 |
| 9 | Walter I. Smith (R) | 27,155 | 56.8 |
| | S. B. Wadsworth (D) | 20,207 | 42.3 |

## IOWA

| | Candidates | Votes | % |
|---|---|---|---|
| 10 | James P. Conner (R) | 36,584 | 62.9 |
| | Robert F. Dale (D) | 20,648 | 35.5 |
| 11 | Lot Thomas (R) | 32,716 | 60.2 |
| | William Muloaney (D) | 20,564 | 37.8 |

### Special Elections

| | | | |
|---|---|---|---|
| 9 | Walter I. Smith (R) | 27,154 | 57.3 |
| | S. B. Wadsworth (D) | 20,229 | 42.7 |
| 10 | James P. Conner (R) | 35,009 | 63.8 |
| | Robert F. Dale (D) | 19,830 | 36.2 |

## KANSAS

| | | | |
|---|---|---|---|
| 1 | Charles Curtis (R) | 28,733 | 59.1 |
| | George W. Glick (D-PP) | 19,915 | 40.9 |
| 2 | Justin D. Bowersock (R) | 28,083 | 52.3 |
| | M. S. Peters (D-PP) | 25,623 | 47.7 |
| 3 | Alfred M. Jackson (D-PP) | 26,760 | 50.0 |
| | George W. Wheatley (R) | 26,492 | 49.5 |
| 4 | James M. Miller (R) | 24,106 | 53.8 |
| | Thomas H. Grisham (D-PP) | 20,670 | 46.2 |
| 5 | William A. Calderhead (R) | 22,436 | 53.9 |
| | W. D. Vincent (D-PP) | 19,211 | 46.1 |
| 6 | William A. Reeder (R) | 19,660 | 48.9 |
| | John B. Dykes (PP) | 15,083 | 37.6 |
| | Tully Scott (D) | 5,430 | 13.5 |
| 7 | Chester I. Long (R) | 31,479 | 51.2 |
| | Claud Duval (D-PP) | 29,960 | 48.8 |
| AL | Charles F. Scott (R) | 180,162 | 52.3 |
| | J. D. Botkin (D-PP) | 160,980 | 46.7 |

## KENTUCKY

| | | | |
|---|---|---|---|
| 1 | Charles K. Wheeler (D) | 25,264 | 59.6 |
| | Keys (R) | 16,809 | 39.7 |
| 2 | Henry D. Allen (D) | 23,410 | 53.9 |
| | Lynch (R) | 19,788 | 45.6 |
| 3 | John S. Rhea (D) | 19,505‡ | 50.0 |
| | J. McKenzie Moss (R) | 19,344 | 49.6 |
| 4 | David H. Smith (D) | 24,920 | 53.2 |
| | Jolly (R) | 21,944 | 46.8 |
| 5 | Harvey S. Irwin (R) | 25,085 | 53.7 |
| | Gregory (D) | 21,374 | 45.8 |
| 6 | Daniel L. Gooch (D) | 22,572 | 56.7 |
| | Shaw (R) | 16,857 | 42.3 |
| 7 | South Trimble (D) | 20,325 | 54.7 |
| | Stoll (R) | 16,810 | 45.3 |
| 8 | George G. Gilbert (D) | 17,646 | 51.2 |
| | Willms (R) | 16,602 | 48.1 |
| 9 | James N. Kehoe (D) | 23,197 | 50.3 |
| | Pugh (R) | 22,961 | 49.7 |
| 10 | James B. White (D) | 19,443 | 51.8 |
| | Hopkins (R) | 18,070 | 48.2 |
| 11 | Vincent Boreing (R) | 34,406 | 69.2 |
| | Smith (D) | 15,281 | 30.8 |

## LOUISIANA

| | | | |
|---|---|---|---|
| 1 | Adolph Meyer (D) | 9,727 | 81.0 |
| | William Brophy (R) | 2,274 | 18.9 |
| 2 | Robert C. Davey (D) | 11,420 | 77.8 |
| | Samuel C. Heaslip (R) | 3,234 | 22.0 |
| 3 | Robert F. Broussard (D) | 9,382 | 62.3 |
| | Frank B. Williams (R) | 5,673 | 37.7 |
| 4 | Phanor Breazeale (D) | 8,592 | 86.9 |
| | F. M. Welch (R) | 1,290 | 13.1 |
| 5 | Joseph E. Ransdell (D) | 6,172 | 90.8 |
| | Henry E. Hardtner (R) | 628 | 9.2 |
| 6 | Samuel M. Robertson (D) | 7,432 | 83.6 |
| | James H. Ducote (R) | 1,455 | 16.4 |

## MAINE

| | | | |
|---|---|---|---|
| 1 | Amos L. Allen (R) | 17,803 | 60.3 |
| | John J. Lynch (D) | 10,040 | 34.0 |
| | D. P. Parker (P) | 1,533 | 5.2 |
| 2 | Charles E. Littlefield (R) | 19,215 | 61.0 |
| | H. H. Monroe (D) | 11,439 | 36.3 |
| 3 | Edwin C. Burleigh (R) | 17,057 | 60.7 |
| | A. F. Gerald (D) | 10,241 | 36.4 |
| 4 | Charles A. Boutelle (R) | 18,826* | 66.3 |
| | Thomas White (D) | 8,765 | 30.9 |

## MARYLAND

| | | | |
|---|---|---|---|
| 1 | William H. Jackson (R) | 19,714 | 50.2 |
| | John P. Moore (D) | 18,173 | 46.3 |
| 2 | Albert A. Blakeney (R) | 27,710 | 48.7 |
| | J. F. C. Talbott (D) | 27,420 | 48.2 |
| 3 | Frank C. Wachter (R) | 21,641 | 51.8 |
| | Robert Fulton Leach Jr. (D) | 19,570 | 46.8 |
| 4 | Charles R. Schirm (R) | 21,932 | 51.4 |
| | James W. Denny (D) | 20,149 | 47.2 |
| 5 | Sydney E. Mudd (R) | 20,936 | 54.2 |
| | Benjamin H. Camalier (D) | 17,305 | 44.8 |
| 6 | George A. Pearre (R) | 23,541 | 53.0 |
| | Charles A. Little (D) | 20,161 | 45.4 |

### Special Election

| | | | |
|---|---|---|---|
| 1 | Josiah L. Kerr (R) | 19,320 | 50.9 |
| | Edwin H. Brown (D) | 18,650 | 49.1 |

## MASSACHUSETTS

| | | | |
|---|---|---|---|
| 1 | George P. Lawrence (R) | 16,520 | 58.0 |
| | James H. Bryan (D) | 10,924 | 38.4 |
| 2 | Frederick H. Gillett (R) | 17,604 | 60.6 |
| | Thomas W. Kenefick (D) | 10,766 | 37.1 |
| 3 | John R. Thayer (D) | 16,039 | 50.2 |
| | Charles G. Washburn (R) | 15,909 | 49.8 |
| 4 | Charles Q. Tirrell (R) | 19,718 | 65.3 |
| | Charles D. Lewis (D) | 10,493 | 34.7 |
| 5 | William S. Knox (R) | 15,887 | 49.4 |
| | Joseph J. Flynn (D) | 15,466 | 48.1 |
| 6 | William H. Moody (R) | 18,328 | 64.6 |
| | Daniel N. Crowley (D) | 6,534 | 23.0 |
| | Albert L. Gillen (D SOCIAL) | 2,725 | 9.6 |
| 7 | Ernest W. Roberts (R) | 19,595 | 60.3 |
| | Henry Winn (D) | 10,815 | 33.3 |
| 8 | Samuel W. McCall (R) | 19,901 | 69.4 |
| | Philip T. Nickerson (D) | 7,970 | 27.8 |
| 9 | Joseph A. Conry (D) | 14,701 | 66.7 |
| | Charles T. Witt (R) | 6,633 | 30.1 |
| 10 | Henry F. Naphen (D) | 23,507 | 59.0 |
| | George B. Pierce (R) | 16,318 | 41.0 |
| 11 | Samuel L. Powers (R) | 21,761 | 60.0 |
| | William H. Baker (D) | 10,885 | 30.0 |
| | Moorfield Storey (I) | 2,858 | 7.9 |
| 12 | William C. Lovering (R) | 17,788 | 61.4 |
| | Charles F. King (D) | 7,434 | 25.7 |
| | Charles E. Lowell (D SOCIAL) | 2,404 | 8.3 |
| 13 | William S. Greene (R) | 16,337 | 69.1 |
| | Charles T. Luce (D) | 5,954 | 25.2 |

## MICHIGAN

| | | | |
|---|---|---|---|
| 1 | John B. Corliss (R) | 24,785 | 54.0 |
| | Rufus W. Jacklin (D) | 20,295 | 44.2 |
| 2 | Henry C. Smith (R) | 26,945 | 52.4 |
| | Martin G. Loennecker (D) | 23,368 | 45.5 |
| 3 | Washington Gardner (R) | 25,998 | 53.3 |
| | Stephen D. Williams (D) | 21,306 | 43.6 |
| 4 | Edward L. Hamilton (R) | 26,883 | 55.6 |
| | Roman I. Jarvis (D) | 20,498 | 42.4 |
| 5 | William Alden Smith (R) | 27,898 | 55.6 |
| | William F. McKnight (D) | 21,497 | 42.8 |
| 6 | Samuel W. Smith (R) | 27,941 | 53.9 |
| | Everett L. Bray (D) | 22,532 | 43.4 |
| 7 | Edgar Weeks (R) | 22,924 | 57.7 |
| | Justin R. Whiting (D) | 15,938 | 40.1 |
| 8 | Joseph W. Fordney (R) | 21,522 | 53.5 |
| | Wellington R. Burt (D) | 17,212 | 42.8 |
| 9 | Roswell P. Bishop (R) | 21,408 | 62.4 |
| | Frank L. Fowler (D) | 12,197 | 35.5 |
| 10 | Rousseau O. Crump (R) | 23,308 | 59.3 |
| | Lee E. Joslyn (D) | 15,241 | 38.8 |
| 11 | Archibald B. Darragh (R) | 29,540 | 66.1 |
| | George Killeen (D) | 15,064 | 33.7 |
| 12 | Carlos D. Shelden (R) | 33,759 | 72.7 |
| | Edward F. Legendre (D) | 11,516 | 24.8 |

## MINNESOTA

| | | | |
|---|---|---|---|
| 1 | James A. Tawney (R) | 23,112 | 56.0 |
| | Brown (PP & D) | 18,130 | 44.0 |
| 2 | James T. McCleary (R) | 30,558 | 59.8 |
| | Mathews (PP & D) | 18,933 | 37.1 |
| 3 | Joel P. Heatwole (R) | 23,110 | 57.7 |
| | Schaller (PP & D) | 16,498 | 41.2 |
| 4 | Frederick C. Stevens (R) | 21,322 | 57.7 |
| | Stone (PP & D) | 14,886 | 40.3 |
| 5 | Loren Fletcher (R) | 24,724 | 59.4 |
| | Stockwell (D) | 14,269 | 34.3 |
| 6 | R. Page W. Morris (R) | 31,792 | 55.5 |
| | Truelson (PP & D) | 24,219 | 42.3 |
| 7 | Frank M. Eddy (R) | 25,738 | 51.8 |
| | Daly (PP & D) | 21,012 | 42.3 |
| | Aaker (P) | 2,483 | 5.0 |

## MISSISSIPPI

| | | | |
|---|---|---|---|
| 1 | Ezekiel S. Candler Jr. (D) | 6,749 | 95.4 |
| 2 | Thomas Speight (D) | 7,548 | 93.8 |
| | John S. Burton (R) | 500 | 6.2 |
| 3 | Patrick Henry (D) | 3,202 | 100.0 |
| 4 | Andrew F. Fox (D) | 8,211 | 86.0 |
| | W. D. Frazee (R) | 688 | 7.2 |
| | Raleigh Brewer (POP) | 653 | 6.8 |
| 5 | John Sharp Williams (D) | 9,385 | 99.9 |
| 6 | Frank A. McLain (D) | 7,032 | 87.0 |
| | H. C. Turley (R) | 1,048 | 13.0 |
| 7 | Charles E. Hooker (D) | 5,722 | 92.6 |
| | N. M. Hollingsmith (MID ROAD) | 457 | 7.4 |

## MISSOURI

| | | | |
|---|---|---|---|
| 1 | James T. Lloyd (D) | 23,920 | 55.4 |
| | Pickler (R) | 19,189 | 44.5 |
| 2 | William W. Rucker (D) | 25,046 | 57.4 |
| | Irwin (R) | 18,485 | 42.4 |
| 3 | John Dougherty (D) | 22,993 | 54.5 |
| | Leeper (R) | 19,131 | 45.3 |
| 4 | Charles F. Cochran (D) | 22,211 | 53.1 |
| | Kennish (R) | 19,595 | 46.9 |
| 5 | William S. Cowherd (D) | 27,644 | 52.7 |
| | Brown (R) | 24,367 | 46.4 |
| 6 | David A. De Armond (D) | 20,017 | 53.9 |
| | Jurden (R) | 16,366 | 44.0 |
| 7 | James Cooney (D) | 26,834 | 55.4 |
| | Parsons (R) | 21,601 | 44.6 |
| 8 | Dorsey W. Shackleford (D) | 23,718 | 53.4 |
| | Moore (R) | 20,634 | 46.5 |
| 9 | James Beauchamp Clark (D) | 19,202 | 53.9 |
| | Flagg (R) | 16,451 | 46.1 |
| 10 | Richard Bartholdt (R) | 24,252 | 55.2 |
| | Bolte (D) | 17,848 | 40.7 |
| 11 | Charles F. Joy (R) | 28,375 | 51.7 |
| | O'Malley (D) | 25,607 | 46.6 |
| 12 | James J. Butler (D) | 22,104‡ | 53.2 |
| | William M. Horton (R) | 18,551 | 44.7 |
| 13 | Edward Robb (D) | 23,798 | 53.7 |
| | Reppy (R) | 20,524 | 46.3 |
| 14 | Willard D. Vandiver (D) | 26,434 | 53.0 |
| | Mozley (R) | 23,364 | 46.8 |
| 15 | Maecenas E. Benton (D) | 26,804 | 53.5 |
| | Holmes (R) | 22,678 | 45.3 |

## MONTANA

| | Candidates | Votes | % |
|---|---|---|---|
| AL | Caldwell Edwards (D) | 28,130 | 45.8 |
| | Samuel G. Murray (R) | 23,207 | 37.8 |
| | Cornielius F. Kelley (ID) | 9,443 | 15.4 |

## NEBRASKA

| | Candidates | Votes | % |
|---|---|---|---|
| 1 | Elmer J. Burkett (R) | 19,449 | 53.1 |
| | George W. Berge (FUS) | 16,548 | 45.2 |
| 2 | David H. Mercer (R) | 16,277 | 51.8 |
| | Edgar Howard (FUS) | 14,807 | 47.1 |
| 3 | John S. Robinson (FUS) | 22,425 | 49.4 |
| | John R. Hays (R) | 22,250 | 49.0 |
| 4 | William L. Stark (FUS) | 21,032 | 49.9 |
| | John D. Pope (R) | 20,435 | 48.5 |
| 5 | Ashton C. Shallenberger (FUS) | 17,688 | 49.4 |
| | Webster L. Morlan (R) | 17,279 | 48.2 |
| 6 | William Neville (FUS) | 17,699 | 48.7 |
| | M. P. Kinkaid (R) | 17,501 | 48.2 |

## NEVADA

| | Candidates | Votes | % |
|---|---|---|---|
| AL | Francis G. Newlands (D & SILVER) | 5,975 | 58.8 |
| | E. S. Farrington (R) | 4,190 | 41.2 |

## NEW HAMPSHIRE

| | Candidates | Votes | % |
|---|---|---|---|
| 1 | Cyrus A. Sulloway (R) | 26,072 | 58.6 |
| | Timothy J. Howard (D) | 17,401 | 39.1 |
| 2 | Frank D. Currier (R) | 27,440 | 60.0 |
| | Henry F. Hollis (D) | 17,517 | 38.3 |

## NEW JERSEY

| | Candidates | Votes | % |
|---|---|---|---|
| 1 | Henry C. Loudenslager (R) | 31,942 | 59.7 |
| | George Pfeiffer Jr. (D) | 19,169 | 35.8 |
| 2 | John J. Gardner (R) | 31,359 | 62.0 |
| | Thomas J. Prickett (D) | 17,351 | 34.3 |
| 3 | Benjamin F. Howell (R) | 24,286 | 55.0 |
| | James J. Bergen (D) | 18,781 | 42.6 |
| 4 | Joshua S. Salmon (D) | 19,661 | 50.1 |
| | H. Burdett Herr (R) | 18,017 | 45.9 |
| 5 | James F. Stewart (R) | 24,323 | 53.6 |
| | John Johnson (D) | 19,708 | 43.4 |
| 6 | Richard Wayne Parker (R) | 32,830 | 60.7 |
| | George H. Lambert (D) | 19,477 | 36.0 |
| 7 | Allan L. McDermott (D) | 33,713 | 50.8 |
| | Marshall Vanwinkle (R) | 30,472 | 46.0 |
| 8 | Charles N. Fowler (R) | 27,121 | 58.8 |
| | Edward A. S. Man (D) | 17,510 | 38.0 |

### Special Election

| | | Votes | % |
|---|---|---|---|
| 7 | Allan L. McDermott (D) | 33,898 | 52.6 |
| | Marshall Vanwinkle (R) | 30,472 | 47.3 |

## NEW YORK

| | Candidates | Votes | % |
|---|---|---|---|
| 1 | Frederick Storm (R) | 28,046 | 51.2 |
| | Rowland Miles (D) | 25,715 | 46.9 |
| 2 | John J. Fitzgerald (D) | 18,387 | 50.1 |
| | Henry B. Ketcham (R) | 18,066 | 49.2 |
| 3 | Henry Bristow (R) | 24,660 | 51.4 |
| | Edmund H. Driggs (D) | 22,904 | 47.7 |
| 4 | Harry A. Hanbury (R) | 28,596 | 50.8 |
| | Bertram T. Clayton (D) | 26,955 | 47.9 |
| 5 | Frank E. Wilson (D) | 22,041 | 49.1 |
| | Jacob Worth (R) | 21,164 | 47.1 |
| 6 | George H. Lindsay (D) | 18,073 | 54.7 |
| | Bert Reiss (R) | 14,460 | 43.8 |
| 7 | Nicholas Muller (D) | 13,654 | 58.5 |
| | James R. O'Beirne (R) | 9,323 | 39.9 |
| 8 | Thomas J. Creamer (D) | 10,330 | 50.1 |
| | Richard Vancott (R) | 10,157 | 49.3 |

| | Candidates | Votes | % |
|---|---|---|---|
| 9 | Henry M. Goldfogle (D) | 13,570 | 57.6 |
| | Theodore Cox (R) | 7,438 | 31.6 |
| | Rudolph Katz (SOC LAB) | 1,261 | 5.4 |
| | Alexander Jones (SOCIAL D) | 1,190 | 5.1 |
| 10 | Amos J. Cummings (D) | 20,585 | 60.9 |
| | John Glass Jr. (R) | 12,886 | 38.1 |
| 11 | William Sulzer (D) | 14,055 | 55.7 |
| | Charles Schwick (R) | 8,976 | 35.6 |
| 12 | George B. McClellan (D) | 15,177 | 57.9 |
| | Herbert Parsons (R) | 10,736 | 41.0 |
| 13 | Oliver H. P. Belmont (D) | 18,021 | 53.7 |
| | William R. Wilcox (R) | 14,781 | 44.0 |
| 14 | William H. Douglas (R) | 36,904 | 52.1 |
| | John Sprunt Hill (D) | 32,167 | 45.5 |
| 15 | Jacob Ruppert Jr. (D) | 31,592 | 49.6 |
| | Elias Goodman (R) | 29,837 | 46.8 |
| 16 | Cornelius A. Pugsley (D) | 37,665 | 48.8 |
| | Norton P. Otis (R) | 36,954 | 47.9 |
| 17 | Arthur S. Tompkins (R) | 22,663 | 54.9 |
| | John D. Blauvelt (D) | 17,953 | 43.5 |
| 18 | John H. Ketcham (R) | 25,618 | 96.4 |
| 19 | William H. Draper (R) | 24,104 | 56.3 |
| | Edward F. McCormick (D) | 17,936 | 41.9 |
| 20 | George N. Southwick (R) | 22,360 | 52.3 |
| | Martin H. Glynn (D) | 19,904 | 46.5 |
| 21 | John K. Stewart (R) | 30,027 | 53.2 |
| | Joseph B. Handy (D) | 24,965 | 44.3 |
| 22 | Lucius N. Littauer (R) | 32,436 | 64.5 |
| | William L. Pert (D) | 16,085 | 32.0 |
| 23 | Louis W. Emerson (R) | 30,604 | 65.7 |
| | Charles A. Burke (D) | 14,977 | 32.1 |
| 24 | Albert D. Shaw (R) | 27,272* | 60.8 |
| | James S. Boyer (D) | 16,385 | 36.5 |
| 25 | James S. Sherman (R) | 26,782 | 57.5 |
| | Henry Martin (D) | 18,831 | 40.5 |
| 26 | George W. Ray (R) | 34,184 | 58.0 |
| | Myron B. Ferris (D) | 22,542 | 38.2 |
| 27 | Michael E. Driscoll (R) | 31,409 | 62.2 |
| | Luke McHenry (D) | 17,993 | 35.6 |
| 28 | Sereno E. Payne (R) | 33,998 | 59.2 |
| | Robert L. Drummond (D) | 21,789 | 37.9 |
| 29 | Charles W. Gillet (R) | 25,330 | 52.4 |
| | Frank J. Nelson (D) | 21,358 | 44.2 |
| 30 | James W. Wadsworth (R) | 29,368 | 56.1 |
| | Charles Ward (D) | 21,196 | 40.5 |
| 31 | James Breck Perkins (R) | 26,187 | 53.6 |
| | Martin S. Mindnich (D) | 20,064 | 41.1 |
| 32 | William H. Ryan (D) | 18,088 | 49.6 |
| | Rowland B. Mahany (R) | 17,772 | 48.7 |
| 33 | De Alva S. Alexander (R) | 29,120 | 59.5 |
| | Harvey W. Richardson (D) | 19,529 | 39.9 |
| 34 | Edward B. Vreeland (R) | 32,357 | 63.7 |
| | Stillman E. Lewis (D) | 16,547 | 32.6 |

## NORTH CAROLINA

| | | Votes | % |
|---|---|---|---|
| 1 | John H. Small (D) | 18,709 | 57.4 |
| | Abner Alexander (R) | 9,493 | 29.1 |
| | Isaac M. Meekins (IR) | 4,355 | 13.4 |
| 2 | Claude Kitchin (D) | 22,901 | 64.6 |
| | Joseph J. Martin (R) | 12,521 | 35.3 |
| 3 | Charles R. Thomas (D) | 13,541 | 53.8 |
| | John E. Fowler (POP) | 11,632 | 46.2 |
| 4 | Edward W. Pou (D) | 18,929 | 57.1 |
| | Jesse A. Giles (R) | 13,057 | 39.4 |
| 5 | William W. Kitchin (D) | 18,538 | 52.5 |
| | John R. Joyce (R) | 16,687 | 47.3 |
| 6 | John D. Bellamy (D) | 18,902 | 72.5 |
| | Oliver H. Dockery (R) | 7,146 | 27.4 |
| 7 | Theodore F. Kluttz (D) | 15,712 | 52.3 |
| | John Q. Holton (R) | 13,380 | 44.5 |
| 8 | Spencer Blackburn (R) | 19,629 | 52.3 |
| | John C. Buxton (D) | 17,778 | 47.4 |
| 9 | James M. Moody (R) | 19,334 | 52.8 |
| | William T. Crawford (D) | 17,250 | 47.1 |

## NORTH DAKOTA

| | | Votes | % |
|---|---|---|---|
| AL | Thomas F. Marshall (R) | 34,887 | 61.0 |
| | Hildreth (D&I) | 21,175 | 37.0 |

## OHIO

| | Candidates | Votes | % |
|---|---|---|---|
| 1 | William B. Shattuc (R) | 26,434 | 58.2 |
| | John B. Peaslee (D) | 18,430 | 40.6 |
| 2 | Jacob H. Bromwell (R) | 28,029 | 54.3 |
| | Henry Ketter (D) | 22,859 | 44.3 |
| 3 | Robert M. Nevin (R) | 28,882 | 49.5 |
| | Ulysses F. Bickley (D) | 28,728 | 49.2 |
| 4 | Robert B. Gordon (D) | 25,870 | 59.9 |
| | Edwin C. Wright (R) | 17,327 | 40.1 |
| 5 | John S. Snook (D) | 22,884 | 54.4 |
| | Frederick L. Hay (R) | 19,176 | 45.6 |
| 6 | Charles Q. Hildebrant (R) | 24,610 | 54.2 |
| | Adam Bridge (D) | 20,407 | 45.0 |
| 7 | Thomas B. Kyle (R) | 24,818 | 54.7 |
| | Stewart L. Tatum (D) | 20,326 | 44.8 |
| 8 | William R. Warnock (R) | 26,287 | 54.4 |
| | William J. Frey (D) | 21,748 | 45.0 |
| 9 | James H. Southard (R) | 29,544 | 51.6 |
| | Negley D. Cochran (D) | 26,697 | 46.6 |
| 10 | Stephen Morgan (R) | 26,244 | 60.2 |
| | James K. McClung (D) | 17,369 | 39.8 |
| 11 | Charles H. Grosvenor (R) | 25,154 | 57.8 |
| | Thomas H. Craig (D) | 18,174 | 41.7 |
| 12 | Emmett Tompkins (R) | 25,705 | 49.5 |
| | John J. Lentz (D) | 25,687 | 49.5 |
| 13 | James A. Norton (D) | 29,672 | 56.1 |
| | Daniel W. Locke (R) | 23,062 | 43.6 |
| 14 | William Woodburn Skiles (R) | 28,021 | 52.6 |
| | William G. Sharp (D) | 25,247 | 47.4 |
| 15 | Henry C. Van Voorhis (R) | 22,623 | 51.3 |
| | L. W. Ellenwood (D) | 21,458 | 48.6 |
| 16 | Joseph J. Gill (R) | 22,838 | 56.0 |
| | Marion Huffman (D) | 17,926 | 44.0 |
| 17 | John W. Cassingham (D) | 26,275 | 55.0 |
| | George Adams (R) | 21,283 | 44.5 |
| 18 | Robert W. Tayler (R) | 31,479 | 54.6 |
| | John H. Morris (D) | 25,026 | 43.4 |
| 19 | Charles Dick (R) | 34,129 | 62.4 |
| | Charles E. Chadman (D) | 20,351 | 37.2 |
| 20 | Jacob A. Beidler (R) | 22,776 | 45.8 |
| | H. B. Harrington (D) | 22,087 | 44.4 |
| | Fremont O. Phillips (I.R.) | 3,973 | 8.0 |
| 21 | Theodore E. Burton (R) | 28,605 | 55.1 |
| | Sylvester V. McMahon (D) | 21,947 | 42.3 |

## OREGON

| | | Votes | % |
|---|---|---|---|
| 1 | Thomas H. Tongue (R) | 21,212 | 49.5 |
| | Bernard Daly (FUS-D-PO) | 18,193 | 42.4 |
| 2 | Malcolm Moody (R) | 22,088 | 55.1 |
| | William Smith (FUS-D-PO) | 12,708 | 31.7 |
| | J. E. Simmons (MID ROAD) | 3,384 | 8.4 |

## PENNSYLVANIA

| | | Votes | % |
|---|---|---|---|
| 1 | Henry H. Bingham (R) | 29,973 | 71.5 |
| | Michael Francis Doyle (D) | 11,765 | 28.1 |
| 2 | Robert Adams Jr (R) | 19,657 | 79.7 |
| | William E. Hooper (D) | 4,998 | 20.3 |
| 3 | Henry Burk (R) | 11,095 | 52.7 |
| | William McAleer (D, MLP) | 9,839 | 46.7 |
| 4 | James Rankin Young (R) | 55,648 | 75.5 |
| | Peter J. Hughes (D) | 17,330 | 23.5 |
| 5 | Edward de V. Morrell (R) | 45,089 | 75.7 |
| | Samuel R. Carter (D) | 13,898 | 23.3 |
| 6 | Thomas S. Butler (R) | 26,379 | 70.2 |
| | Nathaniel M. Ellis (D) | 10,098 | 26.9 |
| 7 | Irving P. Wanger (R) | 25,422 | 57.1 |
| | Christopher Vanartsdalen (D) | 18,542 | 41.7 |
| 8 | Howard Mutchler (D) | 18,448 | 51.3 |
| | Russel C. Stewart (R) | 16,753 | 46.6 |
| 9 | Henry D. Green (D) | 29,160 | 55.9 |
| | William Kerper Stevens (R) | 22,758 | 43.6 |
| 10 | Marriott Brosius (R) | 23,143 | 71.8 |
| | Louis N. Spencer (D) | 8,502 | 26.4 |

## PENNSYLVANIA

| Candidates | Votes | % |
|---|---|---|
| 11 William Connell (R) | 15,536 | 49.5 |
| Michael F. Conry (D) | 13,598 | 43.3 |
| 12 Henry W. Palmer (R) | 18,931 | 54.3 |
| S. W. Davenport (A-TRUST) | 13,698 | 39.3 |
| 13 George R. Patterson (R) | 15,519 | 52.4 |
| James W. Ryan (D) | 13,895 | 46.9 |
| 14 Marlin E. Olmsted (R) | 23,726 | 89.5 |
| Edwin H. Molly (P) | 1,451 | 5.5 |
| Benjamin L. Forster (D) | 1,335 | 5.0 |
| 15 Charles F. Wright (R) | 18,261 | 56.7 |
| William B. Packard (D) | 12,396 | 38.5 |
| 16 Elias Deemer (R) | 19,844 | 52.6 |
| Otto G. Kaupp (D) | 16,509 | 43.8 |
| 17 Rufus K. Polk (D) | 16,615 | 54.3 |
| Clarence F. Huth (R) | 13,071 | 42.7 |
| 18 Thaddeus M. Mahon (R) | 20,756 | 58.9 |
| James G. Heading (D) | 14,464 | 41.1 |
| 19 Robert J. Lewis (R) | 22,266 | 50.3 |
| Harry N. Gitt (D) | 21,280 | 48.1 |
| 20 Alvin Evans (R) | 30,777 | 62.5 |
| James M. Walters (D) | 17,450 | 35.4 |
| 21 Summers M. Jack (R) | 32,909 | 61.6 |
| Curtis H. Gregg (D) | 19,156 | 35.9 |
| 22 John Dalzell (R) | 36,409 | 69.7 |
| John F. Miller (D) | 14,343 | 27.5 |
| 23 William H. Graham (R) | 19,957 | 74.6 |
| John Huckenstine (D) | 6,142 | 23.0 |
| 24 Ernest F. Acheson (R) | 35,939 | 58.7 |
| Wooda N. Carr (D) | 23,568 | 38.5 |
| 25 Joseph B. Showalter (R) | 24,472 | 55.5 |
| M. L. Lockwood (D) | 19,641 | 44.5 |
| 26 Arthur L. Bates (R) | 18,723 | 53.6 |
| Athelston Gaston (D) | 14,918 | 42.7 |
| 27 Joseph C. Sibley (R) | 15,804 | 50.8 |
| Lewis Emery Jr. (D, LIN) | 13,906 | 44.7 |
| 28 J. K. P. Hall (D) | 19,132 | 49.5 |
| A. A. Clearwater (R) | 18,511 | 47.9 |
| AL Galusha A. Grow (R) | 683,941✔ | |
| Robert H. Foerderer (R) | 675,099✔ | |
| Harry E. Grim (D) | 411,552 | |
| Nicholas M. Edwards (D) | 409,918 | |
| William W. Hague (P) | 24,531 | |
| Lee L. Grumbine (P) | 24,412 | |
| John W. Slayton (SOC) | 4,026 | |
| Edward Kuppinger (SOC) | 3,995 | |
| John R. Root (SOC LAB) | 2,660 | |
| Donald L. Monro (SOC LAB) | 2,657 | |
| Robert Bringham (PP) | 795 | |
| George Main (PP) | 775 | |
| Benjamin A. Bubbett | 278 | |

### Special Election

| | | |
|---|---|---|
| 5 Edward de V. Morrell (R) | 34,789 | 100.0 |

## RHODE ISLAND

| | | |
|---|---|---|
| 1 Melville Bull (R) | 16,591 | 59.5 |
| Gorman (D) | 9,498 | 34.0 |
| 2 Adin B. Capron (R) | 13,975 | 57.8 |
| Garvin (D) | 8,870 | 36.7 |

## SOUTH CAROLINA

| | | |
|---|---|---|
| 1 William Elliott (D) | 3,666 | 72.7 |
| W. W. Beckett (R) | 1,378 | 27.3 |
| 2 William J. Talbert (D) | 6,713 | 97.7 |
| 3 Asbury C. Latimer (D) | 7,834 | 97.5 |
| 4 Joseph T. Johnston (D) | 8,189 | 97.1 |
| 5 David E. Finley (D) | 5,634 | 96.8 |
| 6 Robert B. Scarborough (D) | 7,608 | 94.2 |
| R. A. Stuart (R) | 473 | 5.9 |
| 7 J. William Stokes (D) | 7,285 | 93.2 |
| Alexander D. Dantzler (R) | 534 | 6.8 |

## SOUTH DAKOTA

| | | |
|---|---|---|
| AL Charles H. Burke (R) | 53,583✔ | |
| Eben W. Martin (R) | 53,549✔ | |

| Candidates | Votes | % |
|---|---|---|
| Andrew E. Lee (FUS) | 40,560 | |
| Joseph B. Moore (FUS) | 40,151 | |
| O. A. Harpel (P) | 1,323 | |
| M. Rogers (P) | 1,188 | |
| Edm. F. English (POP) | 305 | |
| John M. Pease (POP) | 304 | |

## TENNESSEE

| | | |
|---|---|---|
| 1 Walter P. Brownlow (R) | 22,374 | 62.8 |
| Reaves (D) | 13,107 | 36.8 |
| 2 Henry R. Gibson (R) | 22,062 | 68.7 |
| Park (D) | 9,913 | 30.9 |
| 3 John A. Moon (D) | 18,363 | 52.1 |
| Sharp (R) | 16,591 | 47.1 |
| 4 Charles E. Snodgrass (D) | 15,659 | 59.8 |
| Gore (R) | 10,515 | 40.1 |
| 5 James D. Richardson (D) | 14,653 | 68.0 |
| McClain (R) | 6,895 | 32.0 |
| 6 John W. Gaines (D) | 17,192 | 71.9 |
| Brock (R) | 6,256 | 26.2 |
| 7 Lemuel P. Padgett (D) | 12,636 | 54.4 |
| Fuzzell (I) | 10,610 | 45.6 |
| 8 Thetus W. Sims (D) | 14,509 | 53.1 |
| Hawkins (R) | 12,258 | 44.8 |
| 9 Rice A. Pierce (D) | 16,680 | 71.8 |
| Austin (R) | 6,050 | 26.0 |
| 10 Malcolm R. Patterson (D) | 10,218 | 62.1 |
| Taylor (R) | 6,247 | 37.9 |

## TEXAS

| | | |
|---|---|---|
| 1 Thomas H. Ball (D) | 11,887 | 65.7 |
| S. E. Tracy (R) | 5,391 | 29.8 |
| 2 Samuel B. Cooper (D) | 31,774 | 98.5 |
| 3 Reese C. De Graffenreid (D) | 19,091 | 61.0 |
| C. G. White (R) | 12,230 | 39.1 |
| 4 John L. Sheppard (D) | 17,647 | 57.6 |
| J. C. Gibbons (R) | 9,818 | 32.1 |
| J. L. Darwin (POP) | 3,154 | 10.3 |
| 5 Choice B. Randell (D) | 28,074 | 90.4 |
| J. W. Thomas (R) | 1,790 | 5.8 |
| 6 Robert E. Burke (D) | 33,220 | 77.7 |
| S. H. Lumpkin (POP) | 7,432 | 17.4 |
| 7 Robert L. Henry (D) | 27,243 | 92.1 |
| 8 Samuel W. T. Lanham (D) | 24,093 | 68.2 |
| J. S. Daley (POP) | 6,465 | 18.3 |
| N. A. Dodge (R) | 4,760 | 13.5 |
| 9 Albert S. Burleson (D) | 25,494 | 91.3 |
| Nat Q. Henderson (R) | 2,419 | 8.7 |
| 10 George F. Burgess (D) | 18,203 | 59.5 |
| Walter C. Jones (R) | 12,255 | 40.1 |
| 11 Rudolph Kleberg (D) | 21,329 | 59.2 |
| B. L. Crouch (R) | 14,706 | 40.8 |
| 12 James L. Slayden (D) | 18,421 | 60.8 |
| C. C. Drake (R) | 11,530 | 38.1 |
| 13 John H. Stephens (D) | 30,726 | 85.1 |
| C. W. Johnson (R) | 5,354 | 14.8 |

## UTAH

| | | |
|---|---|---|
| AL George Sutherland (R) | 46,180 | 50.1 |
| W. H. King (D) | 45,939 | 49.9 |

## VERMONT

| | | |
|---|---|---|
| 1 David J. Foster (R) | 22,845 | 68.5 |
| Ozro Meacham (D) | 9,441 | 28.3 |
| 2 Kittredge Haskins (R) | 23,273 | 75.5 |
| George T. Swasey (D) | 7,291 | 23.7 |

## VIRGINIA

| | | |
|---|---|---|
| 1 William A. Jones (D) | 16,076 | 64.1 |
| James Monroe Stubbs (R) | 8,737 | 34.9 |

| Candidates | Votes | % |
|---|---|---|
| 2 Harry L. Maynard (D) | 20,113 | 62.2 |
| R. A. Wise (R) | 10,203 | 31.6 |
| 3 John Lamb (D) | 15,274 | 65.6 |
| Edgar Allan (R) | 7,793 | 33.5 |
| 4 Francis R. Lassiter (D) | 12,796 | 61.4 |
| C. E. Wilson (R) | 8,058 | 38.6 |
| 5 Claude A. Swanson (D) | 14,293 | 58.1 |
| John R. Whitehead (R) | 10,292 | 41.9 |
| 6 Peter J. Otey (D) | 15,948 | 77.5 |
| J. B. Stovall (R) | 2,467 | 12.0 |
| A. E. Fairweather (I) | 2,152 | 10.5 |
| 7 James Hay (D) | 17,276 | 63.4 |
| C. M. Gibbens (R) | 9,995 | 36.7 |
| 8 John F. Rixey (D) | 17,071 | 63.2 |
| William J. Rogers (R) | 9,858 | 36.5 |
| 9 William F. Rhea (D) | 20,164 | 52.3 |
| James A. Walker (R) | 18,412 | 47.7 |
| 10 Henry D. Flood (D) | 16,064 | 54.3 |
| Robert T. Hubard (R) | 12,913 | 43.7 |

### Special Election

| | | |
|---|---|---|
| 4 Francis R. Lassiter (D) | 3,217 | 98.7 |

## WASHINGTON

| | | |
|---|---|---|
| AL Wesley L. Jones (R) | 55,393✔ | |
| Francis W. Cushman (R) | 55,268✔ | |
| J. T. Ronald (D) | 45,448 | |
| F. C. Robertson (D) | 44,882 | |
| Guy Posson (P) | 2,239 | |
| J. A. Adams (P) | 2,059 | |
| William Hogan (SOCIAL D) | 1,954 | |
| Herman F. Titus (SOCIAL D) | 1,916 | |
| Walter Walker (SOC LAB) | 922 | |
| Christian F. Larsen (SOC LAB) | 878 | |

## WEST VIRGINIA

| | | |
|---|---|---|
| 1 Blackburn B. Dovener (R) | 27,767 | 54.2 |
| William E. Haymond (D) | 22,778 | 44.5 |
| 2 Alston G. Dayton (R) | 27,735 | 51.9 |
| Thomas B. Davis (D) | 25,347 | 47.4 |
| 3 Joseph Holt Gaines (R) | 34,243 | 55.1 |
| David E. Johnson (D) | 27,667 | 44.5 |
| 4 James H. Hughes (R) | 28,476 | 53.2 |
| Creed Collins (D) | 24,748 | 46.2 |

## WISCONSIN

| | | |
|---|---|---|
| 1 Henry A. Cooper (R) | 28,256 | 64.1 |
| Gilbert T. Hodges (D) | 14,556 | 33.0 |
| 2 Herman B. Dahle (R) | 22,175 | 52.8 |
| John A. Aylward (D) | 18,819 | 44.8 |
| 3 Joseph W. Babcock (R) | 26,593 | 63.5 |
| Edward L. Luckow (D) | 14,017 | 33.5 |
| 4 Theobold Otjen (R) | 24,637 | 49.5 |
| George W. Peck (D) | 21,691 | 43.5 |
| Robert Meister (SOCIAL D) | 2,991 | 6.0 |
| 5 Samuel S. Barney (R) | 23,089 | 52.4 |
| Charles H. Weisse (D) | 18,066 | 41.0 |
| Henry C. Berger (SOC LAB) | 2,284 | 5.2 |
| 6 James H. Davidson (R) | 26,326 | 55.8 |
| James W. Watson (D) | 19,758 | 41.9 |
| 7 John J. Esch (R) | 22,715 | 65.2 |
| John P. Rice (D) | 11,254 | 32.3 |
| 8 Edward S. Minor (R) | 25,263 | 60.2 |
| Nathan F. Morgan (D) | 16,740 | 39.9 |
| 9 Webster E. Brown (R) | 33,329 | 64.7 |
| Ernest Schweppe (D) | 16,988 | 33.0 |
| 10 John J. Jenkins (R) | 29,144 | 68.7 |
| Frank A. Partlow (D) | 11,930 | 28.1 |

## WYOMING

| | | |
|---|---|---|
| AL Frank W. Mondell (R) | 14,539 | 59.2 |
| John Charles Thompson (D) | 10,017 | 40.8 |

# 1901 House Elections

## PENNSYLVANIA

### Special Election

| Candidates | Votes | % |
|---|---|---|
| 10  Henry B. Cassel (R) | 12,465 | 73.9 |
| Daniel R. McCormick (D) | 4,410 | 26.1 |

## TEXAS

### Special Election

| Candidates | Votes | % |
|---|---|---|
| 6  Dudley G. Wooten (D) | 11,174 | 84.1 |
| Philip Lindsey | 2,063 | 15.5 |

---

# Explanation of Symbols in House Returns

In the returns for House elections *symbols* are used to denote special circumstances. In cases where no symbol is used, the candidate who received the most votes won the election to the House. The following is a key to the symbols used:

✔ Elected to the House. The symbol is used to identify winning candidates in three types of situations: (1) When candidates ran for two or more at-large seats in states which chose all of their at-large representatives in a single election, or ran in a multi-member district; (2) when the vote total and percentage of one or more of the candidates are unavailable and (3) when a candidate who did not receive the highest vote total was seated by the House. *(Explanation of multi-member districts, see p. 916.)*

‡ The symbol is used when an election dispute resulted in the unseating of a representative *after* he was sworn in. *(For discussion of specific cases, consult the* Biographical Directory of the United States Congress, 1774-1989, *U.S. Government Printing Office, Washington, D.C., 1989; hereafter referred to as the* Biographical Directory.)

\* The symbol is used for three types of situations: (1) When a representative-elect died or declined his seat before the constitutionally set date for the beginning of his term—March 4 until 1935, and Jan. 3 thereafter; (2) when the House refused to seat any candidate claiming election to a seat and (3) when state law required a candidate to obtain a popular vote majority for election to the House, but the candidate receiving the most votes failed to receive a majority. *(For discussion of specific cases, consult the* Biographical Directory; *explanation of majority vote requirement, see p. 945.)*

# Information for 1824-1973 returns was obtained from a source other than the Inter-University Consortium for Political and Social Research. *(For a listing of other sources, see p. 1327.)*

**Footnotes.** Numbered footnotes are used to explain unusual situations, such as a series of elections in the same year in the same House district, anomalies resulting from reapportionment and special procedures for conducting House elections in certain states.

# 1902 House Elections

## ALABAMA

| | Candidates | Votes | % |
|---|---|---|---|
| 1 | George W. Taylor (D) | 5,364 | 89.8 |
| | E. B. Hubbard (R) | 545 | 9.1 |
| 2 | Ariosto A. Wiley (D) | 7,696 | 89.9 |
| | Julius Sternfeld (R) | 861 | 10.1 |
| 3 | Henry D. Clayton (D) | 7,595 | 84.1 |
| | M. W. Carden (R) | 905 | 10.0 |
| | J. P. Pelham (R) | 535 | 5.9 |
| 4 | Sydney J. Bowie (D) | 6,880 | 69.3 |
| | J. A. Edwards (R) | 3,048 | 30.7 |
| 5 | Charles W. Thompson (D) | 9,043 | 78.4 |
| | R. S. Nolen (R) | 2,495 | 21.6 |
| 6 | John H. Bankhead (D) | 7,481 | 72.8 |
| | William B. Ford (R) | 2,798 | 27.2 |
| 7 | John L. Burnett (D) | 9,298 | 52.9 |
| | O. D. Street (R) | 8,044 | 45.8 |
| 8 | William Richardson (D) | 7,935 | 80.8 |
| | James Jackson (R) | 1,889 | 19.2 |
| 9 | Oscar W. Underwood (D) | 6,782 | 77.3 |
| | J. Clyde Miller (R) | 1,793 | 20.4 |

## ARKANSAS

| | | | |
|---|---|---|---|
| 1 | Robert B. Macon (D) | 4,796 | 99.8 |
| 2 | Stephen Brundidge Jr. (D) | 4,549 | 84.1 |
| | R. S. Coffman (R) | 858 | 15.9 |
| 3 | Hugh A. Dinsmore (D) | 4,808 | 72.4 |
| | W. L. McPherson (R) | 1,833 | 27.6 |
| 4 | John S. Little (D) | 4,213 | 78.7 |
| | F. A. Youmans (R) | 1,142 | 21.3 |
| 5 | Charles C. Reid (D) | 4,530 | 79.6 |
| | Henry M. Sugg (R) | 1,161 | 20.4 |
| 6 | Joseph T. Robinson (D) | 5,195 | 89.3 |
| | W. H. Carpenter (R) | 622 | 10.7 |
| 7 | Robert Minor Wallace (D) | 4,730 | 83.0 |
| | R. L. Floyd (R) | 971 | 17.0 |

## CALIFORNIA

| | | | |
|---|---|---|---|
| 1 | James N. Gillett (R) | 21,268 | 50.5 |
| | Thomas S. Ford (D) | 19,696 | 46.7 |
| 2 | Theodore A. Bell (D) | 21,536 | 49.2 |
| | Frank L. Coombs (R) | 21,181 | 48.3 |
| 3 | Victor H. Metcalf (R) | 20,532 | 66.2 |
| | Calvin B. White (D) | 8,574 | 27.7 |
| | M. W. Wilkins (SOC) | 1,556 | 5.0 |
| 4 | Edward J. Livernash (D & UN LAB) | 16,146 | 49.2 |
| | Julius Kahn (R) | 16,005 | 48.7 |
| 5 | William J. Wynn (D&UN LAB) | 22,712 | 56.5 |
| | E. F. Loud (R) | 16,577 | 41.2 |
| 6 | James C. Needham (R) | 17,268 | 53.5 |
| | Gaston M. Ashe (D) | 13,732 | 42.6 |
| 7 | James McLachlan (R) | 19,407 | 64.8 |
| | Carl A. Johnson (D) | 8,075 | 27.0 |
| 8 | Milton J. Daniels (R) | 20,135 | 51.9 |
| | William E. Smythe (D) | 15,819 | 40.8 |
| | N. A. Richardson (SOC) | 2,091 | 5.4 |

## COLORADO

| | | | |
|---|---|---|---|
| 1 | John F. Shafroth (D) | 41,440‡ | 49.0 |
| | Robert W. Bonynge (R) | 38,648 | 45.7 |
| 2 | Herschel M. Hogg (R) | 47,546 | 47.6 |
| | John C. Bell (FUS) | 45,234 | 45.3 |
| AL | Franklin E. Brooks (R) | 85,217 | 46.1 |
| | Alva Adams (D) | 84,367 | 45.6 |

## CONNECTICUT

| | | | |
|---|---|---|---|
| 1 | E. Stevens Henry (R) | 20,289 | 52.4 |
| | O'Neil (D) | 17,211 | 44.4 |

| | Candidates | Votes | % |
|---|---|---|---|
| 2 | Nehemiah D. Sperry (R) | 29,658 | 54.7 |
| | Morse (D) | 22,283 | 41.1 |
| 3 | Frank B. Brandegee (R) | 12,547 | 58.7 |
| | Potter (D) | 8,364 | 39.1 |
| 4 | Ebenezer J. Hill (R) | 24,333 | 54.0 |
| | Bishop (D) | 19,888 | 44.2 |
| AL | George L. Lilley (R) | 83,666 | 52.6 |
| | Cummings (D) | 70,590 | 44.3 |

**Special Election**

| | | | |
|---|---|---|---|
| 3 | Frank B. Brandegee (R) | 5,208 | 94.2 |

## DELAWARE

| | | | |
|---|---|---|---|
| AL | Henry A. Houston (D) | 16,396 | 42.9 |
| | William Michael Byrne (UN R) | 12,998 | 34.0 |
| | Lewis Heisler Ball (R) | 8,028 | 21.0 |

## FLORIDA

| | | | |
|---|---|---|---|
| 1 | Stephen M. Sparkman (D) | 5,597 | 100.0 |
| 2 | Robert W. Davis (D) | 6,488 | 100.0 |
| 3 | William B. Lamar (D) | 4,249 | 100.0 |

## GEORGIA

| | | | |
|---|---|---|---|
| 1 | Rufus E. Lester (D) | 4,349 | 100.0 |
| 2 | James M. Griggs (D) | 3,797 | 100.0 |
| 3 | Elijah B. Lewis (D) | 2,957 | 100.0 |
| 4 | William C. Adamson (D) | 2,883 | 100.0 |
| 5 | Leonidas F. Livingston (D) | 2,485 | 100.0 |
| 6 | Charles L. Bartlett (D) | 4,522 | 100.0 |
| 7 | John W. Maddox (D) | 5,305 | 93.2 |
| | S. J. McKnight (POP) | 389 | 6.8 |
| 8 | William M. Howard (D) | 3,139 | 100.0 |
| 9 | F. Carter Tate (D) | 4,749 | 99.6 |
| 10 | Thomas W. Hardwick (D) | 2,675 | 100.0 |
| 11 | William G. Brantley (D) | 3,606 | 100.0 |

## IDAHO

| | | | |
|---|---|---|---|
| AL | Burton L. French (R) | 32,384 | 54.3 |
| | Joseph Henry Hutchinson (D) | 24,878 | 41.7 |

## ILLINOIS

| | | | |
|---|---|---|---|
| 1 | Martin Emerich (D) | 16,591 | 51.3 |
| | Martin B. (R) | 15,339 | 47.4 |
| 2 | James R. Mann (R) | 18,697 | 60.1 |
| | Frank Brust (D) | 9,532 | 30.6 |
| | Bernard Berlyn (SOC) | 2,332 | 7.5 |
| 3 | William Warfield Wilson (R) | 13,977 | 53.5 |
| | Dan Morgan Smith Jr. (D) | 10,517 | 40.3 |
| 4 | George P. Foster (D) | 14,698 | 92.6 |
| | F. Finsterbach (SOC) | 850 | 5.4 |
| 5 | James McAndrews (D) | 12,346 | 88.7 |
| | Jacob Winnen (SOC) | 1,263 | 9.1 |
| 6 | William Lorimer (R) | 16,540 | 49.7 |
| | Allan C. Durborow (D) | 15,555 | 46.7 |
| 7 | Phillip Knopf (R) | 18,167 | 51.1 |
| | John M. Hess (D) | 13,443 | 37.8 |
| | James H. Bard (SOC) | 3,471 | 9.8 |
| 8 | William F. Mahoney (D) | 19,688 | 90.6 |
| | George D. Evans (SOC) | 1,546 | 7.1 |
| 9 | Henry Sherman Boutell (R) | 15,857 | 50.8 |
| | Lockwood Honore (D) | 13,774 | 44.1 |
| 10 | George Edmund Foss (R) | 15,318 | 57.5 |
| | John J. Philbin (D) | 9,733 | 36.6 |

| | Candidates | Votes | % |
|---|---|---|---|
| 11 | Howard M. Snapp (R) | 20,549 | 64.1 |
| | James O. Monroe (D) | 9,968 | 31.1 |
| 12 | Charles E. Fuller (R) | 19,812 | 62.5 |
| | Julian R. Steward (D) | 9,356 | 29.5 |
| | Frank S. Regan (P) | 2,558 | 8.1 |
| 13 | Robert R. Hitt (R) | 19,229 | 65.5 |
| | Louis Dickes (D) | 9,401 | 32.0 |
| 14 | Benjamin F. Marsh (R) | 19,404 | 55.9 |
| | John W. Lusk (D) | 13,195 | 38.0 |
| 15 | George W. Prince (R) | 21,899 | 55.5 |
| | Jonas W. Olson (D) | 16,045 | 40.7 |
| 16 | Joseph V. Graff (R) | 19,360 | 54.5 |
| | John M. Niehaus (D) | 15,623 | 43.9 |
| 17 | John A. Sterling (R) | 18,331 | 54.4 |
| | Z. F. Yost (D) | 14,040 | 41.6 |
| 18 | Joseph G. Cannon (R) | 22,941 | 58.3 |
| | Henry C. Bell (D) | 15,254 | 38.8 |
| 19 | Vespasian Warner (R) | 24,155 | 53.3 |
| | W. B. Hinds (D) | 19,895 | 43.9 |
| 20 | Henry T. Rainey (R) | 20,165 | 56.5 |
| | James H. Danskin (R) | 14,889 | 41.7 |
| 21 | Ben F. Caldwell (D) | 20,774 | 54.0 |
| | Leroy Anderson (R) | 16,998 | 44.2 |
| 22 | William A. Rodenberg (R) | 21,101 | 52.6 |
| | Fred J. Kern (D) | 18,747 | 46.7 |
| 23 | Joseph B. Crowley (D) | 20,735 | 52.4 |
| | Hiram Gilmore Vansandt (R) | 17,557 | 44.4 |
| 24 | James R. Williams (D) | 17,971 | 49.5 |
| | Pleasant T. Chapman (R) | 17,719 | 48.8 |
| 25 | George W. Smith (R) | 18,743 | 51.9 |
| | James Lingle (D) | 16,444 | 45.5 |

## INDIANA

| | | | |
|---|---|---|---|
| 1 | James A. Hemenway (R) | 21,524 | 52.0 |
| | John W. Spencer (D) | 17,833 | 43.1 |
| 2 | Robert W. Miers (D) | 21,162 | 49.5 |
| | John C. Chaney (R) | 20,423 | 47.7 |
| 3 | William T. Zenor (D) | 20,740 | 54.6 |
| | Edmund A. Maginness (R) | 16,784 | 44.2 |
| 4 | Francis M. Griffith (D) | 21,751 | 52.0 |
| | Joshua M. Spencer (R) | 18,894 | 45.2 |
| 5 | Elias S. Holliday (R) | 23,795 | 50.3 |
| | John A. Wiltermood (D) | 21,562 | 45.6 |
| 6 | James E. Watson (R) | 23,641 | 52.9 |
| | James T. Arbuckle (D) | 19,535 | 43.7 |
| 7 | Jesse Overstreet (R) | 25,191 | 52.0 |
| | Jacob P. Dunn (D) | 20,933 | 43.2 |
| 8 | George W. Cromer (R) | 25,842 | 52.0 |
| | James Edward Truesdale (D) | 21,474 | 43.2 |
| 9 | Charles B. Landis (R) | 25,824 | 51.0 |
| | Lex J. Kirkpatrick (D) | 23,317 | 46.0 |
| 10 | Edgar D. Crumpacker (R) | 26,016 | 56.4 |
| | William Guthrie (D) | 19,428 | 42.1 |
| 11 | Frederick K. Landis (R) | 24,390 | 52.6 |
| | John C. Nelson (D) | 19,596 | 42.3 |
| | Bennet L. Shugart (P) | 2,344 | 5.1 |
| 12 | James M. Robinson (D) | 19,320 | 48.1 |
| | Clarence C. Gilhams (R) | 19,035 | 47.4 |
| 13 | Abraham L. Brick (R) | 24,206 | 50.3 |
| | Frank E. Hering (D) | 22,289 | 46.3 |

## IOWA

| | | | |
|---|---|---|---|
| 1 | Thomas Hedge (R) | 15,266 | 51.7 |
| | John E. Craig (D) | 13,343 | 45.2 |
| 2 | Martin J. Wade (D) | 19,825 | 49.6 |
| | William Hoffman (R) | 18,667 | 46.7 |
| 3 | Benjamin P. Birdsall (R) | 22,300 | 54.5 |
| | Horace Boise (D) | 16,761 | 40.9 |
| 4 | Gilbert N. Haugen (R) | 19,303 | 56.1 |
| | A. L. Sortor Jr. (D) | 14,280 | 41.5 |

## IOWA

| | Candidates | Votes | % |
|---|---|---|---|
| 5 | Robert G. Cousins (R) | 19,516 | 56.5 |
| | Anthony P. Daly (D) | 13,733 | 39.8 |
| 6 | John F. Lacey (R) | 18,828 | 51.2 |
| | John P. Reese (D) | 17,015 | 46.2 |
| 7 | John A. T. Hull (R) | 19,037 | 61.6 |
| | Parley Sheldon (D) | 9,914 | 32.1 |
| 8 | William P. Hepburn (R) | 21,657 | 59.4 |
| | F. M. Stuart (D) | 14,796 | 40.6 |
| 9 | Walter I. Smith (R) | 20,997 | 59.6 |
| | George W. Cullison (D) | 13,639 | 38.7 |
| 10 | James P. Connor (R) | 25,596 | 64.1 |
| | Kasper Faltison (D) | 12,822 | 32.1 |
| 11 | Lot Thomas (R) | 21,854 | 62.4 |
| | James M. Parsons (D) | 12,721 | 36.3 |

## KANSAS

| | Candidates | Votes | % |
|---|---|---|---|
| 1 | Charles Curtis (R) | 23,954 | 62.8 |
| | John E. Wagner (D) | 13,774 | 36.1 |
| 2 | Justin D. Bowersock (R) | 23,608 | 54.2 |
| | Noah Bowman (D) | 19,250 | 44.2 |
| 3 | Philip P. Campbell (R) | 22,753 | 53.7 |
| | Alfred M. Jackson (D) | 18,690 | 44.1 |
| 4 | James M. Miller (R) | 20,799 | 58.7 |
| | Thomas H. Grisham (D) | 14,361 | 40.5 |
| 5 | William A. Calderhead (R) | 18,921 | 56.5 |
| | Andrew Sherer (D) | 13,930 | 41.6 |
| 6 | William A. Reeder (R) | 18,307 | 53.2 |
| | C. M. Cole (D) | 15,832 | 46.0 |
| 7 | Chester I. Long (R) | 30,123* | 56.8 |
| | Vernon J. Rose (D) | 22,300 | 42.1 |
| AL | Charles F. Scott (R) | 158,307 | 56.1 |
| | J. D. Botkin (D) | 115,342 | 40.9 |

## KENTUCKY

| | Candidates | Votes | % |
|---|---|---|---|
| 1 | Ollie M. James (D) | 12,731 | 66.4 |
| | C. H. Linn (R) | 5,469 | 28.5 |
| 2 | Augustus O. Stanley (D) | 15,522 | 52.3 |
| | R. W. Slack (R) | 13,675 | 46.1 |
| 3 | John S. Rhea (D) | 16,820 | 50.7 |
| | J. McKenzie Moss (R) | 16,056 | 48.4 |
| 4 | David H. Smith (D) | 14,054 | 93.1 |
| | J. A. Barret (P) | 881 | 5.8 |
| 5 | J. Swagar Sherley (D) | 17,896 | 50.0 |
| | Harvey S. Irwin (R) | 15,892 | 44.4 |
| 6 | Daniel Linn Gooch (D) | 12,978 | 50.8 |
| | Applegate (R) | 10,370 | 40.6 |
| | Breill (SOC) | 1,683 | 6.6 |
| 7 | South Trimble (D) | 12,093 | 59.9 |
| | W. L. Cannon (R) | 7,639 | 37.8 |
| 8 | George G. Gilbert (D) | 13,531 | 53.2 |
| | Lawson Sumrall (R) | 11,458 | 45.1 |
| 9 | James N. Kehoe (D) | 20,823 | 52.4 |
| | W. H. Castner (R) | 18,493 | 46.6 |
| 10 | Frank A. Hopkins (D) | 15,947 | 55.7 |
| | John G. White (R) | 12,458 | 43.5 |
| 11 | Vincent Boreing (R) | 13,443 | 69.2 |
| | J. P. Harrison (D) | 5,076 | 26.1 |

## LOUISIANA

| | Candidates | Votes | % |
|---|---|---|---|
| 1 | Adolph Meyer (D) | 3,910 | 81.9 |
| | Oliver S. Livaudais (R) | 866 | 18.1 |
| 2 | Robert C. Davey (D) | 5,014 | 85.2 |
| | Robert E. Lee (R) | 868 | 14.8 |
| 3 | Robert F. Broussard (D) | 2,725 | 79.4 |
| | William E. Howell (R) | 707 | 20.6 |
| 4 | Phanor Breazeale (D) | 2,567 | 94.3 |
| | S. M. Thomas (R) | 156 | 5.7 |
| 5 | Joseph E. Ransdell (D) | 2,645 | 91.9 |
| | Henry B. Taliaferro (R) | 232 | 8.1 |
| 6 | Samuel M. Robertson (D) | 2,124 | 75.9 |
| | Clarence S. Hebert (R) | 673 | 24.1 |
| 7 | Arsene P. Pujo (D) | 3,233 | 85.6 |
| | Gilbert L. Dupre (R) | 545 | 14.4 |

## MAINE

| | Candidates | Votes | % |
|---|---|---|---|
| 1 | Amos L. Allen (R) | 16,232 | 58.2 |
| | Seth C. Gordon (D) | 11,097 | 39.8 |
| 2 | Charles E. Littlefield (R) | 17,297 | 58.1 |
| | Horatio G. Foss (D) | 11,739 | 39.5 |
| 3 | Edwin C. Burleigh (R) | 15,613 | 64.3 |
| | E. N. Benson (D) | 8,032 | 33.1 |
| 4 | Llewellyn Powers (R) | 16,349 | 64.6 |
| | Thomas White (D) | 7,763 | 30.7 |

## MARYLAND

| | | Votes | % |
|---|---|---|---|
| 1 | William H. Jackson (R) | 17,968 | 50.6 |
| | James E. Ellegood (D) | 16,179 | 45.5 |
| 2 | J. Fred. C. Talbott (D) | 16,971 | 50.8 |
| | William T. Page (R) | 15,422 | 46.2 |
| 3 | Frank C. Wachter (R) | 15,214 | 48.8 |
| | Lee S. Meyer (D) | 15,031 | 48.2 |
| 4 | James W. Denny (D) | 16,105 | 50.0 |
| | Charles R. Schirm (R) | 15,519 | 48.1 |
| 5 | Sydney E. Mudd (R) | 17,621 | 56.9 |
| | B. H. Camalier (D) | 12,781 | 41.3 |
| 6 | George A. Pearre (R) | 18,310 | 54.1 |
| | C. F. Kenneweg (D) | 14,479 | 42.8 |

## MASSACHUSETTS

| | | Votes | % |
|---|---|---|---|
| 1 | George P. Lawrence (R) | 14,093 | 54.0 |
| | Henry M. Fern (D) | 9,949 | 38.1 |
| 2 | Frederick H. Gillett (R) | 14,067 | 58.1 |
| | Arthur F. Nutting (D) | 6,998 | 28.9 |
| | George H. Wrenn (SOC) | 2,779 | 11.5 |
| 3 | John R. Thayer (D) | 14,382 | 49.1 |
| | Rufus B. Dodge (R) | 13,602 | 46.4 |
| 4 | Charles Q. Tirrell (R) | 15,660 | 53.4 |
| | Marcus A. Coolidge (D) | 10,564 | 36.0 |
| | John F. Mullen (SOC) | 2,739 | 9.3 |
| 5 | Butler Ames (R) | 13,648 | 48.4 |
| | John T. Sparks (D) | 12,765 | 45.3 |
| 6 | Augustus P. Gardner (R) | 16,164 | 51.4 |
| | Samuel Roads Jr. (D) | 12,246 | 39.0 |
| | George E. Littlefield (SOC) | 2,679 | 8.5 |
| 7 | Ernest W. Roberts (R) | 15,728 | 54.3 |
| | Arthur Lyman (D) | 9,034 | 31.2 |
| | William B. Turner (SOC) | 2,811 | 9.7 |
| 8 | Samuel W. McCall (R) | 15,077 | 57.6 |
| | Grenville S. MacFarland (D) | 8,872 | 33.9 |
| | Charles W. White (SOC) | 1,634 | 6.2 |
| 9 | John A. Keliher (D CIT) | 10,352 | 38.1 |
| | Joseph A. Conry (DN) | 10,099 | 37.2 |
| | Charles T. Witt (R) | 5,108 | 18.8 |
| | James J. McVey (SOC) | 1,581 | 5.8 |
| 10 | William S. McNary (D) | 17,569 | 54.1 |
| | William W. Towle (R) | 11,374 | 35.1 |
| | John Weaver Sherman (SOC) | 3,506 | 10.8 |
| 11 | John A. Sullivan (D) | 16,333 | 49.4 |
| | Eugene N. Foss (R) | 14,467 | 43.8 |
| | George G. Cutting (SOC) | 2,230 | 6.8 |
| 12 | Samuel L. Powers (R) | 14,807 | 52.6 |
| | Frederic J. Stimson (D) | 10,303 | 36.6 |
| | J. Frank Hayward (SOC) | 2,683 | 9.5 |
| 13 | William S. Greene (R) | 13,565 | 67.9 |
| | Charles T. Luce (D) | 5,241 | 26.2 |
| | Elijah Humphries (P) | 1,178 | 5.9 |
| 14 | William C. Lovering (R) | 14,410 | 57.3 |
| | Charles A. Gilday (D) | 5,447 | 21.7 |
| | Isaac W. Skinner (SOC) | 4,300 | 17.1 |

### Special Election

| | | Votes | % |
|---|---|---|---|
| 6 | Augustus P. Gardner (R) | 15,561 | 52.1 |
| | Samuel Roads Jr. (D) | 11,348 | 38.0 |
| | George E. Littlefield (SOC) | 2,606 | 8.7 |

## MICHIGAN

| | Candidates | Votes | % |
|---|---|---|---|
| 1 | Alfred Lucking (D) | 20,009 | 53.6 |
| | John B. Corliss (R) | 16,743 | 44.9 |
| 2 | Charles E. Townsend (R) | 22,198 | 53.3 |
| | Frederick B. Wood (D) | 18,390 | 44.2 |
| 3 | Washington Gardner (R) | 19,741 | 56.7 |
| | Warner J. Sampson (D) | 13,900 | 40.0 |
| 4 | Edward L. Hamilton (R) | 20,617 | 57.1 |
| | Thomas O'Hara (D) | 15,368 | 42.5 |
| 5 | William Alden Smith (R) | 19,040 | 60.2 |
| | Myron H. Walker (D) | 11,525 | 36.5 |
| 6 | Samuel W. Smith (R) | 23,869 | 56.3 |
| | William H. S. Wood (D) | 18,300 | 43.2 |
| 7 | Henry McMorran (R) | 17,830 | 57.3 |
| | Martin Crocker (D) | 12,481 | 40.1 |
| 8 | Joseph W. Fordney (R) | 17,392 | 56.7 |
| | Henry M. Youmans (D) | 11,380 | 37.1 |
| 9 | Roswell P. Bishop (R) | 14,502 | 66.0 |
| | Daniel W. Goodenough (D) | 6,166 | 28.1 |
| 10 | George A. Loud (R) | 17,069 | 57.9 |
| | Michael O'Brien (D) | 11,846 | 40.2 |
| 11 | Archibald B. Darragh (R) | 18,174 | 69.7 |
| | David J. Erwin (D) | 7,891 | 30.3 |
| 12 | H. Olin Young (R) | 21,224 | 71.5 |
| | John Power (D) | 8,467 | 28.5 |

## MINNESOTA

| | | Votes | % |
|---|---|---|---|
| 1 | James A. Tawney (R) | 19,561 | 60.9 |
| | McGovern (D) | 12,545 | 39.1 |
| 2 | James T. McCleary (R) | 16,100 | 63.4 |
| | Andrews (D) | 9,316 | 36.7 |
| 3 | Charles R. Davis (R) | 16,700 | 58.9 |
| | Kolars (D) | 10,996 | 38.8 |
| 4 | Frederick C. Stevens (R) | 17,404 | 60.4 |
| | Gieske (D) | 11,412 | 39.6 |
| 5 | John Lind (D) | 19,863 | 51.3 |
| | Fletcher (R) | 17,809 | 46.0 |
| 6 | Clarence B. Buckman (R) | 17,894 | 56.6 |
| | Dubois (D) | 13,705 | 43.4 |
| 7 | Andrew J. Volstead (R) | 20,826 | 78.6 |
| | Forsberg (PP) | 5,397 | 20.4 |
| 8 | J. Adam Bede (R) | 14,613 | 60.8 |
| | Fay (D) | 8,882 | 37.0 |
| 9 | Halvor Steenerson (R) | 18,055 | 61.4 |
| | Moen (PP) | 6,784 | 23.1 |
| | McKinnon (D) | 4,572 | 15.6 |

## MISSISSIPPI

| | | Votes | % |
|---|---|---|---|
| 1 | Ezekiel S. Candler Jr. (D) | 3,245 | 100.0 |
| 2 | Thomas Speight (D) | 2,523 | 100.0 |
| 3 | Benjamin G. Humphreys (D) | 1,146 | 100.0 |
| 4 | Wilson S. Hill (D) | 2,834 | 100.0 |
| 5 | Adam M. Byrd (D) | 3,081 | 100.0 |
| 6 | Eaton J. Bowers (D) | 1,774 | 100.0 |
| 7 | Frank A. McLain (D) | 2,022 | 100.0 |
| 8 | John Sharp Williams (D) | 1,433 | 100.0 |

## MISSOURI

| | | Votes | % |
|---|---|---|---|
| 1 | James T. Lloyd (D) | 16,972 | 56.2 |
| | Robison (R) | 13,179 | 43.6 |
| 2 | William W. Rucker (D) | 18,045 | 57.6 |
| | Schmitz (R) | 13,293 | 42.4 |
| 3 | John Dougherty (D) | 17,270 | 54.2 |
| | Ward (R) | 14,618 | 45.8 |
| 4 | Charles F. Cochran (D) | 18,392 | 55.9 |
| | Gilmer (R) | 14,510 | 44.1 |
| 5 | William S. Cowherd (D) | 20,628 | 58.1 |
| | Vanhorn (R) | 14,393 | 40.6 |
| 6 | David A. De Armond (D) | 15,639 | 54.3 |
| | Shafer (R) | 13,124 | 45.6 |
| 7 | Courtney W. Hamlin (D) | 19,277 | 52.7 |
| | Peale (R) | 17,250 | 47.2 |
| 8 | Dorsey W. Shackleford (D) | 14,465 | 52.4 |
| | Enloe (R) | 13,133 | 47.6 |

## MISSOURI

| | Candidates | Votes | % |
|---|---|---|---|
| 9 | James Beauchamp Clark (D) | 18,591 | 55.7 |
| | Tubbs (R) | 14,770 | 44.3 |
| 10 | Richard Bartholdt (R) | 21,516 | 55.1 |
| | Blow (D) | 15,262 | 39.1 |
| 11 | John T. Hunt (D) | 14,913 | 57.5 |
| | Charles F. Joy (R) | 10,077 | 38.9 |
| 12 | James J. Butler (D) | 15,316 | 62.5 |
| | Reynolds (R) | 8,698 | 35.5 |
| 13 | Edward Robb (D) | 15,442 | 52.8 |
| | Raney (R) | 13,793 | 47.2 |
| 14 | Willard D. Vandiver (D) | 19,868 | 54.1 |
| | Kinsalving (R) | 16,788 | 45.7 |
| 15 | Maecenas E. Benton (D) | 20,038 | 51.0 |
| | Lacaff (R) | 18,511 | 47.1 |
| 16 | J. Robert Lamar (D) | 14,102 | 52.0 |
| | Russell (R) | 12,996 | 47.9 |

## MONTANA

| | Candidates | Votes | % |
|---|---|---|---|
| AL | Joseph M. Dixon (R) | 24,626 | 46.2 |
| | John M. Evans (D) | 19,560 | 36.7 |
| | Martin Dee (LAB&POP) | 6,005 | 11.3 |
| | George B. Sproule (SOC) | 3,131 | 5.9 |

## NEBRASKA

| | Candidates | Votes | % |
|---|---|---|---|
| 1 | Elmer J. Burkett (R) | 16,534 | 56.9 |
| | Howard H. Hanks (FUS) | 11,603 | 39.9 |
| 2 | Gilbert M. Hitchcock (FUS) | 13,509 | 50.9 |
| | David H. Mercer (R) | 11,669 | 43.9 |
| | Bernard McCaffery (SOC) | 1,379 | 5.2 |
| 3 | John J. McCarthy (R) | 19,201 | 50.0 |
| | John S. Robinson (FUS) | 18,541 | 48.3 |
| 4 | Edmund H. Hinshaw (R) | 19,337 | 52.4 |
| | William L. Stark (FUS) | 16,838 | 45.6 |
| 5 | George W. Norris (R) | 14,927 | 49.5 |
| | A. C. Shallenberger (FUS) | 14,746 | 48.9 |
| 6 | Moses P. Kinkaid (R) | 16,699 | 52.5 |
| | Patrick H. Barry (FUS) | 13,997 | 44.0 |

## NEVADA

| | Candidates | Votes | % |
|---|---|---|---|
| AL | Clarence D. Van Duzer (D SIL) | 5,848 | 53.6 |
| | E. S. Farrington (R) | 5,073 | 46.5 |

## NEW HAMPSHIRE

| | Candidates | Votes | % |
|---|---|---|---|
| 1 | Cyrus A. Sulloway (R) | 22,491 | 58.0 |
| | Albert S. Langley (D) | 15,218 | 39.2 |
| 2 | Frank D. Currier (R) | 22,138 | 58.0 |
| | George E. Bales (D) | 14,986 | 39.2 |

## NEW JERSEY

| | Candidates | Votes | % |
|---|---|---|---|
| 1 | Henry C. Loudenslager (R) | 20,371 | 55.4 |
| | Richard T. Miller (D) | 15,279 | 41.6 |
| 2 | John J. Gardner (R) | 19,966 | 62.5 |
| | Thomas A. Gash (D) | 9,465 | 29.6 |
| | Marion R. Owen (P) | 2,323 | 7.3 |
| 3 | Benjamin F. Howell (R) | 20,014 | 51.4 |
| | Jacob A. Geisenhainer (D) | 18,345 | 47.2 |
| 4 | William M. Lanning (R) | 18,972 | 51.4 |
| | Lewis Perrine (D) | 16,966 | 46.0 |
| 5 | Charles N. Fowler (R) | 21,030 | 49.6 |
| | Dewitt C. Flanagan (D) | 19,881 | 46.8 |
| 6 | William Hughes (D) | 24,084 | 52.4 |
| | William Barbour (R) | 20,236 | 44.0 |
| 7 | Richard Wayne Parker (R) | 19,878 | 56.6 |
| | George A. Miller (D) | 14,371 | 40.9 |
| 8 | William H. Wiley (R) | 18,814 | 59.3 |
| | Henry G. Atwater (D) | 12,005 | 37.8 |
| 9 | Allan Benny (D) | 14,492 | 49.1 |
| | Robert Carey (R) | 13,700 | 46.4 |
| 10 | Allan L. McDermott (D) | 19,311 | 61.6 |
| | James D. Manning (R) | 10,595 | 33.8 |

## NEW YORK

| | Candidates | Votes | % |
|---|---|---|---|
| 1 | Townsend Scudder (D) | 17,788 | 49.8 |
| | Frederic Storm (R) | 17,681 | 49.5 |
| 2 | George H. Lindsay (D) | 18,728 | 61.9 |
| | James R. Howe (R) | 9,593 | 31.7 |
| 3 | Charles T. Dunwell (R) | 17,457 | 48.3 |
| | Hugh E. Rogers (D) | 17,043 | 47.2 |
| 4 | Frank E. Wilson (D) | 16,415 | 50.9 |
| | William Schnitzpan (R) | 13,695 | 42.5 |
| 5 | Edward M. Bassett (D) | 16,149 | 48.8 |
| | Harry A. Hanbury (R) | 15,216 | 46.0 |
| 6 | Robert Baker (D) | 17,886 | 49.5 |
| | Henry Bristow (R) | 17,420 | 48.2 |
| 7 | John J. Fitzgerald (D) | 23,112 | 67.5 |
| | James T. Williamson (R) | 10,432 | 30.5 |
| 8 | Timothy D. Sullivan (D) | 26,107 | 69.4 |
| | Montague Lessler (R) | 10,386 | 27.6 |
| 9 | Henry M. Goldfogle (D) | 7,739 | 55.6 |
| | Charles S. Adler (R) | 4,235 | 30.5 |
| | Alexander Jonas (SOCIAL D) | 1,355 | 9.7 |
| 10 | William Sulzer (D) | 15,451 | 62.2 |
| | William Blau (R) | 6,088 | 24.5 |
| | H. G. Wilshire (SOCIAL D) | 1,873 | 7.5 |
| | James T. Hunter (SOC LAB) | 1,391 | 5.6 |
| 11 | William Randolph Hearst (D) | 26,953 | 69.1 |
| | Henry Birrell (R) | 10,841 | 27.8 |
| 12 | George B. McClellan (D) | 21,275 | 71.1 |
| | Charles Thongood (R) | 7,039 | 23.5 |
| 13 | Francis Burton Harrison (D) | 15,524 | 51.7 |
| | James W. Perry (R) | 13,987 | 46.5 |
| 14 | Ira Edgar Rider (D) | 20,402 | 63.7 |
| | Andrew J. Anderson (R) | 8,492 | 26.5 |
| | William Ehret (SOCIAL D) | 2,348 | 7.3 |
| 15 | William H. Douglass (R) | 12,575 | 49.8 |
| | Henry B. Martin (D) | 12,161 | 48.2 |
| 16 | Jacob Ruppert Jr (D) | 15,657 | 62.5 |
| | William R. Spooner (R) | 7,485 | 29.9 |
| 17 | Frank E. Shober (D) | 19,248 | 50.6 |
| | Harvey T. Andrews (R) | 17,731 | 46.6 |
| 18 | Joseph A. Goulden (D) | 28,411 | 61.8 |
| | Frank C. Schaeffler (R) | 14,844 | 32.3 |
| 19 | Norton P. Otis (R) | 17,878 | 48.7 |
| | Cornelius A. Pugsley (D) | 17,338 | 47.2 |
| 20 | Thomas W. Bradley (R) | 19,747 | 55.5 |
| | Theodore H. Babcock (D) | 14,874 | 41.8 |
| 21 | John H. Ketcham (R) | 22,363 | 57.3 |
| | Curtis F. Hoag (D) | 15,777 | 40.4 |
| 22 | William H. Draper (R) | 21,689 | 57.5 |
| | John H. Morrison (D) | 15,698 | 41.6 |
| 23 | George N. Southwick (R) | 28,858 | 55.2 |
| | B. Cleveland Sloan (D) | 22,459 | 42.9 |
| 24 | George J. Smith (R) | 26,842 | 55.8 |
| | Clifford Champion (D) | 20,045 | 41.7 |
| 25 | Lucius N. Littauer (R) | 23,018 | 55.1 |
| | Frank Beebe (D) | 18,132 | 43.4 |
| 26 | William H. Flack (R) | 27,816 | 70.8 |
| | Henry Holland (D) | 10,392 | 26.4 |
| 27 | James S. Sherman (R) | 21,743 | 52.4 |
| | Edward Lewis (D) | 18,497 | 44.5 |
| 28 | Charles L. Knapp (R) | 23,196 | 58.9 |
| | C. Frank Smith (D) | 14,883 | 37.8 |
| 29 | Michael E. Driscoll (R) | 27,023 | 60.1 |
| | Martin F. Dillon (D) | 16,330 | 36.3 |
| 30 | John W. Dwight (R) | 28,211 | 62.2 |
| | Charles D. Pratt (D) | 17,176 | 37.8 |
| 31 | Sereno E. Payne (R) | 24,130 | 60.1 |
| | Harry B. Harpending (D) | 14,833 | 37.0 |
| 32 | James Breck Perkins (R) | 22,119 | 52.5 |
| | William Degraff (D) | 15,933 | 37.8 |
| | Charles R. Bach (SOCIAL D) | 2,249 | 5.3 |
| 33 | Charles W. Gillet (R) | 21,587 | 54.5 |
| | Frank P. Frost (D) | 16,494 | 41.7 |
| 34 | James W. Wadsworth (R) | 26,007 | 56.2 |
| | Dean F. Currie (D) | 18,787 | 40.6 |
| 35 | William H. Ryan (D) | 19,884 | 55.3 |
| | John M. Farquhar (R) | 14,715 | 40.9 |

| | Candidates | Votes | % |
|---|---|---|---|
| 36 | De Alva S. Alexander (R) | 21,525 | 55.9 |
| | Ole L. Snyder (D) | 16,016 | 41.6 |
| 37 | Edward B. Vreeland (R) | 27,579 | 67.8 |
| | George J. Ball (D) | 11,470 | 28.2 |

## NORTH CAROLINA

| | Candidates | Votes | % |
|---|---|---|---|
| 1 | John H. Small (D) | 14,086 | 88.5 |
| | H. E. Hodges (R) | 1,834 | 11.5 |
| 2 | Claude Kitchin (D) | 12,705 | 99.0 |
| 3 | Charles R. Thomas (D) | 11,198 | 71.0 |
| | G. E. Butler (R) | 4,567 | 29.0 |
| 4 | Edward W. Pou (D) | 13,799 | 82.7 |
| | John W. Atwater (R) | 2,105 | 12.6 |
| 5 | William W. Kitchin (D) | 17,900 | 65.3 |
| | J. L. Patterson (R) | 9,511 | 34.7 |
| 6 | Gilbert B. Patterson (D) | 9,901 | 69.1 |
| | Albert H. Slocumb (R) | 4,430 | 30.9 |
| 7 | Robert N. Page (D) | 13,269 | 83.5 |
| | E. H. Morris (R) | 2,482 | 15.6 |
| 8 | Theodore F. Kluttz (D) | 15,632 | 52.4 |
| | E. S. Blackburn (R) | 14,158 | 47.4 |
| 9 | Edwin Y. Webb (D) | 14,087 | 61.6 |
| | G. B. Hiss (R) | 8,778 | 38.4 |
| 10 | James M. Gudger Jr. (D) | 12,700 | 50.4 |
| | James M. Moody (R) | 12,517 | 49.6 |

## NORTH DAKOTA

| | Candidates | Votes | % |
|---|---|---|---|
| AL | Thomas F. Marshall (R) | 32,976✔ | |
| | Burleigh F. Spalding (R) | 32,854✔ | |
| | Ueland (D) | 14,775 | |
| | Lovell (D) | 14,392 | |
| | King (SOC) | 1,195 | |

## OHIO

| | Candidates | Votes | % |
|---|---|---|---|
| 1 | Nicholas Longworth (R) | 24,082 | 67.9 |
| | Thomas Bentham (D) | 9,471 | 26.7 |
| 2 | Herman P. Goebel (R) | 24,274 | 61.8 |
| | Harry C. Busch (D) | 12,095 | 30.8 |
| | William R. Fox (SOC) | 2,681 | 6.8 |
| 3 | Robert M. Nevin (R) | 25,406 | 52.8 |
| | Thomas A. Selz (D) | 19,551 | 40.6 |
| 4 | Harvey C. Garber (D) | 18,342 | 54.5 |
| | Lewis H. Rogers (R) | 14,879 | 44.2 |
| 5 | John S. Snook (D) | 19,086 | 53.6 |
| | George Russell (R) | 16,548 | 46.4 |
| 6 | Charles Q. Hildebrant (R) | 19,609 | 55.1 |
| | William G. Thompson (D) | 15,188 | 42.6 |
| 7 | Thomas B. Kyle (R) | 18,381 | 55.0 |
| | Chester Bryan (D) | 13,994 | 41.9 |
| 8 | William R. Warnock (R) | 22,177 | 55.9 |
| | William R. Niven (D) | 16,643 | 42.0 |
| 9 | James H. Southard (R) | 23,815 | 56.6 |
| | Charles I. York (D) | 15,873 | 37.7 |
| 10 | Stephen Morgan (R) | 21,593 | 59.6 |
| | C. E. Belcher (D) | 14,118 | 39.0 |
| 11 | Charles H. Grosvenor (R) | 23,124 | 53.7 |
| | Edward I. Lawrence (D) | 19,487 | 45.3 |
| 12 | De Witt C. Badger (D) | 18,569 | 50.4 |
| | Cyrus Huling (R) | 17,793 | 48.3 |
| 13 | Amos H. Jackson (R) | 22,496 | 49.4 |
| | James A. Norton (D) | 22,169 | 48.7 |
| 14 | William W. Skiles (R) | 22,365 | 54.9 |
| | George B. Neal (D) | 17,615 | 43.2 |
| 15 | Henry C. Van Voorhis (R) | 17,462 | 49.3 |
| | Ernest B. Schneider (D) | 16,850 | 47.6 |
| 16 | Joseph J. Gill (R) | 16,129 | 56.9 |
| | Joseph V. Lawler (D) | 11,501 | 40.6 |
| 17 | John W. Cassingham (D) | 19,753 | 52.9 |
| | W. B. Stevens (R) | 17,563 | 47.1 |
| 18 | James Kennedy (R) | 22,461 | 53.8 |
| | William J. Foley (D) | 10,502 | 25.1 |
| | Thomas J. Duffy (LAB) | 7,923 | 19.0 |
| 19 | Charles Dick (R) | 24,732 | 62.0 |
| | Oliver D. Everhard (D) | 13,261 | 33.3 |
| 20 | Jacob A. Beidler (R) | 20,523 | 52.4 |
| | Charles A. Kohl (D) | 16,885 | 43.1 |

## OHIO

| | Candidates | Votes | % |
|---|---|---|---|
| 21 | Theodore E. Burton (R) | 24,353 | 57.0 |
| | Edmund G. Vail (D) | 16,805 | 39.3 |

## OREGON

| | Candidates | Votes | % |
|---|---|---|---|
| 1 | Thomas H. Tongue (R) | 23,585* | 52.9 |
| | J. K. Weatherford (D) | 16,213 | 36.4 |
| | B. F. Ramp (SOC) | 2,576 | 5.8 |
| 2 | John N. Williamson (R) | 23,397 | 53.5 |
| | W. F. Butcher (D) | 15,598 | 35.7 |
| | Diedrich T. Gerdes (SOC) | 2,753 | 6.3 |

## PENNSYLVANIA

| | Candidates | Votes | % |
|---|---|---|---|
| 1 | Henry H. Bingham (R, UN) | 32,119 | 100.0 |
| 2 | Robert Adams Jr. (R, UN) | 35,274 | 99.4 |
| 3 | Henry Burk (R, UN) | 36,911 | 98.8 |
| 4 | Robert H. Foerderer (R, UN) | 21,094 | 98.3 |
| 5 | Edward de V. Morrell (R, UN) | 25,358 | 98.9 |
| 6 | George D. McCreary (R, BALLOT) | 30,626 | 98.4 |
| 7 | Thomas S. Butler (R) | 20,062 | 65.4 |
| | Frank B. Rhodes (D) | 9,751 | 31.8 |
| 8 | Irving P. Wanger (R, BALLOT) | 22,689 | 52.0 |
| | Charles E. Ingersoll (D) | 20,080 | 46.1 |
| 9 | Henry B. Cassel (R) | 18,287 | 69.7 |
| | James F. McCoy (D) | 7,036 | 26.8 |
| 10 | George Howell (A-MACH) | 13,600‡ | 48.4 |
| | William Connell (R, BALLOT) | 13,139 | 46.8 |
| 11 | Henry W. Palmer (R, P) | 16,787 | 48.3 |
| | T. R. Martin (D, WMP/L) | 14,091 | 40.5 |
| | C. F. Quinn (SOC) | 3,911 | 11.2 |
| 12 | George R. Patterson (R) | 14,151 | 49.2 |
| | James W. Ryan (D) | 12,402 | 43.1 |
| | Thomas J. Lannon (SOC) | 1,928 | 6.7 |
| 13 | Marcus C. L. Kline (D) | 24,771 | 54.1 |
| | William H. Sowden (D) | 19,772 | 43.2 |
| 14 | Charles F. Wright (R) | 14,401 | 54.9 |
| | James West (D) | 10,727 | 40.9 |
| 15 | Elias Deemer (R) | 17,518 | 52.4 |
| | James Mansel (D, P) | 15,012 | 44.9 |
| 16 | Charles H. Dickerman (D) | 14,019 | 50.3 |
| | Fred A. Godcharles (R) | 13,171 | 47.2 |
| 17 | Thaddeus M. Mahon (R) | 21,197 | 55.9 |
| | Harry I. Huber (D) | 16,740 | 44.1 |
| 18 | Marlin E. Olmsted (R) | 22,193 | 59.7 |
| | Benjamin L. Forster (D) | 13,715 | 36.9 |
| 19 | Alvin Evans (R) | 20,814 | 56.8 |
| | Robert E. Creswell (D) | 15,690 | 42.8 |
| 20 | Daniel F. Lafean (R) | 15,553 | 50.5 |
| | William McClean (D) | 14,962 | 48.5 |
| 21 | Solomon R. Dresser (R) | 16,722 | 53.5 |
| | Delos Eugene Hibner (D) | 13,243 | 42.4 |
| 22 | George F. Huff (R) | 18,827 | 57.7 |
| | Charles M. Heineman (D) | 13,014 | 39.9 |
| 23 | Allen F. Cooper (R) | 15,546 | 51.1 |
| | Orram W. Kennedy (D) | 13,791 | 45.3 |
| 24 | E. F. Acheson (REG) | 15,147 | 55.1 |
| | Charles R. Eckert (D) | 9,974 | 36.3 |
| 25 | A. L. Bates (R) | 15,538 | 52.4 |
| | A. B. Osborne (D) | 11,311 | 38.1 |
| | Faye B. Ocamb (SOC) | 1,639 | 5.5 |
| 26 | Joseph H. Shull (D) | 15,765 | 53.3 |
| | Fred Nesbit (R) | 11,599 | 39.2 |
| | James Hughes (SOC) | 1,671 | 5.7 |
| 27 | William O. Smith (R) | 16,018 | 57.9 |
| | Alfred W. Smiley (D) | 10,618 | 38.4 |
| 28 | Joseph C. Sibley (R) | 17,616 | 52.5 |
| | James B. Watson (D) | 12,889 | 38.4 |
| | Richard A. Buzza (P) | 3,042 | 9.1 |
| 29 | George Shiras III (D & CIT) | 14,553 | 49.4 |
| | William H. Graham (R) | 14,535 | 49.4 |
| 30 | John Dalzell (R) | 19,085 | 95.1 |
| 31 | H. Kirke Porter (D & CIT) | 16,241 | 52.6 |
| | James F. Burke (R) | 14,532 | 47.1 |
| 32 | James W. Brown (D & CIT) | 14,517 | 50.8 |
| | A. J. Barchfeld (R) | 13,471 | 47.1 |

### Special Election

| | | | |
|---|---|---|---|
| 17 | Alexander Billmeyer (D) | 14,658 | 54.7 |
| | William K. Lord (R) | 12,143 | 45.3 |

## RHODE ISLAND

| | Candidates | Votes | % |
|---|---|---|---|
| 1 | Daniel L. D. Granger (D) | 15,198 | 49.0 |
| | Melville Bull (R) | 14,535 | 46.9 |
| 2 | Adin B. Capron (R) | 13,680 | 50.2 |
| | Unidentified Candidate (D) | 12,057 | 40.5 |

## SOUTH CAROLINA

| | Candidates | Votes | % |
|---|---|---|---|
| 1 | George S. Legare (D) | 3,749 | 95.5 |
| 2 | George W. Croft (D) | 5,134 | 95.3 |
| 3 | Wyatt Aiken (D) | 5,082 | 98.9 |
| 4 | Joseph T. Johnson (D) | 4,642 | 98.7 |
| 5 | David E. Finley (D) | 4,535 | 99.3 |
| 6 | Robert B. Scarborough (D) | 3,981 | 100.0 |
| 7 | Asbury F. Lever (D) | 4,220 | 96.2 |

## SOUTH DAKOTA

| | Candidates | Votes | % |
|---|---|---|---|
| AL | Eben W. Martin (R) | 48,454✔ | |
| | Charles H. Burke (R) | 48,310✔ | |
| | Wilson (D) | 21,113 | |
| | Robinson (D) | 20,814 | |
| | Knowles (SOC) | 2,738 | |
| | Price (SOC) | 2,578 | |
| | Kelley (P) | 2,319 | |
| | Smith (P) | 2,252 | |

## TENNESSEE

| | Candidates | Votes | % |
|---|---|---|---|
| 1 | Walter P. Brownlow (R) | 15,373 | 61.2 |
| | Lyle (D) | 9,751 | 38.8 |
| 2 | Henry R. Gibson (R) | 11,993 | 55.5 |
| | Hannah (D) | 9,636 | 44.6 |
| 3 | John A. Moon (D) | 14,152 | 97.6 |
| 4 | Morgan C. Fitzpatrick (D) | 11,509 | 64.9 |
| | West (R) | 6,228 | 35.1 |
| 5 | James D. Richardson (D) | 10,314 | 76.8 |
| | Parker (R) | 3,113 | 23.2 |
| 6 | John W. Gaines (D) | 9,422 | 82.3 |
| | Tillman (R) | 2,025 | 17.7 |
| 7 | Lemuel P. Padgett (D) | 9,470 | 75.3 |
| | Gregory (R) | 3,106 | 24.7 |
| 8 | Thetus W. Sims (D) | 9,293 | 52.8 |
| | Davis (R) | 8,317 | 47.2 |
| 9 | Rice A. Pierce (D) | 7,371 | 82.5 |
| | Kellar (R) | 1,567 | 17.5 |
| 10 | Malcolm R. Patterson (D) | 7,869 | 83.2 |
| | Phelan (R) | 1,500 | 15.9 |

## TEXAS

| | Candidates | Votes | % |
|---|---|---|---|
| 1 | Morris Sheppard (D) | 19,214 | 83.2 |
| | John Hurley (R) | 3,875 | 16.8 |
| 2 | Samuel B. Cooper (D) | 17,165 | 86.7 |
| | Warren McDaniel (R) | 2,632 | 13.3 |
| 3 | Gordon J. Russell (D) | 16,628 | 95.0 |
| 4 | Choice B. Randell (D) | 17,464 | 85.1 |
| | C. A. Gray (R) | 3,063 | 14.9 |
| 5 | Jack Beall (D) | 16,310 | 88.4 |
| | S. H. Lumpkin (R) | 1,633 | 8.9 |
| 6 | Scott Field (D) | 16,753 | 100.0 |
| 7 | Alexander W. Gregg (D) | 13,162 | 100.0 |
| 8 | Thomas H. Ball (D) | 14,301 | 68.0 |
| | Lock McDaniel (R) | 6,431 | 30.6 |
| 9 | George F. Burgess (D) | 18,316 | 61.3 |
| | B. R. Burow (R) | 11,574 | 38.7 |
| 10 | Albert S. Burleson (D) | 20,539 | 87.2 |
| | Charles Schenken (R) | 2,990 | 12.7 |
| 11 | Robert L. Henry (D) | 14,548 | 94.2 |
| 12 | Oscar W. Gillespie (D) | 16,220 | 82.6 |
| | S. A. Greenwell (R) | 3,424 | 17.4 |
| 13 | John A. Stephens (D) | 24,027 | 91.8 |
| | R. O. Rector (R) | 2,034 | 7.8 |
| 14 | James L. Slayden (D) | 19,889 | 78.4 |
| | D. H. Meek (R) | 4,915 | 19.4 |
| 15 | John N. Garner (D) | 16,542 | 60.6 |
| | John C. Scott (R) | 10,707 | 39.2 |
| 16 | William R. Smith (D) | 22,118 | 88.0 |
| | D. G. Hunt (R) | 2,911 | 11.6 |

### Special Elections

| | | | |
|---|---|---|---|
| 4 | Morris Sheppard (D) | 8,972 | 86.1 |
| | Frank Lee | 1,426 | 13.7 |
| 14 | Gordon Russell (D) | 13,710 | 100.0 |

## UTAH

| | Candidates | Votes | % |
|---|---|---|---|
| AL | Joseph Howell (R) | 43,710 | 51.5 |
| | William H. King (D) | 38,196 | 45.0 |

## VERMONT

| | Candidates | Votes | % |
|---|---|---|---|
| 1 | David J. Foster (R) | 16,007 | 75.2 |
| | J. Walter Lyons (D) | 4,394 | 20.6 |
| 2 | Kittredge Haskins (R) | 17,532 | 76.8 |
| | Harris Miller (D) | 4,150 | 18.2 |

## VIRGINIA

| | Candidates | Votes | % |
|---|---|---|---|
| 1 | William A. Jones (D) | 7,381 | 72.8 |
| | Malcolm A. Coles (R) | 2,762 | 27.2 |
| 2 | Harry L. Maynard (D) | 9,746 | 75.9 |
| | Robert M. Hughes (R) | 2,917 | 22.7 |
| 3 | John Lamb (D) | 5,300 | 81.1 |
| | B. W. Edwards (R) | 969 | 14.8 |
| 4 | Robert G. Southall (D) | 5,717 | 90.0 |
| | R. T. Vaughan (R) | 507 | 8.0 |
| 5 | Claude A. Swanson (D) | 10,363 | 60.8 |
| | Beverly A. Davis (R) | 6,414 | 37.6 |
| 6 | Carter Glass (D) | 6,345 | 79.4 |
| | Aaron Graham (P) | 1,418 | 17.8 |
| 7 | James Hay (D) | 8,461 | 64.7 |
| | S. J. Hoffman (R) | 4,620 | 35.3 |
| 8 | John F. Rixey (D) | 6,618 | 76.7 |
| | W. K. Skinker (R) | 2,011 | 23.3 |
| 9 | Campbell Slemp (R) | 13,694 | 50.4 |
| | William F. Rhea (D) | 13,476 | 49.6 |
| 10 | Henry D. Flood (D) | 9,119 | 68.3 |
| | James Lyons (R) | 4,235 | 31.7 |

### Special Election

| | | | |
|---|---|---|---|
| 6 | Carter Glass (D) | 6,556 | 95.4 |

## WASHINGTON

| | Candidates | Votes | % |
|---|---|---|---|
| AL | Francis W. Cushman (R) | 58,453✔ | |
| | Wesley L. Jones (R) | 58,193✔ | |
| | William E. Humphrey (R) | 57,435✔ | |
| | George F. Cotterill (D) | 33,435 | |
| | Frank B. Cole (D) | 32,406 | |
| | O. R. Holcomb (D) | 31,497 | |
| | George W. Scott (SOC) | 4,612 | |
| | D. Burgess (SOC) | 4,585 | |
| | J. H. C. Scurlock (SOC) | 4,546 | |
| | O. L. Fowler (P) | 1,732 | |
| | W. J. McKean (P) | 1,725 | |
| | A. H. Sherwood (P) | 1,708 | |
| | William McCormick (SOC LAB) | 817 | |
| | Jense C. Martin (SOC LAB) | 808 | |
| | Hans P. Jorgensen (SOC LAB) | 801 | |

## WEST VIRGINIA

| | Candidates | Votes | % |
|---|---|---|---|
| 1 | Blackburn B. Dovener (R) | 19,962 | 52.1 |
| | Owen S. McKinney (D) | 16,922 | 44.1 |
| 2 | Alston G. Dayton (R) | 20,968 | 50.9 |
| | John T. McGraw (D) | 19,628 | 47.6 |
| 3 | Joseph Holt Gaines (R) | 19,014 | 51.7 |
| | James H. Miller (D) | 17,215 | 46.8 |
| 4 | Harry C. Woodyard (R) | 19,158 | 52.0 |
| | W. N. Chancellor (D) | 16,968 | 46.1 |
| 5 | James A. Hughes (R) | 20,164 | 53.3 |
| | David E. Johnson (D) | 17,617 | 46.6 |

## WISCONSIN

| | Candidates | Votes | % |
|---|---|---|---|
| 1 | Henry Allen Cooper (R) | 20,437 | 60.7 |
| | Lewis C. Baker (D) | 12,122 | 36.0 |
| 2 | Henry C. Adams (R) | 17,519 | 52.8 |
| | John J. Wood Jr (D) | 14,483 | 43.6 |
| 3 | Joseph W. Babcock (R) | 19,405 | 60.8 |
| | Jackson Silbaugh (D) | 11,155 | 35.0 |
| 4 | Theobald Otjen (R) | 15,101 | 44.1 |
| | John F. Donovan (D) | 13,468 | 39.3 |
| | Herman W. Bisborins (SOCIAL D) | 5,167 | 15.1 |
| 5 | William H. Stafford (R) | 14,971 | 45.8 |
| | Henry Smith (D) | 10,971 | 33.6 |
| | H. C. Berger (SOCIAL D) | 6,060 | 18.6 |
| 6 | Charles H. Weisse (D) | 17,991 | 52.2 |
| | William H. Froehlich (R) | 14,575 | 42.3 |
| 7 | John J. Esch (R) | 18,694 | 64.6 |
| | William Cernahan (D) | 9,343 | 32.3 |
| 8 | James H. Davidson (R) | 19,553 | 57.8 |
| | T. H. Patterson (D) | 12,651 | 37.4 |
| 9 | Edward S. Minor (R) | 15,958 | 57.1 |
| | Edward Decker (D) | 11,479 | 41.1 |
| 10 | Webster E. Brown (R) | 19,554 | 55.6 |
| | Burt Williams (D) | 14,935 | 42.5 |
| 11 | John J. Jenkins (R) | 19,329 | 67.4 |
| | Joseph A. Rene (D) | 8,261 | 28.8 |

## WYOMING

| | Candidates | Votes | % |
|---|---|---|---|
| AL | Frank W. Mondell (R) | 15,808 | 64.0 |
| | Charles P. Clemmons (D) | 8,892 | 36.0 |

# 1904 House Elections

## ALABAMA

| Candidates | Votes | % |
|---|---|---|
| 1 George W. Taylor (D) | 7,686 | 100.0 |
| 2 Ariosto A. Wiley (D) | 10,177 | 100.0 |
| 3 Henry D. Clayton (D) | 9,566 | 98.3 |
| 4 Sydney J. Bowie (D) | 7,087 | 76.3 |
| J. W. Kitchens (R) | 2,201 | 23.7 |
| 5 J. Thomas Heflin (D) | 10,105 | 76.3 |
| B. W. Walker (R) | 3,095 | 23.4 |
| 6 John H. Bankhead (D) | 8,873 | 76.6 |
| S. R. Crumpton (R) | 2,718 | 23.5 |
| 7 John L. Burnett (D) | 9,819 | 55.9 |
| T. W. Powell (R) | 7,756 | 44.1 |
| 8 William Richardson (D) | 9,898 | 84.3 |
| J. W. Roberts (R) | 1,040 | 15.7 |
| 9 Oscar W. Underwood (D) | 9,615 | 81.7 |
| J. T. Blakemore (R) | 1,775 | 15.1 |

### Special Election

| | | |
|---|---|---|
| 5 J. Thomas Heflin (D) | 4,065 | 99.7 |

## ARKANSAS

| | | |
|---|---|---|
| 1 Robert B. Macon (D) | 14,391 | 99.3 |
| 2 Stephen Brundidge Jr. (D) | 9,065 | 62.7 |
| F. W. Tucker (R) | 5,388 | 37.3 |
| 3 John C. Floyd (D) | 9,719 | 56.3 |
| J. F. Mayes (R) | 7,547 | 43.7 |
| 4 John S. Little (D) | 9,308 | 59.4 |
| James Brizzolara (R) | 6,352 | 40.6 |
| 5 Charles C. Reid (D) | 11,371 | 60.9 |
| A. S. Fowler (R) | 7,288 | 39.1 |
| 6 Joseph T. Robinson (D) | 9,459 | 62.0 |
| R. C. Thompson (R) | 5,810 | 38.1 |
| 7 Robert Minor Wallace (D) | 14,147 | 99.1 |

## CALIFORNIA

| | | |
|---|---|---|
| 1 James N. Gillett (R) | 21,602 | 54.1 |
| A. Caminetti (D) | 15,706 | 39.3 |
| A. J. Gaylord (SOC) | 2,197 | 5.5 |
| 2 Duncan E. McKinlay (R) | 22,873 | 49.2 |
| Theodore A. Bell (D) | 21,640 | 46.6 |
| 3 Joseph R. Knowland (R) | 24,637 | 68.6 |
| Henry C. McPike (D) | 7,210 | 20.1 |
| M. Lesser (SOC) | 3,617 | 10.1 |
| 4 Julius Kahn (R) | 20,012 | 56.8 |
| Edward J. Livernash (D&UN LAB) | 12,812 | 36.4 |
| William Costley (SOC) | 2,267 | 6.4 |
| 5 E. A. Hayes (R) | 23,701 | 52.3 |
| William J. Wynn (D) | 18,025 | 39.8 |
| 6 James C. Needham (R) | 18,828 | 55.1 |
| William M. Conley (D) | 13,074 | 38.3 |
| 7 James McLachlan (R) | 31,091 | 64.2 |
| W. O. Morton (D) | 11,259 | 23.3 |
| F. I. Wheat (SOC) | 3,594 | 7.4 |
| John Sobieski (P) | 2,467 | 5.1 |
| 8 S. C. Smith (R) | 23,683 | 55.6 |
| William T. Lucas (D) | 12,861 | 30.2 |
| N. A. Richardson (SOC) | 4,636 | 10.9 |

### Special Election

| | | |
|---|---|---|
| 3 Joseph R. Knowland (R) | 24,564 | 77.5 |
| Henry C. McPike (D) | 7,123 | 22.5 |

## COLORADO

| | | |
|---|---|---|
| 1 Robert W. Bonynge (R) | 55,940 | 51.0 |
| Clay B. Whitford (D) | 50,022 | 45.6 |
| 2 Herschel M. Hogg (R) | 68,101 | 52.0 |
| Joseph H. Maupin (D) | 58,554 | 44.7 |
| AL Franklin E. Brooks (R) | 121,236 | 50.2 |
| John F. Shafroth (D) | 112,373 | 46.5 |

## CONNECTICUT

| Candidates | Votes | % |
|---|---|---|
| 1 E. Stevens Henry (R) | 26,363 | 56.9 |
| Morse (D) | 18,218 | 39.3 |
| 2 Nehemiah D. Sperry (R) | 36,832 | 56.9 |
| Fisk (D) | 24,679 | 38.1 |
| 3 Frank B. Brandegee (R) | 15,541 | 60.2 |
| Tanner (D) | 9,718 | 37.7 |
| 4 Ebenezer J. Hill (R) | 31,822 | 59.1 |
| Hallen (D) | 20,760 | 38.6 |
| AL George L. Lilley (R) | 108,918 | 57.1 |
| Kennedy (D) | 75,212 | 39.4 |

## DELAWARE

| | | |
|---|---|---|
| AL Hiram R. Burton (R) | 23,512 | 53.7 |
| Edward D. Hearne (D) | 19,552 | 44.6 |

## FLORIDA

| | | |
|---|---|---|
| 1 Stephen M. Sparkman (D) | 8,418 | 75.1 |
| E. R. Gunby (R) | 2,257 | 20.1 |
| 2 Frank Clark (D) | 10,711 | 77.2 |
| J. M. Cheney (R) | 2,767 | 19.9 |
| 3 William B. Lamar (D) | 6,463 | 84.3 |
| L. M. Ware (R) | 986 | 12.9 |

## GEORGIA

| | | |
|---|---|---|
| 1 Rufus E. Lester (D) | 7,246 | 94.9 |
| 2 James M. Griggs (D) | 8,034 | 99.9 |
| 3 Elijah B. Lewis (D) | 6,908 | 99.0 |
| 4 William C. Adamson (D) | 7,850 | 91.6 |
| J. F. Jones (R) | 722 | 8.4 |
| 5 Leonidas F. Livingston (D) | 9,387 | 71.4 |
| C. P. Goree (R) | 3,760 | 28.6 |
| 6 Charles L. Bartlett (D) | 7,197 | 96.4 |
| 7 Gordon Lee (D) | 10,350 | 69.2 |
| T. Pickett (R) | 4,606 | 30.8 |
| 8 William M. Howard (D) | 7,616 | 88.9 |
| W. M. Hairston (POP) | 877 | 10.2 |
| 9 Thomas M. Bell (D) | 12,813 | 68.1 |
| James Finley (R) | 6,000 | 31.9 |
| 10 Thomas W. Hardwick (D) | 8,606 | 91.6 |
| H. M. Porter (POP) | 788 | 8.4 |
| 11 William G. Brantley (D) | 9,970 | 77.3 |
| A. B. Finley (D) | 2,921 | 22.7 |

## IDAHO

| | | |
|---|---|---|
| AL Burton L. French (R) | 44,813 | 63.7 |
| Benjamin F. Clay (D) | 20,146 | 28.6 |
| John H. Morrison (SOC) | 4,209 | 6.0 |

## ILLINOIS

| | | |
|---|---|---|
| 1 Martin B. Madden (R) | 24,097 | 58.0 |
| John S. Oehmen (D) | 9,166 | 22.1 |
| David S. Geer (IR) | 5,175 | 12.5 |
| Edward Loewenthal (SOC) | 2,334 | 5.6 |
| 2 James R. Mann (R) | 29,010 | 66.3 |
| Charles B. Stafford (D) | 9,221 | 21.1 |
| H. Van Middlesworth (SOC) | 4,817 | 11.0 |
| 3 William W. Wilson (R) | 22,709 | 61.7 |
| Willis C. Stone (D) | 8,749 | 23.8 |
| Edward Dierkes (SOC) | 4,476 | 12.2 |
| 4 Charles S. Wharton (R) | 13,481 | 45.2 |
| George P. Foster (D) | 9,947 | 33.4 |
| James W. Johnson (SOC) | 5,944 | 20.0 |
| 5 Anthony Michalek (R) | 12,904 | 44.9 |
| Charles J. Vopicka (D) | 12,019 | 41.9 |
| Robert W. Schoening (SOC) | 3,480 | 12.1 |

| Candidates | Votes | % |
|---|---|---|
| 6 William Lorimer (R) | 21,824 | 50.8 |
| George P. Gubbins (D) | 12,309 | 28.7 |
| Arthur Gourley (P) | 6,112 | 14.2 |
| A. S. Edwards (SOC) | 2,690 | 6.3 |
| 7 Philip Knopf (R) | 29,100 | 59.4 |
| George S. Foster (D) | 12,490 | 25.5 |
| George Koop (SOC) | 6,540 | 13.4 |
| 8 Charles McGavin (R) | 20,107 | 51.7 |
| William Preston Harrison (D) | 13,025 | 33.5 |
| Marcus H. Taft (SOC) | 4,223 | 10.9 |
| 9 Henry S. Boutell (R) | 22,442 | 57.2 |
| Quin O'Brien (D) | 13,525 | 34.5 |
| Adolph Harrick (SOC) | 2,801 | 7.1 |
| 10 George Edmund Foss (R) | 27,096 | 66.2 |
| James L. Turnock (D) | 10,243 | 25.0 |
| Robert Knox (SOC) | 2,917 | 7.1 |
| 11 Howard M. Snapp (R) | 31,019 | 70.7 |
| James O. Monroe (D) | 9,324 | 21.2 |
| 12 Charles E. Fuller (R) | 33,898 | 70.2 |
| Alex Vaughey (D) | 9,718 | 20.1 |
| David A. Syme (P) | 2,481 | 5.1 |
| 13 Robert R. Hitt (R) | 26,454 | 67.7 |
| John Erwin (D) | 10,049 | 25.7 |
| 14 Benjamin F. Marsh (R) | 24,004 | 58.4 |
| David W. Matthews (D) | 12,256 | 29.8 |
| John Higgins (SOC) | 2,852 | 6.9 |
| 15 George W. Prince (R) | 29,792 | 60.7 |
| Meredith Walker (D) | 15,159 | 30.9 |
| 16 Joseph V. Graff (R) | 25,803 | 60.5 |
| Thomas Cooper (D) | 13,780 | 32.3 |
| 17 John A. Sterling (R) | 23,414 | 58.8 |
| Z. F. Yost (D) | 12,978 | 32.6 |
| William W. Houser (P) | 2,285 | 5.7 |
| 18 Joseph G. Cannon (R) | 30,520 | 62.0 |
| Coulson V. McClenathan (D) | 15,168 | 30.8 |
| 19 William B. McKinley (R) | 30,574 | 56.9 |
| Adolph Sumerlin (D) | 19,931 | 37.1 |
| 20 Henry T. Rainey (D) | 19,881 | 48.9 |
| Cornelius J. Doyle (R) | 18,329 | 45.1 |
| 21 Zeno J. Rives (R) | 21,330 | 47.7 |
| Ben F. Caldwell (D) | 20,238 | 45.2 |
| 22 William A. Rodenberg (R) | 25,770 | 53.5 |
| J. Nick Perrin (D) | 19,494 | 40.5 |
| 23 Frank L. Dickson (R) | 21,931 | 47.7 |
| M. D. Foster (D) | 21,123 | 45.9 |
| William P. Habberton (P) | 2,404 | 5.2 |
| 24 Pleasant T. Chapman (R) | 20,556 | 50.7 |
| J. R. Williams (D) | 18,664 | 46.1 |
| 25 George W. Smith (R) | 22,527 | 55.6 |
| Charles L. Otrich (D) | 14,668 | 36.2 |
| Charles F. Kiest (P) | 2,306 | 5.7 |

## INDIANA

| | | |
|---|---|---|
| 1 James A. Hemenway (R) | 23,158* | 51.1 |
| Albert G. Holcomb (D) | 19,399 | 42.8 |
| 2 John C. Chaney (R) | 25,143 | 49.7 |
| Robert W. Miers (D) | 23,670 | 46.8 |
| 3 William T. Zenor (D) | 22,708 | 53.1 |
| John E. Dillon (R) | 19,119 | 44.7 |
| 4 Lincoln Dixon (D) | 23,451 | 50.8 |
| Anderson Percifield (R) | 21,516 | 46.6 |
| 5 Elias S. Holliday (R) | 28,192 | 52.0 |
| Claude G. Bowers (D) | 23,101 | 42.6 |
| 6 James E. Watson (R) | 29,089 | 56.3 |
| Uriah S. Jackson (D) | 22,046 | 42.7 |
| 7 Jesse Overstreet (R) | 34,178 | 57.1 |
| Levi P. Harlan (D) | 23,334 | 39.0 |
| 8 George W. Cromer (R) | 29,462 | 52.2 |
| Edward C. Dehority (D) | 22,097 | 39.1 |
| Aaron Worth (P) | 3,675 | 6.5 |
| 9 Charles B. Landis (R) | 29,492 | 52.9 |
| Clyde H. Jones (D) | 23,267 | 41.8 |
| 10 Edgar D. Crumpacker (R) | 31,583 | 58.5 |
| Worth W. Pepple (D) | 21,451 | 39.7 |

## INDIANA

| Candidates | Votes | % |
|---|---|---|
| 11 Frederick Landis (R) | 29,591 | 53.6 |
| Clement M. Holderman (D) | 21,406 | 38.8 |
| Edward H. Kennedy (P) | 3,364 | 6.1 |
| 12 Newton W. Gilbert (R) | 23,203 | 50.5 |
| James M. Robinson (D) | 21,322 | 46.4 |
| 13 Abraham L. Brick (R) | 29,361 | 55.1 |
| Frank E. Hering (D) | 21,454 | 40.3 |

## IOWA

| Candidates | Votes | % |
|---|---|---|
| 1 Thomas Hedge (R) | 19,929 | 54.7 |
| John E. Craig (D) | 14,886 | 40.9 |
| 2 Albert F. Dawson (R) | 22,116 | 48.1 |
| Martin J. Wade (D) | 21,930 | 47.7 |
| 3 Benjamin P. Birdsall (R) | 29,297 | 65.3 |
| J. W. Mallon (D) | 14,200 | 31.6 |
| 4 Gilbert N. Haugen (R) | 26,399 | 64.5 |
| W. O. Holman (D) | 13,403 | 32.8 |
| 5 Robert G. Cousins (R) | 25,313 | 59.7 |
| John A. Green (D) | 15,019 | 35.4 |
| 6 John F. Lacey (R) | 23,213 | 58.4 |
| S. A. Brewster (D) | 13,840 | 34.9 |
| 7 John A. T. Hull (R) | 27,637 | 64.3 |
| John T. Mulvaney (D) | 12,046 | 28.0 |
| 8 William P. Hepburn (R) | 26,603 | 63.0 |
| John V. Bennett (D) | 14,518 | 34.4 |
| 9 Walter I. Smith (R) | 27,214 | 63.9 |
| H. Wilcox (D) | 13,907 | 32.7 |
| 10 James P. Conner (R) | 34,977 | 67.3 |
| W. J. Branagan (D) | 14,531 | 28.0 |
| 11 Elbert H. Hubbard (R) | 32,560 | 69.1 |
| P. D. Vanoosterhaut (D) | 13,521 | 28.7 |

## KANSAS

| Candidates | Votes | % |
|---|---|---|
| 1 Charles Curtis (R) | 25,376 | 57.8 |
| A. M. Harvey (D) | 17,808 | 40.6 |
| 2 Justin D. Bowersock (R) | 26,443 | 54.8 |
| C. F. Hutchings (D) | 20,308 | 42.1 |
| 3 Philip P. Campbell (R) | 29,998 | 59.5 |
| William H. Ryan (D) | 15,762 | 31.2 |
| T. C. Davis (SOC) | 4,696 | 9.3 |
| 4 James M. Miller (R) | 24,185 | 62.8 |
| Frank B. Lowrance (D-PP) | 14,326 | 37.2 |
| 5 William A. Calderhead (R) | 22,076 | 65.1 |
| John A. Flack (D-PP) | 11,825 | 34.9 |
| 6 William A. Reeder (R) | 21,808 | 60.5 |
| H. O. Caster (D) | 13,274 | 36.8 |
| 7 Victor Murdock (R) | 35,598 | 60.4 |
| M. Belisle (D) | 19,548 | 33.2 |
| AL Charles F. Scott (R) | 187,983 | 60.3 |
| Francis M. Brady (D) | 105,479 | 33.9 |

## KENTUCKY

| Candidates | Votes | % |
|---|---|---|
| 1 Ollie M. James (D) | 25,558 | 62.3 |
| J. C. Spaight (R) | 13,755 | 33.5 |
| 2 Augustus O. Stanley (D) | 20,732 | 55.7 |
| W. A. Overby (R) | 16,517 | 44.3 |
| 3 James M. Richardson (D) | 18,432 | 50.1 |
| W. H. Jones (R) | 18,332 | 49.9 |
| 4 David H. Smith (D) | 21,979 | 53.1 |
| Ben L. Bruner (R) | 19,419 | 46.9 |
| 5 J. Swagar Sherley (D) | 23,712 | 51.0 |
| William C. Owens (R) | 22,229 | 47.8 |
| 6 Joseph L. Rhinock (D) | 18,854 | 50.7 |
| Leslie T. Applegate (R) | 16,089 | 43.3 |
| 7 South Trimble (D) | 20,356 | 60.0 |
| Joseph W. Calvert (R) | 13,187 | 38.9 |
| 8 George G. Gilbert (D) | 16,481 | 52.4 |
| N. D. Miles (R) | 14,536 | 46.2 |
| 9 Joseph B. Bennett (R) | 21,335 | 50.1 |
| James N. Kehoe (D) | 21,291 | 50.0 |
| 10 Frank A. Hopkins (D) | 19,154 | 51.9 |
| Theodore D. Blakey (R) | 17,736 | 48.1 |
| 11 Don C. Edwards (R) | 31,349 | 70.3 |
| George E. Stone (D) | 13,200 | 29.6 |

## LOUISIANA

| Candidates | Votes | % |
|---|---|---|
| 1 Adolph Meyer (D) | 9,157 | 89.8 |
| Hugh S. Suthon (R) | 791 | 7.8 |
| 2 Robert C. Davey (D) | 9,786 | 91.0 |
| George H. Vennard (R) | 798 | 7.4 |
| 3 Robert F. Broussard (D) | 5,649 | 84.5 |
| Henry N. Pharr (R) | 1,038 | 15.5 |
| 4 John T. Watkins (D) | 6,266 | 99.1 |
| 5 Joseph E. Ransdell (D) | 5,747 | 95.4 |
| 6 Samuel M. Robertson (D) | 5,351 | 88.1 |
| L. E. Bentley (R) | 721 | 11.9 |
| 7 Arsene P. Pujo (D) | 5,432 | 84.2 |
| Joseph Lassalle (R) | 1,007 | 15.6 |

## MAINE

| Candidates | Votes | % |
|---|---|---|
| 1 Amos L. Allen (R) | 18,301 | 57.2 |
| L. R. Moore (D) | 13,320 | 41.6 |
| 2 Charles E. Littlefield (R) | 19,176 | 57.2 |
| Horatio G. Foss (D) | 13,785 | 41.2 |
| 3 Edwin C. Burleigh (R) | 18,541 | 60.3 |
| E. N. Benson (D) | 11,678 | 38.0 |
| 4 Llewellyn Powers (R) | 20,501 | 62.4 |
| William R. Pattangall (D) | 11,600 | 35.3 |

## MARYLAND

| Candidates | Votes | % |
|---|---|---|
| 1 Thomas A. Smith (D) | 17,582 | 49.4 |
| William H. Jackson (R) | 17,072 | 48.0 |
| 2 J. Fred. C. Talbott (D) | 18,922 | 52.2 |
| Robert Garrett (R) | 16,734 | 46.2 |
| 3 Frank C. Wachter (R) | 17,405 | 51.8 |
| Lee S. Meyer (D) | 15,373 | 45.8 |
| 4 John Gill Jr. (D) | 18,464 | 51.8 |
| William C. Smith (R) | 16,754 | 47.0 |
| 5 Sydney E. Mudd (R) | 16,896 | 53.6 |
| Richard S. Hill (D) | 13,762 | 43.6 |
| 6 George A. Pearre (R) | 19,131 | 53.9 |
| Walter A. Johnston (D) | 15,077 | 42.5 |

## MASSACHUSETTS

| Candidates | Votes | % |
|---|---|---|
| 1 George P. Lawrence (R) | 17,217 | 58.0 |
| Charles Giddings (D) | 11,117 | 37.4 |
| 2 Frederick H. Gillett (R) | 17,611 | 63.5 |
| George W. Wheelwright (D) | 7,992 | 28.8 |
| George H. Wrenn (SOC) | 1,744 | 6.3 |
| 3 Rockwood Hoar (R) | 17,796 | 61.1 |
| John B. Ratigan (D) | 10,617 | 36.4 |
| 4 Charles Q. Tirrell (R) | 18,982 | 61.4 |
| Marcus A. Coolidge (D) | 10,478 | 33.9 |
| 5 Butler Ames (R) | 16,287 | 54.6 |
| Alexander B. Bruce (D) | 12,657 | 42.5 |
| 6 Augustus P. Gardner (R) | 18,157 | 61.0 |
| Daniel N. Crowley (D) | 8,880 | 29.8 |
| James F. Carey (SOC) | 2,716 | 9.1 |
| 7 Ernest W. Roberts (R) | 20,821 | 62.9 |
| William A. Kelley (D) | 10,165 | 30.7 |
| 8 Samuel W. McCall (R) | 21,511 | 89.1 |
| Thomas A. Scott (SOC) | 2,623 | 10.9 |
| 9 John A. Keliher (D) | 17,003 | 67.7 |
| Walter L. Sears (R) | 6,895 | 27.5 |
| 10 William S. McNary (D) | 19,211 | 57.3 |
| Jay B. Crawford (R) | 12,740 | 38.0 |
| 11 John A. Sullivan (D) | 18,045 | 51.6 |
| Eugene N. Foss (R) | 15,990 | 45.7 |
| 12 John W. Weeks (R) | 19,312 | 61.3 |
| Augustus Hemenway (D) | 10,813 | 34.3 |
| 13 William S. Greene (R) | 13,631 | 62.8 |
| Francis M. Kennedy (D) | 8,064 | 37.2 |
| 14 William C. Lovering (R) | 18,415 | 60.4 |
| Thomas H. Buttimer (D) | 7,100 | 23.3 |
| Charles H. Coulter (SOC) | 4,279 | 14.0 |

## MICHIGAN

| Candidates | Votes | % |
|---|---|---|
| 1 Edwin Denby (R) | 28,874 | 58.0 |
| Alfred Lucking (D) | 20,490 | 41.2 |
| 2 Charles E. Townsend (R) | 28,797 | 59.2 |
| John P. Kirk (D) | 18,874 | 38.8 |
| 3 Washington Gardner (R) | 28,089 | 63.4 |
| Lloyd C. Feighner (D) | 13,535 | 30.6 |
| 4 Edward L. Hamilton (R) | 28,066 | 66.5 |
| Theodore G. Beaver (D) | 14,143 | 33.5 |
| 5 William Alden Smith (R) | 30,869 | 70.3 |
| Vernon H. Smith (D) | 12,253 | 27.9 |
| 6 Samuel W. Smith (R) | 31,403 | 61.4 |
| Charles A. Durand (D) | 18,224 | 35.6 |
| 7 Henry McMorran (R) | 25,562 | 66.4 |
| Charles Wellman (D) | 12,619 | 32.8 |
| 8 Joseph W. Fordney (R) | 24,417 | 65.2 |
| Henry J. Patterson (D) | 11,898 | 31.8 |
| 9 Roswell P. Bishop (R) | 22,463 | 71.7 |
| George S. Stanley (D) | 7,076 | 22.6 |
| 10 George A. Loud (R) | 27,187 | 70.4 |
| Stephen P. Flynn (D) | 10,527 | 27.3 |
| 11 Archibald B. Darragh (R) | 31,661 | 73.0 |
| William A. Bahlke (D) | 10,639 | 24.5 |
| 12 H. Olin Young (R) | 36,655 | 80.3 |
| John W. Black (D) | 7,915 | 17.3 |

## MINNESOTA

| Candidates | Votes | % |
|---|---|---|
| 1 James A. Tawney (R) | 23,188 | 64.5 |
| Nelson (D) | 12,770 | 35.5 |
| 2 James T. McCleary (R) | 19,246 | 64.1 |
| Jones (D) | 10,784 | 35.9 |
| 3 Charles R. Davis (R) | 20,116 | 66.0 |
| Craven (D) | 10,386 | 34.1 |
| 4 Frederick C. Stevens (R) | 25,631 | 100.0 |
| 5 Loren Fletcher (R) | 21,933 | 51.3 |
| Kohler (D) | 15,923 | 37.2 |
| Hirshfield (LAB) | 3,184 | 7.4 |
| 6 Clarence B. Buckman (R) | 19,309 | 54.0 |
| Vandyke (D) | 16,430 | 46.0 |
| 7 Andrew J. Volstead (R) | 27,060 | 100.0 |
| 8 J. Adam Bede (R) | 22,095 | 76.9 |
| Hughes (D) | 6,626 | 23.1 |
| 9 Halvor Steenerson (R) | 27,061 | 100.0 |

## MISSISSIPPI

| Candidates | Votes | % |
|---|---|---|
| 1 Ezekiel S. Candler Jr. (D) | 8,049 | 100.0 |
| 2 Thomas Spight (D) | 7,279 | 100.0 |
| 3 Benjamin G. Humphreys (D) | 3,744 | 100.0 |
| 4 Wilson S. Hill (D) | 7,135 | 100.0 |
| 5 Adam Byrd (D) | 9,362 | 99.0 |
| 6 Eaton J. Bowers (D) | 6,563 | 93.6 |
| C. W. Baylis (SOC) | 449 | 6.4 |
| 7 Frank McLain (D) | 5,730 | 100.0 |
| 8 John S. Williams (D) | 4,934 | 100.0 |

## MISSOURI

| Candidates | Votes | % |
|---|---|---|
| 1 James T. Lloyd (D) | 20,216 | 51.4 |
| Higbee (R) | 19,131 | 48.6 |
| 2 William W. Rucker (D) | 21,639 | 53.8 |
| Hudson (R) | 18,596 | 46.2 |
| 3 Frank B. Klepper (R) | 19,088 | 50.4 |
| D. Sullinger (D) | 18,791 | 49.6 |
| 4 Frank B. Fulkerson (R) | 19,831 | 51.7 |
| Wilson (D) | 18,531 | 48.3 |
| 5 Edgar C. Ellis (R) | 23,873 | 49.2 |
| Cowherd (D) | 22,912 | 47.2 |
| 6 David A. De Armond (D) | 17,678 | 51.5 |
| Rhodes (R) | 16,637 | 48.5 |
| 7 John Welborn (R) | 23,682 | 51.6 |
| Hamlin (D) | 22,204 | 48.4 |
| 8 Dorsey W. Shackleford (D) | 16,059 | 51.6 |
| Chalfant (R) | 15,091 | 48.5 |
| 9 James Beauchamp Clark (D) | 21,508 | 51.9 |
| Garber (D) | 19,937 | 48.1 |
| 10 Richard Bartholdt (R) | 34,254 | 58.5 |
| Tichacek (D) | 21,271 | 36.3 |
| 11 John T. Hunt (R) | 17,018 | 49.1 |
| Caulfield (R) | 16,326 | 47.1 |

## MISSOURI

| | Candidates | Votes | % |
|---|---|---|---|
| 12 | Ernest E. Wood (D) | 15,134‡ | 50.3 |
| | Harry M. Coudrey (R) | 14,177 | 47.1 |
| 13 | Marion E. Rhodes (R) | 16,166 | 50.6 |
| | Edward Robb (D) | 15,788 | 49.4 |
| 14 | William T. Tyndall (R) | 23,401 | 52.8 |
| | Russell (D) | 20,873 | 47.1 |
| 15 | Cassius M. Shartel (R) | 21,654 | 49.0 |
| | Benton (D) | 19,646 | 44.4 |
| 16 | Arthur P. Murphy (R) | 15,159 | 50.1 |
| | J. Robert Lamar (D) | 15,123 | 49.9 |

## MONTANA

| | Candidates | Votes | % |
|---|---|---|---|
| AL | Joseph M. Dixon (R) | 32,957 | 51.7 |
| | Austin C. Gormley (D-LAB-PP) | 26,729 | 42.0 |
| | John H. Walsh (SOC) | 4,025 | 6.3 |

## NEBRASKA

| | Candidates | Votes | % |
|---|---|---|---|
| 1 | Elmer J. Burkett (R) | 19,786* | 59.7 |
| | Hugh Lamaster (FUS) | 11,863 | 35.8 |
| 2 | John L. Kennedy (R) | 14,417 | 46.8 |
| | Gilbert M. Hitchcock (FUS) | 13,628 | 44.2 |
| | Clark W. Adair (SOC) | 2,534 | 8.2 |
| 3 | John J. McCarthy (R) | 24,151 | 51.9 |
| | Patrick E. McKillip (FUS) | 21,210 | 45.6 |
| 4 | Edmond H. Hinshaw (R) | 23,407 | 57.9 |
| | Charles F. Gilbert (FUS) | 15,702 | 38.8 |
| 5 | George W. Norris (R) | 19,645 | 56.1 |
| | Harry H. Mauck (FUS) | 13,831 | 39.5 |
| 6 | Moses P. Kinkaid (R) | 22,580 | 58.8 |
| | Walter B. McNeel (FUS) | 13,725 | 35.8 |

## NEVADA

| | Candidates | Votes | % |
|---|---|---|---|
| AL | Clarence D. Van Duzer (D & SILVER) | 5,525 | 48.5 |
| | J. A. Yerington (R) | 5,301 | 46.5 |
| | Reinhold Sadler (STAL SIL) | 572 | 5.0 |

## NEW HAMPSHIRE

| | Candidates | Votes | % |
|---|---|---|---|
| 1 | Cyrus A. Sulloway (R) | 25,364 | 58.9 |
| | Napoleon J. Dyer (D) | 16,866 | 39.1 |
| 2 | Frank D. Currier (R) | 26,748 | 60.7 |
| | Harry W. Daniell (D) | 16,462 | 37.4 |

## NEW JERSEY

| | Candidates | Votes | % |
|---|---|---|---|
| 1 | Henry C. Loudenslager (R) | 26,169 | 60.3 |
| | Swackhamer (D) | 15,365 | 35.4 |
| 2 | John J. Gardner (R) | 26,296 | 63.7 |
| | Perry (D) | 13,035 | 31.6 |
| 3 | Benjamin F. Howell (R) | 24,565 | 56.1 |
| | Otis (D) | 17,862 | 40.8 |
| 4 | Ira W. Wood (R) | 22,579 | 54.7 |
| | Stevens (D) | 16,953 | 41.1 |
| 5 | Charles N. Fowler (R) | 24,488 | 52.3 |
| | Martine (D) | 19,254 | 41.1 |
| 6 | Henry C. Allen (R) | 26,612 | 47.8 |
| | William Hughes (D) | 26,102 | 46.9 |
| 7 | Richard W. Parker (R) | 25,578 | 61.4 |
| | Jackson (D) | 14,347 | 34.5 |
| 8 | William H. Wiley (R) | 24,148 | 63.2 |
| | Seymour (D) | 11,607 | 30.4 |
| 9 | Marshall Van Winkle (R) | 19,824 | 50.7 |
| | Benny (D) | 17,399 | 44.5 |
| 10 | Allan L. McDermott (D) | 21,293 | 53.8 |
| | Walker (R) | 15,959 | 40.3 |

## NEW YORK

| | Candidates | Votes | % |
|---|---|---|---|
| 1 | William W. Cocks (R) | 25,481 | 55.7 |
| | William Willett Jr. (D) | 19,362 | 42.3 |
| 2 | George H. Lindsay (D) | 18,506 | 55.8 |
| | Herbert J. Knapp (R) | 12,899 | 38.9 |
| 3 | Charles T. Dunwell (R) | 21,208 | 52.6 |
| | Ephraim Byk (D) | 17,571 | 43.5 |
| 4 | Charles P. Law (R) | 19,418 | 49.4 |
| | Frank E. Wilson (D) | 17,684 | 45.0 |
| 5 | George E. Waldo (R) | 21,299 | 51.8 |
| | John J. Roach (D) | 18,889 | 45.9 |
| 6 | William M. Calder (R) | 22,109 | 52.4 |
| | Robert Baker (D) | 19,430 | 46.0 |
| 7 | John J. Fitzgerald (D) | 23,463 | 62.6 |
| | Robert H. Haskell (R) | 13,282 | 35.4 |
| 8 | Timothy D. Sullivan (D) | 24,532 | 61.5 |
| | Frank L. Frugone (R) | 14,262 | 35.7 |
| 9 | Henry M. Goldfogle (D) | 5,982 | 39.7 |
| | Joseph Levenson (R) | 5,667 | 37.7 |
| | Joseph Barondess (SOCIAL D) | 3,167 | 21.0 |
| 10 | William Sulzer (D) | 13,381 | 51.0 |
| | William Byrnes (R) | 9,383 | 35.8 |
| | Isidor Phillips (SOCIAL D) | 2,789 | 10.6 |
| 11 | William Randolph Hearst (D) | 26,255 | 59.3 |
| | Henry Clay Piercy (R) | 16,594 | 37.5 |
| 12 | William Bourke Cochran (D) | 20,972 | 63.1 |
| | Henry Carey (R) | 10,500 | 31.6 |
| 13 | Herbert Parsons (R) | 18,700 | 52.9 |
| | Edward Swann (D) | 16,038 | 45.4 |
| 14 | Charles A. Towne (D) | 21,627 | 57.1 |
| | Lucian Knapp (R) | 12,664 | 33.4 |
| | William F. Ehret (SOCIAL D) | 2,973 | 7.8 |
| 15 | Jacob Van Vechten Olcott (R) | 16,924 | 51.7 |
| | M. Francis Loughman (D) | 15,199 | 46.4 |
| 16 | Jacob Ruppert Jr. (D) | 15,049 | 52.7 |
| | Theodore Prince (R) | 11,212 | 39.3 |
| | Adolph Groelinger (SOCIAL D) | 1,882 | 6.6 |
| 17 | William S. Bennett (R) | 25,655 | 51.3 |
| | Franklin Leonard Jr (D) | 23,029 | 46.0 |
| 18 | Joseph A. Goulden (D) | 32,266 | 57.2 |
| | William W. Niles (R) | 20,606 | 36.5 |
| 19 | John E. Andrus (R) | 24,199 | 54.1 |
| | J. Harvey Bell (D) | 19,079 | 42.7 |
| 20 | Thomas W. Bradley (R) | 23,224 | 55.5 |
| | Charles C. Dill (D) | 17,562 | 42.0 |
| 21 | John H. Ketcham (R) | 24,791 | 95.9 |
| 22 | William H. Draper (R) | 25,755 | 59.4 |
| | Isaac C. Blandy (D) | 16,261 | 37.5 |
| 23 | George N. Southwick (R) | 33,763 | 55.7 |
| | Daniel C. McElwain (D) | 25,618 | 42.3 |
| 24 | Frank J. Lefevre (R) | 30,980 | 95.5 |
| 25 | Lucius N. Littauer (R) | 27,290 | 54.8 |
| | Joseph A. Kellogg (D) | 20,491 | 41.1 |
| 26 | William H. Flack (R) | 33,564 | 67.5 |
| | Henry Holland (D) | 14,801 | 29.8 |
| 27 | James S. Sherman (R) | 26,657 | 54.5 |
| | William H. Squires (D) | 20,892 | 42.7 |
| 28 | Charles L. Knapp (R) | 27,357 | 60.2 |
| | Henry Purcell (D) | 15,808 | 34.8 |
| 29 | Michael E. Driscoll (R) | 33,738 | 62.6 |
| | Harrison W. Coley (D) | 18,324 | 34.0 |
| 30 | John W. Dwight (R) | 32,272 | 59.8 |
| | George L. Church (D) | 19,846 | 36.8 |
| 31 | Sereno E. Payne (R) | 29,760 | 61.5 |
| | D. J. Vanauken (D) | 17,576 | 36.4 |
| 32 | James Breck Perkins (R) | 30,091 | 58.9 |
| | Henry Selden Bacon (D) | 17,382 | 34.1 |
| 33 | Jacob Sloat Fassett (R) | 26,276 | 57.5 |
| | Frank P. Frost (D) | 18,055 | 39.5 |
| 34 | James W. Wadsworth (R) | 32,364 | 60.5 |
| | James E. Crisfield (D) | 19,328 | 36.2 |
| 35 | William H. Ryan (D) | 20,840 | 49.4 |
| | Warren P. Bender (R) | 19,943 | 47.2 |
| 36 | De Alva S. Alexander (R) | 27,958 | 59.8 |
| | Edwin Gaw Flanigen (D) | 17,569 | 37.6 |
| 37 | Edward B. Vreeland (R) | 33,573 | 67.7 |
| | S. B. McClure (D) | 13,229 | 26.7 |

## NORTH CAROLINA

| | Candidates | Votes | % |
|---|---|---|---|
| 1 | John H. Small (D) | 13,065 | 80.5 |
| | D. O. Newberry (R) | 3,167 | 19.5 |
| 2 | Claude Kitchin (D) | 12,064 | 86.3 |
| | P. C. Jenkins (R) | 1,919 | 13.7 |
| 3 | Charles R. Thomas (D) | 10,645 | 66.0 |
| | W. S. Robinson (R) | 5,496 | 34.1 |
| 4 | Edward W. Pou (D) | 12,658 | 70.9 |
| | Claude Pearson (R) | 5,197 | 29.1 |
| 5 | William W. Kitchin (D) | 16,497 | 58.7 |
| | C. A. Reynolds (R) | 11,546 | 41.1 |
| 6 | Gilbert B. Patterson (D) | 9,770 | 70.0 |
| | O. J. Spears (R) | 4,193 | 30.0 |
| 7 | Robert N. Page (D) | 12,642 | 58.5 |
| | L. D. Mendenhall (R) | 8,986 | 41.6 |
| 8 | E. Spencer Blackburn (R) | 15,566 | 50.3 |
| | W. C. Newland (D) | 15,321 | 49.5 |
| 9 | Edwin Y. Webb (D) | 13,822 | 58.1 |
| | J. F. Newell (R) | 9,957 | 41.9 |
| 10 | James M. Gudger Jr. (D) | 13,554 | 51.7 |
| | H. G. Ewart (R) | 12,666 | 48.3 |

## NORTH DAKOTA

| | Candidates | Votes | % |
|---|---|---|---|
| AL | Thomas F. Marshall (R) | 49,111✔ | |
| | Asle J. Gronna (R) | 47,648✔ | |
| | N. P. Rasmussen (D) | 15,622 | |
| | A. G. Burr (D) | 15,398 | |
| | L. F. Dow (SOC) | 1,734 | |
| | E. D. Herring (SOC) | 1,697 | |
| | B. H. Tibbets (P) | 971 | |
| | N. A. Colby (P) | 967 | |

## OHIO

| | Candidates | Votes | % |
|---|---|---|---|
| 1 | Nicholas Longworth (R) | 32,105 | 68.7 |
| | Braxton W. Campbell (D) | 11,631 | 24.9 |
| | Bishop W. Mason (SOC) | 2,737 | 5.9 |
| 2 | Herman P. Goebel (R) | 31,873 | 62.8 |
| | Charles A. Miller (D) | 14,215 | 28.0 |
| | John F. Ditchen (SOC) | 4,487 | 8.8 |
| 3 | Robert M. Nevin (R) | 31,626 | 53.0 |
| | Charles Conley (D) | 25,594 | 42.9 |
| 4 | Harvey C. Garber (D) | 20,653 | 50.8 |
| | R. D. Kahle (R) | 18,858 | 46.4 |
| 5 | William W. Campbell (D) | 19,707 | 49.4 |
| | Timothy H. Ansberry (D) | 19,383 | 48.6 |
| 6 | Thomas E. Scroggy (R) | 21,485 | 51.4 |
| | James Runyan (D) | 19,148 | 45.8 |
| 7 | J. Warren Keifer (R) | 25,245 | 60.0 |
| | P. E. Montanus (D) | 15,966 | 37.9 |
| 8 | Ralph D. Cole (R) | 27,523 | 60.5 |
| | Henry F. MacCracken (D) | 16,257 | 35.8 |
| 9 | James H. Southard (R) | 35,128 | 63.7 |
| | William H. Althof (D) | 16,488 | 29.9 |
| 10 | Henry Bannon (R) | 25,097 | 62.6 |
| | Matthew S. Merriman (D) | 13,316 | 33.2 |
| 11 | Charles H. Grosvenor (R) | 29,415 | 58.9 |
| | John T. Bridwell (D) | 19,501 | 39.1 |
| 12 | Edward L. Taylor Jr. (R) | 25,178 | 56.6 |
| | Dewitt C. Badger (D) | 17,999 | 40.5 |
| 13 | Grant E. Mouser (R) | 25,054 | 49.5 |
| | D. R. Crissinger (D) | 24,004 | 47.4 |
| 14 | Amos R. Webber (R) | 29,187 | 57.4 |
| | Benjamin F. Long (D) | 19,318 | 38.0 |
| 15 | Beman G. Dawes (R) | 20,763 | 48.4 |
| | Ernest B. Schneider (D) | 20,231 | 47.2 |
| 16 | Capell L. Weems (R) | 23,265 | 59.1 |
| | H. W. Hermann (D) | 13,676 | 34.8 |
| 17 | Martin L. Smyser (R) | 23,847 | 50.7 |
| | J. E. Hurst (D) | 21,571 | 45.8 |
| 18 | James Kennedy (R) | 36,939 | 63.9 |
| | W. J. Foley (D) | 16,472 | 28.5 |
| 19 | W. Aubrey Thomas (R) | 35,676 | 68.9 |
| | Charles J. McCormick (D) | 11,942 | 23.1 |
| | F. N. Prevey (SOC) | 2,927 | 5.7 |
| 20 | Jacob A. Beidler (R) | 29,475 | 59.8 |
| | Charles W. Lapp (D) | 17,106 | 34.7 |
| 21 | Theodore E. Burton (R) | 33,930 | 86.6 |
| | Max S. Hayes (SOC) | 4,144 | 10.6 |

## OHIO
### Special Elections

| | Candidates | Votes | % |
|---|---|---|---|
| 14 | Amos R. Webber (R) | 29,148 | 57.3 |
| | Benjamin F. Long (D) | 19,350 | 38.0 |
| 19 | W. Aubrey Thomas (R) | 35,802 | 83.5 |
| | Charles J. McCormick (D) | 5,467 | 12.8 |

## OREGON

| | Candidates | Votes | % |
|---|---|---|---|
| 1 | Binger Hermann (R) | 23,970 | 51.2 |
| | R. M. Veatch (D) | 17,157 | 36.7 |
| | H. Gould (P) | 2,867 | 6.1 |
| | B. F. Ramp (SOC) | 2,800 | 6.0 |
| 2 | John N. Williamson (R) | 27,126 | 57.6 |
| | J. E. Simmons (D) | 12,773 | 27.1 |
| | George R. Cook (SOC) | 3,678 | 7.8 |
| | H. W. Stone (P) | 3,535 | 7.5 |

## PENNSYLVANIA

| | Candidates | Votes | % |
|---|---|---|---|
| 1 | Henry H. Bingham (R) | 42,228 | 84.7 |
| | Joseph L. Galen (D) | 7,623 | 15.3 |
| 2 | Robert Adams Jr. (R) | 41,637 | 84.9 |
| | John Cadwalader Jr. (D) | 7,010 | 14.3 |
| 3 | George A. Castor (R) | 39,982 | 83.3 |
| | John H. Fow (D, I) | 7,873 | 16.4 |
| 4 | Reuben O. Moon (R) | 25,610 | 81.1 |
| | Charles F. Stilz (D) | 5,253 | 16.6 |
| 5 | Edward de V. Morrell (R) | 28,146 | 78.8 |
| | David Moffet (D) | 6,524 | 18.3 |
| 6 | George D. McCreary (R) | 34,984 | 76.7 |
| | William A. Carr (D) | 8,709 | 19.1 |
| 7 | Thomas S. Butler (R) | 26,145 | 77.5 |
| | Archibald M. Holding (D) | 6,470 | 19.2 |
| 8 | Irving P. Wanger (R) | 26,099 | 60.9 |
| | Joseph J. Broadhurst (D) | 15,847 | 37.0 |
| 9 | Henry B. Cassel (R) | 17,685 | 54.7 |
| | Milton J. Brecht (CI/IC) | 11,526 | 35.6 |
| | Hugh M. North Jr (D) | 2,894 | 8.9 |
| 10 | Thomas H. Dale (R) | 15,003 | 53.2 |
| | George Howell (D) | 12,683 | 44.9 |
| 11 | Henry W. Palmer (R) | 23,324 | 60.8 |
| | William L. Raeder (D) | 14,224 | 37.1 |
| 12 | George R. Patterson (R) | 17,419 | 57.4 |
| | Harry O. Haag (D) | 12,005 | 39.6 |
| 13 | Marcus C. L. Kline (D) | 25,711 | 50.1 |
| | William H. Sowden (R) | 23,781 | 46.4 |
| 14 | Mial E. Lilly (R) | 15,568 | 58.4 |
| | John Kuhbach (D) | 8,696 | 32.6 |
| | William S. H. Heermans (P) | 2,393 | 9.0 |
| 15 | Elias Deemer (R) | 19,807 | 58.3 |
| | George B. McMetzger (D) | 11,959 | 35.2 |
| 16 | E. W. Samuel (R) | 14,969 | 51.6 |
| | Henry E. Davis (D) | 13,191 | 45.5 |
| 17 | Thaddeus M. Mahon (R) | 22,860 | 61.4 |
| | O. C. Bowers (D) | 13,337 | 35.8 |
| 18 | Marlin E. Olmsted (R) | 26,996 | 67.6 |
| | John L. Saylor (D) | 11,663 | 29.2 |
| 19 | John M. Reynolds (R) | 23,164 | 54.9 |
| | Joseph E. Thropp (D, P) | 19,066 | 45.1 |
| 20 | Daniel F. Lafean (R) | 19,088 | 55.8 |
| | William McSherry (D) | 14,782 | 43.2 |
| 21 | Solomon R. Dresser (R) | 18,281 | 59.6 |
| | Charles W. Shaffer (D) | 9,559 | 31.2 |
| | Samuel C. Watts (P) | 2,407 | 7.9 |
| 22 | George F. Huff (R) | 21,547 | 65.5 |
| | Charles M. Heineman (D) | 9,824 | 29.9 |
| 23 | Allen F. Cooper (R) | 18,206 | 58.7 |
| | Charles F. Uhl Jr. (D) | 10,597 | 34.2 |
| | George H. Hocking (P) | 2,226 | 7.2 |
| 24 | Ernest F. Acheson (R) | 23,131 | 69.4 |
| | William J. Mellon (D) | 8,420 | 25.3 |
| | John J. Ashenhurst (P) | 1,798 | 5.4 |
| 25 | Arthur L. Bates (R) | 17,271 | 61.9 |
| | E. W. McArthur (D) | 8,082 | 28.9 |
| | R. C. Loupe (P) | 1,644 | 5.9 |
| 26 | G. A. Schneebeli (R) | 14,763 | 45.3 |
| | J. Davis Brodhead (D, CIT) | 12,895 | 39.6 |

| Candidates | Votes | % |
|---|---|---|
| Joseph H. Shull (PURE POL) | 3,759 | 11.5 |
| 27 William O. Smith (R) | 18,697 | 71.8 |
| A. C. Smith (D) | 7,353 | 28.2 |
| 28 Joseph C. Sibley (R) | 19,861 | 55.2 |
| Salem Heilman (D) | 10,651 | 29.6 |
| John E. Gill (P) | 4,640 | 12.9 |
| 29 William H. Graham (R) | 18,400 | 80.1 |
| W. H. S. Thomson (D) | 3,437 | 15.0 |
| 30 John Dalzell (R) | 17,322 | 79.0 |
| M. L. Thompson (D) | 3,330 | 15.2 |
| 31 James Francis Burke (R) | 18,403 | 75.2 |
| John F. McGrath (D) | 5,289 | 21.6 |
| 32 A. J. Barchfeld (R) | 19,383 | 75.9 |
| John Pierce (D) | 4,690 | 18.4 |

## RHODE ISLAND

| | Candidates | Votes | % |
|---|---|---|---|
| 1 | Daniel L. D. Granger (D) | 15,583 | 49.5 |
| | Stiness (R) | 15,450 | 49.0 |
| 2 | Adin B. Capron (R) | 18,212 | 56.8 |
| | Owen (D) | 13,278 | 41.4 |

## SOUTH CAROLINA

| | Candidates | Votes | % |
|---|---|---|---|
| 1 | George S. Legare (D) | 6,068 | 91.3 |
| | J. A. Noland (R) | 346 | 5.2 |
| 2 | James O'H. Patterson (D) | 7,421 | 94.6 |
| | Isaac Myers (R) | 423 | 5.4 |
| 3 | Wyatt Aiken (D) | 7,659 | 98.1 |
| 4 | Joseph T. Johnson (D) | 8,516 | 97.5 |
| 5 | David E. Finley (D) | 7,928 | 97.9 |
| 6 | J. Edwin Ellerbe (D) | 8,348 | 95.7 |
| 7 | Asbury F. Lever (D) | 8,726 | 93.8 |
| | Charles C. Jocobs (R) | 563 | 6.1 |

## SOUTH DAKOTA

| | Candidates | Votes | % |
|---|---|---|---|
| AL | Eben W. Martin (R) | 70,002✔ | |
| | Charles H. Burke (R) | 69,936✔ | |
| | Wesley A. Stuart (D) | 22,692 | |
| | W. A. Lynch (D) | 22,640 | |
| | H. W. Smith (SOC) | 3,115 | |
| | S. A. Cochrane (SOC) | 3,064 | |
| | A. Jamison (P) | 3,012 | |
| | C. K. Thompson (P) | 2,961 | |
| | A. J. McCain (POP) | 1,216 | |
| | G. W. Lattin (POP) | 1,175 | |

## TENNESSEE

| | Candidates | Votes | % |
|---|---|---|---|
| 1 | Walter P. Brownlow (R) | 19,657 | 68.9 |
| | R. E. Styll (D) | 8,879 | 31.1 |
| 2 | Nathan W. Hale (R) | 14,963 | 70.9 |
| | Staples (D) | 6,013 | 28.5 |
| 3 | John A. Moon (D) | 16,541 | 53.2 |
| | Sharp (R) | 14,285 | 46.0 |
| 4 | Mounce G. Butler (D) | 13,359 | 53.3 |
| | Pickering (R) | 11,596 | 46.2 |
| 5 | William C. Houston (D) | 13,581 | 68.7 |
| | Brown (R) | 6,192 | 31.3 |
| 6 | John W. Gaines (D) | 13,777 | 79.0 |
| | Maxwell (R) | 3,517 | 20.2 |
| 7 | Lemuel P. Padgett (D) | 13,090 | 61.9 |
| | Hughes (R) | 8,027 | 38.0 |
| 8 | Thetus W. Sims (D) | 13,395 | 53.9 |
| | Davis (R) | 11,452 | 46.1 |
| 9 | Finis J. Garrett (D) | 16,222 | 74.9 |
| | Walker (R) | 5,443 | 25.1 |
| 10 | Malcolm R. Patterson (D) | 13,595 | 75.9 |
| | Matthews (R) | 4,307 | 24.1 |

## TEXAS

| | Candidates | Votes | % |
|---|---|---|---|
| 1 | Morris Sheppard (D) | 12,473 | 72.1 |
| | J. A. Armistead (R) | 4,838 | 28.0 |
| 2 | Moses L. Broocks (D) | 13,119 | 76.2 |
| | A. J. Houston (R) | 4,099 | 23.8 |

| | Candidates | Votes | % |
|---|---|---|---|
| 3 | Gordon J. Russell (D) | 12,473 | 73.7 |
| | C. T. White (R) | 4,441 | 26.3 |
| 4 | Choice B. Randell (D) | 14,435 | 90.4 |
| | R. E. Martin (R) | 1,537 | 9.6 |
| 5 | Jack Beall (D) | 14,292 | 86.0 |
| | J. J. Cypert (R) | 2,327 | 14.0 |
| 6 | Scott Field (D) | 9,438 | 100.0 |
| 7 | Alexander W. Gregg (D) | 8,040 | 100.0 |
| 8 | John M. Pinckney (D) | 9,804 | 69.1 |
| | H. F. McGregor (R) | 4,384 | 30.9 |
| 9 | George F. Burgess (D) | 14,316 | 72.3 |
| | B. L. Osgood (R) | 5,484 | 27.7 |
| 10 | Albert S. Burleson (D) | 11,761 | 100.0 |
| 11 | Robert L. Henry (D) | 10,305 | 84.4 |
| | Joe E. Williams (R) | 1,912 | 15.7 |
| 12 | Oscar W. Gillespie (D) | 12,480 | 74.4 |
| | Frank B. Stanley | 2,357 | 14.1 |
| | J. M. Mallett (R) | 1,933 | 11.5 |
| 13 | John H. Stephens (D) | 18,604 | 89.6 |
| | James M. Kindred (R) | 2,157 | 10.4 |
| 14 | James L. Slayden (D) | 15,097 | 98.3 |
| 15 | John N. Garner (D) | 10,647 | 64.9 |
| | J. S. Morin (D) | 5,767 | 35.1 |
| 16 | William R. Smith (D) | 17,488 | 83.1 |
| | Logan McPherson (R) | 3,562 | 16.9 |

## UTAH

| | Candidates | Votes | % |
|---|---|---|---|
| AL | Joseph Howell (R) | 52,675 | 51.8 |
| | Orlando W. Powers (D) | 37,445 | 36.8 |
| | Ogden Hiles (AM) | 6,796 | 6.7 |

## VERMONT

| | Candidates | Votes | % |
|---|---|---|---|
| 1 | David J. Foster (R) | 23,208 | 70.4 |
| | Frank L. Graves (D) | 8,868 | 26.9 |
| 2 | Kittredge Haskins (R) | 23,781 | 74.8 |
| | Harland B. Howe (D) | 7,066 | 22.2 |

## VIRGINIA

| | Candidates | Votes | % |
|---|---|---|---|
| 1 | William A. Jones (D) | 7,826 | 77.1 |
| | Trader (R) | 2,331 | 23.0 |
| 2 | Harry L. Maynard (D) | 10,762 | 78.3 |
| | Robert M. Hughes (R) | 2,800 | 20.4 |
| 3 | John Lamb (D) | 7,121 | 78.0 |
| | Edgar Allan Jr. (R) | 1,020 | 11.2 |
| | George A. Harrison (IR) | 773 | 8.5 |
| 4 | Robert G. Southall (D) | 6,031 | 82.8 |
| | Charles Alexander (R) | 1,248 | 17.1 |
| 5 | Claude A. Swanson (D) | 8,893 | 65.0 |
| | J. B. Stovall (R) | 4,793 | 35.0 |
| 6 | Carter Glass (D) | 7,798 | 69.1 |
| | Samuel H. Hoge (R) | 3,429 | 30.4 |
| 7 | James Hay (D) | 9,051 | 64.7 |
| | Charles M. Kelzel (R) | 4,949 | 35.4 |
| 8 | John F. Rixey (D) | 7,986 | 76.6 |
| | Ernest Linoln Howard (R) | 2,443 | 23.4 |
| 9 | Campbell Slemp (R) | 15,627 | 57.2 |
| | J. C. Wysor (D) | 11,710 | 42.8 |
| 10 | Henry D. Flood (D) | 9,183 | 61.3 |
| | George A. Revercomb (R) | 5,460 | 36.5 |

## WASHINGTON

| | Candidates | Votes | % |
|---|---|---|---|
| AL | Francis W. Cushman (R) | 93,328✔ | |
| | Wesley L. Jones (R) | 92,743✔ | |
| | William E. Humphrey (R) | 92,436✔ | |
| | James J. Anderson (D) | 35,698 | |
| | Howard Hathaway (D) | 35,636 | |
| | W. T. Beck (D) | 35,193 | |
| | T. C. Wiswell (SOC) | 9,005 | |
| | George Croston (SOC) | 8,940 | |
| | H. D. Jory (SOC) | 8,940 | |
| | Ferdinand B. Hawes (P) | 3,059 | |
| | Henry Brown (P) | 3,052 | |
| | William Bonstein (SOC LAB) | 1,320 | |
| | R. McDonald (SOC LAB) | 1,308 | |
| | G. Norling (SOC LAB) | 1,306 | |

## WEST VIRGINIA

| | Candidates | Votes | % |
|---|---|---|---|
| 1 | Blackburn B. Dovener (R) | 27,459 | 54.3 |
| | J. W. Barnes (D) | 21,100 | 41.7 |
| 2 | Alston G. Dayton (R) | 24,225 | 51.6 |
| | Stuart W. Walker (D) | 21,888 | 46.6 |
| 3 | Joseph Holt Gaines (R) | 26,236 | 52.8 |
| | H. B. Davenport (D) | 22,125 | 44.5 |
| 4 | Harry C. Woodyard (D) | 22,942 | 53.6 |
| | Allen C. Murdock (R) | 18,912 | 44.2 |
| 5 | James A. Hughes (R) | 27,593 | 55.8 |
| | S. S. Altezer (D) | 21,276 | 43.0 |

## WISCONSIN

| | Candidates | Votes | % |
|---|---|---|---|
| 1 | Henry Allen Cooper (R) | 25,125 | 59.5 |
| | Calvin Stewart (D) | 13,379 | 31.7 |
| | J. W. Born (SOCIAL D) | 2,461 | 5.8 |
| 2 | Henry C. Adams (R) | 22,773 | 57.7 |
| | John J. Wood (D) | 15,265 | 38.7 |
| 3 | Joseph W. Babcock (R) | 19,047 | 48.8 |
| | Herman Grotophorst (D) | 18,662 | 47.8 |
| 4 | Theobald Otjen (R) | 17,582 | 43.8 |
| | Peter J. Sommers (D) | 12,385 | 30.8 |
| | W. R. Gaylord (SOCIAL D) | 9,625 | 24.0 |
| 5 | William H. Stafford (R) | 17,231 | 44.8 |
| | Victor L. Berger (SOCIAL D) | 10,626 | 27.6 |
| | Arthur Dopp (D) | 9,978 | 26.0 |
| 6 | Charles H. Weisse (D) | 20,665 | 53.4 |
| | Roy L. Morse (R) | 17,687 | 45.7 |
| 7 | John J. Esch (R) | 25,505 | 66.8 |
| | N. C. Basheller (D) | 11,271 | 29.5 |

| | Candidates | Votes | % |
|---|---|---|---|
| 8 | James H. Davidson (R) | 25,233 | 63.1 |
| | C. F. Crane (D) | 12,889 | 32.2 |
| 9 | Edward S. Minor (R) | 19,764 | 58.1 |
| | R. J. McGrehan (D) | 13,124 | 38.6 |
| 10 | Webster E. Brown (R) | 29,392 | 65.4 |
| | Wells M. Ruggles (D) | 14,121 | 31.4 |
| 11 | John J. Jenkins (R) | 31,270 | 74.8 |
| | George C. Cooper (D) | 8,637 | 20.7 |

## WYOMING

| | Candidates | Votes | % |
|---|---|---|---|
| AL | Frank W. Mondell (R) | 19,862 | 64.6 |
| | T. S. Taliaferro Jr (D) | 9,903 | 32.2 |

# 1905 House Election

### ILLINOIS

#### Special Election

| | | Votes | % |
|---|---|---|---|
| 14 | James McKinney (R) | 12,356 | 57.2 |
| | James Howard Pattee | 7,316 | 33.9 |
| | Homer L. Darby | 1,176 | 5.4 |

---

## House Candidates Index

For an index of all House candidates listed in this section (pages 943-1326), see pages 1402-1501. Instructions for use of the House Candidates Index appear on page 1402.

---

# 1906 House Elections

## ALABAMA

| | Candidates | Votes | % |
|---|---|---|---|
| 1 | George W. Taylor (D) | 3,592 | 100.0 |
| 2 | Ariosto A. Wiley (D) | 6,001 | 88.9 |
| | J. C. Fonville (R) | 751 | 11.1 |
| 3 | Henry D. Clayton (D) | 6,922 | 100.0 |
| 4 | William B. Craig (D) | 5,783 | 100.0 |
| 5 | J. Thomas Heflin (D) | 6,940 | 100.0 |
| 6 | Richmond P. Hobson (D) | 8,308 | 100.0 |
| 7 | John L. Burnett (D) | 8,265 | 62.7 |
| | C. B. Kennamer (R) | 4,914 | 37.3 |
| 8 | William Richardson (D) | 5,873 | 94.9 |
| | John T. Masterson (R) | 317 | 5.1 |
| 9 | Oscar W. Underwood (D) | 7,864 | 100.0 |

## ARKANSAS

| | Candidates | Votes | % |
|---|---|---|---|
| 1 | Robert B. Macon (D) | 5,635 | 82.2 |
| | D. F. Taylor (R) | 1,223 | 17.8 |
| 2 | Stephen Brundidge Jr (D) | 5,137 | 80.9 |
| | E. J. Mason (R) | 1,216 | 19.1 |
| 3 | John C. Floyd (D) | 5,715 | 63.8 |
| | W. N. Ivie (R) | 3,246 | 36.2 |
| 4 | William Ben Cravens (D) | 7,290 | 65.5 |
| | George Tilles (R) | 3,840 | 34.5 |
| 5 | Charles C. Reid (D) | 5,967 | 75.1 |
| | Alonzo Hedges (R) | 1,976 | 24.9 |
| 6 | Joseph T. Robinson (D) | 5,473 | 84.4 |
| | R. C. Thompson (R) | 1,010 | 15.6 |
| 7 | Robert M. Wallace (D) | 3,255 | 99.1 |

## CALIFORNIA

| | Candidates | Votes | % |
|---|---|---|---|
| 1 | William F. Englebright (R) | 18,954 | 54.1 |
| | F. W. Taft (D) | 13,984 | 39.9 |
| 2 | Duncan E. McKinlay (R) | 23,411 | 51.8 |
| | W. A. Beard (D) | 20,262 | 44.8 |
| 3 | Joseph R. Knowland (R) | 21,510 | 60.0 |
| | Hugh W. Brunk (D) | 7,716 | 21.5 |
| | Charles C. Boynton (I LEAGUE) | 3,614 | 10.1 |
| | William McDevitt (SOC) | 2,514 | 7.0 |
| 4 | Julius Kahn (R) | 5,678 | 62.4 |
| | David S. Hirshberg (D) | 3,016 | 33.2 |
| 5 | Everis A. Hayes (R) | 22,530 | 52.6 |
| | Hiram G. Davis (D) | 17,925 | 41.9 |
| | Joseph Lawrence (SOC) | 2,343 | 5.5 |
| 6 | James C. Needham (R) | 18,928 | 55.6 |
| | Harry A. Greene (D) | 12,868 | 37.8 |
| 7 | James McLachlan (R) | 22,338 | 56.7 |
| | Robert G. Laucks (D) | 11,197 | 28.4 |
| | Claude Riddle (SOC) | 3,641 | 9.3 |
| | Levi D. Johnson (P) | 2,189 | 5.6 |
| 8 | Sylvester C. Smith (R) | 22,548 | 55.6 |
| | C. A. Barlow (D) | 13,992 | 34.5 |
| | N. A. Richardson (SOC) | 4,001 | 9.9 |

### Special Election

| | Candidates | Votes | % |
|---|---|---|---|
| 1 | William F. Englebright (R) | 18,125 | 95.2 |

## COLORADO

| | Candidates | Votes | % |
|---|---|---|---|
| 1 | Robert William Bonynge (R) | 47,549 | 55.5 |
| | Charles F. Tew (D) | 31,133 | 36.3 |
| | Luella Twining (SOC) | 4,989 | 5.8 |
| 2 | Warren A. Haggott (R) | 54,869 | 49.3 |
| | William W. Rowan (D) | 46,783 | 42.1 |
| | Flavius E. Ashburn (SOC) | 7,666 | 6.9 |
| AL | George W. Cook (R) | 102,426 | 52.2 |
| | Samuel W. Belford (D) | 76,792 | 39.1 |
| | Guy E. Miller (SOC) | 12,668 | 6.5 |

## CONNECTICUT

| | Candidates | Votes | % |
|---|---|---|---|
| 1 | E. Stevens Henry (R) | 21,605 | 56.8 |
| | Holden (D) | 15,039 | 39.6 |
| 2 | Nehemiah D. Sperry (R) | 29,058 | 53.1 |
| | Wallace (D) | 23,757 | 43.4 |
| 3 | Edwin W. Higgins (R) | 12,391 | 57.3 |
| | Larue (D) | 8,833 | 40.8 |
| 4 | Ebenezer J. Hill (R) | 26,484 | 56.9 |
| | Beers (D) | 18,969 | 40.8 |
| AL | George L. Lilley (R) | 88,115 | 54.8 |
| | Donahue (D) | 67,747 | 42.1 |

## DELAWARE

| | Candidates | Votes | % |
|---|---|---|---|
| AL | Hiram R. Burton (R) | 20,210 | 52.8 |
| | David T. Marvel (D) | 17,118 | 44.8 |

## FLORIDA

| | Candidates | Votes | % |
|---|---|---|---|
| 1 | Stephen M. Sparkman (D) | 6,212 | 86.5 |
| | C. C. Allen (SOC) | 967 | 13.5 |
| 2 | Frank Clark (D) | 8,792 | 88.1 |
| | J. F. McClelland (SOC) | 1,179 | 11.8 |
| 3 | William B. Lamar (D) | 5,415 | 93.4 |
| | T. B. Meeker (SOC) | 384 | 6.6 |

## GEORGIA

| | Candidates | Votes | % |
|---|---|---|---|
| 1 | Charles G. Edwards (D) | 4,964 | 92.1 |
| | D. B. Rigdon (R) | 429 | 8.0 |
| 2 | James M. Griggs (D) | 3,425 | 100.0 |
| 3 | Elijah B. Lewis (D) | 2,386 | 100.0 |
| 4 | William C. Adamson (D) | 2,705 | 100.0 |
| 5 | Leonidas F. Livingston (D) | 3,030 | 100.0 |
| 6 | Charles L. Bartlett (D) | 3,374 | 100.0 |
| 7 | Gordon Lee (D) | 3,132 | 100.0 |
| 8 | William M. Howard (D) | 2,246 | 100.0 |
| 9 | Thomas M. Bell (D) | 3,159 | 100.0 |
| 10 | Thomas W. Hardwick (D) | 1,743 | 99.8 |
| 11 | William G. Brantley (D) | 2,748 | 100.0 |

## IDAHO

| | Candidates | Votes | % |
|---|---|---|---|
| AL | Burton L. French (R) | 42,134 | 58.6 |
| | Murray R. Hattabaugh (D) | 23,818 | 33.1 |
| | Edward L. Rigg (SOC) | 4,834 | 6.7 |

## ILLINOIS

| | Candidates | Votes | % |
|---|---|---|---|
| 1 | Martin B. Madden (R) | 17,015 | 59.3 |
| | Martin Emerich (D) | 10,015 | 34.9 |
| 2 | James R. Mann (R) | 20,660 | 63.4 |
| | Herbert J. Friedman (D) | 8,565 | 26.3 |
| | Bernard Berlyn (SOC) | 3,032 | 9.3 |
| 3 | William W. Wilson (R) | 14,130 | 49.7 |
| | Paul A. Dratz (D) | 6,569 | 23.1 |
| | Willis C. Stone (I LG) | 4,775 | 16.8 |
| | James A. Prout (SOC) | 2,457 | 8.6 |
| 4 | James T. McDermott (D) | 9,997 | 46.7 |
| | Charles S. Wharton (R) | 8,377 | 39.1 |
| | James McCarthy (SOC) | 2,859 | 13.3 |
| 5 | Adolph J. Sabath (D) | 9,545 | 46.1 |
| | Anthony Michalek (R) | 8,634 | 41.7 |
| | Joseph Kral (SOC) | 2,373 | 11.5 |
| 6 | William Lorimer (R) | 18,153 | 55.4 |
| | Edmund J. Stack (D) | 10,734 | 32.8 |
| | Walter F. Huggins (SOC) | 2,082 | 6.4 |
| | Edward E. Blake (P) | 1,794 | 5.5 |
| 7 | Philip Knopf (R) | 18,595 | 51.3 |
| | Frank Buchanan (D) | 11,383 | 31.4 |
| | George Koop (SOC) | 5,587 | 15.4 |

| | Candidates | Votes | % |
|---|---|---|---|
| 8 | Charles McGavin (R) | 11,421 | 40.0 |
| | Stanley H. Kunz (D) | 11,336 | 39.7 |
| | Abraham Priess (I LG) | 3,128 | 11.0 |
| | James B. Smiley (SOC) | 2,664 | 9.3 |
| 9 | Henry S. Boutell (R) | 15,316 | 50.6 |
| | Arthur J. Donoghue (D) | 8,504 | 28.1 |
| | John M. Vail (I LG) | 3,607 | 11.9 |
| | Charles L. Breckon (SOC) | 2,592 | 8.6 |
| 10 | George Edmund Foss (R) | 18,886 | 62.7 |
| | Charles L. Young (D) | 7,598 | 25.2 |
| | Lewis W. Hardy (SOC) | 2,777 | 9.2 |
| 11 | Howard M. Snapp (R) | 18,569 | 60.7 |
| | Benjamin P. Alschuler (D) | 9,104 | 29.8 |
| | George McGinnis (P) | 2,201 | 7.2 |
| 12 | Charles E. Fuller (R) | 19,463 | 86.9 |
| | Victor Irving Clark (P) | 1,712 | 7.6 |
| | A. A. Patterson (SOC) | 1,224 | 5.5 |
| 13 | Frank O. Lowden (R) | 16,590 | 51.2 |
| | James P. Wilson (D) | 14,747 | 45.5 |
| 14 | James McKinney (R) | 18,583 | 54.7 |
| | David W. Matthews (D) | 12,978 | 38.2 |
| 15 | George W. Prince (R) | 19,975 | 54.2 |
| | Hiram N. Wheeler (D) | 14,191 | 38.5 |
| 16 | Joseph V. Graff (R) | 16,983 | 50.3 |
| | Louis F. Meek (D) | 13,876 | 41.1 |
| | C. E. Stebbins (P) | 1,966 | 5.8 |
| 17 | John A. Sterling (R) | 16,804 | 55.8 |
| | L. W. MacNeil (D) | 11,377 | 37.8 |
| | James H. Burrows (P) | 1,927 | 6.4 |
| 18 | Joseph G. Cannon (R) | 22,804 | 58.4 |
| | Charles G. Taylor (D) | 12,777 | 32.7 |
| 19 | William B. McKinley (R) | 23,662 | 52.7 |
| | John W. Yantis (D) | 19,247 | 42.9 |
| 20 | Henry T. Rainey (D) | 19,578 | 54.9 |
| | Jacob G. Pope (R) | 14,645 | 41.1 |
| 21 | Benjamin F. Caldwell (D) | 22,429 | 53.5 |
| | Zeno J. Rives (R) | 17,396 | 41.5 |
| 22 | William A. Rodenberg (R) | 23,138 | 56.6 |
| | James J. McInerney (D) | 15,371 | 37.3 |
| 23 | Martin D. Foster (D) | 21,680 | 49.5 |
| | Frank S. Dickson (R) | 20,361 | 46.5 |
| 24 | Pleasant T. Chapman (R) | 17,990 | 51.1 |
| | James R. Williams (D) | 16,241 | 46.2 |
| 25 | George W. Smith (R) | 17,835 | 52.6 |
| | James M. Joplin (D) | 14,240 | 42.0 |

### Special Election

| | Candidates | Votes | % |
|---|---|---|---|
| 13 | Frank O. Lowden (R) | 17,003 | 96.9 |

## INDIANA

| | Candidates | Votes | % |
|---|---|---|---|
| 1 | John H. Foster (R) | 20,278 | 50.0 |
| | Gustavus V. Menzies (D) | 18,959 | 46.7 |
| 2 | John C. Chaney (R) | 22,299 | 48.7 |
| | Cyrus E. Davis (D) | 21,889 | 47.8 |
| 3 | William E. Cox (D) | 18,606 | 49.3 |
| | George H. Hester (R) | 18,151 | 48.1 |
| 4 | Lincoln Dixon (D) | 20,049 | 51.0 |
| | John H. Kamman (R) | 18,181 | 46.2 |
| 5 | Elias S. Holliday (R) | 22,532 | 48.8 |
| | Claud G. Bowers (D) | 21,579 | 46.8 |
| 6 | James E. Watson (R) | 22,135 | 49.5 |
| | Thomas H. Kuhn (D) | 20,629 | 46.2 |
| 7 | Jesse Overstreet (R) | 28,020 | 52.8 |
| | Frank E. Gavin (D) | 23,234 | 43.8 |
| 8 | John A. M. Adair (D) | 24,027 | 51.4 |
| | George W. Cromer (R) | 19,783 | 42.3 |
| 9 | Charles B. Landis (R) | 23,865 | 49.5 |
| | Marion E. Clodfelter (D) | 21,633 | 44.9 |
| 10 | Edgar D. Crumpacker (R) | 24,695 | 54.0 |
| | William Darroch (D) | 20,072 | 43.9 |
| 11 | George W. Rauch (D) | 22,988 | 50.2 |
| | Frederick Landis (R) | 19,833 | 43.3 |
| | Levi T. Pennington (P) | 2,367 | 5.2 |

## INDIANA

| | Candidates | Votes | % |
|---|---|---|---|
| 12 | Clarence C. Gilhams (R) | 19,695 | 48.6 |
| | John W. Morr (D) | 19,345 | 47.7 |
| 13 | Abraham L. Brick (R) | 23,360 | 48.0 |
| | Benjamin F. Shively (D) | 23,153 | 47.5 |

**Special Election**

| | | | |
|---|---|---|---|
| 12 | Clarence C. Gilhams (R) | 19,249 | 50.5 |
| | John W. Morr (D) | 18,870 | 49.5 |

## IOWA

| | Candidate | Votes | % |
|---|---|---|---|
| 1 | Charles A. Kennedy (R) | 16,145 | 49.1 |
| | George S. Tracy (D) | 15,875 | 48.3 |
| 2 | Albert F. Dawson (R) | 20,112 | 50.2 |
| | George W. Ball (D) | 18,520 | 46.2 |
| 3 | Benjamin P. Birdsall (R) | 22,315 | 57.7 |
| | J. C. Murtagh (D) | 15,113 | 39.0 |
| 4 | Gilbert N. Haugen (R) | 20,731 | 60.6 |
| | M. J. Carter (D) | 12,739 | 37.2 |
| 5 | Robert G. Cousins (R) | 19,076 | 54.3 |
| | Robert C. Stinton (D) | 14,612 | 41.6 |
| 6 | Daniel W. Hamilton (D) | 18,987 | 51.8 |
| | John F. Lacey (R) | 16,713 | 45.6 |
| 7 | John A. T. Hull (R) | 19,617 | 59.2 |
| | John Nathan Smith (D) | 11,464 | 34.6 |
| 8 | William Peter Hepburn (R) | 19,516 | 53.0 |
| | Joel S. Estes (D) | 16,074 | 43.7 |
| 9 | Walter I. Smith (R) | 21,863 | 60.7 |
| | William C. Campbell (D) | 13,250 | 36.8 |
| 10 | James Perry Conner (R) | 26,017 | 60.9 |
| | John B. Butler (D) | 15,317 | 35.9 |
| 11 | Elbert H. Hubbard (R) | 22,236 | 55.9 |
| | Charles A. Dickson (D) | 16,893 | 42.5 |

## KANSAS

| | Candidate | Votes | % |
|---|---|---|---|
| 1 | Charles Curtis (R) | 22,790* | 57.5 |
| | W. D. Webb (D) | 16,215 | 40.9 |
| 2 | Charles F. Scott (R) | 23,521 | 53.1 |
| | Mason S. Peters (D) | 19,653 | 44.4 |
| 3 | Philip P. Campbell (R) | 25,669 | 52.5 |
| | Francis M. Brady (D) | 19,807 | 40.5 |
| | Fred D. Warren (SOC) | 2,908 | 5.9 |
| 4 | James Monroe Miller (R) | 17,393 | 53.5 |
| | J. W. Moore (D) | 14,313 | 44.0 |
| 5 | William A. Calderhead (R) | 18,183 | 54.1 |
| | Hugh Alexander (D) | 14,561 | 43.3 |
| 6 | William A. Reeder (R) | 21,212 | 51.9 |
| | John B. Rea (D) | 17,116 | 41.9 |
| 7 | Edmond H. Madison (R) | 21,580 | 55.0 |
| | O. H. Truman (D) | 15,623 | 39.8 |
| 8 | Victor Murdock (R) | 14,862 | 56.5 |
| | F. B. Lawrance (D) | 10,427 | 39.6 |

## KENTUCKY

| | Candidate | Votes | % |
|---|---|---|---|
| 1 | Ollie M. James (D) | 12,870 | 85.9 |
| | J. D. Smith (P) | 2,118 | 14.1 |
| 2 | Augustus O. Stanley (D) | 13,282 | 61.9 |
| | Paul M. Moore (R) | 7,406 | 34.5 |
| 3 | Addison D. James (R) | 14,987 | 50.2 |
| | James M. Richardson (D) | 14,288 | 47.8 |
| 4 | Ben Johnson (D) | 15,128 | 59.1 |
| | M. L. Heavrin (R) | 9,819 | 38.4 |
| 5 | J. Swagar Sherley (D) | 15,698 | 54.8 |
| | William C. Owens (R) | 12,210 | 42.6 |
| 6 | Joseph L. Rhinock (D) | 13,358 | 48.3 |
| | William F. Schuerman (R) | 12,973 | 46.9 |
| 7 | William P. Kimball (D) | 15,658 | 74.0 |
| | Joseph W. Calvert (R) | 5,066 | 23.9 |
| 8 | Harvey Helm (D) | 13,182 | 55.1 |
| | L. W. Bethurum (R) | 10,164 | 42.4 |
| 9 | Joseph B. Bennett (R) | 18,430 | 51.4 |
| | James N. Kehoe (D) | 17,314 | 48.2 |
| 10 | John W. Langley (R) | 17,254 | 50.7 |
| | Frank A. Hopkins (D) | 16,343 | 48.0 |
| 11 | Don C. Edwards (R) | 15,645 | 61.9 |
| | Ancil Gatliff (D) | 8,714 | 34.5 |

## LOUISIANA

| | Candidates | Votes | % |
|---|---|---|---|
| 1 | Adolph Meyer (D) | 8,667 | 90.0 |
| | Henry Seiner (R) | 681 | 7.1 |
| 2 | Robert C. Davey (D) | 6,349 | 91.9 |
| | A. L. Redden (R) | 409 | 5.9 |
| 3 | Robert F. Broussard (D) | 4,267 | 85.0 |
| | S. P. Watts (R) | 753 | 15.0 |
| 4 | John T. Watkins (D) | 3,210 | 97.3 |
| 5 | Joseph E. Ransdell (D) | 3,177 | 100.0 |
| 6 | George K. Favrot (D) | 3,270 | 92.4 |
| | John Deblieux (R) | 269 | 7.6 |
| 7 | Arsene P. Pujo (D) | 3,761 | 66.1 |
| | C. C. Duson (R) | 1,762 | 31.0 |

## MAINE

| | Candidate | Votes | % |
|---|---|---|---|
| 1 | Amos L. Allen (R) | 16,903 | 51.9 |
| | James C. Hamlen (D) | 15,254 | 46.8 |
| 2 | Charles E. Littlefield (R) | 18,708 | 50.9 |
| | Daniel J. McGillicuddy (D) | 17,346 | 47.2 |
| 3 | Edwin C. Burleigh (R) | 16,682 | 51.7 |
| | E. J. Lawrence (D) | 14,891 | 46.2 |
| 4 | Llewellyn Powers (R) | 17,279 | 54.9 |
| | George M. Hanson (D) | 13,705 | 43.6 |

## MARYLAND

| | Candidate | Votes | % |
|---|---|---|---|
| 1 | William H. Jackson (R) | 18,567 | 51.5 |
| | Thomas A. Smith (D) | 16,124 | 44.8 |
| 2 | J. Fred C. Talbott (D) | 17,870 | 50.3 |
| | Robert Garrett (R) | 16,618 | 46.7 |
| 3 | Harry B. Wolf (D) | 15,725 | 49.8 |
| | William W. Johnson (R) | 14,841 | 47.0 |
| 4 | John Gill Jr. (D) | 18,010 | 50.7 |
| | John V. L. Findlay Jr. (R) | 16,306 | 45.9 |
| 5 | Sydney E. Mudd (R) | 16,798 | 53.7 |
| | George M. Smith (D) | 13,405 | 42.8 |
| 6 | George A. Pearre (R) | 16,136 | 55.3 |
| | Harvey R. Spessard (D) | 11,232 | 38.5 |

## MASSACHUSETTS

| | Candidate | Votes | % |
|---|---|---|---|
| 1 | George P. Lawrence (R) | 15,622 | 59.7 |
| | Frank J. Lawler (D) | 9,528 | 36.4 |
| 2 | Frederick H. Gillett (R) | 15,873 | 61.3 |
| | Edward A. Hall (D) | 8,412 | 32.5 |
| | George H. Wrenn (SOC) | 1,622 | 6.3 |
| 3 | Charles G. Washburn (R) | 15,686 | 58.6 |
| | William I. McLoughlin (D) | 10,415 | 38.9 |
| 4 | Charles Q. Tirrell (R) | 20,750 | 79.0 |
| | Timothy Richardson (SOC) | 5,501 | 20.9 |
| 5 | Butler Ames (R) | 15,778 | 54.2 |
| | Joseph J. Flynn (D) | 12,881 | 44.2 |
| 6 | Augustus P. Gardner (R) | 18,390 | 54.8 |
| | George A. Schofield (D) | 14,055 | 41.9 |
| 7 | Ernest W. Roberts (R) | 21,752 | 66.4 |
| | John A. O'Keefe (D) | 9,816 | 30.0 |
| 8 | Samuel W. McCall (R) | 17,952 | 59.4 |
| | Frederick S. Deitrick (D) | 11,690 | 38.7 |
| 9 | John A. Keliher (D) | 15,997 | 68.1 |
| | Edward C. Webb (R) | 6,256 | 26.6 |
| | George W. Galvin (SOC) | 1,242 | 5.3 |
| 10 | Joseph F. O'Connell (D) | 18,979 | 54.9 |
| | Edward B. Callender (R) | 14,621 | 42.3 |
| 11 | Andrew J. Peters (D) | 18,099 | 53.9 |
| | Daniel W. Lane (R) | 14,670 | 43.7 |
| 12 | John W. Weeks (R) | 18,948 | 61.5 |
| | David W. Murray (D) | 10,591 | 34.4 |
| 13 | William S. Greene (R) | 14,236 | 68.3 |
| | Francis M. Kennedy (D) | 6,603 | 31.7 |
| 14 | William C. Lovering (R) | 18,002 | 61.8 |
| | Thomas F. Loorem (D) | 6,815 | 23.4 |
| | Daniel A. White (SOC) | 4,301 | 14.8 |

## MICHIGAN

| | Candidates | Votes | % |
|---|---|---|---|
| 1 | Edwin Denby (R) | 23,741 | 57.5 |
| | Frederick F. Ingram (D) | 16,975 | 41.1 |
| 2 | Charles E. Townsend (R) | 23,397 | 96.2 |
| 3 | Washington Gardner (R) | 16,821 | 58.4 |
| | John B. Shipman (D) | 10,388 | 36.1 |
| 4 | Edward L. Hamilton (R) | 18,553 | 60.6 |
| | George R. Herkimer (D) | 11,561 | 37.8 |
| 5 | William Alden Smith (R) | 18,487* | 88.9 |
| | John E. Nicles (SOC) | 1,302 | 6.3 |
| 6 | Samuel W. Smith (R) | 24,001 | 60.4 |
| | Peter B. Delisle (D) | 14,360 | 36.1 |
| 7 | Henry McMorran (R) | 17,100 | 59.6 |
| | William Springer (D) | 11,028 | 38.4 |
| 8 | Joseph W. Fordney (R) | 16,849 | 92.4 |
| 9 | James C. McLaughlin (R) | 14,374 | 69.8 |
| | Charles G. Wing (D) | 5,288 | 25.7 |
| 10 | George A. Loud (R) | 18,958 | 97.2 |
| 11 | Archibald B. Darragh (R) | 18,110 | 70.7 |
| | Arthur J. Lacy (D) | 7,517 | 29.3 |
| 12 | H. Olin Young (R) | 22,271 | 75.6 |
| | John F. Ryan (D) | 6,315 | 21.4 |

## MINNESOTA

| | Candidate | Votes | % |
|---|---|---|---|
| 1 | James A. Tawney (R) | 17,352 | 57.8 |
| | French (D) | 12,676 | 42.2 |
| 2 | Winfield S. Hammond (D) | 13,526 | 50.5 |
| | McCleary (R) | 12,466 | 46.5 |
| 3 | Charles R. Davis (R) | 19,461 | 100.0 |
| 4 | Frederick C. Stevens (R) | 19,300 | 64.3 |
| | Scholle (D) | 9,179 | 30.6 |
| | Lando (PUB OWN) | 1,544 | 5.1 |
| 5 | Frank M. Nye (R) | 23,742 | 55.6 |
| | Larrabee (D) | 16,448 | 38.5 |
| 6 | Charles A. Lindbergh (R) | 16,752 | 56.1 |
| | Tift (D) | 13,115 | 43.9 |
| 7 | Andrew G. Volstead (R) | 21,491 | 100.0 |
| 8 | J. Adam Bede (R) | 18,640 | 75.6 |
| | Peterson (PUB OWN) | 6,025 | 24.4 |
| 9 | Halvor Steenerson (R) | 22,145 | 80.1 |
| | Boen (PUB OWN) | 5,490 | 19.9 |

## MISSISSIPPI

| | Candidate | Votes | % |
|---|---|---|---|
| 1 | Ezekiel S. Candler Jr. (D) | 2,566 | 100.0 |
| 2 | Thomas Spight (D) | 2,567 | 100.0 |
| 3 | Benjamin G. Humphreys (D) | 1,540 | 100.0 |
| 4 | Wilson S. Hill (D) | 2,536 | 100.0 |
| 5 | Adam Byrd (D) | 2,782 | 100.0 |
| 6 | F. A. McLain (D) | 1,933 | 100.0 |
| 7 | Eaton J. Bowers (D) | 4,077 | 95.9 |
| 8 | John S. Williams (D) | 2,091 | 100.0 |

## MISSOURI

| | Candidate | Votes | % |
|---|---|---|---|
| 1 | James T. Lloyd (D) | 19,796 | 54.3 |
| | Clements (R) | 16,655 | 45.7 |
| 2 | William W. Rucker (D) | 20,732 | 56.7 |
| | Beazell (R) | 15,814 | 43.2 |
| 3 | Joshua W. Alexander (D) | 18,669 | 52.9 |
| | Unidentified Candidate (R) | 16,616 | 47.1 |
| 4 | Charles F. Booher (D) | 18,631 | 51.3 |
| | Fulkerson (R) | 17,458 | 48.1 |
| 5 | Edgar C. Ellis (R) | 21,496 | 52.2 |
| | Wallace (D) | 19,710 | 47.8 |
| 6 | David A. De Armond (D) | 17,574 | 53.0 |
| | Atkeson (R) | 15,579 | 47.0 |
| 7 | Courtney W. Hamlin (D) | 22,248 | 51.3 |
| | Welborn (R) | 20,497 | 47.3 |
| 8 | Dorsey W. Shackleford (D) | 16,245 | 53.4 |
| | Quigley (R) | 14,186 | 46.6 |
| 9 | James Beauchamp Clark (D) | 21,364 | 54.3 |
| | Garber (R) | 17,972 | 45.7 |
| 10 | Richard Bartholdt (R) | 31,639 | 61.9 |
| | Coale (D) | 16,336 | 32.0 |
| | Hoehn (SOC) | 3,102 | 6.1 |

## MISSOURI

| | Candidates | Votes | % |
|---|---|---|---|
| 11 | Henry S. Caulfield (R) | 13,171 | 47.8 |
| | Neville (D) | 13,133 | 47.6 |
| 12 | Harry M. Coudrey (R) | 11,281 | 50.1 |
| | Selph (D) | 10,451 | 46.4 |
| 13 | Madison R. Smith (D) | 16,056 | 50.7 |
| | Rhodes (R) | 15,628 | 49.3 |
| 14 | Joseph J. Russell (D) | 24,288 | 51.4 |
| | Tyndall (R) | 22,799 | 48.3 |
| 15 | Thomas Hackney (D) | 20,677 | 48.3 |
| | Caulkins (R) | 20,402 | 47.6 |
| 16 | J. Robert Lamar (D) | 15,366 | 50.7 |
| | Murphy (R) | 14,939 | 49.3 |

## MONTANA

| | Candidates | Votes | % |
|---|---|---|---|
| AL | Charles N. Pray (R&A-T R) | 28,368 | 50.5 |
| | Thomas J. Walsh (D & LAB) | 22,894 | 40.8 |
| | John Hudson (SOC) | 4,638 | 8.3 |

## NEBRASKA

| | Candidates | Votes | % |
|---|---|---|---|
| 1 | Ernest M. Pollard (R) | 14,771 | 52.8 |
| | T. J. Doyle (D & PPI) | 11,870 | 42.4 |
| 2 | Gilbert M. Hitchcock (D) | 11,644 | 51.0 |
| | John L. Kennedy (R) | 11,136 | 48.8 |
| 3 | John F. Boyd (R) | 18,837 | 49.0 |
| | Guy T. Graves (D & PPI) | 18,546 | 48.2 |
| 4 | Edmund H. Hinshaw (R) | 19,032 | 55.0 |
| | J. J. Thomas (D & PPI) | 15,211 | 44.0 |
| 5 | George W. Norris (R) | 16,450 | 53.1 |
| | Roderick D. Sutherland (D & PPI) | 14,031 | 45.3 |
| 6 | Moses P. Kinkaid (R) | 18,677 | 57.1 |
| | G. L. Shumway (D & PPI) | 13,147 | 40.2 |

## NEVADA

| | Candidates | Votes | % |
|---|---|---|---|
| AL | George A. Bartlett (D&SILVER) | 7,320 | 51.4 |
| | Oscar J. Smith (R) | 5,665 | 39.8 |
| | H. T. Jardine (SOC) | 1,251 | 8.8 |

## NEW HAMPSHIRE

| | Candidates | Votes | % |
|---|---|---|---|
| 1 | Cyrus A. Sulloway (R) | 22,701 | 57.8 |
| | Charles A. Morse (D) | 15,601 | 39.7 |
| 2 | Frank D. Currier (R) | 23,073 | 58.0 |
| | Henri T. Ledoux (D) | 15,669 | 39.4 |

## NEW JERSEY

| | Candidates | Votes | % |
|---|---|---|---|
| 1 | Henry C. Loudenslager (R) | 20,674 | 65.8 |
| | Summerill (D) | 9,308 | 29.6 |
| 2 | John J. Gardner (R) | 19,637 | 63.0 |
| | Perry (D) | 8,921 | 28.6 |
| 3 | Benjamin F. Howell (R) | 20,472 | 54.3 |
| | Harvey (D) | 16,638 | 44.1 |
| 4 | Ira W. Wood (R) | 17,497 | 52.9 |
| | Southwick (D) | 13,989 | 42.3 |
| 5 | Charles N. Fowler (R) | 19,760 | 48.8 |
| | Martine (D & ID) | 19,208 | 47.5 |
| 6 | William Hughes (D) | 25,438 | 50.2 |
| | Burke (R) | 23,335 | 46.1 |
| 7 | Richard W. Parker (R) | 16,493 | 49.5 |
| | Kaemer (D) | 15,983 | 48.0 |
| 8 | Le Gage Pratt (D) | 18,334 | 56.9 |
| | Gottlob (R) | 12,460 | 38.7 |
| 9 | Eugene W. Leake (D) | 18,367 | 55.4 |
| | Pickett (R) | 12,628 | 38.1 |
| 10 | James A. Hamill (D) | 22,882 | 65.2 |
| | Cruse (R) | 9,305 | 26.5 |

## NEW YORK

| | Candidates | Votes | % |
|---|---|---|---|
| 1 | William W. Cocks (R) | 22,569 | 60.3 |
| | Monson Morris (D) | 14,418 | 38.5 |
| 2 | George H. Lindsay (D) | 11,420 | 39.2 |
| | John J. McManus (I LEAGUE) | 9,069 | 31.2 |
| | Ernest C. Wagner (R) | 7,591 | 26.1 |
| 3 | Charles T. Dunwell (R) | 16,546 | 45.5 |
| | Walter B. Raymond (D) | 10,707 | 29.5 |
| | Henry Clay Peters (I LEAGUE) | 8,089 | 22.3 |
| 4 | Charles B. Law (R) | 17,079 | 41.3 |
| | Herman H. Torborg (D) | 12,114 | 29.3 |
| | Edson Lawrence (I LEAGUE) | 10,590 | 25.6 |
| 5 | George E. Waldo (R) | 19,832 | 46.1 |
| | John J. Roach (D) | 11,995 | 27.9 |
| | Michael A. Fitzgerald (I LEAGUE) | 10,575 | 24.6 |
| 6 | William M. Calder (R) | 21,195 | 54.9 |
| | Robert Baker (D & IL) | 17,102 | 44.3 |
| 7 | John J. Fitzgerald (D) | 15,055 | 47.1 |
| | Charles R. Banks (R) | 8,433 | 26.4 |
| | John T. Moran (I LEAGUE) | 8,220 | 25.7 |
| 8 | Daniel J. Riordan (D) | 21,340 | 65.6 |
| | Frank L. Frugone (R) | 10,632 | 32.7 |
| 9 | Henry M. Goldfogle (D) | 7,276 | 53.3 |
| | Morris Hillquit (SOC) | 3,586 | 26.3 |
| | Charles S. Adler (R) | 2,734 | 20.0 |
| 10 | William Sulzer (D & IL) | 15,962 | 71.3 |
| | Frederick J. Etzel (R) | 4,843 | 21.6 |
| | Alexander Jonas (SOC) | 1,560 | 7.0 |
| 11 | Charles V. Fornes (D & IL) | 26,511 | 70.3 |
| | Charles W. Lefler (R) | 10,640 | 28.2 |
| 12 | William Bourke Cockran (D & IL) | 20,481 | 71.4 |
| | Henry Carey (R) | 7,410 | 25.8 |
| 13 | Herbert Parsons (R) | 16,381 | 55.0 |
| | William H. Jackson (D) | 9,881 | 33.2 |
| | Frank Hendrick (I LEAGUE) | 3,172 | 10.7 |
| 14 | William Willett Jr. (D) | 17,675 | 46.3 |
| | Frank E. Losee (R) | 10,006 | 26.2 |
| | Charles E. Shober (I LEAGUE) | 8,110 | 21.3 |
| | Richard Morton (SOC) | 2,328 | 6.1 |
| 15 | Jacob Van Vechten Olcott (R) | 16,210 | 54.8 |
| | John J. Halligan (D & IL) | 13,123 | 44.4 |
| 16 | Francis Burton Harrison (D & IL) | 16,954 | 66.3 |
| | Jacob R. Schiff (R) | 7,062 | 27.6 |
| 17 | William S. Bennet (R) | 27,159 | 53.1 |
| | Francis E. Shober (D & IL) | 23,284 | 45.5 |
| 18 | Joseph A. Goulden (D) | 28,339 | 46.9 |
| | James L. Wells (R) | 17,943 | 29.7 |
| | James T. Farrelly (I LEAGUE) | 12,109 | 20.1 |
| 19 | John E. Andrus (R) | 23,356 | 53.8 |
| | Timothy Healy (D) | 19,218 | 44.3 |
| 20 | Thomas W. Bradley (R) | 21,191 | 55.9 |
| | Victor A. Wilder (D, I LEAGUE) | 16,111 | 42.5 |
| 21 | Samuel McMillan (R) | 20,717 | 51.0 |
| | Percy W. Decker (D, I LEAGUE) | 19,745 | 48.6 |
| 22 | William H. Draper (R) | 22,344 | 55.3 |
| | Thomas A. Paterson (D, I LEAGUE) | 17,188 | 42.5 |
| 23 | George N. Southwick (R) | 29,099 | 50.7 |
| | George C. Hisgen (D, I LEAGUE) | 27,344 | 47.7 |
| 24 | George W. Fairchild (R) | 24,474 | 51.3 |
| | Walter Scott (D, I LEAGUE) | 23,215 | 48.7 |
| 25 | Cyrus Durey (R) | 25,041 | 55.4 |
| | Frank Beebe (D) | 18,385 | 40.7 |
| 26 | George R. Malby (R) | 26,209 | 70.2 |
| | Andrew B. Cooney (D) | 10,931 | 29.3 |
| 27 | James S. Sherman (R) | 24,027 | 53.3 |
| | James K. O'Connor (D, U LAB) | 19,757 | 43.8 |
| 28 | Charles L. Knapp (R) | 23,451 | 60.7 |
| | Jay C. Bardo (D) | 12,573 | 32.5 |
| | Frank H. Lewis (P) | 2,197 | 5.7 |
| 29 | Michael E. Driscoll (R) | 30,350 | 61.4 |
| | William W. Vanbrocklin (D) | 17,385 | 35.2 |
| 30 | John W. Dwight (R) | 27,069 | 59.9 |
| | Amasa G. Genung (D) | 16,269 | 36.0 |
| 31 | Sereno E. Payne (R) | 25,475 | 62.6 |
| | Dudley M. Warner (D) | 14,150 | 34.8 |
| 32 | James Breck Perkins (R) | 25,343 | 52.4 |
| | William L. Manning (D) | 21,393 | 44.2 |
| 33 | Jacob Sloat Fassett (R) | 21,235 | 55.0 |
| | Frank P. Frost (D) | 15,883 | 41.1 |
| 34 | Peter A. Porter (D, IND CONG) | 25,837 | 55.6 |
| | James W. Wadsworth (R) | 19,935 | 42.9 |
| 35 | William H. Ryan (D) | 22,140 | 56.5 |
| | Frank X. Bernhardt (R) | 16,494 | 42.1 |
| 36 | De Alva S. Alexander (R) | 24,457 | 58.0 |
| | John W. Williams (D) | 16,209 | 38.5 |
| 37 | Edward B. Vreeland (R) | 25,468 | 65.2 |
| | Mark Graves (D) | 11,562 | 29.6 |

## NORTH CAROLINA

| | Candidates | Votes | % |
|---|---|---|---|
| 1 | John H. Small (D) | 11,401 | 75.8 |
| | J. Q. A. Wood (R) | 3,610 | 24.0 |
| 2 | Claude Kitchin (D) | 10,057 | 84.6 |
| | J. R. Gaskill (R) | 1,816 | 15.3 |
| 3 | Charles R. Thomas (D) | 10,382 | 66.3 |
| | W. R. Dixon (R) | 5,280 | 33.7 |
| 4 | Edward W. Pou (D) | 12,161 | 69.8 |
| | Berry Godwin (R) | 5,270 | 30.2 |
| 5 | William W. Kitchin (D) | 16,503 | 59.6 |
| | C. A. Reynolds (R) | 11,089 | 40.0 |
| 6 | Hannibal L. Godwin (D) | 9,729 | 67.7 |
| | James B. Schulken (R) | 4,645 | 32.3 |
| 7 | Robert N. Page (D) | 11,780 | 56.7 |
| | G. D. B. Reynolds (R) | 9,008 | 43.3 |
| 8 | Richard N. Hackett (D) | 16,907 | 51.6 |
| | E. S. Blackburn (R) | 15,841 | 48.4 |
| 9 | Edwin Y. Webb (D) | 12,727 | 58.6 |
| | F. Roberts (R) | 8,988 | 41.4 |
| 10 | William T. Crawford (D) | 13,049 | 51.6 |
| | James J. Britt (R) | 12,200 | 48.2 |

## NORTH DAKOTA

| | Candidates | Votes | % |
|---|---|---|---|
| AL | Thomas F. Marshall (R) | 38,923✔ | |
| | Asle J. Gronna (R) | 36,772✔ | |
| | A. G. Burr (D) | 21,350 | |
| | John D. Benton (D) | 21,050 | |
| | H. Halvorson (SOC) | 1,151 | |
| | W. J. Bailey (SOC) | 1,129 | |

## OHIO

| | Candidates | Votes | % |
|---|---|---|---|
| 1 | Nicholas Longworth (R) | 25,161 | 56.9 |
| | Thomas H. Bentham (D) | 18,004 | 40.7 |
| 2 | Herman P. Goebel (R) | 23,219 | 59.1 |
| | John H. Meyer (D) | 12,258 | 31.2 |
| | Harry R. Probasco (I) | 2,259 | 5.8 |
| 3 | J. Eugene Harding (R) | 24,567 | 49.5 |
| | James E. Campbell (D) | 22,837 | 46.0 |
| 4 | William E. Tou Velle (D) | 17,582 | 55.6 |
| | J. C. Rosser (R) | 12,934 | 40.9 |
| 5 | Timothy T. Ansberry (D) | 17,256 | 50.7 |
| | William W. Campbell (R) | 16,241 | 47.7 |
| 6 | Matthew R. Denver (D) | 17,471 | 50.6 |
| | Charles Q. Hildebrant (R) | 16,291 | 47.2 |
| 7 | J. Warren Keifer (R) | 15,975 | 53.8 |
| | William B. Rodgers (D) | 12,387 | 41.8 |
| 8 | Ralph D. Cole (R) | 21,524 | 54.9 |
| | Homer Southard (D) | 16,396 | 41.9 |
| 9 | Isaac R. Sherwood (D, I) | 18,411 | 47.8 |
| | E. G. McClelland (R) | 18,370 | 47.7 |
| 10 | Henry Bannon (R) | 17,979 | 53.3 |
| | Thomas H. B. Jones (D) | 14,686 | 43.5 |
| 11 | Albert Douglas (R) | 21,247 | 50.4 |
| | Oliver W. H. Wright (D) | 19,914 | 47.2 |
| 12 | Edward L. Taylor Jr. (R) | 19,629 | 56.9 |
| | William A. Taylor (D) | 13,351 | 38.7 |
| 13 | Grant E. Mouser (R) | 20,736 | 49.2 |
| | Daniel R. Crissinger (D) | 20,463 | 48.5 |

## OHIO

| | Candidates | Votes | % |
|---|---|---|---|
| 14 | J. Ford Laning (R) | 20,962 | 51.7 |
| | William H. Budd (D) | 18,443 | 45.5 |
| 15 | Beman G. Dawes (R) | 18,364 | 49.6 |
| | George White (D) | 16,945 | 45.8 |
| 16 | Capell L. Weems (R) | 14,712 | 53.9 |
| | Frank A. Summers (D) | 11,347 | 41.6 |
| 17 | William A. Ashbrook (D) | 19,982 | 49.3 |
| | Martin L. Suyser (R) | 19,497 | 48.1 |
| 18 | James Kennedy (R) | 19,684 | 49.5 |
| | John C. Welty (D) | 17,840 | 44.9 |
| 19 | W. Aubrey Thomas (R) | 20,341 | 61.3 |
| | Thaddeus E. Hoyt (D) | 10,926 | 32.9 |
| 20 | Paul Howland (R) | 19,439 | 51.8 |
| | Charles W. Lapp (D) | 16,966 | 45.3 |
| 21 | Theodore E. Burton (R) | 20,826 | 92.9 |
| | Robert Bandlow (SOC) | 1,376 | 6.1 |

## OREGON

| | Candidates | Votes | % |
|---|---|---|---|
| 1 | Willis C. Hawley (R) | 23,120 | 49.1 |
| | Charles V. Galloway (D) | 19,340 | 41.1 |
| | W. W. Myers (SOC) | 2,794 | 5.9 |
| 2 | William R. Ellis (R) | 28,315 | 61.0 |
| | James Harvey Graham (D) | 12,151 | 26.2 |
| | A. M. Paul (SOC) | 3,532 | 7.6 |
| | H. W. Stone (P) | 2,408 | 5.2 |

## PENNSYLVANIA

| | Candidates | Votes | % |
|---|---|---|---|
| 1 | Henry H. Bingham (R, JEFF) | 24,280 | 63.7 |
| | E. Spencer Miller (LINCOLN) | 8,718 | 22.9 |
| | Joseph L. Galen (D) | 4,738 | 12.4 |
| 2 | John E. Reyburn (R, LINCOLN) | 28,140 | 85.7 |
| | G. Frank Stephens (D) | 4,262 | 13.0 |
| 3 | J. Hampton Moore (R, JEFF) | 20,337 | 63.6 |
| | William J. O'Brien (LINCOLN, D) | 11,240 | 35.1 |
| 4 | Reuben O. Moon (R, LINCOLN) | 26,289 | 85.6 |
| | Horace S. Fogel (D) | 3,993 | 13.0 |
| 5 | William W. Foulkrod (R, LINCOLN) | 29,390 | 86.1 |
| | Thomas P. Dolan (D) | 3,987 | 11.7 |
| 6 | George D. McCreary (R, LINCOLN) | 38,269 | 84.6 |
| | Francis X. Ward (D) | 6,425 | 14.2 |
| 7 | Thomas S. Butler (R, BC) | 19,676 | 70.0 |
| | John J. Buckley (D, P) | 8,249 | 29.3 |
| 8 | Irving P. Wanger (R, CP) | 22,416 | 54.6 |
| | Walter F. Leedom (D, LINCOLN) | 18,231 | 44.4 |
| 9 | Henry B. Cassel (R) | 18,903 | 67.7 |
| | J. Harold Wickersham (LINCOLN) | 9,007 | 32.3 |
| 10 | T. D. Nichols (D) | 18,037 | 60.3 |
| | Thomas H. Dale (R, LINCOLN) | 11,796 | 39.4 |
| 11 | John T. Lenahan (D) | 16,176 | 50.6 |
| | Bennett J. Cobleigh (RO SOC D) | 9,627 | 30.1 |
| | William H. Dettry (SOC) | 5,197 | 16.3 |
| 12 | Charles N. Brumm (R) | 15,652 | 58.5 |
| | Watson F. Shepperd (D) | 10,247 | 38.3 |
| 13 | John H. Rothermel (D) | 21,885 | 54.2 |
| | J. Wilmer Fisher (R) | 16,488 | 40.8 |
| | Morris E. Gibson (SOC) | 2,044 | 5.1 |
| 14 | George W. Kipp (D) | 12,091 | 49.2 |
| | Mial E. Lilly (R) | 11,288 | 46.0 |
| 15 | William B. Wilson (D) | 14,582 | 48.2 |
| | Elias Deemer (R) | 14,201 | 47.0 |
| 16 | John G. McHenry (D) | 14,707 | 53.8 |
| | Edmund W. Samuel (R, P) | 12,131 | 44.4 |
| 17 | Benjamin K. Focht (R) | 17,130 | 52.2 |
| | William Alexander (D) | 14,036 | 42.8 |
| 18 | Marlin E. Olmsted (R) | 22,447 | 58.9 |
| | John Lindner (D) | 14,457 | 37.9 |

| | Candidates | Votes | % |
|---|---|---|---|
| 19 | John M. Reynolds (R) | 17,521 | 50.6 |
| | Joseph E. Thropp (D, LINCOLN) | 13,649 | 39.4 |
| | Warren W. Bailey (BRYAN) | 2,140 | 6.2 |
| 20 | Daniel F. Lafean (R) | 15,653 | 50.7 |
| | Horace Keesey (D) | 15,204 | 49.3 |
| 21 | Charles F. Barclay (R, P) | 15,210 | 57.5 |
| | Hugh S. Taylor (D) | 10,572 | 40.0 |
| 22 | George F. Huff (R) | 15,924 | 59.0 |
| | Silas A. Kline (D, LINCOLN) | 10,490 | 38.9 |
| 23 | Allen F. Cooper (R) | 15,008 | 54.7 |
| | Ernest O. Kooser (D, LINCOLN) | 10,309 | 37.6 |
| | John O. Stoner (P) | 1,789 | 6.5 |
| 24 | Ernest F. Acheson (R) | 15,490 | 49.2 |
| | Robert K. Aiken (D, LINCOLN) | 14,163 | 45.0 |
| 25 | Arthur L. Bates (R) | 13,564 | 60.6 |
| | Andrew J. Palm (D, P) | 8,109 | 36.2 |
| 26 | J. Davis Brodhead (D, LINCOLN) | 15,371 | 54.3 |
| | Gustav A. Schneebeli (R) | 12,427 | 43.9 |
| 27 | Joseph G. Beale (R) | 14,646 | 58.3 |
| | S. C. Hepler (D) | 9,101 | 36.2 |
| | Enoch McGary (P) | 1,392 | 5.5 |
| 28 | Nelson P. Wheeler (R) | 16,550 | 52.7 |
| | Earl H. Beshlin (D) | 10,433 | 33.2 |
| | H. E. Horne (P) | 3,750 | 11.9 |
| 29 | William H. Graham (R, CIT) | 17,688 | 91.8 |
| 30 | John Dalzell (R, CIT) | 13,984 | 65.1 |
| | Robert J. Black (D, UN LAB) | 6,452 | 30.0 |
| 31 | James Francis Burke (R, CIT) | 13,364 | 67.5 |
| | Frank Lackner (D) | 5,740 | 29.0 |
| 32 | A. J. Barchfeld (R) | 14,525 | 68.1 |
| | M. C. O'Donovan (D) | 4,811 | 22.6 |

## RHODE ISLAND

| | Candidates | Votes | % |
|---|---|---|---|
| 1 | Daniel L. D. Granger (D) | 16,846 | 50.4 |
| | Dyer (R) | 16,030 | 48.0 |
| 2 | Adin B. Capron (R) | 16,979 | 53.0 |
| | Garvin (D) | 14,593 | 45.5 |

## SOUTH CAROLINA

| | Candidates | Votes | % |
|---|---|---|---|
| 1 | George S. Legare (D) | 3,965 | 99.3 |
| 2 | James O'H. Patterson (D) | 4,588 | 95.3 |
| 3 | Wyatt Aiken (D) | 2,938 | 100.0 |
| 4 | Joseph T. Johnson (D) | 5,124 | 98.7 |
| 5 | David E. Finley (D) | 3,585 | 100.0 |
| 6 | J. Edwin Ellerbe (D) | 3,483 | 100.0 |
| 7 | Asbury F. Lever (D) | 5,191 | 97.5 |

## SOUTH DAKOTA

| | Candidates | Votes | % |
|---|---|---|---|
| AL | Philo Hall (R) | 48,096✓ | |
| | William H. Parker (R) | 48,010✓ | |
| | William S. Elder (D) | 19,976 | |
| | Samuel A. Ramsey (D) | 19,791 | |
| | C. V. Templeton (P) | 3,392 | |
| | R. J. Day (P) | 3,313 | |
| | James Kirwan (SOC) | 2,439 | |
| | Henry A. Berge (SOC) | 2,322 | |

## TENNESSEE

| | Candidates | Votes | % |
|---|---|---|---|
| 1 | Walter P. Brownlow (R) | 17,249 | 52.1 |
| | John H. Coldwell (D) | 9,145 | 27.6 |
| | A. A. Taylor (IR) | 6,700 | 20.2 |
| 2 | Nathan W. Hale (R) | 13,817 | 71.5 |
| | E. L. Foster (D) | 5,125 | 26.5 |
| 3 | John A. Moon (D) | 15,388 | 56.9 |
| | T. W. Peace (R) | 11,409 | 42.2 |
| 4 | Cordell Hull (D) | 11,951 | 53.6 |
| | John E. Oliver (R) | 10,312 | 46.3 |
| 5 | William C. Houston (D) | 11,450 | 71.5 |
| | T. W. Wade (R) | 4,446 | 27.8 |

| | Candidates | Votes | % |
|---|---|---|---|
| 6 | John W. Gaines (D) | 12,546 | 79.8 |
| | J. W. Johnson (R) | 2,981 | 19.0 |
| 7 | Lemuel P. Padgett (D) | 12,750 | 68.7 |
| | Joe P. Kidd (R) | 5,818 | 31.3 |
| 8 | Thetus W. Sims (D) | 11,209 | 50.7 |
| | J. C. R. McCall (R) | 10,874 | 49.2 |
| 9 | Finis J. Garrett (D) | 11,538 | 76.9 |
| | Yandell Hann (R) | 3,437 | 22.9 |
| 10 | George W. Gordon (D) | 10,378 | 95.4 |

## TEXAS

| | Candidates | Votes | % |
|---|---|---|---|
| 1 | Morris Sheppard (D) | 9,479 | 90.6 |
| | Phil E. Baer (R) | 886 | 8.5 |
| 2 | Samuel B. Cooper (D) | 9,593 | 93.0 |
| | J. H. Kurth (R) | 622 | 6.0 |
| 3 | Gordon J. Russell (D) | 8,522 | 89.3 |
| | G. W. L. Smith (R) | 753 | 7.9 |
| 4 | Choice B. Randell (D) | 11,508 | 87.3 |
| | W. G. McGinnis (R) | 1,678 | 12.7 |
| 5 | Jack Beall (D) | 9,060 | 91.9 |
| | A. M. Cochran (R) | 525 | 5.3 |
| 6 | Rufus Hardy (D) | 5,536 | 92.1 |
| 7 | Alexander W. Gregg (D) | 6,590 | 100.0 |
| 8 | John M. Moore (D) | 8,536 | 84.3 |
| | W. A. Matthai (R) | 1,593 | 15.7 |
| 9 | George F. Burgess (D) | 10,257 | 75.6 |
| | A. M. Waugh (R) | 3,043 | 22.4 |
| 10 | Albert S. Burleson (D) | 8,103 | 88.6 |
| | Carl Beck (R) | 1,041 | 11.4 |
| 11 | Robert L. Henry (D) | 7,183 | 100.0 |
| 12 | Oscar W. Gillespie (D) | 9,790 | 95.6 |
| 13 | John H. Stephens (D) | 14,120 | 90.0 |
| | E. E. Diggs (R) | 1,295 | 8.3 |
| 14 | James L. Slayden (D) | 10,811 | 80.1 |
| | D. Doole (R) | 2,692 | 19.9 |
| 15 | John N. Garner (D) | 9,284 | 63.7 |
| | T. W. Moore (R) | 5,281 | 36.3 |
| 16 | William R. Smith (D) | 13,030 | 92.0 |
| | Ben Vantuys (R) | 744 | 5.3 |

## UTAH

| | Candidates | Votes | % |
|---|---|---|---|
| AL | Joseph Howell (R) | 42,620 | 50.1 |
| | Orlando W. Powers (D) | 28,031 | 33.0 |
| | Thomas Weir (AM) | 11,411 | 13.4 |

## VERMONT

| | Candidates | Votes | % |
|---|---|---|---|
| 1 | David J. Foster (R) | 20,660 | 69.0 |
| | Edwin B. Clift (D) | 8,957 | 29.9 |
| 2 | Kittredge Haskins (R) | 20,738 | 70.1 |
| | John H. Fenter (D) | 8,157 | 27.6 |

## VIRGINIA

| | Candidates | Votes | % |
|---|---|---|---|
| 1 | William A. Jones (D) | 5,773 | 81.7 |
| | Bristow (R) | 1,294 | 18.3 |
| 2 | Harry L. Maynard (D) | 4,358 | 74.5 |
| | Hughes (R) | 1,489 | 25.5 |
| 3 | John Lamb (D) | 3,908 | 82.2 |
| | Hanson (R) | 639 | 13.4 |
| 4 | Francis R. Lassiter (D) | 2,615 | 100.0 |
| 5 | Edward W. Saunders (D) | 6,194 | 50.9 |
| | Simmons (R) | 5,972 | 49.1 |
| 6 | Carter Glass (D) | 4,060 | 74.8 |
| | Heermans (R) | 1,336 | 24.6 |
| 7 | James Hay (D) | 5,573 | 70.1 |
| | Beecher (R) | 2,372 | 29.9 |
| 8 | John F. Rixey (D) | 5,059* | 84.0 |
| | Henderson (R) | 962 | 16.0 |
| 9 | Campbell Slemp (R) | 13,798 | 54.0 |
| | Bruce (D) | 11,757 | 46.0 |
| 10 | Henry D. Flood (D) | 5,962 | 68.9 |
| | Gregory (R) | 2,696 | 31.1 |

## WASHINGTON

| | Candidates | Votes | % |
|---|---|---|---|
| AL | Francis W. Cushman (R) | 71,921✓ | |
| | Wesley L. Jones (R) | 71,656✓ | |

## WASHINGTON

| Candidates | Votes | % |
|---|---|---|
| William E. Humphrey (R) | 71,353✔ | |
| William Blackman (D) | 31,811 | |
| Patrick S. Byrne (D) | 30,689 | |
| Dudley Eshleman (D) | 30,369 | |
| Emil Herman (SOC) | 8,431 | |
| J. H. Barkley (SOC) | 8,420 | |
| A. Wagenknecht (SOC) | 8,367 | |
| J. M. Wilkin (P) | 2,584 | |
| A. S. Caton (P) | 2,582 | |
| William Everett (P) | 2,571 | |

## WEST VIRGINIA

| | Candidates | Votes | % |
|---|---|---|---|
| 1 | William P. Hubbard (R) | 19,362 | 52.5 |
| | T. S. Riley (D) | 15,315 | 41.5 |
| 2 | George C. Sturgiss (R) | 20,384 | 53.7 |
| | M. H. Dent (D) | 16,712 | 44.0 |
| 3 | Joseph Holt Gaines (R) | 19,888 | 52.8 |
| | George Byrne (D) | 15,482 | 41.1 |

| | Candidates | Votes | % |
|---|---|---|---|
| 4 | Harry C. Woodyard (R) | 16,310 | 52.3 |
| | George W. Hardman (D) | 13,637 | 43.8 |
| 5 | James A. Hughes (R) | 22,395 | 57.4 |
| | Joseph S. Miller (D) | 15,971 | 40.9 |

## WISCONSIN

| | Candidates | Votes | % |
|---|---|---|---|
| 1 | Henry Allen Cooper (R) | 16,226 | 61.1 |
| | John J. Cunningham (D) | 8,818 | 33.2 |
| | Moses Hull (SOCIAL D) | 1,504 | 5.7 |
| 2 | John M. Nelson (R) | 14,806 | 51.5 |
| | George W. Levis (D) | 12,881 | 44.8 |
| 3 | James W. Murphy (D) | 14,701 | 50.1 |
| | Joseph W. Babcock (R) | 13,690 | 46.6 |
| 4 | William J. Cary (R) | 12,231 | 41.3 |
| | Edmund T. Melms (SOCIAL D) | 8,759 | 29.6 |
| | Thomas J. Fleming (D) | 8,656 | 29.2 |
| 5 | William H. Stafford (R) | 13,948 | 44.3 |
| | Albert J. Welch (SOCIAL D) | 8,870 | 28.1 |
| | Joseph G. Donnelly (D) | 8,192 | 26.0 |

| | Candidates | Votes | % |
|---|---|---|---|
| 6 | Charles H. Weisse (D) | 19,446 | 63.3 |
| | Alvin Dreger (R) | 10,512 | 34.2 |
| 7 | John J. Esch (R) | 18,042 | 72.7 |
| | Charles F. Hulle (D) | 6,779 | 27.3 |
| 8 | James H. Davidson (R) | 16,966 | 59.7 |
| | John E. McMuller (D) | 9,594 | 33.8 |
| 9 | Gustav Kustermann (R) | 14,180 | 60.5 |
| | Phillip A. Badour (D) | 8,689 | 37.1 |
| 10 | Elmer A. Morse (R) | 20,225 | 63.6 |
| | Dennis D. Conway (D) | 10,669 | 33.5 |
| 11 | John J. Jenkins (R) | 19,002 | 74.9 |
| | Francis J. Maguire (D) | 5,147 | 20.3 |

### Special Election

| | | Votes | % |
|---|---|---|---|
| 2 | John M. Nelson (R) | 10,098 | 71.2 |
| | Grant Thomas (PRI R) | 3,703 | 26.1 |

## WYOMING

| | | Votes | % |
|---|---|---|---|
| AL | Frank W. Mondell (R) | 16,813 | 62.2 |
| | John C. Hamm (D) | 8,944 | 33.1 |

# 1907 House Elections

## MICHIGAN

### Special Election

| | Candidates | Votes | % |
|---|---|---|---|
| 5 | Gerrit John Diekema (R) | 11,898 | 51.8 |
| | George P. Hummer (D) | 10,508 | 45.7 |

## OKLAHOMA

(Became a state Nov. 16, 1907)

| | | Votes | % |
|---|---|---|---|
| 1 | Bird S. McGuire (R) | 22,362 | 50.3 |
| | William L. Eagleton (D) | 21,003 | 47.3 |
| 2 | Elmer L. Fulton (D) | 26,006 | 51.0 |
| | Thompson B. Ferguson (R) | 25,028 | 49.0 |
| 3 | James S. Davenport (D) | 26,370 | 52.8 |
| | Henry D. Hubbard (R) | 23,623 | 47.3 |
| 4 | Charles D. Carter (D) | 29,782 | 62.6 |
| | Frank C. Disney (R) | 15,752 | 33.1 |
| 5 | Scott Ferris (D) | 32,935 | 66.2 |
| | Loren G. McKnight (R) | 14,883 | 29.9 |

# 1908 House Elections

## ALABAMA

| | Candidates | Votes | % |
|---|---|---|---|
| 1 | George W. Taylor (D) | 7,457 | 100.0 |
| 2 | S. Hubert Dent Jr. (D) | 10,754 | 100.0 |
| 3 | Henry D. Clayton (D) | 9,993 | 100.0 |
| 4 | William B. Craig (D) | 6,239 | 65.1 |
| | J. Osmond Middleton (R) | 3,341 | 34.9 |
| 5 | J. Thomas Heflin (D) | 8,024 | 83.9 |
| | W. W. Wadsworth | 1,543 | 16.1 |
| 6 | Richmond P. Hobson (D) | 9,211 | 78.0 |
| | Henry T. Nations | 2,593 | 22.0 |
| 7 | John L. Burnett (D) | 8,972 | 56.0 |
| | N. H. Freeman (R) | 7,046 | 44.0 |
| 8 | William Richardson (D) | 9,691 | 82.7 |
| | Jeremiah Murphy (R) | 2,028 | 17.3 |
| 9 | Oscar W. Underwood (D) | 11,288 | 79.4 |
| | J. B. Sloan | 2,567 | 18.1 |

### Special Election

| | Candidates | Votes | % |
|---|---|---|---|
| 2 | Oliver C. Wiley (D) | 7,710 | 100.0 |

## ARKANSAS

| | Candidates | Votes | % |
|---|---|---|---|
| 1 | Robert B. Macon (D) | 12,957 | 66.5 |
| | C. T. Bloodworth (R) | 6,534 | 33.5 |
| 2 | William A. Oldfield (D) | 13,056 | 63.8 |
| | H. H. Myers (R) | 7,421 | 36.2 |
| 3 | John C. Floyd (D) | 13,710 | 59.9 |
| | W. T. Mills (R) | 9,186 | 40.1 |
| 4 | William B. Cravens (D) | 13,064 | 59.8 |
| | Edwin Mechem (R) | 8,779 | 40.2 |
| 5 | Charles C. Reid (D) | 15,331 | 66.1 |
| | Guy W. Caron (R) | 7,849 | 33.9 |
| 6 | Joseph T. Robinson (D) | 24,389 | 100.0 |
| 7 | Robert M. Wallace (D) | 12,354 | 59.8 |
| | S. R. Young (R) | 8,312 | 40.2 |

## CALIFORNIA

| | Candidates | Votes | % |
|---|---|---|---|
| 1 | William F. Englebright (R) | 20,624 | 54.1 |
| | E. W. Holland (D) | 14,031 | 36.8 |
| | D. N. Cunningham (SOC) | 2,898 | 7.6 |
| 2 | Duncan E. McKinlay (R) | 28,627 | 57.4 |
| | W. K. Hays (D) | 19,193 | 38.5 |
| 3 | Joseph R. Knowland (R) | 27,857 | 64.1 |
| | George W. Peckham (D) | 9,889 | 22.8 |
| | O. H. Philbrick (SOC) | 4,052 | 9.3 |
| 4 | Julius Kahn (R) | 9,202 | 52.7 |
| | James G. Maguire (D) | 7,497 | 42.9 |
| 5 | Everis A. Hayes (R) | 28,127 | 49.1 |
| | George A. Tracy (D) | 24,531 | 42.8 |
| | E. H. Misner (SOC) | 3,640 | 6.4 |
| 6 | James C. Needham (R) | 21,323 | 52.0 |
| | Fred P. Feliz (D) | 15,868 | 38.7 |
| | W. M. Pattison (SOC) | 2,288 | 5.6 |
| 7 | James McLachlan (R) | 37,244 | 51.9 |
| | Jud R. Rush (D) | 25,445 | 35.4 |
| | A. R. Holston (SOC) | 4,432 | 6.2 |
| | M. W. Atwood (P) | 3,899 | 5.4 |
| 8 | Sylvester C. Smith (R) | 29,305 | 55.7 |
| | W. E. Shepherd (D) | 18,245 | 34.7 |
| | N. A. Richardson (SOC) | 5,025 | 9.6 |

## COLORADO

| | Candidates | Votes | % |
|---|---|---|---|
| 1 | Atterson W. Rucker (D) | 60,643 | 49.9 |
| | Robert William Bonynge (R) | 57,597 | 47.4 |
| 2 | John A. Martin (D) | 65,814 | 48.7 |
| | Warren A. Haggott (R) | 64,553 | 47.8 |
| AL | Edward T. Taylor (D) | 126,934 | 48.4 |
| | James C. Burger (R) | 121,265 | 46.2 |

## CONNECTICUT

| | Candidates | Votes | % |
|---|---|---|---|
| 1 | E. Stevens Henry (R) | 26,829 | 59.5 |
| | Gerth (D) | 15,595 | 34.6 |
| 2 | Nehemiah D. Sperry (R) | 36,083 | 55.0 |
| | Reilly (D) | 26,832 | 40.9 |
| 3 | Edwin W. Higgins (R) | 14,935 | 60.3 |
| | Hunter (D) | 9,190 | 37.1 |
| 4 | Ebenezer J. Hill (R) | 32,843 | 60.7 |
| | Wilson (D) | 19,423 | 35.9 |
| AL | John Q. Tilson (R) | 111,557 | 58.6 |
| | Avery (D) | 70,029 | 36.8 |

## DELAWARE

| | Candidates | Votes | % |
|---|---|---|---|
| AL | William H. Heald (R) | 24,314 | 50.7 |
| | Levin Irving Handy (D) | 22,515 | 46.9 |

## FLORIDA

| | Candidates | Votes | % |
|---|---|---|---|
| 1 | Stephen M. Sparkman (D) | 9,971 | 75.2 |
| | George W. Allen (R) | 1,990 | 15.0 |
| | C. C. Allen (SOC) | 1,297 | 9.8 |
| 2 | Frank Clark (D) | 10,726 | 75.9 |
| | William R. O'Neal (R) | 2,552 | 18.1 |
| | A. N. Jackson (SOC) | 862 | 6.1 |
| 3 | Dannitte H. Mays (D) | 9,314 | 80.2 |
| | William H. Northup (R) | 1,712 | 14.7 |

## GEORGIA

| | Candidates | Votes | % |
|---|---|---|---|
| 1 | Charles G. Edwards (D) | 9,845 | 95.7 |
| 2 | James M. Griggs (D) | 9,273 | 100.0 |
| 3 | Dudley M. Hughes (D) | 7,627 | 99.7 |
| 4 | William C. Adamson (D) | 7,242 | 100.0 |
| 5 | Leonidas F. Livingston (D) | 8,909 | 100.0 |
| 6 | Charles L. Bartlett (D) | 6,575 | 100.0 |
| 7 | Gordon Lee (D) | 11,396 | 100.0 |
| 8 | William M. Howard (D) | 7,112 | 100.0 |
| 9 | Thomas M. Bell (D) | 11,653 | 100.0 |
| 10 | Thomas W. Hardwick (D) | 6,853 | 100.0 |
| 11 | William G. Brantley (D) | 9,741 | 100.0 |

## IDAHO

| | Candidates | Votes | % |
|---|---|---|---|
| AL | Thomas R. Hamer (R) | 49,983 | 52.0 |
| | James L. McClear (D) | 37,605 | 39.2 |
| | Halbert Barton (SOC) | 6,248 | 6.5 |

## ILLINOIS

| | Candidates | Votes | % |
|---|---|---|---|
| 1 | Martin B. Madden (R) | 23,370 | 60.9 |
| | Matthew L. Mandable (D) | 13,692 | 35.7 |
| 2 | James R. Mann (R) | 32,024 | 64.8 |
| | John T. Donahoe (D) | 14,351 | 29.0 |
| 3 | William Warfield Wilson (R) | 24,979 | 56.0 |
| | Fred J. Crowley (D) | 15,995 | 35.8 |
| 4 | James T. McDermott (D) | 16,606 | 54.7 |
| | Charles S. Wharton (R) | 12,196 | 40.2 |
| 5 | Adolph J. Sabath (D) | 12,997 | 53.3 |
| | Anthony Michalek (R) | 9,876 | 40.5 |
| | Morris Siskind (SOC) | 1,285 | 5.3 |
| 6 | William Lorimer (R) | 32,540 | 61.1 |
| | Frank C. Wood (D) | 17,093 | 32.1 |
| 7 | Fred Lundin (R) | 31,513 | 54.1 |
| | Frank Buchanan (D) | 20,088 | 34.5 |
| | George Koop (SOC) | 4,183 | 7.2 |
| 8 | Thomas Gallagher (D) | 15,963 | 49.2 |
| | Philip M. Ksycki (R) | 14,660 | 45.2 |
| 9 | Henry Sherman Boutell (R) | 21,110 | 56.2 |
| | Charles C. Stilwell (D) | 13,544 | 36.1 |

| | Candidates | Votes | % |
|---|---|---|---|
| 10 | George Edmund Foss (R) | 31,130 | 62.0 |
| | Western Starr (D) | 14,840 | 29.6 |
| 11 | Howard M. Snapp (R) | 29,821 | 61.2 |
| | Coll McNaughton (D) | 15,875 | 32.6 |
| 12 | Charles E. Fuller (R) | 33,340 | 65.4 |
| | M. N. Armstrong (D) | 13,795 | 27.1 |
| 13 | Frank O. Lowden (R) | 24,797 | 61.4 |
| | William C. Green (D) | 13,273 | 32.9 |
| 14 | James McKinney (R) | 23,394 | 54.3 |
| | Matt J. McEniry (D) | 16,745 | 38.9 |
| 15 | George W. Prince (R) | 26,770 | 50.9 |
| | W. Emery Lancaster (D) | 22,410 | 42.6 |
| 16 | Joseph V. Graff (R) | 23,880 | 53.2 |
| | James W. Hill (D) | 18,557 | 41.3 |
| 17 | John A. Sterling (R) | 22,014 | 53.2 |
| | C. S. Schneider (D) | 16,737 | 40.5 |
| | William P. Allin (P) | 2,228 | 5.4 |
| 18 | Joseph G. Cannon (R) | 29,170 | 54.9 |
| | Henry C. Bell (D) | 21,795 | 41.0 |
| 19 | William B. McKinley (R) | 30,588 | 52.9 |
| | Fred B. Hamill (D) | 24,913 | 43.1 |
| 20 | Henry T. Rainey (D) | 24,023 | 55.3 |
| | James H. Danskin (R) | 17,726 | 40.8 |
| 21 | James M. Graham (D) | 23,433 | 47.9 |
| | H. Clay Wilson (R) | 21,716 | 44.4 |
| 22 | William A. Rodenberg (R) | 27,858 | 50.2 |
| | Charles A. Karch (D) | 24,341 | 43.9 |
| 23 | Martin D. Foster (D) | 28,181 | 53.6 |
| | Frank S. Dickson (R) | 23,772 | 45.2 |
| 24 | Pleasant T. Chapman (R) | 21,833 | 52.4 |
| | John Q. A. Ledbetter (D) | 18,333 | 44.0 |
| 25 | Napoleon B. Thistlewood (R) | 24,319 | 51.6 |
| | I. R. Spilman (D) | 20,537 | 43.6 |

### Special Election

| | Candidates | Votes | % |
|---|---|---|---|
| 25 | Napoleon B. Thistlewood (R) | 12,263 | 47.2 |
| | William H. Warder (D) | 8,620 | 33.2 |
| | Sam T. Brush | 3,987 | 15.3 |

## INDIANA

| | Candidates | Votes | % |
|---|---|---|---|
| 1 | John W. Boehne (D) | 23,054 | 48.3 |
| | John H. Foster (R) | 22,965 | 48.1 |
| 2 | William A. Cullop (D) | 27,172 | 50.0 |
| | John C. Chaney (R) | 24,609 | 45.3 |
| 3 | William E. Cox (D) | 24,139 | 54.9 |
| | John W. Lewis (R) | 18,966 | 43.1 |
| 4 | Lincoln Dixon (D) | 25,231 | 53.6 |
| | James A. Cox (R) | 20,726 | 44.0 |
| 5 | Ralph W. Moss (D) | 28,844 | 48.9 |
| | Howard Maxwell (R) | 27,361 | 46.4 |
| 6 | William O. Barnard (R) | 27,053 | 49.2 |
| | Thomas H. Kuhn (D) | 25,905 | 47.2 |
| 7 | Charles A. Korbly (D) | 34,686 | 49.2 |
| | Jesse Overstreet (R) | 34,003 | 48.2 |
| 8 | John A. M. Adair (D) | 29,259 | 52.5 |
| | Nathan B. Hawkins (R) | 23,890 | 42.9 |
| 9 | Martin A. Morrison (D) | 27,540 | 48.9 |
| | Charles B. Landis (R) | 26,449 | 47.0 |
| 10 | Edgar D. Crumpacker (R) | 32,954 | 54.4 |
| | William Darroch (D) | 26,742 | 44.1 |
| 11 | George W. Rauch (D) | 25,526 | 48.3 |
| | Charles H. Good (R) | 24,313 | 46.0 |
| 12 | Cyrus Cline (D) | 25,051 | 50.6 |
| | Clarence L. Gilhams (R) | 22,706 | 45.8 |
| 13 | Henry A. Barnhart (D) | 28,509 | 48.2 |
| | Charles W. Miller (R) | 28,229 | 47.7 |

### Special Election

| | Candidates | Votes | % |
|---|---|---|---|
| 13 | Henry A. Barnhart (D) | 28,131 | 48.4 |
| | Charles W. Miller (R) | 27,708 | 47.7 |

## IOWA

| | Candidates | Votes | % |
|---|---|---|---|
| 1 | Charles A. Kennedy (R) | 18,318 | 51.2 |
| | George S. Tracy (D) | 16,695 | 46.7 |
| 2 | Albert F. Dawson (R) | 22,915 | 51.0 |
| | Mark A. Walsh (D) | 21,050 | 46.9 |
| 3 | Charles E. Pickett (R) | 25,530 | 57.6 |
| | Charles Elliott (D) | 17,362 | 39.2 |
| 4 | Gilbert N. Haugen (R) | 20,929 | 55.3 |
| | M. E. Geiser (D) | 16,296 | 43.1 |
| 5 | James W. Good (R) | 22,773 | 57.3 |
| | Samuel K. Tracy (D) | 15,994 | 40.2 |
| 6 | Nathan E. Kendall (R) | 18,909 | 48.3 |
| | Daniel W. Hamilton (D) | 18,628 | 47.6 |
| 7 | John A. T. Hull (R) | 24,931 | 55.7 |
| | Charles O. Holley (D) | 17,620 | 39.4 |
| 8 | William D. Jamieson (D) | 20,436 | 49.2 |
| | William P. Hepburn (R) | 20,126 | 48.4 |
| 9 | Walter I. Smith (R) | 23,215 | 55.8 |
| | R. C. Spencer (D) | 17,661 | 42.4 |
| 10 | Frank P. Woods (R) | 29,608 | 61.4 |
| | Montague Hakes (D) | 17,256 | 35.8 |
| 11 | Elbert H. Hubbard (R) | 26,572 | 57.1 |
| | W. G. Sears (D) | 19,033 | 40.9 |

## KANSAS

| | | Votes | % |
|---|---|---|---|
| 1 | Daniel R. Anthony Jr. (R) | 27,792 | 57.6 |
| | F. M. Pearl (D) | 19,842 | 41.1 |
| 2 | Charles F. Scott (R) | 28,499 | 50.5 |
| | B. J. Sheridan (D) | 26,242 | 46.5 |
| 3 | Philip P. Campbell (R) | 29,207 | 49.8 |
| | T. J. Hudson (D) | 23,377 | 39.8 |
| | Ben F. Wilson (SOC) | 5,776 | 9.8 |
| 4 | James M. Miller (R) | 20,978 | 55.3 |
| | Thomas M. Grisham (D) | 16,024 | 42.2 |
| 5 | William A. Calderhead (R) | 21,093 | 51.6 |
| | R. A. Lovitt (D) | 18,555 | 45.4 |
| 6 | William A. Reeder (R) | 22,200 | 48.6 |
| | John R. Connelly (D) | 21,923 | 48.0 |
| 7 | Edmond H. Madison (R) | 26,315 | 52.5 |
| | Samuel I. Hale (D) | 21,460 | 42.9 |
| 8 | Victor Murdock (R) | 19,029 | 56.4 |
| | Frank B. Lawrence (D) | 13,477 | 39.9 |

## KENTUCKY

| | | Votes | % |
|---|---|---|---|
| 1 | Ollie M. James (D) | 27,435 | 64.1 |
| | Porter (R) | 15,163 | 35.4 |
| 2 | Augustus O. Stanley (D) | 23,320 | 54.3 |
| | Worsham (R) | 19,302 | 45.0 |
| 3 | Robert Y. Thomas Jr. (D) | 20,079 | 49.8 |
| | James (R) | 19,583 | 48.6 |
| 4 | Ben Johnson (D) | 24,344 | 53.2 |
| | Gaddle (R) | 21,246 | 46.4 |
| 5 | J. Swagar Sherley (D) | 27,953 | 51.7 |
| | Kinkead (R) | 25,513 | 47.1 |
| 6 | Joseph L. Rhinock (D) | 23,945 | 55.4 |
| | Ingils (R) | 18,057 | 41.8 |
| 7 | James C. Cantrill (D) | 21,157 | 59.0 |
| | Bristow (R) | 14,697 | 41.0 |
| 8 | Harvey Helm (D) | 17,725 | 51.8 |
| | Benthrum (R) | 16,049 | 46.9 |
| 9 | Joseph B. Bennett (R) | 22,832 | 50.0 |
| | Kehoe (D) | 22,107 | 48.4 |
| 10 | John W. Langley (R) | 20,092 | 52.0 |
| | Davis (D) | 18,570 | 48.0 |
| 11 | Don C. Edwards (R) | 36,073 | 69.8 |
| | Patterson (D) | 14,729 | 28.5 |

## LOUISIANA

| | | Votes | % |
|---|---|---|---|
| 1 | Albert Estopinal (D) | 13,923 | 87.9 |
| | Henry C. Warmoth (R) | 1,916 | 12.1 |
| 2 | Robert C. Davey (D) | 14,447* | 95.7 |
| 3 | Robert F. Broussard (D) | 5,845 | 75.9 |
| | Carlton R. Beattie (R) | 1,696 | 22.0 |
| 4 | John T. Watkins (D) | 7,188 | 88.2 |
| | W. S. Emmons (SOC) | 513 | 6.3 |

| Candidates | Votes | % |
|---|---|---|
| John F. Slattery (R) | 449 | 5.5 |
| 5 Joseph E. Ransdell (D) | 7,110 | 96.5 |
| 6 Robert C. Wickliffe (D) | 7,108 | 91.8 |
| George J. Reiley (R) | 632 | 8.2 |
| 7 Arsene P. Pujo (D) | 8,270 | 93.4 |
| Alex Hymes (SOC) | 585 | 6.6 |

## MAINE

| | | Votes | % |
|---|---|---|---|
| 1 | Amos L. Allen (R) | 18,887 | 53.5 |
| | John C. Scates (D) | 15,615 | 44.2 |
| 2 | John P. Swasey (R) | 18,479 | 50.7 |
| | Daniel J. McGillicuddy (D) | 17,115 | 46.9 |
| 3 | Edwin C. Burleigh (R) | 18,282 | 53.1 |
| | Samuel W. Gould (D) | 15,611 | 45.3 |
| 4 | Frank E. Guernsey (R) | 19,659 | 54.1 |
| | George M. Hanson (D) | 16,152 | 44.4 |

## MARYLAND

| | | Votes | % |
|---|---|---|---|
| 1 | James Harry Covington (D) | 19,381 | 52.7 |
| | William H. Jackson (R) | 16,547 | 45.0 |
| 2 | J. Fred C. Talbott (D) | 21,526 | 52.2 |
| | Robert Garrett (R) | 19,040 | 46.1 |
| 3 | John Kronmiller (R) | 14,772 | 49.1 |
| | Harry B. Wolf (D) | 14,510 | 48.2 |
| 4 | John Gill Jr. (D) | 18,562 | 52.1 |
| | John P. Hill (R) | 16,626 | 46.7 |
| 5 | Sydney E. Mudd (R) | 15,057 | 49.2 |
| | George M. Smith (D) | 14,740 | 48.2 |
| 6 | George A. Pearre (R) | 18,619 | 49.1 |
| | David J. Lewis (D) | 18,073 | 47.6 |

## MASSACHUSETTS

| | | Votes | % |
|---|---|---|---|
| 1 | George P. Lawrence (R) | 17,990 | 60.2 |
| | David T. Clark (D) | 10,765 | 36.0 |
| 2 | Frederick H. Gillett (R) | 17,515 | 62.0 |
| | John L. Rice (D) | 7,839 | 27.8 |
| | George W. Curtis (I LEAGUE) | 1,623 | 5.8 |
| 3 | Charles G. Washburn (R) | 18,265 | 62.2 |
| | William I. McLoughlin (D) | 9,654 | 32.9 |
| 4 | Charles Q. Tirrell (R) | 18,842 | 55.0 |
| | John J. Mitchell (D) | 15,431 | 45.0 |
| 5 | Butler Ames (R) | 16,251 | 56.0 |
| | Joseph J. Flynn (DI) | 11,910 | 41.1 |
| 6 | Augustus P. Gardner (R) | 22,093 | 69.4 |
| | Arthur Withington (D) | 7,334 | 23.0 |
| | Franklin H. Wentworth (SOC) | 2,418 | 7.6 |
| 7 | Ernest W. Roberts (R) | 22,179 | 68.9 |
| | George Brickett (D) | 7,958 | 24.7 |
| | Clarence L. McIver (I LEAGUE) | 2,078 | 6.5 |
| 8 | Samuel W. McCall (R) | 19,147 | 63.6 |
| | Frederick S. Deitrick (D) | 9,638 | 32.0 |
| 9 | John A. Keliher (D) | 14,060 | 62.3 |
| | John A. Campbell (R) | 6,002 | 26.6 |
| | Junius T. Auerbach (I LEAGUE) | 2,492 | 11.1 |
| 10 | Joseph F. O'Connell (D) | 16,553 | 46.4 |
| | J. Mitchell Galvin (R) | 16,549 | 46.4 |
| 11 | Andrew J. Peters (D) | 15,881 | 48.7 |
| | Daniel W. Lane (R) | 15,447 | 47.4 |
| 12 | John W. Weeks (R) | 21,097 | 66.0 |
| | Jesse C. Ivy (D) | 9,069 | 28.4 |
| | Albert E. George (I LEAGUE) | 1,779 | 5.6 |
| 13 | William S. Greene (R) | 16,870 | 72.5 |
| | John F. McGuinness (D) | 4,977 | 21.4 |
| | Charles W. Copeland (I LEAGUE) | 1,436 | 6.2 |
| 14 | William C. Lovering (R) | 20,959 | 66.8 |
| | Eliot L. Packard (D) | 6,709 | 21.4 |
| | Charles B. Drew (I LEAGUE) | 1,855 | 5.9 |
| | George J. Alcott (SOC) | 1,851 | 5.9 |

## MICHIGAN

| | Candidates | Votes | % |
|---|---|---|---|
| 1 | Edwin Denby (R) | 30,696 | 56.4 |
| | William D. Mahon (D) | 21,695 | 39.9 |
| 2 | Charles E. Townsend (R) | 28,442 | 58.0 |
| | James C. Henderson (D) | 19,306 | 39.4 |
| 3 | Washington Gardner (R) | 24,078 | 53.7 |
| | Hiram C. Blackman (D) | 18,907 | 42.1 |
| 4 | Edward L. Hamilton (R) | 27,074 | 59.4 |
| | Charles H. Kimmerle (D) | 16,731 | 36.7 |
| 5 | Gerrit J. Diekema (R) | 25,030 | 54.1 |
| | Edwin F. Sweet (D) | 19,437 | 42.0 |
| 6 | Samuel W. Smith (R) | 32,043 | 56.8 |
| | Frank L. Dodge (D) | 21,304 | 37.8 |
| 7 | Henry McMorran (R) | 22,879 | 59.4 |
| | William Springer (D) | 13,843 | 36.0 |
| 8 | Joseph W. Fordney (R) | 21,210 | 59.7 |
| | Jenner E. Morse (D) | 13,948 | 39.3 |
| 9 | James C. McLaughlin (R) | 22,459 | 72.1 |
| | Cornelius Gerber (D) | 8,688 | 27.9 |
| 10 | George A. Loud (R) | 24,780 | 64.6 |
| | Lewis P. Coumans (D) | 12,677 | 33.1 |
| 11 | Francis H. Dodds (R) | 29,402 | 70.5 |
| | Leavitt S. Griswold (D) | 12,315 | 29.5 |
| 12 | H. Olin Young (R) | 35,310 | 72.2 |
| | Patrick H. Obrien (D) | 13,586 | 27.8 |

## MINNESOTA

| | | Votes | % |
|---|---|---|---|
| 1 | James A. Tawney (R) | 20,464 | 53.6 |
| | French (D) | 17,708 | 46.4 |
| 2 | Winfield S. Hammond (D) | 17,716 | 55.7 |
| | McCleary (R) | 14,091 | 44.3 |
| 3 | Charles R. Davis (R) | 19,896 | 59.7 |
| 4 | Frederick C. Stevens (R) | 21,818 | 60.8 |
| | Peebles (D) | 12,395 | 34.5 |
| 5 | Frank M. Nye (R) | 24,542 | 61.7 |
| | Thomas P. Dwyer (D) | 13,429 | 33.8 |
| 6 | Charles A. Lindbergh (R) | 22,574 | 63.2 |
| | Gilkinson (D) | 13,174 | 36.9 |
| 7 | Andrew J. Volstead (R) | 26,597 | 100.0 |
| 8 | Clarence B. Miller (R) | 27,873 | 81.6 |
| | Halliday (PUB OWN) | 6,298 | 18.4 |
| 9 | Halvor Steenerson (R) | 17,957 | 50.0 |
| | Sageng (I) | 15,010 | 41.8 |
| | Braaten (PUB OWN) | 2,985 | 8.3 |

## MISSISSIPPI

| | | Votes | % |
|---|---|---|---|
| 1 | Ezekiel S. Candler Jr. (D) | 8,043 | 100.0 |
| 2 | Thomas Spight (D) | 7,511 | 100.0 |
| 3 | Benjamin G. Humphreys (D) | 4,808 | 100.0 |
| 4 | Thomas U. Sisson (D) | 8,039 | 100.0 |
| 5 | Adam M. Byrd (D) | 9,750 | 100.0 |
| 6 | Eaton J. Bowers (D) | 8,702 | 100.0 |
| 7 | William A. Dickson (D) | 6,807 | 94.2 |
| | H. C. Turley (R) | 384 | 5.3 |
| 8 | James W. Collier (D) | 5,657 | 100.0 |

## MISSOURI

| | | Votes | % |
|---|---|---|---|
| 1 | James T. Lloyd (D) | 22,133 | 52.4 |
| | Chamberlain (R) | 19,122 | 45.3 |
| 2 | William W. Rucker (D) | 23,263 | 55.5 |
| | Haley (R) | 18,266 | 43.6 |
| 3 | Joshua W. Alexander (D) | 20,387 | 52.6 |
| | Eads (R) | 18,341 | 47.3 |
| 4 | Charles F. Booher (D) | 21,671 | 53.3 |
| | Reed (R) | 18,908 | 46.4 |
| 5 | William P. Borland (D) | 31,635 | 52.7 |
| | Ellis (R) | 27,289 | 45.5 |
| 6 | David A. De Armond (D) | 18,532 | 52.6 |
| | Atkeson (R) | 16,372 | 46.4 |
| 7 | Courtney W. Hamlin (D) | 24,731 | 49.7 |
| | Whitaker (R) | 23,927 | 48.1 |
| 8 | Dorsey W. Shackleford (D) | 17,230 | 52.1 |
| | Irwin (R) | 15,691 | 47.4 |
| 9 | James Beauchamp Clark (D) | 23,090 | 51.5 |
| | Roy (R) | 21,702 | 48.4 |

## MISSOURI

| District | Candidates | Votes | % |
|---|---|---|---|
| 10 | Richard Bartholdt (R) | 49,127 | 60.4 |
| | Thompson (D) | 28,634 | 35.2 |
| 11 | Patrick F. Gill (D) | 21,001 | 50.9 |
| | Findly (R) | 19,195 | 46.5 |
| 12 | Harry M. Coudrey (R) | 16,471 | 49.7 |
| | Selph (D) | 15,930 | 48.1 |
| 13 | Politte Elvins (R) | 17,125 | 50.3 |
| | Smith (D) | 16,918 | 49.7 |
| 14 | Charles A. Crow (R) | 25,951 | 48.3 |
| | Russell (D) | 25,187 | 46.8 |
| 15 | Charles H. Morgan (R) | 23,040 | 47.9 |
| | Hackney (D) | 22,410 | 46.6 |
| 16 | Arthur P. Murphy (R) | 16,835 | 50.8 |
| | J. Robert Lamar (D) | 16,295 | 49.2 |

## MONTANA

| District | Candidates | Votes | % |
|---|---|---|---|
| AL | Charles N. Pray (R) | 32,819 | 48.9 |
| | Thomas D. Long (D) | 29,032 | 43.2 |
| | Lewis J. Duncan (SOC) | 5,318 | 7.9 |

## NEBRASKA

| District | Candidates | Votes | % |
|---|---|---|---|
| 1 | John A. Maguire (D & PPI) | 19,651 | 51.2 |
| | E. M. Pollard (R) | 18,716 | 48.8 |
| 2 | Gilbert M. Hitchcock (D) | 18,781 | 52.6 |
| | A. W. Jefferies (R) | 16,206 | 45.4 |
| 3 | James P. Latta (D & PPI) | 26,832 | 51.6 |
| | J. F. Boyd (R) | 24,865 | 47.8 |
| 4 | Edmund H. Hinshaw (R) | 22,674 | 50.0 |
| | C. F. Gilbert (D & PPI) | 21,819 | 48.1 |
| 5 | George W. Norris (R) | 20,649# | 49.4 |
| | F. W. Ashton (D & PPI) | 20,627 | 49.4 |
| 6 | Moses P. Kinkaid (R) | 25,786 | 50.7 |
| | W. H. Westover (D & PPI) | 23,317 | 45.8 |

## NEVADA

| District | Candidates | Votes | % |
|---|---|---|---|
| AL | George A. Bartlett (D) | 11,253 | 47.3 |
| | H. B. Maxson (R) | 7,552 | 31.7 |
| | A. L. Fitzgerald (INDEP) | 3,031 | 12.7 |
| | J. Critchfield (SOC) | 1,965 | 8.3 |

## NEW HAMPSHIRE

| District | Candidates | Votes | % |
|---|---|---|---|
| 1 | Cyrus A. Sulloway (R) | 24,413 | 56.9 |
| | Michael J. White (D) | 17,400 | 40.5 |
| 2 | Frank D. Currier (R) | 26,007 | 59.3 |
| | Frederick M. Colby (D) | 16,666 | 38.0 |

## NEW JERSEY

| District | Candidates | Votes | % |
|---|---|---|---|
| 1 | Henry C. Loudenslager (R) | 27,443 | 58.4 |
| | Grosscup (D) | 17,640 | 37.5 |
| 2 | John J. Gardner (R) | 23,906 | 52.2 |
| | Grubb (D) | 20,506 | 44.8 |
| 3 | Benjamin F. Howell (R) | 26,302 | 56.6 |
| | Clark (D) | 19,766 | 42.5 |
| 4 | Ira W. Wood (R) | 23,919 | 56.5 |
| | Steele (D) | 17,210 | 40.7 |
| 5 | Charles N. Fowler (R) | 27,948 | 55.5 |
| | Barber (D) | 20,485 | 40.7 |
| 6 | William Hughes (D) | 29,516 | 49.5 |
| | Foxhall (R) | 27,989 | 46.9 |
| 7 | Richard W. Parker (R) | 24,863 | 56.6 |
| | Townsend (D) | 18,104 | 41.2 |
| 8 | William H. Wiley (R) | 24,536 | 57.9 |
| | Le Gage Pratt (D) | 16,276 | 38.4 |
| 9 | Eugene F. Kinkead (D) | 23,485 | 54.5 |
| | Critchfield (R) | 18,608 | 43.2 |
| 10 | James A. Hamill (D) | 23,820 | 57.7 |
| | Dwyer (R) | 16,105 | 39.0 |

## NEW YORK

| District | Candidates | Votes | % |
|---|---|---|---|
| 1 | William W. Cocks (R) | 29,459 | 56.6 |
| | Monson Morris (D) | 19,519 | 37.5 |
| 2 | George H. Lindsay (D) | 15,455 | 53.9 |
| | William Liebermann (R) | 9,999 | 34.9 |
| | Edward Walsh (I LEAGUE) | 1,886 | 6.6 |
| 3 | Otto Godfrey Foelker (R) | 18,614 | 50.3 |
| | James P. Maher (D) | 15,395 | 41.6 |
| | Otto Wegener (SOC) | 2,707 | 5.6 |
| 4 | Charles B. Law (R) | 23,944 | 49.7 |
| | Edward R. Gilman (D) | 18,910 | 39.2 |
| | Otto Wegener (SOC) | 2,707 | 5.6 |
| | Arthur S. Colborne (I LEAGUE) | 2,542 | 5.3 |
| 5 | Richard Young (R) | 28,075 | 54.2 |
| | J. Harry Snook (D) | 19,897 | 38.4 |
| 6 | William M. Calder (R) | 22,050 | 55.4 |
| 7 | John J. Fitzgerald (D) | 17,773 | 58.5 |
| | William R. A. Koehl (R) | 10,296 | 33.9 |
| | William T. Smith (I LEAGUE) | 1,841 | 6.1 |
| 8 | Daniel J. Riordan (D) | 22,029 | 62.5 |
| | James E. Winterbottom (R) | 11,484 | 32.2 |
| 9 | Henry M. Goldfogle (D) | 6,194 | 53.8 |
| | Morris Hillquit (SOC) | 2,483 | 21.6 |
| | Louis I. Cherey (R) | 2,312 | 20.1 |
| 10 | William Sulzer (D) | 10,602 | 54.4 |
| | Gustave Hartman (R) | 6,511 | 33.4 |
| | Morris Brown (SOC) | 1,754 | 9.0 |
| 11 | Charles V. Fornes (D) | 20,637 | 58.9 |
| | Laurence L. Driggs (R) | 11,700 | 33.4 |
| | Alexander Porter (I LEAGUE) | 1,853 | 5.3 |
| 12 | Michael F. Conroy (D) | 16,757 | 60.9 |
| | Victor H. Duras (R) | 8,090 | 29.4 |
| | James D. Bush (I LEAGUE) | 1,482 | 5.4 |
| 13 | Herbert Parsons (R) | 15,108 | 51.4 |
| | Gerald Hull Gray (D) | 12,380 | 42.2 |
| 14 | William Willett Jr. (D) | 21,643 | 52.2 |
| | Emanuel Castka (R) | 14,189 | 34.2 |
| | Philip H. Schmitt (SOC) | 3,055 | 7.4 |
| | Herbert Wade (I LEAGUE) | 2,485 | 6.0 |
| 15 | Jacob Van Vechten Olcott (R) | 16,921 | 56.5 |
| | Rhinelander Waldo (D) | 12,531 | 41.8 |
| 16 | Francis Burton Harrison (D) | 12,555 | 50.8 |
| | Francis A. Adams (R) | 8,822 | 35.7 |
| | John Parr (SOC) | 1,966 | 8.0 |
| | Edwin D. Ackerman (I LEAGUE) | 1,334 | 5.4 |
| 17 | William S. Bennet (R) | 32,764 | 53.5 |
| | William Madoo (D) | 24,736 | 40.4 |
| 18 | Joseph A. Goulden (D) | 35,569 | 51.5 |
| | Joel Elias Spingarn (R) | 25,590 | 37.1 |
| | Frank McGarry (I LEAGUE) | 4,144 | 6.0 |
| | George B. Staring (SOC) | 3,649 | 5.3 |
| 19 | John E. Andrus (R) | 27,966 | 55.6 |
| | William H. Lynn (D) | 19,851 | 39.4 |
| 20 | Thomas W. Bradley (R) | 23,927 | 55.9 |
| | Richard E. King (D) | 17,979 | 42.0 |
| 21 | Hamilton Fish (R) | 22,832 | 52.0 |
| | Andrew C. Zabriskie (D) | 19,725 | 44.9 |
| 22 | William H. Draper (R) | 22,980 | 52.7 |
| | Winfield A. Huppuch (D) | 19,074 | 43.7 |
| 23 | George N. Southwick (R) | 30,593 | 48.5 |
| | William H. Keeler (D) | 30,008 | 47.6 |
| 24 | George W. Fairchild (R) | 28,496 | 53.8 |
| | G. Hyde Clark (D) | 23,059 | 43.5 |
| 25 | Cyrus Durey (R) | 27,152 | 54.4 |
| | Joseph D. Baucus (D) | 19,927 | 39.9 |
| 26 | George R. Malby (R) | 30,615 | 66.4 |
| | Ellis Woodworth (D) | 14,914 | 32.3 |
| 27 | Charles S. Millington (R) | 26,962 | 54.0 |
| | Curtis F. Alliaume (D) | 21,365 | 42.8 |
| 28 | Charles L. Knapp (R) | 25,948 | 57.9 |
| | Andrew C. Cornwall (D) | 15,756 | 35.1 |
| | Sylvanus V. Barker (P) | 2,372 | 5.3 |
| 29 | Michael E. Driscoll (R) | 33,664 | 59.1 |
| | Alphonso E. Fitch (D) | 20,527 | 36.0 |
| 30 | John W. Dwight (R) | 30,622 | 57.4 |
| | Alexander D. Wales (D) | 19,818 | 37.2 |
| 31 | Sereno E. Payne (R) | 28,990 | 59.7 |
| | John A. Curtis (D) | 17,891 | 36.8 |
| 32 | James B. Perkins (R) | 33,025 | 56.4 |
| | Herman S. Searle (D) | 22,858 | 39.0 |
| 33 | Jacob Sloat Fassett (R) | 24,580 | 52.2 |
| | James A. Parsons (D) | 20,319 | 43.1 |
| 34 | James S. Simmons (R) | 30,298 | 54.7 |
| | Frank W. Brown (D) | 23,298 | 42.1 |
| 35 | Daniel A. Driscoll (D) | 25,866 | 55.2 |
| | L. Bradley Dorr (R) | 20,093 | 42.9 |
| 36 | De Alva S. Alexander (R) | 30,621 | 58.2 |
| | William H. Follette (D) | 20,790 | 39.5 |
| 37 | Edward Butterfield Vreeland (R) | 32,327 | 62.4 |
| | Sanford H. Thorne (D) | 15,718 | 30.4 |

## NORTH CAROLINA

| District | Candidates | Votes | % |
|---|---|---|---|
| 1 | John H. Small (D) | 13,119 | 71.1 |
| | I. M. Meekins (R) | 5,342 | 28.9 |
| 2 | Claude Kitchin (D) | 12,275 | 78.2 |
| | M. Ferguson (R) | 3,361 | 21.4 |
| 3 | Charles R. Thomas (D) | 11,544 | 59.4 |
| | Eli W. Hill (R) | 7,896 | 40.6 |
| 4 | Edward W. Pou (D) | 13,463 | 60.0 |
| | Willis G. Briggs (R) | 8,966 | 40.0 |
| 5 | John M. Morehead (R) | 19,288 | 50.1 |
| | A. L. Brooks (D) | 18,938 | 49.2 |
| 6 | Hannibal L. Godwin (D) | 12,542 | 66.3 |
| | Albert H. Slocumb (R) | 6,385 | 33.7 |
| 7 | Robert N. Page (D) | 15,057 | 56.2 |
| | Z. V. Walser (R) | 11,732 | 43.8 |
| 8 | Charles H. Cowles (R) | 16,863 | 52.1 |
| | R. N. Hackett (D) | 15,488 | 47.8 |
| 9 | Edwin Y. Webb (D) | 16,530 | 55.0 |
| | John A. Smith (R) | 13,514 | 45.0 |
| 10 | John G. Grant (R) | 15,245 | 50.5 |
| | William T. Crawford (D) | 14,884 | 49.3 |

## NORTH DAKOTA

| District | Candidates | Votes | % |
|---|---|---|---|
| AL | Asle J. Gronna (R) | 57,357✔ | |
| | Louis B. Hanna (R) | 55,610✔ | |
| | T. D. Casey (D) | 29,426 | |
| | O. G. Major (D) | 28,448 | |
| | Francis Cooper (I) | 591 | |
| | E. D. Herring (I) | 533 | |

## OHIO

| District | Candidates | Votes | % |
|---|---|---|---|
| 1 | Nicholas Longworth (R) | 30,444 | 55.2 |
| | Thomas P. Hart (D) | 23,224 | 42.1 |
| 2 | Herman P. Goebel (R) | 28,008 | 48.6 |
| | Charles N. Danenhower (D) | 27,904 | 48.4 |
| 3 | James M. Cox (D) | 32,524 | 48.1 |
| | John Eugene Harding (I) | 19,306 | 28.5 |
| | William G. Frizell (R) | 12,593 | 18.6 |
| 4 | William E. Tou Velle (D) | 26,896 | 58.2 |
| | Thomas J. Mulligan (R) | 18,305 | 39.6 |
| 5 | Timothy T. Ansberry (D) | 23,712 | 57.7 |
| | William W. Campbell (R) | 16,745 | 40.7 |
| 6 | Matthew R. Denver (D) | 23,192 | 51.6 |
| | Jesse Taylor (R) | 21,592 | 48.0 |
| 7 | J. Warren Keifer (R) | 24,323 | 51.2 |
| | O. E. Duff (D) | 21,503 | 45.2 |
| 8 | Ralph D. Cole (R) | 24,476 | 50.0 |
| | William H. Niven (D) | 23,271 | 47.5 |
| 9 | Isaac R. Sherwood (D) | 29,171 | 47.8 |
| | James H. Southard (R) | 27,523 | 45.1 |
| | Charles H. Miller (SOC) | 3,285 | 5.4 |
| 10 | Adna R. Johnson (R) | 23,687 | 53.8 |
| | Thomas H. B. Jones (D) | 18,918 | 43.0 |
| 11 | Albert Douglas (R) | 27,796 | 49.9 |
| | L. A. Sears (D) | 26,650 | 47.8 |
| 12 | Edward L. Taylor Jr. (R) | 29,483 | 54.5 |
| | Benjamin F. Gayman (D) | 22,813 | 42.2 |
| 13 | Carl C. Anderson (D) | 29,736 | 53.2 |
| | Grant E. Mouser (R) | 25,019 | 44.7 |
| 14 | William G. Sharp (D) | 28,525 | 50.0 |
| | Frank V. Owen (R) | 26,799 | 47.0 |
| 15 | James Joyce (R) | 22,186 | 48.8 |
| | George White (D) | 22,129 | 48.7 |
| 16 | David A. Hollingsworth (R) | 23,318 | 51.7 |

## OHIO

| | Candidates | Votes | % |
|---|---|---|---|
| | N. A. McCombs (D) | 19,914 | 44.2 |
| 17 | William A. Ashbrook (D) | 28,712 | 55.3 |
| | John F. Harrison (R) | 21,341 | 41.1 |
| 18 | James Kennedy (R) | 32,287 | 48.3 |
| | John J. Whitacre (D) | 29,040 | 43.4 |
| 19 | W. Aubrey Thomas (R) | 32,182 | 55.3 |
| | Stephen A. Robinson (D) | 22,529 | 38.7 |
| 20 | Paul Howland (R) | 32,839 | 55.9 |
| | Charles Lapp (D) | 23,592 | 40.1 |
| 21 | Theodore E. Burton (R) | 31,968* | 59.3 |
| | James E. Wertman (D) | 19,451 | 36.1 |

## OKLAHOMA

| | Candidates | Votes | % |
|---|---|---|---|
| 1 | Bird S. McGuire (R) | 23,312 | 50.6 |
| | Henry S. Johnston (D) | 20,501 | 44.5 |
| 2 | Dick T. Morgan (R) | 26,273 | 46.9 |
| | Elmer L. Fulton (D) | 25,349 | 45.2 |
| | Charles P. Randall (SOC) | 4,443 | 7.9 |
| 3 | Charles E. Creager (R) | 24,952 | 48.3 |
| | James S. Davenport (D) | 23,881 | 46.2 |
| | Winston T. Banks (SOC) | 2,827 | 5.5 |
| 4 | Charles D. Carter (D) | 22,047 | 50.6 |
| | Benjamin F. Hackett (R) | 15,727 | 36.1 |
| | M. C. Carter (SOC) | 5,769 | 13.3 |
| 5 | Scott Ferris (D) | 31,026 | 55.7 |
| | Thompson (R) | 19,149 | 34.4 |
| | Davis (SOC) | 5,478 | 9.8 |

## OREGON

| | Candidates | Votes | % |
|---|---|---|---|
| 1 | Willis C. Hawley (R) | 31,889 | 58.8 |
| | J. J. Whitney (D) | 14,841 | 27.4 |
| | W. S. Richards (SOC) | 4,349 | 8.0 |
| | Daniel Staver (P) | 3,189 | 5.9 |
| 2 | William R. Ellis (R) | 35,579 | 63.6 |
| | John A. Jeffrey (D) | 13,865 | 24.8 |
| | G. E. Sanders (SOC) | 3,855 | 6.9 |

## PENNSYLVANIA

| | Candidates | Votes | % |
|---|---|---|---|
| 1 | Henry H. Bingham (R, CITY) | 27,507 | 76.2 |
| | Michael J. Geraghty (D) | 7,773 | 21.5 |
| 2 | Joel Cook (R, CITY) | 24,579 | 77.4 |
| | William Schlipf Jr. (D) | 6,381 | 20.1 |
| 3 | J. Hampton Moore (R, CITY) | 23,877 | 76.6 |
| | William Beerli (D) | 6,608 | 21.2 |
| 4 | Reuben O. Moon (R) | 17,518 | 66.2 |
| | Haines D. Albright (D, CITY) | 7,613 | 28.8 |
| 5 | William W. Foulkrod (R, CITY) | 21,756 | 66.7 |
| | Michael Donohue (D) | 8,488 | 26.0 |
| 6 | George D. McCreary (R, CITY) | 31,129 | 72.5 |
| | Frederick J. Bailey (D) | 10,205 | 23.8 |
| 7 | Thomas S. Butler (R) | 26,684 | 69.3 |
| | D. P. Hibberd (D) | 10,364 | 26.9 |
| 8 | Irving P. Wanger (R) | 26,384 | 59.9 |
| | Wynne James (D) | 17,684 | 40.1 |
| 9 | William W. Griest (R) | 22,022 | 74.8 |
| | George B. Willson (D) | 7,428 | 25.2 |
| 10 | Thomas D. Nichols (D) | 16,855 | 51.1 |
| | John R. Farr (R) | 16,138 | 48.9 |
| 11 | Henry W. Palmer (R, P) | 21,033 | 51.9 |
| | John H. Bigelow (D) | 18,569 | 45.8 |
| 12 | Alfred B. Garner (R) | 17,446 | 51.9 |
| | Robert E. Lee (D) | 15,339 | 45.6 |
| 13 | John H. Rothermel (D) | 27,655 | 53.3 |
| | Alex N. Ulrich (R) | 21,416 | 41.3 |
| 14 | Charles C. Pratt (R) | 15,024 | 51.2 |
| | George W. Kipp (D) | 12,980 | 44.3 |
| 15 | William B. Wilson (D) | 18,592 | 50.4 |
| | Elias Deemer (R) | 16,577 | 44.9 |
| 16 | John G. McHenry (D) | 18,412 | 57.1 |
| | Edmund W. Samuel (R) | 12,866 | 39.9 |

| | Candidates | Votes | % |
|---|---|---|---|
| 17 | Benjamin K. Focht (R, P) | 23,761 | 62.8 |
| | George C. Bentz (D) | 14,044 | 37.2 |
| 18 | Marlin E. Olmsted (R) | 27,717 | 62.8 |
| | John L. Whisler (D) | 13,876 | 31.5 |
| 19 | John M. Reynolds (R) | 26,157 | 62.2 |
| | Humphrey D. Tate (D) | 15,906 | 37.8 |
| 20 | Daniel F. Lafean (R) | 19,176 | 52.0 |
| | Edward D. Ziegler (D) | 16,928 | 45.9 |
| 21 | Charles F. Barclay (R) | 15,631 | 50.3 |
| | W. Harrison Walker (D) | 12,848 | 41.4 |
| | B. W. McCoy (P) | 1,888 | 6.1 |
| 22 | George F. Huff (R) | 19,339 | 51.0 |
| | Silas W. Kline (D) | 16,234 | 42.8 |
| | R. A. Dornon (P) | 2,338 | 6.2 |
| 23 | Allen F. Cooper (R) | 16,769 | 50.7 |
| | Milton R. Travis (D) | 12,125 | 36.7 |
| | William M. Likins (P) | 3,366 | 10.2 |
| 24 | John K. Tener (R) | 20,538 | 52.2 |
| | Charles H. Akens (D) | 10,985 | 27.9 |
| | Frank Fish (P) | 5,982 | 15.2 |
| 25 | Arthur L. Bates (R) | 16,457 | 52.6 |
| | John B. Brooks (D) | 11,995 | 38.4 |
| | N. J. MacIntyre (P) | 1,849 | 5.9 |
| 26 | A. Mitchell Palmer (D) | 18,865 | 52.8 |
| | Gustav A. Schneebeli (R) | 15,123 | 42.3 |
| 27 | Jonathan N. Langham (R) | 19,010 | 59.7 |
| | John Smith Shirley (D) | 10,088 | 31.7 |
| | J. T. Pender (P) | 2,739 | 8.6 |
| 28 | Nelson P. Wheeler (R) | 18,728 | 55.1 |
| | Till Reiss (D) | 11,256 | 33.1 |
| | J. M. Brown (P) | 4,018 | 11.8 |
| 29 | William H. Graham (R) | 15,616 | 65.5 |
| | John G. Schirmer (D) | 5,401 | 22.6 |
| | J. W. Slayton (SOC) | 1,500 | 6.3 |
| | John A. McConnell (P) | 1,337 | 5.6 |
| 30 | John Dalzell (R) | 15,574 | 58.2 |
| | Edward F. Duffy (D) | 7,512 | 28.1 |
| | William Adams (SOC) | 2,001 | 7.5 |
| | Joseph Fidler (P) | 1,674 | 6.3 |
| 31 | James Francis Burke (R) | 13,380 | 66.6 |
| | Thomas B. Alcorn (D) | 5,320 | 26.5 |
| 32 | Andrew J. Barchfeld (R, UN LAB) | 17,015 | 58.1 |
| | John Murphy (D) | 8,769 | 29.9 |
| | Thomas F. Kennedy (SOC) | 1,871 | 6.4 |
| | H. S. Gleiss (P) | 1,648 | 5.6 |

## RHODE ISLAND

| | Candidates | Votes | % |
|---|---|---|---|
| 1 | William P. Sheffield (R) | 18,222 | 48.6 |
| | Granger (D) | 18,141 | 48.4 |
| 2 | Adin B. Capron (R) | 21,374 | 60.9 |
| | Cooney (D) | 12,634 | 36.0 |

## SOUTH CAROLINA

| | Candidates | Votes | % |
|---|---|---|---|
| 1 | George S. Legare (D) | 5,759 | 90.1 |
| | A. R. Prioleau (R) | 631 | 9.9 |
| 2 | James O'H. Patterson (D) | 8,440 | 99.3 |
| 3 | Wyatt Aiken (D) | 10,274 | 100.0 |
| 4 | Joseph T. Johnston (D) | 10,806 | 100.0 |
| 5 | David E. Finley (D) | 9,468 | 100.0 |
| 6 | J. Edwin Ellebert (D) | 9,035 | 100.0 |
| 7 | Asbury F. Lever (D) | 9,950 | 90.9 |
| | R. H. Richardson (R) | 998 | 9.1 |

## SOUTH DAKOTA

| | Candidates | Votes | % |
|---|---|---|---|
| AL | Eben W. Martin (R) | 67,582✔ | |
| | Charles H. Burke (R) | 67,400✔ | |
| | Robert E. Dowdell (D) | 38,758 | |
| | Andrew H. Olson (D) | 38,624 | |
| | E. S. Chappell (P) | 3,785 | |
| | L. R. Erskine (P) | 3,733 | |
| | T. G. Deffebach (SOC) | 2,676 | |
| | S. H. Goodfellow (SOC) | 2,660 | |
| | L. V. Schneider (SOJ) | 55 | |
| | W. S. Bray (SOJ) | 55 | |

### Special Election

| | Candidates | Votes | % |
|---|---|---|---|
| AL | Eben W. Martin (R) | 65,962 | 62.3 |
| | W. W. Soule (D) | 39,865 | 37.7 |

## TENNESSEE

| | Candidates | Votes | % |
|---|---|---|---|
| 1 | Walter P. Brownlow (R) | 21,998 | 79.5 |
| | J. T. Fugate (D) | 5,686 | 20.5 |
| 2 | Richard W. Austin (R) | 15,337 | 50.9 |
| | N. W. Hale (R) | 14,528 | 48.2 |
| 3 | John A. Moon (D) | 18,403 | 60.2 |
| | John T. Raulston (R) | 12,174 | 39.8 |
| 4 | Cordell Hull (D) | 15,193 | 54.9 |
| | R. Q. Lillard (R) | 12,419 | 44.9 |
| 5 | William C. Houston (D) | 13,123 | 69.7 |
| | Z. T. Cason (R) | 5,697 | 30.2 |
| 6 | Joseph W. Byrns (D) | 18,192 | 97.3 |
| 7 | Lemuel P. Padgett (D) | 14,499 | 64.2 |
| | J. S. Beasley (D) | 8,087 | 35.8 |
| 8 | Thetus W. Sims (D) | 12,874 | 57.5 |
| | R. H. Thrasher (R) | 9,446 | 42.2 |
| 9 | Finis J. Garrett (D) | 14,312 | 73.3 |
| | W. L. Terrell (R) | 5,205 | 26.7 |
| 10 | George W. Gordon (D) | 13,672 | 96.7 |

## TEXAS

| | Candidates | Votes | % |
|---|---|---|---|
| 1 | Morris Sheppard (D) | 14,775 | 84.4 |
| | H. L. McQuiston (R) | 2,304 | 13.2 |
| 2 | Martin Dies (D) | 14,559 | 81.8 |
| | C. E. Smith (R) | 2,719 | 15.3 |
| 3 | Gordon J. Russell (D) | 11,651 | 74.3 |
| | J. A. Harper (R) | 3,289 | 21.0 |
| 4 | Choice B. Randell (D) | 16,017 | 80.0 |
| | R. H. Crabb (R) | 3,205 | 16.0 |
| 5 | Jack Beall (D) | 17,840 | 84.4 |
| | Marion T. Connor (R) | 3,177 | 15.0 |
| 6 | Rufus Hardy (D) | 10,350 | 84.3 |
| | C. L. McCoy (R) | 1,919 | 15.0 |
| 7 | Alexander W. Gregg (D) | 8,625 | 97.0 |
| 8 | John M. Moore (D) | 12,285 | 77.0 |
| | T. M. Kennerly (R) | 3,482 | 22.0 |
| 9 | George F. Burgess (D) | 13,191 | 67.0 |
| | O. S. York (R) | 5,897 | 30.0 |
| 10 | Albert S. Burleson (D) | 13,314 | 80.0 |
| | Joseph W. Burke (R) | 3,185 | 19.0 |
| 11 | Robert L. Henry (D) | 10,114 | 100.0 |
| 12 | Oscar W. Gillespie (D) | 17,778 | 81.0 |
| | W. A. Dodge (R) | 3,095 | 14.0 |
| 13 | John H. Stephens (D) | 24,705 | 84.0 |
| | Jasper W. Haney (R) | 3,715 | 12.0 |
| 14 | James L. Slayden (D) | 16,801 | 99.0 |
| 15 | John N. Garner (D) | 11,682 | 61.0 |
| | W. T. Moore (D) | 7,179 | 37.0 |
| 16 | William R. Smith (D) | 22,159 | 88.0 |
| | G. W. Boynton (R) | 2,544 | 10.0 |

## UTAH

| | Candidates | Votes | % |
|---|---|---|---|
| AL | Joseph Howell (R) | 57,544 | 51.0 |
| | L. R. Martineau (D) | 35,981 | 32.0 |
| | Charles I. Douglas (AM) | 13,484 | 12.0 |

## VERMONT

| | Candidates | Votes | % |
|---|---|---|---|
| 1 | David J. Foster (R) | 22,190 | 71.0 |
| | Emile Blais (D) | 8,028 | 26.0 |
| 2 | Frank Plumley (R) | 22,868 | 75.0 |
| | Andrew J. Sibley (D) | 6,914 | 22.0 |

## VIRGINIA

| | Candidates | Votes | % |
|---|---|---|---|
| 1 | William A. Jones (D) | 9,733 | 74.0 |
| | George N. Wise (R) | 3,287 | 25.0 |
| 2 | Harry L. Maynard (D) | 7,358 | 70.0 |
| | D. L. Groner (R) | 3,026 | 29.0 |
| 3 | John Lamb (D) | 8,105 | 77.0 |
| | J. G. Luce (R) | 2,339 | 22.0 |

## VIRGINIA

| | Candidates | Votes | % |
|---|---|---|---|
| 4 | Francis R. Lassiter (D) | 7,200 | 99.9 |
| 5 | Edward W. Saunders (D) | 7,079 | 50.3 |
| | J. M. Parsons (R) | 6,988 | 49.6 |
| 6 | Carter Glass (D) | 8,807 | 65.9 |
| | M. Hartman (R) | 3,421 | 25.6 |
| | J. M. Parsons | 994 | 7.4 |
| 7 | James Hay (D) | 9,560 | 62.9 |
| | L. Pritchard (R) | 5,652 | 37.2 |
| 8 | Charles C. Carlin (D) | 10,182 | 79.7 |
| | J. W. Gregg (R) | 2,597 | 20.3 |
| 9 | C. Bascom Slemp (R) | 15,693 | 56.3 |
| | J. C. Byars (D) | 12,192 | 43.7 |
| 10 | Henry D. Flood (D) | 10,140 | 65.8 |
| | W. C. Franklin (R) | 5,281 | 34.3 |

## WASHINGTON

| | Candidates | Votes | % |
|---|---|---|---|
| 1 | William E. Humphrey (R) | 39,643 | 63.7 |
| | Charles H. Miller (D) | 21,089 | 33.9 |
| 2 | Francis W. Cushman (R) | 29,850 | 69.8 |
| | Browder D. Brown (D) | 12,006 | 28.1 |
| 3 | Miles Pointdexter (R) | 38,369 | 61.0 |
| | William Goodyear (D) | 23,227 | 36.9 |

## WEST VIRGINIA

| | Candidates | Votes | % |
|---|---|---|---|
| 1 | William P. Hubbard (R) | 27,351 | 51.3 |
| | E. L. Robinson (D) | 23,580 | 44.2 |
| 2 | George C. Sturgiss (R) | 25,322 | 51.1 |
| | B. H. Hines (D) | 22,771 | 45.9 |
| 3 | Joseph Holt Gaines (R) | 29,266 | 53.2 |
| | Andrew Price (D) | 23,355 | 42.5 |
| 4 | Harry C. Woodyard (R) | 21,777 | 51.9 |
| | W. O. Parsons (D) | 19,095 | 45.5 |
| 5 | James A. Hughes (R) | 31,958 | 55.6 |
| | L. H. Clarke (D) | 24,778 | 43.1 |

## WISCONSIN

| | Candidates | Votes | % |
|---|---|---|---|
| 1 | Henry Allen Cooper (R) | 26,728 | 60.6 |
| | H. A. Moehlenpah (D) | 14,018 | 31.8 |
| 2 | John M. Nelson (R) | 20,925 | 53.6 |
| | J. E. Jones (D) | 17,748 | 45.5 |
| 3 | Arthur W. Kopp (R) | 21,409 | 55.8 |
| | J. W. Murphy (D) | 16,010 | 41.7 |
| 4 | William J. Cary (R) | 15,509 | 39.1 |
| | William J. Kershaw (D) | 14,370 | 36.2 |

| | Candidates | Votes | % |
|---|---|---|---|
| | Ed T. Melms (SOCIAL D) | 9,788 | 24.7 |
| 5 | William H. Stafford (R) | 16,394 | 40.4 |
| | G. Holmes Daubner (D) | 12,871 | 31.8 |
| | Albert J. Welch (SOCIAL D) | 11,279 | 27.8 |
| 6 | Charles H. Weisse (D) | 23,317 | 57.8 |
| | George Spratt (R) | 16,184 | 40.1 |
| 7 | John J. Esch (R) | 25,202 | 68.0 |
| | B. F. Keeler (D) | 11,466 | 31.0 |
| 8 | James H. Davidson (R) | 23,097 | 57.3 |
| | Lyman J. Nash (D) | 14,984 | 37.2 |
| 9 | Gustav Kustermann (R) | 18,562 | 53.6 |
| | L. Lindauer (D) | 15,249 | 44.1 |
| 10 | Elmer A. Morse (R) | 26,081 | 60.9 |
| | Wells M. Ruggles (D) | 16,777 | 39.1 |
| 11 | Irvine L. Lenroot (R) | 30,104 | 71.7 |
| | J. S. Konkel (D) | 10,467 | 24.9 |

## WYOMING

| | Candidates | Votes | % |
|---|---|---|---|
| AL | Frank W. Mondell (R) | 21,431 | 57.1 |
| | Hayden M. White (D) | 13,643 | 36.3 |
| | James Morgan (SOC) | 2,486 | 6.6 |

# 1909 House Elections

## ILLINOIS

**Special Election**

| | Candidates | Votes | % |
|---|---|---|---|
| 6 | William J. Moxley (R) | 14,623 | 48.4 |
| | Carl L. Barnes | 8,342 | 27.6 |
| | Frank S. Ryan | 6,435 | 21.3 |

## LOUISIANA

**Special Election**

| | Candidates | Votes | % |
|---|---|---|---|
| 2 | Samuel L. Gilmore (D) | 5,535 | 100.0 |

# 1910 House Elections

## ALABAMA

| Candidates | Votes | % |
|---|---|---|
| 1 George W. Taylor (D) | 7,071 | 97.0 |
| 2 S. Hubert Dent Jr. (D) | 9,593 | 100.0 |
| 3 Henry D. Clayton (D) | 9,573 | 100.0 |
| 4 Fred L. Blackmon (D) | 8,286 | 69.9 |
| J. M. Atkins (R) | 3,572 | 30.1 |
| 5 J. Thomas Heflin (D) | 10,058 | 100.0 |
| 6 Richmond P. Hobson (D) | 9,296 | 81.5 |
| Andrew D. Mitchell (R) | 2,114 | 18.5 |
| 7 John L. Burnett (D) | 9,496 | 51.4 |
| M. W. Howard (R) | 8,977 | 48.6 |
| 8 William Richardson (D) | 8,785 | 98.1 |
| 9 Oscar W. Underwood (D) | 10,114 | 100.0 |

## ARKANSAS

| Candidates | Votes | % |
|---|---|---|
| 1 Robert B. Macon (D) | 2,803 | 100.0 |
| 2 William A. Oldfield (D) | 5,053 | 81.7 |
| J. T. Hall (R) | 1,131 | 18.3 |
| 3 John C. Floyd (D) | 5,131 | 55.6 |
| B. S. Granger (R) | 4,197 | 45.5 |
| 4 William B. Cravens (D) | 3,369 | 100.0 |
| 5 Henderson M. Janeway (D) | 5,505 | 76.4 |
| A. C. Remmel (R) | 1,702 | 23.6 |
| 6 Joseph T. Robinson (D) | 4,701 | 81.6 |
| B. C. Thompson (R) | 1,062 | 18.4 |
| 7 William S. Goodwin (D) | 5,266 | 82.2 |
| A. L. Wilson (R) | 1,143 | 17.8 |

## CALIFORNIA

| Candidates | Votes | % |
|---|---|---|
| 1 John E. Raker (D) | 16,704 | 45.4 |
| William F. Englebright (R) | 16,570 | 45.1 |
| W. M. Morgan (SOC) | 3,231 | 8.8 |
| 2 William Kent (R) | 25,346 | 50.1 |
| I. G. Zumwalt (D) | 22,229 | 44.0 |
| W. H. Ferber (SOC) | 2,647 | 5.2 |
| 3 Joseph R. Knowland (R-D) | 34,291 | 81.9 |
| S. Miller (SOC) | 6,653 | 15.9 |
| 4 Julius Kahn (R) | 10,188 | 56.2 |
| Walter Macarthur (D) | 6,636 | 36.6 |
| Austin Lewis (SOC) | 1,178 | 6.5 |
| 5 Everis Anson Hayes (R) | 33,265 | 59.4 |
| Thomas E. Hayden (D) | 15,345 | 27.4 |
| E. L. Reguin (SOC) | 7,052 | 12.6 |
| 6 James C. Needham (R) | 19,717 | 47.3 |
| A. L. Cowell (D) | 18,408 | 44.1 |
| Richard Kirk (SOC) | 2,568 | 6.2 |
| 7 William D. Stephens (R) | 36,435 | 58.7 |
| Lorin A. Handley (D) | 13,340 | 21.5 |
| T. W. Williams (SOC) | 10,305 | 16.6 |
| 8 Sylvester C. Smith (R) | 28,202 | 50.5 |
| William G. Irving (D) | 18,958 | 34.0 |
| George A. Garrett (SOC) | 7,302 | 13.1 |

## COLORADO

| Candidates | Votes | % |
|---|---|---|
| 1 Atterson W. Rucker (D) | 40,458 | 40.8 |
| James C. Burger (R) | 37,966 | 38.3 |
| George J. Kindel (P) | 17,144 | 17.3 |
| 2 John A. Martin (D) | 60,201 | 48.6 |
| James A. Orr (R) | 57,006 | 46.0 |
| AL Edward T. Taylor (D) | 105,700 | 47.9 |
| Isaac H. Stevens (R) | 101,722 | 46.1 |

## CONNECTICUT

| Candidates | Votes | % |
|---|---|---|
| 1 E. Stevens Henry (R) | 19,367 | 48.1 |
| Augustine Lonergan (D) | 18,132 | 45.0 |
| 2 Thomas L. Reilly (D) | 27,492 | 48.7 |
| Shepard (R) | 24,480 | 43.3 |
| Paecht (SOC) | 3,708 | 6.6 |
| 3 Edwin W. Higgins (R) | 10,011 | 47.8 |
| Raymond J. Jodoin (D) | 9,933 | 47.4 |
| 4 Ebenezer J. Hill (R) | 23,479 | 48.4 |
| Wilson (D) | 20,636 | 42.5 |
| Peach (SOC) | 3,606 | 7.4 |
| AL John Q. Tilson (R) | 79,585 | 47.9 |
| Ingersoll (D) | 73,221 | 44.1 |
| Beardsley (SOC) | 10,304 | 6.2 |

## DELAWARE

| Candidates | Votes | % |
|---|---|---|
| AL William H. Heald (R) | 22,410 | 50.9 |
| Robert C. White (D) | 20,281 | 46.1 |

## FLORIDA

| Candidates | Votes | % |
|---|---|---|
| 1 Stephen M. Sparkman (D) | 10,525 | 81.8 |
| C. C. Allen (SOC) | 2,346 | 18.2 |
| 2 Frank Clark (D) | 11,626 | 78.5 |
| Thomas W. Cox (SOC) | 1,804 | 12.2 |
| Thomas C. Buddington (R) | 1,372 | 9.3 |
| 3 Dannitte H. Mays (D) | 8,844 | 89.6 |
| Eric Vonaxelson (SOC) | 1,032 | 10.5 |

## GEORGIA

| Candidates | Votes | % |
|---|---|---|
| 1 Charles Edwards (D) | 2,019 | 100.0 |
| 2 Seaborn A. Roddenberry (D) | 3,179 | 100.0 |
| 3 Dudley Hughes (D) | 2,855 | 100.0 |
| 4 William C. Adamson (D) | 2,815 | 100.0 |
| 5 William S. Howard (D) | 4,091 | 100.0 |
| 6 Charles L. Bartlett (D) | 3,351 | 100.0 |
| 7 Gordon Lee (D) | 7,146 | 75.8 |
| Walter Akerman (R) | 2,285 | 24.2 |
| 8 Samuel J. Tribble (ID) | 8,635 | 58.1 |
| William Howard (D) | 6,222 | 41.9 |
| 9 Thomas M. Bell (D) | 4,285 | 100.0 |
| 10 Thomas Hardwick (D) | 4,331 | 75.3 |
| C. E. McGregor (ID) | 1,418 | 24.7 |
| 11 William Brantley (D) | 3,160 | 100.0 |

## IDAHO

| Candidates | Votes | % |
|---|---|---|
| AL Burton L. French (R) | 46,401 | 55.4 |
| A. M. Bowen (D) | 31,832 | 38.0 |
| Rolla Myer (SOC) | 5,463 | 6.5 |

## ILLINOIS

| Candidates | Votes | % |
|---|---|---|
| 1 Martin B. Madden (R) | 14,920 | 50.0 |
| Michael E. Maher (D) | 13,466 | 45.1 |
| 2 James R. Mann (R) | 20,128 | 48.4 |
| John Charles Vaughan (D) | 18,717 | 45.0 |
| J. O. Bentall (SOC) | 2,711 | 6.5 |
| 3 William Warfield Wilson (R) | 16,661 | 44.9 |
| Fred J. Crowley (D) | 16,604 | 44.8 |
| J. Clifford Cox (SOC) | 2,920 | 7.9 |
| 4 James T. McDermott (D) | 15,764 | 62.9 |
| Michael G. Walsh (R) | 7,028 | 28.1 |
| Peter Bulthouse (SOC) | 1,994 | 8.0 |
| 5 Adolph J. Sabath (D) | 13,936 | 71.7 |
| Louis H. Clusmann (R) | 3,533 | 18.2 |
| Joseph J. Kral (SOC) | 1,775 | 9.1 |
| 6 Edmund J. Stack (D) | 22,951 | 51.1 |
| William J. Moxley (R) | 17,178 | 38.2 |
| George Chant (SOC) | 3,551 | 7.9 |
| 7 Frank Buchanan (D) | 22,520 | 43.6 |
| Frederick Lundin (R) | 21,096 | 40.8 |
| John Collins (SOC) | 7,016 | 13.6 |
| 8 Thomas Gallagher (D) | 14,281 | 58.7 |
| Daniel D. Coffey (R) | 7,975 | 32.8 |
| John Drexler (SOC) | 1,903 | 7.8 |
| 9 Lynden Evans (D) | 13,501 | 45.7 |
| Frederick H. Gansbergen (R) | 12,991 | 44.0 |
| Frank Shiflersmith (SOC) | 2,650 | 9.0 |
| 10 George Edmund Foss (R) | 20,130 | 47.7 |
| Richard J. Finnegan (D) | 17,541 | 41.5 |
| Robert C. Magisen (SOC) | 3,370 | 8.0 |
| 11 Ira C. Copley (R) | 17,899 | 57.1 |
| Frank O. Hawley (D) | 11,276 | 36.0 |
| 12 Charles E. Fuller (R) | 20,665 | 62.3 |
| J. W. Rausch (D) | 9,185 | 27.7 |
| Thomas Johnson (SOC) | 2,277 | 6.9 |
| 13 John C. McKenzie (R) | 17,249 | 61.3 |
| O. H. Wright (D) | 9,752 | 34.7 |
| 14 James McKinney (R) | 17,004 | 52.3 |
| Clyde H. Tavenner (D) | 12,980 | 40.0 |
| Milton L. Morrill (SOC) | 1,658 | 5.1 |
| 15 George W. Prince (R) | 16,753 | 47.0 |
| Albert E. Bergland (D) | 16,487 | 46.3 |
| 16 Claudius U. Stone (D) | 17,633 | 51.2 |
| Joseph V. Graff (R) | 15,024 | 43.6 |
| 17 John A. Sterling (R) | 16,601 | 52.0 |
| Louis Fitzhenry (D) | 14,215 | 44.5 |
| 18 Joseph G. Cannon (R) | 20,943 | 53.0 |
| William L. Cundiff (D) | 16,186 | 41.0 |
| 19 William B. McKinley (R) | 23,107 | 52.6 |
| I. J. Martin (D) | 19,259 | 43.9 |
| 20 Henry T. Rainey (D) | 20,194 | 59.3 |
| James H. Danskin (R) | 12,961 | 38.0 |
| 21 James M. Graham (D) | 19,886 | 50.1 |
| H. Clay Wilson (R) | 17,318 | 43.6 |
| 22 William A. Rodenberg (R) | 23,024 | 49.7 |
| Bruce A. Campbell (D) | 18,787 | 40.6 |
| Henry Groeteka (SOC) | 3,826 | 8.3 |
| 23 Martin D. Foster (D) | 23,535 | 53.7 |
| J. H. Loy (R) | 18,230 | 41.6 |
| 24 H. Robert Fowler (D) | 17,235 | 48.8 |
| Pleasant T. Chapman (R) | 16,918 | 47.9 |
| 25 Napoleon B. Thistlewood (R) | 18,233 | 49.1 |
| William D. Lyerle (D) | 16,442 | 44.2 |

## INDIANA

| Candidates | Votes | % |
|---|---|---|
| 1 John W. Boehne (D) | 22,420 | 52.3 |
| Francis B. Posey (R) | 18,606 | 43.4 |
| 2 William A. Cullop (D) | 22,960 | 48.4 |
| Oscar E. Bland (R) | 21,419 | 45.2 |
| 3 William E. Cox (D) | 21,670 | 58.4 |
| Harry C. Poindexter (R) | 14,969 | 40.3 |
| 4 Lincoln Dixon (D) | 22,001 | 53.8 |
| John H. Kemman (R) | 17,921 | 43.8 |
| 5 Ralph W. Moss (D) | 25,917 | 51.6 |
| Frank Tilley (R) | 21,267 | 42.4 |
| 6 Finley P. Gray (D) | 23,740 | 49.0 |
| William O. Barnard (R) | 22,242 | 45.9 |
| 7 Charles A. Korbly (D) | 30,330 | 50.3 |
| Linton A. Cox (R) | 26,968 | 44.7 |
| 8 John A. M. Adair (D) | 25,454 | 51.8 |
| Rollin Warner (R) | 19,309 | 39.3 |
| Orville G. Overcarsh (SOC) | 2,910 | 5.9 |
| 9 Martin A. Morrison (D) | 24,434 | 48.0 |
| Everett E. Neal (R) | 23,841 | 46.8 |
| 10 Edgar D. Crumpacker (R) | 27,722 | 50.3 |
| John B. Peterson (D) | 25,692 | 46.6 |
| 11 George W. Rauch (D) | 22,528 | 47.8 |
| John L. Thompson (R) | 21,282 | 45.2 |
| 12 Cyrus Cline (D) | 19,754 | 49.9 |
| Owen N. Heaton (R) | 17,937 | 45.3 |
| 13 Henry A. Barnhart (D) | 25,253 | 48.2 |
| John L. Moorman (R) | 24,153 | 46.1 |

## IOWA

| Candidates | Votes | % |
|---|---|---|
| 1 Charles A. Kennedy (R) | 15,602 | 51.9 |
| J. A. S. Pollard (D) | 13,427 | 44.7 |

## IOWA

| | Candidates | Votes | % |
|---|---|---|---|
| 2 | Irvin S. Pepper (D) | 19,815 | 51.5 |
| | Charles Grilk (R) | 16,971 | 44.1 |
| 3 | Charles E. Pickett (R) | 19,324 | 54.3 |
| | John D. Denison Jr (D) | 15,572 | 43.7 |
| 4 | Gilbert N. Haugen (R) | 16,928 | 49.9 |
| | Daniel D. Murphy (D) | 16,708 | 49.3 |
| 5 | James W. Good (R) | 16,953 | 51.8 |
| | S. C. Huber (D) | 14,676 | 44.8 |
| 6 | Nathan E. Kendall (R) | 16,335 | 48.2 |
| | Daniel W. Hamilton (D) | 15,914 | 47.0 |
| 7 | Solomon F. Prouty (R) | 17,722 | 53.1 |
| | Clint L. Price (D) | 14,534 | 43.5 |
| 8 | Horace M. Towner (R) | 19,548 | 54.9 |
| | Frank Q. Stewart (D) | 15,565 | 43.7 |
| 9 | Walter I. Smith (R) | 18,763 | 52.0 |
| | W. F. Cleeland (D) | 16,916 | 46.9 |
| 10 | Frank P. Woods (Π) | 20,927 | 97.0 |
| 11 | Elbert H. Hubbard (R) | 22,199 | 59.9 |
| | M. M. White (D) | 14,377 | 38.8 |

## KANSAS

| | Candidates | Votes | % |
|---|---|---|---|
| 1 | Daniel R. Anthony Jr. (R) | 21,852 | 72.3 |
| | J. B. Chapman (D) | 7,486 | 24.8 |
| 2 | Alexander C. Mitchell (R) | 23,282 | 50.9 |
| | John Caldwell (D) | 19,852 | 43.4 |
| 3 | Phillip P. Campbell (R) | 20,771 | 44.5 |
| | Jeremiah D. Botkin (D) | 19,943 | 42.7 |
| | C. S. Bendure (SOC) | 5,748 | 12.3 |
| 4 | Fred S. Jackson (R) | 17,111 | 54.9 |
| | Henderson S. Martin (D) | 14,051 | 45.1 |
| 5 | Rollin R. Rees (R) | 17,680 | 51.3 |
| | G. T. Helvering (D) | 15,775 | 45.8 |
| 6 | Isaac D. Young (R) | 21,020 | 50.9 |
| | Frank S. Rockefeller (D) | 18,985 | 46.0 |
| 7 | Edmond H. Madison (R) | 24,925 | 53.1 |
| | George A. Neeley (D) | 20,133 | 42.9 |
| 8 | Victor Murdock (R) | 16,239 | 87.3 |
| | George Burnett (SOC) | 2,354 | 12.7 |

## KENTUCKY

| | Candidates | Votes | % |
|---|---|---|---|
| 1 | Ollie M. James (D) | 11,574 | 89.3 |
| | C. L. Harney (SOC) | 1,389 | 10.7 |
| 2 | Augustus O. Stanley (D) | 12,040 | 62.2 |
| | R. J. Salmon (R) | 6,902 | 35.7 |
| 3 | Robert Y. Thomas Jr. (D) | 16,063 | 51.3 |
| | W. H. Jones (R) | 14,850 | 47.5 |
| 4 | Ben Johnson (D) | 18,263 | 59.2 |
| | D. W. Gaddie (R) | 11,952 | 38.8 |
| 5 | J. Swagar Sherley (D) | 21,437 | 53.2 |
| | J. Wheeler McGee (R) | 17,376 | 43.1 |
| 6 | Arthur B. Rouse (D) | 15,454 | 55.6 |
| | Charles W. Nagel (R) | 11,007 | 39.6 |
| 7 | James C. Cantrill (D) | 13,858 | 56.0 |
| | M. C. Rankin (R) | 10,877 | 44.0 |
| 8 | Harvey Helm (D) | 12,412 | 56.9 |
| | Hugh Miller (R) | 9,385 | 43.1 |
| 9 | William J. Fields (D) | 19,350 | 50.8 |
| | Joseph B. Bennett (R) | 18,737 | 49.2 |
| 10 | John W. Langley (R) | 20,664 | 52.4 |
| | A. Floyd Byrd (D) | 18,766 | 47.6 |
| 11 | Caleb Powers (R) | 25,622 | 60.5 |
| | Elza Bertrand (D) | 16,357 | 38.6 |

## LOUISIANA

| | Candidates | Votes | % |
|---|---|---|---|
| 1 | Albert Estopinal (D) | 11,932 | 89.5 |
| | John A. Wogan (R) | 1,408 | 10.6 |
| 2 | H. Garland Dupre (D) | 10,218 | 83.2 |
| | Victor Loisel (R) | 2,071 | 16.9 |
| 3 | Robert F. Broussard (D) | 4,011 | 91.0 |
| | Jules Dreyfus (R) | 395 | 9.0 |
| 4 | John T. Watkins (D) | 4,244 | 95.9 |
| 5 | Joseph E. Ransdell (D) | 4,469 | 99.0 |
| 6 | Robert C. Wickliffe (D) | 4,016 | 100.0 |
| 7 | Arsene P. Pujo (D) | 7,393 | 91.3 |
| | J. R. Jones (SOC) | 706 | 8.7 |

### Special Election

| | Candidates | Votes | % |
|---|---|---|---|
| 2 | H. Garland Dupre (D) | 10,333 | 82.7 |
| | Victor Loisel (R) | 2,160 | 17.3 |

## MAINE

| | Candidates | Votes | % |
|---|---|---|---|
| 1 | Asher C. Hinds (R) | 17,521 | 49.8 |
| | W. M. Pennell (D) | 16,901 | 48.0 |
| 2 | Daniel J. McGillicuddy (D) | 18,938 | 52.6 |
| | John P. Swasey (R) | 16,227 | 45.1 |
| 3 | Samuel W. Gould (D) | 17,187 | 51.1 |
| | Edwin C. Burleigh (R) | 15,798 | 46.9 |
| 4 | Frank E. Guernsey (R) | 18,017 | 50.3 |
| | George M. Hanson (D) | 17,516 | 48.9 |

## MARYLAND

| | Candidates | Votes | % |
|---|---|---|---|
| 1 | James Harry Covington (D) | 18,341 | 51.6 |
| | A. Lincoln Dryden (R) | 16,066 | 45.2 |
| 2 | Joshua Frederick C. Talbott (D) | 19,352 | 51.8 |
| | William B. Baker (R) | 17,124 | 45.8 |
| 3 | George Konig (D) | 15,028 | 48.4 |
| | Charles W. Main (R) | 14,740 | 47.5 |
| 4 | John Charles Linthicum (D) | 17,478 | 50.8 |
| | Addison E. Mullikin (R) | 15,698 | 45.7 |
| 5 | Thomas Parran (R) | 15,706 | 49.5 |
| | J. Enos Ray Jr. (D) | 14,879 | 46.9 |
| 6 | David J. Lewis (D) | 16,585 | 48.1 |
| | Brainard Henry Warner Jr. (R) | 15,896 | 46.1 |

## MASSACHUSETTS

| | Candidates | Votes | % |
|---|---|---|---|
| 1 | George P. Lawrence (R) | 14,109 | 48.9 |
| | Edward Morgan (D) | 13,244 | 45.9 |
| | Louis B. Clark (SOC) | 1,476 | 5.1 |
| 2 | Frederick H. Gillett (R) | 14,242 | 48.8 |
| | William G. McKechnie (D) | 13,774 | 47.2 |
| 3 | John A. Thayer (D) | 15,243 | 51.2 |
| | Charles G. Washburn (R) | 14,544 | 48.8 |
| 4 | William H. Wilder (R) | 16,965 | 49.1 |
| | John J. Mitchell (D) | 16,835 | 48.7 |
| 5 | Butler Ames (R) | 13,760 | 51.1 |
| | James H. Carmichael (D) | 13,163 | 48.9 |
| 6 | Augustus P. Gardner (R) | 17,272 | 54.0 |
| | William H. O'Brien (D) | 12,038 | 37.6 |
| | James F. Carey (SOC) | 2,667 | 8.3 |
| 7 | Ernest W. Roberts (R) | 16,624 | 50.7 |
| | Walter H. Creamer (D) | 14,337 | 43.7 |
| | W. Lathrop Meaker (DPPC) | 1,837 | 5.6 |
| 8 | Samuel W. McCall (R) | 15,854 | 53.4 |
| | Frederick S. Deitrick (D) | 13,842 | 46.6 |
| 9 | William F. Murray (D) | 11,652 | 49.0 |
| | John A. Keliher (DI) | 10,037 | 42.2 |
| | William H. Oakes (R) | 2,081 | 8.8 |
| 10 | James M. Curley (D) | 20,345 | 56.3 |
| | J. Mitchel Galvin (R) | 15,783 | 43.7 |
| 11 | Andrew J. Peters (D) | 18,933 | 59.2 |
| | William Dudley (R) | 13,033 | 40.8 |
| 12 | John W. Weeks (R) | 19,037 | 56.4 |
| | Daniel J. Daley (D) | 14,696 | 43.6 |
| 13 | William S. Greene (R) | 14,079 | 58.9 |
| | James F. Morris (D) | 9,831 | 41.1 |
| 14 | Robert O. Harris (R) | 15,753 | 47.9 |
| | Thomas C. Thacher (D) | 15,686 | 47.6 |

### Special Election

| | Candidates | Votes | % |
|---|---|---|---|
| 4 | John J. Mitchell (D) | 16,688 | 50.0 |
| | William H. Wilder (R) | 16,664 | 50.0 |

## MICHIGAN

| | Candidates | Votes | % |
|---|---|---|---|
| 1 | Frank E. Doremus (D) | 20,843 | 52.0 |
| | Edwin Denby (R) | 17,676 | 44.1 |
| 2 | William W. Wedemeyer (R) | 21,485 | 57.0 |
| | John V. Sheehan (D) | 15,125 | 40.1 |
| 3 | John M. C. Smith (R) | 18,606 | 57.7 |
| | Nathaniel H. Stewart (D) | 11,935 | 37.0 |
| 4 | Edward L. Hamilton (R) | 17,282 | 56.2 |
| | John E. Barnes (D) | 12,185 | 39.6 |
| 5 | Edwin F. Sweet (D) | 15,219 | 48.4 |
| | Gerrit J. Diekema (R) | 14,589 | 46.4 |
| 6 | Samuel W. Smith (R) | 23,321 | 52.9 |
| | Alva M. Cummins (D) | 18,403 | 41.7 |
| 7 | Henry McMorran (R) | 15,897 | 55.6 |
| | Thomas Wellman (D) | 11,595 | 40.5 |
| 8 | Joseph W. Fordney (R) | 14,878 | 56.5 |
| | James P. Devereaux (D) | 10,571 | 40.2 |
| 9 | James C. McLaughlin (R) | 13,029 | 65.7 |
| | Emery D. Weimer (D) | 6,171 | 31.1 |
| 10 | George A. Loud (R) | 15,060 | 59.8 |
| | Albert Miller (D) | 8,746 | 34.7 |
| 11 | Francis H. Dodds (R) | 16,179 | 64.8 |
| | Hubbard Head (D) | 7,157 | 28.7 |
| 12 | H. Olin Young (R) | 24,661 | 73.6 |
| | Gideon T. Werline (D) | 8,751 | 26.1 |

## MINNESOTA

| | Candidates | Votes | % |
|---|---|---|---|
| 1 | Sydney Anderson (R) | 18,315 | 55.3 |
| | Buck (D) | 14,816 | 44.7 |
| 2 | Winfield S. Hammond (D) | 14,745 | 53.2 |
| | Ellsworth (R) | 12,426 | 44.8 |
| 3 | Charles R. Davis (R) | 21,863 | 100.0 |
| 4 | Frederick C. Stevens (R) | 18,830 | 56.6 |
| | Gieske (D) | 12,495 | 37.6 |
| | Stratton (PUB OWN) | 1,953 | 5.9 |
| 5 | Frank M. Nye (R) | 17,433 | 50.0 |
| | Dyer (D) | 15,113 | 43.3 |
| | Lindsay (PUB OWN) | 2,323 | 6.7 |
| 6 | Charles A. Lindbergh (R) | 25,272 | 100.0 |
| 7 | Andrew J. Volstead (R) | 24,395 | 100.0 |
| 8 | Clarence B. Miller (R) | 17,018 | 53.7 |
| | Jaques (D) | 10,305 | 32.5 |
| | Watkins (PUB OWN) | 4,354 | 13.7 |
| 9 | Halvor Steenerson (R) | 24,572 | 74.5 |
| | Sanders (PUB OWN) | 8,421 | 25.5 |

## MISSISSIPPI

| | Candidates | Votes | % |
|---|---|---|---|
| 1 | Ezekiel S. Candler Jr. (D) | 2,904 | 100.0 |
| 2 | Hubert D. Stephens (D) | 3,304 | 100.0 |
| 3 | Benjamin G. Humphreys (D) | 1,799 | 100.0 |
| 4 | Thomas U. Sisson (D) | 3,719 | 100.0 |
| 5 | Samuel A. Witherspoon (D) | 3,921 | 100.0 |
| 6 | Pat Harrison (D) | 4,011 | 99.4 |
| 7 | William A. Dickson (D) | 2,468 | 100.0 |
| 8 | James W. Collier (D) | 1,739 | 100.0 |

## MISSOURI

| | Candidates | Votes | % |
|---|---|---|---|
| 1 | James T. Lloyd (D) | 19,953 | 54.2 |
| | Higbee (R) | 15,572 | 42.3 |
| 2 | William W. Rucker (D) | 21,090 | 55.6 |
| | Haley (R) | 16,122 | 42.5 |
| 3 | Joshua W. Alexander (D) | 19,213 | 56.3 |
| | Davisson (R) | 14,900 | 43.7 |
| 4 | Charles F. Booher (D) | 20,231 | 55.1 |
| | Amick (R) | 15,825 | 43.1 |
| 5 | William P. Borland (D) | 31,026 | 54.6 |
| | Lea (R) | 23,982 | 42.2 |
| 6 | Clement C. Dickinson (D) | 17,504 | 53.2 |
| | Devol (R) | 14,374 | 43.7 |
| 7 | Courtney W. Hamlin (D) | 22,433 | 49.1 |
| | Hall (R) | 21,951 | 48.0 |
| 8 | Dorsey W. Shackleford (D) | 16,642 | 53.3 |
| | Norfleet (R) | 14,349 | 45.9 |
| 9 | James Beauchamp Clark (D) | 23,124 | 54.5 |
| | Roy (R) | 19,105 | 45.0 |
| 10 | Richard Bartholdt (R) | 53,298 | 60.8 |
| | Charles J. Maurer (D) | 28,054 | 32.0 |
| | Hoehn (SOC) | 5,865 | 6.7 |

## MISSOURI

| | Candidates | Votes | % |
|---|---|---|---|
| 11 | Theron E. Catlin (R) | 20,089‡ | 49.7 |
| | Patrick F. Gill (D) | 18,695 | 46.3 |
| 12 | Leonidas Dyer (R) | 15,965 | 53.1 |
| | Thomas E. Kinney (D) | 13,121 | 43.7 |
| 13 | Walter L. Hensley (D) | 16,020 | 49.3 |
| | Elvins (R) | 15,386 | 47.4 |
| 14 | Joseph J. Russell (D) | 23,612 | 47.8 |
| | Crow (R) | 22,463 | 45.5 |
| | Hafner (SOC) | 2,973 | 6.0 |
| 15 | James A. Daugherty (D) | 21,259 | 47.4 |
| | Morgan (R) | 20,443 | 45.6 |
| 16 | Thomas L. Rubey (D) | 16,239 | 52.1 |
| | Murphy (R) | 14,763 | 47.4 |

## MONTANA

| | Candidates | Votes | % |
|---|---|---|---|
| AL | Charles N. Pray (R) | 32,519 | 49.4 |
| | Charles S. Hartman (D) | 28,071 | 42.7 |
| | J. Frank Mabie (SOC) | 5,184 | 7.9 |

## NEBRASKA

| | Candidates | Votes | % |
|---|---|---|---|
| 1 | John A. Maguire (D & PPI) | 16,501 | 50.4 |
| | William Hayward (R) | 15,763 | 48.2 |
| 2 | C. O. Lobeck (D) | 15,912 | 48.9 |
| | Abraham L. Sutton (R) | 15,673 | 48.1 |
| 3 | James P. Latta (D & PPI) | 25,945 | 57.7 |
| | J. F. Boyd (R) | 18,566 | 41.3 |
| 4 | Charles H. Sloan (R) | 20,807 | 50.8 |
| | Benjamin F. Good (D & PPI) | 19,540 | 47.8 |
| 5 | George W. Norris (R) | 19,929 | 53.7 |
| | Roderick D. Sutherland (D & PPI) | 15,925 | 42.9 |
| 6 | Moses P. Kinkaid (R) | 24,327 | 52.8 |
| | William J. Taylor (D & PPI) | 19,682 | 42.7 |

## NEVADA

| | Candidates | Votes | % |
|---|---|---|---|
| AL | Edwin E. Roberts (R) | 10,066 | 49.9 |
| | Charles S. Sprague (D) | 7,688 | 38.1 |
| | Ashley Grant Miller (SOC) | 2,409 | 12.0 |

## NEW HAMPSHIRE

| | Candidates | Votes | % |
|---|---|---|---|
| 1 | Cyrus A. Sulloway (R) | 20,941 | 50.5 |
| | Eugene E. Reed (D) | 20,093 | 48.5 |
| 2 | Frank D. Currier (R) | 21,639 | 55.1 |
| | Henry H. Metcalf (D) | 16,913 | 43.0 |

## NEW JERSEY

| | Candidates | Votes | % |
|---|---|---|---|
| 1 | Henry C. Loudenslager (R) | 21,394 | 48.6 |
| | Nowrey (D) | 20,554 | 46.7 |
| 2 | John J. Gardner (R) | 22,861 | 51.6 |
| | Hampton (D) | 16,915 | 38.2 |
| | Riddle (I) | 3,508 | 7.9 |
| 3 | Thomas J. Scully (D) | 24,657 | 54.8 |
| | Howell (R) | 20,160 | 44.8 |
| 4 | Ira W. Wood (R) | 19,354 | 49.1 |
| | Libbey (D) | 19,089 | 48.4 |
| 5 | William E. Tuttle Jr. (D) | 23,768 | 51.0 |
| | Runyon (R) | 20,675 | 44.4 |
| 6 | William Hughes (D) | 29,458 | 51.6 |
| | McClave (R) | 25,301 | 44.3 |
| 7 | Edward W. Townsend (D) | 21,962 | 54.0 |
| | Parker (R) | 17,756 | 43.7 |
| 8 | Walter I. McCoy (D) | 19,364 | 51.2 |
| | William H. Wiley (R) | 16,847 | 44.6 |
| 9 | Eugene F. Kinkead (D) | 23,784 | 62.3 |
| | Record (R) | 13,390 | 35.1 |
| 10 | James A. Hamill (D) | 26,266 | 70.2 |
| | Seibel (R) | 10,104 | 27.0 |

## NEW YORK

| | Candidates | Votes | % |
|---|---|---|---|
| 1 | Martin W. Littleton (D & IL) | 26,974 | 54.0 |
| | William W. Cocks (R) | 21,826 | 43.7 |
| 2 | George H. Lindsay (D) | 14,248 | 59.2 |
| | Ladislaus W. Schwenk (R & IL) | 8,304 | 34.5 |
| | Paul Muller Jr. (SOC) | 1,428 | 5.9 |
| 3 | James P. Maher (D) | 15,432 | 48.3 |
| | Alfred T. Hobley (R & IL) | 14,570 | 45.6 |
| | John J. Jennings (SOC) | 1,806 | 5.7 |
| 4 | Frank E. Wilson (D & IL) | 20,676 | 46.6 |
| | Charles B. Law (R) | 20,295 | 45.8 |
| | Barnet Wolff (SOC) | 3,257 | 7.4 |
| 5 | William C. Redfield (D & IL) | 26,220 | 51.7 |
| | Warren I. Lee (R) | 22,576 | 44.5 |
| 6 | William M. Calder (R) | 17,249 | 48.6 |
| | Michael E. Butler (D) | 16,805 | 47.3 |
| 7 | John J. Fitzgerald (D) | 16,847 | 67.3 |
| | William R. A. Koehl (R & IL) | 7,748 | 31.0 |
| 8 | Daniel J. Riordan (D) | 20,683 | 66.2 |
| | George S. Husch (R) | 8,311 | 26.6 |
| 9 | Henry M. Goldfogle (D) | 4,606 | 46.8 |
| | Meyer London (SOC) | 3,322 | 33.8 |
| | Jacob W. Block (R & IL) | 1,850 | 18.8 |
| 10 | William Sulzer (D & IL) | 9,850 | 60.2 |
| | Anthony M. McCabe (R) | 4,807 | 29.4 |
| | John Mullen (SOC) | 1,694 | 10.4 |
| 11 | Charles V. Fornes (D) | 17,384 | 61.2 |
| | Henry H. Curran (R & IL) | 10,171 | 35.8 |
| 12 | Michael Conry (D) | 14,376 | 62.7 |
| | Peter R. Gatens (R & IL) | 7,467 | 32.6 |
| 13 | Jefferson M. Levy (D) | 11,539 | 50.4 |
| | Herbert Parsons (R) | 9,951 | 43.5 |
| 14 | John Joseph Kindred (D) | 20,875 | 54.3 |
| | Victor Hugo Duras (R & IL) | 14,018 | 36.5 |
| | William F. Ehret (SOC) | 3,481 | 9.1 |
| 15 | Thomas G. Patten (D & IL) | 13,838 | 54.4 |
| | William M. Bennett (R) | 11,152 | 43.8 |
| 16 | Francis Burton Harrison (D) | 10,450 | 55.0 |
| | Samuel Bell Thomas (CIV A) | 6,518 | 34.3 |
| | George F. Miner (SOC) | 2,012 | 10.6 |
| 17 | Henry George Jr. (D & IL) | 28,306 | 50.7 |
| | William S. Bennet (R) | 26,010 | 46.6 |
| 18 | Steven B. Ayres (D) | 33,600 | 51.2 |
| | Gottlieb Haneke (R & IL) | 27,607 | 42.0 |
| | Joshua Wauhope (SOC) | 4,354 | 6.6 |
| 19 | John E. Andrus (R) | 23,140 | 49.7 |
| | Cornelius A. Pugsley (D) | 22,247 | 47.7 |
| 20 | Thomas W. Bradley (R) | 19,363 | 51.6 |
| | John Bigelow Jr. (D) | 17,307 | 46.2 |
| 21 | Richard E. Connell (D) | 18,832 | 49.8 |
| | Hamilton Fish (R) | 18,315 | 48.4 |
| 22 | William H. Draper (R) | 20,424 | 51.8 |
| | Elisha C. Tower (D) | 17,277 | 43.8 |
| 23 | Henry S. De Forest (R) | 28,218 | 48.1 |
| | Curtis N. Douglas (D) | 26,228 | 44.7 |
| | Harvey A. Simmons (SOC) | 2,978 | 5.1 |
| 24 | George W. Fairchild (R) | 23,636 | 49.9 |
| | George M. Palmer (D) | 22,416 | 47.3 |
| 25 | Theron Akin (D, I LEAGUE) | 21,754 | 48.9 |
| | Cyrus Durey (R) | 21,442 | 48.2 |
| 26 | George R. Malby (R) | 21,980 | 55.7 |
| | Thomas Cantwell (D) | 15,584 | 39.5 |
| 27 | Charles A. Talcott (D & IL) | 22,458 | 50.8 |
| | Charles S. Millington (R) | 20,242 | 45.8 |
| 28 | Luther W. Mott (R, I LEAGUE) | 18,844 | 50.1 |
| | George W. Reeves (D) | 15,629 | 41.5 |
| | Charles F. Simpson (P) | 2,514 | 6.7 |
| 29 | Michael E. Driscoll (R) | 26,589 | 52.5 |
| | Henry E. Wilson (D & IL) | 20,281 | 40.0 |
| 30 | John W. Dwight (R) | 21,789 | 49.2 |
| | Ira A. Hix (D, I LEAGUE) | 18,346 | 41.4 |
| | Frank Dewitt Reese (P) | 3,521 | 8.0 |
| 31 | Sereno E. Payne (R) | 21,121 | 51.8 |
| | John Colmey (D) | 17,728 | 43.5 |
| 32 | Henry G. Danforth (R) | 26,375 | 52.7 |
| | George P. Decker (D) | 21,176 | 42.3 |
| 33 | Edwin S. Underhill (D) | 19,517 | 49.5 |
| | Jacob Sloat Fassett (R) | 17,556 | 44.5 |
| 34 | James S. Simmons (R) | 25,051 | 54.0 |

| | Candidates | Votes | % |
|---|---|---|---|
| | Elliot W. Horton (D) | 19,307 | 41.6 |
| 35 | Daniel A. Driscoll (D & IL) | 21,727 | 56.9 |
| | Patrick J. Keeler (R) | 14,605 | 38.3 |
| 36 | Charles Bennett Smith (D & IL) | 20,685 | 48.9 |
| | De Alva S. Alexander (R) | 20,684 | 48.8 |
| 37 | Edward Butterfield Vreeland (R) | 20,530 | 53.1 |
| | J. William Sanbury (D, I LEAGUE) | 14,314 | 37.0 |
| | Arthur A. Amidon (P) | 2,099 | 5.4 |

## NORTH CAROLINA

| | Candidates | Votes | % |
|---|---|---|---|
| 1 | John H. Small (D) | 11,544 | 75.3 |
| | Henry T. King (R) | 3,721 | 24.3 |
| 2 | Claude Kitchin (D) | 10,749 | 85.1 |
| | R. H. Norfleet (R) | 1,867 | 14.8 |
| 3 | John M. Faison (D) | 10,428 | 58.1 |
| | George E. Butler (R) | 7,505 | 41.8 |
| 4 | Edward W. Pou (D) | 13,728 | 65.8 |
| | R. A. P. Cooley (R) | 7,110 | 34.1 |
| 5 | Charles M. Stedman (D) | 20,392 | 54.2 |
| | David H. Blair (R) | 17,060 | 45.3 |
| 6 | Hannibal L. Godwin (D) | 10,806 | 71.7 |
| | Iredell Meares (R) | 4,257 | 28.3 |
| 7 | Robert N. Page (D) | 14,367 | 56.5 |
| | John J. Parker (R) | 11,006 | 43.3 |
| 8 | Robert L. Doughton (D) | 16,560 | 51.1 |
| | Charles H. Cowles (R) | 15,801 | 48.8 |
| 9 | Edwin Y. Webb (D) | 16,574 | 59.3 |
| | S. S. McNinch (R) | 11,332 | 40.6 |
| 10 | James M. Gudger Jr. (D) | 15,901 | 51.8 |
| | John G. Grant (R) | 14,771 | 48.1 |

## NORTH DAKOTA

| | Candidates | Votes | % |
|---|---|---|---|
| AL | Louis B. Hanna (R) | 51,556✔ | |
| | Henry T. Helgesen (R) | 50,600✔ | |
| | Tobias D. Casey (D) | 25,880 | |
| | M. A. Hildreth (D) | 25,322 | |
| | Arthur Hagendorf (SOC) | 3,225 | |
| | N. H. Bjornstead (SOC) | 3,179 | |

## OHIO

| | Candidates | Votes | % |
|---|---|---|---|
| 1 | Nicholas Longworth (R) | 24,453 | 51.1 |
| | Thomas P. Hart (D) | 21,497 | 44.9 |
| 2 | Alfred G. Allen (D) | 24,323 | 47.9 |
| | Herman P. Goebel (R) | 23,834 | 47.0 |
| 3 | James M. Cox (D) | 31,539 | 55.5 |
| | George R. Young (R) | 18,730 | 33.0 |
| | Harmon Evans (SOC) | 6,275 | 11.0 |
| 4 | J. Henry Goeke (D) | 20,865 | 58.4 |
| | C. E. Johnston (R) | 13,482 | 37.7 |
| 5 | Timothy T. Ansberry (D) | 21,201 | 60.1 |
| | C. S. Roe (R) | 13,309 | 37.7 |
| 6 | Matthew R. Denver (D) | 20,056 | 54.0 |
| | Jesse Taylor (R) | 17,105 | 46.0 |
| 7 | James D. Post (D) | 20,776 | 52.8 |
| | J. Warren Keifer (R) | 17,569 | 44.6 |
| 8 | Frank B. Willis (R) | 21,030 | 50.0 |
| | Thomas C. Mahon (D) | 19,519 | 46.4 |
| 9 | Isaac R. Sherwood (D) | 21,908 | 48.0 |
| | J. Kent Hamilton (R) | 19,593 | 43.0 |
| | W. F. Ries (SOC) | 3,917 | 8.6 |
| 10 | Robert M. Switzer (R) | 18,548 | 51.3 |
| | Edmond H. Willis (D) | 16,250 | 45.0 |
| 11 | Horatio C. Claypool (D) | 22,894 | 49.9 |
| | Albert Douglas (R) | 20,168 | 44.0 |
| | Austin B. Shinn (SOC) | 2,397 | 5.2 |
| 12 | Edward L. Taylor Jr. (R) | 17,696 | 39.9 |
| | Frank S. Monnett (D) | 15,151 | 34.2 |
| | Jacob L. Bachman (SOC) | 11,142 | 25.1 |
| 13 | Carl C. Anderson (D) | 30,196 | 63.7 |
| | Miles H. McLaughlin (R) | 15,486 | 32.7 |
| 14 | William G. Sharp (D) | 25,287 | 54.6 |
| | George H. Chamberlain (R) | 18,459 | 39.8 |

## OHIO

| | Candidates | Votes | % |
|---|---|---|---|
| 15 | George White (D) | 19,723 | 49.3 |
| | James Joyce (R) | 17,674 | 44.2 |
| | Frank Martin (SOC) | 2,218 | 5.6 |
| 16 | William B. Francis (D) | 15,731 | 46.6 |
| | David A. Hollingsworth (R) | 15,323 | 45.4 |
| | Robert J. Murray (SOC) | 2,325 | 6.9 |
| 17 | William A. Ashbrook (D) | 25,875 | 59.3 |
| | A. B. Critchfield (R) | 14,964 | 34.3 |
| | Edward Schmidt (SOC) | 2,508 | 5.8 |
| 18 | John J. Whitacre (D) | 23,568 | 46.6 |
| | James Kennedy (R) | 20,617 | 40.8 |
| | Thomas Williams (SOC) | 4,907 | 9.7 |
| 19 | Ellsworth R. Bathrick (D) | 19,255 | 46.0 |
| | W. Aubrey Thomas (R) | 18,290 | 43.7 |
| | Paul G. Miller (SOC) | 3,720 | 8.9 |
| 20 | Paul Howland (R) | 20,699 | 46.8 |
| | William Gordon (D) | 20,519 | 46.4 |
| | John G. Willert (SOC) | 2,847 | 6.4 |
| 21 | Robert J. Bulkley (D) | 18,091 | 48.1 |
| | James H. Cassidy (R) | 16,716 | 44.5 |
| | Karl A. Cheyney (SOC) | 2,649 | 7.1 |

## OKLAHOMA

| | Candidates | Votes | % |
|---|---|---|---|
| 1 | Bird S. McGuire (R) | 20,301 | 49.2 |
| | Neil E. McNeill (D) | 18,415 | 44.7 |
| | W. L. Reynolds (SOC) | 2,522 | 6.1 |
| 2 | Dick T. Morgan (R) | 25,134 | 46.1 |
| | Elmer L. Fulton (D) | 24,062 | 44.1 |
| | H. I. Bryant (SOC) | 5,382 | 9.9 |
| 3 | James S. Davenport (D) | 25,312 | 50.0 |
| | Charles E. Creager (R) | 22,367 | 44.2 |
| | G. M. Snyder (SOC) | 2,923 | 5.8 |
| 4 | Charles D. Carter (D) | 21,959 | 55.6 |
| | Charles M. Campbell (R) | 11,979 | 30.4 |
| | J. N. Gilmore (SOC) | 5,534 | 14.0 |
| 5 | Scott Ferris (D) | 28,660 | 58.9 |
| | J. H. Franklin (R) | 13,425 | 27.6 |
| | H. H. Stallard (SOC) | 6,539 | 13.5 |

## OREGON

| | Candidates | Votes | % |
|---|---|---|---|
| 1 | Willis C. Hawley (R) | 26,256 | 48.6 |
| | R. G. Smith (D) | 18,232 | 33.7 |
| | C. W. Sherman (SOC) | 4,971 | 9.2 |
| | W. P. Elmore (P) | 4,585 | 8.5 |
| 2 | Abraham W. Lafferty (R) | 30,642 | 51.8 |
| | John Manning (D) | 19,477 | 32.9 |
| | William A. Crawford (SOC) | 5,583 | 9.4 |
| | George B. Pratt (P) | 3,464 | 5.9 |

## PENNSYLVANIA

| | Candidates | Votes | % |
|---|---|---|---|
| 1 | Henry H. Bingham (R, P) | 28,054 | 69.9 |
| | Henry V. Garrett (KEY, WM PENN) | 8,827 | 22.0 |
| | Michael J. Geraghty (D) | 2,657 | 6.6 |
| 2 | Joel Cook (R, WMP/L) | 24,888* | 69.4 |
| | Daniel W. Simpkins (KEY, WM PENN) | 7,665 | 21.4 |
| | Edward B. Seiberlich (D) | 2,542 | 7.1 |
| 3 | J. Hampton Moore (R, WMP/L) | 23,994 | 69.2 |
| | James G. Ramsdell (KEY) | 7,030 | 20.3 |
| | William A. Hayes (D) | 2,712 | 7.8 |
| 4 | Reuben O. Moon (R, WMP/L) | 16,309 | 72.6 |
| | William C. Mitchell (D) | 2,459 | 10.9 |
| | Albert W. Sanson (WM PENN, CITY) | 2,526 | 11.2 |
| 5 | Michael Donohoe (KEY, D) | 19,209 | 48.4 |
| | William W. Foulkrod (R, WMP/L) | 18,016 | 45.4 |
| | Martin McCue (SOC) | 2,328 | 5.9 |
| 6 | George D. McCreary (R, WMP/L) | 25,747 | 46.2 |
| | Frank H. Hawkins (KEY, WM PENN) | 23,672 | 42.5 |

| | Candidates | Votes | % |
|---|---|---|---|
| | William A. Carr (D) | 4,319 | 7.8 |
| 7 | Thomas S. Butler (R) | 16,490 | 51.7 |
| | Eugene C. Bonniwell (KEY, D) | 14,498 | 45.5 |
| 8 | Robert E. Difenderfer (D, KEY) | 19,683 | 49.6 |
| | Irving P. Wanger (R) | 19,016 | 48.1 |
| 9 | William W. Griest (R) | 14,718 | 79.1 |
| | James G. McSparran (D) | 3,120 | 16.8 |
| 10 | John R. Farr (R) | 13,457 | 50.4 |
| | P. F. Calpin (D) | 11,240 | 42.1 |
| 11 | Charles C. Bowman (R, P) | 14,384‡ | 47.5 |
| | George R. McLean (D) | 13,834 | 45.7 |
| | Charles F. Quinn (SOC, FEDR LAB) | 2,079 | 6.9 |
| 12 | Robert E. Lee (D) | 9,492 | 40.1 |
| | Robert D. Heaton (R) | 9,441 | 39.9 |
| | C. F. Foloy (SOC) | 4,739 | 20.0 |
| 13 | John H. Rothermel (D) | 19,680 | 49.8 |
| | John K. Hahn (R) | 12,939 | 32.7 |
| | Caleb Harrison (SOC) | 6,209 | 15.7 |
| 14 | George W. Kipp (KEY, D) | 10,276 | 49.0 |
| | Charles C. Pratt (R) | 9,481 | 45.2 |
| 15 | William B. Wilson (D) | 13,624 | 49.74 |
| | Clarence L. Peaslee (R) | 10,588 | 38.6 |
| | Clarence C. Ricker (SOC) | 2,004 | 7.3 |
| 16 | John G. McHenry (D, R) | 12,578 | 53.0 |
| | Theodore C. Harter (KEY) | 6,366 | 26.8 |
| | Jacob W. Renn (SOC) | 3,818 | 16.1 |
| 17 | Benjamin K. Focht (R) | 14,473 | 50.8 |
| | J. Murray Africa (D) | 11,681 | 41.0 |
| 18 | Marlin E. Olmsted (R) | 21,221 | 59.7 |
| | W. Jonathan Kiefer (D) | 11,686 | 32.9 |
| 19 | Jesse L. Hartman (R) | 18,133 | 60.4 |
| | Isaiah Scheenline (D) | 7,669 | 25.5 |
| | Stewart C. Cowan (P) | 2,173 | 7.2 |
| | Anslem B. Kirsch (SOC) | 2,048 | 6.8 |
| 20 | Daniel F. Lafean (R) | 15,713 | 50.9 |
| | Andrew R. Brodbeck (D) | 13,786 | 44.7 |
| 21 | Charles E. Patton (R) | 10,493 | 49.6 |
| | William C. Heinle (D) | 6,903 | 32.6 |
| | George W. Fox (SOC) | 2,389 | 11.3 |
| | Charles E. Patton (P) | 1,363 | 6.4 |
| 22 | Curtis H. Gregg (D, KEY) | 12,988 | 42.3 |
| | J. David McJunkin (R) | 12,490 | 40.7 |
| | Robert Dudley (SOC) | 3,242 | 10.6 |
| | E. S. Littell (P) | 1,981 | 6.5 |
| 23 | S. Crago Thomas (R) | 13,665 | 52.9 |
| | Jesse H. Wise (D, KEY) | 8,894 | 34.4 |
| | Washington Herd (SOC) | 2,036 | 7.9 |
| 24 | Charles Matthews (R) | 15,177 | 44.1 |
| | Henry H. Wilson (KEY, D) | 14,372 | 41.8 |
| | Charles A. Collins (SOC) | 3,332 | 9.7 |
| 25 | Arthur L. Bates (R) | 10,668 | 46.4 |
| | John B. Brooks (D, KEY) | 9,632 | 41.9 |
| | George B. Allen (SOC) | 1,377 | 6.0 |
| | Richard A. Buzza (P) | 1,313 | 5.7 |
| 26 | A. Mitchell Palmer (D) | 16,284 | 61.3 |
| | Robert Brown (R) | 8,867 | 33.4 |
| 27 | J. N. Langham (R) | 13,073 | 58.8 |
| | John Smith Shirler (D) | 5,451 | 24.5 |
| | John Houk(P) | 2,479 | 11.1 |
| | M. A. Vanhorn (SOC) | 1,245 | 5.6 |
| 28 | Peter M. Speer (R) | 10,932 | 41.7 |
| | William J. Breene (D) | 9,492 | 36.2 |
| | John E. Gill (P) | 3,047 | 11.6 |
| | John R. McKeown (SOC) | 2,163 | 8.3 |
| 29 | Stephen G. Porter (R) | 14,785 | 74.2 |
| | George T. McConnell (SOC) | 2,468 | 12.4 |
| | Fleming Jamieson (D) | 2,110 | 10.6 |
| 30 | John Dalzell (R) | 13,261 | 46.5 |
| | Robert J. Black (P, UN LAB) | 7,807 | 27.4 |
| | W. J. Wright (SOC) | 2,942 | 10.3 |
| | James A. Wakefield (KEY, D) | 4,208 | 14.8 |
| 31 | James Francis Burke (R) | 12,996 | 64.5 |
| | John J. Thorpe (KEY, D) | 5,798 | 28.8 |
| | John Connor (SOC) | 1,164 | 5.8 |
| 32 | A. J. Barchfeld (R) | 13,483 | 49.7 |
| | Hermann L. Hegner (KEY, D) | 9,933 | 36.6 |
| | Valentine Remmel (SOC) | 3,152 | 11.6 |

## RHODE ISLAND

| | Candidates | Votes | % |
|---|---|---|---|
| 1 | George F. O'Shaunessy (D) | 17,532 | 51.3 |
| | William P. Sheffield (R) | 15,681 | 45.9 |
| 2 | George H. Utter (R) | 18,983 | 57.2 |
| | Cooney (D) | 13,704 | 41.3 |

## SOUTH CAROLINA

| | | Votes | % |
|---|---|---|---|
| 1 | George S. Legare (D) | 3,432 | 97.4 |
| 2 | James F. Byrnes (D) | 4,392 | 100.0 |
| 3 | Wyatt Aiken (D) | 3,381 | 99.9 |
| 4 | Joseph T. Johnston (D) | 7,616 | 98.9 |
| 5 | David E. Finley (D) | 3,470 | 100.0 |
| 6 | J. Edwin Ellerbe (D) | 3,734 | 100.0 |
| 7 | Asbury F. Lever (D) | 4,762 | 95.6 |

## SOUTH DAKOTA

| | | Votes | % |
|---|---|---|---|
| AL | Charles H. Burke (R) | 64,777✔ | |
| | Eben W. Martin (R) | 64,495✔ | |
| | W. W. Soule (D) | 32,655 | |
| | J. E. Kelley (D) | 32,329 | |
| | Knute Lewis (P) | 4,139 | |
| | W. J. Edgar (P) | 4,124 | |
| | Isaac M. Burnside (I) | 1,641 | |

## TENNESSEE

| | | Votes | % |
|---|---|---|---|
| 1 | Sam R. Sells (R) | 20,955 | 74.0 |
| | Cy H. Lyle (D) | 7,380 | 26.1 |
| 2 | Richard W. Austin (R) | 15,761 | 57.3 |
| | N. W. Hale (D) | 11,755 | 42.7 |
| 3 | John A. Moon (D) | 17,654 | 56.9 |
| | Charles R. Evans (R) | 12,953 | 41.7 |
| 4 | Cordell Hull (D) | 19,298 | 78.9 |
| | J. T. Odum (ID) | 5,169 | 21.1 |
| 5 | William C. Houston (D) | 16,697 | 98.9 |
| 6 | Joseph W. Byrns (D) | 16,764 | 87.0 |
| | W. H. Jackson (SOC) | 2,502 | 13.0 |
| 7 | Lemuel P. Padgett (D) | 21,299 | 96.8 |
| 8 | Thetus W. Sims (D) | 13,764 | 57.9 |
| | S. E. Murrey (R) | 9,860 | 41.5 |
| 9 | Finis J. Garrett (D) | 15,000 | 85.8 |
| | J. W. Brown (R) | 1,416 | 8.1 |
| | W. R. Landrum (IR) | 940 | 5.4 |
| 10 | George W. Gordon (D) | 14,862 | 94.8 |
| | T. H. Haines (SOC) | 824 | 5.3 |

### Special Election

| | | Votes | % |
|---|---|---|---|
| 1 | Zachary D. Massey (R) | 19,181 | 77.4 |
| | Cy H. Lyle (D) | 5,618 | 22.7 |

## TEXAS

| | | Votes | % |
|---|---|---|---|
| 1 | Morris Sheppard (D) | 10,707 | 87.4 |
| | Velmar Antle (R) | 1,148 | 9.4 |
| 2 | Martin Dies (D) | 10,898 | 94.4 |
| 3 | James Young (D) | 9,450 | 98.9 |
| 4 | Choice B. Randell (D) | 9,719 | 88.9 |
| | C. A. Gray (R) | 1,208 | 11.1 |
| 5 | Jack Beall (D) | 10,899 | 95.0 |
| 6 | Rufus Hardy (D) | 7,826 | 97.9 |
| 7 | Alexander W. Gregg (D) | 6,566 | 88.2 |
| | Willis Kendall (R) | 843 | 11.3 |
| 8 | John M. Moore (D) | 11,654 | 90.4 |
| | A. M. Lawson (R) | 1,112 | 8.6 |
| 9 | George F. Burgess (D) | 10,244 | 78.0 |
| | E. C. Webster (R) | 2,108 | 16.1 |
| 10 | Albert S. Burleson (D) | 10,118 | 100.0 |
| 11 | Robert L. Henry (D) | 7,384 | 98.6 |
| 12 | Oscar Callaway (D) | 10,525 | 82.0 |
| | Robert G. Martin (SOC) | 1,270 | 9.9 |
| | C. C. Littleton (P) | 836 | 6.5 |
| 13 | John H. Stephens (D) | 19,543 | 83.4 |
| | T. S. Bugbee (R) | 2,039 | 8.7 |
| | John I. Green (SOC) | 1,488 | 6.4 |
| 14 | James L. Slayden (D) | 14,251 | 94.8 |

## TEXAS

| | Candidates | Votes | % |
|---|---|---|---|
| 15 | John N. Garner (D) | 14,300 | 71.7 |
| | Noah Allen (R) | 5,287 | 26.5 |
| 16 | William R. Smith (D) | 18,258 | 85.4 |
| | W. H. Harvey (SOC) | 1,749 | 8.2 |
| | Robert A. Webb (R) | 1,384 | 6.5 |

## UTAH

| | Candidates | Votes | % |
|---|---|---|---|
| AL | Joseph Howell (R) | 50,614 | 49.5 |
| | Ferdinand Erickson (D) | 32,730 | 32.0 |
| | Allen T. Sanford (AM) | 14,042 | 13.7 |

## VERMONT

| | Candidates | Votes | % |
|---|---|---|---|
| 1 | David J. Foster (R) | 18,951 | 68.6 |
| | P. M. Meldon (D) | 8,215 | 29.7 |
| 2 | Frank Plumley (R) | 18,185 | 73.4 |
| | Alexander Cochran (D) | 6,226 | 25.1 |

## VIRGINIA

| | Candidates | Votes | % |
|---|---|---|---|
| 1 | William A. Jones (D) | 5,908 | 80.5 |
| | George N. Wise (R) | 1,431 | 19.5 |
| 2 | Edward E. Holland (D) | 6,649 | 79.6 |
| | H. H. Rumble (R) | 1,703 | 20.4 |
| 3 | John Lamb (D) | 5,408 | 86.9 |
| | W. R. Vawter (R) | 813 | 13.1 |
| 4 | Robert Turnbull (D) | 3,769 | 100.0 |
| 5 | Edward W. Saunders (D) | 7,537 | 50.5 |
| | John M. Parsons (D) | 7,382 | 49.5 |
| 6 | Carter Glass (D) | 5,203 | 87.6 |
| | W. Allison (R) | 734 | 12.4 |
| 7 | James Hay (D) | 5,818 | 58.0 |
| | John Paul (R) | 2,589 | 25.8 |
| | S. Lupton (I) | 1,631 | 16.3 |

| | Candidates | Votes | % |
|---|---|---|---|
| 8 | Charles C. Carlin (D) | 4,669 | 100.0 |
| 9 | Campbell Bascom Slemp (R) | 16,958 | 50.3 |
| | Henry C. Stuart (D) | 16,731 | 49.7 |
| 10 | Henry D. Flood (D) | 5,878 | 100.0 |

## WASHINGTON

| | Candidates | Votes | % |
|---|---|---|---|
| 1 | William E. Humphrey (R) | 27,717 | 51.2 |
| | W. W. Black (D) | 20,116 | 37.2 |
| | W. W. Smith (SOC) | 5,088 | 9.4 |
| 2 | Stanton Warburton (R) | 20,448 | 57.5 |
| | Maurice Langhorne (D) | 10,288 | 28.9 |
| | Leslie E. Aller (SOC) | 3,978 | 11.2 |
| 3 | William L. LaFollette (R) | 30,126 | 62.1 |
| | Harry D. Merritt (D) | 14,423 | 29.7 |
| | David C. Coates (SOC) | 3,998 | 8.2 |

## WEST VIRGINIA

| | Candidates | Votes | % |
|---|---|---|---|
| 1 | John W. Davis (D) | 20,370 | 48.9 |
| | Charles E. Carrigan (R) | 16,962 | 40.7 |
| | A. L. Bauer (SOC) | 3,243 | 7.8 |
| 2 | William G. Brown Jr. (D) | 21,276 | 53.3 |
| | George C. Sturgiss (R) | 16,791 | 42.1 |
| 3 | Adam H. Littlepage (D) | 21,311 | 47.3 |
| | Joseph H. Gaines (R) | 20,105 | 44.6 |
| | L. C. Rogers (SOC) | 2,799 | 6.2 |
| 4 | John M. Hamilton (D) | 17,822 | 51.9 |
| | Harry C. Woodyard (R) | 15,592 | 45.4 |
| 5 | James A. Hughes (R) | 25,007 | 51.8 |
| | Rankin Wiley (D) | 22,154 | 45.9 |

## WISCONSIN

| | Candidates | Votes | % |
|---|---|---|---|
| 1 | Henry Allen Cooper (R) | 15,096 | 57.2 |
| | Calvin Stewart (D) | 8.606 | 32.6 |

| | Candidates | Votes | % |
|---|---|---|---|
| | Michael Yabs (SOCIAL D) | 1,869 | 7.1 |
| 2 | John M. Nelson (R) | 14,009 | 51.5 |
| | Albert C. Schmedeman (D) | 12,090 | 44.4 |
| 3 | Arthur W. Kopp (R) | 13,360 | 56.0 |
| | William Coffland (D) | 9,042 | 37.9 |
| 4 | William J. Cary (R) | 12,261 | 38.0 |
| | William R. Gaylord (SOCIAL D) | 11,814 | 36.7 |
| | William J. Kershaw (D) | 8,081 | 25.1 |
| 5 | Victor L. Berger (SOCIAL D) | 13,497 | 38.3 |
| | Henry F. Cochems (R) | 13,147 | 37.3 |
| | Joseph P. Carney (D) | 8,433 | 23.9 |
| 6 | Michael E. Burke (D) | 15,749 | 51.0 |
| | William H. Froelich (R) | 13,278 | 43.0 |
| | John C. Boll (SOCIAL D) | 1,705 | 5.5 |
| 7 | John J. Esch (R) | 15,365 | 63.1 |
| | Paul W. Mahoney (D) | 7,365 | 30.2 |
| 8 | James H. Davidson (R) | 15,934 | 55.2 |
| | Fred B. Rawson (D) | 10,654 | 36.9 |
| | Richard W. Burke (SOCIAL D) | 2,005 | 7.0 |
| 9 | Thomas F. Konop (D) | 12,140 | 45.6 |
| | Gustav Kustermann (R) | 12,135 | 45.6 |
| | Thomas J. Oliver (SOCIAL D) | 1,777 | 6.7 |
| 10 | Elmer A. Morse (R) | 17,360 | 54.2 |
| | John F. Lamont (D) | 11,798 | 36.8 |
| | Lynn Thompson (SOCIAL D) | 2,882 | 9.0 |
| 11 | Irvine L. Lenroot (R) | 19,224 | 88.5 |
| | Henry M. Parks (SOCIAL D) | 2,473 | 11.4 |

## WYOMING

| | Candidates | Votes | % |
|---|---|---|---|
| AL | Frank W. Mondell (R) | 20,312 | 54.7 |
| | W. B. Ross (D) | 14,659 | 39.5 |
| | J. B. Morgan (SOC) | 2,155 | 5.8 |

# 1911 House Elections

## ARIZONA
(Became a state Feb. 14, 1912)

| | Candidates | Votes | % |
|---|---|---|---|
| AL | Carl Hayden (D) | 11,556 | 54.1 |
| | John S. Williams (R) | 8,485 | 39.7 |
| | John Halberg (SOC) | 1,252 | 5.9 |

## NEW MEXICO
(Became a state Jan. 6, 1912)

| | Candidates | Votes | % |
|---|---|---|---|
| AL | George Curry (R)✔ | 30,162 | |
| | Harvey B. Fergusson (D)✔ | 29,999 | |

| | Candidates | Votes | % |
|---|---|---|---|
| | Elfego Baca (R) | 28,836 | |
| | Paz Valverde (D) | 28,353 | |
| | J. W. Hansen (SOC) | 1,845 | |
| | C. Cutting (SOC) | 1,745 | |

## PENNSYLVANIA
### Special Elections

| | Candidates | Votes | % |
|---|---|---|---|
| 2 | William Stuart Reyburn (R) | 15,470 | 76.3 |
| | Henry Baur (D) | 4,373 | 21.6 |

| | Candidates | Votes | % |
|---|---|---|---|
| 14 | W. D. B. Ainey (R) | 13,860 | 55.6 |
| | Oscar H. Rockwell (D, KEY) | 11,062 | 44.4 |

## TENNESSEE
### Special Election

| | Candidates | Votes | % |
|---|---|---|---|
| 10 | Kenneth D. McKellar (D) | 11,573 | 85.0 |
| | W. A. Weatherall (SOC) | 2,040 | 15.0 |

# 1912 House Elections

## ALABAMA

| Candidates | Votes | % |
|---|---|---|
| 1 George W. Taylor (D) | 7,414 | 97.2 |
| 2 S. Hubert Dent Jr. (D) | 11,197 | 100.0 |
| 3 Henry D. Clayton (D) | 11,225 | 100.0 |
| 4 Fred L. Blackmon (D) | 7,740 | 67.4 |
| A. P. Longshore (PROG) | 3,060 | 26.6 |
| W. H. Sturdivant (R) | 693 | 6.0 |
| 5 J. Thomas Heflin (D) | 10,210 | 100.0 |
| 6 Richmond P. Hobson (D) | 10,065 | 82.0 |
| Charles P. Lunsford (R) | 2,210 | 18.0 |
| 7 John L. Burnett (D) | 9,770 | 54.5 |
| Sumter Cogswell (PROG) | 5,462 | 30.4 |
| John J. Stephens (R) | 2,711 | 15.1 |
| 8 William Richardson (D) | 10,753 | 88.4 |
| William E. Hotchkiss (R) | 1,160 | 9.5 |
| 9 Oscar W. Underwood (D) | 12,584 | 88.7 |
| Frederick B. Parker (R) | 1,598 | 11.3 |
| AL John W. Abercrombie (D) | 87,519 | 87.8 |
| Asa E. Stratton (R) | 9,589 | 9.6 |

## ARIZONA

| Candidates | Votes | % |
|---|---|---|
| AL Carl Hayden (D) | 11,389 | 48.4 |
| Robert S. Fisher (PROG) | 5,819 | 24.7 |
| Thomas E. Campbell (R) | 3,110 | 13.2 |
| A. Charles Smith (SOC) | 3,034 | 12.9 |

## ARKANSAS

| Candidates | Votes | % |
|---|---|---|
| 1 Thaddeus H. Caraway (D) | 15,036 | 100.0 |
| 2 William A. Oldfield (D) | 11,880 | 73.0 |
| G. W. Wells (R) | 4,394 | 27.0 |
| 3 John C. Floyd (D) | 10,849 | 64.6 |
| J. F. Carlton (R) | 5,954 | 35.4 |
| 4 Otis T. Wingo (D) | 11,680 | 67.6 |
| J. O. Livesay (R) | 5,601 | 32.4 |
| 5 Henderson M. Jacoway (D) | 13,438 | 70.3 |
| A. C. Remmel (R) | 5,680 | 29.7 |
| 6 Samuel M. Taylor (D) | 15,879 | 100.0 |
| 7 William S. Goodwin (D) | 10,956 | 69.4 |
| Pat McNalley (R) | 4,824 | 30.6 |

## CALIFORNIA

| Candidates | Votes | % |
|---|---|---|
| 1 William Kent (PROG) | 20,341 | 37.3 |
| I. G. Zumwalt (D) | 18,756 | 34.4 |
| Edward H. Hart (R) | 10,585 | 19.4 |
| Joseph Bredsteen (SOC) | 4,892 | 9.0 |
| 2 John E. Raker (D) | 23,467 | 62.6 |
| Frank M. Rutherford (R) | 10,178 | 27.2 |
| J. C. Williams (SOC) | 3,818 | 10.2 |
| 3 Charles F. Curry (R) | 31,060 | 58.8 |
| Gilbert McMillan Ross (D) | 15,197 | 28.8 |
| William L. Wilson (SOC) | 6,522 | 12.4 |
| 4 Julius Kahn (R) | 25,515 | 56.1 |
| Bert Schlesinger (D) | 14,884 | 32.7 |
| Norman W. Pendleton (SOC) | 5,090 | 11.2 |
| 5 John I. Nolan (R) | 27,902 | 52.3 |
| Stephen V. Costello (D) | 18,516 | 34.7 |
| E. L. Reguin (SOC) | 6,962 | 13.0 |
| 6 Joseph R. Knowland (R) | 35,219 | 53.7 |
| J. Stitt Wilson (SOC) | 26,234 | 40.0 |
| Hiram A. Luttrell (D) | 4,135 | 6.3 |
| 7 Denver S. Church (D) | 23,752 | 44.1 |
| James C. Needham (R) | 22,994 | 42.6 |
| J. S. Cato (SOC) | 7,171 | 13.3 |
| 8 Everis A. Hayes (R) | 29,861 | 50.9 |
| James B. Holohan (D) | 20,620 | 35.2 |
| Robert Whitaker (SOC) | 8,125 | 13.9 |
| 9 Charles W. Bell (R) | 28,845 | 47.2 |
| Thomas N. Kirk (D) | 14,571 | 23.8 |
| Ralph L. Criswell (SOC) | 11,123 | 18.2 |
| George S. Yarnall (P) | 6,510 | 10.7 |
| 10 William D. Stephens (R) | 43,637 | 53.4 |

| Candidates | Votes | % |
|---|---|---|
| George Ringo (D) | 17,890 | 21.9 |
| Fred C. Wheeler (SOC) | 17,126 | 21.0 |
| 11 William Kettner (D) | 24,822 | 42.7 |
| Samuel C. Evans (R) | 21,426 | 36.9 |
| Noble Asa Richardson (SOC) | 7,059 | 12.1 |
| Helen M. Stoddard (P) | 4,842 | 8.3 |

## COLORADO

| | Votes | % |
|---|---|---|
| 1 George J. Kindel (D) | 54,504 | 45.8 |
| W. J. L. Crank (PROG-BMR) | 30,121 | 25.3 |
| Rice W. Means (R) | 24,887 | 20.9 |
| J. W. Martin (SOC) | 6,755 | 5.7 |
| 2 Harry H. Seldomridge (D) | 63,271 | 44.5 |
| Charles A. Ballreich (R) | 40,990 | 28.8 |
| Neil N. McLean (RO PROG) | 27,975 | 19.7 |
| S. A. Van Buskirk (SOC) | 9,993 | 7.0 |
| AL Edward T. Taylor (D) | 115,143✔ | |
| Edward Keating (D) | 110,516✔ | |
| Clarence P. Dodge (PROG-BMR) | 64,835 | |
| Samuel H. Kinsley (R) | 63,714 | |
| Jesse J. Laton (R) | 62,085 | |
| Charles E. Fisher (PROG-BMR) | 58,764 | |
| Robert Knight (SOC) | 16,108 | |
| F. W. Brainard (SOC) | 15,808 | |
| Samuel S. Stutzman (P) | 5,853 | |

## CONNECTICUT

| | Votes | % |
|---|---|---|
| 1 Augustine Lonergan (D) | 17,256 | 40.0 |
| Bissell (R) | 16,726 | 38.7 |
| Alsop (PROG) | 6,445 | 14.9 |
| 2 Bryan F. Mahan (D) | 14,936 | 41.8 |
| King (R) | 14,421 | 40.3 |
| Davis (PROG) | 4,742 | 13.3 |
| 3 Thomas L. Reilly (D) | 16,267 | 42.7 |
| Tilson (R) | 12,989 | 34.1 |
| Henderson (PROG) | 5,480 | 14.4 |
| Applegate (SOC) | 2,658 | 7.0 |
| 4 Jeremiah Donovan (D) | 15,616 | 37.6 |
| Hill (R) | 14,188 | 34.1 |
| Vincent (PROG) | 8,263 | 19.9 |
| Hunter (SOC) | 2,849 | 6.9 |
| 5 William Kennedy (D) | 12,073 | 39.2 |
| Bradstreet (R) | 11,724 | 38.0 |
| Hoadley (PROG) | 4,807 | 15.6 |
| Hull (SOC) | 1,923 | 6.2 |

## DELAWARE

| | Votes | % |
|---|---|---|
| AL Franklin Brockson (D) | 22,485 | 46.2 |
| George H. Hall (R) | 16,740 | 34.4 |
| Hiram R. Burton (N PROG) | 5,497 | 11.3 |
| Louis A. Drexler (PROG) | 2,825 | 5.8 |

## FLORIDA

| | Votes | % |
|---|---|---|
| 1 Stephen M. Sparkman (D) | 12,400 | 78.5 |
| C. C. Allen (SOC) | 1,901 | 12.0 |
| 2 Frank Clark (D) | 14,035 | 80.5 |
| J. J. Collins (SOC) | 1,318 | 7.6 |
| John W. Howell (R) | 1,210 | 6.9 |
| C. E. Speir (PROG) | 875 | 5.0 |
| 3 Emmett Wilson (D) | 9,057 | 86.4 |
| W. N. Lamberry (SOC) | 659 | 6.3 |
| AL Claude L'Engle (D) | 34,324 | 77.4 |
| A. N. Jackson (SOC) | 3,636 | 8.2 |
| George W. Allen (R) | 2,942 | 6.6 |
| E. R. Gunby (PROG) | 2,680 | 6.0 |

## GEORGIA

| Candidates | Votes | % |
|---|---|---|
| 1 Charles G. Edwards (D) | 7,944 | 95.7 |
| 2 Seaborn A. Roddenberry (D) | 7,957 | 100.0 |
| 3 Charles R. Crisp (D) | 7,321 | 100.0 |
| 4 William C. Adamson (D) | 8,904 | 100.0 |
| 5 William Schley Howard (D) | 12,000 | 100.0 |
| 6 Charles L. Bartlett (D) | 13,171 | 100.0 |
| 7 Gordon Lee (D) | 14,099 | 100.0 |
| 8 Samuel J. Tribble (D) | 10,013 | 100.0 |
| 9 Thomas M. Bell (D) | 12,496 | 100.0 |
| 10 Thomas W. Hardwick (D) | 6,474 | 100.0 |
| 11 John R. Walker (D) | 7,922 | 100.0 |
| 12 Dudley M. Hughes (D) | 7,791 | 100.0 |

## IDAHO

| | Votes | % |
|---|---|---|
| AL Burton L. French (R) | 53,542✔ | |
| Addison T. Smith (R) | 43,571✔ | |
| Perry W. Mitchell (D) | 30,172 | |
| Edward M. Pugmire (D) | 30,053 | |
| P. Monroe Smock (PROG) | 12,066 | |
| G. W. Belloit (SOC) | 11,393 | |
| E. L. Riggs (SOC) | 11,389 | |
| John Tucker (P) | 1,176 | |
| Johathan G. Carrick (P) | 1,169 | |

## ILLINOIS

| | Votes | % |
|---|---|---|
| 1 Martin B. Madden (R) | 13,608 | 52.2 |
| Andrew Donovan (D) | 9,967 | 38.2 |
| William F. Barnard (SOC) | 2,217 | 8.5 |
| 2 James R. Mann (R) | 21,374 | 37.4 |
| John Charles Vaughan (D) | 15,827 | 27.7 |
| Thomas D. Knight (PROG) | 15,042 | 26.3 |
| John C. Flora (SOC) | 4,637 | 8.1 |
| 3 George E. Gorman (D) | 16,285 | 33.2 |
| William W. Wilson (R) | 14,133 | 28.8 |
| Franklin P. Simons (PROG) | 13,039 | 26.6 |
| George H. Gibson (SOC) | 5,123 | 10.4 |
| 4 James T. McDermott (D) | 14,225 | 57.3 |
| Charles J. Tomkiewicz (R) | 6,097 | 24.6 |
| Carl F. Gauger (SOC) | 4,503 | 18.1 |
| 5 Adolph J. Sabath (D) | 11,150 | 51.8 |
| Jacob Gartenstein (R) | 4,192 | 19.5 |
| Charles Toepper (SOC) | 3,359 | 15.6 |
| L. H. Clusman (PROG) | 2,825 | 13.1 |
| 6 James McAndrews (D) | 22,520 | 45.3 |
| Arthur W. Fulton (R) | 18,974 | 38.2 |
| John Will (SOC) | 7,776 | 15.6 |
| 7 Frank Buchanan (D) | 19,452 | 28.2 |
| Elton C. Armitage (PROG) | 18,816 | 27.3 |
| Niels Juul (R) | 15,265 | 22.1 |
| Otto C. Christensen (SOC) | 15,043 | 21.8 |
| 8 Thomas Gallagher (D) | 10,922 | 52.4 |
| William G. Herrmann (R) | 6,030 | 29.0 |
| N. F. Holm (SOC) | 3,674 | 17.6 |
| 9 Fred A. Britten (R) | 11,650 | 34.6 |
| Lynden Evans (D) | 10,210 | 30.3 |
| C. O. Ludlow (PROG) | 7,566 | 22.5 |
| Frank Schiflersmith (SOC) | 3,964 | 11.8 |
| 10 Charles M. Thomson (PROG) | 21,028 | 35.2 |
| George Edmund Foss (R) | 17,325 | 29.0 |
| Frank L. Fowler (D) | 15,515 | 26.0 |
| Charles A. Larson (SOC) | 5,311 | 8.9 |
| 11 Ira C. Copley (R) | 25,750 | 61.1 |
| Thomas H. Riley (D) | 14,330 | 34.0 |
| 12 William H. Hinebaugh (PROG) | 18,334 | 36.4 |
| Charles E. Fuller (R) | 16,905 | 33.6 |
| J. W. Rausch (D) | 12,234 | 24.3 |
| 13 John C. McKenzie (R) | 14,398 | 36.5 |
| I. F. Edwards (PROG) | 11,875 | 30.1 |
| Ray Rariden (D) | 11,704 | 29.7 |
| 14 Clyde H. Tavenner (D) | 17,024 | 47.3 |

## ILLINOIS

| Candidates | Votes | % |
|---|---|---|
| Charles J. Searle (R) | 15,816 | 44.0 |
| Charles Block (SOC) | 2,466 | 6.9 |
| 15 Stephen A. Hoxworth (D) | 17,156 | 35.8 |
| Charles F. Kincheloe (PROG) | 15,173 | 31.7 |
| George W. Prince (R) | 12,008 | 25.1 |
| John C. Sjodin (SOC) | 2,642 | 5.5 |
| 16 Claudius U. Stone (D) | 20,956 | 45.7 |
| William E. Cadmus (PROG) | 12,659 | 27.6 |
| Frederick H. Smith (R) | 9,295 | 20.3 |
| Rudolf Pfeiffer (SOC) | 2,474 | 5.4 |
| 17 Louis Fitz Henry (D) | 14,966 | 38.0 |
| John A. Sterling (R) | 13,572 | 34.5 |
| George E. Stump (PROG) | 9,266 | 23.6 |
| 18 Frank T. O'Hair (D) | 19,485 | 38.9 |
| Joseph G. Cannon (R) | 18,707 | 37.3 |
| E. F. Royse (PROG) | 9,511 | 19.0 |
| 19 Charles M. Borchers (D) | 22,166 | 40.2 |
| William B. McKinley (R) | 20,643 | 37.4 |
| John H. Chadwick (PROG) | 10,755 | 19.5 |
| 20 Henry T. Rainey (D) | 21,203 | 54.1 |
| E. E. Brass (R) | 9,478 | 24.2 |
| B. O. Aylesworth (PROG) | 7,007 | 17.9 |
| 21 James M. Graham (D) | 21,361 | 46.8 |
| H. Clay Wilson (R) | 13,556 | 29.7 |
| Robert Johns (PROG) | 7,286 | 16.0 |
| Herman Rahm (SOC) | 2,554 | 5.6 |
| 22 William N. Baltz (D) | 23,112 | 43.5 |
| William A. Rodenberg (R) | 19,438 | 36.6 |
| Utten S. Nixon (PROG) | 5,608 | 10.6 |
| William C. Pierce (SOC) | 4,276 | 8.1 |
| 23 Martin D. Foster (D) | 26,938 | 52.4 |
| Robert B. Clark (R) | 12,837 | 25.0 |
| George W. Jones (PROG) | 9,116 | 17.7 |
| 24 H. Robert Fowler (D) | 19,811 | 47.7 |
| James B. Blackman (R) | 15,004 | 36.1 |
| A. J. Gibbons (PROG) | 5,129 | 12.3 |
| 25 Robert P. Hill (D) | 19,992 | 43.3 |
| Napoleon B. Thistlewood (R) | 16,706 | 36.2 |
| Robert T. Cook (PROG) | 6,545 | 14.2 |
| AL Lawrence B. Stringer (D) | 415,386✔ | |
| William Elza Williams (D) | 401,497✔ | |
| William E. Mason (R) | 313,608 | |
| Lawrence P. Boyle (PROG) | 311,311 | |
| B. M. Maxey (PROG) | 304,072 | |
| Burnett M. Chiperfield (R) | 299,940 | |
| Walter Huggins (SOC) | 84,352 | |
| D. L. Thomas (SOC) | 84,027 | |
| Walter H. Harris (P) | 15,721 | |
| James H. Shaw (P) | 15,590 | |
| George Martin (SOC LAB) | 4,118 | |
| Joseph Fenyves (SOC LAB) | 4,012 | |

## INDIANA

| Candidates | Votes | % |
|---|---|---|
| 1 Charles Lieb (D) | 20,014 | 45.7 |
| D. H. Ortmeyer (R) | 13,158 | 30.0 |
| Humphrey C. Heldt (PROG) | 6,022 | 13.7 |
| William H. Rainey (SOC) | 3,737 | 8.5 |
| 2 William A. Cullop (D) | 22,082 | 45.3 |
| Oscar E. Bland (R) | 15,858 | 32.6 |
| John N. Dyer (PROG) | 6,001 | 12.3 |
| John L. B. Shepherd (SOC) | 3,888 | 8.0 |
| 3 William E. Cox (D) | 23,150 | 51.5 |
| William D. Barnes (R) | 10,049 | 22.4 |
| S. G. Wilkinson (PROG) | 10,005 | 22.3 |
| 4 Lincoln Dixon (D) | 24,250 | 52.4 |
| Rollin A. Turner (R) | 12,436 | 26.9 |
| Charles Zoller Jr. (PROG) | 7,540 | 16.3 |
| 5 Ralph W. Moss (D) | 20,634 | 45.2 |
| F. W. Blankenlaker (R) | 11,995 | 26.3 |
| Joseph W. Amis (SOC) | 8,268 | 18.1 |
| William Houston (PROG) | 3,351 | 7.3 |
| 6 Finly H. Gray (D) | 19,987 | 43.9 |
| William L. Risk (R) | 11,242 | 24.7 |
| Gierluf Jansen (PROG) | 10,797 | 23.7 |
| 7 Charles A. Korbly (D) | 28,901 | 42.8 |
| Joseph V. Zartman (PROG) | 18,402 | 27.3 |
| Thomas R. Shipp (R) | 13,320 | 19.7 |
| Frank J. Hays (SOC) | 5,501 | 8.2 |

| Candidates | Votes | % |
|---|---|---|
| 8 John A. M. Adair (D) | 23,530 | 46.5 |
| E. C. Toner (PROG) | 13,157 | 26.0 |
| I. P. Watts (R) | 8,298 | 16.4 |
| Hunter McDonald (SOC) | 3,611 | 7.1 |
| 9 Martin A. Morrison (D) | 23,574 | 45.1 |
| William Robinson (R) | 15,901 | 30.4 |
| John F. Neil (PROG) | 9,205 | 17.6 |
| 10 John B. Peterson (D) | 18,401 | 38.8 |
| E. D. Crumpacker (R) | 17,294 | 36.5 |
| John O. Bowers (PROG) | 9,793 | 20.6 |
| 11 George W. Rauch (D) | 21,894 | 43.8 |
| John W. G. Stewart (R) | 12,213 | 24.4 |
| Edgar M. Baldwin (PROG) | 10,830 | 21.7 |
| Ernest Malott (SOC) | 2,813 | 5.6 |
| 12 Cyrus Cline (D) | 19,903 | 48.3 |
| Charles R. Lane (R) | 11,147 | 27.1 |
| Louis N. Littman (PROG) | 8,114 | 19.7 |
| 13 Henry A. Barnhart (D) | 24,968 | 43.9 |
| R. Clarence Stephens (PROG) | 13,822 | 24.3 |
| Charles A. Carlisle (R) | 13,787 | 24.3 |
| Ervin H. Cady (SOC) | 2,937 | 5.2 |

## IOWA

| Candidates | Votes | % |
|---|---|---|
| 1 Charles A. Kennedy (R) | 14,167 | 42.1 |
| Joshua F. Elder (D) | 12,114 | 36.0 |
| Joe S. Crail (PROG) | 6,457 | 19.2 |
| 2 Irvin S. Pepper (D) | 24,769 | 85.7 |
| Michael T. Kennedy (SOC) | 3,176 | 11.0 |
| 3 Maurice Connolly (D) | 19,445 | 42.3 |
| Charles E. Picket (R) | 18,166 | 39.6 |
| Robert E. Leach (PROG) | 6,640 | 14.5 |
| 4 William N. Haugen (R) | 19,829 | 52.6 |
| G. A. Meyer (D) | 16,764 | 44.5 |
| 5 James W. Good (R) | 19,030 | 47.7 |
| S. C. Huber (D) | 17,631 | 44.2 |
| 6 Sanford Kirkpatrick (D) | 14,915 | 42.5 |
| M. A. McCord (R) | 13,796 | 39.3 |
| John H. Patton (PROG) | 4,350 | 12.4 |
| Andrew Engle (SOC) | 2,060 | 5.9 |
| 7 Solomon F. Prouty (R) | 17,465 | 43.2 |
| Clint L. Price (D) | 14,075 | 34.8 |
| George C. White (PROG) | 5,944 | 14.7 |
| 8 Horace M. Towner (R) | 18,462 | 49.2 |
| V. R. McGinnis (D) | 15,477 | 41.3 |
| L. W. Laughlin (PROG) | 2,704 | 7.2 |
| 9 William R. Green (R) | 20,030 | 53.3 |
| Orris Mosher (D) | 16,369 | 43.5 |
| 10 Frank P. Woods (R) | 25,263 | 53.9 |
| Nelson L. Rood (D) | 15,242 | 32.5 |
| S. B. Philpot (PROG) | 5,251 | 11.2 |
| 11 George C. Scott (R) | 18,568 | 40.1 |
| A. Vanwagenen (D) | 16,168 | 34.9 |
| J. W. Hallam (PROG) | 10,405 | 22.5 |

### Special Election

| Candidates | Votes | % |
|---|---|---|
| 11 George C. Scott (R) | 18,041 | 41.1 |
| A. Vanwagenen (D) | 15,910 | 36.2 |
| J. W. Hallam (PROG) | 10,003 | 22.8 |

## KANSAS

| Candidates | Votes | % |
|---|---|---|
| 1 Daniel R. Anthony Jr. (R) | 22,978 | 51.8 |
| J. B. Chapman (D) | 20,646 | 46.5 |
| 2 Joseph Taggart (D) | 25,830 | 50.1 |
| J. L. Brady (R) | 21,995 | 42.7 |
| Unidentified Candidate (SOC) | 3,705 | 7.2 |
| 3 Philip P. Campbell (R) | 20,973 | 39.0 |
| Francis M. Brady (D) | 20,142 | 37.4 |
| George D. Brewer (SOC) | 12,732 | 23.6 |
| 4 Dudley Doolittle (D) | 16,997 | 48.6 |
| Fred S. Jackson (R) | 16,479 | 47.1 |
| 5 Guy T. Helvering (D) | 19,618 | 49.8 |
| Rollin R. Rees (R) | 18,098 | 45.9 |

| Candidates | Votes | % |
|---|---|---|
| 6 John R. Connelly (D) | 20,065 | 48.0 |
| I. D. Young (R) | 19,077 | 45.6 |
| Daniel W. Stoner (SOC) | 2,102 | 5.0 |
| 7 George A. Neeley (D) | 26,140 | 51.3 |
| Gordon L. Finley (R) | 21,690 | 42.5 |
| M. L. Amos (SOC) | 2,828 | 5.6 |
| 8 Victor Murdock (R) | 17,958 | 53.4 |
| John I. Saunders (D) | 14,488 | 43.1 |

## KENTUCKY

| Candidates | Votes | % |
|---|---|---|
| 1 Alben W. Barkley (D) | 22,591 | 64.5 |
| Charles Furgeson (R) | 10,664 | 30.4 |
| I. O. Ford (SOC) | 1,787 | 5.1 |
| 2 Augustus O. Stanley (D) | 19,739 | 71.3 |
| L. R. Fox (PROG) | 6,500 | 23.5 |
| Carr Hawkins (SOC) | 1,462 | 5.3 |
| 3 Robert Y. Thomas Jr. (D) | 18,220 | 47.9 |
| T. B. Dixon (R) | 11,181 | 29.4 |
| J. D. Duncan (PROG) | 7,456 | 19.6 |
| 4 Ben Johnson (D) | 22,168 | 53.2 |
| E. R. Bassett (PROG) | 11,907 | 28.6 |
| John C. Thompson (R) | 6,713 | 16.1 |
| 5 J. Swagar Sherley (D) | 24,795 | 46.2 |
| Henry I. Fox (PROG) | 23,115 | 43.0 |
| E. J. Ashcraft (R) | 3,823 | 7.1 |
| 6 Arthur B. Rouse (D) | 20,690 | 57.3 |
| D. B. Wallace (R) | 7,255 | 20.1 |
| J. G. Blackburn (PROG) | 5,701 | 15.8 |
| M. A. Brinkman (SOC) | 2,489 | 6.9 |
| 7 James C. Cantrill (D) | 24,617 | 80.8 |
| J. E. Jones (PROG) | 5,841 | 19.2 |
| 8 Harvey Helm (D) | 18,690 | 71.0 |
| J. W. Dinsmore (PROG) | 7,631 | 29.0 |
| 9 William J. Fields (D) | 27,415 | 50.7 |
| Harry Bailey (R) | 16,608 | 30.7 |
| E. S. Hutchins (PROG) | 8,903 | 16.5 |
| 10 John W. Langley (R) | 12,200 | 69.8 |
| W. T. Stafford (PROG) | 5,286 | 30.2 |
| 11 Caleb Powers (R) | 18,531 | 46.4 |
| Ben V. Smith (D) | 11,760 | 29.5 |
| H. H. Seavey (PROG) | 9,044 | 22.7 |

## LOUISIANA

| Candidates | Votes | % |
|---|---|---|
| 1 Albert Estopinal (D) | 14,770 | 100.0 |
| 2 H. Garland Dupre (D) | 14,406 | 100.0 |
| 3 Robert F. Broussard (D) | 5,035 | 100.0 |
| 4 John T. Watkins (D) | 5,693 | 93.5 |
| Lee Norris (SOC) | 394 | 6.5 |
| 5 Walter Elder (D) | 5,795 | 100.0 |
| 6 Lewis L. Morgan (D) | 6,101 | 100.0 |
| 7 Ladislas Lazaro (D) | 4,943 | 87.4 |
| Otis Putnam (SOC) | 713 | 12.6 |
| 8 James B. Aswell (D) | 6,033 | 77.7 |
| J. R. Jones (SOC) | 1,734 | 22.3 |

## MAINE

| Candidates | Votes | % |
|---|---|---|
| 1 Asher C. Hinds (R) | 17,635 | 51.7 |
| M. T. O'Brien (D) | 15,580 | 45.7 |
| 2 Daniel J. McGillicuddy (D) | 18,077 | 50.4 |
| W. B. Skelton (R) | 16,796 | 46.8 |
| 3 Forrest Goodwin (R) | 17,221 | 49.9 |
| Samuel W. Gould (D) | 16,512 | 47.8 |
| 4 Frank E. Guernsey (R) | 20,198 | 54.4 |
| C. N. Mullen (D) | 16,725 | 45.0 |

## MARYLAND

| Candidates | Votes | % |
|---|---|---|
| 1 James Harry Covington (D) | 17,606 | 85.2 |
| Robert D. Grier (PROG) | 2,303 | 11.2 |
| 2 Joshua Frederick C. Talbott (D) | 22,087 | 59.9 |
| Labin Sparks (R) | 13,732 | 37.2 |
| 3 George Konig (D) | 15,189 | 54.7 |
| Albert M. Sproesser (R) | 11,078 | 39.9 |
| 4 J. Charles Linthicum (D) | 19,075 | 60.9 |
| Jacob F. Murback (R) | 11,257 | 35.9 |

## MARYLAND

| | Candidates | Votes | % |
|---|---|---|---|
| 5 | Frank O. Smith (D) | 13,085 | 49.0 |
| | Thomas Parran (R) | 12,168 | 45.5 |
| 6 | David J. Lewis (D) | 20,434 | 56.0 |
| | Charles D. Wagaman (R) | 14,147 | 38.8 |

## MASSACHUSETTS

| | Candidates | Votes | % |
|---|---|---|---|
| 1 | Allen T. Treadway (R) | 12,920 | 42.8 |
| | Richard J. Morrissey (D) | 12,075 | 40.0 |
| | Samuel P. Blagden (PROG) | 3,883 | 12.9 |
| 2 | Frederick H. Gillett (R) | 12,301 | 42.8 |
| | William G. McKechnie (D) | 10,940 | 38.1 |
| | Thomas L. Hisgen (PROG) | 5,442 | 18.9 |
| 3 | William Henry Wilder (R) | 12,945 | 45.0 |
| | M. Fred O'Connell (D) | 9,742 | 33.8 |
| | Stephen M. Marshall (PROG) | 5,287 | 18.4 |
| 4 | Samuel E. Winslow (R) | 15,153 | 49.6 |
| | John A. Thayer (D) | 11,216 | 36.7 |
| | Burton W. Potter (PROG) | 3,626 | 11.9 |
| 5 | John Jacob Rogers (R) | 12,827 | 44.8 |
| | Humphrey O'Sullivan (D) | 11,037 | 38.5 |
| | William N. Osgood (PROG) | 4,200 | 14.7 |
| 6 | Augustus P. Gardner (R) | 16,918 | 49.8 |
| | George A. Schofield (D) | 9,704 | 28.6 |
| | Arthur L. Nason (PROG) | 7,326 | 21.6 |
| 7 | Michael F. Phelan (D) | 12,964 | 45.9 |
| | Frank P. Bennett Jr. (R) | 8,952 | 31.7 |
| | Lynn M. Ranger (PROG) | 5,086 | 18.0 |
| 8 | Frederick S. Deitrick (D) | 12,484 | 40.5 |
| | Frederick W. Dallinger (R) | 11,209 | 36.4 |
| | Henry C. Long (PROG) | 6,665 | 21.6 |
| 9 | Ernest W. Roberts (R) | 14,021 | 45.1 |
| | Henry C. Rowland (D) | 8,732 | 28.1 |
| | John Herbert (PROG) | 7,364 | 23.7 |
| 10 | William F. Murray (D) | 12,031 | 64.0 |
| | Daniel T. Callahan (PROG) | 3,711 | 19.7 |
| | Loyal L. Jenkins (R) | 2,418 | 12.9 |
| 11 | Andrew J. Peters (D) | 17,875 | 64.0 |
| | Sherwin L. Cook (R) | 8,786 | 31.5 |
| 12 | James M. Curley (D) | 14,875 | 48.8 |
| | James B. Connolly (PROG) | 9,001 | 29.5 |
| | Charles H. S. Robinson (R) | 5,812 | 19.1 |
| 13 | John W. Weeks (R) | 15,934* | 45.1 |
| | John J. Mitchell (D) | 13,583 | 38.4 |
| | George A. Fiel (PROG) | 5,853 | 16.6 |
| 14 | Edward Gilmore (D) | 11,939 | 33.9 |
| | Henry L. Kincaide (PROG) | 11,341 | 32.2 |
| | Robert O. Harris (R) | 9,968 | 28.3 |
| | John McCarty (SOC) | 2,005 | 5.7 |
| 15 | William S. Greene (R) | 11,207 | 45.1 |
| | John W. Coughlin (D) | 8,975 | 36.1 |
| | Alvin G. Weeks (PROG) | 4,172 | 16.8 |
| 16 | Thomas C. Thacher (D) | 10,461 | 40.2 |
| | William J. Bullock (R) | 8,186 | 31.5 |
| | Thomas Thompson (PROG) | 6,540 | 25.1 |

## MICHIGAN

| | Candidates | Votes | % |
|---|---|---|---|
| 1 | Frank E. Doremus (D) | 22,573 | 38.3 |
| | James H. Pound (N PROG) | 16,801 | 28.5 |
| | Ezra P. Beechler (R) | 16,687 | 28.3 |
| 2 | Samuel W. Beakes (D) | 16,761 | 35.0 |
| | William W. Wedemeyer (R) | 16,650 | 34.8 |
| | Hubert F. Probert (N PROG) | 13,660 | 28.5 |
| 3 | John M. C. Smith (R) | 14,609 | 32.7 |
| | Claude S. Carney (D) | 14,482 | 32.4 |
| | Edward N. Dingley (N PROG) | 12,907 | 28.9 |
| | Levant L. Rogers (SOC) | 2,746 | 6.1 |
| 4 | Edward L. Hamilton (R) | 14,788 | 34.2 |
| | Albert E. Beebe (D) | 14,382 | 33.2 |
| | George M. Valentine (N PROG) | 12,712 | 29.4 |
| 5 | Carl E. Mapes (R) | 16,749 | 35.3 |
| | Edwin F. Sweet (D) | 16,148 | 34.0 |
| | Suel A. Sheldon (N PROG) | 11,747 | 24.7 |

| | Candidates | Votes | % |
|---|---|---|---|
| 6 | Samuel W. Smith (R) | 21,686 | 36.9 |
| | Alva M. Cummins (D) | 18,412 | 31.3 |
| | William S. Kellogg (N PROG) | 18,157 | 30.9 |
| 7 | Louis C. Cramton (R) | 15,089 | 37.0 |
| | Loren A. Sherman (N PROG) | 12,588 | 30.8 |
| | John J. Bell (D) | 11,998 | 29.4 |
| 8 | Joseph W. Fordney (R) | 13,215 | 34.4 |
| | Albert L. Chandler (N PROG) | 11,593 | 30.1 |
| | Miles J. Purcell (D) | 11,527 | 30.0 |
| 9 | James C. McLaughlin (R) | 11,966 | 39.1 |
| | William H. Sears (N PROG) | 10,619 | 34.7 |
| | Herman R. O'Connor (D) | 8,020 | 26.2 |
| 10 | Roy O. Woodruff (N PROG) | 12,882 | 35.1 |
| | George A. Loud (R) | 12,141 | 33.1 |
| | Lewis P. Coumans (D) | 10,129 | 27.6 |
| 11 | Francis O. Lindquist (R) | 19,303 | 48.2 |
| | Archie McCall (D) | 9,361 | 23.4 |
| | John W. Patchin (N PROG) | 9,231 | 23.1 |
| 12 | William J. MacDonald (N PROG) | 18,433‡ | 38.4 |
| | H. Olin Young (R) | 18,190 | 37.9 |
| | John Power (D) | 10,322 | 21.5 |
| AL | Patrick H. Kelley (R) | 185,657 | 34.3 |
| | William H. Hill (N PROG) | 174,451 | 32.2 |
| | Edward Frensdorf (D) | 152,188 | 28.1 |

## MINNESOTA

| | Candidates | Votes | % |
|---|---|---|---|
| 1 | Sydney Anderson (R) | 24,681 | 69.6 |
| | Clinton Robinson (D) | 10,786 | 30.4 |
| 2 | Winfield S. Hammond (D) | 14,718 | 50.3 |
| | Franklin F. Ellsworth (R) | 13,093 | 44.7 |
| | John R. Hollister (PUB OWN) | 1,479 | 5.1 |
| 3 | Charles R. Davis (R) | 18,536 | 61.3 |
| | Frank L. Glotzbach (D) | 9,763 | 32.3 |
| | Frank F. Marzahn (P) | 1,919 | 6.4 |
| 4 | Frederick C. Stevens (R) | 15,479 | 36.8 |
| | James J. Regan (D) | 11,333 | 27.0 |
| | H. T. Halbert (PROG) | 9,220 | 21.9 |
| | Albert Rosenquist (PUB OWN) | 6,021 | 14.3 |
| 5 | George R. Smith (R) | 17,861 | 44.3 |
| | Thomas D. Schall (PROG) | 8,574 | 21.3 |
| | Thomas P. Dwyer (D) | 6,987 | 17.3 |
| | Thomas E. Latimer (PUB OWN) | 6,929 | 17.2 |
| 6 | Charles A. Lindbergh (R) | 21,286 | 62.5 |
| | Andrew J. Gilkinson (D) | 9,920 | 29.1 |
| | A. W. Uhl (PUB OWN) | 2,839 | 8.3 |
| 7 | A. J. Volstead (R) | 25,053 | 100.0 |
| 8 | Clarence G. Miller (R) | 20,523 | 50.8 |
| | John Jenswold Jr. (D) | 12,494 | 30.9 |
| | Morris Kaplan (PUB OWN) | 7,398 | 18.3 |
| 9 | Halvor Steenerson (R) | 22,481 | 66.8 |
| | M. A. Brattland (PUB OWN) | 11,190 | 33.2 |
| AL | James Manahan (R) | 154,308 | 55.1 |
| | Carl Johnson Buell (D) | 69,652 | 24.9 |
| | J. S. Ingalls (PUB OWN) | 30,042 | 10.7 |
| | William G. Calderwood (P) | 25,863 | 9.2 |

## MISSISSIPPI

| | Candidates | Votes | % |
|---|---|---|---|
| 1 | Ezekiel S. Candler Jr. (D) | 7,951 | 100.0 |
| 2 | Hubert D. Stephens (D) | 5,801 | 100.0 |
| 3 | Benjamin G. Humphreys (D) | 3,154 | 100.0 |
| 4 | Thomas U. Sisson (D) | 7,402 | 100.0 |
| 5 | Samuel A. Witherspoon (D) | 7,996 | 100.0 |
| 6 | Pat Harrison (D) | 7,347 | 96.1 |
| 7 | Percy E. Quin (D) | 4,486 | 100.0 |
| 8 | James W. Collier (D) | 4,660 | 100.0 |

## MISSOURI

| | Candidates | Votes | % |
|---|---|---|---|
| 1 | James T. Lloyd (D) | 20,874 | 53.9 |
| | Bonfoey (R) | 12,144 | 31.4 |
| | Warner (PROG) | 5,686 | 14.7 |

| | Candidates | Votes | % |
|---|---|---|---|
| 2 | William W. Rucker (D) | 22,786 | 57.3 |
| | Haley (R) | 10,132 | 25.5 |
| | Williams (PROG) | 6,776 | 17.1 |
| 3 | Joshua W. Alexander (D) | 20,179 | 52.8 |
| | Morroway (R) | 11,192 | 29.3 |
| | Wightman (PROG) | 6,812 | 17.8 |
| 4 | Charles F. Booher (D) | 20,232 | 53.8 |
| | Hickman (R) | 11,284 | 30.0 |
| | Robinson (PROG) | 5,347 | 14.2 |
| 5 | William P. Borland (D) | 33,397 | 52.9 |
| | Sumner (PROG) | 21,863 | 34.6 |
| | Kimbrell (R) | 5,759 | 9.1 |
| 6 | Clement C. Dickinson (D) | 17,858 | 52.2 |
| | Dunaway (R) | 9,093 | 26.6 |
| | Theilmann (PROG) | 6,788 | 19.9 |
| 7 | Courtney W. Hamlin (D) | 23,178 | 48.9 |
| | Owen (R) | 15,685 | 33.1 |
| | Blain (PROG) | 7,305 | 15.4 |
| 8 | Dorsey W. Shackleford (D) | 16,219 | 53.0 |
| | Peters (R) | 11,965 | 39.1 |
| | Pemberton (PROG) | 2,391 | 7.8 |
| 9 | James Beauchamp Clark (D) | 21,782 | 56.5 |
| | Cole (R) | 16,283 | 42.2 |
| 10 | Richard Bartholdt (R) | 33,242 | 37.6 |
| | O'Connor (D) | 31,227 | 35.3 |
| | Siebert (PROG) | 16,417 | 18.6 |
| | Hoehn (SOC) | 7,154 | 8.1 |
| 11 | William L. Igoe (D) | 19,653 | 50.4 |
| | Catlin (R) | 12,448 | 31.9 |
| | Ward (PROG) | 4,812 | 12.3 |
| 12 | Leonidas C. Dyer (R) | 11,981‡ | 43.6 |
| | Michael J. Gill (D) | 11,249 | 41.0 |
| | Cotton (PROG) | 3,041 | 11.1 |
| 13 | Walter L. Hensley (D) | 16,079 | 52.1 |
| | Nipper (R) | 13,406 | 43.4 |
| 14 | Joseph J. Russell (D) | 26,081 | 46.5 |
| | Curry (R & PROG) | 25,066 | 44.7 |
| | Bumpas (SOC) | 4,957 | 8.8 |
| 15 | Perl D. Decker (D) | 21,000 | 46.0 |
| | McPherson (R) | 12,850 | 28.2 |
| | Gregg (PROG) | 7,797 | 17.1 |
| | Bedingfield (SOC) | 3,203 | 7.0 |
| 16 | Thomas L. Rubey (D) | 15,908 | 52.3 |
| | O'Bannon (R) | 10,811 | 35.6 |
| | Bradford (PROG) | 3,678 | 12.1 |

## MONTANA

| | Candidates | Votes | % |
|---|---|---|---|
| AL | Thomas Stout (D) | 25,891✔ | |
| | John M. Evans (D) | 24,492✔ | |
| | Charles N. Pray (R) | 23,505 | |
| | William R. Allen (R) | 19,633 | |
| | Thomas M. Everett (PROG) | 16,644 | |
| | George A. Horkan (PROG) | 15,336 | |
| | Henri Labeau (SOC) | 10,271 | |
| | J. Frank Mabie (SOC) | 10,056 | |

## NEBRASKA

| | Candidates | Votes | % |
|---|---|---|---|
| 1 | John A. Maguire (D & PPI) | 17,410 | 50.5 |
| | Paul F. Clark (R & PROG) | 15,706 | 45.6 |
| 2 | Charles O. Lobeck (D & PPI) | 16,075 | 47.4 |
| | Howard H. Baldridge (R & PROG) | 15,662 | 46.2 |
| | J. N. Carter (SOC) | 2,146 | 6.3 |
| 3 | Daniel V. Stephens (D) | 26,229 | 53.1 |
| | Joseph C. Cook (R & PROG) | 21,677 | 43.9 |
| 4 | Charles H. Sloan (R & PROG) | 22,293 | 53.0 |
| | Charles M. Skiles (D & PPI) | 18,279 | 43.4 |
| 5 | Silas R. Barton (R & PROG) | 18,818 | 49.0 |
| | Roderick D. Sutherland (D & PPI) | 17,522 | 45.7 |
| 6 | Moses P. Kinkaid (R) | 24,766 | 47.5 |
| | W. J. Taylor (D & PPI) | 18,529 | 35.5 |
| | Florence Armstrong (P) | 4,997 | 9.6 |
| | Fred J. Warren (SOC) | 3,758 | 7.2 |

## NEVADA

| Candidates | Votes | % |
|---|---|---|
| AL Edwin E. Roberts (R) | 7,380 | 37.3 |
| Clay Tallman (D) | 7,311 | 37.0 |
| John E. Worden (SOC) | 3,011 | 15.2 |
| George Springmeyer (PROG) | 2,072 | 10.5 |

## NEW HAMPSHIRE

| Candidates | Votes | % |
|---|---|---|
| 1 Eugene E. Reed (D) | 18,888 | 45.4 |
| Cyrus A. Sulloway (R) | 17,363 | 41.7 |
| Samuel O. Titus (PROG) | 4,307 | 10.4 |
| 2 Raymond B. Stevens (D) | 21,794 | 53.6 |
| Frank D. Currier (R) | 17,961 | 44.2 |

## NEW JERSEY

| Candidates | Votes | % |
|---|---|---|
| 1 William J. Browning (R) | 14,512 | 39.3 |
| Craven (D) | 13,170 | 35.6 |
| Jess (RO PROG) | 5,891 | 15.9 |
| 2 J. Thompson Baker (D) | 16,130 | 43.1 |
| Gardner (R) | 12,330 | 33.0 |
| Potter (PROG) | 7,384 | 19.7 |
| 3 Thomas J. Scully (D) | 20,596 | 56.9 |
| Brown (R) | 14,363 | 39.7 |
| 4 Allan B. Walsh (D) | 13,222 | 45.0 |
| Blackman (R) | 8,607 | 29.3 |
| Gill (PROG) | 6,685 | 22.7 |
| 5 William E. Tuttle Jr. (D) | 13,920 | 41.0 |
| Runyon (R) | 10,085 | 29.7 |
| Ennis (PROG) | 7,393 | 21.8 |
| Matthews (SOC) | 2,066 | 6.1 |
| 6 Lewis J. Martin (D) | 15,216 | 46.5 |
| McClave (R) | 8,373 | 25.6 |
| Sage (PROG) | 7,007 | 21.4 |
| 7 Robert G. Bremner (D) | 9,990 | 42.2 |
| Smith (R) | 6,666 | 28.2 |
| Marelli (PROG) | 4,746 | 20.0 |
| Luthringer (SOC) | 1,649 | 7.0 |
| 8 Eugene F. Kinkead (D) | 14,058 | 52.3 |
| Bouton (R & PROG) | 9,527 | 35.4 |
| Tew (TAFT) | 2,269 | 8.4 |
| 9 Walter I. McCoy (D) | 10,196 | 42.4 |
| Walker (PROG) | 6,403 | 26.6 |
| Parker (R) | 5,818 | 24.2 |
| Bohm | 1,454 | 6.1 |
| 10 Edward W. Townsend (D) | 10,854 | 39.6 |
| Morgan (PROG) | 7,847 | 28.6 |
| Adams (R) | 7,111 | 25.9 |
| Cairns | 1,514 | 5.5 |
| 11 John J. Eagan (D) | 14,208 | 62.3 |
| Besson (R) | 7,018 | 30.8 |
| Reilly | 1,429 | 6.3 |
| 12 James A. Hamill (D) | 17,980 | 67.5 |
| Record (R & PROG) | 8,089 | 30.4 |

### Special Election

| Candidates | Votes | % |
|---|---|---|
| 6 Archibald C. Hart (D) | 17,197 | 38.8 |
| Smith (R) | 15,325 | 34.6 |
| Shay (PROG) | 11,287 | 25.5 |
| David J. Haney (D) | 3,369 | 7.6 |

## NEW MEXICO

| Candidates | Votes | % |
|---|---|---|
| AL Harvey B. Fergusson (D) | 22,139 | 45.6 |
| Nathan Jaffa (R) | 17,892 | 36.9 |
| Andrew Eggum (SOC) | 5,882 | 12.1 |
| Marcos C. DeBaca (PROG) | 2,644 | 5.5 |

## NEW YORK

| Candidates | Votes | % |
|---|---|---|
| 1 Lathrop Brown (D) | 16,505 | 40.7 |
| Frederick C. Hicks (R) | 11,753 | 29.0 |
| W. Bourke Cockran (N PROG) | 11,306 | 27.9 |
| 2 Denis O'Leary (D) | 23,090 | 57.0 |
| Felix Fritsche (N PROG) | 7,175 | 17.7 |
| Frank E. Hopkins (R) | 6,941 | 17.1 |
| William Danmar (SOC) | 2,918 | 7.2 |
| 3 Frank E. Wilson (D) | 12,658 | 48.0 |
| Frank F. Schulz (R) | 6,633 | 25.1 |
| Westervelt Prentice (N PROG) | 4,918 | 18.6 |
| John H. Jennings (SOC) | 1,801 | 6.8 |
| 4 Harry Howard Dale (D) | 9,059 | 47.1 |
| Samuel Greenblatt (N PROG) | 5,139 | 26.7 |
| William Liebermann (R & IL) | 3,574 | 18.6 |
| Robert J. Nolan (SOC) | 1,441 | 7.5 |
| 5 James P. Maher (D) | 12,504 | 46.0 |
| John S. Gaynor (R) | 7,677 | 28.2 |
| Charles J. Ryan (N PROG) | 5,794 | 21.3 |
| 6 William M. Calder (R) | 21,691 | 47.9 |
| Robert H. Roy (D) | 13,290 | 29.4 |
| Jesse Fuller Jr. (IL & NPR) | 9,310 | 20.6 |
| 7 John J. Fitzgerald (D) | 16,082 | 59.1 |
| Michael A. Fitzgerald (I LEAGUE) | 5,513 | 20.3 |
| John E. Brady (R) | 5,021 | 18.5 |
| 8 Daniel J. Griffin (D) | 17,403 | 52.0 |
| Albert H. T. Banzhaf (IL & NPR) | 8,867 | 26.5 |
| Ernest P. Seelman (R) | 6,027 | 18.0 |
| 9 James H. O'Brien (D) | 15,903 | 41.0 |
| John F. Kennedy (N PROG) | 10,362 | 26.7 |
| Oscar W. Swift (R) | 10,122 | 26.1 |
| William Koenig (SOC) | 2,027 | 5.2 |
| 10 Herman A. Metz (D) | 7,459 | 36.6 |
| Jacob L. Holtzmann (N PROG) | 5,889 | 28.9 |
| Reuben L. Haskell (R & IL) | 5,174 | 25.4 |
| Barnet Wolff (SOC) | 1,785 | 8.8 |
| 11 Daniel J. Riordan (D) | 15,417 | 60.1 |
| William Wirt Mills (IL & NPR) | 5,570 | 21.7 |
| William G. Rose (R) | 4,078 | 15.9 |
| 12 Henry M. Goldfogle (D & IL) | 4,592 | 39.3 |
| Meyer London (SOC) | 3,646 | 31.2 |
| Henry Moskowitz (N PROG) | 2,602 | 22.3 |
| Alexander Wolf (R) | 839 | 7.2 |
| 13 Timothy D. Sullivan (D) | 5,697 | 50.6 |
| Sigmund S. Rotter (N PROG) | 3,615 | 32.1 |
| John B. G. Rinehart (R & IL) | 1,151 | 10.2 |
| Joshua Wauhope (SOC) | 790 | 7.0 |
| 14 Jefferson M. Levy (D) | 8,950 | 49.4 |
| Abraham H. Goodman (N PROG) | 4,457 | 24.6 |
| E. Crosby Kindleberger (R) | 3,468 | 19.1 |
| Marie Macdonald (SOC) | 958 | 5.3 |
| 15 Michael F. Conry (D) | 16,791 | 61.7 |
| James H. Hickey (N PROG) | 4,791 | 17.6 |
| Francis A. O'Neill (R) | 4,721 | 17.4 |
| 16 Peter J. Dooling (D) | 15,036 | 56.3 |
| Francis C. Dale (R & IL) | 5,929 | 22.2 |
| Timothy Healy (N PROG) | 5,019 | 18.8 |
| 17 John F. Carew (D) | 12,350 | 51.8 |
| Lindon Bates Jr. (IL & NPR) | 5,516 | 23.1 |
| Ogden L. Mills (R) | 4,891 | 20.5 |
| 18 Thomas G. Patten (D) | 13,704 | 50.0 |
| Amos R. E. Pinchot (N PROG) | 6,644 | 24.3 |
| S. Walter Kaufman (R & IL) | 4,943 | 18.0 |
| Algernon Lee (SOC) | 2,085 | 7.6 |
| 19 Walter M. Chandler (IL & NPR) | 13,987 | 39.2 |
| Franklin Leonard Jr. (D) | 13,684 | 38.3 |
| Alexander Brough (R) | 7,104 | 19.9 |
| 20 Francis Burton Harrison (D) | 5,221 | 41.7 |
| Julius H. Reiter (N PROG) | 4,694 | 37.5 |
| Abram Goodman (R & IL) | 1,596 | 12.8 |
| Nicholas Aleinikoff (SOC) | 996 | 8.0 |
| 21 Henry George Jr. (D & IL) | 13,189 | 47.0 |
| Jerome F. Reilly (N PROG) | 8,384 | 29.9 |
| Martin C. Ansorge (R) | 5,265 | 18.8 |
| 22 Henry Bruckner (D) | 15,886 | 47.7 |
| Irving M. Crane (N PROG) | 9,462 | 28.4 |
| Rufus P. Johnston (R) | 6,098 | 18.3 |
| Charles Gall (SOC) | 1,835 | 5.5 |
| 23 Joseph A. Goulden (D) | 19,320 | 44.3 |
| Edward J. L. Raldiris (N PROG) | 13,150 | 30.1 |
| Peter Wynne (R & IL) | 8,779 | 20.1 |
| Fred Paulitsch (SOC) | 2,351 | 5.4 |
| 24 Woodson R. Oglesby (D, I LEAGUE) | 17,804 | 44.1 |
| Alfred E. Smith (N PROG) | 12,496 | 30.9 |
| Barton E. Kingman (R) | 8,219 | 20.3 |
| 25 Benjamin Irving Taylor (D, I LEAGUE) | 16,168 | 42.2 |
| James W. Husted (R) | 12,522 | 32.7 |
| John C. Bucher (N PROG) | 8,559 | 22.3 |
| 26 Edmund Platt (R) | 20,618 | 44.5 |
| John K. Sague (D) | 20,191 | 43.6 |
| Augustus B. Gray (N PROG) | 4,418 | 9.5 |
| 27 George McClellan (D) | 23,743 | 48.3 |
| Charles B. Ward (R) | 19,125 | 38.9 |
| Horatio Seymour Manning (N PROG) | 4,779 | 9.7 |
| 28 Peter G. Ten Eyck (D) | 23,193 | 44.1 |
| Daniel H. Prior (R) | 23,076 | 43.9 |
| Joseph F. McLaughlin (N PROG) | 4,918 | 9.4 |
| 29 James S. Parker (R) | 22,348 | 44.0 |
| Milton K. Huppuch (D) | 18,180 | 35.8 |
| Frederick E. Draper Jr. (N PROG) | 8,163 | 16.1 |
| 30 Samuel Wallin (R) | 14,194 | 33.1 |
| R. E. Lee Reynolds (D) | 13,881 | 32.4 |
| George R. Lunn (SOC) | 9,468 | 22.1 |
| Edward Everett Hale (N PROG) | 4,721 | 11.0 |
| 31 Edwin A. Merritt Jr. (R) | 18,458 | 46.1 |
| Dennis B. Lucey (D) | 12,995 | 33.0 |
| John B. Burnham (N PROG) | 7,971 | 20.2 |
| 32 Luther W. Mott (R, P) | 21,607 | 45.6 |
| Robert E. Gregg (D) | 15,848 | 33.4 |
| William W. Kelley (N PROG) | 8,926 | 18.8 |
| 33 Charles A. Talcott (D) | 17,855 | 38.0 |
| Homer P. Snyder (R) | 16,703 | 35.6 |
| Benjamin Thorne Gilbert (N PROG) | 9,914 | 21.1 |
| 34 George W. Fairchild (R) | 22,072 | 43.8 |
| James J. Byard Jr (D, I LEAGUE) | 20,322 | 40.3 |
| Jared C. Estelow (N PROG) | 5,572 | 11.1 |
| 35 John R. Clancy (D) | 18,009 | 35.4 |
| Michael E. Driscoll (R) | 17,874 | 35.1 |
| Giles H. Stilwell (N PROG) | 11,626 | 22.8 |
| 36 Sereno E. Payne (R) | 20,604 | 42.2 |
| Richard C. S. Drummond (D) | 17,900 | 36.7 |
| Wilson M. Gould (N PROG) | 8,151 | 16.7 |
| 37 Edwin S. Underhill (D) | 19,526 | 39.9 |
| Thomas F. Fennell (R) | 18,335 | 37.5 |
| Wiley W. Capron (N PROG) | 7,891 | 16.1 |
| 38 Thomas B. Dunn (R) | 15,776 | 35.4 |
| George P. Decker (D) | 14,440 | 32.4 |
| A. Emerson Babcock (N PROG) | 11,202 | 25.2 |
| Kendrick P. Shedd (SOC) | 2,657 | 6.0 |
| 39 Henry G. Danforth (R) | 17,881 | 39.1 |
| Charles Ward (D) | 15,529 | 33.9 |
| Silas L. Strivings (N PROG) | 10,413 | 22.8 |
| 40 Robert H. Gittins (D) | 16,065 | 37.5 |
| James S. Simmons (R) | 14,450 | 33.7 |
| Frank C. Ferguson (N PROG) | 9,889 | 23.1 |
| 41 Charles B. Smith (D) | 14,866 | 40.5 |
| George A. Davis (R) | 9,578 | 26.1 |

## NEW YORK

| Candidates | Votes | % |
|---|---|---|
| Henry Kobler (N PROG) | 9,471 | 25.8 |
| Edward Simon Jr. (SOC) | 2,528 | 6.9 |
| 42 Daniel A. Driscoll (D) | 14,851 | 45.7 |
| Willard H. Ticknor (R) | 8,613 | 26.5 |
| L. Bradley Dorr (N PROG) | 7,161 | 22.0 |
| 43 Charles M. Hamilton (R) | 17,346 | 37.9 |
| Manton M. Wyvell (D) | 12,479 | 27.3 |
| Samuel A. Carlson (N PROG) | 11,709 | 25.6 |

### Special Elections

| | Candidates | Votes | % |
|---|---|---|---|
| 13 | George W. Loft (D & IL) | 5,945 | 51.2 |
| | Samuel M. Hyman (R) | 2,409 | 20.7 |
| | Victor Tozzi (N PROG) | 2,132 | 18.4 |
| | Joshua Wanhope (SOC) | 828 | 7.1 |
| 20 | Jacob A. Cantor (D & IL) | 5,337 | 41.9 |
| | Isaac A. Hourwich (N PROG) | 3,206 | 25.2 |
| | Louis H. Guterman (R) | 2,991 | 23.5 |
| | Edward F. Cassidy (SOC) | 1,210 | 9.5 |

## NORTH CAROLINA

| | Candidates | Votes | % |
|---|---|---|---|
| 1 | John H. Small (D) | 12,537 | 98.4 |
| 2 | Claude Kitchin (D) | 11,091 | 91.9 |
| | Thomas B. Brown (R) | 982 | 8.1 |
| 3 | John M. Faison (D) | 11,624 | 65.8 |
| | James T. Kennedy (R) | 6,042 | 34.2 |
| 4 | Edward W. Pou (D) | 13,906 | 79.5 |
| | John F. Mitchell (R) | 3,586 | 20.5 |
| 5 | Charles M. Stedman (D) | 21,075 | 56.1 |
| | C. W. Curry (R) | 15,995 | 42.6 |
| 6 | Hannibal L. Godwin (D) | 13,028 | 98.6 |
| 7 | Robert N. Page (D) | 17,873 | 58.9 |
| | R. Don Laws (R) | 12,449 | 41.1 |
| 8 | Robert L. Doughton (D) | 15,180 | 55.6 |
| | George D. B. Reynolds (R) | 12,078 | 44.2 |
| 9 | Edwin Y. Webb (D) | 17,072 | 62.7 |
| | J. A. Smith (PROG) | 7,869 | 28.9 |
| | D. B. Paul (R) | 2,228 | 8.2 |
| 10 | James M. Gudger Jr. (D) | 16,183 | 53.1 |
| | R. Hilliard Staton (R) | 14,237 | 46.7 |

## NORTH DAKOTA

| | Candidates | Votes | % |
|---|---|---|---|
| 1 | Henry T. Helgesen (R) | 17,156 | 61.1 |
| | V. R. Lovell (D) | 9,609 | 34.2 |
| 2 | George M. Young (R) | 16,912 | 64.3 |
| | J. A. Minckler (D) | 7,426 | 28.2 |
| | John A. Yoder (SOC) | 1,922 | 7.3 |
| 3 | Patrick D. Norton (R) | 12,935 | 50.7 |
| | Hal Halvorsen (D) | 7,306 | 28.7 |
| | Arthur Leseuer (SOC) | 5,254 | 20.6 |

## OHIO

| | Candidates | Votes | % |
|---|---|---|---|
| 1 | Stanley E. Bowdle (D) | 22,330 | 42.0 |
| | Nicholas Longworth (R) | 22,229 | 41.8 |
| | Millard F. Andrew (PROG) | 5,771 | 10.9 |
| | Lawrence A. Zitt (SOC) | 2,853 | 5.4 |
| 2 | Alfred G. Allen (D) | 26,066 | 46.6 |
| | Otto J. Renner (R) | 21,113 | 37.7 |
| | William B. Hay (PROG) | 4,940 | 8.8 |
| | R. S. Moore (SOC) | 3,820 | 6.8 |
| 3 | Warren Gard (D) | 26,711 | 42.9 |
| | Bert B. Buckley (R) | 15,339 | 24.7 |
| | Frederick Guy Strickland (SOC) | 12,774 | 20.5 |
| | Edward G. Pease (PROG) | 6,976 | 11.2 |
| 4 | J. Henry Goeke (D) | 21,512 | 53.8 |
| | John L. Cable (R) | 10,267 | 25.7 |
| | William E. Rudy (PROG) | 4,993 | 12.5 |
| | Scott Wilkins (SOC) | 2,132 | 5.3 |
| 5 | Timothy T. Ansberry (D) | 20,091 | 64.0 |
| | Edward Staley (R) | 10,177 | 32.4 |
| 6 | Simeon D. Fess (R) | 18,090 | 49.2 |
| | D. K. Hempstead (D) | 17,300 | 47.0 |

| | Candidates | Votes | % |
|---|---|---|---|
| 7 | James D. Post (D) | 19,301 | 46.7 |
| | R. M. Hughey (R) | 18,595 | 45.0 |
| | Winfield S. Tibbetts (SOC) | 3,002 | 7.3 |
| 8 | Frank B. Willis (R) | 19,379 | 43.8 |
| | W. W. Durbin (D) | 17,965 | 40.6 |
| | Lemuel G. Herbert (PROG) | 5,429 | 12.3 |
| 9 | Isaac R. Sherwood (D) | 26,528 | 53.3 |
| | Holland C. Webster (PROG) | 17,490 | 35.1 |
| | Thomas C. Devine (SOC) | 5,769 | 11.6 |
| 10 | Robert M. Switzer (R) | 13,606 | 37.1 |
| | Charles M. Caldwell (D) | 13,424 | 36.6 |
| | William E. Pricer (PROG) | 7,091 | 19.3 |
| | William Miller (SOC) | 2,581 | 7.0 |
| 11 | Horatio C. Claypool (D) | 21,469 | 49.1 |
| | Albert Douglas (R) | 18,729 | 42.8 |
| | Albert Smith (SOC) | 3,519 | 8.1 |
| 12 | Clement L. Drumbaugh (D) | 24,040 | 52.3 |
| | Edward L. Taylor Jr. (R) | 14,682 | 31.5 |
| | Jacob L. Bachman (SOC) | 7,095 | 15.2 |
| 13 | John A. Key (D) | 26,395 | 53.4 |
| | Miles H. McLaughlin (R) | 13,021 | 26.3 |
| | Benjamin F. Sheidler (PROG) | 6,779 | 13.7 |
| | George P. Maxwell (SOC) | 3,272 | 6.6 |
| 14 | William G. Sharp (D) | 25,523 | 59.0 |
| | W. S. Kerr (R) | 14,142 | 32.7 |
| | George A. Storck (SOC) | 3,569 | 8.3 |
| 15 | George White (D) | 18,169 | 43.9 |
| | James Joyce (R) | 14,678 | 35.5 |
| | Howard E. Buker (PROG) | 4,968 | 12.0 |
| | F. L. Martin (SOC) | 3,033 | 7.3 |
| 16 | William B. Francis (D) | 16,568 | 45.6 |
| | David A. Hollingsworth (R) | 15,781 | 43.5 |
| | Robert Carson (SOC) | 3,953 | 10.9 |
| 17 | William A. Ashbrook (D) | 25,453 | 72.1 |
| | Albert R. Milner (PROG) | 5,895 | 16.7 |
| | Dan McCarton (SOC) | 3,958 | 11.2 |
| 18 | John J. Whitacre (D) | 23,936 | 43.6 |
| | Roscoe C. McCullough (R) | 23,350 | 42.5 |
| | George F. Lelansky (SOC) | 7,617 | 13.9 |
| 19 | Ellsworth R. Bathrick (D) | 20,251 | 35.9 |
| | W. S. Harris (PROG) | 16,035 | 28.4 |
| | Hiram E. Starkey (R) | 11,574 | 20.5 |
| | C. E. Sheplin (SOC) | 7,805 | 13.8 |
| 20 | William Gordon (D) | 24,385 | 40.3 |
| | Frank W. Woods (PROG) | 18,194 | 30.1 |
| | Paul Howland (R) | 12,733 | 21.0 |
| | John G. Willert (SOC) | 5,240 | 8.7 |
| 21 | Robert J. Bulkley (D) | 20,742 | 42.9 |
| | Augustus R. Hatton (PROG) | 13,760 | 28.5 |
| | Frederick L. Taft (R) | 8,811 | 18.2 |
| | Fred C. Ruppel (SOC) | 5,059 | 10.5 |
| AL | Robert M. Crosser (D) | 423,301 | 41.6 |
| | Lawrence K. Langdon (R) | 297,355 | 29.3 |
| | Randolph W. Walton (PROG) | 192,809 | 19.0 |
| | Harry D. Thomas (SOC) | 91,201 | 9.0 |

## OKLAHOMA

| | Candidates | Votes | % |
|---|---|---|---|
| 1 | Bird S. McGuire (R) | 19,035 | 45.0 |
| | John J. Davis (D) | 18,456 | 43.7 |
| | A. W. Renshaw (SOC) | 4,447 | 10.5 |
| 2 | Dick T. Morgan (R) | 24,349 | 43.8 |
| | J. J. Carney (D) | 23,773 | 42.8 |
| | P. D. McKenzie (SOC) | 7,486 | 13.5 |
| 3 | James S. Davenport (D) | 27,184 | 49.5 |
| | R. T. Daniel (R) | 20,884 | 38.0 |
| | Lewis B. Irvin (SOC) | 6,429 | 11.7 |
| 4 | Charles D. Carter (D) | 23,987 | 51.3 |
| | F. W. Holt (SOC) | 11,513 | 24.6 |
| | E. N. Wright (R) | 11,239 | 24.1 |
| 5 | Scott Ferris (D) | 29,574 | 56.2 |
| | C. O. Clark (R) | 11,987 | 22.8 |
| | H. H. Stallard (SOC) | 11,033 | 21.0 |
| AL | William H. Murray (D) | 121,411✔ | |
| | Claude Weaver (D) | 120,753✔ | |
| | Joseph B. Thompson (D) | 120,371✔ | |
| | Alvin D. Allen (R) | 87,468 | |

| Candidates | Votes | % |
|---|---|---|
| James L. Brown (R) | 87,262 | |
| Emory D. Brownlee (R) | 86,883 | |
| Oscar T. Ameringer (SOC) | 41,235 | |
| J. T. Cumbie (SOC) | 41,073 | |
| J. Luther Langston (SOC) | 41,022 | |

## OREGON

| | Candidates | Votes | % |
|---|---|---|---|
| 1 | Willis C. Hawley (R) | 26,925 | 43.1 |
| | R. G. Smith (D) | 15,410 | 24.6 |
| | John W. Campbell (PROG) | 8,679 | 13.9 |
| | W. S. Richards (SOC) | 7,181 | 11.5 |
| | O. A. Stillman (P) | 4,335 | 6.9 |
| 2 | Nicholas J. Sinnott (R) | 15,121 | 53.5 |
| | James H. Graham (D) | 8,322 | 29.4 |
| | C. H. Abercrombie (SOC) | 3,037 | 10.7 |
| | George L. Cleaver (P) | 1,800 | 6.4 |
| 3 | Abraham W. Lafferty (R & PROG) | 16,783 | 42.9 |
| | M. G. Munly (D) | 11,553 | 29.6 |
| | Thomas McCusker (I) | 6,280 | 16.1 |
| | Lee Campbell (SOC) | 3,065 | 7.8 |

## PENNSYLVANIA

| | Candidates | Votes | % |
|---|---|---|---|
| 1 | William S. Vare (R, WASH) | 25,205 | 68.7 |
| | John H. Hall (D, KEY) | 10,492 | 28.6 |
| 2 | George S. Graham (R, LINCOLN) | 14,803 | 50.7 |
| | William Schlipf Jr (D, KEY) | 7,604 | 26.0 |
| | Harry W. Lambirth (WASH) | 5,796 | 19.9 |
| 3 | J. Hampton Moore (R, LINCOLN) | 15,492 | 54.1 |
| | John H. Fow (D) | 6,212 | 21.7 |
| | Harry E. Walter (WASH, KEY) | 5,920 | 20.7 |
| 4 | George W. Edmonds (WASH, R) | 21,728 | 68.5 |
| | Thomas T. Nelson (D) | 8,482 | 26.7 |
| 5 | Michael Donohoe (D, WASH) | 22,001 | 55.2 |
| | Henry S. Borneman (R, LINCOLN) | 15,181 | 38.1 |
| | John Whitehead (SOC) | 2,604 | 6.5 |
| 6 | J. Washington Logue (D, KEY) | 22,091 | 43.5 |
| | Frederick S. Drake (WASH) | 19,642 | 31.0 |
| | Harry A. Mackey (R, RO PROG) | 19,291 | 30.5 |
| 7 | Thomas S. Butler (RO PROG) | 18,276 | 46.7 |
| | Robert E. Difenderfer (D & KEY) | 12,225 | 31.2 |
| | Frederick A. Howard (WASH) | 7,647 | 19.5 |
| 8 | Robert E. Difenderfer (D & KEY) | 18,230 | 38.2 |
| | Oscar O. Bean (R) | 15,840 | 33.2 |
| | Thomas K. Ober Jr. (WASH) | 12,205 | 25.6 |
| 9 | William W. Griest (R K & WASH) | 14,112 | 42.7 |
| | John N. Hetrick (B MOOSE) | 9,947 | 30.1 |
| | Richard M. Reilly (D) | 8,043 | 24.3 |
| 10 | John R. Farr (R & WASH) | 14,939 | 49.6 |
| | Michael A. McGinley (D & KEY) | 12,777 | 42.5 |
| 11 | John J. Casey (D & KEY) | 15,343 | 40.5 |
| | Clarence D. Coughlin (WASH) | 10,597 | 27.9 |
| | Charles C. Bowman (R P & PROG) | 9,864 | 26.0 |
| | C. F. Quinn (SOC) | 2,119 | 5.6 |
| 12 | Robert E. Lee (D K & PROG) | 14,902 | 50.4 |
| | Alfred B. Garner (R & WASH) | 10,463 | 35.4 |
| | Cornelius F. Foley (SOC) | 3,464 | 11.7 |
| 13 | John H. Rothermel (D) | 26,369 | 50.6 |
| | Claude T. Reno (R & WASH) | 20,403 | 39.2 |
| | Clarence T. Wixson (SOC) | 4,938 | 9.5 |
| 14 | William D. B. Ainey (R K & WASH) | 14,747 | 61.1 |

## PENNSYLVANIA

| | Candidates | Votes | % |
|---|---|---|---|
| | Joel G. Hill (D) | 8,384 | 34.7 |
| 15 | Edgar R. Kiess (R & WASH) | 14,211 | 45.9 |
| | William B. Wilson (D & KEY) | 13,643 | 44.1 |
| | Aaron Noll (SOC) | 2,282 | 7.4 |
| 16 | John V. Lesher (D) | 14,209 | 47.1 |
| | I. Clinton Kline (R & WASH) | 12,783 | 42.4 |
| | George W. Dornbach (SOC) | 2,737 | 9.1 |
| 17 | Frank L. Dershem (D & KEY) | 14,073 | 38.9 |
| | Benjamin K. Focht (R & PROG) | 10,978 | 30.3 |
| | Frank B. Clayton (WASH) | 9,442 | 26.1 |
| 18 | Aaron S. Kreider (R BM & PR) | 14,485 | 32.3 |
| | David L. Kaufman (D & KEY) | 14,082 | 31.4 |
| | Henry C. Demming (WASH) | 13,504 | 30.1 |
| 19 | Warren Worth Bailey (D) | 13,626 | 31.8 |
| | Lynn A. Brua (WASH) | 12,688 | 29.6 |
| | Jesse L. Hartman (R & PROG) | 12,633 | 29.5 |
| | D. W. B. Murphy (SOC) | 2,879 | 6.7 |
| 20 | Andrew R. Brodbeck (D) | 16,514 | 46.0 |
| | Daniel F. Lafean (R & BM) | 14,283 | 39.8 |
| | Robert C. Bair (WASH) | 3,186 | 8.9 |
| 21 | Charles E. Patton (R K & WASH) | 13,732 | 50.3 |
| | James A. Gleason (D) | 10,588 | 38.8 |
| | George Fox (SOC) | 2,041 | 7.5 |
| 22 | Abraham L. Keister (R & WASH) | 15,560 | 41.6 |
| | Curtis H. Gregg (D & PROG) | 14,943 | 39.9 |
| | Charles Cunningham (SOC) | 4,735 | 12.7 |
| | Daniel K. Albright (P) | 2,206 | 5.9 |
| 23 | Wooda N. Carr (D) | 12,211 | 38.8 |
| | Thomas S. Crago (R) | 7,836 | 24.9 |
| | Harvey L. Berkeley (WASH) | 7,588 | 24.1 |
| | Charles L. Gans (SOC) | 2,928 | 9.3 |
| 24 | Henry W. Temple (WASH) | 11,495 | 30.8 |
| | Charles Matthews (R) | 10,797 | 28.9 |
| | S. A. Lacock (D) | 8,585 | 23.0 |
| | George C. Frethy (SOC) | 5,082 | 13.6 |
| 25 | Milton W. Shreve (R & WASH) | 13,078 | 47.6 |
| | Turner W. Shacklett (D) | 10,446 | 38.0 |
| | Sidney A. Schwartz (SOC) | 2,727 | 9.9 |
| 26 | A. Mitchell Palmer (D) | 18,201 | 53.4 |
| | Francis A. March Jr. (R & WASH) | 14,451 | 42.4 |
| 27 | J. N. Langham (R & WASH) | 17,138 | 56.7 |
| | Foster M. Mohney (D) | 9,472 | 31.4 |
| | Thomas Jackson Fredericks (SOC) | 1,858 | 6.2 |
| | John Houk (P) | 1,743 | 5.8 |
| 28 | Willis J. Hulings (WASH) | 10,363 | 31.4 |
| | John P. Hines (D) | 9,741 | 29.5 |
| | Peter M. Speer (R) | 7,136 | 21.6 |
| | John R. McKeown (SOC) | 4,097 | 12.4 |
| | J. W. Neilly (P) | 1,692 | 5.1 |
| 29 | Stephen G. Porter (R & WASH) | 15,925 | 61.3 |
| | Joseph Gallagher (D) | 5,509 | 21.2 |
| | George T. McConnell (SOC) | 3,899 | 15.0 |
| 30 | M. Clyde Kelly (RKW & ROPR) | 17,230 | 54.5 |
| | Fred H. Merrick (SOC) | 7,570 | 24.0 |
| | Delmont K. Ferree (D & PROG) | 6,708 | 21.2 |
| 31 | James Francis Burke (R & WASH) | 10,679 | 51.1 |
| | William A. Prosser (SOC) | 5,101 | 24.4 |
| | Joseph F. Joyce (D) | 4,894 | 23.4 |
| 32 | Andrew J. Barchfeld (R & WASH) | 12,265 | 40.8 |
| | Herman L. Hegner (D & PROG) | 7,987 | 26.5 |
| | Thomas F. Kennedy (SOC) | 5,672 | 18.9 |
| | William McClintock Shrodes (KEY) | 4,169 | 13.9 |

| | Candidates | Votes | % |
|---|---|---|---|
| AL | John M. Morin (WASH, R) | 618,537 ✔ | |
| | Anderson H. Walters (WASH, R) | 608,709 ✔ | |
| | Frederick E. Lewis (WASH, R) | 607,702 ✔ | |
| | Arthur R. Rupley (WASH, R) | 606,709 ✔ | |
| | George Benton Shaw (D) | 357,562 | |
| | George R. McLean (D) | 352,396 | |
| | Joseph Howley (D) | 346,814 | |
| | E. E. Greenawalt (D) | 343,163 | |
| | John W. Slayton (SOC) | 81,785 | |
| | William Parker (SOC) | 81,125 | |
| | Charles W. Erwin (SOC) | 80,808 | |
| | E. S. Musser (SOC) | 80.247 | |
| | Howard R. Sheppard (KEY) | 21,553 | |
| | E. L. McKee (P) | 21,074 | |
| | Henry S. Gill (P) | 20,465 | |
| | Howard J. Force (P) | 20,284 | |
| | Thomas H. Hamilton (P) | 20,213 | |
| | Albin Garrett (KEY) | 20,088 | |
| | Charles A. Hawkins (KEY) | 19,701 | |
| | Daniel W. Simkins (KEY) | 18,961 | |
| | William H. Thomas (INDL) | 1,081 | |

### Special Election

| | Candidates | Votes | % |
|---|---|---|---|
| 1 | William S. Vare (R) | 20,461 | 87.8 |
| | Henry V. Garrett (KEY) | 2,762 | 11.9 |

## RHODE ISLAND

| | Candidates | Votes | % |
|---|---|---|---|
| 1 | George F. O'Shaunessy (D) | 13,057 | 50.3 |
| | Sheffield (R) | 9,663 | 37.2 |
| | Bolan (PROG) | 3,044 | 11.7 |
| 2 | Peter G. Gerry (D) | 10,728 | 42.9 |
| | Bliss (R) | 10,335 | 41.4 |
| | Ball (PROG) | 3,642 | 14.6 |
| 3 | Ambrose Kennedy (R) | 11,718 | 49.0 |
| | Rattey (D) | 9,841 | 41.2 |
| | Tuttle (PROG) | 2,158 | 9.0 |

## SOUTH CAROLINA

| | Candidates | Votes | % |
|---|---|---|---|
| 1 | George S. Legare (D) | 4,550* | 97.2 |
| 2 | James F. Byrnes (D) | 6,133 | 100.0 |
| 3 | Wyatt Aiken (D) | 7,458 | 100.0 |
| 4 | Joseph T. Johnson (D) | 10,144 | 100.0 |
| 5 | David E. Finley (D) | 7,901 | 100.0 |
| 6 | J. Willard Ragsdale (D) | 6,446 | 100.0 |
| 7 | Asbury F. Lever (D) | 6,660 | 98.5 |

## SOUTH DAKOTA

| | Candidates | Votes | % |
|---|---|---|---|
| 1 | Charles H. Dillon (R) | 25,498 | 55.9 |
| | Robert E. Dowdell (D) | 18,050 | 39.6 |
| 2 | Charles H. Burke (R) | 23,170 | 57.1 |
| | C. Boyd Barrett Sr. (D) | 14,283 | 35.2 |
| 3 | Eben W. Martin (R) | 15,141 | 52.5 |
| | Harry L. Gandy (D) | 12,154 | 42.1 |
| | J. E. Ballinger (SOC) | 1,564 | 5.4 |

## TENNESSEE

| | Candidates | Votes | % |
|---|---|---|---|
| 1 | Sam R. Sells (R) | 16,660 | 50.9 |
| | Z. D. Massey (PROG R) | 16,053 | 49.0 |
| 2 | Richard W. Austin (R) | 12,712 | 47.6 |
| | W. H. Buttram (PROG R) | 7,025 | 26.3 |
| | J. C. J. Williams (D) | 6,681 | 25.0 |
| 3 | John A. Moon (D) | 18,240 | 67.4 |
| | C. S. Stewart (R) | 6,380 | 23.6 |
| | J. W. Eastman (PROG) | 2,168 | 8.0 |
| 4 | Cordell Hull (D) | 17,077 | 64.9 |
| | I. J. Human (R) | 9,166 | 34.8 |
| 5 | William C. Houston (D) | 12,055 | 54.3 |
| | J. C. Beasley (D) | 8,437 | 38.0 |
| | Doak Aydelott (D) | 1,685 | 7.6 |
| 6 | Joseph W. Byrns (D) | 15,341 | 82.0 |
| | J. A. Althauser (R) | 2,862 | 15.3 |
| 7 | Lemuel P. Padgett (D) | 12,751 | 55.1 |
| | C. W. Turner (D) | 10,380 | 44.8 |

| | Candidates | Votes | % |
|---|---|---|---|
| 8 | Thetus W. Sims (D) | 12,451 | 54.2 |
| | J. W. Ross (R) | 8,368 | 36.4 |
| | C. Grissam (PROG) | 2,017 | 8.8 |
| 9 | Finis J. Garrett (D) | 13,392 | 79.0 |
| | B. C. Cochran (R) | 3,500 | 20.7 |
| 10 | Kenneth D. McKellar (D) | 12,910 | 94.3 |
| | George Pardue (SOC) | 777 | 5.7 |

## TEXAS

| | Candidates | Votes | % |
|---|---|---|---|
| 1 | Horace W. Vaughan (D) | 13,288 | 85.9 |
| | S. L. Willyard | 1,646 | 10.6 |
| 2 | Martin Dies (D) | 14,116 | 80.3 |
| | J. A. Freeland | 2,415 | 13.7 |
| 3 | James Young (D) | 12,158 | 96.6 |
| 4 | Sam Rayburn (D) | 13,900 | 89.6 |
| | C. E. Obsuchain | 1,340 | 8.6 |
| 5 | Jack Beall (D) | 16,915 | 96.6 |
| 6 | Rufus Hardy (D) | 9,743 | 96.0 |
| 7 | Alexander W. Gregg (D) | 9,132 | 100.0 |
| 8 | Joe H. Eagle (D) | 13,762 | 83.3 |
| | Jeff N. Miller (R) | 1,658 | 10.0 |
| | J. E. Curd | 1,111 | 6.7 |
| 9 | George F. Burgess (D) | 13,738 | 99.7 |
| 10 | Albert S. Burleson (D) | 12,383 | 100.0 |
| 11 | Robert L. Henry (D) | 11,429 | 98.1 |
| 12 | Oscar Calloway (D) | 17,283 | 97.6 |
| 13 | John H. Stephens (D) | 25,630 | 89.0 |
| | L. B. Lindsey | 1,656 | 5.8 |
| | H. H. Cooper (R) | 1,465 | 5.1 |
| 14 | James L. Slayden (D) | 17,675 | 97.5 |
| 15 | John N. Garner (D) | 17,231 | 99.9 |
| 16 | William R. Smith (D) | 23,763 | 99.9 |
| AL | Daniel E. Garrett (D) | 235,065 ✔ | |
| | Hatton W. Sumners (D) | 234,591 ✔ | |
| | D. D. Richardson (SOC) | 24,466 | |
| | J. M. Haggard (SOC) | 24,398 | |
| | R. B. Harrison (R) | 22,795 | |
| | J. E. Elgin (R) | 22,656 | |
| | Z. T. White (PROG) | 16,422 | |
| | F. M. Etheridge (PROG) | 16,408 | |
| | E. H. Coniber (P) | 1,195 | |

## UTAH

| | Candidates | Votes | % |
|---|---|---|---|
| AL | Joseph Howell (R) | 43,133 ✔ | |
| | Jacob Johnson (R) | 42,047 ✔ | |
| | Mathonihah Thomas (D) | 37,192 | |
| | T. D. Johnson (D) | 36,640 | |
| | Stephen H. Love (PROG) | 22,358 | |
| | Lewis Larson (PROG) | 21,934 | |
| | Murray E. King (SOC) | 8,971 | |
| | William M. Knerr (SOC) | 8,953 | |
| | Elias Anderson (SOC LAB) | 505 | |
| | Harry S. Joseph (NON PART) | 187 | |

## VERMONT

| | Candidates | Votes | % |
|---|---|---|---|
| 1 | Frank L. Greene (R) | 15,469 | 59.8 |
| | Patrick M. Meldon (D) | 9,154 | 35.4 |
| 2 | Frank Plumley (R) | 13,316 | 58.0 |
| | O. C. Sawyer (D) | 8,268 | 36.0 |

## VIRGINIA

| | Candidates | Votes | % |
|---|---|---|---|
| 1 | William A. Jones (D) | 10,361 | 91.0 |
| | T. E. Coleman (SOC) | 753 | 6.6 |
| 2 | Edward E. Holland (D) | 10,061 | 89.1 |
| | Nathaniel T. Green (PROG) | 1,121 | 9.9 |
| 3 | Andrew Jackson Montague (D) | 10,541 | 97.6 |
| 4 | Walter A. Watson (D) | 7,847 | 96.4 |
| 5 | Edward W. Saunders (D) | 9,479 | 62.1 |
| | A. B. Hamner (R) | 5,449 | 35.7 |
| 6 | Carter Glass (D) | 8,194 | 72.8 |
| | James S. Browning (PROG) | 2,312 | 20.6 |
| 7 | James Hay (D) | 10,015 | 71.5 |
| | George N. Earman (R) | 3,539 | 25.3 |

## VIRGINIA

| | Candidates | Votes | % |
|---|---|---|---|
| 8 | Charles C. Carlin (D) | 9,083 | 90.7 |
| | F. T. Evans (SOC) | 628 | 6.3 |
| 9 | C. Bascom Slemp (R) | 14,868 | 50.0 |
| | R. A. Ayers (D) | 13,857 | 46.6 |
| 10 | Henry D. Flood (D) | 9,615 | 74.5 |
| | E. J. McCulloch (PROG) | 2,458 | 19.0 |
| | Nathan Parkins (SOC) | 842 | 6.5 |

## WASHINGTON

| | Candidates | Votes | % |
|---|---|---|---|
| 1 | William E. Humphrey (R) | 35,252 | 31.0 |
| | Daniel Landon (PROG) | 34,562 | 30.4 |
| | Charles G. Heifner (D) | 26,973 | 23.7 |
| | Joseph Gilbert (SOC) | 16,987 | 14.9 |
| 2 | Albert Johnson (R) | 25,497 | 32.5 |
| | Stanton Warburton (PROG) | 24,214 | 30.9 |
| | James A. Munday (D) | 16,790 | 21.4 |
| | Leslie E. Aller (SOC) | 11,999 | 15.3 |
| 3 | William L. LaFollette (R) | 35,049 | 33.1 |
| | Roscoe M. Drumheller (D) | 31,148 | 29.4 |
| | F. M. Goodwin (PROG) | 29,666 | 28.0 |
| | Robert Burnes Martin (SOC) | 10,138 | 9.6 |
| AL | Jacob A. Falconer (PROG) | 95,049 ✔ | |
| | James W. Bryan (PROG) | 90,348 ✔ | |
| | Henry B. Dewey (R) | 87,613 | |
| | J. E. Frost (R) | 86,300 | |
| | E. O. Connor (D) | 73,133 | |
| | Henry M. White (D) | 72,184 | |

| Candidates | Votes | % |
|---|---|---|
| M. E. Giles (SOC) | 39,772 | |
| Alfred Wagenknecht (SOC) | 39,134 | |
| N. A. Thompson (P) | 8,185 | |

## WEST VIRGINIA

| | Candidates | Votes | % |
|---|---|---|---|
| 1 | John W. Davis (D) | 24,777 | 45.0 |
| | G. A. Laughlin (R) | 24,613 | 44.7 |
| | D. M. S. Holt (SOC) | 4,230 | 7.7 |
| 2 | William G. Brown Jr (D) | 23,669 | 47.5 |
| | W. C. Conley (R) | 23,455 | 47.0 |
| 3 | Samuel B. Avis (R) | 26,041 | 46.1 |
| | A. B. Littlepage (D) | 24,573 | 43.5 |
| | L. C. Rogers (SOC) | 5,213 | 9.2 |
| 4 | Hunter H. Moss Jr (R) | 20,445 | 50.2 |
| | J. M. Hamilton (D) | 19,346 | 47.5 |
| 5 | James A. Hughes (R) | 33,128 | 51.9 |
| | J. F. Beaver (D) | 27,697 | 43.4 |
| AL | Howard Sutherland (R) | 128,467 | 49.2 |
| | Ben H. Hiner (D) | 114,485 | 43.9 |
| | William A. Peter (SOC) | 13,944 | 5.3 |

## WISCONSIN

| | Candidates | Votes | % |
|---|---|---|---|
| 1 | Henry Allen Cooper (R) | 18,914 | 53.2 |
| | Calvin Stewart (D) | 13,816 | 38.8 |
| 2 | Michael E. Burke (D) | 20,665 | 55.2 |
| | Henry J. Grell (R) | 14,698 | 39.3 |

| | Candidates | Votes | % |
|---|---|---|---|
| 3 | John M. Nelson (R) | 22,388 | 52.9 |
| | Albert Long (D) | 18,219 | 43.1 |
| 4 | William J. Cary (D) | 14,906 | 44.9 |
| | Winfield R. Gaylord (SOCIAL D) | 10,840 | 32.6 |
| | John M. Beffel (R) | 6,945 | 20.9 |
| 5 | William H. Stafford (D) | 15,933 | 41.3 |
| | Victor L. Berger (SOCIAL D) | 14,025 | 36.3 |
| | James F. Trottman (R) | 8,251 | 21.4 |
| 6 | Michael K. Reily (D) | 16,742 | 48.7 |
| | James H. Davidson (R) | 15,505 | 45.1 |
| 7 | John J. Esch (R) | 20,065 | 61.0 |
| | William N. Coffland (D) | 10,795 | 32.8 |
| 8 | Edward E. Browne (R) | 17,099 | 54.6 |
| | Arthur J. Plowman (D) | 12,266 | 39.2 |
| 9 | Thomas F. Konop (D) | 16,843 | 48.5 |
| | Elmer A. Morse (R) | 16,139 | 46.4 |
| 10 | James A. Frear (R) | 19,915 | 65.1 |
| | Charles Donohue (D) | 8,794 | 28.7 |
| 11 | Irvine L. Lenroot (R) | 17,466 | 59.6 |
| | Henry A. Johnson (D) | 7,998 | 27.3 |
| | Ellis B. Harris (SOCIAL D) | 3,122 | 10.7 |

## WYOMING

| | Candidates | Votes | % |
|---|---|---|---|
| AL | Frank W. Mondell (R) | 19,130 | 46.4 |
| | Thomas P. Fahey (D) | 14,720 | 35.7 |
| | Charles E. Winter (PROG) | 4,828 | 11.7 |
| | Anthony Carlson (SOC) | 2,230 | 5.4 |

# 1914 House Elections

## ALABAMA

| | Candidates | Votes | % |
|---|---|---|---|
| 1 | Oscar L. Gray (D) | 4,609 | 98.5 |
| 2 | S. Hubert Dent Jr. (D) | 7,470 | 100.0 |
| 3 | Henry B. Steagall (D) | 8,220 | 100.0 |
| 4 | Fred L. Blackmon (D) | 5,441 | 99.9 |
| 5 | J. Thomas Heflin (D) | 8,100 | 100.0 |
| 6 | William B. Oliver (D) | 8,539 | 79.7 |
| | Samuel L. Studdard (R) | 2,178 | 20.3 |
| 7 | John L. Burnett (D) | 8,905 | 53.1 |
| | Thomas H. Stephens (R) | 6,922 | 41.3 |
| 8 | Edward B. Almon (D) | 6,101 | 96.6 |
| 9 | George Huddleston (D) | 6,756 | 83.7 |
| | Robert Fullenweider (R) | 1,316 | 16.3 |
| AL | John W. Abercrombie (D) | 62,830 | 78.0 |
| | James F. Abercrombie (R) | 12,832 | 15.9 |

### Special Election

| | | | |
|---|---|---|---|
| 3 | William O. Mulkey (D) | 6,225 | 53.7 |
| | J. J. Speight | 5,367 | 46.3 |

## ARIZONA

| | | | |
|---|---|---|---|
| Al | Carl Hayden (D) | 33,306 | 74.6 |
| | Henry L. Eads (R) | 7,586 | 17.0 |
| | Ulrich Grill (SOC) | 3,773 | 8.5 |

## ARKANSAS

| | | | |
|---|---|---|---|
| 1 | Thaddeus H. Caraway (D) | 4,806 | 100.0 |
| 2 | William A. Oldfield (D) | 5,253 | 100.0 |
| 3 | John N. Tillman (D) | 7,588 | 61.8 |
| | W. N. Ivie (R) | 4,087 | 33.3 |
| 4 | Otis T. Wingo (D) | 5,166 | 82.0 |
| | L. C. Packard (PROG) | 1,135 | 18.0 |
| 5 | Henderson M. Jacoway (D) | 5,586 | 100.0 |
| 6 | Samuel K. Taylor (D) | 4,110 | 100.0 |
| 7 | William S. Goodwin (D) | 4,757 | 100.0 |

## CALIFORNIA

| | | | |
|---|---|---|---|
| 1 | William Kent (I-PR-SOC) | 35,403 | 47.6 |
| | Edward H. Hart (R) | 28,166 | 37.8 |
| | O. F. Meldon (D) | 7,987 | 10.7 |
| 2 | John E. Raker (D SOC) | 32,575 | 64.6 |
| | James T. Matlock (R & PROG) | 15,716 | 31.2 |
| 3 | Charles F. Curry (R-D-PROG) | 66,034 | 85.0 |
| | David T. Ross (SOC) | 6,752 | 8.7 |
| | Edwin F. Vanvlear (P) | 4,911 | 6.3 |
| 4 | Julius Kahn (R & PROG) | 41,044 | 69.1 |
| | Henry Colombat (D) | 13,550 | 22.8 |
| | A. K. Gifford (SOC) | 3,928 | 6.6 |
| 5 | John I. Nolan (R-D-PROG) | 53,875 | 83.3 |
| | Mads P. Christensen (SOC) | 7,366 | 11.4 |
| | Frederick Head (P) | 3,410 | 5.3 |
| 6 | John A. Elston (PROG) | 36,164 | 44.4 |
| | George H. Derrick (R) | 30,704 | 37.7 |
| | Howard H. Caldwell (SOC) | 11,355 | 13.9 |
| 7 | Denver S. Church (D) | 39,389 | 49.9 |
| | A. M. Drew (R) | 25,106 | 31.8 |
| | Harry M. McKee (SOC) | 7,797 | 9.9 |
| | Don A. Allen (P) | 6,573 | 8.3 |
| 8 | Everis A. Hayes (R) | 36,499 | 49.1 |
| | L. D. Bohnett (PROG D) | 33,706 | 45.3 |
| | Joseph Merritt Horton (P) | 4,157 | 5.6 |
| 9 | Charles H. Randall (P & D) | 28,097 | 30.9 |
| | Charles W. Bell (PROG) | 27,560 | 30.3 |
| | Frank C. Roberts (R) | 25,176 | 27.7 |
| | Henry A. Hart (SOC) | 10,084 | 11.1 |

| | Candidates | Votes | % |
|---|---|---|---|
| 10 | William D. Stephens (PROG) | 44,141 | 38.4 |
| | H. Z. Osborne (R) | 33,172 | 28.9 |
| | Nathan Newby (D) | 17,810 | 15.5 |
| | Ralph L. Criswell (SOC) | 14,900 | 13.0 |
| 11 | William Kettner (D & PROG) | 47,165 | 52.7 |
| | James Carson Needham (R) | 25,001 | 27.9 |
| | James S. Edwards (P) | 11,278 | 12.6 |
| | Kaspar Bauer (SOC) | 6,033 | 6.7 |

## COLORADO

| | | | |
|---|---|---|---|
| 1 | Benjamin C. Hilliard (D) | 26,169 | 44.7 |
| | Horace Phelps (R) | 21,569 | 36.9 |
| | A. W. Rucker (WILSON I) | 5,445 | 9.3 |
| 2 | Charles R. Timberlake (R) | 30,749 | 45.7 |
| | Harry H. Seldomridge (D) | 28,290 | 42.0 |
| | Charles E. Fisher (PROG) | 8,256 | 12.3 |
| 3 | Edward Keating (D) | 37,191 | 53.3 |
| | Neil N. McLean (R & PROG) | 32,567 | 46.7 |
| 4 | Edward T. Taylor (D) | 26,562 | 57.8 |
| | H. J. Baird (R & PROG) | 15,015 | 32.7 |
| | George Kunkle (SOC) | 4,353 | 9.5 |

## CONNECTICUT

| | | | |
|---|---|---|---|
| 1 | P. Davis Oakey (R) | 19,899 | 46.7 |
| | Augustine Lonergan (D) | 19,043 | 44.7 |
| 2 | Richard P. Freeman (R) | 18,255 | 52.5 |
| | Mahan (D) | 14,270 | 41.0 |
| 3 | John Q. Tilson (R) | 16,072 | 46.5 |
| | Reilly (D) | 15,310 | 44.3 |
| 4 | Ebenezer J. Hill (R) | 20,231 | 51.0 |
| | Jeremiah Donovan (D) | 16,610 | 41.8 |
| 5 | James P. Glynn (R) | 14,543 | 48.9 |
| | Kennedy (D) | 12,877 | 43.3 |

## DELAWARE

| | | | |
|---|---|---|---|
| AL | Thomas W. Miller (R) | 22,922 | 50.1 |
| | Franklin Brockson (D) | 20,681 | 45.2 |

## FLORIDA

| | | | |
|---|---|---|---|
| 1 | Stephen M. Sparkman (D) | 5,956 | 99.2 |
| 2 | Frank Clark (D) | 4,577 | 100.0 |
| 3 | Emmett Wilson (D) | 5,484 | 98.8 |
| 4 | William J. Sears (D) | 7,934 | 99.8 |

## GEORGIA

| | | | |
|---|---|---|---|
| 1 | Charles G. Edwards (D) | 5,600 | 100.0 |
| 2 | Frank Park (D) | 5,633 | 100.0 |
| 3 | Charles R. Crisp (D) | 4,357 | 100.0 |
| 4 | William C. Adamson (D) | 4,754 | 100.0 |
| 5 | William S. Howard (D) | 4,780 | 88.2 |
| | Dewar (PROG) | 640 | 11.8 |
| 6 | James W. Wise (D) | 7,100 | 100.0 |
| 7 | Gordon Lee (D) | 10,364 | 100.0 |
| 8 | Samuel J. Tribble (D) | 7,673 | 100.0 |
| 9 | Thomas M. Bell (D) | 12,943 | 100.0 |
| 10 | Carl Vinson (D) | 5,833 | 100.0 |
| 11 | John R. Walker (D) | 4,959 | 100.0 |
| 12 | Dudley M. Hughes (D) | 6,836 | 100.0 |

## IDAHO

| | | | |
|---|---|---|---|
| AL | Addison T. Smith (R) | 45,365✔ | |
| | Robert M. McCracken (R) | 43,918✔ | |
| | James H. Forney (D) | 39,736 | |
| | Bert H. Miller (D) | 37,000 | |
| | Charles W. Luck (EP) | 8,295 | |

| | Candidates | Votes | % |
|---|---|---|---|
| | A. B. Clark (SOC) | 8,093 | |
| | G. W. Beloit (SOC) | 8,061 | |
| | E. H. Rettig (EP) | 7,399 | |
| | R. P. Logan (P) | 1,329 | |
| | J. J. Pugh (P) | 1,276 | |

## ILLINOIS

| | | | |
|---|---|---|---|
| 1 | Martin B. Madden (R) | 13,063 | 53.2 |
| | James M. Quinlan (D) | 9,060 | 36.9 |
| | Henry M. Ashton (PROG) | 1,758 | 7.2 |
| 2 | James R. Mann (R) | 21,612 | 48.5 |
| | Mark B. O'Leary (D) | 11,940 | 26.8 |
| | John C. Vaughan (PROG) | 8,506 | 19.1 |
| | Thomas P. Costello (SOC) | 2,532 | 5.7 |
| 3 | William W. Wilson (R) | 18,511 | 44.9 |
| | Joseph E. Pendergast (D) | 16,614 | 40.3 |
| | William C. Lewis (PROG) | 4,001 | 9.7 |
| | George W. Stone (SOC) | 2,093 | 5.1 |
| 4 | James T. McDermott (D) | 13,313 | 58.2 |
| | William W. Wilcox (R) | 7,019 | 30.7 |
| | Harry P. Turner (SOC) | 1,422 | 6.2 |
| 5 | Adolph J. Sabath (D) | 9,921 | 54.2 |
| | Abram J. Harris (R) | 4,390 | 24.0 |
| | E. F. Napieralski (PROG) | 2,623 | 14.3 |
| | Jacob Danhoff (SOC) | 1,364 | 7.5 |
| 6 | James McAndrews (D) | 23,103 | 45.5 |
| | Frederick E. Coyne (R) | 17,328 | 34.1 |
| | Robert F. Kolb (PROG) | 6,161 | 12.1 |
| | Frank L. Wood (SOC) | 4,162 | 8.2 |
| 7 | Frank Buchanan (D) | 22,377 | 39.3 |
| | Niels Juul (R) | 20,143 | 35.4 |
| | Carl D. Thompson (SOC) | 7,663 | 13.5 |
| | Charles S. Stewart (PROG) | 6,724 | 11.8 |
| 8 | Thomas Gallagher (D) | 12,524 | 69.5 |
| | Edward I. Williams (R) | 3,558 | 19.7 |
| | Henry Anielewski (SOC) | 1,159 | 6.4 |
| 9 | Fred A. Britten (R) | 11,358 | 43.2 |
| | Oscar F. Nelson (D) | 8,242 | 31.4 |
| | R. T. Crane (PROG) | 5,365 | 20.4 |
| | Frank Schiflersmith (SOC) | 1,315 | 5.0 |
| 10 | George Edmund Foss (R) | 18,038 | 38.8 |
| | John F. Waters (D) | 13,096 | 28.2 |
| | Charles M. Thomson (PROG) | 13,039 | 28.0 |
| | John M. Work (SOC) | 2,343 | 5.0 |
| 11 | Ira C. Copley (PROG) | 18,371 | 40.5 |
| | Frank W. Shepherd (R) | 17,197 | 37.9 |
| | John A. Logan (D) | 9,098 | 20.1 |
| 12 | Charles E. Fuller (R) | 20,811 | 50.8 |
| | William H. Hinebaugh (PROG) | 9,700 | 23.7 |
| | George V. B. Weeks (D) | 8,726 | 21.3 |
| 13 | John C. McKenzie (R) | 18,143 | 57.9 |
| | Frank M. Goodwin (D) | 8,735 | 27.9 |
| | Isaac N. Evans (PROG) | 4,054 | 12.9 |
| 14 | Clyde H. Tavenner (D) | 17,221 | 44.1 |
| | Frank E. Abbey (R) | 16,132 | 41.3 |
| | Henry E. Burgess (PROG) | 4,272 | 10.9 |
| 15 | Edward J. King (R) | 16,217 | 41.3 |
| | Edward P. Allen (D) | 14,537 | 37.0 |
| | Julius Kespohl (PROG) | 7,122 | 18.1 |
| 16 | Claude U. Stone (D) | 18,399 | 48.8 |
| | George A. Zeller (R) | 16,462 | 43.7 |
| 17 | John A. Sterling (R) | 16,720 | 48.1 |
| | Louis Fitzhenry (D) | 14,842 | 42.7 |
| | George E. Stump (PROG) | 2,757 | 7.9 |
| 18 | Joseph G. Cannon (R) | 22,035 | 47.1 |
| | Frank T. O'Hair (D) | 20,005 | 42.8 |
| | Wendell P. Kay (PROG) | 4,112 | 8.8 |
| 19 | William B. McKinley (R) | 25,576 | 51.0 |
| | Charles M. Borchers (D) | 19,931 | 39.7 |
| | Frank B. Thomas (PROG) | 4,083 | 8.1 |
| 20 | Henry T. Rainey (D) | 20,340 | 58.0 |
| | Jarvis F. Dubois (R) | 12,885 | 36.8 |
| 21 | Loren E. Wheeler (R) | 20,800 | 47.8 |
| | James M. Graham (D) | 18,361 | 42.2 |
| | Porter Paddock (PROG) | 2,417 | 5.6 |

## ILLINOIS

| | Candidates | Votes | % |
|---|---|---|---|
| 22 | William A. Rodenberg (R) | 23,362 | 46.5 |
| | William N. Baltz (D) | 21,364 | 42.5 |
| | Charles F. Stelzel (PROG) | 2,799 | 5.6 |
| | M. E. Kirkpatrick (SOC) | 2,772 | 5.5 |
| 23 | Martin D. Foster (D) | 24,414 | 53.1 |
| | John J. Bundy (R) | 18,036 | 39.3 |
| | Logan B. Skipper (PROG) | 2,659 | 5.8 |
| 24 | Thomas S. Williams (R) | 18,311 | 49.9 |
| | H. Robert Fowler (D) | 17,369 | 47.3 |
| 25 | Edward E. Dennison (R) | 20,271 | 48.5 |
| | Robert P. Hill (D) | 17,922 | 42.8 |
| | George W. Dowell (PROG) | 2,468 | 5.9 |
| AL | Burnett M. Chiperfield (R) | 388,896 | |
| | William Elza Williams (D) | 375,465 | |
| | J. McLean Davis (R) | 373,682 | |
| | Thomas P. Sullivan (D) | 356,678 | |
| | Harry L. Heer (PROG) | 113,510 | |
| | George N. Kreider (PROG) | 105,088 | |
| | Dan R. Thomas (SOC) | 42,841 | |
| | Carl Strover (SOC) | 41,949 | |
| | Frank E. Herrick (P) | 7,644 | |
| | John A. Shields (P) | 7,275 | |
| | Harry (SOC LAB) | 2,060 | |

## INDIANA

| | Candidates | Votes | % |
|---|---|---|---|
| 1 | Charles Lieb (D) | 20,488 | 46.6 |
| | S. Wallace Cook (R) | 17,661 | 40.1 |
| | U. H. Seider (PROG) | 3,519 | 8.0 |
| 2 | William A. Cullop (D) | 21,451 | 44.3 |
| | O. E. Bland (R) | 19,145 | 39.5 |
| | J. B. Wilson (PROG) | 5,087 | 10.5 |
| 3 | William E. Cox (D) | 23,679 | 56.4 |
| | Edgar D. Bush (R) | 12,260 | 29.2 |
| | Lawson Mace (PROG) | 5,344 | 12.7 |
| 4 | Lincoln Dixon (D) | 22,795 | 50.3 |
| | M. D. Wilson (R) | 16,856 | 37.2 |
| | Roy W. Ewing (PROG) | 4,609 | 10.2 |
| 5 | Ralph W. Moss (D) | 21,785 | 45.9 |
| | R. L. Shattuck (R) | 17,552 | 37.0 |
| | Otis E. Gulley (PROG) | 5,254 | 11.1 |
| 6 | Finly H. Gray (D) | 18,371 | 41.4 |
| | P. J. Lynch (R) | 14,880 | 33.6 |
| | Elbert Russell (PROG) | 9,449 | 21.3 |
| 7 | Merrill Moores (R) | 26,451 | 42.0 |
| | Charles S. Korbly (D) | 21,343 | 33.9 |
| | Paxton Hibben (PROG) | 10,530 | 16.7 |
| | W. H. Henry (SOC) | 4,002 | 6.4 |
| 8 | John A. M. Adair (D) | 21,840 | 44.5 |
| | A. H. Vestal (R) | 13,160 | 26.8 |
| | H. L. Kitselman (PROG) | 10,785 | 22.0 |
| 9 | Martin A. Morrison (D) | 21,992 | 42.8 |
| | F. S. Purnell (R) | 21,035 | 40.9 |
| | C. A. Ford (PROG) | 6,198 | 12.1 |
| 10 | William R. Wood (R) | 22,318 | 45.4 |
| | John B. Peterson (D) | 17,735 | 36.0 |
| | William H. Ade (PROG) | 8,637 | 17.6 |
| 11 | George W. Rauch (D) | 20,666 | 41.6 |
| | S. L. Strickler (R) | 16,999 | 34.3 |
| | B. B. Shively (PROG) | 8,106 | 16.3 |
| 12 | Cyrus Cline (D) | 18,612 | 46.9 |
| | Charles R. Lane (R) | 15,052 | 37.9 |
| | H. M. Widney (P) | 3,976 | 10.0 |
| 13 | Henry A. Barnhart (D) | 25,134 | 44.4 |
| | A. J. Hickney (R) | 19,771 | 34.9 |
| | R. S. Stephens (PROG) | 8,542 | 15.1 |

## IOWA

| | Candidates | Votes | % |
|---|---|---|---|
| 1 | Charles A. Kennedy (R) | 14,866 | 49.2 |
| | F. B. Whittaker (D) | 12,381 | 41.0 |
| | Daniel B. Heller (PROG) | 1,600 | 5.3 |
| 2 | Harry E. Hull (R) | 20,145 | 50.8 |
| | W. J. McDonald (D) | 16,940 | 42.8 |
| 3 | Burton E. Sweet (R) | 22,386 | 56.5 |
| | James C. Murtagh (D) | 15,427 | 39.0 |
| 4 | Gilbert N. Haugen (R) | 20,001 | 56.6 |
| | G. A. Meyer (D) | 13,653 | 38.6 |
| 5 | James W. Good (R) | 20,752 | 56.2 |
| | Joseph Mekota (D) | 14,497 | 39.2 |
| 6 | C. William Ramseyer (R) | 16,616 | 48.1 |
| | W. H. Hamilton (D) | 14,552 | 42.1 |
| 7 | Cassius C. Dowell (R) | 17,225 | 53.8 |
| | John T. Mulvaney (D) | 10,871 | 33.9 |
| | John E. Holmes (PROG) | 2,193 | 6.9 |
| 8 | Horace M. Towner (R) | 19,817 | 54.1 |
| | H. E. Valentine (D) | 14,324 | 39.1 |
| 9 | William R. Green (R) | 19,265 | 53.9 |
| | H. S. Mosher (D) | 14,677 | 41.1 |
| 10 | Frank P. Woods (R) | 24,192 | 54.5 |
| | D. M. Kelleher (D) | 14,401 | 32.5 |
| | William B. Quarton (PROG) | 4,656 | 10.5 |
| 11 | Thomas J. Steele (D) | 21,259 | 48.9 |
| | George C. Scott (R) | 17,000 | 40.5 |
| | Edward H. Crane (PROG) | 3,724 | 8.6 |

### Special Election

| | | Votes | % |
|---|---|---|---|
| 2 | Henry Vollmer (D) | 12,625 | 44.5 |
| | Harry E. Hull (R) | 10,809 | 38.1 |
| | Charles P. Hanley (PROG) | 3,709 | 13.1 |

## KANSAS

| | Candidates | Votes | % |
|---|---|---|---|
| 1 | Daniel R. Anthony Jr. (R) | 31,539 | 51.6 |
| | J. B. Chapman (D) | 20,279 | 33.2 |
| | Sheffield Ingalls (PROG) | 9,259 | 15.2 |
| 2 | Joseph Taggart (D) | 28,412 | 41.7 |
| | John H. Crider (R) | 24,732 | 36.3 |
| | J. L. Brady (PROG) | 12,271 | 18.0 |
| 3 | Philip P. Campbell (R) | 30,644 | 41.2 |
| | P. J. McGinley (D) | 21,492 | 28.9 |
| | L. F. Fuller (SOC) | 11,370 | 15.3 |
| | G. E. Bertch (PROG) | 7,871 | 10.6 |
| 4 | Dudley Doolittle (D) | 23,894 | 47.0 |
| | Howard F. Martindale (R) | 19,331 | 38.0 |
| | N. D. Welty (PROG) | 6,626 | 13.0 |
| 5 | Guy T. Helvering (D) | 25,142 | 45.7 |
| | W. A. Calderhead (R) | 22,756 | 41.4 |
| | Loring Trott (PROG) | 7,083 | 12.9 |
| 6 | John R. Connelly (D) | 27,359 | 47.0 |
| | John B. Dykes (R) | 21,353 | 36.7 |
| | Eva Morley Murphy (PROG) | 6,847 | 11.8 |
| 7 | Jouett Shouse (D) | 27,740 | 39.7 |
| | John S. Simmons (R) | 26,181 | 37.5 |
| | O. W. Dawson (PROG) | 12,537 | 18.0 |
| 8 | William A. Ayres (D) | 21,512 | 46.6 |
| | Charles L. Davidson (PROG) | 11,907 | 25.8 |
| | Ezra Branine (R) | 11,520 | 24.9 |

## KENTUCKY

| | Candidates | Votes | % |
|---|---|---|---|
| 1 | Alben W. Barkley (D) | 18,407 | 65.9 |
| | Edwin Farley (R) | 8,522 | 30.5 |
| 2 | David H. Kincheloe (D) | 15,019 | 57.0 |
| | Alvin H. Clark (R) | 10,593 | 40.2 |
| 3 | Robert Y. Thomas Jr. (D) | 16,020 | 49.7 |
| | J. F. Taylor (R) | 14,414 | 44.7 |
| 4 | Ben Johnson (D) | 17,218 | 56.9 |
| | W. Sherman Ball (R) | 11,496 | 38.0 |
| 5 | J. Swagar Sherley (D) | 23,765 | 60.6 |
| | Charles T. Gardiner (PROG) | 8,106 | 20.7 |
| | Roy Wilhoit (R) | 6,611 | 16.9 |
| 6 | Arthur B. Rouse (D) | 18,018 | 87.9 |
| | Emmett Orr (PROG) | 1,689 | 8.2 |
| 7 | James Campbell Cantrill (D) | 20,040 | 61.2 |
| | Louis L. Bristow (R) | 12,295 | 37.5 |
| 8 | Harvey Helm (D) | 14,393 | 55.0 |
| | James P. Spilman (R) | 10,460 | 40.0 |
| 9 | William J. Fields (D) | 22,739 | 53.0 |
| | H. Glenn Ireland (R) | 19,291 | 45.0 |
| 10 | John W. Langley (R) | 13,150 | 61.5 |
| | F. Tom Hatcher (D) | 7,755 | 36.3 |
| 11 | Caleb Powers (R) | 16,686 | 70.8 |
| | John H. Wilson (I) | 6,893 | 29.2 |

## LOUISIANA

| | Candidates | Votes | % |
|---|---|---|---|
| 1 | Albert Estopinal (D) | 9,657 | 91.4 |
| | Louis Henry Burns (PROG) | 903 | 8.6 |
| 2 | H. Garland Dupre (D) | 8,641 | 81.7 |
| | Louis Lebourgeois (PROG) | 1,939 | 18.3 |
| 3 | Whitmell P. Martin (PROG) | 6,030 | 56.6 |
| | Henri Gueydan (D) | 4,604 | 43.2 |
| 4 | John Thomas Watkins (D) | 3,330 | 96.4 |
| 5 | Riley J. Wilson (D) | 2,865 | 95.1 |
| 6 | Lewis L. Morgan (D) | 3,190 | 99.4 |
| 7 | Ladislas Lazaro (D) | 3,792 | 86.0 |
| | Walter F. Dietz (SOC) | 615 | 14.0 |
| 8 | James B. Aswell (D) | 4,466 | 85.9 |
| | J. R. Jones (SOC) | 729 | 14.0 |

## MAINE

| | Candidates | Votes | % |
|---|---|---|---|
| 1 | Asher C. Hinds (R) | 16,622 | 47.0 |
| | John C. Scates (D) | 16,035 | 45.4 |
| | W. C. Emerson (PROG) | 2,276 | 6.4 |
| 2 | Daniel J. McGillicuddy (D) | 16,508 | 46.9 |
| | H. M. Sewall (R) | 11,335 | 32.2 |
| | A. C. Wheeler (PROG) | 6,539 | 18.6 |
| 3 | John A. Peters (R) | 19,600 | 46.5 |
| | W.R. Pattangall (D) | 18,085 | 42.9 |
| | E. M. Thompson (PROG) | 3,697 | 8.8 |
| 4 | Frank E. Guernsey (R) | 12,707 | 45.0 |
| | C. W. Mullen (D) | 10,021 | 35.5 |
| | Del Merrill (PROG) | 5,371 | 19.0 |

## MARYLAND

| | Candidates | Votes | % |
|---|---|---|---|
| 1 | Jesse D. Price (D) | 17,543 | 49.0 |
| | Robert F. Duer (R) | 17,146 | 47.9 |
| 2 | Joshua Frederick C. Talbott (D) | 23,124 | 53.5 |
| | William J. Heaps (R) | 17,956 | 41.5 |
| 3 | Charles P. Coady (D) | 16,279 | 52.9 |
| | John A. Janetzke (R) | 12,901 | 41.9 |
| 4 | J. Charles Linthicum (D) | 19,791 | 58.2 |
| | Thomas T. Hammond (R) | 12,595 | 37.0 |
| 5 | Sydney E. Mudd (R) | 16,236 | 48.6 |
| | Richard A. Johnson (D) | 15,179 | 45.5 |
| 6 | David J. Lewis (D) | 19,494 | 49.1 |
| | Frederick N. Zihlman (R) | 18,752 | 47.2 |

### Special Election

| | | Votes | % |
|---|---|---|---|
| 1 | Jesse D. Price (D) | 17,858 | 74.7 |
| | Thomas S. Hodson (PROG) | 6,053 | 25.3 |

## MASSACHUSETTS

| | Candidates | Votes | % |
|---|---|---|---|
| 1 | Allen T. Treadway (R) | 15,556 | 55.0 |
| | Morton H. Burdick (D) | 10,695 | 37.8 |
| 2 | Frederick H. Gillett (R) | 15,635 | 56.3 |
| | Edward M. Lewis (D & PROG) | 11,252 | 40.5 |
| 3 | Calvin D. Paige (R) | 15,838 | 56.0 |
| | Owen A. Hoban (D) | 10,539 | 37.2 |
| | Jonas Bemis (PROG) | 1,925 | 6.8 |
| 4 | Samuel E. Winslow (R) | 16,972 | 57.8 |
| | Hugh O'Rourke (D) | 12,373 | 42.2 |
| 5 | John Jacob Rogers (R) | 17,249 | 62.1 |
| | J. Joseph O'Connor (D) | 9,136 | 32.9 |
| | William N. Osgood (PROG) | 1,404 | 5.1 |
| 6 | Augustus P. Gardner (R) | 19,960 | 69.2 |
| | George A. Schofield (D) | 7,692 | 26.7 |
| 7 | Michael F. Phelan (D) | 13,962 | 50.4 |
| | Charles Cabot Johnson (R) | 11,530 | 41.6 |
| 8 | Frederick W. Dallinger (R & PROG) | 15,227 | 49.7 |
| | Frederick S. Deitrick (D) | 14,359 | 46.9 |

## MASSACHUSETTS

| Candidates | Votes | % |
|---|---|---|
| 9 Ernest W. Roberts (R) | 16,087 | 54.8 |
| Peter W. Collins (D) | 9,773 | 33.3 |
| H. Huestis Newton (PROG) | 3,482 | 11.9 |
| 10 Peter F. Tague (D) | 12,409 | 73.7 |
| James A. Cochran (R) | 3,018 | 17.9 |
| Daniel T. Callahan (PROG) | 1,407 | 8.4 |
| 11 George Holden Tinkham (R) | 13,510 | 49.8 |
| Francis J. Horgan (D) | 11,863 | 43.7 |
| Henry Clay Peters (PROG) | 1,765 | 6.5 |
| 12 James A. Gallivan (D) | 18,315 | 66.2 |
| Charles H. S. Robinson (R) | 7,673 | 27.7 |
| Chester R. Lawrence (PROG) | 1,678 | 6.1 |
| 13 William H. Carter (R) | 17,988 | 50.5 |
| John J. Mitchell (D) | 15,935 | 44.7 |
| 14 Richard Olney (D) | 13,246 | 36.5 |
| Harry C. Howard (R) | 12,556 | 34.6 |
| Henry L. Kincaide (PROG) | 9,147 | 25.2 |
| 15 William S. Greene (R) | 12,729 | 57.9 |
| James F. Morris (D) | 7,495 | 34.1 |
| Alvin G. Weeks (PROG) | 1,746 | 8.0 |
| 16 Joseph Walsh (R) | 11,322 | 46.9 |
| Thomas C. Thacher (D) | 10,153 | 42.0 |
| Thomas Thompson (PROG) | 2,669 | 11.1 |

## MICHIGAN

| Candidates | Votes | % |
|---|---|---|
| 1 Frank E. Doremus (D) | 19,197 | 62.5 |
| Charles E. McCarty (R) | 9,483 | 30.9 |
| 2 Samuel W. Beakes (D) | 18,085 | 45.2 |
| Mark R. Bacon (R) | 17,876 | 44.7 |
| Hubert F. Probert (N PROG) | 3,345 | 8.4 |
| 3 John M. C. Smith (R) | 15,644 | 45.6 |
| Orville J. Cornell (D) | 13,245 | 38.6 |
| Edward N. Dingley (N PROG) | 3,846 | 11.2 |
| 4 Edward L. Hamilton (R) | 18,577 | 53.2 |
| Albert E. Beebe (D) | 13,452 | 38.5 |
| J. Mark Harvey (N PROG) | 1,826 | 5.2 |
| 5 Carl E. Mapes (R) | 17,223 | 58.7 |
| Thaddeus B. Taylor (D) | 9,031 | 30.8 |
| Alvin E. Ewing (N PROG) | 1,823 | 6.2 |
| 6 Patrick H. Kelley (R) | 19,154 | 49.3 |
| Frank L. Dodge (D) | 15,013 | 38.7 |
| William S. Kellogg (N PROG) | 3,696 | 9.5 |
| 7 Louis C. Cramton (R) | 20,294 | 60.0 |
| John F. Murphy (D) | 9,488 | 28.0 |
| Jefferson G. Brown (N PROG) | 3,342 | 9.9 |
| 8 Joseph W. Fordney (R) | 20,249 | 52.7 |
| Laurence W. Smith (D) | 15,729 | 40.9 |
| 9 James C. McLaughlin (R) | 16,148 | 55.3 |
| Amos O. White (D) | 6,602 | 22.6 |
| William H. Sears (N PROG) | 4,913 | 16.8 |
| 10 George A. Loud (R) | 13,854 | 44.5 |
| Roy O. Woodruff (N PROG) | 8,167 | 26.8 |
| Charles W. Hitchcock (D) | 7,564 | 24.8 |
| 11 Frank D. Scott (R) | 18,290 | 55.5 |
| Francis T. McDonald (D) | 9,977 | 30.3 |
| Herbert F. Baker (N PROG) | 3,246 | 9.9 |
| 12 W. Frank James (R) | 14,562 | 49.3 |
| William J. Macdonald (N PROG) | 9,205 | 31.1 |
| Frederic J. Bawden (D) | 4,962 | 16.8 |
| 13 Charles A. Nichols (R) | 17,091 | 62.6 |
| Antonio Entenza (D) | 7,417 | 27.2 |
| Ralph Hall Ferris (N PROG) | 2,001 | 7.3 |

## MINNESOTA

| Candidates | Votes | % |
|---|---|---|
| 1 Sydney Anderson (R) | 23,939 | 65.6 |
| Witherstine (D) | 12,540 | 34.4 |
| 2 Franklin F. Ellsworth (R) | 18,888 | 55.3 |
| Flittie (D) | 10,760 | 31.5 |
| Dehual (PROG) | 3,206 | 9.4 |
| 3 Charles R. Davis (R) | 21,151 | 57.4 |
| Avery (D) | 13,791 | 37.4 |
| Mackintosh (PROG) | 1,899 | 5.2 |
| 4 Carl C. Van Dyke (D) | 16,988 | 55.2 |
| Stevens (R) | 11,058 | 35.9 |
| Mahoney (SOC) | 2,221 | 7.2 |
| 5 George R. Smith (R) | 12,576 | 40.7 |
| Van Lear (SOC) | 10,312 | 33.3 |
| Long (D) | 4,423 | 14.3 |
| Powers (PROG) | 3,618 | 11.7 |
| 6 Charles A. Lindbergh (R) | 15,364 | 47.5 |
| Dubois (D) | 11,409 | 35.2 |
| Thomason (SOC) | 3,769 | 11.6 |
| Sharkey (PROG) | 1,836 | 5.7 |
| 7 Andrew J. Volstead (R) | 28,815 | 100.0 |
| 8 Clarence B. Miller (R) | 14,135 | 50.4 |
| Nelson (D) | 8,872 | 31.6 |
| Towne (SOC) | 4,179 | 14.9 |
| 9 Halvor Steenerson (R) | 24,173 | 76.4 |
| Brattland (PUB OWN) | 7,489 | 23.7 |
| 10 Thomas D. Schall (PROG) | 12,786 | 39.1 |
| Jepson (R) | 11,383 | 34.8 |
| Swenson (D) | 8,522 | 26.1 |

## MISSISSIPPI

| Candidates | Votes | % |
|---|---|---|
| 1 Ezekiel S. Candler Jr. (D) | 5,251 | 100.0 |
| 2 Hubert D. Stephens (D) | 5,159 | 100.0 |
| 3 Benjamin G. Humphreys (D) | 2,125 | 98.0 |
| 4 Thomas U. Sisson (D) | 4,684 | 95.6 |
| 5 Samuel A. Witherspoon (D) | 6,451 | 92.8 |
| C. W. Smith (SOC) | 500 | 7.2 |
| 6 Pat Harrison (D) | 6,225 | 95.5 |
| 7 Percy E. Quin (D) | 3,702 | 100.0 |
| 8 James W. Collier (D) | 2,233 | 96.9 |

## MISSOURI

| Candidates | Votes | % |
|---|---|---|
| 1 James T. Lloyd (D) | 18,712 | 56.2 |
| Brown (R) | 12,783 | 38.4 |
| 2 William W. Rucker (D) | 22,243 | 98.7 |
| 3 Joshua W. Alexander (D) | 18,072 | 55.6 |
| Morroway (R) | 11,933 | 36.7 |
| Courtney (PROG) | 2,045 | 6.3 |
| 4 Charles F. Booher (D) | 17,293 | 53.5 |
| Otis (R) | 13,907 | 43.1 |
| 5 William P. Borland (D) | 36,966 | 70.5 |
| Brown (PROG) | 9,309 | 17.8 |
| Orr (R) | 5,387 | 10.3 |
| 6 Clement C. Dickinson (D) | 15,402 | 56.4 |
| Young (R) | 9,474 | 34.7 |
| Theilmann (PROG) | 1,989 | 7.3 |
| 7 Courtney W. Hamlin (D) | 21,953 | 52.0 |
| Lovan (R) | 18,025 | 42.7 |
| 8 Dorsey W. Shackleford (D) | 15,546 | 52.2 |
| Gentry (R) | 13,918 | 46.8 |
| 9 James Beauchamp Clark (D) | 20,058 | 55.8 |
| Brown (R) | 14,733 | 41.0 |
| 10 Jacob E. Meeker (R) | 44,912 | 54.2 |
| Curlee (D) | 30,153 | 36.4 |
| Brandt (SOC) | 5,162 | 6.2 |
| 11 William L. Igoe (D) | 17,163 | 51.1 |
| Hamilton (R) | 15,152 | 45.1 |
| 12 Leonidas C. Dyer (R) | 12,047 | 53.2 |
| Collins (D) | 9,768 | 43.1 |
| 13 Walter L. Hensley (D) | 15,796 | 50.2 |
| Reppy (R) | 14,832 | 47.1 |
| 14 Joseph J. Russell (D) | 23,295 | 47.0 |
| Brown (R) | 22,266 | 44.9 |
| Knecht (SOC) | 3,150 | 6.4 |
| 15 Perl D. Decker (D) | 19,827 | 48.1 |
| Manlove (R) | 18,471 | 44.8 |
| 16 Thomas L. Rubey (D) | 16,340 | 53.0 |
| Diffenderffer (R) | 13,057 | 42.4 |

## MONTANA

| Candidates | Votes | % |
|---|---|---|
| AL John M. Evans (D) | 37,011 ✔ | |
| Thomas Stout (D) | 35,156 ✔ | |

| Candidates | Votes | % |
|---|---|---|
| Wash J. McCormick (R) | 26,161 | |
| Fletcher Maddox (R) | 26,046 | |
| Lewis J. Duncan (SOC) | 12,282 | |
| W. E. Kent (SOC) | 9,424 | |
| Wellington D. Rankin (PROG) | 6,654 | |
| James M. Brinson (PROG) | 6,166 | |

## NEBRASKA

| Candidates | Votes | % |
|---|---|---|
| 1 C. F. Reavis (R) | 15,462 | 48.1 |
| John A. Maguire (D & PPI) | 15,138 | 47.1 |
| 2 Charles O. Lobeck (D) | 16,773 | 58.1 |
| Thomas W. Blackburn (R) | 8,979 | 31.1 |
| Nathan Merriam (PROG) | 1,616 | 5.6 |
| 3 Daniel V. Stephens (D & PPI) | 26,488 | 57.7 |
| O. S. Spillman (R & PROG) | 18,007 | 39.2 |
| 4 Charles H. Sloan (R & PROG) | 22,948 | 54.8 |
| Walter H. Rhodes (D & PPI) | 18,177 | 43.4 |
| 5 Ashton C. Shallenberger (D & PPI) | 16,387 | 48.7 |
| Silas R. Barton (R & PROG) | 16,217 | 48.2 |
| 6 Moses P. Kinkaid (R & PROG) | 29,226 | 57.1 |
| Frank J. Taylor (D & PPI) | 19,346 | 37.8 |

## NEVADA

| Candidates | Votes | % |
|---|---|---|
| AL Edwin E. Roberts (R) | 8,915 | 42.0 |
| Leonard B. Fowler (D) | 8,031 | 37.8 |
| Martin J. Scanlan (SOC) | 4,294 | 20.2 |

## NEW HAMPSHIRE

| Candidates | Votes | % |
|---|---|---|
| 1 Cyrus A. Sulloway (R) | 20,657 | 50.0 |
| Eugene E. Reed (D) | 19,140 | 46.3 |
| 2 Edward H. Wason (R) | 21,793 | 54.8 |
| Charles J. French (D) | 16,101 | 40.5 |

## NEW JERSEY

| Candidates | Votes | % |
|---|---|---|
| 1 William J. Browning (R) | 24,142 | 58.5 |
| Nowrey (D) | 13,271 | 32.1 |
| 2 Isaac Bacharach (R) | 21,448 | 54.3 |
| Baker (D) | 14,352 | 36.3 |
| Bright (RO PROG) | 2,276 | 5.8 |
| 3 Thomas J. Scully (D) | 21,338 | 50.7 |
| Havens (R) | 19,303 | 45.8 |
| 4 Elijah C. Hutchinson (R) | 17,078 | 50.9 |
| Walsh (D) | 13,766 | 41.0 |
| Thorn (RO PROG) | 1,711 | 5.1 |
| 5 John H. Capstick (R) | 16,951 | 45.7 |
| William E. Tuttle Jr. (D) | 15,718 | 42.4 |
| May (RO PROG) | 2,218 | 6.0 |
| Seeholzor (SOC) | 1,854 | 5.0 |
| 6 Archibald C. Hart (D) | 16,286 | 45.4 |
| Prince (R) | 15,880 | 44.3 |
| 7 Dow H. Drukker (R) | 12,664 | 54.7 |
| Cabell (D) | 6,944 | 30.0 |
| Demarest (SOC) | 3,370 | 14.6 |
| 8 Edward W. Gray (R) | 13,438 | 44.9 |
| McDonald (D) | 11,678 | 39.1 |
| Archibald (PROG R) | 2,232 | 7.5 |
| 9 Richard W. Parker (R) | 9,482 | 37.3 |
| Gregory (D) | 8,069 | 31.7 |
| Seymour (D) | 5,672 | 22.3 |
| Bohn (SOC) | 1,342 | 5.3 |
| 10 Frederick R. Lehlbach (R) | 13,765 | 47.5 |
| Edward W. Townsend (D) | 12,278 | 42.4 |
| 11 John J. Eagan (D) | 17,551 | 64.9 |
| Straus (R) | 8,400 | 31.1 |
| 12 James A. Hamill (D) | 16,260 | 62.6 |
| Higginbotham Jr. (R) | 7,379 | 28.4 |
| Anderson (PROG R) | 1,313 | 5.1 |

## NEW JERSEY

### Special Elections

| Candidates | Votes | % |
|---|---|---|
| 7 Dow H. Drukker (R) | 10,613 | 49.0 |
| O'Byrne (D) | 5,240 | 24.2 |
| Demarest (SOC) | 5,064 | 23.4 |
| 9 Richard W. Parker (R) | 4,675 | 50.1 |
| Seymour (D) | 4,178 | 44.8 |
| Bohn (SOC) | 475 | 5.1 |

## NEW MEXICO

| | Candidates | Votes | % |
|---|---|---|---|
| AL | Benigno C. Hernandez (R) | 23,812 | 51.3 |
| | H. B. Fergusson (D) | 19,805 | 42.7 |

## NEW YORK

| | Candidates | Votes | % |
|---|---|---|---|
| 1 | Frederick C. Hicks (R) | 17,726 | 47.6 |
| | Lathrop Brown (D) | 17,722 | 47.5 |
| 2 | Charles Pope Caldwell (D) | 21,330 | 54.5 |
| | Frank E. Hopkins (R) | 10,552 | 27.0 |
| | Lawrence T. Gresser (I) | 3,672 | 9.4 |
| | Benjamin Katz (SOC) | 2,352 | 6.0 |
| 3 | Joseph V. Flynn (D) | 11,298 | 50.1 |
| | George B. Serenbetz (R) | 8,368 | 37.1 |
| | Joseph E. Kleinn (SOC) | 1,559 | 6.9 |
| 4 | Harry Howard Dale (D) | 7,860 | 47.0 |
| | John Kissel (R & IL) | 5,496 | 32.9 |
| | J. Chante Lipes (SOC) | 1,870 | 11.2 |
| | Max Schaffer (PROG) | 1,404 | 8.4 |
| 5 | James P. Maher (D) | 11,754 | 49.5 |
| | Alfred T. Hobley (R) | 8,327 | 35.1 |
| | John S. Gaynor (PROG&IL) | 2,512 | 10.6 |
| 6 | Frederick W. Rowe (R & IL) | 22,262 | 53.8 |
| | Leroy W. Ross (D) | 16,180 | 39.1 |
| 7 | John J. Fitzgerald (D & IL) | 15,065 | 65.9 |
| | C. G. Finney Wilcox (R) | 6,659 | 29.1 |
| 8 | Daniel J. Griffin (D & IL) | 20,213 | 62.0 |
| | Thomas E. Clark (R) | 9,935 | 30.5 |
| 9 | Oscar W. Swift (R & IL) | 18,547 | 48.7 |
| | James H. O'Brien (D) | 15,224 | 40.0 |
| | Anna C. Wright (SOC) | 2,371 | 6.2 |
| 10 | Reuben L. Haskell (R PR IL) | 8,213 | 40.5 |
| | Phillip A. Riley (D) | 6,240 | 30.8 |
| | Alex S. Drescher (A-BOSS) | 2,884 | 14.2 |
| | Harry D. Smith (SOC) | 2,732 | 13.5 |
| 11 | Daniel J. Riordan (D) | 13,200 | 59.0 |
| | George S. Schofield (R) | 7,680 | 34.3 |
| 12 | Meyer London (SOC) | 5,969 | 49.5 |
| | Henry M. Goldfogle (D AM IL) | 4,947 | 41.1 |
| | Benjamin Borowsky (R & PROG) | 1,133 | 9.4 |
| 13 | George W. Loft (D AM IL) | 5,934 | 58.2 |
| | James E. March (R & PROG) | 3,081 | 30.2 |
| | Bouck White (SOC) | 1,177 | 11.6 |
| 14 | Michael F. Farley (D & IL) | 7,310 | 46.5 |
| | Fiorello H. LaGuardia (R) | 5,331 | 33.9 |
| | Henry L. Slobodin (SOC) | 1,534 | 9.8 |
| | John B. Golden (PROG) | 1,456 | 9.3 |
| 15 | Michael F. Conry (D & IL) | 13,846 | 65.1 |
| | Oscar W. Ehrhorn (R & PROG) | 6,698 | 31.5 |
| 16 | Peter J. Dooling (D & IL) | 12,874 | 62.5 |
| | Harry B. Stowell (R) | 6,012 | 29.2 |
| | William J. Moran (PROG) | 1,156 | 5.6 |
| 17 | John F. Carew (D) | 10,243 | 53.7 |
| | Lindon Bates Jr. (R PR IL) | 7,851 | 41.2 |
| 18 | Thomas G. Patten (D & IL) | 12,434 | 53.2 |
| | George B. Francis (R & PROG) | 8,804 | 37.7 |
| | Ernest Ramn (SOC) | 2,047 | 8.8 |
| 19 | Walter M. Chandler (PROG&IL) | 10,682 | 34.1 |
| | Joseph L. Buttenweiser (D) | 10,150 | 32.4 |

| | Candidates | Votes | % |
|---|---|---|---|
| | Albert Ottinger (R) | 9,588 | 30.6 |
| 20 | Isaac Siegel (R PR IL) | 4,923 | 44.1 |
| | Jacob A. Cantor (D) | 4,843 | 43.3 |
| | Ludwig Schmidt (SOC) | 1,356 | 12.1 |
| 21 | Murray Hulbert (D & IL) | 11,575 | 51.2 |
| | Martin Ansorge (R AM&PR) | 9,826 | 43.5 |
| 22 | Henry Buckner (D) | 17,886 | 62.4 |
| | Francis J. Kuerzi (R IL PR) | 8,900 | 31.0 |
| | Maxie McDonald (SOC) | 1,770 | 6.2 |
| 23 | Joseph A. Goulden (D) | 18,822 | 44.1 |
| | Robert L. Niles (R & IL) | 12,060 | 28.3 |
| | Steven B. Ayres (PROG&BUS) | 8,228 | 19.3 |
| | M. Rubinow (SOC) | 3,378 | 7.9 |
| 24 | Woodson R. Oglesby (D) | 17,605 | 43.8 |
| | William Foster (R) | 16,554 | 41.2 |
| | Alfred E. Smith (PROG) | 3,143 | 7.8 |
| | Allen L. Benson (SOC) | 2,238 | 5.6 |
| 25 | James W. Husted (R) | 17,888 | 51.7 |
| | Benjamin Irving Taylor (D) | 14,369 | 41.5 |
| 26 | Edmund Platt (R) | 21,634 | 58.0 |
| | Alonzo F. Albott (D) | 14,412 | 38.6 |
| 27 | Charles B. Ward (R) | 22,505 | 53.0 |
| | George McClellan (D) | 18,074 | 42.6 |
| 28 | Rollin B. Sanford (R) | 27,158 | 51.9 |
| | Peter G. Ten Eyck (D PR&IL) | 24,405 | 46.6 |
| 29 | James S. Parker (R) | 29,454 | 63.7 |
| | James Farrell (D & PROG) | 15,171 | 32.8 |
| 30 | William B. Charles (R) | 16,521 | 42.4 |
| | William C. D. Willson (D) | 9,950 | 25.5 |
| | Philip H. Callery (SOC) | 5,705 | 14.6 |
| | Theron Akin (PROG) | 5,105 | 13.1 |
| 31 | Edwin A. Merritt Jr. (R) | 17,720* | 54.6 |
| | Andrew B. Cooney (D) | 7,850 | 24.2 |
| | Howard D. Hadley (PROG) | 5,351 | 16.5 |
| 32 | Luther W. Mott (R & PROG) | 24,684 | 63.6 |
| | John Fitzgibbons (D) | 11,544 | 29.7 |
| 33 | Homer P. Snyder (R) | 21,144 | 52.6 |
| | Charles A. Talcott (D) | 15,035 | 37.4 |
| | George H. Spitzli (PROG) | 2,582 | 6.4 |
| 34 | George W. Fairchild (R) | 22,786 | 56.2 |
| | George J. West (D) | 12,564 | 31.0 |
| | Albert S. Barnes (PROG, P) | 4,610 | 11.4 |
| 35 | Walter W. Magee (R) | 23,075 | 52.8 |
| | John R. Clancy (D) | 15,131 | 34.6 |
| | Hugh M. Tilroe (PROG) | 3,211 | 7.3 |
| 36 | Sereno E. Payne (R) | 22,523* | 58.9 |
| | Herman L. Kelly (D) | 10,970 | 28.7 |
| | Amasa J. Parker (PROG) | 2,278 | 6.0 |
| | Wallace E. Brown (P) | 1,995 | 5.2 |
| 37 | Harry H. Pratt (R) | 16,081 | 38.9 |
| | John Seeley (D) | 14,056 | 34.0 |
| | Milo Shanks (P) | 8,438 | 20.4 |
| | Jonas S. Vanduzer (PROG) | 2,075 | 5.0 |
| 38 | Thomas B. Dunn (R) | 21,250 | 57.7 |
| | George P. Decker (D) | 8,832 | 24.0 |
| | Oscar M. Arnold (SOC) | 5,324 | 14.5 |
| 39 | Henry G. Danforth (R) | 23,694 | 63.8 |
| | M. A. Bowen (D) | 9,776 | 26.3 |
| | Daniel M. Anthony (PROG) | 2,027 | 5.5 |
| 40 | S. Wallace Dempsey (R) | 22,324 | 57.4 |
| | Robert H. Gittins (D) | 12,857 | 33.1 |
| | Frank C. Ferguson (PROG) | 2,395 | 6.2 |
| 41 | Charles B. Smith (D) | 11,915 | 38.0 |
| | Frank J. Eberle (R) | 11,324 | 36.1 |
| | Conrad J. Meyer (PROG) | 6,488 | 20.7 |
| 42 | Daniel A. Driscoll (D) | 13,081 | 46.9 |
| | Willard H. Ticknor (R) | 12,633 | 45.3 |
| 43 | Charles M. Hamilton (R) | 20,726 | 60.6 |
| | Manton M. Wyvell (D) | 7,619 | 22.3 |
| | Ernest H. Woodruff (P) | 2,159 | 6.3 |
| | Walter N. Renwick (PROG) | 2,119 | 6.2 |

## NORTH CAROLINA

| | Candidates | Votes | % |
|---|---|---|---|
| 1 | John H. Small (D) | 8,940 | 99.8 |
| 2 | Claude Kitchin (D) | 6,964 | 88.6 |

| | Candidates | Votes | % |
|---|---|---|---|
| | W. O. Dixon (D) | 879 | 11.2 |
| 3 | George E. Hood (D) | 8,620 | 57.7 |
| | Buck H. Crumpler (R) | 6,305 | 42.2 |
| 4 | Edward W. Pou (D) | 11,141 | 99.9 |
| 5 | Charles M. Stedman (D) | 18,592 | 55.9 |
| | John T. Benbow (R) | 13,990 | 42.0 |
| 6 | Hannibal L. Godwin (D) | 8,392 | 65.0 |
| | Robert W. Davis (R) | 4,521 | 35.0 |
| 7 | Robert N. Page (D) | 14,789 | 53.5 |
| | Theo E. McCrary (R) | 12,863 | 46.5 |
| 8 | Robert L. Doughton (D) | 14,976 | 53.2 |
| | Frank A. Linney (R) | 13,160 | 46.8 |
| 9 | Edwin Y. Webb (D) | 15,136 | 54.2 |
| | Jacob F. Newell (R) | 12,777 | 45.8 |
| 10 | James M. Britt (R) | 15,347 | 51.3 |
| | James M. Gudger Jr. (D) | 14,579 | 48.7 |

## NORTH DAKOTA

| | Candidates | Votes | % |
|---|---|---|---|
| 1 | Henry T. Helgesen (R) | 16,565 | 56.0 |
| | F. Bartholomew (D) | 12,217 | 41.3 |
| 2 | George M. Young (R) | 18,680 | 68.4 |
| | James J. Weeks (D) | 7,073 | 25.9 |
| | N. H. Bjornstad (SOC) | 1,553 | 5.7 |
| 3 | Patrick D. Norton (R) | 15,547 | 57.1 |
| | Halvor Halvorson (D) | 7,394 | 27.2 |
| | S. Griffith (SOC) | 3,791 | 13.9 |

## OHIO

| | Candidates | Votes | % |
|---|---|---|---|
| 1 | Nicholas Longworth (R) | 29,822 | 52.9 |
| | Stanley E. Bowdle (D) | 24,054 | 42.7 |
| 2 | Alfred G. Allen (D) | 27,811 | 48.6 |
| | Stanley Struble (R) | 26,656 | 46.6 |
| 3 | Warren Gard (D) | 29,707 | 45.9 |
| | Frank I. Brown (R) | 23,535 | 36.3 |
| | Fred Guy Strickland (SOC) | 8,859 | 13.7 |
| 4 | J. E. Russell (R) | 25,096 | 47.9 |
| | N. W. Cunningham (D) | 24,114 | 46.1 |
| 5 | Nelson E. Matthews (R) | 19,859 | 47.8 |
| | T. T. Ansberry (D) | 19,281 | 46.4 |
| | Curtis A. Baxter (PROG) | 2,409 | 5.8 |
| 6 | Charles C. Kearns (R) | 19,456 | 50.6 |
| | William A. Inman (D) | 17,766 | 46.2 |
| 7 | Simeon D. Fess (R) | 37,847 | 58.7 |
| | Charles E. Buroker (D) | 22,544 | 35.0 |
| 8 | John A. Key (D) | 22,490 | 51.0 |
| | John H. Clark (R) | 20,453 | 46.4 |
| 9 | Isaac R. Sherwood (D) | 29,399 | 53.8 |
| | William E. Cordill (R) | 16,152 | 29.5 |
| | Herbert P. Whitney (PROG) | 5,949 | 10.9 |
| | Edward Hoskins (SOC) | 3,200 | 5.9 |
| 10 | Robert M. Switzer (R) | 18,001 | 54.0 |
| | C. L. Martzolff (D) | 12,375 | 37.1 |
| | Edgar Ervin (PROG) | 2,981 | 8.9 |
| 11 | Edwin D. Ricketts (R) | 17,708 | 47.0 |
| | Horatio C. Claypool (D) | 17,598 | 46.7 |
| 12 | Clement L. Brumbaugh (D) | 25,608 | 46.9 |
| | Ralph E. Westfall (R) | 22,499 | 41.2 |
| | Frank E. Hayden (PROG) | 3,278 | 6.0 |
| | Fred P. Zimpfer (SOC) | 3,178 | 5.8 |
| 13 | Arthur W. Overmeyer (D) | 22,085 | 46.8 |
| | Charles S. Hatfield (R) | 22,011 | 46.7 |
| 14 | Seward H. Williams (R) | 21,717 | 41.6 |
| | E. R. Bathrick (D) | 20,339 | 39.0 |
| | Henry M. Hagelbarger (PROG) | 5,602 | 10.7 |
| | C. E. Sheplin (SOC) | 4,079 | 7.8 |
| 15 | William C. Mooney (R) | 21,145 | 45.5 |
| | George White (D) | 21,046 | 45.5 |
| 16 | Roscoe C. McCulloch (R) | 28,609 | 52.5 |
| | Ed J. Meyer (D) | 20,658 | 37.9 |
| | G. A. Kohr (SOC) | 3,933 | 7.2 |
| 17 | William A. Ashbrook (D) | 29,504 | 56.3 |
| | Walter A. Irvine (R) | 21,375 | 40.8 |
| 18 | David A. Hollingsworth (R) | 23,650 | 45.9 |
| | William B. Francis (D) | 22,476 | 43.7 |
| | Fred White (SOC) | 2,936 | 5.7 |
| 19 | John G. Cooper (R) | 24,471 | 52.4 |
| | William S. King (D) | 16,897 | 36.2 |

## OHIO

| Candidates | Votes | % |
|---|---|---|
| G. L. Arner (SOC) | 2,971 | 6.4 |
| W. S. Harris (PROG) | 2,363 | 5.1 |
| 20 William Gordon (D) | 23,541 | 55.7 |
| James E. Mathews (R) | 14,215 | 33.6 |
| C. E. Ruthenberg (SOC) | 2,418 | 5.7 |
| Frank G. Carpenter (PROG) | 2,127 | 5.0 |
| 21 Robert Crosser (D) | 18,962 | 61.1 |
| Harry L. Vail (R) | 9,039 | 29.1 |
| Tom Clifford (SOC) | 1,979 | 6.4 |
| 22 Henry I. Emerson (R) | 17,166 | 39.1 |
| Roy A. Tuttle (D) | 16,093 | 36.7 |
| J.R. McQuigg (PROG) | 9,023 | 20.6 |

## OKLAHOMA

| Candidates | Votes | % |
|---|---|---|
| 1 James S. Davenport (D) | 15,489 | 46.4 |
| Gill (R) | 14,251 | 42.7 |
| Lafayette (SOC) | 3,318 | 9.9 |
| 2 William W. Hastings (D) | 12,719 | 49.1 |
| Cook (R) | 8,569 | 33.1 |
| Crain (SOC) | 4,420 | 17.1 |
| 3 Charles D. Carter (D) | 17,474 | 50.3 |
| Norman (SOC) | 10,588 | 30.5 |
| Elting (R) | 6,479 | 18.7 |
| 4 William H. Murray (D) | 13,758 | 42.2 |
| Flynn (R) | 9,395 | 28.8 |
| Hughes (SOC) | 9,198 | 28.2 |
| 5 Joseph B. Thompson (D) | 14,040 | 47.6 |
| Pope (R) | 9,286 | 31.5 |
| Lurry (SOC) | 5,391 | 18.3 |
| 6 Scott Ferris (D) | 14,578 | 48.1 |
| Campbell (R) | 8,291 | 27.4 |
| J. T. Cumbie (SOC) | 6,671 | 22.0 |
| 7 James V. McClintic (D) | 11,861 | 43.3 |
| Stallard (SOC) | 9,021 | 32.9 |
| Mills (R) | 6,179 | 22.6 |
| 8 Dick T. Morgan (R) | 13,294 | 41.7 |
| Johnston (D) | 12,529 | 39.3 |
| Green (SOC) | 4,231 | 13.3 |
| Alexander (PROG) | 1,645 | 5.2 |

## OREGON

| Candidates | Votes | % |
|---|---|---|
| 1 Willis C. Hawley (R) | 51,295 | 46.4 |
| Frederick Holister (D) | 32,639 | 29.5 |
| Curtis P. Coe (P) | 16,465 | 14.9 |
| W. S. Richards (SOC) | 7,415 | 6.7 |
| 2 Nicholas J. Sinnott (R & PROG) | 24,176 | 47.5 |
| George L. Cleaver (P) | 15,685 | 30.8 |
| Sam Evans (D) | 11,013 | 21.7 |
| 3 Clifton N. McArthur (R) | 26,636 | 35.6 |
| A. F. Flegel (D) | 23,697 | 31.6 |
| A. W. Lafferty (I-PO) | 16,649 | 22.2 |
| Arthur L. Moulton (PROG-P) | 5,770 | 7.7 |

## PENNSYLVANIA

| Candidates | Votes | % |
|---|---|---|
| 1 William S. Vare (R, RO PROG) | 31,800 | 77.6 |
| Lawrence E. McCrossin (D) | 4,220 | 10.3 |
| John Burt (WASH, P) | 4,491 | 11.0 |
| 2 George S. Graham (R, KEY) | 24,371 | 77.4 |
| Patrick P. Conway (D, WASH) | 6,582 | 20.9 |
| 3 J. Hampton Moore (R, KEY) | 24,468 | 79.2 |
| John H. Fow (D) | 3,303 | 10.7 |
| Abraham L. Weinstock (WASH, RO PROG) | 2,642 | 8.6 |
| 4 George W. Edmonds (R, WASH) | 28,460 | 83.2 |
| Patrick H. Lynch (D) | 4,853 | 14.2 |
| 5 Peter E. Costello (R) | 26,352 | 60.8 |
| Michael Donohoe (D, WASH) | 15,113 | 34.9 |
| 6 George P. Darrow (R, B MOOSE) | 38,068 | 56.1 |
| Frederick S. Drake (WASH) | 13,884 | 20.4 |

| Candidates | Votes | % |
|---|---|---|
| J. Washington Logue (D, KEY) | 14,656 | 21.6 |
| 7 Thomas S. Butler (R) | 23,239 | 63.6 |
| Norris B. Slack (D) | 8,340 | 22.8 |
| Arthur H. Tomlinson (WASH) | 4,096 | 11.2 |
| 8 Henry W. Watson (R) | 22,691 | 50.9 |
| Harry E. Grim (D) | 15,706 | 35.2 |
| Harold G. Knight (WASH) | 4,941 | 11.1 |
| 9 William W. Griest (R) | 17,410 | 61.0 |
| John N. Hetrick (D, WASH) | 10,439 | 36.6 |
| 10 John R. Farr (R, WASH) | 16,474 | 54.7 |
| John J. Loftus (D, KEY) | 12,044 | 40.0 |
| 11 John J. Casey (D, B MOOSE) | 22,762 | 57.1 |
| Lewis P. Kniffen (R, WASH) | 16,011 | 40.2 |
| 12 Robert D. Heaton (R) | 17,213 | 53.7 |
| Robert E. Lee (D) | 12,416 | 38.7 |
| William W. Thorn (WASH) | 1,619 | 5.1 |
| 13 Arthur Granville Dewalt (D) | 19,887 | 45.5 |
| John K. Stauffer (R) | 14,850 | 33.9 |
| John L. Stewart (WASH) | 4,516 | 10.3 |
| L. Birch Wilson Jr. (SOC) | 4,138 | 9.5 |
| 14 Louis T. McFadden (R) | 9,153 | 40.3 |
| Fred W. Dean (D) | 6,219 | 27.4 |
| Dana R. Stephens (WASH) | 6,196 | 27.3 |
| 15 Edgar R. Kiess (R) | 11,525 | 41.8 |
| John J. Reardon (D) | 8,118 | 29.5 |
| Montfort T. Stokes (WASH, P) | 6,447 | 23.4 |
| Peter J. Homler (SOC) | 1,472 | 5.3 |
| 16 John V. Lesher (D) | 12,982 | 44.3 |
| Charles H. Robbins (R) | 9,129 | 31.2 |
| W. W. Heffner (WASH) | 4,719 | 16.1 |
| 17 Benjamin K. Focht (R) | 14,176 | 41.4 |
| Frank L. Dershem (D) | 12,597 | 36.8 |
| Charles L. Johnson (WASH) | 5,894 | 17.2 |
| 18 Aaron S. Kreider (R) | 23,789 | 52.3 |
| David L. Kaufman (D) | 13,159 | 28.9 |
| John H. Kreider (WASH) | 6,378 | 14.0 |
| 19 Warren Worth Bailey (D, UN) | 14,993 | 35.8 |
| Jesse L. Hartman (R) | 14,503 | 34.6 |
| Lynn A. Brua (WASH, P) | 10,246 | 24.5 |
| 20 C. William Beales (R) | 14,225 | 45.3 |
| Andrew R. Brodbeck (D) | 13,483 | 43.0 |
| Robert C. Bair (WASH) | 2,419 | 7.7 |
| 21 Charles H. Rowland (R) | 10,403 | 39.3 |
| William E. Tobias (D) | 9,339 | 35.3 |
| Guy B. Mayo (WASH) | 4,574 | 17.3 |
| 22 Abraham L. Keister (R, PERS LIB) | 15,214 | 43.7 |
| James B. Hammond (D, WASH) | 14,802 | 42.5 |
| Joseph B. Slack (SOC) | 2,867 | 8.2 |
| A. P. Hutchison (P) | 1,961 | 5.6 |
| 23 Robert F. Hopwood (R) | 14,308 | 44.7 |
| Wooda N. Carr (D) | 11,801 | 36.9 |
| Charles F. Hood (WASH) | 3,565 | 11.1 |
| 24 William M. Brown (R) | 14,694* | 41.0 |
| Henry W. Temple (WASH) | 10,771 | 30.1 |
| Samuel A. Barnum (D) | 7,051 | 19.7 |
| H. R. Norman (SOC) | 2,370 | 6.6 |
| 25 Michael Liebel Jr. (D) | 10,025 | 36.6 |
| Milton W. Shreve (R) | 9,222 | 33.6 |
| Frank C. Lockwood (WASH, P) | 6,449 | 23.5 |
| F. J. Weaver (SOC) | 1,735 | 6.3 |
| 26 Henry J. Steele (D, PERS LIB) | 15,118 | 51.3 |
| John D. Hoffman (R) | 8,306 | 28.2 |
| Edward Hart (WASH) | 4,671 | 15.8 |
| 27 S. Taylor North (R) | 10,560 | 36.5 |
| R. M. Matson (D) | 8,822 | 30.5 |
| Charles P. Wolfe (WASH) | 6,744 | 23.3 |
| Samuel Dible (P) | 1,673 | 5.8 |
| 28 S. H. Miller (R) | 9,379 | 30.8 |
| William McIntyre (D) | 8,043 | 26.4 |
| Willis J. Hulings (WASH) | 6,825 | 22.4 |

| Candidates | Votes | % |
|---|---|---|
| William P. F. Ferguson (P) | 4,420 | 14.5 |
| William McKay (SOC) | 1,806 | 5.9 |
| 29 Stephen Geyer Porter (R, WASH) | 20,543 | 76.1 |
| John M. Henry (D) | 3,972 | 14.7 |
| Henry Peter (SOC) | 1,879 | 7.0 |
| 30 William H. Coleman (R, PERS LIB) | 16,620 | 48.6 |
| M. Clyde Kelly (WASH, D) | 15,268 | 44.9 |
| Andrew Hunter (SOC) | 2,232 | 6.5 |
| 31 John M. Morin (R, D) | 17,659 | 78.2 |
| William A. Prosser (SOC, P) | 4,333 | 19.2 |
| 32 Andrew J. Barchfeld (R, PERS LIB) | 15,109 | 47.0 |
| W. McClintock (WASH, RO PROG) | 7,938 | 24.7 |
| Guy E. Campbell (D) | 6,626 | 20.6 |
| John W. Slayton (SOC) | 2,464 | 7.7 |
| AL Thomas S. Crago (R, PERS LIB) | 514,270✔ | |
| John R. K. Scott (R, PERS LIB) | 513,676✔ | |
| Mahlon M. Garland (R, PERS LIB) | 507,626✔ | |
| Daniel F. Lafean (R, PERS LIB) | 501,804✔ | |
| Robert S. Bright (D) | 281,154 | |
| Arthur B. Clark (D) | 272,829 | |
| Martin Jennings Caton (D) | 265,474 | |
| Charles N. Crosby (D) | 263,280 | |
| Lex N. Mitchell (WASH, B MOOSE) | 193,106 | |
| Arthur R. Rupley (WASH, B MOOSE) | 185,553 | |
| Anderson H. Walters (WASH, B MOOSE) | 185,028 | |
| Harry Watson (WASH, B MOOSE) | 180,744 | |
| Edward W. Hayden (SOC) | 43,932 | |
| W. S. Greely King (SOC) | 43,188 | |
| Dennis O'Brien Coughlin (SOC) | 43,148 | |
| Charles Sehl (SOC) | 42,048 | |
| George Hart (P) | 27,561 | |
| James J. Patton (P) | 27,038 | |
| S. Harper Smith (P) | 26,075 | |
| B. R. Pike (P) | 24,709 | |
| Joseph B. Holtz (KEY) | 1,462 | |
| Howard S. Welker (KEY) | 1,387 | |
| Albert W. Binz (KEY) | 1,343 | |
| A. M. Fisher (INDL) | 1,124 | |
| John Lipsett (KEY) | 1,080 | |
| James Erwin (INDL) | 759 | |
| H. G. Meinel (INDL) | 558 | |

## RHODE ISLAND

| Candidates | Votes | % |
|---|---|---|
| 1 George F. O'Shaunessy (D) | 12,983 | 49.8 |
| Burchard (R) | 12,080 | 46.3 |
| 2 Walter R. Stiness (R) | 13,072 | 49.0 |
| Gerry (D) | 12,097 | 45.4 |
| 3 Ambrose Kennedy (R) | 13,849 | 55.3 |
| Haven (D) | 10,110 | 40.4 |

## SOUTH CAROLINA

| Candidates | Votes | % |
|---|---|---|
| 1 Richard S. Whaley (D) | 3,018 | 98.5 |
| 2 James F. Byrnes (D) | 4,688 | 100.0 |
| 3 Wyatt Aiken (D) | 4,521 | 100.0 |
| 4 Joseph T. Johnson (D) | 6,175 | 99.5 |
| 5 David E. Finley (D) | 5,180 | 100.0 |
| 6 J. Willard Ragsdale (D) | 4,263 | 100.0 |
| 7 Asbury F. Lever (D) | 5,231 | 95.2 |

## SOUTH DAKOTA

| Candidates | Votes | % |
|---|---|---|
| 1 Charles H. Dillon (R) | 22,058 | 57.9 |
| Theodore Bailey (D) | 13,678 | 35.9 |

## SOUTH DAKOTA

| | Candidates | Votes | % |
|---|---|---|---|
| 2 | Royal C. Johnson (R) | 20,054 | 57.9 |
| | John M. King (D) | 11,810 | 34.1 |
| 3 | Harry L. Gandy (D) | 12,454 | 51.8 |
| | William G. Rice (R) | 10,732 | 44.6 |

## TENNESSEE

| | Candidates | Votes | % |
|---|---|---|---|
| 1 | Sam R. Sells (R) | 15,959 | 61.3 |
| | James B. Cox (PROG) | 7,753 | 29.8 |
| | Cy H. Lyle (D) | 2,337 | 9.0 |
| 2 | Richard W. Austin (R) | 14,870 | 67.0 |
| | H. H. Hannah (D) | 6,949 | 31.3 |
| 3 | John A. Moon (D) | 19,407 | 90.2 |
| | G. W. James (R) | 2,111 | 9.8 |
| 4 | Cordell Hull (D) | 19,152 | 98.2 |
| 5 | William C. Houston (D) | 14,694 | 71.7 |
| | H. C. Watts (ID) | 5,810 | 28.3 |
| 6 | Joseph W. Byrns (D) | 19,319 | 94.4 |
| 7 | Lemuel P. Padgett (D) | 18,227 | 97.3 |
| 8 | Thetus W. Sims (D) | 14,421 | 54.4 |
| | J. E. Deford (R) | 11,930 | 45.0 |
| 9 | Finis J. Garrett (D) | 15,582 | 83.2 |
| | R. C. Cochran (R) | 3,062 | 16.4 |
| 10 | Kenneth D. McKellar (D) | 19,160 | 93.0 |
| | J. O. Davison (SOC) | 1,447 | 7.0 |

## TEXAS

| | Candidates | Votes | % |
|---|---|---|---|
| 1 | Eugene Black (D) | 10,711 | 87.7 |
| | J. C. Thompson (SOC) | 1,498 | 12.3 |
| 2 | Martin Dies (D) | 11,425 | 84.0 |
| | A. Lingan (SOC) | 2,132 | 15.7 |
| 3 | James Young (D) | 11,584 | 75.2 |
| | E. T. Bryant (SOC) | 3,818 | 24.8 |
| 4 | Sam Rayburn (D) | 9,762 | 85.0 |
| | C. E. Obenchain (SOC) | 1,449 | 12.6 |
| 5 | Hatton W. Sumners (D) | 10,430 | 94.9 |
| 6 | Rufus Hardy (D) | 7,772 | 86.4 |
| | W. H. Wilson (R) | 1,229 | 13.7 |
| 7 | Alexander W. Gregg (D) | 7,001 | 100.0 |
| 8 | Joe H. Eagle (D) | 10,078 | 84.7 |
| | E. B. Miller (SOC) | 1,090 | 9.2 |
| | S. L. Hain (R) | 725 | 6.1 |
| 9 | George F. Burgess (D) | 11,083 | 88.5 |
| | B. F. Wright (SOC) | 1,169 | 9.3 |
| 10 | James P. Buchanan (D) | 8,351 | 100.0 |
| 11 | Robert L. Henry (D) | 6,677 | 92.9 |
| | Duncan Carrick (R) | 484 | 6.7 |
| 12 | Oscar Calloway (D) | 11,997 | 85.4 |
| | S. J. Browson (R) | 2,043 | 14.5 |
| 13 | John H. Stephens (D) | 15,680 | 87.0 |
| | C. T. Griffin (R) | 2,335 | 13.0 |
| 14 | James L. Slayden (D) | 13,896 | 90.7 |
| | John A. Currie (SOC) | 921 | 6.0 |
| 15 | John N. Garner (D) | 15,678 | 100.0 |
| 16 | William R. Smith (D) | 15,181 | 99.9 |
| AL | James H. Davis (D) | 173,803✓ | |
| | Atkins Jeff. McLemore (D) | 173,177✓ | |
| | Nat B. Hunt (SOC) | 24,557 | |
| | Reddin Andrews (SOC) | 24,276 | |

| Candidates | Votes | % |
|---|---|---|
| Charles A. Warnken (R) | 10,538 | |
| E. E. Diggs (R) | 10,489 | |
| J. E. Williams (PROG) | 1,542 | |
| H. L. McCuiston (PROG) | 1,541 | |

## UTAH

| | Candidates | Votes | % |
|---|---|---|---|
| 1 | Joseph Howell (R) | 29,481 | 49.4 |
| | Larson (D & PROG) | 27,440 | 45.9 |
| 2 | James H. Mays (D & PROG) | 25,617 | 47.5 |
| | Leatherwood (R) | 25,459 | 47.2 |
| | Kempton (SOC) | 2,861 | 5.3 |

## VERMONT

| | Candidates | Votes | % |
|---|---|---|---|
| 1 | Frank L. Greene (R) | 19,237 | 62.9 |
| | Daniel E. O'Sullivan (D) | 6,817 | 22.3 |
| | Raymond McFarland (PROG, P) | 4,064 | 13.3 |
| 2 | Porter H. Dale (R, P) | 17,743 | 57.5 |
| | John Reardon (D) | 6,868 | 22.2 |
| | Fraser Metzger (PROG) | 5,481 | 17.8 |

## VIRGINIA

| | Candidates | Votes | % |
|---|---|---|---|
| 1 | William A. Jones (D) | 4,742 | 94.3 |
| 2 | Edward E. Holland (D) | 4,039 | 87.9 |
| | E. B. Everton (SOC) | 406 | 8.8 |
| 3 | Andrew J. Montague (D) | 5,054 | 95.8 |
| 4 | Walter A. Watson (D) | 2,887 | 96.2 |
| 5 | Edward W. Saunders (D) | 6,534 | 65.5 |
| | Charles A. Hermans (R) | 2,771 | 27.8 |
| 6 | Carter Glass (D) | 3,823 | 90.7 |
| | B. F. Ginther (SOC) | 391 | 9.3 |
| 7 | James Hay (D) | 4,569 | 87.0 |
| | E. C. Garrison (R) | 685 | 13.0 |
| 8 | Charles C. Carlin (D) | 5,864 | 75.4 |
| | Joseph L. Crupper (R) | 1,753 | 22.5 |
| 9 | C. Bascom Slemp (R) | 15,321 | 51.4 |
| | R. Tate Irvine (D) | 14,153 | 47.5 |
| 10 | Henry D. Flood (D) | 7,105 | 68.4 |
| | George A. Revercomb (R) | 3,124 | 30.1 |

## WASHINGTON

| | Candidates | Votes | % |
|---|---|---|---|
| 1 | William E. Humphrey (R) | 25,320 | 36.9 |
| | William Hickman Moore (D) | 18,336 | 26.7 |
| | Austin E. Griffith (PROG) | 18,134 | 26.4 |
| | Glenn E. Hoover (SOC) | 5,827 | 8.5 |
| 2 | Lindley H. Hadley (R) | 23,551 | 35.8 |
| | Earl W. Husted (D) | 15,032 | 22.9 |
| | J. E. Campbell (PROG) | 14,394 | 21.9 |
| | George E. Boomer (SOC) | 10,099 | 15.4 |
| 3 | Albert Johnson (R) | 33,556 | 42.6 |
| | Charles Drury (D) | 21,978 | 27.9 |
| | S. Warburton (PROG) | 11,677 | 14.8 |
| | Leslie E. Aller (SOC) | 8,775 | 11.1 |
| 4 | William L. LaFollette (R) | 25,541 | 46.2 |
| | Roscoe M. Drumheller (D) | 16,896 | 30.6 |

| | Candidates | Votes | % |
|---|---|---|---|
| | M. A. Peacock (PROG) | 6,952 | 12.6 |
| | John Storland (SOC) | 3,309 | 6.0 |
| 5 | Clarence C. Dill (D) | 24,410 | 36.6 |
| | Harry Rosenhaupt (R) | 20,033 | 30.0 |
| | Thomas Corkery (PROG) | 15,509 | 23.2 |
| | J. C. Harkness (SOC) | 4,502 | 6.8 |

## WEST VIRGINIA

| | Candidates | Votes | % |
|---|---|---|---|
| 1 | Matthew M. Neely (D) | 21,115 | 44.4 |
| | George E. White (R) | 20,654 | 43.5 |
| | M. S. Holt (SOC) | 3,054 | 6.4 |
| 2 | William G. Brown Jr. (D) | 20,666 | 47.5 |
| | George M. Bowers (R) | 19,305 | 44.4 |
| 3 | Adam B. Littlepage (D) | 21,890 | 43.4 |
| | S. B. Avis (R) | 21,457 | 42.5 |
| | H. F. Link (SOC) | 4,769 | 9.5 |
| 4 | Hunter H. Moss Jr. (R) | 18,356 | 48.9 |
| | J. M. Hamilton (D) | 17,532 | 46.7 |
| 5 | Edward Cooper (R) | 27,975 | 49.4 |
| | George S. Neal (D) | 24,839 | 43.9 |
| AL | Howard Sutherland (R) | 110,520 | 47.0 |
| | Hodges (D) | 102,223 | 43.4 |
| | Kintzer (SOC) | 11,944 | 5.1 |

## WISCONSIN

| | Candidates | Votes | % |
|---|---|---|---|
| 1 | Henry Allen Cooper (R) | 16,547 | 58.2 |
| | Calvin Stewart (D) | 9,911 | 34.9 |
| 2 | Michael E. Burke (D) | 16,809 | 52.2 |
| | Edward Voigt (R) | 14,071 | 43.7 |
| 3 | John M. Nelson (R) | 17,511 | 54.8 |
| | W. F. Pierstorff (D) | 13,216 | 41.4 |
| 4 | William G. Cary (R) | 9,911 | 36.5 |
| | Winfield Gaylord (SOCIAL D) | 9,546 | 35.1 |
| | Francis A. Cannon (D) | 7,490 | 27.6 |
| 5 | William H. Stafford (R) | 15,620 | 46.7 |
| | Victor L. Berger (SOCIAL D) | 11,674 | 34.9 |
| | Lawrence McGreal (D) | 5,988 | 17.9 |
| 6 | Michael K. Reilly (D) | 15,115 | 49.5 |
| | James H. Davidson (R) | 13,998 | 45.9 |
| 7 | John J. Esch (R) | 15,113 | 63.5 |
| | Virgil W. Cady (D) | 7,558 | 31.8 |
| 8 | Edward E. Browne (R) | 13,863 | 55.5 |
| | Albert C. Schmidt (D) | 9,880 | 39.6 |
| 9 | Thomas F. Konop (D) | 15,462 | 51.3 |
| | John W. Reynolds (R) | 13,525 | 44.9 |
| 10 | James A. Frear (R) | 13,377 | 60.9 |
| | Andrew Sutherland (D) | 7,326 | 33.4 |
| 11 | Irvine L. Lenroot (R) | 15,834 | 65.3 |
| | John L. Molone (D) | 6,746 | 27.8 |
| | Otto F. Eick (SOCIAL D) | 1,580 | 6.5 |

## WYOMING

| | Candidates | Votes | % |
|---|---|---|---|
| AL | Frank W. Mondell (R) | 21,362 | 51.3 |
| | Douglas A. Preston (D) | 17,246 | 41.5 |

# 1915 House Elections

## PENNSYLVANIA

### Special Election

| | Candidates | Votes | % |
|---|---|---|---|
| 24 | Henry W. Temple (R) | 27,307 | 65.6 |
| | Carl E. Gibson (D) | 9,295 | 22.3 |
| | W. K. Ramsey (SOC) | 3,362 | 8.1 |

# 1916 House Elections

## ALABAMA

| | Candidates | Votes | % |
|---|---|---|---|
| 1 | Oscar L. Gray (D) | 8,538 | 100.0 |
| 2 | S. Hubert Dent Jr. (D) | 12,524 | 97.6 |
| 3 | Henry B. Steagall (D) | 11,761 | 100.0 |
| 4 | Fred L. Blackmon (D) | 8,443 | 67.6 |
| | J. B. Atkinson (R) | 4,055 | 32.5 |
| 5 | J. Thomas Heflin (D) | 8,908 | 81.4 |
| | W. D. Harwell (R) | 2,039 | 18.6 |
| 6 | William B. Oliver (D) | 6,620 | 100.0 |
| 7 | John L. Burnett (D) | 10,894 | 60.1 |
| | T. H. Davidson (R) | 7,231 | 39.9 |
| 8 | Edward B. Almon (D) | 11,862 | 85.2 |
| | W. R. Hutchens (R) | 1,812 | 13.0 |
| 9 | George Huddleston (D) | 11,139 | 86.1 |
| | Francis Latady (R) | 1,565 | 12.1 |
| 10 | William B. Bankhead (D) | 8,091 | 54.3 |
| | Newman H. Freeman (R) | 6,813 | 45.7 |

## ARIZONA

| | Candidates | Votes | % |
|---|---|---|---|
| AL | Carl Hayden (D) | 34,377 | 65.7 |
| | Henry L. Eads (R) | 14,907 | 28.5 |
| | J. R. Barnette (SOC) | 3,060 | 5.9 |

## ARKANSAS

| | Candidates | Votes | % |
|---|---|---|---|
| 1 | Thaddeus H. Caraway (D) | 21,440 | 100.0 |
| 2 | William A. Oldfield (D) | 17,256 | 73.6 |
| | G. W. Wells (R) | 6,205 | 26.5 |
| 3 | John N. Tillman (D) | 16,438 | 62.4 |
| | A. J. Russell (R) | 9,918 | 37.6 |
| 4 | Otis T. Wingo (D) | 25,457 | 100.0 |
| 5 | Henderson M. Jacoway (D) | 19,973 | 74.2 |
| | G. A. McConnell (R) | 6,930 | 25.8 |
| 6 | Samuel M. Taylor (D) | 25,901 | 100.0 |
| 7 | William S. Goodwin (D) | 16,823 | 71.9 |
| | J. G. Brown (R) | 6,573 | 28.1 |

## CALIFORNIA

| | Candidates | Votes | % |
|---|---|---|---|
| 1 | Clarence F. Lea (D) | 32,797 | 48.8 |
| | Edward H. Hart (R) | 28,769 | 42.8 |
| | Mary M. Morgan (SOC) | 3,730 | 5.6 |
| 2 | John E. Raker (D SOC) | 30,042 | 71.0 |
| | James T. Matlock (R) | 12,282 | 29.0 |
| 3 | Charles F. Curry (R) | 48,193 | 66.7 |
| | O. W. Kennedy (D) | 16,900 | 23.4 |
| | Ben Cooper (SOC) | 4,455 | 6.2 |
| 4 | Julius Kahn (R) | 51,968 | 77.2 |
| | J. M. Fernald (D) | 10,579 | 15.7 |
| | A. K. Gifford (SOC) | 3,775 | 5.6 |
| 5 | John I. Nolan (R-D) | 59,333 | 84.6 |
| | Charles A. Preston (SOC) | 6,708 | 9.6 |
| | Frederick Head (P) | 4,046 | 5.8 |
| 6 | John A. Elston (R & PROG) | 56,520 | 64.6 |
| | H. Avery Whitney (D) | 19,787 | 22.6 |
| | Luella Twining (SOC) | 7,588 | 8.7 |
| 7 | Denver S. Church (D) | 38,787 | 51.0 |
| | W. W. Phillips (R) | 27,676 | 36.4 |
| | Harry M. McKee (SOC) | 5,492 | 7.2 |
| | J. F. Butler (P) | 4,042 | 5.3 |
| 8 | Everis A. Hayes (R-D) | 50,659 | 68.6 |
| | George S. Walker (PROG-P) | 17,576 | 23.8 |
| | Cora Pattleton Wilson (SOC) | 5,564 | 7.5 |
| 9 | Charles H. Randall (P D-R&PR) | 58,826 | 57.8 |
| | Charles W. Bell (I) | 33,270 | 32.7 |
| | Ralph L. Criswell (SOC) | 9,661 | 9.5 |
| 10 | Henry Z. Osborne (R) | 63,913 | 49.3 |
| | Rufus V. Bowden (D) | 33,225 | 25.6 |
| | Henry Stanley Benedict (PROG) | 14,305 | 11.0 |

| | Candidates | Votes | % |
|---|---|---|---|
| | James H. Ryckman (SOC) | 9,000 | 6.9 |
| | Henry Clay Needham (P) | 8,781 | 6.8 |
| 11 | William Kettner (D) | 42,051 | 44.5 |
| | Robert C. Harbison (R) | 33,765 | 35.7 |
| | James S. Edwards (P) | 14,759 | 15.6 |

**Special Election**

| | | Votes | % |
|---|---|---|---|
| 10 | Henry Stanley Benedict (PROG) | 19,032 | 56.4 |
| | Joy Clark | 7,147 | 21.2 |

## COLORADO

| | Candidates | Votes | % |
|---|---|---|---|
| 1 | Benjamin C. Hilliard (D) | 30,146 | 48.5 |
| | William N. Vaile (R) | 26,121 | 42.1 |
| | George J. Kindel (L) | 3,306 | 5.3 |
| 2 | Charles B. Timberlake (R) | 42,665 | 55.9 |
| | R. E. Jones (D) | 29,334 | 38.4 |
| | J. Edward Johnson (SOC) | 3,884 | 5.1 |
| 3 | Edward Keating (D) | 40,183 | 53.8 |
| | George E. McClelland (R) | 31,137 | 41.7 |
| 4 | Edward T. Taylor (D) | 30,926 | 65.8 |
| | Henry J. Baird (R) | 13,397 | 28.5 |
| | Emery D. Cox (SOC) | 2,695 | 5.7 |

## CONNECTICUT

| | Candidates | Votes | % |
|---|---|---|---|
| 1 | Augustine Lonergan (D) | 24,565 | 49.6 |
| | Oakey (R) | 22,876 | 46.2 |
| 2 | Richard P. Freeman (R) | 20,406 | 52.7 |
| | Dunn (D) | 17,233 | 44.5 |
| 3 | John Q. Tilson (R) | 20,859 | 48.5 |
| | Reilly (D) | 20,272 | 47.2 |
| 4 | Ebenezer J. Hill (R) | 25,917 | 53.8 |
| | Donovan (D) | 20,700 | 43.0 |
| 5 | James P. Glynn (R) | 16,872 | 49.8 |
| | Kennedy (D) | 15,882 | 46.9 |

## DELAWARE

| | Candidates | Votes | % |
|---|---|---|---|
| AL | Albert F. Polk (D) | 24,395 | 47.6 |
| | Thomas W. Miller (R) | 24,202 | 47.3 |

## FLORIDA

| | Candidates | Votes | % |
|---|---|---|---|
| 1 | Herbert J. Drane (D) | 15,353 | 82.2 |
| | H. W. Bishop (R) | 2,164 | 11.6 |
| | Frank L. Sullivan (SOC) | 1,158 | 6.2 |
| 2 | Frank Clark (D) | 10,047 | 79.9 |
| | W. H. Gober (R) | 1,367 | 10.9 |
| | F. P. Coffin (P) | 1,156 | 9.2 |
| 3 | Walter Kehoe (D) | 12,241 | 83.7 |
| | Peter H. Miller (R) | 2,393 | 16.4 |
| 4 | William J. Sears (D) | 14,748 | 68.9 |
| | D. T. Gerow (R) | 5,071 | 23.7 |
| | A. N. Jackson (SOC) | 1,592 | 7.4 |

## GEORGIA

| | Candidates | Votes | % |
|---|---|---|---|
| 1 | James W. Overstreet (D) | 9,203 | 99.9 |
| 2 | Frank Park (D) | 9,462 | 100.0 |
| 3 | Charles R. Crisp (D) | 8,040 | 100.0 |
| 4 | William C. Adamson (D) | 9,871 | 100.0 |
| 5 | William S. Howard (D) | 13,174 | 88.8 |
| | Moore | 1,656 | 11.2 |
| 6 | James W. Wise (D) | 7,370 | 100.0 |
| 7 | Gordon Lee (D) | 12,831 | 77.9 |
| | Walter Akerman | 3,382 | 20.5 |
| 8 | Samuel J. Tribble (D) | 13,891* | 99.9 |
| 9 | Thomas M. Bell (D) | 15,369 | 88.9 |
| | Adams | 1,926 | 11.1 |
| 10 | Carl Vinson (D) | 5,702 | 100.0 |
| 11 | John R. Walker (D) | 11,826 | 100.0 |
| 12 | William W. Larsen (D) | 9,816 | 95.8 |

## IDAHO

| | Candidates | Votes | % |
|---|---|---|---|
| AL | Burton L. French (R) | 64,648✓ | |
| | Addison T. Smith (R) | 63,790✓ | |
| | Marion J. Kerr (D) | 55,807 | |
| | John V. Stanley (D) | 54,339 | |
| | Albert B. Clark (SOC) | 8,079 | |
| | Sam G. Gilleland (SOC) | 8,033 | |

## ILLINOIS

| | Candidates | Votes | % |
|---|---|---|---|
| 1 | Martin B. Madden (R) | 20,380 | 59.1 |
| | William J. Hennessey (D) | 13,380 | 38.8 |
| 2 | James R. Mann (R) | 44,159 | 63.0 |
| | Philip H. Treacy (D) | 22,722 | 32.4 |
| 3 | William W. Wilson (R) | 35,885 | 55.7 |
| | Bernard McMahon (D) | 25,954 | 40.3 |
| 4 | Charles Martin (D) | 18,722 | 58.5 |
| | John Golombiewski (R) | 11,793 | 36.8 |
| 5 | Adolph J. Sabath (D) | 12,884 | 60.7 |
| | David T. Alexander (R) | 6,850 | 32.3 |
| | Charles Toepper (SOC) | 1,500 | 7.1 |
| 6 | James McAndrews (D) | 39,749 | 48.5 |
| | Arthur W. Fulton (R) | 37,347 | 45.6 |
| | Charles H. Hair (SOC) | 4,586 | 5.6 |
| 7 | Niels Juul (R) | 47,514 | 50.9 |
| | Frank Buchanan (D) | 37,460 | 40.1 |
| | Carl D. Thompson (SOC) | 8,372 | 9.0 |
| 8 | Thomas Gallagher (D) | 14,970 | 63.4 |
| | Frank Sullivan (R) | 8,636 | 36.6 |
| 9 | Fred A. Britten (R) | 20,609 | 59.2 |
| | Eugene L. McGarry (D) | 12,295 | 35.3 |
| | Andrew Lafin (SOC) | 1,891 | 5.4 |
| 10 | George Edmund Foss (R) | 44,749 | 59.3 |
| | Samuel C. Herren (D) | 22,398 | 29.7 |
| | Carl Hjalmar Lundquist (I) | 4,622 | 6.1 |
| 11 | Ira C. Copley (R) | 38,418 | 69.0 |
| | William C. Mooney (D) | 15,715 | 28.2 |
| 12 | Charles E. Fuller (R) | 35,741 | 66.0 |
| | Walter Panneck (D) | 16,033 | 29.6 |
| 13 | John C. McKenzie (R) | 28,123 | 68.1 |
| | F. P. Dudley (D) | 12,436 | 30.1 |
| 14 | William J. Graham (R) | 23,099 | 48.5 |
| | Clyde H. Tavenner (D) | 22,591 | 47.4 |
| 15 | Edward J. King (R) | 28,143 | 54.5 |
| | Edward P. Allen (D) | 21,604 | 41.9 |
| 16 | Clifford Ireland (R) | 25,091 | 49.9 |
| | Claude U. Stone (D) | 24,073 | 47.9 |
| 17 | John A. Sterling (R) | 23,956 | 56.6 |
| | S. A. Rathbun | 17,571 | 41.5 |
| 18 | Joseph G. Cannon (R) | 29,318 | 54.2 |
| | Armand E. Smith (D) | 23,668 | 43.7 |
| 19 | William B. McKinley (R) | 33,162 | 52.7 |
| | F. R. Dove (D) | 28,870 | 45.8 |
| 20 | Henry T. Rainey (D) | 24,364 | 55.6 |
| | Walter B. Sayler (R) | 19,019 | 43.4 |
| 21 | Loren E. Wheeler (R) | 26,367 | 50.0 |
| | Thomas Rees (D) | 23,936 | 45.4 |
| 22 | William A. Rodenberg (R) | 31,958 | 50.4 |
| | D. H. Mudge (D) | 29,451 | 46.5 |
| 23 | Martin D. Foster (D) | 28,805 | 52.9 |
| | Harry C. Ferriman (R) | 24,328 | 44.7 |
| 24 | Thomas S. Williams (R) | 23,766 | 55.0 |
| | Louis W. Goetzman (D) | 18,540 | 42.9 |
| 25 | Edward E. Denison (R) | 27,905 | 52.2 |
| | Andrew J. Rendleman (D) | 24,034 | 44.9 |
| AL | Medill McCormick (R) | 707,958✓ | |
| | William E. Mason (R) | 687,198✓ | |
| | William Elza Williams (D) | 546,471 | |
| | Joseph O. Kosture (D) | 538,756 | |
| | J. Louis Engdahl (SOC) | 49,842 | |
| | Walter Huggins (SOC) | 48,842 | |
| | Charles W. Williams (P) | 9,569 | |
| | Unidentified Candidate (P) | 9,366 | |
| | Frank Hosking (SOC LAB) | 1,790 | |
| | John Kowatzrk (SOC LAB) | 1,739 | |

## INDIANA

| Candidates | Votes | % |
|---|---|---|
| 1 George F. Denton (D) | 23,278 | 48.1 |
| S. Wallace Cook (R) | 22,955 | 47.4 |
| 2 Oscar E. Bland (R) | 24,764 | 47.3 |
| William A. Cullop (D) | 23,759 | 45.4 |
| Z. M. Garten (SOC) | 2,860 | 5.5 |
| 3 William E. Cox (D) | 24,738 | 52.1 |
| John H. Edwards (R) | 21,831 | 46.0 |
| 4 Lincoln Dixon (D) | 24,925 | 51.5 |
| Mauley D. Wilson (R) | 22,730 | 47.0 |
| 5 Everett Sanders (R) | 20,977 | 40.6 |
| Ralph W. Moss (D) | 20,270 | 39.3 |
| E. V. Debs (SOC) | 8,866 | 17.2 |
| 6 Daniel W. Comstock (R) | 23,831 | 48.6 |
| Finley H. Gray (D) | 22,853 | 46.6 |
| 7 Merrill Moores (R) | 40,862 | 51.8 |
| Chalmer Schlosser (D) | 34,732 | 44.1 |
| 8 Albert H. Vestal (R) | 26,135 | 48.0 |
| Jacob F. Denny (D) | 23,854 | 43.8 |
| 9 Fred S. Purnell (R) | 27,712 | 50.4 |
| David F. Maish (D) | 24,547 | 44.6 |
| 10 William R. Wood (R) | 31,895 | 56.9 |
| George E. Hershman (D) | 23,077 | 41.1 |
| 11 Milton Kraus (R) | 25,005 | 46.3 |
| George W. Rauch (D) | 24,578 | 45.5 |
| 12 Louis William Fairfield (R) | 23,863 | 51.2 |
| Cyrus Cline (D) | 20,603 | 44.2 |
| 13 Harry A. Barnhart (D) | 30,537 | 47.7 |
| Andrew J. Hickey (R) | 30,246 | 47.2 |

## IOWA

| Candidates | Votes | % |
|---|---|---|
| 1 Charles A. Kennedy (R) | 20,421 | 58.6 |
| F. B. Whitaker (D) | 14,276 | 41.0 |
| 2 Harry E. Hull (R) | 25,548 | 55.3 |
| M. F. Cronin (D) | 18,591 | 40.3 |
| 3 Burton E. Sweet (R) | 31,567 | 67.0 |
| James C. Murtagh (D) | 14,825 | 31.4 |
| 4 Gilbert N. Haugen (R) | 23,416 | 57.9 |
| Earl Evans (D) | 16,490 | 40.8 |
| 5 James W. Good (R) | 27,438 | 64.1 |
| Robert Melvin Peet (D) | 14,654 | 34.2 |
| 6 C. William Ramseyer (R) | 21,757 | 57.3 |
| S. Kirkpatrick (D) | 14,927 | 39.3 |
| 7 Cassius C. Dowell (R) | 25,993 | 61.7 |
| H. C. Evans (D) | 14,677 | 34.8 |
| 8 Horace M. Towner (R) | 24,195 | 59.0 |
| H. B. Bracewell (D) | 15,940 | 38.9 |
| 9 William R. Green (R) | 23,446 | 55.4 |
| John C. Pryor (D) | 18,743 | 44.3 |
| 10 Frank P. Woods (R) | 32,332 | 63.6 |
| J. R. Files (D) | 17,300 | 34.1 |
| 11 George C. Scott (R) | 26,066 | 49.6 |
| Thomas J. Steele (D) | 25,935 | 49.4 |

## KANSAS

| Candidates | Votes | % |
|---|---|---|
| 1 Daniel R. Anthony Jr. (R) | 37,705 | 55.8 |
| Herbert J. Corwine (D) | 23,272 | 34.4 |
| Eva Harding (I) | 5,144 | 7.6 |
| 2 Edward C. Little (R) | 42,780 | 50.4 |
| Joseph Taggart (D) | 38,815 | 45.7 |
| 3 Phillip P. Campbell (R) | 40,272 | 47.8 |
| William S. Hyatt (D) | 32,837 | 39.0 |
| T. P. Laughlin (SOC) | 9,177 | 10.9 |
| 4 Dudley Doolittle (D) | 29,370 | 51.5 |
| Clyde W. Miller (R) | 26,831 | 47.0 |
| 5 Guy T. Helvering (D) | 32,198 | 50.4 |
| Charles M. Harger (R) | 29,861 | 46.8 |
| 6 John R. Connelly (D) | 40,005 | 56.4 |
| Otis L. Benton (R) | 28,332 | 40.0 |
| 7 Jouett Shouse (D) | 38,099 | 43.9 |
| J. S. Simmons (R) | 31,621 | 36.4 |
| Howard E. Kershner (P) | 13,566 | 15.6 |
| 8 William A. Ayres (D) | 26,993 | 51.0 |
| Thomas C. Wilson (R) | 24,220 | 45.8 |

## KENTUCKY

| Candidates | Votes | % |
|---|---|---|
| 1 Alben W. Barkley (D) | 30,029 | 63.7 |
| Thomas (R) | 16,128 | 34.2 |
| 2 David H. Kincheloe (D) | 24,138 | 54.2 |
| Fowler (R) | 19,953 | 44.8 |
| 3 Robert Y. Thomas Jr. (D) | 22,194 | 49.6 |
| Taylor (R) | 22,180 | 49.6 |
| 4 Ben Johnson (D) | 25,012 | 52.7 |
| Haswell (R) | 21,958 | 46.3 |
| 5 J. Swagar Sherley (D) | 29,204 | 50.1 |
| Owens (R) | 27,861 | 47.8 |
| 6 Arthur B. Rouse (D) | 27,001 | 62.5 |
| Sheppard (R) | 14,959 | 34.7 |
| 7 James C. Cantrill (D) | 28,734 | 59.8 |
| Manby (R) | 19,304 | 40.2 |
| 8 Harvey Helm (D) | 21,187 | 53.7 |
| Neal (R) | 10,030 | 45.7 |
| 9 William J. Fields (D) | 32,957 | 54.3 |
| Pennington (R) | 27,119 | 44.7 |
| 10 John W. Langley (R) | 19,113 | 60.9 |
| Stanton (D) | 11,981 | 38.2 |
| 11 Caleb Powers (R) | 33,867 | 70.0 |
| Dishman (D) | 14,280 | 29.5 |

## LOUISIANA

| Candidates | Votes | % |
|---|---|---|
| 1 Albert Estopinal (D) | 17,939 | 100.0 |
| 2 H. Garland Dupre (D) | 16,328 | 100.0 |
| 3 Whitmell P. Martin (PROG) | 6,481 | 49.0 |
| Wade O. Martin (D) | 6,382 | 48.3 |
| 4 John T. Watkins (D) | 8,306 | 100.0 |
| 5 Riley J. Wilson (D) | 7,650 | 97.6 |
| 6 Jared Y. Sanders (D) | 7,377 | 100.0 |
| 7 Ladislas Lazaro (D) | 7,307 | 94.9 |
| M. McManus (SOC) | 394 | 5.1 |
| 8 James B. Aswell (D) | 7,318 | 94.2 |
| H. O. Bower (SOC) | 449 | 5.8 |

## MAINE

| Candidates | Votes | % |
|---|---|---|
| 1 Louis B. Goodall (R) | 20,357 | 54.2 |
| Stevens (D) | 16,807 | 44.8 |
| 2 Wallace H. White Jr. (R) | 19,338 | 50.1 |
| McGillicuddy (D) | 18,791 | 48.7 |
| 3 John A. Peters (R) | 23,656 | 53.5 |
| Bunker (D) | 20,002 | 45.3 |
| 4 Ira G. Hersey (R) | 17,647 | 57.4 |
| Pierce (D) | 12,969 | 42.2 |

## MARYLAND

| Candidates | Votes | % |
|---|---|---|
| 1 Jesse D. Price (D) | 17,047 | 48.6 |
| Robert F. Duer (R) | 16,981 | 48.4 |
| 2 Joshua Frederick C. Talbott (D) | 24,648 | 50.3 |
| William H. Lawrence (R) | 20,420 | 41.7 |
| John S. Green (P) | 3,513 | 7.2 |
| 3 Charles P. Coady (D) | 16,546 | 52.5 |
| Charles W. Main (R) | 13,857 | 44.0 |
| 4 J. Charles Linthicum (D) | 19,774 | 52.5 |
| J. Frank Fox (R) | 17,030 | 45.2 |
| 5 Sydney E. Mudd (R) | 17,407 | 53.9 |
| Jackson H. Ralston (D) | 13,909 | 43.0 |
| 6 Frederick N. Zihlman (R) | 19,932 | 51.1 |
| Henry Dorsey Etchison (D) | 17,214 | 44.1 |

## MASSACHUSETTS

| Candidates | Votes | % |
|---|---|---|
| 1 Allen T. Treadway (R) | 19,667 | 60.2 |
| Timothy C. Collins (D) | 11,795 | 36.1 |
| 2 Frederick H. Gillett (R) | 20,064 | 60.3 |
| Theobald M. Connor (D) | 11,895 | 35.7 |
| 3 Calvin D. Paige (R) | 19,371 | 66.2 |
| Michael A. Scanlon (D) | 9,905 | 33.8 |
| 4 Samuel E. Winslow (R) | 17,647 | 55.6 |
| John H. Hunt (D) | 13,315 | 41.9 |
| 5 John Jacob Rogers (R) | 20,345 | 64.7 |
| Roger Sherman Hoar (D) | 11,097 | 35.3 |
| 6 Augustus P. Gardner (R) | 21,916 | 67.3 |
| Arthur Howard (D) | 8,578 | 26.4 |
| Charles W. Fitzgerald (SOC) | 2,049 | 6.3 |
| 7 Michael F. Phelan (D) | 16,597 | 51.2 |
| Charles Neal Barney (R) | 14,350 | 44.3 |
| 8 Frederick W. Dallinger (R) | 21,178 | 59.7 |
| Frederick S. Deitrick (D) | 14,308 | 40.3 |
| 9 Alvan T. Fuller (I) | 17,079 | 50.5 |
| Ernest W. Roberts (R) | 16,765 | 49.5 |
| 10 Peter F. Tague (D) | 13,646 | 78.7 |
| James L. Hourihan (R) | 3,684 | 21.3 |
| 11 George Holden Tinkham (R) | 18,424 | 60.1 |
| Francis J. Horgan (D) | 12,244 | 39.9 |
| 12 James A. Gallivan (D) | 22,105 | 67.6 |
| Charles H. S. Robinson (R) | 10,613 | 32.4 |
| 13 William H. Carter (R) | 25,527 | 66.3 |
| William H. Murphy (D) | 12,985 | 33.7 |
| 14 Richard Olney (D) | 21,707 | 53.2 |
| Henry L. Kincaide (R) | 17,702 | 43.4 |
| 15 William S. Greene (R) | 15,788 | 63.2 |
| Arthur J. B. Cartier (D) | 9,203 | 36.8 |
| 16 Joseph Walsh (R) | 18,505 | 68.8 |
| Ralph W. Crosby (D) | 8,392 | 31.2 |

## MICHIGAN

| Candidates | Votes | % |
|---|---|---|
| 1 Frank E. Doremus (D) | 29,571 | 51.2 |
| Hugh Shepherd (R) | 26,679 | 46.2 |
| 2 Mark R. Bacon (R) | 27,182‡ | 49.0 |
| Samuel W. Beakes (D) | 27,133 | 48.9 |
| 3 John M. C. Smith (R) | 24,897 | 49.4 |
| James W. Marsh (D) | 23,117 | 45.8 |
| 4 Edward L. Hamilton (R) | 26,764 | 55.5 |
| Roy J. Wade (D) | 20,445 | 42.4 |
| 5 Carl E. Mapes (R) | 24,258 | 51.1 |
| Peter J. Danhof (D) | 21,639 | 45.6 |
| 6 Patrick H. Kelley (R) | 38,110 | 54.0 |
| William S. Kellogg (D) | 30,664 | 43.5 |
| 7 Louis C. Cramton (R) | 30,101 | 66.9 |
| Varnum J. Bowers (D) | 14,020 | 31.1 |
| 8 Joseph W. Fordney (R) | 28,288 | 53.6 |
| William A. Seegmiller (D) | 23,692 | 44.9 |
| 9 James C. McLaughlin (R) | 24,624 | 58.3 |
| Curtis D. Alway (D) | 15,726 | 37.3 |
| 10 Gilbert A. Currie (R) | 24,240 | 58.1 |
| Henry C. Haller (D) | 16,056 | 38.5 |
| 11 Frank D. Scott (R) | 24,840 | 60.6 |
| John J. Reycraft (D) | 14,499 | 35.4 |
| 12 W. Frank James (R) | 22,998 | 64.1 |
| William J. Macdonald (D & PROG) | 12,882 | 35.9 |
| 13 Charles A. Nichols (R) | 32,317 | 59.3 |
| Eugene P. Berry (D) | 20,921 | 38.4 |

## MINNESOTA

| Candidates | Votes | % |
|---|---|---|
| 1 Sydney Anderson (R) | 25,278 | 65.5 |
| Lamberton (D) | 13,290 | 34.5 |
| 2 Franklin F. Ellsworth (R) | 29,392 | 100.0 |
| 3 Charles R. Davis (R) | 25,527 | 71.1 |
| Kelly Jr. (D) | 10,354 | 28.9 |
| 4 Carl C. Van Dyke (D) | 23,516 | 61.2 |
| Reese (R) | 11,737 | 30.6 |
| 5 Ernest Lundeen (R) | 19,131 | 42.4 |
| Bowler (D) | 11,849 | 26.3 |
| Latimer (SOC) | 7,526 | 16.7 |
| Markve (P) | 6,599 | 14.6 |
| 6 Harold Knutson (R) | 20,889 | 56.8 |
| Donohue (D) | 13,107 | 35.7 |
| Knutsen (P) | 2,766 | 7.5 |
| 7 Andrew J. Volstead (R) | 21,300 | 53.6 |
| Lobeck (P) | 11,961 | 30.1 |
| Townsend (D) | 6,518 | 16.4 |

## MINNESOTA

| Candidates | Votes | % |
|---|---|---|
| 8 Clarence B. Miller (R) | 17,758 | 51.6 |
| Anderson (SOC) | 9,034 | 26.3 |
| Wheeler (P) | 7,621 | 22.2 |
| 9 Halvor Steenerson (R) | 25,429 | 66.8 |
| Swanson (D) | 8,313 | 21.8 |
| Thompson (SOC) | 4,347 | 11.4 |
| 10 Thomas D. Schall (PROG) | 19,696 | 45.0 |
| Jepson (R) | 13,170 | 30.1 |
| Cronin (D) | 7,148 | 16.3 |
| Soltis (SOC) | 3,782 | 8.6 |

## MISSISSIPPI

| Candidates | Votes | % |
|---|---|---|
| 1 Ezekiel S. Candler Jr. (D) | ✔ | |
| 2 Hubert D. Stephens (D) | 10,192 | 97.6 |
| 3 Benjamin G. Humphreys (D) | ✔ | |
| 4 Thomas U. Sisson (D) | ✔ | |
| 5 William A. Venable (D) | 11,966 | 94.5 |
| Charles Evans (SOC) | 692 | 5.5 |
| 6 Pat Harrison (D) | 12,492 | 94.6 |
| F. T. Maxwell (SOC) | 716 | 5.4 |
| 7 Percy E. Quin (D) | ✔ | |
| 8 James W. Collier (D) | 6,147 | 97.6 |

## MISSOURI

| Candidates | Votes | % |
|---|---|---|
| 1 Milton A. Romjue (D) | 22,840 | 54.4 |
| Brown (R) | 18,566 | 44.2 |
| 2 William W. Rucker (D) | 24,964 | 57.7 |
| Pickett (R) | 17,936 | 41.5 |
| 3 Joshua W. Alexander (D) | 21,658 | 54.2 |
| Moulton (R) | 17,769 | 44.5 |
| 4 Charles F. Booher (D) | 22,155 | 53.6 |
| Geiger (R) | 18,632 | 45.1 |
| 5 William P. Borland (D) | 46,065 | 58.7 |
| Kimbrell (R) | 31,292 | 39.9 |
| 6 Clement C. Dickinson (D) | 18,869 | 54.2 |
| Crawford (R) | 15,948 | 45.8 |
| 7 Courtney W. Hamlin (D) | 26,766 | 50.5 |
| Houston (R) | 25,953 | 48.9 |
| 8 Dorsey W. Shackleford (D) | 17,599 | 52.0 |
| Gentry (R) | 16,255 | 48.0 |
| 9 James Beauchamp Clark (D) | 23,755 | 51.9 |
| Cole (R) | 21,704 | 47.5 |
| 10 Jacob E. Meeker (R) | 63,663 | 57.7 |
| Brennan (D) | 43,271 | 39.3 |
| 11 William L. Igoe (D) | 23,928 | 56.8 |
| Barto (R) | 17,434 | 41.4 |
| 12 Leonidas C. Dyer (R) | 16,345 | 55.9 |
| Gill (D) | 12,465 | 42.6 |
| 13 Walter L. Hensley (D) | 17,850 | 49.7 |
| Rhodes (R) | 17,537 | 48.8 |
| 14 Joseph J. Russell (D) | 30,889 | 49.3 |
| Hill (R) | 29,727 | 47.4 |
| 15 Perl D. Decker (D) | 26,240 | 49.8 |
| Manlove (R) | 24,013 | 45.6 |
| 16 Thomas L. Rubey (D) | 17,303 | 51.0 |
| Harrison (R) | 16,058 | 47.3 |

## MONTANA

| Candidates | Votes | % |
|---|---|---|
| AL John M. Evans (D) | 84,499 ✔ | |
| Jeanette Rankin (R) | 76,932 ✔ | |
| Harry B. Mitchell (D) | 70,578 | |
| George W. Farr (R) | 66,974 | |
| John H. McGuffey (SOC) | 9,002 | |
| Albert F. Meissener (SOC) | 8,479 | |

## NEBRASKA

| Candidates | Votes | % |
|---|---|---|
| 1 C. Frank Reavis (R & PROG) | 21,021 | 54.5 |
| John A. Maguire (D & PPI) | 16,894 | 43.8 |
| 2 Charles O. Lobeck (D & PPI) | 25,617 | 55.6 |
| Benjamin S. Baker (R) | 17,578 | 38.1 |
| G. C. Porter (SOC) | 2,922 | 6.3 |

| Candidates | Votes | % |
|---|---|---|
| 3 Daniel V. Stephens (D & PPI) | 28,055 | 51.6 |
| William P. Warner (R & PROG) | 25,541 | 47.0 |
| 4 Charles H. Sloan (R & PROG) | 24,054 | 55.3 |
| William L. Stark (D & PPI) | 18,798 | 43.2 |
| 5 Ashton C. Shallenberger (D PPI&PR) | 22,686 | 54.0 |
| Silas R. Barton (R) | 18,293 | 43.5 |
| 6 Moses P. Kinkaid (R & PROG) | 33,559 | 57.4 |
| Ed B. McDermott (D & PPI) | 22,317 | 38.1 |

## NEVADA

| Candidates | Votes | % |
|---|---|---|
| AL Edwin E. Roberts (R) | 14,106 | 43.6 |
| Edwin E. Caine (D) | 13,100 | 40.5 |
| M. J. Scanlan (SOC) | 5,125 | 15.9 |

## NEW HAMPSHIRE

| Candidates | Votes | % |
|---|---|---|
| 1 Cyrus A. Sulloway (R) | 21,826 | 51.5 |
| Woodbury (D) | 19,806 | 46.8 |
| 2 Edward H. Wason (R) | 22,296 | 51.7 |
| Stevens (D) | 20,145 | 46.7 |

## NEW JERSEY

| Candidates | Votes | % |
|---|---|---|
| 1 William J. Browning (R) | 26,589 | 58.8 |
| Cattell (D) | 15,329 | 33.9 |
| 2 Isaac Bacharach (R) | 24,865 | 59.7 |
| Myers (D) | 14,220 | 34.2 |
| 3 Thomas J. Scully (D) | 21,896 | 48.6 |
| Carson (R) | 21,694 | 48.1 |
| 4 Elijah C. Hutchinson (R) | 18,131 | 50.0 |
| Beekman (D) | 16,926 | 46.6 |
| 5 John H. Capstick (R) | 20,951 | 51.8 |
| Tuttle Jr. (D) | 17,176 | 42.5 |
| 6 John R. Ramsey (R) | 21,464 | 50.8 |
| Heath (D) | 18,770 | 44.4 |
| 7 Dow H. Drukker (R) | 15,931 | 53.0 |
| Beardmore (D) | 7,980 | 26.6 |
| Kershot (SOC) | 3,326 | 11.1 |
| Schweikert (NP) | 2,617 | 8.7 |
| 8 Edward W. Gray (R) | 18,663 | 52.7 |
| Kinkead (D) | 15,395 | 43.5 |
| 9 Richard W. Parker (R) | 14,641 | 47.9 |
| Matthews (D) | 13,625 | 44.6 |
| Wherett (SOC) | 1,923 | 6.3 |
| 10 Frederick R. Lehlbach (R) | 21,822 | 60.7 |
| Flanagan (D) | 12,341 | 34.3 |
| 11 John J. Eagan (D) | 15,769 | 59.2 |
| Brennan (R) | 9,049 | 34.0 |
| 12 James A. Hamill (D) | 17,365 | 57.0 |
| Dear (R) | 12,058 | 39.6 |

## NEW MEXICO

| Candidates | Votes | % |
|---|---|---|
| AL William B. Walton (D) | 32,731 | 49.0 |
| B. C. Hernandez (R) | 32,056 | 48.0 |

## NEW YORK

| Candidates | Votes | % |
|---|---|---|
| 1 Frederick C. Hicks (R IL&NPR) | 29,041 | 63.2 |
| Lathrop Brown (D & AM) | 16,302 | 35.5 |
| 2 Charles Pope Caldwell (D IL) | 24,110 | 51.8 |
| Theron H. Burden (R AM) | 19,504 | 41.9 |
| Benjamin Katz (SOC) | 2,611 | 5.6 |
| 3 Joseph V. Flynn (D & IL) | 11,670 | 49.3 |
| Jared J. Chambers (R NPR AM) | 10,381 | 43.9 |
| William A. Ross (SOC) | 1,552 | 6.6 |

| Candidates | Votes | % |
|---|---|---|
| 4 Harry Howard Dale (D & IL) | 8,861 | 48.2 |
| Michael Stein (R NPR AM) | 7,044 | 38.3 |
| Richard Haffner (SOC) | 2,451 | 13.3 |
| 5 James P. Maher (D & IL) | 12,658 | 49.9 |
| Charles W. Philipbar (R NPR AM) | 11,264 | 44.4 |
| Hans A. Hansen (SOC) | 1,357 | 5.4 |
| 6 Frederick W. Rowe (R NPR) | 29,107 | 60.7 |
| Charles I. Stengle (D & IL) | 17,436 | 36.4 |
| 7 John J. Fitzgerald (D IL NPR) | 15,454 | 63.5 |
| Ralph Waldo Bowman (R) | 8,330 | 34.2 |
| 8 Daniel J. Griffin (D IL NPR) | 22,850 | 60.7 |
| Wilmot L. Morehouse (R) | 13,387 | 35.6 |
| 9 Oscar W. Swift (R & P) | 25,701 | 57.0 |
| Herman H. Torborg (DIL A NP) | 16,575 | 36.8 |
| Ludwig Lore (SOC) | 2,815 | 6.2 |
| 10 Reuben L. Haskell (R IL&NPR) | 11,057 | 45.0 |
| Frank Wasserman (D & AM) | 8,853 | 36.1 |
| William M. Feigenbaum (SOC) | 4,567 | 18.6 |
| 11 Daniel J. Riordan (D IL) | 13,047 | 56.2 |
| Montague Lessler (R NPR) | 9,535 | 41.1 |
| 12 Meyer London (SOC) | 6,103 | 47.4 |
| Leon Sanders (D IL) | 5,763 | 44.8 |
| Louis M. Block (R) | 968 | 7.5 |
| 13 Christopher D. Sullivan (D & IL) | 5,114 | 48.0 |
| Frank Dostal (R NPR AM) | 3,886 | 36.5 |
| Hilda G. Claessens (SOC) | 1,644 | 15.4 |
| 14 Fiorello H. LaGuardia (R NPR AM) | 7,272 | 43.3 |
| Michael F. Farley (D & IL) | 6,915 | 41.2 |
| William I. Sockheim (SOC) | 2,536 | 15.1 |
| 15 Michael F. Conry (D & IL) | 13,362* | 59.9 |
| William Henkel Jr. (R) | 7,996 | 35.8 |
| 16 Peter J. Dooling (D & IL) | 12,115 | 51.6 |
| Walbridge S. Taft (R NPR) | 10,761 | 45.9 |
| 17 John F. Carew (D & IL) | 11,213 | 51.2 |
| Lindell T. Bates (R NPR) | 9,764 | 44.6 |
| 18 George B. Francis (R IL&NPR) | 12,196 | 46.1 |
| Thomas G. Patten (D) | 11,826 | 44.7 |
| Irving Ottenberg (SOC) | 2,407 | 9.1 |
| 19 Walter M. Chandler (R IL&NPR) | 19,922 | 54.8 |
| Michael Schaap (D) | 14,817 | 40.8 |
| 20 Isaac Siegel (R IL&NPR) | 4,542 | 36.0 |
| Morris Hillquit (SOC) | 4,129 | 32.7 |
| Bernard R. Rosenblatt (D) | 3,907 | 31.0 |
| 21 Murray Hulbert (D & IL) | 14,107 | 53.1 |
| Martin Ansorge (R NPR) | 10,953 | 41.3 |
| Alexander Braunstein (SOC) | 1,434 | 5.4 |
| 22 Henry Bruckner (D IL NPR) | 21,284 | 63.5 |
| James A. Francis (R) | 9,878 | 29.5 |
| Max B. Gollin (SOC) | 2,244 | 6.7 |
| 23 Daniel C. Oliver (D) | 25,535 | 46.9 |
| William S. Bennett (RIL A 'NP) | 22,856 | 42.0 |
| J. George Gobsevage (SOC) | 5,810 | 10.7 |
| 24 Benjamin L. Fairchild (RIL P NP) | 25,713 | 53.7 |
| Woodson R. Oglesby (D & AM) | 18,439 | 38.5 |
| Mary G. Schonberg (SOC) | 3,710 | 7.8 |
| 25 James W. Husted (R) | 23,363 | 59.5 |
| Chester D. Pugsley (D IL NPR) | 14,816 | 37.7 |
| 26 Edmund Platt (R IL&NPR) | 23,314 | 54.2 |
| Rosslyn M. Cox (D) | 18,825 | 43.8 |
| 27 Charles B. Ward (RIL A NP) | 24,634 | 56.4 |
| James O. Woodward (D) | 17,674 | 40.5 |
| 28 Rollin B. Sanford (R NPR) | 27,722 | 55.5 |
| Michael F. Collins (D IL) | 21,436 | 42.9 |

## NEW YORK

| Candidates | Votes | % |
|---|---|---|
| 29 James S. Parker (R NPR) | 31,888 | 89.2 |
| Charles E. Robbins (P) | 2,134 | 6.0 |
| 30 George R. Lunn (DIL ANPI) | 19,818 | 47.1 |
| Henry S. Deforest (R) | 19,199 | 45.6 |
| Herbert M. Merrill (SOC) | 2,126 | 5.1 |
| 31 Bertrand H. Snell (R) | 24,938 | 67.2 |
| Louis F. Roberts (D) | 10,934 | 29.5 |
| 32 Luther W. Mott (R IL&NPR) | 28,744 | 62.7 |
| Otto Pfaff (D) | 14,323 | 31.2 |
| 33 Homer P. Snyder (R NPR AM) | 25,299 | 55.6 |
| Charles A. Talcott (D) | 18,944 | 41.6 |
| 34 George W. Fairchild (R IL&NPR) | 27,075 | 58.7 |
| Cortland A. Wilber (D) | 15,895 | 34.5 |
| Levi Hoag (P) | 2,537 | 5.5 |
| 35 Walter W. Magee (R IL&NPR) | 31,429 | 60.9 |
| Arlington H. Mallery (D) | 16,059 | 31.1 |
| 36 Norman J. Gould (R NPR) | 28,325 | 62.3 |
| Hiram G. Hotchkiss (D) | 15,293 | 33.6 |
| 37 Harry H. Pratt (R IL&NPR) | 23,029 | 49.9 |
| Frederick W. Palmer (D & AM) | 20,291 | 44.0 |
| 38 Thomas B. Dunn (R) | 29,894 | 65.1 |
| Jacob Gerling (D) | 13,867 | 30.2 |
| 39 Archie D. Sanders (R) | 28,393 | 65.1 |
| David A. White (D) | 13,424 | 30.8 |
| 40 S. Wallace Dempsey (R) | 27,652 | 61.9 |
| Andrew B. Gilfillan (D NPR) | 15,011 | 33.6 |
| 41 Charles B. Smith (D & AM) | 21,265 | 56.2 |
| William H. Crosby (R P NPR) | 15,508 | 41.0 |
| 42 William F. Waldow (R NPR) | 16,623 | 51.0 |
| Daniel A. Driscoll (D) | 15,411 | 47.3 |
| 43 Charles M. Hamilton (R NPR) | 27,186 | 64.7 |
| A. F. French (D) | 11,414 | 27.2 |

## NORTH CAROLINA

| Candidates | Votes | % |
|---|---|---|
| 1 John H. Small (D) | 13,211 | 72.2 |
| Leslie E. Jones (R) | 5,098 | 27.8 |
| 2 Claude Kitchin (D) | 13,255 | 86.9 |
| W. O. Dixon (R) | 1,999 | 13.1 |
| 3 George E. Hood (D) | 12,269 | 58.0 |
| George E. Butler (R) | 8,889 | 42.0 |
| 4 Edward W. Pou (D) | 15,305 | 64.3 |
| Joseph J. Jenkins (R) | 8,483 | 35.7 |
| 5 Charles M. Stedman (D) | 23,932 | 52.5 |
| Gilliam Grissom (R) | 21,429 | 47.0 |
| 6 Hannibal L. Godwin (D) | 13,337 | 63.9 |
| Alex L. McCaskill (R) | 7,521 | 36.1 |
| 7 Leonidas D. Robinson (D) | 20,518 | 54.7 |
| Presley E. Brown (R) | 17,021 | 45.3 |
| 8 Robert L. Doughton (D) | 17,249 | 52.8 |
| H. Sinclair Williams (R) | 15,411 | 47.2 |
| 9 Edwin Y. Webb (D) | 18,855 | 53.5 |
| Charles E. Greene (R) | 16,381 | 46.5 |
| 10 Zebulon Weaver (D) | 18,023‡ | 50.0 |
| James J. Britt (R) | 18,014 | 50.0 |

## NORTH DAKOTA

| Candidates | Votes | % |
|---|---|---|
| 1 Henry T. Helgesen (R) | 20,709 | 59.9 |
| George A. Bangs (D) | 13,236 | 38.3 |
| 2 George M. Young (R) | 22,227 | 71.7 |
| Hugh McDonald (D) | 7,638 | 24.6 |
| 3 Patrick D. Norton (R) | 20,393 | 65.2 |
| Charles Simon (D) | 8,293 | 26.5 |
| Anton Klemmens (SOC) | 2,586 | 8.3 |

## OHIO

| Candidates | Votes | % |
|---|---|---|
| 1 Nicholas Longworth (R) | 33,903 | 56.7 |
| Edward H. Brink (D) | 24,290 | 40.6 |

| Candidates | Votes | % |
|---|---|---|
| 2 Victor Heintz (R) | 29,612 | 49.4 |
| Stanley E. Bowdle (D) | 28,156 | 47.0 |
| 3 Warren Gard (D) | 37,982 | 53.3 |
| Charles W. Dustin (R) | 28,571 | 40.1 |
| Jeremiah F. Mincker (SOC) | 4,699 | 6.6 |
| 4 Benjamin F. Welty (D) | 29,486 | 53.7 |
| J. E. Russell (R) | 25,378 | 46.3 |
| 5 John S. Snook (D) | 22,852 | 52.8 |
| Nelson E. Matthews (R) | 20,424 | 47.2 |
| 6 Charles C. Kearns (R) | 21,315 | 49.6 |
| A. G. Turnipseed (D) | 20,811 | 48.5 |
| 7 Simeon D. Fess (R) | 39,975 | 94.8 |
| 8 John A. Key (D) | 25,164 | 53.9 |
| John H. Clark (R) | 21,525 | 46.1 |
| 9 Isaac R. Sherwood (D) | 31,921 | 58.2 |
| Frank L. Mulholland (R) | 19,882 | 36.2 |
| Thomas C. Devine (SOC) | 3,091 | 5.6 |
| 10 Robert M. Switzer (R) | 21,185 | 58.0 |
| Charles W. Haslett (D) | 15,375 | 42.1 |
| 11 Horatio C. Claypool (D) | 20,144 | 50.5 |
| Edwin D. Ricketts (R) | 19,022 | 47.7 |
| 12 Clement L. Brumbaugh (D) | 31,362 | 52.8 |
| Hugh Huntington (R) | 26,415 | 44.5 |
| 13 Arthur W. Overmeyer (D) | 26,882 | 54.4 |
| Franklin P. Riegle (R) | 21,523 | 43.6 |
| 14 Ellsworth R. Bathrick (D) | 32,301 | 53.4 |
| S. H. Williams (R) | 26,010 | 43.0 |
| 15 George White (D) | 23,221 | 48.8 |
| W. C. Mooney (R) | 22,934 | 48.2 |
| 16 Roscoe C. McCulloch (R) | 31,945 | 56.2 |
| John J. Whitacre (D) | 24,948 | 43.9 |
| 17 William A. Ashbrook (D) | 31,749 | 56.2 |
| E. Lee Porterfield (R) | 23,705 | 42.0 |
| 18 David A. Hollingsworth (R) | 26,991 | 49.8 |
| William B. Francis (D) | 24,538 | 45.3 |
| 19 John G. Cooper (R) | 26,983 | 55.3 |
| William S. King (D) | 21,828 | 44.7 |
| 20 William Gordon (D) | 26,950 | 58.2 |
| Eugene Quigley (R) | 17,235 | 37.2 |
| 21 Robert Crosser (D) | 22,263 | 65.0 |
| R. S. Taylor (R) | 10,138 | 29.6 |
| Moses Benjamin (SOC) | 1,845 | 5.4 |
| 22 Henry I. Emerson (R) | 29,270 | 55.4 |
| Stephen M. Young (D) | 23,611 | 44.7 |

## OKLAHOMA

| Candidates | Votes | % |
|---|---|---|
| 1 Thomas A. Chandler (R) | 18,218 | 45.6 |
| James S. Davenport (D) | 17,949 | 44.9 |
| Reese (SOC) | 3,671 | 9.2 |
| 2 William W. Hastings (D) | 15,158 | 52.5 |
| Henry Ward (R) | 10,224 | 35.4 |
| J.A.Lewis (SOC) | 3,511 | 12.2 |
| 3 Charles D. Carter (D) | 21,182 | 55.1 |
| Gratton C. McVay (R) | 10,386 | 27.0 |
| H.M.Shelton (SOC) | 6,862 | 17.9 |
| 4 Thomas D. McKeown (D) | 19,076 | 48.3 |
| James E. Gresham (R) | 12,399 | 31.4 |
| Allen C. Adams (SOC) | 8,026 | 20.3 |
| 5 Joseph B. Thompson (D) | 17,828 | 49.5 |
| George H. Dodson (R) | 12,716 | 35.3 |
| Robert L. Allen (SOC) | 5,294 | 14.7 |
| 6 Scott Ferris (D) | 18,212 | 50.8 |
| H.H.Hinkle (R) | 10,930 | 30.5 |
| O.M.Morris (SOC) | 6,727 | 18.8 |
| 7 James V. McClintic (D) | 17,810 | 53.8 |
| H.H. Stallard (SOC) | 8,140 | 24.6 |
| T.W. Jones Jr. (R) | 7,030 | 21.2 |
| 8 Dick T. Morgan (R) | 16,691 | 45.1 |
| Z.A. Harris (D) | 14,816 | 40.0 |
| Joseph Otii (SOC) | 5,158 | 13.9 |

## OREGON

| Candidates | Votes | % |
|---|---|---|
| 1 Willis C. Hawley (R & PROG) | 60,530 | 56.6 |
| Mark V. Weatherford (D & P) | 39,101 | 36.6 |
| W. S. Richards (SOC) | 7,243 | 6.8 |

| Candidates | Votes | % |
|---|---|---|
| 2 Nicholas J. Sinnott (R-D-PROG) | 36,059 | 84.6 |
| James Hickman Barkley (SOC) | 6,028 | 14.1 |
| 3 Clifton N. McArthur (R) | 35,832 | 47.6 |
| A. W. Lafferty (I PROG) | 27,649 | 36.7 |
| John A. Jeffrey (D) | 9,824 | 13.0 |

## PENNSYLVANIA

| Candidates | Votes | % |
|---|---|---|
| 1 William S. Vare (R) | 33,330 | 71.7 |
| Lawrence E. McCrossin (D) | 12,243 | 26.3 |
| 2 George S. Graham (R, WASH) | 23,921 | 76.0 |
| Thomas E. Shea (D) | 7,117 | 22.6 |
| 3 J. Hampton Moore (R, KEY) | 23,753 | 73.6 |
| Joseph Hagerty (D) | 7,611 | 23.6 |
| 4 George W. Edmonds (R, WASH) | 26,122 | 68.2 |
| Patrick H. Lynch (D) | 11,101 | 29.0 |
| 5 Peter E. Costello (R, PERS LIB) | 29,689 | 59.3 |
| Michael Donohoe (D, KEY) | 17,074 | 34.1 |
| 6 George P. Darrow (R, WASH) | 56,207 | 67.6 |
| J. Washington Logue (D, KEY) | 25,665 | 30.9 |
| 7 Thomas S. Butler (R) | 27,879 | 63.0 |
| Edward B. Cassatt (D, WASH) | 15,102 | 34.1 |
| 8 Henry Winfield Watson (R) | 28,852 | 57.0 |
| Joseph Heacock (D) | 20,232 | 40.0 |
| 9 William W. Griest (R) | 20,058 | 64.2 |
| Henry F. Myers (D) | 9,506 | 30.4 |
| 10 John R. Farr (R, B MOOSE) | 17,823 | 53.1 |
| Victor Burschel (D) | 14,694 | 43.7 |
| 11 T. W. Templeton (R) | 24,123 | 53.2 |
| John J. Casey (D, KEY) | 19,185 | 42.3 |
| 12 Robert D. Heaton (R, WASH) | 19,172 | 61.1 |
| Robert E. Lee (D) | 11,340 | 36.1 |
| 13 Arthur G. Dewalt (D) | 28,296 | 49.9 |
| Horace W. Schantz (R, WASH) | 23,412 | 41.3 |
| Elwood W. Leffler (SOC) | 4,507 | 7.9 |
| 14 Louis T. McFadden (R) | 13,638 | 55.6 |
| John D. Brennan (D) | 8,881 | 36.2 |
| William S. H. Heermans (P) | 1,279 | 5.2 |
| 15 Edgar R. Kiess (R, P) | 18,478 | 59.5 |
| Chester H. Ashton (D) | 10,766 | 34.7 |
| P. A. McGowan (SOC) | 1,789 | 5.8 |
| 16 John V. Lesher (D) | 16,490 | 51.8 |
| I. Clinton Kline (R, P) | 14,154 | 44.5 |
| 17 Benjamin K. Focht (R, P) | 18,673 | 50.4 |
| George A. Harris (D) | 17,420 | 47.0 |
| 18 Aaron S. Kreider (R) | 24,630 | 51.6 |
| Harry B. Saussaman (D) | 20,343 | 42.7 |
| 19 John M. Rose (R) | 22,652 | 50.4 |
| Warren Worth Bailey (D, UN) | 21,007 | 46.8 |
| 20 Andrew R. Brodbeck (D) | 18,490 | 50.2 |
| Samuel K. McCall (R, WASH) | 16,327 | 44.3 |
| 21 Charles H. Rowland (R) | 14,150 | 47.6 |
| William E. Tobias (D, P) | 13,938 | 46.9 |
| George Fox (SOC) | 1,605 | 5.4 |
| 22 Edward E. Robbins (R, WASH) | 19,978 | 48.4 |
| Silas A. Kline (D) | 16,165 | 39.2 |
| Charles Cunningham (SOC) | 2,945 | 7.1 |
| R. S. Irwin (P) | 2,153 | 5.2 |
| 23 Bruce F. Sterling (D) | 17,348 | 48.2 |
| Robert F. Hopwood (R, WASH) | 16,453 | 45.7 |
| 24 Henry W. Temple (R, WASH) | 22,839 | 54.3 |
| William J. Mellon (D) | 14,679 | 34.9 |
| W. K. Ramsey (SOC) | 2,839 | 6.8 |
| 25 Henry A. Clark (R) | 13,441 | 43.1 |
| Charles N. Crosby (D) | 13,068 | 41.9 |

## PENNSYLVANIA

| Candidates | Votes | % |
|---|---|---|
| William W. Kincaid (P, WASH) | 3,038 | 9.7 |
| Ralph W. Tillotson (SOC) | 1,612 | 5.2 |
| 26 Henry J. Steele (D, SOC) | 18,374 | 53.5 |
| Winfred D. Lewis (R, WASH) | 14,857 | 43.2 |
| 27 Nathan L. Strong (R, WASH) | 17,702 | 55.9 |
| Harry C. Golden (D) | 10,751 | 34.0 |
| John B. Desantis (P) | 1,793 | 5.7 |
| 28 Orrin D. Bleakley (R) | 16,514 | 47.9 |
| E. H. Beshlin (D) | 12,406 | 36.0 |
| A. R. Rich (P) | 3,470 | 10.1 |
| William E. Ashe (SOC) | 2,102 | 6.1 |
| 29 Stephen Geyer Porter (R, WASH) | 21,123 | 67.8 |
| A. M. Thompson (D) | 7,518 | 24.1 |
| Karl C. Jursek (SOC) | 1,869 | 6.0 |
| 30 M. Clyde Kelly (D, P) | 18,637 | 47.6 |
| William H. Coleman (R, B MOOSE) | 18,386 | 46.9 |
| William Adams (SOC) | 2,147 | 5.5 |
| 31 John M. Morin (R, D) | 20,497 | 87.2 |
| F. C. Brittain (P) | 1,504 | 6.4 |
| James Devlin (SOC) | 1,504 | 6.4 |
| 32 Guy E. Campbell (D, B MOOSE) | 17,134 | 45.8 |
| Andrew J. Barcheld (R) | 17,088 | 45.7 |
| William W. Nooning (SOC) | 2,422 | 6.5 |
| AL Thomas S. Crago (R, RO PROG) | 668,581✔ | |
| John R. K. Scott (R, RO PROG) | 661,930✔ | |
| Mahlon M. Garland (R, PERS LIB) | 654,945✔ | |
| Joseph McLaughlin (R) | 605,657✔ | |
| Thomas Ross (D) | 471,308 | |
| John J. Moore (D) | 439,881 | |
| Joseph T. Kinsley (D) | 439,846 | |
| Jacob B. Waidelich (D) | 427,923 | |
| William A. Prosser (SOC) | 46,896 | |
| Elizabeth N. Baer (SOC) | 45,441 | |
| John W. Slayton (SOC) | 45,330 | |
| Fred Willard Whiteside (SOC) | 43,314 | |
| Fred Groff (P) | 29,937 | |
| Frank L. Morton (P) | 26,483 | |
| B. C. McGrew (P) | 26,116 | |
| J. C. Rummel (P) | 24,952 | |
| Robert C. Bair (WASH) | 24,529 | |
| Arthur G. Graham (WASH) | 24,219 | |
| J. C. Buchanan (KEY) | 3,703 | |
| Michael Donohoe (KEY) | 3,517 | |
| M. J. Lewis (KEY) | 3,382 | |
| Robert C. Bair (B MOOSE) | 3,356 | |
| Arthur G. Graham (B MOOSE) | 3,245 | |
| Oliver Knight (SINGLE T) | 931 | |
| Royd E. Morrison (SINGLE T) | 833 | |
| Jerome C. Reis (SINGLE T) | 769 | |
| Alfred Guerrero (SINGLE T) | 729 | |
| Richard Love (INDL) | 616 | |
| B. H. Brenner (INDL) | 591 | |
| H. G. Meinel (INDL) | 458 | |
| G. W. Ohls (INDL) | 455 | |

## RHODE ISLAND

| Candidates | Votes | % |
|---|---|---|
| 1 George F. O'Shaunessy (D) | 15,996 | 53.9 |
| Dixon (R) | 13,099 | 44.2 |
| 2 Walter R. Stiness (R) | 15,784 | 54.9 |
| Mowry (D) | 12,207 | 42.5 |
| 3 Ambrose Kennedy (R) | 14,376 | 50.4 |
| McDonald (D) | 13,427 | 47.1 |

## SOUTH CAROLINA

| Candidates | Votes | % |
|---|---|---|
| 1 Richard S. Whaley (D) | 4,999 | 95.4 |
| 2 James F. Byrnes (D) | 7,681 | 98.5 |
| 3 Fred H. Dominick (D) | 9,447 | 100.0 |
| 4 Samuel J. Nichols (D) | 11,312 | 99.4 |
| 5 David E. Finley (D) | 8,846* | 100.0 |
| 6 J. Willard Ragsdale (D) | 9,767 | 99.1 |
| 7 Asbury F. Lever (D) | 9,817 | 93.5 |
| I. S. Leevy (R) | 683 | 6.5 |

## SOUTH DAKOTA

| Candidates | Votes | % |
|---|---|---|
| 1 Charles H. Dillon (R) | 28,674 | 58.1 |
| Anderson (D) | 19,846 | 40.2 |
| 2 Royal C. Johnson (R) | 28,366 | 60.2 |
| Batterton (D) | 16,342 | 34.7 |
| 3 Harry L. Gandy (D) | 16,581 | 55.6 |
| Bartine (R) | 12,203 | 41.0 |

## TENNESSEE

| Candidates | Votes | % |
|---|---|---|
| 1 Sam R. Sells (R) | 23,651 | 96.9 |
| 2 Richard W. Austin (R) | 19,835 | 90.0 |
| Fitsgerald (D) | 1,195 | 5.4 |
| 3 John A. Moon (D) | 19,018 | 53.9 |
| Jessie M. Littleton (R) | 16,004 | 45.3 |
| 4 Cordell Hull (D) | 17,170 | 60.2 |
| J. F. Benson (R) | 11,287 | 39.6 |
| 5 William C. Houston (D) | 14,656 | 86.5 |
| Sid Houston (R) | 2,287 | 13.5 |
| 6 Joseph W. Byrns (D) | 17,190 | 83.7 |
| C. E. Tippens (R) | 2,919 | 14.2 |
| 7 Lemuel P. Padgett (D) | 15,313 | 63.0 |
| G. A. Yost (D) | 8,955 | 36.8 |
| 8 Thetus W. Sims (D) | 13,474 | 50.3 |
| L. M. Rhodes (R) | 13,255 | 49.5 |
| 9 Finis J. Garrett (D) | 17,826 | 75.4 |
| W. N. Beasley (R) | 5,817 | 24.6 |
| 10 Hubert F. Fisher (D) | 14,926 | 72.8 |
| W. Wilkerson (COLORED) | 2,677 | 13.1 |
| John W. Farley (R) | 2,089 | 10.2 |

## TEXAS

| Candidates | Votes | % |
|---|---|---|
| 1 Eugene Black (D) | 16,525 | 83.3 |
| David H. Morris (R) | 2,182 | 11.0 |
| J. C. Thompson (SOC) | 1,122 | 5.7 |
| 2 Martin Dies (D) | 16,956 | 86.1 |
| J. B. Truitt (SOC) | 1,462 | 7.4 |
| A. E. Sweatland (R) | 1,266 | 6.4 |
| 3 James Young (D) | 15,168 | 88.3 |
| J. L. Scoggin (SOC) | 2,014 | 11.7 |
| 4 Sam Rayburn (D) | 17,785 | 83.5 |
| G. J. Barlow (R) | 2,043 | 9.6 |
| W. J. Lennon (SOC) | 1,460 | 6.9 |
| 5 Hatton W. Sumners (D) | 24,949 | 88.2 |
| B. F. Crews (R) | 2,879 | 10.2 |
| 6 Rufus Hardy (D) | 12,046 | 95.3 |
| 7 Alexander W. Gregg (D) | 10,921 | 79.5 |
| Theo F. Heiger (R) | 1,541 | 11.2 |
| 8 J. H. Eagle (D) | 18,980 | 82.2 |
| Ira P. Jones (R) | 3,276 | 14.2 |
| 9 Joseph J. Mansfield (D) | 16,453 | 76.2 |
| C. M. Hughes (R) | 4,149 | 19.2 |
| 10 James P. Buchanan (D) | 15,634 | 86.7 |
| Robert A. Brooks (R) | 2,405 | 13.3 |
| 11 Tom Connally (D) | 14,695 | 87.7 |
| John L. Vaughn (R) | 1,443 | 8.6 |
| 12 James C. Wilson (D) | 20,175 | 85.7 |
| Henry Zweifel (R) | 1,843 | 7.8 |
| Leland G. Baker (SOC) | 1,517 | 6.5 |
| 13 Marion Jones (D) | 33,942 | 85.8 |
| J. L. Vannatto (R) | 3,125 | 7.9 |
| J. A. Pressly (SOC) | 2,489 | 6.3 |
| 14 James L. Slayden (D) | 22,435 | 79.4 |
| D. F. Johnson (R) | 5,815 | 20.6 |
| 15 John N. Garner (D) | 16,906 | 73.4 |
| H. M. Wingback (R) | 5,551 | 24.1 |
| 16 Thomas L. Blanton (D) | 30,650 | 85.2 |
| T. B. Holiday (SOC) | 2,826 | 7.9 |
| C. O. Harris (R) | 2,503 | 7.0 |

| Candidates | Votes | % |
|---|---|---|
| AL Atkins Jeff. McLemore (D) | 300,302✔ | |
| Daniel E. Garrett (D) | 298,966✔ | |
| Charles A. Warnken (R) | 46,914 | |
| M. A. Taylor (R) | 46,467 | |
| Arch Lingan (SOC) | 18,583 | |
| W. D. Simpson (SOC) | 18,192 | |
| I. E. Teague (P) | 1,525 | |
| E. G. Cook (P) | 1,457 | |

## UTAH

| Candidates | Votes | % |
|---|---|---|
| 1 Milton H. Welling (D, PROG) | 40,035 | 55.5 |
| Timothy C. Hoyt (R) | 29,902 | 41.5 |
| 2 James H. Mays (D, PROG) | 39,847 | 56.9 |
| Charles R. Mabey (R) | 27,778 | 39.7 |

## VERMONT

| Candidates | Votes | % |
|---|---|---|
| 1 Frank L. Greene (R) | 22,030 | 71.1 |
| Emmett B. Daley (D) | 7,972 | 25.7 |
| 2 Porter H. Dale (R, P) | 22,692 | 72.2 |
| G. Herbert Pape (D) | 7,983 | 25.4 |

## VIRGINIA

| Candidates | Votes | % |
|---|---|---|
| 1 William A. Jones (D) | 9,772 | 76.5 |
| William W. Butzner (R) | 2,823 | 22.1 |
| 2 Edward E. Holland (D) | 10,123 | 82.4 |
| Luther B. Way (R) | 1,939 | 15.8 |
| 3 Andrew Jackson Montague (D) | 10,967 | 93.6 |
| F. E. Maxey (SOC) | 751 | 6.4 |
| 4 Walter A. Watson (D) | 8,119 | 90.8 |
| 5 Edward W. Saunders (D) | 10,614 | 57.8 |
| Beverly A. Davis (R) | 7,601 | 41.4 |
| 6 Carter Glass (D) | 9,119 | 73.6 |
| George W. Wilson (R) | 2,920 | 23.6 |
| 7 Thomas W. Harrison (D) | 10,052 | 61.8 |
| John Paul (R) | 6,064 | 37.3 |
| 8 Charles C. Carlin (D) | 9,168 | 71.8 |
| Joseph L. Crupper (R) | 3,450 | 27.0 |
| 9 C. Bascom Slemp (R) | 17,848 | 51.9 |
| E. Lee Trinkle (D) | 16,430 | 47.8 |
| 10 Henry D. Flood (D) | 11,282 | 69.9 |
| C. P. Nair (R) | 4,583 | 28.4 |

### Special Election

| Candidates | Votes | % |
|---|---|---|
| 7 Thomas W. Harrison (D) | 9,918 | 61.3 |
| John Paul (R) | 6,110 | 37.8 |

## WASHINGTON

| Candidates | Votes | % |
|---|---|---|
| 1 John F. Miller (R) | 38,769 | 50.3 |
| George F. Cotterill (D) | 35,718 | 46.3 |
| 2 Lindley H. Hadley (R) | 31,655 | 47.1 |
| Frances C. Axtell (D) | 28,075 | 41.7 |
| R. J. Olinger (SOC) | 7,537 | 11.2 |
| 3 Albert Johnson (R) | 47,415 | 57.1 |
| George P. Fishburne (D) | 29,949 | 36.1 |
| W. F. Ferguson (SOC) | 5,662 | 6.8 |
| 4 William L. LaFollette (R) | 33,980 | 58.8 |
| Charles W. Masterson (D) | 21,189 | 36.7 |
| 5 Clarence C. Dill (D) | 37,479 | 51.5 |
| Tom Corkery (R) | 32,298 | 44.4 |

## WEST VIRGINIA

| Candidates | Votes | % |
|---|---|---|
| 1 Matthew M. Neely (D) | 22,138 | 50.7 |
| T. W. Fleming (R) | 21,574 | 49.4 |
| 2 George M. Bowers (R) | 24,055 | 50.9 |
| Samuel V. Woods (D) | 23,194 | 49.1 |
| 3 Stuart F. Reed (R) | 23,442 | 50.7 |
| Fleming N. Alderson (D) | 22,762 | 49.3 |
| 4 Harry C. Woodyard (R) | 23,139 | 50.3 |
| T. A. Null (D) | 22,855 | 49.7 |

## WEST VIRGINIA

| Candidates | Votes | % |
|---|---|---|
| 5 Edward Cooper (R) | 25,563 | 51.7 |
| G. R. C. Wiles (D) | 23,857 | 48.3 |
| 6 Adam B. Littlepage (D) | 25,963 | 51.5 |
| M. V. Godbey (R) | 24,415 | 48.5 |

## WISCONSIN

| Candidates | Votes | % |
|---|---|---|
| 1 Henry Allen Cooper (R) | 24,851 | 61.6 |
| Jay W. Page (D) | 12,587 | 31.2 |
| 2 Edward Voigt (R) | 20,718 | 51.3 |
| Michael E. Burke (D) | 18,546 | 45.9 |
| 3 John M. Nelson (R) | 26,785 | 61.8 |
| M. J. Briggs (D) | 15,198 | 35.1 |

| Candidates | Votes | % |
|---|---|---|
| 4 William J. Cary (R) | 12,361 | 35.5 |
| Winfield R. Gaylord (SOCIAL D) | 11,380 | 32.7 |
| Anthony Szczerbinski (D) | 10,757 | 30.9 |
| 5 William H. Stafford (R) | 19,585 | 45.4 |
| Victor L. Berger (SOCIAL D) | 15,936 | 36.9 |
| Lyman H. Browne (D) | 7,420 | 17.2 |
| 6 James H. Davidson (R) | 20,317 | 52.3 |
| Michael K. Reilly (D) | 17,080 | 44.0 |
| 7 John Jacob Esch (R) | 24,157 | 68.2 |
| Herman Grotophorst (D) | 9,549 | 27.0 |
| 8 Edward E. Browne (R) | 23,089 | 67.5 |
| John Kalmes (D) | 10,083 | 29.5 |

| Candidates | Votes | % |
|---|---|---|
| 9 David G. Classon (R) | 20,614 | 52.5 |
| Thomas F. Konop (D) | 18,078 | 46.0 |
| 10 James A. Frear (R) | 23,320 | 69.6 |
| Andrew J. Sutherland (D) | 9,367 | 28.0 |
| 11 Irvine L. Lenroot (R) | 22,740 | 67.4 |
| George C. Cooper (D) | 8,726 | 25.9 |
| Henry M. Parks (SOCIAL D) | 2,252 | 6.7 |

## WYOMING

| Candidates | Votes | % |
|---|---|---|
| AL Frank W. Mondell (R) | 24,693 | 49.0 |
| John D. Clark (D) | 24,156 | 48.0 |

# 1917 House Election

## PENNSYLVANIA

### Special Election

| | Votes | % |
|---|---|---|
| 28 Earl H. Beshlin (D, P) | 12,878 | 47.6 |
| U. G. Lyons (R) | 11,100 | 41.0 |
| Willis J. Hulings (WASH) | 1,622 | 6.0 |
| Richard Crawshaw (SOC) | 1,452 | 5.4 |

---

# House Candidates Index

For an index of all House candidates listed in this section (pages 943-1326), see pages 1402-1501. Instructions for use of the House Candidates Index appear on page 1402.

---

# 1918 House Elections

## ALABAMA

| Candidates | Votes | % |
|---|---|---|
| 1 John McDuffie (D) | 3,721 | 100.0 |
| 2 S. Hubert Dent Jr. (D) | 5,717 | 100.0 |
| 3 Henry B. Steagall (D) | 5,868 | 100.0 |
| 4 Fred L. Blackmon (D) | 4,266 | 66.2 |
| J. A. Bingham (R) | 2,183 | 33.9 |
| 5 J. Thomas Heflin (D) | 6,254 | 100.0 |
| 6 William B. Oliver (D) | 2,741 | 100.0 |
| 7 John L. Burnett (D) | 7,221 | 56.2 |
| O. D. Street (R) | 5,622 | 43.8 |
| 8 Edward B. Almon (D) | 5,598 | 100.0 |
| 9 George Huddleston (D) | 6,338 | 85.8 |
| J. O. Thompson (R) | 1,051 | 14.2 |
| 10 William B. Bankhead (D) | 5,765 | 100.0 |

## ARIZONA

| Candidates | Votes | % |
|---|---|---|
| AL Carl Hayden (D) | 26,805 | 60.4 |
| Thomas Maddock (R) | 16,822 | 37.9 |

## ARKANSAS

| Candidates | Votes | % |
|---|---|---|
| 1 Thaddeus H. Caraway (D) | 10,343 | 100.0 |
| 2 William A. Oldfield (D) | 10,775 | 100.0 |
| 3 John N. Tillman (D) | 14,995 | 100.0 |
| 4 Otis Wingo (D) | 12,279 | 100.0 |
| 5 Henderson M. Jacoway (D) | 11,045 | 100.0 |
| 6 Samuel M. Taylor (D) | 10,444 | 100.0 |
| 7 William S. Goodwin (D) | 8,692 | 100.0 |

## CALIFORNIA

| Candidates | Votes | % |
|---|---|---|
| 1 Clarence F. Lea (DR) | 42,063 | 99.7 |
| 2 John E. Raker (DR SOC P) | 28,249 | 99.9 |
| 3 Charles F. Curry (R-D) | 51,690 | 91.6 |
| A. K. Gifford (SOC) | 4,746 | 8.4 |
| 4 Julius Kahn (R-D-PROG) | 38,278 | 86.6 |
| William Short (SOC) | 5,913 | 13.4 |
| 5 John I. Nolan (R-D) | 40,375 | 87.0 |
| Thomas F. Feeley (SOC) | 6,032 | 13.0 |
| 6 John A. Elston (R-D) | 59,082 | 88.4 |
| Luella Twining (SOC) | 7,721 | 11.6 |
| 7 Henry E. Barbour (R) | 33,476 | 52.1 |
| Henry Hawson (D) | 30,745 | 47.9 |
| 8 Hugh S. Hersman (D) | 31,167 | 53.0 |
| Everis A. Hayes (R) | 27,641 | 47.0 |
| 9 Charles H. Randall (P & D) | 38,782 | 53.0 |
| Montaville Flowers (R) | 31,689 | 43.3 |
| 10 Henry Z. Osborne (R-D-P) | 72,773 | 88.0 |
| James H. Ryckman (SOC) | 9,725 | 11.8 |
| 11 William Kettner (D R&SOC) | 45,915 | 72.2 |
| Stella B. Irvine (P) | 17,642 | 27.8 |

## COLORADO

| Candidates | Votes | % |
|---|---|---|
| 1 William N. Vaile (R) | 27,815 | 54.2 |
| Stack (D) | 16,364 | 31.9 |
| Hilliard (I) | 6,112 | 11.9 |
| 2 Charles B. Timberlake (R) | 41,562 | 61.5 |
| Jones (D) | 26,044 | 38.5 |
| 3 Guy U. Hardy (R) | 31,715 | 51.0 |
| Keating (D) | 29,075 | 46.7 |
| 4 Edward T. Taylor (D) | 22,423 | 65.7 |
| Logan (R) | 11,695 | 34.3 |

## CONNECTICUT

| Candidates | Votes | % |
|---|---|---|
| 1 Augustine Lonergan (D) | 21,169 | 53.5 |
| Quigley (R) | 16,868 | 42.6 |
| 2 Richard P. Freeman (R) | 16,251 | 53.1 |
| Fenton (D) | 13,467 | 44.0 |
| 3 John Q. Tilson (R) | 17,401 | 50.5 |
| O'Keefe (D) | 15,711 | 45.6 |
| 4 Schuyler Merritt (R) | 19,008 | 53.6 |
| Peck (D) | 15,386 | 43.4 |
| 5 James P. Glynn (R) | 13,455 | 50.1 |
| Seery (D) | 12,640 | 47.1 |

## DELAWARE

| Candidates | Votes | % |
|---|---|---|
| AL Caleb R. Layton (R) | 21,226 | 51.4 |
| Albert F. Polk (D) | 19,652 | 47.6 |

## FLORIDA

| Candidates | Votes | % |
|---|---|---|
| 1 Herbert J. Drane (D) | 8,446 | 100.0 |
| 2 Frank Clark (D) | 6,322 | 100.0 |
| 3 John H. Smithwick (D) | 6,644 | 100.0 |
| 4 William J. Sears (D) | 10,401 | 100.0 |

## GEORGIA

| Candidates | Votes | % |
|---|---|---|
| 1 James W. Overstreet (D) | 4,253 | 100.0 |
| 2 Frank Park (D) | 3,953 | 100.0 |
| 3 Charles R. Crisp (D) | 3,244 | 100.0 |
| 4 William C. Wright (D) | 4,991 | 100.0 |
| 5 William D. Upshaw (D) | 5,251 | 100.0 |
| 6 James W. Wise (D) | 4,707 | 100.0 |
| 7 Gordon Lee (D) | 5,960 | 82.5 |
| T. R. Glenn (R) | 1,261 | 17.5 |
| 8 Charles H. Brand (D) | 5,797 | 100.0 |
| 9 Thomas M. Bell (D) | 6,911 | 81.5 |
| John M. Johnson (R) | 1,570 | 18.5 |
| 10 Carl Vinson (D) | 3,440 | 100.0 |
| 11 William C. Lankford (D) | 4,959 | 100.0 |
| 12 William W. Larsen (D) | 3,808 | 100.0 |

## IDAHO

| Candidates | Votes | % |
|---|---|---|
| 1 Burton L. French (R) | 27,084 | 63.4 |
| L. I. Purcell (D) | 15,672 | 36.7 |
| 2 Addison T. Smith (R) | 32,274 | 63.2 |
| C. R. Jeppesen (D) | 18,827 | 36.8 |

## ILLINOIS

| Candidates | Votes | % |
|---|---|---|
| 1 Martin B. Madden (R) | 12,580 | 55.3 |
| George Mayer (D) | 9,776 | 43.0 |
| 2 James R. Mann (R) | 29,099 | 59.5 |
| Leo S. Lebosky (D) | 17,895 | 36.6 |
| 3 William W. Wilson (R) | 24,011 | 52.9 |
| Fred J. Crowley (D) | 19,372 | 42.7 |
| 4 John W. Rainey (D) | 15,514 | 94.6 |
| Carl G. Hoffman (SOC) | 886 | 5.4 |
| 5 Adolph J. Sabath (D) | 10,517 | 69.1 |
| Louis C. Mau (R) | 3,789 | 24.9 |
| Emil Jaeger (SOC) | 919 | 6.0 |
| 6 James McAndrews (D) | 32,638 | 55.9 |
| Hervey C. Foster (R) | 22,692 | 38.8 |
| William F. Kruse (SOC) | 3,101 | 5.3 |
| 7 Niels Juul (R) | 35,428 | 51.3 |
| Frank M. Padden (D) | 26,261 | 38.0 |
| J. Louis Engdahl (SOC) | 7,387 | 10.7 |
| 8 Thomas Gallagher (D) | 11,472 | 78.2 |
| Dan Parrillo (R) | 3,201 | 21.8 |
| 9 Fred A. Britten (R) | 12,654 | 53.0 |
| James H. Poage (D) | 10,074 | 42.2 |
| 10 Carl R. Chindblom (R) | 33,097 | 62.1 |
| Philip J. Finnegan (D) | 16,933 | 31.8 |
| Irving St. John Tucker (SOC) | 3,284 | 6.2 |
| 11 Ira C. Copley (R) | 25,744 | 92.9 |
| Carl F. Schutz (SOC) | 1,954 | 7.1 |
| 12 Charles E. Fuller (R) | 25,623 | 93.1 |
| Oscar Ogren (SOC) | 1,895 | 6.9 |
| 13 John C. McKenzie (R) | 20,861 | 96.2 |
| 14 William J. Graham (R) | 20,635 | 90.6 |
| Edmond B. Passmore (SOC) | 1,791 | 7.9 |
| 15 Edward J. King (R) | 21,334 | 60.2 |
| Edward P. Allen (D) | 13,148 | 37.1 |
| 16 Clifford Ireland (R) | 20,617 | 57.3 |
| Leander O. Eagleton (D) | 14,759 | 41.0 |
| 17 Frank L. Smith (R) | 19,123 | 69.7 |
| C. S. Schneider (D) | 8,321 | 30.3 |
| 18 Joseph G. Cannon (R) | 22,427 | 60.3 |
| Frank M. Crangle (D) | 14,402 | 38.7 |
| 19 William B. McKinley (R) | 26,259 | 60.8 |
| Thomas B. Jack (D) | 16,474 | 38.1 |
| 20 Henry T. Rainey (D) | 17,355 | 55.0 |
| Frank E. Blane (R) | 14,184 | 45.0 |
| 21 Loren E. Wheeler (R) | 20,380 | 50.4 |
| James M. Graham (D) | 19,064 | 47.2 |
| 22 William A. Rodenberg (R) | 21,925 | 51.3 |
| J. Nick Perrin (D) | 18,592 | 43.5 |
| Marshal E. Kirkpatrick (SOC) | 2,240 | 5.2 |
| 23 Edwin B. Brooks (R) | 20,619 | 49.9 |
| Martin D. Foster (D) | 19,397 | 46.9 |
| 24 Thomas S. Williams (R) | 18,689 | 59.4 |
| James R. Campbell (D) | 12,412 | 39.4 |
| 25 Edward E. Denison (R) | 22,886 | 60.4 |
| D. T. Woodard (D) | 15,000 | 39.6 |
| AL Richard Yates (R) | 501,974✓ | |
| William E. Mason (R) | 479,533✓ | |
| William Elza Williams (D) | 361,505 | |
| Michael H. Cleary (D) | 356,168 | |
| Clarence C. Brooks (SOC) | 33,835 | |
| Frank Watts (SOC) | 32,065 | |
| Edward E. Blake (P) | 3,189 | |
| Charles P. Corson (P) | 3,110 | |
| William Hartness (SOC LAB) | 2,956 | |
| Joseph Hamrle (SOC LAB) | 2,790 | |

### Special Election

| Candidates | Votes | % |
|---|---|---|
| 4 John W. Rainey (D) | 13,094 | 65.5 |
| O. W. Christopher (R) | 4,366 | 21.8 |
| Kasimer P. Gugis (SOC) | 2,530 | 12.7 |

## INDIANA

| Candidates | Votes | % |
|---|---|---|
| 1 Oscar R. Luhring (R) | 20,440 | 52.0 |
| George K. Denton (D) | 18,837 | 48.0 |
| 2 Oscar E. Bland (R) | 23,943 | 53.6 |
| Fred F. Bays (D) | 19,731 | 44.2 |
| 3 James W. Dunbar (R) | 20,556 | 50.3 |
| William E. Cox (D) | 19,989 | 48.9 |
| 4 John S. Benham (R) | 20,745 | 50.4 |
| Lincoln Dixon (D) | 20,428 | 49.6 |
| 5 Everett Sanders (R) | 20,271 | 50.5 |
| Ralph W. Moss (D) | 19,213 | 47.9 |
| 6 Richard N. Elliott (R) | 21,266 | 54.2 |
| Harry G. Strickland (D) | 17,755 | 45.3 |
| 7 Merrill Moores (R) | 29,714 | 58.3 |
| Chalmer Schlosser (D) | 20,284 | 39.8 |
| 8 Albert H. Vestal (R) | 24,124 | 53.5 |
| William H. Eichorn (D) | 19,421 | 43.1 |
| 9 Fred S. Purnell (R) | 25,486 | 55.9 |
| Charles F. Howard (D) | 18,948 | 41.6 |
| 10 William R. Wood (R) | 26,384 | 61.4 |
| George R. Kirschman (D) | 16,064 | 37.4 |
| 11 Milton W. Krauss (R) | 24,358 | 54.0 |
| George W. Rauch (D) | 19,849 | 44.0 |
| 12 Louis W. Fairfield (R) | 22,251 | 54.7 |
| Harry H. Hilgeman (D) | 17,538 | 43.1 |
| 13 Andrew J. Hickey (R) | 27,269 | 52.8 |
| Henry A. Barnhart (D) | 23,274 | 45.1 |

## IOWA

| Candidates | Votes | % |
|---|---|---|
| 1 Charles A. Kennedy (R) | 15,921 | 60.6 |
| Edward L. Hirsch (D) | 10,358 | 39.4 |

## IOWA

| Candidates | Votes | % |
|---|---|---|
| 2 Harry E. Hull (R) | 19,958 | 54.7 |
| Nathan D. Ely (D) | 14,395 | 39.5 |
| William E. McIntosh (SOC) | 2,140 | 5.9 |
| 3 Burton E. Sweet (R) | 22,997 | 64.7 |
| Harry B. Clark (D) | 12,527 | 35.3 |
| 4 Gilbert N. Haugen (R) | 20,643 | 64.7 |
| Joseph C. Campbell (D) | 11,283 | 35.3 |
| 5 James W. Good (R) | 20,655 | 65.1 |
| Sherman W. Dewolf (D) | 11,078 | 34.9 |
| 6 C. William Ramseyer (R) | 17,082 | 56.1 |
| Buell McCash (D) | 12,988 | 42.6 |
| 7 Cassius C. Dowell (R) | 18,182 | 66.8 |
| H. C. Evans (D) | 8,493 | 31.2 |
| 8 Horace M. Towner (R) | 20,409 | 64.5 |
| D. Fulton Rice (D) | 11,258 | 35.6 |
| 9 William R. Green (R) | 22,234 | 99.8 |
| 10 Lester J. Dickinson (R) | 23,635 | 64.3 |
| J. R. Files (D) | 13,153 | 35.8 |
| 11 William D. Boies (R) | 21,665 | 56.4 |
| Thomas J. Steele (D) | 16,461 | 42.8 |

## KANSAS

| Candidates | Votes | % |
|---|---|---|
| 1 Daniel R. Anthony Jr. (R) | 33,720 | 65.0 |
| Frank E. Whitney (D) | 17,100 | 33.0 |
| 2 Edward C. Little (R) | 32,653 | 57.2 |
| Henderson S. Martin (D) | 23,262 | 40.8 |
| 3 Phillip P. Campbell (R) | 32,837 | 54.8 |
| C. E. Pile (D) | 22,849 | 38.1 |
| 4 Homer Hoch (R) | 26,880 | 58.8 |
| Dudley Doolittle (D) | 17,787 | 38.9 |
| 5 James G. Strong (R) | 29,703 | 60.8 |
| Guy T. Helvering (D) | 18,112 | 37.1 |
| 6 Hays B. White (R) | 30,427 | 55.4 |
| John R. Connelly (D) | 22,898 | 41.7 |
| 7 Jasper N. Tincher (R) | 37,875 | 56.2 |
| Jouett Shouse (D) | 27,722 | 41.1 |
| 8 William A. Ayres (D) | 22,167 | 51.2 |
| Charles C. Mack (R) | 20,279 | 46.9 |

## KENTUCKY

| Candidates | Votes | % |
|---|---|---|
| 1 Alben W. Barkley (D) | 19,998 | 66.8 |
| W. G. Howard (R) | 9,947 | 33.2 |
| 2 David H. Kincheloe (D) | 18,749 | 57.7 |
| Ben T. Robinson (R) | 13,740 | 42.3 |
| 3 Robert Y. Thomas Jr. (D) | 18,032 | 52.3 |
| Bishop S. Huntsman (R) | 16,443 | 47.7 |
| 4 Ben Johnson (D) | 18,834 | 52.5 |
| John P. Haswell Jr. (R) | 17,075 | 47.6 |
| 5 Charles F. Ogden (R) | 21,788 | 51.3 |
| J. Swager Sherley (D) | 20,703 | 48.7 |
| 6 Arthur B. Rouse (D) | 19,039 | 68.3 |
| Virgil Weaver (R) | 8,842 | 31.7 |
| 7 James C. Cantrill (D) | 19,612 | 60.9 |
| A. B. Hammond (R) | 12,590 | 39.1 |
| 8 Harvey Helm (D) | 15,270* | 52.8 |
| Robert L. Davidson (R) | 13,673 | 47.2 |
| 9 William J. Fields (D) | 21,810 | 54.6 |
| Trumbo Sindegas (R) | 18,106 | 45.4 |
| 10 John W. Langley (R) | 13,284 | 67.1 |
| David Hays (D) | 6,511 | 32.9 |
| 11 John M. Robison (R) | 24,730 | 76.4 |
| Nat W. Elliott (D) | 7,656 | 23.6 |

## LOUISIANA

| Candidates | Votes | % |
|---|---|---|
| 1 Albert Estopinal (D) | 11,060 | 100.0 |
| 2 H. Garland Dupre (D) | 10,391 | 100.0 |
| 3 Whitmell P. Martin (D) | 2,888 | 100.0 |
| 4 John T. Watkins (D) | 5,299 | 100.0 |
| 5 Riley J. Wilson (D) | 3,831 | 100.0 |
| 6 Jared Y. Sanders (D) | 3,659 | 100.0 |
| 7 Ladislas Lazaro (D) | 3,584 | 100.0 |
| 8 James B. Aswell (D) | 4,082 | 100.0 |

## MAINE

| Candidates | Votes | % |
|---|---|---|
| 1 Louis B. Goodall (R) | 15,565 | 53.8 |
| L. B. Swett (D) | 13,388 | 46.2 |
| 2 Wallace H. White Jr. (R) | 17,928 | 54.2 |
| D. J. McGillicuddy (D) | 15,144 | 45.8 |
| 3 John A. Peters (R) | 20,293 | 57.6 |
| Chase (D) | 14,930 | 42.4 |
| 4 Ira G. Hersey (R) | 14,275 | 58.1 |
| L. G. C. Brown (D) | 10,313 | 41.9 |

## MARYLAND

| Candidates | Votes | % |
|---|---|---|
| 1 William N. Andrews (R) | 14,199 | 50.5 |
| Jesse D. Price (D) | 13,913 | 49.5 |
| 2 Carville D. Benson (D) | 17,985 | 54.3 |
| Charles J. Hull (R) | 14,758 | 44.6 |
| 3 Charles P. Coady (D) | 12,422 | 58.4 |
| Charles A. Jording (R) | 8,244 | 38.8 |
| 4 J. Charles Linthicum (D) | 14,689 | 57.0 |
| Walter E. Knickman (R) | 10,718 | 41.6 |
| 5 Sydney E. Mudd (R) | 13,266 | 53.7 |
| Frank M. Duvall (D) | 10,987 | 44.5 |
| 6 Frederick H. Zihlman (R) | 14,872 | 54.9 |
| Henry Dorsey Etchison (D) | 11,489 | 42.4 |

### Special Election

| Candidates | Votes | % |
|---|---|---|
| 2 Carville D. Benson (D) | 17,748 | 54.7 |
| Herbert R. Wooden (R) | 14,674 | 45.3 |

## MASSACHUSETTS

| Candidates | Votes | % |
|---|---|---|
| 1 Allen T. Treadway (R) | 15,933 | 58.3 |
| Thomas F. Cassidy (D) | 11,394 | 41.7 |
| 2 Frederick H. Gillett (R) | 20,277 | 99.9 |
| 3 Calvin D. Paige (R) | 15,267 | 60.5 |
| Eaton D. Sargent (D) | 9,982 | 39.5 |
| 4 Samuel E. Winslow (R) | 14,141 | 52.5 |
| John F. McGrath (D) | 12,792 | 47.5 |
| 5 John Jacob Rogers (R) | 20,496 | 99.2 |
| 6 Willfred W. Lufkin (R) | 21,147 | 88.9 |
| Estus E. Eames (SOC) | 2,648 | 11.1 |
| 7 Michael F. Phelan (D) | 14,437 | 57.3 |
| Charles Cabot Johnson (R) | 10,754 | 42.7 |
| 8 Frederick W. Dallinger (R) | 16,858 | 60.3 |
| James F. Aylward (D) | 11,093 | 39.7 |
| 9 Alvan T. Fuller (R) | 17,597 | 68.7 |
| Henry C. Rowland (D) | 8,022 | 31.3 |
| 10 John F. Fitzgerald (D) | 7,241‡ | 47.3 |
| Peter F. Tague (I) | 7,003 | 45.7 |
| Hammond T. Fletcher (R) | 1,071 | 7.0 |
| 11 George Holden Tinkham (R) | 13,644 | 56.4 |
| Francis J. Horgan (D) | 10,529 | 43.6 |
| 12 James A. Gallivan (D) | 18,349 | 70.4 |
| Harrison H. Atwood (R) | 7,709 | 29.6 |
| 13 Robert Luce (R) | 18,257 | 59.3 |
| Aloysius J. Doon (D) | 12,538 | 40.7 |
| 14 Richard Olney (D) | 18,009 | 56.6 |
| Louis F. R. Langelier (R) | 13,832 | 43.4 |
| 15 William S. Greene (R) | 12,952 | 61.7 |
| Arthur J. B. Cartier (D) | 8,031 | 38.3 |
| 16 Joseph Walsh (R) | 13,874 | 62.4 |
| Frederic Tudor (D) | 8,357 | 37.6 |

## MICHIGAN

| Candidates | Votes | % |
|---|---|---|
| 1 Frank E. Doremus (D) | 22,549 | 60.4 |
| James W. Hanley (R) | 14,063 | 37.6 |
| 2 Earl C. Michener (R) | 20,831 | 55.7 |
| Samuel W. Beakes (D) | 16,276 | 43.5 |
| 3 John M. C. Smith (R) | 20,385 | 61.8 |
| Howard W. Cavanagh (D) | 12,119 | 36.8 |
| 4 Edward L. Hamilton (R) | 20,904 | 65.9 |
| James O'Hara (D) | 10,842 | 34.2 |
| 5 Carl E. Mapes (R) | 22,917 | 66.8 |
| Peter J. Danhof (D) | 10,783 | 31.5 |
| 6 Patrick H. Kelley (R) | 29,183 | 97.3 |
| 7 Louis C. Cramton (R) | 20,573 | 73.3 |
| John W. Scully (D) | 7,155 | 25.5 |
| 8 Joseph W. Fordney (R) | 22,240 | 62.8 |
| Miles J. Purcell (D) | 13,153 | 37.2 |
| 9 James C. McLaughlin (R) | 17,624 | 66.4 |
| Charles M. Black (D) | 8,317 | 31.3 |
| 10 Gilbert A. Currie (R) | 18,409 | 68.0 |
| Henry C. Haller (D) | 8,312 | 30.7 |
| 11 Frank D. Scott (R) | 16,365 | 66.7 |
| Michael J. Doyle (D) | 8,183 | 33.3 |
| 12 W. Frank James (R) | 17,315 | 69.8 |
| Albert S. Ley (D) | 6,681 | 26.9 |
| 13 Charles A. Nichols (R) | 24,525 | 66.9 |
| Louis W. McClear (D) | 11,617 | 31.7 |

## MINNESOTA

| Candidates | Votes | % |
|---|---|---|
| 1 Sydney Anderson (R) | 29,337 | 100.0 |
| 2 Franklin F. Ellsworth (R) | 24,888 | 69.0 |
| Simon (D) | 11,161 | 31.0 |
| 3 Charles R. Davis (R) | 20,092 | 53.4 |
| Farrell (D) | 17,530 | 46.6 |
| 4 Carl C. Van Dyke (D) | 18,736 | 62.0 |
| Mallory (R) | 11,498 | 38.0 |
| 5 Walter H. Newton (R) | 21,607 | 57.6 |
| Robertson (D) | 15,912 | 42.4 |
| 6 Harold Knutson (R) | 22,633 | 72.3 |
| Russell (D) | 8,660 | 27.7 |
| 7 Andrew J. Volstead (R) | 21,406 | 56.3 |
| Lobeck (N) | 16,587 | 43.7 |
| 8 William L. Carss (UN LAB) | 17,266 | 57.1 |
| Miller (D) | 12,964 | 42.9 |
| 9 Halvor Steenerson (R) | 26,303 | 100.0 |
| 10 Thomas D. Schall (R) | 25,866 | 71.1 |
| Finlayson (D) | 10,534 | 28.9 |

## MISSISSIPPI

| Candidates | Votes | % |
|---|---|---|
| 1 Ezekiel S. Candler Jr. (D) | 4,240 | 100.0 |
| 2 Hubert D. Stephens (D) | 4,270 | 100.0 |
| 3 Benjamin G. Humphreys (D) | 2,339 | 100.0 |
| 4 Thomas U. Sisson (D) | 4,135 | 96.3 |
| 5 William W. Venable (D) | 6,174 | 100.0 |
| 6 Paul B. Johnson (D) | 4,972 | 94.3 |
| F. T. Maxwell (SOC) | 303 | 5.7 |
| 7 Percy E. Quin (D) | 3,093 | 93.4 |
| J. B. Sternberger (SOC) | 220 | 6.6 |
| 8 James W. Collier (D) | 2,376 | 98.8 |

## MISSOURI

| Candidates | Votes | % |
|---|---|---|
| 1 Milton A. Romjue (D) | 17,184 | 54.2 |
| Frank C. Millspaugh (R) | 14,255 | 45.0 |
| 2 William W. Rucker (D) | 19,769 | 98.7 |
| 3 Joshua W. Alexander (D) | 15,910 | 52.9 |
| Frost (R) | 14,117 | 46.9 |
| 4 Charles F. Booher (D) | 15,707 | 51.7 |
| McNeeley (R) | 14,597 | 48.0 |
| 5 William T. Bland (D) | 31,561 | 62.7 |
| Reeves (R) | 18,540 | 36.8 |
| 6 Clement C. Dickinson (D) | 14,898 | 52.7 |
| Atkeson (R) | 13,188 | 46.7 |
| 7 Samuel C. Major (D) | 20,300 | 49.8 |
| Salts (R) | 20,222 | 49.6 |
| 8 William L. Nelson (D) | 13,326 | 50.4 |
| Gentry (R) | 13,133 | 49.6 |
| 9 James Beauchamp Clark (D) | 18,248 | 51.7 |
| Dyer (R) | 16,719 | 47.4 |
| 10 Cleveland A. Newton (R) | 50,390 | 60.2 |
| Read (D) | 30,080 | 35.9 |
| 11 William L. Igoe (D) | 16,229 | 96.8 |
| 12 Leonidas C. Dyer (R) | 12,612 | 58.9 |
| Rosenfeld (D) | 8,538 | 39.9 |
| 13 Marion E. Rhodes (R) | 14,776 | 51.4 |
| Brewster (D) | 13,773 | 47.9 |
| 14 Edward D. Hayes (D) | 21,472 | 50.5 |
| Russell (D) | 21,001 | 49.4 |
| 15 Isaac V. McPherson (R) | 19,133 | 51.0 |

## MISSOURI

| Candidates | Votes | % |
|---|---|---|
| Decker (D) | 17,826 | 47.5 |
| 16 Thomas L. Rubey (D) | 13,490 | 49.9 |
| Shelton (R) | 13,320 | 49.2 |

### Special Election

| | Votes | % |
|---|---|---|
| 10 Frederick Essen (R) | 49,416 | 59.6 |
| Read (D) | 30,536 | 36.8 |

## MONTANA

| | Votes | % |
|---|---|---|
| 1 John M. Evans (D) | 25,530 | 47.9 |
| Frank B. Linderman (R) | 22,398 | 42.1 |
| Tom Kane (N) | 5,335 | 10.0 |
| 2 Carl W. Riddick (R) | 24,960 | 49.4 |
| Harry B. Mitchell (D) | 22,826 | 45.1 |
| Joseph Pope (N) | 2,786 | 5.5 |

## NEBRASKA

| | Votes | % |
|---|---|---|
| 1 C. Frank Reavis (R) | 18,097 | 62.3 |
| Frank A. Peterson (D) | 10,945 | 37.7 |
| 2 Albert W. Jefferis (R) | 13,302 | 50.9 |
| Charles Lobeck (D) | 12,839 | 49.1 |
| 3 Robert E. Evans (R) | 22,654 | 52.0 |
| Daniel V. Stephens (D) | 20,903 | 48.0 |
| 4 Melvin O. McLaughlin (R) | 21,041 | 58.1 |
| W. H. Smith (D) | 14,763 | 40.8 |
| 5 William E. Andrews (R) | 17,819 | 50.8 |
| A. C. Shallenberger (D) | 17,268 | 49.2 |
| 6 Moses P. Kinkaid (R) | 28,563 | 60.8 |
| Charles W. Pool (D) | 17,820 | 37.9 |

## NEVADA

| | Votes | % |
|---|---|---|
| AL Charles R. Evans (D) | 12,670 | 51.3 |
| Sylvester S. Downer (R) | 10,660 | 43.2 |
| H. H. Cordill (SOC) | 1,377 | 5.6 |

## NEW HAMPSHIRE

| | Votes | % |
|---|---|---|
| 1 Sherman E. Burroughs (R) | 18,658 | 52.2 |
| William N. Rogers (D) | 17,122 | 47.9 |
| 2 Edward H. Wason (R) | 19,343 | 56.5 |
| Harry F. Lake (D) | 14,923 | 43.6 |

## NEW JERSEY

| | Votes | % |
|---|---|---|
| 1 William J. Browning (R) | 23,785 | 63.8 |
| Dickerson (D) | 10,627 | 28.5 |
| 2 Isaac Bacharach (R) | 20,744 | 67.9 |
| French (D) | 8,610 | 28.2 |
| 3 Thomas J. Scully (D) | 19,965 | 53.1 |
| Carson (R) | 17,068 | 45.4 |
| 4 Elijah C. Hutchinson (R) | 17,875 | 55.1 |
| Vanderbilt (D) | 14,556 | 44.9 |
| 5 Ernest R. Ackerman (R) | 17,510 | 52.7 |
| Clement (D) | 13,545 | 40.7 |
| Furber (SOC) | 1,755 | 5.3 |
| 6 John R. Ramsey (R) | 18,663 | 53.3 |
| Sibbald (D) | 15,542 | 44.4 |
| 7 Amos H. Radcliffe (R) | 12,515 | 53.6 |
| Delaney (D) | 8,581 | 36.8 |
| Derrick (SOC) | 1,657 | 7.1 |
| 8 Cornelius A. McGlennon (D) | 12,436 | 48.7 |
| Ross (R) | 12,137 | 47.6 |
| 9 Daniel F. Minahan (D) | 10,996 | 50.4 |
| Parker (R) | 9,338 | 42.8 |
| Bircher (SOC) | 1,303 | 6.0 |
| 10 Frederick R. Lehlbach (R) | 12,566 | 48.3 |
| Flannagan (D) | 11,979 | 46.1 |
| Poole (SOC) | 1,450 | 5.6 |
| 11 John J. Eagan (D) | 14,281 | 67.5 |
| Brennan (R) | 4,979 | 23.5 |
| Reilly (SOC) | 1,894 | 9.0 |

| Candidates | Votes | % |
|---|---|---|
| 12 James A. Hamill (D) | 17,781 | 70.8 |
| Bierch (R) | 6,048 | 24.1 |
| Bausch (SOC) | 1,277 | 5.1 |

### Special Election

| | Votes | % |
|---|---|---|
| 5 William F. Birch (R) | 17,481 | 53.0 |
| Clement (D) | 13,771 | 41.7 |
| Furber (SOC) | 1,760 | 5.3 |

## NEW MEXICO

| | Votes | % |
|---|---|---|
| AL Bendigno C. Hernandez (R) | 23,862 | 50.7 |
| G. A. Richardson (D) | 22,627 | 48.1 |

## NEW YORK

| | Votes | % |
|---|---|---|
| 1 Frederick C. Hicks (R-D-P) | 53,579 | 96.6 |
| 2 Charles Pope Caldwell (R, D) | 54,394 | 85.9 |
| William Burkle (SOC) | 8,946 | 14.1 |
| 3 John MacCrate (R, D) | 14,720 | 48.9 |
| Michael Fogarty (BUSINESS) | 10,249 | 34.1 |
| Joseph A. Whitehorn (SOC) | 5,107 | 17.0 |
| 4 Thomas H. Cullen (D) | 23,146 | 75.2 |
| Ralph Waldo Bowman (R & P) | 6,599 | 21.4 |
| 5 John B. Johnston (D) | 32,090 | 55.8 |
| George A. Green (R) | 23,844 | 41.5 |
| 6 Frederick W. Rowe (R & P) | 26,806 | 46.6 |
| Franklin Taylor (D) | 26,476 | 46.0 |
| Bernard J. Riley (SOC) | 4,287 | 7.5 |
| 7 James P. Maher (D) | 19,834 | 58.9 |
| John Hill Morgan (R & P) | 9,309 | 27.7 |
| James O'Neal (SOC) | 4,513 | 13.4 |
| 8 William E. Cleary (D) | 24,069 | 54.5 |
| Allison L. Adams (R) | 14,778 | 33.5 |
| Abraham H. Shulman (SOC) | 5,114 | 11.6 |
| 9 David J. O'Connell (D) | 28,882 | 45.8 |
| Oscar W. Swift (R & P) | 27,393 | 43.5 |
| Wilhemus B. Robinson (SOC) | 6,751 | 10.7 |
| 10 Reuben L. Haskell (R) | 17,441 | 40.2 |
| George W. Martin (D) | 15,911 | 36.7 |
| Abraham I. Shiplacoff (SOC) | 9,987 | 23.0 |
| 11 Daniel J. Riordan (D) | 21,525 | 71.2 |
| William H. Michales (R) | 7,080 | 23.4 |
| 12 Henry M. Goldfogle (R, D) | 7,452 | 52.9 |
| Meyer London (SOC) | 6,625 | 47.0 |
| 13 Christopher D. Sullivan (R, D) | 6,962 | 66.4 |
| Algernon Lee (SOC) | 3,502 | 33.4 |
| 14 Fiorello H. LaGuardia (R, D) | 14,523 | 69.7 |
| Scott Nearing (SOC) | 6,214 | 29.8 |
| 15 Peter J. Dooling (D) | 23,492 | 78.4 |
| Jacob I. Wiener (R) | 5,373 | 17.9 |
| 16 Thomas F. Smith (D) | 21,289 | 71.9 |
| Thomas Rock (R) | 6,188 | 20.9 |
| Samuel E. Beardsley (SOC) | 2,057 | 6.9 |
| 17 Herbert C. Pell Jr. (D) | 19,593 | 50.2 |
| Frederick C. Tanner (R) | 17,839 | 45.7 |
| 18 John F. Carew (D) | 23,806 | 71.2 |
| Julius M. Leder (R) | 4,797 | 14.4 |
| Pauline Newman (SOC) | 4,741 | 14.2 |
| 19 Joseph Rowan (D) | 24,961 | 48.3 |
| Walter M. Chandler (R) | 23,125 | 44.8 |
| Theresa Malkiel (SOC) | 3,319 | 6.4 |
| 20 Isaac Siegel (R-D) | 9,417 | 60.9 |
| Morris Hillquit (SOC) | 6,005 | 38.9 |
| 21 Jerome F. Donovan (D) | 33,233 | 53.4 |
| John A. Bolles (R) | 25,677 | 41.2 |
| George Fraser Miller (SOC) | 3,156 | 5.1 |
| 22 Anthony J. Griffin (D) | 22,713 | 69.9 |
| Sadie Kost (R) | 5,269 | 16.2 |
| Patrick J. Murphy (SOC) | 4,323 | 13.3 |

| Candidates | Votes | % |
|---|---|---|
| 23 Richard F. McKiniry (D) | 39,573 | 55.2 |
| Owen A. Haley (R) | 17,975 | 25.1 |
| Max Geisler (SOC) | 14,146 | 19.7 |
| 24 James V. Ganly (D) | 28,636 | 44.3 |
| Benjamin L. Fairchild (R & P) | 27,037 | 41.8 |
| Irvin E. Klein (SOC) | 8,968 | 13.9 |
| 25 James W. Husted (R) | 22,562 | 56.2 |
| Arthur O. Sherman (D) | 16,248 | 40.5 |
| 26 Edmund Platt (R) | 30,010 | 57.1 |
| George A. Coleman (D) | 20,727 | 39.4 |
| 27 Charles B. Ward (R) | 30,839 | 53.9 |
| John K. Evans (D & P) | 25,620 | 44.7 |
| 28 Rollin B. Sanford (R & P) | 41,981 | 54.5 |
| Joseph A. Lawson (D) | 33,712 | 43.8 |
| 29 James S. Parker (R) | 42,035 | 62.3 |
| Gustavus A. Rogers (D) | 23,139 | 34.3 |
| 30 Frank Crowther (R) | 24,443 | 47.9 |
| George R. Lunn (D & P) | 23,820 | 46.7 |
| Herbert M. Merrill (SOC) | 2,786 | 5.5 |
| 31 Bertrand H. Snell (R) | 30,701 | 71.6 |
| Elizabeth Arthur (D) | 10,459 | 24.4 |
| 32 Luther W. Mott (R) | 37,068 | 63.2 |
| Charles A. Hitchcock (D) | 17,742 | 30.2 |
| Stephen R. Lockwood (P) | 3,263 | 5.6 |
| 33 Homer P. Snyder (R) | 31,120 | 54.0 |
| Clarence E. Williams (D) | 23,340 | 40.5 |
| 34 William H. Hill (R) | 38,597 | 57.4 |
| Lavern P. Butts (D) | 21,748 | 32.4 |
| Julius E. Rogers (P) | 6,373 | 9.5 |
| 35 Walter W. Magee (R) | 42,769 | 59.3 |
| Ben Wiles (D) | 23,378 | 32.4 |
| 36 Norman J. Gould (R & P) | 40,991 | 70.9 |
| Everett E. Calman (D) | 16,857 | 29.1 |
| 37 Alanson B. Houghton (R & P) | 38,310 | 62.9 |
| Frederick W. Palmer (D) | 21,800 | 35.8 |
| 38 Thomas B. Dunn (R) | 37,029 | 62.1 |
| Jacob Gerling (D) | 16,563 | 27.8 |
| John W. Dennis (SOC) | 4,098 | 6.9 |
| 39 Archie D. Sanders (R & P) | 35,481 | 68.9 |
| Clara B. Mann (D) | 14,816 | 28.8 |
| 40 S. Wallace Dempsey (R) | 35,710 | 63.0 |
| Matthew P. Young (D) | 17,962 | 31.7 |
| Lee P. Smith (SOC) | 3,045 | 5.4 |
| 41 Clarence MacGregor (R) | 16,492 | 41.2 |
| Charles B. Smith (D & P) | 16,458 | 41.2 |
| Franklin P. Brill (SOC) | 7,038 | 17.6 |
| 42 James M. Mead (D) | 16,453 | 46.2 |
| William F. Waldow (R) | 15,390 | 43.2 |
| Hattie Kreuger (SOC) | 3,099 | 8.7 |
| 43 Daniel A. Reed (R & P) | 35,693 | 73.4 |
| Frank H. Mott (D) | 11,351 | 23.3 |

## NORTH CAROLINA

| | Votes | % |
|---|---|---|
| 1 John H. Small (D) | 10,427 | 75.4 |
| C. R. Pugh (R) | 3,401 | 24.6 |
| 2 Claude Kitchin (D) | 9,986 | 100.0 |
| 3 Samuel L. Brinson (D) | 10,205 | 59.3 |
| Claude R. Wheatley (R) | 7,000 | 40.7 |
| 4 Edward W. Pou (D) | 12,853 | 68.1 |
| Robert H. Dixon (R) | 6,028 | 31.9 |
| 5 Charles M. Stedman (D) | 21,076 | 55.9 |
| John W. Kurfees (R) | 16,635 | 44.1 |
| 6 Hannibal L. Godwin (D) | 9,575 | 72.1 |
| Alexander L. McCaskill (R) | 3,702 | 27.9 |
| 7 Leonidas D. Robinson (D) | 18,275 | 59.3 |
| James D. Gregg (R) | 12,552 | 40.7 |
| 8 Robert L. Doughton (D) | 16,105 | 53.8 |
| Frank A. Linney (R) | 13,826 | 46.2 |
| 9 Edwin Y. Webb (D) | 16,982 | 57.0 |
| Charles A. Jonas (R) | 12,830 | 43.0 |
| 10 Zebulon Weaver (D) | 16,323 | 51.7 |
| James J. Britt (R) | 15,271 | 48.3 |

## NORTH DAKOTA

| | Votes | % |
|---|---|---|
| 1 John M. Baer (R) | 16,428 | 55.1 |
| Fred Bartholomew (D) | 13,416 | 45.0 |

## NORTH DAKOTA

| Candidates | Votes | % |
|---|---|---|
| 2 George M. Young (R) | 20,516 | 74.5 |
| L. N. Torson (D) | 7,038 | 25.5 |
| 3 James H. Sinclair (R) | 17,564 | 66.2 |
| Halvor Halvorson (D) | 8,951 | 33.8 |

## OHIO

| Candidates | Votes | % |
|---|---|---|
| 1 Nicholas Longworth (R) | 27,030 | 56.5 |
| Sidney G. Stricker (D) | 20,826 | 43.5 |
| 2 Ambrose E. B. Stephens (R) | 25,406 | 52.1 |
| Richard A. Powell (D) | 21,867 | 44.8 |
| 3 Warren Gard (D) | 29,653 | 49.2 |
| Charles W. Dustin (R) | 26,625 | 44.2 |
| John M. Cahalane (SOC) | 3,978 | 6.6 |
| 4 Benjamin F. Welty (D) | 22,580 | 50.5 |
| J. E. Russell (R) | 22,136 | 49.5 |
| 5 Charles J. Thompson (R) | 19,071 | 52.6 |
| John S. Snook (D) | 17,162 | 47.4 |
| 6 Charles C. Kearns (R) | 18,592 | 52.8 |
| A. G. Turnipseed (D) | 16,591 | 47.2 |
| 7 Simeon D. Fess (R) | 34,554 | 61.6 |
| George H. Thorne (D) | 21,043 | 37.5 |
| 8 R. Clint Cole (R) | 20,688 | 52.9 |
| John A. Key (R) | 18,441 | 47.1 |
| 9 Isaac R. Sherwood (D) | 25,122 | 55.1 |
| James M. Ashley (R) | 18,398 | 40.3 |
| 10 Israel M. Foster (R) | 18,438 | 100.0 |
| 11 Edwin D. Ricketts (R) | 17,608 | 53.5 |
| H. C. Claypool (D) | 15,287 | 46.5 |
| 12 Clement L. Brumbaugh (D) | 23,444 | 50.5 |
| John C. Speaks (R) | 22,216 | 47.8 |
| 13 James T. Begg (R) | 21,552 | 53.0 |
| Arthur W. Overmeyer (D) | 18,775 | 46.1 |
| 14 Martin L. Davey (D) | 25,932 | 50.3 |
| Charles Dick (R) | 24,170 | 46.9 |
| 15 C. Ellis Moore (R) | 20,063 | 52.5 |
| George White (D) | 18,169 | 47.5 |
| 16 Roscoe C. McCulloch (R) | 29,893 | 61.3 |
| Joseph C. Breitenstein (D) | 17,694 | 36.3 |
| 17 William A. Ashbrook (D) | 24,436 | 52.1 |
| William M. Morgan (R) | 22,499 | 47.9 |
| 18 Frank Murphy (R) | 22,899 | 53.0 |
| William B. Francis (D) | 20,272 | 47.0 |
| 19 John G. Cooper (R) | 26,857 | 95.6 |
| 20 Charles A. Mooney (D) | 19,776 | 55.0 |
| Jerry R. Zmunt (R) | 13,759 | 38.3 |
| C. E. Ruthenberg (SOC) | 2,429 | 6.8 |
| 21 John J. Babka (D) | 15,511 | 55.9 |
| Harry L. Vail (R) | 10,417 | 37.5 |
| Tom Clifford (SOC) | 1,829 | 6.6 |
| 22 Henry I. Emerson (R) | 32,745 | 100.0 |

## OKLAHOMA

| Candidates | Votes | % |
|---|---|---|
| 1 Everette B. Howard (D) | 15,394 | 50.6 |
| T.A. Chandler (R) | 14,506 | 47.6 |
| 2 William W. Hastings (D) | 11,601 | 58.9 |
| Gus H. Tinch (R) | 7,670 | 39.0 |
| 3 Charles D. Carter (D) | 15,635 | 66.8 |
| H.J. Fowler (R) | 6,982 | 29.8 |
| 4 Thomas D. McKeown (D) | 13,861 | 57.0 |
| E.R. Waite (R) | 9,706 | 39.9 |
| 5 Joseph B. Thompson (D) | 13,303 | 57.4 |
| B.A. McAleer (R) | 9,180 | 39.6 |
| 6 Scott Ferris (D) | 12,085 | 54.8 |
| L.A. Holmes (R) | 8,925 | 40.5 |
| 7 James V. McClintic (D) | 11,190 | 59.7 |
| C.B. Leedy (R) | 6,014 | 32.1 |
| Orville E. Enfield (SOC) | 1,526 | 8.2 |
| 8 Dick T. Morgan (R) | 15,261 | 56.3 |
| C.H. Hyde (D) | 10,633 | 39.2 |

## OREGON

| Candidates | Votes | % |
|---|---|---|
| 1 Willis C. Hawley (R-D-P) | 57,245 | 89.6 |
| Harlin Talbert (SOC) | 6,624 | 10.4 |

| Candidates | Votes | % |
|---|---|---|
| 2 Nicholas J. Sinnott (R) | 18,312 | 61.3 |
| James Harvey Graham (D) | 10,461 | 35.0 |
| 3 Clinton N. McArthur (R) | 23,277 | 48.4 |
| John S. Smith (D) | 15,728 | 32.7 |
| A. W. Lafferty (I-N) | 7,661 | 15.9 |

## PENNSYLVANIA

| Candidates | Votes | % |
|---|---|---|
| 1 William S. Vare (R, WASH) | 26,120 | 76.4 |
| Paul B. Cassidy (D) | 7,146 | 20.9 |
| 2 George S. Graham (R, WASH) | 20,578 | 81.5 |
| John H. Berkley (D) | 4,295 | 17.0 |
| 3 J. Hampton Moore (R, P) | 20,099 | 78.8 |
| William A. Hayes (D) | 5,046 | 19.8 |
| 4 George W. Edmonds (R, WASH) | 19,187 | 68.8 |
| Joseph E. Fabian (D) | 7,874 | 28.2 |
| 5 Peter E. Costello (R, SOC) | 25,169 | 69.6 |
| Emanuel R. Clinton (D) | 10,987 | 30.4 |
| 6 George P. Darrow (R, P) | 42,376 | 72.1 |
| John K. Laughlin (D) | 15,722 | 26.8 |
| 7 Thomas S. Butler (R) | 23,882 | 76.1 |
| James G. Milbourn (D) | 6,702 | 21.3 |
| 8 Henry Winfield Watson (R) | 23,127 | 63.4 |
| Harry E. Grim (D, F PLAY) | 12,213 | 33.5 |
| 9 William W. Griest (R) | 17,398 | 77.1 |
| Austin E. McCullough (D) | 4,537 | 20.1 |
| 10 Patrick McLane (D, F PLAY) | 11,765‡ | 50.0 |
| John R. Farr (R, P) | 11,564 | 49.1 |
| 11 John J. Casey (D, SOC) | 16,547 | 50.1 |
| Edmund N. Carpenter (R, P) | 16,505 | 49.9 |
| 12 John Reber (R) | 13,500 | 57.3 |
| James J. Moran (D, F PLAY) | 9,712 | 41.2 |
| 13 Arthur G. Dewalt (D, F PLAY) | 19,776 | 51.9 |
| J. Wilmer Fisher (R, WASH) | 15,608 | 40.9 |
| L. Birch Wilson Jr (SOC) | 2,397 | 6.3 |
| 14 Louis T. McFadden (R) | 11,267 | 66.0 |
| A. M. Cornell (D) | 4,873 | 28.6 |
| 15 Edgar R. Kiess (R, P) | 14,153 | 63.8 |
| Charles E. Spotts (D) | 7,372 | 33.2 |
| 16 John V. Lesher (D) | 11,782 | 48.7 |
| Albert W. Duy (R) | 11,509 | 47.6 |
| 17 Benjamin K. Focht (R) | 16,762 | 59.0 |
| Scott S. Leiby (D, P) | 11,348 | 39.9 |
| 18 Aaron S. Kreider (R) | 24,981 | 86.2 |
| John A. Sprenkle (P) | 2,905 | 10.0 |
| 19 John M. Rose (R, P) | 20,036 | 61.4 |
| Bernard J. Clark (D) | 11,857 | 36.4 |
| 20 Edward S. Brooks (R, WASH) | 15,362 | 52.5 |
| Andrew R. Brodbeck (D, P) | 13,525 | 46.2 |
| 21 Evan J. Jones (R, SOC) | 12,673 | 56.5 |
| William E. Tobias (D) | 8,958 | 39.9 |
| 22 Edward E. Robbins (R, P) | 17,160* | 61.1 |
| George H. McWherter (D, F PLAY) | 9,904 | 35.3 |
| 23 Samuel A. Kendall (R) | 14,550 | 50.1 |
| Bruce F. Sterling (D, P) | 14,029 | 48.3 |
| 24 Henry W. Temple (R, P) | 18,851 | 69.1 |
| William M. Hartman (D) | 7,398 | 27.1 |
| 25 Milton W. Shreve (R, WASH) | 11,164 | 51.0 |
| Charles N. Crosby (D) | 8,766 | 40.0 |
| 26 Henry J. Steele (D, F PLAY) | 11,872 | 49.4 |
| Francis A. March Jr. (R, WASH) | 9,781 | 40.7 |
| Delbert Strader Bachman (P, I PROG) | 2,035 | 8.5 |
| 27 Nathan L. Strong (R, P) | 14,804 | 70.7 |
| Don C. Corbett (D) | 5,686 | 27.2 |
| 28 Willis J. Hulings (R, WASH) | 13,751 | 55.5 |
| Earl H. Beshlin (D, P) | 10,367 | 41.9 |

| Candidates | Votes | % |
|---|---|---|
| 29 Stephen G. Porter (R, D) | 19,045 | 89.0 |
| C. G. Porter (P) | 1,222 | 5.7 |
| Henry Peter (SOC) | 1,138 | 5.3 |
| 30 M. Clyde Kelly (R, D) | 21,559 | 90.5 |
| H. J. Lohr (SOC) | 2,262 | 9.5 |
| 31 John M. Morin (R, D) | 14,081 | 91.4 |
| William A. Prosser (SOC) | 773 | 5.0 |
| 32 Guy E. Campbell (R, D) | 20,567 | 87.2 |
| John W. Slayton (SOC) | 1,553 | 6.6 |
| William C. Wallace (P) | 1,458 | 6.2 |
| AL William J. Burke (R) | 546,373✓ | |
| Mahlon M. Garland (R) | 529,510✓ | |
| Thomas S. Crago (R, WASH) | 527,961✓ | |
| Anderson H. Walters (R, WASH) | 525,615✓ | |
| Joseph F. Gorman (D) | 276,836 | |
| J. Calvin Strayer (D, F PLAY) | 268,533 | |
| Samuel R. Tarner (D, F PLAY) | 264,971 | |
| Fred Ikeler (D, F PLAY) | 264,065 | |
| O. D. Brubaker (P) | 29,309 | |
| Elisha Kent Kane (P) | 26,473 | |
| Albert Gaddis (P) | 25,347 | |
| E. L. McKee (P) | 23,793 | |
| Cora M. Bixler (SOC) | 23,273 | |
| Henry W. Schlegel (SOC) | 21,831 | |
| John C. Euler (SOC) | 21,477 | |
| Harry T. Vaughn (SOC) | 21,143 | |
| John W. Dix (SINGLE T) | 2,211 | |
| Lewis Ryan (SINGLE T) | 2,129 | |
| Oliver McKnight (SINGLE T) | 2,006 | |
| Calvin B. Power (SINGLE T) | 1,631 | |

## RHODE ISLAND

| Candidates | Votes | % |
|---|---|---|
| 1 Clark Burdick (R) | 14,478 | 54.3 |
| Green (D) | 11,556 | 43.4 |
| 2 Walter R. Stiness (R) | 14,710 | 56.0 |
| Casey (D) | 10,914 | 41.6 |
| 3 Ambrose Kennedy (R) | 14,037 | 52.6 |
| Troy (D) | 12,176 | 45.6 |

## SOUTH CAROLINA

| Candidates | Votes | % |
|---|---|---|
| 1 Richard S. Whaley (D) | 2,328 | 100.0 |
| 2 James F. Byrnes (D) | 3,155 | 100.0 |
| 3 Fred H. Dominick (D) | 3,701 | 100.0 |
| 4 Samuel J. Nichols (D) | 4,069 | 100.0 |
| 5 William F. Stevenson (D) | 3,640 | 100.0 |
| 6 J. Willard Ragsdale (D) | 3,626 | 100.0 |
| 7 Asbury F. Lever (D) | 4,761 | 96.4 |

## SOUTH DAKOTA

| Candidates | Votes | % |
|---|---|---|
| 1 Charles A. Christopherson (R) | 19,443 | 54.1 |
| Dowdell (D) | 14,899 | 41.5 |
| 2 Royal C. Johnson (R) | 21,657 | 72.1 |
| McArthur (D) | 8,401 | 28.0 |
| 3 Harry L. Gandy (D) | 10,865 | 50.7 |
| Atwater (R) | 7,805 | 36.4 |
| Ayers (I) | 2,526 | 11.8 |

## TENNESSEE

| Candidates | Votes | % |
|---|---|---|
| 1 Sam R. Sells (R) | 13,752 | 100.0 |
| 2 J. Will Taylor (R) | 13,868 | 73.3 |
| Sam Johnson (D) | 4,879 | 25.8 |
| 3 John A. Moon (D) | 12,566 | 100.0 |
| 4 Cordell Hull (D) | 11,646 | 100.0 |
| 5 Ewen L. Davis (D) | 11,089 | 100.0 |
| 6 Joseph W. Byrns (D) | 10,794 | 100.0 |
| 7 Lemuel P. Padgett (D) | 10,178 | 100.0 |
| 8 Thetus W. Sims (D) | 9,010 | 100.0 |
| 9 Finis J. Garrett (D) | 11,122 | 100.0 |
| 10 Hubert F. Fisher (D) | 11,606 | 100.0 |

## TEXAS

| | Candidates | Votes | % |
|---|---|---|---|
| 1 | Eugene Black (D) | 9,640 | 100.0 |
| 2 | John C. Box (D) | 10,474 | 100.0 |
| 3 | James Young (D) | 10,183 | 100.0 |
| 4 | Sam Rayburn (D) | 9,755 | 100.0 |
| 5 | Hatton W. Sumners (D) | 6,946 | 100.0 |
| 6 | Rufus Hardy (D) | 10,496 | 86.9 |
| | Charles W. Beck (R) | 1,577 | 13.1 |
| 7 | Clay S. Briggs (D) | 6,671 | 100.0 |
| 8 | Joe H. Eagle (D) | 7,554 | 96.1 |
| 9 | Joseph J. Mansfield (D) | 7,672 | 100.0 |
| 10 | James P. Buchanan (D) | 8,576 | 100.0 |
| 11 | Tom T. Connally (D) | 9,304 | 100.0 |
| 12 | James C. Wilson (D) | 9,307 | 100.0 |
| 13 | Lucian W. Parrish (D) | 9,700 | 100.0 |
| 14 | Carlos Bee (D) | 8,038 | 68.4 |
| | John D. Hartman (R) | 3,717 | 31.6 |
| 15 | John N. Garner (D) | 6,814 | 100.0 |
| 16 | Claude Hudspeth (D) | 6,211 | 100.0 |
| 17 | Thomas L. Blanton (D) | 11,194 | 100.0 |
| 18 | Marvin Jones (D) | 10,497 | 95.3 |

## UTAH

| | | Votes | % |
|---|---|---|---|
| 1 | Milton H. Welling (D) | 25,327 | 54.9 |
| | William H. Wattis (R) | 20,478 | 44.4 |
| 2 | James H. Mays (D & PROG) | 23,931 | 58.7 |
| | William Spry (R) | 16,134 | 39.6 |

## VERMONT

| | | Votes | % |
|---|---|---|---|
| 1 | Frank L. Greene (R) | 16,301 | 75.9 |
| | John Higgins (D) | 5,179 | 24.1 |
| 2 | Porter H. Dale (R, P) | 16,145 | 74.5 |
| | John B. Reardon (D) | 5,518 | 25.5 |

## VIRGINIA

| | Candidates | Votes | % |
|---|---|---|---|
| 1 | S. Otis Bland (D) | 4,835 | 99.9 |
| 2 | Edward E. Holland (D) | 3,420 | 100.0 |
| 3 | Andrew Jackson Montague (D) | 3,074 | 100.0 |
| 4 | Walter A. Watson (D) | 2,506 | 99.9 |
| 5 | Edward W. Saunders (D) | 3,880 | 100.0 |
| 6 | Carter Glass (D) | 2,705* | 99.6 |
| 7 | Thomas W. Harrison (D) | 3,767 | 88.8 |
| | John Paul (R) | 466 | 11.0 |
| 8 | Charles C. Carlin (D) | 4,501* | 100.0 |
| 9 | C. Bascom Slemp (R) | 8,089 | 93.9 |
| | D. B. Dale (D) | 515 | 6.0 |
| 10 | Henry D. Flood (D) | 4,699 | 99.7 |

## WASHINGTON

| | | Votes | % |
|---|---|---|---|
| 1 | John F. Miller (R) | 23,326 | 50.6 |
| | J. M. Hawthorne (D) | 20,488 | 44.4 |
| | Hulet M. Wells (SOC) | 2,333 | 5.1 |
| 2 | Lindley H. Hadley (R) | 19,797 | 53.7 |
| | Joseph A. Sloan (D) | 15,059 | 40.8 |
| | James M. Salter (SOC) | 2,045 | 5.5 |
| 3 | Albert Johnson (R) | 29,178 | 66.6 |
| | Theodore Hoss (D) | 12,407 | 28.3 |
| | O. T. Clark (SOC) | 2,243 | 5.1 |
| 4 | John W. Summers (R) | 17,439 | 55.3 |
| | William E. McCroskey (D) | 13,335 | 42.3 |
| 5 | J. Stanley Webster (R) | 22,426 | 52.2 |
| | C. C. Dill (D) | 20,061 | 46.7 |

## WEST VIRGINIA

| | | Votes | % |
|---|---|---|---|
| 1 | Matthew M. Neely (D) | 17,428 | 52.8 |
| | Charles J. Schuck (R) | 15,330 | 46.4 |
| 2 | George M. Bowers (R) | 18,444 | 52.7 |
| | B. H. Hiner (D) | 16,084 | 46.0 |
| 3 | Stuart F. Reed (R) | 19,414 | 53.9 |
| | Ernest Randolph (D) | 16,254 | 45.1 |

| | Candidates | Votes | % |
|---|---|---|---|
| 4 | Harry C. Woodyard (R) | 19,679 | 55.2 |
| | Stuart H. Bowman (D) | 15,799 | 44.3 |
| 5 | Wells Goodykoontz (R) | 19,304 | 54.2 |
| | W. W. McNeal (D) | 16,332 | 45.8 |
| 6 | Leonard S. Echols (R) | 19,851 | 51.5 |
| | Adam B. Littlepage (D) | 18,020 | 46.8 |

## WISCONSIN

| | | Votes | % |
|---|---|---|---|
| 1 | Clifford E. Randall (R) | 13,177 | 42.3 |
| | Cooper (I) | 9,018 | 28.9 |
| | Stewart (D) | 7,718 | 24.8 |
| 2 | Edward Voigt (R) | 15,289 | 44.0 |
| | Clifford (D) | 12,532 | 36.1 |
| | Ameringer (SOC) | 6,936 | 20.0 |
| 3 | James G. Monahan (R) | 18,398 | 73.4 |
| | Warner (I) | 4,397 | 17.5 |
| | Reynolds (I) | 2,232 | 8.9 |
| 4 | John C. Kleczka (R) | 16,524 | 58.1 |
| | Melms (SOC) | 11,890 | 41.8 |
| 5 | Victor L. Berger (SOC) | 17,920* | 43.7 |
| | Joseph P. Carney (D) | 12,450 | 30.3 |
| | Stafford (R) | 10,678 | 26.0 |
| 6 | Florian Lampert (R) | 12,728 | 41.5 |
| | Husting (D) | 10,856 | 35.4 |
| | Thompson (SOC) | 6,737 | 22.0 |
| 7 | John J. Esch (R) | 16,140 | 70.9 |
| | Bentley (D) | 6,109 | 26.8 |
| 8 | Edward E. Browne (R) | 13,755 | 51.8 |
| | Brown (D) | 6,862 | 25.9 |
| | Krzycki (SOC) | 5,904 | 22.3 |
| 9 | David G. Classon (R) | 16,352 | 60.4 |
| | McDonald (D) | 10,702 | 39.6 |
| 10 | James A. Frear (R) | 16,900 | 90.2 |
| | Frawley (I) | 1,814 | 9.7 |
| 11 | Adolphus P. Nelson (R) | 16,413 | 84.3 |
| | Jensen (SOC) | 2,976 | 15.3 |

## WYOMING

| | | Votes | % |
|---|---|---|---|
| AL | Frank W. Mondell (R) | 26,244 | 64.2 |
| | Hayden M. White (D) | 14,639 | 35.8 |

# 1919 House Elections

## OKLAHOMA

### Special Election

| | | Votes | % |
|---|---|---|---|
| 5 | J. W. Harreld (R) | 11,782 | 51.3 |
| | Claude Weaver (D) | 11,076 | 48.2 |

## PENNSYLVANIA

### Special Election

| | | Votes | % |
|---|---|---|---|
| 22 | John H. Wilson (D) | 10,148 | 51.1 |
| | John M. Jamison (R) | 9,721 | 48.9 |

# 1920 House Elections

## ALABAMA

| | Candidates | Votes | % |
|---|---|---|---|
| 1 | John McDuffie (D) | 12,978 | 98.7 |
| 2 | John R. Tyson (D) | 18,469 | 99.6 |
| 3 | Henry B. Steagall (D) | 11,959 | 82.5 |
| | Dallas B. Smith (R) | 2,532 | 17.5 |
| 4 | Fred L. Blackmon (D) | 12,236* | 59.6 |
| | A. P. Longshore (R) | 8,305 | 40.4 |
| 5 | William B. Bolling (D) | 13,290 | 73.5 |
| | W. M. Russell (R) | 4,793 | 26.5 |
| 6 | William B. Oliver (D) | 8,721 | 100.0 |
| 7 | Lilius B. Rainey (D) | 23,709 | 50.5 |
| | Charles B. Kennamer (R) | 22,970 | 49.0 |
| 8 | Edward B. Almon (D) | 17,640 | 76.1 |
| | W. E. Hotchkiss (R) | 5,306 | 23.0 |
| 9 | George Huddleston (D) | 26,776 | 85.4 |
| | Alex Birch (R) | 4,452 | 14.2 |
| 10 | William B. Bankhead (D) | 15,465 | 52.6 |
| | W. L. Chenault (R) | 13,737 | 46.7 |

## ARIZONA

| | Candidates | Votes | % |
|---|---|---|---|
| AL | Carl Hayden (D) | 35,397 | 57.8 |
| | James A. Dunseath (R) | 25,841 | 42.2 |

## ARKANSAS

| | Candidates | Votes | % |
|---|---|---|---|
| 1 | William J. Driver (D) | 19,843 | 73.6 |
| | T. H. Mayes (R) | 7,110 | 26.4 |
| 2 | William A. Oldfield (D) | 16,080 | 66.4 |
| | Thad Rowden (R) | 8,137 | 33.6 |
| 3 | John N. Tillman (D) | 14,341 | 53.3 |
| | John I. Worthington (R) | 12,587 | 46.7 |
| 4 | Otis Wingo (D) | 19,722 | 64.1 |
| | W. H. Dunblazier (R) | 11,031 | 35.9 |
| 5 | Henderson M. Jacoway (D) | 21,948 | 73.2 |
| | G. A. McConnell (R) | 8,039 | 26.8 |
| 6 | Samuel M. Taylor (D) | 18,028 | 69.4 |
| | W. R. Day (R) | 7,956 | 30.6 |
| 7 | Tilman B. Parks (D) | 18,303 | 72.2 |
| | J. C. Russell (R) | 7,064 | 27.9 |

## CALIFORNIA

| | Candidates | Votes | % |
|---|---|---|---|
| 1 | Clarence F. Lea (D-R) | 34,427 | 61.7 |
| | Charles A. Bodwell Jr. (I) | 18,569 | 33.3 |
| 2 | John E. Raker (D R&SOC) | 26,172 | 99.9 |
| 3 | Charles F. Curry (R) | 54,984 | 74.7 |
| | J. W. Struckenbruck (D) | 14,964 | 20.3 |
| 4 | Julius Kahn (R-D) | 50,841 | 84.6 |
| | Milton Harlan (SOC) | 9,289 | 15.5 |
| 5 | John I. Nolan (R-D) | 50,274 | 82.1 |
| | Thomas Conway (SOC) | 10,952 | 17.9 |
| 6 | John A. Elston (R) | 75,610 | 83.3 |
| | Maynard Shipley (SOC) | 15,151 | 16.7 |
| 7 | Henry E. Barbour (R-D) | 57,647 | 87.2 |
| | Harry M. McKee (SOC) | 8,449 | 12.8 |
| 8 | Arthur M. Free (R) | 46,823 | 64.0 |
| | Hugh S. Hersman (D SOC) | 26,311 | 36.0 |
| 9 | Charles F. Van de Water (R) | 62,952* | 59.7 |
| | Charles H. Randall (P & D) | 36,675 | 34.8 |
| | Mary E. Garbutt (SOC) | 5,819 | 5.5 |
| 10 | Henry Z. Osborne (R-D-P) | 97,469 | 82.6 |
| | Upton Sinclair (SOC) | 20,439 | 17.3 |
| 11 | Philip D. Swing (R) | 59,425 | 72.8 |
| | Hugh L. Dickson (D) | 22,144 | 27.1 |

## COLORADO

| | Candidates | Votes | % |
|---|---|---|---|
| 1 | William N. Vaile (R) | 45,658 | 66.9 |
| | Benjamin C. Hilliard (D) | 22,557 | 33.1 |
| 2 | Charles B. Timberlake (R) | 57,512 | 66.4 |
| | A. F. Browns (D) | 29,158 | 33.6 |
| 3 | Guy U. Hardy (R) | 43,426 | 57.7 |
| | Samuel J. Burris (D) | 31,896 | 42.4 |
| 4 | Edward T. Taylor (D) | 25,994 | 55.3 |
| | Merle D. Vincent (R) | 20,991 | 44.7 |

## CONNECTICUT

| | Candidates | Votes | % |
|---|---|---|---|
| 1 | E. Hart Fenn (R) | 53,461 | 60.5 |
| | Joseph F. Dutton (D) | 30,757 | 34.8 |
| 2 | Richard P. Freeman (R) | 39,432 | 63.7 |
| | Thomas R. Murray (D) | 20,868 | 33.7 |
| 3 | John Q. Tilson (R) | 45,406 | 63.7 |
| | William F. Alcorn (D) | 22,357 | 31.4 |
| 4 | Schuyler Merritt (R) | 54,715 | 66.3 |
| | Harry J. Platt (D) | 25,087 | 30.4 |
| 5 | James P. Glynn (R) | 34,621 | 58.7 |
| | Michael L. Caine (D) | 22,950 | 38.9 |

## DELAWARE

| | Candidates | Votes | % |
|---|---|---|---|
| AL | Caleb R. Layton (R) | 52,145 | 55.7 |
| | James R. Clements (D) | 40,206 | 43.0 |

## FLORIDA

| | Candidates | Votes | % |
|---|---|---|---|
| 1 | Herbert J. Drane (D) | 26,385 | 78.1 |
| | H. B. Jeffries (R) | 4,729 | 14.0 |
| 2 | Frank Clark (D) | 15,143 | 84.9 |
| | Fred Cubberly (R) | 2,383 | 13.4 |
| 3 | J. H. Smithwick (D) | 17,199 | 86.2 |
| | Millard M. Owens (R) | 2,753 | 13.8 |
| 4 | William J. Sears (D) | 38,355 | 74.4 |
| | C. D. Bowen (R) | 11,159 | 21.7 |

## GEORGIA

| | Candidates | Votes | % |
|---|---|---|---|
| 1 | James W. Overstreet (D) | 10,156 | 82.5 |
| | E. S. Fuller (R) | 2,161 | 17.5 |
| 2 | Frank Park (D) | 2,217 | 100.0 |
| 3 | Charles R. Crisp (D) | 7,001 | 92.6 |
| | H. E. Locket (R) | 563 | 7.4 |
| 4 | William C. Wright (D) | 10,040 | 100.0 |
| 5 | William D. Upshaw (D) | 10,649 | 70.1 |
| | John W. Martin (R) | 4,544 | 29.9 |
| 6 | James W. Wise (D) | 9,325 | 97.7 |
| 7 | Gordon Lee (D) | 18,385 | 99.6 |
| 8 | Charles H. Brand (D) | 11,708 | 100.0 |
| 9 | Thomas M. Bell (D) | 13,265 | 62.2 |
| | O. L. Barnwell (R) | 8,053 | 37.8 |
| 10 | Carl Vinson (D) | 8,685 | 100.0 |
| 11 | William C. Lankford (D) | 9,012 | 100.0 |
| 12 | William W. Larsen (D) | 8,461 | 100.0 |

## IDAHO

| | Candidates | Votes | % |
|---|---|---|---|
| 1 | Burton L. French (R) | 34,654 | 59.3 |
| | Nell K. Irion (D) | 15,218 | 26.0 |
| | Riley Rice (I) | 8,605 | 14.7 |
| 2 | Addison T. Smith (R) | 49,642 | 63.0 |
| | William P. Whitaker (D) | 29,130 | 37.0 |

## ILLINOIS

| | Candidates | Votes | % |
|---|---|---|---|
| 1 | Martin B. Madden (R) | 41,907 | 75.9 |
| | James A. Gorman (D) | 12,398 | 22.5 |
| 2 | James R. Mann (R) | 92,217 | 72.9 |
| | James J. Leddy (D) | 29,754 | 23.5 |
| 3 | Elliott W. Sproul (R) | 73,547 | 67.4 |
| | Thomas M. Crane (D) | 30,631 | 28.1 |
| 4 | John W. Rainey (D) | 23,230 | 48.9 |
| | John Golombiewski (R) | 21,546 | 45.3 |
| | Charles Beranek (SOC) | 2,750 | 5.8 |
| 5 | Adolph J. Sabath (D) | 14,374 | 45.3 |
| | Jacob Gartenstein (R) | 14,076 | 44.4 |
| | William Neumann (SOC) | 3,290 | 10.4 |
| 6 | John J. Gorman (R) | 88,975 | 63.8 |
| | James McAndrews (D) | 40,576 | 29.1 |
| | William F. Kruse (SOC) | 9,937 | 7.1 |
| 7 | M. A. Michaelson (R) | 110,758 | 70.0 |
| | William J. Cullerton (D) | 34,202 | 21.6 |
| | Samuel Holland (SOC) | 12,097 | 7.7 |
| 8 | Stanley Henry Kunz (D) | 15,432 | 49.2 |
| | Dan Parrillo (R) | 14,627 | 46.6 |
| 9 | Fred A. Britten (R) | 40,548 | 72.5 |
| | Eugene L. McGarry (D) | 13,257 | 23.7 |
| 10 | Carl R. Chindblom (R) | 101,361 | 74.4 |
| | John Haderlin (D) | 30,924 | 22.7 |
| 11 | Ira C. Copley (R) | 68,691 | 80.4 |
| | Anton Nemanich Jr. (D) | 14,885 | 17.4 |
| 12 | Charles E. Fuller (R) | 67,391 | 95.8 |
| 13 | John C. McKenzie (R) | 48,453 | 80.5 |
| | J. L. Dickson (D) | 10,821 | 18.0 |
| 14 | William J. Graham (R) | 49,329 | 67.1 |
| | Andrew Olson (D) | 21,822 | 29.7 |
| 15 | Edward J. King (R) | 49,852 | 69.0 |
| | William F. Gilroy (D) | 20,771 | 28.7 |
| 16 | Clifford Ireland (R) | 47,936 | 67.4 |
| | Jefferson Earle Houston (D) | 21,438 | 30.1 |
| 17 | Frank H. Funk (R) | 42,790 | 70.5 |
| | Frank Gillespie (D) | 17,912 | 29.5 |
| 18 | Joseph G. Cannon (R) | 53,772 | 64.1 |
| | Armand E. Smith (D) | 27,295 | 32.5 |
| 19 | Allen F. Moore (R) | 63,124 | 63.7 |
| | Edward F. Poorman (D) | 35,210 | 35.5 |
| 20 | Guy L. Shaw (R) | 33,375 | 53.1 |
| | Henry T. Rainey (D) | 29,466 | 46.9 |
| 21 | Loren E. Wheeler (R) | 43,223 | 52.0 |
| | J. Earl Major (D) | 29,054 | 34.9 |
| | Duncan McDonald (F-LAB) | 8,970 | 10.8 |
| 22 | William A. Rodenberg (R) | 49,802 | 54.8 |
| | Guy R. McCasland (D) | 26,866 | 29.6 |
| | Cornelius J. Hayes (F-LAB) | 11,929 | 13.1 |
| 23 | Edwin B. Brooks (R) | 44,950 | 54.4 |
| | Albert H. Gravenhorst (D) | 34,740 | 42.1 |
| 24 | Thomas S. Williams (R) | 38,472 | 60.9 |
| | Asher R. Cox (D) | 22,019 | 34.9 |
| 25 | Edward E. Denison (R) | 49,145 | 58.2 |
| | J. Herman Clayton (D) | 28,444 | 33.7 |
| | John H. Reed (F-LAB) | 5,690 | 6.7 |
| AL | Richard Yates (R) | 1,369,673✔ | |
| | William E. Mason (R) | 1,355,392✔ | |
| | William Murphy (D) | 579,799 | |
| | C. S. Schneider (D) | 565,792 | |
| | Frank H. Hall (SOC) | 66,385 | |
| | John Hubert (SOC) | 65,150 | |
| | Gifford Ernest (F-LAB) | 49,432 | |
| | Robert Weber (F-LAB) | 49,191 | |
| | Margaret Wintringer (P) | 19,123 | |
| | W. W. Jones (P) | 9,136 | |
| | Henry Schilling (SOC LAB) | 3,429 | |
| | Frank K. Kuchenbecker (SOC LAB) | 2,985 | |
| | Henry Neil (I) | 627 | |

## INDIANA

| | Candidates | Votes | % |
|---|---|---|---|
| 1 | Oscar R. Luhring (R) | 44,694 | 51.7 |
| | William E. Wilson (D) | 36,834 | 42.6 |
| 2 | Oscar E. Bland (R) | 47,896 | 52.1 |
| | William A. Cullop (D) | 39,349 | 42.8 |
| 3 | James W. Dunbar (R) | 44,743 | 51.0 |
| | John W. Ewing (D) | 42,569 | 48.5 |
| 4 | John S. Benham (R) | 46,360 | 53.0 |
| | Harry C. Canfield (D) | 41,163 | 47.0 |
| 5 | Everett Sanders (R) | 46,464 | 52.1 |
| | Charles S. Batt (D) | 36,403 | 40.8 |

## INDIANA

| | Candidates | Votes | % |
|---|---|---|---|
| 6 | Richard N. Elliott (R) | 48,752 | 55.3 |
| | William A. Yarling (D) | 38,721 | 43.9 |
| 7 | Merrill Moores (R) | 79,782 | 54.9 |
| | Henry N. Spaan (D) | 61,893 | 42.6 |
| 8 | Albert H. Vestal (R) | 54,416 | 56.8 |
| | Charles A. Paddock (D) | 38,725 | 40.4 |
| 9 | Fred S. Purnell (R) | 56,465 | 55.9 |
| | Ben M. Scifres (D) | 42,766 | 42.4 |
| 10 | William R. Wood (R) | 62,438 | 65.5 |
| | Fred Barnett (D) | 26,139 | 27.4 |
| | James H. McGill (F-LAB) | 5,086 | 5.3 |
| 11 | Milton Kraus (R) | 51,106 | 54.7 |
| | Samuel E. Cook (D) | 40,088 | 42.9 |
| 12 | Louis W. Fairfield (R) | 49,709 | 58.6 |
| | Joseph R. Harrison (D) | 31,182 | 36.8 |
| 13 | Andrew J. Hickey (R) | 62,206 | 59.8 |
| | George Y. Hepler (D) | 39,253 | 37.7 |

## IOWA

| | Candidates | Votes | % |
|---|---|---|---|
| 1 | William F. Kopp (R) | 38,100 | 64.5 |
| | E. W. McManus (D) | 20,977 | 35.5 |
| 2 | Harry E. Hull (R) | 50,160 | 89.0 |
| | F. B. Althouse (F-LAB) | 6,058 | 10.8 |
| 3 | Burton E. Sweet (R) | 67,859 | 97.1 |
| 4 | Gilbert N. Haugen (R) | 53,083 | 74.6 |
| | Carl Evans (D) | 18,104 | 25.4 |
| 5 | James W. Good (R) | 58,197 | 99.9 |
| 6 | C. William Ramseyer (R) | 41,644 | 65.9 |
| | O. P. Meyers (D) | 21,538 | 34.1 |
| 7 | Cassius C. Dowell (R) | 66,367 | 98.1 |
| 8 | Horace M. Towner (R) | 49,522 | 99.6 |
| 9 | William R. Green (R) | 48,558 | 82.1 |
| | Hattie T. Harl (I) | 10,607 | 17.9 |
| 10 | Lester J. Dickinson (R) | 67,700 | 96.0 |
| 11 | William D. Boies (R) | 64,342 | 69.7 |
| | E. H. Birmingham (D) | 27,953 | 30.3 |

## KANSAS

| | Candidates | Votes | % |
|---|---|---|---|
| 1 | Daniel R. Anthony Jr. (R) | 42,471 | 67.2 |
| | J. B. Billard (D) | 20,730 | 32.8 |
| 2 | Edward C. Little (R) | 48,307 | 58.9 |
| | C. A. Bowman (D) | 31,862 | 38.9 |
| 3 | Philip P. Campbell (R) | 47,220 | 60.4 |
| | J. D. Turkington (D) | 30,932 | 39.6 |
| 4 | Homer Hoch (R) | 32,619 | 67.0 |
| | Walter W. Austin (D) | 14,944 | 30.7 |
| 5 | James G. Strong (R) | 38,992 | 68.6 |
| | Thomas F. Johnson (D) | 16,303 | 28.7 |
| 6 | Hays B. White (R) | 36,400 | 61.9 |
| | J. C. Ruppenthal (D) | 20,600 | 35.0 |
| 7 | Jasper N. Tincher (R) | 49,601 | 62.9 |
| | J. R. Beeching (D) | 26,992 | 34.2 |
| 8 | Richard E. Bird (R) | 30,076 | 49.4 |
| | W. A. Ayres (D) | 29,899 | 49.1 |

## KENTUCKY

| | Candidates | Votes | % |
|---|---|---|---|
| 1 | Alben W. Barkley (D) | 50,635 | 64.3 |
| | Miller Hughes (R) | 28,070 | 35.7 |
| 2 | David H. Kincheloe (D) | 45,741 | 55.8 |
| | Erskine B. Bassett (R) | 36,280 | 44.2 |
| 3 | Robert Y. Thomas (D) | 36,430 | 50.4 |
| | John H. Gilliam (R) | 35,873 | 49.6 |
| 4 | Ben Johnson (D) | 41,620 | 52.5 |
| | John P. Haswell (R) | 37,702 | 47.5 |
| 5 | Charles F. Ogden (R) | 67,436 | 53.7 |
| | James H. Richmond (D) | 55,037 | 43.9 |
| 6 | Arthur B. Rouse (D) | 39,833 | 53.7 |
| | Rodney G. Bryson (R) | 26,099 | 35.2 |
| | Harry V. Dill (I) | 8,231 | 11.1 |
| 7 | James C. Cantrill (D) | 52,780 | 100.0 |
| 8 | Ralph Gilbert (D) | 37,381 | 52.0 |
| | King Swope (R) | 34,525 | 48.0 |
| 9 | William J. Fields (D) | 51,530 | 52.9 |
| | W. G. Blair (R) | 45,897 | 47.1 |
| 10 | John W. Langley (R) | 33,035 | 100.0 |

| | Candidates | Votes | % |
|---|---|---|---|
| 11 | John M. Robsion (R) | 64,248 | 75.4 |
| | J. E. Sampson (D) | 20,926 | 24.6 |

## LOUISIANA

| | | Votes | % |
|---|---|---|---|
| 1 | James O'Connor (D) | 19,716 | 99.9 |
| 2 | H. Garland Dupre (D) | 19,777 | 100.0 |
| 3 | Whitmell P. Martin (D) | 4,201 | 100.0 |
| 4 | John N. Sandlin (D) | 10,507 | 100.0 |
| 5 | Riley J. Wilson (D) | 9,502 | 100.0 |
| 6 | George K. Favrot (D) | 9,426 | 100.0 |
| 7 | Ladislas Lazaro (D) | 8,551 | 100.0 |
| 8 | James B. Aswell (D) | 10,357 | 100.0 |

## MAINE

| | | Votes | % |
|---|---|---|---|
| 1 | Carroll L. Beedy (R) | 30,810 | 66.6 |
| | F. H. Haskell (D) | 15,456 | 33.4 |
| 2 | Wallace H. White Jr. (R) | 35,015 | 62.5 |
| | W. N. Price (D) | 20,978 | 37.5 |
| 3 | John A. Peters (R) | 38,533 | 66.7 |
| | A. C. Towle (D) | 19,276 | 33.3 |
| 4 | Ira G. Hersey (R) | 30,872 | 72.3 |
| | L. G. C. Brown (D) | 11,805 | 27.7 |

## MARYLAND

| | | Votes | % |
|---|---|---|---|
| 1 | Thomas Alan Goldsborough (D) | 29,969 | 52.5 |
| | William N. Andrews (R) | 27,090 | 47.5 |
| 2 | Albert A. Blakeney (R) | 41,608 | 49.7 |
| | Carville D. Benson (D) | 34,151 | 40.8 |
| | Samuel C. Appleby (I) | 5,679 | 6.8 |
| 3 | John Philip Hill (R) | 24,617 | 49.4 |
| | Charles P. Coady (D) | 23,104 | 46.4 |
| 4 | J. Charles Linthicum (D) | 32,135 | 42.4 |
| | William O. Atwood (R) | 30,891 | 40.8 |
| | Walter E. Knickman (I) | 8,417 | 11.1 |
| 5 | Sydney E. Mudd (R) | 29,867 | 58.9 |
| | Thomas S. Klinger (D) | 18,569 | 36.6 |
| 6 | Frederick N. Zihlman (R) | 35,864 | 56.3 |
| | Frank W. Mish (D) | 25,992 | 40.8 |

## MASSACHUSETTS

| | | Votes | % |
|---|---|---|---|
| 1 | Allen T. Treadway (R) | 36,105 | 61.5 |
| | Thomas F. Cassidy (D) | 22,577 | 38.5 |
| 2 | Frederick H. Gillett (R) | 47,658 | 99.9 |
| 3 | Calvin D. Paige (R) | 38,313 | 71.5 |
| | Nixon Campbell (D) | 15,311 | 28.6 |
| 4 | Samuel E. Winslow (R) | 37,323 | 56.8 |
| | John F. McGrath (D) | 28,438 | 43.2 |
| 5 | John Jacob Rogers (R) | 41,861 | 70.1 |
| | Jackson Palmer (D) | 17,861 | 29.9 |
| 6 | Willfred W. Lufkin (R) | 47,231 | 75.3 |
| | John P. O'Connell (L-LAB D) | 15,523 | 24.7 |
| 7 | Robert S. Maloney (R) | 28,009 | 47.6 |
| | Michael F. Phelan (D) | 25,691 | 43.7 |
| | George F. Hogan (P) | 5,121 | 8.7 |
| 8 | Frederick W. Dallinger (R) | 54,246 | 72.9 |
| | Whitfield L. Tuck (D) | 12,754 | 17.1 |
| | John D. Lynch (I) | 7,407 | 10.0 |
| 9 | Charles L. Underhill (R) | 43,111 | 71.1 |
| | Maurice F. Ahearn (D) | 17,542 | 28.9 |
| 10 | Peter F. Tague (D) | 14,535 | 51.0 |
| | James E. Maguire (D) | 13,995 | 49.1 |
| 11 | George Holden Tinkham (R) | 40,278 | 68.5 |
| | Alfred J. Moore (D) | 18,553 | 31.5 |
| 12 | James A. Gallivan (D) | 32,622 | 58.6 |
| | Harrison H. Atwood (R) | 18,259 | 32.8 |
| | William H. O'Brien (PP CAND) | 4,813 | 8.6 |
| 13 | Robert Luce (R) | 56,451 | 70.9 |
| | Charles F. McCarthy (D) | 23,122 | 29.1 |
| 14 | Louis A. Frothingham (R) | 46,894 | 60.4 |
| | Richard Olney (D) | 28,596 | 36.8 |

| | Candidates | Votes | % |
|---|---|---|---|
| 15 | William S. Greene (R) | 28,095 | 60.2 |
| | Arthur J. B. Cartier (D) | 18,615 | 39.9 |
| 16 | Joseph Walsh (R) | 40,303 | 84.8 |
| | George Richards (LAB) | 7,239 | 15.2 |

## MICHIGAN

| | | Votes | % |
|---|---|---|---|
| 1 | George P. Codd (R) | 89,171 | 80.3 |
| | Frank Murphy (D) | 19,803 | 17.8 |
| 2 | Earl C. Michener (R) | 61,857 | 70.9 |
| | William H. Moore (D) | 25,281 | 29.0 |
| 3 | William H. Frankhauser (R) | 50,778 | 71.4 |
| | Gordon L. Stewart (D) | 19,652 | 27.6 |
| 4 | John C. Ketcham (R) | 47,671 | 75.1 |
| | Roman I. Jarvis Sr. (D) | 15,199 | 23.9 |
| 5 | Carl E. Mapes (R) | 53,379 | 75.0 |
| | Frank C. Jarvis (D) | 15,963 | 22.4 |
| 6 | Patrick H. Kelley (R) | 102,627 | 72.7 |
| | Frank L. Dodge (D) | 33,319 | 23.6 |
| 7 | Louis C. Cramton (R) | 53,416 | 80.1 |
| | John Hooker (D) | 12,755 | 19.1 |
| 8 | Joseph W. Fordney (R) | 54,337 | 72.2 |
| | Austin M. Brown (D) | 20,766 | 27.6 |
| 9 | James C. McLaughlin (R) | 42,992 | 76.3 |
| | Michael B. Danaher (D) | 12,095 | 21.5 |
| 10 | Roy O. Woodruff (R) | 43,678 | 75.5 |
| | David J. Lynch (D) | 13,935 | 24.1 |
| 11 | Frank D. Scott (R) | 41,529 | 100.0 |
| 12 | W. Frank James (R) | 41,783 | 80.4 |
| | Edward C. Anthony (D) | 8,446 | 16.3 |
| 13 | Vincent M. Brennan (R) | 78,116 | 68.1 |
| | James H. Lee (D) | 31,369 | 27.3 |

### Special Election

| | | Votes | % |
|---|---|---|---|
| 13 | Clarence J. McLeod (R) | 77,975 | 72.8 |
| | James H. Lee (D) | 29,110 | 27.2 |

## MINNESOTA

| | | Votes | % |
|---|---|---|---|
| 1 | Sydney Anderson (R) | 50,387 | 70.4 |
| | Julius I. Reiter (F-LAB) | 21,158 | 29.6 |
| 2 | Frank Clague (R) | 49,181 | 65.2 |
| | H. A. Fuller (I) | 19,274 | 25.6 |
| | Frank Simon (D) | 6,934 | 9.2 |
| 3 | Charles R. Davis (R) | 41,678 | 58.8 |
| | James M. Millett (D) | 15,146 | 21.4 |
| | R. A. Pomadt (I) | 14,034 | 19.8 |
| 4 | Oscar E. Keller (R) | 38,792 | 58.7 |
| | Thomas J. Brady (D) | 22,610 | 34.2 |
| | Carl W. Cummins (I) | 4,702 | 7.1 |
| 5 | Walter H. Newton (R) | 54,962 | 57.6 |
| | Lynn Thompson (F-LAB) | 22,584 | 23.7 |
| | Ernest Lundeen (I) | 9,573 | 10.0 |
| | T. O. Dahl (D) | 8,357 | 8.8 |
| 6 | Harold Knutson (R) | 47,954 | 69.0 |
| | Charles A. Lindbergh (I) | 21,587 | 31.0 |
| 7 | Andrew J. Volstead (R) | 36,822 | 47.5 |
| | Ole J. Kvale (I) | 35,370 | 45.6 |
| | James C. Mitchell (D) | 5,358 | 6.9 |
| 8 | Oscar J. Larson (R) | 33,428 | 50.8 |
| | William L. Carss (D) | 32,395 | 49.2 |
| 9 | Halvor Steenerson (R) | 39,122 | 52.7 |
| | N. E. Thormodson (I) | 28,443 | 38.3 |
| | Frank Jeffers (D) | 6,741 | 9.1 |
| 10 | Thomas D. Schall (R) | 54,971 | 68.3 |
| | John G. Soltis (F-LAB) | 18,590 | 23.1 |
| | H. A. Finlayson (D) | 6,917 | 8.6 |

## MISSISSIPPI

| | | Votes | % |
|---|---|---|---|
| 1 | John E. Rankin (D) | 10,400 | 100.0 |
| 2 | Bill G. Lowrey (D) | 6,960 | 100.0 |
| 3 | Benjamin G. Humphreys (D) | 6,338 | 100.0 |
| 4 | Thomas U. Sisson (D) | 8,979 | 93.8 |
| | J. A. Washington (SOC) | 598 | 6.2 |
| 5 | Ross A. Collins (D) | 11,507 | 94.1 |
| 6 | Paul B. Johnson (D) | 9,483 | 86.2 |
| | L. B. Collins (R) | 906 | 8.2 |

## MISSISSIPPI

| Candidates | Votes | % |
|---|---|---|
| T. J. Lyon (SOC) | 610 | 5.6 |
| 7 Percy E. Quin (D) | 6,695 | 92.7 |
| 8 James W. Collier (D) | 5,944 | 95.4 |

## MISSOURI

| Candidates | Votes | % |
|---|---|---|
| 1 Frank C. Millspaugh (R) | 34,259 | 50.5 |
| Milton A. Romjue (D) | 32,952 | 48.6 |
| 2 William W. Rucker (D) | 38,771 | 52.7 |
| B. F. Beazell (R) | 34,645 | 47.1 |
| 3 Henry F. Lawrence (R) | 33,949 | 51.9 |
| Jacob L. Milligan (D) | 31,475 | 48.1 |
| 4 Charles L. Faust (R) | 38,047 | 54.1 |
| L. C. Gabbert (D) | 32,098 | 45.7 |
| 5 Edgar C. Ellis (R) | 79,075 | 50.1 |
| William T. Bland (D) | 77,793 | 49.3 |
| 6 William O. Atkeson (R) | 29,802 | 52.2 |
| Clement C. Dickinson (D) | 26,995 | 47.3 |
| 7 Roscoe C. Patterson (R) | 50,213 | 54.9 |
| Sam C. Major (D) | 40,541 | 44.3 |
| 8 Sidney C. Roach (R) | 30,158 | 53.8 |
| William L. Nelson (D) | 25,733 | 45.9 |
| 9 Theodore W. Hukriede (R) | 39,213 | 52.2 |
| Champ Clark (D) | 35,626 | 47.5 |
| 10 Cleveland A. Newton (R) | 122,100 | 61.1 |
| Hughes (D) | 65,472 | 32.8 |
| 11 Harry B. Hawes (D) | 35,726 | 49.8 |
| Bernard P. Bogy (R) | 33,592 | 46.8 |
| 12 Leonidas C. Dyer (R) | 28,400 | 60.6 |
| Samuel Rosenfeld (D) | 16,901 | 36.1 |
| 13 Marion E. Rhodes (R) | 30,610 | 55.2 |
| A. T. Brewster (D) | 24,394 | 44.0 |
| 14 Edward D. Hays (R) | 56,525 | 56.8 |
| Robert L. Ward (D) | 41,547 | 41.8 |
| 15 Isaac V. McPherson (R) | 44,176 | 55.7 |
| E. M. Roseberry (D) | 33,844 | 42.7 |
| 16 Samuel A. Shelton (R) | 28,500 | 54.5 |
| Thomas L. Rubey (D) | 23,510 | 45.0 |

## MONTANA

| Candidates | Votes | % |
|---|---|---|
| 1 Washington J. McCormick (R) | 39,729 | 57.2 |
| Burton Watson (D) | 29,688 | 42.8 |
| 2 Carl W. Riddick (R) | 68,486 | 64.9 |
| M. McCusker (D) | 37,104 | 35.1 |

## NEBRASKA

| Candidates | Votes | % |
|---|---|---|
| 1 C. Frank Reavis (R) | 35,293 | 67.6 |
| Frank A. Peterson (D) | 16,880 | 32.4 |
| 2 Albert W. Jefferis (R) | 33,196 | 64.4 |
| James O'Hara (D) | 18,346 | 35.6 |
| 3 Robert E. Evans (R) | 38,370 | 54.0 |
| Webb Rice (D) | 17,171 | 24.2 |
| Marie Weekes (I) | 15,516 | 21.8 |
| 4 Melvin O. McLaughlin (R) | 34,384 | 62.5 |
| Albert P. Sprague (D) | 20,662 | 37.5 |
| 5 William E. Andrews (R) | 31,695 | 58.3 |
| Harry S. Dungan (D) | 22,663 | 41.7 |
| 6 Moses P. Kinkaid (R) | 49,122 | 64.5 |
| Thomas C. Grimes (D) | 20,790 | 27.3 |
| Lucien Stebbins (I) | 6,222 | 8.2 |

## NEVADA

| Candidates | Votes | % |
|---|---|---|
| AL Samuel S. Arentz (R) | 13,149 | 48.9 |
| Charles R. Evans (D) | 9,167 | 34.1 |
| Paul Jones (I) | 3,349 | 12.5 |

## NEW HAMPSHIRE

| Candidates | Votes | % |
|---|---|---|
| 1 Sherman E. Burroughs (R) | 46,606 | 59.3 |
| Rosecrans W. Pillsbury (D) | 31,354 | 39.9 |
| 2 Edward H. Wason (R) | 46,720 | 61.4 |
| Charles J. French (D) | 29,376 | 38.6 |

## NEW JERSEY

| Candidates | Votes | % |
|---|---|---|
| 1 Francis F. Patterson Jr. (R) | 55,885 | 65.3 |
| W. P. Kramer (D) | 23,711 | 27.7 |
| 2 Isaac Bacharach (R) | 51,006 | 70.0 |
| William E. Jonah (D) | 21,511 | 29.5 |
| 3 T. Frank Appleby (R) | 55,098 | 64.4 |
| W. E. Ramsay (D) | 29,796 | 34.8 |
| 4 Elijah C. Hutchinson (R) | 39,582 | 55.0 |
| Charles Browne (D) | 31,695 | 44.0 |
| 5 Ernest R. Ackerman (R) | 53,681 | 68.8 |
| R. E. Clement (D) | 21,949 | 28.1 |
| 6 Randolph Perkins (R) | 54,334 | 66.4 |
| Thomas A. Shields (D) | 25,764 | 31.5 |
| 7 Amos H. Radcliff (R) | 33,844 | 64.5 |
| Nicholas Hughes (D) | 15,291 | 29.2 |
| Frank Hubschmitt (SOC) | 2,939 | 5.6 |
| 8 Herbert W. Taylor (R) | 41,898 | 59.3 |
| C. A. McGlennon (D) | 27,822 | 39.4 |
| 9 Richard W. Parker (R) | 32,240 | 59.3 |
| Daniel F. Minahan (D) | 20,244 | 37.3 |
| 10 Frederick R. Lehlbach (R) | 40,965 | 63.6 |
| Dallas Flannagan (D) | 19,548 | 30.4 |
| 11 Archibald E. Olpp (R) | 30,046 | 55.2 |
| John J. Eagan (D) | 23,402 | 43.0 |
| 12 Charles F. X. O'Brien (D) | 34,527 | 53.1 |
| Walter Williams (R) | 29,080 | 44.8 |

### Special Election

| Candidates | Votes | % |
|---|---|---|
| 1 Francis F. Patterson Jr. (R) | 54,971 | 67.2 |
| W. P. Kramer (D) | 23,279 | 28.5 |

## NEW MEXICO

| Candidates | Votes | % |
|---|---|---|
| AL Nestor Montoya (R) | 54,672 | 51.9 |
| Antonio Lucero (D) | 49,426 | 46.9 |

## NEW YORK

| Candidates | Votes | % |
|---|---|---|
| 1 Frederick C. Hicks (R & P) | 61,502 | 69.5 |
| Alfred J. Kennedy (D) | 24,868 | 28.1 |
| 2 John J. Kindred (D) | 42,530 | 47.7 |
| Rudolph Hantusch (R) | 40,201 | 45.1 |
| William Burkle Sr. (SOC) | 5,872 | 6.6 |
| 3 John Kissel (R) | 16,576 | 44.6 |
| Christian J. McWilliams (D) | 15,224 | 40.9 |
| Harry W. Laidler (SOC) | 5,257 | 14.1 |
| 4 Thomas H. Cullen (D) | 21,070 | 56.2 |
| James J. Astorita (R) | 14,686 | 39.2 |
| 5 Ardolph L. Kline (R) | 42,129 | 58.2 |
| Edward Cassin (D) | 27,650 | 38.2 |
| 6 Warren I. Lee (R) | 44,527 | 59.4 |
| William F. X. Geoghan (D) | 22,476 | 30.0 |
| W. W. Passage (SOC) | 6,867 | 9.2 |
| 7 Michael J. Hogan (R) | 20,489 | 46.5 |
| James P. Maher (D) | 16,554 | 37.6 |
| Jean Jacques Coronel (SOC) | 6,561 | 14.9 |
| 8 Charles G. Bond (R) | 30,916 | 49.1 |
| William E. Cleary (D) | 22,586 | 35.8 |
| Victor H. Lawn (SOC) | 9,124 | 14.5 |
| 9 Andrew N. Petersen (R) | 41,399 | 52.1 |
| David J. O'Connell (D) | 30,212 | 38.1 |
| Wilhemus B. Robinson (SOC) | 7,420 | 9.3 |
| 10 Lester D. Volk (R) | 25,808 | 50.0 |
| Gilbert H. Rhoades (D) | 14,071 | 27.3 |
| James O'Neal (SOC) | 11,529 | 22.4 |
| 11 Daniel J. Riordan (D) | 19,097 | 50.7 |
| Wilbur F. Wakeman (R) | 17,358 | 46.1 |
| 12 Meyer London (SOC) | 10,212 | 54.1 |
| Henry M. Goldfogle (D, R) | 8,654 | 45.9 |
| 13 Christopher D. Sullivan (D, R) | 8,979 | 64.6 |
| Charles W. Irwin (SOC) | 4,925 | 35.4 |
| 14 Nathan S. Perlman (R, D) | 18,042 | 67.9 |
| Algernon Lee (SOC) | 8,515 | 32.1 |
| 15 Thomas J. Ryan (R) | 18,936 | 51.6 |
| Peter J. Dooling (D) | 14,971 | 40.8 |
| 16 W. Bourke Cockran (D) | 19,275 | 53.0 |
| Warren S. Fisher (R & P) | 14,336 | 39.4 |
| Bertha H. Mailly (SOC) | 2,748 | 7.6 |
| 17 Ogden L. Mills (R) | 33,659 | 62.0 |
| Herbert C. Pell Jr. (D) | 18,345 | 33.8 |
| 18 John F. Carew (D) | 12,169 | 31.2 |
| Henry J. O'Connor (R) | 11,148 | 28.6 |
| Jeremiah A. O'Leary (F-LAB) | 9,998 | 25.7 |
| Marie MacDonald (SOC) | 5,668 | 14.5 |
| 19 Walter M. Chandler (R) | 41,832 | 59.2 |
| William Kennelly (D) | 23,126 | 32.7 |
| Esther Friedman (SOC) | 5,667 | 8.0 |
| 20 Isaac Siegel (R, D) | 12,605 | 57.2 |
| Morris Hillquit (SOC) | 9,442 | 42.8 |
| 21 Martin C. Ansorge (R) | 48,959 | 58.7 |
| Jerome F. Donovan (D) | 28,535 | 34.2 |
| 22 Anthony J. Griffin (D) | 20,389 | 45.7 |
| Wilbur J. Murphy (R) | 17,657 | 39.6 |
| Patrick J. Murphy (SOC) | 6,580 | 14.7 |
| 23 Albert B. Rossdale (R) | 38,915 | 39.4 |
| Richard F. McKiniry (D) | 36,835 | 37.3 |
| Abraham Josephson (SOC) | 22,949 | 23.3 |
| 24 Benjamin L. Fairchild (R) | 50,409 | 53.7 |
| James V. Ganly (D) | 28,006 | 29.8 |
| George Orr (SOC) | 15,550 | 16.6 |
| 25 James W. Husted (R & P) | 49,829 | 67.4 |
| A. Outram Sherman (D) | 20,632 | 27.9 |
| 26 Hamilton Fish Jr. (R & P) | 43,916 | 63.7 |
| Rosslyn M. Cox (D) | 22,772 | 33.0 |
| 27 Charles B. Ward (R) | 42,504 | 60.8 |
| John R. Green (D) | 23,115 | 33.1 |
| 28 Peter G. Ten Eyck (D) | 51,210 | 53.8 |
| Edward J. Halter (R) | 42,214 | 44.4 |
| 29 James S. Parker (R & P) | 54,313 | 67.9 |
| J. Ward Russell (D) | 23,663 | 29.6 |
| 30 Frank Crowther (R & P) | 41,413 | 61.9 |
| John E. Kelly (D) | 18,687 | 27.9 |
| Harry Christian (SOC) | 6,242 | 9.3 |
| 31 Bertrand H. Snell (R & P) | 45,059 | 74.7 |
| John C. Russell (D) | 14,772 | 24.5 |
| 32 Luther W. Mott (R & P) | 53,249 | 72.6 |
| Newton S. Beebe (D) | 20,085 | 27.4 |
| 33 Homer P. Snyder (R) | 47,251 | 64.6 |
| Roger W. Huntington (D) | 21,732 | 29.7 |
| 34 John Davenport Clarke (R) | 52,809 | 69.8 |
| Charles R. Seymour (D) | 21,496 | 28.4 |
| 35 Walter W. Magee (R) | 60,018 | 65.0 |
| John F. Nash (D) | 25,699 | 27.8 |
| 36 Norman J. Gould (R & P) | 49,160 | 67.6 |
| George K. Shuler (D) | 23,534 | 32.4 |
| 37 Alanson B. Houghton (R & P) | 51,512 | 68.0 |
| Charles L. Durham (D) | 21,762 | 28.7 |
| 38 Thomas B. Dunn (R & P) | 56,796 | 66.0 |
| Hiram R. Wood (D) | 20,281 | 23.6 |
| Charles Messinger (SOC) | 8,369 | 9.7 |
| 39 Archie D. Sanders (R & P) | 53,079 | 71.1 |
| David A. White (D) | 17,602 | 23.6 |
| George Weber (SOC) | 3,943 | 5.3 |
| 40 S. Wallace Dempsey (R & P) | 56,129 | 69.5 |
| Frank S. Nicholson (D) | 19,253 | 23.8 |
| Augustus Meas (SOC) | 5,389 | 6.7 |
| 41 Clarence MacGregor (R & P) | 30,560 | 54.5 |
| Al J. Egloff (D) | 20,692 | 36.9 |
| Martin B. Heisler (SOC) | 4,836 | 8.6 |
| 42 James M. Mead (D) | 22,869 | 48.3 |
| C. Hamilton Cook (R & P) | 21,224 | 44.9 |
| John H. Gibbons (SOC) | 3,218 | 6.8 |
| 43 Daniel A. Reed (R & P) | 52,343 | 74.4 |
| Fred H. Sylvester (D) | 13,720 | 19.5 |
| Gust C. Peterson (SOC) | 4,273 | 6.1 |

## NORTH CAROLINA

| Candidates | Votes | % |
|---|---|---|
| 1 Hallett S. Ward (D) | 21,414 | 74.1 |
| Wheeler Martin (R) | 7,495 | 25.9 |

## NORTH CAROLINA

| Candidates | Votes | % |
|---|---|---|
| 2 Claude Kitchin (D) | 20,890 | 86.1 |
| W. O. Dixon (R) | 3,367 | 13.9 |
| 3 Samuel L. Brinson (D) | 21,547 | 56.9 |
| Richard L. Herring (R) | 16,347 | 43.1 |
| 4 Edward W. Pou (D) | 26,470 | 65.3 |
| James D. Parker (R) | 14,084 | 34.7 |
| 5 Charles M. Stedman (D) | 45,301 | 54.1 |
| William D. Merritt (R) | 38,484 | 45.9 |
| 6 Homer L. Lyon (D) | 24,174 | 68.7 |
| R. S. White (R) | 11,040 | 31.4 |
| 7 William C. Hammer (D) | 37,071 | 53.1 |
| William H. Cox (R) | 32,784 | 46.9 |
| 8 Robert L. Doughton (D) | 32,934 | 51.2 |
| J. Ike Campbell (R) | 31,456 | 48.9 |
| 9 Alfred L. Bulwinkle (D) | 40,195 | 53.0 |
| Jake F. Newell (R) | 35,686 | 47.0 |
| 10 Zebulon Weaver (D) | 36,923 | 51.6 |
| L. L. Jenkins (R) | 34,625 | 48.4 |

## NORTH DAKOTA

| Candidates | Votes | % |
|---|---|---|
| 1 Olger B. Burtness (R) | 43,530 | 57.6 |
| John M. Baer (I N-PART) | 32,072 | 42.4 |
| 2 George M. Young (R) | 34,849 | 51.7 |
| Ole H. Olson (I N-PART) | 32,618 | 48.4 |
| 3 James H. Sinclair (R & | 41,409 | 62.9 |
| R. H. Johnson (D&I) | 24,460 | 37.1 |

## OHIO

| Candidates | Votes | % |
|---|---|---|
| 1 Nicholas Longworth (R) | 57,328 | 57.6 |
| John H. Allen (D) | 40,195 | 40.4 |
| 2 Ambrose E. B. Stephens (R) | 47,797 | 52.6 |
| Thomas H. Morrow (D) | 41,781 | 46.0 |
| 3 Roy G. Fitzgerald (R) | 66,259 | 50.2 |
| William G. Pickrel (D) | 59,214 | 44.9 |
| 4 John S. Cable (R) | 50,478 | 52.6 |
| B. F. Welty (D) | 45,489 | 47.4 |
| 5 Charles J. Thompson (R) | 40,384 | 61.4 |
| Newt Bronson (D) | 25,395 | 38.6 |
| 6 Charles C. Kearns (R) | 38,044 | 55.2 |
| Cleona Searles (D) | 30,903 | 44.8 |
| 7 Simeon D. Fess (R) | 73,794 | 61.0 |
| Paul F. Dye (D) | 47,196 | 39.0 |
| 8 R. Clint Cole (R) | 43,473 | 54.3 |
| Fred E. Guthery (D) | 36,665 | 45.8 |
| 9 William W. Chalmers (R) | 49,732 | 56.5 |
| Isaac R. Sherwood (D) | 38,292 | 43.5 |
| 10 Israel M. Foster (R) | 38,436 | 64.2 |
| Benjamin F. Reynolds (D) | 21,429 | 35.8 |
| 11 Edwin D. Ricketts (R) | 33,524 | 51.7 |
| Mell G. Underwood (D) | 31,359 | 48.3 |
| 12 John C. Speaks (R) | 62,247 | 57.9 |
| Arthur P. Lamneck (D) | 43,845 | 40.8 |
| 13 James T. Begg (R) | 48,416 | 64.5 |
| Alfred Waggoner (D) | 26,646 | 35.5 |
| 14 Charles L. Knight (R) | 63,010 | 52.6 |
| Martin L. Davey (D) | 56,507 | 47.2 |
| 15 C. Ellis Moore (R) | 42,419 | 58.3 |
| John Sherman Talbott (D) | 30,326 | 41.7 |
| 16 Joseph H. Himes (R) | 56,584 | 56.9 |
| John McSweeney Jr. (D) | 42,799 | 43.1 |
| 17 William M. Morgan (R) | 46,968 | 50.2 |
| William A. Ashbrook (D) | 46,675 | 49.8 |
| 18 Frank Murphy (R) | 52,862 | 61.7 |
| Albert O. Barnes (D) | 32,802 | 38.3 |
| 19 John G. Cooper (R) | 60,147 | 70.4 |
| James Kennedy (D) | 25,250 | 29.6 |
| 20 Miner G. Norton (R) | 35,483 | 56.0 |
| Charles A. Mooney (D) | 27,223 | 42.9 |
| 21 Harry C. Gahn (R) | 27,127 | 59.1 |
| John J. Babka (D) | 18,252 | 39.7 |
| 22 Theodore E. Burton (R) | 91,062 | 74.3 |
| Mathew B. Excell (D) | 30,738 | 25.1 |

## OKLAHOMA

| Candidates | Votes | % |
|---|---|---|
| 1 Thomas A. Chandler (R) | 42,782 | 53.3 |
| E. B. Howard (D) | 35,201 | 43.8 |
| 2 Alice M. Robertson (R) | 24,188 | 48.8 |
| W. W. Hastings (D) | 23,979 | 48.4 |
| 3 Charles D. Carter (D) | 33,347 | 51.3 |
| James L. Shinaberger (R) | 27,465 | 42.2 |
| Robert L. Allen (SOC) | 4,227 | 6.5 |
| 4 Joseph C. Pringey (R) | 31,458 | 48.6 |
| Tom D. McKeown (D) | 29,832 | 46.1 |
| J. E. Bartos (SOC) | 3,438 | 5.3 |
| 5 Fletcher B. Swank (D) | 35,067 | 50.6 |
| B. T. Hainer (R) | 31,304 | 45.2 |
| 6 Lorraine M. Gensman (R) | 26,076 | 47.7 |
| Elmer Thomas (D) | 25,304 | 46.3 |
| J. V. Kolachny (SOC) | 3,202 | 5.9 |
| 7 James V. McClintic (D) | 21,422 | 49.4 |
| D. Montgomery (R) | 17,664 | 40.8 |
| O. E. Enfield (SOC) | 4,251 | 9.8 |
| 8 Manuel Herrick (R) | 31,265 | 53.9 |
| Zack A. Harris (D) | 23,405 | 40.4 |
| H. C. Geist (SOC) | 3,304 | 5.7 |

### Special Election

| Candidates | Votes | % |
|---|---|---|
| 8 Charles Swindall (R) | 32,420 | 55.3 |
| Zach A. Harris (D) | 22,389 | 38.2 |
| H. C. Geist (SOC) | 3,835 | 6.5 |

## OREGON

| Candidates | Votes | % |
|---|---|---|
| 1 Willis C. Hawley (R-D-P) | 75,597 | 90.2 |
| Harlin Talbert (SOC) | 8,258 | 9.9 |
| 2 Nicholas J. Sinnott (R) | 29,655 | 69.4 |
| James Harvey Graham (D) | 13,049 | 30.6 |
| 3 Clifton N. McArthur (R) | 37,884 | 51.9 |
| Esther Lovejoy (P) | 31,853 | 43.6 |

## PENNSYLVANIA

| Candidates | Votes | % |
|---|---|---|
| 1 William S. Vare (R) | 43,108 | 73.9 |
| Lawrence E. McCrossin (D) | 11,682 | 20.0 |
| H. J. Nelson (SOC) | 3,509 | 6.0 |
| 2 George S. Graham (R) | 34,848 | 78.7 |
| Herman Becker (D) | 7,877 | 17.8 |
| 3 Harry C. Ransley (R, LAB) | 29,075 | 77.2 |
| Joseph Hagerty (D) | 6,991 | 18.6 |
| 4 George W. Edmonds (R) | 41,102 | 72.3 |
| Harry J. Ruesscamp (D) | 12,003 | 21.1 |
| L. L. Klein (SOC) | 2,969 | 5.2 |
| 5 James J. Connolly (R) | 48,455 | 69.1 |
| Henry J. Burns (D) | 15,671 | 22.4 |
| 6 George P. Darrow (R, P) | 104,576 | 73.5 |
| Harry S. Jeffery (D) | 33,363 | 23.5 |
| 7 Thomas S. Butler (R, P) | 52,863 | 75.6 |
| Freeland S. Brown (D) | 15,942 | 22.8 |
| 8 Henry W. Watson (R) | 44,032 | 67.5 |
| Harvey S. Plummer (D) | 18,605 | 28.5 |
| 9 William W. Griest (R) | 29,252 | 74.2 |
| David F. Magee (D) | 9,504 | 24.1 |
| 10 Charles R. Connell (R) | 35,181 | 52.1 |
| Patrick McLane (D) | 30,411 | 45.0 |
| 11 Clarence D. Coughlin (R, P) | 45,092 | 59.7 |
| John J. Casey (D, SOC) | 30,412 | 40.3 |
| 12 John Reber (R) | 26,816 | 55.2 |
| Thomas J. Butler (D) | 21,787 | 44.8 |
| 13 Fred B. Gernerd (R) | 38,026 | 50.6 |
| Harry J. Dunn (D, LAB) | 29,922 | 39.8 |
| Charles E. Yeager (SOC) | 6,245 | 8.3 |
| 14 Louis T. McFadden (R, P) | 27,782 | 76.0 |
| Thomas A. Doherty (D) | 8,248 | 22.6 |
| 15 Edgar R. Kiess (R, P) | 30,182 | 71.6 |
| C. Edmund Gilmore (D) | 10,802 | 25.6 |
| 16 I. Clinton Kline (R, P) | 25,980 | 52.1 |
| John V. Lesher (D) | 22,417 | 45.0 |
| 17 Benjamin K. Focht (R, P) | 29,874 | 62.6 |
| John C. Dunkle (D) | 17,234 | 36.1 |
| 18 Aaron S. Kreider (R, P) | 42,745 | 64.1 |
| Milton H. Plank (D) | 18,951 | 28.4 |
| George A. Herring (LAB) | 4,110 | 6.2 |
| 19 John M. Rose (R) | 35,068 | 53.5 |
| Warren Worth Bailey (D) | 18,865 | 28.8 |

| Candidates | Votes | % |
|---|---|---|
| William T. Welsh (LAB, SOC) | 9,842 | 15.0 |
| 20 Edward S. Brooks (R) | 22,989 | 51.7 |
| Charles A. Hawkins (D, P) | 20,701 | 46.5 |
| 21 Evan J. Jones (R, P) | 27,780 | 63.4 |
| J. D. Connelly (D, LAB) | 15,000 | 34.2 |
| 22 Adam M. Wyant (R) | 30,540 | 51.6 |
| John H. Wilson (D) | 22,533 | 38.1 |
| S. E. Miller (SOC) | 3,234 | 5.5 |
| 23 Samuel A. Kendall (R, P) | 36,152 | 59.0 |
| Bruce F. Sterling (D) | 23,517 | 38.4 |
| 24 Henry W. Temple (R, P) | 42,402 | 73.3 |
| Samuel Amspoker (D) | 15,405 | 26.7 |
| 25 Milton W. Shreve (P, I) | 19,706 | 43.0 |
| Robert J. Firman (R) | 18,785 | 41.0 |
| Max B. Haibach (D) | 5,442 | 11.9 |
| 26 William H. Kirkpatrick (R) | 25,446 | 56.0 |
| George W. Geiser Jr. (D) | 19,219 | 42.3 |
| 27 Nathan L. Strong (R, P) | 31,209 | 71.4 |
| Lafayette F. Sutter (D, P) | 10,814 | 24.7 |
| 28 Harris J. Bixler (R, D) | 28,718 | 56.4 |
| Willis J. Hulings (P, CIT) | 20,676 | 40.6 |
| 29 Stephen G. Porter (R, P) | 32,766 | 69.5 |
| George J. Shaffer (D) | 10,749 | 22.8 |
| James J. Marshall (SOC) | 3,604 | 7.7 |
| 30 M. Clyde Kelly (R, D) | 51,850 | 91.5 |
| Charles A. Fike (SOC) | 4,847 | 8.6 |
| 31 John M. Morin (R, D) | 29,399 | 89.8 |
| Albert R. Jerling (SOC) | 2,280 | 7.0 |
| 32 Guy E. Campbell (R, D) | 44,307 | 83.9 |
| Earl O. Gunther (SOC) | 4,552 | 8.6 |
| George E. Briggs (P) | 3,953 | 7.5 |
| AL Anderson H. Walters (R) | 1,140,836✔ | |
| William J. Burke (R) | 1,134,013✔ | |
| Mahlon M. Garland (R) | 1,126,406* | |
| Joseph McLaughlin (R) | 1,108,538✔ | |
| John P. Bracken (D) | 466,564 | |
| M. J. Hanlan (D) | 463,866 | |
| Charles M. Bowman (D) | 459,552 | |
| John B. McDonough (D) | 444,306 | |
| Flora J. Diefenderfer (P) | 89,683 | |
| George Hart (P) | 85,771 | |
| Luther S. Kauffman (P) | 85,375 | |
| Charles J. Bauer (SOC) | 67,596 | |
| A. M. Buckwalter (SOC) | 66,628 | |
| Edward W. Hayden (SOC) | 65,928 | |
| Henry W. Schlegel (SOC) | 65,058 | |
| F. E. Whittlesey (P) | 60,278 | |
| Frieda S. Miller (LAB) | 25,265 | |
| Howard Cessna (LAB) | 24,062 | |
| William A. Hagan (SINGLE T) | 1,795 | |
| William R. Kline (SINGLE T) | 1,790 | |
| Thomas A. Kavanagh (SINGLE T) | 1,766 | |
| Joseph E. Robinson (SINGLE T) | 1,727 | |
| Joseph P. Smith (INDL) | 1,197 | |
| Frank Kalcec (INDL) | 977 | |
| Herman Spittal (INDL) | 810 | |
| Joseph Rack (INDL) | 794 | |

### Special Election

| Candidates | Votes | % |
|---|---|---|
| 3 Harry C. Ransley (R, LAB) | 29,097 | 76.6 |
| Joseph Hagerty (D) | 7,041 | 18.6 |

## RHODE ISLAND

| Candidates | Votes | % |
|---|---|---|
| 1 Clark Burdick (R) | 37,116 | 67.9 |
| Patrick J. Boyle (D) | 17,537 | 32.1 |
| 2 Walter R. Stiness (R) | 33,801 | 62.5 |
| Luigi De Pasquale (D) | 19,004 | 35.1 |
| 3 Ambrose Kennedy (R) | 34,775 | 59.7 |
| Herve J. Legace (D) | 22,386 | 38.4 |

## SOUTH CAROLINA

| | Candidates | Votes | % |
|---|---|---|---|
| 1 | W. Turner Logan (D) | 6,301 | 92.6 |
| | Saspartas (R) | 502 | 7.4 |
| 2 | James F. Byrnes (D) | 6,685 | 100.0 |
| 3 | Fred H. Dominick (D) | 9,699 | 100.0 |
| 4 | John J. McSwain (D) | 13,436 | 100.0 |
| 5 | William F. Stevenson (D) | 10,186 | 100.0 |
| 6 | Philip H. Stoll (D) | 8,681 | 100.0 |
| 7 | Hampton P. Fulmer (D) | 9,412 | 91.9 |
| | Hawkins (R) | 834 | 8.1 |

## SOUTH DAKOTA

| | | Votes | % |
|---|---|---|---|
| 1 | Charles A. Christopherson (R) | 39,231 | 56.2 |
| | Engebret J. Holter (NON PART) | 15,810 | 22.6 |
| | Ralph E. Johnson (D) | 14,815 | 21.2 |
| 2 | Royal C. Johnson (R) | 44,759 | 62.3 |
| | Frank Wahlen (NON PART) | 18,357 | 25.5 |
| | Lewis W. Bicknell (D) | 8,770 | 12.2 |
| 3 | William Williamson (R) | 19,335 | 48.0 |
| | Harry L. Gandy (D) | 16,214 | 40.2 |
| | O. E. Farnam (NON PART) | 4,765 | 11.8 |

## TENNESSEE

| | | Votes | % |
|---|---|---|---|
| 1 | B. Carroll Reece (R) | 46,010 | 98.3 |
| 2 | J. Will Taylor (R) | 37,722 | 74.8 |
| | Curtis Gentry (D) | 12,436 | 24.7 |
| 3 | Joseph Brown (R) | 29,366 | 51.6 |
| | John A. Moon (D) | 27,149 | 47.7 |
| 4 | Wynne F. Clouse (R) | 22,440 | 50.3 |
| | Cordell Hull (D) | 22,109 | 49.5 |
| 5 | Ewin L. Davis (D) | 14,845 | 61.9 |
| | Jesse Davenport (R) | 9,102 | 38.0 |
| 6 | Joseph W. Byrns (D) | 24,422 | 82.9 |
| | W. T. Perry (R) | 4,679 | 15.9 |
| 7 | Lemuel P. Padgett (D) | 17,517 | 55.7 |
| | A. M. Hughes (R) | 13,813 | 43.9 |
| 8 | Lon A. Scott (R) | 22,938 | 50.6 |
| | Gordon Browning (D) | 22,279 | 49.1 |
| 9 | Finis J. Garrett (D) | 25,409 | 68.3 |
| | John R. Walker Jr (R) | 11,671 | 31.4 |
| 10 | Hubert F. Fisher (D) | 23,987 | 80.8 |
| | Wayman Wilkerson (I, R) | 4,927 | 16.6 |

## TEXAS

| | | Votes | % |
|---|---|---|---|
| 1 | Eugene Black (D) | 17,814 | 92.3 |
| | G. T. Bartlett (R) | 1,497 | 7.8 |
| 2 | John C. Box (D) | 21,692 | 92.8 |
| | G. E. H. Meyer (AM) | 1,671 | 7.2 |
| 3 | Morgan G. Sanders (D) | 15,575 | 83.2 |
| | J. A. Butler (R) | 3,149 | 16.8 |
| 4 | Sam Rayburn (D) | 17,795 | 77.6 |
| | A. W. Acheson (R) | 5,124 | 22.4 |
| 5 | Hatton W. Sumners (D) | 19,785 | 80.2 |
| | J. O. Burleson (R) | 4,883 | 19.8 |
| 6 | Rufus Hardy (D) | 17,555 | 72.5 |
| | Clyde Essex (AM) | 3,668 | 15.2 |
| | D. H. Merrill (R) | 2,512 | 10.4 |

| | Candidates | Votes | % |
|---|---|---|---|
| 7 | Clay Stone Briggs (D) | 12,656 | 96.6 |
| 8 | Daniel E. Garrett (D) | 18,474 | 55.7 |
| | E. B. Barden (R) | 7,001 | 21.1 |
| | M. H. Broyles (B&T R) | 5,750 | 17.4 |
| | J. M. Gibson (AM) | 1,918 | 5.8 |
| 9 | Joseph J. Mansfield (D) | 12,311 | 58.7 |
| | James W. Rugeley (R) | 8,667 | 41.3 |
| 10 | James P. Buchanan (D) | 14,411 | 65.5 |
| | B. G. Neighbors (AM) | 7,597 | 34.5 |
| 11 | Tom T. Connally (D) | 15,621 | 79.1 |
| | W. D. Lewis (AM) | 4,124 | 20.9 |
| 12 | Fritz G. Lanham (D) | 20,925 | 80.5 |
| | Sam Davidson (R) | 4,203 | 16.2 |
| 13 | Lucian W. Parish (D) | 18,951 | 88.4 |
| | C. W. Johnson (R) | 2,483 | 11.6 |
| 14 | Harry M. Wurzbach (R) | 17,265 | 55.6 |
| | Carlos Bee (D) | 13,771 | 44.4 |
| 15 | John N. Garner (D) | 10,265 | 99.9 |
| 16 | Claude B. Hudspeth (D) | 15,658 | 69.7 |
| | William S. Easterling (R) | 6,796 | 30.3 |
| 17 | Thomas L. Blanton (D) | 22,311 | 83.8 |
| | W. D. Cowan (AM) | 4,298 | 16.2 |
| 18 | Marvin Jones (D) | 25,996 | 97.0 |

## UTAH

| | | Votes | % |
|---|---|---|---|
| 1 | Don B. Colton (R) | 41,749 | 57.3 |
| | James W. Funk (D) | 27,974 | 38.4 |
| 2 | Elmer O. Leatherwood (R) | 39,235 | 54.8 |
| | Mathonihah Thomas (D) | 28,201 | 39.4 |

## VERMONT

| | | Votes | % |
|---|---|---|---|
| 1 | Frank L. Greene (R) | 33,670 | 74.7 |
| | Jeremiah C. Duriok (D) | 11,398 | 25.3 |
| 2 | Porter H. Dale (R, P) | 34,221 | 78.7 |
| | Harry W. Witters (D) | 9,189 | 21.1 |

## VIRGINIA

| | | Votes | % |
|---|---|---|---|
| 1 | Schuyler Otis Bland (D) | 14,646 | 79.8 |
| | S. P. Powell (R) | 3,562 | 19.4 |
| 2 | Joseph T. Deal (D) | 15,318 | 73.6 |
| | Menalcus Lankford (R) | 5,389 | 25.9 |
| 3 | Andrew J. Montague (D) | 20,069 | 72.5 |
| | Walker G. Decourcy (R) | 4,146 | 15.0 |
| | H. H. Price | 2,682 | 9.7 |
| 4 | Patrick Henry Drewry (D) | 11,427 | 92.6 |
| | F. L. Mason (R) | 909 | 7.4 |
| 5 | Rorer A. James (D) | 15,567 | 58.4 |
| | S. Floyd Landreth (R) | 11,109 | 41.6 |
| 6 | James P. Woods (D) | 13,101 | 59.0 |
| | W. M. Doah (R) | 9,114 | 41.0 |
| 7 | Thomas W. Harrison (D) | 13,221‡ | 50.9 |
| | John Paul (R) | 12,773 | 49.1 |
| 8 | R. Walton Moore (D) | 13,142 | 71.7 |
| | F. M. Brooks (R) | 5,200 | 28.4 |
| 9 | C. Bascom Slemp (R) | 28,057 | 54.8 |
| | Bolling H. Handy (D) | 23,100 | 45.2 |
| 10 | Henry D. Flood (D) | 14,811 | 64.8 |
| | James H. C. Grasty (R) | 8,027 | 35.1 |

## WASHINGTON

| | Candidates | Votes | % |
|---|---|---|---|
| 1 | John F. Miller (R) | 51,459 | 56.7 |
| | James A. Duncan (F-LAB) | 28,154 | 31.0 |
| | Hugh C. Todd (D) | 11,184 | 12.3 |
| 2 | Lindley H. Hadley (R) | 39,315 | 59.8 |
| | William Bouck (F-LAB) | 26,398 | 40.2 |
| 3 | Albert Johnson (R) | 50,667 | 55.7 |
| | Homer T. Bone (F-LAB) | 27,824 | 30.6 |
| | George P. Fishburne (D) | 12,553 | 13.8 |
| 4 | John W. Summers (R) | 37,986 | 63.2 |
| | Fred Miller (D) | 11,353 | 18.9 |
| | Knute Hill (F-LAB) | 10,735 | 17.9 |
| 5 | J. Stanley Webster (R) | 39,228 | 58.1 |
| | Charles A. Fleming (D) | 28,300 | 41.9 |

## WEST VIRGINIA

| | | Votes | % |
|---|---|---|---|
| 1 | Benjamin L. Rosenbloom (R) | 40,818 | 50.3 |
| | Matthew M. Neely (D) | 40,393 | 49.7 |
| 2 | George M. Bowers (R) | 43,238 | 56.8 |
| | Forrest W. Brown (D) | 32,896 | 43.2 |
| 3 | Stuart F. Reed (R) | 45,146 | 57.7 |
| | Robert F. Kidd (D) | 33,056 | 42.3 |
| 4 | Harry C. Woodyard (R) | 47,146 | 55.4 |
| | John L. Conner (D) | 37,951 | 44.6 |
| 5 | Wells Goodykoontz (R) | 45,193 | 54.1 |
| | W. W. McNeal (D) | 38,394 | 45.9 |
| 6 | Leonard Sidney Echols (R) | 51,747 | 54.4 |
| | William Edwin Wilson (D) | 43,327 | 45.6 |

## WISCONSIN

| | | Votes | % |
|---|---|---|---|
| 1 | Henry Allen Cooper (R) | 51,144 | 75.9 |
| | Andrew F. Stahl (D) | 13,661 | 20.3 |
| 2 | Edward Voigt (R) | 39,563 | 67.3 |
| | Harry W. Bolens (D) | 14,291 | 24.3 |
| | Jacob F. Miller (SOC) | 4,969 | 8.5 |
| 3 | John M. Nelson (R) | 44,359 | 69.1 |
| | James W. Murphy (D) | 19,794 | 30.8 |
| 4 | John C. Kleczka (R) | 28,854 | 50.2 |
| | Robert Buech (SOC) | 22,137 | 38.6 |
| | Gerald P. Hayes (D) | 6,436 | 11.2 |
| 5 | William H. Stafford (R) | 40,777 | 54.5 |
| | Victor L. Berger (SOC) | 34,004 | 45.5 |
| 6 | Florian Lampert (R) | 38,034 | 68.7 |
| | Leo P. Fox (D) | 11,606 | 21.0 |
| | Edward C. Damrow (SOC) | 5,714 | 10.3 |
| 7 | Joseph D. Beck (R) | 37,137 | 78.4 |
| | Robert H. Clarke (D) | 8,929 | 18.8 |
| 8 | Edward E. Browne (R) | 34,215 | 61.8 |
| | George W. Lippert (SOC) | 14,661 | 26.5 |
| | Leo P. Pasternacki (D) | 6,425 | 11.6 |
| 9 | David G. Classon (R) | 32,027 | 59.2 |
| | Andrew R. McDonald (D) | 20,108 | 37.2 |
| 10 | James A. Frear (R) | 44,658 | 99.4 |
| 11 | Adolphus P. Nelson (R) | 38,057 | 85.3 |
| | John P. Jensen (D) | 6,524 | 14.6 |

## WYOMING

| | | Votes | % |
|---|---|---|---|
| AL | Frank W. Mondell (R) | 34,689 | 61.5 |
| | Wade H. Fowler (D) | 14,952 | 26.5 |
| | James Morgan (F-LAB) | 6,021 | 10.7 |

# 1921 House Election

## PENNSYLVANIA

### Special Election

| | | Votes | % |
|---|---|---|---|
| AL | Thomas S. Crago (R) | 705,876 | 68.2 |
| | John P. Bracken (D) | 225,268 | 21.8 |
| | B. E. P. Prugh (P) | 74,837 | 7.2 |

# 1922 House Elections

## ALABAMA

| | Candidates | Votes | % |
|---|---|---|---|
| 1 | John McDuffie (D) | 13,960 | 100.0 |
| 2 | John R. Tyson (D) | 9,255 | 100.0 |
| 3 | Henry B. Steagall (D) | 9,141 | 90.3 |
| | Charles E. Roberts | 987 | 9.8 |
| 4 | Lamar Jeffers (D) | 9,976 | 81.5 |
| | J. C. Harper | 2,265 | 18.5 |
| 5 | William B. Bowling (D) | 10,411 | 80.4 |
| | W. M. Russell | 2,539 | 19.6 |
| 6 | William B. Oliver (D) | 4,864 | 100.0 |
| 7 | Miles C. Allgood (D) | 18,597 | 62.6 |
| | B. L. Noogin | 11,130 | 37.4 |
| 8 | Edward B. Almon (D) | 12,303 | 96.3 |
| 9 | George Huddleston (D) | 11,300 | 94.7 |
| | G. L. Lemon | 630 | 5.3 |
| 10 | William B. Bankhead (D) | 14,803 | 63.2 |
| | W. A. McMurray | 8,631 | 36.8 |

## ARIZONA

| | Candidates | Votes | % |
|---|---|---|---|
| AL | Carl Hayden (D) | 37,262 | 71.9 |
| | Emma M. Guild (R) | 14 601 | 28.2 |

## ARKANSAS

| | Candidates | Votes | % |
|---|---|---|---|
| 1 | William J. Driver (D) | 1,454 | 100.0 |
| 2 | William A. Oldfield (D) | 5,220 | 86.7 |
| | J. N. Hout | 798 | 13.3 |
| 3 | John N. Tillman (D) | 5,327 | 98.2 |
| 4 | Otis Wingo (D) | 7,330 | 79.5 |
| | George Tillis | 1,896 | 20.6 |
| 5 | Heartsill Ragon (D) | 5,944 | 79.7 |
| | John W. White | 1,513 | 20.3 |
| 6 | Lewis E. Sawyer (D) | 3,232 | 100.0 |
| 7 | Tilman B. Parks (D) | 2,167 | 100.0 |

## CALIFORNIA

| | Candidates | Votes | % |
|---|---|---|---|
| 1 | Clarence F. Lea (DR) | 53,129 | 100.0 |
| 2 | John E. Raker (DR) | 32,981 | 100.0 |
| 3 | Charles F. Curry (R-D) | 71,316 | 91.5 |
| | Marcus H. Steely (SOC) | 6,561 | 8.4 |
| 4 | Julius Kahn (R-D) | 46,527 | 82.9 |
| | Hugo Ernst (SOC) | 9,547 | 17.0 |
| 5 | John I. Nolan (R-D) | 49,414* | 99.8 |
| 6 | James H. MacLafferty (R) | 59,858 | 66.4 |
| | Hugh W. Brunk (D) | 22,711 | 25.2 |
| | Elvina S. Beals (SOC) | 7,616 | 8.4 |
| 7 | Henry E. Barbour (R-D) | 67,000 | 99.9 |
| 8 | Arthur Monroe Free (R-D) | 57,926 | 99.8 |
| 9 | Walter F. Lineberger (R-D) | 66,265 | 59.1 |
| | Charles H. Randall (P & D) | 45,794 | 40.9 |
| 10 | Henry Z. Osborne (R-D-P) | 98,739* | 99.9 |
| 11 | Philip D. Swing (R-D) | 79,039 | 91.3 |
| | George Bauer (SOC) | 7,466 | 8.6 |

### Special Election

| | | Votes | % |
|---|---|---|---|
| 6 | James H. MacLafferty (I) | 53,285 | 68.4 |
| | Hugh W. Brunk (I) | 24,626 | 31.6 |

## COLORADO

| | Candidates | Votes | % |
|---|---|---|---|
| 1 | William N. Vaile (R) | 32,939 | 55.5 |
| | Benjamin C. Hilliard (D) | 25,477 | 42.9 |
| 2 | Charles B. Timberlake (R) | 43,601 | 57.3 |
| | Charles M. Worth (D) | 32,443 | 42.7 |
| 3 | Guy U. Hardy (R) | 43,508 | 52.4 |
| | Chester B. Horn (D) | 39,500 | 47.6 |
| 4 | Edward T. Taylor (D) | 30,331 | 64.3 |
| | Merle D. Vincent (R) | 16,878 | 35.8 |

## CONNECTICUT

| | Candidates | Votes | % |
|---|---|---|---|
| 1 | E. Hart Fenn (R) | 40,124 | 52.2 |
| | Joseph F. Dutton (D) | 35,003 | 45.6 |
| 2 | Richard P. Freeman (R) | 31,484 | 55.4 |
| | Raymond J. Jodoin (D) | 24,732 | 43.5 |
| 3 | John Q. Tilson (R) | 36,247 | 52.3 |
| | Stephen Whitney (D) | 31,674 | 45.7 |
| 4 | Schuyler Merritt (R) | 35,274 | 53.9 |
| | Archibald McNeil (D) | 28,992 | 44.3 |
| 5 | Patrick B. O'Sullivan (D) | 27,359 | 49.7 |
| | James P. Glynn (R) | 27,065 | 49.1 |

## DELAWARE

| | | Votes | % |
|---|---|---|---|
| AL | William H. Boyce (D) | 39,126 | 53.9 |
| | Caleb R. Layton (R) | 32,577 | 44.9 |

## FLORIDA

| | | Votes | % |
|---|---|---|---|
| 1 | Herbert J. Drane (D) | 14,371 | 82.9 |
| | William M. Gober (R) | 2,961 | 17.1 |
| 2 | Frank Clark (D) | 6,931 | 100.0 |
| 3 | John H. Smithwick (D) | 7,564 | 100.0 |
| 4 | William J. Sears (D) | 15,678 | 82.3 |
| | Howard W. McCay (R) | 3,362 | 17.6 |

## GEORGIA

| | | Votes | % |
|---|---|---|---|
| 1 | R. Lee Moore (D) | 5,579 | 90.0 |
| | D. H. Clarke (R) | 426 | 6.9 |
| 2 | Frank Park (D) | 5,449 | 100.0 |
| 3 | Charles R. Crisp (D) | 7,298 | 100.0 |
| 4 | William C. Wright (D) | 4,777 | 100.0 |
| 5 | William D. Upshaw (D) | 4,646 | 93.1 |
| | Max H. Wilensky | 347 | 7.0 |
| 6 | James W. Wise (D) | 6,961 | 100.0 |
| 7 | Gordon Lee (D) | 7,278 | 100.0 |
| 8 | Charles H. Brand (D) | 5,148 | 100.0 |
| 9 | Thomas M. Bell (D) | 11,088 | 94.6 |
| 10 | Carl Vinson (D) | 4,639 | 100.0 |
| 11 | William C. Lankford (D) | 6,879 | 100.0 |
| 12 | William W. Larsen (D) | 5,020 | 100.0 |

## IDAHO

| | | Votes | % |
|---|---|---|---|
| 1 | Burton L. French (R) | 24,167 | 46.8 |
| | George Waters (D) | 13,772 | 26.7 |
| | W. W. Deal (PROG) | 13,673 | 26.5 |
| 2 | Addison T. Smith (R) | 33,206 | 47.8 |
| | W. P. Whitaker (D) | 19,875 | 28.6 |
| | Dow Dunning (PROG) | 16,450 | 23.7 |

## ILLINOIS

| | | Votes | % |
|---|---|---|---|
| 1 | Martin B. Madden (R) | 23,895 | 59.1 |
| | George Mayer (D) | 15,999 | 39.6 |
| 2 | James R. Mann (R) | 58,694* | 58.2 |
| | Adam F. Bloch (D) | 38,487 | 38.2 |
| 3 | Elliott W. Sproul (R) | 48,486 | 48.8 |
| | Thomas M. Crane (D) | 47,335 | 47.7 |
| 4 | John W. Rainey (D) | 32,403 | 69.2 |
| | Henry G. Dobler (R) | 13,328 | 28.5 |
| 5 | Adolph J. Sabath (D) | 20,377 | 66.5 |
| | Jacob Gartenstein (R) | 9,007 | 29.4 |
| 6 | James R. Buckley (D) | 58,928 | 48.2 |
| | John J. Gorman (R) | 58,886 | 48.2 |
| 7 | M. Alfred Michaelson (R) | 69,367 | 49.8 |
| | Frank M. Padden (D) | 61,035 | 43.8 |
| | John M. Collins (SOC) | 7,276 | 5.2 |
| 8 | Stanley Henry Kunz (D) | 18,749 | 65.3 |
| | Fred S. DeCola (R) | 9,311 | 32.5 |
| 9 | Fred A. Britten (R) | 26,143 | 60.0 |
| | James A. Prendergast (D) | 16,223 | 37.3 |

| | Candidates | Votes | % |
|---|---|---|---|
| 10 | Carl R. Chindblom (R) | 62,324 | 61.6 |
| | Bernard Moulton Wiedinger (D) | 35,535 | 35.1 |
| 11 | Frank R. Reid (R) | 43,581 | 68.8 |
| | Edward J. O'Beirne (D) | 18,816 | 29.7 |
| 12 | Charles E. Fuller (R) | 46,893 | 77.6 |
| | John A. Dowdall (D) | 11,733 | 19.4 |
| 13 | John C. McKenzie (R) | 30,064 | 70.0 |
| | William G. Curtiss (D) | 12,319 | 28.7 |
| 14 | William J. Graham (R) | 34,946 | 59.9 |
| | L. S. Mayer (D) | 21,541 | 36.9 |
| 15 | Edward J. King (R) | 36,547 | 60.1 |
| | Charles C. Craig (D) | 23,298 | 38.3 |
| 16 | William E. Hull (R) | 39,372 | 55.2 |
| | Jesse Black Jr. (D) | 30,395 | 42.6 |
| 17 | Frank H. Funk (R) | 28,466 | 55.7 |
| | Frank Gillespie (D) | 22,233 | 43.5 |
| 18 | William P. Holaday (R) | 35,880 | 52.8 |
| | Andrew B. Dennis (D) | 30,123 | 44.4 |
| 19 | Allen F. Moore (R) | 39,636 | 54.4 |
| | Raymond D. Meeker (D) | 32,529 | 44.6 |
| 20 | Henry T. Rainey (D) | 31,430 | 54.2 |
| | Guy L. Shaw (R) | 26,541 | 45.8 |
| 21 | J. Earl Major (D) | 37,661 | 49.3 |
| | Loren E. Wheeler (R) | 33,086 | 43.3 |
| | Duncan McDonald (F-LAB) | 4,438 | 5.8 |
| 22 | Edward E. Miller (R) | 34,224 | 47.6 |
| | Edward E. Campbell (D) | 31,539 | 43.9 |
| | Daniel L. Thomas (F-LAB) | 4,980 | 6.9 |
| 23 | William W. Arnold (D) | 38,908 | 52.5 |
| | Edwin B. Brooks (R) | 34,610 | 46.7 |
| 24 | Thomas S. Williams (R) | 29,141 | 50.8 |
| | Dempsey T. Woodard (D) | 28,252 | 49.2 |
| 25 | Edward E. Denison (R) | 37,907 | 54.4 |
| | A. S. Caldwell (D) | 28,697 | 41.2 |
| AL | Richard Yates (R) | 943,684✔ | |
| | Henry R. Rathborne (R) | 911,599✔ | |
| | Simon J. Gorman (D) | 666,583 | |
| | William Murphy (D) | 662,059 | |
| | Fred W. Wenschoff (SOC) | 36,311 | |
| | Andrew Lafin (SOC) | 35,655 | |
| | Edward Ellis Carr (F-LAB) | 32,595 | |
| | Henry W. Olinger (F-LAB) | 30,756 | |

### Special Election

| | | Votes | % |
|---|---|---|---|
| AL | Winnifred Mason Huck (R) | 865,971 | 52.6 |
| | Allen D. Albert (D) | 710,716 | 43.2 |

## INDIANA

| | | Votes | % |
|---|---|---|---|
| 1 | William E. Wilson (D) | 42,797 | 53.6 |
| | Oscar R. Luhring (R) | 35,835 | 44.9 |
| 2 | Arthur H. Greenwood (D) | 43,632 | 49.5 |
| | Oscar E. Bland (R) | 42,752 | 48.5 |
| 3 | Frank Gardner (D) | 43,344 | 53.5 |
| | Samuel A. Lambdin (R) | 37,202 | 46.0 |
| 4 | Harry C. Canfield (D) | 43,749 | 51.1 |
| | John S. Benham (R) | 41,825 | 48.9 |
| 5 | Everett Sanders (R) | 38,759 | 49.5 |
| | Charles H. Bidaman (D) | 37,748 | 48.2 |
| 6 | Richard N. Elliott (R) | 39,281 | 51.6 |
| | James A. Clifton (D) | 36,818 | 48.4 |
| 7 | Merrill Moores (R) | 49,629 | 53.9 |
| | Joseph P. Turk (D) | 41,118 | 44.6 |
| 8 | Albert H. Vestal (R) | 43,470 | 52.2 |
| | John W. Tyndall (D) | 39,169 | 47.0 |
| 9 | Fred S. Purnell (R) | 46,919 | 51.5 |
| | George Lee Moffett (D) | 42,074 | 46.2 |
| 10 | William R. Wood (R) | 45,590 | 59.2 |
| | William F. Spencer (D) | 30,835 | 40.0 |
| 11 | Samuel E. Cook (D) | 45,389 | 52.8 |
| | Milton Kraus (R) | 39,285 | 45.2 |
| 12 | Louis W. Fairfield (R) | 36,045 | 51.1 |
| | Charles W. Branstrator (D) | 34,457 | 48.9 |

## INDIANA

| | Candidates | Votes | % |
|---|---|---|---|
| 13 | Andrew J. Hickey (R) | 50,003 | 53.7 |
| | Esther Kathleen O'Keefe (D) | 43,053 | 46.3 |

## IOWA

| | Candidates | Votes | % |
|---|---|---|---|
| 1 | William F. Kopp (R) | 26,651 | 65.0 |
| | John M. Lindley (D) | 14,056 | 34.3 |
| 2 | Harry E. Hull (R) | 27,450 | 51.4 |
| | Wayne G. Cook (D) | 25,620 | 47.9 |
| 3 | Thomas J. B. Robinson (R) | 34,518 | 57.6 |
| | Fred P. Hageman (D) | 24,304 | 40.6 |
| 4 | Gilbert N. Haugen (R) | 32,586 | 57.1 |
| | A. M. Schanke (D) | 24,532 | 43.0 |
| 5 | Cyrenus Cole (R) | 33,607 | 68.0 |
| | G. A. Smith (D) | 15,825 | 32.0 |
| 6 | C. William Ramseyer (R) | 28,702 | 61.9 |
| | James E. Craven (D) | 17,489 | 37.7 |
| 7 | Cassius C. Dowell (R) | 34,012 | 62.3 |
| | Winfred E. Robb (D) | 19,987 | 36.6 |
| 8 | Horace M. Towner (R) | 30,551 | 56.6 |
| | J. P. Daughton (D) | 23,478 | 43.5 |
| 9 | William R. Greene (R) | 31,757 | 61.7 |
| | Paul W. Richards (D) | 19,722 | 38.3 |
| 10 | Lester J. Dickinson (R) | 41,290 | 71.1 |
| | Mrs. Jett W. Douglas (D) | 16,781 | 28.9 |
| 11 | William D. Boies (R) | 36,050 | 60.0 |
| | Guy M. Gillette (D) | 24,027 | 40.0 |

## KANSAS

| | Candidates | Votes | % |
|---|---|---|---|
| 1 | Daniel R. Anthony Jr. (R) | 39,463 | 63.7 |
| | Frank Gragg (D) | 22,480 | 36.3 |
| 2 | Edward C. Little (R) | 41,482 | 54.4 |
| | William H. Thompson (D) | 34,816 | 45.6 |
| 3 | William H. Sproul (R) | 38,321 | 49.0 |
| | Charles Stephens (D) | 37,829 | 48.4 |
| 4 | Homer Hoch (R) | 29,657 | 62.0 |
| | Walter W. Austin (D) | 17,294 | 36.2 |
| 5 | James G. Strong (R) | 32,064 | 56.3 |
| | Clarence E. Hatfield (D) | 24,881 | 43.7 |
| 6 | Hays B. White (R) | 33,464 | 54.1 |
| | F. W. Boyd (D) | 26,666 | 43.1 |
| 7 | Jasper N. Tincher (R) | 47,515 | 58.3 |
| | A. S. Allphin (D) | 32,159 | 39.5 |
| 8 | William A. Ayres (D) | 37,581 | 62.3 |
| | Richard E. Bird (R) | 22,721 | 37.7 |

## KENTUCKY

| | Candidates | Votes | % |
|---|---|---|---|
| 1 | Alben W. Barkley (D) | 9,492 | 70.0 |
| | F. M. McClain (R) | 4,075 | 30.0 |
| 2 | David H. Kincheloe (D) | 14,837 | 63.5 |
| | George W. Jolly (R) | 8,541 | 36.5 |
| 3 | Robert Y. Thomas Jr. (D) | 21,189 | 60.9 |
| | W. O. Moats (R) | 13,613 | 39.1 |
| 4 | Ben Johnson (D) | 19,142 | 93.1 |
| | P. N. Woodruff (F-LAB) | 1,429 | 7.0 |
| 5 | Maurice H. Thatcher (R) | 38,806 | 49.1 |
| | Kendrick R. Lewis (D) | 35,124 | 44.4 |
| | Herman F. Young (F-LAB) | 5,154 | 6.5 |
| 6 | Arthur B. Rouse (D) | 18,131 | 63.9 |
| | Leo E. Keller (NON PL) | 9,197 | 32.4 |
| 7 | James C. Cantrill (D) | 9,389 | 100.0 |
| 8 | Ralph Gilbert (D) | 21,296 | 57.4 |
| | D. H. Kincaid (R) | 15,802 | 42.6 |
| 9 | William J. Fields (D) | 22,816 | 65.1 |
| | J. H. Stricklin (R) | 12,249 | 34.9 |
| 10 | John N. Langley (R) | 17,067 | 55.5 |
| | F. T. Hatcher (D) | 13,668 | 44.5 |
| 11 | John M. Robsion (R) | 28,086 | 66.6 |
| | C. J. Sipple (D) | 11,396 | 27.0 |
| | H. H. Seavy (F-LAB) | 2,670 | 6.3 |

## LOUISIANA

| | Candidates | Votes | % |
|---|---|---|---|
| 1 | James O'Connor (D) | 14,760 | 100.0 |
| 2 | H. Garland Dupre (D) | 12,287 | 100.0 |
| 3 | Whitmel P. Martin (D) | 1,954 | 99.7 |
| 4 | John N. Sandlin (D) | 3,618 | 100.0 |
| 5 | Riley J. Wilson (D) | 2,345 | 100.0 |
| 6 | George K. Favrot (D) | 3,317 | 99.5 |
| 7 | Ladislas Lazaro (D) | 3,069 | 99.5 |
| 8 | James B. Aswell (D) | 2,987 | 100.0 |

## MAINE

| | Candidates | Votes | % |
|---|---|---|---|
| 1 | Carroll L. Beedy (R) | 26,050 | 58.7 |
| | Louis A. Donahue (D) | 18,312 | 41.3 |
| 2 | Wallace H. White Jr. (R) | 25,719 | 53.7 |
| | B. G. McIntire (D) | 22,150 | 46.3 |
| 3 | John E. Nelson (R) | 30,654 | 58.4 |
| | Leon O. Tebbetts (D) | 21,828 | 41.6 |
| 4 | Ira G. Hersey (R) | 18,641 | 60.8 |
| | James W. Sewall (D) | 11,997 | 39.2 |

## MARYLAND

| | Candidates | Votes | % |
|---|---|---|---|
| 1 | T. Alan Goldsborough (D) | 27,117 | 55.8 |
| | Charles J. Butler (R) | 21,524 | 44.3 |
| 2 | Millard E. Tydings (D) | 36,565 | 52.8 |
| | Albert Alex Blakeney (R) | 31,053 | 44.8 |
| 3 | John Philip Hill (R) | 27,740 | 67.3 |
| | Antony Dimarco (D) | 12,454 | 30.2 |
| 4 | J. Charles Linthicum (D) | 33,322 | 61.7 |
| | L. Edward Wolf (R) | 18,972 | 35.1 |
| 5 | Sydney E. Mudd (R) | 23,764 | 50.8 |
| | Clarence M. Roberts (D) | 21,112 | 45.1 |
| 6 | Frederick N. Zihlman (R) | 22,261 | 50.7 |
| | Frank W. Mish (D) | 20,838 | 47.5 |

## MASSACHUSETTS

| | Candidates | Votes | % |
|---|---|---|---|
| 1 | Allen T. Treadway (R) | 26,229 | 50.7 |
| | Thomas F. Cassidy (D) | 25,529 | 49.3 |
| 2 | Frederick H. Gillett (R) | 28,639 | 59.6 |
| | Joseph E. Kerigan (D) | 19,376 | 40.4 |
| 3 | Calvin D. Paige (R) | 26,944 | 56.4 |
| | M. Fred O'Connell (D) | 19,311 | 40.4 |
| 4 | Samuel E. Winslow (R) | 32,942 | 52.8 |
| | William H. Dyer (D) | 29,399 | 47.2 |
| 5 | John Jacob Rogers (R) | 33,673 | 64.0 |
| | Andrew E. Barrett (D) | 18,936 | 36.0 |
| 6 | A. Piatt Andrew (R) | 36,426 | 77.0 |
| | Charles I. Pettingell (D) | 10,895 | 23.0 |
| 7 | William P. Connery Jr. (D) | 30,493 | 56.0 |
| | Frederick Butler (R) | 23,978 | 44.0 |
| 8 | Frederick W. Dallinger (R) | 42,248 | 65.9 |
| | John F. Daly (D) | 21,893 | 34.1 |
| 9 | Charles L. Underhill (R) | 31,229 | 57.7 |
| | Arthur D. Healey (D) | 22,867 | 42.3 |
| 10 | Peter F. Tague (D) | 21,029 | 79.5 |
| | Loyal L. Jenkins (R) | 5,422 | 20.5 |
| 11 | George Holden Tinkham (R) | 33,396 | 60.3 |
| | David J. Brickley (D) | 21,999 | 39.7 |
| 12 | James A. Gallivan (D) | 42,779 | 75.9 |
| | Alexander H. Rice (R) | 13,575 | 24.1 |
| 13 | Robert Luce (R) | 50,710 | 100.0 |
| 14 | Louis A. Frothingham (R) | 41,490 | 63.3 |
| | David W. Murray (D) | 24,014 | 36.7 |
| 15 | William S. Greene (R) | 25,179 | 57.4 |
| | Arthur J. B. Cartier (D) | 18,662 | 42.6 |
| 16 | Charles L. Gifford (R) | 23,862 | 54.4 |
| | James P. Doran (D) | 20,021 | 45.6 |

## MICHIGAN

| | Candidates | Votes | % |
|---|---|---|---|
| 1 | Robert H. Clancy (D) | 22,996 | 55.4 |
| | Hugh Shepherd (R) | 17,722 | 42.7 |
| 2 | Earl C. Michener (R) | 31,509 | 57.4 |
| | James W. Helme (D) | 23,393 | 42.6 |
| 3 | John M. C. Smith (R) | 23,869 | 61.1 |
| | George Burr Smith (D) | 15,226 | 39.0 |
| 4 | John C. Ketcham (R) | 26,050 | 65.4 |
| | Homer S. Carr (D) | 13,772 | 34.6 |
| 5 | Carl E. Mapes (R) | 25,853 | 71.1 |
| | Claude O. Taylor (D) | 10,501 | 28.9 |
| 6 | Grant M. Hudson (R) | 46,791 | 61.4 |
| | Charles R. Adair (D) | 29,241 | 38.3 |
| 7 | Louis C. Cramton (R) | 35,328 | 72.3 |
| | Patrick H. Kane (D) | 13,431 | 27.5 |
| 8 | Bird J. Vincent (R) | 33,864 | 63.4 |
| | De Witt Vought (D) | 19,538 | 36.6 |
| 9 | James C. McLaughlin (R) | 21,703 | 95.6 |
| 10 | Roy O. Woodruff (R) | 23,792 | 100.0 |
| 11 | Frank D. Scott (R) | 24,390 | 69.3 |
| | Robert H. Rayburn (D) | 10,823 | 30.7 |
| 12 | W. Frank James (R) | 26,228 | 79.4 |
| | Frederick Kappler (D) | 6,784 | 20.6 |
| 13 | Clarence J. McLeod (R) | 28,871 | 69.8 |
| | Ferris H. Fitch (D) | 11,948 | 28.9 |

## MINNESOTA

| | Candidates | Votes | % |
|---|---|---|---|
| 1 | Sydney Anderson (R) | 36,698 | 57.3 |
| | J. F. Lynn (D) | 27,316 | 42.7 |
| 2 | Frank Clague (R) | 47,591 | 100.0 |
| 3 | Charles R. Davis (R) | 42,708 | 69.8 |
| | Lillien Cox Gault (D) | 18,462 | 30.2 |
| 4 | Oscar E. Keller (R) | 33,259 | 58.7 |
| | Paul E. Doty (D) | 20,187 | 35.6 |
| | O. J. McCartney (I) | 3,243 | 5.7 |
| 5 | Walter H. Newton (R) | 45,221 | 53.9 |
| | John R. Coan (D) | 38,760 | 46.2 |
| 6 | Harold Knutson (R) | 37,201 | 60.9 |
| | Peter J. Seberger (F-LAB) | 19,365 | 31.7 |
| | John Knutsen (I) | 4,550 | 7.4 |
| 7 | Ole J. Kvale (F-LAB) | 42,832 | 59.7 |
| | Andrew J. Volstead (R) | 28,918 | 40.3 |
| 8 | Oscar J. Larson (R) | 32,420 | 53.0 |
| | William L. Carss (D) | 28,757 | 47.0 |
| 9 | Knud Wefald (F-LAB) | 35,551 | 56.3 |
| | Halvor Steenerson (R) | 27,590 | 43.7 |
| 10 | Thomas D. Schall (R) | 53,424 | 80.6 |
| | Henry B. Rutledge (D) | 12,843 | 19.4 |

## MISSISSIPPI

| | Candidates | Votes | % |
|---|---|---|---|
| 1 | John E. Rankin (D) | 9,407 | 99.8 |
| 2 | Bill G. Lowrey (D) | 7,985 | 94.7 |
| | William McDonough (R) | 450 | 5.3 |
| 3 | Benjamin G. Humphreys (D) | 4,403 | 97.0 |
| 4 | T. Jeff Busby (D) | 9,260 | 98.2 |
| 5 | Ross A. Collins (D) | 11,336 | 96.3 |
| 6 | T. Webber Wilson (D) | 12,640 | 98.2 |
| 7 | Percy E. Quin (D) | 5,842 | 97.4 |
| 8 | James W. Collier (D) | 5,609 | 99.0 |

## MISSOURI

| | Candidates | Votes | % |
|---|---|---|---|
| 1 | Milton A. Romjue (D) | 30,102 | 55.8 |
| | Frank C. Millspaugh (R) | 23,577 | 43.7 |
| 2 | Ralph F. Lozier (D) | 34,041 | 61.7 |
| | E. Y. Keiter (R) | 21,016 | 38.1 |
| 3 | Jacob L. Milligan (D) | 25,997 | 52.1 |
| | Henry F. Lawrence (R) | 23,919 | 47.9 |
| 4 | Charles L. Faust (R) | 28,110 | 51.5 |
| | William E. Spratt (D) | 26,394 | 48.4 |
| 5 | Henry L. Jost (D) | 62,702 | 53.0 |
| | Edgar C. Ellis (R) | 55,262 | 46.7 |
| 6 | Clement C. Dickinson (D) | 27,038 | 53.3 |
| | William O. Atkeson (R) | 23,492 | 46.3 |
| 7 | Samuel C. Major (D) | 36,950 | 50.7 |
| | Roscoe C. Patterson (R) | 35,627 | 48.9 |
| 8 | Sidney C. Roach (R) | 25,927 | 54.6 |
| | Mrs. St.Clair Moss (D) | 21,559 | 45.4 |
| 9 | Clarence Cannon (D) | 30,063 | 56.6 |
| | Theodore W. Hukriede (R) | 23,058 | 43.4 |
| 10 | Cleveland A. Newton (R) | 71,827 | 59.4 |
| | A. A. Alexander (D) | 46,704 | 38.7 |
| 11 | Harry B. Hawes (D) | 24,839 | 58.4 |
| | Bernard P. Bogy (R) | 17,188 | 40.4 |
| 12 | Leonidas C. Dyer (R) | 15,667 | 56.7 |
| | David D. Israel (D) | 11,679 | 42.3 |

## MISSOURI

| | Candidates | Votes | % |
|---|---|---|---|
| 13 | J. Scott Wolff (D) | 23,622 | 51.6 |
| | Marion E. Rhodes (R) | 21,870 | 47.8 |
| 14 | James F. Fullbright (D) | 37,896 | 52.0 |
| | Edward D. Hays (R) | 34,573 | 47.4 |
| 15 | Joe J. Manlove (R) | 32,843 | 52.8 |
| | Frank H. Lee (D) | 28,801 | 46.3 |
| 16 | Thomas L. Rubey (D) | 25,989 | 53.7 |
| | Phil A. Bennett (R) | 22,153 | 45.8 |

## MONTANA

| | Candidates | Votes | % |
|---|---|---|---|
| 1 | John M. Evans (D) | 36,589 | 57.0 |
| | Washington J. McCormick (R) | 26,684 | 41.6 |
| 2 | Scott Leavitt (R) | 46,499 | 54.3 |
| | Preston B. Moss (D) | 39,147 | 45.7 |

## NEBRASKA

| | Candidates | Votes | % |
|---|---|---|---|
| 1 | John H. Morehead (D) | 25,079 | 49.2 |
| | Walter L. Anderson (R) | 23,075 | 45.3 |
| 2 | Willis G. Sears (R) | 26,308 | 48.2 |
| | James H. Hanley (D) | 25,251 | 46.2 |
| | Roy M. Harrop (PROG) | 3,048 | 5.6 |
| 3 | Edgar Howard (D) | 34,843 | 48.4 |
| | Robert E. Evans (R) | 32,930 | 45.7 |
| | John Havekost (PROG) | 4,252 | 5.9 |
| 4 | Melvin O. McLaughlin (R) | 29,743 | 51.0 |
| | H. B. Cummins (D) | 25,504 | 43.8 |
| | John O. Schmidt (PROG) | 3,034 | 5.2 |
| 5 | Ashton C. Shallenberger (D) | 26,923 | 45.9 |
| | William E. Andrews (R) | 25,456 | 43.4 |
| | S. J. Franklin (PROG) | 6,250 | 10.7 |
| 6 | Robert G. Simmons (R) | 41,558 | 51.3 |
| | Charles W. Beal (D) | 35,784 | 44.2 |

## NEVADA

| | Candidates | Votes | % |
|---|---|---|---|
| AL | Charles L. Richards (D) | 15,991 | 57.0 |
| | A. Grant Miller (R) | 12,084 | 43.0 |

## NEW HAMPSHIRE

| | Candidates | Votes | % |
|---|---|---|---|
| 1 | William N. Rogers (D) | 36,793 | 54.5 |
| | John Scammon (R) | 30,694 | 45.5 |
| 2 | Edward H. Wason (R) | 31,570 | 53.0 |
| | William H. Barry (D) | 27,980 | 47.0 |

## NEW JERSEY

| | Candidates | Votes | % |
|---|---|---|---|
| 1 | Francis F. Patterson Jr. (R) | 46,505 | 60.5 |
| | Ethan P. Wescott (D) | 29,381 | 38.2 |
| 2 | Isaac Bacharach (R) | 50,925 | 69.8 |
| | Charles S. Stevens (D) | 22,001 | 30.2 |
| 3 | Elmer H. Geran (D) | 44,337 | 50.3 |
| | T. Frank Appleby (R) | 43,809 | 49.7 |
| 4 | Charles Browne (D) | 32,422 | 52.8 |
| | Elijah C. Hutchinson (R) | 28,934 | 47.2 |
| 5 | Ernest R. Ackerman (R) | 43,460 | 56.7 |
| | Monell Sayre (D) | 32,039 | 41.8 |
| 6 | Randolph Perkins (R) | 41,564 | 52.5 |
| | Thomas A. Shields (D) | 37,561 | 47.5 |
| 7 | George N. Seger (R) | 26,613 | 54.6 |
| | Wilmer A. Cadmus (D) | 21,190 | 43.5 |
| 8 | Frank J. McNulty (D) | 40,379# | 58.5 |
| | Warren P. Coon (R) | 27,936 | 40.5 |
| 9 | Daniel F. Minahan (D) | 21,276 | 52.6 |
| | Richard W. Parker (R) | 19,182 | 47.4 |
| 10 | Frederick R. Lehlbach (R) | 28,570 | 57.4 |
| | John F. Cahill (D) | 21,211 | 42.6 |
| 11 | John J. Eagan (D) | 39,957 | 66.8 |
| | Archibald E. Olpp (R) | 18,399 | 30.8 |
| 12 | Charles F. X. O'Brien (D) | 51,596 | 74.3 |
| | William A. O'Brien (R) | 17,372 | 25.0 |

## NEW MEXICO

| | Candidates | Votes | % |
|---|---|---|---|
| AL | John Morrow (D) | 59,254 | 54.0 |
| | Adelina Otero-Warren (R) | 49,698 | 45.3 |

## NEW YORK

| | Candidates | Votes | % |
|---|---|---|---|
| 1 | Robert L. Bacon (R) | 47,191 | 57.6 |
| | S. A. Warner Baltazzi (DFL) | 32,224 | 39.3 |
| 2 | John J. Kindred (D) | 60,306 | 72.1 |
| | Frank E. Hopkins (R) | 19,560 | 23.4 |
| 3 | George W. Lindsay (D) | 21,513 | 65.4 |
| | John Kissel (R) | 8,587 | 26.1 |
| | William W. Passage (SOC &F-L) | 2,716 | 8.3 |
| 4 | Thomas H. Cullen (D) | 27,100 | 76.5 |
| | Dominic E. Picone (R) | 7,104 | 20.1 |
| 5 | Loring M. Black Jr. (D) | 33,840 | 54.9 |
| | Ardolph L. Kline (R) | 25,917 | 42.1 |
| 6 | Charles I. Stengle (D) | 31,363 | 48.3 |
| | Warren I. Lee (R) | 28,240 | 43.5 |
| | Mina Eskenazi (SOC &F-L) | 4,713 | 7.3 |
| 7 | John F. Quayle (D) | 21,688 | 53.4 |
| | Michael J. Hogan (R) | 14,772 | 36.4 |
| | Henry Fruchter (SOC &F-L) | 3,807 | 9.4 |
| 8 | William E. Cleary (D) | 34,622 | 56.4 |
| | Charles G. Bond (R) | 19,745 | 32.1 |
| | David P. Berenberg (SOC &F-L) | 6,804 | 11.1 |
| 9 | David J. O'Connell (D) | 38,833 | 58.1 |
| | Andrew N. Petersen (R) | 23,251 | 34.8 |
| | Wilhelmus B. Robinson (SOC &F-L) | 4,528 | 6.8 |
| 10 | Emanuel Celler (D) | 20,210 | 45.6 |
| | Lester D. Volk (R) | 17,099 | 38.6 |
| | Jerome T. Dehunt (SOC &F-L) | 6,522 | 14.7 |
| 11 | Daniel J. Riordan (D) | 29,134 | 67.6 |
| | Joseph B. Handy (R) | 12,889 | 29.9 |
| 12 | Samuel Dickstein (D) | 11,027 | 60.9 |
| | Meyer London (SOC &F-L) | 5,900 | 32.6 |
| | Louis Zeltner (R) | 1,183 | 6.5 |
| 13 | Christopher D. Sullivan (D) | 11,424 | 66.7 |
| | Murray D. Firstman (R) | 3,041 | 17.8 |
| | Abraham Lefkowitz (SOC &F-L) | 2,659 | 15.5 |
| 14 | Nathan D. Perlman (R) | 8,782 | 37.4 |
| | David H. Knott (D) | 8,173 | 34.8 |
| | Jacob Panken (SOC &F-L) | 6,459 | 27.5 |
| 15 | John J. Boylan (D) | 20,382 | 60.8 |
| | Thomas Jefferson Ryan (R) | 12,205 | 36.4 |
| 16 | W. Bourke Cockran (D) | 23,370* | 70.0 |
| | John C. O'Connor (R) | 8,277 | 24.8 |
| 17 | Ogden L. Mills (R) | 21,274 | 50.5 |
| | Herman A. Metz (D) | 19,355 | 46.0 |
| 18 | John F. Carew (D) | 24,248 | 66.8 |
| | Albert E. Schwartz (R) | 8,398 | 23.1 |
| | Ben Howe (SOC &F-L) | 3,535 | 9.7 |
| 19 | Samuel Marx (D) | 29,798* | 50.3 |
| | Walter M. Chandler (R) | 26,172 | 44.2 |
| 20 | Fiorello H. LaGuardia (P) | 8,492 | 38.3 |
| | Henry Frank (D) | 8,324 | 37.5 |
| | William Karlin (SOC &F-L) | 5,260 | 23.7 |
| 21 | Royal H. Weller (D) | 32,393 | 48.2 |
| | Martin C. Ansorge (R) | 32,053 | 47.6 |
| 22 | Anthony J. Griffin (D) | 29,544 | 72.8 |
| | Charles Francis Connolly (R) | 7,188 | 17.7 |
| | Ernest Bohm (SOC &F-L) | 3,752 | 9.2 |
| 23 | Frank Oliver (D) | 50,382 | 56.5 |
| | Albert B. Rossdale (R) | 25,154 | 28.2 |
| | Salvatore Ninfo (SOC &F-L) | 12,411 | 13.9 |
| 24 | James V. Ganly (D) | 40,058 | 47.4 |
| | Benjamin L. Fairchild (R) | 35,656 | 42.2 |
| | Philip Umstadter (SOC &F-L) | 8,873 | 10.5 |
| 25 | J. Mayhew Wainwright (R & P) | 33,674 | 53.3 |

| | Candidates | Votes | % |
|---|---|---|---|
| | Robert A. Osborn (D) | 27,412 | 43.4 |
| 26 | Hamilton Fish Jr. (R F-L-P) | 34,633 | 61.1 |
| | Thomas Pendell (D) | 20,831 | 36.7 |
| 27 | Charles B. Ward (R) | 30,154 | 46.5 |
| | John J. Burns (DFL) | 27,937 | 43.1 |
| | H. Westlake Coons (P) | 5,830 | 9.0 |
| 28 | Parker Corning (D) | 54,570 | 55.3 |
| | Charles M. Winchester (R) | 42,531 | 43.1 |
| 29 | James S. Parker (R & P) | 45,895 | 60.5 |
| | William H. Faxon (D) | 28,726 | 37.9 |
| 30 | Frank Crowther (R & P) | 32,225 | 53.3 |
| | George H. Derry (D) | 25,261 | 41.8 |
| 31 | Bertrand H. Snell (R F-L-P) | 38,205 | 68.3 |
| | J. Franklin Sharp (D) | 17,257 | 30.9 |
| 32 | Luther W. Mott (R) | 44,091 | 65.1 |
| | M. J. Daley (D) | 22,279 | 32.9 |
| 33 | Homer P. Snyder (R) | 31,978 | 49.6 |
| | Fred J. Sisson (D) | 30,118 | 46.7 |
| 34 | John D. Clarke (R & P) | 40,902 | 62.7 |
| | Clayton L. Wheeler (D) | 23,323 | 35.8 |
| 35 | Walter W. Magee (R) | 47,119 | 54.1 |
| | Frederick W. Thomson (D) | 37,785 | 43.4 |
| 36 | John Taber (R & P) | 43,633 | 65.5 |
| | David J. Sims (D) | 22,980 | 34.5 |
| 37 | Gale H. Stalker (R & P) | 42,144 | 59.2 |
| | Charles P. Smith (DFL) | 28,290 | 39.7 |
| 38 | Meyer Jacobstein (D) | 35,319 | 47.7 |
| | Frederick T. Pierson (R) | 33,690 | 45.5 |
| | Joel Moses (SOC) | 5,101 | 6.9 |
| 39 | Archie D. Sanders (R) | 37,852 | 60.5 |
| | David A. White (DFL) | 22,585 | 36.1 |
| 40 | S. Wallace Dempsey (R-F-LAB) | 41,754 | 63.4 |
| | Philip Clancy (D) | 21,590 | 32.8 |
| 41 | Clarence MacGregor (R) | 25,342 | 55.4 |
| | William P. Greiner (D) | 16,301 | 35.7 |
| | Frank Ehrenfried (SOC) | 4,067 | 8.9 |
| 42 | James M. Mead (DFL) | 25,070 | 61.9 |
| | Louis J. Schwendler (R) | 12,494 | 30.9 |
| | Jacob F. Griesinger (SOC) | 2,913 | 7.2 |
| 43 | Daniel A. Reed (R & P) | 40,374 | 70.5 |
| | Frederick Garfield (D) | 15,261 | 26.7 |

## NORTH CAROLINA

| | Candidates | Votes | % |
|---|---|---|---|
| 1 | Hallett S. Ward (D) | 10,201 | 80.8 |
| | C. E. Kramer (R) | 2,421 | 19.2 |
| 2 | Claude Kitchin (D) | 8,533 | 100.0 |
| 3 | Charles L. Abernethy (D) | 14,101 | 67.1 |
| | Thomas J. Hood (R) | 6,924 | 32.9 |
| 4 | Edward W. Pou (D) | 17,205 | 68.0 |
| | F. Eugene Hester (R) | 8,086 | 32.0 |
| 5 | Charles M. Stedman (D) | 33,694 | 62.3 |
| | Lucy B. Patterson (R) | 20,380 | 37.7 |
| 6 | Homer L. Lyon (D) | 14,996 | 74.0 |
| | William J. McDonald (R) | 5,266 | 26.0 |
| 7 | William C. Hammer (D) | 30,629 | 56.5 |
| | W. B. Love (R) | 23,592 | 43.5 |
| 8 | Robert L. Doughton (D) | 31,340 | 56.1 |
| | J. Ike Campbell (R) | 24,493 | 43.9 |
| 9 | Alfred L. Bulwinkle (D) | 28,596 | 59.9 |
| | R. H. Shuford (R) | 19,168 | 40.1 |
| 10 | Zebulon Weaver (D) | 37,626 | 57.2 |
| | Ralph A. Fisher (R) | 28,192 | 42.8 |

## NORTH DAKOTA

| | Candidates | Votes | % |
|---|---|---|---|
| 1 | Olger B. Burtness (R) | 45,959 | 100.0 |
| 2 | George M. Young (R) | 36,528 | 69.8 |
| | J. W. Deemey (PROG) | 15,834 | 30.2 |
| 3 | James H. Sinclair (R) | 33,499 | 64.2 |
| | E. J. Hughes (IR) | 18,672 | 35.8 |

## OHIO

| | Candidates | Votes | % |
|---|---|---|---|
| 1 | Nicholas Longworth (R) | 45,253 | 57.1 |
| | Sidney G. Stricker (D) | 30,945 | 39.0 |

## OHIO

| Candidates | Votes | % |
|---|---|---|
| 2 Ambrose E. B. Stephens (R) | 39,898 | 54.0 |
| John R. Quane (D) | 30,051 | 40.6 |
| Charles A. Herbst (F-LAB) | 4,001 | 5.4 |
| 3 Roy G. Fitzgerald (R) | 52,111 | 51.8 |
| Warren Gard (D) | 46,127 | 45.9 |
| 4 John C. Cable (R) | 43,251 | 54.6 |
| J. Henry Goeke (D) | 35,916 | 45.4 |
| 5 Charles J. Thompson (R) | 31,700 | 53.0 |
| Frank C. Kniffin (D) | 28,067 | 47.0 |
| 6 Charles C. Kearns (R) | 32,416 | 51.2 |
| William N. Gableman (D) | 30,939 | 48.8 |
| 7 Charles Brand (R) | 54,180 | 58.5 |
| Charles B. Zimmerman (D) | 38,522 | 41.6 |
| 8 R. Clint Cole (R) | 37,065 | 52.1 |
| H. H. Hartman (D) | 34,105 | 47.9 |
| 9 Isaac R. Sherwood (D) | 45,059 | 51.3 |
| William W. Chalmers (R) | 42,712 | 48.7 |
| 10 Israel M. Foster (R) | 30,341 | 63.0 |
| James Sharp (D) | 17,811 | 37.0 |
| 11 Mell G. Underwood (D) | 29,058 | 51.7 |
| Edwin D. Ricketts (R) | 27,162 | 48.3 |
| 12 John C. Speaks (R) | 47,265 | 55.1 |
| H. Sage Valentine (D) | 37,875 | 44.2 |
| 13 James T. Begg (R) | 38,994 | 56.4 |
| Arthur W. Overmeyer (D) | 30,199 | 43.6 |
| 14 Martin L. Davey (D) | 49,935 | 52.0 |
| Frank E. Whittemore (R) | 46,087 | 48.0 |
| 15 C. Ellis Moore (R) | 32,894 | 51.4 |
| James R. Alexander (D) | 30,120 | 47.1 |
| 16 John McSweeney Jr. (D) | 43,590 | 51.8 |
| J. H. Himes (R) | 39,881 | 47.3 |
| 17 William M. Morgan (R) | 42,331 | 50.4 |
| William A. Ashbrook (D) | 41,745 | 49.7 |
| 18 Frank Murphy (R) | 41,572 | 57.0 |
| Marion Huffman (D) | 25,449 | 34.9 |
| Jacob S. Carey Sr. (I) | 5,907 | 8.1 |
| 19 John G. Cooper (R) | 40,492 | 59.3 |
| W. B. Kilpatrick (D) | 27,836 | 40.7 |
| 20 Charles A. Mooney (D) | 23,469 | 54.4 |
| Minor G. Morton (R) | 17,968 | 41.7 |
| 21 Robert Crosser (D) | 18,645 | 55.1 |
| Harry C. Gahn (R) | 14,024 | 41.4 |
| 22 Theodore E. Burton (R) | 57,781 | 73.4 |
| William J. Zoul (D) | 20,511 | 26.1 |

## OKLAHOMA

| Candidates | Votes | % |
|---|---|---|
| 1 Everette B. Howard (D) | 39,135 | 54.7 |
| T. A. Chandler (R) | 32,478 | 45.4 |
| 2 William W. Hastings (D) | 30,418 | 57.7 |
| Alice M. Robertson (R) | 21,973 | 41.7 |
| 3 Charles D. Carter (D) | 39,464 | 71.6 |
| Philas S. Jones (R) | 15,022 | 27.3 |
| 4 Thomas D. McKeown (D) | 39,247 | 65.2 |
| Joseph C. Pringey (R) | 20,568 | 34.2 |
| 5 Fletcher B. Swank (D) | 46,120 | 62.7 |
| U. S. Stone (R) | 26,893 | 36.6 |
| 6 Elmer Thomas (D) | 30,532 | 56.6 |
| L. M. Gensman (R) | 22,757 | 42.2 |
| 7 James V. McClintic (D) | 28,956 | 70.2 |
| W. G. Roe (R) | 11,444 | 27.8 |
| 8 Milton C. Garber (R) | 29,068 | 52.6 |
| Zach A. Harris (D) | 26,111 | 46.7 |

## OREGON

| Candidates | Votes | % |
|---|---|---|
| 1 Willis C. Hawley (R) | 64,567 | 100.0 |
| 2 Nicholas J. Sinnott (R) | 22,861 | 59.2 |
| James Harvey Graham (D) | 15,789 | 40.9 |
| 3 Elton Watkins (D) | 36,690 | 47.6 |
| Clifton N. McArthur (R) | 35,696 | 46.3 |

## PENNSYLVANIA

| Candidates | Votes | % |
|---|---|---|
| 1 William S. Vare (R) | 46,946 | 83.6 |
| Stephen Flanagan (D) | 8,227 | 14.7 |
| 2 George S. Graham (R, P) | 31,470 | 85.4 |
| Ellen Duane Davis (D) | 4,739 | 12.9 |
| 3 Harry C. Ransley (R) | 33,058 | 84.4 |
| Edward P. Carroll (D) | 5,507 | 14.1 |
| 4 George W. Edmonds (R, P) | 28,757 | 74.1 |
| Joseph K. Willing (D) | 8,954 | 23.1 |
| 5 James J. Connolly (R, WELFARE) | 31,357 | 76.6 |
| James J. Sweeney (D) | 7,717 | 18.9 |
| 6 George A. Welsh (R) | 44,159 | 73.4 |
| Robert J. Sterrett (D) | 13,629 | 22.7 |
| 7 George P. Darrow (R, P) | 31,580 | 74.2 |
| John W. Graham (D, VL) | 9,694 | 22.8 |
| 8 Thomas S. Butler (R) | 30,349 | 61.1 |
| William T. Ellis (D, INDL) | 18,306 | 36.9 |
| 9 Henry Winfield Watson (R) | 32,052 | 61.8 |
| C. William Freed (D) | 18,083 | 34.9 |
| 10 William W. Griest (R) | 33,545 | 52.8 |
| Frank C. Musser (D, LANCAST) | 30,017 | 47.2 |
| 11 Laurence H. Watres (R, P) | 23,266 | 50.1 |
| Patrick McLane (D) | 22,540 | 48.5 |
| 12 John J. Casey (D, SOC) | 35,953 | 54.1 |
| Clarence D. Coughlin (R, P) | 30,532 | 45.9 |
| 13 George Franklin Brumm (R, P) | 23,218 | 52.9 |
| Charles F. Ditchey (D) | 19,305 | 44.0 |
| 14 William M. Croll (D) | 31,592 | 48.2 |
| Fred B. Gernerd (R) | 29,617 | 45.2 |
| George W. Snyder (SOC) | 4,294 | 6.6 |
| 15 Louis T. McFadden (R, P) | 20,399 | 64.0 |
| T. Francis Carroll (D) | 11,498 | 36.1 |
| 16 Edgar R. Kiess (R, P) | 17,499 | 57.2 |
| James M. Rook (D) | 12,014 | 39.2 |
| 17 Herbert W. Cummings (D, SOC) | 22,588 | 57.4 |
| I. Clinton Kline (R, P) | 16,796 | 42.6 |
| 18 Edward M. Beers (R, P) | 24,675 | 54.6 |
| King Alexander (D) | 20,069 | 44.4 |
| 19 Frank C. Sites (D) | 33,570 | 53.6 |
| Aaron S. Kreider (R, P) | 28,115 | 44.9 |
| 20 George M. Wertz (R, P) | 12,276 | 41.9 |
| Warren Worth Bailey (D, SOC) | 11,969 | 40.9 |
| Robert M. Palmer (RO) | 2,671 | 9.1 |
| Faber V. McCloskey (LAB) | 2,337 | 8.0 |
| 21 J. Banks Kurtz (R, P) | 13,106 | 47.5 |
| Daniel S. Brumbaugh (D) | 11,425 | 41.4 |
| Earl W. Rothrock (LAB, SOC) | 3,050 | 11.1 |
| 22 Samuel F. Glatfelter (D) | 22,181 | 53.0 |
| Mahlon N. Haines (R, P) | 17,694 | 42.3 |
| 23 William Irvin Swoope (R, SOC) | 16,928 | 48.0 |
| J. Frank Snyder (D) | 14,292 | 40.5 |
| Elisha Kent Kane (P) | 4,041 | 11.5 |
| 24 Samuel A. Kendall (R, P) | 18,261 | 54.0 |
| Harrison N. Boyd (D) | 12,937 | 38.3 |
| Herman G. Lepley (SOC) | 1,985 | 5.9 |
| 25 Henry W. Temple (R, SOC) | 14,098 | 53.5 |
| Charles I. Faddis (D) | 12,242 | 46.5 |
| 26 Thomas W. Phillips Jr (R) | 17,730 | 51.5 |
| John G. Cobler (D, P) | 15,533 | 45.1 |
| 27 Nathan L. Strong (R) | 18,682 | 53.6 |
| Jane E. Leonard (D) | 12,927 | 37.1 |
| 28 Harry J. Bixler (R, P) | 22,631 | 64.4 |
| Charles E. Bordwell (D) | 11,604 | 33.0 |
| 29 Milton W. Shreve (R, P) | 19,043 | 58.9 |
| Charles N. Crosby (D) | 11,917 | 36.9 |
| 30 Everett Kent (D) | 25,644 | 58.2 |
| William H. Kirkpatrick (R) | 17,844 | 40.5 |
| 31 Adam M. Wyant (R, P) | 17,421 | 53.4 |
| James M. Cramer (D) | 13,081 | 40.1 |
| Harry Eckard (SOC) | 2,146 | 6.6 |
| 32 Stephen Geyer Porter (R) | 19,942 | 70.0 |
| P. M. O'Donnell (D) | 5,938 | 20.9 |
| 33 M. Clyde Kelly (R, D) | 21,899 | 87.4 |
| William Adams (SOC) | 3,106 | 12.4 |
| 34 John M. Morin (R) | 15,499 | 72.7 |
| William N. McNair (D, P) | 5,134 | 24.1 |
| 35 James M. Magee (R) | 16,227 | 53.9 |
| Louis K. Manley (D, P) | 12,838 | 42.6 |
| 36 Guy E. Campbell (R, D) | 20,783 | 91.7 |
| William W. Nooning (SOC) | 1,880 | 8.3 |

## RHODE ISLAND

| Candidates | Votes | % |
|---|---|---|
| 1 Clark Burdick (R) | 25,860 | 54.1 |
| George F. O'Shaunessy (D) | 21,935 | 45.9 |
| 2 Richard S. Aldrich (R) | 26,247 | 52.6 |
| Percy J. Cantwell (D) | 23,680 | 47.4 |
| 3 Jeremiah E. O'Connell (D) | 36,147 | 62.6 |
| Isaac Gill (R) | 21,581 | 37.4 |

## SOUTH CAROLINA

| Candidates | Votes | % |
|---|---|---|
| 1 W. Turner Logan (D) | 5,992 | 94.0 |
| S. L. Blomgren (R) | 383 | 6.0 |
| 2 James F. Byrnes (D) | 4,163 | 100.0 |
| 3 Fred H. Dominick (D) | 3,822 | 100.0 |
| 4 John J. McSwain (D) | 8,346 | 97.3 |
| 5 William F. Stevenson (D) | 4,015 | 100.0 |
| 6 Allard H. Gasque (D) | 3,642 | 100.0 |
| 7 Hampton C. Fulmer (D) | 4,411 | 98.5 |

## SOUTH DAKOTA

| Candidates | Votes | % |
|---|---|---|
| 1 Charles A. Christopherson (R) | 31,250 | 48.9 |
| John Stredronsky (D) | 16,372 | 25.6 |
| G. L. Hasvold (NON PART) | 16,230 | 25.4 |
| 2 Royal C. Johnson (R) | 37,208 | 64.5 |
| Andrew Francis Lockhart (NON PART) | 18,968 | 32.9 |
| 3 William Williamson (R) | 18,819 | 49.2 |
| George Philip (D) | 14,857 | 38.8 |
| George H. Smith (NON PART) | 4,581 | 12.0 |

## TENNESSEE

| Candidates | Votes | % |
|---|---|---|
| 1 B. Carroll Reece (R) | 17,050 | 77.0 |
| J. T. Fugate (D) | 5,085 | 23.0 |
| 2 J. Will Taylor (R) | 14,988 | 64.3 |
| J. Rupert Reynolds (D) | 8,330 | 35.7 |
| 3 Sam D. McReynolds (D) | 20,603 | 61.3 |
| R. L. Burnett (R) | 13,027 | 38.7 |
| 4 Cordull Hull (D) | 20,323 | 62.6 |
| W. F. Clouse (R) | 12,125 | 37.4 |
| 5 Ewin L. Davis (D) | 11,634 | 100.0 |
| 6 Joseph W. Byrns (D) | 19,596 | 100.0 |
| 7 William S. Salmon (D) | 13,662 | 78.2 |
| S. A. Vest (R) | 3,818 | 21.8 |
| 8 Gordon Browning (D) | 16,571 | 57.3 |
| Lon A. Scott (R) | 12,328 | 42.7 |
| 9 Finis J. Garrett (D) | 15,822 | 84.8 |
| Homer S. Tatum (R) | 2,846 | 15.3 |
| 10 Hubert F. Fisher (D) | 10,407 | 89.1 |
| Thomas C. Phelen (I) | 1,279 | 10.9 |

### Special Election

| Candidates | Votes | % |
|---|---|---|
| 7 Clarence W. Turner (D) | 12,914 | 86.3 |
| S. W. Williams (R) | 2,053 | 13.7 |

## TEXAS

| Candidates | Votes | % |
|---|---|---|
| 1 Eugene Black (D) | 15,697 | 93.5 |
| G. T. Bartlett (R) | 1,087 | 6.5 |
| 2 John C. Box (D) | 21,216 | 94.8 |
| C. A. Lord (R) | 1,171 | 5.2 |
| 3 Morgan G. Sanders (D) | 16,323 | 91.7 |
| L. B. Crawford (R) | 1,478 | 8.3 |
| 4 Sam Rayburn (D) | 21,327 | 91.1 |
| C. A. Gray (R) | 2,079 | 8.9 |

## TEXAS

| | Candidates | Votes | % |
|---|---|---|---|
| 5 | Hatton W. Sumners (D) | 23,051 | 88.3 |
| | Heber Page (R) | 3,046 | 11.7 |
| 6 | Luther A. Johnson (D) | 18,938 | 94.0 |
| | D. H. Merrill (R) | 1,208 | 6.0 |
| 7 | Clay Stone Briggs (D) | 12,171 | 93.3 |
| | Frank Sneed Camper (R) | 880 | 6.7 |
| 8 | Daniel E. Garrett (D) | 20,058 | 85.3 |
| | E. B. Barden (R) | 3,454 | 14.7 |
| 9 | Joseph J. Mansfield (D) | 17,479 | 64.7 |
| | Willett Wilson (R) | 9,554 | 35.3 |
| 10 | James P. Buchanan (D) | 18,590 | 81.0 |
| | W. J. Kveton (R) | 4,374 | 19.1 |
| 11 | Tom T. Connally (D) | 16,092 | 90.8 |
| | R. A. Hanrick (R) | 1,630 | 9.2 |
| 12 | Fritz G. Lanham (D) | 20,014 | 91.9 |
| | Joe Kingsberry Jr. (R) | 1,772 | 8.1 |
| 13 | Guinn Williams (D) | 21,187 | 93.2 |
| | J. B. Schmitz (R) | 1,538 | 6.8 |
| 14 | Harry M. Wurzbach (R) | 19,083 | 54.8 |
| | Harry Hertzberg (D) | 15,760 | 45.2 |
| 15 | John N. Garner (D) | 14,319 | 100.0 |
| 16 | Claude B. Hudspeth (D) | 18,164 | 81.0 |
| | J. A. Simpson (R) | 4,257 | 19.0 |
| 17 | Thomas L. Blanton (D) | 24,576 | 91.6 |
| | W. D. Girand (R) | 2,266 | 8.4 |
| 18 | Marvin Jones (D) | 24,515 | 93.7 |
| | H. O. Ward (R) | 1,649 | 6.3 |

## UTAH

| | | Votes | % |
|---|---|---|---|
| 1 | Don B. Colton (R) | 33,188 | 52.7 |
| | Milton H. Welling (D) | 27,801 | 44.2 |
| 2 | Elmer O. Leatherwood (R) | 28,591 | 50.5 |
| | David C. Dunbar (D) | 26,145 | 46.1 |

## VERMONT

| | | Votes | % |
|---|---|---|---|
| 1 | Frederick G. Fleetwood (R, P) | 19,359 | 52.1 |
| | James E. Kennedy (D) | 17,821 | 47.9 |
| 2 | Porter H. Dale (R, P) | 25,981 | 78.4 |
| | John J. Wilson (D) | 7,170 | 21.6 |

## VIRGINIA

| | Candidates | Votes | % |
|---|---|---|---|
| 1 | Schuyler Otis Bland (D) | 8,639 | 83.5 |
| | George N. Wise (R) | 1,492 | 14.4 |
| 2 | Joseph T. Deal (D) | 7,367 | 86.5 |
| | Percy S. Stephenson (R) | 1,045 | 12.3 |
| 3 | Andrew Jackson Montague (D) | 7,746 | 90.1 |
| | Channing M. Ward (R) | 847 | 9.9 |
| 4 | Patrick Henry Drewry (D) | 5,737 | 86.2 |
| | Herbert Rogers (R) | 822 | 12.4 |
| 5 | James M. Hooker (D) | 11,458 | 70.9 |
| | Charles P. Smith (R) | 4,699 | 29.1 |
| 6 | Clifton A. Woodrum (D) | 9,505 | 77.9 |
| | J. W. McWane (R) | 2,688 | 22.0 |
| 7 | Thomas W. Harrison (D) | 12,954 | 62.3 |
| | John Paul (R) | 7,841 | 37.7 |
| 8 | R. Walton Moore (D) | 8,702 | 83.3 |
| | John Sidney Wiley (R) | 1,741 | 16.7 |
| 9 | George C. Peery (D) | 32,163 | 52.4 |
| | John H. Hassinger (R) | 29,227 | 47.6 |
| 10 | Henry St.George Tucker (D) | 8,635 | 77.4 |
| | John Martin (R) | 2,521 | 22.6 |

## WASHINGTON

| | | Votes | % |
|---|---|---|---|
| 1 | John F. Miller (R) | 29,579 | 57.4 |
| | Edgar C. Snyder (D) | 13,127 | 25.5 |
| | Fred N. Nelson (F-LAB) | 8,862 | 17.2 |
| 2 | Lindley H. Hadley (R) | 29,906 | 59.0 |
| | Fred A. Clise (D) | 10,608 | 20.9 |
| | P. B. Tyler (F-LAB) | 10,150 | 20.0 |
| 3 | Albert Johnson (R) | 45,482 | 76.3 |
| | J. M. Phillips (F-LAB) | 14,158 | 23.7 |
| 4 | John W. Summers (R) | 29,697 | 68.5 |
| | Charles R. Hill (D) | 10,337 | 23.9 |
| | Elihu Bowles (F-LAB) | 3,292 | 7.6 |
| 5 | J. Stanley Webster (R) | 26,982 | 49.2 |
| | Sam B. Hill (D) | 24,810 | 45.2 |
| | Harry J. Vaughan (F-LAB) | 3,095 | 5.6 |

## WEST VIRGINIA

| | Candidates | Votes | % |
|---|---|---|---|
| 1 | Benjamin L. Rosenbloom (R) | 28,644 | 52.6 |
| | Raymond Kenny (D) | 25,794 | 47.3 |
| 2 | Robert E. L. Allen (D) | 27,320 | 51.5 |
| | George M. Bowers (R) | 24,764 | 46.6 |
| 3 | Stuart F. Reed (R) | 32,066 | 50.5 |
| | Eskridge H. Morton (D) | 31,382 | 49.5 |
| 4 | George W. Johnson (D) | 32,355 | 50.7 |
| | Harry C. Woodyard (R) | 31,448 | 49.3 |
| 5 | Thomas J. Lilly (D) | 35,354 | 51.5 |
| | Wells Goodykoontz (R) | 33,267 | 48.5 |
| 6 | J. Alfred Taylor (D) | 42,320 | 54.2 |
| | Leonard S. Echols (R) | 34,901 | 44.7 |

## WISCONSIN

| | | Votes | % |
|---|---|---|---|
| 1 | Henry Allen Cooper (R) | 37,958 | 94.4 |
| | Niels P. Nielsen (SOC) | 2,179 | 5.4 |
| 2 | Edward Voight (R) | 32,494 | 80.9 |
| | William F. Schanen (D) | 7,667 | 19.1 |
| 3 | John M. Nelson (R) | 33,002 | 79.7 |
| | Martha Riley (ID) | 8,379 | 20.2 |
| 4 | John C. Schafer (R) | 19,179 | 46.0 |
| | Edmund T. Melms (SOC) | 18,548 | 44.5 |
| | Joseph F. Drezdzon (D) | 3,918 | 9.4 |
| 5 | Victor L. Berger (SOC) | 30,045 | 53.3 |
| | William H. Stafford (R) | 26,274 | 46.6 |
| 6 | Florian Lampert (R) | 34,365 | 86.0 |
| | William E. Cavanaugh (ID) | 5,572 | 14.0 |
| 7 | Joseph D. Beck (R) | 27,371 | 87.4 |
| | Bert A. Jolivette (ID) | 3,923 | 12.5 |
| 8 | Edward E. Browne (R) | 33,860 | 91.8 |
| | Herman A. Marth (I SOC) | 2,946 | 8.0 |
| 9 | George J. Schneider (R) | 35,117 | 61.5 |
| | Henry Graass (IR) | 22,015 | 38.5 |
| 10 | James A. Frear (R) | 29,781 | 98.3 |
| 11 | Hubert H. Peavey (R) | 36,635 | 99.0 |

## WYOMING

| | | Votes | % |
|---|---|---|---|
| AL | Charles E. Winter (R) | 30,885 | 53.3 |
| | Robert R. Rose (D) | 27,017 | 46.7 |

# 1923 House Elections

## ALABAMA

**Special Election**

| | | Votes | % |
|---|---|---|---|
| 2 | Lister Hill (D) | 4,483 | 100.0 |

## ARKANSAS

**Special Election**

| | | Votes | % |
|---|---|---|---|
| 6 | James B. Reed (D) | 1,793 | 100.0 |

## ILLINOIS

**Special Elections**

| | | Votes | % |
|---|---|---|---|
| 2 | Morton D. Hull (R) | 56,355 | 53.9 |
| | Barratt O'Hara (D) | 42,427 | 40.6 |
| | Seymorse Stedman (SOC) | 5,759 | 5.5 |
| 4 | Thomas A. Doyle (D) | 17,624 | 95.0 |

## IOWA

**Special Election**

| | | Votes | % |
|---|---|---|---|
| 8 | Hiram K. Evans (R) | 14,334 | 52.6 |
| | J. P. Daughton (D) | 12,901 | 47.4 |

## NEW YORK

**Special Elections**

| | | Votes | % |
|---|---|---|---|
| 11 | Anning S. Prall (D) | 28,215 | 72.9 |
| | Guy O. Walser (R) | 9,972 | 25.8 |
| 16 | John J. O'Connor (D, R) | 27,746 | 96.7 |
| 19 | Sol Bloom (D) | 17,909 | 49.8 |
| | Walter M. Chandler (R) | 17,718 | 49.3 |
| 24 | Benjamin L. Fairchild (R) | 43,475 | 49.0 |
| | Edward R. Koch (D) | 38,435 | 43.3 |
| | Alexander Braunstein (SOC) | 6,913 | 7.8 |
| 32 | Thaddeus C. Sweet (R) | 41,775 | 65.1 |
| | Daniel C. Burke (D) | 21,391 | 33.4 |

# 1924 House Elections

## ALABAMA

| | Candidates | Votes | % |
|---|---|---|---|
| 1 | John McDuffie (D) | 9,932 | 86.1 |
| | Frank J. Thompson (R) | 1,604 | 13.9 |
| 2 | Lister Hill (D) | 15,066 | 100.0 |
| 3 | Henry B. Steagall (D) | 10,425 | 87.7 |
| | Carlos E. Roberts (R) | 1,457 | 12.3 |
| 4 | Lamar Jeffers (D) | 9,945 | 75.6 |
| | J. O. Middleton (R) | 3,208 | 24.4 |
| 5 | William B. Bowling (D) | 8,492 | 78.3 |
| | John C. Walker (R) | 2,355 | 21.7 |
| 6 | William B. Oliver (D) | 6,672 | 100.0 |
| 7 | Miles C. Allgood (D) | 15,984 | 57.1 |
| | B. S. Cooley (R) | 11,907 | 42.9 |
| 8 | Edward B. Almon (D) | 13,353 | 81.5 |
| | G. M. Huckaba (R) | 3,040 | 18.5 |
| 9 | George Huddleston (D) | 18,958 | 99.9 |
| 10 | William B. Bankhead (D) | 11,394 | 59.7 |
| | W. A. McMurray (R) | 7,706 | 40.4 |

## ARIZONA

| | Candidates | Votes | % |
|---|---|---|---|
| AL | Carl Hayden (D) | 40,329 | 82.4 |
| | W. J. Galbraith (R) | 8,628 | 17.6 |

## ARKANSAS

| | Candidates | Votes | % |
|---|---|---|---|
| 1 | William J. Driver (D) | 15,514 | 77.2 |
| | Virgil Greene (R) | 4,580 | 22.8 |
| 2 | William A. Oldfield (D) | 11,412 | 73.8 |
| | M. D. Bowers (R) | 4,057 | 26.2 |
| 3 | John N. Tilman (D) | 13,202 | 60.0 |
| | J. S. Thompson (R) | 8,789 | 40.0 |
| 4 | Otis T. Wingo (D) | 15,935 | 72.5 |
| | Charles A. Darling (R) | 6,060 | 27.6 |
| 5 | Heartsill Ragon (D) | 16,287 | 76.8 |
| | Powell Clayton (R) | 4,922 | 23.2 |
| 6 | James B. Reed (D) | 13,101 | 75.6 |
| | Martin A. Eisele (R) | 4,219 | 24.4 |
| 7 | Tilman B. Parks (D) | 13,975 | 76.5 |
| | J. K. Prescott (R) | 4,302 | 23.5 |

## CALIFORNIA

| | Candidates | Votes | % |
|---|---|---|---|
| 1 | Clarence F. Lea (D-R) | 47,250 | 99.9 |
| 2 | John E. Raker (D-R) | 30,590 | 100.0 |
| 3 | Charles F. Curry (R-D) | 61,512 | 80.7 |
| | James H. Barkley (SOC) | 14,665 | 19.3 |
| 4 | Julius Kahn (R-D) | 44,048* | 81.0 |
| | William McDevitt (SOC) | 10,360 | 19.0 |
| 5 | Lawrence J. Flaherty (R-D) | 38,893 | 76.2 |
| | Isabel C. King (SOC) | 12,175 | 23.8 |
| 6 | Albert E. Carter (R) | 68,547 | 57.5 |
| | John L. Davie (I) | 42,873 | 35.9 |
| | Herbert L. Coggins (SOC) | 7,858 | 6.6 |
| 7 | Henry E. Barbour (R-D) | 65,740 | 99.9 |
| 8 | Arthur Monroe Free (R-D) | 55,713 | 97.9 |
| 9 | Walter F. Lineberger (R) | 119,993 | 63.9 |
| | Charles H. Randall (P D SOC) | 67,735 | 36.1 |
| 10 | John D. Fredericks (R) | 133,780 | 62.3 |
| | Robert W. Richardson (D) | 80,870 | 37.7 |
| 11 | Philip D. Swing (DR SOC P) | 93,811 | 100.0 |

## COLORADO

| | Candidates | Votes | % |
|---|---|---|---|
| 1 | William N. Vaile (R) | 47,155 | 54.2 |
| | James G. Edgeworth (D) | 36,519 | 42.0 |
| 2 | Charles B. Timberlake (R) | 51,028 | 56.9 |
| | James M. Taylor (D) | 31,378 | 35.0 |
| | James A. Ownbey (LAF) | 6,630 | 7.4 |
| 3 | Guy U. Hardy (R) | 53,877 | 58.7 |
| | Charles B. Hughes (D) | 37,976 | 41.3 |

| | Candidates | Votes | % |
|---|---|---|---|
| 4 | Edward T. Taylor (D) | 33,262 | 65.5 |
| | Webster S. Whinnery (R) | 17,486 | 34.5 |

## CONNECTICUT

| | Candidates | Votes | % |
|---|---|---|---|
| 1 | E. Hart Fenn (R) | 61,451 | 66.8 |
| | Johnstone Vance (D) | 29,381 | 31.9 |
| 2 | Richard P. Freeman (R) | 42,161 | 65.0 |
| | Fenton (D) | 22,258 | 34.3 |
| 3 | John Q. Tilson (R) | 48,963 | 67.9 |
| | William T. Hoyt (D) | 21,858 | 30.3 |
| 4 | Schuyler Merritt (R) | 57,966 | 71.1 |
| | Walling (D) | 22,031 | 27.0 |
| 5 | James P. Glynn (R) | 34,548 | 55.0 |
| | Patrick B. O'Sullivan (D, PROG) | 28,248 | 45.0 |

## DELAWARE

| | Candidates | Votes | % |
|---|---|---|---|
| AL | Robert G. Houston (R) | 51,536 | 58.6 |
| | William H. Boyce (D) | 35,943 | 40.9 |

## FLORIDA

| | Candidates | Votes | % |
|---|---|---|---|
| 1 | Herbert J. Drane (D) | 23,244 | 80.0 |
| | A. W. Gage (R) | 5,816 | 20.0 |
| 2 | Robert A. Green (R) | 11,021 | 90.7 |
| | H. O. Brown (R) | 1,137 | 9.4 |
| 3 | John H. Smithwick (D) | 12,660 | 84.1 |
| | J. H. Drummond (R) | 2,389 | 15.9 |
| 4 | William J. Sears (D) | 25,318 | 62.5 |
| | G. W. Bingham (R) | 12,183 | 30.1 |
| | Billy Parker (AM) | 2,993 | 7.4 |

## GEORGIA

| | Candidates | Votes | % |
|---|---|---|---|
| 1 | Charles G. Edwards (D) | 14,694 | 93.2 |
| 2 | E. E. Cox (D) | 10,667 | 100.0 |
| 3 | Charles R. Crisp (D) | 8,138 | 100.0 |
| 4 | William C. Wright (D) | 10,420 | 100.0 |
| 5 | William D. Upshaw (D) | 16,608 | 100.0 |
| 6 | Samuel Rutherford (D) | 12,488 | 100.0 |
| 7 | Gordon Lee (D) | 20,008 | 99.9 |
| 8 | Charles H. Brand (D) | 12,261 | 100.0 |
| 9 | Thomas M. Bell (D) | 17,007 | 87.5 |
| | J. M. Johnson (R) | 2,425# | 12.5 |
| 10 | Carl Vinson (D) | 9,280 | 100.0 |
| 11 | William C. Lankford (D) | 11,590 | 100.0 |
| 12 | William W. Larsen (D) | 11,754 | 100.0 |

## IDAHO

| | Candidates | Votes | % |
|---|---|---|---|
| 1 | Burton L. French (R) | 33,347 | 61.8 |
| | Perry Mitchell (D) | 20,234 | 37.5 |
| 2 | Addison T. Smith (R) | 44,365 | 54.6 |
| | William A. Shuldberg (PROG) | 23,257 | 28.6 |
| | Asher B. Wilson (D) | 13,470 | 16.6 |

## ILLINOIS

| | Candidates | Votes | % |
|---|---|---|---|
| 1 | Martin B. Madden (R) | 43,661 | 73.1 |
| | James F. Doyle (D) | 13,623 | 22.8 |
| 2 | Morton D. Hull (R) | 113,349 | 74.5 |
| | Frank A. Wright (D) | 37,482 | 24.6 |
| 3 | Elliott W. Sproul (R) | 87,563 | 67.0 |
| | Joseph F. Timmis (D) | 42,278 | 32.3 |
| 4 | Thomas A. Doyle (D) | 30,955 | 56.0 |
| | Stanley Jankowski (R) | 23,947 | 43.3 |
| 5 | Adolph J. Sabath (D) | 20,588 | 57.8 |
| | Bernard A. Weaver (R) | 14,730 | 41.4 |
| 6 | John J. Gorman (R) | 116,066 | 67.8 |
| | James R. Buckley (D) | 53,463 | 31.2 |

| | Candidates | Votes | % |
|---|---|---|---|
| 7 | M. Alfred Michaelson (R) | 133,563 | 67.7 |
| | Hynek M. Howell (D) | 46,253 | 23.5 |
| | Edward A. Russell | 13,040 | 6.6 |
| 8 | Stanley Henry Kunz (D) | 17,799 | 53.1 |
| | Ernest D. Potts (R) | 13,853 | 41.3 |
| | Gerard Kasmarek | 1,675 | 5.0 |
| 9 | Fred A. Britten (R) | 42,829 | 76.6 |
| | Urban A. Lavery (D) | 12,541 | 22.4 |
| 10 | Carl R. Chindblom (R) | 126,383 | 80.0 |
| | John P. Reed (D) | 30,474 | 19.3 |
| 11 | Frank R. Reid (R) | 83,696 | 84.2 |
| | Charles L. Schwartz (D) | 15,246 | 15.3 |
| 12 | Charles E. Fuller (R) | 68,696 | 84.5 |
| | Marvin C. Parsons (PROG) | 12,105 | 14.9 |
| 13 | William R. Johnson (R) | 49,717 | 77.8 |
| | William G. Curtiss (D) | 13,887 | 21.7 |
| 14 | John C. Allen (R) | 48,920 | 64.7 |
| | William A. Schaeffer (D) | 26,680 | 35.3 |
| 15 | Edward J. King (R) | 53,123 | 69.2 |
| | Henry E. Schmiedeskamp (D) | 23,051 | 30.0 |
| 16 | William E. Hull (R) | 43,098 | 55.4 |
| | Charles C. Hatcher (D) | 34,185 | 44.0 |
| 17 | Frank H. Funk (R) | 40,226 | 60.1 |
| | Frank Gillespie (D) | 26,497 | 39.6 |
| 18 | William P. Holaday (R) | 52,992 | 64.4 |
| | Andrew B. Dennis (D) | 29,034 | 35.3 |
| 19 | Charles Adkins (R) | 55,605 | 56.5 |
| | Edward F. Poorman (D) | 42,490 | 43.1 |
| 20 | Henry T. Rainey (D) | 36,669 | 53.0 |
| | Guy L. Shaw (R) | 32,569 | 47.0 |
| 21 | Loren E. Wheeler (R) | 45,588 | 50.0 |
| | J. Earl Major (D) | 44,414 | 48.7 |
| 22 | Edward M. Irwin (R) | 56,525 | 57.7 |
| | Edward E. Campbell (D) | 40,604 | 41.5 |
| 23 | William W. Arnold (D) | 45,644 | 53.9 |
| | Charles J. Metzger (R) | 38,670 | 45.7 |
| 24 | Thomas S. Williams (R) | 35,356 | 54.1 |
| | H. Robert Fowler (D) | 29,954 | 45.9 |
| 25 | Edward E. Denison (R) | 47,080 | 58.1 |
| | Philip N. Lewis (D) | 33,638 | 41.5 |
| AL | Richard Yates (R) | 1,519,021✔ | |
| | Henry R. Rathbone (R) | 1,513,708✔ | |
| | Mary Ward Hart (D) | 669,555 | |
| | Allen D. Albert (D) | 658,265 | |
| | Gus C. Sandberg (SOC) | 17,580 | |
| | John C. Flora (SOC) | 17,438 | |
| | J. E. Procum (SOC LAB) | 2,437 | |
| | C. E. Clouse (SOC LAB) | 2,368 | |
| | Robert Minor (WP AM) | 2,235 | |
| | E. B. Hewlett (WP AM) | 2,160 | |
| | Patrick H. Morrissey (IR) | 752 | |
| | Dora Welty (CLP) | 396 | |
| | James W. Hill (CLP) | 363 | |

## INDIANA

| | Candidates | Votes | % |
|---|---|---|---|
| 1 | Harry E. Rowbottom (R) | 48,203 | 52.1 |
| | William E. Wilson (D) | 44,335 | 47.9 |
| 2 | Arthur H. Greenwood (D) | 43,690 | 49.8 |
| | John E. Sedwick (R) | 43,073 | 49.1 |
| 3 | Frank Gardner (D) | 44,376 | 52.8 |
| | Lindley M. Barlow (R) | 39,446 | 46.9 |
| 4 | Harry C. Canfield (D) | 48,803 | 58.2 |
| | James W. Hill (R) | 35,007 | 41.8 |
| 5 | Noble J. Johnson (R) | 46,264 | 55.5 |
| | J. R. Shannon (D) | 28,573 | 34.3 |
| | Jesse Rice Burks (P) | 7,476 | 9.0 |
| 6 | Richard N. Elliott (R) | 46,094 | 55.3 |
| | Lawrence A. Handley (D) | 37,309 | 44.7 |
| 7 | Ralph E. Updike (R) | 94,751 | 60.0 |
| | Joseph P. Turk (D) | 62,279 | 39.4 |
| 8 | Albert H. Vestal (R) | 51,864 | 55.8 |
| | John A. M. Adair (D) | 41,119 | 44.2 |
| 9 | Fred S. Purnell (R) | 51,280 | 54.5 |
| | James P. Davis (D) | 41,973 | 44.6 |

## INDIANA

| | Candidates | Votes | % |
|---|---|---|---|
| 10 | William R. Wood (R) | 67,143 | 66.8 |
| | Harry O. Rhodes (D) | 33,344 | 33.2 |
| 11 | Albert R. Hall (R) | 47,978 | 54.0 |
| | Samuel E. Cook (D) | 39,998 | 45.0 |
| 12 | David Hogg (R) | 49,921 | 58.4 |
| | Charles W. Branstrator (D) | 35,565 | 41.6 |
| 13 | Andrew J. Hickey (R) | 69,042 | 61.7 |
| | James L. Harmon (D) | 42,895 | 38.3 |

## IOWA

| | Candidates | Votes | % |
|---|---|---|---|
| 1 | William F. Kopp (R) | 42,711 | 71.4 |
| | James M. Bell (D) | 17,100 | 28.6 |
| 2 | F. Dickinson Letts (R) | 49,416 | 60.1 |
| | W. Thompson (D) | 32,842 | 39.9 |
| 3 | Thomas J. B. Robinson (R) | 54,921 | 68.5 |
| | Willis N. Birdsall (D) | 25,213 | 31.5 |
| 4 | Gilbert N. Haugen (R) | 50,811 | 71.1 |
| | J. M. Berry (D) | 20,646 | 28.9 |
| 5 | Cyrenus Cole (R) | 52,180 | 70.2 |
| | W. N. Townsend (D) | 22,175 | 29.8 |
| 6 | C. William Ramseyer (R) | 42,848 | 69.3 |
| | James V. Curran (D) | 18,976 | 30.7 |
| 7 | Cassius C. Dowell (R) | 66,550 | 78.3 |
| | William M. Wade (D) | 18,454 | 21.7 |
| 8 | Lloyd Thurston (R) | 42,222 | 62.5 |
| | Le Roy Munyon (D) | 25,321 | 37.5 |
| 9 | William R. Green (R) | 49,153 | 68.4 |
| | Charles F. Paschel (D) | 22,741 | 31.6 |
| 10 | Lester J. Dickinson (R) | 59,954 | 75.4 |
| | R. F. Mitchell (D) | 19,571 | 24.6 |
| 11 | William D. Boies (R) | 56,152 | 61.5 |
| | A. Sykes (D) | 35,086 | 38.5 |

## KANSAS

| | Candidates | Votes | % |
|---|---|---|---|
| 1 | Daniel R. Anthony Jr. (R) | 49,676 | 70.8 |
| | Lee Eppinger (D) | 20,474 | 29.2 |
| 2 | Chauncey B. Little (D) | 43,285 | 48.8 |
| | Russell Dyer (R) | 39,523 | 44.6 |
| | Arthur L. McKenney (I) | 5,895 | 6.7 |
| 3 | William H. Sproul (R) | 49,482 | 57.3 |
| | Charles Stephens (D) | 36,876 | 42.7 |
| 4 | Homer Hoch (R) | 34,731 | 65.0 |
| | R. W. Woodside (D) | 18,728 | 35.0 |
| 5 | James G. Strong (R) | 38,754 | 60.0 |
| | C. E. Hatfield (D) | 25,842 | 40.0 |
| 6 | Hays B. White (R) | 35,690 | 52.5 |
| | John R. Connelly (D) | 32,285 | 47.5 |
| 7 | Jasper N. Tincher (R) | 48,826 | 54.6 |
| | Nellie Cline (D) | 40,583 | 45.4 |
| 8 | William A. Ayres (D) | 44,312 | 60.6 |
| | Chester I. Long (R) | 28,868 | 39.5 |

**Special Election**

| | | | |
|---|---|---|---|
| 2 | U. S. Guyer (R) | 55,765 | 62.0 |
| | Mrs. James A. Cable (D) | 34,170 | 38.0 |

## KENTUCKY

| | Candidates | Votes | % |
|---|---|---|---|
| 1 | Alben W. Barkley (D) | 41,861 | 67.0 |
| | R. L. Myre (R) | 20,669 | 33.1 |
| 2 | David H. Kincheloe (D) | 35,717 | 100.0 |
| 3 | Robert Y. Thomas Jr (D) | 33,084 | 52.7 |
| | George Baker (R) | 29,753 | 47.4 |
| 4 | Ben Johnson (D) | 34,954 | 53.5 |
| | Z. T. Proctor (R) | 29,865 | 45.7 |
| 5 | Maurice Thatcher (R) | 60,403 | 54.5 |
| | Sam H. McMeekin (D) | 50,508 | 45.5 |
| 6 | Arthur B. Rouse (D) | 36,400 | 49.5 |
| | B. S. Landram (R) | 21,951 | 29.8 |
| | William H. Bornhorst (PROG) | 15,219 | 20.7 |
| 7 | Virgil Chapman (D) | 40,654 | 100.0 |
| 8 | Ralph Gilbert (D) | 29,888 | 100.0 |

| | Candidates | Votes | % |
|---|---|---|---|
| 9 | Fred M. Vinson (D) | 45,899 | 54.5 |
| | George Osborne (R) | 38,295 | 45.5 |
| 10 | John W. Langley (R) | 31,057 | 59.7 |
| | Alex L. Ratliff (D) | 20,577 | 39.6 |
| 11 | John M. Robsion (R) | 57,130 | 74.4 |
| | Nat B. Sewell (D) | 19,626 | 25.6 |

**Special Election**

| | | | |
|---|---|---|---|
| 9 | Fred M. Vinson (D) | 15,681 | 72.9 |
| | W. S. Yazell (R) | 5,822 | 27.1 |

## LOUISIANA

| | | Votes | % |
|---|---|---|---|
| 1 | James O'Connor (D) | 20,027 | 100.0 |
| 2 | J. Zach Spearing (D) | 19,503 | 100.0 |
| 3 | Whitmell P. Martin (D) | 6,209 | 100.0 |
| 4 | John N. Sandlin (D) | 9,893 | 100.0 |
| 5 | Riley J. Wilson (D) | 8,523 | 100.0 |
| 6 | Bolivar E. Kemp (D) | 10,216 | 100.0 |
| 7 | Ladislas Lazaro (D) | 10,054 | 100.0 |
| 8 | James B. Aswell (D) | 8,886 | 100.0 |

## MAINE

| | | Votes | % |
|---|---|---|---|
| 1 | Carroll L. Beedy (R) | 39,269 | 59.2 |
| | William M. Ingraham (D) | 27,058 | 40.8 |
| 2 | Wallace H. White Jr. (R) | 34,335 | 57.8 |
| | Bertrand G. McIntire (D) | 25,086 | 42.2 |
| 3 | John E. Nelson (R) | 40,730 | 62.1 |
| | Leon O. Tebbetts (D) | 24,860 | 37.9 |
| 4 | Ira G. Hersey (R) | 34,011 | 62.0 |
| | Clinton C. Stevens (D) | 20,851 | 38.0 |

## MARYLAND

| | | Votes | % |
|---|---|---|---|
| 1 | Thomas Alan Goldsborough (D) | 27,963 | 57.0 |
| | Harry T. Phoebus (R) | 21,060 | 43.0 |
| 2 | Millard E. Tydings (D) | 35,051 | 53.2 |
| | Edward Ridgely Simpson (R) | 29,421 | 44.7 |
| 3 | John Philip Hill (R) | 23,760 | 61.5 |
| | George Heller (D) | 14,217 | 36.8 |
| 4 | J. Charles Linthicum (D) | 28,054 | 59.9 |
| | John R. M. Staum (R) | 17,773 | 38.0 |
| 5 | Stephen W. Gambrill (D) | 24,971 | 51.6 |
| | Thomas B. R. Mudd (R) | 23,412 | 48.4 |
| 6 | Frederick N. Zihlman (R) | 33,800 | 53.8 |
| | David C. Winebrenner (D) | 28,016 | 44.6 |

**Special Election**

| | | | |
|---|---|---|---|
| 5 | Stephen W. Gambrill (D) | 23,474 | 50.3 |
| | Thomas B. R. Mudd (R) | 23,204 | 49.7 |

## MASSACHUSETTS

| | | Votes | % |
|---|---|---|---|
| 1 | Allen T. Treadway (R) | 38,359 | 58.5 |
| | Thomas F. Cassidy (D) | 27,246 | 41.5 |
| 2 | George B. Churchill (R) | 41,126 | 57.3 |
| | Joseph E. Kerigan (D) | 30,703 | 42.7 |
| 3 | Frank H. Foss (R) | 38,626 | 64.4 |
| | Wilfrid J. Lamoureux (D) | 21,368 | 35.6 |
| 4 | George R. Stobbs (R) | 43,221 | 57.3 |
| | William H. Dyer (D) | 31,022 | 41.2 |
| 5 | John Jacob Rogers (R) | 46,841 | 67.4 |
| | Humphrey O'Sullivan (D) | 22,691 | 32.6 |
| 6 | A. Piatt Andrew (R) | 55,023 | 100.0 |
| 7 | William P. Connery Jr (D) | 34,710 | 55.7 |
| | Charles A. Littlefield (R) | 27,600 | 44.3 |
| 8 | Harry I. Thayer (R) | 52,051 | 62.0 |
| | Daniel P. Leahy (D) | 31,844 | 38.0 |
| 9 | Charles L. Underhill (R) | 42,212 | 59.0 |
| | Arthur D. Healey (D) | 29,398 | 41.1 |
| 10 | John J. Douglass (D) | 19,558 | 58.9 |
| | Peter F. Tague | 8,694 | 26.2 |
| | James E. Maguire (R) | 4,168 | 12.6 |

| | Candidates | Votes | % |
|---|---|---|---|
| 11 | George Holden Tinkham (R) | 46,865 | 66.0 |
| | Timothy J. Driscoll (D) | 24,111 | 34.0 |
| 12 | James A. Gallivan (D) | 51,108 | 73.4 |
| | Howard A. Morton (R) | 18,573 | 26.7 |
| 13 | Robert Luce (R) | 61,851 | 69.3 |
| | Edwin F. Tuttle (D) | 27,450 | 30.7 |
| 14 | Louis A. Frothingham (R) | 59,746 | 69.1 |
| | David W. Murray (D) | 26,686 | 30.9 |
| 15 | Joseph W. Martin Jr. (R) | 33,360 | 58.4 |
| | Arthur J. B. Cartier (D) | 23,764 | 41.6 |
| 16 | Charles L. Gifford (R) | 37,913 | 69.5 |
| | John H. Backus Jr. (D) | 14,051 | 25.8 |

## MICHIGAN

| | | Votes | % |
|---|---|---|---|
| 1 | John B. Sosnowski (R) | 76,566 | 67.5 |
| | Robert H. Clancy (D) | 36,516 | 32.2 |
| 2 | Earl C. Michener (R) | 69,680 | 73.8 |
| | James W. Helme (D) | 24,742 | 26.2 |
| 3 | Arthur B. Williams (R) | 50,375 | 65.1 |
| | Claude S. Carney (D) | 27,044 | 34.9 |
| 4 | John C. Ketcham (R) | 49,060 | 70.3 |
| | Fremont Evans (D) | 20,631 | 29.6 |
| 5 | Carl E. Mapes (R) | 58,682 | 81.3 |
| | Harry C. White (D) | 13,497 | 18.7 |
| 6 | Grant M. Hudson (R) | 173,705 | 85.6 |
| | Willis M. Brewer (D) | 29,191 | 14.4 |
| 7 | Louis C. Cramton (R) | 60,404 | 80.8 |
| | Varnum J. Bowers (D) | 14,291 | 19.1 |
| 8 | Bird J. Vincent (R) | 64,749 | 77.5 |
| | William A. Seegmiller (D) | 18,795 | 22.5 |
| 9 | James C. McLaughlin (R) | 47,386 | 84.1 |
| | Charles M. Black (D) | 8,781 | 15.6 |
| 10 | Roy O. Woodruff (R) | 47,555 | 81.3 |
| | Judson E. Richardson (D) | 10,944 | 18.7 |
| 11 | Frank D. Scott (R) | 41,686 | 73.3 |
| | Prentiss M. Brown (D) | 15,222 | 26.8 |
| 12 | W. Frank James (R) | 47,114 | 100.0 |
| 13 | Clarence J. McLeod (R) | 95,747 | 88.4 |
| | Joel R. Moore (D) | 12,526 | 11.6 |

## MINNESOTA

| | | Votes | % |
|---|---|---|---|
| 1 | Allen J. Furlow (R) | 41,484 | 53.4 |
| | Julius J. Reiter (F-LAB) | 28,558 | 36.8 |
| | L. B. Hanna (D) | 7,659 | 9.9 |
| 2 | Frank Clague (R) | 45,730 | 60.5 |
| | O. F. Swanjord (F-LAB) | 29,901 | 39.5 |
| 3 | August H. Andresen (R) | 40,398 | 57.3 |
| | A. C. Welch (F-LAB) | 30,093 | 42.7 |
| 4 | Oscar E. Keller (R) | 39,217 | 47.8 |
| | Dan W. Lawler (D) | 30,277 | 36.9 |
| | Julius F. Emme (F-LAB) | 12,629 | 15.4 |
| 5 | Walter H. Newton (R) | 68,333 | 58.9 |
| | A. G. Bastis (F-LAB) | 36,804 | 31.7 |
| | John S. Crosby (D) | 10,967 | 9.5 |
| 6 | Harold Knutson (R) | 39,800 | 54.1 |
| | S. C. Shipstead (F-LAB) | 33,831 | 46.0 |
| 7 | Ole J. Kvale (F-LAB) | 43,555 | 58.5 |
| | Gunnar B. Bjornson (R) | 30,871 | 41.5 |
| 8 | William L. Carss (F-LAB) | 46,926 | 54.3 |
| | Victor L. Power (D) | 39,505 | 45. |
| 9 | Knud Wefald (F-LAB) | 38,248 | 56.8 |
| | F. H. Peterson (R) | 29,095 | 43.2 |
| 10 | Godfrey G. Goodwin (R) | 47,749 | 53.8 |
| | George D. Brewer (F-LAB) | 36,490 | 41.2 |
| | Frank Hicks (D) | 4,485 | 5.1 |

## MISSISSIPPI

| | | Votes | % |
|---|---|---|---|
| 1 | John E. Rankin (D) | 13,971 | 100.0 |
| 2 | Bill G. Lowery (D) | 10,534 | 100.0 |
| 3 | William M. Whittington (D) | 9,282 | 100.0 |
| 4 | T. Jeff Busby (D) | 12,861 | 95. |
| 5 | Ross A. Collins (D) | 14,738 | 100.0 |
| 6 | T. Webber Wilson (D) | 17,337 | 100.0 |
| 7 | Percy E. Quin (D) | 9,547 | 100.0 |
| 8 | James W. Collier (D) | 10,278 | 100.0 |

## MISSOURI

| Candidates | Votes | % |
|---|---|---|
| 1 Milton A. Romjue (D) | 37,831 | 57.3 |
|   Frank Millspaugh (R) | 28,175 | 42.7 |
| 2 Ralph F. Lozier (D) | 41,643 | 62.8 |
|   Sweeney (R) | 24,195 | 36.5 |
| 3 Jacob L. Milligan (D) | 33,285 | 52.8 |
|   Henry F. Lawrence (R) | 29,773 | 47.2 |
| 4 Charles L. Faust (R) | 35,752 | 51.3 |
|   John McDaniel (D) | 33,948 | 48.7 |
| 5 Edgar C. Ellis (R) | 87,124 | 49.8 |
|   George H. Combs Jr. (D) | 85,581 | 48.9 |
| 6 Clement C. Dickinson (D) | 28,911 | 53.8 |
|   William O. Atkeson (R) | 24,815 | 46.2 |
| 7 Samuel C. Major (D) | 46,264 | 52.0 |
|   O. B. Whitaker (R) | 42,686 | 48.0 |
| 8 William L. Nelson (D) | 28,895 | 50.8 |
|   Sidney C. Hoach (R) | 27,955 | 49.2 |
| 9 Clarence Cannon (D) | 38,228 | 56.1 |
|   George E. Hackmann (R) | 29,509 | 43.3 |
| 10 Cleveland A. Newton (R) | 123,199 | 61.2 |
|   Henry J. Schleper (D) | 70,976 | 35.3 |
| 11 Harry B. Hawes (D) | 31,940 | 50.6 |
|   Michael J. Hart (R) | 29,972 | 47.5 |
| 12 Leonidas C. Dyer (R) | 25,749 | 63.2 |
|   Jerome F. Duggan (D) | 14,022 | 34.4 |
| 13 Charles E. Kiefner (R) | 27,743 | 53.0 |
|   J. Scott Wolff (D) | 24,598 | 47.0 |
| 14 Ralph E. Bailey (R) | 46,541 | 50.3 |
|   James F. Fulbright (D) | 46,020 | 49.7 |
| 15 Joe J. Manlove (R) | 39,148 | 56.4 |
|   William G. Warner (D) | 30,051 | 43.3 |
| 16 Thomas L. Rubey (D) | 28,353 | 55.8 |
|   William P. Elmer (R) | 22,426 | 44.2 |

## MONTANA

| Candidates | Votes | % |
|---|---|---|
| 1 John M. Evans (D) | 44,139 | 63.9 |
|   John O. Davies (R) | 24,012 | 34.8 |
| 2 Scott Leavitt (R) | 55,190 | 61.4 |
|   Joseph Kirschwing (D) | 28,708 | 32.0 |
|   Charles E. Taylor (F-LAB) | 5,938 | 6.6 |

## NEBRASKA

| Candidates | Votes | % |
|---|---|---|
| 1 John H. Morehead (D & PROG) | 33,584 | 51.8 |
|   Roy H. Thorpe (R) | 29,755 | 45.9 |
| 2 Willis G. Sears (R) | 38,382 | 55.5 |
|   William V. Jamieson (D) | 24,756 | 35.8 |
|   Roy M. Harrop (PROG) | 6,059 | 8.8 |
| 3 Edgar Howard (D & PROG) | 46,631 | 57.5 |
|   E. C. Houston (R) | 34,541 | 42.6 |
| 4 Melvin O. McLaughlin (R) | 32,235 | 49.0 |
|   E. E. Placek (D) | 28,962 | 44.0 |
|   John O. Schmidt (PROG) | 4,563 | 6.9 |
| 5 Ashton C. Shallenberger (D & PROG) | 34,766 | 53.8 |
|   William E. Andrews (R) | 29,871 | 46.2 |
| 6 Robert G. Simmons (R) | 54,686 | 59.2 |
|   Charles W. Beal (D) | 32,275 | 34.9 |
|   Jesse Gandy (P) | 5,467 | 5.9 |

## NEVADA

| Candidates | Votes | % |
|---|---|---|
| AL Samuel S. Arentz (R) | 13,107 | 50.4 |
|   Charles L. Richards (D) | 12,880 | 49.6 |

## NEW HAMPSHIRE

| Candidates | Votes | % |
|---|---|---|
| 1 Fletcher Hale (R) | 44,758 | 55.2 |
|   William N. Rogers (D) | 36,306 | 44.8 |
| 2 Edward H. Wason (R) | 47,588 | 61.4 |
|   William H. Barry (D) | 29,880 | 38.6 |

## NEW JERSEY

| Candidates | Votes | % |
|---|---|---|
| 1 Francis F. Patterson Jr. (R) | 64,592 | 69.1 |
|   Robert A. Irving (D) | 25,232 | 27.0 |
| 2 Isaac Bacharach (R) | 67,668 | 76.2 |
|   Charles S. Stevens (D) | 21,185 | 23.8 |
| 3 T. Frank Appleby (R) | 67,445* | 60.3 |
|   Elmer H. Geran (D) | 44,361 | 39.7 |
| 4 Charles A. Eaton (R) | 41,734 | 53.8 |
|   Charles Browne (D) | 35,840 | 46.2 |
| 5 Ernest R. Ackerman (R) | 69,423 | 72.3 |
|   Monell Sayre (D) | 26,662 | 27.8 |
| 6 Randolph Perkins (R) | 66,555 | 66.3 |
|   Alfred T. Holley (D) | 30,954 | 30.8 |
| 7 George N. Seger (R) | 44,932 | 73.0 |
|   Andrew J. Callahan (D) | 13,441 | 21.8 |
| 8 Herbert W. Taylor (R) | 45,744 | 57.0 |
|   Frank J. McNulty (D) | 34,463 | 43.0 |
| 9 Franklin W. Fort (R) | 32,916 | 59.3 |
|   Daniel F. Minahan (D) | 20,356 | 36.7 |
| 10 Frederick R. Lehlbach (R) | 50,890 | 70.1 |
|   Moses Greenwood (D) | 18,578 | 25.6 |
| 11 Oscar L. Auf der Heide (D) | 37,813 | 60.5 |
|   John F. Gardner (R) | 22,085 | 35.3 |
| 12 Mary T. Norton (D) | 44,815 | 61.7 |
|   Douglas D. T. Story (R) | 26,368 | 36.3 |

## NEW MEXICO

| Candidates | Votes | % |
|---|---|---|
| AL John Morrow (D) | 57,802 | 51.2 |
|   J. Felipe Hubbell (R) | 53,960 | 47.8 |

## NEW YORK

| Candidates | Votes | % |
|---|---|---|
| 1 Robert L. Bacon (R) | 87,370 | 67.1 |
|   Ira L. Terry (D) | 39,765 | 30.5 |
| 2 John J. Kindred (D) | 73,757 | 62.6 |
|   Frank E. Hopkins (R) | 40,507 | 34.4 |
| 3 George W. Lindsay (D) | 22,621 | 64.8 |
|   Herman E. Sprigade (R) | 9,804 | 28.1 |
|   Joseph A. Weil (SOC) | 2,488 | 7.1 |
| 4 Thomas H. Cullen (D) | 27,008 | 73.9 |
|   Joseph Rosenbaum (R) | 8,780 | 24.0 |
| 5 Loring M. Black Jr. (D) | 37,200 | 51.1 |
|   William T. Simpson (R) | 33,938 | 46.6 |
| 6 Andrew L. Somers (D) | 42,894 | 47.8 |
|   Warren I. Lee (R) | 41,110 | 45.8 |
|   W. W. Passage (SOC) | 5,779 | 6.4 |
| 7 John F. Quayle (D) | 24,048 | 56.7 |
|   Otis C. Carroll (R) | 14,650 | 34.5 |
|   Jacob Axelrad (SOC) | 3,730 | 8.8 |
| 8 William E. Cleary (D) | 49,479 | 51.3 |
|   Max Perlman (R) | 38,638 | 40.1 |
|   William M. Feigenbaum (SOC) | 8,333 | 8.6 |
| 9 David J. O'Connell (D) | 43,655 | 50.2 |
|   Andrew N. Petersen (R) | 38,708 | 44.5 |
|   Wilhelmus B. Robinson (SOC) | 4,620 | 5.3 |
| 10 Emanuel Celler (D) | 25,251 | 50.0 |
|   James N. Little (R) | 19,444 | 38.5 |
|   Joseph A. Whitehorn (SOC) | 5,449 | 10.8 |
| 11 Anning S. Prall (D) | 34,265 | 68.7 |
|   Frederick W. Lahr (R) | 14,990 | 30.0 |
| 12 Samuel Dickstein (D) | 14,994 | 75.8 |
|   Harry Schlissel (R) | 2,464 | 12.5 |
|   Israel Feinberg (SOC) | 2,164 | 10.9 |
| 13 Christopher D. Sullivan (D) | 13,708 | 71.1 |
|   Murray D. Firstman (R) | 3,960 | 20.6 |
|   Julius Hochman (SOC) | 1,600 | 8.3 |
| 14 Nathan D. Perlman (R) | 12,046 | 44.1 |
|   William Irving Sirovich (D) | 11,920 | 43.6 |
|   William Karlin (SOC) | 3,165 | 11.6 |
| 15 John J. Boylan (D) | 28,132 | 77.0 |
|   Warren Bigelow (R) | 7,732 | 21.2 |
| 16 John J. O'Connor (D) | 27,585 | 72.3 |
|   L. Wilfred Eidt (R) | 9,329 | 24.4 |
| 17 Ogden L. Mills (R) | 31,553 | 57.0 |
|   Charles E. Gehring (D) | 22,526 | 40.7 |
| 18 John F. Carew (D) | 25,975 | 66.1 |
|   Charles W. Ferry (R) | 10,777 | 27.4 |
|   Samuel E. Beardsley (SOC) | 2,519 | 6.4 |
| 19 Sol Bloom (D) | 39,760 | 54.5 |
|   Walter M. Chandler (R) | 31,008 | 42.5 |
| 20 Fiorello H. LaGuardia (SOC) | 10,756 | 42.7 |
|   Henry Frank (D) | 7,141 | 28.4 |
|   Isaac Siegel (R) | 7,099 | 28.2 |
| 21 Royal H. Weller (D) | 43,793 | 52.5 |
|   Charles H. Roberts (R) | 35,881 | 43.1 |
| 22 Anthony J. Griffin (D) | 30,469 | 69.7 |
|   William E. Devlin (R) | 10,169 | 23.3 |
|   Joseph B. Hagerty (SOC) | 3,081 | 7.1 |
| 23 Frank Oliver (D) | 67,650 | 56.3 |
|   Albert B. Rossdale (R) | 35,721 | 29.7 |
|   August Claessens (SOC) | 15,771 | 13.1 |
| 24 Benjamin L. Fairchild (R) | 50,745 | 45.5 |
|   John J. Kinney (D) | 49,948 | 44.7 |
|   Philip Umstadter (SOC&PROG) | 10,937 | 9.8 |
| 25 J. Mayhew Wainwright (R) | 57,539 | 64.8 |
|   A. Outram Sherman (D) | 26,909 | 30.3 |
| 26 Hamilton Fish Jr. (R) | 55,386 | 69.7 |
|   Rosslyn M. Cox (D) | 21,621 | 27.2 |
| 27 Harcourt J. Pratt (R) | 45,764 | 58.6 |
|   William C. DeWitt (R) | 30,805 | 39.4 |
| 28 Parker Corning (D) | 57,194 | 52.7 |
|   Charles H. Johnson (R) | 50,108 | 46.2 |
| 29 James S. Parker (R) | 60,730 | 67.2 |
|   James E. Dwyer (D) | 28,079 | 31.1 |
| 30 Frank Crowther (R) | 47,073 | 62.9 |
|   James P. Boyle (D & PROG) | 24,840 | 33.2 |
| 31 Bertrand H. Snell (R) | 45,372 | 70.5 |
|   John M. Cantwell (D) | 19,018 | 29.5 |
| 32 Thaddeus C. Sweet (R) | 52,506 | 68.9 |
|   Charles R. Lee (D) | 23,715 | 31.1 |
| 33 Frederick M. Davenport (R) | 48,591 | 58.1 |
|   Albert R. Kessinger (D) | 33,068 | 39.5 |
| 34 Harold S. Tolley (R) | 61,547 | 69.7 |
|   Charles R. Seymour (D) | 24,800 | 28.1 |
| 35 Walter W. Magee (R) | 70,268 | 64.7 |
|   John J. Kesel (D) | 35,008 | 32.2 |
| 36 John Taber (R) | 57,865 | 71.7 |
|   Michael J. Maney (D) | 22,890 | 28.3 |
| 37 Gale H. Stalker (R) | 59,498 | 66.9 |
|   Charles L. Durham (D) | 27,763 | 31.2 |
| 38 Meyer Jacobstein (D&SOC) | 63,997 | 65.4 |
|   John J. McInerney (R) | 33,895 | 34.6 |
| 39 Archie D. Sanders (R) | 58,165 | 67.9 |
|   Michael L. Coleman (D) | 23,689 | 27.7 |
| 40 S. Wallace Dempsey (R) | 66,939 | 67.8 |
|   Thurman W. Stoner (D) | 26,382 | 26.7 |
|   Eustace Reynolds (SOC) | 5,478 | 5.5 |
| 41 Clarence MacGregor (R) | 40,449 | 68.1 |
|   Edward C. Dethloff (D) | 13,754 | 23.1 |
|   Frank Ehrenfried (SOC) | 5,237 | 8.8 |
| 42 James M. Mead (D) | 28,152 | 50.1 |
|   Richard S. Persons (R) | 25,256 | 45.0 |
| 43 Daniel A. Reed (R & SOC) | 61,769 | 91.0 |
|   J. Samuel Fowler (PROG) | 6,141 | 9.0 |

## NORTH CAROLINA

| Candidates | Votes | % |
|---|---|---|
| 1 Lindsay C. Warren (D) | 16,387 | 78.5 |
|   Peter D. Burgess (R) | 4,478 | 21.5 |
| 2 John H. Kerr (D) | 16,312 | 93.3 |
|   M. R. Vick (R) | 1,169 | 6.7 |
| 3 Charles L. Abernethy (D) | 17,685 | 67.7 |
|   William H. Fisher (R) | 8,431 | 32.3 |
| 4 Edward W. Pou (D) | 24,057 | 69.6 |
|   Young Z. Parker (R) | 10,505 | 30.4 |
| 5 Charles M. Stedman (D) | 44,048 | 59.3 |
|   Thomas C. Carter (R) | 30,255 | 40.7 |
| 6 Homer L. Lyon (D) | 21,682 | 72.7 |
|   William J. McDonald (R) | 8,153 | 27.3 |
| 7 William C. Hammer (D) | 36,491 | 55.2 |
|   S. Carter Williams (R) | 29,652 | 44.8 |
| 8 Robert L. Doughton (D) | 34,692 | 56.5 |
|   James D. Dorsett (R) | 26,666 | 43.5 |
| 9 Alfred L. Bulwinkle (D) | 37,370 | 57.7 |
|   John A. Hendricks (R) | 27,427 | 42.3 |

## NORTH CAROLINA

| Candidates | Votes | % |
|---|---|---|
| 10 Zebulon Weaver (D) | 41,030 | 55.5 |
| Lewis P. Hamlin (R) | 32,871 | 44.5 |

## NORTH DAKOTA

| | | |
|---|---|---|
| 1 Olger B. Burtness (R) | 44,573 | 75.4 |
| Walter Welford (D) | 14,511 | 24.6 |
| 2 Thomas Hall (R) | 31,212 | 52.1 |
| Gerald P. Nye (PROG) | 28,193 | 47.0 |
| 3 James H. Sinclair (R) | 37,925 | 73.4 |
| R. A. Johnson (D) | 13,730 | 26.6 |

### Special Election

| | | |
|---|---|---|
| 2 Thomas Hall (R) | 33,460 | 51.0 |
| Gerald P. Nye (PROG) | 32,205 | 49.0 |

## OHIO

| | | |
|---|---|---|
| 1 Nicholas Longworth (R) | 58,185 | 61.7 |
| Thomas B. Paxton (D) | 36,065 | 38.3 |
| 2 Ambrose E. B. Stephens (R) | 47,331 | 58.1 |
| Robert J. O'Donnell (D) | 34,118 | 41.9 |
| 3 Roy Fitzgerald (R) | 73,513 | 62.3 |
| John P. Rogers (D) | 43,426 | 36.8 |
| 4 W. T. Fitzgerald (R) | 43,984 | 50.8 |
| Hugh T. Mathers (D) | 42,652 | 49.2 |
| 5 Charles J. Thompson (R) | 31,046 | 51.5 |
| Frank C. Kniffin (D) | 29,245 | 48.5 |
| 6 Charles C. Kearns (R) | 33,064 | 53.0 |
| Ed. N. Kennedy (D) | 29,283 | 47.0 |
| 7 Charles Brand (R) | 61,557 | 63.9 |
| C. K. Wolf (D) | 34,709 | 36.1 |
| 8 Brooks Fletcher (D) | 38,439 | 53.2 |
| R. Clint Cole (R) | 33,258 | 46.0 |
| 9 William W. Chalmers (R) | 54,792 | 51.6 |
| Isaac R. Sherwood (D) | 48,442 | 45.6 |
| 10 Thomas A. Jenkins (R) | 32,617 | 64.5 |
| W. F. Rutherford (D) | 17,923 | 35.5 |
| 11 Mell G. Underwood (D) | 35,696 | 59.5 |
| Edwin D. Ricketts (R) | 24,272 | 40.5 |
| 12 John C. Speaks (R) | 58,705 | 58.7 |
| Lowry F. Sater (D) | 41,291 | 41.3 |
| 13 James T. Begg (R) | 45,307 | 62.1 |
| John Dreitzler (D) | 27,623 | 37.9 |
| 14 Martin L. Davey (D) | 62,314 | 50.8 |
| Arthur W. Doyle (R) | 60,251 | 49.2 |
| 15 C. Ellis Moore (R) | 39,155 | 56.1 |
| James R. Alexander (D) | 30,608 | 43.9 |
| 16 John McSweeney (D) | 51,491 | 51.5 |
| Thomas C. Hunsicker (R) | 45,559 | 45.6 |
| 17 William M. Morgan (R) | 50,226 | 57.9 |
| J. Freer Bittinger (D) | 36,532 | 42.1 |
| 18 Frank Murphy (R) | 56,206 | 66.3 |
| James M. Barton (D) | 26,656 | 31.4 |
| 19 John G. Cooper (R) | 67,581 | 75.5 |
| Phebe T. Sutliff (D) | 21,926 | 24.5 |
| 20 Charles A. Mooney (D) | 34,173 | 59.7 |
| Harvey Drucker (R) | 22,507 | 39.3 |
| 21 Robert Crosser (D) | 24,889 | 53.2 |
| Harry C. Gahn (R) | 21,629 | 46.2 |
| 22 Theodore E. Burton (R) | 95,174# | 61.8 |
| Samuel B. Fitzsimmons (D) | 32,970# | 21.4 |
| Alfred F. Coyle (I) | 25,489# | 16.6 |

## OKLAHOMA

| | | |
|---|---|---|
| 1 Samuel J. Montgomery (R) | 45,949 | 49.3 |
| Wayne B. Bayless (D) | 45,806 | 49.2 |
| 2 William W. Hastings (D) | 30,352 | 54.9 |
| P. E. Reed (R) | 24,413 | 44.2 |
| 3 Charles D. Carter (D) | 38,674 | 68.1 |
| Don Welch (R) | 15,433 | 27.2 |
| 4 Thomas D. McKeown (D) | 36,437 | 58.8 |
| Charles E. Wells (R) | 23,313 | 37.6 |
| 5 Fletcher B. Swank (D) | 44,683 | 59.4 |
| John Golobie (R) | 28,510 | 37.9 |

| Candidates | Votes | % |
|---|---|---|
| 6 Elmer Thomas (D) | 31,188 | 56.4 |
| Lorraine M. Gensman (R) | 21,915 | 39.6 |
| 7 James V. McClintic (D) | 26,582 | 66.6 |
| Walter S. Mills (D) | 10,316 | 25.8 |
| M. Shadid (F-LAB) | 3,041 | 7.6 |
| 8 Milton C. Garber (R) | 34,020 | 51.0 |
| V. P. Crowe (D) | 29,710 | 44.5 |

## OREGON

| | | |
|---|---|---|
| 1 Willis C. Hawley (R) | 72,910 | 63.5 |
| Harvey L. Clark (D) | 25,293 | 22.0 |
| W. J. Butler (I) | 13,494 | 11.8 |
| 2 Nicholas J. Sinnott (R) | 29,937 | 61.6 |
| James H. Graham (D) | 18,652 | 38.4 |
| 3 Maurice E. Crumpacker (R) | 50,834 | 54.7 |
| Elton Watkins (D & PROG) | 39,731 | 42.7 |

## PENNSYLVANIA

| | | |
|---|---|---|
| 1 William S. Vare (R) | 59,287 | 84.4 |
| Joseph A. Robbins (D, PROG) | 7,631 | 10.9 |
| 2 George S. Graham (R) | 37,645 | 82.7 |
| Jessie L. Collet (D, LAB) | 6,355 | 14.0 |
| 3 Harry C. Ransley (R) | 39,171 | 83.9 |
| Edward P. Carroll (D) | 4,092 | 8.8 |
| Jennie Dorriblum (SOC, LAB) | 3,301 | 7.1 |
| 4 Benjamin M. Golder (R) | 40,783 | 77.8 |
| Adolph Class (D) | 8,365 | 16.0 |
| Henry P. Thomas (SOC) | 3,237 | 6.2 |
| 5 James J. Connolly (R) | 47,033 | 81.0 |
| Daniel J. C. O'Donnell (D) | 7,525 | 13.0 |
| Harry Calse (SOC) | 3,118 | 5.4 |
| 6 George A. Welsh (R) | 66,340 | 74.6 |
| Francis I. J. Coyle (D, LAB) | 17,457 | 19.6 |
| 7 George P. Darrow (R, P) | 55,990 | 80.7 |
| Thomas A. O'Hara (D) | 9,999 | 14.4 |
| 8 Thomas S. Butler (R) | 63,480 | 80.7 |
| Gordon H. Cilley (D, PROG) | 12,816 | 16.3 |
| 9 Henry W. Watson (R) | 60,316 | 72.5 |
| C. William Freed (D) | 18,843 | 22.7 |
| 10 William W. Griest (R) | 35,257 | 60.4 |
| Frank C. Musser (D, INDL) | 22,503 | 38.6 |
| 11 Laurence H. Watres (R) | 35,461 | 56.7 |
| David Fowler (D, LAB) | 25,471 | 40.7 |
| 12 Edmund N. Carpenter (R, P) | 44,483 | 55.6 |
| John J. Casey (D, SOC) | 35,562 | 44.4 |
| 13 George Franklin Brumm (R, P) | 35,737 | 69.5 |
| Thomas J. Butler (D) | 14,637 | 28.5 |
| 14 Charles J. Esterly (R) | 43,335 | 50.5 |
| William M. Croll (D) | 36,582 | 42.6 |
| Raymond S. Hofses (SOC) | 5,884 | 6.9 |
| 15 Louis T. McFadden (R, P) | 27,565 | 68.8 |
| Charles M. Driggs (D, LAB) | 11,854 | 29.6 |
| 16 Edgar R. Kiess (R, P) | 26,865 | 55.5 |
| Thomas Wood (D) | 18,246 | 37.7 |
| P. A. McGowan (LAB, SOC) | 3,317 | 6.8 |
| 17 Frederick W. Magrady (R, P) | 27,969 | 53.5 |
| Herbert W. Cummings (D, LAB) | 24,321 | 46.5 |
| 18 Edward M. Beers (R, P) | 35,743 | 66.4 |
| Meredith Meyers (D, LAB) | 18,048 | 33.6 |
| 19 Joshua W. Swartz (R) | 39,465 | 53.9 |
| Frank C. Sites (D, P) | 33,038 | 45.1 |
| 20 Anderson H. Walters (R, P) | 23,519 | 50.1 |
| Warren Worth Bailey (D, LAB) | 23,456 | 49.9 |
| 21 J. Banks Kurtz (R, SOC) | 27,335 | 69.4 |
| Harry K. Filler (D) | 7,290 | 18.5 |
| J. E. Miller (LAB) | 4,748 | 12.1 |

| Candidates | Votes | % |
|---|---|---|
| 22 Franklin Menges (R) | 26,924 | 53.4 |
| Samuel F. Glatfelter (D, P) | 22,784 | 45.2 |
| 23 William Irvin Swoope (R, P) | 31,205 | 64.7 |
| Edward R. Benson (D, LAB) | 17,008 | 35.3 |
| 24 Samuel A. Kendall (R, P) | 31,443 | 68.5 |
| Harrison N. Boyd (D) | 11,810 | 25.7 |
| 25 Henry W. Temple (R, SOC) | 27,192 | 62.5 |
| Grant Furlong (D) | 15,641 | 36.0 |
| 26 Thomas W. Phillips Jr. (R) | 38,723 | 68.8 |
| John G. Cobler (D, P) | 15,307 | 27.2 |
| 27 Nathan L. Strong (R) | 33,267 | 58.9 |
| John H. Murray (P) | 11,208 | 19.8 |
| Harry W. Fee (D) | 10,119 | 17.9 |
| 28 Harris J. Bixler (R, P) | 43,247 | 79.1 |
| William G. Barker (D) | 11,409 | 20.9 |
| 29 Milton W. Shreve (R) | 27,502 | 57.7 |
| Edward M. Murphy (D) | 10,304 | 21.6 |
| Elizabeth R. Culbertson (P, LAB) | 8,261 | 17.3 |
| 30 William R. Coyle (R) | 31,036 | 50.9 |
| Everett Kent (D, LAB) | 28,723 | 47.1 |
| 31 Adam M. Wyant (R, SOC) | 36,314 | 60.4 |
| Chester D. Sensenich (D, LAB) | 23,790 | 39.6 |
| 32 Stephen Geyer Porter (R, P) | 31,102 | 79.5 |
| P. M. O'Donnell (D) | 5,055 | 12.9 |
| 33 M. Clyde Kelly (R, P) | 37,314 | 81.1 |
| Gilbert F. Myer (D) | 6,017 | 13.1 |
| 34 John M. Morin (R, LAB) | 22,669 | 82.5 |
| William N. McNair (D) | 3,289 | 12.0 |
| 35 James M. Magee (R, PROG) | 28,381 | 59.9 |
| John W. Slayton (LAB, SOC) | 9,039 | 19.1 |
| John Murphy (D) | 5,755 | 12.1 |
| Thomas P. Moran (INDL) | 2,544 | 5.4 |
| 36 Guy E. Campbell (R, D) | 34,266 | 87.2 |
| William H. Bright (P) | 5,048 | 12.8 |

## RHODE ISLAND

| | | |
|---|---|---|
| 1 Clark Burdick (R) | 44,952 | 65.2 |
| Alfred H. Jones (D) | 23,958 | 34.8 |
| 2 Richard S. Aldrich (R) | 44,870 | 63.9 |
| Charles M. Hall (D) | 25,361 | 36.1 |
| 3 Jeremiah E. O'Connell (D) | 35,224 | 51.7 |
| Louis Monast (R) | 32,953 | 48.3 |

## SOUTH CAROLINA

| | | |
|---|---|---|
| 1 Thomas S. McMillan (D) | 5,278 | 95.4 |
| 2 Butler B. Hare (D) | 6,695 | 100.0 |
| 3 Fred H. Dominick (D) | 8,331 | 100.0 |
| 4 John J. McSwain (D) | 7,718 | 100.0 |
| 5 William F. Stevenson (D) | 7,689 | 100.0 |
| 6 Allard H. Gasque (D) | 6,278 | 100.0 |
| 7 Hampton P. Fulmer (D) | 7,249 | 100.0 |

## SOUTH DAKOTA

| | | |
|---|---|---|
| 1 Charles A. Christopherson (R) | 39,138 | 53.5 |
| Warren E. Beck (D) | 19,904 | 27.2 |
| William Bartling (I) | 7,206 | 9.9 |
| William T. Jones (F-LAB) | 6,901 | 9.4 |
| 2 Royal C. Johnson (R) | 44,869 | 60.3 |
| Walter P. Wohlheter (F-LAB) | 11,468 | 15.4 |
| Fred H. Hildebrandt (I) | 10,067 | 13.5 |
| Jack P. Reinhard (D) | 8,043 | 10.8 |
| 3 William Williamson (R) | 28,150 | 58.3 |
| John R. Russell (D) | 10,026 | 20.8 |
| Arthur W. Atwood (F-LAB) | 6,950 | 14.4 |

## TENNESSEE

| | Candidates | Votes | % |
|---|---|---|---|
| 1 | B. Carroll Reece (R) | 23,445 | 62.6 |
| | R. M. Barry (D) | 11,362 | 30.3 |
| | F. P. Robinson | 1,970 | 5.3 |
| 2 | J. Will Taylor (R) | 28,975 | 96.3 |
| 3 | Sam D. McReynolds (D) | 22,857 | 56.9 |
| | May Giles Howard (R) | 17,341 | 43.1 |
| 4 | Cordell Hull (D) | 16,908 | 100.0 |
| 5 | Ewin L. Davis (D) | 11,373 | 81.7 |
| | A. L. Davidson (R) | 2,551 | 18.3 |
| 6 | Joseph W. Byrns (D) | 19,756 | 100.0 |
| 7 | Edward E. Eslick (D) | 13,547 | 100.0 |
| 8 | Gordon Browning (D) | 12,940 | 100.0 |
| 9 | Finis J. Garrett (D) | 18,367 | 100.0 |
| 10 | Hubert F. Fisher (D) | 16,306 | 74.0 |
| | George H. Poole | 2,923 | 13.3 |
| | Harry Speers (R) | 2,801 | 12.7 |

## TEXAS

| | | Votes | % |
|---|---|---|---|
| 1 | Eugene Black (D) | 28,218 | 90.9 |
| | R. B. Johnson (R) | 2,826 | 9.1 |
| 2 | John C. Box (D) | 41,188 | 89.9 |
| | A. E. Sweatland (R) | 4,625 | 10.1 |
| 3 | Morgan G. Sanders (D) | 30,618 | 100.0 |
| 4 | Sam Rayburn (D) | 31,825 | 91.1 |
| | C. A. Gray (R) | 3,111 | 8.9 |
| 5 | Hatton W. Sumners (D) | 43,781 | 87.6 |
| | George G. Atkinson (R) | 6,193 | 12.4 |
| 6 | Luther A. Johnson (D) | 33,169 | 93.2 |
| | Tyler Haswell (R) | 2,440 | 6.9 |
| 7 | Clay Stone Briggs (D) | 23,947 | 89.1 |
| | John T. Wheeler (R) | 2,941 | 10.9 |
| 8 | Daniel E. Garrett (D) | 35,189 | 86.0 |
| | Clarence A. Miller (R) | 5,712 | 14.0 |
| 9 | Joseph J. Mansfield (D) | 31,444 | 82.3 |
| | Ed. Franz (R) | 6,742 | 17.7 |
| 10 | James P. Buchanan (D) | 36,681 | 90.5 |
| | Otto Stolley (R) | 3,850 | 9.5 |
| 11 | Tom T. Connally (D) | 29,247 | 88.2 |
| | C. C. Baker (R) | 3,918 | 11.8 |
| 12 | Fritz G. Lanham (D) | 33,186 | 100.0 |
| 13 | Guinn Williams (D) | 32,721 | 88.6 |
| | C. W. Johnson Jr. (R) | 4,197 | 11.4 |
| 14 | Harry M. Wurzbach (R) | 31,784 | 62.4 |
| | D. S. Davenport (D) | 19,165 | 37.6 |
| 15 | John N. Garner (D) | 22,776 | 99.9 |
| 16 | Claude B. Hudspeth (D) | 27,506 | 82.6 |
| | Vernon L. Sullivan (R) | 5,800 | 17.4 |
| 17 | Thomas L. Blanton (D) | 44,377 | 100.0 |
| 18 | Marvin Jones (D) | 42,399 | 89.7 |
| | A. B. Spencer (R) | 4,887 | 10.3 |

## UTAH

| | Candidates | Votes | % |
|---|---|---|---|
| 1 | Don B. Colton (R) | 40,883 | 54.9 |
| | Frank Francis (D) | 33,644 | 45.1 |
| 2 | Elmer O. Leatherwood (R) | 41,888 | 56.7 |
| | James H. Waters (D) | 32,045 | 43.3 |

## VERMONT

| | | Votes | % |
|---|---|---|---|
| 1 | Elbert S. Brigham (R, P) | 36,278 | 76.0 |
| | Allan T. Calhoun (D) | 11,457 | 24.0 |
| 2 | Ernest Willard Gibson (R, P) | 41,099 | 82.8 |
| | Harry C. Shurtleff (D) | 8,479 | 17.1 |

## VIRGINIA

| | | Votes | % |
|---|---|---|---|
| 1 | Schuyler Otis Bland (D) | 16,958 | 99.9 |
| 2 | Joseph T. Deal (D) | 11,795 | 65.8 |
| | Menalcus Lankford (R) | 6,145 | 34.3 |
| 3 | Andrew Jackson Montague (D) | 20,864 | 100.0 |
| 4 | Patrick Henry Drewry (D) | 12,106 | 100.0 |
| 5 | Joseph Whitehead (D) | 16,371 | 76.0 |
| | G. A. De Hart (R) | 5,181 | 24.0 |
| 6 | Clifton A. Woodrum (D) | 13,917 | 69.0 |
| | F. W. McWane (R) | 6,251 | 31.0 |
| 7 | Thomas W. Harrison (D) | 13,013 | 59.2 |
| | J. H. Ruebush (R) | 7,294 | 33.2 |
| | Dabney C. Harrison (I) | 1,692 | 7.7 |
| 8 | R. Walton Moore (D) | 14,113 | 79.9 |
| | John G. Dudley (R) | 3,551 | 20.1 |
| 9 | George C. Peery (D) | 31,407 | 52.6 |
| | C. Henry Harman (R) | 28,341 | 47.4 |
| 10 | Henry St.George Tucker (D) | 14,472 | 69.7 |
| | Henry S. Reid (R) | 6,288 | 30.3 |

## WASHINGTON

| | | Votes | % |
|---|---|---|---|
| 1 | John F. Miller (R) | 53,152 | 78.8 |
| | David J. Williams (D) | 13,922 | 20.6 |
| 2 | Lindley H. Hadley (R) | 37,636 | 57.4 |
| | Lloyd L. Black (D) | 27,154 | 41.4 |
| 3 | Albert Johnson (R) | 60,272 | 70.5 |
| | O. M. Nelson (PROG) | 25,146 | 29.4 |
| 4 | John W. Summers (R) | 36,918 | 65.3 |
| | H. C. Bohlke (D) | 12,254 | 21.7 |
| | Knute Hill (F-LAB) | 7,380 | 13.1 |
| 5 | Sam B. Hill (D) | 36,844 | 50.7 |
| | J. Edward Ferguson (R) | 35,815 | 49.3 |

## WEST VIRGINIA

| | Candidates | Votes | % |
|---|---|---|---|
| 1 | Carl G. Bachmann (R) | 47,318 | 55.2 |
| | George W. Oldham (D) | 38,417 | 44.8 |
| 2 | Frank L. Bowman (R) | 41,825 | 50.1 |
| | Robert E. Lee Allen (D) | 40,474 | 48.5 |
| 3 | John M. Wolverton (R) | 45,995 | 51.9 |
| | Robert H. Kidd (D) | 42,626 | 48.1 |
| 4 | Harry C. Woodyard (R) | 47,136 | 51.2 |
| | George W. Johnson (D) | 44,877 | 48.8 |
| 5 | James French Strother (R) | 50,629 | 51.5 |
| | Thomas Jefferson Lilly (D) | 47,719 | 48.5 |
| 6 | J. Alfred Taylor (D) | 56,570 | 49.8 |
| | Leonard S. Echols (R) | 55,089 | 48.5 |

## WISCONSIN

| | | Votes | % |
|---|---|---|---|
| 1 | Henry Allen Cooper (R) | 60,770 | 72.0 |
| | Calvin Stewart (D) | 23,612 | 28.0 |
| 2 | Edward Voigt (R) | 44,617 | 70.5 |
| | Ernst C. Wrucke (D) | 18,696 | 29.5 |
| 3 | John M. Nelson (R) | 56,868 | 77.0 |
| | William Victora (R) | 16,968 | 23.0 |
| 4 | John C. Schafer (R) | 30,837 | 49.6 |
| | Leo Krzycki (SOC) | 19,770 | 31.8 |
| | Thomas H. Dorr (D) | 11,524 | 18.6 |
| 5 | Victor L. Berger (SOC) | 32,211 | 41.6 |
| | Ernst A. Braun (R) | 31,702 | 41.0 |
| | Raymond Moore (D) | 13,441 | 17.4 |
| 6 | Florian Lampert (R) | 45,982 | 70.6 |
| | Michael K. Reilly (D) | 19,128 | 29.4 |
| 7 | Joseph D. Beck (R) | 47,075 | 80.0 |
| | W. D. Martin (D) | 10,228 | 17.4 |
| 8 | Edward E. Browne (R) | 47,423 | 99.9 |
| 9 | George J. Schneider (R) | 45,159 | 71.0 |
| | T. J. Reinert (D) | 18,449 | 29.0 |
| 10 | James A. Frear (R) | 46,563 | 78.7 |
| | Thomas A. Ryan (D) | 10,481 | 17.7 |
| 11 | Hubert H. Peavey (R) | 48,234 | 78.1 |
| | John Cadigan (D) | 13,455 | 21.8 |

## WYOMING

| | | Votes | % |
|---|---|---|---|
| AL | Charles E. Winter (R) | 43,026 | 60.1 |
| | Theodore Wanerus (D) | 28,537 | 39.9 |

# 1925 House Election

## NEW JERSEY

### Special Election

| | | | |
|---|---|---|---|
| 3 | Stewart H. Appleby (R) | 53,925 | 53.3 |
| | J. Lyle Kinmonth (D) | 47,271 | 46.7 |

# 1926 House Elections

## ALABAMA

| | Candidates | Votes | % |
|---|---|---|---|
| 1 | John McDuffie (D) | 8,297 | 84.0 |
| | Aubrey Boyles (R) | 1,578 | 16.0 |
| 2 | Lister Hill (D) | 10,170 | 100.0 |
| 3 | Henry B. Steagall (D) | 7,619 | 94.6 |
| | C. E. Roberts (R) | 437 | 5.4 |
| 4 | Lamar Jeffers (D) | 8,392 | 68.1 |
| | Omar H. Reynolds (R) | 3,933 | 31.9 |
| 5 | William B. Bowling (D) | 9,012 | 88.4 |
| | John A. Alexander (R) | 1,183 | 11.6 |
| 6 | William B. Oliver (D) | 3,984 | 99.0 |
| 7 | Miles C. Allgood (D) | 14,937 | 64.7 |
| | John J. Stephens (R) | 8,162 | 35.3 |
| 8 | Edward B. Almon (D) | 8,800 | 90.1 |
| | Robert M. Sims (R) | 964 | 9.9 |
| 9 | George Huddleston (D) | 7,260 | 94.4 |
| | Frank H. Lathrop (R) | 430 | 5.6 |
| 10 | William B. Bankhead (D) | 11,895 | 100.0 |

## ARIZONA

| | Candidates | Votes | % |
|---|---|---|---|
| AL | Lewis W. Douglas (D) | 43,725 | 64.1 |
| | Otis J. Baughn (R) | 24,502 | 35.9 |

## ARKANSAS

| | Candidates | Votes | % |
|---|---|---|---|
| 1 | William J. Driver (D) | 3,680 | 100.0 |
| 2 | William A. Oldfield (D) | 4,013 | 78.8 |
| | J. L. McKamey (R) | 1,081 | 21.2 |
| 3 | John N. Tillman (D) | 5,696 | 64.4 |
| | Hardy Kuykendall (R) | 3,146 | 35.6 |
| 4 | Otis T. Wingo (D) | 4,729 | 100.0 |
| 5 | Heartsill Ragon (D) | 4,282 | 88.2 |
| | Harry M. Williams (R) | 574 | 11.8 |
| 6 | James B. Reed (D) | 3,013 | 100.0 |
| 7 | Tillman B. Parks (D) | 3,498 | 100.0 |

## CALIFORNIA

| | Candidates | Votes | % |
|---|---|---|---|
| 1 | Clarence F. Lea (D-R) | 60,207 | 100.0 |
| 2 | Harry L. Englebright (R) | 32,264 | 99.8 |
| 3 | Charles F. Curry (R-D) | 72,912 | 100.0 |
| 4 | Florence P. Kahn (R) | 37,353 | 63.8 |
| | Chauncey F. Tramutolo (D) | 18,210 | 31.1 |
| | William McDevitt (SOC) | 2,960 | 5.1 |
| 5 | Richard J. Welch (R-D) | 47,694 | 100.0 |
| 6 | Albert E. Carter (R) | 91,995 | 100.0 |
| 7 | Henry E. Barbour (R-D) | 73,271 | 100.0 |
| 8 | Arthur Monroe Free (R) | 60,384 | 67.7 |
| | Philip G. Sheehy (D) | 28,836 | 32.3 |
| 9 | William E. Evans (R) | 102,270 | 59.5 |
| | Charles H. Randall (P & D) | 61,719 | 35.9 |
| 10 | Joe Crail (R-D-P) | 144,677 | 86.8 |
| | N. Jackson Wright (SOC) | 21,997 | 13.2 |
| 11 | Philip D. Swing (R-D) | 89,726 | 100.0 |

## COLORADO

| | Candidates | Votes | % |
|---|---|---|---|
| 1 | William N. Vaile (R) | 39,909 | 54.9 |
| | Benjamin C. Hilliard (D) | 30,337 | 41.7 |
| 2 | Charles B. Timberlake (R) | 55,581 | 66.6 |
| | William B. Washburn (D) | 27,939 | 33.5 |
| 3 | Guy U. Hardy (R) | 46,916 | 54.0 |
| | Edmond I. Crockett (D) | 40,009 | 46.0 |
| 4 | Edward T. Taylor (D) | 32,092 | 66.7 |
| | Webster S. Whinnery (R) | 15,990 | 33.3 |

## CONNECTICUT

| | Candidates | Votes | % |
|---|---|---|---|
| 1 | E. Hart Fenn (R) | 45,054 | 63.0 |
| | Henry J. Calnen (D) | 25,777 | 36.0 |
| 2 | Richard P. Freeman (R) | 33,809 | 61.7 |
| | Hermon J. Gibbs (D) | 20,538 | 37.5 |
| 3 | John Q. Tilson (R) | 40,055 | 65.6 |
| | John E. Doughan (D) | 20,281 | 33.2 |
| 4 | Schuyler Merritt (R) | 44,477 | 68.4 |
| | John Held Jr. (D) | 19,623 | 30.2 |
| 5 | James P. Glynn (R) | 28,687 | 58.5 |
| | Arthur F. O'Leary (D) | 20,352 | 41.5 |

## DELAWARE

| | Candidates | Votes | % |
|---|---|---|---|
| AL | Robert G. Houston (R) | 38,909 | 56.9 |
| | Merrill H. Tilghman (D) | 29,424 | 43.1 |

## FLORIDA

| | Candidates | Votes | % |
|---|---|---|---|
| 1 | Herbert J. Drane (D) | 16,034 | 72.8 |
| | Ora E. Chapin (RP & DC) | 6,007 | 27.3 |
| 2 | Robert A. Green (D) | 6,727 | 86.2 |
| | A. F. Knotts (R) | 1,080 | 13.8 |
| 3 | Tom A. Yon (D) | 7,156 | 86.8 |
| | J. H. Drummond (R) | 1,084 | 13.2 |
| 4 | William J. Sears (D) | 19,578 | 73.6 |
| | W. C. Lawson (RDC) | 4,235 | 15.9 |
| | E. D. Housholder (R) | 2,783 | 10.5 |

## GEORGIA

| | Candidates | Votes | % |
|---|---|---|---|
| 1 | Charles G. Edwards (D) | 7,641 | 100.0 |
| 2 | E. E. Cox (D) | 2,384 | 100.0 |
| 3 | Charles R. Crisp (D) | 3,422 | 100.0 |
| 4 | William C. Wright (D) | 2,583 | 100.0 |
| 5 | Leslie J. Steele (D) | 2,919 | 99.9 |
| 6 | Samuel Rutherford (D) | 2,365 | 100.0 |
| 7 | Malcolm C. Tarver (D) | 5,902 | 94.1 |
| | George A. Coffee | 373 | 5.9 |
| 8 | Charles H. Brand (D) | 3,124 | 100.0 |
| 9 | Thomas M. Bell (D) | 7,788 | 100.0 |
| 10 | Carl Vinson (D) | 3,015 | 100.0 |
| 11 | William C. Lankford (D) | 3,461 | 100.0 |
| 12 | William W. Larsen (D) | 2,388 | 100.0 |

## IDAHO

| | Candidates | Votes | % |
|---|---|---|---|
| 1 | Burton L. French (R) | 31,250 | 66.3 |
| | L. L. Burtenshaw (D, PROG) | 15,903 | 33.7 |
| 2 | Addison T. Smith (R) | 40,960 | 60.6 |
| | H. F. Fait (PROG) | 15,368 | 22.7 |
| | Mary George Gray (D) | 11,259 | 16.7 |

## ILLINOIS

| | Candidates | Votes | % |
|---|---|---|---|
| 1 | Martin B. Madden (R) | 26,559 | 68.2 |
| | James F. Doyle (D) | 12,283 | 31.5 |
| 2 | Morton D. Hull (R) | 71,750 | 65.5 |
| | Michael C. Walsh (D) | 37,518 | 34.3 |
| 3 | Elliott W. Sproul (R) | 57,692 | 52.7 |
| | Edward J. Glackin (D) | 51,590 | 47.1 |
| 4 | Thomas A. Doyle (D) | 30,817 | 62.9 |
| | John J. Dever (R) | 18,184 | 37.1 |
| 5 | Adolph J. Sabath (D) | 18,027 | 58.8 |
| | Matt J. Vogel (R) | 12,643 | 41.2 |
| 6 | James T. Igoe (D) | 74,817 | 52.6 |
| | John J. Gorman (R) | 67,419 | 47.4 |
| 7 | M. Alfred Michaelson (R) | 86,405 | 57.8 |
| | John S. Hall (D) | 62,469 | 41.8 |
| 8 | Stanley Henry Kunz (D) | 15,321 | 55.3 |
| | Wencil F. Hetman (R) | 12,388 | 44.7 |
| 9 | Fred A. Britten (R) | 26,530 | 97.8 |
| 10 | Carl R. Chindblom (R) | 68,137 | 66.0 |
| | William X. Meyer (D) | 35,123 | 34.0 |
| 11 | Frank R. Reid (R) | 44,574 | 69.5 |
| | Edward J. O'Beirne (D) | 19,600 | 30.5 |
| 12 | John T. Buckbee (R) | 36,597 | 57.8 |
| | John A. Logan Warren (D) | 26,727 | 42.2 |
| 13 | William R. Johnson (R) | 30,197 | 74.8 |
| | John Ascher (D) | 10,190 | 25.2 |
| 14 | John C. Allen (R) | 33,089 | 68.0 |
| | John W. Casto (D) | 15,572 | 32.0 |
| 15 | Edward J. King (R) | 35,396 | 62.6 |
| | F. William Heckenkamp Jr. (D) | 21,157 | 37.4 |
| 16 | William E. Hull (R) | 37,170 | 63.3 |
| | Carl M. Behrman (D) | 21,530 | 36.7 |
| 17 | Homer W. Hall (R) | 31,874 | 64.9 |
| | Frank Gillespie (D) | 17,220 | 35.1 |
| 18 | William P. Holaday (R) | 44,112 | 65.2 |
| | Wilbur Hickman (D) | 23,569 | 34.8 |
| 19 | Charles Adkins (R) | 40,456 | 62.3 |
| | Joel T. Davis (D) | 24,507 | 37.7 |
| 20 | Henry T. Rainey (D) | 29,935 | 57.8 |
| | Horace H. Bancroft (R) | 21,875 | 42.2 |
| 21 | J. Earl Major (D) | 39,365 | 52.8 |
| | Loren E. Wheeler (R) | 35,191 | 47.2 |
| 22 | Edward M. Irwin (R) | 38,714 | 58.5 |
| | William N. Baltz (D) | 27,428 | 41.5 |
| 23 | William W. Arnold (D) | 38,575 | 55.9 |
| | Erastus D. Telford (R) | 29,896 | 43.3 |
| 24 | Thomas S. Williams (R) | 26,295 | 56.1 |
| | John Marshall Karns (D) | 20,612 | 43.9 |
| 25 | Edward E. Denison (R) | 36,644 | 59.6 |
| | A. F. Gourley (D) | 24,849 | 40.4 |
| AL | Henry R. Rathbone (R) | 987,968 | |
| | Richard Yates (R) | 986,090 | |
| | Frank J. Wise (D) | 631,708 | |
| | Charles A. Karch (D) | 616,713 | |
| | Mrs. P. J. Carlson (PROG) | 5,413 | |
| | Charles Pogoreles (SOC) | 2,662 | |
| | George Koop (SOC) | 2,476 | |
| | James S. O'Rourke (SOC LAB) | 1,977 | |
| | A. H. Otto Beneze (SOC LAB) | 1,746 | |
| | Charles D. Harrison (HL) | 451 | |
| | Andrew A. Gour (CLP) | 431 | |
| | Mary C. Connor (CLP) | 428 | |

## INDIANA

| | Candidates | Votes | % |
|---|---|---|---|
| 1 | Harry E. Rowbottom (R) | 37,503 | 52.4 |
| | William E. Wilson (D) | 34,061 | 47.6 |
| 2 | Arthur H. Greenwood (D) | 44,690 | 55.4 |
| | John E. Sedwick (R) | 35,964 | 44.6 |
| 3 | Frank Gardner (D) | 42,422 | 54.6 |
| | W. Clyde Martin (R) | 35,229 | 45.4 |
| 4 | Harry C. Canfield (D) | 42,882 | 53.9 |
| | John W. Holcomb (R) | 36,655 | 46.1 |
| 5 | Noble J. Johnson (R) | 43,458 | 57.8 |
| | Henry W. Moore (D) | 31,693 | 42.2 |
| 6 | Richard N. Elliott (R) | 38,347 | 55.2 |
| | William H. Myers (D) | 31,107 | 44.8 |
| 7 | Ralph E. Updike (R) | 48,313 | 52.1 |
| | William D. Headrick (D) | 44,142 | 47.6 |
| 8 | Albert H. Vestal (R) | 40,963 | 53.8 |
| | Claude C. Ball (D) | 35,205 | 46.2 |
| 9 | Fred S. Purnell (R) | 43,891 | 52.6 |
| | Roy W. Adney (D) | 39,597 | 47.4 |
| 10 | William R. Wood (R) | 52,286 | 68.2 |
| | Harry O. Rhodes (D) | 24,349 | 31.8 |
| 11 | Albert R. Hall (R) | 42,519 | 54.2 |
| | Samuel E. Cook (D) | 35,870 | 45.8 |
| 12 | David Hogg (R) | 38,936 | 55.3 |
| | Waldemar E. Eickhoff (D) | 31,442 | 44.7 |
| 13 | Andrew J. Hickey (R) | 52,541 | 54.9 |
| | Charles Weidler (D) | 43,119 | 45.1 |

## IOWA

| | Candidates | Votes | % |
|---|---|---|---|
| 1 | William F. Kopp (R) | 27,358 | 70.6 |
| | James M. Bell (D) | 11,408 | 29.4 |
| 2 | F. Dickinson Letts (R) | 29,200 | 59.1 |
| | J. P. Gallagher (D) | 19,612 | 39.7 |
| 3 | Thomas J. B. Robinson (R) | 32,180 | 70.2 |
| | Ellis E. Wilson (D) | 13,696 | 29.9 |
| 4 | Gilbert N. Haugen (R) | 30,611 | 60.4 |
| | Frank E. Howard (D) | 20,076 | 39.6 |
| 5 | Cyrenus Cole (R) | 31,253 | 71.8 |
| | C. E. Watters (D) | 12,263 | 28.2 |
| 6 | C. William Ramseyer (R) | 27,967 | 66.3 |
| | W. L. Etter (D) | 14,193 | 33.7 |
| 7 | Cassius C. Dowell (R) | 34,159 | 76.9 |
| | William M. Wade (D) | 10,255 | 23.1 |
| 8 | Lloyd Thurston (R) | 30,568 | 61.9 |
| | W. S. Bradley (D) | 18,743 | 37.0 |
| 9 | William R. Greene (R) | 30,373 | 67.2 |
| | Charles F. Paschel (D) | 14,837 | 32.8 |
| 10 | Lester J. Dickinson (R) | 39,677 | 97.7 |
| 11 | William D. Boies (R) | 35,381 | 64.4 |
| | R. J. Koehler (D) | 19,542 | 35.6 |

## KANSAS

| | Candidates | Votes | % |
|---|---|---|---|
| 1 | Daniel R. Anthony Jr. (R) | 46,232 | 100.0 |
| 2 | Ulysses S. Guyer (R) | 37,465 | 51.6 |
| | Chauncey B. Little (D) | 35,108 | 48.3 |
| 3 | William H. Sproul (R) | 35,510 | 50.5 |
| | Thurman Hill (D) | 34,765 | 49.5 |
| 4 | Homer Hoch (R) | 29,285 | 65.2 |
| | Edwin F. Hammond (D) | 15,643 | 34.8 |
| 5 | James G. Strong (R) | 33,817 | 62.8 |
| | Rex Montgomery (D) | 20,033 | 37.2 |
| 6 | Hays B. White (R) | 31,159 | 50.1 |
| | W. H. Clark (D) | 31,065 | 49.9 |
| 7 | Clifford R. Hope (R) | 49,072 | 64.1 |
| | Harry F. Brown (D) | 27,374 | 35.8 |
| 8 | William A. Ayres (D) | 32,096 | 60.1 |
| | Fred L. Bell (R) | 21,350 | 40.0 |

## KENTUCKY

| | Candidates | Votes | % |
|---|---|---|---|
| 1 | William V. Gregory (D) | 28,306 | 67.8 |
| | Mrs. William H. Mason (R) | 13,460 | 32.2 |
| 2 | David H. Kincheloe (D) | 23,445 | 56.2 |
| | Ernest Rowe (R) | 18,279 | 43.8 |
| 3 | John W. Moore (D) | 24,303 | 56.2 |
| | Charles E. Whittle (R) | 18,941 | 43.8 |
| 4 | Henry D. Moorman (D) | 24,348 | 55.3 |
| | Pal Garner (R) | 19,658 | 44.7 |
| 5 | Maurice H. Thatcher (R) | 51,328 | 54.8 |
| | S. M. Russell (D) | 42,339 | 45.2 |
| 6 | Orie S. Ware (D) | 26,063 | 57.2 |
| | E. H. Daugherty (R) | 19,487 | 42.8 |
| 7 | Virgil Chapman (D) | 26,924 | 100.0 |
| 8 | Ralph Gilbert (D) | 21,938 | 54.5 |
| | E. W. Draffen (R) | 18,321 | 45.5 |
| 9 | Fred M. Vinson (D) | 31,063 | 59.1 |
| | Trumbo Snedegar (R) | 21,498 | 40.9 |
| 10 | Katherine Langley (R) | 20,463 | 58.4 |
| | Doug Hays (D) | 14,578 | 41.6 |
| 11 | John M. Robsion (R) | 38,474 | 100.0 |

### Special Elections

| | | Votes | % |
|---|---|---|---|
| 3 | John W. Moore (D) | 27,640 | 52.9 |
| | Thurman B. Dixon (R) | 24,580 | 47.1 |
| 10 | Andrew J. Kirk (R) | 10,540 | 60.7 |
| | J. C. Cantrell (D) | 6,838 | 39.4 |

## LOUISIANA

| | Candidates | Votes | % |
|---|---|---|---|
| 1 | James O'Connor (D) | 14,486 | 94.3 |
| | Gus Oertling (R) | 869 | 5.7 |
| 2 | J. Zach Spearing (D) | 15,110 | 100.0 |
| 3 | Whitmell P. Martin (D) | 3,488 | 100.0 |
| 4 | John N. Sandlin (D) | 5,490 | 100.0 |

| | Candidates | Votes | % |
|---|---|---|---|
| 5 | Riley J. Wilson (D) | 2,778 | 100.0 |
| 6 | Bolivar E. Kemp (D) | 4,055 | 100.0 |
| 7 | Ladislas Lazaro (D) | 3,721 | 100.0 |
| 8 | James B. Aswell (D) | 4,192 | 100.0 |

## MAINE

| | | Votes | % |
|---|---|---|---|
| 1 | Carroll L. Beedy (R) | 27,040 | 62.8 |
| | Richard E. Hersom (D) | 16,032 | 37.2 |
| 2 | Wallace H. White Jr. (R) | 26,593 | 56.6 |
| | Charles M. Starbird (D) | 20,422 | 43.4 |
| 3 | John E. Nelson (R) | 30,216 | 64.8 |
| | Edward Chase (D) | 16,421 | 35.2 |
| 4 | Ira G. Hersey (R) | 22,858 | 62.9 |
| | Frank A. Peabody (D) | 13,457 | 37.1 |

## MARYLAND

| | | Votes | % |
|---|---|---|---|
| 1 | T. Alan Goldsborough (D) | 30,845 | 59.1 |
| | Lawrence B. Towers (R) | 21,359 | 40.9 |
| 2 | William P. Cole Jr. (D) | 50,305 | 58.9 |
| | Linwood L. Clark (R) | 34,327 | 40.2 |
| 3 | Vincent L. Palmisano (D) | 21,466 | 58.7 |
| | John J. McGinity (R) | 14,284 | 39.1 |
| 4 | J. Charles Linthicum (D) | 32,620 | 62.0 |
| | Julius F. Diehl (R) | 19,531 | 37.1 |
| 5 | Stephen W. Gambrill (D) | 26,905 | 55.1 |
| | Thomas Brackett Reed Mudd (R) | 21,911 | 44.9 |
| 6 | Frederick N. Zihlman (R) | 35,247 | 58.3 |
| | Frank W. Mish (D) | 24,749 | 40.9 |

## MASSACHUSETTS

| | | Votes | % |
|---|---|---|---|
| 1 | Allen T. Treadway (R) | 37,878 | 58.8 |
| | Eugene A. Lynch (D) | 26,592 | 41.3 |
| 2 | Henry L. Bowles (R) | 36,333 | 64.0 |
| | John Hall (D) | 20,450 | 36.0 |
| 3 | Frank H. Foss (R) | 35,887 | 62.8 |
| | Joseph E. Casey (D) | 21,257 | 37.2 |
| 4 | George R. Stobbs (R) | 37,744 | 57.7 |
| | Peter F. Sullivan (D) | 27,706 | 42.3 |
| 5 | Edith Nourse Rogers (R) | 46,464 | 71.1 |
| | James M. Hurley (D) | 18,846 | 28.9 |
| 6 | A. Piatt Andrew (R) | 39,918 | 76.9 |
| | James McPherson (D) | 11,975 | 23.1 |
| 7 | William P. Connery Jr. (D) | 32,130 | 64.0 |
| | George F. Hogan (R) | 18,045 | 36.0 |
| 8 | Frederick W. Dallinger (R) | 46,642 | 63.7 |
| | John P. Brennan (D) | 26,601 | 36.3 |
| 9 | Charles L. Underhill (R) | 34,468 | 57.8 |
| | Francis X. Tyrrell (D) | 25,211 | 42.2 |
| 10 | John J. Douglass (D) | 29,443 | 100.0 |
| 11 | George Holden Tinkham (R, D) | 48,948 | 100.0 |
| 12 | James A. Gallivan (D) | 49,865 | 100.0 |
| 13 | Robert Luce (R) | 50,463 | 64.0 |
| | John P. Tierney (D) | 28,346 | 36.0 |
| 14 | Louis A. Frothingham (R) | 51,920 | 66.2 |
| | Frank A. Manning (D) | 26,469 | 33.8 |
| 15 | Joseph W. Martin Jr. (R) | 33,687 | 65.2 |
| | Minerva D. Kepple (D) | 17,963 | 34.8 |
| 16 | Charles L. Gifford (R) | 35,235 | 68.0 |
| | George Fox Tucker (D) | 16,570 | 32.0 |

### Special Election

| | | Votes | % |
|---|---|---|---|
| 8 | Frederick W. Dallinger (R) | 44,761# | 64.3 |
| | John P. Brennan (D) | 24,800# | 35.7 |

## MICHIGAN

| | | Votes | % |
|---|---|---|---|
| 1 | Robert H. Clancy (R) | 27,004 | 74.1 |
| | William M. Donnelly (D) | 9,119 | 25.0 |
| 2 | Earl C. Michener (R) | 38,182 | 66.7 |
| | Boyez Dansard (D) | 19,034 | 33.3 |

| | Candidates | Votes | % |
|---|---|---|---|
| 3 | Joseph L. Hooper (R) | 30,704 | 70.2 |
| | Frank L. Willison (D) | 13,034 | 29.8 |
| 4 | John C. Ketcham (R) | 31,881 | 72.3 |
| | Earl B. Sill (D) | 12,223 | 27.7 |
| 5 | Carl E. Mapes (R) | 29,653 | 80.2 |
| | Frank C. Jarvis (D) | 7,339 | 19.8 |
| 6 | Grant M. Hudson (R) | 67,796 | 68.0 |
| | Frank L. Dodge (D) | 31,945 | 32.0 |
| 7 | Louis C. Cramton (R) | 35,967 | 78.1 |
| | Frank W. Merrick (D) | 10,081 | 21.9 |
| 8 | Bird J. Vincent (R) | 39,541 | 100.0 |
| 9 | James C. McLaughlin (R) | 24,927 | 99.3 |
| 10 | Roy O. Woodruff (R) | 23,875 | 100.0 |
| 11 | Frank P. Bohn (R) | 25,816 | 77.6 |
| | Robert H. Wright (D) | 7,468 | 22.4 |
| 12 | W. Frank James (R) | 37,117 | 100.0 |
| 13 | Clarence J. McLeod (R) | 26,190 | 68.0 |
| | Henry A. Behrendt (D) | 12,152 | 31.6 |

## MINNESOTA

| | | Votes | % |
|---|---|---|---|
| 1 | Allen J. Furlow (R) | 46,956 | 74.5 |
| | L. B. Hanna (D) | 16,070 | 25.5 |
| 2 | Frank Clague (R) | 56,679 | 100.0 |
| 3 | August H. Andresen (R) | 40,484 | 63.3 |
| | August M. Gagen (F-LAB) | 13,636 | 21.3 |
| | Charles C. Kolars (D) | 9,825 | 15.4 |
| 4 | Melvin J. Maas (R) | 22,976# | 54.3 |
| | Thomas V. Sullivan (F-LAB) | 17,355# | 41.0 |
| 5 | Walter H. Newton (R) | 47,162 | 64.8 |
| | Albert G. Bastis (F-LAB) | 19,647 | 27.0 |
| | Fred Jensen (D) | 5,942 | 8.2 |
| 6 | Harold Knutson (R) | 39,570 | 59.4 |
| | Joseph B. Himsel (F-LAB) | 27,076 | 40.6 |
| 7 | Ole J. Kvale (F-LAB) | 41,151 | 59.0 |
| | E. E. Howard (R) | 28,641 | 41.0 |
| 8 | William L. Carss (F-LAB) | 41,766 | 55.4 |
| | Oscar J. Larson (R) | 33,606 | 44.6 |
| 9 | Conrad G. Selvig (R) | 33,477 | 50.7 |
| | Knud Wefald (F-LAB) | 32,505 | 49.3 |
| 10 | Godfrey G. Goodwin (R) | 36,897 | 59.1 |
| | Ernest Lundeen (F-LAB) | 21,552 | 34.5 |
| | Henry A. Finlayson (D) | 4,013 | 6.4 |

## MISSISSIPPI

| | | Votes | % |
|---|---|---|---|
| 1 | John E. Rankin (D) | 3,423 | 100.0 |
| 2 | Bill G. Lowrey (D) | 3,167 | 100.0 |
| 3 | William M. Whittington (D) | 2,949 | 100.0 |
| 4 | T. Jeff Busby (D) | 3,945 | 100.0 |
| 5 | Ross A. Collins (D) | 4,832 | 100.0 |
| 6 | T. Webber Wilson (D) | 4,792 | 100.0 |
| 7 | Percy E. Quin (D) | 1,781 | 100.0 |
| 8 | James W. Collier (D) | 2,028 | 100.0 |

## MISSOURI

| | | Votes | % |
|---|---|---|---|
| 1 | Milton A. Romjue (D) | 29,629 | 60.4 |
| | J. Frank Culler (R) | 19,384 | 39.5 |
| 2 | Ralph F. Lozier (D) | 31,999 | 62.4 |
| | Sam A. Clark (R) | 19,243 | 37.5 |
| 3 | Jacob L. Milligan (D) | 26,596 | 56.3 |
| | Charles T. McLaughlin (R) | 20,611 | 43.7 |
| 4 | Charles L. Faust (R) | 30,320 | 56.3 |
| | J. C. Whitsell (D) | 23,573 | 43.7 |
| 5 | George H. Combs Jr. (D) | 78,700 | 56.2 |
| | Edgar C. Ellis (R) | 61,189 | 43.7 |
| 6 | Clement C. Dickinson (D) | 24,161 | 55.2 |
| | Millard E. Lane (R) | 19,524 | 44.6 |
| 7 | Samuel C. Major (D) | 37,392 | 52.1 |
| | Harold T. Lincoln (R) | 34,339 | 47.8 |
| 8 | William L. Nelson (D) | 26,156 | 56.2 |
| | C. W. Thomas (R) | 20,422 | 43.8 |
| 9 | Clarence Cannon (D) | 28,720 | 61.2 |
| | Osmund Haenssler (R) | 18,163 | 38.7 |
| 10 | Henry F. Niedringhaus (R) | 91,419 | 66.1 |
| | Irvin Sale (D) | 46,880 | 33.9 |

## MISSOURI

| Candidates | Votes | % |
|---|---|---|
| 11 John J. Cochran (D) | 22,854 | 52.6 |
| Henri Chouteau (R) | 20,554 | 47.3 |
| 12 Leonidas C. Dyer (R) | 14,494 | 61.3 |
| David D. Israel (D) | 9,120 | 38.6 |
| 13 Clyde Williams (D) | 23,338 | 50.6 |
| Charles E. Kiefner (R) | 22,764 | 49.3 |
| 14 James F. Fullbright (D) | 40,871 | 51.5 |
| James F. Adams (R) | 38,501 | 48.5 |
| 15 Joe J. Manlove (R) | 36,995 | 59.7 |
| Robert W. Moore (D) | 24,786 | 40.0 |
| 16 Thomas L. Rubey (D) | 25,032 | 56.5 |
| Anna Covert (R) | 19,251 | 43.5 |

**Special Election**

| Candidates | Votes | % |
|---|---|---|
| 11 John J. Cochran (D) | 22,971 | 52.8 |
| Henri Chouteau (R) | 20,521 | 47.2 |

## MONTANA

| Candidates | Votes | % |
|---|---|---|
| 1 John M. Evans (D) | 38,527 | 59.4 |
| Ronald Higgins (R) | 25,898 | 39.9 |
| 2 Scott Leavitt (R) | 48,617 | 54.9 |
| Harry B. Mitchell (D) | 37,306 | 42.1 |

## NEBRASKA

| Candidates | Votes | % |
|---|---|---|
| 1 John H. Morehead (D) | 30,840 | 55.3 |
| George W. Marsh (R) | 24,169 | 43.4 |
| 2 Willis G. Sears (R) | 33,211 | 59.5 |
| Grenville P. North (D) | 22,641 | 40.5 |
| 3 Edgar Howard (D) | 43,915 | 60.7 |
| John F. Nesbit (R) | 21,075 | 29.1 |
| Willis E. Reed (LAF I) | 7,383 | 10.2 |
| 4 John N. Norton (D) | 31,107 | 50.6 |
| Melvin O. McLaughlin (R) | 30,397 | 49.4 |
| 5 Ashton C. Shallenberger (D-LAF I) | 36,058 | 60.3 |
| W. E. Andrews (R) | 23,781 | 39.7 |
| 6 Robert G. Simmons (R) | 55,330 | 65.8 |
| Thomas C. Osborne (D) | 28,746 | 34.2 |

## NEVADA

| Candidates | Votes | % |
|---|---|---|
| AL Samuel S. Arentz (R) | 17,598 | 57.7 |
| Maurice J. Sullivan (D) | 12,910 | 42.3 |

## NEW HAMPSHIRE

| Candidates | Votes | % |
|---|---|---|
| 1 Fletcher Hale (R) | 40,566 | 61.4 |
| F. Clyde Keefe (D) | 25,555 | 38.7 |
| 2 Edward H. Wason (R) | 36,598 | 63.2 |
| George H. Duncan (D) | 21,312 | 36.8 |

## NEW JERSEY

| Candidates | Votes | % |
|---|---|---|
| 1 Charles A. Wolverton (R) | 57,522 | 69.7 |
| Edward J. Kelleher (D) | 24,990 | 30.3 |
| 2 Isaac Bacharach (R) | 53,147 | 80.6 |
| Frank Melville (D) | 12,775 | 19.4 |
| 3 Harold Hoffman (R) | 61,484 | 60.7 |
| Fred W. DeVoe (D) | 39,074 | 38.6 |
| 4 Charles A. Eaton (R) | 35,948 | 62.0 |
| William M. Williams (D) | 22,059 | 38.0 |
| 5 Ernest R. Ackerman (R) | 50,209 | 63.7 |
| Frank K. Sauer (D) | 28,644 | 36.3 |
| 6 Randolph Perkins (R) | 58,244 | 62.9 |
| Francis C. Koehler (D) | 33,132 | 35.8 |
| 7 George N. Seger (R) | 29,383 | 70.6 |
| Susan A. McNair (D) | 11,083 | 26.6 |
| 8 Paul J. Moore (D) | 39,436 | 58.1 |
| Herbert W. Taylor (R) | 28,273 | 41.6 |
| 9 Franklin W. Fort (R) | 19,751 | 60.2 |
| James J. Whalen (D) | 13,058 | 39.8 |
| 10 Frederick R. Lehlbach (R) | 28,960 | 64.8 |
| Edward W. Townsend (D) | 15,727 | 35.2 |
| 11 Oscar L. Auf der Heide (D) | 45,877 | 76.1 |
| George M. Eichler (R) | 14,083 | 23.4 |
| 12 Mary T. Norton (D) | 54,082 | 83.1 |
| Philip W. Grece (R) | 11,034 | 17.0 |

## NEW MEXICO

| Candidates | Votes | % |
|---|---|---|
| AL John Morrow (D) | 55,433 | 51.4 |
| Juan A. A. Sedillo (R) | 52,075 | 48.3 |

## NEW YORK

| Candidates | Votes | % |
|---|---|---|
| 1 Robert L. Bacon (R) | 82,090 | 63.4 |
| W. Irving Vanderpoel (D) | 45,699 | 35.3 |
| 2 John J. Kindred (D) | 89,062 | 69.4 |
| Louis C. Gosdorfer (R) | 37,163 | 29.0 |
| 3 George W. Lindsay (D) | 21,713 | 75.1 |
| Walter H. Kreiner (R) | 5,984 | 20.7 |
| 4 Thomas H. Cullen (D) | 24,734 | 78.1 |
| George H. Teommey Sr. (R) | 6,624 | 20.9 |
| 5 Loring M. Black Jr. (D) | 34,488 | 56.0 |
| Robert C. Lee (R) | 26,295 | 42.7 |
| 6 Andrew L. Somers (D) | 47,407 | 57.0 |
| William F. Heissenbuttel (R) | 30,906 | 37.2 |
| William W. Passage (SOC) | 4,799 | 5.8 |
| 7 John F. Quayle (D) | 22,551 | 65.0 |
| Harland B. Tibbetts (R) | 9,747 | 28.1 |
| Mendel Bromberg (SOC) | 2,394 | 6.9 |
| 8 Patrick J. Carley (D) | 62,091 | 61.4 |
| George W. Criss (R) | 30,548 | 30.2 |
| W. M. Feigenbaum (SOC) | 8,526 | 8.4 |
| 9 David J. O'Connell (D) | 45,191 | 57.1 |
| Edward W. Patterson (R) | 31,131 | 39.3 |
| 10 Emanuel Celler (D) | 24,102 | 58.3 |
| Samuel Rubin (R) | 13,428 | 32.5 |
| Abraham I. Shiplacoff (SOC) | 3,576 | 8.6 |
| 11 Anning S. Prall (D) | 34,584 | 72.2 |
| Esli L. Sutton (R) | 12,929 | 27.0 |
| 12 Samuel Dickstein (D) | 13,135 | 79.7 |
| Joseph D. Tarlowe (R) | 2,142 | 13.0 |
| Harry Rogoff (SOC) | 1,201 | 7.3 |
| 13 Christopher D. Sullivan (D) | 12,307 | 75.7 |
| John Fanelle (R) | 3,067 | 18.9 |
| Algernon Lee (SOC) | 846 | 5.2 |
| 14 William Irving Sirovich (D) | 11,809 | 49.4 |
| Nathan D. Perlman (R) | 10,688 | 44.8 |
| Samuel E. Beardsley (SOC) | 1,277 | 5.4 |
| 15 John J. Boylan (D) | 24,083 | 80.8 |
| John J. Curry (R) | 5,312 | 17.8 |
| 16 John J. O'Connor (D) | 24,476 | 76.7 |
| Fred W. Meyer (R) | 6,918 | 21.7 |
| 17 William W. Cohen (D) | 22,401 | 50.4 |
| Louis W. Stotesbury (R) | 21,251 | 47.8 |
| 18 John F. Carew (D) | 25,832 | 77.7 |
| Bernard Katzen (R) | 6,076 | 18.3 |
| 19 Sol Bloom (D) | 36,274 | 64.6 |
| Harold Korn (R) | 18,810 | 33.5 |
| 20 Fiorello H. LaGuardia (R & PROG) | 9,122 | 47.1 |
| H. Warren Hubbard (D) | 9,067 | 46.8 |
| George Dobsevage (SOC) | 1,058 | 5.5 |
| 21 Royal H. Weller (D) | 38,111 | 55.4 |
| Emanuel Hertz (R) | 29,359 | 42.7 |
| 22 Anthony J. Griffin (D) | 26,372 | 73.2 |
| R. Fred Talento (R) | 8,037 | 22.3 |
| 23 Frank Oliver (D) | 78,582 | 65.7 |
| Morris S. Schector (R) | 29,247 | 24.5 |
| Samuel Orr (SOC) | 10,689 | 8.9 |
| 24 James M. Fitzpatrick (D) | 54,153 | 50.6 |
| Benjamin L. Fairchild (R) | 47,439 | 44.3 |
| Patrick J. Murphy (SOC) | 5,509 | 5.1 |
| 25 J. Mayhew Wainwright (R) | 50,080 | 62.3 |
| David L. Frank (D) | 28,853 | 35.9 |
| 26 Hamilton Fish Jr. (R) | 43,173 | 63.1 |
| Walter G. Russell (D) | 23,232 | 34.0 |
| 27 Harcourt J. Pratt (R) | 44,557 | 61.3 |
| Ransom H. Gillett (D) | 28,112 | 38.7 |
| 28 Parker Corning (D) | 63,919 | 58.6 |
| George W. Greene (R) | 43,342 | 39.7 |
| 29 James S. Parker (R, D) | 81,798 | 97.9 |
| 30 Frank Crowther (R) | 38,043 | 57.3 |
| E. Watson Gardiner (D) | 26,510 | 39.9 |
| 31 Bertrand H. Snell (R) | 40,474 | 70.1 |
| Abner D. Whitney (D) | 17,237 | 29.9 |
| 32 Thaddeus C. Sweet (R) | 46,232 | 67.9 |
| John M. Reynolds (D) | 21,007 | 30.8 |
| 33 Frederick M. Davenport (R) | 40,845 | 56.2 |
| Isaac C. Flint (D) | 30,265 | 41.6 |
| 34 John D. Clarke (R) | 52,363 | 71.6 |
| Bernard J. McGuire (D) | 20,792 | 28.4 |
| 35 Walter W. Magee (R) | 62,889 | 62.0 |
| Wilber M. Jones (D) | 38,581 | 38.0 |
| 36 John Taber (R) | 48,793 | 70.0 |
| J. Seldon Brandt (D) | 20,886 | 30.0 |
| 37 Gale H. Stalker (R) | 46,757 | 58.2 |
| Edwin S. Underhill (D) | 32,618 | 40.6 |
| 38 Meyer Jacobstein (D) | 42,803 | 48.9 |
| James E. Cuff (R) | 41,191 | 47.1 |
| 39 Archie D. Sanders (R) | 48,623 | 67.7 |
| David A. White (D) | 20,449 | 28.5 |
| 40 S. Wallace Dempsey (R) | 60,310 | 65.7 |
| William F. Sheehan (D) | 27,751 | 30.3 |
| 41 Clarence MacGregor (R) | 35,739 | 65.1 |
| Robert M. Smyth (D) | 16,913 | 30.8 |
| 42 James M. Mead (D) | 28,873 | 58.1 |
| John Buno McGrath (R) | 19,362 | 38.9 |
| 43 Daniel A. Reed (R & SOC) | 44,073 | 73.9 |
| John B. Leach (D) | 15,555 | 26.1 |

## NORTH CAROLINA

| Candidates | Votes | % |
|---|---|---|
| 1 Lindsay C. Warren (D) | 9,501 | 100.0 |
| 2 John H. Kerr (D) | 7,484 | 100.0 |
| 3 Charles L. Abernethy (D) | 14,520 | 72.5 |
| Roscoe Butler (R) | 5,498 | 27.5 |
| 4 Edward W. Pou (D) | 18,000 | 69.6 |
| Hobart Brantley (R) | 7,881 | 30.5 |
| 5 Charles M. Stedman (D) | 32,727 | 59.8 |
| O. C. Durland (R) | 22,016 | 40.2 |
| 6 Homer L. Lyon (D) | 12,888 | 62.3 |
| Leaman Baggett (R) | 7,810 | 37.7 |
| 7 William C. Hammer (D) | 31,332 | 55.9 |
| S. Carter Williams (R) | 24,769 | 44.2 |
| 8 Robert L. Doughton (D) | 30,520 | 58.6 |
| O. F. Pool (R) | 21,543 | 41.4 |
| 9 Alfred L. Bulwinkle (D) | 26,354 | 56.8 |
| Garrett D. Bailey (R) | 20,045 | 43.2 |
| 10 Zebulon Weaver (D) | 36,829 | 55.8 |
| R. Kenneth Smathers (R) | 29,200 | 44.2 |

## NORTH DAKOTA

| Candidates | Votes | % |
|---|---|---|
| 1 Olger B. Burtness (R) | 37,326 | 79.9 |
| R. E. Smith (D) | 6,136 | 13.1 |
| Donald McDonald (F-LAB) | 3,246 | 7.0 |
| 2 Thomas Hall (R) | 33,607 | 66.3 |
| J. L. Page (D) | 13,735 | 27.1 |
| C. W. Reichert (F-LAB) | 3,350 | 6.6 |
| 3 James H. Sinclair (R) | 42,923 | 87.8 |
| Reuben H. Leavitt (D) | 5,960 | 12.2 |

## OHIO

| Candidates | Votes | % |
|---|---|---|
| 1 Nicholas Longworth (R) | 45,317 | 62.9 |
| John C. Rogers (D) | 26,511 | 36.8 |
| 2 Ambrose E. B. Stephens (R) | 36,608* | 58.2 |
| R. J. O'Donnell (D) | 26,322 | 41.8 |
| 3 Roy Fitzgerald (R) | 50,639 | 60.4 |
| T. A. McCann (D) | 33,253 | 39.6 |
| 4 W. T. Fitzgerald (R) | 32,236 | 50.7 |
| B. F. Welty (D) | 31,293 | 49.3 |

## OHIO

| | Candidates | Votes | % |
|---|---|---|---|
| 5 | Charles J. Thompson (R) | 23,638 | 50.7 |
| | Frank Kniffin (D) | 23,022 | 49.3 |
| 6 | Charles Kearns (R) | 27,688 | 52.9 |
| | B. F. Kennedy (D) | 24,630 | 47.1 |
| 7 | Charles Brand (R) | 45,699 | 67.2 |
| | H. E. Rice (D) | 22,314 | 32.8 |
| 8 | Thomas Brooks Fletcher (D) | 30,167 | 56.5 |
| | James R. Hopley (R) | 23,247 | 43.5 |
| 9 | William W. Chalmers (R) | 47,331 | 64.5 |
| | C. W. Davis (D) | 23,947 | 32.6 |
| 10 | Thomas A. Jenkins (R) | 25,571 | 63.9 |
| | Guy Stevenson (D) | 14,460 | 36.1 |
| 11 | Mell Underwood (D) | 29,950 | 62.1 |
| | Walter S. Barrett (R) | 18,300 | 37.9 |
| 12 | John C. Speaks (R) | 41,119 | 56.5 |
| | H. S. Atkinson (D) | 31,724 | 43.6 |
| 13 | James T. Begg (R) | 36,444 | 65.1 |
| | G. C. Steineman (D) | 19,571 | 34.9 |
| 14 | Martin L. Davey (D) | 53,659 | 65.4 |
| | Arthur Sweeney (R) | 28,446 | 34.7 |
| 15 | C. Ellis Moore (R) | 28,519 | 54.6 |
| | E. B. Schneider (D) | 23,703 | 45.4 |
| 16 | John McSweeney (D) | 40,283 | 59.8 |
| | C. D. McClintock (R) | 27,116 | 40.2 |
| 17 | William M. Morgan (R) | 36,249 | 55.0 |
| | J. F. Bittinger (D) | 29,674 | 45.0 |
| 18 | Frank Murphy (D) | 36,599 | 65.4 |
| | John F. Nolan (D) | 19,341 | 34.6 |
| 19 | John G. Cooper (R) | 45,788 | 72.3 |
| | James Kennedy (D) | 17,513 | 27.7 |
| 20 | Charles Mooney (D) | 22,050 | 100.0 |
| 21 | Robert Crosser (D) | 17,819 | 62.4 |
| | Harry C. Gahn (R) | 10,733 | 37.6 |
| 22 | Theodore E. Burton (R) | 55,589 | 100.0 |

## OKLAHOMA

| | | Votes | % |
|---|---|---|---|
| 1 | Everette B. Howard (D) | 33,475 | 50.6 |
| | Samuel J. Montgomery (R) | 32,692 | 49.4 |
| 2 | William W. Hastings (D) | 24,024 | 56.9 |
| | H. L. Wineland (R) | 18,220 | 43.1 |
| 3 | Wiburn Cartwright (D) | 28,883 | 67.1 |
| | George W. Strawn (R) | 13,964 | 32.5 |
| 4 | Thomas D. McKeown (D) | 29,208 | 59.4 |
| | Charles E. Wells (R) | 19,997 | 40.6 |
| 5 | Fletcher B. Swank (D) | 29,988 | 60.6 |
| | Barritt Galloway (R) | 19,491 | 39.4 |
| 6 | Jed Johnson (D) | 21,838 | 54.2 |
| | Fred W. Lankard (R) | 18,188 | 45.1 |
| 7 | James V. McClintic (D) | 17,962 | 70.4 |
| | Walter S. Mills (R) | 7,416 | 29.1 |
| 8 | Milton C. Garber (R) | 27,377 | 58.8 |
| | C. H. Hyde (D) | 18,957 | 40.7 |

## OREGON

| | | Votes | % |
|---|---|---|---|
| 1 | Willis C. Hawley (R) | 67,020 | 71.1 |
| | Newton W. Borden (D) | 27,273 | 28.9 |
| 2 | Nicholas J. Sinnott (R) | 29,357 | 70.4 |
| | John S. Hodgin (D) | 12,348 | 29.6 |
| 3 | Maurice E. Crumpacker (R) | 51,889 | 71.8 |
| | Joseph K. Carson Jr. (D & PROG) | 20,372 | 28.2 |

## PENNSYLVANIA

| | | Votes | % |
|---|---|---|---|
| 1 | James M. Hazlett (R) | 64,781 | 92.8 |
| | William L. Rooney (D) | 4,799 | 6.9 |
| 2 | George S. Graham (R) | 37,470 | 91.3 |
| | John Joseph Shanahan (D) | 3,223 | 7.9 |
| 3 | Harry C. Ransley (R) | 42,661 | 93.2 |
| | Frank J. McDonnell (D) | 2,827 | 6.2 |
| 4 | Benjamin M. Golder (R) | 34,904 | 82.9 |
| | David Louis Ullman (D) | 5,977 | 14.2 |
| 5 | James J. Connolly (R, P) | 46,997 | 85.9 |
| | Daniel J. C. O'Donnell (D) | 6,507 | 11.9 |

| | Candidates | Votes | % |
|---|---|---|---|
| 6 | George A. Welsh (R) | 51,844 | 79.4 |
| | Thomas A. Logue (D) | 10,344 | 15.8 |
| 7 | George P. Darrow (R) | 44,411 | 80.5 |
| | Harry J. Conway (D) | 9,440 | 17.1 |
| 8 | Thomas S. Butler (R, SOC) | 44,664 | 82.2 |
| | Frank B. Rhodes (D) | 8,802 | 16.2 |
| 9 | Henry W. Watson (R) | 38,350 | 71.3 |
| | Richard J. Hamilton (D, LAB) | 14,337 | 26.7 |
| 10 | William W. Griest (R, LAB) | 28,664 | 66.8 |
| | W. W. Heidelbaugh (D, I) | 14,272 | 33.2 |
| 11 | Laurence H. Watres (R, P) | 32,091 | 70.1 |
| | Joseph J. Walsh (D) | 13,662 | 29.9 |
| 12 | John J. Casey (R, D) | 49,467 | 76.5 |
| | Edmund N. Carpenter (P) | 15,166 | 23.5 |
| 13 | Cyrus M. Palmer (R) | 22,850 | 54.3 |
| | Neal J. Ferry (D) | 18,480 | 43.9 |
| 14 | Robert Grey Bushong (R) | 30,240 | 50.2 |
| | Arthur G. Dewalt (D) | 26,930 | 44.7 |
| | Raymond S. Hofses (SOC, LAB) | 3,050 | 5.1 |
| 15 | Louis T. McFadden (R, P) | 19,864 | 69.4 |
| | C. M. Driggs (D) | 8,763 | 30.6 |
| 16 | Edgar R. Kiess (R, D) | 26,047 | 99.9 |
| 17 | Frederick W. Magrady (R, P) | 19,717 | 52.7 |
| | Herbert W. Cummings (D, SOC) | 17,695 | 47.3 |
| 18 | Edward M. Beers (R, P) | 26,067 | 67.8 |
| | Frederick A. Rupp (D) | 12,349 | 32.1 |
| 19 | Isaac H. Doutrich (R, LAB) | 32,833 | 60.1 |
| | Frank C. Sites (D) | 21,563 | 39.5 |
| 20 | J. Russell Leech (R) | 16,254 | 54.8 |
| | Warren Worth Bailey (D, LAB) | 11,182 | 37.7 |
| | Harry Crichton (P) | 2,217 | 7.5 |
| 21 | J. Banks Kurtz (R, P) | 18,094 | 74.7 |
| | Harry K. Filler (D) | 4,799 | 19.8 |
| | Charles Kutz (LAB) | 1,215 | 5.0 |
| 22 | Franklin Menges (R, P) | 20,485 | 57.0 |
| | Samuel F. Glatfelter (D) | 15,268 | 42.5 |
| 23 | J. Mitchell Chase (R, P) | 22,337 | 69.8 |
| | Clarence R. Kramer (D) | 9,664 | 30.2 |
| 24 | Samuel Austin Kendall (R, SOC) | 20,097 | 75.7 |
| | Clark W. Martin (D) | 6,464 | 24.3 |
| 25 | Henry W. Temple (R, P) | 17,004 | 58.8 |
| | James S. Pates (D, LAB) | 11,890 | 41.2 |
| 26 | J. Howard Swick (R, LAB) | 22,062 | 62.0 |
| | James P. Leaf (D, P) | 13,516 | 38.0 |
| 27 | Nathan L. Strong (R, LAB) | 27,757 | 74.5 |
| | D. A. Dorn (D) | 9,038 | 24.3 |
| 28 | Thomas C. Cochran (R, D) | 30,520 | 99.7 |
| 29 | Milton W. Shreve (R) | 17,870 | 82.6 |
| | William H. Kerschner (P) | 3,758 | 17.4 |
| 30 | Everett Kent (D, LAB) | 24,392 | 50.9 |
| | William R. Coyle (R) | 22,981 | 47.9 |
| 31 | Adam M. Wyant (R) | 24,911 | 65.7 |
| | Albert H. Bell (D, P) | 12,175 | 32.1 |
| 32 | Stephen G. Porter (R, LAB) | 28,290 | 82.3 |
| | Walter P. Berner (D) | 4,680 | 13.6 |
| 33 | M. Clyde Kelly (R, D) | 31,886 | 96.1 |
| 34 | John M. Morin (R, D) | 28,783 | 98.8 |
| 35 | Harry A. Estep (R) | 23,881 | 77.5 |
| | John Murphy (D) | 4,242 | 13.8 |
| | James Magee (LAB, P) | 2,191 | 7.1 |
| 36 | Guy C. Campbell (R, D) | 25,474 | 84.2 |
| | Ellsworth C. Trott (P) | 3,264 | 10.8 |

## RHODE ISLAND

| | | Votes | % |
|---|---|---|---|
| 1 | Clark Burdick (R) | 32,459 | 63.0 |
| | Arthur L. Conaty (D) | 19,066 | 37.0 |
| 2 | Richard S. Aldrich (R) | 33,542 | 61.8 |
| | Clarence E. Palmer (D) | 20,738 | 38.2 |
| 3 | Louis Monast (R) | 29,366 | 50.4 |
| | Jeremiah E. O'Connell (D) | 28,909 | 49.6 |

## SOUTH CAROLINA

| | Candidates | Votes | % |
|---|---|---|---|
| 1 | Thomas S. McMillan (D) | 2,244 | 100.0 |
| 2 | Butler B. Hare (D) | 1,766 | 100.0 |
| 3 | Fred H. Dominick (D) | 2,374 | 100.0 |
| 4 | John J. McSwain (D) | 2,057 | 100.0 |
| 5 | William F. Stevenson (D) | 2,416 | 100.0 |
| 6 | Allard H. Gasque (D) | 1,532 | 100.0 |
| 7 | Hampton P. Fulmer (D) | 1,933 | 100.0 |

## SOUTH DAKOTA

| | | Votes | % |
|---|---|---|---|
| 1 | Charles A. Christopherson (R) | 37,185 | 56.3 |
| | J. E. House (D) | 26,103 | 39.5 |
| 2 | Royal C. Johnson (R) | 38,928 | 64.3 |
| | Fred H. Hildebrandt (D) | 21,505 | 35.7 |
| 3 | William Williamson (R) | 22,932 | 52.3 |
| | Arthur W. Watwood (D) | 20,902 | 47.7 |

## TENNESSEE

| | | Votes | % |
|---|---|---|---|
| 1 | B. Carroll Reece (R) | 10,553 | 88.0 |
| | W. L. Giles (D) | 1,439 | 12.0 |
| 2 | J. Will Taylor (R) | 11,789 | 99.8 |
| 3 | Sam D. McReynolds (D) | 13,012 | 75.6 |
| | L. D. Copeland (R) | 4,194 | 24.4 |
| 4 | Cordell Hull (D) | 10,726 | 71.4 |
| | Mrs. Wilson Thompson (R) | 4,292 | 28.6 |
| 5 | Ewin L. Davis (D) | 5,481 | 100.0 |
| 6 | Joseph W. Byrns (D) | 10,271 | 100.0 |
| 7 | Edward E. Eslick (D) | 8,049 | 100.0 |
| 8 | Gordon Browning (D) | 9,456 | 100.0 |
| 9 | Finis J. Garrett (D) | 9,180 | 100.0 |
| 10 | Hubert F. Fisher (D) | 4,217 | 100.0 |

## TEXAS

| | | Votes | % |
|---|---|---|---|
| 1 | Eugene Black (D) | 9,828 | 94.4 |
| | D. F. Wimmer (R) | 579 | 5.6 |
| 2 | John C. Box (D) | 11,955 | 95.6 |
| 3 | Morgan G. Sanders (D) | 11,336 | 91.2 |
| | Enoch G. Fletcher (R) | 1,098 | 8.8 |
| 4 | Sam Rayburn (D) | 13,499 | 89.9 |
| | Henry C. Barlow (R) | 1,524 | 10.1 |
| 5 | Hatton W. Sumners (D) | 29,687 | 96.5 |
| 6 | Luther A. Johnson (D) | 10,162 | 96.1 |
| 7 | Clay Stone Briggs (D) | 7,678 | 94.1 |
| | S. R. Halstead (R) | 478 | 5.9 |
| 8 | Daniel E. Garrett (D) | 8,459 | 91.0 |
| | J. M. Gibson (R) | 842 | 9.1 |
| 9 | Joseph J. Mansfield (D) | 10,577 | 82.6 |
| | E. F. Glaze (R) | 2,228 | 17.4 |
| 10 | James P. Buchanan (D) | 12,051 | 93.2 |
| | W. H. Matthaei (R) | 886 | 6.9 |
| 11 | Tom T. Connally (D) | 8,481 | 94.2 |
| | W. H. Black (R) | 526 | 5.8 |
| 12 | Fritz G. Lanham (D) | 10,466 | 94.4 |
| | David Sutton (R) | 620 | 5.6 |
| 13 | Guinn Williams (D) | 12,406 | 94.0 |
| | Mel E. Peters (R) | 797 | 6.0 |
| 14 | Harry M. Wurzbach (R) | 14,224 | 57.2 |
| | A. D. Rogers (D) | 10,633 | 42.8 |
| 15 | John N. Garner (D) | 13,551 | 82.8 |
| | Hardie H. Jeffries (R) | 2,825 | 17.3 |
| 16 | Claude B. Hudspeth (D) | 15,732 | 86.1 |
| | A. W. Norcop (R) | 2,542 | 13.9 |
| 17 | Thomas L. Blanton (D) | 15,935 | 93.7 |
| | H. B. Tanner (R) | 1,065 | 6.3 |
| 18 | Marvin Jones (D) | 18,027 | 93.6 |
| | S. E. Fish (R) | 1,237 | 6.4 |

## UTAH

| | | Votes | % |
|---|---|---|---|
| 1 | Don B. Colton (R) | 44,007 | 61.4 |
| | Ephraim Bergeson (D) | 27,198 | 38.0 |
| 2 | Elmer O. Leatherwood (R) | 42,073 | 60.2 |
| | William R. Wallace Jr. (D) | 27,006 | 38.6 |

## VERMONT

| | Candidates | Votes | % |
|---|---|---|---|
| 1 | Elbert S. Brigham (R) | 27,419 | 72.3 |
| | Allan T. Calhoun (D) | 10,529 | 27.7 |
| 2 | Ernest Willard Gibson (R) | 27,711 | 80.4 |
| | George F. Root (D) | 6,753 | 19.6 |

## VIRGINIA

| | | Votes | % |
|---|---|---|---|
| 1 | Schuyler Otis Bland (D) | 3,847 | 99.9 |
| 2 | Joseph T. Deal (D) | 7,741 | 65.4 |
| | L. S. Parsons (R) | 4,093 | 34.6 |
| 3 | Andrew Jackson Montague (D) | 3,738 | 99.8 |
| 4 | Patrick Henry Drewry (D) | 2,694 | 99.3 |
| 5 | Joseph Whitehead (D) | 6,491 | 100.0 |
| 6 | Clifton A. Woodrum (D) | 2,936 | 99.8 |
| 7 | Thomas W. Harrison (D) | 8,302 | 64.9 |
| | Walter R. Talbot (R) | 3,758 | 29.4 |
| | Dabney C. Harrison (I) | 727 | 5.7 |
| 8 | R. Walton Moore (D) | 5,655 | 95.4 |
| 9 | George C. Peery (D) | 28,304 | 53.4 |
| | S. R. Hurley (R) | 24,685 | 46.6 |
| 10 | Henry St.George Tucker (D) | 4,657 | 99.8 |

## WASHINGTON

| | Candidates | Votes | % |
|---|---|---|---|
| 1 | John F. Miller (R) | 35,944 | 51.1 |
| | Stephen F. Chadwick (D) | 34,401 | 48.9 |
| 2 | Lindley H. Hadley (R) | 35,510 | 68.5 |
| | Frances C. Axtell (D) | 15,876 | 30.6 |
| 3 | Albert Johnson (R) | 58,361 | 100.0 |
| 4 | John W. Summers (R) | 34,199 | 99.8 |
| 5 | Sam B. Hill (D) | 29,157 | 52.1 |
| | Jack T. Fancher (R) | 26,783 | 47.9 |

## WEST VIRGINIA

| | | Votes | % |
|---|---|---|---|
| 1 | Carl G. Bachmann (R) | 31,839 | 52.2 |
| | George W. Oldham (D) | 29,117 | 47.8 |
| 2 | Frank L. Bowman (R) | 32,803 | 54.0 |
| | Robert E. Lee Allen (D) | 27,744 | 45.7 |
| 3 | William S. O'Brien (D) | 31,954 | 51.7 |
| | John M. Wolverton (R) | 29,819 | 48.3 |
| 4 | James A. Hughes (R) | 36,394 | 52.4 |
| | John D. Sweeney (D) | 33,065 | 47.6 |
| 5 | James F. Strother (R) | 44,263 | 53.3 |
| | Emmet F. Scaggs (D) | 38,723 | 46.7 |
| 6 | Edward T. England (R) | 45,898 | 50.1 |
| | J. Alfred Taylor (D) | 45,681 | 49.9 |

## WISCONSIN

| | Candidates | Votes | % |
|---|---|---|---|
| 1 | Henry Allen Cooper (R) | 50,531 | 100.0 |
| 2 | Charles A. Kading (R) | 29,785 | 69.5 |
| | Ernest C. Wrucke (D) | 8,285 | 19.3 |
| | John H. Kaiser (I-PROG-R) | 4,817 | 11.2 |
| 3 | John Mandt Nelson (R) | 41,666 | 99.9 |
| 4 | John C. Schafer (R) | 20,324 | 48.0 |
| | Edmund T. Melms (SOC) | 14,911 | 35.2 |
| | William J. Kershaw (D) | 7,099 | 16.8 |
| 5 | Victor L. Berger (SOC) | 26,377 | 48.8 |
| | William H. Stafford (R) | 24,297 | 44.8 |
| | Rose Horwitz (D) | 3,394 | 6.3 |
| 6 | Florian Lampert (R) | 34,445 | 75.9 |
| | B. F. Sheridan (D) | 10,895 | 24.0 |
| 7 | Joseph D. Beck (R) | 32,479 | 86.1 |
| | A. H. Schubert (ID) | 3,628 | 9.6 |
| 8 | Edward E. Browne (R) | 35,472 | 91.8 |
| | R. J. Walsh (ID) | 3,130 | 8.1 |
| 9 | George J. Schneider (R) | 41,498 | 99.9 |
| 10 | James A. Frear (R) | 40,888 | 97.4 |
| 11 | Hubert H. Peavey (R) | 31,105 | 70.1 |
| | Theodore M. Thomas (I-PROG-R) | 11,860 | 26.7 |

## WYOMING

| | | Votes | % |
|---|---|---|---|
| AL | Charles E. Winter (R) | 39,392 | 60.8 |
| | Thomas M. Fagan (D) | 25,082 | 38.7 |

# 1927 House Elections

## LOUISIANA

### Special Election

| | | | |
|---|---|---|---|
| 7 | Rene L. DeRouen (D) | 3,699 | 98.5 |

## NEW YORK

### Special Election

| | | | |
|---|---|---|---|
| 35 | Clarence E. Hancock (R) | 68,502 | 69.0 |
| | Henry B. Brewster (D) | 29,302 | 29.5 |

## Explanation of Symbols in House Returns

In the returns for House elections *symbols* are used to denote special circumstances. In cases where no symbol is used, the candidate who received the most votes won the election to the House. The following is a key to the symbols used:

✔ Elected to the House. The symbol is used to identify winning candidates in three types of situations: (1) When candidates ran for two or more at-large seats in states which chose all of their at-large representatives in a single election, or ran in a multi-member district; (2) when the vote total and percentage of one or more of the candidates are unavailable and (3) when a candidate who did not receive the highest vote total was seated by the House. (*Explanation of multi-member districts, see p. 916.*)

‡ The symbol is used when an election dispute resulted in the unseating of a representative *after* he was sworn in. (*For discussion of specific cases, consult the* Biographical Directory of the United States Congress 1774-1989, *U.S. Government Printing Office, Washington, D.C., 1989; hereafter referred to as the* Biographical Directory.)

* The symbol is used for three types of situations: (1) When a representative-elect died or declined his seat before the constitutionally set date for the beginning of his term—March 4 until 1935, and Jan. 3 thereafter; (2) when the House refused to seat any candidate claiming election to a seat and (3) when state law required a candidate to obtain a popular vote majority for election to the House, but the candidate receiving the most votes failed to receive a majority. (*For discussion of specific cases, consult the* Biographical Directory; *explanation of majority vote requirement, see p. 945.*)

# Information for 1824-1973 returns was obtained from a source other than the Inter-University Consortium for Political and Social Research. (*For a listing of other sources, see p. 1327.*)

**Footnotes.** Numbered footnotes are used to explain unusual situations, such as a series of elections in the same year in the same House district, anomalies resulting from reapportionment and special procedures for conducting House elections in certain states.

# 1928 House Elections

## ALABAMA

| | Candidates | Votes | % |
|---|---|---|---|
| 1 | John McDuffie (D) | 16,712 | 100.0 |
| 2 | Lister Hill (D) | 20,945 | 100.0 |
| 3 | Henry B. Steagall (D) | 14,611 | 100.0 |
| 4 | Lamar Jeffers (D) | 13,271 | 63.1 |
| | A. B. Baxley (R) | 7,768 | 36.9 |
| 5 | Lafayette L. Patterson (D) | 13,067 | 100.0 |
| 6 | William B. Oliver (D) | 9,539 | 100.0 |
| 7 | Miles C. Allgood (D) | 18,186 | 51.7 |
| | Wallace M. Sloan (R) | 16,983 | 48.3 |
| 8 | Edward B. Almon (D) | 20,006 | 100.0 |
| 9 | George Huddleston (D) | 23,553 | 100.0 |
| 10 | William B. Bankhead (D) | 15,133 | 58.2 |
| | John A. Posey (R) | 10,862 | 41.8 |

### Special Election

| | | Votes | % |
|---|---|---|---|
| 5 | Lafayette L. Patterson (D) | 7,683 | 99.9 |

## ARIZONA

| | | Votes | % |
|---|---|---|---|
| AL | Lewis W. Douglas (D) | 50,231 | 61.6 |
| | Guy Axline (R) | 31,382 | 38.5 |

## ARKANSAS

| | | Votes | % |
|---|---|---|---|
| 1 | William J. Driver (D) | 24,844 | 83.9 |
| | S. E. Simonson (R) | 4,770 | 16.1 |
| 2 | William A. Oldfield (D) | 18,772* | 77.4 |
| | J. L. McKamey (R) | 5,471 | 22.6 |
| 3 | Claude A. Fuller (D) | 18,160 | 57.7 |
| | Sam B. Cecil (R) | 13,129 | 41.7 |
| 4 | Otis Wingo (D) | 21,494 | 71.9 |
| | G. W. Johnston (R) | 8,397 | 28.1 |
| 5 | Heartsill Ragon (D) | 25,583 | 78.2 |
| | Alonzo A. Ross (R) | 7,144 | 21.8 |
| 6 | David D. Glover (D) | 28,101 | 100.0 |
| 7 | Tilman B. Parks (D) | 20,954 | 81.5 |
| | Pat McNally (R) | 4,759 | 18.5 |

## CALIFORNIA

| | | Votes | % |
|---|---|---|---|
| 1 | Clarence F. Lea (D-R) | 56,381 | 100.0 |
| 2 | Harry L. Englebright (R-D) | 32,455 | 100.0 |
| 3 | Charles F. Curry (R-D) | 77,750 | 100.0 |
| 4 | Florence P. Kahn (R) | 50,206 | 74.9 |
| | Harry W. Hutton (I) | 16,838 | 25.1 |
| 5 | Richard J. Welch (R-D) | 51,708 | 100.0 |
| 6 | Albert E. Carter (R) | 113,579 | 99.9 |
| 7 | Henry E. Barbour (R-D) | 71,195 | 99.9 |
| 8 | Arthur Monroe Free (R) | 80,613 | 68.0 |
| | Cecelia C. Casserly (D) | 37,947 | 32.0 |
| 9 | William E. Evans (R) | 222,261 | 77.0 |
| | James B. Ogg (D) | 58,263 | 20.2 |
| 10 | Joe Crail (R-D) | 301,028 | 93.5 |
| | Harry Sherr (SOC) | 19,659 | 6.1 |
| 11 | Philip D. Swing (R-D) | 127,115 | 100.0 |

## COLORADO

| | | Votes | % |
|---|---|---|---|
| 1 | William R. Eaton (R) | 63,258 | 58.1 |
| | S. Harrison White (D) | 44,713 | 41.1 |
| 2 | Charles B. Timberlake (R) | 62,375 | 66.5 |
| | Earl E. House (D) | 31,480 | 33.5 |
| 3 | Guy U. Hardy (R) | 64,116 | 64.9 |
| | Harry A. McIntyre (D) | 34,670 | 35.1 |
| 4 | Edward T. Taylor (D) | 30,142 | 58.8 |
| | William P. Dale (R) | 21,089 | 41.2 |

## CONNECTICUT

| | Candidates | Votes | % |
|---|---|---|---|
| 1 | E. Hart Fenn (R) | 75,743 | 53.1 |
| | Herman P. Kopplemann (D) | 65,922 | 46.2 |
| 2 | Richard P. Freeman (R) | 48,590 | 56.0 |
| | William M. Citron (D) | 37,786 | 43.5 |
| 3 | John Q. Tilson (R) | 58,337 | 52.3 |
| | Nicholas Moseley (D) | 52,358 | 46.9 |
| 4 | Schuyler Merritt (R) | 71,649 | 56.1 |
| | Anthony Sunderland (D) | 55,106 | 43.2 |
| 5 | James P. Glynn (R) | 43,332 | 52.4 |
| | Edward Mascolo (D) | 39,354 | 47.6 |

## DELAWARE

| | | Votes | % |
|---|---|---|---|
| AL | Robert G. Houston (R) | 66,361 | 63.6 |
| | John M. Richardson (D) | 38,045 | 36.4 |

## FLORIDA

| | | Votes | % |
|---|---|---|---|
| 1 | Herbert J. Drane (D) | 42,003 | 58.4 |
| | Abner B. Brown (R) | 29,871 | 41.6 |
| 2 | Robert A. Green (D) | 17,228 | 83.9 |
| | Thomas Peter Chaires (R) | 3,310 | 16.1 |
| 3 | Tom A. Yon (D) | 22,167 | 100.0 |
| 4 | Ruth Bryan Owen (D) | 67,130 | 64.9 |
| | William C. Lawson (R) | 36,288 | 35.1 |

## GEORGIA

| | | Votes | % |
|---|---|---|---|
| 1 | Charles G. Edwards (D) | 16,438 | 100.0 |
| 2 | E. E. Cox (D) | 15,235 | 100.0 |
| 3 | Charles R. Crisp (D) | 11,183 | 100.0 |
| 4 | William C. Wright (D) | 16,037 | 100.0 |
| 5 | Leslie J. Steele (D) | 19,328 | 100.0 |
| 6 | Samuel Rutherford (D) | 15,310 | 100.0 |
| 7 | Malcolm C. Tarver (D) | 23,251 | 100.0 |
| 8 | Charles H. Brand (D) | 15,940 | 100.0 |
| 9 | Thomas M. Bell (D) | 22,916 | 100.0 |
| 10 | Carl Vinson (D) | 12,644 | 100.0 |
| 11 | William C. Lankford (D) | 18,044 | 100.0 |
| 12 | William W. Larsen (D) | 13,862 | 100.0 |

## IDAHO

| | | Votes | % |
|---|---|---|---|
| 1 | Burton L. French (R) | 43,770 | 68.9 |
| | Joe Tyler (D) | 19,064 | 30.0 |
| 2 | Addison T. Smith (R) | 53,236 | 64.1 |
| | Ralph W. Harding (D) | 29,422 | 35.4 |

## ILLINOIS

| | | Votes | % |
|---|---|---|---|
| 1 | Oscar De Priest (R) | 24,479 | 47.8 |
| | Harry Baker (D) | 20,664 | 40.3 |
| | William Harrison | 5,861 | 11.4 |
| 2 | Morton D. Hull (R) | 126,005 | 62.1 |
| | Michael C. Walsh (D) | 76,909 | 37.9 |
| 3 | Elliott W. Sproul (R) | 101,384 | 51.4 |
| | Henry P. Bergen (D) | 95,999 | 48.6 |
| 4 | Thomas A. Doyle (D) | 40,940 | 64.3 |
| | Frank George Zelezinski (R) | 22,741 | 35.7 |
| 5 | Adolph J. Sabath (D) | 25,225 | 69.8 |
| | Edward J. Gates (R) | 10,799 | 29.9 |
| 6 | James T. Igoe (D) | 143,989 | 60.3 |
| | Samuel L. Golan (R) | 94,941 | 39.7 |
| 7 | M. Alfred Michaelson (R) | 164,447 | 57.8 |
| | Emil Selten (D) | 119,933 | 42.2 |
| 8 | Stanley Henry Kunz (D) | 24,517 | 70.8 |
| | Edward Walz (R) | 10,110 | 29.2 |
| 9 | Fred A. Britten (R) | 43,394 | 62.0 |
| | James T. McDermott (D) | 26,450 | 37.8 |

| | Candidates | Votes | % |
|---|---|---|---|
| 10 | Carl R. Chindblom (R) | 138,386 | 62.6 |
| | Joseph A. Weber (D) | 82,598 | 37.4 |
| 11 | Frank R. Reid (R) | 97,938 | 68.9 |
| | Edwin H. Wilson (D) | 44,306 | 31.2 |
| 12 | John T. Buckbee (R) | 82,938 | 73.8 |
| | Jules Vallatt (D) | 29,385 | 26.2 |
| 13 | William R. Johnson (R) | 53,985 | 73.7 |
| | William G. Curtis (D) | 19,209 | 26.2 |
| 14 | John C. Allen (R) | 53,680 | 64.3 |
| | William H. Hartzell (D) | 29,768 | 35.7 |
| 15 | Edward J. King (R) | 57,284* | 64.2 |
| | James H. Andrews (D) | 31,944 | 35.8 |
| 16 | William F. Hull (R) | 60,100 | 61.1 |
| | George H. Rinkenberger (D) | 37,662 | 38.9 |
| 17 | Homer W. Hall (R) | 47,266 | 65.0 |
| | Frank Gillespie (D) | 25,480 | 35.0 |
| 18 | William P. Holaday (R) | 57,373 | 62.0 |
| | James H. Elliott (D) | 35,213 | 38.0 |
| 19 | Charles Adkins (R) | 73,243 | 66.2 |
| | W. W. Reeves (D) | 37,358 | 33.8 |
| 20 | Henry T. Rainey (D) | 38,409 | 56.0 |
| | E. T. Hunter (R) | 30,100 | 43.9 |
| 21 | Frank M. Ramey (R) | 52,320 | 50.1 |
| | J. Earl Major (D) | 52,183 | 49.9 |
| 22 | Edward M. Irwin (R) | 72,448 | 56.0 |
| | Eugene W. Kreitner (D) | 56,825 | 44.0 |
| 23 | William W. Arnold (D) | 49,378 | 53.9 |
| | C. T. Wade (R) | 42,263 | 46.1 |
| 24 | Thomas S. Williams (R) | 36,239 | 58.4 |
| | Val B. Campbell (D) | 25,773 | 41.6 |
| 25 | Edward E. Denison (R) | 51,025 | 54.4 |
| | A. F. Gourley (D) | 42,799 | 45.6 |
| AL | Ruth Hanna McCormick (R) | 1,711,651✓ | |
| | Richard Yates (R) | 1,673,962✓ | |
| | Charles F. Brown (D) | 1,171,520 | |
| | C. D. Joplin (D) | 1,111,253 | |
| | Florence Kirkpatrick (SOC) | 11,958 | |
| | John E. Mahoney (SOC) | 11,538 | |
| | Elizabeth G. Doty (WCP AM) | 2,887 | |
| | Frank Gushes (WCP AM) | 2,802 | |
| | James S. O'Rourke (SOC LAB) | 1,384 | |
| | Thomas Buckley (SOC LAB) | 1,340 | |

## INDIANA

| | | Votes | % |
|---|---|---|---|
| 1 | Harry E. Rowbottom (R) | 49,013 | 50.8 |
| | John W. Boehne Jr. (D) | 47,404 | 49.2 |
| 2 | Arthur H. Greenwood (D) | 45,901 | 50.2 |
| | Orville T. Stout (R) | 44,941 | 49.1 |
| 3 | James W. Dunbar (R) | 47,768 | 51.1 |
| | Frank Gardner (D) | 45,718 | 48.9 |
| 4 | Harry C. Canfield (D) | 44,671 | 52.5 |
| | Charles S. Hisey (R) | 40,345 | 47.5 |
| 5 | Noble J. Johnson (R) | 51,138 | 56.1 |
| | Henry W. Moore (D) | 39,538 | 43.3 |
| 6 | Richard N. Elliott (R) | 50,795 | 57.0 |
| | William H. Larrabee (D) | 38,326 | 43.0 |
| 7 | Louis Ludlow (D) | 94,643 | 51.5 |
| | Ralph E. Updike (R) | 88,263 | 48.0 |
| 8 | Albert H. Vestal (R) | 59,704 | 58.3 |
| | Don C. Ward (D) | 42,645 | 41.7 |
| 9 | Fred S. Purnell (R) | 53,998 | 57.2 |
| | George L. Mackintosh (D) | 40,357 | 42.8 |
| 10 | William R. Wood (R) | 87,972 | 62.0 |
| | John W. Sobraske (D) | 53,874 | 38.0 |
| 11 | Albert R. Hall (R) | 49,326 | 54.1 |
| | M. Clifford Townsend (D) | 41,836 | 45.9 |
| 12 | David Hogg (R) | 56,436 | 55.3 |
| | Samuel D. Jackson (D) | 45,592 | 44.7 |
| 13 | Andrew J. Hickey (R) | 90,618 | 59.8 |
| | Chester A. Perkins (D) | 60,993 | 40.2 |

## IOWA

| Candidates | Votes | % |
|---|---|---|
| 1 William F. Kopp (R) | 45,806 | 100.0 |
| 2 F. Dickinson Letts (R) | 49,691 | 57.0 |
| Frank C. Titzell (D) | 37,442 | 43.0 |
| 3 Thomas J. B. Robinson (R) | 60,025 | 60.9 |
| Leo F. Tierney (D) | 38,469 | 39.1 |
| 4 Gilbert N. Haugen (R) | 50,938 | 61.4 |
| Erwin Larson (D) | 31,968 | 38.6 |
| 5 Cyrenus Cole (R) | 54,603 | 66.3 |
| Maurice Cahill (D) | 27,793 | 33.7 |
| 6 C. William Ramseyer (R) | 43,259 | 65.2 |
| C. Ver Ploeg (D) | 23,065 | 34.8 |
| 7 Cassius C. Dowell (R) | 72,404 | 100.0 |
| 8 Lloyd Thurston (R) | 43,050 | 60.0 |
| James Pearson (D) | 28,686 | 40.0 |
| 9 Charles E. Swanson (R) | 47,632 | 63.2 |
| W. J. Burke (D) | 27,760 | 36.8 |
| 10 Lester J. Dickinson (R) | 59,374 | 100.0 |
| 11 Ed H. Campbell (R) | 49,279 | 70.9 |
| George Finch (D) | 20,244 | 29.1 |

## KANSAS

| Candidates | Votes | % |
|---|---|---|
| 1 William P. Lambertson (R) | 48,543 | 68.3 |
| Maurice P. O'Keefe (D) | 22,492 | 31.7 |
| 2 Ulysses S. Guyer (R) | 66,044 | 70.2 |
| Lee R. Hettick (D) | 28,106 | 29.9 |
| 3 William H. Sproul (R) | 45,121 | 53.4 |
| Joe E. Gaitskill (D) | 39,323 | 46.6 |
| 4 Homer Hoch (R) | 38,664 | 74.2 |
| C. T. Neihart (D) | 13,450 | 25.8 |
| 5 James G. Strong (R) | 45,053 | 69.9 |
| John F. Corder (D) | 19,425 | 30.1 |
| 6 Charles I. Sparks (R) | 41,272 | 63.4 |
| William H. Clark (D) | 23,836 | 36.6 |
| 7 Clifford R. Hope (R) | 58,001 | 69.5 |
| W. C. Dickey (D) | 25,433 | 30.5 |
| 8 William A. Ayres (D) | 46,117 | 58.4 |
| Richard E. Bird (R) | 32,802 | 41.6 |

## KENTUCKY

| Candidates | Votes | % |
|---|---|---|
| 1 William V. Gregory (D) | 36,325 | 56.8 |
| Miller Hughes (R) | 27,581 | 43.2 |
| 2 David H. Kincheloe (D) | 38,093 | 52.7 |
| Clark M. Donald (R) | 34,194 | 47.3 |
| 3 Charles W. Roark (R) | 37,216 | 52.8 |
| John W. Moore (D) | 33,210 | 47.2 |
| 4 John D. Craddock (R) | 39,244 | 53.1 |
| Henry D. Moorman (D) | 34,639 | 46.9 |
| 5 Maurice H. Thatcher (R) | 96,926 | 60.2 |
| Arthur Yager (D) | 64,201 | 39.8 |
| 6 J. Lincoln Newhall (R) | 48,009 | 53.1 |
| Brent Spence (D) | 42,309 | 46.8 |
| 7 Robert E. Lee Blackburn (R) | 43,604 | 53.5 |
| Virgil Chapman (D) | 37,936 | 46.5 |
| 8 Lewis L. Walker (R) | 33,931 | 52.7 |
| Ralph Gilbert (D) | 30,424 | 47.3 |
| 9 Elva R. Kendall (R) | 51,019 | 52.9 |
| Fred M. Vinson (D) | 45,426 | 47.1 |
| 10 Katherine Langley (R) | 39,541 | 56.1 |
| A. J. May (D) | 30,919 | 43.9 |
| 11 John M. Robsion (R) | 74,929 | 79.8 |
| H. F. Reed (D) | 18,939 | 20.2 |

## LOUISIANA

| Candidates | Votes | % |
|---|---|---|
| 1 James O'Connor (D) | 28,066 | 100.0 |
| 2 J. Zach Spearing (D) | 33,176 | 69.4 |
| Peter I. J. Fletchinger (R) | 14,661 | 30.7 |
| 3 Whitmell P. Martin (D) | 15,219 | 100.0 |
| 4 John N. Sandlin (D) | 14,949 | 100.0 |
| 5 Riley J. Wilson (D) | 11,827 | 100.0 |
| 6 Bolivar E. Kemp (D) | 18,379 | 100.0 |
| 7 Rene L. DeRouen (D) | 16,582 | 100.0 |
| 8 James B. Aswell (D) | 14,618 | 100.0 |

## MAINE

| Candidates | Votes | % |
|---|---|---|
| 1 Carroll L. Beedy (R) | 40,255 | 67.7 |
| Elvington P. Spinney (D) | 19,219 | 32.3 |
| 2 Wallace H. White Jr. (R) | 36,791 | 65.5 |
| Albert Beliveau (D) | 19,420 | 34.6 |
| 3 John E. Nelson (R) | 36,686 | 74.6 |
| S. Curtis C. Ward (D) | 12,498 | 25.4 |
| 4 Donald F. Snow (R) | 32,223 | 75.0 |
| Clinton C. Stevens (D) | 10,753 | 25.0 |

## MARYLAND

| | Votes | % |
|---|---|---|
| 1 T. Alan Goldsborough (D) | 28,795 | 50.7 |
| A. Stengle Marine (R) | 28,059 | 49.4 |
| 2 Linwood L. Clark (R) | 69,267 | 53.3 |
| William P. Cole Jr. (D) | 59,912 | 46.1 |
| 3 Vincent L. Palmisano (D) | 27,377 | 49.8 |
| John Philip Hill (R) | 27,047 | 49.2 |
| 4 J. Charles Linthicum (D) | 41,432 | 54.5 |
| John P. Brandau (R) | 34,112 | 44.8 |
| 5 Stephen W. Gambrill (D) | 31,403 | 51.9 |
| Oliver Metzerott (R) | 28,574 | 47.2 |
| 6 Frederick N. Zihlman (R) | 47,789 | 56.2 |
| David J. Lewis (D) | 37,197 | 43.8 |

## MASSACHUSETTS

| | Votes | % |
|---|---|---|
| 1 Allen T. Treadway (R) | 51,791 | 55.7 |
| Daniel A. Martin (D) | 41,216 | 44.3 |
| 2 William Kirk Kaynor (R) | 52,344 | 54.4 |
| John D. O'Connor (D) | 43,856 | 45.6 |
| 3 Frank H. Foss (R) | 46,204 | 57.1 |
| Joseph E. Casey (D) | 34,776 | 42.9 |
| 4 George R. Stobbs (R) | 51,145 | 54.8 |
| Freeman M. Saltus (D) | 42,115 | 45.2 |
| 5 Edith Nourse Rogers (R) | 56,004 | 61.1 |
| Cornelius F. Cronin (D) | 35,713 | 38.9 |
| 6 A. Piatt Andrew (R) | 58,293 | 68.2 |
| George J. Ferguson (D) | 27,130 | 31.8 |
| 7 William P. Connery Jr. (R-D) | 61,697 | 100.0 |
| 8 Frederick W. Dallinger (R) | 71,850 | 57.2 |
| James P. Brennan (D) | 53,721 | 42.8 |
| 9 Charles L. Underhill (R) | 48,947 | 50.3 |
| Arthur D. Healey (D) | 48,290 | 49.7 |
| 10 John J. Douglass (D) | 42,594 | 85.0 |
| Edward L. Donnelly (R) | 7,498 | 15.0 |
| 11 George Holden Tinkham (R) | 52,576 | 58.4 |
| Maurice J. Tobin (D) | 37,514 | 41.6 |
| 12 John W. McCormack (D) | 64,351 | 76.4 |
| Herbert W. Burr (R) | 19,937 | 23.7 |
| 13 Robert Luce (R) | 74,097 | 58.2 |
| Thomas D. Lavelle (D) | 53,266 | 41.8 |
| 14 Richard B. Wigglesworth (R) | 73,598 | 61.3 |
| Christopher M. Clifford (D) | 46,498 | 38.7 |
| 15 Joseph W. Martin Jr. (R) | 39,905 | 56.8 |
| John F. Trainor (D) | 30,373 | 43.2 |
| 16 Charles L. Gifford (R) | 49,202 | 63.1 |
| Willard E. Boyden (D) | 23,590 | 30.3 |
| Frank J. Manning (SOC) | 5,115 | 6.6 |

## MICHIGAN

| | Votes | % |
|---|---|---|
| 1 Robert H. Clancy (R) | 64,606 | 61.5 |
| William M. Donnelly (D) | 39,870 | 38.0 |
| 2 Earl C. Michener (R) | 86,804 | 73.6 |
| Grover L. Morden (D) | 31,223 | 26.5 |
| 3 Joseph Hooper (R) | 71,650 | 79.5 |
| William Fitzgerald (D) | 18,535 | 20.6 |
| 4 John C. Ketcham (R) | 60,334 | 75.4 |
| Roman I. Jarvis Sr. (D) | 19,708 | 24.6 |
| 5 Carl E. Mapes (R) | 73,241 | 78.8 |
| Frank C. Jarvis (D) | 19,627 | 21.1 |
| 6 Grant M. Hudson (R) | 238,223 | 72.5 |
| A. Bruce Atwell (D) | 89,085 | 27.1 |

| Candidates | Votes | % |
|---|---|---|
| 7 Louis C. Cramton (R) | 61,439 | 73.9 |
| Varnum J. Bowers (D) | 21,659 | 26.1 |
| 8 Bird J. Vincent (R) | 65,600 | 75.4 |
| Burnett J. Abbott (D) | 21,387 | 24.6 |
| 9 James C. McLaughlin (R) | 51,246 | 99.8 |
| 10 Roy O. Woodruff (R) | 43,800 | 73.7 |
| Judson E. Richardson (D) | 15,598 | 26.3 |
| 11 Frank P. Bohn (R) | 44,546 | 67.2 |
| Carl R. Henry (D) | 21,760 | 32.8 |
| 12 W. Frank James (R) | 47,069 | 69.1 |
| L. A. Barry (D) | 21,039 | 30.9 |
| 13 Clarence J. McLeod (R) | 70,513 | 64.9 |
| John S. Hall (D) | 37,574 | 34.6 |

## MINNESOTA

| | Votes | % |
|---|---|---|
| 1 Victor Christgau (R) | 59,628 | 64.8 |
| James F. Lynn (D) | 32,398 | 35.2 |
| 2 Frank Clague (R) | 60,259 | 69.4 |
| J. A. Cashel (D) | 26,606 | 30.6 |
| 3 August H. Andresen (R) | 52,526 | 58.8 |
| Charles C. Kolars (D) | 19,844 | 22.2 |
| Henry Arens (F-LAB) | 15,749 | 17.6 |
| 4 Melvin Joseph Maas (R) | 39,648 | 36.0 |
| John P. J. Dolan (D) | 31,521 | 28.6 |
| Howard Y. Williams (F-LAB) | 23,068 | 21.0 |
| Fred A. Snyder (I) | 15,365 | 14.0 |
| 5 Walter H. Newton (R) | 80,856 | 58.6 |
| James Robertson (D) | 31,528 | 22.9 |
| Ferdinand Johnson (F-LAB) | 24,869 | 18.0 |
| 6 Harold Knutson (R) | 55,663 | 66.3 |
| John Knutsen (F-LAB) | 28,276 | 33.7 |
| 7 Ole J. Kvale (F-LAB) | 56,029 | 66.9 |
| Lawrence M. Carlson (R) | 27,735 | 33.1 |
| 8 William A. Pittenger (R) | 43,777 | 44.2 |
| William L. Carss (F-LAB) | 42,508 | 42.9 |
| Dana C. Reed (D) | 9,784 | 9.9 |
| 9 Conrad G. Selvig (R) | 45,319 | 55.2 |
| Knud Wefald (F-LAB) | 36,853 | 44.9 |
| 10 Godfrey G. Goodwin (R) | 60,100 | 56.4 |
| C. R. Hedlund (F-LAB) | 23,774 | 22.3 |
| Ernest W. Erickson (D) | 22,702 | 21.3 |

## MISSISSIPPI

| | Votes | % |
|---|---|---|
| 1 John E. Rankin (D) | 13,816 | 100.0 |
| 2 Wall Doxey (D) | 12,276 | 100.0 |
| 3 William M. Whittington (D) | 13,039 | 100.0 |
| 4 T. Jeff Busby (D) | 13,456 | 100.0 |
| 5 Ross A. Collins (D) | 17,967 | 100.0 |
| 6 Robert S. Hall (D) | 18,212 | 100.0 |
| 7 Percy E. Quin (D) | 12,338 | 100.0 |
| 8 James W. Collier (D) | 11,442 | 100.0 |

## MISSOURI

| | Votes | % |
|---|---|---|
| 1 Milton A. Romjue (D) | 35,702 | 52.9 |
| J. Frank Culler (R) | 31,751 | 47.1 |
| 2 Ralph Lozier (D) | 37,829 | 53.2 |
| Lloyd V. Harmon (R) | 33,273 | 46.8 |
| 3 Jacob L. Milligan (D) | 32,665 | 50.0 |
| H. F. Lawrence (R) | 32,626 | 50.0 |
| 4 Charles L. Faust (R) | 43,733* | 57.1 |
| Richard M. Duncan (D) | 32,892 | 42.9 |
| 5 Edgar C. Ellis (R) | 113,043 | 50.5 |
| Floyd E. Jacobs (D) | 110,529 | 49.4 |
| 6 Thomas J. Halsey (R) | 30,557 | 53.2 |
| C. C. Dickinson (D) | 26,838 | 46.8 |
| 7 John W. Palmer (R) | 52,317 | 53.3 |
| Samuel C. Major (D) | 45,832 | 46.7 |
| 8 William L. Nelson (D) | 32,877 | 55.3 |
| David W. Peters (R) | 26,619 | 44.7 |
| 9 Clarence Cannon (D) | 41,036 | 54.5 |
| A. H. Steinbeck (R) | 34,248 | 45.5 |
| 10 Henry F. Niedringhaus (R) | 164,083 | 55.0 |
| John R. Green (D) | 134,324 | 45.0 |

## MISSOURI

| | Candidates | Votes | % |
|---|---|---|---|
| 11 | John J. Cochran (D) | 44,130 | 57.4 |
| | William Gray (R) | 32,706 | 42.6 |
| 12 | Leonidas C. Dyer (R) | 24,701 | 58.4 |
| | Joseph L. McLemore (D) | 17,609 | 41.6 |
| 13 | Charles E. Kiefner (R) | 30,535 | 50.6 |
| | Clyde Williams (D) | 29,842 | 49.4 |
| 14 | Dewey Short (R) | 57,880 | 53.9 |
| | James F. Fulbright (D) | 49,495 | 46.1 |
| 15 | Joe J. Manlove (R) | 52,142 | 64.6 |
| | George B. Lang (D) | 28,551 | 35.4 |
| 16 | Rowland L. Johnston (R) | 29,848 | 53.5 |
| | S. A. Cunningham (D) | 25,899 | 46.5 |

## MONTANA

| 1 | John M. Evans (D) | 44,018 | 57.3 |
|---|---|---|---|
| | Mark D. Fitzgerrald (R) | 32,796 | 42.1 |
| 2 | Scott Leavitt (R) | 70,682 | 67.9 |
| | B. A. Taylor (D) | 33,033 | 31.7 |

## NEBRASKA

| 1 | John H. Morehead (D) | 39,202 | 50.4 |
|---|---|---|---|
| | Elmer J. Burkett (R) | 38,583 | 49.6 |
| 2 | Willis G. Sears (R) | 52,801 | 56.0 |
| | Harry B. Fleharty (D) | 41,424 | 44.0 |
| 3 | Edgar Howard (D) | 50,974 | 54.9 |
| | James Nichols (R) | 41,967 | 45.2 |
| 4 | Charles H. Sloan (R) | 37,114 | 50.2 |
| | J. N. Norton (D) | 36,896 | 49.9 |
| 5 | Fred G. Johnson (R) | 37,853 | 51.0 |
| | Ashton C. Shallenberger (D) | 36,383 | 49.0 |
| 6 | Robert G. Simmons (R) | 81,581 | 74.3 |
| | John McCoy (D) | 28,215 | 25.7 |

## NEVADA

| AL | Samuel S. Arentz (R) | 18,815 | 58.6 |
|---|---|---|---|
| | Charles Lee Horsey (D) | 13,287 | 41.4 |

## NEW HAMPSHIRE

| 1 | Fletcher Hale (R) | 53,642 | 57.5 |
|---|---|---|---|
| | Francis C. Keefe (D) | 39,568 | 42.4 |
| 2 | Edward H. Wason (R) | 54,642 | 60.0 |
| | Alfred W. Levensaler (D) | 36,275 | 39.9 |

## NEW JERSEY

| 1 | Charles A. Wolverton (R) | 109,510 | 74.9 |
|---|---|---|---|
| | Alfred R. White (D) | 36,778 | 25.1 |
| 2 | Isaac Bacharach (R) | 99,109 | 76.3 |
| | George R. Greis (D) | 30,856 | 23.7 |
| 3 | Harold G. Hoffman (R) | 95,669 | 63.0 |
| | John R. Phillips Jr. (D) | 56,290 | 37.0 |
| 4 | Charles A. Eaton (R) | 65,149 | 63.6 |
| | Orren Jack Turner (D) | 37,341 | 36.4 |
| 5 | Ernest R. Ackerman (R) | 95,458 | 67.4 |
| | Roswell S. Nichols (D) | 46,211 | 32.6 |
| 6 | Randolph Perkins (R) | 98,859 | 61.7 |
| | Frank L. Sample (D) | 60,988 | 38.1 |
| 7 | George N. Seger (R) | 54,896 | 57.0 |
| | Abram Klenert (D) | 41,012 | 42.6 |
| 8 | Fred A. Hartley Jr. (R) | 64,915# | 50.1 |
| | Paul J. Moore (D) | 64,594# | 49.9 |
| 9 | Franklin W. Fort (R) | 46,685 | 56.5 |
| | Francis X. Purcell (D) | 35,730 | 43.3 |
| 10 | Frederick R. Lehlbach (R) | 74,154 | 62.1 |
| | Eugene J. O'Mara (D) | 45,287 | 37.9 |
| 11 | Oscar L. Auf der Heide (D) | 51,982 | 62.1 |
| | George M. Eichler (R) | 31,728 | 37.9 |
| 12 | Mary T. Norton (D) | 56,748 | 62.0 |
| | Philip W. Grece (R) | 34,817 | 38.0 |

## NEW MEXICO

| | Candidates | Votes | % |
|---|---|---|---|
| AL | Albert Gallatin Simms (R) | 61,208 | 52.2 |
| | John Morrow (D) | 56,045 | 47.8 |

## NEW YORK

| 1 | Robert L. Bacon (R) | 143,230 | 62.0 |
|---|---|---|---|
| | Thomas J. Cuff (D) | 83,535 | 36.2 |
| 2 | William F. Brunner (D) | 137,214 | 62.4 |
| | Jacob A. Visel (R) | 78,536 | 35.7 |
| 3 | George W. Lindsay (D) | 26,626 | 72.2 |
| | Francis J. Nicosia (R) | 9,139 | 24.8 |
| 4 | Thomas H. Cullen (D) | 34,496 | 75.0 |
| | Charles O. Winnie (R) | 10,696 | 23.2 |
| 5 | Loring M. Black Jr. (D) | 50,158 | 56.7 |
| | Robert C. Lee (R) | 35,935 | 40.6 |
| 6 | Andrew L. Somers (D) | 70,953 | 53.9 |
| | John L. Lotsch (R) | 53,700 | 40.8 |
| | Bernard J. Riley (SOC) | 7,026 | 5.3 |
| 7 | John F. Quayle (D) | 30,897 | 67.2 |
| | Peter S. Gehris (R) | 13,211 | 28.7 |
| 8 | Patrick J. Carley (D) | 108,028 | 58.5 |
| | William A. Blank (R) | 66,180 | 35.8 |
| | William M. Feigenbaum (SOC) | 10,551 | 5.7 |
| 9 | David J. O'Connell (D) | 60,097 | 51.1 |
| | Ernest C. Wagner (R) | 53,552 | 45.5 |
| 10 | Emanuel Celler (D) | 31,152 | 58.0 |
| | William G. Bushell (R) | 18,411 | 34.3 |
| | Abraham I. Shiplacoff (SOC) | 3,645 | 6.8 |
| 11 | Anning S. Prall (D) | 44,820 | 66.4 |
| | James A. Simonson (R) | 22,099 | 32.7 |
| 12 | Samuel Dickstein (D) | 15,093 | 78.7 |
| | Samuel K. Beier (R) | 3,321 | 17.3 |
| 13 | Christopher D. Sullivan (D) | 16,062 | 77.3 |
| | Jacob Rosenberg (R) | 4,076 | 19.6 |
| 14 | William I. Sirovich (D) | 16,602 | 54.4 |
| | Sol Ullman (R) | 11,974 | 39.2 |
| | August Claessens (SOC) | 1,648 | 5.4 |
| 15 | John J. Boylan (D) | 30,849 | 77.6 |
| | Gabriel L. Kaplan (R) | 8,294 | 20.9 |
| 16 | John J. O'Connor (D) | 29,351 | 68.7 |
| | Michael G. Panzer (R) | 12,600 | 29.5 |
| 17 | Ruth Baker Pratt (R) | 36,655 | 51.8 |
| | Philip Berolzheimer (D) | 32,466 | 45.9 |
| 18 | John F. Carew (D) | 30,030 | 74.0 |
| | Bernard Katzen (R) | 9,562 | 23.6 |
| 19 | Sol Bloom (D) | 48,054 | 59.4 |
| | David Steinhardt (R) | 30,617 | 37.8 |
| 20 | Fiorello H. LaGuardia (R) | 11,956 | 50.1 |
| | Saul J. Dickheiser (D) | 10,856 | 45.5 |
| 21 | Royal H. Weller (D) | 56,992* | 53.3 |
| | Edward A. Johnson (R) | 45,610 | 42.7 |
| 22 | Anthony J. Griffin (D) | 35,711 | 71.5 |
| | Thomas J. Burke (R) | 12,868 | 25.7 |
| 23 | Frank Oliver (D) | 128,372 | 66.6 |
| | Henry H. Spitz (R) | 52,588 | 27.3 |
| 24 | James M. Fitzpatrick (D) | 96,556 | 54.2 |
| | Benjamin F. Fairchild (R) | 72,408 | 40.6 |
| | Louis Painken (SOC) | 9,347 | 5.2 |
| 25 | J. Mayhew Wainwright (R) | 79,228 | 59.9 |
| | Herbert McKennis (D) | 50,589 | 38.3 |
| 26 | Hamilton Fish Jr. (R) | 69,445 | 63.6 |
| | George C. Rogers (D) | 36,591 | 33.5 |
| 27 | Harcourt J. Pratt (R) | 59,183 | 62.8 |
| | Robert R. Livingston (D) | 34,993 | 37.2 |
| 28 | Parker Corning (D) | 77,365 | 58.2 |
| | Franklin D. Sargent (R) | 53,383 | 40.1 |
| 29 | James S. Parker (R) | 71,326 | 62.8 |
| | Theodore A. Knapp (D) | 40,541 | 35.7 |
| 30 | Frank Crowther (R) | 58,022 | 59.8 |
| | E. Watson Gardiner (D) | 36,956 | 38.1 |
| 31 | Bertrand H. Snell (R) | 52,702 | 63.3 |
| | John C. Howard (D) | 30,602 | 36.7 |
| 32 | Francis D. Culkin (R) | 65,009 | 67.5 |
| | Frank Bowman (D) | 30,201 | 31.3 |
| 33 | Frederick M. Davenport (R) | 62,746 | 56.5 |

| | Candidates | Votes | % |
|---|---|---|---|
| 34 | John D. Clarke (R) | 80,531 | 71.0 |
| | William W. Lampman (D) | 32,925 | 29.0 |
| 35 | Clarence E. Hancock (R) | 90,370 | 61.8 |
| | Augustus C. Stevens (D) | 52,926 | 36.2 |
| 36 | John Taber (R) | 68,095 | 69.1 |
| | Joseph P. Craugh (D) | 30,503 | 30.9 |
| 37 | Gale H. Stalker (R & SOC) | 78,789 | 70.4 |
| | Paul Smith (D) | 33,212 | 29.7 |
| 38 | James L. Whitley (R) | 47,298 | 36.0 |
| | Charles Stanton (D) | 43,009 | 32.7 |
| | William MacFarlane (I) | 38,324 | 29.2 |
| 39 | Archie D. Sanders (R) | 69,615 | 65.0 |
| | Frank L. Morris (D) | 34,175 | 31.9 |
| 40 | S. Wallace Dempsey (R) | 99,896 | 65.4 |
| | John M. Powers (D) | 46,860 | 30.7 |
| 41 | Edmund F. Cooke (R) | 44,641 | 52.2 |
| | Fred C. Fornes (D) | 37,057 | 43.7 |
| 42 | James M. Mead (D) | 44,373 | 56.1 |
| | C. Hamilton Cook (R) | 31,785 | 40.2 |
| 43 | Daniel A. Reed (R) | 73,571 | 76.0 |
| | Arthur E. Towne (D) | 23,176 | 24.0 |

## NORTH CAROLINA

| 1 | Lindsay C. Warren (D) | 23,140 | 76.3 |
|---|---|---|---|
| | Marion B. Prescott (R) | 7,209 | 23.8 |
| 2 | John H. Kerr (D) | 24,129 | 88.9 |
| | J. L. Johnston (R) | 3,005 | 11.1 |
| 3 | Charles L. Abernethy (D) | 21,740 | 55.7 |
| | William G. Mebane (R) | 17,307 | 44.3 |
| 4 | Edward W. Pou (D) | 31,288 | 65.6 |
| | Lossing L. Wrenn (R) | 16,434 | 34.4 |
| 5 | Charles M. Stedman (D) | 54,980 | 50.1 |
| | Junius H. Harden (R) | 54,813 | 49.8 |
| 6 | J. Bayard Clark (D) | 26,061 | 61.4 |
| | W. C. Downing (R) | 16,364 | 38.6 |
| 7 | William C. Hammer (D) | 41,124 | 51.3 |
| | A. I. Ferree (R) | 39,106 | 48.7 |
| 8 | Robert L. Doughton (D) | 37,535 | 50.9 |
| | W. S. Bogle (R) | 36,251 | 49.1 |
| 9 | Charles A. Jonas (R) | 49,799 | 51.6 |
| | Alfred L. Bulwinkle (D) | 46,756 | 48.4 |
| 10 | George M. Pritchard (R) | 49,045 | 50.2 |
| | Zebulon Weaver (D) | 48,607 | 49.8 |

## NORTH DAKOTA

| 1 | Olger B. Burtness (R) | 53,941 | 77.5 |
|---|---|---|---|
| | W. S. Hooper (D) | 15,646 | 22.5 |
| 2 | Thomas Hall (R) | 42,844 | 61.7 |
| | J. L. Page (D) | 26,566 | 38.3 |
| 3 | James H. Sinclair (R) | 52,220 | 84.8 |
| | Reuben H. Leavitt (D) | 9,335 | 15.2 |

## OHIO

| 1 | Nicholas Longworth (R) | 80,812 | 61.8 |
|---|---|---|---|
| | Arthur Espy (D) | 49,880 | 38.2 |
| 2 | William E. Hess (R) | 63,605 | 53.9 |
| | James H. Cleveland (D) | 54,332 | 46.1 |
| 3 | Roy Fitzgerald (R) | 101,050 | 64.4 |
| | Frank L. Humphrey (D) | 55,767 | 35.6 |
| 4 | John L. Cable (R) | 56,291 | 57.5 |
| | William Klinger (D) | 41,677 | 42.5 |
| 5 | Charles J. Thompson (R) | 36,096 | 53.5 |
| | Frank C. Kniffin (D) | 31,385 | 46.5 |
| 6 | Charles C. Kearns (R) | 43,519 | 56.9 |
| | George D. Nye (D) | 33,020 | 43.1 |
| 7 | Charles Brand (R) | 75,753 | 68.8 |
| | Harry E. Rice (D) | 34,323 | 31.2 |
| 8 | Grant E. Mouser Jr. (R) | 42,199 | 52.2 |
| | Brooks Fletcher (D) | 38,651 | 47.8 |
| 9 | William W. Chalmers (R) | 82,560 | 61.9 |
| | William P. Clarke (D) | 50,601 | 38.0 |
| 10 | Thomas A. Jenkins (R) | 38,347 | 69.9 |
| | Charles E. Poston (D) | 16,551 | 30.2 |
| 11 | Mell G. Underwood (D) | 34,257 | 52.8 |
| | Edwin D. Ricketts (R) | 30,574 | 47.2 |

## OHIO

| | Candidates | Votes | % |
|---|---|---|---|
| 12 | John C. Speaks (R) | 82,574 | 62.2 |
| | Carl H. Valentine (D) | 50,216 | 37.8 |
| 13 | Joe E. Baird (R) | 54,174 | 61.4 |
| | William C. Martin (D) | 34,015 | 38.6 |
| 14 | Francis Seiberling (R) | 106,253 | 64.4 |
| | A. F. O'Neil (D) | 58,848 | 35.6 |
| 15 | C. Ellis Moore (R) | 50,941 | 65.8 |
| | Frank H. Ward (D) | 26,441 | 34.2 |
| 16 | C. B. McClintock (R) | 73,966 | 56.4 |
| | John McSweeney (D) | 55,778 | 42.5 |
| 17 | William M. Morgan (R) | 56,823 | 58.2 |
| | Charles West (D) | 40,846 | 41.8 |
| 18 | B. Frank Murphy (R) | 71,378 | 69.2 |
| | John J. Whitacre (D) | 31,422 | 30.5 |
| 19 | John G. Cooper (R) | 89,731 | 68.7 |
| | Locke Miller (D) | 40,948 | 31.3 |
| 20 | Charles A. Mooney (D) | 47,313 | 62.3 |
| | Oscar V. Hensley (R) | 28,381 | 37.4 |
| 21 | Robert Crosser (D) | 39,090 | 59.8 |
| | Joseph F. Lange (R) | 26,267 | 40.2 |
| 22 | Chester C. Bolton (R) | 151,565 | 69.8 |
| | Simon B. Fitzsimmons (D) | 65,742 | 30.3 |

## OKLAHOMA

| | Candidates | Votes | % |
|---|---|---|---|
| 1 | Charles O'Connor (R) | 63,641 | 52.2 |
| | Everette B. Howard (D) | 58,148 | 47.7 |
| 2 | William W. Hastings (D) | 31,287 | 51.9 |
| | E. L. Kirby (R) | 28,959 | 48.0 |
| 3 | Wilburn Cartwright (D) | 39,467 | 64.1 |
| | Robert N. Allen (R) | 21,804 | 35.4 |
| 4 | Thomas D. McKeown (D) | 37,191 | 50.5 |
| | Fred L. Patrick (R) | 36,151 | 49.1 |
| 5 | Ulysses S. Stone (R) | 44,814 | 50.9 |
| | Fletcher B. Swank (D) | 42,856 | 48.7 |
| 6 | Jed Johnson (D) | 32,820 | 53.4 |
| | Walter C. Stephens (R) | 28,304 | 46.0 |
| 7 | James V. McClintic (D) | 27,670 | 55.6 |
| | Walter S. Mills (R) | 21,758 | 43.7 |
| 8 | Milton C. Garber (R) | 48,445 | 63.8 |
| | J. P. Battenberg (D) | 27,135 | 35.7 |

## OREGON

| | Candidates | Votes | % |
|---|---|---|---|
| 1 | Willis C. Hawley (R) | 91,839 | 70.9 |
| | Harvey G. Starkweather (D) | 33,772 | 26.1 |
| 2 | Robert R. Butler (R) | 28,865 | 55.7 |
| | Walter M. Pierce (D) | 22,108 | 42.6 |
| 3 | Franklin F. Korell (R) | 75,835 | 67.6 |
| | William C. Culbertson (D) | 29,673# | 26.5 |

## PENNSYLVANIA

| | Candidates | Votes | % |
|---|---|---|---|
| 1 | James M. Beck (R) | 45,070 | 49.8 |
| | William L. Rooney (D) | 44,956 | 49.7 |
| 2 | George S. Graham (R) | 34,432 | 64.6 |
| | John J. Shanahan (D) | 18,697 | 35.1 |
| 3 | Harry C. Ransley (R) | 30,458 | 57.4 |
| | James J. Hayes (D) | 22,559 | 42.5 |
| 4 | Benjamin M. Golder (R) | 49,877 | 61.2 |
| | Thomas J. Carroll (D, LAB) | 31,082 | 38.1 |
| 5 | James J. Connolly (R, D) | 110,648 | 99.4 |
| 6 | George A. Welsh (R) | 89,362 | 59.8 |
| | Bruce A. Metzger (D) | 59,410 | 39.7 |
| 7 | George P. Darrow (R) | 91,305 | 68.0 |
| | Thomas A. O'Hara (D) | 42,217 | 31.5 |
| 8 | James Wolfenden (R) | 116,266 | 76.2 |
| | Henry W. Davis (D) | 34,607 | 22.7 |
| 9 | Henry W. Watson (R) | 102,019 | 76.3 |
| | Richard Vaux (D) | 31,389 | 23.5 |
| 10 | William W. Griest (R, LAB) | 55,623 | 82.5 |
| | John A. McSparran (D) | 11,395 | 16.9 |
| 11 | Laurence H. Watres (R, P) | 48,626 | 50.3 |
| | Frank M. Walsh (D) | 48,017 | 49.7 |

| | Candidates | Votes | % |
|---|---|---|---|
| 12 | John J. Casey (D, LAB) | 70,943 | 51.6 |
| | Henry W. Merritt (R, P) | 66,661 | 48.4 |
| 13 | George Franklin Brumm (R) | 46,486 | 55.5 |
| | Bernard V. O'Hare (D) | 37,243 | 44.5 |
| 14 | Charles J. Esterly (R) | 76,670 | 61.9 |
| | Abraham H. Rothermel (D) | 36,176 | 29.2 |
| | Howard McDonough (SOC, LAB) | 10,950 | 8.8 |
| 15 | Louis T. McFadden (R, D) | 50,770 | 93.8 |
| | Cornelia Bryce Pinchot (P) | 3,348 | 6.2 |
| 16 | Edgar R. Kiess (R, P) | 48,041 | 74.0 |
| | Thomas Wood (D) | 16,693 | 25.7 |
| 17 | Frederick W. Magrady (R) | 45,437 | 60.0 |
| | Samuel M. Shipman (D, P) | 30,290 | 40.0 |
| 18 | Edward M. Beers (R, LAB) | 55,736 | 81.0 |
| | Frederick A. Rupp (D) | 13,070 | 19.0 |
| 19 | Isaac H. Doutrich (R, LAB) | 80,291 | 80.3 |
| | John E. Blair (D) | 19,032 | 19.1 |
| 20 | J. Russell Leech (R) | 29,383 | 53.3 |
| | George E. Wolfe (D, LAB) | 25,737 | 46.7 |
| 21 | J. Banks Kurtz (R, LAB) | 42,965 | 76.2 |
| | Harry K. Filler (D) | 13,420 | 23.8 |
| 22 | Franklin Menges (R, P) | 44,198 | 63.3 |
| | John H. Myers (D) | 25,622 | 36.7 |
| 23 | J. Mitchell Chase (R, LAB) | 43,294 | 74.0 |
| | T. E. Costello (D) | 15,219 | 26.0 |
| 24 | Samuel A. Kendall (R, P) | 42,118 | 64.3 |
| | J. Calvin Core (D) | 23,176 | 35.4 |
| 25 | Henry W. Temple (R, P) | 34,806 | 59.6 |
| | James S. Pates (D) | 23,260 | 39.9 |
| 26 | J. Howard Swick (R, P) | 64,160 | 72.2 |
| | C. Hale Sipe (D) | 24,352 | 27.4 |
| 27 | Nathan L. Strong (R, P) | 52,868 | 75.2 |
| | Harry W. Fee (D) | 17,433 | 24.8 |
| 28 | Thomas C. Cochran (R, P) | 59,143 | 74.3 |
| | Harry B. Mitchell (D) | 20,443 | 25.7 |
| 29 | Milton W. Shreve (R, P) | 42,747 | 60.4 |
| | Albert L. Thomas (D) | 28,004 | 39.6 |
| 30 | William R. Coyle (R) | 48,421 | 56.9 |
| | Everett Kent (D, LAB) | 36,612 | 43.1 |
| 31 | Adam M. Wyant (R, P) | 50,981 | 95.8 |
| 32 | Stephen G. Porter (R) | 48,837 | 64.6 |
| | Edward S. Michalowski (D) | 26,145 | 34.6 |
| 33 | M. Clyde Kelly (R, D) | 81,328 | 99.0 |
| 34 | Patrick J. Sullivan (R, D) | 48,638 | 97.4 |
| 35 | Harry A. Estep (R) | 42,450 | 57.3 |
| | John J. Murray (D) | 30,619 | 41.4 |
| 36 | Guy E. Campbell (R, P) | 48,190 | 60.3 |
| | William E. Madden Jr. (D) | 31,151 | 39.0 |

### Special Election

| | | Votes | % |
|---|---|---|---|
| 8 | James Wolfenden (R) | 116,504 | 97.8 |

## RHODE ISLAND

| | Candidates | Votes | % |
|---|---|---|---|
| 1 | Clark Burdick (R) | 42,366 | 55.6 |
| | John J. Cooney (D) | 33,902 | 44.5 |
| 2 | Richard S. Aldrich (R) | 43,772 | 55.6 |
| | Sumner Mowry (D) | 34,947 | 44.4 |
| 3 | Jeremiah E. O'Connell (D) | 45,605 | 57.1 |
| | Louis Monast (R) | 34,223 | 42.9 |

## SOUTH CAROLINA

| | Candidates | Votes | % |
|---|---|---|---|
| 1 | Thomas S. McMillan (D) | 8,469 | 100.0 |
| 2 | Butler B. Hare (D) | 7,648 | 100.0 |
| 3 | Fred H. Dominick (D) | 10,917 | 100.0 |
| 4 | John J. McSwain (D) | 8,873 | 100.0 |
| 5 | William F. Stevenson (D) | 8,911 | 100.0 |
| 6 | Allard H. Gasque (D) | 7,757 | 100.0 |
| 7 | Hampton P. Fulmer (D) | 8,772 | 100.0 |

## SOUTH DAKOTA

| | Candidates | Votes | % |
|---|---|---|---|
| 1 | Charles A. Christopherson (R) | 54,573 | 58.4 |
| | A. O. Steensland (D) | 38,055 | 40.7 |

| | Candidates | Votes | % |
|---|---|---|---|
| 2 | Royal C. Johnson (R) | 54,846 | 57.2 |
| | Fred Hildebrandt (D) | 39,970 | 41.7 |
| 3 | William Williamson (R) | 33,245 | 55.7 |
| | Arthur W. Watwood (D) | 26,412 | 44.3 |

## TENNESSEE

| | Candidates | Votes | % |
|---|---|---|---|
| 1 | B. Carroll Reece (R) | 28,142 | 78.6 |
| | W. I. Giles (D) | 7,646 | 21.4 |
| 2 | J. Will Taylor (R) | 30,917 | 68.9 |
| | Leon Jourolmon (D) | 13,968 | 31.1 |
| 3 | Sam D. McReynolds (D) | 25,667 | 53.4 |
| | Silas Williams (R) | 22,405 | 46.6 |
| 4 | Cordell Hull (D) | 17,141 | 68.2 |
| | S. H. Justice (R) | 7,999 | 31.8 |
| 5 | Ewin L. Davis (D) | 12,847 | 80.4 |
| | John F. Aplinger | 3,126# | 19.6 |
| 6 | Joseph W. Byrns (D) | 24,738 | 79.9 |
| | E. L. Bradbury (R) | 6,220 | 20.1 |
| 7 | Edward E. Eslick (D) | 16,893 | 93.0 |
| | S. E. Stephens (R) | 1,268 | 7.0 |
| 8 | Gordon Browning (D) | 17,868 | 66.1 |
| | Harvey E. Cantrell (R) | 9,184 | 34.0 |
| 9 | Jere Cooper (D) | 20,184 | 90.1 |
| | Carmack Murchison (R) | 2,222 | 9.9 |
| 10 | Hubert F. Fisher (D) | 21,524 | 81.3 |
| | R. L. Harper (R) | 4,964 | 18.7 |

## TEXAS

| | Candidates | Votes | % |
|---|---|---|---|
| 1 | Wright Patman (D) | 24,267 | 87.9 |
| | Richard E. Stephens (R) | 3,349 | 12.1 |
| 2 | John C. Box (D) | 38,901 | 100.0 |
| 3 | Morgan G. Sanders (D) | 22,221 | 100.0 |
| 4 | Sam Rayburn (D) | 23,847 | 84.2 |
| | Floyd Harry (R) | 4,488 | 15.8 |
| 5 | Hatton W. Sumners (D) | 42,482 | 100.0 |
| 6 | Luther A. Johnson (D) | 26,412 | 90.7 |
| | H. Lee Monroe (R) | 2,714 | 9.3 |
| 7 | Clay Stone Briggs (D) | 21,461 | 88.4 |
| | A. J. Long (R) | 2,827 | 11.6 |
| 8 | Daniel E. Garrett (D) | 43,891 | 81.8 |
| | George E. Kepple (R) | 9,739 | 18.2 |
| 9 | Joseph J. Mansfield (D) | 24,742 | 86.9 |
| | Louis B. Allen (R) | 3,718 | 13.1 |
| 10 | James P. Buchanan (D) | 27,890 | 91.9 |
| | David H. Morris (R) | 2,457 | 8.1 |
| 11 | Oliver H. Crass (D) | 21,484 | 90.9 |
| | R. C. Bush (R) | 2,141 | 9.1 |
| 12 | Fritz G. Lanham (D) | 30,905 | 79.6 |
| | David Sutter (R) | 7,921 | 20.4 |
| 13 | Guinn Williams (D) | 30,926 | 88.5 |
| | Mrs. P. A. Welty (R) | 4,026 | 11.5 |
| 14 | Augustus McCloskey (D) | 29,085‡ | 50.3 |
| | Harry M. Wurzbach (R) | 28,766 | 49.7 |
| 15 | John N. Garner (D) | 28,417 | 100.0 |
| 16 | Claude B. Hudspeth (D) | 31,132 | 100.0 |
| 17 | Robert Q. Lee (D) | 41,727 | 100.0 |
| 18 | Marvin Jones (D) | 58,667 | 86.5 |
| | V. C. Nelson (R) | 9,137 | 13.5 |

## UTAH

| | Candidates | Votes | % |
|---|---|---|---|
| 1 | Don B. Colton (R) | 50,274 | 60.9 |
| | Knox Patterson (D) | 31,889 | 38.6 |
| 2 | Elmer O. Leatherwood (R) | 46,866 | 50.2 |
| | Joshua H. Paul (D) | 46,025 | 49.3 |

## VERMONT

| | Candidates | Votes | % |
|---|---|---|---|
| 1 | Elbert S. Brigham (R) | 44,082 | 63.0 |
| | Jeremiah C. Durick (D) | 25,095 | 35.9 |
| 2 | Ernest Willard Gibson (R) | 47,141 | 79.3 |
| | Harry W. Witters (D) | 11,356 | 19.1 |

## VIRGINIA

| | Candidates | Votes | % |
|---|---|---|---|
| 1 | Schuyler Otis Bland (D) | 23,912 | 99.7 |
| 2 | Menalcus Lankford (R) | 18,614 | 55.9 |
| | Joseph T. Deal (D) | 14,668 | 44.1 |
| 3 | Andrew J. Montague (D) | 23,350 | 75.9 |
| | J. D. Peake (I) | 5,854 | 19.0 |
| | James E. Maynard (I) | 1,561 | 5.1 |
| 4 | Patrick Henry Drewry (D) | 16,904 | 99.7 |
| 5 | Joseph Whitehead (D) | 16,672 | 54.3 |
| | Taylor G. Vaughan (R) | 14,049 | 45.7 |
| 6 | Clifton A. Woodrum (D) | 25,091 | 99.7 |
| 7 | Jacob A. Garber (R) | 15,243 | 50.4 |
| | Thomas W. Harrison (D) | 15,009 | 49.6 |
| 8 | R. Walton Moore (D) | 24,368 | 99.1 |
| 9 | Joseph C. Shaffer (R) | 32,696 | 50.8 |
| | William H. Rouse (D) | 31,722 | 49.2 |
| 10 | Henry St.George Tucker (D) | 14,817 | 56.9 |
| | M. J. Putnam (R) | 11,230 | 43.1 |

## WASHINGTON

| | Candidates | Votes | % |
|---|---|---|---|
| 1 | John F. Miller (R) | 70,703 | 65.5 |
| | Hugh Todd (D) | 36,858 | 34.1 |
| 2 | Lindley H. Hadley (R) | 59,534 | 99.3 |
| 3 | Albert Johnson (R) | 77,314 | 70.0 |
| | O. M. Nelson (D) | 33,217 | 30.1 |

| | Candidates | Votes | % |
|---|---|---|---|
| 4 | John W. Summers (R) | 48,766 | 77.1 |
| | H. C. Bohlke (D) | 14,512 | 22.9 |
| 5 | Sam B. Hill (D) | 50,323 | 58.5 |
| | Thomas Corkery (R) | 35,660 | 41.5 |

## WEST VIRGINIA

| | Candidates | Votes | % |
|---|---|---|---|
| 1 | Carl G. Bachmann (R) | 62,646 | 60.6 |
| | Paul R. Wellman (D) | 40,666 | 39.4 |
| 2 | Frank L. Bowman (R) | 52,424 | 55.7 |
| | Ben H. Hiner (D) | 41,640 | 44.2 |
| 3 | John M. Wolverton (R) | 45,167 | 50.4 |
| | William S. O'Brien (D) | 44,477 | 49.6 |
| 4 | James A. Hughes (R) | 55,672 | 57.0 |
| | Harry H. Darnall (D) | 42,057 | 43.0 |
| 5 | Hugh Ike Shott (R) | 63,559 | 53.4 |
| | John Kee (D) | 55,376 | 46.0 |
| 6 | Joe L. Smith (D) | 67,845 | 50.1 |
| | Edward T. England (R) | 67,617 | 49.9 |

## WISCONSIN

| | Candidates | Votes | % |
|---|---|---|---|
| 1 | Henry Allen Cooper (R) | 83,069 | 80.2 |
| | William C. Kiernan (D) | 20,534 | 19.8 |
| 2 | Charles A. Kading (R) | 53,530 | 69.9 |
| | Eugene A. Clifford (D) | 23,101 | 30.1 |

| | Candidates | Votes | % |
|---|---|---|---|
| 3 | John Mandt Nelson (R) | 62,938 | 74.7 |
| | William Victora (D) | 20,262 | 24.1 |
| 4 | John C. Schafer (R) | 37,685 | 44.1 |
| | William J. Kershaw (D) | 28,956 | 33.9 |
| | Walter Polakowski (SOC) | 18,885 | 22.1 |
| 5 | William H. Stafford (R) | 41,265 | 38.9 |
| | Victor L. Berger (SOC) | 40,536 | 38.2 |
| | Thomas O'Malley (D) | 24,037 | 22.7 |
| 6 | Florian Lampert (R) | 53,952 | 69.2 |
| | Morley G. Kelly (D) | 24,009 | 30.8 |
| 7 | Merlin Hull (R) | 49,590 | 72.4 |
| | A. H. Schubert (D) | 18,530 | 27.0 |
| 8 | Edward E. Browne (R) | 47,848 | 74.0 |
| | R. J. Walsh (D) | 16,316 | 25.2 |
| 9 | George J. Schneider (R) | 52,300 | 60.4 |
| | James H. McGillan (D) | 33,302 | 38.5 |
| 10 | James A. Frear (R) | 59,314 | 81.4 |
| | Miles H. McNally (D) | 13,590 | 18.6 |
| 11 | Hubert H. Peavey (R) | 56,586 | 80.8 |
| | Frank P. Kennedy (D) | 11,962 | 17.1 |

## WYOMING

| | Candidates | Votes | % |
|---|---|---|---|
| AL | Vincent M. Carter (R) | 38,935 | 51.8 |
| | W. S. Kimball (D) | 35,972 | 47.8 |

# 1929 House Elections

## KENTUCKY

### Special Election

| | | Votes | % |
|---|---|---|---|
| 3 | John W. Moore (D) | 19,669 | 51.3 |
| | Homer Beliles (R) | 18,644 | 48.7 |

## LOUISIANA
### Special Election

| | | Votes | % |
|---|---|---|---|
| 3 | Numa F. Montet (D) | 11,460 | 57.7 |
| | M. E. Norman (R) | 8,399 | 42.3 |

## MISSOURI
### Special Election

| | | Votes | % |
|---|---|---|---|
| 4 | David Hopkins (R) | 23,898 | 53.0 |
| | Louis V. Stigall (D) | 21,179 | 47.0 |

## NEW YORK

### Special Election

| | | Votes | % |
|---|---|---|---|
| 21 | Joseph A. Gavagan (D) | 39,893 | 56.7 |
| | Hubert T. Delany (R&SQDEAL) | 26,666 | 37.9 |
| | Frank Crosswaith (SOC) | 3,561 | 5.1 |

---

## House Candidates Index

For an index of all House candidates listed in this section (pages 943-1326), see pages 1402-1501. Instructions for use of the House Candidates Index appear on page 1402.

---

# 1930 House Elections

## ALABAMA

| | Candidates | Votes | % |
|---|---|---|---|
| 1 | John McDuffie (D) | 16,839 | 100.0 |
| 2 | Lister Hill (D) | 22,630 | 100.0 |
| 3 | Henry B. Steagall (D) | 13,398 | 100.0 |
| 4 | Lamar Jeffers (D) | 13,502 | 65.2 |
| | E. D. Banks (I) | 7,209 | 34.8 |
| 5 | Lafayette L. Patterson (D) | 13,221 | 100.0 |
| 6 | William B. Oliver (D) | 9,439 | 100.0 |
| 7 | Miles C. Allgood (D) | 18,932 | 61.1 |
| | John B. Isbell (R) | 12,062 | 38.9 |
| 8 | Edward B. Almon (D) | 18,570 | 100.0 |
| 9 | George Huddleston (D) | 24,484 | 81.0 |
| | Hollis B. Parris (I) | 5,750 | 19.0 |
| 10 | William B. Bankhead (D) | 14,388 | 64.2 |
| | Charles P. G. Lunsford (R) | 8,009 | 35.8 |

## ARIZONA

| | Candidates | Votes | % |
|---|---|---|---|
| AL | Lewis W. Douglas (D) | 52,342 | 100.0 |

## ARKANSAS

| | Candidates | Votes | % |
|---|---|---|---|
| 1 | William J. Driver (D) | 19,103 | 100.0 |
| 2 | John E. Miller (D) | 18,623 | 100.0 |
| 3 | Claude A. Fuller (D) | 28,809 | 100.0 |
| 4 | Effiegene Wingo (D) | 21,753 | 100.0 |
| 5 | Heartsill Ragon (D) | 21,896 | 100.0 |
| 6 | David D. Glover (D) | 18,127 | 100.0 |
| 7 | Tilman B. Parks (D) | 15,860 | 100.0 |

## CALIFORNIA

| | Candidates | Votes | % |
|---|---|---|---|
| 1 | Clarence F. Lea (D-R) | 66,703 | 100.0 |
| 2 | Harry L. Englebright (R-D) | 35,941 | 99.9 |
| 3 | Charles F. Curry | 43,336 | 53.4 |
| | J. M. Inman (R) | 26,785# | 33.0 |
| | Frank H. Buck (D) | 9,172# | 11.3 |
| 4 | Florence P. Kahn (R-D) | 47,397 | 100.0 |
| 5 | Richard J. Welch (R-D) | 59,853 | 100.0 |
| 6 | Albert E. Carter (R-D) | 110,190 | 100.0 |
| 7 | Henry E. Barbour (R-D) | 79,041 | 100.0 |
| 8 | Arthur Monroe Free (R-D) | 93,377 | 99.9 |
| 9 | William E. Evans (R) | 182,176 | 99.9 |
| 10 | Joe Crail (R) | 162,502 | 75.0 |
| | John F. Dockweiler (D) | 54,231 | 25.0 |
| 11 | Philip D. Swing (R-D) | 124,092 | 100.0 |

## COLORADO

| | Candidates | Votes | % |
|---|---|---|---|
| 1 | William R. Eaton (R) | 39,907 | 50.3 |
| | Lawrence Lewis (D) | 38,152 | 48.1 |
| 2 | Charles B. Timberlake (R) | 55,099 | 59.3 |
| | O. E. Webb (D) | 37,760 | 40.7 |
| 3 | Guy U. Hardy (R) | 55,170 | 60.7 |
| | Guy M. Weybright (D) | 35,744 | 39.3 |
| 4 | Edward T. Taylor (D) | 34,536 | 67.0 |
| | Webster S. Whinnery (R) | 17,051 | 33.1 |

## CONNECTICUT

| | Candidates | Votes | % |
|---|---|---|---|
| 1 | Augustine Lonergan (D) | 51,551 | 50.3 |
| | Clarence W. Seymour (R) | 50,877 | 49.7 |
| 2 | Richard P. Freeman (R) | 37,801 | 53.1 |
| | William C. Fox (D) | 33,329 | 46.9 |
| 3 | John Q. Tilson (R) | 45,329 | 52.1 |
| | James A. Shanley (D) | 40,269 | 46.3 |
| 4 | William L. Tierney (D) | 50,769 | 49.7 |
| | Schuyler Merritt (R) | 49,209 | 48.2 |
| 5 | Edward W. Goss (R) | 33,302 | 50.5 |
| | Martin E. Gormley (D) | 32,584 | 49.5 |

### Special Election

| | Candidates | Votes | % |
|---|---|---|---|
| 5 | Edward W. Goss (R) | 33,284 | 50.6 |
| | Martin E. Gormley (D) | 32,479 | 49.4 |

## DELAWARE

| | Candidates | Votes | % |
|---|---|---|---|
| AL | Robert G. Houston (R) | 48,493 | 55.4 |
| | John P. Le Fevre (D) | 38,891 | 44.4 |

## FLORIDA

| | Candidates | Votes | % |
|---|---|---|---|
| 1 | Herbert J. Drane (D) | 24,792 | 67.7 |
| | L. E. Womack (R) | 11,819 | 32.3 |
| 2 | Robert A. Green (D) | 7,060 | 100.0 |
| 3 | Tom A. Yon (D) | 11,796 | 99.8 |
| 4 | Ruth Bryan Owen (D) | 40,422 | 99.9 |

## GEORGIA

| | Candidates | Votes | % |
|---|---|---|---|
| 1 | Charles G. Edwards (D) | 2,465 | 100.0 |
| 2 | E. E. Cox (D) | 2,518 | 100.0 |
| 3 | Charles R. Crisp (D) | 2,440 | 100.0 |
| 4 | William C. Wright (D) | 2,721 | 100.0 |
| 5 | Robert Ramspeck (D) | 10,752 | 100.0 |
| 6 | Samuel Rutherford (D) | 4,333 | 100.0 |
| 7 | Malcolm C. Tarver (D) | 5,590 | 100.0 |
| 8 | Charles H. Brand (D) | 5,058 | 93.2 |
| | W. N. Phillips (I) | 369# | 6.8 |
| 9 | John S. Wood (D) | 7,089 | 100.0 |
| 10 | Carl Vinson (D) | 2,691 | 100.0 |
| 11 | William C. Lankford (D) | 6,462 | 80.9 |
| | H. J. Carswell (R) | 1,526# | 19.1 |
| 12 | William W. Larsen (D) | 2,444 | 100.0 |

## IDAHO

| | Candidates | Votes | % |
|---|---|---|---|
| 1 | Burton L. French (R) | 34,527 | 64.9 |
| | Compton I. White (D) | 18,657 | 35.1 |
| 2 | Addison T. Smith (R) | 46,342 | 63.2 |
| | W. F. Alworth (D) | 27,002 | 36.8 |

## ILLINOIS

| | Candidates | Votes | % |
|---|---|---|---|
| 1 | Oscar De Priest (R) | 23,719 | 58.4 |
| | Harry Baker (D) | 16,747 | 41.2 |
| 2 | Morton D. Hull (R) | 76,665 | 54.4 |
| | Michael C. Walsh (D) | 63,341 | 44.9 |
| 3 | Edward A. Kelly (D) | 83,028 | 58.1 |
| | Elliott W. Sproul (R) | 59,644 | 41.8 |
| 4 | Harry P. Beam (D) | 36,736 | 69.3 |
| | Frank George Zelezinski (R) | 16,192 | 30.5 |
| 5 | Adolph J. Sabath (D) | 21,460 | 66.2 |
| | Frank V. Kara (R) | 10,816 | 33.3 |
| 6 | James T. Igoe (D) | 120,408 | 66.7 |
| | Henry R. Lundblad (R) | 59,052 | 32.7 |
| 7 | Leonard W. Schuetz (D) | 111,525 | 55.0 |
| | James C. Moreland (R) | 90,844 | 44.8 |
| 8 | Peter C. Granata (R) | 16,565 | 51.8 |
| | Stanley H. Kunz (D) | 15,394 | 48.1 |
| 9 | Fred A. Britten (R) | 24,028 | 99.4 |
| 10 | Carl R. Chindblom (R) | 72,938 | 50.8 |
| | John E. Hesse (D) | 70,621 | 49.2 |
| 11 | Frank R. Reid (R) | 56,957 | 63.1 |
| | Elmer P. Schaefer (D) | 33,169 | 36.8 |
| 12 | John T. Buckbee (R) | 55,754 | 76.1 |
| | Richard J. O'Halloran (D) | 17,497 | 23.9 |
| 13 | William R. Johnson (R) | 28,113 | 70.2 |
| | John A. Ascher (D) | 11,937 | 29.8 |
| 14 | John C. Allen (R) | 36,370 | 56.9 |
| | William H. Hartzell (D) | 27,592 | 43.1 |
| 15 | Burnett M. Chiperfield (R) | 35,114 | 56.5 |
| | J. Hays Paxton (D) | 27,031 | 43.5 |
| 16 | William E. Hull (R) | 36,572 | 52.8 |
| | Edwin S. Carr (D) | 32,692 | 47.2 |
| 17 | Homer W. Hall (R) | 27,696 | 58.4 |
| | C. S. Schneider (D) | 19,711 | 41.6 |
| 18 | William P. Holaday (R) | 38,102 | 56.8 |
| | Charles R. Hill (D) | 29,012 | 43.2 |
| 19 | Charles Adkins (R) | 43,794 | 55.4 |
| | Charles M. Borchers (D) | 35,310 | 44.6 |
| 20 | Henry T. Rainey (D) | 37,537 | 64.9 |
| | William J. Thornton (R) | 20,262 | 35.1 |
| 21 | J. Earl Major (D) | 46,058 | 57.1 |
| | Roger E. Chapin (R) | 34,521 | 42.8 |
| 22 | Charles A. Karch (D) | 48,281 | 50.3 |
| | Ed. M. Irwin (R) | 47,715 | 49.7 |
| 23 | William W. Arnold (D) | 49,111 | 62.6 |
| | Joe Frank Allen (R) | 29,291 | 37.4 |
| 24 | Claude V. Parsons (D) | 27,325 | 50.0 |
| | James V. Heidinger (R) | 27,296 | 50.0 |
| 25 | Kent E. Keller (D) | 38,796 | 52.6 |
| | Edward E. Denison (R) | 34,927 | 47.4 |
| AL | William H. Dieterich (D) | 1,062,606✔ | |
| | Richard Yates (R) | 991,083✔ | |
| | Walter Nesbit (D) | 975,422 | |
| | Frank L. Smith (R) | 890,327 | |
| | Emil Z. Levitin (SOC) | 9,526 | |
| | Morris A. Gold (SOC) | 9,207 | |
| | William S. Feinberg (AM NAT) | 1,337 | |
| | John W. McLain (AM NAT) | 1,228 | |
| | I. J. Brown (LIB) | 884 | |
| | Charles A. Reinhart (LIB) | 824 | |

### Special Elections

| | Candidates | Votes | % |
|---|---|---|---|
| 15 | Burnett M. Chiperfield (R) | 34,063 | 56.2 |
| | J. Hays Paxton (D) | 26,467 | 43.7 |
| 24 | Claude V. Parsons (D) | 26,929 | 50.2 |
| | James V. Heidinger (R) | 26,732 | 49.8 |

## INDIANA

| | Candidates | Votes | % |
|---|---|---|---|
| 1 | John W. Boehne Jr. (D) | 46,836 | 53.9 |
| | Harry E. Rowbottom (R) | 40,015 | 46.1 |
| 2 | Arthur H. Greenwood (D) | 52,452 | 59.5 |
| | Ray S. Sisson (R) | 35,689 | 40.5 |
| 3 | Eugene B. Crowe (D) | 45,070 | 50.2 |
| | James W. Dunbar (R) | 44,808 | 49.9 |
| 4 | Harry C. Canfield (D) | 46,396 | 57.1 |
| | Scott Thompson (R) | 34,856 | 42.9 |
| 5 | Courtland C. Gillen (D) | 43,355 | 51.5 |
| | Noble J. Johnson (R) | 40,919 | 48.6 |
| 6 | William H. Larrabee (D) | 40,803 | 51.8 |
| | Richard N. Elliott (R) | 37,969 | 48.2 |
| 7 | Louis Ludlow (D) | 87,777 | 61.6 |
| | Archibald M. Hall (R) | 53,822 | 37.8 |
| 8 | Albert H. Vestal (R) | 44,203 | 50.0 |
| | Claude C. Ball (D) | 44,194 | 50.0 |
| 9 | Fred S. Purnell (R) | 43,681 | 50.2 |
| | Harry L. Matlock (D) | 43,346 | 49.8 |
| 10 | William R. Wood (R) | 53,702 | 53.3 |
| | Charles J. Murphy (D) | 47,057 | 46.7 |
| 11 | Glenn Griswold (D) | 41,823 | 51.3 |
| | Albert R. Hall (R) | 39,771 | 48.7 |
| 12 | David R. Hogg (R) | 43,286 | 52.3 |
| | Thomas P. Riddle (D) | 39,488 | 47.7 |
| 13 | Samuel B. Pettengill (D) | 62,609 | 51.3 |
| | Andrew J. Hickey (R) | 59,361 | 48.7 |

## IOWA

| | Candidates | Votes | % |
|---|---|---|---|
| 1 | William F. Kopp (R) | 27,053 | 63.3 |
| | Max A. Conrad (D) | 15,538 | 36.4 |
| 2 | Bernhard M. Jacobsen (D) | 30,006 | 55.4 |
| | F. D. Letts (R) | 24,113 | 44.6 |

## IOWA

| | Candidates | Votes | % |
|---|---|---|---|
| 3 | Thomas J. B. Robinson (R) | 27,098 | 63.0 |
| | W. L. Beecher (D) | 15,908 | 37.0 |
| 4 | Gilbert N. Haugen (R) | 29,224 | 59.1 |
| | Wilbur L. Peck (D) | 20,236 | 40.9 |
| 5 | Cyrenus Cole (R) | 23,221 | 53.8 |
| | H. M. Cooper (D) | 19,931 | 46.2 |
| 6 | C. William Ramseyer (R) | 25,875 | 60.6 |
| | S. F. McConnell (D) | 16,811 | 39.4 |
| 7 | Cassius C. Dowell (R) | 36,715 | 76.5 |
| | Carl Evans (D) | 11,272 | 23.5 |
| 8 | Lloyd Thurston (R) | 27,960 | 51.5 |
| | James Pearson (D) | 26,373 | 48.5 |
| 9 | Charles E. Swanson (R) | 27,873 | 57.1 |
| | June M. Fickel (D) | 20,587 | 42.2 |
| 10 | Fred C. Gilchrist (R) | 34,915 | 66.1 |
| | Paul Anderson (D) | 17,540 | 33.2 |
| 11 | Ed H. Campbell (R) | 37,659 | 73.8 |
| | Fordyce W. Bisbee (D) | 13,382 | 26.2 |

## KANSAS

| | | Votes | % |
|---|---|---|---|
| 1 | William P. Lambertson (R) | 53,799 | 100.0 |
| 2 | Ulysses S. Guyer (R) | 49,844 | 56.8 |
| | Chauncey B. Little (D) | 37,991 | 43.3 |
| 3 | Harold McGugin (R) | 42,106 | 52.7 |
| | Earl Knight (D) | 37,807 | 47.3 |
| 4 | Homer Hoch (R) | 30,840 | 58.4 |
| | James E. Hilkey (D) | 21,933 | 41.6 |
| 5 | James G. Strong (R) | 33,871 | 53.9 |
| | Clyde Short (D) | 28,971 | 46.1 |
| 6 | Charles I. Sparks (R) | 40,132 | 61.6 |
| | Robert Good (D) | 24,975 | 38.4 |
| 7 | Clifford R. Hope (R) | 52,858 | 61.1 |
| | A. S. Allphin (D) | 33,627 | 38.9 |
| 8 | William A. Ayres (D) | 57,173 | 74.7 |
| | Stella B. Haines (R) | 19,325 | 25.3 |

## KENTUCKY

| | | Votes | % |
|---|---|---|---|
| 1 | William V. Gregory (D) | 24,622 | 100.0 |
| 2 | Glover H. Cary (D) | 21,685 | 100.0 |
| 3 | John W. Moore (D) | 25,981 | 99.7 |
| 4 | Cap R. Carden (D) | 30,910 | 52.3 |
| | John Craddock (R) | 28,220 | 47.7 |
| 5 | Maurice H. Thatcher (R) | 61,832 | 97.9 |
| 6 | Brent Spence (D) | 31,520 | 56.9 |
| | J. Lincoln Newhall (R) | 18,891 | 34.1 |
| | Blaine McLaughlin (I) | 4,746 | 8.6 |
| 7 | Virgil Chapman (D) | 33,402 | 57.8 |
| | Robert Blackburn (R) | 24,380 | 42.2 |
| 8 | Ralph Gilbert (D) | 25,688 | 57.5 |
| | Patrick H. Taylor (R) | 19,023 | 42.6 |
| 9 | Fred M. Vinson (D) | 42,671 | 59.7 |
| | Elva R. Kendall (R) | 28,850 | 40.3 |
| 10 | Andrew J. May (D) | 27,159 | 52.9 |
| | Katherine Langley (R) | 24,172 | 47.1 |
| 11 | Charles Finley (R) | 48,535 | 66.3 |
| | Will Ward Duffield (D) | 24,716 | 33.7 |

### Special Elections

| | | Votes | % |
|---|---|---|---|
| 2 | John L. Dorsey Jr. (D) | 21,406# | 100.0 |
| 11 | Charles Finley (R) | 14,148 | 76.0 |
| | M. B. Sewell (D) | 4,471 | 24.0 |

## LOUISIANA

| | | Votes | % |
|---|---|---|---|
| 1 | Joachim O. Fernandez (D) | 30,629 | 95.8 |
| 2 | Paul H. Maloney (D) | 30,739 | 97.2 |
| 3 | Numa F. Montet (D) | 8,517 | 100.0 |
| 4 | John N. Sandlin (D) | 11,833 | 100.0 |
| 5 | Riley J. Wilson (D) | 11,168 | 100.0 |
| 6 | Bolivar E. Kemp (D) | 15,524 | 100.0 |
| 7 | Rene L. DeRouen (D) | 9,293 | 100.0 |
| 8 | James B. Aswell (D) | 12,383 | 100.0 |

## MAINE

| | Candidates | Votes | % |
|---|---|---|---|
| 1 | Carroll L. Beedy (R) | 23,434 | 61.4 |
| | Thomas F. Locke (D) | 14,741 | 38.6 |
| 2 | Donald B. Partridge (R) | 24,338 | 56.2 |
| | Albert Beliveau (D) | 18,943 | 43.8 |
| 3 | John E. Nelson (R) | 25,099 | 64.3 |
| | Leo D. Lamond (D) | 13,948 | 35.7 |
| 4 | Donald F. Snow (R) | 15,199 | 66.0 |
| | Clinton C. Stevens (D) | 7,839 | 34.0 |

## MARYLAND

| | | Votes | % |
|---|---|---|---|
| 1 | T. Alan Goldsborough (D) | 34,553 | 57.3 |
| | A. Stengle Marine (R) | 25,792 | 42.7 |
| 2 | William P. Cole Jr. (D) | 79,963 | 59.3 |
| | Linwood L. Clark (R) | 54,914 | 40.7 |
| 3 | Vincent L. Palmisano (D) | 28,633 | 53.4 |
| | John Philip Hill (R) | 24,170 | 45.1 |
| 4 | J. Charles Linthicum (D) | 49,471 | 65.0 |
| | W. O. Atwood (R) | 26,661 | 35.0 |
| 5 | Stephen Warfield Gambrill (D) | 40,315 | 65.3 |
| | A. Kingsley Love (R) | 21,463 | 34.7 |
| 6 | David J. Lewis (D) | 42,526 | 53.6 |
| | Frederick N. Zihlman (R) | 36,815 | 46.4 |

## MASSACHUSETTS

| | | Votes | % |
|---|---|---|---|
| 1 | Allen T. Treadway (R) | 41,334 | 54.9 |
| | Hugh McLean (D) | 33,934 | 45.1 |
| 2 | William J. Granfield (D) | 46,432 | 55.5 |
| | Joshua L. Brooks (R) | 37,247 | 44.5 |
| 3 | Frank H. Foss (R) | 36,620 | 57.1 |
| | Frank W. Barr (D) | 27,568 | 43.0 |
| 4 | Pehr G. Holmes (R) | 42,996 | 54.7 |
| | David Goldstein (D) | 35,661 | 45.3 |
| 5 | Edith Nourse Rogers (R) | 50,541 | 66.3 |
| | Joseph M. Halloran (D) | 25,742 | 33.8 |
| 6 | A. Piatt Andrew (R) | 50,814 | 76.4 |
| | Charles D. Smith (D) | 15,683 | 23.6 |
| 7 | William P. Connery Jr. (D) | 45,521 | 67.6 |
| | Charles W. Lovett (R) | 21,821 | 32.4 |
| 8 | Frederick W. Dallinger (R) | 57,428 | 56.6 |
| | John P. Brennan (D) | 44,041 | 43.4 |
| 9 | Charles L. Underhill (R) | 41,040 | 50.7 |
| | Joseph J. Borgatti (D) | 39,948 | 49.3 |
| 10 | John J. Douglass (D) | 33,218 | 87.3 |
| | Edward L. Donnelly (R) | 4,815 | 12.7 |
| 11 | George Holden Tinkham (R) | 40,417 | 63.0 |
| | John Joseph Kelleher (D) | 23,739 | 37.0 |
| 12 | John W. McCormack (D) | 50,894 | 76.7 |
| | Samuel Abrams (R) | 15,422 | 23.3 |
| 13 | Robert Luce (R) | 55,470 | 55.9 |
| | Donald M. Hill (D) | 43,800 | 44.1 |
| 14 | Richard B. Wigglesworth (R) | 56,803 | 57.3 |
| | Edward G. Morris (D) | 42,307 | 42.7 |
| 15 | Joseph W. Martin Jr. (R) | 37,100 | 64.1 |
| | William J. Murphy (D) | 20,780 | 35.9 |
| 16 | Charles L. Gifford (R) | 39,953 | 69.6 |
| | John D. W. Bodfish (I) | 17,467 | 30.4 |

## MICHIGAN

| | | Votes | % |
|---|---|---|---|
| 1 | Robert H. Clancy (R) | 44,021 | 82.2 |
| | William M. Donnelly (D) | 8,758 | 16.4 |
| 2 | Earl C. Michener (R) | 41,478 | 58.0 |
| | Edward Frensdorf (D) | 29,979 | 41.9 |
| 3 | Joseph L. Hooper (R) | 36,190 | 71.1 |
| | Rosslyn L. Sowers (D) | 14,737 | 28.9 |
| 4 | John C. Ketcham (R) | 34,980 | 66.1 |
| | Roman I. Jarvis Sr. (D) | 17,953 | 33.9 |
| 5 | Carl E. Mapes (R) | 31,297 | 98.7 |
| 6 | Seymour H. Person (R) | 124,797 | 70.2 |
| | Patrick H. O'Brien (D) | 50,221 | 28.2 |

| | Candidates | Votes | % |
|---|---|---|---|
| 7 | Jesse P. Wolcott (R) | 42,256 | 94.3 |
| | Emerald B. Dixon (D) | 2,534 | 5.7 |
| 8 | Bird J. Vincent (R) | 38,891 | 67.4 |
| | Michael J. Hart (D) | 18,838 | 32.6 |
| 9 | James C. McLaughlin (R) | 31,318 | 75.0 |
| | Loren N. O'Brien (D) | 10,462 | 25.0 |
| 10 | Roy O. Woodruff (R) | 31,033 | 78.8 |
| | Henry C. Haller (D) | 8,345 | 21.2 |
| 11 | Frank P. Bohn (R) | 34,971 | 100.0 |
| 12 | W. Frank James (R) | 36,909 | 98.1 |
| 13 | Clarence J. McLeod (R) | 39,064 | 78.8 |
| | Walter I. McKenzie (D) | 9,575 | 19.3 |

## MINNESOTA

| | | Votes | % |
|---|---|---|---|
| 1 | Victor Christgau (R) | 45,330 | 65.1 |
| | Matt Fitzpatrick (F-LAB) | 24,357 | 35.0 |
| 2 | Frank Clague (R) | 38,431 | 53.7 |
| | L. A. Fritsche (F-LAB) | 33,092 | 46.3 |
| 3 | August H. Andresen (R) | 35,704 | 48.1 |
| | Francis H. Shoemaker (F-LAB) | 21,118 | 28.4 |
| | Joseph J. Moriarity (D) | 17,485 | 23.5 |
| 4 | Melvin J. Maas (R) | 48,633 | 66.5 |
| | Claus V. Hammerstrom (F-LAB) | 16,180 | 22.1 |
| | Frank Munger Sr. (D) | 6,593 | 9.0 |
| 5 | W. I. Nolan (R) | 55,502 | 61.3 |
| | Silas M. Bryan (D) | 32,215 | 35.6 |
| 6 | Harold Knutson (R) | 44,058 | 60.6 |
| | John Knutsen (F-LAB) | 19,461 | 26.8 |
| | P. J. Russell (D) | 9,197 | 12.7 |
| 7 | Paul John Kvale (F-LAB) | 58,334 | 81.2 |
| | Frank Hopkins (R) | 13,506 | 18.8 |
| 8 | William A. Pittenger (R) | 55,802 | 63.3 |
| | William L. Carss (F-LAB) | 29,001 | 32.9 |
| 9 | Conrad G. Selvig (R) | 37,531 | 53.3 |
| | Knud Wefald (F-LAB) | 32,874 | 46.7 |
| 10 | Godfrey G. Goodwin (R) | 38,391 | 49.5 |
| | Erling Swenson (F-LAB) | 37,182 | 48.0 |

## MISSISSIPPI

| | | Votes | % |
|---|---|---|---|
| 1 | John E. Rankin (D) | 5,378 | 100.0 |
| 2 | Wall Doxey (D) | 4,202 | 100.0 |
| 3 | William M. Whittington (D) | 4,282 | 100.0 |
| 4 | Jeff Busby (D) | 4,017 | 100.0 |
| 5 | Ross A. Collins (D) | 5,107 | 100.0 |
| 6 | Robert S. Hall (D) | 5,995 | 100.0 |
| 7 | Percy E. Quinn (D) | 3,356 | 100.0 |
| 8 | James W. Collier (D) | 2,560 | 100.0 |

## MISSOURI

| | | Votes | % |
|---|---|---|---|
| 1 | Milton A. Romjue (D) | 28,974 | 61.8 |
| | J. F. Culler (R) | 17,898 | 38.2 |
| 2 | Ralph F. Lozier (D) | 30,020 | 62.8 |
| | Pearl Gehrig (R) | 17,746 | 37.1 |
| 3 | Jacob L. Milligan (D) | 25,853 | 58.9 |
| | H. F. Lawrence (R) | 18,074 | 41.2 |
| 4 | David Hopkins (R) | 33,284 | 50.8 |
| | Romulus E. Culver (D) | 32,208 | 49.2 |
| 5 | Joseph B. Shannon (D) | 102,569 | 64.3 |
| | Edgar C. Ellis (R) | 56,918 | 35.7 |
| 6 | Clement C. Dickinson (D) | 24,713 | 54.9 |
| | Thomas J. Halsey (R) | 20,249 | 45.0 |
| 7 | Samuel C. Major (D) | 36,543 | 51.8 |
| | John W. Palmer (R) | 33,964 | 48.2 |
| 8 | William L. Nelson (D) | 27,321 | 57.9 |
| | E. J. Melton (R) | 19,850 | 42.1 |
| 9 | Clarence Cannon (D) | 25,796 | 62.4 |
| | Frank H. Hollmann (R) | 15,472 | 37.5 |
| 10 | Henry F. Niedringhaus (R) | 93,433 | 99.8 |
| 11 | John J. Cochran (D) | 17,726 | 99.9 |
| 12 | Leonidas C. Dyer (R) | 14,195 | 99.8 |
| 13 | Clyde Williams (D) | 27,563 | 53.1 |
| | Charles E. Kiefner (R) | 24,378 | 46.9 |
| 14 | James F. Fulbright (D) | 45,332 | 51.6 |
| | Dewey Short (R) | 42,579 | 48.4 |

## MISSOURI

| | Candidates | Votes | % |
|---|---|---|---|
| 15 | Joe J. Manlove (R) | 37,788 | 57.8 |
| | Frank H. Lee (D) | 27,387 | 41.9 |
| 16 | William E. Barton (D) | 25,392 | 52.4 |
| | Rowland L. Johnston (R) | 23,025 | 47.6 |

## MONTANA

| | | Votes | % |
|---|---|---|---|
| 1 | John M. Evans (D) | 39,166 | 56.1 |
| | Mark D. Fitzgarrald (R) | 29,793 | 42.7 |
| 2 | Scott Leavitt (R) | 52,943 | 52.8 |
| | Tom Stout (D) | 45,438 | 45.3 |

## NEBRASKA

| | | Votes | % |
|---|---|---|---|
| 1 | John H. Morehead (D) | 34,662 | 63.9 |
| | Ralph S. Moseley (R) | 19,589 | 36.1 |
| 2 | Malcolm Baldridge (R) | 34,114 | 50.6 |
| | Edward R. Burke (D) | 33,276 | 49.4 |
| 3 | Edgar Howard (D) | 53,221 | 69.3 |
| | H. Halderson (R) | 23,599 | 30.7 |
| 4 | John N. Norton (D) | 35,812 | 56.0 |
| | Charles H. Sloan (R) | 28,196 | 44.1 |
| 5 | Ashton C. Shallenberger (D) | 34,915 | 55.6 |
| | Fred G. Johnson (R) | 27,932 | 44.4 |
| 6 | Robert G. Simmons (R) | 65,766 | 72.8 |
| | John McCoy (D) | 24,519 | 27.2 |

## NEVADA

| | | Votes | % |
|---|---|---|---|
| AL | Samuel S. Arentz (R) | 18,279 | 54.4 |
| | Maurice J. Sullivan (D) | 15,343 | 45.6 |

## NEW HAMPSHIRE

| | | Votes | % |
|---|---|---|---|
| 1 | Fletcher Hale (R) | 37,570 | 56.3 |
| | Napoleon J. Dyer (D) | 29,166 | 43.7 |
| 2 | Edward H. Wason (R) | 34,253 | 59.7 |
| | Eaton D. Sargent (D) | 23,157 | 40.3 |

## NEW JERSEY

| | | Votes | % |
|---|---|---|---|
| 1 | Charles A. Wolverton (R) | 78,019 | 79.1 |
| | Francis G. Homan (D) | 19,486 | 19.8 |
| 2 | Isaac Bacharach (R) | 67,729 | 79.7 |
| | Hans Froehlicher Jr. (D) | 17,125 | 20.1 |
| 3 | William H. Sutphin (D) | 57,911 | 51.1 |
| | Thomas M. Gopsill (R) | 54,889 | 48.5 |
| 4 | Charles A. Eaton (R) | 39,019 | 57.6 |
| | Charles Browne (D) | 28,330 | 41.9 |
| 5 | Ernest R. Ackerman (R) | 65,178 | 65.3 |
| | Warren N. Gaffney (D) | 33,851 | 33.9 |
| 6 | Randolph Perkins (R) | 72,868 | 56.5 |
| | Archibald C. Hart (D) | 55,283 | 42.8 |
| 7 | George N. Seger (R) | 35,636 | 53.7 |
| | Harry Joelson (D) | 29,879 | 45.0 |
| 8 | Fred A. Hartley Jr. (R) | 44,038 | 50.4 |
| | Paul J. Moore (D) | 43,195 | 49.4 |
| 9 | Peter A. Cavicchia (R) | 24,312 | 53.8 |
| | Daniel F. Minahan (D) | 20,497 | 45.4 |
| 10 | Frederick R. Lehlbach (R) | 44,435 | 66.6 |
| | Edward W. Simms (D) | 21,539 | 32.3 |
| 11 | Oscar L. Auf der Heide (D) | 44,691 | 73.0 |
| | Irving W. Taft (R) | 16,087 | 26.3 |
| 12 | Mary T. Norton (D) | 53,565 | 75.9 |
| | Douglas D. T. Story (R) | 16,715 | 23.7 |

## NEW MEXICO

| | | Votes | % |
|---|---|---|---|
| AL | Dennis Chavez (D) | 65,228 | 57.5 |
| | Albert G. Simms (R) | 47,955 | 42.3 |

## NEW YORK

| | Candidates | Votes | % |
|---|---|---|---|
| 1 | Robert L. Bacon (R) | 96,390 | 58.4 |
| | James S. Shevlin (D) | 64,172 | 38.9 |
| 2 | William F. Brunner (D) | 110,081 | 67.5 |
| | James C. MacDevitt (R) | 45,651 | 28.0 |
| 3 | George W. Lindsay (D) | 20,525 | 75.1 |
| | James A. Campbell (R) | 5,159 | 18.9 |
| | Joseph A. Weil (SOC) | 1,443 | 5.3 |
| 4 | Thomas H. Cullen (D) | 25,935 | 79.8 |
| | Charles A. Walter (R) | 5,713 | 17.6 |
| 5 | Loring M. Black Jr. (D) | 35,580 | 63.4 |
| | Henry C. Reiners (R) | 18,150 | 32.3 |
| 6 | Andrew L. Somers (D) | 46,681 | 47.0 |
| | Joseph G. Myerson (R) | 29,862 | 30.1 |
| | Norman Thomas (SOC) | 21,938 | 22.1 |
| 7 | John F. Quayle (D) | 22,387* | 65.0 |
| | Louis F. Arnold Jr. (R) | 8,884 | 25.8 |
| | Benjamin Jackson (SOC) | 2,749 | 8.0 |
| 8 | Patrick J. Carley (D) | 80,119 | 57.2 |
| | Benjamin Ammerman (R) | 36,421 | 26.0 |
| | Baruch C. Vladeck (SOC) | 23,662 | 16.9 |
| 9 | David J. O'Connell (D) | 48,065* | 58.9 |
| | William Koch (R) | 27,698 | 34.0 |
| | Wilhelmus B. Robinson (SOC) | 5,783 | 7.1 |
| 10 | Emanuel Celler (D) | 23,711 | 58.0 |
| | George J. Beldock (R) | 11,532 | 28.2 |
| | Abraham I. Shiplacoff (SOC) | 5,050 | 12.4 |
| 11 | Anning S. Prall (D) | 37,148 | 71.1 |
| | Wilbur F. Wakeman (R) | 13,856 | 26.5 |
| 12 | Samuel Dickstein (D) | 14,327 | 79.1 |
| | Gustave J. Landau (R) | 2,663 | 14.7 |
| | Marx Lewis (SOC) | 941 | 5.2 |
| 13 | Christopher D. Sullivan (D) | 13,034 | 76.6 |
| | Michael R. Matteo (R) | 3,192 | 18.8 |
| 14 | William I. Sirovich (D) | 12,431 | 47.3 |
| | Jacob Panken (SOC) | 6,793 | 25.9 |
| | Edward E. Spafford (R) | 6,658 | 25.4 |
| 15 | John J. Boylan (D) | 21,758 | 81.3 |
| | Alexander Todd (R) | 4,377 | 16.4 |
| 16 | John J. O'Connor (D) | 20,707 | 72.1 |
| | Irwin Ira Rackoff (R) | 7,081 | 24.7 |
| 17 | Ruth Baker Pratt (R) | 19,913 | 43.3 |
| | Louis B. Brodsky (D) | 19,218 | 41.8 |
| | Heywood Broun (SOC) | 6,841 | 14.9 |
| 18 | Martin J. Kennedy (D) | 22,131 | 77.0 |
| | Patrick S. Hickey (R) | 5,288 | 18.4 |
| 19 | Sol Bloom (D) | 35,322 | 66.9 |
| | Julius D. Tobias (R) | 14,919 | 28.3 |
| 20 | Fiorello H. LaGuardia (R) | 10,606 | 52.1 |
| | Vincent H. Auleta (D) | 8,709 | 42.8 |
| 21 | Joseph A. Gavagan (D) | 42,468 | 60.2 |
| | Mortimer Kraus (R) | 24,202 | 34.3 |
| | Frank R. Crosswaith (SOC) | 3,699 | 5.2 |
| 22 | Anthony J. Griffin (D) | 25,198 | 73.9 |
| | William E. Devlin (R) | 7,060 | 20.7 |
| | Andrew A. MacLean (SOC) | 1,832 | 5.4 |
| 23 | Frank Oliver (D) | 93,426 | 67.1 |
| | George M. Fayles (R) | 27,456 | 19.7 |
| | Samuel Orr (SOC) | 16,539 | 11.9 |
| 24 | James M. Fitzpatrick (D) | 79,917 | 57.0 |
| | Benjamin L. Fairchild (R) | 48,154 | 34.3 |
| | Louis Weil (SOC) | 12,224 | 8.7 |
| 25 | Charles D. Millard (R) | 51,332 | 50.3 |
| | Thomas George Barnes (D) | 34,940 | 34.2 |
| | John M. Holzworth (REPEAL L) | 14,086 | 13.8 |
| 26 | Hamilton Fish Jr. (R) | 46,082 | 61.1 |
| | John K. Sague (D) | 26,545 | 35.2 |
| 27 | Harcourt J. Pratt (R) | 41,423 | 52.9 |
| | Guernsey T. Cross (D) | 35,574 | 45.4 |
| 28 | Parker Corning (D) | 74,386 | 63.5 |
| | Laura B. Treadwell (R) | 40,628 | 34.7 |
| 29 | James S. Parker (R) | 51,341 | 58.5 |
| | Theodore A. Knapp (D) | 35,316 | 40.2 |
| 30 | Frank Crowther (R) | 36,190 | 52.1 |
| | Izetta Jewel Miller (D) | 31,567 | 45.4 |
| 31 | Bertrand H. Snell (R) | 36,308 | 61.8 |
| | Rufus A. Prescott (D) | 21,811 | 37.1 |

## NEW YORK (continued)

| | Candidates | Votes | % |
|---|---|---|---|
| 32 | Francis D. Culkin (R) | 43,625 | 66.6 |
| | Walter W. Wilcox (D) | 20,905 | 31.9 |
| 33 | Frederick M. Davenport (R) | 39,810 | 50.3 |
| | James J. Loftis (D&SOC) | 39,340 | 49.7 |
| 34 | John D. Clarke (R) | 51,460 | 68.2 |
| | James F. Byrne (D) | 23,968 | 31.8 |
| 35 | Clarence E. Hancock (R) | 63,955 | 57.6 |
| | Frederick B. Northrup (D) | 44,336 | 40.0 |
| 36 | John Taber (R) | 43,132 | 63.3 |
| | Joseph P. Craugh (D) | 23,763 | 34.9 |
| 37 | Gale H. Stalker (R) | 44,374 | 59.4 |
| | Julian P. Bretz (D) | 28,723 | 38.4 |
| 38 | James L. Whitley (R) | 50,083 | 55.3 |
| | Nelson E. Spencer (D) | 37,500 | 41.4 |
| 39 | Archie D. Sanders (R) | 40,069 | 55.8 |
| | James M. Dwyer (D) | 29,610 | 41.2 |
| 40 | Walter Gresham Andrews (R) | 61,333 | 63.1 |
| | Roland Crangle (D) | 27,268 | 28.0 |
| | Frank C. Perkins (I CIT AL) | 5,126 | 5.3 |
| 41 | Edmund F. Cooke (R) | 26,995 | 48.9 |
| | Henry F. Jerge (D) | 25,861 | 46.9 |
| 42 | James M. Mead (D) | 33,195 | 65.6 |
| | Frank A. Dorn (R) | 16,072 | 31.8 |
| 43 | Daniel A. Reed (R) | 38,913 | 70.6 |
| | Mattie C. Dellone (D) | 14,755 | 26.8 |

**Special Election**

| | | Votes | % |
|---|---|---|---|
| 18 | Martin J. Kennedy (D) | 8,716 | 80.5 |
| | Bernard Katzen (R) | 1,898 | 17.5 |

## NORTH CAROLINA

| | | Votes | % |
|---|---|---|---|
| 1 | Lindsay C. Warren (D) | 17,985 | 100.0 |
| 2 | John H. Kerr (D) | 15,987 | 93.4 |
| | E. Dana Dickens (R) | 1,124 | 6.6 |
| 3 | Charles L. Abernethy (D) | 20,197 | 66.4 |
| | W. G. Mebane (R) | 10,215 | 33.6 |
| 4 | Edward W. Pou (D) | 25,724 | 73.4 |
| | John C. Matthews (R) | 9,339 | 26.6 |
| 5 | Franklin W. Hancock Jr. (D) | 54,277 | 61.3 |
| | John F. Reynolds (R) | 34,259 | 38.7 |
| 6 | J. Bayard Clark (D) | 20,786 | 71.4 |
| | C. Ed Taylor (R) | 8,348 | 28.7 |
| 7 | J. Walter Lambeth (D) | 38,229 | 59.0 |
| | Colin G. Spencer (R) | 26,583 | 41.0 |
| 8 | Robert L. Doughton (D) | 44,068 | 60.1 |
| | E. F. Wakefield (R) | 29,307 | 39.9 |
| 9 | Alfred L. Bulwinkle (D) | 44,699 | 54.1 |
| | Charles A. Jonas (R) | 37,911 | 45.9 |
| 10 | Zebulon Weaver (D) | 52,964 | 56.2 |
| | Brownlow Jackson (R) | 41,224 | 43.8 |

## NORTH DAKOTA

| | | Votes | % |
|---|---|---|---|
| 1 | Olger B. Burtness (R) | 42,598 | 75.0 |
| | J. E. Garvey (D) | 14,208 | 25.0 |
| 2 | Thomas Hall (R) | 33,863 | 55.6 |
| | P. W. Lanier (D) | 25,780 | 42.3 |
| 3 | James H. Sinclair (R) | 50,917 | 77.8 |
| | R. H. Leavitt (D) | 12,296 | 18.8 |

## OHIO

| | | Votes | % |
|---|---|---|---|
| 1 | Nicholas Longworth (R) | 50,481 | 51.8 |
| | John W. Pattison (D) | 46,974 | 48.2 |
| 2 | William E. Hess (R) | 46,347 | 50.3 |
| | Charles Sawyer (D) | 45,761 | 49.7 |
| 3 | Byron B. Harlan (D) | 62,107 | 50.8 |
| | Roy G. Fitzgerald (R) | 60,249 | 49.2 |
| 4 | John L. Cable (R) | 43,104 | 53.4 |
| | Gainor Jennings (D) | 37,673 | 46.6 |
| 5 | Frank C. Kniffin (D) | 29,117 | 51.4 |
| | Charles J. Thompson (R) | 27,497 | 48.6 |

## OHIO

| | Candidates | Votes | % |
|---|---|---|---|
| 6 | James G. Polk (D) | 37,158 | 52.7 |
| | Charles C. Kearns (R) | 33,300 | 47.3 |
| 7 | Charles Brand (R) | 50,595 | 56.4 |
| | John L. Zimmerman Jr. (D) | 39,142 | 43.6 |
| 8 | Grant E. Mouser Jr. (R) | 35,663 | 51.3 |
| | Carl W. Smith (D) | 33,906 | 48.7 |
| 9 | Wilbur M. White (R) | 49,498 | 57.6 |
| | Scott Stahl (D) | 36,375 | 42.4 |
| 10 | Thomas A. Jenkins (R) | 31,836 | 62.4 |
| | H. L. Crary (D) | 19,157 | 37.6 |
| 11 | Mell G. Underwood (D) | 37,887 | 64.0 |
| | Ned Thacher (R) | 21,339 | 36.0 |
| 12 | Arthur P. Lamneck (D) | 59,330 | 57.5 |
| | John C. Speaks (R) | 43,840 | 42.5 |
| 13 | William L. Fiesinger (D) | 38,067 | 52.0 |
| | Joe E. Baird (R) | 35,199 | 48.0 |
| 14 | Francis Seiberling (R) | 61,628 | 50.3 |
| | Dow W. Harter (D) | 60,951 | 49.7 |
| 15 | C. Ellis Moore (R) | 35,611 | 51.2 |
| | H. R. McClintock (D) | 33,968 | 48.8 |
| 16 | C. B. McClintock (R) | 51,113 | 52.0 |
| | William R. Thom (D) | 47,237 | 48.0 |
| 17 | Charles West (D) | 45,633 | 51.4 |
| | William M. Morgan (R) | 43,197 | 48.6 |
| 18 | B. Frank Murphy (R) | 47,096 | 60.5 |
| | Emerson Campbell (D) | 30,815 | 39.6 |
| 19 | John G. Cooper (R) | 53,966 | 56.9 |
| | W. B. Kilpatrick (D) | 40,960 | 43.2 |
| 20 | Charles A. Mooney (D) | 42,123 | 75.3 |
| | Max D. Gustin (R) | 13,824 | 24.7 |
| 21 | Robert Crosser (D) | 30,722 | 51.3 |
| | George H. Bender (R) | 29,081 | 48.6 |
| 22 | Chester C. Bolton (R) | 91,222 | 56.9 |
| | Edw. F. Carran (D) | 55,868 | 34.8 |
| | Helen Green (I) | 13,372 | 8.3 |

## OKLAHOMA

| | Candidates | Votes | % |
|---|---|---|---|
| 1 | Wesley E. Disney (D) | 41,902 | 50.2 |
| | Charles O'Connor (R) | 41,642 | 49.8 |
| 2 | William W. Hastings (D) | 31,093 | 61.5 |
| | E. L. Kirby (R) | 19,464 | 38.5 |
| 3 | Wilburn Cartwright (D) | 39,943 | 80.4 |
| | Palestine Brice (R) | 9,721 | 19.6 |
| 4 | Thomas D. McKeown (D) | 42,885 | 69.7 |
| | M. L. Matson (R) | 18,616 | 30.3 |
| 5 | Fletcher B. Swank (D) | 38,215 | 58.7 |
| | U. S. Stone (R) | 26,943 | 41.4 |
| 6 | Jed Johnson (D) | 35,969 | 71.7 |
| | Ann W. Dillard (R) | 14,233 | 28.4 |
| 7 | James V. McClintic (D) | 29,829 | 78.2 |
| | R. C. Holt (R) | 8,298 | 21.8 |
| 8 | Milton C. Garber (R) | 35,027 | 60.4 |
| | H. B. King (D) | 22,784 | 39.3 |

## OREGON

| | Candidates | Votes | % |
|---|---|---|---|
| 1 | Willis C. Hawley (R) | 55,855 | 55.5 |
| | William A. Delzell (D) | 44,810 | 44.5 |
| 2 | Robert R. Butler (R) | 25,304 | 66.0 |
| | Robert E. Bradford (D) | 13,061 | 34.0 |
| 3 | Charles H. Martin (D) | 49,316 | 55.1 |
| | F. F. Korell (R) | 35,483 | 39.7 |
| | Peter Streiff Jr. (I SOC) | 4,690 | 5.2 |

## PENNSYLVANIA

| | Candidates | Votes | % |
|---|---|---|---|
| 1 | James M. Beck (R) | 57,382 | 78.9 |
| | John P. Mulrenan (D) | 14,918 | 20.5 |
| 2 | George S. Graham (R) | 34,387 | 84.6 |
| | Charles S. Hill (D) | 6,084 | 15.0 |
| 3 | Harry C. Ransley (R) | 38,346 | 84.4 |
| | Edward P. Carroll (D) | 6,921 | 15.2 |
| 4 | Benjamin M. Golder (R) | 41,549 | 78.0 |
| | Thomas J. Carroll (D) | 11,084 | 20.8 |
| 5 | James J. Connolly (R) | 57,501 | 76.6 |
| | Frank W. Dougherty (D) | 17,182 | 22.9 |
| 6 | George A. Welsh (R) | 66,799 | 76.1 |
| | John P. Boylan (D) | 21,004 | 23.9 |
| 7 | George P. Darrow (R) | 61,573 | 77.5 |
| | Robert V. Bolger (D) | 17,860 | 22.5 |
| 8 | James Wolfenden (R) | 84,521 | 80.5 |
| | Harry D. Wescott (D) | 20,443 | 19.5 |
| 9 | Henry W. Watson (R) | 63,286 | 73.0 |
| | John F. Headly (D) | 23,375 | 27.0 |
| 10 | J. Roland Kinzer (R) | 32,455 | 77.3 |
| | William A. Brinkman (D) | 9,547 | 22.7 |
| 11 | Patrick J. Boland (D, R) | 62,994 | 100.0 |
| 12 | C. Murray Turpin (R) | 53,336 | 57.8 |
| | John T. Kmetz (D, LAB) | 38,938 | 42.2 |
| 13 | George Franklin Brumm (R, D) | 47,344 | 92.3 |
| | William Wilhelm (U) | 3,968 | 7.7 |
| 14 | Norton L. Lichtenwalner (D) | 44,546 | 52.4 |
| | Robert Grey Bushong (R) | 29,164 | 34.3 |
| | Andrew P. Bower (SOC) | 11,309 | 13.3 |
| 15 | Louis T. McFadden (R, P) | 29,150 | 72.6 |
| | Frank J. Price (D) | 10,998 | 27.4 |
| 16 | Robert F. Rich (R) | 32,964 | 75.5 |
| | J. Drew Fague (D) | 10,719 | 24.5 |
| 17 | Frederick W. Magrady (R) | 31,247 | 60.5 |
| | Samuel M. Shipman (D, L) | 20,413 | 39.5 |
| 18 | Edward M. Beers (R) | 39,116 | 68.0 |
| | T. Z. Minehart (D) | 18,389 | 32.0 |
| 19 | Isaac H. Doutrich (R) | 64,345 | 79.4 |
| | Harold V. McNair (D) | 16,685 | 20.6 |
| 20 | J. Russell Leech (R, P) | 20,361 | 54.9 |
| | George E. Wolfe (D, LAB) | 16,740 | 45.1 |
| 21 | J. Banks Kurtz (R) | 25,619 | 71.8 |
| | Bernard J. Clark (D) | 10,045 | 28.2 |
| 22 | Harry L. Haines (D) | 27,943 | 54.4 |
| | Franklin Menges (R) | 22,716 | 44.2 |
| 23 | J. Mitchell Chase (R) | 28,916 | 70.8 |
| | Maxwell J. Moore (D) | 11,954 | 29.3 |
| 24 | Samuel A. Kendall (R) | 28,279 | 67.6 |
| | Milton M. Brooke (D) | 13,581 | 32.4 |
| 25 | Henry W. Temple (R, LAB) | 27,561 | 69.8 |
| | James S. Pates (D) | 11,910 | 30.2 |
| 26 | J. Howard Swick (R, D) | 50,858 | 100.0 |
| 27 | Nathan L. Strong (R) | 42,569 | 79.2 |
| | D. R. Tomb (D) | 11,200 | 20.8 |
| 28 | Thomas C. Cochran (R) | 36,367 | 70.9 |
| | Guy Thorne (D) | 14,953 | 29.1 |
| 29 | Milton W. Shreve (R) | 24,511 | 54.5 |
| | Charles N. Crosby (D) | 20,470 | 45.5 |
| 30 | William R. Coyle (R) | 28,503 | 50.8 |
| | Everett Kent (D) | 27,621 | 49.2 |
| 31 | Adam M. Wyant (R, P) | 38,999 | 70.5 |
| | James M. Cramer (D) | 15,022 | 27.2 |
| 32 | Edmund F. Erk (R) | 36,355 | 82.6 |
| | Edward S. Michalowski (D) | 7,294 | 16.6 |
| 33 | M. Clyde Kelly (R, D) | 47,187 | 96.4 |
| 34 | Patrick J. Sullivan (R, D) | 29,074 | 97.6 |
| 35 | Harry A. Estep (R) | 31,172 | 81.6 |
| | John Murphy (D) | 7,005 | 18.3 |
| 36 | Guy E. Campbell (R, D) | 46,172 | 99.9 |

**Special Elections**

| | | Votes | % |
|---|---|---|---|
| 16 | Robert F. Rich (R) | 32,393 | 99.5 |
| 32 | Edmund F. Erk (R) | 35,176 | 99.9 |

## RHODE ISLAND

| | Candidates | Votes | % |
|---|---|---|---|
| 1 | Clark Burdick (R) | 39,712 | 57.5 |
| | Samuel W. Smith Jr. (D) | 29,341 | 42.5 |
| 2 | Richard S. Aldrich (R) | 40,037 | 54.7 |
| | Arthur L. Conaty (D) | 33,164 | 45.3 |
| 3 | Francis B. Condon (D) | 43,463 | 56.4 |
| | William R. Fortin (R) | 33,605 | 43.6 |

**Special Election**

| | | Votes | % |
|---|---|---|---|
| 3 | Francis Condon (D) | 43,429 | 56.5 |
| | William R. Fortin (R) | 33,387 | 43.5 |

## SOUTH CAROLINA

| | Candidates | Votes | % |
|---|---|---|---|
| 1 | Thomas S. McMillan (D) | 2,536 | 100.0 |
| 2 | Butler B. Hare (D) | 2,149 | 100.0 |
| 3 | Fred H. Dominick (D) | 2,221 | 100.0 |
| 4 | John J. McSwain (D) | 3,685 | 100.0 |
| 5 | William F. Stevenson (D) | 2,319 | 100.0 |
| 6 | Allard H. Gasque (D) | 1,881 | 100.0 |
| 7 | Hampton P. Fulmer (D) | 1,372 | 100.0 |

## SOUTH DAKOTA

| | Candidates | Votes | % |
|---|---|---|---|
| 1 | Charles A. Christopherson (R) | 41,151 | 84.7 |
| | Henry Borman (I) | 7,451 | 15.3 |
| 2 | Royal C. Johnson (R) | 38,195 | 52.4 |
| | Fred H. Hildebrandt (D) | 34,245 | 47.0 |
| 3 | William Williamson (R) | 27,083 | 55.8 |
| | Theodore B. Werner (D) | 21,473 | 44.2 |

## TENNESSEE

| | Candidates | Votes | % |
|---|---|---|---|
| 1 | Oscar B. Lovette (IR) | 20,893 | 53.4 |
| | B. Carroll Reece (R) | 18,241 | 46.6 |
| 2 | J. Will Taylor (R) | 17,831 | 55.5 |
| | E. E. Patton (IR) | 13,355 | 41.6 |
| 3 | Sam D. McReynolds (D) | 21,401 | 100.0 |
| 4 | John R. Mitchell (D) | 15,269 | 100.0 |
| 5 | Ewin L. Davis (D) | 11,792 | 92.0 |
| | George Motlow (R) | 1,032 | 8.1 |
| 6 | Joseph W. Byrns (D) | 13,879 | 93.3 |
| | E. L. Bradbury (I) | 990 | 6.7 |
| 7 | Edward E. Eslick (D) | 13,927 | 100.0 |
| 8 | Gordon Browning (D) | 14,024 | 100.0 |
| 9 | Jere Cooper (D) | 17,979 | 100.0 |
| 10 | Edward H. Crump (D) | 23,746 | 93.7 |

## TEXAS

| | Candidates | Votes | % |
|---|---|---|---|
| 1 | Wright Patman (D) | 9,160 | 94.7 |
| | Thomas A. Clark (R) | 515 | 5.3 |
| 2 | Martin Dies (D) | 14,236 | 100.0 |
| 3 | Morgan G. Sanders (D) | 8,162 | 100.0 |
| 4 | Sam Rayburn (D) | 9,385 | 88.8 |
| | Floyd Harry (R) | 1,189 | 11.2 |
| 5 | Hatton W. Sumners (D) | 9,924 | 88.1 |
| | Clinton S. Bailey (R) | 1,344 | 11.9 |
| 6 | Luther A. Johnson (D) | 12,396 | 100.0 |
| 7 | Clay Stone Briggs (D) | 9,357 | 100.0 |
| 8 | Daniel E. Garrett (D) | 12,877 | 100.0 |
| 9 | Joseph J. Mansfield (D) | 14,855 | 86.9 |
| | George Seydler Sr. (R) | 2,239 | 13.1 |
| 10 | James P. Buchanan (D) | 12,780 | 100.0 |
| 11 | Oliver H. Cross (D) | 10,381 | 100.0 |
| 12 | Fritz G. Lanham (D) | 9,846 | 100.0 |
| 13 | Guinn Williams (D) | 12,840 | 91.1 |
| | W. C. Witcher (R) | 1,257 | 8.9 |
| 14 | Harry M. Wurzbach (R) | 27,206 | 59.3 |
| | Henry B. Dielmann (D) | 18,707 | 40.7 |
| 15 | John N. Garner (D) | 20,733 | 77.5 |
| | Carlos G. Watson (R) | 6,016 | 22.5 |
| 16 | R. Ewing Thomason (D) | 18,915 | 84.1 |
| | Mitchell Waldrop (R) | 3,581 | 15.9 |
| 17 | Thomas L. Blanton (D) | 17,199 | 100.0 |
| 18 | Marvin Jones (D) | 26,697 | 93.3 |
| | S. E. Fish (R) | 1,934 | 6.8 |

**Special Election**

| | | Votes | % |
|---|---|---|---|
| 17 | Thomas L. Blanton (D) | 10,225 | 56.1 |
| | Mrs. R. Q. Lee | 8,012 | 43.9 |

## UTAH

| | Candidates | Votes | % |
|---|---|---|---|
| 1 | Don B. Colton (R) | 45,875 | 60.8 |
| | Joseph Ririe (D) | 29,210 | 38.7 |
| 2 | Frederick C. Loofbourow (R) | 35,106 | 44.3 |
| | Joshua H. Paul (D) | 33,618 | 42.4 |
| | George N. Lawrence (LIB) | 10,303 | 13.0 |

## UTAH

### Special Election

| | | | |
|---|---|---|---|
| 2 | Frederick C. Loofbourow (R) | 35,349 | *44.1* |
| | Joshua H. Paul (D) | 33,915 | *42.3* |
| | George N. Lawrence (LIB) | 10,591 | *13.2* |

## VERMONT

| | | | |
|---|---|---|---|
| 1 | John E. Weeks (R) | 25,170 | *58.0* |
| | Joseph A. McNamara (D) | 18,205 | *42.0* |
| 2 | Ernest W. Gibson (R) | 23,904 | *81.2* |
| | James Cosgrove (D) | 5,536 | *18.8* |

## VIRGINIA

| | | | |
|---|---|---|---|
| 1 | Schuyler Otis Bland (D) | 7,324 | *91.0* |
| | W. A. Rowe | 705 | *8.8* |
| 2 | Menalcus Lankford (R) | 14,678 | *54.4* |
| | Joseph T. Deal (D) | 12,297 | *45.6* |
| 3 | Andrew Jackson Montague (D) | 6,134 | *87.4* |
| | R. Houston Brett (IR) | 853 | *12.2* |
| 4 | Patrick Henry Drewry (D) | 4,296 | *99.9* |
| 5 | Thomas G. Burch (D) | 7,095 | *99.9* |
| 6 | Clifton A. Woodrum (D) | 5,979 | *99.7* |
| 7 | John W. Fishburne (D) | 13,951 | *58.4* |
| | Jacob A. Garber (R) | 9,934 | *41.6* |
| 8 | Howard W. Smith (D) | 11,201 | *79.3* |
| | F. M. Brooks (R) | 2,742 | *19.4* |
| 9 | John W. Flannagan Jr. (D) | 32,802 | *55.6* |
| | Joseph C. Shaffer (R) | 26,244 | *44.5* |

| Candidates | | Votes | % |
|---|---|---|---|
| 10 | Henry St.George Tucker (D) | 7,229 | *85.9* |
| | Carney Kelly Rosser (IR) | 620 | *7.4* |
| | M. J. Putman (R) | 563 | *6.7* |

## WASHINGTON

| | | | |
|---|---|---|---|
| 1 | Ralph A. Horr (R) | 43,998 | *55.8* |
| | Charles G. Heifner (D) | 32,365 | *41.0* |
| 2 | Lindley H. Hadley (R) | 47,679 | *89.7* |
| | William M. Bouck (F-LAB) | 3,428 | *6.5* |
| 3 | Albert Johnson (R) | 63,451 | *100.0* |
| 4 | John W. Summers (R) | 35,917 | *100.0* |
| 5 | Sam B. Hill (D) | 43,059 | *74.3* |
| | T. W. Symons Jr. (R) | 14,892 | *25.7* |

## WEST VIRGINIA

| | | | |
|---|---|---|---|
| 1 | Carl G. Bachmann (R) | 43,919 | *56.1* |
| | Robert L. Ramsey (D) | 34,368 | *43.9* |
| 2 | Frank L. Bowman (R) | 36,079 | *50.8* |
| | Jennings Randolph (D) | 34,968 | *49.2* |
| 3 | Lynn S. Hornor (D) | 37,970 | *51.4* |
| | John M. Wolverton (R) | 35,853 | *48.6* |
| 4 | Robert L. Hogg (R) | 43,152 | *50.3* |
| | Mary M. Johnson (D) | 42,677 | *49.7* |
| 5 | Hugh Ike Shott (R) | 44,978 | *52.2* |
| | T. J. Lilly (D) | 41,162 | *47.8* |
| 6 | Joe L. Smith (D) | 80,648 | *56.6* |
| | Fred O. Blue (R) | 61,876 | *43.4* |

### Special

| | | | |
|---|---|---|---|
| 4 | Robert L. Hogg (R) | 41,455 | *53.8* |
| | Mary M. Johnson (D) | 35,649 | *46.2* |

## WISCONSIN

| Candidates | | Votes | % |
|---|---|---|---|
| 1 | Henry Allen Cooper (R) | 46,272* | *95.7* |
| 2 | Charles A. Kading (R) | 37,071 | *71.5* |
| | A. A. Nowak (D) | 14,780 | *28.5* |
| 3 | John M. Nelson (R) | 43,184 | *95.1* |
| 4 | John C. Schafer (R) | 26,763 | *46.6* |
| | William F. Quick Sr. (SOC) | 20,789 | *36.2* |
| | William J. Kershaw (D) | 8,871 | *15.5* |
| 5 | William H. Stafford (R) | 27,533 | *42.2* |
| | James P. Sheehan (SOC) | 26,357# | *40.4* |
| | Thomas O'Malley (D) | 10,947 | *16.8* |
| 6 | Michael K. Reilly (D) | 25,605 | *50.2* |
| | Philip Lehner (R) | 24,986 | *49.0* |
| 7 | Gardner R. Withrow (R) | 31,530 | *82.3* |
| | Merlin Hull | 5,606 | *14.6* |
| 8 | Gerald J. Boileau (R) | 30,045 | *79.1* |
| | William F. Collins (D) | 7,927 | *20.9* |
| 9 | George J. Schneider (R) | 43,080 | *100.0* |
| 10 | James A. Frear (R) | 36,804 | *97.5* |
| 11 | Hubert H. Peavey (R) | 43,004 | *100.0* |

### Special Election

| | | | |
|---|---|---|---|
| 6 | Michael K. Reilly (D) | 25,400 | *50.6* |
| | Philip Lehner (R) | 24,825 | *49.4* |

## WYOMING

| | | | |
|---|---|---|---|
| AL | Vincent M. Carter (R) | 44,890 | *65.6* |
| | John P. Rusk (D) | 23,519 | *34.4* |

# 1931 House Elections

## LOUISIANA

### Special Elections

| | | | |
|---|---|---|---|
| 8 | John H. Overton (D) | 4,674 | *99.9* |

## NEW YORK[1]

### Special Elections

| | | | |
|---|---|---|---|
| 7 | Matthew V. O'Malley (D) | 9,969 | *70.0* |
| | Leonard Greenstone (R) | 4,014 | *28.2* |
| 7 | John J. Delaney (D) | 24,587 | *69.3* |
| | William L. Padgett (R) | 7,840 | *22.1* |
| | Abraham Zucker (SOC) | 2,724 | *7.7* |

| | | | |
|---|---|---|---|
| 9 | Stephen A. Rudd (D) | 15,342 | *71.5* |
| | William Koch (R) | 5,605 | *26.1* |

## TEXAS

### Special Election

| | | | |
|---|---|---|---|
| 14 | Richard M. Kleberg (D) | 19,038 | *46.9* |
| | C. W. Johnson | 13,945 | *34.4* |
| | C. W. Anderson | 5,759 | *14.2* |

## WISCONSIN

### Special Election

| | | | |
|---|---|---|---|
| 1 | Thomas R. Amlie (R) | 14,447 | *54.4* |
| | O. J. Bouma (SOC) | 7,282 | *27.4* |
| | G. H. Herzog (ID) | 3,440 | *13.0* |

*1. Rep. John F. Quayle died Nov. 27, 1930, following his re-election to the 72nd Congress (1931-33). According to the Biographical Directory, Matthew V. O'Malley was elected Feb. 17, 1931 to fill Quayle's seat for the term beginning March 4, 1931. O'Malley died May 26, 1931. In a second special election, John J. Delaney was elected to fill the seat for the remainder of the term.*

# 1932 House Elections

## ALABAMA

| | Candidates | Votes | % |
|---|---|---|---|
| 1 | John D. McDuffie (D) | 20,675 | 100.0 |
| 2 | Lister Hill (D) | 28,250 | 95.7 |
| 3 | Henry B. Steagall (D) | 20,959 | 100.0 |
| 4 | Lamar Jeffers (D) | 20,960 | 83.9 |
| | Hogan D. Stewart (R) | 4,016 | 16.1 |
| 5 | Miles C. Allgood (D) | 24,783 | 80.2 |
| | Joe Brown (R) | 6,135 | 19.8 |
| 6 | William B. Oliver (D) | 15,296 | 100.0 |
| 7 | William B. Bankhead (D) | 21,322 | 73.5 |
| | James B. Sloan (R) | 7,699 | 26.5 |
| 8 | Edward B. Almon (D) | 23,705 | 100.0 |
| 9 | George Huddleston (D) | 31,539 | 86.2 |
| | Paul G. Parsons (R) | 3,701 | 10.1 |

## ARIZONA

| | Candidates | Votes | % |
|---|---|---|---|
| AL | Lewis W. Douglas (D) | 75,469* | 70.8 |
| | H. B. Wilkinson (R) | 29,710 | 27.9 |

## ARKANSAS

| | Candidates | Votes | % |
|---|---|---|---|
| 1 | William J. Driver (D) | 35,975 | 100.0 |
| 2 | John E. Miller (D) | 23,351 | 92.1 |
| | Ira J. Mock (R) | 1,995 | 7.9 |
| 3 | Claude A. Fuller (D) | 30,337 | 100.0 |
| 4 | William B. Cravens (D) | 30,443 | 100.0 |
| 5 | Heartsill Ragon (D) | 29,240 | 90.7 |
| | A. L. Barber (R) | 3,001 | 9.3 |
| 6 | David D. Glover (D) | 33,503 | 100.0 |
| 7 | Tilman B. Parks (D) | 30,340 | 100.0 |

## CALIFORNIA

| | Candidates | Votes | % |
|---|---|---|---|
| 1 | Clarence F. Lea (D-R) | 73,400 | 99.9 |
| 2 | Harry L. Englebright (R-D) | 43,146 | 100.0 |
| 3 | Frank H. Buck (D) | 61,694 | 56.8 |
| | Charles F. Curry (R) | 46,887 | 43.1 |
| 4 | Florence P. Kahn (R-D) | 67,425 | 85.3 |
| | Milen C. Dempster (SOC) | 11,603 | 14.7 |
| 5 | Richard J. Welch (R-D) | 67,349 | 100.0 |
| 6 | Albert E. Carter (R-D) | 75,528 | 99.9 |
| 7 | Ralph R. Eltse (R) | 45,944 | 45.5 |
| | Frank V. Cornish (D) | 32,365 | 32.0 |
| | J. Stitt Wilson (SOC) | 22,767 | 22.5 |
| 8 | John J. McGrath (D) | 65,455 | 56.9 |
| | Arthur M. Free (R) | 49,487 | 43.1 |
| 9 | Denver S. Church (D) | 50,125 | 61.6 |
| | Henry E. Barbour (R) | 31,209 | 38.4 |
| 10 | Henry E. Stubbs (D) | 50,390 | 55.3 |
| | Arthur S. Crites (R) | 40,794 | 44.7 |
| 11 | William E. Evans (R) | 57,739 | 51.8 |
| | Albert D. Hadley (D) | 38,240 | 34.3 |
| | Marshall V. Hartranft (LIB) | 15,520 | 13.9 |
| 12 | John H. Hoeppel (D) | 43,122 | 45.8 |
| | Frederick F. Houser (R) | 40,674 | 43.2 |
| | Richard M. Cannon (P) | 10,308 | 11.0 |
| 13 | Charles Kramer (D) | 65,261 | 52.6 |
| | Charles H. Randall (R) | 53,449 | 43.1 |
| 14 | Thomas F. Ford (D) | 47,368 | 57.1 |
| | William D. Campbell (R) | 35,598 | 42.9 |
| 15 | William L. Traeger (R) | 67,390 | 52.8 |
| | John M. Costello (D) | 57,518 | 45.1 |
| 16 | John F. Dockweiler (D) | 70,333 | 54.9 |
| | Clyde Woodworth (R) | 57,718 | 45.1 |
| 17 | Charles J. Colden (D) | 50,720 | 62.2 |
| | A. E. Henning (R) | 26,868 | 32.9 |
| 18 | John H. Burke (D) | 48,179 | 53.2 |
| | Robert Henderson (R) | 33,817 | 37.4 |
| | William E. Hinshaw (I) | 8,399 | 9.3 |

## Candidates (continued)

| | Candidates | Votes | % |
|---|---|---|---|
| 19 | Sam L. Collins (R) | 56,889 | 51.0 |
| | B. Z. McKinney (D) | 51,796 | 46.4 |
| 20 | George Burnham (R) | 43,757 | 50.3 |
| | Claude Chandler (D) | 43,304 | 49.7 |

## COLORADO

| | Candidates | Votes | % |
|---|---|---|---|
| 1 | Lawrence Lewis (D) | 70,826 | 54.4 |
| | William R. Eaton (R) | 56,601 | 43.5 |
| 2 | Fred Cummings (D) | 63,399 | 52.9 |
| | George H. Bradfield (R) | 56,516 | 47.1 |
| 3 | John A. Martin (D) | 59,882 | 50.9 |
| | Guy U. Hardy (R) | 57,793 | 49.1 |
| 4 | Edward T. Taylor (D) | 40,736 | 66.0 |
| | Richard C. Callen (R) | 20,993 | 34.0 |

## CONNECTICUT

| | Candidates | Votes | % |
|---|---|---|---|
| 1 | Herman P. Kopplemann (D) | 72,807 | 48.8 |
| | Clarence W. Seymour (R) | 70,920 | 47.5 |
| 2 | William L. Higgins (R) | 45,232 | 49.4 |
| | William C. Fox (D) | 45,011 | 49.2 |
| 3 | Francis T. Maloney (D) | 57,881 | 48.4 |
| | T. A. D. Jones (R) | 55,254 | 46.2 |
| 4 | Schuyler Merritt (R) | 71,670 | 49.7 |
| | William M. Tierney (D) | 64,268 | 44.5 |
| | Arnold E. Freese (SOC) | 7,237 | 5.0 |
| 5 | Edward W. Goss (R) | 42,132 | 49.3 |
| | Martin E. Gormley (D) | 42,054 | 49.2 |
| AL | Charles M. Bakewell (R) | 284,438 | 48.5 |
| | William M. Citron (D) | 282,557 | 48.2 |

## DELAWARE

| | Candidates | Votes | % |
|---|---|---|---|
| AL | Wilbur L. Adams (D) | 51,698 | 46.1 |
| | Reuben Satterthwaite Jr (R) | 48,841 | 43.6 |
| | Francis Burgette Short (P) | 10,560 | 9.4 |

## FLORIDA

| | Candidates | Votes | % |
|---|---|---|---|
| 1 | J. Hardin Peterson (D) | 61,381 | 76.4 |
| | Arthur R. Thompson (R) | 19,010 | 23.7 |
| 2 | Robert A. Green (D) | 22,213 | 100.0 |
| 3 | Millard F. Caldwell (D) | 28,208 | 100.0 |
| 4 | J. Mark Wilcox (D) | 86,101 | 99.6 |
| AL | William J. Sears (D) | 186,284 | 75.2 |
| | Glenn B. Skipper (R) | 61,300 | 24.8 |

## GEORGIA

| | Candidates | Votes | % |
|---|---|---|---|
| 1 | Homer C. Parker (D) | 24,429 | 93.4 |
| | E. K. Overstreet Jr. (R) | 1,726 | 6.6 |
| 2 | E. E. Cox (D) | 22,446 | 100.0 |
| 3 | B. T. Castellow (D) | 22,691 | 100.0 |
| 4 | Emmett M. Owen (D) | 24,783 | 99.9 |
| 5 | Robert Ramspeck (D) | 26,657 | 100.0 |
| 6 | Carl Vinson (D) | 19,615 | 99.9 |
| 7 | M. C. Tarver (D) | 24,689 | 85.2 |
| | Regina Rambo Benson (I) | 4,295 | 14.8 |
| 8 | Braswell Deen (D) | 20,021 | 95.6 |
| 9 | John S. Wood (D) | 24,673 | 80.6 |
| | J. M. Johnson (R) | 5,898 | 19.3 |
| 10 | Charles H. Brand (D) | 23,911 | 100.0 |

## IDAHO

| | Candidates | Votes | % |
|---|---|---|---|
| 1 | Compton I. White (D) | 42,784 | 54.9 |
| | Burton L. French (R) | 32,545 | 41.8 |
| 2 | Thomas C. Coffin (D) | 58,138 | 55.0 |
| | Addison T. Smith (R) | 46,293 | 43.8 |

## ILLINOIS

| | Candidates | Votes | % |
|---|---|---|---|
| 1 | Oscar De Priest (R) | 33,672 | 54.8 |
| | Harry Baker (D) | 26,959 | 43.9 |
| 2 | P. H. Moynihan (R) | 113,447 | 50.8 |
| | Victor L. Schlaeger (D) | 102,099 | 45.7 |
| 3 | Edward A. Kelly (D) | 120,093 | 55.8 |
| | Elliott W. Sproul (R) | 95,282 | 44.2 |
| 4 | Harry P. Beam (D) | 53,722 | 74.2 |
| | Casimir T. Janowski (R) | 18,659 | 25.8 |
| 5 | Adolph J. Sabath (D) | 30,747 | 70.9 |
| | Samuel S. Epstein (R) | 12,254 | 28.3 |
| 6 | Thomas J. O'Brien (D) | 164,187 | 63.2 |
| | Alfred F. Rueben (R) | 95,637 | 36.8 |
| 7 | Leonard W. Schuetz (D) | 190,446 | 58.1 |
| | M. A. Michaelson (R) | 134,801 | 41.1 |
| 8 | Leo Kocialkowski (D) | 30,147 | 72.2 |
| | Peter C. Granata (R) | 11,625 | 27.8 |
| 9 | Fred A. Britten (R) | 40,253 | 52.0 |
| | James McAndrews (D) | 36,596 | 47.3 |
| 10 | James Simpson Jr. (R) | 101,671 | 41.1 |
| | Charles H. Weber (D) | 100,449 | 40.6 |
| | Ralph E. Church (I) | 45,067 | 18.2 |
| 11 | Frank R. Reid (R) | 82,195 | 50.4 |
| | James A. Howell (D) | 80,862 | 49.6 |
| 12 | John T. Buckbee (R) | 65,122 | 53.1 |
| | Charles H. Linscott (D) | 57,578 | 46.9 |
| 13 | Leo E. Allen (R) | 44,655 | 56.1 |
| | Orestes H. Wright (D) | 34,917 | 43.9 |
| 14 | Chester Thompson (D) | 50,277 | 53.9 |
| | John C. Allen (R) | 43,082 | 46.2 |
| 15 | J. Leroy Adair (D) | 55,739 | 56.9 |
| | Burnett M. Chiperfield (R) | 42,255 | 43.1 |
| 16 | Everett M. Dirksen (R) | 67,949 | 60.3 |
| | Edwin S. Carr (D) | 44,802 | 39.7 |
| 17 | Frank Gillespie (D) | 43,198 | 53.5 |
| | Homer W. Hall (R) | 37,594 | 46.5 |
| 18 | James A. Meeks (D) | 58,483 | 56.6 |
| | William P. Holaday (R) | 44,787 | 43.4 |
| 19 | D. C. Dobbins (D) | 72,366 | 57.7 |
| | Charles Adkins (R) | 53,151 | 42.4 |
| 20 | Henry T. Rainey (D) | 48,612 | 63.8 |
| | William J. Thornton (R) | 27,540 | 36.2 |
| 21 | J. Earl Major (D) | 66,213 | 59.8 |
| | Roy M. Seeley (R) | 44,430 | 40.1 |
| 22 | Edwin M. Schaefer (D) | 88,151 | 63.8 |
| | Stewart Campbell (R) | 49,965 | 36.2 |
| 23 | William W. Arnold (D) | 64,551 | 64.3 |
| | T. Edward Austin (R) | 35,885 | 35.7 |
| 24 | Claude V. Parsons (D) | 43,107 | 58.8 |
| | Arthur A. Miles (R) | 30,175 | 41.2 |
| 25 | Kent E. Keller (D) | 64,286 | 59.6 |
| | Edward E. Denison (R) | 43,580 | 40.4 |
| AL | Martin A. Brennan (D) | 1,676,274✔ | |
| | Walter Nesbit (D) | 1,655,147✔ | |
| | Richard Yates | 1,421,221 | |
| | Julius Klein (R) | 1,406,771 | |
| | Hyman Schneid (SOC) | 38,486 | |
| | George Koop (SOC) | 36,324 | |
| | Anthony Pszczolkowski (COM) | 11,243 | |
| | Leslie Raymond Hurt (COM) | 11,019 | |
| | W. F. Alexander (SOC LAB) | 2,837 | |
| | Clifton Crawford (SOC LAB) | 2,684 | |
| | Pasquale Iovino (I) | 1,067 | |

## INDIANA

| | Candidates | Votes | % |
|---|---|---|---|
| 1 | William T. Schulte (D) | 45,473 | 50.0 |
| | Oscar A. Ahlgren (R) | 42,575 | 46.8 |
| 2 | George R. Durgan (D) | 73,357 | 54.0 |
| | William R. Wood (R) | 61,897 | 45.6 |
| 3 | Samuel B. Pettengill (D) | 67,686 | 55.1 |
| | Andrew J. Hickey (R) | 52,965 | 43.2 |

## INDIANA

| Candidates | Votes | % |
|---|---|---|
| 4 James I. Farley (D) | 73,258 | 56.1 |
| David Hogg (R) | 56,602 | 43.3 |
| 5 Glenn Griswold (D) | 70,698 | 53.5 |
| J. Raymond Schutz (R) | 59,904 | 45.3 |
| 6 Virginia E. Jenckes (D) | 74,827 | 53.6 |
| Fred S. Purnell (R) | 64,081 | 45.9 |
| 7 Arthur H. Greenwood (D) | 78,356 | 56.7 |
| George W. Henley (R) | 59,949 | 43.4 |
| 8 John W. Boehne Jr. (D) | 83,396 | 63.5 |
| French Clements (R) | 48,031 | 36.6 |
| 9 Eugene B. Crowe (D) | 76,157 | 57.5 |
| Chester A. Davis (R) | 55,868 | 42.2 |
| 10 Finly H. Gray (D) | 68,974 | 52.0 |
| Ephriam F. Bowen (R) | 63,398 | 47.8 |
| 11 William H. Larrabee (D) | 67,871 | 54.2 |
| Dale B. Spencer (R) | 57,006 | 45.5 |
| 12 Louis Ludlow (D) | 70,128 | 52.1 |
| William H. Harrison (R) | 61,241 | 45.5 |

## IOWA

| Candidates | Votes | % |
|---|---|---|
| 1 Edward C. Eicher (D) | 55,378 | 54.2 |
| W. F. Kopp (R) | 46,738 | 45.8 |
| 2 Bernhard M. Jacobsen (D) | 71,914 | 58.7 |
| Frank Elliott (R) | 50,636 | 41.3 |
| 3 Albert C. Willford (D) | 48,939 | 50.6 |
| T. J. B. Robinson (R) | 47,776 | 49.4 |
| 4 Fred Biermann (D) | 62,598 | 59.7 |
| Gilbert N. Haugen (R) | 42,217 | 40.3 |
| 5 Lloyd Thurston (R) | 51,909 | 50.1 |
| Lloyd Ellis (D) | 51,732 | 49.9 |
| 6 Cassius C. Dowell (R) | 56,962 | 56.5 |
| Charles S. Cooter (D) | 43,891 | 43.5 |
| 7 Otha D. Wearin (D) | 57,803 | 56.3 |
| Charles E. Swanson (R) | 44,925 | 43.7 |
| 8 Fred C. Gilchrist (R) | 47,834 | 53.4 |
| William T. Branagan (D) | 41,772 | 46.6 |
| 9 Guy M. Gillette (D) | 61,755 | 54.9 |
| Ed. H. Campbell (R) | 50,796 | 45.1 |

## KANSAS

| Candidates | Votes | % |
|---|---|---|
| 1 William P. Lambertson (R) | 59,241 | 57.8 |
| M. R. Howard (D) | 34,244 | 33.4 |
| George C. Hall (I) | 9,019 | 8.8 |
| 2 Ulysses S. Guyer (R) | 60,902 | 51.7 |
| B. J. Sheridan (D) | 56,805 | 48.3 |
| 3 Harold McGugin (R) | 52,881 | 52.9 |
| E. W. Patterson (D) | 44,910 | 44.9 |
| 4 William Randolph Carpenter (D) | 45,246 | 50.2 |
| Homer Hoch (R) | 44,621 | 49.5 |
| 5 William A. Ayres (D) | 65,713 | 73.9 |
| W. L. Farquharson (R) | 23,176 | 26.1 |
| 6 Kathryn E. O'Loughlin (D) | 62,818 | 55.6 |
| Charles I. Sparks (R) | 50,242 | 44.4 |
| 7 Clifford R. Hope (R) | 59,269 | 55.6 |
| Aaron Coleman (D) | 47,418 | 44.5 |

## KENTUCKY

| Candidates | Votes | % |
|---|---|---|
| AL Fred M. Vinson (D) | 575,289 ✔ | |
| John Young Brown (D) | 574,278 ✔ | |
| Brent Spence (D) | 574,035 ✔ | |
| Andrew J. May (D) | 573,966 ✔ | |
| Virgil Chapman (D) | 573,719 ✔ | |
| Glover H. Cary (D) | 573,504 ✔ | |
| William V. Gregory (D) | 573,233 ✔ | |
| Cap R. Carden (D) | 573,219 ✔ | |
| Finley Hamilton (D) | 573,061 ✔ | |
| Hillard H. Smith (R) | 391,878 | |
| Robert Blackburn (R) | 391,673 | |
| William Lewis (R) | 390,977 | |
| George P. Ellison (R) | 390,839 | |
| D. E. McClure (R) | 390,474 | |
| J. C. Speight (R) | 390,370 | |
| Hugh H. Asher (R) | 390,148 | |
| B. T. Rountree (R) | 390,141 | |

| Candidates | Votes | % |
|---|---|---|
| Frank B. Russell (R) | 389,950 | |
| J. T. Scopes (SOC) | 3,273 | |
| W. G. Haag (SOC) | 3,261 | |
| C. E. Trimble (SOC) | 3,260 | |
| E. L. Nance (SOC) | 3,256 | |
| E. C. Schulz (SOC) | 3,256 | |
| J. J. Thobe (SOC) | 3,246 | |
| J. M. Woodward (SOC) | 3,237 | |
| H. L. Harwood (SOC) | 3,236 | |
| D. S. Bennett (SOC) | 3,234 | |
| Frank Reynolds (COM) | 241 | |
| George N. Conway (COM) | 236 | |

## LOUISIANA

| Candidates | Votes | % |
|---|---|---|
| 1 Joachim O. Fernandez (D) | 48,784 | 100.0 |
| 2 Paul H. Maloney (D) | 50,327 | 100.0 |
| 3 Numa F. Montet (D) | 18,340 | 100.0 |
| 4 John N. Sandlin (D) | 26,262 | 100.0 |
| 5 Riley J. Wilson (D) | 25,853 | 100.0 |
| 6 Bolivar E. Kemp (D) | 25,238 | 100.0 |
| 7 Rene L. DeRouen (D) | 24,233 | 100.0 |
| 8 Cleveland Dear (D) | 25,644 | 100.0 |

## MAINE

| Candidates | Votes | % |
|---|---|---|
| 1 Carroll L. Beedy (R) | 41,034 | 51.0 |
| Joseph E. F. Connolly (D) | 39,381 | 49.0 |
| 2 Edward C. Moran (R) | 44,490 | 51.8 |
| John E. Nelson (R) | 40,703 | 47.4 |
| 3 John G. Utterback (D) | 34,520 | 50.1 |
| Ralph O. Brewster (R) | 34,226 | 49.6 |

## MARYLAND

| Candidates | Votes | % |
|---|---|---|
| 1 T. Alan Goldsborough (D) | 39,471 | 64.9 |
| Harry T. Phoebus (R) | 21,387 | 35.1 |
| 2 William P. Cole Jr. (D) | 87,841 | 67.3 |
| David L. Elliott (R) | 42,740 | 32.7 |
| 3 Vincent L. Palmisano (D) | 34,724 | 72.8 |
| R. Palmer Ingram (R) | 11,370 | 23.8 |
| 4 Ambrose J. Kennedy (D) | 46,463 | 66.0 |
| Claude B. Sweezey (R) | 22,231 | 31.6 |
| 5 Stephen W. Gambrill (D) | 42,329 | 70.4 |
| A. Kingsley Love (R) | 17,835 | 29.6 |
| 6 David J. Lewis (D) | 49,126 | 58.4 |
| Harold C. Smith (R) | 34,989 | 41.6 |

### Special Election

| Candidates | Votes | % |
|---|---|---|
| 4 Ambrose J. Kennedy (D) | 46,781 | 100.0 |

## MASSACHUSETTS

| Candidates | Votes | % |
|---|---|---|
| 1 Allen T. Treadway (R) | 56,767 | 54.7 |
| Thomas F. Cassidy (D) | 44,211 | 42.6 |
| 2 William J. Granfield (D) | 52,346 | 49.9 |
| Joshua L. Brooks (R) | 47,920 | 45.7 |
| 3 Frank H. Foss (R) | 50,617 | 51.5 |
| M. Fred O'Connell (D) | 47,632 | 48.5 |
| 4 Pehr G. Holmes (R) | 56,408 | 55.0 |
| John Walsh (D) | 46,081 | 45.0 |
| 5 Edith Nourse Rogers (R) | 74,459 | 59.9 |
| James J. Bruin (D) | 49,788 | 40.1 |
| 6 A. Piatt Andrew (R) | 65,728 | 67.7 |
| James D. Burns (D) | 31,416 | 32.3 |
| 7 William P. Connery Jr. (D) | 61,591 | 56.6 |
| Charles W. Lovett (R) | 44,331 | 40.7 |
| 8 Arthur D. Healey (D) | 50,266 | 51.1 |
| George H. Norton (R) | 48,070 | 48.9 |
| 9 Robert Luce (R) | 61,178 | 51.4 |
| Frederick S. Deitrick (D) | 56,425 | 47.4 |
| 10 George Holden Tinkham (R) | 60,926 | 60.3 |
| John Crehan (D) | 40,099 | 39.7 |
| 11 John J. Douglass (D) | 45,343 | 85.7 |
| William F. McDonald (R) | 7,583 | 14.3 |
| 12 John W. McCormack (D) | 69,994 | 72.9 |
| Bernard Ginsburg (R) | 25,995 | 27.1 |

| Candidates | Votes | % |
|---|---|---|
| 13 Richard B. Wigglesworth (R) | 64,589 | 58.4 |
| Edward G. Morris (D) | 45,964 | 41.6 |
| 14 Joseph William Martin Jr. (R) | 51,680 | 56.8 |
| Andrew J. McGraw (D) | 39,259 | 43.2 |
| 15 Charles L. Gifford (R) | 53,066 | 57.5 |
| Thomas H. Buckley (D) | 36,556 | 39.6 |

## MICHIGAN

| Candidates | Votes | % |
|---|---|---|
| 1 George G. Sadowski (D) | 51,620 | 68.1 |
| Charles H. Mahoney (R) | 21,764 | 28.7 |
| 2 John C. Lehr (D) | 51,592 | 50.6 |
| Earl C. Michener (R) | 49,257 | 48.3 |
| 3 Joseph L. Hooper (R) | 49,383 | 50.2 |
| Charles E. Gauss (D) | 46,093 | 46.9 |
| 4 George Foulkes (D) | 46,927 | 51.6 |
| John C. Ketcham (R) | 42,922 | 47.2 |
| 5 Carl E. Mapes (R) | 52,870 | 51.3 |
| Winfield H. Caslow (D) | 48,686 | 47.3 |
| 6 Claude E. Cady (D) | 55,478 | 47.8 |
| Seymour H. Person (R) | 45,818 | 39.5 |
| Grant M. Hudson (R) | 14,541 | 12.5 |
| 7 Jesse P. Wolcott (R) | 51,974 | 56.1 |
| James G. Tucker (D) | 38,738 | 41.8 |
| 8 Michael J. Hart (D) | 53,959 | 53.5 |
| William M. Smith (R) | 45,263 | 44.9 |
| 9 Harry W. Musselwhite (D) | 40,200 | 52.2 |
| James C. McLaughlin (R) | 36,434 | 47.3 |
| 10 Roy O. Woodruff (R) | 38,937 | 54.0 |
| William J. Kelly (D) | 32,376 | 44.9 |
| 11 Prentiss M. Brown (D) | 39,261 | 50.1 |
| Frank P. Bohn (R) | 37,311 | 47.6 |
| 12 W. Frank James (R) | 48,014 | 62.5 |
| Levi S. Rice (D) | 26,925 | 35.0 |
| 13 Clarence J. McLeod (R) | 50,437 | 52.4 |
| Clarence E. Seebaldt (D) | 43,374 | 45.1 |
| 14 Carl M. Weideman (D) | 53,789 | 50.4 |
| Robert H. Clancy (R) | 50,491 | 47.3 |
| 15 John D. Dingell (D) | 52,376 | 48.3 |
| Charles Bowles (R) | 49,801 | 46.0 |
| 16 John Lesinski (D) | 43,369 | 53.0 |
| Frank P. Darin (R) | 36,174 | 44.2 |
| 17 George A. Dondero (R) | 51,918 | 52.4 |
| Harry Mitchell (D) | 44,325 | 44.9 |

## MINNESOTA

| Candidates | Votes | % |
|---|---|---|
| AL Magnus Johnson (F-LAB) | 388,616 ✔ | |
| Paul John Kvale (F-LAB) | 380,444 ✔ | |
| Henry Arens (F-LAB) | 361,724 ✔ | |
| Ernest Lundeen (F-LAB) | 350,455 ✔ | |
| Theodore Christianson (R) | 337,110 ✔ | |
| Einar Hoidale (D) | 321,949 ✔ | |
| Ray P. Chase (R) | 321,102 ✔ | |
| Francis H. Shoemaker (F-LAB) | 317,109 ✔ | |
| Harold Knutson (R) | 313,221 ✔ | |
| August H. Andresen (R) | 312,198 | |
| W. I. Nolan (R) | 306,266 | |
| Conrad G. Selvig (R) | 304,846 | |
| J. A. A. Burnquist (R) | 302,356 | |
| J. L. Peterson (F-LAB) | 298,331 | |
| Henry G. Teigan (F-LAB) | 291,837 | |
| C. F. Gaarenstroom (F-LAB) | 291,687 | |
| William A. Pittenger (R) | 291,478 | |
| N. J. Holmberg (R) | 287,381 | |
| A. C. Townley (F-LAB) | 261,120 | |
| Robert C. Bell (D) | 237,881 | |
| John P. Coughlin (D) | 214,462 | |
| Silas M. Bryan (D) | 207,419 | |
| Emil E. Holmes (D) | 205,673 | |
| James R. Bennett (D) | 198,421 | |
| Donald A. Chapman (D) | 190,530 | |
| Hugh T. Kennedy (D) | 186,466 | |
| John Bowe (D) | 184,587 | |
| Victor Christgau (STICKER) | 82,826 | |

## MINNESOTA

| Candidates | Votes | % |
|---|---|---|
| J. W. Anderson (COM) | 16,299 | |
| M. Karson (COM) | 9,573 | |
| Fred Lequier (COM) | 8,927 | |
| Melvin Maas (STICKER) | 784 | |

## MISSISSIPPI

| | Candidates | Votes | % |
|---|---|---|---|
| 1 | John E. Rankin (D) | 19,549 | 97.0 |
| 2 | Wall Doxey (D) | 15,092 | 98.5 |
| 3 | Will M. Whittington (D) | 13,562 | 95.8 |
| 4 | Jeff Busby (D) | 14,072 | 97.8 |
| 5 | Ross A. Collins (D) | 19,123 | 97.1 |
| 6 | William M. Colmer (D) | 22,831 | 94.5 |
| 7 | Russell Ellzey (D) | 25,725 | 95.6 |

## MISSOURI

| | Candidates | Votes | % |
|---|---|---|---|
| AL | John J. Cochran (D) | 1,013,824 ✓ | |
| | James R. Claiborne (D) | 1,004,170 ✓ | |
| | Joseph B. Shannon (D) | 1,002,545 ✓ | |
| | Clyde Williams (D) | 1,000,218 ✓ | |
| | Clarence Cannon (D) | 997,642 ✓ | |
| | Frank H. Lee (D) | 997,148 ✓ | |
| | James E. Ruffin (D) | 996,969 ✓ | |
| | Ralph F. Lozier (D) | 995,676 ✓ | |
| | Jacob L. Milligan (D) | 995,002 ✓ | |
| | Reuben T. Wood (D) | 994,487 ✓ | |
| | Milton A. Romjue (D) | 994,123 ✓ | |
| | Richard M. Duncan (D) | 988,200 ✓ | |
| | Clement C. Dickinson (D) | 981,847 ✓ | |
| | Leonidas C. Dyer (R) | 609,268 | |
| | Henry F. Niedringhaus (R) | 603,345 | |
| | James Stewart (R) | 589,615 | |
| | John M. Hadley (R) | 589,205 | |
| | Carl Otto (R) | 588,647 | |
| | Louis E. Miller (R) | 588,246 | |
| | Phil A. Bennett (R) | 586,272 | |
| | Sam A. Clark (R) | 586,215 | |
| | Joe J. Manlove (R) | 585,840 | |
| | Rowland L. Johnston (R) | 584,256 | |
| | David Hopkins (R) | 582,662 | |
| | John W. Palmer (R) | 582,324 | |
| | Manvel H. Davis (R) | 578,995 | |
| | Phillips (SOC) | 11,658 | |
| | Morrison (SOC) | 11,637 | |
| | Langley (SOC) | 11,625 | |
| | Becker (SOC) | 11,606 | |
| | Elliff (SOC) | 11,598 | |
| | Anderson (SOC) | 11,573 | |
| | Henschel (SOC) | 11,571 | |
| | Davidson (SOC) | 11,543 | |
| | Turner (SOC) | 11,493 | |
| | Hill (SOC) | 11,459 | |
| | Harrison (SOC) | 11,417 | |
| | Shumaker (SOC) | 11,356 | |
| | Thayer (SOC) | 11,324 | |
| | Benz (COM) | 627 | |

## MONTANA

| | Candidates | Votes | % |
|---|---|---|---|
| 1 | Joseph P. Monaghan (D) | 51,159 | 59.0 |
| | Mark D. Fitzgarrald (R) | 33,333 | 38.4 |
| 2 | Roy E. Ayers (D) | 64,103 | 52.5 |
| | Scott Leavitt (R) | 53,890 | 44.1 |

## NEBRASKA

| | Candidates | Votes | % |
|---|---|---|---|
| 1 | John H. Morehead (D) | 63,022 | 58.0 |
| | Marcus L. Poteet (R) | 43,653 | 40.2 |
| 2 | Edward R. Burke (D) | 51,728 | 51.3 |
| | Malcolm Baldridge (R) | 44,209 | 43.8 |
| 3 | Edgar Howard (D) | 74,207 | 66.0 |
| | H. Halderson (R) | 32,954 | 29.3 |
| 4 | Ashton C. Shallenberger (D) | 53,713 | 44.8 |
| | Fred G. Johnson (R) | 38,938 | 32.5 |
| | Charles G. Binderup | 21,100 | 17.6 |

| | Candidates | Votes | % |
|---|---|---|---|
| 5 | Terry Carpenter (D) | 53,586 | 51.3 |
| | Robert G. Simmons (R) | 49,200 | 47.1 |

## NEVADA

| | Candidates | Votes | % |
|---|---|---|---|
| AL | James G. Scrugham (D) | 24,979 | 60.8 |
| | Samuel S. Arentz (R) | 16,133 | 39.2 |

## NEW HAMPSHIRE

| | Candidates | Votes | % |
|---|---|---|---|
| 1 | William N. Rogers (D) | 50,306 | 51.3 |
| | William P. Straw (R) | 47,646 | 48.6 |
| 2 | Charles W. Tobey (R) | 50,156 | 52.8 |
| | Jeremiah J. Doyle (D) | 44,459 | 46.8 |

## NEW JERSEY

| | Candidates | Votes | % |
|---|---|---|---|
| 1 | Charles A. Wolverton (R) | 89,816 | 60.2 |
| | Samuel T. French (D) | 54,701 | 36.7 |
| 2 | Isaac Bacharach (R) | 60,963 | 62.9 |
| | Harry R. Coulomb (D) | 35,257 | 36.4 |
| 3 | William H. Sutphin (D) | 61,253 | 50.9 |
| | Stanley Washburn (R) | 58,217 | 48.4 |
| 4 | D. Lane Powers (R) | 51,794 | 55.0 |
| | Monell Sayre (D) | 40,705 | 43.2 |
| 5 | Charles A. Eaton (R) | 60,713 | 53.2 |
| | Frederick M. P. Pearse (D) | 51,964 | 45.6 |
| 6 | Donald H. McLean (R) | 65,653 | 57.4 |
| | Fred C. Hyer (D) | 47,938 | 41.9 |
| 7 | Randolph Perkins (R) | 52,003 | 51.6 |
| | Hamilton Cross (D) | 47,688 | 47.3 |
| 8 | George N. Seger (R) | 50,997 | 49.2 |
| | Harry Joelson (D) | 50,759 | 48.9 |
| 9 | Edward A. Kenney (D) | 53,822 | 47.6 |
| | Joseph W. Marini (R) | 52,968 | 46.8 |
| 10 | Fred A. Hartley Jr. (R) | 53,316 | 55.2 |
| | William W. Harrison (D) | 41,901 | 43.4 |
| 11 | Peter A. Cavicchia (R) | 47,495 | 49.8 |
| | John J. McCloskey (D) | 46,540 | 48.8 |
| 12 | Frederick R. Lehlbach (R) | 54,783 | 56.1 |
| | Joseph M. Degnan (D) | 40,746 | 41.7 |
| 13 | Mary T. Norton (D) | 73,779 | 72.1 |
| | Mortimer Neuman (R) | 27,964 | 27.3 |
| 14 | Oscar L. Auf der Heide (D) | 77,519 | 75.1 |
| | Vincent P. McGann (R) | 24,448 | 23.7 |

## NEW MEXICO

| | Candidates | Votes | % |
|---|---|---|---|
| AL | Dennis Chavez (D) | 95,363 | 63.5 |
| | Jose E. Armijo (R) | 52,905 | 35.2 |

## NEW YORK

| | Candidates | Votes | % |
|---|---|---|---|
| 1 | Robert L. Bacon (R) | 153,435 | 54.0 |
| | Cornelius V. Whitney (D) | 121,909 | 42.9 |
| 2 | William F. Brunner (D) | 172,512 | 68.6 |
| | Horace A. Demarest (R) | 68,525 | 27.3 |
| 3 | George W. Lindsay (D) | 33,750 | 80.8 |
| | Edgar H. Hazelwood (R) | 5,799 | 13.9 |
| 4 | Thomas H. Cullen (D) | 39,562 | 82.1 |
| | Conrad F. Printzlien (R) | 7,429 | 15.4 |
| 5 | Loring M. Black Jr. (D) | 51,932 | 64.8 |
| | Irving C. Maltz (R) | 24,814 | 31.0 |
| 6 | Andrew L. Somers (D) | 81,011 | 57.0 |
| | Joseph P. Byrne (R) | 42,221 | 29.7 |
| | Harry W. Laidler (SOC) | 15,568 | 11.0 |
| 7 | John J. Delaney (D) | 36,088 | 72.5 |
| | Richard W. Thomas (R) | 9,696 | 19.5 |
| | David M. Cory (SOC) | 3,181 | 6.4 |
| 8 | Patrick J. Carley (D) | 140,853 | 62.1 |
| | Daniel Adelman (R) | 49,471 | 21.8 |
| | Baruch C. Vladeck (SOC) | 31,930 | 14.1 |
| 9 | Stephen A. Rudd (D) | 69,634 | 59.9 |
| | James Virdone (R) | 38,047 | 32.7 |
| | Abraham I. Shiplacoff (SOC) | 7,496 | 6.5 |

| | Candidates | Votes | % |
|---|---|---|---|
| 10 | Emanuel Celler (D) | 36,460 | 63.9 |
| | William A. Ronalds (R) | 14,167 | 24.8 |
| | Louis Sadoff (SOC) | 5,334 | 9.3 |
| 11 | Anning S. Prall (D) | 50,418 | 69.2 |
| | Frank Homer Fay (R) | 20,323 | 27.9 |
| 12 | Samuel Dickstein (D) | 21,248 | 86.5 |
| | Henry Steinberg (R) | 2,068 | 8.4 |
| 13 | Christopher D. Sullivan (D) | 21,939 | 86.5 |
| | John Rosenberg (R) | 2,513 | 9.9 |
| 14 | William I. Sirovich (D) | 20,668 | 60.7 |
| | Henry A. Lowenberg (R) | 9,651 | 28.3 |
| | August Claessens (SOC) | 2,735 | 8.0 |
| 15 | John J. Boylan (D) | 30,112 | 80.9 |
| | Charles Coudert Nast (R) | 5,987 | 16.1 |
| 16 | John J. O'Connor (D) | 29,485 | 67.1 |
| | Eugene S. Taliaferro (R) | 12,449 | 28.3 |
| 17 | Theodore A. Peyser (D) | 36,397 | 52.9 |
| | Ruth Pratt (R) | 29,776 | 43.3 |
| 18 | Martin J. Kennedy (D) | 30,245 | 75.1 |
| | Patrick S. Hickey (R) | 7,997 | 19.9 |
| 19 | Sol Bloom (D) | 57,400 | 69.0 |
| | William L. Carns (R) | 21,758 | 26.2 |
| 20 | James J. Lanzetta (D) | 16,447 | 50.7 |
| | Fiorello H. LaGuardia (R) | 15,227 | 47.0 |
| 21 | Joseph A. Gavagan (D) | 67,583 | 64.6 |
| | Oscar J. Smith (R) | 28,955 | 27.7 |
| | Frank R. Crosswaith (SOC) | 7,390 | 7.1 |
| 22 | Anthony J. Griffin (D) | 38,172 | 76.7 |
| | Wilbur J. Murphy (R) | 8,768 | 17.6 |
| 23 | Frank Oliver (D) | 131,852 | 69.5 |
| | Samuel J. Krinn (R) | 31,753 | 16.7 |
| | Samuel Orr (SOC) | 21,349 | 11.3 |
| 24 | James M. Fitzpatrick (D) | 128,881 | 60.1 |
| | Benjamin L. Fairchild (R & LP) | 65,189 | 30.4 |
| | Esther Friedman (SOC) | 15,389 | 7.2 |
| 25 | Charles D. Millard (R) | 80,909 | 54.3 |
| | Jesse B. Perlman (D) | 63,345 | 42.5 |
| 26 | Hamilton Fish Jr. (R) | 61,687 | 58.3 |
| | Roslyn M. Cox (D) | 43,174 | 40.8 |
| 27 | Philip A. Goodwin (R & LP) | 52,099 | 52.5 |
| | Clifford L. Miller (D) | 46,154 | 46.5 |
| 28 | Parker Corning (D) | 89,096 | 64.7 |
| | Isaac G. Braman (R) | 47,706 | 34.7 |
| 29 | James S. Parker (R & LP) | 65,359 | 57.8 |
| | John J. Nyhoff (D) | 46,935 | 41.5 |
| 30 | Frank Crowther (R & LP) | 55,981 | 55.5 |
| | George D. Lamberton (D) | 42,632 | 42.3 |
| 31 | Bertrand H. Snell (R) | 47,937 | 57.5 |
| | Kenneth Gardner (D) | 35,153 | 42.1 |
| 32 | Francis D. Culkin (R & LP) | 56,654 | 61.9 |
| | John C. Purcell (D) | 34,199 | 37.3 |
| 33 | Fred J. Sisson (D) | 53,427 | 50.0 |
| | Frederick M. Davenport (R & LP) | 52,398 | 49.0 |
| 34 | John D. Clarke (R) | 58,735 | 53.3 |
| | Charles R. Seymour (D) | 44,174 | 40.1 |
| | Leon Ray Steenburg (LAW PRES) | 6,676 | 6.1 |
| 35 | Clarence E. Hancock (R) | 79,345 | 55.6 |
| | Edmund L. Weston (D) | 60,376 | 42.3 |
| 36 | John Taber (R & LP) | 58,484 | 60.9 |
| | Lithgow Osborne (D) | 36,648 | 38.2 |
| 37 | Gale H. Stalker (R & LP) | 55,305 | 52.5 |
| | Julian P. Bretz (D) | 48,048 | 45.6 |
| 38 | James L. Whitley (R) | 64,003 | 46.2 |
| | Charles Stanton (D) | 58,775 | 42.4 |
| | Arthur Rathjen (LAW PRES) | 12,097 | 8.7 |
| 39 | James W. Wadsworth (R) | 50,855 | 47.1 |
| | David A. White (D) | 35,367 | 32.8 |
| | Ernest R. Clark (LAW PRES) | 20,209 | 18.7 |
| 40 | Walter Gresham Andrews (R) | 92,929 | 61.8 |
| | Ralph W. Nolan (D) | 54,363 | 36.1 |
| 41 | Alfred F. Beiter (D) | 45,120 | 50.1 |
| | Edmund F. Cooke (R) | 42,743 | 47.4 |
| 42 | James M. Mead (D) | 51,516 | 62.0 |
| | Henry Adsit Bull (R) | 30,230 | 36.4 |

## NEW YORK

| | Candidates | Votes | % |
|---|---|---|---|
| 43 | Daniel A. Reed (R & LP) | 55,988 | 60.1 |
| | Gerald A. Herrick (D) | 34,561 | 37.1 |
| AL | Elmer E. Studley (D) | 2,363,627✔ | |
| | John Fitzgibbons (D) | 2,333,787✔ | |
| | Nicholas Howard Pinto (R) | 1,756,343 | |
| | Sherman J. Lowell (R) | 1,740,325 | |
| | G. August Gerber (SOC) | 166,781 | |
| | Fred Sander (SOC) | 163,648 | |
| | Elizabeth Smart (LAW PRES) | 74,436 | |
| | J. Elmer Cates (LAW PRES) | 68,622 | |
| | Jacob Berlin (SOC LAB) | 12,546 | |
| | O. Martin Olson (SOC LAB) | 11,623 | |

## NORTH CAROLINA

| | Candidates | Votes | % |
|---|---|---|---|
| 1 | Lindsay C. Warren (D) | 32,790 | 90.8 |
| | John B. Respass (R) | 3,313 | 9.2 |
| 2 | John H. Kerr (D) | 34,325 | 96.0 |
| 3 | Charles L. Abernethy (D) | 30,395 | 73.2 |
| | H. B. Ivey (R) | 11,146 | 26.8 |
| 4 | Edward W. Pou (D) | 51,103 | 76.0 |
| | L. P. Dixon (R) | 16,129 | 24.0 |
| 5 | Franklin W. Hancock Jr. (D) | 40,825 | 70.2 |
| | L. L. Wall (R) | 17,326 | 29.8 |
| 6 | William B. Umstead (D) | 38,074 | 67.8 |
| | William I. Ward (R) | 18,093 | 32.2 |
| 7 | J. Bayard Clark (D) | 35,416 | 80.4 |
| | J. M. Byrd (R) | 8,657 | 19.6 |
| 8 | J. Walter Lambeth (D) | 49,584 | 65.4 |
| | A. H. Ragan (R) | 26,260 | 34.6 |
| 9 | Robert L. Doughton (D) | 51,145 | 63.5 |
| | P. P. Dulin (R) | 29,421 | 36.5 |
| 10 | Alfred L. Bulwinkle (D) | 63,776 | 59.7 |
| | Charles A. Jonas (R) | 43,067 | 40.3 |
| 11 | Zebulon Weaver (D) | 64,667 | 62.3 |
| | Crawford F. James (R) | 39,180 | 37.7 |

## NORTH DAKOTA

| | Candidates | Votes | % |
|---|---|---|---|
| AL | James H. Sinclair (R) | 144,339✔ | |
| | William Lemke (R) | 135,339✔ | |
| | W. D. Lynch | 72,659 | |
| | R. B. Murphy (D) | 71,695 | |
| | Pat J. Barrett (I) | 690 | |
| | Ella Reeve Bloor (I) | 678 | |

## OHIO

| | Candidates | Votes | % |
|---|---|---|---|
| 1 | John B. Hollister (R) | 66,018 | 54.4 |
| | Edward H. Brink (D) | 55,416 | 45.6 |
| 2 | William E. Hess (R) | 58,971 | 50.7 |
| | Ed. F. Alexander (D) | 57,258 | 49.3 |
| 3 | Byron B. Harlan (D) | 85,069 | 54.8 |
| | Edith McClure Patterson (R) | 66,107 | 42.6 |
| 4 | Frank L. Kloeb (D) | 59,003 | 54.6 |
| | John L. Cable (R) | 49,100 | 45.4 |
| 5 | Frank C. Kniffin (D) | 44,433 | 60.0 |
| | William L. Manahan (R) | 29,605 | 40.0 |
| 6 | James G. Polk (D) | 50,913 | 56.2 |
| | Mack Sauer (R) | 39,668 | 43.8 |
| 7 | L. T. Marshall (R) | 65,064 | 53.0 |
| | Aaron J. Halloran (D) | 57,715 | 47.0 |
| 8 | Brooks Fletcher (D) | 45,930 | 52.7 |
| | Grant E. Mouser Jr. (R) | 41,234 | 47.3 |
| 9 | Warren J. Duffey (D) | 56,755 | 47.7 |
| | Wilbur M. White (R) | 54,078 | 45.4 |
| 10 | Thomas A. Jenkins (R) | 41,654 | 58.9 |
| | Charles M. Hogan (D) | 29,027 | 41.1 |
| 11 | Mell G. Underwood (D) | 44,380 | 63.0 |
| | David J. Lewis (R) | 26,075 | 37.0 |
| 12 | Arthur P. Lamneck (D) | 63,135 | 50.2 |
| | John C. Speaks (R) | 62,704 | 49.8 |
| 13 | William L. Fiesinger (D) | 56,070 | 58.9 |
| | Walter E. Kruger (R) | 39,122 | 41.1 |
| 14 | Dow W. Harter (D) | 93,057 | 53.9 |
| | Francis Seiberling (R) | 78,852 | 45.7 |

| | Candidates | Votes | % |
|---|---|---|---|
| 15 | Robert T. Secrest (D) | 50,313 | 56.6 |
| | C. Ellis Moore (R) | 38,113 | 42.9 |
| 16 | William R. Thom (D) | 67,670 | 51.6 |
| | C. B. McClintock (R) | 63,609 | 48.5 |
| 17 | Charles West (D) | 55,396 | 51.8 |
| | William M. Morgan (R) | 51,611 | 48.2 |
| 18 | Lawrence E. Imhoff (D) | 56,576 | 50.3 |
| | Frank Murphy (R) | 56,013 | 49.8 |
| 19 | John G. Cooper (R) | 74,534 | 53.3 |
| | D. F. Dunlavy (D) | 65,024 | 46.5 |
| 20 | Martin L. Sweeney (D) | 52,933 | 98.8 |
| 21 | Robert Crosser (D) | 49,436 | 65.2 |
| | Gerard Pilliod (R) | 25,527 | 33.7 |
| 22 | Chester C. Bolton (R) | 141,296 | 58.7 |
| | Florence E. Allen (D) | 98,427 | 40.9 |
| AL | Charles V. Truax (D) | 1,206,631✔ | |
| | Stephen M. Young (D) | 1,200,946✔ | |
| | George H. Bender (R) | 1,109,562 | |
| | L. T. Palmer (R) | 1,102,567 | |
| | Edward R. Stafford (P) | 24,625 | |
| | Alfred H. Stratton (P) | 18,844 | |
| | John Rehms (COM) | 7,053 | |
| | William Hughey (COM) | 6,010 | |

## OKLAHOMA

| | Candidates | Votes | % |
|---|---|---|---|
| 1 | Wesley E. Disney (D) | 81,080 | 63.3 |
| | Frank Frantz (R) | 46,472 | 36.3 |
| 2 | William W. Hastings (D) | 46,710 | 70.5 |
| | William F. Head (R) | 19,567 | 29.5 |
| 3 | Wilburn Cartwright (D) | 59,090 | 85.3 |
| | Walter Colbert (R) | 10,225 | 14.8 |
| 4 | Thomas D. McKeown (D) | 61,867 | 75.5 |
| | E. W. Kemp (R) | 20,069 | 24.5 |
| 5 | Fletcher B. Swank (D) | 64,303 | 64.3 |
| | Paul Huston (R) | 35,785 | 35.8 |
| 6 | Jed Johnson (D) | 53,869 | 79.3 |
| | George E. Young (R) | 14,048 | 20.7 |
| 7 | James V. McClintic (D) | 43,809 | 77.9 |
| | W. G. Roe (R) | 8,756 | 15.6 |
| | T. H. McLemore (I) | 3,651 | 6.5 |
| 8 | E. W. Marland (D) | 51,404 | 61.3 |
| | M. C. Garber (R) | 31,677 | 37.8 |
| AL | Will Rogers (D) | 467,644 | 72.8 |
| | R. A. Howard (R) | 171,415 | 26.7 |

## OREGON

| | Candidates | Votes | % |
|---|---|---|---|
| 1 | James W. Mott (R) | 82,443 | 51.2 |
| | Harvey G. Starkweather (D) | 60,066 | 37.3 |
| | W. J. Butler (I) | 12,417 | 7.7 |
| 2 | Walter M. Pierce (D) | 30,219 | 48.2 |
| | Robert R. Butler (R) | 25,169 | 40.1 |
| | Hugh E. Brady (I) | 5,133 | 8.2 |
| 3 | Charles H. Martin (D) | 74,397 | 59.0 |
| | Homer D. Angell (R) | 40,650 | 32.2 |

## PENNSYLVANIA

| | Candidates | Votes | % |
|---|---|---|---|
| 1 | Harry C. Ransley (R, D) | 65,508 | 91.5 |
| | Harry T. Glenn (F PLAY) | 4,933 | 6.9 |
| 2 | James M. Beck (R, R&P) | 42,233 | 59.2 |
| | John J. Shanahan (D, LAB) | 27,571 | 38.7 |
| 3 | Alfred M. Waldron (R, R&P) | 53,044 | 57.4 |
| | Frank M. O'Brien (D) | 37,487 | 40.6 |
| 4 | George W. Edmonds (R) | 43,086 | 52.9 |
| | William J. O'Rourke (D) | 36,198 | 44.4 |
| 5 | James J. Connolly (R, L) | 49,516 | 55.3 |
| | Carroll J. Agnew (D, A-CB) | 36,240 | 40.5 |
| 6 | Edward Lowber Stokes (R, L) | 44,884 | 51.0 |
| | Harry V. Dougherty (D, R&P) | 40,440 | 45.9 |
| 7 | George P. Darrow (R) | 62,031 | 62.2 |
| | James C. Crumlish (D) | 35,096 | 35.2 |
| 8 | James Wolfenden (R, L) | 70,177 | 65.8 |
| | Matthew Randall (D) | 32,139 | 30.1 |

| | Candidates | Votes | % |
|---|---|---|---|
| 9 | Henry W. Watson (R) | 40,726 | 50.3 |
| | Norton L. Lichtenwalner (D) | 37,490 | 46.3 |
| 10 | J. Roland Kinzer (R, P) | 62,682 | 61.5 |
| | Richard P. McGrann (D, REPEAL) | 36,841 | 36.2 |
| 11 | Patrick J. Boland (D, R) | 69,684 | 95.9 |
| 12 | C. Murray Turpin (R) | 57,377 | 50.8 |
| | John J. Casey (D, SOC) | 55,650 | 49.2 |
| 13 | George Franklin Brumm (R, D) | 97,120 | 90.8 |
| 14 | William E. Richardson (D) | 29,386 | 41.0 |
| | Thomas L. Rhodes (R) | 22,898 | 31.9 |
| | Raymond S. Hofses (SOC) | 19,319 | 27.0 |
| 15 | Louis T. McFadden (R, D) | 71,345 | 95.9 |
| 16 | Robert F. Rich (R, P) | 46,044 | 63.5 |
| | Paul A. Rothfuss (D) | 24,671 | 34.0 |
| 17 | J. William Ditter (R, L) | 59,693 | 59.9 |
| | Phillip Childs Pendleton (D, R&P) | 32,706 | 32.8 |
| 18 | Benjamin K. Focht (R) | 28,749 | 48.3 |
| | J. G. Harry Rippman (D) | 19,230 | 32.3 |
| | Omer B. Poulson (CIT) | 11,568 | 19.4 |
| 19 | Isaac H. Doutrich (R) | 59,120 | 58.1 |
| | Carl K. Deen (D) | 37,752 | 37.1 |
| 20 | Thomas C. Cochran (R, P) | 44,754 | 53.6 |
| | D. J. Driscoll (D) | 38,798 | 46.4 |
| 21 | Francis E. Walter (D) | 39,996 | 52.7 |
| | William R. Coyle (R) | 34,189 | 45.1 |
| 22 | Harry L. Haines (D, P) | 51,894 | 57.2 |
| | Leighton C. Taylor (R) | 37,434 | 41.3 |
| 23 | J. Banks Kurtz (R, P) | 35,342 | 49.2 |
| | Frederick B. Kerr (D) | 33,948 | 47.2 |
| 24 | J. Buell Snyder (D) | 33,633 | 53.0 |
| | Samuel A. Kendall (R, P) | 28,498 | 44.9 |
| 25 | Charles I. Faddis (D) | 36,781 | 56.1 |
| | Henry W. Temple (R, P) | 27,351 | 41.7 |
| 26 | J. Howard Swick (R, P) | 45,029 | 54.0 |
| | Sam B. Wilson (D) | 38,402 | 46.0 |
| 27 | Nathan L. Strong (R, P) | 52,884 | 50.7 |
| | D. A. Dorn (D) | 42,763 | 41.0 |
| 28 | William M. Berlin (D, JOBLESS) | 43,619 | 55.2 |
| | Adam M. Wyant (R, P) | 32,177 | 40.8 |
| 29 | Charles N. Crosby (D, I) | 30,106 | 50.1 |
| | Milton W. Shreve (R, P) | 27,949 | 46.5 |
| 30 | Twing Brooks (D) | 35,186 | 47.2 |
| | Edward F. Erk (R, I) | 35,045 | 47.0 |
| 31 | Clyde Kelly (R, D) | 68,944 | 85.5 |
| | Leo O. Guthrie (REPEAL) | 6,031 | 7.5 |
| | William B. Kane (SOC) | 5,620 | 7.0 |
| 32 | Michael J. Muldowney (R, JOBLESS) | 24,785 | 53.3 |
| | Anne E. Felix (D) | 18,986 | 40.9 |
| 33 | Henry Ellenbogen (D, JOBLESS) | 35,612 | 52.0 |
| | Harry A. Estep (R) | 30,076 | 43.9 |
| 34 | Matthew A. Dunn (D, JOBLESS) | 40,651 | 49.9 |
| | Guy E. Campbell (R, L) | 36,101 | 44.3 |

| Special Elections | | Votes | % |
|---|---|---|---|
| 6 | Robert L. Davis (R) | 63,929 | 54.1 |
| | Leo J. Horton (D) | 54,178 | 45.9 |
| 18 | Joseph F. Biddle (R) | 38,584 | 59.3 |
| | Meredith Meyers (D) | 26,370 | 40.6 |

## RHODE ISLAND

| | Candidates | Votes | % |
|---|---|---|---|
| 1 | Francis B. Condon (D) | 70,566 | 55.6 |
| | Clark Burdick (R) | 56,153 | 44.2 |
| 2 | John M. O'Connell (D) | 73,086 | 54.7 |
| | Thomas P. Hazard (R) | 60,153 | 45.0 |

## SOUTH CAROLINA

| | Candidates | Votes | % |
|---|---|---|---|
| 1 | Thomas S. McMillan (D) | 14,415 | 95.9 |
| 2 | Hampton P. Fulmer (D) | 18,699 | 97.9 |
| 3 | John C. Taylor (D) | 19,286 | 99.2 |

## SOUTH CAROLINA

| Candidates | Votes | % |
|---|---|---|
| 4 John J. McSwain (D) | 23,041 | 98.4 |
| 5 James P. Richards (D) | 15,046 | 98.5 |
| 6 Allard H. Gasque (D) | 14,159 | 98.7 |

## SOUTH DAKOTA

| Candidates | Votes | % |
|---|---|---|
| 1 Fred H. Hildebrandt (D) | 110,047 | 53.1 |
| C. A. Christopherson (R) | 92,062 | 44.4 |
| 2 Theodore B. Werner (D) | 36,839 | 55.7 |
| William Williamson (R) | 29,066 | 43.9 |

## TENNESSEE

| Candidates | Votes | % |
|---|---|---|
| 1 B. Carroll Reece (R) | 30,336 | 45.7 |
| O. B. Lovette (I) | 27,888 | 42.0 |
| Albert C. Tipton (D) | 7,950 | 12.0 |
| 2 J. Will Taylor (R) | 32,460 | 57.7 |
| Hamilton S. Burnett (D) | 22,818 | 40.5 |
| 3 Sam D. McReynolds (D) | 28,758 | 91.6 |
| 4 Ridley Mitchell (D) | 30,580 | 82.6 |
| W. H. Crowell (R) | 5,882 | 15.9 |
| 5 Joseph W. Byrns (D) | 33,833 | 87.6 |
| J. Y. Freeman (R) | 4,066 | 10.5 |
| 6 Clarence W. Turner (D) | 15,779 | 79.1 |
| G. C. Stephenson (R) | 3,915 | 19.6 |
| 7 Gordon Browning (D) | 20,315 | 77.8 |
| Willoughy Stewart (R) | 5,485 | 21.0 |
| 8 Jere Cooper (D) | 19,871 | 88.2 |
| Mary Burnett (R) | 2,307 | 10.2 |
| 9 Edward H. Crump (D) | 38,001 | 90.1 |
| S. A. Godsey (R) | 2,953 | 7.0 |

## TEXAS

| Candidates | Votes | % |
|---|---|---|
| 1 Wright Patman (D) | 30,854 | 98.0 |
| 2 Martin Dies (D) | 51,999 | 95.4 |
| 3 M. G. Sanders (D) | 36,507 | 100.0 |
| 4 Sam Rayburn (D) | 23,440 | 95.2 |
| 5 Hatton W. Sumners (D) | 52,598 | 92.1 |
| G. J. McManus (R) | 4,539 | 7.9 |
| 6 Luther A. Johnson (D) | 32,966 | 100.0 |
| 7 Clay S. Briggs (D) | 28,490 | 95.3 |
| 8 Daniel E. Garrett (D) | 57,882* | 92.0 |
| W. E. Long (R) | 5,015 | 8.0 |
| 9 J. J. Mansfield (D) | 33,366 | 97.5 |
| 10 J. P. Buchanan (D) | 33,232 | 100.0 |
| 11 O. H. Cross (D) | 35,186 | 96.6 |
| 12 Fritz G. Lanham (D) | 41,151 | 93.3 |
| George Calvert (R) | 2,968 | 6.7 |
| 13 W. D. McFarlane (D) | 33,023 | 100.0 |
| 14 Richard M. Kleberg (D) | 69,471 | 91.5 |
| Frank B. Vaughn (R) | 6,456 | 8.5 |
| 15 John N. Garner (D) | 44,300* | 88.4 |
| C. G. Watson (R) | 5,785 | 11.6 |
| 16 R. E. Thomason (D) | 49,068 | 99.7 |
| 17 Thomas L. Blanton (D) | 43,959 | 100.0 |
| 18 Marvin Jones (D) | 76,918 | 96.1 |

| Candidates | Votes | % |
|---|---|---|
| AL George B. Terrell (D) | 794,521 | ✔ |
| Sterling P. Strong (D) | 794,333 | ✔ |
| Joseph W. Bailey Jr. (D) | 790,024 | ✔ |
| Enoch J. Fletcher (R) | 62,957 | |
| F. A. Blankenbeckler (R) | 60,360 | |
| J. A. Simpson (R) | 59,390 | |
| H. M. Shelton (SOC) | 2,534 | |
| P. L. Petersen (SOC) | 2,530 | |
| Ben O. Miller (SOC) | 2,424 | |
| P. A. Spain (LIB) | 188 | |
| H. G. Eastridge (LIB) | 172 | |

## UTAH

| Candidates | Votes | % |
|---|---|---|
| 1 Abe Murdock (D) | 47,776 | 50.7 |
| Don B. Colton (R) | 44,827 | 47.6 |
| 2 J. W. Robinson (D) | 62,400 | 56.0 |
| Frederick C. Loofbourow (R) | 46,919 | 42.1 |

## VERMONT

| Candidates | Votes | % |
|---|---|---|
| AL Ernest Willard Gibson (R) | 86,194 | 64.4 |
| Joseph A. McNamara (D) | 47,591 | 35.6 |

## VIRGINIA

| Candidates | Votes | % |
|---|---|---|
| AL Clifton A. Woodrum (D) | 206,631 | ✔ |
| Andrew J. Montague (D) | 205,133 | ✔ |
| Schuyler Otis Bland (D) | 204,372 | ✔ |
| Thomas G. Burch (D) | 204,069 | ✔ |
| A. Willis Robertson (D) | 203,727 | ✔ |
| Howard W. Smith (D) | 203,023 | ✔ |
| Patrick Henry Drewry (D) | 202,800 | ✔ |
| Colgate W. Darden Jr. (D) | 202,759 | ✔ |
| John W. Flannagan Jr. (D) | 201,474 | ✔ |
| Menalcus Lankford (R) | 92,586 | |
| J. A. Garber (R) | 84,464 | |
| Fred W. McWane (R) | 82,480 | |
| Roland E. Chase (R) | 81,909 | |
| George Cole Scott (R) | 81,025 | |
| Henry A. Wise (R) | 78,622 | |
| W. M. Brown (I) | 43,936 | |
| C. C. Berkeley (I) | 43,202 | |
| R. Lindsay Gordon Jr. (I) | 16,504 | |
| A. J. Dunning Jr. (P) | 16,392 | |
| Albon James Royal (SOC) | 4,782 | |
| Winston F. Dawson (SOC) | 4,629 | |
| Herman R. Ansell (SOC) | 4,603 | |
| David G. George (SOC) | 4,165 | |
| Angie M. Norris (SOC) | 3,956 | |
| J. F. Spaulding (R) | 3,601 | |
| Frank Lyon | 207 | |

### Special Election

| Candidates | Votes | % |
|---|---|---|
| 10 Joel W. Flood (D) | 23,129 | 99.9 |

## WASHINGTON

| Candidates | Votes | % |
|---|---|---|
| 1 Marion A. Zioncheck (D) | 80,665 | 55.6 |
| John F. Miller (R) | 62,283 | 42.9 |
| 2 Monrad C. Wallgren (D) | 49,002 | 56.1 |
| Lindley H. Hadley (R) | 30,780 | 35.2 |
| Floyd Hatfield (LIB) | 6,687 | 7.7 |
| 3 Martin F. Smith (D) | 38,713 | 46.9 |
| Albert Johnson (R) | 28,388 | 34.4 |
| J. T. Sullivan (LIB) | 15,427 | 18.7 |
| 4 Knute Hill (D) | 41,708 | 56.3 |
| John W. Summers (R) | 32,360 | 43.7 |
| 5 Sam B. Hill (D) | 73,041 | 96.8 |
| 6 Wesley Lloyd (D) | 44,573 | 50.1 |
| John T. McCutcheon (R) | 32,760 | 36.8 |
| Tom Martin (LIB) | 11,554 | 13.0 |

## WEST VIRGINIA

| Candidates | Votes | % |
|---|---|---|
| 1 Robert L. Ramsay (D) | 58,060 | 50.9 |
| Carl G. Bachmann (R) | 55,023 | 48.3 |
| 2 Jennings Randolph (D) | 55,556 | 53.4 |
| Frank L. Bowman (R) | 48,055 | 46.2 |
| 3 Lynn S. Hornor (D) | 52,287 | 53.6 |
| John M. Wolverton (R) | 45,274 | 46.4 |
| 4 George W. Johnson (D) | 62,848 | 52.3 |
| Robert L. Hogg (R) | 56,993 | 47.4 |
| 5 John Kee (D) | 61,277 | 52.1 |
| Hugh Ike Shott (R) | 56,355 | 47.9 |
| 6 Joe L. Smith (D) | 102,896 | 56.4 |
| James O. Lakin (R) | 79,470 | 43.6 |

## WISCONSIN

| Candidates | Votes | % |
|---|---|---|
| 1 George W. Blanchard (R) | 50,874 | 48.5 |
| William D. Thompson (D) | 48,093 | 45.8 |
| 2 Charles W. Henney (D) | 63,091 | 56.2 |
| John B. Gay (R) | 47,193 | 42.0 |
| 3 Gardner R. Withrow (R) | 59,535 | 61.1 |
| John J. Boyle (D) | 37,846 | 38.9 |
| 4 Raymond J. Cannon (D) | 61,058 | 51.0 |
| John C. Schafer (R) | 33,609 | 28.1 |
| Walter Polakowski (SOC) | 24,377 | 20.4 |
| 5 Thomas O'Malley (D) | 57,294 | 43.8 |
| Joseph A. Padway (R) | 32,559 | 24.9 |
| Herman O. Kent (SOC) | 30,534 | 23.3 |
| 6 Michael K. Reilly (D) | 59,055 | 59.1 |
| Louis J. Fellenz (R) | 38,708 | 38.7 |
| 7 Gerald J. Boileau (R) | 49,322 | 51.4 |
| Frank D. Chapman (D) | 46,737 | 48.7 |
| 8 James Hughes (D) | 53,414 | 50.7 |
| George J. Schneider (R) | 51,932 | 49.3 |
| 9 James A. Frear (R) | 52,680 | 56.9 |
| Miles H. McNally (D) | 39,874 | 43.1 |
| 10 Hubert H. Peavey (R) | 49,764 | 59.2 |
| Peter B. Cadigan (D) | 33,448 | 39.8 |

## WYOMING

| Candidates | Votes | % |
|---|---|---|
| AL Vincent M. Carter (R) | 44,816 | 49.7 |
| Paul R. Greever (D) | 43,056 | 47.7 |

# 1933 House Elections

## ARIZONA

### Special Election

| Candidates | Votes | % |
|---|---|---|
| AL Isabella S. Greenway (D) | 24,163 | 73.6 |
| D. E. Sumpter (SOC) | 5,556 | 16.9 |
| H. B. Wilkinson (R) | 3,123 | 9.5 |

## LOUISIANA

### Special Election

| Candidates | Votes | % |
|---|---|---|
| 6 Mrs. Bolivar E. Kemp (D) | 5,029* | 99.8 |

## NEW YORK

### Special Election

| Candidates | Votes | % |
|---|---|---|
| 34 Marian W. Clarke (R) | 16,806 | 59.3 |
| John J. Burns (D) | 11,559 | 40.8 |

# 1934 House Elections

## ALABAMA

| | Candidates | Votes | % |
|---|---|---|---|
| 1 | John McDuffie (D) | 13,076 | 99.7 |
| 2 | Lister Hill (D) | 18,592 | 100.0 |
| 3 | Henry B. Steagall (D) | 13,191 | 100.0 |
| 4 | Sam Hobbs (D) | 14,728 | 87.6 |
| | Charles R. Robinson (R) | 2,086 | 12.4 |
| 5 | Joe Starnes (D) | 22,040 | 75.2 |
| | J. C. Swann (R) | 7,282 | 24.8 |
| 6 | William B. Oliver (D) | 12,342 | 100.0 |
| 7 | William B. Bankhead (D) | 22,001 | 80.4 |
| | J. W. Dodd (I) | 5,361 | 19.6 |
| 8 | Archibald H. Carmichael (D) | 13,817 | 100.0 |
| 9 | George Huddleston (D) | 19,317 | 95.0 |

## ARIZONA

| | Candidates | Votes | % |
|---|---|---|---|
| AL | Isabella S. Greenway (D) | 65,914 | 68.6 |
| | H. A. Smith (R) | 28,283 | 29.5 |

## ARKANSAS

| | Candidates | Votes | % |
|---|---|---|---|
| 1 | William J. Driver (D) | 20,136 | 100.0 |
| 2 | John E. Miller (D) | 18,629 | 100.0 |
| 3 | Claude A. Fuller (D) | 17,363 | 66.3 |
| | Pat W. Murphy (R) | 8,823 | 33.7 |
| 4 | William B. Cravens (D) | 21,157 | 100.0 |
| 5 | David D. Terry (D) | 20,209 | 100.0 |
| 6 | John L. McClellan (D) | 19,078 | 100.0 |
| 7 | Tilman B. Parks (D) | 13,887 | 95.8 |

## CALIFORNIA

| | Candidates | Votes | % |
|---|---|---|---|
| 1 | Clarence F. Lea (D-R) | 98,661 | 93.6 |
| | Allen K. Gifford (SOC) | 6,698 | 6.4 |
| 2 | Harry L. Englebright (R-D-PROG) | 66,370 | 100.0 |
| 3 | Frank H. Buck (D) | 65,566 | 53.3 |
| | J. M. Inman (R & PROG) | 56,222 | 45.7 |
| 4 | Florence P. Kahn (R) | 50,491 | 48.0 |
| | Chauncey Tramutolo (D) | 46,871 | 44.5 |
| 5 | Richard J. Welch (R-D-PROG) | 89,751 | 93.8 |
| | Alexander Noral (COM) | 5,933 | 6.2 |
| 6 | Albert E. Carter (R-D-PROG) | 48,180 | 99.8 |
| 7 | John H. Tolan (D) | 51,962 | 52.3 |
| | Ralph R. Eltse (R) | 47,414 | 47.7 |
| 8 | John J. McGrath (R-D-PROG) | 107,325 | 99.9 |
| 9 | B. W. Gearhart (R-D) | 77,650 | 100.0 |
| 10 | Henry E. Stubbs (D) | 68,475 | 64.4 |
| | George R. Bliss (R) | 37,860 | 35.6 |
| 11 | John Steven McGroarty (D) | 66,999 | 53.5 |
| | William E. Evans (R) | 56,350 | 45.0 |
| 12 | John Henry Hoeppel (D) | 52,555 | 50.6 |
| | Frederick F. Houser (R) | 51,216 | 49.3 |
| 13 | Charles Kramer (D) | 83,384 | 62.4 |
| | Thomas K. Case (R) | 27,993 | 21.0 |
| | Charles H. Randall (PROG) | 18,760 | 14.0 |
| 14 | Thomas F. Ford (D) | 52,761 | 57.7 |
| | William D. Campbell (R) | 33,945 | 37.1 |
| 15 | John M. Costello (D) | 67,247 | 50.5 |
| | William I. Traeger (R) | 65,858 | 49.5 |
| 16 | John F. Dockweiler (D-R) | 119,332 | 98.8 |
| 17 | Charles J. Colden (D) | 60,045 | 70.3 |
| | C. P. Wright (R) | 20,508 | 24.0 |
| | Richard Pomeroy (SOC) | 4,721 | 5.5 |
| 18 | Byron N. Scott (D) | 52,377 | 56.3 |
| | William Brayton (R) | 40,179 | 43.2 |
| 19 | Sam L. Collins (R-D) | 97,119 | 88.6 |
| | A. B. Hillabold | 12,301 | 11.2 |
| 20 | George Burnham (R) | 51,682 | 52.4 |
| | Ed V. Izac (D & PROG) | 46,957 | 47.6 |

## COLORADO

| | Candidates | Votes | % |
|---|---|---|---|
| 1 | Lawrence Lewis (D) | 59,744 | 56.0 |
| | William R. Eaton (R) | 34,073 | 32.0 |
| | Charles W. Varnum (OLD AGE) | 9,511 | 8.9 |
| 2 | Fred Cummings (D) | 64,719 | 55.9 |
| | George H. Bradfield (R) | 49,142 | 42.4 |
| 3 | John A. Martin (D) | 73,281 | 64.2 |
| | W. O. Peterson (R) | 39,753 | 34.8 |
| 4 | Edward T. Taylor (D) | 39,747 | 67.3 |
| | Harry McDevitt (R) | 17,234 | 29.2 |

## CONNECTICUT

| | Candidates | Votes | % |
|---|---|---|---|
| 1 | Herman P. Kopplemann (D) | 74,533 | 54.3 |
| | Anson T. McCook (R) | 59,240 | 43.2 |
| 2 | William L. Higgins (R) | 44,899 | 49.6 |
| | John M. Dowe (D) | 43,816 | 48.4 |
| 3 | James A. Shanley (D) | 55,894 | 48.8 |
| | Joseph F. Morrissey (R) | 52,832 | 46.1 |
| 4 | Schuyler Merritt (R) | 54,178 | 44.1 |
| | Edward T. Buckingham (D) | 45,835 | 37.3 |
| | Arnold E. Freese (SOC) | 21,021 | 17.1 |
| 5 | J. Joseph Smith (D) | 42,594 | 51.4 |
| | Edward W. Goss (R) | 38,547 | 46.5 |
| AL | William M. Citron (D) | 263,794 | 51.4 |
| | Charles M. Bakewell (R) | 249,146 | 48.6 |

## DELAWARE

| | Candidates | Votes | % |
|---|---|---|---|
| AL | John George Stewart (R) | 52,468 | 53.1 |
| | John C. Hazzard (D) | 45,927 | 46.5 |

## FLORIDA

| | Candidates | Votes | % |
|---|---|---|---|
| 1 | J. Hardin Peterson (D) | 42,051 | 100.0 |
| 2 | Robert A. Green (D) | 13,740 | 100.0 |
| 3 | Millard F. Caldwell (D) | 16,740 | 100.0 |
| 4 | J. Mark Wilcox (D) | 59,286 | 100.0 |
| AL | William J. Sears (D) | 125,263 | 100.0 |

## GEORGIA

| | Candidates | Votes | % |
|---|---|---|---|
| 1 | Hugh Peterson Jr. (D) | 5,392 | 100.0 |
| 2 | E. E. Cox (D) | 3,369 | 100.0 |
| 3 | Bryant T. Castellow (D) | 4,078 | 100.0 |
| 4 | E. M. Owen (D) | 5,131 | 95.5 |
| 5 | Robert Ramspeck (D) | 5,206 | 100.0 |
| 6 | Carl Vinson (D) | 3,067 | 100.0 |
| 7 | Malcolm C. Tarver (D) | 5,179 | 100.0 |
| 8 | Braswell Deen (D) | 4,501 | 100.0 |
| 9 | B. Frank Whelchel (D) | 8,391 | 100.0 |
| 10 | Paul Brown (D) | 8,129 | 100.0 |

## IDAHO

| | Candidates | Votes | % |
|---|---|---|---|
| 1 | Compton I. White (D) | 42,223 | 61.9 |
| | Burton L. French (R) | 25,969 | 38.1 |
| 2 | D. Worth Clark (D) | 57,547 | 60.5 |
| | Heber Q. Hale (R) | 37,200 | 39.1 |

## ILLINOIS

| | Candidates | Votes | % |
|---|---|---|---|
| 1 | Arthur W. Mitchell (D) | 27,963 | 53.0 |
| | Oscar De Priest (R) | 24,829 | 47.0 |
| 2 | Raymond S. McKeough (D) | 104,479 | 56.3 |
| | P. H. Moynihan (R) | 81,034 | 43.7 |
| 3 | Edward A. Kelly (D) | 122,109 | 63.5 |
| | Frank M. Fulton (R) | 70,329 | 36.6 |
| 4 | Harry P. Beam (D) | 53,448 | 78.8 |
| | Frank George Zelezinski (R) | 14,401 | 21.2 |
| 5 | Adolph J. Sabath (D) | 29,107 | 72.5 |
| | John A. Stanek (R) | 10,923 | 27.2 |
| 6 | Thomas J. O'Brien (D) | 148,645 | 65.7 |
| | Arnold L. Lund (R) | 77,462 | 34.3 |
| 7 | Leonard W. Schuetz (D) | 185,658 | 64.0 |
| | Raymond J. Peacock (R) | 104,079 | 35.9 |
| 8 | Leo Kocialkowski (D) | 27,682 | 74.1 |
| | Edward Richard Piszatowski (R) | 9,671 | 25.9 |
| 9 | James McAndrews (D) | 36,949 | 56.3 |
| | Fred A. Britten (R) | 28,663 | 43.7 |
| 10 | Ralph E. Church (R) | 100,161 | 51.3 |
| | David B. Maloney (D) | 94,993 | 48.7 |
| 11 | Chauncey W. Reed (R) | 69,469 | 50.3 |
| | James A. Howell (D) | 68,748 | 49.7 |
| 12 | John T. Buckbee (R) | 57,126 | 55.3 |
| | C. H. Smith (D) | 46,111 | 44.7 |
| 13 | Leo S. Allen (R) | 40,423 | 60.5 |
| | Edward S. Nicholas (D) | 26,427 | 39.5 |
| 14 | Chester Thompson (D) | 44,965 | 53.3 |
| | John C. Allen (R) | 39,330 | 46.7 |
| 15 | J. Leroy Adair (D) | 48,682 | 54.9 |
| | Burnett M. Chiperfield (R) | 40,035 | 45.1 |
| 16 | Everett M. Dirksen (R) | 58,716 | 65.4 |
| | Rayburn L. Russell (D) | 31,044 | 34.6 |
| 17 | Leslie C. Arends (R) | 36,552 | 52.1 |
| | Frank Gillespie (D) | 33,621 | 47.9 |
| 18 | James A. Meeks (D) | 48,791 | 52.0 |
| | Elmer A. Taylor (R) | 44,617 | 47.6 |
| 19 | Donald C. Dobbins (D) | 59,179 | 53.9 |
| | Charles H. Fletcher (R) | 50,571 | 46.1 |
| 20 | Scott W. Lucas (D) | 39,761 | 56.9 |
| | Warren W. Wright (R) | 30,085 | 43.1 |
| 21 | Harry H. Mason (D) | 49,825 | 51.0 |
| | Frank M. Ramey (R) | 47,330 | 48.4 |
| 22 | Edwin M. Schaefer (D) | 62,161 | 56.3 |
| | Jesse R. Brown (R) | 48,285 | 43.7 |
| 23 | William W. Arnold (D) | 51,712 | 55.5 |
| | Ben O. Sumner (R) | 41,520 | 44.5 |
| 24 | Claude V. Parsons (D) | 39,442 | 51.7 |
| | James V. Heidinger (R) | 36,891 | 48.3 |
| 25 | Kent E. Keller (D) | 55,824 | 54.8 |
| | J. Lester Buford (R) | 45,955 | 45.2 |
| AL | Michael L. Igoe (D) | 1,507,714✔ | |
| | Martin A. Brennan (D) | 1,459,890✔ | |
| | C. Wayland Brooks (R) | 1,201,373 | |
| | Milton E. Jones (R) | 1,112,802 | |
| | Walter Nesbit (N PROG) | 19,329 | |
| | Arthur McDowell (SOC) | 13,586 | |
| | Harold O. Hatcher (SOC) | 13,580 | |
| | Martin Powroznik (N PROG) | 7,778 | |
| | Frank Earl Herrick (P) | 4,863 | |
| | Clay F. Gaumer (P) | 4,659 | |
| | John L. Lindsey (SOC LAB) | 3,396 | |
| | Frank Schnur (SOC LAB) | 3,195 | |

## INDIANA

| | Candidates | Votes | % |
|---|---|---|---|
| 1 | William T. Schulte (D) | 44,983 | 53.5 |
| | E. Miles Norton (R) | 38,531 | 45.9 |
| 2 | Frederick Landis (R) | 72,552* | 53.9 |
| | George R. Durgan (D) | 61,610 | 45.8 |
| 3 | Samuel B. Pettengill (D) | 55,283 | 50.7 |
| | Andrew J. Hickey (R) | 52,410 | 48.1 |
| 4 | James I. Farley (D) | 58,625 | 51.7 |
| | David Hogg (R) | 54,510 | 48.1 |
| 5 | Glenn Griswold (D) | 68,079 | 54.1 |
| | Albert R. Hall (R) | 56,420 | 44.8 |
| 6 | Virginia E. Jenckes (D) | 67,521 | 49.8 |
| | Fred S. Purnell (R) | 67,138 | 49.6 |
| 7 | Arthur H. Greenwood (D) | 73,324 | 51.5 |
| | Gerald W. Landis (R) | 67,987 | 47.7 |
| 8 | John W. Boehne Jr. (D) | 75,268 | 56.9 |
| | Charles F. Werner (R) | 56,470 | 42.7 |
| 9 | Eugene B. Crowe (D) | 68,329 | 52.1 |
| | Chester A. Davis (R) | 62,403 | 47.6 |

## INDIANA

| | Candidates | Votes | % |
|---|---|---|---|
| 10 | Finly H. Gray (D) | 64,939 | 51.5 |
| | Robert F. Murray (R) | 60,693 | 48.1 |
| 11 | William H. Larrabee (D) | 61,476 | 54.4 |
| | Ralph A. Scott (R) | 50,350 | 44.5 |
| 12 | Louis Ludlow (D) | 60,358 | 55.6 |
| | Delbert O. Wilmeth (R) | 47,134 | 43.4 |

## IOWA

| | | Votes | % |
|---|---|---|---|
| 1 | Edward C. Eicher (D) | 48,544 | 55.4 |
| | E. R. Hicklin (R) | 39,047 | 44.6 |
| 2 | Bernhard M. Jacobsen (D) | 60,654 | 64.0 |
| | M. B. Andelfinger (R) | 34,153 | 36.0 |
| 3 | John W. Gwynne (R) | 42,063 | 54.5 |
| | Albert C. Willford (D) | 35,159 | 45.5 |
| 4 | Fred Biermann (D) | 49,504 | 53.1 |
| | C. A. Benson (R) | 43,794 | 46.9 |
| 5 | Lloyd Thurston (R) | 54,699 | 53.0 |
| | Ernest H. Fabritz (D) | 48,449 | 47.0 |
| 6 | Hubert Utterback (D) | 50,828 | 52.5 |
| | Cassius C. Dowell (R) | 46,084 | 47.6 |
| 7 | Otha D. Wearin (D) | 51,395 | 52.0 |
| | Charles E. Swanson (R) | 47,508 | 48.0 |
| 8 | Fred C. Gilchrist (R) | 45,875 | 53.2 |
| | Joseph J. Meyers (D) | 40,434 | 46.9 |
| 9 | Guy M. Gillette (D) | 58,598 | 64.2 |
| | Thomas H. McBride (R) | 32,639 | 35.8 |

## KANSAS

| | | Votes | % |
|---|---|---|---|
| 1 | William P. Lambertson (R) | 66,293 | 60.5 |
| | John H. Arnett (D) | 43,205 | 39.5 |
| 2 | Ulysses S. Guyer (R) | 60,401 | 49.7 |
| | Howard E. Payne (D) | 59,698 | 49.1 |
| 3 | Edward W. Patterson (D) | 51,793 | 50.0 |
| | Harold McGugin (R) | 49,710 | 48.0 |
| 4 | William Randolph Carpenter (D) | 50,309 | 52.6 |
| | Hal E. Harlan (R) | 45,346 | 47.4 |
| 5 | John M. Houston (D) | 49,610 | 57.0 |
| | Ira C. Watson (R) | 31,511 | 36.2 |
| | C. F. Whitson | 4,661 | 5.4 |
| 6 | Frank Carlson (R) | 62,824 | 51.1 |
| | Kathryn O'Loughlin McCarthy (D) | 60,028 | 48.8 |
| 7 | Clifford R. Hope (R) | 63,952 | 54.6 |
| | L. E. Webb (D) | 53,104 | 45.4 |

## KENTUCKY

| | | Votes | % |
|---|---|---|---|
| 1 | William V. Gregory (D) | 18,868 | 61.1 |
| | John W. Taylor (R) | 12,008 | 38.9 |
| 2 | Glover H. Cary (D) | 18,410 | 75.1 |
| | William M. Likins (P) | 5,188 | 21.2 |
| 3 | Emmet O'Neal (D) | 48,664 | 56.2 |
| | Frank M. Drake (R) | 36,922 | 42.6 |
| 4 | Cap R. Carden (D) | 25,669 | 52.1 |
| | James Tudor (R) | 23,644 | 48.0 |
| 5 | Brent Spence (D) | 24,666 | 65.1 |
| | J. L. Newhall (R) | 11,576 | 30.6 |
| 6 | Virgil Chapman (D) | 34,641 | 60.0 |
| | W. D. Rogers (R) | 23,070 | 40.0 |
| 7 | Andrew J. May (D) | 35,642 | 52.9 |
| | Harry H. Ramey (R) | 31,799 | 47.2 |
| 8 | Fred M. Vinson (D) | 35,288 | 59.2 |
| | George R. Ellison (R) | 24,358 | 40.8 |
| 9 | John M. Robsion (R) | 42,741 | 77.0 |
| | L. L. Terrell (D) | 12,736 | 23.0 |

## LOUISIANA

| | | Votes | % |
|---|---|---|---|
| 1 | Joachim O. Fernandez (D) | 45,678 | 99.9 |
| 2 | Paul H. Maloney (D) | 45,793 | 100.0 |
| 3 | Numa F. Montet (D) | 12,636 | 100.0 |
| 4 | John N. Sandlin (D) | 14,680 | 100.0 |
| 5 | Riley J. Wilson (D) | 14,158 | 100.0 |
| 6 | Jared Y. Sanders Jr. (D) | 19,377 | 100.0 |

| | Candidates | Votes | % |
|---|---|---|---|
| 7 | Rene L. DeRouen (D) | 16,528 | 100.0 |
| 8 | Cleveland Dear (D) | 17,213 | 100.0 |

### Special Election

| | | Votes | % |
|---|---|---|---|
| 6 | Jared Y. Sanders Jr. (D) | 9,649 | 99.6 |

## MAINE

| | | Votes | % |
|---|---|---|---|
| 1 | Simon M. Hamlin (D) | 48,235 | 50.8 |
| | Carroll L. Beedy (R) | 46,635 | 49.2 |
| 2 | Edward C. Moran Jr. (D) | 52,491 | 53.2 |
| | Zelma M. Dwinal (R) | 46,200 | 46.8 |
| 3 | Ralph O. Brewster (R) | 44,024 | 51.4 |
| | J. G. Utterback (D) | 41,710 | 48.7 |

## MARYLAND

| | | Votes | % |
|---|---|---|---|
| 1 | T. Alan Goldsborough (D) | 41,627 | 64.0 |
| | H. Burdett Messenger (R) | 23,378 | 36.0 |
| 2 | William P. Cole (D) | 75,244 | 57.7 |
| | Theodore F. Brown (R) | 51,303 | 39.3 |
| 3 | Vincent L. Palmisano (D) | 27,988 | 66.4 |
| | F. Stanley Porter (R) | 13,042 | 30.9 |
| 4 | Ambrose J. Kennedy (D) | 37,006 | 59.1 |
| | William J. Stocksdale (R) | 24,162 | 38.6 |
| 5 | Stephen W. Gambrill (D) | 39,734 | 61.4 |
| | Joseph Allison Wilmer (R) | 24,364 | 37.7 |
| 6 | David J. Lewis (D) | 45,605 | 50.3 |
| | Frederick N. Zihlman (R) | 44,244 | 48.8 |

## MASSACHUSETTS

| | | Votes | % |
|---|---|---|---|
| 1 | Allen T. Treadway (R) | 51,046 | 57.6 |
| | George E. Haggerty (D) | 35,061 | 39.6 |
| 2 | William J. Granfield (D) | 47,894 | 51.2 |
| | Charles R. Clason (R) | 42,495 | 45.5 |
| 3 | Joseph E. Casey (D) | 46,830 | 50.1 |
| | Frank H. Foss (R) | 46,572 | 49.9 |
| 4 | Pehr G. Holmes (R) | 54,601 | 57.5 |
| | James H. Ferguson (D) | 38,984 | 41.0 |
| 5 | Edith Nourse Rogers (R) | 75,754 | 62.2 |
| | Jeremiah J. O'Sullivan (D) | 46,124 | 37.8 |
| 6 | A. Piatt Andrew (R) | 64,610 | 100.0 |
| 7 | William P. Connery Jr. (D) | 62,666 | 59.1 |
| | C. F. Nelson Pratt (R) | 40,988 | 38.6 |
| 8 | Arthur D. Healey (D) | 53,581 | 58.6 |
| | William S. Howe (R) | 37,873 | 41.4 |
| 9 | Richard M. Russell (D) | 60,141 | 52.6 |
| | Robert Luce (R) | 54,198 | 47.4 |
| 10 | George Holden Tinkham (R, D) | 84,244 | 100.0 |
| 11 | John P. Higgins (D) | 46,383 | 100.0 |
| 12 | John W. McCormack (D) | 78,783 | 82.8 |
| | Francis A. Pentoney (R) | 16,370 | 17.2 |
| 13 | Richard B. Wigglesworth (R) | 58,653 | 54.9 |
| | Francis H. Foy (D) | 48,241 | 45.1 |
| 14 | Joseph W. Martin Jr. (R) | 46,411 | 54.8 |
| | Arthur E. Seagrave (D) | 38,325 | 45.2 |
| 15 | Charles L. Gifford (R) | 46,446 | 53.4 |
| | John D. W. Bodfish (D) | 38,336 | 44.0 |

## MICHIGAN

| | | Votes | % |
|---|---|---|---|
| 1 | George G. Sadowski (D) | 40,054 | 65.8 |
| | Charles A. Roxborough (R) | 19,194 | 31.5 |
| 2 | Earl C. Michener (R) | 40,119 | 50.2 |
| | John C. Lehr (D) | 38,972 | 48.7 |
| 3 | Henry M. Kimball (R) | 41,587 | 55.0 |
| | Paul H. Todd (D) | 32,928 | 43.6 |
| 4 | Clare E. Hoffman (R) | 45,224 | 58.2 |
| | George Foulkes (D) | 31,646 | 40.7 |
| 5 | Carl E. Mapes (R) | 39,682 | 50.5 |
| | Thomas F. McAllister (D) | 37,847 | 48.2 |
| 6 | William W. Blackney (R) | 42,424 | 50.6 |
| | Claude E. Cady (D) | 41,100 | 49.0 |

| | Candidates | Votes | % |
|---|---|---|---|
| 7 | Jesse P. Wolcott (R) | 42,857 | 59.9 |
| | Frank J. Wiegand (D) | 27,690 | 38.7 |
| 8 | Fred L. Crawford (R) | 40,333 | 51.5 |
| | Michael J. Hart (D) | 35,945 | 45.9 |
| 9 | Albert J. Engel (R) | 33,222 | 52.0 |
| | Harry W. Musselwhite (D) | 30,513 | 47.7 |
| 10 | Roy O. Woodruff (R) | 36,719 | 59.5 |
| | Hubert J. Gaffney (D) | 24,526 | 39.8 |
| 11 | Prentiss M. Brown (D) | 39,293 | 54.8 |
| | John J. O'Hara (R) | 32,460 | 45.2 |
| 12 | Frank E. Hook (D) | 37,298 | 52.1 |
| | W. Frank James (R) | 34,281 | 47.9 |
| 13 | Clarence J. McLeod (R) | 35,879 | 56.7 |
| | John H. Slevin (D) | 25,869 | 40.9 |
| 14 | Louis C. Rabaut (D) | 45,301 | 62.2 |
| | John H. McPherson (R) | 26,006 | 35.7 |
| 15 | John D. Dingell (D) | 40,110 | 54.4 |
| | Charles Bowles (R) | 32,011 | 43.4 |
| 16 | John Lesinski (D) | 32,269 | 52.7 |
| | Clyde M. Ford (R) | 27,487 | 44.9 |
| 17 | George A. Dondero (R) | 35,562 | 53.8 |
| | Charles P. Webster (D) | 29,250 | 44.2 |

## MINNESOTA

| | | Votes | % |
|---|---|---|---|
| 1 | August H. Andresen (R) | 51,099 | 46.6 |
| | John W. Feller (D) | 29,581 | 27.0 |
| | Otto Baudler (F-LAB) | 29,038 | 26.5 |
| 2 | Elmer J. Ryan (D) | 43,677 | 37.2 |
| | Henry Arens (F-LAB) | 37,663 | 32.1 |
| | L. P. Johnson (R) | 35,968 | 30.7 |
| 3 | Ernest Lundeen (F-LAB) | 59,097 | 53.3 |
| | Josiah H. Chase (R) | 28,637 | 25.8 |
| | John W. Schmidt (D) | 22,556 | 20.3 |
| 4 | Melvin J. Maas (R) | 37,933 | 36.8 |
| | A. E. Smith (F-LAB) | 30,354 | 29.5 |
| | John J. McDonough (D) | 24,122 | 23.4 |
| | Charles J. Andre (I) | 10,180 | 9.9 |
| 5 | Theodore Christianson (R) | 45,875 | 39.3 |
| | Dewey W. Johnson (F-LAB) | 42,322 | 36.2 |
| | Sidney Benson (D) | 27,814 | 23.8 |
| 6 | Harold Knutson (R) | 56,642 | 46.2 |
| | Magnus Johnson (F-LAB) | 46,346 | 37.8 |
| | Frank R. Weber (D) | 19,572 | 16.0 |
| 7 | Paul John Kvale (F-LAB) | 65,261 | 59.3 |
| | Richard T. Daly (D) | 44,762 | 40.7 |
| 8 | William A. Pittenger (R) | 39,513 | 35.7 |
| | F. H. Shoemaker (I) | 25,386 | 23.0 |
| | A. L. Winterquist (F-LAB) | 25,024 | 22.6 |
| | Jerry A. Harri (D) | 18,707 | 16.9 |
| 9 | Richard T. Buckler (F-LAB) | 41,822 | 44.2 |
| | Ole O. Sageng (R) | 27,522 | 29.1 |
| | Martin Oscar Brandon (D) | 25,210 | 26.7 |

## MISSISSIPPI

| | | Votes | % |
|---|---|---|---|
| 1 | John E. Rankin (D) | 6,825 | 100.0 |
| 2 | Wall Doxey (D) | 5,721 | 100.0 |
| 3 | William M. Whittington (D) | 3,586 | 100.0 |
| 4 | Aaron Lane Ford (D) | 8,051 | 100.0 |
| 5 | Aubert C. Dunn (D) | 9,412 | 100.0 |
| 6 | William M. Colmer (D) | 9,002 | 100.0 |
| 7 | Dan R. McGehee (D) | 14,730 | 100.0 |

## MISSOURI

| | | Votes | % |
|---|---|---|---|
| 1 | Milton A. Romjue (D) | 52,273 | 54.8 |
| | J. Grover Morgan (R) | 42,513 | 44.5 |
| 2 | William L. Nelson (D) | 59,557 | 58.6 |
| | Logan (R) | 41,916 | 41.2 |
| 3 | Richard M. Duncan (D) | 61,548 | 60.6 |
| | William A. Black (R) | 39,953 | 39.3 |
| 4 | C. Jasper Bell (D) | 82,995 | 81.7 |
| | Horace Guffin (R) | 18,368 | 18.1 |
| 5 | Joseph B. Shannon (D) | 96,798 | 84.3 |
| | Claude E. Sowers (R) | 17,889 | 15.6 |
| 6 | Reuben T. Wood (D) | 58,902 | 55.1 |
| | Oliver J. Page (R) | 47,769 | 44.7 |

## MISSOURI

| Candidates | Votes | % |
|---|---|---|
| 7 Dewey Short (R) | 65,211 | 52.9 |
| Frank H. Lee (D) | 57,446 | 46.6 |
| 8 Clyde Williams (D) | 54,006 | 54.4 |
| Breuer (R) | 45,354 | 45.7 |
| 9 Clarence Cannon (D) | 41,514 | 62.4 |
| Voelkerding (R) | 24,380 | 36.7 |
| 10 Orville Zimmerman (D) | 42,865 | 58.2 |
| McAnally (R) | 29,949 | 40.7 |
| 11 Thomas C. Hennings (D) | 59,119 | 56.4 |
| Leonidas C. Dyer (R) | 44,693 | 42.6 |
| 12 James R. Claiborne (D) | 70,754 | 51.0 |
| Cleveland A. Newton (R) | 66,108 | 47.7 |
| 13 John J. Cochran (D) | 60,198 | 65.5 |
| George W. Strodtman (R) | 31,165 | 33.9 |

## MONTANA

| Candidates | Votes | % |
|---|---|---|
| 1 Joseph P. Monaghan (D) | 55,877 | 67.8 |
| D. D. Evans (R) | 25,567 | 31.0 |
| 2 Roy E. Ayers (D) | 79,856 | 69.8 |
| Stanley E. Felt (R) | 33,703 | 29.5 |

## NEBRASKA

| Candidates | Votes | % |
|---|---|---|
| 1 Henry C. Luckey (D) | 55,897 | 52.8 |
| Marcus L. Poteet (R) | 45,258 | 42.8 |
| 2 Charles F. McLaughlin (D) | 46,790 | 54.2 |
| Herbert Rhoades (R) | 36,743 | 42.5 |
| 3 Karl Stefan (R) | 69,363 | 57.8 |
| Edgar Howard (D) | 50,707 | 42.2 |
| 4 C. G. Binderup (D) | 69,275 | 58.4 |
| James W. Hammond (R) | 49,357 | 41.6 |
| 5 Harry B. Coffee (D) | 55,709 | 52.1 |
| Albert N. Mathers (R) | 49,161 | 45.9 |

## NEVADA

| Candidates | Votes | % |
|---|---|---|
| AL James G. Scrugham (D) | 29,691 | 71.2 |
| George B. Russell (R) | 11,992 | 28.8 |

## NEW HAMPSHIRE

| Candidates | Votes | % |
|---|---|---|
| 1 William N. Rogers (D) | 48,568 | 53.9 |
| Arthur B. Jenks (R) | 41,425 | 46.0 |
| 2 Charles W. Tobey (R) | 42,706 | 53.3 |
| Harry B. Metcalf (D) | 37,122 | 46.3 |

## NEW JERSEY

| Candidates | Votes | % |
|---|---|---|
| 1 Charles A. Wolverton (R) | 81,634 | 61.2 |
| Willis Tullis Porch (D) | 48,770 | 36.6 |
| 2 Isaac Bacharach (R) | 49,824 | 50.4 |
| Charles W. Ackley (D) | 48,743 | 49.3 |
| 3 William H. Sutphin (D) | 58,670 | 52.2 |
| Oliver F. Van Camp (R) | 53,170 | 47.3 |
| 4 D. Lane Powers (R) | 48,760 | 56.7 |
| Walter Lincoln Whittlesey (D) | 36,326 | 42.2 |
| 5 Charles A. Eaton (R) | 54,938 | 51.7 |
| Charles S. MacKenzie (D) | 50,395 | 47.4 |
| 6 Donald H. McLean (R) | 51,528 | 52.5 |
| Richard U. Strong (D) | 45,581 | 46.4 |
| 7 Randolph Perkins (R) | 47,083 | 51.4 |
| Hamilton Cross (D) | 43,771 | 47.7 |
| 8 George N. Seger (R) | 45,123 | 53.6 |
| Frank J. Van Noort (D) | 37,119 | 44.1 |
| 9 Edward A. Kenney (D) | 54,941 | 54.6 |
| John Pollock (R) | 44,704 | 44.4 |
| 10 Fred A. Hartley Jr. (R) | 40,205 | 52.9 |
| William Herda Smith (D) | 35,261 | 46.4 |
| 11 Peter A. Cavicchia (R) | 34,110 | 50.0 |
| Edward L. O'Neill (D) | 33,531 | 49.1 |
| 12 Frederick R. Lehlbach (R) | 39,817 | 54.3 |
| Charles P. McCann (D) | 32,546 | 44.4 |
| 13 Mary T. Norton (D) | 73,342 | 73.2 |
| Anthony L. Montelli (R) | 26,447 | 26.4 |

| Candidates | Votes | % |
|---|---|---|
| 14 Edward J. Hart (D) | 77,020 | 77.7 |
| Fred G. Tauber (R) | 21,081 | 21.3 |

## NEW MEXICO

| Candidates | Votes | % |
|---|---|---|
| AL John J. Dempsey (D) | 76,833 | 51.8 |
| M. F. Miera (R) | 70,659 | 47.7 |

## NEW YORK

| Candidates | Votes | % |
|---|---|---|
| 1 Robert L. Bacon (RCF & LP) | 127,082 | 56.0 |
| Gerald Morrell (D) | 93,794 | 41.4 |
| 2 William F. Brunner (D) | 140,520 | 69.6 |
| Thomas J. Styles (R & VIC) | 48,306 | 23.9 |
| 3 Joseph L. Pfeifer (D) | 26,738 | 72.8 |
| Alex Pisciotta (R CF&REC) | 8,179 | 22.3 |
| 4 Thomas H. Cullen (D & REC) | 29,858 | 74.5 |
| Charles E. Miller (R VIC&CF) | 8,935 | 22.3 |
| 5 Marcellus H. Evans (D & REC) | 41,154 | 64.7 |
| Frank E. Davis (RCF & LP) | 19,010 | 29.9 |
| 6 Andrew L. Somers (D & LP) | 70,164 | 60.9 |
| Donald C. Strachan (R & CF) | 30,671 | 26.6 |
| Jacob Axelrad (SOC) | 10,327 | 9.0 |
| 7 John J. Delaney (D) | 28,945 | 67.9 |
| Joseph M. Aimee (RCF & LP) | 9,897 | 23.2 |
| Alexander Kahn (SOC & LP) | 2,503 | 5.9 |
| 8 Richard J. Tonry (D & REC) | 111,247 | 59.2 |
| Sigurd J. Arnesen (R & CF) | 44,423 | 23.6 |
| Baruch C. Vladeck (SOC) | 22,149 | 11.8 |
| 9 Stephen A. Rudd (D) | 56,617 | 60.6 |
| Murray Rosof (R & CF) | 30,462 | 32.6 |
| Theodore Shapiro (SOC) | 4,738 | 5.1 |
| 10 Emanuel Celler (D LP & L) | 31,193 | 60.9 |
| Michael C. Antonelli (R CF&REC) | 14,770 | 28.8 |
| Samuel H. Friedman (SOC) | 3,470 | 6.8 |
| 11 James A. O'Leary (D) | 36,393 | 59.9 |
| Arthur L. Willshaw (R) | 15,595 | 25.7 |
| Vernon B. Hampton (RC I) | 6,666 | 11.0 |
| 12 Samuel Dickstein (D) | 14,895 | 76.8 |
| Solomon Siss (R & CF) | 3,029 | 15.6 |
| 13 Christopher D. Sullivan (D) | 13,090 | 72.3 |
| John Rosenberg (R) | 3,828 | 21.1 |
| 14 William I. Sirovich (D) | 15,437 | 52.8 |
| Frederick J. Groehl (R) | 9,744 | 33.4 |
| Rachel Panken (SOC) | 2,259 | 7.7 |
| Peter E. Cacchione (COM) | 1,612 | 5.5 |
| 15 John J. Boylan (D) | 23,482 | 80.2 |
| Frank J. McCoy (R) | 4,726 | 16.1 |
| 16 John J. O'Connor (D) | 22,528 | 66.3 |
| J. Homer Cudmore (R) | 9,735 | 28.6 |
| 17 Theodore A. Peyser (D) | 29,338 | 53.9 |
| George A. Spiegelberg (R CST&CF) | 22,688 | 41.7 |
| 18 Martin J. Kennedy (D) | 23,480 | 69.0 |
| Charles W. Ferry (R) | 8,832 | 26.0 |
| 19 Sol Bloom (D & LP) | 42,614 | 65.3 |
| Harold Goldman (R & CF) | 18,612 | 28.5 |
| 20 Vito Marcantonio (R & CF) | 13,083 | 46.6 |
| James J. Lanzetta (LAW PRES) | 12,836 | 45.8 |
| 21 Joseph A. Gavagan (D) | 62,042 | 68.2 |
| Kenneth Cameron (R & CF) | 23,534 | 25.9 |
| 22 Anthony J. Griffin (D) | 28,535 | 69.3 |
| John J. Sochurek (R & IV) | 9,162 | 22.3 |
| 23 Charles A. Buckley (D) | 109,319 | 64.2 |
| Isaac F. Becker (R) | 31,028 | 18.2 |
| Samuel Orr (SOC) | 14,333 | 8.4 |
| 24 James M. Fitzpatrick (D) | 104,652 | 60.1 |
| John H. Nichols (R) | 51,535 | 29.6 |

| Candidates | Votes | % |
|---|---|---|
| Solomon Perrin (SOC) | 11,256 | 6.5 |
| 25 Charles D. Millard (R) | 63,782 | 54.8 |
| Homer A. Stebbins (D) | 49,469 | 42.5 |
| 26 Hamilton Fish Jr. (R SOC&LP) | 50,849 | 61.9 |
| Thomas Pendell (D) | 31,292 | 38.1 |
| 27 Philip A. Goodwin (R & SOC) | 46,924 | 55.7 |
| Willis G. Nash (D & LP) | 37,295 | 44.3 |
| 28 Parker Corning (D) | 89,511 | 70.1 |
| Frank R. Lanagan (R) | 36,117 | 28.3 |
| 29 William D. Thomas (R & LP) | 56,401 | 58.4 |
| Buell G. Brayton (D) | 38,054 | 39.4 |
| 30 Frank Crowther (R & LP) | 42,740 | 50.8 |
| Carroll A. Gardner (D) | 39,048 | 46.4 |
| 31 Bertrand H. Snell (R) | 43,942 | 62.0 |
| Kenneth Gardner (D) | 26,308 | 37.1 |
| 32 Francis D. Culkin (R & LP) | 49,055 | 67.0 |
| Annie D. Mills (D) | 22,959 | 31.3 |
| 33 Fred J. Sisson (D) | 45,831 | 49.1 |
| Frederick M. Davenport (R) | 45,579 | 48.9 |
| 34 Bert Lord (R) | 50,528 | 60.2 |
| Charles C. Flaesch (D) | 32,075 | 38.2 |
| 35 Clarence E. Hancock (R) | 65,732 | 54.7 |
| Richard P. Byrne (D) | 50,599 | 42.1 |
| 36 John Taber (R) | 45,431 | 61.0 |
| Dennis F. Sullivan (D) | 27,129 | 36.4 |
| 37 W. Sterling Cole (R) | 48,964 | 59.8 |
| Julian P. Bretz (D) | 28,979 | 35.4 |
| 38 James P. B. Duffy (D) | 64,434 | 54.2 |
| James L. Whitley (R & LP) | 50,066 | 42.1 |
| 39 James W. Wadsworth Jr. (R & LP) | 49,915 | 56.2 |
| David A. White (D) | 36,658 | 41.3 |
| 40 Walter G. Andrews (R) | 69,353 | 55.7 |
| Frank S. Anderson (D) | 50,532 | 40.6 |
| 41 Alfred F. Beiter (D) | 45,830 | 55.7 |
| Carlton A. Fisher (R) | 33,793 | 41.1 |
| 42 James M. Mead (D) | 49,251 | 63.8 |
| Walter J. Lohr (R & LP) | 26,036 | 33.7 |
| 43 Daniel A. Reed (R & LP) | 42,513 | 63.3 |
| Peter B. Hogan (D) | 21,856 | 32.6 |
| AL Caroline O'Day (D) | 1,978,670✔ | |
| Matthew J. Merritt (D) | 1,952,039✔ | |
| Natalie F. Couch (R) | 1,417,271 | |
| William B. Groat Jr (R) | 1,387,460 | |
| Charles W. Noonan (SOC) | 141,799 | |
| August Claessens (SOC) | 138,778 | |
| Henry Sheppard (COM) | 48,851 | |
| Emanuel Levin (COM) | 47,812 | |
| Dorothy Frooks (LAW PRES) | 19,853 | |
| William E. Barron (LAW PRES) | 16,770 | |
| Jeremiah D. Crowley (SOC LAB) | 7,529 | |
| Jacob Berlin (SOC LAB) | 6,701 | |

### Special Election

| | Votes | % |
|---|---|---|
| 29 William D. Thomas (R) | 25,048 | 60.1 |
| John J. Nyhoff (D) | 16,030 | 38.5 |

## NORTH CAROLINA

| Candidates | Votes | % |
|---|---|---|
| 1 Lindsay C. Warren (D) | 11,786 | 87.8 |
| R. C. Dozier (R) | 1,637 | 12.2 |
| 2 John H. Kerr (D) | 11,329 | 100.0 |
| 3 Graham A. Barden (D) | 20,218 | 67.1 |
| W. B. Rouse (R) | 9,922 | 32.9 |
| 4 Harold D. Cooley (D) | 29,431 | 68.5 |
| Hobart Brantley (R) | 13,507 | 31.5 |
| 5 Franklin W. Hancock Jr. (D) | 28,221 | 100.0 |
| 6 William B. Umstead (D) | 21,241 | 69.0 |
| B. C. Campbell (R) | 9,543 | 31.0 |
| 7 J. Bayard Clark (D) | 17,774 | 78.9 |
| Louis Goodman (R) | 4,747 | 21.1 |

## NORTH CAROLINA

| | Candidates | Votes | % |
|---|---|---|---|
| 8 | J. Walter Lambeth (D) | 35,794 | 58.0 |
| | Avalon E. Hall (R) | 25,974 | 42.1 |
| 9 | Robert L. Doughton (D) | 44,780 | 58.2 |
| | J. M. Prevette (R) | 32,171 | 41.8 |
| 10 | Alfred L. Bulwinkle (D) | 43,483 | 53.5 |
| | Calvin R. Edney (R) | 37,820 | 46.5 |
| 11 | Zebulon Weaver (D) | 56,199 | 59.6 |
| | Halsey B. Leavitt (R) | 38,126 | 40.4 |

### Special Election

| | | Votes | % |
|---|---|---|---|
| 4 | Harold D. Cooley (D) | 16,881 | 93.8 |
| | Hobart Brantley (R) | 1,110 | 6.2 |

## NORTH DAKOTA

| | | Votes | |
|---|---|---|---|
| AL | William Lemke (R) | 144,705 | |
| | Usher L. Burdick (R) | 114,841 | |
| | William D. Lynch (D) | 85,771 | |
| | G. F. Lamb (D) | 79,338 | |
| | J. H. Sinclair (I) | 46,304 | |
| | Jasper Haaland (I) | 1,299 | |
| | Effie Kjorstad (I) | 1,090 | |

## OHIO

| | | Votes | % |
|---|---|---|---|
| 1 | John B. Hollister (R) | 53,985 | 55.8 |
| | Edwin G. Becker (D) | 42,723 | 44.2 |
| 2 | William E. Hess (R) | 51,171 | 55.1 |
| | Charles E. Miller (D) | 41,701 | 44.9 |
| 3 | Byron B. Harlan (D) | 67,695 | 53.6 |
| | Howard F. Heald (R) | 56,480 | 44.8 |
| 4 | Frank L. Kloeb (D) | 48,613 | 53.9 |
| | Guy D. Hawley (R) | 41,504 | 46.1 |
| 5 | Frank C. Kniffin (D) | 34,249 | 55.5 |
| | Davis B. Johnson (R) | 27,423 | 44.5 |
| 6 | James G. Polk (D) | 42,340 | 52.2 |
| | Albert L. Daniels (R) | 38,538 | 47.5 |
| 7 | Leroy T. Marshall (R) | 56,453 | 56.6 |
| | C. W. Rich (D) | 43,226 | 43.4 |
| 8 | Brooks Fletcher (D) | 39,466 | 52.2 |
| | Gertrude Jones (R) | 36,112 | 47.8 |
| 9 | Warren J. Duffey (D) | 61,037 | 62.3 |
| | Frank L. Mulholland (R) | 35,732 | 36.5 |
| 10 | Thomas A. Jenkins (R) | 36,824 | 58.4 |
| | W. F. Marting (D) | 26,278 | 41.6 |
| 11 | Mell G. Underwood (D) | 36,020 | 57.4 |
| | Renick W. Dunlap (R) | 26,723 | 42.6 |
| 12 | Arthur P. Lamneck (D) | 63,396 | 55.7 |
| | John C. Speaks (R) | 50,386 | 44.3 |
| 13 | William L. Fiesinger (D) | 43,617 | 54.3 |
| | Walter E. Kruger (R) | 35,889 | 44.7 |
| 14 | Dow W. Harter (D) | 65,152 | 49.1 |
| | Carl D. Sheppard (R) | 63,274 | 47.7 |
| 15 | Robert T. Secrest (D) | 42,722 | 55.7 |
| | Kenneth C. Ray (R) | 33,950 | 44.3 |
| 16 | William R. Thom (D) | 59,354 | 56.7 |
| | C. B. McClintock (R) | 45,390 | 43.3 |
| 17 | William A. Ashbrook (D) | 49,211 | 54.0 |
| | James A. Glenn (R) | 41,954 | 46.0 |
| 18 | Lawrence E. Imhoff (D) | 49,160 | 55.4 |
| | Frank Murphy (R) | 39,642 | 44.6 |
| 19 | John G. Cooper (R) | 56,200 | 51.2 |
| | Locke Miller (D) | 52,023 | 47.4 |
| 20 | Martin L. Sweeney (D) | 50,611 | 67.9 |
| | Joseph E. Cassidy (R) | 21,952 | 29.4 |
| 21 | Robert W. Crosser (D) | 47,540 | 63.8 |
| | Frank W. Sotak (R) | 25,253 | 33.9 |
| 22 | Chester C. Bolton (R) | 99,535 | 52.1 |
| | William C. Dixon (D) | 88,551 | 46.3 |
| AL | Charles V. Truax (D) | 1,061,857 | |
| | Stephen M. Young (D) | 1,050,089 | |
| | George H. Bender (R) | 905,233 | |
| | L. L. Marshall (R) | 871,432 | |
| | Ben Atkins (COM) | 13,972 | |
| | John Marshall (COM) | 13,808 | |

## OKLAHOMA

| | Candidates | Votes | % |
|---|---|---|---|
| 1 | Wesley E. Disney (D) | 61,470 | 60.1 |
| | Robert W. Kellough (R) | 39,085 | 38.2 |
| 2 | Jack Nichols (D) | 40,210 | 62.2 |
| | C. E. Creager (R) | 24,001 | 37.1 |
| 3 | Wilburn Cartwright (D) | 50,435 | 76.9 |
| | John D. Morrison (R) | 14,202 | 21.7 |
| 4 | P. L. Gassaway (D) | 47,140 | 67.5 |
| | James S. Davidson (R) | 19,875 | 28.5 |
| 5 | Josh Lee (D) | 58,322 | 74.6 |
| | Paul Huston (R) | 18,640 | 23.9 |
| 6 | Jed Johnson (D) | 37,567 | 67.2 |
| | George E. Young (R) | 15,567 | 27.8 |
| 7 | Sam C. Massingale (D) | 35,210 | 76.0 |
| | Fred Langley (R) | 8,214 | 17.7 |
| | Orville E. Enfield (SOC) | 2,891 | 6.2 |
| 8 | Phil Fergucon (D) | 40,248 | 56.8 |
| | T. J. Sargent (R) | 30,019 | 42.4 |
| AL | Will Rogers (D) | 354,542 | 66.9 |
| | U. S. Stone (R) | 162,991 | 30.7 |

## OREGON

| | | Votes | % |
|---|---|---|---|
| 1 | James W. Mott (R) | 67,286 | 49.9 |
| | R. R. Turner (D) | 51,443 | 38.1 |
| | Emmett W. Gulley (I) | 12,963 | 9.6 |
| 2 | Walter M. Pierce (D) | 29,221 | 56.7 |
| | Jay H. Upton (R) | 21,255 | 41.3 |
| 3 | William A. Ekwall (R) | 43,900 | 41.1 |
| | Walter B. Gleason (D) | 41,152 | 38.5 |
| | Andrew C. Smith (I) | 9,968 | 9.3 |

## PENNSYLVANIA

| | | Votes | % |
|---|---|---|---|
| 1 | Harry C. Ransley (R) | 46,039 | 52.1 |
| | Joseph Marinelli (D) | 41,733 | 47.2 |
| 2 | William H. Wilson (R) | 44,478 | 54.7 |
| | James P. McGranery (D) | 36,212 | 44.6 |
| 3 | Clare Gerald Fenerty (R) | 53,512 | 52.0 |
| | Michael Joseph Bradley (D) | 48,141 | 46.8 |
| 4 | J. Burrwood Daly (D) | 45,901 | 49.7 |
| | George W. Edmonds (R) | 45,526 | 49.2 |
| 5 | Frank J. G. Dorsey (D) | 50,650 | 52.2 |
| | James J. Connolly (R) | 45,287 | 46.7 |
| 6 | Michael J. Stack (D) | 50,977 | 50.8 |
| | Robert L. Davis (R) | 48,308 | 48.2 |
| 7 | George P. Darrow (R) | 56,990 | 52.7 |
| | James C. Crumlich (D) | 50,207 | 46.4 |
| 8 | James Wolfenden (R) | 60,139 | 57.2 |
| | John E. McDonough (D) | 43,426 | 41.3 |
| 9 | Oliver W. Frey (D) | 40,494 | 50.2 |
| | Theodore R. Gardner (R) | 38,427 | 47.6 |
| 10 | J. Roland Kinzer (R, P) | 58,773 | 57.6 |
| | Charles T. Carpenter (D) | 42,540 | 41.7 |
| 11 | Patrick J. Boland (R, D) | 76,568 | 98.1 |
| 12 | C. Murray Turpin (R) | 60,608 | 51.4 |
| | John J. Casey (D, SOC) | 56,554 | 48.0 |
| 13 | James H. Gildea (D) | 54,309 | 50.1 |
| | David W. Bechtel (R) | 49,584 | 45.7 |
| 14 | William E. Richardson (D, R) | 39,134 | 63.3 |
| | Raymond S. Hofses (SOC) | 19,871 | 32.2 |
| 15 | C. Elmer Dietrich (D) | 39,566 | 50.1 |
| | Louis T. McFadden (R, P) | 38,905 | 49.3 |
| 16 | Robert F. Rich (R, P) | 38,761 | 53.0 |
| | Paul A. Rothfuss (D, SOC) | 32,464 | 44.4 |
| 17 | J. William Ditter (R) | 50,149 | 56.2 |
| | Howard J. Dager (D) | 37,541 | 42.1 |
| 18 | Benjamin K. Focht (R, P) | 37,992 | 55.6 |
| | B. Stiles Duncan (D) | 30,320 | 44.4 |
| 19 | Isaac H. Doutrich (R) | 62,576 | 55.1 |
| | Forrest Mercer (D) | 48,743 | 42.9 |
| 20 | D. J. Driscoll (D) | 48,245 | 52.7 |
| | Leon H. Gavin (R) | 40,050 | 43.7 |
| 21 | Francis E. Walter (D, P) | 41,789 | 58.6 |
| | T. Fred Woodley (R) | 28,520 | 40.0 |
| 22 | Harry L. Haines (D) | 49,629 | 54.6 |
| | Emanuel C. Beck (R) | 39,719 | 43.7 |

| | Candidates | Votes | % |
|---|---|---|---|
| 23 | Don Gingery (D) | 41,088 | 52.4 |
| | J. Banks Kurtz (R, P) | 34,631 | 44.2 |
| 24 | J. Buell Snyder (D) | 43,530 | 57.3 |
| | Paul H. Griffith (R, P) | 31,904 | 42.0 |
| 25 | Charles I. Faddis (D, SOC) | 39,122 | 59.4 |
| | Albert S. Sickman (R) | 25,435 | 38.6 |
| 26 | Charles R. Eckert (D) | 52,243 | 59.1 |
| | J. Howard Swick (R, P) | 35,302 | 40.0 |
| 27 | Joseph Gray (D) | 59,891 | 54.4 |
| | Nathan L. Strong (R, P) | 49,005 | 44.5 |
| 28 | William M. Berlin (D, R) | 63,262 | 92.5 |
| 29 | Charles N. Crosby (D) | 32,530 | 52.5 |
| | Will Rose (R) | 28,292 | 45.6 |
| 30 | J. Twing Brooks (D) | 40,864 | 53.4 |
| | Edmund F. Erk (R, RO) | 34,412 | 45.0 |
| 31 | James L. Quinn (D) | 44,711 | 52.3 |
| | Clyde Kelly (R, P) | 38,984 | 45.6 |
| 32 | Theodore L. Moritz (D) | 24,275 | 43.3 |
| | Michael J. Muldowney (R) | 19,134 | 34.1 |
| | Alexander H. Schullman (I) | 8,441 | 15.0 |
| | Anne E. Felix (HE) | 2,865 | 5.1 |
| 33 | Henry Ellenbogen (D, R) | 72,584 | 95.2 |
| 34 | Matthew A. Dunn (D, R) | 72,215 | 89.2 |
| | Guy E. Campbell (LFD) | 5,474 | 6.8 |

## RHODE ISLAND

| | | Votes | % |
|---|---|---|---|
| 1 | Francis Bernard Condon (D) | 70,516 | 59.0 |
| | John C. Cosseboom (R) | 49,087 | 41.0 |
| 2 | John Matthew O'Connell (D) | 69,765 | 55.8 |
| | George C. Clark (R) | 55,191 | 44.2 |

## SOUTH CAROLINA

| | | Votes | % |
|---|---|---|---|
| 1 | Thomas S. McMillan (D) | 4,264 | 97.7 |
| 2 | Hampton P. Fulmer (D) | 3,518 | 99.2 |
| 3 | John C. Taylor (D) | 3,830 | 99.4 |
| 4 | John J. McSwain (D) | 4,681 | 99.4 |
| 5 | James P. Richards (D) | 2,645 | 98.7 |
| 6 | Allard H. Gasque (D) | 2,983 | 99.3 |

## SOUTH DAKOTA

| | | Votes | % |
|---|---|---|---|
| 1 | Fred H. Hildebrandt (D) | 122,932 | 58.5 |
| | C. A. Christopherson (R) | 84,830 | 40.4 |
| 2 | Theodore B. Werner (D) | 35,467 | 52.5 |
| | Francis H. Case (R) | 32,105 | 47.5 |

## TENNESSEE

| | | Votes | % |
|---|---|---|---|
| 1 | B. Carroll Reece (R) | 22,156 | 56.8 |
| | W. A. S. Furlow (D) | 13,708 | 35.2 |
| 2 | J. Will Taylor (R) | 25,729 | 58.7 |
| | T. C. Drinnon (D) | 9,740 | 22.2 |
| | E. E. Patton (I) | 7,081 | 16.2 |
| 3 | Sam D. McReynolds (D) | 21,559 | 60.0 |
| | Pat H. Thach (R) | 14,387 | 40.0 |
| 4 | J. Ridley Mitchell (D) | 26,064 | 78.4 |
| | H. E. McLean (R) | 7,182 | 21.6 |
| 5 | Joseph W. Byrns (D) | 26,856 | 100.0 |
| 6 | Clarence W. Turner (D) | 16,102 | 100.0 |
| 7 | Herron Pearson (D) | 15,808 | 100.0 |
| 8 | Jere Cooper (D) | 18,112 | 100.0 |
| 9 | Walter Chandler (D) | 46,363 | 100.0 |

## TEXAS

| | | Votes | % |
|---|---|---|---|
| 1 | Wright Patman (D) | 18,608 | 98.5 |
| 2 | Martin Dies (D) | 16,628 | 100.0 |
| 3 | Morgan G. Sanders (D) | 14,790 | 100.0 |
| 4 | Sam Rayburn (D) | 16,684 | 96.8 |
| 5 | Hatton Sumners (D) | 27,302 | 96.9 |
| 6 | Luther Johnson (D) | 16,294 | 100.0 |
| 7 | Nat Patton (D) | 18,063 | 99.1 |
| 8 | Joe H. Eagle (D) | 40,400 | 99.5 |
| 9 | Joseph J. Mansfield (D) | 23,257 | 100.0 |
| 10 | James P. Buchanan (D) | 19,306 | 100.0 |
| 11 | Oliver H. Cross (D) | 20,383 | 100.0 |

## TEXAS

| | Candidates | Votes | % |
|---|---|---|---|
| 12 | Fritz G. Lanham (D) | 24,984 | 98.4 |
| 13 | W. D. McFarlane (D) | 21,005 | 100.0 |
| 14 | Richard M. Kleberg (D) | 26,276 | 100.0 |
| 15 | Milton H. West (D) | 20,102 | 88.0 |
| | G. C. Mann (R) | 2,739 | 12.0 |
| 16 | R. Ewing Thomason (D) | 11,063 | 100.0 |
| 17 | Thomas L. Blanton (D) | 17,266 | 100.0 |
| 18 | Marvin Jones (D) | 23,202 | 96.9 |
| 19 | George Mahon (D) | 20,169 | 100.0 |
| 20 | Maury Maverick (D) | 17,810 | 98.6 |
| 21 | Charles L. South (D) | 26,093 | 100.0 |

## UTAH

| | | Votes | % |
|---|---|---|---|
| 1 | Abe Murdock (D) | 55,800 | 64.4 |
| | Arthur Woolley (R) | 29,878 | 34.5 |
| 2 | J. Will Robinson (D) | 58,175 | 62.3 |
| | Frederick Loofbourow (R) | 34,007 | 36.4 |

## VERMONT

| | | Votes | % |
|---|---|---|---|
| AL | Charles A. Plumley (R) | 73,809 | 56.9 |
| | Carroll E. Jenkins (D) | 54,967 | 42.4 |

## VIRGINIA

| | | Votes | % |
|---|---|---|---|
| 1 | Schuyler Otis Bland (D) | 7,637 | 91.4 |
| 2 | Colgate W. Darden Jr. (D) | 11,102 | 76.1 |
| | Gerould M. Rumble (R) | 3,321 | 22.8 |
| 3 | Andrew Jackson Montague (D) | 9,738 | 80.5 |
| | Roy C. Parks (R) | 2,129 | 17.6 |
| 4 | Patrick Henry Drewry (D) | 7,850 | 93.4 |
| 5 | Thomas G. Burch (D) | 11,964 | 88.2 |
| | Henry P. Wilder | 1,168 | 8.6 |
| 6 | Clifton A. Woodrum (D) | 10,738 | 67.1 |
| | Thomas J. Wilson Jr. (R) | 5,060 | 31.6 |

| | Candidates | Votes | % |
|---|---|---|---|
| 7 | A. Willis Robertson (D) | 14,903 | 68.3 |
| | J. Everett Will (R) | 6,562 | 30.1 |
| 8 | Howard W. Smith (D) | 14,191 | 78.8 |
| | John Locke Green (R) | 3,583 | 19.9 |
| 9 | John W. Flannagan Jr. (D) | 20,532 | 58.1 |
| | Fred C. Parks (R) | 12,355 | 35.0 |
| | Bruce Crawford (I) | 2,402 | 6.8 |

## WASHINGTON

| | | Votes | % |
|---|---|---|---|
| 1 | Marion A. Zioncheck (D) | 68,395 | 57.7 |
| | Bert C. Ross (R) | 38,350 | 32.4 |
| | Cecil R. Fuller (CNM) | 8,500 | 7.2 |
| 2 | Mon C. Wallgren (D) | 50,486 | 67.0 |
| | Payson Peterson (R) | 23,638 | 31.4 |
| 3 | Martin F. Smith (D) | 48,887 | 69.2 |
| | Russell V. Mack (R) | 21,750 | 30.8 |
| 4 | Knute Hill (D) | 35,702 | 56.4 |
| | John W. Summers (R) | 27,637 | 43.6 |
| 5 | Sam B. Hill (D) | 58,901 | 76.2 |
| | Mansfield E. Mack (R) | 18,397 | 23.8 |
| 6 | Wesley Lloyd (D) | 52,314 | 70.5 |
| | Emery Asbury (R) | 21,883 | 29.5 |

## WEST VIRGINIA

| | | Votes | % |
|---|---|---|---|
| 1 | Robert L. Ramsay (D) | 52,714 | 53.3 |
| | Carl G. Bachmann (R) | 45,442 | 45.9 |
| 2 | Jennings Randolph (D) | 54,531 | 57.6 |
| | Herbert E. Hannis (R) | 39,832 | 42.1 |
| 3 | Andrew Edmiston (D) | 54,885 | 53.6 |
| | James A. Rusmisell (R) | 46,978 | 45.9 |
| 4 | George W. Johnson (D) | 60,684 | 50.4 |
| | Robert B. McDougle (R) | 59,013 | 49.1 |
| 5 | John Kee (D) | 54,659 | 58.5 |
| | C. M. (Casey) Jones (R) | 38,599 | 41.3 |
| 6 | Joe L. Smith (D) | 67,671 | 61.4 |
| | Frank C. Burdette (R) | 42,147 | 38.3 |

## WISCONSIN

| | Candidates | Votes | % |
|---|---|---|---|
| 1 | Thomas R. Amlie (PROG) | 32,397 | 37.4 |
| | Judson W. Staplekamp (R) | 28,459 | 32.9 |
| | Ralph V. Brown (D) | 23,532 | 27.2 |
| 2 | Harry Sauthoff (PROG) | 41,458 | 41.8 |
| | Charles W. Henney (D) | 33,347 | 33.6 |
| | John B. Gay (R) | 22,995 | 23.2 |
| 3 | Gardner R. Withrow (PROG) | 47,311 | 52.1 |
| | Levi H. Bancroft (R) | 25,851 | 28.5 |
| | Bart E. McGonigle (D) | 17,222 | 19.0 |
| 4 | Raymond J. Cannon (D) | 33,886 | 38.6 |
| | John C. Schafer (R) | 19,840 | 22.6 |
| | Marvin V. Baxter (SOC) | 18,166 | 20.7 |
| | Laurence C. Gram (PROG) | 15,364 | 17.5 |
| 5 | Thomas O'Malley (D) | 32,931 | 34.7 |
| | Otto Hauser (SOC) | 23,334 | 24.6 |
| | Arthur T. Spence (R) | 21,533 | 22.7 |
| | Carl J. Ludwig (PROG) | 16,693 | 17.6 |
| 6 | Michael K. Reilly (D) | 34,664 | 42.3 |
| | Walter D. Corrigan (PROG) | 28,477 | 34.7 |
| | William J. Campbell (R) | 18,825 | 23.0 |
| 7 | Gerald J. Boileau (PROG) | 41,321 | 48.5 |
| | Frank D. Chapman (D) | 24,871 | 29.2 |
| | Caspar Wallrich (R) | 17,461 | 20.5 |
| 8 | George J. Schneider (PROG) | 39,505 | 43.8 |
| | Gerald F. Clifford (D) | 34,397 | 38.2 |
| | L. Herman Waite (R) | 15,748 | 17.5 |
| 9 | Merlin Hull (PROG) | 42,422 | 49.6 |
| | Willis E. Donley (D) | 20,828 | 24.3 |
| | Knute Anderson (R) | 20,043 | 23.4 |
| 10 | Bernard J. Gehrmann (PROG) | 29,397 | 35.4 |
| | Hubert H. Peavey (R) | 24,850 | 29.9 |
| | Charles P. Cadigan (D) | 24,689 | 29.7 |

## WYOMING

| | | Votes | % |
|---|---|---|---|
| AL | Paul R. Greever (D) | 53,288 | 58.3 |
| | Charles E. Winter (R) | 37,492 | 41.0 |

# 1935 House Election

## INDIANA

### Special Election

| | | Votes | % |
|---|---|---|---|
| 2 | Charles A. Halleck (R) | 50,324 | 52.7 |
| | George R. Durgan (D) | 45,089 | 47.3 |

# 1936 House Elections

## ALABAMA

| | Candidates | Votes | % |
|---|---|---|---|
| 1 | Frank W. Boykin (D) | 23,421 | 100.0 |
| 2 | Lister Hill (D) | 32,452 | 99.1 |
| 3 | Henry B. Steagall (D) | 22,535 | 100.0 |
| 4 | Sam Hobbs (D) | 22,615 | 86.4 |
| | Charles R. Robinson (R) | 3,556 | 13.6 |
| 5 | Joe Starnes (D) | 29,891 | 100.0 |
| 6 | Pete Jarman (D) | 18,325 | 100.0 |
| 7 | William B. Bankhead (D) | 25,126 | 73.0 |
| | J. B. Weaver (R) | 9,311 | 27.0 |
| 8 | John J. Sparkman (D) | 27,788 | 99.7 |
| 9 | Luther Patrick (D) | 36,405 | 91.8 |
| | J. G. Bass (R) | 3,177 | 8.0 |

## ARIZONA

| | | Votes | % |
|---|---|---|---|
| AL | John R. Murdock (D) | 84,403 | 77.6 |
| | G. L. Burgess (R) | 20,383 | 18.7 |

## ARKANSAS

| | | Votes | % |
|---|---|---|---|
| 1 | William J. Driver (D) | 32,066 | 100.0 |
| 2 | John E. Miller (D) | 19,146 | 85.6 |
| | J. N. Hout Jr. (R) | 3,224 | 14.4 |
| 3 | Claude A. Fuller (D) | 18,417 | 65.3 |
| | J. S. Thompson (R) | 9,796 | 34.7 |
| 4 | William B. Cravens (D) | 25,902 | 100.0 |
| 5 | David D. Terry (D) | 26,102 | 100.0 |
| 6 | John L. McClellan (D) | 25,411 | 100.0 |
| 7 | Wade Kitchens (D) | 20,117 | 95.4 |

## CALIFORNIA

| | | Votes | % |
|---|---|---|---|
| 1 | Clarence F. Lea (D) | 58,073 | 53.8 |
| | Nelson B. Van Matre (R) | 48,647 | 45.1 |
| 2 | Harry L. Englebright (R-D-PROG) | 51,416 | 100.0 |
| 3 | Frank H. Buck (D-R) | 93,110 | 90.4 |
| | Walter Schaefer | 5,310 | 5.2 |
| 4 | Franck R. Havenner (D & PROG) | 64,063 | 58.5 |
| | Florence P. Kahn (R) | 43,805 | 40.0 |
| 5 | Richard J. Welch (R-D-PROG) | 82,910 | 94.8 |
| | Lawrence Ross (COM) | 4,545 | 5.2 |
| 6 | Albert E. Carter (R-D) | 103,712 | 91.0 |
| | Clarence E. Rust (SOC) | 8,247 | 7.2 |
| 7 | John H. Tolan (D) | 69,463 | 59.8 |
| | Charles W. Fisher (R) | 46,647 | 40.2 |
| 8 | John Joseph McGrath (D & PROG) | 78,557 | 57.6 |
| | Alonzo L. Baker (R) | 57,808 | 42.4 |
| | Bertrand W. Gearhart (R-D) | 82,360 | 97.0 |
| | Henry E. Stubbs (D) | 72,367 | 69.5 |
| | George R. Bliss (R) | 31,700 | 30.4 |
| | John Steven McGroarty (D) | 69,679 | 50.5 |
| | Carl Hinshaw (R) | 54,914 | 39.8 |
| | Robert S. Funk (PROG) | 12,340 | 8.9 |
| | H. Jerry Voorhis (D) | 62,034 | 53.7 |
| | Frederick F. Houser (R) | 53,445 | 46.3 |
| | Charles Kramer (D-R) | 119,251 | 89.4 |
| | Floyd Seaman | 6,946 | 5.2 |
| | Thomas F. Ford (D) | 63,365 | 61.0 |
| | William D. Campbell (R) | 25,497 | 24.6 |
| | Albert L. Johnson (PROG) | 12,874 | 12.4 |
| | John M. Costello (D & PROG) | 99,107 | 69.0 |
| | Ernest Walker Sawyer (R) | 44,559 | 31.0 |
| | John F. Dockweiler (D) | 90,986 | 57.7 |
| | Raymond V. Darby (R) | 66,583 | 42.2 |
| | Charles J. Colden (D) | 68,189 | 71.9 |
| | Leonard Roach (R) | 24,981 | 26.3 |
| | Byron N. Scott (D) | 61,415 | 58.9 |
| | James F. Collins (R) | 42,748 | 41.0 |

| | Candidates | Votes | % |
|---|---|---|---|
| 19 | Harry R. Sheppard (D) | 70,339 | 53.8 |
| | Sam L. Collins (R) | 59,071 | 45.2 |
| 20 | Edouard V. M. Izac (D) | 59,208 | 56.4 |
| | Ed P. Sample (R) | 44,925 | 42.8 |

## COLORADO

| | | Votes | % |
|---|---|---|---|
| 1 | Lawrence Lewis (D) | 100,704 | 69.0 |
| | Harry Zimmerhackel (R) | 41,574 | 28.5 |
| 2 | Fred Cummings (D) | 66,420 | 53.3 |
| | George H. Bradfield (R) | 57,145 | 45.8 |
| 3 | John A. Martin (D) | 74,013 | 60.2 |
| | J. Arthur Phelps (R) | 48,871 | 39.8 |
| 4 | Edward T. Taylor (D) | 42,010 | 65.5 |
| | John S. Woody (R) | 22,175 | 34.6 |

## CONNECTICUT

| | | Votes | % |
|---|---|---|---|
| 1 | Herman P. Kopplemann (D) | 101,766 | 57.9 |
| | Walter E. Batterson (R) | 66,005 | 37.6 |
| 2 | William J. Fitzgerald (D) | 55,369 | 50.9 |
| | William L. Higgins (R) | 50,369 | 46.3 |
| 3 | James A. Shanley (D) | 77,295 | 54.6 |
| | John F. Lynch (R) | 57,243 | 40.4 |
| 4 | Alfred N. Phillips Jr. (D) | 80,875 | 50.0 |
| | Schuyler Merritt (R) | 67,768 | 41.9 |
| 5 | J. Joseph Smith (D) | 55,897 | 58.6 |
| | J. Warren Upson (R) | 39,230 | 41.1 |
| AL | William N. Citron (D) | 371,572 | 53.9 |
| | Francis Pallotti (R) | 282,618 | 41.0 |

## DELAWARE

| | | Votes | % |
|---|---|---|---|
| AL | William F. Allen (D) | 65,485 | 51.7 |
| | John George Stewart (R) | 55,664 | 44.0 |

## FLORIDA

| | | Votes | % |
|---|---|---|---|
| 1 | J. Hardin Peterson (D) | 61,855 | 74.5 |
| | B. L. Hamner (R) | 21,215 | 25.5 |
| 2 | R. A. Green (D) | 47,520 | 100.0 |
| 3 | Millard Caldwell (D) | 34,239 | 100.0 |
| 4 | J. Mark Wilcox (D) | 46,854 | 70.6 |
| | Thomas E. Swanson (R) | 19,515 | 29.4 |
| 5 | Joe Hendricks (D) | 42,937 | 79.9 |
| | C. F. Batchelder (R) | 10,802 | 20.1 |

## GEORGIA

| | | Votes | % |
|---|---|---|---|
| 1 | Hugh Peterson Jr. (D) | 25,846 | 100.0 |
| 2 | E. E. Cox (D) | 21,405 | 100.0 |
| 3 | Stephen Pace (D) | 25,613 | 100.0 |
| 4 | E. M. Owen (D) | 24,643 | 100.0 |
| 5 | Robert Ramspeck (D) | 35,540 | 89.4 |
| | H. H. Alexander (R) | 4,213 | 10.6 |
| 6 | Carl Vinson (D) | 20,595 | 100.0 |
| 7 | Malcolm C. Tarver (D) | 31,343 | 92.6 |
| | L. Mitchell Johnson (R) | 2,493 | 7.4 |
| 8 | Braswell Deen (D) | 24,695 | 94.9 |
| | Ben J. Ford (R) | 1,320 | 5.1 |
| 9 | B. Frank Whelchel (D) | 23,682 | 75.4 |
| | John M. Johnson (R) | 7,739 | 24.6 |
| 10 | Paul Brown (D) | 27,147 | 100.0 |

## IDAHO

| | | Votes | % |
|---|---|---|---|
| 1 | Compton I. White (D) | 58,941 | 70.3 |
| | John S. Heckathorn (R) | 24,959 | 29.8 |
| 2 | D. Worth Clark (D) | 67,238 | 60.5 |
| | Henry C. Dworshak (R) | 43,834 | 39.5 |

## ILLINOIS

| | Candidates | Votes | % |
|---|---|---|---|
| 1 | Arthur W. Mitchell (D) | 35,376 | 55.1 |
| | Oscar De Priest (R) | 28,640 | 44.6 |
| 2 | Raymond S. McKeough (D) | 163,198 | 55.6 |
| | P. H. Moynihan (R) | 130,197 | 44.4 |
| 3 | Edward A. Kelly (D) | 156,425 | 59.3 |
| | Frank M. Fulton (R) | 106,300 | 40.3 |
| 4 | Harry P. Beam (D) | 69,931 | 80.8 |
| | Irene A. Tomas (R) | 16,591 | 19.2 |
| 5 | Adolph J. Sabath (D) | 35,019 | 77.4 |
| | Max Price (R) | 10,252 | 22.6 |
| 6 | Thomas J. O'Brien (D) | 204,548 | 65.5 |
| | Frederick A. Virkus (R) | 107,649 | 34.5 |
| 7 | Leonard W. Schuetz (D) | 248,835 | 59.2 |
| | James C. Moreland (R) | 158,755 | 37.7 |
| 8 | Leo Kocialkowski (D) | 34,452 | 78.6 |
| | Edw. Richard Piszatowski (R) | 8,945 | 20.4 |
| 9 | James McAndrews (D) | 60,307 | 59.2 |
| | Bertha Baur (R) | 41,587 | 40.8 |
| 10 | Ralph E. Church (R) | 158,497 | 51.4 |
| | Charles J. Wightman (D) | 140,225 | 45.5 |
| 11 | Chauncey W. Reed (R) | 99,027 | 56.0 |
| | John R. Barber (D) | 77,938 | 44.0 |
| 12 | Noah M. Mason (R) | 69,721 | 51.6 |
| | D. O. Thompson (D) | 58,263 | 43.1 |
| | D. S. Gishwiller (TOWN OAP) | 7,203 | 5.3 |
| 13 | Leo E. Allen (R) | 52,495 | 58.4 |
| | David L. Trunck (D) | 37,346 | 41.6 |
| 14 | Chester Thompson (D) | 58,809 | 54.4 |
| | Clinton Searle (R) | 49,250 | 45.6 |
| 15 | Lewis L. Boyer (D) | 54,703 | 49.4 |
| | Joe E. Anderson (R) | 53,531 | 48.3 |
| 16 | Everett M. Dirksen (R) | 68,964 | 53.2 |
| | Charles C. Dickman (D) | 60,559 | 46.8 |
| 17 | Leslie C. Arends (R) | 46,646 | 52.6 |
| | Frank Gillespie (D) | 42,071 | 47.4 |
| 18 | James A. Meeks (D) | 61,286 | 53.8 |
| | Hugh M. Luckey (R) | 52,730 | 46.3 |
| 19 | Hugh M. Rigney (D) | 77,446 | 55.7 |
| | William H. Wheat (R) | 61,535 | 44.3 |
| 20 | Scott W. Lucas (D) | 48,128 | 56.7 |
| | Harry C. Montgomery (R) | 36,732 | 43.3 |
| 21 | Frank W. Fries (D) | 62,769 | 51.7 |
| | Frank M. Ramey (R) | 58,573 | 48.2 |
| 22 | Edwin M. Schaefer (D) | 96,589 | 59.1 |
| | Jesse R. Brown (R) | 66,960 | 40.9 |
| 23 | Laurence F. Arnold (D) | 62,044 | 55.2 |
| | Ben O. Sumner (R) | 50,354 | 44.8 |
| 24 | Claude V. Parsons (D) | 45,740 | 51.7 |
| | W. A. Spence (R) | 42,764 | 48.3 |
| 25 | Kent E. Keller (D) | 68,995 | 53.9 |
| | J. Lester Buford (R) | 59,101 | 46.1 |
| AL | Lewis M. Long (D) | 2,062,886✓ | |
| | Edwin V. Champion (D) | 2,032,432✓ | |
| | Rodney H. Brandon (R) | 1,568,552 | |
| | John T. Dempsey (R) | 1,564,889 | |
| | Severin H. Hanson (UN PROG) | 83,886 | |
| | Rad Burnett (UN PROG) | 81,551 | |
| | Ina M. White (SOC) | 7,817 | |
| | Nate Egnor (SOC) | 7,651 | |
| | Mary Morgan Williams (P) | 3,269 | |
| | Frank Earl Herrick (P) | 3,262 | |
| | Edward K. Schooley (SOC LAB) | 2,374 | |
| | Mathilda M. Deavers (SOC LAB) | 2,235 | |

## INDIANA

| | | Votes | % |
|---|---|---|---|
| 1 | William T. Schulte (D) | 68,210 | 66.4 |
| | Fred F. Schultz (R) | 34,259 | 33.3 |
| 2 | Charles A. Halleck (R) | 73,072 | 51.5 |
| | Hugh A. Barnhart (D) | 68,318 | 48.2 |

## INDIANA

| Candidates | Votes | % |
|---|---|---|
| 3 Samuel B. Pettingill (D) | 71,315 | 56.2 |
| Andrew J. Hickey (R) | 52,462 | 41.4 |
| 4 James I. Farley (D) | 72,210 | 55.2 |
| David Hogg (R) | 58,519 | 44.8 |
| 5 Glenn Griswold (D) | 70,854 | 52.6 |
| Benjamin J. Brown (R) | 63,517 | 47.2 |
| 6 Virginia A. Jenckes (D) | 82,096 | 54.9 |
| Noble J. Johnson (R) | 66,942 | 44.8 |
| 7 Arthur Greenwood (D) | 81,901 | 53.8 |
| Gerald W. Landis (R) | 69,928 | 45.9 |
| 8 John W. Boehne Jr. (D) | 89,548 | 62.6 |
| Charles F. Werner (R) | 50,590 | 35.4 |
| 9 Eugene B. Crowe (D) | 74,486 | 54.2 |
| Chester A. Davis (R) | 62,714 | 45.7 |
| 10 Finly H. Gray (D) | 73,547 | 52.6 |
| Clarence M. Brown (R) | 66,299 | 47.4 |
| 11 William H. Larrabee (D) | 80,856 | 59.4 |
| Don Roberts (R) | 53,801 | 39.5 |
| 12 Louis Ludlow (D) | 77,510 | 57.7 |
| Homer Elliott (R) | 54,885 | 40.9 |

## IOWA

| | Votes | % |
|---|---|---|
| 1 Edward C. Eicher (D) | 55,721 | 51.0 |
| John N. Calhoun (R) | 53,474 | 49.0 |
| 2 William S. Jacobsen (D) | 70,923 | 54.6 |
| Charles Penningroth (R) | 55,255 | 42.5 |
| 3 John W. Gwynne (R) | 53,928 | 53.2 |
| A. C. Willford (D) | 47,391 | 46.8 |
| 4 Fred Biermann (D) | 56,308 | 50.6 |
| Henry O. Talle (R) | 51,805 | 46.6 |
| 5 Lloyd Thurston (R) | 63,802 | 51.5 |
| Kenneth F. Baldridge (D) | 58,971 | 47.6 |
| 6 Cassius C. Dowell (R) | 63,026 | 52.4 |
| Harry B. Dunlap (D) | 55,975 | 46.5 |
| 7 Otha D. Wearin (D) | 61,398 | 50.4 |
| Henry K. Peterson (R) | 59,834 | 49.2 |
| 8 Fred C. Gilchrist (R) | 56,076 | 52.5 |
| Ray Murray (D) | 48,403 | 45.3 |
| 9 Vincent F. Harrington (D) | 63,995 | 53.5 |
| Fred B. Wolf (R) | 53,675 | 44.9 |

## KANSAS

| | Votes | % |
|---|---|---|
| 1 William P. Lambertson (R) | 66,158 | 58.3 |
| Howard S. Miller (D) | 47,303 | 41.7 |
| 2 Ulysses S. Guyer (R) | 72,038 | 53.3 |
| David C. Doten (D) | 60,049 | 44.5 |
| 3 Edward W. Patterson (D) | 55,541 | 48.4 |
| Harold McGugin (R) | 52,235 | 45.5 |
| L. P. Beard (I) | 6,921 | 6.0 |
| 4 Edward H. Rees (R) | 51,732 | 54.5 |
| C. D. Hill (D) | 42,818 | 45.1 |
| 5 John M. Houston (D) | 62,501 | 60.0 |
| J. B. Patterson (R) | 41,656 | 40.0 |
| 6 Frank Carlson (R) | 61,669 | 52.0 |
| Arthur Connelly (D) | 56,850 | 48.0 |
| 7 Clifford R. Hope (R) | 66,553 | 56.0 |
| Thomas A. Ralston (D) | 52,370 | 44.0 |

## KENTUCKY

| | Votes | % |
|---|---|---|
| 1 Noble J. Gregory (D) | 58,265 | 71.9 |
| R. N. Brumfield (R) | 22,757 | 28.1 |
| 2 Glover H. Cary (D) | 70,949* | 64.0 |
| Claude E. Smith (R) | 39,887 | 36.0 |
| 3 Emmet O'Neal (D) | 85,034 | 60.3 |
| W. A. Armstrong (R) | 52,600 | 37.3 |
| 4 Edward W. Creal (D) | 54,616 | 59.0 |
| Stanley Jaggers (R) | 37,979 | 41.0 |
| 5 Brent Spence (D) | 57,842 | 66.7 |
| Ervin L. Bramlage (R) | 25,011 | 28.8 |
| 6 Virgil Chapman (D) | 70,094 | 57.9 |
| A. R. Anderson (R) | 48,771 | 40.3 |
| 7 Andrew J. May (D) | 40,366 | 55.9 |
| John B. Mollette (R) | 31,865 | 44.1 |
| 8 Fred M. Vinson (D) | 60,474 | 58.7 |
| W. Hoffman Wood (R) | 42,507 | 41.3 |

| Candidates | Votes | % |
|---|---|---|
| 9 John M. Robsion (R) | 67,199 | 61.6 |
| George L. Tye (D) | 41,958 | 38.4 |

## LOUISIANA

| | Votes | % |
|---|---|---|
| 1 Joachim O. Fernandez (D) | 61,142 | 100.0 |
| 2 Paul H. Maloney (D) | 65,345 | 100.0 |
| 3 Robert L. Mouton (D) | 20,605 | 100.0 |
| 4 Overton Brooks (D) | 26,152 | 99.9 |
| 5 Newton V. Mills (D) | 29,144 | 100.0 |
| 6 John K. Griffith (D) | 34,908 | 100.0 |
| 7 Rene L. DeRouen (D) | 27,563 | 100.0 |
| 8 A. Leonard Allen (D) | 27,071 | 100.0 |

## MAINE

| | Votes | % |
|---|---|---|
| 1 James C. Oliver (R) | 60,565 | 57.9 |
| Simon M. Hamlin (D) | 44,106 | 42.1 |
| 2 Clyde H. Smith (R) | 53,822 | 51.6 |
| Ernest L. McLean (D) | 38,986 | 37.4 |
| J. C. Leckemby (IR) | 8,197 | 7.9 |
| 3 Ralph O. Brewster (R) | 56,044 | 60.8 |
| Wallace F. Mabee (D) | 36,103 | 39.2 |

## MARYLAND

| | Votes | % |
|---|---|---|
| 1 T. Alan Goldsborough (D) | 38,705 | 60.0 |
| O. Straughn Lloyd (R) | 25,780 | 40.0 |
| 2 William P. Cole Jr. (D) | 98,515 | 61.7 |
| Henry C. Whiteford (R) | 60,003 | 37.6 |
| 3 Vincent L. Palmisano (D) | 37,446 | 60.5 |
| John Philip Hill (R) | 23,941 | 38.7 |
| 4 Ambrose J. Kennedy (D) | 46,132 | 51.5 |
| Daniel Ellison (R) | 39,653 | 44.3 |
| 5 Stephen Warfield Gambrill (D) | 47,145 | 64.7 |
| Roscoe C. Rowe (R) | 25,036 | 34.4 |
| 6 David J. Lewis (D) | 53,504 | 56.4 |
| Harry W. Le Gore (R) | 40,823 | 43.0 |

## MASSACHUSETTS

| | Votes | % |
|---|---|---|
| 1 Allen T. Treadway (R) | 60,043 | 50.5 |
| Owen Johnson (D) | 52,342 | 44.0 |
| 2 Charles R. Clason (R) | 57,618 | 49.0 |
| Agnes C. Reavey (D) | 52,197 | 44.3 |
| 3 Joseph E. Casey (D) | 64,960 | 54.1 |
| Bernard W. Doyle (R) | 54,154 | 45.1 |
| 4 Pehr G. Holmes (R) | 61,624 | 51.5 |
| Edward A. Ryan (D) | 56,770 | 47.4 |
| 5 Edith Nourse Rogers (R) | 90,845 | 62.8 |
| Daniel J. Coughlin (D) | 48,701 | 33.7 |
| 6 George J. Bates (R) | 79,145 | 68.6 |
| John E. Taffe (TOWN-SJD) | 36,171 | 31.4 |
| 7 William P. Connery Jr. (D) | 76,521 | 59.1 |
| C. F. Nelson Pratt (R) | 51,009 | 39.4 |
| 8 Arthur D. Healey (D) | 60,211 | 52.6 |
| William S. Howe (R) | 46,446 | 40.5 |
| Nelson F. Wright (UN) | 6,010 | 5.3 |
| 9 Robert Luce (R) | 70,852 | 50.6 |
| Richard M. Russell (D) | 61,582 | 44.0 |
| 10 George Holden Tinkham (R) | 74,251 | 59.5 |
| William F. Madden (D) | 39,112 | 31.4 |
| John McLaren (TOWN-C-L) | 11,349 | 9.1 |
| 11 John P. Higgins (D) | 53,129 | 81.3 |
| Joseph M. De Napoli (R) | 8,523 | 13.1 |
| 12 John W. McCormack (D) | 78,711 | 68.7 |
| Albert P. McCulloch (FACP R) | 35,827 | 31.3 |
| 13 Richard B. Wigglesworth (R) | 76,793 | 58.5 |
| Harry J. Dowd (D) | 54,576 | 41.5 |
| 14 Joseph W. Martin Jr. (R) | 58,758 | 53.3 |
| Arthur E. Seagrave (D) | 38,609 | 35.0 |
| Lawrence O. Witter (UN) | 12,872 | 11.7 |
| 15 Charles L. Gifford (R) | 58,355 | 50.1 |
| John D. W. Bodfish (D) | 42,538 | 36.5 |

| Candidates | Votes | % |
|---|---|---|
| John Henry McNeece (TOWN SJ) | 12,419 | 10.7 |

## MICHIGAN

| | Votes | % |
|---|---|---|
| 1 George G. Sadowski (D) | 72,713 | 80.4 |
| Charles A. Roxborough (R) | 17,265 | 19.1 |
| 2 Earl C. Michener (R) | 53,845 | 51.7 |
| Charles E. Downing (D) | 50,238 | 48.3 |
| 3 Paul W. Shafer (R) | 54,767 | 51.8 |
| Rosslyn L. Sowers (D) | 50,956 | 48.2 |
| 4 Clare E. Hoffman (R) | 49,641 | 50.5 |
| Guy M. Tyler (D) | 44,365 | 45.1 |
| 5 Carl E. Mapes (R) | 49,860 | 48.2 |
| Thomas F. McAllister (D) | 48,998 | 47.4 |
| 6 Andrew J. Transue (D) | 72,556 | 57.7 |
| William W. Blackney (R) | 53,140 | 42.3 |
| 7 Jesse P. Wolcott (R) | 54,693 | 59.9 |
| Albert A. Wagner (D) | 36,462 | 39.9 |
| 8 Fred L. Crawford (R) | 45,379 | 46.8 |
| Michael J. Hart (D) | 44,309 | 45.7 |
| Clarence J. Brainerd (UN) | 7,249 | 7.5 |
| 9 Albert J. Engel (R) | 40,675 | 50.2 |
| Jack Eliasohn (D) | 40,095 | 49.5 |
| 10 Roy O. Woodruff (R) | 41,997 | 57.6 |
| William J. Kelly (D) | 30,784 | 42.3 |
| 11 John Luecke (D) | 44,528 | 52.8 |
| Herbert J. Rushton (R) | 39,602 | 46.9 |
| 12 Frank E. Hook (D) | 46,284 | 54.7 |
| W. Frank James (R) | 37,714 | 44.6 |
| 13 George D. O'Brien (D) | 63,479 | 55.1 |
| Clarence J. McLeod (R) | 49,910 | 43.3 |
| 14 Louis C. Rabaut (D) | 66,791 | 55.9 |
| Frederick M. Alger Jr. (R) | 41,130 | 34.4 |
| Edgar J. Auclair (THIRD) | 10,660 | 8.9 |
| 15 John D. Dingell (D) | 68,264 | 57.5 |
| Nathaniel H. Goldstick (R) | 49,443 | 41.6 |
| 16 John Lesinski (D) | 56,589 | 58.3 |
| Clyde M. Ford (R) | 35,223 | 36.3 |
| 17 George A. Dondero (R) | 51,603 | 47.3 |
| Draper Allen (D) | 50,463 | 46.4 |
| Maynard Seibert (UN) | 5,593 | 5.2 |

## MINNESOTA

| | Votes | % |
|---|---|---|
| 1 August H. Andresen (R) | 60,980 | 50.9 |
| Chester Watson (F-LAB) | 27,753 | 23.2 |
| Richard W. Morin (D) | 26,058 | 21.8 |
| 2 Elmer J. Ryan (D) | 47,567 | 39.4 |
| Henry Arens (F-LAB) | 39,489 | 32.7 |
| Christian J. Laurisch (R) | 34,268 | 28.4 |
| 3 Henry G. Teigan (F-LAB) | 58,023 | 46.9 |
| Milton Lindbloom (R) | 40,775 | 32.9 |
| Martin A. Hogan (D) | 15,170 | 12.2 |
| Mrs. Frank McConville (I) | 11,476 | 9.2 |
| 4 Melvin J. Maas (R) | 48,399 | 38.6 |
| Howard Y. Williams (F-LAB) | 48,039 | 38.3 |
| A. B. C. Doherty (D) | 28,957 | 22.1 |
| 5 Dewey W. Johnson (F-LAB) | 67,349 | 47.9 |
| Walter H. Newton (R) | 58,110 | 41.3 |
| M. J. Dillon (D) | 15,337 | 10.9 |
| 6 Harold Knutson (R) | 55,504 | 46.7 |
| C. A. Ryan (F-LAB) | 47,707 | 39.2 |
| Joseph H. Kowalkowski (D) | 17,235 | 14.1 |
| 7 Paul John Kvale (F-LAB) | 56,310 | 49.5 |
| H. Carl Andersen (R) | 37,190 | 32.7 |
| C. L. Cole (D) | 19,878 | 17.5 |
| 8 John T. Bernard (F-LAB) | 69,788 | 55.6 |
| William A. Pittenger (R) | 53,914 | 43.0 |
| 9 Richard Thompson Buckler (F-LAB) | 48,256 | 48.4 |
| Elmer A. Haugen (R) | 31,181 | 31.3 |
| Martin O. Brandon (D) | 20,165 | 20.2 |

## MISSISSIPPI

| | Votes | % |
|---|---|---|
| 1 John E. Rankin (D) | 19,208 | 98.9 |
| 2 Wall Doxey (D) | 13,632 | 98.9 |

## MISSISSIPPI

| Candidates | Votes | % |
|---|---|---|
| 3 William M. Whittington (D) | 15,688 | 97.5 |
| 4 A. L. Ford (D) | 14,444 | 100.0 |
| 5 Ross A. Collins (D) | 26,150 | 99.4 |
| 6 William M. Colmer (D) | 25,385 | 100.0 |
| 7 Daniel R. McGehee (D) | 32,004 | 97.5 |

## MISSOURI

| | | |
|---|---|---|
| 1 Milton A. Romjue (D) | 68,447 | 55.4 |
| James G. Morgan (R) | 55,032 | 44.5 |
| 2 William L. Nelson (D) | 81,293 | 58.1 |
| O. B. Whitaker (R) | 58,610 | 41.9 |
| 3 Richard M. Duncan (D) | 86,199 | 58.8 |
| Miles Elliott (R) | 60,411 | 41.2 |
| 4 C. Jasper Bell (D) | 103,492 | 74.6 |
| Paul R. Byrum (R) | 35,081 | 25.3 |
| 5 Joseph B. Shannon (D) | 113,946 | 73.7 |
| Lowell R. Johnson (R) | 40,546 | 26.2 |
| 6 Reuben T. Wood (D) | 74,202 | 53.0 |
| Thomas H. Douglas (R) | 65,679 | 46.9 |
| 7 Dewey Short (R) | 73,861 | 52.5 |
| Gene Frost (D) | 66,695 | 47.4 |
| 8 Clyde Williams (D) | 65,780 | 56.6 |
| C. M. Becker (R) | 50,216 | 43.2 |
| 9 Clarence Cannon (D) | 62,623 | 61.8 |
| Herschel Schooley (R) | 38,706 | 38.2 |
| 10 Orville Zimmerman (D) | 65,168 | 61.4 |
| Linder Deimund (R) | 40,860 | 38.5 |
| 11 Thomas C. Hennings (D) | 94,330 | 61.1 |
| L. C. Dyer (R) | 59,536 | 38.6 |
| 12 C. Arthur Anderson (D) | 125,333 | 56.2 |
| Harry P. Rosecan (R) | 97,151 | 43.5 |
| 13 John J. Cochran (D) | 85,630 | 68.2 |
| Harry E. Wiehe (R) | 39,714 | 31.6 |

## MONTANA

| | | |
|---|---|---|
| 1 Jerry J. O'Connell (D) | 54,816 | 63.4 |
| H. L. Hart (R) | 31,231 | 36.1 |
| 2 James F. O'Connor (D) | 79,190 | 64.9 |
| T. S. Stockdal (R) | 42,454 | 34.8 |

## NEBRASKA

| | | |
|---|---|---|
| 1 Henry C. Luckey (D) | 61,104 | 53.3 |
| Ernest B. Perry (R) | 52,137 | 45.5 |
| 2 Charles F. McLaughlin (D) | 66,833 | 62.0 |
| Jackson B. Chase (R) | 38,511 | 35.7 |
| 3 Karl Stefan (R) | 83,587 | 70.5 |
| John Havekost (D) | 31,967 | 27.0 |
| 4 Charles Binderup (D) | 66,763 | 55.3 |
| Arthur J. Denney (R) | 51,524 | 42.7 |
| 5 Harry B. Coffee (D) | 62,714 | 58.3 |
| Cullen N. Wright (R) | 36,396 | 33.8 |
| Frank Brown (UN) | 7,912 | 7.4 |

## NEVADA

| | | |
|---|---|---|
| AL James G. Scrugham (D) | 25,575 | 58.4 |
| Ed C. Peterson (R) | 11,785 | 26.9 |
| Harry H. Austin (I) | 6,444 | 14.7 |

## NEW HAMPSHIRE

| | | |
|---|---|---|
| 1 Arthur B. Jenks (R) | 51,920‡ | 50.0 |
| Alphonse Roy (D) | 51,370 | 49.5 |
| 2 Charles W. Tobey (R) | 53,706 | 53.7 |
| Daniel J. Hagerty (D) | 45,437 | 45.4 |

## NEW JERSEY

| | | |
|---|---|---|
| 1 Charles A. Wolverton (R) | 84,980 | 51.8 |
| Guy Lee Jr. (D) | 75,631 | 46.1 |
| 2 Elmer H. Wene (D) | 55,580 | 50.0 |
| Isaac Bacharach (R) | 50,958 | 45.8 |

| Candidates | Votes | % |
|---|---|---|
| 3 William H. Sutphin (D) | 68,189 | 50.6 |
| Albert B. Hermann (R) | 64,237 | 47.7 |
| 4 D. Lane Powers (R) | 58,258 | 52.3 |
| Joseph A. Daly (D) | 52,735 | 47.4 |
| 5 Charles A. Eaton (R) | 65,459 | 50.9 |
| Charles S. Mackenzie (D) | 62,904 | 48.9 |
| 6 Donald H. McLean (R) | 62,525 | 50.2 |
| Frank Moore (D) | 61,351 | 49.3 |
| 7 J. Parnell Thomas (R) | 58,021 | 51.6 |
| H. P. J. Hoffmann (D) | 54,163 | 48.2 |
| 8 George N. Seger (R) | 57,778 | 50.8 |
| Leo V. Becker (D) | 52,430 | 46.1 |
| 9 Edward A. Kenney (D) | 67,874 | 53.9 |
| Lawrence A. Cavinato (R) | 57,547 | 45.7 |
| 10 Fred A. Hartley Jr. (R) | 52,197 | 50.2 |
| Lindsay H. Rudd (D) | 51,532 | 49.6 |
| 11 Edward L. O'Neill (D) | 54,402 | 52.6 |
| Peter A. Cavicchia (R) | 48,672 | 47.1 |
| 12 Frank W. Towey Jr. (D) | 54,688 | 49.9 |
| Frederick R. Lehlbach (R) | 54,363 | 49.6 |
| 13 Mary T. Norton (D) | 93,702 | 75.8 |
| John J. Grossi (R) | 27,615 | 22.3 |
| 14 Edward J. Hart (D) | 96,053 | 79.3 |
| Fred G. Tauber (R) | 23,985 | 19.8 |

## NEW MEXICO

| | | |
|---|---|---|
| AL John J. Dempsey (D) | 106,951 | 63.1 |
| M. Ralph Brown (R) | 62,375 | 36.8 |

## NEW YORK

| | | |
|---|---|---|
| 1 Robert L. Bacon (R) | 185,891 | 55.2 |
| Gerald Morrell (D, UN) | 144,562 | 42.9 |
| 2 William B. Barry (D) | 222,217 | 69.2 |
| Allen E. R. Craig (R) | 90,437 | 28.2 |
| 3 Joseph L. Pfeifer (D) | 40,640 | 80.3 |
| Jerome G. Licari (R) | 8,680 | 17.2 |
| 4 Thomas H. Cullen (D) | 43,917 | 77.7 |
| William G. Nolan (R) | 11,594 | 20.5 |
| 5 Marcellus H. Evans (D) | 63,661 | 64.9 |
| Frank A. Dalton (R) | 30,995 | 31.6 |
| 6 Andrew L. Somers (D) | 126,024 | 69.1 |
| Donald C. Strachan (R) | 43,862 | 24.1 |
| 7 John J. Delaney (D) | 46,154 | 75.5 |
| Joseph M. Aimee (R) | 12,085 | 19.8 |
| 8 Donald L. O'Toole (D) | 217,568 | 72.2 |
| Nathan Greenbaum (R) | 64,002 | 21.2 |
| 9 Eugene J. Keogh (D) | 91,803 | 65.6 |
| Robert E. Hower (R) | 42,456 | 30.4 |
| 10 Emanuel Celler (D) | 47,872 | 68.8 |
| Mortimer H. Michaels (R) | 17,643 | 25.4 |
| 11 James A. O'Leary (D) | 56,307 | 66.7 |
| Archibald Cooper (R) | 25,553 | 30.3 |
| 12 Samuel Dickstein (D) | 19,280 | 86.5 |
| Joseph Levine (R) | 2,136 | 9.6 |
| 13 Christopher D. Sullivan (D) | 20,456 | 79.7 |
| Vincent A. Marsicano (R) | 4,254 | 16.6 |
| 14 William I. Sirovich (D) | 25,528 | 61.5 |
| Emanuel A. Manginelli (R) | 13,059 | 31.4 |
| 15 John J. Boylan (D) | 32,435 | 77.5 |
| Arthur Wyler (R) | 7,953 | 19.0 |
| 16 John J. O'Connor (D) | 33,082 | 60.0 |
| J. Homer Cudmore (R) | 17,832 | 32.3 |
| 17 Theodore A. Peyser (D) | 48,611 | 52.1 |
| Frederick F. Greenman (R) | 41,430 | 44.4 |
| 18 Martin J. Kennedy (D) | 36,317 | 72.9 |
| William I. Cohen (R) | 11,851 | 23.8 |
| 19 Sol Bloom (D) | 74,160 | 69.5 |
| William S. Bennet (R) | 24,835 | 23.3 |
| 20 James J. Lanzetta (D) | 18,772 | 51.2 |
| Vito Marcantonio (R, ALL PP) | 17,212 | 46.9 |
| 21 Joseph A. Gavagan (D) | 114,626 | 73.7 |
| Melinda Alexander (R) | 31,504 | 20.3 |
| 22 Edwin W. Curley (D) | 49,495 | 77.6 |
| Victor Santini (R) | 12,220 | 19.2 |
| 23 Charles A. Buckley (D) | 202,730 | 74.3 |
| Isaac F. Becker (R) | 51,623 | 18.9 |

| Candidates | Votes | % |
|---|---|---|
| 24 James M. Fitzpatrick (D) | 183,823 | 65.2 |
| Oliver C. Carpenter (R) | 82,759 | 29.4 |
| 25 Charles D. Millard (R) | 97,953 | 56.3 |
| Homer A. Stebbins (D) | 73,132 | 42.0 |
| 26 Hamilton Fish (R) | 72,302 | 58.5 |
| Alpha R. Whiton (D, AM LAB) | 49,137 | 39.7 |
| 27 Philip A. Goodwin (R) | 61,748 | 57.2 |
| D. Roy Shafer (D) | 44,220 | 40.9 |
| 28 William T. Byrne (D) | 85,004 | 58.4 |
| Colin D. Macrae (R) | 52,498 | 36.1 |
| 29 E. Harold Cluett (R) | 74,644 | 61.3 |
| John J. Nyhoff (D) | 44,567 | 36.6 |
| 30 Frank Crowther (R) | 57,482 | 51.6 |
| Earl E. Cummins (D, AM LAB) | 51,590 | 46.3 |
| 31 Bertrand H. Snell (R) | 54,160 | 58.8 |
| George C. Owens (D) | 31,752 | 34.5 |
| Jesse W. Williams (TOWN) | 6,185 | 6.7 |
| 32 Francis D. Culkin (R) | 65,761 | 66.1 |
| Paul J. Woodard (D) | 32,318 | 32.5 |
| 33 Fred J. Douglas (R) | 63,281 | 53.1 |
| Fred J. Sisson (D, AM LAB) | 45,969 | 38.6 |
| William D. Arquint | 8,479 | 7.1 |
| 34 Bert Lord (R) | 75,580 | 60.6 |
| John T. Buckley (D) | 47,857 | 38.4 |
| 35 Clarence E. Hancock (R) | 85,702 | 54.3 |
| Arthur R. Perrin (D) | 59,540 | 37.8 |
| Robert H. Anderson (YP) | 9,798 | 6.2 |
| 36 John Taber (R) | 61,271 | 59.2 |
| William A. Aiken (D) | 32,318 | 31.2 |
| John E. DuBois (TOWN) | 8,003 | 7.7 |
| 37 W. Sterling Cole (R) | 73,018 | 64.5 |
| Paul Smith (D) | 38,560 | 34.1 |
| 38 George B. Kelly (D) | 82,708 | 51.6 |
| Joseph Fritsch Jr (R) | 72,910 | 45.5 |
| 39 James W. Wadsworth (R) | 66,869 | 58.5 |
| Donald J. Corbett (D) | 41,699 | 36.5 |
| 40 Walter Gresham Andrews (R) | 94,682 | 52.5 |
| John L. Beyer (D) | 68,241 | 37.8 |
| Melvin L. Payne (UN&SQD) | 13,593 | 7.5 |
| 41 Alfred F. Beiter (D, AM LAB) | 55,508 | 50.4 |
| Fred Kohler (R) | 45,113 | 41.0 |
| 42 James M. Mead (D, AM LAB) | 57,132 | 56.4 |
| Eugene D. Crooker (R) | 32,395 | 32.0 |
| Anthony Fitzgibbons (UN) | 6,840 | 6.8 |
| 43 Daniel A. Reed (R) | 56,129 | 54.9 |
| Clare Barnes (D) | 44,585 | 43.6 |
| AL Matthew J. Merritt (D) | 3,013,931✔ | |
| Caroline O'Day (D) | 2,992,057✔ | |
| Natalie F. Couch (R) | 2,078,803 | |
| Anthony J. Contiguglia (R) | 2,028,865 | |
| Edna Mitchell Blue (SOC) | 102,133 | |
| Frank R. Crosswaith (SOC) | 101,184 | |
| Roy Hudson (COM) | 69,336 | |
| Simon W. Gerson (COM) | 68,868 | |

## NORTH CAROLINA

| | | |
|---|---|---|
| 1 Lindsay C. Warren (D) | 35,333 | 90.2 |
| John Wilkinson (R) | 3,833 | 9.8 |
| 2 John H. Kerr (D) | 37,771 | 95.2 |
| 3 Graham A. Barden (D) | 34,524 | 74.3 |
| Julian T. Gaskill (R) | 11,967 | 25.7 |
| 4 Harold D. Cooley (D) | 56,703 | 76.8 |
| A. I. Ferree (R) | 17,179 | 23.3 |
| 5 Frank W. Hancock Jr. (D) | 48,500 | 73.3 |
| Edward F. Butler (R) | 17,671 | 26.7 |
| 6 William B. Umstead (D) | 46,329 | 69.8 |
| Willis H. Slane (R) | 20,092 | 30.3 |
| 7 J. Bayard Clark (D) | 41,549 | 83.2 |
| W. C. Downing (R) | 8,396 | 16.8 |
| 8 J. Walter Lambeth (D) | 54,846 | 64.1 |
| Kyle Hayes (R) | 30,699 | 35.9 |
| 9 Robert L. Doughton (D) | 60,223 | 64.8 |
| Watt Gragg (R) | 32,659 | 35.2 |

## NORTH CAROLINA

| | Candidates | Votes | % |
|---|---|---|---|
| 10 | Alfred L. Bulwinkle (D) | 79,059 | 65.0 |
| | Calvin R. Edney (R) | 42,650 | 35.0 |
| 11 | Zebulon Weaver (D) | 73,645 | 63.0 |
| | Clyde H. Jarrett (R) | 43,346 | 37.1 |

## NORTH DAKOTA

| | | Votes | |
|---|---|---|---|
| AL | William Lemke (R) | 131,117 ✓ | |
| | Usher L. Burdick (R) | 115,913 ✓ | |
| | Henry Holt (D) | 100,609 | |
| | J. J. Nygaard (D) | 89,713 | |
| | I. J. Moe (I) | 3,310 | |
| | P. H. Miller (I) | 3,273 | |
| | E. A. Johansson (I) | 2,697 | |
| | Jasper Haaland (I) | 540 | |
| | W. D. Webster (I) | 461 | |

## OHIO

| | | Votes | % |
|---|---|---|---|
| 1 | Joseph A. Dixon (D) | 71,935 | 52.1 |
| | John B. Hollister (R) | 66,082 | 47.9 |
| 2 | Herbert S. Bigelow (D) | 67,213 | 51.8 |
| | William E. Hess (R) | 62,546 | 48.2 |
| 3 | Byron B. Harlan (D) | 101,115 | 55.9 |
| | Robert N. Brumbaugh (R) | 70,023 | 38.7 |
| | Leonidas E. Speer (I) | 9,886 | 5.5 |
| 4 | Frank L. Kloeb (D) | 61,927 | 53.7 |
| | Robert W. Turner (R) | 53,352 | 46.3 |
| 5 | Frank C. Kniffin (D) | 41,693 | 53.1 |
| | Stephen S. Beard (R) | 33,212 | 42.3 |
| 6 | James G. Polk (D) | 54,904 | 54.6 |
| | Emory F. Smith (R) | 45,733 | 45.4 |
| 7 | Arthur W. Aleshire (D) | 68,456 | 50.4 |
| | L. T. Marshall (R) | 67,454 | 49.6 |
| 8 | Brooks Fletcher (D) | 49,668 | 53.9 |
| | Grant E. Mouser Jr. (R) | 42,565 | 46.2 |
| 9 | John F. Hunter (D) | 75,737 | 56.3 |
| | Raymond E. Hilderbrand (R) | 55,043 | 40.9 |
| 10 | Thomas A. Jenkins (R) | 46,965 | 57.7 |
| | O. J. Kleffner (D) | 34,477 | 42.3 |
| 11 | Harold K. Claypool (D) | 41,773 | 53.4 |
| | L. P. Mooney (R) | 33,249 | 42.5 |
| 12 | Arthur P. Lamneck (D) | 88,222 | 57.7 |
| | Grant P. Ward (R) | 64,766 | 42.3 |
| 13 | Dudley A. White (R) | 46,623 | 47.3 |
| | Forrest R. Black (D) | 39,042 | 39.6 |
| | Merrell E. Martin (I) | 12,959 | 13.1 |
| 14 | Dow W. Harter (D) | 118,659 | 58.1 |
| | Carl D. Sheppard (R) | 77,039 | 37.7 |
| 15 | Robert T. Secrest (D) | 53,263 | 55.7 |
| | Kenneth C. Ray (R) | 42,053 | 44.0 |
| 16 | William R. Thom (D) | 89,911 | 59.2 |
| | H. Ross Ake (R) | 54,979 | 36.2 |
| 17 | William A. Ashbrook (D) | 69,446 | 57.7 |
| | James A. Glenn (R) | 48,270 | 40.1 |
| 18 | Lawrence E. Imhoff (D) | 83,052 | 60.6 |
| | Earl R. Lewis (R) | 54,119 | 39.5 |
| 19 | Michael J. Kirwan (D) | 93,636 | 58.4 |
| | John G. Cooper (R) | 65,926 | 41.1 |
| 20 | Martin L. Sweeney (D) | 54,295 | 54.4 |
| | Blase A. Buonpane (R) | 23,367 | 23.4 |
| | John L. Mihelich (I) | 22,158 | 22.2 |
| 21 | Robert Crosser (D) | 70,596 | 74.8 |
| | Harry C. Gahn (R) | 23,811 | 25.2 |
| 22 | Anthony A. Fleger (D) | 131,250 | 51.3 |
| | Chester C. Bolton (R) | 124,446 | 48.7 |
| AL | John McSweeney (D) | 1,553,059 ✓ | |
| | Harold G. Mosier (D) | 1,493,053 ✓ | |
| | George H. Bender (R) | 1,226,247 | |
| | L. L. Marshall (R) | 1,121,370 | |
| | William C. Sandberg (COM) | 8,945 | |

### Special Elections

| | | Votes | % |
|---|---|---|---|
| 11 | Peter F. Hammond (D) | 41,310 | 56.5 |
| | John L. Moriarty (R) | 31,864 | 43.6 |
| AL | Daniel S. Earhart (D) | 1,479,284 | 58.3 |
| | Benson Ogier (R) | 1,057,473 | 41.7 |

## OKLAHOMA

| | Candidates | Votes | % |
|---|---|---|---|
| 1 | Wesley E. Disney (D) | 81,286 | 57.7 |
| | Jo O. Ferguson (R) | 58,983 | 41.9 |
| 2 | Jack Nichols (D) | 45,724 | 63.5 |
| | V. S. Cannon (R) | 26,310 | 36.5 |
| 3 | Wilburn Cartwright (D) | 58,261 | 79.9 |
| | John D. Morrison (R) | 14,672 | 20.1 |
| 4 | Lyle H. Boren (D) | 63,306 | 72.7 |
| | Fred L. Patrick (R) | 23,615 | 27.1 |
| 5 | Robert P. Hill (D) | 78,873 | 70.2 |
| | John William Mee (R) | 33,071 | 29.4 |
| 6 | Jed Johnson (D) | 52,373 | 72.8 |
| | L. M. Gensman (R) | 19,495 | 27.1 |
| 7 | Sam C. Massingale (D) | 46,940 | 83.3 |
| | Clyde J. Matherly (R) | 9,396 | 16.7 |
| 8 | Phil Ferguson (D) | 47,497 | 58.9 |
| | T. J. Sargent (R) | 32,858 | 40.7 |
| AL | Will Rogers (D) | 475,567 | 70.7 |
| | John C. Burns (R) | 193,487 | 28.8 |

## OREGON

| | | Votes | % |
|---|---|---|---|
| 1 | James W. Mott (R) | 114,073 | 65.6 |
| | E. W. Kirkpatrick (D) | 59,788 | 34.4 |
| 2 | Walter M. Pierce (D) | 46,412 | 68.0 |
| | Roy W. Ritner (R) | 21,813 | 32.0 |
| 3 | Nan Wood Honeyman (D) | 78,624 | 53.2 |
| | William A. Ekwall (R) | 45,872 | 31.0 |
| | John A. Jeffrey (I) | 21,848 | 14.8 |

## PENNSYLVANIA

| | | Votes | % |
|---|---|---|---|
| 1 | Leon Sacks (D, D-OP) | 67,276 | 64.6 |
| | Harry C. Ransley (R, R-OP) | 34,813 | 33.4 |
| 2 | James P. McGranery (D, D-OP) | 65,779 | 59.8 |
| | William H. Wilson (R, R-OP) | 41,267 | 37.5 |
| 3 | Michael J. Bradley (D) | 75,445 | 60.8 |
| | Clare Gerald Fenerty (R, R-OP) | 48,035 | 38.7 |
| 4 | J. Burrwood Daly (D, D-OP) | 77,406 | 62.8 |
| | Boies Penrose Jr. (R, R-OP) | 41,545 | 33.7 |
| 5 | Frank J. G. Dorsey (D, D-OP) | 72,210 | 56.6 |
| | James J. Connolly (R, R-OP) | 46,238 | 36.2 |
| 6 | Michael J. Stack (D, D-OP) | 84,487 | 61.1 |
| | George F. Holmes (R, R-OP) | 51,892 | 37.5 |
| 7 | Ira Walton Drew (D, D-OP) | 77,949 | 51.8 |
| | George P. Darrow (R) | 71,749 | 47.7 |
| 8 | James Wolfenden (R) | 73,335 | 52.2 |
| | Howard Kirk (D, D-OP) | 66,119 | 47.1 |
| 9 | Oliver W. Frey (D) | 56,108 | 51.0 |
| | Theodore R. Gardner (R) | 50,361 | 45.8 |
| 10 | J. Roland Kinzer (R) | 72,181 | 52.7 |
| | H. Clay Burkholder (D) | 62,768 | 45.8 |
| 11 | Patrick J. Boland (D) | 75,905 | 57.5 |
| | John J. Owens (R) | 50,123 | 38.0 |
| 12 | J. Harold Flannery (D) | 99,161 | 53.7 |
| | C. Murray Turpin (R) | 84,902 | 46.0 |
| 13 | James H. Gildea (D, D-OP) | 83,662 | 54.6 |
| | James H. Kirchner (R) | 68,772 | 44.9 |
| 14 | Guy L. Moser (D, D-OP) | 46,192 | 53.2 |
| | Charles E. Roth (R) | 28,001 | 32.3 |
| 15 | Albert G. Rutherford (R) | 55,268 | 54.3 |
| | C. Elmer Dietrich (D) | 45,808 | 45.0 |
| 16 | Robert F. Rich (R) | 54,040 | 51.8 |
| | Paul A. Rothfuss (D, D-OP) | 49,249 | 47.2 |
| 17 | J. William Ditter (R) | 67,850 | 53.9 |
| | George H. Bartholomew (D) | 55,083 | 43.8 |
| 18 | Benjamin K. Focht (R) | 49,243 | 54.0 |
| | John M. Keichline (D) | 41,881 | 46.0 |
| 19 | Guy J. Swope (D) | 73,374 | 51.4 |
| | Isaac H. Doutrich (R, R-OP) | 67,884 | 47.5 |
| 20 | Benjamin Jarrett (R) | 58,738 | 48.4 |
| | D. J. Driscoll (D) | 56,941 | 46.9 |
| 21 | Francis E. Walter (D) | 56,566 | 56.8 |
| | William R. Coyle (R) | 39,537 | 39.7 |
| 22 | Harry L. Haines (D) | 66,306 | 54.7 |
| | Frank S. Magill (R, R-OP) | 49,273 | 40.6 |
| 23 | Don Gingery (D) | 53,629 | 48.9 |
| | Benjamin C. Jones (R) | 46,726 | 42.6 |
| 24 | J. Buell Snyder (D) | 62,009 | 60.5 |
| | Davis W. Henderson (R) | 40,067 | 39.1 |
| 25 | Charles I. Faddis (D) | 61,988 | 65.5 |
| | John C. Judson (R) | 30,208 | 31.9 |
| 26 | Charles R. Eckert (D) | 71,332 | 56.0 |
| | Orville Brown (R) | 52,925 | 41.5 |
| 27 | Joseph Gray (D) | 83,908 | 54.1 |
| | Walter E. Morris (R) | 67,809 | 43.7 |
| 28 | Robert G. Allen (D) | 67,169 | 60.2 |
| | James B. Weaver (R, R-OP) | 42,259 | 37.9 |
| 29 | Charles N. Crosby (D, D-OP) | 48,993 | 53.7 |
| | Will Rose (R) | 40,687 | 44.6 |
| 30 | Peter J. Demuth (D, D-OP) | 65,465 | 59.4 |
| | James A. Geltz (R, R-OP) | 43,878 | 39.8 |
| 31 | James L. Quinn (D, D-OP) | 81,544 | 63.0 |
| | James H. McClure (R) | 45,742 | 35.3 |
| 32 | Herman P. Eberharter (D, D-OP) | 49,722 | 66.2 |
| | Jacob E. Kalson (R, R-OP) | 21,067 | 28.0 |
| 33 | Henry Ellenbogen (D, D-OP) | 70,601 | 64.5 |
| | Edward O. Tabor (R) | 38,383 | 35.1 |
| 34 | Matthew A. Dunn (D, D-OP) | 80,194 | 64.4 |
| | Elmer A. Barchfeld (R, R-OP) | 43,827 | 35.2 |

## RHODE ISLAND

| | | Votes | % |
|---|---|---|---|
| 1 | Aime J. Forand (D) | 74,058 | 50.5 |
| | Charles F. Risk (R) | 62,199 | 42.4 |
| | Dunn (UN) | 9,973 | 6.8 |
| 2 | John M. O'Connell (D) | 75,899 | 47.8 |
| | Harry Sandager (R) | 71,981 | 45.3 |
| | Dougherty (UN) | 10,689 | 6.7 |

## SOUTH CAROLINA

| | | Votes | % |
|---|---|---|---|
| 1 | Thomas S. McMillan (D) | 15,772 | 96.9 |
| 2 | H. P. Fulmer (D) | 21,653 | 98.3 |
| 3 | John C. Taylor (D) | 18,983 | 99.0 |
| 4 | G. Heyward Mahon Jr. (D) | 25,468 | 98.9 |
| 5 | James P. Richards (D) | 15,748 | 99.2 |
| 6 | Allard H. Gasque (D) | 16,027 | 99.3 |

### Special Election

| | | Votes | % |
|---|---|---|---|
| 4 | G. Heyward Mahon Jr. (D) | 24,715 | 100.0 |

## SOUTH DAKOTA

| | | Votes | % |
|---|---|---|---|
| 1 | Fred H. Hildebrandt (D) | 110,829 | 50.6 |
| | Karl Mundt (R) | 108,259 | 49.4 |
| 2 | Francis H. Case (R) | 34,812 | 51.7 |
| | Theodore B. Werner (D) | 32,549 | 48.3 |

## TENNESSEE

| | | Votes | % |
|---|---|---|---|
| 1 | B. Carroll Reece (R) | 33,501 | 60.4 |
| | William M. Crawford (D) | 17,289 | 31.2 |
| | Charles W. Clark | 4,684 | 8.4 |
| 2 | J. Will Taylor (R) | 40,595 | 50.8 |
| | John T. O'Connor (D) | 38,991 | 48.8 |
| 3 | Sam D. McReynolds (D) | 32,065 | 68.0 |
| | William Hillery (R) | 15,096 | 32.0 |
| 4 | J. Ridley Mitchell (D) | 33,154 | 81.8 |
| | H. E. McLean (R) | 7,382 | 18.2 |

## TENNESSEE

| | Candidates | Votes | % |
|---|---|---|---|
| 5 | Richard M. Atkinson (D) | 34,277 | 94.1 |
| | E. L. Bradbury (R) | 2,163 | 5.9 |
| 6 | Clarence W. Turner (D) | 20,390 | 80.9 |
| | M. C. Ridings (R) | 4,819 | 19.1 |
| 7 | Herron Pearson (D) | 20,432 | 100.0 |
| 8 | Jere Cooper (D) | 27,032 | 93.8 |
| | Allen J. Strawbridge (R) | 1,780 | 6.2 |
| 9 | Walter Chandler (D) | 58,034 | 99.2 |

## TEXAS

| | | Votes | % |
|---|---|---|---|
| 1 | Wright Patman (D) | 29,351 | 97.6 |
| 2 | Martin Dies (D) | 39,484 | 100.0 |
| 3 | Morgan G. Sanders (D) | 29,482 | 96.3 |
| 4 | Sam Rayburn (D) | 33,355 | 97.5 |
| 5 | Hatton W. Sumners (D) | 43,954 | 88.5 |
| | D. C. Humphrey (R) | 5,579 | 11.2 |
| 6 | Luther A. Johnson (D) | 29,574 | 97.3 |
| 7 | Nat Patton (D) | 29,011 | 97.6 |
| 8 | Albert Thomas (D) | 61,616 | 91.8 |
| | R. B. Nichols (R) | 5,456 | 8.1 |
| 9 | Joseph J. Mansfield (D) | 36,968 | 93.2 |
| | F. W. Dusek (R) | 2,700 | 6.8 |
| 10 | James P. Buchanan (D) | 33,631 | 99.5 |
| 11 | W. R. Poage (D) | 31,227 | 100.0 |
| 12 | Fritz Lanham (D) | 39,708 | 93.3 |
| | Arnold Davis (R) | 2,845 | 6.7 |
| 13 | William D. McFarlane (D) | 40,935 | 95.2 |
| 14 | Richard M. Kleberg (D) | 39,576 | 92.1 |
| | Howell Ward (R) | 3,408 | 7.9 |
| 15 | Milton H. West (D) | 29,598 | 82.6 |
| | J. A. Simpson (R) | 6,244 | 17.4 |
| 16 | R. Ewing Thomason (D) | 26,353 | 100.0 |
| 17 | Clyde L. Garrett (D) | 35,386 | 100.0 |
| 18 | Marvin Jones (D) | 44,652 | 94.1 |
| | S. E. Fish (R) | 2,526 | 5.3 |
| 19 | George H. Mahon (D) | 39,059 | 100.0 |
| 20 | Maury Maverick (D) | 34,478 | 71.6 |
| | E. W. Clements (R) | 12,056 | 25.0 |
| 21 | Charles L. South (D) | 37,964 | 88.6 |
| | M. J. Bierschwale (R) | 4,891 | 11.4 |

## UTAH

| | | Votes | % |
|---|---|---|---|
| 1 | Abe Murdock (D) | 68,877 | 69.2 |
| | Charles W. Dunn (R) | 30,415 | 30.6 |
| 2 | J. Will Robinson (D) | 81,119 | 69.8 |
| | A. V. Watkins (R) | 34,855 | 30.0 |

## VERMONT

| | Candidates | Votes | % |
|---|---|---|---|
| AL | Charles A. Plumley (R) | 83,091 | 59.2 |
| | John B. Candon (D) | 56,334 | 40.1 |

## VIRGINIA

| | | Votes | % |
|---|---|---|---|
| 1 | S. Otis Bland (D) | 20,012 | 80.9 |
| | William A. Dickinson (R) | 4,592 | 18.6 |
| 2 | Norman R. Hamilton (D) | 29,269 | 88.7 |
| | G. M. Rumble (R) | 3,287 | 10.0 |
| 3 | Andrew Jackson Montague (D) | 28,803 | 84.4 |
| | Charles G. Wilson (R) | 4,936 | 14.5 |
| 4 | Patrick Henry Drewry (D) | 19,539 | 90.4 |
| | John Martin (R) | 1,832 | 8.5 |
| 5 | Thomas G. Burch (D) | 25,752 | 64.9 |
| | Taylor G. Vaughan (R) | 13,890 | 35.0 |
| 6 | Clifton A. Woodrum (D) | 25,327 | 60.7 |
| | T. X. Parsons (R) | 16,404 | 39.3 |
| 7 | A. Willis Robertson (D) | 24,790 | 63.9 |
| | J. Everett Will (R) | 13,814 | 35.6 |
| 8 | Howard W. Smith (D) | 28,052 | 75.4 |
| | John Locke Green (R) | 8,685 | 23.3 |
| 9 | John W. Flannagan Jr. (D) | 31,918 | 62.2 |
| | Luther E. Fuller (R) | 19,400 | 37.8 |

## WASHINGTON

| | | Votes | % |
|---|---|---|---|
| 1 | Warren G. Magnuson (D) | 103,967 | 63.7 |
| | Frederick J. Wettrick (R) | 58,794 | 36.0 |
| 2 | Mon C. Wallgren (D) | 64,214 | 63.6 |
| | Payson Peterson (R) | 36,508 | 36.2 |
| 3 | Martin F. Smith (D) | 67,159 | 72.0 |
| | Herbert H. Sieler (R) | 25,717 | 27.6 |
| 4 | Knute Hill (D) | 48,264 | 57.9 |
| | John W. Summers (R) | 35,063 | 42.0 |
| 5 | Charles H. Leavy (D) | 76,048 | 70.8 |
| | Warren O. Dow (R) | 31,218 | 29.1 |
| 6 | John M. Coffee (D) | 66,333 | 67.3 |
| | Paul A. Preus (R) | 31,724 | 32.2 |

## WEST VIRGINIA

| | | Votes | % |
|---|---|---|---|
| 1 | Robert L. Ramsay (D) | 75,859 | 59.9 |
| | Charles J. Shuck (R) | 50,885 | 40.2 |

| | Candidates | Votes | % |
|---|---|---|---|
| 2 | Jennings Randolph (D) | 78,856 | 59.9 |
| | C. S. Musser (R) | 52,847 | 40.1 |
| 3 | Andrew Edmiston (D) | 82,059 | 59.3 |
| | John M. Wolverton (R) | 56,251 | 40.7 |
| 4 | George W. Johnson (D) | 80,856 | 53.5 |
| | Raymond V. Humphreys (R) | 70,304 | 46.5 |
| 5 | John Kee (D) | 79,855 | 64.5 |
| | C. M. Jones (R) | 44,010 | 35.5 |
| 6 | Joe L. Smith (D) | 98,148 | 63.9 |
| | M. F. Matheny (R) | 55,536 | 36.1 |

## WISCONSIN

| | | Votes | % |
|---|---|---|---|
| 1 | Thomas R. Amlie (PROG) | 49,402 | 43.1 |
| | Paul E. Jorgensen (R) | 44,687 | 39.0 |
| | Wolf (D) | 20,597 | 18.0 |
| 2 | Harry Sauthoff (PROG) | 57,874 | 47.9 |
| | Frank R. Bentley (R) | 34,565 | 28.6 |
| | Dempsey (D) | 28,326 | 23.5 |
| 3 | Gardner R. Withrow (PROG) | 56,141 | 51.2 |
| | J. Charles Pile (R) | 38,698 | 35.3 |
| | McGonigle (D) | 14,920 | 13.6 |
| 4 | Raymond J. Cannon (D) | 63,565 | 47.3 |
| | Paul Gauer (PROG) | 42,029 | 31.2 |
| | Schafer (R) | 28,930 | 21.5 |
| 5 | Thomas O'Malley (D) | 60,716 | 41.5 |
| | Carl P. Dietz (PROG) | 50,466 | 34.5 |
| | Spence (R) | 35,121 | 24.0 |
| 6 | Michael K. Reilly (D) | 41,688 | 39.3 |
| | Frank B. Keefe (R) | 38,904 | 36.7 |
| | Poltl (PROG) | 25,395 | 24.0 |
| 7 | Gerald J. Boileau (PROG) | 48,637 | 47.0 |
| | Arthur W. Prehn (R) | 30,555 | 29.5 |
| | Coleman (D) | 24,315 | 23.5 |
| 8 | George J. Schneider (PROG) | 38,721 | 33.5 |
| | John E. Cashman (D) | 38,138 | 33.0 |
| | Farrell (R) | 33,459 | 28.9 |
| 9 | Merlin Hull (PROG) | 61,593 | 80.7 |
| | Edwin J. Larkin (D) | 14,702 | 19.3 |
| 10 | Bernard J. Gehrmann (PROG) | 49,005 | 51.5 |
| | Philip E. Nelson (R) | 30,121 | 31.7 |
| | Bostrom (D) | 15,956 | 16.8 |

## WYOMING

| | | Votes | % |
|---|---|---|---|
| AL | Paul R. Greever (D) | 56,204 | 57.2 |
| | Frank A. Barrett (R) | 41,362 | 42.1 |

# 1937 House Elections

## NEW YORK
### Special Election

| | | | |
|---|---|---|---|
| 17 | Bruce Barton (R) | 35,314# | 47.6 |
| | Stanley Osserman (D) | 21,599# | 29.1 |
| | George Backer (AM LAB) | 9,325# | 12.6 |

## OKLAHOMA
### Special Election

| | | | |
|---|---|---|---|
| 5 | Gomer Smith (D) | 21,131 | 74.5 |
| | Harlan Deupree (R) | 7,132 | 25.2 |

## PENNSYLVANIA
### Special Election

| | | | |
|---|---|---|---|
| 18 | Richard M. Simpson (R) | 34,104 | 58.0 |
| | Lowell H. Alexander (D) | 24,735 | 42.0 |

## TEXAS
### Special Election

| | | | |
|---|---|---|---|
| 10 | Lyndon B. Johnson (D) | 8,280 | 27.7 |
| | Morton Harris | 5,111 | 17.1 |
| | Polk Shelton | 4,420 | 14.8 |
| | Sam V. Stone | 4,048 | 13.5 |
| | C. N. Avery | 3,951 | 13.2 |
| | Houghton Brownell | 3,019 | 10.1 |

# 1938 House Elections

## ALABAMA

| | Candidates | Votes | % |
|---|---|---|---|
| 1 | Frank W. Boykin (D) | 9,853 | 100.0 |
| 2 | George Grant (D) | 15,569 | 100.0 |
| 3 | Henry B. Steagall (D) | 10,089 | 100.0 |
| 4 | Sam Hobbs (D) | 11,113 | 88.2 |
| | C. W. McKay (R) | 1,488 | 11.8 |
| 5 | Joe Starnes (D) | 16,587 | 99.7 |
| 6 | Pete Jarman (D) | 10,246 | 100.0 |
| 7 | William B. Bankhead (D) | 17,903 | 71.3 |
| | E. M. Reed (R) | 7,207 | 28.7 |
| 8 | John J. Sparkman (D) | 10,266 | 100.0 |
| 9 | Luther Patrick (D) | 12,627 | 93.5 |
| | J. G. Bass (R) | 878 | 6.5 |

## ARIZONA

| | Candidates | Votes | % |
|---|---|---|---|
| AL | John R. Murdock (D) | 83,556 | 80.3 |
| | M. E. Cassidy (R) | 20,502 | 19.7 |

## ARKANSAS

| | Candidates | Votes | % |
|---|---|---|---|
| 1 | Ezekiel C. Gathings (D) | 23,274 | 100.0 |
| 2 | Wilbur D. Mills (D) | 18,913 | 100.0 |
| 3 | Clyde T. Ellis (D) | 22,141 | 100.0 |
| 4 | William B. Cravens (D) | 22,272 | 100.0 |
| 5 | David D. Terry (D) | 23,949 | 100.0 |
| 6 | William F. Norrell (D) | 17,662 | 100.0 |
| 7 | Wade Kitchens (D) | 16,145 | 100.0 |

## CALIFORNIA

| | Candidates | Votes | % |
|---|---|---|---|
| 1 | Clarence F. Lea (D-R) | 73,636 | 62.9 |
| | Ernest S. Mitchell (TOWN) | 43,320 | 37.0 |
| 2 | Harry L. Englebright (R D P T) | 71,496 | 99.9 |
| 3 | Frank H. Buck (D-R) | 119,236 | 92.7 |
| | Nora Conklin (COM) | 8,271 | 6.4 |
| 4 | Franck R. Havenner (D & PROG) | 64,452 | 61.2 |
| | Kennett B. Dawson (R) | 40,842 | 38.8 |
| 5 | Richard J. Welch (R-D-PROG) | 91,868 | 100.0 |
| 6 | Albert E. Carter (R D P T) | 118,632 | 94.1 |
| | Dave L. Saunders (COM) | 7,015 | 5.6 |
| 7 | John H. Tolan (D) | 62,599 | 55.3 |
| | Charles Wade Snook (R) | 50,504 | 44.6 |
| 8 | John Z. Anderson (R) | 84,084 | 55.0 |
| | John J. McGrath (D) | 68,681 | 45.0 |
| 9 | Bertrand W. Gearhart (R-D) | 91,128 | 96.2 |
| 10 | Alfred J. Elliott (D) | 84,791 | 67.2 |
| | F. Fred Hoelscher (R) | 41,194 | 32.7 |
| 11 | Carl Hinshaw (R) | 68,712 | 47.0 |
| | Carl Stuart Hamblen (D) | 59,993 | 41.0 |
| | Ralph D. Horton (TOWN) | 12,713 | 8.7 |
| 12 | H. Jerry Voorhis (D) | 75,003 | 60.7 |
| | Eugene W. Nixon (R) | 40,457 | 32.8 |
| | Russell R. Hand (TOWN) | 7,903 | 6.4 |
| 13 | Charles Kramer (D & PROG) | 96,258 | 65.6 |
| | K. L. Stockton (R T) | 44,808 | 30.6 |
| 14 | Thomas F. Ford (D) | 67,588 | 67.8 |
| | William D. Campbell (R) | 31,375 | 31.5 |
| 15 | John M. Costello (D) | 83,086 | 60.2 |
| | O. D. Thomas (R) | 51,483 | 37.3 |
| 16 | Leland M. Ford (R-D) | 97,407 | 62.8 |
| | John F. Dockweiler (D) | 32,863 | 21.2 |
| | Ted E. Felt (TOWN) | 16,045 | 10.3 |
| 17 | Lee E. Geyer (D) | 56,513 | 58.6 |
| | Clifton A. Hix (R) | 26,891 | 27.9 |
| | Fred C. Wagner (TOWN) | 8,870 | 9.2 |
| 18 | Thomas M. Eaton (R) | 52,216 | 48.5 |
| | Byron N. Scott (D) | 51,874 | 48.2 |

| | Candidates | Votes | % |
|---|---|---|---|
| 19 | Harry R. Sheppard (D) | 75,819 | 53.3 |
| | C. T. Johnson (R T) | 66,402 | 46.7 |
| 20 | Edouard V. M. Izac (D) | 65,243 | 60.4 |
| | John L. Bacon (R) | 42,710 | 39.5 |

## COLORADO

| | Candidates | Votes | % |
|---|---|---|---|
| 1 | Lawrence Lewis (D) | 83,517 | 65.3 |
| | William I. Reilly (R) | 42,758 | 33.4 |
| 2 | Fred Cummings (D) | 65,448 | 51.7 |
| | William S. Hill (R) | 60,259 | 47.6 |
| 3 | John A. Martin (D) | 72,736 | 57.4 |
| | Henry Leonard (R) | 54,007 | 42.6 |
| 4 | Edward T. Taylor (D) | 43,596 | 63.7 |
| | John S. Woody (R) | 24,805 | 36.3 |

## CONNECTICUT

| | Candidates | Votes | % |
|---|---|---|---|
| 1 | William J. Miller (R) | 68,229 | 43.2 |
| | Herman P. Kopplemann (D) | 64,483 | 40.8 |
| | Edward C. Roffler (SOC) | 24,718 | 15.7 |
| 2 | Thomas R. Ball (R) | 48,180 | 48.3 |
| | William J. Fitzgerald (D) | 45,056 | 45.2 |
| | Thomas E. Bowman (SOC) | 6,333 | 6.4 |
| 3 | James A. Shanley (D) | 55,893 | 43.4 |
| | Ranulf Compton (R) | 55,501 | 43.1 |
| | Harry Watstein (SOC) | 17,111 | 13.3 |
| 4 | Albert E. Austin (R) | 61,161 | 43.1 |
| | Alfred N. Phillips Jr. (D) | 44,626 | 31.4 |
| | Charles H. McLevy (SOC) | 35,328 | 24.9 |
| 5 | J. Joseph Smith (D) | 39,824 | 42.0 |
| | Roy E. Rice (R) | 39,652 | 41.8 |
| | John W. Ring (SOC) | 15,369 | 16.2 |
| AL | Boleslaus J. Monkiewicz (R) | 271,329 | 43.1 |
| | William M. Citron (D) | 250,013 | 39.7 |
| | Arthur F. King (SOC) | 99,717 | 15.8 |

## DELAWARE

| | Candidates | Votes | % |
|---|---|---|---|
| AL | George S. Williams (R) | 60,661 | 55.9 |
| | William F. Allen (D) | 46,989 | 43.3 |

## FLORIDA

| | Candidates | Votes | % |
|---|---|---|---|
| 1 | J. Hardin Peterson (D) | 43,837 | 100.0 |
| 2 | Robert A. Green (D) | 24,830 | 100.0 |
| 3 | Millard Caldwell (D) | 20,174 | 100.0 |
| 4 | Arthur P. Cannon (D) | 29,621 | 81.5 |
| | J. S. G. Gallagher (R) | 6,705 | 18.5 |
| 5 | Joe Hendricks (D) | 27,894 | 100.0 |

## GEORGIA

| | Candidates | Votes | % |
|---|---|---|---|
| 1 | Hugh Peterson (D) | 10,920 | 99.3 |
| 2 | E. E. Cox (D) | 5,137 | 100.0 |
| 3 | Stephen Pace (D) | 5,987 | 100.0 |
| 4 | E. M. Owen (D) | 5,413 | 100.0 |
| 5 | Robert Ramspeck (D) | 6,906 | 97.2 |
| 6 | Carl Vinson (D) | 4,360 | 100.0 |
| 7 | Malcoln Tarver (D) | 5,622 | 100.0 |
| 8 | W. Benjamin Gibbs (D) | 4,929 | 100.0 |
| 9 | B. Frank Whelchel (D) | 8,934 | 100.0 |
| 10 | Paul Brown (D) | 9,044 | 94.4 |

## IDAHO

| | Candidates | Votes | % |
|---|---|---|---|
| 1 | Compton I. White (D) | 48,318 | 62.8 |
| | Rex T. Henson (R) | 28,640 | 37.2 |
| 2 | Henry C. Dworshak (R) | 54,527 | 53.6 |
| | Bert H. Miller (D) | 47,199 | 46.4 |

## ILLINOIS

| | Candidates | Votes | % |
|---|---|---|---|
| 1 | Arthur W. Mitchell (D) | 30,207 | 53.4 |
| | William L. Dawson (R) | 26,396 | 46.6 |
| 2 | Raymond S. McKeough (D) | 129,620 | 54.4 |
| | Noble W. Lee (R) | 108,483 | 45.6 |
| 3 | Edward A. Kelly (D) | 127,597 | 56.0 |
| | Goodwin L. Dosland (R) | 100,357 | 44.0 |
| 4 | Harry P. Beam (D) | 61,504 | 76.4 |
| | Dominic M. Janec Jr. (R) | 18,962 | 23.6 |
| 5 | Adolph J. Sabath (D) | 32,104 | 74.8 |
| | Max Price (R) | 10,842 | 25.3 |
| 6 | A. F. Maciejewski (D) | 154,818 | 58.5 |
| | Robert Isham Randolph (R) | 109,031 | 41.3 |
| 7 | Leonard W. Schuetz (D) | 192,750 | 54.3 |
| | James C. Moreland (R) | 162,069 | 45.7 |
| 8 | Leo Kocialkowski (D) | 31,823 | 75.0 |
| | Rena E. Pikiel (R) | 10,440 | 24.7 |
| 9 | James McAndrews (D) | 44,064 | 52.7 |
| | Charles S. Dewey (R) | 39,512 | 47.3 |
| 10 | Ralph E. Church (R) | 141,685 | 58.1 |
| | Joseph F. Elward (D) | 102,234 | 41.9 |
| 11 | Chauncey W. Reed (R) | 94,565 | 65.9 |
| | William J. Bossingham (D) | 48,876 | 34.1 |
| 12 | Noah M. Mason (R) | 67,326 | 60.7 |
| | Edward C. Hunter (D) | 43,631 | 39.3 |
| 13 | Leo E. Allen (R) | 45,177 | 65.6 |
| | Theodore A. Secker (D) | 23,708 | 34.4 |
| 14 | Anton J. Johnson (R) | 44,243 | 51.5 |
| | Chester Thompson (D) | 41,682 | 48.5 |
| 15 | Robert B. Chiperfield (R) | 47,703 | 54.5 |
| | Lewis L. Boyer (D) | 39,779 | 45.5 |
| 16 | Everett M. Dirksen (R) | 61,012 | 63.5 |
| | James C. Dillon (D) | 35,081 | 36.5 |
| 17 | Leslie C. Arends (R) | 45,235 | 60.9 |
| | Thomas V. Watson (D) | 29,023 | 39.1 |
| 18 | Jessie Sumner (R) | 56,587 | 55.3 |
| | James A. Meeks (D) | 45,691 | 44.7 |
| 19 | William H. Wheat (R) | 59,446 | 51.5 |
| | Hugh M. Rigney (D) | 55,956 | 48.5 |
| 20 | James M. Barnes (D) | 37,184 | 55.4 |
| | Stuart E. Pierson (R) | 29,907 | 44.6 |
| 21 | Frank W. Fries (D) | 52,173 | 50.3 |
| | Frank H. Ramey (R) | 51,651 | 49.8 |
| 22 | Edwin M. Schaefer (D) | 66,743 | 52.5 |
| | Jesse R. Brown (R) | 60,518 | 47.6 |
| 23 | Laurence F. Arnold (D) | 49,537 | 53.8 |
| | O. A. James (R) | 42,572 | 46.2 |
| 24 | Claude V. Parsons (D) | 40,633 | 51.1 |
| | R. R. Randolph (R) | 38,889 | 48.9 |
| 25 | Kent E. Keller (D) | 59,203 | 52.3 |
| | R. G. Crisenberry (R) | 53,999 | 47.7 |
| AL | Thomas V. Smith (D) | 1,572,870✔ | |
| | John C. Martin (D) | 1,560,283✔ | |
| | Stephen A. Day (R) | 1,472,638 | |
| | Simon E. Lantz (R) | 1,456,535 | |
| | Harmon W. Reed (P) | 9,337 | |
| | A. G. Carnine (P) | 8,808 | |

## INDIANA

| | Candidates | Votes | % |
|---|---|---|---|
| 1 | William T. Schulte (D) | 56,630 | 54.9 |
| | M. Elliott Belshaw (R) | 46,370 | 45.0 |
| 2 | Charles A. Halleck (R) | 79,304 | 57.8 |
| | Homer Stonebraker (D) | 57,860 | 42.2 |
| 3 | Robert A. Grant (R) | 61,836 | 51.0 |
| | George N. Beamer (D) | 59,359 | 49.0 |
| 4 | George W. Gillie (R) | 72,567 | 58.1 |
| | James I. Farley (D) | 52,293 | 41.9 |
| 5 | Forest A. Harness (R) | 73,102 | 54.7 |
| | Glenn Griswold (D) | 60,643 | 45.3 |
| 6 | Noble J. Johnson (R) | 71,883 | 50.6 |
| | Virginia E. Jenckes (D) | 70,128 | 49.4 |
| 7 | Gerald W. Landis (R) | 78,870 | 51.6 |
| | Arthur H. Greenwood (D) | 74,001 | 48.4 |
| 8 | John W. Boehne Jr. (D) | 76,780 | 56.4 |
| | Charles F. Werner (R) | 59,254 | 43.6 |

## INDIANA

| Candidates | Votes | % |
|---|---|---|
| 9 Eugene B. Crowe (D) | 70,237 | 52.1 |
| Clifford H. Long (R) | 64,541 | 47.9 |
| 10 Raymond S. Springer (R) | 73,782 | 53.5 |
| Finly H. Gray (D) | 64,176 | 46.5 |
| 11 William H. Larrabee (D) | 65,646 | 51.6 |
| William O. Nelson (R) | 61,627 | 48.4 |
| 12 Louis Ludlow (D) | 65,368 | 53.7 |
| Charles Jewett (R) | 56,319 | 46.3 |

## IOWA

| Candidates | Votes | % |
|---|---|---|
| 1 Thomas E. Martin (R) | 46,636 | 57.7 |
| James P. Gaffney (D) | 33,765 | 41.8 |
| 2 William S. Jacobsen (D) | 48,155 | 50.3 |
| Alfred C. Mueller (R) | 47,535 | 49.7 |
| 3 John W. Gwynne (R) | 45,541 | 59.7 |
| W. F. Hayes (D) | 30,158 | 39.5 |
| 4 Henry O. Talle (R) | 48,640 | 51.9 |
| Fred Biermann (D) | 44,601 | 47.6 |
| 5 Karl M. LeCompte (R) | 50,860 | 53.9 |
| Ruth F. Hollingshead (D) | 43,452 | 46.1 |
| 6 Cassius C. Dowell (R) | 53,505 | 58.5 |
| Hubert Utterback (D) | 37,056 | 40.5 |
| 7 Ben F. Jensen (R) | 54,922 | 59.0 |
| Roger F. Warin (D) | 37,992 | 40.8 |
| 8 Fred C. Gilchrist (R) | 51,934 | 62.5 |
| H. Lloyd Eveland (D) | 30,632 | 36.9 |
| 9 Vincent F. Harrington (D) | 46,705 | 49.7 |
| Albert F. Swanson (R) | 46,366 | 49.3 |

## KANSAS

| Candidates | Votes | % |
|---|---|---|
| 1 William P. Lambertson (R) | 65,945 | 60.3 |
| H. N. Hensley (D) | 43,374 | 39.7 |
| 2 Ulysses S. Guyer (R) | 70,605 | 56.4 |
| W. F. Jackson (D) | 54,582 | 43.6 |
| 3 Thomas D. Winter (R) | 56,361 | 53.4 |
| Edward W. Patterson (D) | 49,117 | 46.6 |
| 4 Edward H. Rees (R) | 55,419 | 63.1 |
| J. Donald Coffin (D) | 32,443 | 36.9 |
| 5 John M. Houston (D) | 43,990 | 50.3 |
| Stanley Taylor (R) | 43,480 | 49.7 |
| 6 Frank Carlson (R) | 69,989 | 63.4 |
| Roy L. Hamilton (D) | 40,466 | 36.6 |
| 7 Clifford R. Hope (R) | 72,893 | 65.5 |
| Claude E. Main (D) | 38,357 | 34.5 |

## KENTUCKY

| Candidates | Votes | % |
|---|---|---|
| 1 Noble J. Gregory (D) | 35,332 | 76.0 |
| Alvin Schutz (R) | 11,153 | 24.0 |
| 2 Beverly M. Vincent (D) | 36,170 | 63.8 |
| Richard Slack (R) | 20,566 | 36.3 |
| 3 Emmet O'Neal (D) | 57,227 | 61.2 |
| Frank A. Ropke (R) | 36,361 | 38.9 |
| 4 Edward W. Creal (D) | 32,179 | 59.2 |
| Harry H. Wilson (R) | 22,139 | 40.8 |
| 5 Brent Spence (D) | 28,383 | 68.4 |
| Joseph A. Kreke (R) | 13,095 | 31.6 |
| 6 Virgil Chapman (D) | 38,148 | 64.9 |
| Chester D. Silvers (R) | 20,471 | 34.8 |
| 7 Andrew J. May (D) | 27,655 | 53.2 |
| Hillard H. Smith (R) | 24,337 | 46.8 |
| 8 Joe B. Bates (D) | 39,006 | 58.8 |
| H. Clell Hayes (R) | 27,308 | 41.2 |
| 9 John M. Robsion (R) | 42,901 | 66.8 |
| Bert Rowland (D) | 21,327 | 33.2 |

### Special Election

| | | |
|---|---|---|
| 8 Joe B. Bates (D) | 21,318 | 52.9 |
| James C. Sparks (R) | 18,972 | 47.1 |

## LOUISIANA

| | | |
|---|---|---|
| 1 Joachim O. Fernandez (D) | 50,453 | 100.0 |
| 2 Paul H. Maloney (D) | 47,746 | 100.0 |
| 3 Robert L. Mouton (D) | 5,236 | 100.0 |
| 4 Overton Brooks (D) | 10,661 | 99.6 |
| 5 Newt V. Mills (D) | 11,644 | 100.0 |
| 6 John K. Griffith (D) | 12,225 | 100.0 |
| 7 Rene L. DeRouen (D) | 5,313 | 100.0 |
| 8 A. Leonard Allen (D) | 9,088 | 100.0 |

## MAINE

| | | |
|---|---|---|
| 1 James C. Oliver (R) | 57,642 | 59.0 |
| H. B. Emery (D) | 40,103 | 41.0 |
| 2 Clyde H. Smith (R) | 55,718 | 48.9 |
| F. H. Dubord (D) | 46,900 | 41.1 |
| J. C. Leckemby (R) | 8,197 | 7.2 |
| 3 Ralph O. Brewster (R) | 51,485 | 63.4 |
| Melvin P. Roberts (D) | 29,771 | 36.6 |

## MARYLAND

| | | |
|---|---|---|
| 1 T. Alan Goldsborough (D) | 38,926 | 62.8 |
| Charles H. Gibson (R) | 23,096 | 37.2 |
| 2 William P. Cole Jr. (D) | 91,231 | 66.3 |
| Irving H. Mezger (R) | 44,699 | 32.5 |
| 3 Thomas D'Alesandro Jr. (D) | 29,891 | 56.6 |
| John A. Janetzke Jr. (R) | 22,909 | 43.4 |
| 4 Ambrose J. Kennedy (D) | 37,416 | 50.2 |
| Daniel Ellison (R) | 37,126 | 49.8 |
| 5 Stephen W. Gambrill (D) | 46,678* | 68.0 |
| A. Kingsley Love (R) | 19,604 | 28.6 |
| 6 William D. Byron (D) | 46,200 | 50.8 |
| A. Charles Stewart (R) | 44,734 | 49.2 |

## MASSACHUSETTS

| | | |
|---|---|---|
| 1 Allen T. Treadway (R) | 64,886 | 58.8 |
| Owen Johnson (D) | 45,397 | 41.2 |
| 2 Charles R. Clason (R) | 68,106 | 61.9 |
| James F. Egan (D) | 41,935 | 38.1 |
| 3 Joseph E. Casey (D) | 58,600 | 51.8 |
| J. Walton Tuttle (R) | 54,557 | 48.2 |
| 4 Pehr G. Holmes (R) | 62,874 | 54.1 |
| Edward A. Ryan (D) | 53,266 | 45.9 |
| 5 Edith Nourse Rogers (R) | 104,912 | 74.8 |
| Francis J. Roane (D) | 35,323 | 25.2 |
| 6 George J. Bates (R) | 82,434 | 74.7 |
| James D. Burns (D) | 27,967 | 25.3 |
| 7 Lawrence J. Connery (D) | 83,618 | 63.7 |
| George W. Eastman (R) | 47,533 | 36.2 |
| 8 Arthur D. Healey (D) | 62,152 | 55.1 |
| Rufus H. Bond (R) | 50,711 | 44.9 |
| 9 Robert Luce (R) | 70,059 | 50.7 |
| Thomas H. Eliot (D) | 68,258 | 49.4 |
| 10 George Holden Tinkham (R) | 78,052 | 64.4 |
| Martin J. Kelly (D) | 43,093 | 35.6 |
| 11 Thomas A. Flaherty (D) | 56,939 | 100.0 |
| 12 John W. McCormack (D) | 86,618 | 77.1 |
| Henry J. Allen (R) | 25,678 | 22.9 |
| 13 Richard B. Wigglesworth (R) | 86,389 | 68.4 |
| Andrew T. Clancy (D) | 39,939 | 31.6 |
| 14 Joseph W. Martin Jr. (R) | 63,608 | 58.7 |
| Lawrence J. Bresnahan (D) | 43,876 | 40.5 |
| 15 Charles L. Gifford (R) | 66,054 | 59.0 |
| John D. W. Bodfish (D) | 45,867 | 41.0 |

## MICHIGAN

| | | |
|---|---|---|
| 1 Rudolph G. Tenerowicz (D) | 71,533 | 80.4 |
| Charles A. Roxborough (R) | 16,752 | 18.8 |
| 2 Earl C. Michener (R) | 58,921 | 64.4 |
| Walter C. Averill Jr. (D) | 32,468 | 35.5 |
| 3 Paul W. Shafer (R) | 58,128 | 66.1 |
| Gordon L. Stewart (D) | 29,832 | 33.9 |
| 4 Clare E. Hoffman (R) | 49,279 | 59.2 |
| Felix A. Racette (D) | 33,912 | 40.8 |
| 5 Carl E. Mapes (R) | 50,473 | 59.1 |
| Tunis Johnson (D) | 34,991 | 40.9 |
| 6 William W. Blackney (R) | 66,612 | 55.0 |
| Andrew J. Transue (D) | 54,491 | 45.0 |
| 7 Jesse P. Wolcott (R) | 62,910 | 69.0 |
| Charles F. Mann (D) | 28,259 | 31.0 |
| 8 Fred L. Crawford (R) | 52,250 | 58.7 |
| Louis C. Schwinger (D) | 36,758 | 41.3 |
| 9 Albert J. Engel (R) | 40,849 | 58.2 |
| Noel P. Fox (D) | 29,397 | 41.9 |
| 10 Roy O. Woodruff (R) | 44,818 | 66.4 |
| Harold C. Bellows (D) | 22,615 | 33.5 |
| 11 Fred Bradley (R) | 40,904 | 51.4 |
| John Luecke (D) | 38,707 | 48.6 |
| 12 Frank E. Hook (D) | 43,453 | 51.7 |
| John B. Bennett (R) | 40,587 | 48.3 |
| 13 Clarence J. McLeod (R) | 50,123 | 50.6 |
| George D. O'Brien (D) | 48,443 | 48.9 |
| 14 Louis C. Rabaut (D) | 62,872 | 57.6 |
| O. Z. Ide (R) | 45,967 | 42.1 |
| 15 John D. Dingell (D) | 57,401 | 54.0 |
| Archie C. Fraser (R) | 48,429 | 45.6 |
| 16 John Lesinski (D) | 49,101 | 55.1 |
| John L. Carey (R) | 39,623 | 44.5 |
| 17 George A. Dondero (R) | 63,769 | 61.4 |
| Samuel G. Backus (D) | 39,784 | 38.3 |

## MINNESOTA

| | | |
|---|---|---|
| 1 August H. Andresen (R) | 74,493 | 64.9 |
| Ray G. Moonan (D) | 40,340 | 35.1 |
| 2 Elmer J. Ryan (D) | 53,258 | 43.6 |
| Joseph P. O'Hara (R) | 43,919 | 35.9 |
| C. F. Gaarenstroom (F-LAB) | 25,060 | 20.5 |
| 3 John G. Alexander (R) | 53,442 | 45.3 |
| Henry G. Teigan (F-LAB) | 50,505 | 42.8 |
| Martin A. Hogan (D) | 14,073 | 11.9 |
| 4 Melvin J. Maas (R) | 60,252 | 53.1 |
| Howard Y. Williams (F-LAB) | 40,558 | 35.8 |
| A. B. C. Doherty (D) | 12,619 | 11.1 |
| 5 Oscar Youngdahl (R) | 67,722 | 54.7 |
| Dewey W. Johnson (F-LAB) | 45,568 | 36.8 |
| John L. Gleason (D) | 10,598 | 8.6 |
| 6 Harold Knutson (R) | 79,900 | 63.2 |
| Harry W. Christenson (F-LAB) | 36,023 | 28.5 |
| Harold F. Deering (D) | 10,448 | 8.3 |
| 7 H. Carl Andersen (R) | 49,394 | 42.6 |
| Paul John Kvale (F-LAB) | 42,572 | 36.7 |
| J. L. O'Connor (D) | 19,330 | 16.7 |
| 8 William A. Pittenger (R) | 67,960 | 51.8 |
| John T. Bernard (F-LAB) | 54,381 | 41.4 |
| Merle J. McKeon (D) | 8,945 | 6.8 |
| 9 Richard Thompson Buckler (F-LAB) | 44,017 | 42.0 |
| Ole O. Sageng (R) | 40,383 | 38.5 |
| Martin O. Brandon (D) | 20,425 | 19.5 |

## MISSISSIPPI

| | | |
|---|---|---|
| 1 John E. Rankin (D) | 4,384 | 100.0 |
| 2 Wall Doxey (D) | 4,134 | 100.0 |
| 3 William M. Whittington (D) | 2,172 | 100.0 |
| 4 Aaron Lane Ford (D) | 3,502 | 100.0 |
| 5 Ross A. Collins (D) | 11,540 | 100.0 |
| 6 William M. Colmer (D) | 4,873 | 100.0 |
| 7 Dan R. McGehee (D) | 4,834 | 100.0 |

## MISSOURI

| | | |
|---|---|---|
| 1 Milton A. Romjue (D) | 43,607 | 54.7 |
| J. G. Morgan (R) | 36,064 | 45.2 |
| 2 William L. Nelson (D) | 51,451 | 57.9 |
| Mrs. George B. Simmons (R) | 37,294 | 42.0 |
| 3 Richard M. Duncan (D) | 50,501 | 55.3 |
| Fred Maughmer (R) | 40,801 | 44.7 |

## MISSOURI

| Candidates | Votes | % |
|---|---|---|
| 4 C. Jasper Bell (D) | 71,940 | 80.4 |
| George E. Kimball (R) | 17,560 | 19.6 |
| 5 Joseph B. Shannon (D) | 75,810 | 81.0 |
| Leslie J. Lyons (R) | 17,809 | 19.0 |
| 6 Reuben T. Wood (D) | 52,774 | 50.3 |
| Phil A. Bennett (R) | 52,159 | 49.7 |
| 7 Dewey Short (R) | 63,758 | 56.3 |
| Frank H. Lee (D) | 49,396 | 43.6 |
| 8 Clyde Williams (D) | 56,489 | 55.3 |
| Homer S. Cotton (R) | 45,673 | 44.7 |
| 9 Clarence Cannon (D) | 40,686 | 60.5 |
| F. B. Meyer (R) | 26,510 | 39.4 |
| 10 Orville Zimmerman (D) | 44,182 | 58.9 |
| Ralph Hutchison (R) | 30,804 | 41.1 |
| 11 Thomas C. Hennings (D) | 63,332 | 61.8 |
| William E. Buder (R) | 38,866 | 37.9 |
| 12 C. Arthur Anderson (D) | 78,481 | 52.0 |
| Russell J. Horsefield (R) | 71,831 | 47.6 |
| 13 John J. Cochran (D) | 59,202 | 69.0 |
| William Gray (R) | 26,476 | 30.9 |

## MONTANA

| Candidates | Votes | % |
|---|---|---|
| 1 Jacob Thorkelson (R) | 49,253 | 54.4 |
| Jerry J. O'Connell (D) | 41,319 | 45.6 |
| 2 James F. O'Connor (D) | 63,506 | 53.8 |
| W. C. Husband (R) | 54,632 | 46.2 |

## NEBRASKA

| Candidates | Votes | % |
|---|---|---|
| 1 George H. Heinke (R) | 45,527 | 47.0 |
| Henry C. Luckey (D) | 45,178 | 46.6 |
| Catherine E. McGerr | 6,153 | 6.4 |
| 2 Charles F. McLaughlin (D) | 46,927 | 57.3 |
| M. F. Mulvaney (R) | 32,685 | 39.9 |
| 3 Karl Stefan (R) | 78,765 | 75.3 |
| Edgar Howard (D) | 25,862 | 24.7 |
| 4 Carl T. Curtis (R) | 59,794 | 58.2 |
| Charles G. Binderup (D) | 42,957 | 41.8 |
| 5 Harry B. Coffee (D) | 57,192 | 62.4 |
| William E. Shuman (R) | 31,225 | 34.1 |

## NEVADA

| Candidates | Votes | % |
|---|---|---|
| AL James G. Scrugham (D) | 30,156 | 66.4 |
| Harry E. Stewart (R) | 15,285 | 33.6 |

## NEW HAMPSHIRE

| Candidates | Votes | % |
|---|---|---|
| 1 Arthur B. Jenks (R) | 52,444 | 54.0 |
| Alphonse Roy (D) | 44,681 | 46.0 |
| 2 Foster Stearns (R) | 49,696 | 59.1 |
| Alvin A. Lucier (D) | 34,452 | 40.9 |

## NEW JERSEY

| Candidates | Votes | % |
|---|---|---|
| 1 Charles A. Wolverton (R) | 96,518 | 62.0 |
| Thomas M. Madden (D) | 58,450 | 37.5 |
| 2 Walter Sooy Jeffries (R) | 57,090 | 50.6 |
| Elmer H. Wene (D) | 55,344 | 49.1 |
| 3 Walter H. Sutphin (D) | 64,621 | 50.5 |
| James K. Allardice (R) | 63,345 | 49.5 |
| 4 D. Lane Powers (R) | 62,123 | 61.3 |
| Richard J. Hughes (D) | 38,921 | 38.4 |
| 5 Charles A. Eaton (R) | 71,661 | 56.7 |
| Franklin W. Rice (D) | 54,690 | 43.2 |
| 6 Donald H. McLean (R) | 63,583 | 61.4 |
| Richard F. Green (D) | 38,667 | 37.4 |
| 7 J. Parnell Thomas (R) | 64,147 | 64.0 |
| Edward W. Wildrick (D) | 35,628 | 35.6 |
| 8 George N. Seger (R) | 61,988 | 59.2 |
| Fred Hoelscher (D) | 42,030 | 40.2 |
| 9 Frank C. Osmers Jr. (R) | 64,903 | 59.3 |
| Vincent Clausen (D) | 43,641 | 39.9 |
| 10 Fred A. Hartley Jr. (R) | 51,025 | 55.6 |
| Lindsay H. Rudd (D) | 36,273 | 39.5 |

| Candidates | Votes | % |
|---|---|---|
| 11 Albert L. Vreeland (R) | 43,747 | 50.4 |
| Edward L. O'Neill (D) | 38,885 | 44.8 |
| 12 Robert W. Kean (R) | 48,854 | 55.0 |
| Frank W. Towey Jr (D) | 36,736 | 41.3 |
| 13 Mary T. Norton (D) | 89,287 | 79.8 |
| T. Burton Coyle (R) | 22,459 | 20.1 |
| 14 Edward J. Hart (D) | 86,128 | 78.6 |
| Henry T. Stuhr (R) | 23,166 | 21.1 |

## NEW MEXICO

| Candidates | Votes | % |
|---|---|---|
| AL John J. Dempsey (D) | 90,608 | 58.4 |
| Pearce Rodey (R) | 64,281 | 41.4 |

## NEW YORK

| Candidates | Votes | % |
|---|---|---|
| 1 Leonard W. Hall (R) | 184,539 | 63.0 |
| John F. Kiernan (D) | 99,521 | 34.0 |
| 2 William B. Barry (D, AM LAB) | 175,009 | 67.6 |
| George Archinal (R, C) | 81,534 | 31.5 |
| 3 Joseph L. Pfeifer (D) | 28,317 | 64.8 |
| Philip Tirone (R) | 10,174 | 23.3 |
| Bernard Kleban (AM LAB) | 4,898 | 11.2 |
| 4 Thomas H. Cullen (D, AM LAB) | 31,881 | 74.5 |
| Edwin R. Kaprat (R) | 10,620 | 24.8 |
| 5 Marcellus H. Evans (D) | 45,387 | 58.3 |
| Francis H. Warland (R, CITY FUS) | 23,410 | 30.1 |
| Joseph Dermody (AM LAB) | 8,352 | 10.7 |
| 6 Andrew L. Somers (D, PROG) | 78,530 | 52.0 |
| Gustav Drews (R, AM LAB) | 69,793 | 46.2 |
| 7 John J. Delaney (D) | 29,823 | 59.6 |
| John J. Blust (R) | 9,930 | 19.8 |
| Bernard Reswick (AM LAB) | 9,734 | 19.5 |
| 8 Donald L. O'Toole (D) | 134,461 | 54.1 |
| Dorothy J. Bellanca (AM LAB, R) | 111,252 | 44.7 |
| 9 Eugene J. Keogh (D, CITY FUS) | 60,164 | 54.1 |
| Nelson S. Kirk II (R) | 37,740 | 34.0 |
| Spencer K. Binyon (AM LAB) | 12,199 | 11.0 |
| 10 Emanuel Celler (D, AM LAB) | 43,881 | 73.5 |
| Arthur H. J. MacMullen (R) | 14,852 | 24.9 |
| 11 James A. O'Leary (D) | 40,407 | 58.9 |
| Percy C. Ryder (R) | 23,220 | 33.9 |
| John V. Murphy (AM LAB) | 4,527 | 6.6 |
| 12 Samuel Dickstein (D, AM LAB) | 17,295 | 89.0 |
| Hyman Hecht (R) | 1,865 | 9.6 |
| 13 Christopher D. Sullivan (D) | 13,313 | 63.8 |
| John Rosenberg (R) | 3,809 | 18.3 |
| Eugene P. Connolly (AM LAB) | 3,541 | 17.0 |
| 14 William I. Sirovich (D, AM LAB) | 23,722 | 68.4 |
| Maurice Wahl (R) | 10,392 | 30.0 |
| 15 Michael J. Kennedy (D) | 22,237 | 67.3 |
| John Kane Jr. (R) | 7,477 | 22.6 |
| Daniel L. McDonough (AM LAB) | 3,103 | 9.4 |
| 16 James H. Fay (D, AM LAB) | 24,500 | 52.1 |
| John J. O'Connor (R, AJAC) | 22,037 | 46.9 |
| 17 Bruce Barton (R, I PROG) | 40,421 | 55.0 |
| Walter H. Liebman (D) | 26,581 | 36.2 |
| George Backer (AM LAB) | 6,120 | 8.3 |
| 18 Martin J. Kennedy (D) | 25,817 | 60.8 |
| Raymond S. Fanning (R) | 12,952 | 30.5 |
| Martin C. Kyne (AM LAB) | 3,440 | 8.1 |
| 19 Sol Bloom (D) | 43,134 | 53.3 |
| Robert P. Levis (R, I PROG) | 22,741 | 28.1 |
| Joseph Schlossberg (AM LAB, SOC) | 15,033 | 18.6 |

| Candidates | Votes | % |
|---|---|---|
| 20 Vito Marcantonio (R, AM LAB) | 18,960 | 59.7 |
| James J. Lanzetta (D) | 12,376 | 39.0 |
| 21 Joseph A. Gavagan (D, AM LAB) | 84,629 | 69.5 |
| Lorenzo H. King (R) | 36,034 | 29.6 |
| 22 Edward W. Curley (D, CITY FUS) | 34,094 | 64.5 |
| Arthur D. Fisher (R) | 12,177 | 23.0 |
| Thomas C. O'Leary (AM LAB) | 6,141 | 11.6 |
| 23 Charles A. Buckley (D, L) | 120,474 | 50.8 |
| Isidore Nagler (AM LAB, SOC) | 67,273 | 28.4 |
| Robert H. Brennen (R, I PROG) | 49,235 | 20.8 |
| 24 James M. Fitzpatrick (D, CITY FUS) | 116,733 | 48.7 |
| Louis Goldrich (R) | 79,537 | 33.2 |
| Bartholomew F. Murphy (AM LAB) | 40,931 | 17.1 |
| 25 Ralph A. Gamble (R) | 94,865 | 64.9 |
| Homer A. Stebbins (D) | 46,730 | 32.0 |
| 26 Hamilton Fish (R) | 67,837 | 64.3 |
| Ben Martin (D, AM LAB) | 36,937 | 35.0 |
| 27 Lewis K. Rockefeller (R, SOC) | 58,565 | 61.0 |
| George W. Markey (D, AM LAB) | 37,452 | 39.0 |
| 28 William T. Byrne (D) | 88,037 | 60.5 |
| William B. Cornell (R) | 54,610 | 37.5 |
| 29 E. Harold Cluett (R) | 74,888 | 65.0 |
| Harry M. Brooks (D, AM LAB) | 40,004 | 34.7 |
| 30 Frank Crowther (R) | 58,691 | 60.1 |
| C. Dorothea Greene (D) | 38,535 | 39.4 |
| 31 Wallace E. Pierce (R) | 49,240 | 64.1 |
| George C. Owens (D) | 19,784 | 25.7 |
| Jesse W. Williams (TOWN) | 7,638 | 9.9 |
| 32 Francis D. Culkin (R) | 60,947 | 75.5 |
| Virginia A. Spencer (D) | 19,631 | 24.3 |
| 33 Fred J. Douglas (R) | 63,857 | 61.2 |
| Ralph A. Peters (D) | 37,195 | 35.7 |
| 34 Bert Lord (R) | 67,330 | 65.3 |
| John V. Johnson (D, AM LAB) | 35,456 | 34.4 |
| 35 Clarence E. Hancock (R) | 90,078 | 64.1 |
| Caleb Candee Brown Jr. (D, AM LAB) | 50,083 | 35.6 |
| 36 John Taber (R) | 48,344 | 54.7 |
| George F. Davie (D) | 20,636 | 23.3 |
| Charles P. Russell (AM LAB, TOWN) | 19,020 | 21.5 |
| 37 W. Sterling Cole (R) | 57,648 | 60.5 |
| David Moses (D, AM LAB) | 37,216 | 39.1 |
| 38 Joseph J. O'Brien (R) | 80,963 | 55.8 |
| George B. Kelly (D, AM LAB) | 63,325 | 43.7 |
| 39 James W. Wadsworth (R) | 65,489 | 65.8 |
| J. Frank Gilligan (D) | 28,292 | 28.4 |
| Edward J. Wagner (AM LAB) | 5,460 | 5.5 |
| 40 Walter G. Andrews (R) | 92,271 | 62.6 |
| John L. Beyer (D) | 50,705 | 34.4 |
| 41 J. Francis Harter (R) | 46,784 | 50.5 |
| Alfred F. Beiter (D, AM LAB) | 45,516 | 49.1 |
| 42 Pius L. Schwert (D, AM LAB) | 39,287 | 45.8 |
| John C. Butler (R) | 36,326 | 42.3 |
| John A. Ulinski (OB) | 9,537 | 11.1 |
| 43 Daniel A. Reed (R) | 53,261 | 65.3 |
| Samuel A. Carlson (D, AM LAB) | 28,289 | 34.7 |
| AL Caroline O'Day (D, AM LAB) | 2,363,463 ✓ | |
| Matthew J. Merritt (D, AM LAB) | 2,352,159 ✓ | |
| Helen Z. M. Rodgers (R, I PROG) | 2,011,507 | |
| Richard B. Scandrett Jr. (R, I PROG) | 1,990,455 | |

## NEW YORK

| Candidates | Votes | % |
|---|---|---|
| Israel Amter (COM) | 105,681 | |
| Edna Mitchell Blue (SOC) | 25,214 | |
| Brendan Sexton (SOC) | 24,990 | |
| Jeremiah D. Crowley (IND GOVT) | 5,080 | |
| William Herlet (IND GOVT) | 4,291 | |

## NORTH CAROLINA

| | Candidates | Votes | % |
|---|---|---|---|
| 1 | Lindsay C. Warren (D) | 12,083 | 100.0 |
| 2 | John H. Kerr (D) | 9,955 | 100.0 |
| 3 | Graham A. Barden (D) | 17,507 | 100.0 |
| 4 | Harold D. Cooley (D) | 26,932 | 63.9 |
| | Willis G. Briggs (R) | 15,209 | 36.1 |
| 5 | Alonzo D. Folger (D) | 25,472 | 09.7 |
| | John W. Kurfees Jr. (R) | 11,087 | 30.3 |
| 6 | Carl T. Durham (D) | 15,730 | 75.2 |
| | Oscar G. Barker (D) | 5,188 | 24.8 |
| 7 | J. Bayard Clark (D) | 17,175 | 75.7 |
| | Edgar C. Geddie (R) | 5,501 | 24.3 |
| 8 | William O. Burgin (D) | 34,757 | 55.2 |
| | John R. Jones (R) | 28,187 | 44.8 |
| 9 | Robert L. Doughton (D) | 43,912 | 60.9 |
| | Monroe Adams (R) | 28,202 | 39.1 |
| 10 | Alfred L. Bulwinkle (D) | 48,590 | 56.5 |
| | Frank C. Patton (R) | 37,360 | 43.5 |
| 11 | Zebulon Weaver (D) | 61,508 | 63.8 |
| | Vonno L. Gudger (R) | 34,912 | 36.2 |

## NORTH DAKOTA

| | Candidates | Votes | % |
|---|---|---|---|
| AL | William Lemke (R) | 153,288✔ | |
| | Usher L. Burdick (R) | 149,047✔ | |
| | Howard I. Henry (D) | 55,125 | |
| | Alfred S. Dale (D) | 44,691 | |
| | J. B. Field (I) | 8,109 | |

## OHIO

| | Candidates | Votes | % |
|---|---|---|---|
| 1 | Charles H. Elston (R) | 63,285 | 58.2 |
| | Joseph A. Dixon (D) | 45,536 | 41.8 |
| 2 | William E. Hess (R) | 61,480 | 59.0 |
| | Herbert S. Bigelow (D) | 42,773 | 41.0 |
| 3 | Harry N. Routzohn (R) | 73,534 | 55.9 |
| | Byron B. Harlan (D) | 58,139 | 44.2 |
| 4 | Robert F. Jones (R) | 56,399 | 59.8 |
| | William B. Swonger (D) | 33,284 | 35.3 |
| 5 | Cliff Clevenger (R) | 37,027 | 56.9 |
| | Frank C. Kniffin (D) | 28,109 | 43.2 |
| 6 | James G. Polk (D) | 43,646 | 50.5 |
| | Emory F. Smith (R) | 42,847 | 49.5 |
| 7 | Clarence J. Brown (R) | 68,185 | 57.6 |
| | Arthur W. Aleshire (D) | 50,163 | 42.4 |
| 8 | Frederick C. Smith (R) | 40,772 | 54.6 |
| | Brooks Fletcher (D) | 33,972 | 45.5 |
| 9 | John F. Hunter (D) | 56,306 | 50.4 |
| | Homer A. Ramey (R) | 55,441 | 49.6 |
| 10 | Thomas A. Jenkins (R) | 47,036 | 66.0 |
| | Elsie Stanton (D) | 24,198 | 34.0 |
| 11 | Harold K. Claypool (D) | 33,764 | 52.1 |
| | Tom P. White (R) | 31,004 | 47.9 |
| 12 | John M. Vorys (R) | 64,409 | 50.9 |
| | Arthur P. Lamneck (D) | 62,026 | 49.1 |
| 13 | Dudley A. White (R) | 56,204 | 69.4 |
| | William L. Fiesinger (D) | 24,749 | 30.6 |
| 14 | Dow W. Harter (D) | 87,303 | 53.4 |
| | Edward S. Sheck (R) | 76,346 | 46.7 |
| 15 | Robert T. Secrest (D) | 42,573 | 52.3 |
| | P. W. Griffiths (R) | 38,903 | 47.8 |
| 16 | Jim Seccombe (R) | 62,176 | 50.7 |
| | William R. Thom (D) | 60,382 | 49.3 |
| 17 | William A. Ashbrook (D) | 51,305 | 52.6 |
| | Walter B. Woodward (R) | 46,300 | 47.4 |
| 18 | Earl R. Lewis (R) | 56,468 | 50.3 |
| | Lawrence E. Imhoff (D) | 55,809 | 49.7 |
| 19 | Michael J. Kirwan (D) | 76,268 | 52.4 |
| | William P. Barnum (R) | 69,214 | 47.6 |

| | Candidates | Votes | % |
|---|---|---|---|
| 20 | Martin L. Sweeney (D) | 54,185 | 70.4 |
| | Thomas F. McCafferty (R) | 22,775 | 29.6 |
| 21 | Robert Crosser (D) | 53,180 | 68.7 |
| | J. E. Chizek (R) | 24,240 | 31.3 |
| 22 | Chester C. Bolton (R) | 109,494 | 55.5 |
| | Anthony A. Fleger (D) | 87,635 | 44.5 |
| AL | George H. Bender (R) | 1,177,982✔ | |
| | Lycurgus L. Marshall (R) | 1,101,194✔ | |
| | John McSweeney (D) | 1,068,916 | |
| | Stephen M. Young (D) | 1,015,035 | |

### Special Election

| | | Votes | % |
|---|---|---|---|
| 4 | Walter H. Albaugh (R) | 47,631 | 54.9 |
| | Roy E. Layton (D) | 39,112 | 45.1 |

## OKLAHOMA

| | Candidates | Votes | % |
|---|---|---|---|
| 1 | Wesley E. Disney (D) | 55,253 | 63.2 |
| | A. M. Armstrong (R) | 31,755 | 36.3 |
| 2 | Jack Nichols (D) | 38,058 | 71.3 |
| | Bruce L. Keenan (R) | 15,335 | 28.7 |
| 3 | Wilburn Cartwright (D) | 42,616 | 85.4 |
| | Frank D. McSherry (R) | 7,286 | 14.6 |
| 4 | Lyle H. Boren (D) | 44,233 | 71.7 |
| | Ed Ball (R) | 17,506 | 28.4 |
| 5 | A. S. Mike Monroney (D) | 47,692 | 71.9 |
| | Harlan Deupree (R) | 18,271 | 27.6 |
| 6 | Jed Johnson (D) | 33,808 | 69.5 |
| | James F. Rowell (R) | 14,617 | 30.1 |
| 7 | Sam C. Massingale (D) | 24,986 | 76.1 |
| | A. L. Smith (R) | 7,862 | 23.9 |
| 8 | Phil Ferguson (D) | 34,113 | 50.2 |
| | Charles E. Knox (R) | 33,438 | 49.2 |
| AL | Will Rogers (D) | 306,241 | 68.7 |
| | R. R. Wilson (R) | 137,733 | 30.9 |

## OREGON

| | Candidates | Votes | % |
|---|---|---|---|
| 1 | James W. Mott (R) | 119,965 | 70.7 |
| | Andrew C. Burk (D) | 49,666 | 29.3 |
| 2 | Walter M. Pierce (D) | 35,200 | 57.9 |
| | U. S. Balentine (R) | 25,557 | 42.1 |
| 3 | Homer D. Angell (R) | 69,049 | 50.9 |
| | Nan Wood Honeyman (D) | 66,498 | 49.1 |

## PENNSYLVANIA

| | Candidates | Votes | % |
|---|---|---|---|
| 1 | Leon Sachs (D, D-OP) | 54,819 | 53.5 |
| | John Alessandroni (R) | 47,692 | 46.5 |
| 2 | James P. McGranery (D) | 51,565 | 52.4 |
| | Edward W. Henry (R) | 46,248 | 47.0 |
| 3 | Michael J. Bradley (D) | 61,686 | 52.0 |
| | William T. Connor (R, R-OP) | 56,958 | 48.0 |
| 4 | J. Burrwood Daly (D) | 60,514 | 53.8 |
| | Edward F. Roberts (R) | 51,343 | 45.7 |
| 5 | Fred C. Gartner (R) | 63,877 | 52.5 |
| | Frank J. G. Dorsey (D) | 56,492 | 46.5 |
| 6 | Francis J. Myers (D) | 62,524 | 49.9 |
| | J. Howard Berry Jr. (R) | 59,548 | 47.5 |
| 7 | George P. Darrow (R) | 84,077 | 59.3 |
| | Ira W. Drew (D) | 57,046 | 40.2 |
| 8 | James Wolfenden (R) | 84,103 | 67.6 |
| | C. Fenno Hoffman (D) | 40,324 | 32.4 |
| 9 | Charles L. Gerlach (R) | 56,589 | 56.7 |
| | Oliver W. Frey (D) | 43,055 | 43.1 |
| 10 | J. Roland Kinzer (R) | 78,986 | 64.1 |
| | Thomas Jefferson McClelland (D) | 43,928 | 35.7 |
| 11 | Patrick J. Boland (D) | 66,626 | 52.5 |
| | William F. Hallstead (R, R-OP) | 60,307 | 47.5 |
| 12 | J. Harold Flannery (D) | 98,715 | 51.2 |
| | Michael A. Yeosock (D) | 94,108 | 48.8 |
| 13 | Ivor D. Fenton (R, R-OP) | 79,468 | 53.2 |
| | James H. Gildea (D) | 69,817 | 46.8 |
| 14 | Guy L. Moser (D) | 34,678 | 52.7 |
| | John C. Evans (R) | 31,068 | 47.3 |

| | Candidates | Votes | % |
|---|---|---|---|
| 15 | Albert G. Rutherford (R) | 58,571 | 61.6 |
| | Harry M. Turrell (D, D-OP) | 36,096 | 37.9 |
| 16 | Robert F. Rich (R, R-OP) | 63,241 | 61.5 |
| | Paul A. Rothfuss (D) | 38,908 | 37.8 |
| 17 | J. William Ditter (R) | 72,225 | 68.5 |
| | Carroll L. Rutter (D) | 32,921 | 31.2 |
| 18 | Richard M. Simpson (R) | 53,067 | 60.5 |
| | Richard L. Schroyer (D) | 34,578 | 39.5 |
| 19 | John C. Kunkel (R, R-OP) | 77,354 | 55.0 |
| | Guy J. Swope (D) | 63,180 | 45.0 |
| 20 | Benjamin Jarrett (R) | 65,547 | 61.8 |
| | Earl H. Beshlin (D, D-OP) | 40,511 | 38.2 |
| 21 | Francis E. Walter (D) | 43,276 | 50.2 |
| | Alonzo L. Reinhard (R) | 41,665 | 48.4 |
| 22 | Chester H. Gross (R) | 55,565 | 50.3 |
| | Harry L. Haines (D, D-OP) | 54,880 | 49.7 |
| 23 | James E. Van Zandt (R) | 61,372 | 57.1 |
| | Don Gingery (D, D-OP) | 45,694 | 42.5 |
| 24 | J. Buell Snyder (D) | 47,045 | 51.2 |
| | J. C. Glassburn (R) | 44,604 | 48.5 |
| 25 | Charles I. Faddis (D, D-OP) | 43,604 | 53.1 |
| | Warren S. Burchinal (R) | 38,549 | 46.9 |
| 26 | Louis E. Graham (R) | 59,754 | 52.4 |
| | Charles R. Eckert (D, D-OP) | 53,434 | 46.8 |
| 27 | Harve Tibbott (R, R-OP) | 81,690 | 55.8 |
| | Joseph H. Gray (D, D-OP) | 63,790 | 43.5 |
| 28 | Robert G. Allen (D, D-OP) | 52,034 | 53.9 |
| | Roy C. McKenna (R) | 44,196 | 45.8 |
| 29 | Robert L. Rodgers (R) | 46,856 | 53.8 |
| | Norbert James Fitzgerald (D) | 39,762 | 45.6 |
| 30 | Robert J. Corbett (R) | 53,541 | 51.2 |
| | Peter J. DeMuth (D, D-OP) | 51,028 | 48.8 |
| 31 | John McDowell (R, R-OP) | 57,392 | 50.7 |
| | James J. Quinn (D) | 55,211 | 48.8 |
| 32 | Herman P. Eberharter (D) | 48,025 | 63.3 |
| | Jacob E. Kalson (R) | 27,440 | 36.2 |
| 33 | Joseph A. McArdle (D, D-OP) | 54,888 | 51.6 |
| | James I. Marsh (R) | 51,427 | 48.4 |
| 34 | Matthew A. Dunn (D, D-OP) | 55,502 | 50.0 |
| | Robert B. McKinley (R) | 55,055 | 49.6 |

## RHODE ISLAND

| | Candidates | Votes | % |
|---|---|---|---|
| 1 | Charles F. Risk (R) | 73,394 | 50.3 |
| | Aime J. Forand (D) | 72,484 | 49.7 |
| 2 | Harry Sandager (R, GOOD GOV) | 87,932 | 57.0 |
| | Edward J. Fenelon Jr. (D) | 66,408 | 43.0 |

## SOUTH CAROLINA

| | Candidates | Votes | % |
|---|---|---|---|
| 1 | Thomas S. McMillan (D) | 7,649 | 98.2 |
| 2 | Hampton P. Fulmer (D) | 7,236 | 98.8 |
| 3 | Butler B. Hare (D) | 10,028 | 99.6 |
| 4 | Joseph R. Bryson (D) | 8,995 | 99.4 |
| 5 | James P. Richards (D) | 6,191 | 99.8 |
| 6 | John L. McMillan (D) | 5,707 | 99.2 |

## SOUTH DAKOTA

| | Candidates | Votes | % |
|---|---|---|---|
| 1 | Karl E. Mundt (R) | 111,805 | 54.0 |
| | Emil Loriks (D) | 95,353 | 46.0 |
| 2 | Francis H. Case (R) | 41,335 | 61.5 |
| | Theodore B. Werner (D) | 25,932 | 38.6 |

## TENNESSEE

| | Candidates | Votes | % |
|---|---|---|---|
| 1 | B. Carroll Reece (R) | 23,251 | 58.0 |
| | John A. Armstrong (D) | 10,609 | 26.5 |
| | James P. Kinett | 4,382 | 10.9 |
| 2 | J. Will Taylor (R) | 32,312 | 64.1 |
| | Judd Acuff (I) | 16,079 | 31.9 |

## TENNESSEE

| | Candidates | Votes | % |
|---|---|---|---|
| 3 | Sam D. McReynolds (D) | 21,804 | 73.9 |
| | Joe F. Benson (R) | 7,708 | 26.1 |
| 4 | Albert Gore (D) | 25,220 | 100.0 |
| 5 | Joseph Byrns (D) | 16,819 | 90.6 |
| | William I. Love (I) | 1,749 | 9.4 |
| 6 | Clarence W. Turner (D) | 14,318 | 82.2 |
| | John U. McDonough (I) | 1,957 | 11.2 |
| | Maurice C. Riding | 1,146 | 6.6 |
| 7 | Herron Pearson (D) | 19,554 | 100.0 |
| 8 | Jere Cooper (D) | 18,173 | 95.4 |
| 9 | Walter Chandler (D) | 43,976 | 98.4 |

## TEXAS

| | | Votes | % |
|---|---|---|---|
| 1 | Wright Patman (D) | 14,833 | 98.8 |
| 2 | Martin Dies (D) | 12,816 | 100.0 |
| 3 | Lindley Beckworth (D) | 17,115 | 100.0 |
| 4 | Sam Rayburn (D) | 16,523 | 97.9 |
| 5 | Hatton W. Sumners (D) | 10,344 | 95.3 |
| 6 | Luther A. Johnson (D) | 15,619 | 100.0 |
| 7 | Nat Patton (D) | 16,467 | 100.0 |
| 8 | Albert Thomas (D) | 36,989 | 98.3 |
| 9 | Joseph J. Mansfield (D) | 16,680 | 100.0 |
| 10 | Lyndon B. Johnson (D) | 14,476 | 100.0 |
| 11 | W. R. Poage (D) | 14,664 | 100.0 |
| 12 | Fritz G. Lanham (D) | 12,972 | 100.0 |
| 13 | Ed Gossett (D) | 20,620 | 100.0 |
| 14 | Richard M. Kleberg (D) | 23,438 | 100.0 |
| 15 | Milton H. West (D) | 18,995 | 100.0 |
| 16 | R. Ewing Thomason (D) | 9,237 | 100.0 |
| 17 | Clyde L. Garrett (D) | 17,107 | 100.0 |
| 18 | Marvin Jones (D) | 18,048 | 100.0 |
| 19 | George H. Mahon (D) | 16,372 | 100.0 |
| 20 | Paul J. Kilday (D) | 16,703 | 100.0 |
| 21 | Charles L. South (D) | 21,671 | 93.0 |
| | M. J. Bierschwale (R) | 1,621 | 7.0 |

## UTAH

| | | Votes | % |
|---|---|---|---|
| 1 | Abe Murdock (D) | 52,927 | 59.7 |
| | LeRoy B. Young (R) | 35,790 | 40.3 |
| 2 | J. W. Robinson (D) | 58,456 | 62.3 |
| | Dean F. Brayton (R) | 35,359 | 37.7 |

## VERMONT

| | Candidates | Votes | % |
|---|---|---|---|
| AL | Charles A. Plumley (R) | 71,901 | 64.0 |
| | James P. Leamy (D) | 40,483 | 36.0 |

## VIRGINIA

| | | Votes | % |
|---|---|---|---|
| 1 | Schuyler Otis Bland (D) | 7,191 | 99.7 |
| 2 | Colgate W. Darden Jr. (D) | 15,276 | 87.2 |
| | Carl P. Spaeth | 2,142 | 12.2 |
| 3 | David E. Satterfield Jr. (D) | 5,560 | 99.7 |
| 4 | Patrick Henry Drewry (D) | 5,805 | 99.9 |
| 5 | Thomas G. Burch (D) | 5,761 | 99.6 |
| 6 | Clifton A. Woodrum (D) | 11,509 | 55.9 |
| | Fred W. McWane (R) | 9,083 | 44.1 |
| 7 | A. Willis Robertson (D) | 11,398 | 63.9 |
| | Charles C. Leap (R) | 6,449 | 36.1 |
| 8 | Howard W. Smith (D) | 13,796 | 99.6 |
| 9 | John W. Flannagan Jr. (D) | 21,235 | 66.7 |
| | L. E. Gulliford (R) | 10,612 | 33.3 |

## WASHINGTON

| | | Votes | % |
|---|---|---|---|
| 1 | Warren G. Magnuson (D) | 90,768 | 61.7 |
| | Matthew W. Hill (R) | 56,293 | 38.3 |
| 2 | Mon C. Wallgren (D) | 58,313 | 61.5 |
| | Charles A. Sather (R) | 36,442 | 38.5 |
| 3 | Martin F. Smith (D) | 52,305 | 60.3 |
| | Walter S. Talbott (R) | 34,394 | 39.7 |
| 4 | Knute Hill (D) | 38,647 | 50.4 |
| | Frank Miller (R) | 37,969 | 49.6 |
| 5 | Charles H. Leavy (D) | 52,782 | 57.1 |
| | Norman A. Ericson (R) | 38,858 | 42.0 |
| 6 | John M. Coffee (D) | 64,871 | 73.0 |
| | Willard V. Young (R) | 24,002 | 27.0 |

## WEST VIRGINIA

| | | Votes | % |
|---|---|---|---|
| 1 | Andrew C. Schiffler (R) | 57,043 | 54.8 |
| | Robert L. Ramsey (D) | 47,051 | 45.2 |
| 2 | Jennings Randolph (D) | 53,277 | 54.6 |
| | Melvin C. Snyder (R) | 44,334 | 45.4 |
| 3 | Andrew Edmiston (D) | 53,722 | 55.3 |
| | H. Roy Waugh (R) | 43,407 | 44.7 |

| | Candidates | Votes | % |
|---|---|---|---|
| 4 | George W. Johnson (D) | 65,965 | 52.9 |
| | Raymond V. Humphreys (R) | 58,749 | 47.1 |
| 5 | John Kee (D) | 55,501 | 61.3 |
| | Hartley Sanders (R) | 34,989 | 38.7 |
| 6 | Joe L. Smith (D) | 67,818 | 62.3 |
| | R. E. O'Connor (R) | 40,965 | 37.7 |

## WISCONSIN

| | | Votes | % |
|---|---|---|---|
| 1 | Stephen Bolles (R) | 45,247 | 49.1 |
| | Francis H. Wendt (PROG) | 29,478 | 32.0 |
| | Calvin Stewart (D) | 14,573 | 15.8 |
| 2 | Charles Hawks Jr. (R) | 42,154 | 44.9 |
| | Harry Sauthoff (PROG) | 40,656 | 43.3 |
| | Reinhold A. Gerth (D) | 11,185 | 11.9 |
| 3 | Harry W. Griswold (R) | 43,495 | 50.1 |
| | Gardner R. Withrow (PROG) | 36,509 | 42.0 |
| | Bart E. McGonigle (D) | 6,887 | 7.9 |
| 4 | John C. Schafer (R) | 34,196 | 32.0 |
| | Thaddeus F. B. Wasielewski (D) | 33,559 | 31.4 |
| | Paul Gauer (PROG) | 30,817 | 28.8 |
| | Raymond J. Cannon (I) | 7,498 | 7.0 |
| 5 | Lewis D. Thill (R) | 47,032 | 43.1 |
| | Thomas O'Malley (D) | 31,154 | 28.6 |
| | Alfred Benson (PROG) | 29,874 | 27.4 |
| 6 | Frank B. Keefe (R) | 46,082 | 53.6 |
| | Michael K. Reilly (D) | 25,842 | 30.1 |
| | Adam F. Poltl (PROG) | 13,258 | 15.4 |
| 7 | Reid F. Murray (R) | 41,662 | 48.9 |
| | Gerald J. Boileau (PROG) | 32,442 | 38.0 |
| | James J. Cavanaugh (D) | 9,727 | 11.4 |
| 8 | Joshua L. Johns (R) | 33,354 | 36.2 |
| | George J. Schneider (PROG) | 29,035 | 31.5 |
| | John E. Cashman (D) | 28,221 | 30.6 |
| 9 | Merlin Hull (PROG) | 42,880 | 53.4 |
| | Hugh M. Jones (R) | 32,375 | 40.3 |
| | William F. Crane (D) | 5,066 | 6.3 |
| 10 | Bernard J. Gehrmann (PROG) | 45,874 | 57.5 |
| | James H. Carroll (R) | 33,854 | 42.5 |

## WYOMING

| | | Votes | % |
|---|---|---|---|
| AL | Frank O. Horton (R) | 49,975 | 52.9 |
| | Paul R. Greever (D) | 44,525 | 47.1 |

# 1939 House Election

### PENNSYLVANIA

**Special Election**

| | | Votes | % |
|---|---|---|---|
| 4 | John Edward Sheridan (D) | 52,250 | 51.8 |
| | Boies Penrose (R) | 48,648 | 48.2 |

# 1940 House Elections

## ALABAMA

| Candidates | Votes | % |
|---|---|---|
| 1 Frank W. Boykin (D) | 25,993 | 100.0 |
| 2 George Grant (D) | 33,433 | 100.0 |
| 3 Henry B. Steagall (D) | 22,906 | 100.0 |
| 4 Sam Hobbs (D) | 24,870 | 87.9 |
| Thomas G. McNaron (R) | 3,428 | 12.1 |
| 5 Joe Starnes (D) | 31,966 | 100.0 |
| 6 Pete Jarman (D) | 18,881 | 100.0 |
| 7 Walter Will Bankhead (D) | 27,696 | 70.9 |
| A. W. Hargett (R) | 11,368 | 29.1 |
| 8 John J. Sparkman (D) | 29,020 | 100.0 |
| 9 Luther Patrick (D) | 39,660 | 99.2 |

## ARIZONA

| Candidates | Votes | % |
|---|---|---|
| AL John R. Murdock (D) | 99,424 | 71.1 |
| K. T. Palmer (R) | 40,360 | 28.9 |

## ARKANSAS

| Candidates | Votes | % |
|---|---|---|
| 1 Ezekiel C. Gathings (D) | 33,127 | 100.0 |
| 2 Wilbur D. Mills (D) | 25,718 | 100.0 |
| 3 Clyde E. Ellis (D) | 21,060 | 71.1 |
| Clyde M. Williams (R) | 8,566 | 28.9 |
| 4 Fadjo Cravens (D) | 28,999 | 100.0 |
| 5 David D. Terry (D) | 36,067 | 100.0 |
| 6 William F. Norrell (D) | 27,972 | 100.0 |
| 7 Oren Harris (D) | 26,994 | 100.0 |

## CALIFORNIA

| Candidates | Votes | % |
|---|---|---|
| 1 Clarence F. Lea (D-R) | 103,547 | 93.0 |
| Albert J. Lima (COM) | 5,647 | 5.1 |
| 2 Harry L. Englebright (R D P T) | 71,033 | 100.0 |
| 3 Frank H. Buck (D-R) | 135,461 | 91.0 |
| C. H. Farman (P) | 10,539 | 7.1 |
| 4 Thomas Rolph (R) | 75,369 | 54.6 |
| Franck R. Havenner (D & PROG) | 61,341 | 44.4 |
| 5 Richard J. Welch (R-D) | 119,122 | 95.8 |
| 6 Albert E. Carter (R D P T) | 131,584 | 96.0 |
| 7 John H. Tolan (D) | 72,838 | 55.5 |
| Ralph R. Eltse (R) | 56,808 | 43.3 |
| 8 John Z. Anderson (R-D) | 148,180 | 96.5 |
| 9 Bertrand W. Gearhart (R-D) | 99,708 | 99.9 |
| 10 Alfred J. Elliott (D-R) | 125,845 | 96.8 |
| 11 Carl Hinshaw (R-D-PROG) | 170,504 | 96.2 |
| 12 H. Jerry Voorhis (D) | 99,494 | 64.0 |
| Irwin W. Minger (R) | 54,731 | 35.2 |
| 13 Charles Kramer (D-R) | 127,167 | 75.6 |
| Charles H. Randall (PROG-P) | 36,406 | 21.7 |
| 14 Thomas F. Ford (D-R) | 73,137 | 64.2 |
| Herbert L. Herberts (R) | 37,939 | 33.3 |
| 15 John M. Costello (D) | 94,435 | 56.2 |
| Norris J. Nelson (R & PROG) | 71,667 | 42.6 |
| 16 Leland Merritt Ford (R-D) | 188,004 | 96.2 |
| 17 Lee E. Geyer (D) | 75,109 | 65.5 |
| Clifton A. Hix (R) | 32,862 | 28.6 |
| 18 Ward Johnson (R) | 73,932 | 54.3 |
| Byron N. Scott (D) | 60,764 | 44.6 |
| 19 Harry R. Sheppard (D) | 84,931 | 52.9 |
| Lotus H. Loudon (R) | 75,495 | 47.0 |
| 20 Edouard V. M. Izac (D) | 69,874 | 51.1 |
| Ed Fletcher (R) | 66,132 | 48.3 |

## COLORADO

| Candidates | Votes | % |
|---|---|---|
| 1 Lawrence Lewis (D) | 110,078 | 64.6 |
| James D. Parriott (R) | 59,427 | 34.9 |
| 2 William S. Hill (R) | 76,859 | 53.3 |
| Fred Cummings (D) | 66,662 | 46.2 |
| 3 J. Edgar Chenoweth (R) | 70,842 | 52.1 |
| Byron G. Rogers (D) | 65,269 | 48.0 |
| 4 Edward T. Taylor (D) | 44,095 | 59.4 |
| Paul W. Crawford (R) | 30,126 | 40.6 |

### Special Election

| Candidates | Votes | % |
|---|---|---|
| 3 William E. Burney (D) | 68,225 | 51.0 |
| Henry Leonard (R) | 65,675 | 49.1 |

## CONNECTICUT

| Candidates | Votes | % |
|---|---|---|
| 1 Herman P. Kopplemann (D) | 109,880 | 54.2 |
| William J. Miller (R, SOC) | 92,980 | 45.8 |
| 2 William J. Fitzgerald (D) | 63,021 | 52.4 |
| Thomas R. Ball (R) | 56,825 | 47.3 |
| 3 James A. Shanley (D) | 84,439 | 53.6 |
| Ranulf Compton (R, UN) | 73,078 | 46.4 |
| 4 Le Roy D. Downs (D) | 90,942 | 49.0 |
| Albert E. Austin (R) | 90,239 | 48.6 |
| 5 J. Joseph Smith (D) | 62,783 | 54.9 |
| Frank T. Johnson (R) | 51,049 | 44.7 |
| AL Lucien J. Maciora (D) | 407,868 | 52.1 |
| Boleslaus J. Monkiewicz (R) | 365,851 | 46.8 |

## DELAWARE

| Candidates | Votes | % |
|---|---|---|
| AL Philip A. Traynor (D) | 68,205 | 50.6 |
| George S. Williams (R) | 64,384 | 47.8 |

## FLORIDA

| Candidates | Votes | % |
|---|---|---|
| 1 J. Hardin Peterson (D) | 88,158 | 100.0 |
| 2 Robert A. Green (D) | 68,797 | 89.1 |
| Francis McHale (R) | 8,382 | 10.9 |
| 3 Robert L. F. Sikes (D) | 36,573 | 100.0 |
| 4 Arthur P. Cannon (D) | 84,594 | 75.3 |
| Bert L. Acker (R) | 27,815 | 24.7 |
| 5 Joe Hendricks (D) | 49,715 | 75.4 |
| Emory Akerman (R) | 16,214 | 24.6 |

## GEORGIA

| Candidates | Votes | % |
|---|---|---|
| 1 Hugh Peterson (D) | 28,601 | 99.5 |
| 2 E. E. Cox (D) | 19,443 | 96.8 |
| 3 Stephen Pace (D) | 22,882 | 100.0 |
| 4 A. Sidney Camp (D) | 25,609 | 100.0 |
| 5 Robert Ramspeck (D, I) | 41,677 | 99.9 |
| 6 Carl Vinson (D) | 21,966 | 99.9 |
| 7 Malcolm C. Tarver (D) | 32,280 | 86.4 |
| Lewis H. Crawford (R) | 5,062 | 13.6 |
| 8 John S. Gibson (D, R) | 24,454 | 100.0 |
| 9 B. Frank Whelchel (D) | 25,461 | 84.4 |
| William C. Horton (R) | 4,025 | 13.3 |
| 10 Paul Brown (D) | 18,291 | 98.7 |

## IDAHO

| Candidates | Votes | % |
|---|---|---|
| 1 Compton I. White (D) | 62,107 | 62.0 |
| Edward Gaffney (R) | 37,999 | 38.0 |
| 2 Henry C. Dworshak (R) | 69,804 | 53.1 |
| Ira H. Masters (D) | 61,726 | 46.9 |

## ILLINOIS

| Candidates | Votes | % |
|---|---|---|
| 1 Arthur W. Mitchell (D) | 34,641 | 53.0 |
| William E. King (R) | 30,698 | 47.0 |
| 2 Raymond S. McKeough (D) | 155,698 | 51.5 |
| P. H. Moynihan (R) | 146,927 | 48.6 |
| 3 Edward A. Kelly (D) | 148,382 | 51.1 |
| Waldemar J. Roehler (R) | 141,768 | 48.9 |
| 4 Harry P. Beam (D) | 74,977 | 77.4 |
| Henry F. Schmudde (R) | 21,858 | 22.6 |
| 5 Adolph J. Sabath (D) | 35,637 | 71.0 |
| Martin Dykema (R) | 14,540 | 29.0 |
| 6 A. F. Maciejewski (D) | 187,393 | 56.2 |
| Joseph Wagner (R) | 146,253 | 43.8 |
| 7 Leonard W. Schuetz (D) | 229,161 | 50.9 |
| James C. Moreland (R) | 220,793 | 49.1 |
| 8 Leo Kocialkowski (D) | 40,074 | 78.1 |
| Anthony V. Champagne (R) | 11,232 | 21.9 |
| 9 Charles S. Dewey (R) | 56,806 | 53.3 |
| James McAndrews (D) | 49,816 | 46.7 |
| 10 George A. Paddock (R) | 199,418 | 61.3 |
| John Haderlein (D) | 125,827 | 38.7 |
| 11 Chauncey W. Reed (R) | 128,645 | 64.6 |
| Edgar O. Eakin (D) | 70,581 | 35.4 |
| 12 Noah M. Mason (R) | 90,744 | 60.6 |
| August C. Engh (D) | 58,945 | 39.4 |
| 13 Leo E. Allen (R) | 65,698 | 67.6 |
| John B. Hayes (D) | 31,502 | 32.4 |
| 14 Anton J. Johnson (R) | 60,909 | 52.4 |
| Forest Dizotell (D) | 55,451 | 47.7 |
| 15 Robert B. Chiperfield (R) | 65,639 | 56.4 |
| Russell M. Gunn (D) | 50,820 | 43.6 |
| 16 Everett M. Dirksen (R) | 79,780 | 58.1 |
| M. R. Clark (D) | 57,567 | 41.9 |
| 17 Leslie C. Arends (R) | 56,712 | 61.1 |
| J. Joseph Pitts (D) | 36,102 | 38.9 |
| 18 Jessie Sumner (R) | 64,409 | 53.2 |
| James A. Meeks (D) | 56,744 | 46.8 |
| 19 William H. Wheat (R) | 75,933 | 50.6 |
| Alfred D. Huston (D) | 74,091 | 49.4 |
| 20 James M. Barnes (D) | 44,824 | 51.7 |
| Hardin E. Hanks (R) | 41,806 | 48.3 |
| 21 Evan Howell (R) | 67,896 | 51.6 |
| Frank W. Fries (D) | 63,740 | 48.4 |
| 22 Edwin M. Schaefer (D) | 98,162 | 53.8 |
| Calvin D. Johnson (R) | 84,381 | 46.2 |
| 23 Laurence F. Arnold (D) | 65,062 | 51.4 |
| Ben O. Sumner (R) | 61,521 | 48.6 |
| 24 James V. Heidinger (R) | 49,731 | 53.6 |
| Claude V. Parsons (D) | 43,050 | 46.4 |
| 25 Cecil W. Bishop (R) | 69,165 | 50.5 |
| Kent E. Keller (D) | 67,891 | 49.5 |
| AL William G. Stratton (R) | 2,050,493 | |
| Stephen A. Day (R) | 2,020,008 | |
| Thomas V. Smith (D) | 1,968,143 | |
| Walter J. Orlikoski (D) | 1,913,950 | |
| Harry Fleischman (SOC) | 7,377 | |
| Lee S. Gregory (SOC) | 7,191 | |
| Willis Ray Wilson (P) | 6,786 | |
| Lena Duell Vincent (P) | 6,621 | |

## INDIANA

| Candidates | Votes | % |
|---|---|---|
| 1 William T. Schulte (D) | 71,606 | 60.8 |
| Elliot Belshaw (R) | 45,947 | 39.0 |
| 2 Charles A. Halleck (R) | 87,652 | 58.1 |
| James O. Cox (D) | 63,290 | 41.9 |
| 3 Robert A. Grant (R) | 73,914 | 51.3 |
| George Sands (D) | 70,208 | 48.7 |
| 4 George W. Gillie (R) | 80,259 | 58.0 |
| Frank E. Corbett (D) | 58,157 | 42.0 |
| 5 Forest A. Harness (R) | 78,691 | 54.7 |
| George W. Wolf (D) | 65,200 | 45.3 |
| 6 Noble J. Johnson (R) | 80,595 | 52.3 |
| Lenhardt E. Bauer (D) | 73,449 | 47.7 |
| 7 Gerald W. Landis (R) | 81,632 | 52.2 |
| Charles H. Bedwell (D) | 74,746 | 47.8 |
| 8 John W. Boehne Jr. (D) | 87,141 | 55.5 |
| Charles F. Werner (R) | 69,761 | 44.5 |
| 9 Earl Wilson (R) | 71,624 | 50.9 |
| Eugene B. Crowe (D) | 69,227 | 49.2 |
| 10 Raymond S. Springer (R) | 80,725 | 53.0 |
| Don C. Ward (D) | 71,478 | 47.0 |
| 11 William H. Larrabee (D) | 79,070 | 51.7 |
| Maurice G. Robinson (R) | 73,867 | 48.3 |

## INDIANA

| | Candidates | Votes | % |
|---|---|---|---|
| 12 | Louis Ludlow (D) | 80,954 | *52.9* |
| | James A. Collins (R) | 72,174 | *47.1* |

## IOWA

| | Candidates | Votes | % |
|---|---|---|---|
| 1 | Thomas E. Martin (R) | 70,120 | *60.4* |
| | Zoe S. Nabers (D) | 46,040 | *39.6* |
| 2 | William S. Jacobsen (D) | 75,774 | *52.2* |
| | W. A. McCullough (R) | 69,298 | *47.8* |
| 3 | John W. Gwynne (R) | 65,425 | *60.0* |
| | Ernest J. Seemann (D) | 43,709 | *40.1* |
| 4 | Henry O. Taile (R) | 66,691 | *56.4* |
| | Morgan J. McEnaney (D) | 51,558 | *43.6* |
| 5 | Karl M. LeCompte (R) | 66,940 | *53.3* |
| | Roy E. Stevens (D) | 58,718 | *46.7* |
| 6 | Paul Cunningham (R) | 70,707 | *52.3* |
| | E. Frank Fox (D) | 64,314 | *47.6* |
| 7 | Ben F. Jensen (R) | 71,633 | *58.6* |
| | Ernest M. Miller (D) | 50,644 | *41.4* |
| 8 | Fred C. Gilchrist (R) | 64,687 | *58.1* |
| | Frank J. Lund (D) | 46,597 | *41.9* |
| 9 | Vincent F. Harrington (D) | 67,017 | *50.8* |
| | Albert F. Swanson (R) | 64,877 | *49.2* |

## KANSAS

| | Candidates | Votes | % |
|---|---|---|---|
| 1 | William P. Lambertson (R) | 64,766 | *61.0* |
| | Clive R. Lane (D) | 41,375 | *39.0* |
| 2 | Ulysses S. Guyer (R) | 73,659 | *54.0* |
| | Harold H. Harding (D) | 62,787 | *46.0* |
| 3 | Thomas D. Winter (R) | 60,381 | *55.2* |
| | W. E. Ledbetter (D) | 48,971 | *44.8* |
| 4 | Edward H. Rees (R) | 58,183 | *62.5* |
| | Dudley Doolittle (D) | 34,957 | *37.5* |
| 5 | John M. Houston (D) | 58,486 | *52.5* |
| | Stanley Taylor (R) | 52,901 | *47.5* |
| 6 | Frank Carlson (R) | 69,627 | *60.9* |
| | Max Jones (D) | 44,702 | *39.1* |
| 7 | Clifford R. Hope (R) | 75,349 | *63.9* |
| | Claude E. Main (D) | 42,518 | *36.1* |

## KENTUCKY

| | Candidates | Votes | % |
|---|---|---|---|
| 1 | Noble J. Gregory (D) | 60,777 | *100.0* |
| 2 | Beverly M. Vincent (D) | 69,905 | *100.0* |
| 3 | Emmet O'Neal (D) | 96,253 | *60.0* |
| | Ben J. Brumleve (R) | 64,053 | *40.0* |
| 4 | Edward W. Creal (D) | 55,561 | *58.5* |
| | Lewis H. Mather (R) | 39,447 | *41.5* |
| 5 | Brent Spence (D) | 51,954 | *61.2* |
| | Henry J. Cook (R) | 32,981 | *38.8* |
| 6 | Virgil Chapman (D) | 74,463 | *60.5* |
| | William D. Rogers (R) | 48,700 | *39.5* |
| 7 | Andrew J. May (D) | 44,185 | *56.8* |
| | James W. Turner (R) | 33,574 | *43.2* |
| 8 | Joe B. Bates (D) | 61,881 | *58.0* |
| | H. Clell Hayes (R) | 44,736 | *42.0* |
| 9 | John M. Robsion (R) | 71,750 | *62.5* |
| | Bert Rowland (D) | 43,013 | *37.5* |

## LOUISIANA

| | Candidates | Votes | % |
|---|---|---|---|
| 1 | F. Edward Hebert (D) | 58,234 | *100.0* |
| 2 | Hale Boggs (D) | 56,026 | *100.0* |
| 3 | James Domengeaux (D) | 27,081 | *66.0* |
| | David W. Pipes Jr. (R) | 13,933 | *34.0* |
| 4 | Overton Brooks (D) | 33,704 | *100.0* |
| 5 | Newt V. Mills (D) | 33,462 | *100.0* |
| 6 | Jared Y. Sanders Jr. (D) | 41,173 | *100.0* |
| 7 | Vance Plauche (D) | 28,518 | *100.0* |
| 8 | A. Leonard Allen (D) | 28,904 | *100.0* |

## MAINE

| | Candidates | Votes | % |
|---|---|---|---|
| 1 | James C. Oliver (R) | 55,503 | *63.4* |
| | Peter M. McDonald (D) | 32,018 | *36.6* |
| 2 | Margaret Chase Smith (R) | 57,152 | *64.6* |
| | Edward J. Beauchamp (D) | 31,334 | *35.4* |
| 3 | Frank Fellows (R) | 46,732 | *66.1* |
| | Thomas N. Curran (D) | 23,934 | *33.9* |

## MARYLAND

| | Candidates | Votes | % |
|---|---|---|---|
| 1 | David J. Ward (D) | 36,057 | *53.9* |
| | Robert F. Duer (R) | 30,810 | *46.1* |
| 2 | William P. Cole Jr. (D) | 113,495 | *65.7* |
| | Theodore F. Brown (R) | 59,223 | *34.3* |
| 3 | Thomas D'Alesandro Jr. (D) | 38,540 | *61.5* |
| | John A. Janetzke (R) | 24,153 | *38.5* |
| 4 | John A. Meyer (D) | 50,120 | *56.6* |
| | Daniel Ellison (R) | 38,444 | *43.4* |
| 5 | Lansdale Sasscer (D) | 58,418 | *71.0* |
| | John N. Torvestad (R) | 23,857 | *29.0* |
| 6 | William D. Byron (D) | 60,037 | *53.5* |
| | Walter P. Johnson (R) | 52,258 | *46.5* |

## MASSACHUSETTS

| | Candidates | Votes | % |
|---|---|---|---|
| 1 | Allen T. Treadway (R) | 72,750 | *57.1* |
| | Clifford J. Akey (D) | 54,634 | *42.9* |
| 2 | Charles R. Clason (R) | 76,373 | *58.4* |
| | Patrick A. Doyle (D) | 54,428 | *41.6* |
| 3 | Joseph E. Casey (D) | 72,839 | *54.6* |
| | Edward T. Simoneau (R) | 60,676 | *45.4* |
| 4 | Pehr G. Holmes (R) | 70,542 | *53.2* |
| | Frank J. McGrail (D) | 60,988 | *46.0* |
| 5 | Edith Nourse Rogers (R) | 120,435 | *76.2* |
| | Francis J. Roane (D) | 37,593 | *23.8* |
| 6 | George J. Bates (R) | 88,834 | *71.6* |
| | James D. Burns (D) | 35,214 | *28.4* |
| 7 | Lawrence J. Connery (D) | 89,966 | *62.1* |
| | William Henry Haskell (R) | 52,701 | *36.4* |
| 8 | Arthur D. Healey (D) | 71,127 | *55.4* |
| | John J. Irwin (R) | 57,217 | *44.6* |
| 9 | Thomas H. Eliot (D) | 81,523 | *52.1* |
| | Robert Luce (R) | 74,922 | *47.9* |
| 10 | George Holden Tinkham (R) | 78,029 | *59.1* |
| | David M. Owens (D) | 54,093 | *40.9* |
| 11 | Thomas A. Flaherty (D) | 58,041 | *81.5* |
| | Benjamin J. Green (R) | 13,176 | *18.5* |
| 12 | John W. McCormack (D) | 97,588 | *78.1* |
| | Henry J. Allen (R) | 27,302 | *21.9* |
| 13 | Richard B. Wigglesworth (R) | 92,651 | *65.0* |
| | Francis G. O'Neill (D) | 48,606 | *34.1* |
| 14 | Joseph W. Martin Jr. (R) | 65,780 | *54.4* |
| | Harold E. Cole (D) | 55,241 | *45.7* |
| 15 | Charles L. Gifford (R) | 73,358 | *57.8* |
| | George F. Backus (D) | 53,581 | *42.2* |

## MICHIGAN

| | Candidates | Votes | % |
|---|---|---|---|
| 1 | Rudolph G. Tenerowicz (D) | 87,451 | *79.9* |
| | Donald J. Marshall (R) | 21,399 | *19.5* |
| 2 | Earl C. Michener (R) | 72,235 | *62.3* |
| | Redmond M. Burr (D) | 43,733 | *37.7* |
| 3 | Paul W. Shafer (R) | 74,614 | *62.1* |
| | Charles T. McSherry (D) | 45,138 | *37.6* |
| 4 | Clare E. Hoffman (R) | 65,666 | *61.8* |
| | Harvey Hope Jarvis (D) | 40,443 | *38.1* |
| 5 | Bartel J. Jonkman (R) | 65,240 | *53.7* |
| | Garrett Heyns (D) | 56,172 | *46.3* |
| 6 | William W. Blackney (R) | 77,340 | *51.1* |
| | Charles R. Adair (D) | 73,629 | *48.6* |
| 7 | Jesse P. Wolcott (R) | 73,926 | *65.2* |
| | Albert A. Wagner (D) | 39,416 | *34.8* |
| 8 | Fred L. Crawford (R) | 68,265 | *61.2* |
| | Louis C. Schwinger (D) | 43,297 | *38.8* |
| 9 | Albert J. Engel (R) | 52,343 | *56.9* |
| | Noel P. Fox (D) | 39,667 | *43.1* |
| 10 | Roy O. Woodruff (R) | 52,685 | *61.9* |
| | William J. Kelly (D) | 32,289 | *37.9* |
| 11 | Fred Bradley (R) | 48,087 | *51.1* |
| | Wendell L. Lund (D) | 45,826 | *48.7* |
| 12 | Frank E. Hook (D) | 47,429 | *51.3* |
| | John B. Bennett (R) | 44,733 | *48.4* |
| 13 | George D. O'Brien (D) | 66,985 | *54.6* |
| | Clarence J. McLeod (R) | 55,115 | *44.9* |
| 14 | Louis C. Rabaut (D) | 80,463 | *59.0* |
| | George B. Shaeffer (R) | 55,910 | *41.0* |
| 15 | John D. Dingell (D) | 85,239 | *61.9* |
| | Archie C. Fraser (R) | 52,131 | *37.9* |
| 16 | John Lesinski (D) | 73,956 | *58.8* |
| | Robert Ford (R) | 51,276 | *40.8* |
| 17 | George A. Dondero (R) | 82,809 | *54.7* |
| | Draper Allen (D) | 68,195 | *45.1* |

## MINNESOTA

| | Candidates | Votes | % |
|---|---|---|---|
| 1 | August H. Andresen (R) | 88,814 | *64.8* |
| | Francis L. Murphy (D) | 27,479 | *20.1* |
| | Endre B. Anderson (F-LAB) | 20,700 | *15.1* |
| 2 | Joseph P. O'Hara (R) | 66,610 | *49.0* |
| | Elmer J. Ryan (D) | 57,673 | *42.5* |
| | C. E. McNaught (F-LAB) | 11,534 | *8.5* |
| 3 | Richard P. Gale (R) | 63,854 | *43.5* |
| | Henry G. Teigan (F-LAB) | 50,222 | *34.2* |
| | Martin A. Hogan (D) | 28,321 | *19.3* |
| 4 | Melvin J. Maas (R) | 68,525 | *58.8* |
| | George L. Siegel (F-LAB) | 32,898 | *28.3* |
| | Willard J. Moran (D) | 15,050 | *12.9* |
| 5 | Oscar Youngdahl (R) | 79,491 | *52.1* |
| | Dewey W. Johnson (F-LAB) | 52,289 | *34.3* |
| | Lamoine Montgomery Dowling (D) | 20,720 | *13.6* |
| 6 | Harold Knutson (R) | 84,023 | *61.5* |
| | E. Thomas O'Brien (D) | 52,504 | *38.5* |
| 7 | H. Carl Andersen (R) | 65,958 | *50.7* |
| | Harold L. Peterson (F-LAB) | 42,356 | *32.6* |
| | J. L. O'Connor (D) | 21,796 | *16.8* |
| 8 | William A. Pittenger (R) | 74,521 | *54.2* |
| | John T. Bernard (F-LAB) | 39,252 | *28.5* |
| | M. W. Raihala (D) | 23,845 | *17.3* |
| 9 | Richard Thompson Buckler (F-LAB) | 48,999 | *43.4* |
| | Colvin G. Butler (R) | 48,324 | *42.8* |
| | Frank H. Timm (D) | 15,507 | *13.7* |

## MISSISSIPPI

| | Candidates | Votes | % |
|---|---|---|---|
| 1 | John E. Rankin (D) | 19,390 | *100.0* |
| 2 | Wall Doxey (D) | 16,939 | *100.0* |
| 3 | William M. Whittington (D) | 16,597 | *100.0* |
| 4 | Aaron Lane Ford (D) | 15,329 | *100.0* |
| 5 | Ross A. Collins (D) | 24,079 | *100.0* |
| 6 | William M. Colmer (D) | 26,679 | *100.0* |
| 7 | Dan R. McGehee (D) | 29,799 | *100.0* |

## MISSOURI

| | Candidates | Votes | % |
|---|---|---|---|
| 1 | Milton A. Romjue (D) | 62,461 | *50.5* |
| | Henry S. Beardsley (R) | 61,123 | *49.5* |
| 2 | William L. Nelson (D) | 77,922 | *53.8* |
| | Roy O. Miller (R) | 66,794 | *46.2* |
| 3 | Richard M. Duncan (D) | 77,424 | *53.3* |
| | Fred Maughmer (R) | 67,757 | *46.7* |
| 4 | C. Jasper Bell (D) | 72,331 | *60.0* |
| | John W. Mitchell (R) | 48,181 | *40.0* |
| 5 | Joseph B. Shannon (D) | 63,202 | *54.2* |
| | Forest W. Hanna (R) | 53,390 | *45.8* |
| 6 | Philip A. Bennett (R) | 78,746 | *53.7* |
| | Reuben T. Wood (D) | 67,902 | *46.3* |
| 7 | Dewey Short (R) | 86,547 | *59.3* |
| | Vernon Sigars (D) | 59,344 | *40.7* |
| 8 | Clyde Williams (D) | 64,263 | *51.1* |
| | Parke M. Banta (R) | 61,587 | *48.9* |
| 9 | Clarence Cannon (D) | 60,204 | *55.3* |
| | F. B. Meyer (R) | 48,704 | *44.7* |
| 10 | Orville Zimmerman (D) | 69,859 | *57.4* |
| | C. E. Davenport (R) | 51,755 | *42.6* |

## MISSOURI

| | Candidates | Votes | % |
|---|---|---|---|
| 11 | John B. Sullivan (D) | 85,722 | 55.7 |
| | Charles J. Riley (R) | 68,088 | 44.3 |
| 12 | Walter C. Ploeser (R) | 127,005 | 53.9 |
| | C. Arthur Anderson (D) | 108,605 | 46.1 |
| 13 | John J. Cochran (D) | 82,417 | 64.5 |
| | W. S. Sanford (R) | 45,262 | 35.5 |

## MONTANA

| | Candidates | Votes | % |
|---|---|---|---|
| 1 | Jeanette Rankin (R) | 56,616 | 54.5 |
| | Jerry J. O'Connell (D) | 47,352 | 45.5 |
| 2 | James F. O'Connor (D) | 83,101 | 62.0 |
| | Melvin N. Hoiness (R) | 49,710 | 37.1 |

## NEBRASKA

| | Candidates | Votes | % |
|---|---|---|---|
| 1 | Oren S. Copeland (R) | 64,431 | 55.6 |
| | Henry C. Luckey (D) | 51,524 | 44.4 |
| 2 | Charles F. McLaughlin (D) | 68,760 | 56.6 |
| | Theodore W. Metcalfe (R) | 52,669 | 43.4 |
| 3 | Karl Stefan (R) | 90,561 | 80.0 |
| | Victor J. McGonigle (D) | 19,253 | 17.0 |
| 4 | Carl T. Curtis (R) | 66,966 | 57.7 |
| | R. O. Canaday (D) | 29,311 | 25.3 |
| | Charles G. Binderup | 19,807 | 17.1 |
| 5 | Harry B. Coffee (D) | 63,025 | 58.1 |
| | Bert Howard (R) | 45,548 | 42.0 |

## NEVADA

| | Candidates | Votes | % |
|---|---|---|---|
| AL | James G. Scrugham (D) | 32,714 | 64.5 |
| | Ralph W. Lattin (R) | 18,032 | 35.5 |

## NEW HAMPSHIRE

| | Candidates | Votes | % |
|---|---|---|---|
| 1 | Arthur B. Jenks (R) | 57,982 | 51.1 |
| | Alphonse Roy (D) | 55,434 | 48.9 |
| 2 | Foster Stearns (R) | 55,530 | 53.0 |
| | Daniel J. Moriarty (D) | 49,260 | 47.0 |

## NEW JERSEY

| | Candidates | Votes | % |
|---|---|---|---|
| 1 | Charles A. Wolverton (R) | 97,547 | 55.5 |
| | Harry Roye (D) | 77,931 | 44.3 |
| 2 | Elmer H. Wene (D) | 60,392 | 52.2 |
| | Walter Sooy Jeffries (R) | 55,382 | 47.8 |
| 3 | William H. Sutphin (D) | 76,048 | 51.7 |
| | Joseph F. Irwin (R) | 70,890 | 48.2 |
| 4 | D. Lane Powers (R) | 69,834 | 55.9 |
| | Thomas S. Dignan (D) | 54,909 | 44.0 |
| 5 | Charles A. Eaton (R) | 82,840 | 55.9 |
| | Charles R. M. Tuttle (D) | 65,200 | 44.0 |
| 6 | Donald H. McLean (R) | 78,361 | 54.9 |
| | James E. Downes (D) | 62,888 | 44.1 |
| 7 | J. Parnell Thomas (R) | 82,287 | 64.6 |
| | Mort L. O'Connell (D) | 44,527 | 35.0 |
| 8 | Gordon Canfield (R) | 72,197 | 58.6 |
| | Addison P. Rosenkrans (D) | 50,622 | 41.1 |
| 9 | Frank C. Osmers Jr. (R) | 91,352 | 62.7 |
| | Abram A. Lebson (D) | 54,254 | 37.2 |
| 10 | Fred A. Hartley Jr. (R) | 64,699 | 56.8 |
| | William E. Holmwood (D) | 46,934 | 41.2 |
| 11 | Albert L. Vreeland (R) | 61,606 | 55.8 |
| | Mary C. Duffy (D) | 46,130 | 41.8 |
| 12 | Robert Winthrop Kean (R) | 67,996 | 53.7 |
| | Thomas J. Halleran (D) | 53,677 | 42.4 |
| 13 | Mary T. Norton (D) | 92,356 | 70.2 |
| | Raymond J. Cuddy (R) | 39,274 | 29.8 |
| 14 | Edward J. Hart (D) | 84,538 | 65.3 |
| | Otto Trankler (R) | 44,893 | 34.7 |

## NEW MEXICO

| | Candidates | Votes | % |
|---|---|---|---|
| AL | Clinton P. Anderson (D) | 106,972 | 58.8 |
| | Herman R. Crile (R) | 75,085 | 41.2 |

## NEW YORK

| | Candidates | Votes | % |
|---|---|---|---|
| 1 | Leonard W. Hall (R) | 267,873 | 63.7 |
| | Frederic S. Farah (D) | 141,774 | 33.7 |
| 2 | William B. Barry (D) | 216,309 | 52.8 |
| | Thomas J. Styles (R) | 170,004 | 41.5 |
| | Matthew Napear (AM LAB) | 20,827 | 5.1 |
| 3 | Joseph L. Pfeifer (D, AM LAB) | 42,884 | 70.6 |
| | Samuel Rosenthal (R) | 17,839 | 29.4 |
| 4 | Thomas H. Cullen (D) | 36,995 | 56.2 |
| | Alfred A. Larossa (R) | 25,207 | 38.3 |
| | Michael Giaratano (AM LAB) | 3,636 | 5.5 |
| 5 | James J. Heffernan (D, AM LAB) | 63,295 | 55.2 |
| | Marcellus H. Evans (R) | 51,428 | 44.8 |
| 6 | Andrew L. Somers (D) | 130,391 | 57.7 |
| | Alfred E. Buck (R) | 58,507 | 25.9 |
| | Irving B. Altman (AM LAB) | 31,945 | 14.1 |
| 7 | John J. Delaney (D, AM LAB) | 50,189 | 72.8 |
| | Julius Reinlieb (R) | 18,765 | 27.2 |
| 8 | Donald L. O'Toole (D) | 217,599 | 56.8 |
| | Jacob M. Offenhender (R) | 103,753 | 27.1 |
| | Benjamin Brenner (AM LAB) | 52,972 | 13.8 |
| 9 | Eugene J. Keogh (D, AM LAB) | 92,559 | 57.7 |
| | William J. McGahie (R) | 67,901 | 42.3 |
| 10 | Emanuel Celler (D, AM LAB) | 57,286 | 71.4 |
| | Edward H. Wilson (R) | 21,358 | 26.6 |
| 11 | James A. O'Leary (D) | 46,616 | 49.4 |
| | Thomas Garrett (R) | 42,631 | 45.1 |
| | Wellington Roe (AM LAB) | 5,193 | 5.5 |
| 12 | Samuel Dickstein (D) | 17,176 | 72.1 |
| | Bernard Harkavy (AM LAB) | 3,664 | 15.4 |
| | Joseph Levine (R) | 2,976 | 12.5 |
| 13 | Louis J. Capozzoli (D) | 18,334 | 62.7 |
| | John Rosenberg (R) | 8,367 | 28.6 |
| | Gino Bardi (AM LAB) | 2,534 | 8.7 |
| 14 | M. Michael Edelstein (D) | 26,455 | 56.9 |
| | Peter J. Bakanatch (R) | 13,940 | 30.0 |
| | Samuel Burt (AM LAB) | 6,103 | 13.1 |
| 15 | Michael J. Kennedy (D) | 26,314 | 59.7 |
| | Arthur A. Wyler (R) | 13,158 | 29.8 |
| | Joseph Curran (AM LAB) | 4,623 | 10.5 |
| 16 | William T. Pheiffer (R) | 31,020 | 48.7 |
| | James H. Fay (D) | 28,837 | 45.3 |
| | Thomas Darcy (AM LAB) | 3,874 | 6.1 |
| 17 | Kenneth F. Simpson (R) | 54,636 | 50.8 |
| | Samuel Kramer (D) | 47,155 | 43.8 |
| | Morris Watson (AM LAB) | 5,845 | 5.4 |
| 18 | Martin J. Kennedy (D) | 31,151 | 52.7 |
| | James B. Walker Jr. (R) | 24,312 | 41.2 |
| | Shaemas O'Sheal (AM LAB) | 3,612 | 6.1 |
| 19 | Sol Bloom (D) | 71,018 | 62.8 |
| | Daniel J. Riesner (R) | 32,821 | 29.0 |
| | Benjamin M. Zelman (AM LAB) | 9,209 | 8.2 |
| 20 | Vito Marcantonio (R, AM LAB) | 25,254 | 62.5 |
| | James J. Lanzetta (D) | 15,160 | 37.5 |
| 21 | Joseph A. Gavagan (D) | 108,139 | 63.2 |
| | Charles H. Roberts (R) | 46,324 | 27.1 |
| | Alfred K. Stern (AM LAB) | 16,529 | 9.7 |
| 22 | Walter A. Lynch (D) | 44,296 | 60.1 |
| | F. Shepard Cornell (R) | 23,532 | 31.9 |
| | Frank R. Crosswaith (AM LAB) | 5,931 | 8.0 |
| 23 | Charles A. Buckley (D) | 190,396 | 56.5 |
| | Lowell H. Brown (R) | 88,083 | 26.1 |
| | Jack Altman (AM LAB) | 50,293 | 14.9 |
| 24 | James M. Fitzpatrick (D) | 161,577 | 47.7 |
| | Ralph W. Gwinn (R) | 136,835 | 40.4 |
| | George Thomas (AM LAB) | 35,233 | 10.4 |
| 25 | Ralph A. Gamble (R) | 125,411 | 64.0 |
| | Homer A. Stebbins (D) | 64,889 | 33.1 |
| 26 | Hamilton Fish (R) | 68,715 | 51.9 |
| | Hardy Steeholm (D) | 59,739 | 45.1 |
| 27 | Lewis K. Rockefeller (R) | 65,618 | 58.0 |
| | George J. Mutari (D, AM LAB) | 47,610 | 42.1 |
| 28 | William T. Byrne (D) | 89,592 | 57.8 |
| | William V. A. Waterman (R) | 59,344 | 38.3 |
| 29 | E. Harold Cluett (R) | 82,328 | 63.7 |
| | Salvatore J. Leombruno (D) | 43,588 | 33.7 |
| 30 | Frank Crowther (R) | 66,159 | 54.8 |
| | Burlin G. McKillip (D) | 51,270 | 42.5 |
| 31 | Clarence E. Kilburn (R) | 58,727 | 62.5 |
| | Horatio W. Thomas (D, AM LAB) | 35,307 | 37.5 |
| 32 | Francis D. Culkin (R) | 71,782 | 68.8 |
| | Frank M. McCormack (D) | 30,105 | 28.8 |
| 33 | Fred J. Douglas (R) | 72,412 | 50.5 |
| | Samuel H. Miller (D) | 52,469 | 40.9 |
| 34 | Edwin Arthur Hall (R) | 93,990 | 68.3 |
| | Donald W. Kramer (D) | 41,027 | 29.8 |
| 35 | Clarence E. Hancock (R) | 97,688 | 56.8 |
| | Flora D. Johnson (D) | 69,730 | 40.6 |
| 36 | John Taber (R) | 64,507 | 59.6 |
| | John W. Kennelly (D) | 40,929 | 37.8 |
| 37 | W. Sterling Cole (R) | 76,630 | 64.9 |
| | David Moses (D) | 38,878 | 32.9 |
| 38 | Joseph J. O'Brien (R) | 92,866 | 51.9 |
| | George B. Kelly (D, AM LAB) | 86,197 | 48.1 |
| 39 | James W. Wadsworth (R) | 73,316 | 60.4 |
| | J. Frederick Colson (D, AM LAB) | 48,133 | 39.6 |
| 40 | Walter Gresham Andrews (R) | 119,972 | 61.1 |
| | Robert A. Hoffman (D, AM LAB) | 76,468 | 38.9 |
| 41 | Alfred F. Beiter (D, AM LAB) | 62,843 | 52.3 |
| | J. Francis Harter (R) | 57,335 | 47.7 |
| 42 | Pius L. Schwert (D, AM LAB) | 64,250 | 58.8 |
| | Edward F. Moss (R) | 44,866 | 41.0 |
| 43 | Daniel A. Reed (R) | 67,520 | 62.2 |
| | Milton A. Bissell (D, AM LAB) | 40,980 | 37.8 |
| AL | Caroline O'Day (D, AM LAB) | 3,199,019✔ | |
| | Matthew J. Merritt (D, AM LAB) | 3,182,936✔ | |
| | Mary Donlon (R) | 2,830,517 | |
| | Messmore Kendall (R) | 2,812,066 | |
| | Helen G. H. Estella (P) | 5,679 | |
| | Neil Dow Cranmer (P) | 5,212 | |

## NORTH CAROLINA

| | Candidates | Votes | % |
|---|---|---|---|
| 1 | Herbert C. Bonner (D) | 36,722 | 92.8 |
| | John A. Wilkinson (R) | 2,851 | 7.2 |
| 2 | John H. Kerr (D) | 41,217 | 100.0 |
| 3 | Graham A. Barden (D) | 33,760 | 75.0 |
| | Julian T. Gaskill (R) | 11,248 | 25.0 |
| 4 | Harold D. Cooley (D) | 57,610 | 79.4 |
| | Ezra Parker (R) | 14,926 | 20.6 |
| 5 | Alonzo D. Folger (D) | 53,778 | 77.2 |
| | Ottis James Reynolds (R) | 15,872 | 22.8 |
| 6 | Carl T. Durham (D) | 55,549 | 78.5 |
| | Gilliam Grissom (R) | 15,259 | 21.6 |
| 7 | J. Bayard Clark (D) | 41,663 | 85.3 |
| | Fred R. Keith (R) | 7,168 | 14.7 |
| 8 | William O. Burgin (D) | 57,879 | 67.2 |
| | F. D. B. Harding (R) | 28,232 | 32.8 |
| 9 | Robert L. Doughton (D) | 60,875 | 68.3 |
| | Monroe Adams (R) | 28,287 | 31.7 |
| 10 | Alfred L. Bulwinkle (D) | 87,156 | 69.8 |
| | Ernest M. Morgan (R) | 37,736 | 30.2 |
| 11 | Zebulon Weaver (D) | 75,763 | 69.0 |
| | Robert Frank Jarrett (R) | 34,104 | 31.0 |

## NORTH DAKOTA

| | Candidates | Votes | % |
|---|---|---|---|
| AL | Usher L. Burdick (R) | 148,227✔ | |
| | Charles R. Robertson (R) | 111,125✔ | |
| | R. J. Downey (D) | 63,662 | |
| | Adolph Michelson (D) | 63,028 | |
| | Thomas Hall (I) | 23,399 | |
| | John Omdahl (I) | 20,845 | |

## OHIO

| | Candidates | Votes | % |
|---|---|---|---|
| 1 | Charles H. Elston (R) | 84,622 | 58.0 |
| | Joseph A. Dixon (D) | 61,382 | 42.0 |
| 2 | William E. Hess (R) | 77,769 | 56.3 |
| | James E. O'Connell (D) | 60,410 | 43.7 |
| 3 | Greg Holbrock (D) | 103,291 | 52.6 |
| | Harry N. Routzohn (R) | 93,002 | 47.4 |
| 4 | Robert F. Jones (R) | 65,603 | 57.8 |
| | Clarence C. Miller (D) | 47,820 | 42.2 |
| 5 | Cliff Clevenger (R) | 48,040 | 60.7 |
| | C. H. Armbruster (D) | 31,063 | 39.3 |
| 6 | Jacob E. Davis (D) | 52,769 | 52.2 |
| | Chester P. Fitch (R) | 48,257 | 47.8 |
| 7 | Clarence J. Brown (R) | 83,415 | 58.3 |
| | J. Fuller Trump (D) | 59,667 | 41.7 |
| 8 | Frederick C. Smith (R) | 49,218 | 52.5 |
| | Kenneth M. Petri (D) | 44,605 | 47.5 |
| 9 | John F. Hunter (D) | 86,956 | 54.7 |
| | Wilbur M. White (R) | 71,927 | 45.3 |
| 10 | Thomas A. Jenkins (R) | 48,217 | 58.9 |
| | John P. Kelso (D) | 33,698 | 41.1 |
| 11 | Harold K. Claypool (D) | 43,548 | 53.8 |
| | Ray W. Davis (R) | 37,398 | 46.2 |
| 12 | John M. Vorys (R) | 91,767 | 51.3 |
| | A. P. Lammeck (D) | 87,115 | 48.7 |
| 13 | A. D. Baumhart Jr. (R) | 62,442 | 60.8 |
| | Werner S. Haslinger (D) | 40,274 | 39.2 |
| 14 | Dow W. Harter (D) | 121,037 | 52.3 |
| | Walter B. Wanamaker (R) | 108,016 | 46.6 |
| 15 | Robert T. Secrest (D) | 57,359 | 58.8 |
| | Clair A. Young (R) | 40,233 | 41.2 |
| 16 | William R. Thom (D) | 92,469 | 56.4 |
| | Jim Seccombe (R) | 71,629 | 43.7 |
| 17 | J. Harry McGregor (R) | 69,102 | 55.1 |
| | Ralph C. Lutz (D) | 56,343 | 44.9 |
| 18 | Lawrence E. Imhoff (D) | 79,718 | 54.5 |
| | Earl R. Lewis (R) | 66,666 | 45.5 |
| 19 | Michael J. Kirwan (D) | 122,075 | 61.9 |
| | Charles H. Anderson (R) | 75,016 | 38.1 |
| 20 | Martin L. Sweeney (D) | 72,385 | 67.7 |
| | George Pillersdorf (R) | 34,609 | 32.4 |
| 21 | Robert Crosser (D) | 79,602 | 77.1 |
| | J. E. Chizek (R) | 23,658 | 22.9 |
| 22 | Frances P. Bolton (R) | 165,322 | 56.7 |
| | Anthony A. Fleger (D) | 126,273 | 43.3 |
| AL | George H. Bender (R) | 1,519,628✔ | |
| | Stephen M. Young (D) | 1,483,934✔ | |
| | L. L. Marshall (R) | 1,386,696 | |
| | Francis W. Durbin (D) | 1,384,800 | |

## OKLAHOMA

| | Candidates | Votes | % |
|---|---|---|---|
| 1 | Wesley E. Disney (D) | 93,366 | 62.2 |
| | W. R. Boyd (R) | 56,112 | 37.4 |
| 2 | Jack Nichols (D) | 50,351 | 62.2 |
| | E. O. Clark (R) | 30,630 | 37.8 |
| 3 | Wilburn Cartwright (D) | 68,344 | 79.0 |
| | Frank D. McSherry (R) | 18,145 | 21.0 |
| 4 | Lyle H. Boren (D) | 69,040 | 71.1 |
| | Clyde T. Patrick (R) | 28,046 | 28.9 |
| 5 | A. S. Mike Monroney (D) | 93,457 | 72.4 |
| | U. S. Stone (R) | 34,942 | 27.1 |
| 6 | Jed Johnson (D) | 52,338 | 70.1 |
| | Walter Hubbell (R) | 22,343 | 29.9 |
| 7 | Sam C. Massingale (D) | 39,884 | 70.0 |
| | Place Montgomery (R) | 16,246 | 28.5 |
| 8 | Ross Rizley (R) | 48,737 | 53.8 |
| | Phil Ferguson (D) | 41,417 | 45.7 |
| AL | Will Rogers (D) | 479,433 | 65.7 |
| | John W. Harreld (R) | 245,384 | 33.6 |

## OREGON

| | Candidates | Votes | % |
|---|---|---|---|
| 1 | James W. Mott (R) | 145,675 | 68.4 |
| | Charles A. Robertson (D) | 63,940 | 30.0 |
| 2 | Walter M. Pierce (D) | 44,832 | 56.3 |
| | Rex Ellis (R) | 33,529 | 42.1 |
| 3 | Homer D. Angell (R) | 84,275 | 49.9 |
| | Nan Wood Honeyman (D) | 80,930 | 47.9 |

## PENNSYLVANIA

| | Candidates | Votes | % |
|---|---|---|---|
| 1 | Leon Sacks (D) | 64,599 | 61.7 |
| | Emanuel W. Beloff (R) | 39,770 | 38.0 |
| 2 | James P. McGranery (D) | 62,844 | 60.9 |
| | Augustus Trask Ashton (R) | 39,489 | 38.3 |
| 3 | Michael J. Bradley (D) | 77,436 | 63.1 |
| | Frank J. Kownacki (R) | 44,757 | 36.5 |
| 4 | John Edward Sheridan (D) | 74,458 | 63.0 |
| | Benjamin M. Golder (R) | 42,578 | 36.1 |
| 5 | Francis R. Smith (D) | 76,724 | 55.8 |
| | Fred C. Gartner (R) | 60,109 | 43.7 |
| 6 | Francis J. Myers (D) | 82,550 | 61.1 |
| | Frank F. Truscott (R) | 51,313 | 38.0 |
| 7 | Hugh Scott (R) | 79,416 | 50.9 |
| | Gilbert Cassidy (D) | 76,054 | 48.8 |
| 8 | James Wolfenden (R) | 69,649 | 59.6 |
| | E. Adele Scott Saul (D) | 46,960 | 40.2 |
| 9 | Charles L. Gerlach (R) | 55,919 | 52.4 |
| | Henry V. Scheirer (D) | 50,632 | 47.4 |
| 10 | J. Roland Kinzer (R) | 72,843 | 57.7 |
| | George M. May (D) | 53,333 | 42.2 |
| 11 | Patrick J. Boland (D) | 65,368 | 52.6 |
| | Joseph F. Gunster (R) | 58,831 | 47.4 |
| 12 | J. Harold Flannery (D) | 101,854 | 57.8 |
| | J. Henry Pool (R) | 74,305 | 42.2 |
| 13 | Ivor D. Fenton (R) | 70,647 | 50.5 |
| | James H. Gildea (D) | 68,501 | 48.9 |
| 14 | Guy L. Moser (D) | 48,140 | 56.0 |
| | Joseph C. Evans (R) | 31,839 | 37.1 |
| | Raymond S. Hofses (SOC) | 4,980 | 5.8 |
| 15 | Albert G. Rutherford (R) | 46,740 | 59.3 |
| | F. R. Clark (D) | 31,675 | 40.2 |
| 16 | Robert F. Rich (R) | 61,167 | 60.5 |
| | Hugh Gilmore (D) | 39,988 | 39.5 |
| 17 | J. William Ditter (R) | 75,006 | 62.2 |
| | Victor Eppstein (D) | 45,616 | 37.8 |
| 18 | Richard M. Simpson (R) | 46,595 | 57.6 |
| | John W. Keichline (D) | 34,328 | 42.4 |
| 19 | John C. Kunkel (R) | 74,420 | 54.4 |
| | John A. Smith (D) | 62,298 | 45.6 |
| 20 | Benjamin Jarrett (R) | 64,189 | 58.2 |
| | John R. Boland Jr. (D) | 44,919 | 40.8 |
| 21 | Francis E. Walter (D) | 52,530 | 56.2 |
| | T. Fred Woodley (R) | 40,863 | 43.7 |
| 22 | Harry L. Haines (D) | 60,848 | 54.8 |
| | Chester H. Gross (R) | 49,532 | 44.6 |
| 23 | James E. Van Zandt (R) | 57,027 | 56.3 |
| | William M. Aukerman (D) | 44,263 | 43.7 |
| 24 | J. Buell Snyder (D) | 54,631 | 56.6 |
| | J. Clark Glassburn (R) | 41,641 | 43.2 |
| 25 | Charles I. Faddis (D) | 58,442 | 61.0 |
| | Lucius McK. Crumrine (R) | 37,357 | 39.0 |
| 26 | Louis E. Graham (R) | 64,669 | 50.9 |
| | Peter P. Reising (D) | 62,273 | 49.1 |
| 27 | Harve Tibbott (R) | 75,243 | 51.6 |
| | Joseph Gray (D) | 69,736 | 47.9 |
| 28 | Augustine B. Kelley (D) | 58,772 | 55.5 |
| | James M. Underwood (R) | 44,528 | 42.0 |
| 29 | Robert L. Rodgers (R) | 50,147 | 54.3 |
| | James F. Lavery (D) | 41,924 | 45.4 |
| 30 | Thomas E. Scanlon (D) | 62,450 | 50.1 |
| | Robert J. Corbett (R) | 62,097 | 49.9 |
| 31 | Samuel A. Weiss (D) | 76,819 | 55.7 |
| | John McDowell (R) | 59,960 | 43.5 |
| 32 | Herman P. Eberharter (D) | 62,121 | 68.6 |
| | Samuel M. Jackson (R) | 28,196 | 31.1 |
| 33 | Joseph A. McArdle (D) | 70,824 | 55.0 |
| | James I. Marsh (R) | 57,737 | 44.9 |
| 34 | James A. Wright (D) | 75,004 | 53.8 |
| | Robert B. McKinley (R) | 64,336 | 46.2 |

## RHODE ISLAND

| | Candidates | Votes | % |
|---|---|---|---|
| 1 | Aime J. Forand (D) | 87,530 | 57.6 |
| | Charles F. Risk (R) | 64,539 | 42.4 |
| 2 | John E. Fogarty (D) | 87,332 | 53.8 |
| | Harry Sandager (R) | 74,987 | 46.2 |

## SOUTH CAROLINA

| | | Votes | % |
|---|---|---|---|
| 1 | L. Mendel Rivers (D) | 16,626 | 98.4 |
| 2 | Hampton P. Fulmer (D) | 14,920 | 98.6 |
| 3 | Butler B. Hare (D) | 15,977 | 98.9 |
| 4 | Joseph R. Bryson (D) | 23,825 | 97.3 |
| 5 | James P. Richards (D) | 14,754 | 99.2 |
| 6 | John L. McMillan (D) | 12,074 | 99.0 |

## SOUTH DAKOTA

| | | Votes | % |
|---|---|---|---|
| 1 | Karl E. Mundt (R) | 135,406 | 59.6 |
| | Oscar Fosheim (D) | 91,967 | 40.5 |
| 2 | Francis H. Case (R) | 47,051 | 66.1 |
| | Arthur W. Watwood (D) | 24,177 | 33.9 |

## TENNESSEE

| | | Votes | % |
|---|---|---|---|
| 1 | B. Carroll Reece (R) | 39,577 | 68.7 |
| | R. E. Walker (D) | 18,051 | 31.3 |
| 2 | John Jennings Jr. (R) | 41,274 | 56.6 |
| | Clay Jones (D) | 31,663 | 43.4 |
| 3 | Estes Kefauver (D) | 35,332 | 68.7 |
| | Jerome Taylor (R) | 16,099 | 31.3 |
| 4 | Albert Gore (D) | 38,278 | 88.9 |
| | H. E. McLean (R) | 4,777 | 11.1 |
| 5 | J. Percy Priest (I) | 24,565 | 50.2 |
| | Joseph W. Byrns Jr. (D) | 20,933 | 42.8 |
| | Julian H. Campbell (R) | 3,459 | 7.1 |
| 6 | Wirt Courtney (D) | 24,536 | 100.0 |
| 7 | Herron Pearson (D) | 25,590 | 100.0 |
| 8 | Jere Cooper (D) | 32,002 | 92.1 |
| | Julian Palmer | 2,760 | 7.9 |
| 9 | Clifford Davis (D) | 55,952 | 96.0 |

## TEXAS

| | | Votes | % |
|---|---|---|---|
| 1 | Wright Patman (D) | 27,030 | 100.0 |
| 2 | Martin Dies (D) | 43,597 | 100.0 |
| 3 | Lindley Beckworth (D) | 47,292 | 100.0 |
| 4 | Sam Rayburn (D) | 46,333 | 100.0 |
| 5 | Hatton W. Sumners (D) | 57,789 | 87.5 |
| | Floyd E. Royer (R) | 8,273 | 12.5 |
| 6 | Luther A. Johnson (D) | 33,546 | 100.0 |
| 7 | Nat Patton (D) | 30,384 | 98.2 |
| 8 | Albert Thomas (D) | 89,796 | 95.2 |
| 9 | Joseph J. Mansfield (D) | 52,754 | 100.0 |
| 10 | Lyndon B. Johnson (D) | 48,442 | 100.0 |
| 11 | W. R. Poage (D) | 41,432 | 99.9 |
| 12 | Fritz G. Lanham (D) | 54,108 | 100.0 |
| 13 | Ed Gossett (D) | 50,076 | 96.5 |
| 14 | Richard M. Kleberg (D) | 59,016 | 100.0 |
| 15 | Milton H. West (D) | 32,300 | 92.5 |
| | J. A. Simpson (R) | 2,628 | 7.5 |
| 16 | R. Ewing Thomason (D) | 34,515 | 99.9 |
| 17 | Sam Russell (D) | 45,456 | 100.0 |
| 18 | Eugene Worley (D) | 51,660 | 96.5 |
| 19 | George H. Mahon (D) | 56,343 | 100.0 |
| 20 | Paul J. Kilday (D) | 47,075 | 83.4 |
| | Harry Hotchkin (R) | 9,296 | 16.5 |
| 21 | Charles L. South (D) | 49,468 | 92.8 |
| | Ray Ridenhower (R) | 3,832 | 7.2 |

## UTAH

| | | Votes | % |
|---|---|---|---|
| 1 | Walter K. Granger (D) | 62,654 | 57.1 |
| | LeRoy B. Young (R) | 47,021 | 42.9 |
| 2 | J. W. Robinson (D) | 84,874 | 62.8 |
| | A. Sherman Christensen (R) | 50,332 | 37.2 |

## VERMONT

| Candidates | Votes | % |
|---|---|---|
| AL Charles A. Plumley (R) | 89,637 | 63.8 |
| Michael J. Rock (D) | 50,804 | 36.2 |

## VIRGINIA

| | Candidates | Votes | % |
|---|---|---|---|
| 1 | Schuyler Otis Bland (D) | 22,493 | 99.9 |
| 2 | Colgate W. Darden Jr. (D) | 29,788 | 100.0 |
| 3 | Dave E. Satterfield Jr. (D) | 34,885 | 96.8 |
| 4 | Patrick Henry Drewry (D) | 19,043 | 96.0 |
| 5 | Thomas G. Burch (D) | 25,631 | 100.0 |
| 6 | Clifton.A. Woodrum (D) | 30,046 | 68.1 |
| | Fred W. McWane (R) | 13,864 | 31.4 |
| 7 | A. Willis Robertson (D) | 26,233 | 65.1 |
| | J. A. Garber (R) | 13,964 | 34.7 |
| 8 | Howard W. Smith (D) | 33,031 | 79.0 |
| | Henry B. Goodloe (R) | 8,794 | 21.0 |
| 9 | John W. Flannagan Jr. (D) | 32,412 | 57.3 |
| | Fred C. Parks (R) | 24,109 | 42.7 |

## WASHINGTON

| | Candidates | Votes | % |
|---|---|---|---|
| 1 | Warren G. Magnuson (D) | 113,988 | 61.6 |
| | Fred J. Wettrick (R) | 71,110 | 38.4 |
| 2 | Henry M. Jackson (D) | 66,314 | 57.4 |
| | Payson Peterson (R) | 49,209 | 42.6 |
| 3 | Martin F. Smith (D) | 60,529 | 55.3 |
| | Russell V. Mack (R) | 48,700 | 44.5 |

| | Candidates | Votes | % |
|---|---|---|---|
| 4 | Knute Hill (D) | 50,493 | 51.3 |
| | Frank Miller (R) | 48,003 | 48.7 |
| 5 | Charles H. Leavy (D) | 67,582 | 55.5 |
| | Walt Horan (R) | 54,258 | 44.5 |
| 6 | John M. Coffee (D) | 71,536 | 62.8 |
| | Paul A. Preus (R) | 42,334 | 37.2 |

## WEST VIRGINIA

| | Candidates | Votes | % |
|---|---|---|---|
| 1 | Robert L. Ramsay (D) | 72,717 | 53.2 |
| | A. C. Schiffler (R) | 63,906 | 46.8 |
| 2 | Jennings Randolph (D) | 77,045 | 57.5 |
| | Summers H. Sharp (R) | 56,911 | 42.5 |
| 3 | Andrew Edmiston (D) | 79,441 | 56.6 |
| | H. Roy Waugh (R) | 60,810 | 43.4 |
| 4 | George W. Johnson (D) | 82,979 | 52.7 |
| | Harry O. Hiteshew (R) | 74,491 | 47.3 |
| 5 | John Kee (D) | 81,903 | 62.9 |
| | Hartley Sanders (R) | 48,223 | 37.1 |
| 6 | Joe L. Smith (D) | 105,927 | 61.7 |
| | R. E. O'Connor (R) | 65,762 | 38.3 |

## WISCONSIN

| | Candidates | Votes | % |
|---|---|---|---|
| 1 | Stephen Bolles (R) | 69,276 | 55.8 |
| | Stanley W. Slagg (PROG) | 28,308 | 22.8 |
| | Jacob M. Weisman (D) | 26,520 | 21.4 |
| 2 | Harry Sauthoff (PROG) | 60,481 | 44.2 |
| | Charles Hawks Jr. (R) | 58,121 | 42.5 |
| | Thomas R. Brooks (D) | 18,237 | 13.3 |

| | Candidates | Votes | % |
|---|---|---|---|
| 3 | William H. Stevenson (R) | 54,457 | 46.0 |
| | Gardner R. Withrow (PROG) | 52,131 | 44.0 |
| | George T. Doherty (D) | 11,806 | 10.0 |
| 4 | Thaddeus F.B. Wasielewski (D) | 57,381 | 35.6 |
| | Leonard C. Fons (PROG) | 52,907 | 32.8 |
| | John C. Schafer (R) | 50,796 | 31.5 |
| 5 | Lewis D. Thill (R) | 73,728 | 44.4 |
| | James M. Pasch (PROG) | 54,501 | 32.8 |
| | Francis T. Murphy (D) | 37,872 | 22.8 |
| 6 | Frank B. Keefe (R) | 66,821 | 57.4 |
| | Jacob A. Fessler (D) | 30,162 | 25.9 |
| | Walter D. Corrigan (PROG) | 19,387 | 16.7 |
| 7 | Reid F. Murray (R) | 58,696 | 51.6 |
| | Gerald J. Boileau (PROG) | 40,558 | 35.7 |
| | Wallace A. Bloedorn (D) | 14,495 | 12.7 |
| 8 | Joshua L. Johns (R) | 61,987 | 55.9 |
| | Michael F. Kresky (PROG) | 49,005 | 44.2 |
| 9 | Merlin Hull (PROG) | 61,009 | 52.8 |
| | John R. Nygaard (R) | 47,825 | 41.4 |
| | James E. Hughes (D) | 6,763 | 5.9 |
| 10 | Bernard J. Gehrmann (PROG) | 50,776 | 48.0 |
| | Peter Van Nostrand (R) | 37,819 | 35.7 |
| | John G. Green (D) | 17,284 | 16.3 |

## WYOMING

| | Candidates | Votes | % |
|---|---|---|---|
| AL | John J. McIntyre (D) | 57,030 | 53.4 |
| | Frank O. Horton (R) | 49,701 | 46.5 |

# 1941 House Elections

## MISSISSIPPI

**Special Election**

| | Candidates | Votes | % |
|---|---|---|---|
| 2 | Jamie L. Whitten (D) | 8,703 | 69.3 |
| | L. A. Plye | 3,865 | 30.8 |

## NEW YORK

**Special Elections**

| | Candidates | Votes | % |
|---|---|---|---|
| 14 | Arthur G. Klein (D, LIB) | 8,615 | 68.0 |
| | George A. Hastings (R) | 3,337 | 26.3 |

| | Candidates | Votes | % |
|---|---|---|---|
| | Leonard H. Wacker (AM LAB) | 714 | 5.6 |
| 17 | Joseph Clark Baldwin (R) | 23,254 | 52.9 |
| | Dean Alfange (D) | 16,690 | 38.0 |
| | Eugene P. Connolly (AM LAB) | 3,985 | 9.1 |
| 42 | John C. Butler (R) | 15,065 | 40.6 |
| | Hattie E. Schwert (D, AM LAB) | 13,554 | 36.5 |
| | Edmund P. Radwan (NEW DEAL) | 7,787 | 21.0 |

## OKLAHOMA

**Special Election**

| | Candidates | Votes | % |
|---|---|---|---|
| 7 | Victor Wickersham (D) | 19,884 | 82.5 |
| | George Davidson (R) | 4,004 | 16.6 |

## WISCONSIN

**Special Election**

| | Candidates | Votes | % |
|---|---|---|---|
| 1 | Lawrence H. Smith (R) | 29,638 | 63.6 |
| | Thomas R. Amlie (D) | 16,949 | 36.4 |

---

# House Candidates Index

For an index of all House candidates listed in this section (pages 943-1326), see pages 1402-1501. Instructions for use of the House Candidates Index appear on page 1402.

---

# 1942 House Elections

## ALABAMA

| Candidates | Votes | % |
|---|---|---|
| 1 Frank W. Boykin (D) | 5,600 | 100.0 |
| 2 George Grant (D) | 6,672 | 100.0 |
| 3 Henry B. Steagall (D) | 5,043 | 100.0 |
| 4 Sam Hobbs (D) | 7,468 | 100.0 |
| 5 Joe Starnes (D) | 11,841 | 100.0 |
| 6 Pete Jarman (D) | 7,556 | 100.0 |
| 7 Carter Manasco (D) | 9,788 | 100.0 |
| 8 John J. Sparkman (D) | 5,954 | 100.0 |
| 9 John P. Newsome (D) | 8,802 | 95.6 |

## ARIZONA

| Candidates | Votes | % |
|---|---|---|
| AL Richard F. Harless (D) | 56,357✔ | |
| John R. Murdock (D) | 55,825✔ | |
| George R. Darnell (R) | 23,015 | |
| Joseph S. Jenckes Jr. (R) | 18,205 | |
| Morris Graham (COM) | 375 | |

## ARKANSAS

| Candidates | Votes | % |
|---|---|---|
| 1 Ezekiel C. Gathings (D) | 13,998 | 100.0 |
| 2 Wilbur D. Mills (D) | 11,380 | 100.0 |
| 3 J. William Fulbright (D) | 16,111 | 100.0 |
| 4 Fadjo Cravens (D) | 14,733 | 100.0 |
| 5 Brooks Hays (D) | 16,850 | 100.0 |
| 6 William F. Norrell (D) | 13,166 | 100.0 |
| 7 Oren Harris (D) | 12,108 | 100.0 |

## CALIFORNIA

| Candidates | Votes | % |
|---|---|---|
| 1 Clarence F. Lea (D-R) | 78,281 | 93.2 |
| Albert Jason Lima (COM) | 5,703 | 6.8 |
| 2 Harry L. Englebright (R D T) | 50,094 | 99.8 |
| 3 J. Leroy Johnson (R) | 63,982 | 54.5 |
| Joseph B. O'Neil (D) | 53,521 | 45.6 |
| 4 Thomas Rolph (R-D) | 62,735 | 98.2 |
| 5 Richard J. Welch (R-D) | 85,747 | 92.7 |
| Walter Raymond Lambert (COM) | 6,749 | 7.3 |
| 6 Albert E. Carter (R-D) | 108,585 | 92.4 |
| Clarence Paton (COM) | 8,532 | 7.3 |
| 7 John H. Tolan (D-R) | 77,292 | 99.4 |
| 8 John Z. Anderson (R-D) | 91,536 | 99.6 |
| 9 Bertrand W. Gearhart (R-D) | 65,791 | 99.9 |
| 10 Alfred J. Elliott (D-R) | 43,864 | 99.8 |
| 11 George E. Outland (D) | 31,611 | 50.7 |
| A. J. Dingeman (R) | 30,781 | 49.3 |
| 12 H. Jerry Voorhis (D) | 53,705 | 56.8 |
| Robert P. Shuler (R & P) | 40,780 | 43.2 |
| 13 Norris Poulson (R) | 38,577 | 49.2 |
| Charles Kramer (D) | 33,060 | 42.2 |
| Calvert S. Wilson (TOWN) | 6,306 | 8.0 |
| 14 Thomas F. Ford (D) | 49,326 | 66.9 |
| Herbert L. Herberts (R) | 24,349 | 33.0 |
| 15 John M. Costello (D-R) | 88,798 | 86.1 |
| B. Tarkington Dowden (PRC TOWN) | 10,185 | 9.9 |
| 16 Will Rogers Jr. (D) | 61,437 | 53.7 |
| Leland Merritt Ford (R) | 52,023 | 45.4 |
| 17 Cecil R. King (D-R) | 92,260 | 99.8 |
| 18 Ward Johnson (R) | 53,136 | 56.8 |
| Francis H. Gentry (D) | 40,339 | 43.1 |
| 19 Chet Holifield (D) | 34,918 | 63.1 |
| Carlton H. Casjens (R) | 20,446 | 36.9 |
| 20 Carl Hinshaw (R) | 62,628 | 48.4 |
| Joseph O. Donovan (D) | 55,479 | 42.9 |
| Virgil G. Hinshaw (P) | 6,864 | 5.3 |
| 21 Harry R. Sheppard (D-R) | 38,419 | 96.4 |
| 22 John Phillips (R) | 42,765 | 57.6 |
| N. E. West (D) | 31,440 | 42.4 |
| 23 Edouard V. M. Izac (D) | 42,864 | 50.5 |
| James B. Abbey (R) | 42,087 | 49.5 |

## COLORADO

| Candidates | Votes | % |
|---|---|---|
| 1 Lawrence Lewis (D) | 58,143 | 53.4 |
| Olaf H. Jacobson (R) | 50,083 | 46.0 |
| 2 William S. Hill (R) | 64,984 | 67.7 |
| Julian E. Hall (D) | 30,485 | 31.7 |
| 3 J. Edgar Chenoweth (R) | 55,838 | 62.7 |
| J. C. Jarrett (D) | 33,154 | 37.3 |
| 4 Robert F. Rockwell (R) | 28,460 | 58.8 |
| Elizabeth E. Pellet (D) | 19,979 | 41.3 |

## CONNECTICUT

| Candidates | Votes | % |
|---|---|---|
| 1 William J. Miller (R) | 72,306 | 51.4 |
| Herman P. Kopplemann (D) | 68,435 | 48.6 |
| 2 John D. McWilliams (R) | 46,426 | 51.3 |
| William J. Fitzgerald (D) | 43,934 | 48.6 |
| 3 Ranulf Compton (R) | 57,612 | 51.7 |
| James J. Shanley (D) | 53,825 | 48.3 |
| 4 Clare Boothe Luce (R) | 63,719 | 46.5 |
| LeRoy D. Downs (D) | 56,861 | 41.5 |
| David Mansell (SOC) | 15,573 | 11.4 |
| 5 Joseph E. Talbot (R) | 42,602 | 53.6 |
| William A. Patten (D) | 36,327 | 45.7 |
| AL Boleslaus J. Monkiewicz (R) | 283,280 | 49.8 |
| Lucien J. Maciora (D) | 257,941 | 45.3 |

## DELAWARE

| Candidates | Votes | % |
|---|---|---|
| AL Earle D. Willey (R) | 45,376 | 53.6 |
| Philip A. Traynor (D) | 38,791 | 45.8 |

## FLORIDA

| Candidates | Votes | % |
|---|---|---|
| 1 J. Hardin Peterson (D) | 25,037 | 100.0 |
| 2 Emory H. Price (D) | 15,777 | 100.0 |
| 3 Robert L. F. Sikes (D) | 11,739 | 100.0 |
| 4 Arthur P. Cannon (D) | 25,056 | 81.4 |
| Bert Leigh Acker (R) | 5,725 | 18.6 |
| 5 Joe Hendricks (D) | 16,850 | 70.9 |
| Emory Akerman (R) | 6,906 | 29.1 |
| AL Robert A. Green (D) | 91,120 | 100.0 |

## GEORGIA

| Candidates | Votes | % |
|---|---|---|
| 1 Hugh Peterson (D) | 6,980 | 98.2 |
| 2 E. E. Cox (D) | 3,793 | 100.0 |
| 3 Stephen Pace (D) | 4,818 | 100.0 |
| 4 A. Sidney Camp (D) | 5,106 | 100.0 |
| 5 Robert Ramspeck (D) | 9,176 | 96.0 |
| 6 Carl Vinson (D) | 5,725 | 100.0 |
| 7 Malcolm Tarver (D) | 5,172 | 100.0 |
| 8 John Gibson (D) | 4,785 | 100.0 |
| 9 B. Frank Whelchel (D) | 7,404 | 71.1 |
| Roscoe Pickett (I) | 3,013 | 28.9 |
| 10 Paul Brown (D) | 5,393 | 100.0 |

## IDAHO

| Candidates | Votes | % |
|---|---|---|
| 1 Compton I. White (D) | 30,105 | 54.1 |
| H. C. Baldridge (R) | 25,562 | 45.9 |
| 2 Henry C. Dworshak (R) | 45,805 | 54.8 |
| Ira H. Masters (D) | 37,815 | 45.2 |

## ILLINOIS

| Candidates | Votes | % |
|---|---|---|
| 1 William L. Dawson (D) | 26,280 | 52.8 |
| William E. King (R) | 23,537 | 47.3 |
| 2 William A. Rowan (D) | 110,069 | 50.8 |
| Thomas J. Downs (R) | 106,552 | 49.2 |
| 3 Fred E. Busbey (R) | 115,390 | 51.3 |
| Edward A. Kelly (D) | 109,409 | 48.7 |
| 4 Martin Gorski (D) | 60,623 | 78.7 |
| Arthur Joseph Rutshaw (R) | 16,396 | 21.3 |
| 5 Adolph J. Sabath (D) | 29,167 | 72.2 |
| Clem Graver (R) | 11,255 | 27.8 |
| 6 Thomas J. O'Brien (D) | 149,342 | 57.4 |
| Raymond E. Trafelet (R) | 110,823 | 42.6 |
| 7 Leonard W. Schuetz (D) | 179,906 | 50.3 |
| James C. Moreland (R) | 177,931 | 49.7 |
| 8 Thomas S. Gordon (D) | 33,425 | 78.8 |
| Rena E. Pikiel (R) | 8,995 | 21.2 |
| 9 Charles S. Dewey (R) | 40,803 | 51.3 |
| Irwin N. Walker (D) | 38,679 | 48.7 |
| 10 Ralph E. Church (R) | 150,558 | 63.0 |
| Jack Bairstow (D) | 88,266 | 37.0 |
| 11 Chauncey W. Reed (R) | 97,316 | 71.0 |
| Joseph S. Perry (D) | 39,829 | 29.0 |
| 12 Noah M. Mason (R) | 68,426 | 71.4 |
| Tony R. Berrettini (D) | 27,405 | 28.6 |
| 13 Leo E. Allen (R) | 48,500 | 79.4 |
| Michael M. Kinney (D) | 12,596 | 20.6 |
| 14 Anton J. Johnson (R) | 47,294 | 59.3 |
| Robert M. Harper (D) | 32,450 | 40.7 |
| 15 Robert B. Chiperfield (R) | 48,677 | 62.1 |
| Montgomery B. Carrott (D) | 29,741 | 37.9 |
| 16 Everett M. Dirksen (R) | 55,135 | 68.8 |
| James D. Carrigan (D) | 24,969 | 31.2 |
| 17 Leslie C. Arends (R) | 44,563 | 72.4 |
| Frank Gillespie (D) | 17,023 | 27.6 |
| 18 Jessie Sumner (R) | 51,281 | 62.4 |
| Fred E. Butcher (D) | 30,852 | 37.6 |
| 19 William H. Wheat (R) | 56,657 | 57.3 |
| Alfred D. Huston (D) | 42,171 | 42.7 |
| 20 Sid Simpson (R) | 31,360 | 51.0 |
| James M. Barnes (D) | 30,131 | 49.0 |
| 21 Evan Howell (R) | 54,585 | 58.1 |
| William P. Roberts (D) | 39,318 | 41.9 |
| 22 Calvin D. Johnson (R) | 67,313 | 55.7 |
| Harry C. Odum (D) | 53,470 | 44.3 |
| 23 Charles W. Vursell (R) | 47,526 | 52.7 |
| Laurence F. Arnold (D) | 42,736 | 47.4 |
| 24 James V. Heidinger (R) | 37,008 | 58.4 |
| Leroy Barham (D) | 26,377 | 41.6 |
| 25 C. W. Bishop (R) | 49,965 | 55.1 |
| Kent E. Keller (D) | 40,762 | 44.9 |
| AL Stephen A. Day (R) | 1,481,419 | 51.3 |
| Benjamin S. Adamowski (D) | 1,395,053 | 48.3 |

## INDIANA

| Candidates | Votes | % |
|---|---|---|
| 1 Ray J. Madden (D) | 44,334 | 53.6 |
| Samuel W. Cullison (R) | 38,450 | 46.5 |
| 2 Charles A. Halleck (R) | 63,120 | 61.2 |
| Emmett Ferguson (D) | 39,943 | 38.8 |
| 3 Robert A. Grant (R) | 66,434 | 55.2 |
| Lewis J. Murphy (D) | 53,992 | 44.8 |
| 4 George W. Gillie (R) | 61,032 | 61.0 |
| Samuel C. Cleland (D) | 39,032 | 39.0 |
| 5 Forest A. Harness (R) | 80,464 | 55.7 |
| Edward C. Hays (D) | 63,994 | 44.3 |
| 6 Noble J. Johnson (R) | 65,764 | 58.1 |
| Floyd I. McMurray (D) | 47,363 | 41.9 |
| 7 Gerald W. Landis (R) | 69,044 | 56.9 |
| O. A. Noland (D) | 52,386 | 43.1 |
| 8 Charles M. LaFollette (R) | 67,237 | 53.7 |
| John W. Boehne Jr. (D) | 57,868 | 46.3 |
| 9 Earl Wilson (R) | 55,949 | 55.9 |
| Roy Huckleberry (D) | 44,096 | 44.1 |
| 10 Raymond S. Springer (R) | 67,201 | 57.4 |
| William H. Larrabee (D) | 49,963 | 42.6 |
| 11 Louis Ludlow (D) | 79,932 | 50.3 |
| Howard M. Meyer (R) | 79,136 | 49.8 |

## IOWA

| Candidates | Votes | % |
|---|---|---|
| 1 Thomas E. Martin (R) | 55,139 | 61.5 |
| Vern W. Nall (D) | 32,893 | 36.7 |

## IOWA

| | Candidates | Votes | % |
|---|---|---|---|
| 2 | Henry O. Talle (R) | 62,290 | 57.4 |
| | William S. Jacobsen (D) | 46,310 | 42.6 |
| 3 | John W. Gwynne (R) | 54,124 | 60.7 |
| | William D. Kearney (D) | 35,065 | 39.3 |
| 4 | Karl M. LeCompte (R) | 52,258 | 64.5 |
| | Thomas L. Curran (D) | 28,745 | 35.5 |
| 5 | Paul Cunningham (R) | 48,578 | 63.2 |
| | E. Frank Fox (D) | 28,287 | 36.8 |
| 6 | Fred C. Gilchrist (R) | 46,843 | 60.3 |
| | Edward Breen (D) | 30,802 | 39.7 |
| 7 | Ben F. Jensen (R) | 49,086 | 64.2 |
| | Jess Alton (D) | 27,409 | 35.8 |
| 8 | Charles B. Hoeven (R) | 42,154 | 64.6 |
| | Walter T. Mahoney (D) | 23,059 | 35.4 |

## KANSAS

| | Candidates | Votes | % |
|---|---|---|---|
| 1 | William P. Lambertson (R) | 49,962 | 59.2 |
| | John E. Barrett (D) | 34,404 | 40.8 |
| 2 | Ulysses S. Guyer (R) | 48,594 | 59.1 |
| | Herbert L. Drake (D) | 33,625 | 40.9 |
| 3 | Thomas D. Winter (R) | 40,789 | 59.9 |
| | William E. Murphy (D) | 27,364 | 40.2 |
| 4 | Edward H. Rees (R) | 55,612 | 55.7 |
| | John M. Houston (D) | 44,313 | 44.4 |
| 5 | Clifford R. Hope (R) | 54,655 | 66.6 |
| | S. S. Alexander (D) | 27,381 | 33.4 |
| 6 | Frank Carlson (R) | 49,403 | 64.2 |
| | Lud W. Strnad (D) | 27,590 | 35.8 |

## KENTUCKY

| | Candidates | Votes | % |
|---|---|---|---|
| 1 | Noble J. Gregory (D) | 17,027 | 67.5 |
| | Walter L. Prince (R) | 8,195 | 32.5 |
| 2 | Beverly M. Vincent (D) | 21,866 | 100.0 |
| 3 | Emmet O'Neal (D) | 39,866 | 55.2 |
| | J. R. Todd (R) | 32,404 | 44.8 |
| 4 | Edward W. Creal (D) | 23,871 | 55.7 |
| | Don Victor Drye (R) | 19,015 | 44.3 |
| 5 | Brent Spence (D) | 18,510 | 53.5 |
| | Lewis R. Kimberly (R) | 12,073 | 34.9 |
| | Ed Wimmer (I) | 3,806 | 11.0 |
| 6 | Virgil Chapman (D) | 27,382 | 100.0 |
| 7 | Andrew J. May (D) | 22,160 | 50.6 |
| | Elmer E. Gabbard (R) | 21,620 | 49.4 |
| 8 | Joe B. Bates (D) | 22,499 | 56.0 |
| | F. A. Easterling (R) | 17,644 | 44.0 |
| 9 | John M. Robsion (R) | 34,440 | 100.0 |

## LOUISIANA

| | Candidates | Votes | % |
|---|---|---|---|
| 1 | F. Edward Hebert (D) | 20,973 | 100.0 |
| 2 | Paul H. Maloney (D) | 19,007 | 100.0 |
| 3 | James Domengeaux (D) | 6,260 | 100.0 |
| 4 | Overton Brooks (D) | 7,184 | 100.0 |
| 5 | Charles E. McKenzie (D) | 7,949 | 100.0 |
| 6 | James H. Morrison (D) | 9,313 | 100.0 |
| 7 | Henry D. Larcade Jr. (D) | 6,201 | 100.0 |
| 8 | A. Leonard Allen (D) | 8,100 | 100.0 |

## MAINE

| | Candidates | Votes | % |
|---|---|---|---|
| 1 | Robert Hale (R) | 38,128 | 57.0 |
| | Louis J. Brann (D) | 28,759 | 43.0 |
| 2 | Margaret Chase Smith (R) | 42,062 | 67.6 |
| | Bradford C. Redonnett (D) | 20,164 | 32.4 |
| 3 | Frank Fellows (R) | 31,728 | 100.0 |

## MARYLAND

| | Candidates | Votes | % |
|---|---|---|---|
| 1 | David Jenkins Ward (D) | 25,270 | 55.9 |
| | William H. Lloyd (R) | 19,938 | 44.1 |
| 2 | Harry Streett Baldwin (D) | 57,865 | 62.2 |
| | George R. Norris (R) | 35,228 | 37.8 |
| 3 | Thomas D'Alesandro Jr. (D) | 20,450 | 73.3 |
| | Edward S. Panetti (R) | 7,469 | 26.8 |

| | Candidates | Votes | % |
|---|---|---|---|
| 4 | Daniel Ellison (R) | 22,673 | 50.9 |
| | John M. Wyatt (D) | 21,845 | 49.1 |
| 5 | Lansdale G. Sasscer (D) | 33,191 | 66.7 |
| | John Torvestad (D) | 16,596 | 33.3 |
| 6 | J. Glenn Beall (R) | 45,724 | 59.5 |
| | E. Brooke Lee (D) | 31,187 | 40.6 |

## MASSACHUSETTS

| | Candidates | Votes | % |
|---|---|---|---|
| 1 | Allen T. Treadway (R) | 50,302 | 56.7 |
| | Frank Hurley (D) | 36,257 | 40.9 |
| 2 | Charles R. Clason (R) | 58,781 | 61.6 |
| | John J. Granfield (D) | 36,675 | 38.4 |
| 3 | Philip J. Philbin (D) | 46,412 | 50.4 |
| | Alfred Woollacott (R) | 45,689 | 49.6 |
| 4 | Pehr G. Holmes (R) | 57,323 | 57.2 |
| | John S. Sullivan (D) | 42,895 | 42.8 |
| 5 | Edith Nourse Rogers (R) | 95,231 | 100.0 |
| 6 | George J. Bates (R) | 68,739 | 75.3 |
| | James D. Burns (D) | 22,523 | 24.7 |
| 7 | Thomas J. Lane (D) | 68,073 | 100.0 |
| 8 | Angier L. Goodwin (R) | 57,016 | 56.2 |
| | Frederick McDermott (D) | 44,401 | 43.8 |
| 9 | Charles L. Gifford (R) | 50,902 | 58.8 |
| | George F. Backus (D) | 35,633 | 41.2 |
| 10 | Christian A. Herter (R) | 64,247 | 51.2 |
| | William A. Carey (D) | 61,359 | 48.9 |
| 11 | James M. Curley (D) | 60,850 | 69.3 |
| | Vincent Mottola (R) | 27,008 | 30.7 |
| 12 | John W. McCormack (D) | 76,043 | 78.7 |
| | Francis P. O'Neill (R) | 20,600 | 21.3 |
| 13 | Richard B. Wigglesworth (R) | 62,608 | 59.3 |
| | Francis H. Foy (D) | 42,995 | 40.7 |
| 14 | Joseph W. Martin Jr. (R) | 54,977 | 59.4 |
| | Terrance J. Lomax Jr. (D) | 37,598 | 40.6 |

## MICHIGAN

| | Candidates | Votes | % |
|---|---|---|---|
| 1 | George G. Sadowski (D) | 48,620 | 78.0 |
| | John B. Sosnowski (R) | 13,691 | 22.0 |
| 2 | Earl C. Michener (R) | 40,439 | 63.1 |
| | Redmond M. Burr (D) | 23,277 | 36.3 |
| 3 | Paul Shafer (R) | 41,002 | 65.7 |
| | Harold E. Steinbacher (D) | 20,334 | 32.6 |
| 4 | Clare E. Hoffman (R) | 42,653 | 68.6 |
| | Dean Morley (D) | 19,065 | 30.7 |
| 5 | Bartel J. Jonkman (R) | 37,020 | 54.0 |
| | Herman J. Wierenga (D) | 30,840 | 45.0 |
| 6 | William W. Blackney (R) | 48,364 | 57.6 |
| | David M. Martin (D) | 34,893 | 41.6 |
| 7 | Jesse P. Wolcott (R) | 46,946 | 67.3 |
| | Leroy S. Wilson (D) | 22,775 | 32.7 |
| 8 | Fred L. Crawford (R) | 45,182 | 66.9 |
| | Michael J. Hart (D) | 21,689 | 32.1 |
| 9 | Albert J. Engel (R) | 34,548 | 65.4 |
| | Arnold B. Coxhill (D) | 17,954 | 34.0 |
| 10 | Roy O. Woodruff (R) | 31,895 | 60.1 |
| | John E. Morrison (D) | 20,852 | 39.3 |
| 11 | Fred Bradley (R) | 32,579 | 58.0 |
| | Paul L. Adams (D) | 23,555 | 42.0 |
| 12 | John B. Bennett (R) | 31,643 | 51.5 |
| | Frank E. Hook (D) | 27,983 | 45.6 |
| 13 | George D. O'Brien (D) | 33,807 | 51.1 |
| | Clarence J. McLeod (R) | 32,298 | 48.9 |
| 14 | Louis C. Rabaut (D) | 50,707 | 58.7 |
| | Claude G. McDonald (R) | 35,638 | 41.3 |
| 15 | John D. Dingell (D) | 52,384 | 64.6 |
| | Ivan L. Bowman (R) | 28,694 | 35.4 |
| 16 | John Lesinski (D) | 42,911 | 58.5 |
| | Robert W. Ford (R) | 30,480 | 41.5 |
| 17 | George A. Dondero (R) | 56,607 | 56.8 |
| | Dorothy K. Roosevelt (D) | 43,036 | 43.2 |

## MINNESOTA

| | Candidates | Votes | % |
|---|---|---|---|
| 1 | August H. Andresen (R) | 58,387 | 66.2 |
| | Harold R. Atwood (D) | 29,771 | 33.8 |
| 2 | Joseph P. O'Hara (R) | 60,028 | 70.0 |
| | R. J. Neunsinger (D) | 13,866 | 16.2 |

| | Candidates | Votes | % |
|---|---|---|---|
| | Charles D. Peterson (F-LAB) | 11,819 | 13.8 |
| 3 | Richard P. Gale (R) | 44,662 | 49.0 |
| | Charles Munn (F-LAB) | 29,936 | 32.9 |
| | William J. Gallagher (D) | 16,505 | 18.1 |
| 4 | Melvin J. Maas (R) | 45,903 | 65.1 |
| | William Mahoney (F-LAB) | 17,071 | 24.2 |
| | Edward K. Delaney (D) | 6,938 | 9.8 |
| 5 | Walter H. Judd (R) | 60,883 | 63.8 |
| | Joseph Gilbert (F-LAB) | 18,566 | 19.5 |
| | Thomas P. Ryan (D) | 15,976 | 16.7 |
| 6 | Harold Knutson (R) | 49,295 | 57.1 |
| | E. Thomas O'Brien (D) | 37,070 | 43.0 |
| 7 | H. Carl Andersen (R) | 46,570 | 54.8 |
| | Theodor S. Slen (D) | 21,192 | 24.9 |
| | Francis H. Shoemaker (F-LAB) | 17,241 | 20.3 |
| 0 | William A. Pittenger (R) | 51,803 | 58.2 |
| | Rudolph Rautio (F-LAB) | 21,786 | 24.5 |
| | E. J. Larsen (R) | 10,284 | 11.6 |
| | S. B. Ruohoniemi (D) | 5,148 | 5.8 |
| 9 | Harold C. Hagen (F-LAB) | 35,265 | 50.4 |
| | John W. Padden (R) | 34,661 | 49.6 |

## MISSISSIPPI

| | Candidates | Votes | % |
|---|---|---|---|
| 1 | John E. Rankin (D) | 7,079 | 100.0 |
| 2 | Jamie L. Whitten (D) | 5,698 | 100.0 |
| 3 | William M. Whittington (D) | 5,552 | 100.0 |
| 4 | Thomas G. Abernethy (D) | 5,660 | 100.0 |
| 5 | W. Arthur Winstead (D) | 10,548 | 100.0 |
| 6 | William M. Colmer (D) | 7,462 | 100.0 |
| 7 | Dan R. McGehee (D) | 9,699 | 100.0 |

## MISSOURI

| | Candidates | Votes | % |
|---|---|---|---|
| 1 | Samuel W. Arnold (R) | 41,809 | 55.5 |
| | Milton A. Romjue (D) | 33,465 | 44.5 |
| 2 | Max Schwabe (R) | 37,635 | 50.4 |
| | William L. Nelson (D) | 37,069 | 49.6 |
| 3 | William C. Cole (R) | 40,227 | 56.4 |
| | Richard M. Duncan (D) | 31,108 | 43.6 |
| 4 | C. Jasper Bell (D) | 30,227 | 60.5 |
| | John W. Mitchell (R) | 19,709 | 39.5 |
| 5 | Roger C. Slaughter (D) | 27,243 | 50.9 |
| | Ralph B. Innis (R) | 26,163 | 48.9 |
| 6 | Philip A. Bennett (R) | 46,735* | 54.6 |
| | Sam M. Wear (D) | 38,946 | 45.5 |
| 7 | Dewey Short (R) | 49,595 | 63.5 |
| | Ralph C. Max (D) | 28,542 | 36.5 |
| 8 | William P. Elmer (R) | 39,422 | 51.5 |
| | Clyde Williams (D) | 37,072 | 48.5 |
| 9 | Clarence Cannon (D) | 30,082 | 54.6 |
| | Carl E. Starkloff (R) | 24,912 | 45.2 |
| 10 | Orville Zimmerman (D) | 29,514 | 56.7 |
| | Merrill Spitler (R) | 22,555 | 43.3 |
| 11 | Louis E. Miller (R) | 36,133 | 50.4 |
| | John B. Sullivan (D) | 35,510 | 49.6 |
| 12 | Walter C. Ploeser (R) | 68,329 | 57.0 |
| | Martin L. Neaf (D) | 51,649 | 43.1 |
| 13 | John J. Cochran (D) | 37,651 | 61.3 |
| | D. E. Horn (R) | 23,770 | 38.7 |

## MONTANA

| | Candidates | Votes | % |
|---|---|---|---|
| 1 | Mike Mansfield (D) | 42,754 | 59.0 |
| | H. K. Hazelbaker (R) | 28,603 | 39.5 |
| 2 | James F. O'Connor (D) | 50,489 | 52.0 |
| | F. F. Haynes (R) | 45,051 | 46.4 |

## NEBRASKA

| | Candidates | Votes | % |
|---|---|---|---|
| 1 | Carl T. Curtis (R) | 69,651 | 66.6 |
| | Ralph G. Brooks (D) | 31,422 | 30.0 |
| 2 | Howard Buffett (R) | 40,646 | 53.2 |
| | Charles F. McLaughlin (D) | 35,743 | 46.8 |
| 3 | Karl Stefan (R) | 61,813 | 66.3 |
| | George Hally (D) | 27,708 | 29.7 |

## NEBRASKA

| Candidates | Votes | % |
|---|---|---|
| 4 Arthur L. Miller (R) | 55,914 | 67.1 |
| Tom Lanigan (D) | 27,406 | 32.9 |

## NEVADA

| Candidates | Votes | % |
|---|---|---|
| AL Maurice J. Sullivan (D) | 21,100 | 53.6 |
| Ernest Brooks (R) | 18,289 | 46.4 |

## NEW HAMPSHIRE

| Candidates | Votes | % |
|---|---|---|
| 1 Chester E. Merrow (R) | 43,281 | 52.1 |
| Thomas A. Murray (D) | 39,743 | 47.9 |
| 2 Foster Stearns (R) | 42,718 | 58.4 |
| Henry J. Proulx (D) | 30,473 | 41.6 |

## NEW JERSEY

| Candidates | Votes | % |
|---|---|---|
| 1 Charles A. Wolverton (R) | 74,867 | 61.4 |
| Ralph W. Wescott (D) | 46,445 | 38.1 |
| 2 Elmer H. Wene (D) | 40,478 | 53.0 |
| Benjamin D. Foulois (R) | 35,930 | 47.0 |
| 3 James C. Auchincloss (R) | 51,573 | 53.4 |
| William H. Sutphin (D) | 45,037 | 46.6 |
| 4 D. Lane Powers (R) | 51,498 | 63.8 |
| William H. Thompson Jr. (D) | 29,088 | 36.0 |
| 5 Charles A. Eaton (R) | 61,896 | 64.7 |
| J. Ellis Kirkham (D) | 32,999 | 34.5 |
| 6 Donald H. McLean (R) | 52,211 | 57.8 |
| George R. Walsh (D) | 36,425 | 40.4 |
| 7 J. Parnell Thomas (R) | 55,424 | 68.8 |
| Emil M. Wulster (D) | 25,171 | 31.2 |
| 8 Gordon Canfield (R) | 56,582 | 66.6 |
| Irving Abramson (D) | 28,060 | 33.0 |
| 9 Harry L. Towe (R) | 51,692 | 61.8 |
| Frank H. Hennessy (D) | 32,021 | 38.3 |
| 10 Fred A. Hartley Jr. (R) | 37,189 | 53.0 |
| Frederic Bigelow (D) | 31,504 | 44.9 |
| 11 Frank L. Sundstrom (R) | 36,500 | 58.9 |
| William Freiday (D) | 23,630 | 38.2 |
| 12 Robert W. Kean (R) | 43,942 | 60.8 |
| Joseph Siegler (D) | 26,188 | 36.3 |
| 13 Mary T. Norton (D) | 73,766 | 79.6 |
| Raymond J. Cuddy (R) | 18,894 | 20.4 |
| 14 Edward J. Hart (D) | 75,322 | 78.9 |
| Otto A. Trankler (R) | 20,161 | 21.1 |

## NEW MEXICO

| Candidates | Votes | % |
|---|---|---|
| AL Clinton P. Anderson (D) | 62,320✔ | |
| Antonio M. Fernandez (D) | 57,474✔ | |
| William A. Sutherland (R) | 43,627 | |
| Reese P. Fullerton (R) | 43,071 | |

## NEW YORK

| Candidates | Votes | % |
|---|---|---|
| 1 Leonard W. Hall (R) | 197,473 | 68.1 |
| Rene A. Carreau (D) | 83,453 | 28.8 |
| 2 William B. Barry (D) | 125,090 | 50.3 |
| William D. Rawlins (R) | 95,240 | 38.3 |
| William F. Brunner (AM LAB) | 28,224 | 11.4 |
| 3 Joseph L. Pfeifer (D) | 18,700 | 59.6 |
| Samuel Rosenthal (R) | 8,979 | 28.6 |
| Joseph A. Weil (AM LAB) | 3,693 | 11.8 |
| 4 Thomas H. Cullen (D) | 21,456 | 63.3 |
| Frederick H. Gutkes (R) | 10,070 | 29.7 |
| Matthew P. Coleman (AM LAB) | 2,370 | 7.0 |
| 5 James J. Heffernan (D, AM LAB) | 44,522 | 65.7 |
| Charles G. Jochum (R) | 23,285 | 34.3 |
| 6 Andrew L. Somers (D, AM LAB) | 96,990 | 72.2 |
| Theodore R. Studwell (R) | 37,427 | 27.8 |
| 7 John J. Delaney (D, AM LAB) | 27,688 | 72.8 |
| Harry Boyarsky (R) | 10,353 | 27.2 |
| 8 Donald L. O'Toole (D, AM LAB) | 158,685 | 72.8 |
| George F. Picken (R) | 59,408 | 27.2 |
| 9 Eugene J. Keogh (D) | 44,064 | 45.7 |
| William J. Drake (R) | 41,491 | 43.0 |
| Albert Slade (AM LAB) | 10,957 | 11.4 |
| 10 Emanuel Celler (D, AM LAB) | 32,026 | 68.5 |
| Jerome Lewis (R) | 14,693 | 31.5 |
| 11 James A. O'Leary (D, AM LAB) | 31,723 | 57.9 |
| Robert S. Woodward (R) | 23,029 | 42.1 |
| 12 Samuel Dickstein (D, AM LAB) | 13,584 | 87.0 |
| Hyman Hecht (R) | 2,031 | 13.0 |
| 13 Louis J. Capozzoli (D, AM LAB) | 11,245 | 74.0 |
| John Rosenberg (R) | 3,947 | 26.0 |
| 14 Arthur G. Klein (D, AM LAB) | 17,652 | 63.7 |
| Stuart Scheftel (R) | 10,037 | 36.3 |
| 15 Thomas F. Burchill (D) | 14,746 | 58.7 |
| Walter A. Lockwood (R) | 7,566 | 30.1 |
| John Rogan (AM LAB) | 2,798 | 11.1 |
| 16 James H. Fay (D, AM LAB) | 18,710 | 50.1 |
| William T. Pheiffer (R) | 18,630 | 49.9 |
| 17 Joseph Clark Baldwin (R, AM LAB) | 38,079 | 61.0 |
| Carl Sherman (D) | 24,365 | 39.0 |
| 18 Martin J. Kennedy (D) | 18,636 | 52.8 |
| Garrow T. Geer Jr. (R, AM LAB) | 16,665 | 47.2 |
| 19 Sol Bloom (D, AM LAB) | 41,566 | 67.5 |
| Clarence McMillan (R) | 20,000 | 32.5 |
| 20 Vito Marcantonio (R, D) | 18,924 | 100.0 |
| 21 Joseph A. Gavagan (D, AM LAB) | 60,588 | 66.3 |
| Herbert Malkin (R) | 30,796 | 33.7 |
| 22 Walter A. Lynch (D, AM LAB) | 25,933 | 67.1 |
| Richard C. Califano (R) | 12,714 | 32.9 |
| 23 Charles A. Buckley (D, AM LAB) | 142,395 | 74.0 |
| William J. Waterman (R) | 50,063 | 26.0 |
| 24 James M. Fitzpatrick (D, AM LAB) | 117,198 | 57.5 |
| Ralph W. Gwinn (R) | 86,506 | 42.5 |
| 25 Ralph A. Gamble (R) | 85,024 | 69.7 |
| James J. Butterly (D) | 33,040 | 27.1 |
| 26 Hamilton Fish (R) | 48,793 | 52.2 |
| Ferdinand A. Hoyt (D, AM LAB) | 44,751 | 47.8 |
| 27 Jay LeFevre (R) | 53,626 | 63.1 |
| Sharon J. Mauhs (D, AM LAB) | 31,426 | 36.9 |
| 28 William T. Byrne (D, AM LAB) | 86,767 | 62.9 |
| Ernest B. Morris (R) | 51,190 | 37.1 |
| 29 Dean P. Taylor (R, AM LAB) | 69,794 | 68.8 |
| John T. Degnan (D) | 31,616 | 31.2 |
| 30 Bernard W. Kearney (R) | 53,147 | 62.6 |
| Burlin G. McKillip (D) | 29,414 | 34.6 |
| 31 Clarence E. Kilburn (R) | 43,197 | 69.0 |
| Thomas Q. Ryan (D, AM LAB) | 19,448 | 31.0 |
| 32 Francis D. Culkin (R) | 50,970 | 73.2 |
| Vanche F. Milligan (D) | 17,631 | 25.3 |
| 33 Fred J. Douglas (R) | 53,030 | 60.3 |
| Stanard Dow Butler (D, AM LAB) | 34,965 | 39.7 |
| 34 Edwin Arthur Hall (R) | 53,762 | 60.8 |
| Arthur J. Ruland (D) | 33,276 | 37.6 |
| 35 Clarence E. Hancock (R) | 82,021 | 64.5 |
| Arthur B. McGuire (D) | 42,270 | 33.2 |
| 36 John Taber (R) | 47,620 | 62.6 |
| Charles Osborne (D, AM LAB) | 28,502 | 37.4 |
| 37 W. Sterling Cole (R) | 54,700 | 70.9 |
| Daniel Crowley (D, AM LAB) | 22,452 | 29.1 |
| 38 Joseph J. O'Brien (R) | 77,970 | 59.1 |
| Walden Moore (D, AM LAB) | 53,889 | 40.9 |
| 39 James W. Wadsworth (R, D) | 83,195 | 100.0 |
| 40 Walter Gresham Andrews (R) | 91,222 | 68.8 |
| Julian Park (D, AM LAB) | 41,459 | 31.2 |
| 41 Joseph Mruk (R) | 49,239 | 57.4 |
| Alfred F. Beiter (D, AM LAB) | 36,589 | 42.6 |
| 42 John C. Butler (R) | 39,650 | 53.7 |
| Frank J. Caffery (D, AM LAB) | 34,248 | 46.3 |
| 43 Daniel Reed (R) | 43,730 | 64.3 |
| Clare Barnes (D) | 20,867 | 30.7 |
| Nelson M. Fuller (AM LAB) | 3,466 | 5.1 |
| AL Winifred C. Stanley (R) | 1,965,794✔ | |
| Matthew J. Merritt (D, AM LAB) | 1,909,706✔ | |
| Charles Muzzicato (R) | 1,887,688 | |
| Flora D. Johnson (D, AM LAB) | 1,872,321 | |
| Benjamin J. Davis Jr. (COM) | 52,002 | |
| Elizabeth Gurley Flynn (COM) | 50,305 | |
| Layle Lane (SOC) | 22,361 | |
| Amicus Most (SOC) | 19,249 | |

## NORTH CAROLINA

| Candidates | Votes | % |
|---|---|---|
| 1 Herbert C. Bonner (D) | 8,444 | 92.6 |
| J. C. Meekins Jr. (R) | 671 | 7.4 |
| 2 John H. Kerr (D) | 7,124 | 100.0 |
| 3 Graham A. Barden (D) | 9,596 | 100.0 |
| 4 Harold D. Cooley (D) | 20,703 | 65.2 |
| Wiley L. Ward (R) | 11,064 | 34.8 |
| 5 John Hamlin Folger (D) | 20,601 | 67.5 |
| S. Evan Hall (R) | 9,899 | 32.5 |
| 6 Carl T. Durham (D) | 16,548 | 74.5 |
| Hobart M. Patterson (R) | 5,660 | 25.5 |
| 7 J. Bayard Clark (D) | 12,112 | 100.0 |
| 8 William O. Burgin (D) | 27,146 | 56.5 |
| A. D. Barber (R) | 20,868 | 43.5 |
| 9 Robert L. Doughton (D) | 29,213 | 100.0 |
| 10 Cameron Morrison (D) | 26,785 | 55.4 |
| Charles A. Jonas (R) | 21,535 | 44.6 |
| 11 Alfred L. Bulwinkle (D) | 20,270 | 100.0 |
| 12 Zebulon Weaver (D) | 30,438 | 65.3 |
| Gola P. Ferguson (R) | 16,150 | 34.7 |

## NORTH DAKOTA

| Candidates | Votes | % |
|---|---|---|
| AL Usher L. Burdick (R) | 85,936✔ | |
| William Lemke (R) | 65,905✔ | |
| Charles R. Robertson (IR) | 48,472 | |
| Halvor L. Halvorson (D) | 47,972 | |
| E. A. Johanson (D) | 31,547 | |

## OHIO

| Candidates | Votes | % |
|---|---|---|
| 1 Charles H. Elston (R) | 54,120 | 61.5 |
| William H. Hessler (D) | 33,884 | 38.5 |
| 2 William E. Hess (R) | 53,083 | 64.0 |
| Nicholas Bauer (D) | 29,823 | 36.0 |
| 3 Harry P. Jeffrey (R) | 51,477 | 51.6 |
| Greg Holbrock (D) | 48,338 | 48.4 |
| 4 Robert F. Jones (R) | 39,275 | 63.5 |
| Clarence C. Miller (D) | 22,567 | 36.5 |
| 5 Cliff Clevenger (R) | 30,667 | 63.7 |
| Ferdinand E. Warren (D) | 17,514 | 36.4 |
| 6 Edward O. McCowen (R) | 33,171 | 51.1 |
| Jacob E. Davis (D) | 31,793 | 48.9 |
| 7 Clarence J. Brown (R) | 52,270 | 69.1 |
| George H. Smith (D) | 23,384 | 30.9 |
| 8 Frederick C. Smith (R) | 33,797 | 59.8 |
| Brooks Fletcher (D) | 22,753 | 40.2 |
| 9 Homer A. Ramey (R) | 47,377 | 51.8 |
| John F. Hunter (D) | 44,027 | 48.2 |

## OHIO

| | Candidates | Votes | % |
|---|---|---|---|
| 10 | Thomas A. Jenkins (R) | 29,691 | 64.2 |
| | Oral Daugherty (D) | 16,582 | 35.8 |
| 11 | Walter E. Brehm (R) | 31,385 | 61.3 |
| | Harold K. Claypool (D) | 19,817 | 38.7 |
| 12 | John M. Vorys (R) | 56,558 | 58.4 |
| | A. P. Lamneck (D) | 40,290 | 41.6 |
| 13 | Alvin Weichel (R) | 37,923 | 61.6 |
| | E. C. Alexander (D) | 23,618 | 38.4 |
| 14 | Ed Rowe (R) | 60,868 | 51.3 |
| | Dow W. Harter (D) | 57,759 | 48.7 |
| 15 | P. W. Griffiths (R) | 35,137 | 60.2 |
| | Charles W. Lynch (D) | 23,213 | 39.8 |
| 16 | Henderson H. Carson (R) | 50,657 | 52.7 |
| | William R. Thom (D) | 45,531 | 47.3 |
| 17 | J. Harry McGregor (R) | 47,565 | 62.8 |
| | Samuel A. Anderson (D) | 28,235 | 37.3 |
| 18 | Earl R. Lewis (R) | 43,279 | 53.3 |
| | Lawrence E. Imhoff (D) | 37,951 | 46.7 |
| 19 | Michael J. Kirwan (D) | 60,248 | 56.4 |
| | James T. Begg (R) | 46,567 | 43.6 |
| 20 | Michael A. Feighan (D) | 34,462 | 61.8 |
| | Harry T. Marshall (R) | 14,001 | 25.1 |
| | Marie R. Sweeney (I) | 7,289 | 13.1 |
| 21 | Robert Crosser (D) | 35,109 | 63.9 |
| | William J. Rogers (R) | 19,137 | 34.8 |
| 22 | Frances P. Bolton (R) | 92,644 | 57.1 |
| | James Metzenbaum (D) | 69,601 | 42.9 |
| AL | George H. Bender (R) | 945,995 | 56.9 |
| | Stephen M. Young (D) | 717,692 | 43.1 |

## OKLAHOMA

| | | | |
|---|---|---|---|
| 1 | Wesley E. Disney (D) | 42,907 | 54.2 |
| | W. R. Boyd (R) | 35,174 | 44.4 |
| 2 | Jack Nichols (D) | 21,651 | 50.5 |
| | E. O. Clark (R) | 21,266 | 49.6 |
| 3 | Paul Stewart (D) | 23,317 | 78.6 |
| | Frank D. McSherry (R) | 6,346 | 21.4 |
| 4 | Lyle H. Boren (D) | 23,921 | 56.8 |
| | Charles E. Wells (R) | 18,177 | 43.2 |
| 5 | A. S. Mike Monroney (D) | 36,736 | 69.7 |
| | George Wesley Colvert (R) | 15,738 | 29.9 |
| 6 | Jed Johnson (D) | 19,945 | 57.9 |
| | J. L. Hart Jr. (R) | 14,532 | 42.2 |
| 7 | Victor Wickersham (D) | 14,042 | 70.0 |
| | Roscoe C. Holt (R) | 6,009 | 30.0 |
| 8 | Ross Rizley (R) | 30,522 | 60.3 |
| | Julius W. Cox (D) | 19,765 | 39.1 |

## OREGON

| | | | |
|---|---|---|---|
| 1 | James W. Mott (R) | 49,021 | 64.3 |
| | Earl A. Nott (D) | 27,208 | 35.7 |
| 2 | Lowell Stockman (R) | 26,723 | 61.4 |
| | Walter M. Pierce (D) | 16,809 | 38.6 |
| 3 | Homer D. Angell (R) | 55,775 | 51.8 |
| | Thomas R. Mahoney (D) | 51,870 | 48.2 |
| 4 | Harris Ellsworth (R) | 29,385 | 60.0 |
| | Edward C. Kelly (D) | 19,632 | 40.0 |

## PENNSYLVANIA

| | | | |
|---|---|---|---|
| 1 | James Gallagher (R) | 44,519 | 53.5 |
| | Leon Sacks (D) | 38,768 | 46.6 |
| 2 | James P. McGranery (D) | 36,258 | 50.5 |
| | Augustus Trask Ashton (R) | 35,545 | 49.5 |
| 3 | Michael J. Bradley (D) | 47,515 | 51.4 |
| | John R. K. Scott (R) | 45,014 | 48.7 |
| 4 | John Edward Sheridan (D) | 43,284 | 53.2 |
| | Howard T. Scott (R) | 36,689 | 45.1 |
| 5 | C. Frederick Pracht (R) | 48,781 | 51.1 |
| | Francis R. Smith (D) | 46,691 | 48.9 |
| 6 | Francis J. Myers (D) | 53,284 | 55.3 |
| | William H. Sylk (R) | 42,995 | 44.7 |
| 7 | Hugh Scott (R) | 60,836 | 55.7 |
| | Thomas Z. Minehart (D) | 48,373 | 44.3 |

| | Candidates | Votes | % |
|---|---|---|---|
| 8 | James Wolfenden (R) | 48,210 | 58.5 |
| | Vernon A. O'Rourke (D) | 34,164 | 41.5 |
| 9 | Charles L. Gerlach (R) | 41,282 | 62.0 |
| | Francis L. Collum (D) | 25,284 | 38.0 |
| 10 | J. Roland Kinzer (R) | 52,380 | 68.8 |
| | Daniel J. C. O'Donnell (D) | 23,784 | 31.2 |
| 11 | John W. Murphy (D) | 43,585 | 55.8 |
| | James K. Peck (R) | 34,527 | 44.2 |
| 12 | Thomas Byron Miller (R) | 55,679 | 54.5 |
| | Daniel J. Flood (D) | 46,550 | 45.5 |
| 13 | Ivor D. Fenton (R) | 50,721 | 58.2 |
| | J. Noble Hirsch (D) | 36,466 | 41.8 |
| 14 | Daniel K. Hoch (D) | 23,247 | 51.0 |
| | John C. Griesemer (R) | 19,498 | 42.8 |
| | Raymond Hofses (SOC) | 2,783 | 6.1 |
| 15 | Wilson D. Gillette (R) | 63,077 | 65.7 |
| | Michael E. Yurkovsky (D) | 32,953 | 34.3 |
| 16 | Thomas E. Scanlon (D) | 47,920 | 51.3 |
| | Robert Van Der Voort (R) | 45,472 | 48.7 |
| 17 | J. William Ditter (R) | 52,661 | 69.2 |
| | Charles W. Moyer (D) | 23,492 | 30.9 |
| 18 | Richard M. Simpson (R) | 33,147 | 62.0 |
| | John W. Mann (D, I) | 20,340 | 38.0 |
| 19 | John C. Kunkel (R) | 62,119 | 66.0 |
| | A. S. Beshore (D) | 31,969 | 34.0 |
| 20 | Leon H. Gavin (R) | 37,738 | 64.5 |
| | John C. Brecht (D) | 20,171 | 34.5 |
| 21 | Francis E. Walter (D) | 32,498 | 53.5 |
| | William Radford Coyle (R) | 28,272 | 46.5 |
| 22 | Chester H. Gross (R) | 34,202 | 50.0 |
| | Harry L. Haines (D) | 34,131 | 49.9 |
| 23 | James E. Van Zandt (R) | 38,235 | 61.0 |
| | Harry E. Diehl (D) | 24,432 | 39.0 |
| 24 | J. Buell Snyder (D) | 33,480 | 51.1 |
| | Carl H. Hoffman (R) | 32,014 | 48.9 |
| 25 | Grant Furlong (D) | 38,316 | 50.3 |
| | M. B. Armstrong (R) | 37,903 | 49.7 |
| 26 | Louis E. Graham (R) | 41,730 | 58.5 |
| | Peter P. Reising (D) | 29,652 | 41.5 |
| 27 | Harve Tibbott (R) | 50,153 | 55.6 |
| | Eddie McCloskey (D) | 40,096 | 44.4 |
| 28 | Augustine B. Kelley (D) | 32,886 | 53.5 |
| | Edward P. Stirling (R) | 28,543 | 46.5 |
| 29 | Robert L. Rodgers (R) | 40,243 | 59.3 |
| | James F. Lavery (D) | 27,573 | 40.7 |
| 30 | Samuel A. Weiss (D) | 43,482 | 56.4 |
| | John McDowell (R) | 33,568 | 43.6 |
| 31 | Herman P. Eberharter (D) | 50,316 | 58.1 |
| | Robert Garland (R) | 36,239 | 41.9 |
| 32 | James A. Wright (D) | 41,798 | 51.6 |
| | James Grove Fulton (R) | 39,262 | 48.4 |
| AL | William I. Troutman (R) | 1,360,664 | 54.7 |
| | Inez B. Peel (D) | 1,105,992 | 44.4 |

## RHODE ISLAND

| | | | |
|---|---|---|---|
| 1 | Aime J. Forand (D) | 68,242 | 59.0 |
| | Charles H. Eden (R) | 47,480 | 41.0 |
| 2 | John E. Fogarty (D) | 69,411 | 57.4 |
| | Harry Sandager (R) | 51,471 | 42.6 |

## SOUTH CAROLINA

| | | | |
|---|---|---|---|
| 1 | L. Mendel Rivers (D) | 5,452 | 100.0 |
| 2 | Hampton P. Fulmer (D) | 4,448 | 100.0 |
| 3 | Butler B. Hare (D) | 3,201 | 100.0 |
| 4 | Joseph R. Bryson (D) | 4,228 | 100.0 |
| 5 | James P. Richards (D) | 3,122 | 100.0 |
| 6 | John L. McMillan (D) | 2,905 | 100.0 |

## SOUTH DAKOTA

| | | | |
|---|---|---|---|
| 1 | Karl E. Mundt (R) | 81,373 | 59.9 |
| | Fred Hildebrandt (D) | 54,457 | 40.1 |
| 2 | Francis H. Case (R) | 30,389 | 71.9 |
| | George M. Bailey (D) | 11,892 | 28.1 |

## TENNESSEE

| | Candidates | Votes | % |
|---|---|---|---|
| 1 | B. Carroll Reece (R) | 19,777 | 96.1 |
| 2 | John Jennings Jr. (R) | 18,613 | 53.6 |
| | John T. O'Connor (D) | 16,132 | 46.4 |
| 3 | Estes Kefauver (D) | 14,704 | 75.7 |
| | Walter M. Higgins (R) | 3,831 | 19.7 |
| 4 | Albert Gore (D) | 7,667 | 68.9 |
| | H. E. McLean (R) | 3,463 | 31.1 |
| 5 | Jim Nance McCord (D) | 9,841 | 100.0 |
| 6 | J. Percy Priest (D) | 4,945 | 100.0 |
| 7 | Wirt Courtney (D) | 8,689 | 100.0 |
| 8 | Thomas J. Murray (D) | 9,151 | 61.2 |
| | P. W. Maddox (D) | 5,801 | 38.8 |
| 9 | Jere Cooper (D) | 7,354 | 89.3 |
| | S. Homer Tatum (R) | 882 | 10.7 |
| 10 | Clifford Davis (D) | 23,660 | 100.0 |

## TEXAS

| | | | |
|---|---|---|---|
| 1 | Wright Patman (D) | 9,502 | 100.0 |
| 2 | Martin Dies (D) | 10,128 | 100.0 |
| 3 | Lindley Beckworth (D) | 10,929 | 100.0 |
| 4 | Sam Rayburn (D) | 11,768 | 100.0 |
| 5 | Hatton W. Sumners (D) | 10,568 | 100.0 |
| 6 | Luther A. Johnson (D) | 10,726 | 100.0 |
| 7 | Nat Patton (D) | 11,043 | 99.1 |
| 8 | Albert Thomas (D) | 31,038 | 96.9 |
| 9 | Joseph J. Mansfield (D) | 13,852 | 100.0 |
| 10 | Lyndon B. Johnson (D) | 12,799 | 100.0 |
| 11 | W. R. Poage (D) | 7,554 | 100.0 |
| 12 | Fritz Lanham (D) | 25,894 | 100.0 |
| 13 | Ed Gossett (D) | 12,677 | 98.1 |
| 14 | Richard M. Kleberg (D) | 16,212 | 100.0 |
| 15 | Milton H. West (D) | 12,169 | 100.0 |
| 16 | R. Ewing Thomason (D) | 6,612 | 100.0 |
| 17 | Sam Russell (D) | 13,261 | 100.0 |
| 18 | Eugene Worley (D) | 10,739 | 100.0 |
| 19 | George Mahon (D) | 12,216 | 100.0 |
| 20 | Paul J. Kilday (D) | 8,860 | 81.7 |
| | W. H. Turner (R) | 1,980 | 18.3 |
| 21 | O. Clark Fisher (D) | 16,554 | 100.0 |

## UTAH

| | | | |
|---|---|---|---|
| 1 | Walter K. Granger (D) | 36,297 | 50.2 |
| | J. Bracken Lee (R) | 36,028 | 49.8 |
| 2 | J. W. Robinson (D) | 43,582 | 55.8 |
| | Reed E. Vetterli (R) | 34,586 | 44.3 |

## VERMONT

| | | | |
|---|---|---|---|
| AL | Charles A. Plumley (R) | 40,751 | 70.2 |
| | John B. Candon (D) | 17,304 | 29.8 |

## VIRGINIA

| | | | |
|---|---|---|---|
| 1 | Schuyler Otis Bland (D) | 5,207 | 100.0 |
| 2 | Winder R. Harris (D) | 5,369 | 100.0 |
| 3 | David E. Satterfield Jr. (D) | 5,822 | 99.9 |
| 4 | Patrick Henry Drewry (D) | 4,457 | 99.8 |
| 5 | Thomas G. Burch (D) | 8,166 | 93.1 |
| | Howard H. Carwile (SOC) | 601 | 6.9 |
| 6 | Clifton A. Woodrum (D) | 10,510 | 93.4 |
| | Stephen A. Moore (SOC) | 724 | 6.4 |
| 7 | A. Willis Robertson (D) | 7,521 | 99.7 |
| 8 | Howard W. Smith (D) | 13,380 | 86.6 |
| | Harrie Byrd Conlin (R) | 1,757 | 11.4 |
| 9 | John W. Flannagan Jr. (D) | 16,655 | 63.6 |
| | Cary Ingram Crockett (R) | 9,534 | 36.4 |

## WASHINGTON

| | | | |
|---|---|---|---|
| 1 | Warren G. Magnuson (D) | 69,010 | 65.5 |
| | Harold H. Stewart (R) | 35,910 | 34.1 |
| 2 | Henry M. Jackson (D) | 39,628 | 59.9 |
| | Payson Peterson (R) | 26,573 | 40.1 |

## WASHINGTON

| | Candidates | Votes | % |
|---|---|---|---|
| 3 | Fred Norman (R) | 34,462 | 57.1 |
| | Martin F. Smith (D) | 25,894 | 42.9 |
| 4 | Hal Holmes (R) | 34,495 | 63.6 |
| | Knute Hill (D) | 19,751 | 36.4 |
| 5 | Walt Horan (R) | 47,242 | 62.7 |
| | C. C. Dill (D) | 28,076 | 37.3 |
| 6 | John M. Coffee (D) | 42,666 | 64.0 |
| | Ralph Woods (R) | 23,650 | 35.5 |

## WEST VIRGINIA

| | Candidates | Votes | % |
|---|---|---|---|
| 1 | Andrew C. Schiffler (R) | 42,787 | 54.7 |
| | Robert L. Ramsey (D) | 35,498 | 45.3 |
| 2 | Jennings Randolph (D) | 32,935 | 50.2 |
| | Charles G. Baker (R) | 32,676 | 49.8 |
| 3 | Edward G. Rohrbough (R) | 37,135 | 53.2 |
| | Andrew Edmiston (D) | 32,682 | 46.8 |
| 4 | Hubert S. Ellis (R) | 48,697 | 52.2 |
| | George W. Johnson (D) | 44,528 | 47.8 |

| | Candidates | Votes | % |
|---|---|---|---|
| 5 | John Kee (D) | 36,625 | 57.2 |
| | B. F. Howard (R) | 27,400 | 42.8 |
| 6 | Joe L. Smith (D) | 46,281 | 51.8 |
| | Houston G. Young (R) | 43,043 | 48.2 |

## WISCONSIN

| | Candidates | Votes | % |
|---|---|---|---|
| 1 | Lawrence H. Smith (R) | 46,453 | 71.9 |
| | Bernard F. Magruder (D) | 16,848 | 26.1 |
| 2 | Harry Sauthoff (PROG) | 43,412 | 50.2 |
| | Charles Hawks Jr. (R) | 34,272 | 39.6 |
| | Thomas R. Brooks (D) | 8,315 | 9.6 |
| 3 | William H. Stevenson (R) | 34,177 | 46.9 |
| | Gardner R. Withrow (PROG) | 31,092 | 42.6 |
| | William D. Carroll (D) | 7,385 | 10.1 |
| 4 | Thaddeus F. B. Wasielewski (D) | 46,819 | 48.8 |
| | John C. Schafer (R) | 29,104 | 30.3 |
| | John C. Brophy (PROG) | 17,468 | 18.2 |
| 5 | Howard J. McMurray (D) | 44,337 | 43.2 |
| | Lewis D. Thill (R) | 38,345 | 37.4 |

| | Candidates | Votes | % |
|---|---|---|---|
| | Roy A. Roush (PROG) | 16,409 | 16.0 |
| 6 | Frank B. Keefe (R) | 41,385 | 62.2 |
| | Eugene Schallern (D) | 13,364 | 20.1 |
| | Adam F. Poltl (PROG) | 10,645 | 16.0 |
| 7 | Reid F. Murray (R) | 40,520 | 71.9 |
| | John A. Kennedy (D) | 15,821 | 28.1 |
| 8 | LaVern R. Dilweg (D) | 40,002 | 54.5 |
| | Joshua H. Johns (R) | 33,441 | 45.5 |
| 9 | Merlin Hull (PROG) | 37,919 | 61.8 |
| | George H. Hipke (R) | 19,972 | 32.6 |
| | Jack E. Joyce (D) | 3,448 | 5.6 |
| 10 | Alvin E. O'Konski (R) | 33,143 | 48.4 |
| | Bernard J. Gehrmann (PROG) | 28,169 | 41.1 |
| | John G. Green (D) | 7,198 | 10.5 |

## WYOMING

| | Candidates | Votes | % |
|---|---|---|---|
| AL | Frank A. Barrett (R) | 37,965 | 50.7 |
| | John J. McIntyre (D) | 36,892 | 49.3 |

# 1943 House Elections

## KANSAS

**Special Election**

| | Candidates | Votes | % |
|---|---|---|---|
| 2 | Errett P. Scrivner (R) | 19,798 | 69.1 |
| | Herbert L. Drake (D) | 8,859 | 30.9 |

## KENTUCKY

**Special Election**

| | Candidates | Votes | % |
|---|---|---|---|
| 4 | Chester O. Carrier (R) | 29,855 | 63.4 |
| | J. Dan Talbott (D) | 17,218 | 36.6 |

## MISSOURI

**Special Election**

| | Candidates | Votes | % |
|---|---|---|---|
| 6 | Marion T. Bennett (R) | 36,448 | 62.9 |
| | Sam M. Wear (D) | 21,496 | 37.1 |

# 1944 House Elections

## ALABAMA

| | Candidates | Votes | % |
|---|---|---|---|
| 1 | Frank W. Boykin (D) | 19,082 | 100.0 |
| 2 | George M. Grant (D) | 24,180 | 100.0 |
| 3 | George W. Andrews (D) | 20,470 | 100.0 |
| 4 | Sam Hobbs (D) | 19,391 | 84.5 |
| | O. D. Beard (R) | 3,554 | 15.5 |
| 5 | Albert Rains (D) | 25,317 | 100.0 |
| 6 | Pete Jarman (D) | 14,561 | 100.0 |
| 7 | Carter Manasco (D) | 21,671 | 34.1 |
| | I. B. Burdick (R) | 11,202 | 34.1 |
| 8 | John J. Sparkman (D) | 24,023 | 100.0 |
| 9 | Luther Patrick (D) | 31,767 | 81.7 |
| | H. H. Grooms (R) | 7,120 | 18.3 |

## ARIZONA

| | Candidates | Votes | % |
|---|---|---|---|
| AL | John R. Murdock (D) | 88,532✓ | |
| | Richard F. Harless (D) | 86,691✓ | |
| | Margaret Adams Rockwell (R) | 39,035 | |
| | A. M. Ward (R) | 36,352 | |
| | A. Walter Gehres (P) | 469 | |

## ARKANSAS

| | Candidates | Votes | % |
|---|---|---|---|
| 1 | Ezekiel C. Gathings (D) | 32,501 | 100.0 |
| 2 | Wilbur D. Mills (D) | 24,977 | 100.0 |
| 3 | James W. Trimble (D) | 20,061 | 63.3 |
| | Lonzo A. Ross (R) | 11,613 | 36.7 |
| 4 | Fadjo Cravens (D) | 30,310 | 100.0 |
| 5 | Brooks Hays (D) | 33,215 | 87.1 |
| | Ross (R) | 4,902 | 12.9 |
| 6 | William F. Norrell (D) | 31,785 | 100.0 |
| 7 | Oren Harris (D) | 27,851 | 100.0 |

## CALIFORNIA

| | Candidates | Votes | % |
|---|---|---|---|
| 1 | Clarence F. Lea (D-R) | 92,706 | 99.9 |
| 2 | Clair Engle (D) | 48,201 | 63.8 |
| | Jesse M. Mayo (R) | 27,312 | 36.2 |
| 3 | J. Leroy Johnson (R-D) | 131,705 | 99.9 |
| 4 | Franck R. Havenner (D) | 73,582 | 50.1 |
| | Thomas Rolph (R) | 73,367 | 49.9 |
| 5 | Richard J. Welch (R-D) | 112,151 | 100.0 |
| 6 | George P. Miller (D) | 104,441 | 52.0 |
| | Albert E. Carter (R) | 96,395 | 48.0 |
| 7 | John H. Tolan (D-R) | 81,762 | 57.9 |
| | Chesley M. Walter (R) | 59,360 | 42.0 |
| 8 | John Z. Anderson (R) | 94,218 | 56.5 |
| | Arthur L. Johnson (D) | 72,420 | 43.5 |
| 9 | Bertrand W. Gearhart (R-D) | 66,845 | 99.5 |
| 10 | Alfred J. Elliott (D-R) | 60,001 | 99.9 |
| 11 | George E. Outland (D) | 52,218 | 56.0 |
| | Fred J. Hart (R) | 41,005 | 44.0 |
| 12 | H. Jerry Voorhis (D) | 77,385 | 55.3 |
| | Roy P. McLaughlin (R) | 62,524 | 44.7 |
| 13 | Ned R. Healy (D) | 66,854 | 54.9 |
| | Norris Poulson (R) | 54,792 | 45.0 |
| 14 | Helen Gahagan Douglas (D) | 65,729 | 51.5 |
| | William D. Campbell (R) | 61,767 | 48.4 |
| 15 | Gordon L. McDonough (R) | 100,305 | 56.6 |
| | Hal Styles (D) | 73,655 | 41.6 |
| 16 | Ellis E. Patterson (D) | 105,835 | 54.1 |
| | Jesse Randolph Kellems (R) | 89,700 | 45.9 |
| 17 | Cecil R. King (D-R) | 147,217 | 99.8 |
| 18 | Clyde G. Doyle (D) | 95,090 | 55.6 |
| | Ward Johnson (R) | 75,749 | 44.3 |
| 19 | Chet Holifield (D) | 65,758 | 71.7 |
| | Carlton H. Casjens (R) | 25,852 | 28.2 |
| 20 | Carl Hinshaw (R) | 112,663 | 51.8 |
| | Archibald B. Young (D) | 101,090 | 46.5 |

| | Candidates | Votes | % |
|---|---|---|---|
| 21 | Harry R. Sheppard (D) | 48,539 | 58.5 |
| | Earl S. Webb (R) | 34,409 | 41.5 |
| 22 | John Phillips (R-D) | 88,537 | 99.8 |
| 23 | Edouard V. M. Izac (D) | 86,707 | 55.1 |
| | James B. Abbey (R) | 70,787 | 45.0 |

## COLORADO

| | | Votes | % |
|---|---|---|---|
| 1 | Dean M. Gillespie (R) | 90,151 | 51.8 |
| | Charles A. Graham (D) | 83,253 | 47.8 |
| 2 | William S. Hill (R) | 83,264 | 62.3 |
| | David J. Miller (D) | 49,079 | 36.8 |
| 3 | J. Edgar Chenoweth (R) | 69,492 | 56.3 |
| | Arthur M. Wimmell (D) | 53,904 | 43.7 |
| 4 | Robert F. Rockwell (R) | 38,671 | 61.7 |
| | John L. Heuschkel (D) | 24,039 | 38.3 |

## CONNECTICUT

| | | Votes | % |
|---|---|---|---|
| 1 | Herman P. Kopplemann (D) | 120,100 | 54.0 |
| | William J. Miller (R) | 102,257 | 46.0 |
| 2 | Chase Going Woodhouse (D) | 63,013 | 51.2 |
| | John D. McWilliams (R) | 59,973 | 48.8 |
| 3 | James P. Geelan (D) | 82,472 | 51.5 |
| | Ranulf Compton (R) | 77,753 | 48.5 |
| 4 | Clare Boothe Luce (R) | 102,043 | 49.9 |
| | Margaret Connor (D) | 100,035 | 48.9 |
| 5 | Joseph E. Talbot (R) | 60,137 | 52.2 |
| | Peter M. Higgins (D) | 54,885 | 47.7 |
| AL | Joseph F. Ryter (D) | 424,146 | 51.2 |
| | Boleslaus J. Monkiewicz (R) | 397,725 | 48.1 |

## DELAWARE

| | | Votes | % |
|---|---|---|---|
| AL | Philip A. Traynor (D) | 63,649 | 50.3 |
| | Earle D. Willey (R) | 62,378 | 49.3 |

## FLORIDA

| | | Votes | % |
|---|---|---|---|
| 1 | J. Hardin Peterson (D) | 84,280 | 100.0 |
| 2 | Emory H. Price (D) | 66,604 | 100.0 |
| 3 | Robert L. F. Sikes (D) | 51,693 | 100.0 |
| 4 | Pat Cannon (D) | 65,900 | 72.0 |
| | Edith Shaffer Stearn (R) | 25,643 | 28.0 |
| 5 | Joe Hendricks (D) | 48,602 | 67.5 |
| | Emory Akerman (R) | 23,406 | 32.5 |
| 6 | Dwight L. Rogers (D) | 32,491 | 69.7 |
| | Edward W. Greb (R) | 14,134 | 30.3 |

## GEORGIA

| | | Votes | % |
|---|---|---|---|
| 1 | Hugh Peterson (D) | 24,468 | 100.0 |
| 2 | E. E. Cox (D) | 21,791 | 100.0 |
| 3 | Stephen Pace (D) | 25,276 | 100.0 |
| 4 | A. Sidney Camp (D) | 27,375 | 100.0 |
| 5 | Robert Ramspeck (D) | 50,257 | 94.5 |
| | H. A. Alexander (I) | 2,929 | 5.5 |
| 6 | Carl Vinson (D) | 18,989 | 100.0 |
| 7 | Malcolm Tarver (D) | 31,400 | 100.0 |
| 8 | John S. Gibson (D) | 21,916 | 100.0 |
| 9 | John S. Wood (D) | 25,880 | 100.0 |
| 10 | Paul Brown (D) | 25,102 | 100.0 |

## IDAHO

| | | Votes | % |
|---|---|---|---|
| 1 | Compton I. White (D) | 49,581 | 56.6 |
| | Robert L. Brainard (R) | 37,998 | 43.4 |
| 2 | Henry C. Dworshak (R) | 61,751 | 52.3 |
| | Phil J. Evans (D) | 56,249 | 47.7 |

## ILLINOIS

| | Candidates | Votes | % |
|---|---|---|---|
| 1 | William L. Dawson (D) | 42,713 | 62.0 |
| | William E. King (R) | 26,204 | 38.0 |
| 2 | William A. Rowan (D) | 186,089 | 57.3 |
| | Thomas J. Downs (R) | 138,579 | 42.7 |
| 3 | Edward A. Kelly (D) | 158,944 | 52.0 |
| | Fred E. Busbey (R) | 146,961 | 48.0 |
| 4 | Martin Gorski (D) | 79,243 | 80.4 |
| | Leo J. Kozicki (R) | 19,346 | 19.6 |
| 5 | Adolph J. Sabath (D) | 38,370 | 76.3 |
| | Max Price (R) | 11,929 | 23.7 |
| 6 | Thomas J. O'Brien (D) | 211,056 | 59.9 |
| | Charles J. Anderson, Jr (R) | 140,069 | 39.7 |
| 7 | William W. Link (D) | 261,473 | 54.6 |
| | Charles H. Garland (R) | 217,207 | 45.4 |
| 8 | Thomas S. Gordon (D) | 39,866 | 79.2 |
| | John F. Uczciwek (R) | 10,474 | 20.8 |
| 9 | Alexander J. Resa (D) | 61,168 | 52.8 |
| | Charles S. Dewey (R) | 54,698 | 47.2 |
| 10 | Ralph E. Church (R) | 193,948 | 55.8 |
| | Curtis D. MacDougall (D) | 153,644 | 44.2 |
| 11 | Chauncey W. Reed (R) | 128,064 | 66.2 |
| | Otto Joseph Hruby Jr. (D) | 65,296 | 33.8 |
| 12 | Noah M. Mason (R) | 86,228 | 61.0 |
| | Herbert J. Max (D) | 55,236 | 39.1 |
| 13 | Leo E. Allen (R) | 59,372 | 70.0 |
| | Garret J. Schutt (D) | 25,482 | 30.0 |
| 14 | Anton J. Johnson (R) | 55,812 | 54.4 |
| | Carl M. Seaberg (D) | 46,759 | 45.6 |
| 15 | Robert B. Chiperfield (R) | 58,358 | 59.3 |
| | Ray Simpkins (D) | 40,093 | 40.7 |
| 16 | Everett M. Dirksen (R) | 70,301 | 59.0 |
| | M. R. Clark (D) | 48,779 | 41.0 |
| 17 | Leslie C. Arends (R) | 52,706 | 66.4 |
| | Ruth G. Fillingham (D) | 26,732 | 33.7 |
| 18 | Jessie Sumner (R) | 58,617 | 56.9 |
| | Carl B. Jewell (D) | 44,340 | 43.1 |
| 19 | Rolla C. McMillen (R) | 70,942 | 55.8 |
| | George M. Brown (D) | 56,247 | 44.2 |
| 20 | Sid Simpson (R) | 38,922 | 55.6 |
| | Don Irving (D) | 31,092 | 44.4 |
| 21 | Evan Howell (R) | 62,879 | 55.7 |
| | Thomas L. Jarrett (D) | 50,050 | 44.3 |
| 22 | Melvin Price (D) | 83,311 | 50.8 |
| | Calvin D. Johnson (R) | 80,616 | 49.2 |
| 23 | Charles W. Vursell (R) | 56,712 | 54.7 |
| | J. E. McMackin (D) | 46,957 | 45.3 |
| 24 | James V. Heidinger (R) | 42,927 | 58.2 |
| | Early C. Phelps (D) | 30,808 | 41.8 |
| 25 | C. W. Bishop (R) | 57,672 | 53.5 |
| | Kent E. Keller (D) | 50,140 | 46.5 |
| AL | Emily Taft Douglas (D) | 2,030,755 | 52.3 |
| | Stephen A. Day (R) | 1,839,518 | 47.4 |

### Special Election

| | | Votes | % |
|---|---|---|---|
| 19 | Rolla McMillen (R) | 4,722 | 98.7 |

## INDIANA

| | | Votes | % |
|---|---|---|---|
| 1 | Ray J. Madden (D) | 75,635 | 61.3 |
| | Otto G. Fifield (R) | 46,969 | 38.1 |
| 2 | Charles A. Halleck (R) | 78,061 | 61.6 |
| | James O. Cox (D) | 48,103 | 37.9 |
| 3 | Robert A. Grant (R) | 85,362 | 51.8 |
| | Marshall A. Kizer (D) | 78,621 | 47.7 |
| 4 | George W. Gillie (R) | 81,110 | 59.9 |
| | Robert W. Bushee (D) | 53,636 | 39.6 |
| 5 | Forest A. Harness (R) | 94,274 | 53.1 |
| | Bennett H. Rockey (D) | 80,208 | 45.1 |
| 6 | Noble J. Johnson (R) | 75,517 | 55.2 |
| | Otis G. Jamison (D) | 60,758 | 44.5 |
| 7 | Gerald W. Landis (R) | 73,417 | 53.9 |
| | Arthur H. Greenwood (D) | 62,136 | 45.6 |

## INDIANA

| Candidates | Votes | % |
|---|---|---|
| 8 Charles M. LaFollette (R) | 84,095 | 52.0 |
| Charles J. Eichel (D) | 76,905 | 47.6 |
| 9 Earl Wilson (R) | 62,831 | 55.6 |
| George W. Elliott (D) | 49,380 | 43.7 |
| 10 Raymond S. Springer (R) | 82,582 | 54.3 |
| Sidney E. Baker (D) | 67,724 | 44.5 |
| 11 Louis Ludlow (D) | 114,051 | 51.1 |
| Judson L. Stark (R) | 108,503 | 48.6 |

## IOWA

| Candidates | Votes | % |
|---|---|---|
| 1 Thomas E. Martin (R) | 78,729 | 56.7 |
| Clair A. Williams (D) | 60,048 | 43.3 |
| 2 Henry O. Talle (R) | 86,903 | 55.9 |
| George C. Classen (D) | 68,489 | 44.1 |
| 3 John W. Gwynne (R) | 74,901 | 56.8 |
| William D. Kearney (D) | 56,985 | 43.2 |
| 4 Karl M. LeCompte (R) | 59,658 | 54.9 |
| Harold J. Fleck (D) | 49,098 | 45.2 |
| 5 Paul Cunningham (R) | 66,260 | 54.1 |
| Ralph N. Lynch (D) | 56,138 | 45.8 |
| 6 James I. Dolliver (R) | 60,153 | 58.8 |
| Charles Hanna (D) | 42,098 | 41.1 |
| 7 Ben F. Jensen (R) | 66,905 | 61.5 |
| Albert McGinn (D) | 41,802 | 38.4 |
| 8 Charles B. Hoeven (R) | 58,537 | 56.2 |
| Lester S. Gillette (D) | 45,682 | 43.8 |

## KANSAS

| Candidates | Votes | % |
|---|---|---|
| 1 Albert M. Cole (R) | 71,565 | 67.3 |
| Ralph Ulm (D) | 34,731 | 32.7 |
| 2 Errett P. Scrivner (R) | 68,815 | 59.1 |
| Albert Baker (D) | 47,676 | 40.9 |
| 3 Thomas D. Winter (R) | 52,361 | 60.2 |
| Herman L. Gees (D) | 34,645 | 39.8 |
| 4 Edward H. Rees (R) | 90,186 | 58.6 |
| William J. Kropp (D) | 63,843 | 41.5 |
| 5 Clifford R. Hope (R) | 72,370 | 69.0 |
| A. E. Hawes (D) | 32,557 | 31.0 |
| 6 Frank Carlson (R) | 63,035 | 66.0 |
| Dan M. McCarthy (D) | 32,408 | 34.0 |

## KENTUCKY

| Candidates | Votes | % |
|---|---|---|
| 1 Noble J. Gregory (D) | 51,369 | 69.3 |
| A. R. Anderson (R) | 22,196 | 29.9 |
| 2 Earle C. Clements (D) | 57,948 | 57.3 |
| Otis White (R) | 42,802 | 42.4 |
| 3 Emmet O'Neal (D) | 79,922 | 57.3 |
| Garland R. Hubbard (R) | 59,190 | 42.5 |
| 4 Frank L. Chelf (D) | 48,671 | 54.5 |
| Chester O. Carrier (R) | 40,317 | 45.2 |
| 5 Brent Spence (D) | 45,228 | 58.0 |
| Olin W. Davis (R) | 32,606 | 41.8 |
| 6 Virgil Chapman (D) | 63,404 | 58.8 |
| George W. Boner (R) | 44,214 | 41.0 |
| 7 Andrew J. May (D) | 33,406 | 52.5 |
| Elmer Gabbard (R) | 30,165 | 47.4 |
| 8 Joe B. Bates (D) | 48,969 | 54.3 |
| Thomas S. Yates (R) | 41,154 | 45.6 |
| 9 John M. Robsion (R) | 68,908 | 68.8 |
| H. F. Reed (D) | 31,019 | 31.0 |

## LOUISIANA

| Candidates | Votes | % |
|---|---|---|
| 1 F. Edward Hebert (D) | 55,887 | 100.0 |
| 2 Paul H. Maloney (D) | 56,636 | 100.0 |
| 3 James Domengeaux (D) | 28,123 | 100.0 |
| 4 Overton Brooks (D) | 27,886 | 100.0 |
| 5 Charles E. McKenzie (D) | 25,462 | 100.0 |
| 6 James H. Morrison (D) | 38,561 | 100.0 |
| 7 Henry D. Larcade Jr. (D) | 26,931 | 100.0 |
| 8 A. Leonard Allen (D) | 23,083 | 100.0 |

### Special Election

| | Votes | % |
|---|---|---|
| 3 James Domengaux (D) | 26,093 | 100.0 |

## MAINE

| Candidates | Votes | % |
|---|---|---|
| 1 Robert Hale (R) | 47,721 | 68.8 |
| Andrew A. Pettis (D) | 21,620 | 31.2 |
| 2 Margaret Chase Smith (R) | 46,545 | 67.8 |
| David H. Staples (D) | 22,139 | 32.2 |
| 3 Frank Fellows (R) | 35,644 | 77.9 |
| Ralph E. Graham (D) | 10,102 | 22.1 |

## MARYLAND

| | Votes | % |
|---|---|---|
| 1 Dudley G. Roe (D) | 30,257 | 50.8 |
| Wilmer F. Davis (R) | 29,298 | 49.2 |
| 2 H. S. Baldwin (D) | 97,239 | 57.0 |
| Wilfred T. McQuaid (R) | 73,469 | 43.0 |
| 3 Thomas D'Alesandro Jr. (D) | 39,032 | 73.5 |
| John W. Benson (R) | 14,046 | 26.5 |
| 4 George Fallon (D) | 47,088 | 59.2 |
| Daniel Ellison (R) | 32,416 | 40.8 |
| 5 Lansdale Sasscer (D) | 51,318 | 64.9 |
| C. Maurice Weidemeyer (R) | 27,821 | 35.2 |
| 6 J. Glenn Beall (R) | 63,079 | 57.9 |
| Daniel F. McMullen (D) | 45,877 | 42.1 |

## MASSACHUSETTS

| | Votes | % |
|---|---|---|
| 1 John W. Heselton (R) | 63,693 | 50.5 |
| James P. McAndrews (D) | 62,525 | 49.5 |
| 2 Charles R. Clason (R) | 75,571 | 55.7 |
| Michael W. Albano (D) | 60,195 | 44.3 |
| 3 Philip J. Philbin (D) | 78,848 | 61.5 |
| Wilfred P. Bazinet (R) | 49,300 | 38.5 |
| 4 Pehr G. Holmes (R) | 76,097 | 55.5 |
| Frank J. McGrail (D) | 60,967 | 44.5 |
| 5 Edith Nourse Rogers (R) | 109,242 | 73.2 |
| Milton A. Wesson (D) | 39,911 | 26.8 |
| 6 George J. Bates (R) | 87,211 | 67.0 |
| John M. Bresnahan (D) | 42,937 | 33.0 |
| 7 Thomas J. Lane (D) | 78,008 | 67.9 |
| Ernest Bentley (R) | 36,877 | 32.1 |
| 8 Angier L. Goodwin (R) | 79,912 | 57.5 |
| Frederick J. McDermott (D) | 59,058 | 42.5 |
| 9 Charles L. Gifford (R) | 75,803 | 58.5 |
| William McAuliffe (D) | 53,820 | 41.5 |
| 10 Christian A. Herter (R) | 100,334 | 55.8 |
| William A. Carey (D) | 79,380 | 44.2 |
| 11 James M. Curley (D) | 75,469 | 65.6 |
| Lester W. Bowen (R) | 39,523 | 34.4 |
| 12 John W. McCormack (D) | 97,469 | 75.8 |
| Henry J. Allen (R) | 31,178 | 24.2 |
| 13 Richard B. Wigglesworth (R) | 97,013 | 65.8 |
| Andrew T. Clancy (D) | 50,377 | 34.2 |
| 14 Joseph W. Martin Jr. (R) | 79,928 | 62.0 |
| Edmond P. Talbot (D) | 48,993 | 38.0 |

## MICHIGAN

| | Votes | % |
|---|---|---|
| 1 George G. Sadowski (D) | 103,782 | 80.6 |
| John B. Sosnowski (R) | 24,542 | 19.1 |
| 2 Earl C. Michener (R) | 80,594 | 64.8 |
| Redmond M. Burr (D) | 43,536 | 35.0 |
| 3 Paul W. Shafer (R) | 73,134 | 62.5 |
| Charles V. Hampton (D) | 42,902 | 36.7 |
| 4 Clare E. Hoffman (R) | 68,233 | 64.1 |
| Bernard T. Foley (D) | 37,754 | 35.5 |
| 5 Bartel J. Jonkman (R) | 73,034 | 57.8 |
| J. Neal Lamoreaux (D) | 53,437 | 42.3 |
| 6 William W. Blackney (R) | 87,105 | 55.2 |
| Robert B. McLaughlin (D) | 70,104 | 44.5 |
| 7 Jesse P. Wolcott (R) | 79,455 | 65.9 |
| Charles F. Mann (D) | 40,298 | 33.4 |
| 8 Fred L. Crawford (R) | 75,700 | 67.5 |
| William A. Hemmer (D) | 35,982 | 32.1 |
| 9 Albert J. Engel (R) | 56,308 | 62.6 |
| Arnold B. Coxhill (D) | 33,705 | 37.4 |
| 10 Roy O. Woodruff (R) | 54,066 | 64.8 |
| William J. Kelly (D) | 29,108 | 34.9 |

| Candidates | Votes | % |
|---|---|---|
| 11 Fred Bradley (R) | 46,985 | 59.0 |
| Cecil W. Bailey (D) | 32,400 | 40.7 |
| 12 Frank E. Hook (D) | 41,481 | 50.6 |
| John B. Bennett (R) | 40,573 | 49.5 |
| 13 George D. O'Brien (D) | 80,565 | 57.9 |
| Clarence J. McLeod (R) | 58,101 | 41.8 |
| 14 Louis C. Rabaut (D) | 98,988 | 56.4 |
| Claude G. McDonald (R) | 76,358 | 43.5 |
| 15 John D. Dingell (D) | 100,879 | 63.7 |
| Harry Henderson (R) | 57,070 | 36.1 |
| 16 John Lesinski (D) | 95,483 | 61.4 |
| Albert A. Riddering (R) | 59,456 | 38.2 |
| 17 George A. Dondero (R) | 116,242 | 56.4 |
| John W. L. Hicks (D) | 87,767 | 42.6 |

## MINNESOTA

| | Votes | % |
|---|---|---|
| 1 August H. Andresen (R) | 77,798 | 61.7 |
| Andrew Meldahl (DFL) | 48,301 | 38.3 |
| 2 Joseph P. O'Hara (R) | 91,867 | 75.7 |
| L. J. Kilbride (DFL) | 29,548 | 24.3 |
| 3 William J. Gallagher (DFL) | 71,856 | 50.9 |
| Richard P. Gale (R) | 69,277 | 49.1 |
| 4 Frank T. Starkey (DFL) | 64,434 | 51.8 |
| Melvin J. Maas (R) | 59,994 | 48.2 |
| 5 Walter H. Judd (R) | 81,798 | 56.6 |
| Edgar T. Buckley (DFL) | 62,761 | 43.4 |
| 6 Harold Knutson (R) | 76,421 | 64.6 |
| Harry J. O'Brien (DFL) | 38,947 | 32.9 |
| 7 H. Carl Andersen (R) | 75,315 | 65.9 |
| Arthur F. Nellermoe (DFL) | 38,949 | 34.1 |
| 8 William A. Pittinger (R) | 62,600 | 51.9 |
| William McKinnon (DFL) | 58,131 | 48.2 |
| 9 Harold C. Hagen (R) | 58,080 | 59.2 |
| Halvor Langslet (DFL) | 40,018 | 40.7 |

## MISSISSIPPI

| | Votes | % |
|---|---|---|
| 1 John E. Rankin (D) | 17,793 | 96.9 |
| 2 Jamie L. Whitten (D) | 16,251 | 98.7 |
| 3 William M. Whittington (D) | 16,222 | 96.4 |
| 4 Thomas G. Abernethy (D) | 13,343 | 100.0 |
| 5 W. Arthur Winstead (D) | 22,924 | 100.0 |
| 6 William M. Colmer (D) | 31,742 | 95.7 |
| 7 Dan R. McGehee (D) | 29,594 | 92.8 |
| L. R. Collins (R) | 2,313 | 7.3 |

## MISSOURI

| | Votes | % |
|---|---|---|
| 1 Samuel W. Arnold (R) | 52,561 | 50.8 |
| Edward M. Jayne (D) | 50,910 | 49.2 |
| 2 Max Schwabe (R) | 60,857 | 50.1 |
| Lue C. Lozier (D) | 60,587 | 49.9 |
| 3 William C. Cole (R) | 61,720 | 50.6 |
| Maurice Hoffman (D) | 60,273 | 49.4 |
| 4 C. Jasper Bell (D) | 60,594 | 57.2 |
| John W. Mitchell (R) | 45,381 | 42.8 |
| 5 Roger C. Slaughter (D) | 53,320 | 52.6 |
| Ralph B. Innis (R) | 48,127 | 47.4 |
| 6 Marion T. Bennett (R) | 71,705 | 57.0 |
| George A. Clason (D) | 54,095 | 43.0 |
| 7 Dewey Short (R) | 76,180 | 64.0 |
| A. L. McCawley (D) | 42,929 | 36.0 |
| 8 Albert S. J. Carnahan (D) | 54,010 | 50.5 |
| William P. Elmer (R) | 52,924 | 49.5 |
| 9 Clarence Cannon (D) | 50,594 | 53.2 |
| William Barton (R) | 44,476 | 46.8 |
| 10 Orville Zimmerman (D) | 55,243 | 56.7 |
| Ralph Hutchison (R) | 42,129 | 43.3 |
| 11 John B. Sullivan (D) | 69,351 | 58.9 |
| Louis E. Miller (R) | 48,435 | 41.1 |
| 12 Walter C. Ploeser (R) | 118,394 | 51.8 |
| Phelim O'Toole (D) | 110,060 | 48.2 |
| 13 John J. Cochran (D) | 76,408 | 100.0 |

## MONTANA

| | Candidates | Votes | % |
|---|---|---|---|
| 1 | Mike Mansfield (D) | 57,008 | 67.9 |
| | M. S. Galasso (R) | 26,141 | 31.1 |
| 2 | James F. O'Connor (D) | 61,123 | 54.0 |
| | F. F. Haynes (R) | 51,372 | 45.4 |

## NEBRASKA

| | Candidates | Votes | % |
|---|---|---|---|
| 1 | Carl T. Curtis (R) | 100,816 | 69.9 |
| | Charles A. Chappell (D) | 43,341 | 30.1 |
| 2 | Howard Buffett (R) | 78,686 | 59.5 |
| | Mabel Gillespie (D) | 53,637 | 40.5 |
| 3 | Karl Stefan (R) | 84,251 | 68.4 |
| | George Hally (D) | 34,317 | 27.8 |
| 4 | Arthur L. Miller (R) | 72,647 | 63.1 |
| | Tom Lanigan (D) | 34,394 | 29.9 |
| | Willis B. Furman | 8,102 | 7.0 |

## NEVADA

| | Candidates | Votes | % |
|---|---|---|---|
| AL | Berkeley L. Bunker (D) | 32,648 | 63.1 |
| | Rex Bell (R) | 19,096 | 36.9 |

## NEW HAMPSHIRE

| | Candidates | Votes | % |
|---|---|---|---|
| 1 | Chester E. Merrow (R) | 57,537 | 50.9 |
| | Fortunat E. Normandin (D) | 55,492 | 49.1 |
| 2 | Sherman Adams (R) | 55,911 | 54.4 |
| | Harry Carlson (D) | 46,872 | 45.6 |

## NEW JERSEY

| | Candidates | Votes | % |
|---|---|---|---|
| 1 | Charles A. Wolverton (R) | 87,950 | 50.4 |
| | John F. Gorman (D) | 86,178 | 49.4 |
| 2 | T. Millet Hand (R) | 51,194 | 54.4 |
| | Edison Hedges (D) | 42,862 | 45.6 |
| 3 | James C. Auchincloss (R) | 80,438 | 57.0 |
| | Arnold E. Ascherfeld (D) | 60,769 | 43.0 |
| 4 | D. Lane Powers (R) | 68,647 | 55.6 |
| | Don Guinness (D) | 54,680 | 44.3 |
| 5 | Charles A. Eaton (R) | 87,129 | 58.4 |
| | Andrew D. Desmond (D) | 61,153 | 41.0 |
| 6 | Clifford P. Case (R) | 84,143 | 55.5 |
| | Walter H. Van Hoesen (D) | 65,344 | 43.1 |
| 7 | J. Parnell Thomas (R) | 86,759 | 66.0 |
| | James J. Cannon (D) | 44,423 | 33.8 |
| 8 | Gordon Canfield (R) | 75,479 | 58.5 |
| | Harry Smith (D) | 53,136 | 41.2 |
| 9 | Harry L. Towe (R) | 93,687 | 63.5 |
| | Elmer I. Zabriskie (D) | 53,847 | 36.5 |
| 10 | Fred A. Hartley Jr. (R) | 62,004 | 53.0 |
| | Luke A. Kiernan Jr. (D) | 53,577 | 45.8 |
| 11 | Frank L. Sundstrom (R) | 58,586 | 51.7 |
| | John J. Francis (D) | 52,376 | 46.3 |
| 12 | Robert W. Kean (R) | 67,680 | 50.6 |
| | John W. Suling (D) | 63,087 | 47.2 |
| 13 | Mary T. Norton (D) | 89,736 | 69.9 |
| | Frank J. V. Gimino (R) | 38,336 | 29.9 |
| 14 | Edward J. Hart (D) | 79,158 | 63.2 |
| | Otto Trankler (R) | 46,076 | 36.8 |

## NEW MEXICO

| | Candidates | Votes | % |
|---|---|---|---|
| AL | Clinton P. Anderson (D) | 85,244✔ | |
| | Antonio M. Fernandez (D) | 80,752✔ | |
| | Manuel Lujan (R) | 66,644 | |
| | Ben F. Meyer (R) | 66,309 | |

## NEW YORK

| | Candidates | Votes | % |
|---|---|---|---|
| 1 | Edgar A. Sharp (R) | 92,044 | 69.6 |
| | Edward Hudson (D, AM LAB) | 40,294 | 30.4 |
| 2 | Leonard W. Hall (R) | 131,906 | 67.9 |
| | John S. Thorp (D, AM LAB) | 62,242 | 32.1 |
| 3 | Henry J. Latham (R) | 108,118 | 60.6 |
| | George H. Bruns (D, AM LAB) | 70,163 | 39.4 |
| 4 | William B. Barry (D, AM LAB) | 73,098 | 52.8 |
| | Alfred J. Phillips (R) | 65,390 | 47.2 |
| 5 | James A. Roe (D, AM LAB) | 90,338 | 54.3 |
| | Raymond S. Richmond (R) | 76,014 | 45.7 |
| 6 | James J. Delaney (D, AM LAB) | 81,228 | 55.2 |
| | Otto Schuler (R) | 65,821 | 44.8 |
| 7 | John J. Delaney (D, AM LAB) | 73,868 | 63.4 |
| | Roy M. D. Richardson (R) | 42,716 | 36.6 |
| 8 | Joseph L. Pfeifer (D, AM LAB) | 55,565 | 59.5 |
| | Frank W. Porcaro (R) | 37,816 | 40.5 |
| 9 | Eugene J. Keogh (D, L) | 63,400 | 55.4 |
| | Harry Chiert (R) | 34,517 | 30.2 |
| | Jacob A. Salzman (AM LAB) | 16,521 | 14.4 |
| 10 | Andrew L. Somers (D, AM LAB) | 78,753 | 57.8 |
| | Philip Kahaner (R) | 36,854 | 27.0 |
| | Louis P. Goldberg (L) | 20,719 | 15.2 |
| 11 | James J. Heffernan (D, AM LAB) | 95,213 | 65.8 |
| | John Patrick Devery (R) | 49,442 | 34.2 |
| 12 | John J. Rooney (D, AM LAB) | 51,411 | 55.0 |
| | William G. Nolan (R) | 42,007 | 45.0 |
| 13 | Donald L. O'Toole (D, AM LAB) | 81,640 | 60.3 |
| | Clarence W. Archibald (R) | 53,854 | 39.8 |
| 14 | Leo F. Rayfiel (D, L) | 85,534 | 58.3 |
| | Bernard P. Levy (R) | 32,393 | 22.1 |
| | James V. King (AM LAB) | 28,766 | 19.6 |
| 15 | Emanuel Celler (D, AM LAB) | 105,943 | 81.1 |
| | Nathan J. Paulson (R) | 24,650 | 18.9 |
| 16 | Ellsworth B. Buck (R) | 55,647 | 53.5 |
| | Rae L. Egbert (D, AM LAB) | 48,411 | 46.5 |
| 17 | Joseph Clark Baldwin (R) | 77,196 | 52.4 |
| | Max Waterman (D) | 57,769 | 39.2 |
| | Seon Felshin (AM LAB) | 12,278 | 8.3 |
| 18 | Vito Marcantonio (D, R) | 82,316 | 100.0 |
| 19 | Samuel Dickstein (D, AM LAB) | 69,973 | 73.3 |
| | William I. Lehrfeld (R) | 25,494 | 26.7 |
| 20 | Sol Bloom (D, AM LAB) | 87,724 | 70.8 |
| | Lawrence S. Mayers (R) | 36,197 | 29.2 |
| 21 | James H. Torrens (D, AM LAB) | 91,747 | 69.3 |
| | Herbert Malkin (R) | 40,718 | 30.7 |
| 22 | Adam C. Powell Jr. (D, R) | 83,140 | 100.0 |
| 23 | Walter A. Lynch (D, AM LAB) | 126,245 | 79.5 |
| | William J. Waterman (R) | 32,594 | 20.5 |
| 24 | Benjamin J. Rabin (D, AM LAB) | 102,684 | 84.8 |
| | Morris Schaeffer (R) | 18,461 | 15.2 |
| 25 | Charles A. Buckley (D, AM LAB) | 114,248 | 62.1 |
| | Roderick Stephens (R) | 50,274 | 27.3 |
| | John A. Devany Jr (CST) | 19,561 | 10.6 |
| 26 | Peter A. Quinn (D, AM LAB) | 91,665 | 56.4 |
| | Samuel T. Shay (R) | 70,746 | 43.6 |
| 27 | Ralph W. Gwinn (R) | 90,699 | 61.9 |
| | Joseph E. Venuti (D, AM LAB) | 55,756 | 38.1 |
| 28 | Ralph A. Gamble (R) | 90,623 | 65.5 |
| | John H. Jackson (D, AM LAB) | 47,646 | 34.5 |
| 29 | Augustus W. Bennet (D, AM LAB) | 70,630 | 53.0 |
| | Hamilton Fish (R, JEFF) | 62,583 | 47.0 |
| 30 | Jay LeFevre (R) | 88,067 | 63.0 |
| | Sharon J. Mauhs (D, AM LAB) | 51,725 | 37.0 |
| 31 | Bernard W. Kearney (R) | 85,178 | 60.0 |
| | Alexander Grasso (D, AM LAB) | 56,706 | 40.0 |
| 32 | William T. Byrne (D, AM LAB) | 85,147 | 57.2 |
| | Miles A. McGrane Jr. (R) | 63,603 | 42.8 |
| 33 | Dean P. Taylor (R) | 95,299 | 62.6 |
| | Thomas P. McLoughlin (D) | 52,354 | 34.4 |
| 34 | Clarence E. Kilburn (R) | 75,532 | 62.9 |
| | John D. Van Kennen (D) | 44,557 | 37.1 |
| 35 | Hadwen C. Fuller (R) | 65,857 | 52.3 |
| | Samuel H. Miller Jr. (D, AM LAB) | 60,025 | 47.7 |
| 36 | Clarence E. Hancock (R) | 79,535 | 53.2 |
| | George M. Haight (D, AM LAB) | 70,012 | 46.8 |
| 37 | Edwin Arthur Hall (R) | 75,246 | 69.2 |
| | James S. Byrne (D, AM LAB) | 33,465 | 30.8 |
| 38 | John Taber (R) | 75,432 | 65.6 |
| | Frank J. Erwin (D) | 36,327 | 31.6 |
| 39 | W. Sterling Cole (R) | 75,740 | 68.1 |
| | Charlotte D. Curren (D) | 31,152 | 28.0 |
| 40 | George F. Rogers (D, AM LAB) | 90,369 | 50.4 |
| | Joseph J. O'Brien (R) | 88,782 | 49.6 |
| 41 | James W. Wadsworth (R) | 71,988 | 63.2 |
| | Jean Walrath (D, AM LAB) | 41,991 | 36.8 |
| 42 | Walter Gresham Andrews (R) | 83,781 | 57.2 |
| | William Haeseler Jr. (D, AM LAB) | 62,590 | 42.8 |
| 43 | Edward J. Elsaesser (R) | 74,366 | 51.1 |
| | Raymond J. Barnes (D, AM LAB) | 71,216 | 48.9 |
| 44 | John C. Butler (R) | 72,402 | 50.1 |
| | Leon A. Dombrowski (D, AM LAB) | 72,164 | 49.9 |
| 45 | Daniel A. Reed (R) | 64,456 | 64.1 |
| | Orrin H. Parker (D, AM LAB) | 36,050 | 35.9 |

## NORTH CAROLINA

| | Candidates | Votes | % |
|---|---|---|---|
| 1 | Herbert C. Bonner (D) | 30,149 | 90.6 |
| | R. Clarence Dozier (R) | 3,139 | 9.4 |
| 2 | John H. Kerr (D) | 34,949 | 95.9 |
| 3 | Graham A. Barden (D) | 30,447 | 71.6 |
| | H. B. Kornegay (R) | 12,055 | 28.4 |
| 4 | Harold D. Cooley (D) | 53,340 | 74.7 |
| | J. Ira Lee (R) | 18,046 | 25.3 |
| 5 | John H. Folger (D) | 42,982 | 66.5 |
| | John J. Ingle (R) | 21,669 | 33.5 |
| 6 | Carl T. Durham (D) | 50,003 | 73.3 |
| | Worth Henderson (R) | 18,195 | 26.7 |
| 7 | J. Bayard Clark (D) | 39,342 | 79.3 |
| | Josiah A. Maultsby (R) | 10,260 | 20.7 |
| 8 | William O. Burgin (D) | 48,244 | 59.8 |
| | B. C. Brock (R) | 32,450 | 40.2 |
| 9 | Robert L. Doughton (D) | 50,595 | 58.8 |
| | Emory C. McCall (R) | 35,506 | 41.2 |
| 10 | Joe W. Ervin (D) | 50,605 | 65.4 |
| | Loomis F. Klutz (R) | 26,757 | 34.6 |
| 11 | Alfred L. Bulwinkle (D) | 41,576 | 65.6 |
| | C. V. Moss (R) | 21,829 | 34.4 |
| 12 | Zebulon Weaver (D) | 52,042 | 64.2 |
| | Lewis P. Hamlin (R) | 28,965 | 35.8 |

## NORTH DAKOTA

| | Candidates | Votes | % |
|---|---|---|---|
| AL | William Lemke (R) | 101,007✔ | |
| | Charles R. Robertson (R) | 91,419✔ | |
| | Halvor L. Halvorson (D) | 56,699 | |
| | J. R. Kennedy (D) | 44,708 | |
| | Usher L. Burdick (IR) | 39,888 | |
| | George McClellan | 3,135 | |
| | A. C. Townley | 2,307 | |

## OHIO

| | Candidates | Votes | % |
|---|---|---|---|
| 1 | Charles H. Elston (R) | 82,373 | 56.8 |
| | Frank J. Richter (D) | 62,617 | 43.2 |
| 2 | William E. Hess (R) | 78,185 | 56.0 |
| | J. Harry Moore (D) | 61,473 | 44.0 |

## OHIO

| | Candidates | Votes | % |
|---|---|---|---|
| 3 | Edward J. Gardner (D) | 104,247 | 52.6 |
| | Harry P. Jeffrey (R) | 94,064 | 47.4 |
| 4 | Robert F. Jones (R) | 67,829 | 61.2 |
| | Earl Ludwig (D) | 42,983 | 38.8 |
| 5 | Cliff Clevenger (R) | 48,490 | 68.1 |
| | T. Walter Williams (D) | 22,740 | 31.9 |
| 6 | Edward O. McCowen (R) | 45,284 | 51.8 |
| | John W. Bush (D) | 42,167 | 48.2 |
| 7 | Clarence J. Brown (R) | 84,770 | 61.7 |
| | John L. Cashin (D) | 52,403 | 38.1 |
| 8 | Frederick C. Smith (R) | 51,253 | 59.8 |
| | Roy Warren Roof (D) | 34,494 | 40.2 |
| 9 | Homer A. Ramey (R) | 82,735 | 51.6 |
| | John F. Hunter (D) | 77,693 | 48.4 |
| 10 | Thomas A. Jenkins (R) | 43,388 | 64.4 |
| | Elsie Stanton (D) | 23,986 | 35.6 |
| 11 | Walter E. Brehm (R) | 38,263 | 53.6 |
| | Mell G. Underwood Jr. (D) | 33,098 | 46.4 |
| 12 | John M. Vorys (R) | 97,856 | 54.3 |
| | Forrest F. Smith (D) | 82,503 | 45.7 |
| 13 | Alvin F. Weichel (R) | 67,298 | 100.0 |
| 14 | Walter B. Huber (D) | 117,770 | 50.6 |
| | Ed Rowe (R) | 115,145 | 49.4 |
| 15 | P. W. Griffiths (R) | 47,710 | 60.0 |
| | Olney R. Gillogly (D) | 31,756 | 40.0 |
| 16 | William R. Thom (D) | 85,755 | 52.7 |
| | Henderson H. Carson (R) | 75,948 | 46.6 |
| 17 | J. Harry McGregor (R) | 73,206 | 62.9 |
| | Thomas A. Wilson (D) | 43,271 | 37.2 |
| 18 | Earl R. Lewis (R) | 65,847 | 51.1 |
| | Ross Michener (D) | 63,098 | 48.9 |
| 19 | Michael J. Kirwan (D) | 120,191 | 63.4 |
| | Herschel Hunt (R) | 69,403 | 36.6 |
| 20 | Michael A. Feighan (D) | 75,218 | 75.9 |
| | A. R. McNamara (R) | 23,945 | 24.2 |
| 21 | Robert Crosser (D) | 77,525 | 77.7 |
| | Harry C. Gahn (R) | 22,288 | 22.3 |
| 22 | Frances P. Bolton (R) | 185,187 | 57.4 |
| | Don O. Cameron (D) | 137,546 | 42.6 |
| AL | George H. Bender (R) | 1,542,422 | 53.1 |
| | William Glass (D) | 1,362,843 | 46.9 |

## OKLAHOMA

| | Candidates | Votes | % |
|---|---|---|---|
| 1 | George B. Schwabe (R) | 71,545 | 51.1 |
| | Dennis Bushyhead (D) | 68,561 | 48.9 |
| 2 | William G. Stigler (D) | 39,052 | 58.0 |
| | E. O. Clark (R) | 28,282 | 42.0 |
| 3 | Paul Stewart (D) | 51,135 | 76.2 |
| | Russell Overstreet (R) | 16,016 | 23.9 |
| 4 | Lyle H. Boren (D) | 47,733 | 61.7 |
| | Ralph R. Kirchner (R) | 29,582 | 38.3 |
| 5 | A. S. Mike Monroney (D) | 85,132 | 62.7 |
| | Howard B. Hopps (R) | 50,207 | 37.0 |
| 6 | Jed Johnson (D) | 41,987 | 60.0 |
| | Ted R. Fisher (R) | 27,979 | 40.0 |
| 7 | Victor Wickersham (D) | 35,895 | 70.8 |
| | J. Warren White (R) | 14,790 | 29.2 |
| 8 | Ross Rizley (R) | 43,878 | 57.6 |
| | Philip C. Ferguson (D) | 31,737 | 41.6 |

### Special Election

| | | Votes | % |
|---|---|---|---|
| 2 | William G. Stigler (D) | 22,036 | 54.4 |
| | Ralph R. Kirchner (R) | 18,502 | 45.6 |

## OREGON

| | Candidates | Votes | % |
|---|---|---|---|
| 1 | James W. Mott (R) | 80,106 | 66.7 |
| | O. Henry Oleen (D) | 39,928 | 33.3 |
| 2 | Lowell Stockman (R) | 43,145 | 65.7 |
| | C. J. Shorb (D) | 22,498 | 34.3 |
| 3 | Homer D. Angell (R) | 95,605 | 55.1 |
| | Lester Sheeley (D) | 77,814 | 44.9 |
| 4 | Harris Ellsworth (R) | 53,356 | 64.0 |
| | Floyd K. Dover (D) | 30,024 | 36.0 |

## PENNSYLVANIA

| | Candidates | Votes | % |
|---|---|---|---|
| 1 | William A. Barrett (D) | 73,289 | 58.4 |
| | James Gallagher (R) | 52,159 | 41.6 |
| 2 | William T. Granahan (D) | 97,351 | 62.7 |
| | Charles M. Mosser (R) | 57,849 | 37.3 |
| 3 | Michael J. Bradley (D) | 80,920 | 58.3 |
| | Joseph M. Pratt (R) | 57,856 | 41.7 |
| 4 | John Edward Sheridan (D) | 80,367 | 66.2 |
| | Franklin J. Maloney (R) | 41,018 | 33.8 |
| 5 | William J. Green Jr. (D) | 74,744 | 54.2 |
| | C. Frederick Pracht (R) | 63,085 | 45.8 |
| 6 | Herbert J. McGlinchey (D) | 78,123 | 50.7 |
| | Hugh Scott (R) | 75,794 | 49.2 |
| 7 | James Wolfenden (R) | 72,289 | 51.5 |
| | Vernon A. O'Rourke (D) | 68,161 | 48.5 |
| 8 | Charles J. Gerlach (R) | 59,497 | 58.0 |
| | Marie M. Bickert (D) | 43,073 | 42.0 |
| 9 | J. Roland Kinzer (R) | 71,129 | 61.3 |
| | H. Clay Burkholder (D) | 44,952 | 38.7 |
| 10 | John W. Murphy (D) | 59,047 | 56.4 |
| | Walter W. Kohler (R) | 45,593 | 43.6 |
| 11 | Daniel J. Flood (D) | 71,843 | 52.2 |
| | Thomas Byron Miller (R) | 65,922 | 47.9 |
| 12 | Ivor D. Fenton (R) | 65,960 | 56.8 |
| | Charles E. Klinger (D) | 50,153 | 43.2 |
| 13 | Daniel K. Hoch (D) | 43,233 | 54.1 |
| | Randolph Stauffer (R) | 33,240 | 41.6 |
| 14 | Wilson D. Gillette (R) | 51,333 | 65.0 |
| | Clement J. Reap (D) | 27,653 | 35.0 |
| 15 | Robert F. Rich (R) | 52,826 | 61.0 |
| | Richard F. Hartzell (D) | 33,750 | 39.0 |
| 16 | Samuel K. McConnell Jr. (R) | 79,555 | 63.7 |
| | Marvin B. Brunner (D) | 45,392 | 36.3 |
| 17 | Richard M. Simpson (R) | 45,198 | 64.5 |
| | John W. Mann (D, I) | 24,875 | 35.5 |
| 18 | John C. Kunkel (R) | 81,814 | 62.5 |
| | Howard K. Beard (D) | 49,080 | 37.5 |
| 19 | Leon H. Gavin (R) | 49,670 | 63.3 |
| | John C. Brecht (D) | 27,655 | 35.2 |
| 20 | Francis E. Walter (D) | 51,594 | 57.3 |
| | Charles A. P. Bartlett (R) | 38,460 | 42.7 |
| 21 | Chester H. Gross (R) | 55,984 | 52.6 |
| | Josiah W. Gitt (D) | 50,548 | 47.5 |
| 22 | D. Emmert Brumbaugh (R) | 50,000 | 57.8 |
| | Bernard J. D. Clark (D) | 36,476 | 42.2 |
| 23 | J. Buell Snyder (D) | 44,585 | 54.6 |
| | Carl H. Hoffman (R) | 37,062 | 45.4 |
| 24 | Thomas E. Morgan (D) | 52,500 | 62.2 |
| | Gilbert E. Koedel (R) | 31,940 | 37.8 |
| 25 | Louis E. Graham (R) | 61,544 | 50.4 |
| | Samuel G. Neff (D) | 60,473 | 49.6 |
| 26 | Harve Tibbott (R) | 58,743 | 52.6 |
| | Eddie McCloskey (D) | 52,994 | 47.4 |
| 27 | Augustine B. Kelley (D) | 61,263 | 59.7 |
| | Edward J. Howard (R) | 41,289 | 40.3 |
| 28 | Robert L. Rodgers (R) | 68,675 | 54.6 |
| | James F. Lavery (D) | 57,044 | 45.4 |
| 29 | Howard E. Campbell (R) | 63,086 | 50.2 |
| | John F. Lowers (D) | 62,592 | 49.8 |
| 30 | Robert J. Corbett (R) | 60,391 | 51.7 |
| | Thomas E. Scanlon (D) | 56,423 | 48.3 |
| 31 | James G. Fulton (R) | 71,222 | 53.8 |
| | James A. Wright (D) | 61,104 | 46.2 |
| 32 | Herman P. Eberharter (D) | 83,724 | 71.6 |
| | Gregory Zatkovich (R) | 33,221 | 28.4 |
| 33 | Samuel A. Weiss (D) | 75,796 | 69.3 |
| | Ray A. Liddle (R) | 33,651 | 30.8 |

## RHODE ISLAND

| | Candidates | Votes | % |
|---|---|---|---|
| 1 | Aime J. Forand (D) | 88,179 | 61.9 |
| | Charles A. Curran (R) | 54,233 | 38.1 |
| 2 | John E. Fogarty (D) | 87,189 | 57.8 |
| | Charles T. Algren (R) | 63,778 | 42.3 |

## SOUTH CAROLINA

| | Candidates | Votes | % |
|---|---|---|---|
| 1 | L. Mendel Rivers (D) | 15,326 | 92.8 |
| | O. H. Wilcox (R) | 1,190 | 7.2 |
| 2 | John J. Riley (D) | 19,342 | 98.0 |
| 3 | Butler B. Hare (D) | 13,105 | 97.0 |
| 4 | Joseph R. Bryson (D) | 20,988 | 95.7 |
| 5 | James P. Richards (D) | 14,435 | 98.1 |
| 6 | John L. McMillan (D) | 14,164 | 98.0 |

## SOUTH DAKOTA

| | Candidates | Votes | % |
|---|---|---|---|
| 1 | Karl E. Mundt (R) | 113,769 | 64.0 |
| | Grover Lothrop (D) | 63,981 | 36.0 |
| 2 | Francis H. Case (R) | 33,119 | 69.0 |
| | H. W. Clarkson (D) | 14,869 | 31.0 |

## TENNESSEE

| | Candidates | Votes | % |
|---|---|---|---|
| 1 | B. Carroll Reece (R) | 45,498 | 100.0 |
| 2 | John Jennings Jr. (R) | 45,416 | 55.5 |
| | Lowell Blanchard (D) | 36,441 | 44.5 |
| 3 | Estes Kefauver (D) | 32,497 | 67.8 |
| | Foster Johnson (R) | 11,541 | 24.1 |
| | Ernest W. Forstner (I) | 3,894 | 8.1 |
| 4 | Albert Gore (D) | 20,684 | 65.1 |
| | E. M. Shelley (R) | 9,642 | 30.4 |
| 5 | Harold H. Earthman (D) | 27,087 | 85.5 |
| | W. H. Crowell (R) | 4,598 | 14.5 |
| 6 | J. Percy Priest (D) | 28,752 | 97.0 |
| 7 | Wirt Courtney (D) | 22,592 | 100.0 |
| 8 | Thomas J. Murray (D) | 19,822 | 63.3 |
| | A. Bradley Frazier (R) | 11,509 | 36.7 |
| 9 | Jere Cooper (D) | 25,250 | 87.8 |
| | Homer Tatum (R) | 3,510 | 12.2 |
| 10 | Clifford Davis (D) | 47,569 | 100.0 |

## TEXAS

| | Candidates | Votes | % |
|---|---|---|---|
| 1 | Wright Patman (D) | 39,404 | 100.0 |
| 2 | Jesse M. Combs (D) | 54,258 | 94.0 |
| | Lanar Cecil (R) | 3,442 | 6.0 |
| 3 | Lindley Beckworth (D) | 36,954 | 93.3 |
| | O. P. Stephens (R) | 2,668 | 6.7 |
| 4 | Sam Rayburn (D) | 40,039 | 100.0 |
| 5 | Hatton W. Sumners (D) | 62,459 | 71.4 |
| | C. D. Turner (R) | 25,027 | 28.6 |
| 6 | Luther A. Johnson (D) | 36,884 | 100.0 |
| 7 | Tom Pickett (D) | 32,850 | 96.1 |
| 8 | Albert Thomas (D) | 90,963 | 92.3 |
| | L. B. Robinson (R) | 7,555 | 7.7 |
| 9 | Joseph J. Mansfield (D) | 56,194 | 93.4 |
| | Lewis Allen (R) | 3,967 | 6.6 |
| 10 | Lyndon B. Johnson (D) | 44,602 | 92.9 |
| | A. H. Bartelt (R) | 3,423 | 7.1 |
| 11 | W. R. Poage (D) | 39,866 | 95.3 |
| 12 | Fritz Lanham (D) | 59,119 | 100.0 |
| 13 | Ed Gossett (D) | 53,503 | 95.4 |
| 14 | John E. Lyle (D) | 53,756 | 100.0 |
| 15 | Milton H. West (D) | 35,862 | 100.0 |
| 16 | R. Ewing Thomason (D) | 31,658 | 100.0 |
| 17 | Sam Russell (D) | 43,785 | 96.8 |
| 18 | Eugene Worley (D) | 47,588 | 93.3 |
| | M. C. P. Bybee (R) | 3,435 | 6.7 |
| 19 | George H. Mahon (D) | 53,326 | 100.0 |
| 20 | Paul J. Kilday (D) | 39,394 | 100.0 |
| 21 | O. Clark Fisher (D) | 47,796 | 88.1 |
| | M. J. Lehman (R) | 6,474 | 11.9 |

## UTAH

| | Candidates | Votes | % |
|---|---|---|---|
| 1 | Walter K. Granger (D) | 59,755 | 57.8 |
| | B. H. Stringham (R) | 43,642 | 42.2 |
| 2 | J. Will Robinson (D) | 89,844 | 62.3 |
| | Quayle Cannon Jr. (R) | 54,440 | 37.7 |

## VERMONT

| | Candidates | Votes | % |
|---|---|---|---|
| AL | Charles A. Plumley (R) | 76,800 | 62.4 |
| | Robert W. Ready (D) | 46,230 | 37.6 |

## VIRGINIA

| | Candidates | Votes | % |
|---|---|---|---|
| 1 | S. Otis Bland (D) | 23,284 | 81.2 |
| | Walter Johnson (R) | 5,391 | 18.8 |

## VIRGINIA

| | Candidates | Votes | % |
|---|---|---|---|
| 2 | Ralph H. Daughton (D) | 21,268 | 57.7 |
| | Thomas L. Woodward (R) | 9,304 | 25.2 |
| | W. B. Shafer Jr. (I) | 6,302 | 17.1 |
| 3 | David E. Satterfield Jr. (D) | 32,918 | 100.0 |
| 4 | Patrick Henry Drewry (D) | 15,724 | 100.0 |
| 5 | Thomas G. Burch (D) | 24,781 | 84.6 |
| | Howard H. Carwile (I) | 4,509 | 15.4 |
| 6 | Clifton A. Woodrum (D) | 30,844 | 68.7 |
| | John Strickler (R) | 13,798 | 30.8 |
| 7 | A. Willis Robertson (D) | 24,967 | 59.9 |
| | D. Wampler Earman (R) | 16,738 | 40.1 |
| 8 | Howard W. Smith (D) | 31,618 | 60.1 |
| | Elizabeth Chilton Murray (ID) | 11,019 | 21.0 |
| | Lawrence Michael (IR) | 9,019 | 17.2 |
| 9 | John W. Flannagan Jr. (D) | 33,943 | 56.3 |
| | Ralph L. Lincoln (R) | 26,373 | 43.7 |

## WASHINGTON

| | Candidates | Votes | % |
|---|---|---|---|
| 1 | Hugh De Lacy (D) | 118,354 | 53.1 |
| | Robert H. Harlin (R) | 103,099 | 46.2 |
| 2 | Henry M. Jackson (D) | 74,676 | 60.4 |
| | Payson Peterson (R) | 48,974 | 39.6 |
| 3 | Charles Savage (D) | 57,942 | 52.0 |
| | Fred Norman (R) | 53,503 | 48.0 |

| | Candidates | Votes | % |
|---|---|---|---|
| 4 | Hal Holmes (R) | 56,211 | 60.2 |
| | Al McCoy (D) | 37,150 | 39.8 |
| 5 | Walt Horan (R) | 62,648 | 52.3 |
| | Edward J. Reilly (D) | 57,235 | 47.7 |
| 6 | John M. Coffee (D) | 80,679 | 61.2 |
| | Thor C. Tollefson (R) | 51,119 | 38.8 |

## WEST VIRGINIA

| | Candidates | Votes | % |
|---|---|---|---|
| 1 | Matthew M. Neely (D) | 58,313 | 50.4 |
| | A. C. Schiffler (R) | 57,363 | 49.6 |
| 2 | Jennings Randolph (D) | 58,695 | 54.1 |
| | Melvin C. Muntzing (R) | 49,722 | 45.9 |
| 3 | Cleveland M. Bailey (D) | 57,912 | 52.5 |
| | Edward G. Rohrbough (R) | 52,457 | 47.5 |
| 4 | Hubert S. Ellis (R) | 68,204 | 51.2 |
| | E. B. Pennybacker (D) | 64,986 | 48.8 |
| 5 | John Kee (D) | 65,463 | 61.7 |
| | Hartley Sanders (R) | 40,568 | 38.3 |
| 6 | E. H. Hedrick (D) | 84,369 | 58.3 |
| | J. W. Maxwell (R) | 60,457 | 41.7 |

## WISCONSIN

| | Candidates | Votes | % |
|---|---|---|---|
| 1 | Lawrence H. Smith (R) | 74,223 | 74.8 |
| | John K. Kyle (PROG) | 24,013 | 24.2 |

| | Candidates | Votes | % |
|---|---|---|---|
| 2 | Robert K. Henry (R) | 74,937 | 56.8 |
| | John W. Nash (D) | 34,145 | 25.9 |
| | Herbert C. Schenk (PROG) | 22,095 | 16.7 |
| 3 | William H. Stevenson (R) | 74,092 | 69.9 |
| | William D. Carroll (D) | 26,978 | 25.4 |
| 4 | Thaddeus F.B. Wasielewski (D) | 103,583 | 63.5 |
| | Robert Blackwood (R) | 55,375 | 34.0 |
| 5 | Andrew J. Biemiller (D) | 88,606 | 50.8 |
| | Lewis D. Thill (R) | 78,834 | 45.2 |
| 6 | Frank B. Keefe (R) | 74,487 | 66.5 |
| | Henry Danes (D) | 36,180 | 32.3 |
| 7 | Reid F. Murray (R) | 73,531 | 69.3 |
| | William H. Ludwig (D) | 31,991 | 30.1 |
| 8 | John W. Byrnes (R) | 64,623# | 51.1 |
| | La Vern R. Dilweg (R) | 57,458# | 45.5 |
| 9 | Merlin Hull (PROG) | 48,064 | 98.5 |
| 10 | Alvin E. O'Konski (R) | 54,731 | 57.8 |
| | Elizabeth Hawkes (D) | 29,773 | 31.4 |
| | Harry P. Van Guilder (PROG) | 9,567 | 10.1 |

## WYOMING

| | Candidates | Votes | % |
|---|---|---|---|
| AL | Frank A. Barrett (R) | 53,533 | 55.7 |
| | Charles E. Norris (D) | 42,569 | 44.3 |

# 1945 House Elections

## ILLINOIS

### Special Election

| | Candidates | Votes | % |
|---|---|---|---|
| 24 | Roy Clippinger (R) | 5,617 | 98.9 |

## MONTANA

### Special Election

| | Candidates | Votes | % |
|---|---|---|---|
| 2 | Wesley A. D'Ewart (R) | 26,158 | 50.4 |
| | Leo C. Graybill (D) | 22,126 | 42.6 |
| | Robert Yellowtail (I) | 3,417 | 6.6 |

# 1946 House Elections

## ALABAMA

| | Candidates | Votes | % |
|---|---|---|---|
| 1 | Frank W. Boykin (D) | 12,448 | 100.0 |
| 2 | George M. Grant (D) | 17,711 | 100.0 |
| 3 | George W. Andrews (D) | 13,397 | 100.0 |
| 4 | Sam Hobbs (D) | 16,299 | 88.1 |
| | Roger S. Bingham (R) | 2,207 | 11.9 |
| 5 | Albert Rains (D) | 21,560 | 100.0 |
| 6 | Pete Jarman (D) | 13,551 | 100.0 |
| 7 | Carter Manasco (D) | 22,853 | 72.7 |
| | M. H. Woodward (R) | 8,565 | 27.3 |
| 8 | John J. Sparkman (D) | 17,624* | 92.4 |
| | Arthur South (R) | 1,453 | 7.6 |
| 9 | Laurie C. Battle (D) | 29,940 | 94.1 |
| | J. G. Bass (R) | 1,880 | 5.9 |

## ARIZONA

| | | Votes | % |
|---|---|---|---|
| AL | John R. Murdock (D) | 74,948✔ | |
| | Richard F. Harless (D) | 71,836✔ | |
| | Denver C. Henson (R) | 37,033 | |
| | John H. Curnutte (R) | 36,185 | |
| | Karl M. Wilson (COM) | 831 | |

## ARKANSAS

| | | Votes | % |
|---|---|---|---|
| 1 | Ezekiel C. Gathings (D) | 20,250 | 100.0 |
| 2 | Wilbur D. Mills (D) | 22,955 | 100.0 |
| 3 | James W. Trimble (D) | 24,950 | 100.0 |
| 4 | Fadjo Cravens (D) | 13,844 | 100.0 |
| 5 | Brooks Hays (D) | 21,777 | 85.2 |
| | James R. Harris (R) | 2,881 | 11.3 |
| 6 | William F. Norrell (D) | 23,892 | 84.7 |
| | M. O. Evans (I) | 4,305 | 15.3 |
| 7 | Oren Harris (D) | 15,584 | 100.0 |

## CALIFORNIA

| | | Votes | % |
|---|---|---|---|
| 1 | Clarence F. Lea (D-R) | 77,653 | 99.8 |
| 2 | Clair Engle (D-R) | 57,895 | 100.0 |
| 3 | Leroy Johnson (R-D) | 116,792 | 100.0 |
| 4 | Franck R. Havenner (D) | 60,655 | 52.9 |
| | Truman R. Young (R) | 54,113 | 47.2 |
| 5 | Richard J. Welch (R-D) | 94,293 | 100.0 |
| 6 | George P. Miller (D-R) | 118,548 | 99.9 |
| 7 | John J. Allen Jr. (R) | 61,508 | 56.2 |
| | Patrick W. McDonough (D) | 47,988 | 43.8 |
| 8 | John Z. Anderson (R-D) | 113,325 | 99.9 |
| 9 | Bertrand W. Gearhart (R) | 50,171 | 53.7 |
| | Hubert Phillips (D) | 43,244 | 46.3 |
| 10 | Alfred J. Elliott (D-R) | 51,843 | 99.8 |
| 11 | Ernest K. Bramblett (R) | 41,902 | 53.1 |
| | George E. Outland (D) | 36,996 | 46.9 |
| 12 | Richard M. Nixon (R) | 65,586 | 56.0 |
| | H. Jerry Voorhis (D) | 49,994 | 42.7 |
| 13 | Norris Poulson (R) | 48,071 | 51.8 |
| | Ned R. Healy (D) | 44,712 | 48.2 |
| 14 | Helen Gahagan Douglas (D) | 53,536 | 54.3 |
| | Frederick M. Roberts (R) | 44,914 | 45.6 |
| 15 | Gordon L. McDonough (R-D) | 106,020 | 99.4 |
| 16 | Donald L. Jackson (R) | 78,264 | 53.9 |
| | Harold Harby (D) | 45,951 | 31.6 |
| | Ellis E. Patterson | 20,945 | 14.4 |
| 17 | Cecil R. King (D-R) | 110,654 | 99.4 |
| 18 | Willis W. Bradley (R) | 67,363 | 52.8 |
| | Clyde Doyle (D) | 60,218 | 47.2 |
| 19 | Chet Holifield (D-R) | 50,666 | 97.2 |
| 20 | Carl Hinshaw (R) | 98,283 | 59.3 |
| | Everett G. Burkhalter (D) | 67,317 | 40.6 |
| 21 | Harry R. Sheppard (D) | 37,229 | 52.7 |
| | Lowell E. Lathrop (R) | 33,395 | 47.3 |
| 22 | John Phillips (R) | 59,935 | 62.1 |
| | Ray Adkinson (D) | 36,649 | 37.9 |
| 23 | Charles K. Fletcher (R) | 69,411 | 56.3 |
| | Ed V. Izac (D) | 53,898 | 43.7 |

## COLORADO

| | Candidates | Votes | % |
|---|---|---|---|
| 1 | John A. Carroll (D) | 60,513 | 51.8 |
| | Dean M. Gillespie (R) | 55,724 | 47.7 |
| 2 | William S. Hill (R) | 54,768 | 65.7 |
| | Frank A. Safranek (D) | 27,393 | 32.9 |
| 3 | J. Edgar Chenoweth (R) | 45,043 | 54.6 |
| | Walter W. Johnson (D) | 37,496 | 45.4 |
| 4 | Robert F. Rockwell (R) | 28,894 | 58.8 |
| | Thomas Matthews (D) | 20,290 | 41.3 |

## CONNECTICUT

| | | Votes | % |
|---|---|---|---|
| 1 | William J. Miller (R) | 93,006 | 53.1 |
| | Herman P. Kopplemann (D) | 82,231 | 46.9 |
| 2 | Horace Seely-Brown Jr. (R) | 59,828 | 55.3 |
| | Chase Going Woodhouse (D) | 48,376 | 44.7 |
| 3 | Ellsworth B. Foote (R) | 76,408 | 58.9 |
| | James P. Geelan (D) | 53,404 | 41.1 |
| 4 | John Davis Lodge (R) | 93,513 | 57.1 |
| | Henry A. Mucci (D) | 57,913 | 35.4 |
| | Stanley W. Mayhew (SOC) | 9,427 | 5.8 |
| 5 | James T. Patterson (R) | 51,790 | 53.1 |
| | Thomas Radzevich (D) | 39,785 | 40.8 |
| | John C. Cluney (SOC, CLUNEY) | 5,984 | 6.1 |
| AL | Antoni N. Sadlak (R) | 377,972 | 55.6 |
| | Joseph F. Ryter (D) | 277,872 | 40.9 |

## DELAWARE

| | | Votes | % |
|---|---|---|---|
| AL | J. Caleb Boggs (R) | 63,516 | 56.4 |
| | Philip A. Traynor (D) | 49,105 | 43.6 |

## FLORIDA

| | | Votes | % |
|---|---|---|---|
| 1 | J. Hardin Peterson (D) | 31,145 | 100.0 |
| 2 | Emory H. Price (D) | 26,093 | 100.0 |
| 3 | Robert L. F. Sikes (D) | 18,455 | 100.0 |
| 4 | George A. Smathers (D) | 37,002 | 71.9 |
| | Norman N. Curtis (R) | 14,458 | 28.1 |
| 5 | Joe Hendricks (D) | 24,695 | 61.3 |
| | M. J. Moss Jr. (R) | 15,591 | 38.7 |
| 6 | Dwight L. Rogers (D) | 13,733 | 71.1 |
| | Joseph P. Moe (R) | 5,591 | 28.9 |

## GEORGIA

| | | Votes | % |
|---|---|---|---|
| 1 | Prince H. Preston (D) | 20,937 | 99.8 |
| 2 | E. E. Cox (D) | 10,805 | 100.0 |
| 3 | Stephen Pace (D) | 8,961 | 100.0 |
| 4 | A. Sidney Camp (D) | 8,476 | 100.0 |
| 5 | James C. Davis (D) | 31,444 | 61.6 |
| | Helen Douglas Mankin (I) | 19,527# | 38.3 |
| 6 | Carl Vinson (D) | 13,566 | 100.0 |
| 7 | Henderson Lanham (D) | 7,573 | 100.0 |
| 8 | W. M. Wheeler (D) | 8,986 | 100.0 |
| 9 | John Wood (D) | 14,815 | 100.0 |
| 10 | Paul Brown (D) | 16,398 | 100.0 |

### Special Election

| | | Votes | % |
|---|---|---|---|
| 5 | Helen Douglas Mankin (D) | 11,067 | 36.5 |
| | Thomas L. Camp | 10,275 | 33.9 |
| | Ben T. Huiet | 2,724 | 9.0 |
| | J. E. B. Stewart | 2,363 | 7.8 |

## IDAHO

| | | Votes | % |
|---|---|---|---|
| 1 | Abe McGregor Goff (R) | 37,326 | 50.6 |
| | Compton I. White (D) | 36,509 | 49.5 |
| 2 | John Sanborn (R) | 63,692 | 60.7 |
| | Pete Leguineche (D) | 41,231 | 39.3 |

## ILLINOIS

| | Candidates | Votes | % |
|---|---|---|---|
| 1 | William L. Dawson (D) | 38,040 | 56.8 |
| | William E. King (R) | 28,945 | 43.2 |
| 2 | Richard B. Vail (R) | 156,697 | 51.3 |
| | William A. Rowan (D) | 148,995 | 48.7 |
| 3 | Fred E. Busbey (R) | 169,543 | 57.2 |
| | Edward A. Kelly (D) | 126,638 | 42.8 |
| 4 | Martin Gorski (D) | 68,113 | 70.7 |
| | John T. Parsons (R) | 28,251 | 29.3 |
| 5 | Adolph J. Sabath (D) | 34,904 | 71.6 |
| | Michael A. Francisco (R) | 13,859 | 28.4 |
| 6 | Thomas J. O'Brien (D) | 171,778 | 52.0 |
| | Harold C. Woodward (R) | 158,702 | 48.0 |
| 7 | Thomas L. Owens (R) | 252,981 | 55.0 |
| | William W. Link (D) | 206,963 | 45.0 |
| 8 | Thomas S. Gordon (D) | 38,317 | 77.3 |
| | Scott John Vitell (R) | 11,266 | 22.7 |
| 9 | Robert J. Twyman (R) | 54,615 | 51.3 |
| | Alexander J. Resa (D) | 51,788 | 48.7 |
| 10 | Ralph E. Church (R) | 201,010 | 64.7 |
| | Harold H. Kolbe (D) | 109,712 | 35.3 |
| 11 | Chauncey W. Reed (R) | 120,640 | 74.9 |
| | Louis William Oswald (D) | 40,355 | 25.1 |
| 12 | Noah M. Mason (R) | 73,431 | 69.1 |
| | Richard G. Myrland (D) | 32,816 | 30.9 |
| 13 | Leo E. Allen (R) | 48,238 | 77.8 |
| | Michael M. Kinney (D) | 13,767 | 22.2 |
| 14 | Anton J. Johnson (R) | 45,723 | 62.1 |
| | Carl E. Wright Jr. (D) | 27,877 | 37.9 |
| 15 | Robert B. Chiperfield (R) | 49,895 | 64.3 |
| | Henry D. Sullivan (D) | 27,667 | 35.7 |
| 16 | Everett M. Dirksen (R) | 64,534 | 67.5 |
| | Hans A. Spading (D) | 31,091 | 32.5 |
| 17 | Leslie C. Arends (R) | 45,969 | 71.2 |
| | Carl Vrooman (D) | 18,617 | 28.8 |
| 18 | Edward H. Jenison (R) | 56,537 | 65.1 |
| | C. E. Spang (D) | 30,305 | 34.9 |
| 19 | Rolla C. McMillen (R) | 64,063 | 62.5 |
| | Olive Remington Goldman (D) | 38,485 | 37.5 |
| 20 | Sidney E. Simpson (R) | 34,923 | 58.8 |
| | Don Irving (D) | 24,508 | 41.2 |
| 21 | Evan Howell (R) | 55,609 | 55.1 |
| | Roscoe Bonjean (D) | 45,293 | 44.9 |
| 22 | Melvin Price (D) | 69,669 | 50.7 |
| | Calvin D. Johnson (R) | 67,665 | 49.3 |
| 23 | Charles W. Vursell (R) | 51,440 | 54.9 |
| | Homer Kasserman (D) | 42,237 | 45.1 |
| 24 | Roy Clippinger (R) | 37,909 | 58.9 |
| | Edward Hines (D) | 26,483 | 41.1 |
| 25 | C. W. Bishop (R) | 53,831 | 59.8 |
| | Sherman S. Carr (D) | 36,217 | 40.2 |
| AL | William G. Stratton (R) | 1,906,717 | 55.1 |
| | Emily Taft Douglas (D) | 1,539,248 | 44.5 |

## INDIANA

| | | Votes | % |
|---|---|---|---|
| 1 | Ray J. Madden (D) | 51,809 | 51.9 |
| | Charles W. Gannon (R) | 46,677 | 46.8 |
| 2 | Charles A. Halleck (R) | 66,423 | 61.3 |
| | Margaret A. Afflis (D) | 40,847 | 37.7 |
| 3 | Robert A. Grant (R) | 73,239 | 55.6 |
| | John S. Gonas (D) | 57,425 | 43.6 |
| 4 | George W. Gillie (R) | 59,790 | 59.4 |
| | Walter E. Frederick (D) | 39,766 | 39.5 |
| 5 | Forest A. Harness (R) | 79,752 | 55.0 |
| | William W. Welsh (D) | 61,364 | 42.3 |
| 6 | Noble J. Johnson (R) | 65,926 | 57.4 |
| | Thomas A. Sigler (D) | 47,972 | 41.7 |
| 7 | Gerald W. Landis (R) | 63,667 | 50.7 |
| | James E. Noland (D) | 59,908 | 47.7 |
| 8 | Edward A. Mitchell (R) | 66,050 | 51.8 |
| | Winfield K. Denton (D) | 60,385 | 47.3 |
| 9 | Earl Wilson (R) | 58,384 | 55.8 |
| | Oliver O. Dixon (D) | 45,316 | 43.3 |

## INDIANA

| Candidates | Votes | % |
|---|---|---|
| 10 Raymond S. Springer (R) | 70,969 | 59.3 |
| Frank C. Unger (D) | 44,807 | 37.4 |
| 11 Louis Ludlow (D) | 79,040 | 51.1 |
| Albert J. Beveridge (R) | 74,745 | 48.3 |

## IOWA

| Candidates | Votes | % |
|---|---|---|
| 1 Thomas E. Martin (R) | 52,488 | 61.5 |
| Clair A. Williams (D) | 32,849 | 38.5 |
| 2 Henry O. Talle (R) | 60,111 | 59.1 |
| Richard V. Bernhart (D) | 41,544 | 40.9 |
| 3 John W. Gwynne (R) | 48,346 | 62.0 |
| Dan J. P. Ryan (D) | 29,661 | 38.0 |
| 4 Karl M. LeCompte (R) | 43,753 | 58.4 |
| A. E. Augustine (D) | 31,203 | 41.6 |
| 5 Paul Cunningham (R) | 41,679 | 59.4 |
| Vince L. Browner (D) | 28,490 | 40.6 |
| 6 James I. Dolliver (R) | 40,595 | 63.4 |
| Oscar E. Johnson (D) | 23,422 | 36.6 |
| 7 Ben F. Jensen (R) | 40,152 | 63.0 |
| Philip A. Allen (D) | 23,567 | 37.0 |
| 8 Charles B. Hoeven (R) | 37,868 | 68.6 |
| George A. Heikens (D) | 17,303 | 31.4 |

## KANSAS

| Candidates | Votes | % |
|---|---|---|
| 1 Albert M. Cole (R) | 63,076 | 64.3 |
| James W. Lowry (D) | 35,045 | 35.7 |
| 2 Errett P. Scrivner (R) | 56,363 | 58.8 |
| Murray H. Hodges (D) | 39,484 | 41.2 |
| 3 Herbert A. Meyer (R) | 41,624 | 55.4 |
| Jo E. Gaitskill (D) | 33,578 | 44.7 |
| 4 Edward H. Rees (R) | 68,658 | 56.2 |
| William P. Warren (D) | 53,617 | 43.9 |
| 5 Clifford R. Hope (R) | 54,578 | 62.7 |
| Arthur L. Sparks (D) | 32,538 | 37.4 |
| 6 Wint Smith (R) | 44,343 | 58.1 |
| G. E. Bengtson (D) | 28,911 | 37.9 |

## KENTUCKY

| Candidates | Votes | % |
|---|---|---|
| 1 Noble J. Gregory (D) | 32,121 | 66.2 |
| William E. Porter (R) | 16,064 | 33.1 |
| 2 Earle C. Clements (D) | 38,020 | 56.6 |
| Thomas W. Hines (R) | 29,124 | 43.4 |
| 3 Thruston B. Morton (R) | 61,899 | 58.1 |
| Emmet O'Neal (D) | 44,599 | 41.9 |
| 4 Frank L. Chelf (D) | 33,116 | 53.1 |
| Don Victor Drye Sr. (R) | 29,304 | 47.0 |
| 5 Brent Spence (D) | 26,444 | 51.2 |
| Marion W. Moore (R) | 25,240 | 48.8 |
| 6 Virgil Chapman (D) | 43,176 | 55.0 |
| W. D. Rogers (R) | 35,368 | 45.0 |
| 7 W. Howes Meade (D) | 30,070 | 59.4 |
| A. J. May (D) | 20,596 | 40.7 |
| 8 Joe B. Bates (D) | 33,408 | 52.6 |
| Ray Schmauch (R) | 30,127 | 47.4 |
| 9 John M. Robsion (R) | 54,306 | 100.0 |

## LOUISIANA

| Candidates | Votes | % |
|---|---|---|
| 1 F. Edward Hebert (D) | 29,329 | 91.8 |
| Dennison Suarez (R) | 2,614 | 8.2 |
| 2 Hale Boggs (D) | 29,457 | 90.7 |
| Harold M. Herbst (R) | 3,037 | 9.4 |
| 3 James Domengeaux (D) | 4,595 | 100.0 |
| 4 Overton Brooks (D) | 8,499 | 100.0 |
| 5 Otto E. Passman (D) | 6,049 | 100.0 |
| 6 James H. Morrison (D) | 8,781 | 100.0 |
| 7 Henry D. Larcade Jr. (D) | 5,907 | 100.0 |
| 8 A. Leonard Allen (D) | 7,740 | 100.0 |

## MAINE

| Candidates | Votes | % |
|---|---|---|
| 1 Robert Hale (R) | 38,975 | 59.6 |
| John C. Fitzgerald (D) | 26,378 | 40.4 |
| 2 Margaret Chase Smith (R) | 39,791 | 60.7 |
| Edward J. Beauchamp (D) | 25,739 | 39.3 |
| 3 Frank Fellows (R) | 31,622 | 72.9 |
| John M. Coghill (D) | 11,743 | 27.1 |

## MARYLAND

| Candidates | Votes | % |
|---|---|---|
| 1 Edward T. Miller (R) | 27,364 | 50.9 |
| Dudley George Roe (D) | 26,360 | 49.1 |
| 2 Hugh A. Meade (D) | 69,211 | 52.4 |
| David G. Harry (R) | 62,760 | 47.6 |
| 3 Thomas D'Alesandro Jr. (D) | 24,347 | 63.9 |
| Edward N. Kowzan (R) | 13,761 | 36.1 |
| 4 George H. Fallon (D) | 31,453 | 57.2 |
| Paul Robertson (R) | 23,499 | 42.8 |
| 5 Lansdale G. Sasscer (D) | 40,929 | 58.2 |
| Edwin A. Glenn (R) | 29,406 | 41.8 |
| 6 J. Glenn Beall (R) | 55,667 | 58.1 |
| Arch McDonald (D) | 40,198 | 41.9 |

## MASSACHUSETTS

| Candidates | Votes | % |
|---|---|---|
| 1 John W. Heselton (R) | 59,222 | 58.0 |
| John J. Falvey (D) | 40,549 | 39.7 |
| 2 Charles R. Clason (R) | 59,754 | 51.4 |
| Foster Furcolo (D) | 56,459 | 48.6 |
| 3 Philip J. Philbin (D) | 69,038 | 62.2 |
| Carroll H. Balcom (R) | 42,033 | 37.8 |
| 4 Harold D. Donohue (D) | 59,847 | 49.5 |
| Pehr G. Holmes (R) | 58,663 | 48.5 |
| 5 Edith Nourse Rogers (R) | 98,488 | 71.6 |
| Oliver S. Allen (D) | 38,575 | 28.0 |
| 6 George J. Bates (R) | 79,709 | 70.2 |
| Richard B. O'Keefe (D) | 33,823 | 29.8 |
| 7 Thomas J. Lane (D) | 59,871 | 60.8 |
| Ernest Bentley (R) | 37,250 | 37.8 |
| 8 Angier L. Goodwin (R) | 76,305 | 63.5 |
| Anthony M. Roche (D) | 43,827 | 36.5 |
| 9 Charles L. Gifford (R) | 69,831 | 60.8 |
| William McAuliffe (D) | 43,367 | 37.8 |
| 10 Christian A. Herter (R) | 96,607 | 64.0 |
| Paul J. McCarty (D) | 54,421 | 36.0 |
| 11 John F. Kennedy (D) | 69,093 | 71.9 |
| Lester W. Bowen (R) | 26,007 | 27.1 |
| 12 John W. McCormack (D) | 92,622 | 100.0 |
| 13 Richard B. Wigglesworth (R) | 87,839 | 67.5 |
| James J. Goode Jr. (D) | 42,274 | 32.5 |
| 14 Joseph W. Martin Jr. (R) | 71,566 | 63.6 |
| Martha Sharp (D) | 40,999 | 36.4 |

## MICHIGAN

| Candidates | Votes | % |
|---|---|---|
| 1 George G. Sadowski (D) | 57,753 | 65.9 |
| John B. Sosnowski (R) | 29,293 | 33.4 |
| 2 Earl C. Michener (R) | 66,486 | 71.2 |
| William R. Kelley (D) | 26,141 | 28.0 |
| 3 Paul W. Shafer (R) | 59,823 | 68.9 |
| Herschel W. Carney (D) | 25,914 | 29.9 |
| 4 Clare E. Hoffman (R) | 58,798 | 72.5 |
| Harvey Hope Jarvis (D) | 21,514 | 26.5 |
| 5 Bartel J. Jonkman (R) | 63,093 | 71.6 |
| Earle W. Reynolds (D) | 25,022 | 28.4 |
| 6 William W. Blackney (R) | 69,203 | 57.3 |
| Arthur Elliott (D) | 50,684 | 42.0 |
| 7 Jesse P. Wolcott (R) | 64,404 | 74.2 |
| Earl J. Tallman (D) | 21,708 | 25.0 |
| 8 Fred L. Crawford (R) | 58,725 | 72.6 |
| J. Charles Mottashed (D) | 21,375 | 26.4 |
| 9 Albert J. Engel (R) | 49,017 | 71.8 |
| J. Willard Krause (D) | 18,828 | 27.6 |
| 10 Roy O. Woodruff (R) | 44,853 | 71.1 |
| Herman N. Butler (D) | 17,737 | 28.1 |
| 11 Fred Bradley (R) | 41,436 | 65.9 |
| Cecil W. Bailey (D) | 21,340 | 33.9 |
| 12 John B. Bennett (R) | 40,717 | 54.4 |
| Frank E. Hook (D) | 33,799 | 45.2 |

## MICHIGAN (cont.)

| Candidates | Votes | % |
|---|---|---|
| 13 Howard A. Coffin (R) | 50,539 | 52.8 |
| George D. O'Brien (D) | 44,883 | 46.9 |
| 14 Harold F. Youngblood (R) | 69,968 | 53.3 |
| Louis C. Rabaut (D) | 60,808 | 46.3 |
| 15 John D. Dingell (D) | 59,111 | 51.9 |
| Harry Henderson (R) | 54,296 | 47.7 |
| 16 John Lesinski (D) | 57,773 | 51.9 |
| Albert A. Riddering (R) | 52,376 | 47.1 |
| 17 George A. Dondero (R) | 102,336 | 64.7 |
| John W. L. Hicks (D) | 54,928 | 34.7 |

## MINNESOTA

| Candidates | Votes | % |
|---|---|---|
| 1 August H. Andresen (R) | 65,906 | 68.4 |
| Karl F. Rolvaag (DFL) | 30,439 | 31.6 |
| 2 Joseph P. O'Hara (R) | 69,487 | 76.0 |
| L. J. Kilbride (DFL) | 21,947 | 24.0 |
| 3 George MacKinnon (R) | 57,397 | 51.5 |
| Roy W. Wier (DFL) | 52,797 | 47.3 |
| 4 Edward J. Devitt (R) | 45,667 | 51.5 |
| Frank T. Starkey (DFL) | 41,897 | 47.2 |
| 5 Walter H. Judd (R) | 66,837 | 58.3 |
| Douglas Hall (DFL) | 47,777 | 41.7 |
| 6 Harold Knutson (R) | 55,401 | 57.4 |
| J. Edward Anderson (DFL) | 41,147 | 42.6 |
| 7 H. Carl Andersen (R) | 57,869 | 65.4 |
| Donald M. Lawson (DFL) | 30,667 | 34.6 |
| 8 John A. Blatnik (DFL) | 62,876 | 57.7 |
| William A. Pittenger (R) | 46,189 | 42.4 |
| 9 Harold C. Hagen (R) | 50,031 | 63.9 |
| Verner Nelson (DFL) | 28,211 | 36.1 |

## MISSISSIPPI

| Candidates | Votes | % |
|---|---|---|
| 1 John E. Rankin (D) | 5,429 | 100.0 |
| 2 Jamie L. Whitten (D) | 6,411 | 100.0 |
| 3 William M. Whittington (D) | 4,265 | 100.0 |
| 4 Thomas G. Abernethy (D) | 10,017 | 100.0 |
| 5 W. Arthur Winstead (D) | 7,122 | 100.0 |
| 6 William M. Colmer (D) | 6,448 | 100.0 |
| 7 John Bell Williams (D) | 10,345 | 100.0 |

## MISSOURI

| Candidates | Votes | % |
|---|---|---|
| 1 Samuel W. Arnold (R) | 37,584 | 50.3 |
| Walter G. Stillwell (D) | 37,105 | 49.7 |
| 2 Max Schwabe (R) | 44,292 | 51.1 |
| Will L. Nelson Jr. (D) | 42,437 | 48.9 |
| 3 William C. Cole (R) | 38,828 | 52.8 |
| William Orr Sawyers (D) | 34,730 | 47.2 |
| 4 C. Jasper Bell (D) | 41,843 | 55.1 |
| Vernon D. Fulcrut (R) | 34,066 | 44.9 |
| 5 Albert L. Reeves Jr. (R) | 42,065 | 53.7 |
| Enos A. Axtell (D) | 36,324 | 46.3 |
| 6 Marion T. Bennett (R) | 54,034 | 58.6 |
| Tom B. Hembree (D) | 38,113 | 41.4 |
| 7 Dewey Short (R) | 50,588 | 65.4 |
| Don Ervin (D) | 26,712 | 34.6 |
| 8 Parke M. Banta (R) | 42,076 | 51.1 |
| A. S. J. Carnahan (D) | 40,241 | 48.9 |
| 9 Clarence Cannon (D) | 35,253 | 53.9 |
| William Barton (R) | 30,199 | 46.1 |
| 10 Orville Zimmerman (D) | 37,236 | 60.6 |
| Walter K. Dillon (R) | 24,164 | 39.4 |
| 11 Claude I. Bakewell (R) | 41,202 | 50.8 |
| John B. Sullivan (D) | 39,879 | 49.2 |
| 12 Walter C. Ploeser (R) | 93,136 | 58.2 |
| Henry W. Simpson (D) | 66,878 | 41.8 |
| 13 Frank M. Karsten (D) | 41,229 | 54.8 |
| Alfred L. Grattendick (R) | 34,062 | 45.2 |

## MONTANA

| Candidates | Votes | % |
|---|---|---|
| 1 Mike Mansfield (D) | 47,418 | 57.6 |
| W. R. Rankin (R) | 34,958 | 42.4 |
| 2 Wesley A. D'Ewart (R) | 58,307 | 54.1 |
| John J. Holmes (D) | 48,564 | 45.1 |

## NEBRASKA

| Candidates | Votes | % |
|---|---|---|
| 1 Carl T. Curtis (R) | 73,602 | 66.4 |
| William H. Meier (D) | 37,280 | 33.6 |
| 2 Howard Buffett (R) | 53,398 | 58.3 |
| Frank A. Jelen (D) | 38,125 | 41.7 |
| 3 Karl Stefan (R) | 64,016 | 72.2 |
| Hans O. Jensen (D) | 20,161 | 22.7 |
| Paul Burke (I) | 4,516# | 5.1 |
| 4 Arthur L. Miller (R) | 57,708 | 71.3 |
| Stanley D. Long (D) | 23,234 | 28.7 |

## NEVADA

| Candidates | Votes | % |
|---|---|---|
| AL Charles H. Russell (R) | 28,859 | 58.8 |
| Malcolm McEachin (D) | 20,187 | 41.2 |

## NEW HAMPSHIRE

| Candidates | Votes | % |
|---|---|---|
| 1 Chester E. Merrow (R) | 53,909 | 59.8 |
| Josaphet T. Benoit (D) | 36,316 | 40.3 |
| 2 Norris Cotton (R) | 45,963 | 64.9 |
| Patrick J. Hinchey (D) | 24,904 | 35.1 |

## NEW JERSEY

| Candidates | Votes | % |
|---|---|---|
| 1 Charles A. Wolverton (R) | 82,919 | 63.5 |
| George F. Neutze (D) | 47,631 | 36.5 |
| 2 T. Millet Hand (R) | 54,511 | 67.1 |
| Edward T. Keeley (D) | 26,740 | 32.9 |
| 3 James C. Auchincloss (R) | 70,302 | 64.9 |
| John W. Zimmermann (D) | 36,177 | 33.4 |
| 4 Frank A. Mathews Jr. (R) | 50,221 | 52.6 |
| Charles R. Howell (D) | 45,225 | 47.4 |
| 5 Charles A. Eaton (R) | 69,338 | 61.3 |
| John J. George (D) | 43,593 | 38.6 |
| 6 Clifford P. Case (R) | 69,395 | 64.7 |
| Walter H. Van Hoesen (D) | 35,378 | 33.0 |
| 7 J. Parnell Thomas (R) | 65,426 | 69.0 |
| Robert B. Meyner (D) | 29,418 | 31.0 |
| 8 Gordon Canfield (R) | 57,616 | 70.5 |
| John V. Breslin (D) | 23,007 | 28.2 |
| 9 Harry L. Towe (R) | 74,870 | 69.1 |
| John M. Mehler (D) | 33,553 | 31.0 |
| 10 Fred A. Hartley Jr. (R) | 44,619 | 52.5 |
| Peter W. Rodino Jr. (D) | 38,889 | 45.7 |
| 11 Frank L. Sundstrom (R) | 46,034 | 60.4 |
| Robert F. J. McGarry (D) | 28,545 | 37.5 |
| 12 Robert W. Kean (R) | 55,732 | 63.6 |
| Raymond C. Connell (D) | 30,389 | 34.7 |
| 13 Mary T. Norton (D) | 69,440 | 64.4 |
| John A. Jones (R) | 36,270 | 33.7 |
| 14 Edward J. Hart (D) | 65,979 | 63.2 |
| Edward P. Nicolay (R) | 38,008 | 36.4 |

## NEW MEXICO

| Candidates | Votes | % |
|---|---|---|
| AL Georgia L. Lusk (D) | 66,420✔ | |
| Antonio M. Fernandez (D) | 65,242✔ | |
| Earl Douglas (R) | 60,519 | |
| Herman G. Baca (R) | 58,937 | |

## NEW YORK

| Candidates | Votes | % |
|---|---|---|
| 1 W. Kingsland Macy (R) | 83,877 | 77.3 |
| Eugene T. O'Neill (D) | 22,855 | 21.1 |
| 2 Leonard W. Hall (R) | 123,873 | 78.4 |
| Josephine U. Mayes (D, AM LAB) | 34,217 | 21.6 |
| 3 Henry J. Latham (R) | 98,722 | 69.7 |
| Aloysius J. Maickel (D) | 32,002 | 22.6 |
| 4 Gregory McMahon (R) | 57,176 | 53.3 |
| Emily B. Barry (D) | 38,227 | 35.6 |
| George H. Rooney (AM LAB) | 7,439 | 6.9 |
| 5 Robert Tripp Ross (R) | 66,754 | 53.0 |
| James A. Phillips (D, AM LAB) | 59,092 | 47.0 |
| 6 Robert J. Nodar Jr. (R) | 59,438 | 53.9 |
| James J. Delaney (D, AM LAB) | 50,944 | 46.1 |
| 7 John J. Delaney (D, AM LAB) | 49,449 | 57.5 |
| Roy M. D. Richardson (R) | 36,510 | 42.5 |
| 8 Joseph L. Pfeifer (D, AM LAB) | 34,876 | 53.9 |
| Paul W. Williams (R) | 29,851 | 46.1 |
| 9 Eugene J. Keogh (D, L) | 41,304 | 48.6 |
| Samuel R. Scialabba (R) | 27,289 | 32.1 |
| Anthony Scimeca (AM LAB) | 16,359 | 19.3 |
| 10 Andrew L. Somers (D, AM LAB) | 57,658 | 57.9 |
| Victor Wichum (R) | 33,642 | 33.8 |
| August Claessens (L) | 8,314 | 8.4 |
| 11 James J. Heffernan (D, AM LAB) | 69,089 | 60.4 |
| Alfred C. McKenzie (R) | 45,279 | 39.6 |
| 12 John J. Rooney (D) | 36,399 | 54.0 |
| Vincent J. Longhi (R, AM LAB) | 31,052 | 46.0 |
| 13 Donald L. O'Toole (D, AM LAB) | 51,406 | 53.5 |
| Charles H. Weadon (R) | 44,674 | 46.5 |
| 14 Leo F. Rayfiel (D, AM LAB) | 79,336 | 75.0 |
| Robert H. Thayer (R) | 26,450 | 25.0 |
| 15 Emanuel Celler (D, AM LAB) | 78,543 | 78.7 |
| Lauri T. Laisi (R) | 21,094 | 21.1 |
| 16 Ellsworth B. Buck (R, VETS V) | 49,758 | 61.2 |
| John Burry (D, AM LAB) | 31,583 | 38.8 |
| 17 Frederic R. Coudert Jr. (R) | 66,063 | 57.5 |
| Myron Sulzberger (D) | 39,216 | 34.2 |
| Joseph Clark Baldwin (AM LAB) | 9,527 | 8.3 |
| 18 Vito Marcantonio (D, AM LAB) | 42,229 | 54.2 |
| Frederick V. P. Bryan (R) | 35,693 | 45.8 |
| 19 Arthur G. Klein (D, AM LAB) | 48,437 | 71.4 |
| William I. Lehrfeld (R) | 19,410 | 28.6 |
| 20 Sol Bloom (D, AM LAB) | 57,208 | 61.1 |
| Jules J. Justin (R) | 36,450 | 38.9 |
| 21 Jacob K. Javits (R, L) | 46,897 | 46.0 |
| Daniel Flynn (D) | 40,652 | 39.9 |
| Eugene P. Connolly (AM LAB) | 14,359 | 14.1 |
| 22 Adam Clayton Powell Jr. (D, AM LAB) | 32,573 | 62.5 |
| Grant Reynolds (R) | 19,514 | 37.5 |
| 23 Walter A. Lynch (D) | 52,616 | 43.4 |
| Peter Wynne (R) | 30,534 | 25.2 |
| David A. Schlossberg (AM LAB) | 25,229 | 20.8 |
| William Wacks (L) | 12,803 | 10.6 |
| 24 Benjamin J. Rabin (D) | 39,316 | 44.2 |
| Roy Soden (AM LAB) | 24,249 | 27.3 |
| David Scher (R) | 16,931 | 19.0 |
| Bernice Benedick (L) | 8,504 | 9.6 |
| 25 Charles A. Buckley (D) | 47,142 | 32.5 |
| Charles Garside (R) | 46,853 | 32.3 |
| Edward V. Morand (AM LAB) | 25,353 | 17.5 |
| Ira J. Palestine (L) | 15,814 | 10.9 |
| John A. Devany (VETS V) | 9,791 | 6.8 |
| 26 David Potts (R) | 58,061 | 44.1 |
| Peter A. Quinn (D) | 49,067 | 37.3 |
| Gerald O'Reilly (AM LAB) | 17,379 | 13.2 |
| Augustus Batten (L) | 7,140 | 5.4 |
| 27 Ralph W. Gwinn (R) | 84,882 | 68.6 |
| Francis X. Nulty (D, AM LAB) | 38,950 | 31.5 |
| 28 Ralph A. Gamble (R) | 83,533 | 75.4 |
| Morris Karnes (D, AM LAB) | 27,236 | 24.6 |
| 29 Katharine St.George (R) | 60,769 | 58.2 |
| James K. Welsh (D, VETS F) | 40,174 | 38.4 |
| 30 Jay LeFevre (R) | 80,469 | 69.5 |
| John F. Killgrew (D, AM LAB) | 35,240 | 30.5 |
| 31 Bernard W. Kearney (R) | 66,395 | 59.2 |
| Carroll A. Gardner (D, AM LAB) | 45,777 | 40.8 |
| 32 William T. Byrne (D, AM LAB) | 79,042 | 55.1 |
| William K. Sanford (R) | 64,325 | 44.9 |
| 33 Dean P. Taylor (R) | 89,778 | 69.9 |
| David J. Fitzgerald (D, AM LAB) | 38,666 | 30.1 |
| 34 Clarence E. Kilburn (R) | 64,217 | 73.0 |
| William G. Houk (D) | 22,368 | 25.4 |
| 35 Hadwen C. Fuller (R) | 58,040 | 54.3 |
| Frank A. Emma (D, AM LAB) | 48,854 | 45.7 |
| 36 R. Walter Riehlman (R) | 76,372 | 63.3 |
| Lawson Barnes (D, AM LAB) | 44,371 | 36.7 |
| 37 Edwin Arthur Hall (R) | 59,920 | 71.7 |
| Charles R. Wilson (D, AM LAB) | 23,687 | 28.3 |
| 38 John Taber (R) | 63,382 | 72.1 |
| George T. Franklin (D) | 24,576 | 27.9 |
| 39 W. Sterling Cole (R) | 61,330 | 72.6 |
| William Heidt Jr. (D, AM LAB) | 23,205 | 27.4 |
| 40 Kenneth B. Keating (R) | 84,852 | 60.5 |
| George F. Rogers (D, AM LAB) | 55,321 | 39.5 |
| 41 James W. Wadsworth (R) | 65,975 | 71.5 |
| Charles J. Reap (D, AM LAB) | 26,332 | 28.5 |
| 42 Walter Gresham Andrews (R) | 71,862 | 62.6 |
| William R. Lupton (D, AM LAB) | 43,028 | 37.4 |
| 43 Edward J. Elsaesser (R) | 71,758 | 62.6 |
| Charles P. McCabe (D) | 38,108 | 33.2 |
| 44 John C. Butler (R) | 67,495 | 57.5 |
| James B. Downey (D, AM LAB) | 49,798 | 42.5 |
| 45 Daniel A. Reed (R) | 53,327 | 70.4 |
| Joseph E. Proudman (D, AM LAB) | 20,205 | 26.7 |

### Special Election

| Candidates | Votes | % |
|---|---|---|
| 19 Arthur G. Klein (D) | 17,360 | 49.5 |
| Johannes Stell (AM LAB) | 13,415 | 38.2 |
| William S. Shea (R) | 4,314 | 12.3 |

## NORTH CAROLINA

| Candidates | Votes | % |
|---|---|---|
| 1 Herbert C. Bonner (D) | 9,993 | 89.2 |
| Zeno O. Ratcliff (R) | 1,208 | 10.8 |
| 2 John H. Kerr (D) | 9,426 | 100.0 |
| 3 Graham A. Barden (D) | 14,798 | 66.7 |
| H. B. Kornegay (R) | 7,385 | 33.3 |
| 4 Harold D. Cooley (D) | 22,977 | 65.7 |
| Ben L. Spence (R) | 12,005 | 34.3 |
| 5 John H. Folger (D) | 26,316 | 62.9 |
| S. Evan Hall (R) | 15,521 | 37.1 |
| 6 Carl T. Durham (D) | 18,564 | 63.4 |
| A. A. McDonald (R) | 10,721 | 36.6 |
| 7 J. Bayard Clark (D) | 15,428 | 73.9 |
| H. Edmund Rodgers (R) | 5,445 | 26.1 |
| 8 Charles B. Deane (D) | 29,920 | 54.2 |
| Joseph H. Whicker Sr. (R) | 25,305 | 45.8 |
| 9 Robert L. Doughton (D) | 36,007 | 54.9 |
| Clyde R. Greene (R) | 29,585 | 45.1 |
| 10 Hamilton C. Jones (D) | 24,614 | 53.9 |
| P. C. Burkholder (R) | 21,096 | 46.2 |
| 11 Alfred L. Bulwinkle (D) | 25,544 | 58.5 |
| C. Y. Nanney Jr. (R) | 18,143 | 41.5 |
| 12 Monroe M. Redden (D) | 43,690 | 60.5 |
| Guy Weaver (R) | 28,531 | 39.5 |

### Special Elections

| Candidates | Votes | % |
|---|---|---|
| 8 Jane Pratt (D) | 31,058 | 79.5 |
| H. Frank Hulin (R) | 8,017 | 20.5 |
| 10 Sam J. Ervin Jr. (D) | 2,303 | 99.7 |

## NORTH DAKOTA

| Candidates | Votes | % |
|---|---|---|
| AL William Lemke (R) | 103,205✓ | |
| Charles R. Robertson (R) | 102,087✓ | |
| James M. Hanley (D) | 41,189 | |
| Edwin Cooper (D) | 29,865 | |

## OHIO

| | Candidates | Votes | % |
|---|---|---|---|
| 1 | Charles H. Elston (R) | 72,909 | 64.2 |
| | G. Andrews Espy (D) | 40,594 | 35.8 |
| 2 | William E. Hess (R) | 67,067 | 63.2 |
| | Francis G. Davis (D) | 39,112 | 36.8 |
| 3 | Raymond H. Burke (R) | 71,171 | 52.0 |
| | Edward J. Gardner (D) | 65,749 | 48.0 |
| 4 | Robert F. Jones (R) | 46,718 | 59.2 |
| | Merl J. Bragg (D) | 32,160 | 40.8 |
| 5 | Cliff Clevenger (R) | 30,623 | 60.3 |
| | Willard Thomas (D) | 20,163 | 39.7 |
| 6 | Edward O. McCowen (R) | 39,992 | 54.8 |
| | Franklin E. Smith (D) | 33,013 | 45.2 |
| 7 | Clarence J. Brown (R) | 63,390 | 68.0 |
| | Carl H. Ehl (D) | 29,824 | 32.0 |
| 8 | Frederick C. Smith (R) | 40,755 | 64.0 |
| | John T. Siemon (D) | 22,945 | 36.0 |
| 9 | Homer A. Ramey (R) | 59,394 | 50.1 |
| | Michael V. DiSalle (D) | 59,057 | 49.9 |
| 10 | Thomas A. Jenkins (R) | 35,406 | 66.7 |
| | H. A. McCown (D) | 17,719 | 33.4 |
| 11 | Walter E. Brehm (R) | 31,576 | 60.6 |
| | Lester S. Reid (D) | 20,543 | 39.4 |
| 12 | John M. Vorys (R) | 74,691 | 62.0 |
| | Arthur P. Lamneck (D) | 45,779 | 38.0 |
| 13 | Alvin F. Weichel (R) | 49,725 | 72.1 |
| | Frank W. Thomas (D) | 19,237 | 27.9 |
| 14 | Walter B. Huber (D) | 88,178 | 52.6 |
| | Fred W. Danner (R) | 77,674 | 46.4 |
| 15 | Percy W. Griffiths (R) | 36,564 | 53.2 |
| | Robert T. Secrest (D) | 32,159 | 46.8 |
| 16 | Henderson H. Carson (R) | 65,639 | 55.8 |
| | William R. Thom (D) | 51,931 | 44.2 |
| 17 | J. Harry McGregor (R) | 57,167 | 65.3 |
| | Wesley W. Purdy (D) | 30,406 | 34.7 |
| 18 | Earl R. Lewis (R) | 55,140 | 58.8 |
| | Eugene A. Blum (D) | 38,606 | 41.2 |
| 19 | Michael J. Kirwan (D) | 88,872 | 59.9 |
| | Norman W. Adams (R) | 59,607 | 40.2 |
| 20 | Michael A. Feighan (D) | 49,670 | 67.0 |
| | Walter E. Obert (R) | 24,476 | 33.0 |
| 21 | Robert Crosser (D) | 49,111 | 64.0 |
| | James S. Hudec (R) | 27,657 | 36.0 |
| 22 | Frances P. Bolton (R) | 174,823 | 69.1 |
| | Earl Heffley (D) | 69,050 | 27.3 |
| AL | George H. Bender (R) | 1,281,864 | 59.5 |
| | William M. Boyd (D) | 871,660 | 40.5 |

## OKLAHOMA

| | Candidates | Votes | % |
|---|---|---|---|
| 1 | George B. Schwabe (R) | 61,205 | 54.5 |
| | Oras A. Shaw (D) | 51,041 | 45.5 |
| 2 | William G. Stigler (D) | 32,559 | 63.1 |
| | Ferd P. Snider (R) | 19,029 | 36.9 |
| 3 | Carl Albert (D) | 38,699 | 85.0 |
| | Eleanor L. Watson (R) | 6,835 | 15.0 |
| 4 | Glen D. Johnson (D) | 36,559 | 64.4 |
| | Pliney S. Frye (R) | 20,230 | 35.6 |
| 5 | A. S. Mike Monroney (D) | 47,173 | 52.0 |
| | Carmon C. Harris (R) | 43,508 | 48.0 |
| 6 | Toby Morris (D) | 30,408 | 65.7 |
| | Joe Hart Jr. (R) | 15,912 | 34.4 |
| 7 | Preston E. Peden (D) | 26,585 | 78.7 |
| | J. Warren White (R) | 7,204 | 21.3 |
| 8 | Ross Rizley (R) | 30,240 | 54.8 |
| | Tom Hieronymus (D) | 24,954 | 45.2 |

## OREGON

| | Candidates | Votes | % |
|---|---|---|---|
| 1 | Walter Norblad (R) | 67,535 | 72.0 |
| | Lyman Ross (D) | 26,278 | 28.0 |

| | Candidates | Votes | % |
|---|---|---|---|
| 2 | Lowell Stockman (R) | 32,541 | 67.4 |
| | Lamar Townsend (D) | 15,744 | 32.6 |
| 3 | Homer D. Angell (R) | 74,061 | 56.7 |
| | Lew Wallace (D) | 56,525 | 43.3 |
| 4 | Harris Ellsworth (R) | 42,868 | 69.2 |
| | Louis A. Wood (D) | 19,118 | 30.8 |

## PENNSYLVANIA

| | Candidates | Votes | % |
|---|---|---|---|
| 1 | James Gallagher (R) | 70,680 | 57.3 |
| | William Barrett (D) | 52,593 | 42.7 |
| 2 | Robert N. McGarvey (R) | 70,474 | 51.4 |
| | William T. Granahan (D) | 66,674 | 48.6 |
| 3 | Hardie Scott (R) | 83,618 | 62.1 |
| | Albert S. Townsend (D) | 50,962 | 37.9 |
| 4 | Franklin J. Maloney (R) | 55,239 | 50.2 |
| | John Edward Sheridan (D) | 49,025 | 44.6 |
| | John K. Rice (U CIT) | 5,688 | 5.2 |
| 5 | George W. Sarbacher Jr. (R) | 73,946 | 56.9 |
| | William J. Green Jr. (D) | 56,086 | 43.1 |
| 6 | Hugh Scott (R) | 82,671 | 58.5 |
| | Herbert J. McGlinchey (D) | 58,557 | 41.5 |
| 7 | E. Wallace Chadwick (R) | 76,021 | 66.5 |
| | Vernon A. O'Rourke (D) | 38,253 | 33.5 |
| 8 | Charles L. Gerlach (R) | 49,196 | 59.0 |
| | Henry Chapin (D) | 34,260 | 41.1 |
| 9 | Paul B. Dague (R) | 64,311 | 72.7 |
| | Edgar Campbell (D) | 24,175 | 27.3 |
| 10 | James P. Scoblick (R) | 47,704 | 51.0 |
| | Frank X. Murray (D) | 45,843 | 49.0 |
| 11 | Mitchell Jenkins (R) | 58,413 | 50.8 |
| | Daniel J. Flood (D) | 56,570 | 49.2 |
| 12 | Ivor D. Fenton (R) | 62,151 | 62.7 |
| | Ralph M. Bashore (D) | 36,954 | 37.3 |
| 13 | Frederick A. Muhlenberg (R) | 33,409 | 54.6 |
| | Daniel K. Hoch (D) | 25,073 | 41.0 |
| 14 | Wilson D. Gillette (R) | 43,142 | 67.4 |
| | James S. Fields (D) | 20,842 | 32.6 |
| 15 | Robert F. Rich (R) | 44,264 | 68.5 |
| | Richard F. Hartzell (D) | 20,376 | 31.5 |
| 16 | Samuel K. McConnell Jr. (R) | 76,314 | 74.4 |
| | William L. Batt Jr. (D) | 26,305 | 25.6 |
| 17 | Richard M. Simpson (R) | 37,194 | 66.2 |
| | Lowell H. Alexander (D) | 18,972 | 33.8 |
| 18 | John C. Kunkel (R) | 77,349 | 69.0 |
| | William B. Freeland (D) | 34,708 | 31.0 |
| 19 | Leon H. Gavin (R) | 41,500 | 68.0 |
| | Lloyd N. Huth (D) | 18,199 | 29.8 |
| 20 | Francis E. Walter (D) | 39,751 | 52.5 |
| | Norman A. Peil (R) | 36,008 | 47.5 |
| 21 | Chester H. Gross (R) | 45,559 | 52.0 |
| | John W. Brehm (D) | 42,118 | 48.0 |
| 22 | James E. Van Zandt (R) | 42,217 | 65.9 |
| | John A. Shartle (D) | 21,853 | 34.1 |
| 23 | William J. Crow (R) | 34,194 | 52.9 |
| | John W. Rankin (D) | 30,493 | 47.1 |
| 24 | Thomas E. Morgan (D) | 39,749 | 56.8 |
| | Roy A. Purviance (R) | 30,231 | 43.2 |
| 25 | Louis E. Graham (R) | 53,932 | 58.8 |
| | Samuel G. Neff (D) | 37,723 | 41.2 |
| 26 | Harve Tibbott (R) | 49,573 | 54.6 |
| | Thomas A. Owens (D) | 41,224 | 45.4 |
| 27 | Augustine B. Kelley (D) | 46,137 | 52.9 |
| | Roy C. McKenna (R) | 41,030 | 47.1 |
| 28 | Carroll D. Kearns (R) | 56,835 | 63.9 |
| | Charles W. Webb (D) | 32,166 | 36.1 |
| 29 | John McDowell (R) | 55,329 | 53.5 |
| | Harry J. Davenport (D) | 48,091 | 46.5 |
| 30 | Robert J. Corbett (R) | 57,827 | 60.1 |
| | James W. Knox (D) | 38,362 | 39.9 |
| 31 | James G. Fulton (R) | 70,419 | 63.8 |
| | Edward A. Schultz (D) | 40,010 | 36.2 |
| 32 | Herman P. Eberharter (D) | 62,963 | 62.8 |
| | Ignatius J. Pillart (R) | 37,247 | 37.2 |
| 33 | Frank Buchanan (D) | 51,656 | 57.9 |
| | John Robert Brown Jr. (R) | 37,555 | 42.1 |

## RHODE ISLAND

| | Candidates | Votes | % |
|---|---|---|---|
| 1 | Aime J. Forand (D) | 74,324 | 56.7 |
| | Raymond A. Mailloux (R) | 55,900 | 42.6 |
| 2 | John E. Fogarty (D) | 74,349 | 52.6 |
| | John J. Kelly Jr. (R) | 66,987 | 47.4 |

## SOUTH CAROLINA

| | | Votes | % |
|---|---|---|---|
| 1 | L. Mendel Rivers (D) | 5,354 | 99.5 |
| 2 | John J. Riley (D) | 4,795 | 98.6 |
| 3 | W. J. Bryan Dorn (D) | 3,527 | 99.9 |
| 4 | Joseph R. Bryson (D) | 3,363 | 99.6 |
| 5 | James P. Richards (D) | 3,357 | 100.0 |
| 6 | John L. McMillan (D) | 5,671 | 96.9 |

## SOUTH DAKOTA

| | | Votes | % |
|---|---|---|---|
| 1 | Karl E. Mundt (R) | 76,720 | 61.5 |
| | Merton B. Tice (D) | 48,065 | 38.5 |
| 2 | Francis H. Case (R) | 28,011 | 73.7 |
| | John B. Reinhard (D) | 10,008 | 26.3 |

## TENNESSEE

| | | Votes | % |
|---|---|---|---|
| 1 | Dayton E. Phillips (R) | 24,144 | 100.0 |
| 2 | John Jennings Jr. (R) | 28,752 | 84.0 |
| | James Douglas Wyrick (I) | 5,485 | 16.0 |
| 3 | Estes Kefauver (D) | 26,779 | 90.8 |
| | George Bagwell (I) | 2,725 | 9.2 |
| 4 | Albert A. Gore (D) | 7,624 | 67.5 |
| | H. E. McLean (R) | 3,673 | 32.5 |
| 5 | Joe L. Evins (D) | 11,646 | 100.0 |
| 6 | J. Percy Priest (D) | 7,178 | 77.1 |
| | Will T. Perry (R) | 2,135 | 22.9 |
| 7 | Wirt Courtney (D) | 11,658 | 100.0 |
| 8 | Thomas J. Murray (D) | 11,891 | 100.0 |
| 9 | Jere Cooper (D) | 12,685 | 100.0 |
| 10 | Clifford Davis (D) | 37,069 | 100.0 |

## TEXAS

| | | Votes | % |
|---|---|---|---|
| 1 | Wright Patman (D) | 11,929 | 100.0 |
| 2 | Jesse M. Combs (D) | 19,909 | 96.2 |
| 3 | Lindley Beckworth (D) | 10,686 | 100.0 |
| 4 | Sam Rayburn (D) | 11,957 | 93.7 |
| | Floyd Harry (R) | 800 | 6.3 |
| 5 | J. Frank Wilson (D) | 12,267 | 75.8 |
| | L. W. Stayart (R) | 3,921 | 24.2 |
| 6 | Olin E. Teague (D) | 11,421 | 100.0 |
| 7 | Tom Pickett (D) | 14,810 | 100.0 |
| 8 | Albert Thomas (D) | 42,163 | 90.8 |
| | R. F. Burns (R) | 4,253 | 9.2 |
| 9 | Joseph J. Mansfield (D) | 16,712 | 100.0 |
| 10 | Lyndon B. Johnson (D) | 16,947 | 100.0 |
| 11 | W. R. Poage (D) | 9,178 | 100.0 |
| 12 | Wingate H. Lucas (D) | 15,266 | 87.7 |
| | E. M. Hyder (R) | 2,146 | 12.3 |
| 13 | Ed Gossett (D) | 17,714 | 100.0 |
| 14 | John E. Lyle (D) | 30,064 | 100.0 |
| 15 | Milton H. West (D) | 16,674 | 100.0 |
| 16 | R. Ewing Thomason (D) | 8,114 | 100.0 |
| 17 | Omar Burleson (D) | 14,874 | 100.0 |
| 18 | Eugene Worley (D) | 12,475 | 74.1 |
| | F. T. O'Brien (R) | 4,357 | 25.9 |
| 19 | George H. Mahon (D) | 15,791 | 94.6 |
| | M. D. Temple (R) | 905 | 5.4 |
| 20 | Paul J. Kilday (D) | 10,543 | 100.0 |
| 21 | O. Clark Fisher (D) | 15,943 | 100.0 |

## UTAH

| | | Votes | % |
|---|---|---|---|
| 1 | Walter K. Granger (D) | 44,888 | 50.1 |
| | David J. Wilson (R) | 44,784 | 49.9 |
| 2 | William A. Dawson (R) | 56,402 | 52.7 |
| | J. Will Robinson (D) | 50,598 | 47.3 |

## VERMONT

| | Candidates | Votes | % |
|---|---|---|---|
| AL | Charles A. Plumley (R) | 46,985 | 64.3 |
| | Matthew J. Caldbeck (D) | 26,056 | 35.7 |

## VIRGINIA

| | Candidates | Votes | % |
|---|---|---|---|
| 1 | S. Otis Bland (D) | 13,863 | 75.0 |
| | Walter Johnson (R) | 4,628 | 25.0 |
| 2 | Porter Hardy Jr. (D) | 19,267 | 65.7 |
| | Sidney H. Kelsey (R) | 10,078 | 34.3 |
| 3 | J. Vaughan Gary (D) | 21,947 | 73.3 |
| | Earle Lutz (R) | 7,974 | 26.7 |
| 4 | Patrick Henry Drewry (D) | 13,636 | 87.1 |
| | Andrew S. Condrey (P) | 2,012 | 12.9 |
| 5 | Thomas B. Stanley (D) | 17,741 | 73.5 |
| | William L. Creasy (R) | 6,390 | 26.5 |
| 6 | J. Lindsay Almond Jr. (D) | 20,068 | 64.8 |
| | Frank R. Angell (R) | 10,641 | 34.4 |
| 7 | Burr P. Harrison (D) | 19,535 | 62.3 |
| | Karl Jenkins (R) | 11,813 | 37.7 |
| 8 | Howard Worth Smith (D) | 21,252 | 62.1 |
| | Lawrence Michael (R) | 12,950 | 37.9 |
| 9 | John W. Flannagan Jr. (D) | 20,610 | 51.8 |
| | S. H. Sutherland (R) | 17,152 | 43.1 |
| | John Albert Goodpasture Jr. (I) | 2,026 | 5.1 |

### Special Elections

| | | | |
|---|---|---|---|
| 5 | Thomas B. Stanley (D) | 17,862 | 75.4 |
| | William L. Creasy (R) | 5,829 | 24.6 |

| | Candidates | Votes | % |
|---|---|---|---|
| 7 | Burr P. Harrison (D) | 19,711 | 62.5 |
| | Karl Jenkins (R) | 11,809 | 37.5 |

## WASHINGTON

| | | Votes | % |
|---|---|---|---|
| 1 | Homer R. Jones (R) | 113,289 | 63.8 |
| | Hugh De Lacy (D) | 64,155 | 36.2 |
| 2 | Henry M. Jackson (D) | 54,089 | 53.1 |
| | Payson Peterson (R) | 47,838 | 46.9 |
| 3 | Fred Norman (R) | 47,875 | 53.9 |
| | Charles R. Savage (D) | 40,980 | 46.1 |
| 4 | Hal Holmes (R) | 51,476 | 67.6 |
| | Earl S. Coe (D) | 24,662 | 32.4 |
| 5 | Walt Horan (R) | 58,535 | 61.3 |
| | John T. Little (D) | 34,870 | 36.5 |
| 6 | Thor C. Tollefson (R) | 56,702 | 53.9 |
| | John M. Coffee (D) | 48,431 | 46.1 |

## WEST VIRGINIA

| | | | |
|---|---|---|---|
| 1 | Francis J. Love (R) | 45,691 | 53.1 |
| | Matthew M. Neely (D) | 40,370 | 46.9 |
| 2 | Melvin C. Snyder (R) | 41,224 | 51.4 |
| | Jennings Randolph (D) | 39,041 | 48.6 |
| 3 | Edward G. Rohrbough (R) | 42,386 | 51.5 |
| | Cleveland M. Bailey (D) | 39,872 | 48.5 |
| 4 | Hubert S. Ellis (R) | 54,932 | 52.7 |
| | M. G. Burnside (D) | 49,408 | 47.4 |

| | Candidates | Votes | % |
|---|---|---|---|
| 5 | John Kee (D) | 43,154 | 56.9 |
| | Hartley Sanders (R) | 32,754 | 43.2 |
| 6 | Erland H. Hedrick (D) | 57,461 | 53.0 |
| | Harold H. Neff (R) | 51,064 | 47.1 |

## WISCONSIN

| | | | |
|---|---|---|---|
| 1 | Lawrence H. Smith (R) | 58,344 | 56.5 |
| | John R. Redstrom (D) | 44,188 | 42.8 |
| 2 | Robert K. Henry (R) | 68,794* | 62.9 |
| | William G. Rice (D) | 39,657 | 36.3 |
| 3 | William H. Stevenson (R) | 65,177 | 96.1 |
| 4 | John C. Brophy (R) | 49,144 | 36.5 |
| | Edmund V. Bobrowicz (D) | 44,398 | 33.0 |
| | Thaddeus F. B. Wasielewski (I) | 38,502 | 28.6 |
| 5 | Charles J. Kersten (R) | 76,364 | 54.1 |
| | Andrew J. Biemiller (D) | 59,764 | 42.3 |
| 6 | Frank B. Keefe (R) | 58,444 | 64.2 |
| | Edwin W. Webster (D) | 31,550 | 34.7 |
| 7 | Reid F. Murray (R) | 60,390 | 71.6 |
| | Elmer E. Fraley (D) | 23,481 | 27.8 |
| 8 | John W. Byrnes (R) | 67,840 | 64.7 |
| | Martin J. Young (D) | 37,013 | 35.3 |
| 9 | Merlin Hull (R) | 70,527 | 99.0 |
| 10 | Alvin E. O'Konski (R) | 40,263 | 53.0 |
| | Henry J. Berquist (D) | 32,238 | 42.4 |

## WYOMING

| | | | |
|---|---|---|---|
| AL | Frank A. Barrett (R) | 44,512 | 56.0 |
| | John J. McIntyre (D) | 34,946 | 44.0 |

# 1947 House Elections

## NEW YORK

### Special Election

| | | | |
|---|---|---|---|
| 14 | Abraham J. Multer (D, L) | 47,849 | 58.2 |
| | Victor J. Rabinowitz (AM LAB) | 20,800 | 25.3 |
| | Jacob P. Fefkowitz (R) | 13,597 | 16.5 |

## WISCONSIN

### Special Election

| | | | |
|---|---|---|---|
| 2 | Glenn R. Davis (R) | 24,023 | 50.6 |
| | Thompson (D) | 23,181 | 48.8 |

# 1948 House Elections

## ALABAMA

| | Candidates | Votes | % |
|---|---|---|---|
| 1 | Frank W. Boykin (D) | 19,778 | 100.0 |
| 2 | George M. Grant (D) | 21,271 | 100.0 |
| 3 | George W. Andrews (D) | 16,279 | 100.0 |
| 4 | Sam Hobbs (D) | 17,282 | 85.0 |
| | B. Hogan Stewart (R) | 3,054 | 15.0 |
| 5 | Albert Rains (D) | 20,548 | 100.0 |
| 6 | Edward deGraffenried (D) | 13,968 | 82.4 |
| | W. P. Ivey (R) | 2,994 | 17.7 |
| 7 | Carl A. Elliott (D) | 21,552 | 100.0 |
| 8 | Robert E. Jones Jr. (D) | 19,060 | 88.4 |
| | Harry J. Frahn (R) | 2,510 | 11.6 |
| 9 | Laurie C. Battle (D) | 33,781 | 87.1 |
| | Hiram Dodd (R) | 5,006 | 12.9 |

## ARIZONA

| | | Votes | % |
|---|---|---|---|
| 1 | John R. Murdock (D) | 42,565 | 58.4 |
| | John H. Udall (R) | 29,864 | 41.0 |
| 2 | Harold A. Patten (D) | 54,066 | 62.8 |
| | Albert R. Buehman (R) | 30,140 | 35.0 |

## ARKANSAS

| | | Votes | % |
|---|---|---|---|
| 1 | Ezekiel C. Gathings (D) | 34,676 | 100.0 |
| 2 | Wilbur D. Mills (D) | 29,922 | 100.0 |
| 3 | James W. Trimble (D) | 27,278 | 68.6 |
| | Dalton Dotson (R) | 12,462 | 31.4 |
| 4 | Boyd Tackett (D) | 29,338 | 87.8 |
| | C. R. Starbird (R) | 4,094 | 12.3 |
| 5 | Brooks Hays (D) | 36,440 | 87.0 |
| | Thad Tisdale (R) | 5,471 | 13.1 |
| 6 | William F. Norrell (D) | 40,291 | 100.0 |
| 7 | Oren Harris (D) | 32,982 | 100.0 |

## CALIFORNIA

| | | Votes | % |
|---|---|---|---|
| 1 | Hubert B. Scudder (R) | 82,947 | 54.5 |
| | Sterling J. Norgard (D-IP) | 68,951 | 45.3 |
| 2 | Clair Engle (D-R) | 78,555 | 100.0 |
| 3 | Leroy Johnson (R-D) | 166,571 | 84.4 |
| | James B. Willard (I PROG) | 30,878 | 15.6 |
| 4 | Franck R. Havenner (D) | 73,704 | 51.0 |
| | William S. Mailliard (R) | 68,875 | 47.7 |
| 5 | Richard J. Welch (R-D) | 116,347 | 100.0 |
| 6 | George P. Miller (D-R) | 194,985 | 99.9 |
| 7 | John J. Allen Jr. (R) | 78,534 | 51.4 |
| | Buel G. Gallagher (D-IP) | 74,318 | 48.6 |
| 8 | Jack Z. Anderson (R-D) | 161,743 | 79.9 |
| | Paul Taylor (I PROG) | 40,670 | 20.1 |
| 9 | Cecil F. White (D) | 72,826 | 51.3 |
| | Bertrand W. Gearhart (R) | 66,563 | 46.9 |
| 10 | Thomas H. Werdel (R-D) | 67,448 | 71.3 |
| | Sam James Miller (I PROG) | 27,168 | 28.7 |
| 11 | Ernest K. Bramblett (R-D) | 87,143 | 80.7 |
| | Cole Weston (I PROG) | 14,582 | 13.5 |
| | George E. Outland | 6,157 | 5.7 |
| 12 | Richard M. Nixon (R-D) | 141,509 | 86.9 |
| | Una W. Rice (I PROG) | 19,631 | 12.1 |
| 13 | Norris Poulson (R) | 62,951 | 52.6 |
| | Ned R. Healy (D-IP) | 56,624 | 47.3 |
| 14 | Helen Gahagan Douglas (D) | 89,581 | 65.3 |
| | W. Wallace Braden (R) | 44,611 | 32.5 |
| 15 | Gordon L. McDonough (R-D) | 131,933 | 83.0 |
| | Maynard J. Omerberg (I PROG) | 27,007 | 17.0 |
| 16 | Donald L. Jackson (R) | 121,198 | 57.0 |
| | Ellis E. Patterson (D-IP) | 91,268 | 42.9 |
| 17 | Cecil R. King (D-R) | 194,782 | 99.9 |
| 18 | Clyde Doyle (D) | 105,687 | 51.1 |
| | Willis W. Bradley (R) | 92,721 | 44.9 |
| 19 | Chet Holifield (D) | 72,900 | 69.7 |
| | Joseph Francis Quigley (R) | 28,698 | 27.5 |

## COLORADO

| | | Votes | % |
|---|---|---|---|
| 1 | John A. Carroll (D) | 106,096 | 64.8 |
| | Christopher F. Cusack (R) | 57,541 | 35.2 |
| 2 | William S. Hill (R) | 71,868 | 51.9 |
| | George L. Bickel (D) | 66,579 | 48.1 |
| 3 | John H. Marsalis (D) | 65,114 | 50.7 |
| | J. Edgar Chenoweth (R) | 63,312 | 49.3 |
| 4 | Wayne N. Aspinall (D) | 34,695 | 51.9 |
| | Robert F. Rockwell (R) | 32,206 | 48.1 |

## CONNECTICUT

| | | Votes | % |
|---|---|---|---|
| 1 | Abraham A. Ribicoff (D) | 127,802 | 54.7 |
| | William J. Miller (R) | 103,294 | 44.2 |
| 2 | Chase Going Woodhouse (D) | 69,339 | 51.7 |
| | Horace Seely-Brown Jr. (R) | 64,916 | 48.4 |
| 3 | John A. McGuire (D) | 84,449 | 49.7 |
| | Ellsworth B. Foote (R) | 83,310 | 49.0 |
| 4 | John Davis Lodge (R) | 117,727 | 55.2 |
| | William Gaston (D) | 92,618 | 43.4 |
| 5 | James T. Patterson (R) | 62,804 | 51.1 |
| | Vincent P. Kiernan (D) | 58,300 | 47.4 |
| AL | Antoni N. Sadlak (R) | 433,311 | 49.3 |
| | Fred Trotta (D) | 429,348 | 48.8 |

## DELAWARE

| | | Votes | % |
|---|---|---|---|
| AL | J. Caleb Boggs (R) | 71,127 | 50.6 |
| | J. Carl McGuigan (D) | 68,909 | 49.0 |

## FLORIDA

| | | Votes | % |
|---|---|---|---|
| 1 | J. Hardin Peterson (D) | 66,348 | 100.0 |
| 2 | Charles E. Bennett (D) | 55,715 | 91.1 |
| | Camille Geneau (R) | 5,413 | 8.9 |
| 3 | Robert L. F. Sikes (D) | 30,730 | 100.0 |
| 4 | George A. Smathers (D) | 63,665 | 81.0 |
| | J. L. Wambaugh (R) | 14,912 | 19.0 |
| 5 | A. S. Herlong Jr. (D) | 46,939 | 70.7 |
| | M. J. Moss Jr. (R) | 19,501 | 29.4 |
| 6 | Dwight L. Rogers (D) | 31,933 | 66.7 |
| | Rolf Kaltenborn (R) | 15,977 | 33.4 |

## GEORGIA

| | | Votes | % |
|---|---|---|---|
| 1 | Prince H. Preston (D) | 42,677 | 100.0 |
| 2 | E. E. Cox (D) | 26,815 | 100.0 |
| 3 | Stephen Pace (D) | 32,098 | 100.0 |
| 4 | A. Sidney Camp (D) | 33,522 | 100.0 |
| 5 | James C. Davis (D) | 54,637 | 99.6 |
| 6 | Carl Vinson (D) | 29,446 | 100.0 |
| 7 | Henderson Lanham (D) | 45,195 | 100.0 |
| 8 | W. M. Wheeler (D) | 35,608 | 100.0 |
| 9 | John S. Wood (D) | 29,699 | 100.0 |
| 10 | Paul Brown (D) | 35,479 | 100.0 |

## IDAHO

| | | Votes | % |
|---|---|---|---|
| 1 | Compton I. White (D) | 46,846 | 51.8 |
| | Abe McGregor Goff (R) | 41,404 | 45.7 |
| 2 | John C. Sanborn (R) | 61,690 | 50.7 |
| | Asael Lyman (D) | 59,006 | 48.5 |

---

| | Candidates | Votes | % |
|---|---|---|---|
| 20 | Carl Hinshaw (R-D) | 204,710 | 81.5 |
| | William B. Esterman (I PROG) | 46,232 | 18.4 |
| 21 | Harry R. Sheppard (D) | 61,383 | 55.2 |
| | Lowell E. Lathrop (R) | 47,411 | 42.6 |
| 22 | John Phillips (R-D) | 115,697 | 99.9 |
| 23 | Clinton D. McKinnon (D) | 112,534 | 55.8 |
| | Charles K. Fletcher (R) | 87,138 | 43.2 |

## ILLINOIS

| | Candidates | Votes | % |
|---|---|---|---|
| 1 | William L. Dawson (D) | 98,690 | 67.0 |
| | William E. King (R) | 43,034 | 29.2 |
| 2 | Barratt O'Hara (D) | 91,648 | 50.5 |
| | Richard B. Vail (R) | 85,119 | 46.9 |
| 3 | Neil J. Linehan (D) | 91,204 | 52.9 |
| | Fred E. Busbey (R) | 81,175 | 47.1 |
| 4 | James V. Buckley (D) | 89,557 | 52.1 |
| | Leslie E. Salter (R) | 82,310 | 47.9 |
| 5 | Martin Gorski (D) | 114,660 | 72.5 |
| | John L. Waner (R) | 43,610 | 27.6 |
| 6 | Thomas J. O'Brien (D) | 127,918 | 68.4 |
| | John M. Coan (R) | 53,548 | 28.6 |
| 7 | Adolph J. Sabath (D) | 133,199 | 73.7 |
| | Francis C. Sperry (R) | 47,602 | 26.3 |
| 8 | Thomas S. Gordon (D) | 101,098 | 65.1 |
| | Herbert F. Geisler (R) | 54,316 | 35.0 |
| 9 | Sidney R. Yates (D) | 91,271 | 54.5 |
| | Robert J. Twyman (R) | 73,301 | 43.8 |
| 10 | Richard W. Hoffman (R) | 109,031 | 58.1 |
| | Marvin J. Peters (D) | 78,533 | 41.9 |
| 11 | Chester A. Chesney (D) | 80,750 | 50.8 |
| | James C. Moreland (R) | 78,269 | 49.2 |
| 12 | Edgar A. Jonas (R) | 98,956 | 51.4 |
| | Blair L. Varnes (D) | 88,795 | 46.1 |
| 13 | Ralph E. Church (R) | 123,978 | 68.0 |
| | Willard C. Walters (D) | 58,340 | 32.0 |
| 14 | Chauncey W. Reed (R) | 94,962 | 68.3 |
| | Richard Plum (D) | 44,050 | 31.7 |
| 15 | Noah M. Mason (R) | 74,213 | 56.4 |
| | G. M. Wells (D) | 57,296 | 43.6 |
| 16 | Leo E. Allen (R) | 76,840 | 58.5 |
| | Albert H. Manus Jr. (D) | 54,481 | 41.5 |
| 17 | Leslie C. Arends (R) | 71,220 | 62.8 |
| | Carl Vrooman (D) | 42,226 | 37.2 |
| 18 | Harold H. Velde (R) | 61,652 | 52.1 |
| | Dale E. Sutton (D) | 56,688 | 47.9 |
| 19 | Robert B. Chiperfield (R) | 69,733 | 54.0 |
| | Fred J. Brown (D) | 59,397 | 46.0 |
| 20 | Sid Simpson (R) | 59,067 | 53.1 |
| | Henry D. Sullivan (D) | 52,235 | 46.9 |
| 21 | Peter F. Mack Jr. (D) | 69,619 | 53.1 |
| | Joseph L. Moore (R) | 61,452 | 46.9 |
| 22 | Rolla C. McMillen (R) | 64,625 | 53.2 |
| | Olive Remington Goldman (D) | 56,893 | 46.8 |
| 23 | Edward H. Jenison (R) | 57,800 | 51.8 |
| | Wayne R. Cook (D) | 53,885 | 48.3 |
| 24 | Charles W. Vursell (R) | 57,732 | 50.6 |
| | John David Upchurch (D) | 56,262 | 49.4 |
| 25 | Melvin Price (D) | 101,927 | 69.5 |
| | Russell H. Classen (R) | 44,728 | 30.5 |
| 26 | C. W. Bishop (R) | 54,993 | 51.9 |
| | Kent E. Keller (D) | 51,028 | 48.1 |

## INDIANA

| | | Votes | % |
|---|---|---|---|
| 1 | Ray J. Madden (D) | 78,898 | 60.7 |
| | Theodore L. Sendak (R) | 50,194 | 38.6 |
| 2 | Charles A. Halleck (R) | 71,907 | 55.2 |
| | Theodore J. Smith (D) | 57,245 | 44.0 |
| 3 | Thurman C. Crook (D) | 86,382 | 51.9 |
| | Robert A. Grant (R) | 78,935 | 47.5 |
| 4 | Edward H. Kruse Jr. (D) | 66,689 | 50.8 |
| | George W. Gillie (R) | 63,403 | 48.3 |
| 5 | John R. Walsh (D) | 91,861 | 51.9 |
| | Forest A. Harness (R) | 82,730 | 46.8 |
| 6 | Cecil M. Harden (R) | 66,414 | 49.9 |
| | Jack J. O'Grady (D) | 65,931 | 49.5 |
| 7 | James E. Noland (D) | 74,396 | 53.7 |
| | Gerald W. Landis (R) | 62,855 | 45.4 |
| 8 | Winfield K. Denton (D) | 89,990 | 55.4 |
| | Edward A. Mitchell (R) | 71,634 | 44.1 |
| 9 | Earl Wilson (R) | 59,787 | 51.6 |
| | Christopher D. Moritz (D) | 55,333 | 47.7 |

## INDIANA

| Candidates | Votes | % |
|---|---|---|
| 10 Ralph Harvey (R) | 76,036 | 52.5 |
| Robert C. Oliver (D) | 67,081 | 46.3 |
| 11 Andrew Jacobs Sr. (D) | 103,046 | 50.6 |
| George L. Denny (R) | 98,451 | 48.4 |

## IOWA

| Candidates | Votes | % |
|---|---|---|
| 1 Thomas E. Martin (R) | 70,959 | 53.6 |
| James D. France (D) | 60,860 | 45.9 |
| 2 Henry O. Talle (R) | 82,139 | 53.6 |
| T. W. Mullaney (D) | 70,272 | 45.9 |
| 3 H. R. Gross (R) | 78,838 | 58.3 |
| Dan J. P. Ryan (D) | 56,002 | 41.4 |
| 4 Karl LeCompte (R) | 53,384 | 51.5 |
| Steven V. Carter (D) | 49,894 | 48.2 |
| 5 Paul Cunningham (R) | 60,103 | 50.8 |
| Vincent L. Browner (D) | 57,370 | 48.5 |
| 6 James I. Dolliver (R) | 55,641 | 55.8 |
| James E. Irwin (D) | 43,997 | 44.2 |
| 7 Ben F. Jensen (R) | 59,173 | 56.9 |
| W. A. Byers (D) | 44,857 | 43.1 |
| 8 Charles B. Hoeven (R) | 56,970 | 55.2 |
| L. J. McGivern (D) | 45,796 | 44.4 |

## KANSAS

| Candidates | Votes | % |
|---|---|---|
| 1 Albert M. Cole (R) | 68,395 | 60.5 |
| James L. Quinn (D) | 44,711 | 39.5 |
| 2 Errett P. Scrivner (R) | 68,324 | 51.9 |
| Philip A. Dergance (D) | 63,431 | 48.1 |
| 3 Herbert A. Meyer (R) | 46,935 | 55.0 |
| Marcus C. Black (D) | 38,391 | 45.0 |
| 4 Edward H. Rees (R) | 88,605 | 55.6 |
| William J. Kropp (D) | 70,778 | 44.4 |
| 5 Clifford R. Hope (R) | 77,160 | 65.0 |
| Henry D. Parkinson (D) | 41,614 | 35.0 |
| 6 Wint Smith (R) | 55,013 | 57.6 |
| Leslie E. Davis (D) | 40,553 | 42.4 |

## KENTUCKY

| Candidates | Votes | % |
|---|---|---|
| 1 Noble J. Gregory (D) | 50,720 | 100.0 |
| 2 John Whitaker (D) | 54,586 | 63.4 |
| Mallam Lake (R) | 31,527 | 36.6 |
| 3 Thruston B. Morton (R) | 74,168 | 53.0 |
| Ralph H. Logan (D) | 64,877 | 46.3 |
| 4 Frank L. Chelf (D) | 45,538 | 59.5 |
| Stanley Jaggers (R) | 31,062 | 40.6 |
| 5 Brent Spence (D) | 47,518 | 66.2 |
| George T. Smith (R) | 24,240 | 33.8 |
| 6 Thomas R. Underwood (D) | 60,659 | 60.7 |
| John N. Menefee (R) | 39,251 | 39.3 |
| 7 Carl D. Perkins (D) | 39,788 | 60.5 |
| W. Howes Meade (R) | 26,007 | 39.5 |
| 8 Joe B. Bates (D) | 52,328 | 58.6 |
| Hubert Counts (R) | 34,127 | 38.2 |
| 9 James S. Golden (R) | 60,309 | 100.0 |

## LOUISIANA

| Candidates | Votes | % |
|---|---|---|
| 1 F. Edward Hebert (D) | 36,748 | 100.0 |
| 2 Hale Boggs (D) | 61,316 | 100.0 |
| 3 Edwin E. Willis (D) | 26,587 | 66.4 |
| J. Paulin Duhe (R) | 13,437 | 33.6 |
| 4 Overton Brooks (D) | 32,045 | 100.0 |
| 5 Otto E. Passman (D) | 34,362 | 100.0 |
| 6 James H. Morrison (D) | 47,515 | 100.0 |
| 7 Henry D. Larcade Jr. (D) | 36,053 | 100.0 |
| 8 A. Leonard Allen (D) | 33,613 | 100.0 |

## MAINE

| Candidates | Votes | % |
|---|---|---|
| 1 Robert Hale (R) | 52,536 | 62.5 |
| James A. McVicar (D) | 31,528 | 37.5 |
| 2 Charles P. Nelson (R) | 50,552 | 67.2 |
| Benjamin J. Arena (D) | 24,698 | 32.8 |

| Candidates | Votes | % |
|---|---|---|
| 3 Frank Fellows (R) | 38,692 | 70.9 |
| F. Davis Clark (D) | 15,888 | 29.1 |

## MARYLAND

| Candidates | Votes | % |
|---|---|---|
| 1 Edward T. Miller (R) | 29,700 | 52.4 |
| S. Scott Beck Jr. (D) | 27,024 | 47.6 |
| 2 William P. Bolton (D) | 99,157 | 55.2 |
| A. Earl Shipley (R) | 76,235 | 42.5 |
| 3 Edward A. Garmatz (D) | 32,138 | 68.8 |
| John A. Janetzke Jr. (R) | 13,131 | 28.1 |
| 4 George H. Fallon (D) | 38,486 | 58.2 |
| James W. Miller (R) | 21,084 | 31.9 |
| John E. T. Camper (PROG) | 6,552 | 9.9 |
| 5 Lansdale G. Sasscer (D) | 45,902 | 59.7 |
| C. Maurice Weidemeyer (R) | 30,997 | 40.3 |
| 6 J. Glenn Beall (R) | 59,856 | 55.3 |
| F. Byrne Austin (D) | 48,304 | 44.7 |

## MASSACHUSETTS

| Candidates | Votes | % |
|---|---|---|
| 1 John W. Heselton (R) | 75,582 | 57.2 |
| Patrick J. O'Malley (D) | 56,604 | 42.8 |
| 2 Foster Furcolo (D) | 81,775 | 54.9 |
| Charles R. Clason (R) | 67,267 | 45.1 |
| 3 Philip J. Philbin (D) | 104,601 | 73.9 |
| Carroll H. Balcom (R) | 36,855 | 26.1 |
| 4 Harold D. Donohue (D) | 89,064 | 59.2 |
| John J. Maginnis (R) | 61,448 | 40.8 |
| 5 Edith Nourse Rogers (R) | 139,288 | 100.0 |
| 6 George J. Bates (R) | 108,179 | 100.0 |
| 7 Thomas J. Lane (D) | 100,333 | 79.2 |
| A. Prescott Barker (R) | 26,339 | 20.8 |
| 8 Angier L. Goodwin (R) | 75,844 | 51.0 |
| Anthony M. Roche (D) | 72,767 | 49.0 |
| 9 Donald W. Nicholson (R) | 82,750 | 56.7 |
| Jacinto F. Diniz (D) | 63,275 | 43.3 |
| 10 Christian A. Herter (R) | 118,741 | 69.5 |
| Walter A. O'Brien Jr. (D) | 52,022 | 30.5 |
| 11 John F. Kennedy (D) | 106,366 | 100.0 |
| 12 John W. McCormack (D) | 125,015 | 100.0 |
| 13 Richard B. Wigglesworth (R) | 89,913 | 56.6 |
| David J. Concannon (D) | 69,050 | 43.4 |
| 14 Joseph W. Martin Jr. (R) | 87,973 | 61.4 |
| Joseph M. Mendonca (D) | 55,369 | 38.6 |

## MICHIGAN

| Candidates | Votes | % |
|---|---|---|
| 1 George G. Sadowski (D) | 101,954 | 83.5 |
| Rudolph G. Tenerowicz (R) | 19,609 | 16.1 |
| 2 Earl C. Michener (R) | 65,006 | 55.8 |
| Preston W. Slosson (D) | 50,148 | 43.0 |
| 3 Paul W. Shafer (R) | 64,637 | 59.4 |
| Leeman J. McCarty (D) | 42,146 | 38.7 |
| 4 Clare E. Hoffman (R) | 61,059 | 64.9 |
| Tom Surprise (D) | 31,429 | 33.4 |
| 5 Gerald R. Ford Jr. (R) | 74,191 | 60.5 |
| Fred J. Barr Jr. (D) | 46,972 | 38.3 |
| 6 William W. Blackney (R) | 73,465 | 49.8 |
| George D. Stevens (D) | 72,681 | 49.3 |
| 7 Jesse P. Wolcott (R) | 68,903 | 59.0 |
| Harvey C. Whetzel (D) | 47,040 | 40.3 |
| 8 Fred L. Crawford (R) | 61,394 | 61.3 |
| Louis C. Schwinger (D) | 37,125 | 37.1 |
| 9 Albert J. Engel (R) | 51,771 | 58.5 |
| John George Hosko (D) | 35,805 | 40.5 |
| 10 Roy O. Woodruff (R) | 49,206 | 63.3 |
| Edward J. Daugherty (D) | 27,742 | 35.7 |
| 11 Charles E. Potter (R) | 48,633 | 63.6 |
| Violet L. Patterson (D) | 27,265 | 35.6 |
| 12 John B. Bennett (R) | 42,955 | 56.6 |
| Gene A. Saari (D) | 32,485 | 42.8 |
| 13 George D. O'Brien (D) | 76,947 | 62.5 |
| Howard A. Coffin (R) | 45,761 | 37.1 |
| 14 Louis C. Rabaut (D) | 99,227 | 57.0 |
| Harold F. Youngblood (R) | 74,474 | 42.7 |
| 15 John D. Dingell (D) | 92,579 | 65.0 |
| Charles G. Burns (R) | 49,286 | 34.6 |

| Candidates | Votes | % |
|---|---|---|
| 16 John Lesinski (D) | 97,826 | 62.5 |
| Kirby L. Wilson Jr. (R) | 57,730 | 36.9 |
| 17 George A. Dondero (R) | 116,427 | 52.7 |
| John J. Brown (D) | 103,390 | 46.8 |

## MINNESOTA

| Candidates | Votes | % |
|---|---|---|
| 1 August H. Andresen (R) | 80,345 | 61.4 |
| Karl F. Rolvaag (DFL) | 50,533 | 38.6 |
| 2 Joseph P. O'Hara (R) | 82,886 | 63.9 |
| Milton F. Maxwell (DFL) | 46,894 | 36.1 |
| 3 Roy W. Wier (DFL) | 87,111 | 54.6 |
| George MacKinnon (R) | 72,402 | 45.4 |
| 4 Eugene J. McCarthy (DFL) | 78,476 | 59.4 |
| Edward J. Devitt (R) | 53,574 | 40.6 |
| 5 Walter H. Judd (R) | 76,313 | 54.0 |
| Marcella F. Killen (DFL) | 65,113 | 46.0 |
| 6 Fred Marshall (DFL) | 66,601 | 51.7 |
| Harold Knutson (R) | 62,194 | 48.3 |
| 7 H. Carl Andersen (R) | 63,879 | 52.5 |
| James M. Youngdale (DFL) | 57,863 | 47.5 |
| 8 John A. Blatnik (DFL) | 88,501 | 66.6 |
| William A. Berlin (R) | 44,306 | 33.4 |
| 9 Harold C. Hagen (DFL) | 57,189 | 54.6 |
| Oscar A. Johnson (DFL) | 47,476 | 45.4 |

## MISSISSIPPI

| Candidates | Votes | % |
|---|---|---|
| 1 John E. Rankin (D) | 16,800 | 100.0 |
| 2 Jamie L. Whitten (D) | 13,771 | 100.0 |
| 3 William M. Whittington (D) | 17,369 | 100.0 |
| 4 Thomas G. Abernethy (D) | 15,290 | 98.4 |
| 5 W. Arthur Winstead (D) | 22,641 | 100.0 |
| 6 William M. Colmer (D) | 29,751 | 100.0 |
| 7 John Bell Williams (D) | 36,663 | 100.0 |

## MISSOURI

| Candidates | Votes | % |
|---|---|---|
| 1 Clare Magee (D) | 56,226 | 57.6 |
| Wat Arnold (R) | 41,365 | 42.4 |
| 2 Morgan M. Moulder (D) | 66,062 | 56.7 |
| Max Schwabe (R) | 50,372 | 43.2 |
| 3 Philip J. Welch (D) | 69,599 | 57.1 |
| William C. Cole (R) | 52,290 | 42.9 |
| 4 Theodore Leonard Irving (D) | 74,752 | 64.1 |
| Richard A. Erickson (R) | 41,576 | 35.7 |
| 5 Richard W. Bolling (D) | 59,961 | 55.9 |
| Albert L. Reeves Jr. (R) | 47,371 | 44.1 |
| 6 George H. Christopher (D) | 63,390 | 51.4 |
| Marion T. Bennett (R) | 59,959 | 48.6 |
| 7 Dewey Short (R) | 61,242 | 54.0 |
| Thomas A. Johnson (D) | 52,255 | 46.0 |
| 8 Albert S. J. Carnahan (D) | 60,081 | 57.2 |
| Parke M. Banta (R) | 44,887 | 42.8 |
| 9 Clarence Cannon (D) | 56,669 | 61.7 |
| Robert V. Niedner (R) | 35,232 | 38.3 |
| 10 Paul C. Jones (D) | 67,564 | 71.6 |
| W. K. Dillon (R) | 26,760 | 28.4 |
| 11 John B. Sullivan (D) | 78,162 | 64.7 |
| Claude I. Bakewell (R) | 40,719 | 33.7 |
| 12 Raymond W. Karst (D) | 132,920 | 55.0 |
| Walter C. Ploeser (R) | 107,861 | 44.6 |
| 13 Frank M. Karsten (D) | 77,245 | 70.6 |
| Charles P. McBride (R) | 32,217 | 29.4 |

## MONTANA

| Candidates | Votes | % |
|---|---|---|
| 1 Mike Mansfield (D) | 64,276 | 67.9 |
| Albert H. Angstman (R) | 29,937 | 31.6 |
| 2 Wesley A. D'Ewart (R) | 61,124 | 51.0 |
| Willard E. Fraser (D) | 58,711 | 49.0 |

## NEBRASKA

| Candidates | Votes | % |
|---|---|---|
| 1 Carl T. Curtis (R) | 76,359 | 57.2 |
| Frank B. Morrison (D) | 57,031 | 42.8 |

## NEBRASKA

| Candidates | Votes | % |
|---|---|---|
| 2 Eugene D. O'Sullivan (D) | 58,443 | 51.4 |
| Howard Buffett (R) | 55,199 | 48.6 |
| 3 Karl Stefan (R) | 71,513 | 64.8 |
| Duane K. Peterson (D) | 38,846 | 35.2 |
| 4 Arthur L. Miller (R) | 65,549 | 63.6 |
| C. Edgar Leafdale (D) | 37,511 | 36.4 |

## NEVADA

| Candidates | Votes | % |
|---|---|---|
| AL Walter S. Baring (D) | 29,733 | 50.7 |
| Charles H. Russell (R) | 28,972 | 49.4 |

## NEW HAMPSHIRE

| Candidates | Votes | % |
|---|---|---|
| 1 Chester E. Merrow (R) | 64,794 | 55.5 |
| Peter R. Poirier (D) | 51,262 | 43.9 |
| 2 Norris Cotton (R) | 59,505 | 57.4 |
| Richard W. Leonard (D) | 43,289 | 41.8 |

## NEW JERSEY

| Candidates | Votes | % |
|---|---|---|
| 1 Charles A. Wolverton (R) | 89,211 | 53.0 |
| John W. Donges (D) | 77,012 | 45.8 |
| 2 T. Millet Hand (R) | 62,804 | 61.7 |
| William E. Stringer (D) | 38,194 | 37.5 |
| 3 James C. Auchincloss (R) | 87,538 | 58.5 |
| Charles F. Sullivan (D) | 59,810 | 40.0 |
| 4 Charles R. Howell (D) | 77,018 | 61.5 |
| Albert C. Jones (R) | 48,204 | 38.5 |
| 5 Charles A. Eaton (R) | 92,286 | 57.4 |
| George C. Miller (D) | 66,387 | 41.3 |
| 6 Clifford P. Case (R) | 83,285 | 55.3 |
| H. Frank Pettit (D) | 61,465 | 40.8 |
| 7 J. Parnell Thomas (R) | 72,873 | 56.2 |
| John J. Carlin (D) | 56,095 | 43.2 |
| 8 Gordon Canfield (R) | 59,191 | 47.5 |
| Charles S. Joelson (D) | 59,043 | 47.4 |
| 9 Harry L. Towe (R) | 90,153 | 62.3 |
| James S. Brown (D) | 54,682 | 37.8 |
| 10 Peter W. Rodino Jr. (D) | 58,668 | 50.7 |
| Anthony Guiliano (R) | 52,898 | 45.7 |
| 11 Hugh J. Addonizio (D) | 52,644 | 47.7 |
| Frank L. Sundstrom (R) | 50,920 | 46.2 |
| 12 Robert W. Kean (R) | 63,232 | 48.6 |
| Harry Dudkin (D) | 58,495 | 44.9 |
| 13 Mary T. Norton (D) | 84,487 | 68.1 |
| Leon Banach (R) | 39,661 | 32.0 |
| 14 Edward J. Hart (D) | 76,881 | 62.8 |
| Michael Bongiovanni (R) | 45,564 | 37.2 |

## NEW MEXICO

| Candidates | Votes | % |
|---|---|---|
| AL John E. Miles (D) | 108,529 ✔ | |
| Antonio M. Fernandez (D) | 105,300 ✔ | |
| Ben F. Meyer (R) | 76,695 | |
| Herman G. Baca (R) | 73,661 | |
| Clinton E. Jencks (PROG) | 805 | |

## NEW YORK

| Candidates | Votes | % |
|---|---|---|
| 1 W. Kingsland Macy (R) | 101,924 | 66.0 |
| Harold W. Worzel (D) | 48,816 | 31.6 |
| 2 Leonard W. Hall (R) | 144,052 | 68.1 |
| Richard T. Mayes (D, L) | 62,142 | 29.4 |
| 3 Henry J. Latham (R) | 104,476 | 56.5 |
| George G. Gross (D) | 65,247 | 35.3 |
| 4 L. Gary Clemente (D) | 62,190 | 46.9 |
| Gregory McMahon (R) | 58,192 | 43.8 |
| Thomas J. McCabe (AM LAB) | 7,681 | 5.8 |
| 5 T. Vincent Quinn (D, L) | 83,213 | 49.8 |
| Robert Tripp Ross (R) | 72,012 | 43.1 |
| Morris Pottish (AM LAB) | 11,994 | 7.2 |
| 6 James J. Delaney (D, L) | 76,828 | 54.2 |
| Robert Nodar Jr. (R) | 55,844 | 39.4 |
| Irma Lindheim (AM LAB) | 9,092 | 6.4 |
| 7 John J. Delaney (D, AM LAB) | 65,162* | 60.0 |
| Francis E. Dorn (R, L) | 43,483 | 40.0 |
| 8 Joseph L. Pfeifer (D, AM LAB) | 61,037 | 67.7 |
| Benjamin F. Westervelt Jr (R) | 25,773 | 28.6 |
| 9 Eugene J. Keogh (D, L) | 59,711 | 56.2 |
| Philip Hodes (R) | 26,700 | 25.1 |
| Murray Rosof (AM LAB) | 19,803 | 18.6 |
| 10 Andrew L. Somers (D, L) | 69,502 | 56.1 |
| Arthur S. Hirsch (R) | 32,290 | 26.1 |
| Ada B. Jackson (AM LAB) | 22,067 | 17.8 |
| 11 James J. Heffernan (D, L) | 74,974 | 54.9 |
| Alfred C. McKenzie (R) | 41,289 | 30.2 |
| Frank Serri (AM LAB) | 20,340 | 14.9 |
| 12 John J. Rooney (D, L) | 55,021 | 60.4 |
| John J. Miller (R) | 29,061 | 31.9 |
| Vincent J. Longhi (AM LAB) | 6,968 | 7.7 |
| 13 Donald L. O'Toole (D, L) | 66,111 | 52.8 |
| Charles A. Fisher (R) | 44,718 | 35.7 |
| James Griesi (AM LAB) | 14,440 | 11.5 |
| 14 Abraham J. Multer (D, R) | 103,676 | 77.8 |
| Lee Pressman (AM LAB) | 29,502 | 22.2 |
| 15 Emanuel Celler (D, AM LAB) | 94,828 | 81.4 |
| Henry D. Dorfman (R) | 21,703 | 18.6 |
| 16 James J. Murphy (D, L) | 51,185 | 49.3 |
| Frank A. Pavis (R) | 45,623 | 44.0 |
| Frank Cremonesi (AM LAB) | 6,991 | 6.7 |
| 17 Frederic R. Coudert Jr. (R) | 74,581 | 53.2 |
| Arthur T. Sawyer (D, L) | 52,101 | 37.2 |
| Alvin Udell (AM LAB) | 13,401 | 9.6 |
| 18 Vito Marcantonio (AM LAB) | 36,278 | 36.9 |
| John P. Morrissey (D) | 31,211 | 31.7 |
| John Ellis (R, L) | 30,899 | 31.4 |
| 19 Arthur G. Klein (D, AM LAB) | 77,426 | 74.4 |
| Herbert Lasky (R) | 20,697 | 19.9 |
| Stephen C. Vladeck (L) | 5,886 | 5.7 |
| 20 Sol Bloom (D, L) | 73,866 | 59.4 |
| Jules J. Justin (R) | 34,819 | 28.0 |
| Eugene P. Connolly (AM LAB) | 15,727 | 12.6 |
| 21 Jacob K. Javits (R, L) | 66,527 | 50.7 |
| Paul O'Dwyer (D, AM LAB) | 64,654 | 49.3 |
| 22 Adam Clayton Powell Jr. (D, AM LAB) | 63,523 | 76.4 |
| Harold C. Burton (R) | 14,012 | 16.9 |
| Edna C. Moseley (L) | 5,583 | 6.7 |
| 23 Walter A. Lynch (D, R) | 121,523 | 83.0 |
| Leon Straus (AM LAB) | 24,903 | 17.0 |
| 24 Isidore Dollinger (D, R) | 74,971 | 63.1 |
| Leo Isacson (AM LAB) | 43,933 | 37.0 |
| 25 Charles A. Buckley (D, R) | 138,706 | 82.2 |
| Albert E. Kahn (AM LAB) | 30,112 | 17.8 |
| 26 Christopher C. McGrath (D, L) | 91,456 | 54.8 |
| David M. Potts (R) | 57,061 | 34.2 |
| Nicholas Carnes (AM LAB) | 18,379 | 11.0 |
| 27 Ralph W. Gwinn (R) | 81,144 | 52.1 |
| Richard W. McSpedon (D, L) | 67,541 | 43.4 |
| 28 Ralph A. Gamble (R) | 88,822 | 62.7 |
| Charles J. Nager (D, L) | 46,335 | 32.7 |
| 29 Katharine St. George (R) | 79,229 | 60.1 |
| William G. Pendergast (D, L) | 48,063 | 36.5 |
| 30 Jay LeFevre (R) | 91,649 | 64.8 |
| Robert R. Decormier (D, AM LAB) | 49,691 | 35.2 |
| 31 Bernard W. Kearney (R) | 77,725 | 55.3 |
| William M. Murphy (D, L) | 58,215 | 41.4 |
| 32 William T. Byrne (D, L) | 88,476 | 55.6 |
| Lawrence J. Collins (R) | 65,341 | 41.1 |
| 33 Dean P. Taylor (R) | 98,618 | 63.7 |
| Joseph T. Hammer (D, L) | 52,059 | 33.6 |
| 34 Clarence E. Kilburn (R) | 70,715 | 60.7 |
| Francis K. Purcell (D) | 43,777 | 37.6 |
| 35 John C. Davies (D, L) | 62,855 | 48.9 |
| Hadwen C. Fuller (R) | 62,717 | 48.8 |
| 36 R. Walter Riehlman (R) | 78,409 | 50.5 |
| Richard T. Mosher (D, L) | 71,847 | 46.3 |
| 37 Edwin Arthur Hall (R) | 65,848 | 63.4 |
| Myron C. Sloat (D) | 35,503 | 34.2 |
| 38 John Taber (R) | 66,695 | 58.0 |
| Francis J. Souhan (D) | 48,222 | 42.0 |
| 39 W. Sterling Cole (R) | 70,656 | 64.3 |
| Donald J. O'Connor (D, L) | 37,272 | 33.9 |
| 40 Kenneth B. Keating (R) | 90,305 | 51.4 |
| George F. Rogers (D, AM LAB) | 85,505 | 48.6 |
| 41 James W. Wadsworth Jr. (R) | 67,882 | 59.1 |
| Bernard E. Hart (D) | 45,155 | 39.3 |
| 42 William L. Pfeiffer (R) | 75,842 | 51.1 |
| Mary Louise Nice (D, L) | 69,290 | 46.6 |
| 43 Anthony F. Tauriello (D, L) | 72,388 | 50.8 |
| Edward J. Elsaesser (R) | 66,729 | 46.9 |
| 44 Chester C. Gorski (D, L) | 79,795 | 51.8 |
| John C. Butler (R) | 71,275 | 46.2 |
| 45 Daniel A. Reed (R) | 58,340 | 60.1 |
| Hubert D. Bliss (D) | 35,406 | 36.5 |

### Special Election

| Candidates | Votes | % |
|---|---|---|
| 24 Leo Isacson (AM LAB) | 22,697 | 55.9 |
| Karl Propper (D) | 12,598 | 31.0 |
| Dean Alfange (L) | 3,843 | 9.5 |

## NORTH CAROLINA

| Candidates | Votes | % |
|---|---|---|
| 1 Herbert C. Bonner (D) | 31,850 | 92.7 |
| Zeno O. Ratcliff (R) | 2,507 | 7.3 |
| 2 John H. Kerr (D) | 36,227 | 96.0 |
| 3 Graham A. Barden (D) | 34,997 | 78.8 |
| Perry G. Crumpler (R) | 9,407 | 21.2 |
| 4 Harold D. Cooley (D) | 57,658 | 78.1 |
| Joel A. Johnson (R) | 15,866 | 21.5 |
| 5 Richard Thurmond Chatham (D) | 47,575 | 72.7 |
| John Tucker Day (R) | 17,041 | 26.1 |
| 6 Carl T. Durham (D) | 50,659 | 72.1 |
| Ralph O. Smith (R) | 17,906 | 25.5 |
| 7 F. Ertel Carlyle (D) | 43,292 | 84.3 |
| J. O. West (R) | 7,839 | 15.3 |
| 8 Charles B. Deane (D) | 46,941 | 62.7 |
| Lafayette Williams (R) | 27,924 | 37.3 |
| 9 Robert L. Doughton (D) | 51,586 | 59.6 |
| Clyde R. Greene (R) | 35,008 | 40.4 |
| 10 Hamilton C. Jones (D) | 48,043 | 59.6 |
| Roy A. Harmon (R) | 32,321 | 40.1 |
| 11 Alfred L. Bulwinkle (D) | 40,009 | 64.9 |
| Calvin R. Edney (R) | 21,614 | 35.1 |
| 12 Monroe M. Redden (D) | 52,036 | 63.1 |
| W. W. Candler (R) | 30,456 | 36.9 |

## NORTH DAKOTA

| Candidates | Votes | % |
|---|---|---|
| AL William Lemke (R) | 132,343 ✔ | |
| Usher L. Burdick (R) | 128,454 ✔ | |
| Alfred Dale (D) | 56,702 | |
| John M. Weiler | 1,758 | |

## OHIO

| Candidates | Votes | % |
|---|---|---|
| 1 Charles H. Elston (R) | 73,952 | 51.7 |
| Morse Johnson (D) | 69,240 | 48.4 |
| 2 Earl T. Wagner (R) | 75,062 | 52.9 |
| William E. Hess (R) | 66,968 | 47.2 |
| 3 Edward Breen (D) | 110,204 | 58.2 |
| Raymond H. Burke (R) | 79,162 | 41.8 |
| 4 William M. McCulloch (R) | 57,321 | 55.7 |
| Earl Ludwig (D) | 45,534 | 44.3 |
| 5 Cliff Clevenger (R) | 34,950 | 52.1 |
| Dan Batt (D) | 32,076 | 47.9 |
| 6 James G. Polk (D) | 46,944 | 53.1 |
| Edward O. McCowen (R) | 41,492 | 46.9 |
| 7 Clarence J. Brown (R) | 71,737 | 100.0 |
| 8 Frederick C. Smith (R) | 43,929 | 54.5 |
| Andrew T. Durbin (D) | 36,685 | 45.5 |

## OHIO

| | Candidates | Votes | % |
|---|---|---|---|
| 9 | Thomas H. Burke (D) | 85,409 | 53.8 |
| | Homer A. Ramey (R) | 73,394 | 46.2 |
| 10 | Thomas A. Jenkins (R) | 38,330 | 57.9 |
| | Delmar A. Canaday (D) | 27,913 | 42.1 |
| 11 | Walter E. Brehm (R) | 33,796 | 50.9 |
| | Joseph C. Allen (D) | 32,667 | 49.2 |
| 12 | John M. Vorys (R) | 95,575 | 52.1 |
| | Robert M. Draper (D) | 87,770 | 47.9 |
| 13 | Alvin F. Weichel (R) | 55,408 | 59.2 |
| | Dwight A. Blackmore (D) | 38,264 | 40.9 |
| 14 | Walter B. Huber (D) | 125,346 | 57.2 |
| | Ed Rowe (R) | 92,535 | 42.2 |
| 15 | Robert T. Secrest (D) | 45,575 | 56.4 |
| | P. W. Griffiths (R) | 35,294 | 43.6 |
| 16 | John McSweeney (D) | 79,859 | 52.6 |
| | Henderson H. Carson (R) | 71,871 | 47.4 |
| 17 | J. Harry McGregor (R) | 60,234 | 52.9 |
| | Robert W. Levering (D) | 53,651 | 47.1 |
| 18 | Wayne L. Hays (D) | 65,475 | 54.1 |
| | Earl R. Lewis (R) | 55,455 | 45.9 |
| 19 | Michael J. Kirwan (D) | 134,448 | 68.1 |
| | William Bacon (R) | 63,079 | 31.9 |
| 20 | Michael A. Feighan (D) | 64,241 | 100.0 |
| 21 | Robert Crosser (D) | 72,417 | 76.0 |
| | Harry W. Mitchell (R) | 22,932 | 24.1 |
| 22 | Frances P. Bolton (R) | 170,085 | 54.7 |
| | Jack G. Day (D) | 141,018 | 45.3 |
| AL | Stephen M. Young (D) | 1,455,972 | 52.0 |
| | George H. Bender (R) | 1,342,409 | 48.0 |

## OKLAHOMA

| | Candidates | Votes | % |
|---|---|---|---|
| 1 | William Franklin Gilmer (D) | 77,949 | 53.3 |
| | George B. Schwabe (R) | 68,423 | 46.8 |
| 2 | William G. Stigler (D) | 43,801 | 70.6 |
| | George T. Balch (R) | 18,236 | 29.4 |
| 3 | Carl Albert (D) | 57,300 | 83.9 |
| | Russell Overstreet (R) | 11,007 | 16.1 |
| 4 | Tom Steed (D) | 53,419 | 72.1 |
| | Clyde T. Patrick (R) | 20,716 | 27.9 |
| 5 | A. S. Mike Monroney (D) | 95,248 | 67.4 |
| | Carmon C. Harris (R) | 45,985 | 32.6 |
| 6 | Toby Morris (D) | 47,857 | 73.7 |
| | George E. Young (R) | 17,100 | 26.3 |
| 7 | Victor E. Wickersham (D) | 39,380 | 79.4 |
| | J. Warren White (R) | 10,236 | 20.6 |
| 8 | George H. Wilson (D) | 42,417 | 58.0 |
| | Martin Garber (R) | 30,687 | 42.0 |

## OREGON

| | Candidates | Votes | % |
|---|---|---|---|
| 1 | Walter Norblad (R) | 88,587 | 63.3 |
| | Edward E. Gideon (D) | 45,904 | 32.8 |
| 2 | Lowell Stockman (R) | 42,730 | 58.2 |
| | C. J. Shorb (D) | 30,743 | 41.8 |
| 3 | Homer D. Angell (R) | 99,464 | 55.5 |
| | Roland C. Bartlett (D) | 66,436 | 37.1 |
| | Peggy T. Carlson (PROG) | 13,171 | 7.4 |
| 4 | Harris Ellsworth (R) | 65,606 | 66.6 |
| | William F. Tanton (D & PROG) | 32,931 | 33.4 |

## PENNSYLVANIA

| | Candidates | Votes | % |
|---|---|---|---|
| 1 | William A. Barrett (D) | 70,165 | 53.4 |
| | John De Nero (R) | 61,165 | 46.6 |
| 2 | William T. Granahan (D) | 82,863 | 54.4 |
| | Robert H. McGarvey (R) | 69,604 | 45.7 |
| 3 | Hardie Scott (R) | 76,009 | 52.0 |
| | Maurice S. Osser (D) | 70,075 | 48.0 |
| 4 | Earl Chudoff (D) | 70,129 | 55.7 |
| | Franklin J. Maloney (R) | 50,236 | 39.9 |
| 5 | William J. Green Jr. (D) | 77,221 | 50.7 |
| | George W. Sarbacher Jr. (R) | 75,007 | 49.3 |
| 6 | Hugh Scott (R) | 86,755 | 57.0 |
| | Herbert J. McGlinchey (D) | 65,535 | 43.0 |
| 7 | Benjamin F. James (R) | 91,394 | 61.3 |
| | Arnold M. Snyder (D) | 56,263 | 37.8 |
| 8 | Franklin H. Lichtenwalter (R) | 62,229 | 59.2 |
| | Wynne James Jr. (D) | 42,878 | 40.8 |
| 9 | Paul B. Dague (R) | 74,726 | 67.1 |
| | W. Roger Simpson (D) | 36,677 | 32.9 |
| 10 | Harry P. O'Neill (D) | 64,289 | 58.5 |
| | Nelson Nichols (R) | 45,587 | 41.5 |
| 11 | Daniel J. Flood (D) | 68,628 | 51.8 |
| | Robert H. Stroh (R) | 63,797 | 48.2 |
| 12 | Ivor D. Fenton (R) | 68,089 | 60.6 |
| | John Oshinskie (D) | 44,345 | 39.4 |
| 13 | George M. Rhodes (D) | 40,415 | 50.3 |
| | Frederick A. Muhlenberg (R) | 37,261 | 46.4 |
| 14 | Wilson D. Gillette (R) | 47,715 | 65.2 |
| | David Burchell (D) | 25,484 | 34.8 |
| 15 | Robert F. Rich (R, P) | 48,760 | 61.6 |
| | Patrick A. McGowan (D) | 30,457 | 38.5 |
| 16 | Samuel K. McConnell Jr. (R) | 84,997 | 66.9 |
| | Harry Hellar Kelly (D) | 42,118 | 33.1 |
| 17 | Richard M. Simpson (R) | 38,735 | 64.5 |
| | Ira Garman (D) | 21,339 | 35.5 |
| 18 | John C. Kunkel (R) | 81,704 | 63.7 |
| | Theodore C. Frederick Jr. (D) | 46,586 | 36.3 |
| 19 | Leon H. Gavin (R) | 43,520 | 63.7 |
| | Francis J. Manno (D) | 24,800 | 36.3 |
| 20 | Francis E. Walter (D) | 54,041 | 58.8 |
| | Roy E. James (R) | 37,904 | 41.2 |
| 21 | James F. Lind (D) | 54,152 | 53.7 |
| | Chester H. Gross (R) | 46,701 | 46.3 |
| 22 | James E. Van Zandt (R) | 46,451 | 60.4 |
| | Julia Luigia Maietta (D) | 30,454 | 39.6 |
| 23 | Anthony Cavalcante (D) | 42,084 | 54.3 |
| | William J. Crow (R) | 35,384 | 45.7 |
| 24 | Thomas E. Morgan (D) | 56,282 | 65.4 |
| | Roy A. Purviance (R) | 29,768 | 34.6 |
| 25 | Louis E. Graham (R) | 56,966 | 52.6 |
| | Andrew G. Katcher (D) | 51,391 | 47.4 |
| 26 | Robert L. Coffey Jr. (D) | 62,061 | 55.4 |
| | Harve Tibbott (R) | 50,005 | 44.6 |
| 27 | Augustine B. Kelley (D) | 64,943 | 62.2 |
| | W. Urban Gillespie (R) | 39,517 | 37.8 |
| 28 | Carroll D. Kearns (R) | 65,276 | 54.5 |
| | James A. Kennedy (D) | 54,402 | 45.5 |
| 29 | Harry J. Davenport (D) | 63,454 | 54.2 |
| | John McDowell (R) | 53,609 | 45.8 |
| 30 | Robert J. Corbett (R) | 56,932 | 50.3 |
| | J. R. Montgomery (D) | 56,233 | 49.7 |
| 31 | James G. Fulton (R) | 75,147 | 56.4 |
| | John J. Kane Jr. (D) | 58,113 | 43.6 |
| 32 | Herman P. Eberharter (D) | 80,600 | 72.7 |
| | Albert J. Weilersbacher (R) | 30,328 | 27.3 |
| 33 | Frank Buchanan (D) | 74,508 | 69.2 |
| | Albert G. Brown (R) | 33,107 | 30.8 |

## RHODE ISLAND

| | Candidates | Votes | % |
|---|---|---|---|
| 1 | Aime J. Forand (D) | 95,045 | 62.0 |
| | Oscar J. V. Hurteau (R) | 58,209 | 38.0 |
| 2 | John E. Fogarty (D) | 98,586 | 59.7 |
| | Thomas J. Paolino (R) | 66,672 | 40.3 |

## SOUTH CAROLINA

| | Candidates | Votes | % |
|---|---|---|---|
| 1 | L. Mendel Rivers (D) | 24,529 | 89.1 |
| | W. T. Baggott (R) | 2,989 | 10.9 |
| 2 | Hugo S. Sims Jr. (D) | 27,677 | 96.5 |
| 3 | James B. Hare (D) | 19,181 | 97.8 |
| 4 | Joseph R. Bryson (D) | 26,098 | 94.9 |
| | James B. Gaston (D) | 1,410 | 5.1 |
| 5 | James P. Richards (D) | 14,544 | 97.1 |
| 6 | John L. McMillan (D) | 21,703 | 97.1 |

## SOUTH DAKOTA

| | Candidates | Votes | % |
|---|---|---|---|
| 1 | Harold O. Lovre (R) | 99,062 | 53.5 |
| | Merton B. Tice (D) | 85,957 | 46.5 |

| | Candidates | Votes | % |
|---|---|---|---|
| 2 | Francis H. Case (R) | 36,713 | 65.9 |
| | Jessie E. Sanders (D) | 18,988 | 34.1 |

## TENNESSEE

| | Candidates | Votes | % |
|---|---|---|---|
| 1 | Dayton E. Phillips (R) | 54,439 | 84.7 |
| | Arthur W. Bright (D) | 9,806 | 15.3 |
| 2 | John Jennings Jr. (R) | 43,849 | 58.0 |
| | Thomas P. Fowler (IR) | 31,743 | 42.0 |
| 3 | James B. Frazier Jr. (D) | 44,683 | 67.3 |
| | W. E. Michael (R) | 20,740 | 31.3 |
| 4 | Albert Gore (D) | 21,445 | 64.3 |
| | Tom T. Tucker Jr. (R) | 11,910 | 35.7 |
| 5 | Joe L. Evins (D) | 27,777 | 100.0 |
| 6 | J. Percy Priest (D) | 28,951 | 81.4 |
| | Jesse L. Perry (R) | 6,056 | 17.0 |
| 7 | James P. Sutton (D) | 28,058 | 100.0 |
| 8 | Thomas J. Murray (D) | 25,170 | 69.2 |
| | J. Sam Johnson Jr. (R) | 11,229 | 30.9 |
| 9 | Jere Cooper (D) | 26,033 | 91.1 |
| | S. Homer Tatum (R) | 2,555 | 8.9 |
| 10 | Clifford Davis (D) | 49,371 | 93.1 |
| | Dwight V. Kyle (R) | 3,670 | 6.9 |

## TEXAS

| | Candidates | Votes | % |
|---|---|---|---|
| 1 | Wright Patman (D) | 40,162 | 100.0 |
| 2 | Jesse M. Combs (D) | 55,072 | 93.3 |
| | Don Parker (R) | 3,978 | 6.7 |
| 3 | Lindley Beckworth (D) | 36,361 | 88.7 |
| | R. E. Kennedy (R) | 4,642 | 11.3 |
| 4 | Sam Rayburn (D) | 38,211 | 100.0 |
| 5 | J. Frank Wilson (D) | 66,484 | 98.4 |
| 6 | Olin E. Teague (D) | 18,731 | 99.8 |
| 7 | Tom Pickett (D) | 27,945 | 100.0 |
| 8 | Albert Thomas (D) | 100,721 | 85.5 |
| | Joe Ingraham (R) | 17,124 | 14.5 |
| 9 | Clark W. Thompson (D) | 55,606 | 100.0 |
| 10 | Homer Thornberry (D) | 45,007 | 100.0 |
| 11 | W. R. Poage (D) | 39,795 | 96.2 |
| 12 | Wingate H. Lucas (D) | 61,206 | 89.1 |
| | Elton M. Hyder (R) | 7,480 | 10.9 |
| 13 | Ed Gossett (D) | 44,274 | 100.0 |
| 14 | John E. Lyle Jr. (D) | 59,163 | 88.9 |
| | J. M. Swafford (R) | 7,202 | 10.8 |
| 15 | Lloyd M. Bentsen Jr. (D) | 27,402 | 100.0 |
| 16 | Ken Regan (D) | 37,173 | 99.5 |
| 17 | Omar Burleson (D) | 34,078 | 100.0 |
| 18 | Eugene Worley (D) | 48,985 | 88.7 |
| | J. Evetts Haley (R) | 6,266 | 11.3 |
| 19 | George Mahon (D) | 58,585 | 95.6 |
| 20 | Paul J. Kilday (D) | 43,709 | 75.3 |
| | J. P. Ledvina (R) | 14,376 | 24.8 |
| 21 | O. Clark Fisher (D) | 45,274 | 100.0 |

## UTAH

| | Candidates | Votes | % |
|---|---|---|---|
| 1 | Walter K. Granger (D) | 66,641 | 59.0 |
| | David J. Wilson (R) | 46,229 | 41.0 |
| 2 | Reva Beck Bosone (D) | 92,770 | 57.5 |
| | William A. Dawson (R) | 68,693 | 42.5 |

## VERMONT

| | Candidates | Votes | % |
|---|---|---|---|
| AL | Charles A. Plumley (R) | 74,076 | 60.7 |
| | Robert W. Ready (D) | 47,767 | 39.2 |

## VIRGINIA

| | Candidates | Votes | % |
|---|---|---|---|
| 1 | S. Otis Bland (D) | 24,746 | 80.0 |
| | Stanley G. Adams (R) | 5,753 | 18.6 |
| 2 | Porter Hardy Jr. (D) | 28,071 | 61.2 |
| | Walter E. Hoffman (R) | 15,800 | 34.4 |
| 3 | J. Vaughan Gary (D) | 33,950 | 72.9 |
| | Richard C. Poage (R) | 11,291 | 24.3 |
| 4 | Watkins M. Abbitt (D) | 22,029 | 100.0 |

## VIRGINIA

| | Candidates | Votes | % |
|---|---|---|---|
| 5 | Thomas B. Stanley (D) | 23,879 | 99.5 |
| 6 | Clarence G. Burton (D) | 29,589 | 64.7 |
| | John Strickler (R) | 15,854 | 34.7 |
| 7 | Burr P. Harrison (D) | 25,799 | 60.4 |
| | Stephen D. Timberlake (R) | 16,890 | 39.6 |
| 8 | Howard W. Smith (D) | 33,563 | 54.8 |
| | Tyrrell Krum (R) | 25,420 | 41.5 |
| 9 | Thomas B. Fugate (D) | 33,550 | 52.4 |
| | T. Eugene Worrell (R) | 30,466 | 47.6 |

### Special Election

| | | | |
|---|---|---|---|
| 6 | Clarence G. Burton (D) | 30,841 | 65.2 |
| | John Strickler (R) | 16,435 | 34.8 |

## WASHINGTON

| | | | |
|---|---|---|---|
| 1 | Hugh B. Mitchell (D) | 100,030 | 50.8 |
| | Homer R. Jones (R) | 92,215 | 46.8 |
| 2 | Henry M. Jackson (D) | 83,824 | 61.6 |
| | Payson Peterson (R) | 48,413 | 35.6 |
| 3 | Russell V. Mack (R) | 61,856 | 52.1 |
| | Charles R. Savage (D) | 56,947 | 47.9 |

| | Candidates | Votes | % |
|---|---|---|---|
| 4 | Hal Holmes (R) | 58,105 | 53.2 |
| | John F. Eubank (D) | 51,195 | 46.8 |
| 5 | Walt Horan (R) | 67,757 | 54.6 |
| | John F. McKay (D) | 56,343 | 45.4 |
| 6 | Thor C. Tollefson (R) | 72,988 | 55.1 |
| | Jack E. Knudsen (D) | 54,166 | 40.9 |

## WEST VIRGINIA

| | | | |
|---|---|---|---|
| 1 | Robert L. Ramsay (D) | 68,829 | 57.3 |
| | Francis J. Love (R) | 51,381 | 42.7 |
| 2 | Harley O. Staggers (D) | 61,786 | 54.7 |
| | Melvin C. Snyder (R) | 51,226 | 45.3 |
| 3 | Cleveland M. Bailey (D) | 68,055 | 57.1 |
| | Edward G. Rohrbough (R) | 51,123 | 42.9 |
| 4 | Maurice G. Burnside (D) | 72,378 | 53.1 |
| | Hubert S. Ellis (R) | 64,001 | 46.9 |
| 5 | John Kee (D) | 71,664 | 65.1 |
| | Hartley Sanders (R) | 38,446 | 34.9 |
| 6 | Erland H. Hedrick (D) | 99,842 | 62.5 |
| | D. L. Salisbury (R) | 59,900 | 37.5 |

## WISCONSIN

| | Candidates | Votes | % |
|---|---|---|---|
| 1 | Lawrence H. Smith (R) | 67,387 | 51.9 |
| | Jack Harvey (D) | 61,791 | 47.6 |
| 2 | Glenn R. Davis (R) | 74,306 | 53.9 |
| | Horace W. Wilkie (D) | 62,953 | 45.6 |
| 3 | Gardner R. Withrow (R) | 69,727 | 69.2 |
| | Frank J. Antoine (D) | 30,650 | 30.4 |
| 4 | Clement J. Zablocki (D) | 89,391 | 55.9 |
| | John C. Brophy (R) | 63,161 | 39.5 |
| 5 | Andrew J. Biemiller (D) | 91,072 | 53.1 |
| | Charles J. Kersten (R) | 76,782 | 44.8 |
| 6 | Frank B. Keefe (R) | 60,675 | 55.5 |
| | Kenneth Kunde (D) | 47,844 | 43.8 |
| 7 | Reid F. Murray (R) | 64,531 | 62.5 |
| | Ralph E. Kronenwetter (D) | 37,307 | 36.1 |
| 8 | John W. Byrnes (R) | 70,905 | 56.7 |
| | Martin J. Young (D) | 53,287 | 42.6 |
| 9 | Merlin Hull (R) | 76,903 | 98.1 |
| 10 | Alvin E. O'Konski (R) | 52,124 | 54.8 |
| | Daniel W. Hoan (D) | 39,523 | 41.6 |

## WYOMING

| | | | |
|---|---|---|---|
| AL | Frank A. Barrett (R) | 50,218 | 51.5 |
| | L. G. Flannery (D) | 47,246 | 48.5 |

# 1949 House Elections

## NEW YORK

### Special Election

| | Candidates | Votes | % |
|---|---|---|---|
| 7 | Louis B. Heller (D, L) | 22,939 | 54.8 |
| | Francis E. Dorn (R) | 16,179 | 38.7 |
| | Minneola Ingersoll (AM LAB) | 2,712 | 6.5 |
| 10 | Edna F. Kelly (D) | 48,945 | 55.1 |
| | Jules Cohen (L) | 24,419 | 27.5 |
| | George H. Fankuchen (R) | 15,514 | 17.5 |
| 20 | Franklin D. Roosevelt Jr (L, FF) | 40,822 | 50.7 |
| | Benjamin Shalleck (D) | 24,352 | 30.2 |
| | William H. McIntyre (R) | 10,026 | 12.5 |
| | Annette T. Rubinstein (AM LAB) | 5,348 | 6.6 |

---

## House Candidates Index

For an index of all House candidates listed in this section (pages 943-1326), see pages 1402-1501. Instructions for use of the House Candidates Index appear on page 1402.

---

# 1950 House Elections

## ALABAMA

| Candidates | Votes | % |
|---|---|---|
| 1 Frank W. Boykin (D) | 14,206 | 100.0 |
| 2 George M. Grant (D) | 17,441 | 100.0 |
| 3 George W. Andrews (D) | 10,914 | 100.0 |
| 4 Kenneth A. Roberts (D) | 14,608 | 93.7 |
| J. P. Carter (R) | 980 | 6.3 |
| 5 Albert Rains (D) | 17,269 | 100.0 |
| 6 Edward deGraffenried (D) | 11,709 | 100.0 |
| 7 Carl A. Elliott (D) | 20,580 | 100.0 |
| 8 Robert E. Jones Jr. (D) | 13,742 | 100.0 |
| 9 Laurie C. Battle (D) | 30,743 | 100.0 |

## ARIZONA

| Candidates | Votes | % |
|---|---|---|
| 1 John R. Murdock (D) | 51,526 | 60.6 |
| Carl W. Divelbiss (R) | 33,528 | 39.4 |
| 2 Harold A. Patten (D) | 63,991 | 69.1 |
| John H. Curnutte (R) | 28,622 | 30.9 |

## ARKANSAS

| Candidates | Votes | % |
|---|---|---|
| 1 Ezekiel C. Gathings (D) | 47,238 | 100.0 |
| 2 Wilbur D. Mills (D) | 31,048 | 100.0 |
| 3 James W. Trimble (D) | 34,434 | 100.0 |
| 4 Boyd Tackett (D) | 43,156 | 100.0 |
| 5 Brooks Hays (D) | 54,338 | 100.0 |
| 6 William F. Norrell (D) | 46,467 | 100.0 |
| 7 Oren Harris (D) | 39,121 | 100.0 |

## CALIFORNIA

| Candidates | Votes | % |
|---|---|---|
| 1 Hubert B. Scudder (R) | 85,122 | 54.0 |
| Roger Kent (D) | 72,584 | 46.0 |
| 2 Clair Engle (D-R) | 85,103 | 100.0 |
| 3 Leroy Johnson (R-D) | 177,269 | 100.0 |
| 4 Franck R. Havenner (D) | 83,078 | 67.2 |
| Raymond D. Smith (R) | 40,569 | 32.8 |
| 5 John F. Shelley (D-R) | 117,888 | 100.0 |
| 6 George P. Miller (D-R) | 192,342 | 100.0 |
| 7 John J. Allen Jr. (R) | 74,069 | 55.3 |
| Lyle E. Cook (D) | 59,976 | 44.7 |
| 8 Jack Z. Anderson (R-D) | 168,510 | 83.1 |
| John A. Peterson (I PROG) | 34,176 | 16.9 |
| 9 Allan Oakley Hunter (R) | 76,015 | 52.0 |
| Cecil F. White (D) | 70,201 | 48.0 |
| 10 Thomas H. Werdel (R) | 59,313 | 53.6 |
| Ardis M. Walker (D) | 51,409 | 46.4 |
| 11 Ernest K. Bramblett (R) | 59,780 | 52.1 |
| Marion R. Walker (D) | 55,020 | 47.9 |
| 12 Patrick J. Hillings (R) | 107,933 | 60.1 |
| Steve Zetterberg (D) | 71,682 | 39.9 |
| 13 Norris Poulson (R-D) | 83,296 | 84.8 |
| Ellen P. Davidson (I PROG) | 14,789 | 15.1 |
| 14 Samuel William Yorty (D) | 47,653 | 49.4 |
| Jack W. Hardy (R) | 35,543 | 36.8 |
| Charlotta A. Bass (I PROG) | 13,364 | 13.8 |
| 15 Gordon L. McDonough (R-D) | 112,704 | 87.1 |
| Jeanne Cole (I PROG) | 16,559 | 12.8 |
| 16 Donald L. Jackson (R) | 115,970 | 59.2 |
| Esther Murray (D) | 79,744 | 40.7 |
| 17 Cecil R. King (D-R) | 166,334 | 99.9 |
| 18 Clyde Doyle (D) | 97,177 | 50.5 |
| Craig Hosmer (R) | 95,308 | 49.5 |
| 19 Chet Holifield (D-R) | 73,317 | 90.9 |
| Myra Tanner Weiss (I) | 7,329 | 9.1 |
| 20 Carl Hinshaw (R-D) | 211,012 | 85.1 |
| William B. Esterman (I PROG) | 26,508 | 10.7 |
| 21 Harry R. Sheppard (D) | 62,994 | 57.4 |
| R. E. Reynolds (R) | 46,693 | 42.6 |
| 22 John Phillips (R-D) | 114,497 | 99.9 |
| 23 Clinton D. McKinnon (D) | 94,137 | 51.0 |
| Leslie E. Gehres (R) | 90,398 | 49.0 |

## COLORADO

| Candidates | Votes | % |
|---|---|---|
| 1 Byron Rogers (D) | 70,165 | 50.3 |
| Richard Luxford (R) | 67,436 | 48.4 |
| 2 William S. Hill (R) | 73,045 | 57.5 |
| George L. Bickel (D) | 53,313 | 42.0 |
| 3 J. Edgar Chenoweth (R) | 58,831 | 51.6 |
| John H. Marsalis (D) | 55,110 | 48.4 |
| 4 Wayne N. Aspinall (D) | 35,797 | 57.3 |
| Jack Evans (R) | 26,674 | 42.7 |

## CONNECTICUT

| Candidates | Votes | % |
|---|---|---|
| 1 Abraham A. Ribicoff (D) | 134,258 | 58.1 |
| Harry Schwolsky (R) | 96,251 | 41.7 |
| 2 Horace Seely-Brown Jr. (R) | 68,747 | 50.8 |
| Chase Going Woodhouse (D) | 66,523 | 49.2 |
| 3 John A. McGuire (D) | 89,391 | 51.9 |
| Ellsworth B. Foote (R) | 82,304 | 47.8 |
| 4 Albert P. Morano (R) | 111,939 | 53.1 |
| Dennis M. Carroll (D) | 88,682 | 42.1 |
| 5 James T. Patterson (R) | 65,915 | 53.0 |
| J. Gregory Lynch (D) | 56,752 | 45.7 |
| AL Antoni N. Sadlak (R) | 433,912 | 49.4 |
| Joseph W. Bogdanski (D) | 426,485 | 48.6 |

## DELAWARE

| Candidates | Votes | % |
|---|---|---|
| AL J. Caleb Boggs (R) | 73,313 | 56.7 |
| Henry M. Winchester (D) | 56,091 | 43.4 |

## FLORIDA

| Candidates | Votes | % |
|---|---|---|
| 1 Chester B. McMullen (D) | 40,466 | 100.0 |
| 2 Charles E. Bennett (D) | 34,334 | 100.0 |
| 3 Robert L. F. Sikes (D) | 24,548 | 100.0 |
| 4 Bill Lantaff (D) | 65,758 | 82.1 |
| Joseph Edward Worton (R) | 14,305 | 17.9 |
| 5 A. S. Herlong Jr. (D) | 32,475 | 76.5 |
| Carl K. Landes (R) | 9,958 | 23.5 |
| 6 Dwight L. Rogers (D) | 31,205 | 100.0 |

## GEORGIA

| Candidates | Votes | % |
|---|---|---|
| 1 Prince H. Preston (D) | 29,716 | 100.0 |
| 2 E. E. Cox (D) | 18,920 | 100.0 |
| 3 E. L. Forrester (D) | 24,221 | 100.0 |
| 4 A. Sidney Camp (D) | 21,900 | 100.0 |
| 5 James C. Davis (D) | 49,317 | 100.0 |
| 6 Carl Vinson (D) | 22,402 | 100.0 |
| 7 Henderson Lanham (D) | 23,595 | 100.0 |
| 8 W. M. Wheeler (D) | 21,573 | 100.0 |
| 9 John S. Wood (D) | 20,943 | 100.0 |
| 10 Paul Brown (D) | 27,568 | 100.0 |

## IDAHO

| Candidates | Votes | % |
|---|---|---|
| 1 John T. Wood (R) | 41,823 | 50.5 |
| Gracie Pfost (D) | 41,040 | 49.5 |
| 2 Hamer Budge (R) | 66,966 | 57.1 |
| James H. Hawley Jr. (D) | 50,255 | 42.9 |

## ILLINOIS

| Candidates | Votes | % |
|---|---|---|
| 1 William L. Dawson (D) | 69,056 | 61.6 |
| Archibald James Carey Jr. (R) | 41,944 | 37.4 |
| 2 Richard B. Vail (R) | 83,023 | 53.6 |
| Barratt O'Hara (D) | 71,945 | 46.4 |
| 3 Fred E. Busbey (R) | 87,241 | 54.5 |
| Neil J. Linehan (D) | 72,676 | 45.4 |
| 4 William E. McVey (R) | 73,542 | 55.8 |
| James V. Buckley (D) | 58,190 | 44.2 |
| 5 John C. Kluczynski (D) | 91,589 | 65.6 |
| Edward M. Gaynor (R) | 48,052 | 34.4 |
| 6 Thomas J. O'Brien (D) | 106,701 | 64.5 |
| John M. Fay (R) | 58,534 | 35.4 |
| 7 Adolph J. Sabath (D) | 109,841 | 71.8 |
| Henry E. Hayes (R) | 43,211 | 28.2 |
| 8 Thomas S. Gordon (D) | 77,736 | 59.3 |
| Philip Grontkowski (R) | 53,305 | 40.7 |
| 9 Sidney R. Yates (D) | 74,699 | 51.8 |
| Maxwell A. Goodwin (R) | 69,552 | 48.2 |
| 10 Richard W. Hoffman (R) | 117,498 | 66.5 |
| Charles J. Michal (D) | 59,127 | 33.5 |
| 11 Timothy P. Sheehan (R) | 81,358 | 56.7 |
| Chester A. Chesney (D) | 62,050 | 43.3 |
| 12 Edgar A. Jonas (R) | 96,489 | 56.2 |
| Charles J. Komaiko (D) | 75,226 | 43.8 |
| 13 Marguerite Stitt Church (R) | 140,750 | 74.1 |
| Thomas F. Dolan (D) | 49,187 | 25.9 |
| 14 Chauncey W. Reed (R) | 103,312 | 74.2 |
| Homer R. McElroy (D) | 35,856 | 25.8 |
| 15 Noah M. Mason (R) | 82,155 | 63.3 |
| Wayne F. Caskey (D) | 47,633 | 36.7 |
| 16 Leo E. Allen (R) | 82,190 | 67.3 |
| Russell J. Goldman (D) | 39,944 | 32.7 |
| 17 Leslie C. Arends (R) | 74,643 | 66.8 |
| Joe W. Russell (D) | 37,096 | 33.2 |
| 18 Harold H. Velde (R) | 72,499 | 61.6 |
| Walter Durley Boyle (D) | 45,214 | 38.4 |
| 19 Robert B. Chiperfield (R) | 69,379 | 59.0 |
| John Michael Kerwin Jr. (D) | 48,286 | 41.0 |
| 20 Sid Simpson (R) | 62,138 | 59.3 |
| Howard Manning (D) | 42,647 | 40.7 |
| 21 Peter F. Mack Jr. (D) | 67,704 | 52.8 |
| Benjamin S. Deboice (R) | 60,530 | 47.2 |
| 22 William L. Springer (R) | 67,668 | 60.7 |
| Robert B. Borchers (D) | 43,795 | 39.3 |
| 23 Edward H. Jenison (R) | 63,669 | 55.9 |
| Laurence F. Arnold (D) | 50,143 | 44.1 |
| 24 Charles W. Vursell (R) | 62,692 | 55.3 |
| John David Upchurch (D) | 50,638 | 44.7 |
| 25 Melvin Price (D) | 78,812 | 64.9 |
| Rogers D. Jones (R) | 42,696 | 35.1 |
| 26 C. W. Bishop (R) | 53,207 | 51.2 |
| Kent E. Keller (D) | 50,759 | 48.8 |

## INDIANA

| Candidates | Votes | % |
|---|---|---|
| 1 Ray J. Madden (D) | 62,666 | 52.6 |
| Paul Cyr (R) | 56,063 | 47.0 |
| 2 Charles A. Halleck (R) | 74,872 | 57.2 |
| Dale E. Beck (D) | 55,153 | 42.2 |
| 3 Shepard J. Crumpacker Jr. (R) | 83,816 | 52.8 |
| Thurman C. Crook (D) | 73,646 | 46.4 |
| 4 E. Ross Adair (R) | 69,741 | 56.2 |
| Edward H. Kruse Jr. (D) | 53,550 | 43.1 |
| 5 John V. Beamer (R) | 91,929 | 54.1 |
| John R. Walsh (D) | 76,878 | 45.3 |
| 6 Cecil M. Harden (R) | 69,789 | 52.4 |
| Jack H. Mankin (D) | 62,915 | 47.2 |
| 7 William G. Bray (R) | 68,885 | 50.0 |
| James E. Noland (D) | 67,992 | 49.3 |
| 8 Winfield K. Denton (D) | 78,750 | 51.1 |
| Herman L. McCray (R) | 74,573 | 48.3 |
| 9 Earl Wilson (R) | 63,229 | 54.9 |
| Charles W. Long (D) | 51,350 | 44.6 |
| 10 Ralph Harvey (R) | 81,392 | 58.7 |
| Vernon J. Dwyer (D) | 56,149 | 40.5 |
| 11 Charles B. Brownson (R) | 116,068 | 56.5 |
| Andrew Jacobs Sr. (D) | 88,418 | 43.0 |

## IOWA

| Candidates | Votes | % |
|---|---|---|
| 1 Thomas E. Martin (R) | 70,058 | 61.7 |
| James D. France (D) | 43,140 | 38.0 |

## IOWA

| Candidates | Votes | % |
|---|---|---|
| Henry O. Talle (R) | 79,066 | 58.8 |
| Eugene J. Kean (D) | 55,359 | 41.2 |
| Harold R. Gross (R) | 73,490 | 64.0 |
| James O. Babcock (D) | 40,786 | 35.5 |
| Karl M. LeCompte (R) | 51,168 | 56.7 |
| Steven V. Carter (D) | 38,649 | 42.8 |
| Paul Cunningham (R) | 57,429 | 56.9 |
| Gibson C. Holliday (D) | 43,105 | 42.7 |
| James I. Dolliver (R) | 56,982 | 64.6 |
| Maurice O'Reilly (D) | 30,877 | 35.0 |
| Ben F. Jensen (R) | 55,291 | 62.1 |
| James A. Hart (D) | 33,617 | 37.7 |
| Charles B. Hoeven (R) | 56,942 | 64.1 |
| L. J. McGivern (D) | 31,689 | 35.7 |

## KANSAS

| | Votes | % |
|---|---|---|
| Albert M. Cole (R) | 66,607 | 66.5 |
| Ewell Steward (D) | 33,562 | 33.5 |
| Errett P. Scrivner (R) | 56,862 | 52.2 |
| Milton Sullivant (D) | 52,015 | 47.8 |
| Myron V. George (R) | 42,263 | 54.7 |
| Barnes Griffith (D) | 35,028 | 45.3 |
| Edward H. Rees (R) | 77,856 | 58.9 |
| Louis A. Donnell (D) | 54,438 | 41.2 |
| Clifford R. Hope (R) | 60,608 | 61.0 |
| Robert L. Bock (D) | 38,767 | 39.0 |
| Wint Smith (R) | 51,653 | 59.6 |
| F. F. Wasinger (D) | 35,087 | 40.5 |

### Special Election

| | Votes | % |
|---|---|---|
| Myron V. George (R) | 41,676 | 54.5 |
| Barnes Griffith (D) | 34,845 | 45.5 |

## KENTUCKY

| | Votes | % |
|---|---|---|
| Noble J. Gregory (D) | 34,970 | 100.0 |
| John A. Whitaker (D) | 41,226 | 100.0 |
| Thruston B. Morton (R) | 62,363 | 55.5 |
| Alex P. Humphrey (D) | 49,935 | 44.5 |
| Frank L. Chelf (D) | 35,529 | 100.0 |
| Brent Spence (D) | 33,920 | 63.3 |
| Thomas W. Hardesty (R) | 19,670 | 36.7 |
| Thomas R. Underwood (D) | 39,762 | 100.0 |
| Carl D. Perkins (D) | 34,767 | 56.1 |
| D. W. Thompson (R) | 27,190 | 43.9 |
| Joe B. Bates (D) | 37,727 | 60.5 |
| Elmer C. Roberts (R) | 24,627 | 39.5 |
| James S. Golden (R) | 46,928 | 100.0 |

## LOUISIANA

| | Votes | % |
|---|---|---|
| F. Edward Hebert (D) | 35,456 | 100.0 |
| Hale Boggs (D) | 39,232 | 100.0 |
| Edwin E. Willis (D) | 21,591 | 100.0 |
| Overton Brooks (D) | 25,529 | 100.0 |
| Otto E. Passman (D) | 22,478 | 100.0 |
| James H. Morrison (D) | 34,718 | 100.0 |
| Henry D. Larcade Jr. (D) | 22,931 | 100.0 |
| A. Leonard Allen (D) | 25,140 | 100.0 |

## MAINE

| | Votes | % |
|---|---|---|
| Robert Hale (R) | 48,869 | 54.0 |
| Lucia M. Cormier (D) | 41,620 | 46.0 |
| Charles P. Nelson (R) | 49,743 | 57.7 |
| John J. Maloney Jr. (D) | 36,506 | 42.3 |
| Frank Fellows (R) | 38,289 | 62.9 |
| John V. Keenan (D) | 22,605 | 37.1 |

## MARYLAND

| | Votes | % |
|---|---|---|
| Edward T. Miller (R) | 36,005 | 57.0 |
| Thomas F. Johnson (D) | 27,122 | 43.0 |
| James P. S. Devereux (R) | 99,497 | 50.2 |
| William P. Bolton (D) | 96,498 | 48.7 |

| Candidates | Votes | % |
|---|---|---|
| 3 Edward A. Garmatz (D) | 27,646 | 65.7 |
| Louis R. Milio (R) | 14,430 | 34.3 |
| 4 George H. Fallon (D) | 34,769 | 56.8 |
| James W. Miller (R) | 25,287 | 41.3 |
| 5 Lansdale G. Sasscer (D) | 54,152 | 57.5 |
| Thomas S. Carr (R) | 40,031 | 42.5 |
| 6 J. Glenn Beall (R) | 70,707 | 61.9 |
| Russell Peter Hartle (D) | 43,540 | 38.1 |

## MASSACHUSETTS

| | Votes | % |
|---|---|---|
| 1 John W. Heselton (R) | 88,018 | 68.9 |
| Anna Sullivan (D) | 39,717 | 31.1 |
| 2 Foster Furcolo (D) | 76,497 | 54.6 |
| Chester T. Skibinski (R) | 63,493 | 45.4 |
| 3 Philip J. Philbin (D) | 93,591 | 71.5 |
| John F. Fuller (R) | 37,258 | 28.5 |
| 4 Harold D. Donohue (D) | 76,881 | 56.9 |
| John Winslow (R) | 57,483 | 42.6 |
| 5 Edith Nourse Rogers (R) | 116,474 | 76.1 |
| Clement Gregory McDonough (D) | 36,530 | 23.9 |
| 6 William H. Bates (R) | 94,162 | 73.7 |
| Richard M. Russell (D) | 33,578 | 26.3 |
| 7 Thomas J. Lane (D) | 91,854 | 78.5 |
| Laurence A. Doyle (R) | 24,307 | 20.8 |
| 8 Angier L. Goodwin (R) | 71,938 | 53.9 |
| John B. Carr (D) | 61,559 | 46.1 |
| 9 Donald W. Nicholson (R) | 78,655 | 58.1 |
| August J. Cormier (D) | 55,949 | 41.3 |
| 10 Christian A. Herter (R) | 88,549 | 57.8 |
| Francis X. Hurley (D) | 63,618 | 41.5 |
| 11 John F. Kennedy (D) | 87,699 | 82.3 |
| Vincent J. Celeste (R) | 18,302 | 17.2 |
| 12 John W. McCormack (D) | 102,940 | 84.0 |
| John J. Biggins (R) | 16,746 | 13.7 |
| 13 Richard B. Wigglesworth (R) | 90,387 | 62.2 |
| David J. Concannon (D) | 54,243 | 37.3 |
| 14 Joseph W. Martin Jr. (R) | 84,508 | 64.3 |
| Edward P. Grace (D) | 46,332 | 35.3 |

## MICHIGAN

| | Votes | % |
|---|---|---|
| 1 Thaddeus M. Machrowicz (D) | 75,478 | 82.2 |
| Rudolph G. Tenerowicz (R) | 14,619 | 15.9 |
| 2 George Meader (R) | 61,574 | 60.4 |
| John P. Dawson (D) | 39,771 | 39.0 |
| 3 Paul W. Shafer (R) | 58,489 | 61.4 |
| Thomas B. Woodworth (D) | 35,877 | 37.6 |
| 4 Clare E. Hoffman (R) | 58,625 | 68.6 |
| Forest A. Schoonard (D) | 26,301 | 30.8 |
| 5 Gerald R. Ford Jr. (R) | 72,829 | 66.7 |
| James H. McLaughlin (D) | 35,927 | 32.9 |
| 6 William W. Blackney (R) | 70,100 | 52.8 |
| Herbert W. Devine (D) | 61,435 | 46.3 |
| 7 Jesse P. Wolcott (R) | 66,951 | 63.0 |
| Roy E. Visnaw (D) | 38,953 | 36.6 |
| 8 Fred L. Crawford (R) | 55,001 | 60.5 |
| Leland S. Jennings (D) | 35,164 | 38.7 |
| 9 Ruth Thompson (R) | 43,910 | 54.5 |
| Noel P. Fox (D) | 36,222 | 45.0 |
| 10 Roy O. Woodruff (R) | 47,489 | 66.2 |
| William J. Kelly (D) | 24,198 | 33.8 |
| 11 Charles E. Potter (R) | 50,523 | 66.5 |
| Fred L. Hanscom (D) | 25,254 | 33.2 |
| 12 John B. Bennett (R) | 43,010 | 61.7 |
| John Sabol (D) | 26,667 | 38.3 |
| 13 George D. O'Brien (D) | 56,388 | 61.4 |
| Clarence J. McLeod (R) | 35,178 | 38.3 |
| 14 Louis C. Rabaut (D) | 76,938 | 51.5 |
| Richard Durant (R) | 72,137 | 48.3 |
| 15 John D. Dingell (D) | 73,238 | 64.1 |
| Robert L. Berry (R) | 40,866 | 35.7 |
| 16 John Lesinski Jr. (D) | 80,229 | 60.7 |
| Kirby L. Wilson Jr. (R) | 50,873 | 38.5 |
| 17 George A. Dondero (R) | 114,274 | 55.6 |
| Eugene G. Donohoe (D) | 90,712 | 44.1 |

## MINNESOTA

| Candidates | Votes | % |
|---|---|---|
| 1 August H. Andresen (R) | 75,016 | 67.1 |
| Burton Chambers (DFL) | 36,839 | 32.9 |
| 2 Joseph P. O'Hara (R) | 69,304 | 59.9 |
| Harry Sieben (DFL) | 46,452 | 40.1 |
| 3 Roy W. Wier (DFL) | 73,786 | 51.7 |
| Alfred D. Lindley (R) | 68,947 | 48.3 |
| 4 Eugene J. McCarthy (DFL) | 59,930 | 60.4 |
| Ward Fleming (R) | 39,307 | 39.6 |
| 5 Walter H. Judd (R) | 71,243 | 58.7 |
| Marcella F. Killen (DFL) | 48,759 | 40.2 |
| 6 Fred Marshall (DFL) | 63,911 | 56.2 |
| Robert F. Lee (R) | 49,879 | 43.8 |
| 7 H. Carl Andersen (R) | 65,644 | 61.7 |
| Carl J. Eastvold (DFL) | 40,785 | 38.3 |
| 8 John A. Blatnik (DFL) | 72,440 | 62.9 |
| William A. Pittongor (R) | 42,705 | 37.1 |
| 9 Harold C. Hagen (DFL) | 56,928 | 61.9 |
| Curtiss Olson (DFL) | 30,808 | 33.5 |

## MISSISSIPPI

| | Votes | % |
|---|---|---|
| 1 John E. Rankin (D) | 8,994 | 92.5 |
| Glenn Haynes (R) | 730 | 7.5 |
| 2 Jamie L. Whitten (D) | 5,891 | 100.0 |
| 3 Frank E. Smith (D) | 6,529 | 92.5 |
| Nelson E. Taylor (R) | 529 | 7.5 |
| 4 Thomas G. Abernethy (D) | 12,602 | 95.8 |
| 5 W. Arthur Winstead (D) | 13,395 | 97.6 |
| 6 William M. Colmer (D) | 15,964 | 87.9 |
| Frank H. Harper (I) | 2,199 | 12.1 |
| 7 John Bell Williams (D) | 19,321 | 96.4 |

## MISSOURI

| | Votes | % |
|---|---|---|
| 1 Clare Magee (D) | 43,384 | 54.4 |
| Wat Arnold (R) | 36,403 | 45.6 |
| 2 Morgan M. Moulder (D) | 49,408 | 53.0 |
| Max Schwabe (R) | 43,816 | 47.0 |
| 3 Philip J. Welch (D) | 48,244 | 51.1 |
| William C. Cole (R) | 46,154 | 48.9 |
| 4 Theodore Leonard Irving (D) | 53,424 | 61.6 |
| Vernon D. Fulcrut (R) | 33,367 | 38.5 |
| 5 Richard W. Bolling (D) | 45,762 | 54.5 |
| Richard C. Jensen (R) | 38,276 | 45.6 |
| 6 Orland K. Armstrong (R) | 55,176 | 50.7 |
| George H. Christopher (D) | 53,593 | 49.3 |
| 7 Dewey Short (R) | 60,557 | 58.7 |
| Daniel J. Leary (D) | 42,629 | 41.3 |
| 8 Albert S. J. Carnahan (D) | 49,894 | 54.7 |
| Parke M. Banta (R) | 41,406 | 45.4 |
| 9 Clarence Cannon (D) | 43,950 | 61.5 |
| John H. Fahien (R) | 27,573 | 38.6 |
| 10 Paul C. Jones (D) | 44,469 | 100.0 |
| 11 John B. Sullivan (D) | 57,225 | 64.5 |
| Sidney J. Redman (R) | 31,163 | 35.2 |
| 12 Thomas B. Curtis (R) | 110,757 | 50.9 |
| Raymond W. Karst (D) | 106,728 | 49.0 |
| 13 Frank M. Karsten (D) | 58,832 | 68.2 |
| Hal A. Hamilton (R) | 27,366 | 31.7 |

## MONTANA

| | Votes | % |
|---|---|---|
| 1 Mike Mansfield (D) | 54,394 | 60.3 |
| Ralph Y. McGinnis (R) | 34,945 | 38.7 |
| 2 Wesley A. D'Ewart (R) | 65,003 | 54.1 |
| John J. Holmes (D) | 53,854 | 44.8 |

## NEBRASKA

| | Votes | % |
|---|---|---|
| 1 Carl T. Curtis (R) | 67,164 | 54.5 |
| Clarence G. Miles (D) | 55,972 | 45.5 |
| 2 Howard Buffett (R) | 71,126 | 63.5 |
| Eugene D. O'Sullivan (D) | 40,939 | 36.5 |
| 3 Karl Stefan (R) | 68,889 | 66.9 |
| Duane K. Peterson (D) | 34,017 | 33.1 |
| 4 Arthur L. Miller (R) | 64,661 | 65.8 |
| Hans J. Holtorf Jr. (D) | 33,562 | 34.2 |

## NEVADA

| Candidates | Votes | % |
|---|---|---|
| AL Walter S. Baring (D) | 31,843 | 52.8 |
| A. E. MacKenzie (R) | 28,485 | 47.2 |

## NEW HAMPSHIRE

| | Votes | % |
|---|---|---|
| 1 Chester E. Merrow (R) | 57,371 | 57.5 |
| Frank L. Sullivan (D) | 42,371 | 42.5 |
| 2 Norris Cotton (R) | 55,116 | 64.5 |
| George Brummer (D) | 30,389 | 35.5 |

## NEW JERSEY

| | Votes | % |
|---|---|---|
| 1 Charles A. Wolverton (R) | 85,100 | 56.8 |
| John J. Crean (D) | 64,868 | 43.3 |
| 2 T. Millet Hand (R) | 54,897 | 54.3 |
| Elmer H. Wene (D) | 46,121 | 45.7 |
| 3 James C. Auchincloss (R) | 79,374 | 62.4 |
| John C. Applegate (D) | 47,055 | 37.0 |
| 4 Charles R. Howell (D) | 60,364 | 52.2 |
| Gill Robb Wilson (R) | 55,364 | 47.8 |
| 5 Charles A. Eaton (R) | 80,678 | 61.6 |
| Thomas Chabrak (D) | 50,220 | 38.4 |
| 6 Clifford P. Case (R) | 74,739 | 62.2 |
| Harry Mopsick (D) | 45,376 | 37.8 |
| 7 William B. Widnall (R) | 79,421 | 69.7 |
| Emil M. Wulster (D) | 34,578 | 30.3 |
| 8 Gordon Canfield (R) | 60,420 | 63.6 |
| Charles H. Roemer (D) | 34,194 | 36.0 |
| 9 Harry L. Towe (R) | 67,712 | 57.8 |
| Karl D. Van Wagner (D) | 38,431 | 32.8 |
| Carl E. Ring (I) | 10,932 | 9.3 |
| 10 Peter W. Rodino Jr. (D) | 60,432 | 61.0 |
| William H. Rawson (R) | 38,613 | 39.0 |
| 11 Hugh J. Addonizio (D) | 46,242 | 51.6 |
| Albert L. Vreeland (R) | 42,581 | 47.5 |
| 12 Robert Winthrop Kean (R) | 54,123 | 53.1 |
| Harry Dudkin (D) | 45,525 | 44.7 |
| 13 Alfred D. Sieminski (D) | 55,008 | 51.9 |
| Edward S. Binkowski (R) | 43,851 | 41.4 |
| Michael A. Fiore (IPP CH) | 7,072 | 6.7 |
| 14 Edward J. Hart (D) | 61,410 | 59.2 |
| Michael Bongiovanni (R) | 42,272 | 40.8 |

## NEW MEXICO

| | Votes | % |
|---|---|---|
| AL John J. Dempsey (D) | 97,187✔ | |
| Antonio M. Fernandez (D) | 96,291✔ | |
| Steiner Mason (R) | 75,447 | |
| Jose E. Armijo (R) | 68,762 | |

## NEW YORK

| | Votes | % |
|---|---|---|
| 1 Ernest Greenwood (D, L) | 76,375 | 49.2 |
| W. Kingsland Macy (R) | 76,240 | 49.1 |
| 2 Leonard W. Hall (R) | 129,291 | 67.1 |
| Lawrence W. McKeown (D, L) | 60,152 | 31.2 |
| 3 Henry J. Latham (R) | 92,466 | 56.3 |
| James Pasta (D) | 55,285 | 33.6 |
| Mark Starr (L) | 11,122 | 6.8 |
| 4 L. Gary Clemente (D, L) | 55,793 | 54.2 |
| Gregory McMahon (R) | 43,055 | 41.8 |
| 5 T. Vincent Quinn (D) | 63,620 | 48.4 |
| Robert Tripp Ross (R) | 54,061 | 41.1 |
| Bernard Brown (L) | 7,857 | 6.0 |
| 6 James J. Delaney (D, L) | 60,725 | 56.8 |
| Herbert Suppan (R) | 41,615 | 38.9 |
| 7 Louis B. Heller (D, L) | 47,466 | 57.0 |
| Francis E. Dorn (R) | 30,379 | 36.5 |
| Lester Zirin (AM LAB) | 5,454 | 6.6 |
| 8 Victor L. Anfuso (D) | 42,305 | 61.9 |
| Joseph R. Fontanetta (R) | 18,551 | 27.2 |
| Antonio Iandiorio (AM LAB) | 4,119 | 6.0 |
| 9 Eugene J. Keogh (D, R) | 73,280 | 91.0 |
| Helen Wishnofsky (AM LAB) | 7,267 | 9.0 |

| Candidates | Votes | % |
|---|---|---|
| 10 Edna F. Kelly (D, L) | 66,847 | 67.1 |
| David L. Samuels (R) | 25,485 | 25.6 |
| Gerald Root (AM LAB) | 7,327 | 7.4 |
| 11 James J. Heffernan (D, L) | 67,560 | 62.9 |
| Alfred C. McKenzie (R) | 31,558 | 29.4 |
| Blanche Katz (AM LAB) | 8,270 | 7.7 |
| 12 John J. Rooney (D, L) | 42,396 | 61.6 |
| Joseph J. Petito (R) | 22,796 | 33.1 |
| Vincent J. Longhi (AM LAB) | 3,628 | 5.3 |
| 13 Donald L. O'Toole (D, L) | 54,919 | 59.6 |
| James F. O'Hara (R) | 35,418 | 36.7 |
| Ralph Shapiro (AM LAB) | 6,247 | 6.5 |
| 14 Abraham J. Multer (D, L) | 75,020 | 70.6 |
| P. Vincent Landi (R) | 21,350 | 20.1 |
| Helen Phillips (AM LAB) | 9,859 | 9.3 |
| 15 Emanuel Celler (D, L) | 72,396 | 72.8 |
| Louis H. Heiger (R) | 17,144 | 17.2 |
| William Podell (AM LAB) | 9,916 | 10.0 |
| 16 James J. Murphy (D, L) | 42,516 | 50.5 |
| Edward J. McCormick (R) | 37,363 | 44.4 |
| Frank Cremonesi (AM LAB) | 4,340 | 5.2 |
| 17 Frederic R. Coudert Jr. (R) | 57,247 | 53.4 |
| Irving M. Engel (D, L) | 44,502 | 41.5 |
| Robert T. Leicester (AM LAB) | 5,492 | 5.1 |
| 18 James G. Donovan (D, R) | 49,448 | 57.8 |
| Vito Marcantonio (AM LAB) | 36,095 | 42.2 |
| 19 Arthur G. Klein (D, L) | 58,616 | 66.4 |
| Edward I. Goldberg (R) | 21,034 | 23.8 |
| Bernard Harkavy (AM LAB) | 8,597 | 9.7 |
| 20 Franklin D. Roosevelt Jr. (D, L) | 57,432 | 62.1 |
| Henry V. Poor (R) | 29,305 | 31.7 |
| John W. Darr Jr. (AM LAB) | 5,717 | 6.2 |
| 21 Jacob K. Javits (R, L) | 62,604 | 61.7 |
| Bennett I. Schlessel (D) | 33,349 | 32.9 |
| William M. Mandel (AM LAB) | 5,419 | 5.4 |
| 22 Adam Clayton Powell Jr. (D) | 35,233 | 63.5 |
| Elmer A. Carter (R, L) | 15,208 | 27.4 |
| John Quillian (AM LAB) | 5,050 | 9.1 |
| 23 Sidney A. Fine (D) | 64,270 | 56.3 |
| William J. Waterman (R) | 22,103 | 19.4 |
| Harold Bauman (L) | 17,882 | 15.7 |
| Robert Diamond (AM LAB) | 9,847 | 8.6 |
| 24 Isidore Dollinger (D) | 54,628 | 62.5 |
| Barnett Levy (R) | 11,303 | 12.9 |
| Herman Woskow (L) | 10,774 | 12.3 |
| Stephen J. White (AM LAB) | 10,755 | 12.3 |
| 25 Charles A. Buckley (D) | 64,353 | 46.8 |
| Solon S. Kane (R) | 40,552 | 29.5 |
| Max Bloom (L) | 20,929 | 15.2 |
| Charles J. Hendley (AM LAB) | 11,707 | 8.5 |
| 26 Christopher C. McGrath (D) | 69,152 | 51.4 |
| Fred E. Schiemann (R) | 44,598 | 33.1 |
| Ernest Doerfler (L) | 11,518 | 8.6 |
| August Buhr (AM LAB) | 9,333 | 6.9 |
| 27 Ralph W. Gwinn (R) | 78,221 | 55.9 |
| George A. Brenner (D, L) | 59,759 | 42.7 |
| 28 Ralph A. Gamble (R) | 79,490 | 67.5 |
| Morris E. Lasker (D) | 35,059 | 29.8 |
| 29 Katharine St. George (R) | 72,721 | 61.8 |
| Harry O. Prince (D, L) | 43,315 | 36.8 |
| 30 James Ernest Wharton (R) | 86,053 | 65.8 |
| James R. Bourne (D) | 41,833 | 32.0 |
| 31 Bernard W. Kearney (R) | 79,007 | 64.1 |
| John H. Peterson (D) | 41,680 | 33.8 |
| 32 William T. Byrne (D) | 90,420 | 58.8 |
| John T. Casey (R) | 60,087 | 39.1 |
| 33 Dean P. Taylor (R) | 100,425 | 69.0 |
| Joseph T. Hammer (D) | 42,680 | 29.3 |
| 34 Clarence E. Kilburn (R) | 67,739 | 66.4 |
| Mildred McGill (D) | 32,446 | 31.8 |
| 35 William R. Williams (R) | 60,657 | 51.6 |
| John C. Davies (D, L) | 54,284 | 46.2 |
| 36 R. Walter Riehlman (R) | 81,508 | 61.9 |
| Alfred W. Haight (D, L) | 50,107 | 38.9 |

| Candidates | Votes | % |
|---|---|---|
| 37 Edwin Arthur Hall (R) | 60,278 | 64.6 |
| John J. Burns (D, L) | 33,018 | 35.4 |
| 38 John Taber (R) | 68,474 | 68.8 |
| Robert G. Gordon (D, L) | 31,115 | 31.2 |
| 39 W. Sterling Cole (R) | 64,377 | 66.3 |
| Donald J. O'Connor (D, L) | 31,639 | 32.6 |
| 40 Kenneth B. Keating (R) | 103,710 | 65.8 |
| A. Roger Clarke (D, L) | 52,363 | 33.2 |
| 41 Harold C. Ostertag (R) | 64,801 | 64.1 |
| Bernard E. Hart (D, L) | 35,370 | 35.0 |
| 42 William E. Miller (R) | 75,377 | 58.6 |
| Mary Louise Nice (D, L) | 53,310 | 41.4 |
| 43 Edmund P. Radwan (R) | 61,781 | 50.8 |
| Anthony F. Tauriello (D, L) | 58,327 | 48.0 |
| 44 John C. Butler (R) | 69,260 | 50.3 |
| Chester C. Gorski (D, L) | 66,541 | 48.3 |
| 45 Daniel A. Reed (R) | 54,490 | 66.0 |
| Frederick S. Buck (D) | 27,317 | 33.1 |

## NORTH CAROLINA

| | Votes | % |
|---|---|---|
| 1 Herbert C. Bonner (D) | 14,698 | 92.8 |
| Zeno O. Ratcliff (R) | 1,147 | 7.2 |
| 2 John H. Kerr (D) | 15,602 | 100.0 |
| 3 Graham A. Barden (D) | 21,287 | 100.0 |
| 4 Harold D. Cooley (D) | 34,580 | 72.8 |
| Ray F. Swain (R) | 12,945 | 27.2 |
| 5 Richard Thurmond Chatham (D) | 29,598 | 100.0 |
| 6 Carl T. Durham (D) | 27,751 | 75.4 |
| A. A. McDonald (R) | 9,075 | 24.6 |
| 7 F. Ertel Carlyle (D) | 21,911 | 84.0 |
| Irvin B. Tucker Jr. (R) | 4,171 | 16.0 |
| 8 Charles B. Deane (D) | 40,834 | 59.6 |
| T. E. Story (R) | 27,688 | 40.4 |
| 9 Robert L. Doughton (D) | 47,183 | 61.2 |
| Fate J. Beal (R) | 29,982 | 38.9 |
| 10 Hamilton C. Jones (D) | 33,591 | 52.3 |
| Louis G. Rogers (R) | 30,591 | 47.7 |
| 11 Woodrow W. Jones (D) | 31,712 | 68.9 |
| A. W. Whitehurst (R) | 14,293 | 31.1 |
| 12 Monroe M. Redden (D) | 46,851 | 63.7 |
| John A. Wagner (R) | 26,710 | 36.3 |

### Special Election

| | Votes | % |
|---|---|---|
| 11 Woodrow W. Jones (D) | 31,460 | 67. |
| A. W. Whitehurst (R) | 15,295 | 32. |

## NORTH DAKOTA

| | Votes | % |
|---|---|---|
| AL Fred G. Aandahl (R) | 119,047✔ | |
| Usher L. Burdick (R) | 110,534✔ | |
| Ervin Schumacher (D) | 62,322 | |
| E. A. Johansson (D) | 32,946 | |

## OHIO

| | Votes | % |
|---|---|---|
| 1 Charles H. Elston (R) | 77,507 | 59 |
| Rollin H. Everett (D) | 53,760 | 41 |
| 2 William E. Hess (R) | 69,543 | 52 |
| Earl T. Wagner (D) | 62,542 | 47 |
| 3 Edward Breen (D) | 92,840 | 54 |
| Paul F. Schenck (R) | 77,634 | 45 |
| 4 William M. McCulloch (R) | 65,640 | 66 |
| Carleton Carl Reiser (D) | 32,686 | 33 |
| 5 Cliff Clevenger (R) | 36,096 | 57 |
| Dan Batt (D) | 26,689 | 42 |
| 6 James G. Polk (D) | 40,335 | 50 |
| Edward O. McCowen (R) | 38,996 | 49 |
| 7 Clarence J. Brown (R) | 77,660 | 68 |
| Ben J. Goldman (D) | 35,818 | 31 |
| 8 Jackson E. Betts (R) | 47,761 | 62 |
| W. Dexter Hazen (D) | 28,379 | 37 |
| 9 Frazier Reams (I) | 51,024 | 36 |
| Thomas H. Burke (D) | 45,268 | 32 |
| Homer A. Ramey (R) | 43,301 | 31 |

## OHIO

| | Candidates | Votes | % |
|---|---|---|---|
| 10 | Thomas A. Jenkins (R) | 39,584 | 65.2 |
| | William J. Curry (D) | 21,117 | 34.8 |
| 11 | Walter E. Brehm (R) | 33,648 | 53.1 |
| | Mell G. Underwood Jr. (D) | 29,687 | 46.9 |
| 12 | John M. Vorys (R) | 117,396 | 64.1 |
| | John W. Guy (D) | 65,860 | 35.9 |
| 13 | Alvin F. Weichel (R) | 58,484 | 70.9 |
| | Dwight A. Blackmore (D) | 24,042 | 29.1 |
| 14 | William H. Ayres (R) | 102,868 | 48.7 |
| | Walter B. Huber (D) | 100,947 | 47.8 |
| 15 | Robert T. Secrest (D) | 47,448 | 61.6 |
| | Holland M. Gary (R) | 29,573 | 38.4 |
| 16 | Frank T. Bow (R) | 77,306 | 50.7 |
| | John McSweeney (D) | 75,255 | 49.3 |
| 17 | J. Harry McGregor (R) | 71,382 | 64.3 |
| | Robert W. Levering (D) | 39,726 | 35.8 |
| 18 | Wayne L. Hays (D) | 58,295 | 50.8 |
| | Robert L. Quinn (R) | 56,508 | 49.2 |
| 19 | Michael J. Kirwan (D) | 119,245 | 63.8 |
| | Henry P. Kosling (R) | 67,661 | 36.2 |
| 20 | Michael A. Feighan (D) | 60,565 | 74.2 |
| | Paul W. Cassidy (R) | 21,044 | 25.8 |
| 21 | Robert Crosser (D) | 66,341 | 75.5 |
| | William Hodge (R) | 21,588 | 24.6 |
| 22 | Frances P. Bolton (R) | 219,788 | 62.7 |
| | Chat Paterson (D) | 130,623 | 37.3 |
| AL | George H. Bender (R) | 1,447,154 | 53.9 |
| | Stephen M. Young (D) | 1,237,409 | 46.1 |

## OKLAHOMA

| | Candidates | Votes | % |
|---|---|---|---|
| 1 | George B. Schwabe (R) | 72,367 | 52.9 |
| | Dixie Gilmer (D) | 64,481 | 47.1 |
| 2 | William G. Stigler (D) | 36,552 | 66.2 |
| | Cleo Crain (D) | 18,687 | 33.8 |
| 3 | Carl Albert (D) | 46,404 | 82.8 |
| | Charles Powell (R) | 9,639 | 17.2 |
| 4 | Tom Steed (D) | 43,838 | 68.1 |
| | Glenn O. Young (R) | 20,527 | 31.9 |
| 5 | John Jarman (D) | 72,877 | 58.8 |
| | C. E. Barnes (R) | 51,008 | 41.2 |
| 6 | Toby Morris (D) | 38,166 | 67.1 |
| | George Campbell (R) | 18,743 | 32.9 |
| 7 | Victor Wickersham (D) | 28,733 | 67.1 |
| | K. B. Cornell (R) | 14,078 | 32.9 |
| 8 | Page H. Belcher (R) | 38,285 | 64.2 |
| | George H. Wilson (D) | 32,401 | 45.8 |

## OREGON

| | Candidates | Votes | % |
|---|---|---|---|
| 1 | Walter Norblad (R) | 93,547 | 66.5 |
| | Roy R. Hewitt (D) | 47,155 | 33.5 |
| 2 | Lowell Stockman (R) | 41,365 | 55.4 |
| | Vernon Bull (D) | 33,282 | 44.6 |
| 3 | Homer D. Angell (R) | 90,232 | 50.7 |
| | Carl C. Donaugh (D) | 77,606 | 43.6 |
| 4 | Harris Ellsworth (R) | 63,211 | 59.5 |
| | David C. Shaw (D) | 43,053 | 40.5 |

## PENNSYLVANIA

| | Candidates | Votes | % |
|---|---|---|---|
| 1 | William A. Barrett (D) | 69,300 | 53.8 |
| | Robert Sebastian (R) | 59,593 | 46.2 |
| 2 | William T. Granahan (D) | 83,344 | 57.0 |
| | Max Slepin (R) | 62,970 | 43.0 |
| 3 | Hardie Scott (R) | 68,217 | 50.3 |
| | Maurice S. Osser (D) | 67,286 | 49.7 |
| 4 | Earl Chudoff (D) | 65,255 | 57.5 |
| | Theodore O. Spaulding (R) | 48,280 | 42.5 |
| 5 | William J. Green Jr. (D) | 84,177 | 55.5 |
| | George W. Sarbacher Jr. (R) | 67,525 | 44.5 |
| 6 | Hugh Scott (R) | 74,316 | 50.0 |
| | Ethan Allen Doty (D) | 73,913 | 49.7 |
| 7 | Benjamin F. James (R) | 91,387 | 62.7 |
| | Hubert P. Earle (D) | 54,425 | 37.3 |
| 8 | Albert C. Vaughn (R) | 56,300 | 58.2 |
| | George F. Kanc (D) | 40,502 | 41.8 |

| | Candidates | Votes | % |
|---|---|---|---|
| 9 | Paul B. Dague (R) | 70,368 | 67.2 |
| | Philip Ragan (D) | 34,317 | 32.8 |
| 10 | Harry P. O'Neill (D) | 56,158 | 51.5 |
| | Fraser P. Donlan (R) | 52,859 | 48.5 |
| 11 | Daniel J. Flood (D) | 77,466 | 54.4 |
| | Elwood H. Jones (R) | 65,015 | 45.6 |
| 12 | Ivor D. Fenton (R) | 67,135 | 56.8 |
| | James H. Gildea (D) | 51,028 | 43.2 |
| 13 | George M. Rhodes (D) | 36,335 | 49.8 |
| | James W. Bertolet (R) | 34,640 | 47.5 |
| 14 | Wilson D. Gillette (R) | 45,986 | 60.9 |
| | John E. Snedeker (D) | 29,538 | 39.1 |
| 15 | Alvin R. Bush (R) | 47,697 | 60.7 |
| | Paul A. Rothfuss (D) | 28,759 | 36.6 |
| 16 | Samuel K. McConnell Jr (R) | 81,366 | 66.2 |
| | Leon C. MacMullen (D) | 41,642 | 33.9 |
| 17 | Richard M. Simpson (R) | 40,029 | 62.8 |
| | James L. Gatins (D) | 23,762 | 37.3 |
| 18 | Walter M. Mumma (R) | 78,577 | 63.7 |
| | James M. Quigley (D) | 44,871 | 36.4 |
| 19 | Leon H. Gavin (R) | 42,719 | 62.8 |
| | Fred C. Barr (D) | 25,348 | 37.2 |
| 20 | Francis E. Walter (D) | 49,660 | 58.3 |
| | George M. Berg (R) | 35,487 | 41.7 |
| 21 | James F. Lind (D) | 48,550 | 52.2 |
| | Francis Worley (D) | 44,465 | 47.8 |
| 22 | James E. Van Zandt (R) | 42,701 | 59.5 |
| | Arthur H. Reede (D) | 29,080 | 40.5 |
| 23 | Edward L. Sittler Jr. (R) | 39,431 | 51.8 |
| | Anthony Cavalcante (D) | 36,740 | 48.2 |
| 24 | Thomas E. Morgan (D) | 46,875 | 59.1 |
| | John J. Cairns Jr. (R) | 32,470 | 40.9 |
| 25 | Louis E. Graham (R) | 55,866 | 52.4 |
| | Samuel Gunnett Neff (D) | 50,686 | 47.6 |
| 26 | John P. Saylor (R) | 63,445 | 52.5 |
| | Lewis E. Evans (D) | 57,396 | 47.5 |
| 27 | Augustine B. Kelley (D) | 53,229 | 57.1 |
| | George E. Berry Jr. (R) | 40,037 | 42.9 |
| 28 | Carroll D. Kearns (R) | 67,604 | 57.0 |
| | Steve Filipkowski (D) | 51,060 | 43.0 |
| 29 | Harmar D. Denny Jr. (R) | 54,076 | 52.6 |
| | Harry J. Davenport (D) | 48,198 | 46.9 |
| 30 | Robert J. Corbett (R) | 58,096 | 56.5 |
| | J. R. Montgomery (D) | 44,778 | 43.5 |
| 31 | James G. Fulton (R) | 82,525 | 67.5 |
| | Wilber I. Newstetter Jr. (D) | 39,776 | 32.5 |
| 32 | Herman P. Eberharter (D) | 66,077 | 68.7 |
| | James E. Dougherty (R) | 30,088 | 31.3 |
| 33 | Frank Buchanan (D) | 63,257 | 65.8 |
| | Cornelius McLaughlin Sr. (R) | 32,858 | 34.2 |

## RHODE ISLAND

| | Candidates | Votes | % |
|---|---|---|---|
| 1 | Aime J. Forand (D) | 90,065 | 63.2 |
| | Francis R. Foley (R) | 52,553 | 36.9 |
| 2 | John E. Fogarty (D) | 93,039 | 60.8 |
| | Wilford S. Budlong (R) | 60,036 | 39.2 |

## SOUTH CAROLINA

| | Candidates | Votes | % |
|---|---|---|---|
| 1 | L. Mendel Rivers (D) | 6,753 | 100.0 |
| 2 | John J. Riley (D) | 9,747 | 100.0 |
| 3 | W. J. Bryan Dorn (D) | 8,126 | 100.0 |
| 4 | Joseph R. Bryson (D) | 7,976 | 99.9 |
| 5 | James P. Richards (D) | 10,648 | 100.0 |
| 6 | John L. McMillan (D) | 7,131 | 100.0 |

## SOUTH DAKOTA

| | Candidates | Votes | % |
|---|---|---|---|
| 1 | Harold O. Lovre (R) | 116,173 | 60.8 |
| | Merton B. Tice (D) | 74,983 | 39.2 |
| 2 | E. Y. Berry (R) | 34,533 | 60.3 |
| | Sam H. Bober (D) | 22,737 | 39.7 |

## TENNESSEE

| | Candidates | Votes | % |
|---|---|---|---|
| 1 | B. Carroll Reece (R) | 33,308 | 46.5 |
| | Dayton Phillips (IR) | 20,121 | 28.1 |
| | Kyle K. King (D) | 18,260 | 25.5 |
| 2 | Howard H. Baker (R) | 38,585 | 52.2 |
| | Frank W. Wilson (D) | 35,349 | 47.8 |
| 3 | James B. Frazier Jr. (D) | 23,807 | 100.0 |
| 4 | Albert Gore (D) | 11,112 | 100.0 |
| 5 | Joe L. Evins (D) | 15,283 | 100.0 |
| 6 | J. Percy Priest (D) | 10,047 | 65.9 |
| | James W. Perkins (I) | 5,189 | 34.1 |
| 7 | James P. Sutton (D) | 13,520 | 100.0 |
| 8 | Thomas J. Murray (D) | 13,623 | 100.0 |
| 9 | Jere Cooper (D) | 9,276 | 100.0 |
| 10 | Clifford Davis (D) | 15,128 | 100.0 |

## TEXAS

| | Candidates | Votes | % |
|---|---|---|---|
| 1 | Wright Patman (D) | 12,444 | 100.0 |
| 2 | Jesse M. Combs (D) | 16,900 | 100.0 |
| 3 | Lindley Beckworth (D) | 11,784 | 91.1 |
| | R. E. Kennedy (R) | 1,145 | 8.9 |
| 4 | Sam Rayburn (D) | 11,546 | 100.0 |
| 5 | J. Frank Wilson (D) | 23,568 | 100.0 |
| 6 | Olin Teague (D) | 8,118 | 98.1 |
| 7 | Tom Pickett (D) | 12,537 | 100.0 |
| 8 | Albert Thomas (D) | 19,068 | 77.8 |
| | B. F. Hanna (R) | 5,427 | 22.2 |
| 9 | Clark W. Thompson (D) | 20,200 | 100.0 |
| 10 | Homer Thornberry (D) | 13,703 | 100.0 |
| 11 | W. R. Poage (D) | 10,576 | 100.0 |
| 12 | Wingate H. Lucas (D) | 13,179 | 80.7 |
| | H. G. Neely (D) | 3,162 | 19.4 |
| 13 | Ed Gossett (D) | 14,761 | 100.0 |
| 14 | John E. Lyle Jr. (D) | 31,201 | 100.0 |
| 15 | Lloyd M. Bentsen Jr. (D) | 18,524 | 100.0 |
| 16 | Ken Regan (D) | 8,928 | 100.0 |
| 17 | Omar Burleson (D) | 10,228 | 100.0 |
| 18 | Walter Rogers (D) | 25,666 | 52.5 |
| | B. H. Guill (R) | 23,259 | 47.5 |
| 19 | George Mahon (D) | 17,828 | 93.9 |
| | M. D. Temple (R) | 1,162 | 6.1 |
| 20 | Paul J. Kilday (D) | 9,138 | 100.0 |
| 21 | O. Clark Fisher (D) | 16,334 | 100.0 |

### Special Election

| | | Votes | % |
|---|---|---|---|
| 18 | Ben H. Guill (R) | ✔ | # |

## UTAH

| | Candidates | Votes | % |
|---|---|---|---|
| 1 | Walter K. Granger (D) | 54,161 | 51.1 |
| | Preston L. Jones (R) | 51,868 | 48.9 |
| 2 | Reva B. Bosone (D) | 84,283 | 53.4 |
| | Ivy B. Priest (R) | 73,535 | 46.6 |

## VERMONT

| | Candidates | Votes | % |
|---|---|---|---|
| AL | Winston L. Prouty (R) | 65,248 | 73.4 |
| | Herbert B. Comings (D) | 22,709 | 25.6 |

## VIRGINIA

| | Candidates | Votes | % |
|---|---|---|---|
| 1 | Edward J. Robeson Jr. (D) | 18,741 | 81.0 |
| | Nile Straughan (R) | 2,518 | 10.9 |
| | Stanley S. Garner (I) | 1,878 | 8.1 |
| 2 | Porter Hardy Jr. (D) | 14,846 | 99.9 |
| 3 | J. Vaughan Gary (D) | 15,300 | 89.6 |
| | Phronia A. McNeill (PROG) | 1,095 | 6.4 |
| 4 | Watkins M. Abbitt (D) | 8,325 | 99.9 |
| 5 | Thomas B. Stanley (D) | 9,433 | 99.9 |
| 6 | Clarence G. Burton (D) | 12,287 | 99.3 |
| 7 | Burr P. Harrison (D) | 19,932 | 69.4 |
| | J. A. Garber (R) | 8,786 | 30.6 |
| 8 | Howard W. Smith (D) | 29,730 | 57.2 |
| | Tyrrell Krum (R) | 21,071 | 40.6 |
| 9 | Thomas B. Fugate (D) | 26,802 | 58.4 |
| | George C. Sutherland (R) | 19,118 | 41.6 |

### Special Election

| | Candidates | Votes | % |
|---|---|---|---|
| 1 | Edward J. Robeson Jr (D) | 10,988 | 42.5 |
| | William A. Wright | 7,667 | 29.6 |
| | Blake T. Newton | 5,425 | 21.0 |
| | Nile Straughan (R) | 1,792 | 6.9 |

*Footnote, see p. 1218.*

## WASHINGTON

| Candidates | Votes | % |
|---|---|---|
| 1 Hugh B. Mitchell (D) | 90,053 | 51.4 |
| F. F. Powell (R) | 84,024 | 47.9 |
| 2 Henry M. Jackson (D) | 73,296 | 61.2 |
| Herb Wilson (R) | 45,737 | 38.2 |
| 3 Russell V. Mack (R) | 55,056 | 52.9 |
| Gordon M. Quarnstrom (D) | 48,623 | 46.8 |
| 4 Hal Holmes (R) | 61,544 | 64.3 |
| Ted Little (D) | 34,174 | 35.7 |
| 5 Walt Horan (R) | 60,273 | 54.8 |
| Robert Dellwo (D) | 49,767 | 45.2 |
| 6 Thor C. Tollefson (R) | 71,785 | 60.5 |
| John M. Coffee (D) | 46,249 | 39.0 |

## WEST VIRGINIA

| Candidates | Votes | % |
|---|---|---|
| 1 Robert L. Ramsay (D) | 53,584 | 51.7 |
| Francis J. Love (R) | 49,987 | 48.3 |
| 2 Harley O. Staggers (D) | 53,485 | 54.4 |
| Melvin C. Snyder (R) | 44,925 | 45.7 |
| 3 Cleveland M. Bailey (D) | 56,794 | 54.4 |
| Rush D. Holt (R) | 47,589 | 45.6 |
| 4 Maurice G. Burnside (D) | 64,265 | 51.7 |
| Hubert S. Ellis (R) | 60,171 | 48.4 |
| 5 John Kee (D) | 61,000 | 65.8 |
| Arnold G. Porterfield (R) | 31,777 | 34.3 |
| 6 Erland H. Hedrick (D) | 85,793 | 61.6 |
| Latelle M. LaFollette Jr. (R) | 53,466 | 38.4 |

## WISCONSIN

| Candidates | Votes | % |
|---|---|---|
| 1 Lawrence H. Smith (R) | 70,883 | 57.2 |
| Jack Harvey (D) | 53,071 | 42.8 |
| 2 Glenn R. Davis (R) | 75,281 | 57.6 |
| Horace W. Wilkie (D) | 55,117 | 42.2 |
| 3 Gardner R. Withrow (R) | 54,783 | 58.8 |
| Patrick J. Lucey (D) | 38,265 | 41.0 |
| 4 Clement J. Zablocki (D) | 83,564 | 60.9 |
| John C. Brophy (R) | 53,702 | 39.1 |
| 5 Charles J. Kersten (R) | 75,955 | 51.6 |
| Andrew J. Biemiller (D) | 71,203 | 48.4 |
| 6 William K. Van Pelt (R) | 66,289 | 65.1 |
| Kenneth Kunde (D) | 35,618 | 35.0 |
| 7 Reid F. Murray (R) | 63,433 | 68.3 |
| Edward G. Gilbertson (D) | 29,408 | 31.7 |
| 8 John W. Byrnes (R) | 71,908 | 62.1 |
| John W. Reynolds Jr. (D) | 43,877 | 37.9 |
| 9 Merlin Hull (R) | 60,337 | 70.8 |
| Arthur L. Henning (D) | 24,871 | 29.2 |
| 10 Alvin E. O'Konski (R) | 46,722 | 57.0 |
| Rodney J. Edwards (D) | 35,281 | 43.0 |

## WYOMING

| Candidates | Votes | % |
|---|---|---|
| AL William Henry Harrison (R) | 50,865 | 54.5 |
| John B. Clark (D) | 42,483 | 45.5 |

1. Guill received 7,717 votes (23.2 percent) for a plurality victory over a field of 11 candidates. The election is significant as he became the first Republican elected from the South (not including the two easternmost Tennessee districts that had been Republican since the Civil War) since 1930.

# 1951 House Elections

## KENTUCKY

**Special Election**

| | Votes | % |
|---|---|---|
| 6 John C. Watts (D) | 28,599 | 55.3 |
| Otis C. Thomas (R) | 23,108 | 44.7 |

## MISSOURI

**Special Election**

| | Votes | % |
|---|---|---|
| 11 Claude I. Bakewell (R) | 25,849# | 57.3 |
| Harry Schendel (D) | 19,275# | 42.7 |

## NEW YORK

**Special Election**

| | Votes | % |
|---|---|---|
| 5 Robert Tripp Ross (R) | 17,300 | 53.1 |
| Hugh Quinn (D) | 11,438 | 35.1 |
| George Cranmore (L) | 2,641 | 8.1 |

## TEXAS

**Special Election**

| | Votes | % |
|---|---|---|
| 13 Frank Ikard (D) | 8,970 | 31.0 |
| Jenkins | 5,363 | 18.5 |
| Jackson | 5,101 | 17.6 |
| Wagonseller | 4,225 | 14.6 |
| McFarland | 2,786 | 9.6 |
| Crouch | 2,423 | 8.4 |

# 1952 House Elections

## ALABAMA

| | Candidates | Votes | % |
|---|---|---|---|
| 1 | Frank W. Boykin (D) | 30,758 | 100.0 |
| 2 | George Grant (D) | 38,421 | 100.0 |
| 3 | George W. Andrews (D) | 29,321 | 100.0 |
| 4 | Kenneth A. Roberts (D) | 31,389 | 100.0 |
| 5 | Albert Rains (D) | 43,843 | 100.0 |
| 6 | Armistead I. Selden Jr. (D) | 24,058 | 100.0 |
| 7 | Carl Elliott (D) | 33,533 | 72.6 |
| | Cyrus Kitchens (R) | 12,689 | 27.5 |
| 8 | Robert E. Jones Jr. (D) | 41,293 | 87.3 |
| | H. G. Williams (R) | 5,984 | 12.7 |
| 9 | Laurie C. Battle (D) | 51,537 | 100.0 |

## ARIZONA

| | | Votes | % |
|---|---|---|---|
| 1 | John J. Rhodes (R) | 66,512 | 54.0 |
| | John R. Murdock (D) | 56,622 | 46.0 |
| 2 | Harold A. Patten (D) | 71,245 | 56.9 |
| | William C. Frey (R) | 54,021 | 43.1 |

## ARKANSAS

| | | Votes | % |
|---|---|---|---|
| 1 | Ezekiel C. Gathings (D) | 42,494 | 100.0 |
| 2 | Wilbur D. Mills (D) | 36,252 | 100.0 |
| 3 | James W. Trimble (D) | 49,284 | 56.0 |
| | Jack Joyce (R) | 38,784 | 44.0 |
| 4 | Oren Harris (D) | 65,374 | 100.0 |
| 5 | Brooks Hays (D) | 53,056 | 78.8 |
| | Alonzo A. Ross (R) | 13,105 | 19.5 |
| 6 | William F. Norrell (D) | 62,378 | 100.0 |

## CALIFORNIA

| | | Votes | % |
|---|---|---|---|
| 1 | Hubert B. Scudder (R-D) | 137,801 | 86.3 |
| | Carl Sullivan (I PROG) | 21,734 | 13.6 |
| 2 | Clair Engle (D-R) | 124,179 | 100.0 |
| 3 | John E. Moss Jr. (D) | 87,335 | 50.8 |
| | Leslie E. Wood (R) | 82,133 | 47.8 |
| 4 | William S. Mailliard (R) | 102,359 | 55.0 |
| | Franck R. Havenner (D) | 83,748 | 45.0 |
| 5 | John F. Shelley (D-R) | 107,542 | 100.0 |
| 6 | Robert L. Condon (D) | 87,768 | 50.6 |
| | John F. Baldwin Jr. (R) | 85,756 | 49.4 |
| 7 | John J. Allen Jr. (R-D) | 120,666 | 84.2 |
| | John Allen Johnson (I PROG) | 22,408 | 15.6 |
| 8 | George P. Miller (D-R) | 156,445 | 99.9 |
| 9 | J. Arthur Younger (R) | 71,426 | 53.1 |
| | Harold F. Taggart (D) | 61,028 | 45.3 |
| 10 | Charles S. Gubser (R) | 106,375 | 59.2 |
| | Arthur L. Johnson (D) | 70,271 | 39.1 |
| 11 | Leroy Johnson (R-D) | 101,052 | 87.1 |
| | Leslie B. Schlingheyde (I PROG) | 14,999 | 12.9 |
| 12 | A. Oakley Hunter (R-D) | 103,587 | 99.3 |
| 13 | Ernest K. Bramblett (R) | 79,496 | 51.0 |
| | Will Hayes (D) | 76,516 | 49.0 |
| 14 | Harlan Hagen (D) | 70,809 | 51.0 |
| | Thomas H. Werdel (R) | 68,011 | 49.0 |
| 15 | Gordon L. McDonough (R-D) | 142,545 | 99.7 |
| 16 | Donald L. Jackson (R) | 79,127 | 59.7 |
| | Jerry K. Harter (D) | 53,337 | 40.2 |
| 17 | Cecil R. King (D) | 114,650 | 54.6 |
| | Robert H. Finch (R) | 92,587 | 44.1 |
| 18 | Craig Hosmer (R) | 90,438 | 55.5 |
| | Joseph M. Kennick (D) | 72,457 | 44.5 |
| 19 | Chet Holifield (D-R) | 126,606 | 87.0 |
| | Ida Alvarez (I PROG) | 13,724 | 9.4 |
| 20 | Carl Hinshaw (R-D) | 109,509 | 99.7 |
| 21 | Edgar W. Hiestand (R) | 112,100 | 53.6 |
| | Everett G. Burkhalter (D) | 97,007 | 46.4 |
| 22 | Joseph F. Holt (R) | 85,039 | 60.5 |
| | Dean E. McHenry (D) | 55,534 | 39.5 |

| | Candidates | Votes | % |
|---|---|---|---|
| 23 | Clyde Doyle (D-R) | 138,356 | 87.3 |
| | Olive T. Thompson (I PROG) | 17,501 | 11.1 |
| 24 | Norris Poulson (R-D) | 119,799 | 87.2 |
| | Bertram L. Sharp (I PROG) | 17,307 | 12.6 |
| 25 | Patrick J. Hillings (R) | 135,465 | 64.3 |
| | Woodrow Wilson Sayre (D) | 75,125 | 35.7 |
| 26 | Samuel William Yorty (D-R) | 157,973 | 88.0 |
| | Horace V. Alexander (I PROG) | 21,465 | 12.0 |
| 27 | Harry R. Sheppard (D) | 68,773 | 55.0 |
| | Carl B. Hilliard (R) | 56,202 | 45.0 |
| 28 | James B. Utt (R) | 106,972 | 63.0 |
| | Lionel Van Deerlin (D) | 62,779 | 37.0 |
| 29 | John Phillips (R-D) | 73,144 | 99.7 |
| 30 | Bob Wilson (R) | 121,332 | 59.6 |
| | Degraff Austin (D) | 82,311 | 40.4 |

## COLORADO

| | | Votes | % |
|---|---|---|---|
| 1 | Byron G. Rogers (D) | 101,864 | 50.8 |
| | Mason Knuckles (R) | 97,442 | 48.6 |
| 2 | William S. Hill (R) | 113,566 | 63.1 |
| | Ralph L. Williams (D) | 66,300 | 36.9 |
| 3 | J. Edgar Chenoweth (R) | 84,739 | 57.7 |
| | John H. Marsalis (D) | 62,025 | 42.3 |
| 4 | Wayne N. Aspinall (D) | 39,676 | 50.0 |
| | Howard M. Shults (R) | 39,647 | 50.0 |

## CONNECTICUT

| | | Votes | % |
|---|---|---|---|
| 1 | Thomas J. Dodd (D) | 160,080 | 54.0 |
| | John Ashmead (R) | 136,540 | 46.0 |
| 2 | Horace Seely-Brown Jr. (R) | 90,827 | 55.5 |
| | William M. Citron (D) | 72,868 | 44.5 |
| 3 | Albert W. Cretella (R) | 111,018 | 52.8 |
| | John A. McGuire (D) | 99,408 | 47.2 |
| 4 | Albert P. Morano (R) | 164,689 | 60.1 |
| | Joseph P. Lyford (D) | 107,881 | 39.4 |
| 5 | James T. Patterson (R) | 83,848 | 56.7 |
| | John A. Speziale (D) | 64,020 | 43.3 |
| AL | Antoni N. Sadlak (R) | 601,238 | 55.0 |
| | Stanley J. Pribyson (D) | 489,645 | 44.8 |

## DELAWARE

| | | Votes | % |
|---|---|---|---|
| AL | Herbert B. Warburton (R) | 88,285 | 51.9 |
| | Joseph J. Scannel (D) | 81,730 | 48.1 |

## FLORIDA

| | | Votes | % |
|---|---|---|---|
| 1 | Courtney Campbell (D) | 69,149 | 50.7 |
| | William C. Cramer (R) | 67,286 | 49.3 |
| 2 | Charles E. Bennett (D) | 64,080 | 100.0 |
| 3 | Robert L. F. Sikes (D) | 74,909 | 100.0 |
| 4 | Bill Lantaff (D) | 115,611 | 66.0 |
| | Dorothea M. B. Vermorel (R) | 59,458 | 34.0 |
| 5 | A. S. Herlong Jr. (D) | 89,943 | 100.0 |
| 6 | Dwight L. Rogers (D) | 55,901 | 60.8 |
| | Janet H. Fitzgerald (R) | 36,113 | 39.3 |
| 7 | James A. Haley (D) | 36,973 | 56.3 |
| | Kent S. McKinley (R) | 28,725 | 43.7 |
| 8 | D. R. Matthews (D) | 43,447 | 100.0 |

## GEORGIA

| | | Votes | % |
|---|---|---|---|
| 1 | Prince H. Preston (D) | 57,088 | 100.0 |
| 2 | E. E. Cox (D) | 42,226* | 100.0 |
| 3 | E. L. Forrester (D) | 53,161 | 100.0 |
| 4 | A. Sidney Camp (D) | 52,327 | 100.0 |
| 5 | James C. Davis (D) | 83,920 | 100.0 |

| | Candidates | Votes | % |
|---|---|---|---|
| 6 | Carl Vinson (D) | 49,635 | 100.0 |
| 7 | Henderson Lanham (D) | 65,416 | 99.9 |
| 8 | W. M. Wheeler (D) | 51,349 | 99.9 |
| 9 | Phil M. Landrum (D) | 47,327 | 100.0 |
| 10 | Paul Brown (D) | 44,646 | 100.0 |

## IDAHO

| | | Votes | % |
|---|---|---|---|
| 1 | Gracie Pfost (D) | 54,725 | 50.3 |
| | John T. Wood (R) | 54,134 | 49.7 |
| 2 | Hamer H. Budge (R) | 103,047 | 66.2 |
| | W. H. Jensen (D) | 52,692 | 33.8 |

## ILLINOIS

| | | Votes | % |
|---|---|---|---|
| 1 | William L. Dawson (D) | 95,899 | 73.5 |
| | Edgar G. Brown (R) | 34,571 | 26.5 |
| 2 | Barratt O'Hara (D) | 94,253 | 51.4 |
| | Richard B. Vail (R) | 89,080 | 48.6 |
| 3 | Fred E. Busbey (R) | 102,328 | 54.5 |
| | Neil J. Linehan (D) | 85,539 | 45.5 |
| 4 | William E. McVey (R) | 131,215 | 56.6 |
| | Arthur E. Dillner (D) | 100,809 | 43.5 |
| 5 | John C. Kluczynski (D) | 104,900 | 64.5 |
| | Ernest L. Kaysen (R) | 57,775 | 35.5 |
| 6 | Thomas J. O'Brien (D) | 112,121 | 63.1 |
| | John L. Roach (R) | 65,537 | 36.9 |
| 7 | Adolph J. Sabath (D) | 111,960* | 70.0 |
| | Louis F. Capuzi (R) | 48,000 | 30.0 |
| 8 | Thomas S. Gordon (D) | 87,871 | 59.0 |
| | William F. Cooper (R) | 61,048 | 41.0 |
| 9 | Sidney R. Yates (D) | 87,285 | 52.4 |
| | Robert R. Siegrist (R) | 79,429 | 47.6 |
| 10 | Richard W. Hoffman (R) | 138,560 | 65.0 |
| | John Schaffenegger (D) | 74,467 | 35.0 |
| 11 | Timothy P. Sheehan (R) | 103,265 | 59.4 |
| | Stanley W. Morten (D) | 70,691 | 40.6 |
| 12 | Edgar A. Jonas (R) | 113,762 | 55.7 |
| | Philip A. Fleischman (D) | 90,444 | 44.3 |
| 13 | Marguerite Stitt Church (R) | 184,696 | 70.6 |
| | Lawrence I. Hayes (D) | 77,068 | 29.4 |
| 14 | Chauncey W. Reed (R) | 137,881 | 71.5 |
| | William E. Hartnett (D) | 54,953 | 28.5 |
| 15 | Noah M. Mason (R) | 103,398 | 63.7 |
| | Stanley Hubbs (D) | 59,050 | 36.4 |
| 16 | Leo E. Allen (R) | 110,182 | 66.5 |
| | John P. Barton (D) | 55,399 | 33.5 |
| 17 | Leslie C. Arends (R) | 105,042 | 63.6 |
| | John A. Kinneman (D) | 60,112 | 36.4 |
| 18 | Harold H. Velde (R) | 83,706 | 55.2 |
| | John T. McNaughton (D) | 67,905 | 44.8 |
| 19 | Robert B. Chiperfield (R) | 94,141 | 60.8 |
| | Ray Simkins (D) | 60,619 | 39.2 |
| 20 | Sidney E. Simpson (R) | 84,994 | 61.8 |
| | John R. Roy (D) | 52,586 | 38.2 |
| 21 | Peter F. Mack Jr. (D) | 94,026 | 52.5 |
| | Edward H. Jenison (R) | 85,248 | 47.6 |
| 22 | William L. Springer (R) | 92,851 | 63.0 |
| | David W. Beggs Jr. (D) | 54,576 | 37.0 |
| 23 | Charles Vursell (R) | 89,428 | 57.7 |
| | W. Carl Johnson (D) | 65,442 | 42.3 |
| 24 | Melvin Price (D) | 117,408 | 64.8 |
| | Phyllis Stewart Schlafly (R) | 63,778 | 35.2 |
| 25 | C. W. Bishop (R) | 88,810 | 56.2 |
| | C. Edwin Hair (D) | 69,245 | 43.8 |

## INDIANA

| | | Votes | % |
|---|---|---|---|
| 1 | Ray J. Madden (D) | 93,187 | 56.4 |
| | Elliott Belshaw (R) | 71,617 | 43.3 |
| 2 | Charles A. Halleck (R) | 94,795 | 63.3 |
| | L. Dewey Burham (D) | 54,025 | 36.1 |
| 3 | Shepard J. Crumpacker Jr. (R) | 107,839 | 54.5 |
| | Charles C. Price (D) | 88,776 | 44.9 |

## INDIANA

| | Candidates | Votes | % |
|---|---|---|---|
| 4 | E. Ross Adair (R) | 95,613 | 63.7 |
| | Howard L. Morrison (D) | 53,154 | 35.4 |
| 5 | John V. Beamer (R) | 114,081 | 56.9 |
| | Philip C. Dermond (D) | 84,825 | 42.3 |
| 6 | Cecil M. Harden (R) | 86,899 | 55.7 |
| | Jack H. Mankin (D) | 68,709 | 44.0 |
| 7 | William G. Bray (R) | 85,601 | 56.1 |
| | Thomas J. Courtney (D) | 66,218 | 43.4 |
| 8 | D. Bailey Merrill (R) | 98,226 | 52.6 |
| | Winfield K. Denton (D) | 87,770 | 47.0 |
| 9 | Earl Wilson (R) | 74,052 | 56.4 |
| | Edward Lewis (D) | 56,759 | 43.2 |
| 10 | Ralph Harvey (R) | 103,937 | 59.9 |
| | Fred V. Culp (D) | 67,932 | 39.1 |
| 11 | Charles B. Brownson (R) | 160,929 | 59.4 |
| | John C. Carvey (D) | 109,403 | 40.4 |

## IOWA

| | Candidates | Votes | % |
|---|---|---|---|
| 1 | Thomas E. Martin (R) | 105,526 | 62.9 |
| | Clair A. Williams (D) | 62,011 | 36.9 |
| 2 | Henry O. Talle (R) | 114,553 | 62.2 |
| | T. W. Mullaney (D) | 69,421 | 37.7 |
| 3 | H. R. Gross (R) | 109,992 | 65.8 |
| | George R. Laub (D) | 56,871 | 34.0 |
| 4 | Karl M. LeCompte (R) | 73,317 | 61.9 |
| | Earl E. Glassburner (D) | 44,900 | 37.9 |
| 5 | Paul Cunningham (R) | 95,057 | 58.8 |
| | Alvin P. Meyer (D) | 66,303 | 41.0 |
| 6 | James I. Dolliver (R) | 86,842 | 68.7 |
| | Francis G. Cutler (D) | 39,245 | 31.1 |
| 7 | Ben F. Jensen (R) | 82,462 | 67.3 |
| | Thomas J. Keleher (D) | 39,999 | 32.6 |
| 8 | Charles B. Hoeven (R) | 94,561 | 99.7 |

## KANSAS

| | Candidates | Votes | % |
|---|---|---|---|
| 1 | Howard S. Miller (D) | 68,909 | 51.5 |
| | Albert M. Cole (R) | 64,963 | 48.5 |
| 2 | Errett P. Scrivner (R) | 91,676 | 57.3 |
| | Claude L. Rice (D) | 68,396 | 42.7 |
| 3 | Myron V. George (R) | 57,126 | 59.5 |
| | Fred L. Hedges (D) | 38,960 | 40.6 |
| 4 | Edward H. Rees (R) | 118,206 | 59.4 |
| | Bill Porter (D) | 80,697 | 40.6 |
| 5 | Clifford R. Hope (R) | 90,967 | 70.9 |
| | Art McAnarney (D) | 37,361 | 29.1 |
| 6 | Wint Smith (R) | 66,723 | 62.6 |
| | Horace A. Santry (D) | 39,955 | 37.5 |

## KENTUCKY

| | Candidates | Votes | % |
|---|---|---|---|
| 1 | Noble J. Gregory (D) | 66,106 | 65.8 |
| | W. Mallam Lake (R) | 34,360 | 34.2 |
| 2 | Garrett L. Withers (D) | 57,518 | 54.4 |
| | David C. Brodie (R) | 48,191 | 45.6 |
| 3 | John M. Robsion Jr. (R) | 95,041 | 54.0 |
| | B. L. Shamburger (D) | 80,347 | 45.7 |
| 4 | Frank L. Chelf (D) | 55,670 | 55.9 |
| | R. H. Hutchison Jr. (R) | 43,981 | 44.1 |
| 5 | Brent Spence (D) | 78,431 | 55.4 |
| | William D. Cochran (R) | 63,058 | 44.6 |
| 6 | John C. Watts (D) | 68,554 | 56.3 |
| | Leslie A. Henderson (R) | 53,297 | 43.7 |
| 7 | Carl D. Perkins (D) | 53,238 | 58.2 |
| | Curtis Clark (R) | 38,290 | 41.8 |
| 8 | James S. Golden (R) | 78,584 | 68.9 |
| | W. D. Scalf (D) | 35,556 | 31.2 |

## LOUISIANA

| | Candidates | Votes | % |
|---|---|---|---|
| 1 | F. Edward Hebert (D) | 71,448 | 66.4 |
| | George W. Reese Jr. (R) | 36,161 | 33.6 |
| 2 | Hale Boggs (D) | 68,112 | 100.0 |
| 3 | Edwin E. Willis (D) | 33,184 | 100.0 |
| 4 | Overton Brooks (D) | 40,724 | 100.0 |
| 5 | Otto E. Passman (D) | 32,743 | 100.0 |

| | Candidates | Votes | % |
|---|---|---|---|
| 6 | James H. Morrison (D) | 61,744 | 100.0 |
| 7 | T. A. Thompson (D) | 40,811 | 100.0 |
| 8 | George S. Long (D) | 31,476 | 100.0 |

## MAINE

| | Candidates | Votes | % |
|---|---|---|---|
| 1 | Robert Hale (R) | 56,239 | 61.6 |
| | James A. McVicar (D) | 35,078 | 38.4 |
| 2 | Charles P. Nelson (R) | 55,393 | 66.8 |
| | Leland B. Currier (D) | 27,527 | 33.2 |
| 3 | Clifford G. McIntire (R) | 45,095 | 76.2 |
| | Philip R. Sharpe (D) | 14,103 | 23.8 |

## MARYLAND

| | Candidates | Votes | % |
|---|---|---|---|
| 1 | Edward T. Miller (R) | 47,164 | 61.0 |
| | Dudley George Roe (D) | 30,162 | 39.0 |
| 2 | James P. S. Devereux (R) | 95,811 | 61.4 |
| | A. Gordon Boone (D) | 60,121 | 38.6 |
| 3 | Edward A. Garmatz (D) | 60,659 | 70.9 |
| | Jerry Toula (R) | 24,879 | 29.1 |
| 4 | George H. Fallon (D) | 54,215 | 54.7 |
| | Samuel Hopkins (R) | 44,974 | 45.3 |
| 5 | Frank Small Jr. (R) | 68,405 | 50.4 |
| | Richard E. Lankford (D) | 67,366 | 49.6 |
| 6 | DeWitt S. Hyde (R) | 94,603 | 57.8 |
| | Stella B. Werner (D) | 69,050 | 42.2 |
| 7 | Samuel N. Friedel (D) | 63,652 | 51.4 |
| | William F. Laukaitis (R) | 60,277 | 48.6 |

## MASSACHUSETTS

| | Candidates | Votes | % |
|---|---|---|---|
| 1 | John W. Heselton (R) | 101,512 | 67.1 |
| | William H. Burns (D) | 49,379 | 32.7 |
| 2 | Edward P. Boland (D) | 88,424 | 51.8 |
| | Troy T. Murray (R) | 81,847 | 48.0 |
| 3 | Philip J. Philbin (D) | 108,743 | 67.3 |
| | Frank D. Walker (R) | 52,348 | 32.4 |
| 4 | Harold D. Donohue (D) | 93,530 | 54.4 |
| | Carl A. Sheridan (R) | 77,536 | 45.1 |
| 5 | Edith Nourse Rogers (R) | 146,269 | 75.9 |
| | Helen M. Fitzgerald (D) | 45,650 | 23.7 |
| 6 | William H. Bates (R) | 139,657 | 95.1 |
| 7 | Thomas J. Lane (D) | 105,662 | 74.7 |
| | John L. Southwick Jr. (R) | 34,663 | 24.5 |
| 8 | Angier L. Goodwin (R) | 85,918 | 50.9 |
| | John C. Carr Jr. (D) | 82,114 | 48.7 |
| 9 | Donald W. Nicholson (R) | 103,708 | 59.2 |
| | James F. O'Neill (D) | 71,129 | 40.6 |
| 10 | Laurence Curtis (R) | 101,221 | 54.3 |
| | Frederick C. Hailer Jr. (D) | 84,021 | 45.1 |
| 11 | Thomas P. O'Neill (D) | 86,532 | 69.3 |
| | Jesse A. Rogers (R) | 37,816 | 30.3 |
| 12 | John W. McCormack (D) | 111,986 | 82.2 |
| | James S. Tremblay (R) | 24,271 | 17.8 |
| 13 | Richard B. Wigglesworth (R) | 114,761 | 60.6 |
| | David J. Crowley (D) | 74,730 | 39.4 |
| 14 | Joseph W. Martin Jr. (R) | 108,215 | 63.2 |
| | Edward F. Doolan (D) | 62,554 | 36.5 |

## MICHIGAN

| | Candidates | Votes | % |
|---|---|---|---|
| 1 | Thaddeus M. Machrowicz (D) | 118,695 | 84.2 |
| | Rudolph G. Tenerowicz (R) | 21,442 | 15.2 |
| 2 | George Meader (R) | 101,341 | 63.4 |
| | John P. Dawson (D) | 58,024 | 36.3 |
| 3 | Paul W. Shafer (R) | 95,061 | 62.0 |
| | Kenneth G. Brown (D) | 57,666 | 37.6 |
| 4 | Clare E. Hoffman (R) | 87,703 | 66.6 |
| | Murle E. Gorton (D) | 43,450 | 33.0 |
| 5 | Gerald R. Ford Jr. (R) | 109,807 | 66.3 |
| | Vincent E. O'Neill (D) | 55,147 | 33.3 |
| 6 | Kit Clardy (R) | 108,263 | 52.6 |
| | Donald Hayworth (D) | 96,682 | 47.0 |
| 7 | Jesse P. Wolcott (R) | 101,936 | 60.3 |
| | Ira D. McCoy (D) | 66,699 | 39.5 |

| | Candidates | Votes | % |
|---|---|---|---|
| 8 | Alvin M. Bentley (R) | 91,731 | 66.6 |
| | Clarence V. Smazel (D) | 45,431 | 33.0 |
| 9 | Ruth Thompson (R) | 70,456 | 59.5 |
| | John H. Piercey (D) | 47,456 | 40.1 |
| 10 | Elford A. Cederberg (R) | 69,727 | 67.5 |
| | William J. Kelly (D) | 33,602 | 32.5 |
| 11 | Victor A. Knox (R) | 54,883 | 59.3 |
| | Prentiss M. Brown Jr. (D) | 37,701 | 40.7 |
| 12 | John B. Bennett (R) | 47,160 | 58.2 |
| | E. Burr Sherwood (D) | 33,892 | 41.8 |
| 13 | George D. O'Brien (D) | 88,473 | 64.8 |
| | Clarence J. McLeod (R) | 47,881 | 35.1 |
| 14 | Louis C. Rabaut (D) | 117,027 | 53.1 |
| | Richard Durant (R) | 103,366 | 46.9 |
| 15 | John D. Dingell (D) | 109,109 | 66.7 |
| | Gregory M. Pillon (R) | 54,236 | 33.2 |
| 16 | John Lesinski Jr. (D) | 139,011 | 60.6 |
| | Harold J. Smith (R) | 89,159 | 38.9 |
| 17 | Charles G. Oakman (R) | 94,517 | 52.9 |
| | Martha W. Griffiths (D) | 84,001 | 47.0 |
| 18 | George A. Dondero (R) | 108,673 | 56.2 |
| | Arthur J. Law (D) | 84,308 | 43.6 |

## MINNESOTA

| | Candidates | Votes | % |
|---|---|---|---|
| 1 | August H. Andresen (R) | 103,218 | 69.4 |
| | George Alfson (DFL) | 45,496 | 30.6 |
| 2 | Joseph P. O'Hara (R) | 101,641 | 67.7 |
| | Richard T. Malone (DFL) | 48,404 | 32.3 |
| 3 | Roy W. Wier (DFL) | 115,008 | 52.2 |
| | Ed Willow (R) | 105,320 | 47.8 |
| 4 | Eugene J. McCarthy (DFL) | 98,015 | 61.7 |
| | Roger G. Kennedy (R) | 60,827 | 38.3 |
| 5 | Walter H. Judd (R) | 99,027 | 59.2 |
| | Karl F. Rolvaag (DFL) | 68,326 | 40.8 |
| 6 | Fred Marshall (DFL) | 74,041 | 52.6 |
| | J. Arthur Bensen (R) | 66,764 | 47.4 |
| 7 | H. Carl Andersen (R) | 87,460 | 62.7 |
| | James M. Youngdale (DFL) | 52,144 | 37.4 |
| 8 | John A. Blatnik (DFL) | 91,465 | 62.6 |
| | Ernest R. Orchard (R) | 54,756 | 37.5 |
| 9 | Harold C. Hagen (R) | 70,402 | 60.6 |
| | Curtiss T. Olson (DFL) | 45,874 | 39.5 |

## MISSISSIPPI

| | Candidates | Votes | % |
|---|---|---|---|
| 1 | Thomas G. Abernethy (D) | 40,333 | 100.0 |
| 2 | Jamie L. Whitten (D) | 29,025 | 100.0 |
| 3 | Frank E. Smith (D) | 23,906 | 87.2 |
| | Paul Clark (R) | 3,523 | 12.8 |
| 4 | John Bell Williams (D) | 50,318 | 100.0 |
| 5 | Arthur Winstead (D) | 39,919 | 94.1 |
| | Henry J. Maddox (R) | 2,501 | 5.9 |
| 6 | William M. Colmer (D) | 51,227 | 100.0 |

## MISSOURI

| | Candidates | Votes | % |
|---|---|---|---|
| 1 | Frank M. Karsten (D) | 126,583 | 64.2 |
| | Eugene A. Miller (R) | 70,479 | 35.8 |
| 2 | Thomas B. Curtis (R) | 125,625 | 56.9 |
| | Donald McClanahan (D) | 95,208 | 43.1 |
| 3 | Leonor K. Sullivan (D) | 107,428 | 64.8 |
| | Claude I. Bakewell (R) | 58,413 | 35.2 |
| 4 | Jeffrey P. Hillelson (R) | 96,988 | 53.3 |
| | Leonard Irving (D) | 84,899 | 46.7 |
| 5 | Richard Bolling (D) | 90,357 | 56.0 |
| | Frank C. Rayburn (R) | 70,898 | 44.0 |
| 6 | William C. Cole (R) | 89,428 | 52.4 |
| | Robert O. Richardson (D) | 81,237 | 47.6 |
| 7 | Dewey Short (R) | 115,842 | 61.7 |
| | John Hosmer (D) | 71,936 | 38.3 |
| 8 | A. S. J. Carnahan (D) | 69,068 | 52.9 |
| | Francis E. Howard (R) | 61,621 | 47.2 |
| 9 | Clarence Cannon (D) | 98,965 | 54.8 |
| | S. W. (Wat) Arnold (R) | 81,806 | 45.3 |
| 10 | Paul C. Jones (D) | 71,156 | 60.7 |
| | Andrew Sandegren (R) | 46,033 | 39.3 |
| 11 | Morgan M. Moulder (D) | 74,362 | 50.4 |
| | Max Schwabe (R) | 73,104 | 49.6 |

## MONTANA

| | Candidates | Votes | % |
|---|---|---|---|
| 1 | Lee Metcalf (D) | 55,679 | 50.3 |
| | Wellington D. Rankin (R) | 54,086 | 48.9 |
| 2 | Wesley A. D'Ewart (R) | 90,210 | 62.0 |
| | Willard E. Fraser (D) | 55,203 | 38.0 |

## NEBRASKA

| | Candidates | Votes | % |
|---|---|---|---|
| 1 | Carl T. Curtis (R) | 117,336 | 72.1 |
| | Samuel Freeman (D) | 45,523 | 28.0 |
| 2 | Roman L. Hruska (R) | 81,185 | 56.1 |
| | James A. Hart (D) | 63,485 | 43.9 |
| 3 | Robert D. Harrison (R) | 89,879 | 71.9 |
| | Alan A. Dusatko (D) | 35,213 | 28.2 |
| 4 | Arthur L. Miller (R) | 98,032 | 73.3 |
| | Francis D. Lee (D) | 35,628 | 26.7 |

## NEVADA

| | Candidates | Votes | % |
|---|---|---|---|
| AL | Clifton Young (R) | 40,683 | 50.5 |
| | Walter S. Baring (D) | 39,912 | 49.5 |

## NEW HAMPSHIRE

| | Candidates | Votes | % |
|---|---|---|---|
| 1 | Chester E. Merrow (R) | 82,689 | 60.2 |
| | Peter R. Poirier (D) | 54,746 | 39.8 |
| 2 | Norris Cotton (R) | 80,061 | 66.5 |
| | John Guay (D) | 40,373 | 33.5 |

## NEW JERSEY

| | Candidates | Votes | % |
|---|---|---|---|
| 1 | Charles A. Wolverton (R) | 118,367 | 55.0 |
| | Alfred R. Pierce (D) | 96,162 | 44.7 |
| 2 | T. Millet Hand (R) | 79,955 | 63.4 |
| | Charles Edward Rupp (D) | 46,174 | 36.6 |
| 3 | James C. Auchincloss (R) | 124,292 | 64.4 |
| | John W. Zimmermann (D) | 67,642 | 35.0 |
| 4 | Charles R. Howell (D) | 84,733 | 54.7 |
| | John J. Inglesby (R) | 70,076 | 45.3 |
| 5 | Peter H. B. Frelinghuysen Jr. (R) | 133,276 | 62.2 |
| | Aldona L. Appleton (D) | 80,922 | 37.8 |
| 6 | Clifford P. Case (R) | 121,252 | 63.9 |
| | H. Frank Pettit (D) | 67,159 | 35.4 |
| 7 | William B. Widnall (R) | 130,603 | 68.3 |
| | Vito A. Concilio (D) | 60,553 | 31.7 |
| 8 | Gordon Canfield (R) | 97,338 | 62.6 |
| | John J. Winberry (D) | 54,367 | 35.0 |
| 9 | Frank C. Osmers Jr. (R) | 125,402 | 66.2 |
| | William H. McNulty (D) | 63,175 | 33.4 |
| 10 | Peter W. Rodino Jr. (D) | 78,612 | 56.9 |
| | Alexander J. Matturri (R) | 57,740 | 41.8 |
| 11 | Hugh J. Addonizio (D) | 68,273 | 52.2 |
| | William O. Barnes Jr. (R) | 60,461 | 46.3 |
| 12 | Robert Winthrop Kean (R) | 84,949 | 54.8 |
| | Martin S. Fox (D) | 70,046 | 45.2 |
| 13 | Alfred D. Sieminski (D) | 72,987 | 55.2 |
| | Julius D. Canter (R) | 54,581 | 41.2 |
| 14 | Edward J. Hart (D) | 67,109 | 51.5 |
| | William J. Bozzuffi (R) | 59,112 | 45.4 |

## NEW MEXICO

| | Candidates | Votes | % |
|---|---|---|---|
| AL | John J. Dempsey (D) | 121,477 | |
| | Antonio M. Fernandez (D) | 119,925 | |
| | Homer J. Berkshire (R) | 112,297 | |
| | Ed Guthmann (R) | 109,595 | |

## NEW YORK

| | Candidates | Votes | % |
|---|---|---|---|
| 1 | Stuyvesant Wainwright (R) | 114,135 | 60.4 |
| | Ernest Greenwood (D, L) | 74,174 | 39.3 |
| 2 | Steven B. Derounian (R) | 132,512 | 68.8 |
| | Joseph Liff (D) | 54,725 | 28.4 |
| 3 | Frank J. Becker (R) | 128,007 | 65.4 |
| | Richard A. O'Leary (D) | 60,800 | 31.0 |
| 4 | Henry J. Latham (R) | 123,132 | 62.6 |
| | Joseph J. Perrini (D, L) | 70,755 | 36.0 |
| 5 | Albert H. Bosch (R) | 86,168 | 53.5 |
| | L. Gary Clemente (D, L) | 73,083 | 45.3 |
| 6 | Lester Holtzman (D, L) | 105,261 | 49.2 |
| | Robert Tripp Ross (R) | 104,720 | 48.9 |
| 7 | James J. Delaney (D, L) | 87,204 | 51.0 |
| | William Adam Schulz (R) | 80,896 | 47.3 |
| 8 | Louis B. Heller (D, L) | 75,772 | 65.3 |
| | Benjamin F. Westervelt Jr. (R) | 37,884 | 32.6 |
| 9 | Eugene J. Keogh (D, L) | 83,841 | 61.1 |
| | Joseph M. Soviero (R) | 48,998 | 35.7 |
| 10 | Edna F. Kelly (D, L) | 105,302 | 71.2 |
| | George W. Thomas (R) | 42,498 | 28.8 |
| 11 | Emanuel Celler (D, L) | 127,091 | 73.8 |
| | Henry D. Dorfman (R) | 37,244 | 21.6 |
| 12 | Francis E. Dorn (R) | 75,895 | 52.7 |
| | Donald L. O'Toole (D, L) | 65,650 | 45.6 |
| 13 | Abraham J. Multer (D, L) | 112,152 | 68.3 |
| | P. Vincent Landi (R) | 45,664 | 27.8 |
| 14 | John J. Rooney (D, L) | 86,952 | 64.2 |
| | Jacob P. Lefkowitz (R) | 45,004 | 33.2 |
| 15 | John H. Ray (R) | 97,023 | 57.9 |
| | James J. Murphy (D, L) | 69,538 | 41.5 |
| 16 | Adam Clayton Powell Jr. (D) | 72,562 | 73.9 |
| | Richard L. Baltimore Jr. (R) | 15,937 | 16.2 |
| | Clarence Francis (L) | 7,125 | 7.3 |
| 17 | Frederic R. Coudert Jr. (R) | 84,821 | 57.0 |
| | Harry Grossman (D, L) | 60,624 | 40.7 |
| 18 | James G. Donovan (D, R) | 88,629 | 92.6 |
| | Vito Magli (AM LAB) | 7,047 | 7.4 |
| 19 | Arthur G. Klein (D, L) | 77,267 | 66.0 |
| | Edward I. Goldberg (R) | 34,795 | 29.7 |
| 20 | Franklin D. Roosevelt Jr. (D, L) | 81,591 | 60.2 |
| | Clarence C. Vambell (R) | 49,905 | 36.8 |
| 21 | Jacob K. Javits (R, L) | 89,866 | 63.4 |
| | John C. Hart (D) | 47,637 | 33.6 |
| 22 | Sidney A. Fine (D) | 90,474 | 58.0 |
| | Martin Greene (R) | 38,681 | 24.8 |
| | David Wells (L) | 21,606 | 13.9 |
| 23 | Isidore Dollinger (D) | 78,350 | 63.8 |
| | Sidney S. Flaum (R) | 23,238 | 18.9 |
| | Harry Kavesh (L) | 14,393 | 11.7 |
| | Howard Fast (AM LAB) | 6,834 | 5.6 |
| 24 | Charles A. Buckley (D) | 82,343 | 46.5 |
| | Solon S. Kane (R) | 58,096 | 32.8 |
| | Herman Woskow (L) | 29,425 | 16.6 |
| 25 | Paul A. Fino (R) | 85,308 | 50.1 |
| | Bernard J. O'Connell (D) | 68,862 | 40.4 |
| | Louis Schifrin (L) | 13,325 | 7.8 |
| 26 | Ralph A. Gamble (R) | 116,091 | 67.3 |
| | Flora Chudson (D, L) | 55,184 | 32.0 |
| 27 | Ralph W. Gwinn (R) | 108,575 | 58.5 |
| | George A. Brenner (D, L) | 75,781 | 40.9 |
| 28 | Katharine St. George (R) | 102,476 | 65.6 |
| | Marion K. Sanders (D, L) | 52,994 | 33.9 |
| 29 | J. Ernest Wharton (R) | 115,502 | 69.8 |
| | Walter Donnaruma (D) | 46,727 | 28.2 |
| 30 | Leo W. O'Brien (D, L) | 101,178 | 53.7 |
| | John F. Forner Jr. (R) | 86,651 | 46.0 |
| 31 | Dean P. Taylor (R) | 114,656 | 70.6 |
| | Helen Nolan Neil (D) | 44,367 | 27.3 |
| 32 | Bernard W. Kearney (R) | 111,025 | 67.4 |
| 33 | Clarence E. Kilburn (R) | 98,653 | 69.0 |
| | Maurice N. McGrath (D) | 41,803 | 29.2 |
| 34 | William R. Williams (R) | 97,488 | 58.8 |
| | Charles Ray Wilson (D) | 65,080 | 39.3 |
| 35 | R. Walter Riehlman (R) | 113,778 | 63.2 |
| | Arthur B. McGuire (D, L) | 65,763 | 36.5 |
| 36 | John Taber (R) | 110,304 | 69.9 |
| | Donald J. O'Connor (D, L) | 47,189 | 29.9 |
| 37 | W. Sterling Cole (R) | 131,172 | 69.4 |
| | Jean Ivory (D, L) | 57,474 | 30.4 |
| 38 | Kenneth B. Keating (R) | 128,566 | 69.3 |
| | Victor Kruppenbacher (D, L) | 56,177 | 30.3 |
| 39 | Harold C. Ostertag (R) | 107,501 | 65.8 |
| | O. Richard Judson (D, L) | 55,483 | 34.0 |
| 40 | William E. Miller (R) | 102,565 | 59.6 |
| | E. Dent Lackey (D, L) | 69,087 | 40.2 |
| 41 | Edmund P. Radwan (R) | 95,755 | 55.9 |
| | Anthony F. Tauriello (D, L) | 75,552 | 44.1 |
| 42 | John R. Pillion (R) | 100,434 | 55.2 |
| | Chester C. Gorski (D, L) | 81,201 | 44.6 |
| 43 | Daniel A. Reed (R) | 91,534 | 66.2 |
| | Harry D. Johnson (D) | 44,276 | 32.0 |

**Special Election**

| | Candidates | Votes | % |
|---|---|---|---|
| 32 | Leo W. O'Brien (D, L) | 66,849 | 70.8 |
| | John F. Forner Jr. (R) | 27,276 | 28.9 |

## NORTH CAROLINA

| | Candidates | Votes | % |
|---|---|---|---|
| 1 | Herbert C. Bonner (D) | 43,104 | 100.0 |
| 2 | L. H. Fountain (D) | 51,213 | 94.8 |
| | W. B. White (R) | 2,822 | 5.2 |
| 3 | Graham A. Barden (D) | 45,458 | 76.2 |
| | Everette L. Peterson (R) | 14,239 | 23.9 |
| 4 | Harold D. Cooley (D) | 79,520 | 75.3 |
| | Paul C. West (R) | 26,039 | 24.7 |
| 5 | Thurmond Chatham (D) | 74,884 | 98.2 |
| 6 | Carl T. Durham (D) | 84,203 | 69.5 |
| | Louis F. Ferree (R) | 36,912 | 30.5 |
| 7 | F. Ertel Carlyle (D) | 62,884 | 98.5 |
| 8 | Charles B. Deane (D) | 67,764 | 59.9 |
| | Walter B. Love (R) | 45,451 | 40.2 |
| 9 | Hugh Q. Alexander (D) | 68,624 | 51.5 |
| | Walter P. Johnson (R) | 64,662 | 48.5 |
| 10 | Charles Raper Jonas (R) | 82,428 | 57.4 |
| | Hamilton C. Jones (D) | 61,149 | 42.6 |
| 11 | Woodrow W. Jones (D) | 61,540 | 63.0 |
| | George M. Pritchard (R) | 36,157 | 37.0 |
| 12 | George A. Shuford (D) | 63,045 | 56.9 |
| | Hugh Montieth (R) | 47,752 | 43.1 |

## NORTH DAKOTA

| | Candidates | Votes | % |
|---|---|---|---|
| AL | Usher L. Burdick (R) | 181,218 | |
| | Otto Krueger (R) | 156,829 | |
| | Edward Nesemeier (D) | 49,829 | |

## OHIO

| | Candidates | Votes | % |
|---|---|---|---|
| 1 | Gordon H. Scherer (R) | 96,385 | 61.6 |
| | Walter A. Kelly (D) | 60,015 | 38.4 |
| 2 | William E. Hess (R) | 90,417 | 56.6 |
| | Earl T. Wagner (D) | 69,341 | 43.4 |
| 3 | Paul F. Schenck (R) | 112,325 | 51.1 |
| | Thomas B. Talbot (D) | 107,561 | 48.9 |
| 4 | William M. McCulloch (R) | 93,442 | 68.3 |
| | Carleton Carl Reiser (D) | 43,426 | 31.7 |
| 5 | Cliff Clevenger (R) | 72,168 | 63.2 |
| | Dan Batt (D) | 42,104 | 36.9 |
| 6 | James G. Polk (D) | 67,220 | 50.1 |
| | Leo Blackburn (R) | 66,896 | 49.9 |
| 7 | Clarence J. Brown (R) | 98,354 | 100.0 |
| 8 | Jackson E. Betts (R) | 75,768 | 68.7 |
| | Henry P. Drake (D) | 34,474 | 31.3 |
| 9 | Frazier Reams (I) | 74,821 | 40.9 |
| | Thomas H. Burke (D) | 61,047 | 33.4 |
| | Gilmore Flues (R) | 46,989 | 25.7 |
| 10 | Thomas A. Jenkins (R) | 63,339 | 64.0 |
| | Delmar A. Canaday (D) | 35,666 | 36.0 |
| 11 | Oliver P. Bolton (R) | 91,204 | 58.8 |
| | Robert J. Kilpatrick (D) | 63,930 | 41.2 |
| 12 | John M. Vorys (R) | 134,693 | 62.3 |
| | George T. Tarbutton (D) | 81,665 | 37.8 |
| 13 | Alvin F. Weichel (R) | 63,344 | 58.8 |
| | George C. Steinemann (D) | 44,467 | 41.3 |
| 14 | William H. Ayres (R) | 117,475 | 58.5 |
| | Walter B. Huber (D) | 83,463 | 41.5 |
| 15 | Robert T. Secrest (D) | 62,913 | 64.3 |
| | P. W. Griffiths (R) | 34,966 | 35.7 |
| 16 | Frank T. Bow (R) | 98,447 | 54.4 |
| | John McSweeney (D) | 82,522 | 45.6 |

## OHIO

| Candidates | Votes | % |
|---|---|---|
| 17 J. Harry McGregor (R) | 94,624 | 68.2 |
| James J. Mayer (D) | 44,117 | 31.8 |
| 18 Wayne L. Hays (D) | 78,277 | 55.8 |
| Clarence L. Wetzel (R) | 62,081 | 44.2 |
| 19 Michael J. Kirwan (D) | 91,074 | 66.3 |
| Allen Russell (R) | 46,202 | 33.7 |
| 20 Michael A. Feighan (D) | 109,211 | 65.2 |
| John H. Ferguson (R) | 58,271 | 34.8 |
| 21 Robert Crosser (D) | 100,340 | 68.6 |
| Lawrence O. Payne (R) | 45,896 | 31.4 |
| 22 Frances P. Bolton (R) | 87,316 | 58.8 |
| Chat Paterson (D) | 61,197 | 41.2 |
| 23 George H. Bender (R) | 85,752 | 64.6 |
| Michael P. O'Brien (D) | 47,090 | 35.5 |

## OKLAHOMA

| Candidates | Votes | % |
|---|---|---|
| 1 Page Belcher (R) | 121,442 | 58.6 |
| H. G. Dickey (D) | 85,647 | 41.4 |
| 2 Ed Edmondson (D) | 92,407 | 59.2 |
| Edward E. Easton (R) | 60,550 | 38.8 |
| 3 Carl Albert (D) | 73,185 | 77.9 |
| Frank D. McSherry (R) | 20,735 | 22.1 |
| 4 Tom Steed (D) | 67,024 | 58.7 |
| John L. Goode (R) | 46,446 | 40.7 |
| 5 John Jarman (D) | 128,627 | 62.4 |
| Edwin Whitney Burch (R) | 77,425 | 37.6 |
| 6 Victor E. Wickersham (D) | 98,823 | 63.3 |
| K. B. Cornell (R) | 57,261 | 36.7 |

## OREGON

| Candidates | Votes | % |
|---|---|---|
| 1 Walter Norblad (R) | 124,720 | 68.0 |
| Robert B. Jones (D) | 58,796 | 32.0 |
| 2 Sam Coon (R) | 57,155 | 58.5 |
| John G. Jones (D) | 40,550 | 41.5 |
| 3 Homer D. Angell (R) | 125,504 | 54.0 |
| Alfred H. Corbett (D) | 107,099 | 46.0 |
| 4 Harris Ellsworth (R) | 100,970 | 66.3 |
| Walter A. Swanson (D) | 51,298 | 33.7 |

## PENNSYLVANIA

| Candidates | Votes | % |
|---|---|---|
| 1 William A. Barrett (D) | 89,879 | 68.2 |
| James Iannucci (R) | 41,948 | 31.8 |
| 2 William T. Granahan (D) | 105,553 | 61.8 |
| Daniel J. McCauley Jr. (R) | 65,159 | 38.2 |
| 3 James A. Byrne (D) | 81,837 | 58.4 |
| Morton Witkin (R) | 58,191 | 41.6 |
| 4 Earl Chudoff (D) | 90,077 | 69.9 |
| Joseph R. Burns (R) | 38,228 | 29.7 |
| 5 William J. Green Jr (D) | 104,112 | 54.2 |
| Philip Richman (R) | 88,040 | 45.8 |
| 6 Hugh Scott (R) | 93,368 | 51.7 |
| Harrington Herr (D) | 87,124 | 48.2 |
| 7 Benjamin F. James (R) | 127,918 | 61.7 |
| Murray P. Zealor (D) | 79,423 | 38.3 |
| 8 Karl C. King (R) | 83,966 | 59.3 |
| Wilson H. Stephenson (D) | 57,723 | 40.7 |
| 9 Paul B. Dague (R) | 100,578 | 66.2 |
| Philip E. Ragan (D) | 51,268 | 33.8 |
| 10 Joseph L. Carrigg (R) | 89,820 | 53.6 |
| Harry P. O'Neill (D) | 77,758 | 46.4 |
| 11 Edward J. Bonin (R) | 80,310 | 50.2 |
| Daniel J. Flood (D) | 79,722 | 49.8 |
| 12 Ivor D. Fenton (R) | 79,859 | 60.7 |
| Peter Krehel (D) | 51,736 | 39.3 |
| 13 Samuel K. McConnell Jr. (R) | 114,672 | 66.4 |
| Frank A. Keegan (D) | 57,974 | 33.6 |
| 14 George M. Rhodes (D) | 48,427 | 49.7 |
| James W. Bertolet (R) | 48,019 | 49.2 |
| 15 Francis E. Walter (D) | 61,566 | 54.8 |
| John Russell Craig (R) | 50,871 | 45.2 |
| 16 Walter M. Mumma (R) | 83,493 | 61.7 |
| David V. Randall (D) | 51,825 | 38.3 |
| 17 Alvin R. Bush (R) | 82,058 | 64.2 |
| Patrick A. McGowan (D) | 44,376 | 34.7 |

| Candidates | Votes | % |
|---|---|---|
| 18 Richard M. Simpson (R) | 75,723 | 63.5 |
| Philip R. Shoemaker (D) | 43,555 | 36.5 |
| 19 S. Walter Stauffer (R) | 72,466 | 52.3 |
| James F. Lind (D) | 66,165 | 47.7 |
| 20 James E. Van Zandt (R) | 62,804 | 62.8 |
| Joseph A. Moran (D) | 37,152 | 37.2 |
| 21 Augustine B. Kelley (D) | 73,223 | 52.9 |
| J. Cleveland McKenna (R) | 65,252 | 47.1 |
| 22 John P. Saylor (R) | 77,391 | 52.4 |
| William D. Shettig (D) | 70,218 | 47.6 |
| 23 Leon H. Gavin (R) | 73,001 | 67.8 |
| Fred C. Barr (D) | 34,633 | 32.2 |
| 24 Carroll D. Kearns (R) | 90,276 | 57.1 |
| Clinton J. Bebell (D) | 67,790 | 42.9 |
| 25 Louis E. Graham (R) | 77,577 | 50.4 |
| Frank M. Clark (D) | 76,214 | 49.6 |
| 26 Thomas E. Morgan (D) | 105,581 | 59.1 |
| Edward J. Sittler Jr. (R) | 72,981 | 40.9 |
| 27 James C. Fulton (R) | 118,915 | 62.6 |
| Thomas J. O'Toole (D) | 71,039 | 37.4 |
| 28 Herman P. Eberharter (D) | 98,432 | 58.7 |
| Harmar D. Denny (R) | 69,288 | 41.3 |
| 29 Robert J. Corbett (R) | 115,069 | 61.7 |
| Lee T. Sellars (D) | 71,573 | 38.4 |
| 30 Vera Buchanan (D) | 115,292 | 63.6 |
| Peter F. Bender (R) | 65,926 | 36.4 |

## RHODE ISLAND

| Candidates | Votes | % |
|---|---|---|
| 1 Aime J. Forand (D) | 105,404 | 54.9 |
| Berthelot Leclaire (R) | 86,523 | 45.1 |
| 2 John E. Fogarty (D) | 115,057 | 53.4 |
| James O. Watts (R) | 100,305 | 46.6 |

## SOUTH CAROLINA

| Candidates | Votes | % |
|---|---|---|
| 1 L. Mendel Rivers (D) | 30,483 | 100.0 |
| 2 John J. Riley (D) | 42,201 | 100.0 |
| 3 W. J. Bryan Dorn (D) | 44,237 | 93.8 |
| David Dows (R) | 2,849 | 6.0 |
| 4 Joseph R. Bryson (D) | 77,850 | 100.0 |
| 5 James P. Richards (D) | 42,081 | 93.9 |
| Herbert L. Crosland (R) | 2,722 | 6.1 |
| 6 John L. McMillan (D) | 41,328 | 100.0 |

## SOUTH DAKOTA

| Candidates | Votes | % |
|---|---|---|
| 1 Harold O. Lovre (R) | 151,449 | 68.5 |
| Goldie Wells (D) | 69,777 | 31.5 |
| 2 E. Y. Berry (R) | 45,688 | 69.0 |
| George A. Bangs (D) | 20,561 | 31.0 |

## TENNESSEE

| Candidates | Votes | % |
|---|---|---|
| 1 B. Carroll Reece (R) | 70,556 | 65.9 |
| Arthur W. Bright (D) | 36,477 | 34.1 |
| 2 Howard H. Baker (R) | 84,977 | 69.0 |
| Boyd W. Cox (D) | 38,268 | 31.1 |
| 3 James B. Frazier Jr. (D) | 56,473 | 70.0 |
| Joseph M. Parker (R) | 24,177 | 30.0 |
| 4 Joe L. Evins (D) | 65,787 | 100.0 |
| 5 J. Percy Priest (D) | 49,925 | 67.5 |
| Homer P. Wall (R) | 24,056 | 32.5 |
| 6 Pat Sutton (D) | 56,878 | 100.0 |
| 7 Tom Murray (D) | 39,529 | 100.0 |
| 8 Jere Cooper (D) | 34,877 | 100.0 |
| 9 Clifford Davis (D) | 101,427 | 85.7 |
| William P. Chenault (I) | 16,972 | 14.3 |

## TEXAS

| Candidates | Votes | % |
|---|---|---|
| 1 Wright Patman (D) | 56,491 | 100.0 |
| 2 Jack Brooks (D) | 83,267 | 79.0 |
| R. C. Reed (R) | 22,108 | 21.0 |
| 3 Brady Gentry (D) | 57,033 | 100.0 |
| 4 Sam Rayburn (D) | 47,888 | 100.0 |
| 5 J. Frank Wilson (D) | 172,539 | 100.0 |
| 6 Olin E. Teague (D) | 49,461 | 100.0 |

| Candidates | Votes | % |
|---|---|---|
| 7 John Dowdy (D) | 52,420 | 100.0 |
| 8 Albert Thomas (D) | 200,608 | 100.0 |
| 9 Clark W. Thompson (D) | 96,214 | 100.0 |
| 10 Homer Thornberry (D) | 65,924 | 100.0 |
| 11 W. R. Poage (D) | 59,088 | 100.0 |
| 12 Wingate Lucas (D) | 101,964 | 100.0 |
| 13 Frank Ikard (D) | 72,373 | 100.0 |
| 14 John E. Lyle Jr. (D) | 94,866 | 100.0 |
| 15 Lloyd M. Bentsen Jr. (D) | 63,753 | 99.9 |
| 16 Ken Regan (D) | 67,782 | 100.0 |
| 17 Omar Burleson (D) | 59,386 | 100.0 |
| 18 Walter Rogers (D) | 77,661 | 100.0 |
| 19 George Mahon (D) | 87,894 | 100.0 |
| 20 Paul J. Kilday (D) | 64,841 | 100.0 |
| 21 O. C. Fisher (D) | 65,762 | 100.0 |
| AL Martin Dies (D, R) | 1,979,811 | 100.0 |

## UTAH

| Candidates | Votes | % |
|---|---|---|
| 1 Douglas R. Stringfellow (R) | 76,545 | 60.5 |
| Ernest R. McKay (D) | 49,898 | 39.5 |
| 2 William A. Dawson (R) | 105,296 | 52.6 |
| Reva Beck Bosone (D) | 95,084 | 47.5 |

## VERMONT

| Candidates | Votes | % |
|---|---|---|
| AL Winston L. Prouty (R) | 109,871 | 71.8 |
| Herbert B. Comings (D) | 43,187 | 28.2 |

## VIRGINIA

| Candidates | Votes | % |
|---|---|---|
| 1 Edward J. Robeson Jr. (D) | 24,836 | 99.6 |
| 2 Porter Hardy Jr. (D) | 28,948 | 99.9 |
| 3 J. Vaughan Gary (D) | 36,085 | 57.5 |
| Walter R. Gambill (R) | 26,488 | 42.2 |
| 4 Watkins M. Abbitt (D) | 23,806 | 99.8 |
| 5 Thomas B. Stanley (D) | 19,971 | 99.9 |
| 6 Richard H. Poff (R) | 34,041 | 51.5 |
| Clarence G. Burton (D) | 31,997 | 48.4 |
| 7 Burr P. Harrison (D) | 37,360 | 79.1 |
| Glenn W. Ruebush (R) | 9,876 | 20.9 |
| 8 Howard W. Smith (D) | 29,670 | 75.7 |
| Homer G. Richey (I) | 9,495 | 24.2 |
| 9 William C. Wampler (R) | 35,047 | 51.7 |
| M. M. Long (D) | 32,735 | 48.3 |
| 10 Joel T. Broyhill (R) | 33,152 | 50.2 |
| Edmund D. Campbell (D) | 32,830 | 49.7 |

## WASHINGTON

| Candidates | Votes | % |
|---|---|---|
| 1 Thomas M. Pelly (R) | 121,926 | 51.4 |
| Stimson Bullitt (D) | 114,617 | 48.3 |
| 2 Jack Westland (R) | 91,853 | 54.2 |
| Harry F. Henson (D) | 77,179 | 45.6 |
| 3 Russell V. Mack (R) | 75,165 | 53.3 |
| Gordon M. Quarnstrom (D) | 65,715 | 46.6 |
| 4 Hal Holmes (R) | 92,551 | 67.6 |
| William Bryan (D) | 44,464 | 32.5 |
| 5 Walter F. Horan (R) | 82,530 | 56.0 |
| Robert D. Dellwo (D) | 64,820 | 44.0 |
| 6 Thor C. Tollefson (R) | 110,169 | 59.8 |
| John J. O'Connell (D) | 74,143 | 40.2 |
| AL Don Magnuson (D) | 515,213 | 50.5 |
| Al Canwell (R) | 504,783 | 49.5 |

## WEST VIRGINIA

| Candidates | Votes | % |
|---|---|---|
| 1 Robert H. Mollohan (D) | 72,218 | 52.9 |
| Francis J. Love (R) | 64,216 | 47.1 |
| 2 Harley O. Staggers (D) | 67,172 | 51.5 |
| Kermit R. Mason (R) | 63,320 | 48.5 |
| 3 Cleveland M. Bailey (D) | 71,926 | 53.4 |
| Frank Love (D) | 62,839 | 46.6 |
| 4 Will E. Neal (R) | 82,104 | 53.3 |
| M. G. Burnside (D) | 71,819 | 46.7 |

## WEST VIRGINIA

| Candidates | Votes | % |
|---|---|---|
| 5 Elizabeth Kee (D) | 83,653 | 63.8 |
| Cyrus H. Gadd (R) | 47,519 | 36.2 |
| 6 Robert C. Byrd (D) | 104,387 | 55.6 |
| Latelle M. LaFollette (R) | 83,429 | 44.4 |

## WISCONSIN

| Candidates | Votes | % |
|---|---|---|
| 1 Lawrence H. Smith (R) | 99,742 | 59.4 |
| Arnie W. Agnew (D) | 68,269 | 40.6 |
| 2 Glenn R. Davis (R) | 116,542 | 62.9 |
| Horace W. Wilkie (D) | 68,665 | 37.1 |

| Candidates | Votes | % |
|---|---|---|
| 3 Gardner R. Withrow (R) | 96,908 | 75.1 |
| Edna Bowen (D) | 32,165 | 24.9 |
| 4 Clement J. Zablocki (D) | 131,098 | 64.3 |
| John C. Schafer (R) | 72,869 | 35.7 |
| 5 Charles J. Kersten (R) | 112,048 | 51.6 |
| Andrew J. Biemiller (D) | 105,013 | 48.4 |
| 6 William K. Van Pelt (R) | 103,464 | 71.7 |
| Ralph A. Norem (D) | 40,910 | 28.3 |
| 7 Melvin R. Laird (R) | 95,049 | 72.3 |
| Ernest Kluck (D) | 36,387 | 27.7 |
| 8 John W. Byrnes (R) | 114,183 | 73.6 |
| Robert C. Schultz (D) | 40,980 | 26.4 |

| Candidates | Votes | % |
|---|---|---|
| 9 Merlin Hull (R) | 81,258 | 65.2 |
| Kent L. Pillsbury (D) | 43,437 | 34.8 |
| 10 Alvin E. O'Konski (R) | 73,527 | 67.4 |
| Roland Kannenberg (D) | 35,597 | 32.6 |

## WYOMING

| Candidates | Votes | % |
|---|---|---|
| AL William Henry Harrison (R) | 76,161 | 60.1 |
| Robert R. Ross Jr. (D) | 50,559 | 39.9 |

# 1953 House Elections

## GEORGIA

### Special Election

| Candidates | Votes | % |
|---|---|---|
| 2 J. L. Pilcher (D) | 10,936 | 35.5 |
| H. Grady Rawls | 9,764 | 31.7 |
| H. L. Wingate Jr. | 6,073 | 19.7 |
| John E. Sheffield Jr. | 3,130 | 10.2 |

## ILLINOIS
### Special Election

| Candidates | Votes | % |
|---|---|---|
| 7 James B. Bowler (D) | 31,600 | 83.5 |
| Philip J. Boffa (R) | 6,239 | 16.5 |

## NEW JERSEY
### Special Election

| Candidates | Votes | % |
|---|---|---|
| 6 Harrison A. Williams Jr. (D) | 68,871 | 50.8 |
| George F. Hetfield (R) | 66,796 | 49.2 |

## VIRGINIA
### Special Election

| Candidates | Votes | % |
|---|---|---|
| 5 William M. Tuck (D) | 16,693 | 57.8 |
| Lorne R. Campbell | 12,182 | 42.2 |

## WISCONSIN
### Special Election

| Candidates | Votes | % |
|---|---|---|
| 9 Lester R. Johnson (D) | 27,852 | 56.9 |
| Arthur L. Padrutt (R) | 21,127 | 43.1 |

# 1954 House Elections

## ALABAMA

| | Candidates | Votes | % |
|---|---|---|---|
| 1 | Frank W. Boykin (D) | 27,462 | 100.0 |
| 2 | George Grant (D) | 30,661 | 100.0 |
| 3 | George Andrews (D) | 22,371 | 100.0 |
| 4 | Kenneth A. Roberts (D) | 28,660 | 100.0 |
| 5 | Albert Rains (D) | 38,257 | 100.0 |
| 6 | Armistead I. Selden Jr. (D) | 18,753 | 100.0 |
| 7 | Carl Elliott (D) | 31,988 | 78.9 |
| | W. B. Engle (D) | 8,547 | 21.1 |
| 8 | Robert E. Jones Jr. (D) | 29,414 | 91.6 |
| | Adin Batson (R) | 2,689 | 8.4 |
| 9 | George Huddleston Jr. (D) | 40,986 | 100.0 |

## ARIZONA

| | Candidates | Votes | % |
|---|---|---|---|
| 1 | John J. Rhodes (R) | 60,423 | 53.1 |
| | L. S. Adams (D) | 53,307 | 46.9 |
| 2 | Stewart L. Udall (D) | 68,085 | 62.1 |
| | Henry Zipf (R) | 41,587 | 37.9 |

## ARKANSAS

| | Candidates | Votes | % |
|---|---|---|---|
| 1 | Ezekiel C. Gathings (D) | 38,951 | 100.0 |
| 2 | Wilbur D. Mills (D) | 33,038 | 100.0 |
| 3 | James W. Trimble (D) | 60,035 | 100.0 |
| 4 | Oren Harris (D) | 51,579 | 100.0 |
| 5 | Brooks Hays (D) | 51,828 | 100.0 |
| 6 | William F. Norrell (D) | 44,833 | 100.0 |

## CALIFORNIA

| | Candidates | Votes | % |
|---|---|---|---|
| 1 | Hubert B. Scudder (R) | 83,762 | 59.1 |
| | Max Kortum (D) | 58,004 | 40.9 |
| 2 | Clair Engle (D-R) | 113,104 | 100.0 |
| 3 | John E. Moss Jr. (D) | 96,238 | 65.3 |
| | James H. Phillips (R) | 51,111 | 34.7 |
| 4 | William S. Mailliard (R) | 88,439 | 61.2 |
| | Philip A. O'Rourke (D) | 52,980 | 36.7 |
| 5 | John F. Shelley (D-R) | 86,428 | 100.0 |
| 6 | John F. Baldwin Jr. (R) | 72,336 | 50.9 |
| | Robert L. Condon (D) | 69,776 | 49.1 |
| 7 | John J. Allen Jr. (R) | 64,083 | 53.0 |
| | Stanley K. Crook (D) | 56,807 | 47.0 |
| 8 | George P. Miller (D) | 101,803 | 65.4 |
| | Jess M. Ritchie (R) | 53,869 | 34.6 |
| 9 | J. Arthur Younger (R) | 60,648 | 54.5 |
| | Harold F. Taggart (D) | 50,619 | 45.5 |
| 10 | Charles S. Gubser (R) | 94,418 | 61.2 |
| | Paul V. Birmingham (D) | 59,843 | 38.8 |
| 11 | Leroy Johnson (R) | 54,716 | 52.6 |
| | Carl Sugar (D) | 49,388 | 47.4 |
| 12 | B. F. Sisk (D) | 63,911 | 53.8 |
| | Oakley Hunter (R) | 54,903 | 46.2 |
| 13 | Charles M. Teague (R) | 69,287 | 52.5 |
| | Timothy I. O'Reilly (D) | 62,786 | 47.5 |
| 14 | Harlan Hagen (D) | 75,194 | 65.1 |
| | Al Blain (R) | 40,270 | 34.9 |
| 15 | Gordon L. McDonough (R) | 77,651 | 56.9 |
| | Frank P. O'Sullivan (D) | 58,785 | 43.1 |
| 16 | Donald L. Jackson (R) | 63,124 | 60.8 |
| | S. Mark Hogue (D) | 40,659 | 39.2 |
| 17 | Cecil R. King (D) | 97,828 | 60.1 |
| | Robert H. Finch (R) | 64,967 | 39.9 |
| 18 | Craig Hosmer (R) | 71,731 | 55.0 |
| | Joseph M. Kennick (D) | 58,647 | 45.0 |
| 19 | Chet Holifield (D) | 90,269 | 74.8 |
| | Raymond R. Pritchard (R) | 30,404 | 25.2 |
| 20 | Carl Hinshaw (R) | 71,213 | 71.2 |
| | Eugene Radding (D) | 28,838 | 28.8 |
| 21 | Edgar W. Hiestand (R) | 100,258 | 58.7 |
| | William E. Roskam (D) | 70,486 | 41.3 |
| 22 | Joe Holt (R) | 65,165 | 58.2 |
| | William M. Costley (D) | 46,875 | 41.8 |

| | Candidates | Votes | % |
|---|---|---|---|
| 23 | Clyde Doyle (D) | 90,729 | 70.9 |
| | Frank G. Bussing (R) | 34,911 | 27.3 |
| 24 | Glenard P. Lipscomb (R) | 65,431 | 56.9 |
| | George Arnold (D) | 49,592 | 43.1 |
| 25 | Patrick J. Hillings (R) | 113,027 | 65.2 |
| | John G. Sobieski (D) | 60,370 | 34.8 |
| 26 | James Roosevelt (D) | 94,261 | 60.1 |
| | Theodore R. Owings (R) | 62,585 | 39.9 |
| 27 | Harry R. Sheppard (D) | 65,389 | 64.8 |
| | Martin K. Barrett (R) | 35,594 | 35.3 |
| 28 | James B. Utt (R) | 95,680 | 66.2 |
| | Harriet Enderle (D) | 48,785 | 33.8 |
| 29 | John Phillips (R) | 42,420 | 57.9 |
| | Bruce Shangle (D) | 30,781 | 42.1 |
| 30 | Bob Wilson (R) | 94,623 | 60.4 |
| | Ross T. McIntire (D) | 61,994 | 39.6 |

## COLORADO

| | Candidates | Votes | % |
|---|---|---|---|
| 1 | Byron G. Rogers (D) | 84,745 | 55.6 |
| | Ellen G. Harris (R) | 67,210 | 44.1 |
| 2 | William S. Hill (R) | 80,162 | 55.3 |
| | Lacy L. Wilkinson (D) | 64,776 | 44.7 |
| 3 | J. Edgar Chenoweth (R) | 62,884 | 53.0 |
| | Alva B. Adams (D) | 55,750 | 47.0 |
| 4 | Wayne N. Aspinall (D) | 34,294 | 53.5 |
| | Charles E. Wilson (R) | 29,818 | 46.5 |

## CONNECTICUT

| | Candidates | Votes | % |
|---|---|---|---|
| 1 | Thomas J. Dodd (D) | 148,935 | 57.0 |
| | Wallace Barnes (R) | 112,526 | 43.0 |
| 2 | Horace Seely-Brown Jr. (R) | 72,833 | 50.7 |
| | Henry H. Pierce Jr. (D) | 70,853 | 49.3 |
| 3 | Albert W. Cretella (R) | 94,977 | 52.7 |
| | James F. Gartland (D) | 85,369 | 47.3 |
| 4 | Albert P. Morano (R) | 123,890 | 56.2 |
| | Edward R. Fay Jr. (D) | 91,184 | 41.4 |
| 5 | James T. Patterson (R) | 68,451 | 52.8 |
| | David Brady (D) | 61,313 | 47.3 |
| AL | Antoni N. Sadlak (R) | 474,585 | 51.0 |
| | Joseph P. Lyford (D) | 455,887 | 49.0 |

## DELAWARE

| | Candidates | Votes | % |
|---|---|---|---|
| AL | Harris B. McDowell Jr. (D) | 79,201 | 54.9 |
| | Lillian I. Martin (R) | 65,035 | 45.1 |

## FLORIDA

| | Candidates | Votes | % |
|---|---|---|---|
| 1 | William C. Cramer (R) | 52,287 | 50.8 |
| | Courtney Campbell (D) | 50,744 | 49.3 |
| 2 | Charles E. Bennett (D) | 14,376 | 100.0 |
| 3 | Robert L. F. Sikes (D) | 27,013 | 100.0 |
| 4 | Dante B. Fascell (D) | 47,697 | 100.0 |
| 5 | A. S. Herlong Jr. (D) | 35,971 | 100.0 |
| 6 | Dwight L. Rogers (D) | 39,148 | 100.0 |
| 7 | James A. Haley (D) | 23,469 | 55.5 |
| | E. B. Sutton (R) | 18,850 | 44.5 |
| 8 | D. R. Matthews (D) | 16,732 | 100.0 |

## GEORGIA

| | Candidates | Votes | % |
|---|---|---|---|
| 1 | Prince H. Preston (D) | 26,205 | 83.7 |
| | Frank Downing | 5,100 | 16.3 |
| 2 | J. L. Pilcher (D) | 26,705 | 99.9 |
| 3 | E. L. Forrester (D) | 34,973 | 100.0 |
| 4 | John J. Flynt Jr. (D) | 32,400 | 100.0 |
| 5 | James C. Davis (D) | 54,069 | 64.4 |
| | Charles A. Moye Jr. (D) | 29,911 | 35.6 |
| 6 | Carl Vinson (D) | 26,250 | 100.0 |
| 7 | Henderson L. Lanham (D) | 35,147 | 100.0 |

| | Candidates | Votes | % |
|---|---|---|---|
| 8 | Iris Faircloth Blitch (D) | 27,037 | 100.0 |
| 9 | Phil M. Landrum (D) | 26,849 | 100.0 |
| 10 | Paul Brown (D) | 28,068 | 100.0 |

## IDAHO

| | Candidates | Votes | % |
|---|---|---|---|
| 1 | Gracie B. Pfost (D) | 50,214 | 54.9 |
| | Erwin H. Schwiebert (R) | 41,293 | 45.1 |
| 2 | Hamer H. Budge (R) | 81,824 | 60.8 |
| | William P. Whitaker (D) | 52,681 | 39.2 |

## ILLINOIS

| | Candidates | Votes | % |
|---|---|---|---|
| 1 | William L. Dawson (D) | 71,472 | 75.3 |
| | Genoa S. Washington (R) | 23,470 | 24.7 |
| 2 | Barratt O'Hara (D) | 80,016 | 61.6 |
| | Richard B. Vail (R) | 49,970 | 38.4 |
| 3 | James C. Murray (D) | 77,675 | 53.8 |
| | Fred E. Busbey (R) | 66,767 | 46.2 |
| 4 | William E. McVey (R) | 94,125 | 52.2 |
| | William A. Rowan (D) | 86,372 | 47.9 |
| 5 | John C. Kluczynski (D) | 92,780 | 73.2 |
| | S. Charles Bubacz (R) | 33,987 | 26.8 |
| 6 | Thomas J. O'Brien (D) | 99,590 | 71.7 |
| | Orville F. Corbin (R) | 39,289 | 28.3 |
| 7 | James B. Bowler (D) | 97,398 | 78.4 |
| | Charles M. Barrett (R) | 26,763 | 21.6 |
| 8 | Thomas S. Gordon (D) | 74,837 | 68.4 |
| | James L. Doherty (R) | 34,535 | 31.6 |
| 9 | Sidney R. Yates (D) | 73,187 | 60.3 |
| | Ralph Lee Goodman (R) | 48,130 | 39.7 |
| 10 | Richard W. Hoffman (R) | 90,961 | 57.3 |
| | Helen J. Kelleher (D) | 67,903 | 42.7 |
| 11 | Timothy P. Sheehan (R) | 67,141 | 50.9 |
| | Harry H. Semrow (D) | 64,788 | 49.1 |
| 12 | Charles A. Boyle (D) | 82,518 | 54.1 |
| | Edgar A. Jonas (R) | 69,999 | 45.9 |
| 13 | Marguerite Stitt Church (R) | 146,184 | 69.6 |
| | Richard A. Griffin (D) | 63,852 | 30.4 |
| 14 | Chauncey W. Reed (R) | 100,024 | 72.4 |
| | Richard Plum (D) | 38,161 | 27.6 |
| 15 | Noah M. Mason (R) | 72,576 | 62.8 |
| | Richard A. Mohan (D) | 42,934 | 37.2 |
| 16 | Leo E. Allen (R) | 77,557 | 100.0 |
| 17 | Leslie C. Arends (R) | 79,044 | 65.0 |
| | Branson Wright (D) | 42,600 | 35.0 |
| 18 | Harold H. Velde (R) | 59,963 | 57.5 |
| | Howard S. Beeney (D) | 44,408 | 42.6 |
| 19 | Robert B. Chiperfield (R) | 64,772 | 56.5 |
| | John M. Kerwin Jr. (D) | 49,876 | 43.5 |
| 20 | Sidney E. Simpson (R) | 68,104 | 62.9 |
| | James A. Barry (D) | 40,165 | 37.1 |
| 21 | Peter F. Mack Jr. (D) | 83,501 | 54.8 |
| | Edward H. Jenison (R) | 68,924 | 45.2 |
| 22 | William L. Springer (R) | 66,797 | 62.0 |
| | Robert W. Martin (D) | 40,873 | 38.0 |
| 23 | Charles W. Vursell (R) | 69,179 | 52.9 |
| | Albert R. Imle (D) | 61,493 | 47.1 |
| 24 | Melvin Price (D) | 90,482 | 69.2 |
| | John T. Thomas (R) | 40,358 | 30.9 |
| 25 | Kenneth J. Gray (D) | 69,562 | 52.6 |
| | C. W. Bishop (R) | 62,659 | 47.4 |

## INDIANA

| | Candidates | Votes | % |
|---|---|---|---|
| 1 | Ray J. Madden (D) | 81,217 | 61.4 |
| | Robert H. Moore (R) | 50,439 | 38.2 |
| 2 | Charles A. Halleck (R) | 73,717 | 59.6 |
| | James H. Berg (D) | 49,996 | 40.4 |
| 3 | Shepard J. Crumpacker Jr. (R) | 85,884 | 50.4 |
| | John Brademas (D) | 83,851 | 49.2 |
| 4 | E. Ross Adair (R) | 71,436 | 59.8 |
| | Fred W. Greene (D) | 47,384 | 39.7 |

## INDIANA

| Candidates | Votes | % |
|---|---|---|
| 5 John V. Beamer (R) | 88,428 | 53.1 |
| John R. Walsh (D) | 76,972 | 46.2 |
| 6 Cecil M. Harden (R) | 67,371 | 52.5 |
| John W. King (D) | 60,896 | 47.5 |
| 7 William G. Bray (R) | 75,608 | 55.4 |
| George D. Gettinger (D) | 60,594 | 44.4 |
| 8 Winfield K. Denton (D) | 82,264 | 52.1 |
| D. Bailey Merrill (R) | 74,960 | 47.5 |
| 9 Earl Wilson (R) | 61,285 | 51.7 |
| Wilfrid J. Ullrich (D) | 57,350 | 48.3 |
| 10 Ralph Harvey (R) | 76,132 | 55.9 |
| Inez M. Scholl (D) | 59,103 | 43.4 |
| 11 Charles B. Brownson (R) | 108,044 | 54.9 |
| Charles H. Boswell (D) | 88,173 | 44.8 |

## IOWA

| Candidates | Votes | % |
|---|---|---|
| 1 Fred Schwengel (R) | 67,128 | 57.0 |
| John O'Connor (D) | 50,577 | 43.0 |
| 2 Henry O. Talle (R) | 72,231 | 55.4 |
| Ruben V. Austin (D) | 58,092 | 44.6 |
| 3 H. R. Gross (R) | 68,307 | 62.1 |
| George R. Laub (D) | 41,622 | 37.9 |
| 4 Karl M. LeCompte (R) | 49,608 | 55.6 |
| Herschel C. Loveless (D) | 39,652 | 44.4 |
| 5 Paul Cunningham (R) | 61,355 | 55.6 |
| James A. McLaughlin (D) | 49,063 | 44.4 |
| 6 James I. Dolliver (R) | 53,457 | 60.3 |
| Lumund F. Wilcox (D) | 35,137 | 39.7 |
| 7 Ben F. Jensen (R) | 51,022 | 60.4 |
| Elmer G. Carlson (D) | 33,492 | 39.6 |
| 8 Charles B. Hoeven (R) | 55,214 | 63.8 |
| Roy B. Holland (D) | 31,296 | 36.2 |

## KANSAS

| Candidates | Votes | % |
|---|---|---|
| 1 William H. Avery (R) | 56,079 | 54.3 |
| Howard S. Miller (D) | 47,165 | 45.7 |
| 2 Errett P. Scrivner (R) | 64,263 | 54.7 |
| Newell A. George (D) | 53,302 | 45.3 |
| 3 Myron V. George (R) | 41,342 | 55.4 |
| William W. Monypeny (D) | 33,307 | 44.6 |
| 4 Ed H. Rees (R) | 77,920 | 56.2 |
| Robert M. Green (D) | 60,697 | 43.8 |
| 5 Clifford R. Hope (R) | 64,023 | 64.9 |
| Robert L. Bock (D) | 34,691 | 35.1 |
| 6 Wint Smith (R) | 43,831 | 53.3 |
| Elmo J. Mahoney (D) | 38,369 | 46.7 |

## KENTUCKY

| Candidates | Votes | % |
|---|---|---|
| 1 Noble J. Gregory (D) | 62,210 | 100.0 |
| 2 William H. Natcher (D) | 49,231 | 100.0 |
| 3 John M. Robsion Jr. (R) | 72,073 | 50.2 |
| Harrison M. Robertson (D) | 71,500 | 49.8 |
| 4 Frank Chelf (D) | 49,496 | 100.0 |
| 5 Brent Spence (D) | 63,640 | 61.0 |
| M. J. See (R) | 40,679 | 39.0 |
| 6 John C. Watts (D) | 59,434 | 60.9 |
| Robert L. Milby (R) | 38,145 | 39.1 |
| 7 Carl D. Perkins (D) | 44,353 | 60.4 |
| Curtis Clark (R) | 29,115 | 39.6 |
| 8 Eugene T. Siler (R) | 56,182 | 63.4 |
| Mitchel S. Fannin (D) | 32,128 | 36.3 |

## LOUISIANA

| Candidates | Votes | % |
|---|---|---|
| 1 F. Edward Hebert (D) | 38,213 | 82.3 |
| George W. Reese Jr. (R) | 8,212 | 17.7 |
| 2 Hale Boggs (D) | 37,583 | 100.0 |
| 3 Edwin E. Willis (D) | 15,808 | 100.0 |
| 4 Overton Brooks (D) | 24,587 | 100.0 |
| 5 Otto E. Passman (D) | 21,831 | 100.0 |
| 6 James H. Morrison (D) | 30,082 | 100.0 |
| 7 T. Ashton Thompson (D) | 21,525 | 100.0 |
| 8 George S. Long (D) | 18,482 | 100.0 |

## MAINE

| Candidates | Votes | % |
|---|---|---|
| 1 Robert Hale (R) | 47,327 | 52.1 |
| James C. Oliver (D) | 43,561 | 47.9 |
| 2 Charles P. Nelson (R) | 45,819 | 54.0 |
| Thomas E. Delahanty (D) | 39,075 | 46.0 |
| 3 Clifford G. McIntire (R) | 39,749 | 60.5 |
| Kenneth B. Colbath (D) | 25,912 | 39.5 |

## MARYLAND

| Candidates | Votes | % |
|---|---|---|
| 1 Edward T. Miller (R) | 35,221 | 55.6 |
| Edward Turner (D) | 28,184 | 44.5 |
| 2 James P. S. Devereux (R) | 67,179 | 56.1 |
| William P. Bolton (D) | 52,540 | 43.9 |
| 3 Edward A. Garmatz (D) | 45,531 | 97.2 |
| 4 George H. Fallon (D) | 40,029 | 57.2 |
| Arthur W. Sherwood (R) | 29,921 | 42.8 |
| 5 Richard E. Lankford (D) | 60,850 | 53.7 |
| Frank Small Jr. (R) | 52,420 | 46.3 |
| 6 DeWitt S. Hyde (R) | 69,658 | 51.4 |
| Edward J. Ryan (D) | 65,760 | 48.6 |
| 7 Samuel N. Friedel (D) | 49,221 | 54.5 |
| Edward C. Dukehart (R) | 41,027 | 45.5 |

## MASSACHUSETTS

| Candidates | Votes | % |
|---|---|---|
| 1 John W. Heselton (R) | 68,420 | 55.6 |
| John J. Dwyer (D) | 54,675 | 44.4 |
| 2 Edward P. Boland (D) | 77,899 | 59.6 |
| Vernon E. Bradley (R) | 52,725 | 40.4 |
| 3 Philip J. Philbin (D) | 110,013 | 100.0 |
| 4 Harold D. Donohue (D) | 83,053 | 57.1 |
| Andrew B. Holmstrom (R) | 62,318 | 42.9 |
| 5 Edith Nourse Rogers (R) | 139,989 | 100.0 |
| 6 William H. Bates (R) | 91,916 | 71.2 |
| Andrew J. Gillis (D) | 37,216 | 28.8 |
| 7 Thomas J. Lane (D, R) | 102,659 | 100.0 |
| 8 Torbert H. Macdonald (D) | 74,568 | 53.2 |
| Angier L. Goodwin (R) | 65,614 | 46.8 |
| 9 Donald W. Nicholson (R) | 81,378 | 56.6 |
| James F. O'Neill (D) | 62,445 | 43.4 |
| 10 Laurence Curtis (R) | 72,502 | 50.7 |
| Jackson J. Holtz (D) | 70,608 | 49.3 |
| 11 Thomas P. O'Neill Jr. (D) | 75,613 | 78.2 |
| Charles S. Bolster (R) | 21,039 | 21.8 |
| 12 John W. McCormack (D) | 79,073 | 100.0 |
| 13 Richard B. Wigglesworth (R) | 90,924 | 58.0 |
| James F. Gardner (D) | 65,854 | 42.0 |
| 14 Joseph W. Martin Jr. (R) | 87,840 | 62.0 |
| Edward F. Doolan (D) | 53,818 | 38.0 |

## MICHIGAN

| Candidates | Votes | % |
|---|---|---|
| 1 Thaddeus M. Machrowicz (D) | 91,435 | 88.3 |
| Rudolph G. Tenerowicz (R) | 11,731 | 11.3 |
| 2 George Meader (R) | 69,825 | 59.8 |
| J. Henry Owens (D) | 46,817 | 40.1 |
| 3 August E. Johansen (R) | 65,942 | 59.4 |
| Charles C. Wickett (D) | 44,574 | 40.2 |
| 4 Clare E. Hoffman (R) | 62,025 | 62.3 |
| Gordon A. Elferdink (D) | 37,500 | 37.7 |
| 5 Gerald R. Ford Jr. (R) | 81,702 | 63.3 |
| Robert S. McAllister (D) | 47,453 | 36.7 |
| 6 Don Hayworth (D) | 80,325 | 51.1 |
| Kit Clardy (R) | 76,335 | 48.6 |
| 7 Jesse P. Wolcott (R) | 71,651 | 52.8 |
| Ira D. McCoy (D) | 63,797 | 47.0 |
| 8 Alvin M. Bentley (R) | 65,813 | 62.7 |
| Clarence V. Smazel (D) | 38,828 | 37.0 |
| 9 Ruth Thompson (R) | 50,659 | 55.7 |
| Theodore E. A. Engstrom (D) | 39,966 | 44.0 |
| 10 Elford A. Cederberg (R) | 50,570 | 61.4 |
| William J. Kelly (D) | 31,794 | 38.6 |
| 11 Victor A. Knox (R) | 41,665 | 54.9 |
| Harold Beaton (D) | 34,204 | 45.1 |

| Candidates | Votes | % |
|---|---|---|
| 12 John B. Bennett (R) | 39,531 | 55.9 |
| Frank E. Hook (D) | 31,187 | 44.1 |
| 13 Charles C. Diggs Jr. (D) | 64,716 | 65.8 |
| Landon Knight (R) | 33,127 | 33.7 |
| 14 Louis C. Rabaut (D) | 97,297 | 58.2 |
| Joseph A. Moynihan Jr. (R) | 69,503 | 41.6 |
| 15 John D. Dingell (D) | 85,100 | 72.7 |
| Gregory M. Pillon (R) | 31,815 | 27.2 |
| 16 John Lesinski (D) | 121,557 | 67.9 |
| Stanley A. Grendel (R) | 56,815 | 31.7 |
| 17 Martha W. Griffiths (D) | 75,258 | 52.2 |
| Charles G. Oakman (R) | 68,613 | 47.6 |
| 18 George A. Dondero (R) | 80,771 | 53.9 |
| Paul Sutton (D) | 69,131 | 46.1 |

## MINNESOTA

| Candidates | Votes | % |
|---|---|---|
| 1 August H. Andresen (R) | 72,686 | 60.9 |
| Robert C. Olson (DFL) | 46,678 | 39.1 |
| 2 Joseph P. O'Hara (R) | 71,592 | 57.9 |
| Harry Sieben (DFL) | 52,089 | 42.1 |
| 3 Roy W. Wier (DFL) | 98,407 | 54.4 |
| Edward Willow (R) | 82,389 | 45.6 |
| 4 Eugene J. McCarthy (DFL) | 81,651 | 63.0 |
| Richard C. Hansen (R) | 47,933 | 37.0 |
| 5 Walter H. Judd (R) | 69,901 | 55.8 |
| Anders Thompson (DFL) | 55,452 | 44.2 |
| 6 Fred Marshall (DFL) | 72,922 | 61.9 |
| Oscar J. Jerde (R) | 44,850 | 38.1 |
| 7 H. Carl Andersen (R) | 60,120 | 52.6 |
| Douglas P. Hunt (DFL) | 54,140 | 47.4 |
| 8 John A. Blatnik (DFL) | 89,778 | 71.8 |
| Ernie Orchard (R) | 35,241 | 28.2 |
| 9 Coya Knutson (DFL) | 48,999 | 51.2 |
| Harold C. Hagen (R) | 46,664 | 48.8 |

## MISSISSIPPI

| Candidates | Votes | % |
|---|---|---|
| 1 Thomas G. Abernethy (D) | 15,944 | 100.0 |
| 2 Jamie L. Whitten (D) | 13,516 | 100.0 |
| 3 Frank E. Smith (D) | 13,468 | 100.0 |
| 4 John Bell Williams (D) | 19,164 | 100.0 |
| 5 Arthur Winstead (D) | 17,400 | 100.0 |
| 6 William M. Colmer (D) | 21,806 | 100.0 |

## MISSOURI

| Candidates | Votes | % |
|---|---|---|
| 1 Frank M. Karsten (D) | 89,649 | 66.3 |
| Bill Bangert (R) | 45,653 | 33.7 |
| 2 Thomas B. Curtis (R) | 83,861 | 54.7 |
| Eugene H. Buder (D) | 69,450 | 45.3 |
| 3 Leonor K. Sullivan (D) | 67,715 | 71.0 |
| George W. Curran (R) | 27,598 | 29.0 |
| 4 George H. Christopher (D) | 62,012 | 51.6 |
| Jeffrey P. Hillelson (R) | 58,152 | 48.4 |
| 5 Richard Bolling (D) | 50,874 | 58.9 |
| Samuel Lee Chaney (R) | 35,477 | 41.1 |
| 6 W. R. Hull Jr. (D) | 60,380 | 53.6 |
| William C. Cole (R) | 52,203 | 46.4 |
| 7 Dewey Short (R) | 67,918 | 53.6 |
| J. M. Lowry (D) | 58,729 | 46.4 |
| 8 A. S. J. Carnahan (D) | 52,658 | 57.3 |
| Dorman L. Steelman (R) | 39,326 | 42.8 |
| 9 Clarence Cannon (D) | 65,862 | 59.0 |
| Noel Carpenter (R) | 45,765 | 41.0 |
| 10 Paul C. Jones (D) | 34,009 | 63.9 |
| Clyde Whaley (R) | 19,179 | 36.1 |
| 11 Morgan M. Moulder (D) | 54,384 | 55.3 |
| L. C. Davis (R) | 43,959 | 44.7 |

## MONTANA

| Candidates | Votes | % |
|---|---|---|
| 1 Lee Metcalf (D) | 52,614 | 56.0 |
| Winfield E. Page (R) | 41,375 | 44.0 |
| 2 Orvin B. Fjare (R) | 66,103 | 50.6 |
| LeRoy H. Anderson (D) | 64,495 | 49.4 |

## NEBRASKA

| | Candidates | Votes | % |
|---|---|---|---|
| 1 | Phil Weaver (R) | 68,563 | 58.6 |
| | Frank B. Morrison (D) | 48,457 | 41.4 |
| 2 | Jackson B. Chase (R) | 52,471 | 53.0 |
| | James A. Hart (D) | 46,629 | 47.1 |
| 3 | Robert D. Harrison (R) | 61,124 | 65.2 |
| | Ernest M. Luther (D) | 32,562 | 34.8 |
| 4 | Arthur L. Miller (R) | 68,189 | 70.4 |
| | Carlton W. Laird (D) | 28,695 | 29.6 |

## NEVADA

| | | Votes | % |
|---|---|---|---|
| AL | Clifton Young (R) | 42,321 | 54.5 |
| | Walter S. Baring (D) | 35,318 | 45.5 |

## NEW HAMPSHIRE

| | | Votes | % |
|---|---|---|---|
| 1 | Chester E. Merrow (R) | 54,052 | 50.2 |
| | Thomas J. McIntyre (D) | 53,584 | 49.8 |
| 2 | Perkins Bass (R) | 51,010 | 60.4 |
| | George F. Brown (D) | 33,415 | 39.6 |

## NEW JERSEY

| | | Votes | % |
|---|---|---|---|
| 1 | Charles A. Wolverton (R) | 92,070 | 54.4 |
| | J. Frank Crawford (D) | 77,100 | 45.5 |
| 2 | T. Millet Hand (R) | 65,551 | 63.6 |
| | Clayton E. Burdick (D) | 37,541 | 36.4 |
| 3 | James C. Auchincloss (R) | 89,085 | 57.6 |
| | Charles F. Sullivan (D) | 65,685 | 42.4 |
| 4 | Frank Thompson Jr. (D) | 72,884 | 58.4 |
| | William G. Freeman (R) | 51,998 | 41.6 |
| 5 | Peter H. B. Frelinghuysen (R) | 99,946 | 59.3 |
| | Luther H. Martin (D) | 68,702 | 40.7 |
| 6 | Harrison A. Williams Jr. (D) | 85,784 | 56.1 |
| | Fred E. Shepard (R) | 64,164 | 41.9 |
| 7 | William B. Widnall (R) | 99,977 | 63.2 |
| | Eugene E. Demarest (D) | 58,211 | 36.8 |
| 8 | Gordon Canfield (R) | 65,359 | 54.8 |
| | Charles S. Joelson (D) | 53,844 | 45.1 |
| 9 | Frank C. Osmers Jr. (R) | 87,008 | 60.2 |
| | Walter J. O'Connell (D) | 57,445 | 39.8 |
| 10 | Peter W. Rodino Jr. (D) | 62,384 | 63.4 |
| | William E. McGlynn (R) | 36,056 | 36.6 |
| 11 | Hugh J. Addonizio (D) | 52,311 | 56.3 |
| | Philip Insabella (R) | 38,351 | 41.2 |
| 12 | Robert Winthrop Kean (R) | 59,151 | 53.1 |
| | Martin S. Fox (D) | 52,314 | 46.9 |
| 13 | Alfred D. Sieminski (D) | 60,108 | 60.8 |
| | Norman Roth (R) | 26,638 | 26.9 |
| | Jeremiah J. O'Callaghan (I) | 12,174 | 12.3 |
| 14 | T. James Tumulty (D) | 58,069 | 62.4 |
| | Vincent J. Dellay (R) | 32,485 | 34.9 |

## NEW MEXICO

| | | Votes | % |
|---|---|---|---|
| AL | John J. Dempsey (D) | 111,713✔ | |
| | Antonio M. Fernandez (D) | 109,837✔ | |
| | Thomas J. Childers (R) | 77,151 | |
| | Warren R. Cobean (R) | 76,528 | |

## NEW YORK

| | | Votes | % |
|---|---|---|---|
| 1 | Stuyvesant Wainwright (R) | 108,130 | 63.1 |
| | Ernest Greenwood (D, L) | 62,853 | 36.7 |
| 2 | Steven B. Derounian (R) | 98,610 | 63.7 |
| | William R. Brennan Jr. (D, L) | 55,477 | 35.8 |
| 3 | Frank J. Becker (R) | 93,396 | 58.3 |
| | John T. Cogley (D, L) | 66,703 | 41.7 |
| 4 | Henry J. Latham (R) | 74,621 | 54.2 |
| | Thomas A. Dent (D) | 55,479 | 40.3 |
| | Robert A. Rose (L) | 7,526 | 5.5 |

| | Candidates | Votes | % |
|---|---|---|---|
| 5 | Albert H. Bosch (R) | 50,778 | 51.7 |
| | William Kerwick (D) | 43,086 | 43.9 |
| 6 | Lester Holtzman (D, L) | 81,033 | 54.4 |
| | Seymour Halpern (R) | 67,681 | 45.5 |
| 7 | James J. Delaney (D, L) | 62,541 | 59.0 |
| | Joseph Stockinger (R) | 43,525 | 41.0 |
| 8 | Victor L. Anfuso (D, L) | 51,993 | 77.7 |
| | Eugene J. Renne (R) | 14,948 | 22.3 |
| 9 | Eugene J. Keogh (D, L) | 59,392 | 71.1 |
| | Harry Keller (R) | 22,808 | 27.3 |
| 10 | Edna F. Kelly (D, L) | 80,541 | 76.8 |
| | Abraham Sher (R) | 22,479 | 21.4 |
| 11 | Emanuel Celler (D, L) | 103,788 | 83.5 |
| | Henry D. Dorfman (R) | 20,452 | 16.5 |
| 12 | Francis E. Dorn (R) | 49,449 | 51.3 |
| | Donald L. O'Toole (D, L) | 46,926 | 48.7 |
| 13 | Abraham J. Multer (D, L) | 89,907 | 78.8 |
| | Joseph Moriber (R) | 21,881 | 19.2 |
| 14 | John J. Rooney (D, L) | 61,879 | 73.1 |
| | Alfred A. Manti (R) | 21,598 | 25.5 |
| 15 | John H. Ray (R) | 56,020 | 51.6 |
| | Vincent R. Fitzpatrick (D, L) | 52,292 | 48.1 |
| 16 | Adam Clayton Powell Jr. (D) | 43,545 | 77.6 |
| | Harold C. Burton (R) | 8,904 | 15.9 |
| | Formington Taylor (L) | 3,701 | 6.6 |
| 17 | Frederic R. Coudert Jr. (R) | 48,999 | 50.2 |
| | Anthony B. Akers (D, L) | 48,685 | 49.8 |
| 18 | James G. Donovan (D, R) | 49,850 | 86.8 |
| | Amos Basel (L) | 6,219 | 10.8 |
| 19 | Arthur G. Klein (D, L) | 56,634 | 74.6 |
| | Henry E. Delrosso (R) | 19,310 | 25.4 |
| 20 | Irwin D. Davidson (D, L) | 58,030 | 67.2 |
| | Warren L. Schnur (R) | 26,462 | 30.7 |
| 21 | Herbert Zelenko (D, L) | 63,284 | 67.8 |
| | Floyd Cramer (R) | 29,995 | 32.2 |
| 22 | Sidney A. Fine (D) | 72,091 | 67.9 |
| | Henry Rose (R) | 18,952 | 17.8 |
| | Louis Schifrin (L) | 13,249 | 12.5 |
| 23 | Isidore Dollinger (D) | 58,490 | 75.6 |
| | Philip Myer (R) | 9,976 | 12.9 |
| | Bernice Benedick (L) | 8,869 | 11.5 |
| 24 | Charles A. Buckley (D) | 69,552 | 58.3 |
| | Charles V. Scanlan (R) | 31,670 | 26.6 |
| | Elias Rosenblatt (L) | 18,067 | 15.2 |
| 25 | Paul A. Fino (R) | 59,409 | 50.4 |
| | Salvatore J. Milano (D) | 50,818 | 43.1 |
| | Ernest Doerfler (L) | 7,624 | 6.5 |
| 26 | Ralph A. Gamble (R) | 81,608 | 64.0 |
| | Julia L. Crews (D, L) | 45,892 | 36.0 |
| 27 | Ralph W. Gwinn (R) | 83,866 | 57.2 |
| | John R. Harold (D, L) | 62,797 | 42.8 |
| 28 | Katharine St. George (R) | 79,587 | 64.9 |
| | Paul G. Reilly (D) | 40,109 | 32.7 |
| 29 | J. Ernest Wharton (R) | 88,227 | 66.5 |
| | Robert D. Byron (D) | 42,084 | 31.7 |
| 30 | Leo W. O'Brien (D, L) | 104,585 | 61.2 |
| | James W. Smith (R) | 66,319 | 38.8 |
| 31 | Dean P. Taylor (R) | 86,768 | 66.3 |
| | Joseph R. MacLaren (D, L) | 44,212 | 33.8 |
| 32 | Bernard W. Kearney (R) | 77,891 | 61.5 |
| | David C. Prince (D, L) | 48,808 | 38.5 |
| 33 | Clarence E. Kilburn (R) | 70,708 | 68.1 |
| | Harold Blake (D) | 31,279 | 30.1 |
| 34 | William R. Williams (R) | 77,659 | 59.3 |
| | Vernon E. Olin (D, L) | 53,112 | 40.6 |
| 35 | R. Walter Riehlman (R) | 90,002 | 63.5 |
| | James H. O'Connor (D, L) | 51,358 | 36.3 |
| 36 | John Taber (R) | 79,850 | 68.4 |
| | Daniel J. Carey (D, L) | 36,910 | 31.6 |
| 37 | W. Sterling Cole (R) | 94,840 | 71.7 |
| | John E. Bloomer (D, L) | 37,525 | 28.3 |
| 38 | Kenneth B. Keating (R) | 103,293 | 71.9 |
| | Rubin Brodsky (D, L) | 40,400 | 28.1 |
| 39 | Harold C. Ostertag (R) | 82,769 | 64.8 |
| | George W. Cooke (D, L) | 45,000 | 35.2 |
| 40 | William E. Miller (R) | 77,016 | 60.9 |
| | Mariano A. Lucca (D) | 46,956 | 37.1 |
| 41 | Edmund P. Radwan (R) | 77,259 | 63.1 |
| | Bernard J. Wojtkowiak (D, L) | 45,144 | 36.9 |

| | Candidates | Votes | % |
|---|---|---|---|
| 42 | John R. Pillion (R) | 82,707 | 57.6 |
| | John J. Zablotny (D, L) | 60,880 | 42.4 |
| 43 | Daniel A. Reed (R) | 66,852 | 64.8 |
| | James F. Crowley (D) | 34,590 | 33.5 |

## NORTH CAROLINA

| | | Votes | % |
|---|---|---|---|
| 1 | Herbert C. Bonner (D) | 20,650 | 92.5 |
| | W. T. Love (R) | 1,685 | 7.5 |
| 2 | L. H. Fountain (D) | 14,471 | 100.0 |
| 3 | Graham A. Barden (D) | 24,837 | 77.3 |
| | Christine P. Odom (R) | 7,301 | 22.7 |
| 4 | Harold D. Cooley (D) | 34,406 | 100.0 |
| 5 | Thurmond Chatham (D) | 31,781 | 66.2 |
| | Joe New (R) | 16,194 | 33.8 |
| 6 | Carl T. Durham (D) | 30,118 | 74.3 |
| | Rufus K. Haworth Jr. (R) | 10,446 | 25.8 |
| 7 | F. Ertel Carlyle (D) | 21,669 | 81.3 |
| | J. O. West (R) | 5,001 | 18.8 |
| 8 | Charles B. Deane (D) | 39,028 | 59.1 |
| | Harold W. Gavin (R) | 26,966 | 40.9 |
| 9 | Hugh Q. Alexander (D) | 54,103 | 52.2 |
| | William E. Stevens Jr. (R) | 49,555 | 47.8 |
| 10 | Charles Raper Jonas (R) | 51,492 | 57.5 |
| | J. C. Sedberry (D) | 38,080 | 42.5 |
| 11 | Woodrow W. Jones (D) | 36,766 | 67.5 |
| | R. R. Ramsey (R) | 17,721 | 32.5 |
| 12 | George A. Shuford (D) | 44,258 | 61.6 |
| | Charles Cunningham (R) | 27,651 | 38.5 |

## NORTH DAKOTA

| | | Votes | % |
|---|---|---|---|
| AL | Usher L. Burdick (R) | 124,845✔ | |
| | Otto Krueger (R) | 106,341✔ | |
| | P. W. Lanier (D) | 64,089 | |
| | Raymond G. Vendsel (D) | 49,183 | |

## OHIO

| | | Votes | % |
|---|---|---|---|
| 1 | Gordon H. Scherer (R) | 71,042 | 64.3 |
| | Mrs. Warwick B. Hobart (D) | 39,421 | 35.7 |
| 2 | William E. Hess (R) | 69,695 | 58.4 |
| | Earl T. Wagner (D) | 49,690 | 41.6 |
| 3 | Paul F. Schenck (R) | 82,701 | 52.6 |
| | Thomas B. Talbot (D) | 74,585 | 47.4 |
| 4 | William M. McCulloch (R) | 67,762 | 67.6 |
| | Forrest L. Blankenship (D) | 32,474 | 32.4 |
| 5 | Cliff Clevenger (R) | 49,265 | 59.5 |
| | Martin W. Feigert (D) | 33,483 | 40.5 |
| 6 | James G. Polk (D) | 54,044 | 52.2 |
| | Leo Blackburn (R) | 49,531 | 47.8 |
| 7 | Clarence J. Brown (R) | 62,821 | 63.9 |
| | G. Louie Wren (D) | 35,504 | 36.1 |
| 8 | Jackson E. Betts (R) | 52,196 | 63.1 |
| | Thomas M. Dowd (D) | 30,592 | 37.0 |
| 9 | Thomas L. Ashley (D) | 48,471 | 36.4 |
| | Frazier Reams (I) | 44,656 | 33.6 |
| | Irving C. Reynolds (R) | 39,933 | 30.0 |
| 10 | Thomas A. Jenkins (R) | 45,277 | 61.7 |
| | Truman A. Morris (D) | 28,150 | 38.3 |
| 11 | Oliver P. Bolton (R) | 74,065 | 65.3 |
| | Edward C. Kaley (D) | 39,404 | 34.7 |
| 12 | John M. Vorys (R) | 94,585 | 61.5 |
| | Jacob F. Myers (D) | 59,210 | 38.5 |
| 13 | A. D. Baumhart Jr. (R) | 46,524 | 59.1 |
| | George C. Steinemann (D) | 32,177 | 40.9 |
| 14 | William H. Ayres (R) | 82,086 | 54.6 |
| | John L. Smith (D) | 68,204 | 45.4 |
| 15 | John E. Henderson (R) | 38,524 | 54.0 |
| | Max Lewis Underwood (D) | 32,795 | 46.0 |
| 16 | Frank T. Bow (R) | 79,371 | 58.3 |
| | Thomas H. Nichols (D) | 56,787 | 41.7 |
| 17 | J. Harry McGregor (R) | 63,301 | 64.6 |
| | Robert W. Levering (D) | 34,638 | 35.4 |
| 18 | Wayne L. Hays (D) | 59,165 | 57.3 |
| | Walter J. Hunston (R) | 44,143 | 42.7 |
| 19 | Michael J. Kirwan (D) | 69,324 | 67.5 |
| | David S. Edwards (R) | 33,352 | 32.5 |

## OHIO

| | Candidates | Votes | % |
|---|---|---|---|
| 20 | Michael A. Feighan (D) | 81,304 | 67.7 |
| | John H. Ferguson (R) | 38,865 | 32.3 |
| 21 | Charles A. Vanik (D) | 76,201 | 76.0 |
| | Francis E. Young (R) | 24,076 | 24.0 |
| 22 | Frances P. Bolton (R) | 61,738 | 58.4 |
| | Chat Paterson (D) | 44,072 | 41.7 |
| 23 | William E. Minshall Jr. (R) | 69,994 | 67.5 |
| | Bernice S. Pyke (D) | 33,639 | 32.5 |

## OKLAHOMA

| | | Votes | % |
|---|---|---|---|
| 1 | Page Belcher (R) | 79,151 | 58.8 |
| | Ben Crowley (D) | 55,391 | 41.2 |
| 2 | Ed Edmondson (D) | 67,872 | 64.7 |
| | Percy Butler (R) | 37,030 | 35.3 |
| 3 | Carl Albert (D) | 52,662 | 83.3 |
| | Jasper N. Butler (R) | 10,554 | 16.7 |
| 4 | Tom Steed (D) | 43,915 | 100.0 |
| 5 | John Jarman (D) | 72,380 | 66.0 |
| | George E. Young (R) | 37,223 | 34.0 |
| 6 | Victor E. Wickersham (D) | 62,119 | 69.3 |
| | Reece L. Russell (R) | 27,492 | 30.7 |

## OREGON

| | | Votes | % |
|---|---|---|---|
| 1 | Walter Norblad (R) | 98,592 | 63.0 |
| | Donnell Mitchell (D) | 57,882 | 37.0 |
| 2 | Sam Coon (R) | 43,731 | 52.6 |
| | Al Ullman (D) | 39,475 | 47.4 |
| 3 | Edith Green (D) | 103,976 | 52.4 |
| | Tom McCall (R) | 94,368 | 47.6 |
| 4 | Harris Ellsworth (R) | 70,695 | 55.9 |
| | Charles O. Porter (D) | 55,775 | 44.1 |

## PENNSYLVANIA

| | | Votes | % |
|---|---|---|---|
| 1 | William A. Barrett (D) | 68,531 | 61.5 |
| | Joseph A. Graham Jr. (R) | 42,893 | 38.5 |
| 2 | William T. Granahan (D) | 80,377 | 61.3 |
| | Albert A. Ciardi (R) | 50,857 | 38.8 |
| 3 | James A. Byrne (D) | 61,639 | 55.4 |
| | Charles H. Sporkin (R) | 49,702 | 44.6 |
| 4 | Earl Chudoff (D) | 60,564 | 65.7 |
| | W. Beverly Carter Jr. (R) | 31,551 | 34.2 |
| 5 | William J. Green Jr. (D) | 87,435 | 55.0 |
| | Francis P. McCusker (R) | 71,462 | 45.0 |
| 6 | Hugh Scott (R) | 74,328 | 50.6 |
| | Alexander Hemphill (D) | 72,587 | 49.4 |
| 7 | Benjamin F. James (R) | 101,282 | 60.9 |
| | O. Arthur Cappiello (D) | 65,086 | 39.1 |
| 8 | Karl C. King (R) | 62,897 | 51.2 |
| | John P. Fullam (D) | 59,848 | 48.8 |
| 9 | Paul B. Dague (R) | 76,163 | 62.7 |
| | Edward G. Wilson (D) | 45,402 | 37.4 |
| 10 | Joseph L. Carrigg (R) | 74,515 | 50.5 |
| | Robert H. Jones (D) | 73,046 | 49.5 |
| 11 | Daniel J. Flood (D) | 70,254 | 50.9 |
| | Edward J. Bonin (R) | 67,682 | 49.1 |
| 12 | Ivor D. Fenton (R) | 62,779 | 55.5 |
| | Charles E. Lotz (D) | 50,373 | 44.5 |
| 13 | Samuel K. McConnell Jr. (R) | 91,639 | 64.3 |
| | Joseph C. Mansfield (D) | 50,796 | 35.7 |
| 14 | George M. Rhodes (D) | 50,765 | 62.0 |
| | Donald F. Spang (R) | 31,136 | 38.0 |
| 15 | Francis E. Walter (D) | 56,871 | 61.6 |
| | LeRoy Mikels (R) | 35,464 | 38.4 |
| 16 | Walter M. Mumma (R) | 69,240 | 59.8 |
| | Richard A. Swank (D) | 46,619 | 40.2 |
| 17 | Alvin R. Bush (R) | 57,928 | 56.5 |
| | William T. Longe (D) | 44,543 | 43.5 |
| 18 | Richard M. Simpson (R) | 58,959 | 55.9 |
| | Robert M. Meyers (D) | 46,463 | 44.1 |
| 19 | James M. Quigley (D) | 62,108 | 51.0 |
| | S. Walter Stauffer (R) | 59,594 | 49.0 |
| 20 | James E. Van Zandt (R) | 48,561 | 56.3 |
| | John R. Stewart (D) | 37,725 | 43.7 |

| | Candidates | Votes | % |
|---|---|---|---|
| 21 | Augustine B. Kelley (D) | 70,224 | 61.1 |
| | Herbert O. Morrison (R) | 44,789 | 38.9 |
| 22 | John P. Saylor (R) | 66,270 | 51.9 |
| | Robert S. Glass (D) | 61,474 | 48.1 |
| 23 | Leon H. Gavin (R) | 53,616 | 61.9 |
| | Fred C. Barr (D) | 33,044 | 38.1 |
| 24 | Carroll D. Kearns (R) | 66,005 | 52.0 |
| | Edmund T. Rogers (D) | 60,842 | 48.0 |
| 25 | Frank M. Clark (D) | 66,223 | 53.5 |
| | Louis E. Graham (R) | 57,657 | 46.5 |
| 26 | Thomas E. Morgan (D) | 95,531 | 65.3 |
| | Branko Stupar (R) | 50,768 | 34.7 |
| 27 | James G. Fulton (R) | 92,533 | 62.8 |
| | Charles J. Chamberlin (D) | 54,876 | 37.2 |
| 28 | Herman P. Eberharter (D) | 85,550 | 65.1 |
| | Guy C. Read (R) | 45,913 | 34.9 |
| 29 | Robert J. Corbett (R) | 83,846 | 60.6 |
| | William G. Foley (D) | 54,511 | 39.4 |
| 30 | Vera D. Buchanan (D) | 98,318 | 69.0 |
| | David J. Smith (R) | 44,157 | 31.0 |

## RHODE ISLAND

| | | Votes | % |
|---|---|---|---|
| 1 | Aime J. Forand (D) | 89,678 | 59.1 |
| | Arthur Carrelas (R) | 61,990 | 40.9 |
| 2 | John E. Fogarty (D) | 105,522 | 60.5 |
| | James O. Watts (R) | 68,869 | 39.5 |

## SOUTH CAROLINA

| | | Votes | % |
|---|---|---|---|
| 1 | L. Mendel Rivers (D) | 33,402 | 97.8 |
| 2 | John J. Riley (D) | 44,484 | 97.7 |
| 3 | W. J. Bryan Dorn (D) | 30,790 | 99.3 |
| 4 | Robert T. Ashmore (D) | 43,857 | 99.2 |
| 5 | James P. Richards (D) | 26,950 | 100.0 |
| 6 | John L. McMillan (D) | 31,141 | 98.9 |

## SOUTH DAKOTA

| | | Votes | % |
|---|---|---|---|
| 1 | Harold O. Lovre (R) | 102,797 | 58.0 |
| | Francis G. Dunn (D) | 74,450 | 42.0 |
| 2 | E. Y. Berry (R) | 34,476 | 63.9 |
| | Ray Satterlee (D) | 19,444 | 36.1 |

## TENNESSEE

| | | Votes | % |
|---|---|---|---|
| 1 | B. Carroll Reece (R) | 32,991 | 62.5 |
| | Arthur Bright (D) | 19,828 | 37.5 |
| 2 | Howard H. Baker (R) | 47,989 | 58.0 |
| | C. Howard Bozeman (D) | 34,688 | 42.0 |
| 3 | James B. Frazier Jr. (D) | 30,558 | 59.2 |
| | O. M. Spence (R) | 21,081 | 40.8 |
| 4 | Joe L. Evins (D) | 27,613 | 100.0 |
| 5 | J. Percy Priest (D) | 20,849 | 90.8 |
| | Robert M. Donihi (R) | 2,123 | 9.2 |
| 6 | Ross Bass (D) | 26,081 | 99.4 |
| 7 | Tom Murray (D) | 17,708 | 100.0 |
| 8 | Jere Cooper (D) | 15,078 | 100.0 |
| 9 | Clifford Davis (D) | 40,121 | 83.5 |
| | W. A. Danielson (R) | 7,926 | 16.5 |

## TEXAS

| | | Votes | % |
|---|---|---|---|
| 1 | Wright Patman (D) | 18,104 | 100.0 |
| 2 | Jack Brooks (D) | 25,008 | 100.0 |
| 3 | Brady Gentry (D) | 20,767 | 100.0 |
| 4 | Sam Rayburn (D) | 15,177 | 100.0 |
| 5 | Bruce Alger (R) | 27,982 | 52.9 |
| | Wallace Savage (D) | 24,904 | 47.1 |
| 6 | Olin E. Teague (D) | 15,161 | 100.0 |
| 7 | John Dowdy (D) | 18,361 | 100.0 |
| 8 | Albert Thomas (D) | 60,374 | 62.1 |
| | W. B. Butler (R) | 36,405 | 37.4 |
| 9 | Clark W. Thompson (D) | 29,972 | 100.0 |
| 10 | Homer Thornberry (D) | 23,752 | 100.0 |
| 11 | W. R. Poage (D) | 17,739 | 100.0 |
| 12 | Jim Wright (D) | 35,611 | 98.8 |

| | Candidates | Votes | % |
|---|---|---|---|
| 13 | Frank Ikard (D) | 25,085 | 100.0 |
| 14 | John J. Bell (D) | 36,284 | 93.8 |
| | D. C. DeWitt (R) | 2,384 | 6.2 |
| 15 | Joe M. Kilgore (D) | 29,113 | 100.0 |
| 16 | J. T. Rutherford (D) | 25,122 | 100.0 |
| 17 | Omar Burleson (D) | 18,484 | 100.0 |
| 18 | Walter Rogers (D) | 25,430 | 64.9 |
| | Leroy LaMaster (R) | 13,756 | 35.1 |
| 19 | George Mahon (D) | 26,829 | 100.0 |
| 20 | Paul J. Kilday (D) | 23,533 | 100.0 |
| 21 | O. C. Fisher (D) | 25,381 | 100.0 |
| AL | Martin Dies (D) | 555,446 | 88.0 |
| | Tom Nolan (R) | 75,472 | 12.0 |

## UTAH

| | | Votes | % |
|---|---|---|---|
| 1 | Henry Aldous Dixon (R) | 55,542 | 53.4 |
| | Walter K. Granger (D) | 48,535 | 46.6 |
| 2 | William A. Dawson (R) | 90,864 | 57.2 |
| | Reva Beck Bosone (D) | 68,090 | 42.8 |

## VERMONT

| | | Votes | % |
|---|---|---|---|
| AL | Winston L. Prouty (R) | 70,143 | 61.4 |
| | John J. Boylan Jr. (D) | 44,141 | 38.6 |

## VIRGINIA

| | | Votes | % |
|---|---|---|---|
| 1 | Edward J. Robeson Jr. (D) | 16,029 | 99.8 |
| 2 | Porter Hardy Jr. (D) | 18,190 | 74.4 |
| | George V. Credle Jr. (R) | 6,243 | 25.6 |
| 3 | J. Vaughan Gary (D) | 19,466 | 58.0 |
| | J. Calvitt Clarke Jr. (R) | 14,088 | 42.0 |
| 4 | Watkins M. Abbitt (D) | 14,728 | 99.9 |
| 5 | William M. Tuck (D) | 13,042 | 99.9 |
| 6 | Richard H. Poff (R) | 32,855 | 62.3 |
| | Ernest Robertson (D) | 19,727 | 37.4 |
| 7 | Burr P. Harrison (D) | 22,025 | 74.2 |
| | John Paul Ruddick (R) | 7,669 | 25.8 |
| 8 | Howard W. Smith (D) | 17,321 | 66.6 |
| | C. S. Lenhart (I) | 8,679 | 33.4 |
| 9 | W. Pat Jennings (D) | 39,238 | 50.5 |
| | William C. Wampler (R) | 38,239 | 49.2 |
| 10 | Joel T. Broyhill (R) | 29,221 | 53.8 |
| | John C. Webb (D) | 24,667 | 45.4 |

## WASHINGTON

| | | Votes | % |
|---|---|---|---|
| 1 | Thomas M. Pelly (R) | 101,913 | 52.6 |
| | Hugh B. Mitchell (D) | 91,721 | 47.4 |
| 2 | Jack Westland (R) | 73,264 | 52.2 |
| | Harry F. Henson (D) | 67,232 | 47.9 |
| 3 | Russell V. Mack (R) | 70,844 | 64.9 |
| | Clyde V. Tisdale (D) | 38,344 | 35.1 |
| 4 | Hal Holmes (R) | 67,171 | 61.0 |
| | Fred Yoder (D) | 42,911 | 39.0 |
| 5 | Walt Horan (R) | 68,628 | 58.6 |
| | Art Garton (D) | 48,542 | 41.4 |
| 6 | Thor C. Tollefson (R) | 80,241 | 55.2 |
| | John T. McCutcheon (D) | 65,011 | 44.8 |
| AL | Don Magnuson (D) | 464,045 | 57.3 |
| | Al Canwell (R) | 342,089 | 42.2 |

## WEST VIRGINIA

| | | Votes | % |
|---|---|---|---|
| 1 | Robert H. Mollohan (D) | 52,609 | 52.7 |
| | Arch A. Moore Jr. (R) | 47,199 | 47.3 |
| 2 | Harley O. Staggers (D) | 50,283 | 55.0 |
| | Albert M. Morgan (R) | 41,171 | 45.0 |
| 3 | Cleveland M. Bailey (D) | 54,684 | 58.9 |
| | Joseph B. Lightburn (R) | 38,218 | 41.1 |
| 4 | M. G. Burnside (D) | 56,498 | 50.2 |
| | Will E. Neal (R) | 55,994 | 49.8 |
| 5 | Elizabeth Kee (D) | 52,349 | 67.5 |
| | Fred O. Blue (R) | 25,267 | 32.6 |
| 6 | Robert C. Byrd (D) | 73,535 | 62.7 |
| | Pat B. Withrow Jr. (R) | 43,685 | 37.3 |

## WISCONSIN

| Candidates | Votes | % |
|---|---|---|
| 1 Lawrence H. Smith (R) | 65,562 | 54.4 |
| Edward A. Krenzke (D) | 54,864 | 45.6 |
| 2 Glenn R. Davis (R) | 74,460 | 54.0 |
| Gaylord A. Nelson (D) | 63,449 | 46.0 |
| 3 Gardner R. Withrow (R) | 56,228 | 62.1 |
| Joseph A. Seep (D) | 34,375 | 37.9 |

| Candidates | Votes | % |
|---|---|---|
| 4 Clement J. Zablocki (D) | 100,120 | 71.1 |
| John C. Schafer (R) | 40,723 | 28.9 |
| 5 Henry S. Reuss (D) | 77,208 | 52.3 |
| Charles J. Kersten (R) | 70,565 | 47.8 |
| 6 William K. Van Pelt (R) | 68,653 | 62.5 |
| Russell S. Johnson (D) | 41,191 | 37.5 |
| 7 Melvin R. Laird (R) | 57,581 | 59.1 |
| Kenneth E. Anderson (D) | 39,828 | 40.9 |
| 8 John W. Byrnes (R) | 73,588 | 62.0 |
| Jerome J. Reinke (D) | 45,037 | 38.0 |

| Candidates | Votes | % |
|---|---|---|
| 9 Lester R. Johnson (D) | 52,485 | 55.4 |
| William E. Owen (R) | 42,234 | 44.6 |
| 10 Alvin E. O'Konski (R) | 49,325 | 59.8 |
| Basil G. Kennedy (D) | 33,219 | 40.2 |

## WYOMING

| Candidates | Votes | % |
|---|---|---|
| AL E. Keith Thomson (R) | 61,111 | 56.2 |
| Sam Tully (D) | 47,660 | 43.8 |

# 1956 House Elections

## ALABAMA

| Candidates | Votes | % |
|---|---|---|
| 1 Frank W. Boykin (D) | 31,469 | 100.0 |
| 2 George Grant (D) | 36,613 | 100.0 |
| 3 George W. Andrews (D) | 29,547 | 100.0 |
| 4 Kenneth A. Roberts (D) | 33,591 | 73.4 |
| Roy Banks (R) | 12,166 | 26.6 |
| 5 Albert Rains (D) | 45,281 | 100.0 |
| 6 Armistead I. Selden Jr. (D) | 22,513 | 100.0 |
| 7 Carl Elliott (D) | 31,988 | 100.0 |
| 8 Robert E. Jones Jr. (D) | 46,730 | 80.1 |
| Mrs. James G. Fortney (R) | 11,634 | 19.9 |
| 9 George Huddleston Jr. (D) | 56,414 | 65.9 |
| W. L. Longshore Jr. (R) | 29,222 | 34.1 |

## ARIZONA

| Candidates | Votes | % |
|---|---|---|
| 1 John J. Rhodes (R) | 78,998 | 54.9 |
| William P. Mahoney Jr. (D) | 64,805 | 45.1 |
| 2 Stewart L. Udall (D) | 82,110 | 60.1 |
| John G. Speiden (R) | 54,596 | 39.9 |

## ARKANSAS

| Candidates | Votes | % |
|---|---|---|
| 1 Ezekiel C. Gathings (D) | 25,622 | 100.0 |
| 2 Wilbur D. Mills (D) | 19,540 | 100.0 |
| 3 James W. Trimble (D) | 54,481 | 61.4 |
| William S. Spicer (R) | 34,318 | 38.7 |
| 4 Oren Harris (D) | 37,284 | 100.0 |
| 5 Brooks Hays (D) | 56,271 | 100.0 |
| 6 William F. Norrell (D) | 42,447 | 100.0 |

## CALIFORNIA

| Candidates | Votes | % |
|---|---|---|
| 1 Hubert B. Scudder (R) | 102,604 | 53.6 |
| Clement W. Miller (D) | 88,962 | 46.4 |
| 2 Clair Engle (D-R) | 136,544 | 100.0 |
| 3 John E. Moss Jr. (D) | 132,930 | 68.6 |
| Noel C. Stevenson (R) | 60,889 | 31.4 |
| 4 William S. Mailliard (R) | 109,188 | 61.9 |
| James L. Quigley (D) | 67,132 | 38.1 |
| 5 John F. Shelley (D-R) | 104,358 | 100.0 |
| 6 John F. Baldwin Jr. (R) | 98,683 | 53.7 |
| H. Roberts Quinney (D) | 84,965 | 46.3 |
| 7 John J. Allen Jr. (R) | 75,932 | 52.8 |
| Laurence L. Cross (D) | 67,931 | 47.2 |
| 8 George P. Miller (D) | 136,720 | 65.6 |
| Robert Lee Watkins (R) | 71,700 | 34.4 |
| 9 J. Arthur Younger (R) | 96,388 | 60.3 |
| James T. McKay (D) | 63,504 | 39.7 |
| 10 Charles S. Gubser (R) | 128,891 | 60.7 |
| William H. Vatcher Jr. (D) | 83,586 | 39.3 |
| 11 John J. McFall (D) | 70,630 | 53.1 |
| Leroy Johnson (R) | 62,448 | 46.9 |
| 12 B. F. Sisk (D) | 109,920 | 73.0 |
| Robert B. Moore (R) | 40,663 | 27.0 |
| 13 Charles M. Teague (R) | 104,009 | 59.6 |
| William Kirk Stewart (D) | 70,567 | 40.4 |
| 14 Harlan Hagan (D) | 94,461 | 63.0 |
| Myron D. Tisdel (R) | 55,509 | 37.0 |
| 15 Gordon L. McDonough (R) | 97,182 | 57.9 |
| Emery S. Petty (D) | 70,681 | 42.1 |
| 16 Donald L. Jackson (R) | 83,050 | 60.8 |
| G. Robert Fleming (D) | 53,624 | 39.2 |
| 17 Cecil R. King (D) | 157,270 | 64.9 |
| Charles A. Franklin (R) | 84,900 | 35.1 |
| 18 Craig Hosmer (R) | 103,108 | 59.3 |
| Raymond C. Simpson (D) | 70,911 | 40.8 |
| 19 Chet Holifield (D) | 116,287 | 73.8 |
| Roy E. Reynolds (R) | 41,269 | 26.2 |
| 20 H. Allen Smith (R) | 85,459 | 70.8 |
| Eugene Radding (D) | 35,249 | 29.2 |

| Candidates | Votes | % |
|---|---|---|
| 21 Edgar W. Hiestand (R) | 153,679 | 62.6 |
| W. C. Stethem (D) | 91,683 | 37.4 |
| 22 Joe Holt (R) | 97,317 | 59.8 |
| Irving Glasband (D) | 65,314 | 40.2 |
| 23 Clyde Doyle (D & P) | 120,109 | 70.9 |
| E. Elgie Calvin (R) | 49,198 | 29.1 |
| 24 Glenard P. Lipscomb (R) | 84,120 | 61.9 |
| Fay Porter (D) | 51,692 | 38.1 |
| 25 Patrick J. Hillings (R) | 166,305 | 63.8 |
| John G. Sobieski (D) | 94,180 | 36.2 |
| 26 James Roosevelt (D) | 133,036 | 68.8 |
| Edward H. Gibbons (R) | 60,230 | 31.2 |
| 27 Harry R. Sheppard (D-П) | 124,662 | 99.8 |
| 28 James B. Utt (R) | 159,456 | 64.5 |
| Gordon T. Shepard (D) | 87,691 | 35.5 |
| 29 Dalip S. Saund (D) | 54,989 | 51.5 |
| Jacqueline Cochran Odlum (R) | 51,690 | 48.4 |
| 30 Bob Wilson (R) | 142,753 | 66.8 |
| George A. Cheney (D) | 71,112 | 33.3 |

## COLORADO

| Candidates | Votes | % |
|---|---|---|
| 1 Byron G. Rogers (D) | 116,487 | 57.8 |
| Robert S. McCollum (R) | 85,127 | 42.2 |
| 2 William S. Hill (R) | 107,153 | 53.4 |
| Byron L. Johnson (D) | 93,572 | 46.6 |
| 3 J. Edgar Chenoweth (R) | 74,196 | 50.2 |
| Alva B. Adams (D) | 73,503 | 49.8 |
| 4 Wayne N. Aspinall (D) | 48,489 | 61.8 |
| Hugh L. Caldwell (R) | 30,026 | 38.2 |

## CONNECTICUT

| Candidates | Votes | % |
|---|---|---|
| 1 Edwin H. May Jr. (R) | 161,360 | 53.5 |
| Patrick J. Ward (D) | 139,147 | 46.1 |
| 2 Horace Seely-Brown Jr. (R) | 99,274 | 59.1 |
| Douglas J. Bennet (D) | 68,847 | 41.0 |
| 3 Albert W. Cretella (R) | 126,850 | 60.0 |
| Robert N. Giaimo (D) | 84,568 | 40.0 |
| 4 Albert P. Morano (R) | 194,333 | 68.4 |
| Jack Stock (D) | 88,487 | 31.1 |
| 5 James T. Patterson (R) | 91,690 | 61.9 |
| Luke F. Martin (D) | 56,375 | 38.1 |
| AL Antoni N. Sadlak (R) | 683,387 | 61.5 |
| Matthew P. Kuta (D) | 428,709 | 38.6 |

## DELAWARE

| Candidates | Votes | % |
|---|---|---|
| AL Harry G. Haskell Jr. (R) | 91,538 | 52.0 |
| Harris B. Mcdowell Jr. (D) | 84,644 | 48.0 |

## FLORIDA

| Candidates | Votes | % |
|---|---|---|
| 1 William C. Cramer (R) | 105,958 | 56.4 |
| Winton H. King (D) | 82,075 | 43.7 |
| 2 Charles E. Bennett (D) | 66,614 | 100.0 |
| 3 Robert L. F. Sikes (D) | 86,272 | 89.6 |
| Arthur Barker Sr. (R) | 10,042 | 10.4 |
| 4 Dante B. Fascell (D) | 120,509 | 60.9 |
| Leland Hyzer (R) | 77,301 | 39.1 |
| 5 A. S. Herlong Jr. (D) | 73,498 | 51.4 |
| Arnold L. Lund (R) | 69,378 | 48.6 |
| 6 Paul G. Rogers (D) | 73,259 | 54.7 |
| Dorothy A. Smith (R) | 60,570 | 45.3 |
| 7 James A. Haley (D) | 47,985 | 62.4 |
| G. M. Nelson (R) | 28,900 | 37.6 |
| 8 Donald R. Matthews (D) | 39,362 | 100.0 |

## GEORGIA

| Candidates | Votes | % |
|---|---|---|
| 1 Prince H. Preston (D) | 40,360 | 78.3 |
| Harry P. Anestos (I) | 10,931 | 21.2 |
| 2 J. L. Pilcher (D) | 41,270 | 100.0 |
| 3 E. L. Forrester (D) | 51,703 | 100.0 |

| Candidates | Votes | % |
|---|---|---|
| 4 John J. Flynt Jr. (D) | 51,568 | 100.0 |
| 5 James C. Davis (D) | 85,292 | 59.2 |
| Randolph W. Thrower (R) | 58,777 | 40.8 |
| 6 Carl Vinson (D) | 42,766 | 100.0 |
| 7 Henderson Lanham (D) | 69,873 | 99.5 |
| 8 Iris Faircloth Blitch (D) | 50,068 | 100.0 |
| 9 Phil M. Landrum (D) | 47,360 | 100.0 |
| 10 Paul Brown (D) | 41,812 | 99.8 |

## IDAHO

| Candidates | Votes | % |
|---|---|---|
| 1 Gracie B. Pfost (D) | 60,170 | 55.1 |
| Louise Shadduck (H) | 48,974 | 44.9 |
| 2 Hamer H. Budge (R) | 90,738 | 60.0 |
| J. W. Reynolds (D) | 60,552 | 40.0 |

## ILLINOIS

| Candidates | Votes | % |
|---|---|---|
| 1 William L. Dawson (D) | 66,704 | 64.4 |
| George W. Lawrence (R) | 36,847 | 35.6 |
| 2 Barratt O'Hara (D) | 86,386 | 55.3 |
| George B. McKibbin (R) | 69,892 | 44.7 |
| 3 Emmet F. Byrne (R) | 92,907 | 51.5 |
| James C. Murray (D) | 87,677 | 48.6 |
| 4 William E. McVey (R) | 155,447 | 60.0 |
| Michael Hinko (D) | 103,494 | 40.0 |
| 5 John C. Kluczynski (D) | 96,399 | 61.8 |
| Lawrence Welnowski (R) | 59,608 | 38.2 |
| 6 Thomas J. O'Brien (D) | 94,281 | 62.0 |
| John J. Dillon (R) | 57,750 | 38.0 |
| 7 James B. Bowler (D) | 93,732 | 71.7 |
| Gabriel L. Grimaldi (R) | 37,068 | 28.3 |
| 8 Thomas S. Gordon (D) | 73,628 | 59.5 |
| Victor O. Wright (R) | 50,055 | 40.5 |
| 9 Sidney R. Yates (D) | 75,511 | 54.0 |
| Johann S. Ackerman (R) | 64,237 | 46.0 |
| 10 Harold R. Collier (R) | 132,928 | 64.5 |
| Marvin E. Lore (D) | 73,331 | 35.6 |
| 11 Timothy P. Sheehan (R) | 95,140 | 55.5 |
| Roman C. Pucinski (D) | 76,400 | 44.5 |
| 12 Charles A. Boyle (D) | 100,273 | 53.2 |
| Edgar A. Jonas (R) | 88,315 | 46.8 |
| 13 Marguerite Stitt Church (R) | 229,358 | 71.6 |
| Helen Benson Leys (D) | 91,059 | 28.4 |
| 14 Russell W. Keeney (R) | 151,236 | 70.6 |
| Harold J. Spelman (D) | 63,067 | 29.4 |
| 15 Noah M. Mason (R) | 103,557 | 64.6 |
| Stanley Hubbs (D) | 56,802 | 35.4 |
| 16 Leo E. Allen (R) | 106,734 | 63.7 |
| Glen F. Kunkle (D) | 60,748 | 36.3 |
| 17 Leslie C. Arends (R) | 106,463 | 64.9 |
| C. E. Spang (D) | 57,467 | 35.1 |
| 18 Robert H. Michel (R) | 87,187 | 58.8 |
| Fred Allen (D) | 61,099 | 41.2 |
| 19 Robert B. Chiperfield (R) | 85,497 | 55.8 |
| Martin P. Sutor (D) | 67,691 | 44.2 |
| 20 Sidney E. Simpson (R) | 79,641 | 59.7 |
| Henry W. Pollock (D) | 53,882 | 40.4 |
| 21 Peter F. Mack Jr. (D) | 94,565 | 53.5 |
| Frederic S. O'Hara (R) | 82,251 | 46.5 |
| 22 William L. Springer (R) | 93,399 | 62.3 |
| E. H. Winegarner (D) | 56,612 | 37.7 |
| 23 Charles W. Vursell (R) | 79,862 | 52.6 |
| Albert R. Imle (D) | 72,070 | 47.4 |
| 24 Melvin Price (D) | 121,381 | 68.2 |
| Waldo E. Schellenger (R) | 56,568 | 31.8 |
| 25 Kenneth J. Gray (D) | 82,845 | 53.8 |
| Samuel J. Scott (R) | 71,048 | 46.2 |

## INDIANA

| Candidates | Votes | % |
|---|---|---|
| 1 Ray J. Madden (D) | 93,658 | 52.6 |
| Donald K. Stimson Jr. (R) | 84,125 | 47.2 |
| 2 Charles A. Halleck (R) | 94,852 | 62.2 |
| Thurman C. Crook (D) | 57,049 | 37.4 |

## INDIANA

| | Candidates | Votes | % |
|---|---|---|---|
| 3 | F. Jay Nimtz (R) | 109,907 | 53.1 |
| | John Brademas (D) | 97,196 | 46.9 |
| 4 | E. Ross Adair (R) | 96,531 | 63.5 |
| | F. Dean Bechtol (D) | 55,284 | 36.3 |
| 5 | John V. Beamer (R) | 113,586 | 56.4 |
| | William C. Whitehead (D) | 86,797 | 43.1 |
| 6 | Cecil M. Harden (R) | 86,020 | 55.0 |
| | John W. King (D) | 70,035 | 44.8 |
| 7 | William G. Bray (R) | 87,635 | 57.2 |
| | Vernon R. Hill (D) | 65,482 | 42.8 |
| 8 | Winfield K. Denton (D) | 95,699 | 50.1 |
| | D. Bailey Merrill (R) | 95,003 | 49.7 |
| 9 | Earl Wilson (R) | 70,926 | 53.4 |
| | Wilfrid J. Ullrich (D) | 61,465 | 46.3 |
| 10 | Ralph Harvey (R) | 98,301 | 56.3 |
| | Gerald C. Carmony (D) | 75,665 | 43.3 |
| 11 | Charles B. Brownson (R) | 155,541 | 59.4 |
| | John C. Carvey (D) | 106,021 | 40.5 |

## IOWA

| | Candidates | Votes | % |
|---|---|---|---|
| 1 | Fred D. Schwengel (R) | 94,223 | 58.0 |
| | Ronald O. Bramhall (D) | 68,287 | 42.0 |
| 2 | Henry O. Talle (R) | 95,999 | 51.4 |
| | Leonard G. Wolf (D) | 90,843 | 48.6 |
| 3 | H. R. Gross (R) | 97,590 | 58.6 |
| | Michael Micich (D) | 69,076 | 41.5 |
| 4 | Karl M. LeCompte (R) | 58,024 | 50.7 |
| | Steven V. Carter (D) | 56,406 | 49.3 |
| 5 | Paul Cunningham (R) | 85,178 | 51.1 |
| | William F. Denman (D) | 81,418 | 48.9 |
| 6 | Merwin Coad (D) | 64,625 | 50.1 |
| | James I. Dolliver (R) | 64,427 | 49.9 |
| 7 | Ben F. Jensen (R) | 64,967 | 55.4 |
| | John L. Jensen (D) | 52,389 | 44.6 |
| 8 | Charles B. Hoeven (R) | 76,165 | 60.1 |
| | Robert J. Salem (D) | 50,597 | 39.9 |

## KANSAS

| | Candidates | Votes | % |
|---|---|---|---|
| 1 | William H. Avery (R) | 69,841 | 53.1 |
| | Howard S. Miller (D) | 60,313 | 45.8 |
| 2 | Errett P. Scrivner (R) | 93,609 | 54.9 |
| | Newell A. George (D) | 77,049 | 45.2 |
| 3 | Myron V. George (R) | 48,246 | 55.0 |
| | Denver D. Hargis (D) | 39,407 | 45.0 |
| 4 | Edward H. Rees (R) | 111,970 | 53.8 |
| | John D. Montgomery (D) | 96,002 | 46.2 |
| 5 | J. Floyd Breeding (D) | 64,392 | 50.5 |
| | John W. Crutcher (R) | 63,057 | 49.5 |
| 6 | Wint Smith (R) | 52,145 | 51.1 |
| | Elmo J. Mahoney (D) | 49,933 | 48.9 |

## KENTUCKY

| | Candidates | Votes | % |
|---|---|---|---|
| 1 | Noble J. Gregory (D) | 75,726 | 100.0 |
| 2 | William H. Natcher (D) | 55,103 | 52.3 |
| | R. B. Blankenship (R) | 50,266 | 47.7 |
| 3 | John M. Robsion Jr. (R) | 111,598 | 56.8 |
| | Philip Ardery (D) | 84,912 | 43.2 |
| 4 | Frank Chelf (D) | 51,675 | 56.3 |
| | John B. Preston (R) | 40,129 | 43.7 |
| 5 | Brent Spence (D) | 59,402 | 55.9 |
| | Jule Appel (R) | 46,821 | 44.1 |
| 6 | John C. Watts (D) | 69,468 | 52.7 |
| | Wallace Jones (R) | 62,313 | 47.3 |
| 7 | Carl D. Perkins (D) | 77,564 | 52.4 |
| | Scott Craft (R) | 70,450 | 47.6 |
| 8 | Eugene Siler (R) | 80,067 | 71.7 |
| | W. D. Scalf (D) | 31,632 | 28.3 |

## LOUISIANA

| | Candidates | Votes | % |
|---|---|---|---|
| 1 | F. Edward Hebert (D) | 69,500 | 100.0 |
| 2 | Hale Boggs (D) | 69,715 | 64.5 |
| | George R. Blue (R) | 38,344 | 35.5 |
| 3 | Edwin E. Willis (D) | 19,075 | 100.0 |
| 4 | Overton Brooks (D) | 40,583 | 68.1 |
| | Calhoun Allen Jr. (R) | 19,041 | 31.9 |
| 5 | Otto E. Passman (D) | 18,210 | 100.0 |
| 6 | James H. Morrison (D) | 58,414 | 100.0 |
| 7 | T. A. Thompson (D) | 36,432 | 100.0 |
| 8 | George S. Long (D) | 18,341 | 100.0 |

## MAINE

| | Candidates | Votes | % |
|---|---|---|---|
| 1 | Robert Hale (R) | 58,028 | 50.0 |
| | James C. Oliver (D) | 57,999 | 50.0 |
| 2 | Frank M. Coffin (D) | 55,430 | 53.4 |
| | James L. Reid (R) | 48,292 | 46.6 |
| 3 | Clifford G. McIntire (R) | 44,095 | 60.7 |
| | Kenneth B. Colbath (D) | 28,612 | 39.4 |

## MARYLAND

| | Candidates | Votes | % |
|---|---|---|---|
| 1 | Edward T. Miller (R) | 42,731 | 55.7 |
| | Hamilton P. Fox (D) | 33,961 | 44.3 |
| 2 | James P. S. Devereux (R) | 103,103 | 58.1 |
| | A. Gordon Boone (D) | 74,224 | 41.9 |
| 3 | Edward A. Garmatz (D) | 48,397 | 69.8 |
| | Harry Kemper (R) | 20,990 | 30.3 |
| 4 | George H. Fallon (D) | 44,260 | 53.8 |
| | George Denys Hubbard (R) | 37,957 | 46.2 |
| 5 | Richard E. Lankford (D) | 88,227 | 56.8 |
| | William B. Prendergast (R) | 67,072 | 43.2 |
| 6 | Dewitt S. Hyde (R) | 100,580 | 54.3 |
| | John R. Foley (D) | 84,837 | 45.8 |
| 7 | Samuel N. Friedel (D) | 70,512 | 59.0 |
| | David A. Halley (R) | 48,949 | 41.0 |

## MASSACHUSETTS

| | Candidates | Votes | % |
|---|---|---|---|
| 1 | John W. Heselton (R) | 92,269 | 63.6 |
| | Howard W. Shea (D) | 52,213 | 36.0 |
| 2 | Edward P. Boland (D) | 103,563 | 61.2 |
| | Foster W. Doty (R) | 65,598 | 38.8 |
| 3 | Philip J. Philbin (D) | 114,848 | 70.9 |
| | Robert A. Parker (R) | 47,041 | 29.1 |
| 4 | Harold D. Donohue (D) | 104,653 | 59.4 |
| | Mary R. Wheeler (R) | 71,437 | 40.6 |
| 5 | Edith Nourse Rogers (R) | 150,957 | 73.3 |
| | Lawrence E. Corcoran (D) | 55,038 | 26.7 |
| 6 | William H. Bates (R) | 131,310 | 100.0 |
| 7 | Thomas J. Lane (D) | 87,415 | 64.5 |
| | Robert T. Breed (R) | 48,173 | 35.5 |
| 8 | Torbert H. Macdonald (D) | 92,463 | 54.8 |
| | C. Eugene Farnam (R) | 76,312 | 45.2 |
| 9 | Donald W. Nicholson (R) | 111,860 | 61.1 |
| | William McAuliffe (D) | 71,245 | 38.9 |
| 10 | Laurence Curtis (R) | 93,327 | 53.0 |
| | Jackson J. Holtz (D) | 82,882 | 47.0 |
| 11 | Thomas P. O'Neill Jr. (D) | 83,532 | 75.3 |
| | Rudolph E. Mottola (R) | 27,384 | 24.7 |
| 12 | John W. McCormack (D) | 89,943 | 82.5 |
| | James S. Tremblay (R) | 19,099 | 17.5 |
| 13 | Richard B. Wigglesworth (R) | 109,950 | 55.6 |
| | Richard E. McCormack (D) | 87,719 | 44.4 |
| 14 | Joseph W. Martin Jr. (R) | 111,420 | 62.4 |
| | Edward F. Doolan (D) | 67,183 | 37.6 |

## MICHIGAN

| | Candidates | Votes | % |
|---|---|---|---|
| 1 | Thaddeus M. Machrowicz (D) | 112,290 | 86.1 |
| | Walter Czarnecki (R) | 18,137 | 13.9 |
| 2 | George Meader (R) | 105,940 | 63.1 |
| | Franklin J. Shepherd (D) | 61,456 | 36.6 |
| 3 | August E. Johansen (R) | 100,056 | 63.8 |
| | Truman Barkhuff (D) | 56,119 | 35.8 |
| 4 | Clare E. Hoffman (R) | 83,876 | 62.0 |
| | Samuel I. Clark (D) | 51,491 | 38.0 |
| 5 | Gerald R. Ford Jr. (R) | 120,349 | 67.1 |
| | George E. Clay (D) | 58,899 | 32.9 |
| 6 | Charles E. Chamberlain (R) | 116,570 | 50.8 |
| | Don Hayworth (D) | 112,603 | 49.0 |
| 7 | Robert J. McIntosh (R) | 114,674 | 53.7 |
| | Ira D. McCoy (D) | 98,928 | 46.3 |
| 8 | Alvin M. Bentley (R) | 93,357 | 64.1 |
| | William R. Hart (D) | 51,897 | 35.6 |
| 9 | Robert P. Griffin (R) | 68,166 | 56.0 |
| | William E. Baker (D) | 53,609 | 44.0 |
| 10 | Elford A. Cederberg (R) | 72,781 | 65.6 |
| | William J. Kelly (D) | 38,166 | 34.4 |
| 11 | Victor A. Knox (R) | 53,117 | 56.1 |
| | Prentiss M. Brown Jr. (D) | 41,600 | 43.9 |
| 12 | John B. Bennett (R) | 45,721 | 56.3 |
| | Joseph S. Mack (D) | 35,434 | 43.7 |
| 13 | Charles C. Diggs Jr. (D) | 87,353 | 69.8 |
| | Willis F. Ward (R) | 37,860 | 30.2 |
| 14 | Louis C. Rabaut (D) | 122,079 | 56.8 |
| | Harold F. Youngblood (R) | 92,933 | 43.2 |
| 15 | John D. Dingell (D) | 111,827 | 74.1 |
| | Larry Middleton (R) | 38,973 | 25.8 |
| 16 | John Lesinski (D) | 176,663 | 64.1 |
| | Arthur Kurtz (R) | 98,172 | 35.6 |
| 17 | Martha W. Griffiths (D) | 112,811 | 53.3 |
| | George E. Smith (R) | 98,432 | 46.5 |
| 18 | William S. Broomfield (R) | 141,058 | 56.7 |
| | Paul Sutton (D) | 107,609 | 43.3 |

## MINNESOTA

| | Candidates | Votes | % |
|---|---|---|---|
| 1 | August H. Andresen (R) | 92,092 | 61.5 |
| | Arnold L. Fredriksen (DFL) | 57,747 | 38.5 |
| 2 | Joseph P. O'Hara (R) | 97,520 | 63.8 |
| | Harold Zupp (DFL) | 55,336 | 36.2 |
| 3 | Roy W. Wier (DFL) | 127,356 | 52.0 |
| | George Mikan (R) | 117,716 | 48.0 |
| 4 | Eugene J. McCarthy (DFL) | 103,320 | 64.1 |
| | Edward C. Slettedahl (R) | 57,947 | 35.9 |
| 5 | Walter H. Judd (R) | 82,258 | 56.0 |
| | Joseph Robbie (DFL) | 64,602 | 44.0 |
| 6 | Fred Marshall (DFL) | 76,396 | 56.2 |
| | Joseph L. Kaczmarek (R) | 59,568 | 43.8 |
| 7 | H. Carl Andersen (R) | 76,271 | 55.9 |
| | Clint Haroldson (DFL) | 60,168 | 44.1 |
| 8 | John A. Blatnik (DFL) | 108,565 | 73.2 |
| | Alfred J. Weinberg (R) | 39,795 | 26.8 |
| 9 | Coya Knutson (DFL) | 58,916 | 52.7 |
| | Harold C. Hagen (R) | 52,937 | 47.3 |

## MISSISSIPPI

| | Candidates | Votes | % |
|---|---|---|---|
| 1 | Thomas G. Abernethy (D) | 38,021 | 100.0 |
| 2 | Jamie L. Whitten (D) | 23,513 | 100.0 |
| 3 | Frank E. Smith (D) | 19,369 | 100.0 |
| 4 | John Bell Williams (D) | 42,085 | 100.0 |
| 5 | Arthur Winstead (D) | 35,461 | 100.0 |
| 6 | William M. Colmer (D) | 47,083 | 100.0 |

## MISSOURI

| | Candidates | Votes | % |
|---|---|---|---|
| 1 | Frank M. Karsten (D) | 136,873 | 66.3 |
| | Bill Bangert (R) | 69,661 | 33.7 |
| 2 | Thomas B. Curtis (R) | 123,596 | 51.8 |
| | James L. Sullivan (D) | 114,837 | 48.2 |
| 3 | Leonor K. Sullivan (D) | 96,416 | 69.7 |
| | Sidney R. Redmond (R) | 42,023 | 30.4 |
| 4 | George H. Christopher (D) | 98,106 | 51.8 |
| | Jeffrey P. Hillelson (R) | 91,392 | 48.2 |
| 5 | Richard Bolling (D) | 77,287 | 57.2 |
| | Lemot Jones Jr. (R) | 57,778 | 42.8 |
| 6 | W. R. Hull Jr. (D) | 85,021 | 52.0 |
| | Stanley I. Dale (R) | 78,637 | 48.1 |
| 7 | Charles H. Brown (D) | 90,986 | 50.3 |
| | Dewey Short (R) | 89,926 | 49.7 |
| 8 | A. S. J. Carnahan (D) | 69,336 | 54.3 |
| | Frank W. May (R) | 58,425 | 45.7 |
| 9 | Clarence Cannon (D) | 100,065 | 100.0 |
| 10 | Paul C. Jones (D) | 69,536 | 100.0 |

### MISSOURI

| Candidates | Votes | % |
|---|---|---|
| 11 Morgan M. Moulder (D) | 72,594 | 50.8 |
| George H. Miller (R) | 70,286 | 49.2 |

### MONTANA

| | Votes | % |
|---|---|---|
| 1 Lee Metcalf (D) | 69,644 | 62.1 |
| W. D. McDonald (R) | 42,591 | 38.0 |
| 2 Leroy H. Anderson (D) | 76,805 | 50.9 |
| Orvin B. Fjare (R) | 74,164 | 49.1 |

### NEBRASKA

| | Votes | % |
|---|---|---|
| 1 Phil Weaver (R) | 102,012 | 67.0 |
| Samuel Freeman (D) | 50,351 | 33.1 |
| 2 Glenn Cunningham (R) | 77,253 | 53.4 |
| Joseph V. Benesch (D) | 65,039 | 45.0 |
| 3 Robert D. Harrison (R) | 62,645 | 50.1 |
| Lawrence Brock (D) | 62,399 | 49.9 |
| 4 Arthur L. Miller (R) | 81,731 | 65.8 |
| Carlton W. Laird (D) | 42,583 | 34.3 |

### NEVADA

| | Votes | % |
|---|---|---|
| AL Walter S. Baring (D) | 51,100 | 54.2 |
| Richard W. Horton (R) | 43,154 | 45.8 |

### NEW HAMPSHIRE

| | Votes | % |
|---|---|---|
| 1 Chester E. Merrow (R) | 78,296 | 57.4 |
| James B. Sullivan (D) | 58,104 | 42.6 |
| 2 Perkins Bass (R) | 77,019 | 66.0 |
| George F. Brown (D) | 39,726 | 34.0 |

### NEW JERSEY

| | Votes | % |
|---|---|---|
| 1 Charles A. Wolverton (R) | 133,153 | 58.3 |
| J. Frank Crawford (D) | 94,758 | 41.5 |
| 2 T. Millet Hand (R) | 83,433* | 67.9 |
| Thomas E. Stewart (D) | 39,383 | 32.0 |
| 3 James C. Auchincloss (R) | 136,780 | 65.3 |
| Sidney Shiff (D) | 72,617 | 34.7 |
| 4 Frank Thompson Jr. (D) | 89,646 | 54.5 |
| William H. Wells (R) | 74,737 | 45.5 |
| 5 Peter H. B. Frelinghuysen Jr. (R) | 153,829 | 64.5 |
| Francis C. Foley Jr. (D) | 84,374 | 35.4 |
| 6 Florence P. Dwyer (R) | 106,414 | 50.6 |
| Harrison A. Williams Jr. (D) | 102,015 | 48.5 |
| 7 William B. Widnall (R) | 151,573 | 70.7 |
| Daniel Amster (D) | 62,924 | 29.3 |
| 8 Gordon Canfield (R) | 96,494 | 60.8 |
| Walter H. Gardner (D) | 61,464 | 38.7 |
| 9 Frank C. Osmers Jr. (R) | 135,498 | 67.8 |
| Robert D. Gruen (D) | 63,728 | 31.9 |
| 10 Peter W. Rodino Jr. (D) | 71,311 | 56.1 |
| G. George Addonizio (R) | 55,761 | 43.9 |
| 11 Hugh J. Addonizio (D) | 63,482 | 51.7 |
| Chester K. Ligham (R) | 57,447 | 46.8 |
| 12 Robert Winthrop Kean (R) | 90,032 | 59.7 |
| Irving L. Hodes (D) | 58,364 | 38.7 |
| 13 Alfred D. Sieminski (D) | 54,841 | 45.0 |
| Norman H. Roth (R) | 54,784 | 44.9 |
| 14 Vincent J. Dellay (D) | 61,600 | 52.3 |
| T. James Tumulty (D) | 53,713 | 45.6 |

### NEW MEXICO

| | Votes | % |
|---|---|---|
| AL John J. Dempsey (D) | 129,625✔ | |
| Antonio M. Fernandez (D) | 128,330* | |
| Dudley Cornell (R) | 114,719 | |
| Forrest Atchley (R) | 112,531 | |

### NEW YORK

| Candidates | Votes | % |
|---|---|---|
| 1 Stuyvesant Wainwright (R) | 191,356 | 65.8 |
| T. Bronson O'Reilly (D, L) | 99,304 | 34.2 |
| 2 Steven B. Derounian (R) | 148,098 | 67.5 |
| Julius J. Damato (D, L) | 71,422 | 32.5 |
| 3 Frank J. Becker (R) | 143,559 | 61.9 |
| Francis X. Hardiman (D, L) | 88,245 | 38.1 |
| 4 Henry J. Latham (R) | 116,470 | 55.8 |
| Joseph J. Perrini (D, L) | 92,217 | 44.2 |
| 5 Albert H. Bosch (R) | 87,154 | 58.6 |
| John J. Quinn (D, L) | 61,678 | 41.4 |
| 6 Lester Holtzman (D, L) | 128,545 | 56.9 |
| Albert H. Buschmann (R) | 97,558 | 43.2 |
| 7 James J. Delaney (D, L) | 78,030 | 50.0 |
| Joseph Stockinger (R) | 77,928 | 50.0 |
| 8 Victor L. Anfuso (D, L) | 59,998 | 65.6 |
| Julius Reinlieb (R) | 31,399 | 34.4 |
| 9 Eugene J. Keogh (D, L) | 75,814 | 62.8 |
| Benjamin W. Feldman (R) | 44,016 | 37.2 |
| 10 Edna F. Kelly (D, L) | 100,808 | 73.2 |
| Abraham Sher (R) | 36,878 | 26.8 |
| 11 Emanuel Celler (D, L) | 131,508 | 77.7 |
| Henry D. Dorfman (R) | 37,651 | 22.3 |
| 12 Francis E. Dorn (R) | 76,137 | 57.6 |
| Donald L. O'Toole (D, L) | 56,035 | 42.4 |
| 13 Abraham J. Multer (D, L) | 110,469 | 71.2 |
| Joseph Moriber (R) | 44,771 | 28.8 |
| 14 John J. Rooney (D, L) | 77,706 | 64.2 |
| Jacob P. Lefkowitz (R) | 43,343 | 35.8 |
| 15 John H. Ray (R) | 98,093 | 61.4 |
| Ralph Di Iorio (D, L) | 60,989 | 38.2 |
| 16 Adam Clayton Powell Jr. (D) | 59,339 | 69.7 |
| Joseph A. Bailey (R) | 16,960 | 19.9 |
| Formington Taylor (L) | 8,801 | 10.3 |
| 17 Frederic R. Coudert Jr. (R) | 68,874 | 50.9 |
| Anthony B. Akers (D, L) | 66,396 | 49.1 |
| 18 Alfred E. Santangelo (D, L) | 47,953 | 58.0 |
| James G. Donovan (R) | 34,748 | 42.0 |
| 19 Leonard Farbstein (D, L) | 68,411 | 68.4 |
| Maurice G. Henry Jr. (R) | 31,546 | 31.6 |
| 20 Ludwig Teller (D, L) | 70,726 | 63.8 |
| Milton H. Adler (R) | 40,191 | 36.2 |
| 21 Herbert Zelenko (D, L) | 81,464 | 66.5 |
| Dalton J. Shapo (R) | 41,070 | 33.5 |
| 22 James C. Healey (D) | 88,441 | 64.1 |
| Henry Rose (R) | 34,084 | 24.7 |
| David I. Wells (L) | 15,524 | 11.3 |
| 23 Isidore Dollinger (D) | 70,238 | 68.5 |
| Philip Myer (R) | 22,414 | 21.9 |
| Hyman Fromowitz (L) | 9,880 | 9.6 |
| 24 Charles A. Buckley (D) | 90,076 | 54.7 |
| Harold Grosberg (R) | 53,172 | 32.3 |
| Elias Rosenblatt (L) | 21,444 | 13.0 |
| 25 Paul A. Fino (R) | 104,771 | 59.4 |
| Edward A. Cunningham (D) | 62,729 | 35.5 |
| Bernard Tobacman (L) | 8,989 | 5.1 |
| 26 Edwin B. Dooley (R) | 123,996 | 67.5 |
| Julia L. Crews (D, L) | 59,842 | 32.6 |
| 27 Ralph W. Gwinn (R) | 117,100 | 58.1 |
| William D. Carlebach (D, L) | 84,568 | 41.9 |
| 28 Katharine St.George (R) | 103,114 | 62.2 |
| William H. Mauldin (D, L) | 62,770 | 37.8 |
| 29 J. Ernest Wharton (R) | 124,211 | 71.4 |
| Vincent di Gennaro (D, L) | 49,725 | 28.6 |
| 30 Leo W. O'Brien (D, L) | 104,022 | 55.8 |
| Robert E. Gray (R) | 82,429 | 44.2 |
| 31 Dean P. Taylor (R) | 116,682 | 71.8 |
| Theodore A. Knapp (D, L) | 45,767 | 28.2 |
| 32 Bernard W. Kearney (R) | 107,959 | 67.5 |
| R. Joseph Giblin (D, L) | 52,064 | 32.5 |
| 33 Clarence E. Kilburn (R) | 103,419 | 72.7 |
| Louis C. Britton (D, L) | 38,793 | 27.3 |
| 34 William R. Williams (R) | 95,681 | 57.5 |
| Edwin L. Slusarczyk (D, L) | 70,837 | 42.5 |
| 35 R. Walter Riehlman (R) | 124,108 | 67.1 |
| Thomas J. Lowery (D) | 59,534 | 32.2 |
| 36 John Taber (R) | 109,101 | 69.6 |
| Lewis S. Bell (D, L) | 47,764 | 30.4 |
| 37 Sterling Cole (R) | 136,044 | 71.7 |
| Francis P. Hogan (D, L) | 53,830 | 28.4 |
| 38 Kenneth B. Keating (R) | 135,572 | 71.7 |
| Reed Harding (D, L) | 53,477 | 28.3 |
| 39 Harold C. Ostertag (R) | 116,043 | 70.5 |
| William H. Mostyn (D, L) | 48,634 | 29.5 |
| 40 William E. Miller (R) | 117,051 | 64.3 |
| A. Thorne Hills (D, L) | 64,872 | 35.7 |
| 41 Edmund P. Radwan (R) | 99,151 | 64.4 |
| Edward P. Jehle (D, L) | 54,776 | 35.6 |
| 42 John R. Pillion (R) | 117,178 | 58.7 |
| James Kane Jr. (D) | 80,568 | 40.3 |
| 43 Daniel A. Reed (R) | 93,079 | 68.7 |
| T. Joseph Lynch (D, L) | 42,476 | 31.3 |

#### Special Election

| | Votes | % |
|---|---|---|
| 22 James C. Healey (D) | 9,473 | 72.3 |
| Sidney Burnstein (L) | 1,943 | 14.8 |
| Barnett Davis (R) | 1,691 | 12.9 |

### NORTH CAROLINA

| | Votes | % |
|---|---|---|
| 1 Herbert C. Bonner (D) | 44,271 | 88.6 |
| Zeno O. Ratcliff (R) | 5,693 | 11.4 |
| 2 L. H. Fountain (D) | 49,812 | 100.0 |
| 3 Graham A. Barden (D) | 47,251 | 78.8 |
| Joe Reynolds (R) | 12,698 | 21.2 |
| 4 Harold D. Cooley (D) | 76,560 | 100.0 |
| 5 Ralph J. Scott (D) | 58,552 | 59.7 |
| Joe New (R) | 39,561 | 40.3 |
| 6 Carl T. Durham (D) | 73,111 | 100.0 |
| 7 Alton Lennon (D) | 65,424 | 84.0 |
| C. Dana Malpass (R) | 12,477 | 16.0 |
| 8 A. Paul Kitchin (D) | 64,220 | 59.5 |
| Fred Myers (R) | 43,732 | 40.5 |
| 9 Hugh Q. Alexander (D) | 68,181 | 53.9 |
| A. M. Miller (R) | 58,407 | 46.1 |
| 10 Charles Raper Jonas (R) | 89,743 | 62.7 |
| Ben E. Douglas (D) | 53,475 | 37.3 |
| 11 Basil L. Whitener (D) | 59,417 | 100.0 |
| 12 George A. Shuford (D) | 55,927 | 54.5 |
| Richard C. Clarke Jr. (R) | 46,760 | 45.5 |

### NORTH DAKOTA

| | Votes | % |
|---|---|---|
| AL Usher L. Burdick (R) | 143,514✔ | |
| Otto Krueger (R) | 136,003✔ | |
| Agnes Geelan (D) | 85,743 | |
| S. B. Hocking (D) | 83,284 | |

### OHIO

| | Votes | % |
|---|---|---|
| 1 Gordon H. Scherer (R) | 91,181 | 64.7 |
| Leonard D. Slutz (D) | 49,701 | 35.3 |
| 2 William E. Hess (R) | 109,099 | 65.5 |
| James T. Dewan (D) | 57,554 | 34.5 |
| 3 Paul F. Schenck (R) | 135,152 | 59.0 |
| R. William Patterson (D) | 93,782 | 41.0 |
| 4 William M. McCulloch (R) | 93,607 | 68.8 |
| Ortha O. Barr Jr. (D) | 42,416 | 31.2 |
| 5 Cliff Clevenger (R) | 69,774 | 62.3 |
| George E. Rafferty (D) | 42,181 | 37.7 |
| 6 James G. Polk (D) | 72,229 | 54.5 |
| Albert L. Daniels (R) | 60,300 | 45.5 |
| 7 Clarence J. Brown (R) | 91,439 | 66.0 |
| Joseph A. Sullivan (D) | 47,220 | 34.1 |
| 8 Jackson E. Betts (R) | 70,690 | 63.5 |
| Robert M. Corry (D) | 40,716 | 36.6 |
| 9 Thomas L. Ashley (D) | 100,696 | 55.3 |
| Harvey G. Straub (R) | 81,562 | 44.8 |
| 10 Thomas A. Jenkins (R) | 71,295 | 100.0 |
| 11 David S. Dennison Jr. (R) | 96,707 | 58.4 |
| James P. Bennett (D) | 68,831 | 41.6 |
| 12 John M. Vorys (R) | 128,682 | 61.8 |
| Walter J. Shapter Jr. (D) | 79,597 | 38.2 |
| 13 A. D. Baumhart Jr. (R) | 79,324 | 70.7 |
| J. P. Henderson (D) | 32,900 | 29.3 |
| 14 William H. Ayres (R) | 123,105 | 58.9 |
| Bernard Rosen (D) | 85,946 | 41.1 |
| 15 John E. Henderson (R) | 55,126 | 60.5 |
| Herbert U. Smith (D) | 35,954 | 39.5 |

## OHIO

| | Candidates | Votes | % |
|---|---|---|---|
| 16 | Frank T. Bow (R) | 101,324 | 55.2 |
| | John McSweeney (D) | 82,206 | 44.8 |
| 17 | J. Harry McGregor (R) | 88,931 | 66.5 |
| | Robert W. Levering (D) | 44,806 | 33.5 |
| 18 | Wayne L. Hays (D) | 78,962 | 59.6 |
| | Joseph Miller (R) | 53,627 | 40.5 |
| 19 | Michael J. Kirwan (D) | 92,924 | 68.7 |
| | Ralph E. Turner (R) | 42,293 | 31.3 |
| 20 | Michael A. Feighan (D) | 105,562 | 65.3 |
| | John H. Ferguson (R) | 56,209 | 34.8 |
| 21 | Charles A. Vanik (D) | 96,106 | 71.6 |
| | Charles H. Loeb (R) | 38,060 | 28.4 |
| 22 | Frances P. Bolton (R) | 96,468 | 66.7 |
| | Harry A. Blachman (D) | 48,169 | 33.3 |
| 23 | William E. Minshall Jr. (R) | 102,707 | 69.0 |
| | George A. Hurley (D) | 46,247 | 31.1 |

## OKLAHOMA

| | Candidates | Votes | % |
|---|---|---|---|
| 1 | Page Belcher (R) | 114,896 | 57.2 |
| | Harry B. Moreland (D) | 86,123 | 42.8 |
| 2 | Ed Edmondson (D) | 83,976 | 60.2 |
| | Percy Butler (R) | 55,416 | 39.8 |
| 3 | Carl Albert (D) | 60,620 | 76.5 |
| | Chapin Wallace (R) | 18,182 | 23.0 |
| 4 | Tom Steed (D) | 57,416 | 61.1 |
| | Harold H. Potter (R) | 36,534 | 38.9 |
| 5 | John Jarman (D) | 110,416 | 63.7 |
| | Hobart H. Hobbs (R) | 62,812 | 36.3 |
| 6 | Toby Morris (D) | 86,770 | 68.9 |
| | Fred L. Coogan (R) | 39,153 | 31.1 |

## OREGON

| | Candidates | Votes | % |
|---|---|---|---|
| 1 | Walter Norblad (R) | 109,360 | 54.7 |
| | Jason Lee (D) | 90,567 | 45.3 |
| 2 | Al Ullman (D) | 53,219 | 50.7 |
| | Sam Coon (R) | 51,844 | 49.4 |
| 3 | Edith Green (D) | 146,250 | 61.6 |
| | Phil J. Roth (R) | 91,239 | 38.4 |
| 4 | Charles O. Porter (D) | 90,355 | 51.3 |
| | Harris Ellsworth (R) | 85,860 | 48.7 |

## PENNSYLVANIA

| | Candidates | Votes | % |
|---|---|---|---|
| 1 | William A. Barrett (D) | 74,511 | 62.7 |
| | A. J. Cammarota (R) | 44,333 | 37.3 |
| 2 | Kathryn E. Granahan (D) | 95,567 | 62.3 |
| | Robert F. Frankenfield (R) | 57,773 | 37.7 |
| 3 | James A. Byrne (D) | 71,161 | 59.9 |
| | Charles J. Sporkin (R) | 47,550 | 40.1 |
| 4 | Earl Chudoff (D) | 75,374 | 69.1 |
| | Horace C. Scott (R) | 33,672 | 30.9 |
| 5 | William J. Green Jr. (D) | 107,021 | 53.3 |
| | James J. Schissler (R) | 93,612 | 46.7 |
| 6 | Hugh Scott (R) | 90,966 | 51.5 |
| | Herbert J. McGlinchey (D) | 85,541 | 48.5 |
| 7 | Benjamin F. James (R) | 137,764 | 61.9 |
| | William A. Welsh (D) | 84,764 | 38.1 |
| 8 | Willard S. Curtin (R) | 98,023 | 55.9 |
| | John P. Fullam (D) | 77,229 | 44.1 |
| 9 | Paul B. Dague (R) | 110,230 | 68.4 |
| | Edward G. Wilson (D) | 50,947 | 31.6 |
| 10 | Joseph L. Carrigg (R) | 91,103 | 55.8 |
| | Jerome P. Casey (D) | 72,178 | 44.2 |
| 11 | Daniel J. Flood (D) | 83,178 | 53.1 |
| | Enoch H. Thomas Jr. (R) | 73,606 | 47.0 |
| 12 | Ivor D. Fenton (R) | 72,125 | 56.5 |
| | George G. Lindsay (D) | 55,642 | 43.6 |
| 13 | Samuel K. McConnell Jr. (R) | 127,627 | 66.7 |
| | Alfred M. Klein (D) | 63,610 | 33.3 |
| 14 | George M. Rhodes (D) | 51,088 | 51.3 |
| | Thomas K. Leinbach (R) | 48,129 | 48.4 |
| 15 | Francis E. Walter (D) | 63,204 | 55.6 |
| | George M. Berg (R) | 50,491 | 44.4 |
| 16 | Walter M. Mumma (R) | 84,617 | 60.5 |
| | Guy J. Swope (D) | 55,260 | 39.5 |
| 17 | Alvin R. Bush (R) | 74,748 | 58.6 |
| | Dean R. Fisher (D) | 52,900 | 41.4 |
| 18 | Richard M. Simpson (R) | 77,833 | 59.9 |
| | Ross E. Hershberger (D) | 52,180 | 40.1 |
| 19 | S. Walter Stauffer (R) | 79,448 | 53.8 |
| | James M. Quigley (D) | 68,171 | 46.2 |
| 20 | James E. Van Zandt (R) | 65,457 | 63.0 |
| | John R. Stewart (D) | 38,483 | 37.0 |
| 21 | Augustine B. Kelley (D) | 78,744 | 56.8 |
| | Herbert O. Morrison (R) | 59,786 | 43.2 |
| 22 | John P. Saylor (R) | 85,540 | 56.9 |
| | Joseph C. Dolan (D) | 64,689 | 43.1 |
| 23 | Leon H. Gavin (R) | 72,365 | 66.1 |
| | Grace M. Sloan (D) | 37,122 | 33.9 |
| 24 | Carroll D. Kearns (R) | 93,824 | 57.8 |
| | William D. Thomas (D) | 68,625 | 42.2 |
| 25 | Frank M. Clark (D) | 81,339 | 51.3 |
| | Sidney L. Lockley (R) | 77,150 | 48.7 |
| 26 | Thomas E. Morgan (D) | 104,049 | 61.9 |
| | I. Willits McCaskey (R) | 64,129 | 38.1 |
| 27 | James G. Fulton (R) | 126,247 | 66.0 |
| | Kenneth L. Stilley (D) | 64,917 | 34.0 |
| 28 | Herman P. Eberharter (D) | 88,725 | 57.8 |
| | Richard C. Witt (R) | 64,905 | 42.3 |
| 29 | Robert J. Corbett (R) | 114,109 | 64.7 |
| | Joseph A. Guerrier (D) | 62,225 | 35.3 |
| 30 | Elmer J. Holland (D) | 103,389 | 59.8 |
| | Ross V. Walker (R) | 69,495 | 40.2 |

## RHODE ISLAND

| | Candidates | Votes | % |
|---|---|---|---|
| 1 | Aime J. Forand (D) | 96,732 | 55.8 |
| | Samuel H. Ramsay (R) | 76,714 | 44.2 |
| 2 | John E. Fogarty (D) | 105,496 | 52.2 |
| | Thomas H. Needham (R) | 96,568 | 47.8 |

## SOUTH CAROLINA

| | Candidates | Votes | % |
|---|---|---|---|
| 1 | L. Mendel Rivers (D) | 31,112 | 100.0 |
| 2 | John J. Riley (D) | 49,284 | 100.0 |
| 3 | W. J. Bryan Dorn (D) | 39,270 | 92.9 |
| | Mrs. Maka Knox (R) | 2,885 | 6.8 |
| 4 | Robert T. Ashmore (D) | 53,722 | 85.1 |
| | Dan H. Wallace Jr (R) | 9,393 | 14.9 |
| 5 | Robert Hemphill (D) | 36,454 | 100.0 |
| 6 | John L. McMillan (D) | 39,749 | 100.0 |

## SOUTH DAKOTA

| | Candidates | Votes | % |
|---|---|---|---|
| 1 | George McGovern (D) | 116,516 | 52.4 |
| | Harold O. Lovre (R) | 105,835 | 47.6 |
| 2 | E. Y. Berry (R) | 36,681 | 55.9 |
| | Tom Eastman Jr. (D) | 28,984 | 44.1 |

## TENNESSEE

| | Candidates | Votes | % |
|---|---|---|---|
| 1 | B. Carroll Reece (R) | 86,531 | 72.1 |
| | Arthur Bright (D) | 33,403 | 27.9 |
| 2 | Howard H. Baker (R) | 90,127 | 100.0 |
| 3 | James B. Frazier Jr. (D) | 55,715 | 53.7 |
| | P. H. Wood (R) | 47,954 | 46.3 |
| 4 | Joe L. Evins (D) | 56,191 | 98.4 |
| 5 | J. Carlton Loser (D) | 54,318 | 74.5 |
| | George S. Spence (R) | 18,585 | 25.5 |
| 6 | Ross Bass (D) | 47,098 | 100.0 |
| 7 | Tom Murray (D) | 36,301 | 100.0 |
| 8 | Jere Cooper (D) | 27,485 | 100.0 |
| 9 | Clifford Davis (D) | 90,874 | 71.8 |
| | Herbert Harper (R) | 35,783 | 28.3 |

## TEXAS

| | Candidates | Votes | % |
|---|---|---|---|
| 1 | Wright Patman (D) | 54,837 | 100.0 |
| 2 | Jack Brooks (D) | 81,343 | 100.0 |
| 3 | Lindley Beckworth (D) | 47,570 | 83.5 |
| | R. E. Kennedy (R) | 9,402 | 16.5 |
| 4 | Sam Rayburn (D) | 41,867 | 100.0 |
| 5 | Bruce Alger (R) | 102,380 | 55.6 |
| | Henry Wade (D) | 81,705 | 44.4 |
| 6 | Olin Teague (D) | 42,383 | 100.0 |
| 7 | John Dowdy (D) | 44,456 | 100.0 |
| 8 | Albert Thomas (D) | 137,950 | 60.5 |
| | C. A. Friloux Jr. (R) | 86,640 | 38.0 |
| 9 | Clark W. Thompson (D) | 88,487 | 100.0 |
| 10 | Homer Thornberry (D) | 68,697 | 100.0 |
| 11 | W. R. Poage (D) | 56,990 | 100.0 |
| 12 | Jim Wright (D) | 110,196 | 100.0 |
| 13 | Frank Ikard (D) | 66,108 | 100.0 |
| 14 | John Young (D) | 85,922 | 87.3 |
| | Olive B. Stichter (R) | 12,517 | 12.7 |
| 15 | Joe M. Kilgore (D) | 64,011 | 100.0 |
| 16 | J. T. Rutherford (D) | 50,704 | 64.6 |
| | Charles H. Gibson (R) | 27,821 | 35.4 |
| 17 | Omar Burleson (D) | 53,003 | 100.0 |
| 18 | Walter Rogers (D) | 75,243 | 100.0 |
| 19 | George Mahon (D) | 85,566 | 100.0 |
| 20 | Paul J. Kilday (D) | 67,707 | 100.0 |
| 21 | O. C. Fisher (D) | 60,344 | 100.0 |
| AL | Martin Dies (D) | 1,436,831 | 98.5 |

## UTAH

| | Candidates | Votes | % |
|---|---|---|---|
| 1 | Henry Aldous Dixon (R) | 74,107 | 60.9 |
| | Carlyle F. Gronning (D) | 47,533 | 39.1 |
| 2 | William A. Dawson (R) | 119,683 | 57.6 |
| | Oscar W. McConkie Jr. (D) | 87,970 | 42.4 |

## VERMONT

| | Candidates | Votes | % |
|---|---|---|---|
| AL | Winston L. Prouty (R) | 103,736 | 67.1 |
| | Camille E. St. Amour (D) | 50,797 | 32.9 |

## VIRGINIA

| | Candidates | Votes | % |
|---|---|---|---|
| 1 | Edward J. Robeson Jr. (D) | 31,839 | 50.8 |
| | Horace E. Henderson (R) | 30,799 | 49.2 |
| 2 | Porter Hardy Jr. (D) | 46,958 | 76.4 |
| | William R. Burns (R) | 14,483 | 23.6 |
| 3 | J. Vaughan Gary (D) | 46,109 | 59.1 |
| | Roy E. Cabell Jr. (R) | 31,947 | 40.9 |
| 4 | Watkins M. Abbitt (D) | 51,434 | 99.9 |
| 5 | William M. Tuck (D) | 39,771 | 67.4 |
| | Jackson L. Kiser (R) | 19,263 | 32.6 |
| 6 | Richard H. Poff (R) | 51,279 | 62.1 |
| | John L. Whitehead (D) | 31,043 | 37.6 |
| 7 | Burr P. Harrison (D) | 40,069 | 69.0 |
| | A. R. Dunning (R) | 17,970 | 31.0 |
| 8 | Howard W. Smith (D) | 38,648 | 67.3 |
| | Horace B. Clay (R) | 18,813 | 32.7 |
| 9 | W. Pat Jennings (D) | 49,448 | 54.1 |
| | William C. Wampler (R) | 41,957 | 45.9 |
| 10 | Joel T. Broyhill (R) | 53,149 | 56.2 |
| | Warren D. Quenstedt (D) | 40,553 | 42.9 |

## WASHINGTON

| | Candidates | Votes | % |
|---|---|---|---|
| 1 | Thomas M. Pelly (R) | 129,768 | 58.1 |
| | James B. Wilson (D) | 93,492 | 41.9 |
| 2 | Jack Westland (R) | 105,975 | 56.0 |
| | Payson Peterson (D) | 83,195 | 44.0 |
| 3 | Russell V. Mack (R) | 80,520 | 56.5 |
| | Al McCoy (D) | 61,962 | 43.5 |
| 4 | Hal Holmes (R) | 76,769 | 50.4 |
| | Frank LeRoux (D) | 75,519 | 49.6 |
| 5 | Walt Horan (R) | 83,230 | 53.8 |
| | Tom Delaney (D) | 71,571 | 46.2 |
| 6 | Thor C. Tollefson (R) | 108,014 | 54.0 |
| | John T. McCutcheon (D) | 91,878 | 46.0 |
| AL | Don Magnuson (D) | 621,118 | 58.5 |
| | Philip Evans (R) | 439,896 | 41.5 |

### WEST VIRGINIA

| Candidates | Votes | % |
|---|---|---|
| 1 Arch A. Moore Jr. (R) | 65,096 | 50.3 |
| C. Lee Spillers (D) | 64,334 | 49.7 |
| 2 Harley O. Staggers (D) | 63,327 | 52.4 |
| Mary Elkins (R) | 57,597 | 47.6 |
| 3 Cleveland M. Bailey (D) | 62,240 | 51.5 |
| Daniel L. Louchery (R) | 58,623 | 48.5 |
| 4 Will E. Neal (R) | 78,225 | 52.8 |
| M. G. Burnside (D) | 69,871 | 47.2 |
| 5 Elizabeth Kee (D) | 68,638 | 60.7 |
| William H. Sanders (R) | 44,479 | 39.3 |
| 6 Robert C. Byrd (D) | 99,854 | 57.4 |
| Cleo S. Jones (R) | 74,110 | 42.6 |

### WISCONSIN

| Candidates | Votes | % |
|---|---|---|
| 1 Lawrence H. Smith (R) | 94,882 | 57.1 |
| Gerald T. Flynn (D) | 71,379 | 42.9 |
| 2 Donald E. Tewes (R) | 101,444 | 55.3 |
| Robert W. Kastenmeier (D) | 81,922 | 44.7 |
| 3 Gardner R. Withrow (R) | 74,000 | 61.2 |
| Norman M. Clapp (D) | 46,911 | 38.8 |
| 4 Clement J. Zablocki (D) | 128,213 | 65.7 |
| William J. Burke (R) | 67,063 | 34.3 |
| 5 Henry S. Reuss (D) | 118,603 | 57.8 |
| Russell Wirth Jr. (R) | 86,764 | 42.3 |
| 6 William K. Van Pelt (R) | 96,783 | 67.2 |
| Rudolph J. Ploetz (D) | 47,277 | 32.8 |

| Candidates | Votes | % |
|---|---|---|
| 7 Melvin R. Laird (R) | 80,143 | 61.9 |
| Margaret Anderson (D) | 49,442 | 38.2 |
| 8 John W. Byrnes (R) | 97,952 | 64.7 |
| Milo Singler (D) | 53,567 | 35.4 |
| 9 Lester R. Johnson (D) | 62,476 | 51.4 |
| Arthur L. Peterson (R) | 59,024 | 48.6 |
| 10 Alvin E. O'Konski (R) | 67,250 | 64.5 |
| Carl E. Lauri (D) | 36,941 | 35.5 |

### WYOMING

| | Votes | % |
|---|---|---|
| AL Keith Thomson (R) | 69,903 | 58.2 |
| Jerry A. O'Callaghan (D) | 50,225 | 41.8 |

# 1957 House Elections

### ILLINOIS

**Special Election**

| | Votes | % |
|---|---|---|
| 7 Roland V. Libonati (D) | 32,221 | 88.1 |
| Anthony C. Catena (R) | 4,353 | 11.9 |

### NEW JERSEY

**Special Election**

| | Votes | % |
|---|---|---|
| 2 Milton W. Glenn (R) | 58,129 | 54.8 |
| Joseph G. Hancock (D) | 47,647 | 44.9 |

---

## House Candidates Index

For an index of all House candidates listed in this section (pages 943-1326), see pages 1402-1501. Instructions for use of the House Candidates Index appear on page 1402.

---

# 1958 House Elections

## ALABAMA

| | Candidates | Votes | % |
|---|---|---|---|
| 1 | Frank W. Boykin (D) | 19,499 | 100.0 |
| 2 | George Grant (D) | 27,972 | 100.0 |
| 3 | George W. Andrews (D) | 17,389 | 100.0 |
| 4 | Kenneth A. Roberts (D) | 25,133 | 100.0 |
| 5 | Albert Rains (D) | 31,687 | 100.0 |
| 6 | Armistead I. Selden Jr. (D) | 18,557 | 100.0 |
| 7 | Carl Elliott (D) | 29,936 | 100.0 |
| 8 | Robert E. Jones (D) | 22,710 | 100.0 |
| 9 | George Huddleston Jr. (D) | 38,229 | 86.3 |
| | Frank L. Mason (R) | 6,050 | 13.7 |

## ALASKA

(Became a state Jan. 3, 1959)

| | Candidates | Votes | % |
|---|---|---|---|
| AL | Ralph J. Rivers (D) | 27,945 | 57.5 |
| | Henry A. Benson (R) | 20,699 | 42.6 |

## ARIZONA

| | Candidates | Votes | % |
|---|---|---|---|
| 1 | John J. Rhodes (R) | 86,959 | 59.3 |
| | Joe Haldiman Jr. (D) | 59,816 | 40.8 |
| 2 | Stewart L. Udall (D) | 79,651 | 60.9 |
| | John G. Speiden (R) | 51,140 | 39.1 |

## ARKANSAS

| | Candidates | Votes | % |
|---|---|---|---|
| 1 | Ezekiel C. Gathings (D) | | 100.0 |
| 2 | Wilbur D. Mills (D) | | 100.0 |
| 3 | James W. Trimble (D) | | 100.0 |
| 4 | Oren Harris (D) | | 100.0 |
| 5 | Dale Alford (WRITE IN) | 30,739 | 51.0 |
| | Brooks Hays (D) | 29,483 | 49.0 |
| 6 | William F. Norrell (D) | | 100.0 |

## CALIFORNIA

| | Candidates | Votes | % |
|---|---|---|---|
| 1 | Clem W. Miller (D) | 102,096 | 54.9 |
| | Frederick G. Dupuis (R) | 83,807 | 45.1 |
| 2 | Harold T. Johnson (D) | 90,850 | 61.0 |
| | Curtis W. Tarr (R) | 58,199 | 39.1 |
| 3 | John E. Moss (D-R) | 169,727 | 100.0 |
| 4 | William S. Mailliard (R) | 98,574 | 60.0 |
| | George D. Collins Jr. (D) | 65,798 | 40.0 |
| 5 | John F. Shelley (D-R) | 99,171 | 100.0 |
| 6 | John F. Baldwin Jr. (R) | 92,669 | 51.0 |
| | Howard H. Jewel (D) | 89,192 | 49.0 |
| 7 | Jeffery Cohelan (D) | 65,699 | 50.9 |
| | John J. Allen Jr. (R) | 63,270 | 49.1 |
| 8 | George P. Miller (D-R) | 181,437 | 100.0 |
| 9 | J. Arthur Younger (R) | 90,735 | 58.8 |
| | Elma D. Oddstad (D) | 63,597 | 41.2 |
| 10 | Charles S. Gubser (R) | 118,715 | 54.6 |
| | Russell B. Bryan (D) | 98,894 | 45.4 |
| 11 | John J. McFall (D) | 86,924 | 69.3 |
| | Fredrick S. Van Dyke (R) | 38,427 | 30.7 |
| 12 | B. F. Sisk (D) | 112,702 | 81.1 |
| | Daniel K. Halpin (R) | 26,228 | 18.9 |
| 13 | Charles M. Teague (R) | 98,381 | 57.0 |
| | William Kirk Stewart (D) | 74,160 | 43.0 |
| 14 | Harlan Hagen (D-R) | 120,347 | 99.9 |
| 15 | Gordon L. McDonough (R) | 77,267 | 52.0 |
| | Emery S. Petty (D) | 71,192 | 48.0 |
| 16 | Donald L. Jackson (R) | 70,724 | 57.8 |
| | Melvin Lennard (D) | 51,616 | 42.2 |
| 17 | Cecil R. King (D) | 182,965 | 75.3 |
| | Leonard Di Miceli (R) | 59,973 | 24.7 |
| 18 | Craig Hosmer (R) | 95,682 | 60.0 |
| | Harry S. May (D) | 63,684 | 40.0 |
| 19 | Chet Holifield (D) | 131,421 | 83.4 |
| | Harry Vincent Leppek (R) | 26,092 | 16.6 |
| 20 | H. Allen Smith (R) | 72,311 | 66.0 |
| | Raymond Robert Farrell (D) | 37,331 | 34.1 |

| | Candidates | Votes | % |
|---|---|---|---|
| 21 | Edgar W. Hiestand (R) | 127,238 | 51.9 |
| | Mrs. Rudd Brown (D) | 118,141 | 48.1 |
| 22 | Joe Holt (R) | 87,785 | 55.4 |
| | Irving Glasband (D) | 70,777 | 44.6 |
| 23 | Clyde Doyle (D-R) | 140,817 | 100.0 |
| 24 | Glenard P. Lipscomb (R) | 68,184 | 56.4 |
| | William H. Ware Jr. (D) | 52,804 | 43.6 |
| 25 | George A. Kasem (D) | 135,009 | 50.1 |
| | Prescott O. Lieberg (R) | 134,406 | 49.9 |
| 26 | James Roosevelt (D) | 125,495 | 72.2 |
| | Crispus Wright (R) | 48,248 | 27.8 |
| 27 | Harry R. Sheppard (D) | 105,062 | 72.3 |
| | Robert M. Castle (R) | 40,317 | 27.7 |
| 28 | James B. Utt (R) | 152,855 | 58.2 |
| | T. R. Boyett (D) | 109,794 | 41.8 |
| 29 | Dalip S. Saund (D) | 64,518 | 62.4 |
| | John Babbage (R) | 38,899 | 37.6 |
| 30 | Bob Wilson (R) | 112,290 | 55.3 |
| | Lionel Van Deerlin (D) | 90,641 | 44.7 |

## COLORADO

| | Candidates | Votes | % |
|---|---|---|---|
| 1 | Byron G. Rogers (D) | 107,567 | 66.7 |
| | John L. Harpel (R) | 53,801 | 33.3 |
| 2 | Byron L. Johnson (D) | 95,409 | 53.9 |
| | John G. Mackie (R) | 80,467 | 45.5 |
| 3 | J. Edgar Chenoweth (R) | 63,655 | 50.2 |
| | Fred M. Betz (D) | 63,112 | 49.8 |
| 4 | Wayne N. Aspinall (D) | 43,785 | 63.6 |
| | J. R. (Dick) Wells (R) | 25,048 | 36.4 |

## CONNECTICUT

| | Candidates | Votes | % |
|---|---|---|---|
| 1 | Emilio Q. Daddario (D) | 146,115 | 54.3 |
| | Edwin H. May Jr. (R) | 122,770 | 45.7 |
| 2 | Chester Bowles (D) | 79,672 | 53.3 |
| | Horace Seely-Brown Jr. (R) | 69,837 | 46.7 |
| 3 | Robert N. Giaimo (D) | 101,028 | 56.2 |
| | Albert W. Cretella (R) | 78,665 | 43.8 |
| 4 | Donald J. Irwin (D) | 119,766 | 50.9 |
| | Albert P. Morano (R) | 115,505 | 49.1 |
| 5 | John S. Monagan (D) | 72,604 | 53.8 |
| | James T. Patterson (R) | 62,353 | 46.2 |
| AL | Frank Kowalski (D) | 542,315 | 56.0 |
| | Antoni N. Sadlak (R) | 425,452 | 44.0 |

## DELAWARE

| | Candidates | Votes | % |
|---|---|---|---|
| AL | Harris B. McDowell Jr. (D) | 76,797 | 50.2 |
| | Harry G. Haskell Jr. (R) | 76,099 | 49.8 |

## FLORIDA

| | Candidates | Votes | % |
|---|---|---|---|
| 1 | William C. Cramer (R) | 79,876 | 58.8 |
| | Winton H. King (D) | 56,005 | 41.2 |
| 2 | Charles E. Bennett (D) | 32,975 | 100.0 |
| 3 | Robert L. F. Sikes (D) | 27,855 | 100.0 |
| 4 | Dante B. Fascell (D) | 56,051 | 100.0 |
| 5 | A. Sydney Herlong Jr. (D) | 63,245 | 67.0 |
| | William C. Coleman (R) | 31,188 | 33.0 |
| 6 | Paul G. Rogers (D) | 71,189 | 71.5 |
| | Charles P. Ware (R) | 28,355 | 28.5 |
| 7 | James A. Haley (D) | 28,953 | 100.0 |
| 8 | D. R. Matthews (D) | 18,669 | 100.0 |

## GEORGIA

| | Candidates | Votes | % |
|---|---|---|---|
| 1 | Prince H. Preston (D) | 13,488 | 100.0 |
| 2 | John L. Pilcher (D) | 8,712 | 100.0 |
| 3 | E. L. Forrester (D) | 16,703 | 100.0 |
| 4 | John J. Flynt Jr. (D) | 17,054 | 100.0 |
| 5 | James C. Davis (D) | 32,135 | 100.0 |

| | Candidates | Votes | % |
|---|---|---|---|
| 6 | Carl Vinson (D) | 15,569 | 100.0 |
| 7 | Harlan Erwin Mitchell (D) | 13,913 | 100.0 |
| 8 | Iris Faircloth Blitch (D) | 12,940 | 100.0 |
| 9 | Phil M. Landrum (D) | 14,019 | 100.0 |
| 10 | Paul Brown (D) | 14,103 | 100.0 |

### Special Election

| | Candidates | Votes | % |
|---|---|---|---|
| 7 | Harlan Erwin Mitchell (D) | 16,426 | 95.5 |

## IDAHO

| | Candidates | Votes | % |
|---|---|---|---|
| 1 | Gracie B. Pfost (D) | 60,083 | 62.4 |
| | A. B. Curtis (R) | 36,178 | 37.6 |
| 2 | Hamer H. Budge (R) | 78,553 | 55.0 |
| | Tim Brennan (D) | 64,214 | 45.0 |

## ILLINOIS

| | Candidates | Votes | % |
|---|---|---|---|
| 1 | William L. Dawson (D) | 60,778 | 72.2 |
| | Theodore R. M. Howard (R) | 23,384 | 27.8 |
| 2 | Barratt O'Hara (D) | 75,691 | 68.3 |
| | Harold E. Marks (R) | 34,203 | 30.9 |
| 3 | William T. Murphy (D) | 79,886 | 56.5 |
| | Emmet F. Byrne (R) | 55,513 | 39.2 |
| 4 | Edward J. Derwinski (R) | 106,691 | 52.0 |
| | Leland H. Rayson (D) | 98,657 | 48.0 |
| 5 | John C. Kluczynski (D) | 96,591 | 76.1 |
| | Theodore Wozniak (R) | 30,374 | 23.9 |
| 6 | Thomas J. O'Brien (D) | 90,796 | 73.1 |
| | Frank S. Estes (R) | 33,392 | 26.9 |
| 7 | Roland V. Libonati (D) | 90,974 | 83.0 |
| | Anthony C. Catena (R) | 18,595 | 17.0 |
| 8 | Daniel D. Rostenkowski (D) | 73,413 | 74.6 |
| | William F. H. Schmidt (R) | 25,011 | 25.4 |
| 9 | Sidney R. Yates (D) | 70,989 | 67.0 |
| | Homer P. Hargraves Jr. (R) | 34,909 | 33.0 |
| 10 | Harold R. Collier (R) | 84,045 | 54.3 |
| | William J. McGah Jr. (D) | 70,621 | 45.7 |
| 11 | Roman C. Pucinski (D) | 79,167 | 56.7 |
| | Timothy P. Sheehan (R) | 60,347 | 43.3 |
| 12 | Charles A. Boyle (D) | 85,129 | 60.8 |
| | Allen A. Freeman (R) | 54,967 | 39.2 |
| 13 | Marguerite Stitt Church (R) | 165,910 | 67.1 |
| | Laurence A. Kusek (D) | 81,326 | 32.9 |
| 14 | Elmer J. Hoffman (R) | 96,381 | 64.3 |
| | Peter J. Fiefer (D) | 53,449 | 35.7 |
| 15 | Noah M. Mason (R) | 58,829 | 52.5 |
| | Dorothy G. O'Brien (D) | 53,196 | 47.5 |
| 16 | Leo E. Allen (R) | 71,049 | 61.4 |
| | Milton A. Lundstrom (D) | 44,723 | 38.6 |
| 17 | Leslie C. Arends (R) | 70,125 | 61.0 |
| | William T. Larkin (D) | 44,821 | 39.0 |
| 18 | Robert H. Michel (R) | 57,929 | 59.5 |
| | James W. McGee (D) | 39,464 | 40.5 |
| 19 | Robert B. Chiperfield (R) | 52,049 | 50.5 |
| | John C. Watson (D) | 51,104 | 49.5 |
| 20 | Edna Simpson (R) | 57,412 | 55.3 |
| | Henry W. Pollock (D) | 46,076 | 44.4 |
| 21 | Peter F. Mack Jr. (D) | 87,134 | 58.8 |
| | Norma Eaton (R) | 61,137 | 41.2 |
| 22 | William L. Springer (R) | 65,080 | 60.5 |
| | Carlton H. Myers (D) | 42,533 | 39.5 |
| 23 | George E. Shipley (D) | 65,114 | 50.1 |
| | Charles W. Vursell (R) | 64,927 | 49.9 |
| 24 | Melvin Price (D) | 94,231 | 76.1 |
| | Alex Chouinard (R) | 29,670 | 24.0 |
| 25 | Kenneth J. Gray (D) | 78,385 | 58.2 |
| | Carl D. Sneed (R) | 56,257 | 41.8 |

## INDIANA

| | Candidates | Votes | % |
|---|---|---|---|
| 1 | Ray J. Madden (D) | 95,801 | 66.4 |
| | Edward P. Keck (R) | 47,588 | 33.0 |
| 2 | Charles A. Halleck (R) | 71,933 | 52.2 |
| | George H. Bowers (D) | 65,792 | 47.8 |

## INDIANA

| | Candidates | Votes | % |
|---|---|---|---|
| 3 | John Brademas (D) | 101,802 | 56.9 |
| | F. Jay Nimtz (R) | 77,014 | 43.1 |
| 4 | E. Ross Adair (R) | 69,745 | 50.1 |
| | W. Robert Fleming (D) | 69,478 | 49.9 |
| 5 | J. Edward Roush (D) | 97,184 | 53.7 |
| | John V. Beamer (R) | 83,852 | 46.3 |
| 6 | Fred Wampler (D) | 71,669 | 51.5 |
| | Cecil M. Harden (R) | 67,549 | 48.5 |
| 7 | William G. Bray (R) | 77,045 | 53.8 |
| | Thomas L. Lemon (D) | 66,217 | 46.2 |
| 8 | Winfield K. Denton (D) | 100,611 | 61.5 |
| | Franklin E. Katterjohn (R) | 63,005 | 38.5 |
| 9 | Earl Hogan (D) | 62,810 | 50.3 |
| | Earl Wilson (R) | 62,064 | 49.7 |
| 10 | Randall S. Harmon (D) | 76,757 | 50.8 |
| | Ralph Harvey (R) | 74,500 | 49.3 |
| 11 | Joseph W. Barr (D) | 113,674 | 52.1 |
| | Charles B. Brownson (R) | 104,555 | 47.9 |

## IOWA

| | | Votes | % |
|---|---|---|---|
| 1 | Fred Schwengel (R) | 59,577 | 53.4 |
| | Thomas J. Dailey (D) | 51,996 | 46.6 |
| 2 | Leonard G. Wolf (D) | 67,022 | 51.1 |
| | Henry O. Talle (R) | 64,073 | 48.9 |
| 3 | H. R. Gross (R) | 61,920 | 53.7 |
| | Michael Micich (D) | 53,467 | 46.3 |
| 4 | Steven V. Carter (D) | 42,479 | 52.0 |
| | John Kyl (R) | 39,233 | 48.0 |
| 5 | Neal Smith (D) | 61,693 | 52.3 |
| | Paul Cunningham (R) | 56,320 | 47.7 |
| 6 | Merwin Coad (D) | 57,491 | 58.3 |
| | Robert E. Waggoner (R) | 41,204 | 41.8 |
| 7 | Ben F. Jensen (R) | 41,053 | 51.5 |
| | Ellsworth O. Hays (D) | 38,660 | 48.5 |
| 8 | Charles B. Hoeven (R) | 49,418 | 52.7 |
| | Donald E. O'Brien (D) | 44,310 | 47.3 |

## KANSAS

| | | Votes | % |
|---|---|---|---|
| 1 | William H. Avery (R) | 60,198 | 51.2 |
| | Robert W. Domme (D) | 55,749 | 47.4 |
| 2 | Newell A. George (D) | 69,954 | 50.8 |
| | Errett P. Scrivner (R) | 67,882 | 49.3 |
| 3 | Denver D. Hargis (D) | 42,718 | 51.7 |
| | Myron V. George (R) | 39,872 | 48.3 |
| 4 | Edward H. Rees (R) | 89,611 | 50.7 |
| | Warner Moore (D) | 87,244 | 49.3 |
| 5 | J. Floyd Breeding (D) | 60,549 | 53.1 |
| | Clifford R. Hope Jr. (R) | 53,387 | 46.9 |
| 6 | Wint Smith (R) | 43,782 | 49.2 |
| | Elmo J. Mahoney (D) | 43,549 | 49.0 |

## KENTUCKY

| | | Votes | % |
|---|---|---|---|
| 1 | Frank Stubblefield (D) | 41,214 | 85.0 |
| | James G. Bondy (R) | 7,263 | 15.0 |
| 2 | William H. Natcher (D) | 38,941 | 76.1 |
| | Wayland Render (R) | 12,239 | 23.9 |
| 3 | Frank W. Burke (D) | 73,121 | 52.2 |
| | John M. Robsion Jr. (R) | 67,059 | 47.8 |
| 4 | Frank Chelf (D) | 19,310 | 100.0 |
| 5 | Brent Spence (D) | 34,919 | 71.9 |
| | Jule Appel (R) | 13,631 | 28.1 |
| 6 | John C. Watts (D) | 29,199 | 94.7 |
| | Wallace Jones | 1,622 | 5.3 |
| 7 | Carl D. Perkins (D) | 56,756 | 65.8 |
| | E. L. Raybourn (R) | 29,505 | 34.2 |
| 8 | Eugene Siler (R) | 34,728 | 68.0 |
| | W. D. Scalf (D) | 16,311 | 32.0 |

## LOUISIANA

| | | Votes | % |
|---|---|---|---|
| 1 | F. Edward Hebert (D) | 41,861 | 100.0 |
| 2 | Hale Boggs (D) | 46,614 | 91.8 |
| | John Patrick Conway (R) | 4,160 | 8.2 |

| | Candidates | Votes | % |
|---|---|---|---|
| 3 | Edwin E. Willis (D) | 8,692 | 100.0 |
| 4 | Overton Brooks (D) | 23,844 | 100.0 |
| 5 | Otto E. Passman (D) | 14,900 | 100.0 |
| 6 | James H. Morrison (D) | 20,599 | 100.0 |
| 7 | T. A. Thompson (D) | 10,328 | 100.0 |
| 8 | Harold B. McSween (D) | 11,125 | 100.0 |

## MAINE

| | | Votes | % |
|---|---|---|---|
| 1 | James C. Oliver (D) | 55,686 | 52.1 |
| | Robert Hale (R) | 51,231 | 47.9 |
| 2 | Frank M. Coffin (D) | 59,054 | 61.3 |
| | Neil Bishop (R) | 37,219 | 38.7 |
| 3 | Clifford G. McIntire (R) | 40,156 | 56.0 |
| | Gerald J. Grady (D) | 31,616 | 44.1 |

## MARYLAND

| | | Votes | % |
|---|---|---|---|
| 1 | Thomas F. Johnson (D) | 32,328 | 50.6 |
| | Edward T. Miller (R) | 31,610 | 49.4 |
| 2 | Daniel B. Brewster (D) | 87,667 | 61.0 |
| | Fife Symington (R) | 56,165 | 39.1 |
| 3 | Edward A. Garmatz (D) | 49,649 | 84.0 |
| | Harry Kemper (R) | 9,470 | 16.0 |
| 4 | George H. Fallon (D) | 45,646 | 71.6 |
| | Louis W. Collier (R) | 18,094 | 28.4 |
| 5 | Richard E. Lankford (D) | 96,919 | 75.1 |
| | Robert E. Ennis (R) | 32,072 | 24.9 |
| 6 | John R. Foley (D) | 78,987 | 51.4 |
| | DeWitt S. Hyde (R) | 74,683 | 48.6 |
| 7 | Samuel N. Friedel (D) | 72,692 | 73.6 |
| | Elizabeth P. Brown (R) | 26,144 | 26.5 |

## MASSACHUSETTS

| | | Votes | % |
|---|---|---|---|
| 1 | Silvio O. Conte (R) | 66,067 | 55.3 |
| | James M. Burns (D) | 52,853 | 44.2 |
| 2 | Edward P. Boland (D) | 103,079 | 100.0 |
| 3 | Phillip J. Philbin (D) | 114,483 | 100.0 |
| 4 | Harold D. Donohue (D) | 93,993 | 63.8 |
| | Charles D. Briggs Jr. (R) | 53,359 | 36.2 |
| 5 | Edith Nourse Rogers (R) | 116,072 | 66.0 |
| | William H. Sullivan (D) | 59,746 | 34.0 |
| 6 | William H. Bates (R) | 106,807 | 100.0 |
| 7 | Thomas J. Lane (D) | 84,243 | 75.6 |
| | Robert T. Breed (R) | 27,215 | 24.4 |
| 8 | Torbert H. Macdonald (D) | 91,263 | 66.4 |
| | Gordon F. Hughes (R) | 46,274 | 33.6 |
| 9 | Hastings Keith (R) | 82,659 | 54.7 |
| | John Almeida Jr. (D) | 68,486 | 45.3 |
| 10 | Laurence Curtis (R) | 71,100 | 52.2 |
| | John L. Saltonstall Jr. (D) | 65,159 | 47.8 |
| 11 | Thomas P. O'Neill Jr. (D) | 68,353 | 80.4 |
| | Elliott H. Stone (R) | 16,669 | 19.6 |
| 12 | John W. McCormack (D) | 72,523 | 100.0 |
| 13 | James A. Burke (D) | 89,073 | 53.5 |
| | William W. Jenness (R) | 77,400 | 46.5 |
| 14 | Joseph W. Martin Jr. (R) | 90,751 | 61.0 |
| | Edward F. Doolan (D) | 57,920 | 39.0 |

## MICHIGAN

| | | Votes | % |
|---|---|---|---|
| 1 | Thaddeus M. Machrowicz (D) | 82,288 | 90.4 |
| | Walter Czarnecki (R) | 8,502 | 9.3 |
| 2 | George Meader (R) | 73,954 | 58.8 |
| | Robert G. Hall (D) | 51,323 | 40.8 |
| 3 | August E. Johansen (R) | 68,144 | 60.4 |
| | John R. O'Meara (D) | 44,189 | 39.2 |
| 4 | Clare E. Hoffman (R) | 59,780 | 59.9 |
| | Gordon A. Elferdink (D) | 39,765 | 39.8 |
| 5 | Gerald R. Ford Jr. (R) | 88,156 | 63.6 |
| | Richard F. Vander Veen (D) | 50,203 | 36.2 |
| 6 | Charles E. Chamberlain (R) | 92,313 | 52.1 |
| | Don Hayworth (D) | 84,418 | 47.7 |
| 7 | James G. O'Hara (D) | 87,299 | 50.7 |
| | Robert J. McIntosh (R) | 84,531 | 49.1 |

| | Candidates | Votes | % |
|---|---|---|---|
| 8 | Alvin M. Bentley (R) | 69,858 | 62.2 |
| | James O. Pino (D) | 42,467 | 37.8 |
| 9 | Robert P. Griffin (R) | 56,780 | 56.7 |
| | Jan B. Vanderploeg (D) | 43,196 | 43.1 |
| 10 | Elford A. Cederberg (R) | 54,316 | 61.1 |
| | Daniel E. Reed (D) | 34,390 | 38.7 |
| 11 | Victor A. Knox (R) | 41,689 | 52.3 |
| | Prentiss M. Brown Jr. (D) | 37,995 | 47.6 |
| 12 | John B. Bennett (R) | 39,239 | 57.0 |
| | Joseph S. Mack (D) | 29,506 | 42.9 |
| 13 | Charles C. Diggs Jr. (D) | 57,354 | 72.7 |
| | Charles P. White (R) | 21,280 | 27.0 |
| 14 | Louis C. Rabaut (D) | 97,236 | 64.2 |
| | Lois V. Nair (R) | 53,987 | 35.7 |
| 15 | John D. Dingell (D) | 79,216 | 78.5 |
| | Austin W. Curtis Jr. (R) | 21,414 | 21.2 |
| 16 | John Lesinski (D) | 145,665 | 71.8 |
| | Ralph B. Guy (H) | 50,400 | 27.8 |
| 17 | Martha W. Griffiths (D) | 96,660 | 60.3 |
| | Lucas S. Miel (R) | 63,323 | 39.5 |
| 18 | William S. Broomfield (R) | 101,100 | 52.6 |
| | Leslie H. Hudson (D) | 90,526 | 47.1 |

## MINNESOTA

| | | Votes | % |
|---|---|---|---|
| 1 | Albert H. Quie (R) | 73,345 | 57.0 |
| | Eugene P. Foley (DFL) | 55,445 | 43.1 |
| 2 | Ancher Nelsen (R) | 71,623 | 57.1 |
| | Conrad H. Hammar (DFL) | 53,869 | 42.9 |
| 3 | Roy W. Wier (DFL) | 98,449 | 51.6 |
| | Leonard E. Lindquist (R) | 92,190 | 48.4 |
| 4 | Joseph E. Karth (DFL) | 72,952 | 56.4 |
| | Frank S. Farrell (R) | 56,484 | 43.6 |
| 5 | Walter H. Judd (R) | 59,739 | 57.3 |
| | Joseph Robbie (DFL) | 44,453 | 42.7 |
| 6 | Fred Marshall (DFL) | 73,881 | 64.3 |
| | Hugo Holmstrom (R) | 41,018 | 35.7 |
| 7 | H. Carl Andersen (R) | 61,265 | 53.3 |
| | A. I. Johnson (DFL) | 53,689 | 46.7 |
| 8 | John A. Blatnik (DFL) | 97,046 | 75.6 |
| | Roy W. Ranum (R) | 31,343 | 24.4 |
| 9 | Odin Langen (R) | 47,863 | 50.7 |
| | Coya Knutson (DFL) | 46,473 | 49.3 |

#### Special Election

| | | Votes | % |
|---|---|---|---|
| 1 | Albert H. Quie (R) | 44,276 | 50.3 |
| | Eugene P. Foley (DFL) | 43,674 | 49.7 |

## MISSISSIPPI

| | | Votes | % |
|---|---|---|---|
| 1 | Thomas G. Abernethy (D) | 12,413 | 100.0 |
| 2 | Jamie L. Whitten (D) | 7,982 | 100.0 |
| 3 | Frank E. Smith (D) | 4,644 | 100.0 |
| 4 | John Bell Williams (D) | 8,665 | 100.0 |
| 5 | Arthur Winstead (D) | 14,517 | 100.0 |
| 6 | William M. Colmer (D) | 13,243 | 100.0 |

## MISSOURI

| | | Votes | % |
|---|---|---|---|
| 1 | Frank M. Karsten (D) | 99,368 | 75.8 |
| | Paul E. Corning Jr. (R) | 31,804 | 24.3 |
| 2 | Thomas B. Curtis (R) | 88,321 | 51.9 |
| | James L. Sullivan (D) | 81,811 | 48.1 |
| 3 | Leonor K. Sullivan (D) | 63,679 | 79.2 |
| | Josiah C. Thomas (R) | 16,753 | 20.8 |
| 4 | George H. Christopher (D) | 72,792 | 64.0 |
| | James A. Rahm (R) | 40,912 | 36.0 |
| 5 | Richard Bolling (D) | 53,622 | 70.0 |
| | Richard W. Byrne (R) | 22,953 | 30.0 |
| 6 | W. R. Hull Jr. (D) | 64,277 | 64.9 |
| | Clyde M. Kirk (R) | 34,758 | 35.1 |
| 7 | Charles H. Brown (D) | 76,239 | 53.7 |
| | Noel Cox (R) | 65,666 | 46.3 |
| 8 | A. S. J. Carnahan (D) | 58,628 | 64.3 |
| | Francis Howard (R) | 32,543 | 35.7 |
| 9 | Clarence Cannon (D) | 67,555 | 64.8 |
| | Anthony Schroeder (R) | 36,758 | 35.2 |

## MISSOURI

| Candidates | Votes | % |
|---|---|---|
| 10 Paul C. Jones | 44,892 | 70.7 |
| Gilbert Degenhardt (R) | 18,633 | 29.3 |
| 11 Morgan M. Moulder (D) | 54,014 | 56.9 |
| Don W. Owensby (R) | 40,839 | 43.1 |

## MONTANA

| | | |
|---|---|---|
| Lee Metcalf (D) | 68,586 | 69.5 |
| Jean Walterskirschen (R) | 30,111 | 30.5 |
| 2 LeRoy H. Anderson (D) | 79,140 | 61.0 |
| Ashton Jones (R) | 50,633 | 39.0 |

## NEBRASKA

| | | |
|---|---|---|
| 1 Phil Weaver (R) | 62,770 | 53.4 |
| Clair A. Callan (D) | 54,705 | 46.6 |
| 2 Glenn Cunningham (R) | 67,660 | 64.8 |
| Francis M. Casey (D) | 36,842 | 35.3 |
| 3 Lawrence Brock (D) | 53,033 | 55.1 |
| Robert D. Harrison (R) | 43,236 | 44.9 |
| 4 Donald F. McGinley (D) | 50,870 | 52.3 |
| Arthur L. Miller (R) | 46,474 | 47.7 |

## NEVADA

| | | |
|---|---|---|
| AL Walter S. Baring (D) | 55,053 | 66.9 |
| Robert C. Horton (R) | 27,275 | 33.1 |

## NEW HAMPSHIRE

| | | |
|---|---|---|
| 1 Chester E. Merrow (R) | 62,734 | 58.5 |
| Alphonse Roy (D) | 44,051 | 41.0 |
| 2 Perkins Bass (R) | 52,636 | 58.4 |
| Stuart V. Nims (D) | 37,212 | 41.3 |

## NEW JERSEY

| | | |
|---|---|---|
| 1 William T. Cahill (R) | 96,619 | 50.3 |
| Alexander Feinberg (D) | 94,790 | 49.3 |
| 2 Milton W. Glenn (R) | 58,621 | 53.4 |
| Joseph G. Hancock (D) | 50,558 | 46.1 |
| 3 James C. Auchincloss (R) | 98,826 | 56.1 |
| Thomas F. Guthrie Jr. (D) | 77,423 | 43.9 |
| 4 Frank Thompson Jr. (D) | 83,388 | 63.0 |
| A. Jerome Moore (R) | 48,990 | 37.0 |
| 5 Peter H. B. Frelinghuysen Jr. (R) | 111,250 | 55.7 |
| David S. North (D) | 87,966 | 44.0 |
| 6 Florence P. Dwyer (R) | 88,084 | 51.1 |
| Jack B. Dunn (D) | 80,779 | 46.9 |
| 7 William B. Widnall (R) | 103,169 | 59.6 |
| J. Emmet Cassidy (D) | 69,250 | 40.0 |
| 8 Gordon Canfield (R) | 68,385 | 58.1 |
| Joseph R. Brumale (D) | 48,481 | 41.2 |
| 9 Frank C. Osmers Jr. (R) | 92,513 | 57.4 |
| Daniel W. Allen (D) | 67,633 | 42.0 |
| 10 Peter W. Rodino Jr. (D) | 60,482 | 63.9 |
| G. George Addonizio (R) | 32,946 | 34.8 |
| 11 Hugh J. Addonizio (D) | 50,821 | 59.3 |
| John P. Langan (R) | 34,821 | 40.7 |
| 12 George M. Wallhauser (R) | 57,510 | 52.7 |
| Thomas J. Holleran (D) | 49,463 | 45.3 |
| 13 Cornelius E. Gallagher (D) | 61,094 | 66.1 |
| Samuel F. Kanis (R) | 23,001 | 24.9 |
| 14 Dominick V. Daniels (D) | 56,475 | 62.9 |
| Frank A. Musto (R) | 29,614 | 33.0 |

## NEW MEXICO

| | | |
|---|---|---|
| AL Joseph M. Montoya (D) | 124,924✔ | |
| Thomas G. Morris (D) | 115,928✔ | |
| William A. Thompson (R) | 72,922 | |
| George W. McKim (R) | 70,925 | |

## NEW YORK

| Candidates | Votes | % |
|---|---|---|
| 1 Stuyvesant Wainwright (R) | 155,387 | 57.5 |
| Otis G. Pike (D, L) | 115,019 | 42.5 |
| 2 Steven B. Derounian (R) | 113,820 | 60.5 |
| Walter A. Lynch Jr. (D, L) | 74,194 | 39.5 |
| 3 Frank J. Becker (R) | 109,245 | 54.4 |
| A. William Larson (D, L) | 91,514 | 45.6 |
| 4 Seymour Halpern (R) | 78,054 | 52.6 |
| Joseph J. Perrini (D, L) | 70,437 | 47.4 |
| 5 Albert A. Bosch (R) | 56,839 | 52.1 |
| William Kerwick (D) | 47,661 | 43.7 |
| 6 Lester Holtzman (D, L) | 106,762 | 63.6 |
| George T. Reilly (R) | 61,204 | 36.4 |
| 7 James J. Delaney (D, L) | 71,007 | 61.1 |
| Edward V. Lisoski (R) | 45,135 | 38.9 |
| 8 Victor L. Anfuso (D, L) | 43,656 | 71.7 |
| Leon F. Nadrowski (R) | 17,271 | 28.4 |
| 9 Eugene J. Keogh (D, L) | 61,816 | 72.1 |
| Anton Eyring (R) | 23,957 | 27.9 |
| 10 Edna F. Kelly (D, L) | 77,351 | 76.1 |
| Jerome P. Schneider (R) | 24,286 | 23.9 |
| 11 Emanuel Celler (D, L) | 105,011 | 81.4 |
| Jesse M. Browser (R) | 24,034 | 18.6 |
| 12 Francis E. Dorn (R) | 51,861 | 52.7 |
| Thomas J. Cuite (D) | 39,275 | 39.9 |
| Leroy Bowman (L) | 7,322 | 7.4 |
| 13 Abraham J. Multer (D, L) | 88,406 | 76.1 |
| Hyman D. Siegel (R) | 27,701 | 23.9 |
| 14 John J. Rooney (D, L) | 60,703 | 70.6 |
| Anthony D'Allessandro (R) | 25,319 | 29.4 |
| 15 John H. Ray (R, U TAX) | 65,318 | 52.8 |
| Vincent R. Fitzpatrick (D, L) | 58,351 | 47.2 |
| 16 Adam Clayton Powell Jr. (D, R) | 56,383 | 90.8 |
| Earl Brown (L) | 5,705 | 9.2 |
| 17 John V. Lindsay (R) | 54,459 | 53.9 |
| Anthony B. Akers (D, L) | 46,570 | 46.1 |
| 18 Alfred E. Santangelo (D) | 36,601 | 59.4 |
| George A. Eyer Jr. (R) | 20,848 | 33.8 |
| Manuel Velazquez (L) | 4,201 | 6.8 |
| 19 Leonard Farbstein (D, L) | 55,069 | 73.1 |
| Gonzales Suarez (R) | 20,232 | 26.9 |
| 20 Ludwig Teller (D, L) | 50,735 | 67.0 |
| Milton H. Adler (R) | 24,933 | 33.0 |
| 21 Herbert Zelenko (D, L) | 67,743 | 72.5 |
| Carl Medonick (R) | 25,699 | 27.5 |
| 22 James C. Healey (D) | 65,996 | 65.2 |
| Alex J. Soled (R) | 20,777 | 20.5 |
| David I. Wells (L) | 14,391 | 14.2 |
| 23 Isidore Dollinger (D) | 49,452 | 71.5 |
| Simon M. Koenig (R) | 12,278 | 17.7 |
| Hector Mathew (L) | 7,469 | 10.8 |
| 24 Charles A. Buckley (D) | 71,616 | 56.2 |
| Charles V. Scanlan (R) | 35,993 | 28.3 |
| Murray Koenig (L) | 19,759 | 15.5 |
| 25 Paul A. Fino (R) | 79,857 | 57.8 |
| Neal P. Bottiglieri (D, L) | 58,396 | 42.2 |
| 26 Edwin B. Dooley (R) | 98,677 | 63.2 |
| Phil E. Gilbert Jr. (D, L) | 57,465 | 36.8 |
| 27 Robert R. Barry (R) | 104,240 | 58.2 |
| Richard W. McSpedon (D, L) | 74,883 | 41.8 |
| 28 Katharine St.George (R) | 84,536 | 59.7 |
| David Sive (D) | 53,981 | 38.1 |
| 29 J. Ernest Wharton (R) | 93,667 | 63.4 |
| Christopher D. Morris (D, L) | 54,153 | 36.6 |
| 30 Leo W. O'Brien (D, L) | 109,744 | 64.7 |
| George H. Witbeck Jr. (R) | 59,958 | 35.3 |
| 31 Dean P. Taylor (R) | 87,704 | 63.8 |
| John R. Cummins (D, L) | 49,777 | 36.2 |
| 32 Samuel S. Stratton (D, L) | 73,384 | 54.0 |
| Walter C. Shaw (R) | 62,443 | 46.0 |
| 33 Clarence E. Kilburn (R) | 73,698 | 64.8 |
| Robert P. McDonald (D, L) | 40,010 | 35.2 |
| 34 Alexander Pirnie (R) | 70,482 | 50.8 |
| Edwin L. Slusarczyk (D, L) | 68,271 | 49.2 |

| Candidates | Votes | % |
|---|---|---|
| 35 R. Walter Riehlman (R) | 90,285 | 53.8 |
| Caryl M. Kline (D, L) | 77,449 | 46.2 |
| 36 John Taber (R) | 84,019 | 64.7 |
| Frank B. Lent (D, L) | 45,822 | 35.3 |
| 37 Howard W. Robison (R) | 101,279 | 65.8 |
| Francis P. Hogan (D, L) | 52,636 | 34.2 |
| 38 Jessica McC Weis (R) | 92,944 | 58.2 |
| Alphonse L. Cassetti (D, L) | 66,806 | 41.8 |
| 39 Harold C. Ostertag (R) | 90,004 | 65.2 |
| Harold L. Rakov (D, L) | 48,144 | 34.8 |
| 40 William E. Miller (R) | 90,066 | 60.8 |
| Mariano A. Lucca (D) | 54,728 | 36.9 |
| 41 Thaddeus J. Dulski (D, L) | 60,360 | 50.3 |
| James O. Moore Jr. (R) | 59,634 | 49.7 |
| 42 John R. Pillion (R) | 99,799 | 58.9 |
| Joseph R. Stiglmeier (D, L) | 69,747 | 41.1 |
| 43 Daniel A. Reed (R) | 68,896 | 63.8 |
| T. Joseph Lynch (D) | 36,799 | 34.1 |

### Special Election

| | | |
|---|---|---|
| 37 Howard W. Robison (R) | 45,920 | 59.8 |
| Francis P. Hogan (D, L) | 30,891 | 40.2 |

## NORTH CAROLINA

| | | |
|---|---|---|
| 1 Herbert C. Bonner (D) | 12,743 | 100.0 |
| 2 L. H. Fountain (D) | 17,061 | 100.0 |
| 3 Graham A. Barden (D) | 22,446 | 79.1 |
| Joe A. Dunn (D) | 5,927 | 20.9 |
| 4 Harold D. Cooley (D) | 30,505 | 75.6 |
| L. T. Dark Jr. (R) | 9,863 | 24.4 |
| 5 Ralph J. Scott (D) | 40,544 | 71.6 |
| William E. Morrow (R) | 16,048 | 28.4 |
| 6 Carl T. Durham (D) | 35,715 | 100.0 |
| 7 Alton Lennon (D) | 27,902 | 89.0 |
| C. Dana Malpass (R) | 3,461 | 11.0 |
| 8 A. Paul Kitchin (D) | 43,793 | 63.4 |
| F. D. B. Harding (R) | 25,276 | 36.6 |
| 9 Hugh Q. Alexander (D) | 57,672 | 66.5 |
| William White (R) | 29,065 | 33.5 |
| 10 Charles Raper Jonas (R) | 56,487 | 51.9 |
| David Clark (D) | 52,306 | 48.1 |
| 11 Basil L. Whitener (D) | 37,926 | 100.0 |
| 12 David M. Hall (D) | 52,609 | 62.5 |
| W. Harold Sams (R) | 31,524 | 37.5 |

## NORTH DAKOTA

| | | |
|---|---|---|
| AL Quentin N. Burdick (D) | 99,562✔ | |
| Don L. Short (R) | 97,862✔ | |
| Orris G. Nordhougen (R) | 92,124 | |
| S. B. Hocking (D) | 78,889 | |

## OHIO

| | | |
|---|---|---|
| 1 Gordon H. Scherer (R) | 70,686 | 56.6 |
| W. Ted Osborne (D) | 54,119 | 43.4 |
| 2 William E. Hess (R) | 86,656 | 54.7 |
| James O. Bradley (D) | 71,674 | 45.3 |
| 3 Paul F. Schenck (R) | 102,806 | 52.4 |
| Thomas B. Talbot (D) | 93,401 | 47.6 |
| 4 William M. McCulloch (R) | 73,448 | 61.0 |
| Marjorie Conrad Struna (D) | 46,933 | 39.0 |
| 5 Delbert L. Latta (R) | 52,612 | 53.9 |
| George Rafferty (D) | 44,971 | 46.1 |
| 6 James G. Polk (D) | 76,566 | 62.0 |
| Elmer S. Barrett (R) | 46,924 | 38.0 |
| 7 Clarence J. Brown (R) | 75,085 | 60.5 |
| Joseph A. Sullivan (D) | 48,994 | 39.5 |
| 8 Jackson E. Betts (R) | 62,232 | 61.3 |
| Virgil M. Gase (D) | 39,343 | 38.7 |
| 9 Thomas L. Ashley (D) | 102,115 | 61.6 |
| William K. Gernheuser (R) | 63,660 | 38.4 |
| 10 Walter H. Moeller (D) | 47,939 | 52.9 |
| Homer E. Abele (R) | 42,607 | 47.1 |

## OHIO

| | Candidates | Votes | % |
|---|---|---|---|
| 11 | Robert E. Cook (D) | 79,468 | 50.3 |
| | David Dennison Jr. (R) | 78,501 | 49.7 |
| 12 | Samuel L. Devine (R) | 100,684 | 54.4 |
| | Walter J. Shapter Jr. (D) | 84,470 | 45.6 |
| 13 | Albert D. Baumhart Jr. (R) | 65,169 | 58.9 |
| | J. William McCray (D) | 45,390 | 41.1 |
| 14 | William H. Ayres (R) | 114,827 | 60.1 |
| | Jack B. Arnold (D) | 76,138 | 39.9 |
| 15 | John E. Henderson (R) | 48,316 | 57.3 |
| | Herbert U. Smith (D) | 36,062 | 42.7 |
| 16 | Frank T. Bow (R) | 100,678 | 57.4 |
| | John G. Freedom (D) | 74,660 | 42.6 |
| 17 | Robert W. Levering (D) | 63,650 | 51.7 |
| | Lawrence Burns (R) | 59,490 | 48.3 |
| 18 | Wayne L. Hays (D) | 88,813 | 71.6 |
| | Francis Wallace (R) | 35,322 | 28.5 |
| 19 | Michael J. Kirwan (D) | 93,660 | 75.0 |
| | Loren E. Van Brocklin (R) | 31,192 | 25.0 |
| 20 | Michael A. Feighan (D) | 113,200 | 79.4 |
| | Malvern E. Schultz (R) | 29,308 | 20.6 |
| 21 | Charles A. Vanik (D) | 93,987 | 80.4 |
| | Ermer L. Watson (R) | 22,956 | 19.6 |
| 22 | Frances P. Bolton (R) | 71,139 | 55.3 |
| | Chat Paterson (D) | 57,508 | 44.7 |
| 23 | William E. Minshall Jr. (R) | 95,267 | 66.5 |
| | Daniel Winston (D) | 47,953 | 33.5 |

## OKLAHOMA

| | Candidates | Votes | % |
|---|---|---|---|
| 1 | Page H. Belcher (R) | 74,853 | 50.8 |
| | Herbert William Wright Jr. (D) | 71,190 | 48.3 |
| 2 | Ed Edmondson (D) | 75,492 | 79.1 |
| | Milo Ritter (R) | 19,996 | 20.9 |
| 3 | Carl Albert (D) | 43,868 | 90.9 |
| | Chapin Wallace (R) | 4,398 | 9.1 |
| 4 | Tom Steed (D) | 43,837 | 74.1 |
| | Rolla C. Calkins (R) | 15,359 | 26.0 |
| 5 | John Jarman (D) | 79,917 | 82.3 |
| | Hobart H. Hobbs (R) | 17,137 | 17.7 |
| 6 | Toby Morris (D) | 54,967 | 66.7 |
| | Fred L. Coogan (R) | 27,425 | 33.3 |

## OREGON

| | Candidates | Votes | % |
|---|---|---|---|
| 1 | Walter Norblad (R) | 95,420 | 54.9 |
| | Robert Y. Thornton (D) | 78,362 | 45.1 |
| 2 | Al Ullman (D) | 50,166 | 61.1 |
| | Marion T. Weatherford (R) | 31,987 | 38.9 |
| 3 | Edith Green (D) | 131,164 | 65.8 |
| | John Johnston (R) | 68,235 | 34.2 |
| 4 | Charles O. Porter (D) | 79,166 | 56.3 |
| | Paul Geddes (R) | 61,386 | 43.7 |

## PENNSYLVANIA

| | Candidates | Votes | % |
|---|---|---|---|
| 1 | William A. Barrett (D) | 67,531 | 64.7 |
| | Gerard Iannelli (R) | 36,854 | 35.3 |
| 2 | Kathryn E. Granahan (D) | 84,058 | 66.3 |
| | Maurice M. Green (R) | 42,759 | 33.7 |
| 3 | James A. Byrne (D) | 65,201 | 63.5 |
| | James Thomas McDermott (R) | 37,420 | 36.5 |
| 4 | Robert N. C. Nix (D) | 63,031 | 72.6 |
| | Cecil B. Moore (R) | 23,845 | 27.5 |
| 5 | William J. Green Jr. (D) | 100,680 | 55.3 |
| | D. Donald Jamieson (R) | 81,530 | 44.8 |
| 6 | Herman Toll (D) | 83,491 | 55.4 |
| | Fred C. Gartner (R) | 67,205 | 44.6 |
| 7 | William H. Milliken Jr. (R) | 114,275 | 59.2 |
| | Hubert P. Earle (D) | 78,747 | 40.8 |
| 8 | Willard S. Curtin (R) | 85,010 | 54.3 |
| | Harold Lefcourt (D) | 71,583 | 45.7 |
| 9 | Paul B. Dague (R) | 88,193 | 61.9 |
| | James C. N. Paul (D) | 54,220 | 38.1 |
| 10 | Stanley A. Prokop (D) | 74,890 | 50.4 |
| | Joseph L. Carrigg (R) | 73,601 | 49.6 |

| | Candidates | Votes | % |
|---|---|---|---|
| 11 | Daniel J. Flood (D) | 89,167 | 61.7 |
| | Herman C. Kersteen (R) | 55,349 | 38.3 |
| 12 | Ivor D. Fenton (R) | 64,960 | 54.9 |
| | Charles E. Lotz (D) | 53,402 | 45.1 |
| 13 | John A. Lafore Jr. (R) | 104,156 | 62.9 |
| | John T. Synnestvedt (D) | 61,475 | 37.1 |
| 14 | George M. Rhodes (D) | 51,281 | 58.3 |
| | Thomas C. Anthony Jr. (R) | 36,170 | 41.1 |
| 15 | Francis E. Walter (D) | 60,742 | 61.1 |
| | Luther M. Ackerman (R) | 38,726 | 38.9 |
| 16 | Walter M. Mumma (R) | 70,810 | 56.6 |
| | John H. Bream (D) | 54,245 | 43.4 |
| 17 | Alvin Bush (R) | 65,071 | 56.0 |
| | C. Max Hess (D) | 51,053 | 44.0 |
| 18 | Richard M. Simpson (R) | 67,719 | 56.3 |
| | Ross E. Hershberger (D) | 52,514 | 43.7 |
| 10 | James M. Quigley (D) | 67,603 | 51.5 |
| | S. Walter Stauffer (R) | 63,749 | 48.5 |
| 20 | James E. Van Zandt (R) | 61,010 | 64.9 |
| | Julia L. Maietta (D) | 33,060 | 35.1 |
| 21 | John H. Dent (D) | 70,828 | 59.2 |
| | Edward S. Stiteler (R) | 48,925 | 40.9 |
| 22 | John P. Saylor (R) | 77,407 | 57.0 |
| | Robert S. Glass (D) | 58,434 | 43.0 |
| 23 | Leon H. Gavin (R) | 60,080 | 61.1 |
| | Thomas P. Kennedy (D) | 38,179 | 38.9 |
| 24 | Carroll D. Kearns (R) | 76,870 | 53.8 |
| | James P. O'Brien (D) | 65,937 | 46.2 |
| 25 | Frank M. Clark (D) | 80,704 | 58.9 |
| | Thomas W. King Jr. (R) | 56,375 | 41.1 |
| 26 | Thomas E. Morgan (D) | 92,755 | 64.8 |
| | Harry T. Zimmer Jr. (R) | 50,403 | 35.2 |
| 27 | James G. Fulton (R) | 105,998 | 64.1 |
| | Emery F. Bacon (D) | 59,283 | 35.9 |
| 28 | William S. Moorhead (D) | 82,081 | 67.3 |
| | Harry L. Verbofsky (R) | 39,900 | 32.7 |
| 29 | Robert J. Corbett (R) | 97,203 | 63.6 |
| | Lee T. Sellars (D) | 55,575 | 36.4 |
| 30 | Elmer J. Holland (D) | 98,244 | 66.7 |
| | Harold E. Morgan (R) | 49,093 | 33.3 |

## RHODE ISLAND

| | Candidates | Votes | % |
|---|---|---|---|
| 1 | Aime J. Forand (D) | 97,425 | 62.9 |
| | Francis E. Martineau (R) | 57,581 | 37.2 |
| 2 | John E. Fogarty (D) | 117,506 | 63.3 |
| | Robert L. Gammell (R) | 67,942 | 36.6 |

## SOUTH CAROLINA

| | Candidates | Votes | % |
|---|---|---|---|
| 1 | L. Mendel Rivers (D) | 13,538 | 100.0 |
| 2 | John J. Riley (D) | 13,677 | 100.0 |
| 3 | W. J. Bryan Dorn (D) | 9,528 | 99.9 |
| 4 | Robert T. Ashmore (D) | 17,247 | 100.0 |
| 5 | Robert W. Hemphill (D) | 9,780 | 100.0 |
| 6 | John L. McMillan (D) | 12,862 | 100.0 |

## SOUTH DAKOTA

| | Candidates | Votes | % |
|---|---|---|---|
| 1 | George McGovern (D) | 107,202 | 53.4 |
| | Joe Foss (R) | 93,388 | 46.6 |
| 2 | E. Y. Berry (R) | 31,908 | 55.6 |
| | J. T. McCullen (D) | 25,491 | 44.4 |

## TENNESSEE

| | Candidates | Votes | % |
|---|---|---|---|
| 1 | B. Carroll Reece (R) | 42,615 | 58.7 |
| | Mayne W. Miller (D) | 29,999 | 41.3 |
| 2 | Howard H. Baker (R) | 49,420 | 67.7 |
| | John Grady O'Hara Sr. (D) | 23,470 | 32.2 |
| 3 | James B. Frazier Jr. (D) | 31,267 | 100.0 |
| 4 | Joe L. Evins (D) | 38,062 | 100.0 |
| 5 | J. Carlton Loser (D) | 30,879 | 94.4 |
| | Porter Freeman (R) | 1,824# | 5.6 |
| 6 | Ross Bass (D) | 33,445 | 97.2 |
| 7 | Tom Murray (D) | 24,053 | 100.0 |
| 8 | Robert A. Everett (D) | 19,145 | 100.0 |
| 9 | Clifford Davis (D) | 46,550 | 100.0 |

## TEXAS

| | Candidates | Votes | % |
|---|---|---|---|
| 1 | Wright Patman (D) | 19,203 | 100.0 |
| 2 | Jack Brooks (D) | 47,092 | 100.0 |
| 3 | Lindley Beckworth (D) | 22,751 | 100.0 |
| 4 | Sam Rayburn (D) | 15,942 | 100.0 |
| 5 | Bruce Alger (R) | 62,722 | 52.6 |
| | Barefoot Sanders (D) | 56,566 | 47.4 |
| 6 | Olin Teague (D) | 25,827 | 100.0 |
| 7 | John Dowdy (D) | 22,733 | 96.7 |
| 8 | Albert Thomas (D) | 33,393 | 88.2 |
| | R. E. Nesmith (R) | 4,477 | 11.8 |
| 9 | Clark W. Thompson (D) | 36,012 | 100.0 |
| 10 | Homer Thornberry (D) | 28,990 | 100.0 |
| 11 | W. R. Poage (D) | 21,900 | 100.0 |
| 12 | Jim Wright (D) | 38,180 | 100.0 |
| 13 | Frank Ikard (D) | 27,671 | 100.0 |
| 14 | John Young (D) | 37,861 | 100.0 |
| 15 | Joe M. Kilgore (D) | 28,404 | 100.0 |
| 16 | J. T. Rutherford (D) | 28,744 | 100.0 |
| 17 | Omar Burleson (D) | 25,123 | 100.0 |
| 18 | Walter Rogers (D) | 34,617 | 100.0 |
| 19 | George Mahon (D) | 29,068 | 100.0 |
| 20 | Paul J. Kilday (D) | 23,539 | 100.0 |
| 21 | O. C. Fisher (D) | 26,497 | 100.0 |
| 22 | Bob Casey (D) | 43,660 | 61.7 |
| | T. Everton Kennerly (R) | 23,317 | 33.0 |
| | Jack Gardner | 3,789 | 5.4 |

## UTAH

| | | Votes | % |
|---|---|---|---|
| 1 | Henry Aldous Dixon (R) | 58,141 | 53.9 |
| | M. Blaine Peterson (D) | 49,735 | 46.1 |
| 2 | David S. King (D) | 91,213 | 51.1 |
| | William A. Dawson (R) | 87,234 | 48.9 |

## VERMONT

| | | Votes | % |
|---|---|---|---|
| AL | William H. Meyer (D) | 63,131 | 51.5 |
| | Harold J. Arthur (R) | 59,536 | 48.5 |

## VIRGINIA

| | | Votes | % |
|---|---|---|---|
| 1 | Thomas N. Downing (D) | 31,765 | 99.9 |
| 2 | Porter Hardy Jr. (D) | 32,758 | 100.0 |
| 3 | J. Vaughan Gary (D) | 34,040 | 76.1 |
| | Richard R. Ryder (R) | 10,668 | 23.9 |
| 4 | Watkins M. Abbitt (D) | 37,679 | 87.1 |
| | Frank M. McCann (I) | 5,556 | 12.9 |
| 5 | William M. Tuck (D) | 26,322 | 100.0 |
| 6 | Richard H. Poff (R) | 37,779 | 56.7 |
| | Richard F. Pence (D) | 28,530 | 42.9 |
| 7 | Burr P. Harrison (D) | 30,486 | 76.6 |
| | Henry A. Oder Jr. (I) | 9,294 | 23.4 |
| 8 | Howard W. Smith (D) | 28,815 | 99.7 |
| 9 | W. Pat Jennings (D) | 34,685 | 76.6 |
| | T. L. Maness (I) | 10,615 | 23.4 |
| 10 | Joel T. Broyhill (R) | 37,764 | 52.3 |
| | Joseph H. Freehill (D) | 33,553 | 46.5 |

## WASHINGTON

| | | Votes | % |
|---|---|---|---|
| 1 | Thomas M. Pelly (R) | 98,897 | 70.1 |
| | Robert Odman (D) | 42,128 | 29.9 |
| 2 | Jack Westland (R) | 62,152 | 53.6 |
| | Hugh B. Mitchell (D) | 53,436 | 46.1 |
| 3 | Russell V. Mack (R) | 69,745 | 60.9 |
| | Victor A. Meyers (D) | 44,515 | 38.9 |
| 4 | Catherine May (R) | 66,544 | 54.0 |
| | Frank LeRoux (D) | 56,308 | 45.7 |
| 5 | Walt Horan (R) | 67,072 | 53.2 |
| | Tom Delaney (D) | 58,431 | 46.3 |
| 6 | Thor C. Tollefson (R) | 63,560 | 53.5 |
| | John M. Coffee (D) | 54,536 | 45.9 |
| 7 | Don Magnuson (D) | 96,841 | 70.9 |
| | Bob Jones (R) | 39,708 | 29.1 |

## WEST VIRGINIA

| | Candidates | Votes | % |
|---|---|---|---|
| 1 | Arch A. Moore Jr. (R) | 55,613 | 54.6 |
| | Robert H. Mollohan (D) | 46,262 | 45.4 |
| 2 | Harley O. Staggers (D) | 57,761 | 62.7 |
| | Ward W. Keesecker (R) | 34,436 | 37.4 |
| 3 | Cleveland M. Bailey (D) | 59,084 | 59.9 |
| | Rex Keith Bumgardner (R) | 39,507 | 40.1 |
| 4 | Ken Hechler (D) | 60,794 | 51.5 |
| | Will E. Neal (R) | 57,291 | 48.5 |
| 5 | Elizabeth Kee (D) | 63,873 | 99.8 |
| 6 | John M. Slack Jr. (D) | 93,209 | 66.1 |
| | F. O'Dair Duff (R) | 47,852 | 33.9 |

## WISCONSIN

| | Candidates | Votes | % |
|---|---|---|---|
| 1 | Gerald T. Flynn (D) | 63,065 | 50.6 |
| | Eleanor J. Smith (R) | 61,615 | 49.4 |
| 2 | Robert W. Kastenmeier (D) | 78,009 | 52.1 |
| | Donald E. Tewes (R) | 71,748 | 47.9 |
| 3 | Gardner R. Withrow (R) | 47,858 | 51.2 |
| | Norman M. Clapp (D) | 45,608 | 48.8 |
| 4 | Clement J. Zablocki (D) | 112,226 | 74.1 |
| | James J. Arnold (R) | 39,167 | 25.9 |
| 5 | Henry S. Reuss (D) | 104,374 | 69.5 |
| | Otto R. Werkmeister (R) | 45,901 | 30.5 |
| 6 | William K. Van Pelt (R) | 61,490 | 52.8 |
| | James Megellas (D) | 55,031 | 47.2 |

| | Candidates | Votes | % |
|---|---|---|---|
| 7 | Melvin R. Laird (R) | 59,186 | 60.5 |
| | Kenneth Traeger (D) | 38,702 | 39.5 |
| 8 | John W. Byrnes (R) | 69,682 | 57.3 |
| | Milo Singler (D) | 51,887 | 42.7 |
| 9 | Lester R. Johnson (D) | 55,420 | 63.1 |
| | Charles A. Hornbeck (R) | 32,425 | 36.9 |
| 10 | Alvin E. O'Konski (R) | 58,801 | 67.1 |
| | Basil G. Kennedy (D) | 28,830 | 32.9 |

## WYOMING

| | Candidates | Votes | % |
|---|---|---|---|
| AL | Keith Thomson (R) | 59,894 | 53.6 |
| | Ray Whitaker (D) | 51,886 | 46.4 |

# 1959 House Elections

## HAWAII

(Became a state Aug. 21, 1959)

| | Candidates | Votes | % |
|---|---|---|---|
| AL | Daniel K. Inouye (D) | 111,727 | 68.2 |
| | Charles H. Silva (R) | 51,058 | 31.2 |

## IOWA

### Special Election

| | | Votes | % |
|---|---|---|---|
| 4 | John Henry Kyl (R)# | 28,326 | 52.3 |
| | C. Edwin Gilmour (D) | 25,809 | 47.7 |

## NEW YORK

### Special Election

| | | Votes | % |
|---|---|---|---|
| 43 | Charles E. Goodell (R) | 27,454 | 65.0 |
| | Robert E. McCaffery (D) | 14,250 | 33.8 |

# Explanation of Symbols in House Returns

In the returns for House elections *symbols* are used to denote special circumstances. In cases where no symbol is used, the candidate who received the most votes won the election to the House. The following is a key to the symbols used:

✔ Elected to the House. The symbol is used to identify winning candidates in three types of situations: (1) When candidates ran for two or more at-large seats in states which chose all of their at-large representatives in a single election, or ran in a multi-member district; (2) when the vote total and percentage of one or more of the candidates are unavailable and (3) when a candidate who did not receive the highest vote total was seated by the House. *(Explanation of multi-member districts, see p. 916.)*

‡ The symbol is used when an election dispute resulted in the unseating of a representative *after* he was sworn in. *(For discussion of specific cases, consult the Biographical Directory of the United States Congress 1774-1989, U.S. Government Printing Office, Washington, D.C., 1989; hereafter referred to as the Biographical Directory.)*

\* The symbol is used for three types of situations: (1) When a representative-elect died or declined his seat before the constitutionally set date for the beginning of his term—March 4 until 1935, and Jan. 3 thereafter; (2) when the House refused to seat any candidate claiming election to a seat and (3) when state law required a candidate to obtain a popular vote majority for election to the House, but the candidate receiving the most votes failed to receive a majority. *(For discussion of specific cases, consult the Biographical Directory; explanation of majority vote requirement, see p. 945.)*

\# Information for 1824-1973 returns was obtained from a source other than the Inter-University Consortium for Political and Social Research. *(For a listing of other sources, see p. 1327.)*

**Footnotes.** Numbered footnotes are used to explain unusual situations, such as a series of elections in the same year in the same House district, anomalies resulting from reapportionment and special procedures for conducting House elections in certain states.

# 1960 House Elections

## ALABAMA

| | Candidates | Votes | % |
|---|---|---|---|
| 1 | Frank W. Boykin (D) | 45,225 | 100.0 |
| 2 | George Grant (D) | 44,487 | 100.0 |
| 3 | George Andrews (D) | 33,881 | 100.0 |
| 4 | Kenneth A. Roberts (D) | 34,855 | 99.9 |
| 5 | Albert Rains (D) | 48,772 | 100.0 |
| 6 | Armistead I. Selden Jr. (D) | 23,245 | 100.0 |
| 7 | Carl Elliott (D) | 36,124 | 100.0 |
| 8 | Robert E. Jones (D) | 52,411 | 79.2 |
| | H. G. Williams (R) | 13,800 | 20.8 |
| 9 | George Huddleston Jr. (D) | 70,507 | 67.3 |
| | William P. Ivey (R) | 34,317 | 32.7 |

## ALASKA

| | | Votes | % |
|---|---|---|---|
| AL | Ralph J. Rivers (D) | 33,546 | 56.8 |
| | R. L. (Ron) Rettig (R) | 25,517 | 43.2 |

## ARIZONA

| | | Votes | % |
|---|---|---|---|
| 1 | John J. Rhodes (R) | 121,563 | 59.2 |
| | Richard F. Harless (D) | 83,676 | 40.8 |
| 2 | Stewart L. Udall (D) | 95,512 | 55.8 |
| | Mac C. Matheson (R) | 75,811 | 44.3 |

## ARKANSAS

| | | Votes | % |
|---|---|---|---|
| 1 | Ezekiel C. Gathings (D) | | 100.0 |
| 2 | Wilbur D. Mills (D) | | 100.0 |
| 3 | James W. Trimble (D) | | 100.0 |
| 4 | Oren Harris (D) | | 100.0 |
| 5 | Dale Alford (D) | 57,617 | 82.7 |
| | L. J. Churchill (R) | 12,054 | 17.3 |
| 6 | William F. Norrell (D) | | 100.0 |

## CALIFORNIA

| | | Votes | % |
|---|---|---|---|
| 1 | Clem Miller (D) | 115,829 | 51.6 |
| | Fred G. Dupuis (R) | 108,505 | 48.4 |
| 2 | Harold T. Johnson (D) | 109,565 | 62.7 |
| | Fredric H. Nagel Jr. (R) | 65,198 | 37.3 |
| 3 | John E. Moss Jr. (D) | 200,439 | 100.0 |
| 4 | William S. Mailliard (R) | 118,249 | 65.3 |
| | Phillips S. Davies (D) | 62,814 | 34.7 |
| 5 | John F. Shelley (D) | 104,507 | 83.7 |
| | Nick Verreos (R) | 20,305 | 16.3 |
| 6 | John F. Baldwin (R) | 128,418 | 58.7 |
| | Douglas R. Page (D) | 90,260 | 41.3 |
| 7 | Jeffery Cohelan (D) | 79,776 | 57.0 |
| | Lewis F. Sherman (R) | 60,065 | 43.0 |
| 8 | George P. Miller (D) | 152,476 | 62.0 |
| | Robert E. Hannon (R) | 93,403 | 38.0 |
| 9 | J. Arthur Younger (R) | 116,589 | 59.2 |
| | John D. Kaster (D) | 80,227 | 40.8 |
| 10 | Charles S. Gubser (R) | 170,063 | 58.9 |
| | Russell B. Bryan (D) | 118,520 | 41.1 |
| 11 | John J. McFall (D) | 97,368 | 65.4 |
| | Clifford B. Bull (R) | 51,473 | 34.6 |
| 12 | B. F. Sisk (D-R) | 141,974 | 99.9 |
| 13 | Charles M. Teague (R) | 146,072 | 65.0 |
| | L. Boyd Finch (D) | 78,597 | 35.0 |
| 14 | Harlen Hagen (D) | 97,026 | 56.5 |
| | G. Ray Arnett (R) | 74,800 | 43.5 |
| 15 | Gordon L. McDonough (R) | 89,234 | 51.3 |
| | Norman H. Martell (D) | 84,650 | 48.6 |
| 16 | Alphonzo Bell (R) | 83,601 | 55.4 |
| | Jerry Pacht (D) | 67,318 | 44.6 |
| 17 | Cecil R. King (D) | 206,620 | 67.7 |
| | Tom Coffee (R) | 98,510 | 32.3 |
| 18 | Craig Hosmer (R) | 129,851 | 70.0 |
| | D. Patrick Ahern (D) | 55,735 | 30.0 |
| 19 | Chet Holifield (D) | 145,479 | 78.2 |
| | Gordon S. McWilliams (R) | 40,491 | 21.8 |

| | Candidates | Votes | % |
|---|---|---|---|
| 20 | H. Allen Smith (R) | 90,214 | 70.1 |
| | Gareth W. Sadler (D) | 38,497 | 29.9 |
| 21 | Edgar W. Hiestand (R) | 179,376 | 58.4 |
| | Mrs. Rudd Brown (D) | 127,591 | 41.6 |
| 22 | James C. Corman (D) | 104,919 | 51.1 |
| | Lemoine Blanchard (R) | 100,321 | 48.9 |
| 23 | Clyde Doyle (D) | 148,415 | 74.2 |
| | Emmett A. Schwartz (R) | 51,548 | 25.8 |
| 24 | Glenard P. Lipscomb (R) | 82,497 | 59.7 |
| | Norman Hass (D) | 55,613 | 40.3 |
| 25 | John H. Rousselot (R) | 182,545 | 53.6 |
| | George A. Kasem (D) | 158,289 | 46.4 |
| 26 | James Roosevelt (D) | 150,318 | 73.4 |
| | William E. McIntyre (R) | 54,540 | 26.6 |
| 27 | Harry R. Sheppard (D) | 123,645 | 66.8 |
| | Robert M. Castle (R) | 61,484 | 33.2 |
| 28 | James B. Utt (R) | 241,765 | 60.9 |
| | Max E. Woods (D) | 155,221 | 39.1 |
| 29 | D. S. Saund (D) | 76,139 | 57.1 |
| | Charles H. Jameson (R) | 57,319 | 43.0 |
| 30 | Bob Wilson (R) | 158,679 | 59.3 |
| | Walter Wencke (D) | 108,882 | 40.7 |

## COLORADO

| | | Votes | % |
|---|---|---|---|
| 1 | Byron G. Rogers (D) | 121,610 | 60.0 |
| | Robert D. Rolander (R) | 81,042 | 40.0 |
| 2 | Peter H. Dominick (R) | 150,964 | 57.6 |
| | Byron L. Johnson (D) | 111,077 | 42.4 |
| 3 | J. Edgar Chenoweth (R) | 85,825 | 52.1 |
| | Franklin R. Stewart (D) | 79,069 | 48.0 |
| 4 | Wayne N. Aspinall (D) | 58,731 | 68.5 |
| | Charles P. Casteel (R) | 26,961 | 31.5 |

## CONNECTICUT

| | | Votes | % |
|---|---|---|---|
| 1 | Emilio Q. Daddario (D) | 193,330 | 58.5 |
| | Thomas F. Brennan (R) | 137,386 | 41.5 |
| 2 | Horace Seely-Brown Jr. (R) | 93,971 | 50.1 |
| | William L. St. Onge (D) | 93,515 | 49.9 |
| 3 | Robert N. Giaimo (D) | 124,547 | 54.9 |
| | Albert W. Cretella (R) | 102,271 | 45.1 |
| 4 | Abner W. Sibal (R) | 160,654 | 51.3 |
| | Donald J. Irwin (D) | 150,205 | 48.0 |
| 5 | John S. Monagan (D) | 88,310 | 55.1 |
| | James T. Patterson (R) | 71,964 | 44.9 |
| AL | Frank Kowalski (D) | 657,680 | 54.0 |
| | Antoni N. Sadlak (R) | 560,803 | 46.0 |

## DELAWARE

| | | Votes | % |
|---|---|---|---|
| AL | Harris B. McDowell Jr. (D) | 98,227 | 50.5 |
| | James T. McKinstry (R) | 96,337 | 49.5 |

## FLORIDA

| | | Votes | % |
|---|---|---|---|
| 1 | William C. Cramer (R) | 159,515 | 58.4 |
| | James M. McEwen (D) | 113,504 | 41.6 |
| 2 | Charles E. Bennett (D) | 94,570 | 82.5 |
| | J. Edward Musser (R) | 20,090 | 17.5 |
| 3 | Robert L. F. Sikes (D) | 95,062 | 100.0 |
| 4 | Dante B. Fascell (D) | 194,023 | 70.5 |
| | Hugh M. Tartaglia (R) | 81,209 | 29.5 |
| 5 | A. Sydney Herlong Jr. (D) | 113,938 | 100.0 |
| 6 | Paul G. Rogers (D) | 138,226 | 62.0 |
| | John D. Kruse (R) | 84,776 | 38.0 |
| 7 | James A. Haley (D) | 65,144 | 61.4 |
| | Henry S. Bartholomew (R) | 40,923 | 38.6 |
| 8 | D. R. Matthews (D) | 46,794 | 100.0 |

## GEORGIA

| | | Votes | % |
|---|---|---|---|
| 1 | G. Elliott Hagan (D) | 53,749 | 100.0 |
| 2 | J. L. Pilcher (D) | 43,596 | 100.0 |

| | Candidates | Votes | % |
|---|---|---|---|
| 3 | E. L. Forrester (D) | 55,005 | 99.7 |
| 4 | John J. Flynt Jr. (D) | 53,394 | 100.0 |
| 5 | James C. Davis (D) | 80,023 | 99.7 |
| 6 | Carl Vinson (D) | 44,237 | 100.0 |
| 7 | John W. Davis (D) | 69,717 | 74.2 |
| | E. Ralph Ivey (R) | 24,285 | 25.8 |
| 8 | Iris Faircloth Blitch (D) | 50,456 | 99.8 |
| 9 | Phil M. Landrum (D) | 57,549 | 100.0 |
| 10 | Robert G. Stephens Jr. (D) | 41,679 | 99.9 |

## HAWAII

| | | Votes | % |
|---|---|---|---|
| AL | Daniel K. Inouye (D) | 135,827 | 74.4 |
| | Fred Titcomb (R) | 46,812 | 25.6 |

## IDAHO

| | | Votes | % |
|---|---|---|---|
| 1 | Gracie B. Pfost (D) | 68,863 | 60.4 |
| | Thomas A. Leupp (R) | 45,166 | 39.6 |
| 2 | Ralph R. Harding (D) | 90,161 | 51.2 |
| | Hamer H. Budge (R) | 86,100 | 48.9 |

## ILLINOIS

| | | Votes | % |
|---|---|---|---|
| 1 | William L. Dawson (D) | 75,938 | 77.8 |
| | Genoa S. Washington (R) | 21,660 | 22.2 |
| 2 | Barratt O'Hara (D) | 103,535 | 66.6 |
| | Bernard E. Epton (R) | 52,028 | 33.4 |
| 3 | William T. Murphy (D) | 114,523 | 59.1 |
| | Emmet F. Byrne (R) | 79,307 | 40.9 |
| 4 | Edward J. Derwinski (R) | 179,480 | 55.7 |
| | Frank G. Sulewski (D) | 142,772 | 44.3 |
| 5 | John C. Kluczynski (D) | 121,240 | 71.2 |
| | Edward J. Tomek (R) | 49,030 | 28.8 |
| 6 | Thomas J. O'Brien (D) | 107,474 | 71.7 |
| | Frank Estes (R) | 42,361 | 28.3 |
| 7 | Roland Victor Libonati (D) | 28,494 | 54.5 |
| | Lawrence J. Blasi (R) | 23,840 | 45.6 |
| 8 | Dan Rostenkowski (D) | 81,092 | 67.2 |
| | Henry Klinger Jr. (R) | 39,651 | 32.8 |
| 9 | Sidney R. Yates (D) | 80,681 | 60.1 |
| | Chester E. Emanuelson (R) | 53,686 | 40.0 |
| 10 | Harold R. Collier (R) | 126,671 | 57.1 |
| | Edward V. Hanrahan (D) | 95,214 | 42.9 |
| 11 | Roman C. Pucinski (D) | 101,224 | 54.0 |
| | Timothy P. Sheehan (R) | 86,305 | 46.0 |
| 12 | Edward R. Finnegan (D) | 94,907 | 50.8 |
| | Theodore P. Fields (R) | 91,978 | 49.2 |
| 13 | Marguerite Stitt Church (R) | 268,647 | 66.0 |
| | Tyler Thompson (D) | 138,348 | 34.0 |
| 14 | Elmer J. Hoffman (R) | 167,128 | 63.8 |
| | Hayes Beall (D) | 94,945 | 36.2 |
| 15 | Noah M. Mason (R) | 93,986 | 50.5 |
| | Dorothy Q. O'Brien (D) | 92,301 | 49.6 |
| 16 | John B. Anderson (R) | 115,693 | 62.3 |
| | Edwin M. Nelson (D) | 69,944 | 37.7 |
| 17 | Leslie C. Arends (R) | 107,896 | 61.3 |
| | William T. Larkin (D) | 68,020 | 38.7 |
| 18 | Robert H. Michel (R) | 94,388 | 59.3 |
| | Richard A. Estep (D) | 64,885 | 40.7 |
| 19 | Robert B. Chiperfield (R) | 82,622 | 50.6 |
| | John C. Watson (D) | 80,700 | 49.4 |
| 20 | Paul Findley (R) | 77,286 | 55.6 |
| | Montgomery B. Carrott (D) | 61,790 | 44.4 |
| 21 | Peter F. Mack Jr. (D) | 102,154 | 54.7 |
| | J. Waldo Ackerman Jr. (R) | 84,471 | 45.3 |
| 22 | William L. Springer (R) | 98,438 | 61.4 |
| | James T. Nally (D) | 61,837 | 38.6 |
| 23 | George E. Shipley (D) | 80,718 | 51.6 |
| | Frank H. Walker (R) | 75,809 | 48.4 |
| 24 | Melvin Price (D) | 144,560 | 72.2 |
| | Phyllis Schlafly (R) | 55,620 | 27.8 |
| 25 | Kenneth J. Gray (D) | 92,227 | 57.9 |
| | Gordon E. Kerr (R) | 67,067 | 42.1 |

## INDIANA

| | Candidates | Votes | % |
|---|---|---|---|
| 1 | Ray J. Madden (D) | 136,443 | 64.7 |
| | Philip P. Parker (R) | 73,984 | 35.1 |
| 2 | Charles A. Halleck (R) | 95,920 | 57.5 |
| | George H. Bowers (D) | 70,464 | 42.2 |
| 3 | John Brademas (D) | 115,070 | 52.4 |
| | F. Jay Nimtz (R) | 104,430 | 47.6 |
| 4 | E. Ross Adair (R) | 100,419 | 58.2 |
| | Byron McCammon (D) | 72,251 | 41.8 |
| 5 | J. Edward Roush (D) | 107,357# | 50.0 |
| | George O. Chambers (R) | 107,258# | 50.0 |
| 6 | Richard L. Roudebush (R) | 84,662 | 52.0 |
| | Fred Wampler (D) | 78,247 | 48.0 |
| 7 | William G. Bray (R) | 95,998 | 60.1 |
| | Thomas C. Cravens (D) | 63,646 | 39.9 |
| 8 | Winfield K. Denton (D) | 108,058 | 53.2 |
| | Alvan V. Burch (R) | 94,694 | 46.6 |
| 9 | Earl Wilson (R) | 71,402 | 50.6 |
| | Earl Hogan (D) | 69,761 | 49.4 |
| 10 | Ralph Harvey (R) | 104,885 | 57.1 |
| | Randall S. Harmon (D) | 78,716 | 42.9 |
| 11 | Donald Cogley Bruce (R) | 154,676 | 53.7 |
| | Joseph W. Barr (D) | 133,153 | 46.2 |

## IOWA

| | Candidates | Votes | % |
|---|---|---|---|
| 1 | Fred Schwengel (R) | 104,737 | 60.9 |
| | Walter J. Guenther (D) | 67,287 | 39.1 |
| 2 | James E. Bromwell (R) | 108,137 | 52.6 |
| | Leonard G. Wolf (D) | 97,608 | 47.4 |
| 3 | H. R. Gross (R) | 99,046 | 56.3 |
| | Edward J. Gallagher Jr. (D) | 76,837 | 43.7 |
| 4 | John Kyl (R) | 65,016 | 56.6 |
| | C. Edwin Gilmour (D) | 49,918 | 43.4 |
| 5 | Neal Smith (D) | 91,808 | 53.0 |
| | Floyd M. Burgeson (R) | 81,474 | 47.0 |
| 6 | Merwin Coad (D) | 70,353 | 53.6 |
| | Curtis G. Riehm (R) | 60,834 | 46.4 |
| 7 | Ben F. Jensen (R) | 66,037 | 55.8 |
| | Duane Orton (D) | 52,214 | 44.2 |
| 8 | Charles B. Hoeven (R) | 77,583 | 57.5 |
| | Donald E. O'Brien (D) | 57,333 | 42.5 |

## KANSAS

| | Candidates | Votes | % |
|---|---|---|---|
| 1 | William H. Avery (R) | 84,816 | 63.1 |
| | Marshall G. Gardiner (D) | 49,598 | 36.9 |
| 2 | Robert F. Ellsworth (R) | 95,346 | 52.3 |
| | Newell A. George (D) | 86,905 | 47.7 |
| 3 | Walter L. McVey (R) | 49,429 | 51.2 |
| | Denver D. Hargis (D) | 47,127 | 48.8 |
| 4 | Garner E. Shriver (R) | 119,275 | 55.2 |
| | William I. Robinson (D) | 96,706 | 44.8 |
| 5 | J. Floyd Breeding (D) | 75,687 | 55.5 |
| | Joe W. Hunter (R) | 60,794 | 44.5 |
| 6 | Bob Dole (R) | 62,335 | 59.3 |
| | William A. Davis (D) | 42,869 | 40.8 |

## KENTUCKY

| | Candidates | Votes | % |
|---|---|---|---|
| 1 | Frank A. Stubblefield (D) | 66,248 | 100.0 |
| 2 | William H. Natcher (D) | 55,877 | 100.0 |
| 3 | Frank W. Burke (D) | 115,421 | 50.3 |
| | Henry R. Heyburn (R) | 114,263 | 49.8 |
| 4 | Frank Chelf (D) | 48,743 | 100.0 |
| 5 | Brent Spence (D) | 63,555 | 55.4 |
| | Jule Appel (R) | 51,125 | 44.6 |
| 6 | John C. Watts (D) | 74,500 | 54.7 |
| | Howard A. Dickey (R) | 61,795 | 45.3 |
| 7 | Carl D. Perkins (D) | 82,746 | 56.1 |
| | Herbert Rowland (R) | 64,687 | 43.9 |
| 8 | Eugene Siler (R) | 81,903 | 71.8 |
| | Donald R. Shepherd (D) | 32,163 | 28.2 |

## LOUISIANA

| | Candidates | Votes | % |
|---|---|---|---|
| 1 | F. Edward Hebert (D) | 70,465 | 82.2 |
| | Norman W. Prendergast (R) | 15,314 | 17.9 |
| 2 | Hale Boggs (D) | 81,034 | 78.0 |
| | Elliot Ross Buckley (R) | 22,818 | 22.0 |
| 3 | Edwin E. Willis (D) | 52,428 | 83.6 |
| | Floyd J. Duplantis (R) | 10,286 | 16.4 |
| 4 | Overton Brooks (D) | 48,286 | 74.2 |
| | Fred C. McClanahan (R) | 16,827 | 25.8 |
| 5 | Otto E. Passman (D) | 22,181 | 100.0 |
| 6 | James H. Morrison (D) | 78,640 | 85.6 |
| | Charles H. Dillemuth (R) | 13,233 | 14.4 |
| 7 | T. A. Thompson (D) | 60,007 | 100.0 |
| 8 | Harold B. McSween (D) | 28,492 | 100.0 |

## MAINE

| | Candidates | Votes | % |
|---|---|---|---|
| 1 | Peter Garland (R) | 85,821 | 53.8 |
| | James C. Oliver (D) | 73,826 | 46.2 |
| 2 | Stanley R. Tupper (R) | 71,271 | 53.2 |
| | John C. Donovan (D) | 62,309 | 46.5 |
| 3 | Clifford G. McIntire (R) | 73,742 | 64.1 |
| | David G. Roberts (D) | 41,307 | 35.9 |

## MARYLAND

| | Candidates | Votes | % |
|---|---|---|---|
| 1 | Thomas F. Johnson (D) | 42,219 | 53.6 |
| | Edward T. Miller (R) | 36,508 | 46.4 |
| 2 | Daniel B. Brewster (D) | 126,452 | 58.6 |
| | Fife Symington (R) | 89,262 | 41.4 |
| 3 | Edward A. Garmatz (D) | 57,154 | 80.3 |
| | Robert J. Gerstung (R) | 14,026 | 19.7 |
| 4 | George H. Fallon (D) | 48,145 | 65.5 |
| | Melvin H. Kenney (R) | 25,394 | 34.5 |
| 5 | Richard E. Lankford (D) | 120,773 | 62.2 |
| | Carlyle J. Lancaster (R) | 73,433 | 37.8 |
| 6 | Charles McC. Mathias Jr. (R) | 115,088 | 52.0 |
| | John R. Foley (D) | 106,098 | 48.0 |
| 7 | Samuel N. Friedel (D) | 81,474 | 64.5 |
| | David M. Blum (R) | 44,779 | 35.5 |

## MASSACHUSETTS

| | Candidates | Votes | % |
|---|---|---|---|
| 1 | Silvio O. Conte (R) | 102,921 | 68.5 |
| | William H. Burns (D) | 46,863 | 31.2 |
| 2 | Edward P. Boland (D) | 135,815 | 100.0 |
| 3 | Philip J. Philbin (D) | 145,237 | 100.0 |
| 4 | Harold D. Donohue (D) | 122,364 | 64.5 |
| | Robert N. Scola (R) | 67,270 | 35.5 |
| 5 | F. Bradford Morse (R) | 123,161 | 54.5 |
| | William C. Madden (D) | 102,765 | 45.5 |
| 6 | William H. Bates (R) | 112,835 | 65.9 |
| | Mary Kennedy (D) | 58,312 | 34.1 |
| 7 | Thomas J. Lane (D) | 117,237 | 100.0 |
| 8 | Torbert H. Macdonald (D) | 114,333 | 65.8 |
| | Ward Collins Cramer (R) | 59,550 | 34.3 |
| 9 | Hastings Keith (R) | 110,955 | 55.7 |
| | Edward F. Harrington (D) | 88,222 | 44.3 |
| 10 | Laurence Curtis (R) | 98,257 | 58.2 |
| | Joseph J. Mulhern (D) | 70,510 | 41.8 |
| 11 | Thomas P. O'Neill Jr. (D) | 87,866 | 100.0 |
| 12 | John W. McCormack (D) | 86,057 | 100.0 |
| 13 | James A. Burke (D) | 126,936 | 58.5 |
| | Charles J. Gabriel (R) | 89,921 | 41.5 |
| 14 | Joseph W. Martin Jr. (R) | 115,209 | 60.3 |
| | Edward F. Doolan (D) | 75,815 | 39.7 |

## MICHIGAN

| | Candidates | Votes | % |
|---|---|---|---|
| 1 | Thaddeus M. Machrowicz (D) | 102,948 | 88.4 |
| | Walter Czarnecki (R) | 13,157 | 11.3 |
| 2 | George Meader (R) | 110,124 | 59.6 |
| | Thomas P. Payne (D) | 74,276 | 40.2 |
| 3 | August E. Johansen (R) | 100,918 | 60.6 |
| | Samuel I. Clark (D) | 65,402 | 39.2 |
| 4 | Clare E. Hoffman (R) | 90,831 | 62.3 |
| | Edward Burns (D) | 54,655 | 37.5 |
| 5 | Gerald R. Ford Jr. (R) | 131,461 | 66.8 |
| | William S. Reamon (D) | 65,064 | 33.1 |
| 6 | Charles E. Chamberlain (R) | 138,355 | 56.6 |
| | Jerome F. O'Rourke (D) | 105,864 | 43.3 |
| 7 | James G. O'Hara (D) | 142,795 | 53.3 |
| | Robert J. McIntosh (R) | 124,750 | 46.6 |
| 8 | James Harvey (R) | 94,405 | 62.2 |
| | Mary M. Harden (D) | 57,126 | 37.6 |
| 9 | Robert P. Griffin (R) | 77,541 | 59.6 |
| | Donald G. Jennings (D) | 52,375 | 40.3 |
| 10 | Elford A. Cederberg (R) | 75,846 | 62.1 |
| | Daniel E. Reed (D) | 46,140 | 37.8 |
| 11 | Victor A. Knox (R) | 54,300 | 54.9 |
| | Prentiss M. Brown Jr. (D) | 44,650 | 45.1 |
| 12 | John B. Bennett (R) | 48,422 | 60.8 |
| | Robert C. McCarthy (D) | 31,137 | 39.1 |
| 13 | Charles C. Diggs Jr. (D) | 76,812 | 71.4 |
| | Robert B. Blackwell (R) | 30,369 | 28.2 |
| 14 | Louis C. Rabaut (D) | 132,602 | 62.7 |
| | Lois V. Nair (R) | 78,548 | 37.1 |
| 15 | John D. Dingell (D) | 111,671 | 79.4 |
| | Robert J. Robbins (R) | 28,532 | 20.3 |
| 16 | John Lesinski (D) | 211,733 | 66.0 |
| | Lee H. Clark (R) | 108,332 | 33.8 |
| 17 | Martha W. Griffiths (D) | 134,660 | 57.6 |
| | Richard E. Morell (R) | 98,721 | 42.2 |
| 18 | William S. Broomfield (R) | 163,233 | 55.9 |
| | James Kellis (D) | 128,678 | 44.0 |

## MINNESOTA

| | Candidates | Votes | % |
|---|---|---|---|
| 1 | Albert H. Quie (R) | 100,381 | 60.5 |
| | George Shepherd (DFL) | 65,422 | 39.5 |
| 2 | Ancher Nelsen (R) | 96,471 | 57.2 |
| | Russel Schwandt (DFL) | 72,239 | 42.8 |
| 3 | Clark MacGregor (R) | 154,847 | 51.6 |
| | Roy W. Wier (DFL) | 139,908 | 46.6 |
| 4 | Joseph E. Karth (DFL) | 108,738 | 61.0 |
| | Joseph J. Mitchell (R) | 69,635 | 39.0 |
| 5 | Walter H. Judd (R) | 86,223 | 60.9 |
| | George W. Matthews (DFL) | 55,377 | 39.1 |
| 6 | Fred Marshall (DFL) | 87,332 | 59.6 |
| | Frank L. King (R) | 59,305 | 40.4 |
| 7 | H. Carl Andersen (R) | 73,487 | 52.5 |
| | Gordon E. Duenow (DFL) | 66,609 | 47.6 |
| 8 | John A. Blatnik (DFL) | 107,154 | 69.5 |
| | Jerry H. Ketola (R) | 47,099 | 30.5 |
| 9 | Odin Langen (R) | 62,322 | 52.2 |
| | Coya Knutson (DFL) | 57,114 | 47.8 |

## MISSISSIPPI

| | Candidates | Votes | % |
|---|---|---|---|
| 1 | Thomas G. Abernethy (D) | 44,381 | 93.6 |
| | Edward W. Scott (R) | 3,018 | 6.4 |
| 2 | Jamie L. Whitten (D) | 23,942 | 100.0 |
| 3 | Frank E. Smith (D) | 25,592 | 92.7 |
| | W. A. Clark (R) | 2,018 | 7.3 |
| 4 | John Bell Williams (D) | 58,974 | 100.0 |
| 5 | Arthur Winstead (D) | 40,480 | 100.0 |
| 6 | William M. Colmer (D) | 59,372 | 100.0 |

## MISSOURI

| | Candidates | Votes | % |
|---|---|---|---|
| 1 | Frank M. Karsten (D) | 161,394 | 70.8 |
| | Sam J. Kallaos (R) | 66,640 | 29.2 |
| 2 | Thomas B. Curtis (R) | 150,327 | 56.7 |
| | Richard L. Carp (D) | 114,803 | 43.3 |
| 3 | Leonor K. Sullivan (D) | 87,637 | 73.3 |
| | Morton L. Schwartz (R) | 31,902 | 26.7 |
| 4 | William J. Randall (D) | 111,557 | 54.0 |
| | Kenneth K. Lowe (R) | 95,070 | 46.0 |
| 5 | Richard Bolling (D) | 74,834 | 61.0 |
| | Clinton H. Gates (R) | 47,810 | 39.0 |
| 6 | W. R. Hull Jr. (D) | 93,285 | 54.6 |
| | Ethan H. Campbell (R) | 77,638 | 45.4 |
| 7 | Durward G. Hall (R) | 107,208 | 54.9 |
| | Charles H. Brown (D) | 88,162 | 45.1 |
| 8 | Richard Ichord (D) | 79,020 | 58.0 |
| | Curtis J. Tindel (R) | 57,234 | 42.0 |
| 9 | Clarence Cannon (D) | 107,384 | 59.8 |
| | Anthony C. Schroeder (R) | 72,098 | 40.2 |
| 10 | Paul C. Jones (D) | 69,997 | 100.0 |
| 11 | Morgan M. Moulder (D) | 74,866 | 50.1 |
| | Robert A. Bartel (R) | 74,505 | 49.9 |

## MONTANA

| | Candidates | Votes | % |
|---|---|---|---|
| 1 | Arnold Olsen (D) | 63,081 | 53.3 |
| | George P. Sarsfield (R) | 55,347 | 46.7 |
| 2 | James F. Battin (R) | 78,277 | 50.9 |
| | Leo Graybill Jr. (D) | 75,507 | 49.1 |

## NEBRASKA

| | | Votes | % |
|---|---|---|---|
| 1 | Phil Weaver (R) | 89,016 | 55.8 |
| | Gerald T. Whelan (D) | 70,626 | 44.2 |
| 2 | Glenn Cunningham (R) | 101,347 | 66.6 |
| | Joseph V. Benesch (D) | 50,768 | 33.4 |
| 3 | Ralph F. Beermann (R) | 67,129 | 51.3 |
| | Lawrence Brock (D) | 63,838 | 48.7 |
| 4 | Dave Martin (R) | 69,754 | 51.1 |
| | Donald F. McGinley (D) | 66,609 | 48.9 |

## NEVADA

| | | Votes | % |
|---|---|---|---|
| AL | Walter S. Baring (D) | 59,616 | 57.5 |
| | George W. Malone (R) | 43,986 | 42.5 |

## NEW HAMPSHIRE

| | | Votes | % |
|---|---|---|---|
| 1 | Chester E. Merrow (R) | 88,118 | 56.6 |
| | Romeo J. Champagne (D) | 67,717 | 43.5 |
| 2 | Perkins Bass (R) | 77,701 | 60.3 |
| | Stuart V. Nims (D) | 51,145 | 39.7 |

## NEW JERSEY

| | | Votes | % |
|---|---|---|---|
| 1 | William T. Cahill (R) | 153,817 | 57.6 |
| | John A. Healey (D) | 112,802 | 42.2 |
| 2 | Milton W. Glenn (R) | 77,894 | 56.6 |
| | John A. Miller (D) | 59,520 | 43.2 |
| 3 | James C. Auchincloss (R) | 139,590 | 53.1 |
| | Katharine E. White (D) | 123,280 | 46.9 |
| 4 | Frank Thompson Jr. (D) | 115,761 | 60.2 |
| | A. Jerome Moore (R) | 76,067 | 39.6 |
| 5 | Peter H. B. Frelinghuysen Jr. (R) | 170,859 | 58.6 |
| | Jerome H. Taub (D) | 120,302 | 41.3 |
| 6 | Florence P. Dwyer (R) | 136,723 | 57.7 |
| | Jack B. Dunn (D) | 98,043 | 41.4 |
| 7 | William B. Widnall (R) | 156,758 | 63.7 |
| | James Dobbins (D) | 88,649 | 36.0 |
| 8 | Charles S. Joelson (D) | 88,100 | 52.0 |
| | Walter P. Kennedy (R) | 74,165 | 43.8 |
| 9 | Frank C. Osmers Jr. (R) | 127,088 | 58.1 |
| | Vincent T. McKenna (D) | 91,065 | 41.6 |
| 10 | Peter W. Rodino Jr. (D) | 84,859 | 65.3 |
| | Alphonse A. Miele (R) | 43,238 | 33.3 |
| 11 | Hugh J. Addonizio (D) | 75,533 | 61.4 |
| | Frank A. Palmieri (R) | 44,580 | 36.2 |
| 12 | George M. Wallhauser (R) | 76,945 | 50.2 |
| | Robert R. Peacock (D) | 73,119 | 47.7 |
| 13 | Cornelius E. Gallagher (D) | 80,490 | 68.3 |
| | Samuel J. Kanis (R) | 37,350 | 31.7 |
| 14 | Dominick V. Daniels (D) | 64,359 | 57.4 |
| | Frank A. Musto (R) | 46,770 | 41.7 |

## NEW MEXICO

| | | Votes | % |
|---|---|---|---|
| AL | Thomas C. Morris (D) | 172,577 | 58.0 |
| | John D. Robb (R) | 124,101 | 41.7 |
| AL | Joseph M. Montoya (D) | 176,514 | 58.6 |
| | Edward W. Balcomb (R) | 123,683 | 41.1 |

## NEW YORK

| | | Votes | % |
|---|---|---|---|
| 1 | Otis G. Pike (D, L) | 187,286 | 50.4 |
| | Stuyvesant Wainwright (R) | 184,549 | 49.6 |
| 2 | Steven B. Derounian (R) | 139,423 | 61.0 |
| | John J. Drury (D, L) | 89,176 | 39.0 |
| 3 | Frank J. Becker (R) | 133,416 | 54.1 |
| | Julius J. Rosen (D, L) | 113,143 | 45.9 |
| 4 | Seymour Halpern (R) | 115,736 | 55.1 |
| | Bernard A. Helfat (D, L) | 94,390 | 44.9 |
| 5 | Joseph P. Addabbo (D, L) | 60,453 | 54.2 |
| | George Archinal (R) | 51,129 | 45.8 |
| 6 | Lester Holtzman (D, L) | 155,904 | 65.6 |
| | Vincent L. Pitaro (R) | 81,694 | 34.4 |
| 7 | James J. Delaney (D, L) | 92,424 | 60.7 |
| | Edward V. Lisoski (R) | 59,882 | 39.3 |
| 8 | Victor L. Anfuso (D, L) | 60,030 | 72.9 |
| | Leon F. Nadrowski (R) | 22,318 | 27.1 |
| 9 | Eugene J. Keogh (D, L) | 84,941 | 72.3 |
| | Herman Sanders (R) | 32,538 | 27.7 |
| 10 | Edna F. Kelly (D, L) | 98,938 | 76.6 |
| | Jerome P. Schneider (R) | 30,243 | 23.4 |
| 11 | Emanuel Celler (D, L) | 139,397 | 81.6 |
| | Seymour Besunder (R) | 31,378 | 18.4 |
| 12 | Hugh L. Carey (D, L) | 65,996 | 50.4 |
| | Francis E. Dorn (R) | 64,800 | 49.6 |
| 13 | Abraham J. Multer (D, L) | 117,087 | 75.4 |
| | Joseph A. DeMarco (R) | 38,189 | 24.6 |
| 14 | John J. Rooney (D, L) | 80,972 | 70.6 |
| | Carlo M. Colavito (R) | 33,769 | 29.4 |
| 15 | John H. Ray (R) | 80,218 | 48.7 |
| | John M. Murphy (D) | 77,812 | 47.2 |
| 16 | Adam Clayton Powell Jr. (D) | 59,957 | 71.6 |
| | Joseph A. Bailey (R) | 14,706 | 17.6 |
| | Arthur O. Boyer (L) | 9,093 | 10.9 |
| 17 | John V. Lindsay (R) | 81,006 | 60.2 |
| | William J. Vanden Heuvel (D, L) | 53,574 | 39.8 |
| 18 | Alfred E. Santangelo (D) | 47,749 | 58.3 |
| | Charles Muzzicato (R) | 27,419 | 33.5 |
| | Faustino Louis Garcia (L) | 6,680 | 8.2 |
| 19 | Leonard Farbstein (D) | 68,445 | 72.4 |
| | Thomas P. O'Callaghan (R) | 26,054 | 27.6 |
| 20 | William F. Ryan (D) | 55,272 | 55.7 |
| | Morris Aarons (R) | 30,046 | 30.3 |
| | Ludwig Teller (L) | 13,884 | 14.0 |
| 21 | Herbert Zelenko (D, L) | 87,775 | 74.6 |
| | Thomas H. Bartzos (R) | 29,835 | 25.4 |
| 22 | James C. Healey (D) | 78,717 | 65.0 |
| | Dominick A. Fusco (R) | 24,958 | 20.6 |
| | David I. Wells (L) | 17,438 | 14.4 |
| 23 | Jacob H. Gilbert (D) | 61,474 | 70.6 |
| | Benjamin Thornley (R) | 15,208 | 17.5 |
| | Nicholas B. Gyory (L) | 10,420 | 12.0 |
| 24 | Charles A. Buckley (D) | 89,140 | 56.6 |
| | Michael R. Cappelli (R) | 43,110 | 27.4 |
| | Murray Koenig (L) | 25,283 | 16.1 |
| 25 | Paul A. Fino (R) | 112,187 | 59.8 |
| | Eugene L. Sugarman (D) | 66,539 | 35.5 |
| 26 | Edwin B. Dooley (R) | 98,506 | 52.6 |
| | Phil E. Gilbert Jr. (D, L) | 88,879 | 47.4 |
| 27 | Robert R. Barry (R) | 121,533 | 56.3 |
| | John R. Harold (D) | 86,997 | 40.3 |
| 28 | Katharine St.George (R) | 107,179 | 58.7 |
| | James E. Truex (D, L) | 75,448 | 41.3 |
| 29 | J. Ernest Wharton (R) | 103,966 | 56.7 |
| | Gore Vidal (D, L) | 79,252 | 43.3 |
| 30 | Leo W. O'Brien (D, L) | 117,692 | 62.9 |
| | Irving I. Waxman (R) | 69,549 | 37.1 |
| 31 | Carleton J. King (R) | 99,604 | 60.4 |
| | Louis E. Wolfe (D, L) | 65,305 | 39.6 |
| 32 | Samuel S. Stratton (D, L) | 98,990 | 62.3 |
| | W. Clyde Wright (R) | 59,890 | 37.7 |
| 33 | Clarence E. Kilburn (R) | 91,710 | 61.9 |
| | Edward J. Gosier (D) | 53,130 | 35.9 |
| 34 | Alexander Pirnie (R) | 98,063 | 55.3 |
| | Edwin L. Slusarczyk (D, L) | 79,153 | 44.7 |
| 35 | R. Walter Riehlman (R) | 105,241 | 53.8 |
| | Jerome M. Wilson (D) | 87,347 | 44.6 |
| 36 | John Taber (R) | 84,441 | 52.6 |
| | Francis J. Souhan (D, L) | 76,120 | 47.4 |
| 37 | Howard W. Robison (R) | 123,782 | 63.4 |
| | Joseph V. Julian (D, L) | 71,354 | 36.6 |
| 38 | Jessica McC. Weis (R) | 114,871 | 57.6 |
| | Arthur B. Curran Jr. (D, L) | 84,716 | 42.4 |
| 39 | Harold C. Ostertag (R) | 103,162 | 59.7 |
| | Henry R. Dutcher Jr. (D, L) | 69,704 | 40.3 |
| 40 | William E. Miller (R) | 104,752 | 53.6 |
| | Mariano A. Lucca (D) | 85,005 | 43.5 |
| 41 | Thaddeus J. Dulski (D, L) | 82,114 | 56.2 |
| | Ralph J. Radwan (R) | 63,889 | 43.8 |
| 42 | John R. Pillion (R) | 122,073 | 55.4 |
| | Charles J. McCabe (D) | 93,492 | 42.4 |
| 43 | Charles E. Goodell (R) | 87,585 | 62.8 |
| | T. Joseph Lynch (D) | 48,423 | 34.7 |

### Special Election

| | | Votes | % |
|---|---|---|---|
| 23 | Jacob H. Gilbert (D) | 4,594 | 82.3 |
| | Simon M. Koenig (R) | 574 | 10.3 |
| | Hector Mathew (L) | 411 | 7.4 |

## NORTH CAROLINA

| | | Votes | % |
|---|---|---|---|
| 1 | Herbert C. Bonner (D) | 48,809 | 86.6 |
| | Zeno O. Ratcliff (R) | 7,587 | 13.5 |
| 2 | L. H. Fountain (D) | 51,156 | 87.8 |
| | L. Paul Gooding (R) | 7,135 | 12.2 |
| 3 | David N. Henderson (D) | 51,193 | 71.2 |
| | Jack D. Brinson (R) | 20,674 | 28.8 |
| 4 | Harold D. Cooley (D) | 75,464 | 66.6 |
| | Elam Reamuel Temple Jr. (R) | 37,821 | 33.4 |
| 5 | Ralph J. Scott (D) | 66,079 | 57.6 |
| | Russell F. Biggam (R) | 48,572 | 42.4 |
| 6 | Horace R. Kornegay (D) | 79,809 | 59.6 |
| | Holland L. Robb (R) | 54,028 | 40.4 |
| 7 | Alton Lennon (D) | 71,726 | 76.5 |
| | Joel C. Clifton (R) | 21,997 | 23.5 |
| 8 | A. Paul Kitchin (D) | 71,429 | 56.3 |
| | A. M. Snipes (R) | 55,372 | 43.7 |
| 9 | Hugh Q. Alexander (D) | 75,909 | 53.1 |
| | W. S. Bogle (R) | 67,033 | 46.9 |
| 10 | Charles Raper Jonas (R) | 97,138 | 58.6 |
| | David Clark (D) | 68,761 | 41.5 |
| 11 | Basil L. Whitener (D) | 65,478 | 61.1 |
| | Kelly Dixon (R) | 41,763 | 38.9 |
| 12 | Roy A. Taylor (D) | 61,170 | 52.0 |
| | Heinz Rollman (R) | 56,368 | 48.0 |

### Special Election

| | | Votes | % |
|---|---|---|---|
| 12 | Roy A. Taylor (D) | 28,744 | 98.6 |

## NORTH DAKOTA

| | | Votes | % |
|---|---|---|---|
| AL | Don L. Short (R) | 135,579✔ | |
| | Hjalmar Nygaard (R) | 127,118✔ | |
| | Raymond Vendsel (D) | 120,773 | |
| | Anson J. Anderson (D) | 109,207 | |

## OHIO

| | | Votes | % |
|---|---|---|---|
| 1 | Gordon H. Scherer (R) | 88,899 | 58.9 |
| | W. Ted Osborne (D) | 62,043 | 41.1 |
| 2 | Donald D. Clancy (R) | 118,046 | 57.4 |
| | H. A. Sand (D) | 87,531 | 42.6 |
| 3 | Paul F. Schenck (R) | 167,117 | 62.0 |
| | R. William Patterson (D) | 102,237 | 38.0 |
| 4 | William M. McCulloch (R) | 99,683 | 65.4 |
| | Joseph J. Murphy (D) | 52,797 | 34.6 |
| 5 | Delbert L. Latta (R) | 85,175 | 67.3 |
| | Tom P. McRitchie (D) | 41,375 | 32.7 |
| 6 | William H. Harsha Jr. (R) | 80,124 | 55.2 |
| | Franklin E. Smith (D) | 65,045 | 44.8 |
| 7 | Clarence J. Brown (R) | 105,026 | 65.5 |
| | Joseph A. Sullivan (D) | 55,451 | 34.6 |
| 8 | Jackson E. Betts (R) | 81,373 | 67.7 |
| | Virgil M. Gase (D) | 38,871 | 32.3 |
| 9 | Thomas Ludlow Ashley (D) | 108,688 | 56.9 |
| | Howard C. Cook (R) | 82,433 | 43.1 |
| 10 | Walter H. Moeller (D) | 58,085 | 52.5 |
| | Oakley C. Collins (R) | 52,479 | 47.5 |
| 11 | Robert E. Cook (D) | 104,183 | 51.0 |
| | David S. Dennison Jr. (R) | 99,991 | 49.0 |
| 12 | Samuel L. Devine (R) | 140,236 | 60.7 |
| | Richard E. Liming (D) | 90,894 | 39.3 |

## OHIO

| | Candidates | Votes | % |
|---|---|---|---|
| 13 | Charles A. Mosher (R) | 73,110 | 51.4 |
| | J. William McCray (D) | 69,033 | 48.6 |
| 14 | William H. Ayres (R) | 145,526 | 61.5 |
| | John H. Mihaly (D) | 91,103 | 38.5 |
| 15 | Tom V. Moorehead (R) | 49,742 | 51.2 |
| | Herbert U. Smith (D) | 47,366 | 48.8 |
| 16 | Frank T. Bow (R) | 130,542 | 62.5 |
| | John G. Freedom (D) | 78,257 | 37.5 |
| 17 | John M. Ashbrook (R) | 79,609 | 53.0 |
| | Robert W. Levering (D) | 70,470 | 47.0 |
| 18 | Wayne L. Hays (D) | 96,474 | 65.6 |
| | Walter Jay Hunston (R) | 50,698 | 34.5 |
| 19 | Michael J. Kirwan (D) | 102,874 | 68.9 |
| | Paul E. Stevens (R) | 46,537 | 31.2 |
| 20 | Michael A. Feighan (D) | 113,302 | 67.8 |
| | Leonard G. Richter (R) | 53,845 | 32.2 |
| 21 | Charles A. Vanik (D) | 103,460 | 73.0 |
| | William O. Walker (R) | 38,326 | 27.0 |
| 22 | Frances P. Bolton (R) | 88,389 | 56.9 |
| | Chat Paterson (D) | 66,930 | 43.1 |
| 23 | William E. Minshall (R) | 123,364 | 67.3 |
| | Daniel Winston (D) | 59,893 | 32.7 |

### Special Election

| | | Votes | % |
|---|---|---|---|
| 6 | Ward M. Miller (R) | 76,520 | 55.4 |
| | Gladys E. Davis (D) | 61,713 | 44.6 |

## OKLAHOMA

| | | Votes | % |
|---|---|---|---|
| 1 | Page Belcher (R) | 133,964 | 63.8 |
| | Yates Land (D) | 75,934 | 36.2 |
| 2 | Ed Edmondson (D) | 79,732 | 57.0 |
| | Bill Sharp (R) | 60,253 | 43.0 |
| 3 | Carl Albert (D) | 56,138 | 74.9 |
| | George B. Sherritt (R) | 18,799 | 25.1 |
| 4 | Tom Steed (D) | 54,181 | 60.7 |
| | Don H. Crall (R) | 35,028 | 39.3 |
| 5 | John Jarman (D) | 125,286 | 66.6 |
| | Hobart H. Hobbs (R) | 62,971 | 33.5 |
| 6[1] | Victor Wickersham (D) | 68,192 | 50.4 |
| | Clyde Wheeler Jr. (R) | 67,116 | 49.6 |

## OREGON

| | | Votes | % |
|---|---|---|---|
| 1 | Walter Norblad (R) | 144,743 | 65.1 |
| | Marv Owens (D) | 77,689 | 34.9 |
| 2 | Al Ullman (D) | 62,690 | 59.6 |
| | Ronald E. Phair (R) | 42,516 | 40.4 |
| 3 | Edith Green (D) | 157,243 | 63.9 |
| | Wallace L. Lee (R) | 88,906 | 36.1 |
| 4 | Edwin R. Durno (R) | 96,022 | 51.1 |
| | Charles O. Porter (D) | 91,947 | 48.9 |

## PENNSYLVANIA

| | | Votes | % |
|---|---|---|---|
| 1 | William A. Barrett (D) | 88,805 | 77.0 |
| | Michael Grasso Jr. (R) | 26,601 | 23.1 |
| 2 | Kathryn E. Granahan (D) | 109,452 | 72.3 |
| | Joseph C. Bruno (R) | 42,019 | 27.7 |
| 3 | James A. Byrne (D) | 80,258 | 69.7 |
| | Joseph Patrick Gorham (R) | 34,956 | 30.3 |
| 4 | Robert N. C. Nix (D) | 84,053 | 78.4 |
| | Clarence M. Smith (R) | 23,146 | 21.6 |
| 5 | William J. Green Jr. (D) | 140,658 | 61.0 |
| | James W. Gilmour (R) | 90,087 | 39.0 |
| 6 | Herman Toll (D) | 109,275 | 59.6 |
| | David O. Maxwell (R) | 74,132 | 40.4 |
| 7 | William H. Milliken Jr.(R) | 136,021 | 53.0 |
| | Henry Gouley (D) | 120,839 | 47.0 |
| 8 | Willard S. Curtin (R) | 121,564 | 56.1 |
| | Donald V. Hock (D) | 95,140 | 43.9 |
| 9 | Paul B. Dague (R) | 128,917 | 66.6 |
| | Howard H. Halsey (D) | 64,659 | 33.4 |
| 10 | William W. Scranton (R) | 97,012 | 54.8 |
| | Stanley A. Prokop (D) | 80,097 | 45.2 |
| 11 | Daniel J. Flood (D) | 115,042 | 67.1 |
| | Donald B. Ayers (R) | 56,428 | 32.9 |

| | Candidates | Votes | % |
|---|---|---|---|
| 12 | Ivor D. Fenton (R) | 72,061 | 52.4 |
| | William H. Deitman (D) | 65,585 | 47.7 |
| 13 | Richard S. Schweiker (R) | 142,966 | 61.8 |
| | Warren M. Ballard (D) | 88,486 | 38.2 |
| 14 | George M. Rhodes (D) | 60,211 | 53.8 |
| | James H. Mantis (R) | 51,746 | 46.2 |
| 15 | Francis E. Walter (D) | 67,830 | 55.2 |
| | Woodrow A. Horn (R) | 55,125 | 44.8 |
| 16 | Walter M. Mumma (R) | 93,831 | 62.5 |
| | Miles Albright (D) | 56,267 | 37.5 |
| 17 | Herman T. Schneebeli (R) | 82,040 | 56.7 |
| | Dean R. Fisher (D) | 62,695 | 43.3 |
| 18 | J. Irving Whalley (R) | 88,397 | 62.3 |
| | Robert M. Meyers (D) | 53,453 | 37.7 |
| 19 | George A. Goodling (R) | 88,776 | 53.2 |
| | James M. Quigley (D) | 78,043 | 46.8 |
| 20 | James E. Van Zandt (R) | 77,776 | 67.8 |
| | Robert N. Hendershot (D) | 36,997 | 32.2 |
| 21 | John H. Dent (D) | 85,853 | 56.0 |
| | William L. Batten (R) | 65,551 | 42.8 |
| 22 | John P. Saylor (R) | 89,261 | 57.4 |
| | William D. Patton (D) | 66,383 | 42.7 |
| 23 | Leon H. Gavin (R) | 74,542 | 62.4 |
| | John H. Cartwright (D) | 43,927 | 36.8 |
| 24 | Carroll D. Kearns (R) | 95,149 | 51.0 |
| | Chester C. Hampton (D) | 91,498 | 49.0 |
| 25 | Frank M. Clark (D) | 102,750 | 58.1 |
| | Fred A. Obley (R) | 74,217 | 41.9 |
| 26 | Thomas E. Morgan (D) | 111,362 | 63.6 |
| | Bartley P. Osborne (R) | 63,702 | 36.4 |
| 27 | James G. Fulton (R) | 127,995 | 59.1 |
| | Margaret Lee Walgren (D) | 88,660 | 40.9 |
| 28 | William S. Moorhead (D) | 99,491 | 67.8 |
| | Arthur O. Sharron (R) | 47,232 | 32.2 |
| 29 | Robert J. Corbett (R) | 117,009 | 59.2 |
| | Russell M. Douthett (D) | 80,497 | 40.8 |
| 30 | Elmer J. Holland (D) | 126,619 | 68.6 |
| | Jerome M. Meyers (R) | 58,063 | 31.4 |

### Special Election

| | | Votes | % |
|---|---|---|---|
| 18 | J. Irving Whalley (R) | 86,527 | 62.3 |
| | Robert M. Meyers (D) | 52,324 | 37.7 |

## RHODE ISLAND

| | | Votes | % |
|---|---|---|---|
| 1 | Fernard J. St.Germain (D) | 117,162 | 66.2 |
| | Theophile Martin (R) | 59,737 | 33.8 |
| 2 | John E. Fogarty (D) | 151,544 | 70.4 |
| | Robert L. Gammell (R) | 63,795 | 29.6 |

## SOUTH CAROLINA

| | | Votes | % |
|---|---|---|---|
| 1 | L. Mendel Rivers (D) | 47,153 | 100.0 |
| 2 | John J. Riley (D) | 63,207 | 100.0 |
| 3 | William J. Bryan Dorn (D) | 52,398 | 100.0 |
| 4 | Robert T. Ashmore (D) | 68,973 | 100.0 |
| 5 | Robert W. Hemphill (D) | 46,815 | 99.8 |
| 6 | John L. McMillan (D) | 49,780 | 100.0 |

## SOUTH DAKOTA

| | | Votes | % |
|---|---|---|---|
| 1 | Ben Reifel (R) | 126,033 | 54.9 |
| | Ray Fitzgerald (D) | 103,755 | 45.2 |
| 2 | E. Y. Berry (R) | 42,550 | 59.8 |
| | W. H. Raff (D) | 28,666 | 40.3 |

## TENNESSEE

| | | Votes | % |
|---|---|---|---|
| 1 | B. Carroll Reece (R) | 103,872 | 75.4 |
| | Arthur Bright (D) | 33,873 | 24.6 |
| 2 | Howard H. Baker (R) | 98,839 | 100.0 |
| 3 | James B. Frazier Jr. (D) | 62,827 | 100.0 |
| 4 | Joe L. Evins (D) | 60,730 | 100.0 |
| 5 | J. Carlton Loser (D) | 42,524 | 100.0 |
| 6 | Ross Bass (D) | 55,736 | 100.0 |
| 7 | Tom Murray (D) | 34,130 | 100.0 |
| 8 | Robert A. Everett (D) | 30,124 | 100.0 |
| 9 | Clifford Davis (D) | 120,159 | 100.0 |

## TEXAS

| | Candidates | Votes | % |
|---|---|---|---|
| 1 | Wright Patman (D) | 58,674 | 100.0 |
| 2 | Jack Brooks (D) | 75,657 | 69.7 |
| | F. S. Newmann (R) | 32,473 | 29.9 |
| 3 | Lindley Beckworth (D) | 59,386 | 100.0 |
| 4 | Sam Rayburn (D) | 44,902 | 100.0 |
| 5 | Bruce Alger (R) | 129,886 | 57.3 |
| | Joe Pool (D) | 96,709 | 42.7 |
| 6 | Olin Teague (D) | 56,603 | 100.0 |
| 7 | John Dowdy (D) | 61,586 | 100.0 |
| 8 | Albert Thomas (D) | 76,767 | 68.6 |
| | Anthony J. P. Farris (R) | 24,486 | 21.9 |
| | Robert Nesmith (CST) | 10,684 | 9.5 |
| 9 | Clark Thompson (D) | 98,586 | 94.3 |
| | P. D. Rogers (CST) | 5,981 | 5.7 |
| 10 | Homer Thornberry (D) | 75,165 | 98.1 |
| 11 | W. R. Poage (D) | 64,351 | 100.0 |
| 12 | Jim Wright (D) | 115,797 | 100.0 |
| 13 | Frank Ikard (D) | 75,972 | 100.0 |
| 14 | John Young (D) | 105,792 | 100.0 |
| 15 | Joe Kilgore (D) | 76,421 | 100.0 |
| 16 | J. T. Rutherford (D) | 63,634 | 58.9 |
| | Dorothy Wynell (CST) | 24,996 | 23.1 |
| | Ford Chapman (R) | 19,491 | 18.0 |
| 17 | Omar Burleson (D) | 60,401 | 77.6 |
| | Max Mossholder (CST) | 17,400 | 22.4 |
| 18 | Walter Rogers (D) | 79,675 | 100.0 |
| 19 | George Mahon (D) | 77,415 | 85.7 |
| | J. R. Anderson (CST) | 12,953 | 14.3 |
| 20 | Paul J. Kilday (D) | 84,487 | 100.0 |
| 21 | O. C. Fisher (D) | 63,277 | 100.0 |
| 22 | Bob Casey (D) | 109,418 | 58.3 |
| | J. C. Noonan (R) | 73,503 | 39.2 |

## UTAH

| | | Votes | % |
|---|---|---|---|
| 1 | M. Blaine Peterson (D) | 65,939 | 50.0 |
| | A. Walter Stevenson (R) | 65,871 | 50.0 |
| 2 | David S. King (D) | 120,771 | 50.8 |
| | Sherman P. Lloyd (R) | 116,881 | 49.2 |

## VERMONT

| | | Votes | % |
|---|---|---|---|
| AL | Robert T. Stafford (R) | 94,905 | 57.2 |
| | William H. Meyer (D) | 71,111 | 42.8 |

## VIRGINIA

| | | Votes | % |
|---|---|---|---|
| 1 | Thomas N. Downing (D) | 53,768 | 82.4 |
| | Richard A. May (R) | 11,429 | 17.5 |
| 2 | Porter Hardy Jr. (D) | 49,750 | 75.8 |
| | Louis B. Fine (R) | 15,758 | 24.0 |
| 3 | J. Vaughan Gary (D) | 52,908 | 77.8 |
| | T. Coleman Andrews | 14,907 | 21.9 |
| 4 | Watkins M. Abbitt (D) | 39,408 | 99.5 |
| 5 | William M. Tuck (D) | 30,154 | 98.9 |
| 6 | Richard H. Poff (R) | 60,371 | 82.4 |
| | J. B. Brayman (SOCIAL D) | 12,700 | 17.3 |
| 7 | Burr P. Harrison (D) | 42,199 | 99.6 |
| 8 | Howard W. Smith (D) | 42,809 | 75.7 |
| | Lawrence M. Traylor (R) | 13,410 | 23.7 |
| 9 | W. Pat Jennings (D) | 47,372 | 58.0 |
| | E. Summers Sheffey (R) | 34,280 | 42.0 |
| 10 | Joel T. Broyhill (R) | 64,408 | 55.0 |
| | Ralph Kaul (D) | 52,647 | 45.0 |

## WASHINGTON

| | | Votes | % |
|---|---|---|---|
| 1 | Thomas M. Pelly (R) | 124,721 | 70.2 |
| | Carl Viking Holman (D) | 53,009 | 29.8 |
| 2 | Jack Westland (R) | 87,802 | 60.2 |
| | Payson Peterson (D) | 58,154 | 39.8 |
| 3 | Julia Butler Hansen (D) | 76,930 | 53.4 |
| | Dale M. Nordquist (R) | 67,060 | 46.6 |
| 4 | Catherine May (R) | 94,210 | 58.8 |
| | Roy Mundy (D) | 65,964 | 41.2 |
| 5 | Walt Horan (R) | 94,042 | 59.4 |
| | Bernard J. Gallagher (D) | 64,321 | 40.6 |

1. Figures are for December recount. Election was contested after initial vote tally had Wheeler winning by 188 votes.

## WASHINGTON

| Candidates | Votes | % |
|---|---|---|
| 6 Thor C. Tollefson (R) | 83,158 | 56.5 |
| John G. McCutcheon (D) | 64,167 | 43.6 |
| 7 Don Magnuson (D) | 95,663 | 50.0 |
| John Stender (R) | 95,524 | 50.0 |

### Special Election

| | | |
|---|---|---|
| 3 Julia Butler Hansen (D) | 71,416 | 53.1 |
| Dale M. Nordquist (R) | 63,058 | 46.9 |

## WEST VIRGINIA

| | | |
|---|---|---|
| 1 Arch A. Moore Jr. (R) | 81,018 | 60.3 |
| Steven D. Narick (D) | 53,318 | 39.7 |
| 2 Harley O. Staggers (D) | 74,184 | 60.3 |
| Charles J. Whiston (R) | 48,903 | 39.7 |

| Candidates | Votes | % |
|---|---|---|
| 3 Cleveland M. Bailey (D) | 71,718 | 59.8 |
| James M. Knowles Jr. (R) | 48,258 | 40.2 |
| 4 Ken Hechler (D) | 82,931 | 53.2 |
| Clyde Pinson (R) | 73,052 | 46.8 |
| 5 Elizabeth Kee (D) | 77,524 | 69.5 |
| L. M. LaFollette (R) | 34,052 | 30.5 |
| 6 John M. Slack Jr. (D) | 108,452 | 61.8 |
| George W. King (R) | 67,070 | 38.2 |

## WISCONSIN

| | | |
|---|---|---|
| 1 Henry C. Schadeberg (R) | 97,662 | 52.7 |
| Gerald T. Flynn (D) | 87,646 | 47.3 |
| 2 Robert W. Kastenmeier (D) | 119,885 | 53.4 |
| Donald E. Tewes (R) | 104,744 | 46.6 |
| 3 Vernon W. Thomson (R) | 71,677 | 54.6 |
| Norman M. Clapp (D) | 59,527 | 45.4 |

| Candidates | Votes | % |
|---|---|---|
| 4 Clement J. Zablocki (D) | 155,789 | 71.7 |
| Samuel P. Murray (R) | 61,468 | 28.3 |
| 5 Henry S. Reuss (D) | 126,314 | 57.7 |
| Kirby Hendee (R) | 92,526 | 42.3 |
| 6 William K. Van Pelt (R) | 91,450 | 55.8 |
| James Megellas (D) | 72,442 | 44.2 |
| 7 Melvin R. Laird (R) | 95,152 | 67.1 |
| Kenneth Traeger (D) | 46,606 | 32.9 |
| 8 John W. Byrnes (R) | 101,132 | 58.8 |
| Milo Singler (D) | 70,740 | 41.2 |
| 9 Lester R. Johnson (D) | 74,268 | 56.6 |
| Perry M. Hull (R) | 57,069 | 43.5 |
| 10 Alvin E. O'Konski (R) | 73,114 | 95.0 |

## WYOMING

| | | |
|---|---|---|
| AL William Henry Harrison (R) | 70,241 | 52.3 |
| Hepburn T. Armstrong (D) | 64,090 | 47.7 |

# 1961 House Elections

## ARIZONA

### Special Election

| | | |
|---|---|---|
| 2 Morris K. Udall (D) | 51,304# | 51.0 |
| Mac C. Matheson (R) | 49,297# | 49.0 |

## ARKANSAS

### Special Election

| | | |
|---|---|---|
| 6 Catherine D. Norrell (D) | 10,209# | 43.1 |
| John Harris Jones (D) | 5,955# | 25.1 |
| M. C. Lewis Jr. (D) | 5,499# | 23.2 |
| James F. Cross (D) | 1,727# | 7.3 |

## LOUISIANA

### Special Election

| | | |
|---|---|---|
| 4 Joe D. Waggonner Jr. (D) | 33,892 | 54.5 |
| Charlton H. Lyons (R) | 28,250 | 45.5 |

## MICHIGAN

### Special Election

| | | |
|---|---|---|
| 1 Lucien N. Nedzi (D) | 33,690# | 85.5 |
| Walter Czarnecki (R) | 5,729# | 14.5 |

## PENNSYLVANIA

### Special Election

| | | |
|---|---|---|
| 16 John C. Kunkel (R) | 43,220 | 65.6 |
| Kathryn Z. Vanderslice (D) | 22,698 | 34.4 |

## TENNESSEE

### Special Election

| | | |
|---|---|---|
| 1 Louise G. Reece (R) | 29,819# | 62.9 |
| William W. Faw (D) | 15,718# | 33.2 |

## TEXAS [1]

### Special Elections

| | | |
|---|---|---|
| 4 Ray Roberts (D) | 8,154 | 36.9 |
| R. C. Slagle (D) | 5,945 | 26.9 |
| David Brown (D) | 2,393 | 10.8 |
| Conner Harrington (R) | 2,353 | 10.6 |
| Jack Finney (D) | 2,211 | 10.0 |
| 13 Graham B. Purcell Jr. (D) | 8,960 | 33.6 |
| Joe Meissner (R) | 6,740 | 25.3 |
| Jack Hightower (D) | 6,157 | 23.1 |
| Vernon Stewart (D) | 2,706 | 10.2 |
| Jimmy P. Horany (D) | 2,076 | 7.8 |
| 20 Henry B. Gonzalez (D) | 52,696 | 54.6 |
| John Goode | 42,511 | 44.0 |

1. In Texas special elections for the House held prior to 1961, all candidates ran against each other in one election regardless of party; the candidate receiving the most votes was the winner. Thus Lyndon B. Johnson won a 1937 special election with 27.7 percent of the vote (see p. 1183).

The Texas law was changed in 1961 to require that in a special election, if no candidate received a majority, a special election runoff would be held between the top two candidates.

Thus, in the three House special elections held in Texas in 1961, only the election in the 20th district produced a majority vote winner. In the 4th and 13th districts, no candidate received a majority. Runoff special elections between the top two candidates in each district were held in 1962; see page 1247.

# 1962 House Elections

## ALABAMA

| | Candidates | Votes | % |
|---|---|---|---|
| AL | George Huddleston Jr. (D) | 304,210✔ | |
| | Armistead I. Selden Jr. (D) | 295,882✔ | |
| | George Andrews (D) | 293,182✔ | |
| | George Grant (D) | 288,074✔ | |
| | Albert Rains (D) | 271,075✔ | |
| | Kenneth A. Roberts (D) | 269,410✔ | |
| | Robert E. Jones (D) | 258,674✔ | |
| | Carl Elliott (D) | 257,299✔ | |
| | John H. Buchanan Jr. (R) | 141,202 | |
| | Tom Abernethy (R) | 138,963 | |
| | Evan Foreman Jr. (R) | 136,339 | |
| | J. Chester Robinson (NSR) | 32,446 | |

## ALASKA

| | Candidates | Votes | % |
|---|---|---|---|
| AL | Ralph J. Rivers (D) | 31,953 | 54.5 |
| | Lowell Thomas Jr. (R) | 26,638 | 45.5 |

## ARIZONA

| | Candidates | Votes | % |
|---|---|---|---|
| 1 | John J. Rhodes (R) | 113,240 | 58.7 |
| | Howard V. Peterson (D) | 79,763 | 41.3 |
| 2 | Morris K. Udall (D) | 64,510 | 58.3 |
| | Richard K. Burke (R) | 46,219 | 41.7 |
| 3 | George F. Senner Jr. (D) | 25,359 | 56.0 |
| | John P. Clark (R) | 19,933 | 44.0 |

## ARKANSAS

| | Candidates | Votes | % |
|---|---|---|---|
| 1 | Ezekiel C. Gathings (D) | | 100.0 |
| 2 | Wilbur D. Mills (D) | | 100.0 |
| 3 | James W. Trimble (D) | 58,786 | 69.4 |
| | Cy Carney Jr. (R) | 25,987 | 30.7 |
| 4 | Oren Harris (D) | 74,972 | 77.4 |
| | Warren Lieblong (R) | 21,818 | 22.5 |

## CALIFORNIA

| | Candidates | Votes | % |
|---|---|---|---|
| 1 | Clem Miller (D) | 100,962* | 50.8 |
| | Don H. Clausen (R) | 97,949 | 49.2 |
| 2 | Harold T. Johnson (D) | 106,239 | 64.6 |
| | Fredric H. Nagel Jr. (R) | 58,150 | 35.4 |
| 3 | John E. Moss Jr (D) | 138,257 | 74.8 |
| | George W. S. Smith (R) | 46,510 | 25.2 |
| 4 | Robert L. Leggett (D) | 55,560 | 56.5 |
| | L. V. Honsinger (R) | 42,762 | 43.5 |
| 5 | John F. Shelley (D) | 64,493 | 80.4 |
| | Roland S. Charles (R) | 15,670 | 19.5 |
| 6 | William S. Mailliard (R) | 105,762 | 58.7 |
| | John A. O'Connell (D) | 74,429 | 41.3 |
| 7 | Jeffery Cohelan (D) | 86,215 | 64.5 |
| | Leonard L. Cantando (R) | 47,409 | 35.5 |
| 8 | George P. Miller (D) | 97,014 | 72.5 |
| | Harold Petersen (R) | 36,810 | 27.5 |
| 9 | Don Edwards (D) | 79,616 | 65.9 |
| | Joseph Francis Donovan (R) | 41,104 | 34.0 |
| 10 | Charles S. Gubser (R) | 106,419 | 60.7 |
| | James P. Thurber Jr. (D) | 68,885 | 39.3 |
| 11 | J. Arthur Younger (R) | 101,963 | 62.3 |
| | William J. Keller (D) | 61,623 | 37.7 |
| 12 | Burt L. Talcott (R) | 75,424 | 61.3 |
| | William K. Stewart (D) | 47,576 | 38.7 |
| 13 | Charles M. Teague (R) | 84,743 | 64.9 |
| | George J. Holgate (D) | 45,746 | 35.1 |
| 14 | John F. Baldwin (R) | 99,040 | 62.9 |
| | Charles R. Weidner (D) | 58,369 | 37.1 |
| 15 | John J. McFall (D) | 97,322 | 70.0 |
| | Arthur L. Young (R) | 41,726 | 30.0 |
| 16 | B. F. Sisk (D) | 108,339 | 71.9 |
| | Arthur L. Selland (R) | 42,401 | 28.1 |

| | Candidates | Votes | % |
|---|---|---|---|
| 17 | Cecil R. King (D) | 74,964 | 67.2 |
| | Ted Bruinsma (R) | 36,663 | 32.8 |
| 18 | Harlan Hagen (D) | 91,684 | 58.9 |
| | Ray Arnett (R) | 64,037 | 41.1 |
| 19 | Chet Holifield (D) | 78,436 | 61.6 |
| | Robert T. Ramsay (R) | 48,976 | 38.4 |
| 20 | H. Allen Smith (R) | 119,938 | 70.6 |
| | Leon Mayer (D) | 49,850 | 29.4 |
| 21 | Augustus F. Hawkins (D) | 73,465 | 84.5 |
| | Herman Smith (R) | 13,371 | 15.4 |
| 22 | James C. Corman (D) | 75,294 | 53.6 |
| | Charles S. Foote (R) | 65,087 | 46.4 |
| 23 | Clyde Doyle (D) | 83,269 | 64.2 |
| | Del Clawson (R) | 46,488 | 35.8 |
| 24 | Glenard P. Lipscomb (R) | 120,884 | 70.3 |
| | Knox Mellon (D) | 50,970 | 29.7 |
| 25 | Ronald Brooks Cameron (D) | 62,371 | 53.1 |
| | John H. Rousselot (R) | 53,961 | 45.9 |
| 26 | James Roosevelt (D) | 112,162 | 68.3 |
| | Daniel Beltz (R) | 52,063 | 31.7 |
| 27 | Everett G. Burkhalter (D) | 66,979 | 52.1 |
| | Edgar W. Hiestand (R) | 61,538 | 47.9 |
| 28 | Alphonzo Bell (R) | 162,233 | 64.0 |
| | Robert J. Felixson (D) | 91,305 | 36.0 |
| 29 | George E. Brown Jr. (D) | 73,740 | 55.6 |
| | H. L. Richardson (R) | 58,760 | 44.3 |
| 30 | Edward R. Roybal (D) | 69,008 | 56.5 |
| | Gordon L. McDonough (R) | 53,104 | 43.5 |
| 31 | Charles H. Wilson (D) | 76,631 | 52.2 |
| | Gordon Hahn (R) | 70,154 | 47.8 |
| 32 | Craig Hosmer (R) | 115,915 | 70.7 |
| | J. J. Johovich (D) | 47,917 | 29.2 |
| 33 | Harry R. Sheppard (D) | 96,192 | 59.0 |
| | William R. Thomas (R) | 66,764 | 41.0 |
| 34 | Richard T. Hanna (D) | 90,758 | 55.9 |
| | Robert A. Geier (R) | 71,478 | 44.1 |
| 35 | James B. Utt (R) | 133,737 | 68.5 |
| | Burton Shamsky (D) | 61,395 | 31.5 |
| 36 | Bob Wilson (R) | 91,626 | 61.8 |
| | William C. Godfrey (D) | 56,637 | 38.2 |
| 37 | Lionel Van Deerlin (D) | 63,821 | 51.3 |
| | Dick Wilson (R) | 60,460 | 48.6 |
| 38 | Patrick Minor Martin (R) | 68,583 | 55.9 |
| | Dalip S. Saund (D) | 54,022 | 44.1 |

## COLORADO

| | Candidates | Votes | % |
|---|---|---|---|
| 1 | Byron G. Rogers (D) | 94,680 | 56.0 |
| | William B. Chenoweth (R) | 74,392 | 44.0 |
| 2 | Donald G. Brotzman (R) | 134,939 | 61.9 |
| | Conrad L. McBride (D) | 83,235 | 38.2 |
| 3 | J. Edgar Chenoweth (R) | 74,848 | 54.7 |
| | Albert J. Tomsic (D) | 62,097 | 45.3 |
| 4 | Wayne N. Aspinall (D) | 42,462 | 58.7 |
| | Leo R. Sommerville (R) | 29,943 | 41.4 |

## CONNECTICUT

| | Candidates | Votes | % |
|---|---|---|---|
| 1 | Emilio Q. Daddario (D) | 162,844 | 57.5 |
| | James F. Collins (R) | 118,767 | 41.9 |
| 2 | William L. St.Onge (D) | 83,652 | 50.8 |
| | Moses A. Savin (R) | 81,010 | 49.2 |
| 3 | Robert Giaimo (D) | 104,728 | 56.0 |
| | Daniel Reinhardsen Jr. (R) | 82,215 | 44.0 |
| 4 | Abner W. Sibal (R) | 132,595 | 52.0 |
| | Francis X. Lennon Jr. (D) | 122,362 | 48.0 |
| 5 | John S. Monagan (D) | 83,321 | 58.5 |
| | John A. Rand (R) | 59,072 | 41.5 |
| AL | Bernard F. Grabowski (D) | 543,424 | 52.7 |
| | John M. Lupton (R) | 487,575 | 47.3 |

## DELAWARE

| | Candidates | Votes | % |
|---|---|---|---|
| AL | Harris B. McDowell Jr. (D) | 81,166 | 52.9 |
| | Wilmer F. Williams (R) | 71,934 | 46.9 |

## FLORIDA

| | Candidates | Votes | % |
|---|---|---|---|
| 1 | Robert L. F. Sikes (D) | 35,781 | 81.9 |
| | M. M. Woolley (R) | 7,902 | 18.1 |
| 2 | Charles E. Bennett (D) | 41,378 | 99.7 |
| 3 | Claude Pepper (D) | 59,985 | 57.6 |
| | Bob Peterson (R) | 44,164 | 42.4 |
| 4 | Dante B. Fascell (D) | 67,136 | 64.5 |
| | J. C. McGlon Jr. (R) | 36,981 | 35.5 |
| 5 | A. Sydney Herlong Jr. (D) | 54,383 | 65.2 |
| | Hubert H. Hevey Jr. (R) | 29,008 | 34.8 |
| 6 | Paul G. Rogers (D) | 102,396 | 64.2 |
| | Frederick A. Kibbe (R) | 57,112 | 35.8 |
| 7 | James A. Haley (D) | 52,417 | 66.8 |
| | F. Onell Rogells (R) | 26,042 | 33.2 |
| 8 | D. R. Matthews (D) | 23,387 | 100.0 |
| 9 | Don Fuqua (D) | 23,651 | 75.3 |
| | Wilfred C. Varn (R) | 7,735 | 24.6 |
| 10 | Sam M. Gibbons (D) | 41,426 | 70.6 |
| | Victor A. Rule (R) | 17,214 | 29.4 |
| 11 | Edward J. Gurney (R) | 46,814 | 51.9 |
| | John A. Sutton (D) | 43,348 | 48.1 |
| 12 | William C. Cramer (R) | 78,982 | 64.5 |
| | Grover C. Criswell Jr. (D) | 43,431 | 35.5 |

## GEORGIA

| | Candidates | Votes | % |
|---|---|---|---|
| 1 | G. Elliott Hagan (D) | 25,229 | 97.6 |
| 2 | John L. Pilcher (D) | 18,967 | 96.3 |
| 3 | E. L. Forrester (D) | 25,001 | 100.0 |
| 4 | John J. Flynt Jr. (D) | 21,214 | 100.0 |
| 5 | Charles L. Weltner (D) | 60,583 | 55.6 |
| | L. J. O'Callaghan (R) | 48,466 | 44.4 |
| 6 | Carl Vinson (D) | 19,701 | 100.0 |
| 7 | John W. Davis (D) | 28,994 | 72.4 |
| | Ralph Ivey (R) | 11,048 | 27.6 |
| 8 | J. Russell Tuten (D) | 19,694 | 100.0 |
| 9 | Phil M. Landrum (D) | 25,942 | 100.0 |
| 10 | Robert G. Stephens Jr. (D) | 27,169 | 100.0 |

## HAWAII

| | Candidates | Votes | % |
|---|---|---|---|
| AL | Thomas P. Gill (D) | 123,649✔ | |
| | Spark M. Matsunaga (D) | 123,599✔ | |
| | Albert W. Evensen (R) | 70,880 | |
| | Richard Ike Sutton (R) | 46,292 | |

## IDAHO

| | Candidates | Votes | % |
|---|---|---|---|
| 1 | Compton I. White Jr. (D) | 51,422 | 53.. |
| | Erwin H. Schwiebert (R) | 45,552 | 47.. |
| 2 | Ralph R. Harding (D) | 83,152 | 52.. |
| | Orval Hansen (R) | 74,203 | 47.. |

## ILLINOIS

| | Candidates | Votes | % |
|---|---|---|---|
| 1 | William L. Dawson (D) | 98,305 | 74. |
| | Benjamin C. Duster (R) | 34,379 | 25. |
| 2 | Barratt O'Hara (D) | 78,119 | 62. |
| | Philip G. Bixler (R) | 47,336 | 37. |
| 3 | William T. Murphy (D) | 82,866 | 51. |
| | Ernest E. Michaels (R) | 77,814 | 48. |
| 4 | Edward J. Derwinski (R) | 114,954 | 64. |
| | Richard E. Friedman (D) | 62,189 | 35. |
| 5 | John C. Kluczynski (D) | 84,455 | 63. |
| | Joseph Potempa (R) | 48,825 | 36. |
| 6 | Thomas J. O'Brien (D) | 72,183 | 77. |
| | Adolph Herda (R) | 20,690 | 22. |
| 7 | Roland Victor Libonati (D) | 86,677 | 78. |
| | Joseph D. Day (R) | 23,285 | 21. |
| 8 | Dan Rostenkowski (D) | 112,778 | 60. |
| | Irvin R. Tchon (R) | 72,726 | 39. |

## ILLINOIS

| Candidates | Votes | % |
|---|---|---|
| 9 Edward R. Finnegan (D) | 80,378 | 54.8 |
| Thomas E. Ward (R) | 66,196 | 45.2 |
| 10 Harold R. Collier (R) | 149,761 | 66.6 |
| Joseph A. Salerno (D) | 74,986 | 33.4 |
| 11 Roman C. Pucinski (D) | 103,677 | 52.7 |
| Henry J. Hyde (R) | 92,910 | 47.3 |
| 12 Robert McClory (R) | 76,335 | 63.9 |
| John Clark Kimball (D) | 43,200 | 36.1 |
| 13 Donald Rumsfeld (R) | 139,230 | 63.5 |
| John A. Kennedy (D) | 79,419 | 36.2 |
| 14 Elmer J. Hoffman (R) | 107,285 | 59.7 |
| Jerome M. Ziegler (D) | 72,390 | 40.3 |
| 15 Charlotte T. Reid (R) | 77,718 | 60.3 |
| Stanley H. Cowan (D) | 49,444 | 38.3 |
| 16 John B. Anderson (R) | 78,594 | 66.9 |
| Walter S. Busky (D) | 38,853 | 33.1 |
| 17 Leslie C. Arends (R) | 87,612 | 62.5 |
| Donald M. Laughlin (D) | 52,592 | 37.5 |
| 18 Robert H. Michel (R) | 75,957 | 61.2 |
| Francis D. Nash (D) | 48,177 | 38.8 |
| 19 Robert T. McLoskey (R) | 66,547 | 55.9 |
| David Dedoncker (D) | 52,482 | 44.1 |
| 20 Paul Findley (R) | 100,558 | 52.9 |
| Peter F. Mack Jr. (D) | 89,522 | 47.1 |
| 21 Kenneth J. Gray (D) | 96,971 | 60.0 |
| Frank H. Walker (R) | 64,687 | 40.0 |
| 22 William L. Springer (R) | 70,870 | 59.8 |
| Bob Wilson (D) | 47,745 | 40.3 |
| 23 George E. Shipley (D) | 99,133 | 51.7 |
| Edward H. Jenison (R) | 92,562 | 48.3 |
| 24 Melvin Price (D) | 95,522 | 73.8 |
| Kurt Glaser (R) | 33,993 | 26.3 |

## INDIANA

| Candidates | Votes | % |
|---|---|---|
| 1 Ray J. Madden (D) | 104,212 | 60.5 |
| Harold Moody (R) | 67,230 | 39.0 |
| 2 Charles A. Halleck (R) | 82,971 | 57.6 |
| John J. Murray (D) | 61,076 | 42.4 |
| 3 John Brademas (D) | 92,609 | 51.9 |
| Charles W. Ainlay (R) | 85,845 | 48.1 |
| 4 E. Ross Adair (R) | 80,693 | 55.6 |
| Ronald R. Ross (D) | 64,553 | 44.4 |
| 5 J. Edward Roush (D) | 92,264 | 51.6 |
| George O. Chambers (R) | 86,403 | 48.4 |
| 6 Richard L. Roudebush (R) | 76,506 | 52.7 |
| Fred Wampler (D) | 68,777 | 47.3 |
| 7 William G. Bray (R) | 82,160 | 57.8 |
| Elden C. Tipton (D) | 59,953 | 42.2 |
| 8 Winfield K. Denton (D) | 95,126 | 55.7 |
| Earl J. Heseman (R) | 75,731 | 44.3 |
| 9 Earl Wilson (R) | 65,287 | 52.1 |
| John Pritchard (D) | 59,985 | 47.9 |
| 10 Ralph Harvey (R) | 81,007 | 52.9 |
| John E. Mitchell (D) | 72,009 | 47.1 |
| 11 Donald Cogley Bruce (R) | 127,763 | 54.3 |
| Andrew Jacobs Jr. (D) | 107,747 | 45.8 |

## IOWA

| Candidates | Votes | % |
|---|---|---|
| 1 Fred Schwengel (R) | 65,975 | 61.1 |
| Harold Stephens (D) | 42,000 | 38.9 |
| 2 James E. Bromwell (R) | 67,475 | 52.8 |
| Frank W. Less (D) | 60,296 | 47.2 |
| 3 H. R. Gross (R) | 66,337 | 56.7 |
| Neel F. Hill (D) | 50,580 | 43.3 |
| 4 John Kyl (R) | 65,538 | 55.9 |
| Gene W. Glenn (D) | 51,810 | 44.2 |
| 5 Neal Smith (D) | 73,963 | 62.8 |
| Sonja C. Egenes (R) | 43,877 | 37.2 |
| 6 Charles B. Hoeven (R) | 66,940 | 58.5 |
| Donald W. Murray (D) | 47,542 | 41.5 |
| 7 Ben F. Jensen (R) | 56,341 | 56.1 |
| Edward J. Peters (D) | 44,171 | 44.0 |

## KANSAS

| Candidates | Votes | % |
|---|---|---|
| 1 Bob Dole (R) | 102,499 | 55.8 |
| J. Floyd Breeding (D) | 81,092 | 44.2 |

| Candidates | Votes | % |
|---|---|---|
| 2 William H. Avery (R) | 72,945 | 65.2 |
| Harry F. Kehoe (D) | 38,923 | 34.8 |
| 3 Robert F. Ellsworth (R) | 60,865 | 63.4 |
| Bill Sparks (D) | 35,166 | 36.6 |
| 4 Garner E. Shriver (R) | 72,712 | 66.9 |
| Lawrence J. Wetzel (D) | 35,922 | 33.1 |
| 5 Joe Skubitz (R) | 66,705 | 53.3 |
| Wade A. Myers (D) | 58,453 | 46.7 |

## KENTUCKY

| Candidates | Votes | % |
|---|---|---|
| 1 Frank A. Stubblefield (D) | 53,240 | 100.0 |
| 2 William H. Natcher (D) | 45,999 | 100.0 |
| 3 M. G. (Gene) Snyder (R) | 94,579 | 50.8 |
| Frank W. Burke (D) | 91,544 | 49.2 |
| 4 Frank Chelf (D) | 57,956 | 52.9 |
| Clyde Middleton (R) | 51,637 | 47.1 |
| 5 Eugene Siler (R) | 59,326 | 100.0 |
| 6 John C. Watts (D) | 53,454 | 100.0 |
| 7 Carl D. Perkins (D) | 70,195 | 56.8 |
| C. Alex Parker Jr. (R) | 52,640 | 42.6 |

## LOUISIANA

| Candidates | Votes | % |
|---|---|---|
| 1 F. Edward Hebert (D) | 57,326 | 100.0 |
| 2 Hale Boggs (D) | 57,395 | 67.2 |
| David C. Treen (R) | 27,971 | 32.8 |
| 3 Edwin E. Willis (D) | 26,170 | 100.0 |
| 4 Joe D. Waggonner Jr. (D) | 29,754 | 100.0 |
| 5 Otto E. Passman (D) | 24,609 | 100.0 |
| 6 James H. Morrison (D) | 48,894 | 100.0 |
| 7 T. Ashton Thompson (D) | 33,983 | 100.0 |
| 8 Gillis W. Long (D) | 25,682 | 64.0 |
| John W. Lewis Jr. (R) | 14,448 | 36.0 |

## MAINE

| Candidates | Votes | % |
|---|---|---|
| 1 Stanley R. Tupper (R) | 85,864 | 59.6 |
| Ronald Kellam (D) | 58,129 | 40.4 |
| 2 Clifford G. McIntire (R) | 72,349 | 51.1 |
| William D. Hathaway (D) | 69,159 | 48.9 |

## MARYLAND

| Candidates | Votes | % |
|---|---|---|
| 1 Rogers C. B. Morton (R) | 33,674 | 53.2 |
| Thomas F. Johnson (D) | 29,653 | 46.8 |
| 2 Clarence D. Long (D) | 85,383 | 51.9 |
| Fife Symington (R) | 79,075 | 48.1 |
| 3 Edward A. Garmatz (D) | 41,446 | 100.0 |
| 4 George H. Fallon (D) | 35,077 | 72.3 |
| John E. Brondau (R) | 13,425 | 27.7 |
| 5 Richard E. Lankford (D) | 85,612 | 59.5 |
| Joseph E. Baker Jr. (R) | 58,332 | 40.5 |
| 6 Charles McC. Mathias Jr. (R) | 106,212 | 60.9 |
| John Foley (D) | 68,116 | 39.1 |
| 7 Samuel N. Friedel (D) | 57,958 | 70.0 |
| Caroline R. Ramsay (R) | 24,825 | 30.0 |
| AL Carlton R. Sickles (D) | 388,107 | 55.7 |
| Newton Steers (R) | 308,792 | 44.3 |

## MASSACHUSETTS

| Candidates | Votes | % |
|---|---|---|
| 1 Silvio O. Conte (R) | 106,498 | 74.4 |
| William K. Hefner (D) | 36,711 | 25.6 |
| 2 Edward P. Boland (D) | 92,340 | 67.8 |
| Samuel S. Rodman (R) | 43,873 | 32.2 |
| 3 Philip J. Philbin (D) | 129,326 | 72.4 |
| Frank Anthony (R) | 49,418 | 27.7 |
| 4 Harold D. Donohue (D) | 145,166 | 90.4 |
| Stanley Shogren (P) | 15,310 | 9.5 |
| 5 F. Bradford Morse (R) | 112,455 | 57.4 |
| Thomas J. Lane (D) | 83,504 | 42.6 |
| 6 William H. Bates (R) | 113,104 | 56.2 |
| George J. O'Shea (D) | 88,187 | 43.8 |
| 7 Torbert H. Macdonald (D) | 119,117 | 71.6 |
| Gordon F. Hughes (R) | 47,289 | 28.4 |
| 8 Thomas P. O'Neill Jr. (D) | 100,814 | 73.0 |
| Howard Greyber (R) | 37,374 | 27.1 |

| Candidates | Votes | % |
|---|---|---|
| 9 John W. McCormack (D) | 105,565 | 100.0 |
| 10 Joseph W. Martin Jr. (R) | 124,091 | 65.5 |
| Edward F. Doolan (D) | 65,443 | 34.5 |
| 11 James A. Burke (D) | 121,030 | 64.3 |
| Harry F. Stimpson (R) | 67,138 | 35.7 |
| 12 Hastings Keith (R) | 107,000 | 64.2 |
| Alexander Byron (D) | 59,681 | 35.8 |

## MICHIGAN

| Candidates | Votes | % |
|---|---|---|
| 1 Lucien N. Nedzi (D) | 82,321 | 89.3 |
| Walter Czarnecki (R) | 9,916 | 10.8 |
| 2 George Meader (R) | 88,427 | 58.4 |
| Thomas P. Payne (D) | 63,036 | 41.6 |
| 3 August E. Johansen (R) | 77,316 | 59.5 |
| Paul H. Todd Jr. (D) | 52,667 | 40.5 |
| 4 Edward Hutchinson (R) | 73,308 | 63.8 |
| Leland D. Mitchell (D) | 41,620 | 30.2 |
| 5 Gerald R. Ford Jr. (R) | 110,043 | 67.0 |
| William G. Reamon (D) | 54,112 | 33.0 |
| 6 Charles E. Chamberlain (R) | 112,861 | 54.5 |
| Don Hayworth (D) | 94,157 | 45.5 |
| 7 James G. O'Hara (D) | 127,067 | 56.3 |
| H. Charles Knill (R) | 98,742 | 43.7 |
| 8 James Harvey (R) | 77,022 | 60.5 |
| Jerome T. Hart (D) | 50,376 | 39.5 |
| 9 Robert P. Griffin (R) | 66,645 | 59.4 |
| Donald G. Jennings (D) | 45,536 | 40.6 |
| 10 Elford A. Cederberg (R) | 63,452 | 61.5 |
| Hubert C. Evans (D) | 39,771 | 38.5 |
| 11 Victor A. Knox (R) | 48,244 | 56.7 |
| Warren P. Cleary (D) | 36,886 | 43.3 |
| 12 John B. Bennett (R) | 41,784 | 63.3 |
| William J. Bolognesi (D) | 24,240 | 36.7 |
| 13 Charles C. Diggs Jr. (D) | 59,688 | 71.2 |
| Robert B. Blackwell (R) | 24,134 | 28.8 |
| 14 Harold M. Ryan (D) | 108,025 | 61.8 |
| Lois V. Nair (R) | 66,889 | 38.2 |
| 15 John D. Dingell (D) | 94,197 | 83.0 |
| Ernest Richards (R) | 19,258 | 17.0 |
| 16 John Lesinski Jr. (D) | 180,626 | 67.9 |
| Laverne O. Elliott (R) | 85,485 | 32.1 |
| 17 Martha W. Griffiths (D) | 122,021 | 59.3 |
| James F. O'Neil (R) | 83,870 | 40.7 |
| 18 William S. Broomfield (R) | 149,863 | 59.6 |
| George J. Fulkerson (D) | 101,468 | 40.4 |
| AL Neil Staebler (D) | 1,392,221 | 52.0 |
| Alvin M. Bentley (R) | 1,282,082 | 47.9 |

### Special Election

| Candidates | Votes | % |
|---|---|---|
| 14 Harold M. Ryan (D) | 30,367# | 50.5 |
| Robert E. Waldron (R) | 29,600# | 49.2 |

## MINNESOTA

| Candidates | Votes | % |
|---|---|---|
| 1 Albert H. Quie (R) | 90,632 | 57.5 |
| David L. Graven (DFL) | 66,956 | 42.5 |
| 2 Ancher Nelsen (R) | 81,557 | 62.2 |
| Conrad H. Hammar (DFL) | 49,543 | 37.8 |
| 3 Clark MacGregor (R) | 87,730 | 60.2 |
| Irving R. Keldsen (DFL) | 58,066 | 39.8 |
| 4 Joseph E. Karth (DFL) | 93,519 | 59.5 |
| Harry Strong (R) | 63,766 | 40.5 |
| 5 Donald M. Fraser (DFL) | 87,002 | 51.8 |
| Walter H. Judd (R) | 80,865 | 48.2 |
| 6 Alec G. Olson (DFL) | 77,310 | 50.1 |
| Robert J. Odegard (R) | 76,962 | 49.9 |
| 7 Odin Langen (R) | 70,546 | 52.0 |
| Harding C. Noblitt (DFL) | 65,161 | 48.0 |
| 8 John A. Blatnik (DFL) | 101,567 | 65.7 |
| Jerry H. Ketola (R) | 52,996 | 34.3 |

## MISSISSIPPI

| Candidates | Votes | % |
|---|---|---|
| 1 Thomas G. Abernathy (D) | 26,251 | 100.0 |
| 2 Jamie L. Whitten (D) | 31,344 | 100.0 |
| 3 John Bell Williams (D) | 38,093 | 100.0 |

## MISSISSIPPI

| Candidates | Votes | % |
|---|---|---|
| 4 Arthur Winstead (D) | 21,730 | 83.0 |
| Sterling P. Davis (I) | 4,461 | 17.0 |
| 5 William M. Colmer (D) | 39,735 | 100.0 |

## MISSOURI

| Candidates | Votes | % |
|---|---|---|
| 1 Frank M. Karsten (D) | 82,216 | 70.7 |
| Charles F. Cherry (R) | 34,089 | 29.3 |
| 2 Thomas B. Curtis (R) | 102,861 | 56.3 |
| Philip V. Maher (D) | 79,732 | 43.7 |
| 3 Leonor K. Sullivan (D) | 81,346 | 70.5 |
| J. Marvin Krause (R) | 34,031 | 29.5 |
| 4 William J. Randall (D) | 59,599 | 53.9 |
| John D. Fox (R) | 50,945 | 46.1 |
| 5 Richard Bolling (D) | 54,166 | 58.9 |
| Walter McCarty (R) | 37,835 | 41.1 |
| 6 W. R. Hull Jr. (D) | 62,366 | 55.3 |
| Ethan H. Campbell (R) | 50,339 | 44.7 |
| 7 Durward G. Hall (R) | 84,631 | 57.7 |
| Jim Thomas (D) | 62,082 | 42.3 |
| 8 Richard Ichord (D) | 77,535 | 59.0 |
| David W. Bernhardt (R) | 53,862 | 41.0 |
| 9 Clarence Cannon (D) | 74,254 | 61.2 |
| Anthony C. Schroeder (R) | 47,026 | 38.8 |
| 10 Paul C. Jones (D) | 50,581 | 60.6 |
| Truman Farrow (R) | 32,828 | 39.4 |

## MONTANA

| Candidates | Votes | % |
|---|---|---|
| 1 Arnold Olsen (D) | 55,611 | 52.8 |
| Wayne Montgomery (R) | 49,760 | 47.2 |
| 2 James F. Battin (R) | 79,315 | 55.4 |
| Leo Graybill Jr. (D) | 63,755 | 44.6 |

## NEBRASKA

| Candidates | Votes | % |
|---|---|---|
| 1 Ralph F. Beermann (R) | 85,559 | 50.9 |
| Clair A. Callan (D) | 73,768 | 43.9 |
| George C. Menkens | 8,794 | 5.2 |
| 2 Glenn Cunningham (R) | 83,139 | 69.5 |
| Thomas N. Bonner (D) | 36,577 | 30.6 |
| 3 Dave Martin (R) | 103,079 | 65.6 |
| John A. Hoffman (D) | 54,058 | 34.4 |

## NEVADA

| Candidates | Votes | % |
|---|---|---|
| AL Walter S. Baring (D) | 66,866 | 71.7 |
| J. Carlton Adair (R) | 26,458 | 28.4 |

## NEW HAMPSHIRE

| Candidates | Votes | % |
|---|---|---|
| 1 Louis C. Wyman (R) | 65,651 | 53.1 |
| J. Oliva Huot (D) | 57,910 | 46.9 |
| 2 James C. Cleveland (R) | 56,152 | 57.5 |
| Eugene S. Daniell (D) | 41,539 | 42.5 |

## NEW JERSEY

| Candidates | Votes | % |
|---|---|---|
| 1 William T. Cahill (R) | 119,633 | 58.8 |
| Neil F. Deighan Jr. (D) | 83,405 | 41.0 |
| 2 Milton W. Glenn (R) | 61,285 | 52.7 |
| Paul R. Porreca (D) | 54,317 | 46.7 |
| 3 James C. Auchincloss (R) | 82,220 | 56.9 |
| Peter J. Gannon (D) | 62,258 | 43.1 |
| 4 Frank Thompson Jr. (D) | 88,668 | 63.8 |
| Ephraim Tomlinson (R) | 49,952 | 35.9 |
| 5 Peter H. B. Frelinghuysen Jr. (R) | 86,133 | 66.0 |
| Eugene M. Friedman (D) | 43,347 | 33.2 |
| 6 Florence P. Dwyer (R) | 110,143 | 59.6 |
| Lillian Walsh Egolf (D) | 73,436 | 39.8 |
| 7 William B. Widnall (R) | 110,926 | 61.4 |
| J. Emmet Cassidy (D) | 68,330 | 37.8 |
| 8 Charles S. Joelson (D) | 75,820 | 65.0 |
| Walter W. Porter Jr. (R) | 39,903 | 34.2 |

| Candidates | Votes | % |
|---|---|---|
| 9 Frank C. Osmers Jr. (R) | 89,345 | 56.9 |
| Donald R. Sorkow (D) | 66,140 | 42.2 |
| 10 Peter W. Rodino Jr. (D) | 62,616 | 72.8 |
| Charles Allan Baretski (R) | 22,819 | 26.5 |
| 11 Joseph G. Minish (D) | 48,102 | 59.5 |
| Frank A. Palmieri (R) | 30,244 | 37.4 |
| 12 George M. Wallhauser (R) | 57,169 | 52.5 |
| Robert R. Peacock (D) | 50,783 | 46.6 |
| 13 Cornelius E. Gallagher (D) | 62,636 | 77.1 |
| Eugene P. Kenny (R) | 17,063 | 21.0 |
| 14 Dominick V. Daniels (D) | 54,000 | 70.6 |
| Michael J. Bell (R) | 21,303 | 27.9 |
| 15 Edward J. Patten (D) | 86,651 | 56.7 |
| Bernard F. Rodgers (R) | 66,142 | 43.3 |

## NEW MEXICO

| Candidates | Votes | % |
|---|---|---|
| AL Thomas G. Morris (D) | 152,684 | 64.4 |
| Junio Lopez (R) | 84,457 | 35.6 |
| AL Joseph M. Montoya (D) | 128,651 | 52.5 |
| Jack C. Redman (R) | 116,262 | 47.5 |

## NEW YORK

| Candidates | Votes | % |
|---|---|---|
| 1 Otis G. Pike (D, L) | 85,619 | 61.7 |
| Walter M. Ormsby (R) | 53,133 | 38.3 |
| 2 James R. Grover Jr. (R) | 70,352 | 55.7 |
| Robert J. Flynn (D, L) | 55,963 | 44.3 |
| 3 Steven B. Derounian (R) | 86,430 | 59.2 |
| George Soll (D, L) | 59,635 | 40.8 |
| 4 John W. Wydler (R) | 74,508 | 56.4 |
| Joseph A. Daley (D, L) | 56,438 | 42.7 |
| 5 Frank J. Becker (R) | 89,964 | 57.5 |
| Franklin Bear (D, L) | 66,502 | 42.5 |
| 6 Seymour Halpern (R) | 96,475 | 63.3 |
| Leonard L. Finz (D, L) | 55,883 | 36.7 |
| 7 Joseph P. Addabbo (D, L) | 80,983 | 59.3 |
| George Archinal (R) | 55,654 | 40.7 |
| 8 Benjamin S. Rosenthal (D, L) | 104,895 | 66.4 |
| Arthur McCrossen (R) | 53,122 | 33.6 |
| 9 James J. Delaney (D) | 85,987 | 58.8 |
| Charles H. Cohen (R) | 51,325 | 35.1 |
| Mark Starr (L) | 9,051 | 6.2 |
| 10 Emanuel Celler (D, L) | 90,216 | 80.0 |
| Seymour Besunder (R) | 21,210 | 19.0 |
| 11 Eugene J. Keogh (D, L) | 60,082 | 71.6 |
| Abraham L. Banner (R) | 23,844 | 28.4 |
| 12 Edna F. Kelly (D, L) | 106,375 | 70.0 |
| Louis London Goldberg (R) | 45,492 | 30.0 |
| 13 Abraham J. Multer (D, L) | 116,753 | 74.6 |
| Melvyn M. Rothman (R) | 39,765 | 25.4 |
| 14 John J. Rooney (D, L) | 54,298 | 70.9 |
| Leon F. Nadrowski (R) | 22,287 | 29.1 |
| 15 Hugh L. Carey (D, L) | 55,602 | 50.2 |
| Francis E. Dorn (R) | 55,219 | 49.8 |
| 16 John M. Murphy (D) | 57,666 | 47.5 |
| Robert T. Connor (R) | 55,821 | 45.9 |
| George B. Murphy (L) | 8,043 | 6.6 |
| 17 John V. Lindsay (R) | 98,024 | 68.7 |
| Martin B. Dworkis (D, L) | 44,728 | 31.3 |
| 18 Adam Clayton Powell Jr. (D) | 59,125 | 69.6 |
| Ramon A. Martinez (R) | 18,313 | 21.6 |
| Mae P. Watts (L) | 7,457 | 8.8 |
| 19 Leonard Farbstein (D) | 59,880 | 58.5 |
| Richard S. Aldrich (R, OP) | 31,244 | 30.5 |
| Bentley Kassal (L) | 11,233 | 11.0 |
| 20 William F. Ryan (D, L) | 94,425 | 72.6 |
| Gilbert A. Robinson (R) | 35,664 | 27.4 |
| 21 James C. Healey (D) | 65,242 | 67.4 |
| Stanley L. Slater (R) | 20,354 | 21.0 |
| Lillian Gulker (L) | 11,187 | 11.6 |
| 22 Jacob H. Gilbert (D) | 51,241 | 70.4 |
| Oscar Gonzalez-Suarez (R) | 14,901 | 20.5 |
| David Grand (L) | 6,629 | 9.1 |

| Candidates | Votes | % |
|---|---|---|
| 23 Charles A. Buckley (D) | 69,836 | 54.4 |
| John J. Parker (R) | 39,692 | 30.9 |
| John P. Hagan (L) | 18,749 | 14.6 |
| 24 Paul A. Fino (R) | 77,785 | 60.1 |
| Alfred E. Santangelo (D) | 46,455 | 35.9 |
| 25 Robert R. Barry (R) | 109,989 | 61.5 |
| A. Frank Reel (D, L) | 68,859 | 38.5 |
| 26 Ogden R. Reid (R) | 93,064 | 60.9 |
| Stanley W. Church (D, L) | 59,725 | 39.1 |
| 27 Katharine St.George (R) | 86,958 | 57.9 |
| William F. Ward Jr. (D, L) | 63,306 | 42.1 |
| 28 J. Ernest Wharton (R) | 94,531 | 64.1 |
| Morton E. Gilday (D, L) | 52,994 | 35.9 |
| 29 Leo W. O'Brien (D, L) | 126,313 | 60.1 |
| Wolfgang J. Riemer (R) | 83,719 | 39.9 |
| 30 Carleton J. King (R) | 108,860 | 63.8 |
| William W. Egan (D) | 57,822 | 33.9 |
| 31 Clarence E. Kilburn (R) | 66,283 | 60.0 |
| Francis G. Healey (D, L) | 44,171 | 40.0 |
| 32 Alexander Pirnie (R) | 77,875 | 57.6 |
| Virgil C. Crisafulli (D, L) | 57,414 | 42.4 |
| 33 Howard W. Robison (R) | 92,460 | 66.6 |
| Theodore W. Maurer (D) | 41,412 | 29.9 |
| 34 R. Walter Riehlman (R) | 84,780 | 54.8 |
| Lee Alexander (D) | 67,149 | 43.4 |
| 35 Samuel S. Stratton (D, L) | 78,560 | 54.5 |
| Janet Hill Gordon (R) | 65,697 | 45.5 |
| 36 Frank J. Horton (R) | 96,581 | 59.3 |
| Robert R. Bickal (D, L) | 66,371 | 40.7 |
| 37 Harold C. Ostertag (R) | 101,821 | 64.3 |
| Norman C. Katner (D, L) | 56,428 | 35.7 |
| 38 Charles E. Goodell (R) | 83,361 | 68.4 |
| T. Joseph Lynch (D) | 36,992 | 30.3 |
| 39 John R. Pillion (R) | 99,527 | 62.6 |
| Angelo S. Deloia (D) | 55,774 | 35.1 |
| 40 William E. Miller (R) | 72,706 | 52.0 |
| E. Dent Lackey (D, L) | 67,004 | 48.0 |
| 41 Thaddeus J. Dulski (D, L) | 93,982 | 71.5 |
| Daniel J. Kij (R) | 37,544 | 28.5 |

### Special Election

| Candidates | Votes | % |
|---|---|---|
| 6 Benjamin S. Rosenthal (D, L) | 16,115# | 44.5 |
| Thomas F. Galvin (R) | 15,851# | 43.8 |
| Emil Levin (I) | 4,245# | 11.7 |

## NORTH CAROLINA

| Candidates | Votes | % |
|---|---|---|
| 1 Herbert C. Bonner (D) | 17,898 | 100.0 |
| 2 L. H. Fountain (D) | 21,050 | 100.0 |
| 3 David N. Henderson (D) | 34,056 | 100.0 |
| 4 Harold D. Cooley (D) | 45,249 | 58.1 |
| George E. Ward (R) | 32,593 | 41.9 |
| 5 Ralph J. Scott (D) | 47,009 | 59.2 |
| A. M. Snipes (R) | 32,427 | 40.8 |
| 6 Horace R. Kornegay (D) | 43,021 | 59.9 |
| Blackwell P. Robinson (R) | 28,827 | 40.1 |
| 7 Alton Lennon (D) | 33,173 | 77.0 |
| James E. Walsh Jr. (R) | 9,895 | 23.0 |
| 8 Charles R. Jonas (R) | 64,703 | 56.0 |
| A. Paul Kitchin (D) | 50,926 | 44.0 |
| 9 James T. Broyhill (R) | 67,608 | 50.5 |
| Hugh Q. Alexander (D) | 66,332 | 49.5 |
| 10 Basil L. Whitener (D) | 52,641 | 55.1 |
| Carrol M. Barringer (R) | 42,908 | 44.9 |
| 11 Roy A. Taylor (D) | 70,791 | 55.2 |
| Robert Brown (R) | 57,422 | 44.8 |

## NORTH DAKOTA

| Candidates | Votes | % |
|---|---|---|
| 1 Hjalmar C. Nygaard (R) | 61,330 | 54.6 |
| Scott Anderson (D) | 50,924 | 45.4 |
| 2 Don L. Short (R) | 56,203 | 54.0 |
| Robert Vogel (D) | 47,825 | 46.0 |

## OHIO

| Candidates | Votes | % |
|---|---|---|
| 1 Carl W. Rich (R) | 74,320 | 62.7 |
| Monica Nolan (D) | 44,264 | 37.3 |
| 2 Donald D. Clancy (R) | 105,750 | 62.8 |
| H. A. Sand (D) | 62,733 | 37.2 |
| 3 Paul F. Schenck (R) | 113,584 | 57.0 |
| Martin A. Evers (D) | 85,573 | 43.0 |
| 4 William H. McCulloch (R) | 77,790 | 70.3 |
| Marjorie Conrad Struna (D) | 32,866 | 29.7 |
| 5 Delbert L. Latta (R) | 69,272 | 70.4 |
| William T. Hunt (D) | 29,114 | 29.6 |
| 6 William H. Harsha (R) | 72,743 | 60.4 |
| Jerry C. Rasor (D) | 47,737 | 39.6 |
| 7 Clarence J. Brown (R) | 83,680 | 67.7 |
| Robert A. Riley (D) | 39,908 | 32.3 |
| 8 Jackson E. Betts (R) | 66,458 | 70.1 |
| Morris Laderman (D) | 28,400 | 29.9 |
| 9 Thomas L. Ashley (D) | 86,443 | 57.4 |
| Martin A. Janis (R) | 64,279 | 42.7 |
| 10 Homer E. Abele (R) | 46,158 | 52.3 |
| Walter H. Moeller (D) | 42,131 | 47.7 |
| 11 Oliver P. Bolton (R) | 74,573 | 50.6 |
| Robert E. Cook (D) | 72,936 | 49.5 |
| 12 Samuel L. Devine (R) | 130,316 | 68.3 |
| Paul D. Cassidy (D) | 60,563 | 31.7 |
| 13 Charles A. Mosher (R) | 63,858 | 55.1 |
| J. Grant Keys (D) | 52,030 | 44.9 |
| 14 William H. Ayres (R) | 100,909 | 53.7 |
| Oliver Ocasek (D) | 86,947 | 46.3 |
| 15 Robert T. Secrest (D) | 41,856 | 52.4 |
| Tom V. Moorehead (R) | 38,095 | 47.7 |
| 16 Frank T. Bow (R) | 96,512 | 60.1 |
| Ed Witmer (D) | 64,213 | 40.0 |
| 17 John M. Ashbrook (R) | 69,976 | 58.6 |
| Robert W. Levering (D) | 49,415 | 41.4 |
| 18 Wayne L. Hays (D) | 66,327 | 61.0 |
| John J. Carrigg (R) | 42,336 | 39.0 |
| 19 Michael J. Kirwan (D) | 75,967 | 62.2 |
| William Vincent Williams (R) | 46,200 | 37.8 |
| 20 Michael A. Feighan (D) | 91,544 | 71.0 |
| Leonard G. Richter (R) | 37,325 | 29.0 |
| 21 Charles A. Vanik (D) | 79,514 | 79.9 |
| Leodis Harris (R) | 20,027 | 20.1 |
| 22 Frances P. Bolton (R) | 74,603 | 64.6 |
| Edward Corrigan (D) | 35,353 | 30.6 |
| 23 William E. Minshall (R) | 107,510 | 71.5 |
| Emil C. Weber (D) | 42,907 | 28.5 |
| AL Robert Taft Jr. (R) | 1,786,018 | 60.5 |
| Richard D. Kennedy (D) | 1,164,776 | 39.5 |

## OKLAHOMA

| Candidates | Votes | % |
|---|---|---|
| 1 Page Belcher (R) | 102,585 | 68.6 |
| Herbert W. Wright Jr. (D) | 46,949 | 31.4 |
| 2 Ed Edmondson (D) | 65,968 | 56.7 |
| Bill Sharp (R) | 50,481 | 43.4 |
| 3 Carl Albert (D) | 56,010 | 100.0 |
| 4 Tom Steed (D) | 66,000 | 100.0 |
| 5 John Jarman (D) | 90,392 | 68.9 |
| William P. Pointon Jr. (R) | 40,825 | 31.1 |
| 6 Victor Wickersham (D) | 56,508 | 53.6 |
| Glenn L. Gibson (R) | 48,985 | 46.4 |

## OREGON

| Candidates | Votes | % |
|---|---|---|
| 1 Walter Norblad (R) | 119,263 | 61.8 |
| R. Blaine Whipple (D) | 73,641 | 38.2 |
| 2 Al Ullman (D) | 53,335 | 64.0 |
| Robert W. Chandler (R) | 29,995 | 36.0 |
| 3 Edith Green (D) | 131,573 | 66.0 |
| Stanley E. Hartman (R) | 67,830 | 34.0 |
| 4 Robert B. Duncan (D) | 83,660 | 53.9 |
| Carl Fisher (R) | 71,483 | 46.1 |

## PENNSYLVANIA

| Candidates | Votes | % |
|---|---|---|
| 1 William A. Barrett (D) | 102,722 | 63.5 |
| Winifred H. Malinowsky (R) | 58,953 | 36.5 |
| 2 Robert N. C. Nix (D) | 86,812 | 67.1 |
| Arthur C. Thomas (R) | 42,607 | 32.9 |
| 3 James A. Byrne (D) | 81,405 | 59.3 |
| Joseph R. Burns (R) | 55,827 | 40.7 |
| 4 Herman Toll (D) | 104,300 | 56.0 |
| Frank J. Barbera (R) | 82,014 | 44.0 |
| 5 William J. Green Jr. (D) | 94,501 | 55.9 |
| Michael J. Bednarek (R) | 74,557 | 44.1 |
| 6 George M. Rhodes (D) | 112,959 | 51.2 |
| Ivor D. Fenton (R) | 107,724 | 48.8 |
| 7 William H. Milliken (R) | 136,965 | 60.8 |
| John A. Reilly (D) | 88,482 | 39.3 |
| 8 Willard S. Curtin (R) | 101,853 | 54.8 |
| James A. Michener (D) | 84,043 | 45.2 |
| 9 Paul B. Dague (R) | 113,880 | 67.2 |
| Richard C. Keller (D) | 55,565 | 32.8 |
| 10 Joseph M. McDade (R) | 95,754 | 52.5 |
| William D. Combar (D) | 86,680 | 47.5 |
| 11 Daniel J. Flood (D) | 101,754 | 66.5 |
| Donald B. Ayers (R) | 51,263 | 33.5 |
| 12 J. Irving Whalley (R) | 98,190 | 60.5 |
| A. Reed Hayes (D) | 64,227 | 39.5 |
| 13 Richard S. Schweiker (R) | 135,847 | 66.6 |
| Lee F. Driscoll Jr. (D) | 68,234 | 33.4 |
| 14 William S. Moorhead (D) | 93,130 | 65.7 |
| Joseph M. Beatty (R) | 48,726 | 34.4 |
| 15 Francis E. Walter (D) | 63,574 | 57.5 |
| Woodrow A. Horn (R) | 46,928 | 42.5 |
| 16 John C. Kunkel (R) | 90,113 | 66.7 |
| John A. Walter (D) | 44,932 | 33.3 |
| 17 Herman T. Schneebeli (R) | 96,088 | 62.9 |
| William W. Litke (D) | 56,692 | 37.1 |
| 18 Robert J. Corbett (R) | 108,433 | 64.3 |
| Edward F. Cook (D) | 60,260 | 35.7 |
| 19 George A. Goodling (R) | 82,924 | 56.8 |
| Earl D. Warner (D) | 62,995 | 43.2 |
| 20 Elmer J. Holland (D) | 106,971 | 67.4 |
| Budd Edward Sheppard (R) | 51,688 | 32.6 |
| 21 John H. Dent (D) | 80,410 | 59.6 |
| Charles E. Scalf (R) | 54,543 | 40.4 |
| 22 John P. Saylor (R) | 82,584 | 57.5 |
| Donald J. Perry (D) | 61,054 | 42.5 |
| 23 Leon H. Gavin (R) | 79,158 | 58.6 |
| Frank M. O'Neil (D) | 54,798 | 40.6 |
| 24 James D. Weaver (R) | 82,213 | 51.4 |
| Peter J. Joyce (D) | 77,749 | 48.6 |
| 25 Frank M. Clark (D) | 87,552 | 56.4 |
| Harvey R. Robinson (R) | 67,630 | 43.6 |
| 26 Thomas E. Morgan (D) | 94,932 | 61.7 |
| Jerome Hahn (R) | 58,945 | 38.3 |
| 27 James G. Fulton (R) | 112,034 | 65.5 |
| Margaret Lee Walgren (D) | 58,984 | 34.5 |

## RHODE ISLAND

| Candidates | Votes | % |
|---|---|---|
| 1 Fernard J. St.Germain (D) | 80,333 | 56.8 |
| R. Gordon Butler (R) | 61,186 | 43.2 |
| 2 John E. Fogarty (D) | 127,184 | 71.8 |
| John F. Kennedy (R) | 49,955 | 28.2 |

## SOUTH CAROLINA

| Candidates | Votes | % |
|---|---|---|
| 1 L. Mendel Rivers (D) | 39,176 | 100.0 |
| 2 Albert W. Watson (D) | 39,149 | 52.8 |
| Floyd D. Spence (R) | 34,947 | 47.2 |
| 3 W. J. Bryan Dorn (D) | 34,545 | 100.0 |
| 4 Robert T. Ashmore (D) | 47,044 | 100.0 |
| 5 Robert W. Hemphill (D) | 28,989 | 93.9 |
| Robert M. Doster (R) | 1,861 | 6.0 |
| 6 John L. McMillan (D) | 36,811 | 100.0 |

### Special Election

| | | |
|---|---|---|
| 2 Corinne B. Riley (D) | 3,626# | 100.0 |

## SOUTH DAKOTA

| Candidates | Votes | % |
|---|---|---|
| 1 Ben Reifel (R) | 113,975 | 59.2 |
| Ralph A. Nauman (D) | 78,421 | 40.8 |
| 2 E. Y. Berry (R) | 37,092 | 61.5 |
| M. W. Morrie Clarkson (D) | 23,243 | 38.5 |

## TENNESSEE [1]

| Candidates | Votes | % |
|---|---|---|
| 1 James Quillen (R) | 49,320 | 53.9 |
| Herbert Silvers (D) | 40,113 | 43.8 |
| 2 Howard H. Baker (R) | 61,306 | 70.6 |
| Tally R. Livingston (D) | 25,579 | 29.4 |
| 3 Bill Brock (R) | 47,604 | 51.1 |
| Wilkes T. Thrasher Jr. (D) | 45,597 | 48.9 |
| 4 Joe L. Evins (D) | 46,005 | 87.9 |
| Arch M. Eaton Sr. (I) | 6,310 | 12.1 |
| 5 Richard Fulton | 47,756 | 60.4 |
| J. Carleton Loser | 30,182 | 38.2 |
| 6 Ross Bass (D) | 36,404 | 81.8 |
| J. J. Underwood Jr. (I) | 8,120 | 18.2 |
| 7 Tom Murray (D) | 24,746 | 100.0 |
| 8 Robert A. Everett (D) | 23,521 | 97.3 |
| 9 Clifford Davis (D) | 55,345 | 50.6 |
| Robert B. James (R) | 54,132 | 49.5 |

## TEXAS

| Candidates | Votes | % |
|---|---|---|
| 1 Wright Patman (D) | 26,669 | 67.3 |
| James Timberlake (R) | 12,938 | 32.7 |
| 2 Jack Brooks (D) | 47,137 | 68.8 |
| Roy James Jr. (R) | 21,385 | 31.2 |
| 3 Lindley Beckworth (D) | 26,915 | 52.0 |
| William Steger (R) | 24,803 | 48.0 |
| 4 Ray Roberts (D) | 23,573 | 72.0 |
| Conner Harrington (R) | 9,165 | 28.0 |
| 5 Bruce Alger (R) | 89,938 | 56.3 |
| Bill Jones (D) | 69,813 | 43.7 |
| 6 Olin E. Teague (D) | 33,617 | 100.0 |
| 7 John Dowdy (D) | 37,756 | 88.2 |
| Raymond Ramage (R) | 5,045 | 11.8 |
| 8 Albert Thomas (D) | 51,285 | 71.5 |
| Anthony Farris (R) | 20,475 | 28.5 |
| 9 Clark W. Thompson (D) | 56,179 | 66.3 |
| Dave Oaks (R) | 28,594 | 33.7 |
| 10 Homer Thornberry (D) | 43,396 | 63.3 |
| Jim Dobbs (R) | 25,165 | 36.7 |
| 11 W. R. Poage (D) | 41,698 | 100.0 |
| 12 Jim Wright (D) | 53,705 | 60.6 |
| Del Barron (R) | 34,879 | 39.4 |
| 13 Graham B. Purcell (D) | 37,941 | 67.1 |
| Joe Meissner (R) | 18,578 | 32.9 |
| 14 John Young (D) | 60,803 | 70.4 |
| Lawrence E. Hoover (R) | 25,623 | 29.7 |
| 15 Joe Kilgore (D) | 53,552 | 100.0 |
| 16 Ed Foreman (R) | 44,095 | 53.8 |
| J. T. Rutherford (D) | 37,821 | 46.2 |
| 17 Omar Burleson (D) | 46,895 | 100.0 |
| 18 Walter Rogers (D) | 43,389 | 58.8 |
| Jack Seale (R) | 30,393 | 41.2 |
| 19 George Mahon (D) | 46,925 | 67.1 |
| Dennis Taylor (R) | 23,022 | 32.9 |
| 20 Henry B. Gonzalez (D) | 62,776 | 100.0 |
| 21 O. C. Fisher (D) | 39,261 | 76.1 |
| E. S. Mayer Jr. (R) | 12,310 | 23.9 |
| 22 Bob Casey (D) | 73,141 | 53.6 |
| Ross Baker (R) | 63,452 | 46.5 |
| AL Joe Pool (D) | 870,860 | 56.1 |
| Desmond A. Barry (R) | 680,569 | 43.9 |

### Special Runoff Elections [2]

| | | |
|---|---|---|
| 4 Ray Roberts (D) | 16,109 | 54.3 |
| R. C. Slagle Jr. (D) | 13,572 | 45.7 |
| 13 Graham B. Purcell Jr. (D) | 23,905 | 62.9 |
| Joe Meissner (R) | 14,098 | 37.1 |

## UTAH

| Candidates | Votes | % |
|---|---|---|
| 1 Laurence J. Burton (R) | 59,032 | 50.9 |
| Morris Blaine Peterson (D) | 56,989 | 49.1 |

*Footnotes, see p. 1248.*

## UTAH

| | Candidates | Votes | % |
|---|---|---|---|
| 2 | Sherman P. Lloyd (R) | 108,355 | 53.9 |
| | Bruce S. Jenkins (D) | 92,631 | 46.1 |

## VERMONT

| | | Votes | % |
|---|---|---|---|
| AL | Robert T. Stafford (R) | 68,822 | 56.7 |
| | Harold Raynolds (D) | 52,535 | 43.3 |

## VIRGINIA

| | | Votes | % |
|---|---|---|---|
| 1 | Thomas N. Downing (D) | 21,664 | 99.7 |
| 2 | Porter Hardy Jr. (D) | 30,306 | 75.0 |
| | Louis B. Fine (R) | 10,121 | 25.0 |
| 3 | J. Vaughan Gary (D) | 28,914 | 49.8 |
| | Louis H. Williams (R) | 28,566 | 49.2 |
| 4 | Watkins M. Abbitt (D) | 30,642 | 99.5 |
| 5 | William M. Tuck (D) | 13,827 | 99.8 |
| 6 | Richard H. Poff (R) | 44,060 | 65.2 |
| | John P. Wheeler (D) | 23,280 | 34.5 |
| 7 | John O. Marsh Jr. (D) | 26,302 | 50.6 |
| | J. Kenneth Robinson (R) | 25,704 | 49.4 |
| 8 | Howard W. Smith (D) | 20,931 | 98.7 |
| 9 | W. Pat Jennings (D) | 32,893 | 61.2 |
| | Leon Owens (R) | 20,851 | 38.8 |
| 10 | Joel T. Broyhill (R) | 49,611 | 55.4 |
| | Augustus C. Johnson (D) | 39,940 | 44.6 |

## WASHINGTON

| | Candidates | Votes | % |
|---|---|---|---|
| 1 | Thomas M. Pelly (R) | 108,561 | 73.7 |
| | Alice Franklin Bryant (D) | 38,669 | 26.3 |
| 2 | Jack Westland (R) | 70,498 | 59.8 |
| | Milo Moore (D) | 47,333 | 40.2 |
| 3 | Julia Butler Hansen (D) | 69,045 | 65.3 |
| | Edwin J. Alexander (R) | 36,629 | 34.7 |
| 4 | Catherine May (R) | 83,182 | 67.0 |
| | David A. Gallant (D) | 40,887 | 33.0 |
| 5 | Walt Horan (R) | 78,504 | 64.4 |
| | Bernard J. Gallagher (D) | 43,333 | 35.6 |
| 6 | Thor C. Tollefson (R) | 79,838 | 71.1 |
| | Dawn Olson (D) | 32,513 | 28.9 |
| 7 | K. W. Stinson (R) | 86,106 | 56.6 |
| | Don Magnuson (D) | 66,052 | 43.4 |

## WEST VIRGINIA

| | | Votes | % |
|---|---|---|---|
| 1 | Arch A. Moore Jr. (R) | 97,556 | 59.9 |
| | Cleveland M. Bailey (D) | 65,328 | 40.1 |
| 2 | Harley O. Staggers (D) | 62,291 | 58.7 |
| | Cooper P. Benedict (R) | 43,769 | 41.3 |
| 3 | John M. Slack Jr. (D) | 74,743 | 61.7 |
| | M. G. Guthrie (R) | 46,344 | 38.3 |
| 4 | Ken Hechler (D) | 83,507 | 57.8 |
| | Clyde B. Pinson (R) | 60,931 | 42.2 |
| 5 | Elizabeth Kee (D) | 57,405 | 73.1 |
| | James Strother Crockett (R) | 21,144 | 26.9 |

## WISCONSIN

| | Candidates | Votes | % |
|---|---|---|---|
| 1 | Henry C. Schadeberg (R) | 71,657 | 53.3 |
| | Gerald T. Flynn (D) | 62,800 | 46.7 |
| 2 | Robert W. Kastenmeier (D) | 89,740 | 52.5 |
| | Ivan H. Kindschi (R) | 81,274 | 47.5 |
| 3 | Vernon W. Thomson (R) | 54,237 | 61.3 |
| | Walter P. Thoresen (D) | 34,240 | 38.7 |
| 4 | Clement J. Zablocki (D) | 117,029 | 72.5 |
| | David F. Tillotson (R) | 44,368 | 27.5 |
| 5 | Henry S. Reuss (D) | 103,705 | 63.6 |
| | Thomas F. Nelson (R) | 59,441 | 36.4 |
| 6 | William K. Van Pelt (R) | 71,298 | 59.2 |
| | John A. Race (D) | 49,238 | 40.9 |
| 7 | Melvin R. Laird (R) | 68,418 | 66.1 |
| | John E. Evans (D) | 35,151 | 33.9 |
| 8 | John W. Byrnes (R) | 80,808 | 62.8 |
| | Owen F. Monfils (D) | 47,833 | 37.2 |
| 9 | Lester R. Johnson (D) | 50,025 | 55.6 |
| | Dennis B. Danielson (R) | 39,955 | 44.4 |
| 10 | Alvin E. O'Konski (R) | 52,451 | 63.2 |
| | J. Louis Hanson (D) | 30,556 | 36.8 |

## WYOMING

| | | Votes | % |
|---|---|---|---|
| AL | William Henry Harrison (R) | 71,489 | 61.4 |
| | Louis A. Mankus (D) | 44,985 | 38.6 |

# 1963 House Elections

## CALIFORNIA

**Special Elections**

| | | Votes | % |
|---|---|---|---|
| 1 | Don Clausen (R) | 79,292 | 54.2 |
| | William F. Grader (D) | 65,339 | 44.7 |
| 23 | Del Clawson (R) | 33,042 | 53.2 |
| | Carley V. Porter (D) | 21,969 | 35.4 |

## NORTH DAKOTA

**Special Election**

| | | Votes | % |
|---|---|---|---|
| 1 | Mark Andrews (R) | 47,062# | 49.1 |
| | John Hove (D) | 42,470# | 44.3 |
| | John W. Scott (CR) | 5,995# | 6.3 |

## PENNSYLVANIA

**Special Elections**

| | | Votes | % |
|---|---|---|---|
| 15 | Fred B. Rooney (D) | 48,846# | 53.5 |
| | Robert G. Bartlett (R) | 42,374# | 46.5 |
| 23 | Albert W. Johnson (R) | 64,137# | 58.4 |
| | William T. Hagerty (D) | 45,677# | 41.6 |

## TEXAS [1]

**Special Election**

| | | Votes | % |
|---|---|---|---|
| 10 | J. J. Pickle (D) | 14,389# | 35.0 |
| | Jim Dobbs (R) | 13,702# | 33.3 |
| | Jack Ritter (D) | 13,027# | 31.7 |

**Special Runoff Election**

| | | Votes | % |
|---|---|---|---|
| 10 | J. J. Pickle (D) | 27,228# | 62.9 |
| | Jim Dobbs (R) | 16,052# | 37.1 |

**1962 Elections**

1. The race in Tennessee's 5th district was held without party affiliation. It was an outgrowth of a disputed Democratic primary between Fulton and Loser. Neither was given the Democratic nomination and the general election was conducted on a non-partisan basis.

2. These elections were runoffs between the two candidates who finished with the most votes in special primaries held in 1961, but failed to win a majority. (See Texas 1961, p. 1243.)

**1963 Elections**

1. Under Texas's special election law, a majority was required to win the House seat. Since no candidate had a majority in the initial special election, a runoff special election was held between the top two finishers. (See Texas 1961 for explanation of Texas special election law, p. 1243.)

# 1964 House Elections

## ALABAMA

| | Candidates | Votes | % |
|---|---|---|---|
| 1 | Jack Edwards (R) | 54,522 | 59.9 |
| | John Tyson (D) | 36,482 | 40.1 |
| 2 | William L. Dickinson (R) | 49,936 | 61.7 |
| | George M. Grant (D) | 29,628 | 36.6 |
| 3 | George Andrews (D) | 27,939 | 100.0 |
| 4 | Glenn Andrews (R) | 40,143 | 58.6 |
| | Kenneth A. Roberts (D) | 27,800 | 40.6 |
| 5 | Armistead I. Selden Jr. (D) | 42,784 | 53.0 |
| | Robert French (R) | 37,960 | 47.0 |
| 6 | John Buchanan (R) | 69,246 | 60.6 |
| | George Huddleston Jr. (D) | 45,090 | 39.4 |
| 7 | James D. Martin (R) | 65,353 | 59.6 |
| | George C. Hawkins (D) | 44,386 | 40.5 |
| 8 | Robert E. Jones (D) | 43,842 | 100.0 |

## ALASKA

| | Candidates | Votes | % |
|---|---|---|---|
| AL | Ralph J. Rivers (D) | 34,605 | 51.5 |
| | Lowell Thomas Jr. (R) | 32,566 | 48.5 |

## ARIZONA

| | Candidates | Votes | % |
|---|---|---|---|
| 1 | John J. Rhodes (R) | 140,507 | 55.3 |
| | John Ahearn (D) | 113,669 | 44.7 |
| 2 | Morris K. Udall (D) | 86,499 | 58.7 |
| | William E. Kimble (R) | 60,782 | 41.3 |
| 3 | George F. Senner Jr. (D) | 30,565 | 51.5 |
| | Sam Steiger (R) | 28,802 | 48.5 |

## ARKANSAS

| | Candidates | Votes | % |
|---|---|---|---|
| 1 | E. C. Gathings (D) | | 100.0 |
| 2 | Wilbur D. Mills (D) | | 100.0 |
| 3 | James W. Trimble (D) | 71,228 | 54.7 |
| | J. E. Hinshaw (R) | 58,884 | 45.3 |
| 4 | Oren Harris (D) | | 100.0 |

## CALIFORNIA

| | Candidates | Votes | % |
|---|---|---|---|
| 1 | Don H. Clausen (R) | 141,018 | 59.1 |
| | George McCabe (D) | 97,651 | 40.9 |
| 2 | Harold T. Johnson (D) | 125,774 | 64.6 |
| | Chester C. Merriam (R) | 68,835 | 35.4 |
| 3 | John E. Moss (D) | 166,688 | 74.3 |
| | Einar B. Gjelsteen (R) | 57,630 | 25.7 |
| 4 | Robert L. Leggett (D) | 84,949 | 71.9 |
| | Ivan Norris (R) | 33,160 | 28.1 |
| 5 | Phillip Burton (D) | 71,638 | 100.0 |
| 6 | William S. Mailliard (R) | 125,869 | 63.7 |
| | Thomas P. O'Toole (D) | 71,894 | 36.4 |
| 7 | Jeffery Cohelan (D) | 100,901 | 66.1 |
| | Lawrence E. McNutt (R) | 51,675 | 33.9 |
| 8 | George P. Miller (D) | 108,771 | 70.3 |
| | Donald R. McKay (R) | 46,063 | 29.8 |
| 9 | Don Edwards (D) | 115,954 | 69.8 |
| | William P. Hyde (R) | 50,261 | 30.2 |
| 10 | Charles S. Gubser (R) | 151,027 | 63.1 |
| | E. Day Carman (D) | 88,240 | 36.9 |
| 11 | J. Arthur Younger (R) | 116,022 | 54.8 |
| | W. Mark Sullivan (D) | 95,747 | 45.2 |
| 12 | Burt L. Talcott (R) | 93,112 | 61.9 |
| | Sanford Bolz (D) | 57,243 | 38.1 |
| 13 | Charles M. Teague (R) | 104,744 | 57.4 |
| | George E. Taylor (D) | 77,763 | 42.6 |
| 14 | John F. Baldwin (R) | 117,272 | 64.9 |
| | Russell M. Koch (D) | 63,469 | 35.1 |
| 15 | John J. McFall (D) | 109,560 | 70.9 |
| | Kenneth B. Gibson (R) | 44,977 | 29.1 |
| 16 | B. F. Sisk (D) | 117,727 | 66.8 |
| | David T. Harris (R) | 58,604 | 33.2 |
| 17 | Cecil R. King (D) | 95,640 | 67.7 |
| | Robert Muncaster (R) | 45,688 | 32.3 |
| 18 | Harlan Hagen (D) | 121,304 | 66.7 |
| | James E. Williams Jr. (R) | 60,523 | 33.3 |

| | Candidates | Votes | % |
|---|---|---|---|
| 19 | Chet Holifield (D) | 97,934 | 65.4 |
| | C. Everett Hunt (R) | 51,747 | 34.6 |
| 20 | H. Allen Smith (R) | 132,402 | 67.9 |
| | C. Bernard Kaufman (D) | 62,645 | 32.1 |
| 21 | Augustus F. Hawkins (D) | 106,231 | 90.3 |
| | Rayfield Lundy (R) | 11,374 | 9.7 |
| 22 | James C. Corman (D) | 94,141 | 50.5 |
| | Robert C. Cline (R) | 92,133 | 49.5 |
| 23 | Del Clawson (R) | 90,721 | 55.4 |
| | H. O. Van Petten (D) | 72,903 | 44.5 |
| 24 | Glenard P. Lipscomb (R) | 139,784 | 67.9 |
| | Bryan W. Stevens (D) | 65,967 | 32.1 |
| 25 | Ronald Brooks Cameron (D) | 81,320 | 55.4 |
| | Frank J. Walton (R) | 65,344 | 44.6 |
| 26 | James Roosevelt (D) | 136,025 | 70.4 |
| | Gil Seton (R) | 57,209 | 29.6 |
| 27 | Ed Reinecke (R) | 83,141 | 51.7 |
| | Tom Bane (D) | 77,587 | 48.3 |
| 28 | Alphonzo Bell (R) | 205,473 | 65.6 |
| | Gerald H. Gottlieb (D) | 107,852 | 34.4 |
| 29 | George E. Brown Jr. (D) | 90,208 | 58.6 |
| | Charles J. Farrington Jr. (R) | 63,836 | 41.4 |
| 30 | Edward R. Roybal (D) | 90,329 | 66.3 |
| | Alfred J. Feder (R) | 45,912 | 33.7 |
| 31 | Charles H. Wilson (D) | 114,246 | 64.0 |
| | Norman G. Shanahan (R) | 64,256 | 36.0 |
| 32 | Craig Hosmer (R) | 132,603 | 68.9 |
| | Michael Cullen (D) | 59,765 | 31.1 |
| 33 | Kenneth W. Dyal (D) | 109,047 | 51.7 |
| | Jerry L. Pettis (R) | 101,742 | 48.3 |
| 34 | Richard T. Hanna (D) | 137,588 | 58.3 |
| | Robert A. Geier (R) | 98,606 | 41.8 |
| 35 | James B. Utt (R) | 167,791 | 65.0 |
| | Paul B. Carpenter (D) | 90,295 | 35.0 |
| 36 | Bob Wilson (R) | 105,346 | 59.1 |
| | Quinton Whelan (D) | 73,034 | 40.9 |
| 37 | Lionel Van Deerlin (D) | 85,624 | 58.2 |
| | Dick Wilson (R) | 61,373 | 41.8 |
| 38 | John V. Tunney (D) | 85,661 | 52.8 |
| | Patrick Minor Martin (R) | 76,525 | 47.2 |

**Special Election**

| | Candidates | Votes | % |
|---|---|---|---|
| 5 | Phillip Burton (D) | 26,698 | 53.6 |
| | Nick A. Verreos (R) | 12,777 | 25.7 |
| | Tom Flowers (D) | 3,841 | 7.7 |
| | Joe Bortin (D) | 3,327 | 6.7 |

## COLORADO

| | Candidates | Votes | % |
|---|---|---|---|
| 1 | Byron G. Rogers (D) | 138,475 | 67.5 |
| | Glenn R. Jones (R) | 65,423 | 31.9 |
| 2 | Roy H. McVicker (D) | 109,526 | 50.6 |
| | Donald G. Brotzman (R) | 106,788 | 49.4 |
| 3 | Frank E. Evans (D) | 85,404 | 51.2 |
| | J. Edgar Chenoweth (R) | 81,544 | 48.8 |
| 4 | Wayne N. Aspinall (D) | 106,685 | 63.0 |
| | Edwin S. Lamm (R) | 62,617 | 37.0 |

## CONNECTICUT

| | Candidates | Votes | % |
|---|---|---|---|
| 1 | Emilio Q. Daddario (D) | 141,310 | 70.0 |
| | James F. Collins (R) | 60,654 | 30.0 |
| 2 | William L. St.Onge (D) | 119,530 | 63.3 |
| | Belton A. Copp (R) | 69,403 | 36.7 |
| 3 | Robert N. Giaimo (D) | 126,353 | 63.9 |
| | Bernard J. Burns (R) | 71,393 | 36.1 |
| 4 | Donald J. Irwin (D) | 117,220 | 51.8 |
| | Abner W. Sibal (R) | 109,027 | 48.2 |
| 5 | John S. Monagan (D) | 133,072 | 67.3 |
| | Charles W. Terrell Jr. (R) | 64,651 | 32.7 |
| 6 | Bernard F. Grabowski (D) | 115,498 | 58.7 |
| | Thomas J. Meskill Jr. (R) | 81,105 | 41.2 |

## DELAWARE

| | Candidates | Votes | % |
|---|---|---|---|
| AL | Harris B. McDowell Jr. (D) | 112,361 | 56.6 |
| | James H. Snowden (R) | 86,254 | 43.4 |

## FLORIDA

| | Candidates | Votes | % |
|---|---|---|---|
| 1 | Robert L. F. Sikes (D) | 74,615 | 98.0 |
| 2 | Charles E. Bennett (D) | 99,191 | 72.7 |
| | William T. Stockton Jr. | 37,283 | 27.3 |
| 3 | Claude Pepper (D) | 101,162 | 65.7 |
| | Paul J. O'Neil (R) | 52,758 | 34.3 |
| 4 | Dante B. Fascell (D) | 94,726 | 63.9 |
| | Jay McGlon (R) | 53,468 | 36.1 |
| 5 | A. Sydney Herlong Jr. (D) | 85,851 | 100.0 |
| 6 | Paul G. Rogers (D) | 168,573 | 66.1 |
| | John D. Steele (R) | 86,657 | 34.0 |
| 7 | James A. Haley (D) | 79,504 | 100.0 |
| 8 | D. R. Matthews (D) | 49,374 | 99.9 |
| 9 | Don Fuqua (D) | 44,917 | 98.8 |
| 10 | Sam M. Gibbons (D) | 69,860 | 99.6 |
| 11 | Edward J. Gurney (R) | 91,731 | 60.6 |
| | Thomas S. Kenney (D) | 59,746 | 39.4 |
| 12 | William C. Cramer (R) | 98,959 | 60.6 |
| | F. Marion Harrelson (D) | 64,378 | 39.4 |

## GEORGIA

| | Candidates | Votes | % |
|---|---|---|---|
| 1 | G. Elliott Hagan (D) | 65,146 | 72.3 |
| | J. Milton Lent (I) | 25,006 | 27.7 |
| 2 | Maston O'Neal (D) | 37,634 | 99.9 |
| 3 | Howard H. Callaway (R) | 45,545 | 57.4 |
| | Garland T. Byrd (D) | 33,733 | 42.5 |
| 4 | James A. Mackay (D) | 66,488 | 56.9 |
| | Roscoe Pickett (R) | 50,326 | 43.1 |
| 5 | Charles L. Weltner (D) | 65,803 | 54.0 |
| | L. J. O'Callaghan (R) | 55,983 | 46.0 |
| 6 | John J. Flynt Jr. (D) | 69,712 | 100.0 |
| 7 | John W. Davis (D) | 69,575 | 54.7 |
| | Ed Chapin (R) | 57,562 | 45.3 |
| 8 | J. Russell Tuten (D) | 49,727 | 100.0 |
| 9 | Phil M. Landrum (D) | 59,186 | 60.5 |
| | Jack Prince (R) | 38,608 | 39.5 |
| 10 | Robert G. Stephens Jr. (D) | 45,418 | 100.0 |

## HAWAII

| | Candidates | Votes | % |
|---|---|---|---|
| AL | Spark M. Matsunaga (D) | 140,224✔ | |
| | Patsy Takemoto Mink (D) | 106,909✔ | |
| | John E. Milligan (R) | 89,425 | |
| | Richard Ike Sutton (R) | 56,147 | |

## IDAHO

| | Candidates | Votes | % |
|---|---|---|---|
| 1 | Compton I. White Jr. (D) | 56,203 | 51.7 |
| | John N. Mattmiller (R) | 52,468 | 48.3 |
| 2 | George V. Hansen (R) | 91,838 | 52.2 |
| | Ralph R. Harding (D) | 84,022 | 47.8 |

## ILLINOIS

| | Candidates | Votes | % |
|---|---|---|---|
| 1 | William L. Dawson (D) | 150,953 | 84.9 |
| | Wilbur N. Daniel (R) | 26,823 | 15.1 |
| 2 | Barratt O'Hara (D) | 107,795 | 67.3 |
| | William F. Scannell (R) | 52,416 | 32.7 |
| 3 | William T. Murphy (D) | 120,711 | 59.1 |
| | Emmet F. Byrne (R) | 83,404 | 40.9 |
| 4 | Edward J. Derwinski (R) | 144,762 | 58.9 |
| | Ray J. Rybacki (D) | 100,895 | 41.1 |
| 5 | John C. Kluczynski (D) | 101,626 | 63.7 |
| | Robert V. Kotowski (R) | 57,871 | 36.3 |

## ILLINOIS

| Candidates | Votes | % |
|---|---|---|
| 6 Daniel J. Ronan (D) | 89,850 | 83.4 |
| Joseph W. Halac (R) | 17,918 | 16.6 |
| 7 Frank Annunzio (D) | 106,708 | 85.9 |
| Ray Wolfram (R) | 17,471 | 14.1 |
| 8 Dan Rostenkowski (D) | 137,715 | 66.1 |
| Eugene L. Ebrom (R) | 70,624 | 33.9 |
| 9 Sidney R. Yates (D) | 113,851 | 63.9 |
| Robert S. Decker (R) | 64,428 | 36.1 |
| 10 Harold R. Collier (R) | 172,499 | 60.8 |
| Thomas E. Gause (D) | 111,029 | 39.2 |
| 11 Roman C. Pucinski (D) | 129,337 | 56.9 |
| Chester T. Podgorski (R) | 98,132 | 43.1 |
| 12 Robert McClory (R) | 97,003 | 58.6 |
| John Clark Kimball (D) | 68,555 | 41.4 |
| 13 Donald Rumsfeld (R) | 165,129 | 57.8 |
| Lynn A. Williams (D) | 120,449 | 42.2 |
| 14 John N. Erlenborn (R) | 145,830 | 59.0 |
| Jerome M. Ziegler (D) | 101,432 | 41.0 |
| 15 Charlotte T. Reid (R) | 103,709 | 58.4 |
| Poppy X. Mitchell (D) | 73,741 | 41.6 |
| 16 John B. Anderson (R) | 93,051 | 56.4 |
| Robert E. Brinkmeier (D) | 71,992 | 43.6 |
| 17 Leslie C. Arends (R) | 96,209 | 56.4 |
| Bernard J. Hughes (D) | 74,261 | 43.6 |
| 18 Robert H. Michel (R) | 91,173 | 54.0 |
| Edward P. Kohlbacher (D) | 77,711 | 46.0 |
| 19 Gale Schisler (D) | 81,800 | 52.4 |
| Robert T. McLoskey (R) | 74,290 | 47.6 |
| 20 Paul Findley (R) | 119,184 | 54.8 |
| Lester E. Collins (D) | 98,256 | 45.2 |
| 21 Kenneth J. Gray (D) | 117,701 | 65.0 |
| Mrs. Stillman J. Stanard (R) | 63,431 | 35.0 |
| 22 William L. Springer (R) | 80,895 | 53.0 |
| John J. Desmond (D) | 71,875 | 47.1 |
| 23 George E. Shipley (D) | 119,447 | 54.6 |
| Wayne S. Jones (R) | 99,496 | 45.4 |
| 24 Melvin Price (D) | 144,743 | 75.7 |
| G. S. Mirza (R) | 46,419 | 24.3 |

## INDIANA

| Candidates | Votes | % |
|---|---|---|
| 1 Ray J. Madden (D) | 133,089 | 63.7 |
| Arthur F. Endres (R) | 75,226 | 36.0 |
| 2 Charles A. Halleck (R) | 88,204 | 52.9 |
| John C. Raber (D) | 78,566 | 47.1 |
| 3 John Brademas (D) | 121,209 | 60.7 |
| Robert Lowell Miller (R) | 78,642 | 39.4 |
| 4 E. Ross Adair (R) | 89,437 | 52.1 |
| Max E. Hobbs (D) | 82,284 | 47.9 |
| 5 J. Edward Roush (D) | 114,252 | 55.2 |
| John R. Feighner (R) | 92,802 | 44.8 |
| 6 Richard L. Roudebush (R) | 86,168 | 54.1 |
| Karl O'Lessker (D) | 73,002 | 45.9 |
| 7 William G. Bray (R) | 84,427 | 54.2 |
| Elden C. Tipton (D) | 71,461 | 45.8 |
| 8 Winfield K. Denton (D) | 109,134 | 56.5 |
| Roger H. Zion (R) | 84,135 | 43.5 |
| 9 Lee H. Hamilton (D) | 74,939 | 54.4 |
| Earl Wilson (R) | 62,780 | 45.6 |
| 10 Ralph Harvey (R) | 89,303 | 50.5 |
| Russell E. Davis (D) | 87,721 | 49.6 |
| 11 Andrew Jacobs Jr. (D) | 149,342 | 50.5 |
| Don A. Tabbert (R) | 146,424 | 49.5 |

## IOWA

| Candidates | Votes | % |
|---|---|---|
| 1 John R. Schmidhauser (D) | 84,042 | 51.0 |
| Fred Schwengel (R) | 80,697 | 48.9 |
| 2 John C. Culver (D) | 97,470 | 52.2 |
| James E. Bromwell (R) | 89,299 | 47.8 |
| 3 H. R. Gross (R) | 83,455 | 50.1 |
| Stephen M. Peterson (D) | 83,036 | 49.9 |
| 4 Bert Bandstra (D) | 85,518 | 53.6 |
| John Kyl (R) | 73,898 | 46.4 |
| 5 Neal Smith (D) | 108,212 | 69.6 |
| Benjamin J. Gibson Jr. (R) | 46,160 | 29.7 |
| 6 Stanley L. Greigg (D) | 86,323 | 53.2 |
| Howard N. Sokol (R) | 75,478 | 46.5 |

| Candidates | Votes | % |
|---|---|---|
| 7 John R. Hansen (D) | 78,243 | 53.5 |
| Ben F. Jensen (R) | 67,942 | 46.5 |

## KANSAS

| Candidates | Votes | % |
|---|---|---|
| 1 Bob Dole (R) | 113,212 | 51.2 |
| Bill Bork (D) | 108,086 | 48.8 |
| 2 Chester L. Mize (R) | 80,806 | 51.1 |
| John Montgomery (D) | 77,189 | 48.9 |
| 3 Robert F. Ellsworth (R) | 89,588 | 62.2 |
| A. Clayton Dial (D) | 54,522 | 37.8 |
| 4 Garner Shriver (R) | 84,800 | 59.4 |
| Jack Glaves (D) | 58,057 | 40.6 |
| 5 Joe Skubitz (R) | 83,120 | 56.4 |
| Reb Russell (D) | 64,308 | 43.6 |

## KENTUCKY

| Candidates | Votes | % |
|---|---|---|
| 1 Frank Stubblefield (D) | 84,574 | 100.0 |
| 2 William H. Natcher (D) | 79,519 | 68.4 |
| Rhodes Bratcher (R) | 36,664 | 31.6 |
| 3 Charles P. Farnsley (D) | 117,892 | 53.8 |
| M. G. (Gene) Snyder (R) | 101,168 | 46.2 |
| 4 Frank Chelf (D) | 88,337 | 61.7 |
| Clyde Middleton (R) | 54,937 | 38.3 |
| 5 Tim Lee Carter (R) | 61,137 | 53.1 |
| Francis Jones Mills (D) | 53,916 | 46.9 |
| 6 John C. Watts (D) | 93,322 | 70.6 |
| John W. Swope (R) | 38,869 | 29.4 |
| 7 Carl D. Perkins (D) | 100,929 | 69.7 |
| Walter Clay Van Hoose (R) | 43,921 | 30.3 |

## LOUISIANA

| Candidates | Votes | % |
|---|---|---|
| 1 F. Edward Hebert (D) | 76,455 | 100.0 |
| 2 Hale Boggs (D) | 77,009 | 55.1 |
| David C. Treen (R) | 62,881 | 45.0 |
| 3 Edwin E. Willis (D) | 52,532 | 62.3 |
| Robert J. Angers Jr. (R) | 31,806 | 37.7 |
| 4 Joe D. Waggonner Jr. (D) | 44,599 | 100.0 |
| 5 Otto E. Passman (D) | 24,544 | 100.0 |
| 6 James H. Morrison (D) | 82,686 | 62.9 |
| Floyd O. Crawford (R) | 48,715 | 37.1 |
| 7 T. A. Thompson (D) | 38,492 | 100.0 |
| 8 Speedy O. Long (D) | 33,250 | 54.5 |
| William S. Walker (R) | 27,735 | 45.5 |

## MAINE

| Candidates | Votes | % |
|---|---|---|
| 1 Stanley R. Tupper (R) | 95,398 | 50.1 |
| Kenneth M. Curtis (D) | 95,195 | 50.0 |
| 2 William D. Hathaway (D) | 110,931 | 62.0 |
| Kenneth P. MacLeod (R) | 67,978 | 38.0 |

## MARYLAND

| Candidates | Votes | % |
|---|---|---|
| 1 Rogers C. B. Morton (R) | 40,762 | 53.1 |
| Harry R. Hughes (D) | 36,013 | 46.9 |
| 2 Clarence D. Long (D) | 143,132 | 65.9 |
| George A. Price (R) | 74,067 | 34.1 |
| 3 Edward A. Garmatz (D) | 56,295 | 100.0 |
| 4 George H. Fallon (D) | 57,229 | 77.8 |
| Charles O'D. Evans (R) | 16,372 | 22.2 |
| 5 Hervey G. Machen (D) | 131,712 | 61.0 |
| Edward A. Potts (R) | 84,318 | 39.0 |
| 6 Charles McC. Mathias Jr. (R) | 134,521 | 54.5 |
| Royce Hanson (D) | 112,410 | 45.5 |
| 7 Samuel N. Friedel (D) | 99,654 | 79.5 |
| Thomas C. Hofstetter (R) | 25,706 | 20.5 |
| AL Carlton R. Sickles (D) | 683,143 | 69.4 |
| David Scull (R) | 301,250 | 30.6 |

## MASSACHUSETTS

| Candidates | Votes | % |
|---|---|---|
| 1 Silvio O. Conte (R) | 139,503 | 100.0 |
| 2 Edward P. Boland (D) | 125,894 | 100.0 |

| Candidates | Votes | % |
|---|---|---|
| 3 Philip J. Philbin (D) | 177,917 | 100.0 |
| 4 Harold D. Donohue (D) | 142,339 | 71.8 |
| Dudley B. Dumaine (R) | 56,034 | 28.3 |
| 5 F. Bradford Morse (R) | 137,735 | 65.0 |
| George W. Arvanitis (D) | 74,133 | 35.0 |
| 6 William H. Bates (R) | 141,733 | 64.6 |
| James E. Zafris Jr. (D) | 77,646 | 35.4 |
| 7 Torbert H. Macdonald (D) | 139,095 | 77.0 |
| Gordon F. Hughes (R) | 41,671 | 23.1 |
| 8 Thomas P. O'Neill Jr. (D) | 122,050 | 100.0 |
| 9 John W. McCormack (D) | 118,385 | 80.3 |
| Jack E. Molesworth (R) | 21,557 | 14.6 |
| Noel A. Day (I) | 7,440 | 5.1 |
| 10 Joseph W. Martin Jr. (R) | 133,403 | 63.0 |
| Edward F. Doolan (D) | 78,415 | 37.0 |
| 11 James A. Burke (D) | 179,261 | 100.0 |
| 12 Hastings Keith (R) | 115,656 | 59.6 |
| Alexander Byron (D) | 78,313 | 40.4 |

## MICHIGAN

| Candidates | Votes | % |
|---|---|---|
| 1 John Conyers Jr. (D) | 138,589 | 83.6 |
| Robert B. Blackwell (R) | 25,735 | 15.5 |
| 2 Weston E. Vivian (D) | 77,806 | 50.4 |
| George Meader (R) | 76,280 | 49.4 |
| 3 Paul H. Todd (D) | 85,001 | 52.7 |
| August E. Johansen (R) | 76,350 | 47.3 |
| 4 Edward Hutchinson (R) | 83,391 | 54.3 |
| Russell W. Holcomb (D) | 70,212 | 45.7 |
| 5 Gerald R. Ford (R) | 101,810 | 61.2 |
| William G. Reamon (D) | 64,488 | 38.8 |
| 6 Charles E. Chamberlain (R) | 88,882 | 56.6 |
| Boyd K. Benedict (D) | 68,265 | 43.4 |
| 7 John C. Mackie (D) | 104,115 | 65.7 |
| Claude E. Sadler (R) | 54,307 | 34.3 |
| 8 James Harvey (R) | 84,588 | 54.7 |
| Sanford A. Brown (D) | 69,931 | 45.3 |
| 9 Robert P. Griffin (R) | 95,376 | 57.4 |
| Daniel Griffen (D) | 70,693 | 42.6 |
| 10 Elford A. Cederberg (R) | 87,232 | 56.6 |
| Hubert C. Evans (D) | 66,835 | 43.4 |
| 11 Raymond F. Clevenger (D) | 86,557 | 53.3 |
| Victor A. Knox (R) | 75,955 | 46.7 |
| 12 James G. O'Hara (D) | 126,769 | 74.8 |
| Robert G. Powell (R) | 42,615 | 25.2 |
| 13 Charles C. Diggs Jr. (D) | 102,413 | 85.8 |
| Bruce Watson (R) | 16,585 | 13.9 |
| 14 Lucien N. Nedzi (D) | 120,308 | 66.9 |
| George Bashara (R) | 59,487 | 33.1 |
| 15 William D. Ford (D) | 103,724 | 71.0 |
| John F. Fellrath Jr. (R) | 42,464 | 29.1 |
| 16 John D. Dingell (D) | 112,763 | 73.4 |
| Raymond B. Leonard (R) | 40,673 | 26.5 |
| 17 Martha W. Griffiths (D) | 136,230 | 72.8 |
| William P. Harrington (D) | 50,580 | 27.0 |
| 18 William S. Broomfield (R) | 109,777 | 59.5 |
| Frank J. Sierawski (D) | 74,576 | 40.4 |
| 19 Billie S. Farnum (D) | 88,441 | 53.4 |
| Richard D. Kuhn (R) | 77,204 | 46.6 |

## MINNESOTA

| Candidates | Votes | % |
|---|---|---|
| 1 Albert H. Quie (R) | 108,639 | 55. |
| George Daley (DFL) | 87,789 | 44. |
| 2 Ancher Nelsen (R) | 97,804 | 58. |
| Charles V. Simpson (DFL) | 69,801 | 41. |
| 3 Clark MacGregor (R) | 125,464 | 57. |
| Richard J. Parish (DFL) | 94,682 | 43. |
| 4 Joseph E. Karth (DFL) | 144,801 | 73. |
| John M. Drexler (R) | 52,221 | 26. |
| 5 Donald M. Fraser (DFL) | 127,963 | 61. |
| John W. Johnson (R) | 78,767 | 38. |
| 6 Alec G. Olson (DFL) | 95,848 | 51. |
| Robert J. Odegard (R) | 89,228 | 48. |
| 7 Odin Langen (R) | 84,300 | 50. |
| Ben M. Wichterman (DFL) | 81,718 | 49. |
| 8 John A. Blatnik (DFL) | 124,277 | 69. |
| David W. Glossbrenner (R) | 54,691 | 30. |

## MISSISSIPPI

| | Candidates | Votes | % |
|---|---|---|---|
| 1 | Thomas G. Abernethy (D) | 60,052 | 100.0 |
| 2 | Jamie L. Whitten (D) | 70,218 | 100.0 |
| 3 | John Bell Williams (D) | 84,503 | 100.0 |
| 4 | Prentiss Walker (R) | 35,277 | 55.7 |
| | Arthur Winstead (D) | 28,057 | 44.3 |
| 5 | William M. Colmer (D) | 83,120 | 100.0 |

## MISSOURI

| | | Votes | % |
|---|---|---|---|
| 1 | Frank M. Karsten (D) | 140,848 | 76.9 |
| | Theodore J. Fischer (R) | 42,351 | 23.1 |
| 2 | Thomas B. Curtis (R) | 130,894 | 53.1 |
| | Sidney B. McClanahan (D) | 115,446 | 46.9 |
| 3 | Leonor K. Sullivan (D) | 123,193 | 71.7 |
| | Howard C. Ohlendorf (R) | 48,709 | 28.3 |
| 4 | William J. Randall (D) | 109,375 | 63.9 |
| | James M. Taylor (R) | 61,854 | 36.1 |
| 5 | Richard Bolling (D) | 91,721 | 67.9 |
| | Robert B. Langworthy (R) | 43,314 | 32.1 |
| 6 | W. R. Hull Jr. (D) | 110,532 | 64.7 |
| | Henry E. Wurst (R) | 60,356 | 35.3 |
| 7 | Durward G. Hall (R) | 102,926 | 51.7 |
| | Jim Thomas (D) | 96,120 | 48.3 |
| 8 | Richard Ichord (D) | 117,672 | 65.2 |
| | Ben A. Rogers (R) | 62,823 | 34.8 |
| 9 | William L. Hungate (D) | 112,907 | 62.3 |
| | Anthony C. Schroeder (R) | 68,032 | 37.6 |
| 10 | Paul C. Jones (D) | 89,698 | 67.4 |
| | Carl F. Painter (R) | 43,304 | 32.6 |

### Special Election

| | | Votes | % |
|---|---|---|---|
| | William L. Hungate (D) | 102,422 | 62.5 |
| | Anthony C. Schroeder (R) | 61,439 | 37.5 |

## MONTANA

| | | Votes | % |
|---|---|---|---|
| 1 | Arnold Olsen (D) | 64,847 | 53.6 |
| | Wayne Montgomery (R) | 55,417 | 45.8 |
| 2 | James F. Battin (R) | 84,241 | 54.1 |
| | Jack C. Toole (D) | 71,461 | 45.9 |

## NEBRASKA

| | | Votes | % |
|---|---|---|---|
| 1 | Clair A. Callan (D) | 107,683 | 51.3 |
| | Ralph F. Beermann (R) | 102,113 | 48.7 |
| 2 | Glenn Cunningham (R) | 81,660 | 53.1 |
| | John Richard Swenson (D) | 72,003 | 46.9 |
| 3 | Dave Martin (R) | 104,380 | 52.8 |
| | William E. Colwell (D) | 93,236 | 47.2 |

## NEVADA

| | | Votes | % |
|---|---|---|---|
| AL | Walter S. Baring (D) | 82,748 | 63.3 |
| | George Von Tobel (R) | 47,989 | 36.7 |

## NEW HAMPSHIRE

| | | Votes | % |
|---|---|---|---|
| 1 | J. Oliva Huot (D) | 79,097 | 51.4 |
| | Louis C. Wyman (R) | 74,939 | 48.7 |
| 2 | James C. Cleveland (R) | 62,680 | 50.1 |
| | Charles B. Officer (D) | 62,382 | 49.9 |

## NEW JERSEY

| | | Votes | % |
|---|---|---|---|
| 1 | William T. Cahill (R) | 150,805 | 56.2 |
| | William J. Procacci (D) | 117,227 | 43.7 |
| 2 | Thomas C. McGrath Jr. (D) | 73,264 | 50.8 |
| | Milton W. Glenn (R) | 70,997 | 49.2 |
| 3 | James J. Howard (D) | 105,803 | 50.4 |
| | Marcus Daly (R) | 104,063 | 49.6 |
| 4 | Frank Thompson Jr. (D) | 134,747 | 67.5 |
| | Ephraim Tomlinson (R) | 64,447 | 32.3 |
| 5 | Peter H. B. Frelinghuysen (R) | 122,168 | 63.6 |
| | Eugene M. Friedman (D) | 70,001 | 36.4 |
| 6 | Florence P. Dwyer (R) | 140,999 | 59.7 |
| | Richard J. Traynor (D) | 95,021 | 40.3 |
| 7 | William B. Widnall (R) | 144,585 | 56.5 |
| | Edward H. Ihnen (D) | 110,328 | 43.1 |
| 8 | Charles S. Joelson (D) | 112,483 | 67.5 |
| | J. Palmer Murphy (R) | 53,732 | 32.3 |
| 9 | Henry Helstoski (D) | 111,741 | 50.1 |
| | Frank C. Osmers Jr. (R) | 109,313 | 49.0 |
| 10 | Peter W. Rodino Jr. (D) | 92,488 | 74.0 |
| | Raymond W. Schroeder (R) | 31,306 | 25.1 |
| 11 | Joseph G. Minish (D) | 82,457 | 69.6 |
| | William L. Stubbs (R) | 35,956 | 30.4 |
| 12 | Paul J. Krebs (D) | 82,726 | 52.4 |
| | David H. Wiener (R) | 72,601 | 46.0 |
| 13 | Cornelius E. Gallagher (D) | 89,360 | 77.1 |
| | Cresenzi W. Castaldo (R) | 24,874 | 21.5 |
| 14 | Dominick V. Daniels (D) | 73,635 | 74.0 |
| | Cecil T. Woolsey (R) | 25,068 | 25.4 |
| 15 | Edward J. Patten (D) | 131,393 | 63.2 |
| | Bernard F. Rodgers (R) | 76,686 | 36.9 |

## NEW MEXICO

| | | Votes | % |
|---|---|---|---|
| AL | Thomas G. Morris (D) | 194,407 | 61.8 |
| | Mike Sims (R) | 120,349 | 38.2 |
| AL | E. S. Johnny Walker (D) | 164,863 | 51.6 |
| | Jack C. Redman (R) | 154,780 | 48.4 |

## NEW YORK

| | | Votes | % |
|---|---|---|---|
| 1 | Otis G. Pike (D, L) | 126,529 | 64.9 |
| | John J. Hart Jr. (R) | 68,362 | 35.1 |
| 2 | James R. Grover Jr. (R) | 88,390 | 51.7 |
| | Edwyn Silberling (D, L) | 82,757 | 48.4 |
| 3 | Lester L. Wolff (D, L) | 96,503 | 50.7 |
| | Steven B. Derounian (R) | 93,883 | 49.3 |
| 4 | John W. Wydler (R) | 89,971 | 53.2 |
| | Joseph L. Marino (D) | 73,148 | 43.2 |
| 5 | Herbert Tenzer (D, L) | 112,899 | 55.8 |
| | Ralph J. Edsell Jr. (R) | 89,455 | 44.2 |
| 6 | Seymour Halpern (R) | 100,069 | 57.1 |
| | Emil Levin (D) | 75,327 | 43.0 |
| 7 | Joseph P. Addabbo (D, L) | 121,091 | 69.8 |
| | Robert L. Nelson (R) | 49,151 | 28.3 |
| 8 | Benjamin S. Rosenthal (D, L) | 148,696 | 75.0 |
| | Vincent P. Brevetti (R) | 44,398 | 22.4 |
| 9 | James J. Delaney (D) | 109,973 | 65.9 |
| | Charles H. Cohen (R) | 48,878 | 29.3 |
| 10 | Emanuel Celler (D, L) | 118,941 | 87.5 |
| | Samuel W. Held (R) | 16,941 | 12.5 |
| 11 | Eugene J. Keogh (D, L) | 75,073 | 78.8 |
| | Herman Sanders (R) | 17,732 | 18.6 |
| 12 | Edna F. Kelly (D, L) | 141,570 | 81.7 |
| | Carlo G. Colavito (R) | 31,737 | 18.3 |
| 13 | Abraham J. Multer (D, L) | 129,414 | 69.1 |
| | Gerald S. Held (R) | 34,809 | 18.6 |
| | Gerard M. Weisberg (L) | 23,148 | 12.4 |
| 14 | John J. Rooney (D, L) | 68,165 | 77.4 |
| | Victor J. Tirabasso Jr. (R) | 19,861 | 22.6 |
| 15 | Hugh L. Carey (D, L) | 66,567 | 53.6 |
| | Luigi R. Marano (R, C) | 57,626 | 46.4 |
| 16 | John M. Murphy (D, L) | 89,438 | 61.4 |
| | David D. Smith (R, C) | 56,238 | 38.6 |
| 17 | John V. Lindsay (R) | 135,807 | 71.5 |
| | Eleanor C. French (D, L) | 44,533 | 23.5 |
| | Kieran O'Doherty (C) | 9,491 | 5.0 |
| 18 | Adam Clayton Powell Jr. (D) | 94,222 | 84.6 |
| | Joseph A. Bailey (R) | 11,621 | 10.4 |
| 19 | Leonard Farbstein (D) | 84,781 | 68.9 |
| | Henry E. Delrosso (R) | 24,829 | 20.2 |
| | Edward A. Morrison (L) | 12,129 | 9.9 |
| 20 | William F. Ryan (D, L) | 124,128 | 82.5 |
| | Ronald N. Gottlieb (R) | 23,409 | 15.6 |
| 21 | James H. Scheuer (D, L) | 91,898 | 84.3 |
| | Henry Rose (R) | 15,380 | 14.1 |
| 22 | Jacob H. Gilbert (D) | 70,147 | 81.6 |
| | Manuel R. Roque (R) | 10,134 | 11.8 |
| | Joseph A. Mazar (L) | 5,026 | 5.8 |
| 23 | Jonathan B. Bingham (D) | 108,205 | 71.3 |
| | Patrick J. Foley (R) | 30,476 | 20.1 |
| | John P. Hagan (L) | 10,602 | 7.0 |
| 24 | Paul A. Fino (R) | 89,814 | 61.2 |
| | Robert J. Malang (D) | 51,740 | 35.3 |
| 25 | Richard Ottinger (D, L) | 122,260 | 56.2 |
| | Robert R. Barry (R) | 95,214 | 43.8 |
| 26 | Ogden R. Reid (R) | 102,064 | 54.9 |
| | Frank Conniff (D, L) | 78,546 | 42.2 |
| 27 | John G. Dow (D) | 97,337 | 51.6 |
| | Katherine St.George (R) | 91,172 | 48.4 |
| 28 | Joseph Y. Resnick (D) | 95,820 | 51.7 |
| | J. Ernest Wharton (R, C) | 84,008 | 45.3 |
| 29 | Leo W. O'Brien (D, L) | 158,797 | 69.2 |
| | John D. Meader (R, C) | 70,518 | 30.8 |
| 30 | Carleton J. King (R) | 100,950 | 50.3 |
| | Joseph J. Martin (D, L) | 99,841 | 49.7 |
| 31 | Robert C. McEwen (R, C) | 74,380 | 54.6 |
| | Raymond E. Bishop (D, L) | 61,726 | 45.4 |
| 32 | Alexander Pirnie (R) | 86,717 | 53.4 |
| | Robert Castle (D) | 75,660 | 46.6 |
| 33 | Howard W. Robison (R) | 97,213 | 58.4 |
| | John L. Joy (D, L) | 69,277 | 41.6 |
| 34 | James M. Hanley (D, L) | 96,219 | 51.2 |
| | R. Walter Riehlman (R, C) | 91,697 | 48.8 |
| 35 | Samuel S. Stratton (D, L) | 110,948 | 64.0 |
| | Robert M. Quigley (R, C) | 62,463 | 36.0 |
| 36 | Frank J. Horton (R) | 107,406 | 56.0 |
| | John C. Williams (D) | 81,509 | 42.5 |
| 37 | Barber B. Conable Jr. (R) | 98,923 | 54.2 |
| | Neil F. Bubel (D) | 80,411 | 44.0 |
| 38 | Charles E. Goodell (R) | 90,201 | 58.4 |
| | Robert V. Kelley (D, L) | 64,179 | 41.6 |
| 39 | Richard D. McCarthy (D, L) | 108,235 | 52.8 |
| | John R. Pillion (R) | 96,934 | 47.3 |
| 40 | Henry P. Smith III (R) | 90,745 | 51.5 |
| | Wesley J. Hilts (D) | 81,531 | 46.3 |
| 41 | Thaddeus J. Dulski (D, L) | 130,961 | 82.1 |
| | Joseph A. Klawon (R) | 28,578 | 17.9 |

## NORTH CAROLINA

| | | Votes | % |
|---|---|---|---|
| 1 | Herbert C. Bonner (D) | 52,567 | 82.6 |
| | Zeno O. Ratcliff (R) | 11,108 | 17.4 |
| 2 | L. H. Fountain (D) | 62,406 | 100.0 |
| 3 | David N. Henderson (D) | 63,235 | 67.4 |
| | Sherman T. Rock (R) | 30,557 | 32.6 |
| 4 | Harold D. Cooley (D) | 73,470 | 51.8 |
| | James C. Gardner (R) | 68,387 | 48.2 |
| 5 | Ralph J. Scott (D) | 72,254 | 51.6 |
| | W. A. Armfield (R) | 67,781 | 48.4 |
| 6 | Horace R. Kornegay (D) | 84,151 | 61.4 |
| | Walter G. Green (R) | 52,964 | 38.6 |
| 7 | Alton Lennon (D) | 71,357 | 100.0 |
| 8 | Charles R. Jonas (R) | 85,869 | 54.3 |
| | W. D. James (D) | 72,269 | 45.7 |
| 9 | James T. Broyhill (R) | 88,195 | 55.2 |
| | Robert M. Davis (D) | 71,629 | 44.8 |
| 10 | Basil L. Whitener (D) | 78,684 | 58.7 |
| | W. Hall Young (R) | 55,483 | 41.4 |
| 11 | Roy A. Taylor (D) | 85,880 | 60.5 |
| | Clyde M. Roberts (R) | 55,996 | 39.5 |

## NORTH DAKOTA

| | | Votes | % |
|---|---|---|---|
| 1 | Mark Andrews (R) | 69,575 | 52.1 |
| | George A. Sinner (D) | 63,208 | 47.4 |
| 2 | Rolland Redlin (D) | 60,751 | 52.5 |
| | Don L. Short (R) | 54,878 | 47.5 |

## OHIO

| | | Votes | % |
|---|---|---|---|
| 1 | John J. Gilligan (D) | 74,525 | 51.9 |
| | Carl W. Rich (R) | 69,114 | 48.1 |
| 2 | Donald D. Clancy (R) | 122,487 | 60.5 |
| | H. A. Sand (D) | 79,824 | 39.5 |
| 3 | Rodney M. Love (D) | 129,469 | 52.0 |
| | Paul F. Schenck (R) | 119,400 | 48.0 |

## OHIO

| | Candidates | Votes | % |
|---|---|---|---|
| 4 | William M. McCulloch (R) | 81,204 | 55.7 |
| | Robert H. Mihlbaugh (D) | 64,667 | 44.3 |
| 5 | Delbert L. Latta (R) | 80,394 | 65.9 |
| | Milford Landis (D) | 41,621 | 34.1 |
| 6 | William H. Harsha (R) | 86,015 | 60.1 |
| | Frank E. Smith (D) | 57,223 | 40.0 |
| 7 | Clarence J. Brown (R) | 93,022 | 56.8 |
| | Jerry R. Graham (D) | 70,857 | 43.2 |
| 8 | Jackson E. Betts (R) | 73,395 | 61.8 |
| | Frank Bennett (D) | 45,445 | 38.2 |
| 9 | Thomas L. Ashley (D) | 109,167 | 62.9 |
| | John O. Celusta (R) | 64,401 | 37.1 |
| 10 | Walter H. Moeller (D) | 54,729 | 52.4 |
| | Homer E. Abele (R) | 49,744 | 47.6 |
| 11 | J. William Stanton (R) | 102,619 | 55.4 |
| | C. D. Lambros (D) | 82,728 | 44.6 |
| 12 | Samuel L. Devine (R) | 146,971 | 55.4 |
| | Robert L. Van Heyde (D) | 118,299 | 44.6 |
| 13 | Charles A. Mosher (R) | 75,945 | 54.7 |
| | Louis G. Frey (D) | 62,780 | 45.3 |
| 14 | William H. Ayres (R) | 126,088 | 54.7 |
| | Frances McGovern (D) | 104,547 | 45.3 |
| 15 | Robert T. Secrest (D) | 62,438 | 66.1 |
| | Randall Metcalf (R) | 31,983 | 33.9 |
| 16 | Frank T. Bow (R) | 101,802 | 52.2 |
| | Robert D. Freeman (D) | 93,255 | 47.8 |
| 17 | John M. Ashbrook (R) | 75,674 | 51.5 |
| | Robert W. Levering (D) | 71,291 | 48.5 |
| 18 | Wayne L. Hays (D) | 94,768 | 68.8 |
| | Allen J. Dalrymple (R) | 42,960 | 31.2 |
| 19 | Michael J. Kirwan (D) | 111,682 | 76.3 |
| | Albert H. James (R) | 34,654 | 23.7 |
| 20 | Michael A. Feighan (D) | 115,675 | 74.4 |
| | Joseph A. Cipollone (R) | 39,747 | 25.6 |
| 21 | Charles A. Vanik (D) | 113,157 | 90.1 |
| | Eugene E. Smith (R) | 12,416 | 9.9 |
| 22 | Frances P. Bolton (R) | 84,183 | 56.6 |
| | Chat Paterson (D) | 64,454 | 43.4 |
| 23 | William E. Minshall (R) | 131,554 | 67.2 |
| | Norbert G. Dennerll Jr. (D) | 64,162 | 32.8 |
| AL | Robert E. Sweeney (D) | 1,872,351 | 52.2 |
| | Oliver P. Bolton (R) | 1,716,480 | 47.8 |

## OKLAHOMA

| | | Votes | % |
|---|---|---|---|
| 1 | Page Belcher (R) | 125,377 | 63.5 |
| | Doug Martin (D) | 71,998 | 36.5 |
| 2 | Ed Edmondson (D) | 90,466 | 61.4 |
| | George L. Lange (R) | 56,843 | 38.6 |
| 3 | Carl Albert (D) | 62,952 | 79.0 |
| | Frank D. McSherry (R) | 16,706 | 21.0 |
| 4 | Tom Steed (D) | 98,419 | 100.0 |
| 5 | John Jarman (D) | 130,014 | 70.8 |
| | Homer Cowan (R) | 53,596 | 29.2 |
| 6 | Jed Johnson Jr. (D) | 75,879 | 56.7 |
| | Bayard C. Auchincloss (R) | 58,041 | 43.3 |

## OREGON

| | | Votes | % |
|---|---|---|---|
| 1 | Wendell Wyatt (R) | 122,010 | 53.1 |
| | R. Blaine Whipple (D) | 107,920 | 46.9 |
| 2 | Al Ullman (D) | 70,136 | 68.1 |
| | Everett J. Thoren (R) | 32,916 | 31.9 |
| 3 | Edith Green (D) | 157,882 | 65.6 |
| | Lyle Dean (R) | 82,468 | 34.3 |
| 4 | Robert B. Duncan (D) | 125,752 | 64.8 |
| | Paul Jaffarian (R) | 68,288 | 35.2 |

### Special Election

| | | Votes | % |
|---|---|---|---|
| 1 | Wendell Wyatt (R) | 125,473 | 52.8 |
| | R. Blaine Whipple (D) | 112,112 | 47.2 |

## PENNSYLVANIA

| | | Votes | % |
|---|---|---|---|
| 1 | William A. Barrett (D) | 129,471 | 71.8 |
| | Alvin J. Bello (R) | 50,780 | 28.2 |

| | Candidates | Votes | % |
|---|---|---|---|
| 2 | Robert N. C. Nix (D) | 125,100 | 80.2 |
| | Melvin C. Howell (R) | 30,801 | 19.8 |
| 3 | James A. Byrne (D) | 111,885 | 72.0 |
| | John J. Poserina Jr. (R) | 43,471 | 28.0 |
| 4 | Herman Toll (D) | 135,681 | 64.1 |
| | James R. Cavanaugh (R) | 75,901 | 35.9 |
| 5 | William J. Green III (D) | 117,049 | 65.2 |
| | Edward H. Rovner (R) | 62,446 | 34.8 |
| 6 | George M. Rhodes (D) | 144,697# | 62.1 |
| | James B. Bamford (R) | 88,495# | 37.9 |
| 7 | G. Robert Watkins (R) | 129,572 | 51.2 |
| | Leonard Bachman (D) | 123,750 | 48.9 |
| 8 | Willard S. Curtin (R) | 112,472 | 51.1 |
| | Ralph O. Samuel (D) | 107,670 | 48.9 |
| 9 | Paul B. Dague (R) | 111,545 | 57.7 |
| | John A. O'Brien (D) | 81,823 | 42.3 |
| 10 | Joseph M. McDade (R) | 90,903 | 50.8 |
| | James J. Haggerty (D) | 88,082 | 49.2 |
| 11 | Daniel J. Flood (D) | 116,875 | 77.4 |
| | Charles R. Thomas (R) | 34,057 | 22.6 |
| 12 | J. Irving Whalley (R) | 97,114 | 58.6 |
| | Paul A. Stephens (D) | 68,703 | 41.4 |
| 13 | Richard S. Schweiker (R) | 139,817 | 59.1 |
| | William D. Searle (D) | 96,849 | 40.9 |
| 14 | William S. Moorhead (D) | 117,525 | 74.8 |
| | Alvin D. Capozzi (R) | 39,513 | 25.2 |
| 15 | Fred B. Rooney (D) | 81,062 | 66.1 |
| | Leo W. McCormick (R) | 41,656 | 33.9 |
| 16 | John C. Kunkel (R) | 90,331 | 64.1 |
| | William F. Stefanic (D) | 50,509 | 35.9 |
| 17 | Herman T. Schneebeli (R) | 91,504 | 58.0 |
| | William F. Plankenhorn (D) | 66,266 | 42.0 |
| 18 | Robert J. Corbett (R) | 119,938 | 62.6 |
| | Frank J. Reed (D) | 71,621 | 37.4 |
| 19 | N. Neiman Craley Jr. (D) | 82,498 | 50.8 |
| | George A. Goodling (R) | 79,809 | 49.2 |
| 20 | Elmer J. Holland (D) | 126,846 | 74.4 |
| | Ronald Bryan (R) | 43,591 | 25.6 |
| 21 | John H. Dent (D) | 97,379 | 65.8 |
| | Thomas M. Schooley Jr. (R) | 50,513 | 34.2 |
| 22 | John P. Saylor (R) | 81,400 | 57.0 |
| | James E. McCaffery (D) | 61,482 | 43.0 |
| 23 | Albert W. Johnson (R) | 76,575 | 54.9 |
| | John Still (D) | 62,932 | 45.1 |
| 24 | Joseph P. Vigorito (D) | 92,612 | 50.8 |
| | James D. Weaver (R) | 89,828 | 49.2 |
| 25 | Frank M. Clark (D) | 121,140 | 70.3 |
| | John Loth (R) | 51,071 | 29.7 |
| 26 | Thomas E. Morgan (D) | 109,532 | 68.1 |
| | Paul B. Riggle (R) | 51,219 | 31.9 |
| 27 | James G. Fulton (R) | 120,395 | 62.7 |
| | John A. Young (D) | 71,519 | 37.3 |

### Special Election

| | | Votes | % |
|---|---|---|---|
| 5 | William J. Green III (D) | 30,904# | 58.6 |
| | Edward H. Rovner (R) | 21,832# | 41.4 |

## RHODE ISLAND

| | | Votes | % |
|---|---|---|---|
| 1 | Fernard J. St.Germain (D) | 110,056 | 66.3 |
| | Roland H. Blanchette (R) | 56,056 | 33.8 |
| 2 | John E. Fogarty (D) | 168,374 | 81.4 |
| | Guy J. Wells (R) | 38,601 | 18.7 |

## SOUTH CAROLINA

| | | Votes | % |
|---|---|---|---|
| 1 | L. Mendel Rivers (D) | 64,804 | 99.6 |
| 2 | Albert W. Watson (D) | 88,682 | 97.6 |
| 3 | W. J. Bryan Dorn (D) | 65,920 | 99.9 |
| 4 | Robert T. Ashmore (D) | 81,727 | 100.0 |
| 5 | Tom S. Gettys (D) | 44,859 | 66.7 |
| | Robert M. Doster (R) | 22,384 | 33.3 |
| 6 | John L. McMillan (D) | 49,398 | 65.0 |
| | E. R. Kirkland (R) | 26,586 | 35.0 |

### Special Election

| | | Votes | % |
|---|---|---|---|
| 5 | Tom S. Gettys (D) | 44,241 | 66.8 |
| | Robert M. Doster (R) | 22,031 | 33.2 |

## SOUTH DAKOTA

| | Candidates | Votes | % |
|---|---|---|---|
| 1 | Ben Reifel (R) | 124,791 | 57.6 |
| | George May (D) | 92,057 | 42.5 |
| 2 | E. Y. Berry (R) | 39,657 | 56.0 |
| | Byron T. Brown (D) | 31,208 | 44.0 |

## TENNESSEE

| | | Votes | % |
|---|---|---|---|
| 1 | James H. Quillen (R) | 94,535 | 71.7 |
| | Arthur Bright (D) | 37,252 | 28.3 |
| 2 | John J. Duncan (R) | 84,868 | 53.8 |
| | Willard V. Yarbrough (D) | 70,119 | 44.5 |
| 3 | Bill Brock (R) | 71,005 | 54.6 |
| | Robert M. Summitt (D) | 59,027 | 45.4 |
| 4 | Joe L. Evins (D) | 85,286 | 100.0 |
| 5 | Richard Fulton (D) | 74,597 | 59.8 |
| | William R. Wills (R) | 50,210 | 40.2 |
| 6 | William R. Anderson (D) | 66,817 | 78.2 |
| | Cecil R. Hill (R) | 18,595 | 21.8 |
| 7 | Tom Murray (D) | 35,612 | 53.6 |
| | Julius Hurst (IR) | 24,496 | 36.8 |
| | Earl Maclin (I) | 6,382 | 9.6 |
| 8 | Robert A. Everett (D) | 43,876 | 93.9 |
| | Sarah Flannary (I) | 2,865 | 6.1 |
| 9 | George W. Grider (D) | 108,425 | 52.7 |
| | Robert James (R) | 97,537 | 47.3 |

### Special Election

| | | Votes | % |
|---|---|---|---|
| 2 | Irene Baker (R) | 40,708# | 55.? |
| | Willard V. Yarbrough (D) | 31,763# | 43.? |

## TEXAS

| | | Votes | % |
|---|---|---|---|
| 1 | Wright Patman (D) | 52,698 | 74.? |
| | Mrs. William E. Jones (R) | 17,967 | 25.? |
| 2 | Jack Brooks (D) | 75,226 | 62.? |
| | John Greco (R) | 44,772 | 37.? |
| 3 | Lindley Beckworth (D) | 53,331 | 59.? |
| | James Warren (R) | 36,566 | 40.? |
| 4 | Ray Roberts (D) | 46,782 | 81.? |
| | Fred Banfield (R) | 10,707 | 18.? |
| 5 | Earle Cabell (D) | 172,287 | 57.? |
| | Bruce Alger (R) | 127,568 | 42.? |
| 6 | Olin Teague (D) | 55,155 | 82.? |
| | William Van Winkle (R) | 11,967 | 17.? |
| 7 | John Dowdy (D) | 64,456 | 83.? |
| | James W. Orr (R) | 12,606 | 16.? |
| 8 | Albert Thomas (D) | 103,595 | 76.? |
| | Bob Gilbert (R) | 31,351 | 23.? |
| 9 | Clark Thompson (D) | 105,631 | 75.? |
| | Dave Oakes (R) | 34,692 | 24.? |
| 10 | Jake Pickle (D) | 80,045 | 75.? |
| | Billie Pratt (R) | 25,594 | 24.? |
| 11 | W. R. Poage (D) | 62,175 | 81.? |
| | Charles M. Isenhower (R) | 14,094 | 18.? |
| 12 | Jim Wright (D) | 107,896 | 68.? |
| | Fred Dielman (R) | 49,633 | 31.? |
| 13 | Graham Purcell (D) | 67,947 | 75.? |
| | George Corse (R) | 22,429 | 24.? |
| 14 | John Young (D) | 105,352 | 77.? |
| | Billy Patton (R) | 30,522 | 22.? |
| 15 | Eligio de la Garza (D) | 66,897 | 69.? |
| | Joe Coulter (R) | 29,551 | 30.? |
| 16 | Richard C. White (D) | 70,262 | 55.? |
| | Ed Foreman (R) | 55,951 | 44.? |
| 17 | Omar Burleson (D) | 59,769 | 76.? |
| | Phil M. Bridges (R) | 18,440 | 23.? |
| 18 | Walter Rogers (D) | 58,701 | 55.? |
| | Robert Price (R) | 48,054 | 45.? |
| 19 | George Mahon (D) | 87,555 | 77.? |
| | Joe B. Phillips (R) | 25,243 | 22.? |
| 20 | Henry B. Gonzalez (D) | 103,464 | 64.? |
| | John M. O'Connell (R) | 56,601 | 35.? |
| 21 | O. C. Fisher (D) | 61,785 | 78.? |
| | Harry Claypool (R) | 17,295 | 21.? |
| 22 | Bob Casey (D) | 136,289 | 58.? |
| | Desmond Barry (R) | 98,287 | 41.? |
| AL | Joe Pool (D) | 1,690,674 | 66.? |
| | Bill Hayes (R) | 826,991 | 32.? |

## UTAH

| Candidates | Votes | % |
|---|---|---|
| 1 Laurence J. Burton (R) | 75,986 | 56.0 |
| William G. Bruhn (D) | 59,768 | 44.0 |
| 2 David S. King (D) | 149,754 | 57.5 |
| Thomas G. Judd (R) | 110,512 | 42.5 |

## VERMONT

| | Votes | % |
|---|---|---|
| AL Robert T. Stafford (R, I) | 92,252 | 56.4 |
| Bernard G. O'Shea (D) | 71,193 | 43.6 |

## VIRGINIA

| Candidates | Votes | % |
|---|---|---|
| 1 Thomas N. Downing (D) | 72,819 | 78.7 |
| Wayne C. Thiessen (R) | 19,698 | 21.3 |
| 2 Porter Hardy Jr. (D) | 54,315 | 68.7 |
| Wayne Lustig (R) | 17,082 | 21.6 |
| H. W. Grady Speers Jr. (I) | 7,635 | 9.7 |
| 3 David E. Satterfield III (D) | 43,880 | 34.5 |
| Richard D. Obenshain (R) | 43,226 | 34.0 |
| Edward E. Haddock (I) | 39,223 | 30.8 |
| 4 Watkins M. Abbitt (D) | 53,857 | 69.5 |
| S. W. Tucker (R) | 23,682 | 30.5 |
| 5 William M. Tuck (D) | 39,867 | 63.5 |
| Robert L. Gilliam (R) | 22,946 | 36.5 |
| 6 Richard H. Poff (R) | 57,987 | 56.2 |
| William B. Hopkins (D) | 45,113 | 43.8 |
| 7 John O. Marsh Jr. (D) | 47,888 | 69.6 |
| Roy Erickson (R) | 20,911 | 30.4 |

| Candidates | Votes | % |
|---|---|---|
| 8 Howard W. Smith (D) | 49,440 | 69.4 |
| Floyd Caldwell Bagley (I) | 21,813 | 30.6 |
| 9 W. Pat Jennings (D) | 51,106 | 58.2 |
| Glen M. Williams (R) | 36,668 | 41.8 |
| 10 Joel T. Broyhill (R) | 80,370 | 50.7 |
| Augustus C. Johnson (D) | 78,242 | 49.3 |

## WASHINGTON

| | Votes | % |
|---|---|---|
| 1 Thomas M. Pelly (R) | 117,851 | 59.9 |
| Edward Palmason (D) | 78,876 | 40.1 |
| 2 Lloyd Meeds (D) | 88,551 | 54.9 |
| Jack Westland (R) | 72,830 | 45.1 |
| 3 Julia Butler Hansen (D) | 102,080 | 70.2 |
| Harold L. Anderson (R) | 43,415 | 29.8 |
| 4 Catherine May (R) | 102,964 | 65.3 |
| Stephen H. Huza (D) | 54,819 | 34.7 |
| 5 Thomas S. Foley (D) | 84,830 | 53.5 |
| Walt Horan (R) | 73,884 | 46.6 |
| 6 Floyd V. Hicks (D) | 79,042 | 52.1 |
| Thor C. Tollefson (R) | 72,702 | 47.9 |
| 7 Brock Adams (D) | 125,222 | 55.5 |
| William Stinson (R) | 100,119 | 44.4 |

## WEST VIRGINIA

| | Votes | % |
|---|---|---|
| 1 Arch A. Moore Jr. (R) | 115,799 | 61.4 |
| John L. Bailey (D) | 72,714 | 38.6 |
| 2 Harley O. Staggers (D) | 87,928 | 65.0 |
| Stanley R. Cox Jr. (R) | 47,457 | 35.1 |
| 3 John M. Slack Jr. (D) | 103,117 | 65.4 |
| Jim Comstock (R) | 54,566 | 34.6 |

| Candidates | Votes | % |
|---|---|---|
| 4 Ken Hechler (D) | 109,287 | 61.2 |
| Jack L. Miller (R) | 69,253 | 38.8 |
| 5 James Kee (D) | 77,156 | 70.0 |
| Wade Hampton Ballard III (R) | 33,108 | 30.0 |

## WISCONSIN

| | Votes | % |
|---|---|---|
| 1 Lynn E. Stalbaum (D) | 90,450 | 51.5 |
| Henry C. Schadeberg (R) | 85,117 | 48.5 |
| 2 Robert W. Kastenmeier (D) | 108,148 | 63.6 |
| Carl V. Kolata (R) | 61,865 | 36.4 |
| 3 Vernon W. Thomson (R) | 91,092 | 60.6 |
| Harold C. Ristow (D) | 59,173 | 39.4 |
| 4 Clement J. Zablocki (D) | 125,683 | 74.2 |
| Edward E. Estkowski (R) | 43,773 | 25.8 |
| 5 Henry S. Reuss (D) | 107,610 | 75.9 |
| Robert Taylor (R) | 34,059 | 24.0 |
| 6 John A. Race (D) | 84,690 | 50.8 |
| William K. Van Pelt (R) | 82,103 | 49.2 |
| 7 Melvin R. Laird (R) | 98,110 | 61.8 |
| Thomas E. Martin (D) | 60,758 | 38.2 |
| 8 John W. Byrnes (R) | 96,160 | 59.6 |
| Cletus J. Johnson (D) | 65,292 | 40.4 |
| 9 Glenn R. Davis (R) | 105,332 | 55.3 |
| James P. Buckley (D) | 85,071 | 44.7 |
| 10 Alvin E. O'Konski (R) | 92,198 | 56.2 |
| Edmund A. Nix (D) | 71,983 | 43.8 |

## WYOMING

| | Votes | % |
|---|---|---|
| AL Teno Roncalio (D) | 70,693 | 50.8 |
| William Henry Harrison (R) | 68,482 | 49.2 |

# 1965 House Elections

## CALIFORNIA

### Special Election

| | | Votes | % |
|---|---|---|---|
| 26 | Thomas M. Rees (D) | 40,430 | 59.4 |
| | Edward M. Marshall (R) | 27,579 | 40.5 |

## LOUISIANA
### Special Election

| | | |
|---|---|---|
| 7 | Edwin W. Edwards (D) | ✔ |

### OHIO
#### Special Election

| | | Votes | % |
|---|---|---|---|
| 7 | Clarence J. Brown Jr. (R) | 70,573 | 59.6 |
| | James A. Berry (D) | 47,830 | 40.4 |

## SOUTH CAROLINA

### Special Election

| | | Votes | % |
|---|---|---|---|
| 2 | Albert W. Watson (R) | 55,977# | 69.3 |
| | Preston H. Callison (D) | 24,761# | 30.7 |

---

## House Candidates Index

For an index of all House candidates listed in this section (pages 943-1326), see pages 1402-1501. Instructions for use of the House Candidates Index appear on page 1402.

# 1966 House Elections

## ALABAMA

| Candidates | Votes | % |
|---|---|---|
| 1 Jack Edwards (R) | 58,515 | 65.8 |
| Warren L. Finch (D) | 30,474 | 34.2 |
| 2 William L. Dickinson (R) | 49,203 | 54.7 |
| Robert F. Whaley (D) | 40,832 | 45.4 |
| 3 George Andrews (D) | 61,015 | 100.0 |
| 4 Bill Nichols (D) | 54,515 | 58.7 |
| Glenn Andrews (R) | 38,402 | 41.3 |
| 5 Armistead I. Selden Jr. (D) | 68,486 | 100.0 |
| 6 John Buchanan (R) | 64,435 | 63.4 |
| Walter Emmett Perry (D) | 37,131 | 36.6 |
| 7 Tom Bevill (D) | 73,987 | 64.4 |
| Wayman Sherrer (R) | 40,972 | 35.6 |
| 8 Robert E. Jones (D) | 65,982 | 71.3 |
| Don Mayhall (R) | 26,561 | 28.7 |

## ALASKA

| Candidates | Votes | % |
|---|---|---|
| AL Howard W. Pollock (R) | 34,040 | 51.7 |
| Ralph J. Rivers (D) | 31,867 | 48.4 |

## ARIZONA

| Candidates | Votes | % |
|---|---|---|
| 1 John J. Rhodes (R) | 102,007 | 67.2 |
| L. Alton Riggs (D) | 49,913 | 32.9 |
| 2 Morris K. Udall (D) | 66,813 | 59.6 |
| G. Alfred McGinnis (R) | 45,326 | 40.4 |
| 3 Sam Steiger (R) | 57,145 | 56.9 |
| George F. Senner Jr. (D) | 43,219 | 43.1 |

## ARKANSAS

| Candidates | Votes | % |
|---|---|---|
| 1 E. C. Gathings (D) | | 100.0 |
| 2 Wilbur Mills (D) | | 100.0 |
| 3 John P. Hammerschmidt (R) | 83,938 | 53.1 |
| James W. Trimble (D) | 74,009 | 46.9 |
| 4 David Pryor (D) | 86,887 | 65.0 |
| Lynn Lowe (R) | 46,804 | 35.0 |

### Special Election

| | | | |
|---|---|---|---|
| 4 David Pryor (D) | 85,125 | 64.5 |
| Lynn Lowe (R) | 46,764 | 35.0 |

## CALIFORNIA

| Candidates | Votes | % |
|---|---|---|
| 1 Don H. Clausen (R) | 143,755 | 64.9 |
| Thomas T. Storer (D) | 77,000 | 34.7 |
| 2 Harold T. Johnson (D) | 131,145 | 70.9 |
| William H. Romack (R) | 53,753 | 29.1 |
| 3 John E. Moss Jr. (D) | 143,177 | 67.5 |
| Terry G. Feil (R) | 69,057 | 32.5 |
| 4 Robert L. Leggett (D) | 67,942 | 59.5 |
| Tom McHatton (R) | 46,337 | 40.5 |
| 5 Phillip Burton (D) | 56,476 | 71.3 |
| Terry R. Macken (R) | 22,778 | 28.7 |
| 6 William S. Mailliard (R) | 132,506 | 76.6 |
| Lerue Grim (D) | 40,514 | 23.4 |
| 7 Jeffery Cohelan (D) | 84,644 | 63.9 |
| Malcolm M. Champlin (R) | 46,763 | 35.3 |
| 8 George P. Miller (D) | 92,263 | 65.4 |
| Raymond P. Britton (R) | 48,727 | 34.6 |
| 9 Don Edwards (D) | 97,311 | 63.1 |
| Wilbur G. Durkee (R) | 56,784 | 36.9 |
| 10 Charles S. Gubser (R) | 156,549 | 69.1 |
| George Leppert (D) | 70,013 | 30.9 |
| 11 J. Arthur Younger (R) | 113,679 | 59.4 |
| Mark Sullivan (D) | 77,605 | 40.6 |
| 12 Burt L. Talcott (R) | 108,070 | 77.2 |
| Gerald V. Barron (D) | 31,787 | 22.7 |
| 13 Charles M. Teague (R) | 116,701 | 67.5 |
| Charles A. Storke (D) | 56,240 | 32.5 |

| Candidates | Votes | % |
|---|---|---|
| 14 Jerome R. Waldie (D) | 108,668 | 56.4 |
| Frank J. Newman (R) | 83,878 | 43.5 |
| 15 John J. McFall (D) | 81,733 | 57.0 |
| Sam Van Dyken (R) | 61,550 | 43.0 |
| 16 B. F. Sisk (D) | 118,063 | 71.3 |
| Cecil F. White (R) | 47,329 | 28.6 |
| 17 Cecil R. King (D) | 76,962 | 60.8 |
| Don Cortum (R) | 49,615 | 39.2 |
| 18 Robert B. Mathias (R) | 96,699 | 55.9 |
| Harlan Hagen (D) | 76,346 | 44.1 |
| 19 Chet Holifield (D) | 82,592 | 62.2 |
| William R. Sutton (R) | 50,068 | 37.7 |
| 20 H. Allen Smith (R) | 128,896 | 73.4 |
| Raymond Freschi (D) | 46,730 | 26.6 |
| 21 Augustus F. Hawkins (D) | 74,216 | 84.8 |
| Norman A. Hodges (R) | 13,294 | 15.2 |
| 22 James C. Corman (D) | 94,420 | 53.5 |
| Robert C. Cline (R) | 82,207 | 46.5 |
| 23 Del Clawson (R) | 93,320 | 67.4 |
| Ed O'Connor (D) | 45,141 | 32.6 |
| 24 Glenard P. Lipscomb (R) | 148,190 | 76.2 |
| Earl G. McNall (D) | 46,115 | 23.7 |
| 25 Charles E. Wiggins (R) | 70,154 | 52.6 |
| Ronald Brooks Cameron (D) | 63,345 | 47.5 |
| 26 Thomas M. Rees (D) | 103,289 | 62.3 |
| Irving Teichner (R) | 62,441 | 37.7 |
| 27 Ed Reinecke (R) | 93,890 | 65.3 |
| John A. Howard (D) | 49,785 | 34.6 |
| 28 Alphonzo Bell (R) | 211,404 | 72.3 |
| Lawrence Sherman (D) | 81,007 | 27.7 |
| 29 George E. Brown Jr. (D) | 69,115 | 51.1 |
| Bill Orozco (R) | 66,079 | 48.9 |
| 30 Edward R. Roybal (D) | 72,173 | 66.4 |
| Henri O'Bryant Jr. (R) | 36,506 | 33.6 |
| 31 Charles H. Wilson (D) | 92,875 | 63.4 |
| Theodore Smith (R) | 53,708 | 36.6 |
| 32 Craig Hosmer (R) | 139,328 | 80.1 |
| Tracy Odell (D) | 34,609 | 19.9 |
| 33 Jerry L. Pettis (R) | 102,401 | 53.5 |
| Kenneth W. Dyal (D) | 89,071 | 46.5 |
| 34 Richard T. Hanna (D) | 127,976 | 55.8 |
| Frank La Magna (R) | 101,410 | 44.2 |
| 35 James B. Utt (R) | 189,582 | 73.1 |
| Thomas B. Lenhart (D) | 69,873 | 26.9 |
| 36 Bob Wilson (R) | 119,274 | 72.7 |
| William C. Godfrey (D) | 44,365 | 27.1 |
| 37 Lionel Van Deerlin (D) | 80,060 | 61.1 |
| Samuel S. Vener (R) | 50,817 | 38.8 |
| 38 John V. Tunney (D) | 83,216 | 54.5 |
| Robert R. Barry (R) | 69,444 | 45.5 |

### Special Election

| | Votes | % |
|---|---|---|
| 14 Jerome R. Waldie (D) | 71,501# | 51.2 |
| Frank J. Newman (R) | 43,539# | 31.2 |
| John A. Richardson (R) | 14,693# | 10.5 |

## COLORADO

| Candidates | Votes | % |
|---|---|---|
| 1 Byron G. Rogers (D) | 92,688 | 56.0 |
| Greg Pearson (R) | 72,732 | 44.0 |
| 2 Donald G. Brotzman (R) | 95,123 | 51.7 |
| Roy H. McVicker (D) | 86,685 | 47.1 |
| 3 Frank E. Evans (D) | 76,270 | 51.7 |
| David W. Enoch (R) | 71,213 | 48.3 |
| 4 Wayne N. Aspinall (D) | 84,107 | 58.6 |
| James P. Johnson (R) | 59,404 | 41.4 |

## CONNECTICUT

| Candidates | Votes | % |
|---|---|---|
| 1 Emilio Q. Daddario (D) | 100,447 | 58.0 |
| John L. Bonee (R) | 71,353 | 41.2 |
| 2 William L. St.Onge (D) | 90,298 | 56.2 |
| Joseph H. Goldberg (R) | 69,402 | 43.2 |
| 3 Robert Giaimo (D) | 86,029 | 53.1 |
| Stelio Salmona (R) | 67,226 | 41.5 |

| Candidates | Votes | % |
|---|---|---|
| Robert M. Cook (AM I) | 8,730 | 5.4 |
| 4 Donald J. Irwin (D) | 89,709 | 50.9 |
| Abner W. Sibal (R) | 86,337 | 49.0 |
| 5 John S. Monagan (D) | 96,801 | 59.1 |
| Romeo G. Petroni (R) | 67,094 | 40.9 |
| 6 Thomas J. Meskill Jr. (R) | 81,907 | 48.9 |
| Bernard F. Grabowski (D) | 79,865 | 47.7 |

## DELAWARE

| Candidates | Votes | % |
|---|---|---|
| AL William V. Roth (R) | 90,961 | 55.8 |
| Harris B. McDowell Jr. (D) | 72,132 | 44.2 |

## FLORIDA

| Candidates | Votes | % |
|---|---|---|
| 1 Robert L. F. Sikes (D) | 55,547 | 95.1 |
| 2 Don Fuqua (D) | 71,565 | 76.3 |
| Harold Hill (R) | 22,281 | 23.7 |
| 3 Charles E. Bennett (D) | 72,038 | 99.9 |
| 4 A. Sydney Herlong Jr. (D) | 70,155 | 100.0 |
| 5 Edward J. Gurney (R) | 75,875 | 99.7 |
| 6 Sam M. Gibbons (D) | 50,772 | 99.8 |
| 7 James A. Haley (D) | 64,498 | 63.2 |
| Joe Z. Lovingood (R) | 37,586 | 36.8 |
| 8 William C. Cramer (R) | 105,019 | 70.8 |
| Roy L. Reynolds (D) | 43,275 | 29.2 |
| 9 Paul G. Rogers (D) | 76,328 | 100.0 |
| 10 J. Herbert Burke (R) | 80,989 | 60.6 |
| Joe Varon (D) | 51,636 | 38.7 |
| 11 Claude Pepper (D) | 62,195 | 99.9 |
| 12 Dante B. Fascell (D) | 62,457 | 56.9 |
| Mike Thompson (R) | 47,226 | 43.1 |

## GEORGIA

| Candidates | Votes | % |
|---|---|---|
| 1 G. Elliott Hagan (D) | 53,413 | 58.0 |
| Porter W. Carswell (R) | 38,619 | 41.9 |
| 2 Maston O'Neal (D) | 54,487 | 100.0 |
| 3 Jack Brinkley (D) | 42,424 | 61.2 |
| Billy Mixon (R) | 26,255 | 37.9 |
| 4 Ben B. Blackburn (R) | 55,249 | 50.2 |
| James A. Mackay (D) | 54,889 | 49.8 |
| 5 Fletcher Thompson (R) | 55,423 | 60.1 |
| Archie Lindsey (D) | 36,751 | 39.9 |
| 6 John J. Flynt Jr. (D) | 74,175 | 67.9 |
| G. Paul Jones Jr. (R) | 35,048 | 32.1 |
| 7 John W. Davis (D) | 65,614 | 65.0 |
| E. Y. Chapin III (R) | 35,383 | 35.0 |
| 8 W. S. Stuckey Jr. (D) | 60,059 | 77.0 |
| Mack F. Mattingly (R) | 17,926 | 23.0 |
| 9 Phil M. Landrum (D) | 61,930 | 100.0 |
| 10 Robert G. Stephens Jr. (D) | 54,141 | 65.7 |
| Leroy H. Simkins Jr. (R) | 28,247 | 34.3 |

## HAWAII

| Candidates | Votes | % |
|---|---|---|
| AL Patsy T. Mink (D) | 140,880✔ | |
| Spark M. Matsunaga (D) | 140,110✔ | |
| John S. Carroll (R) | 67,281 | |
| James K. Kealoha (R) | 62,473 | |

## IDAHO

| Candidates | Votes | % |
|---|---|---|
| 1 James A. McClure (R) | 70,410 | 51.8 |
| Compton I. White Jr. (D) | 65,446 | 48.2 |
| 2 George V. Hansen (R) | 79,024 | 70.3 |
| A. W. Brunt (D) | 33,348 | 29.7 |

## ILLINOIS

| Candidates | Votes | % |
|---|---|---|
| 1 William L. Dawson (D) | 91,119 | 72.6 |
| David R. Reed (R) | 34,421 | 27.4 |

## ILLINOIS

| Candidates | Votes | % |
|---|---|---|
| 2 Barratt O'Hara (D) | 83,471 | 59.2 |
| Philip G. Bixler (R) | 57,629 | 40.8 |
| 3 William T. Murphy (D) | 83,857 | 52.0 |
| Albert F. Manion (R) | 77,442 | 48.0 |
| 4 Edward J. Derwinski (R) | 125,365 | 72.0 |
| Ray J. Rybacki (D) | 48,673 | 28.0 |
| 5 John C. Kluczynski (D) | 85,770 | 56.2 |
| Walter K. Kiltz (R) | 66,735 | 43.8 |
| 6 Daniel J. Ronan (D) | 84,126 | 57.0 |
| Samuel A. Decaro (R) | 63,374 | 43.0 |
| 7 Frank Annunzio (D) | 82,962 | 80.9 |
| Joseph H. Day (R) | 19,650 | 19.2 |
| 8 Daniel D. Rostenkowski (D) | 94,631 | 59.9 |
| John H. Leszynski (R) | 63,377 | 40.1 |
| 9 Sydney R. Yates (D) | 96,746 | 59.9 |
| Richard C. Storey Jr. (R) | 64,875 | 40.1 |
| 10 Harold R. Collier (R) | 132,650 | 69.4 |
| Frank J. Jirka Jr. (D) | 58,376 | 30.6 |
| 11 Roman C. Pucinski (D) | 105,996 | 50.9 |
| John J. Hoellen (R) | 102,244 | 49.1 |
| 12 Robert McClory (R) | 90,483 | 69.1 |
| Herbert L. Stern (D) | 40,502 | 30.9 |
| 13 Donald Rumsfeld (R) | 158,769 | 76.0 |
| James L. McCabe (D) | 50,107 | 24.0 |
| 14 John N. Erlenborn (R) | 130,442 | 71.7 |
| Kenneth McCleary (D) | 51,385 | 28.3 |
| 15 Charlotte T. Reid (R) | 102,018 | 72.3 |
| Selwyn L. Boyer (D) | 39,123 | 27.7 |
| 16 John B. Anderson (R) | 89,990 | 73.0 |
| Robert M. Whiteford (D) | 33,274 | 27.0 |
| 17 Leslie C. Arends (R) | 104,240 | 67.4 |
| Bernard J. Hughes (D) | 50,350 | 32.6 |
| 18 Robert H. Michel (R) | 80,293 | 58.4 |
| Thomas V. Cassidy (D) | 57,100 | 41.6 |
| 19 Tom Railsback (R) | 77,895 | 52.3 |
| Gale Schisler (D) | 71,050 | 47.7 |
| 20 Paul Findley (R) | 102,609 | 62.2 |
| Richard R. Wolfe (D) | 62,343 | 37.8 |
| 21 Kenneth J. Gray (D) | 103,128 | 56.2 |
| Bob Beckmeyer (R) | 80,382 | 43.8 |
| 22 William L. Springer (R) | 96,453 | 63.3 |
| Cameron B. Satterthwaite (D) | 55,818 | 36.7 |
| 23 George E. Shipley (D) | 95,156 | 56.4 |
| Leslie N. Jones (R) | 73,463 | 43.6 |
| 24 Melvin Price (D) | 82,513 | 71.5 |
| John S. Guthrie (R) | 32,915 | 28.5 |

## INDIANA

| Candidates | Votes | % |
|---|---|---|
| 1 Ray J. Madden (D) | 71,040 | 58.3 |
| Albert F. Harrigan (R) | 50,804 | 41.7 |
| 2 Charles A. Halleck (R) | 97,161 | 57.5 |
| Ralph G. McFadden (D) | 71,825 | 42.5 |
| 3 John Brademas (D) | 75,321 | 55.8 |
| Robert A. Ehlers (R) | 59,731 | 44.2 |
| 4 E. Ross Adair (R) | 94,457 | 63.5 |
| J. Byron Hayes (D) | 54,331 | 36.5 |
| 5 J. Edward Roush (D) | 76,176 | 51.1 |
| Kenneth Bowman (R) | 72,873 | 48.9 |
| 6 William G. Bray (R) | 124,087 | 65.7 |
| James M. Nicholson (D) | 63,342 | 33.6 |
| 7 John T. Myers (R) | 79,864 | 54.3 |
| Elden C. Tipton (D) | 67,135 | 45.7 |
| 8 Roger H. Zion (R) | 94,924 | 51.1 |
| Winfield K. Denton (D) | 90,887 | 48.9 |
| 9 Lee H. Hamilton (D) | 89,392 | 53.8 |
| John W. Lewis (R) | 76,661 | 46.2 |
| 10 Richard L. Roudebush (R) | 94,428 | 63.4 |
| Robert H. Staton (D) | 54,515 | 36.6 |
| 11 Andrew Jacobs Jr. (D) | 65,624 | 55.8 |
| Paul R. Oakes (R) | 52,096 | 44.3 |

## IOWA

| Candidates | Votes | % |
|---|---|---|
| 1 Fred Schwengel (R) | 64,795 | 51.3 |
| John R. Schmidhauser (D) | 60,534 | 47.9 |
| 2 John C. Culver (D) | 76,281 | 54.0 |
| Robert M. L. Johnson (R) | 65,079 | 46.0 |
| 3 H. R. Gross (R) | 79,343 | 62.1 |
| L. A. Touchae (D) | 48,530 | 38.0 |
| 4 John Kyl (R) | 65,259 | 51.7 |
| Bert Bandstra (D) | 61,074 | 48.3 |
| 5 Neal Smith (D) | 72,875 | 60.4 |
| Don Mahon (R) | 46,981 | 39.0 |
| 6 Wiley Mayne (R) | 73,274 | 57.4 |
| Stanley L. Greigg (D) | 53,917 | 42.3 |
| 7 William J. Scherle (R) | 64,217 | 59.0 |
| John R. Hansen (D) | 44,529 | 40.9 |

## KANSAS

| Candidates | Votes | % |
|---|---|---|
| 1 Bob Dole (R) | 97,487 | 68.6 |
| Berniece Henkle (D) | 44,569 | 31.4 |
| 2 Chester L. Mize (R) | 85,128 | 62.8 |
| Harry Wiles (D) | 50,336 | 37.2 |
| 3 Larry Winn Jr. (R) | 60,107 | 52.9 |
| Marvin E. Rainey (D) | 51,108 | 45.0 |
| 4 Garner E. Shriver (R) | 86,944 | 68.7 |
| Paul H. Gerling (D) | 39,625 | 31.3 |
| 5 Joe Skubitz (R) | 86,944 | 60.9 |
| Delno E. Bass (D) | 55,933 | 39.2 |

## KENTUCKY

| Candidates | Votes | % |
|---|---|---|
| 1 Frank A. Stubblefield (D) | 57,736 | 70.6 |
| Richard Nicholson (R) | 24,085 | 29.4 |
| 2 William H. Natcher (D) | 51,311 | 58.9 |
| R. Douglas Ford (R) | 35,770 | 41.1 |
| 3 William O. Cowger (R) | 66,577 | 59.0 |
| Norbert Blume (D) | 46,240 | 41.0 |
| 4 M. G. (Gene) Snyder (R) | 66,801 | 53.9 |
| Frank Chelf (D) | 56,902 | 46.0 |
| 5 Tim Lee Carter (R) | 65,596 | 75.4 |
| Eugene C. Harter (D) | 21,452 | 24.6 |
| 6 John C. Watts (D) | 58,182 | 65.1 |
| William McKinley Hendren (R) | 31,266 | 35.0 |
| 7 Carl D. Perkins (D) | 65,522 | 68.9 |
| C. F. See (R) | 29,541 | 31.1 |

## LOUISIANA

| Candidates | Votes | % |
|---|---|---|
| 1 F. Edward Hebert (D) | 68,523 | 100.0 |
| 2 Hale Boggs (D) | 90,149 | 68.6 |
| Leonard L. Limes (R) | 41,209 | 31.4 |
| 3 Edwin E. Willis (D) | 46,533 | 59.7 |
| Hall M. Lyons (R) | 31,444 | 40.3 |
| 4 Joe D. Waggonner Jr. (D) | 48,345 | 100.0 |
| 5 Otto E. Passman (D) | 38,660 | 100.0 |
| 6 John R. Rarick (D) | 86,958 | 76.6 |
| Crayton G. Hall (R) | 26,599 | 23.4 |
| 7 Edwin W. Edwards (D) | 34,655 | 100.0 |
| 8 Speedy O. Long (D) | 33,183 | 100.0 |

## MAINE

| Candidates | Votes | % |
|---|---|---|
| 1 Peter N. Kyros (D) | 81,302 | 50.4 |
| Peter A. Garland (R) | 72,984 | 45.2 |
| 2 William D. Hathaway (D) | 85,956 | 56.8 |
| Howard M. Foley (R) | 65,476 | 43.2 |

## MARYLAND

| Candidates | Votes | % |
|---|---|---|
| 1 Rogers C. B. Morton (R) | 69,940 | 71.4 |
| H. C. Byrd (D) | 28,025 | 28.6 |
| 2 Clarence D. Long (D) | 79,963 | 69.3 |
| Paul T. McHenry Jr. (R) | 35,476 | 30.7 |
| 3 Edward A. Garmatz (D) | 56,980 | 100.0 |
| 4 George H. Fallon (D) | 57,572 | 74.3 |
| G. Neilson Sigler (R) | 19,930 | 25.7 |
| 5 Hervey G. Machen (D) | 55,676 | 53.9 |
| Lawrence J. Hogan (R) | 47,703 | 46.1 |
| 6 Charles McC. Mathias Jr. (R) | 72,360 | 70.9 |
| Walter G. Finch (D) | 29,637 | 29.1 |
| 7 Samuel N. Friedel (D) | 61,959 | 76.0 |
| Stephen L. Rosenstein (R) | 19,584 | 24.0 |
| 8 Gilbert Gude (R) | 71,050 | 54.4 |
| Royce Hanson (D) | 59,568 | 45.6 |

## MASSACHUSETTS

| Candidates | Votes | % |
|---|---|---|
| 1 Silvio O. Conte (R) | 109,370 | 100.0 |
| 2 Edward P. Boland (D) | 95,985 | 100.0 |
| 3 Philip J. Philbin (D) | 126,664 | 71.0 |
| Howard A. Miller (R) | 51,646 | 29.0 |
| 4 Harold D. Donohue (D) | 137,681 | 100.0 |
| 5 F. Bradford Morse (R) | 140,702 | 74.8 |
| Charles N. Tsapatsaris (D) | 47,377 | 25.2 |
| 6 William H. Bates (R) | 127,744 | 65.7 |
| Daniel L. Parent (D) | 66,675 | 34.3 |
| 7 Torbert H. Macdonald (D) | 119,543 | 74.5 |
| Gordon F. Hughes (R) | 40,930 | 25.5 |
| 8 Thomas P. O'Neill Jr. (D) | 102,104 | 100.0 |
| 9 John W. McCormack (D) | 87,879 | 100.0 |
| 10 Margaret M. Heckler (R) | 96,675 | 51.1 |
| Patrick H. Harrington Jr. (D) | 92,516 | 48.9 |
| 11 James A. Burke (D) | 141,465 | 74.8 |
| James L. Hofford (R) | 47,705 | 25.2 |
| 12 Hastings Keith (R) | 98,372 | 55.0 |
| Edward F. Harrington (D) | 80,473 | 45.0 |

## MICHIGAN

| Candidates | Votes | % |
|---|---|---|
| 1 John Conyers (D) | 89,908 | 84.2 |
| Rhecha R. Ross (R) | 16,853 | 15.8 |
| 2 Marvin L. Esch (R) | 65,205 | 51.0 |
| Weston E. Vivian (D) | 62,536 | 49.0 |
| 3 Garry Brown (R) | 68,912 | 52.3 |
| Paul H. Todd Jr. (D) | 62,984 | 47.8 |
| 4 Edward Hutchinson (R) | 78,190 | 67.8 |
| John V. Martin (D) | 37,177 | 32.2 |
| 5 Gerald R. Ford (R) | 88,108 | 68.5 |
| James Mathew Catchick (D) | 40,435 | 31.5 |
| 6 Charles E. Chamberlain (R) | 85,669 | 67.3 |
| Lee H. Wenke (D) | 41,695 | 32.7 |
| 7 Donald W. Riegle Jr. (R) | 71,166 | 54.1 |
| John C. Mackie (D) | 60,408 | 45.9 |
| 8 James Harvey (R) | 85,657 | 69.9 |
| Wager F. Clunis (D) | 36,967 | 30.2 |
| 9 Guy Vander Jagt (R) | 92,710 | 66.7 |
| Henry J. Dongvillo (D) | 46,266 | 33.3 |
| 10 Elford A. Cederberg (R) | 85,754 | 67.4 |
| Hubert C. Evans (D) | 41,410 | 32.6 |
| 11 Phillip E. Ruppe (R) | 70,820 | 51.8 |
| Raymond F. Clevenger (D) | 65,875 | 48.2 |
| 12 James G. O'Hara (D) | 84,379 | 65.1 |
| Patrick J. Driscoll (R) | 45,199 | 34.9 |
| 13 Charles C. Diggs Jr. (D) | 60,660 | 83.0 |
| Frank Daniels (R) | 12,393 | 17.0 |
| 14 Lucien N. Nedzi (D) | 77,851 | 59.7 |
| William J. Kennedy (R) | 52,490 | 40.3 |
| 15 William D. Ford (D) | 72,987 | 67.8 |
| Arpo Yemen (R) | 34,619 | 32.2 |
| 16 John D. Dingell Jr. (D) | 71,787 | 62.7 |
| John T. Dempsey (R) | 42,738 | 37.3 |
| 17 Martha W. Griffiths (D) | 90,541 | 69.2 |
| William P. Harrington (R) | 40,334 | 30.8 |
| 18 William S. Broomfield (R) | 102,501 | 67.8 |
| William H. Merrill (D) | 48,627 | 32.2 |
| 19 Jack H. McDonald (R) | 76,884 | 57.0 |
| Billie S. Farnum (D) | 57,907 | 43.0 |

### Special Election

| Candidates | Votes | % |
|---|---|---|
| 9 Guy Vander Jagt (R) | 91,056 | 66.6 |
| Henry J. Dongvillo (D) | 45,699 | 33.4 |

## MINNESOTA

| Candidates | Votes | % |
|---|---|---|
| 1 Albert H. Quie (R) | 109,312 | 65.9 |
| George Daley (DFL) | 56,547 | 34.1 |
| 2 Ancher Nelson (R) | 93,855 | 66.2 |
| Charles M. Christensen (DFL) | 47,899 | 33.8 |

## MINNESOTA

| | Candidates | Votes | % |
|---|---|---|---|
| 3 | Clark MacGregor (R) | 122,775 | 65.4 |
| | Elva D. Walker (DFL) | 64,861 | 34.6 |
| 4 | Joseph Karth (DFL) | 91,271 | 53.4 |
| | Stephan Maxwell (R) | 79,667 | 46.6 |
| 5 | Donald M. Fraser (DFL) | 86,953 | 59.7 |
| | William Hathaway (R) | 58,816 | 40.4 |
| 6 | John M. Zwach (R) | 80,710 | 51.4 |
| | Alec G. Olson (DFL) | 76,439 | 48.6 |
| 7 | Odin Langen (R) | 84,914 | 63.2 |
| | Keith C. Davison (DFL) | 49,388 | 36.8 |
| 8 | John A. Blatnik (DFL) | 116,969 | 100.0 |

## MISSISSIPPI

| | | | |
|---|---|---|---|
| 1 | Thomas G. Abernethy (D) | 47,359 | 68.8 |
| | W. B. Alexander (I) | 14,700 | 21.4 |
| | Dock Drummond (I) | 6,805 | 9.9 |
| 2 | Jamie L. Whitten (D) | 53,620 | 83.5 |
| | S. B. Wise (R) | 10,622 | 16.5 |
| 3 | John Bell Williams (D) | 71,377 | 82.4 |
| | Emma Sanders (I) | 15,218 | 17.6 |
| 4 | G. V. (Sonny) Montgomery (D) | 52,138 | 65.3 |
| | L. L. McAllister Jr. (R) | 26,027 | 32.6 |
| 5 | William M. Colmer (D) | 58,080 | 70.0 |
| | James M. Moye (R) | 24,865 | 30.0 |

## MISSOURI

| | | | |
|---|---|---|---|
| 1 | Frank M. Karsten (D) | 62,143 | 63.9 |
| | Robert L. Sharp (R) | 35,053 | 36.1 |
| 2 | Thomas B. Curtis (R) | 102,985 | 66.2 |
| | William B. Milius (D) | 52,527 | 33.8 |
| 3 | Leonor K. Sullivan (D) | 59,014 | 71.1 |
| | Homer McCracken (R) | 23,953 | 28.9 |
| 4 | William J. Randall (D) | 54,330 | 60.9 |
| | Forest Nave Jr. (R) | 34,952 | 39.2 |
| 5 | Richard Bolling (D) | 46,674 | 61.2 |
| | Willis Earl Salyers (R) | 29,641 | 38.8 |
| 6 | W. R. Hull Jr. (D) | 55,418 | 58.0 |
| | John L. Leims (R) | 40,185 | 42.0 |
| 7 | Durward G. Hall (R) | 86,626 | 62.3 |
| | Arch M. Skelton (D) | 52,421 | 37.7 |
| 8 | Richard Ichord (D) | 61,128 | 58.1 |
| | Ben Rogers (R) | 44,035 | 41.9 |
| 9 | William L. Hungate (D) | 68,472 | 55.3 |
| | Anthony C. Schroeder (R) | 55,405 | 44.7 |
| 10 | Paul C. Jones (D) | 48,985 | 61.0 |
| | William Bruckerhoff (R) | 31,263 | 39.0 |

## MONTANA

| | | | |
|---|---|---|---|
| 1 | Arnold Olsen (D) | 67,123 | 50.8 |
| | Richard Smiley (R) | 64,925 | 49.2 |
| 2 | James F. Battin (R) | 76,015 | 60.2 |
| | John Melcher (D) | 50,308 | 39.8 |

## NEBRASKA

| | | | |
|---|---|---|---|
| 1 | Robert V. Denney (R) | 93,628 | 51.2 |
| | Clair A. Callan (D) | 89,363 | 48.8 |
| 2 | Glenn Cunningham (R) | 83,082 | 64.3 |
| | Richard Fellman (D) | 46,235 | 35.8 |
| 3 | David Martin (R) | 115,893 | 73.0 |
| | John Homan (D) | 42,920 | 27.0 |

## NEVADA

| | | | |
|---|---|---|---|
| AL | Walter S. Baring (D) | 86,467 | 67.6 |
| | Ralph L. Kraemer (R) | 41,383 | 32.4 |

## NEW HAMPSHIRE

| | | | |
|---|---|---|---|
| 1 | Louis C. Wyman (R) | 72,909 | 56.2 |
| | J. Oliva Huot (D) | 56,750 | 43.8 |
| 2 | James C. Cleveland (R) | 66,176 | 66.7 |
| | William H. Barry Jr. (D) | 32,838 | 33.1 |

## NEW JERSEY

| | Candidates | Votes | % |
|---|---|---|---|
| 1 | John E. Hunt (R) | 68,248 | 51.4 |
| | Michael J. Piarulli (D) | 61,469 | 46.3 |
| 2 | Charles W. Sandman Jr. (R) | 72,014 | 51.5 |
| | Thomas C. McGrath Jr. (D) | 65,494 | 46.9 |
| 3 | James J. Howard (D) | 81,382 | 52.7 |
| | James M. Coleman (R) | 72,043 | 46.6 |
| 4 | Frank Thompson Jr. (D) | 82,271 | 56.2 |
| | Ralph Clark Chandler (R) | 63,730 | 43.5 |
| 5 | Peter H. B. Frelinghuysen (R) | 108,375 | 70.8 |
| | Carter Jefferson (D) | 41,476 | 27.1 |
| 6 | William T. Cahill (R) | 106,406 | 66.9 |
| | Walter Dubrow (D) | 48,738 | 30.7 |
| 7 | William B. Widnall (R) | 101,253 | 66.4 |
| | Robert E. Hamer (D) | 51,204 | 33.6 |
| 8 | Charles S. Joelson (D) | 80,725 | 59.6 |
| | Richard M. DeMarco (R) | 51,784 | 38.2 |
| 9 | Henry Helstoski (D) | 74,320 | 50.9 |
| | Frank C. Osmers Jr. (R) | 71,756 | 49.1 |
| 10 | Peter W. Rodino Jr. (D) | 71,699 | 64.3 |
| | Earl Harris (R) | 36,508 | 32.7 |
| 11 | Joseph G. Minish (D) | 64,023 | 58.3 |
| | Leonard J. Felzenberg (R) | 44,803 | 40.8 |
| 12 | Florence P. Dwyer (R) | 116,701 | 73.9 |
| | Robert F. Allen (D) | 37,790 | 23.9 |
| 13 | Cornelius E. Gallagher (D) | 90,488 | 71.8 |
| | Ruth Swayze (R) | 35,486 | 28.2 |
| 14 | Dominick V. Daniels (D) | 87,741 | 68.0 |
| | Thomas R. McSherry (R) | 36,828 | 28.5 |
| 15 | Edward J. Patten (D) | 81,959 | 57.0 |
| | C. John Stroumtsos (R) | 59,706 | 41.5 |

## NEW MEXICO

| | | | |
|---|---|---|---|
| AL | Thomas G. Morris (D) | 140,057 | 55.9 |
| | Schuble C. Cook (R) | 110,441 | 44.1 |
| AL | E. S. Johnny Walker (D) | 126,984 | 50.5 |
| | Robert C. Davidson (R) | 124,536 | 49.5 |

## NEW YORK

| | | | |
|---|---|---|---|
| 1 | Otis G. Pike (D, L) | 101,963 | 58.9 |
| | James M. Catterson Jr. (R) | 58,296 | 33.7 |
| | Domenico Crachi Jr. (C) | 12,731 | 7.4 |
| 2 | James R. Grover Jr. (R) | 79,649 | 54.7 |
| | Frank M. Corso (D, L) | 49,743 | 34.1 |
| | Edward Campbell (C) | 14,820 | 10.2 |
| 3 | Lester L. Wolff (D, L) | 81,959 | 50.3 |
| | Steven B. Derounian (R) | 81,122 | 49.7 |
| 4 | John W. Wydler (R) | 86,677 | 59.7 |
| | Martin J. Steadman (D, L) | 46,555 | 32.0 |
| | Donald H. Serrell (C) | 10,035 | 6.9 |
| 5 | Herbert Tenzer (D, L) | 88,602 | 49.9 |
| | Thomas M. Brennan (R, C) | 86,356 | 48.6 |
| 6 | Seymour Halpern (R, L) | 91,526 | 59.0 |
| | Gilbert T. Redleaf (D) | 45,621 | 29.4 |
| | Ronald E. Weiss (C) | 17,863 | 11.5 |
| 7 | Joseph P. Addabbo (D, L) | 93,758 | 64.9 |
| | Louis R. Mercogliano (R) | 34,644 | 24.0 |
| | Raymond G. Carpenter (C) | 16,070 | 11.1 |
| 8 | Benjamin S. Rosenthal (D, L) | 115,310 | 69.6 |
| | Thomas C. Gowlan (R) | 36,573 | 22.1 |
| | Cyrus S. Julien (C) | 13,726 | 8.3 |
| 9 | James J. Delaney (D) | 75,915 | 53.5 |
| | John F. Haggerty (R, C) | 56,754 | 40.0 |
| | David Green (L) | 9,182 | 6.5 |
| 10 | Emanuel Celler (D, L) | 76,439 | 82.1 |
| | Irwin A. Rosenberg (R) | 16,702 | 17.9 |
| 11 | Frank J. Brasco (D) | 39,386 | 70.6 |
| | Benjamin W. Feldman (R) | 12,200 | 21.9 |
| | Edward L. Johnson (L) | 4,174 | 7.5 |
| 12 | Edna F. Kelley (D, L) | 87,651 | 72.7 |
| | Alfred Grant Walton (R) | 29,390 | 24.4 |

| | Candidates | Votes | % |
|---|---|---|---|
| 13 | Abraham J. Multer (D) | 95,511 | 61.9 |
| | Mary Gravina (R) | 28,750 | 18.6 |
| | Herschell Chanin (L) | 20,557 | 13.3 |
| | Michael J. Spadaro (C) | 9,463 | 6.1 |
| 14 | John J. Rooney (D, L) | 43,142 | 76.2 |
| | Leon F. Nadrowski (R) | 13,482 | 23.8 |
| 15 | Hugh L. Carey (D, U TAX) | 52,919 | 56.8 |
| | Herbert F. Ryan (R, C) | 40,181 | 43.2 |
| 16 | John M. Murphy (D, L) | 71,889 | 57.4 |
| | Frank J. Biondolillo (R, C) | 53,346 | 42.6 |
| 17 | Theodore R. Kupferman (R) | 69,492 | 47.7 |
| | Jerome L. Wilson (D, L) | 67,334 | 46.2 |
| | Richard J. Callahan (C) | 8,818 | 6.1 |
| 18 | Adam C. Powell (D) | 45,308* | 74.1 |
| | Lassen L. Walsh (R) | 10,711 | 17.5 |
| | Richard Prideaux (L) | 3,954 | 6.5 |
| 19 | Leonard Farbstein (D) | 53,581 | 57.8 |
| | Henry E. Del Rosso (R, C) | 24,340 | 26.2 |
| | Elaine M. Morrison (L) | 11,349 | 12.2 |
| 20 | William F. Ryan (D, L) | 74,215 | 74.8 |
| | Norman C. Harlowe (R) | 20,560 | 20.7 |
| 21 | James H. Scheuer (D, L) | 63,173 | 83.6 |
| | Burton Siegel (R) | 12,414 | 16.4 |
| 22 | Jacob H. Gilbert (D) | 40,787 | 74.2 |
| | Pedro Luis Rodriguez (R, ALL PP) | 10,603 | 19.3 |
| | Carlos Rosario (L) | 3,552 | 6.5 |
| 23 | Jonathan B. Bingham (D, L) | 84,540 | 73.4 |
| | Harold Grosberg (R) | 21,735 | 18.9 |
| | Walter A. Quinn Jr. (C) | 8,949 | 7.8 |
| 24 | Paul A. Fino (R, C) | 80,882 | 63.9 |
| | Aileen B. Ryan (D) | 42,291 | 33.4 |
| 25 | Richard L. Ottinger (D, L) | 106,952 | 54.6 |
| | Frederick J. Martin Jr. (R) | 88,769 | 45.4 |
| 26 | Ogden R. Reid (R) | 107,031 | 69.3 |
| | Joseph L. Hutner (D) | 39,203 | 25.4 |
| | Albert M. Gants (C) | 8,159 | 5.3 |
| 27 | John G. Dow (D, L) | 79,424 | 47.2 |
| | Louis V. Mills (R) | 74,816 | 44.5 |
| | Frederick P. Roland (C) | 13,946 | 8.3 |
| 28 | Joseph Y. Resnick (D, L) | 84,940 | 50.3 |
| | Hamilton Fish Jr. (R) | 78,258 | 46.3 |
| 29 | Daniel E. Button (R, L) | 107,671 | 53.3 |
| | Richard J. Conners (D) | 91,174 | 45.1 |
| 30 | Carleton J. King (R) | 113,759 | 65.0 |
| | John S. Hall (D, L) | 61,216 | 35.0 |
| 31 | Robert C. McEwen (R) | 75,680 | 67.6 |
| | Raymond E. Bishop (D, L) | 36,273 | 32.4 |
| 32 | Alexander Pirnie (R, L) | 94,331 | 72.3 |
| | Robert Castle (D) | 36,195 | 27.7 |
| 33 | Howard W. Robison (R) | 88,378 | 65.7 |
| | Blair G. Ewing (D, L) | 45,761 | 34.0 |
| 34 | James M. Hanley (D) | 90,044 | 55.1 |
| | Stewart F. Hancock Jr. (R) | 62,559 | 38.3 |
| 35 | Samuel S. Stratton (D, L) | 93,746 | 65.8 |
| | Frederick D. Dugan (R) | 48,668 | 34.2 |
| 36 | Frank J. Horton (R) | 110,514 | 67.3 |
| | Milo Thomas (D) | 37,129 | 22.6 |
| | Robert H. Detig (C) | 10,493 | 6.4 |
| 37 | Barber B. Conable Jr (R) | 104,342 | 67.7 |
| | Kenneth Hed (D) | 46,201 | 30.0 |
| 38 | Charles E. Goodell (R) | 82,137 | 67.2 |
| | Edison Leroy Jr (D) | 35,785 | 29.3 |
| 39 | Richard D. McCarthy (D, L) | 95,671 | 52.3 |
| | John R. Pillion (R, C) | 87,230 | 47.7 |
| 40 | Henry P. Smith III (R) | 85,801 | 61.2 |
| | William Levitt (D, L) | 54,303 | 38.8 |
| 41 | Thaddeus J. Dulski (D, L) | 92,222 | 76.4 |
| | Frank X. Schwab (R, C) | 28,491 | 23.6 |

### Special Election

| | | | |
|---|---|---|---|
| 17 | Theodore R. Kupferman (R) | 44,125 | 46.4 |
| | Orin Lehman (D) | 43,206 | 45.4 |
| | Jeffrey St.John (C) | 7,796 | 8.2 |

## NORTH CAROLINA

| | Candidates | Votes | % |
|---|---|---|---|
| 1 | Walter B. Jones (D) | 43,539 | 61.4 |
| | John P. East (R) | 27,434 | 38.7 |
| 2 | L. H. Fountain (D) | 36,849 | 65.0 |
| | Reece B. Gardiner (R) | 19,888 | 35.1 |
| 3 | David N. Henderson (D) | 33,809 | 100.0 |
| 4 | James C. Gardner (R) | 60,686 | 56.5 |
| | Harold D. Cooley (D) | 46,673 | 43.5 |
| 5 | Nick Galifianakis (D) | 46,035 | 53.1 |
| | G. Fred Steele Jr. (R) | 40,729 | 46.9 |
| 6 | Horace R. Kornegay (D) | 42,677 | 51.6 |
| | Richard B. Barnwell (R) | 40,000 | 48.4 |
| 7 | Alton Lennon (D) | 40,512 | 100.0 |
| 8 | Charles Raper Jonas (R) | 56,382 | 71.5 |
| | John G. Plumides (D) | 22,465 | 28.5 |
| 9 | James T. Broyhill (R) | 80,989 | 63.3 |
| | Robert Bingham (D) | 46,882 | 36.7 |
| 10 | Basil L. Whitener (D) | 52,117 | 56.1 |
| | W. Hall Young (R) | 40,741 | 43.9 |
| 11 | Roy A. Taylor (D) | 72,855 | 52.8 |
| | W. Scott Harvey (R) | 65,187 | 47.2 |

### Special Election

| | | | |
|---|---|---|---|
| 1 | Walter B. Jones (D) | 21,773 | 60.3 |
| | John P. East (R) | 14,308 | 39.7 |

## NORTH DAKOTA

| | | | |
|---|---|---|---|
| 1 | Mark Andrews (R) | 66,011 | 66.2 |
| | S. F. (Buckshot) Hoffner (D) | 33,694 | 33.8 |
| 2 | Thomas S. Kleppe (R) | 50,801 | 52.0 |
| | Rolland Redlin (D) | 46,993 | 48.1 |

## OHIO

| | | | |
|---|---|---|---|
| 1 | Robert Taft Jr. (R) | 70,366 | 52.9 |
| | John J. Gilligan (D) | 62,580 | 47.1 |
| 2 | Donald D. Clancy (R) | 102,313 | 70.7 |
| | Thomas E. Anderson (D) | 42,367 | 29.3 |
| 3 | Charles W. Whalen Jr. (R) | 62,471 | 53.8 |
| | Rodney M. Love (D) | 53,658 | 46.2 |
| 4 | William M. McCulloch (R) | 66,142 | 63.6 |
| | Robert H. Mihlbaugh (D) | 37,855 | 36.4 |
| 5 | Delbert L. Latta (R) | 80,906 | 75.3 |
| | John H. Shock (D) | 26,503 | 24.7 |
| 6 | William H. Harsha (R) | 74,847 | 67.9 |
| | Ottie W. Reno (D) | 35,345 | 32.1 |
| 7 | Clarence J. Brown Jr. (R) | 81,225 | 100.0 |
| 8 | Jackson E. Betts (R) | 78,933 | 67.1 |
| | Frank B. Bennett (D) | 38,787 | 33.0 |
| 9 | Thomas L. Ashley (D) | 83,261 | 60.8 |
| | Jane M. Kuebbeler (R) | 53,777 | 39.2 |
| 10 | Clarence E. Miller (R) | 56,659 | 52.0 |
| | Walter H. Moeller (D) | 52,258 | 48.0 |
| 11 | J. William Stanton (R) | 86,273 | 69.3 |
| | James F. Henderson (D) | 38,206 | 30.7 |
| 12 | Samuel L. Devine (R) | 70,102 | 64.2 |
| | Robert N. Shamansky (D) | 39,140 | 35.8 |
| 13 | Charles A. Mosher (R) | 69,862 | 65.5 |
| | Thomas E. Wolfe (D) | 36,751 | 34.5 |
| 14 | William H. Ayres (R) | 77,819 | 59.7 |
| | Charles F. Madden Jr. (D) | 52,646 | 40.4 |
| 15 | Chalmers P. Wylie (R) | 57,993 | 59.9 |
| | Robert L. Van Heyde (D) | 38,805 | 40.1 |
| 16 | Frank T. Bow (R) | 87,597 | 61.1 |
| | Robert D. Freeman (D) | 55,775 | 38.9 |
| 17 | John M. Ashbrook (R) | 73,132 | 55.3 |
| | Robert T. Secrest (D) | 59,031 | 44.7 |
| 18 | Wayne L. Hays (D) | 73,657 | 64.2 |
| | William H. Weir (R) | 41,165 | 35.9 |
| 19 | Michael J. Kirwan (D) | 86,975 | 71.9 |
| | Donald J. Lewis (R) | 34,037 | 28.1 |
| 20 | Michael A. Feighan (D) | 63,629 | 76.1 |
| | Clarence E. McLeod (R) | 20,034 | 24.0 |
| 21 | Charles A. Vanik (D) | 81,210 | 81.7 |
| | Frederick M. Coleman (R) | 18,205 | 18.3 |

| | Candidates | Votes | % |
|---|---|---|---|
| 22 | Frances P. Bolton (R) | 71,927 | 55.9 |
| | Anthony O. Calabrese Jr. (D) | 56,803 | 44.1 |
| 23 | William E. Minshall (R) | 102,513 | 73.2 |
| | Sheldon D. Clark (D) | 37,489 | 26.8 |
| 24 | Donald E. Lukens (R) | 61,194 | 58.5 |
| | James H. Pelley (D) | 43,418 | 41.5 |

## OKLAHOMA

| | | | |
|---|---|---|---|
| 1 | Page Belcher (R) | 106,259 | 69.7 |
| | Ed Cadenhead (D) | 46,286 | 30.3 |
| 2 | Ed Edmondson (D) | 62,324 | 53.6 |
| | Denzil D. Garrison (R) | 53,919 | 46.4 |
| 3 | Carl Albert (D) | 43,049 | 77.2 |
| | Whit Pate (R) | 12,697 | 22.8 |
| 4 | Tom Steed (D) | 36,719 | 50.3 |
| | Truman T. Branscum (R) | 36,355 | 49.8 |
| 5 | John Jarman (D) | 96,464 | 69.6 |
| | Melvin H. Gragg (R) | 42,088 | 30.4 |
| 6 | James V. Smith (R) | 51,474 | 51.4 |
| | Jed Johnson Jr. (D) | 48,755 | 48.6 |

## OREGON

| | | | |
|---|---|---|---|
| 1 | Wendell Wyatt (R) | 144,361 | 74.3 |
| | Malcolm H. Cross (D) | 49,841 | 25.7 |
| 2 | Al Ullman (D) | 94,346 | 63.3 |
| | Everett J. Thoren (R) | 54,789 | 36.7 |
| 3 | Edith Green (D) | 114,687 | 66.9 |
| | Lyle Dean (R) | 56,598 | 33.0 |
| 4 | John R. Dellenback (R) | 94,154 | 62.7 |
| | Charles O. Porter (D) | 56,007 | 37.3 |

## PENNSYLVANIA

| | | | |
|---|---|---|---|
| 1 | William A. Barrett (D) | 90,100 | 66.1 |
| | Beatrice K. Chernock (R) | 46,280 | 33.9 |
| 2 | Robert N. C. Nix (D) | 76,372 | 59.9 |
| | Herbert R. Cain Jr. (R) | 51,079 | 40.1 |
| 3 | James A. Byrne (D) | 64,575 | 56.6 |
| | Walter T. Darmopray (R) | 49,434 | 43.4 |
| 4 | Joshua Eilberg (D) | 98,793 | 51.9 |
| | Robert Baer Cohen (R) | 91,620 | 48.1 |
| 5 | William J. Green III (D) | 86,128 | 59.1 |
| | Michael J. Bednarek (R) | 59,515 | 40.9 |
| 6 | George M. Rhodes (D) | 91,538 | 56.1 |
| | Daniel B. Boyer Jr. (R) | 71,508 | 43.9 |
| 7 | Lawrence G. Williams (R) | 101,042 | 63.2 |
| | John J. Logue (D) | 58,766 | 36.8 |
| 8 | Edward G. Biester Jr. (R) | 70,435 | 59.6 |
| | Walter S. Farley Jr. (D) | 47,845 | 40.5 |
| 9 | G. Robert Watkins (R) | 81,516 | 62.6 |
| | Louis F. Waldmann (D) | 48,656 | 37.4 |
| 10 | Joseph M. McDade (R) | 115,765 | 66.8 |
| | Neil Trama (D) | 57,615 | 33.2 |
| 11 | Daniel J. Flood (D) | 110,877 | 67.2 |
| | Gerald C. Broadt (R) | 54,032 | 32.8 |
| 12 | J. Irving Whalley (R) | 107,374 | 66.9 |
| | J. Robert Rohm (D) | 53,044 | 33.1 |
| 13 | Richard S. Schweiker (R) | 134,414 | 72.5 |
| | William D. Searle (D) | 51,024 | 27.5 |
| 14 | William S. Moorhead (D) | 83,967 | 68.3 |
| | Richard L. Thornburgh (R) | 39,024 | 31.7 |
| 15 | Fred B. Rooney (D) | 80,407 | 52.3 |
| | George J. Joseph (R) | 73,404 | 47.7 |
| 16 | Edwin D. Eshleman (R) | 82,527 | 69.2 |
| | Richard F. Charles (D) | 36,721 | 30.8 |
| 17 | Herman T. Schneebeli (R) | 109,169 | 66.2 |
| | William Conrad Reuter (D) | 55,761 | 33.8 |
| 18 | Robert J. Corbett (R) | 107,677 | 67.1 |
| | John R. Wohlfarth (D) | 52,714 | 32.9 |
| 19 | George A. Goodling (R) | 70,445 | 51.7 |
| | N. Neiman Craley Jr. (D) | 65,907 | 48.3 |
| 20 | Elmer J. Holland (D) | 93,068 | 65.9 |
| | Joseph Sabol Jr. (R) | 48,229 | 34.1 |
| 21 | John H. Dent (D) | 80,472 | 64.2 |
| | Edward B. Byrne (R) | 44,800 | 35.8 |

| | Candidates | Votes | % |
|---|---|---|---|
| 22 | John P. Saylor (R) | 103,808 | 67.5 |
| | Frank H. Buck (D) | 50,017 | 32.5 |
| 23 | Albert W. Johnson (R) | 81,658 | 62.8 |
| | Robert W. Mitchell (D) | 48,373 | 37.2 |
| 24 | Joseph P. Vigorito (D) | 85,193 | 55.3 |
| | James D. Weaver (R) | 68,955 | 44.7 |
| 25 | Frank M. Clark (D) | 92,073 | 64.5 |
| | John F. Heath (R) | 50,639 | 35.5 |
| 26 | Thomas E. Morgan (D) | 83,687 | 64.1 |
| | Paul P. Riggle (R) | 46,957 | 35.9 |
| 27 | James G. Fulton (R) | 108,731 | 67.7 |
| | Stephen J. Arnold (D) | 51,928 | 32.3 |

## RHODE ISLAND

| | | | |
|---|---|---|---|
| 1 | Fernand J. St Germain (D) | 79,046 | 56.6 |
| | Raymond W. Houghton (R) | 60,093 | 43.0 |
| 2 | John E. Fogarty (D) | 117,911 | 64.7 |
| | Everett C. Sammartino (R) | 64,438 | 35.3 |

## SOUTH CAROLINA

| | | | |
|---|---|---|---|
| 1 | L. Mendel Rivers (D) | 59,055 | 100.0 |
| 2 | Albert W. Watson (R) | 48,742 | 64.3 |
| | Fred Leclercq (D) | 27,013 | 35.7 |
| 3 | William J. Bryan Dorn (D) | 42,834 | 57.8 |
| | John Grisso (R) | 31,331 | 42.2 |
| 4 | Robert T. Ashmore (D) | 43,611 | 100.0 |
| 5 | Thomas S. Gettys (D) | 41,550 | 99.2 |
| 6 | John L. McMillan (D) | 43,090 | 61.7 |
| | Archie C. Odom (R) | 26,702 | 38.3 |

## SOUTH DAKOTA

| | | | |
|---|---|---|---|
| 1 | Ben Reifel (R) | 80,592 | 66.7 |
| | Francis C. Richter (D) | 40,236 | 33.3 |
| 2 | E. Y. Berry (R) | 63,063 | 60.5 |
| | Jack Allmon (D) | 41,155 | 39.5 |

## TENNESSEE

| | | | |
|---|---|---|---|
| 1 | James A. Quillen (R) | 86,421 | 87.1 |
| | Temus Bright (I) | 12,819 | 12.9 |
| 2 | John J. Duncan (R) | 87,777 | 78.9 |
| | Jake Armstrong (D) | 23,538 | 21.2 |
| 3 | Bill Brock (R) | 67,705 | 64.2 |
| | Franklin Haney (D) | 37,720 | 35.8 |
| 4 | Joe L. Evins (D) | 72,621 | 90.0 |
| | William Bean (I) | 8,061 | 10.0 |
| 5 | Richard H. Fulton (D) | 55,685 | 63.0 |
| | George Kelly (R) | 32,706 | 37.0 |
| 6 | William R. Anderson (D) | 50,758 | 79.6 |
| | Cecil Hill (I) | 12,987 | 20.4 |
| 7 | Ray Blanton (D) | 45,083 | 50.6 |
| | Julius Hurst (R) | 43,118 | 48.4 |
| 8 | Robert A. Everett (D) | 53,338 | 75.2 |
| | Jim Boyd (R) | 17,608 | 24.8 |
| 9 | Dan H. Kuykendall (R) | 47,489 | 52.2 |
| | George W. Grider (D) | 43,553 | 47.8 |

## TEXAS

| | | | |
|---|---|---|---|
| 1 | Wright Patman (D) | 50,072 | 100.0 |
| 2 | John Dowdy (D) | 55,134 | 99.9 |
| 3 | Joe Pool (D) | 35,081 | 53.4 |
| | James M. Collins (R) | 30,588 | 46.6 |
| 4 | Ray Roberts (D) | 51,895 | 100.0 |
| 5 | Earle Cabell (D) | 39,977 | 61.0 |
| | Duke Burgess (R) | 25,563 | 39.0 |
| 6 | Olin Teague (D) | 42,017 | 100.0 |
| 7 | George Bush (R) | 53,756 | 57.1 |
| | Frank Briscoe (D) | 39,958 | 42.4 |
| 8 | Bob Eckhardt (D) | 38,497 | 92.3 |
| | W. D. Spayne (CONST) | 3,207 | 7.7 |
| 9 | Jack Brooks (D) | 47,604 | 100.0 |
| 10 | J. J. Pickle (D) | 55,424 | 74.3 |
| | Jane Sumner (R) | 18,343 | 24.6 |

## TEXAS

| | Candidates | Votes | % |
|---|---|---|---|
| 11 | W. R. Poage (D) | 39,140 | 94.9 |
| | Laurel N. Dunn (C) | 2,102 | 5.1 |
| 12 | Jim Wright (D) | 27,070 | 100.0 |
| 13 | Graham Purcell (D) | 43,820 | 57.1 |
| | D. C. Norwood (R) | 32,960 | 42.9 |
| 14 | John Young (D) | 52,861 | 100.0 |
| 15 | Eligio de la Garza (D) | 33,129 | 100.0 |
| 16 | Richard C. White (D) | 33,179 | 100.0 |
| 17 | Omar Burleson (D) | 52,169 | 100.0 |
| 18 | Bob Price (R) | 45,209 | 59.5 |
| | Dee D. Miller (D) | 30,822 | 40.5 |
| 19 | George Mahon (D) | 56,792 | 100.0 |
| 20 | Henry Gonzalez (D) | 41,067 | 87.1 |
| | Robert C. Moore (C) | 3,671 | 7.8 |
| | Bert Ellis (CONST) | 2,390 | 5.1 |
| 21 | O. C. Fisher (D) | 60,497 | 100.0 |
| 22 | Bob Casey (D) | 60,817 | 100.0 |
| 23 | Abraham Kazen (D) | 50,322 | 96.4 |

### Special Election

| | | Votes | % |
|---|---|---|---|
| 8 | Lera M. Thomas (D) | 6,120# | 74.0 |
| | Louis Leman (R) | 2,147# | 26.0 |

## UTAH

| | | Votes | % |
|---|---|---|---|
| 1 | Laurence J. Burton (R) | 99,750 | 66.5 |
| | J. Keith Melville (D) | 50,260 | 33.5 |
| 2 | Sherman P. Lloyd (R) | 96,426 | 61.3 |
| | David S. King (D) | 61,001 | 38.8 |

## VERMONT

| | | Votes | % |
|---|---|---|---|
| AL | Robert T. Stafford (R) | 89,097 | 65.6 |
| | William J. Ryan (D) | 46,643 | 34.4 |

## VIRGINIA

| | Candidates | Votes | % |
|---|---|---|---|
| 1 | Thomas N. Downing (D) | 51,016 | 99.8 |
| 2 | Porter Hardy Jr. (D) | 33,761 | 100.0 |
| 3 | David E. Satterfield III (D) | 51,576 | 99.6 |
| 4 | Watkins M. Abbitt (D) | 45,226 | 66.6 |
| | Edward J. Silverman (C) | 14,827 | 21.8 |
| 5 | William M. Tuck (D) | 32,312 | 56.2 |
| | Robert L. Gilliam (R) | 25,203 | 43.8 |
| 6 | Richard H. Poff (R) | 55,342 | 80.8 |
| | Murray A. Stoller (D) | 13,113 | 19.2 |
| 7 | John O. Marsh Jr. (D) | 42,532 | 59.2 |
| | Edward O. McCue (R) | 29,249 | 40.7 |
| 8 | William Lloyd Scott (R) | 50,782 | 57.2 |
| | George C. Rawlings Jr (D) | 37,929 | 42.8 |
| 9 | William C. Wampler (R) | 49,413 | 53.7 |
| | W. Pat Jennings (D) | 42,571 | 46.3 |
| 10 | Joel T. Broyhill (R) | 58,105 | 58.3 |
| | Clive L. Duval II (D) | 41,502 | 41.7 |

## WASHINGTON

| | | Votes | % |
|---|---|---|---|
| 1 | Thomas M. Pelly (R) | 120,747 | 80.3 |
| | Alice Franklin Bryant (D) | 29,686 | 19.7 |
| 2 | Lloyd Meeds (D) | 75,357 | 60.7 |
| | Eugene M. Smith (R) | 44,727 | 36.0 |
| 3 | Julia Butler Hansen (D) | 78,601 | 65.8 |
| | Keith Kisor (R) | 40,946 | 34.3 |
| 4 | Catherine May (R) | 77,929 | 62.1 |
| | Gustav Bansmer (D) | 38,029 | 30.3 |
| | Floyd Paxton (C) | 9,585 | 7.6 |
| 5 | Thomas S. Foley (D) | 74,571 | 56.5 |
| | Dorothy R. Powers (R) | 57,310 | 43.5 |
| 6 | Floyd V. Hicks (D) | 73,164 | 60.4 |
| | George Mahler (R) | 48,041 | 39.6 |
| 7 | Brock Adams (D) | 104,613 | 62.8 |
| | James Munn (R) | 60,065 | 36.0 |

## WEST VIRGINIA

| | Candidates | Votes | % |
|---|---|---|---|
| 1 | Arch A. Moore Jr. (R) | 88,364 | 70.9 |
| | William M. Kidd (D) | 36,242 | 29.1 |
| 2 | Harley O. Staggers (D) | 51,235 | 60.3 |
| | George L. Strader (R) | 33,676 | 39.7 |
| 3 | John M. Slack (D) | 60,073 | 61.6 |
| | Mal Guthrie (R) | 37,416 | 38.4 |
| 4 | Ken Hechler (D) | 71,751 | 59.7 |
| | Harry D. Humphreys (R) | 48,396 | 40.3 |
| 5 | James Kee (D) | 42,722 | 63.6 |
| | Elizabeth Ann Bowen (R) | 24,470 | 36.4 |

## WISCONSIN

| | | Votes | % |
|---|---|---|---|
| 1 | Henry C. Schadeberg (R) | 65,041 | 51.0 |
| | Lynn E. Stalbaum (D) | 62,398 | 49.0 |
| 2 | Robert W. Kastenmeier (D) | 70,311 | 58.0 |
| | William B. Smith (R) | 50,850 | 42.0 |
| 3 | Vernon W. Thomson (R) | 72,586 | 68.8 |
| | John D. Rice (D) | 32,849 | 31.2 |
| 4 | Clement J. Zablocki (D) | 77,690 | 74.3 |
| | James E. Laessig (R) | 26,863 | 25.7 |
| 5 | Henry S. Reuss (D) | 52,332 | 70.0 |
| | Curtis T. Pechtel (R) | 22,167 | 29.7 |
| 6 | William A. Steiger (R) | 67,941 | 52.4 |
| | John A. Race (D) | 61,761 | 47.6 |
| 7 | Melvin R. Laird (R) | 74,942 | 65.2 |
| | Norman L. Myhra (D) | 40,093 | 34.9 |
| 8 | John W. Byrnes (R) | 75,817 | 61.3 |
| | Marvin S. Kagen (D) | 47,926 | 38.7 |
| 9 | Glenn R. Davis (R) | 85,297 | 64.1 |
| | James P. Buckley (D) | 47,674 | 35.9 |
| 10 | Alvin E. O'Konski (R) | 79,282 | 66.5 |
| | Carl E. Lauri (D) | 39,863 | 33.5 |

## WYOMING

| | | Votes | % |
|---|---|---|---|
| AL | William Henry Harrison (R) | 62,984 | 52.3 |
| | Al Christian (D) | 57,442 | 47.? |

# 1967 House Elections

## CALIFORNIA

### Special Primary Election [1]

| | | Votes | % |
|---|---|---|---|
| 11 | Paul N. McCloskey Jr. (R) | 52,882 | 34.3 |
| | Shirley Temple Black (R) | 34,521 | 22.4 |
| | William H. Draper III (R) | 19,566 | 12.7 |
| | Roy Archibald (D) | 15,069 | 9.8 |
| | Earl B. Whitmore (R) | 12,823 | 8.3 |
| | Edward M. Keating (D) | 8,813 | 5.7 |

### Special Election

| | | Votes | % |
|---|---|---|---|
| 11 | Paul N. McCloskey Jr. (R) | 66,385# | 57.8 |
| | Roy Archibald (D) | 44,319# | 38.6 |

## NEW YORK

### Special Election [2]

| | | Votes | % |
|---|---|---|---|
| 18 | Adam C. Powell (D) | 27,963# | 86.3 |
| | Lucille P. Williams (R) | 3,999# | 12.3 |

## RHODE ISLAND

### Special Election

| | | Votes | % |
|---|---|---|---|
| 2 | Robert O. Tiernan (D) | 56,051# | 48.8 |
| | James DiPrete (R) | 55,748# | 48.5 |

1. Under California's special election law, a majority of the total vote cast was required for election. If no candidate achieved it, another election would be held with the top candidates from each party competing. In the 11th District, McCloskey had more votes than any other Republican, but not a majority of the total vote, so he became the Republican nominee against Archibald, the top Democrat, in the special election.

2. Following his re-election to the 90th Congress (1967-69) in 1966, Powell was not allowed to take the oath of office in January 1967 and was subsequently excluded by vote of the House March 1, 1967. A special election was held April 11, 1967, to fill the vacancy. Powell was again a candidate and won easily, but he never attempted to claim the seat and it remained vacant for the remainder of the Congress.

# 1968 House Elections

## ALABAMA

| | Candidates | Votes | % |
|---|---|---|---|
| 1 | Jack Edwards (R) | 60,318 | 57.1 |
| | Arnold Debrow (D) | 40,593 | 38.4 |
| 2 | William L. Dickinson (R) | 60,743 | 55.4 |
| | Robert Whaley (D) | 37,533 | 34.2 |
| | Richard Boone (NDPA) | 11,446 | 10.4 |
| 3 | George Andrews (D) | 86,796 | 90.8 |
| | Wilbur Johnston (NDPA) | 8,031 | 8.4 |
| 4 | Bill Nichols (D) | 94,726 | 81.4 |
| | Robert Kerr (R) | 12,427 | 10.7 |
| | T. Clemons (NDPA) | 9,248 | 7.9 |
| 5 | Walter Flowers (D) | 69,110 | 56.2 |
| | William McKinley Branch (NDPA) | 28,040 | 22.8 |
| | Frank Donaldson (R) | 14,582 | 11.9 |
| | Mike Simpson (I) | 9,429 | 7.7 |
| 6 | John Buchanan (R) | 69,445 | 59.3 |
| | Quinton Bowers (D) | 34,608 | 29.6 |
| | Thomas Wrenn (NDPA) | 12,976 | 11.1 |
| 7 | Tom Bevill (D) | 106,132 | 76.1 |
| | Jodie Connell (R) | 29,923 | 21.5 |
| 8 | Robert E. Jones (D) | 85,528 | 76.1 |
| | Ken Hearn (C) | 16,900 | 15.0 |
| | Charlie Burgess (NDPA) | 7,140 | 6.4 |

## ALASKA

| | Candidates | Votes | % |
|---|---|---|---|
| AL | Howard W. Pollock (R) | 43,577 | 54.2 |
| | Nick Begich (D) | 36,785 | 45.8 |

## ARIZONA

| | Candidates | Votes | % |
|---|---|---|---|
| 1 | John J. Rhodes (R) | 137,761 | 71.6 |
| | Robert E. Miller (D) | 54,594 | 28.4 |
| 2 | Morris K. Udall (D) | 102,301 | 70.3 |
| | G. Alfred McGinnis (R) | 43,235 | 29.7 |
| 3 | Sam Steiger (R) | 79,667 | 63.4 |
| | Ralph Watkins Jr. (D) | 46,072 | 36.6 |

## ARKANSAS

| | Candidates | Votes | % |
|---|---|---|---|
| 1 | Bill Alexander (D) | 80,293 | 68.9 |
| | Guy Newcomb (R) | 36,284 | 31.1 |
| 2 | Wilbur D. Mills (D) | | 100.0 |
| 3 | John Paul Hammerschmidt (R) | 121,771 | 67.1 |
| | Hardy Croxton (D) | 59,642 | 32.9 |
| 4 | David Pryor (D) | | 100.0 |

## CALIFORNIA

| | Candidates | Votes | % |
|---|---|---|---|
| 1 | Don H. Clausen (R) | 133,597 | 75.2 |
| | Donald W. Graham (D) | 37,756 | 21.3 |
| 2 | Harold T. Johnson (D) | 127,744 | 60.7 |
| | Osmer E. Dunaway (R) | 78,986 | 37.6 |
| 3 | John E. Moss (D) | 107,446 | 56.0 |
| | Elmore J. Duffy (R) | 80,193 | 41.8 |
| 4 | Robert L. Leggett (D) | 90,126 | 55.6 |
| | James M. Shumway (R) | 67,225 | 41.5 |
| 5 | Phillip Burton (D) | 95,630 | 72.8 |
| | Waldo Velasquez (R) | 31,157 | 23.7 |
| 6 | William S. Mailliard (R) | 151,336 | 73.4 |
| | Phillip Drath (D) | 54,928 | 26.6 |
| 7 | Jeffery Cohelan (D) | 102,689 | 62.9 |
| | Barney E. Hilburn (R) | 48,397 | 29.6 |
| | Huey P. Newton (PFP) | 12,279 | 7.5 |
| 8 | George P. Miller (D) | 104,768 | 64.0 |
| | Raymond P. Britton (R) | 58,887 | 36.0 |
| 9 | Don Edwards (D) | 101,329 | 56.6 |
| | Larry Fargher (R) | 77,847 | 43.5 |
| 10 | Charles S. Gubser (R) | 160,563 | 67.3 |
| | Grayson S. Taketa (D) | 73,720 | 30.9 |
| 11 | Paul N. McCloskey Jr. (R) | 166,252 | 79.4 |
| | Urban G. Whitaker (D) | 40,957 | 19.6 |

| | Candidates | Votes | % |
|---|---|---|---|
| 12 | Burt L. Talcott (R) | 143,222 | 92.6 |
| 13 | Charles M. Teague (R) | 151,608 | 65.9 |
| | Stanley K. Sheinbaum (D) | 78,628 | 34.2 |
| 14 | Jerome R. Waldie (D) | 152,847 | 71.6 |
| | David W. Schuh (R) | 56,730 | 26.6 |
| 15 | John J. McFall (D) | 86,386 | 53.8 |
| | Sam Van Dyken (R) | 74,058 | 46.2 |
| 16 | B. F. Sisk (D) | 97,476 | 62.5 |
| | Dave Harris (R) | 55,188 | 35.4 |
| 17 | Glenn M. Anderson (D) | 77,250 | 50.7 |
| | Joe Blatchford (R) | 73,351 | 48.1 |
| 18 | Robert B. Mathias (R) | 100,115 | 65.2 |
| | Harlan Hagen (D) | 51,373 | 33.5 |
| 19 | Chet Holifield (D) | 99,069 | 63.1 |
| | Bill Jones (R) | 53,842 | 34.3 |
| 20 | H. Allen Smith (R) | 136,238 | 69.4 |
| | Don White (D) | 57,064 | 29.1 |
| 21 | Augustus F. Hawkins (D) | 89,536 | 91.6 |
| | Rayfield Lundy (R) | 8,244 | 8.4 |
| 22 | James C. Corman (D) | 103,695 | 56.9 |
| | Joe Holt (R) | 75,457 | 41.4 |
| 23 | Del Clawson (R) | 97,232 | 65.1 |
| | Jim Sperrazzo (D) | 52,202 | 34.9 |
| 24 | Glenard P. Lipscomb (R) | 155,443 | 72.8 |
| | Fred W. Neal (D) | 57,972 | 27.2 |
| 25 | Charles E. Wiggins (R) | 145,245 | 68.7 |
| | Keith F. Shirey (D) | 66,263 | 31.3 |
| 26 | Thomas M. Rees (D) | 134,642 | 65.4 |
| | Irving Teichner (R) | 64,505 | 31.4 |
| 27 | Ed Reinecke (R) | 162,854 | 72.2 |
| | John T. Butchko (D) | 62,824 | 27.8 |
| 28 | Alphonzo Bell (R) | 173,680 | 71.3 |
| | John M. Pratt (D) | 65,233 | 26.8 |
| 29 | George E. Brown Jr. (D) | 76,091 | 52.3 |
| | Bill Orozco (R) | 69,485 | 47.7 |
| 30 | Edward R. Roybal (D) | 76,967 | 67.4 |
| | Samuel M. Cavnar (R) | 37,234 | 32.6 |
| 31 | Charles H. Wilson (D) | 97,855 | 58.9 |
| | James R. Dunn (R) | 65,004 | 39.1 |
| 32 | Craig Hosmer (R) | 142,401 | 73.9 |
| | Arthur J. Gottlieb (D) | 46,404 | 24.1 |
| 33 | Jerry L. Pettis (R) | 123,507 | 66.3 |
| | Al C. Ballard (D) | 59,649 | 32.0 |
| 34 | Richard T. Hanna (D) | 107,113 | 50.9 |
| | William J. Teague (R) | 103,470 | 49.1 |
| 35 | James B. Utt (R) | 216,093 | 72.5 |
| | Thomas B. Lenhart (D) | 74,798 | 25.1 |
| 36 | Bob Wilson (R) | 148,854 | 71.6 |
| | Don Lindgren (D) | 59,011 | 28.4 |
| 37 | Lionel Van Deerlin (D) | 96,130 | 64.7 |
| | Mike Schaefer (R) | 52,547 | 35.3 |
| 38 | John V. Tunney (D) | 121,749 | 62.7 |
| | Robert O. Hunter (R) | 68,887 | 35.5 |

## COLORADO

| | Candidates | Votes | % |
|---|---|---|---|
| 1 | Byron G. Rogers (D) | 91,199 | 45.7 |
| | Frank A. Kemp (R) | 82,677 | 41.5 |
| | Gordon G. Barnewall (DENVER I) | 25,499 | 12.8 |
| 2 | Donald G. Brotzman (R) | 152,153 | 62.9 |
| | Roy H. McVicker (D) | 89,917 | 37.2 |
| 3 | Frank E. Evans (D) | 88,368 | 52.1 |
| | Paul Bradley (R) | 81,173 | 47.9 |
| 4 | Wayne N. Aspinall (D) | 92,680 | 54.7 |
| | Fred E. Anderson (R) | 76,776 | 45.3 |

## CONNECTICUT

| | Candidates | Votes | % |
|---|---|---|---|
| 1 | Emilio Q. Daddario (D) | 124,966 | 62.4 |
| | Roger B. Ladd (R) | 74,615 | 37.3 |
| 2 | William L. St.Onge (D) | 106,203 | 54.1 |
| | Peter P. Mariani (R) | 89,098 | 45.4 |
| 3 | Robert Giaimo (D) | 102,636 | 54.0 |
| | Stelio Salmona (R) | 80,696 | 42.5 |
| 4 | Lowell P. Weicker Jr. (R) | 113,749 | 51.4 |
| | Donald J. Irwin (D) | 104,723 | 47.3 |
| 5 | John S. Monagan (D) | 110,337 | 56.3 |
| | Gaetano A. Russo Jr. (R) | 85,591 | 43.7 |
| 6 | Thomas J. Meskill (R) | 126,208 | 62.3 |
| | Robert M. Sharaf (D) | 76,413 | 37.7 |

## DELAWARE

| | Candidates | Votes | % |
|---|---|---|---|
| AL | William V. Roth (R) | 117,827 | 58.7 |
| | Harris B. McDowell Jr. (D) | 82,993 | 41.3 |

## FLORIDA

| | Candidates | Votes | % |
|---|---|---|---|
| 1 | Robert L. F. Sikes (D) | 116,215 | 84.7 |
| | John Drzazga (R) | 21,063 | 15.3 |
| 2 | Don Fuqua (D) | 87,313 | 100.0 |
| 3 | Charles E. Bennett (D) | 103,540 | 78.9 |
| | Bill Parsons (R) | 27,696 | 21.1 |
| 4 | Bill Chappell Jr. (D) | 86,251 | 52.8 |
| | William F. Herlong Jr. (R) | 76,974 | 47.2 |
| 5 | Louis Frey (R) | 108,620 | 61.7 |
| | James C. Robinson (D) | 67,505 | 38.3 |
| 6 | Sam M. Gibbons (D) | 84,193 | 62.0 |
| | Paul A. Saad (R) | 51,637 | 38.0 |
| 7 | James A. Haley (D) | 91,539 | 55.0 |
| | Joe Z. Lovingood (R) | 74,896 | 45.0 |
| 8 | William C. Cramer (R) | 117,747 | 100.0 |
| 9 | Paul G. Rogers (D) | 111,539 | 56.2 |
| | Robert W. Rust (R) | 87,074 | 43.8 |
| 10 | J. Herbert Burke (R) | 99,844 | 54.9 |
| | Elton J. Gissendanner (D) | 82,138 | 45.1 |
| 11 | Claude Pepper (D) | 99,154 | 76.6 |
| | Ronald I. Strauss (R) | 30,324 | 23.4 |
| 12 | Dante B. Fascell (D) | 82,362 | 57.0 |
| | Mike Thompson (R) | 62,032 | 43.0 |

## GEORGIA

| | Candidates | Votes | % |
|---|---|---|---|
| 1 | G. Elliott Hagan (D) | 77,403 | 68.2 |
| | Joseph J. Tribble (R) | 36,118 | 31.8 |
| 2 | Maston O'Neal (D) | 72,830 | 100.0 |
| 3 | Jack Brinkley (D) | 55,759 | 100.0 |
| 4 | Ben B. Blackburn (R) | 78,753 | 57.5 |
| | James A. Mackay (D) | 58,154 | 42.5 |
| 5 | Fletcher Thompson (R) | 79,258 | 55.6 |
| | Charles L. Weltner (D) | 63,183 | 44.4 |
| 6 | John J. Flynt Jr. (D) | 97,289 | 100.0 |
| 7 | John W. Davis (D) | 96,565 | 99.8 |
| 8 | W. S. Stuckey Jr. (D) | 64,912 | 100.0 |
| 9 | Phil M. Landrum (D) | 83,829 | 100.0 |
| 10 | Robert G. Stephens (D) | 80,674 | 100.0 |

## HAWAII

| | Candidates | Votes | % |
|---|---|---|---|
| AL | Spark M. Matsunaga (D) | 161,954✔ | |
| | Patsy T. Mink (D) | 149,207✔ | |
| | Neal S. Blaisdell (R) | 78,733 | |
| | George Dubois (R) | 39,233 | |
| | Jon D. Olsen (PFP) | 2,432 | |
| | Peter O. Lombardi (PFP) | 2,026 | |

## IDAHO

| | Candidates | Votes | % |
|---|---|---|---|
| 1 | James A. McClure (R) | 90,870 | 59.4 |
| | Compton I. White (D) | 62,002 | 40.6 |
| 2 | Orval Hansen (R) | 65,029 | 52.6 |
| | Darrell Manning (D) | 54,256 | 43.9 |

## ILLINOIS

| | Candidates | Votes | % |
|---|---|---|---|
| 1 | William L. Dawson (D) | 119,207 | 84.6 |
| | Janet Roberts Jenning (R) | 21,758 | 15.4 |
| 2 | Abner J. Mikva (D) | 106,642 | 65.4 |
| | Thomas R. Ireland (R) | 56,513 | 34.6 |
| 3 | William T. Murphy (D) | 101,729 | 54.0 |
| | Robert A. Podesta (R) | 86,535 | 46.0 |
| 4 | Edward J. Derwinski (R) | 151,216 | 68.3 |
| | Robert E. Creighton (D) | 70,145 | 31.7 |
| 5 | John C. Kluczynski (D) | 96,584 | 55.4 |
| | Joseph J. Krasowski (R) | 77,887 | 44.6 |
| 6 | Daniel J. Ronan (D) | 94,779 | 59.7 |
| | Gerald Dolezal (R) | 63,999 | 40.3 |
| 7 | Frank Annunzio (D) | 86,769 | 83.1 |
| | Thomas J. Lento (R) | 17,594 | 16.9 |
| 8 | Daniel Rostenkowski (D) | 105,003 | 62.8 |
| | Henry S. Kaplinski (R) | 62,254 | 37.2 |
| 9 | Sidney R. Yates (D) | 119,032 | 64.4 |
| | Edward V. Notz (R) | 65,687 | 35.6 |
| 10 | Harold R. Collier (R) | 148,398 | 66.8 |
| | Seymour C. Axelrood (D) | 73,766 | 33.2 |
| 11 | Roman C. Pucinski (D) | 128,152 | 55.8 |
| | John J. Hoellen (R) | 101,665 | 44.2 |
| 12 | Robert McClory (R) | 120,370 | 70.4 |
| | Albert S. Salvi (D) | 50,525 | 29.6 |
| 13 | Donald Rumsfeld (R) | 186,714 | 72.7 |
| | David C. Baylor (D) | 69,987 | 27.3 |
| 14 | John N. Erlenborn (R) | 163,332 | 71.1 |
| | Marc Karson (D) | 66,293 | 28.9 |
| 15 | Charlotte T. Reid (R) | 121,432 | 68.7 |
| | Benjamin P. Alschuler (D) | 55,291 | 31.3 |
| 16 | John B. Anderson (R) | 111,037 | 67.4 |
| | Stan Major (D) | 53,838 | 32.7 |
| 17 | Leslie C. Arends (R) | 122,513 | 65.3 |
| | Lester A. Hawthorne (D) | 65,192 | 34.7 |
| 18 | Robert H. Michel (R) | 106,122 | 60.9 |
| | James G. Hatcher (D) | 68,173 | 39.1 |
| 19 | Tom Railsback (R) | 114,948 | 63.5 |
| | Craig Lovitt (D) | 66,135 | 36.5 |
| 20 | Paul Findley (R) | 124,121 | 66.2 |
| | Donald L. Schilson (D) | 63,412 | 33.8 |
| 21 | Kenneth J. Gray (D) | 111,425 | 54.2 |
| | Val Oshel (R) | 94,363 | 45.9 |
| 22 | William L. Springer (R) | 115,258 | 64.3 |
| | Carl F. Firley (D) | 63,957 | 35.7 |
| 23 | George E. Shipley (D) | 104,349 | 54.0 |
| | Bert Hopper (R) | 88,945 | 46.0 |
| 24 | Melvin Price (D) | 113,507 | 71.3 |
| | John S. Guthrie (R) | 45,649 | 28.7 |

## INDIANA

| | | Votes | % |
|---|---|---|---|
| 1 | Ray J. Madden (D) | 90,055 | 56.7 |
| | Donald E. Taylor (R) | 68,318 | 43.0 |
| 2 | Earl F. Landgrebe (R) | 104,238 | 55.1 |
| | Edward F. Kelly (D) | 85,084 | 44.9 |
| 3 | John Brademas (D) | 94,452 | 52.2 |
| | William W. Erwin (R) | 86,354 | 47.8 |
| 4 | E. Ross Adair (R) | 98,977 | 51.4 |
| | J. Edward Roush (D) | 93,515 | 48.6 |
| 5 | Richard L. Roudebush (R) | 114,537 | 63.0 |
| | Robert C. Ford (D) | 67,370 | 37.0 |
| 6 | William G. Bray (R) | 142,207 | 64.9 |
| | Phillip L. Bayt (D) | 76,940 | 35.1 |
| 7 | John T. Myers (R) | 115,921 | 59.8 |
| | Elden C. Tipton (D) | 78,045 | 40.2 |
| 8 | Roger H. Zion (R) | 109,585 | 54.5 |
| | K. Wayne Kent (D) | 91,642 | 45.5 |
| 9 | Lee H. Hamilton (D) | 102,707 | 54.4 |
| | Robert D. Garton (R) | 86,012 | 45.6 |
| 10 | David W. Dennis (R) | 98,090 | 53.9 |
| | William J. Norton (D) | 83,981 | 46.1 |
| 11 | Andrew Jacobs Jr. (D) | 80,015 | 53.1 |
| | W. W. Hill Jr. (R) | 70,725 | 46.9 |

## IOWA

| | | Votes | % |
|---|---|---|---|
| 1 | Fred Schwengel (R) | 91,419 | 53.0 |
| | John R. Schmidhauser (D) | 81,049 | 47.0 |
| 2 | John C. Culver (D) | 103,651 | 55.1 |
| | Tom Riley (R) | 84,634 | 45.0 |
| 3 | H. R. Gross (R) | 101,839 | 64.1 |
| | John E. Van Eschen (D) | 57,164 | 36.0 |
| 4 | John Kyl (R) | 83,259 | 53.9 |
| | Bert Bandstra (D) | 71,134 | 46.1 |
| 5 | Neal Smith (D) | 99,586 | 62.1 |
| | Don Mahon (R) | 60,710 | 37.9 |
| 6 | Wiley Mayne (R) | 100,802 | 65.0 |
| | Jerry O'Sullivan (D) | 54,171 | 35.0 |
| 7 | William Scherle (R) | 86,212 | 64.8 |
| | Richard Oshlo (D) | 46,774 | 35.2 |

## KANSAS

| | | Votes | % |
|---|---|---|---|
| 1 | Keith G. Sebelius (R) | 87,012 | 51.5 |
| | George W. Meeker (D) | 82,102 | 48.6 |
| 2 | Chester L. Mize (R) | 110,768 | 67.6 |
| | Robert A. Swan (D) | 53,151 | 32.4 |
| 3 | Larry Winn (R) | 100,877 | 62.8 |
| | Newell A. George (D) | 59,672 | 37.2 |
| 4 | Garner E. Shriver (R) | 101,991 | 64.7 |
| | Patrick F. Kelly (D) | 55,621 | 35.3 |
| 5 | Joe Skubitz (R) | 107,085 | 64.5 |
| | A. F. Bramble (D) | 59,005 | 35.5 |

## KENTUCKY

| | | Votes | % |
|---|---|---|---|
| 1 | Frank A. Stubblefield (D) | 72,072 | 100.0 |
| 2 | William H. Natcher (D) | 65,860 | 56.4 |
| | Robert D. Simmons (R) | 50,904 | 43.6 |
| 3 | William O. Cowger (R) | 70,318 | 56.0 |
| | Tom Ray (D) | 55,366 | 44.1 |
| 4 | M. G. (Gene) Snyder (R) | 103,793 | 65.0 |
| | Gus Sheehan (D) | 55,971 | 35.0 |
| 5 | Tim Lee Carter (R) | 86,391 | 72.8 |
| | Thomas J. Roberts (D) | 30,575 | 25.8 |
| 6 | John C. Watts (D) | 78,536 | 56.5 |
| | Russell G. Mobley (R) | 58,905 | 42.4 |
| 7 | Carl D. Perkins (D) | 82,594 | 62.0 |
| | James D. Nickell (R) | 50,699 | 38.0 |

## LOUISIANA

| | | Votes | % |
|---|---|---|---|
| 1 | F. Edward Hebert (D) | 70,658 | 100.0 |
| 2 | Hale Boggs (D) | 81,537 | 51.2 |
| | David C. Treen (R) | 77,633 | 48.8 |
| 3 | Patrick T. Caffery (D) | 39,215 | 100.0 |
| 4 | Joe D. Waggonner Jr. (D) | 63,788 | 100.0 |
| 5 | Otto E. Passman (D) | 34,901 | 100.0 |
| 6 | John R. Rarick (D) | 100,461 | 79.5 |
| | Loyd J. Rockhold (R) | 25,867 | 20.5 |
| 7 | Edwin W. Edwards (D) | 79,709 | 85.0 |
| | Vance W. Plauche (R) | 14,126 | 15.1 |
| 8 | Speedy O. Long (D) | 41,086 | 100.0 |

## MAINE

| | | Votes | % |
|---|---|---|---|
| 1 | Peter N. Kyros (D) | 113,501 | 56.6 |
| | Horace A. Hildreth Jr. (R) | 86,949 | 43.4 |
| 2 | William D. Hathaway (D) | 102,369 | 55.7 |
| | Elden H. Shute (R) | 81,398 | 44.3 |

## MARYLAND

| | | Votes | % |
|---|---|---|---|
| 1 | Rogers C. B. Morton (R) | 87,078 | 73.6 |
| | E. Homer White Jr. (D) | 31,250 | 26.4 |
| 2 | Clarence D. Long (D) | 86,025 | 59.1 |
| | John E. Mudd (R) | 59,635 | 40.9 |
| 3 | Edward A. Garmatz (D) | 63,269 | 81.3 |
| | James E. Chew (R) | 14,604 | 18.8 |
| 4 | George H. Fallon (D) | 60,651 | 65.6 |
| | Thomas Paul Raimondi (R) | 31,813 | 34.4 |
| 5 | Lawrence J. Hogan (R) | 89,073 | 52.7 |
| | Hervey G. Machen (D) | 79,870 | 47.3 |
| 6 | J. Glenn Beall Jr. (R) | 71,714 | 53.0 |
| | Goodloe E. Byron (D) | 63,597 | 47.0 |

| | Candidates | Votes | % |
|---|---|---|---|
| 7 | Samuel N. Friedel (D) | 81,048 | 79.6 |
| | Arthur W. Downs (R) | 20,745 | 20.4 |
| 8 | Gilbert Gude (R) | 109,167 | 60.9 |
| | Margaret C. Schweinhaut (D) | 70,109 | 39.1 |

## MASSACHUSETTS

| | | Votes | % |
|---|---|---|---|
| 1 | Silvio O. Conte (R) | 140,419 | 99.8 |
| 2 | Edward P. Boland (D) | 126,485 | 73.7 |
| | Frederick M. Whitney Jr. (R) | 45,262 | 26.4 |
| 3 | Philip J. Philbin (D) | 91,587 | 47.8 |
| | Chandler Harrison Stevens (I) | 53,047 | 27.7 |
| | Laurence Curtis (R) | 46,860 | 24.5 |
| 4 | Harold D. Donohue (D) | 121,211 | 61.0 |
| | Howard A. Miller Jr. (R) | 77,658 | 39.1 |
| 5 | F. Bradford Morse (R) | 124,930 | 60.4 |
| | Robert C. Maguire (D) | 81,875 | 39.6 |
| 6 | William H. Bates (R) | 136,951 | 66.1 |
| | Deirdre Henderson (D) | 70,304 | 33.9 |
| 7 | Torbert H. Macdonald (D) | 119,562 | 62.5 |
| | William S. Abbot (R) | 71,689 | 34.8 |
| 8 | Thomas P. O'Neill Jr. (D) | 107,645 | 100.0 |
| 9 | John W. McCormack (D) | 77,347 | 89.2 |
| | Allan C. Freeman (R) | 15,906 | 17.1 |
| 10 | Margaret M. Heckler (R) | 138,220 | 67.4 |
| | Edmund Dinis (D) | 66,949 | 32.6 |
| 11 | James A. Burke (D) | 169,766 | 100.0 |
| 12 | Hastings Keith (R) | 173,295 | 99.9 |

## MICHIGAN

| | | Votes | % |
|---|---|---|---|
| 1 | John Conyers Jr. (D) | 127,847 | 100.0 |
| 2 | Marvin L. Esch (R) | 90,804 | 54.4 |
| | Weston E. Vivian (D) | 75,009 | 44.9 |
| 3 | Garry Brown (R) | 109,754 | 65.2 |
| | Thomas L. Keenan (D) | 58,692 | 34.8 |
| 4 | Edward Hutchinson (R) | 100,128 | 65.6 |
| | John V. Martin (D) | 52,441 | 34.4 |
| 5 | Gerald R. Ford (R) | 105,085 | 62.8 |
| | Laurence E. Howard (D) | 62,219 | 37.2 |
| 6 | Charles E. Chamberlain (R) | 103,423 | 64.1 |
| | James A. Harrison (D) | 57,839 | 35.9 |
| 7 | Donald W. Riegle Jr. (R) | 104,502 | 60.6 |
| | William R. Blue (D) | 67,779 | 39.3 |
| 8 | James Harvey (R) | 105,238 | 68.8 |
| | Richard E. Davies (D) | 47,639 | 31.2 |
| 9 | Guy Vander Jagt (R) | 111,774 | 67.5 |
| | Jay A. Wabeke (D) | 53,886 | 32.5 |
| 10 | Elford A. Cederberg (R) | 104,791 | 65.9 |
| | Wayne Miller (D) | 54,152 | 34.1 |
| 11 | Philip E. Ruppe (R) | 94,513 | 58.8 |
| | Raymond F. Clevenger (D) | 66,251 | 41.2 |
| 12 | James G. O'Hara (D) | 131,517 | 70.3 |
| | Max B. Harris Jr. (R) | 54,760 | 29.3 |
| 13 | Charles C. Diggs Jr. (D) | 81,951 | 86.4 |
| | Eugene Beauregard (R) | 12,873 | 13.6 |
| 14 | Lucien N. Nedzi (D) | 101,961 | 63.1 |
| | Peter O'Rourke (R) | 59,757 | 37.0 |
| 15 | William D. Ford (D) | 106,960 | 71.1 |
| | John F. Boyle (R) | 43,582 | 29.0 |
| 16 | John D. Dingell Jr. (D) | 105,690 | 73.9 |
| | Monte R. Bona (R) | 37,000 | 25.9 |
| 17 | Martha W. Griffiths (D) | 123,376 | 74.8 |
| | John M. Siviter (R) | 40,906 | 24.8 |
| 18 | William S. Broomfield (R) | 124,025 | 59.9 |
| | Allen Zemmol (D) | 82,234 | 39.7 |
| 19 | Jack McDonald (R) | 104,057 | 58.0 |
| | Garry F. Frink (D) | 75,250 | 42.0 |

## MINNESOTA

| | | Votes | % |
|---|---|---|---|
| 1 | Albert H. Quie (R) | 138,400 | 68.8 |
| | George Daley (DFL) | 62,916 | 31.3 |
| 2 | Ancher Nelsen (R) | 100,623 | 59.5 |
| | Jon Wefald (DFL) | 68,528 | 40.5 |

## MINNESOTA

| Candidates | Votes | % |
|---|---|---|
| 3 Clark MacGregor (R) | 158,989 | 64.8 |
| Eugene E. Stokowski (DFL) | 86,434 | 35.2 |
| 4 Joseph E. Karth (DFL) | 129,082 | 61.3 |
| Emery Barrette (R) | 81,392 | 38.7 |
| 5 Donald M. Fraser (DFL) | 108,588 | 57.5 |
| Harmon T. Ogdahl (R) | 78,819 | 41.8 |
| 6 John M. Zwach (R) | 104,664 | 56.2 |
| J. Buford Johnson (DFL) | 81,578 | 43.8 |
| 7 Odin Langen (R) | 83,113 | 51.3 |
| Bob Bergland (DFL) | 79,067 | 48.8 |
| 8 John A. Blatnik (DFL) | 115,343 | 67.6 |
| James A. Hennen (R) | 55,209 | 32.4 |

## MISSISSIPPI

| Candidates | Votes | % |
|---|---|---|
| 1 Thomas G. Abernethy (D) | 73,800 | 100.0 |
| 2 Jamie L. Whitten (D) | 71,260 | 100.0 |
| 3 Charles H. Griffin (D) | 82,896 | 100.0 |
| 4 G. V. (Sonny) Montgomery (D) | 78,768 | 70.1 |
| Prentiss Walker (R) | 33,683 | 30.0 |
| 5 William M. Colmer (D) | 108,297 | 100.0 |

### Special Runoff Election[1]

| Candidates | Votes | % |
|---|---|---|
| 3 Charles H. Griffin (D) | 87,713# | 66.9 |
| Charles Evers (D) | 43,303# | 33.1 |

## MISSOURI

| Candidates | Votes | % |
|---|---|---|
| 1 William Clay (D) | 79,295 | 64.2 |
| Curtis C. Crawford (R) | 44,316 | 35.9 |
| 2 James W. Symington (D) | 115,476 | 53.2 |
| Hugh Scott (R) | 101,500 | 46.8 |
| 3 Leonor K. Sullivan (D) | 106,150 | 73.4 |
| Homer McCracken (R) | 38,439 | 26.6 |
| 4 William B. Randall (D) | 104,056 | 57.9 |
| Leslie O. Olson (R) | 75,790 | 42.1 |
| 5 Richard Bolling (D) | 86,681 | 65.4 |
| Harold Masters (R) | 45,951 | 34.7 |
| 6 W. R. Hull Jr. (D) | 102,315 | 54.6 |
| James E. Austin (R) | 85,237 | 45.5 |
| 7 Durward G. Hall (R) | 123,958 | 63.8 |
| Edward J. Bonitt (D) | 70,455 | 36.2 |
| 8 Richard Ichord (D) | 108,416 | 57.5 |
| Eugene E. Northern (R) | 79,179 | 42.0 |
| 9 William L. Hungate (D) | 108,184 | 52.2 |
| Christopher S. Bond (R) | 98,923 | 47.8 |
| 10 Bill D. Burlison (D) | 78,326 | 54.0 |
| Vernon H. Landgraf (R) | 66,830 | 46.0 |

## MONTANA

| Candidates | Votes | % |
|---|---|---|
| 1 Arnold Olsen (D) | 74,974 | 53.6 |
| Richard Smiley (R) | 64,862 | 46.4 |
| 2 James F. Battin (R) | 83,888 | 67.9 |
| Robert L. Kelleher (D) | 39,752 | 32.2 |

## NEBRASKA

| Candidates | Votes | % |
|---|---|---|
| 1 Robert V. Denney (R) | 97,697 | 54.1 |
| Clair A. Callan (D) | 78,374 | 43.4 |
| 2 Glenn Cunningham (R) | 87,683 | 55.2 |
| Mrs. Frank B. Morrison (D) | 71,254 | 44.8 |
| 3 Dave Martin (R) | 123,838 | 67.8 |
| J. B. Dean (D) | 58,728 | 32.2 |

## NEVADA

| Candidates | Votes | % |
|---|---|---|
| AL Walter S. Baring (D) | 104,136 | 72.1 |
| James Michael Slattery (R) | 40,209 | 27.9 |

## NEW HAMPSHIRE

| Candidates | Votes | % |
|---|---|---|
| 1 Louis C. Wyman (R) | 100,269 | 63.4 |
| James T. Keefe (D) | 57,959 | 36.6 |

| Candidates | Votes | % |
|---|---|---|
| 2 James C. Cleveland (R) | 88,609 | 71.1 |
| David C. Hoeh (D) | 35,942 | 28.9 |

## NEW JERSEY

| Candidates | Votes | % |
|---|---|---|
| 1 John E. Hunt (R) | 105,856 | 58.0 |
| Thomas S. Higgins (D) | 74,703 | 41.0 |
| 2 Charles W. Sandman Jr. (R) | 91,218 | 55.3 |
| David Dichter (D) | 73,361 | 44.4 |
| 3 James J. Howard (D) | 113,587 | 57.8 |
| Richard R. Stout (R) | 82,441 | 41.9 |
| 4 Frank Thompson Jr. (R) | 106,504 | 53.4 |
| Sydney S. Souter (D) | 92,710 | 46.4 |
| 5 Peter H. B. Frelinghuysen Jr. (Π) | 143,963 | 68.2 |
| Robert F. Allen (D) | 63,208 | 29.9 |
| 6 William T. Cahill (R) | 138,060 | 65.7 |
| Robert A. Gasser (D) | 71,338 | 34.0 |
| 7 William B. Widnall (R) | 120,523 | 62.2 |
| Charles S. Gregg (D) | 71,123 | 36.7 |
| 8 Charles S. Joelson (D) | 100,653 | 61.4 |
| Richard M. DeMarco (R) | 62,661 | 38.2 |
| 9 Henry Helstoski (D) | 97,599 | 49.8 |
| Peter Moraites (R) | 95,267 | 48.7 |
| 10 Peter W. Rodino Jr. (D) | 89,109 | 63.8 |
| Celestino Clemente (R) | 47,989 | 34.4 |
| 11 Joseph G. Minish (D) | 91,496 | 65.5 |
| George M. Wallhauser Jr. (R) | 46,426 | 33.2 |
| 12 Florence P. Dwyer (R) | 146,264 | 71.6 |
| John B. Duff (D) | 58,112 | 28.4 |
| 13 Cornelius E. Gallagher (D) | 83,151 | 55.5 |
| Marion D. Dwyer (R) | 52,159 | 34.8 |
| Jeremiah J. O'Callaghan (VI) | 9,399 | 6.3 |
| 14 Dominick V. Daniels (D) | 87,187 | 58.5 |
| Joseph Bartletta (R) | 50,829 | 34.1 |
| Mervin Murray (C) | 7,634 | 5.1 |
| 15 Edward J. Patten (D) | 107,316 | 54.6 |
| George W. Luke (R) | 88,043 | 44.8 |

## NEW MEXICO

| Candidates | Votes | % |
|---|---|---|
| 1 Manuel Lujan Jr. (R) | 88,517 | 52.9 |
| Thomas G. Morris (D) | 78,117 | 46.6 |
| 2 Ed Foreman (R) | 71,857 | 50.5 |
| E. S. Johnny Walker (D) | 69,858 | 49.1 |

## NEW YORK

| Candidates | Votes | % |
|---|---|---|
| 1 Otis G. Pike (D) | 118,913 | 53.9 |
| James M. Catterson Jr. (R) | 79,208 | 35.9 |
| Harold Haar (C) | 19,470 | 8.8 |
| 2 James R. Grover Jr. (R, C) | 129,731 | 69.0 |
| Charles A. Heeg (D) | 53,552 | 28.5 |
| 3 Lester L. Wolff (D, L) | 98,226 | 52.1 |
| Abe Seldin (R) | 75,910 | 40.2 |
| Daniel L. Rice (C) | 14,556 | 7.7 |
| 4 John W. Wydler (R, C) | 116,190 | 70.1 |
| Michael J. Delguidice (D) | 45,130 | 27.2 |
| 5 Allard K. Lowenstein (D, L) | 99,193 | 50.7 |
| Mason L. Hampton Jr. (R, C) | 96,427 | 49.3 |
| 6 Seymour Halpern (R, L) | 95,016 | 57.5 |
| Franklin Miller (D) | 49,676 | 30.1 |
| Thomas J. Adams (C) | 20,511 | 12.4 |
| 7 Joseph P. Addabbo (D, L) | 90,204# | 66.3 |
| Louis R. Mercogliano (R, C) | 45,813# | 33.7 |
| 8 Benjamin S. Rosenthal (D, L) | 120,257 | 69.8 |
| Jack M. Weinstein (R) | 37,314 | 21.7 |
| Charles Witteck Jr. (C) | 14,714 | 8.5 |
| 9 James J. Delaney (D) | 69,462 | 49.7 |
| John F. Haggerty (R, C) | 59,690 | 42.7 |
| Rose L. Rubin (L) | 8,935 | 6.4 |

| Candidates | Votes | % |
|---|---|---|
| 10 Emanuel Celler (D, L) | 106,622 | 70.5 |
| Frank L. Martano (R, C) | 44,551 | 29.5 |
| 11 Frank J. Brasco (D) | 40,460 | 69.7 |
| Robert J. Hower (R) | 10,708 | 18.4 |
| Basil E. Reynolds (C) | 3,807 | 6.6 |
| Edward L. Johnson (L) | 3,101 | 5.3 |
| 12 Shirley Chisholm (D) | 34,885 | 66.5 |
| James Farmer (R, L) | 13,777 | 26.3 |
| Ralph J. Carrano (C) | 3,771 | 7.2 |
| 13 Bertram L. Podell (D) | 107,960 | 68.2 |
| Jack Sterngass (R) | 25,499 | 16.1 |
| Kenneth Haber (L) | 15,392 | 9.7 |
| Robert C. Laborde (C) | 9,504 | 6.0 |
| 14 John J. Rooney (D, L) | 42,149 | 63.9 |
| Victor J. Tirabasso (R) | 18,396 | 27.9 |
| Alice A. Capatosto (C) | 5,422 | 8.2 |
| 15 Hugh L. Carey (D) | 59,707 | 57.6 |
| Frank C. Spinner (R) | 31,802 | 30.7 |
| Stephen P. Marion (C) | 7,920 | 7.6 |
| 16 John M. Murphy (D) | 73,253 | 48.8 |
| Frank J. Biondolillo (R, C) | 69,126 | 46.0 |
| Joseph Kottler (L) | 7,883 | 5.3 |
| 17 Edward I. Koch (D, L) | 84,627 | 51.7 |
| Whitney North Seymour Jr. (R) | 70,086 | 42.8 |
| Richard J. Callahan (C) | 9,030 | 5.5 |
| 18 Adam Clayton Powell Jr. (D) | 37,146 | 80.8 |
| Henry L. Hall (R) | 7,215 | 15.7 |
| 19 Leonard Farbstein (D) | 44,843 | 53.3 |
| Donald E. Weeden (R) | 27,959 | 33.2 |
| 20 William F. Ryan (D, L) | 66,192 | 78.8 |
| John G. Proudfit (R) | 13,968 | 16.6 |
| 21 James H. Scheuer (D, L) | 55,129 | 82.6 |
| Stanley L. Shapiro (R) | 8,778 | 13.2 |
| 22 Jacob H. Gilbert (D) | 45,144 | 76.2 |
| James N. Harris (R) | 7,087 | 12.0 |
| Sergio S. Pena (L) | 4,402 | 7.4 |
| 23 Jonathan B. Bingham (D, L) | 94,108 | 71.9 |
| Alexander Sacks (R, C) | 36,823 | 28.1 |
| 24 Mario Biaggi (D, C) | 83,234 | 60.5 |
| Andrew Mantovani (R) | 46,510 | 33.8 |
| John Patrick Hagan (L) | 7,758 | 5.6 |
| 25 Richard L. Ottinger (D, L) | 125,415 | 58.6 |
| Samuel Nakasian (R) | 74,275 | 34.7 |
| Anthony J. DeVito (C) | 14,463 | 6.8 |
| 26 Ogden R. Reid (R, L) | 130,229 | 68.1 |
| Paul Davidoff (D) | 44,084 | 23.1 |
| A. Lining Burnet (C) | 16,877 | 8.8 |
| 27 Martin B. McKneally (R) | 94,689 | 47.9 |
| John G. Dow (D, L) | 88,894 | 44.9 |
| Frederick P. Roland (C) | 14,239 | 7.2 |
| 28 Hamilton Fish Jr. (R) | 91,590 | 48.2 |
| John S. Dyson (D) | 86,827 | 45.6 |
| 29 Daniel E. Button (R, CIT) | 119,039 | 56.9 |
| Jacob H. Herzog (D, C) | 87,896 | 42.0 |
| 30 Carleton J. King (R, C) | 124,995 | 66.5 |
| Orlando B. Potter (D, L) | 62,897 | 33.5 |
| 31 Robert C. McEwen (R, C) | 88,562 | 58.4 |
| K. Daniel Haley (D) | 61,947 | 40.9 |
| 32 Alexander Pirnie (R, L) | 95,793 | 64.1 |
| Anthony J. Montoya (D) | 43,254 | 28.9 |
| Albert J. Bushong (C) | 10,393 | 7.0 |
| 33 Howard W. Robison (R) | 110,080 | 68.5 |
| Benjamin Nichols (D, L) | 50,549 | 31.5 |
| 34 James M. Hanley (D) | 96,520 | 51.3 |
| David V. O'Brien (R) | 82,333 | 43.8 |
| 35 Samuel S. Stratton (D) | 112,640 | 69.4 |
| George R. Metcalf (R) | 47,849 | 29.5 |
| 36 Frank J. Horton (R) | 138,400 | 70.4 |
| Augustine J. Marvin (D) | 46,008 | 23.4 |
| Leo J. Kesselring (C) | 9,916 | 5.0 |
| 37 Barber B. Conable Jr (R) | 129,697 | 71.1 |
| Norman M. Gerhard (D) | 50,930 | 27.9 |
| 38 James F. Hastings (R) | 90,281 | 63.4 |
| Wilbur White Jr (D) | 47,093 | 33.1 |
| 39 Richard D. McCarthy (D) | 120,509 | 54.6 |
| Daniel E. Weber (R, L) | 92,589 | 42.0 |

*Footnote, see p. 1263.*

## NEW YORK

| | Candidates | Votes | % |
|---|---|---|---|
| 40 | Henry P. Smith III (R, C) | 106,984 | 64.8 |
| | Eugene O'Connor (D) | 56,201 | 34.0 |
| 41 | Thaddeus J. Dulski (D, L) | 96,703 | 77.6 |
| | Edward P. Matter (R) | 27,920 | 22.4 |

**Special Election**

| | | | |
|---|---|---|---|
| 13 | Bertram L. Podell (D) | 36,093# | 49.7 |
| | Melvin Dubin (NEW LEAD) | 27,856# | 38.4 |
| | Gerald S. Held (D) | 4,848# | 6.7 |
| | Michael V. Ajello (C) | 3,806# | 5.2 |

## NORTH CAROLINA

| | | | |
|---|---|---|---|
| 1 | Walter B. Jones (D) | 75,796 | 66.2 |
| | Reece B. Gardner (R) | 38,660 | 33.8 |
| 2 | L. H. Fountain (D) | 92,542 | 100.0 |
| 3 | David N. Henderson (D) | 57,244 | 54.0 |
| | Herbert H. Howell (R) | 48,815 | 46.0 |
| 4 | Nick Galifianakis (D) | 77,871 | 51.5 |
| | G. Fred Steele Jr. (R) | 73,471 | 48.6 |
| 5 | Wilmer Mizell (R) | 84,905 | 52.4 |
| | Smith Bagley (D) | 77,112 | 47.6 |
| 6 | Richardson Preyer (D) | 76,028 | 53.6 |
| | William L. Osteen (R) | 65,703 | 46.4 |
| 7 | Alton A. Lennon (D) | 77,419 | 100.0 |
| 8 | Earl B. Ruth (R) | 70,480 | 51.2 |
| | Voit Gilmore (D) | 67,281 | 48.8 |
| 9 | Charles Raper Jonas (R) | 94,510 | 100.0 |
| 10 | James T. Broyhill (R) | 87,811 | 54.9 |
| | Basil L. Whitener (D) | 72,295 | 45.2 |
| 11 | Roy A. Taylor (D) | 91,477 | 56.3 |
| | W. Scott Harvey (R) | 71,041 | 43.7 |

## NORTH DAKOTA

| | | | |
|---|---|---|---|
| 1 | Mark Andrews (R) | 84,114 | 66.8 |
| | Bruce Hagen (D) | 39,692 | 31.5 |
| 2 | Thomas S. Kleppe (R) | 55,962 | 49.9 |
| | Rolland Redlin (D) | 54,655 | 48.7 |

## OHIO

| | | | |
|---|---|---|---|
| 1 | Robert Taft Jr. (R) | 102,219 | 67.2 |
| | Karl F. Heiser (D) | 49,830 | 32.8 |
| 2 | Donald D. Clancy (R) | 108,157 | 67.4 |
| | Don Driehaus (D) | 52,327 | 32.6 |
| 3 | Charles W. Whalen Jr. (R) | 114,549 | 78.2 |
| | Paul Tipps (D) | 32,012 | 21.8 |
| 4 | William M. McCulloch (R) | 129,435 | 99.9 |
| 5 | Delbert L. Latta (R) | 113,381 | 71.2 |
| | Louis Richard Batzler (D) | 45,884 | 28.8 |
| 6 | William H. Harsha (R) | 107,289 | 72.4 |
| | Kenneth L. Kirby (D) | 40,964 | 27.6 |
| 7 | Clarence J. Brown Jr. (R) | 97,581 | 63.8 |
| | Robert E. Cecile (D) | 55,386 | 36.2 |
| 8 | Jackson E. Betts (R) | 101,974 | 71.4 |
| | Marie Baker (D) | 40,898 | 28.6 |
| 9 | Thomas L. Ashley (D) | 85,280 | 57.4 |
| | Ben Marsh (R) | 63,290 | 42.6 |
| 10 | Clarence E. Miller (R) | 102,890 | 69.3 |
| | Harry B. Crewson (D) | 45,686 | 30.8 |
| 11 | J. William Stanton (R) | 116,323 | 75.4 |
| | Alan D. Wright (D) | 38,063 | 24.7 |
| 12 | Samuel L. Devine (R) | 106,664 | 67.6 |
| | Herbert J. Pfeifer (D) | 51,202 | 32.4 |
| 13 | Charles A. Mosher (R) | 97,158 | 61.9 |
| | Adrian F. Betleski (D) | 59,864 | 38.1 |
| 14 | William H. Ayres (R) | 84,561 | 55.1 |
| | Oliver Ocasek (D) | 68,889 | 44.9 |
| 15 | Chalmers P. Wylie (R) | 98,499 | 73.1 |
| | Russell H. Volkema (D) | 35,861 | 26.6 |
| 16 | Frank T. Bow (R) | 101,495 | 59.6 |
| | Virgil L. Musser (D) | 68,916 | 40.4 |
| 17 | John M. Ashbrook (R) | 100,148 | 64.9 |
| | Robert W. Levering (D) | 54,127 | 35.1 |
| 18 | Wayne L. Hays (D) | 96,711 | 60.3 |
| | James F. Sutherland (R) | 63,747 | 39.7 |

| | Candidates | Votes | % |
|---|---|---|---|
| 19 | Michael J. Kirwan (D) | 101,813 | 69.7 |
| | Donald J. Lewis (R) | 44,363 | 30.4 |
| 20 | Michael A. Feighan (D) | 72,918 | 72.4 |
| | J. William Petro (R) | 27,827 | 27.6 |
| 21 | Louis Stokes (D) | 85,509 | 74.7 |
| | Charles P. Lucas (R) | 28,931 | 25.3 |
| 22 | Charles A. Vanik (D) | 102,656 | 54.7 |
| | Frances P. Bolton (R) | 84,975 | 45.3 |
| 23 | William E. Minshall (R) | 106,852 | 52.0 |
| | James V. Stanton (D) | 98,825 | 48.1 |
| 24 | Donald E. Lukens (R) | 105,350 | 70.4 |
| | Lloyd D. Miller (D) | 44,400 | 29.7 |

## OKLAHOMA

| | | | |
|---|---|---|---|
| 1 | Page Belcher (R) | 92,513 | 59.3 |
| | John B. Jarboe (D) | 63,451 | 40.7 |
| 2 | Ed Edmondson (D) | 77,192 | 54.9 |
| | Robert G. Smith (R) | 63,437 | 45.1 |
| 3 | Carl Albert (D) | 85,981 | 68.4 |
| | Gerald L. Beasley Jr. (R) | 39,740 | 31.6 |
| 4 | Tom Steed (D) | 67,352 | 53.6 |
| | James V. Smith (R) | 58,253 | 46.4 |
| 5 | John Jarman (D) | 86,420 | 73.6 |
| | Bob Leeper (R) | 30,931 | 26.4 |
| 6 | John N. Happy Camp (R) | 79,992 | 55.3 |
| | John W. Goodwin (D) | 64,599 | 44.7 |

## OREGON

| | | | |
|---|---|---|---|
| 1 | Wendell Wyatt (R) | 189,023 | 80.6 |
| | Thomas M. Baggs (D) | 45,479 | 19.4 |
| 2 | Al Ullman (D) | 114,232 | 63.9 |
| | Marv Root (R) | 64,478 | 36.1 |
| 3 | Edith Green (D) | 137,746 | 69.8 |
| | Douglas S. Warren (R) | 59,447 | 30.1 |
| 4 | John Dellenback (R) | 104,159 | 58.9 |
| | Edward N. Fadely (D) | 72,579 | 41.1 |

## PENNSYLVANIA

| | | | |
|---|---|---|---|
| 1 | William A. Barrett (D) | 113,696 | 74.7 |
| | Leslie J. Carson Jr. (R) | 38,432 | 25.3 |
| 2 | Robert N. C. Nix (D) | 102,869 | 70.0 |
| | Herbert R. McMaster (R) | 44,041 | 30.0 |
| 3 | James A. Byrne (D) | 75,728 | 61.3 |
| | Richard R. Block (R) | 47,813 | 38.7 |
| 4 | Joshua Eilberg (D) | 131,810 | 59.3 |
| | Alexander Kaptik Jr. (R) | 88,229 | 39.7 |
| 5 | William J. Green III (D) | 108,243 | 69.1 |
| | Gregory J. Meade (R) | 48,455 | 30.9 |
| 6 | Gus Yatron (D) | 94,247 | 51.4 |
| | Peter Yonavick (R) | 87,090 | 47.5 |
| 7 | Lawrence G. Williams (R) | 105,699 | 56.5 |
| | Edward J. O'Halloran (D) | 79,782 | 42.7 |
| 8 | Edward G. Biester Jr. (R) | 94,254 | 58.0 |
| | Richard M. Hepburn (D) | 60,324 | 37.1 |
| 9 | G. Robert Watkins (R) | 100,399 | 62.9 |
| | Philip L. Harding (D) | 56,532 | 35.4 |
| 10 | Joseph M. McDade (R) | 125,916 | 66.6 |
| | Robert J. Landy (D) | 61,960 | 32.8 |
| 11 | Daniel J. Flood (D) | 128,794 | 70.0 |
| | Stanley Bunn (R) | 52,475 | 28.5 |
| 12 | J. Irving Whalley (R) | 119,522 | 67.5 |
| | H. Richard Hostetler (D) | 55,838 | 31.5 |
| 13 | R. Lawrence Coughlin (R) | 141,764 | 62.0 |
| | Robert D. Gates (D) | 84,137 | 36.8 |
| 14 | William S. Moorhead (D) | 96,117 | 69.4 |
| | Algia Gary (R) | 39,671 | 28.7 |
| 15 | Fred B. Rooney (D) | 106,877 | 58.8 |
| | Paul E. Henderson (R) | 70,333 | 38.7 |
| 16 | Edwin D. Eshleman (R) | 98,877 | 68.9 |
| | Robert M. Going (D) | 39,507 | 27.5 |
| 17 | Herman T. Schneebeli (R, YOUNGMAN) | 119,003 | 66.2 |
| | Donald J. Rippon (D) | 57,093 | 31.7 |
| 18 | Robert J. Corbett (R) | 121,664 | 62.7 |
| | William T. Sherman (D) | 68,434 | 35.3 |

| | Candidates | Votes | % |
|---|---|---|---|
| 19 | George A. Goodling (R) | 93,352 | 57.7 |
| | Robert L. Myers (D) | 65,903 | 40.8 |
| 20 | Joseph M. Gaydos (D) | 109,236 | 70.2 |
| | Joseph Sabol Jr. (R) | 44,037 | 28.3 |
| 21 | John H. Dent (D) | 93,033 | 62.8 |
| | Thomas H. Young (R, CONST) | 55,099 | 37.2 |
| 22 | John P. Saylor (R) | 98,576 | 58.0 |
| | John P. Murtha (D) | 71,297 | 42.0 |
| 23 | Albert W. Johnson (R) | 87,968 | 61.5 |
| | Alan R. Cleeton (D) | 54,453 | 38.0 |
| 24 | Joseph P. Vigorito (D) | 106,869 | 61.1 |
| | John V. Edwards (R) | 66,429 | 38.0 |
| 25 | Frank M. Clark (D) | 105,048 | 63.1 |
| | Richard L. Doolittle (R) | 59,576 | 35.8 |
| 26 | Thomas E. Morgan (D) | 95,898 | 63.6 |
| | Paul P. Riggle (R) | 50,594 | 33.6 |
| 27 | James G. Fulton (R) | 130,784 | 66.7 |
| | Joseph L. Cosetti (D) | 62,638 | 31.9 |

## RHODE ISLAND

| | | | |
|---|---|---|---|
| 1 | Fernand J. St.Germain (D) | 97,945 | 60.4 |
| | Lincoln C. Almond (R) | 62,394 | 38.5 |
| 2 | Robert O. Tiernan (D) | 124,044 | 61.2 |
| | Howard E. Russell Jr. (R) | 78,502 | 38.8 |

## SOUTH CAROLINA

| | | | |
|---|---|---|---|
| 1 | L. Mendel Rivers (D) | 95,428 | 100.0 |
| 2 | Albert W. Watson (R) | 63,877 | 57.6 |
| | Frank K. Sloan (D) | 47,053 | 42.4 |
| 3 | William J. Bryan Dorn (D) | 74,104 | 66.1 |
| | John K. Grisso (R) | 35,463 | 31.7 |
| 4 | James R. Mann (D) | 68,437 | 61.2 |
| | Charles Bradshaw (R) | 43,440 | 38.8 |
| 5 | Thomas S. Gettys (D) | 72,805 | 74.7 |
| | Hugh J. Boyd (R) | 21,246 | 21.8 |
| 6 | John L. McMillan (D) | 58,304 | 58.3 |
| | Ray Harris (R) | 39,876 | 39.9 |

## SOUTH DAKOTA

| | | | |
|---|---|---|---|
| 1 | Ben Reifel (R) | 85,232 | 58.0 |
| | Frank E. Denholm (D) | 61,738 | 42.0 |
| 2 | E. Y. Berry (R) | 73,987 | 59.4 |
| | David Garner (D) | 50,683 | 40.7 |

## TENNESSEE

| | | | |
|---|---|---|---|
| 1 | James H. Quillen (R) | 100,712 | 85.2 |
| | Arthur Bright (D) | 17,441 | 14.8 |
| 2 | John J. Duncan (R) | 97,832 | 82.4 |
| | Jake Armstrong (D) | 17,547 | 14.8 |
| 3 | Bill Brock (R) | 76,390 | 57.0 |
| | J. William Pope Jr. (D) | 57,565 | 43.0 |
| 4 | Joe L. Evins (D) | 74,041 | 75.9 |
| | J. D. Boles (R) | 23,553 | 24.1 |
| 5 | Richard Fulton (D) | 61,045 | 48.7 |
| | George Kelley (R) | 52,836 | 42.2 |
| | William F. Burton Jr. (I) | 11,412 | 9.1 |
| 6 | William Anderson (D) | 61,223 | 59.4 |
| | Ronnie Page (R) | 41,923 | 40.6 |
| 7 | Ray Blanton (D) | 80,893 | 66.1 |
| | John T. Williams (R) | 41,457 | 33.9 |
| 8 | Robert A. Everett (D) | 70,644 | 100.0 |
| 9 | Dan Kuykendall (R) | 73,293 | 59.4 |
| | James E. Irwin (D) | 45,434 | 36.8 |

## TEXAS

| | | | |
|---|---|---|---|
| 1 | Wright Patman (D) | 87,038 | 100.0 |
| 2 | John Dowdy (D) | 87,565 | 100.0 |
| 3 | James M. Collins (R) | 81,696 | 59.4 |
| | Robert H. Hughes (D) | 55,939 | 46.0 |
| 4 | Ray Roberts (D) | 95,413 | 100.0 |
| 5 | Earle Cabell (D) | 79,317 | 61.4 |
| | Roy Wagoner (R) | 49,821 | 38.6 |

## TEXAS

| | Candidates | Votes | % |
|---|---|---|---|
| 6 | Olin E. Teague (D) | 90,889 | 100.0 |
| 7 | George Bush (R) | 110,455 | 100.0 |
| 8 | Bob Eckhardt (D) | 63,256 | 70.6 |
| | Joe Stevens (R) | 26,402 | 29.5 |
| 9 | Jack Brooks (D) | 71,937 | 60.6 |
| | Henry Pressler (R) | 46,829 | 39.4 |
| 10 | J. J. (Jake) Pickle (D) | 85,037 | 62.1 |
| | Ray Gabler (R) | 51,933 | 37.9 |
| 11 | W. R. Poage (D) | 78,127 | 96.5 |
| 12 | Jim Wright (D) | 86,069 | 100.0 |
| 13 | Graham Purcell (D) | 83,839 | 55.8 |
| | Frank Crowley (R) | 66,477 | 44.2 |
| 14 | John Young (D) | 89,868 | 100.0 |
| 15 | Eligio de la Garza (D) | 57,618 | 100.0 |
| 16 | Richard C. White (D) | 62,491 | 73.5 |
| | Donald Slaughter (R) | 22,510 | 26.5 |
| 17 | Omar Burleson (D) | 90,856 | 100.0 |
| 18 | Bob Price (R) | 81,715 | 65.2 |
| | J. R. Brown (D) | 43,568 | 34.8 |
| 19 | George Mahon (D) | 79,161 | 100.0 |
| 20 | Henry B. Gonzalez (D) | 64,112 | 81.5 |
| | Robert Schneider (R) | 14,569 | 18.5 |
| 21 | O. C. Fisher (D) | 91,784 | 60.8 |
| | W. J. Alexander (R) | 59,082 | 39.2 |
| 22 | Bob Casey (D) | 101,498 | 62.4 |
| | Walter Blaney (R) | 61,278 | 37.7 |
| 23 | Abraham Kazen Jr. (D) | 75,026 | 100.0 |

**Special Election**

| | | Votes | % |
|---|---|---|---|
| 3 | James M. Collins (R) | 13,828# | 60.0 |
| | Mrs. Joe Pool (D) | 9,209# | 40.0 |

## UTAH

| | | Votes | % |
|---|---|---|---|
| 1 | Laurence J. Burton (R) | 139,456 | 68.1 |
| | Richard J. Maughan (D) | 65,265 | 31.9 |
| 2 | Sherman P. Lloyd (R) | 130,127 | 61.7 |
| | Galen J. Ross (D) | 80,948 | 38.4 |

## VERMONT

| | | Votes | % |
|---|---|---|---|
| AL | Robert T. Stafford (R, D) | 156,956 | 99.9 |

## VIRGINIA

| | Candidates | Votes | % |
|---|---|---|---|
| 1 | Thomas N. Downing (D) | 96,265 | 72.9 |
| | J. Cornelius Fauntleroy Jr. (I) | 19,229 | 14.6 |
| | James S. Stafford (R) | 16,456 | 12.5 |
| 2 | G. William Whitehurst (R) | 51,184 | 54.2 |
| | Frederick T. Stant Jr. (D) | 43,229 | 45.8 |
| 3 | David E. Satterfield III (D) | 94,118 | 60.3 |
| | John S. Hansen (R) | 62,082 | 39.7 |
| 4 | Watkins M. Abbitt (D) | 81,723 | 71.5 |
| | S. W. Tucker (R) | 32,548 | 28.5 |
| 5 | W. C. (Dan) Daniel (D) | 70,681 | 54.6 |
| | Weldon W. Tuck (R) | 34,608 | 26.7 |
| | Ruth L. Harvey (I) | 24,196 | 18.7 |
| 6 | Richard H. Poff (R) | 91,549 | 92.2 |
| | Tom Hufford (D) | 7,221 | 7.3 |
| 7 | John O. Marsh Jr. (D) | 64,717 | 54.4 |
| | A. R. (Pete) Giesen Jr. (R) | 51,349 | 43.2 |
| 8 | William L. Scott (R) | 92,121 | 64.9 |
| | Andrew H. McCutcheon (D) | 49,731 | 35.1 |
| 9 | William C. Wampler (R) | 71,531 | 59.9 |
| | Joseph P. Johnson Jr. (D) | 47,906 | 40.1 |
| 10 | Joel T. Broyhill (R) | 97,465 | 59.8 |
| | David Kinney (D) | 65,474 | 40.2 |

## WASHINGTON

| | | Votes | % |
|---|---|---|---|
| 1 | Thomas M. Pelly (R) | 124,513 | 61.4 |
| | Don Cole (D) | 76,456 | 37.7 |
| 2 | Lloyd Meeds (D) | 102,522 | 56.2 |
| | Wally Turner (R) | 79,800 | 43.8 |
| 3 | Julia Butler Hansen (D) | 89,777 | 56.8 |
| | Wayne N. Adams (R) | 68,387 | 43.2 |
| 4 | Catherine May (R) | 99,840 | 66.8 |
| | Lee Lukson (D) | 49,601 | 33.2 |
| 5 | Thomas S. Foley (D) | 88,446 | 56.8 |
| | Richard M. Bond (R) | 67,304 | 43.2 |
| 6 | Floyd V. Hicks (D) | 93,399 | 55.8 |
| | Anthony Chase (R) | 72,177 | 43.1 |
| 7 | Brock Adams (D) | 123,429 | 65.6 |
| | Robert Eberle (R) | 64,051 | 34.0 |

## WEST VIRGINIA

| | Candidates | Votes | % |
|---|---|---|---|
| 1 | Robert H. Mollohan (D) | 85,436 | 53.9 |
| | Tom Sweeney (R) | 73,176 | 46.1 |
| 2 | Harley O. Staggers (D) | 91,022 | 61.5 |
| | George L. Strader (R) | 56,911 | 38.5 |
| 3 | John Slack (D) | 82,911 | 60.5 |
| | Neal A. Kinsolving (R) | 54,164 | 39.5 |
| 4 | Ken Hechler (D) | 94,507 | 64.2 |
| | Ralph Lewis Shannon (R) | 52,636 | 35.8 |
| 5 | James Kee (D) | 80,204 | 66.2 |
| | J. Donald Clark (R) | 41,038 | 33.9 |

## WISCONSIN

| | | Votes | % |
|---|---|---|---|
| 1 | Henry C. Schadeberg (R) | 89,182 | 50.9 |
| | Lynn E. Stalbaum (D) | 86,067 | 49.1 |
| 2 | Robert W. Kastenmeier (D) | 107,804 | 59.9 |
| | Richard D. Murray (R) | 72,229 | 40.1 |
| 3 | Vernon W. Thomson (R) | 95,606 | 63.7 |
| | Gunnar A. Gundersen (D) | 54,517 | 36.3 |
| 4 | Clement J. Zablocki (D) | 118,203 | 72.6 |
| | Walter McCullough (R) | 44,558 | 27.4 |
| 5 | Henry S. Reuss (D) | 76,607 | 67.8 |
| | Robert J. Dwyer (R) | 35,536 | 31.4 |
| 6 | William A. Steiger (R) | 111,934 | 64.0 |
| | John A. Race (D) | 60,059 | 34.3 |
| 7 | Melvin R. Laird (R) | 101,808 | 64.1 |
| | Lawrence Dahl (D) | 56,964 | 35.9 |
| 8 | John W. Byrnes (R) | 111,859 | 68.0 |
| | John E. Nixon (D) | 52,660 | 32.0 |
| 9 | Glenn R. Davis (R) | 126,392 | 63.1 |
| | Carol E. Baumann (D) | 73,891 | 36.9 |
| 10 | Alvin E. O'Konski (R) | 106,266 | 65.9 |
| | Timothy J. Hirsch (D) | 54,889 | 34.1 |

## WYOMING

| | | Votes | % |
|---|---|---|---|
| AL | John Wold (R) | 77,363 | 62.7 |
| | Velma Linford (D) | 45,950 | 37.3 |

# 1969 House Elections

## CALIFORNIA[1]

**Special Primary**

| | | Votes | % |
|---|---|---|---|
| 7 | Barry Goldwater Jr. (R) | 39,580# | 31.3 |
| | John K. Van de Kamp (D) | 17,356# | 13.7 |
| | James B. Potter Jr. (R) | 16,908# | 13.4 |
| | Jack B. Lindsey (R) | 13,818# | 10.9 |
| | Gary Schlessinger (D) | 12,278# | 9.7 |
| | Patrick D. McGee (R) | 8,532# | 6.7 |

**Special Election**

| | | Votes | % |
|---|---|---|---|
| 7 | Barry M. Goldwater Jr. (R) | 64,734 | 56.9 |
| | John K. Van de Kamp (D) | 48,983 | 43.1 |

## ILLINOIS

**Special Election**

| | | Votes | % |
|---|---|---|---|
| 3 | Philip M. Crane (R) | 68,418 | 58.4 |
| | Edward A. Warman (D) | 48,759 | 41.6 |

## MASSACHUSETTS

**Special Election**

| | | Votes | % |
|---|---|---|---|
| 6 | Michael J. Harrington (D) | 72,092# | 52.4 |
| | William Saltonstall (R) | 65,452# | 47.6 |

## MONTANA

**Special Election**

| | | Votes | % |
|---|---|---|---|
| 2 | John Melcher (D) | 45,473# | 50.8 |
| | W. S. Mather (R) | 43,441# | 48.6 |

## NEW JERSEY

**Special Election**

| | | Votes | % |
|---|---|---|---|
| 8 | Robert A. Roe (D) | 67,188 | 49.2 |
| | Eugene Boyle Jr. (R) | 66,228 | 48.5 |

## TENNESSEE

**Special Election**

| | | Votes | % |
|---|---|---|---|
| 8 | Ed Jones (D) | 33,028# | 47.6 |
| | W. J. Davis (AM) | 16,375# | 23.6 |
| | Leonard Dunavant (R) | 15,773# | 22.7 |

## WISCONSIN

**Special Election**

| | | Votes | % |
|---|---|---|---|
| 7 | David R. Obey (D) | 63,567 | 51.6 |
| | Walter J. Chilsen (R) | 59,512 | 48.4 |

*1968 Elections*

*1. The election returns shown from Mississippi's 3rd District were from a special runoff between Griffin and Evers, who had finished with the highest number of votes in an earlier special election. Both elections were held under a provision of Mississippi law requiring that all candidates in a special election for the House run against each other, regardless of party affiliations, with a majority required for election. Since neither Evers nor Griffin had a majority, the runoff was required.*

*The returns from the first special election were as follows: Charles Evers (D), 33,706, 29.3%; Charles H. Griffin (D), 28,927, 25.2; Ellis Bodron (D), 22,842, 19.9; Troy Watkins (D), 10,476, 9.1; Joe Pigott (D), 8,314, 7.2; Hagan Thompson (R), 7,978, 6.9. Source: Mississippi Secretary of State.*

*1969 Elections*

*1. No candidate received a majority of the vote, which was required to win in the first special election. Under California's special election law, the highest vote recipients from the first election from each party then faced each other in another election. In this case, Goldwater became the Republican nominee against Van de Kamp, the Democratic nominee.*

# 1970 House Elections

## ALABAMA

| | Candidates | Votes | % |
|---|---|---|---|
| 1 | Jack Edwards (R) | 63,457 | 60.6 |
| | John Tyson (D) | 27,457 | 26.2 |
| | Noble Beasley (NDPA) | 13,798 | 13.2 |
| 2 | William L. Dickinson (R) | 62,316 | 61.4 |
| | Jack Winfield (D) | 25,966 | 25.6 |
| | Percy Smith Jr. (NDPA) | 13,281 | 13.1 |
| 3 | George Andrews (D) | 70,015 | 89.1 |
| | Detroit Lee (NDPA) | 8,537 | 10.9 |
| 4 | Bill Nichols (D) | 77,701 | 83.7 |
| | Glenn Andrews (R) | 13,217 | 14.2 |
| 5 | Walter Flowers (D) | 78,368 | 75.9 |
| | T. Y. Rogers (NDPA) | 24,863 | 24.1 |
| 6 | John Buchanan (R) | 50,060 | 60.1 |
| | John C. Schmarkey (D) | 31,378 | 37.7 |
| 7 | Tom Bevill (D) | 87,797 | 100.0 |
| 8 | Robert E. Jones (D) | 76,413 | 84.9 |
| | Ken Hearn (C) | 7,599 | 8.4 |
| | Thornton Stanley (NDPA) | 4,846 | 5.4 |

## ALASKA

| | | Votes | % |
|---|---|---|---|
| AL | Nick Begich (D) | 44,137 | 55.1 |
| | Frank H. Murkowski (R) | 35,947 | 44.9 |

## ARIZONA

| | | Votes | % |
|---|---|---|---|
| 1 | John J. Rhodes (R) | 99,706 | 68.5 |
| | Gerald A. Pollock (D) | 45,870 | 31.5 |
| 2 | Morris K. Udall (D) | 86,760 | 69.0 |
| | Morris Herring (R) | 37,561 | 29.9 |
| 3 | Sam Steiger (R) | 81,239 | 62.1 |
| | Orren Beaty (D) | 49,626 | 37.9 |

## ARKANSAS

| | | Votes | % |
|---|---|---|---|
| 1 | Bill Alexander (D) | | 100.0 |
| 2 | Wilbur D. Mills (D) | | 100.0 |
| 3 | John Paul Hammerschmidt (R) | 115,532 | 66.7 |
| | Donald Poe (D) | 57,679 | 33.3 |
| 4 | David Pryor (D) | | 100.0 |

## CALIFORNIA

| | | Votes | % |
|---|---|---|---|
| 1 | Don H. Clausen (R) | 108,358 | 63.4 |
| | William M. Kortum (D) | 62,688 | 36.7 |
| 2 | Harold T. Johnson (D) | 151,070 | 77.9 |
| | Lloyd E. Gilbert (R) | 37,223 | 19.2 |
| 3 | John E. Moss (D) | 117,496 | 61.6 |
| | Elmore J. Duffy (R) | 69,811 | 36.6 |
| 4 | Robert L. Leggett (D) | 103,485 | 68.0 |
| | Andrew Gyorke (R) | 48,783 | 32.0 |
| 5 | Phillip Burton (D) | 76,567 | 70.8 |
| | John E. Parks (R) | 31,570 | 29.2 |
| 6 | William S. Mailliard (R) | 96,393 | 53.4 |
| | Russell R. Miller (D) | 84,255 | 46.6 |
| 7 | Ronald V. Dellums (D) | 89,784 | 57.3 |
| | John E. Healy (R) | 64,691 | 41.3 |
| 8 | George P. Miller (D) | 104,311 | 69.0 |
| | Michael A. Crane (R) | 46,872 | 31.0 |
| 9 | Don Edwards (D) | 120,041 | 69.2 |
| | Mark Guerra (R) | 49,556 | 28.6 |
| 10 | Charles S. Gubser (R) | 135,864 | 62.0 |
| | Stuart D. McLean (D) | 80,530 | 36.8 |
| 11 | Paul N. McCloskey Jr. (R) | 144,500 | 77.5 |
| | Robert E. Gomperts (D) | 39,188 | 21.0 |
| 12 | Burt L. Talcott (R) | 95,549 | 63.6 |
| | O'Brien Riordan (D) | 50,942 | 33.9 |
| 13 | Charles M. Teague (R) | 127,507 | 59.1 |
| | Gary K. Hart (D) | 87,980 | 40.8 |
| 14 | Jerome R. Waldie (D) | 148,655 | 74.6 |
| | Byron D. Athan (R) | 50,750 | 25.5 |

| | Candidates | Votes | % |
|---|---|---|---|
| 15 | John J. McFall (D) | 98,442 | 63.1 |
| | Sam Van Dyken (R) | 55,546 | 35.6 |
| 16 | B. F. Sisk (D) | 95,118 | 66.4 |
| | Phillip V. Sanchez (R) | 43,843 | 30.6 |
| 17 | Glenn M. Anderson (D) | 83,739 | 62.2 |
| | Michael C. Donaldson (R) | 47,778 | 35.5 |
| 18 | Robert B. Mathias (R) | 86,071 | 63.2 |
| | Milton S. Miller (D) | 48,415 | 35.6 |
| 19 | Chet Holifield (D) | 98,578 | 70.4 |
| | Bill Jones (R) | 41,462 | 29.6 |
| 20 | H. Allen Smith (R) | 116,437 | 69.1 |
| | Michael M. Stolzberg (D) | 50,033 | 29.7 |
| 21 | Augustus F. Hawkins (D) | 75,127 | 94.5 |
| | Southey M. Johnson (R) | 4,349 | 5.5 |
| 22 | James C. Corman (D) | 95,256 | 59.4 |
| | Tom Hayden (R) | 63,297 | 39.5 |
| 23 | Del Clawson (R) | 77,346 | 63.3 |
| | G. L. Chapman (D) | 44,767 | 36.7 |
| 24 | John H. Rousselot (R) | 124,071 | 65.1 |
| | Myrlie B. Evers (D) | 61,777 | 32.4 |
| 25 | Charles E. Wiggins (R) | 116,169 | 63.3 |
| | Leslie W. Craven (D) | 64,386 | 35.1 |
| 26 | Thomas M. Rees (D) | 130,499 | 71.3 |
| | Nathaniel Jay Friedman (R) | 47,260 | 25.8 |
| 27 | Barry M. Goldwater Jr. (R) | 139,326 | 66.7 |
| | N. (Toni) Kimmel (D) | 63,652 | 30.5 |
| 28 | Alphonzo Bell (R) | 154,691 | 69.3 |
| | Don McLaughlin (D) | 57,882 | 25.9 |
| 29 | George E. Danielson (D) | 71,308 | 62.6 |
| | Tom McMann (R) | 42,620 | 37.4 |
| 30 | Edward R. Roybal (D) | 63,903 | 68.3 |
| | Samuel M. Cavnar (R) | 28,038 | 30.0 |
| 31 | Charles H. Wilson (D) | 102,071 | 73.2 |
| | Fred L. Casmir (R) | 37,416 | 26.8 |
| 32 | Craig Hosmer (R) | 119,340 | 71.5 |
| | Walter L. Mallonee (D) | 44,278 | 26.5 |
| 33 | Jerry L. Pettis (R) | 116,093 | 72.2 |
| | Chester M. Wright (D) | 44,764 | 27.8 |
| 34 | Richard T. Hanna (D) | 101,664 | 54.5 |
| | William J. Teague (R) | 82,167 | 44.0 |
| 35 | John G. Schmitz (R) | 192,765 | 67.0 |
| | Thomas B. Lenhart (D) | 87,019 | 30.3 |
| 36 | Bob Wilson (R) | 132,446 | 71.5 |
| | Daniel K. Hostetter (D) | 44,841 | 24.2 |
| 37 | Lionel Van Deerlin (D) | 93,952 | 72.1 |
| | James B. Kuhn (R) | 31,968 | 24.5 |
| 38 | Victor V. Veysey (R) | 87,479 | 49.8 |
| | David A. Tunno (D) | 85,684 | 48.8 |

### Special Elections [1]

| | | Votes | % |
|---|---|---|---|
| 24 | John H. Rousselot (R) | 62,749 | 68.2 |
| | Myrlie B. Evers (D) | 29,248 | 31.8 |
| 35 | John G. Schmitz (R) | 67,209 | 72.4 |
| | David N. Hartman (D) | 25,655 | 27.6 |

## COLORADO

| | | Votes | % |
|---|---|---|---|
| 1 | James D. McKevitt (R) | 84,843 | 51.6 |
| | Craig S. Barnes (D) | 74,444 | 45.3 |
| 2 | Donald G. Brotzman (R) | 125,274 | 63.4 |
| | Richard G. Gebhardt (D) | 72,339 | 36.6 |
| 3 | Frank E. Evans (D) | 87,090 | 63.7 |
| | John C. Mitchell Jr. (R) | 45,610 | 33.4 |
| 4 | Wayne N. Aspinall (D) | 76,244 | 55.1 |
| | Bill Gossard (R) | 62,169 | 44.9 |

## CONNECTICUT

| | | Votes | % |
|---|---|---|---|
| 1 | William R. Cotter (D) | 88,374 | 48.7 |
| | Antonina P. Uccello (R) | 87,209 | 48.1 |
| 2 | Robert H. Steele (R) | 92,846 | 53.3 |
| | John F. Pickett (D) | 81,492 | 46.7 |

| | Candidates | Votes | % |
|---|---|---|---|
| 3 | Robert Giaimo (D) | 89,042 | 52.9 |
| | Robert J. Dunn (R) | 69,084 | 41.1 |
| 4 | Stewart B. McKinney (R) | 104,494 | 56.6 |
| | T. F. Gilroy Daly (D) | 78,699 | 42.6 |
| 5 | John S. Monagan (D) | 96,947 | 54.8 |
| | James T. Patterson (R) | 78,414 | 44.3 |
| 6 | Ella T. Grasso (D) | 96,969 | 51.1 |
| | Richard C. Kilbourne (R) | 92,906 | 48.9 |

### Special Election

| | | Votes | % |
|---|---|---|---|
| 2 | Robert H. Steele (R) | 92,816 | 53.3 |
| | John F. Pickett (D) | 81,333 | 46.7 |

## DELAWARE

| | | Votes | % |
|---|---|---|---|
| AL | Pierre S. duPont IV (R) | 86,125 | 53.7 |
| | John Daniello (D) | 71,429 | 44.6 |

## FLORIDA

| | | Votes | % |
|---|---|---|---|
| 1 | Robert L. F. Sikes (D) | 88,744 | 80.2 |
| | H. D. Shuemake (R) | 21,951 | 19.8 |
| 2 | Don Fuqua (D) | | 100.0 |
| 3 | Charles E. Bennett (D) | | 100.0 |
| 4 | Bill Chappell (D) | 75,673 | 57.8 |
| | Leonard V. Wood (R) | 55,311 | 42.2 |
| 5 | Louis Frey Jr. (R) | 110,841 | 75.8 |
| | Roy Girod (D) | 35,398 | 24.2 |
| 6 | Sam M. Gibbons (D) | 78,832 | 72.3 |
| | Robert A. Carter (R) | 30,252 | 27.7 |
| 7 | James A. Haley (D) | 78,535 | 53.4 |
| | Joe Z. Lovingood (R) | 68,646 | 46.6 |
| 8 | C. W. Bill Young (R) | 120,466 | 67.2 |
| | Ted A. Bailey (D) | 58,904 | 32.8 |
| 9 | Paul G. Rogers (D) | 120,565 | 70.6 |
| | Emil F. Danciu (R) | 50,146 | 29.4 |
| 10 | J. Herbert Burke (R) | 81,170 | 54.1 |
| | James J. Ward Jr. (D) | 68,847 | 45.9 |
| 11 | Claude Pepper (D) | | 100.0 |
| 12 | Dante B. Fascell (D) | 75,895 | 71.7 |
| | Robert A. Zinzell (R) | 29,935 | 28.3 |

## GEORGIA

| | | Votes | % |
|---|---|---|---|
| 1 | G. Elliot Hagan (D) | 70,856 | 100.0 |
| 2 | Dawson Mathis (D) | 59,994 | 91.8 |
| | Thomas Ragsdale (R) | 5,376 | 8.2 |
| 3 | Jack Brinkley (D) | 54,588 | 99.5 |
| 4 | Ben B. Blackburn (R) | 85,848 | 65.2 |
| | Franklin Shumake (D) | 45,908 | 34.8 |
| 5 | Fletcher Thompson (R) | 78,540 | 57.4 |
| | Andrew Young (D) | 58,394 | 42.6 |
| 6 | John J. Flynt Jr. (D) | 92,500 | 100.0 |
| 7 | John W. Davis (D) | 80,149 | 72.5 |
| | Dick Fullerton (R) | 30,392 | 27.5 |
| 8 | W. S. Stuckey Jr. (D) | 52,446 | 100.0 |
| 9 | Phil M. Landrum (D) | 64,603 | 71.7 |
| | Bob Cooper (R) | 25,476 | 28.3 |
| 10 | Robert G. Stephens Jr. (D) | 74,075 | 100.0 |

## HAWAII

| | | Votes | % |
|---|---|---|---|
| 1 | Spark M. Matsunaga (D) | 85,411 | 72.9 |
| | Richard K. Cockey (R) | 31,764 | 27.1 |
| 2 | Patsy T. Mink (D) | 91,038 | 100.0 |

## IDAHO

| | | Votes | % |
|---|---|---|---|
| 1 | James A. McClure (R) | 77,515 | 58.2 |
| | William J. Brauner (D) | 55,743 | 41.8 |
| 2 | Orval Hansen (R) | 66,428 | 65.8 |
| | Marden E. Wells (D) | 31,872 | 31.6 |

*Footnote, see p. 1268.*

## ILLINOIS

| Candidates | Votes | % |
|---|---|---|
| 1 Ralph H. Metcalfe (D) | 93,272 | 91.0 |
| Janet Roberts Jennings (R) | 9,267 | 9.0 |
| 2 Abner J. Mikva (D) | 88,252 | 74.7 |
| Harold E. Marks (R) | 29,853 | 25.3 |
| 3 Morgan F. Murphy (D) | 97,693 | 68.9 |
| Robert P. Rowan (R) | 44,013 | 31.1 |
| 4 Edward J. Derwinski (R) | 117,590 | 68.0 |
| Melvin W. Morgan (D) | 55,328 | 32.0 |
| 5 John C. Kluczynski (D) | 97,278 | 68.8 |
| Edmund W. Ochenkowski (R) | 44,049 | 31.2 |
| 6 George W. Collins (D) | 68,182 | 56.2 |
| Alex J. Zabrosky (R) | 53,240 | 43.9 |
| 7 Frank Annunzio (D) | 70,112 | 87.3 |
| Thomas J. Lento (R) | 10,235 | 12.7 |
| 8 Dan Rostenkowski (D) | 98,453 | 73.9 |
| Henry S. Kaplinski (R) | 34,841 | 26.1 |
| 9 Sidney R. Yates (D) | 111,955 | 75.8 |
| Edward Wolbank (R) | 35,795 | 24.2 |
| 10 Harold R. Collier (R) | 107,416 | 62.2 |
| R. G. Logan (D) | 65,170 | 37.8 |
| 11 Roman C. Pucinski (D) | 137,090 | 71.9 |
| James R. Mason (R) | 53,461 | 28.1 |
| 12 Robert McClory (R) | 84,356 | 62.1 |
| James J. Cone (D) | 51,499 | 37.9 |
| 13 Philip M. Crane (R) | 124,649 | 58.0 |
| Edward A. Warman (D) | 90,364 | 42.0 |
| 14 John N. Erlenborn (R) | 122,115 | 65.5 |
| William J. Adelman (D) | 64,231 | 34.5 |
| 15 Charlotte T. Reid (R) | 95,222 | 68.9 |
| James E. Todd (D) | 43,014 | 31.1 |
| 16 John B. Anderson (R) | 83,296 | 66.8 |
| John E. Devine Jr. (D) | 41,459 | 33.2 |
| 17 Leslie C. Arends (R) | 92,917 | 62.3 |
| Lester A. Hawthorne (D) | 56,340 | 37.8 |
| 18 Robert H. Michel (R) | 84,864 | 66.1 |
| Rosa Lee Fox (D) | 43,601 | 33.9 |
| 19 Tom Railsback (R) | 92,247 | 68.2 |
| James L. Shaw (D) | 43,094 | 31.8 |
| 20 Paul Findley (R) | 103,485 | 67.5 |
| Billie M. Cox (D) | 49,727 | 32.5 |
| 21 Kenneth J. Gray (D) | 110,374 | 62.5 |
| Fred Evans (R) | 66,273 | 37.5 |
| 22 William L. Springer (R) | 83,131 | 59.0 |
| Robert C. Miller (D) | 57,781 | 41.0 |
| 23 George E. Shipley (D) | 91,158 | 54.0 |
| Phyllis Schlafly (R) | 77,762 | 46.0 |
| 24 Melvin Price (D) | 88,637 | 74.2 |
| Scott R. Randolph (R) | 30,784 | 25.8 |

### Special Election

| | Votes | % |
|---|---|---|
| 6 George W. Collins (D) | 68,949 | 55.7 |
| Alex J. Zabrosky (R) | 54,746 | 44.3 |

## INDIANA

| | Votes | % |
|---|---|---|
| 1 Ray J. Madden (D) | 73,145 | 65.6 |
| Eugene M. Kirtland (R) | 38,294 | 34.4 |
| 2 Earl F. Landgrebe (R) | 79,163 | 50.4 |
| Philip A. Sprague (D) | 77,959 | 49.6 |
| 3 John Brademas (D) | 87,064 | 57.5 |
| Don M. Newman (R) | 64,249 | 42.5 |
| 4 J. Edward Roush (D) | 86,582 | 51.9 |
| E. Ross Adair (R) | 80,326 | 48.1 |
| 5 Elwood H. Hillis (R) | 86,199 | 56.0 |
| Kathleen Z. Williams (D) | 67,740 | 44.0 |
| 6 William G. Bray (R) | 115,113 | 60.7 |
| Terrence D. Straub (D) | 74,599 | 39.3 |
| 7 John T. Myers (R) | 97,152 | 57.1 |
| William D. Roach (D) | 73,042 | 42.9 |
| 8 Roger H. Zion (R) | 93,088 | 52.6 |
| J. David Huber (D) | 83,911 | 47.4 |
| 9 Lee H. Hamilton (D) | 104,599 | 62.5 |
| Richard B. Wathen (R) | 62,772 | 37.5 |
| 10 David W. Dennis (R) | 81,439 | 50.8 |
| Philip S. Sharp (D) | 78,871 | 49.2 |
| 11 Andrew Jacobs Jr. (D) | 71,329 | 58.3 |
| Danny L. Burton (R) | 50,990 | 41.7 |

## IOWA

| Candidates | Votes | % |
|---|---|---|
| 1 Fred Schwengel (R) | 60,270 | 49.8 |
| Edward Mezvinsky (D) | 59,505 | 49.2 |
| 2 John C. Culver (D) | 84,049 | 60.5 |
| Cole McMartin (R) | 54,932 | 39.5 |
| 3 H. R. Gross (R) | 66,087 | 59.0 |
| Lyle D. Taylor (D) | 45,958 | 41.0 |
| 4 John Kyl (R) | 59,396 | 54.6 |
| Roger Blobaum (D) | 49,369 | 45.4 |
| 5 Neal Smith (D) | 73,820 | 64.9 |
| Don Mahon (R) | 37,374 | 32.9 |
| 6 Wiley Mayne (R) | 57,285 | 57.0 |
| Fred H. Moore (D) | 43,257 | 43.0 |
| 7 William J. Scherle (R) | 53,084 | 62.7 |
| Lou Galetich (D) | 31,552 | 37.3 |

## KANSAS

| | Votes | % |
|---|---|---|
| 1 Keith G. Sebelius (R) | 83,923 | 56.8 |
| Billy D. Jellison (D) | 63,791 | 43.2 |
| 2 William R. Roy (D) | 80,161 | 52.3 |
| Chester L. Mize (R) | 68,843 | 45.0 |
| 3 Larry Winn Jr. (R) | 74,603 | 53.0 |
| James H. DeCoursey Jr. (D) | 64,344 | 45.7 |
| 4 Garner E. Shriver (R) | 85,058 | 63.2 |
| James C. Junhke (D) | 47,004 | 34.9 |
| 5 Joe Skubitz (R) | 94,837 | 66.1 |
| T. D. Saar Jr. (D) | 48,688 | 33.9 |

## KENTUCKY

| | Votes | % |
|---|---|---|
| 1 Frank A. Stubblefield (D) | 27,829 | 100.0 |
| 2 William H. Natcher (D) | 21,024 | 100.0 |
| 3 Romano L. Mazzoli (D) | 50,102 | 48.5 |
| William O. Cowger (R) | 49,891 | 48.3 |
| 4 M. G. (Gene) Snyder (R) | 83,037 | 66.6 |
| Charles W. Webster (D) | 41,659 | 33.4 |
| 5 Tim Lee Carter (R) | 49,266 | 80.4 |
| Lyle Leonard Willis (D) | 11,977 | 19.6 |
| 6 John C. Watts (D) | 44,322 | 64.9 |
| Gerald G. Gregory (R) | 23,971 | 35.1 |
| 7 Carl D. Perkins (D) | 50,672 | 75.3 |
| Herbert E. Myers (R) | 16,648 | 24.7 |

## LOUISIANA

| | Votes | % |
|---|---|---|
| 1 F. Edward Hebert (D) | 66,284 | 87.4 |
| Luke J. Fontana (I) | 9,602 | 12.7 |
| 2 Hale Boggs (D) | 51,812 | 69.3 |
| Robert E. Lee (R) | 19,703 | 26.3 |
| 3 Patrick T. Caffery (D) | 48,677 | 100.0 |
| 4 Joe D. Waggonner Jr. (D) | 44,848 | 100.0 |
| 5 Otto E. Passman (D) | 31,087 | 100.0 |
| 6 John R. Rarick (D) | 36,632 | 100.0 |
| 7 Edwin W. Edwards (D) | 24,517 | 100.0 |
| 8 Speedy O. Long (D) | 26,607 | 100.0 |

## MAINE

| | Votes | % |
|---|---|---|
| 1 Peter N. Kyros (D) | 99,483 | 59.2 |
| Ronald T. Speers (R) | 68,671 | 40.8 |
| 2 William D. Hathaway (D) | 96,235 | 64.2 |
| Maynard G. Conners (R) | 53,642 | 35.8 |

## MARYLAND

| | Votes | % |
|---|---|---|
| 1 Rogers C. B. Morton (R) | 79,594 | 75.6 |
| David S. Aland (D) | 24,923 | 23.7 |
| 2 Clarence D. Long (D) | 87,224 | 68.5 |
| Ross Z. Pierpont (R) | 40,177 | 31.5 |
| 3 Edward A. Garmatz (D) | 52,374 | 100.0 |
| 4 Paul S. Sarbanes (D) | 54,936 | 70.1 |
| David Fentress (R) | 23,491 | 30.0 |
| 5 Lawrence J. Hogan (R) | 84,314 | 61.4 |
| Royal Hart (D) | 52,979 | 38.6 |

| Candidates | Votes | % |
|---|---|---|
| 6 Goodloe E. Byron (D) | 59,267 | 50.8 |
| George R. Hughes Jr. (R) | 55,511 | 47.6 |
| 7 Parren J. Mitchell (D) | 60,390 | 58.7 |
| Peter Parker (R) | 42,566 | 41.3 |
| 8 Gilbert Gude (R) | 104,647 | 63.4 |
| Thomas Hale Boggs Jr. (D) | 60,453 | 36.6 |

## MASSACHUSETTS

| | Votes | % |
|---|---|---|
| 1 Silvio O. Conte (R) | 117,045 | 100.0 |
| 2 Edward P. Boland (D) | 111,430 | 100.0 |
| 3 Robert F. Drinan (D) | 63,942 | 37.7 |
| John McGlennon (R) | 60,575 | 35.7 |
| Philip J. Philbin (WRITE IN) | 45,278 | 26.7 |
| 4 Harold D. Donohue (D) | 95,016 | 54.3 |
| Howard A. Miller Jr. (R) | 79,870 | 45.7 |
| 5 F. Bradford Morse (R) | 116,660 | 63.3 |
| Richard Williams (D) | 67,646 | 36.7 |
| 6 Michael J. Harrington (D) | 114,276 | 61.7 |
| Howard Phillips (R) | 70,955 | 38.3 |
| 7 Torbert H. Macdonald (D) | 115,597 | 72.2 |
| Gordon F. Hughes (R) | 44,463 | 27.8 |
| 8 Thomas P. O'Neill Jr. (D) | 89,875 | 100.0 |
| 9 Louise Day Hicks (D) | 50,269 | 59.2 |
| Daniel J. Houton (I) | 17,395 | 20.5 |
| Laurence Curtis (R) | 17,324 | 20.4 |
| 10 Margaret M. Heckler (R) | 102,895 | 57.0 |
| Bertram A. Yaffe (D) | 77,497 | 43.0 |
| 11 James A. Burke (D) | 143,026 | 100.0 |
| 12 Hastings Keith (R) | 100,432 | 50.4 |
| Gerry E. Studds (D) | 98,910 | 49.6 |

## MICHIGAN

| | Votes | % |
|---|---|---|
| 1 John Conyers Jr. (D) | 93,075 | 88.2 |
| Howard L. Johnson (R) | 11,876 | 11.3 |
| 2 Marvin L. Esch (R) | 88,071 | 62.5 |
| R. Michael Stillwagon (D) | 52,782 | 37.5 |
| 3 Garry Brown (R) | 80,447 | 56.3 |
| Richard A. Enslen (D) | 62,530 | 43.7 |
| 4 Edward Hutchinson (R) | 74,471 | 61.9 |
| David R. McCormack (D) | 45,838 | 38.1 |
| 5 Gerald R. Ford Jr (R) | 88,208 | 61.4 |
| Jean McKee (D) | 55,337 | 38.5 |
| 6 Charles E. Chamberlain (R) | 84,276 | 60.3 |
| John A. Cihon (D) | 55,591 | 39.8 |
| 7 Donald W. Riegle Jr. (R) | 97,683 | 69.2 |
| Richard J. Ruhala (D) | 41,235 | 29.2 |
| 8 James Harvey (R) | 85,634 | 65.9 |
| Richard E. Davies (D) | 44,400 | 34.1 |
| 9 Guy A. Vander Jagt (R) | 94,027 | 64.4 |
| Charles Arthur Rogers (D) | 51,223 | 35.1 |
| 10 Elford A. Cederberg (R) | 82,528 | 59.1 |
| Gerald J. Parent (D) | 57,031 | 40.9 |
| 11 Philip E. Ruppe (R) | 85,323 | 61.6 |
| Nino Green (D) | 53,146 | 38.4 |
| 12 James G. O'Hara (D) | 129,287 | 76.1 |
| Patrick Driscoll (R) | 38,946 | 22.9 |
| 13 Charles C. Diggs Jr. (D) | 56,872 | 86.2 |
| Fred Engel (R) | 9,141 | 13.9 |
| 14 Lucien N. Nedzi (D) | 91,111 | 70.1 |
| John L. Owen (R) | 38,956 | 30.0 |
| 15 William D. Ford (D) | 101,018 | 80.0 |
| Ernest C. Fackler (R) | 25,340 | 20.1 |
| 16 John D. Dingell (D) | 90,540 | 79.1 |
| William E. Rostron (R) | 23,867 | 20.9 |
| 17 Martha W. Griffiths (D) | 108,176 | 79.7 |
| Thomas E. Klunzinger (R) | 27,608 | 20.3 |
| 18 William S. Broomfield (R) | 113,309 | 64.6 |
| August Scholle (D) | 62,081 | 35.4 |
| 19 Jack McDonald (R) | 91,763 | 58.9 |
| Fred L. Harris (D) | 63,175 | 40.5 |

## MINNESOTA

| | Votes | % |
|---|---|---|
| 1 Albert H. Quie (R) | 121,802 | 69.3 |
| B. A. Lundeen (DFL) | 53,995 | 30.7 |
| 2 Ancher Nelsen (R) | 94,080 | 63.3 |
| Clifford R. Adams (DFL) | 54,498 | 36.7 |

## MINNESOTA

| Candidates | Votes | % |
|---|---|---|
| 3 Bill Frenzel (R) | 110,921 | 50.6 |
| George Rice (DFL) | 108,141 | 49.4 |
| 4 Joseph E. Karth (DFL) | 131,263 | 74.2 |
| Frank L. Loss (R) | 45,680 | 25.8 |
| 5 Donald M. Fraser (DFL) | 83,207 | 57.1 |
| Dick Enroth (R) | 61,682 | 42.3 |
| 6 John M. Zwach (R) | 88,753 | 51.8 |
| Terry Montgomery (DFL) | 81,004 | 47.3 |
| 7 Bob Bergland (DFL) | 79,378 | 54.1 |
| Odin Langen (R) | 67,296 | 45.9 |
| 8 John A. Blatnik (DFL) | 118,149 | 78.0 |
| Paul Reed (R) | 38,369 | 25.3 |

## MISSISSIPPI

| Candidates | Votes | % |
|---|---|---|
| 1 Thomas G. Abernethy (D) | 42,367 | 100.0 |
| 2 Jamie L. Whitten (D) | 51,689 | 86.5 |
| Eugene Carter (I) | 8,092 | 13.5 |
| 3 Charles H. Griffin (D) | 50,527 | 63.7 |
| Ray Lee (R) | 28,847 | 36.3 |
| 4 G. V. (Sonny) Montgomery (D) | 66,064 | 100.0 |
| 5 William M. Colmer (D) | 58,546 | 90.4 |
| Earnest J. Creel (I) | 6,225 | 9.6 |

## MISSOURI

| Candidates | Votes | % |
|---|---|---|
| 1 William Clay (D) | 58,082 | 90.5 |
| Gerald G. Frischer (AM MO) | 6,078 | 9.5 |
| 2 James W. Symington (D) | 93,294 | 57.6 |
| Philip R. Hoffman (R) | 66,503 | 41.1 |
| 3 Leonor K. Sullivan (D) | 73,021 | 74.8 |
| Dale F. Troske (R) | 24,651 | 25.2 |
| 4 William J. Randall (D) | 80,153 | 60.1 |
| Leslie O. Olsen (R) | 53,204 | 39.9 |
| 5 Richard Bolling (D) | 51,668 | 61.3 |
| Randall Vanet (R) | 31,806 | 37.8 |
| 6 W. R. Hull Jr. (D) | 74,496 | 53.6 |
| Hugh A. Sprague (R) | 63,789 | 45.9 |
| 7 Durward G. Hall (R) | 92,965 | 100.0 |
| 8 Richard Ichord (D) | 97,560 | 64.4 |
| John L. Caskanett (R) | 53,181 | 35.1 |
| 9 William L. Hungate (D) | 100,988 | 63.0 |
| Anthony C. Schroeder (R) | 58,103 | 36.3 |
| 10 Bill D. Burlison (D) | 62,764 | 56.0 |
| Gary Rust (R) | 49,355 | 44.0 |

## MONTANA

| Candidates | Votes | % |
|---|---|---|
| 1 Richard G. Shoup (R) | 64,388 | 50.5 |
| Arnold Olsen (D) | 63,175 | 49.5 |
| 2 John Melcher (D) | 78,082 | 64.1 |
| Jack Rehberg (R) | 43,752 | 35.9 |

## NEBRASKA

| Candidates | Votes | % |
|---|---|---|
| 1 Charles Thone (R) | 79,131 | 50.6 |
| Clair A. Callan (I) | 40,919 | 26.2 |
| George Burrows (D) | 36,240 | 23.2 |
| 2 John Y. McCollister (R) | 69,671 | 51.8 |
| John Hlavacek (D) | 64,520 | 48.0 |
| 3 Dave Martin (R) | 93,705 | 59.5 |
| Donald Searcy (D) | 63,698 | 40.5 |

## NEVADA

| Candidates | Votes | % |
|---|---|---|
| AL Walter S. Baring (D) | 113,496 | 82.5 |
| J. Robert Charles (R) | 24,147 | 17.5 |

## NEW HAMPSHIRE

| Candidates | Votes | % |
|---|---|---|
| 1 Louis C. Wyman (R) | 72,170 | 67.4 |
| Chester E. Merrow (D) | 34,882 | 32.6 |
| 2 James C. Cleveland (R) | 74,219 | 69.6 |
| Eugene S. Daniell Jr. (D) | 32,374 | 30.4 |

## NEW JERSEY

| Candidates | Votes | % |
|---|---|---|
| 1 John E. Hunt (R) | 83,726 | 61.2 |
| Salvatore T. Mansi (D) | 52,567 | 38.4 |
| 2 Charles W. Sandman Jr. (R) | 69,392 | 51.7 |
| William J. Hughes (D) | 64,882 | 48.3 |
| 3 James J. Howard (D) | 87,973 | 55.2 |
| William F. Dowd (R) | 68,675 | 43.1 |
| 4 Frank Thompson Jr. (D) | 91,670 | 58.4 |
| Edward A. Costigan (R) | 65,030 | 41.4 |
| 5 Peter H. B. Frelinghuysen (R) | 111,553 | 66.4 |
| Ronald C. Eisele (D) | 53,436 | 31.8 |
| 6 Edwin B. Forsythe (R) | 88,051 | 53.6 |
| Charles B. Yates (D) | 72,347 | 44.1 |
| 7 William B. Widnall (R) | 90,410 | 58.6 |
| Arthur J. Lesemann (D) | 63,928 | 41.4 |
| 8 Robert A. Roe (D) | 75,056 | 61.0 |
| Alfred E. Fontanella (R) | 48,011 | 39.0 |
| 9 Henry Helstoski (D) | 91,589 | 56.6 |
| Henry L. Hoebel (R) | 68,974 | 42.6 |
| 10 Peter W. Rodino Jr. (D) | 71,003 | 70.0 |
| Griffith H. Jones (R) | 30,460 | 30.0 |
| 11 Joseph G. Minish (D) | 68,075 | 68.5 |
| James W. Shue (R) | 31,369 | 31.5 |
| 12 Florence P. Dwyer (R) | 109,537 | 66.2 |
| Daniel F. Lundy (D) | 55,930 | 33.8 |
| 13 Cornelius E. Gallagher (D) | 77,789 | 71.1 |
| Raul E. L. Comesanas (R) | 27,929 | 25.5 |
| 14 Dominick V. Daniels (D) | 77,771 | 69.7 |
| Carlo N. DeGennaro (R) | 31,161 | 27.9 |
| 15 Edward J. Patten (D) | 94,772 | 61.1 |
| Peter P. Garibaldi (R) | 60,450 | 38.9 |

### Special Election

| Candidates | Votes | % |
|---|---|---|
| 6 Edwin B. Forsythe (R) | 89,565 | 54.8 |
| Charles B. Yates (D) | 73,821 | 45.2 |

## NEW MEXICO

| Candidates | Votes | % |
|---|---|---|
| 1 Manuel Lujan Jr. (R) | 91,187 | 57.6 |
| Fabian Chavez Jr. (D) | 64,598 | 40.8 |
| 2 Harold Runnels (D) | 64,518 | 50.8 |
| Ed Foreman (R) | 61,074 | 48.1 |

## NEW YORK

| Candidates | Votes | % |
|---|---|---|
| 1 Otis G. Pike (D, L) | 108,746 | 52.2 |
| Malcolm E. Smith Jr. (R, C) | 99,503 | 47.8 |
| 2 James R. Grover Jr. (R, C) | 107,443 | 66.1 |
| Harvey W. Sherman (D, L) | 54,996 | 33.9 |
| 3 Lester L. Wolff (D, L) | 94,414 | 54.4 |
| Raymond J. Rice (R, ENVIRON) | 66,196 | 38.1 |
| Lola Camardi (C) | 12,925 | 7.5 |
| 4 John W. Wydler (R) | 91,787 | 57.1 |
| Karen S. Burstein (D, L) | 56,411 | 35.1 |
| Donald A. Derham (C) | 12,701 | 7.9 |
| 5 Norman F. Lent (R, C) | 93,824 | 51.0 |
| Allard K. Lowenstein (D, L) | 84,738 | 46.1 |
| 6 Seymour Halpern (R, L) | 89,250 | 77.3 |
| John J. Flynn (C) | 26,244 | 22.7 |
| 7 Joseph P. Addabbo (D, R) | 112,983 | 90.8 |
| Christopher T. Acer (C) | 11,515 | 9.3 |
| 8 Benjamin S. Rosenthal (D, L) | 93,666 | 62.8 |
| Cosmo J. DiTucci (R, C) | 55,406 | 37.2 |
| 9 James J. Delaney (D, R) | 102,205 | 91.9 |
| Rose L. Rubin (L) | 9,025 | 8.1 |
| 10 Emanuel Celler (D, L) | 78,324 | 73.0 |
| Frank J. Occhiogrosso (R, C) | 29,012 | 27.0 |
| 11 Frank J. Brasco (D) | 60,919 | 78.6 |
| William Sampol (C) | 9,462 | 12.2 |
| Paul Myrowitz (L) | 7,156 | 9.2 |

| Candidates | Votes | % |
|---|---|---|
| 12 Shirley Chisholm (D, L) | 31,500 | 81.8 |
| John Coleman (R) | 5,816 | 15.1 |
| 13 Bertram L. Podell (D) | 102,247 | 77.0 |
| George W. McKenzie (R) | 20,550 | 15.5 |
| Herbert Dicker (L) | 9,925 | 7.5 |
| 14 John J. Rooney (D) | 31,586 | 55.2 |
| John F. Jacobs (R, C) | 15,222 | 26.6 |
| Peter E. Eikenberry (L) | 10,452 | 18.3 |
| 15 Hugh L. Carey (D) | 50,767 | 64.7 |
| Frank C. Spinner (R) | 17,931 | 22.8 |
| Stephen P. Marion (C) | 5,307 | 6.8 |
| Carl Saks (L) | 4,506 | 5.7 |
| 16 John M. Murphy (D, CSI) | 71,553 | 51.6 |
| David D. Smith (R, C) | 62,597 | 45.2 |
| 17 Edward I. Koch (D, L) | 98,300 | 62.0 |
| Peter J. Sprague (R) | 50,647 | 32.0 |
| Richard J. Callahan (C) | 9,586 | 6.1 |
| 18 Charles B. Rangel (D, R) | 52,651 | 86.8 |
| Charles Taylor (C) | 6,385 | 10.5 |
| 19 Bella S. Abzug (D) | 46,947 | 52.3 |
| Barry Farber (R, L) | 38,460 | 42.8 |
| 20 William F. Ryan (D, L) | 73,509 | 78.7 |
| William Goldstein (R) | 13,527 | 14.5 |
| Francis C. Saunders (C) | 6,315 | 6.8 |
| 21 Herman Badillo (D, L) | 38,866 | 83.7 |
| George B. Smaragdas (C) | 7,561 | 16.3 |
| 22 James H. Scheuer (D, L) | 50,372 | 71.6 |
| Robert M. Schneck (R, C) | 19,994 | 28.4 |
| 23 Jonathan B. Bingham (D, L) | 78,723 | 76.2 |
| George E. Sweeney (R) | 16,172 | 15.7 |
| Nora M. Kardian (C) | 8,456 | 8.2 |
| 24 Mario Biaggi (D, C) | 106,942 | 69.9 |
| Joseph F. Periconi (R, SILENT) | 38,173 | 24.9 |
| John Patrick Hagan (L) | 7,970 | 5.2 |
| 25 Peter A. Peyser (R) | 76,611 | 42.5 |
| William Dretzin (D) | 66,688 | 37.0 |
| Anthony J. DeVito (C) | 31,250 | 17.3 |
| 26 Ogden R. Reid (R, L) | 109,783 | 66.4 |
| Michael A. Coffey (C) | 29,702 | 18.0 |
| G. Russell James (D) | 25,909 | 15.7 |
| 27 John G. Dow (D, L) | 89,787 | 52.2 |
| Martin B. McKneally (R, C) | 82,191 | 47.8 |
| 28 Hamilton Fish Jr. (R) | 119,954 | 70.8 |
| John J. Greaney (D) | 41,908 | 24.7 |
| 29 Samuel S. Stratton (D) | 128,017 | 66.2 |
| Daniel E. Button (R, L) | 65,339 | 33.8 |
| 30 Carleton J. King (R, C) | 95,470 | 57.1 |
| Edward W. Pattison (D, L) | 71,832 | 42.9 |
| 31 Robert C. McEwen (R, C) | 90,585 | 72.4 |
| Erwin L. Bornstein (D) | 34,568 | 27.6 |
| 32 Alexander Pirnie (R, L) | 90,884 | 65.8 |
| Joseph Simmons (D) | 47,306 | 34.2 |
| 33 Howard W. Robison (R) | 90,196 | 66.5 |
| David Bernstein (D, L) | 45,373 | 33.5 |
| 34 John H. Terry (R, C) | 88,786 | 59.5 |
| Neal J. McCurn (D) | 60,452 | 40.5 |
| 35 James M. Hanley (D) | 82,425 | 51.9 |
| John F. O'Connor (R, C) | 76,381 | 48.1 |
| 36 Frank J. Horton (R) | 123,209 | 70.5 |
| Jordan E. Pappas (D) | 38,898 | 22.3 |
| David F. Hampson (C) | 10,442 | 6.0 |
| 37 Barber B. Conable Jr. (R) | 107,677 | 65.9 |
| Richard N. Anderson (D, L) | 48,061 | 29.4 |
| 38 James F. Hastings (R, C) | 94,906 | 71.4 |
| James G. Cretekos (D) | 37,961 | 28.6 |
| 39 Jack F. Kemp (R, C) | 96,989 | 51.6 |
| Thomas P. Flaherty (D, L) | 90,949 | 48.4 |
| 40 Henry P. Smith III (R, C) | 87,183 | 63.4 |
| Edward Cuddy (D) | 50,418 | 36.6 |
| 41 Thaddeus J. Dulski (D, L) | 79,151 | 79.7 |
| William M. Johns (R, C) | 20,108 | 20.3 |

## NORTH CAROLINA

| Candidates | Votes | % |
|---|---|---|
| 1 Walter B. Jones (D) | 41,674 | 70.2 |
| R. Frank Everett (R) | 16,217 | 27.3 |

## NORTH CAROLINA

| | Candidates | Votes | % |
|---|---|---|---|
| 2 | L. H. Fountain (D) | 38,891 | 100.0 |
| 3 | David N. Henderson (D) | 41,065 | 60.1 |
| | Herbert H. Howell (R) | 27,224 | 39.9 |
| 4 | Nick Galifianakis (D) | 49,866 | 52.4 |
| | R. Jack Hawke (R) | 45,386 | 47.7 |
| 5 | Wilmer D. Mizell (R) | 68,937 | 58.1 |
| | James G. White (D) | 49,663 | 41.9 |
| 6 | Richardson Preyer (D) | 47,693 | 66.0 |
| | Clifton B. Barham Jr. (R) | 20,739 | 28.7 |
| | Lynwood Bullock (AM) | 3,849 | 5.3 |
| 7 | Alton A. Lennon (D) | 37,377 | 72.0 |
| | Frederick R. Weber (R) | 14,529 | 28.0 |
| 8 | Earl B. Ruth (R) | 51,873 | 56.1 |
| | H. Clifton Blue (D) | 40,563 | 43.9 |
| 9 | Charles Raper Jonas (R) | 57,525 | 66.6 |
| | Cy N. Bahakel (D) | 28,801 | 33.4 |
| 10 | James T. Broyhill (R) | 63,936 | 57.1 |
| | Basil L. Whitener (D) | 48,113 | 42.9 |
| 11 | Roy A. Taylor (D) | 90,199 | 67.0 |
| | Luke Atkinson (R) | 44,376 | 33.0 |

## NORTH DAKOTA

| | | Votes | % |
|---|---|---|---|
| 1 | Mark Andrews (R) | 72,168 | 65.7 |
| | James E. Brooks (D) | 37,688 | 34.3 |
| 2 | Arthur A. Link (D) | 50,416 | 50.3 |
| | Robert P. McCarney (R) | 49,888 | 49.7 |

## OHIO

| | | Votes | % |
|---|---|---|---|
| 1 | William J. Keating (R) | 89,169 | 69.1 |
| | Bailey W. Turner (D) | 39,820 | 30.9 |
| 2 | Donald D. Clancy (R) | 77,071 | 55.9 |
| | Gerald N. Springer (D) | 60,860 | 44.1 |
| 3 | Charles W. Whalen Jr. (R) | 86,973 | 74.2 |
| | Dempsey A. Kerr (D) | 26,735 | 22.8 |
| 4 | William M. McCulloch (R) | 82,521 | 64.4 |
| | Donald B. Laws (D) | 45,619 | 35.6 |
| 5 | Delbert L. Latta (R) | 92,577 | 71.2 |
| | Carl G. Sherer (D) | 37,545 | 28.9 |
| 6 | William H. Harsha (R) | 82,772 | 67.8 |
| | Raymond H. Stevens (D) | 39,265 | 32.2 |
| 7 | Clarence J. Brown Jr. (R) | 84,448 | 69.4 |
| | Joseph D. Lewis (D) | 37,294 | 30.6 |
| 8 | Jackson E. Betts (R) | 90,916 | 100.0 |
| 9 | Thomas L. Ashley (D) | 82,777 | 70.9 |
| | Allen H. Shapiro (R) | 33,947 | 29.1 |
| 10 | Clarence E. Miller (R) | 80,838 | 66.5 |
| | Doug Arnett (D) | 40,669 | 33.5 |
| 11 | J. William Stanton (R) | 91,437 | 68.3 |
| | Ralph Rudd (D) | 42,542 | 31.8 |
| 12 | Samuel L. Devine (R) | 82,486 | 57.7 |
| | James W. Goodrich (D) | 60,538 | 42.3 |
| 13 | Charles A. Mosher (R) | 85,858 | 61.7 |
| | Joseph J. Bartolomeo (D) | 53,271 | 38.3 |
| 14 | John F. Seiberling Jr. (D) | 71,282 | 56.4 |
| | William H. Ayres (R) | 55,038 | 43.6 |
| 15 | Chalmers P. Wylie (R) | 81,536 | 70.6 |
| | Manley L. McGee (D) | 34,018 | 29.4 |
| 16 | Frank T. Bow (R) | 81,208 | 56.2 |
| | Virgil L. Musser (D) | 63,187 | 43.8 |
| 17 | John M. Ashbrook (R) | 79,472 | 62.2 |
| | James C. Hood (D) | 44,066 | 34.5 |
| 18 | Wayne L. Hays (D) | 82,071 | 68.3 |
| | Robert Stewart (R) | 38,104 | 31.7 |
| 19 | Charles J. Carney (D) | 73,222 | 58.5 |
| | Margaret Dennison (R) | 52,057 | 41.6 |
| 20 | James V. Stanton (D) | 70,140 | 81.3 |
| | J. William Petro (R) | 16,118 | 18.7 |
| 21 | Louis Stokes (D) | 74,340 | 77.6 |
| | Bill Mack (R) | 21,440 | 22.4 |
| 22 | Charles A. Vanik (D) | 114,790 | 71.5 |
| | Adrian Fink (R) | 45,657 | 28.5 |
| 23 | William E. Minshall (R) | 111,218 | 60.0 |
| | Ronald M. Mottl (D) | 73,765 | 39.8 |
| 24 | Walter E. Powell (R) | 63,344 | 51.5 |
| | James D. Ruppert (D) | 55,455 | 45.1 |

### Special Election

| | Candidates | Votes | % |
|---|---|---|---|
| 19 | Charles J. Carney (D) | 70,161 | 58.4 |
| | Margaret Dennison (R) | 50,005 | 41.6 |

## OKLAHOMA

| | | Votes | % |
|---|---|---|---|
| 1 | Page Belcher (R) | 67,386 | 55.7 |
| | James R. Jones (D) | 53,598 | 44.3 |
| 2 | Ed Edmondson (D) | 87,131 | 70.8 |
| | Gene Humphries (R) | 35,989 | 29.2 |
| 3 | Carl Albert (D) | 112,458 | 100.0 |
| 4 | Tom Steed (D) | 67,743 | 63.7 |
| | Jay G. Wilkinson (R) | 37,081 | 34.9 |
| 5 | John Jarman (D) | 62,034 | 73.1 |
| | Terry L. Campbell (R) | 22,801 | 26.9 |
| 6 | John N. Happy Camp (R) | 81,959 | 64.2 |
| | R. O. Cassity Jr. (D) | 45,742 | 35.8 |

## OREGON

| | | Votes | % |
|---|---|---|---|
| 1 | Wendell Wyatt (R) | 147,239 | 71.8 |
| | Vern Cook (D) | 57,837 | 28.2 |
| 2 | Al Ullman (D) | 100,943 | 71.2 |
| | Everett Thoren (R) | 40,620 | 28.7 |
| 3 | Edith Green (D) | 118,919 | 73.7 |
| | Robert E. Dugdale (R) | 42,391 | 26.3 |
| 4 | John Dellenback (R) | 84,474 | 58.3 |
| | James Weaver (D) | 60,299 | 41.7 |

## PENNSYLVANIA

| | | Votes | % |
|---|---|---|---|
| 1 | William A. Barrett (D) | 79,425 | 69.2 |
| | Joseph S. Ziccardi (R) | 34,649 | 30.2 |
| 2 | Robert N. C. Nix (D) | 70,530 | 68.2 |
| | Edward L. Taylor (R) | 32,858 | 31.8 |
| 3 | James A. Byrne (D) | 54,755 | 56.4 |
| | Gustine J. Pelagatti (R) | 42,393 | 43.6 |
| 4 | Joshua Eilberg (D) | 113,920 | 59.4 |
| | Charles F. Dougherty (R) | 77,817 | 40.6 |
| 5 | William J. Green III (D) | 80,142 | 66.9 |
| | James H. Ring (R) | 38,955 | 32.5 |
| 6 | Gus Yatron (D) | 96,453 | 65.0 |
| | Michael Kitsock (R) | 48,397 | 32.6 |
| 7 | Lawrence G. Williams (R) | 91,042 | 59.2 |
| | Joseph R. Breslin (D) | 62,722 | 40.8 |
| 8 | Edward G. Biester Jr. (R) | 73,041 | 56.4 |
| | Arthur Leo Hennessy Jr. (D) | 51,464 | 39.7 |
| 9 | John H. Ware III (R) | 76,535 | 59.2 |
| | Louis F. Waldman (D) | 52,852 | 40.9 |
| 10 | Joseph M. McDade (R) | 102,716 | 65.4 |
| | Edward J. Smith (D) | 51,506 | 32.8 |
| 11 | Daniel J. Flood (D) | 146,789 | 96.6 |
| 12 | J. Irving Whalley (R) | 93,385 | 64.0 |
| | Victor J. Karycki Jr. (D) | 48,738 | 33.4 |
| 13 | R. Lawrence Coughlin (R) | 101,953 | 58.3 |
| | Frank R. Romano (D) | 68,743 | 39.3 |
| 14 | William S. Moorhead (D) | 72,509 | 76.5 |
| | Barry Levine (R) | 21,572 | 22.8 |
| 15 | Fred B. Rooney (D) | 93,169 | 66.9 |
| | Charles H. Roberts (R) | 44,103 | 31.7 |
| 16 | Edwin D. Eshleman (R) | 74,006 | 66.5 |
| | John E. Pflum (D) | 33,986 | 30.5 |
| 17 | Herman T. Schneebeli (R) | 88,173 | 57.9 |
| | William P. Zurick (D) | 60,714 | 39.9 |
| 18 | Robert J. Corbett (R) | 87,246 | 60.2 |
| | Ronald E. Leslie (D) | 54,639 | 37.7 |
| 19 | George A. Goodling (R) | 71,497 | 53.9 |
| | Arthur L. Berger (D) | 58,399 | 44.0 |
| 20 | Joseph M. Gaydos (D) | 84,911 | 77.0 |
| | Joseph Honeygosky (R) | 22,553 | 20.5 |
| 21 | John H. Dent (D) | 76,915 | 68.5 |
| | Glenn G. Anderson (R) | 33,396 | 29.7 |
| 22 | John P. Saylor (R) | 81,675 | 57.7 |
| | Joseph F. O'Kicki (D) | 58,720 | 41.5 |
| 23 | Albert W. Johnson (R) | 70,074 | 57.9 |
| | Cecil R. Harrington (D) | 50,908 | 42.1 |
| 24 | Joseph P. Vigorito (D) | 94,029 | 66.8 |
| | Wayne R. Merrick (R) | 44,395 | 31.5 |

| | Candidates | Votes | % |
|---|---|---|---|
| 25 | Frank M. Clark (D) | 92,638 | 69.7 |
| | John Loth (R) | 37,355 | 28.1 |
| 26 | Thomas E. Morgan (D) | 80,734 | 68.4 |
| | Domenick A. Cupelli (R) | 35,083 | 29.7 |
| 27 | James G. Fulton (R) | 86,932 | 60.5 |
| | Douglas Walgren (D) | 55,050 | 38.3 |

### Special Election

| | | Votes | % |
|---|---|---|---|
| 9 | John H. Ware III (R) | 44,077 | 57.0 |
| | Louis F. Waldman (D) | 31,353 | 40.5 |

## RHODE ISLAND

| | | Votes | % |
|---|---|---|---|
| 1 | Fernand J. St.Germain (D) | 86,283 | 61.0 |
| | Walter J. Miska (R) | 52,962 | 37.4 |
| 2 | Robert O. Tiernan (D) | 121,704 | 67.2 |
| | William A. Dimitri Jr. (R) | 61,819 | 34.2 |

## SOUTH CAROLINA

| | | Votes | % |
|---|---|---|---|
| 1 | L. Mendel Rivers (D) | 63,891* | 100.0 |
| 2 | Floyd Spence (R) | 48,093 | 53.1 |
| | Heyward McDonald (D) | 42,005 | 46.4 |
| 3 | William Jennings Bryan Dorn (D) | 60,708 | 75.2 |
| | H. Grady Ballard (R) | 19,981 | 24.8 |
| 4 | James R. Mann (D) | 52,175 | 100.0 |
| 5 | Thomas S. Gettys (D) | 43,742 | 65.9 |
| | B. Leonard Phillips (R) | 21,911 | 33.0 |
| 6 | John L. McMillan (D) | 46,966 | 64.1 |
| | Edward B. Baskin (R) | 25,546 | 34.9 |

## SOUTH DAKOTA

| | | Votes | % |
|---|---|---|---|
| 1 | Frank E. Denholm (D) | 71,636 | 56.0 |
| | Dexter H. Gunderson (R) | 56,330 | 44.0 |
| 2 | James Abourezk (D) | 55,925 | 52.3 |
| | Fred D. Brady (R) | 51,092 | 47.7 |

## TENNESSEE

| | | Votes | % |
|---|---|---|---|
| 1 | James H. Quillen (R) | 78,896 | 67.9 |
| | David Bruce Shine (D) | 37,348 | 32.1 |
| 2 | John J. Duncan (D) | 85,849 | 73.3 |
| | Roger Cowan (D) | 30,146 | 25.7 |
| 3 | LaMar Baker (R) | 61,527 | 51.3 |
| | Richard Winningham (D) | 54,662 | 45.6 |
| 4 | Joe L. Evins (D) | 86,437 | 82.6 |
| | J. Durelle Boles (R) | 18,180 | 17.4 |
| 5 | Richard Fulton (D) | 89,900 | 70.6 |
| | George Kelly (R) | 37,522 | 29.5 |
| 6 | William R. Anderson (D) | 87,517 | 81.7 |
| | Elmer Davies Jr. (R) | 19,622 | 18.3 |
| 7 | Ray Blanton (D) | 83,904 | 74.2 |
| | W. G. Doss (R) | 29,139 | 25.8 |
| 8 | Ed Jones (D) | 66,590 | 100.0 |
| 9 | Dan Kuykendall (R) | 72,498 | 62.6 |
| | Michael Osborn (D) | 43,279 | 37.4 |

## TEXAS

| | | Votes | % |
|---|---|---|---|
| 1 | Wright Patman (D) | 67,883 | 78.9 |
| | James Hogan (R) | 18,614 | 21.6 |
| 2 | John Dowdy (D) | 52,634 | 73.6 |
| | Eugene Hoyt (WRITE IN) | 11,987# | 17.2 |
| | Joe Runnels (WRITE IN) | 4,693# | 6.8 |
| 3 | James M. Collins (R) | 63,690 | 60.6 |
| | John Mead (D) | 41,425 | 39.4 |
| 4 | Ray Roberts (D) | 70,103 | 100.0 |
| 5 | Earle Cabell (D) | 57,058 | 59.7 |
| | Frank Crowley (R) | 38,481 | 40.3 |
| 6 | Olin E. Teague (D) | 74,038 | 100.0 |
| 7 | Bill Archer (R) | 93,457 | 64.8 |
| | Jim Greenwood (D) | 50,750 | 35.2 |
| 8 | Bob Eckhardt (D) | 26,294 | 100.0 |

## TEXAS

| | Candidates | Votes | % |
|---|---|---|---|
| 9 | Jack Brooks (D) | 57,180 | 64.5 |
| | Henry Pressler (R) | 31,483 | 35.5 |
| 10 | J. J. Pickle (D) | 78,872 | 100.0 |
| 11 | W. R. Poage (D) | 59,641 | 99.9 |
| 12 | Jim Wright (D) | 62,057 | 100.0 |
| 13 | Graham B. Purcell (D) | 80,070 | 64.9 |
| | Joe Staley (R) | 43,319 | 35.1 |
| 14 | John Young (D) | 62,560 | 100.0 |
| 15 | Eligio de la Garza (D) | 54,498 | 76.2 |
| | Ben A. Martinez (R) | 17,049 | 23.8 |
| 16 | Richard C. White (D) | 54,617 | 82.7 |
| | J. R. Provencio (R) | 11,420 | 17.3 |
| 17 | Omar Burleson (D) | 70,040 | 100.0 |
| 18 | Bob Price (R) | 52,845 | 99.9 |
| 19 | George Mahon (D) | 59,996 | 100.0 |
| 20 | Henry B. Gonzalez (D) | 48,710 | 100.0 |
| 21 | O. C. Fisher (D) | 76,004 | 61.4 |
| | Richardson B. Gill (R) | 47,868 | 38.6 |
| 22 | Bob Casey (D) | 73,514 | 55.7 |
| | A. W. Busch (R) | 58,598 | 44.4 |
| 23 | Abraham Kazen Jr. (D) | 61,068 | 100.0 |

## UTAH

| | Candidates | Votes | % |
|---|---|---|---|
| 1 | K. Gunn McKay (D) | 95,499 | 51.3 |
| | Richard Richards (R) | 89,269 | 47.9 |
| 2 | Sherman P. Lloyd (R) | 97,549 | 52.3 |
| | A. H. (Bob) Nance (D) | 87,000 | 46.6 |

## VERMONT

| | Candidates | Votes | % |
|---|---|---|---|
| AL | Robert T. Stafford (R) | 103,806 | 68.0 |
| | Bernard O'Shea (D) | 44,415 | 29.1 |

## VIRGINIA

| | Candidates | Votes | % |
|---|---|---|---|
| 1 | Thomas N. Downing (D) | 71,465 | 100.0 |
| 2 | G. William Whitehurst (R) | 44,108 | 61.7 |
| | Joseph T. Fitzpatrick (D) | 27,367 | 38.3 |
| 3 | David E. Satterfield III (D) | 73,123 | 65.2 |
| | J. Harvie Wilkinson III (R) | 35,258 | 31.5 |
| 4 | Watkins M. Abbitt (D) | 55,246 | 61.0 |
| | Ben Ragsdale (I) | 25,403 | 28.1 |
| | James M. Helms (R) | 9,883 | 10.9 |
| 5 | W. C. (Dan) Daniel (D) | 54,274 | 73.0 |
| | Allen T. St.Clair Jr. (R) | 20,039 | 27.0 |
| 6 | Richard H. Poff (R) | 62,350 | 74.6 |
| | Roy R. White (D) | 21,241 | 25.4 |
| 7 | J. Kenneth Robinson (R) | 52,716 | 61.8 |
| | Murat Williams (D) | 32,642 | 38.2 |
| 8 | William L. Scott (R) | 68,311 | 63.7 |
| | Darrel H. Stearns (D) | 38,848 | 36.3 |
| 9 | William C. Wampler (R) | 53,960 | 60.9 |
| | Tate C. Buchanan (D) | 34,609 | 39.1 |
| 10 | Joel T. Broyhill (R) | 67,650 | 54.5 |
| | Harold O. Miller (D) | 56,603 | 45.6 |

## WASHINGTON

| | Candidates | Votes | % |
|---|---|---|---|
| 1 | Thomas M. Pelly (R) | 107,072 | 64.4 |
| | David A. Hughes (D) | 53,156 | 32.0 |
| 2 | Lloyd Meeds (D) | 117,562 | 72.7 |
| | Edward A. McBride (R) | 44,049 | 27.3 |
| 3 | Julia Butler Hansen (D) | 81,892 | 59.2 |
| | R. C. (Skip) McConkey (R) | 56,566 | 40.9 |
| 4 | Mike McCormack (D) | 70,119 | 52.6 |
| | Catherine May (R) | 63,244 | 47.4 |
| 5 | Thomas S. Foley (D) | 88,189 | 67.0 |
| | George Gamble (R) | 43,376 | 33.0 |
| 6 | Floyd V. Hicks (D) | 98,282 | 69.4 |
| | John Jarstad (R) | 42,213 | 29.8 |
| 7 | Brock Adams (D) | 99,308 | 66.6 |
| | Brian Lewis (R) | 47,426 | 31.8 |

## WEST VIRGINIA

| | Candidates | Votes | % |
|---|---|---|---|
| 1 | Robert H. Mollohan (D) | 61,296 | 61.5 |
| | Ken Doll (R) | 38,327 | 38.5 |
| 2 | Harvey O. Staggers (D) | 56,263 | 62.7 |
| | Richard M. Reddecliff (R) | 33,509 | 37.3 |
| 3 | John Slack (D) | 57,630 | 65.4 |
| | Neal A. Kinsolving (R) | 30,525 | 34.6 |
| 4 | Ken Hechler (D) | 62,531 | 67.4 |
| | Ralph Shannon (R) | 30,255 | 32.6 |
| 5 | James Kee (D) | 48,286 | 70.4 |
| | Marian McQuade (R) | 20,261 | 29.6 |

## WISCONSIN

| | Candidates | Votes | % |
|---|---|---|---|
| 1 | Les Aspin (D) | 87,428 | 60.9 |
| | Henry C. Schadeberg (R) | 56,067 | 39.1 |
| 2 | Robert W. Kastenmeier (D) | 102,879 | 68.5 |
| | Norman Anderson (R) | 46,620 | 31.0 |
| 3 | Vernon W. Thomson (R) | 64,891 | 55.5 |
| | Ray Short (D) | 52,085 | 44.5 |
| 4 | Clement J. Zablocki (D) | 102,464 | 81.6 |
| | Phillip D. Mrozinski (R) | 23,081 | 18.4 |
| 5 | Henry S. Reuss (D) | 60,630 | 75.9 |
| | Robert J. Dwyer (R) | 18,360 | 23.0 |
| 6 | William A. Steiger (R) | 98,587 | 67.7 |
| | Franklin R. Utech (D) | 44,794 | 30.8 |
| 7 | David R. Obey (D) | 88,746 | 67.6 |
| | Andre E. Le Tendre (R) | 41,330 | 31.5 |
| 8 | John W. Byrnes (R) | 76,893 | 55.5 |
| | Robert J. Cornell (D) | 60,345 | 43.6 |
| 9 | Glenn R. Davis (R) | 84,732 | 52.0 |
| | Fred N. Tabak (D) | 78,123 | 48.0 |
| 10 | Alvin E. O'Konski (R) | 66,014 | 50.9 |
| | Walter Thoresen (D) | 62,991 | 48.6 |

## WYOMING

| | Candidates | Votes | % |
|---|---|---|---|
| AL | Teno Roncalio (D) | 58,456 | 50.3 |
| | Harry Roberts (R) | 57,848 | 49.7 |

# 1971 House Elections

## KENTUCKY

### Special Election

| | Candidates | Votes | % |
|---|---|---|---|
| 6 | William P. Curlin (D) | 29,778# | 52.6 |
| | Raymond Nutter (R) | 21,584# | 38.1 |
| | Edgar A. Wallace | 4,070# | 7.2 |

## MARYLAND

### Special Election

| | Candidates | Votes | % |
|---|---|---|---|
| 1 | William O. Mills (R) | 31,165 | 53.4 |
| | Elroy G. Boyer (D) | 27,234 | 46.6 |

## PENNSYLVANIA

### Special Election

| | | Votes | % |
|---|---|---|---|
| 18 | H. John Heinz III (R) | 103,543 | 66.6 |
| | John E. Connelly (D) | 49,269 | 31.7 |

## SOUTH CAROLINA

### Special Election

| | Candidates | Votes | % |
|---|---|---|---|
| 1 | Mendel J. Davis (D) | 38,012 | 48.6 |
| | James B. Edwards (R) | 32,227 | 41.2 |
| | Victoria DeLee (I) | 7,965 | 10.2 |

*1970 Elections*

  [1] *These two California special elections were held to fill unexpired terms in the 91st Congress (1969-71).*

  *The returns for special House elections in the 24th and 35th Districts are from elections held after no candidate received a majority of the vote in the initial special primary elections. (California special primary law, see p. 1258)*

  *Special Primary Election returns, 24th District: John H. Rousselot (R), 37,348, 29.0; Bill McColl (R), 35,682, 27.7; Myrlie B. Evers (D), 23,688, 18.4; Patrick J. Hillings (R), 22,394, 17.4; Jack Alex (R), 8,230, 6.4. Rousselot, the top Republican, and Evers, the top Democrat, thus qualified to meet in the special election. Source: California Secretary of State.*

  *Special Primary Election returns, 35th District: Congressional Quarterly was unable to obtain complete official returns. Seven candidates competed for the seat, five Republicans and two Democrats. Schmitz, the Republican receiving the highest number of votes, and Hartman, the top Democrat, qualified to meet in the special election.*

# 1972 House Elections

## ALABAMA

| | Candidates | Votes | % |
|---|---|---|---|
| 1 | Jack Edwards (R) | 104,606 | 76.5 |
| | O. W. McCrory (D) | 24,357 | 17.8 |
| | Thomas McAboy Jr. (NDPA) | 7,747 | 5.7 |
| 2 | William L. Dickinson (R) | 80,362 | 54.9 |
| | Ben C. Reeves (D) | 60,769 | 41.5 |
| 3 | Bill Nichols (D) | 100,045 | 75.6 |
| | Robert M. Kerr (R) | 27,253 | 20.6 |
| 4 | Tom Bevill (D) | 108,039 | 69.6 |
| | Ed Nelson (R) | 46,551 | 30.0 |
| 5 | Robert E. Jones (D) | 101,303 | 74.2 |
| | Digter J. Schrader (R) | 33,352 | 24.4 |
| 6 | John H. Buchanan Jr. (R) | 91,499 | 59.8 |
| | Ben Erdroich (D) | 54,497 | 35.0 |
| 7 | Walter Flowers (D) | 95,060 | 84.8 |
| | Lewis Black (NDPA) | 15,703 | 14.0 |

**Special Election**

| | | |
|---|---|---|
| 3 | Elizabeth Andrews (D) | ✔ |

## ALASKA

| | | Votes | % |
|---|---|---|---|
| AL | Nick Begich (D) | 53,651* | 56.2 |
| | Don Young (R) | 41,750 | 43.8 |

## ARIZONA

| | | Votes | % |
|---|---|---|---|
| 1 | John J. Rhodes (R) | 80,453 | 57.3 |
| | Gerald A. Pollock (D) | 59,900 | 42.7 |
| 2 | Morris K. Udall (D) | 97,616 | 63.5 |
| | Gene Savoie (R) | 56,188 | 36.5 |
| 3 | Sam Steiger (R) | 90,710 | 63.0 |
| | Ted Wyckoff (D) | 53,220 | 37.0 |
| 4 | John B. Conlan (R) | 82,511 | 53.0 |
| | Jack E. Brown (D) | 73,309 | 47.1 |

## ARKANSAS

| | | Votes | % |
|---|---|---|---|
| 1 | Bill Alexander (D) | ✔ | |
| 2 | Wilbur D. Mills (D) | ✔ | |
| 3 | John Paul Hammerschmidt (R) | 144,571 | 77.3 |
| | Guy W. Hatfield (D) | 42,481 | 22.7 |
| 4 | Ray Thornton (D) | ✔ | |

## CALIFORNIA

| | | Votes | % |
|---|---|---|---|
| 1 | Don H. Clausen (R) | 141,226 | 62.3 |
| | William A. Nighswonger (D) | 77,610 | 34.2 |
| 2 | Harold T. Johnson (D) | 149,590 | 68.4 |
| | Frances X. Callahan (R) | 62,727 | 28.7 |
| 3 | John E. Moss (D) | 151,706 | 69.9 |
| | John Rakus (R) | 65,298 | 30.1 |
| 4 | Robert L. Leggett (D) | 115,038 | 67.4 |
| | Benjamin Chang (R) | 55,540 | 32.6 |
| 5 | Phillip Burton (D) | 124,164 | 81.8 |
| | Edlo E. Powell (R) | 27,474 | 18.1 |
| 6 | William S. Mailliard (R) | 119,704 | 52.1 |
| | Roger Boas (D) | 110,144 | 47.9 |
| 7 | Ronald V. Dellums (D) | 126,913 | 55.9 |
| | Peter Hannaford (R) | 86,587 | 38.1 |
| | Frank V. Cortese (AM I) | 13,550 | 6.0 |
| 8 | Fortney H. (Pete) Stark Jr. (D) | 102,153 | 52.9 |
| | Lew M. Warden Jr. (R) | 90,970 | 47.1 |
| 9 | Don Edwards (D) | 123,994 | 72.3 |
| | Herb Smith (R) | 43,140 | 25.2 |
| 10 | Charles S. Gubser (R) | 140,342 | 64.6 |
| | B. Frank Gillette (D) | 76,839 | 35.4 |
| 11 | Leo J. Ryan (D) | 114,134 | 60.5 |
| | Charles E. Chase (R) | 69,632 | 36.9 |
| 12 | Burt L. Talcott (R) | 105,556 | 51.4 |
| | Julian Camacho (D) | 84,174 | 41.0 |
| 13 | Charles M. Teague (R) | 153,877 | 73.9 |
| | Lester D. Cleveland (D) | 54,299 | 26.1 |
| 14 | Jerome R. Waldie (D) | 159,335 | 77.6 |
| | Floyd E. Sims (R) | 46,082 | 22.4 |
| 15 | John J. McFall (D) | 146,358 | 100.0 |
| 16 | B. F. Sisk (D) | 134,132 | 79.1 |
| | Carol O. Harner (R) | 35,385 | 20.9 |
| 17 | Paul N. McCloskey Jr. (R) | 110,988 | 54.5 |
| | James Stewart (D) | 73,123 | 35.9 |
| | James Gordon Knapp (WRITE IN) | 19,377 | 9.5 |
| 18 | Bob Mathias (R) | 110,153 | 66.4 |
| | Vincent J. Lavery (D) | 55,829 | 33.6 |
| 19 | Chet Holifield (D) | 105,699 | 67.2 |
| | Kenneth M. Fisher (R) | 43,792 | 27.9 |
| 20 | Carlos J. Moorhead (R) | 122,309 | 57.4 |
| | John Binkley (D) | 90,842 | 42.6 |
| 21 | Augustus F. Hawkins (D) | 95,050 | 82.9 |
| | Rayfield Lundy (R) | 19,569 | 17.1 |
| 22 | James C. Corman (D) | 123,863 | 67.6 |
| | Bruce P. Wolfe (R) | 53,603 | 29.3 |
| 23 | Del Clawson (R) | 120,313 | 61.4 |
| | Conrad G. Tuohey (D) | 75,546 | 38.6 |
| 24 | John H. Rousselot (R) | 144,057 | 70.1 |
| | Luther Mandell (D) | 61,326 | 29.9 |
| 25 | Charles E. Wiggins (R) | 118,631 | 65.0 |
| | Leslie W. Craven (D) | 58,323 | 31.9 |
| 26 | Thomas M. Rees (D) | 164,351 | 68.7 |
| | Philip Robert Rutta (R) | 66,731 | 27.9 |
| 27 | Barry Goldwater Jr. (R) | 119,475 | 57.4 |
| | Mark S. Novak (D) | 88,548 | 42.6 |
| 28 | Alphonzo Bell (R) | 144,815 | 60.7 |
| | Michael Shapiro (D) | 89,517 | 37.5 |
| 29 | George E. Danielson (D) | 92,856 | 62.7 |
| | Richard E. Ferraro (R) | 49,590 | 33.5 |
| 30 | Edward R. Roybal (D) | 78,193 | 68.4 |
| | Bill Brophy (R) | 32,717 | 28.6 |
| 31 | Charles H. Wilson (D) | 87,975 | 52.3 |
| | Ben Valentine (R) | 71,395 | 42.5 |
| | Roberta Lynn Wood (PFP) | 8,788 | 5.2 |
| 32 | Craig Hosmer (R) | 149,514 | 65.9 |
| | Dennis Murray (D) | 72,481 | 32.0 |
| 33 | Jerry L. Pettis (R) | 140,868 | 75.0 |
| | Ken Thompson (D) | 46,911 | 25.0 |
| 34 | Richard T. Hanna (D) | 115,880 | 67.1 |
| | John D. Ratterree (R) | 49,971 | 29.0 |
| 35 | Glenn M. Anderson (D) | 105,667 | 74.8 |
| | Vernon E. Brown (R) | 35,614 | 25.2 |
| 36 | William M. Ketchum (R) | 88,071 | 52.7 |
| | Timothy Lemucchi (D) | 72,623 | 43.5 |
| 37 | Yvonne Brathwaite Burke (D) | 123,468 | 60.2 |
| | Gregg Tria (R) | 41,562 | 20.3 |
| 38 | George E. Brown Jr. (D) | 77,922 | 55.9 |
| | Howard J. Snider (R) | 60,459 | 43.4 |
| 39 | Andrew J. Hinshaw (R) | 149,081 | 65.7 |
| | John W. Black (D) | 77,817 | 34.3 |
| 40 | Bob Wilson (R) | 155,269 | 67.8 |
| | Frank Caprio (D) | 69,377 | 30.3 |
| 41 | Lionel Van Deerlin (D) | 116,980 | 74.1 |
| | D. Richard Kau (R) | 40,997 | 26.0 |
| 42 | Clair W. Burgener (R) | 158,475 | 67.5 |
| | Bob Lowe (D) | 68,381 | 29.1 |
| 43 | Victor V. Veysey (R) | 118,536 | 62.7 |
| | Ernest Z. Robles (D) | 70,455 | 37.3 |

## COLORADO

| | | Votes | % |
|---|---|---|---|
| 1 | Patricia Schroeder (D) | 101,832 | 52.0 |
| | James D. McKevitt (R) | 93,733 | 47.9 |
| 2 | Donald G. Brotzman (R) | 132,562 | 66.3 |
| | Francis W. Brush (D) | 66,817 | 33.4 |
| 3 | Frank E. Evans (D) | 107,511 | 66.3 |
| | Chuck Brady (R) | 54,556 | 33.7 |
| 4 | James P. Johnson (R) | 94,994 | 51.0 |
| | Alan Merson (D) | 91,151 | 49.0 |
| 5 | William L. Armstrong (R) | 104,214 | 62.3 |
| | Byron L. Johnson (D) | 60,948 | 36.5 |

## CONNECTICUT

| | Candidates | Votes | % |
|---|---|---|---|
| 1 | William R. Cotter (D) | 130,701 | 56.9 |
| | Richard M. Rittenband (R) | 96,188 | 41.9 |
| 2 | Robert H. Steele (R) | 142,094 | 65.9 |
| | Roger Hilsman (D) | 73,400 | 34.1 |
| 3 | Robert N. Giaimo (D) | 121,217 | 53.3 |
| | Henry A. Povinelli (R) | 106,313 | 46.7 |
| 4 | Stewart B. McKinney (R) | 135,883 | 63.1 |
| | James P. McLoughlin (D) | 79,515 | 36.9 |
| 5 | Ronald A. Sarasin (R) | 117,578 | 51.2 |
| | John S. Monagan (D) | 112,142 | 48.8 |
| 6 | Ella T. Grasso (D) | 140,290 | 60.2 |
| | John F. Walsh (R) | 92,783 | 39.8 |

## DELAWARE

| | | Votes | % |
|---|---|---|---|
| AL | Pierre S. duPont IV (R) | 141,237 | 62.5 |
| | Norma Handloff (D) | 83,230 | 36.9 |

## FLORIDA

| | | Votes | % |
|---|---|---|---|
| 1 | Robert L. F. Sikes (D) | ✔ | |
| 2 | Don Fuqua (D) | ✔ | |
| 3 | Charles E. Bennett (D) | 101,441 | 82.0 |
| | John F. Bowen (R) | 22,219 | 18.0 |
| 4 | Bill Chappell (D) | 92,541 | 55.9 |
| | P. T. Fleuchaus (R) | 72,960 | 44.1 |
| 5 | William D. Gunter Jr. (D) | 97,902 | 55.5 |
| | Jack P. Insco (R) | 78,463 | 44.5 |
| 6 | C. W. Bill Young (R) | 156,150 | 76.0 |
| | Michael O. Plunkett (D) | 49,399 | 24.0 |
| 7 | Sam Gibbons (D) | 91,931 | 68.0 |
| | Robert A. Carter (R) | 43,343 | 32.0 |
| 8 | James A. Haley (D) | 89,068 | 57.8 |
| | Roy Thompson Jr. (R) | 64,920 | 42.2 |
| 9 | Louis Frey Jr. (R) | ✔ | |
| 10 | L. A. (Skip) Bafalis (R) | 113,461 | 62.0 |
| | Bill Sikes (D) | 69,502 | 38.0 |
| 11 | Paul G. Rogers (D) | 116,157 | 60.2 |
| | Joel Karl Gustafson (R) | 76,739 | 39.8 |
| 12 | J. Herbert Burke (R) | 110,750 | 62.8 |
| | James T. Stephanis (D) | 65,526 | 37.2 |
| 13 | William Lehman (D) | 92,258 | 61.6 |
| | Paul D. Bethel (R) | 57,418 | 38.4 |
| 14 | Claude Pepper (D) | 75,131 | 67.7 |
| | Evelio S. Estrella (R) | 35,935 | 32.4 |
| 15 | Dante B. Fascell (D) | 89,961 | 56.8 |
| | Ellis S. Rubin (R) | 68,320 | 43.2 |

## GEORGIA

| | | Votes | % |
|---|---|---|---|
| 1 | Ronald B. (Bo) Ginn (D) | 55,256 | 100.0 |
| 2 | Dawson Mathis (D) | 65,997 | 100.0 |
| 3 | Jack Brinkley (D) | 71,756 | 100.0 |
| 4 | Ben B. Blackburn (R) | 103,155 | 75.9 |
| | F. Odell Welborn (D) | 32,731 | 24.1 |
| 5 | Andrew Young (D) | 72,289 | 52.8 |
| | Rodney M. Cook (R) | 64,495 | 47.1 |
| 6 | John J. Flynt Jr. (D) | 70,586 | 100.0 |
| 7 | John W. Davis (D) | 59,031 | 58.3 |
| | Charles B. Sherrill (R) | 42,265 | 41.7 |
| 8 | W. S. Stuckey Jr. (D) | 71,283 | 62.4 |
| | Ronnie Thompson (R) | 42,986 | 37.6 |
| 9 | Phil M. Landrum (D) | 71,801 | 100.0 |
| 10 | Robert G. Stephens Jr. (D) | 68,096 | 100.0 |

## HAWAII

| | | Votes | % |
|---|---|---|---|
| 1 | Spark M. Matsunaga (D) | 73,826 | 54.7 |
| | Fred W. Rohlfing (R) | 61,138 | 45.3 |
| 2 | Patsy T. Mink (D) | 79,856 | 57.1 |
| | Diana Hansen (R) | 60,043 | 42.9 |

## IDAHO

| | Candidates | Votes | % |
|---|---|---|---|
| 1 | Steven D. Symms (R) | 85,270 | 55.6 |
| | Edward Williams (D) | 68,106 | 44.4 |
| 2 | Orval Hansen (R) | 102,537 | 69.2 |
| | Willis H. Ludlow (D) | 40,081 | 27.1 |

## ILLINOIS

| | | Votes | % |
|---|---|---|---|
| 1 | Ralph H. Metcalfe (D) | 136,755 | 91.4 |
| | Louis H. Coggs (R) | 12,877 | 8.6 |
| 2 | Morgan F. Murphy (D) | 115,306 | 75.0 |
| | James E. Doyle (R) | 38,391 | 25.0 |
| 3 | Robert P. Hanrahan (R) | 128,329 | 62.3 |
| | Daniel P. Coman (D) | 77,814 | 37.8 |
| 4 | Edward J. Derwinski (R) | 141,402 | 70.5 |
| | C. F. Dore (D) | 59,057 | 29.5 |
| 5 | John C. Kluczynski (D) | 121,278 | 72.8 |
| | Leonard C. Jarzab (R) | 45,264 | 27.2 |
| 6 | Harold R. Collier (R) | 124,486 | 61.2 |
| | Michael R. Galasso (D) | 79,002 | 38.8 |
| 7 | George W. Collins (D) | 95,018* | 82.8 |
| | Thomas J. Lento (R) | 19,758 | 17.2 |
| 8 | Daniel D. Rostenkowski (D) | 110,457 | 74.0 |
| | Edward L. Stepnowski (R) | 38,758 | 26.0 |
| 9 | Sidney R. Yates (D) | 131,777 | 68.3 |
| | Clark W. Fetridge (R) | 61,083 | 31.7 |
| 10 | Samuel H. Young (R) | 120,681 | 51.6 |
| | Abner J. Mikva (D) | 113,222 | 48.4 |
| 11 | Frank Annunzio (D) | 118,637 | 53.3 |
| | John J. Hoellen (R) | 103,773 | 46.7 |
| 12 | Philip M. Crane (R) | 152,938 | 74.2 |
| | E. L. Frank (D) | 53,055 | 25.8 |
| 13 | Robert McClory (R) | 98,201 | 61.5 |
| | Stanley W. Beetham (D) | 61,537 | 38.5 |
| 14 | John N. Erlenborn (R) | 154,794 | 72.8 |
| | James M. Wall (D) | 57,874 | 27.2 |
| 15 | Leslie C. Arends (R) | 111,022 | 57.2 |
| | Tim L. Hall (D) | 82,925 | 42.8 |
| 16 | John B. Anderson (R) | 129,640 | 71.9 |
| | John E. Devine Jr. (D) | 50,649 | 28.1 |
| 17 | George M. O'Brien (R) | 100,175 | 55.7 |
| | John J. Houlihan (D) | 79,840 | 44.4 |
| 18 | Robert H. Michel (R) | 124,407 | 64.8 |
| | Stephen L. Nordvall (D) | 67,514 | 35.2 |
| 19 | Thomas F. Railsback (R) | 138,123 | 100.0 |
| 20 | Paul Findley (R) | 148,419 | 68.8 |
| | Robert S. O'Shea (D) | 67,445 | 31.2 |
| 21 | Edward R. Madigan (R) | 99,966 | 54.8 |
| | Lawrence E. Johnson (D) | 82,523 | 45.2 |
| 22 | George E. Shipley (D) | 124,589 | 56.5 |
| | Robert B. Lamkin (R) | 90,390 | 41.0 |
| 23 | Melvin Price (D) | 121,682 | 75.1 |
| | Robert Mays (R) | 40,428 | 24.9 |
| 24 | Kenneth J. Gray (D) | 138,867 | 93.7 |
| | Hugh Muldoon (I) | 9,398 | 6.3 |

### Special Election

| | | Votes | % |
|---|---|---|---|
| 15 | Clifford D. Carlson (R) | 31,543 | 54.8 |
| | Tim L. Hall (D) | 26,030 | 45.2 |

## INDIANA

| | | Votes | % |
|---|---|---|---|
| 1 | Ray J. Madden (D) | 95,873 | 56.9 |
| | Bruce R. Haller (R) | 72,662 | 43.1 |
| 2 | Earl F. Landgrebe (R) | 110,406 | 54.7 |
| | Floyd Fithian (D) | 91,533 | 45.3 |
| 3 | John Brademas (D) | 103,949 | 55.2 |
| | Don M. Newman (R) | 81,369 | 43.2 |
| 4 | J. Edward Roush (D) | 100,327 | 51.5 |
| | Allan Bloom (R) | 94,492 | 48.5 |
| 5 | Elwood Hillis (R) | 124,692 | 64.1 |
| | Kathleen Z. Williams (D) | 69,746 | 35.9 |
| 6 | William G. Bray (R) | 112,525 | 64.8 |
| | David W. Evans (D) | 61,070 | 35.2 |
| 7 | John T. Myers (R) | 128,688 | 61.6 |
| | Warren Henegar (D) | 80,145 | 38.4 |

| | Candidates | Votes | % |
|---|---|---|---|
| 8 | Roger H. Zion (R) | 133,850 | 63.3 |
| | Richard L. Deen (D) | 77,371 | 36.6 |
| 9 | Lee Hamilton (D) | 122,698 | 62.9 |
| | William A. Johnson (R) | 72,325 | 37.1 |
| 10 | David W. Dennis (R) | 106,798 | 57.3 |
| | Philip R. Sharp (D) | 79,756 | 42.8 |
| 11 | William H. Hudnut III (R) | 95,839 | 51.2 |
| | Andrew Jacobs Jr. (D) | 91,238 | 48.8 |

## IOWA

| | | Votes | % |
|---|---|---|---|
| 1 | Edward Mezvinsky (D) | 107,099 | 53.4 |
| | Fred Schwengel (R) | 91,609 | 45.7 |
| 2 | John C. Culver (D) | 115,489 | 59.2 |
| | Theodore R. Ellsworth (R) | 79,667 | 40.8 |
| 3 | H. R. Gross (R) | 109,113 | 55.7 |
| | Lyle Taylor (D) | 86,848 | 44.3 |
| 4 | Neal Smith (D) | 125,431 | 59.6 |
| | John Kyl (R) | 85,156 | 40.4 |
| 5 | William J. Scherle (R) | 108,596 | 55.3 |
| | Tom Harkin (D) | 87,937 | 44.7 |
| 6 | Wiley Mayne (R) | 103,284 | 52.5 |
| | Berkley Bedell (D) | 93,574 | 47.5 |

## KANSAS

| | | Votes | % |
|---|---|---|---|
| 1 | Keith G. Sebelius (R) | 145,712 | 77.2 |
| | Morris Coover (D) | 40,678 | 21.6 |
| 2 | William R. Roy (D) | 106,276 | 60.6 |
| | Charles D. McAtee (R) | 65,071 | 37.1 |
| 3 | Larry Winn Jr. (R) | 122,358 | 71.0 |
| | Charles Barsotti (D) | 43,777 | 25.4 |
| 4 | Garner E. Shriver (R) | 120,120 | 73.2 |
| | John S. Stevens (D) | 40,753 | 24.8 |
| 5 | Joe Skubitz (R) | 128,639 | 72.3 |
| | Lloyd L. Kitch (D) | 49,169 | 27.7 |

## KENTUCKY

| | | Votes | % |
|---|---|---|---|
| 1 | Frank A. Stubblefield (D) | 81,456 | 64.8 |
| | Charles T. Banken (R) | 42,286 | 33.7 |
| 2 | William H. Natcher (D) | 75,871 | 61.5 |
| | J. C. Carter (R) | 47,436 | 38.5 |
| 3 | Romano L. Mazzoli (D) | 86,810 | 62.2 |
| | Phil Kaelin Jr. (R) | 51,634 | 37.0 |
| 4 | M. G. (Gene) Snyder (R) | 110,902 | 73.8 |
| | James W. Rogers (D) | 39,332 | 26.2 |
| 5 | Tim Lee Carter (R) | 109,264 | 73.6 |
| | Lyle L. Willis (D) | 39,301 | 26.5 |
| 6 | John Breckinridge (D) | 76,185 | 52.4 |
| | Laban P. Jackson (R) | 68,012 | 46.8 |
| 7 | Carl D. Perkins (D) | 94,840 | 61.9 |
| | Robert Holcomb (R) | 58,286 | 38.1 |

## LOUISIANA

| | | Votes | % |
|---|---|---|---|
| 1 | F. Edward Hebert (D) | 78,156 | 100.0 |
| 2 | Hale Boggs (D) | 68,093* | 100.0 |
| 3 | David C. Treen (R) | 71,090 | 54.0 |
| | J. Louis Watkins Jr. (D) | 60,521 | 46.0 |
| 4 | Joe D. Waggonner Jr. (D) | 74,397 | 100.0 |
| 5 | Otto E. Passman (D) | 64,027 | 100.0 |
| 6 | John R. Rarick (D) | 84,275 | 100.0 |
| 7 | John B. Breaux (D) | 71,901 | 100.0 |
| 8 | Gillis W. Long (D) | 72,607 | 68.5 |
| | R. S. Abramson (AM) | 17,844 | 16.8 |
| | Roy C. Strickland (R) | 15,517 | 14.6 |

### Special Election

| | | Votes | % |
|---|---|---|---|
| 7 | John B. Breaux (D) | ✔ | |

## MAINE

| | | Votes | % |
|---|---|---|---|
| 1 | Peter N. Kyros (D) | 129,408 | 59.4 |
| | L. Robert Porteous Jr. (R) | 88,588 | 40.6 |
| 2 | William S. Cohen (R) | 106,280 | 54.4 |
| | Elmer H. Violette (D) | 89,135 | 45.6 |

## MARYLAND

| | Candidates | Votes | % |
|---|---|---|---|
| 1 | William O. Mills (R) | 86,326 | 70.5 |
| | John R. Hargreaves (D) | 36,139 | 29.5 |
| 2 | Clarence D. Long (D) | 123,346 | 65.8 |
| | John J. Bishop Jr. (R) | 64,119 | 34.2 |
| 3 | Paul S. Sarbanes (D) | 93,093 | 69.7 |
| | Robert D. Morrow (R) | 40,442 | 30.3 |
| 4 | Marjorie S. Holt (R) | 87,534 | 59.4 |
| | Werner Fornos (D) | 59,877 | 40.6 |
| 5 | Lawrence J. Hogan (R) | 90,016 | 62.9 |
| | Edward T. Conroy (D) | 53,049 | 37.1 |
| 6 | Goodloe E. Byron (D) | 107,283 | 64.8 |
| | Edward J. Mason (R) | 58,259 | 35.2 |
| 7 | Parren J. Mitchell (D) | 83,749 | 80.1 |
| | Verdell Adair (R) | 20,876 | 20.0 |
| 8 | Gilbert Gude (R) | 137,287 | 63.9 |
| | Joseph G. Anastasi (D) | 77,551 | 36.1 |

## MASSACHUSETTS

| | | Votes | % |
|---|---|---|---|
| 1 | Silvio O. Conte (R) | 159,282 | 99.9 |
| 2 | Edward P. Boland (D) | 137,616 | 100.0 |
| 3 | Harold D. Donohue (D) | 156,703 | 99.9 |
| 4 | Robert F. Drinan (D) | 101,714 | 49.5 |
| | Martin A. Linsky (R) | 92,250 | 44.9 |
| | John T. Collins (IC) | 11,141 | 5.4 |
| 5 | Paul W. Cronin (R) | 110,970 | 53.5 |
| | John F. Kerry (D) | 92,847 | 44.7 |
| 6 | Michael J. Harrington (D) | 139,697 | 64.1 |
| | James Brady Moseley (R) | 78,381 | 35.9 |
| 7 | Torbert H. Macdonald (D) | 135,193 | 67.7 |
| | Joan M. Aliberti (R) | 64,357 | 32.3 |
| 8 | Thomas P. O'Neill Jr. (D) | 142,470 | 88.7 |
| | John E. Powers Jr. (SOC WORK) | 18,169 | 11.3 |
| 9 | John Joseph Moakley (I) | 70,571 | 43.2 |
| | Louise Day Hicks (D) | 67,143 | 41.1 |
| | Howard M. Miller (R) | 23,177 | 14.2 |
| 10 | Margaret M. Heckler (R) | 161,708 | 100.0 |
| 11 | James A. Burke (D) | 154,397 | 100.0 |
| 12 | Gerry E. Studds (D) | 117,710 | 50.2 |
| | William D. Weeks (R) | 116,592 | 49.8 |

## MICHIGAN

| | | Votes | % |
|---|---|---|---|
| 1 | John Conyers Jr. (D) | 131,353 | 88.4 |
| | Walter F. Girardot (R) | 16,096 | 10.8 |
| 2 | Marvin L. Esch (R) | 103,321 | 56.0 |
| | Marvin R. Stempien (D) | 79,762 | 43.3 |
| 3 | Garry Brown (R) | 110,082 | 59.2 |
| | James T. Brignall (D) | 74,114 | 39.9 |
| 4 | Edward Hutchinson (R) | 111,185 | 67.3 |
| | Charles W. Jameson (D) | 54,141 | 32.8 |
| 5 | Gerald Ford (R) | 118,027 | 61.1 |
| | Jean McKee (D) | 72,782 | 37.7 |
| 6 | Charles E. Chamberlain (R) | 97,666 | 50.6 |
| | Bob Carr (D) | 95,209 | 49.4 |
| 7 | Donald W. Riegle Jr. (R) | 114,656 | 71.4 |
| | Eugene L. Mattison (D) | 48,883 | 30.5 |
| 8 | James Harvey (R) | 100,597 | 59.3 |
| | Jerome Hart (D) | 66,873 | 39.4 |
| 9 | Guy A. Vander Jagt (R) | 132,268 | 69.4 |
| | Larry H. Olson (D) | 56,236 | 29.5 |
| 10 | Elford A. Cederberg (R) | 121,368 | 66.7 |
| | Bennie D. Graves (D) | 56,149 | 30.9 |
| 11 | Philip E. Ruppe (R) | 135,786 | 69.4 |
| | James Edward McNamara (D) | 58,334 | 29.8 |
| 12 | James G. O'Hara (D) | 83,351 | 50.7 |
| | David M. Serotkin (R) | 80,667 | 49.0 |
| 13 | Charles C. Diggs Jr. (D) | 97,562 | 85.6 |
| | Leonard T. Edwards (R) | 15,180 | 13.3 |
| 14 | Lucien N. Nedzi (D) | 93,923 | 54.9 |
| | Robert V. McGrath (R) | 77,273 | 45.1 |
| 15 | William D. Ford (D) | 97,054 | 65.8 |
| | Ernest D. Fackler (R) | 48,504 | 32.9 |
| 16 | John D. Dingell Jr. (D) | 110,715 | 68.1 |
| | William E. Rostron (R) | 48,414 | 29.8 |
| 17 | Martha W. Griffiths (D) | 123,331 | 66.4 |
| | Ralph E. Judd (R) | 60,337 | 32.5 |

## MICHIGAN

| | Candidates | Votes | % |
|---|---|---|---|
| 18 | Robert J. Huber (R) | 95,053 | 52.6 |
| | Daniel S. Cooper (D) | 85,580 | 47.4 |
| 19 | William S. Broomfield (R) | 123,697 | 70.4 |
| | George F. Montgomery (D) | 50,355 | 28.6 |

## MINNESOTA

| | | | |
|---|---|---|---|
| 1 | Albert H. Quie (R) | 142,698 | 70.7 |
| | Charles S. Thompson (DFL) | 59,106 | 29.3 |
| 2 | Ancher Nelsen (R) | 124,350 | 57.1 |
| | Charles V. Turnbull (DFL) | 93,433 | 42.9 |
| 3 | Bill Frenzel (R) | 132,638 | 62.9 |
| | Jim Bell (DFL) | 66,070 | 31.3 |
| | Donald Wright (MINN TAX) | 12,234 | 5.8 |
| 4 | Joseph E. Karth (DFL) | 138,292 | 72.4 |
| | Steve Thompson (R) | 52,786 | 27.6 |
| 5 | Donald M. Fraser (DFL) | 135,108 | 65.8 |
| | Allan Davisson (R) | 50,014 | 24.4 |
| | Norm Selby (MINN TAX) | 15,845 | 7.7 |
| 6 | John M. Zwach (R) | 114,537 | 51.0 |
| | Richard M. Nolan (DFL) | 109,955 | 49.0 |
| 7 | Bob Bergland (DFL) | 133,067 | 59.1 |
| | Jon O. Haaven (R) | 92,283 | 41.0 |
| 8 | John A. Blatnik (DFL) | 161,823 | 75.9 |
| | Edward Johnson (R) | 51,314 | 24.1 |

## MISSISSIPPI

| | | | |
|---|---|---|---|
| 1 | Jamie L. Whitten (D) | 87,526 | 100.0 |
| 2 | David R. Bowen (D) | 69,892 | 61.9 |
| | Carl Butler (R) | 39,117 | 34.7 |
| 3 | G. V. (Sonny) Montgomery (D) | 105,722 | 100.0 |
| 4 | Thad Cochran (R) | 67,655 | 47.9 |
| | Ellis B. Bodron (D) | 62,148 | 44.0 |
| | Eddie L. McBride (I) | 11,571 | 8.2 |
| 5 | Trent Lott (R) | 77,826 | 55.4 |
| | Ben Stone (D) | 62,101 | 44.2 |

## MISSOURI

| | | | |
|---|---|---|---|
| 1 | William Clay (D) | 95,098 | 64.0 |
| | Richard O. Funsch (R) | 53,596 | 36.0 |
| 2 | James W. Symington (D) | 134,332 | 63.5 |
| | John W. Cooper Jr. (R) | 77,192 | 36.5 |
| 3 | Leonor K. Sullivan (D) | 124,365 | 69.3 |
| | Albert Holst (R) | 54,523 | 30.4 |
| 4 | William J. Randall (D) | 108,131 | 57.4 |
| | Raymond E. Barrows (R) | 80,228 | 42.6 |
| 5 | Richard Bolling (D) | 93,812 | 62.8 |
| | Vernon E. Rice (R) | 53,257 | 35.6 |
| 6 | Jerry Litton (D) | 110,047 | 52.2 |
| | Russell Sloan (R) | 91,610 | 43.5 |
| 7 | Gene Taylor (R) | 132,780 | 63.7 |
| | William Thomas (D) | 75,613 | 36.3 |
| 8 | Richard Ichord (D) | 112,556 | 62.1 |
| | David R. Countie (R) | 68,580 | 37.9 |
| 9 | William L. Hungate (D) | 132,150 | 66.5 |
| | Robert L. Prange (R) | 66,528 | 33.5 |
| 10 | Bill D. Burlison (D) | 106,301 | 64.3 |
| | M. Francis Svendrowski (R) | 59,083 | 35.7 |

## MONTANA

| | | | |
|---|---|---|---|
| 1 | Richard G. Shoup (R) | 88,373 | 53.7 |
| | Arnold Olsen (D) | 76,073 | 46.3 |
| 2 | John Melcher (D) | 114,524 | 76.1 |
| | Richard L. Forester (R) | 36,063 | 24.0 |

## NEBRASKA

| | | | |
|---|---|---|---|
| 1 | Charles Thone (R) | 126,789 | 64.2 |
| | Darrel E. Berg (D) | 70,570 | 35.8 |
| 2 | John Y. McCollister (R) | 114,669 | 63.9 |
| | Patrick L. Cooney (D) | 64,696 | 36.1 |
| 3 | Dave Martin (R) | 133,607 | 69.6 |
| | Warren Fitzgerald (D) | 58,378 | 30.4 |

## NEVADA

| | Candidates | Votes | % |
|---|---|---|---|
| AL | David Towell (R) | 94,113 | 52.2 |
| | James H. Bilbray (D) | 86,349 | 47.9 |

## NEW HAMPSHIRE

| | | | |
|---|---|---|---|
| 1 | Louis C. Wyman (R) | 115,732 | 72.9 |
| | Chester E. Merrow (D) | 42,996 | 27.1 |
| 2 | James C. Cleveland (R) | 107,021 | 67.6 |
| | Charles B. Officer (D) | 51,259 | 32.4 |

## NEW JERSEY

| | | | |
|---|---|---|---|
| 1 | John E. Hunt (R) | 97,650 | 52.5 |
| | James J. Florio (D) | 87,492 | 47.0 |
| 2 | Charles W. Sandman Jr. (R) | 133,096 | 65.7 |
| | John D. Rose (D) | 69,374 | 34.3 |
| 3 | James J. Howard (D) | 103,893 | 53.0 |
| | William F. Dowd (R) | 92,285 | 47.0 |
| 4 | Frank Thompson Jr (D) | 98,206 | 58.0 |
| | Peter P. Garibaldi (R) | 71,030 | 42.0 |
| 5 | Peter H. B. Frelinghuysen Jr. (R) | 127,310 | 62.0 |
| | Frederick M. Bohen (D) | 78,076 | 38.0 |
| 6 | Edwin B. Forsythe (R) | 123,610 | 62.8 |
| | Francis P. Brennen (D) | 71,113 | 36.1 |
| 7 | William B. Widnall (R) | 124,365 | 57.9 |
| | Arthur J. Lesemann (D) | 85,712 | 39.9 |
| 8 | Robert A. Roe (D) | 104,381 | 63.1 |
| | Walter E. Johnson (R) | 61,073 | 36.9 |
| 9 | Henry Helstoski (D) | 119,543 | 55.8 |
| | Alfred D. Schiaffo (R) | 94,747 | 44.2 |
| 10 | Peter W. Rodino Jr. (D) | 94,308 | 79.8 |
| | Kenneth C. Miller (R) | 23,949 | 20.3 |
| 11 | Joseph G. Minish (D) | 120,227 | 57.5 |
| | Milton A. Waldor (R) | 82,957 | 39.7 |
| 12 | Matthew J. Rinaldo (R) | 127,690 | 63.5 |
| | Jerry Fitzgerald English (D) | 72,758 | 36.2 |
| 13 | Joseph J. Maraziti (R) | 109,640 | 55.7 |
| | Helen S. Meyner (D) | 84,492 | 42.9 |
| 14 | Dominick V. Daniels (D) | 103,089 | 61.2 |
| | Richard T. Bozzone (R) | 57,683 | 34.3 |
| 15 | Edward J. Patten (D) | 98,155 | 52.3 |
| | Fuller H. Brooks (R) | 89,400 | 47.7 |

## NEW MEXICO

| | | | |
|---|---|---|---|
| 1 | Manuel Lujan Jr. (R) | 118,403 | 55.7 |
| | Eugene Gallegos (D) | 94,239 | 44.3 |
| 2 | Harold Runnels (D) | 116,152 | 72.2 |
| | George E. Presson (R) | 44,784 | 27.8 |

## NEW YORK

| | | | |
|---|---|---|---|
| 1 | Otis G. Pike (D) | 102,628 | 52.5 |
| | Joseph H. Boyd (R) | 72,133 | 36.9 |
| | Robert D. L. Gardiner (C) | 18,627 | 9.5 |
| 2 | James R. Grover Jr. (R) | 99,348 | 65.8 |
| | Fern Coste Dennison (D) | 49,454 | 32.8 |
| 3 | Angelo D. Roncallo (R) | 103,620 | 57.0 |
| | Carter F. Bales (D) | 73,429 | 40.4 |
| | Lawrence P. Russo (C) | 14,768 | 8.1 |
| 4 | Norman F. Lent (R) | 125,422 | 62.4 |
| | Elaine B. Horowitz (D) | 72,280 | 36.0 |
| 5 | John W. Wydler (R) | 133,332 | 62.4 |
| | Ferne M. Steckler (D) | 67,709 | 31.7 |
| 6 | Lester L. Wolff (D, L) | 109,620 | 51.5 |
| | John T. Gallagher (R, C) | 103,038 | 48.5 |
| 7 | Joseph P. Addabbo (D, L) | 103,110 | 75.0 |
| | John E. Hall (R) | 28,296 | 20.6 |
| 8 | Benjamin S. Rosenthal (D, L) | 110,293 | 64.7 |
| | Frank A. La Pina (R, C) | 60,166 | 35.3 |
| 9 | James J. Delaney (D, R) | 141,323 | 93.4 |
| | Loretta E. Gressey (L) | 9,965 | 6.6 |
| 10 | Mario Biaggi (D, R) | 130,200 | 93.9 |
| | Michael S. Bank (L) | 8,397 | 6.1 |

| | Candidates | Votes | % |
|---|---|---|---|
| 11 | Frank J. Brasco (D) | 87,869 | 63.9 |
| | Melvin Solomon (R, C) | 43,105 | 31.3 |
| 12 | Shirley Chisholm (D, L) | 57,821 | 87.9 |
| | John M. Coleman (R) | 6,373 | 9.7 |
| 13 | Bertram L. Podell (D) | 113,294 | 65.2 |
| | Joseph F. Marcucci (R) | 44,293 | 25.5 |
| | Leonard M. Simon (L) | 9,173 | 5.3 |
| 14 | John J. Rooney (D, C) | 45,515 | 53.9 |
| | Allard K. Lowenstein (L) | 23,732 | 28.1 |
| | Francis J. Voyticky (R) | 14,813 | 17.5 |
| 15 | Hugh L. Carey (D) | 77,019 | 52.2 |
| | John F. Gangemi (R) | 63,446 | 43.0 |
| 16 | Elizabeth Holtzman (D) | 96,984 | 65.6 |
| | Nicholas R. Macchio (R) | 33,828 | 22.9 |
| | Emanuel Celler (L) | 10,337 | 7.0 |
| 17 | John N. Murphy (D) | 92,252 | 60.3 |
| | Mario D. Belardino (R, C) | 60,812 | 39.7 |
| 18 | Edward I. Koch (D, L) | 125,117 | 69.9 |
| | Jane P. Langley (R, C) | 52,379 | 29.3 |
| 19 | Charles Rangel (D, R) | 104,427 | 96.0 |
| 20 | Bella S. Abzug (D) | 85,558 | 55.7 |
| | Priscilla M. Ryan (L) | 43,045 | 28.0 |
| | Annette Flatto Levy (R) | 18,024 | 11.7 |
| 21 | Herman Badillo (D, L) | 48,441 | 86.9 |
| | Manuel A. Ramos (R) | 6,366 | 11.4 |
| 22 | Jonathan B. Bingham (D, L) | 107,448 | 76.5 |
| | Charles A. Avarello (R, C) | 33,045 | 23.5 |
| 23 | Peter A. Peyser (R, C) | 99,737 | 50.4 |
| | Richard L. Ottinger (D, L) | 98,335 | 49.6 |
| 24 | Ogden R. Reid (D, L) | 107,979 | 52.2 |
| | Carl A. Vergari (R, C) | 98,818 | 47.8 |
| 25 | Hamilton Fish Jr. (R, C) | 144,386 | 71.6 |
| | John M. Burns III (D) | 54,271 | 26.9 |
| 26 | Benjamin A. Gilman (R) | 90,922 | 47.8 |
| | John G. Dow (D) | 74,906 | 39.3 |
| | Yale Rapkin (C, NEW I) | 24,569 | 12.9 |
| 27 | Howard W. Robison (R) | 114,902 | 62.2 |
| | David H. Blazer (D) | 55,076 | 29.8 |
| | Patrick M. O'Neil (C) | 9,521 | 5.2 |
| 28 | Samuel S. Stratton (D) | 182,395 | 80.0 |
| | John F. Ryan Jr. (R, C) | 45,623 | 20.0 |
| 29 | Carleton J. King (R, C) | 148,170 | 69.9 |
| | Harold B. Gordon (D, L) | 63,920 | 30.1 |
| 30 | Robert C. McEwen (R, C) | 114,193 | 66.0 |
| | Ernest J. Labaff (D, L) | 58,788 | 34.0 |
| 31 | Donald J. Mitchell (R, C) | 98,454 | 51.0 |
| | Robert Castle (D) | 75,513 | 39.1 |
| | Franklin Nichols (AP) | 12,075 | 6.3 |
| 32 | James M. Hanley (D) | 111,481 | 57.2 |
| | Leonard C. Koldin (R, C) | 83,451 | 42.8 |
| 33 | William F. Walsh (R, C) | 132,139 | 71.4 |
| | Clarence Kadys (D) | 53,039 | 28.6 |
| 34 | Frank Horton (R) | 142,803 | 72.1 |
| | Jack Rubens (D) | 46,509 | 23.5 |
| 35 | Barber B. Conable (R) | 127,298 | 67.9 |
| | Terence J. Spencer (D) | 53,321 | 28.4 |
| 36 | Henry P. Smith III (R, C) | 110,238 | 57.3 |
| | Richard D. (Max) McCarthy (D, L) | 82,095 | 42.7 |
| 37 | Thaddeus J. Dulski (D, L) | 114,603 | 72.2 |
| | William F. McLaughlin (R, C) | 44,103 | 27.8 |
| 38 | Jack F. Kemp (R, C) | 156,967 | 73.2 |
| | Anthony P. Lo Russo (D, L) | 57,585 | 26.8 |
| 39 | James F. Hastings (R, C) | 126,147 | 71.9 |
| | Wilbur White Jr (D) | 49,253 | 28.1 |

## NORTH CAROLINA

| | | | |
|---|---|---|---|
| 1 | Walter, B. Jones (D) | 77,438 | 68.8 |
| | J. Jordan Bonner (R) | 35,063 | 31.2 |
| 2 | L. H. Fountain (D) | 88,798 | 71.6 |
| | Erick P. Little (R) | 35,193 | 28.4 |
| 3 | David N. Henderson (D) | 56,968 | 100.0 |

## NORTH CAROLINA

| Candidates | Votes | % |
|---|---|---|
| 4 Ike F. Andrews (D) | 72,972 | 50.3 |
| R. Jack Hawke (R) | 71,972 | 49.7 |
| 5 Wilmer D. Mizell (R) | 101,375 | 64.8 |
| Brooks Hays (D) | 54,986 | 35.2 |
| 6 L. Richardson Preyer (D) | 82,158 | 93.9 |
| Lynwood Bullock (AM) | 5,331 | 6.1 |
| 7 Charles Rose (D) | 57,348 | 60.4 |
| Jerry C. Scott (R) | 36,726 | 38.7 |
| 8 Earl B. Ruth (R) | 82,060 | 60.2 |
| Richard Clark (D) | 54,198 | 39.8 |
| 9 James G. Martin (R) | 80,356 | 58.9 |
| James Beatty (D) | 56,171 | 41.1 |
| 10 James T. Broyhill (R) | 103,119 | 72.6 |
| Paul L. Beck (D) | 39,025 | 27.5 |
| 11 Roy A. Taylor (D) | 94,465 | 59.6 |
| Jesse I. Ledbetter (R) | 64,062 | 40.4 |

## NORTH DAKOTA

| Candidates | Votes | % |
|---|---|---|
| AL Mark Andrews (R) | 195,360 | 72.7 |
| Richard Ista (D) | 72,850 | 27.1 |

## OHIO

| Candidates | Votes | % |
|---|---|---|
| 1 William J. Keating (R) | 119,469 | 70.3 |
| Karl F. Heiser (D) | 50,575 | 29.7 |
| 2 Donald D. Clancy (R) | 109,961 | 62.8 |
| Penny Manes (D) | 65,237 | 37.2 |
| 3 Charles W. Whalen Jr. (R) | 111,253 | 76.2 |
| John W. Lelack Jr. (D) | 34,819 | 23.8 |
| 4 Tennyson Guyer (R) | 109,612 | 62.7 |
| Dimitri Nicholas (D) | 65,216 | 37.3 |
| 5 Delbert L. Latta (R) | 132,032 | 72.8 |
| Bruce Edwards (D) | 49,465 | 27.3 |
| 6 William H. Harsha (R) | 128,394 | 100.0 |
| 7 Clarence J. Brown (R) | 112,350 | 73.3 |
| Dorothy Franke (I) | 40,945 | 26.7 |
| 8 Walter E. Powell (R) | 80,050 | 52.2 |
| James D. Ruppert (D) | 73,344 | 47.8 |
| 9 Thomas L. Ashley (D) | 110,450 | 69.1 |
| Joseph C. Richards (R) | 49,388 | 30.9 |
| 10 Clarence E. Miller (R) | 129,683 | 73.2 |
| Robert H. Wheatley (D) | 47,456 | 26.8 |
| 11 J. William Stanton (R) | 106,841 | 68.2 |
| Dennis M. Callahan (D) | 49,891 | 31.8 |
| 12 Samuel L. Devine (R) | 103,655 | 56.1 |
| James W. Goodrich (D) | 81,074 | 43.9 |
| 13 Charles A. Mosher (R) | 111,242 | 68.2 |
| John Michael Ryan (D) | 51,991 | 31.9 |
| 14 John F. Seiberling (D) | 135,068 | 74.4 |
| Norman W. Holt (R) | 46,490 | 25.6 |
| 15 Chalmers P. Wylie (R) | 115,779 | 65.8 |
| M. L. McGee (D) | 55,314 | 31.4 |
| 16 Ralph S. Regula (R) | 102,013 | 57.3 |
| Virgil L. Musser (D) | 75,929 | 42.7 |
| 17 John M. Ashbrook (R) | 92,666 | 57.4 |
| Raymond C. Beck (D) | 62,512 | 38.7 |
| 18 Wayne L. Hays (D) | 128,663 | 70.2 |
| Robert Stewart (R) | 54,572 | 29.8 |
| 19 Charles J. Carney (D) | 109,979 | 64.0 |
| Norman M. Parr (R) | 61,934 | 36.0 |
| 20 James V. Stanton (D) | 117,302 | 84.3 |
| Thomas E. Vilt (R) | 16,624 | 11.9 |
| 21 Louis Stokes (D) | 99,190 | 81.1 |
| James D. Johnson (R) | 13,861 | 11.3 |
| 22 Charles A. Vanik (D) | 126,462 | 63.9 |
| Donald W. Gropp (R) | 64,577 | 32.6 |
| 23 William E. Minshall (R) | 98,594 | 49.4 |
| Dennis J. Kucinich (D) | 94,366 | 47.3 |

## OKLAHOMA

| Candidates | Votes | % |
|---|---|---|
| 1 James R. Jones (D) | 91,684 | 54.4 |
| J. M. Hewgley (R) | 73,786 | 43.8 |
| 2 Clem Rogers McSpadden (D) | 105,110 | 71.1 |
| Emery H. Toliver (R) | 42,632 | 28.9 |
| 3 Carl Albert (D) | 101,732 | 93.4 |
| Harold J. Marshall (I) | 7,242 | 6.7 |

| Candidates | Votes | % |
|---|---|---|
| 4 Tom Steed (D) | 85,578 | 71.3 |
| William E. Crozier (R) | 34,484 | 28.7 |
| 5 John Jarman (D) | 69,710 | 60.4 |
| Llewllyn L. Keller (R) | 45,711 | 39.6 |
| 6 John N. Happy Camp (R) | 113,567 | 72.7 |
| William Patrick Schmitt (D) | 42,663 | 27.3 |

## OREGON

| Candidates | Votes | % |
|---|---|---|
| 1 Wendell Wyatt (R) | 166,476 | 68.6 |
| Ralph E. Bunch (D) | 76,307 | 31.4 |
| 2 Al Ullman (D) | 178,537 | 99.9 |
| 3 Edith Green (D) | 141,086 | 62.4 |
| Mike Walsh (R) | 84,697 | 37.5 |
| 4 John Dellenback (R) | 138,965 | 62.0 |
| Charles O. Porter (D) | 83,134 | 37.1 |

## PENNSYLVANIA

| Candidates | Votes | % |
|---|---|---|
| 1 William A. Barrett (D) | 118,953 | 66.1 |
| Gus A. Pedicone (R) | 59,807 | 33.2 |
| 2 Robert N. C. Nix (D) | 107,509 | 70.2 |
| Frederick D. Bryant (R) | 45,753 | 29.9 |
| 3 William J. Green III (D) | 101,144 | 63.3 |
| Alfred Marroletti (R) | 57,787 | 36.2 |
| 4 Joshua Eilberg (D) | 129,105 | 55.9 |
| William Pfender (R) | 102,013 | 44.1 |
| 5 John H. Ware III (R) | 121,346 | 64.7 |
| Brower B. Yerger (D) | 66,329 | 35.3 |
| 6 Gus Yatron (D) | 119,557 | 64.5 |
| Eugene W. Hubler (R) | 64,076 | 34.6 |
| 7 Lawrence G. Williams (R) | 122,622 | 60.6 |
| Stuart S. Bowie (D) | 79,578 | 39.4 |
| 8 Edward G. Biester (R) | 115,799 | 64.4 |
| Alan Williams (D) | 64,069 | 35.6 |
| 9 E. G. Shuster (R) | 95,913 | 61.7 |
| Earl D. Collins (D) | 59,386 | 38.2 |
| 10 Joseph M. McDade (R) | 143,670 | 73.6 |
| Stanley R. Coveleskie (D) | 51,550 | 26.4 |
| 11 Daniel J. Flood (D) | 124,336 | 68.3 |
| Donald B. Ayers (R) | 57,809 | 31.7 |
| 12 John P. Saylor (R) | 122,628 | 68.2 |
| Joseph Murphy (D) | 57,314 | 31.9 |
| 13 R. Lawrence Coughlin (R) | 139,085 | 66.6 |
| Katherine L. Camp (D) | 69,728 | 33.4 |
| 14 William S. Moorhead (D) | 106,158 | 59.3 |
| Roland S. Catarinella (R) | 72,275 | 40.4 |
| 15 Fred B. Rooney (D) | 99,937 | 60.8 |
| Wardell F. Steigerwalt (R) | 64,560 | 39.3 |
| 16 Edwin D. Eshleman (R) | 112,292 | 73.5 |
| Shirley S. Garrett (D) | 40,534 | 26.5 |
| 17 Herman T. Schneebeli (R) | 120,214 | 72.2 |
| Donald J. Rippon (D) | 44,202 | 26.6 |
| 18 H. John Heinz III (R) | 144,521 | 72.8 |
| Douglas Walgren (D) | 53,929 | 27.2 |
| 19 George A. Goodling (R) | 93,536 | 57.5 |
| Richard P. Noll (D) | 67,018 | 41.2 |
| 20 Joseph M. Gaydos (D) | 117,933 | 61.5 |
| William R. Hunt (R) | 73,817 | 38.5 |
| 21 John H. Dent (D) | 104,203 | 62.0 |
| Thomas H. Young (R) | 63,812 | 38.0 |
| 22 Thomas E. Morgan (D) | 100,918 | 60.8 |
| James R. Montgomery (R) | 65,005 | 39.2 |
| 23 Albert W. Johnson (R) | 90,615 | 56.5 |
| Ernest A. Kassab (D) | 69,813 | 43.5 |
| 24 Joseph P. Vigorito (D) | 122,092 | 68.8 |
| Alvin W. Levenhagen (R) | 55,406 | 31.2 |
| 25 Frank M. Clark (D) | 97,549 | 55.8 |
| Gary A. Myers (R) | 77,123 | 44.2 |

### Special Election[1]

| Candidates | Votes | % |
|---|---|---|
| 27 William S. Conover (R) | 28,647# | 51.1 |
| Douglas Walgren (D) | 25,956# | 46.3 |

## RHODE ISLAND

| Candidates | Votes | % |
|---|---|---|
| 1 Fernand J. St.Germain (D) | 120,705 | 62.4 |
| John M. Feeley (R) | 67,125 | 34.7 |
| 2 Robert O. Tiernan (D) | 122,739 | 63.1 |
| Donald P. Ryan (R) | 77,661 | 40.0 |

## SOUTH CAROLINA

| Candidates | Votes | % |
|---|---|---|
| 1 Mendel J. Davis (D) | 61,625 | 54.5 |
| J. Sidi Limehouse (R) | 51,469 | 45.5 |
| 2 Floyd Spence (R) | 83,543 | 99.9 |
| 3 William Jennings Bryan Dorn (D) | 82,579 | 75.2 |
| Roy Ethridge (R) | 27,173 | 24.8 |
| 4 James R. Mann (D) | 64,989 | 66.1 |
| Wayne N. Whatley (R) | 33,363 | 33.9 |
| 5 Tom S. Gettys (D) | 66,343 | 60.9 |
| B. Leonard Phillips (R) | 42,620 | 39.1 |
| 6 Edward L. Young (R) | 63,527 | 54.4 |
| John W. Jenrette Jr (D) | 53,324 | 45.6 |

## SOUTH DAKOTA

| Candidates | Votes | % |
|---|---|---|
| 1 Frank E. Denholm (D) | 94,442 | 60.5 |
| John Vickerman (R) | 61,589 | 39.5 |
| 2 James Abdnor (R) | 79,546 | 54.9 |
| Pat McKeever (D) | 65,415 | 45.1 |

## TENNESSEE

| Candidates | Votes | % |
|---|---|---|
| 1 James H. Quillen (R) | 110,868 | 79.4 |
| Bernard Cantor (D) | 28,736 | 20.6 |
| 2 John J. Duncan (R) | 109,925 | 100.0 |
| 3 LaMar Baker (R) | 82,561 | 55.3 |
| Howard Sompayrac (D) | 62,536 | 41.9 |
| 4 Joe L. Evins (D) | 93,042 | 81.1 |
| Billy Joe Finney (R) | 21,689 | 18.9 |
| 5 Richard Fulton (D) | 93,555 | 62.6 |
| Alfred Adams (R) | 55,067 | 36.8 |
| 6 Robin L. Beard (R) | 77,263 | 55.3 |
| William R. Anderson (D) | 60,254 | 43.1 |
| 7 Ed Jones (D) | 92,419 | 70.5 |
| Stockton Adkins (R) | 38,726 | 29.5 |
| 8 Dan Kuykendall (R) | 93,173 | 55.4 |
| J. O. Patterson Jr. (D) | 74,240 | 44.1 |

## TEXAS

| Candidates | Votes | % |
|---|---|---|
| 1 Wright Patman (D) | 93,891 | 100.0 |
| 2 Charles Wilson (D) | 100,345 | 73.8 |
| Charles O. Brightwell (R) | 35,600 | 26.2 |
| 3 James Collins (R) | 122,984 | 73.3 |
| George A. Hughes (D) | 44,708 | 26.7 |
| 4 Ray Roberts (D) | 95,674 | 70.2 |
| James Russell (R) | 40,548 | 29.8 |
| 5 Alan Steelman (R) | 74,932 | 55.7 |
| Earle Cabell (D) | 59,601 | 44.3 |
| 6 Olin E. Teague (D) | 100,917 | 72.6 |
| Carl Nigliazzo (R) | 38,086 | 27.4 |
| 7 Bill Archer (R) | 171,127 | 82.3 |
| Jim Brady (D) | 36,899 | 17.7 |
| 8 Bob Eckhardt (D) | 73,909 | 64.6 |
| Lewis Emerich (R) | 39,686 | 34.7 |
| 9 Jack Brooks (D) | 89,111 | 66.2 |
| Randolph Reed (R) | 45,462 | 33.8 |
| 10 J. J. Pickle (D) | 130,973 | 91.2 |
| Melissa Singler (SOC WORK) | 12,682 | 8.8 |
| 11 W. R. Poage (D) | 88,861 | 100.0 |
| 12 Jim Wright (D) | 84,356 | 100.0 |
| 13 Bob Price (R) | 87,084 | 54.8 |
| Graham Purcell (D) | 71,730 | 45.2 |
| 14 John Young (D) | 89,725 | 100.0 |
| 15 Eligio de la Garza (D) | 73,994 | 100.0 |
| 16 Richard C. White (D) | 81,347 | 100.0 |
| 17 Omar Burleson (D) | 95,122 | 100.0 |

*1. Pennsylvania lost two House seats between the 1970 and 1972 general elections due to redistricting. The special election in the 27th District, held April 25, 1972, was for a partial term expiring Jan. 3, 1973, after which the district ceased to exist.*

## TEXAS

| | Candidates | Votes | % |
|---|---|---|---|
| 18 | Barbara C. Jordan (D) | 85,672 | 80.6 |
| | Paul Merritt (R) | 19,355 | 18.2 |
| 19 | George Mahon (D) | 97,084 | 100.0 |
| 20 | Henry B. Gonzalez (D) | 81,443 | 96.9 |
| 21 | O. C. Fisher (D) | 91,180 | 56.8 |
| | Douglas S. Harlan (R) | 69,374 | 43.2 |
| 22 | Bob Casey (D) | 101,786 | 70.2 |
| | James Griffin (R) | 42,094 | 29.0 |
| 23 | Abraham Kazen (D) | 72,799 | 100.0 |
| 24 | Dale Milford (D) | 91,054 | 65.1 |
| | Courtney Roberts (R) | 48,853 | 34.9 |

## UTAH

| | Candidates | Votes | % |
|---|---|---|---|
| 1 | K. Gunn McKay (D) | 127,027 | 55.4 |
| | Robert K. Wolthuis (R) | 96,296 | 42.0 |
| 2 | Wayne Owens (D) | 132,832 | 54.5 |
| | Sherman P. Lloyd (R) | 107,185 | 44.0 |

## VERMONT

| | Candidates | Votes | % |
|---|---|---|---|
| AL | Richard W. Mallary (R) | 120,924 | 65.0 |
| | William H. Meyer (D) | 65,062 | 35.0 |

### Special Election

| | Candidates | Votes | % |
|---|---|---|---|
| AL | Richard W. Mallary (R) | 39,903# | 55.8 |
| | J. William O'Brien (D) | 26,889# | 37.6 |

## VIRGINIA

| | Candidates | Votes | % |
|---|---|---|---|
| 1 | Thomas N. Downing (D) | 100,901 | 78.1 |
| | Kenneth D. Wells (R) | 28,310 | 21.9 |
| 2 | G. William Whitehurst (R) | 79,672 | 73.4 |
| | L. Charles Burlage (D) | 28,803 | 26.6 |
| 3 | David E. Satterfield III (D) | 102,523 | 99.9 |

| | Candidates | Votes | % |
|---|---|---|---|
| 4 | Robert W. Daniel Jr. (R) | 57,520 | 47.1 |
| | Robert E. Gibson (D) | 45,776 | 37.5 |
| | Robert R. Hardy (I) | 8,668 | 7.1 |
| | William E. Ward | 6,172 | 5.1 |
| 5 | W. C. (Dan) Daniel (D) | 83,772 | 99.9 |
| 6 | M. Caldwell Butler (R) | 75,189 | 54.6 |
| | Willis N. Anderson (D) | 53,928 | 39.2 |
| | Roy R. White (I) | 8,531 | 6.2 |
| 7 | J. Kenneth Robinson (R) | 89,120 | 66.2 |
| | Murat Wills Williams (D) | 45,513 | 33.8 |
| 8 | Stanford E. Parris (R) | 60,446 | 44.4 |
| | Robert F. Horan (D) | 51,444 | 37.8 |
| | William R. Durland (I) | 18,654 | 13.7 |
| 9 | William C. Wampler (R) | 98,178 | 71.9 |
| | Zane Dale Christian (D) | 36,000 | 26.4 |
| 10 | Joel T. Broyhill (R) | 101,138 | 56.3 |
| | Harold O. Miller (D) | 78,638 | 43.7 |

### Special Election

| | Candidates | Votes | % |
|---|---|---|---|
| 6 | M. Caldwell Butler (R) | 61,898 | 51.8 |
| | Willis M. Anderson (D) | 47,588 | 39.8 |
| | Roy R. White (I) | 10,098 | 8.4 |

## WASHINGTON

| | Candidates | Votes | % |
|---|---|---|---|
| 1 | Joel Pritchard (R) | 107,581 | 50.9 |
| | John Hempelmann (D) | 104,959 | 49.7 |
| 2 | Lloyd Meeds (D) | 114,900 | 60.5 |
| | Bill Reams (R) | 75,181 | 39.6 |
| 3 | Julia Butler Hansen (D) | 122,933 | 66.3 |
| | R. C. (Skip) McConkey (R) | 62,564 | 33.7 |
| 4 | Mike McCormack (D) | 97,593 | 52.1 |
| | Stewart Bledsoe (R) | 89,812 | 47.9 |
| 5 | Thomas Foley (D) | 150,580 | 81.3 |
| | Clarice L. R. Privette (R) | 34,742 | 18.8 |
| 6 | Floyd V. Hicks (D) | 126,349 | 72.1 |
| | Thomas C. Lowry (R) | 48,914 | 27.9 |

| | Candidates | Votes | % |
|---|---|---|---|
| 7 | Brock Adams (D) | 140,307 | 85.4 |
| | J. J. (Tiny) Freeman (R) | 19,889 | 12.1 |

## WEST VIRGINIA

| | Candidates | Votes | % |
|---|---|---|---|
| 1 | Robert H. Mollohan (D) | 130,062 | 69.4 |
| | George E. Kapnicky (R) | 57,724 | 30.8 |
| 2 | Harley O. Staggers (D) | 128,286 | 70.0 |
| | David Dix (R) | 54,949 | 30.0 |
| 3 | John M. Slack (D) | 118,346 | 63.7 |
| | T. David Higgins (R) | 67,441 | 36.3 |
| 4 | Ken Hechler (D) | 100,600 | 61.0 |
| | Joe Neal (R) | 64,242 | 39.0 |

## WISCONSIN

| | Candidates | Votes | % |
|---|---|---|---|
| 1 | Les Aspin (D) | 122,973 | 64.4 |
| | Merrill E. Stalbaum (R) | 66,665 | 34.9 |
| 2 | Robert W. Kastenmeier (D) | 148,136 | 68.2 |
| | J. Michael Kelly (R) | 68,167 | 31.4 |
| 3 | Vernon W. Thomson (R) | 112,905 | 54.7 |
| | Walter Thoresen (D) | 91,953 | 44.6 |
| 4 | Clement J. Zablocki (D) | 149,078 | 75.7 |
| | Phillip D. Mrozinski (R) | 45,003 | 22.8 |
| 5 | Henry S. Reuss (D) | 127,273 | 77.3 |
| | Frederick Van Hecke (R) | 33,627 | 20.4 |
| 6 | William A. Steiger (R) | 130,701 | 65.8 |
| | James A. Adams (D) | 63,643 | 32.0 |
| 7 | David R. Obey (D) | 135,385 | 62.8 |
| | Alvin E. O'Konski (R) | 80,207 | 37.2 |
| 8 | Harold V. Froehlich (R) | 101,634 | 50.4 |
| | Robert J. Cornell (D) | 97,795 | 48.5 |
| 9 | Glenn R. Davis (R) | 128,230 | 61.4 |
| | Ralph A. Fine (D) | 76,585 | 36.7 |

## WYOMING

| | Candidates | Votes | % |
|---|---|---|---|
| AL | Teno Roncalio (D) | 75,632 | 51.7 |
| | Bill Kidd (R) | 70,667 | 48.3 |

# 1973 House Elections

## ALASKA

### Special Election

| | Candidates | Votes | % |
|---|---|---|---|
| AL | Don Young (R) | 35,044 | 51.4 |
| | Emil Notti (D) | 33,123 | 48.6 |

## ILLINOIS

### Special Election

| | Candidates | Votes | % |
|---|---|---|---|
| 7 | Cardiss Collins (D) | 33,875# | 92.5 |

## LOUISIANA

### Special Election

| | Candidates | Votes | % |
|---|---|---|---|
| 2 | Corinne (Lindy) Boggs (D) | 42,583 | 80.4 |
| | Robert E. Lee (R) | 10,352 | 19.6 |

## MARYLAND

### Special Election

| | Candidates | Votes | % |
|---|---|---|---|
| 1 | Robert E. Bauman (R) | 27,248 | 51.2 |
| | Frederick C. Malkus (D) | 26,001 | 48.8 |

# 1974 House Elections

## ALABAMA

| Candidates | Votes | % |
|---|---|---|
| 1 Jack Edwards (R) | 60,710 | 59.5 |
| Augusta E. Wilson (D) | 37,718 | 37.0 |
| 2 William L. Dickinson (R) | 54,089 | 66.1 |
| Clair Chisler (D) | 27,729 | 33.9 |
| 3 Bill Nichols (D) | 63,582 | 95.9 |
| 4 Tom Bevill (D) | 77,925 | 99.8 |
| 5 Robert E. Jones (D) | 56,375 | 100.0 |
| 6 John Buchanan (R) | 54,505 | 56.6 |
| Nina Miglionico (D) | 39,444 | 41.0 |
| 7 Walter Flowers (D) | 73,203 | 91.0 |
| Frank P. Walls (C) | 5,175 | 6.4 |

## ALASKA

| Candidates | Votes | % |
|---|---|---|
| AL Donald E. Young (R) | 51,641 | 53.8 |
| William L. Hensley (D) | 44,280 | 46.2 |

## ARIZONA[1]

| Candidates | Votes | % |
|---|---|---|
| 1 John J. Rhodes (R) | 63,847 | 51.1 |
| Patricia M. Fullinwider (D) | 52,897 | 42.3 |
| J. M. Sanders (LLJ) | 8,199 | 6.6 |
| 2 Morris K. Udall (D) | 84,491 | 62.0 |
| Keith Dolgaard (R) | 51,886 | 38.0 |
| 3 Sam Steiger (R) | 71,497 | 51.1 |
| Pat Bosch (D) | 68,424 | 48.9 |
| 4 John B. Conlan (R) | 78,887 | 55.3 |
| Byron T. Brown (D) | 63,677 | 44.7 |

## ARKANSAS

| Candidates | Votes | % |
|---|---|---|
| 1 Bill Alexander (D) | 104,247 | 90.6 |
| James Lawrence Dauer (R) | 10,821 | 9.4 |
| 2 Wilbur D. Mills (D) | 80,296 | 58.9 |
| Judy Petty (R) | 56,038 | 41.1 |
| 3 John Paul Hammerschmidt (R) | 89,324 | 51.8 |
| Bill Clinton (D) | 83,030 | 48.2 |
| 4 Ray Thornton (D) | | 100.0 |

## CALIFORNIA

| Candidates | Votes | % |
|---|---|---|
| 1 Harold T. Johnson (D) | 138,082 | 85.8 |
| Dorothy D. Paradis (AIP) | 22,881 | 14.2 |
| 2 Don H. Clausen (R) | 95,929 | 53.0 |
| Oscar H. Klee (D) | 77,232 | 42.7 |
| 3 John E. Moss (D) | 122,134 | 72.3 |
| Ivaldo Lenci (R) | 46,712 | 27.7 |
| 4 Robert L. Leggett (D) | 101,152 | 100.0 |
| 5 John L. Burton (D) | 88,909 | 59.6 |
| Thomas Caylor (R) | 56,274 | 37.7 |
| 6 Phillip Burton (D) | 85,712 | 71.3 |
| Tom Spinosa (R) | 26,260 | 21.8 |
| 7 George Miller (D) | 83,054 | 55.6 |
| Gary Fernandez (R) | 66,325 | 44.4 |
| 8 Ronald V. Dellums (D) | 95,041 | 56.6 |
| Jack Redden (R) | 66,386 | 39.6 |
| 9 Fortney H. (Pete) Stark Jr. (D) | 92,436 | 70.6 |
| Edson Adams (R) | 38,521 | 29.4 |
| 10 Don Edwards (D) | 87,978 | 77.0 |
| John M. Enright (R) | 26,288 | 23.0 |
| 11 Leo J. Ryan (D) | 106,429 | 75.8 |
| Brainard G. Merdinger (R) | 29,861 | 21.3 |
| 12 Paul N. McCloskey Jr. (R) | 103,692 | 69.1 |
| Gary G. Gillmor (D) | 46,383 | 30.9 |
| 13 Norman Y. Mineta (D) | 78,858 | 52.6 |
| George W. Milias (R) | 63,573 | 42.4 |
| 14 John J. McFall (D) | 102,180 | 70.9 |
| Charles M. Gibson (R) | 34,775 | 24.1 |
| 15 B. F. Sisk (D) | 80,897 | 72.0 |
| Carol O. Harner (R) | 31,439 | 28.0 |
| 16 Burt L. Talcott (R) | 76,356 | 49.2 |
| Julian Camacho (D) | 74,168 | 47.8 |

| Candidates | Votes | % |
|---|---|---|
| 17 John Krebs (D) | 66,675 | 51.9 |
| Robert B. Mathias (R) | 61,812 | 48.1 |
| 18 William M. Ketchum (R) | 67,650 | 52.7 |
| George A. Seielstad (D) | 60,733 | 47.3 |
| 19 Robert J. Lagomarsino (R) | 84,249 | 56.3 |
| James D. Loebl (D) | 65,469 | 43.7 |
| 20 Barry M. Goldwater Jr. (R) | 98,410 | 61.2 |
| Arline Mathews (D) | 62,326 | 38.8 |
| 21 James C. Corman (D) | 88,915 | 73.5 |
| Mel Nadell (R) | 32,038 | 26.5 |
| 22 Carlos J. Moorhead (R) | 81,641 | 55.8 |
| Richard Hallin (D) | 64,691 | 44.2 |
| 23 Thomas M. Rees (D) | 122,076 | 71.4 |
| Jack E. Roberts (R) | 48,826 | 28.6 |
| 24 Henry A. Waxman (D) | 87,521 | 64.0 |
| Elliott Stone Graham (R) | 45,128 | 33.0 |
| 25 Edward R. Roybal (D) | 45,059 | 100.0 |
| 26 John H. Rousselot (R) | 82,735 | 58.9 |
| Paul A. Conforti (D) | 57,685 | 41.1 |
| 27 Alphonzo Bell (R) | 102,663 | 63.9 |
| John Dalessio (D) | 52,236 | 32.5 |
| 28 Yvonne Burke (D) | 88,655 | 80.1 |
| Tom Neddy (R) | 21,957 | 19.9 |
| 29 Augustus F. Hawkins (D) | 47,204 | 100.0 |
| 30 George E. Danielson (D) | 67,328 | 74.2 |
| John J. Perez (R) | 23,383 | 25.8 |
| 31 Charles H. Wilson (D) | 61,322 | 70.4 |
| Norman A. Hodges (R) | 23,359 | 26.8 |
| 32 Glenn M. Anderson (D) | 84,428 | 87.7 |
| Virgil V. Badalich (AIP) | 8,874 | 9.2 |
| 33 Del Clawson (R) | 72,471 | 53.4 |
| Robert E. White (D) | 58,492 | 43.1 |
| 34 Mark W. Hannaford (D) | 81,151 | 49.8 |
| Bill Bond (R) | 75,426 | 46.3 |
| 35 Jim Lloyd (D) | 61,903 | 50.3 |
| Victor V. Veysey (R) | 61,168 | 49.7 |
| 36 George E. Brown Jr. (D) | 69,766 | 62.6 |
| Jim Osgood (R) | 35,938 | 32.3 |
| William E. Pasley (AIP) | 5,711 | 5.1 |
| 37 Jerry L. Pettis (R) | 89,849 | 63.2 |
| Bobby Ray Vincent (D) | 46,783 | 32.9 |
| 38 Jerry M. Patterson (D) | 68,335 | 54.0 |
| David Rehmann (R) | 52,207 | 41.3 |
| 39 Charles E. Wiggins (R) | 89,220 | 55.3 |
| William E. Farris (D) | 65,170 | 40.4 |
| 40 Andrew J. Hinshaw (R) | 116,449 | 63.4 |
| Roderick J. Wilson (D) | 56,850 | 30.9 |
| Grayson L. Watkins (AIP) | 10,498 | 5.7 |
| 41 Bob Wilson (R) | 94,709 | 54.5 |
| Colleen M. O'Connor (D) | 74,823 | 43.0 |
| 42 Lionel Van Deerlin (D) | 70,579 | 69.9 |
| Wes Marden (R) | 30,435 | 30.1 |
| 43 Clair W. Burgener (R) | 115,275 | 60.4 |
| Bill Bandes (D) | 75,629 | 39.6 |

### Special Elections [2]

| Candidates | Votes | % |
|---|---|---|
| 6 John L. Burton (D) | 73,114 | 50.0 |
| Thomas Caylor (R) | 30,908 | 21.2 |
| Terence McGuire (D) | 12,777 | 8.7 |
| Jean Wall (R) | 8,501 | 5.8 |
| Sean McCarthy (R) | 7,783 | 5.3 |
| 13 Robert J. Lagomarsino (R) | 52,140 | 53.6 |
| James D. Loebl (D) | 18,223 | 18.8 |
| James A. Browning (D) | 7,536 | 7.8 |
| Roger I. Ikola (D) | 6,155 | 6.3 |
| E.T. Jolicoeur (D) | 5,786 | 6.0 |

## COLORADO

| Candidates | Votes | % |
|---|---|---|
| 1 Patricia Schroeder (D) | 94,583 | 58.5 |
| Frank K. Southworth (R) | 66,046 | 40.8 |
| 2 Timothy W. Wirth (D) | 93,728 | 51.9 |
| Donald G. Brotzman (R) | 86,720 | 48.0 |
| 3 Frank E. Evans (D) | 91,783 | 67.9 |
| E. Keith Records (R) | 43,298 | 32.1 |

| Candidates | Votes | % |
|---|---|---|
| 4 James P. Johnson (R) | 82,982 | 52.0 |
| John S. Carroll (D) | 76,452 | 48.0 |
| 5 William L. Armstrong (R) | 85,326 | 57.7 |
| Ben Galloway (D) | 56,888 | 38.5 |

## CONNECTICUT

| Candidates | Votes | % |
|---|---|---|
| 1 William R. Cotter (D) | 117,038 | 62.7 |
| F. Mac Buckley (R) | 67,080 | 35.9 |
| 2 Christopher J. Dodd (D) | 104,436 | 59.0 |
| Samuel B. Hellier (R) | 69,380 | 39.2 |
| 3 Robert N. Giaimo (D) | 114,316 | 65.1 |
| James F. Altham Jr. (R) | 55,177 | 31.4 |
| 4 Stewart B. McKinney (R) | 83,630 | 53.2 |
| James G. Kellis (D) | 71,047 | 45.2 |
| 5 Ronald A. Sarasin (R) | 94,998 | 50.4 |
| William R. Ratchford (D) | 90,407 | 48.0 |
| 6 Anthony J. Moffett (D) | 122,785 | 63.4 |
| Patsy J. Piscopo (R) | 69,942 | 36.1 |

## DELAWARE

| Candidates | Votes | % |
|---|---|---|
| AL Pierre S. duPont IV (R) | 93,826 | 58.5 |
| James R. Soles (D) | 63,490 | 39.6 |

## FLORIDA

| Candidates | Votes | % |
|---|---|---|
| 1 Robert L. F. Sikes (D) | | 100.0 |
| 2 Don Fuqua (D) | | 100.0 |
| 3 Charles E. Bennett (D) | | 100.0 |
| 4 Bill Chappell Jr. (D) | 74,720 | 68.2 |
| Warren A. Hauser (R) | 34,867 | 31.8 |
| 5 Richard Kelly (R) | 74,954 | 52.8 |
| JoAnn Saunders (D) | 63,610 | 44.8 |
| 6 C. W. Bill Young (R) | 109,302 | 75.8 |
| Herbert M. Monrose (D) | 34,886 | 24.2 |
| 7 Sam Gibbons (D) | | 100.0 |
| 8 James A. Haley (D) | 63,283 | 56.7 |
| Joe Z. Lovingood (R) | 48,240 | 43.3 |
| 9 Louis Frey Jr. (R) | 86,226 | 76.7 |
| William D. Rowland (D) | 26,255 | 23.3 |
| 10 L. A. (Skip) Bafalis (R) | 117,368 | 73.7 |
| Evelyn Tucker (D) | 41,925 | 26.3 |
| 11 Paul G. Rogers (D) | | 100.0 |
| 12 J. Herbert Burke (R) | 61,191 | 51.0 |
| Charles Friedman (D) | 58,899 | 49.0 |
| 13 William Lehman (D) | | 100.0 |
| 14 Claude Pepper (D) | 45,479 | 69.1 |
| Michael A. Carricarte (R) | 20,383 | 30.9 |
| 15 Dante B. Fascell (D) | 68,064 | 70.5 |
| S. Peter Capua (R) | 28,444 | 29.5 |

## GEORGIA

| Candidates | Votes | % |
|---|---|---|
| 1 Ronald B. (Bo) Ginn (D) | 64,958 | 86.1 |
| Bill Gowan (R) | 10,485 | 13.9 |
| 2 Dawson Mathis (D) | 59,514 | 100.0 |
| 3 Jack Brinkley (D) | 67,438 | 87.7 |
| Carl Savage (R) | 9,453 | 12.3 |
| 4 Elliott H. Levitas (D) | 61,211 | 55.1 |
| Ben B. Blackburn (R) | 49,922 | 44.9 |
| 5 Andrew Young (D) | 69,221 | 71.6 |
| Wyman C. Lowe (R) | 27,397 | 28.3 |
| 6 John J. Flynt Jr. (D) | 49,082 | 51.5 |
| Newt Gingrich (R) | 46,308 | 48.5 |
| 7 Lawrence P. McDonald (D) | 47,993 | 50.3 |
| Quincy Collins (R) | 47,450 | 49.7 |
| 8 W. S. (Bill) Stuckey Jr. (D) | 59,182 | 100.0 |
| 9 Phil M. Landrum (D) | 64,096 | 74.8 |
| Ronald D. Reeves (R) | 21,540 | 25.2 |
| 10 Robert G. Stephens Jr. (D) | 45,843 | 68.4 |
| Gary Pleger (R) | 21,214 | 31.6 |

*Footnotes, see p. 1278.*

## HAWAII

| | Candidates | Votes | % |
|---|---|---|---|
| 1 | Spark M. Matsunaga (D) | 71,552 | 59.3 |
| | William B. Paul (R) | 49,065 | 40.7 |
| 2 | Patsy T. Mink (D) | 86,916 | 62.6 |
| | Carla W. Coray (R) | 51,894 | 37.4 |

## IDAHO

| | | Votes | % |
|---|---|---|---|
| 1 | Steven D. Symms (R) | 75,414 | 58.3 |
| | J. Ray Cox (D) | 54,001 | 41.7 |
| 2 | George V. Hansen (R) | 67,274 | 55.7 |
| | Max Hanson (D) | 53,599 | 44.3 |

## ILLINOIS

| | | Votes | % |
|---|---|---|---|
| 1 | Ralph H. Metcalfe (D) | 75,206 | 03.7 |
| | Oscar H. Haynes (R) | 4,399 | 5.5 |
| 2 | Morgan F. Murphy (D) | 65,812 | 87.5 |
| | James Ginderske (R) | 9,386 | 12.5 |
| 3 | Martin A. Russo (D) | 65,336 | 52.6 |
| | Robert P. Hanrahan (R) | 58,891 | 47.4 |
| 4 | Edward J. Derwinski (R) | 68,428 | 59.2 |
| | Ronald A. Rodger (D) | 47,096 | 40.8 |
| 5 | John C. Kluczynski (D) | 93,069 | 86.0 |
| | William H. G. Toms (R) | 15,108 | 14.0 |
| 6 | Henry J. Hyde (R) | 66,027 | 53.4 |
| | Edward V. Hanrahan (D) | 57,654 | 46.6 |
| 7 | Cardiss Collins (D) | 63,962 | 87.9 |
| | Donald L. Metzger (R) | 8,800 | 12.1 |
| 8 | Dan Rostenkowski (D) | 75,011 | 86.5 |
| | Salvatore E. Oddo (R) | 11,664 | 13.5 |
| 9 | Sidney R. Yates (D) | 93,864 | 100.0 |
| 10 | Abner J. Mikva (D) | 83,457 | 50.9 |
| | Samuel H. Young (R) | 80,597 | 49.1 |
| 11 | Frank Annunzio (D) | 102,541 | 72.4 |
| | Mitchell S. Zadrozny (R) | 39,182 | 27.6 |
| 12 | Philip M. Crane (R) | 70,731 | 61.1 |
| | Betty C. Spence (D) | 45,049 | 38.9 |
| 13 | Robert McClory (R) | 51,405 | 54.5 |
| | Stanley W. Beetham (D) | 42,903 | 45.5 |
| 14 | John N. Erlenborn (R) | 77,718 | 66.6 |
| | Robert H. Renshaw (D) | 38,981 | 33.4 |
| 15 | Tim L. Hall (D) | 61,912 | 52.0 |
| | Clifford D. Carlson (R) | 54,278 | 45.6 |
| 16 | John B. Anderson (R) | 65,175 | 55.5 |
| | Marshall Hungness (D) | 33,724 | 28.7 |
| | W. John Schade Jr. (IND) | 18,580 | 15.8 |
| 17 | George M. O'Brien (R) | 59,984 | 51.5 |
| | John J. Houlihan (D) | 56,541 | 48.5 |
| 18 | Robert H. Michel (R) | 71,681 | 54.8 |
| | Stephen L. Nordvall (D) | 59,225 | 45.2 |
| 19 | Tom Railsback (R) | 84,049 | 65.3 |
| | Jim Gende (D) | 44,677 | 34.7 |
| 20 | Paul Findley (R) | 84,426 | 54.8 |
| | Peter F. Mack (D) | 69,551 | 45.2 |
| 21 | Edward R. Madigan (R) | 78,640 | 65.8 |
| | Richard N. Small (D) | 40,896 | 34.2 |
| 22 | George E. Shipley (D) | 97,921 | 59.8 |
| | William A. Young (R) | 65,731 | 40.2 |
| 23 | Melvin Price (D) | 78,347 | 80.5 |
| | Scott R. Randolph (R) | 18,987 | 19.5 |
| 24 | Paul Simon (D) | 108,417 | 59.6 |
| | Val Oshel (R) | 73,634 | 40.4 |

## INDIANA

| | | Votes | % |
|---|---|---|---|
| 1 | Ray J. Madden (D) | 71,759 | 68.6 |
| | Joseph D. Harkin (R) | 32,793 | 31.4 |
| 2 | Floyd J. Fithian (D) | 101,856 | 61.1 |
| | Earl F. Landgrebe (R) | 64,950 | 38.9 |
| 3 | John Brademas (D) | 89,306 | 64.1 |
| | Virginia R. Black (R) | 50,116 | 35.9 |
| 4 | J. Edward Roush (D) | 83,604 | 51.9 |
| | Walter P. Helmke (R) | 75,031 | 46.5 |
| 5 | Elwood Hillis (R) | 95,331 | 56.6 |
| | William T. Sebree (D) | 73,239 | 43.4 |
| 6 | David W. Evans (D) | 78,414 | 52.4 |
| | William G. Bray (R) | 71,134 | 47.6 |

| | Candidates | Votes | % |
|---|---|---|---|
| 7 | John T. Myers (R) | 100,128 | 57.1 |
| | Elden C. Tipton (D) | 73,802 | 42.1 |
| 8 | Philip H. Hayes (D) | 100,121 | 53.4 |
| | Roger H. Zion (R) | 87,296 | 46.6 |
| 9 | Lee H. Hamilton (D) | 117,648 | 71.1 |
| | Delson Cox Jr. (R) | 47,881 | 28.9 |
| 10 | Philip R. Sharp (D) | 85,418 | 54.4 |
| | David W. Dennis (R) | 71,701 | 45.6 |
| 11 | Andrew Jacobs Jr. (D) | 81,508 | 52.5 |
| | William H. Hudnut III (R) | 73,793 | 47.5 |

## IOWA

| | | Votes | % |
|---|---|---|---|
| 1 | Edward Mezvinsky (D) | 75,687 | 54.4 |
| | James A. S. Leach (R) | 63,540 | 45.6 |
| 2 | Michael T. Blouin (D) | 73,416 | 51.1 |
| | Tom Riley (R) | 69,088 | 48.1 |
| 3 | Charles E. Grassley (R) | 77,468 | 50.8 |
| | Stephen J. Rapp (D) | 74,895 | 49.2 |
| 4 | Neal Smith (D) | 96,755 | 63.9 |
| | Chuck Dick (R) | 53,756 | 35.5 |
| 5 | Tom Harkin (D) | 81,186 | 51.1 |
| | William J. Scherle (R) | 77,683 | 48.9 |
| 6 | Berkley Bedell (D) | 86,315 | 54.6 |
| | Wiley Mayne (R) | 71,695 | 45.4 |

## KANSAS

| | | Votes | % |
|---|---|---|---|
| 1 | Keith G. Sebelius (R) | 101,565 | 58.4 |
| | Donald C. Smith (D) | 57,326 | 33.0 |
| | Thelma Morgan (A) | 13,009 | 7.5 |
| 2 | Martha E. Keys (D) | 84,864 | 55.0 |
| | John C. Peterson (R) | 67,650 | 43.9 |
| 3 | Larry Winn Jr. (R) | 89,694 | 62.9 |
| | Samuel J. Wells (D) | 49,976 | 35.0 |
| 4 | Garner E. Shriver (R) | 70,401 | 48.8 |
| | Bert Chaney (D) | 61,210 | 42.5 |
| | John S. Stevens (A) | 12,520 | 8.7 |
| 5 | Joe Skubitz (R) | 88,646 | 55.2 |
| | Franklin D. Gaines (D) | 72,024 | 44.8 |

## KENTUCKY

| | | Votes | % |
|---|---|---|---|
| 1 | Carroll Hubbard Jr. (D) | 70,723 | 78.2 |
| | Charles T. Banken Jr. (R) | 16,937 | 18.7 |
| 2 | William H. Natcher (D) | 56,502 | 73.0 |
| | Art Eddleman (R) | 18,312 | 23.7 |
| 3 | Romano L. Mazzoli (D) | 75,571 | 69.7 |
| | Vincent N. Barclay (R) | 28,813 | 26.6 |
| 4 | M. G. (Gene) Snyder (R) | 63,845 | 51.7 |
| | Kyle Hubbard (D) | 59,539 | 48.3 |
| 5 | Tim Lee Carter (R) | 66,709 | 68.2 |
| | Lyle L. Willis (D) | 28,706 | 29.3 |
| 6 | John B. Breckinridge (D) | 63,010 | 72.1 |
| | Thomas F. Rogers III (R) | 21,039 | 24.1 |
| 7 | Carl D. Perkins (D) | 71,221 | 75.6 |
| | Granville Thomas (R) | 22,982 | 24.4 |

## LOUISIANA [3]

| | | Votes | % |
|---|---|---|---|
| 1 | F. Edward Hebert (D) | 48,452 | 100.0 |
| 2 | Corinne C. Boggs (D) | 58,802 | 81.8 |
| | Diane Morphos (R) | 9,632 | 14.6 |
| 3 | David C. Treen (R) | 55,574 | 58.5 |
| | Charles Grisbaum Jr. (D) | 39,412 | 41.5 |
| 4 | Joe D. Waggonner Jr. (D) | 47,371 | 100.0 |
| 5 | Otto E. Passman (D) | 43,068 | 100.0 |
| 6 | W. Henson Moore (R) | | |
| | Jeff LaCaze (D) | | |
| 7 | John B. Breaux (D) | 59,406 | 89.3 |
| | Jeremy J. Millett (IND) | 7,131 | 10.7 |
| 8 | Gillis W. Long (D) | 41,704 | 100.0 |

## MAINE [4]

| | | Votes | % |
|---|---|---|---|
| 1 | David F. Emery (R) | 94,203 | 50.2 |
| | Peter N. Kyros (D) | 93,524 | 49.8 |

| | Candidates | Votes | % |
|---|---|---|---|
| 2 | William S. Cohen (R) | 118,154 | 71.4 |
| | Markham L. Gartley (D) | 47,399 | 28.6 |

## MARYLAND

| | | Votes | % |
|---|---|---|---|
| 1 | Robert E. Bauman (R) | 59,570 | 53.0 |
| | Thomas J. Hatem (D) | 52,853 | 47.0 |
| 2 | Clarence D. Long (D) | 103,222 | 77.1 |
| | John M. Seney (R) | 30,639 | 22.9 |
| 3 | Paul S. Sarbanes (D) | 93,218 | 83.8 |
| | William H. Mathews (R) | 17,967 | 16.2 |
| 4 | Marjorie S. Holt (R) | 61,208 | 58.1 |
| | Fred L. Wineland (D) | 44,059 | 41.9 |
| 5 | Gladys N. Spellman (D) | 45,211 | 52.6 |
| | John B. Burcham Jr. (R) | 40,805 | 47.4 |
| 6 | Goodloe E. Byron (D) | 90,882 | 73.7 |
| | Elton R. Wampler (R) | 32,416 | 26.3 |
| 7 | Parren J. Mitchell (D) | 43,252 | 100.0 |
| 8 | Gilbert Gude (R) | 104,675 | 65.9 |
| | Sidney Kramer (D) | 54,112 | 34.1 |

## MASSACHUSETTS

| | | Votes | % |
|---|---|---|---|
| 1 | Silvio O. Conte (R) | 107,285 | 71.1 |
| | Thomas R. Manning (D) | 43,524 | 28.9 |
| 2 | Edward P. Boland (D) | 105,763 | 100.0 |
| 3 | Joseph D. Early (D) | 78,244 | 49.5 |
| | David J. Lionett (R) | 60,717 | 38.4 |
| | Douglas J. Rowe (IND) | 19,018 | 12.0 |
| 4 | Robert F. Drinan (D) | 77,286 | 50.8 |
| | Jon Rotenberg (IND) | 52,785 | 34.7 |
| | Alvin Mandell (R) | 21,922 | 14.4 |
| 5 | Paul E. Tsongas (D) | 99,518 | 60.6 |
| | Paul W. Cronin (R) | 64,596 | 39.4 |
| 6 | Michael J. Harrington (D) | 119,278 | 100.0 |
| 7 | Torbert H. Macdonald (D) | 122,165 | 79.8 |
| | James J. Murphy (IND) | 30,959 | 20.2 |
| 8 | Thomas P. O'Neill Jr. (D) | 107,042 | 87.9 |
| | James Kiggin (USLP) | 8,363 | 6.9 |
| | Laura Ross (COM) | 6,421 | 5.3 |
| 9 | John Joseph Moakley (D) | 94,804 | 89.3 |
| | L. R. Sherman (USLP) | 11,344 | 10.7 |
| 10 | Margaret M. Heckler (R) | 99,993 | 64.2 |
| | Barry F. Monahan (D) | 55,871 | 35.8 |
| 11 | James A. Burke (D) | 125,978 | 100.0 |
| 12 | Gerry E. Studds (D) | 138,779 | 74.8 |
| | J. Alan MacKay (R) | 46,787 | 25.2 |

## MICHIGAN

| | | Votes | % |
|---|---|---|---|
| 1 | John Conyers Jr. (D) | 97,620 | 90.7 |
| | Walter F. Girardot (R) | 9,358 | 8.7 |
| 2 | Marvin L. Esch (R) | 72,245 | 52.3 |
| | John S. Reuther (D) | 62,755 | 45.4 |
| 3 | Garry Brown (R) | 70,157 | 51.2 |
| | Paul H. Todd Jr. (D) | 65,212 | 47.6 |
| 4 | Edward Hutchinson (R) | 64,731 | 53.1 |
| | Richard E. Daugherty (D) | 55,469 | 45.5 |
| 5 | Richard F. Vander Veen (D) | 80,778 | 52.6 |
| | Paul G. Goebel Jr. (R) | 66,659 | 43.4 |
| 6 | Bob Carr (D) | 73,956 | 49.3 |
| | Clifford W. Taylor (R) | 73,309 | 48.9 |
| 7 | Donald W. Riegle Jr. (D) | 81,014 | 64.7 |
| | Robert E. Eastman (R) | 41,603 | 33.2 |
| 8 | Bob Traxler (D) | 77,795 | 54.8 |
| | James M. Sparling Jr. (R) | 61,578 | 43.4 |
| 9 | Guy A. Vander Jagt (R) | 87,551 | 56.6 |
| | Norman C. Halbower (D) | 65,235 | 42.1 |
| 10 | Elford A. Cederberg (R) | 78,897 | 53.7 |
| | Samuel D. Marble (D) | 67,467 | 45.9 |
| 11 | Philip E. Ruppe (R) | 83,293 | 50.9 |
| | Francis D. Brouillette (D) | 79,793 | 48.8 |
| 12 | James G. O'Hara (D) | 89,822 | 72.2 |
| | Eugene J. Tyza (R) | 34,293 | 27.6 |
| 13 | Charles C. Diggs Jr. (D) | 63,246 | 87.4 |
| | George E. McCall (R) | 8,036 | 11.1 |
| 14 | Lucien N. Nedzi (D) | 93,973 | 71.2 |
| | Herbert O. Steiger (R) | 35,723 | 27.1 |
| 15 | William D. Ford (D) | 86,601 | 78.1 |
| | Jack A. Underwood (R) | 23,028 | 20.8 |

*Footnotes, see p. 1278.*

## MICHIGAN

| Candidates | Votes | % |
|---|---|---|
| 16 John D. Dingell (D) | 95,834 | 77.7 |
| Wallace D. English (R) | 25,248 | 20.5 |
| 17 William M. Brodhead (D) | 94,242 | 69.5 |
| Kenneth C. Gallagher (R) | 39,856 | 29.4 |
| 18 James J. Blanchard (D) | 83,523 | 58.7 |
| Robert J. Huber (R) | 57,133 | 40.2 |
| 19 William S. Broomfield (R) | 86,846 | 62.9 |
| George F. Montgomery (D) | 50,924 | 36.9 |

### Special Elections

| | Votes | % |
|---|---|---|
| 5 Richard F. Vander Veen (D) | 53,083 | 50.9 |
| Robert Vander Laan (R) | 46,160 | 44.3 |
| 8 Bob Traxler (D) | 59,993 | 51.5 |
| James M. Sparling Jr. (R) | 56,548 | 48.5 |

## MINNESOTA

| Candidates | Votes | % |
|---|---|---|
| 1 Albert H. Quie (R) | 95,138 | 62.6 |
| Uric Scott (D) | 56,868 | 37.4 |
| 2 Tom Hagedorn (R) | 88,071 | 53.1 |
| Steve Babcock (D) | 77,780 | 46.9 |
| 3 Bill Frenzel (R) | 83,325 | 60.4 |
| Bob Riggs (D) | 54,630 | 39.6 |
| 4 Joseph E. Karth (D) | 95,437 | 76.0 |
| Joseph A. Rheinberger (R) | 30,083 | 24.0 |
| 5 Donald M. Fraser (D) | 90,012 | 73.8 |
| Phil Ratte (R) | 30,146 | 24.7 |
| 6 Richard Nolan (D) | 96,465 | 55.4 |
| Jon Grunseth (R) | 77,797 | 44.6 |
| 7 Bob Bergland (D) | 129,207 | 75.0 |
| Dan Reber (R) | 43,045 | 25.0 |
| 8 James L. Oberstar (D) | 104,740 | 62.0 |
| Jerome Arnold (R) | 44,298 | 26.2 |
| William R. Ojala (EJ) | 16,932 | 10.0 |

## MISSISSIPPI

| Candidates | Votes | % |
|---|---|---|
| 1 Jamie L. Whitten (D) | 39,158 | 88.2 |
| Jack Benney (IND) | 5,250 | 11.8 |
| 2 David R. Bowen (D) | 37,909 | 66.1 |
| Ben F. Hilbun Jr. (R) | 15,876 | 27.7 |
| H. B. Wells (D) | 3,573 | 6.2 |
| 3 G. V. (Sonny) Montgomery (D) | 43,020 | 100.0 |
| 4 Thad Cochran (R) | 62,634 | 70.2 |
| Kenneth L. Dean (D) | 25,699 | 28.8 |
| 5 Trent Lott (R) | 52,489 | 73.0 |
| Walter W. Murphey (D) | 10,333 | 14.4 |
| Claudia Mertz (IND) | 6,404 | 8.9 |

## MISSOURI

| Candidates | Votes | % |
|---|---|---|
| 1 William (Bill) Clay (D) | 61,933 | 68.3 |
| Arthur O. Martin (R) | 28,707 | 31.7 |
| 2 James W. Symington (D) | 85,977 | 61.0 |
| Howard C. Ohlendorf (R) | 55,026 | 39.0 |
| 3 Leonor K. Sullivan (D) | 96,201 | 74.3 |
| Jo Ann P. Raisch (R) | 31,489 | 24.3 |
| 4 William J. Randall (D) | 82,447 | 67.9 |
| Claude Patterson (R) | 39,055 | 32.1 |
| 5 Richard Bolling (D) | 57,081 | 69.1 |
| John J. McDonough (R) | 24,669 | 29.9 |
| 6 Jerry Litton (D) | 101,609 | 78.9 |
| Grover H. Speers (R) | 27,147 | 21.1 |
| 7 Gene Taylor (R) | 79,787 | 52.3 |
| Richard L. Franks (D) | 72,653 | 47.7 |
| 8 Richard H. Ichord (D) | 86,595 | 69.9 |
| James A. Noland Jr. (R) | 37,369 | 30.1 |
| 9 William L. Hungate (D) | 87,546 | 66.4 |
| Milton Bischof Jr. (R) | 44,318 | 33.6 |
| 10 Bill D. Burlison (D) | 77,677 | 72.8 |
| Truman Farrow (R) | 29,050 | 27.2 |

## MONTANA

| Candidates | Votes | % |
|---|---|---|
| 1 Max S. Baucus (D) | 74,304 | 54.8 |
| Richard G. Shoup (R) | 61,309 | 45.2 |
| 2 John Melcher (D) | 74,680 | 63.0 |
| John K. McDonald (R) | 43,853 | 37.0 |

## NEBRASKA

| Candidates | Votes | % |
|---|---|---|
| 1 Charles Thone (R) | 82,353 | 53.3 |
| Hess Dyas (D) | 72,099 | 46.7 |
| 2 John Y. McCollister (R) | 72,731 | 55.2 |
| Daniel C. Lynch (D) | 59,142 | 44.8 |
| 3 Virginia Smith (R) | 80,992 | 50.2 |
| Wayne W. Ziebarth (D) | 80,255 | 49.8 |

## NEVADA

| Candidates | Votes | % |
|---|---|---|
| AL James Santini (D) | 93,665 | 55.8 |
| David Towell (R) | 61,182 | 36.4 |
| Joel F. Hansen (IA) | 13,119 | 7.8 |

## NEW HAMPSHIRE

| Candidates | Votes | % |
|---|---|---|
| 1 Norman E. D'Amours (D) | 58,388 | 52.1 |
| David A. Banks (R) | 53,610 | 47.9 |
| 2 James C. Cleveland (R) | 69,068 | 64.2 |
| Helen L. Bliss (D) | 38,463 | 35.8 |

## NEW JERSEY

| Candidates | Votes | % |
|---|---|---|
| 1 James J. Florio (D) | 80,768 | 57.5 |
| John E. Hunt (R) | 54,069 | 38.5 |
| 2 William J. Hughes (D) | 109,763 | 57.3 |
| Charles W. Sandman Jr. (R) | 79,064 | 41.3 |
| 3 James J. Howard (D) | 105,979 | 68.9 |
| Kenneth W. Clark (R) | 45,932 | 29.8 |
| 4 Frank Thompson Jr. (D) | 82,195 | 66.8 |
| Henry J. Keller (R) | 40,797 | 33.2 |
| 5 Millicent Fenwick (R) | 81,498 | 53.4 |
| Frederick M. Bohen (D) | 66,380 | 43.5 |
| 6 Edwin B. Forsythe (R) | 81,190 | 52.5 |
| Charles B. Yates (D) | 70,353 | 45.5 |
| 7 Andrew Maguire (D) | 79,808 | 49.7 |
| William B. Widnall (R) | 71,377 | 44.4 |
| Milton Gralla (IND) | 9,520 | 5.9 |
| 8 Robert A. Roe (D) | 83,724 | 73.9 |
| Herman Schmidt (R) | 27,839 | 24.6 |
| 9 Henry Helstoski (D) | 99,592 | 64.5 |
| Harold A. Pareti (R) | 50,859 | 32.9 |
| 10 Peter W. Rodino Jr. (D) | 53,094 | 81.0 |
| John R. Taliaferro (R) | 9,936 | 15.2 |
| 11 Joseph G. Minish (D) | 98,957 | 69.2 |
| William B. Grant (R) | 42,036 | 29.4 |
| 12 Matthew J. Rinaldo (R) | 92,829 | 65.0 |
| Adam K. Levin (D) | 46,246 | 32.4 |
| 13 Helen S. Meyner (D) | 86,043 | 57.3 |
| Joseph J. Maraziti (R) | 64,166 | 42.7 |
| 14 Dominick V. Daniels (D) | 85,438 | 79.9 |
| Claire J. Sheridan (R) | 17,231 | 16.1 |
| 15 Edward J. Patten (D) | 92,593 | 71.0 |
| E. J. Hammesfahr (R) | 35,875 | 27.5 |

## NEW MEXICO

| Candidates | Votes | % |
|---|---|---|
| 1 Manuel Lujan Jr. (R) | 106,268 | 58.6 |
| Robert A. Mondragon (D) | 71,968 | 39.7 |
| 2 Harold Runnels (D) | 90,127 | 66.7 |
| Donald W. Trubey (R) | 43,045 | 31.9 |

## NEW YORK

| Candidates | Votes | % |
|---|---|---|
| 1 Otis G. Pike (D-L) | 101,130 | 65.0 |
| Donald R. Sallah (R) | 44,513 | 28.6 |
| Seth C. Morgan (C) | 10,038 | 6.4 |
| 2 Thomas J. Downey (D) | 58,289 | 48.8 |
| James R. Grover Jr. (R) | 53,344 | 44.7 |
| Neil Greene (C) | 7,818 | 6.5 |
| 3 Jerome A. Ambro Jr. (D) | 76,383 | 51.8 |
| Angelo D. Roncalio (R-C) | 67,986 | 46.1 |
| 4 Norman F. Lent (R-C) | 85,382 | 53.6 |
| Franklin Ornstein (D-L) | 73,822 | 46.4 |
| 5 John W. Wydler (R-C) | 91,677 | 54.2 |
| Allard K. Lowenstein (D-L) | 77,356 | 45.8 |
| 6 Lester L. Wolff (D-L) | 101,237 | 66.7 |
| Edythe Layne (R-C) | 50,528 | 33.3 |
| 7 Joseph P. Addabbo (D-R-L) | 83,972 | 100.0 |
| 8 Benjamin S. Rosenthal (D-L) | 90,200 | 79.0 |
| Albert Lemishow (R-C) | 23,980 | 21.0 |
| 9 James J. Delaney (D-R-C) | 92,231 | 93.0 |
| Theodore E. Garrison (L) | 6,924 | 7.0 |
| 10 Mario Biaggi (D-R) | 75,375 | 82.4 |
| Francis L. McHugh (R) | 10,250 | 11.2 |
| John P. Hagan (L) | 5,797 | 6.3 |
| 11 James H. Scheuer (D) | 62,388 | 72.2 |
| E. G. Desborough (R) | 12,297 | 14.2 |
| Christopher Acer (C) | 7,181 | 8.3 |
| Tibby Blum (L) | 4,485 | 5.2 |
| 12 Shirley Chisholm (D-L) | 26,468 | 80.2 |
| Francis J. Voyticky (R) | 4,577 | 13.9 |
| 13 Stephen J. Solarz (D-L) | 91,008 | 81.8 |
| Jack N. Dobosh (R-C) | 20,229 | 18.2 |
| 14 Frederick W. Richmond (D) | 33,195 | 71.3 |
| Michael Carbajal Jr. (R) | 5,360 | 11.5 |
| Donald H. Elliott (L) | 6,186 | 13.3 |
| 15 Leo C. Zeferetti (D-C) | 53,733 | 58.4 |
| Austen D. Canade (R) | 34,814 | 37.9 |
| 16 Elizabeth Holtzman (D-L) | 74,010 | 78.9 |
| Joseph L. Gentili (R-C) | 19,806 | 21.1 |
| 17 John M. Murphy (D) | 63,805 | 57.7 |
| Frank J. Biondolillo (R) | 28,269 | 25.6 |
| Jerome Kretchmer (L) | 10,622 | 9.6 |
| Michael Ajello (C) | 7,808 | 7.1 |
| 18 Edward I. Koch (D-L) | 91,985 | 76.7 |
| John Boogaerts Jr. (R) | 22,560 | 18.8 |
| 19 Charles B. Rangel (D-R-L) | 63,146 | 96.9 |
| 20 Bella S. Abzug (D-L) | 76,074 | 78.7 |
| Stephen Posner (R) | 15,053 | 15.6 |
| 21 Herman Badillo (D-L) | 28,025 | 96.7 |
| 22 Jonathan B. Bingham (D-L) | 77,157 | 85.1 |
| Robert Black (R) | 8,142 | 9.0 |
| John DiGiovanni (C) | 5,333 | 5.9 |
| 23 Peter A. Peyser (R-C) | 80,361 | 57.6 |
| W. S. Greenawalt (D-L) | 59,108 | 42.4 |
| 24 Richard L. Ottinger (D) | 82,542 | 57.8 |
| Charles J. Stephens (R-C) | 60,180 | 42.2 |
| 25 Hamilton Fish Jr. (R-C) | 103,799 | 65.3 |
| Nicholas B. Angell (D) | 53,357 | 33.6 |
| 26 Benjamin A. Gilman (R) | 81,562 | 54.0 |
| John G. Dow (D-L) | 58,161 | 38.5 |
| Thomas Moore (C) | 11,345 | 7.5 |
| 27 Matthew F. McHugh (D-L) | 83,562 | 52.8 |
| Alfred J. Libous (R) | 68,273 | 43.1 |
| 28 Samuel S. Stratton (D) | 156,849 | 80.6 |
| Wayne E. Wagner (R) | 33,493 | 17.3 |
| 29 Edward W. Pattison (D-L) | 100,324 | 54.5 |
| Carleton J. King (R-C) | 83,768 | 45.5 |
| 30 Robert C. McEwen (R) | 78,117 | 55.0 |
| Roger W. Tubby (D-L) | 63,893 | 45.0 |
| 31 Donald J. Mitchell (R-C) | 94,319 | 59.6 |
| Donald J. Reile (D) | 59,639 | 37.7 |
| 32 James M. Hanley (D) | 88,660 | 59.1 |
| William E. Bush (R-C) | 61,379 | 40.9 |
| 33 William F. Walsh (R) | 97,380 | 65.3 |
| Robert H. Bockman (D) | 45,043 | 30.2 |
| 34 Frank Horton (R) | 105,585 | 67.5 |
| Irene Gossin (D) | 45,408 | 29.0 |
| 35 Barber B. Conable Jr. (R) | 90,269 | 56.8 |
| Margaret Costanza (D) | 63,012 | 39.6 |
| 36 John J. LaFalce (D-L) | 90,498 | 59.6 |
| Russell A. Rourke (R-C) | 61,442 | 40.4 |
| 37 Henry J. Nowak (D-L) | 84,064 | 75.0 |
| Joseph R. Bala (R-C) | 27,531 | 24.6 |
| 38 Jack F. Kemp (R-C) | 126,687 | 72.1 |
| Barbara C. Wicks (D-L) | 48,929 | 27.9 |
| 39 James F. Hastings (R) | 87,321 | 60.2 |
| W. L. Parment (D-L) | 53,866 | 37.1 |

## NORTH CAROLINA

| | Candidates | Votes | % |
|---|---|---|---|
| 1 | Walter B. Jones (D) | 55,323 | 77.5 |
| | Harry McMullan (R) | 16,097 | 22.5 |
| 2 | L. H. Fountain (D) | 52,786 | 100.0 |
| 3 | David N. Henderson (D) | 50,931 | 100.0 |
| 4 | Ike F. Andrews (D) | 62,600 | 64.7 |
| | Ward Purrington (R) | 33,521 | 34.6 |
| 5 | Stephen L. Neal (D) | 64,634 | 52.0 |
| | Wilmer Mizell (R) | 59,182 | 47.6 |
| 6 | Richardson Preyer (D) | 56,507 | 63.7 |
| | R. S. Ritchie (R) | 31,906 | 35.9 |
| 7 | Charles G. Rose III (D) | 49,780 | 100.0 |
| 8 | W. G. (Bill) Hefner (D) | 61,591 | 57.0 |
| | Earl B. Ruth (R) | 46,500 | 43.0 |
| 9 | James G. Martin (R) | 51,032 | 54.4 |
| | Milton Short (D) | 41,387 | 44.1 |
| 10 | James T. Broyhill (R) | 63,382 | 54.4 |
| | Jack L. Rhyne (D) | 53,131 | 45.6 |
| 11 | Roy A. Taylor (D) | 89,163 | 66.0 |
| | Albert F. Gilman (R) | 45,983 | 34.0 |

## NORTH DAKOTA

| | Candidates | Votes | % |
|---|---|---|---|
| AL | Mark Andrews (R) | 130,184 | 55.7 |
| | Byron Dorgan (D) | 103,504 | 44.3 |

## OHIO

| | Candidates | Votes | % |
|---|---|---|---|
| 1 | Willis D. Gradison Jr. (R) | 70,284 | 50.9 |
| | Thomas A. Luken (D) | 67,685 | 49.1 |
| 2 | Donald D. Clancy (R) | 71,512 | 53.4 |
| | Edward W. Wolterman (D) | 62,530 | 46.6 |
| 3 | Charles W. Whalen Jr. (R) | 82,159 | 100.0 |
| 4 | Tennyson Guyer (R) | 81,674 | 61.5 |
| | James L. Gehrlich (D) | 51,065 | 38.5 |
| 5 | Delbert L. Latta (R) | 89,161 | 62.5 |
| | Bruce Edwards (D) | 53,391 | 37.5 |
| 7 | William H. Harsha (R) | 93,400 | 68.2 |
| | Lloyd Allen Wood (D) | 42,316 | 31.2 |
| 7 | Clarence J. Brown (R) | 73,503 | 60.5 |
| | Patrick L. Nelson (D) | 34,828 | 28.7 |
| | Dorothy Franke (IND) | 13,088 | 10.8 |
| 8 | Thomas N. Kindness (R) | 51,097 | 42.4 |
| | T. Edward Strinko (D) | 45,701 | 38.0 |
| | Don Gingerich (IND) | 23,616 | 19.6 |
| 9 | Thomas L. Ashley (D) | 64,831 | 52.8 |
| | C. S. Finkbeiner Jr. (R) | 57,892 | 47.2 |
| 10 | Clarence E. Miller (R) | 100,521 | 70.4 |
| | H. Kent Bumpass (D) | 42,333 | 29.6 |
| 11 | J. William Stanton (R) | 79,756 | 60.5 |
| | Michael D. Coffey (D) | 52,017 | 39.5 |
| 12 | Samuel L. Devine (R) | 73,303 | 50.9 |
| | Fran Ryan (D) | 70,818 | 49.1 |
| 13 | Charles A. Mosher (R) | 72,881 | 57.5 |
| | Fred M. Ritenauer (D) | 53,766 | 42.5 |
| 14 | John F. Seiberling (D) | 93,931 | 75.4 |
| | Mark Figetakis (R) | 30,603 | 24.6 |
| 15 | Chalmers P. Wylie (R) | 79,376 | 61.5 |
| | Mike McGee (D) | 49,683 | 38.5 |
| 16 | Ralph S. Regula (R) | 92,986 | 65.6 |
| | John G. Freedom (D) | 48,754 | 34.4 |
| 17 | John M. Ashbrook (R) | 70,708 | 52.7 |
| | David D. Noble (D) | 63,342 | 47.3 |
| 18 | Wayne L. Hays (D) | 90,447 | 65.6 |
| | Ralph H. Romig (R) | 47,385 | 34.4 |
| 19 | Charles J. Carney (D) | 97,709 | 72.7 |
| | James L. Ripple (R) | 36,649 | 27.3 |
| 20 | James V. Stanton (D) | 86,405 | 86.9 |
| | Robert A. Frantz (R) | 12,991 | 13.1 |
| 21 | Louis Stokes (D) | 58,969 | 82.0 |
| | Bill Mack (R) | 12,986 | 18.0 |
| 22 | Charles A. Vanik (D) | 112,671 | 78.7 |
| | William J. Franz (R) | 30,585 | 21.3 |
| 23 | Ronald M. Mottl (D) | 53,338 | 34.8 |
| | George E. Mastics (R) | 46,810 | 30.5 |
| | Dennis J. Kucinich (IND) | 45,186 | 29.4 |

**Special Election**

| | Candidates | Votes | % |
|---|---|---|---|
| 1 | Thomas A. Luken (D) | 55,134 | 51.9 |
| | Willis D. Gradison Jr. (R) | 51,063 | 48.1 |

## OKLAHOMA

| | | Votes | % |
|---|---|---|---|
| 1 | James R. Jones (D) | 88,159 | 67.9 |
| | George Alfred Mizer Jr. (R) | 41,697 | 32.1 |
| 2 | Theodore Risenhoover (D) | 78,046 | 59.1 |
| | Ralph F. Keen (R) | 54,110 | 40.9 |
| 3 | Carl Albert (D) | | 100.0 |
| 4 | Tom Steed (D) | | 100.0 |
| 5 | John Jarman (D) | 52,107 | 51.7 |
| | M. H. Edwards (R) | 48,705 | 48.3 |
| 6 | Glenn English (D) | 76,392 | 53.2 |
| | John N. Happy Camp (R) | 63,731 | 44.4 |

## OREGON

| | | Votes | % |
|---|---|---|---|
| 1 | Les AuCoin (D) | 114,629 | 56.0 |
| | Diarmuid O'Scannlain (R) | 89,848 | 43.9 |
| 2 | Al Ullman (D) | 140,963 | 78.1 |
| | Kenneth Brown (R) | 39,441 | 21.9 |
| 3 | Robert Duncan (D) | 129,290 | 70.4 |
| | John Piacentini (R) | 54,080 | 29.5 |
| 4 | James Weaver (D) | 97,580 | 52.9 |
| | John Dellenback (R) | 86,950 | 47.1 |

## PENNSYLVANIA

| | | Votes | % |
|---|---|---|---|
| 1 | William A. Barrett (D) | 96,988 | 75.8 |
| | Russell M. Nigro (R) | 29,772 | 23.3 |
| 2 | Robert N. C. Nix (D) | 75,033 | 74.0 |
| | Jesse W. Woods Jr. (R) | 26,353 | 26.0 |
| 3 | William J. Green III (D) | 84,675 | 75.4 |
| | Richard P. Colbert (R) | 27,692 | 24.6 |
| 4 | Joshua Eilberg (D) | 123,952 | 71.0 |
| | Isadore Einhorn (R) | 50,688 | 29.0 |
| 5 | Richard T. Schulze (R) | 83,526 | 59.6 |
| | Leo D. McDermott (D) | 56,626 | 40.4 |
| 6 | Gus Yatron (D) | 111,127 | 74.6 |
| | Stephen Postupack (R) | 35,805 | 24.0 |
| 7 | Robert W. Edgar (D) | 89,680 | 55.3 |
| | Stephen J. McEwen Jr. (R) | 70,894 | 43.7 |
| 8 | Edward G. Biester Jr. (R) | 75,313 | 56.3 |
| | William B. Moyer (D) | 54,815 | 40.9 |
| 9 | E. G. Shuster (R) | 73,881 | 56.5 |
| | Robert D. Ford (D) | 56,844 | 43.5 |
| 10 | Joseph M. McDade (R) | 100,793 | 64.9 |
| | Thomas J. Hanlon (D) | 54,401 | 35.1 |
| 11 | Daniel J. Flood (D) | 111,572 | 74.5 |
| | Richard A. Muzyka (R) | 38,106 | 25.5 |
| 12 | John P. Murtha (D) | 89,193 | 58.1 |
| | Harry M. Fox (R) | 64,416 | 41.9 |
| 13 | R. Lawrence Coughlin (R) | 98,985 | 62.5 |
| | Lawrence H. Curry (D) | 59,433 | 37.5 |
| 14 | William S. Moorhead (D) | 93,169 | 77.4 |
| | Zachary Taylor Davis (R) | 27,116 | 22.5 |
| 15 | Fred B. Rooney (D) | 85,905 | 100.0 |
| 16 | Edwin D. Eshleman (R) | 73,130 | 63.5 |
| | Michael J. Minney (D) | 40,273 | 35.0 |
| 17 | Herman T. Schneebeli (R) | 70,274 | 52.1 |
| | Peter C. Wambach (D) | 64,576 | 47.9 |
| 18 | H. John Heinz III (R) | 107,723 | 72.1 |
| | Francis J. McArdle (D) | 41,706 | 27.9 |
| 19 | William F. Goodling (R) | 66,417 | 51.4 |
| | Arthur L. Berger (D) | 61,414 | 47.6 |
| 20 | Joseph M. Gaydos (D) | 112,237 | 81.7 |
| | Joseph J. Anderko (R) | 25,129 | 18.3 |
| 21 | John H. Dent (D) | 88,701 | 69.9 |
| | C. L. Sconing (R) | 38,111 | 30.1 |
| 22 | Thomas E. Morgan (D) | 83,654 | 63.6 |
| | J. R. Montgomery (R) | 41,706 | 31.7 |
| 23 | Albert W. Johnson (R) | 67,192 | 52.7 |
| | Yates Mast (D) | 60,211 | 47.3 |
| 24 | Joseph P. Vigorito (D) | 76,920 | 58.6 |
| | Clement R. Scalzitti (R) | 54,277 | 41.4 |
| 25 | Gary A. Myers (R) | 74,645 | 53.8 |
| | Frank M. Clark (D) | 64,049 | 46.2 |

**Special Election**

| | Candidates | Votes | % |
|---|---|---|---|
| 12 | John P. Murtha (D) | 60,538 | 49.9 |
| | Harry M. Fox (R) | 60,416 | 49.8 |

## RHODE ISLAND

| | | Votes | % |
|---|---|---|---|
| 1 | Fernand J. St Germain (D) | 105,288 | 72.9 |
| | Ernest Barone (R) | 39,096 | 27.1 |
| 2 | Edward P. Beard (D) | 124,759 | 78.2 |
| | Vincent J. Rotondo (R) | 34,728 | 21.8 |

## SOUTH CAROLINA

| | | Votes | % |
|---|---|---|---|
| 1 | Mendel J. Davis (D) | 63,111 | 72.7 |
| | George B. Rast (R) | 22,450 | 25.9 |
| 2 | Floyd Spence (R) | 58,936 | 56.1 |
| | Matthew J. Perry (D) | 45,205 | 43.0 |
| 3 | Butler C. Derrick Jr. (D) | 55,120 | 61.8 |
| | Marshall J. Parker (R) | 34,046 | 38.2 |
| 4 | James R. Mann (D) | 45,070 | 63.3 |
| | Robert L. Watkins (R) | 26,185 | 36.7 |
| 5 | Kenneth L. Holland (D) | 47,614 | 61.4 |
| | Len Phillips (R) | 29,294 | 37.8 |
| 6 | John W. Jenrette Jr. (D) | 45,396 | 52.0 |
| | Edward L. Young (R) | 41,982 | 48.0 |

## SOUTH DAKOTA

| | | Votes | % |
|---|---|---|---|
| 1 | Larry Pressler (R) | 78,266 | 55.3 |
| | Frank E. Denholm (D) | 63,339 | 44.7 |
| 2 | James Abdnor (R) | 88,746 | 67.8 |
| | Jack M. Weiland (D) | 42,119 | 32.2 |

## TENNESSEE

| | | Votes | % |
|---|---|---|---|
| 1 | James H. Quillen (R) | 76,394 | 64.2 |
| | Lloyd Blevins (D) | 42,523 | 35.8 |
| 2 | John J. Duncan (R) | 87,419 | 70.9 |
| | Jesse James Brown (D) | 35,920 | 29.1 |
| 3 | Marilyn Lloyd (D) | 61,926 | 51.1 |
| | LaMar Baker (R) | 55,580 | 45.9 |
| 4 | Joe L. Evins (D) | 94,847 | 99.9 |
| 5 | Richard Fulton (D) | 88,206 | 99.8 |
| 6 | Robin L. Beard Jr. (R) | 76,928 | 56.7 |
| | Tim Schaeffer (D) | 58,824 | 43.3 |
| 7 | Ed Jones (D) | 83,231 | 100.0 |
| 8 | Harold E. Ford (D) | 67,925 | 49.9 |
| | Dan Kuykendall (R) | 67,181 | 49.4 |

## TEXAS

| | | Votes | % |
|---|---|---|---|
| 1 | Wright Patman (D) | 49,426 | 68.6 |
| | James W. Farris (R) | 22,619 | 31.4 |
| 2 | Charles Wilson (D) | 57,096 | 100.0 |
| 3 | James M. Collins (R) | 63,489 | 64.7 |
| | Harold Collum (D) | 34,623 | 35.3 |
| 4 | Ray Roberts (D) | 48,209 | 74.9 |
| | Dick LeTourneau (R) | 16,113 | 25.1 |
| 5 | Alan Steelman (R) | 28,446 | 52.1 |
| | Mike McKool (D) | 26,190 | 47.9 |
| 6 | Olin E. Teague (D) | 53,345 | 83.0 |
| | Carl A. Nigliazzo (R) | 10,908 | 17.0 |
| 7 | Bill Archer (R) | 70,363 | 79.2 |
| | Jim Brady (D) | 18,524 | 20.8 |
| 8 | Bob Eckhardt (D) | 30,158 | 72.2 |
| | Donald D. Whitefield (R) | 11,605 | 27.8 |
| 9 | Jack Brooks (D) | 37,275 | 61.9 |
| | Coleman R. Ferguson (R) | 22,935 | 38.1 |
| 10 | J. J. Pickle (D) | 76,240 | 80.4 |
| | Paul A. Weiss (R) | 18,560 | 19.6 |
| 11 | W. R. Poage (D) | 46,828 | 81.6 |
| | Don Clements (R) | 9,883 | 17.2 |
| 12 | Jim Wright (D) | 42,632 | 78.7 |
| | James S. Garvey (R) | 11,543 | 21.3 |

| | Candidates | Votes | % |
|---|---|---|---|
| 13 | Jack Hightower (D) | 53,094 | 57.6 |
| | Robert Price (R) | 39,087 | 42.4 |
| 14 | John Young (D) | 41,066 | 100.0 |
| 15 | Eligio de la Garza (D) | 42,567 | 100.0 |
| 16 | Richard C. White (D) | 42,880 | 100.0 |
| 17 | Omar Burleson (D) | 64,595 | 100.0 |
| 18 | Barbara C. Jordan (D) | 36,597 | 84.8 |
| | Robbins Mitchell (R) | 6,053 | 14.0 |
| 19 | George Mahon (D) | 49,610 | 100.0 |
| 20 | Henry B. Gonzalez (D) | 39,358 | 100.0 |
| 21 | Robert Krueger (D) | 53,543 | 52.6 |
| | Douglas S. Harlan (R) | 45,959 | 45.2 |
| 22 | Bob Casey (D) | 47,783 | 69.5 |
| | Ron Paul (R) | 19,483 | 28.4 |
| 23 | Abraham Kazen Jr. (D) | 47,249 | 100.0 |
| 24 | Dale Milford (D) | 36,085 | 76.1 |
| | Joseph Beaman Jr. (R) | 9,698 | 20.4 |

## UTAH

| | | Votes | % |
|---|---|---|---|
| 1 | K. Gunn McKay (D) | 124,793 | 62.6 |
| | Ronald W. Inkley (R) | 62,807 | 31.5 |
| | L. S. Brown (A) | 11,664 | 5.9 |
| 2 | Allan T. Howe (D) | 105,739 | 49.5 |
| | Stephen M. Harmsen (R) | 100,259 | 46.9 |

## VERMONT

| | | Votes | % |
|---|---|---|---|
| AL | James M. Jeffords (R) | 74,561 | 52.9 |
| | Francis J. Cain (D I VT) | 56,342 | 40.0 |
| | Michael Parenti (LU) | 9,961 | 7.1 |

## VIRGINIA

| | Candidates | Votes | % |
|---|---|---|---|
| 1 | Thomas N. Downing (D) | 58,338 | 99.8 |
| 2 | G. William Whitehurst (R) | 49,369 | 60.0 |
| | Robert R. Richards (D) | 32,923 | 40.0 |
| 3 | David E. Satterfield III (D) | 64,627 | 88.5 |
| | A. R. Ogden (IND) | 7,574 | 10.4 |
| 4 | Robert W. Daniel Jr. (R) | 48,032 | 47.2 |
| | Lester E. Schlitz (D) | 36,489 | 35.9 |
| | Curtis W. Harris (IND) | 17,224 | 16.9 |
| 5 | W. C. (Dan) Daniel (D) | 52,459 | 99.4 |
| 6 | M. Caldwell Butler (R) | 45,805 | 45.1 |
| | Paul J. Puckett (D) | 27,350 | 27.0 |
| | Warren D. Saunders (IND) | 26,466 | 26.1 |
| 7 | J. Kenneth Robinson (R) | 54,267 | 52.6 |
| | George H. Gilliam (D) | 48,611 | 47.1 |
| 8 | Herbert E. Harris (D) | 53,074 | 57.6 |
| | Stanford E. Parris (R) | 38,997 | 42.4 |
| 9 | William C. Wampler (R) | 68,183 | 50.9 |
| | Charles J. Horne (D) | 65,783 | 49.1 |
| 10 | Joseph L. Fisher (D) | 67,184 | 53.6 |
| | Joel T. Broyhill (R) | 56,649 | 45.2 |

## WASHINGTON

| | | Votes | % |
|---|---|---|---|
| 1 | Joel Pritchard (R) | 108,391 | 69.5 |
| | W. R. Knedlik (D) | 44,655 | 28.6 |
| 2 | Lloyd Meeds (D) | 81,565 | 59.7 |
| | Ronald C. Reed (R) | 53,157 | 38.9 |
| 3 | Don Bonker (D) | 93,980 | 60.9 |
| | A. Ludlow Kramer (R) | 58,774 | 38.1 |
| 4 | Mike McCormack (D) | 84,949 | 58.9 |
| | Floyd Paxton (R) | 59,249 | 41.1 |
| 5 | Thomas S. Foley (D) | 87,959 | 64.3 |
| | Gary G. Gage (R) | 48,739 | 35.7 |
| 6 | Floyd V. Hicks (D) | 95,354 | 71.8 |
| | George M. Nalley (R) | 37,400 | 28.2 |
| 7 | Brock Adams (D) | 85,593 | 71.1 |
| | Raymond Pritchard (R) | 34,847 | 28.9 |

## WEST VIRGINIA

| | Candidates | Votes | % |
|---|---|---|---|
| 1 | Robert H. Mollohan (D) | 72,457 | 59.7 |
| | Joe Laurita Jr. (R) | 48,966 | 40.3 |
| 2 | Harley O. Staggers (D) | 73,683 | 64.4 |
| | William H. Loy (R) | 40,779 | 35.6 |
| 3 | John M. Slack (D) | 77,586 | 68.5 |
| | William L. Larcamp (R) | 35,623 | 31.5 |
| 4 | Ken Hechler (D) | 66,420 | 100.0 |

## WISCONSIN

| | | Votes | % |
|---|---|---|---|
| 1 | Les Aspin (D) | 81,902 | 70.5 |
| | Leonard W. Smith (R) | 34,288 | 29.5 |
| 2 | Robert W. Kastenmeier (D) | 93,561 | 64.8 |
| | Elizabeth T. Miller (R) | 50,890 | 35.2 |
| 3 | Alvin J. Baldus (D) | 76,668 | 51.1 |
| | Vernon W. Thomson (R) | 71,171 | 47.4 |
| 4 | Clement J. Zablocki (D) | 84,768 | 72.5 |
| | Lewis H. Collison (R) | 27,818 | 23.8 |
| 5 | Henry S. Reuss (D) | 65,060 | 80.0 |
| | Mildred A. Morries (R) | 16,293 | 20.0 |
| 6 | William A. Steiger (R) | 86,652 | 59.5 |
| | Nancy J. Simenz (D) | 51,571 | 35.4 |
| | Harvey C. LeRoy (A) | 7,432 | 5.1 |
| 7 | David R. Obey (D) | 104,468 | 70.5 |
| | Josef Burger (R) | 43,558 | 29.4 |
| 8 | Robert J. Cornell (D) | 79,923 | 54.4 |
| | Howard V. Froehlich (R) | 66,889 | 45.6 |
| 9 | Robert W. Kasten Jr. (R) | 77,733 | 52.9 |
| | Lynn S. Adelman (D) | 66,071 | 45.0 |

## WYOMING

| | | Votes | % |
|---|---|---|---|
| AL | Teno Roncalio (D) | 69,434 | 54.7 |
| | Tom Stroock (R) | 57,499 | 45.3 |

# 1975 House Elections

## CALIFORNIA

### Special Election

| | Candidates | Votes | % |
|---|---|---|---|
| 37 | Shirley N. Pettis (R) | 53,165 | 60.5 |
| | Ron Pettis (D) | 12,940 | 14.7 |
| | James L. Mayfield (D) | 11,140 | 12.7 |
| | Frank M. Bogert (R) | 4,773 | 5.4 |

## ILLINOIS

### Special Election

| | | Votes | % |
|---|---|---|---|
| 5 | John G. Fary (D) | 55,036 | 71.9 |
| | Francis X. Lawlor (R) | 21,491 | 28.1 |

## LOUISIANA

### Special Election [1]

| | | Votes | % |
|---|---|---|---|
| 6 | W. Henson Moore (R) | 74,802 | 54.1 |
| | Jeff LaCaze (D) | 63,366 | 45.9 |

## TENNESSEE

### Special Election

| | | Votes | % |
|---|---|---|---|
| 5 | Clifford Allen (D) | 46,593 | 64.6 |
| | Bob Olsen (R) | 24,901 | 34.5 |

**1974 Election**

*1. LLJ, the party affiliation of the 1st District candidate, J. M. Sanders, stands for "Life, Liberty, Justice."*

*2. In the 6th District special election, 146,147 votes were were cast. To win outright without a second election, a candidate needed 73,074 votes. John L. Burton received 73,114 votes, 40 more than needed.*

*California was redistricted in 1974 for the November general election, changing the numbers of many of the districts. Burton was re-elected to the 94th Congress (1975-77) from the 5th District and Robert J. Lagomarsino from the 19th.*

*3. There are no reliable final returns for the House race in the 6th District. Post-election results showed Moore leading LaCaze by a handful of votes, but the outcome could not be determined because one voting machine had malfunctioned and did not record votes for LaCaze.*

*The case went to the Louisiana courts for resolution. LaCaze asked that persons who voted on the malfunctioning machine be polled again in court under oath and their votes added to the total, but the Louisiana Supreme Court rejected this plan and ordered a new election. Moore won easily. (See Louisiana 1975.)*

*4. The returns from the 1st District House race are not final. Kyros challenged Emery's election before the House Administration Committee, which conducted a partial recount of the returns until Kyros conceded defeat. The recount changed the total votes received by each candidate, but not the result.*

**1975 Election**

*1. This election, Jan. 7, 1975, was a court-ordered rerun held after it was found impossible to determine who won the November 1974 House race between the same two candidates. (See Louisiana 1974.)*

# 1976 House Elections

## ALABAMA

| Candidates | Votes | % |
|---|---|---|
| 1 Jack Edwards (R) | 98,257 | 62.5 |
| Bill Davenport (D) | 58,906 | 37.5 |
| 2 William L. Dickinson (R) | 90,069 | 57.6 |
| J. Carole Keahey (D) | 66,288 | 42.4 |
| 3 Bill Nichols (D) | 106,935 | 99.0 |
| 4 Tom Bevill (D) | 141,490 | 80.4 |
| Leonard Wilson (R) | 34,531 | 19.6 |
| 5 Ronnie G. Flippo (D) | 113,553 | 100.0 |
| 6 John Buchanan (R) | 92,113 | 56.7 |
| Mel Bailey (D) | 69,384 | 42.7 |
| 7 Walter Flowers (D) | 110,496 | 100.0 |

## ALASKA

| Candidates | Votes | % |
|---|---|---|
| AL Donald E. Young (R) | 83,722 | 70.8 |
| Eben Hopson (D) | 34,194 | 28.9 |

## ARIZONA

| Candidates | Votes | % |
|---|---|---|
| 1 John J. Rhodes (R) | 96,397 | 57.3 |
| Patricia Fullinwider (D) | 68,404 | 40.7 |
| 2 Morris K. Udall (D) | 106,054 | 58.2 |
| Laird Guttersen (R) | 71,765 | 39.4 |
| 3 Bob Stump (D) | 88,854 | 47.5 |
| Fred Koory Jr. (R) | 79,162 | 42.3 |
| Bill McCune (NON PART I) | 19,149 | 10.2 |
| 4 Eldon Rudd (R) | 93,154 | 48.6 |
| Tony Mason (D) | 92,435 | 48.2 |

## ARKANSAS

| Candidates | Votes | % |
|---|---|---|
| 1 Bill Alexander (D) | 116,217 | 68.9 |
| Harlan (Bo) Holleman (R) | 52,565 | 31.1 |
| 2 Jim Guy Tucker (D) | 144,780 | 86.4 |
| James J. Kelly (R) | 22,819 | 13.6 |
| 3 John Paul Hammerschmidt (R) [1] | | 100.0 |
| 4 Ray Thornton (D) [1] | | 100.0 |

## CALIFORNIA

| Candidates | Votes | % |
|---|---|---|
| 1 Harold T. (Bizz) Johnson (D) | 160,477 | 73.9 |
| James E. Taylor (R) | 56,539 | 26.1 |
| 2 Don H. Clausen (R) | 121,290 | 56.0 |
| Oscar H. Klee (D) | 88,829 | 41.0 |
| 3 John E. Moss (D) | 139,779 | 72.9 |
| George R. Marsh Jr. (R) | 52,075 | 27.1 |
| 4 Robert L. Leggett (D) | 75,844 | 46.7 |
| Albert Dehr (R) | 75,193 | 46.3 |
| Joseph E. (Ted) Sheedy (WRITE IN) | 11,279 | 6.9 |
| 5 John L. Burton (D) | 103,746 | 61.8 |
| Branwell Fanning (R) | 64,008 | 38.2 |
| 6 Phillip Burton (D) | 86,493 | 66.1 |
| Tom Spinosa (R) | 35,359 | 27.0 |
| Emily Siegel (PFP) | 6,570 | 5.0 |
| 7 George Miller (D) | 147,064 | 74.7 |
| Robert L. Vickers (R) | 45,863 | 23.3 |
| 8 Ronald V. Dellums (D) | 122,342 | 62.1 |
| Philip S. Breck Jr. (R) | 68,374 | 34.7 |
| 9 Fortney H. Stark Jr. (D) | 116,398 | 70.8 |
| James K. Mills (R) | 44,607 | 27.1 |
| 10 Don Edwards (D) | 111,992 | 72.0 |
| Herb Smith (R) | 38,088 | 24.5 |
| 11 Leo J. Ryan (D) | 107,618 | 61.1 |
| Bob Jones (R) | 62,435 | 35.4 |
| 12 Paul N. McCloskey Jr. (R) | 130,332 | 66.2 |
| David Harris (D) | 61,526 | 31.3 |
| 13 Norman Y. Mineta (D) | 135,291 | 66.8 |
| Ernest L. Konnyu (R) | 63,130 | 31.2 |
| 14 John J. McFall (D) | 123,285 | 72.5 |
| Roger A. Blain (R) | 46,674 | 27.5 |
| 15 B. F. Sisk (D) | 92,735 | 72.2 |
| Carol O. Harner (R) | 35,700 | 27.8 |

| Candidates | Votes | % |
|---|---|---|
| 16 Leon E. Panetta (D) | 104,545 | 53.4 |
| Burt L. Talcott (R) | 91,160 | 46.6 |
| 17 John Krebs (D) | 103,898 | 65.7 |
| Henry J. Andreas (R) | 54,270 | 34.3 |
| 18 William M. Ketchum (R) | 101,658 | 64.2 |
| Dean Close (D) | 56,683 | 35.8 |
| 19 Robert J. Lagomarsino (R) | 124,201 | 64.4 |
| Dan Sisson (D) | 68,722 | 35.6 |
| 20 Barry M. Goldwater Jr. (R) | 146,158 | 67.2 |
| Patti Lear Corman (D) | 71,193 | 32.8 |
| 21 James C. Corman (D) | 101,837 | 66.5 |
| Erwin G. (Ed) Hogan (R) | 44,094 | 28.8 |
| 22 Carlos J. Moorhead (R) | 114,769 | 62.6 |
| Robert L. Salley (D) | 68,543 | 37.4 |
| 32 Anthony C. (Tony) Beilenson (D) | 130,619 | 60.2 |
| Thomas F. Bartman (R) | 86,434 | 39.8 |
| 24 Henry A. Waxman (D) | 108,296 | 67.8 |
| David I. Simmons (R) | 51,478 | 32.2 |
| 25 Edward R. Roybal (D) | 57,966 | 71.9 |
| Jim Madrid (R) | 17,737 | 22.0 |
| Marilyn Seals (PFP) | 4,922 | 6.1 |
| 26 John H. Rousselot (R) | 112,619 | 65.6 |
| Bruce Latta (D) | 59,093 | 34.4 |
| 27 Robert K. Dornan (R) | 114,623 | 54.7 |
| Gary Familian (D) | 94,988 | 45.3 |
| 28 Yvonne Brathwaite Burke (D) | 114,612 | 80.2 |
| Edward S. Skinner (R) | 28,303 | 19.8 |
| 29 Augustus F. Hawkins (D) | 82,515 | 85.4 |
| Michael D. Germonprez (R) | 10,852 | 11.2 |
| 30 George E. Danielson (D) | 82,767 | 74.4 |
| Harry Couch (R) | 28,503 | 25.6 |
| 31 Charles H. Wilson (D) | 83,155 | 100.0 |
| 32 Glenn M. Anderson (D) | 92,034 | 72.2 |
| Clifford O. Young (R) | 35,394 | 27.8 |
| 33 Del Clawson (R) | 95,398 | 55.1 |
| Ted Snyder (D) | 77,807 | 44.9 |
| 34 Mark W. Hannaford (D) | 100,988 | 50.7 |
| Daniel E. Lungren (R) | 98,147 | 49.3 |
| 35 Jim Lloyd (D) | 87,472 | 53.3 |
| Louis Brutocao (R) | 76,765 | 46.7 |
| 36 George E. Brown Jr. (D) | 90,830 | 61.6 |
| Grant C. Carner (R) | 49,368 | 33.5 |
| William E. Pasley (AMI) | 7,358 | 5.0 |
| 37 Shirley N. Pettis (R) | 133,634 | 71.1 |
| Douglas C. Nilson Jr. (D) | 49,021 | 26.1 |
| 38 Jerry M. Patterson (D) | 103,317 | 63.6 |
| James Combs (R) | 59,092 | 36.4 |
| 39 Charles E. Wiggins (R) | 122,657 | 58.6 |
| William E. Farris (D) | 86,745 | 41.4 |
| 40 Robert E. Badham (R) | 148,512 | 59.3 |
| Vivian Hall (D) | 102,132 | 40.7 |
| 41 Bob Wilson (R) | 128,784 | 57.7 |
| King Golden Jr. (D) | 94,590 | 42.3 |
| 42 Lionel Van Deerlin (D) | 103,062 | 76.0 |
| Wes Marden (D) | 32,565 | 24.0 |
| 43 Clair W. Burgener (R) | 173,576 | 65.0 |
| Pat Kelly (D) | 93,475 | 35.0 |

## COLORADO

| Candidates | Votes | % |
|---|---|---|
| 1 Patricia Schroeder (D) | 103,037 | 53.2 |
| Don Friedman (R) | 89,384 | 46.2 |
| 2 Timothy E. Wirth (D) | 121,336 | 50.5 |
| Ed Scott (R) | 118,936 | 49.5 |
| 3 Frank E. Evans (D) | 89,308 | 51.0 |
| Melvin H. Takaki (R) | 82,269 | 47.0 |
| 4 James P. Johnson (R) | 119,408 | 53.7 |
| Dan Ogden (D) | 78,355 | 35.2 |
| Dick Davis (I) | 20,398 | 9.2 |
| 5 William L. Armstrong (R) | 126,784 | 66.4 |
| Dorothy Hores (D) | 64,067 | 33.6 |

## CONNECTICUT

| Candidates | Votes | % |
|---|---|---|
| 1 William R. Cotter (D) | 128,479 | 57.1 |
| Lucien P. DiFazio Jr. (R) | 94,106 | 41.8 |
| 2 Christopher J. Dodd (D) | 142,684 | 65.1 |
| Richard M. Jackson (R) | 74,743 | 34.1 |
| 3 Robert N. Giaimo (D) | 121,623 | 54.6 |
| John G. Pucciano (R) | 96,714 | 43.4 |
| 4 Stewart B. McKinney (R) | 126,314 | 61.0 |
| Geoffrey G. Peterson (R) | 76,722 | 37.1 |
| 5 Ronald A. Sarasin (R) | 157,009 | 66.5 |
| Michael J. Adanti (D) | 77,308 | 32.7 |
| 6 Anthony J. Moffett (D) | 134,914 | 56.6 |
| Thomas F. Upson (R) | 102,364 | 43.0 |

## DELAWARE

| Candidates | Votes | % |
|---|---|---|
| AL Thomas B. Evans Jr. (R) | 110,677 | 51.5 |
| Samuel L. Shipley (D) | 102,431 | 47.7 |

## FLORIDA

| Candidates | Votes | % |
|---|---|---|
| 1 Robert L. F. Sikes (D) [1] | | 100.0 |
| 2 Don Fuqua (D) [1] | | 100.0 |
| 3 Charles E. Bennett (D) [1] | | 100.0 |
| 4 Bill Chappell Jr. (D) [1] | | 100.0 |
| 5 Richard Kelly (R) | 138,371 | 59.0 |
| Jo Ann Saunders (D) | 96,260 | 41.0 |
| 6 C. W. Bill Young (R) | 151,371 | 65.2 |
| Gabriel Cazares (D) | 80,821 | 34.8 |
| 7 Sam M. Gibbons (D) | 102,739 | 65.7 |
| Dusty Owens (R) | 53,599 | 34.3 |
| 8 Andy Ireland (D) | 103,360 | 58.0 |
| Robert Johnson (R) | 74,794 | 42.0 |
| 9 Louis Frey Jr. (R) | 130,509 | 78.1 |
| Joseph A. Rosier (D) | 36,630 | 21.9 |
| 10 L. A. (Skip) Bafalis (R) | 164,273 | 66.3 |
| Bill Sikes (D) | 83,413 | 33.7 |
| 11 Paul G. Rogers (D) | 199,031 | 91.1 |
| Clyde Adams (AM) | 19,406 | 8.9 |
| 12 J. Herbert Burke (R) | 107,268 | 53.9 |
| Charles Friedman (D) | 91,749 | 46.1 |
| 13 William Lehman (D) | 127,822 | 78.3 |
| Lee Arnold Spiegelman (R) | 35,357 | 21.7 |
| 14 Claude Pepper (D) | 82,665 | 72.9 |
| Evelio S. Estrella (R) | 30,774 | 27.1 |
| 15 Dante B. Fascell (D) | 121,292 | 70.4 |
| Paul R. Cobb (R) | 50,941 | 29.6 |

## GEORGIA

| Candidates | Votes | % |
|---|---|---|
| 1 Ronald B. Ginn (D) | 73,826 | 99.9 |
| 2 Dawson Mathis (D) | 95,807 | 99.8 |
| 3 Jack Brinkley (D) | 93,174 | 88.7 |
| Steve Dugan (R) | 11,829 | 11.3 |
| 4 Elliott H. Levitas (D) | 110,261 | 68.3 |
| George Warren (R) | 51,140 | 31.7 |
| 5 Andrew Young (D) | 96,056 | 66.7 |
| Ed Gadrix (R) | 47,998 | 33.3 |
| 6 John J. Flynt Jr. (D) | 77,532 | 51.7 |
| Newt Gingrich (R) | 72,400 | 48.3 |
| 7 Lawrence P. McDonald (D) | 84,587 | 55.1 |
| Quincy Collins (R) | 68,947 | 44.9 |
| 8 Billy Lee Evans (D) | 91,351 | 69.7 |
| Billy Adams (R) | 39,623 | 30.3 |
| 9 Ed Jenkins (D) | 113,245 | 79.0 |
| Louise Wofford (R) | 29,954 | 20.9 |
| 10 Doug Barnard (D) | 94,782 | 99.9 |

## HAWAII

| Candidates | Votes | % |
|---|---|---|
| 1 Cecil (Cec) Heftel (D) | 60,050 | 43.6 |
| Fred W. Rohlfing (R) | 53,745 | 39.1 |
| Kathy Hoshijo (I GOD GOV) | 23,807 | 17.3 |
| 2 Daniel K. Akaka (D) | 124,116 | 79.5 |
| Hank Inouye (R) | 23,917 | 15.3 |

## IDAHO

| Candidates | Votes | % |
|---|---|---|
| 1 Steven D. Symms (R) | 95,833 | 54.6 |
| Ken Pursley (D) | 79,662 | 45.4 |

| Candidates | Votes | % |
|---|---|---|
| 2 George V. Hansen (R) | 84,175 | 50.6 |
| Stan Kress (D) | 82,237 | 49.4 |

### ILLINOIS

| Candidates | Votes | % |
|---|---|---|
| 1 Ralph H. Metcalfe (D) | 126,632 | 92.3 |
| A. A. Rayner (R) | 10,147 | 7.4 |
| 2 Morgan F. Murphy (D) | 127,297 | 84.7 |
| Spencer Leak (R) | 23,037 | 15.3 |
| 3 Martin A. Russo (D) | 115,591 | 58.9 |
| Ronald Buikema (R) | 79,434 | 40.5 |
| 4 Edward J. Derwinski (R) | 124,847 | 65.8 |
| Ronald A. Rodger (D) | 64,924 | 34.2 |
| 5 John G. Fary (D) | 119,336 | 76.9 |
| Vincent Krok (R) | 35,756 | 23.1 |
| 6 Henry J. Hyde (R) | 106,667 | 60.6 |
| Marilyn D. Clancy (D) | 69,359 | 39.4 |
| 7 Cardiss Collins (D) | 88,239 | 84.8 |
| Newell Ward (R) | 15,854 | 15.2 |
| 8 Dan Rostenkowski (D) | 105,595 | 80.5 |
| John F. Urbaszewski (R) | 25,512 | 19.5 |
| 9 Sidney R. Yates (D) | 121,915 | 72.1 |
| Thomas J. Wajerski (R) | 47,054 | 27.8 |
| 10 Abner J. Mikva (D) | 106,804 | 50.0 |
| Samuel H. Young (R) | 106,603 | 50.0 |
| 11 Frank Annunzio (D) | 135,755 | 67.4 |
| Daniel C. Reber (R) | 65,680 | 32.6 |
| 12 Philip M. Crane (R) | 151,899 | 72.8 |
| E. L. Frank (D) | 56,644 | 27.2 |
| 13 Robert McClory (R) | 109,726 | 66.8 |
| James J. Cummings (D) | 49,777 | 30.3 |
| 14 John N. Erlenborn (R) | 176,076 | 74.4 |
| Marie Agnes Fese (D) | 60,505 | 25.6 |
| 15 Tom Corcoran (R) | 102,555 | 53.9 |
| Tim L. Hall (D) | 37,676 | 46.1 |
| 16 John B. Anderson (R) | 114,324 | 67.9 |
| Stephen Eytalis (D) | 54,002 | 32.1 |
| 17 George M. O'Brien (R) | 113,145 | 58.2 |
| Merlin E. Karlock (D) | 81,220 | 41.8 |
| 18 Robert H. Michel (R) | 108,028 | 57.7 |
| Matthew Ryan (D) | 79,102 | 42.3 |
| 19 Thomas F. Railsback (R) | 132,571 | 68.5 |
| John Craver (D) | 60,967 | 31.5 |
| 20 Paul Findley (R) | 137,223 | 63.6 |
| Peter F. Mack Jr. (D) | 78,634 | 36.4 |
| 21 Edward R. Madigan (R) | 137,037 | 74.5 |
| Anna Wall Scott (D) | 46,996 | 25.5 |
| 22 George E. Shipley (D) | 129,187 | 61.4 |
| Ralph Y. McGinnis (R) | 81,102 | 38.6 |
| 23 Melvin Price (D) | 128,113 | 78.6 |
| Sam P. Drenovac (R) | 34,825 | 21.4 |
| 24 Paul Simon (D) | 152,344 | 67.4 |
| Peter G. Prineas (R) | 73,766 | 32.6 |

### INDIANA

| Candidates | Votes | % |
|---|---|---|
| 1 Adam Benjamin Jr. (D) | 121,155 | 71.3 |
| Robert J. Billings (R) | 48,756 | 28.7 |
| 2 Floyd Fithian (D) | 117,617 | 54.8 |
| William W. Erwin (R) | 95,505 | 44.5 |
| 3 John Brademas (D) | 101,777 | 56.9 |
| Thomas L. Thorson (R) | 77,094 | 43.1 |
| 4 Dan Quayle (R) | 107,762 | 54.4 |
| J. Edward Roush (D) | 88,361 | 44.6 |
| 5 Elwood H. Hillis (R) | 127,194 | 61.7 |
| William C. Stout (D) | 78,807 | 38.3 |
| 6 David W. Evans (D) | 105,773 | 54.9 |
| David G. Crane (R) | 86,854 | 45.1 |
| 7 John T. Myers (R) | 130,005 | 62.7 |
| John Elden Tipton (D) | 77,355 | 37.3 |
| 8 David L. Cornwell (D) | 109,013 | 50.5 |
| Belden Bell (R) | 107,013 | 49.5 |
| 9 Lee H. Hamilton (D) | 136,056 | 100.0 |
| 10 Philip R. Sharp (D) | 114,559 | 59.8 |
| William G. Frazier (R) | 76,890 | 40.2 |
| 11 Andrew Jacobs Jr. (D) | 115,895 | 60.4 |
| Lawrence L. Buell (R) | 74,829 | 39.0 |

### IOWA

| Candidates | Votes | % |
|---|---|---|
| 1 James A. S. Leach (R) | 109,694 | 51.9 |
| Edward Mezvinsky (D) | 101,024 | 47.8 |
| 2 Michael T. Blouin (D) | 102,980 | 50.3 |
| Tom Riley (R) | 100,344 | 49.1 |
| 3 Charles E. Grassley (R) | 117,957 | 56.5 |
| Stephen J. Rapp (D) | 90,981 | 43.5 |
| 4 Neal Smith (D) | 145,343 | 69.1 |
| Charles E. Minor (R) | 65,013 | 30.9 |
| 5 Tom Harkin (D) | 135,600 | 64.9 |
| Kenneth R. Fulk (R) | 71,377 | 34.1 |
| 6 Berkley Bedell (D) | 133,507 | 67.4 |
| Joanne D. Soper (R) | 62,292 | 31.5 |

### KANSAS

| Candidates | Votes | % |
|---|---|---|
| 1 Keith G. Sebelius (R) | 142,311 | 73.1 |
| Randy D. Yowell (D) | 52,459 | 26.9 |
| 2 Martha E. Keys (D) | 88,645 | 50.7 |
| Ross R. Freeman (R) | 82,946 | 47.4 |
| 3 Larry Winn Jr. (R) | 123,578 | 68.7 |
| Philip S. Rhoads (D) | 52,110 | 29.0 |
| 4 Dan Glickman (D) | 90,067 | 50.3 |
| Garner E. Shriver (R) | 86,832 | 48.5 |
| 5 Joe Skubitz (R) | 109,573 | 60.7 |
| Virgil L. Olson (D) | 65,340 | 36.2 |

### KENTUCKY

| Candidates | Votes | % |
|---|---|---|
| 1 Carroll Hubbard Jr. (D) | 118,886 | 82.0 |
| Bob Bersky (R) | 26,089 | 18.0 |
| 2 William H. Natcher (D) | 79,016 | 60.4 |
| Walter A. Baker (R) | 51,900 | 39.6 |
| 3 Romano L. Mazzoli (D) | 80,496 | 57.2 |
| Denzil J. Ramsey (R) | 58,019 | 41.2 |
| 4 M. G. (Gene) Snyder (R) | 97,493 | 55.9 |
| Edward J. Winterberg (D) | 77,009 | 44.1 |
| 5 Tim Lee Carter (R) | 100,204 | 66.6 |
| Charles C. Smith (D) | 49,128 | 32.6 |
| 6 John Breckinridge (D) | 90,695 | 94.0 |
| Anthony A. McCord (AM) | 5,795 | 6.0 |
| 7 Carl D. Perkins (D) | 110,450 | 73.2 |
| Granville Thomas (R) | 40,381 | 26.8 |

### LOUISIANA

| Candidates | Votes | % |
|---|---|---|
| 1 Richard A. Tonry (D) | 61,652 | 47.2 |
| Bob Livingston (R) | 56,679 | 43.4 |
| John R. Rarick (I) | 12,227 | 9.4 |
| 2 Corinne (Lindy) (Mrs. Hale) Boggs (D) | 85,923 | 92.6 |
| Jules W. Hillery (I) | 6,904 | 7.4 |
| 3 David C. Treen (R) | 109,135 | 73.3 |
| David H. Scheuermann Sr. (D) | 39,728 | 26.7 |
| 4 Joe D. Waggonner Jr. (D) | 76,406 | 100.0 |
| 5 Jerry Huckaby (D) | 83,696 | 52.5 |
| Frank Spooner (R) | 75,574 | 47.5 |
| 6 W. Henson Moore III (R) | 99,780 | 65.2 |
| J. D. DeBlieux (D) | 53,212 | 34.8 |
| 7 John B. Breaux (D) | 117,196 | 83.3 |
| Charles F. Huff (R) | 23,414 | 16.7 |
| 8 Gillis W. Long (D) | 106,285 | 94.2 |
| Kent Courtney (I) | 6,526 | 5.8 |

### MAINE

| Candidates | Votes | % |
|---|---|---|
| 1 David F. Emery (R) | 145,523 | 57.4 |
| Frederick D. Barton (D) | 108,105 | 42.6 |
| 2 William S. Cohen (R) | 169,292 | 77.1 |
| Leighton Cooney (D) | 43,150 | 19.7 |

### MARYLAND

| Candidates | Votes | % |
|---|---|---|
| 1 Robert E. Bauman (R) | 85,919 | 54.1 |
| Roy Dyson (D) | 72,993 | 45.9 |
| 2 Clarence D. Long (D) | 139,196 | 70.9 |
| John M. Seney (R) | 35,258 | 18.0 |
| Ronald A. Meroney (I) | 21,849 | 11.1 |
| 3 Barbara Mikulski (D) | 107,014 | 74.6 |
| Samuel A. Culotta (R) | 36,447 | 25.4 |
| 4 Marjorie S. Holt (R) | 95,158 | 57.7 |
| Werner Fornos (D) | 69,855 | 42.3 |
| 5 Gladys N. Spellman (D) | 77,836 | 57.7 |
| John B. Burcham Jr. (R) | 57,057 | 42.3 |
| 6 Goodloe E. Bryon (D) | 126,801 | 70.8 |
| Arthur T. Bond (R) | 52,203 | 29.2 |
| 7 Parren J. Mitchell (D) | 94,991 | 94.4 |
| William Salisbury (I) | 5,642 | 5.6 |
| 8 Newton Steers (R) | 111,274 | 46.8 |
| Lanny Davis (D) | 100,343 | 42.2 |
| Robin Ficker (I) | 26,035 | 11.0 |

### MASSACHUSETTS

| Candidates | Votes | % |
|---|---|---|
| 1 Silvio O. Conte (R) | 137,652 | 63.8 |
| Edward A. McColgan (D) | 78,181 | 36.2 |
| 2 Edward P. Boland (D) | 134,408 | 72.4 |
| Thomas P. Swank (R) | 41,563 | 22.4 |
| John D. McCarthy (USLP) | 9,776 | 5.3 |
| 3 Joseph D. Early (D) | 168,520 | 100.0 |
| 4 Robert F. Drinan (D) | 109,268 | 52.1 |
| Arthur D. Mason (R) | 100,562 | 47.9 |
| 5 Paul E. Tsongas (D) | 144,217 | 67.3 |
| Roger P. Durkin (R) | 70,036 | 32.7 |
| 6 Michael J. Harrington (D) | 121,562 | 54.8 |
| William E. Bronson (R) | 91,655 | 41.3 |
| 7 Edward J. Markey (D) | 162,126 | 76.9 |
| Richard W. Daly (R) | 37,063 | 17.6 |
| 8 Thomas P. O'Neill Jr. (D) | 133,131 | 74.4 |
| William A. Barnstead (R) | 33,437 | 18.7 |
| 9 John Joseph Moakley (D) | 103,901 | 69.6 |
| Robert G. Cunningham (R) | 34,547 | 23.1 |
| Joseph M. O'Loughlin (I) | 7,862 | 5.3 |
| 10 Margaret M. Heckler (R) | 176,604 | 100.0 |
| 11 James A. Burke (D) | 131,789 | 69.0 |
| Danielle DeBenedictis (I) | 59,240 | 31.0 |
| 12 Gerry E. Studds (D) | 222,418 | 100.0 |

### MICHIGAN

| Candidates | Votes | % |
|---|---|---|
| 1 John Conyers Jr. (D) | 126,161 | 92.4 |
| Isaac Hood (R) | 8,927 | 6.5 |
| 2 Carl D. Pursell (R) | 95,397 | 49.8 |
| Edward C. Pierce (D) | 95,053 | 49.6 |
| 3 Garry Brown (R) | 99,231 | 50.6 |
| Howard Wolpe (D) | 95,261 | 48.6 |
| 4 Dave Stockman (R) | 107,881 | 60.0 |
| Richard E. Daugherty (D) | 69,655 | 38.8 |
| 5 Harold S. Sawyer (R) | 109,589 | 53.3 |
| Richard F. Vander Veen (D) | 94,973 | 46.2 |
| 6 Bob Carr (D) | 108,909 | 52.7 |
| Clifford W. Taylor (R) | 96,008 | 46.3 |
| 7 Dale E. Kildee (D) | 124,260 | 70.6 |
| Robin Widgery (R) | 50,301 | 28.3 |
| 8 Bob Traxler (D) | 110,127 | 59.2 |
| E. Brady Denton (R) | 75,323 | 40.4 |
| 9 Guy A. Vander Jagt (R) | 146,712 | 70.6 |
| Stephen Fawley (D) | 61,641 | 29.4 |
| 10 Elford A. Cederberg (R) | 118,726 | 56.3 |
| Donald J. Albosta (D) | 89,980 | 42.3 |
| 11 Philip E. Ruppe (R) | 118,871 | 54.4 |
| Francis D. Brouillette (D) | 97,325 | 44.6 |
| 12 David E. Bonior (D) | 94,815 | 52.4 |
| David M. Serotkin (R) | 85,326 | 47.2 |
| 13 Charles C. Diggs Jr. (D) | 83,387 | 89.4 |
| Richard A. Golden (R) | 9,002 | 9.6 |
| 14 Lucien N. Nedzi (D) | 107,503 | 66.9 |
| John Edward Getz (R) | 52,995 | 32.9 |
| 15 William D. Ford (D) | 117,313 | 74.4 |
| James D. Walaskay (R) | 39,177 | 24.8 |
| 16 John D. Dingell Jr. (D) | 121,682 | 75.9 |
| William E. Rostron (R) | 36,378 | 22.7 |
| 17 William M. Brodhead (D) | 112,746 | 64.4 |
| James W. Burdick (R) | 60,476 | 34.6 |
| 18 James J. Blanchard (D) | 123,113 | 66.9 |
| John E. Olsen (R) | 60,995 | 32.6 |
| 19 William S. Broomfield (R) | 131,799 | 66.9 |
| Dorothea Becker (D) | 64,337 | 32.6 |

### MINNESOTA

| Candidates | Votes | % |
|---|---|---|
| 1 Albert H. Quie (I-R) | 158,177 | 68.8 |
| Robert C. Olson Jr. (DFL) | 70,630 | 30.6 |

| Candidates | Votes | % |
|---|---|---|
| 2 Tom Hagedorn (I-R) | 148,322 | 60.3 |
| Gloria Griffin (DFL) | 97,488 | 39.7 |
| 3 Bill Frenzel (I-R) | 149,013 | 66.1 |
| Jerome W. Coughlin (DFL) | 72,044 | 32.0 |
| 4 Bruce F. Vento (DFL) | 133,282 | 66.4 |
| Andrew Engebretson (I-R) | 59,767 | 29.8 |
| 5 Donald M. Fraser (DFL) | 138,213 | 70.7 |
| Richard M. Erdall (I-R) | 50,764 | 26.0 |
| 6 Richard M. Nolan (DFL) | 147,507 | 59.8 |
| James Anderson (I-R) | 99,201 | 40.2 |
| 7 Bob Bergland (DFL) | 174,080 | 72.0 |
| Bob Leiseth (I-R) | 64,333 | 26.6 |
| 8 James L. Oberstar (DFL) | 206,755 | 100.0 |

## MISSISSIPPI

| | Votes | % |
|---|---|---|
| 1 Jamie L. Whitten (D) | 03,687 | 100.0 |
| 2 David R. Bowen (D) | 75,092 | 63.0 |
| Roland Byrd (R) | 42,601 | 35.7 |
| 3 G. V. (Sonny) Montgomery (D) | 129,088 | 93.9 |
| Dorothy Colby Cleveland (R) | 8,321 | 6.1 |
| 4 Thad Cochran (R) | 101,132 | 76.0 |
| Sterling P. Davis (D) | 28,737 | 21.6 |
| 5 Trent Lott (R) | 104,554 | 68.2 |
| Gerald Blessey (D) | 48,724 | 31.8 |

## MISSOURI

| | Votes | % |
|---|---|---|
| 1 William Clay (D) | 87,310 | 65.5 |
| Robert L. Witherspoon (R) | 45,874 | 34.4 |
| 2 Robert A. Young (D) | 111,568 | 51.1 |
| Robert O. Snyder (R) | 106,811 | 48.9 |
| 3 Richard A. Gephardt (D) | 115,109 | 63.7 |
| Joseph L. Badaracco (R) | 65,623 | 36.3 |
| 4 Ike Skelton (D) | 115,955 | 55.9 |
| Richard A. King (R) | 91,605 | 44.1 |
| 5 Richard Bolling (D) | 100,876 | 68.0 |
| Joanne M. Collins (R) | 41,681 | 28.1 |
| 6 E. Thomas Coleman (R) | 120,969 | 58.5 |
| Morgan Maxfield (D) | 83,755 | 40.5 |
| 7 Gene Taylor (R) | 133,656 | 62.0 |
| Dolan G. Hawkins (D) | 81,848 | 38.0 |
| 8 Richard Ichord (D) | 132,386 | 67.3 |
| Charles R. Leick(R) | 60,179 | 30.6 |
| 9 Harold L. Volkmer (D) | 120,325 | 55.9 |
| J. H. Frappier (R) | 94,816 | 44.1 |
| 10 Bill D. Burlison (D) | 131,675 | 72.1 |
| Joe Carron (R) | 51,024 | 27.9 |

## MONTANA

| | Votes | % |
|---|---|---|
| 1 Max S. Baucus (D) | 111,487 | 66.4 |
| W. D. (Bill) Diehl (R) | 56,297 | 33.6 |
| 2 Ron Marlenee (R) | 84,149 | 55.0 |
| Thomas E. Towe (D) | 68,972 | 45.0 |

## NEBRASKA

| | Votes | % |
|---|---|---|
| 1 Charles Thone (R) | 146,558 | 73.2 |
| Pauline F. Anderson (D) | 53,703 | 26.8 |
| 2 John J. Cavanaugh (D) | 106,296 | 54.6 |
| Lee Terry (R) | 88,352 | 45.4 |
| 3 Virginia Smith (R) | 150,720 | 72.9 |
| James T. Hansen (D) | 51,012 | 24.7 |

## NEVADA

| | Votes | % |
|---|---|---|
| AL James Santini (D) | 153,996 | 77.1 |
| Walden Charles Earhart (R) | 24,124 | 12.1 |
| Janine M. Hansen (IA) | 12,038 | 6.0 |

## NEW HAMPSHIRE

| | Votes | % |
|---|---|---|
| 1 Norman E. D'Amours (D) | 107,806 | 68.0 |
| John Adams (R) | 48,087 | 30.3 |
| 2 James C. Cleveland (R) | 100,911 | 60.5 |
| J. Joseph Grandmaison (D) | 65,792 | 39.5 |

## NEW JERSEY

| Candidates | Votes | % |
|---|---|---|
| 1 James J. Florio (D) | 136,624 | 70.1 |
| Joseph I. McCullough Jr. (R) | 56,363 | 28.9 |
| 2 William J. Hughes (D) | 141,753 | 61.7 |
| James R. Hurley (R) | 87,915 | 38.3 |
| 3 James J. Howard (D) | 127,164 | 62.1 |
| Ralph A. Siciliano(R) | 75,934 | 37.1 |
| 4 Frank Thompson Jr. (D) | 113,281 | 66.3 |
| Joseph S. Indyk (R) | 54,789 | 32.1 |
| 5 Millicent Fenwick (R) | 137,803 | 66.9 |
| Frank R. Nero (D) | 64,598 | 31.3 |
| 6 Edwin B. Forsythe (R) | 125,920 | 58.8 |
| Catherine A. Costa (D) | 85,053 | 39.7 |
| 7 Andrew Maguire (D) | 120,526 | 56.5 |
| James J. Sheehan (R) | 92,624 | 43.5 |
| 8 Robert A. Roe (D) | 108,841 | 70.6 |
| Bessie Doty (R) | 44,775 | 29.0 |
| 9 Harold C. Hollenbeck (R) | 107,454 | 53.1 |
| Henry Helstoski (D) | 89,723 | 44.3 |
| 10 Peter W. Rodino Jr. (D) | 88,245 | 82.6 |
| Tony Grandison (R) | 17,129 | 16.0 |
| 11 Joseph G. Minish (D) | 129,026 | 67.6 |
| Charles A. Poekel Jr. (R) | 59,397 | 31.1 |
| 12 Matthew J. Rinaldo (R) | 136,973 | 73.1 |
| Richard A. Buggelli (D) | 49,189 | 26.3 |
| 13 Helen S. Meyner (D) | 105,291 | 50.4 |
| William E. Schluter (R) | 100,050 | 47.9 |
| 14 Joseph A. LeFante (D) | 73,174 | 49.9 |
| Anthony L. Campenni (R) | 66,319 | 45.2 |
| 15 Edward J. Patten (D) | 106,170 | 59.0 |
| Charles W. Wiley (R) | 54,487 | 30.3 |
| Dennis Adams Sr. (I) | 14,543 | 8.1 |

## NEW MEXICO

| | Votes | % |
|---|---|---|
| 1 Manuel Lujan Jr. (R) | 162,587 | 72.1 |
| Raymond Garcia (D) | 61,800 | 27.4 |
| 2 Harold Runnels (D) | 123,563 | 70.3 |
| Donald W. Trubey (R) | 52,131 | 29.7 |

## NEW YORK

| | Votes | % |
|---|---|---|
| 1 Otis G. Pike (D,L) | 135,528 | 65.3 |
| Salvatore Nicosia (R) | 61,671 | 29.7 |
| 2 Thomas J. Downey (D,I) | 91,241 | 57.1 |
| Peter Cohalan (R,C) | 67,755 | 42.4 |
| 3 Jerome A. Ambro Jr. (D) | 94,265 | 52.0 |
| Howard T. Hogan Jr. (R,C) | 84,824 | 46.8 |
| 4 Norman F. Lent (R,C) | 106,058 | 55.8 |
| Gerald P. Halpern (D,L) | 83,971 | 44.2 |
| 5 John W. Wydler (R,C) | 110,366 | 55.7 |
| Ailard K. Lowenstein (D,L) | 87,868 | 44.3 |
| 6 Lester L. Wolff (D,L) | 112,422 | 61.8 |
| Vincent R. Balletta Jr. (R) | 60,567 | 33.3 |
| 7 Joseph P. Addabbo (D,R,L) | 107,312 | 94.7 |
| 8 Benjamin S. Rosenthal (D,L) | 107,295 | 77.8 |
| Albert Lemishow (R,C) | 30,191 | 21.9 |
| 9 James J. Delaney (D,R,C) | 109,552 | 95.1 |
| 10 Mario Biaggi (D,R) | 106,222 | 91.6 |
| Joanne S. Fuchs (C) | 5,868 | 5.1 |
| 11 James H. Scheuer (D) | 84,770 | 74.1 |
| Arthur Cuccia (R) | 19,203 | 16.8 |
| Bryan F. Levinson (C) | 6,316 | 5.5 |
| 12 Shirley Chisholm (D,L) | 43,203 | 87.0 |
| Horace Morancie (R) | 5,336 | 10.8 |
| 13 Stephen J. Solarz (D,L) | 110,624 | 83.7 |
| Jack N. Dobosh (R,C) | 21,600 | 16.3 |
| 14 Frederick W. Richmond (D,L) | 55,723 | 85.0 |
| Frank X. Gargiulo (R,C) | 8,977 | 13.7 |
| 15 Leo C. Zeferetti (D,C) | 69,242 | 63.2 |
| Ronald J. D'Angelo (R) | 33,641 | 30.7 |
| Arthur J. Paone (L) | 6,604 | 6.0 |
| 16 Elizabeth Holtzman (D,L) | 93,995 | 82.9 |
| Gladys Pemberton (R,C) | 19,423 | 17.1 |
| 17 John M. Murphy (D) | 89,126 | 65.6 |
| Kenneth J. Grossberger (R) | 27,734 | 20.4 |
| John M. Peters (C) | 10,399 | 7.7 |
| Ned Schneir (L) | 8,656 | 6.4 |
| 18 Edward I. Koch (D,L) | 112,187 | 75.1 |
| Sonia Landau (R) | 29,728 | 19.9 |

| Candidates | Votes | % |
|---|---|---|
| 19 Charles B. Rangel (D,R,L) | 91,672 | 97.0 |
| 20 Theodore S. Weiss (D,L) | 91,977 | 83.2 |
| Denise Weiseman (R) | 14,114 | 12.8 |
| 21 Herman Badillo (D,R,L) | 41,285 | 98.6 |
| 22 Jonathan B. Bingham (D,L) | 92,044 | 86.4 |
| Paul Slotkin (R) | 11,130 | 10.4 |
| 23 Bruce F. Caputo (R,C) | 93,006 | 53.6 |
| J. Edward Meyer (D,L) | 80,424 | 46.4 |
| 24 Richard L. Ottinger (D) | 99,761 | 54.5 |
| David V. Hicks (R,C) | 81,111 | 44.3 |
| 25 Hamilton Fish Jr. (R,C) | 139,434 | 70.5 |
| Minna Post Peyser (D) | 58,216 | 29.5 |
| 26 Benjamin A. Gilman (R) | 120,049 | 65.3 |
| John R. Maloney (D) | 60,511 | 32.9 |
| 27 Matthew F. McHugh (D,L) | 127,048 | 66.6 |
| William H. Harter (R,C) | 63,626 | 33.4 |
| 28 Samuel S. Stratton (D) | 170,034 | 79.0 |
| Mary A. Bradt (R,C) | 44,053 | 20.5 |
| 29 Edward W. Pattison (D,L) | 100,663 | 47.0 |
| Joseph A. Martino (R) | 96,476 | 45.0 |
| James E. DeYoung (C) | 15,337 | 7.2 |
| 30 Robert C. McEwen (R,C) | 95,564 | 55.7 |
| Norma A. Bartle (D) | 75,951 | 44.3 |
| 31 Donald J. Mitchell (R,C) | 123,143 | 66.5 |
| Anita Maxwell (D) | 62,032 | 33.5 |
| 32 James M. Hanley (D) | 101,419 | 54.8 |
| George C. Wortley (R,C) | 81,597 | 44.1 |
| 33 William F. Walsh (R) | 125,163 | 68.5 |
| Charles R. Welch (D) | 48,855 | 26.7 |
| 34 Frank J. Horton (R) | 126,566 | 65.9 |
| William C. Larsen (D) | 58,247 | 30.3 |
| 35 Barber B. Conable Jr. (R) | 120,738 | 64.3 |
| Michael Macaluso (D,C) | 67,177 | 35.7 |
| 36 John J. LaFalce (D,L) | 123,246 | 66.6 |
| Ralph J. Argen (R,C) | 61,701 | 33.4 |
| 37 Henry J. Nowak (D,L) | 100,042 | 78.2 |
| Calvin Kimbrough (R) | 23,660 | 18.5 |
| 38 Jack F. Kemp (R,C) | 165,702 | 78.2 |
| Peter J. Geraci (D,L) | 46,307 | 21.8 |
| 39 Stanley N. Lundine (D) | 109,986 | 61.8 |
| Richard A. Snowden (R,C) | 68,018 | 38.2 |

| **Special Election** | | |
|---|---|---|
| 39 Stanley N. Lundine (D) | 55,402 | 61.2 |
| John T. Calkins (R) | 35,107 | 38.8 |

## NORTH CAROLINA

| | Votes | % |
|---|---|---|
| 1 Walter B. Jones (D) | 98,611 | 75.9 |
| Joseph M. Ward (R) | 29,295 | 22.5 |
| 2 L. H. Fountain (D) | 113,368 | 99.8 |
| 3 Charlie Whitley (D) | 77,193 | 68.7 |
| Willard J. Blanchard (R) | 35,089 | 31.2 |
| 4 Ike F. Andrews (D) | 92,165 | 60.6 |
| Johnnie L. Gallemore Jr. (R) | 59,917 | 39.4 |
| 5 Stephen L. Neal (D) | 98,789 | 54.2 |
| Wilmer D. Mizell (R) | 83,129 | 45.6 |
| 6 Richardson Preyer (D) | 103,851 | 96.3 |
| 7 Charles Rose (D) | 95,463 | 81.3 |
| M.H. (Mike) Vaughan (R) | 21,955 | 18.7 |
| 8 W. G. (Bill) Hefner (D) | 99,296 | 65.7 |
| Carl Eagle (R) | 49,094 | 32.5 |
| 9 James G. Martin (R) | 82,297 | 53.5 |
| Arthur Goodman Jr. (D) | 70,847 | 46.1 |
| 10 James T. Broyhill (R) | 99,882 | 59.8 |
| John J. Hunt (D) | 67,190 | 40.2 |
| 11 Lamar Gudger (D) | 93,857 | 50.9 |
| Bruce B. Briggs (R) | 88,752 | 48.1 |

## NORTH DAKOTA

| | Votes | % |
|---|---|---|
| AL Mark Andrews (R) | 181,018 | 62.4 |
| Lloyd Omdahl (D) | 104,263 | 36.0 |

## OHIO

| | Votes | % |
|---|---|---|
| 1 Willis D. Gradison Jr. (R) | 109,789 | 64.8 |
| William F. Bowen (D) | 56,995 | 33.6 |
| 2 Thomas A. Luken (D) | 88,178 | 51.4 |
| Donald D. Clancy (R) | 83,459 | 48.6 |

| Candidates | Votes | % |
|---|---|---|
| 3 Charles W. Whalen Jr. (R) | 100,871 | 69.4 |
| Leonard Stubbs (D) | 33,873 | 23.3 |
| 4 Tennyson Guyer (R) | 121,173 | 70.1 |
| Clinton G. Dorsey (D) | 51,784 | 29.9 |
| 5 Delbert L. Latta (R) | 124,910 | 67.4 |
| Bruce Edwards (D) | 60,304 | 32.6 |
| 6 William H. Harsha (R) | 107,064 | 61.5 |
| Ted Strickland (D) | 67,067 | 38.5 |
| 7 Clarence J. Brown Jr. (R) | 101,027 | 64.9 |
| Dorothy Franke (D) | 54,755 | 35.1 |
| 8 Thomas N. Kindness (R) | 110,775 | 68.7 |
| John W. Griffin (D) | 46,424 | 28.8 |
| 9 Thomas L. Ashley (D) | 91,040 | 54.2 |
| C. S. Finkbeiner (R) | 73,919 | 44.0 |
| 10 Clarence E. Miller (R) | 127,147 | 68.8 |
| James A. Plummer (D) | 57,757 | 31.2 |
| 11 J. William Stanton (R) | 120,716 | 71.7 |
| Thomas R. West Jr. (D) | 47,548 | 28.3 |
| 12 Samuel L. Devine (R) | 90,987 | 46.5 |
| Fran Ryan (D) | 89,424 | 45.7 |
| William R. Moss (I) | 15,429 | 7.9 |
| 13 Don J. Pease (D) | 108,061 | 66.0 |
| Woodrow W. Mathna (R) | 49,828 | 30.4 |
| 14 John F. Seiberling Jr. (D) | 121,652 | 74.1 |
| James E. Houston (R) | 39,917 | 24.3 |
| 15 Chalmers P. Wylie (R) | 109,630 | 65.5 |
| Mike McGee (D) | 57,741 | 34.5 |
| 16 Ralph S. Regula (R) | 116,374 | 66.8 |
| John G. Freedom (D) | 55,671 | 32.0 |
| 17 John M. Ashbrook (R) | 94,874 | 56.8 |
| John C. McDonald (D) | 72,168 | 43.2 |
| 18 Douglas Applegate (D) | 116,901 | 62.9 |
| Ralph R. McCoy (R) | 45,735 | 24.6 |
| William Crabbe (I) | 21,537 | 11.6 |
| 19 Charles J. Carney (D) | 90,386 | 50.2 |
| Jack C. Hunter (R) | 86,162 | 47.9 |
| 20 Mary Rose Oakar (D) | 98,785 | 81.0 |
| Raymond J. Grabow (I) | 20,553 | 16.9 |
| 21 Louis Stokes (D) | 91,903 | 83.8 |
| Barbara Sparks (R) | 12,434 | 11.3 |
| 22 Charles A. Vanik (D) | 128,535 | 72.7 |
| Harry A. Hanna (R) | 42,727 | 24.2 |
| 32 Ronald M. Mottl (D) | 130,576 | 73.2 |
| Michael T. Scanlon (R) | 47,804 | 26.8 |

## OKLAHOMA

| Candidates | Votes | % |
|---|---|---|
| 1 James R. Jones (D) | 100,945 | 54.0 |
| James M. Inhofe (R) | 84,374 | 45.1 |
| 2 Theodore Risenhoover (D) | 102,402 | 54.0 |
| E. L. (Bud) Stewart (R) | 87,341 | 46.0 |
| 3 Wes Watkins (D) | 151,271 | 82.0 |
| Gerald L. Beasley Jr. (R) | 31,732 | 17.2 |
| 4 Tom Steed (D) | 116,425 | 74.9 |
| M. C. Stanley (R) | 34,170 | 22.0 |
| 5 M. H. Edwards (R) | 78,651 | 49.9 |
| Tom Dunlap (D) | 74,752 | 47.4 |
| 6 Glenn English (D) | 137,498 | 71.1 |
| Carol McCurley (R) | 55,953 | 28.9 |

## OREGON

| Candidates | Votes | % |
|---|---|---|
| 1 Les AuCoin (D) | 154,844 | 58.7 |
| Philip N. Bladine (R) | 109,140 | 41.3 |
| 2 Al Ullman (D) | 173,313 | 72.0 |
| Thomas H. Mercer (R) | 67,431 | 28.0 |
| 3 Robert Duncan (D) | 148,503 | 83.9 |
| Martin Simon (I) | 28,245 | 16.0 |
| 4 James Weaver (D) | 122,475 | 50.0 |
| Jerry Lausmann (R) | 85,943 | 35.1 |
| Jim Howard (I) | 22,104 | 9.0 |
| Theodora Nathan (I) | 14,307 | 5.8 |

## PENNSYLVANIA

| Candidates | Votes | % |
|---|---|---|
| 1 Michael (Ozzie) Myers (D) | 117,087 | 73.5 |
| Samuel N. Fanelli (R) | 40,191 | 25.2 |
| 2 Robert N. C. Nix (D) | 109,855 | 73.5 |
| Jesse W. Woods Jr. (R) | 37,907 | 25.4 |

| Candidates | Votes | % |
|---|---|---|
| 3 Raymond F. Lederer (D) | 98,627 | 73.2 |
| Terrence J. Schade (R) | 35,491 | 26.3 |
| 4 Joshua Eilberg (D) | 144,890 | 67.5 |
| James E. Mugford (R) | 69,700 | 32.5 |
| 5 Richard T. Schulze (R) | 119,682 | 59.5 |
| Anthony Campolo (D) | 81,299 | 40.5 |
| 6 Gus Yatron (D) | 133,624 | 73.8 |
| Stephen Postupack (R) | 46,103 | 25.5 |
| 7 Robert W. Edgar (D) | 109,436 | 54.1 |
| John N. Kenney (R) | 92,788 | 45.9 |
| 8 Peter H. Kostmayer (D) | 93,855 | 49.5 |
| John S. Renninger (R) | 92,543 | 48.8 |
| 9 E. G. Shuster (R,D) | 154,359 | 100.0 |
| 10 Joseph M. McDade (R) | 125,218 | 62.6 |
| Edward Mitchell (D) | 74,925 | 37.4 |
| 11 Daniel J. Flood (D) | 130,175 | 70.8 |
| Howard G. Williams (R) | 53,621 | 29.2 |
| 12 John P. Murtha (D) | 122,504 | 67.7 |
| Ted Humes (R) | 58,489 | 32.3 |
| 13 R. Lawrence Coughlin (R) | 130,705 | 63.4 |
| Gertrude Strick (D) | 75,435 | 36.6 |
| 14 William S. Moorhead (D) | 114,472 | 71.7 |
| John F. Bradley (R) | 43,308 | 27.1 |
| 15 Fred B. Rooney (D) | 108,844 | 65.2 |
| Alice Sivulich (R) | 57,616 | 34.5 |
| 16 Robert S. Walker (R) | 97,527 | 62.3 |
| Michael J. Minney (D) | 57,836 | 37.0 |
| 17 Allen E. Ertel (D) | 86,158 | 50.7 |
| H. Joseph Hepford (R) | 82,370 | 48.5 |
| 18 Douglas Walgren (D) | 113,787 | 59.5 |
| Robert J. Casey (R) | 77,594 | 40.5 |
| 19 William F. Goodling (R) | 124,098 | 70.6 |
| Richard P. Noll (D) | 51,686 | 29.4 |
| 20 Joseph M. Gaydos (D) | 134,961 | 75.0 |
| John P. Kostelac (R) | 44,432 | 24.7 |
| 21 John H. Dent (D) | 99,160 | 59.4 |
| Robert H. Miller (R) | 67,763 | 40.6 |
| 22 Austin J. Murphy (D) | 97,036 | 55.3 |
| Roger Fischer (R) | 77,030 | 43.9 |
| 23 Joseph S. Ammerman (D) | 95,821 | 56.5 |
| Albert W. Johnson (R) | 73,641 | 43.5 |
| 24 Marc L. Marks (R) | 101,048 | 55.4 |
| Joseph P. Vigorito (D) | 79,937 | 43.8 |
| 25 Gary A. Myers (R) | 103,632 | 56.8 |
| Eugene V. Atkinson (D) | 78,857 | 43.2 |

## RHODE ISLAND

| Candidates | Votes | % |
|---|---|---|
| 1 Fernand J. St Germain (D) | 116,674 | 62.4 |
| John J. Slocum Jr. (R) | 68,080 | 36.4 |
| 2 Edward P. Beard (D) | 154,453 | 76.5 |
| Thomas V. Iannitti (R) | 45,438 | 22.5 |

## SOUTH CAROLINA

| Candidates | Votes | % |
|---|---|---|
| 1 Mendel J. Davis (D) | 89,891 | 68.9 |
| Lonnie Rowell (R) | 40,598 | 31.1 |
| 2 Floyd D. Spence (R) | 83,426 | 57.5 |
| Clyde B. Livingston (D) | 60,602 | 41.8 |
| 3 Butler C. Derrick (D) | 117,740 | 99.9 |
| 4 James R. Mann (D) | 91,721 | 73.5 |
| Robert L. Watkins (R) | 32,983 | 26.4 |
| 5 Kenneth L. Holland (D) | 66,073 | 51.4 |
| Bobby Richardson (R) | 62,095 | 48.3 |
| 6 John W. Jenrette Jr. (D) | 75,916 | 55.5 |
| Edward L. Young (R) | 60,288 | 44.0 |

## SOUTH DAKOTA

| Candidates | Votes | % |
|---|---|---|
| 1 Larry Pressler (R) | 121,587 | 79.8 |
| James V. Guffey (D) | 29,533 | 19.4 |
| 2 James Abdnor (R) | 99,601 | 69.9 |
| Grace Mickelson (D) | 42,968 | 30.1 |

## TENNESSEE

| Candidates | Votes | % |
|---|---|---|
| 1 James H. (Jimmy) Quillen (R) | 97,781 | 57.9 |
| Lloyd Blevins (D) | 69,507 | 41.2 |

| Candidates | Votes | % |
|---|---|---|
| 2 John J. Duncan (R) | 117,256 | 62.8 |
| Mike Rowland (D) | 69,449 | 37.2 |
| 3 Marilyn Lloyd (D) | 123,872 | 67.5 |
| LaMar Baker (R) | 57,116 | 31.1 |
| 4 Albert Gore Jr. (D) | 115,392 | 94.0 |
| William H. McGlamery (I) | 7,320 | 6.0 |
| 5 Clifford R. Allen (D) | 125,830 | 92.4 |
| Roger E. Bissell (I) | 10,292 | 7.6 |
| 6 Robin L. Beard (R) | 116,905 | 64.5 |
| Ross Bass (D) | 64,462 | 35.5 |
| 7 Ed Jones (D) | 105,832 | 100.0 |
| 8 Harold E. Ford (D) | 100,683 | 60.7 |
| A. D. Alissandratos (R) | 63,819 | 38.5 |

## TEXAS

| Candidates | Votes | % |
|---|---|---|
| 1 Sam B. Hall Jr. (D) | 135,384 | 83.7 |
| James Hogan (R) | 26,334 | 16.3 |
| 2 Charles Wilson (D) | 133,910 | 95.0 |
| James William Doyle III (AM) | 6,992 | 5.0 |
| 3 James M. Collins (R) | 171,343 | 74.0 |
| Les E. Shackelford Jr. (D) | 60,070 | 26.0 |
| 4 Ray Roberts (D) | 105,394 | 62.7 |
| Frank S. Glenn (R) | 62,641 | 37.3 |
| 5 Jim Mattox (D) | 67,871 | 54.0 |
| Nancy Judy (R) | 56,056 | 44.6 |
| 6 Olin E. Teague (D) | 119,025 | 65.9 |
| Wes Mowery (R) | 60,316 | 33.4 |
| 7 Bill Archer (R) | 193,127 | 100.0 |
| 8 Bob Eckhardt (D) | 84,404 | 60.7 |
| Nick Gearhart (R) | 54,566 | 39.2 |
| 9 Jack Brooks (D) | 112,945 | 99.9 |
| 10 J. J. (Jake) Pickle (D) | 160,683 | 76.8 |
| Paul McClure (R) | 48,482 | 23.2 |
| 11 W. R. Poage (D) | 92,142 | 57.4 |
| Jack Burgess (R) | 68,373 | 42.6 |
| 12 Jim Wright (D) | 101,814 | 75.8 |
| W. R. Durham (R) | 31,941 | 23.8 |
| 13 Jack Hightower (D) | 101,798 | 59.3 |
| Bob Price (R) | 69,328 | 40.4 |
| 14 John Young (D) | 93,589 | 61.4 |
| L. Dean Holford (R) | 58,788 | 38.6 |
| 15 Eligio de la Garza (D) | 102,837 | 74.4 |
| R. L. (Lendy) McDonald (R) | 35,446 | 25.6 |
| 16 Richard C. White (D) | 71,876 | 57.8 |
| Vic Shackelford (R) | 52,499 | 42.2 |
| 17 Omar Burleson (D) | 127,613 | 99.9 |
| 18 Barbara C. Jordan (D) | 93,953 | 85.5 |
| Sam H. Wright (R) | 15,381 | 14.0 |
| 19 George Mahon (D) | 87,908 | 54.6 |
| Jim Reese (R) | 72,991 | 45.4 |
| 20 Henry B. Gonzalez (D) | 90,173 | 100.0 |
| 21 Robert Krueger (D) | 149,395 | 71.0 |
| Bobby A. Locke (R) | 56,211 | 26.7 |
| 22 Bob Gammage (D) | 96,535 | 50.1 |
| Ron Paul (R) | 96,267 | 49.9 |
| 23 Abraham Kazen Jr. (D) | 96,481 | 100.0 |
| 24 Dale Milford (D) | 82,743 | 63.4 |
| Leo Berman (R) | 47,075 | 36.1 |

### Special Elections [2]

| Candidates | Votes | % |
|---|---|---|
| 1 Sam B. Hall Jr. (D) | 20,556 | 72.0 |
| Glen Jones (D) | 6,327 | 22.2 |
| 22 Bob Gammage (D) | 15,287 | 42.1 |
| Ron Paul (R) | 14,386 | 39.6 |
| John S. Brunson (D) | 3,670 | 10.1 |

### Special Runoff Election

| Candidates | Votes | % |
|---|---|---|
| 22 Ron Paul (R) | 39,041 | 56.2 |
| Bob Gammage (D) | 30,483 | 43.8 |

## UTAH

| Candidates | Votes | % |
|---|---|---|
| 1 K. Gunn McKay (D) | 155,631 | 58.2 |
| Joe H. Ferguson (R) | 106,542 | 39.8 |
| 2 Dan Marriott (R) | 144,861 | 52.4 |
| Allan T. Howe (D) | 110,931 | 40.1 |
| D. J. McCarty (WRITE IN) | 20,508 | 7.4 |

## VERMONT

| Candidates | Votes | % |
|---|---|---|
| AL James M. Jeffords (R) | 124,458 | 67.4 |
| John A. Burgess (D,I VT) | 60,202 | 32.6 |

## VIRGINIA

| | Candidates | Votes | % |
|---|---|---|---|
| 1 | Paul S. Trible Jr. (R) | 71,789 | 48.6 |
| | Robert E. Quinn (D) | 70,159 | 47.5 |
| 2 | G. William Whitehurst (R) | 79,381 | 65.7 |
| | Robert E. Washington (D) | 41,464 | 34.3 |
| 3 | David E. Satterfield III (D) | 129,066 | 87.9 |
| | A. R. Ogden (I) | 17,503 | 11.9 |
| 4 | Robert W. Daniel Jr. (R) | 74,495 | 53.0 |
| | J. W. (Billy) O'Brien (D) | 65,982 | 47.0 |
| 5 | W. C. (Dan) Daniel (D) | 101,038 | 100.0 |
| 6 | M. Caldwell Butler (R) | 90,830 | 62.2 |
| | Warren D. Saunders (I) | 55,115 | 37.8 |
| 7 | J. Kenneth Robinson (R) | 115,508 | 81.6 |
| | James B. Hutt Jr. (I) | 25,731 | 18.2 |
| 8 | Herbert E. Harris (D) | 83,245 | 51.6 |
| | James R. Tate (R) | 68,729 | 42.6 |
| | Michael D. Cannon (I) | 9,292 | 5.8 |
| 9 | William C. Wampler (R) | 96,052 | 57.3 |
| | Charles J. Horne (D) | 71,439 | 42.6 |
| 10 | Joseph L. Fisher (D) | 103,689 | 54.7 |
| | Vincent F. Callahan Jr. (R) | 73,616 | 38.8 |
| | E. Stanley Rittenhouse (I) | 12,124 | 6.4 |

## WASHINGTON

| | Candidates | Votes | % |
|---|---|---|---|
| 1 | Joel Pritchard (R) | 161,354 | 71.9 |
| | Dave Wood (D) | 58,006 | 25.8 |
| 2 | Lloyd Meeds (D) | 107,328 | 49.3 |
| | John Nance Garner (R) | 106,786 | 49.0 |
| 3 | Don Bonker (D) | 145,198 | 70.8 |
| | Chuck Elhart (R) | 57,517 | 28.0 |
| 4 | Mike McCormack (D) | 115,364 | 57.8 |
| | Dick Granger (R) | 81,813 | 41.0 |
| 5 | Thomas S. Foley (D) | 120,415 | 58.0 |
| | Duane Alton (R) | 84,262 | 40.6 |
| 6 | Norman D. Dicks (D) | 137,964 | 73.5 |
| | Robert M. Reynolds (R) | 47,539 | 25.3 |
| 7 | Brock Adams (D) | 133,673 | 73.0 |
| | Raymond Pritchard (R) | 46,448 | 25.4 |

## WEST VIRGINIA

| | Candidates | Votes | % |
|---|---|---|---|
| 1 | Robert H. Mollohan (D) | 108,103 | 58.0 |
| | John F. McCuskey (R) | 78,159 | 42.0 |
| 2 | Harley O. Staggers (D) | 136,749 | 73.2 |
| | Jim Sloan (R) | 50,079 | 26.8 |
| 3 | John M. Slack (D) | 128,086 | 99.7 |
| 4 | Nick J. Rahall (D) | 73,626 | 45.6 |
| | Ken Hechler (WRITE IN) | 59,067 | 36.6 |
| | E. S. (Steve) Goodman (R) | 28,825 | 17.8 |

## WISCONSIN

| | Candidates | Votes | % |
|---|---|---|---|
| 1 | Les Aspin (D) | 136,162 | 64.9 |
| | William W. Petrie (R) | 71,427 | 34.0 |
| 2 | Robert W. Kastenmeier (D) | 155,158 | 65.6 |
| | Elizabeth T. Miller (R) | 81,350 | 34.4 |
| 3 | Alvin J. Baldus (D) | 139,083 | 58.1 |
| | Adolf L. Gundersen (R) | 100,218 | 41.9 |
| 4 | Clement J. Zablocki (D) | 172,166 | 100.0 |
| 5 | Henry S. Reuss (D) | 134,935 | 77.8 |
| | Robert L. Hicks (R) | 36,413 | 21.0 |
| 6 | William A. Steiger (R) | 139,541 | 63.3 |
| | Joseph C. Smith (D) | 80,715 | 36.6 |
| 7 | David R. Obey (D) | 171,366 | 73.3 |
| | Frank A. Savino (R) | 60,952 | 26.1 |
| 8 | Robert J. Cornell (D) | 115,996 | 50.9 |
| | Harold V. Froehlich (R) | 107,048 | 46.9 |
| 9 | Robert W. Kasten Jr. (R) | 163,791 | 65.9 |
| | Lynn M. McDonald (D) | 84,706 | 34.1 |

## WYOMING

| | Candidates | Votes | % |
|---|---|---|---|
| AL | Teno Roncalio (D) | 85,721 | 56.4 |
| | Larry Joe Hart (R) | 66,147 | 43.6 |

**1976 Election**
1. Arkansas and Florida did not record the votes for unopposed candidates.
2. Texas election law required all candidates in special elections to run against each other, regardless of party. If no candidate received a majority, a special election runoff was held between the two candidates receiving the most votes in the special election.

# 1977 House Elections

## GEORGIA

**Special Election** [1]

| | Candidates | Votes | % |
|---|---|---|---|
| 5 | Wyche Fowler Jr. (D) | 29,898 | 39.6 |
| | John Lewis (D) | 21,531 | 28.6 |
| | Paul D. Coverdell (R) | 16,509 | 21.9 |

**Special Runoff Election**

| | Candidates | Votes | % |
|---|---|---|---|
| 5 | Wyche Fowler Jr. (D) | 54,378 | 62.4 |
| | John Lewis (D) | 32,732 | 37.6 |

## LOUISIANA

**Special Election**

| | Candidates | Votes | % |
|---|---|---|---|
| 1 | Robert L. Livingston (R) | 56,121 | 51.2 |
| | Ron Faucheux (D) | 40,802 | 37.2 |
| | Sanford Krasnoff (I) | 12,665 | 11.6 |

## MINNESOTA

**Special Election**

| | Candidates | Votes | % |
|---|---|---|---|
| 7 | Arlan Stangeland (I-R) | 71,340 | 57.6 |
| | Michael J. Sullivan (DFL) | 45,490 | 36.7 |

## WASHINGTON

**Special Election**

| | Candidates | Votes | % |
|---|---|---|---|
| 7 | John E. Cunningham (R) | 42,650 | 54.0 |
| | Marvin Durning (D) | 35,525 | 45.0 |

**1977 Election**
1. Georgia election law required all candidates in special elections to run against each other, regardless of party. If no candidate received a majority, a special election runoff was held between the two candidates receiving the most votes in the special election.

# 1978 House Elections

## ALABAMA

| Candidates | Votes | % |
|---|---|---|
| 1 Jack Edwards (R) | 71,711 | 63.9 |
| L. W. (Red) Noonan (D) | 40,450 | 36.1 |
| 2 William L. Dickinson (R) | 57,924 | 54.0 |
| Wendell Mitchell (D) | 49,341 | 46.0 |
| 3 Bill Nichols (D) | 74,895 | 100.0 |
| 4 Tom Bevill (D) | 87,380 | 100.0 |
| 5 Ronnie G. Flippo (D) | 68,985 | 96.8 |
| 6 John Buchanan (R) | 65,700 | 61.7 |
| Don Hawkins (D) | 40,771 | 38.3 |
| 7 Richard C. Shelby (D) | 77,742 | 93.8 |

## ALASKA

| Candidates | Votes | % |
|---|---|---|
| AL Don Young (R) | 68,811 | 55.4 |
| Patrick Rodey (D) | 55,176 | 44.4 |

## ARIZONA

| Candidates | Votes | % |
|---|---|---|
| 1 John J. Rhodes (R) | 81,108 | 71.0 |
| Ken Graves (D) | 33,178 | 29.0 |
| 2 Morris K. Udall (D) | 67,878 | 52.5 |
| Tom Richey (R) | 58,697 | 45.4 |
| 3 Bob Stump (D) | 111,850 | 85.0 |
| Kathleen Cooke (LIBERT) | 19,813 | 15.0 |
| 4 Eldon Rudd (R) | 90,768 | 63.1 |
| Michael L. McCormick (D) | 48,661 | 33.8 |

## ARKANSAS

| Candidates | Votes | % |
|---|---|---|
| 1 Bill Alexander (D) | | 100.0 |
| 2 Ed Bethune (R) | 65,285 | 51.2 |
| Doug Brandon (D) | 62,140 | 48.8 |
| 3 John Paul Hammerschmidt (R) | 130,086 | 78.4 |
| William C. Mears (D) | 35,748 | 21.6 |
| 4 Beryl F. Anthony Jr. (D) | | 100.0 |

## CALIFORNIA

| Candidates | Votes | % |
|---|---|---|
| 1 Harold T. Johnson (D) | 125,122 | 59.4 |
| James E. Taylor (R) | 85,690 | 40.6 |
| 2 Don H. Clausen (R) | 114,451 | 52.0 |
| Norma Bork (D) | 99,712 | 45.3 |
| 3 Robert T. Matsui (D) | 105,537 | 53.4 |
| Sandy Smoley (R) | 91,966 | 46.6 |
| 4 Vic Fazio (D) | 87,764 | 55.4 |
| Rex Hime (R) | 70,733 | 44.6 |
| 5 John L. Burton (D) | 106,046 | 66.8 |
| Dolores Skore (R) | 52,603 | 33.2 |
| 6 Phillip Burton (D) | 81,801 | 68.3 |
| Tom Spinosa (R) | 33,515 | 27.9 |
| 7 George Miller (D) | 109,676 | 63.4 |
| Paula Gordon (R) | 58,332 | 33.7 |
| 8 Ronald V. Dellums (D) | 94,824 | 57.4 |
| Charles V. Hughes (R) | 70,481 | 42.6 |
| 9 Fortney H. (Pete) Stark (D) | 88,179 | 65.4 |
| Robert S. Allen (R) | 41,138 | 30.5 |
| 10 Don Edwards (D) | 84,488 | 67.1 |
| Rudy Hansen (R) | 41,374 | 32.9 |
| 11 Leo J. Ryan (D) | 92,882 | 60.5 |
| David Welch (R) | 54,621 | 35.6 |
| 12 Paul N. McCloskey Jr. (R) | 116,982 | 73.1 |
| Kirsten Olsen (D) | 34,472 | 21.5 |
| 13 Norman Y. Mineta (D) | 100,809 | 57.5 |
| Dan O'Keefe (R) | 69,306 | 39.5 |
| 14 Norman D. Shumway (R) | 95,962 | 53.4 |
| John J. McFall (D) | 76,602 | 42.6 |
| 15 Tony Coelho (D) | 75,212 | 60.1 |
| Chris Patterakis (R) | 49,914 | 39.9 |
| 16 Leon E. Panetta (D) | 104,550 | 61.4 |
| Eric Seastrand (R) | 65,808 | 38.6 |
| 17 Charles (Chip) Pashayan Jr. (R) | 81,296 | 54.5 |
| John Krebs (D) | 67,885 | 45.5 |
| 18 William Thomas (R) | 85,663 | 59.2 |
| Bob Sogge (D) | 58,900 | 40.7 |

| Candidates | Votes | % |
|---|---|---|
| 19 Robert J. Lagomarsino (R) | 123,192 | 71.7 |
| Jerome Zamos (D) | 41,672 | 24.3 |
| 20 Barry M. Goldwater Jr. (R) | 129,714 | 66.4 |
| Pat Lear (D) | 65,695 | 33.6 |
| 21 James C. Corman (D) | 73,869 | 59.5 |
| G. (Rod) Walsh (R) | 44,519 | 35.9 |
| 22 Carlos J. Moorehead (R) | 99,502 | 64.6 |
| Robert S. Henry (D) | 54,442 | 35.4 |
| 23 Anthony C. (Tony) Beilenson | 117,498 | 65.6 |
| Joseph Barbara (R) | 61,496 | 34.4 |
| 24 Henry A. Waxman (D) | 85,075 | 62.7 |
| Howard G. Schaefer (R) | 44,243 | 32.6 |
| 25 Edward R. Roybal (D) | 45,881 | 67.4 |
| Robert K. Watson (R) | 22,205 | 32.6 |
| 26 John H. Rousselot (R) | 113,059 | 100.0 |
| 27 Robert K. Dornan (R) | 89,392 | 51.0 |
| Carey Peck (D) | 85,880 | 49.0 |
| 28 Julian C. Dixon (D) | 97,592 | 100.0 |
| 29 Augustus F. Hawkins (D) | 65,214 | 85.0 |
| Uriah J. Fields (R) | 11,512 | 15.0 |
| 30 George E. Danielson (D) | 66,241 | 71.4 |
| Henry Ares (R) | 26,511 | 28.6 |
| 31 Charles H. Wilson (D) | 55,667 | 67.7 |
| Don Grimshaw (R) | 26,490 | 32.2 |
| 32 Glenn M. Anderson (D) | 74,004 | 71.4 |
| Sonya (Sonny) Mathison (R) | 23,242 | 22.4 |
| Ida Bader (AM I) | 6,363 | 6.1 |
| 33 Wayne Grisham (R) | 79,533 | 56.0 |
| Dennis S. Kazarian (D) | 62,540 | 44.0 |
| 34 Daniel E. Lungren (R) | 90,554 | 53.7 |
| Mark W. Hannaford (D) | 73,608 | 43.7 |
| 35 Jim Lloyd (D) | 80,388 | 54.0 |
| David Dreier (R) | 68,442 | 46.0 |
| 36 George E. Brown Jr. (D) | 80,448 | 62.9 |
| Dana Warren Carmody (R) | 47,417 | 37.1 |
| 37 Jerry Lewis (R) | 106,581 | 61.4 |
| Dan Corcoran (D) | 60,463 | 34.8 |
| 38 Jerry M. Patterson (D) | 75,471 | 58.6 |
| Don Goedeke (R) | 53,298 | 41.4 |
| 39 William E. Dannemeyer (R) | 112,160 | 63.7 |
| William E. Farris (D) | 63,891 | 36.3 |
| 40 Robert E. Badham (R) | 147,882 | 65.9 |
| Jim McGuy (D) | 76,358 | 34.1 |
| 41 Bob Wilson (R) | 107,685 | 58.1 |
| King Golden Jr. (D) | 77,540 | 41.9 |
| 42 Lionel Van Deerlin (D) | 85,126 | 73.7 |
| Lawrence C. Mattera (R) | 30,319 | 26.3 |
| 43 Clair W. Burgener (R) | 167,150 | 68.7 |
| Ruben B. Brooks (D) | 76,308 | 31.3 |

## COLORADO

| Candidates | Votes | % |
|---|---|---|
| 1 Patricia Schroeder (D) | 82,742 | 61.5 |
| Gene Hutcheson (R) | 49,845 | 37.0 |
| 2 Timothy E. Wirth (D) | 98,889 | 52.9 |
| Ed Scott (R) | 88,072 | 47.1 |
| 3 Ray Kogovsek (D) | 69,669 | 49.3 |
| Harold L. McCormick (R) | 69,303 | 49.0 |
| 4 James P. (Jim) Johnson (R) | 103,121 | 61.2 |
| Morgan Smith (D) | 65,241 | 38.8 |
| 5 Ken Kramer (R) | 91,933 | 59.8 |
| Gerry Frank (D) | 52,914 | 34.4 |
| L. W. Dan Bridges (I) | 8,933 | 5.8 |

## CONNECTICUT

| Candidates | Votes | % |
|---|---|---|
| 1 William R. Cotter (D) | 102,749 | 59.5 |
| Ben F. Andrews Jr. (R) | 67,828 | 39.3 |
| 2 Christopher J. Dodd (D) | 116,624 | 69.9 |
| Thomas H. Connell (R) | 50,167 | 30.1 |
| 3 Robert N. Giaimo (D) | 96,830 | 58.1 |
| John G. Pucciano (R) | 66,663 | 40.0 |
| 4 Stewart B. McKinney (R) | 83,990 | 58.4 |
| Michael G. Morgan (D) | 59,918 | 41.6 |
| 5 William R. Ratchford (D) | 96,738 | 52.3 |
| George C. Guidera (R) | 88,162 | 47.7 |

| Candidates | Votes | % |
|---|---|---|
| 6 Toby Moffett (D) | 119,537 | 64.2 |
| Daniel F. MacKinnon (R) | 66,664 | 35.8 |

## DELAWARE

| Candidates | Votes | % |
|---|---|---|
| AL Thomas B. Evans Jr. (R) | 91,689 | 58.2 |
| Gary E. Hindes (D) | 64,863 | 41.2 |

## FLORIDA

| Candidates | Votes | % |
|---|---|---|
| 1 Earl D. Hutto (D) | 85,608 | 63.3 |
| Warren Briggs (R) | 49,715 | 36.7 |
| 2 Don Fuqua (D) | 112,649 | 81.7 |
| Peter L. W. Brathwaite (R) | 25,148 | 18.3 |
| 3 Charles E. Bennett (D) | | 100.0 |
| 4 Bill Chappell Jr. (D) | 113,302 | 73.1 |
| Tom Boney (R) | 41,647 | 26.9 |
| 5 Richard Kelly (R) | 106,319 | 51.1 |
| David R. Best (D) | 101,867 | 48.9 |
| 6 C. W. Bill Young (R) | 150,694 | 78.8 |
| James A. Christison (D) | 40,654 | 21.2 |
| 7 Sam Gibbons (D) | | 100.0 |
| 8 Andy Ireland (D) | | 100.0 |
| 9 Bill Nelson (D) | 89,543 | 61.5 |
| Edward J. Gurney (R) | 56,074 | 38.5 |
| 10 L. A. (Skip) Bafalis (R) | | 100.0 |
| 11 Dan Mica (D) | 123,346 | 55.3 |
| Bill James (R) | 99,757 | 44.7 |
| 12 Edward J. Stack (D) | 107,037 | 61.6 |
| J. Herbert Burke (R) | 66,610 | 38.4 |
| 13 William Lehman (D) | | 100.0 |
| 14 Claude Pepper (D) | 65,202 | 63.1 |
| Al Cardenas (R) | 38,081 | 36.9 |
| 15 Dante B. Fascell (D) | 108,837 | 74.2 |
| Herbert J. Hoodwin (R) | 37,897 | 25.8 |

## GEORGIA

| Candidates | Votes | % |
|---|---|---|
| 1 Bo Ginn (D) | 36,961 | 100.0 |
| 2 Dawson Mathis (D) | 42,234 | 100.0 |
| 3 Jack Brinkley (D) | 54,881 | 100.0 |
| 4 Elliott H. Levitas (D) | 60,284 | 80.9 |
| Homer Cheung (R) | 14,221 | 19.1 |
| 5 Wyche Fowler Jr. (D) | 52,739 | 75.5 |
| Thomas P. Bowles Jr. (R) | 17,132 | 24.5 |
| 6 Newt Gingrich (R) | 47,078 | 54.4 |
| Virginia Shapard (D) | 39,451 | 45.6 |
| 7 Larry P. McDonald (D) | 47,090 | 66.5 |
| Ernie Norsworthy (R) | 23,698 | 33.5 |
| 8 Billy Lee Evans (D) | 41,184 | 100.0 |
| 9 Ed Jenkins (D) | 47,264 | 76.9 |
| David G. Ashworth (R) | 14,172 | 23.1 |
| 10 Doug Barnard (D) | 50,122 | 100.0 |

## HAWAII

| Candidates | Votes | % |
|---|---|---|
| 1 Cecil (Cec) Heftel (D) | 84,552 | 73.3 |
| William D. Spillane (R) | 24,470 | 21.2 |
| 2 Daniel K. Akaka (D) | 118,272 | 85. |
| Charles Isaak (R) | 15,697 | 11. |

## IDAHO

| Candidates | Votes | % |
|---|---|---|
| 1 Steven D. Symms (R) | 86,680 | 59. |
| Roy Truby (D) | 57,972 | 40. |
| 2 George Hansen (R) | 80,591 | 57. |
| Stan Kress (D) | 60,040 | 42. |

## ILLINOIS

| Candidates | Votes | % |
|---|---|---|
| 1 Bennett Stewart (D) | 47,581 | 58. |
| A. A. Rayner (R) | 33,540 | 41. |
| 2 Morgan F. Murphy (D) | 80,906 | 86. |
| James Wognum (R) | 11,104 | 11. |

| Candidates | Votes | % |
|---|---|---|
| 3 Marty Russo (D) | 95,701 | 65.2 |
| Robert L. Dunne (R) | 51,098 | 34.8 |
| 4 Edward J. Derwinski (R) | 94,435 | 66.9 |
| Andrew D. Thomas (D) | 46,788 | 33.1 |
| 5 John G. Fary (D) | 98,702 | 84.0 |
| Joseph A. Barracca (R) | 18,802 | 16.0 |
| 6 Henry J. Hyde (R) | 87,193 | 66.2 |
| Jeanne P. Quinn (D) | 44,543 | 33.8 |
| 7 Cardiss Collins (D) | 64,716 | 86.3 |
| James C. Holt (R) | 10,273 | 13.7 |
| 8 Dan Rostenkowski (D) | 81,457 | 86.0 |
| Carl C. LoDico (R) | 13,302 | 14.0 |
| 9 Sidney R. Yates (D) | 87,543 | 75.3 |
| John M. Collins (R) | 28,673 | 24.7 |
| 10 Abner J. Mikva (D) | 89,479 | 50.2 |
| John E. Porter (R) | 88,829 | 49.8 |
| 11 Frank Annunzio (D) | 112,365 | 73.7 |
| John Hoeger (R) | 40,044 | 26.3 |
| 12 Philip M. Crane (R) | 110,503 | 79.5 |
| Gilbert Bogen (D) | 28,424 | 20.5 |
| 13 Robert McClory (R) | 64,060 | 61.2 |
| Frederick J. Steffen (D) | 40,675 | 38.8 |
| 14 John N. Erlenborn (R) | 118,741 | 75.1 |
| James A. Romanyak (D) | 39,438 | 24.9 |
| 15 Tom Corcoran (R) | 80,856 | 62.4 |
| Tim L. Hall (D) | 48,756 | 37.6 |
| 16 John B. Anderson (R) | 76,752 | 65.4 |
| Ernest W. Dahlin (D) | 40,471 | 34.5 |
| 17 George M. O'Brien (R) | 94,375 | 70.6 |
| Clifford J. Sinclair (D) | 39,260 | 29.4 |
| 18 Robert H. Michel (R) | 85,973 | 65.9 |
| Virgil R. Grunkemeyer (D) | 44,527 | 34.1 |
| 19 Tom Railsback (R) | 89,770 | 100.0 |
| 20 Paul Findley (R) | 111,054 | 69.6 |
| Victor W. Roberts (D) | 48,426 | 30.4 |
| 21 Edward R. Madigan (R) | 97,473 | 78.3 |
| Kenneth E. Baughman (D) | 27,054 | 21.7 |
| 22 Daniel B. Crane (R) | 86,051 | 54.0 |
| Terry L. Bruce (D) | 73,331 | 46.0 |
| 23 Melvin Price (D) | 74,247 | 74.2 |
| Daniel J. Stack (R) | 25,858 | 25.8 |
| 24 Paul Simon (D) | 110,298 | 65.6 |
| John T. Anderson (R) | 57,763 | 34.4 |

### INDIANA

| Candidates | Votes | % |
|---|---|---|
| 1 Adam Benjamin Jr. (D) | 72,367 | 80.3 |
| Owen W. Crumpacker (R) | 17,419 | 19.3 |
| 2 Floyd Fithian (D) | 82,402 | 56.5 |
| J. Philip Oppenheim (R) | 52,842 | 36.2 |
| William Costas (I) | 9,368 | 6.4 |
| 3 John Brademas (D) | 64,336 | 55.5 |
| Thomas L. Thorson (R) | 50,145 | 43.3 |
| 4 Dan Quayle (R) | 80,527 | 64.4 |
| John D. Walda (D) | 42,238 | 33.8 |
| 5 Elwood Hillis (R) | 94,950 | 67.6 |
| Max E. Heiss (D) | 45,479 | 32.4 |
| 6 David W. Evans (D) | 66,421 | 52.2 |
| David G. Crane (R) | 60,630 | 47.6 |
| 7 John T. Myers (R) | 86,955 | 56.3 |
| Charlotte Zietlow (D) | 67,469 | 43.7 |
| 8 H. Joel Deckard (R) | 83,019 | 52.0 |
| David L. Cornwell (D) | 76,654 | 48.0 |
| 9 Lee H. Hamilton Jr. (D) | 99,727 | 65.6 |
| Frank I. Hamilton Jr. (R) | 52,218 | 34.4 |
| 10 Phil Sharp (D) | 73,343 | 56.1 |
| William G. Frazier (R) | 55,999 | 42.8 |
| 11 Andy Jacobs Jr. (D) | 61,504 | 57.2 |
| Charles F. Bosma (R) | 45,809 | 42.6 |

### IOWA

| Candidates | Votes | % |
|---|---|---|
| 1 Jim Leach (R) | 79,940 | 63.5 |
| Dick Myers (D) | 45,037 | 35.8 |
| 2 Tom Tauke (R) | 72,644 | 52.3 |
| Michael T. Blouin (D) | 65,450 | 47.1 |
| 3 Charles E. Grassley (R) | 103,659 | 74.8 |
| John Knudson (D) | 34,880 | 25.2 |
| 4 Neal Smith (D) | 88,526 | 64.7 |
| Charles E. Minor (R) | 48,308 | 35.3 |

| Candidates | Votes | % |
|---|---|---|
| 5 Tom Harkin (D) | 82,333 | 58.9 |
| Julian B. Garrett (R) | 57,377 | 41.1 |
| 6 Berkley Bedell (D) | 87,139 | 66.3 |
| Willis E. Junker (R) | 44,320 | 33.7 |

### KANSAS

| Candidates | Votes | % |
|---|---|---|
| 1 Keith G. Sebelius (R) | 131,037 | 100.0 |
| 2 Jim Jeffries (R) | 76,419 | 52.0 |
| Martha Keys (D) | 70,460 | 48.0 |
| 3 Larry Winn Jr. (R) | 103,265 | 100.0 |
| 4 Dan Glickman (D) | 100,139 | 69.5 |
| James P. Litsey (R) | 43,854 | 30.5 |
| 5 Robert Whittaker (R) | 86,011 | 57.0 |
| Donald L. Allegrucci (D) | 62,402 | 41.4 |

### KENTUCKY

| Candidates | Votes | % |
|---|---|---|
| 1 Carroll Hubbard Jr. (D) | 44,090 | 100.0 |
| 2 William H. Natcher (D) | 36,441 | 100.0 |
| 3 Romano L. Mazzoli (D) | 37,346 | 65.7 |
| Norbert D. Leveronne (R) | 17,785 | 31.3 |
| 4 Gene Snyder (R) | 62,087 | 65.8 |
| George C. Martin (D) | 32,212 | 34.2 |
| 5 Tim Lee Carter (R) | 59,743 | 79.2 |
| Jesse M. Ramey (D) | 15,714 | 20.8 |
| 6 Larry J. Hopkins (R) | 52,092 | 50.6 |
| Tom Easterly (D) | 47,436 | 46.1 |
| 7 Carl D. Perkins (D) | 51,559 | 76.5 |
| Granville Thomas (R) | 15,861 | 23.5 |

### LOUISIANA [1]

| Candidates | Votes | % |
|---|---|---|
| 1 Robert L. Livingston (R) | | 100.0 |
| 2 Lindy Boggs (D) | | 100.0 |
| 3 David C. Treen (R) | | 100.0 |
| 4 Claude (Buddy) Leach (D) | 65,583 | 50.1 |
| Jimmy Wilson (R) | 65,317 | 49.9 |
| 5 Jerry Huckaby (D) | | 100.0 |
| 6 W. Henson Moore (R) | | 100.0 |
| 7 John B. Breaux (D) | | 100.0 |
| 8 Gillis W. Long (D) | | 100.0 |

### MAINE

| Candidates | Votes | % |
|---|---|---|
| 1 David F. Emery (R) | 120,791 | 61.5 |
| John Quinn (D) | 70,348 | 35.8 |
| 2 Olympia J. Snowe (R) | 87,939 | 50.8 |
| Markham L. Gartley (D) | 70,691 | 40.8 |

### MARYLAND

| Candidates | Votes | % |
|---|---|---|
| 1 Robert E. Bauman (R) | 80,202 | 63.5 |
| Joseph D. Quinn (D) | 46,093 | 36.5 |
| 2 Clarence D. Long (D) | 98,601 | 66.4 |
| Malcolm M. McKnight (R) | 49,886 | 33.6 |
| 3 Barbara A. Mikulski (D) | 91,189 | 100.0 |
| 4 Marjorie S. Holt (R) | 71,374 | 62.0 |
| Sue F. Ward (D) | 43,663 | 38.0 |
| 5 Gladys Noon Spellman (D) | 64,868 | 77.2 |
| Saul J. Harris (R) | 19,160 | 22.8 |
| 6 Beverly Byron (D) | 126,196 | 89.7 |
| Melvin Perkins (R) | 14,545 | 10.3 |
| 7 Parren J. Mitchell (D) | 51,996 | 88.7 |
| Debra Hanania Freeman (I) | 6,626 | 11.3 |
| 8 Michael D. Barnes (D) | 81,851 | 51.3 |
| Newton I. Steers Jr. (R) | 77,807 | 48.7 |

### MASSACHUSETTS

| Candidates | Votes | % |
|---|---|---|
| 1 Silvio O. Conte (R) | 131,773 | 100.0 |
| 2 Edward P. Boland (D) | 101,570 | 72.8 |
| Thomas P. Swank (R) | 37,681 | 27.2 |
| 3 Joseph D. Early (D) | 119,391 | 75.2 |
| Charles Kevin MacLeod (R) | 39,259 | 24.7 |
| 4 Robert F. Drinan (D) | 111,353 | 100.0 |
| 5 James M. Shannon (D) | 90,156 | 52.2 |

| Candidates | Votes | % |
|---|---|---|
| John J. Buckley (R) | 48,685 | 28.2 |
| James J. Gaffney III (I) | 33,835 | 19.6 |
| 6 Nicholas Mavroules (D) | 97,099 | 53.8 |
| William E. Bronson (R) | 83,511 | 46.2 |
| 7 Edward J. Markey (D) | 145,615 | 84.8 |
| James J. Murphy (I) | 26,017 | 15.2 |
| 8 Thomas P. O'Neill Jr. (D) | 102,160 | 74.6 |
| William A. Barnstead (R) | 28,566 | 20.9 |
| 9 Joe Moakley (D) | 106,805 | 91.8 |
| Brenda Lee Franklin (SOC WORK) | 6,794 | 5.8 |
| 10 Margaret M. Heckler (R) | 102,080 | 61.1 |
| John J. Marino (D) | 64,868 | 38.9 |
| 11 Brian J. Donnelly (D) | 133,644 | 91.7 |
| H. Graham Lowry (USLP) | 12,044 | 8.3 |
| 12 Gerry E. Studds (D) | 176,704 | 99.9 |

### MICHIGAN

| Candidates | Votes | % |
|---|---|---|
| 1 John Conyers Jr. (D) | 89,646 | 92.9 |
| Robert S. Arnold (R) | 6,878 | 7.1 |
| 2 Carl D. Pursell (R) | 97,503 | 67.6 |
| Earl Greene (D) | 45,631 | 31.6 |
| 3 Howard Wolpe (D) | 83,932 | 51.3 |
| Garry Brown (R) | 79,572 | 48.7 |
| 4 Dave Stockman (R) | 95,440 | 70.6 |
| Morgan L. Hager Jr. (D) | 38,204 | 28.3 |
| 5 Harold S. Sawyer (R) | 81,794 | 49.4 |
| Dale R. Sprik (D) | 80,622 | 48.7 |
| 6 Bob Carr (D) | 97,971 | 56.7 |
| Mike Conlin (R) | 74,718 | 43.3 |
| 7 Dale E. Kildee (D) | 105,402 | 76.6 |
| Gale M. Cronk (R) | 29,958 | 21.8 |
| 8 Bob Traxler (D) | 103,346 | 66.6 |
| Norman R. Hughes (R) | 51,900 | 33.4 |
| 9 Guy Vander Jagt (R) | 122,363 | 69.6 |
| Howard M. Leroux (D) | 53,450 | 30.4 |
| 10 Donald J. Albosta (D) | 94,913 | 51.5 |
| Elford A. Cederberg (R) | 89,451 | 48.5 |
| 11 Robert W. Davis (R) | 96,351 | 54.9 |
| Keith McLeod (D) | 79,081 | 45.1 |
| 12 David E. Bonior (D) | 82,892 | 54.9 |
| Kirby Holmes (R) | 68,063 | 45.1 |
| 13 Charles C. Diggs Jr. (D) | 44,771 | 79.2 |
| Dovie T. Pickett (R) | 11,749 | 20.8 |
| 14 Lucien N. Nedzi (D) | 84,032 | 67.4 |
| John Edward Getz (R) | 40,716 | 32.6 |
| 15 William D. Ford (D) | 95,137 | 79.6 |
| Edgar Nieten (R) | 23,177 | 19.4 |
| 16 John D. Dingell (D) | 93,387 | 76.5 |
| Melvin E. Heuer (R) | 26,827 | 22.0 |
| 17 William M. Brodhead (D) | 106,303 | 95.2 |
| 18 James J. Blanchard (D) | 113,037 | 74.5 |
| Robert J. Salloum (R) | 36,913 | 24.3 |
| 19 William S. Broomfield (R) | 117,122 | 71.3 |
| Betty F. Collier (D) | 47,165 | 28.7 |

### MINNESOTA

| Candidates | Votes | % |
|---|---|---|
| 1 Arlen Erdahl (I-R) | 110,090 | 56.2 |
| Gerry Sikorski (DFL) | 83,271 | 42.5 |
| 2 Tom Hagedorn (I-R) | 145,415 | 70.4 |
| John F. Considine (DFL) | 61,173 | 29.6 |
| 3 Bill Frenzel (I-R) | 128,759 | 65.7 |
| Michael O. Freeman (DFL) | 67,120 | 34.3 |
| 4 Bruce F. Vento (DFL) | 95,989 | 58.0 |
| John R. Berg (I-R) | 69,396 | 42.0 |
| 5 Martin Olav Sabo (DFL) | 91,673 | 62.3 |
| Michael Till (I-R) | 55,412 | 37.7 |
| 6 Richard Nolan (DFL) | 115,880 | 55.3 |
| Russ Bjorhus (I-R) | 93,742 | 44.7 |
| 7 Arlan Stangeland (I-R) | 109,456 | 52.4 |
| Gene R. Wenstrom (DFL) | 93,055 | 44.5 |
| 8 James L. Oberstar (DFL) | 171,125 | 87.2 |
| John W. Hull (AM) | 25,015 | 12.7 |

### MISSISSIPPI

| Candidates | Votes | % |
|---|---|---|
| 1 Jamie L. Whitten (D) | 57,358 | 66.6 |
| T. K. Moffett (R) | 26,734 | 31.0 |

| Candidates | Votes | % |
|---|---|---|
| 2 David R. Bowen (D) | 57,678 | 61.7 |
| Roland Byrd (R) | 35,730 | 38.2 |
| 3 G. V. (Sonny) Montgomery (D) | 101,685 | 92.3 |
| Dorothy Cleveland (R) | 8,408 | 7.6 |
| 4 Jon C. Hinson (R) | 68,225 | 51.6 |
| John Hampton Stennis (D) | 34,837 | 26.4 |
| Evan Doss (I) | 25,134 | 19.0 |
| 5 Trent Lott (R) | 97,177 | 100.0 |

### MISSOURI

| Candidates | Votes | % |
|---|---|---|
| 1 William (Bill) Clay (D) | 65,950 | 66.6 |
| William E. White (R) | 30,995 | 31.3 |
| 2 Robert A. Young (D) | 102,911 | 56.4 |
| Robert C. Chase (R) | 79,495 | 43.6 |
| 3 Richard A. Gephardt (D) | 121,565 | 81.9 |
| Lee Buchschacher (R) | 26,881 | 18.1 |
| 4 Ike Skelton (D) | 120,748 | 72.8 |
| William D. Baker (R) | 45,116 | 27.2 |
| 5 Richard Bolling (D) | 82,140 | 72.0 |
| Steven L. Walter (R) | 30,360 | 26.6 |
| 6 E. Thomas Coleman (R) | 96,574 | 55.9 |
| Phil Snowden (D) | 76,061 | 44.1 |
| 7 Gene Taylor (R) | 104,566 | 61.2 |
| Jim Thomas (D) | 66,351 | 38.8 |
| 8 Richard H. Ichord (D) | 96,509 | 60.5 |
| Donald D. Meyer (R) | 63,109 | 39.5 |
| 9 Harold L. Volkmer (D) | 135,170 | 74.7 |
| Jerry A. Dent (R) | 45,795 | 25.3 |
| 10 Bill D. Burlison (D) | 99,148 | 65.3 |
| James A. Weir (R) | 52,687 | 34.7 |

### MONTANA

| Candidates | Votes | % |
|---|---|---|
| 1 Pat Williams (D) | 86,016 | 57.3 |
| Jim Waltermire (R) | 64,093 | 42.7 |
| 2 Ron Marlenee (R) | 75,766 | 56.9 |
| Thomas G. Monahan (D) | 57,480 | 43.1 |

### NEBRASKA

| Candidates | Votes | % |
|---|---|---|
| 1 Douglas K. Bereuter (R) | 99,013 | 58.1 |
| Hess Dyas (D) | 71,311 | 41.9 |
| 2 John J. Cavanaugh (D) | 77,135 | 52.3 |
| Harold J. Daub Jr. (R) | 70,309 | 47.7 |
| 3 Virginia Smith (R) | 141,597 | 80.0 |
| Marilyn Fowler (D) | 35,371 | 20.0 |

### NEVADA

| Candidates | Votes | % |
|---|---|---|
| AL Jim Santini (D) | 132,513 | 69.5 |
| Bill O'Mara (R) | 44,425 | 23.3 |

### NEW HAMPSHIRE

| Candidates | Votes | % |
|---|---|---|
| 1 Norman E. D'Amours (D) | 82,697 | 61.6 |
| Daniel M. Hughes (R) | 49,131 | 36.6 |
| 2 James C. Cleveland (R) | 84,535 | 68.1 |
| Edgar J. Helms (D) | 39,546 | 31.9 |

### NEW JERSEY

| Candidates | Votes | % |
|---|---|---|
| 1 James J. Florio (D) | 106,096 | 79.4 |
| Robert M. Deitch (R) | 26,853 | 20.1 |
| 2 William J. Hughes (D) | 112,768 | 66.4 |
| James H. Biggs (R) | 56,997 | 33.6 |
| 3 James J. Howard (D) | 83,349 | 56.0 |
| Bruce G. Coe (R) | 64,730 | 43.5 |
| 4 Frank Thompson Jr. (D) | 69,259 | 61.1 |
| Christopher H. Smith (R) | 41,833 | 36.9 |
| 5 Millicent Fenwick (R) | 100,739 | 72.6 |
| John T. Fahy (D) | 38,108 | 27.4 |
| 6 Edwin B. Forsythe (R) | 89,446 | 60.4 |
| W. Thomas McGann (D) | 56,874 | 38.4 |
| 7 Andrew Maguire (D) | 78,358 | 52.5 |
| Margaret S. Roukema (R) | 69,543 | 46.6 |

| Candidates | Votes | % |
|---|---|---|
| 8 Robert A. Roe (D) | 69,496 | 74.5 |
| Thomas Melani (R) | 23,842 | 25.5 |
| 9 Harold C. Hollenback (R) | 73,478 | 48.9 |
| Nicholas S. Mastorelli (D) | 56,888 | 37.9 |
| Henry Helstoski (I) | 19,126 | 12.7 |
| 10 Peter W. Rodino Jr. (D) | 55,074 | 86.4 |
| John L. Pelt (R) | 8,066 | 12.6 |
| 11 Joseph G. Minish (D) | 88,294 | 70.5 |
| Julius George Feld (R) | 35,642 | 28.5 |
| 12 Matthew J. Rinaldo (R) | 94,850 | 73.4 |
| Richard McCormack (D) | 34,423 | 26.6 |
| 13 James A. Courter (R) | 77,301 | 51.8 |
| Helen Meyner (D) | 71,808 | 48.2 |
| 14 Frank J. Guarini (D) | 67,008 | 63.6 |
| Henry J. Hill (R) | 21,355 | 20.3 |
| Thomas E. McDonough (I) | 15,015 | 14.3 |
| 15 Edward J. Patten (D) | 55,944 | 48.3 |
| Charles W. Wiley (R) | 53,108 | 45.8 |

### NEW MEXICO

| Candidates | Votes | % |
|---|---|---|
| 1 Manuel Lujan Jr. (R) | 118,075 | 62.5 |
| Robert Hawk (D) | 70,761 | 37.5 |
| 2 Harold Runnels (D) | 95,710 | 100.0 |

### NEW YORK

| Candidates | Votes | % |
|---|---|---|
| 1 William Carney (R, C) | 90,115 | 56.3 |
| John F. Randolph (D) | 67,180 | 41.9 |
| 2 Thomas J. Downey (D) | 64,807 | 54.9 |
| Harold J. Withers Jr. (R, C) | 53,322 | 45.1 |
| 3 Jerome A. Ambro (D) | 70,526 | 50.9 |
| Gregory W. Carman (R, C) | 66,458 | 47.9 |
| 4 Norman F. Lent (R, C) | 94,711 | 66.1 |
| Everett A. Rosenblum (D) | 46,508 | 32.5 |
| 5 John W. Wydler (R, C) | 84,864 | 58.4 |
| John W. Matthews (D, L) | 60,519 | 41.6 |
| 6 Lester L. Wolff (D, L) | 80,799 | 60.0 |
| Stuart L. Ain (R) | 44,304 | 32.9 |
| Howard Horowitz (C) | 9,503 | 7.1 |
| 7 Joseph P. Addabbo (D, R, L) | 73,066 | 94.9 |
| Mark Elliott Scott (C) | 3,935 | 5.1 |
| 8 Benjamin S. Rosenthal (D, L) | 74,872 | 78.6 |
| Albert Lemishow (R) | 15,165 | 15.9 |
| Paul C. Ruebenacker (C) | 5,165 | 5.4 |
| 9 Geraldine A. Ferraro (D) | 51,350 | 54.2 |
| Alfred A. DelliBovi (R, C) | 42,108 | 44.4 |
| 10 Mario Biaggi (D, R, L) | 77,979 | 95.0 |
| Carmen Ricciardi (C) | 4,082 | 5.0 |
| 11 James H. Scheuer (D, L) | 58,997 | 78.5 |
| Kenneth Huhn (R, C) | 16,206 | 21.5 |
| 12 Shirley Chisholm (D, L) | 25,697 | 87.8 |
| Charles Gibb (R) | 3,580 | 12.2 |
| 13 Stephen J. Solarz (D, L) | 68,837 | 81.1 |
| Max Carasso (R, C) | 16,002 | 18.9 |
| 14 Frederick Richmond (D. L) | 31,339 | 76.9 |
| Arthur Bramwell (R) | 7,516 | 18.4 |
| 15 Leo C. Zeferetti (D, C) | 49,272 | 68.1 |
| Robert P. Whelan (R) | 20,508 | 28.4 |
| 16 Elizabeth Holtzman (D, L) | 59,703 | 81.9 |
| Larry Penner (R, UT) | 9,405 | 12.9 |
| John H. Fox (C) | 3,782 | 5.2 |
| 17 John M. Murphy (D) | 54,228 | 54.2 |
| John Michael Peters (R, C) | 33,071 | 33.1 |
| Thomas H. Stokes (L) | 12,662 | 12.7 |
| 18 S. William Green (R) | 60,867 | 53.3 |
| Carter Burden (D, L) | 53,434 | 46.7 |
| 19 Charles B. Rangel (D, R, L) | 59,731 | 96.4 |
| 20 Ted Weiss (D. L) | 64,275 | 84.6 |
| Harry Torczyner (R) | 11,661 | 15.4 |
| 21 Robert Garcia (D, R, L) | 23,950 | 98.0 |
| 22 Jonathan B. Bingham (D, L) | 58,727 | 84.1 |
| Anthony J. Geidel Jr. (R, C) | 11,110 | 15.9 |
| 23 Peter A. Peyser (D) | 66,354 | 51.6 |
| Angelo R. Martinelli (R, C) | 59,455 | 46.2 |
| 24 Richard L. Ottinger (D) | 75,397 | 56.1 |
| Michael R. Edelman (R, C) | 57,451 | 42.7 |
| 25 Hamilton Fish Jr. (R) | 114,641 | 78.2 |
| Gunars M. Ozols (D) | 31,213 | 21.3 |
| 26 Benjamin A. Gilman (R) | 87,059 | 62.3 |

| Candidates | Votes | % |
|---|---|---|
| Charles E. Holbrook (D, L) | 41,870 | 30. |
| William R. Schaeffer Jr. (C) | 10,708 | 7. |
| 27 Matthew F. McHugh (D) | 83,413 | 55. |
| Neil Tyler Wallace (R, C) | 66,177 | 44. |
| 28 Samuel S. Stratton (D) | 139,575 | 76. |
| Paul H. Tocker (R, C) | 36,017 | 19. |
| 29 Gerald B. Solomon (R, C) | 99,518 | 54. |
| Edward W. Pattison (D, L) | 84,705 | 46. |
| 30 Robert C. McEwen (R. C) | 85,478 | 60. |
| Norma A. Bartle (D, L) | 55,785 | 39. |
| 31 Donald J. Mitchell (R, C) | 107,791 | 100. |
| 32 James M. Hanley (D) | 76,251 | 52. |
| Peter J. Del Giorno (R, C) | 67,071 | 46. |
| 33 Gary A. Lee (R) | 82,501 | 56. |
| Roy A. Bernardi (D) | 58,286 | 39. |
| 34 Frank Horton (R, D) | 122,785 | 87. |
| Leo J. Kesselring (C) | 18,127 | 12. |
| 35 Barber B. Conable Jr. (R) | 96,119 | 69. |
| Francis C. Repicci (D) | 36,428 | 26. |
| 36 John J. LaFalce (D) | 99,497 | 74. |
| Francina J. Cartonia (R) | 31,527 | 23. |
| 37 Henry J. Nowak (D, L) | 70,911 | 78. |
| Charles Roth III (R) | 17,585 | 19. |
| 38 Jack F. Kemp (R, C) | 113,928 | 94. |
| James A. Peck (L) | 6,204 | 5. |
| 39 Stanley N. Lundine (D) | 79,385 | 58. |
| Crispin M. Maguire (R, C) | 56,431 | 41. |

#### Special Elections

| Candidates | Votes | % |
|---|---|---|
| 18 S. William Green (R) | 30,332 | 50. |
| Bella S. Abzug (D, L) | 29,189 | 48. |
| 21 Robert Garcia (R, L) | 7,959 | 55. |
| Louis Nine (D, C) | 3,514 | 24. |
| Ramon S. Valez (I) | 2,280 | 15. |

### NORTH CAROLINA

| Candidates | Votes | % |
|---|---|---|
| 1 Walter B. Jones (D) | 67,716 | 80. |
| James Newcomb (R) | 16,814 | 19. |
| 2 L. H. Fountain (D) | 61,851 | 78. |
| Barry L. Gardner (R) | 15,988 | 20. |
| 3 Charlie Whitley (D) | 54,452 | 71. |
| Willard J. Blanchard (R) | 22,150 | 28. |
| 4 Ike F. Andrews (D) | 74,249 | 94. |
| Naudeen Beek (LIBERT) | 4,436 | 5. |
| 5 Stephen L. Neal (D) | 68,778 | 54. |
| Hamilton C. Horton Jr. (R) | 58,161 | 45. |
| 6 Richardson Preyer (D) | 58,193 | 6. |
| George Bemus (R) | 26,882 | 3. |
| 7 Charlie Rose (D) | 53,696 | 68. |
| Raymond C. Schrump (R) | 23,146 | 3. |
| 8 W. G. (Bill) Hefner (D) | 63,168 | 5. |
| Roger Austin (R) | 43,942 | 4. |
| 9 James G. Martin (R) | 66,157 | 6. |
| Charles Maxwell (D) | 29,761 | 3. |
| 10 James T. Broyhill (R) | 67,004 | 100. |
| 11 Lamar Gudger (D) | 75,460 | 5. |
| R. Curtis Ratcliff (R) | 65,832 | 4. |

### NORTH DAKOTA

| Candidates | Votes | % |
|---|---|---|
| AL Mark Andrews (R) | 147,746 | 6. |
| Bruce Hagen (D) | 68,016 | 3. |

### OHIO

| Candidates | Votes | % |
|---|---|---|
| 1 Bill Gradison (R) | 73,593 | 6. |
| Timothy M. Burke (D) | 38,669 | 3. |
| 2 Thomas A. Luken (D) | 64,522 | 5. |
| Stanley J. Aronoff (R) | 58,716 | 4. |
| 3 Tony P. Hall (D) | 62,849 | 5. |
| Dudley P. Kircher (R) | 51,833 | 4. |
| 4 Tennyson Guyer (R) | 88,575 | 6. |
| John W. Griffin (D) | 39,360 | 3. |
| 5 Delbert L. Latta (R) | 85,547 | 6. |
| James R. Sherck (D) | 51,071 | 3. |
| 6 William H. Harsha (R) | 85,592 | 6. |
| Ted Strickland (D) | 46,318 | 3. |

| Candidates | Votes | % |
|---|---|---|
| Clarence J. Brown (R) | 92,507 | 100.0 |
| Thomas N. Kindness (R) | 81,156 | 71.4 |
| Lou Schroeder (D) | 32,493 | 28.6 |
| Thomas L. Ashley (D) | 71,709 | 63.4 |
| John C. Hoyt (R) | 34,326 | 30.3 |
| Clarence E. Miller (R) | 99,329 | 73.9 |
| James A. Plummer (D) | 35,039 | 26.1 |
| J. William Stanton (R) | 89,327 | 68.1 |
| Patrick J. Donlin (D) | 37,131 | 28.3 |
| Samuel L. Devine (R) | 81,573 | 56.9 |
| James L. Baumann (D) | 61,698 | 43.1 |
| Don J. Pease (D) | 80,875 | 65.1 |
| Mark W. Whitfield (R) | 43,269 | 34.9 |
| John F. Seiberling (D) | 82,356 | 72.5 |
| Walter J. Vogel (R) | 31,311 | 27.5 |
| Chalmers P. Wylie (R) | 91,023 | 71.1 |
| Henry W. Eckhart (D) | 37,000 | 28.9 |
| Ralph S. Regula (R) | 105,152 | 78.0 |
| Owen S. Hand Jr. (D) | 29,640 | 22.0 |
| John M. Ashbrook (R) | 87,010 | 67.4 |
| Kenneth R. Grier (D) | 42,117 | 32.6 |
| Douglas Applegate (D) | 71,894 | 59.5 |
| Bill Ress (R) | 48,931 | 40.5 |
| Lyle Williams (R) | 71,890 | 50.7 |
| Charles J. Carney (D) | 69,977 | 49.3 |
| Mary Rose Oakar (D) | 76,973 | 100.0 |
| Louis Stokes (D) | 58,934 | 86.1 |
| Bill Mack (R) | 9,533 | 13.9 |
| Charles A. Vanik (D) | 87,551 | 66.0 |
| Richard W. Sander (R) | 30,935 | 23.3 |
| James F. Sexton (I) | 7,126 | 5.4 |
| Robert E. Lehman (I) | 6,960 | 5.2 |
| Ronald M. Mottl (D) | 99,975 | 74.8 |
| Homes S. Taft (R) | 33,732 | 25.2 |

## OKLAHOMA

| Candidates | Votes | % |
|---|---|---|
| James R. Jones (D) | 73,886 | 59.9 |
| Paula Unruh (R) | 49,404 | 40.1 |
| Mike Synar (D) | 72,583 | 54.8 |
| Gary L. Richardson (R) | 59,853 | 45.2 |
| Wes Watkins (D) | | 100.0 |
| Tom Steed (D) | 62,993 | 60.3 |
| Scotty Robb (R) | 41,421 | 39.7 |
| Mickey Edwards (R) | 71,451 | 79.9 |
| Jesse D. Knipp (D) | 17,978 | 20.1 |
| Glenn English (D) | 103,512 | 74.2 |
| Harold Hunter (R) | 36,031 | 25.8 |

## OREGON

| Candidates | Votes | % |
|---|---|---|
| Les AuCoin (D) | 158,706 | 62.9 |
| Nick Bunick (R) | 93,640 | 37.1 |
| Al Ullman (D) | 152,099 | 69.1 |
| Terry L. Hicks (R) | 67,547 | 30.7 |
| Robert Duncan (D) | 151,895 | 84.6 |
| Martin Simon (USLP) | 27,120 | 15.1 |
| James Weaver (D) | 124,745 | 56.3 |
| Jerry L. Lausmann (R) | 96,953 | 43.7 |

## PENNSYLVANIA

| Candidates | Votes | % |
|---|---|---|
| Michael (Ozzie) Myers (D) | 104,412 | 71.9 |
| Samuel N. Fanelli (R) | 37,913 | 26.1 |
| William H. Gray III (D) | 132,594 | 82.0 |
| Roland J. Atkins (R) | 25,785 | 15.9 |
| Raymond F. Lederer (D) | 86,915 | 71.8 |
| Raymond A. Kauffman (R) | 33,750 | 28.2 |
| Charles F. Dougherty (R) | 119,445 | 55.8 |
| Joshua Eilberg (D) | 87,555 | 44.2 |
| Richard T. Schulze (R) | 119,565 | 75.1 |
| Murray P. Zealor (D) | 36,704 | 24.9 |
| Gus Yatron (D) | 196,432 | 73.8 |
| Stephen Mazur (R) | 37,746 | 26.2 |
| Robert W. Edgar (D) | 79,771 | 50.3 |
| Eugene D. Kane (R) | 78,403 | 49.4 |
| Peter H. Kostmayer (D) | 89,276 | 61.1 |
| S. Roger Bowers (R) | 56,776 | 38.9 |
| Bud Shuster (R) | 101,151 | 74.9 |
| Elaine L. Havice Jr. (D) | 33,882 | 25.1 |

| Candidates | Votes | % |
|---|---|---|
| 10 Joseph M. McDade (R) | 116,003 | 76.5 |
| Gene Basalyga (D) | 35,721 | 23.5 |
| 11 Daniel J. Flood (D) | 61,433 | 57.5 |
| Robert P. Hudock (R) | 45,335 | 42.5 |
| 12 John P. Murtha (D) | 194,216 | 68.7 |
| Luther V. Elkins (R) | 47,442 | 31.3 |
| 13 Lawrence Coughlin (R) | 112,711 | 70.5 |
| Alan B. Rubenstein (D) | 47,151 | 29.5 |
| 14 William S. Moorhead (D) | 68,004 | 57.0 |
| Stan Thomas (R) | 49,992 | 41.9 |
| 15 Donald L. Ritter (R) | 65,986 | 53.2 |
| Fred B. Rooney (D) | 58,077 | 46.8 |
| 16 Robert S. Walker (R) | 91,910 | 77.0 |
| Charles W. Boohar (D) | 27,386 | 23.0 |
| 17 Allen E. Ertel (D) | 79,234 | 59.6 |
| Thomas R. Rippon (R) | 53,613 | 40.4 |
| 18 Doug Walgren (D) | 88,299 | 57.1 |
| Ted Jacob (R) | 65,088 | 42.1 |
| 19 Bill Goodling (R) | 105,424 | 78.7 |
| Rajeshwar Kumar (D) | 28,577 | 21.3 |
| 20 Joseph M. Gaydos (D) | 97,745 | 72.1 |
| Kathleen M. Meyer (R) | 37,745 | 27.9 |
| 21 Don Bailey (D) | 73,712 | 52.9 |
| Robert H. Miller (R) | 65,622 | 47.1 |
| 22 Austin J. Murphy (D) | 99,559 | 71.6 |
| Marilyn C. Ecoff (R) | 39,518 | 28.4 |
| 23 William F. Clinger Jr. (R) | 73,194 | 54.3 |
| Joseph S. Ammerman (D) | 61,657 | 45.7 |
| 24 Marc L. Marks (R) | 87,041 | 64.0 |
| Joseph F. Vigorito (D) | 48,894 | 36.0 |
| 25 Eugene V. Atkinson (D) | 68,293 | 46.5 |
| Tim Shaffer (R) | 62,160 | 42.3 |
| Robert Morris (I) | 10,588 | 7.2 |

## RHODE ISLAND

| Candidates | Votes | % |
|---|---|---|
| 1 Fernand J. St Germain (D) | 86,768 | 61.2 |
| John J. Slocum Jr. (R) | 54,912 | 38.8 |
| 2 Edward P. Beard (D) | 87,397 | 52.6 |
| Claudine Schneider (R) | 78,725 | 47.4 |

## SOUTH CAROLINA

| Candidates | Votes | % |
|---|---|---|
| 1 Mendel J. Davis (D) | 65,835 | 60.6 |
| C. C. Wannamaker (R) | 42,811 | 39.4 |
| 2 Floyd Spence (R) | 71,208 | 57.3 |
| Jack Bass (D) | 53,021 | 42.7 |
| 3 Butler Derrick (D) | 81,638 | 82.0 |
| Anthony Panuccio (R) | 17,973 | 18.0 |
| 4 Carroll A. Campbell Jr. (R) | 51,377 | 52.1 |
| Max M. Heller (D) | 45,484 | 46.2 |
| 5 Ken Holland (D) | 63,538 | 82.7 |
| Harold Hough (I) | 13,251 | 17.3 |
| 6 John W. Jenrette Jr. (D) | 69,372 | 100.0 |

## SOUTH DAKOTA

| Candidates | Votes | % |
|---|---|---|
| 1 Thomas A. Daschle (D) | 64,683 | 50.1 |
| Leo K. Thorsness (R) | 64,544 | 49.9 |
| 2 James Abdnor (R) | 70,780 | 56.0 |
| Bob Samuelson (D) | 55,516 | 44.0 |

## TENNESSEE

| Candidates | Votes | % |
|---|---|---|
| 1 James H. (Jimmy) Quillen (R) | 92,143 | 64.5 |
| Gordon Ball (D) | 50,694 | 35.5 |
| 2 John J. Duncan (R) | 125,082 | 81.8 |
| Margaret Francis (D) | 27,745 | 18.2 |
| 3 Marilyn Lloyd (D) | 108,282 | 88.9 |
| Dan East (I) | 13,535 | 11.1 |
| 4 Albert Gore Jr. (D) | 108,695 | 100.0 |
| 5 Bill Boner (D) | 68,608 | 51.4 |
| Bill Goodwin (R) | 47,288 | 35.4 |
| Henry Haile (I) | 17,674 | 13.2 |
| 6 Robin L. Beard Jr. (R) | 114,630 | 74.6 |
| Ron Arline (D) | 38,954 | 25.4 |
| 7 Ed Jones (D) | 96,863 | 72.9 |
| Ross Cook (R) | 36,003 | 27.1 |
| 8 Harold E. Ford (D) | 80,776 | 69.7 |
| Duncan Ragsdale (R) | 33,679 | 29.1 |

## TEXAS

| Candidates | Votes | % |
|---|---|---|
| 1 Sam B. Hall Jr. (D) | 73,708 | 78.1 |
| Fred Hudson (R) | 20,700 | 21.9 |
| 2 Charles Wilson (D) | 66,986 | 70.1 |
| Jim (Matt) Dillon (R) | 28,584 | 29.9 |
| 3 James M. Collins (R) | 96,406 | 100.0 |
| 4 Ray Roberts (D) | 58,336 | 61.5 |
| Frank S. Glenn (R) | 36,582 | 38.5 |
| 5 Jim Mattox (D) | 35,524 | 50.3 |
| Tom Pauken (R) | 34,672 | 49.1 |
| 6 Phil Gramm (D) | 66,025 | 65.1 |
| Wesley H. Mowrey (R) | 35,393 | 34.9 |
| 7 Bill Archer (R) | 128,214 | 85.1 |
| Robert L. Hutchings (D) | 22,415 | 14.9 |
| 8 Bob Eckhardt (D) | 39,429 | 61.5 |
| Nick Gearhart (R) | 24,673 | 38.5 |
| 9 Jack Brooks (D) | 50,792 | 63.3 |
| Randy Evans (R) | 29,473 | 36.7 |
| 10 J. J. Pickle (D) | 94,529 | 76.3 |
| Emmett L. Hudspeth (R) | 29,328 | 23.7 |
| 11 J. Marvin Leath (D) | 53,354 | 51.6 |
| Jack Burgess (R) | 49,965 | 48.4 |
| 12 Jim Wright (D) | 46,456 | 68.5 |
| Claude K. Brown (R) | 21,364 | 31.5 |
| 13 Jack Hightower (D) | 75,271 | 74.9 |
| Clifford A. Jones (R) | 25,275 | 25.1 |
| 14 Joe Wyatt (D) | 63,953 | 72.4 |
| Joy Yates (R) | 24,325 | 27.6 |
| 15 E. (Kika) de la Garza (D) | 54,560 | 66.2 |
| Robert L. McDonald (R) | 27,853 | 33.8 |
| 16 Richard C. White (D) | 53,090 | 70.0 |
| Michael Giere (R) | 22,743 | 30.0 |
| 17 Charles W. Stenholm (D) | 69,030 | 68.1 |
| Billy Lee Fisher (R) | 32,302 | 31.9 |
| 18 Mickey Leland (D) | 36,783 | 96.8 |
| 19 Kent Hance (D) | 54,729 | 53.2 |
| George W. Bush (R) | 48,070 | 46.8 |
| 20 Henry B. Gonzalez (D) | 51,584 | 100.0 |
| 21 Tom Loeffler (R) | 84,336 | 57.0 |
| Nelson W. Wolff (R) | 63,501 | 43.0 |
| 22 Ron Paul (R) | 54,643 | 50.6 |
| Bob Gammage (D) | 53,443 | 49.4 |
| 23 Abraham Kazen Jr. (D) | 62,649 | 89.7 |
| Augustin Mata (LRU) | 7,185 | 10.3 |
| 24 Martin Frost (D) | 39,201 | 54.1 |
| Leo Berman (R) | 33,314 | 45.9 |

## UTAH

| Candidates | Votes | % |
|---|---|---|
| 1 Gunn McKay (D) | 93,892 | 51.0 |
| Jed J. Richardson (R) | 85,028 | 46.2 |
| 2 Dan Marriott (R) | 121,492 | 62.3 |
| Edwin B. Firmage (D) | 68,899 | 35.3 |

## VERMONT

| Candidates | Votes | % |
|---|---|---|
| AL James M. Jeffords (R) | 90,688 | 75.3 |
| S. Marie Dietz (D) | 23,228 | 19.3 |
| Peter Diamondstone (LU) | 6,505 | 5.4 |

## VIRGINIA

| Candidates | Votes | % |
|---|---|---|
| 1 Paul S. Trible Jr. (R) | 89,158 | 72.1 |
| Lew Puller (D) | 34,578 | 27.9 |
| 2 G. William Whitehurst (R) | 63,512 | 100.0 |
| 3 David E. Satterfield III (D) | 104,550 | 87.7 |
| Alan R. Ogden (I) | 14,453 | 12.1 |
| 4 Robert W. Daniel Jr. (R) | 77,827 | 99.9 |
| 5 Dan Daniel (D) | 83,575 | 99.9 |
| 6 M. Caldwell Butler (R) | 88,647 | 99.8 |
| 7 J. Kenneth Robinson (R) | 84,517 | 64.3 |
| Lewis Fickett (D) | 46,950 | 35.7 |
| 8 Herbert E. Harris II (D) | 56,137 | 50.5 |
| John F. Herrity (D) | 52,396 | 47.1 |
| 9 William C. Wampler (R) | 76,877 | 61.9 |
| Champ Clark (D) | 47,367 | 38.1 |
| 10 Joseph L. Fisher (D) | 70,892 | 53.3 |
| Frank Wolf (R) | 61,981 | 46.6 |

## WASHINGTON

| Candidates | Votes | % |
|---|---|---|
| 1 Joel Pritchard (R) | 99,942 | 64.0 |
| Janice Niemi (D) | 52,706 | 33.7 |
| 2 Al Swift (D) | 70,620 | 51.4 |
| John Nance Garner (R) | 66,793 | 48.6 |
| 3 Don Bonker (D) | 82,616 | 58.6 |
| Rick Bennett (R) | 58,270 | 41.4 |
| 4 Mike McCormack (D) | 85,602 | 61.1 |
| Susan Roylance (R) | 54,389 | 38.9 |
| 5 Thomas S. Foley (D) | 77,201 | 48.0 |
| Duane Alton (R) | 68,761 | 42.7 |
| Mel Tonasket (I) | 14,887 | 9.3 |
| 6 Norman D. Dicks (D) | 71,057 | 60.9 |
| James E. Beaver (R) | 43,640 | 37.4 |
| 7 Mike Lowry (D) | 67,450 | 53.3 |
| John E. Cunningham (R) | 59,052 | 46.7 |

## WEST VIRGINIA

| | Votes | % |
|---|---|---|
| 1 Robert H. Mollohan (D) | 76,372 | 63.4 |
| Gene A. Haynes (R) | 44,062 | 36.6 |

| Candidates | Votes | % |
|---|---|---|
| 2 Harley O. Staggers (D) | 69,683 | 55.3 |
| Cleveland K. Benedict (R) | 56,272 | 44.7 |
| 3 John M. Slack (D) | 74,837 | 59.2 |
| David M. Staton (R) | 51,584 | 40.8 |
| 4 Nick J. Rahall (D) | 70,035 | 100.0 |

## WISCONSIN

| | Votes | % |
|---|---|---|
| 1 Les Aspin (D) | 77,146 | 54.5 |
| William W. Petrie (R) | 64,437 | 45.5 |
| 2 Robert W. Kastenmeier (D) | 99,631 | 57.7 |
| James A. Wright (R) | 71,412 | 41.3 |
| 3 Alvin Baldus (D) | 96,326 | 62.8 |
| Michael S. Ellis (R) | 57.060 | 37.2 |
| 4 Clement J. Zablocki (D) | 101,575 | 66.1 |
| Elroy G. Honadel (R) | 52,125 | 33.9 |
| 5 Henry S. Reuss (D) | 85,067 | 73.1 |
| James R. Medina (R) | 30,185 | 25.9 |

| Candidates | Votes | % |
|---|---|---|
| 6 William A. Steiger (R) | 114,742 | 69. |
| Robert J. Steffes (D) | 48,785 | 29. |
| 7 David R. Obey (D) | 110,874 | 62. |
| Vinton A. Vesta (R) | 65,750 | 36. |
| 8 Tobias A. Roth (R) | 101,856 | 57. |
| Robert J. Cornell (D) | 73,925 | 42. |
| 9 F. James Sansenbrenner Jr. (R) | 118,386 | 61. |
| Matthew J. Flynn (D) | 75,207 | 38. |

## WYOMING

| | Votes | % |
|---|---|---|
| AL Richard Cheney (R) | 75,855 | 58 |
| Bill Bagley (D) | 53,522 | 4 |

1. For the 1978 House elections in Louisiana, an open primary was held with candidates from all parties running on the same ballot. Any candidate who received a majority was elected unopposed without any further appearance on the general election ballot. Where no candidate received 50 percent, there was a general election runoff between the top two finishers regardless of party. This condition prevailed only in Congressional District 4.

# 1979 House Elections

## CALIFORNIA

### Special Election

| Candidates | Votes | % |
|---|---|---|
| 11 Bill Royer (R) | 52,585 | 57.3 |
| G. W. Holsinger (D) | 37,685 | 41.1 |

## WISCONSIN

### Special Election

| | Votes | % |
|---|---|---|
| 6 Thomas E. Petri (R) | 71,715 | 50.0 |
| Gary R. Goyke (D) | 70,492 | 49.5 |

# 1980 House Elections

## ALABAMA

| Candidates | Votes | % |
|---|---|---|
| 1 Jack Edwards (R) | 111,089 | 94.8 |
| Steve Smith (LIBERT) | 6,130 | 5.2 |
| 2 William L. Dickinson (R) | 104,796 | 60.6 |
| Cecil Wyatt (D) | 63,447 | 36.7 |
| 3 Bill Nichols (D) | 107,654 | 100.0 |
| 4 Tom Bevill (D) | 129,365 | 97.9 |
| 5 Ronnie G. Flippo (D) | 117,626 | 94.1 |
| Betty T. Benson (LIBERT) | 7,341 | 5.9 |
| 6 Albert Lee Smith Jr. (R) | 95,019 | 50.5 |
| W.B. (Pete) Clifford (D) | 87,536 | 46.6 |
| 7 Richard C. Shelby (D) | 122,505 | 72.6 |
| James E. Bacon (R) | 43,320 | 25.7 |

## ALASKA

| Candidates | Votes | % |
|---|---|---|
| AL Don Young (R) | 114,089 | 73.8 |
| Kevin (Pat) Parnell (D) | 39,922 | 25.8 |

## ARIZONA

| Candidates | Votes | % |
|---|---|---|
| 1 John J. Rhodes (R) | 136,961 | 73.3 |
| Steve Jancek (D) | 40,045 | 21.4 |
| 2 Morris K. Udall (D) | 127,736 | 58.1 |
| Richard H. Huff (R) | 88,653 | 40.4 |
| 3 Bob Stump (D) | 141,448 | 64.3 |
| Bob Croft (R) | 65,845 | 30.0 |
| Sharon Hayse (LIBERT) | 12,529 | 5.7 |
| 4 Eldon Rudd (R) | 142,565 | 62.6 |
| Les Miller (D) | 85,046 | 37.4 |

## ARKANSAS

| Candidates | Votes | % |
|---|---|---|
| 1 Bill Alexander (D) | | 100.0 |
| 2 Ed Bethune (R) | 159,148 | 78.9 |
| James G. Reid (D) | 42,278 | 21.0 |
| 3 John Paul Hammerschmidt (R) | | 100.0 |
| 4 Beryl Anthony Jr. (D) | | 100.0 |

## CALIFORNIA

| Candidates | Votes | % |
|---|---|---|
| 1 Eugene A. Chappie (R) | 145,585 | 53.7 |
| Harold T. Johnson (D) | 107,993 | 39.8 |
| Jim McClarin (LIBERT) | 17,497 | 6.5 |
| 2 Don H. Clausen (R) | 141,698 | 54.2 |
| Norma K. Bork (D) | 109,789 | 42.0 |
| 3 Robert T. Matsui (D) | 170,670 | 70.6 |
| Joseph Murphy (R) | 64,215 | 26.5 |
| 4 Vic Fazio (D) | 133,853 | 65.1 |
| Albert Dehr (R) | 60,935 | 29.6 |
| Robert J. Burnside (LIBERT) | 10,267 | 5.0 |
| 5 John L. Burton (D) | 101,105 | 51.1 |
| Dennis McQuaid (R) | 89,624 | 45.3 |
| 6 Phillip Burton (D) | 93,400 | 69.4 |
| Tom Spinosa (R) | 34,500 | 25.6 |
| Roy Childs (LIBERT) | 6,750 | 5.0 |
| 7 George Miller (D) | 142,044 | 63.3 |
| Giles St. Clair (R) | 70,479 | 31.4 |
| 8 Ronald V. Dellums (D) | 108,380 | 55.5 |
| Charles V. Hughes (R) | 76,580 | 39.2 |
| Tom Mikuriya (LIBERT) | 10,465 | 5.3 |
| 9 Fortney H. (Pete) Stark (D) | 90,504 | 55.3 |
| William J. Kennedy (R) | 67,265 | 41.1 |
| 10 Don Edwards (D) | 102,231 | 62.1 |
| John M. Lutton (R) | 45,987 | 27.9 |
| Joseph Fuhrig (LIBERT) | 11,904 | 7.2 |
| 11 Tom Lantos (D) | 85,823 | 46.4 |
| Bill Royer (R) | 80,100 | 43.3 |
| Wilson Branch (PFP) | 13,723 | 7.4 |
| 12 Paul N. McCloskey Jr. (R) | 143,817 | 72.2 |
| Kirsten Olsen (D) | 37,009 | 18.6 |
| Bill Evers (LIBERT) | 15,073 | 7.6 |
| 13 Norman Y. Mineta (D) | 132,246 | 58.9 |
| W.E. (Ted) Gagne (R) | 79,766 | 35.5 |
| 14 Norman D. Shumway (R) | 133,979 | 60.7 |
| Ann Cerney (D) | 79,883 | 36.2 |

| Candidates | Votes | % |
|---|---|---|
| 15 Tony Coelho (D) | 108,072 | 71.8 |
| Ron Schwartz (R) | 37,895 | 25.2 |
| 16 Leon E. Panetta (D) | 158,360 | 71.0 |
| W.A. (Jack) Roth (R) | 54,675 | 24.5 |
| 17 Charles Pashayan Jr. (R) | 129,159 | 70.6 |
| Willard H. Johnson (D) | 53,780 | 29.4 |
| 18 William M. Thomas (R) | 126,046 | 71.0 |
| Mary (Pat) Timmermans (D) | 51,415 | 29.0 |
| 19 Robert J. Lagomarsino (R) | 162,854 | 77.7 |
| Carmen Lodise (D) | 36,990 | 17.6 |
| 20 Barry Goldwater Jr. (R) | 199,681 | 78.8 |
| Matt Miller (D) | 43,025 | 17.0 |
| 21 Dobbi Fiedler (R) | 74,843 | 48.7 |
| James C. Corman (D) | 74,091 | 48.2 |
| 22 Carlos J. Moorhead (R) | 115,241 | 63.9 |
| Pierce O'Donnell (D) | 57,477 | 31.9 |
| 23 Anthony C. Beilenson (D) | 126,020 | 63.2 |
| Robert Winckler (R) | 62,742 | 31.5 |
| Jeffrey P. Lieb (LIBERT) | 10,623 | 5.3 |
| 24 Henry A. Waxman (D) | 93,569 | 63.8 |
| Roland Cayard (R) | 39,744 | 27.1 |
| 25 Edward R. Roybal (D) | 49,080 | 66.0 |
| Richard L. Ferraro Jr. (R) | 21,116 | 28.4 |
| William D. Mitchell (LIBERT) | 4,169 | 5.6 |
| 26 Joseph L. Lisoni (D) | 40,099 | 24.4 |
| John H. Rousselot (R) | 116,715 | 70.9 |
| 27 Robert K. Dornan (R) | 109,807 | 51.0 |
| Carey Peck (D) | 100,061 | 46.5 |
| 28 Julian C. Dixon (D) | 108,725 | 79.2 |
| Robert Reid (R) | 23,179 | 16.9 |
| 29 Augustus F. Hawkins (D) | 80,095 | 86.1 |
| Michael A. Hirt (R) | 10,282 | 11.1 |
| 30 George E. Danielson (D) | 74,119 | 72.1 |
| J. Arthur Platten (R) | 24,136 | 23.5 |
| 31 Mervyn M. Dymally (D) | 69,146 | 64.4 |
| Don Grimshaw (R) | 38,203 | 35.6 |
| 32 Glenn M. Anderson (D) | 84,057 | 65.9 |
| John R. Adler (R) | 39,260 | 30.8 |
| 33 Wayne Grisham (R) | 122,439 | 70.9 |
| Fred L. Anderson (D) | 50,365 | 29.1 |
| 34 Dan Lungren (R) | 138,024 | 71.8 |
| Simone (D) | 46,351 | 24.1 |
| 35 David Dreier (R) | 100,743 | 51.8 |
| Jim Lloyd (D) | 88,279 | 45.4 |
| 36 George E. Brown Jr. (D) | 88,634 | 52.5 |
| John Paul Stark (R) | 73,252 | 43.4 |
| 37 Jerry Lewis (R) | 166,640 | 71.6 |
| Donald M. Rusk (D) | 58,462 | 25.1 |
| 38 Jerry M. Patterson (D) | 91,880 | 55.5 |
| Art Jacobson (R) | 66,256 | 40.0 |
| 39 William Dannemeyer (R) | 175,228 | 76.3 |
| Leonard L. Lahtinen (D) | 54,504 | 23.7 |
| 40 Robert E. Badham (R) | 213,999 | 70.2 |
| Michael F. Dow (D) | 66,512 | 21.8 |
| Dan Mahaffey (LIBERT) | 24,486 | 8.0 |
| 41 Bill Lowery (R) | 123,187 | 52.7 |
| Bob Wilson (D) | 101,191 | 43.2 |
| 42 Duncan L. Hunter (R) | 79,713 | 53.3 |
| Lionel Van Deerlin (D) | 69,936 | 46.7 |
| 43 Clair W. Burgener (R) | 299,037 | 86.5 |
| Tom Metzger (D) | 46,383 | 13.4 |

## COLORADO

| Candidates | Votes | % |
|---|---|---|
| 1 Patricia Schroeder (D) | 107,364 | 59.8 |
| Naomi Bradford (R) | 67,804 | 37.7 |
| 2 Timothy E. Wirth (D) | 153,618 | 56.4 |
| John McElderry (R) | 111,825 | 41.1 |
| 3 Ray Kogovsek (D) | 105,820 | 54.9 |
| Harold McCormick (R) | 84,292 | 43.7 |
| 4 Hank Brown (R) | 178,221 | 68.4 |
| Polly Baca Barragan (D) | 76,849 | 29.5 |
| 5 Ken Kramer (R) | 177,319 | 72.4 |
| Ed Schreiber (D) | 62,003 | 25.3 |

## CONNECTICUT

| Candidates | Votes | % |
|---|---|---|
| 1 William R. Cotter (D) | 137,849 | 63.0 |
| Marjorie D. Anderson (R) | 80,816 | 37.0 |
| 2 Samuel Gejdenson (D) | 119,176 | 53.4 |
| Tony Guglielmo (R) | 104,107 | 46.6 |
| 3 Lawrence J. DeNardis (R) | 117,024 | 52.3 |
| Joseph I. Lieberman (D) | 103,903 | 46.5 |
| 4 Stewart B. McKinney (R) | 124,285 | 62.6 |
| John A. Phillips (D) | 74,326 | 37.4 |
| 5 William R. Ratchford (D) | 117,316 | 50.4 |
| Edward M. Donahue (R) | 115,614 | 49.6 |
| 6 Toby Moffett (D) | 142,685 | 59.0 |
| Nicholas Schaus (R) | 98,331 | 40.6 |

## DELAWARE

| Candidates | Votes | % |
|---|---|---|
| AL Thomas B. Evans Jr. (R) | 133,842 | 61.8 |
| Robert L. Maxwell (D) | 81,227 | 37.5 |

## FLORIDA

| Candidates | Votes | % |
|---|---|---|
| 1 Earl Hutto (D) | 119,829 | 61.2 |
| Warren Briggs (R) | 75,939 | 38.8 |
| 2 Don Fuqua (D) | 138,252 | 70.6 |
| John R. LaCapra (R) | 57,588 | 29.4 |
| 3 Charles E. Bennett (D) | 104,672 | 77.0 |
| Harry Radcliffe (R) | 31,208 | 23.0 |
| 4 Bill Chappell Jr. (D) | 147,775 | 65.8 |
| Barney E. Dillard Jr. (R) | 76,924 | 34.2 |
| 5 Bill McCollum (R) | 177,603 | 55.8 |
| David Best (D) | 140,903 | 44.2 |
| 6 C.W. Bill Young (R) | | 100.0 |
| 7 Sam Gibbons (D) | 132,529 | 71.8 |
| Charles P. Jones (R) | 52,138 | 28.2 |
| 8 Andy Ireland (D) | 151,613 | 69.3 |
| Scott Nicholson (R) | 61,820 | 28.2 |
| 9 Bill Nelson (D) | 139,468 | 70.4 |
| Stan Dowiat (R) | 58,734 | 29.6 |
| 10 L.A. (Skip) Bafalis (R) | 272,393 | 78.9 |
| Richard D. Sparkman (D) | 72,646 | 21.1 |
| 11 Dan Mica (D) | 201,713 | 59.5 |
| Al Coogler (R) | 137,520 | 40.5 |
| 12 Clay Shaw (R) | 128,561 | 54.5 |
| Alan S. Becker (D) | 107,164 | 45.5 |
| 13 William Lehman (D) | 127,828 | 74.9 |
| Alvin E. Entin (R) | 42,830 | 25.1 |
| 14 Claude Pepper (D) | 95,820 | 74.9 |
| Evelio S. Estrella (R) | 32,027 | 25.1 |
| 15 Dante B. Fascell (D) | 132,952 | 65.4 |
| Herbert J. Hoodwin (R) | 70,433 | 34.6 |

## GEORGIA

| Candidates | Votes | % |
|---|---|---|
| 1 Bo Ginn (D) | 82,145 | 100.0 |
| 2 Charles F. Hatcher (D) | 92,264 | 73.6 |
| Jack E. Harrell Jr. (R) | 33,107 | 26.4 |
| 3 Jack Brinkley (D) | 89,040 | 100.0 |
| 4 Elliott H. Levitas (D) | 117,091 | 69.4 |
| Barry E. Billington (R) | 51,546 | 30.6 |
| 5 Wyche Fowler Jr. (D) | 101,646 | 74.0 |
| F. William Dowda (D) | 35,640 | 26.0 |
| 6 Newt Gingrich (R) | 96,071 | 59.1 |
| Dock H. Davis (D) | 66,606 | 40.9 |
| 7 Larry P. McDonald (D) | 115,892 | 68.1 |
| Richard L. Castellucis (R) | 54,242 | 31.9 |
| 8 Billy Lee Evans (D) | 91,103 | 74.6 |
| Darwin Carter (R) | 31,033 | 25.4 |
| 9 Ed Jenkins (D) | 115,576 | 68.0 |
| David G. Ashworth (R) | 54,341 | 32.0 |
| 10 Doug Barnard (D) | 102,177 | 80.2 |
| Bruce J. Neubauer (R) | 25,194 | 19.8 |

## HAWAII

| Candidates | Votes | % |
|---|---|---|
| 1 Cecil Heftel (D) | 98,256 | 79.8 |
| Aloma Keen Noble (R) | 19,819 | 16.1 |
| 2 Daniel K. Akaka (D) | 141,477 | 89.9 |
| Don G. Smith (LIBERT) | 15,903 | 10.1 |

## IDAHO

| Candidates | Votes | % |
|---|---|---|
| 1 Larry Craig (R) | 116,845 | 53.7 |
| Glenn W. Nichols (D) | 100,697 | 46.3 |
| 2 George Hansen (R) | 116,196 | 58.8 |
| Diane Bilyeu (D) | 81,364 | 41.2 |

## ILLINOIS

| Candidates | Votes | % |
|---|---|---|
| 1 Harold Washington (D) | 119,562 | 95.5 |
| 2 Gus Savage (D) | 129,771 | 88.1 |
| Marsha A. Harris (R) | 17,428 | 11.8 |
| 3 Marty Russo (D) | 137,283 | 68.9 |
| Lawrence C. Sarsoun (R) | 61,955 | 31.1 |
| 4 Edward J. Derwinski (R) | 152,377 | 68.0 |
| Richard S. Jalovec (D) | 71,814 | 32.0 |
| 5 John G. Fary (D) | 106,142 | 79.6 |
| Robert V. Kotowski (R) | 27,136 | 20.4 |
| 6 Henry J. Hyde (R) | 123,593 | 67.0 |
| Mario Raymond Reda (D) | 60,951 | 33.0 |
| 7 Cardiss Collins (D) | 80,056 | 85.1 |
| Ruth R. Hooper (R) | 14,041 | 14.9 |
| 8 Dan Rostenkowski (D) | 98,524 | 84.7 |
| Walter F. Zilke (R) | 17,845 | 15.3 |
| 9 Sidney R. Yates (D) | 106,543 | 73.1 |
| John D. Andrica (R) | 39,244 | 26.9 |
| 10 John E. Porter (R) | 137,707 | 60.7 |
| Robert A. Weinberger (D) | 89,008 | 39.3 |
| 11 Frank Annunzio (D) | 121,166 | 69.8 |
| Michael R. Zanillo (R) | 52,417 | 30.2 |
| 12 Philip M. Crane (R) | 185,080 | 74.1 |
| David McCartney (D) | 64,729 | 25.9 |
| 13 Robert McClory (R) | 131,448 | 71.7 |
| Michael Reese (D) | 52,000 | 28.3 |
| 14 John N. Erlenborn (R) | 202,583 | 76.8 |
| LeRoy E. Kennel (D) | 61,224 | 23.2 |
| 15 Tom Corcoran (R) | 150,898 | 76.7 |
| John P. Quillin (D) | 45,721 | 23.3 |
| 16 Lynn M. Martin (R) | 132,905 | 67.4 |
| Douglas R. Aurand (D) | 64,224 | 32.6 |
| 17 George M. O'Brien (R) | 125,806 | 65.8 |
| Michael A. Murer (D) | 65,305 | 34.2 |
| 18 Robert H. Michel (R) | 125,741 | 62.1 |
| John L. Knuppel (D) | 76,471 | 37.9 |
| 19 Tom Railsback (R) | 142,616 | 73.4 |
| Thomas J. Hand (D) | 51,753 | 26.6 |
| 20 Paul Findley (R) | 123,427 | 56.0 |
| David L. Robinson (D) | 96,950 | 44.0 |
| 21 Edward R. Madigan (R) | 132,186 | 67.6 |
| Penny L. Severns (D) | 63,476 | 32.4 |
| 22 Daniel B. Crane (R) | 146,014 | 68.8 |
| Peter M. Voelz (D) | 66,065 | 31.2 |
| 23 Melvin Price (D) | 107,786 | 64.4 |
| Ronald L. Davinroy (R) | 59,644 | 35.6 |
| 24 Paul Simon (D) | 112,134 | 49.1 |
| John T. Anderson (R) | 110,176 | 48.3 |

**Special Election**

| | | |
|---|---|---|
| 10 John E. Porter (R) | 36,981 | 54.0 |
| Robert Weinberger (D) | 30,929 | 46.0 |

## INDIANA

| Candidates | Votes | % |
|---|---|---|
| 1 Adam Benjamin Jr. (D) | 112,016 | 72.0 |
| Joseph D. Harkin (R) | 43,537 | 28.0 |
| 2 Floyd Fithian (D) | 122,326 | 54.1 |
| Ernest Niemeyer (R) | 103,957 | 45.9 |
| 3 John P. Hiler (R) | 103,972 | 55.0 |
| John Brademas (D) | 85,136 | 45.0 |
| 4 Daniel R. Coats (R) | 120,055 | 60.5 |
| John D. Walda (D) | 77,542 | 39.1 |
| 5 Elwood Hillis (R) | 129,474 | 61.7 |
| Nels J. Ackerson (D) | 80,378 | 38.3 |
| 6 David W. Evans (D) | 98,482 | 50.2 |
| David G. Crane (R) | 97,582 | 49.8 |
| 7 John T. Myers (R) | 137,604 | 66.1 |
| Patrick D. Carroll (D) | 69,051 | 33.2 |
| 8 H. Joel Deckard (R) | 119,415 | 55.2 |
| Kenneth C. Snider (D) | 97,059 | 44.8 |
| 9 Lee H. Hamilton (D) | 136,574 | 64.4 |
| George Meyers Jr. (R) | 75,601 | 35.6 |
| 10 Phil Sharp (D) | 103,083 | 53.4 |

| Candidates | Votes | % |
|---|---|---|
| William G. Frazier (R) | 90,051 | 46.6 |
| 11 Andy Jacobs Jr. (D) | 105,468 | 57.3 |
| Sheila Suess (R) | 78,743 | 42.7 |

## IOWA

| Candidates | Votes | % |
|---|---|---|
| 1 Jim Leach (R) | 133,349 | 64.1 |
| Jim Larew (D) | 72,602 | 34.9 |
| 2 Tom Tauke (R) | 111,587 | 54.0 |
| Steve Sovern (D) | 93,175 | 45.1 |
| 3 Cooper Evans (R) | 107,869 | 51.4 |
| Lynn G. Cutler (D) | 101,735 | 48.4 |
| 4 Neal Smith (D) | 117,896 | 53.9 |
| Donald C. Young (R) | 100,335 | 45.9 |
| 5 Tom Harkin (D) | 127,895 | 60.2 |
| Cal Hultman (R) | 84,472 | 39.8 |
| 6 Berkley Bedell (D) | 129,460 | 64.3 |
| Clarence S. Carney (R) | 71,866 | 35.7 |

## KANSAS

| Candidates | Votes | % |
|---|---|---|
| 1 Pat Roberts (R) | 121,545 | 62.3 |
| Phil Martin (D) | 73,586 | 37.7 |
| 2 Jim Jeffries (R) | 92,107 | 53.9 |
| Sam Keys (D) | 78,859 | 46.1 |
| 3 Larry Winn Jr. (R) | 109,294 | 55.5 |
| Dan Watkins (D) | 82,414 | 41.8 |
| 4 Dan Glickman (D) | 124,014 | 68.9 |
| Clay Hunter (R) | 55,899 | 31.1 |
| 5 Bob Whittaker (R) | 141,029 | 74.2 |
| David L. Miller (D) | 45,676 | 24.0 |

## KENTUCKY

| Candidates | Votes | % |
|---|---|---|
| 1 Carroll Hubbard Jr. (D) | 118,565 | 100.0 |
| 2 William H. Natcher (D) | 99,670 | 65.7 |
| Mark T. Watson (R) | 52,110 | 34.3 |
| 3 Romano L. Mazzoli (D) | 85,873 | 63.7 |
| Richard Cesler (R) | 46,681 | 34.6 |
| 4 Gene Snyder (R) | 126,049 | 67.0 |
| Phil M. McGary (D) | 62,138 | 33.0 |
| 5 Harold Rogers (R) | 112,093 | 67.5 |
| Ted R. Marcum (D) | 54,027 | 32.5 |
| 6 Larry J. Hopkins (R) | 105,376 | 58.9 |
| Tom Easterly (D) | 72,473 | 40.5 |
| 7 Carl D. Perkins (D) | 117,665 | 100.0 |

## LOUISIANA[1]

| Candidates | Votes | % |
|---|---|---|
| 1 Robert L. Livingston (R) | | 100.0 |
| 2 Lindy Boggs (D) | | 100.0 |
| 3 W. J. (Billy) Tauzin (D) | | 100.0 |
| 4 Buddy Roemer (D) | 103,625 | 63.8 |
| Claude (Buddy) Leach (D) | 58,705 | 36.2 |
| 5 Jerry Huckaby (D) | | 100.0 |
| 6 W. Henson Moore (R) | | 100.0 |
| 7 John B. Breaux (D) | | 100.0 |
| 8 Gillis W. Long (D) | | 100.0 |

**Special Election**

| | | |
|---|---|---|
| 3. W. J. (Billy) Tauzin (D) | 62,108 | 53.0 |
| James Donelon (R) | 54,815 | 47.0 |

## MAINE

| Candidates | Votes | % |
|---|---|---|
| 1 David F. Emery (R) | 188,667 | 68.5 |
| Harold C. Pachios (D) | 86,819 | 31.5 |
| 2 Olympia J. Snowe (R) | 186,406 | 78.5 |
| Harold L. Silverman (D) | 51,026 | 21.5 |

## MARYLAND

| Candidates | Votes | % |
|---|---|---|
| 1 Roy Dyson (D) | 97,743 | 51.7 |
| Robert E. Bauman (R) | 91,143 | 48.3 |
| 2 Clarence D. Long (D) | 121,017 | 57.4 |
| Helen D. Bentley (R) | 89,961 | 42.6 |
| 3 Barbara A. Mikulski (D) | 102,293 | 76.1 |
| Russell T. Schaffer (R) | 32,074 | 23.9 |
| 4 Marjorie S. Holt (R) | 120,985 | 71.9 |
| James J. Riley (D) | 47,375 | 28.1 |
| 5 Gladys Noon Spellman (D) | 106,035 | 80.5 |

| Candidates | Votes | % |
|---|---|---|
| Kevin R. Igoe (R) | 25,693 | 19.5 |
| 6 Beverly B. Byron (D) | 146,101 | 69.9 |
| Raymond E. Beck (R) | 62,913 | 30.1 |
| 7 Parren J. Mitchell (D) | 97,104 | 88.5 |
| Victor Clark Jr. (R) | 12,650 | 11.5 |
| 8 Michael D. Barnes (D) | 148,301 | 59.3 |
| Newton I. Steers Jr. (R) | 101,659 | 40.7 |

## MASSACHUSETTS

| Candidates | Votes | % |
|---|---|---|
| 1 Silvio O. Conte (R) | 156,415 | 74.9 |
| Helen Poppy Doyle (D) | 52,457 | 25.1 |
| 2 Edward P. Boland (D) | 120,711 | 67.2 |
| Thomas P. Swank (R) | 38,672 | 21.5 |
| John B. Aubuchon (I) | 20,247 | 11.3 |
| 3 Joseph D. Early (D) | 141,560 | 72.3 |
| David G. Skehan (R) | 54,123 | 27.7 |
| 4 Barney Frank (D) | 103,466 | 51.9 |
| Richard A. Jones (R) | 95,898 | 48.1 |
| 5 James M. Shannon (D) | 136,758 | 66.0 |
| William C. Sawyer (R) | 70,547 | 34.0 |
| 6 Nicholas Mavroules (D) | 111,393 | 50.8 |
| Thomas H. Trimarco (R) | 103,192 | 47.1 |
| 7 Edward J. Markey (D) | 155,759 | 100.0 |
| 8 Thomas P. O'Neill Jr. (D) | 128,689 | 78.4 |
| William A. Barnstead (R) | 35,477 | 21.6 |
| 9 Joe Moakley (D) | 104,010 | 100.0 |
| 10 Margaret M. Heckler (R) | 131,794 | 60.6 |
| Robert E. McCarthy (D) | 85,629 | 39.4 |
| 11 Brian J. Donnelly (D) | 137,066 | 100.0 |
| 12 Gerry E. Studds (D) | 195,791 | 73.2 |
| Paul V. Doane (R) | 71,620 | 26.8 |

## MICHIGAN

| Candidates | Votes | % |
|---|---|---|
| 1 John Conyers Jr. (D) | 123,286 | 94.7 |
| 2 Carl D. Pursell (R) | 115,562 | 57.3 |
| Kathleen F. O'Reilly (D) | 83,550 | 41.4 |
| 3 Howard Wolpe (D) | 113,080 | 52.0 |
| James S. Gilmore (R) | 102,591 | 47.2 |
| 4 Dave Stockman (R) | 148,950 | 74.7 |
| Lyndon G. Furst (D) | 47,777 | 24.0 |
| 5 Harold S. Sawyer (R) | 118,061 | 53.1 |
| Dale R. Sprik (D) | 101,737 | 45.8 |
| 6 Jim Dunn (R) | 111,272 | 50.6 |
| Bob Carr (D) | 108,548 | 49.4 |
| 7 Dale E. Kildee (D) | 147,280 | 92.7 |
| Dennis L. Berry (LIBERT) | 11,507 | 7.2 |
| 8 Bob Traxler (D) | 124,155 | 60.7 |
| Norman R. Hughes (R) | 77,009 | 37.7 |
| 9 Guy Vander Jagt (R) | 168,713 | 96.5 |
| 10 Don Albosta (D) | 126,962 | 52.4 |
| Richard J. Allen (R) | 111,496 | 46.0 |
| 11 Robert W. Davis (R) | 146,205 | 65.5 |
| Dan Dorrity (D) | 75,515 | 33.8 |
| 12 David E. Bonior (D) | 112,698 | 55.3 |
| Kirk Walsh (R) | 90,931 | 44.7 |
| 13 George W. Crockett Jr. (D) | 79,719 | 91.5 |
| M. Michael Hurd (R) | 6,473 | 7.4 |
| 14 Dennis M. Hertel (D) | 90,362 | 53.3 |
| Vic Caputo (R) | 78,395 | 46.2 |
| 15 William D. Ford (D) | 113,492 | 67.6 |
| Gerald R. Carlson (R) | 53,046 | 31.6 |
| 16 John D. Dingell (D) | 105,844 | 69.9 |
| Pamella A. Seay (R) | 42,735 | 28.2 |
| 17 William M. Brodhead (D) | 127,525 | 73.3 |
| Alfred L. Patterson (R) | 44,313 | 25.4 |
| 18 James J. Blanchard (D) | 135,705 | 65.3 |
| Betty J. Suida (R) | 68,575 | 33.0 |
| 19 William S. Broomfield (R) | 168,530 | 72.7 |
| Wayne E. Daniels (D) | 60,100 | 25.3 |

## MINNESOTA[2]

| Candidates | Votes | % |
|---|---|---|
| 1 Arlen Erdahl (I-R) | 171,099 | 71.4 |
| Russell V. Smith (DFL) | 67,279 | 28.1 |
| 2 Tom Hagedorn (I-R) | 158,082 | 60.5 |
| Harold J. Bergquist (DFL) | 102,586 | 39.3 |
| 3 Bill Frenzel (I-R) | 179,393 | 75.4 |
| Joel Alexander Saliterman (DFL) | 57,868 | 24.3 |
| 4 Bruce F. Vento (DFL) | 119,182 | 58.5 |

*Footnotes, see p. 1293.*

| Candidates | Votes | % |
|---|---|---|
| John Berg (I-R) | 82,537 | 40.5 |
| 5 Martin Olav Sabo (DFL) | 126,451 | 70.1 |
| John Doherty (I-R) | 48,200 | 26.7 |
| 6 Vin Weber (I-R) | 140,402 | 52.7 |
| Archie Baumann (DFL) | 126,173 | 47.3 |
| 7 Arlan Stangeland (I-R) | 135,084 | 52.1 |
| Gene Wenstrom (DFL) | 124,026 | 47.9 |
| 8 James L. Oberstar (DFL) | 182,228 | 70.4 |
| Edward Fiore (I-R) | 72,350 | 28.0 |

### MISSISSIPPI

| Candidates | Votes | % |
|---|---|---|
| 1 Jamie L. Whitten (D) | 104,269 | 63.0 |
| T.K. Moffett (R) | 61,292 | 37.0 |
| 2 David R. Bowen (D) | 96,750 | 69.6 |
| Frank Drake (R) | 42,300 | 30.4 |
| 3 G.V. Montgomery (D) | 128,035 | 100.0 |
| 4 Jon C. Hinson (R) | 69,321 | 39.0 |
| Leslie Burl McLemore (I) | 52,959 | 29.8 |
| Britt R. Singletary (D) | 52,303 | 29.4 |
| 5 Trent Lott (R) | 131,559 | 73.9 |
| Jimmy McVeay (D) | 46,416 | 26.1 |

### MISSOURI

| Candidates | Votes | % |
|---|---|---|
| 1 William Clay (D) | 91,272 | 70.2 |
| Bill White (R) | 38,667 | 29.8 |
| 2 Robert A. Young (D) | 148,227 | 64.4 |
| John O. Shields (R) | 81,762 | 35.6 |
| 3 Richard A. Gephardt (D) | 143,132 | 77.6 |
| Robert A. Cedarburg (R) | 41,277 | 22.4 |
| 4 Ike Skelton (D) | 151,459 | 67.8 |
| Bill Baker (R) | 71,869 | 32.2 |
| 5 Richard Bolling (D) | 110,957 | 70.1 |
| Vincent E. Baker (R) | 47,309 | 29.9 |
| 6 E. Thomas Coleman (R) | 149,281 | 70.6 |
| Vernon A. Young (D) | 62,048 | 29.4 |
| 7 Gene Taylor (R) | 161,668 | 67.8 |
| Ken Young (D) | 76,844 | 32.2 |
| 8 Wendell Bailey (R) | 127,675 | 57.1 |
| Steve Gardner (D) | 95,751 | 42.9 |
| 9 Harold L. Volkmer (D) | 135,905 | 56.5 |
| John W. Turner (R) | 104,835 | 43.5 |
| 10 Bill Emerson (R) | 116,167 | 55.2 |
| Bill D. Burlison (D) | 94,465 | 44.8 |

### MONTANA

| Candidates | Votes | % |
|---|---|---|
| 1 Pat Williams (D) | 112,866 | 61.4 |
| John K. McDonald (R) | 70,874 | 38.6 |
| 2 Ron Marlenee (R) | 91,431 | 59.1 |
| Tom Monahan (D) | 63,370 | 40.9 |

### NEBRASKA

| Candidates | Votes | % |
|---|---|---|
| 1 Douglas K. Bereuter (R) | 160,705 | 78.6 |
| Rex S. Story (D) | 43,605 | 21.3 |
| 2 Hal Daub (R) | 107,736 | 53.1 |
| Richard M. Fellman (D) | 88,843 | 43.8 |
| 3 Virginia Smith (R) | 182,887 | 83.9 |
| Stan Ditus (D) | 34,967 | 16.0 |

### NEVADA

| Candidates | Votes | % |
|---|---|---|
| AL Jim Santini (D) | 165,107 | 67.5 |
| Vince Saunders (R) | 63,163 | 25.8 |

### NEW HAMPSHIRE

| Candidates | Votes | % |
|---|---|---|
| 1 Norman E. D'Amours (D) | 114,061 | 60.8 |
| Marshall W. Cobleigh (R) | 73,565 | 39.2 |
| 2 Judd Gregg (R) | 113,304 | 64.1 |
| Maurice L. Arel (D) | 63,350 | 35.9 |

### NEW JERSEY

| Candidates | Votes | % |
|---|---|---|
| 1 James J. Florio (D) | 147,352 | 76.7 |
| Scott L. Sibert (R) | 42,154 | 21.9 |
| 2 William J. Hughes (D) | 135,437 | 57.5 |
| Beech N. Fox (R) | 97,072 | 41.2 |
| 3 James J. Howard (D) | 106,269 | 49.9 |
| Marie Sheehan Muhler (R) | 104,184 | 49.0 |

| Candidates | Votes | % |
|---|---|---|
| 4 Christopher H. Smith (R) | 95,447 | 56.6 |
| Frank Thompson Jr. (D) | 68,480 | 40.6 |
| 5 Millicent Fenwick (R) | 156,016 | 77.5 |
| Kieran E. Pillion Jr. (D) | 41,269 | 20.5 |
| 6 Edwin B. Forsythe (R) | 125,792 | 56.3 |
| Lewis M. Weinstein (D) | 92,227 | 41.3 |
| 7 Marge Roukema (R) | 108,760 | 50.7 |
| Andrew Maguire (D) | 99,737 | 46.5 |
| 8 Robert A. Roe (D) | 95,493 | 67.2 |
| William R. Cleveland (R) | 44,625 | 31.4 |
| 9 Harold C. Hollenbeck (R) | 116,128 | 59.1 |
| Gabriel Ambrosio (D) | 75,321 | 38.3 |
| 10 Peter W. Rodino Jr. (D) | 76,154 | 85.3 |
| Everett J. Jennings (R) | 11,778 | 13.2 |
| 11 Joseph G. Minish (D) | 106,155 | 63.0 |
| Robert A. Davis (R) | 57,772 | 34.3 |
| 12 Matthew J. Rinaldo (R) | 134,973 | 77.1 |
| Rose Zeidwerg Monyek (D) | 36,577 | 20.9 |
| 13 Jim Courter (R) | 152,862 | 71.6 |
| Dave Stickle (D) | 56,251 | 26.4 |
| 14 Frank J. Guarini (D) | 86,921 | 64.2 |
| Dennis E. Teti (R) | 45,606 | 33.7 |
| 15 Bernard J. Dwyer (D) | 92,457 | 53.4 |
| William O'Sullivan Jr. (R) | 75,812 | 43.8 |

### NEW MEXICO

| Candidates | Votes | % |
|---|---|---|
| 1 Manuel Lujan Jr. (R) | 125,910 | 51.0 |
| Bill Richardson (D) | 120,903 | 49.0 |
| 2 Joe Skeen (WRITE IN) | 61,564 | 38.0 |
| David King (D) | 55,085 | 34.0 |
| Dorothy Runnels (WRITE IN) | 45,343 | 28.0 |

### NEW YORK

| Candidates | Votes | % |
|---|---|---|
| 1 William Carney (R,C,RTL) | 115,213 | 56.3 |
| Thomas A. Twomey (D) | 85,629 | 41.9 |
| 2 Thomas J. Downey (D) | 84,035 | 56.3 |
| Louis J. Modica (R,RTL) | 65,106 | 43.7 |
| 3 Gregory W. Carman (R,C) | 87,952 | 50.1 |
| Jerome A. Ambro (D,RTL) | 83,389 | 47.5 |
| 4 Norman F. Lent (R,C,RTL) | 117,455 | 66.8 |
| Charles F. Brennan (D,L) | 58,270 | 33.2 |
| 5 Raymond McGrath (R,C,RTL) | 105,140 | 57.7 |
| Karen S. Burstein (D,L) | 77,228 | 42.3 |
| 6 John LeBoutillier (R,C,RTL) | 89,762 | 52.8 |
| Lester L. Wolff (D,L) | 80,209 | 47.2 |
| 7 Joseph Addabbo (D,R,L) | 96,131 | 95.3 |
| 8 Benjamin Rosenthal (D,L) | 84,273 | 75.6 |
| Albert Lemishow (R,C,RTL) | 27,156 | 24.4 |
| 9 Geraldine A. Ferraro (D) | 63,796 | 58.3 |
| Vito P. Battista (R,C,RTL) | 44,473 | 40.7 |
| 10 Mario Biaggi (D,R,L) | 95,322 | 94.5 |
| 11 James H. Scheuer (D,L) | 72,798 | 74.1 |
| Andrew E. Carlan (R,C,RTL) | 25,424 | 25.9 |
| 12 Shirley Chisholm (D,L) | 35,446 | 87.1 |
| Charles Gibbs (R) | 3,372 | 8.3 |
| 13 Stephen J. Solarz (D,L) | 81,954 | 79.4 |
| Harry DeMell (R,C) | 19,536 | 18.9 |
| 14 Fred Richmond (D,L) | 45,029 | 76.1 |
| Christopher Lovell (R,C) | 8,257 | 14.0 |
| Moses S. Harris (I) | 4,151 | 7.0 |
| 15 Leo C. Zeferetti (D) | 49,684 | 50.2 |
| Paul M. Atanasio (R,C,RTL) | 46,467 | 46.9 |
| 16 Charles E. Schumer (D,L) | 67,343 | 77.5 |
| Theodore Silverman (R,C) | 17,050 | 19.6 |
| 17 Guy V. Molinari (R,C) | 69,573 | 47.8 |
| John M. Murphy (D,RTL) | 50,954 | 35.0 |
| Mary T. Codd (L) | 25,118 | 17.2 |
| 18 S. William Green (R) | 91,341 | 56.7 |
| Mark J. Green (D,L) | 68,786 | 42.7 |
| 19 Charles B. Rangel (D,R,L) | 84,062 | 96.2 |
| 20 Ted Weiss (D,L) | 86,454 | 82.4 |
| James E. Greene (R) | 15,350 | 14.6 |
| 21 Robert Garcia (D,R,L) | 32,173 | 98.2 |
| 22 Jonathan B. Bingham (D,L) | 66,301 | 83.9 |
| Steve S. Black (R) | 9,943 | 12.6 |
| 23 Peter A. Peyser (D) | 85,549 | 56.2 |
| Andrew Albanese (R,C) | 66,771 | 43.8 |
| 24 Richard L. Ottinger (D) | 100,182 | 59.4 |

| Candidates | Votes | % |
|---|---|---|
| Joseph Christiana (R,C,RTL) | 66,689 | 39.6 |
| 25 Hamilton Fish Jr. (R,C) | 158,936 | 81.0 |
| Gunars Ozols (D) | 37,369 | 19.0 |
| 26 Benjamin A. Gilman (R) | 137,159 | 74.3 |
| Eugene Victor (D) | 37,475 | 20.3 |
| 27 Matthew F. McHugh (D) | 103,863 | 55.0 |
| Neil T. Wallace (R,C) | 83,096 | 44.0 |
| 28 Samuel S. Stratton (D) | 164,088 | 77.9 |
| Frank Wicks (R) | 37,504 | 17.8 |
| 29 Gerald Solomon (R,C,RTL) | 141,631 | 66.7 |
| Rodger L. Hurley (D,L) | 70,697 | 33.3 |
| 30 David O'B. Martin (R,C) | 111,008 | 63.8 |
| Mary Anne Krupsak (D,L) | 54,896 | 31.6 |
| 31 Donald J. Mitchell (R,RTL) | 135,976 | 77.5 |
| Irving A. Schwartz (D,L) | 39,589 | 22.5 |
| 32 George Wortley (R,C) | 108,128 | 60.4 |
| Jeffery S. Brooks (D, L) | 56,535 | 31.6 |
| Peter J. Del Giorno (RTL) | 11,978 | 6.7 |
| 33 Gary A. Lee (R,C) | 132,831 | 75.8 |
| Dolores M. Reed (D,L) | 39,542 | 22.6 |
| 34 Frank Horton (R) | 133,278 | 72.9 |
| James Toole (D) | 37,883 | 20.7 |
| 35 Barber B. Conable Jr. (R) | 127,623 | 72.2 |
| John M. Owens (D,C) | 44,754 | 25.3 |
| 36 John J. LaFalce (D,L) | 122,929 | 71.7 |
| H. William Feder (R,C,RTL) | 48,428 | 28.3 |
| 37 Henry J. Nowak (D,L) | 94,890 | 83.0 |
| Roger Heymanowski (R,C) | 16,560 | 14.5 |
| 38 Jack F. Kemp (R,C,RTL) | 167,434 | 81.6 |
| Gale A. Denn (D,L) | 37,875 | 18.4 |
| 39 Stanley N. Lundine (D) | 93,839 | 54.7 |
| James Abdella (R,C) | 75,039 | 43.8 |

### NORTH CAROLINA

| Candidates | Votes | % |
|---|---|---|
| 1 Walter B. Jones (D) | 108,738 | 100.0 |
| 2 L. H. Fountain (D) | 99,297 | 73.4 |
| Barry L. Gardner (R) | 35,946 | 26.6 |
| 3 Charles Whitley (D) | 84,862 | 68.3 |
| Larry J. Parker (R) | 39,393 | 31.7 |
| 4 Ike F. Andrews (D) | 97,167 | 52.6 |
| Thurman Hogan (R) | 84,631 | 45.8 |
| 5 Stephen L. Neal (D) | 99,117 | 51.0 |
| Anne Bagnal (R) | 94,894 | 48.8 |
| 6 Eugene Johnston (R) | 80,275 | 51.1 |
| Richardson Preyer (D) | 76,957 | 48.9 |
| 7 Charlie Rose (D) | 88,564 | 68.7 |
| Vivian S. Wright (R) | 40,270 | 31.3 |
| 8 W.G. (Bill) Hefner (D) | 95,013 | 58.5 |
| L.E. (Larry) Harris (R) | 67,317 | 41.5 |
| 9 James G. Martin (R) | 101,156 | 58.6 |
| Randall R. Kincaid (D) | 71,504 | 41.4 |
| 10 James T. Broyhill (R) | 120,777 | 69.7 |
| James O. Icenhour (D) | 52,485 | 30.3 |
| 11 William M. Hendon (R) | 104,485 | 53.5 |
| Lamar Gudger (D) | 90,789 | 46.5 |

### NORTH DAKOTA

| Candidates | Votes | % |
|---|---|---|
| AL Byron L. Dorgan (D) | 166,437 | 56.8 |
| Jim Smykowski (R) | 124,707 | 42.6 |

### OHIO

| Candidates | Votes | % |
|---|---|---|
| 1 Bill Gradison (R) | 124,080 | 74.7 |
| Donald J. Zwick (D) | 38,529 | 23.2 |
| 2 Thomas A. Luken (D) | 103,423 | 58.7 |
| Tom Atkins (R) | 72,693 | 41.3 |
| 3 Tony P. Hall (D) | 95,558 | 57.3 |
| Albert H. Sealy (R) | 66,698 | 40.0 |
| 4 Tennyson Guyer (R) | 133,795 | 72.3 |
| Geraldine Tebben (D) | 51,150 | 27.7 |
| 5 Delbert L. Latta (R) | 137,003 | 70.4 |
| James R. Sherck (D) | 57,704 | 29.6 |
| 6 Bob McEwen (R) | 101,288 | 54.6 |
| Ted Strickland (D) | 84,235 | 45.4 |
| 7 Clarence J. Brown (R) | 124,137 | 76.1 |
| Donald Hollister (D) | 38,952 | 23.9 |
| 8 Thomas N. Kindness (R) | 139,590 | 76.0 |
| John W. Griffin (D) | 44,162 | 24.0 |

| Candidates | Votes | % |
|---|---|---|
| 9 Ed Weber (R) | 96,927 | 56.2 |
| Thomas L. Ashley (D) | 68,728 | 39.9 |
| 10 Clarence E. Miller (R) | 143,403 | 74.4 |
| Jack E. Stecher (D) | 49,433 | 25.6 |
| 11 J. William Stanton (R) | 128,507 | 69.3 |
| Patrick J. Donlin (D) | 51,224 | 27.6 |
| 12 Robert N. Shamansky (D) | 108,690 | 52.6 |
| Samuel L. Devine (R) | 98,110 | 47.4 |
| 13 Don J. Pease (D) | 113,439 | 63.8 |
| David E. Armstrong (R) | 64,296 | 36.2 |
| 14 John F. Seiberling (D) | 103,336 | 64.9 |
| Louis A. Mangels (R) | 55,962 | 35.1 |
| 15 Chalmers P. Wylie (R) | 129,025 | 72.6 |
| Terry Freeman (D) | 48,708 | 27.4 |
| 16 Ralph S. Regula (R) | 149,960 | 79.3 |
| Larry V. Slagle (D) | 39,219 | 20.7 |
| 17 John M. Ashbrook (R) | 128,870 | 72.9 |
| Donald E. Yunker (D) | 47,900 | 27.1 |
| 18 Douglas Applegate (D) | 134,835 | 76.1 |
| Gary L. Hammersley (R) | 42,354 | 23.9 |
| 19 Lyle Williams (R) | 107,032 | 58.1 |
| Harry Meshel (D) | 77,272 | 41.9 |
| 20 Mary Rose Oakar (D) | 96,217 | 100.0 |
| 21 Louis Stokes (D) | 83,188 | 88.2 |
| Robert L. Woodall (R) | 11,103 | 11.8 |
| 22 Dennis E. Eckart (D) | 108,137 | 55.2 |
| Joseph J. Nahra (R) | 80,836 | 41.3 |
| 23 Ronald M. Mottl (D) | 144,317 | 100.0 |

## OKLAHOMA

| Candidates | Votes | % |
|---|---|---|
| 1 James R. Jones (D) | 115,381 | 58.4 |
| Richard C. Freeman (R) | 82,293 | 41.6 |
| 2 Mike Synar (D) | 101,516 | 54.0 |
| Gary Richardson (R) | 86,544 | 46.0 |
| 3 Wes Watkins (D) | | 100.0 |
| 4 Dave McCurdy (D) | 74,245 | 51.0 |
| Howard Rutledge (R) | 71,339 | 49.0 |
| 5 Mickey Edwards (R) | 90,053 | 68.4 |
| David C. Hood (D) | 36,815 | 28.0 |
| 6 Glenn English (D) | 111,694 | 64.7 |
| Carol McCurley (R) | 60,980 | 35.3 |

## OREGON

| Candidates | Votes | % |
|---|---|---|
| 1 Les AuCoin (D) | 203,532 | 65.9 |
| Lynn Engdahl (R) | 105,083 | 34.0 |
| 2 Denny Smith (R) | 141,854 | 48.8 |
| Al Ullman (D) | 138,089 | 47.5 |
| 3 Ron Wyden (D) | 156,371 | 71.9 |
| Darrell R. Conger (R) | 60,940 | 28.0 |
| 4 James Weaver (D) | 158,745 | 54.8 |
| Michael Fitzgerald (R) | 130,861 | 45.2 |

## PENNSYLVANIA

| Candidates | Votes | % |
|---|---|---|
| 1 Thomas M. Foglietta (I) | 58,737 | 37.8 |
| Michael (Ozzie) Myers (D) | 52,956 | 34.1 |
| Robert R. Burke (R) | 37,893 | 24.4 |
| 2 William H. Gray III (D) | 127,106 | 96.4 |
| 3 Raymond F. Lederer (D) | 67,942 | 54.5 |
| William J. Phillips (R) | 40,866 | 32.8 |
| Max Weiner (CONSU) | 11,849 | 9.5 |
| 4 Charles F. Dougherty (R) | 127,475 | 63.3 |
| Thomas J. Magrann (D) | 73,895 | 36.7 |
| 5 Richard T. Schulze (R) | 148,898 | 75.1 |
| Grady G. Brickhouse (D) | 47,092 | 23.8 |
| 6 Gus Yatron (D) | 117,965 | 67.1 |
| George Hulshart (R) | 57,844 | 32.9 |
| 7 Robert W. Edgar (D) | 99,381 | 53.1 |
| Dennis J. Rochford (R) | 87,643 | 46.9 |
| 8 James K. Coyne (R) | 103,585 | 50.7 |
| Peter H. Kostmayer (D) | 99,593 | 48.7 |
| 9 Bud Shuster (R,D) | 157,241 | 100.0 |
| 10 Joseph M. McDade (R) | 145,703 | 76.6 |
| Gene Basalyga (D) | 43,152 | 22.7 |
| 11 James L. Nelligan (R) | 93,621 | 51.9 |
| Raphael Musto (D) | 86,703 | 48.1 |
| 12 John P. Murtha (D) | 106,750 | 59.4 |
| Charles A. Getty (R) | 72,999 | 40.6 |
| 13 Lawrence Coughlin (R) | 138,212 | 70.0 |
| Pete Slawek (D) | 57,745 | 29.2 |

| Candidates | Votes | % |
|---|---|---|
| 14 William J. Coyne (D) | 102,545 | 68.5 |
| Stan Thomas (R) | 44,071 | 29.5 |
| 15 Don Ritter (R) | 99,874 | 59.6 |
| Jeanette Reibman (D) | 66,626 | 39.7 |
| 16 James A. Woodcock (D) | 38,891 | 23.1 |
| Robert S. Walker (R) | 129,765 | 76.9 |
| 17 Allen E. Ertel (D) | 97,995 | 60.6 |
| Daniel S. Seiverling (R) | 63,790 | 39.4 |
| 18 Doug Walgren (D) | 127,641 | 68.5 |
| Steven R. Snyder (R) | 58,821 | 31.5 |
| 19 Bill Goodling (R) | 136,873 | 76.0 |
| Richard P. Noll (D) | 41,584 | 23.1 |
| 20 Joseph M. Gaydos (D) | 122,100 | 72.5 |
| Kathleen M. Meyer (R) | 46,313 | 27.5 |
| 21 Don Bailey (D) | 112,427 | 68.4 |
| Dirk Matson (R) | 51,821 | 31.6 |
| 22 Austin J. Murphy (D) | 118,084 | 69.5 |
| Marilyn C. Ecoff (R) | 50,020 | 29.5 |
| 23 William F. Clinger Jr. (R) | 122,855 | 73.5 |
| Peter Atigan (D) | 41,033 | 24.6 |
| 24 Marc L. Marks (R) | 86,687 | 49.7 |
| David C. DiCarlo (D) | 86,567 | 49.6 |
| 25 Eugene V. Atkinson (D) | 119,817 | 67.1 |
| Robert H. Morris (R) | 58,768 | 32.9 |

### Special Election

| Candidates | Votes | % |
|---|---|---|
| 11 Raphael Musto (D) | 32,073 | 27.3 |
| James Nelligan (R) | 27,496 | 23.4 |
| Frank Harrison (I) | 20,475 | 17.4 |
| Paul Kanjorski (I) | 18,241 | 15.5 |
| Ted Mitchell (I) | 12,009 | 10.2 |

## RHODE ISLAND

| Candidates | Votes | % |
|---|---|---|
| 1 Fernand J. St Germain (D) | 120,756 | 67.6 |
| William P. Montgomery (R) | 57,844 | 32.4 |
| 2 Claudine Schneider (R) | 115,057 | 55.3 |
| Edward P. Beard (D) | 92,970 | 44.7 |

## SOUTH CAROLINA

| Candidates | Votes | % |
|---|---|---|
| 1 Thomas F. Hartnett (R) | 81,988 | 51.6 |
| Charles D. Ravenel (D) | 76,743 | 48.3 |
| 2 Floyd Spence (R) | 92,306 | 55.7 |
| Tom Turnipseed (D) | 73,353 | 44.3 |
| 3 Butler Derrick (D) | 87,680 | 59.8 |
| Marshall Parker (R) | 57,840 | 39.4 |
| 4 Carroll Campbell Jr. (R) | 90,941 | 92.6 |
| Thomas Waldenfels (LIBERT) | 6,984 | 7.1 |
| 5 Ken Holland (D) | 99,773 | 87.5 |
| Thomas Campbell (LIBERT) | 14,252 | 12.5 |
| 6 John L. Napier (R) | 75,964 | 51.7 |
| John W. Jenrette Jr. (D) | 70,747 | 48.2 |

## SOUTH DAKOTA

| Candidates | Votes | % |
|---|---|---|
| 1 Thomas A. Daschle (D) | 109,910 | 65.8 |
| Bart Kull (R) | 57,155 | 34.2 |
| 2 Clint Roberts (R) | 88,991 | 58.4 |
| Kenneth D. Stofferahn (D) | 63,447 | 41.6 |

## TENNESSEE

| Candidates | Votes | % |
|---|---|---|
| 1 James H. Quillen (R) | 130,296 | 86.2 |
| John Curtis (I) | 20,816 | 13.8 |
| 2 John J. Duncan (R) | 147,947 | 76.1 |
| Dave Dunaway (D) | 46,578 | 23.9 |
| 3 Marilyn Lloyd Bouquard (D) | 117,355 | 61.1 |
| Glen M. Byers (R) | 74,761 | 38.9 |
| 4 Albert Gore Jr. (D) | 137,612 | 79.3 |
| James Beau Seigneur (R) | 35,954 | 20.7 |
| 5 Bill Boner (D) | 118,506 | 65.4 |
| Mike Adams (R) | 62,746 | 34.6 |
| 6 Robin L. Beard Jr. (R) | 127,945 | 99.6 |
| 7 Ed Jones (D) | 133,606 | 77.3 |
| Daniel Campbell (R) | 39,227 | 22.7 |
| 8 Harold E. Ford (D) | 110,139 | 99.9 |

## TEXAS

| Candidates | Votes | % |
|---|---|---|
| 1 Sam B. Hall Jr. (D) | 137,665 | 100.0 |

| Candidates | Votes | % |
|---|---|---|
| 2 Charles Wilson (D) | 142,496 | 69.3 |
| F. H. Pannill Sr. (R) | 60,742 | 29.5 |
| 3 James M. Collins (R) | 218,228 | 79.3 |
| Earle S. Porter (D) | 49,667 | 18.0 |
| 4 Ralph M. Hall (D) | 102,787 | 52.3 |
| John H. Wright (R) | 93,915 | 47.7 |
| 5 Jim Mattox (D) | 70,892 | 51.0 |
| Tom Pauken (R) | 67,848 | 48.8 |
| 6 Phil Gramm (D) | 144,816 | 70.9 |
| Dave (Buster) Haskins (R) | 59,503 | 29.1 |
| 7 Bill Archer (R) | 242,810 | 82.1 |
| Robert L. Hutchings (D) | 48,594 | 16.4 |
| 8 Jack Fields (R) | 72,856 | 51.8 |
| Bob Eckhardt (D) | 67,921 | 48.2 |
| 9 Jack Brooks (D) | 103,225 | 99.7 |
| 10 J. J. Pickle (D) | 135,618 | 59.1 |
| John Biggar (R) | 88,940 | 38.8 |
| 11 Marvin Leath (D) | 128,520 | 100.0 |
| 12 Jim Wright (D) | 99,104 | 59.9 |
| Jim Bradshaw (R) | 65,005 | 39.3 |
| 13 Jack Hightower (D) | 98,779 | 55.0 |
| Ron Slover (R) | 80,819 | 45.0 |
| 14 William N. Patman (D) | 93,884 | 56.8 |
| Charles L. Concklin (R) | 71,495 | 43.2 |
| 15 E. (Kika) de la Garza (D) | 105,325 | 70.0 |
| Lendy McDonald (R) | 45,090 | 30.0 |
| 16 Richard C. White (D) | 104,734 | 84.6 |
| Catherine McDivitt (LIBERT) | 19,010 | 15.4 |
| 17 Charles W. Stenholm (D) | 130,465 | 100.0 |
| 18 Mickey Leland (D) | 71,985 | 79.9 |
| C. L. Kennedy (R) | 16,128 | 17.9 |
| 19 Kent Hance (D) | 126,632 | 93.5 |
| J. D. Webster (LIBERT) | 8,792 | 6.5 |
| 20 Henry B. Gonzalez (D) | 84,113 | 81.9 |
| Merle W. Nash (R) | 17,725 | 17.3 |
| 21 Tom Loeffler (R) | 196,424 | 76.5 |
| Joe Sullivan (D) | 58,425 | 22.8 |
| 22 Ron Paul (R) | 106,797 | 51.0 |
| Mike Andrews (D) | 101,094 | 48.3 |
| 23 Abraham Kazen Jr. (D) | 104,595 | 69.8 |
| Bobby Locke (R) | 45,139 | 30.1 |
| 24 Martin Frost (D) | 93,690 | 61.3 |
| Clay Smothers (R) | 59,172 | 38.7 |

## UTAH

| Candidates | Votes | % |
|---|---|---|
| 1 James V. Hansen (R) | 157,111 | 52.1 |
| Gunn McKay (D) | 144,459 | 47.9 |
| 2 Dan Marriott (R) | 194,885 | 67.0 |
| Arthur L. Monson (D) | 87,967 | 30.3 |

## VERMONT

| Candidates | Votes | % |
|---|---|---|
| AL James M. Jeffords (R) | 154,274 | 79.2 |
| Robin Lloyd (CIT) | 24,758 | 12.7 |
| Peter Diamondstone (LU) | 15,218 | 7.8 |

## VIRGINIA

| Candidates | Votes | % |
|---|---|---|
| 1 Paul S. Trible Jr. (R) | 130,130 | 90.5 |
| Sharon D. Grant (I) | 13,688 | 9.5 |
| 2 G. William Whitehurst (R) | 97,319 | 89.8 |
| Kenneth Morrison (LIBERT) | 11,003 | 10.2 |
| 3 Thomas J. Bliley Jr. (R) | 96,524 | 51.6 |
| John A. Mapp (D) | 60,962 | 32.6 |
| Howard H. Carwile (I) | 19,549 | 10.5 |
| James B. Turney (LIBERT) | 9,852 | 5.3 |
| 4 Robert W. Daniel Jr. (R) | 92,557 | 60.7 |
| Cecil Y. Jenkins (D) | 59,930 | 39.3 |
| 5 Dan Daniel (D) | 112,143 | 99.9 |
| 6 M. Caldwell Butler (R) | 123,125 | 99.2 |
| 7 J. Kenneth Robinson (R) | 139,957 | 99.7 |
| 8 Stanford E. Parris (R) | 95,624 | 48.8 |
| Herbert E. Harris II (D) | 94,530 | 48.3 |
| 9 William C. Wampler (R) | 119,196 | 69.4 |
| Roosevelt Ferguson (D) | 52,636 | 30.6 |
| 10 Frank R. Wolf (R) | 110,840 | 51.1 |
| Joseph L. Fisher (D) | 105,883 | 48.9 |

## WASHINGTON

| Candidates | Votes | % |
|---|---|---|
| 1 Joel Pritchard (R) | 180,475 | 78.3 |
| Robin Drake (D) | 41,830 | 18.1 |

| Candidates | Votes | % | Candidates | Votes | % | Candidates | Votes | % |
|---|---|---|---|---|---|---|---|---|
| 2 Al Swift (D) | 162,002 | 63.9 | Pat R. Hamilton (D) | 80,940 | 44.1 | Alvin Baldus (D) | 126,859 | 49.0 |
| Neal Snider (R) | 82,639 | 32.6 | 3 Mick Staton (R) | 94,583 | 52.7 | 4 Clement J. Zablocki (D) | 146,437 | 70.0 |
| 3 Don Bonker (D) | 155,906 | 62.7 | John G. Hutchinson (D) | 84,980 | 47.3 | Elroy C. Honadel (R) | 61,027 | 29.2 |
| Rod Culp (R) | 92,872 | 37.3 | 4 Nick J. Rahall (D) | 117,595 | 76.6 | 5 Henry S. Reuss (D) | 129,574 | 77.0 |
| 4 Sid Morrison (R) | 134,691 | 57.4 | Winton G. Covey Jr. (R) | 36,020 | 23.4 | David Bathke (R) | 37,267 | 22.2 |
| Mike McCormack (D) | 100,114 | 42.6 | | | | 6 Thomas E. Petri (R) | 143,980 | 59.3 |
| 5 Thomas S. Foley (D) | 120,530 | 51.9 | **Special Election** | | | Gary R. Goyke (D) | 98,628 | 40.7 |
| John Sonneland (R) | 111,705 | 48.1 | | | | 7 David R. Obey (D) | 164,340 | 64.7 |
| 6 Norman D. Dicks (D) | 122,903 | 53.6 | 3 John G. Hutchinson (D) | 51,169 | 53.8 | Vinton A. Vesta (R) | 89,745 | 35.3 |
| Jim Beaver (R) | 106,236 | 46.4 | David Staton (R) | 43,950 | 46.2 | 8 Toby Roth (R) | 169,664 | 67.7 |
| 7 Mike Lowry (D) | 112,848 | 57.3 | | | | Michael R. Monfils (D) | 81,043 | 32.3 |
| Ron Dunlap (R) | 84,218 | 42.7 | | | | 9 F. James Sensenbrenner (R) | 206,227 | 78.4 |
| | | | **WISCONSIN** | | | Gary C. Benedict (D) | 56,838 | 21.6 |
| **WEST VIRGINIA** | | | I Les Aspin (D) | 126,222 | 56.2 | **WYOMING** | | |
| 1 Robert H. Mollohan (D) | 107,471 | 63.6 | Kathryn H. Canary (R) | 96,047 | 42.8 | AL Richard B. Cheney (R) | 116,361 | 68.6 |
| Joe Bartlett (R) | 61,438 | 36.4 | 2 Robert W. Kastenmeier (D) | 142,037 | 54.0 | Jim Rogers (D) | 53,338 | 31.4 |
| 2 Cleve Benedict (R) | 102,805 | 55.9 | James A. Wright (R) | 119,514 | 45.4 | David G. Glancy (D) | 24,390 | 42.8 |
| | | | 3 Steven Gunderson (R) | 132,001 | 51.0 | | | |

# 1981 House Elections

## MARYLAND

**Special Election**

| Candidates | Votes | % |
|---|---|---|
| 5 Steny H. Hoyer (D) | 42,573 | 55.2 |
| Audrey Scott (R) | 33,708 | 43.5 |

## MICHIGAN

**Special Election**

| Candidates | Votes | % |
|---|---|---|
| 4 Mark Siljander (R) | 36,046 | 72.6 |
| Johnie Rodebush (D) | 12,461 | 25.1 |

## MISSISSIPPI

**Special Election**

| | Votes | % |
|---|---|---|
| 4 Wayne Dowdy (D) | 55,656 | 50.4 |
| Liles Williams (R) | 54,744 | 49.6 |

## OHIO

**Special Election**

| Candidates | Votes | % |
|---|---|---|
| 4 Michael Oxley (R) | 41,987 | 50.2 |
| Dale Locker (D) | 41,646 | 49.8 |

## PENNSYLVANIA

**Special Election**

| | Votes | % |
|---|---|---|
| 3 Joseph F. Smith (R, I) | 29,907 | 52.5 |
| David G. Glancy (D) | 24,390 | 42.8 |

**1980 Elections**

*1. For the 1980 House elections in Louisiana, an open primary election was held with candidates from all parties running on the same ballot. Any candidate who received a majority was elected unopposed, with no further appearance on the general election ballot. If no candidate received 50 percent, a runoff was held between the two top finishers.*

*2. In Minnesota the Democratic Party is known as the Democratic-Farmer-Labor Party and the Republican Party as the Independent-Republican Party; candidates appear on the ballot with these designations.*

# 1982 House Elections

## ALABAMA

| Candidates | Votes | % |
|---|---|---|
| 1 Jack Edwards (R) | 87,901 | 61.0 |
| Steve Gudac (D) | 54,315 | 37.7 |
| 2 William L. Dickinson (R) | 83,290 | 50.4 |
| Billy Joe Camp (D) | 81,904 | 49.6 |
| 3 Bill Nichols (D) | 100,864 | 96.3 |
| 4 Tom Bevill (D) | 118,595 | 100.0 |
| 5 Ronnie G. Flippo (D) | 108,807 | 80.7 |
| Leopold Yambrek (R) | 24,593 | 18.2 |
| 6 Ben Erdreich (D) | 88,029 | 53.2 |
| Albert Lee Smith Jr. (R) | 76,726 | 46.4 |
| 7 Richard C. Shelby (D) | 124,070 | 96.8 |

## ALASKA

| | Votes | % |
|---|---|---|
| AL Don Young (R) | 128,274 | 70.8 |
| Dave Carlson (D) | 52,001 | 28.7 |

## ARIZONA

| | Votes | % |
|---|---|---|
| 1 John McCain (R) | 89,116 | 65.9 |
| William E. Hegarty (D) | 41,261 | 30.5 |
| 2 Morris K. Udall (D) | 73,468 | 70.9 |
| Roy B. Laos (R) | 28,407 | 27.4 |
| 3 Bob Stump (R) | 101,198 | 63.3 |
| Pat Bosch (D) | 58,644 | 36.7 |
| 4 Eldon Rudd (R) | 95,620 | 65.7 |
| Wayne O. Earley (D) | 44,182 | 30.4 |
| 5 Jim McNulty (D) | 82,938 | 49.7 |
| Jim Kolbe (R) | 80,531 | 48.3 |

## ARKANSAS

| | Votes | % |
|---|---|---|
| 1 Bill Alexander (D) | 124,208 | 64.8 |
| Chuck Banks (R) | 67,427 | 35.2 |
| 2 Ed Bethune (R) | 96,775 | 53.9 |
| Charles L. George (D) | 82,913 | 46.1 |
| 3 John Paul Hammerschmidt (R) | 133,909 | 66.0 |
| Jim McDougal (D) | 69,089 | 34.0 |
| 4 Beryl Anthony Jr. (D) | 121,256 | 65.6 |
| Bob Leslie (R) | 63,661 | 34.4 |

## CALIFORNIA

| | Votes | % |
|---|---|---|
| 1 Douglas H. Bosco (D) | 107,749 | 49.8 |
| Don H. Clausen (R) | 102,043 | 47.2 |
| 2 Gene Chappie (R) | 116,172 | 57.9 |
| John A. Newmeyer (D) | 81,314 | 40.5 |
| 3 Robert T. Matsui (D) | 194,680 | 89.6 |
| Bruce A. Daniel (LIBERT) | 16,222 | 7.5 |
| 4 Vic Fazio (D) | 118,476 | 63.9 |
| Roger B. Canfield (R) | 67,047 | 36.1 |
| 5 Phillip Burton (D) | 103,268 | 57.9 |
| Milton Marks (R) | 72,139 | 40.5 |
| 6 Barbara Boxer (D) | 96,379 | 52.4 |
| Dennis McQuaid (R) | 82,128 | 44.6 |
| 7 George Miller (D) | 126,952 | 67.2 |
| Paul E. Vallely (R) | 56,960 | 30.2 |
| 8 Ronald V. Dellums (D) | 121,537 | 55.9 |
| Claude B. Hutchison Jr. (R) | 95,694 | 44.0 |
| 9 Fortney H. (Pete) Stark (D) | 104,393 | 60.7 |
| Bill J. Kennedy (R) | 67,702 | 39.3 |
| 10 Don Edwards (D) | 77,263 | 62.7 |
| Bob Herriott (R) | 41,506 | 33.7 |
| 11 Tom Lantos (D) | 109,812 | 57.1 |
| Bill Royer (R) | 76,462 | 39.7 |
| 12 Ed Zschau (R) | 115,365 | 62.9 |
| Emmett Lynch (D) | 61,372 | 33.5 |
| 13 Norman Y. Mineta (D) | 110,805 | 65.9 |
| Tom Kelly (R) | 52,806 | 31.4 |
| 14 Norman D. Shumway (R) | 134,225 | 63.4 |
| Baron Reed (D) | 77,400 | 36.6 |
| 15 Tony Coelho (D) | 86,022 | 63.7 |

| Candidates | Votes | % |
|---|---|---|
| Ed Bates (R) | 45,948 | 34.0 |
| 16 Leon E. Panetta (D) | 142,630 | 83.5 |
| G. Richard Arnold (R) | 24,448 | 14.3 |
| 17 Charles Pashayan Jr. (R) | 80,271 | 54.0 |
| Gene Tackett (D) | 68,364 | 46.0 |
| 18 Richard Lehman (D) | 92,762 | 59.5 |
| Adrian C. Fondse (R) | 59,664 | 38.3 |
| 19 Robert J. Lagomarsino (R) | 112,486 | 61.1 |
| Frank Frost (D) | 66,042 | 35.8 |
| 20 William M. Thomas (R) | 123,312 | 68.1 |
| Robert J. Bethea (D) | 57,769 | 31.9 |
| 21 Bobbi Fiedler (R) | 138,474 | 71.8 |
| George Henry Margolis (D) | 46,412 | 24.1 |
| 22 Carlos J. Moorhead (R) | 145,831 | 73.6 |
| Harvey L. Goldhammer (D) | 46,521 | 23.5 |
| 23 Anthony C. Beilenson (D) | 120,788 | 59.6 |
| David Armor (R) | 82,031 | 40.4 |
| 24 Henry A. Waxman (D) | 88,516 | 65.1 |
| Jerry Zerg (R) | 42,133 | 31.0 |
| 25 Edward R. Roybal (D) | 71,106 | 85.5 |
| Daniel John Gorham (LIBERT) | 12,060 | 14.5 |
| 26 Howard L. Berman (D) | 97,383 | 59.6 |
| Hal Phillips (R) | 66,072 | 40.4 |
| 27 Mel Levine (D) | 108,347 | 59.5 |
| Bart W. Christensen (R) | 67,479 | 37.0 |
| 28 Julian C. Dixon (D) | 103,469 | 78.9 |
| David Goerz (R) | 24,473 | 18.7 |
| 29 Augustus F. Hawkins (D) | 97,028 | 79.8 |
| Milton R. MacKaig (R) | 24,568 | 20.2 |
| 30 Matthew G. (Marty) Martinez (D) | 60,905 | 53.9 |
| John H. Rousselot (R) | 52,177 | 46.1 |
| 31 Mervyn M. Dymally (D) | 86,718 | 72.4 |
| Henry C. Minturn (R) | 33,043 | 27.6 |
| 32 Glenn M. Anderson (D) | 84,663 | 58.0 |
| Brian Lungren (R) | 57,863 | 39.6 |
| 33 David Dreier (R) | 112,362 | 65.2 |
| Paul Servelle (D) | 55,514 | 32.2 |
| 34 Esteban Torres (D) | 68,316 | 57.2 |
| Paul R. Jackson (R) | 51,026 | 42.8 |
| 35 Jerry Lewis (R) | 112,786 | 68.3 |
| Robert E. Erwin (D) | 52,349 | 31.7 |
| 36 George E. Brown Jr. (D) | 76,546 | 54.3 |
| John Paul Stark (R) | 64,361 | 45.7 |
| 37 Al McCandless (R) | 105,065 | 59.1 |
| Curtis P. (Sam) Cross (D) | 68,510 | 38.5 |
| 38 Jerry M. Patterson (D) | 73,914 | 52.4 |
| William F. Dohr (R) | 61,279 | 43.4 |
| 39 William E. Dannemeyer (R) | 129,539 | 72.2 |
| Frank G. Verges (D) | 46,681 | 26.0 |
| 40 Robert E. Badham (R) | 144,228 | 71.5 |
| Paul Haseman (D) | 52,546 | 26.1 |
| 41 Bill Lowery (R) | 140,130 | 68.9 |
| Tony Brandenburg (D) | 58,677 | 28.8 |
| 42 Dan Lungren (R) | 142,845 | 69.0 |
| James P. Spellman (D) | 58,690 | 28.3 |
| 43 Ron Packard (R WRITE-IN) | 66,444 | 36.8 |
| Roy (Pat) Archer (D) | 57,995 | 32.1 |
| Johnnie R. Crean (R) | 56,297 | 31.1 |
| 44 Jim Bates (D) | 78,474 | 64.9 |
| Shirley M. Gissendanner (R) | 38,447 | 31.8 |
| 45 Duncan L. Hunter (R) | 117,771 | 68.6 |
| Richard Hill (D) | 50,148 | 29.2 |

### Special Election

| | Votes | % |
|---|---|---|
| 30 Matthew G. (Marty) Martinez (D) | 22,572 | 32.0 |
| Dennis S. Kazarian (D) | 20,313 | 29.0 |
| Ralph Ramirez (R) | 11,033 | 16.0 |

### Special Runoff Election

| | Votes | % |
|---|---|---|
| 30 Matthew G. (Marty) Martinez (D) | 14,593 | 51.0 |
| Ralph Ramirez (R) | 14,043 | 49.0 |

## COLORADO

| Candidates | Votes | % |
|---|---|---|
| 1 Patricia Schroeder (D) | 94,969 | 60.3 |
| Arch Decker (R) | 59,009 | 37.4 |
| 2 Timothy E. Wirth (D) | 101,202 | 61.8 |
| John C. Buechner (R) | 59,590 | 36.4 |
| 3 Ray Kogovsek (D) | 92,384 | 53.4 |
| Tom Wiens (R) | 77,410 | 44.8 |
| 4 Hank Brown (R) | 105,550 | 69.8 |
| Charles L. (Bud) Bishopp (D) | 45,750 | 30.2 |
| 5 Ken Kramer (R) | 84,479 | 59.5 |
| Tom Cronin (D) | 57,392 | 40.5 |
| 6 Jack Swigert (R) | 98,909 | 62.2 |
| Steve Hogan (D) | 56,598 | 35.6 |

## CONNECTICUT

| | Votes | % |
|---|---|---|
| 1 Barbara B. Kennelly (D) | 126,798 | 68.1 |
| Herschel A. Klein (R) | 58,075 | 31.2 |
| 2 Sam Gejdenson (D) | 95,254 | 55.8 |
| Tony Guglielmo (R) | 74,294 | 43.5 |
| 3 Bruce A. Morrison (D) | 90,638 | 49.9 |
| Lawrence J. DeNardis (R) | 88,951 | 49.0 |
| 4 Stewart B. McKinney (R) | 93,660 | 56.5 |
| John A. Phillips (D) | 71,110 | 42.9 |
| 5 William R. Ratchford (D) | 101,362 | 58.5 |
| Neal B. Hanlon (R) | 70,808 | 40.8 |
| 6 Nancy L. Johnson (R) | 99,703 | 51.7 |
| William E. Curry Jr. (D) | 92,178 | 47.8 |

### Special Election

| | Votes | % |
|---|---|---|
| 1 Barbara B. Kennelly (D) | 51,431 | 58.8 |
| Ann P. Uccello (R) | 36,085 | 41.2 |

## DELAWARE

| | Votes | % |
|---|---|---|
| AL Thomas R. Carper (D) | 98,533 | 52.4 |
| Thomas B. Evans Jr. (R) | 87,153 | 46.3 |

## FLORIDA

| | Votes | % |
|---|---|---|
| 1 Earl Hutto (D) | 82,569 | 74. |
| J. Terry Bechtol (R) | 28,373 | 25. |
| 2 Don Fuqua (D) | 79,143 | 61. |
| Ron McNeil (R) | 49,101 | 38. |
| 3 Charles E. Bennett (D) | 73,802 | 84. |
| George Grimsley (R) | 13,972 | 15. |
| 4 Bill Chappell Jr. (D) | 83,895 | 66. |
| Larry Gaudet (R) | 41,457 | 33. |
| 5 Bill McCollum (R) | 69,993 | 58. |
| Dick Batchelor (D) | 49,070 | 41. |
| 6 Kenneth H. (Buddy) MacKay (D) | 85,825 | 61. |
| Ed Havill (R) | 54,059 | 38. |
| 7 Sam Gibbons (D) | 85,331 | 74. |
| Ken Ayers (R) | 29,632 | 25 |
| 8 C. W. Bill Young (R) | | 100 |
| 9 Michael Bilirakis (R) | 95,009 | 51 |
| George H. Sheldon (D) | 90,697 | 48 |
| 10 Andy Ireland (D) | | 100 |
| 11 Bill Nelson (D) | 101,746 | 70 |
| Joel Robinson (R) | 42,422 | 29 |
| 12 Tom Lewis (R) | 81,893 | 52 |
| Brad Culverhouse (D) | 73,913 | 47 |
| 13 Connie Mack III (R) | 132,951 | 65 |
| Dana N. Stevens (D) | 71,239 | 34 |
| 14 Daniel A. Mica (D) | 128,646 | 73 |
| Steve Mitchell (R) | 47,560 | 27 |
| 15 E. Clay Shaw Jr. (R) | 89,158 | 57 |
| Edward J. Stack (D) | 67,083 | 4. |
| 16 Larry Smith (D) | 91,888 | 6 |
| Maurice Berkowitz (R) | 43,458 | 3. |
| 17 William Lehman (D) | | 10 |
| 18 Claude Pepper (D) | 72,183 | 7 |
| Ricardo Nunez (R) | 29,196 | 2 |

| Candidates | Votes | % |
|---|---|---|
| 9 Dante B. Fascell (D) | 74,312 | 58.8 |
| Glenn Rinker (R) | 51,969 | 41.2 |

## GEORGIA

| Candidates | Votes | % |
|---|---|---|
| 1 Lindsay Thomas (D) | 65,625 | 64.1 |
| Herb Jones (R) | 36,799 | 35.9 |
| 2 Charles Hatcher (D) | 73,897 | 100.0 |
| 3 Richard Ray (D) | 74,626 | 71.0 |
| Tyron Elliott (R) | 30,537 | 29.0 |
| 4 Elliott H. Levitas (D) | 38,758 | 65.5 |
| Dick Winder (R) | 20,418 | 34.5 |
| 5 Wyche Fowler Jr. (D) | 53,264 | 80.8 |
| J. E. (Billy) McKinney (I) | 9,049 | 13.7 |
| Paul Jones (R) | 3,633 | 5.5 |
| 6 Newt Gingrich (R) | 62,352 | 55.3 |
| Jim Wood (D) | 50,459 | 44.7 |
| 7 Larry P. McDonald (D) | 71,647 | 61.1 |
| Dave Sellers (R) | 45,569 | 38.9 |
| 8 J. Roy Rowland (D) | 75,009 | 100.0 |
| 9 Ed Jenkins (D) | 86,514 | 77.0 |
| Charles Sherwood (R) | 25,907 | 23.0 |
| 10 Doug Barnard Jr. (D) | 80,311 | 100.0 |

## HAWAII

| Candidates | Votes | % |
|---|---|---|
| 1 Cecil Heftel (D) | 134,779 | 89.9 |
| Rockne H. Johnson (LIBERT) | 15,128 | 10.1 |
| 2 Daniel K. Akaka (D) | 132,072 | 89.2 |
| Gregory B. Mills (NP) | 9,080 | 6.2 |

## IDAHO

| Candidates | Votes | % |
|---|---|---|
| 1 Larry E. Craig (R) | 86,277 | 53.7 |
| Larry LaRocco (D) | 74,388 | 46.3 |
| 2 George Hansen (R) | 83,873 | 52.3 |
| Richard Stallings (D) | 76,608 | 47.7 |

## ILLINOIS

| Candidates | Votes | % |
|---|---|---|
| 1 Harold Washington (D) | 172,641 | 97.3 |
| 2 Gus Savage (D) | 140,827 | 87.0 |
| Kevin Walker Sparks (R) | 20,670 | 12.8 |
| 3 Marty Russo (D) | 137,391 | 74.0 |
| Richard D. Murphy (R) | 48,268 | 26.0 |
| 4 George M. O'Brien (R) | 79,842 | 54.6 |
| Michael A. Murer (D) | 66,323 | 45.4 |
| 5 William O. Lipinski (D) | 110,351 | 75.4 |
| Daniel J. Partyka (R) | 35,970 | 24.6 |
| 6 Henry J. Hyde (R) | 97,918 | 68.4 |
| Leroy E. Kennel (D) | 45,237 | 31.6 |
| 7 Cardiss Collins (D) | 133,978 | 86.5 |
| Dansby Cheeks (R) | 20,994 | 13.5 |
| 8 Dan Rostenkowski (D) | 124,318 | 83.4 |
| Bonnie Hickey (R) | 24,666 | 16.6 |
| 9 Sidney R. Yates (D) | 114,083 | 66.5 |
| Catherine Bertini (R) | 54,851 | 32.0 |
| 10 John Edward Porter (R) | 90,750 | 59.0 |
| Eugenia S. Chapman (D) | 63,115 | 41.0 |
| 11 Frank Annunzio (D) | 134,755 | 72.6 |
| James F. Moynihan (R) | 50,967 | 27.4 |
| 12 Philip M. Crane (R) | 86,487 | 66.2 |
| Daniel G. DeFosse (D) | 40,108 | 30.7 |
| 13 John N. Erlenborn (R) | 113,423 | 69.8 |
| Robert Bily (D) | 49,105 | 30.2 |
| 14 Tom Corcoran (R) | 98,262 | 64.6 |
| Dan McGrath (D) | 53,914 | 35.4 |
| 15 Edward R. Madigan (R) | 105,038 | 66.3 |
| Tim L. Hall (D) | 53,303 | 33.7 |
| 16 Lynn Martin (R) | 89,405 | 57.2 |
| Carl R. Schwerdtfeger (D) | 66,877 | 42.8 |
| 17 Lane Evans (D) | 94,483 | 52.8 |
| Kenneth G. McMillan (R) | 84,347 | 47.2 |
| 18 Robert H. Michel (R) | 97,406 | 51.6 |
| G. Douglas Stephens (D) | 91,281 | 48.4 |
| 19 Daniel B. Crane (R) | 94,833 | 52.1 |
| John Gwinn (D) | 87,231 | 47.9 |
| 20 Richard J. Durbin (D) | 100,758 | 50.4 |
| Paul Findley (R) | 99,348 | 49.6 |

| Candidates | Votes | % |
|---|---|---|
| 21 Melvin Price (D) | 89,500 | 63.7 |
| Robert H. Gaffner (R) | 46,764 | 33.3 |
| 22 Paul Simon (D) | 123,693 | 66.2 |
| Peter G. Prineas (R) | 63,279 | 33.8 |

## INDIANA

| Candidates | Votes | % |
|---|---|---|
| 1 Katie Hall (D) | 87,369 | 56.3 |
| Thomas H. Krieger (R) | 66,921 | 43.1 |
| 2 Philip R. Sharp (D) | 107,298 | 56.2 |
| Ralph W. Van Natta (R) | 83,593 | 43.8 |
| 3 John Hiler (R) | 86,958 | 51.2 |
| Richard C. Bodine (D) | 83,046 | 48.8 |
| 4 Dan Coats (R) | 110,155 | 64.3 |
| Roger M. Miller (D) | 60,054 | 35.1 |
| 5 Elwood Hillis (R) | 105,469 | 61.1 |
| Allen B. Maxwell (D) | 67,238 | 38.9 |
| 6 Dan Burton (R) | 131,100 | 64.9 |
| George E. Grabianowski (D) | 70,764 | 35.1 |
| 7 John T. Myers (R) | 115,884 | 62.3 |
| Stephen S. Bonney (D) | 70,249 | 37.7 |
| 8 Francis X. McCloskey (D) | 100,592 | 51.4 |
| Joel Deckard (R) | 94,127 | 48.1 |
| 9 Lee H. Hamilton (D) | 121,094 | 67.1 |
| Floyd E. Coates (R) | 58,532 | 32.4 |
| 10 Andrew Jacobs Jr. (D) | 114,674 | 66.7 |
| Michael A. Carroll (R) | 56,992 | 33.2 |

## IOWA

| Candidates | Votes | % |
|---|---|---|
| 1 Jim Leach (R) | 89,585 | 59.2 |
| William E. Gluba (D) | 61,734 | 40.8 |
| 2 Tom Tauke (R) | 99,478 | 58.8 |
| Brent Appel (D) | 69,539 | 41.1 |
| 3 Cooper Evans (R) | 104,072 | 55.5 |
| Lynn G. Cutler (D) | 83,581 | 44.5 |
| 4 Neal Smith (D) | 118,849 | 66.0 |
| Dave Readinger (R) | 60,534 | 33.6 |
| 5 Tom Harkin (D) | 93,333 | 58.9 |
| Arlyn E. Danker (R) | 65,200 | 41.1 |
| 6 Berkley Bedell (D) | 101,690 | 64.3 |
| Al Bremer (R) | 56,487 | 35.7 |

## KANSAS

| Candidates | Votes | % |
|---|---|---|
| 1 Pat Roberts (R) | 115,749 | 68.4 |
| Kent Roth (D) | 51,079 | 30.2 |
| 2 Jim Slattery (D) | 86,286 | 57.4 |
| Morris Kay (R) | 63,942 | 42.6 |
| 3 Larry Winn Jr. (R) | 82,117 | 59.2 |
| William L. Kostar (D) | 53,140 | 38.3 |
| 4 Dan Glickman (D) | 107,326 | 73.9 |
| Gerald Caywood (R) | 35,478 | 24.4 |
| 5 Bob Whittaker (R) | 103,551 | 67.6 |
| Lee Rowe (D) | 47,676 | 31.1 |

## KENTUCKY

| Candidates | Votes | % |
|---|---|---|
| 1 Carroll Hubbard Jr. (D) | 48,342 | 100.0 |
| 2 William H. Natcher (D) | 49,571 | 73.8 |
| Mark T. Watson (R) | 17,561 | 26.2 |
| 3 Romano L. Mazzoli (D) | 92,849 | 65.1 |
| Carl Brown (R) | 45,900 | 32.2 |
| 4 Gene Snyder (R) | 74,109 | 54.2 |
| Terry L. Mann (D) | 61,937 | 45.3 |
| 5 Harold Rogers (R) | 52,928 | 65.2 |
| Doye Davenport (D) | 28,285 | 34.8 |
| 6 Larry J. Hopkins (R) | 68,418 | 56.8 |
| Don Mills (D) | 49,839 | 41.4 |
| 7 Carl D. Perkins (D) | 82,463 | 79.4 |
| Tom Hamby (R) | 21,436 | 20.6 |

## LOUISIANA

| Candidates | Votes | % |
|---|---|---|
| 1 Bob Livingston (R) | | 100.0 |
| 2 Lindy (Mrs. Hale) Boggs (D) | | 100.0 |
| 3 W. J. (Billy) Tauzin (D) | | 100.0 |
| 4 Buddy Roemer (D) | | 100.0 |

| Candidates | Votes | % |
|---|---|---|
| 5 Jerry Huckaby (D) | | 100.0 |
| 6 Henson Moore (R) | | 100.0 |
| 7 John B. Breaux (D) | | 100.0 |
| 8 Gillis W. Long (D) | | 100.0 |

## MAINE

| Candidates | Votes | % |
|---|---|---|
| 1 John R. McKernan Jr. (R) | 124,850 | 50.3 |
| John M. Kerry (D) | 118,884 | 47.9 |
| 2 Olympia J. Snowe (R) | 136,075 | 66.6 |
| James Patrick Dunleavy (D) | 68,086 | 33.3 |

## MARYLAND

| Candidates | Votes | % |
|---|---|---|
| 1 Roy Dyson (D) | 89,503 | 69.3 |
| C. A. Porter Hopkins (R) | 30,656 | 30.7 |
| 2 Clarence D. Long (D) | 83,318 | 52.6 |
| Helen Delich Bentley (R) | 75,062 | 47.4 |
| 3 Barbara A. Mikulski (D) | 110,042 | 74.2 |
| H. Robert Scherr (R) | 38,259 | 25.8 |
| 4 Marjorie S. Holt (R) | 75,617 | 61.2 |
| Patricia O'Brien Aiken (D) | 47,947 | 38.8 |
| 5 Steny H. Hoyer (D) | 83,937 | 79.6 |
| William P. Guthrie (R) | 21,533 | 20.4 |
| 6 Beverly B. Byron (D) | 102,596 | 74.4 |
| Roscoe Bartlett (R) | 35,321 | 25.6 |
| 7 Parren J. Mitchell (D) | 103,496 | 87.9 |
| M. Leonora Jones (R) | 14,203 | 12.1 |
| 8 Michael D. Barnes (D) | 121,761 | 71.3 |
| Elizabeth W. Spencer (R) | 48,910 | 28.7 |

## MASSACHUSETTS

| Candidates | Votes | % |
|---|---|---|
| 1 Silvio O. Conte (R, D) | 145,417 | 100.0 |
| 2 Edward P. Boland (D) | 118,215 | 72.6 |
| Thomas P. Swank (R) | 44,544 | 27.4 |
| 3 Joseph D. Early (D) | 142,611 | 100.0 |
| 4 Barney Frank (D) | 121,802 | 59.5 |
| Margaret M. Heckler (R) | 82,804 | 40.5 |
| 5 James M. Shannon (D) | 140,177 | 84.6 |
| Angelo Laudani (LIBERT) | 25,224 | 15.2 |
| 6 Nicholas Mavroules (D) | 117,723 | 57.8 |
| Thomas H. Trimarco (R) | 85,849 | 42.2 |
| 7 Edward J. Markey (D) | 151,305 | 77.8 |
| David Basile (R) | 43,063 | 22.2 |
| 8 Thomas P. O'Neill Jr. (D) | 123,296 | 74.9 |
| Frank Luke McNamara Jr. (R) | 41,370 | 25.1 |
| 9 Joe Moakley (D) | 102,665 | 64.1 |
| Deborah R. Cochran (R) | 55,030 | 34.3 |
| 10 Gerry E. Studds (D) | 138,418 | 68.7 |
| John E. Conway (R) | 63,014 | 31.3 |
| 11 Brian J. Donnelly (D) | 144,132 | 100.0 |

## MICHIGAN

| Candidates | Votes | % |
|---|---|---|
| 1 John Conyers Jr. (D) | 125,517 | 96.7 |
| 2 Carl D. Pursell (R) | 106,960 | 65.5 |
| George Wahr Sallade (D) | 53,040 | 32.5 |
| 3 Howard Wolpe (D) | 96,842 | 56.3 |
| Richard L. Milliman (R) | 73,315 | 42.6 |
| 4 Mark Siljander (R) | 87,489 | 59.7 |
| David A. Masiokas (D) | 56,877 | 38.8 |
| 5 Harold S. Sawyer (R) | 98,650 | 53.1 |
| Stephen V. Monsma (D) | 87,229 | 46.9 |
| 6 Bob Carr (D) | 84,778 | 51.4 |
| Jim Dunn (R) | 78,388 | 47.5 |
| 7 Dale E. Kildee (D) | 118,538 | 75.4 |
| George R. Darrah (R) | 36,303 | 23.1 |
| 8 Bob Traxler (D) | 113,515 | 91.0 |
| Sheila M. Hart (LIBERT) | 11,219 | 9.0 |
| 9 Guy Vander Jagt (R) | 112,504 | 64.9 |
| Gerald D. Warner (D) | 60,932 | 35.1 |
| 10 Don Albosta (D) | 102,048 | 60.1 |
| Lawrence W. Reed (R) | 66,080 | 38.9 |
| 11 Robert W. Davis (R) | 106,039 | 60.5 |
| Kent Bourland (D) | 69,181 | 39.5 |
| 12 David E. Bonior (D) | 103,851 | 65.9 |
| Ray Contesti (R) | 52,312 | 33.2 |

*Footnote, see p. 1298.*

| Candidates | Votes | % |
|---|---|---|
| 13 George W. Crockett Jr. (D) | 108,351 | 88.0 |
| Letty Gupta (R) | 13,732 | 11.1 |
| 14 Dennis M. Hertel (D) | 116,421 | 94.9 |
| Harold H. Dunn (LIBERT) | 6,175 | 5.0 |
| 15 William D. Ford (D) | 94,950 | 72.8 |
| Mitchell Moran (R) | 33,904 | 26.0 |
| 16 John D. Dingell (D) | 114,006 | 73.7 |
| David K. Haskins (R) | 39,227 | 25.3 |
| 17 Sander Levin (D) | 116,901 | 66.6 |
| Gerald E. Rosen (R) | 55,620 | 31.7 |
| 18 Allen J. Sipher (D) | 46,545 | 25.7 |
| William S. Broomfield (R) | 132,902 | 73.3 |

## MINNESOTA

| Candidates | Votes | % |
|---|---|---|
| 1 Timothy J. Penny (DFL) | 109,257 | 51.2 |
| Tom Hagedorn (I-R) | 102,298 | 47.9 |
| 2 Vin Weber (I-R) | 123,508 | 54.5 |
| James W. Nichols (DFL) | 103,243 | 45.5 |
| 3 Bill Frenzel (I-R) | 166,891 | 72.2 |
| Joel Saliterman (DFL) | 60,993 | 26.4 |
| 4 Bruce F. Vento (DFL) | 153,494 | 73.2 |
| Bill James (I-R) | 56,248 | 26.8 |
| 5 Martin Olav Sabo (DFL) | 136,634 | 65.5 |
| Keith W. Johnson (I-R) | 61,184 | 29.4 |
| 6 Gerry Sikorski (DFL) | 109,246 | 50.8 |
| Arlen Erdahl (I-R) | 105,734 | 49.2 |
| 7 Arlan Stangeland (I-R) | 108,254 | 50.3 |
| Gene Wenstrom (DFL) | 107,062 | 49.7 |
| 8 James L. Oberstar (DFL) | 176,392 | 76.7 |
| Marjory L. Luce (I-R) | 53,467 | 23.3 |

## MISSISSIPPI

| Candidates | Votes | % |
|---|---|---|
| 1 Jamie L. Whitten (D) | 79,726 | 70.9 |
| Fran Fawcett (R) | 32,750 | 29.1 |
| 2 Webb Franklin (R) | 74,450 | 50.3 |
| Robert G. Clark (D) | 71,536 | 48.4 |
| 3 G. V. (Sonny) Montgomery (D) | 114,530 | 93.1 |
| James Bradshaw (I) | 8,519 | 6.9 |
| 4 Wayne Dowdy (D) | 79,977 | 52.5 |
| Liles Williams (R) | 69,469 | 45.6 |
| 5 Trent Lott (R) | 82,884 | 78.5 |
| Arlon (Blackie) Coate (D) | 22,634 | 21.5 |

## MISSOURI

| Candidates | Votes | % |
|---|---|---|
| 1 William Clay (D) | 102,656 | 66.1 |
| William E. White (R) | 52,599 | 33.9 |
| 2 Robert A. Young (D) | 100,770 | 56.5 |
| Harold L. Dielmann (R) | 77,433 | 43.5 |
| 3 Richard A. Gephardt (D) | 131,566 | 77.9 |
| Richard Foristel (R) | 37,388 | 22.1 |
| 4 Ike Skelton (D) | 96,388 | 54.8 |
| Wendell Bailey (R) | 79,565 | 45.2 |
| 5 Alan Wheat (D) | 96,059 | 57.9 |
| John A. Sharp (R) | 66,664 | 40.2 |
| 6 E. Thomas Coleman (R) | 97,993 | 55.3 |
| Jim Russell (D) | 79,053 | 44.7 |
| 7 Gene Taylor (R) | 91,391 | 50.5 |
| David A. Geisler (D) | 89,549 | 49.5 |
| 8 Bill Emerson (R) | 86,493 | 53.1 |
| Jerry Ford (D) | 76,413 | 46.9 |
| 9 Harold L. Volkmer (D) | 99,228 | 60.8 |
| Larry E. Mead (R) | 63,942 | 39.2 |

## MONTANA

| Candidates | Votes | % |
|---|---|---|
| 1 Pat Williams (D) | 100,087 | 59.7 |
| Bob Davies (R) | 62,402 | 37.2 |
| 2 Howard Lyman (D) | 65,815 | 44.2 |
| Ron Marlenee (R) | 79,968 | 53.7 |

## NEBRASKA

| Candidates | Votes | % |
|---|---|---|
| 1 Douglas K. Bereuter (R) | 137,675 | 75.1 |
| Curt Donaldson (D) | 45,676 | 24.9 |
| 2 Hal Daub (R) | 92,639 | 56.7 |
| Richard M. Fellman (D) | 70,431 | 43.1 |
| 3 Virginia Smith (R) | 171,853 | 100.0 |

## NEVADA

| Candidates | Votes | % |
|---|---|---|
| 1 Harry Reid (D) | 61,901 | 57.5 |
| Peggy Cavnar (R) | 45,675 | 42.5 |
| 2 Barbara Vucanovich (R) | 70,188 | 55.5 |
| Mary Gojack (D) | 52,265 | 41.3 |

## NEW HAMPSHIRE

| Candidates | Votes | % |
|---|---|---|
| 1 Norman E. D'Amours (D) | 76,281 | 54.9 |
| Robert C. Smith (R) | 61,876 | 44.5 |
| 2 Judd Gregg (R) | 92,098 | 70.8 |
| Robert L. Dupay (D) | 37,906 | 29.2 |

## NEW JERSEY

| Candidates | Votes | % |
|---|---|---|
| 1 James J. Florio (D) | 110,570 | 73.3 |
| John A. Dramesi (R) | 39,501 | 26.2 |
| 2 William J. Hughes (D) | 102,826 | 68.0 |
| John J. Mahoney (R) | 47,069 | 31.1 |
| 3 James J. Howard (D) | 104,055 | 62.3 |
| Marie Sheehan Muhler (R) | 60,515 | 36.2 |
| 4 Christopher H. Smith (R) | 85,660 | 52.7 |
| Joseph P. Merlino (D) | 75,658 | 46.5 |
| 5 Marge Roukema (R) | 104,695 | 65.3 |
| Fritz Cammerzell (D) | 53,659 | 33.5 |
| 6 Bernard J. Dwyer (D) | 100,419 | 68.1 |
| Bertram L. Buckler (R) | 46,095 | 31.3 |
| 7 Matthew J. Rinaldo (R) | 91,837 | 56.0 |
| Adam K. Levin (D) | 70,978 | 43.3 |
| 8 Robert A. Roe (D) | 89,980 | 70.7 |
| Norm Robertson (R) | 36,317 | 28.5 |
| 9 Robert G. Torricelli (D) | 99,090 | 53.0 |
| Harold C. Hollenbeck (R) | 86,022 | 46.0 |
| 10 Peter W. Rodino Jr. (D) | 76,684 | 82.6 |
| Timothy Lee Jr. (R) | 14,551 | 15.7 |
| 11 Joseph G. Minish (D) | 105,607 | 64.3 |
| Rey Redington (R) | 57,099 | 34.8 |
| 12 Jim Courter (R) | 117,793 | 66.8 |
| Jeff Connor (D) | 57,049 | 32.3 |
| 13 Edwin B. Forsythe (R) | 100,061 | 59.5 |
| George Callas (D) | 65,820 | 39.1 |
| 14 Frank J. Guarini (D) | 94,021 | 74.3 |
| Charles J. Catrillo (R) | 28,257 | 22.3 |

## NEW MEXICO

| Candidates | Votes | % |
|---|---|---|
| 1 Manuel Lujan Jr. (R) | 74,459 | 52.4 |
| Jan Alan Hartke (D) | 67,534 | 47.6 |
| 2 Joe Skeen (R) | 71,021 | 58.4 |
| Caleb Chandler (D) | 50,599 | 41.6 |
| 3 Bill Richardson (D) | 84,669 | 64.5 |
| Marjorie Bell Chambers (R) | 46,466 | 35.4 |

## NEW YORK

| Candidates | Votes | % |
|---|---|---|
| 1 William Carney (R, C, RTL) | 88,234 | 63.9 |
| Ethan C. Eldon (D) | 49,787 | 36.1 |
| 2 Thomas J. Downey (D) | 80,951 | 63.9 |
| Paul G. Costello (R, C) | 42,790 | 33.8 |
| 3 Robert J. Mrazek (D) | 93,846 | 51.8 |
| John LeBoutillier (R, C) | 83,238 | 46.0 |
| 4 Norman F. Lent (R, C) | 105,241 | 60.4 |
| Robert P. Zimmerman (D, L) | 63,390 | 36.4 |
| 5 Raymond J. McGrath (R, C) | 100,485 | 58.1 |
| Arnold J. Miller (D, L) | 67,002 | 38.8 |
| 6 Joseph P. Addabbo (D, R, L) | 95,483 | 95.9 |
| 7 Benjamin S. Rosenthal (D, L) | 84,013 | 77.2 |
| Albert Lemishow (R, C, RTL) | 24,832 | 22.8 |
| 8 James H. Scheuer (D, L) | 91,830 | 89.5 |
| John T. Blume (C) | 10,741 | 10.5 |
| 9 Geraldine A. Ferraro (D) | 75,286 | 73.2 |
| John J. Weigandt (R) | 20,352 | 19.8 |
| Ralph G. Groves (C, RTL) | 6,011 | 5.9 |
| 10 Charles E. Schumer (D, L) | 89,852 | 79.2 |
| Stephen Marks (R, C) | 21,726 | 19.2 |
| 11 Edolphus Towns (D) | 39,357 | 83.7 |
| James W. Smith (R) | 4,449 | 9.5 |
| 12 Major R. Owens (D, L) | 44,586 | 90.5 |
| David Katan Sr. (R) | 3,215 | 6.5 |
| 13 Stephen J. Solarz (D, L) | 68,549 | 80.5 |
| Leon F. Nadrowski (R, RTL) | 14,257 | 16.7 |
| 14 Guy V. Molinari (R, C, RTL) | 67,626 | 56.1 |
| Leo C. Zeferetti (D) | 51,728 | 42.9 |
| 15 Bill Green (R) | 66,262 | 53.6 |
| Betty G. Lall (D, L) | 55,483 | 44.9 |
| 16 Charles B. Rangel (D, R, L) | 76,626 | 97.5 |
| 17 Ted Weiss (D, L) | 113,172 | 85.0 |
| Louis S. Antonelli (R, C, RTL) | 19,928 | 15.0 |
| 18 Robert Garcia (D, R, L) | 57,009 | 98.9 |
| 19 Mario Biaggi (D, R, L, RTL) | 118,803 | 93.7 |
| Michael J. McSherry (C) | 7,438 | 5.9 |
| 20 Richard L. Ottinger (D) | 98,425 | 56.5 |
| Jon S. Fossel (R, C) | 72,005 | 41.3 |
| 21 Hamilton Fish Jr. (R, C) | 117,460 | 75.2 |
| J. Morgan Strong (D) | 38,664 | 24.8 |
| 22 Benjamin A. Gilman (R) | 92,266 | 52.9 |
| Peter A. Peyser (D) | 73,124 | 42.0 |
| 23 Samuel S. Stratton (D) | 164,427 | 76.1 |
| Frank Wicks (R, NF) | 41,386 | 19.2 |
| 24 Gerald B. H. Solomon (R, C, RTL) | 140,296 | 73.9 |
| Roy Esiason (D) | 49,441 | 26.1 |
| 25 Sherwood L. Boehlert (R) | 93,071 | 55.8 |
| Anita Maxwell (D) | 70,793 | 42.4 |
| 26 David O'B. Martin (R, C) | 108,962 | 71.6 |
| David P. Landy (D) | 43,208 | 28.4 |
| 27 George C. Wortley (R) | 95,290 | 53.2 |
| Elaine Lytel (D, L) | 79,209 | 44.2 |
| 28 Matthew F. McHugh (D, L) | 100,665 | 56.3 |
| David F. Crowley (R, C) | 75,991 | 42.5 |
| 29 Frank Horton (R) | 104,412 | 66.4 |
| William C. Larsen (D) | 47,463 | 30.2 |
| 30 Barber B. Conable Jr. (R) | 119,105 | 68.2 |
| Bill Benet (D) | 48,764 | 27.9 |
| 31 Jack F. Kemp (R, C) | 133,462 | 75.3 |
| James A. Martin (D, L) | 43,843 | 24.1 |
| 32 John J. LaFalce (D) | 116,386 | 91.4 |
| Raymond R. Walker (R, C) | 8,638 | 6.8 |
| 33 Henry J. Nowak (D, L) | 126,091 | 84.1 |
| Walter J. Pillich (R, C) | 19,791 | 13.2 |
| 34 Stanley N. Lundine (D) | 99,502 | 60.2 |
| James J. Snyder (R, C) | 63,972 | 38.7 |

## NORTH CAROLINA

| Candidates | Votes | % |
|---|---|---|
| 1 Walter B. Jones (D) | 79,954 | 81.3 |
| James F. McIntyre III (R) | 17,478 | 17.8 |
| 2 I. T. (Tim) Valentine Jr. (D) | 59,617 | 53.6 |
| John W. Marin (R) | 34,293 | 30.8 |
| H. M. Michaux Jr. (WRITE IN) | 15,990 | 14.4 |
| 3 Charles Whitley (D) | 68,936 | 63.4 |
| Eugene (Red) McDaniel (R) | 39,046 | 36.0 |
| 4 Ike Andrews (D) | 70,369 | 51.3 |
| William Cobey Jr. (R) | 64,955 | 47.4 |
| 5 Stephen L. Neal (D) | 87,819 | 60.3 |
| Anne Bagnal (R) | 57,083 | 39.2 |
| 6 Charles Robin Britt (D) | 68,696 | 53.8 |
| Eugene Johnston (R) | 58,244 | 45.6 |
| 7 Charlie Rose (D) | 68,529 | 71.6 |
| Edward Johnson (R) | 27,015 | 28.0 |
| 8 W. G. (Bill) Hefner (D) | 71,691 | 57.4 |
| Harris D. Blake (R) | 52,417 | 42.0 |
| 9 James G. Martin (R) | 64,297 | 57.0 |
| Preston Cornelius (D) | 47,258 | 41.9 |
| 10 James T. Broyhill (R) | 80,904 | 92.2 |
| Jhon Rankin (LIBERT) | 6,360 | 7.3 |
| 11 James McClure Clarke (D) | 85,410 | 49.3 |
| Bill Hendon (R) | 84,085 | 49.2 |

## NORTH DAKOTA

| Candidates | Votes | % |
|---|---|---|
| AL Byron L. Dorgan (D) | 186,534 | 71.1 |
| Kent H. Jones (R) | 72,241 | 27.6 |

## OHIO

| Candidates | Votes | % |
|---|---|---|
| Thomas A. Luken (D) | 99,143 | 63.5 |
| John (Jake) Held (R) | 52,658 | 33.7 |
| Bill Gradison (R) | 97,434 | 62.7 |
| William J. Luttmer (D) | 53,169 | 34.2 |
| Tony P. Hall (D) | 119,926 | 87.7 |
| Kathryn E. Brown (LIBERT) | 16,828 | 12.3 |
| Michael G. Oxley (R) | 105,087 | 64.6 |
| Robert W. Moon (D) | 57,564 | 35.4 |
| Delbert L. Latta (R) | 86,450 | 55.2 |
| James R. Sherck (D) | 70,120 | 44.8 |
| Bob McEwen (R) | 92,135 | 59.2 |
| Lynn Alan Grimshaw (D) | 63,435 | 40.8 |
| Michael Dewine (R) | 87,842 | 56.3 |
| Roger D. Tackett (D) | 65,543 | 42.0 |
| Thomas N. Kindness (R) | 98,527 | 66.4 |
| John W. Griffin (D) | 49,877 | 33.6 |
| Marcy Kaptur (D) | 95,162 | 57.9 |
| Ed Weber (R) | 64,459 | 39.3 |
| Clarence E. Miller (R) | 100,044 | 63.3 |
| John M. Buchanan (D) | 57,983 | 36.7 |
| Dennis E. Eckart (D) | 93,302 | 60.9 |
| Glen W. Warner (R) | 56,616 | 36.9 |
| John R. Kasich (R) | 88,335 | 50.5 |
| Bob Shamansky (D) | 82,753 | 47.3 |
| Don J. Pease (D) | 92,296 | 61.2 |
| Timothy Paul Martin (R) | 53,376 | 35.4 |
| John F. Seiberling (D) | 115,629 | 70.5 |
| Louis A. Mangels (R) | 48,421 | 29.5 |
| Chalmers P. Wylie (R) | 104,678 | 66.3 |
| Greg Kostelac (D) | 47,070 | 29.8 |
| Ralph Regula (R) | 110,485 | 65.8 |
| Jeffrey R. Orenstein (D) | 57,386 | 34.2 |
| Lyle Williams (R) | 98,476 | 55.1 |
| George D. Tablack (D) | 80,375 | 44.9 |
| Douglas Applegate (D) | 128,665 | 100.0 |
| Edward F. Feighan (D) | 111,760 | 58.8 |
| Richard G. Anter II (R) | 72,682 | 38.3 |
| Mary Rose Oakar (D) | 133,603 | 85.6 |
| Paris T. LeJeune (R) | 17,675 | 11.3 |
| Louis Stokes (D) | 132,544 | 86.1 |
| Alan G. Shatteen (R) | 21,332 | 13.9 |

### Special Election

| | Votes | % |
|---|---|---|
| Jean Ashbrook (R) | 18,106 | 73.4 |
| Jack Koelbe (D) | 6,385 | 25.9 |

## OKLAHOMA

| | Votes | % |
|---|---|---|
| James R. Jones (D) | 76,379 | 54.1 |
| Richard C. Freeman (R) | 64,704 | 45.9 |
| Mike Synar (D) | 111,895 | 72.6 |
| Lou Striegel (R) | 42,298 | 27.4 |
| Wes Watkins (D) | 121,670 | 82.2 |
| Patrick K. Miller (R) | 26,335 | 17.8 |
| Dave McCurdy (D) | 84,205 | 65.0 |
| Howard Rutledge (R) | 44,351 | 34.2 |
| Mickey Edwards (R) | 98,979 | 67.2 |
| Dan Lane (D) | 42,453 | 28.8 |
| Glenn English (D) | 102,811 | 75.4 |
| Ed Moore (R) | 33,519 | 24.6 |

## OREGON

| | Votes | % |
|---|---|---|
| Les AuCoin (D) | 118,638 | 53.8 |
| Bill Moshofsky (R) | 101,720 | 46.2 |
| Bob Smith (R) | 106,912 | 55.6 |
| Larryann Willis (D) | 85,495 | 44.4 |
| Ron Wyden (D) | 159,416 | 78.3 |
| Thomas H. Phelan (R) | 44,162 | 21.7 |
| James Weaver (D) | 115,448 | 59.0 |
| Ross Anthony (R) | 80,054 | 40.9 |
| Denny Smith (R) | 103,906 | 51.2 |
| J. Ruth McFarland (D) | 98,952 | 48.8 |

## PENNSYLVANIA

| | Votes | % |
|---|---|---|
| Thomas M. Foglietta (D) | 103,626 | 72.3 |
| Michael Marino (R) | 38,155 | 26.6 |
| 2 William H. Gray III (D) | 120,744 | 76.1 |
| Milton Street (I) | 35,205 | 22.2 |
| 3 Robert A. Borski (D) | 97,161 | 50.1 |
| Charles F. Dougherty (R) | 94,497 | 48.7 |
| 4 Joseph P. Kolter (D) | 100,481 | 60.1 |
| Eugene V. Atkinson (R) | 64,539 | 38.6 |
| 5 Richard T. Schulze (R) | 90,648 | 67.2 |
| Bob Burger (D) | 44,170 | 32.8 |
| 6 Gus Yatron (D) | 108,230 | 72.0 |
| Harry B. Martin (R) | 42,155 | 28.0 |
| 7 Robert W. Edgar (D) | 105,775 | 55.4 |
| Steve Joachim (R) | 85,023 | 44.6 |
| 8 Peter H. Kostmayer (D) | 83,242 | 50.3 |
| Jim Coyne (R) | 80,928 | 48.9 |
| 9 Bud Shuster (R) | 92,322 | 65.1 |
| Eugene J. Duncan (D) | 49,583 | 34.9 |
| 10 Joseph M. McDade (R) | 103,617 | 67.5 |
| Robert J. Rafalko (D) | 49,868 | 32.5 |
| 11 Frank Harrison (D) | 90,371 | 53.5 |
| James L. Nelligan (R) | 78,485 | 46.5 |
| 12 John P. Murtha (D) | 96,369 | 61.1 |
| William N. Tuscano (R) | 54,212 | 34.4 |
| 13 Lawrence Coughlin (R) | 109,198 | 64.3 |
| Martin J. Cunningham Jr. (D) | 59,709 | 35.2 |
| 14 William J. Coyne (D) | 120,980 | 74.9 |
| John R. Clark (R) | 32,780 | 20.3 |
| 15 Don Ritter (R) | 79,455 | 57.8 |
| Richard J. Orloski (D) | 58,002 | 42.2 |
| 16 Robert S. Walker (R) | 93,034 | 71.3 |
| Jean D. Mowery (D) | 37,364 | 28.7 |
| 17 George W. Gekas (R) | 84,291 | 57.6 |
| Larry J. Hochendoner (D) | 61,974 | 42.4 |
| 18 Doug Walgren (D) | 101,807 | 54.2 |
| Ted Jacob (R) | 84,428 | 45.0 |
| 19 Bill Goodling (R) | 101,163 | 70.8 |
| Larry Becker (D) | 41,787 | 29.2 |
| 20 Joseph M. Gaydos (D) | 127,281 | 76.0 |
| Terry T. Ray (R) | 38,212 | 22.8 |
| 21 Thomas J. Ridge (R) | 80,180 | 50.2 |
| Anthony (Buzz) Andrezeski (D) | 79,451 | 49.8 |
| 22 Austin J. Murphy (D) | 123,716 | 78.7 |
| Frank J. Paterra (R) | 32,176 | 20.5 |
| 23 William F. Clinger Jr. (R) | 92,424 | 65.2 |
| Joseph J. Calla Jr. (D) | 49,297 | 34.8 |

## RHODE ISLAND

| | Votes | % |
|---|---|---|
| 1 Fernand J. St Germain (D) | 97,254 | 60.7 |
| Burton Stallwood (R) | 61,253 | 38.3 |
| 2 Claudine Schneider (R) | 96,282 | 55.6 |
| James V. Aukerman (D) | 76,769 | 44.4 |

## SOUTH CAROLINA

| | Votes | % |
|---|---|---|
| 1 Thomas F. Hartnett (R) | 63,945 | 54.3 |
| W. Mullins McLeod (D) | 52,916 | 44.9 |
| 2 Floyd Spence (R) | 71,569 | 58.5 |
| Ken Mosely (D) | 50,749 | 41.5 |
| 3 Butler Derrick (D) | 77,125 | 90.4 |
| Gordon T. Davis (LIBERT) | 8,214 | 9.6 |
| 4 Carroll A. Campbell Jr. (R) | 69,802 | 63.3 |
| Marion E. Tyus (D) | 40,394 | 36.7 |
| 5 John Spratt (D) | 69,345 | 67.6 |
| John S. Wilkerson (R) | 33,191 | 32.4 |
| 6 Robert M. Tallon Jr. (D) | 62,582 | 52.5 |
| John L. Napier (R) | 56,653 | 47.5 |

## SOUTH DAKOTA

| | Votes | % |
|---|---|---|
| AL Thomas A. Daschle (D) | 142,122 | 51.6 |
| Clint Roberts (R) | 133,530 | 48.4 |

## TENNESSEE

| | Votes | % |
|---|---|---|
| 1 James H. Quillen (R) | 89,497 | 74.1 |
| Jessie J. Cable (D) | 27,580 | 22.8 |
| 2 John J. Duncan (R) | 109,045 | 100.0 |
| 3 Marilyn Lloyd Bouquard (D) | 84,967 | 61.8 |
| Glen Byers (R) | 49,885 | 36.3 |
| 4 Jim Cooper (D) | 93,453 | 66.1 |
| Cissy Baker (R) | 47,865 | 33.9 |
| 5 Bill Boner (D) | 109,282 | 80.1 |
| Laural Steinhice (R) | 27,061 | 19.8 |
| 6 Albert Gore Jr. (D) | 104,094 | 100.0 |
| 7 Don Sundquist (R) | 73,835 | 50.5 |
| Bob Clement (D) | 72,359 | 49.5 |
| 8 Ed Jones (D) | 93,945 | 74.9 |
| Bruce Benson (R) | 31,527 | 25.1 |
| 9 Harold E. Ford (D) | 112,143 | 72.4 |
| Joe Crawford (R) | 40,812 | 26.4 |

## TEXAS

| | Votes | % |
|---|---|---|
| 1 Sam B. Hall Jr. (D) | 100,685 | 97.5 |
| 2 Charles Wilson (D) | 91,762 | 94.3 |
| Ed Richbourg (LIBERT) | 5,584 | 5.7 |
| 3 Steve Bartlett (R) | 99,852 | 77.1 |
| James L. McNees Jr. (D) | 28,223 | 21.8 |
| 4 Ralph M. Hall (D) | 94,134 | 73.8 |
| Peter J. Collumb (R) | 32,221 | 25.3 |
| 5 John Bryant (D) | 52,214 | 64.8 |
| Joe Devaney (R) | 27,121 | 33.7 |
| 6 Phil Gramm (D) | 91,546 | 94.5 |
| Ron Hard (LIBERT) | 5,288 | 5.5 |
| 7 Bill Archer (R) | 108,718 | 85.0 |
| Dennis Scoggins (D) | 17,866 | 14.0 |
| 8 Jack Fields (R) | 50,630 | 56.7 |
| Henry E. Allee (D) | 38,041 | 42.6 |
| 9 Jack Brooks (D) | 78,965 | 67.6 |
| John W. Lewis (R) | 35,422 | 30.3 |
| 10 J. J. Pickle (D) | 121,030 | 90.1 |
| William G. Kelsey (LIBERT) | 8,735 | 6.5 |
| 11 Marvin Leath (D) | 83,236 | 96.3 |
| 12 Jim Wright (D) | 78,913 | 68.9 |
| Jim Ryan (R) | 34,879 | 30.5 |
| 13 Jack Hightower (D) | 86,376 | 63.6 |
| Ron Slover (R) | 47,877 | 35.3 |
| 14 Bill Patman (D) | 76,851 | 60.7 |
| Joe Wyatt Jr. (R) | 48,942 | 38.6 |
| 15 E. (Kika) de la Garza (D) | 76,544 | 95.7 |
| 16 Ronald Coleman (D) | 44,024 | 53.9 |
| Pat B. Haggerty (R) | 36,064 | 44.2 |
| 17 Charles W. Stenholm (D) | 109,359 | 97.1 |
| 18 Mickey Leland (D) | 68,014 | 82.6 |
| C. Leon Pickett (R) | 12,104 | 14.7 |
| 19 Kent Hance (D) | 89,702 | 81.6 |
| E. L. Hicks (R) | 19,062 | 17.3 |
| 20 Henry B. Gonzalez (D) | 68,544 | 91.5 |
| Roger V. Gary (LIBERT) | 4,163 | 5.6 |
| 21 Tom Loeffler (R) | 106,515 | 74.6 |
| Charles S. Stough (D) | 35,112 | 24.6 |
| 22 Ron Paul (R) | 66,536 | 100.0 |
| 23 Abraham Kazen Jr. (D) | 51,690 | 55.3 |
| Jeff Wentworth (R) | 41,363 | 44.2 |
| 24 Martin Frost (D) | 63,857 | 72.9 |
| Lucy P. Patterson (R) | 22,798 | 26.0 |
| 25 Mike Andrews (D) | 63,974 | 60.4 |
| Mike Faubion (R) | 40,112 | 37.9 |
| 26 Tom Vandergriff (D) | 69,782 | 50.1 |
| Jim Bradshaw (R) | 69,438 | 49.9 |
| 27 Solomon P. Ortiz (D) | 66,604 | 64.0 |
| Jason Luby (R) | 35,209 | 33.8 |

## UTAH

| | Votes | % |
|---|---|---|
| 1 James V. Hansen (R) | 111,416 | 62.8 |
| A. Stephen Dirks (D) | 66,006 | 37.2 |
| 2 Dan Marriott (R) | 92,109 | 53.8 |
| Frances Farley (D) | 78,981 | 46.2 |
| 3 Howard C. Nielson (R) | 108,478 | 76.9 |
| Henry A. Huish (I) | 32,661 | 23.1 |

## VERMONT

| | Votes | % |
|---|---|---|
| AL James M. Jeffords (R) | 114,191 | 69.2 |
| Mark A. Kaplan (D) | 38,296 | 23.2 |

## VIRGINIA

| Candidates | Votes | % |
|---|---|---|
| 1 Herbert H. Bateman (R) | 76,926 | 53.9 |
| John J. McGlennon (D) | 62,379 | 43.7 |
| 2 G. William Whitehurst (R) | 78,108 | 99.9 |
| 3 Thomas J. Bliley Jr. (R) | 92,928 | 59.2 |
| John A. Waldrop Jr. (D) | 63,946 | 40.8 |
| 4 Norman Sisisky (D) | 80,695 | 54.4 |
| Robert W. Daniel Jr. (R) | 67,708 | 45.6 |
| 5 Dan Daniel (D) | 88,293 | 100.0 |
| 6 James R. Olin (D) | 68,192 | 49.7 |
| Kevin G. Miller (R) | 66,537 | 48.5 |
| 7 J. Kenneth Robinson (R) | 76,752 | 59.9 |
| Lindsay G. Dorrier Jr. (D) | 46,514 | 36.3 |
| 8 Stan Parris (R) | 69,620 | 49.7 |
| Herbert E. Harris II (D) | 68,071 | 48.6 |
| 9 Frederick C. Boucher (D) | 76,205 | 50.4 |
| William C. Wampler (R) | 75,082 | 49.6 |
| 10 Frank R. Wolf (R) | 86,506 | 52.7 |
| Ira M. Lechner (D) | 75,361 | 45.9 |

## WASHINGTON

| | Votes | % |
|---|---|---|
| 1 Joel Pritchard (R) | 123,956 | 67.6 |
| Brian Long (D) | 59,444 | 32.4 |

| Candidates | Votes | % |
|---|---|---|
| 2 Al Swift (D) | 101,383 | 59.6 |
| Joan Houchen (R) | 68,622 | 40.4 |
| 3 Don Bonker (D) | 97,323 | 60.1 |
| J. T. Quigg (R) | 59,686 | 36.8 |
| 4 Sid Morrison (R) | 112,148 | 69.8 |
| Charles D. Kilbury (D) | 45,990 | 28.6 |
| 5 Thomas S. Foley (D) | 109,549 | 64.3 |
| John Sonneland (R) | 60,816 | 35.7 |
| 6 Norman D. Dicks (D) | 89,985 | 62.5 |
| Ted Haley (R) | 47,720 | 33.2 |
| 7 Mike Lowry (D) | 126,313 | 70.9 |
| Bob Dorse (R) | 51,759 | 29.1 |
| 8 Rodney Chandler (R) | 79,209 | 57.0 |
| Beth Bland (D) | 59,824 | 43.0 |

## WEST VIRGINIA

| | Votes | % |
|---|---|---|
| 1 Alan B. Mollohan (D) | 79,529 | 53.2 |
| John F. McCuskey (R) | 70,069 | 46.8 |
| 2 Harley O. Staggers Jr. (D) | 87,904 | 64.0 |
| J. D. Hinkle Jr. (R) | 49,413 | 36.0 |
| 3 Bob Wise (D) | 84,619 | 57.9 |
| David Michael Staton (R) | 60,844 | 41.6 |
| 4 Nick J. Rahall II (D) | 91,184 | 80.5 |
| Homer L. Harris (R) | 22,054 | 19.5 |

## WISCONSIN

| Candidates | Votes | % |
|---|---|---|
| 1 Les Aspin (D) | 95,055 | 61.0 |
| Peter N. Jannson (R) | 59,309 | 38.1 |
| 2 Robert W. Kastenmeier (D) | 112,677 | 60.6 |
| Jim Johnson (R) | 71,989 | 38.7 |
| 3 Steve Gunderson (R) | 99,304 | 56.6 |
| Paul Offner (D) | 75,132 | 42.8 |
| 4 Clement J. Zablocki (D) | 129,557 | 94.6 |
| 5 Jim Moody (D) | 99,713 | 63.5 |
| Rod K. Johnston (R) | 54,826 | 34.9 |
| 6 Thomas E. Petri (R) | 111,348 | 65.0 |
| Gordon E. Loehr (D) | 59,922 | 35.0 |
| 7 David R. Obey (D) | 122,124 | 68.0 |
| Bernard A. Zimmerman (R) | 57,535 | 32.0 |
| 8 Toby Roth (R) | 101,379 | 57.2 |
| Ruth C. Clusen (D) | 74,436 | 42.0 |
| 9 F. James Sensenbrenner Jr. (R) | 111,503 | 100.0 |

## WYOMING

| | Votes | % |
|---|---|---|
| AL Dick Cheney (R) | 113,236 | 71.1 |
| Ted Hommel (D) | 46,041 | 28.9 |

**1982 Elections**

1. For the 1982 House elections in Louisiana, an open primary election was held with candidates from all parties running on the same ballot. Any candidate who received a majority was elected unopposed, with no further appearance on the general election ballot. If no candidate received 50 percent, a runoff was held between the two top finishers.

# 1983 House Elections

## CALIFORNIA

| Candidates | Votes | % |
|---|---|---|
| **Special Election** | | |
| 5 Sala Burton (D) | 44,790 | 56.9 |
| Dunan Howard (R) | 18,305 | 23.3 |
| Richard Doyle (D) | 6,582 | 8.4 |

## COLORADO

| Special Election | | |
|---|---|---|
| 6 Daniel S. Schaefer (R) | 49,816 | 63.3 |
| Steve Hogan (D) | 27,779 | 35.3 |

## GEORGIA

### Special Election (Non-partisan)

| Candidates | Votes | % |
|---|---|---|
| 7 Kathryn McDonald | 25,468 | 30.6 |
| George W. (Buddy) Darden | 22,894 | 27.6 |
| George A. Sellers | 20,970 | 25.2 |
| George Pullen | 4,578 | 5.5 |
| Dan H. Fincher | 4,278 | 5.1 |

### Special Runoff Election (Non-partisan)

| | Votes | % |
|---|---|---|
| 7 George W. (Buddy) Darden | 56,267 | 59.1 |
| Kathryn McDonald | 38,949 | 40.9 |

## ILLINOIS

### Special Election

| | Votes | % |
|---|---|---|
| 1 Charles A. Hayes (D) | 39,623 | 93.7 |
| Diane Preacely (R) | 2,272 | 5.4 |

## NEW YORK

| Candidates | Votes | % |
|---|---|---|
| **Special Election** | | |
| 7 Gary L. Ackerman (D, L) | 18,388 | 48.7 |
| Albert Lemishow (R, C) | 8,331 | 22.1 |
| Douglas F. Schoen (NEIGH) | 5,997 | 15.9 |
| Sheldon Loeffler (I) | 4,318 | 11.4 |

## TEXAS

| Special Election | | |
|---|---|---|
| 6 Phil Gramm (R) | 46,371 | 55.3 |
| Dan Kubiak (D) | 33,201 | 39.6 |

# 1984 House Elections

## ALABAMA

| Candidates | Votes | % |
|---|---|---|
| Sonny Callahan (R) | 102,479 | 51.0 |
| Frank McRight (D) | 98,455 | 49.0 |
| William L. Dickinson (R) | 118,153 | 60.3 |
| Larry Lee (D) | 75,506 | 38.6 |
| Bill Nichols (D) | 120,357 | 96.2 |
| Tom Bevill (D) | 120,106 | 100.0 |
| Ronnie G. Flippo (D) | 140,542 | 95.9 |
| Ben Erdreich (D) | 130,973 | 59.6 |
| J. T. (Jabo) Waggoner (R) | 87,550 | 39.8 |
| Richard C. Shelby (D) | 135,834 | 96.8 |

## ALASKA

| | Votes | % |
|---|---|---|
| Don Young (R) | 113,582 | 55.0 |
| Pegge Begich (D) | 86,052 | 41.7 |

## ARIZONA

| | Votes | % |
|---|---|---|
| John McCain (R) | 162,418 | 78.1 |
| Harry W. Braun III (D) | 45,609 | 21.9 |
| Morris K. Udall (D) | 106,332 | 87.7 |
| Lorenzo Torrez (I) | 14,869 | 12.3 |
| Bob Stump (R) | 156,686 | 71.8 |
| Bob Schuster (D) | 57,748 | 26.4 |
| Eldon Rudd (R) | 167,558 | 100.0 |
| Jim Kolbe (R) | 116,075 | 50.9 |
| James F. McNulty Jr. (D) | 109,871 | 48.2 |

## ARKANSAS

| | Votes | % |
|---|---|---|
| Bill Alexander (D) | 121,047 | 97.2 |
| Tommy F. Robinson (D) | 103,165 | 47.1 |
| Judy Petty (R) | 90,841 | 41.5 |
| Jim Taylor (I) | 25,073 | 11.4 |
| John Paul Hammerschmidt (R) | | 100.0 |
| Beryl Anthony Jr. (D) | 117,123 | 97.9 |

## CALIFORNIA

| | Votes | % |
|---|---|---|
| Douglas H. Bosco (D) | 157,037 | 62.3 |
| David Redick (R) | 95,186 | 37.7 |
| Gene Chappie (R) | 158,679 | 69.5 |
| Harry Cozad (D) | 69,793 | 30.5 |
| Robert T. Matsui (D) | 131,369 | 100.0 |
| Vic Fazio (D) | 130,109 | 61.4 |
| Roger Canfield (R) | 77,773 | 36.7 |
| Sala Burton (D) | 139,692 | 72.3 |
| Tom Spinosa (R) | 45,930 | 23.8 |
| Barbara Boxer (D) | 162,511 | 68.0 |
| Douglas Binderup (R) | 71,011 | 29.7 |
| George Miller (D) | 158,306 | 66.7 |
| Rosemary Thakar (R) | 78,985 | 33.3 |
| Ronald V. Dellums (D) | 144,316 | 60.3 |
| Charles Connor (R) | 94,907 | 39.7 |
| Fortney H. (Pete) Stark (D) | 136,511 | 69.9 |
| J. T. Eager Beaver (R) | 51,399 | 26.3 |
| Don Edwards (D) | 102,469 | 62.4 |
| Robert P. Herriott (R) | 56,256 | 34.3 |
| Tom Lantos (D) | 147,607 | 69.9 |
| John J. Hickey (R) | 59,625 | 28.3 |
| Ed Zschau (R) | 155,795 | 61.7 |
| Martin Carnoy (D) | 91,026 | 36.0 |
| Norman Y. Mineta (D) | 139,851 | 65.2 |
| John D. Williams (R) | 70,666 | 33.0 |
| Norman D. Shumway (R) | 179,238 | 73.3 |
| Ruth (Paula) Carlson (D) | 58,384 | 23.9 |
| Tony Coelho (D) | 109,590 | 65.5 |
| Carol Harner (R) | 54,730 | 32.7 |
| Leon E. Panetta (D) | 153,377 | 70.8 |
| Patricia Smith Ramsey (R) | 60,065 | 27.7 |
| Charles Pashayan Jr. (R) | 128,802 | 72.5 |
| Simon Lakritz (D) | 48,888 | 27.5 |
| Richard H. Lehman (D) | 128,186 | 67.3 |

| | Candidates | Votes | % |
|---|---|---|---|
| | Dale L. Ewen (R) | 62,339 | 32.7 |
| 19 | Robert J. Lagomarsino (R) | 153,187 | 67.3 |
| | James C. Carey Jr. (D) | 70,278 | 30.9 |
| 20 | William M. Thomas (R) | 151,732 | 70.9 |
| | Mike LeSage (D) | 62,307 | 29.1 |
| 21 | Bobbi Fiedler (R) | 173,504 | 72.3 |
| | Charles Davis (D) | 62,085 | 25.9 |
| 22 | Carlos J. Moorhead (R) | 184,981 | 85.2 |
| | Michael B. Yauch (LIBERT) | 32,036 | 14.8 |
| 23 | Anthony C. Beilenson (D) | 140,461 | 61.6 |
| | Claude Parrish (R) | 84,093 | 36.9 |
| 24 | Henry A. Waxman (D) | 97,340 | 63.4 |
| | Jerry Zerg (R) | 51,010 | 33.2 |
| 25 | Edward R. Roybal (D) | 74,261 | 71.7 |
| | Roy D. (Bill) Bloxom (R) | 24,968 | 24.1 |
| 26 | Howard L. Berman (D) | 117,080 | 62.8 |
| | Miriam Ojeda (R) | 69,372 | 37.2 |
| 27 | Mel Levine (D) | 116,933 | 54.9 |
| | Robert B. Scribner (R) | 88,896 | 41.8 |
| 28 | Julian C. Dixon (D) | 113,076 | 75.6 |
| | Beatrice M. Jett (R) | 33,511 | 22.4 |
| 29 | Augustus F. Hawkins (D) | 108,777 | 86.6 |
| | Echo Y. Goto (R) | 16,781 | 13.4 |
| 30 | Matthew G. Martinez (D) | 64,378 | 51.8 |
| | Richard Gomez (R) | 53,900 | 43.3 |
| 31 | Mervyn M. Dymally (D) | 100,658 | 70.7 |
| | Henry C. Minturn (R) | 41,691 | 29.3 |
| 32 | Glenn M. Anderson (D) | 102,961 | 60.7 |
| | Roger E. Fiola (R) | 62,176 | 36.6 |
| 33 | David Dreier (R) | 147,363 | 70.6 |
| | Claire K. McDonald (D) | 54,147 | 26.0 |
| 34 | Esteban Edward Torres (D) | 87,060 | 59.8 |
| | Paul R. Jackson (R) | 58,467 | 40.2 |
| 35 | Jerry Lewis (R) | 176,477 | 85.5 |
| | Kevin Akin (PFP) | 29,990 | 14.5 |
| 36 | George E. Brown Jr. (D) | 104,438 | 56.6 |
| | John Paul Stark (R) | 80,212 | 43.4 |
| 37 | Al McCandless (R) | 149,955 | 63.6 |
| | David E. Skinner (D) | 85,908 | 36.4 |
| 38 | Bob Dornan (R) | 86,545 | 53.2 |
| | Jerry M. Patterson (D) | 73,231 | 45.0 |
| 39 | William E. Dannemeyer (R) | 175,788 | 76.2 |
| | Robert E. Ward (D) | 54,889 | 23.8 |
| 40 | Robert E. Badham (R) | 164,257 | 64.4 |
| | Carol Ann Bradford (D) | 86,748 | 34.0 |
| 41 | Bill Lowery (R) | 161,068 | 63.4 |
| | Robert L. Simmons (D) | 85,475 | 33.7 |
| 42 | Dan Lungren (R) | 177,783 | 73.0 |
| | Mary Lou Brophy (D) | 60,025 | 24.6 |
| 43 | Ron Packard (R) | 165,643 | 74. |
| | Lois E. Humphreys (D) | 50,996 | 22.J |
| 44 | Jim Bates (D) | 99,378 | 69.7 |
| | Neill Campbell (R) | 39,977 | 28.0 |
| 45 | Duncan L. Hunter (R) | 149,011 | 75.1 |
| | David W. Guthrie (D) | 45,325 | 22.9 |

## COLORADO

| | | Votes | % |
|---|---|---|---|
| 1 | Patricia Schroeder (D) | 126,348 | 62.0 |
| | Mary Downs (R) | 73,993 | 36.3 |
| 2 | Timothy E. Wirth (D) | 118,580 | 53.2 |
| | Michael J. Norton (R) | 101,488 | 45.5 |
| 3 | Mike Strang (R) | 122,669 | 57.1 |
| | W. Mitchell (D) | 90,063 | 41.9 |
| 4 | Hank Brown (R) | 146,469 | 71.1 |
| | Mary Fagan Bates (D) | 56,462 | 27.4 |
| 5 | Ken Kramer (R) | 163,654 | 78.6 |
| | William Geffen (D) | 44,588 | 21.4 |
| 6 | Dan L. Schaefer (R) | 171,427 | 89.4 |
| | John Heckman (I) | 20,333 | 10.6 |

## CONNECTICUT

| | | Votes | % |
|---|---|---|---|
| 1 | Barbara B. Kennelly (D) | 147,748 | 61.7 |
| | Herschel A. Klein (R) | 90,823 | 37.9 |
| 2 | Sam Gejdenson (D) | 124,110 | 54.4 |
| | Roberta F. Koontz (R) | 103,119 | 45.2 |

| | Candidates | Votes | % |
|---|---|---|---|
| 3 | Bruce A. Morrison (D) | 129,230 | 52.6 |
| | Lawrence J. DeNardis (R) | 115,939 | 47.2 |
| 4 | Stewart B. McKinney (R) | 165,644 | 70.4 |
| | John M. Ormon (D) | 69,666 | 29.6 |
| 5 | John G. Rowland (R) | 130,700 | 54.3 |
| | William R. Ratchford (D) | 109,425 | 45.5 |
| 6 | Nancy L. Johnson (R) | 155,422 | 64.0 |
| | Arthur H. House (D) | 87,489 | 36.0 |

## DELAWARE

| | | Votes | % |
|---|---|---|---|
| AL | Thomas R. Carper (D) | 142,070 | 58.5 |
| | Elise R. W. du Pont (R) | 100,650 | 41.4 |

## FLORIDA

| | | Votes | % |
|---|---|---|---|
| 1 | Earl Hutto (D) | | 100.0 |
| 2 | Don Fuqua (D) | | 100.0 |
| 3 | Charles E. Bennett (D) | | 100.0 |
| 4 | Bill Chappell Jr. (D) | 134,694 | 64.8 |
| | Alton H. (Bill) Starling (R) | 73,218 | 35.2 |
| 5 | Bill McCollum (R) | | 100.0 |
| 6 | Buddy MacKay (D) | 167,409 | 99.3 |
| 7 | Sam Gibbons (D) | 100,430 | 58.8 |
| | Michael N. Kavouklis (R) | 70,280 | 41.2 |
| 8 | C. W. Bill Young (R) | 184,553 | 80.3 |
| | Robert Kent (D) | 45,393 | 19.7 |
| 9 | Michael Bilirakis (R) | 191,343 | 78.6 |
| | Jack Wilson (D) | 52,150 | 21.4 |
| 10 | Andy Ireland (R) | 126,206 | 61.9 |
| | Patricia M. Glass (D) | 77,635 | 38.1 |
| 11 | Bill Nelson (D) | 145,764 | 60.5 |
| | Rob Quartel (R) | 95,115 | 39.5 |
| 12 | Tom Lewis (R) | | 100.0 |
| 13 | Connie Mack (R) | | 100.0 |
| 14 | Daniel A. Mica (D) | 153,935 | 55.4 |
| | Don Ross (R) | 123,926 | 44.6 |
| 15 | E. Clay Shaw Jr. (R) | 128,097 | 65.7 |
| | Bill Humphrey (D) | 66,833 | 34.3 |
| 16 | Larry Smith (D) | 108,410 | 56.4 |
| | Tom Bush (R) | 83,903 | 43.6 |
| 17 | William Lehman (D) | | 100.0 |
| 18 | Claude Pepper (D) | 76,404 | 60.5 |
| | Ricardo Nunez (R) | 49,818 | 39.5 |
| 19 | Dante B. Fascell (D) | 115,631 | 64.3 |
| | Bill Flanagan (R) | 64,317 | 35.7 |

## GEORGIA

| | | Votes | % |
|---|---|---|---|
| 1 | Robert Lindsay Thomas (D) | 126,082 | 81.6 |
| | Erie Lee Downing (R) | 28,460 | 18.4 |
| 2 | Charles Hatcher (D) | 110,561 | 100.0 |
| 3 | Richard Ray (D) | 111,061 | 81.4 |
| | Mitchell Cantu (R) | 25,410 | 18.6 |
| 4 | Pat Swindall (R) | 120,456 | 53.1 |
| | Elliott H. Levitas (D) | 106,376 | 46.9 |
| 5 | Wyche Fowler Jr. (D) | 151,233 | 100.0 |
| 6 | Newt Gingrich (R) | 116,655 | 69.1 |
| | Gerald Johnson (D) | 52,061 | 30.9 |
| 7 | George (Buddy) Darden (D) | 106,586 | 55.2 |
| | William E. Bronson (R) | 86,431 | 44.8 |
| 8 | J. Roy Rowland (D) | 100,936 | 100.0 |
| 9 | Ed Jenkins (D) | 109,422 | 67.5 |
| | Frank H. Cofer Jr. (R) | 52,731 | 32.5 |
| 10 | Doug Barnard Jr. (D) | 116,364 | 100.0 |

## HAWAII

| | | Votes | % |
|---|---|---|---|
| 1 | Cecil Heftel (D) | 114,844 | 82.7 |
| | William F. Beard (R) | 20,608 | 14.8 |
| 2 | Daniel K. Akaka (D) | 112,377 | 82.2 |
| | A. D. Shipley (R) | 20,000 | 14.6 |

## IDAHO

| | | Votes | % |
|---|---|---|---|
| 1 | Larry E. Craig (R) | 139,085 | 68.6 |
| | Bill Hellar (D) | 63,591 | 31.4 |

| Candidates | Votes | % |
|---|---|---|
| 2 Richard H. Stallings (D) | 101,287 | 50.0 |
| George Hansen (R) | 101,117 | 50.0 |

## ILLINOIS

| Candidates | Votes | % |
|---|---|---|
| 1 Charles A. Hayes (D) | 177,438 | 95.6 |
| 2 Gus Savage (D) | 155,349 | 83.0 |
| Dale F. Harman (R) | 31,865 | 17.0 |
| 3 Marty Russo (D) | 143,363 | 64.4 |
| Richard D. Murphy (R) | 79,218 | 35.6 |
| 4 George M. O'Brien (R) | 121,744 | 64.0 |
| Dennis E. Marlow (D) | 68,547 | 36.0 |
| 5 William O. Lipinski (D) | 106,597 | 63.6 |
| John M. Paczkowski (R) | 61,109 | 36.4 |
| 6 Henry J. Hyde (R) | 157,370 | 75.1 |
| Robert H. Renshaw (D) | 52,189 | 24.9 |
| 7 Cardiss Collins (D) | 135,493 | 78.4 |
| James L. Bevel (R) | 37,411 | 21.6 |
| 8 Dan Rostenkowski (D) | 114,385 | 71.3 |
| Spiro F. Georgeson (R) | 46,030 | 28.7 |
| 9 Sidney R. Yates (D) | 144,879 | 67.5 |
| Herbert Sohn (R) | 69,613 | 32.5 |
| 10 John Edward Porter (R) | 153,330 | 72.6 |
| Ruth C. Braver (D) | 57,809 | 27.4 |
| 11 Frank Annunzio (D) | 138,171 | 62.6 |
| Charles J. Theusch (R) | 82,518 | 37.4 |
| 12 Philip M. Crane (R) | 159,582 | 77.8 |
| Edward J. LaFlamme (D) | 45,537 | 22.2 |
| 13 Harris W. Fawell (R) | 157,603 | 67.0 |
| Michael J. Donohue (D) | 77,623 | 33.0 |
| 14 John E. Grotberg (R) | 135,967 | 62.2 |
| Dan McGrath (D) | 82,756 | 37.8 |
| 15 Edward R. Madigan (R) | 149,096 | 73.2 |
| John M. Hoffman (D) | 54,516 | 26.8 |
| 16 Lynn Martin (R) | 127,684 | 58.4 |
| Carl R. Schwerdtfeger (D) | 90,850 | 41.6 |
| 17 Lane Evans (D) | 128,273 | 56.7 |
| Kenneth G. McMillan (R) | 98,069 | 43.3 |
| 18 Robert H. Michel (R) | 136,183 | 61.0 |
| Gerald A. Bradley (D) | 86,884 | 38.9 |
| 19 Terry L. Bruce (D) | 117,634 | 52.3 |
| Daniel B. Crane (R) | 107,463 | 47.7 |
| 20 Richard J. Durbin (D) | 145,092 | 61.3 |
| Richard G. Austin (R) | 91,728 | 38.7 |
| 21 Melvin Price (D) | 127,046 | 60.2 |
| Robert H. Gaffner (R) | 84,148 | 39.8 |
| 22 Kenneth J. Gray (D) | 116,952 | 50.3 |
| Randy Patchett (R) | 115,775 | 49.7 |

## INDIANA

| Candidates | Votes | % |
|---|---|---|
| 1 Peter J. Visclosky (D) | 147,035 | 70.7 |
| Joseph B. Grenchik (R) | 59,986 | 28.8 |
| 2 Philip R. Sharp (D) | 118,965 | 53.4 |
| Ken MacKenzie (R) | 103,061 | 46.3 |
| 3 John Hiler (R) | 115,139 | 52.4 |
| Michael P. Barnes (D) | 103,961 | 47.3 |
| 4 Dan Coats (R) | 129,674 | 60.8 |
| Michael H. Barnard (D) | 82,053 | 38.5 |
| 5 Elwood Hillis (R) | 143,560 | 67.9 |
| Allen B. Maxwell (D) | 66,631 | 31.5 |
| 6 Dan Burton (R) | 178,814 | 72.7 |
| Howard O. Campbell (D) | 65,772 | 26.8 |
| 7 John T. Myers (R) | 147,787 | 67.3 |
| Arthur E. Smith (D) | 69,097 | 31.5 |
| 8[1] Richard D. McIntyre (R) | 114,278 | 49.9 |
| Frank McCloskey (D) | 113,860 | 49.8 |
| 9 Lee H. Hamilton (D) | 137,018 | 65.1 |
| Floyd E. Coates (R) | 72,652 | 34.5 |
| 10 Andrew Jacobs Jr. (D) | 115,274 | 59.0 |
| Joseph P. Watkins (R) | 79,342 | 40.6 |

## IOWA

| Candidates | Votes | % |
|---|---|---|
| 1 Jim Leach (R) | 131,182 | 66.8 |
| Kevin Ready (D) | 65,293 | 33.2 |
| 2 Tom Tauke (R) | 136,893 | 63.9 |
| Joe Welsh (D) | 77,335 | 36.1 |
| 3 Cooper Evans (R) | 133,737 | 60.7 |
| Joe Johnston (D) | 86,574 | 39.3 |
| 4 Neal Smith (D) | 136,922 | 60.7 |
| Robert R. Lockard (R) | 88,717 | 39.3 |
| 5 Jim Lightfoot (R) | 104,632 | 50.8 |
| Jerome D. Fitzgerald (D) | 101,435 | 49.2 |
| 6 Berkley Bedell (D) | 127,706 | 62.0 |
| Darrel Rensink (R) | 78,182 | 38.0 |

## KANSAS

| Candidates | Votes | % |
|---|---|---|
| 1 Pat Roberts (R) | 159,931 | 76.0 |
| Darrell Ringer (D) | 49,015 | 23.3 |
| 2 Jim Slattery (D) | 112,263 | 60.0 |
| Jim Van Slyke (R) | 73,045 | 39.1 |
| 3 Jan Meyers (R) | 117,159 | 54.8 |
| John E. Reardon (D) | 85,441 | 39.9 |
| John S. Ralph Jr. (I) | 11,302 | 5.3 |
| 4 Dan Glickman (D) | 138,917 | 74.4 |
| William V. Krause (R) | 47,776 | 25.6 |
| 5 Bob Whittaker (R) | 144,075 | 73.5 |
| John A. Barnes (D) | 49,435 | 25.2 |

## KENTUCKY

| Candidates | Votes | % |
|---|---|---|
| 1 Carroll Hubbard Jr. (D) | 112,180 | 100.0 |
| 2 William H. Natcher (D) | 93,042 | 62.1 |
| Timothy A. Morrison (R) | 56,700 | 37.9 |
| 3 Romano L. Mazzoli (D) | 145,680 | 67.7 |
| Suzanne M. Warner (R) | 68,185 | 31.7 |
| 4 Gene Snyder (R) | 108,398 | 53.7 |
| William P. Mulloy II (D) | 93,640 | 46.3 |
| 5 Harold Rogers (R) | 125,164 | 75.9 |
| Sherman W. McIntosh (D) | 39,783 | 24.1 |
| 6 Larry J. Hopkins (R) | 126,525 | 71.4 |
| Jerry Hammond (D) | 49,657 | 28.0 |
| 7[2] Carl C. (Chris) Perkins (D) | 122,679 | 73.7 |
| Aubrey Russell (R) | 43,890 | 26.3 |

## LOUISIANA[3]

| Candidates | Votes | % |
|---|---|---|
| 1 Bob Livingston (R) | | 100.0 |
| 2 Lindy (Mrs. Hale) Boggs (D) | | 100.0 |
| 3 W. J. (Billy) Tauzin (D) | | 100.0 |
| 4 Buddy Roemer (D) | | 100.0 |
| 5 Jerry Huckaby (D) | | 100.0 |
| 6 W. Henson Moore (R) | | 100.0 |
| 7 John B. Breaux (D) | | 100.0 |
| 8 Gillis W. Long (D) | | 100.0 |

## MAINE

| Candidates | Votes | % |
|---|---|---|
| 1 John R. McKernan Jr. (R) | 182,785 | 63.5 |
| Barry J. Hobbins (D) | 104,972 | 36.5 |
| 2 Olympia J. Snowe (R) | 192,166 | 75.7 |
| Chipman C. Bull (D) | 57,347 | 22.6 |

## MARYLAND

| Candidates | Votes | % |
|---|---|---|
| 1 Roy Dyson (D) | 96,673 | 58.4 |
| Harlan C. Williams (R) | 68,865 | 41.6 |
| 2 Helen Delich Bentley (R) | 111,517 | 51.4 |
| Clarence D. Long (D) | 105,571 | 48.6 |
| 3 Barbara A. Mikulski (D) | 133,189 | 68.2 |
| Ross Z. Pierpont (R) | 59,493 | 30.5 |
| 4 Marjorie S. Holt (R) | 114,430 | 66.2 |
| Howard M. Greenebaum (D) | 58,312 | 33.8 |
| 5 Steny H. Hoyer (D) | 116,310 | 72.2 |
| John E. Ritchie (R) | 44,839 | 27.8 |
| 6 Beverly B. Byron (D) | 123,383 | 65.1 |
| Robin Ficker (R) | 66,056 | 34.9 |
| 7 Parren J. Mitchell (D) | 139,488 | 100.0 |
| 8 Michael D. Barnes (D) | 181,947 | 71.5 |
| Albert Ceccone (R) | 70,715 | 27.8 |

## MASSACHUSETTS

| Candidates | Votes | % |
|---|---|---|
| 1 Silvio O. Conte (R) | 162,646 | 72.9 |
| Mary L. Wentworth (D) | 60,372 | 27.1 |
| 2 Edward P. Boland (D) | 132,693 | 68.7 |
| Thomas P. Swank (R) | 60,463 | 31.3 |
| 3 Joseph D. Early (D) | 148,461 | 67.4 |
| Kenneth J. Redding (R) | 71,765 | 32.6 |
| 4 Barney Frank (D) | 172,903 | 74.2 |
| Jim Forte (R) | 60,121 | 25.8 |
| 5 Chester G. Atkins (D) | 120,008 | 53.4 |
| Gregory S. Hyatt (R) | 104,912 | 46.6 |
| 6 Nicholas Mavroules (D) | 168,662 | 70.4 |
| Frederick S. Leber (R) | 63,363 | 26.4 |
| 7 Edward J. Markey (D) | 167,211 | 71.4 |
| S. Lester Ralph (R) | 66,930 | 28.6 |
| 8 Thomas P. O'Neill Jr. (D) | 179,617 | 91.8 |
| Laura Ross (COM) | 15,810 | 8.1 |
| 9 Joe Moakley (D) | 153,132 | 99.9 |
| 10 Gerry E. Studds (D) | 143,062 | 55.7 |
| Lewis Crampton (R) | 113,745 | 44.3 |
| 11 Brian J. Donnelly (D) | 172,010 | 100.0 |

## MICHIGAN

| Candidates | Votes | % |
|---|---|---|
| 1 John Conyers Jr. (D) | 152,432 | 89.4 |
| Edward J. Mack (R) | 17,393 | 10.2 |
| 2 Carl D. Pursell (R) | 140,688 | 68.6 |
| Mike McCauley (D) | 62,374 | 30.4 |
| 3 Howard Wolpe (D) | 106,505 | 52.9 |
| Jackie McGregor (R) | 94,714 | 47.1 |
| 4 Mark D. Siljander (R) | 127,907 | 66.9 |
| Charles S. Rodebaugh (D) | 63,159 | 33.1 |
| 5 Paul B. Henry (R) | 140,131 | 61.8 |
| Gary J. McInerney (D) | 85,232 | 37.6 |
| 6 Bob Carr (D) | 106,705 | 52.4 |
| Tom Ritter (R) | 95,113 | 46.7 |
| 7 Dale E. Kildee (D) | 145,070 | 93.1 |
| Samuel Johnston (I) | 10,663 | 6.8 |
| 8 Bob Traxler (D) | 126,161 | 64.4 |
| John Heussner (R) | 69,683 | 35.6 |
| 9 Guy Vander Jagt (R) | 150,885 | 70.9 |
| John M. Senger (D) | 61,233 | 28.8 |
| 10 Bill Schuette (R) | 104,950 | 50.1 |
| Donald J. Albosta (D) | 103,636 | 49.4 |
| 11 Robert W. Davis (R) | 126,992 | 58.6 |
| Tom Stewart (D) | 89,640 | 41.4 |
| 12 David E. Bonior (D) | 113,772 | 58.3 |
| Eugene J. Tyza (R) | 79,824 | 40.9 |
| 13 George W. Crockett Jr. (D) | 132,222 | 86.6 |
| Robert Murphy (R) | 20,416 | 13.4 |
| 14 Dennis M. Hertel (D) | 113,610 | 59.1 |
| John Lauve (R) | 77,427 | 40.3 |
| 15 William D. Ford (D) | 98,973 | 59.9 |
| Gerald R. Carlson (R) | 66,172 | 40.1 |
| 16 John D. Dingell (D) | 121,463 | 63.7 |
| Frank Grzywacki (R) | 68,116 | 35.7 |
| 17 Sander M. Levin (D) | 133,064 | 100.0 |
| 18 William S. Broomfield (R) | 186,505 | 79.4 |
| Vivian H. Smargon (D) | 46,191 | 19.7 |

## MINNESOTA[4]

| Candidates | Votes | % |
|---|---|---|
| 1 Timothy J. Penny (DFL) | 140,095 | 57.0 |
| Keith Spicer (I-R) | 105,723 | 43.0 |
| 2 Vin Weber (I-R) | 153,308 | 63.1 |
| Todd Lundquist (DFL) | 89,770 | 36.9 |
| 3 Bill Frenzel (I-R) | 207,819 | 73.2 |
| Dave Peterson (DFL) | 76,132 | 26.8 |
| 4 Bruce F. Vento (DFL) | 167,678 | 73.5 |
| Mary Jane Rachner (I-R) | 57,450 | 25.2 |
| 5 Martin Olav Sabo (DFL) | 165,075 | 70.1 |
| Richard D. Wieblen (I-R) | 62,642 | 26.6 |
| 6 Gerry Sikorski (DFL) | 154,661 | 60.5 |
| Patrick Trueman (I-R) | 101,058 | 39.5 |
| 7 Arlan Stangeland (I-R) | 135,087 | 57.0 |
| Collin C. Peterson (DFL) | 101,720 | 42.9 |
| 8 James L. Oberstar (DFL) | 165,727 | 67.2 |
| Dave Rued (I-R) | 79,181 | 32.1 |

## MISSISSIPPI

| Candidates | Votes | % |
|---|---|---|
| 1 Jamie L. Whitten (D) | 136,530 | 88.4 |
| John Hargett (I) | 17,991 | 11.6 |

*Footnotes, see p. 1303.*

| Candidates | Votes | % |
|---|---|---|
| 2 Webb Franklin (R) | 92,392 | 50.6 |
|   Robert G. Clark (D) | 89,154 | 48.9 |
| 3 G. V. (Sonny) Montgomery (D) | 158,002 | 100.0 |
| 4 Wayne Dowdy (D) | 113,635 | 55.3 |
|   David Armstrong (R) | 91,797 | 45.6 |
| 5 Trent Lott (R) | 142,637 | 84.7 |
|   Arlon (Blackie) Coate (D) | 25,840 | 15.3 |

### MISSOURI

| Candidates | Votes | % |
|---|---|---|
| 1 William L. Clay (D) | 147,436 | 68.3 |
|   Eric Rathbone (R) | 68,538 | 31.7 |
| 2 Robert A. Young (D) | 139,123 | 51.8 |
|   John Buechner (R) | 127,710 | 47.5 |
| 3 Richard A. Gephardt (D) | 193,537 | 100.0 |
| 4 Ike Skelton (D) | 150,624 | 66.9 |
|   Carl D. Russell (R) | 74,434 | 33.1 |
| 5 Alan Wheat (D) | 150,675 | 66.0 |
|   Jim Kenworthy (R) | 72,477 | 31.8 |
| 6 E. Thomas Coleman (R) | 150,996 | 64.8 |
|   Kenneth C. Hensley (D) | 81,917 | 35.2 |
| 7 Gene Taylor (R) | 164,586 | 69.6 |
|   Ken Young (D) | 71,867 | 30.4 |
| 8 Bill Emerson (R) | 134,186 | 65.4 |
|   Bill Blue (D) | 70,922 | 34.6 |
| 9 Harold L. Volkmer (D) | 123,588 | 52.9 |
|   Carrie Francke (R) | 110,100 | 47.1 |

### MONTANA

| Candidates | Votes | % |
|---|---|---|
| 1 Pat Williams (D) | 126,998 | 65.6 |
|   Gary K. Carlson (R) | 61,794 | 31.9 |
| 2 Ron Marlenee (R) | 116,932 | 65.9 |
|   Chet Blaylock (D) | 60,445 | 34.1 |

### NEBRASKA

| Candidates | Votes | % |
|---|---|---|
| 1 Doug Bereuter (R) | 158,836 | 74.1 |
|   Monica Bauer (D) | 55,508 | 25.9 |
| 2 Hal Daub (R) | 139,384 | 64.9 |
|   Thomas F. Cavanaugh (D) | 75,210 | 35.0 |
| 3 Virginia Smith (R) | 183,901 | 83.3 |
|   Tom Vickers (D) | 36,899 | 16.7 |

### NEVADA

| Candidates | Votes | % |
|---|---|---|
| 1 Harry Reid (D) | 73,242 | 56.1 |
|   Peggy Cavnar (R) | 55,391 | 42.4 |
| 2 Barbara F. Vucanovich (R) | 99,775 | 71.2 |
|   Andrew Barbano (D) | 36,130 | 25.8 |

### NEW HAMPSHIRE

| Candidates | Votes | % |
|---|---|---|
| 1 Robert C. Smith (R) | 111,627 | 58.6 |
|   Dudley Dudley (D) | 76,854 | 40.3 |
| 2 Judd Gregg (R) | 138,975 | 76.2 |
|   Larry Converse (D) | 42,257 | 23.2 |

### NEW JERSEY

| Candidates | Votes | % |
|---|---|---|
| 1 James J. Florio (D) | 152,125 | 71.9 |
|   Frederick A. Busch Jr. (R) | 58,800 | 27.8 |
| 2 William J. Hughes (D) | 132,841 | 63.2 |
|   Raymond G. Massie (R) | 77,231 | 36.7 |
| 3 James J. Howard (D) | 122,291 | 53.3 |
|   Brian T. Kennedy (R) | 105,028 | 45.8 |
| 4 Christopher H. Smith (R) | 139,295 | 61.3 |
|   James C. Hedden (D) | 87,908 | 38.7 |
| 5 Marge Roukema (R) | 171,979 | 71.2 |
|   Rose Brunetto (D) | 69,666 | 28.8 |
| 6 Bernard J. Dwyer (D) | 118,532 | 55.9 |
|   Dennis Adams (R) | 90,862 | 42.8 |
| 7 Matthew J. Rinaldo (R) | 165,685 | 74.2 |
|   John F. Feeley (D) | 56,798 | 25.4 |
| 8 Robert A. Roe (D) | 118,793 | 62.7 |
|   Marguerite A. Page (R) | 69,973 | 36.9 |

| Candidates | Votes | % |
|---|---|---|
| 9 Robert G. Torricelli (D) | 149,493 | 62.6 |
|   Neil Romano (R) | 89,166 | 37.4 |
| 10 Peter W. Rodino Jr. (D) | 111,244 | 83.7 |
|   Howard E. Berkeley (R) | 21,712 | 16.3 |
| 11 Dean A. Gallo (R) | 133,662 | 55.8 |
|   Joseph G. Minish (D) | 106,038 | 44.2 |
| 12 Jim Courter (R) | 148,042 | 65.0 |
|   Peter Bearse (D) | 78,167 | 34.3 |
| 13⁵ H. James Saxton (R) | 141,136 | 60.7 |
|   James B. Smith (D) | 89,307 | 38.4 |
| 14 Frank J. Guarini (D) | 115,117 | 65.7 |
|   Edward T. Magee (R) | 58,265 | 33.3 |

### NEW MEXICO

| Candidates | Votes | % |
|---|---|---|
| 1 Manuel Lujan Jr. (R) | 115,808 | 64.9 |
|   Charles Ted Asbury (D) | 60,598 | 34.0 |
| 2 Joe Skeen (R) | 116,006 | 74.3 |
|   Peter R. York (D) | 40,063 | 25.7 |
| 3 Bill Richardson (D) | 100,470 | 60.8 |
|   Louis H. Gallegos (R) | 62,351 | 37.7 |

### NEW YORK

| Candidates | Votes | % |
|---|---|---|
| 1 William Carney (R, C, RTL) | 107,029 | 53.1 |
|   George J. Hochbrueckner (D, RP) | 94,551 | 46.9 |
| 2 Thomas J. Downey (D, IP) | 97,648 | 54.7 |
|   Paul Aniboli (R, C, RTL) | 80,855 | 45.3 |
| 3 Robert J. Mrazek (D) | 120,191 | 51.0 |
|   Robert P. Quinn (R, C) | 112,909 | 47.9 |
| 4 Norman F. Lent (R, C) | 154,875 | 68.9 |
|   Sheldon Engelhard (D, L) | 65,678 | 29.2 |
| 5 Raymond J. McGrath (R, C) | 138,560 | 62.4 |
|   Michael d'Innocenzo (D, IV) | 78,429 | 35.3 |
| 6 Joseph P. Addabbo (D, L) | 120,098 | 82.7 |
|   Philip J. Veltre (R, C, RTL) | 25,040 | 17.3 |
| 7 Gary L. Ackerman (D, L) | 97,674 | 69.3 |
|   Gustave A. Reifenkugel (R, C) | 43,370 | 30.7 |
| 8 James H. Scheuer (D, L) | 104,558 | 62.8 |
|   Robert L. Brandofino (R, C) | 62,015 | 37.2 |
| 9 Thomas J. Manton (D) | 71,420 | 52.8 |
|   Serphin R. Maltese (R, C, RTL) | 63,910 | 47.2 |
| 10 Charles E. Schumer (D, L) | 115,867 | 72.4 |
|   John H. Fox (R, C) | 42,009 | 26.3 |
| 11 Edolphus Towns (D, L) | 81,002 | 85.2 |
|   Nathaniel Hendricks (R) | 12,494 | 13.1 |
| 12 Major R. Owens (D, L) | 82,047 | 90.5 |
|   Joseph N. O. Caesar (R, C, RTL) | 8,609 | 9.5 |
| 13 Stephen J. Solarz (D, L) | 82,610 | 65.9 |
|   Lew Y. Levin (R, C, RTL) | 42,737 | 34.1 |
| 14 Guy V. Molinari (R, C, RTL) | 117,041 | 70.2 |
|   Kevin L. Sheehy (D) | 49,776 | 29.8 |
| 15 Bill Green (R, I) | 107,644 | 56.1 |
|   Andrew J. Stein (D, L) | 84,404 | 43.9 |
| 16 Charles B. Rangel (D, R) | 117,759 | 97.0 |
| 17 Ted Weiss (D, L) | 162,489 | 81.5 |
|   Kenneth Katzman (R) | 33,316 | 16.7 |
| 18 Robert Garcia (D, L) | 85,960 | 89.2 |
|   Curtis Johnson (R) | 8,970 | 9.3 |
| 19 Mario Biaggi (D, R, L, RTL) | 155,067 | 94.8 |
|   Alice Farrell (C) | 8,472 | 5.2 |
| 20 Joseph J. DioGuardi (R, C) | 106,958 | 50.1 |
|   Oren J. Teicher (D) | 102,842 | 48.2 |
| 21 Hamilton Fish Jr. (R, C, RTL) | 160,053 | 78.3 |
|   Lawrence W. Grunberger (D) | 44,274 | 21.7 |
| 22 Benjamin A. Gilman (R) | 144,278 | 68.5 |
|   Bruce M. Levine (D, L) | 57,934 | 27.5 |
| 23 Samuel S. Stratton (D) | 188,144 | 77.8 |
|   Frank Wicks (R, NF) | 53,060 | 21.9 |
| 24 Gerald B. H. Solomon (R, C, RTL) | 164,019 | 73.2 |
|   Edward J. Bloch (D) | 60,188 | 26.8 |
| 25 Sherwood Boehlert (R) | 140,256 | 72.8 |
|   James J. Ball (D) | 52,434 | 27.2 |
| 26 David O'B. Martin (R, C) | 131,257 | 70.6 |
|   Bernard J. Lammers (D) | 54,663 | 29.4 |

| Candidates | Votes | % |
|---|---|---|
| 27 George C. Wortley (R, C) | 122,215 | 56.6 |
|   Thomas C. Buckel Jr. (D, L) | 93,601 | 43.4 |
| 28 Matthew F. McHugh (D) | 123,334 | 56.6 |
|   Constance E. Cook (R) | 90,324 | 41.4 |
| 29 Frank Horton (R) | 138,362 | 69.6 |
|   James R. Toole (D) | 48,301 | 24.3 |
| 30 Fred J. Eckert (R, C, RTL) | 119,844 | 54.4 |
|   W. Douglas Call (R) | 100,066 | 45.4 |
| 31 Jack F. Kemp (R, C, RTL) | 168,332 | 75.0 |
|   Peter J. Martinelli (D, L) | 56,156 | 25.0 |
| 32 John J. LaFalce (D, L) | 139,979 | 69.4 |
|   Anthony J. Murty (R, C, RTL) | 61,797 | 30.6 |
| 33 Henry J. Nowak (D, L) | 155,198 | 77.6 |
|   David S. Lewandowski (R, C, RTL) | 44,880 | 22.4 |
| 34 Stan Lundine (D) | 110,902 | 54.2 |
|   Jill Houghton Emery (R, C) | 91,016 | 44.5 |

### NORTH CAROLINA

| Candidates | Votes | % |
|---|---|---|
| 1 Walter B. Jones (D) | 122,815 | 67.1 |
|   Herbert W. Lee (R) | 60,153 | 32.9 |
| 2 Tim Valentine (D) | 122,292 | 67.7 |
|   Frank H. Hill (R) | 58,312 | 32.3 |
| 3 Charles Whitley (D) | 100,185 | 64.1 |
|   Danny G. Moody (R) | 56,096 | 35.9 |
| 4 Bill Cobey (R) | 117,436 | 50.6 |
|   Ike Andrews (D) | 114,462 | 49.4 |
| 5 Stephen L. Neal (D) | 109,831 | 50.7 |
|   Stuart Epperson (R) | 106,599 | 49.3 |
| 6 Howard Coble (R) | 102,925 | 50.6 |
|   Robin Britt (D) | 100,263 | 49.3 |
| 7 Charlie Rose (D) | 92,157 | 59.2 |
|   S. Thomas Rhodes (R) | 63,625 | 40.8 |
| 8 W. G. (Bill) Hefner (D) | 99,731 | 50.9 |
|   Harris D. Blake (R) | 96,354 | 49.1 |
| 9 J. Alex McMillan (R) | 109,420 | 50.1 |
|   D. G. Martin (D) | 109,099 | 49.9 |
| 10 James T. Broyhill (R) | 142,873 | 73.4 |
|   Ted A. Poovey (D) | 51,860 | 26.6 |
| 11 Bill Hendon (R) | 112,598 | 51.0 |
|   James McClure Clarke (D) | 108,284 | 49.0 |

### NORTH DAKOTA

| Candidates | Votes | % |
|---|---|---|
| AL Byron L. Dorgan (D) | 242,968 | 78.7 |
|   Lois Ivers Altenburg (R) | 65,761 | 21.3 |

### OHIO

| Candidates | Votes | % |
|---|---|---|
| 1 Thomas A. Luken (D) | 121,577 | 55.1 |
|   Norman A. Murdock (R) | 88,859 | 40.3 |
| 2 Bill Gradison (R) | 149,856 | 68.6 |
|   Thomas D. Porter (D) | 68,597 | 31.4 |
| 3 Tony P. Hall (D) | 151,398 | 100.0 |
| 4 Michael G. Oxley (R) | 162,199 | 77.5 |
|   William O. Sutton (D) | 47,018 | 22.5 |
| 5 Delbert L. Latta (R) | 132,582 | 62.7 |
|   James R. Sherck (D) | 78,809 | 37.3 |
| 6 Bob McEwen (R) | 150,101 | 74.0 |
|   Bob Smith (D) | 52,727 | 26.0 |
| 7 Michael DeWine (R) | 147,885 | 76.7 |
|   Donald E. Scott (D) | 40,621 | 21.1 |
| 8 Thomas N. Kindness (R) | 155,200 | 76.9 |
|   John T. Francis (D) | 46,673 | 23.1 |
| 9 Marcy Kaptur (D) | 117,985 | 54.9 |
|   Frank Venner (R) | 93,210 | 43.4 |
| 10 Clarence E. Miller (R) | 149,337 | 73.0 |
|   John M. Buchanan (D) | 55,172 | 27.0 |
| 11 Dennis E. Eckart (D) | 133,096 | 66.8 |
|   Dean Beagle (R) | 66,278 | 33.2 |
| 12 John R. Kasich (R) | 148,899 | 69.5 |
|   Richard Sloan (D) | 65,215 | 30.5 |
| 13 Don J. Pease (D) | 131,923 | 66.4 |
|   William G. Schaffner (R) | 59,610 | 30.0 |
| 14 John F. Seiberling (D) | 155,729 | 71.4 |
|   Jean E. Bender (R) | 62,366 | 28.6 |
| 15 Chalmers P. Wylie (R) | 148,311 | 71.6 |
|   Duane Jager (D) | 58,870 | 28.4 |

| | Candidates | Votes | % |
|---|---|---|---|
| 16 | Ralph Regula (R) | 152,399 | 72.4 |
| | James Gwin (D) | 58,048 | 27.6 |
| 17 | James A. Traficant Jr. (D) | 123,014 | 53.3 |
| | Lyle Williams (R) | 105,449 | 45.7 |
| 18 | Douglas Applegate (D) | 155,759 | 75.9 |
| | Kenneth P. Burt Jr. (R) | 49,356 | 24.1 |
| 19 | Edward F. Feighan (D) | 139,605 | 55.2 |
| | Matthew J. Hatchadorian (R) | 107,957 | 42.7 |
| 20 | Mary Rose Oakar (D) | 167,115 | 100.0 |
| 21 | Louis Stokes (D) | 165,247 | 82.4 |
| | Robert L. Woodall (R) | 29,500 | 14.7 |

## OKLAHOMA

| | Candidates | Votes | % |
|---|---|---|---|
| 1 | James R. Jones (D) | 113,919 | 52.2 |
| | Frank Keating (R) | 103,098 | 47.3 |
| 2 | Mike Synar (D) | 148,124 | 74.1 |
| | Gary K. Rice (R) | 51,889 | 25.9 |
| 3 | Wes Watkins (D) | 137,964 | 77.8 |
| | Patrick K. Miller (R) | 39,454 | 22.2 |
| 4 | Dave McCurdy (D) | 109,447 | 63.6 |
| | Jerry Smith (R) | 60,844 | 35.4 |
| 5 | Mickey Edwards (R) | 135,167 | 75.6 |
| | Allen Greeson (D) | 39,089 | 21.9 |
| 6 | Glenn English (D) | 96,994 | 58.9 |
| | Craig Dodd (R) | 67,601 | 41.1 |

## OREGON

| | Candidates | Votes | % |
|---|---|---|---|
| 1 | Les AuCoin (D) | 138,393 | 53.1 |
| | Bill Moshofsky (R) | 122,247 | 46.9 |
| 2 | Robert F. Smith (R) | 132,649 | 57.0 |
| | Larryann C. Willis (D) | 100,152 | 43.0 |
| 3 | Ron Wyden (D) | 173,438 | 72.3 |
| | Drew Davis (R) | 66,394 | 27.7 |
| 4 | James Weaver (D) | 134,190 | 58.2 |
| | Bruce Long (R) | 96,487 | 41.8 |
| | Ruth McFarland (D) | 108,919 | 45.5 |
| 5 | Denny Smith (R) | 130,424 | 54.5 |

## PENNSYLVANIA

| | Candidates | Votes | % |
|---|---|---|---|
| 1 | Thomas M. Foglietta (D) | 148,123 | 74.9 |
| | Carmine DiBiase (R) | 49,559 | 25.1 |
| 2 | William H. Gray III (D) | 200,484 | 91.0 |
| | Ronald J. Sharper (R) | 18,224 | 8.3 |
| 3 | Robert A. Borski (D) | 152,598 | 63.9 |
| | Flora L. Becker (R) | 85,358 | 35.7 |
| 4 | Joe Kolter (D) | 114,040 | 56.8 |
| | James Kunder (R) | 86,769 | 43.2 |
| 5 | Richard T. Schulze (R) | 141,965 | 72.6 |
| | Louis J. Fanti (D) | 53,586 | 27.4 |
| 6 | Gus Yatron (D) | 181,165 | 100.0 |
| 7 | Bob Edgar (D) | 124,458 | 50.1 |
| | Curt Weldon (R) | 124,046 | 49.9 |
| 8 | Peter H. Kostmayer (D) | 112,648 | 50.9 |
| | David A. Christian (R) | 108,696 | 49.1 |
| 9 | Bud Shuster (R) | 118,437 | 66.5 |
| | Nancy Kulp (D) | 59,549 | 33.5 |
| 10 | Joseph M. McDade (R) | 150,166 | 77.1 |
| | Gene Basalyga (D) | 44,571 | 22.9 |
| 11 | Paul E. Kanjorski (D) | 108,430 | 58.6 |
| | Robert P. Hudock (R) | 76,692 | 41.4 |
| 12 | John P. Murtha (D) | 134,384 | 69.1 |
| | Thomas J. Fullard III (R) | 57,466 | 29.5 |
| 13 | Lawrence Coughlin (R) | 133,948 | 56.1 |
| | Joseph M. Hoeffel (D) | 104,756 | 43.9 |
| 14 | William J. Coyne (D) | 163,818 | 76.6 |
| | John Robert Clark (R) | 42,616 | 19.9 |
| 15 | Don Ritter (R) | 110,338 | 58.1 |
| | Jane Wells-Schooley (D) | 79,490 | 41.9 |
| 16 | Robert S. Walker (R) | 138,477 | 77.8 |
| | Martin L. Bard (D) | 39,515 | 22.2 |
| 17 | George W. Gekas (R) | 129,716 | 80.3 |
| | Stephen A. Anderson (D) | 31,770 | 19.7 |
| 18 | Doug Walgren (D) | 149,628 | 62.7 |
| | John G. Maxwell (R) | 87,521 | 36.7 |
| 19 | Bill Goodling (R) | 141,196 | 75.6 |
| | F. John Rarig (D) | 44,117 | 23.6 |
| 20 | Joseph M. Gaydos (D) | 158,751 | 76.0 |
| | Daniel Lloyd (R) | 50,247 | 24.0 |

| | Candidates | Votes | % |
|---|---|---|---|
| 21 | Tom Ridge (R) | 125,730 | 65.4 |
| | James A. Young (D) | 65,594 | 34.1 |
| 22 | Austin J. Murphy (D) | 153,514 | 79.0 |
| | Nancy S. Pryor (R) | 39,752 | 20.0 |
| 23 | William F. Clinger Jr. (R) | 94,952 | 51.6 |
| | Bill Wachob (D) | 88,957 | 48.4 |

## RHODE ISLAND

| | Candidates | Votes | % |
|---|---|---|---|
| 1 | Fernand J. St Germain (D) | 130,584 | 68.5 |
| | Alfred Rego Jr. (R) | 60,026 | 31.5 |
| 2 | Claudine Schneider (R) | 135,161 | 67.7 |
| | Richard Sinapi (D) | 64,341 | 32.3 |

## SOUTH CAROLINA

| | Candidates | Votes | % |
|---|---|---|---|
| 1 | Thomas F. Hartnett (R) | 103,288 | 61.7 |
| | Ed Pendarvis (D) | 64,022 | 38.3 |
| 2 | Floyd Spence (R) | 108,085 | 62.1 |
| | Ken Mosely (D) | 63,932 | 36.7 |
| 3 | Butler Derrick (D) | 88,917 | 58.4 |
| | Clarence E. Taylor (R) | 61,739 | 40.6 |
| 4 | Carroll A. Campbell Jr. (R) | 105,139 | 63.9 |
| | Jeff Smith (D) | 57,854 | 35.2 |
| 5 | John M. Spratt Jr. (D) | 98,513 | 96.3 |
| 6 | Robin Tallon (D) | 97,329 | 59.9 |
| | Lois Eargle (R) | 63,005 | 38.8 |

## SOUTH DAKOTA

| | Candidates | Votes | % |
|---|---|---|---|
| AL | Thomas A. Daschle (D) | 181,401 | 57.4 |
| | Dale Bell (R) | 134,821 | 42.6 |

## TENNESSEE

| | Candidates | Votes | % |
|---|---|---|---|
| 1 | James H. Quillen (R) | 113,407 | 100.0 |
| 2 | John J. Duncan (R) | 132,604 | 77.3 |
| | John F. Bowen (D) | 38,846 | 22.7 |
| 3 | Marilyn Lloyd (D) | 99,465 | 52.4 |
| | John Davis (R) | 90,216 | 47.6 |
| 4 | Jim Cooper (D) | 93,848 | 75.2 |
| | James Beau Seigneur (R) | 31,011 | 24.8 |
| 5 | Bill Boner (D) | 138,233 | 100.0 |
| 6 | Bart Gordon (D) | 103,989 | 62.8 |
| | Joe Simpkins (R) | 61,559 | 37.2 |
| 7 | Don Sundquist (R) | 107,257 | 100.0 |
| 8 | Ed Jones (D) | 118,653 | 100.0 |
| 9 | Harold E. Ford (D) | 133,428 | 71.5 |
| | William B. Thompson Jr. (R) | 53,064 | 28.5 |

## TEXAS

| | Candidates | Votes | % |
|---|---|---|---|
| 1 | Sam B. Hall Jr. (D) | 139,829 | 100.0 |
| 2 | Charles Wilson (D) | 113,225 | 59.3 |
| | Louis Dugas Jr. (R) | 77,842 | 40.7 |
| 3 | Steve Bartlett (R) | 228,819 | 83.0 |
| | Jim Westbrook (D) | 46,890 | 17.0 |
| 4 | Ralph M. Hall (D) | 120,749 | 58.0 |
| | Thomas Blow (R) | 87,553 | 42.0 |
| 5 | John Bryant (D) | 94,391 | 100.0 |
| 6 | Joe L. Barton (R) | 131,482 | 56.6 |
| | Dan Kubiak (D) | 100,799 | 43.4 |
| 7 | Bill Archer (R) | 213,480 | 86.7 |
| | Billy Willibey (D) | 32,835 | 13.3 |
| 8 | Jack Fields (R) | 113,031 | 64.6 |
| | Don Buford (D) | 62,072 | 35.4 |
| 9 | Jack Brooks (D) | 120,559 | 58.9 |
| | Jim Mahan (R) | 84,306 | 41.2 |
| 10 | J. J. Pickle (D) | 186,447 | 99.8 |
| 11 | Marvin Leath (D) | 112,940 | 100.0 |
| 12 | Jim Wright (D) | 106,299 | 100.0 |
| 13 | Beau Boulter (R) | 107,600 | 53.0 |
| | Jack Hightower (D) | 95,367 | 47.0 |
| 14 | Mac Sweeney (R) | 104,181 | 51.3 |
| | Bill Patman (D) | 98,885 | 48.7 |
| 15 | E. (Kika) de la Garza (D) | 104,863 | 100.0 |
| 16 | Ronald D. Coleman (D) | 76,375 | 57.4 |
| | Jack Hammond (R) | 56,589 | 42.6 |

| | Candidates | Votes | % |
|---|---|---|---|
| 17 | Charles W. Stenholm (D) | 143,012 | 100.0 |
| 18 | Mickey Leland (D) | 109,626 | 78.8 |
| | Glen E. Beaman (R) | 26,400 | 19.0 |
| 19 | Larry Combest (R) | 102,805 | 58.1 |
| | Don R. Richards (D) | 74,044 | 41.9 |
| 20 | Henry B. Gonzalez (D) | 100,443 | 100.0 |
| 21 | Tom Loeffler (R) | 199,909 | 80.6 |
| | Joe Sullivan (D) | 48,039 | 19.4 |
| 22 | Thomas D. DeLay (R) | 125,225 | 65.3 |
| | Doug Williams (D) | 66,495 | 34.7 |
| 23 | Albert G. Bustamante (D) | 95,721 | 100.0 |
| 24 | Martin Frost (D) | 105,210 | 59.5 |
| | Bob Burk (R) | 71,703 | 40.5 |
| 25 | Michael A. Andrews (D) | 113,946 | 64.0 |
| | Jerry Patterson (R) | 63,974 | 36.0 |
| 26 | Dick Armey (R) | 126,641 | 51.3 |
| | Tom Vandergriff (D) | 120,451 | 48.7 |
| 27 | Solomon P. Ortiz (D) | 105,516 | 63.6 |
| | Richard Moore (R) | 60,283 | 36.4 |

## UTAH

| | Candidates | Votes | % |
|---|---|---|---|
| 1 | James V. Hansen (R) | 142,952 | 71.2 |
| | Milton C. Abrams (D) | 56,619 | 28.2 |
| 2 | David S. Monson (R) | 105,540 | 49.4 |
| | Frances Farley (D) | 105,044 | 49.1 |
| 3 | Howard C. Nielson (R) | 138,918 | 74.5 |
| | Bruce R. Baird (D) | 46,560 | 25.0 |

## VERMONT

| | Candidates | Votes | % |
|---|---|---|---|
| AL | James M. Jeffords (R) | 148,025 | 65.4 |
| | Anthony Pollina (D) | 60,360 | 26.7 |

## VIRGINIA

| | Candidates | Votes | % |
|---|---|---|---|
| 1 | Herbert H. Bateman (R) | 118,085 | 59.1 |
| | John McGlennon (D) | 79,577 | 39.8 |
| 2 | G. William Whitehurst (R) | 136,632 | 99.8 |
| 3 | Thomas J. Bliley Jr. (R) | 169,987 | 85.6 |
| | Roger L. Coffey (I) | 28,556 | 14.4 |
| 4 | Norman Sisisky (D) | 120,093 | 99.9 |
| 5 | Dan Daniel (D) | 117,738 | 100.0 |
| 6 | James R. Olin (D) | 105,207 | 53.5 |
| | Ray Garland (R) | 91,344 | 46.5 |
| 7 | D. French Slaughter Jr. (R) | 109,110 | 56.5 |
| | Lewis M. Costello (D) | 77,624 | 40.2 |
| 8 | Stan Parris (R) | 125,015 | 55.8 |
| | Richard L. Saslaw (D) | 97,250 | 43.4 |
| 9 | Frederick C. Boucher (D) | 102,446 | 52.0 |
| | Jefferson Stafford (R) | 94,510 | 48.0 |
| 10 | Frank R. Wolf (R) | 158,528 | 62.5 |
| | John P. Flannery II (D) | 95,074 | 37.5 |

## WASHINGTON

| | Candidates | Votes | % |
|---|---|---|---|
| 1 | John R. Miller (R) | 147,926 | 56.3 |
| | Brock Evans (D) | 115,001 | 43.7 |
| 2 | Al Swift (D) | 142,065 | 58.6 |
| | Jim Klauder (R) | 93,472 | 38.6 |
| 3 | Don Bonker (D) | 150,432 | 71.1 |
| | Herb Elder (R) | 61,219 | 28.9 |
| 4 | Sid Morrison (R) | 150,322 | 76.1 |
| | Mark Epperson (D) | 47,158 | 23.9 |
| 5 | Thomas S. Foley (D) | 154,988 | 69.7 |
| | Jack Hebner (R) | 67,438 | 30.3 |
| 6 | Norman D. Dicks (D) | 124,367 | 66.1 |
| | Mike Lonergan (R) | 60,721 | 32.3 |
| 7 | Mike Lowry (D) | 174,560 | 70.4 |
| | Robert O. Dorse (R) | 71,576 | 28.9 |
| 8 | Rod Chandler (R) | 146,891 | 62.4 |
| | Bob Lamson (D) | 88,379 | 37.6 |

## WEST VIRGINIA

| | Candidates | Votes | % |
|---|---|---|---|
| 1 | Alan B. Mollohan (D) | 104,639 | 54.4 |
| | James Altmeyer (R) | 87,622 | 45.6 |
| 2 | Harley O. Staggers Jr. (D) | 100,345 | 56.0 |
| | Cleve Benedict (R) | 78,936 | 44.0 |

| Candidates | Votes | % | | Candidates | Votes | % | | Candidates | Votes | % |
|---|---|---|---|---|---|---|---|---|---|---|
| 3 Bob Wise (D) | 125,306 | *67.9* | 3 | Steve Gunderson (R) | 160,437 | *68.4* | 9 | F. James Sensenbrenner Jr. (R) | 180,247 | *73.4* |
| Margaret Miller (R) | 59,128 | *32.1* | | Charles F. Dahl (D) | 74,253 | *31.6* | | John Krause (D) | 64,157 | *26.1* |
| 4 Nick J. Rahall II (D) | 98,919 | *66.7* | 4 | Gerald D. Kleczka (D) | 158,722 | *66.6* | | **Special Election** | | |
| Jess T. Shumate (R) | 49,474 | *33.3* | | Robert V. Nolan (R) | 78,056 | *32.8* | | | | |
| **WISCONSIN** | | | 5 | Jim Moody (D) | 175,243 | *98.0* | 4 | Gerald D. Kleczka (D) | 76,384 | *65.0* |
| | | | 6 | Thomas E. Petri (R) | 170,271 | *75.8* | | Robert V. Nolan (R) | 41,007 | *34.9* |
| 1 Les Aspin (D) | 127,184 | *56.2* | | David L. Iaquinta (D) | 54,266 | *24.2* | | **WYOMING** | | |
| Pete Jansson (R) | 99,080 | *43.8* | 7 | David R. Obey (D) | 146,131 | *61.2* | | | | |
| 2 Robert W. Kastenmeier (D) | 159,987 | *63.6* | | Mark G. Michaelsen (R) | 92,507 | *38.8* | AL | Dick Cheney (R) | 138,234 | *73.6* |
| Albert E. Wiley Jr. (R) | 91,345 | *36.3* | 8 | Toby Roth (R) | 161,005 | *67.9* | | Hugh B. McFadden Jr. (D) | 45,857 | *24.4* |
| | | | | Paul Willems (D) | 73,090 | *30.8* | | | | |

**1984 Elections**

1. *Contested election. A recount by a House Administration Committee task force determined that McCloskey defeated McIntyre by a four-vote margin, 116,645 (50.00085 percent) to 116,641 (49.99914 percent). On May 1, 1985, the House voted 236-190 to seat McCloskey.*

2. *A special election was held in conjunction with the November election. Perkins was elected to fill both the unexpired term of his father, Rep. Carl D. Perkins, D, who died Aug. 3, 1984, and the two-year term beginning Jan. 3, 1985.*

3. *For the 1984 House elections in Louisiana, an open primary election was held with candidates from all parties running on the same ballot. Any candidate who received a majority*

*was elected unopposed, with no further appearance on the general election ballot. If no candidate received 50 percent, a runoff was held between the two top finishers.*

4. *In Minnesota the Democratic Party is known as the Democratic-Farmer-Labor Party and the Republican Party as the Independent-Republican Party; candidates appear on the ballot with these designations.*

5. *A special election was held in conjunction with the November election. Saxton was elected to serve both the unexpired term of Rep. Edwin B. Forsythe, R, who died March 29, 1984, and the two-year term beginning Jan. 3, 1985.*

# 1985 House Elections

## LOUISIANA

### Special Election [1]

| Candidates | Votes | % |
|---|---|---|
| 8 Cathy (Mrs. Gillis) Long (D) | 61,791 | *55.7* |
| John E. (Jock) Scott (D) | 27,138 | *24.5* |
| Clyde C. Holloway (R) | 18,013 | *16.3* |

## TEXAS

### Special Election [2]

| Candidates | Votes | % |
|---|---|---|
| 1 Edd Hargett (R) | 29,720 | *42.0* |
| Jim Chapman (D) | 21,382 | *30.2* |
| Sam Russell (D) | 13,090 | *18.5* |

### Special Runoff Election

| | Votes | % |
|---|---|---|
| 1 Jim Chapman (D) | 52,665 | *50.9* |
| Edd Hargett (R) | 50,741 | *49.1* |

**1985 Elections**

1. *Long was elected to serve the unexpired term of her husband, Rep. Gillis W. Long, D, who died Jan. 20, 1985.*

2. *A special election was held to fill the unexpired term of Rep. Sam B. Hall Jr., D, who resigned May 27, 1985, to accept a federal judgeship.*

1303

# 1986 House Elections

## ALABAMA

| | Candidates | Votes | % |
|---|---|---|---|
| 1 | Sonny Callahan (R) | 96,469 | 100.0 |
| 2 | William L. Dickinson (R) | 115,302 | 66.7 |
| | Mercer Stone (D) | 57,568 | 33.3 |
| 3 | Bill Nichols (D) | 115,127 | 80.6 |
| | Whit Guerin (R) | 27,769 | 19.4 |
| 4 | Tom Bevill (D) | 132,881 | 77.5 |
| | Al DeShazo (R) | 38,588 | 22.5 |
| 5 | Ronnie G. Flippo (D) | 125,406 | 78.9 |
| | Herb McCarley (R) | 33,528 | 21.1 |
| 6 | Ben Erdreich (D) | 139,608 | 72.7 |
| | L. Morgan Williams (R) | 51,924 | 27.1 |
| 7 | Claude Harris (D) | 108,126 | 59.8 |
| | Bill McFarland (R) | 72,777 | 40.2 |

## ALASKA

| | Candidates | Votes | % |
|---|---|---|---|
| AL | Don Young (R) | 101,799 | 56.5 |
| | Pegge Begich (D) | 74,053 | 41.1 |

## ARIZONA

| | Candidates | Votes | % |
|---|---|---|---|
| 1 | John J. Rhodes III (R) | 127,370 | 71.3 |
| | Harry Braun III (D) | 51,163 | 28.7 |
| 2 | Morris K. Udall (D) | 77,239 | 73.3 |
| | Sheldon Clark (R) | 24,522 | 23.3 |
| 3 | Bob Stump (R) | 146,462 | 100.0 |
| 4 | Jon Kyl (R) | 121,939 | 43.6 |
| | Philip R. Davis (D) | 66,894 | 35.4 |
| 5 | Jim Kolbe (R) | 119,647 | 64.9 |
| | Joel Ireland (D) | 64,848 | 35.1 |

## ARKANSAS

| | Candidates | Votes | % |
|---|---|---|---|
| 1 | Bill Alexander (D) | 105,773 | 64.2 |
| | Rick H. Albin (R) | 58,937 | 35.8 |
| 2 | Tommy F. Robinson (D) | 128,814 | 75.7 |
| | Keith Hamaker (R) | 41,244 | 24.2 |
| 3 | John Hammerschmidt (R) | 145,113 | 79.8 |
| | Su Sargent (D) | 36,726 | 20.2 |
| 4 | Beryl Anthony Jr. (D) | 115,335 | 77.5 |
| | Lamar Keels (R) | 22,980 | 15.4 |
| | Stephen A. Bitely (I) | 10,604 | 7.1 |

## CALIFORNIA

| | Candidates | Votes | % |
|---|---|---|---|
| 1 | Douglas H. Bosco (D) | 138,174 | 67.5 |
| | Floyd G. Sampson (R) | 54,436 | 26.6 |
| | Elden McFarland (PFP) | 12,149 | 5.9 |
| 2 | Wally Herger (R) | 109,758 | 58.3 |
| | Stephen C. Swendiman (D) | 74,602 | 39.6 |
| 3 | Robert T. Matsui (D) | 158,709 | 75.9 |
| | Lowell P. Landowski (R) | 50,265 | 24.1 |
| 4 | Vic Fazio (D) | 128,364 | 70.2 |
| | Jack D. Hite (R) | 54,596 | 29.8 |
| 5 | Sala Burton (D) | 122,688 | 75.1 |
| | Mike Garza (R) | 36,039 | 22.1 |
| 6 | Barbara Boxer (D) | 142,946 | 73.9 |
| | Franklin H. Ernst III (R) | 50,606 | 26.1 |
| 7 | George Miller (D) | 124,174 | 66.6 |
| | Rosemary Thakar (R) | 62,379 | 33.4 |
| 8 | Ronald V. Dellums (D) | 121,790 | 60.0 |
| | Steven Eigenberg (R) | 76,850 | 37.9 |
| 9 | Fortney H. Stark (D) | 113,490 | 69.7 |
| | David M. Williams (R) | 49,300 | 30.3 |
| 10 | Don Edwards (D) | 84,240 | 70.5 |
| | Michael R. La Crone (R) | 31,826 | 26.6 |
| 11 | Tom Lantos (D) | 112,380 | 74.1 |
| | G. M. ''Bill'' Quraishi (R) | 39,315 | 25.9 |
| 12 | Ernest L. Konnyu (R) | 111,252 | 59.5 |
| | Lance T. Weil (D) | 69,564 | 37.2 |

| | Candidates | Votes | % |
|---|---|---|---|
| 13 | Norman Y. Mineta (D) | 107,696 | 69.7 |
| | Bob Nash (R) | 46,754 | 30.3 |
| 14 | Norman D. Shumway (R) | 146,906 | 71.6 |
| | Bill Steele (D) | 53,597 | 26.1 |
| 15 | Tony Coelho (D) | 93,600 | 71.0 |
| | Carol Harner (R) | 35,793 | 27.2 |
| 16 | Leon E. Panetta (D) | 128,151 | 78.4 |
| | Louis Darrigo (R) | 31,386 | 19.2 |
| 17 | Charles Pashayan Jr. (R) | 88,787 | 60.2 |
| | John Hartnett (D) | 58,682 | 39.8 |
| 18 | Richard H. Lehman (D) | 101,480 | 71.3 |
| | David C. Crevelt (R) | 40,907 | 28.7 |
| 19 | Robert J. Lagomarsino (R) | 122,578 | 71.9 |
| | Wayne B. Norris (D) | 45,619 | 26.7 |
| 20 | William M. Thomas (R) | 129,989 | 72.6 |
| | Jules H. Moquin (D) | 49,027 | 27.4 |
| 21 | Elton Gallegly (R) | 132,090 | 68.4 |
| | Gilbert R. Saldana (D) | 54,497 | 28.2 |
| 22 | Carlos J. Moorhead (R) | 141,096 | 73.8 |
| | John G. Simmons (D) | 44,036 | 23.1 |
| 23 | Anthony C. Beilenson (D) | 121,468 | 65.7 |
| | George Woolverton (R) | 58,746 | 31.8 |
| 24 | Henry A. Waxman (D) | 103,914 | 87.9 |
| | George Abrahams (LIBERT) | 8,871 | 7.5 |
| 25 | Edward R. Roybal (D) | 62,692 | 76.1 |
| | Gregory L. Hardy (R) | 17,558 | 21.3 |
| 26 | Howard L. Berman (D) | 98,091 | 65.1 |
| | Robert M. Kerns (R) | 52,662 | 34.9 |
| 27 | Mel Levine (D) | 110,403 | 63.7 |
| | Robert B. Scribner (R) | 59,410 | 34.3 |
| 28 | Julian C. Dixon (D) | 92,635 | 76.4 |
| | George Z. Adams (R) | 25,858 | 21.3 |
| 29 | Augustus F. Hawkins (D) | 78,132 | 84.6 |
| | John Van de Brooke (R) | 13,432 | 14.5 |
| 30 | Matthew G. Martinez (D) | 59,369 | 62.5 |
| | John W. Almquist (R) | 33,705 | 35.5 |
| 31 | Mervyn M. Dymally (D) | 77,126 | 70.3 |
| | Jack McMurray (R) | 30,322 | 27.6 |
| 32 | Glenn M. Anderson (D) | 90,739 | 68.5 |
| | Joyce M. Robertson (R) | 39,003 | 29.4 |
| 33 | David Dreier (R) | 118,541 | 71.7 |
| | Monty Hempel (D) | 44,312 | 26.8 |
| 34 | Esteban E. Torres (D) | 66,404 | 60.3 |
| | Charles M. House (R) | 43,659 | 39.7 |
| 35 | Jerry Lewis (R) | 127,235 | 76.9 |
| | R. ''Sarge'' Hall (D) | 33,322 | 23.1 |
| 36 | George E. Brown Jr. (D) | 78,118 | 57.1 |
| | Bob Henley (R) | 58,660 | 42.9 |
| 37 | Al McCandless (R) | 122,416 | 63.7 |
| | David E. Skinner (D) | 69,808 | 36.3 |
| 38 | Bob Dornan (R) | 66,032 | 55.3 |
| | Richard Robinson (D) | 50,625 | 42.4 |
| 39 | William E. Dannemeyer (R) | 137,603 | 74.5 |
| | David D. Vest (D) | 42,377 | 24.0 |
| 40 | Robert E. Badham (R) | 119,829 | 59.8 |
| | Bruce W. Sumner (D) | 75,664 | 37.7 |
| 41 | Bill Lowery (R) | 133,566 | 67.8 |
| | Dan Kripke (D) | 59,816 | 30.4 |
| 42 | Dan Lungren (R) | 140,364 | 72.8 |
| | Michael P. Blackburn (D) | 47,586 | 24.7 |
| 43 | Ron Packard (R) | 137,341 | 73.1 |
| | Joseph Chirra (D) | 45,078 | 24.0 |
| 44 | Jim Bates (D) | 70,557 | 64.3 |
| | Bill Mitchell (R) | 36,359 | 33.1 |
| 45 | Duncan Hunter (R) | 118,900 | 76.9 |
| | Hewitt Fitts Ryan (D) | 32,800 | 21.2 |

## COLORADO

| | Candidates | Votes | % |
|---|---|---|---|
| 1 | Patricia Schroeder (D) | 106,113 | 68.4 |
| | Joy Wood (R) | 49,095 | 31.6 |
| 2 | David E. Skaggs (D) | 91,223 | 51.5 |
| | Michael J. Norton (R) | 86,032 | 48.5 |
| 3 | Ben Nighthorse Campbell (D) | 95,353 | 51.9 |

| | Candidates | Votes | % |
|---|---|---|---|
| | Mike Strang (R) | 88,508 | 48.1 |
| 4 | Hank Brown (R) | 117,089 | 69.8 |
| | David Sprague (D) | 50,672 | 30.2 |
| 5 | Joel Hefley (R) | 121,153 | 69.8 |
| | Bill Story (D) | 52,488 | 30.2 |
| 6 | Dan Schaefer (R) | 104,359 | 65.0 |
| | Chuck Norris (D) | 53,834 | 33.5 |

## CONNECTICUT

| | Candidates | Votes | % |
|---|---|---|---|
| 1 | Barbara B. Kennelly (D) | 128,930 | 74.2 |
| | Herschel A. Klein (R) | 44,122 | 25.4 |
| 2 | Sam Gejdenson (D) | 109,229 | 67.4 |
| | Francis M. ''Bud'' Mullen (R) | 52,869 | 32.6 |
| 3 | Bruce A. Morrison (D) | 114,276 | 69.6 |
| | Ernest J. Diette Jr. (R) | 49,806 | 30.4 |
| 4 | Stewart B. McKinney (R) | 77,212 | 53.5 |
| | Christine M. Niedermeier (D) | 66,999 | 46.5 |
| 5 | John G. Rowland (R) | 98,664 | 60.9 |
| | Jim Cohen (D) | 63,371 | 39.1 |
| 6 | Nancy L. Johnson (R) | 111,304 | 64.2 |
| | Paul S. Amenta (D) | 62,133 | 35.8 |

## DELAWARE

| | Candidates | Votes | % |
|---|---|---|---|
| AL | Thomas R. Carper (D) | 106,351 | 66.2 |
| | Thomas Stephen Neuberger (R) | 53,767 | 33.4 |

## FLORIDA

| | Candidates | Votes | % |
|---|---|---|---|
| 1 | Earl Hutto (D) | 97,465 | 63. |
| | Greg Neubeck (R) | 55,415 | 36. |
| 2 | Bill Grant (D) | 110,120 | 99. |
| 3 | Charles E. Bennett (D) | | 100. |
| 4 | Bill Chappell Jr. (D) | | 100. |
| 5 | Bill McCollum (R) | | 100. |
| 6 | Buddy MacKay (D) | 143,583 | 70. |
| | Larry Gallagher (R) | 61,053 | 29. |
| 7 | Sam Gibbons (D) | | 100. |
| 8 | C. W. Bill Young (R) | | 100. |
| 9 | Michael Bilirakis (R) | 166,504 | 70. |
| | Gabe Cazares (D) | 68,574 | 29. |
| 10 | Andy Ireland (R) | 122,368 | 71. |
| | David B. Higginbottom (D) | 49,559 | 28. |
| 11 | Bill Nelson (D) | 149,036 | 72. |
| | Scott Ellis (R) | 55,904 | 27. |
| 12 | Tom Lewis (R) | 150,222 | 99. |
| 13 | Connie Mack (R) | 187,794 | 75. |
| | Addison S. Gilbert III (D) | 62,694 | 25. |
| 14 | Daniel A. Mica (D) | 171,961 | 73 |
| | Rick Martin (R) | 61,185 | 26 |
| 15 | E. Clay Shaw Jr. (R) | | 100 |
| 16 | Lawrence J. Smith (D) | 121,213 | 69 |
| | Mary Collins (R) | 52,807 | 30 |
| 17 | William Lehman (D) | | 100 |
| 18 | Claude Pepper (D) | 80,047 | 73 |
| | Tom Brodie (R) | 28,803 | 26 |
| 19 | Dante B. Fascell (D) | 99,203 | 69 |
| | Bill Flanagan (R) | 44,455 | 30 |

## GEORGIA

| | Candidates | Votes | % |
|---|---|---|---|
| 1 | Lindsay Thomas (D) | 69,440 | 100 |
| 2 | Charles Hatcher (D) | 72,482 | 100 |
| 3 | Richard Ray (D) | 75,850 | 99 |
| 4 | Pat Swindall (R) | 86,366 | 53 |
| | Ben Jones (D) | 75,892 | 46 |
| 5 | John Lewis (D) | 93,229 | 75 |
| | Portia A. Scott (R) | 30,562 | 24 |
| 6 | Newt Gingrich (R) | 75,583 | 59 |
| | Crandle Bray (D) | 51,352 | 40 |
| 7 | George ''Buddy'' Darden (D) | 88,636 | 60 |

| Candidates | Votes | % |
|---|---|---|
| Joe Morecraft (R) | 44,891 | 33.6 |
| 8 J. Roy Rowland (D) | 82,254 | 86.4 |
| Eddie McDowell (R) | 12,952 | 13.6 |
| 9 Ed Jenkins (D) | 84,303 | 100.0 |
| 10 Doug Barnard Jr. (D) | 79,548 | 67.3 |
| Jim Hill (R) | 38,714 | 32.7 |

### HAWAII

| | Votes | % |
|---|---|---|
| 1 Patricia Saiki (R) | 99,683 | 59.2 |
| Mufi Hannemann (D) | 63,061 | 37.5 |
| 2 Daniel K. Akaka (D) | 123,830 | 76.1 |
| Maria M. Hustace (R) | 35,371 | 21.7 |

#### Special Election [1]

| | Votes | % |
|---|---|---|
| 1 Neil Abercrombie (D) | 42,031 | 29.9 |
| Patricia Saiki (R) | 41,067 | 29.2 |
| Mufi Hannemann (D) | 39,800 | 28.3 |
| Steve Cobb (D) | 16,721 | 11.9 |

### IDAHO

| | Votes | % |
|---|---|---|
| 1 Larry E. Craig (R) | 120,553 | 65.1 |
| Bill Currie (D) | 59,723 | 32.3 |
| 2 Richard H. Stallings (D) | 103,035 | 54.4 |
| Mel Richardson (R) | 86,528 | 45.6 |

### ILLINOIS

| | Votes | % |
|---|---|---|
| 1 Charles A. Hayes (D) | 122,376 | 96.4 |
| 2 Gus Savage (D) | 99,268 | 83.8 |
| Ron Taylor (R) | 19,149 | 16.2 |
| 3 Marty Russo (D) | 102,964 | 66.2 |
| James J. Tierney (R) | 52,618 | 33.8 |
| 4 Jack Davis (R) | 61,633 | 51.6 |
| Shawn Collins (D) | 57,925 | 48.4 |
| 5 William O. Lipinski (D) | 82,466 | 70.4 |
| Daniel John Sobieski (R) | 34,738 | 29.6 |
| 6 Henry J. Hyde (R) | 98,196 | 75.4 |
| Robert H. Renshaw (D) | 32,064 | 24.6 |
| 7 Cardiss Collins (D) | 90,761 | 80.2 |
| Caroline K. Kallas (R) | 21,055 | 18.6 |
| 8 Dan Rostenkowski (D) | 82,873 | 78.7 |
| Thomas J. DeFazio (R) | 22,383 | 21.3 |
| 9 Sidney R. Yates (D) | 92,738 | 71.6 |
| Herbert Sohn (R) | 36,715 | 28.4 |
| 10 John Edward Porter (R) | 87,530 | 75.1 |
| Robert A. Cleland (D) | 28,990 | 24.9 |
| 11 Frank Annunzio (D) | 106,970 | 70.7 |
| George S. Gottlieb (R) | 44,341 | 29.3 |
| 12 Philip M. Crane (R) | 89,044 | 77.7 |
| John A. Leonardi (D) | 25,536 | 22.3 |
| 13 Harris W. Fawell (R) | 107,227 | 73.4 |
| Dominick J. Jeffrey (D) | 38,874 | 26.6 |
| 14 Dennis Hastert (R) | 77,288 | 52.4 |
| Mary Lou Kearns (D) | 70,293 | 47.6 |
| 15 Edward R. Madigan (R) | 115,284 | 100.0 |
| 16 Lynn Martin (R) | 92,982 | 66.9 |
| Kenneth F. Bohnsack (D) | 46,087 | 33.1 |
| 17 Lane Evans (D) | 85,442 | 55.6 |
| Sam McHard (R) | 68,101 | 44.4 |
| 18 Robert H. Michel (R) | 94,308 | 62.6 |
| Jim Dawson (D) | 56,331 | 37.4 |
| 19 Terry L. Bruce (D) | 111,105 | 66.4 |
| Al Salvi (R) | 56,186 | 33.6 |
| 20 Richard J. Durbin (D) | 126,556 | 68.1 |
| Kevin B. McCarthy (R) | 59,291 | 31.9 |
| 21 Melvin Price (D) | 65,722 | 50.4 |
| Robert H. Gaffner (R) | 64,779 | 49.6 |
| 22 Kenneth J. Gray (D) | 97,585 | 53.2 |
| Randy Patchett (R) | 85,733 | 46.8 |

### INDIANA

| | Votes | % |
|---|---|---|
| 1 Peter J. Visclosky (D) | 86,983 | 73.4 |
| William Costas (R) | 30,395 | 25.7 |
| 2 Philip R. Sharp (D) | 102,456 | 61.9 |
| Donald J. Lynch (R) | 62,013 | 37.4 |

| Candidates | Votes | % |
|---|---|---|
| 3 John Hiler (R) | 75,979 | 49.8 |
| Thomas W. Ward (D) | 75,932 | 49.8 |
| 4 Daniel R. Coats (R) | 99,865 | 69.6 |
| Gregory Alan Scher (D) | 43,105 | 30.0 |
| 5 Jim Jontz (D) | 80,772 | 51.4 |
| James R. Butcher (R) | 75,507 | 48.1 |
| 6 Dan Burton (R) | 118,363 | 68.3 |
| Thomas F. McKenna (D) | 53,431 | 30.9 |
| 7 John T. Myers (R) | 104,965 | 66.8 |
| L. Eugene Smith (D) | 49,675 | 31.6 |
| 8 Frank McCloskey (D) | 106,662 | 53.0 |
| Richard D. McIntyre (R) | 93,586 | 46.5 |
| 9 Lee H. Hamilton (D) | 120,586 | 71.9 |
| Robert Walter Kilroy (R) | 46,398 | 27.7 |
| 10 Andrew Jacobs Jr. (D) | 68,817 | 57.7 |
| Jim Eynon (R) | 49,064 | 41.2 |

### IOWA

| | Votes | % |
|---|---|---|
| 1 Jim Leach (R) | 86,834 | 66.4 |
| John R. Whitaker (D) | 43,985 | 33.6 |
| 2 Tom Tauke (R) | 88,708 | 61.3 |
| Eric Tabor (D) | 55,903 | 38.7 |
| 3 David R. Nagle (D) | 83,504 | 54.6 |
| John McIntee (R) | 69,386 | 45.4 |
| 4 Neal Smith (D) | 107,271 | 68.4 |
| Bob Lockard (R) | 49,641 | 31.6 |
| 5 Jim Ross Lightfoot (R) | 85,025 | 59.2 |
| Scott Hughes (D) | 58,552 | 40.8 |
| 6 Fred Grandy (R) | 81,861 | 50.9 |
| Clayton Hodgson (D) | 78,807 | 49.0 |

### KANSAS

| | Votes | % |
|---|---|---|
| 1 Pat Roberts (R) | 141,297 | 76.5 |
| Dale Lyon (D) | 43,359 | 23.5 |
| 2 Jim Slattery (D) | 110,737 | 70.6 |
| Phill Kline (R) | 46,029 | 29.4 |
| 3 Jan Meyers (R) | 109,266 | 100.0 |
| 4 Dan Glickman (D) | 111,164 | 64.5 |
| Bob Knight (R) | 61,178 | 35.5 |
| 5 Bob Whittaker (R) | 116,800 | 71.1 |
| Kym E. Myers (D) | 47,540 | 28.9 |

### KENTUCKY

| | Votes | % |
|---|---|---|
| 1 Carroll Hubbard Jr. (D) | 64,315 | 100.0 |
| 2 William H. Natcher (D) | 57,644 | 100.0 |
| 3 Romano L. Mazzoli (D) | 81,943 | 73.0 |
| Lee Holmes (R) | 29,348 | 26.2 |
| 4 Jim Bunning (R) | 67,626 | 55.1 |
| Terry L. Mann (D) | 53,906 | 43.9 |
| 5 Harold Rogers (R) | 56,760 | 100.0 |
| 6 Larry J. Hopkins (R) | 75,906 | 74.3 |
| Jerry W. Hammond (D) | 26,315 | 25.7 |
| 7 Carl C. Perkins (D) | 90,619 | 79.6 |
| James T. Polley (R) | 23,209 | 20.4 |

### LOUISIANA [2]

| | Votes | % |
|---|---|---|
| 1 Robert L. Livingston (R) | | 100.0 |
| 2 Lindy (Mrs. Hale) Boggs (D) | | 100.0 |
| 3 W. J. "Billy" Tauzin (D) | | 100.0 |
| 4 Buddy Roemer (D) | | 100.0 |
| 5 Jerry Huckaby (D) | | 100.0 |
| 6 Richard H. Baker (R) | | 100.0 |
| 7 Jimmy Hayes (D) | 109,205 | 57.0 |
| Margaret Lowenthal (D) | 82,293 | 43.0 |
| 8 Clyde C. Holloway (R) | 102,276 | 51.4 |
| Faye Williams (D) | 96,864 | 48.6 |

### MAINE

| | Votes | % |
|---|---|---|
| 1 Joseph E. Brennan (D) | 121,848 | 53.2 |
| H. Rollin Ives (R) | 100,260 | 43.7 |
| 2 Olympia J. Snowe (R) | 148,770 | 77.3 |
| Richard R. Charette (D) | 43,614 | 22.7 |

*Footnote, see p. 1308.*

### MARYLAND

| Candidates | Votes | % |
|---|---|---|
| 1 Roy Dyson (D) | 88,113 | 66.8 |
| Harlan C. Williams (R) | 43,764 | 33.2 |
| 2 Helen Delich Bentley (R) | 96,745 | 58.7 |
| Kathleen Kennedy Townsend (D) | 68,200 | 41.3 |
| 3 Benjamin L. Cardin (D) | 100,161 | 79.1 |
| Ross Z. Pierpont (R) | 26,452 | 20.9 |
| 4 Tom McMillen (D) | 65,075 | 50.2 |
| Robert R. Neall (R) | 64,651 | 49.8 |
| 5 Steny H. Hoyer (D) | 82,098 | 81.9 |
| John Eugene Sellner (R) | 18,102 | 18.1 |
| 6 Beverly B. Byron (D) | 102,975 | 72.2 |
| John Vandenberge (R) | 39,600 | 27.8 |
| 7 Kweisi Mfume (D) | 79,226 | 86.7 |
| Saint George I. B. Crosse III (R) | 12,170 | 13.3 |
| 8 Constance A. Morella (R) | 92,917 | 52.9 |
| Stewart Bainum Jr. (D) | 82,825 | 47.1 |

### MASSACHUSETTS

| | Votes | % |
|---|---|---|
| 1 Silvio O. Conte (R) | 113,653 | 77.8 |
| Robert S. Weiner (D) | 32,396 | 22.2 |
| 2 Edward P. Boland (D) | 91,033 | 65.9 |
| Brian P. Lees (R) | 47,022 | 34.1 |
| 3 Joseph D. Early (D) | 120,222 | 100.0 |
| 4 Barney Frank (D) | 134,387 | 88.8 |
| Thomas D. DeVisscher (AM) | 16,857 | 11.2 |
| 5 Chester G. Atkins (D) | 113,690 | 99.9 |
| 6 Nicholas Mavroules (D) | 131,051 | 99.9 |
| 7 Edward J. Markey (D) | 124,183 | 100.0 |
| 8 Joseph P. Kennedy II (D) | 104,651 | 72.0 |
| Clark C. Abt (R) | 40,259 | 27.7 |
| 9 Joe Moakley (D) | 110,026 | 83.8 |
| Robert W. Horan (I) | 21,292 | 16.2 |
| 10 Gerry E. Studds (D) | 121,578 | 65.1 |
| Ricardo M. Barros (R) | 49,451 | 26.5 |
| Alexander Byron (I) | 15,687 | 8.4 |
| 11 Brian J. Donnelly (D) | 114,926 | 100.0 |

### MICHIGAN

| | Votes | % |
|---|---|---|
| 1 John Conyers Jr. (D) | 94,307 | 89.2 |
| Bill Ashe (R) | 10,407 | 9.8 |
| 2 Carl D. Pursell (R) | 79,567 | 59.0 |
| Dean Baker (D) | 55,204 | 41.0 |
| 3 Howard Wolpe (D) | 78,720 | 60.4 |
| Jackie McGregor (R) | 51,678 | 39.6 |
| 4 Fred Upton (R) | 70,331 | 61.9 |
| Dan Roche (D) | 41,624 | 36.6 |
| 5 Paul B. Henry (R) | 100,577 | 71.2 |
| Teresa S. Decker (D) | 40,608 | 28.8 |
| 6 Bob Carr (D) | 74,927 | 56.7 |
| Jim Dunn (R) | 57,283 | 43.3 |
| 7 Dale E. Kildee (D) | 101,225 | 79.6 |
| Trudie Callihan (D) | 24,848 | 19.5 |
| 8 Bob Traxler (D) | 97,406 | 72.6 |
| John A. Levi (R) | 36,695 | 27.4 |
| 9 Guy Vander Jagt (R) | 89,991 | 64.4 |
| Richard J. Anderson (D) | 49,702 | 35.6 |
| 10 Bill Schuette (R) | 78,475 | 51.2 |
| Donald J. Albosta (D) | 74,941 | 48.8 |
| 11 Robert W. Davis (R) | 91,575 | 63.0 |
| Robert C. Anderson (D) | 53,180 | 36.6 |
| 12 David E. Bonior (D) | 87,643 | 66.4 |
| Candice S. Miller (R) | 44,442 | 33.6 |
| 13 George W. Crockett Jr. (D) | 76,435 | 85.2 |
| Mary Griffin (R) | 12,395 | 13.8 |
| 14 Dennis M. Hertel (D) | 92,328 | 72.9 |
| Stanley T. Grot (R) | 33,831 | 26.7 |
| 15 William D. Ford (D) | 77,950 | 75.2 |
| Glen Kassel (R) | 25,078 | 24.2 |
| 16 John D. Dingell (D) | 101,659 | 77.8 |
| Frank W. Grzywacki (R) | 28,971 | 22.2 |
| 17 Sander M. Levin (D) | 105,031 | 76.4 |
| Calvin Williams (R) | 30,879 | 22.5 |
| 18 William S. Broomfield (R) | 110,099 | 73.8 |
| Gary L. Kohut (D) | 39,144 | 26.2 |

## MINNESOTA [3]

| | Candidates | Votes | % |
|---|---|---|---|
| 1 | Timothy J. Penny (DFL) | 125,115 | 72.4 |
| | Paul H. Grawe (I-R) | 47,750 | 27.6 |
| 2 | Vin Weber (I-R) | 100,249 | 51.6 |
| | Dave Johnson (DFL) | 94,048 | 48.4 |
| 3 | Bill Frenzel (I-R) | 127,434 | 70.1 |
| | Ray Stock (DFL) | 54,261 | 29.9 |
| 4 | Bruce F. Vento (DFL) | 112,662 | 72.9 |
| | Harold Stassen (I-R) | 41,926 | 27.1 |
| 5 | Martin Olav Sabo (DFL) | 105,410 | 72.7 |
| | Rick Serra (I-R) | 37,583 | 25.9 |
| 6 | Gerry Sikorski (DFL) | 110,598 | 65.8 |
| | Barbara Zwach Sykora (I-R) | 57,460 | 34.2 |
| 7 | Arlan Stangeland (I-R) | 94,024 | 49.7 |
| | Collin C. Peterson (DFL) | 93,903 | 49.6 |
| 8 | James L. Oberstar (DFL) | 135,718 | 72.6 |
| | Dave Rued (I-R) | 51,315 | 27.4 |

## MISSISSIPPI

| | Candidates | Votes | % |
|---|---|---|---|
| 1 | Jamie L. Whitten (D) | 59,870 | 66.4 |
| | Larry Cobb (R) | 30,267 | 33.6 |
| 2 | Mike Espy (D) | 73,119 | 51.7 |
| | Webb Franklin (R) | 68,292 | 48.3 |
| 3 | G. V. "Sonny" Montgomery (D) | 80,575 | 100.0 |
| 4 | Wayne Dowdy (D) | 85,819 | 71.5 |
| | Gail Healy (R) | 34,190 | 28.5 |
| 5 | Trent Lott (R) | 75,288 | 82.3 |
| | Larry L. Albritton (D) | 16,143 | 17.7 |

## MISSOURI

| | Candidates | Votes | % |
|---|---|---|---|
| 1 | William L. Clay (D) | 91,044 | 66.1 |
| | Robert J. Wittmann (R) | 46,599 | 33.9 |
| 2 | Jack Buechner (R) | 101,010 | 51.9 |
| | Robert A. Young (D) | 93,538 | 48.1 |
| 3 | Richard A. Gephardt (D) | 116,403 | 69.0 |
| 4 | Ike Skelton (D) | 129,471 | 100.0 |
| 5 | Alan Wheat (D) | 101,030 | 70.9 |
| | Greg Fisher (R) | 39,340 | 27.6 |
| 6 | E. Thomas Coleman (R) | 95,865 | 56.7 |
| | Doug R. Hughes (D) | 73,155 | 43.3 |
| 7 | Gene Taylor (R) | 114,210 | 67.0 |
| | Ken Young (D) | 56,291 | 33.0 |
| 8 | Bill Emerson (R) | 79,142 | 52.5 |
| | Wayne Cryts (D) | 71,532 | 47.5 |
| 9 | Harold L. Volkmer (D) | 95,939 | 57.5 |
| | Ralph Uthlaut Jr. (R) | 70,972 | 42.5 |

## MONTANA

| | Candidates | Votes | % |
|---|---|---|---|
| 1 | Pat Williams (D) | 98,501 | 61.7 |
| | Don Allen (R) | 61,230 | 38.3 |
| 2 | Ron Marlenee (R) | 84,548 | 53.5 |
| | Richard "Buck" O'Brien (D) | 73,583 | 46.5 |

## NEBRASKA

| | Candidates | Votes | % |
|---|---|---|---|
| 1 | Doug Bereuter (R) | 121,772 | 64.4 |
| | Steve Burns (D) | 67,137 | 35.5 |
| 2 | Hal Daub (R) | 99,569 | 58.5 |
| | Walter M. Calinger (D) | 70,372 | 41.3 |
| 3 | Virginia Smith (R) | 136,985 | 69.8 |
| | Scott E. Sidwell (D) | 59,182 | 30.2 |

## NEVADA

| | Candidates | Votes | % |
|---|---|---|---|
| 1 | James H. Bilbray (D) | 61,830 | 54.1 |
| | Bob Ryan (R) | 50,342 | 44.0 |
| 2 | Barbara F. Vucanovich (R) | 83,479 | 58.4 |
| | Pete Sferrazza (D) | 59,433 | 41.6 |

## NEW HAMPSHIRE

| | Candidates | Votes | % |
|---|---|---|---|
| 1 | Robert C. Smith (R) | 70,739 | 56.4 |
| | James M. Demers (D) | 54,787 | 43.6 |
| 2 | Judd Gregg (R) | 85,479 | 74.2 |
| | Laurence Craig-Green (D) | 29,688 | 25.8 |

## NEW JERSEY

| | Candidates | Votes | % |
|---|---|---|---|
| 1 | James J. Florio (D) | 93,497 | 75.6 |
| | Fred A. Busch (R) | 29,175 | 23.6 |
| 2 | William J. Hughes (D) | 83,821 | 68.3 |
| | Alfred J. Bennington Jr. (R) | 35,167 | 28.6 |
| 3 | James J. Howard (D) | 73,743 | 58.7 |
| | Brian T. Kennedy (R) | 51,882 | 41.3 |
| 4 | Christopher H. Smith (R) | 78,699 | 61.1 |
| | Jeffrey Laurenti (D) | 49,290 | 38.3 |
| 5 | Marge Roukema (R) | 94,253 | 74.6 |
| | H. Vernon Jolley (D) | 32,145 | 25.4 |
| 6 | Bernard J. Dwyer (D) | 67,460 | 69.0 |
| | John D. Scalamonti (R) | 28,286 | 28.9 |
| 7 | Matthew J. Rinaldo (R) | 92,254 | 79.0 |
| | June S. Fischer (D) | 24,462 | 21.0 |
| 8 | Robert A. Roe (D) | 57,820 | 62.8 |
| | Thomas P. Zampino (R) | 34,268 | 37.2 |
| 9 | Robert G. Torricelli (D) | 89,634 | 69.0 |
| | Arthur F. Jones (R) | 40,226 | 31.0 |
| 10 | Peter W. Rodino Jr. (D) | 46,666 | 95.9 |
| 11 | Dean A. Gallo (R) | 75,037 | 68.0 |
| | Frank Askin (D) | 35,280 | 32.0 |
| 12 | Jim Courter (R) | 72,966 | 63.5 |
| | David B. Crabiel (D) | 41,967 | 36.5 |
| 13 | H. James Saxton (R) | 82,866 | 65.4 |
| | John Wydra (D) | 43,920 | 34.6 |
| 14 | Frank J. Guarini (D) | 63,057 | 70.7 |
| | Albio Sires (R) | 23,822 | 26.7 |

## NEW MEXICO

| | Candidates | Votes | % |
|---|---|---|---|
| 1 | Manuel Lujan Jr. (R) | 90,476 | 70.9 |
| | Manny Garcia (D) | 37,138 | 29.1 |
| 2 | Joe Skeen (R) | 77,787 | 62.9 |
| | Mike Runnels (D) | 45,924 | 37.1 |
| 3 | Bill Richardson (D) | 95,760 | 71.3 |
| | David F. Cargo (R) | 38,552 | 28.7 |

## NEW YORK

| | Candidates | Votes | % |
|---|---|---|---|
| 1 | George J. Hochbrueckner (D) | 67,139 | 51.2 |
| | Gregory J. Blass (R) | 55,413 | 42.3 |
| 2 | Thomas J. Downey (D) | 69,771 | 64.3 |
| | Jeffrey A. Butzke (R, C) | 35,132 | 32.4 |
| 3 | Robert J. Mrazek (D) | 83,985 | 56.4 |
| | Joseph A. Guarino (R, C) | 60,367 | 40.6 |
| 4 | Norman F. Lent (R, C) | 92,214 | 64.8 |
| | Patricia Sullivan (D, L) | 43,581 | 30.6 |
| 5 | Raymond J. McGrath (R, C) | 93,473 | 65.3 |
| | Michael T. Sullivan (D, L, RTL) | 49,728 | 34.7 |
| 6 | Floyd H. Flake (D) | 58,317 | 67.7 |
| | Richard Dietl (R) | 27,773 | 32.3 |
| 7 | Gary L. Ackerman (D) | 62,836 | 77.4 |
| | Edward Nelson Rodriguez (R, C) | 18,384 | 22.6 |
| 8 | James H. Scheuer (D, L) | 70,605 | 90.2 |
| | Gustave Reifenkugel (C) | 7,679 | 9.8 |
| 9 | Thomas J. Manton (D) | 50,738 | 69.4 |
| | Salvatore J. Calise (R) | 18,040 | 24.7 |
| | Thomas V. Ognibene (C) | 4,348 | 5.9 |
| 10 | Charles E. Schumer (D, L) | 76,318 | 93.3 |
| | Alice E. Gaffney (C) | 5,472 | 6.7 |
| 11 | Edolphus Towns (D, L) | 41,689 | 89.4 |
| | Nathaniel Hendricks (R) | 4,053 | 8.7 |
| 12 | Major R. Owens (D, L) | 42,138 | 91.5 |
| | Owen Augustin (R) | 2,752 | 6.0 |
| 13 | Stephen J. Solarz (D, L) | 61,089 | 82.4 |
| | Leon Nadrowski (R) | 10,941 | 14.8 |
| 14 | Guy V. Molinari (R, C) | 64,647 | 68.8 |
| | Barbara Walla (D) | 27,950 | 29.7 |
| 15 | Bill Green (R) | 58,214 | 58.0 |
| | George A. Hirsch (D, L) | 42,147 | 42.0 |
| 16 | Charles B. Rangel (D, R, L) | 61,262 | 96.4 |
| 17 | Ted Weiss (D) | 95,094 | 85.5 |

| | Candidates | Votes | % |
|---|---|---|---|
| | Thomas A. Chorba (R, C) | 15,587 | 14.0 |
| 18 | Robert Garcia (D, L) | 43,343 | 93.5 |
| | Melanie Chase (R) | 2,479 | 5.4 |
| 19 | Mario Biaggi (D, R, L) | 87,774 | 90.2 |
| | Alice Farrell (C) | 6,906 | 7.1 |
| 20 | Joseph J. DioGuardi (R, C) | 80,220 | 53.9 |
| | Bella S. Abzug (D) | 66,359 | 44.5 |
| 21 | Hamilton Fish Jr. (R, C) | 102,070 | 76.5 |
| | Lawrence W. Grunberger (D) | 28,339 | 21.3 |
| 22 | Benjamin A. Gilman (R) | 94,244 | 69.5 |
| | Eleanor F. Burlingham (D) | 36,852 | 27.2 |
| 23 | Samuel S. Stratton (D) | 140,759 | 96.4 |
| 24 | Gerald B. H. Solomon (R, C, RTL) | 117,285 | 70.4 |
| | Ed Bloch (D) | 49,225 | 29.6 |
| 25 | Sherwood Boehlert (R) | 104,216 | 69.0 |
| | Kevin J. Conway (D) | 33,864 | 22.4 |
| | Robert S. Barstow (C, RTL) | 12,999 | 8.6 |
| 26 | David O'B. Martin (R, C) | 94,840 | 100.0 |
| 27 | George C. Wortley (R) | 83,430 | 49.7 |
| | Rosemary S. Pooler (D) | 82,491 | 49.1 |
| 28 | Matthew F. McHugh (D) | 103,908 | 68.3 |
| | Mark R. Masterson (R, C, RTL) | 48,213 | 31.7 |
| 29 | Frank Horton (R) | 99,704 | 70.7 |
| | James R. Vogel (D) | 34,194 | 24.2 |
| 30 | Louise M. Slaughter (D) | 86,777 | 51.0 |
| | Fred J. Eckert (R, C) | 83,402 | 49.0 |
| 31 | Jack F. Kemp (R, C, RTL) | 92,508 | 57.4 |
| | James P. Keane (D) | 67,574 | 42.0 |
| 32 | John J. LaFalce (D, L) | 99,745 | 91.0 |
| | Dean L. Walker (R) | 6,234 | 5.7 |
| 33 | Henry J. Nowak (D, L) | 109,256 | 85.1 |
| | Charles A. Walker (R, C) | 19,147 | 14.9 |
| 34 | Amo Houghton (R, C) | 85,856 | 60.1 |
| | Larry M. Himelein (D) | 56,898 | 39.9 |

### Special Election [4]

| | Candidates | Votes | % |
|---|---|---|---|
| 6 | Alton R. Waldon Jr. (D) | 12,654 | 31.0 |
| | Floyd H. Flake (UT) | 12,376 | 30.3 |
| | Richard Dietl (R, C) | 8,700 | 21.3 |
| | Kevin McCabe (GOOD GOV) | 3,738 | 9.2 |
| | Andrew Jenkins (L) | 3,323 | 8.1 |

## NORTH CAROLINA

| | Candidates | Votes | % |
|---|---|---|---|
| 1 | Walter B. Jones (D) | 91,122 | 69.5 |
| | Howard Moye (R) | 39,912 | 30.5 |
| 2 | Tim Valentine (D) | 95,320 | 74.6 |
| | Bud McElhaney (R) | 32,515 | 25.4 |
| 3 | H. Martin Lancaster (D) | 71,460 | 64.5 |
| | Gerald B. Hurst (R) | 39,408 | 35.5 |
| 4 | David E. Price (D) | 92,216 | 55.7 |
| | William Cobey Jr. (R) | 73,469 | 44.3 |
| 5 | Stephen L. Neal (D) | 86,410 | 54.1 |
| | Stuart Epperson (R) | 73,261 | 45.9 |
| 6 | Howard Coble (R) | 72,329 | 50.0 |
| | Robin Britt (D) | 72,250 | 50.0 |
| 7 | Charlie Rose (D) | 70,471 | 64.2 |
| | Thomas J. Harrelson (R) | 39,289 | 35.8 |
| 8 | W. G. "Bill" Hefner (D) | 80,959 | 57.9 |
| | William G. Hamby Jr. (R) | 58,941 | 42.1 |
| 9 | Alex McMillan (R) | 80,352 | 51.3 |
| | D. G. Martin (D) | 76,240 | 48.7 |
| 10 | Cass Ballenger (R) | 83,902 | 57.5 |
| | Lester D. Roark (D) | 62,035 | 42.5 |
| 11 | James McClure Clarke (D) | 91,575 | 50.7 |
| | Bill Hendon (R) | 89,069 | 49.3 |

### Special Election [5]

| | Candidates | Votes | % |
|---|---|---|---|
| 10 | Cass Ballenger (R) | 82,973 | 57.5 |
| | Lester D. Roark (D) | 61,205 | 42.5 |

## NORTH DAKOTA

| | Candidates | Votes | % |
|---|---|---|---|
| AL | Byron L. Dorgan (D) | 216,258 | 75.5 |
| | Syver Vinje (R) | 66,989 | 23.4 |

## OHIO

| | Candidates | Votes | % |
|---|---|---|---|
| 1 | Thomas A. Luken (D) | 90,477 | 61.7 |
| | Fred E. Morr (R) | 56,100 | 38.3 |
| 2 | Bill Gradison (R) | 105,061 | 70.7 |
| | William F. Stineman (D) | 43,448 | 29.3 |
| 3 | Tony P. Hall (D) | 98,311 | 73.7 |
| | Ron Crutcher (R) | 35,167 | 26.3 |
| 4 | Michael G. Oxley (R) | 115,751 | 75.1 |
| | Clem T. Cratty (D) | 26,320 | 17.1 |
| | Raven L. Workman (I) | 11,997 | 7.8 |
| 5 | Delbert L. Latta (R) | 102,016 | 65.0 |
| | Tom Murray (D) | 54,864 | 35.0 |
| 6 | Bob McEwen (R) | 106,354 | 70.3 |
| | Gordon Roberts (D) | 42,155 | 27.8 |
| 7 | Michael DeWine (R) | 119,238 | 100.0 |
| 8 | Donald E. Lukens (R) | 98,475 | 68.1 |
| | John W. Griffin (D) | 46,195 | 31.9 |
| 9 | Marcy Kaptur (D) | 105,646 | 77.5 |
| | Mike Shufeldt (R) | 30,643 | 22.5 |
| 10 | Clarence E. Miller (R) | 106,870 | 70.4 |
| | John M. Buchanan (D) | 44,847 | 29.6 |
| 11 | Dennis E. Eckart (D) | 104,740 | 72.4 |
| | Margaret Mueller (R) | 35,944 | 24.9 |
| 12 | John R. Kasich (R) | 117,905 | 73.4 |
| | Timothy C. Jochim (D) | 42,727 | 26.6 |
| 13 | Don J. Pease (D) | 88,612 | 62.8 |
| | William D. Nielsen (R) | 52,452 | 37.2 |
| 14 | Thomas C. Sawyer (D) | 83,257 | 53.7 |
| | Lynn Slaby (R) | 71,713 | 46.3 |
| 15 | Chalmers P. Wylie (R) | 97,745 | 63.7 |
| | David L. Jackson (D) | 55,750 | 36.3 |
| 16 | Ralph Regula (R) | 118,206 | 76.3 |
| | William J. Kennick (D) | 36,639 | 23.7 |
| 17 | James A. Traficant Jr. (D) | 112,855 | 72.3 |
| | James H. Fulks (R) | 43,334 | 27.7 |
| 18 | Douglas Applegate (D) | 126,526 | 100.0 |
| 19 | Edward F. Feighan (D) | 97,814 | 54.8 |
| | Gary C. Suhadolnik (R) | 80,743 | 45.2 |
| 20 | Mary Rose Oakar (D) | 110,976 | 84.9 |
| | Bill Smith (R) | 19,794 | 15.1 |
| 21 | Louis Stokes (D) | 99,878 | 81.6 |
| | Franklin H. Roski (R) | 22,594 | 18.4 |

## OKLAHOMA

| | Candidates | Votes | % |
|---|---|---|---|
| 1 | James M. Inhofe (R) | 78,919 | 54.8 |
| | Gary D. Allison (D) | 61,663 | 42.8 |
| 2 | Mike Synar (D) | 114,543 | 73.3 |
| | Gary K. Rice (R) | 41,795 | 26.7 |
| 3 | Wes Watkins (D) | 114,008 | 78.1 |
| | Patrick K. Miller (R) | 31,913 | 21.9 |
| 4 | Dave McCurdy (D) | 94,984 | 76.2 |
| | Larry Humphreys (R) | 29,697 | 23.8 |
| 5 | Mickey Edwards (R) | 108,774 | 70.6 |
| | Donna Compton (D) | 45,256 | 29.4 |
| 6 | Glenn English (D) | | 100.0 |

## OREGON

| | Candidates | Votes | % |
|---|---|---|---|
| 1 | Les AuCoin (D) | 141,585 | 61.7 |
| | Tony Meeker (R) | 87,874 | 38.3 |
| 2 | Robert F. Smith (R) | 113,566 | 60.2 |
| | Larry Tuttle (D) | 75,124 | 39.8 |
| 3 | Ron Wyden (D) | 180,067 | 85.9 |
| | Thomas H. Phelan (R) | 29,321 | 14.0 |
| 4 | Peter A. DeFazio (D) | 105,697 | 54.1 |
| | Bruce Long (R) | 89,795 | 45.9 |
| 5 | Denny Smith (R) | 125,906 | 60.5 |
| | Barbara Ross (D) | 82,290 | 39.5 |

## PENNSYLVANIA

| | Candidates | Votes | % |
|---|---|---|---|
| 1 | Thomas M. Foglietta (D) | 88,224 | 74.7 |
| | Anthony J. Mucciolo (R) | 29,811 | 25.3 |
| 2 | William H. Gray III (D) | 128,399 | 98.4 |
| 3 | Robert A. Borski (D) | 107,804 | 61.8 |
| | Robert A. Rovner (R) | 66,693 | 38.2 |
| 4 | Joe Kolter (D) | 86,133 | 60.4 |

| | Candidates | Votes | % |
|---|---|---|---|
| | Al Lindsay (R) | 55,165 | 38.7 |
| 5 | Richard T. Schulze (R) | 87,593 | 65.7 |
| | Tim Ringgold (D) | 45,648 | 34.3 |
| 6 | Gus Yatron (D) | 98,142 | 69.1 |
| | Norm Bertasavage (R) | 43,858 | 30.9 |
| 7 | Curt Weldon (R) | 110,118 | 61.3 |
| | Bill Spingler (D) | 69,557 | 38.7 |
| 8 | Peter H. Kostmayer (D) | 85,731 | 55.0 |
| | David A. Christian (R) | 70,047 | 45.0 |
| 9 | Bud Shuster (R) | 120,890 | 100.0 |
| 10 | Joseph M. McDade (R) | 118,603 | 74.7 |
| | Robert C. Bolus (D) | 40,248 | 25.3 |
| 11 | Paul E. Kanjorski (D) | 112,405 | 70.6 |
| | Marc Holtzman (R) | 46,785 | 29.4 |
| 12 | John P. Murtha (D) | 97,135 | 67.4 |
| | Kathy Holtzman (R) | 46,937 | 32.6 |
| 13 | Lawrence Coughlin (R) | 100,701 | 58.5 |
| | Joseph M. Hoeffel (D) | 71,381 | 41.5 |
| 14 | William J. Coyne (D) | 104,726 | 89.6 |
| | Richard Edward Caligiuri (LIBERT) | 6,058 | 5.2 |
| 15 | Don Ritter (R) | 74,829 | 56.8 |
| | Joe Simonetta (D) | 56,972 | 43.2 |
| 16 | Robert S. Walker (R) | 100,784 | 74.6 |
| | James D. Hagelgans (D) | 34,399 | 25.4 |
| 17 | George W. Gekas (R) | 101,027 | 73.6 |
| | Michael S. Ogden (D) | 36,157 | 26.4 |
| 18 | Doug Walgren (D) | 104,164 | 63.0 |
| | Ernie Buckman (R) | 61,164 | 37.0 |
| 19 | Bill Goodling (R) | 100,055 | 72.9 |
| | Richard F. Thornton (D) | 37,223 | 27.1 |
| 20 | Joseph M. Gaydos (D) | 136,638 | 98.5 |
| 21 | Tom Ridge (R) | 111,148 | 80.9 |
| | Joylyn Blackwell (D) | 26,324 | 19.1 |
| 22 | Austin J. Murphy (D) | 131,650 | 100.0 |
| 23 | William F. Clinger Jr. (R) | 79,595 | 55.5 |
| | Bill Wachob (D) | 63,875 | 44.5 |

## RHODE ISLAND

| | Candidates | Votes | % |
|---|---|---|---|
| 1 | Fernand J. St Germain (D) | 85,077 | 57.7 |
| | John A. Holmes Jr. (R) | 62,397 | 42.3 |
| 2 | Claudine Schneider (R) | 113,603 | 71.8 |
| | Donald J. Ferry (D) | 44,586 | 28.2 |

## SOUTH CAROLINA

| | Candidates | Votes | % |
|---|---|---|---|
| 1 | Arthur Ravenel Jr. (R) | 59,969 | 52.0 |
| | Jimmy Stuckey (D) | 55,262 | 48.0 |
| 2 | Floyd D. Spence (R) | 73,455 | 53.6 |
| | Fred Zeigler (D) | 63,592 | 46.4 |
| 3 | Butler Derrick (D) | 79,109 | 68.4 |
| | Richard Dickison (R) | 36,495 | 31.5 |
| 4 | Liz J. Patterson (D) | 67,012 | 51.4 |
| | Bill Workman (R) | 61,648 | 47.3 |
| 5 | John M. Spratt Jr. (D) | 95,859 | 99.7 |
| 6 | Robin Tallon (D) | 92,398 | 75.5 |
| | Robbie Cunningham (R) | 29,922 | 24.5 |

## SOUTH DAKOTA

| | Candidates | Votes | % |
|---|---|---|---|
| AL | Tim Johnson (D) | 171,462 | 59.2 |
| | Dale Bell (R) | 118,261 | 40.8 |

## TENNESSEE

| | Candidates | Votes | % |
|---|---|---|---|
| 1 | James H. Quillen (R) | 80,289 | 68.9 |
| | John B. Russell (D) | 36,278 | 31.1 |
| 2 | John J. Duncan (R) | 96,396 | 76.2 |
| | John F. Bowen (D) | 30,088 | 23.8 |
| 3 | Marilyn Lloyd (D) | 75,034 | 53.9 |
| | Jim Golden (R) | 64,084 | 46.1 |
| 4 | Jim Cooper (D) | 86,997 | 100.0 |
| 5 | Bill Boner (D) | 85,126 | 57.9 |
| | Terry Holcomb (R) | 58,701 | 39.9 |
| 6 | Bart Gordon (D) | 102,180 | 76.8 |
| | Fred Vail (R) | 30,823 | 23.2 |
| 7 | Don Sundquist (R) | 93,902 | 72.3 |
| | M. Lloyd Hiler (D) | 35,966 | 27.7 |

| | Candidates | Votes | % |
|---|---|---|---|
| 8 | Ed Jones (D) | 101,699 | 80.4 |
| | Dan H. Campbell (R) | 24,792 | 19.6 |
| 9 | Harold E. Ford (D) | 83,006 | 83.4 |
| | Isaac Richmond (I) | 16,221 | 16.3 |

## TEXAS

| | Candidates | Votes | % |
|---|---|---|---|
| 1 | Jim Chapman (D) | 84,445 | 100.0 |
| 2 | Charles Wilson (D) | 78,529 | 56.7 |
| | Julian Gordon (R) | 55,986 | 40.5 |
| 3 | Steve Bartlett (R) | 143,381 | 94.1 |
| 4 | Ralph M. Hall (D) | 97,540 | 71.7 |
| | Thomas Blow (R) | 38,578 | 28.3 |
| 5 | John Bryant (D) | 57,410 | 58.5 |
| | Tom Carter (R) | 39,945 | 40.7 |
| 6 | Joe L. Barton (R) | 86,190 | 55.8 |
| | Pete Geren (D) | 68,270 | 44.2 |
| 7 | Bill Archer (R) | 129,673 | 87.4 |
| | Harry Kniffen (D) | 17,635 | 11.9 |
| 8 | Jack Fields (R) | 66,280 | 68.4 |
| | Blaine Mann (D) | 30,617 | 31.6 |
| 9 | Jack Brooks (D) | 73,285 | 61.5 |
| | Lisa D. Duperier (R) | 45,834 | 38.5 |
| 10 | J. J. "Jake" Pickle (D) | 135,863 | 72.3 |
| | Carole Keeton Rylander (R) | 52,000 | 27.7 |
| 11 | Marvin Leath (D) | 84,201 | 100.0 |
| 12 | Jim Wright (D) | 84,831 | 68.7 |
| | Don McNeil (R) | 38,620 | 31.3 |
| 13 | Beau Boulter (R) | 84,980 | 64.9 |
| | Doug Seal (D) | 45,907 | 35.1 |
| 14 | Mac Sweeney (R) | 74,471 | 52.3 |
| | Greg H. Laughlin (D) | 67,852 | 47.7 |
| 15 | E. "Kika" de la Garza (D) | 70,777 | 100.0 |
| 16 | Ronald D. Coleman (D) | 50,590 | 65.7 |
| | Roy Gillia (R) | 26,421 | 34.3 |
| 17 | Charles W. Stenholm (D) | 97,791 | 100.0 |
| 18 | Mickey Leland (D) | 63,335 | 90.2 |
| | Joanne Kuniansky (I) | 6,884 | 9.8 |
| 19 | Larry Combest (R) | 68,695 | 62.0 |
| | Gerald McCathern (D) | 42,129 | 38.0 |
| 20 | Henry B. Gonzalez (D) | 55,363 | 100.0 |
| 21 | Lamar Smith (R) | 100,346 | 60.6 |
| | Pete Snelson (D) | 63,779 | 38.5 |
| 22 | Thomas D. DeLay (R) | 76,459 | 71.8 |
| | Susan Director (D) | 30,079 | 28.2 |
| 23 | Albert G. Bustamante (D) | 68,131 | 90.7 |
| | Ken Hendrix (LIBERT) | 7,001 | 9.3 |
| 24 | Martin Frost (D) | 69,368 | 67.2 |
| | Bob Burk (R) | 33,819 | 32.8 |
| 25 | Michael A. Andrews (D) | 67,435 | 100.0 |
| 26 | Dick Armey (R) | 101,735 | 68.1 |
| | George Richardson (D) | 47,651 | 31.9 |
| 27 | Solomon P. Ortiz (D) | 64,165 | 100.0 |

## UTAH

| | Candidates | Votes | % |
|---|---|---|---|
| 1 | James V. Hansen (R) | 82,151 | 51.6 |
| | Gunn McKay (D) | 77,180 | 48.4 |
| 2 | Wayne Owens (D) | 76,921 | 55.2 |
| | Tom Shimizu (R) | 60,967 | 43.7 |
| 3 | Howard C. Nielson (R) | 86,599 | 66.6 |
| | Dale F. Gardiner (D) | 42,582 | 32.7 |

## VERMONT

| | Candidates | Votes | % |
|---|---|---|---|
| AL | James M. Jeffords (R) | 168,403 | 89.1 |

## VIRGINIA

| | Candidates | Votes | % |
|---|---|---|---|
| 1 | Herbert H. Bateman (R) | 80,713 | 56.0 |
| | Robert C. Scott (D) | 63,364 | 44.0 |
| 2 | Owen B. Pickett (D) | 54,491 | 49.5 |
| | A. J. "Joe" Canada Jr. (R) | 46,137 | 41.9 |
| | Stephen P. Shao (I) | 9,492 | 8.6 |
| 3 | Thomas J. Bliley Jr. (R) | 74,525 | 67.0 |
| | Kenneth E. Powell (D) | 32,961 | 29.7 |
| 4 | Norman Sisisky (D) | 64,699 | 99.8 |
| 5 | Dan Daniel (D) | 73,085 | 81.5 |
| | J. F. "Frank" Cole (I) | 16,551 | 18.5 |

| Candidates | Votes | % |
|---|---|---|
| 6 Jim Olin (D) | 88,230 | 69.9 |
| Flo Neher Traywick (R) | 38,051 | 30.1 |
| 7 D. French Slaughter Jr. (R) | 58,927 | 98.3 |
| 8 Stan Parris (R) | 72,670 | 61.8 |
| James H. Boren (D) | 44,965 | 38.2 |
| 9 Rick Boucher (D) | 59,864 | 99.0 |
| 10 Frank R. Wolf (R) | 95,724 | 60.2 |
| John G. Milliken (D) | 63,292 | 39.8 |

### WASHINGTON

| Candidates | Votes | % |
|---|---|---|
| 1 John R. Miller (R) | 97,969 | 51.4 |
| Reese Lindquist (D) | 92,697 | 48.6 |
| 2 Al Swift (D) | 124,840 | 72.2 |
| Thomas S. Talman (R) | 48,077 | 27.8 |
| 3 Don Bonker (D) | 114,775 | 73.6 |
| Joe Illing (R) | 41,275 | 26.4 |
| 4 Sid Morrison (R) | 107,593 | 72.1 |
| Robert Goedecke (D) | 41,709 | 27.9 |
| 5 Thomas S. Foley (D) | 121,732 | 74.7 |
| Floyd L. Wakefield (R) | 41,179 | 25.3 |

| Candidates | Votes | % |
|---|---|---|
| 6 Norm Dicks (D) | 90,063 | 71.2 |
| Kenneth W. Braaten (R) | 36,410 | 28.8 |
| 7 Mike Lowry (D) | 124,317 | 72.6 |
| Don McDonald (R) | 46,831 | 27.4 |
| 8 Rod Chandler (R) | 107,824 | 65.2 |
| David E. Giles (D) | 57,545 | 34.8 |

### WEST VIRGINIA

| Candidates | Votes | % |
|---|---|---|
| 1 Alan B. Mollohan (D) | 90,715 | 100.0 |
| 2 Harley O. Staggers Jr. (D) | 76,355 | 69.5 |
| Michele Golden (R) | 33,554 | 30.5 |
| 3 Bob Wise (D) | 73,669 | 64.9 |
| Tim Sharp (R) | 39,820 | 35.1 |
| 4 Nick J. Rahall II (D) | 58,217 | 71.3 |
| Martin Miller (R) | 23,490 | 28.7 |

### WISCONSIN

| Candidates | Votes | % |
|---|---|---|
| 1 Les Aspin (D) | 106,288 | 74.3 |
| Iris Peterson (R) | 34,495 | 24.1 |

| Candidates | Votes | % |
|---|---|---|
| 2 Robert W. Kastenmeier (D) | 106,919 | 55.6 |
| Ann J. Haney (R) | 85,156 | 44.2 |
| 3 Steve Gunderson (R) | 104,393 | 64.1 |
| Leland E. Mulder (D) | 58,445 | 35.9 |
| 4 Gerald D. Kleczka (D) | 120,354 | 99.6 |
| 5 Jim Moody (D) | 109,506 | 99.0 |
| 6 Thomas E. Petri (R) | 124,328 | 96.7 |
| 7 David R. Obey (D) | 106,700 | 62.2 |
| Kevin J. Hermening (R) | 63,408 | 36.9 |
| 8 Toby Roth (R) | 118,162 | 67.4 |
| Paul F. Willems (D) | 57,265 | 32.6 |
| 9 F. James Sensenbrenner Jr. (R) | 138,766 | 78.2 |
| Thomas G. Popp (D) | 38,636 | 21.8 |

### WYOMING

| Candidates | Votes | % |
|---|---|---|
| AL Dick Cheney (R) | 111,007 | 69.5 |
| Rick Gilmore (D) | 48,780 | 30.5 |

**1986 Elections**

1. A special election was held to fill the unexpired term of Rep. Cecil Heftel (D), who resigned July 11, 1986.
2. For the 1986 House elections in Louisiana, an open primary election was held with candidates from all parties running on the same ballot. Any candidate who received a majority was elected unopposed, with no further appearance on the general election ballot. If no candidate received 50 percent, a runoff was held between the two top finishers.

3. In Minnesota the Democratic Party is known as the Democratic-Farmer-Labor Party and the Republican Party as the Independent-Republican Party; candidates appear on the ballot with these designations.
4. A special election was held to fill the unexpired term of Rep. Joseph P. Addabbo (D), who died April 10, 1986.
5. A special election was held to fill the unexpired term of Rep. James T. Broyhill (R), who resigned in July 1986, having been appointed to the Senate.

# 1987 House Elections

### CALIFORNIA

**Special Election [1]**

| Candidates | Votes | % |
|---|---|---|
| 5 Nancy Pelosi (D) | 46,428 | 63.3 |
| Harriet Ross (R) | 22,478 | 30.7 |

### CONNECTICUT

**Special Election [2]**

| Candidates | Votes | % |
|---|---|---|
| 4 Christopher Shays (R) | 50,518 | 57.2 |
| Christine M. Niedermeier (D) | 37,293 | 42.2 |

**1987 Elections**

1. A special election was held to fill the unexpired term of Rep. Sala Burton (D), who died Feb. 1, 1987.

2. A special election was held to fill the unexpired term of Rep. Stewart B. McKinney (R), who died May 7, 1987.

# 1988 House Elections

## ALABAMA

| | Candidates | Votes | % |
|---|---|---|---|
| 1 | Sonny Callahan (R) | 115,173 | 59.2 |
| | John M. Tyson Jr. (D) | 77,670 | 40.0 |
| 2 | Bill Dickinson (R) | 120,408 | 94.2 |
| | Brooke King (LIBERT) | 7,352 | 5.8 |
| 3 | Bill Nichols (D) | 117,514 | 96.1 |
| | Shockley (LIBERT) | 4,793 | 3.9 |
| 4 | Tom Bevill (D) | 131,880 | 96.2 |
| | John Sebastian (LIBERT) | 5,264 | 3.8 |
| 5 | Ronnie G. Flippo (D) | 120,142 | 64.4 |
| | Stan McDonald (R) | 64,491 | 34.5 |
| 6 | Ben Erdreich (D) | 138,920 | 66.5 |
| | Charles Caddis (R) | 68,788 | 32.9 |
| 7 | Claude Harris (D) | 136,074 | 67.7 |
| | James E. "Jim" Bacon (R) | 63,372 | 31.5 |

## ALASKA

| | Candidates | Votes | % |
|---|---|---|---|
| AL | Don Young (R) | 120,595 | 62.5 |
| | Peter Gruenstein (D) | 71,881 | 37.3 |

## ARIZONA

| | Candidates | Votes | % |
|---|---|---|---|
| 1 | John J. Rhodes III (R) | 184,639 | 72.1 |
| | John M. Fillmore (D) | 71,388 | 27.9 |
| 2 | Morris K. Udall (D) | 99,895 | 73.3 |
| | Joseph D. Sweeney (R) | 36,309 | 26.7 |
| 3 | Bob Stump (R) | 174,453 | 68.9 |
| | Dave Moss (D) | 72,417 | 28.6 |
| 4 | Jon Kyl (R) | 206,248 | 87.1 |
| | Gary Sprunk (LIBERT) | 30,430 | 12.9 |
| 5 | Jim Kolbe (R) | 164,462 | 67.8 |
| | Judith E. Belcher (D) | 78,115 | 32.2 |

## ARKANSAS

| | Candidates | Votes | % |
|---|---|---|---|
| 1 | Bill Alexander (D) | | 100.0 |
| 2 | Tommy F. Robinson (D) | 168,889 | 83.5 |
| | Warren D. Carpenter (R) | 33,475 | 16.5 |
| 3 | John Paul Hammerschmidt (R) | 161,623 | 74.7 |
| | David Stewart (D) | 54,767 | 25.3 |
| 4 | Beryl Anthony Jr. (D) | 129,508 | 69.2 |
| | Roger N. Bell (R) | 57,658 | 30.8 |

## CALIFORNIA

| | Candidates | Votes | % |
|---|---|---|---|
| 1 | Douglas H. Bosco (D) | 159,815 | 62.9 |
| | Samuel "Mark" Vanderbilt (R) | 72,189 | 28.4 |
| | Eric Fried (PFP) | 22,150 | 8.7 |
| 2 | Wally Herger (R) | 139,010 | 58.8 |
| | Wayne Meyer (D) | 91,088 | 38.5 |
| 3 | Robert T. Matsui (D) | 183,470 | 71.2 |
| | Lowell P. Landowski (R) | 74,296 | 28.8 |
| 4 | Vic Fazio (D) | 181,184 | 99.3 |
| 5 | Nancy Pelosi (D) | 133,530 | 76.4 |
| | Bruce Michael O'Neill (R) | 33,692 | 19.3 |
| 6 | Barbara Boxer (D) | 176,645 | 73.4 |
| | William Steinmetz (R) | 64,174 | 26.6 |
| 7 | George Miller (D) | 170,006 | 68.4 |
| | Jean Last (R) | 78,478 | 31.6 |
| 8 | Ronald V. Dellums (D) | 163,221 | 66.6 |
| | John J. Cuddihy Jr. (R) | 76,531 | 31.2 |
| 9 | Pete Stark (D) | 152,866 | 73.0 |
| | Howard Hertz (R) | 56,656 | 27.0 |
| 10 | Don Edwards (D) | 142,500 | 86.2 |
| | Kennita Watson (LIBERT) | 22,801 | 13.8 |
| 11 | Tom Lantos (D) | 145,484 | 71.0 |
| | G. M. "Bill" Quraishi (R) | 50,050 | 24.4 |
| 12 | Tom Campbell (R) | 136,384 | 51.7 |
| | Anna G. Eshoo (D) | 121,523 | 46.0 |
| 13 | Norman Y. Mineta (D) | 143,980 | 67.1 |

| | Candidates | Votes | % |
|---|---|---|---|
| | Luke Sommer (R) | 63,959 | 29.8 |
| 14 | Norman D. Shumway (R) | 173,876 | 62.6 |
| | Patricia Malberg (D) | 103,899 | 37.4 |
| 15 | Tony Coelho (D) | 118,710 | 69.7 |
| | Carol Harner (R) | 47,957 | 28.2 |
| 16 | Leon E. Panetta (D) | 177,452 | 78.6 |
| | Stanley Monteith (R) | 48,375 | 21.4 |
| 17 | Charles Pashayan Jr. (R) | 129,568 | 71.5 |
| | Vincent Lavery (D) | 51,730 | 28.5 |
| 18 | Richard H. Lehman (D) | 125,715 | 69.9 |
| | David A. Linn (R) | 54,034 | 30.1 |
| 19 | Robert J. Lagomarsino (R) | 116,026 | 50.2 |
| | Gary K. Hart (D) | 112,033 | 48.5 |
| 20 | William M. Thomas (R) | 162,779 | 71.1 |
| | Lita Reid (D) | 62,037 | 27.1 |
| 21 | Elton Gallegly (R) | 181,413 | 69.1 |
| | Donald E. Stevens (D) | 75,739 | 28.8 |
| 22 | Carlos J. Moorhead (R) | 164,699 | 69.5 |
| | John G. Simmons (D) | 61,555 | 26.0 |
| 23 | Anthony C. Beilenson (D) | 147,858 | 63.5 |
| | Jim Salomon (R) | 77,184 | 33.1 |
| 24 | Henry A. Waxman (D) | 112,038 | 72.3 |
| | John N. Cowles (R) | 36,835 | 23.7 |
| 25 | Edward R. Roybal (D) | 85,378 | 85.5 |
| | Raul Reyes (PFP) | 8,746 | 8.8 |
| | John C. Thie (LIBERT) | 5,752 | 5.8 |
| 26 | Howard L. Berman (D) | 126,930 | 70.3 |
| | G. C. "Brodie" Broderson (R) | 53,518 | 29.7 |
| 27 | Mel Levine (D) | 148,814 | 67.5 |
| | Dennis Galbraith (R) | 65,307 | 29.6 |
| 28 | Julian C. Dixon (D) | 109,801 | 76.1 |
| | George Z. Adams (R) | 28,645 | 19.8 |
| 29 | Augustus F. Hawkins (D) | 88,169 | 82.8 |
| | Reuben D. Franco (R) | 14,543 | 13.7 |
| 30 | Matthew G. Martinez (D) | 72,253 | 59.9 |
| | Ralph R. Ramirez (R) | 43,833 | 36.3 |
| 31 | Mervyn M. Dymally (D) | 100,919 | 71.6 |
| | Arnold C. May (R) | 36,017 | 25.5 |
| 32 | Glenn M. Anderson (D) | 114,666 | 66.9 |
| | Sanford W. Kahn (R) | 50,710 | 29.6 |
| 33 | David Dreier (R) | 151,704 | 69.2 |
| | Nelson Gentry (D) | 57,586 | 26.2 |
| 34 | Esteban E. Torres (D) | 92,087 | 63.2 |
| | Charles M. House (R) | 50,954 | 35.0 |
| 35 | Jerry Lewis (R) | 181,203 | 70.4 |
| | Paul Sweeney (D) | 71,186 | 27.7 |
| 36 | George E. Brown Jr. (D) | 103,493 | 54.0 |
| | John Paul Stark (R) | 81,413 | 42.5 |
| 37 | Al McCandless (R) | 174,284 | 64.3 |
| | Johnny Pearson (D) | 89,666 | 33.1 |
| 38 | Robert K. Dornan (R) | 87,690 | 59.5 |
| | Jerry Yudelson (D) | 52,399 | 35.6 |
| 39 | William E. Dannemeyer (R) | 169,360 | 73.8 |
| | Don E. Marquis (D) | 52,162 | 22.7 |
| 40 | C. Christopher Cox (R) | 181,269 | 67.0 |
| | Lida Lenney (D) | 80,782 | 29.9 |
| 41 | Bill Lowery (R) | 187,380 | 65.6 |
| | Dan Kripke (D) | 88,192 | 30.8 |
| 42 | Dana Rohrabacher (R) | 153,280 | 64.2 |
| | Guy C. Kimbrough (D) | 78,778 | 33.0 |
| 43 | Ron Packard (R) | 202,478 | 71.7 |
| | Howard Greenebaum (D) | 72,499 | 25.6 |
| 44 | Jim Bates (D) | 90,796 | 59.7 |
| | Rob Butterfield (R) | 55,511 | 36.5 |
| 45 | Duncan Hunter (R) | 166,451 | 74.0 |
| | Pete Lepiscopo (D) | 54,012 | 24.0 |

## COLORADO

| | Candidates | Votes | % |
|---|---|---|---|
| 1 | Patricia Schroeder (D) | 133,922 | 69.9 |
| | Joy Wood (R) | 57,587 | 30.1 |
| 2 | David E. Skaggs (D) | 147,437 | 62.7 |
| | David Bath (R) | 87,578 | 37.3 |
| 3 | Ben Nighthorse Campbell (D) | 169,284 | 78.0 |
| | Jim Zartman (R) | 47,625 | 22.0 |

| | Candidates | Votes | % |
|---|---|---|---|
| 4 | Hank Brown (R) | 156,202 | 73.1 |
| | Charles S. Vigil (D) | 57,552 | 26.9 |
| 5 | Joel Hefley (R) | 181,612 | 75.1 |
| | John J. Mitchell (D) | 60,116 | 24.9 |
| 6 | Dan Schaefer (R) | 136,487 | 63.0 |
| | Martha M. Ezzard (D) | 77,158 | 35.6 |

## CONNECTICUT

| | Candidates | Votes | % |
|---|---|---|---|
| 1 | Barbara B. Kennelly (D) | 176,463 | 77.2 |
| | Mario Robloo Jr. (R) | 51,985 | 22.8 |
| 2 | Sam Gejdenson (D) | 143,326 | 63.6 |
| | Glenn Carberry (R) | 81,965 | 36.4 |
| 3 | Bruce A. Morrison (D) | 147,394 | 66.5 |
| | Gerard B. Patton (R) | 74,275 | 33.5 |
| 4 | Christopher Shays (R) | 147,843 | 71.8 |
| | Roger Pearson (D) | 55,751 | 27.1 |
| 5 | John G. Rowland (R) | 163,729 | 73.6 |
| | Joseph Marinan Jr. (D) | 58,612 | 26.4 |
| 6 | Nancy L. Johnson (R) | 157,020 | 66.3 |
| | James L. Griffin (D) | 78,814 | 33.3 |

## DELAWARE

| | Candidates | Votes | % |
|---|---|---|---|
| AL | Thomas R. Carper (D) | 158,338 | 67.5 |
| | James P. Krapf Sr. (R) | 76,179 | 32.5 |

## FLORIDA

| | Candidates | Votes | % |
|---|---|---|---|
| 1 | Earl Hutto (D) | 142,449 | 66.9 |
| | E. D. Armbruster (R) | 70,534 | 33.1 |
| 2 | Bill Grant (D) | 134,269 | 99.7 |
| 3 | Charles E. Bennett (D) | | 100.0 |
| 4 | Craig T. James (R) | 125,608 | 50.2 |
| | Bill Chappell Jr. (D) | 124,817 | 49.8 |
| 5 | Bill McCollum (R) | | 100.0 |
| 6 | Cliff Stearns (R) | 136,415 | 53.5 |
| | Jon Mills (D) | 118,756 | 46.5 |
| 7 | Sam Gibbons (D) | | 100.0 |
| 8 | C. W. Bill Young (R) | 169,165 | 73.0 |
| | C. Bette Wimbish (D) | 62,539 | 27.0 |
| 9 | Michael Bilirakis (R) | 223,925 | 99.9 |
| 10 | Andy Ireland (R) | 156,563 | 73.5 |
| | David B. Higginbottom (D) | 56,536 | 26.5 |
| 11 | Bill Nelson (D) | 168,390 | 60.8 |
| | Bill Tolley (R) | 108,373 | 39.2 |
| 12 | Tom Lewis (R) | | 100.0 |
| 13 | Porter J. Goss (R) | 231,170 | 71.2 |
| | Jack Conway (D) | 93,700 | 28.8 |
| 14 | Harry A. Johnston (D) | 173,292 | 54.9 |
| | Ken Adams (R) | 142,635 | 45.1 |
| 15 | E. Clay Shaw Jr. (R) | 132,090 | 66.1 |
| | Michael A. "Mike" Kuhle (D) | 67,746 | 33.9 |
| 16 | Lawrence J. Smith (D) | 153,032 | 69.4 |
| | Joseph Smith (R) | 67,461 | 30.6 |
| 17 | William Lehman (D) | | 100.0 |
| 18 | Claude Pepper (D) | | 100.0 |
| 19 | Dante B. Fascell (D) | 135,355 | 72.4 |
| | Ralph Carlos Rocheteau (R) | 51,628 | 27.6 |

## GEORGIA

| | Candidates | Votes | % |
|---|---|---|---|
| 1 | Lindsay Thomas (D) | 94,531 | 67.0 |
| | Chris Meredith (R) | 46,552 | 33.0 |
| 2 | Charles Hatcher (D) | 85,029 | 61.7 |
| | Ralph T. Hudgens (R) | 52,807 | 38.3 |
| 3 | Richard Ray (D) | 97,663 | 100.0 |
| 4 | Ben Jones (D) | 148,394 | 60.3 |
| | Pat Swindall (R) | 97,745 | 39.7 |
| 5 | John Lewis (D) | 135,194 | 78.2 |
| | J. W. Tibbs Jr. (R) | 37,693 | 21.8 |
| 6 | Newt Gingrich (R) | 110,169 | 58.9 |
| | David Worley (D) | 76,824 | 41.1 |
| 7 | George "Buddy" Darden (D) | 135,056 | 64.8 |

| Candidates | Votes | % |
|---|---|---|
| Robert Lamutt (R) | 73,425 | 35.2 |
| 8 J. Roy Rowland (D) | 102,696 | 100.0 |
| 9 Ed Jenkins (D) | 121,800 | 62.9 |
| Joe Hoffman (R) | 71,905 | 37.1 |
| 10 Doug Barnard Jr. (D) | 118,156 | 64.0 |
| Mark Myers (R) | 66,521 | 36.0 |

### HAWAII

| Candidates | Votes | % |
|---|---|---|
| 1 Patricia Saiki (R) | 96,848 | 54.7 |
| Mary Bitterman (D) | 76,394 | 43.2 |
| 2 Daniel K. Akaka (D) | 144,802 | 88.9 |
| Lloyd "Jeff" Mallan (LIBERT) | 18,006 | 11.1 |

### IDAHO

| Candidates | Votes | % |
|---|---|---|
| 1 Larry E. Craig (R) | 135,221 | 65.8 |
| Jeanne Givens (D) | 70,328 | 34.2 |
| 2 Richard H. Stallings (D) | 127,956 | 63.4 |
| Dane Watkins (R) | 68,226 | 33.8 |

### ILLINOIS

| Candidates | Votes | % |
|---|---|---|
| 1 Charles A. Hayes (D) | 164,125 | 96.0 |
| 2 Gus Savage (D) | 138,256 | 82.7 |
| William T. Hespel (R) | 28,831 | 17.3 |
| 3 Marty Russo (D) | 132,111 | 62.2 |
| Joseph J. McCarthy (R) | 80,181 | 37.8 |
| 4 George E. Sangmeister (D) | 91,282 | 50.3 |
| Jack Davis (R) | 90,243 | 49.7 |
| 5 William O. Lipinski (D) | 93,567 | 61.3 |
| John J. Holowinski (R) | 59,128 | 38.7 |
| 6 Henry J. Hyde (R) | 153,425 | 73.7 |
| William J. Andrle (D) | 54,804 | 26.3 |
| 7 Cardiss Collins (D) | 135,331 | 100.0 |
| 8 Dan Rostenkowski (D) | 107,728 | 74.6 |
| V. Stephen Vetter (R) | 34,659 | 24.0 |
| 9 Sidney R. Yates (D) | 135,583 | 66.1 |
| Herbert Sohn (R) | 67,604 | 32.9 |
| 10 John Edward Porter (R) | 158,519 | 72.5 |
| Eugene F. Friedman (D) | 60,187 | 27.5 |
| 11 Frank Annunzio (D) | 131,753 | 64.5 |
| George S. Gottlieb (R) | 72,489 | 35.5 |
| 12 Philip M. Crane (R) | 165,913 | 75.2 |
| John A. Leonardi (D) | 54,769 | 24.8 |
| 13 Harris W. Fawell (R) | 174,992 | 70.2 |
| Evelyn E. Craig (D) | 74,424 | 29.8 |
| 14 Dennis Hastert (R) | 161,146 | 73.7 |
| Stephen Youhanaie (D) | 57,482 | 26.3 |
| 15 Edward R. Madigan (R) | 140,171 | 71.7 |
| Thomas J. "Tom" Curl (D) | 55,260 | 28.3 |
| 16 Lynn Martin (R) | 128,365 | 63.9 |
| Steven E. Mahan (D) | 72,431 | 36.1 |
| 17 Lane Evans (D) | 132,130 | 64.9 |
| William E. Stewart (R) | 71,560 | 35.1 |
| 18 Robert H. Michel (R) | 114,458 | 54.7 |
| G. Douglas Stephens (D) | 94,763 | 45.3 |
| 19 Terry L. Bruce (D) | 132,889 | 64.2 |
| Robert F. Kerans (R) | 73,981 | 35.8 |
| 20 Richard J. Durbin (D) | 153,341 | 68.9 |
| Paul E. Jurgens (R) | 69,303 | 31.1 |
| 21 Jerry F. Costello (D) | 105,836 | 52.6 |
| Robert H. Gaffner (R) | 95,385 | 47.4 |
| 22 Glenn Poshard (D) | 139,392 | 64.9 |
| Patrick J. Kelley (R) | 75,462 | 35.1 |

#### Special Election [1]

| Candidates | Votes | % |
|---|---|---|
| 21 Jerry F. Costello (D) | 33,144 | 51.5 |
| Robert H. Gaffner (R) | 31,257 | 48.5 |

### INDIANA

| Candidates | Votes | % |
|---|---|---|
| 1 Peter J. Visclosky (D) | 138,251 | 77.1 |
| Owen W. Crumpacker (R) | 41,076 | 22.9 |
| 2 Philip R. Sharp (D) | 116,915 | 53.2 |
| Mike Pence (R) | 102,846 | 46.8 |
| 3 John Hiler (R) | 116,309 | 54.3 |

| Candidates | Votes | % |
|---|---|---|
| Thomas W. Ward (D) | 97,934 | 45.7 |
| 4 Daniel R. Coats (R) | 132,843 | 62.1 |
| Jill Long (D) | 80,915 | 37.9 |
| 5 Jim Jontz (D) | 116,240 | 56.3 |
| Patricia L. Williams (R) | 90,163 | 43.7 |
| 6 Dan Burton (R) | 192,064 | 72.9 |
| George Thomas Holland (D) | 71,447 | 27.1 |
| 7 John T. Myers (R) | 130,578 | 61.8 |
| Mark Richard Waterfill (D) | 80,738 | 38.2 |
| 8 Frank McCloskey (D) | 141,355 | 61.8 |
| John L. Myers (R) | 87,321 | 38.2 |
| 9 Lee H. Hamilton (D) | 147,193 | 70.7 |
| Floyd Eugene Coates (R) | 60,946 | 29.3 |
| 10 Andrew Jacobs Jr. (D) | 105,846 | 60.5 |
| James C. Cummings (R) | 68,978 | 39.5 |

### IOWA

| Candidates | Votes | % |
|---|---|---|
| 1 Jim Leach (R) | 112,746 | 60.7 |
| Bill Gluba (D) | 71,280 | 38.4 |
| 2 Tom Tauke (R) | 113,543 | 56.8 |
| Eric Tabor (D) | 86,438 | 43.2 |
| 3 Dave Nagle (D) | 129,204 | 63.4 |
| Donald B. Redfern (R) | 74,682 | 36.6 |
| 4 Neal Smith (D) | 157,065 | 71.6 |
| Paul Lunde (R) | 62,056 | 28.3 |
| 5 Jim Ross Lightfoot (R) | 117,761 | 63.9 |
| Gene Freund (D) | 66,599 | 36.1 |
| 6 Fred Grandy (R) | 125,859 | 64.4 |
| Dave O'Brien (D) | 69,614 | 35.6 |

### KANSAS

| Candidates | Votes | % |
|---|---|---|
| 1 Pat Roberts (R) | 168,700 | 100.0 |
| 2 Jim Slattery (D) | 135,694 | 73.3 |
| Phil Meinhardt (R) | 49,498 | 26.7 |
| 3 Jan Meyers (R) | 150,223 | 73.6 |
| Lionel Kunst (D) | 53,959 | 26.4 |
| 4 Dan Glickman (D) | 122,777 | 64.0 |
| Lee Thompson (R) | 69,165 | 36.0 |
| 5 Bob Whittaker (R) | 127,722 | 70.2 |
| John A. Barnes (D) | 54,327 | 29.8 |

### KENTUCKY

| Candidates | Votes | % |
|---|---|---|
| 1 Carroll Hubbard Jr. (D) | 117,288 | 95.0 |
| 2 William H. Natcher (D) | 92,184 | 60.6 |
| Martin A. Tori (R) | 59,907 | 39.4 |
| 3 Romano L. Mazzoli (D) | 131,981 | 69.7 |
| Philip Dunnagan (R) | 57,387 | 30.3 |
| 4 Jim Bunning (R) | 145,609 | 74.2 |
| Richard V. Beliles (D) | 50,575 | 25.8 |
| 5 Harold Rogers (R) | 104,467 | 100.0 |
| 6 Larry J. Hopkins (R) | 128,898 | 74.0 |
| Milton Patton (D) | 45,339 | 26.0 |
| 7 Carl C. Perkins (D) | 96,946 | 58.7 |
| Will T. Scott (R) | 68,165 | 41.3 |

### LOUISIANA [2]

| Candidates | Votes | % |
|---|---|---|
| 1 Robert L. Livingston (R) | | 100.0 |
| 2 Lindy (Mrs. Hale) Boggs (D) | | 100.0 |
| 3 W. J. "Billy" Tauzin (D) | | 100.0 |
| 4 Jim McCrery (R) | | 100.0 |
| 5 Jerry Huckaby (D) | | 100.0 |
| 6 Richard H. Baker (R) | | 100.0 |
| 7 Jimmy Hayes (D) | | 100.0 |
| 8 Clyde C. Holloway (R) | 116,241 | 56.8 |
| Faye Williams (D) | 88,564 | 43.2 |

#### Special Election [3]

| Candidates | Votes | % |
|---|---|---|
| 4 Jim McCrery (R) | 63,590 | 50.5 |
| Foster Campbell (D) | 62,214 | 49.5 |

### MAINE

| Candidates | Votes | % |
|---|---|---|
| 1 Joseph E. Brennan (D) | 190,989 | 63.2 |
| Edward S. O'Meara Jr. (R) | 111,125 | 36.8 |
| 2 Olympia J. Snowe (R) | 167,229 | 66.2 |
| Kenneth P. Hayes (D) | 85,346 | 33.8 |

### MARYLAND

| Candidates | Votes | % |
|---|---|---|
| 1 Roy Dyson (D) | 96,128 | 50.4 |
| Wayne T. Gilchrest (R) | 94,588 | 49.6 |
| 2 Helen Delich Bentley (R) | 157,956 | 71.5 |
| Joseph Bartenfelder (D) | 63,114 | 28.5 |
| 3 Benjamin L. Cardin (D) | 133,779 | 72.9 |
| Ross Z. Pierpont (R) | 49,733 | 27.1 |
| 4 Tom McMillen (D) | 128,624 | 68.3 |
| Bradlyn McClanahan (R) | 59,688 | 31.7 |
| 5 Steny H. Hoyer (D) | 128,437 | 78.6 |
| John Eugene Sellner (R) | 34,909 | 21.4 |
| 6 Beverly B. Byron (D) | 166,753 | 75.4 |
| Kenneth W. Halsey (R) | 54,528 | 24.6 |
| 7 Kweisi Mfume (D) | 117,650 | 100.0 |
| 8 Constance A. Morella (R) | 172,619 | 62.7 |
| Peter Franchot (D) | 102,478 | 37.3 |

### MASSACHUSETTS

| Candidates | Votes | % |
|---|---|---|
| 1 Silvio O. Conte (R) | 186,356 | 82. |
| John R. Arden (D) | 38,907 | 17. |
| 2 Richard E. Neal (D) | 156,262 | 80. |
| Louis R. Godena (I) | 38,446 | 19. |
| 3 Joseph D. Early (D) | 191,005 | 99. |
| 4 Barney Frank (D) | 169,729 | 70. |
| Debra R. Tucker (R) | 71,661 | 29. |
| 5 Chester G. Atkins (D) | 181,860 | 84. |
| T. David Hudson (LIBERT) | 34,339 | 15. |
| 6 Nicholas Mavroules (D) | 177,643 | 69. |
| Paul McCarthy (R) | 77,186 | 30. |
| 7 Edward J. Markey (D) | 188,647 | 100. |
| 8 Joseph P. Kennedy II (D) | 165,745 | 80. |
| Glenn W. Fiscus (R) | 40,316 | 19. |
| 9 Joe Moakley (D) | 160,799 | 99. |
| 10 Gerry E. Studds (D) | 187,178 | 66. |
| Jon L. Bryan (R) | 93,564 | 33. |
| 11 Brian J. Donnelly (D) | 169,692 | 80. |
| Michael C. Gilleran (R) | 40,277 | 19. |

### MICHIGAN

| Candidates | Votes | % |
|---|---|---|
| 1 John Conyers Jr. (D) | 127,800 | 91. |
| Bill Ashe (R) | 10,979 | 7. |
| 2 Carl D. Pursell (R) | 120,070 | 54. |
| Lana Pollack (D) | 98,290 | 44. |
| 3 Howard Wolpe (D) | 112,605 | 57. |
| Cal Allgaier (R) | 83,769 | 42. |
| 4 Fred Upton (R) | 132,270 | 70. |
| Norman J. Rivers (D) | 54,428 | 29. |
| 5 Paul B. Henry (R) | 166,569 | 72. |
| James M. Catchick (D) | 62,868 | 27. |
| 6 Bob Carr (D) | 120,581 | 58. |
| Scott Schultz (R) | 81,079 | 39. |
| 7 Dale E. Kildee (D) | 150,832 | 75. |
| Jeff Coad (R) | 47,071 | 24. |
| 8 Bob Traxler (D) | 139,904 | 72. |
| Lloyd F. Buhl (R) | 54,195 | 27. |
| 9 Guy Vander Jagt (R) | 149,748 | 69. |
| David John Gawron (D) | 64,843 | 30. |
| 10 Bill Schuette (R) | 152,646 | 72. |
| Mathias G. Forbes (D) | 55,398 | 26. |
| 11 Robert W. Davis (R) | 129,085 | 59. |
| Mitch Irwin (D) | 86,526 | 40. |
| 12 David E. Bonior (D) | 108,158 | 53. |
| Douglas Carl (R) | 91,780 | 45. |
| 13 George W. Crockett Jr. (D) | 99,751 | 87. |
| John Wright Savage II (R) | 13,196 | 11. |
| 14 Dennis M. Hertel (D) | 111,612 | 62. |
| Kenneth C. McNealy (R) | 64,750 | 36. |
| 15 William D. Ford (D) | 104,596 | 63. |
| Burl C. Adkins (R) | 56,963 | 34. |

*Footnote, see p. 1313.*

| | Candidates | Votes | % |
|---|---|---|---|
| 16 | John D. Dingell (D) | 132,775 | 97.4 |
| 17 | Sander M. Levin (D) | 135,493 | 70.2 |
| | Dennis M. Flessland (R) | 55,197 | 28.6 |
| 18 | William S. Broomfield (R) | 195,579 | 76.0 |
| | Gary L. Kohut (D) | 57,643 | 22.4 |

## MINNESOTA [4]

| | Candidates | Votes | % |
|---|---|---|---|
| 1 | Timothy J. Penny (DFL) | 161,118 | 70.1 |
| | Curt Schrimpf (I-R) | 67,709 | 29.5 |
| 2 | Vin Weber (I-R) | 131,639 | 57.8 |
| | Doug Peterson (DFL) | 96,016 | 42.2 |
| 3 | Bill Frenzel (I-R) | 215,322 | 68.2 |
| | Dave Carlson (DFL) | 99,770 | 31.6 |
| 4 | Bruce F. Vento (DFL) | 181,227 | 72.4 |
| | Ian Maitland (I-R) | 67,073 | 26.8 |
| 5 | Martin Olav Sabo (DFL) | 174,416 | 72.1 |
| | Raymond C. Gilbertson (I-R) | 60,646 | 25.1 |
| 6 | Gerry Sikorski (DFL) | 169,486 | 65.4 |
| | Ray Ploetz (I-R) | 89,209 | 34.4 |
| 7 | Arlan Stangeland (I-R) | 121,396 | 54.6 |
| | Marv Hanson (DFL) | 101,011 | 45.4 |
| 8 | James L. Oberstar (DFL) | 165,656 | 74.5 |
| | Jerry Shuster (I-R) | 56,630 | 25.5 |

## MISSISSIPPI

| | Candidates | Votes | % |
|---|---|---|---|
| 1 | Jamie L. Whitten (D) | 137,445 | 78.2 |
| | Jim Bush (R) | 38,381 | 21.8 |
| 2 | Mike Espy (D) | 112,401 | 64.7 |
| | Jack Coleman (R) | 59,827 | 34.5 |
| 3 | G. V. "Sonny" Montgomery (D) | 164,651 | 88.8 |
| | Jimmie Ray Bourland (R) | 20,729 | 11.2 |
| 4 | Mike Parker (D) | 110,184 | 54.8 |
| | Thomas Collins (R) | 88,433 | 44.0 |
| 5 | Larkin Smith (R) | 100,185 | 55.0 |
| | Gene Taylor (D) | 82,034 | 45.0 |

## MISSOURI

| | Candidates | Votes | % |
|---|---|---|---|
| 1 | William L. Clay (D) | 140,751 | 71.6 |
| | Joseph A. Schwan (R) | 53,109 | 27.0 |
| 2 | Jack Buechner (R) | 186,450 | 66.3 |
| | Bob Feigenbaum (D) | 91,645 | 32.6 |
| 3 | Richard A. Gephardt (D) | 150,205 | 62.8 |
| | Mark F. "Thor" Hearne (R) | 86,763 | 36.3 |
| 4 | Ike Skelton (D) | 166,480 | 71.8 |
| | David Eyerly (R) | 65,393 | 28.2 |
| 5 | Alan Wheat (D) | 149,166 | 70.3 |
| | Mary Ellen Lobb (R) | 60,453 | 28.5 |
| 6 | E. Thomas Coleman (R) | 135,883 | 59.3 |
| | Doug R. Hughes (D) | 93,128 | 40.7 |
| 7 | Mel Hancock (R) | 127,939 | 53.1 |
| | Max E. Bacon (D) | 111,244 | 46.2 |
| 8 | Bill Emerson (R) | 117,601 | 58.1 |
| | Wayne Cryts (D) | 84,801 | 41.9 |
| 9 | Harold L. Volkmer (D) | 160,872 | 67.9 |
| | Ken Dudley (R) | 76,008 | 32.1 |

## MONTANA

| | Candidates | Votes | % |
|---|---|---|---|
| 1 | Pat Williams (D) | 115,278 | 60.8 |
| | Jim Fenlason (R) | 74,405 | 39.2 |
| 2 | Ron Marlenee (R) | 97,465 | 55.5 |
| | Richard "Buck" O'Brien (D) | 78,069 | 44.5 |

## NEBRASKA

| | Candidates | Votes | % |
|---|---|---|---|
| 1 | Doug Bereuter (R) | 146,231 | 66.9 |
| | Corky Jones (D) | 72,167 | 33.0 |
| 2 | Peter Hoagland (D) | 112,174 | 50.5 |
| | Jerry Schenken (R) | 109,193 | 49.1 |
| 3 | Virginia Smith (R) | 170,302 | 79.0 |
| | John D. Racek (D) | 45,183 | 21.0 |

## NEVADA

| | Candidates | Votes | % |
|---|---|---|---|
| 1 | James H. Bilbray (D) | 101,764 | 64.0 |
| | Lucille Lusk (R) | 53,588 | 33.7 |
| 2 | Barbara F. Vucanovich (R) | 105,981 | 57.3 |
| | James Spoo (D) | 75,163 | 40.6 |

## NEW HAMPSHIRE

| | Candidates | Votes | % |
|---|---|---|---|
| 1 | Robert C. Smith (R) | 131,824 | 60.3 |
| | Joseph F. Keefe (D) | 86,623 | 39.6 |
| 2 | Chuck Douglas (R) | 119,742 | 56.8 |
| | James W. Donchess (D) | 89,677 | 42.5 |

## NEW JERSEY

| | Candidates | Votes | % |
|---|---|---|---|
| 1 | James J. Florio (D) | 141,988 | 69.9 |
| | Frank A. Cristaudo (R) | 60,037 | 29.5 |
| 2 | William J. Hughes (D) | 134,505 | 65.7 |
| | Kirk W. Conover (R) | 67,759 | 33.1 |
| 3 | Frank Pallone Jr. (D) | 117,024 | 51.6 |
| | Joseph Azzolina (R) | 107,479 | 47.4 |
| 4 | Christopher H. Smith (R) | 155,283 | 65.7 |
| | Betty Holland (D) | 79,006 | 33.4 |
| 5 | Marge Roukema (R) | 175,562 | 75.7 |
| | Lee Monaco (D) | 54,828 | 23.6 |
| 6 | Bernard J. Dwyer (D) | 120,125 | 61.1 |
| | Peter J. Sica (R) | 74,824 | 38.1 |
| 7 | Matthew J. Rinaldo (R) | 153,350 | 74.6 |
| | James Hely (D) | 52,189 | 25.4 |
| 8 | Robert A. Roe (D) | 96,036 | 100.0 |
| 9 | Robert G. Torricelli (D) | 142,012 | 67.1 |
| | Roger J. Lane (R) | 68,363 | 32.3 |
| 10 | Donald M. Payne (D) | 84,681 | 77.4 |
| | Michael Webb (R) | 13,848 | 12.6 |
| | Anthony Imperiale (I) | 5,422 | 5.0 |
| 11 | Dean A. Gallo (R) | 154,654 | 70.5 |
| | John C. Shaw (D) | 64,773 | 29.5 |
| 12 | Jim Courter (R) | 165,918 | 69.3 |
| | Norman J. Weinstein (D) | 71,596 | 29.9 |
| 13 | H. James Saxton (R) | 167,470 | 69.5 |
| | James B. Smith (D) | 73,561 | 30.5 |
| 14 | Frank J. Guarini (D) | 104,001 | 67.3 |
| | Fred J. Theemling Jr. (R) | 47,293 | 30.6 |

### Special Election [5]

| | Candidates | Votes | % |
|---|---|---|---|
| 3 | Frank Pallone Jr. (D) | 116,988 | 52.0 |
| | Joseph Azzolina (R) | 106,489 | 47.3 |

## NEW MEXICO

| | Candidates | Votes | % |
|---|---|---|---|
| 1 | Steven H. Schiff (R) | 89,985 | 50.6 |
| | Tom Udall (D) | 84,138 | 47.3 |
| 2 | Joe Skeen (R) | 100,324 | 100.0 |
| 3 | Bill Richardson (D) | 124,938 | 73.1 |
| | Cecilia M. Salazar (R) | 45,954 | 26.9 |

## NEW YORK

| | Candidates | Votes | % |
|---|---|---|---|
| 1 | George J. Hochbrueckner (D) | 105,624 | 50.8 |
| | Edward P. Romaine (R, C, RTL) | 102,327 | 49.2 |
| 2 | Thomas J. Downey (D) | 107,646 | 61.6 |
| | Joseph Cardino Jr. (R, C, RTL) | 66,972 | 38.4 |
| 3 | Robert J. Mrazek (D) | 128,336 | 57.2 |
| | Robert Previdi (R, C) | 91,122 | 40.6 |
| 4 | Norman F. Lent (R, C) | 151,038 | 70.1 |
| | Francis T. Goban (D, L) | 59,479 | 27.6 |
| 5 | Raymond J. McGrath (R, C) | 134,881 | 65.1 |
| | William G. Kelly (D) | 68,930 | 33.2 |
| 6 | Floyd H. Flake (D, L) | 94,506 | 85.9 |
| | Robert L. Brandofino (C) | 15,547 | 14.1 |
| 7 | Gary L. Ackerman (D, L) | 93,120 | 100.0 |
| 8 | James H. Scheuer (D, L) | 100,240 | 100.0 |
| 9 | Thomas J. Manton (D) | 72,851 | 100.0 |
| 10 | Charles E. Schumer (D, L) | 107,056 | 78.4 |
| | George S. Popielarski (R) | 24,313 | 17.8 |

*Footnote, see p. 1313.*

| | Candidates | Votes | % |
|---|---|---|---|
| 11 | Edolphus Towns (D, L) | 73,755 | 88.7 |
| | Riaz B. Hussain (R) | 7,418 | 8.9 |
| 12 | Major R. Owens (D, L) | 74,304 | 93.0 |
| | Owen Augustin (R, C) | 5,582 | 7.0 |
| 13 | Stephen J. Solarz (D, L) | 81,305 | 74.7 |
| | Anthony M. Curci (R, C) | 27,536 | 25.3 |
| 14 | Guy V. Molinari (R, C, RTL) | 99,179 | 63.3 |
| | Jerome X. O'Donovan (D) | 57,503 | 36.7 |
| 15 | Bill Green (R) | 107,599 | 61.3 |
| | Peter G. Doukas (D) | 64,425 | 36.7 |
| 16 | Charles B. Rangel (D, R, L) | 107,620 | 97.1 |
| 17 | Ted Weiss (D, L) | 157,339 | 84.4 |
| | Myrna C. Albert (R, C) | 29,156 | 15.6 |
| 18 | Robert Garcia (D, L) | 75,459 | 91.1 |
| | Fred Brown (R) | 5,764 | 6.9 |
| 19 | Eliot L. Engel (D, L) | 77,158 | 56.0 |
| | Mario Biaggi (R) | 37,454 | 27.2 |
| | Martin J. O'Grady (RTL) | 11,271 | 8.2 |
| | Robert Blumetti (C) | 11,182 | 8.1 |
| 20 | Nita M. Lowey (D) | 102,235 | 50.3 |
| | Joseph J. DioGuardi (R, C) | 96,465 | 47.5 |
| 21 | Hamilton Fish Jr. (R, C) | 150,443 | 74.6 |
| | Lawrence W. Grunberger (D) | 47,294 | 23.5 |
| 22 | Benjamin A. Gilman (R) | 144,227 | 70.8 |
| | Eleanor F. Burlingham (D) | 54,312 | 26.7 |
| 23 | Michael R. McNulty (D) | 145,040 | 61.7 |
| | Peter M. Bakal (R, C) | 89,858 | 38.3 |
| 24 | Gerald B. H. Solomon (R, C, RTL) | 162,962 | 72.4 |
| | Fred Baye (D) | 62,177 | 27.6 |
| 25 | Sherwood Boehlert (R) | 130,122 | 100.0 |
| 26 | David O'B. Martin (R, C) | 131,043 | 75.0 |
| | Donald R. Ravenscroft (D) | 43,585 | 25.0 |
| 27 | James T. Walsh (R) | 124,928 | 57.5 |
| | Rosemary S. Pooler (D) | 90,854 | 41.8 |
| 28 | Matthew F. McHugh (D) | 141,976 | 93.2 |
| | Mary C. Dixon (RTL) | 10,395 | 6.8 |
| 29 | Frank Horton (R) | 132,608 | 68.8 |
| | James R. Vogel (D) | 51,243 | 26.6 |
| 30 | Louise M. Slaughter (D) | 128,364 | 56.9 |
| | John D. Bouchard (R) | 89,126 | 39.5 |
| 31 | Bill Paxon (R, C, RTL) | 117,710 | 53.4 |
| | David J. Swarts (D, L) | 102,777 | 46.6 |
| 32 | John J. LaFalce (D, L) | 133,917 | 72.7 |
| | Emil K. Everett (R, C, RTL) | 50,229 | 27.3 |
| 33 | Henry J. Nowak (D, L) | 139,604 | 100.0 |
| 34 | Amo Houghton (R, C) | 131,078 | 96.5 |

## NORTH CAROLINA

| | Candidates | Votes | % |
|---|---|---|---|
| 1 | Walter B. Jones (D) | 118,027 | 65.2 |
| | Howard Moye (R) | 63,013 | 34.8 |
| 2 | Tim Valentine (D) | 128,832 | 100.0 |
| 3 | H. Martin Lancaster (D) | 95,323 | 100.0 |
| 4 | David E. Price (D) | 131,896 | 58.0 |
| | Tom Fetzer (R) | 95,482 | 42.0 |
| 5 | Stephen L. Neal (D) | 110,516 | 52.6 |
| | Lyons Gray (R) | 99,540 | 47.4 |
| 6 | Howard Coble (R) | 116,534 | 62.5 |
| | Tom Gilmore (D) | 70,008 | 37.5 |
| 7 | Charlie Rose (D) | 102,392 | 67.3 |
| | George "Jerry" Thompson (R) | 49,855 | 32.7 |
| 8 | W. G. "Bill" Hefner (D) | 99,214 | 51.5 |
| | Ted Blanton (R) | 93,463 | 48.5 |
| 9 | Alex McMillan (R) | 139,014 | 65.9 |
| | Mark Sholander (D) | 71,802 | 34.1 |
| 10 | Cass Ballenger (R) | 112,554 | 61.0 |
| | Jack L. Rhyne (D) | 71,865 | 39.0 |
| 11 | James McClure Clarke (D) | 108,436 | 50.4 |
| | Charles H. Taylor (R) | 106,907 | 49.6 |

## NORTH DAKOTA

| | Candidates | Votes | % |
|---|---|---|---|
| AL | Byron L. Dorgan (D) | 212,583 | 70.9 |
| | Steve Sydness (R) | 84,475 | 28.1 |

# OHIO

| | Candidates | Votes | % |
|---|---|---|---|
| 1 | Thomas A. Luken (D) | 117,682 | 56.5 |
| | Steve Chabot (R) | 90,738 | 43.5 |
| 2 | Bill Gradison (R) | 153,162 | 72.3 |
| | Chuck R. Stidham (D) | 58,637 | 27.7 |
| 3 | Tony P. Hall (D) | 141,953 | 76.9 |
| | Ron Crutcher (R) | 42,664 | 23.1 |
| 4 | Michael G. Oxley (R) | 160,099 | 99.7 |
| 5 | Paul E. Gillmor (R) | 123,838 | 60.7 |
| | Tom Murray (D) | 80,292 | 39.3 |
| 6 | Bob McEwen (R) | 152,235 | 74.3 |
| | Gordon Roberts (D) | 52,635 | 25.7 |
| 7 | Michael DeWine (R) | 142,597 | 73.9 |
| | Jack Schira (D) | 50,423 | 26.1 |
| 8 | Donald E. Lukens (R) | 154,164 | 75.9 |
| | John W. Griffin (D) | 49,084 | 24.1 |
| 9 | Marcy Kaptur (D) | 157,557 | 81.3 |
| | Al Hawkins (R) | 36,183 | 18.7 |
| 10 | Clarence E. Miller (R) | 143,673 | 71.6 |
| | John M. Buchanan (D) | 56,893 | 28.4 |
| 11 | Dennis E. Eckart (D) | 124,600 | 61.5 |
| | Margaret Mueller (R) | 78,028 | 38.5 |
| 12 | John R. Kasich (R) | 154,727 | 79.0 |
| | Mark P. Brown (D) | 41,178 | 21.0 |
| 13 | Don J. Pease (D) | 137,074 | 69.8 |
| | Dwight Brown (R) | 59,287 | 30.2 |
| 14 | Thomas C. Sawyer (D) | 148,951 | 74.7 |
| | Loretta A. Lang (R) | 50,356 | 25.3 |
| 15 | Chalmers P. Wylie (R) | 146,854 | 74.8 |
| | Mark S. Froehlich (D) | 49,441 | 25.2 |
| 16 | Ralph Regula (R) | 158,824 | 78.6 |
| | Melvin J. Gravely (D) | 43,356 | 21.4 |
| 17 | James A. Traficant Jr. (D) | 162,526 | 77.2 |
| | Frederick W. Lenz (R) | 47,929 | 22.8 |
| 18 | Douglas Applegate (D) | 151,306 | 76.6 |
| | William C. Abraham (R) | 46,130 | 23.4 |
| 19 | Edward F. Feighan (D) | 168,065 | 70.5 |
| | Noel F. Roberts (R) | 70,359 | 29.5 |
| 20 | Mary Rose Oakar (D) | 146,715 | 82.6 |
| | Michael Sajna (R) | 30,944 | 17.4 |
| 21 | Louis Stokes (D) | 148,388 | 85.7 |
| | Franklin H. Roski (R) | 24,804 | 14.3 |

# OKLAHOMA

| | | | |
|---|---|---|---|
| 1 | James M. Inhofe (R) | 103,458 | 52.6 |
| | Kurt Glassco (D) | 93,101 | 47.4 |
| 2 | Mike Synar (D) | 136,009 | 64.9 |
| | Ira Phillips (R) | 73,659 | 35.1 |
| 3 | Wes Watkins (D) | | 100.0 |
| 4 | Dave McCurdy (D) | | 100.0 |
| 5 | Mickey Edwards (R) | 139,182 | 72.2 |
| | Terry J. Montgomery (D) | 53,668 | 27.8 |
| 6 | Glenn English (D) | 122,887 | 73.1 |
| | Mike Brown (R) | 45,239 | 26.9 |

# OREGON

| | | | |
|---|---|---|---|
| 1 | Les AuCoin (D) | 179,915 | 69.6 |
| | Earl Molander (R) | 78,626 | 30.4 |
| 2 | Robert F. Smith (R) | 125,366 | 62.7 |
| | Larry Tuttle (D) | 74,700 | 37.3 |
| 3 | Ron Wyden (D) | 190,684 | 99.4 |
| 4 | Peter A. DeFazio (D) | 108,483 | 72.0 |
| | Jim Howard (R) | 42,220 | 28.0 |
| 5 | Denny Smith (R) | 111,489 | 50.2 |
| | Mike Kopetski (D) | 110,782 | 49.8 |

# PENNSYLVANIA

| | | | |
|---|---|---|---|
| 1 | Thomas M. Foglietta (D) | 128,076 | 76.3 |
| | William J. O'Brien (R) | 39,749 | 23.7 |
| 2 | William H. Gray III (D) | 184,322 | 93.7 |
| | Richard L. Harsch (R) | 12,365 | 6.3 |
| 3 | Robert A. Borski (D) | 135,590 | 63.2 |
| | Mark Matthews (R) | 78,909 | 36.8 |
| 4 | Joe Kolter (D) | 124,041 | 69.8 |
| | Gordon R. Johnston (R) | 52,402 | 29.5 |

| | Candidates | Votes | % |
|---|---|---|---|
| 5 | Richard T. Schulze (R) | 153,453 | 78.2 |
| | Donald A. Hadley (D) | 42,758 | 21.8 |
| 6 | Gus Yatron (D) | 114,119 | 63.1 |
| | James R. Erwin (R) | 65,278 | 36.1 |
| 7 | Curt Weldon (R) | 155,387 | 67.8 |
| | David Landau (D) | 73,745 | 32.2 |
| 8 | Peter H. Kostmayer (D) | 128,153 | 56.8 |
| | Ed Howard (R) | 93,648 | 41.5 |
| 9 | Bud Shuster (R, D) | 158,702 | 100.0 |
| 10 | Joseph M. McDade (R) | 140,096 | 73.2 |
| | Robert C. Cordaro (D) | 51,179 | 26.8 |
| 11 | Paul E. Kanjorski (D) | 120,706 | 100.0 |
| 12 | John P. Murtha (D) | 133,081 | 100.0 |
| 13 | Lawrence Coughlin (R) | 152,191 | 66.6 |
| | Bernard Tomkin (D) | 76,424 | 33.4 |
| 14 | William J. Coyne (D) | 135,181 | 78.6 |
| | Richard Edward Caligiuri (R) | 36,719 | 21.4 |
| 15 | Don Ritter (R) | 106,951 | 57.5 |
| | Ed Reibman (D) | 79,127 | 42.5 |
| 16 | Robert S. Walker (R) | 136,944 | 74.0 |
| | Ernest Eric Guyll (D) | 48,169 | 26.0 |
| 17 | George W. Gekas (R, D) | 166,289 | 100.0 |
| 18 | Doug Walgren (D) | 136,924 | 62.7 |
| | John A. Newman (R) | 80,975 | 37.0 |
| 19 | Bill Goodling (R) | 145,381 | 77.2 |
| | Paul E. Ritchey (D) | 42,819 | 22.8 |
| 20 | Joseph M. Gaydos (D) | 137,472 | 98.5 |
| 21 | Tom Ridge (R) | 141,832 | 78.7 |
| | George R. H. Elder (D) | 38,288 | 21.3 |
| 22 | Austin J. Murphy (D) | 123,428 | 72.4 |
| | William Hodgkiss (R) | 47,039 | 27.6 |
| 23 | William F. Clinger Jr. (R) | 105,575 | 62.0 |
| | Howard Shakespeare (D) | 63,476 | 37.3 |

# RHODE ISLAND

| | | | |
|---|---|---|---|
| 1 | Ronald K. Machtley (R) | 105,506 | 55.6 |
| | Fernand J. St Germain (D) | 84,141 | 44.4 |
| 2 | Claudine Schneider (R) | 145,218 | 72.1 |
| | Ruth S. Morgenthau (D) | 56,129 | 27.9 |

# SOUTH CAROLINA

| | | | |
|---|---|---|---|
| 1 | Arthur Ravenel Jr. (R) | 101,572 | 63.8 |
| | Wheeler Tillman (D) | 57,691 | 36.2 |
| 2 | Floyd D. Spence (R) | 94,960 | 52.8 |
| | Jim Leventis (D) | 83,978 | 46.6 |
| 3 | Butler Derrick (D) | 89,071 | 53.7 |
| | Henry S. Jordan (R) | 75,571 | 45.6 |
| 4 | Liz J. Patterson (D) | 90,234 | 52.2 |
| | Knox White (R) | 82,794 | 47.8 |
| 5 | John M. Spratt Jr. (D) | 107,959 | 69.8 |
| | Robert K. "Bob" Carley (R) | 46,622 | 30.2 |
| 6 | Robin Tallon (D) | 120,719 | 76.1 |
| | Robert Cunningham Sr. (R) | 37,958 | 23.9 |

# SOUTH DAKOTA

| | | | |
|---|---|---|---|
| AL | Tim Johnson (D) | 223,759 | 71.7 |
| | David Volk (R) | 88,157 | 28.3 |

# TENNESSEE

| | | | |
|---|---|---|---|
| 1 | James H. Quillen (R) | 119,526 | 80.2 |
| | Sidney S. Smith (D) | 29,469 | 19.8 |
| 2 | John J. Duncan (R) | 99,631 | 56.2 |
| | Dudley W. Taylor (D) | 77,540 | 43.8 |
| 3 | Marilyn Lloyd (D) | 108,264 | 57.4 |
| | Harold L. Coker (R) | 80,372 | 42.6 |
| 4 | Jim Cooper (D) | 94,129 | 100.0 |
| 5 | Bob Clement (D) | 155,068 | 100.0 |
| 6 | Bart Gordon (D) | 123,652 | 76.5 |
| | Wallace Embry (R) | 38,033 | 23.5 |
| 7 | Don Sundquist (R) | 142,025 | 80.1 |
| | Ken Bloodworth (D) | 35,237 | 19.9 |
| 8 | John Tanner (D) | 94,571 | 62.4 |
| | Ed Bryant (R) | 56,893 | 37.6 |
| 9 | Harold E. Ford (D) | 126,280 | 81.6 |
| | Isaac Richmond (I) | 28,522 | 18.4 |

| | Candidates | Votes | % |
|---|---|---|---|
| | **Special Elections** | | |
| 2 | John J. "Jimmy" Duncan Jr. [6] (R) | 92,929 | 56. |
| | Dudley W. Taylor (D) | 70,576 | 42. |
| 5 | Bob Clement (D) [7] | 56,323 | 62. |
| | Terry Holcomb (R) | 32,847 | 36. |

# TEXAS

| | | | |
|---|---|---|---|
| 1 | Jim Chapman (D) | 122,566 | 62. |
| | Horace McQueen (R) | 74,357 | 37. |
| 2 | Charles Wilson (D) | 145,614 | 87. |
| | Gary W. Nelson (LIBERT) | 20,475 | 12. |
| 3 | Steve Bartlett (R) | 227,882 | 81. |
| | Blake Cowden (D) | 50,627 | 18. |
| 4 | Ralph M. Hall (D) | 139,379 | 66. |
| | Randy Sutton (R) | 67,337 | 32. |
| 5 | John Bryant (D) | 95,376 | 60. |
| | Lon Williams (R) | 59,877 | 38. |
| 6 | Joe L. Barton (R) | 164,692 | 67. |
| | N. P. "Pat" Kendrick (D) | 78,786 | 32. |
| 7 | Bill Archer (R) | 185,203 | 79. |
| | Diane Richards (D) | 48,824 | 20. |
| 8 | Jack Fields (R) | 90,503 | 100. |
| 9 | Jack Brooks (D) | 137,270 | 100. |
| 10 | J. J. "Jake" Pickle (D) | 232,213 | 93. |
| | Vincent J. May (LIBERT) | 16,281 | 6. |
| 11 | Marvin Leath (D) | 134,207 | 95. |
| 12 | Jim Wright (D) | 135,459 | 99. |
| 13 | Bill Sarpalius (D) | 98,345 | 52. |
| | Larry S. Milner (R) | 89,105 | 47. |
| 14 | Greg H. Laughlin (D) | 111,395 | 53. |
| | Mac Sweeney (R) | 96,042 | 45. |
| 15 | E. "Kika" de la Garza (D) | 93,672 | 93. |
| | Gloria Joyce Hendrix (LIBERT) | 6,133 | 6. |
| 16 | Ronald D. Coleman (D) | 104,514 | 100. |
| 17 | Charles W. Stenholm (D) | 149,064 | 100. |
| 18 | Mickey Leland (D) | 94,408 | 92. |
| | J. Alejandro Snead (LIBERT) | 7,235 | 7. |
| 19 | Larry Combest (R) | 113,068 | 67. |
| | Gerald McCathern (D) | 53,932 | 32. |
| 20 | Henry B. Gonzalez (D) | 94,527 | 70. |
| | Lee Trevino (R) | 36,801 | 27. |
| 21 | Lamar Smith (R) | 203,989 | 93. |
| | James A. Robinson (LIBERT) | 14,801 | 6. |
| 22 | Thomas D. DeLay (R) | 125,733 | 67. |
| | Wayne Walker (D) | 58,471 | 31. |
| 23 | Albert G. Bustamante (D) | 116,423 | 64. |
| | Jerome L. Gonzales (R) | 60,559 | 33. |
| 24 | Martin Frost (D) | 135,794 | 92. |
| | Leo Sadovy (LIBERT) | 10,841 | 7. |
| 25 | Michael A. Andrews (D) | 113,499 | 71. |
| | George H. Loefflor Jr. (R) | 44,043 | 27. |
| 26 | Dick Armey (R) | 194,944 | 69. |
| | Jo Ann Reyes (D) | 86,490 | 30. |
| 27 | Solomon P. Ortiz (D) | 105,085 | 100. |

# UTAH

| | | | |
|---|---|---|---|
| 1 | James V. Hansen (R) | 130,893 | 59. |
| | Gunn McKay (D) | 87,976 | 40. |
| 2 | Wayne Owens (D) | 112,129 | 57. |
| | Richard Snelgrove (R) | 80,212 | 41. |
| 3 | Howard C. Nielson (R) | 129,951 | 66. |
| | Robert W. Stringham (D) | 60,018 | 30. |

# VERMONT

| | | | |
|---|---|---|---|
| AL | Peter Smith (R) | 98,937 | 41. |
| | Bernard Sanders (I) | 90,026 | 37. |
| | Paul N. Poirier (D) | 45,330 | 18. |

# VIRGINIA

| | | | |
|---|---|---|---|
| 1 | Herbert H. Bateman (R) | 135,937 | 73. |
| | James S. Ellenson (D) | 49,614 | 26. |
| 2 | Owen B. Pickett (D) | 106,666 | 60. |

*Footnote, see p. 1313.*

| Candidates | Votes | % |
|---|---|---|
| Jerry R. Curry (R) | 62,564 | 35.5 |
| Stephen P. Shao (I) | 4,255 | 2.4 |
| Robert A. Smith (I) | 2,691 | 1.5 |
| 3 Thomas J. Bliley Jr. (R) | 187,354 | 99.7 |
| 4 Norman Sisisky (D) | 134,786 | 99.9 |
| 5 Lewis F. Payne Jr. (D) | 97,242 | 54.2 |
| Charles Hawkins (R) | 78,396 | 43.7 |
| 6 Jim Olin (D) | 118,369 | 63.9 |
| Charles E. Judd (R) | 66,935 | 36.1 |
| 7 D. French Slaughter Jr. (R) | 136,988 | 99.6 |
| 8 Stan Parris (R) | 154,761 | 62.3 |
| David G. Brickley (D) | 93,561 | 37.7 |
| 9 Rick Boucher (D) | 113,309 | 63.4 |
| John C. Brown (R) | 65,410 | 36.6 |
| 10 Frank R. Wolf (R) | 188,550 | 68.1 |
| Robert L. Weinberg (D) | 88,284 | 31.9 |

### Special Election [8]

| | Votes | % |
|---|---|---|
| Lewis F. Payne Jr. (D) | 55,469 | 59.3 |
| Linda Arey (R) | 38,063 | 40.7 |

## WASHINGTON

| | Votes | % |
|---|---|---|
| 1 John R. Miller (R) | 152,265 | 55.4 |
| Reese Lindquist (D) | 122,646 | 44.6 |

| Candidates | Votes | % |
|---|---|---|
| 2 Al Swift (D) | 175,191 | 100.0 |
| 3 Jolene Unsoeld (D) | 109,412 | 50.1 |
| Bill Wight (R) | 108,794 | 49.9 |
| 4 Sid Morrison (R) | 142,938 | 74.5 |
| J. Richard Golob (D) | 48,850 | 25.5 |
| 5 Thomas S. Foley (D) | 160,654 | 76.4 |
| Marlyn A. Derby (R) | 49,657 | 23.6 |
| 6 Norm Dicks (D) | 125,904 | 67.6 |
| Kevin P. Cook (R) | 60,346 | 32.4 |
| 7 Jim McDermott (D) | 173,809 | 76.3 |
| Robert Edwards (R) | 53,902 | 23.7 |
| 8 Rod Chandler (R) | 174,942 | 70.9 |
| Jim Kean (D) | 71,920 | 29.1 |

## WEST VIRGINIA

| | Votes | % |
|---|---|---|
| 1 Alan B. Mollohan (D) | 119,256 | 74.5 |
| Howard K. Tuck (R) | 40,732 | 25.5 |
| 2 Harley O. Staggers Jr. (D) | 118,356 | 100.0 |
| 3 Bob Wise (D) | 120,192 | 74.3 |
| Paul W. Hart (R) | 41,478 | 25.7 |
| 4 Nick J. Rahall II (D) | 78,812 | 61.3 |
| Marianne R. Brewster (R) | 49,753 | 38.7 |

## WISCONSIN

| Candidates | Votes | % |
|---|---|---|
| 1 Les Aspin (D) | 158,552 | 76.2 |
| Bernie Weaver (R) | 49,620 | 23.8 |
| 2 Robert W. Kastenmeier (D) | 151,501 | 58.5 |
| Ann J. Haney (R) | 107,457 | 41.5 |
| 3 Steve Gunderson (R) | 157,513 | 68.3 |
| Karl E. Krueger (D) | 72,935 | 31.6 |
| 4 Gerald D. Kleczka (D) | 177,283 | 99.7 |
| 5 Jim Moody (D) | 140,518 | 64.1 |
| Helen Barnhill (R) | 78,307 | 35.7 |
| 6 Thomas E. Petri (R) | 165,923 | 74.2 |
| Joe Garrett (D) | 57,552 | 25.8 |
| 7 David R. Obey (D) | 142,197 | 61.8 |
| Kevin J. Hermening (R) | 86,077 | 37.4 |
| 8 Toby Roth (R) | 167,275 | 69.7 |
| Robert Baron (D) | 72,708 | 30.3 |
| 9 F. James Sensenbrenner Jr. (R) | 185,093 | 74.9 |
| Tom Hickey (D) | 62,003 | 25.1 |

## WYOMING

| | Votes | % |
|---|---|---|
| AL Dick Cheney (R) | 118,350 | 66.6 |
| Bryan Sharratt (D) | 56,527 | 31.8 |

**1988 Elections**

1. A special election was held to fill the unexpired term of Rep. Melvin Price (D), who died April 22, 1988.

2. For the 1988 House elections in Louisiana, an open primary election was held with candidates from all parties running on the same ballot. Any candidate who received a majority was elected unopposed, with no further appearance on the general election ballot. If no candidate received 50 percent, a runoff was held between the two top finishers.

3. A special election was held to fill the unexpired term of Rep. Buddy Roemer (D), who resigned March 14, 1988, having been elected governor.

4. In Minnesota the Democratic Party is known as the Democratic-Farmer-Labor Party and

the Republican Party as the Independent-Republican Party; candidates appear on the ballot with these designations.

5. A special election was held to fill the unexpired term of Rep. James J. Howard (D), who died March 25, 1988.

6. A special election was held to fill the unexpired term of Rep. John J. Duncan (R), who died June 21, 1988.

7. A special election was held to fill the unexpired term of Rep. Bill Bonor (D), who resigned Oct. 5, 1987, having been elected mayor of Nashville.

8. A special election was held to fill the unexpired term of Rep. W. C. Daniel (D), who died Jan. 23, 1988.

# 1989 House Elections

## ALABAMA

**Special Election [1]**

| | Candidates | Votes | % |
|---|---|---|---|
| 3 | Glen Browder (D) | 47,294 | *65.3* |
| | John Rice (R) | 25,142 | *34.7* |

## CALIFORNIA

**Special Election [2]**

| | | Votes | % |
|---|---|---|---|
| 15 | Gary Condit (D) | 51,543 | *57.1* |
| | Clare Berryhill (R) | 1,592 | *35.0* |

## FLORIDA

**Special Election [3]**

| | | Votes | % |
|---|---|---|---|
| 18 | Ileana Ros-Lehtinen (R) | 49,298 | *53.3* |
| | Gerald Richman (D) | 43,274 | *46.7* |

## INDIANA

**Special Election [4]**

| | | Votes | % |
|---|---|---|---|
| 4 | Jill L. Long (D) | 65,272 | *50.7* |
| | Dan Heath (R) | 63,494 | *49.3* |

## MISSISSIPPI

**Special Election [5]**

| | Candidates | Votes | % |
|---|---|---|---|
| 5 | Gene Taylor (D) | 51,561 | *42.0* |
| | Tom Anderson Jr. (R) | 45,727 | *37.2* |
| | Mike Moore (D) | 25,579 | *20.8* |

**Special Runoff Election**

| | | Votes | % |
|---|---|---|---|
| 5 | Gene Taylor (D) | 83,296 | *65.2* |
| | Tom Anderson Jr. (R) | 44,494 | *34.8* |

## TEXAS [6]

**Special Election [7]**

| | | Votes | % |
|---|---|---|---|
| 12 | Bob Lanier (R) | 21,978 | *39.4* |
| | Pete Geren (D) | 17,751 | *31.8* |
| | Jim Lane (D) | 12,308 | *22.1* |

**Special Runoff Election**

| | Candidates | Votes | % |
|---|---|---|---|
| 12 | Pete Geren (D) | 40,210 | *51* |
| | Bob Lanier (R) | 38,590 | *49* |

**Special Election [8]**

| | | Votes | % |
|---|---|---|---|
| 18 | Craig Washington (D) | 27,367 | *41* |
| | Anthony Hall (D) | 22,797 | *34* |
| | Ron Wilson (D) | 4,948 | *7* |

**Special Runoff Election**

| | | Votes | % |
|---|---|---|---|
| 18 | Craig Washington (D) | 24,140 | *56.6* |
| | Anthony Hall (D) | 18,484 | *43.4* |

## WYOMING

**Special Election [9]**

| | | Votes | % |
|---|---|---|---|
| AL | Craig Thomas (R) | 74,384 | *52* |
| | John P. Vinich (D) | 60,845 | *43* |

**1989 Elections**

*1. A special election was held to fill the unexpired term of Rep. Bill Nichols (D), who died Dec. 13, 1988.*

*2. A special election was held to fill the unexpired term of Rep. Tony Coelho (D), who resigned June 15, 1989.*

*3. A special election was held to fill the unexpired term of Rep. Claude Pepper (D), who died May 30, 1989.*

*4. A special election was held to fill the unexpired term of Rep. Daniel R. Coats (R), who resigned in January 1989, having been appointed to the U.S. Senate.*

*5. A special election was held to fill the unexpired term of Rep. Larkin Smith (R), who died Aug. 15, 1989.*

*6. Texas election law required all candidates in special elections to run against each other, regardless of party. If no candidate received a majority, a special runoff election was held between the two candidates receiving the most votes in the special election.*

*7. A special election was held to fill the unexpired term of Rep. Jim Wright (D), who resigned June 30, 1989.*

*8. A special election was held to fill the unexpired term of Rep. Mickey Leland (D), who died Aug. 7, 1989.*

*9. A special election was held to fill the unexpired term of Rep. Dick Cheney (R), who resigned March 17, 1989, having been appointed defense secretary.*

# 1990 House Elections

## ALABAMA

| Candidates | Votes | % |
|---|---|---|
| Sonny Callahan (R) | 82,185 | 99.6 |
| Bill Dickinson (R) | 87,649 | 51.3 |
| Faye Baggiano (D) | 83,243 | 48.7 |
| Glen Browder (D) | 101,923 | 73.7 |
| Don Sledge (R) | 36,317 | 26.3 |
| Tom Bevill (D) | 129,872 | 99.7 |
| Robert E. "Bud" Cramer (D) | 113,047 | 67.1 |
| Albert McDonald (R) | 55,326 | 32.9 |
| Ben Erdreich (D) | 134,112 | 92.8 |
| David A. Alvarez (I) | 8,640 | 6.0 |
| Claude Harris (D) | 127,490 | 70.5 |
| Michael D. Barker (R) | 53,258 | 29.5 |

## ALASKA

| | Votes | % |
|---|---|---|
| Don Young (R) | 99,003 | 51.7 |
| John E. Devens (D) | 91,677 | 47.8 |

## ARIZONA

| | Votes | % |
|---|---|---|
| John J. Rhodes III (R) | 166,223 | 99.5 |
| Morris K. Udall (D) | 76,549 | 65.9 |
| Joseph D. Sweeney (R) | 39,586 | 34.1 |
| Bob Stump (R) | 134,279 | 56.6 |
| Roger Hartstone (D) | 103,018 | 43.4 |
| Jon Kyl (R) | 141,843 | 61.3 |
| Mark Ivey Jr. (D) | 89,395 | 38.7 |
| Jim Kolbe (R) | 138,975 | 64.8 |
| Chuck Phillips (D) | 75,642 | 35.2 |

## ARKANSAS

| | Votes | % |
|---|---|---|
| Bill Alexander (D) | 101,026 | 64.3 |
| Terry Hayes (R) | 56,071 | 35.7 |
| Ray Thornton (D) | 103,471 | 60.4 |
| Jim Keet (R) | 67,800 | 39.6 |
| John Paul Hammerschmidt (R) | 129,876 | 70.5 |
| Dan Ivy (D) | 54,332 | 29.5 |
| Beryl Anthony Jr. (D) | 110,365 | 72.4 |
| Roy Rood (R) | 42,130 | 27.6 |

## CALIFORNIA

| | Votes | % |
|---|---|---|
| Frank Riggs (R) | 99,782 | 43.3 |
| Douglas H. Bosco (D) | 96,468 | 41.9 |
| Darlene G. Comingore (PF) | 34,011 | 14.8 |
| Wally Herger (R) | 133,315 | 63.7 |
| Erwin E. "Bill" Rush (D) | 65,333 | 31.2 |
| Ross Crain (LIBERT) | 10,753 | 5.1 |
| Robert T. Matsui (D) | 132,143 | 60.3 |
| Lowell P. Landowski (R) | 76,148 | 34.8 |
| Vic Fazio (D) | 115,090 | 54.7 |
| Mark Baughman (R) | 82,738 | 39.3 |
| Bryce Bigwood (LIBERT) | 12,626 | 6.0 |
| Nancy Pelosi (D) | 120,633 | 77.2 |
| Alan Nichols (R) | 35,671 | 22.8 |
| Barbara Boxer (D) | 137,306 | 68.1 |
| Bill Boerum (R) | 64,402 | 31.9 |
| George Miller (D) | 121,080 | 60.5 |
| Roger A. Payton (R) | 79,031 | 39.5 |
| Ronald V. Dellums (D) | 119,645 | 61.3 |
| Barbara Galewski (R) | 75,544 | 38.7 |
| Pete Stark (D) | 94,739 | 58.4 |
| Victor Romero (R) | 67,412 | 41.6 |
| Don Edwards (D) | 81,875 | 62.7 |
| Mark Patrosso (R) | 48,747 | 37.3 |
| Tom Lantos (D) | 105,029 | 65.9 |
| G. M. "Bill" Quraishi (R) | 45,818 | 28.8 |
| June R. Genis (LIBERT) | 8,518 | 5.3 |
| Tom Campbell (R) | 125,157 | 60.8 |
| Robert Palmer (D) | 69,270 | 33.7 |

| Candidates | Votes | % |
|---|---|---|
| Chuck Olson (LIBERT) | 11,271 | 5.5 |
| 13 Norman Y. Mineta (D) | 97,286 | 58.0 |
| David E. Smith (R) | 59,773 | 35.7 |
| John H. Webster (LIBERT) | 10,587 | 6.3 |
| 14 John T. Doolittle (R) | 128,309 | 51.5 |
| Patricia Malberg (D) | 120,742 | 48.5 |
| 15 Gary Condit (D) | 97,147 | 66.2 |
| Cliff Burris (R) | 49,634 | 33.8 |
| 16 Leon E. Panetta (D) | 134,236 | 74.2 |
| Jerry M. Reiss (R) | 39,885 | 22.0 |
| 17 Calvin Dooley (D) | 82,611 | 54.5 |
| Charles Pashayan Jr. (R) | 68,848 | 45.5 |
| 18 Richard H. Lehman (D) | 98,804 | 100 |
| 19 Robert J. Lagomarsino (R) | 94,599 | 54.6 |
| Anita Perez Ferguson (D) | 76,991 | 44.4 |
| 20 William M. Thomas (R) | 112,962 | 59.8 |
| Michael A. Thomas (D) | 65,101 | 34.4 |
| William H. Dilbeck (LIBERT) | 10,555 | 5.6 |
| 21 Elton Gallegly (R) | 118,326 | 58.4 |
| Richard D. Freiman (D) | 68,921 | 34.0 |
| Peggy Christensen (LIBERT) | 15,364 | 7.6 |
| 22 Carlos J. Moorhead (R) | 108,634 | 60.0 |
| David Bayer (D) | 61,630 | 34.1 |
| 23 Anthony C. Beilenson (D) | 103,141 | 61.7 |
| Jim Salomon (R) | 57,118 | 34.2 |
| 24 Henry A. Waxman (D) | 71,562 | 68.9 |
| John N. Cowles (R) | 26,607 | 25.6 |
| Maggie Phair (PF) | 5,706 | 5.5 |
| 25 Edward R. Roybal (D) | 48,120 | 70.0 |
| Steven J. Renshaw (R) | 17,021 | 24.8 |
| Robert H. Scott (LIBERT) | 3,576 | 5.2 |
| 26 Howard L. Berman (D) | 78,031 | 61.1 |
| Roy Dahlson (R) | 44,492 | 34.8 |
| 27 Mel Levine (D) | 90,857 | 58.2 |
| David Barrett Cohen (R) | 58,140 | 37.2 |
| 28 Julian C. Dixon (D) | 69,482 | 72.7 |
| George Z. Adams (R) | 21,245 | 22.2 |
| 29 Maxine Waters (D) | 51,350 | 79.4 |
| Bill DeWitt (R) | 12,054 | 18.6 |
| 30 Matthew G. Martinez (D) | 45,456 | 58.2 |
| Reuben D. Franco (R) | 28,914 | 37.0 |
| 31 Mervyn M. Dymally (D) | 56,394 | 67.1 |
| Eunice A. Sato (R) | 27,593 | 32.9 |
| 32 Glenn M. Anderson (D) | 68,268 | 61.5 |
| Sanford W. Kahn (R) | 42,692 | 38.5 |
| 33 David Dreier (R) | 101,336 | 63.7 |
| Georgia Houston Webb (D) | 49,981 | 31.4 |
| 34 Esteban E. Torres (D) | 55,646 | 60.7 |
| John Eastman (R) | 36,024 | 39.3 |
| 35 Jerry Lewis (R) | 121,602 | 60.6 |
| Barry Norton (D) | 66,100 | 32.9 |
| Jerry Johnson (LIBERT) | 13,020 | 6.5 |
| 36 George E. Brown Jr. (D) | 72,409 | 52.7 |
| Robert Hammock (R) | 64,961 | 47.3 |
| 37 Al McCandless (R) | 115,469 | 49.7 |
| Ralph Waite (D) | 103,961 | 44.8 |
| 38 Robert K. Dornan (R) | 60,561 | 58.1 |
| Barbara Jackson (D) | 43,693 | 41.9 |
| 39 William E. Dannemeyer (R) | 113,849 | 65.3 |
| Francis X. Hoffman (D) | 53,670 | 30.8 |
| 40 C. Christopher Cox (R) | 142,299 | 67.6 |
| Eugene C. Gratz (D) | 68,087 | 32.4 |
| 41 Bill Lowery (R) | 105,723 | 49.2 |
| Dan Kripke (D) | 93,586 | 43.6 |
| Karen S. R. Works (PF) | 15,428 | 7.2 |
| 42 Dana Rohrabacher (R) | 109,353 | 59.3 |
| Guy C. Kimbrough (D) | 67,189 | 36.5 |
| 43 Ron Packard (R) | 151,206 | 68.1 |
| Doug Hansen (PF) | 40,212 | 18.1 |
| Richard L. Arnold (LIBERT) | 30,720 | 13.8 |
| 44 Randy "Duke" Cunningham (R) | 50,377 | 46.3 |
| Jim Bates (D) | 48,712 | 44.8 |
| 45 Duncan Hunter (R) | 123,591 | 72.8 |
| Joe Shea (LIBERT) | 46,068 | 27.2 |

## COLORADO

| Candidates | Votes | % |
|---|---|---|
| 1 Patricia Schroeder (D) | 82,176 | 63.7 |
| Gloria Gonzales Roemer (R) | 46,802 | 36.3 |
| 2 David E. Skaggs (D) | 105,248 | 60.7 |
| Jason Lewis (R) | 68,226 | 39.3 |
| 3 Ben Nighthorse Campbell (D) | 124,487 | 70.2 |
| Bob Ellis (R) | 49,961 | 28.2 |
| 4 Wayne Allard (R) | 89,285 | 54.1 |
| Dick Bond (D) | 75,901 | 45.9 |
| 5 Joel Hefley (R) | 127,740 | 66.4 |
| Cal Johnston (D) | 57,776 | 30.0 |
| 6 Dan Schaefer (R) | 105,312 | 64.5 |
| Don Jarrett (D) | 57,961 | 35.5 |

## CONNECTICUT

| | Votes | % |
|---|---|---|
| 1 Barbara B. Kennelly (D) | 126,566 | 71.4 |
| James M. Garvey (R) | 50,690 | 28.6 |
| 2 Sam Gejdenson (D) | 105,085 | 59.7 |
| John M. Ragsdale (R) | 70,922 | 40.3 |
| 3 Rosa DeLauro (D) | 90,772 | 52.1 |
| Thomas Scott (R) | 83,440 | 47.9 |
| 4 Christopher Shays (R) | 105,682 | 76.5 |
| Al Smith (D) | 32,352 | 23.4 |
| 5 Gary Franks (R) | 93,912 | 51.7 |
| Toby Moffett (D) | 85,803 | 47.2 |
| 6 Nancy L. Johnson (R) | 141,105 | 74.4 |
| Paul Kulas (D) | 48,628 | 25.6 |

## DELAWARE

| | Votes | % |
|---|---|---|
| AL Thomas R. Carper (D) | 116,274 | 65.5 |
| Ralph O. Williams (R) | 58,037 | 32.7 |

## FLORIDA

| | Votes | % |
|---|---|---|
| 1 Earl Hutto (D) | 88,416 | 52.2 |
| Terry Ketchel (R) | 80,851 | 47.8 |
| 2 Pete Peterson (D) | 103,032 | 56.9 |
| Bill Grant (R) | 77,939 | 43.1 |
| 3 Charles E. Bennett (D) | 84,280 | 72.7 |
| Rod Sullivan (R) | 31,727 | 27.3 |
| 4 Craig T. James (R) | 120,895 | 55.9 |
| Reid Hughes (D) | 95,320 | 44.1 |
| 5 Bill McCollum (R) | 94,453 | 59.9 |
| Bob Fletcher (D) | 63,253 | 40.1 |
| 6 Cliff Stearns (R) | 138,588 | 59.2 |
| Art Johnson (D) | 95,421 | 40.8 |
| 7 Sam Gibbons (D) | 99,464 | 67.6 |
| Charles D. Prout (R) | 47,765 | 32.4 |
| 8 C. W. Bill Young (R) | | 100.0 |
| 9 Michael Bilirakis (R) | 142,163 | 58.1 |
| Cheryl Davis Knapp (D) | 102,503 | 41.9 |
| 10 Andy Ireland (R) | | 100.0 |
| 11 Jim Bacchus (D) | 120,991 | 51.9 |
| Bill Tolley (R) | 111,970 | 48.1 |
| 12 Tom Lewis (R) | | 100.0 |
| 13 Porter J. Goss (R) | | 100.0 |
| 14 Harry A. Johnston (D) | 156,055 | 66.0 |
| Scott Shore (R) | 80,249 | 34.0 |
| 15 E. Clay Shaw Jr. (R) | 104,295 | 97.8 |
| 16 Lawrence J. Smith (D) | | 100.0 |
| 17 William Lehman (D) | 79,569 | 78.3 |
| Earl Rodney (R) | 22,029 | 21.7 |
| 18 Ileana Ros-Lehtinen (R) | 56,364 | 60.4 |
| Bernard Anscher (D) | 36,978 | 39.6 |
| 19 Dante B. Fascell (D) | 87,696 | 62.0 |
| Bob Allen (R) | 53,796 | 38.0 |

## GEORGIA

| | Candidates | Votes | % |
|---|---|---|---|
| 1 | Lindsay Thomas (D) | 80,515 | 71.2 |
| | Chris Meredith (R) | 32,532 | 28.8 |
| 2 | Charles Hatcher (D) | 77,910 | 73.0 |
| | Jonathan Perry Waters (R) | 28,781 | 27.0 |
| 3 | Richard Ray (D) | 72,961 | 63.2 |
| | Paul Broun (R) | 42,561 | 36.8 |
| 4 | Ben Jones (D) | 96,526 | 52.4 |
| | John Linder (R) | 87,569 | 47.6 |
| 5 | John Lewis (D) | 86,037 | 75.6 |
| | J. W. Tibbs Jr. (R) | 27,781 | 24.4 |
| 6 | Newt Gingrich (R) | 78,768 | 50.3 |
| | David Worley (D) | 77,794 | 49.7 |
| 7 | George "Buddy" Darden (D) | 95,817 | 60.1 |
| | Al Beverly (R) | 63,588 | 39.9 |
| 8 | J. Roy Rowland (D) | 81,344 | 68.7 |
| | Bob Cunningham (R) | 36,980 | 31.3 |
| 9 | Ed Jenkins (D) | 96,197 | 55.8 |
| | Joe Hoffman (R) | 76,121 | 44.2 |
| 10 | Doug Barnard Jr. (D) | 89,683 | 58.3 |
| | Sam Jones (R) | 64,184 | 41.7 |

## HAWAII

| | | Votes | % |
|---|---|---|---|
| 1 | Neil Abercrombie (D) | 97,622 | 60.0 |
| | Mike Liu (R) | 62,982 | 38.7 |
| 2 | Patsy T. Mink (D) | 118,155 | 66.3 |
| | Andy Poepoe (R) | 54,625 | 30.6 |

### Special Election [1]

| | | Votes | % |
|---|---|---|---|
| 2 | Patsy T. Mink (D) | 51,841 | 37.4 |
| | Mufi Hannemann (D) | 50,164 | 36.1 |
| | Ron Menor (D) | 23,629 | 17.0 |
| | Andy Poepoe (R) | 8,872 | 6.4 |

## IDAHO

| | | Votes | % |
|---|---|---|---|
| 1 | Larry LaRocco (D) | 85,054 | 53.0 |
| | C. A. "Skip" Smyser (R) | 75,406 | 47.0 |
| 2 | Richard H. Stallings (D) | 98,008 | 63.6 |
| | Sean McDevitt (R) | 56,044 | 36.4 |

## ILLINOIS

| | | Votes | % |
|---|---|---|---|
| 1 | Charles A. Hayes (D) | 100,890 | 93.8 |
| | Babette Peyton (R) | 6,708 | 6.2 |
| 2 | Gus Savage (D) | 80,245 | 78.2 |
| | William T. Hespel (R) | 22,350 | 21.8 |
| 3 | Marty Russo (D) | 110,512 | 70.9 |
| | Carl L. Klein (R) | 45,299 | 29.1 |
| 4 | George E. Sangmeister (D) | 77,290 | 59.2 |
| | Manny Hoffman (R) | 53,258 | 40.8 |
| 5 | William O. Lipinski (D) | 73,805 | 66.3 |
| | David J. Shestokas (R) | 34,440 | 31.0 |
| 6 | Henry J. Hyde (R) | 96,410 | 66.7 |
| | Robert J. Cassidy (D) | 48,155 | 33.3 |
| 7 | Cardiss Collins (D) | 80,021 | 79.9 |
| | Michael Dooley (R) | 20,099 | 20.1 |
| 8 | Dan Rostenkowski (D) | 70,151 | 79.1 |
| | Robert Marshall (LIBERT) | 18,529 | 20.9 |
| 9 | Sidney R. Yates (D) | 96,557 | 71.2 |
| | Herbert Sohn (R) | 39,031 | 28.8 |
| 10 | John Edward Porter (R) | 104,070 | 67.7 |
| | Peg McNamara (D) | 47,286 | 30.8 |
| 11 | Frank Annunzio (D) | 82,703 | 53.6 |
| | Walter W. Dudycz (R) | 68,850 | 44.6 |
| | Larry Saska (IS) | 2,692 | 1.7 |
| 12 | Philip M. Crane (R) | 113,081 | 82.2 |
| | Steve Pedersen (IS) | 24,450 | 17.8 |
| 13 | Harris W. Fawell (R) | 116,048 | 65.8 |
| | Steven Thomas (D) | 60,305 | 34.2 |
| 14 | Dennis Hastert (R) | 112,383 | 66.9 |
| | Donald J. Westphal (D) | 55,592 | 33.1 |
| 15 | Edward R. Madigan (R) | 119,812 | 100 |
| 16 | John W. Cox Jr. (D) | 83,061 | 54.6 |
| | John W. Hallock Jr. (R) | 69,105 | 45.4 |

| | Candidates | Votes | % |
|---|---|---|---|
| 17 | Lane Evans (D) | 102,062 | 66.5 |
| | Dan Lee (R) | 51,380 | 33.5 |
| 18 | Robert H. Michel (R) | 105,693 | 98.4 |
| 19 | Terry L. Bruce (D) | 113,958 | 66.3 |
| | Robert F. Kerans (R) | 55,680 | 32.4 |
| 20 | Richard J. Durbin (D) | 130,114 | 66.2 |
| | Paul E. Jurgens (R) | 66,433 | 33.8 |
| 21 | Jerry F. Costello (D) | 95,208 | 66.0 |
| | Robert H. Gaffner (R) | 48,949 | 34.0 |
| 22 | Glenn Poshard (D) | 138,425 | 83.7 |
| | Jim Wham (I) | 26,896 | 16.3 |

## INDIANA

| | | Votes | % |
|---|---|---|---|
| 1 | Peter J. Visclosky (D) | 68,920 | 66.0 |
| | William Costas (R) | 35,450 | 34.0 |
| 2 | Philip R. Sharp (D) | 93,495 | 59.4 |
| | Mike Pence (R) | 63,980 | 40.6 |
| 3 | Tim Roemer (D) | 80,740 | 50.9 |
| | John Hiler (R) | 77,911 | 49.1 |
| 4 | Jill Long (D) | 99,347 | 60.7 |
| | Rick Hawks (R) | 64,415 | 39.3 |
| 5 | Jim Jontz (D) | 81,373 | 53.1 |
| | John A. Johnson (R) | 71,750 | 46.9 |
| 6 | Dan Burton (R) | 116,470 | 63.5 |
| | James P. Fadely (D) | 67,024 | 36.5 |
| 7 | John T. Myers (R) | 88,584 | 57.6 |
| | John W. Riley Sr. (D) | 65,248 | 42.4 |
| 8 | Frank McCloskey (D) | 97,465 | 54.7 |
| | Richard E. Mourdock (R) | 80,645 | 45.3 |
| 9 | Lee H. Hamilton (D) | 107,526 | 69.0 |
| | Floyd Eugene Coates (R) | 48,325 | 31.0 |
| 10 | Andrew Jacobs Jr. (D) | 69,362 | 66.4 |
| | Janos Horvath (R) | 35,049 | 33.6 |

## IOWA

| | | Votes | % |
|---|---|---|---|
| 1 | Jim Leach (R) | 90,042 | 99.8 |
| 2 | Jim Nussle (R) | 82,650 | 49.8 |
| | Eric Tabor (D) | 81,008 | 48.8 |
| 3 | David R. Nagle (D) | 100,947 | 99.2 |
| 4 | Neal Smith (D) | 127,812 | 97.9 |
| 5 | Jim Ross Lightfoot (R) | 99,978 | 68.0 |
| | Rod Powell (D) | 47,022 | 32.0 |
| 6 | Fred Grandy (R) | 112,333 | 71.8 |
| | Mike D. Earll (D) | 44,063 | 28.2 |

## KANSAS

| | | Votes | % |
|---|---|---|---|
| 1 | Pat Roberts (R) | 102,974 | 62.6 |
| | Duane West (D) | 61,396 | 37.4 |
| 2 | Jim Slattery (D) | 99,093 | 62.8 |
| | Scott Morgan (R) | 58,643 | 37.2 |
| 3 | Jan Meyers (R) | 88,725 | 60.1 |
| | Leroy Jones (D) | 58,923 | 39.9 |
| 4 | Dan Glickman (D) | 112,015 | 70.8 |
| | Roger M. Grund (R) | 46,283 | 29.2 |
| 5 | Dick Nichols (R) | 90,555 | 59.3 |
| | George Wingert (D) | 62,244 | 40.7 |

## KENTUCKY

| | | Votes | % |
|---|---|---|---|
| 1 | Carroll Hubbard Jr. (D) | 85,323 | 86.9 |
| | Marvin H. Seat (POP) | 12,879 | 13.1 |
| 2 | William H. Natcher (D) | 77,057 | 66.0 |
| | Martin A. Tori (R) | 39,624 | 34.0 |
| 3 | Romano L. Mazzoli (D) | 84,750 | 60.6 |
| | Al Brown (R) | 55,188 | 39.4 |
| 4 | Jim Bunning (R) | 101,680 | 69.3 |
| | Galen Martin (D) | 44,979 | 30.7 |
| 5 | Harold Rogers (R) | 64,660 | 100 |
| 6 | Larry J. Hopkins (R) | 76,859 | 100 |
| 7 | Carl C. Perkins (D) | 61,330 | 50.8 |
| | Will T. Scott (R) | 59,377 | 49.2 |

## LOUISIANA [2]

| | Candidates | Votes | % |
|---|---|---|---|
| 1 | Bob Livingston (R) | X | |
| 2 | William J. Jefferson (D) | 55,621 | 52 |
| | Marc H. Morial (D) | 50,232 | 47 |
| 3 | W. J. "Billy" Tauzin (D) | | |
| 4 | Jim McCrery (R) | | 100 |
| 5 | Jerry Huckaby (D) | | 100 |
| 6 | Richard H. Baker (R) | | 100 |
| 7 | Jimmy Hayes (D) | | 100 |
| 8 | Clyde C. Holloway (R) | | 100 |

## MAINE

| | | Votes | % |
|---|---|---|---|
| 1 | Thomas H. Andrews (D) | 167,623 | 60 |
| | David F. Emery (R) | 110,836 | 39 |
| 2 | Olympia J. Snowe (R) | 121,704 | 51 |
| | Patrick K. McGowan (D) | 116,798 | 49 |

## MARYLAND

| | | Votes | % |
|---|---|---|---|
| 1 | Wayne T. Gilchrest (R) | 88,920 | 56 |
| | Roy Dyson (D) | 67,518 | 4. |
| 2 | Helen Delich Bentley (R) | 115,398 | 74 |
| | Ronald P. Bowers (D) | 39,785 | 25 |
| 3 | Benjamin L. Cardin (D) | 82,545 | 69 |
| | Harwood Nichols (R) | 35,841 | 30 |
| 4 | Tom McMillen (D) | 85,601 | 58 |
| | Robert P. Duckworth (R) | 59,846 | 4 |
| 5 | Steny H. Hoyer (D) | 84,747 | 80 |
| | Lee F. Breuer (R) | 20,314 | 1. |
| 6 | Beverly B. Byron (D) | 106,502 | 6. |
| | Christopher P. Fiotes Jr. (R) | 56,479 | 3. |
| 7 | Kweisi Mfume (D) | 59,628 | 8. |
| | Kenneth Kondner (R) | 10,529 | 1. |
| 8 | Constance A. Morella (R) | 130,059 | 7. |
| | James Walker Jr. (D) | 39,343 | 2. |

## MASSACHUSETTS

| | | Votes | % |
|---|---|---|---|
| 1 | Silvio O. Conte (R) | 150,748 | 7. |
| | John R. Arden (D) | 43,611 | 2. |
| 2 | Richard E. Neal (D) | 134,152 | 9. |
| 3 | Joseph D. Early (D) | 150,992 | 9. |
| 4 | Barney Frank (D) | 143,473 | 6. |
| | John R. Soto (R) | 75,454 | 3. |
| 5 | Chester G. Atkins (D) | 110,232 | 5. |
| | John F. MacGovern (R) | 101,017 | 4. |
| 6 | Nicholas Mavroules (D) | 149,284 | 6. |
| | Edgar L. Kelley (R) | 80,177 | 3. |
| 7 | Edward J. Markey (D) | 155,380 | 9. |
| 8 | Joseph P. Kennedy II (D) | 125,479 | 7. |
| | Glenn W. Fiscus (R) | 39,310 | 2. |
| | Susan C. Davies (NA) | 8,806 | |
| 9 | Joe Moakley (D) | 124,534 | 7. |
| | Robert W. Horan (I) | 52,660 | 2. |
| 10 | Larry E. Studds (D) | 137,805 | 5. |
| | Jon L. Bryan (R) | 120,217 | 4. |
| 11 | Brian J. Donnelly (D) | 145,480 | 9. |

## MICHIGAN

| | | Votes | % |
|---|---|---|---|
| 1 | John Conyers Jr. (D) | 76,556 | 8. |
| | Ray Shoulders (R) | 7,298 | |
| 2 | Carl D. Pursell (R) | 95,962 | 5. |
| | Elmer White (D) | 49,678 | 3. |
| 3 | Howard Wolpe (D) | 82,376 | 5. |
| | Brad Haskins (R) | 60,007 | 4. |
| 4 | Fred Upton (R) | 75,850 | 5. |
| | JoAnne McFarland (D) | 55,449 | 5. |
| 5 | Paul B. Henry (R) | 126,308 | 7. |
| | Thomas Trzybinski (D) | 41,170 | 4. |
| 6 | Bob Carr (D) | 97,547 | 5. |
| 7 | Dale E. Kildee (D) | 90,307 | 5. |
| | David J. Morrill (D) | 41,759 | 5. |
| 8 | Bob Traxler (D) | 98,903 | 5. |
| | James White (R) | 45,259 | 5. |
| 9 | Guy Vander Jagt (R) | 89,078 | |

*Footnote, see p. 1319.*

| Candidates | Votes | % |
|---|---|---|
| Geraldine Greene (D) | 73,604 | 45.2 |
| 10 Dave Camp (R) | 99,952 | 65.0 |
| Joan Louise Dennison (D) | 50,923 | 33.1 |
| 11 Robert W. Davis (R) | 94,555 | 61.3 |
| Marcia Gould (D) | 59,759 | 38.7 |
| 12 David E. Bonior (D) | 98,232 | 64.7 |
| Jim Dingeman (R) | 51,119 | 33.7 |
| 13 Barbara-Rose Collins (D) | 54,345 | 80.1 |
| Carl R. Edwards Sr. (R) | 11,203 | 16.5 |
| 14 Dennis M. Hertel (D) | 78,506 | 63.6 |
| Kenneth C. McNealy (R) | 40,499 | 32.8 |
| 15 William D. Ford (D) | 68,742 | 61.2 |
| Burl C. Adkins (R) | 41,092 | 36.6 |
| 16 John D. Dingell (D) | 88,962 | 66.6 |
| Frank Beaumont (R) | 42,629 | 31.9 |
| 17 Sander M. Levin (D) | 92,205 | 69.7 |
| Blaine L. Lankford (R) | 40,100 | 30.3 |
| 18 William S. Broomfield (R) | 126,629 | 66.4 |
| Walter Briggs (D) | 64,185 | 33.6 |

### MINNESOTA [3]

| Candidates | Votes | % |
|---|---|---|
| 1 Timothy J. Penny (DFL) | 156,749 | 78.1 |
| Doug Andersen (I-R) | 43,856 | 21.9 |
| 2 Vin Weber (I-R) | 126,367 | 61.8 |
| Jim Stone (DFL) | 77,935 | 38.1 |
| 3 Jim Ramstad (I-R) | 195,833 | 66.9 |
| Lewis DeMars (DFL) | 96,395 | 32.9 |
| 4 Bruce F. Vento (DFL) | 143,353 | 64.7 |
| Ian Maitland (I-R) | 77,639 | 35.1 |
| 5 Martin Olav Sabo (DFL) | 144,682 | 72.9 |
| Raymond C. Gilbertson (I-R) | 53,720 | 27.1 |
| 6 Gerry Sikorski (DFL) | 164,816 | 64.6 |
| Bruce D. Anderson (I-R) | 90,138 | 35.3 |
| 7 Collin C. Peterson (DFL) | 107,126 | 53.5 |
| Arlan Stangeland (I-R) | 92,876 | 46.4 |
| 8 James L. Oberstar (DFL) | 151,145 | 72.9 |
| Jerry Shuster (I-R) | 56,068 | 27.0 |

### MISSISSIPPI

| Candidates | Votes | % |
|---|---|---|
| 1 Jamie L. Whitten (D) | 43,668 | 64.9 |
| Bill Bowlin (R) | 23,650 | 35.1 |
| 2 Mike Espy (D) | 59,393 | 84.1 |
| Dorothy Benford (R) | 11,224 | 15.9 |
| 3 G. V. "Sonny" Montgomery (D) | 49,162 | 100.0 |
| 4 Mike Parker (D) | 57,137 | 80.6 |
| Jerry "Rev" Parks (R) | 13,754 | 19.4 |
| 5 Gene Taylor (D) | 89,926 | 81.4 |
| Sheila Smith (R) | 20,588 | 18.6 |

### MISSOURI

| Candidates | Votes | % |
|---|---|---|
| 1 William L. Clay (D) | 62,550 | 60.9 |
| Wayne G. Piotrowski (R) | 40,160 | 39.1 |
| 2 Joan Kelly Horn (D) | 94,378 | 50.0 |
| Jack Buechner (R) | 94,324 | 50.0 |
| 3 Richard A. Gephardt (D) | 88,950 | 56.8 |
| Malcolm L. Holekamp (R) | 67,659 | 43.2 |
| 4 Ike Skelton (D) | 105,527 | 61.8 |
| David Eyerly (R) | 65,095 | 38.2 |
| 5 Alan Wheat (D) | 71,890 | 62.1 |
| Robert H. Gardner (R) | 43,897 | 37.9 |
| 6 E. Thomas Coleman (R) | 78,956 | 51.9 |
| Bob McClure (D) | 73,093 | 48.1 |
| 7 Mel Hancock (R) | 83,600 | 52.1 |
| Thomas Patrick Deaton (D) | 76,725 | 47.9 |
| 8 Bill Emerson (R) | 81,452 | 57.3 |
| Russ Carnahan (D) | 60,751 | 42.7 |
| 9 Harold L. Volkmer (D) | 94,156 | 57.5 |
| Don Curtis (R) | 69,514 | 42.5 |

### MONTANA

| Candidates | Votes | % |
|---|---|---|
| 1 Pat Williams (D) | 100,409 | 61.1 |
| Brad Johnson (R) | 63,837 | 38.9 |
| 2 Ron Marlenee (R) | 96,449 | 63.0 |
| Don Burris (D) | 56,739 | 37.0 |

### NEBRASKA

| Candidates | Votes | % |
|---|---|---|
| 1 Doug Bereuter (R) | 129,654 | 64.7 |
| Larry Hall (D) | 70,587 | 35.2 |
| 2 Peter Hoagland (D) | 111,903 | 57.9 |
| Ally Milder (R) | 80,845 | 41.8 |
| 3 Bill Barrett (R) | 98,607 | 51.1 |
| Sandra K. Scofield (D) | 94,234 | 48.8 |

### NEVADA

| Candidates | Votes | % |
|---|---|---|
| 1 James H. Bilbray (D) | 84,650 | 61.4 |
| Bob Dickinson (R) | 47,377 | 34.4 |
| 2 Barbara F. Vucanovich (R) | 103,508 | 59.1 |
| Jane Wisdom (D) | 60,581 | 34.0 |
| Dan Becan (LIBERT) | 12,120 | 6.9 |

### NEW HAMPSHIRE

| Candidates | Votes | % |
|---|---|---|
| 1 Bill Zeliff (R) | 81,684 | 55.1 |
| Joseph F. Keefe (D) | 66,176 | 44.6 |
| 2 Dick Swett (D) | 74,829 | 52.7 |
| Chuck Douglas (R) | 67,063 | 47.2 |

### NEW JERSEY

| Candidates | Votes | % |
|---|---|---|
| 1 Robert E. Andrews (D) | 73,522 | 54.3 |
| Daniel J. Mangini (R) | 57,801 | 42.7 |
| 2 William J. Hughes (D) | 98,734 | 88.2 |
| William A. Kanengiser (POP) | 13,246 | 11.8 |
| 3 Frank Pallone Jr. (D) | 77,709 | 49.1 |
| Paul A. Kapalko (R) | 73,451 | 46.4 |
| 4 Christopher H. Smith (R) | 101,508 | 62.9 |
| Mark Setaro (D) | 55,454 | 34.4 |
| 5 Marge Roukema (R) | 118,101 | 75.7 |
| Lawrence Wayne Olsen (D) | 35,010 | 22.4 |
| 6 Bernard J. Dwyer (D) | 63,696 | 50.5 |
| Paul Danielczyk (R) | 58,209 | 46.2 |
| 7 Matthew J. Rinaldo (R) | 100,274 | 74.6 |
| Bruce H. Bergen (D) | 31,114 | 23.2 |
| 8 Robert A. Roe (D) | 55,212 | 76.9 |
| Stephen Sibilia (IC) | 13,239 | 18.4 |
| 9 Robert G. Torricelli (D) | 82,736 | 57.0 |
| Peter J. Russo (R) | 59,759 | 41.2 |
| 10 Donald M. Payne (D) | 42,616 | 81.5 |
| Howard E. Berkeley (R) | 9,072 | 17.3 |
| 11 Dean A. Gallo (R) | 95,198 | 64.9 |
| Michael Gordon (D) | 47,782 | 32.6 |
| 12 Dick Zimmer (R) | 108,173 | 64.0 |
| Marguerite Chandler (D) | 52,498 | 31.1 |
| 13 H. James Saxton (R) | 100,537 | 58.1 |
| John H. Adler (D) | 68,286 | 39.5 |
| 14 Frank J. Guarini (D) | 57,581 | 66.1 |
| Fred J. Theemling Jr. (R) | 25,473 | 29.2 |

#### Special Election [4]

| Candidates | Votes | % |
|---|---|---|
| 1 Robert E. Andrews (D) | 72,324 | 55.3 |
| Daniel J. Mangini (R) | 58,671 | 44.7 |

### NEW MEXICO

| Candidates | Votes | % |
|---|---|---|
| 1 Steven H. Schiff (R) | 97,375 | 70.2 |
| Rebecca Vigil-Giron (D) | 41,306 | 29.8 |
| 2 Joe Skeen (R) | 80,677 | 100.0 |
| 3 Bill Richardson (D) | 104,225 | 74.5 |
| Phil T. Archuletta (R) | 35,751 | 25.5 |

### NEW YORK

| Candidates | Votes | % |
|---|---|---|
| 1 George J. Hochbrueckner (D, Tax Break) | 75,211 | 56.3 |
| Francis W. Creighton (R) | 46,380 | 34.7 |
| Clayton Baldwin Jr. (C) | 6,883 | 5.2 |
| 2 Thomas J. Downey (D) | 56,722 | 55.8 |
| John W. Bugler (R, RTL, Tax Cut) | 36,859 | 36.2 |
| Dominic A. Curcio (C) | 8,150 | 8.0 |
| 3 Robert J. Mrazek (D, L) | 73,029 | 53.3 |
| Robert Previdi (R, C) | 59,089 | 43.1 |
| 4 Norman F. Lent (R, C) | 79,304 | 61.2 |
| Francis T. Goban (D) | 41,308 | 31.8 |
| John J. Dunkle (RTL) | 6,706 | 5.2 |
| 5 Raymond J. McGrath (R, C) | 71,948 | 54.6 |
| Mark S. Epstein (D, L) | 53,920 | 40.9 |
| 6 Floyd H. Flake (D, L) | 44,306 | 73.1 |
| William Sampol (R) | 13,224 | 21.8 |
| John Cronin (RTL) | 3,111 | 5.1 |
| 7 Gary L. Ackerman (D, L) | 51,091 | 100 |
| 8 James H. Scheuer (D, L) | 56,396 | 72.3 |
| Gustave Reifenkugel (R) | 21,646 | 27.7 |
| 9 Thomas J. Manton (D) | 35,177 | 64.4 |
| Ann Pfoser Darby (R, AC) | 13,330 | 24.4 |
| Thomas V. Ognibene (C) | 6,137 | 11.2 |
| 10 Charles E. Schumer (D, L) | 61,468 | 80.4 |
| Patrick J. Kinsella (R, C) | 14,963 | 19.6 |
| 11 Edolphus Towns (D, L) | 36,286 | 92.9 |
| 12 Major R. Owens (D, L) | 40,570 | 94.9 |
| 13 Stephen J. Solarz (D, L) | 47,446 | 80.4 |
| Edwin Ramos (R, C) | 11,557 | 19.6 |
| 14 Susan Molinari (R, C) | 58,616 | 60.0 |
| Anthony J. Pocchia (D, L, SIS) | 34,625 | 35.5 |
| 15 Bill Green (R) | 52,919 | 58.8 |
| Frances L. Reiter (D) | 33,464 | 37.2 |
| 16 Charles B. Rangel (D, R, L) | 55,882 | 97.2 |
| Alvaader Frazier (NA) | 1,592 | 2.8 |
| 17 Ted Weiss (D, L) | 79,161 | 80.4 |
| William W. Koeppel (R) | 15,219 | 15.5 |
| 18 Jose E. Serrano (D, L) | 38,024 | 93.2 |
| 19 Eliot L. Engel (D, L) | 45,758 | 61.2 |
| William J. Gouldman (R) | 17,135 | 22.9 |
| Kevin Brawley (C, RTL) | 11,868 | 15.9 |
| 20 Nita M. Lowey (D) | 82,203 | 62.8 |
| Glenn D. Belitto (R) | 35,575 | 27.2 |
| John M. Schafer (C, RTL) | 13,030 | 10.0 |
| 21 Hamilton Fish Jr. (R, C) | 99,866 | 71.4 |
| Richard L. Barbuto (D) | 34,128 | 24.4 |
| 22 Benjamin A. Gilman (R) | 95,495 | 68.6 |
| John G. Dow (D) | 37,034 | 26.6 |
| 23 Michael R. McNulty (D, C) | 117,239 | 64.1 |
| Margaret B. Buhrmaster (R) | 65,760 | 35.9 |
| 24 Gerald B. H. Solomon (R, C, RTL) | 121,206 | 68.1 |
| Bob Lawrence (D) | 56,671 | 31.9 |
| 25 Sherwood Boehlert (R) | 91,348 | 83.9 |
| William L. Griffen (L) | 17,481 | 16.1 |
| 26 David O'B. Martin (R, C) | 97,340 | 100 |
| 27 James T. Walsh (R, C) | 95,220 | 63.2 |
| Peggy L. Murray (D, L) | 52,438 | 34.8 |
| 28 Matthew F. McHugh (D) | 97,815 | 64.8 |
| Seymour Krieger (R) | 53,077 | 35.2 |
| 29 Frank Horton (R) | 89,105 | 63.0 |
| Alton F. Eber (D) | 34,835 | 24.6 |
| Peter DeMauro (C) | 12,599 | 8.9 |
| 30 Louise M. Slaughter (D) | 97,280 | 59.0 |
| John M. Regan Jr. (R, C, RTL) | 67,534 | 41.0 |
| 31 Bill Paxon (R, C, RTL) | 90,237 | 56.6 |
| Kevin P. Gaughan (D, L) | 69,328 | 43.4 |
| 32 John J. LaFalce (D, L) | 68,367 | 55.0 |
| Michael T. Waring (R) | 39,053 | 31.4 |
| Kenneth J. Kowalski (C, RTL) | 16,853 | 13.6 |
| 33 Henry J. Nowak (D, L) | 84,905 | 77.5 |
| Thomas K. Kepfer (R) | 18,181 | 16.6 |
| Louis P. Corrigan Jr. (C) | 6,460 | 5.9 |
| 34 Amo Houghton (R, C) | 89,831 | 69.6 |
| Joseph P. Leahey (D) | 37,421 | 29.0 |

#### Special Elections

| Candidates | Votes | % |
|---|---|---|
| 14 Susan Molinari (R) [5] | 29,336 | 59.0 |
| Robert Gigante (D) | 17,302 | 34.8 |
| Barbara Bollaert (RTL) | 2,649 | 5.3 |
| 18 Jose E. Serrano (D, L) [6] | 26,928 | 92.4 |
| Simeon Golar (R) | 2,079 | 7.1 |

*Footnote, see p. 1319.*

## NORTH CAROLINA

| | Candidates | Votes | % |
|---|---|---|---|
| 1 | Walter B. Jones (D) | 105,832 | 64.8 |
| | Howard Moye (R) | 57,526 | 35.2 |
| 2 | Tim Valentine (D) | 130,979 | 74.7 |
| | Hal C. Sharpe (R) | 44,263 | 25.3 |
| 3 | H. Martin Lancaster (D) | 83,930 | 59.3 |
| | Don Davis (R) | 57,605 | 40.7 |
| 4 | David E. Price (D) | 139,396 | 58.1 |
| | John Carrington (R) | 100,661 | 41.9 |
| 5 | Stephen L. Neal (D) | 113,814 | 59.1 |
| | Ken Bell (R) | 78,747 | 40.9 |
| 6 | Howard Coble (R) | 125,392 | 66.6 |
| | Helen R. Allegrone (D) | 62,913 | 33.4 |
| 7 | Charlie Rose (D) | 94,946 | 65.6 |
| | Robert C. Anderson (R) | 49,681 | 34.4 |
| 8 | W. G. "Bill" Hefner (D) | 98,700 | 55.0 |
| | Ted Blanton (R) | 80,852 | 45.0 |
| 9 | Alex McMillan (R) | 131,936 | 62.0 |
| | David P. McKnight (D) | 80,802 | 38.0 |
| 10 | Cass Ballenger (R) | 106,400 | 61.8 |
| | Daniel R. Green Jr. (D) | 65,710 | 38.2 |
| 11 | Charles H. Taylor (R) | 101,991 | 50.7 |
| | James McClure Clarke (D) | 99,318 | 49.3 |

## NORTH DAKOTA

| | Candidates | Votes | % |
|---|---|---|---|
| AL | Byron L. Dorgan (D) | 152,530 | 65.2 |
| | Edward T. Schafer (R) | 81,443 | 34.8 |

## OHIO

| | Candidates | Votes | % |
|---|---|---|---|
| 1 | Charles Luken (D) | 83,932 | 51.1 |
| | J. Kenneth Blackwell (R) | 80,362 | 48.9 |
| 2 | Bill Gradison (R) | 103,817 | 64.4 |
| | Tyrone K. Yates (D) | 57,345 | 35.6 |
| 3 | Tony P. Hall (D) | 116,797 | 100 |
| 4 | Michael G. Oxley (R) | 103,897 | 61.7 |
| | Thomas E. Burkhart (D) | 64,467 | 38.3 |
| 5 | Paul E. Gillmor (R) | 113,615 | 68.5 |
| | P. Scott Mange (D) | 41,693 | 25.1 |
| | John E. Jackson (I) | 10,612 | 6.4 |
| 6 | Bob McEwen (R) | 117,220 | 71.2 |
| | Ray Mitchell (D) | 47,415 | 28.8 |
| 7 | David L. Hobson (R) | 97,123 | 62.1 |
| | Jack Schira (D) | 59,349 | 37.9 |
| 8 | John A. Boehner (R) | 99,955 | 61.1 |
| | Gregory V. Jolivette (D) | 63,584 | 38.9 |
| 9 | Marcy Kaptur (D) | 117,681 | 77.7 |
| | Jerry D. Lammers (R) | 33,791 | 22.3 |
| 10 | Clarence E. Miller (R) | 106,009 | 63.2 |
| | John M. Buchanan (D) | 61,656 | 36.8 |
| 11 | Dennis E. Eckart (D) | 111,923 | 65.7 |
| | Margaret Mueller (R) | 58,372 | 34.3 |
| 12 | John R. Kasich (R) | 130,495 | 72.0 |
| | Mike Gelpi (D) | 50,784 | 28.0 |
| 13 | Don J. Pease (D) | 93,431 | 56.7 |
| | William D. Nielsen (R) | 60,925 | 36.9 |
| | John Michael Ryan (I) | 10,506 | 6.4 |
| 14 | Thomas C. Sawyer (D) | 97,875 | 59.6 |
| | Jean E. Bender (R) | 66,460 | 40.4 |
| 15 | Chalmers P. Wylie (R) | 99,251 | 59.1 |
| | Thomas V. Erney (D) | 68,510 | 40.8 |
| 16 | Ralph Regula (R) | 101,097 | 58.9 |
| | Warner D. Mendenhall (D) | 70,516 | 41.1 |
| 17 | James A. Traficant Jr. (D) | 133,207 | 77.7 |
| | Robert R. DeJulio Jr. (R) | 38,199 | 22.3 |
| 18 | Douglas Applegate (D) | 120,782 | 74.3 |
| | John A. Hales (R) | 41,823 | 25.7 |
| 19 | Edward F. Feighan (D) | 132,951 | 64.8 |
| | Susan M. Lawko (R) | 72,315 | 35.2 |
| 20 | Mary Rose Oakar (D) | 109,390 | 73.3 |
| | Bill Smith (R) | 39,749 | 26.7 |
| 21 | Louis Stokes (D) | 103,338 | 80.0 |
| | Franklin H. Roski (R) | 25,906 | 20.0 |

## OKLAHOMA

| | Candidates | Votes | % |
|---|---|---|---|
| 1 | James M. Inhofe (R) | 75,618 | 56.0 |
| | Kurt Glassco (D) | 59,521 | 44.0 |
| 2 | Mike Synar (D) | 90,820 | 61.3 |
| | Terry M. Gorham (R) | 57,331 | 38.7 |
| 3 | Bill Brewster (D) | 107,641 | 80.4 |
| | Patrick K. Miller (R) | 26,261 | 19.6 |
| 4 | Dave McCurdy (D) | 100,879 | 73.6 |
| | Howard Bell (R) | 36,232 | 26.4 |
| 5 | Mickey Edwards (R) | 114,608 | 69.6 |
| | Bryce Baggett (D) | 50,086 | 30.4 |
| 6 | Glenn English (D) | 110,100 | 80.0 |
| | Robert Burns (R) | 27,540 | 20.0 |

## OREGON

| | Candidates | Votes | % |
|---|---|---|---|
| 1 | Les AuCoin (D) | 150,292 | 63.1 |
| | Earl Molander (R) | 72,382 | 30.4 |
| | Rick Livingston (I) | 15,585 | 6.5 |
| 2 | Robert F. Smith (R) | 127,998 | 68.0 |
| | Jim Smiley (D) | 60,131 | 32.0 |
| 3 | Ron Wyden (D) | 169,731 | 80.8 |
| | Philip E. Mooney (R) | 40,216 | 19.1 |
| 4 | Peter A. DeFazio (D) | 162,494 | 85.8 |
| | Tonie Nathan (LIBERT) | 26,432 | 14.0 |
| 5 | Mike Kopetski (D) | 124,610 | 55.0 |
| | Denny Smith (R) | 101,650 | 44.9 |

## PENNSYLVANIA

| | Candidates | Votes | % |
|---|---|---|---|
| 1 | Thomas M. Foglietta (D) | 73,423 | 79.4 |
| | James Love Jackson (R) | 19,018 | 20.6 |
| 2 | William H. Gray III (D) | 94,584 | 92.1 |
| | Donald Bakove (R) | 8,118 | 7.9 |
| 3 | Robert A. Borski (D) | 89,908 | 60.0 |
| | Joseph Marc McColgan (R) | 59,901 | 40.0 |
| 4 | Joe Kolter (D) | 74,114 | 55.9 |
| | Gordon R. Johnston (R) | 58,469 | 44.1 |
| 5 | Richard T. Schulze (R) | 75,097 | 57.1 |
| | Samuel C. Stretton (D) | 50,597 | 38.5 |
| 6 | Gus Yatron (D) | 74,394 | 57.0 |
| | John F. Hicks (R) | 56,093 | 43.0 |
| 7 | Curt Weldon (R) | 105,868 | 65.3 |
| | John Innelli (D) | 56,292 | 34.7 |
| 8 | Peter H. Kostmayer (D) | 85,015 | 56.6 |
| | Audrie Zettick Schaller (R) | 65,100 | 43.4 |
| 9 | Bud Shuster (R, D) | 106,632 | 100.0 |
| 10 | Joseph M. McDade (R, D) | 113,490 | 100.0 |
| 11 | Paul E. Kanjorski (D) | 88,219 | 100.0 |
| 12 | John P. Murtha (D) | 80,686 | 61.7 |
| | William Choby (R) | 50,007 | 38.3 |
| 13 | Lawrence Coughlin (R) | 89,577 | 60.3 |
| | Bernard Tomkin (D) | 58,967 | 39.7 |
| 14 | William J. Coyne (D) | 77,636 | 71.8 |
| | Richard Edward Caligiuri (R) | 30,497 | 28.2 |
| 15 | Don Ritter (R) | 77,178 | 60.6 |
| | Richard J. Orloski (D) | 50,233 | 39.4 |
| 16 | Robert S. Walker (R) | 85,596 | 66.1 |
| | Ernest Eric Guyll (D) | 43,849 | 33.9 |
| 17 | George W. Gekas (R, D) | 110,317 | 100 |
| 18 | Rick Santorum (R) | 85,697 | 51.4 |
| | Doug Walgren (D) | 80,880 | 48.6 |
| 19 | Bill Goodling (R) | 96,336 | 100.0 |
| 20 | Joseph M. Gaydos (D) | 82,080 | 65.6 |
| | Robert C. Lee (R) | 43,054 | 34.4 |
| 21 | Tom Ridge (R) | 92,732 | 100.0 |
| 22 | Austin J. Murphy (D) | 78,375 | 63.3 |
| | Suzanne Hayden (R) | 45,509 | 36.7 |
| 23 | William F. Clinger Jr. (R) | 78,189 | 59.4 |
| | Daniel J. Shannon (D) | 53,465 | 40.6 |

## RHODE ISLAND

| | Candidates | Votes | % |
|---|---|---|---|
| 1 | Ronald K. Machtley (R) | 89,963 | 55.2 |
| | Scott Wolf (D) | 73,131 | 44.8 |
| 2 | Jack Reed (D) | 108,818 | 59.2 |
| | Gertrude M. "Trudy" Coxe (R) | 74,953 | 40.8 |

## SOUTH CAROLINA

| | Candidates | Votes | % |
|---|---|---|---|
| 1 | Arthur Ravenel Jr. (R) | 80,839 | 65.5 |
| | Eugene Platt (D) | 42,555 | 34.5 |
| 2 | Floyd D. Spence (R) | 90,054 | 88.7 |
| | Geb Sommer (LIBERT) | 11,101 | 10.9 |
| 3 | Butler Derrick (D) | 72,561 | 58.0 |
| | Ray Haskett (R) | 52,419 | 41.9 |
| 4 | Liz J. Patterson (D) | 81,927 | 61.4 |
| | Terry E. Haskins (R) | 51,338 | 38.4 |
| 5 | John M. Spratt Jr. (D) | 91,775 | 99.9 |
| 6 | Robin Tallon (D) | 94,121 | 99.6 |

## SOUTH DAKOTA

| | Candidates | Votes | % |
|---|---|---|---|
| AL | Tim Johnson (D) | 173,814 | 67.6 |
| | Don Frankenfeld (R) | 83,484 | 32.4 |

## TENNESSEE

| | Candidates | Votes | % |
|---|---|---|---|
| 1 | James H. Quillen (R) | 47,796 | 99.9 |
| 2 | John J. Duncan (R) | 62,797 | 80.6 |
| | Peter Hebert (I) | 15,127 | 19.4 |
| 3 | Marilyn Lloyd (D) | 49,662 | 53.0 |
| | Grady L. Rhoden (R) | 36,855 | 39.3 |
| | Peter T. Melcher (I) | 5,598 | 6.0 |
| 4 | Jim Cooper (D) | 52,101 | 67.4 |
| | Claiborne "Clay" Sanders (R) | 22,890 | 29.6 |
| 5 | Bob Clement (D) | 55,607 | 72.4 |
| | Tom Stone (I) | 13,577 | 17.7 |
| | Al Borgman (I) | 5,383 | 7.0 |
| 6 | Bart Gordon (D) | 60,538 | 66.7 |
| | Gregory Cochran (R) | 26,424 | 29.1 |
| 7 | Don Sundquist (R) | 66,141 | 62.0 |
| | Ken Bloodworth (D) | 40,516 | 38.0 |
| 8 | John Tanner (D) | 62,241 | 100.0 |
| 9 | Harold E. Ford (D) | 48,629 | 58.1 |
| | Aaron C. Davis (R) | 25,730 | 30.8 |
| | Thomas M. Davidson (I) | 7,249 | 8.7 |

## TEXAS

| | Candidates | Votes | % |
|---|---|---|---|
| 1 | Jim Chapman (D) | 89,241 | 61.0 |
| | Hamp Hodges (R) | 56,954 | 39.0 |
| 2 | Charles Wilson (D) | 76,974 | 55.6 |
| | Donna Peterson (R) | 61,555 | 44.4 |
| 3 | Steve Bartlett (R) | 153,857 | 99.6 |
| 4 | Ralph M. Hall (D) | 108,300 | 99.6 |
| 5 | John Bryant (D) | 65,228 | 59.6 |
| | Jerry Rucker (R) | 41,307 | 37.7 |
| 6 | Joe L. Barton (R) | 125,049 | 66.5 |
| | John E. Welch (D) | 62,344 | 33.1 |
| 7 | Bill Archer (R) | 114,254 | 100.0 |
| 8 | Jack Fields (R) | 60,603 | 100.0 |
| 9 | Jack Brooks (D) | 79,786 | 57.1 |
| | Maury Meyers (R) | 58,399 | 42.3 |
| 10 | J. J. "Jake" Pickle (D) | 152,784 | 64.5 |
| | David Beilharz (R) | 73,766 | 31.3 |
| 11 | Chet Edwards (D) | 73,810 | 53.3 |
| | Hugh D. Shine (R) | 64,269 | 46.3 |
| 12 | Pete Geren (D) | 98,026 | 71.3 |
| | Mike McGinn (R) | 39,438 | 28.2 |
| 13 | Bill Sarpalius (D) | 81,815 | 56.5 |
| | Dick Waterfield (R) | 63,045 | 43.3 |
| 14 | Greg H. Laughlin (D) | 89,241 | 54.4 |
| | Joe Dial (R) | 75,098 | 45.5 |
| 15 | E. "Kika" de la Garza (D) | 72,461 | 100.0 |
| 16 | Ronald D. Coleman (D) | 62,455 | 95.6 |
| 17 | Charles W. Stenholm (D) | 104,100 | 100.0 |
| 18 | Craig Washington (D) | 54,477 | 99.6 |
| 19 | Larry Combest (R) | 83,795 | 100.0 |
| 20 | Henry B. Gonzalez (D) | 56,318 | 100.0 |
| 21 | Lamar Smith (R) | 144,570 | 74.4 |
| | Kirby J. Roberts (D) | 48,585 | 25.2 |
| 22 | Thomas D. DeLay (R) | 93,425 | 71.1 |
| | Bruce Director (D) | 37,721 | 28.7 |
| 23 | Albert G. Bustamante (D) | 71,052 | 63.3 |
| | Jerome L. Gonzales (R) | 40,856 | 36.4 |
| 24 | Martin Frost (D) | 86,297 | 100.0 |

| Candidates | Votes | % |
|---|---|---|
| 25 Michael A. Andrews (D) | 67,427 | 100.0 |
| 26 Dick Armey (R) | 147,856 | 70.4 |
| John Wayne Caton (D) | 62,158 | 29.6 |
| 27 Solomon P. Ortiz (D) | 62,822 | 100.0 |

## UTAH

| | | |
|---|---|---|
| 1 James V. Hansen (R) | 82,746 | 52.1 |
| Kenley Brunsdale (D) | 69,491 | 43.8 |
| 2 Wayne Owens (D) | 85,167 | 57.6 |
| Genevieve Atwood (R) | 58,869 | 39.8 |
| 3 Bill Orton (D) | 79,163 | 58.3 |
| Karl Snow (R) | 49,452 | 36.4 |

## VERMONT

| | | |
|---|---|---|
| L Bernard Sanders (I) | 117,522 | 56.0 |
| Peter Smith (R) | 82,938 | 39.5 |

## VIRGINIA

| | | |
|---|---|---|
| 1 Herbert H. Bateman (R) | 72,000 | 51.0 |
| Andrew H. Fox (D) | 69,194 | 49.0 |
| 2 Owen B. Pickett (D) | 55,179 | 75.0 |
| Harry G. Broskie (I) | 15,915 | 21.6 |
| 3 Thomas J. Bliley Jr. (R) | 77,125 | 65.3 |
| Jay Starke (D) | 36,253 | 30.7 |
| 4 Norman Sisisky (D) | 71,051 | 78.3 |
| Don L. Reynolds (I) | 12,295 | 13.6 |
| Loretta F. Chandler (I) | 7,102 | 7.8 |
| 5 Lewis F. Payne Jr. (D) | 66,532 | 99.4 |

| Candidates | Votes | % |
|---|---|---|
| 6 Jim Olin (D) | 92,968 | 82.7 |
| Gerald E. Berg (I) | 18,148 | 16.1 |
| 7 D. French Slaughter Jr. (R) | 81,688 | 58.1 |
| David M. Smith (D) | 58,684 | 41.7 |
| 8 James P. Moran Jr. (D) | 88,475 | 51.7 |
| Stan Parris (R) | 76,367 | 44.6 |
| 9 Rick Boucher (D) | 67,215 | 97.1 |
| 10 Frank R. Wolf (R) | 103,761 | 61.5 |
| N. MacKenzie Canter III (D) | 57,249 | 33.9 |

## WASHINGTON

| | | |
|---|---|---|
| 1 John R. Miller (R) | 100,339 | 52.0 |
| Cynthia Sullivan (D) | 92,447 | 48.0 |
| 2 Al Swift (D) | 92,837 | 50.5 |
| Doug Smith (R) | 75,669 | 41.2 |
| William L. McCord (LIBERT) | 15,165 | 8.3 |
| 3 Jolene Unsoeld (D) | 95,645 | 53.8 |
| Bob Williams (R) | 82,269 | 46.2 |
| 4 Sid Morrison (R) | 106,545 | 70.7 |
| Ole Hougen (D) | 44,241 | 29.3 |
| 5 Thomas S. Foley (D) | 110,234 | 68.8 |
| Marlyn A. Derby (R) | 49,965 | 31.2 |
| 6 Norm Dicks (D) | 79,079 | 61.4 |
| Norbert Mueller (R) | 49,786 | 38.6 |
| 7 Jim McDermott (D) | 106,761 | 72.3 |
| Larry Penberthy (R) | 35,511 | 24.1 |
| 8 Rod Chandler (R) | 96,323 | 56.2 |
| David E. Giles (D) | 75,031 | 43.8 |

## WEST VIRGINIA

| Candidates | Votes | % |
|---|---|---|
| 1 Alan B. Mollohan (D) | 72,849 | 67.1 |
| Howard K. Tuck (R) | 35,657 | 32.9 |
| 2 Harley O. Staggers Jr. (D) | 63,174 | 55.5 |
| Oliver Luck (R) | 50,708 | 44.5 |
| 3 Bob Wise (D) | 75,327 | 100.0 |
| 4 Nick J. Rahall II (D) | 39,948 | 52.0 |
| Marianne R. Brewster (R) | 36,946 | 48.0 |

## WISCONSIN

| | | |
|---|---|---|
| 1 Les Aspin (D) | 93,961 | 99.4 |
| 2 Scott L. Klug (R) | 96,938 | 53.2 |
| Robert W. Kastenmeier (D) | 85,156 | 46.8 |
| 3 Steve Gunderson (R) | 94,509 | 61.0 |
| James L. Ziegeweid (D) | 60,409 | 39.0 |
| 4 Gerald D. Kleczka (D) | 96,981 | 69.2 |
| Joseph L. Cook (R) | 43,001 | 30.7 |
| 5 Jim Moody (D) | 77,557 | 68.0 |
| Donalda Hammersmith (R) | 31,255 | 27.4 |
| 6 Thomas E. Petri (R) | 111,036 | 99.5 |
| 7 David R. Obey (D) | 100,069 | 62.1 |
| John L. McEwen (R) | 60,961 | 37.9 |
| 8 Toby Roth (R) | 95,902 | 53.5 |
| Jerome Van Sistine (D) | 83,199 | 46.4 |
| 9 F. James Sensenbrenner Jr. (R) | 117,967 | 99.7 |

## WYOMING

| | | |
|---|---|---|
| AL Craig Thomas (R) | 87,078 | 55.1 |
| Pete Maxfield (D) | 70,977 | 44.9 |

**90 Elections**

*1. A special election was held to fill the unexpired term of Rep. Daniel K. Akaka (D), who signed May 16, 1990, having been appointed to the U.S. Senate.*

*2. For the 1990 House elections in Louisiana, an open primary election was held with candidates from all parties running on the same ballot. Any candidate who received a majority as elected unopposed, with no further appearance on the general election ballot. If no candidate received 50 percent, a runoff was held between the two top finishers.*

*3. In Minnesota the Democratic Party is known as the Democratic-Farmer-Labor Party and the Republican Party as the Independent-Republican Party; candidates appear on the ballot with these designations.*

*4. A special election was held to fill the unexpired term of Rep. James J. Florio (D), who resigned Jan. 16, 1990, having been elected governor.*

*5. A special election was held to fill the unexpired term of Rep. Guy V. Molinari (R), who resigned Jan. 1, 1990.*

*6. A special election was held to fill the unexpired term of Rep. Robert Garcia (D), who resigned Jan. 7, 1990.*

# 1991 House Elections

## ARIZONA

### Special Election [1]

| | Candidates | Votes | % |
|---|---|---|---|
| 2 | Ed Pastor (D) | 32,289 | 55.5 |
| | Pat Conner (R) | 25,814 | 44.4 |

## ILLINOIS

### Special Election [2]

| | | Votes | % |
|---|---|---|---|
| 15 | Thomas W. Ewing (R) | 25,675 | 66.4 |
| | Gerald Bradley (D) | 13,011 | 33.6 |

## MASSACHUSETTS

### Special Election [3]

| | Candidates | Votes | % |
|---|---|---|---|
| 1 | John Olver (D) | 70,022 | 49.6 |
| | Steven D. Pierce (R) | 68,052 | 48.2 |

## PENNSYLVANIA

### Special Election [4]

| | | Votes | % |
|---|---|---|---|
| 2 | Lucien E. Blackwell (D) | 51,820 | 39.2 |
| | Chaka Fattah (D) | 37,068 | 28.0 |
| | John F. White Jr. (D) | 36,469 | 27.6 |
| | Nadine G. Smith-Bulford (R) | 6,928 | 5.2 |

## TEXAS

### Special Election [5]

| | Candidates | Votes | % |
|---|---|---|---|
| 3 | Sam Johnson (R) | 24,004 | 52.6 |
| | Tom Pauken (R) | 21,647 | 47.4 |

## VIRGINIA

### Special Election [6]

| | | Votes | % |
|---|---|---|---|
| 7 | George F. Allen (R) | 106,745 | 62. |
| | Kay Slaughter (D) | 59,655 | 34. |

**1991 Elections**

1. A special election was held to fill the unexpired term of Rep. Morris K. Udall (D), who resigned May 4, 1991.

2. A special election was held to fill the unexpired term of Rep. Edward R. Madigan (R), who resigned March 8, 1991, having been appointed agriculture secretary.

3. A special election was held to fill the unexpired term of Rep. Silvio O. Conte (R), who died Feb. 8, 1991.

4. A special election was held to fill the unexpired term of Rep. William H. Gray III (D), who resigned Sept. 11, 1991.

5. A special election was held to fill the unexpired term of Rep. Steve Bartlett (R), who resigned March 11, 1991.

6. A special election was held to fill the unexpired term of Rep. D. French Slaughter Jr. (R), who resigned Nov. 5, 1991.

# 1992 House Elections

## ALABAMA

| | Candidates | Votes | % |
|---|---|---|---|
| 1 | Sonny Callahan (R) | 128,874 | 60.2 |
| | William A. Brewer (D) | 78,742 | 36.8 |
| 2 | Terry Everett (R) | 112,906 | 49.5 |
| | George C. Wallace Jr. (D) | 109,335 | 47.9 |
| 3 | Glen Browder (D) | 119,175 | 60.3 |
| | Don Sledge (R) | 73,800 | 37.4 |
| 4 | Tom Bevill (D) | 157,907 | 68.5 |
| | Mickey Strickland (R) | 66,934 | 29.0 |
| 5 | Robert E. "Bud" Cramer (D) | 160,060 | 65.6 |
| | Terry Smith (R) | 77,951 | 31.9 |
| 6 | Spencer Bachus (R) | 146,599 | 52.4 |
| | Ben Erdreich (D) | 126,062 | 45.0 |
| 7 | Earl F. Hilliard (D) | 144,320 | 69.5 |
| | Kervin Jones (R) | 36,086 | 17.4 |
| | James M. Lewis (I) | 12,461 | 6.0 |
| | James Chambliss (I) | 11,466 | 5.5 |

## ALASKA

| | | Votes | % |
|---|---|---|---|
| | Don Young (R) | 111,849 | 46.8 |
| | John E. Devens (D) | 102,378 | 42.8 |
| | Michael A. States (ALI) | 15,049 | 6.3 |

## ARIZONA

| | | Votes | % |
|---|---|---|---|
| | Sam Coppersmith (D) | 130,715 | 51.3 |
| | John J. Rhodes III (R) | 113,613 | 44.6 |
| | Ed Pastor (D) | 90,693 | 66.0 |
| | Don Shooter (R) | 41,257 | 30.0 |
| | Bob Stump (R) | 158,906 | 61.5 |
| | Roger Hartstone (D) | 88,830 | 34.4 |
| | Jon Kyl (R) | 156,330 | 59.2 |
| | Walter R. Mybeck II (D) | 70,572 | 26.7 |
| | Debbie Collings (I) | 25,553 | 9.7 |
| | Jim Kolbe (R) | 172,867 | 66.5 |
| | Jim Toevs (D) | 77,256 | 29.7 |
| | Karan English (D) | 124,251 | 53.0 |
| | Doug Wead (R) | 97,074 | 41.4 |
| | Sarah Stannard (I) | 13,047 | 5.6 |

## ARKANSAS

| | | Votes | % |
|---|---|---|---|
| | Blanche Lambert (D) | 149,558 | 69.8 |
| | Terry Hayes (R) | 64,618 | 30.2 |
| | Ray Thornton (D) | 154,946 | 74.2 |
| | Dennis Scott (R) | 53,978 | 25.8 |
| | Tim Hutchinson (R) | 125,295 | 50.2 |
| | John VanWinkle (D) | 117,775 | 47.2 |
| | Jay Dickey (R) | 113,009 | 52.3 |
| | W. J. "Bill" McCuen (D) | 102,918 | 47.7 |

## CALIFORNIA

| | | Votes | % |
|---|---|---|---|
| | Dan Hamburg (D) | 119,676 | 47.6 |
| | Frank Riggs (R) | 113,266 | 45.1 |
| | Wally Herger (R) | 167,247 | 65.2 |
| | Elliot Roy Freedman (D) | 71,780 | 28.0 |
| | Harry H. Pendery (LIBERT) | 17,529 | 6.8 |
| | Vic Fazio (D) | 122,149 | 51.2 |
| | H. L. "Bill" Richardson (R) | 96,092 | 40.3 |
| | Ross Crain (LIBERT) | 20,444 | 8.6 |
| | John T. Doolittle (R) | 141,155 | 49.8 |
| | Patricia Malberg (D) | 129,489 | 45.7 |
| | Robert T. Matsui (D) | 158,250 | 68.6 |
| | Robert S. Dinsmore (R) | 58,698 | 25.5 |
| | Lynn Woolsey (D) | 190,322 | 65.2 |
| | Bill Filante (R) | 98,171 | 33.6 |
| | George Miller (D) | 153,320 | 70.3 |
| | Dave Scholl (R) | 54,822 | 25.1 |
| | Nancy Pelosi (D) | 191,906 | 82.5 |
| | Marc Wolin (R) | 25,693 | 11.0 |

| | Candidates | Votes | % |
|---|---|---|---|
| 9 | Ronald V. Dellums (D) | 164,265 | 71.9 |
| | G. William Hunter (R) | 53,707 | 23.5 |
| 10 | Bill Baker (R) | 145,702 | 52.0 |
| | Wendell H. Williams (D) | 134,635 | 48.0 |
| 11 | Richard W. Pombo (R) | 94,453 | 47.6 |
| | Patricia Garamendi (D) | 90,539 | 45.6 |
| | Christine Roberts (LIBERT) | 13,498 | 6.8 |
| 12 | Tom Lantos (D) | 157,205 | 68.8 |
| | Jim Tomlin (R) | 53,278 | 23.3 |
| 13 | Pete Stark (D) | 123,795 | 60.2 |
| | Verne Teyler (R) | 64,953 | 31.6 |
| | Roslyn A. Allen (PFP) | 16,768 | 8.2 |
| 14 | Anna G. Eshoo (D) | 146,873 | 56.7 |
| | Tom Huening (R) | 101,202 | 39.0 |
| 15 | Norman Y. Mineta (D) | 168,617 | 63.5 |
| | Robert Wick (R) | 82,875 | 31.2 |
| | Duggan Dieterly (LIBERT) | 13,293 | 5.0 |
| 16 | Don Edwards (D) | 96,661 | 62.0 |
| | Ted Bundesen (R) | 49,843 | 32.0 |
| | Amani S. Kuumba (PFP) | 9,370 | 6.0 |
| 17 | Leon E. Panetta (D) | 151,561 | 72.0 |
| | Bill McCampbell (R) | 49,947 | 23.7 |
| 18 | Gary Condit (D) | 139,704 | 84.7 |
| | Kim R. Almstrom (LIBERT) | 25,307 | 15.3 |
| 19 | Richard H. Lehman (D) | 101,619 | 46.9 |
| | Tal L. Cloud (R) | 100,590 | 46.4 |
| | Dorothy L. Wells (PFP) | 13,334 | 6.2 |
| 20 | Calvin Dooley (D) | 72,679 | 64.9 |
| | Ed Hunt (R) | 39,388 | 35.1 |
| 21 | William M. Thomas (R) | 127,758 | 65.2 |
| | Deborah A. Vollmer (D) | 68,058 | 34.7 |
| 22 | Michael Huffington (R) | 131,242 | 52.5 |
| | Gloria Ochoa (D) | 87,328 | 34.9 |
| | Mindy Lorenz (GREEN) | 23,699 | 9.5 |
| 23 | Elton Gallegly (R) | 115,504 | 54.3 |
| | Anita Perez Ferguson (D) | 88,225 | 41.4 |
| 24 | Anthony C. Beilenson (D) | 141,742 | 55.5 |
| | Tom McClintock (R) | 99,835 | 39.1 |
| | John Paul Lindblad (PFP) | 13,690 | 5.4 |
| 25 | Howard P. "Buck" McKeon (R) | 113,611 | 51.9 |
| | James H. "Gil" Gilmartin (D) | 72,233 | 33.0 |
| | Rick Pamplin (I) | 13,930 | 6.4 |
| 26 | Howard L. Berman (D) | 73,807 | 61.0 |
| | Gary Forsch (R) | 36,453 | 30.1 |
| | Margery Hinds (PFP) | 7,180 | 5.9 |
| 27 | Carlos J. Moorhead (R) | 105,521 | 49.7 |
| | Doug Kahn (D) | 83,805 | 39.4 |
| | Jesse A. Moorman (GREEN) | 11,003 | 5.2 |
| 28 | David Dreier (R) | 122,353 | 58.4 |
| | Al Wachtel (D) | 76,525 | 36.5 |
| 29 | Henry A. Waxman (D) | 160,312 | 61.3 |
| | Mark A. Robbins (R) | 67,141 | 25.7 |
| | David Davis (I) | 15,445 | 5.9 |
| | Susan C. Davies (PFP) | 13,888 | 5.3 |
| 30 | Xavier Becerra (D) | 48,800 | 58.4 |
| | Morry Waksberg (R) | 20,034 | 24.0 |
| | Blase Bonpane (GREEN) | 6,315 | 7.6 |
| | Elizabeth A. Nakano (PFP) | 6,173 | 7.4 |
| 31 | Matthew G. Martinez (D) | 68,324 | 62.6 |
| | Reuben D. Franco (R) | 40,873 | 37.4 |
| 32 | Julian C. Dixon (D) | 150,644 | 87.2 |
| | Bob Weber (LIBERT) | 12,384 | 7.2 |
| | William R. Williams (PFP) | 9,782 | 5.7 |
| 33 | Lucille Roybal-Allard (D) | 32,010 | 63.0 |
| | Robert Guzman (R) | 15,428 | 30.4 |
| 34 | Esteban E. Torres (D) | 91,738 | 61.3 |
| | J. "Jay" Hernandez (R) | 50,907 | 34.0 |
| 35 | Maxine Waters (D) | 102,941 | 82.5 |
| | Nate Truman (R) | 17,417 | 14.0 |
| 36 | Jane Harman (D) | 125,751 | 48.4 |
| | Joan Milke Flores (R) | 109,684 | 42.2 |
| | Richard H. Greene (GREEN) | 13,297 | 5.1 |
| 37 | Walter R. Tucker (D) | 97,159 | 85.7 |
| | B. Kwaku Duren (PFP) | 16,178 | 14.3 |
| 38 | Steve Horn (R) | 92,038 | 48.6 |

| | Candidates | Votes | % |
|---|---|---|---|
| | Evan Anderson Braude (D) | 82,108 | 43.4 |
| 39 | Ed Royce (R) | 122,472 | 57.3 |
| | Molly McClanahan (D) | 81,728 | 38.2 |
| 40 | Jerry Lewis (R) | 129,563 | 63.1 |
| | Donald M. Rusk (D) | 63,881 | 31.1 |
| | Margie Akin (PFP) | 11,839 | 5.8 |
| 41 | Jay C. Kim (R) | 101,753 | 59.6 |
| | Bob Baker (D) | 58,777 | 34.4 |
| | Mike Noonan (PFP) | 10,136 | 5.9 |
| 42 | George E. Brown Jr. (D) | 79,780 | 50.7 |
| | Dick Rutan (R) | 69,251 | 44.0 |
| | Fritz R. Ward (LIBERT) | 8,424 | 5.4 |
| 43 | Ken Calvert (R) | 88,987 | 46.7 |
| | Mark A. Takano (D) | 88,468 | 46.4 |
| 44 | Al McCandless (R) | 110,333 | 54.2 |
| | Georgia Smith (D) | 81,693 | 40.1 |
| | Phil Turner (LIBERT) | 11,515 | 5.7 |
| 45 | Dana Rohrabacher (R) | 123,731 | 54.5 |
| | Patricia McCabe (D) | 88,508 | 39.0 |
| | Gary D. Copeland (LIBERT) | 14,777 | 6.5 |
| 46 | Robert K. Dornan (R) | 55,659 | 50.2 |
| | Robert John Banuelos (D) | 45,435 | 41.0 |
| | Richard G. Newhouse (LIBERT) | 9,712 | 8.8 |
| 47 | C. Christopher Cox (R) | 165,004 | 64.9 |
| | John F. Anwiler (D) | 76,924 | 30.3 |
| 48 | Ron Packard (R) | 140,935 | 61.1 |
| | Michael Farber (D) | 67,415 | 29.2 |
| | Donna White (PFP) | 13,396 | 5.8 |
| 49 | Lynn Schenk (D) | 127,280 | 51.1 |
| | Judy Jarvis (R) | 106,170 | 42.7 |
| 50 | Bob Filner (D) | 77,293 | 56.6 |
| | Tony Valencia (R) | 39,531 | 28.9 |
| | Barbara Hutchinson (LIBERT) | 15,489 | 11.3 |
| 51 | Randy "Duke" Cunningham (R) | 141,890 | 56.1 |
| | Bea Herbert (D) | 85,148 | 33.7 |
| 52 | Duncan Hunter (R) | 112,995 | 52.9 |
| | Janet M. Gastil (D) | 88,076 | 41.2 |

## COLORADO

| | | Votes | % |
|---|---|---|---|
| 1 | Patricia Schroeder (D) | 156,629 | 68.8 |
| | Raymond Diaz Aragon (R) | 70,902 | 31.2 |
| 2 | David E. Skaggs (D) | 164,790 | 60.7 |
| | Bryan Day (R) | 88,470 | 32.6 |
| | Vern Tharp (AGA) | 18,101 | 6.7 |
| 3 | Scott McInnis (R) | 143,293 | 54.7 |
| | Mike Callihan (D) | 114,480 | 43.7 |
| 4 | Wayne Allard (R) | 139,884 | 57.8 |
| | Tom Redder (D) | 101,957 | 42.2 |
| 5 | Joel Hefley (R) | 173,096 | 71.1 |
| | Charles A. Oriez (D) | 62,550 | 25.7 |
| 6 | Dan Schaefer (R) | 142,021 | 60.9 |
| | Tom Kolbe (D) | 91,073 | 39.1 |

## CONNECTICUT

| | | Votes | % |
|---|---|---|---|
| 1 | Barbara B. Kennelly (D, ACP) | 164,735 | 67.1 |
| | Philip L. Steele (R) | 75,113 | 30.6 |
| 2 | Sam Gejdenson (D, ACP) | 123,291 | 50.8 |
| | Edward W. Munster (R) | 119,416 | 49.2 |
| 3 | Rosa DeLauro (D, ACP) | 162,568 | 65.7 |
| | Thomas Scott (R) | 84,952 | 34.3 |
| 4 | Christopher Shays (R) | 147,816 | 67.3 |
| | Dave Schropfer (D) | 58,666 | 26.7 |
| | Al Smith (ACP) | 11,679 | 5.3 |
| 5 | Gary Franks (R) | 104,891 | 43.7 |
| | James J. Lawlor (D) | 74,791 | 31.1 |
| | Lynn H. Taborsak (ACP) | 54,022 | 22.5 |
| 6 | Nancy L. Johnson (R) | 166,967 | 69.7 |
| | Eugene F. Slason (D) | 60,373 | 25.2 |

## DELAWARE

| Candidates | Votes | % |
|---|---|---|
| AL Michael N. Castle (R) | 153,037 | 55.4 |
| S. B. Woo (D) | 117,426 | 42.5 |

## FLORIDA

| | Candidates | Votes | % |
|---|---|---|---|
| 1 | Earl Hutto (D) | 118,941 | 52.0 |
| | Terry Ketchel (R) | 100,349 | 43.9 |
| 2 | Pete Peterson (D) | 167,215 | 73.4 |
| | Ray Wagner (R) | 60,425 | 26.5 |
| 3 | Corrine Brown (D) | 91,915 | 59.3 |
| | Don Weidner (R) | 63,115 | 40.7 |
| 4 | Tillie Fowler (R) | 135,883 | 56.7 |
| | Mattox Hair (D) | 103,531 | 43.2 |
| 5 | Karen L. Thurman (D) | 129,698 | 49.2 |
| | Tom Hogan (R) | 114,356 | 43.4 |
| | Cindy Munkittrick (I) | 19,462 | 7.4 |
| 6 | Cliff Stearns (R) | 144,195 | 65.4 |
| | Phil Denton (D) | 76,419 | 34.6 |
| 7 | John L. Mica (R) | 125,823 | 56.4 |
| | Dan Webster (D) | 96,945 | 43.5 |
| 8 | Bill McCollum (R) | 141,977 | 68.5 |
| | Chuck Kovaleski (D) | 65,145 | 31.5 |
| 9 | Michael Bilirakis (R) | 158,028 | 58.9 |
| | Cheryl Davis Knapp (D) | 110,135 | 41.1 |
| 10 | C. W. Bill Young (R) | 149,606 | 56.6 |
| | Karen Moffitt (D) | 114,809 | 43.4 |
| 11 | Sam Gibbons (D) | 100,984 | 52.8 |
| | Mark Sharpe (R) | 77,640 | 40.6 |
| | Joe De Minico (I) | 12,730 | 6.7 |
| 12 | Charles T. Canady (R) | 100,484 | 52.1 |
| | Tom Mims (D) | 92,346 | 47.9 |
| 13 | Dan Miller (R) | 158,881 | 57.8 |
| | Rand Snell (D) | 115,767 | 42.2 |
| 14 | Porter J. Goss (R) | 220,351 | 82.1 |
| | James H. King (I) | 48,160 | 17.9 |
| 15 | Jim Bacchus (D) | 132,412 | 50.7 |
| | Bill Tolley (R) | 128,873 | 49.3 |
| 16 | Tom Lewis (R) | 157,322 | 60.8 |
| | John P. Comerford (D) | 101,237 | 39.2 |
| 17 | Carrie Meek (D) | 102,784 | 100.0 |
| 18 | Ileana Ros-Lehtinen (R) | 104,755 | 66.8 |
| | Magda Montiel Davis (D) | 52,142 | 33.2 |
| 19 | Harry A. Johnston (D) | 177,423 | 63.1 |
| | Larry Metz (R) | 103,867 | 36.9 |
| 20 | Peter Deutsch (D) | 130,959 | 55.1 |
| | Beverly Kennedy (R) | 91,589 | 38.5 |
| | James M. Blackburn (I) | 15,341 | 6.4 |
| 21 | Lincoln Diaz-Balart (R) | | 100.0 |
| 22 | E. Clay Shaw Jr. (R) | 128,400 | 52.0 |
| | Gwen Margolis (D) | 91,625 | 37.1 |
| | Richard "Even" Stephens (I) | 15,469 | 6.3 |
| 23 | Alcee L. Hastings (D) | 84,249 | 58.5 |
| | Ed Fielding (R) | 44,807 | 31.1 |
| | Al Woods (I) | 14,879 | 10.3 |

## GEORGIA

| | Candidates | Votes | % |
|---|---|---|---|
| 1 | Jack Kingston (R) | 103,932 | 57.8 |
| | Barbara Christmas (D) | 75,808 | 42.2 |
| 2 | Sanford Bishop (D) | 95,789 | 63.7 |
| | Jim Dudley (R) | 54,593 | 36.3 |
| 3 | Mac Collins (R) | 114,107 | 54.8 |
| | Richard Ray (D) | 94,271 | 45.2 |
| 4 | John Linder (R) | 126,495 | 50.5 |
| | Cathey Steinberg (D) | 123,819 | 49.5 |
| 5 | John Lewis (D) | 147,445 | 72.1 |
| | Paul R. Stabler (R) | 56,960 | 27.9 |
| 6 | Newt Gingrich (R) | 158,761 | 57.7 |
| | Tony Center (D) | 116,196 | 42.3 |
| 7 | George "Buddy" Darden (D) | 111,374 | 57.3 |
| | Al Beverly (R) | 82,915 | 42.7 |
| 8 | J. Roy Rowland (D) | 108,472 | 55.7 |
| | Bob Cunningham (R) | 86,220 | 44.3 |
| 9 | Nathan Deal (D) | 113,024 | 59.2 |
| | Daniel Becker (R) | 77,919 | 40.8 |
| 10 | Don Johnson (D) | 108,426 | 53.8 |
| | Ralph T. Hudgens (R) | 93,059 | 46.2 |

| | Candidates | Votes | % |
|---|---|---|---|
| 11 | Cynthia McKinney (D) | 120,168 | 73.1 |
| | Woodrow Lovett (R) | 44,221 | 26.9 |

## HAWAII

| | Candidates | Votes | % |
|---|---|---|---|
| 1 | Neil Abercrombie (D) | 129,332 | 72.9 |
| | Warner C. Kimo Sutton (R) | 41,575 | 23.4 |
| 2 | Patsy T. Mink (D) | 131,454 | 72.6 |
| | Kamuela Price (R) | 40,070 | 22.1 |
| | Lloyd "Jeff" Mallan (LIBERT) | 9,431 | 5.2 |

## IDAHO

| | | | |
|---|---|---|---|
| 1 | Larry LaRocco (D) | 140,985 | 58.1 |
| | Rachel S. Gilbert (R) | 90,983 | 37.5 |
| 2 | Michael D. Crapo (R) | 139,783 | 60.8 |
| | J. D. Williams (D) | 81,450 | 35.4 |

## ILLINOIS

| | | | |
|---|---|---|---|
| 1 | Bobby L. Rush (D) | 209,258 | 82.8 |
| | Jay Walker (R) | 43,453 | 17.2 |
| 2 | Mel Reynolds (D) | 182,614 | 78.1 |
| | Ron Blackstone (R) | 31,957 | 13.7 |
| | Louanner Peters (I) | 19,293 | 8.2 |
| 3 | William O. Lipinski (D) | 162,165 | 63.5 |
| | Harry C. Lepinske (R) | 93,128 | 36.5 |
| 4 | Luis V. Gutierrez (D) | 90,452 | 77.6 |
| | Hildegarde Rodriguez-Schieman (R) | 26,154 | 22.4 |
| 5 | Dan Rostenkowski (D) | 132,889 | 57.3 |
| | Elias R. Zenkich (R) | 90,738 | 39.1 |
| 6 | Henry J. Hyde (R) | 165,009 | 65.5 |
| | Barry W. Watkins (D) | 86,891 | 34.5 |
| 7 | Cardiss Collins (D) | 182,811 | 81.1 |
| | Norman G. Boccio (R) | 35,346 | 15.7 |
| 8 | Philip M. Crane (R) | 132,887 | 55.7 |
| | Sheila A. Smith (D) | 96,419 | 40.4 |
| 9 | Sidney R. Yates (D) | 162,942 | 68.0 |
| | Herbert Sohn (R) | 64,760 | 27.0 |
| | Sheila A. Jones (ECR) | 12,001 | 5.0 |
| 10 | John Edward Porter (R) | 155,230 | 64.5 |
| | Michael J. Kennedy (D) | 85,400 | 35.5 |
| 11 | George E. Sangmeister (D) | 135,387 | 55.7 |
| | Robert T. Herbolsheimer (R) | 107,860 | 44.3 |
| 12 | Jerry F. Costello (D) | 168,762 | 71.2 |
| | Mike Starr (R) | 68,115 | 28.8 |
| 13 | Harris W. Fawell (R) | 179,257 | 68.4 |
| | Dennis Michael Temple (D) | 82,985 | 31.6 |
| 14 | Dennis Hastert (R) | 155,271 | 67.3 |
| | Jonathan Abram Reich (D) | 75,294 | 32.6 |
| 15 | Thomas W. Ewing (R) | 142,167 | 59.3 |
| | Charles D. Mattis (D) | 97,190 | 40.6 |
| 16 | Donald Manzullo (R) | 142,388 | 55.6 |
| | John W. Cox Jr. (D) | 113,555 | 44.4 |
| 17 | Lane Evans (D) | 156,233 | 60.1 |
| | Ken Schloemer (R) | 103,719 | 39.9 |
| 18 | Robert H. Michel (R) | 156,533 | 57.8 |
| | Ronald C. Hawkins (D) | 114,413 | 42.2 |
| 19 | Glenn Poshard (D) | 187,156 | 69.1 |
| | Douglas E. Lee (R) | 83,526 | 30.9 |
| 20 | Richard J. Durbin (D) | 154,869 | 56.5 |
| | John M. Shimkus (R) | 119,219 | 43.5 |

## INDIANA

| | | | |
|---|---|---|---|
| 1 | Peter J. Visclosky (D) | 147,054 | 69.4 |
| | David J. Vucich (R) | 64,770 | 30.6 |
| 2 | Philip R. Sharp (D) | 130,881 | 57.1 |
| | William G. Frazier (R) | 90,593 | 39.5 |
| 3 | Tim Roemer (D) | 121,269 | 57.4 |
| | Carl H. Baxmeyer (R) | 89,834 | 42.6 |
| 4 | Jill Long (D) | 134,907 | 62.1 |
| | Charles W. Pierson (R) | 82,468 | 37.9 |
| 5 | Steve Buyer (R) | 112,492 | 51.0 |
| | Jim Jontz (D) | 107,973 | 49.0 |
| 6 | Dan Burton (R) | 186,49☐ | 72.2 |
| | Natalie M. Bruner (D) | 71,952 | 27.8 |

| | Candidates | Votes | % |
|---|---|---|---|
| 7 | John T. Myers (R) | 129,189 | 59☐ |
| | Ellen E. Wedum (D) | 88,005 | 40☐ |
| 8 | Frank McCloskey (D) | 125,244 | 52☐ |
| | Richard E. Mourdock (R) | 108,054 | 45☐ |
| 9 | Lee H. Hamilton (D) | 160,980 | 69☐ |
| | Michael E. Bailey (R) | 70,057 | 30☐ |
| 10 | Andrew Jacobs Jr. (D) | 117,604 | 64☐ |
| | Janos Horvath (R) | 64,378 | 35☐ |

## IOWA

| | | | |
|---|---|---|---|
| 1 | Jim Leach (R) | 178,042 | 68☐ |
| | Jan J. Zonneveld (D) | 81,600 | 31☐ |
| 2 | Jim Nussle (R) | 134,536 | 50☐ |
| | David R. Nagle (D) | 131,570 | 49☐ |
| 3 | Jim Ross Lightfoot (R) | 125,931 | 48☐ |
| | Elaine Baxter (D) | 121,063 | 47☐ |
| 4 | Neal Smith (D) | 158,610 | 61☐ |
| | Paul Lunde (R) | 94,045 | 36☐ |
| 5 | Fred Grandy (R) | 196,942 | 99☐ |

## KANSAS

| | | | |
|---|---|---|---|
| 1 | Pat Roberts (R) | 194,912 | 68☐ |
| | Duane West (D) | 83,620 | 29☐ |
| 2 | Jim Slattery (D) | 151,019 | 58☐ |
| | Jim Van Slyke (R) | 109,801 | 40☐ |
| 3 | Jan Meyers (R) | 169,925 | 58☐ |
| | Tom Love (D) | 110,076 | 37☐ |
| 4 | Dan Glickman (D) | 143,671 | 5☐ |
| | Eric R. Yost (R) | 117,070 | 4☐ |
| | Seth L. Warren (LIBERT) | 17,275 | ☐ |

## KENTUCKY

| | | | |
|---|---|---|---|
| 1 | Tom Barlow (D) | 128,524 | 6☐ |
| | Steve Hamrick (R) | 83,088 | 3☐ |
| 2 | William H. Natcher (D) | 126,894 | 6☐ |
| | Bruce R. Bartley (R) | 79,684 | 3☐ |
| 3 | Romano L. Mazzoli (D) | 148,066 | 5☐ |
| | Susan B. Stokes (R) | 132,689 | 4☐ |
| 4 | Jim Bunning (R) | 139,634 | 6☐ |
| | Dr. Floyd G. Poore (D) | 86,890 | 3☐ |
| 5 | Harold Rogers (R) | 115,255 | 5☐ |
| | John Doug Hays (D) | 95,760 | 4☐ |
| 6 | Scotty Baesler (D) | 135,613 | 6☐ |
| | Charles W. Ellinger (R) | 87,816 | 3☐ |

## LOUISIANA [1]

| | | | |
|---|---|---|---|
| 1 | Robert L. Livingston (R) | | 10☐ |
| 2 | William J. Jefferson (D) | | 10☐ |
| 3 | W. J. "Billy" Tauzin (D) | | 10☐ |
| 4 | Cleo Fields (D) | 143,980 | ☐ |
| | Charles Jones (D) | 50,851 | ☐ |
| 5 | Jim McCrery (R) | 153,501 | 6☐ |
| | Jerry Huckaby (D) | 90,079 | 3☐ |
| 6 | Richard H. Baker (R) | 123,953 | ☐ |
| | Clyde C. Holloway (R) | 121,225 | 4☐ |
| 7 | Jimmy Hayes (D) | | 10☐ |

## MAINE

| | | | |
|---|---|---|---|
| 1 | Thomas H. Andrews (D) | 232,696 | 6☐ |
| | Linda Bean (R) | 125,236 | 3☐ |
| 2 | Olympia J. Snowe (R) | 153,022 | 4☐ |
| | Patrick K. McGowan (D) | 130,824 | 4☐ |
| | Jonathan K. Carter (GREEN) | 27,526 | |

## MARYLAND

| | | | |
|---|---|---|---|
| 1 | Wayne T. Gilchrest (R) | 120,084 | 5☐ |
| | Tom McMillen (D) | 112,771 | 4☐ |
| 2 | Helen Delich Bentley (R) | 165,443 | 6☐ |
| | Michael C. Hickey Jr. (D) | 88,658 | 3☐ |
| 3 | Benjamin L. Cardin (D) | 163,354 | 7☐ |
| | William T. S. Bricker (R) | 58,869 | 2☐ |
| 4 | Albert R. Wynn (D) | 136,902 | 7☐ |

| Candidates | Votes | % |
|---|---|---|
| Michele Dyson (R) | 45,166 | 24.8 |
| Steny H. Hoyer (D) | 118,312 | 53.0 |
| Lawrence J. Hogan Jr. (R) | 97,982 | 43.9 |
| Roscoe G. Bartlett (R) | 125,564 | 54.2 |
| Thomas H. Hattery (D) | 106,224 | 45.8 |
| Kweisi Mfume (D) | 152,689 | 85.3 |
| Kenneth Kondner (R) | 26,304 | 14.7 |
| Constance A. Morella (R) | 203,377 | 72.5 |
| Edward J. Heffernan (D) | 77,042 | 27.5 |

## MASSACHUSETTS

| | | |
|---|---|---|
| John W. Olver (D) | 135,049 | 51.5 |
| Patrick Larkin (R) | 113,828 | 43.4 |
| Richard E. Neal (D) | 131,215 | 53.1 |
| Anthony W. Ravosa Jr. (R) | 76,795 | 31.1 |
| Thomas R. Sheehan (FTP) | 38,963 | 15.8 |
| Peter I. Blute (R) | 131,473 | 50.4 |
| Joseph D. Early (D) | 115,587 | 44.3 |
| Barney Frank (D) | 182,633 | 67.7 |
| Edward J. McCormick III (R) | 70,665 | 26.2 |
| Luke Lumina (IV) | 13,670 | 5.1 |
| Martin T. Meehan (D) | 133,844 | 52.2 |
| Paul W. Cronin (R) | 96,206 | 37.5 |
| Mary J. Farinelli (I) | 19,077 | 7.4 |
| Peter G. Torkildsen (R) | 159,165 | 54.8 |
| Nicholas Mavroules (D) | 130,248 | 44.9 |
| Edward J. Markey (D) | 174,837 | 62.1 |
| Stephen A. Sohn (R) | 78,262 | 27.8 |
| Robert B. Antonelli (I) | 28,421 | 10.1 |
| Joseph P. Kennedy II (D) | 149,903 | 83.1 |
| Alice Harriett Nakash (I) | 30,402 | 16.8 |
| Joe Moakley (D) | 175,550 | 69.2 |
| Martin D. Conboy (R) | 54,291 | 21.4 |
| Lawrence C. Mackin (I) | 15,637 | 6.2 |
| Gerry E. Studds (D) | 189,342 | 60.8 |
| Daniel W. Daly (R) | 75,887 | 24.4 |
| Jon L. Bryan (I) | 39,265 | 12.6 |

## MICHIGAN

| | | |
|---|---|---|
| Bart Stupak (D) | 144,857 | 53.9 |
| Philip E. Ruppe (R) | 117,056 | 43.6 |
| Peter Hoekstra (R) | 155,577 | 63.0 |
| John H. Miltner (D) | 86,265 | 35.0 |
| Paul B. Henry (R) | 162,451 | 61.3 |
| Carol S. Kooistra (D) | 95,927 | 36.2 |
| Dave Camp (R) | 157,337 | 62.5 |
| Lisa A. Donaldson (D) | 87,573 | 34.8 |
| James A. Barcia (D) | 147,618 | 60.3 |
| Keith Muxlow (R) | 93,098 | 38.0 |
| Fred Upton (R) | 144,083 | 61.8 |
| Andy Davis (D) | 89,020 | 38.2 |
| Nick Smith (R) | 133,972 | 87.6 |
| Kenneth Proctor (LIBERT) | 18,751 | 12.3 |
| Bob Carr (D) | 135,517 | 47.6 |
| Dick Chrysler (R) | 131,906 | 46.3 |
| Dale E. Kildee (D) | 133,956 | 53.7 |
| Megan O'Neill (R) | 111,798 | 44.8 |
| David E. Bonior (D) | 138,193 | 53.1 |
| Douglas Carl (R) | 114,918 | 44.2 |
| Joe Knollenberg (R) | 168,940 | 57.6 |
| Walter Briggs (D) | 117,725 | 40.2 |
| Sander M. Levin (D) | 137,514 | 52.6 |
| John Pappageorge (R) | 119,357 | 45.7 |
| William D. Ford (D) | 127,642 | 51.9 |
| Robert Geake (R) | 105,169 | 42.8 |
| John Conyers Jr. (D) | 165,496 | 82.4 |
| John W. Gordon (R) | 32,036 | 15.9 |
| Barbara-Rose Collins (D) | 148,908 | 80.5 |
| Charles C. Vincent (R) | 31,849 | 17.2 |
| John D. Dingell (D) | 156,964 | 65.1 |
| Frank Beaumont (R) | 75,694 | 31.4 |

## MINNESOTA [2]

| | Candidates | Votes | % |
|---|---|---|---|
| 1 | Timothy J. Penny (DFL) | 206,369 | 73.9 |
| | Timothy R. Droogsma (I-R) | 72,367 | 25.9 |
| 2 | David Minge (DFL) | 132,156 | 47.8 |
| | Cal R. Ludeman (I-R) | 131,587 | 47.6 |
| 3 | Jim Ramstad (I-R) | 200,240 | 63.6 |
| | Paul Mandell (DFL) | 104,606 | 33.2 |
| 4 | Bruce F. Vento (DFL) | 159,796 | 57.5 |
| | Ian Maitland (I-R) | 101,744 | 36.6 |
| 5 | Martin Olav Sabo (DFL) | 174,139 | 62.8 |
| | Stephen A. Moriarty (I-R) | 77,093 | 27.8 |
| 6 | Rod Grams (I-R) | 133,564 | 44.4 |
| | Gerry Sikorski (DFL) | 100,016 | 33.2 |
| | Dean Barkley (I) | 48,329 | 16.1 |
| | James H. Peterson (IFP) | 16,411 | 5.5 |
| 7 | Collin C. Peterson (DFL) | 133,886 | 50.4 |
| | Bernie Omann (I-R) | 130,396 | 49.1 |
| 8 | James L. Oberstar (DFL) | 167,104 | 59.0 |
| | Phil Herwig (I-R) | 83,823 | 29.6 |
| | Harry Robb Welty (Perot Choice) | 22,619 | 8.0 |

## MISSISSIPPI

| | | Votes | % |
|---|---|---|---|
| 1 | Jamie L. Whitten (D) | 121,664 | 59.5 |
| | Clyde E. Whitaker (R) | 82,952 | 40.5 |
| 2 | Mike Espy (D) | 133,361 | 76.4 |
| | Dorothy Benford (R) | 41,248 | 23.6 |
| 3 | G. V. "Sonny" Montgomery (D) | 162,864 | 81.2 |
| | Michael E. Williams (R) | 37,710 | 18.8 |
| 4 | Mike Parker (D) | 130,927 | 67.3 |
| | Jack L. McMillan (R) | 43,705 | 22.5 |
| | Liz Gilchrist (I) | 10,523 | 5.4 |
| 5 | Gene Taylor (D) | 120,766 | 63.2 |
| | Paul Harvey (R) | 67,619 | 35.4 |

## MISSOURI

| | | Votes | % |
|---|---|---|---|
| 1 | William L. Clay (D) | 158,693 | 68.1 |
| | Arthur S. Montgomery (R) | 74,482 | 31.9 |
| 2 | James M. Talent (R) | 157,594 | 50.4 |
| | Joan Kelly Horn (D) | 148,729 | 47.6 |
| 3 | Richard A. Gephardt (D) | 174,000 | 64.0 |
| | Malcolm L. Holekamp (R) | 90,006 | 33.1 |
| 4 | Ike Skelton (D) | 176,977 | 70.4 |
| | John Carley (R) | 74,475 | 29.6 |
| 5 | Alan Wheat (D) | 151,014 | 59.1 |
| | Edward "Gomer" Moody (R) | 93,562 | 36.6 |
| 6 | Pat Danner (D) | 148,887 | 55.4 |
| | E. Thomas Coleman (R) | 119,637 | 44.6 |
| 7 | Mel Hancock (R) | 160,303 | 61.6 |
| | Thomas Patrick Deaton (D) | 99,762 | 38.4 |
| 8 | Bill Emerson (R) | 147,398 | 62.9 |
| | Thad Bullock (D) | 86,730 | 37.0 |
| 9 | Harold L. Volkmer (D) | 124,694 | 47.7 |
| | Rick Hardy (R) | 118,811 | 45.5 |

## MONTANA

| | | Votes | % |
|---|---|---|---|
| AL | Pat Williams (D) | 203,711 | 50.5 |
| | Ron Marlenee (R) | 189,570 | 47.0 |

## NEBRASKA

| | | Votes | % |
|---|---|---|---|
| 1 | Doug Bereuter (R) | 142,713 | 59.7 |
| | Gerry Finnegan (D) | 96,309 | 40.3 |
| 2 | Peter Hoagland (D) | 119,512 | 51.2 |
| | Ronald L. Staskiewicz (R) | 113,828 | 48.8 |
| 3 | Bill Barrett (R) | 170,857 | 71.7 |
| | Lowell Fisher (D) | 67,457 | 28.3 |

## NEVADA

| | | Votes | % |
|---|---|---|---|
| 1 | James H. Bilbray (D) | 128,278 | 57.9 |
| | J. Coy Pettyjohn (R) | 84,217 | 38.0 |
| 2 | Barbara F. Vucanovich (R) | 129,575 | 47.9 |
| | Pete Sferrazza (D) | 117,199 | 43.3 |

## NEW HAMPSHIRE

| | Candidates | Votes | % |
|---|---|---|---|
| 1 | Bill Zeliff (R) | 135,936 | 53.1 |
| | Bob Preston (D) | 108,578 | 42.4 |
| 2 | Dick Swett (D) | 157,328 | 61.7 |
| | Bill Hatch (R) | 91,126 | 35.7 |

## NEW JERSEY

| | | Votes | % |
|---|---|---|---|
| 1 | Robert E. Andrews (D) | 153,525 | 67.3 |
| | Lee A. Solomon (R) | 65,123 | 28.6 |
| 2 | William J. Hughes (D) | 132,465 | 55.9 |
| | Frank A. LoBiondo (R) | 98,315 | 41.5 |
| 3 | H. James Saxton (R) | 151,368 | 59.2 |
| | Timothy E. Ryan (D) | 94,012 | 36.8 |
| 4 | Christopher H. Smith (R) | 149,095 | 61.8 |
| | Brian M. Hughes (D) | 84,514 | 35.0 |
| 5 | Marge Roukema (R) | 196,198 | 71.5 |
| | Frank R. Lucas (D) | 67,579 | 24.6 |
| 6 | Frank Pallone Jr. (D) | 118,266 | 52.3 |
| | Joseph M. Kyrillos (R) | 100,949 | 44.6 |
| 7 | Bob Franks (R) | 132,174 | 53.3 |
| | Leonard R. Sendelsky (D) | 105,761 | 42.6 |
| 8 | Herbert C. Klein (D) | 96,742 | 47.0 |
| | Joseph L. Bubba (R) | 84,674 | 41.1 |
| | Gloria J. Kolodziej (IFC) | 16,170 | 7.9 |
| 9 | Robert G. Torricelli (D) | 139,188 | 58.3 |
| | Patrick J. Roma (R) | 88,179 | 36.9 |
| 10 | Donald M. Payne (D) | 117,287 | 78.4 |
| | Alfred D. Palermo (R) | 30,160 | 20.2 |
| 11 | Dean A. Gallo (R) | 188,165 | 70.1 |
| | Ona Spiridellis (D) | 68,871 | 25.7 |
| 12 | Dick Zimmer (R) | 174,216 | 63.9 |
| | Frank Abate (D) | 83,035 | 30.4 |
| 13 | Robert Menendez (D) | 93,670 | 64.3 |
| | Fred J. Theemling Jr. (R) | 44,529 | 30.6 |

## NEW MEXICO

| | | Votes | % |
|---|---|---|---|
| 1 | Steven H. Schiff (R) | 128,426 | 62.6 |
| | Robert J. Aragon (D) | 76,600 | 37.3 |
| 2 | Joe Skeen (R) | 94,838 | 56.4 |
| | Dan Sosa Jr. (D) | 73,157 | 43.5 |
| 3 | Bill Richardson (D) | 122,850 | 67.4 |
| | F. Gregg Bemis Jr. (R) | 54,569 | 29.9 |

## NEW YORK

| | | Votes | % |
|---|---|---|---|
| 1 | George J. Hochbrueckner (D, LIF) | 117,940 | 51.7 |
| | Edward P. Romaine (R, C, RTL, TCP-LI) | 110,043 | 48.3 |
| 2 | Rick A. Lazio (R, C, TCP-LI) | 109,386 | 53.2 |
| | Thomas J. Downey (D, LIF) | 96,328 | 46.8 |
| 3 | Peter T. King (R, C) | 124,727 | 49.6 |
| | Steve A. Orlins (D) | 116,915 | 46.5 |
| 4 | David A. Levy (R, C) | 110,710 | 50.2 |
| | Philip Schiliro (D, L) | 100,386 | 45.5 |
| 5 | Gary L. Ackerman (D, L) | 110,476 | 52.4 |
| | Allan E. Binder (R, C) | 94,907 | 45.0 |
| 6 | Floyd H. Flake (D) | 96,972 | 81.0 |
| | Dianand D. Bhagwandin (R, C) | 22,687 | 19.0 |
| 7 | Thomas J. Manton (D) | 72,280 | 56.9 |
| | Dennis C. Shea (R, C) | 54,639 | 43.1 |
| 8 | Jerrold Nadler (D, L) | 138,296 | 81.2 |
| | David L. Askren (R) | 25,548 | 15.0 |
| 9 | Charles E. Schumer (D, L) | 116,545 | 88.6 |
| | Alice E. Gaffney (R) | 14,985 | 11.4 |
| 10 | Edolphus Towns (D, L) | 97,509 | 95.8 |
| 11 | Major R. Owens (D, L) | 80,028 | 93.6 |
| | Michael Gaffney (C) | 4,287 | 5.0 |
| 12 | Nydia M. Velázquez (D) | 55,926 | 76.5 |
| | Angel Diaz (R, C, RTL) | 14,976 | 20.5 |
| 13 | Susan Molinari (R, C) | 107,903 | 56.1 |
| | Sal F. Albanese (D, L) | 73,520 | 38.2 |
| | Kathleen M. Murphy (RTL) | 10,825 | 5.6 |

| Candidates | Votes | % |
|---|---|---|
| 14 Carolyn B. Maloney (D, L) | 101,652 | 50.4 |
| Bill Green (R, INS) | 97,215 | 48.2 |
| 15 Charles B. Rangel (D) | 105,011 | 94.9 |
| 16 Jose E. Serrano (D, L) | 85,222 | 91.4 |
| Michael Walters (R, C) | 7,975 | 8.6 |
| 17 Eliot L. Engel (D, L) | 98,068 | 80.1 |
| Martin Richman (R) | 16,511 | 13.5 |
| 18 Nita M. Lowey (D) | 115,841 | 55.6 |
| Joseph J. DioGuardi | | |
| (R, C, RTL) | 92,687 | 44.4 |
| 19 Hamilton Fish Jr. (R, C) | 139,610 | 60.1 |
| Neil McCarthy (D) | 92,854 | 39.9 |
| 20 Benjamin A. Gilman (R) | 150,301 | 66.1 |
| Jonathan L. Levine (D) | 66,826 | 29.4 |
| 21 Michael R. McNulty (D, C) | 166,371 | 62.7 |
| Nancy Norman (R, L) | 91,184 | 34.4 |
| 22 Gerald B. H. Solomon | | |
| (R, C, RTL) | 164,436 | 65.4 |
| David Roberts (D) | 86,896 | 34.6 |
| 23 Sherwood Boehlert (R) | 139,774 | 63.6 |
| Paula DiPerna (D) | 61,835 | 28.2 |
| 24 John M. McHugh (R, VR) | 122,257 | 60.8 |
| Margaret M. Ravenscroft (D) | 47,675 | 23.7 |
| Morrison J. Hosley Jr. (C, RTL) | 26,763 | 13.3 |
| 25 James T. Walsh (R, C) | 135,076 | 55.7 |
| Rhea Jezer (D, CS) | 107,310 | 44.3 |
| 26 Maurice D. Hinchey (D, L) | 119,557 | 50.4 |
| Bob Moppert (R, C) | 110,738 | 46.7 |
| 27 Bill Paxon (R, C, RTL) | 156,596 | 63.5 |
| W. Douglas Call (D) | 89,906 | 36.5 |
| 28 Louise M. Slaughter (D) | 140,908 | 55.2 |
| William P. Polito (R, C) | 112,273 | 44.0 |
| 29 John J. LaFalce (D, L) | 128,230 | 54.5 |
| William E. Miller Jr. (R, C) | 98,031 | 41.6 |
| 30 Jack Quinn (R, CC) | 125,734 | 51.7 |
| Dennis Gorski (D, C) | 111,445 | 45.8 |
| 31 Amo Houghton (R, C) | 150,696 | 70.6 |
| Joseph P. Leahey (D) | 52,010 | 24.4 |
| Gretchen S. McManus (RTL) | 10,848 | 5.1 |

**Special Election [3]**

| | | |
|---|---|---|
| 17 Jerrold Nadler (D, L) | 151,122 | 100.0 |

## NORTH CAROLINA

| | | |
|---|---|---|
| 1 Eva Clayton (D) | 116,078 | 67.0 |
| Ted Tyler (R) | 54,457 | 31.4 |
| 2 Tim Valentine (D) | 113,693 | 53.7 |
| Don Davis (R) | 93,893 | 44.4 |
| 3 H. Martin Lancaster (D) | 101,739 | 54.4 |
| Tommy Pollard (R) | 80,759 | 43.2 |
| 4 David E. Price (D) | 171,299 | 64.6 |
| LaVinia "Vicky" Rothrock Goudie (R) | 89,345 | 33.7 |
| 5 Stephen L. Neal (D) | 117,835 | 52.7 |
| Richard M. Burr (R) | 102,086 | 45.6 |
| 6 Howard Coble (R) | 162,822 | 70.8 |
| Robin Hood (D) | 67,200 | 29.2 |
| 7 Charlie Rose (D) | 92,414 | 56.7 |
| Robert C. Anderson (R) | 66,536 | 40.8 |
| 8 W. G. "Bill" Hefner (D) | 113,162 | 59.3 |
| Coy C. Privette (R) | 71,842 | 37.6 |
| 9 Alex McMillan (R) | 153,650 | 67.3 |
| Rory Blake (D) | 74,583 | 32.7 |
| 10 Cass Ballenger (R) | 149,033 | 63.4 |
| Ben Neill (D) | 79,206 | 33.7 |
| 11 Charles H. Taylor (R) | 130,158 | 54.7 |
| John S. Stevens (D) | 108,003 | 45.3 |
| 12 Melvin Watt (D) | 127,262 | 70.4 |
| Barbara Gore Washington (R) | 49,402 | 27.3 |

**Special Election [4]**

| | | |
|---|---|---|
| 1 Eva Clayton (D) | 118,324 | 56.7 |
| Ted Tyler (R) | 86,273 | 41.3 |

## NORTH DAKOTA

| Candidates | Votes | % |
|---|---|---|
| AL Earl Pomeroy (D) | 169,273 | 56.8 |
| John T. Korsmo (R) | 117,442 | 39.4 |

## OHIO

| | | |
|---|---|---|
| 1 David Mann (D) | 120,190 | 51.3 |
| Steve Grote (I) | 101,498 | 43.3 |
| James A. Berns (I) | 12,734 | 5.4 |
| 2 Bill Gradison (R) | 177,720 | 70.1 |
| Thomas R. Chandler (D) | 75,924 | 29.9 |
| 3 Tony P. Hall (D) | 146,072 | 59.7 |
| Peter W. Davis (R) | 98,733 | 40.3 |
| 4 Michael G. Oxley (R) | 147,346 | 61.3 |
| Raymond M. Ball (D) | 92,608 | 38.5 |
| 5 Paul E. Gillmor (R) | 187,860 | 100.0 |
| 6 Ted Strickland (D) | 122,720 | 50.7 |
| Bob McEwen (R) | 119,252 | 49.3 |
| 7 David L. Hobson (R) | 164,195 | 71.3 |
| Clifford S. Heskett (D) | 66,237 | 28.7 |
| 8 John A. Boehner (R) | 176,362 | 74.0 |
| Fred Sennet (D) | 62,033 | 26.0 |
| 9 Marcy Kaptur (D) | 178,879 | 73.6 |
| Ken D. Brown (R) | 53,011 | 21.8 |
| 10 Martin R. Hoke (R) | 136,433 | 56.8 |
| Mary Rose Oakar (D) | 103,788 | 43.2 |
| 11 Louis Stokes (D) | 154,718 | 69.2 |
| Beryl E. Rothschild (R) | 43,866 | 19.6 |
| Edmund Gudenas (I) | 19,773 | 8.8 |
| 12 John R. Kasich (R) | 170,297 | 71.2 |
| Bob Fitrakis (D) | 68,761 | 28.8 |
| 13 Sherrod Brown (D) | 134,486 | 53.3 |
| Margaret Mueller (R) | 88,889 | 35.2 |
| Mark Miller (I) | 20,320 | 8.1 |
| 14 Thomas C. Sawyer (D) | 165,335 | 67.8 |
| Robert Morgan (R) | 78,659 | 32.2 |
| 15 Deborah Pryce (R) | 110,390 | 44.1 |
| Richard Cordray (D) | 94,907 | 37.9 |
| Linda S. Reidelbach (I) | 44,906 | 17.9 |
| 16 Ralph Regula (R) | 158,489 | 63.7 |
| Warner D. Mendenhall (D) | 90,224 | 36.3 |
| 17 James A. Traficant Jr. (D) | 216,503 | 84.2 |
| Salvatore Pansino (R) | 40,743 | 15.8 |
| 18 Douglas Applegate (D) | 166,189 | 68.3 |
| Bill Ress (R) | 77,229 | 31.7 |
| 19 Eric D. Fingerhut (D) | 138,465 | 52.6 |
| Robert A. Gardner (R) | 124,606 | 47.4 |

## OKLAHOMA

| | | |
|---|---|---|
| 1 James M. Inhofe (R) | 119,211 | 52.8 |
| John Selph (D) | 106,619 | 47.2 |
| 2 Mike Synar (D) | 118,542 | 55.5 |
| Jerry Hill (R) | 87,657 | 41.1 |
| 3 Bill Brewster (D) | 155,934 | 75.1 |
| Robert W. Stokes (R) | 51,725 | 24.9 |
| 4 Dave McCurdy (D) | 140,841 | 70.7 |
| Howard Bell (R) | 58,235 | 29.3 |
| 5 Ernest Jim Istook (R) | 123,237 | 53.4 |
| Laurie Williams (D) | 107,579 | 46.6 |
| 6 Glenn English (D) | 134,734 | 67.8 |
| Bob Anthony (R) | 64,068 | 32.2 |

## OREGON

| | | |
|---|---|---|
| 1 Elizabeth Furse (D) | 152,917 | 52.0 |
| Tony Meeker (R) | 140,986 | 47.9 |
| 2 Robert F. Smith (R) | 184,163 | 67.1 |
| Denzel Ferguson (D) | 90,036 | 32.8 |
| 3 Ron Wyden (D) | 208,043 | 77.1 |
| Al Ritter (R) | 50,235 | 18.6 |
| 4 Peter A. DeFazio (D) | 199,372 | 71.4 |
| Richard L. Schulz (R) | 79,733 | 28.5 |
| 5 Mike Kopetski (D) | 174,443 | 63.9 |
| Jim Seagraves (R) | 97,984 | 35.9 |

## PENNSYLVANIA

| Candidates | Votes | % |
|---|---|---|
| 1 Thomas M. Foglietta (D) | 150,172 | 8 |
| Craig Snyder (R) | 35,419 | |
| 2 Lucien E. Blackwell (D) | 164,355 | 2 |
| Larry Hollin (R) | 47,906 | 2 |
| 3 Robert A. Borski (D) | 130,828 | 5 |
| Charles F. Dougherty (R) | 86,787 | 3 |
| 4 Ron Klink (D) | 186,684 | 2 |
| Gordon R. Johnston (R) | 48,484 | 2 |
| 5 William F. Clinger Jr. (R, D) | 188,911 | 10 |
| 6 Tim Holden (D) | 108,312 | 5 |
| John E. Jones (R) | 99,694 | |
| 7 Curt Weldon (R) | 180,648 | 6 |
| Frank Daly (D) | 91,623 | |
| 8 Jim Greenwood (R) | 129,593 | 5 |
| Peter H. Kostmayer (D) | 114,095 | |
| 9 Bud Shuster (R, D) | 182,406 | 10 |
| 10 Joseph M. McDade (R, D) | 189,414 | 8 |
| Albert A. Smith (LIBERT) | 20,134 | |
| 11 Paul E. Kanjorski (D) | 138,875 | |
| Michael A. Fescina (R) | 68,112 | |
| 12 John P. Murtha (D) | 166,916 | 1 |
| 13 Marjorie Margolies-Mezvinsky (D) | 127,685 | |
| Jon D. Fox (R) | 126,312 | |
| 14 William J. Coyne (D) | 165,633 | |
| Byron W. King (R) | 61,311 | |
| 15 Paul McHale (D) | 111,419 | |
| Don Ritter (R) | 99,520 | |
| 16 Robert S. Walker (R) | 137,823 | |
| Robert Peters (D) | 74,741 | |
| 17 George W. Gekas (R) | 150,158 | |
| Bill Sturges (D) | 65,881 | |
| 18 Rick Santorum (R) | 154,024 | |
| Frank A. Pecora (D) | 96,655 | |
| 19 Bill Goodling (R) | 98,599 | |
| Paul V. Kilker (D) | 74,798 | |
| Thomas M. Humbert (I) | 44,190 | |
| 20 Austin J. Murphy (D) | 114,898 | |
| Bill Townsend (R) | 111,591 | |
| 21 Tom Ridge (R) | 150,729 | |
| John C. Harkins (D) | 70,802 | |

## RHODE ISLAND

| | | |
|---|---|---|
| 1 Ronald K. Machtley (R) | 135,982 | |
| David R. Carlin Jr. (D) | 48,092 | |
| Frederick E. Dick (RPI) | 6,012 | |
| Norman J. Jacques (I) | 4,003 | |
| 2 Jack Reed (D) | 144,450 | |
| James W. Bell (R) | 49,998 | |

## SOUTH CAROLINA

| | | |
|---|---|---|
| 1 Arthur Ravenel Jr. (R) | 121,938 | |
| Bill Oberst Jr. (D) | 59,908 | |
| 2 Floyd D. Spence (R) | 148,667 | |
| Geb Sommer (LIBERT) | 20,816 | |
| 3 Butler Derrick (D) | 119,119 | |
| Jim Bland (R) | 75,660 | |
| 4 Bob Inglis (R) | 99,879 | |
| Liz J. Patterson (D) | 94,182 | |
| 5 John M. Spratt Jr. (D) | 112,031 | |
| Bill Horne (R) | 70,866 | |
| 6 James E. Clyburn (D) | 120,647 | |
| John Chase (R) | 64,149 | |

## SOUTH DAKOTA

| | | |
|---|---|---|
| AL Tim Johnson (D) | 230,070 | |
| John Timmer (R) | 89,375 | |

## TENNESSEE

| | | |
|---|---|---|
| 1 James H. Quillen (R) | 114,797 | |
| J. Carr "Jack" Christian (D) | 47,809 | |

*Footnote, see p. 1325.*

| Candidates | Votes | % |
|---|---|---|
| 2 John J. Duncan (R) | 148,377 | 72.2 |
| Troy Goodale (D) | 52,887 | 25.7 |
| 3 Marilyn Lloyd (D) | 105,693 | 48.8 |
| Zach Wamp (R) | 102,763 | 47.5 |
| 4 Jim Cooper (D) | 98,984 | 64.1 |
| Dale Johnson (R) | 50,340 | 32.6 |
| 5 Bob Clement (D) | 125,233 | 66.8 |
| Tom Stone (R) | 49,417 | 26.3 |
| 6 Bart Gordon (D) | 120,177 | 56.6 |
| Marsha Blackburn (R) | 86,289 | 40.6 |
| 7 Don Sundquist (D) | 125,101 | 61.7 |
| David R. Davis (D) | 72,062 | 35.5 |
| 8 John Tanner (D) | 136,852 | 83.7 |
| Lawrence J. Barnes (I) | 9,605 | 5.9 |
| 9 Harold E. Ford (D) | 123,276 | 57.9 |
| Charles L. Black (R) | 60,606 | 28.5 |
| Richard Liptock (I) | 14,075 | 6.6 |
| James Vandergriff (I) | 12,265 | 5.8 |

## TEXAS

| Candidates | Votes | % |
|---|---|---|
| 1 Jim Chapman (D) | 152,209 | 100.0 |
| 2 Charles Wilson (D) | 118,625 | 56.1 |
| Donna Peterson (R) | 92,176 | 43.6 |
| 3 Sam Johnson (R) | 201,569 | 86.1 |
| Noel Kopala (LIBERT) | 32,570 | 13.9 |
| 4 Ralph M. Hall (D) | 128,008 | 58.1 |
| David L. Bridges (R) | 83,875 | 38.1 |
| 5 John Bryant (D) | 98,567 | 58.9 |
| Richard Stokley (R) | 62,419 | 37.3 |
| 6 Joe L. Barton (R) | 189,140 | 71.9 |
| John Dietrich (D) | 73,933 | 28.1 |
| 7 Bill Archer (R) | 169,407 | 100.0 |
| 8 Jack Fields (R) | 179,349 | 77.0 |
| Chas. Robinson (D) | 53,473 | 23.0 |
| 9 Jack Brooks (D) | 118,690 | 53.6 |
| Steve Stockman (R) | 96,270 | 43.5 |
| 10 J. J. "Jake" Pickle (D) | 177,233 | 67.7 |
| Herbert Spiro (R) | 68,646 | 26.2 |
| 11 Chet Edwards (D) | 119,999 | 67.4 |
| James W. Broyles (R) | 58,033 | 32.6 |
| 12 Pete Geren (D) | 125,492 | 62.8 |
| David Hobbs (R) | 74,432 | 37.2 |
| 13 Bill Sarpalius (D) | 117,892 | 60.3 |
| Beau Boulter (R) | 77,514 | 39.7 |
| 14 Greg H. Laughlin (D) | 135,930 | 68.1 |
| Humberto J. Garza (R) | 54,412 | 27.3 |
| 15 E. "Kika" de la Garza (D) | 86,351 | 60.4 |
| Tom Haughey (R) | 56,549 | 39.6 |
| 16 Ronald D. Coleman (D) | 66,731 | 51.9 |
| Chip Taberski (R) | 61,870 | 48.1 |
| 17 Charles W. Stenholm (D) | 136,213 | 66.1 |
| Jeannie Sadowski (R) | 69,958 | 33.9 |
| 18 Craig Washington (D) | 111,422 | 64.7 |
| Edward Blum (R) | 56,080 | 32.6 |
| 19 Larry Combest (R) | 162,057 | 77.4 |
| Terry Lee Moser (D) | 47,325 | 22.6 |
| 20 Henry B. Gonzalez (D) | 103,755 | 100.0 |
| 21 Lamar Smith (R) | 190,979 | 72.2 |
| James M. Gaddy (D) | 62,827 | 23.7 |

| Candidates | Votes | % |
|---|---|---|
| 22 Thomas D. DeLay (R) | 150,221 | 68.9 |
| Richard Konrad (D) | 67,812 | 31.1 |
| 23 Henry Bonilla (R) | 98,259 | 59.1 |
| Albert G. Bustamante (D) | 63,797 | 38.4 |
| 24 Martin Frost (D) | 104,174 | 59.8 |
| Steve Masterson (R) | 70,042 | 40.2 |
| 25 Michael A. Andrews (D) | 98,975 | 56.0 |
| Dolly Madison McKenna (R) | 73,192 | 41.4 |
| 26 Dick Armey (R) | 150,209 | 73.1 |
| John Wayne Caton (D) | 55,237 | 26.9 |
| 27 Solomon P. Ortiz (D) | 87,022 | 55.5 |
| Jay Kimbrough (R) | 66,853 | 42.6 |
| 28 Frank Tejeda (D) | 122,457 | 87.1 |
| David C. Slatter (LIBERT) | 18,128 | 12.9 |
| 29 Gene Green (D) | 64,064 | 64.9 |
| Clark Kent Ervin (R) | 34,609 | 35.1 |
| 30 Eddie Bernice Johnson (D) | 107,831 | 71.5 |
| Lucy Cain (R) | 37,853 | 25.1 |

## UTAH

| Candidates | Votes | % |
|---|---|---|
| 1 James V. Hansen (R) | 160,037 | 65.3 |
| Ron Holt (D) | 68,712 | 28.0 |
| William J. Lawrence (IP) | 16,505 | 6.7 |
| 2 Karen Shepherd (D) | 127,738 | 50.5 |
| Enid Greene (R) | 118,307 | 46.8 |
| 3 Bill Orton (D) | 135,029 | 58.9 |
| Richard R. Harrington (R) | 84,019 | 36.7 |

## VERMONT

| Candidates | Votes | % |
|---|---|---|
| AL Bernard Sanders (I) | 162,724 | 57.8 |
| Tim Philbin (R) | 86,901 | 30.9 |
| Lewis E. Young (D) | 22,279 | 7.9 |

## VIRGINIA

| Candidates | Votes | % |
|---|---|---|
| 1 Herbert H. Bateman (R) | 133,537 | 57.5 |
| Andrew H. Fox (D) | 89,814 | 38.7 |
| 2 Owen B. Pickett (D) | 99,253 | 56.0 |
| J.L. "Jim" Chapman IV (R) | 77,797 | 43.9 |
| 3 Robert C. Scott (D) | 132,432 | 78.6 |
| Daniel Jenkins (R) | 35,780 | 21.2 |
| 4 Norman Sisisky (D) | 147,649 | 68.4 |
| A.J. "Tony" Zevgolis (R) | 68,286 | 31.6 |
| 5 Lewis F. Payne Jr. (D) | 133,031 | 68.9 |
| W. A. "Bill" Hurlburt (R) | 60,030 | 31.1 |
| 6 Robert W. Goodlatte (R) | 127,309 | 60.0 |
| Stephen Alan Musselwhite (D) | 84,618 | 39.9 |
| 7 Thomas J. Bliley Jr. (R) | 211,618 | 82.9 |
| Gerald E. Berg (I) | 43,267 | 16.9 |
| 8 James P. Moran Jr. (D) | 138,542 | 56.1 |
| Kyle E. McSlarrow (R) | 102,717 | 41.6 |
| 9 Rick Boucher (D) | 133,284 | 63.1 |
| L. Garrett Weddle (R) | 77,985 | 36.9 |
| 10 Frank R. Wolf (R) | 144,471 | 63.6 |
| Raymond E. Vickery (D) | 75,775 | 33.4 |
| 11 Leslie L. Byrne (D) | 114,172 | 50.0 |
| Henry N. Butler (R) | 103,119 | 45.2 |

## WASHINGTON

| Candidates | Votes | % |
|---|---|---|
| 1 Maria Cantwell (D) | 148,844 | 54.9 |
| Gary Nelson (R) | 113,897 | 42.0 |
| 2 Al Swift (D) | 133,207 | 52.1 |
| Jack Metcalf (R) | 107,365 | 42.0 |
| 3 Jolene Unsoeld (D) | 138,043 | 56.0 |
| Pat Fiske (R) | 108,583 | 44.0 |
| 4 Jay Inslee (D) | 106,556 | 50.8 |
| Richard "Doc" Hastings (R) | 103,028 | 49.2 |
| 5 Thomas S. Foley (D) | 135,965 | 55.2 |
| John Sonneland (R) | 110,443 | 44.8 |
| 6 Norm Dicks (D) | 152,933 | 64.2 |
| Lauri J. Phillips (R) | 66,664 | 28.0 |
| Tom Donnelly (D) | 14,490 | 6.1 |
| 7 Jim McDermott (D) | 222,604 | 78.4 |
| Glenn C. Hampson (R) | 54,149 | 19.1 |
| 8 Jennifer Dunn (R) | 155,874 | 60.4 |
| George O. Tamblyn (D) | 87,611 | 33.9 |
| Bob Adams (I) | 14,686 | 5.7 |
| 9 Mike Kreidler (D) | 110,902 | 52.1 |
| Pete von Reichbauer (R) | 91,910 | 43.2 |

## WEST VIRGINIA

| Candidates | Votes | % |
|---|---|---|
| 1 Alan B. Mollohan (D) | 172,924 | 100.0 |
| 2 Bob Wise (D) | 143,988 | 70.9 |
| Samuel A. Cravotta (R) | 59,102 | 29.1 |
| 3 Nick J. Rahall II (D) | 122,279 | 65.6 |
| Ben Waldman (R) | 64,012 | 34.4 |

## WISCONSIN

| Candidates | Votes | % |
|---|---|---|
| 1 Les Aspin (D) | 147,495 | 57.6 |
| Mark Neumann (R) | 104,352 | 40.7 |
| 2 Scott L. Klug (R) | 183,366 | 62.6 |
| Ada E. Deer (D) | 108,291 | 37.0 |
| 3 Steve Gunderson (R) | 146,903 | 56.4 |
| Paul Sacia (D) | 108,664 | 41.7 |
| 4 Gerald D. Kleczka (D) | 173,482 | 65.8 |
| Joseph L. Cook (R) | 84,872 | 32.2 |
| 5 Thomas M. Barrett (D) | 162,344 | 69.3 |
| Donalda Hammersmith (R) | 71,085 | 30.4 |
| 6 Thomas E. Petri (R) | 143,875 | 52.9 |
| Peggy A. Lautenschlager (D) | 128,232 | 47.1 |
| 7 David R. Obey (D) | 166,200 | 64.4 |
| Dale R. Vannes (R) | 91,772 | 35.6 |
| 8 Toby Roth (R) | 191,704 | 70.1 |
| Catherine L. Helms (D) | 81,792 | 29.9 |
| 9 F. James Sensenbrenner Jr. (R) | 192,898 | 69.7 |
| Ingrid K. Buxton (D) | 77,362 | 28.0 |

## WYOMING

| Candidates | Votes | % |
|---|---|---|
| AL Craig Thomas (R) | 113,882 | 57.8 |
| Jon Herschler (D) | 77,418 | 39.3 |

**1992 Elections**

*1. For the 1992 House elections in Louisiana, an open primary election was held with candidates from all parties running on the same ballot. Any candidate who received a majority was elected unopposed, with no further appearance on the general election ballot. If no candidate received 50 percent, a runoff was held between the two top finishers.*

*2. In Minnesota the Democratic Party is known as the Democratic-Farmer-Labor Party and the Republican Party as the Independent-Republican Party; candidates appear on the ballot with these designations.*

*3. A special election was held in conjunction with the November election. Nadler was elected to serve both the unexpired term of Rep. Ted Weiss, D, who died Sept. 14, 1992, and the two-year term beginning Jan. 5, 1993 in a newly renumbered district.*

*4. A special election was held in conjunction with the November election. Clayton was elected to serve both the unexpired term of Rep. Walter B. Jones, who died Sept. 15, 1992, and the two-year term beginning Jan. 5, 1993.*

# 1993 House Elections

## CALIFORNIA

**Special Election** [1]

| Candidates | Votes | % |
|---|---|---|
| 17 Sam Farr (D) | 53,675 | 52.3 |
| Bill McCampbell (R) | 43,774 | 42.6 |

## MICHIGAN

**Special Election** [2]

| Candidates | Votes | % |
|---|---|---|
| 3 Vernon J. Ehlers (R) | 57,484 | 66.4 |
| Dale R. Sprik (D) | 19,993 | 23.1 |
| Dawn Ida Krupp (I) | 8,759 | 10.1 |

## MISSISSIPPI

**Special Election** [3]

| Candidates | Votes | % |
|---|---|---|
| 2 Bennie Thompson (D) | 72,561 | 55.2 |
| Hayes Dent (R) | 58,995 | 44.8 |

## OHIO

**Special Election** [4]

| Candidates | Votes | % |
|---|---|---|
| 2 Rob Portman (R) | 53,020 | 70.1 |
| Lee Hornberger (D) | 22,652 | 29.9 |

## WISCONSIN

**Special Election** [5]

| Candidates | Votes | % |
|---|---|---|
| 1 Peter W. Barca (D) | 55,605 | 49.9 |
| Mark W. Neumann (R) | 54,930 | 49.3 |

**1993 Elections**

1. A special election was held to fill the unexpired term of Rep. Leon E. Panetta (D), who resigned Jan. 21, 1993, having been appointed director of the White House Office of Management and Budget.

2. A special election was held to fill the unexpired term of Rep. Paul B. Henry (R), who died July 31, 1993.

3. A special election was held to fill the unexpired term of Rep. Mike Espy (D), who resigned Jan. 21, 1993, having been appointed agriculture secretary.

4. A special election was held to fill the unexpired term of Rep. Bill Gradison (R), who resigned Jan. 31, 1993.

5. A special election was held to fill the unexpired term of Rep. Les Aspin (D), who resigned Jan. 20, 1993, having been appointed defense secretary.

# House Returns: Other Sources

In the preceding pages of House popular election returns (943-1326) the symbol # is used to denote returns for the years 1824-1973 that were taken from a source other than the Inter-University Consortium for Political and Social Research (ICPSR). This page lists the source for each of those returns. *(For description of ICPSR data, see pp. x, 942.)*

The two most frequently used alternative sources were *Statistics of the Congressional Elections of* _____,

published by the Clerk of the House of Representatives for every general election year since 1920, and the Elections Research Center, which compiles the biennial *America Votes* series under the direction of Richard M. Scammon and Alice V. McGillivray.

For elections 1974-93, Congressional Quarterly obtained the returns for the state secretaries of state. Where discrepancies existed between these figures and *America Votes*, the latter's figures were used.

**1840—Georgia** (at-large special):
Georgia Secretary of State.

**1844—Ohio** (10th District special):
Ohio Historical Society Archives.

**1845—Tennessee** (8th District):
Tennessee Secretary of State.

**1872—Georgia** (4th District special):
Georgia Secretary of State.

**1872—Pennsylvania** (13th District special):
Pennsylvania Secretary of State.

**1873—Louisiana** (4th District special):
Louisiana State University Library.

**1874—Tennessee** (4th District special):
Tennessee Secretary of State.

**1884—Pennsylvania** (19th District special):
Pennsylvania Secretary of State.

**1884—South Carolina** (4th District special):
South Carolina Secretary of State.

**1886—Louisiana** (2nd District special):
*Biographical Directory of the American Congress, 1774-1971* (Washington, D. C.: Government Printing Office, 1971).

**1892—Texas** (9th District special):
*Official Texas Election Register.*

**1908—Nebraska** (5th District):
*1910 World Almanac,* published by *The New York World* newspaper.

**1922—New Jersey** (8th District):
*Statistics of the Congressional Election of Nov. 7, 1922.*

**1924—Georgia** (9th District) **Ohio** (22nd District):
*Statistics of the Congressional and Presidential Election of Nov. 4, 1924.*

**1926—Massachusetts** (8th District special); **Minnesota** (4th District):
*Statistics of the Congressional Election of Nov. 2, 1926.*

**1928—New Jersey** (8th District); **Oregon** (3rd District); **Tennessee** (5th District):
*Statistics of the Congressional and Presidential Election of Nov. 6, 1928.*

**1930—California** (3rd District); **Georgia** (8th and 11th districts); **Kentucky** (2nd District special); **Wisconsin** (5th District):
*Statistics of the Congressional Election of Nov. 4, 1930.*

**1937—New York** (17th District special):
New York Secretary of State.

**1944—Wisconsin** (8th District):
*Statistics of the Presidential and Congressional Election of Nov. 7, 1944.*

**1946—Georgia** (5th District); **Nebraska** (3rd District):
*Statistics of the Congressional Election of Nov. 5, 1946.*

**1950—Tennessee** (5th District):
*Statistics of the Congressional Election of Nov. 4, 1958.*

**1950—Texas** (18th District special):
Texas Secretary of State.

**1951—Missouri** (11th District special):
Missouri Secretary of State.

**1959—Iowa** (4th District special):
Iowa Secretary of State.

**1960—Indiana** (5th District):
Richard M. Scammon (ed.), *America Votes 4* (Pittsburgh: University of Pittsburgh Press, 1962), p. 123

**1961—Arizona, Arkansas, Michigan, Tennessee** (special elections):
Elections Research Center.

**1962—Michigan** (14th District special); **New York** (6th District special); **South Carolina** (2nd District special):
Elections Research Center.

**1963—North Dakota, Pennsylvania, Texas** (special elections):
Elections Research Center.

**1964—Pennsylvania** (5th District special); **Tennessee** (2nd District special):
Elections Research Center.

**1964—Pennsylvania** (6th District):
Pennsylvania Secretary of State.

**1965—South Carolina** (special):
Elections Research Center.

**1966—California** (4th District special); **Texas** (8th District special):
Elections Research Center.

**1967—California** (11th District special primary):
California Secretary of State.

**1967—California** (11th District special):
Elections Research Center.

**1967—New York; Rhode Island** (special elections):
Elections Research Center.

**1968—New York** (7th District):
Richard M. Scammon (ed.), *America Votes 8* (Washington, D.C.: Congressional Quarterly, 1970), p. 274.

**1968—New York** (13th District special): **Texas** (3rd District special):
Elections Research Center.

**1968—Mississippi** (3rd District special):
Mississippi Secretary of State.

**1969—California** (27th District special primary):
California Secretary of State.

**1969—Massachusetts; Montana; Tennessee** (special elections):
Elections Research Center.

**1970—Texas** (2nd District):
Texas Secretary of State.

**1971—Kentucky** (special):
Kentucky Secretary of State.

**1972—Pennsylvania** (27th District special):
Pennsylvania Secretary of State.

**1972—Vermont** (special):
Elections Research Center.

**1973—Illinois** (special):
Illinois Secretary of State.

# Appendix

# Sessions of the U.S. Congress, 1789-1991

| Con-gress | Ses-sion | Date of beginning[1] | Date of adjournment[2] | Length in days | Senate Recesses | House Recesses | President pro tempore of the Senate[3] | Speaker of the House of Representatives |
|---|---|---|---|---|---|---|---|---|
| 1st | 1 | March 4, 1789 | Sept. 29, 1789 | 210 | | | John Langdon, N.H.[4] | Frederick Augustus Conrad Muhlenberg, Pa. |
| | 2 | Jan. 4, 1790 | Aug. 12, 1790 | 221 | | | | |
| | 3 | Dec. 6, 1790 | March 3, 1791 | 88 | | | | |
| 2nd | 1 | Oct. 24, 1791 | May 8, 1792 | 197 | | | Richard Henry Lee, Va. | Jonathan Trumbull, Jr., Conn. |
| | 2 | Nov. 5, 1792 | March 2, 1793 | 119 | | | John Langdon, N.H. | |
| 3rd | 1 | Dec. 2, 1793 | June 9, 1794 | 190 | | | Langdon Ralph Izard, S.C. | Frederick Augustus Conrad Muhlenberg, Pa. |
| | 2 | Nov. 3, 1794 | March 3, 1795 | 121 | | | Henry Tazewell, Va. | |
| 4th | 1 | Dec. 7, 1795 | June 1, 1796 | 177 | | | Tazewell Samuel Livermore, N.H. | Jonathan Dayton, N.J. |
| | 2 | Dec. 5, 1796 | March 3, 1797 | 89 | | | William Bingham, Pa. | |
| 5th | 1 | May 15, 1797 | July 10, 1797 | 57 | | | William Bradford, R.I. | Dayton |
| | 2 | Nov. 13, 1797 | July 16, 1798 | 246 | | | Jacob Read, S.C. Theodore Sedgwick, Mass. | George Dent, Md.[5] |
| | 3 | Dec. 3, 1798 | March 3, 1799 | 91 | | | John Laurence, N.Y. James Ross, Pa. | |
| 6th | 1 | Dec. 2, 1799 | May 14, 1800 | 164 | | | Samuel Livermore, N.H. Uriah Tracy, Conn. | Theodore Sedgwick, Mass. |
| | 2 | Nov. 17, 1800 | March 3, 1801 | 107 | Dec. 23-Dec. 30, 1800 | Dec. 23-Dec. 30, 1800 | John Eager Howard, Md. James Hillhouse, Conn. | |
| 7th | 1 | Dec. 7, 1801 | May 3, 1802 | 148 | | | Abraham Baldwin, Ga. | Nathaniel Macon, N.C. |
| | 2 | Dec. 6, 1802 | March 3, 1803 | 88 | | | Stephen Row Bradley, Vt. | |
| 8th | 1 | Oct. 17, 1803 | March 27, 1804 | 163 | | | John Brown, Ky. Jesse Franklin, N.C. | Macon |
| | 2 | Nov. 5, 1804 | March 3, 1805 | 119 | | | Joseph Anderson, Tenn. | |
| 9th | 1 | Dec. 2, 1805 | April 21, 1806 | 141 | | | Samuel Smith, Md. | Macon |
| | 2 | Dec. 1, 1806 | March 3, 1807 | 93 | | | Smith | |
| 10th | 1 | Oct. 26, 1807 | April 25, 1808 | 182 | | | Smith | Joseph Bradley Varnum, Mass. |
| | 2 | Nov. 7, 1808 | March 3, 1809 | 117 | | | Stephen Row Bradley, Vt. John Milledge, Ga. | |
| 11th | 1 | May 22, 1809 | June 28, 1809 | 38 | | | Andrew Gregg, Pa. | Varnum |
| | 2 | Nov. 27, 1809 | May 1, 1810 | 156 | | | John Gaillard, S.C. | |
| | 3 | Dec. 3, 1810 | March 3, 1811 | 91 | | | John Pope, Ky. | |
| 12th | 1 | Nov. 4, 1811 | July 6, 1812 | 245 | | | William Harris Crawford, Ga. | Henry Clay, Ky. |
| | 2 | Nov. 2, 1812 | March 3, 1813 | 122 | | | Crawford | |
| 13th | 1 | May 24, 1813 | Aug. 2, 1813 | 71 | | | Crawford | Clay |
| | 2 | Dec. 6, 1813 | April 18, 1814 | 134 | | | Joseph Bradley Varnum, Mass. | |
| | 3 | Sept. 19, 1814 | March 3, 1815 | 166 | | | John Gaillard, S.C. | Langdon Cheves, S.C.[6] |
| 14th | 1 | Dec. 4, 1815 | April 30, 1816 | 148 | | | Gaillard | Henry Clay, Ky. |
| | 2 | Dec. 2, 1816 | March 3, 1817 | 92 | | | Gaillard | |
| 15th | 1 | Dec. 1, 1817 | April 20, 1818 | 141 | Dec. 24-Dec. 29, 1817 | Dec. 24-Dec. 29, 1817 | Gaillard | Clay |
| | 2 | Nov. 16, 1818 | March 3, 1819 | 108 | | | James Barbour, Va. | |
| 16th | 1 | Dec. 6, 1819 | May 15, 1820 | 162 | | | John Gaillard, S.C. | Clay |
| | 2 | Nov. 13, 1820 | March 3, 1821 | 111 | | | Gaillard | John W. Taylor, N.Y.[7] |
| 17th | 1 | Dec. 3, 1821 | May 8, 1822 | 157 | | | Gaillard | Philip Pendelton Barbour, Va. |
| | 2 | Dec. 2, 1822 | March 3, 1823 | 92 | | | Gaillard | |
| 18th | 1 | Dec. 1, 1823 | May 27, 1824 | 178 | | | Gaillard | Henry Clay, Ky. |
| | 2 | Dec. 6, 1824 | March 3, 1825 | 88 | | | Gaillard | |

| Con-gress | Ses-sion | Date of beginning[1] | Date of adjournment[2] | Length in days | Senate Recesses | House Recesses | President pro tempore of the Senate[3] | Speaker of the House of Representatives |
|---|---|---|---|---|---|---|---|---|
| 19th | 1 | Dec. 5, 1825 | May 22, 1826 | 169 | | | Nathaniel Macon, N.C. | John W. Taylor, N.Y. |
| | 2 | Dec. 4, 1826 | March 3, 1827 | 90 | | | Macon | |
| 20th | 1 | Dec. 3, 1827 | May 26, 1828 | 175 | | | Samuel Smith, Md. | Andrew Stevenson, Va. |
| | 2 | Dec. 1, 1828 | March 3, 1829 | 93 | Dec. 24-Dec. 29, 1828 | Dec. 24-Dec. 29, 1828 | Smith | |
| 21st | 1 | Dec. 7, 1829 | May 31, 1830 | 176 | | | Smith | Stevenson |
| | 2 | Dec. 6, 1830 | March 3, 1831 | 88 | | | Littleton Waller Tazewell, Va. | |
| 22nd | 1 | Dec. 5, 1831 | July 16, 1832 | 225 | | | Tazewell | Stevenson |
| | 2 | Dec. 3, 1832 | March 2, 1833 | 91 | | | Hugh Lawson White, Tenn. | |
| 23rd | 1 | Dec. 2, 1833 | June 30, 1834 | 211 | | | George Poindexter, Miss. | Stevenson |
| | 2 | Dec. 1, 1834 | March 3, 1835 | 93 | | | John Tyler, Va. | John Bell, Tenn.[8] |
| 24th | 1 | Dec. 7, 1835 | July 4, 1836 | 211 | | | William Rufus deVane King, Ala. | James Knox Polk, Tenn. |
| | 2 | Dec. 5, 1836 | March 3, 1837 | 89 | | | King | |
| 25th | 1 | Sept. 4, 1837 | Oct. 16, 1837 | 43 | | | King | Polk |
| | 2 | Dec. 4, 1837 | July 9, 1838 | 218 | | | King | |
| | 3 | Dec. 3, 1838 | March 3, 1839 | 91 | | | King | |
| 26th | 1 | Dec. 2, 1839 | July 21, 1840 | 233 | | | King | Robert Mercer Taliaferro Hunter, Va. |
| | 2 | Dec. 7, 1840 | March 3, 1841 | 87 | | | King | |
| 27th | 1 | May 31, 1841 | Sept. 13, 1841 | 106 | | | Samuel Lewis Southard, N.J. | John White, Ky. |
| | 2 | Dec. 6, 1841 | Aug. 31, 1842 | 269 | | | Willie Person Mangum, N.C. | |
| | 3 | Dec. 5, 1842 | March 3, 1843 | 89 | | | Mangum | |
| 28th | 1 | Dec. 4, 1843 | June 17, 1844 | 196 | | | Mangum | John Winston Jones, Va. |
| | 2 | Dec. 2, 1844 | March 3, 1845 | 92 | | | Mangum | |
| 29th | 1 | Dec. 1, 1845 | Aug. 10, 1846 | 253 | | | David Rice Atchison, Mo. | John Wesley Davis, Ind. |
| | 2 | Dec. 7, 1846 | March 3, 1847 | 87 | | | Atchison | |
| 30th | 1 | Dec. 6, 1847 | Aug. 14, 1848 | 254 | | | Atchison | Robert Charles Winthrop, Mass. |
| | 2 | Dec. 4, 1848 | March 3, 1849 | 90 | | | Atchison | |
| 31st | 1 | Dec. 3, 1849 | Sept. 30, 1850 | 302 | | | William Rufus deVane King, Ala. | Howell Cobb, Ga. |
| | 2 | Dec. 2, 1850 | March 3, 1851 | 92 | | | King | |
| 32nd | 1 | Dec. 1, 1851 | Aug. 31, 1852 | 275 | | | King | Linn Boyd, Ky. |
| | 2 | Dec. 6, 1852 | March 3, 1853 | 88 | | | David Rice Atchison, Mo. | |
| 33rd | 1 | Dec. 5, 1853 | Aug. 7, 1854 | 246 | | | Atchison | Boyd |
| | 2 | Dec. 4, 1854 | March 3, 1855 | 90 | | | Jesse David Bright, Ind. Lewis Cass, Mich. | |
| 34th | 1 | Dec. 3, 1855 | Aug. 18, 1856 | 260 | | | Jesse David Bright, Ind. | Nathaniel Prentice Banks, Mass. |
| | 2 | Aug. 21, 1856 | Aug. 30, 1856 | 10 | | | Bright | |
| | 3 | Dec. 1, 1856 | March 3, 1857 | 93 | | | James Murray Mason, Va. Thomas Jefferson Rusk, Texas | |
| 35th | 1 | Dec. 7, 1857 | June 14, 1858 | 189 | Dec. 23, 1857-Jan. 4, 1858 | Dec. 23, 1857-Jan. 4, 1858 | Benjamin Fitzpatrick, Ala. | James Lawrence Orr, S.C. |
| | 2 | Dec. 6, 1858 | March 3, 1859 | 88 | Dec. 23, 1858-Jan. 4, 1859 | Dec. 23, 1858-Jan. 4, 1859 | Fitzpatrick | |
| 36th | 1 | Dec. 5, 1859 | June 25, 1860 | 202 | | | Fitzpatrick Jesse David Bright, Ind. | William Pennington, N.J. |
| | 2 | Dec. 3, 1860 | March 3, 1861 | 93 | | | Solomon Foot, Vt. | |
| 37th | 1 | July 4, 1861 | Aug. 6, 1861 | 34 | | | Foot | Galusha Aaron Grow, Pa. |
| | 2 | Dec. 2, 1861 | July 17, 1862 | 228 | | | Foot | |
| | 3 | Dec. 1, 1862 | March 3, 1863 | 93 | Dec. 23, 1862-Jan. 5, 1863 | Dec. 23, 1862-Jan. 5, 1863 | Foot | |

| Con-gress | Ses-sion | Date of beginning[1] | Date of adjournment[2] | Length in days | Senate Recesses | House Recesses | President pro tempore of the Senate[3] | Speaker of the House of Representatives |
|---|---|---|---|---|---|---|---|---|
| 38th | 1 | Dec. 7, 1863 | July 4, 1864 | 209 | Dec. 23, 1863-Jan. 5, 1864 | Dec. 23, 1863-Jan. 5, 1864 | Foot<br>Daniel Clark, N.H. | Schuyler Colfax, Ind. |
|  | 2 | Dec. 5, 1864 | March 3, 1865 | 89 | Dec. 22, 1864-Jan. 5, 1865 | Dec. 22, 1864-Jan. 5, 1865 | Clark |  |
| 39th | 1 | Dec. 4, 1865 | July 28, 1866 | 237 | Dec. 6-Dec. 11, 1865<br>Dec. 21, 1865-Jan. 5, 1866 | Dec. 6-Dec. 11, 1865<br>Dec. 21, 1865-Jan. 5, 1866 | Lafayette Sabine Foster, Conn. | Colfax |
|  | 2 | Dec. 3, 1866 | March 3, 1867 | 91 | Dec. 20, 1866-Jan. 3, 1867 | Dec. 20, 1866-Jan. 3, 1867 | Benjamin Franklin Wade, Ohio |  |
| 40th | 1 | March 4, 1867 | Dec. 1, 1867 | 273 | March 30-July 3, 1867<br>July 20-Nov. 21, 1867 | March 30-July 3, 1867<br>July 20-Nov. 21, 1867 | Wade | Colfax |
|  | 2 | Dec. 2, 1867 | Nov. 10, 1868 | 345 | Dec. 20, 1867-Jan. 6, 1868<br>July 27-Sept. 21, 1868<br>Sept. 21-Oct. 16, 1868<br>Oct. 16-Nov. 10, 1868 | Dec. 20, 1867-Jan. 6, 1868<br>July 27-Sept. 21, 1868<br>Sept. 21-Oct. 16, 1868<br>Oct. 16-Nov. 10, 1868 | Wade |  |
|  | 3 | Dec. 7, 1868 | March 3, 1869 | 87 | Dec. 21, 1868-Jan. 5, 1869 | Dec. 21, 1868-Jan. 5, 1869 | Wade | Theodore Medad Pomeroy, N.Y.[9] |
| 41st | 1 | March 4, 1869 | April 10, 1869 | 38 |  |  | Henry Bowen Anthony, R.I. | James Gillespie Blaine, Maine |
|  | 2 | Dec. 6, 1869 | July 15, 1870 | 222 | Dec. 22, 1869-Jan. 10, 1870 | Dec. 22, 1869-Jan. 10, 1870 | Anthony |  |
|  | 3 | Dec. 5, 1870 | March 3, 1871 | 89 | Dec. 23, 1870-Jan. 4, 1871 | Dec. 22, 1870-Jan. 4, 1871 | Anthony |  |
| 42nd | 1 | March 4, 1871 | April 20, 1871 | 48 |  |  | Anthony | Blaine |
|  | 2 | Dec. 4, 1871 | June 10, 1872 | 190 | Dec. 21, 1871-Jan. 8, 1872 | Dec. 21, 1871-Jan. 8, 1872 | Anthony |  |
|  | 3 | Dec. 2, 1872 | March 3, 1873 | 92 | Dec. 20, 1872-Jan. 6, 1873 | Dec. 20, 1872-Jan. 6, 1873 | Anthony |  |
| 43rd | 1 | Dec. 1, 1873 | June 23, 1874 | 204 | Dec. 19, 1873-Jan. 5, 1874 | Dec. 19, 1873-Jan. 5, 1874 | Matthew Hale Carpenter, Wis. | Blaine |
|  | 2 | Dec. 7, 1874 | March 3, 1875 | 87 | Dec. 23, 1874-Jan. 5, 1875 | Dec. 23, 1874-Jan. 5, 1875 | Carpenter<br>Henry Bowen Anthony, R.I. |  |
| 44th | 1 | Dec. 6, 1875 | Aug. 15, 1876 | 254 | Dec. 20, 1875-Jan. 5, 1876 | Dec. 21, 1875-Jan. 5, 1876 | Thomas White Ferry, Mich. | Michael Crawford Kerr, Ind.[10]<br>Samuel Sullivan Cox, N.Y., pro tempore[11]<br>Milton Sayler, Ohio, pro tempore[12] |
|  | 2 | Dec. 4, 1876 | March 3, 1877 | 90 |  |  | Ferry | Samuel Jackson Randall, Pa. |
| 45th | 1 | Oct. 15, 1877 | Dec. 3, 1877 | 50 |  |  | Ferry | Randall |
|  | 2 | Dec. 3, 1877 | June 20, 1878 | 200 | Dec. 15, 1877-Jan. 10, 1878 | Dec. 15, 1877-Jan. 10, 1878 | Ferry |  |
|  | 3 | Dec. 2, 1878 | March 3, 1879 | 92 | Dec. 20, 1878-Jan. 7, 1879 | Dec. 20, 1878-Jan. 7, 1879 | Ferry |  |
| 46th | 1 | March 18, 1879 | July 1, 1879 | 106 |  |  | Allen Granberry Thurman, Ohio | Randall |
|  | 2 | Dec. 1, 1879 | June 16, 1880 | 199 | Dec. 19, 1879-Jan. 6, 1880 | Dec. 19, 1879-Jan. 6, 1880 | Thurman |  |
|  | 3 | Dec. 6, 1880 | March 3, 1881 | 88 | Dec. 23, 1880-Jan. 5, 1881 | Dec. 23, 1880-Jan. 5, 1881 | Thurman |  |
| 47th | 1 | Dec. 5, 1881 | Aug. 8, 1882 | 247 | Dec. 22, 1881-Jan. 5, 1882 | Dec. 22, 1881-Jan. 5, 1882 | Thomas Francis Bayard, Sr., Del.<br>David Davis, Ill.<br>George Franklin Edmunds, Vt. | Joseph Warren Keifer, Ohio |
|  | 2 | Dec. 4, 1882 | March 3, 1883 | 90 |  |  | Edmunds |  |
| 48th | 1 | Dec. 3, 1883 | July 7, 1884 | 218 | Dec. 24, 1883-Jan. 7, 1884 | Dec. 24, 1883-Jan. 7, 1884 | Edmunds | John Griffin Carlisle, Ky. |
|  | 2 | Dec. 1, 1884 | March 3, 1885 | 93 | Dec. 24, 1884-Jan. 5, 1885 | Dec. 24, 1884-Jan. 5, 1885 | Edmunds |  |
| 49th | 1 | Dec. 7, 1885 | Aug. 5, 1886 | 242 | Dec. 21, 1885-Jan. 5, 1886 | Dec. 21, 1885-Jan. 5, 1886 | John Sherman, Ohio | Carlisle |
|  | 2 | Dec. 6, 1886 | March 3, 1887 | 88 | Dec. 22, 1886-Jan. 4, 1887 | Dec. 22, 1886-Jan. 4, 1887 | John James Ingalls, Kan. |  |
| 50th | 1 | Dec. 5, 1887 | Oct. 20, 1888 | 321 | Dec. 22, 1887-Jan. 4, 1888 | Dec. 22, 1887-Jan. 4, 1888 | Ingalls | Carlisle |
|  | 2 | Dec. 3, 1888 | March 3, 1889 | 91 | Dec. 21, 1888-Jan. 2, 1889 | Dec. 21, 1888-Jan. 2, 1889 | Ingalls |  |
| 51st | 1 | Dec. 2, 1889 | Oct. 1, 1890 | 304 | Dec. 21, 1889-Jan. 6, 1890 | Dec. 21, 1889-Jan. 6, 1890 | Ingalls | Thomas Brackett Reed, Maine |
|  | 2 | Dec. 1, 1890 | March 3, 1891 | 93 |  |  | Charles Frederick Manderson, Neb. |  |
| 52nd | 1 | Dec. 7, 1891 | Aug. 5, 1892 | 251 |  |  | Manderson | Charles Frederick Crisp, Ga. |
|  | 2 | Dec. 5, 1892 | March 3, 1893 | 89 | Dec. 22, 1892-Jan. 4, 1893 | Dec. 22, 1892-Jan. 4, 1893 | Isham Green Harris, Tenn. |  |
| 53rd | 1 | Aug. 7, 1893 | Nov. 3, 1893 | 89 |  |  | Harris | Crisp |
|  | 2 | Dec. 4, 1893 | Aug. 28, 1894 | 268 |  | Dec. 21, 1893-Jan. 3, 1894 | Harris |  |

| Con-gress | Ses-sion | Date of beginning[1] | Date of adjournment[2] | Length in days | Senate Recesses | House Recesses | President pro tempore of the Senate[3] | Speaker of the House of Representatives |
|---|---|---|---|---|---|---|---|---|
| | 3 | Dec. 3, 1894 | March 3, 1895 | 97 | | Dec. 23, 1894-Jan. 3, 1895 | Matt Whitaker Ransom, N.C. Isham Green Harris, Tenn. | |
| 54th | 1 | Dec. 2, 1895 | June 11, 1896 | 193 | | | William Pierce Frye, Maine | Thomas Brackett Reed, Maine |
| | 2 | Dec. 7, 1896 | March 3, 1897 | 87 | Dec. 22, 1896-Jan. 5, 1897 | Dec. 22, 1896-Jan. 5, 1897 | Frye | |
| 55th | 1 | March 15, 1897 | July 24, 1897 | 131 | | | Frye | Reed |
| | 2 | Dec. 6, 1897 | July 8, 1898 | 215 | Dec. 18, 1897-Jan. 5, 1898 | Dec. 18, 1897-Jan. 5, 1898 | Frye | |
| | 3 | Dec. 5, 1898 | March 3, 1899 | 89 | Dec. 21, 1898-Jan. 4, 1899 | Dec. 21, 1898-Jan. 4, 1899 | Frye | |
| 56th | 1 | Dec. 4, 1899 | June 7, 1900 | 186 | Dec. 20, 1899-Jan. 3, 1900 | Dec. 20, 1899-Jan. 3, 1900 | Frye | David Bremner Henderson, Iowa |
| | 2 | Dec. 3, 1900 | March 3, 1901 | 91 | Dec. 20, 1900-Jan. 3, 1901 | Dec. 21, 1900-Jan. 3, 1901 | Frye | |
| 57th | 1 | Dec. 2, 1901 | July 1, 1902 | 212 | Dec. 19, 1901-Jan. 6, 1902 | Dec. 19, 1901-Jan. 6, 1902 | Frye | Henderson |
| | 2 | Dec. 1, 1902 | March 3, 1903 | 93 | Dec. 20, 1902-Jan. 5, 1903 | Dec. 20, 1902-Jan. 5, 1903 | Frye | |
| 58th | 1 | Nov. 9, 1903 | Dec. 7, 1903 | 29 | | | Frye | Joseph Gurney Cannon, Ill. |
| | 2 | Dec. 7, 1903 | April 28, 1904 | 144 | Dec. 19, 1903-Jan. 4, 1904 | Dec. 19, 1903-Jan. 4, 1904 | Frye | |
| | 3 | Dec. 5, 1904 | March 3, 1905 | 89 | Dec. 21, 1904-Jan. 4, 1905 | Dec. 21, 1904-Jan. 4, 1905 | Frye | |
| 59th | 1 | Dec. 4, 1905 | June 30, 1906 | 209 | Dec. 21, 1905-Jan. 4, 1906 | Dec. 21, 1905-Jan. 4, 1906 | Frye | Cannon |
| | 2 | Dec. 3, 1906 | March 3, 1907 | 91 | Dec. 20, 1906-Jan. 3, 1907 | Dec. 20, 1906-Jan. 3, 1907 | Frye | |
| 60th | 1 | Dec. 2, 1907 | May 30, 1908 | 181 | Dec. 21, 1907-Jan. 6, 1908 | Dec. 21, 1907-Jan. 6, 1908 | Frye | Cannon |
| | 2 | Dec. 7, 1908 | March 3, 1909 | 87 | Dec. 19, 1908-Jan. 4, 1909 | Dec. 19, 1908-Jan. 4, 1909 | Frye | |
| 61st | 1 | March 15, 1909 | Aug. 5, 1909 | 144 | | | Frye | Cannon |
| | 2 | Dec. 6, 1909 | June 25, 1910 | 202 | Dec. 21, 1909-Jan. 4, 1910 | Dec. 21, 1909-Jan. 4, 1910 | Frye | |
| | 3 | Dec. 5, 1910 | March 3, 1911 | 89 | Dec. 21, 1910-Jan. 5, 1911 | Dec. 21, 1910-Jan. 5, 1911 | Frye | |
| 62nd | 1 | April 4, 1911 | Aug. 22, 1911 | 141 | | | Frye[13] | James Beauchamp "Champ" Clark, Mo. |
| | 2 | Dec. 4, 1911 | Aug. 26, 1912 | 267 | Dec. 21, 1911-Jan. 3, 1912 | Dec. 21, 1911-Jan. 3, 1912 | Augustus Octavious Bacon, Ga.[14]; Frank Bosworth Brandegee, Conn.[15]; Charles Curtis, Kan.[16]; Jacob Harold Gallinger, N.H.[17]; Henry Cabot Lodge, Mass.[18] | |
| | 3 | Dec. 2, 1912 | March 3, 1913 | 92 | Dec. 19, 1912-Jan. 2, 1913 | Dec. 19, 1912-Jan. 2, 1913 | Bacon[19]; Gallinger[20] | |
| 63rd | 1 | April 7, 1913 | Dec. 1, 1913 | 239 | | | James Paul Clarke, Ark. | Clark |
| | 2 | Dec. 1, 1913 | Oct. 24, 1914 | 328 | Dec. 23, 1913-Jan. 12, 1914 | Dec. 23, 1913-Jan. 12, 1914 | Clarke | |
| | 3 | Dec. 7, 1914 | March 3, 1915 | 87 | Dec. 23-Dec. 28, 1914 | Dec. 23-Dec. 28, 1914 | Clarke | |
| 64th | 1 | Dec. 6, 1915 | Sept. 8, 1916 | 278 | Dec. 17, 1915-Jan. 4, 1916 | Dec. 17, 1915-Jan. 4, 1916 | Clarke[21] | Clark |
| | 2 | Dec. 4, 1916 | March 3, 1917 | 90 | Dec. 22, 1916-Jan. 2, 1917 | Dec. 22, 1916-Jan. 2, 1917 | Willard Saulsbury, Jr., Del. | |
| 65th | 1 | April 2, 1917 | Oct. 6, 1917 | 188 | | | Saulsbury | Clark |
| | 2 | Dec. 3, 1917 | Nov. 21, 1918 | 354 | Dec. 18, 1917-Jan. 3, 1918 | Dec. 18, 1917-Jan. 3, 1918 | Saulsbury | |
| | 3 | Dec. 2, 1918 | March 3, 1919 | 92 | | | Saulsbury | |
| 66th | 1 | May 19, 1919 | Nov. 19, 1919 | 185 | July 1-July 8, 1919 | July 1-July 8, 1919 | Albert Baird Cummins, Iowa | Frederick Huntington Gillett, Mass. |
| | 2 | Dec. 1, 1919 | June 5, 1920 | 188 | Dec. 20, 1919-Jan. 5, 1920 | Dec. 20, 1919-Jan. 5, 1920 | Cummins | |
| | 3 | Dec. 6, 1920 | March 3, 1921 | 88 | | | Cummins | |
| 67th | 1 | April 11, 1921 | Nov. 23, 1921 | 227 | | | Cummins | Gillett |
| | 2 | Dec. 5, 1921 | Sept. 22, 1922 | 292 | Dec. 22, 1921-Jan. 3, 1922 | Dec. 22, 1921-Jan. 3, 1922 | Cummins | |
| | 3 | Nov. 20, 1922 | Dec. 4, 1922 | 15 | | | Cummins | |
| | 4 | Dec. 4, 1922 | March 3, 1923 | 90 | | | Cummins | |
| 68th | 1 | Dec. 3, 1923 | June 7, 1924 | 188 | Dec. 20, 1923-Jan. 3, 1924 | Dec. 20, 1923-Jan. 3, 1924 | Cummins | Gillett |
| | 2 | Dec. 1, 1924 | March 3, 1925 | 93 | Dec. 20-Dec. 29, 1924 | Dec. 20-Dec. 29, 1924 | Cummins | |
| 69th | 1 | Dec. 7, 1925 | July 3, 1926 | 209 | Dec. 22, 1925-Jan. 4, 1926 | Dec. 22, 1925-Jan. 4, 1926 | George Higgins Moses, N.H. | Nicholas Longworth, Ohio |
| | 2 | Dec. 6, 1926 | March 4, 1927 | 88 | Dec. 22, 1926-Jan. 3, 1927 | Dec. 22, 1926-Jan. 3, 1927 | Moses | |
| 70th | 1 | Dec. 5, 1927 | May 29, 1928 | 177 | Dec. 21, 1927-Jan. 4, 1928 | Dec. 21, 1927-Jan. 4, 1928 | Moses | Longworth |
| | 2 | Dec. 3, 1928 | March 3, 1929 | 91 | Dec. 22, 1928-Jan. 3, 1929 | Dec. 22, 1928-Jan. 3, 1929 | Moses | |
| 71st | 1 | April 15, 1929 | Nov. 22, 1929 | 222 | June 19-Aug. 19, 1929 | June 19-Sept. 23, 1929 | Moses | Longworth |
| | 2 | Dec. 2, 1929 | July 3, 1930 | 214 | Dec. 21, 1929-Jan. 6, 1930 | Dec. 21, 1929-Jan. 6, 1930 | Moses | |
| | 3 | Dec. 1, 1930 | March 3, 1931 | 93 | Dec. 20, 1930-Jan. 5, 1931 | Dec. 20, 1930-Jan. 5, 1931 | Moses | |

| Con-gress | Ses-sion | Date of beginning[1] | Date of adjournment[2] | Length in days | Senate Recesses | House Recesses | President pro tempore of the Senate[3] | Speaker of the House of Representatives |
|---|---|---|---|---|---|---|---|---|
| 72nd | 1 | Dec. 7, 1931 | July 16, 1932 | 223 | Dec. 22, 1931-Jan. 4, 1932 | Dec. 22, 1931-Jan. 4, 1932 | Moses | John Nance Garner, Texas |
| | 2 | Dec. 5, 1932 | March 3, 1933 | 89 | | | Moses | |
| 73rd | 1 | March 9, 1933 | June 15, 1933 | 99 | | | Key Pittman, Nev. | Henry Thomas Rainey, Ill.[22] |
| | 2 | Jan. 3, 1934 | June 18, 1934 | 167 | | | Pittman | |
| 74th | 1 | Jan. 3, 1935 | Aug. 26, 1935 | 236 | | | Pittman | Joseph Wellington Byrns, Tenn.[23] |
| | 2 | Jan. 3, 1936 | June 20, 1936 | 170 | June 8-June 15, 1936 | June 8-June 15, 1936 | Pittman | William Brockman Bankhead, Ala.[24] |
| 75th | 1 | Jan. 5, 1937 | Aug. 21, 1937 | 229 | | | Pittman | Bankhead |
| | 2 | Nov. 15, 1937 | Dec. 21, 1937 | 37 | | | Pittman | |
| | 3 | Jan. 3, 1938 | June 16, 1938 | 165 | | | Pittman | |
| 76th | 1 | Jan. 3, 1939 | Aug. 5, 1939 | 215 | | | Pittman | Bankhead[25] |
| | 2 | Sept. 21, 1939 | Nov. 3, 1939 | 44 | | | Pittman | |
| | 3 | Jan. 3, 1940 | Jan. 3, 1941 | 366 | July 11-July 22, 1940 | July 11-July 22, 1940 | Pittman[26] William Henry King, Utah[28] | Samuel Taliaferro Rayburn, Texas[27] |
| 77th | 1 | Jan. 3, 1941 | Jan. 2, 1942 | 365 | | | Byron Patton "Pat" Harrison, Miss.[29]; Carter Glass, Va.[30] | Rayburn |
| | 2 | Jan. 5, 1942 | Dec. 16, 1942 | 346 | | | Glass | |
| 78th | 1 | Jan. 6, 1943 | Dec. 21, 1943 | 350 | July 8-Sept. 14, 1943 | July 8-Sept. 14, 1943 | Glass | Rayburn |
| | 2 | Jan. 10, 1944 | Dec. 19, 1944 | 345 | April 1-April 12, 1944 June 23-Aug. 1, 1944 Sept. 21-Nov. 14, 1944 | April 1-April 12, 1944 June 23-Aug. 1, 1944 Sept. 21-Nov. 14, 1944 | Glass | |
| 79th | 1 | Jan. 3, 1945 | Dec. 21, 1945 | 353 | Aug. 1-Sept. 5, 1945 | July 21-Sept. 5, 1945 | Kenneth Douglas McKellar, Tenn. | Rayburn |
| | 2 | Jan. 14, 1946 | Aug. 2, 1946 | 201 | | April 18-April 30, 1946 | McKellar | |
| 80th | 1 | Jan. 3, 1947 | Dec. 19, 1947 | 351 | July 27-Nov. 17, 1947 | July 27-Nov. 17, 1947 | Arthur Hendrick Vandenberg, Mich. | Joseph William Martin, Jr., Mass. |
| | 2 | Jan. 6, 1948 | Dec. 31, 1948 | 361 | June 20-July 26, 1948 Aug. 7-Dec. 31, 1948 | June 20-July 26, 1948 Aug. 7-Dec. 31, 1948 | Vandenberg | |
| 81st | 1 | Jan. 3, 1949 | Oct. 19, 1949 | 290 | | | Kenneth Douglas McKellar, Tenn. | Samuel Taliaferro Rayburn, Texas |
| | 2 | Jan. 3, 1950 | Jan. 2, 1951 | 365 | Sept. 23-Nov. 27, 1950 | April 6-April 18, 1950 Sept. 23-Nov. 27, 1950 | McKellar | |
| 82nd | 1 | Jan. 3, 1951 | Oct. 20, 1951 | 291 | | March 22-April 2, 1951 Aug. 23-Sept. 12, 1951 | McKellar | Rayburn |
| | 2 | Jan. 8, 1952 | July 7, 1952 | 182 | | April 10-April 22, 1952 | McKellar | |
| 83rd | 1 | Jan. 3, 1953 | Aug. 3, 1953 | 213 | | April 2-April 13, 1953 | Henry Styles Bridges, N.H. | Joseph William Martin, Jr., Mass. |
| | 2 | Jan. 6, 1954 | Dec. 2, 1954 | 331 | Aug. 20-Nov. 8, 1954 Nov. 18-Nov. 29, 1954 | April 15-April 22, 1954 Adjourned sine die Aug. 20, 1954 | Bridges | |
| 84th | 1 | Jan. 5, 1955 | Aug. 2, 1955 | 210 | April 4-April 13, 1955 | April 4-April 13, 1955 | Walter Franklin George, Ga. | Samuel Taliaferro Rayburn, Texas |
| | 2 | Jan. 3, 1956 | July 27, 1956 | 207 | March 29-April 9, 1956 | March 29-April 9, 1956 | George | |
| 85th | 1 | Jan. 3, 1957 | Aug. 30, 1957 | 239 | April 18-April 29, 1957 | April 18-April 29, 1957 | Carl Trumbull Hayden, Ariz. | Rayburn |
| | 2 | Jan. 7, 1958 | Aug. 24, 1958 | 230 | April 3-April 14, 1958 | April 3-April 14, 1958 | Hayden | |
| 86th | 1 | Jan. 7, 1959 | Sept. 15, 1959 | 252 | March 26-April 7, 1959 | March 26-April 7, 1959 | Hayden | Rayburn |
| | 2 | Jan. 6, 1960 | Sept. 1, 1960 | 240 | April 14-April 18, 1960 May 27-May 31, 1960 July 3-Aug. 8, 1960 | April 14-April 18, 1960 May 27-May 31, 1960 July 3-Aug. 15, 1960 | Hayden | |
| 87th | 1 | Jan. 3, 1961 | Sept. 27, 1961 | 268 | | March 30-April 10, 1961 | Hayden | Rayburn[31] |
| | 2 | Jan. 10, 1962 | Oct. 13, 1962 | 277 | | April 19-April 30, 1962 | Hayden | John William Mc-Cormack, Mass.[32] |
| 88th | 1 | Jan. 9, 1963 | Dec. 30, 1963 | 356 | | April 11-April 22, 1963 | Hayden | McCormack |
| | 2 | Jan. 7, 1964 | Oct. 3, 1964 | 270 | July 10-July 20, 1964 Aug. 21-Aug. 31, 1964 | March 26-April 6, 1964 July 2-July 20, 1964 Aug. 21-Aug. 31, 1964 | Hayden | |
| 89th | 1 | Jan. 4, 1965 | Oct. 23, 1965 | 293 | | | Hayden | McCormack |
| | 2 | Jan. 10, 1966 | Oct. 22, 1966 | 286 | April 7-April 13, 1966 June 30-July 11, 1966 | April 7-April 18, 1966 June 30-July 11, 1966 | Hayden | |

| Con-gress | Ses-sion | Date of beginning[1] | Date of adjournment[2] | Length in days | Senate Recesses | House Recesses | President pro tempore of the Senate[3] | Speaker of the House of Representatives |
|---|---|---|---|---|---|---|---|---|
| 90th | 1 | Jan. 10, 1967 | Dec. 15, 1967 | 340 | March 23-April 3, 1967<br>June 29-July 10, 1967<br>Aug. 31-Sept. 11, 1967<br>Nov. 22-Nov. 27, 1967 | March 23-April 3, 1967<br>June 29-July 10, 1967<br>Aug. 31-Sept. 11, 1967<br>Nov. 22-Nov. 27, 1967 | Hayden | McCormack |
| | 2 | Jan. 15, 1968 | Oct. 14, 1968 | 274 | April 11-April 17, 1968<br>May 29-June 3, 1968<br>June 3-July 8, 1968<br>Aug. 2-Sept. 4, 1968 | April 11-April 22, 1968<br>May 29-June 3, 1968<br>June 3-July 8, 1968<br>Aug. 2-Sept. 4, 1968 | Hayden | |
| 91st | 1 | Jan. 3, 1969 | Dec. 23, 1969 | 355 | Feb. 7-Feb. 17, 1969<br>April 3-April 14, 1969<br>July 2-July 7, 1969<br>Aug. 13-Sept. 3, 1969<br>Nov. 26-Dec. 1, 1969 | Feb. 7-Feb. 17, 1969<br>April 3-April 14, 1969<br>May 28-June 2, 1969<br>July 2-July 7, 1969<br>Aug. 13-Sept. 3, 1969<br>Nov. 6-Nov. 12, 1969<br>Nov. 26-Dec. 1, 1969 | Richard Brevard Russell, Jr., Ga. | McCormack |
| | 2 | Jan. 19, 1970 | Jan. 2, 1971 | 349 | Feb. 10-Feb. 16, 1970<br>March 26-March 31, 1970<br>Sept. 2-Sept. 8, 1970<br>Oct. 14-Nov. 16, 1970<br>Nov. 25-Nov. 30, 1970<br>Dec. 22-Dec. 28, 1970 | Feb. 10-Feb. 16, 1970<br>March 26-March 31, 1970<br>May 27-June 1, 1970<br>July 1-July 6, 1970<br>Aug. 14-Sept. 9, 1970<br>Oct. 14-Nov. 16, 1970<br>Nov. 25-Nov. 30, 1970<br>Dec. 22-Dec. 29, 1970 | Russell | |
| 92nd | 1 | Jan. 21, 1971 | Dec. 17, 1971 | 331 | Feb. 11-Feb. 17, 1971<br>April 7-April 14, 1971<br>May 26-June 1, 1971<br>June 30-July 6, 1971<br>Aug. 6-Sept. 8, 1971<br>Oct. 21-Oct. 26, 1971<br>Nov. 24-Nov. 29, 1971 | Feb. 10-Feb. 17, 1971<br>April 7-April 19, 1971<br>May 27-June 1, 1971<br>July 1-July 6, 1971<br>Aug. 6-Sept. 8, 1971<br>Oct. 7-Oct. 12, 1971<br>Oct. 21-Oct. 26, 1971<br>Nov. 19-Nov. 29, 1971 | Russell[33]; Allen Joseph Ellender, La.[34] | Carl Bert Albert, Okla. |
| | 2 | Jan. 18, 1972 | Oct. 18, 1972 | 275 | Feb. 9-Feb. 14, 1972<br>March 30-April 4, 1972<br>May 25-May 30, 1972<br>June 30-July 17, 1972<br>Aug. 18-Sept. 5, 1972 | Feb. 9-Feb. 16, 1972<br>March 29-April 10, 1972<br>May 24-May 30, 1972<br>June 30-July 17, 1972<br>Aug. 18-Sept. 5, 1972 | Ellender[35]; James Oliver Eastland, Miss.[36] | |
| 93rd | 1 | Jan. 3, 1973 | Dec. 22, 1973 | 354 | Feb. 8-Feb. 15, 1973<br>April 18-April 30, 1973<br>May 23-May 29, 1973<br>June 30-July 9, 1973<br>Aug. 3-Sept. 5, 1973<br>Oct. 18-Oct. 23, 1973<br>Nov. 21-Nov. 26, 1973 | Feb. 8-Feb. 19, 1973<br>April 19-April 30, 1973<br>May 24-May 29, 1973<br>June 30-July 10, 1973<br>Aug. 3-Sept. 5, 1973<br>Oct. 4-Oct. 9, 1973<br>Oct. 18-Oct. 23, 1973<br>Nov. 15-Nov. 26, 1973 | Eastland | Albert |
| | 2 | Jan. 21, 1974 | Dec. 20, 1974 | 334 | Feb. 8-Feb. 18, 1974<br>March 13-March 19, 1974<br>April 11-April 22, 1974<br>May 23-May 28, 1974<br>Aug. 22-Sept. 4, 1974<br>Oct. 17-Nov. 18, 1974<br>Nov. 26-Dec. 2, 1974 | Feb. 7-Feb. 13, 1974<br>April 11-April 22, 1974<br>May 23-May 28, 1974<br>Aug. 22-Sept. 11, 1974<br>Oct. 17-Nov. 18, 1974<br>Nov. 26-Dec. 3, 1974 | Eastland | |
| 94th | 1 | Jan. 14, 1975 | Dec. 19, 1975 | 340 | March 26-April 7, 1975<br>May 22-June 2, 1975<br>June 27-July 7, 1975<br>Aug. 1-Sept. 3, 1975<br>Oct. 9-Oct. 20, 1975<br>Oct. 23-Oct. 28, 1975<br>Nov. 20-Dec. 1, 1975 | March 26-April 7, 1975<br>May 22-June 2, 1975<br>June 26-July 8, 1975<br>Aug. 1-Sept. 3, 1975<br>Oct. 9-Oct. 20, 1975<br>Oct. 23-Oct. 28, 1975<br>Nov. 20-Dec. 1, 1975 | Eastland | Albert |
| | 2 | Jan. 19, 1976 | Oct. 2, 1976 | 258 | Feb. 6-Feb. 16, 1976<br>April 14-April 26, 1976<br>May 28-June 2, 1976<br>July 2-July 19, 1976<br>Aug. 10-Aug. 23, 1976<br>Sept. 1-Sept. 7, 1976 | Feb. 11-Feb. 16, 1976<br>April 14-April 26, 1976<br>May 27-June 1, 1976<br>July 2-July 19, 1976<br>Aug. 10-Aug. 23, 1976<br>Sept. 2-Sept. 8, 1976 | Eastland | |
| 95th | 1 | Jan. 4, 1977 | Dec. 15, 1977 | 346 | Feb. 11-Feb. 21, 1977<br>April 7-April 18, 1977<br>May 27-June 6, 1977<br>July 1-July 11, 1977<br>Aug. 6-Sept. 7, 1977 | Feb. 9-Feb. 16, 1977<br>April 6-April 18, 1977<br>May 26-June 1, 1977<br>June 30-July 11, 1977<br>Aug. 5-Sept. 7, 1977<br>Oct. 6-Oct. 11, 1977 | Eastland | Thomas Phillip O'Neill, Jr., Mass. |
| | 2 | Jan. 19, 1978 | Oct. 15, 1978 | 270 | Feb. 10-Feb. 20, 1978<br>March 23-April 3, 1978<br>May 26-June 5, 1978<br>June 29-July 10, 1978<br>Aug. 25-Sept. 6, 1978 | Feb. 9-Feb. 14, 1978<br>March 22-April 3, 1978<br>May 25-May 31, 1978<br>June 29-July 10, 1978<br>Aug. 17-Sept. 6, 1978 | Eastland | |

| Con-gress | Ses-sion | Date of beginning[1] | Date of adjournment[2] | Length in days | Senate Recesses | House Recesses | President pro tempore of the Senate[3] | Speaker of the House of Representatives |
|---|---|---|---|---|---|---|---|---|
| 96th | 1 | Jan. 15, 1979 | Jan. 3, 1980 | 354 | Feb. 9-Feb. 19, 1979<br>April 10-April 23, 1979<br>May 24-June 4, 1979<br>June 27-July 9, 1979<br>Aug. 3-Sept. 5, 1979<br>Nov. 20-Nov. 26, 1979<br>Adjourned sine die Dec. 20, 1979 | Feb. 8-Feb. 13, 1979<br>April 10-April 23, 1979<br>May 24-May 30, 1979<br>June 29-July 9, 1979<br>Aug. 2-Sept. 5, 1979<br>Nov. 20-Nov. 26, 1979<br>Adjourned sine die Jan. 3, 1980 | Warren Grant Magnuson, Wash. | O'Neill |
| | 2 | Jan. 3, 1980 | Dec. 16, 1980 | 349 | April 3-April 15, 1980<br>May 22-May 28, 1980<br>July 2-July 21, 1980<br>Aug. 6-Aug. 18, 1980<br>Aug. 27-Sept. 3, 1980<br>Oct. 1-Nov. 12, 1980<br>Nov. 25-Dec. 1, 1980 | Feb. 13-Feb. 19, 1980<br>April 2-April 15, 1980<br>May 22-May 28, 1980<br>July 2-July 21, 1980<br>Aug. 1-Aug. 18, 1980<br>Aug. 28-Sept. 3, 1980<br>Oct. 2-Nov. 12, 1980<br>Nov. 21-Dec. 1, 1980 | Magnuson | |
| 97th | 1 | Jan. 5, 1981 | Dec. 16, 1981 | 347 | Feb. 6-Feb. 16, 1981<br>April 10-April 27, 1981<br>June 25-July 8, 1981<br>Aug. 3-Sept. 9, 1981<br>Oct. 7-Oct. 14, 1981<br>Nov. 24-Nov. 30, 1981 | Feb. 6-Feb. 17, 1981<br>April 10-April 27, 1981<br>June 26-July 8, 1981<br>Aug. 4-Sept. 9, 1981<br>Oct. 7-Oct. 13, 1981<br>Nov. 23-Nov. 30, 1981 | James Strom Thurmond, S.C. | O'Neill |
| | 2 | Jan. 25, 1982 | Dec. 23, 1982 | 333 | Feb. 11-Feb. 22, 1982<br>April 1-April 13, 1982<br>May 27-June 8, 1982<br>July 1-July 12, 1982<br>Aug. 20-Sept. 8, 1982<br>Oct. 1-Nov. 29, 1982 | Feb. 10-Feb. 22, 1982<br>April 6-April 20, 1982<br>May 27-June 2, 1982<br>July 1-July 12, 1982<br>Aug. 20-Sept. 8, 1982<br>Oct. 1-Nov. 29, 1982 | Thurmond | |
| 98th | 1 | Jan. 3, 1983 | Nov. 18, 1983 | 320 | Jan. 3-Jan. 25, 1983<br>Feb. 3-Feb. 14, 1983<br>March 24-April 5, 1983<br>May 26-June 6, 1983<br>June 29-July 11, 1983<br>Aug. 4-Sept. 12, 1983<br>Oct. 7-Oct. 17, 1983 | Jan. 6-Jan. 25, 1983<br>Feb. 17-Feb. 22, 1983<br>March 24-April 5, 1983<br>May 26-June 1, 1983<br>June 30-July 11, 1983<br>Aug. 4-Sept. 12, 1983<br>Oct. 6-Oct. 17, 1983 | Thurmond | O'Neill |
| | 2 | Jan. 23, 1984 | Oct. 12, 1984 | 264 | Feb. 9-Feb. 20, 1984<br>April 12-April 24, 1984<br>May 24-May 31, 1984<br>June 29-July 23, 1984<br>Aug. 10-Sept. 5, 1984 | Feb. 9-Feb. 21, 1984<br>April 12-April 24, 1984<br>May 24-May 30, 1984<br>June 29-July 23, 1984<br>Aug. 10-Sept. 5, 1984 | Thurmond | |
| 99th | 1 | Jan. 3, 1985 | Dec. 20, 1985 | 352 | Jan. 7-Jan. 21, 1985<br>Feb. 7-Feb. 18, 1985<br>April 4-April 15, 1985<br>May 9-May 14, 1985<br>May 24-June 3, 1985<br>June 27-July 8, 1985<br>Aug. 1-Sept. 9, 1985<br>Nov. 23-Dec. 2, 1985 | Jan. 3-Jan. 21, 1985<br>Feb. 7-Feb. 19, 1985<br>March 7-March 19, 1985<br>April 4-April 15, 1985<br>May 23-June 3, 1985<br>June 27-July 8, 1985<br>Aug. 1-Sept. 4, 1985<br>Nov. 21-Dec. 2, 1985 | Thurmond | O'Neill |
| | 2 | Jan. 21, 1986 | Oct. 18, 1986 | 278 | Feb. 7-Feb. 17, 1986<br>March 27-April 8, 1986<br>May 21-June 2, 1986<br>June 26-July 7, 1986<br>Aug. 15-Sept. 8, 1986 | Feb. 6-Feb. 18, 1986<br>March 25-April 8, 1986<br>May 22-June 3, 1986<br>June 26-July 14, 1986<br>Aug. 16-Sept. 8, 1986 | Thurmond | |
| 100th | 1 | Jan. 6, 1987 | Dec. 22, 1987 | 351 | Jan. 6-Jan. 12, 1987<br>Feb. 5-Feb. 16, 1987<br>April 10-April 21, 1987<br>May 21-May 27, 1987<br>July 1-July 7, 1987<br>Aug. 7-Sept. 9, 1987<br>Nov. 20-Nov. 30, 1987 | Jan. 8-Jan. 20, 1987<br>Feb. 11-Feb. 18, 1987<br>April 9-April 21, 1987<br>May 21-May 27, 1987<br>July 1-July 7, 1987<br>July 15-July 20, 1987<br>Aug. 7-Sept. 9, 1987<br>Nov. 10-Nov. 16, 1987<br>Nov. 20-Nov. 30, 1987 | John Cornelius Stennis, Miss. | James Claude Wright, Jr., Texas |
| | 2 | Jan. 25, 1988 | Oct. 22, 1988 | 272 | Feb. 4-Feb. 15, 1988<br>March 4-March 14, 1988<br>March 31-April 11, 1988<br>April 29-May 9, 1988<br>May 27-June 6, 1988<br>June 29-July 6, 1988<br>July 14-July 25, 1988<br>Aug. 11-Sept. 7, 1988 | Feb. 9-Feb. 16, 1988<br>March 31-April 11, 1988<br>May 26-June 1, 1988<br>June 30-July 7, 1988<br>July 14-July 26, 1988<br>Aug. 11-Sept. 7, 1988 | Stennis | |

| Con-gress | Ses-sion | Date of beginning[1] | Date of adjournment[2] | Length in days | Senate Recesses | House Recesses | President pro tempore of the Senate[3] | Speaker of the House of Representatives |
|---|---|---|---|---|---|---|---|---|
| 101st | 1 | Jan. 3, 1989 | Nov. 22, 1989 | 324 | Jan. 4-Jan. 20, 1989<br>Jan. 20-Jan. 25, 1989<br>Feb. 9-Feb. 21, 1989<br>March 17-April 4, 1989<br>April 19-May 1, 1989<br>May 18-May 31, 1989<br>June 23-July 11, 1989<br>Aug. 4-Sept. 6, 1989 | Jan. 4-Jan. 19, 1989<br>Feb. 9-Feb. 21, 1989<br>March 23-April 3, 1989<br>April 18-April 25, 1989<br>May 25-May 31, 1989<br>June 29-July 10, 1989<br>Aug. 5-Sept. 6, 1989 | Robert Carlyle Byrd, W.Va. | Wright; Thomas Stephen Foley, Wash.[37] |
| | 2 | Jan. 23, 1990 | Oct. 28, 1990 | 260 | Feb. 8-Feb. 20, 1990<br>March 9-March 20, 1990<br>April 5-April 18, 1990<br>May 24-June 5, 1990<br>June 28-July 10, 1990<br>Aug. 4-Sept. 10, 1990 | June 28-July 10, 1990<br>Aug. 4-Sept. 5, 1990<br>Feb. 7-Feb. 20, 1990<br>Apr. 4-Apr. 18, 1990<br>May 25-June 5, 1990 | Byrd | Foley |
| 102nd | 1 | Jan. 3, 1991 | Jan. 3, 1992 | 365 | Feb. 6-Feb. 19, 1991<br>March 22-April 9, 1991<br>April 25-May 6, 1991<br>May 24-June 3, 1991<br>June 28-July 8, 1991<br>Aug. 2-Sept. 10, 1991<br>Nov. 27, 1991-Jan. 3, 1992 | Feb. 7-Feb. 19, 1991<br>March 22-April 9, 1991<br>May 23-May 29, 1991<br>June 27-July 9, 1991<br>Aug. 2-Sept. 11, 1991<br>Nov. 27, 1991-Jan. 3, 1992 | Byrd | Foley |
| | 2 | Jan. 3, 1992 | Oct. 9, 1992 | 281 | Jan. 3-Jan. 21, 1992<br>Feb. 7-Feb. 18, 1992<br>Apr. 10-Apr. 28, 1992<br>May 21-June 1, 1992<br>July 2-July 20, 1992<br>Aug. 12-Sept. 8, 1992<br>Jan. 7-Jan. 20, 1992 | Jan. 3-Jan. 22, 1992<br>Apr. 10-Apr. 28, 1992<br>May 21-May 26, 1992<br>July 2-July 7, 1992<br>July 9-July 21, 1992<br>Aug. 12-Sept. 9, 1992<br>Jan. 6-Jan. 20, 1993 | Byrd | Foley |
| 103rd | 1 | Jan. 5, 1993 | Nov. 26, 1993 | 295 | Feb. 4-Feb. 16, 1993<br>Apr. 7-Apr. 19, 1993<br>May 28-June 7, 1993<br>July 1-July 13, 1993<br>Aug. 6-Sept. 7, 1993<br>Nov. 10-Nov. 16, 1993 | Jan. 27-Feb. 2, 1993<br>Feb. 4-Feb. 16, 1993<br>Apr. 7-Apr. 19, 1993<br>May 27-June 8, 1993<br>July 1-July 13, 1993<br>Aug. 6-Sept. 8, 1993<br>Nov. 10-Nov. 14, 1993 | Byrd | Foley |
| | 2 | Jan. 25, 1994 | | | Jan. 28-Jan. 31, 1994<br>Feb. 11-Feb. 22, 1994<br>Mar. 25-Apr. 11, 1994 | Jan. 26-Feb. 1, 1994<br>Feb. 11-Feb. 22, 1994<br>Mar. 24-Apr. 12, 1994[38] | Byrd | Foley |

1. The Constitution (Article I, Section 4) provided that "The Congress shall assemble at least once in every year ... on the first Monday in December, unless they shall by law appoint a different day." Pursuant to a resolution of the Continental Congress, the first session of the First Congress convened March 4, 1789. Up to and including May 20, 1820, eighteen acts were passed providing for the meeting of Congress on other days in the year. After 1820 Congress met regularly on the first Monday in December until 1934, when the 20th Amendment to the Constitution became effective changing the meeting date to Jan. 3. (Until then, brief special sessions of the Senate only were held at the beginning of each presidential term to confirm cabinet and other nominations—and occasionally at other times for other purposes. The Senate last met in special session from March 4 to March 6, 1933. *List, p. 135-A*.)

   The first and second sessions of the First Congress were held in New York City. Subsequently, including the first session of the Sixth Congress, Philadelphia was the meeting place; since then, Congress has convened in Washington.
2. Until adoption of the 20th Amendment, the deadline for adjournment of Congress in odd-numbered years was March 3. However, the expiring Congress often extended the "legislative day" of March 3 up to noon of March 4, when the new Congress came officially into being. After ratification of the 20th Amendment, the deadline for adjournment of Congress in odd-numbered years was noon on Jan. 3.
3. At one time the appointment or election of a president pro tempore was considered by the Senate to be for the occasion only, so that more than one appears in several sessions and in others none was chosen. Since March 12, 1890, they have served until "the Senate otherwise ordered."
4. Elected to count the vote for president and vice president, which was done April 6, 1789, because there was a quorum of the Senate for the first time. John Adams, vice president, appeared April 21, 1789, and took his seat as president of the Senate.
5. Elected Speaker pro tempore for April 20, 1798, and for May 28, 1798.
6. Elected Speaker Jan. 19, 1814, to succeed Henry Clay, who resigned Jan. 19, 1814.
7. Elected Speaker Nov. 15, 1820, to succeed Henry Clay, who resigned Oct. 28, 1820.

8. Elected Speaker June 2, 1834, to succeed Andrew Stevenson of Virginia, who resigned.
9. Elected Speaker March 3, 1869, and served one day.
10. Died Aug. 19, 1876.
11. Appointed Speaker pro tempore Feb. 17, May 12, June 19.
12. Appointed Speaker pro tempore June 4.
13. Resigned as president pro tempore April 27, 1911.
14. Elected to serve Jan. 11-17, March 11-12, April 8, May 10, May 30 to June 1 and 3, June 13 to July 5, Aug. 1-10, and Aug. 27 to Dec. 15, 1912.
15. Elected to serve May 25, 1912.
16. Elected to serve Dec. 4-Dec. 12, 1911.
17. Elected to serve Feb. 12-Feb. 14, April 26-April 27, May 7, July 6-July 31, Aug. 12-Aug. 26, 1912.
18. Elected to serve March 25-March 26, 1912.
19. Elected to serve Aug. 27 to Dec. 15, 1912, Jan. 5-18, and Feb. 2-15, 1913.
20. Elected to serve Dec. 16, 1912, to Jan. 4, 1913, Jan. 19 to Feb. 1, and Feb. 16 to March 3, 1913.
21. Died Oct. 1, 1916.
22. Died Aug. 19, 1934.
23. Died June 4, 1936.
24. Elected June 4, 1936.
25. Died Sept. 15, 1940.
26. Died Nov. 10, 1940.
27. Elected Sept. 16, 1940.
28. Elected Nov. 19, 1940.
29. Elected Jan. 6, 1941; died June 22, 1941.
30. Elected July 10, 1941.
31. Died Nov. 16, 1961.
32. Elected Jan. 10, 1962.
33. Died Jan. 21, 1971.
34. Elected Jan. 22, 1971.
35. Died July 27, 1972.
36. Elected July 28, 1972.
37. Elected Speaker June 6, 1989, to succeed James Claude Wright, Jr., who resigned June 6, 1989.
38. Senate and House recesses for the 103rd Congress as of May 23, 1994.

*Sources: 1993-1994 Congressional Directory, 103rd Congress* (Washington, D.C.: Government Printing Office, 1993); *Congressional Quarterly Weekly Report; Congressional Record.*

# Leaders of the House since 1899

| Congress | | House Floor Leaders | | House Whips | |
|---|---|---|---|---|---|
| | | Majority | Minority | Majority | Minority |
| 56th | (1899-1901) | Sereno E. Payne (R N.Y.) | James D. Richardson (D Tenn.) | James A. Tawney (R Minn.) | Oscar W. Underwood (D Ala.)[6] |
| 57th | (1901-1903) | Payne | Richardson | Tawney | James T. Lloyd (D Mo.) |
| 58th | (1903-1905) | Payne | John Sharp Williams (D Miss.) | Tawney | Lloyd |
| 59th | (1905-1907) | Payne | Williams | James E. Watson (R Ind.) | Lloyd |
| 60th | (1907-1909) | Payne | Williams/Champ Clark (D Mo.)[1] | Watson | Lloyd[7] |
| 61st | (1909-1911) | Payne | Clark | John W. Dwight (R N.Y.) | None |
| 62nd | (1911-1913) | Oscar W. Underwood (D Ala.) | James R. Mann (R Ill.) | None | John W. Dwight (R N.Y.) |
| 63rd | (1913-1915) | Underwood | Mann | Thomas M. Bell (D Ga.) | Charles H. Burke (R S.D.) |
| 64th | (1915-1917) | Claude Kitchin (D N.C.) | Mann | None | Charles M. Hamilton (R N.Y.) |
| 65th | (1917-1919) | Kitchin | Mann | None | Hamilton |
| 66th | (1919-1921) | Franklin W. Mondell (R Wyo.) | Clark | Harold Knutson (R Minn.) | None |
| 67th | (1921-1923) | Mondell | Claude Kitchin (D N.C.) | Knutson | William A. Oldfield (D Ark.) |
| 68th | (1923-1925) | Nicholas Longworth (R Ohio) | Finis J. Garrett (D Tenn.) | Albert H. Vestal (R Ind.) | Oldfield |
| 69th | (1925-1927) | John Q. Tilson (R Conn.) | Garrett | Vestal | Oldfield |
| 70th | (1927-1929) | Tilson | Garrett | Vestal | Oldfield/John McDuffie (D Ala.)[8] |
| 71st | (1929-1931) | Tilson | John N. Garner (D Texas) | Vestal | McDuffie |
| 72nd | (1931-1933) | Henry T. Rainey (D Ill.) | Bertrand H. Snell (R N.Y.) | John McDuffie (D Ala.) | Carl G. Bachmann (R W.Va.) |
| 73rd | (1933-1935) | Joseph W. Byrns (D Tenn.) | Snell | Arthur H. Greenwood (D Ind.) | Harry L. Englebright (R Calif.) |
| 74th | (1935-1937) | William B. Bankhead (D Ala.)[2] | Snell | Patrick J. Boland (D Pa.) | Englebright |
| 75th | (1937-1939) | Sam Rayburn (D Texas) | Snell | Boland | Englebright |
| 76th | (1939-1941) | Rayburn/John W. McCormack (D Mass.)[3] | Joseph W. Martin Jr. (R Mass.) | Boland | Englebright |
| 77th | (1941-1943) | McCormack | Martin | Boland/Robert Ramspeck (D Ga.)[9] | Englebright |
| 78th | (1943-1945) | McCormack | Martin | Ramspeck | Leslie C. Arends (R Ill.) |
| 79th | (1945-1947) | McCormack | Martin | Ramspeck/John J. Sparkman (D Ala.)[10] | Arends |
| 80th | (1947-1949) | Charles A. Halleck (R Ind.) | Sam Rayburn (D Texas) | Leslie C. Arends (R Ill.) | John W. McCormack (D Mass.) |
| 81st | (1949-1951) | McCormack | Martin | J. Percy Priest (D Tenn.) | Arends |
| 82nd | (1951-1953) | McCormack | Martin | Priest | Arends |
| 83rd | (1953-1955) | Halleck | Rayburn | Arends | McCormack |
| 84th | (1955-1957) | McCormack | Martin | Carl Albert (D Okla.) | Arends |
| 85th | (1957-1959) | McCormack | Martin | Albert | Arends |
| 86th | (1959-1961) | McCormack | Charles A. Halleck (R Ind.) | Albert | Arends |
| 87th | (1961-1963) | McCormack/Carl Albert (D Okla.)[4] | Halleck | Albert/Hale Boggs (D La.)[11] | Arends |
| 88th | (1963-1965) | Albert | Halleck | Boggs | Arends |
| 89th | (1965-1967) | Albert | Gerald R. Ford (R Mich.) | Boggs | Arends |
| 90th | (1967-1969) | Albert | Ford | Boggs | Arends |
| 91st | (1969-1971) | Albert | Ford | Boggs | Arends |
| 92nd | (1971-1973) | Hale Boggs (D La.) | Ford | Thomas P. O'Neill Jr. (D Mass.) | Arends |
| 93rd | (1973-1975) | Thomas P. O'Neill Jr. (D Mass.) | Ford/John J. Rhodes (R Ariz.)[5] | John J. McFall (D Calif.) | Arends |
| 94th | (1975-1977) | O'Neill | Rhodes | McFall | Robert H. Michel (R Ill.) |
| 95th | (1977-1979) | Jim Wright (D Texas) | Rhodes | John Brademas (D Ind.) | Michel |
| 96th | (1979-1981) | Wright | Rhodes | Brademas | Michel |
| 97th | (1981-1983) | Wright | Robert H. Michel (R Ill.) | Thomas S. Foley (D Wash.) | Trent Lott (R Miss.) |
| 98th | (1983-1985) | Wright | Michel | Foley | Lott |
| 99th | (1985-1987) | Wright | Michel | Foley | Lott |
| 100th | (1987-1989) | Thomas S. Foley (D Wash.) | Michel | Tony Coelho (D Calif.) | Lott |
| 101st | (1989-1991) | Foley/Richard A. Gephardt (D Mo.)[12] | Michel | Coelho/William H. Gray III (D Pa.)[13] | Dick Cheney (R Wyo.)/Newt Gingrich (R Ga.)[14] |
| 102nd | (1991-1993) | Gephardt | Michel | Gray/David E. Bonior (D Mich.)[15] | Gingrich |
| 103rd | (1993-1995) | Gephardt | Michel | Bonior | Gingrich |

1. Clark became minority leader in 1908.
2. Bankhead became Speaker of the House on June 4, 1936. The post of majority leader remained vacant until the next Congress.
3. McCormack became majority leader on Sept. 26, 1940, filling the vacancy caused by the elevation of Rayburn to the post of Speaker of the House on Sept. 16, 1940.
4. Albert became majority leader on Jan. 10, 1962, filling the vacancy caused by the elevation of McCormack to the post of Speaker of the House on Jan. 10, 1962.

5. Rhodes became minority leader on Dec. 7, 1973, filling the vacancy caused by the resignation of Ford on Dec. 6, 1973, to become vice president.
6. Underwood did not become minority whip until 1901.
7. Lloyd resigned to become chairman of the Democratic Congressional Campaign Committee in 1908. The post of minority whip remained vacant until the beginning of the 62nd Congress.
8. McDuffie became minority whip after the death of Oldfield on Nov. 19, 1928.
9. Ramspeck became majority whip on June 8, 1942, filling the vacancy caused by the death of Boland on May 18, 1942.
10. Sparkman became majority whip on Jan. 14, 1946, filling the vacancy caused by the resignation of Ramspeck on Dec. 31, 1945.

11. Boggs became majority whip on Jan. 10, 1962, filling the vacancy caused by the elevation of Albert to the post of majority leader on Jan. 10, 1962.
12. Gephardt became majority leader on June 14, 1989, filling the vacancy created when Foley succeeded Wright as Speaker of the House on June 6, 1989.
13. Gray became majority whip on June 14, 1989, filling the vacancy caused by Coehlo's resignation from Congress on June 15, 1989.
14. Gingrich became minority whip on March 23, 1989, filling the vacancy caused by the resignation of Cheney on March 17, 1989, to become secretary of defense.
15. Bonior became majority whip on Sept. 11, 1991, filling the vacancy caused by Gray's resignation from Congress on Sept. 11, 1991.

*Sources:* Randall B. Ripley, *Party Leaders in the House of Representatives* (Washington, D.C.: Brookings Institution), 1967; *Congressional Directory* (Washington, D.C.: Government Printing Office), various years; *Biographical Directory of the American Congress, 1774-1971,* comp. Lawrence F. Kennedy, 92nd Cong., 1st sess., 1971, S Doc 8; *Congressional Quarterly Weekly Report.*

# Leaders of the Senate since 1911

| Congress | | Senate Floor Leaders | | Senate Whips | |
|---|---|---|---|---|---|
| | | Majority | Minority | Majority | Minority |
| 62nd | (1911-1913) | Shelby M. Cullom (R Ill.) | Thomas S. Martin (D Va.) | None | None |
| 63rd | (1913-1915) | John W. Kern (D Ind.) | Jacob H. Gallinger (R N.H.) | J. Hamilton Lewis (D Ill.) | None |
| 64th | (1915-1917) | Kern | Gallinger | Lewis | James W. Wadsworth Jr. (R N.Y.)/Charles Curtis (R Kan.)[8] |
| 65th | (1917-1919) | Thomas S. Martin (D Va.) | Gallinger/Henry Cabot Lodge (R Mass.)[1] | Lewis | Curtis |
| 66th | (1919-1921) | Henry Cabot Lodge (R Mass.) | Martin/Oscar W. Underwood (D Ala.)[2] | Charles Curtis (R Kan.) | Peter G. Gerry (D R.I.) |
| 67th | (1921-1923) | Lodge | Underwood | Curtis | Gerry |
| 68th | (1923-1925) | Lodge/Charles Curtis (R Kan.)[3] | Joseph T. Robinson (D Ark.) | Curtis/Wesley L. Jones (R Wash.)[9] | Gerry |
| 69th | (1925-1927) | Curtis | Robinson | Jones | Gerry |
| 70th | (1927-1929) | Curtis | Robinson | Jones | Gerry |
| 71st | (1929-1931) | James E. Watson (R Ind.) | Robinson | Simeon D. Fess (R Ohio) | Morris Sheppard (D Texas) |
| 72nd | (1931-1933) | Watson | Robinson | Fess | Sheppard |
| 73rd | (1933-1935) | Joseph T. Robinson (D Ark.) | Charles L. McNary (R Ore.) | Lewis | Felix Hebert (R R.I.) |
| 74th | (1935-1937) | Robinson | McNary | Lewis | None |
| 75th | (1937-1939) | Robinson/Alben W. Barkley (D Ky.)[4] | McNary | Lewis | None |
| 76th | (1939-1941) | Barkley | McNary | Sherman Minton (D Ind.) | None |
| 77th | (1941-1943) | Barkley | McNary | Lister Hill (D Ala.) | None |
| 78th | (1943-1945) | Barkley | McNary | Hill | Kenneth Wherry (R Neb.) |
| 79th | (1945-1947) | Barkley | Wallace H. White Jr. (R Maine) | Hill | Wherry |

| Congress | | Senate Floor Leaders | | Senate Whips | |
|---|---|---|---|---|---|
| | | Majority | Minority | Majority | Minority |
| 80th | (1947-1949) | Wallace H. White Jr. (R Maine) | Alben W. Barkley (D Ky.) | Kenneth Wherry (R Neb.) | Scott Lucas (D Ill.) |
| 81st | (1949-1951) | Scott W. Lucas (D Ill.) | Kenneth S. Wherry (R Neb.) | Francis Myers (D Pa.) | Leverett Saltonstall (R Mass.) |
| 82nd | (1951-1953) | Ernest W. McFarland (D Ariz.) | Wherry/Styles Bridges (R N.H.)[5] | Lyndon B. Johnson (D Texas) | Saltonstall |
| 83rd | (1953-1955) | Robert A. Taft (R Ohio)/ William F. Knowland (R Calif.)[6] | Lyndon B. Johnson (D Texas) | Leverett Saltonstall (R Mass.) | Earle Clements (D Ky.) |
| 84th | (1955-1957) | Lyndon B. Johnson (D Texas) | William F. Knowland (R Calif.) | Earle Clements (D Ky.) | Saltonstall |
| 85th | (1957-1959) | Johnson | Knowland | Mike Mansfield (D Mont.) | Everett McKinley Dirksen (R Ill.) |
| 86th | (1959-1961) | Johnson | Everett McKinley Dirksen (R Ill.) | Mansfield | Thomas H. Kuchel (R Calif.) |
| 87th | (1961-1963) | Mike Mansfield (D Mont.) | Dirksen | Hubert H. Humphrey (D Minn.) | Kuchel |
| 88th | (1963-1965) | Mansfield | Dirksen | Humphrey | Kuchel |
| 89th | (1965-1967) | Mansfield | Dirksen | Russell Long (D La.) | Kuchel |
| 90th | (1967-1969) | Mansfield | Dirksen | Long | Kuchel |
| 91st | (1969-1971) | Mansfield | Dirksen/Hugh Scott (R Pa.)[7] | Edward M. Kennedy (D Mass.) | Hugh Scott (R Pa.)/Robert P. Griffin (R Mich.)[10] |
| 92nd | (1971-1973) | Mansfield | Scott | Robert C. Byrd (D W.Va.) | Griffin |
| 93rd | (1973-1975) | Mansfield | Scott | Byrd | Griffin |
| 94th | (1975-1977) | Mansfield | Scott | Byrd | Griffin |
| 95th | (1977-1979) | Robert C. Byrd (D W.Va.) | Howard H. Baker Jr. (R Tenn.) | Alan Cranston (D Calif.) | Ted Stevens (R Alaska) |
| 96th | (1979-1981) | Byrd | Baker | Cranston | Stevens |
| 97th | (1981-1983) | Howard H. Baker Jr. (R Tenn.) | Robert C. Byrd (D W.Va.) | Ted Stevens (R Alaska) | Alan Cranston (D Calif.) |
| 98th | (1983-1985) | Baker | Byrd | Stevens | Cranston |
| 99th | (1985-1987) | Robert Dole (R Kan.) | Byrd | Alan K. Simpson (R Wyo.) | Cranston |
| 100th | (1987-1989) | Byrd | Robert Dole (R Kan.) | Cranston | Alan K. Simpson (R Wyo.) |
| 101st | (1989-1991) | George J. Mitchell (D Maine) | Dole | Cranston | Simpson |
| 102nd | (1991-1993) | Mitchell | Dole | Wendell H. Ford (D Ky.) | Simpson |
| 103rd | (1993-1995) | Mitchell | Dole | Ford | Simpson |

1. Lodge became minority leader on Aug. 24, 1918, filling the vacancy caused by the death of Gallinger on Aug. 17, 1918.
2. Underwood became minority leader on April 27, 1920, filling the vacancy caused by the death of Martin on Nov. 12, 1919. Gilbert M. Hitchcock (D Neb.) served as acting minority leader in the interim.
3. Curtis became majority leader on Nov. 28, 1924, filling the vacancy caused by the death of Lodge on Nov. 9, 1924.
4. Barkley became majority leader on July 22, 1937, filling the vacancy caused by the death of Robinson on July 14, 1937.
5. Bridges became minority leader on Jan. 8, 1952, filling the vacancy caused by the death of Wherry on Nov. 29, 1951.
6. Knowland became majority leader on Aug. 4, 1953, filling the vacancy caused by the death of Taft on July 31, 1953. Taft's

vacant seat was filled by a Democrat, Thomas Burke, on Nov. 10, 1953. The division of the Senate changed to 48 Democrats, 47 Republicans, and 1 Independent, thus giving control of the Senate to the Democrats. However, Knowland remained as majority leader until the end of the 83rd Congress.
7. Scott became minority leader on Sept. 24, 1969, filling the vacancy caused by the death of Dirksen on Sept. 7, 1969.
8. Wadsworth served as minority whip for only one week, from Dec. 6 to Dec. 13, 1915.
9. Jones became majority whip filling the vacancy caused by the elevation of Curtis to the post of majority leader.
10. Griffin became minority whip on Sept. 24, 1969, filling the vacancy caused by the elevation of Scott to the post of minority leader.

*Sources:* Walter J. Oleszek, "Party Whips in the United States Senate," *Journal of Politics* 33 (November 1971): 955-979; *Congressional Directory* (Washington, D.C.: Government Printing Office), various years; *Biographical Directory of the American Congress, 1774-1971*, comp. Lawrence F. Kennedy, 92nd Cong., 1st sess., 1971, S Doc 8; *Majority and Minority Leaders of the Senate*, comp. Floyd M. Riddick, 94th Cong., 1st ses., 1975, S Doc 66; *Congressional Quarterly Weekly Report.*

# Changing Methods of Electing . . .

**Note:** The following chart shows the changing methods used by the states to elect presidential electors from 1788 to 1836. *(Additional detail, p. 345)*

| State | 1788-1789 | 1792 | 1796 | 1800 | 1804 | 1808 |
|---|---|---|---|---|---|---|
| Alabama | - | - | - | - | - | - |
| Arkansas | - | - | - | - | - | - |
| Connecticut | L | L | L | L | L | L |
| Delaware | D(3) [1] | L | L | L | L | L |
| Georgia | L | L | GT | L | L | L |
| Illinois | - | - | - | - | - | - |
| Indiana | - | - | - | - | - | - |
| Kentucky | - | D(4) | D(4) | D(4) | D(2) [2] | D(2) [2] |
| Louisiana | - | - | - | - | - | - |
| Maine | - | - | - | - | - | - |
| Maryland | GT | GT | D(10) | D(10) | D(9) [4] | D(9) [4] |
| Massachusetts | D(8) and L [6] | D(4) and L [7] | D(14) and L [8] | L | D(17) and A(2) | L |
| Michigan | - | - | - | - | - | - |
| Mississippi | - | - | - | - | - | - |
| Missouri | - | - | - | - | - | - |
| New Hampshire | GT and L [10] | GT [11] | GT and L [10] | L | GT | GT |
| New Jersey | L | L | L | L | GT | GT |
| New York | - | L | L | L | L | L |
| North Carolina | - | L [13] | D(12) | D(12) | D(14) | D(14) |
| Ohio | - | - | - | - | GT | GT |
| Pennsylvania | GT | GT | GT | L | GT | GT |
| Rhode Island | - | L | L | GT | GT | GT |
| South Carolina | L | L | L | L | L | L |
| Tennessee | - | - | E [14] | E [14] | D(5) | D(5) |
| Vermont | - | L | L | L | L | L |
| Virginia | D(12) | D(21) | D(21) | GT | GT | GT |

**Explanation of Symbols:** L—by Legislature; GT—by people, on general ticket; D—by people, in districts; A—by people, in the state at large; E—by electors. The number in parentheses following the symbol "D" is the number of districts into which the state was divided. As a rule, each district elected 1 elector. The number in parentheses following the symbol "A" is the number of electors elected at large.

1. Each qualified voter voted for 1 elector. The 3 electors who received most votes in the State were elected.
2. Each district elected 4 electors.
3. 2 districts chose 5 electors each, and 1 chose 4 electors.
4. During the years 1804-1828, Maryland chose 11 electors in 9 districts, 2 of the districts elected 2 members each.
5. 1 district chose 4 electors; 1, 3 electors; 1, 2 electors; 1, 1 elector.
6. Each of the 8 districts chose 2 electors, from which the General Court (i.e., the legislature) selected 1. It also elected 2 electors at large.
7. 2 of the districts voted for 5 members each, and 2 for 3 members each. A majority of votes was necessary for a choice. In case of a failure to elect by popular vote the General Court supplied the deficiency. In the election of 1792, the people chose 5 electors and the General Court, 11.

# ...Presidential Electors: 1788-1836

Source: Bureau of the Census, *Historical Statistics of the United States; Colonial Times to 1970* (Washington, D.C.: Government Printing Office, 1975).

| | 1812 | 1816 | 1820 | 1824 | 1828 | 1832 | 1836 |
|---|---|---|---|---|---|---|---|
| **Ala.** | - | - | L | GT | GT | GT | GT |
| **Ark.** | - | - | - | - | - | - | GT |
| **Conn.** | L | L | GT | GT | GT | GT | GT |
| **Del.** | L | L | L | L | L | GT | GT |
| **Ga.** | L | L | L | L | GT | GT | GT |
| **Ill.** | - | - | D(3) | D(3) | GT | GT | GT |
| **Ind.** | - | L | L | GT | GT | GT | GT |
| **Ky.** | D(3) [2] | D(3) [2] | D(3) [2] | D(3) [3] | GT | GT | GT |
| **La.** | L | L | L | L | GT | GT | GT |
| **Maine** | - | - | D(7) and A(2) | D(7) and A(2) | D(7) and A(2) | GT | GT |
| **Md.** | D(9) [4] | D(9) [4] | D(9) [4] | D(9) [4] | D(9) [4] | D(4) [5] | GT |
| **Mass.** | D(6) [9] | L | D(13) and A(2) | GT | GT | GT | GT |
| **Mich.** | - | - | - | - | - | - | GT |
| **Miss.** | - | - | GT | GT | GT | GT | GT |
| **Mo.** | - | - | L | D(3) | GT | GT | GT |
| **N.H.** | GT | GT | GT | GT | GT | GT | GT |
| **N.J.** | L | GT | GT | GT | GT | GT | GT |
| **N.Y.** | L | L | L | L | D(30) and E [12] | GT | GT |
| **N.C.** | L | GT | GT | GT | GT | GT | GT |
| **Ohio** | GT | GT | GT | GT | GT | GT | GT |
| **Pa.** | GT | GT | GT | GT | GT | GT | GT |
| **R.I.** | GT | GT | GT | GT | GT | GT | GT |
| **S.C.** | L | L | L | L | L | L | L |
| **Tenn.** | D(8) | D(8) | D(8) | D(11) | D(11) | GT | GT |
| **Vt.** | L | L | L | L | GT | GT | GT |
| **Va.** | GT | GT | GT | GT | GT | GT | GT |

8. *A majority of votes was necessary for a popular choice. Deficiencies were filled by the General Court, as in 1792. It also chose 2 electors at large. In 1796 it chose 9 electors, and the people, 7.*

9. *1 district chose 6 electors; 1, 5 electors; 1, 4 electors; 2, 3 electors each; and 1, 1 elector.*

10. *A majority of the popular vote was necessary for a choice. In case of a failure to elect, the legislature supplied the deficiency.*

11. *A majority of votes was necessary for a choice. In case of a failure to elect 1 or more electors a second election was held by the people, at which choice was made from the candidates in the first election who had the most votes. The*

*number of candidates in the second election was limited to twice the number of electors wanted.*

12. *1 district elected 3 electors; 2, 2 electors each; and 27, 1 elector each. The 34 electors thus elected chose 2 presidential electors.*

13. *The State was divided into 4 districts, and the members of the legislature residing in each district chose 3 electors.*

14. *In 1796 and 1800, Tennessee choose 3 presidential electors—1 each for the districts of Washington, Hamilton, and Mero. 3 "electors" for each county in the State were appointed by the legislature, and the "electors" residing in each of the 3 districts chose 1 of the 3 presidential electors.*

# Election Results, Congress and Presidency, 1860-1992

| Election Year | Congress Elected | House Members Elected Dem. | House Members Elected Rep. | House Members Elected Misc. | House Gains/Losses Dem. | House Gains/Losses Rep. | Senate Members Elected Dem. | Senate Members Elected Rep. | Senate Members Elected Misc. | Senate Gains/Losses Dem. | Senate Gains/Losses Rep. | Presidency Elected | Presidency Popular Vote Plurality |
|---|---|---|---|---|---|---|---|---|---|---|---|---|---|
| 1860 | 37th | 42 | 106 | 28 | − 59 | − 7 | 11 | 31 | 7 | −27 | + 5 | Lincoln (R) | 485,706 |
| 1862 | 38th | 80 | 103 | | + 38 | − 3 | 12 | 39 | | + 1 | + 8 | | |
| 1864 | 39th | 46 | 145 | | − 34 | + 42 | 10 | 42 | | − 2 | + 3 | Lincoln (R) | 405,581 |
| 1866 | 40th | 49 | 143 | | + 3 | − 2 | 11 | 42 | | + 1 | 0 | Johnson (R) | |
| 1868 | 41st | 73 | 170 | | + 24 | + 27 | 11 | 61 | | 0 | +19 | Grant (R) | 304,906 |
| 1870 | 42nd | 104 | 139 | | + 31 | − 31 | 17 | 57 | | + 6 | − 4 | | |
| 1872 | 43rd | 88 | 203 | | − 16 | + 64 | 19 | 54 | | + 2 | − 3 | Grant (R) | 763,474 |
| 1874 | 44th | 181 | 107 | 3 | + 93 | − 96 | 29 | 46 | | +10 | − 8 | | |
| 1876 | 45th | 156 | 137 | | − 25 | + 30 | 36 | 39 | 1 | + 7 | − 7 | Hayes (R) | −254,235 |
| 1878 | 46th | 150 | 128 | 14 | − 6 | − 9 | 43 | 33 | | + 7 | − 6 | | |
| 1880 | 47th | 130 | 152 | 11 | − 20 | + 24 | 37 | 37 | 2 | − 6 | + 4 | Garfield (R) | 1,898 |
| 1882 | 48th | 200 | 119 | 6 | + 70 | − 33 | 36 | 40 | | − 1 | + 3 | Arthur (R) | |
| 1884 | 49th | 182 | 140 | 2 | − 18 | + 21 | 34 | 41 | | − 2 | + 2 | Cleveland (D) | 25,685 |
| 1886 | 50th | 170 | 151 | 4 | − 12 | + 11 | 37 | 39 | | + 3 | − 2 | | |
| 1888 | 51st | 156 | 173 | 1 | − 14 | + 22 | 37 | 47 | | 0 | + 8 | Harrison (R) | −90,596 |
| 1890 | 52nd | 231 | 88 | 14 | + 75 | − 85 | 39 | 47 | 2 | + 2 | 0 | | |
| 1892 | 53rd | 220 | 126 | 8 | − 11 | + 38 | 44 | 38 | 3 | + 5 | − 9 | Cleveland (D) | 372,639 |
| 1894 | 54th | 104 | 246 | 7 | −116 | +120 | 30 | 44 | 5 | − 5 | + 6 | | |
| 1896 | 55th | 134 | 206 | 16 | + 30 | − 40 | 34 | 46 | 10 | − 5 | + 2 | McKinley (R) | 596,985 |
| 1898 | 56th | 163 | 185 | 9 | + 29 | − 21 | 26 | 53 | 11 | − 8 | + 7 | | |
| 1900 | 57th | 153 | 198 | 5 | − 10 | + 13 | 29 | 56 | 3 | + 3 | + 3 | McKinley (R) | 859,694 |
| 1902 | 58th | 178 | 207 | | + 25 | + 9 | 32 | 58 | | + 3 | + 2 | Roosevelt (R) | |
| 1904 | 59th | 136 | 250 | | − 42 | + 43 | 32 | 58 | | 0 | 0 | Roosevelt (R) | 2,543,695 |
| 1906 | 60th | 164 | 222 | | + 28 | − 28 | 29 | 61 | | − 3 | − 3 | | |
| 1908 | 61st | 172 | 219 | | + 8 | − 3 | 32 | 59 | | + 3 | − 2 | Taft (R) | 1,269,457 |
| 1910 | 62nd | 228 | 162 | 1 | + 56 | − 57 | 42 | 49 | | +10 | −10 | | |
| 1912 | 63rd | 290 | 127 | 18 | + 62 | − 35 | 51 | 44 | 1 | + 9 | − 5 | Wilson (D) | 2,173,945 |
| 1914 | 64th | 231 | 193 | 8 | − 59 | + 66 | 56 | 39 | 1 | + 5 | − 5 | | |
| 1916 | 65th | 210 | 216 | 9 | − 21 | + 23 | 53 | 42 | 1 | − 3 | + 3 | Wilson (D) | 579,511 |
| 1918 | 66th | 191 | 237 | 7 | − 19 | + 21 | 47 | 48 | 1 | − 6 | + 6 | | |
| 1920 | 67th | 132 | 300 | 1 | − 59 | + 63 | 37 | 59 | | −10 | +11 | Harding (R) | 7,020,023 |
| 1922 | 68th | 207 | 225 | 3 | + 75 | − 75 | 43 | 51 | 2 | + 6 | − 8 | Coolidge (R) | |
| 1924 | 69th | 183 | 247 | 5 | − 24 | + 22 | 40 | 54 | 1 | − 3 | + 3 | Coolidge (R) | 7,333,217 |
| 1926 | 70th | 195 | 237 | 3 | + 12 | − 10 | 47 | 48 | 1 | + 7 | − 6 | | |
| 1928 | 71st | 167 | 267 | 1 | − 28 | + 30 | 39 | 56 | 1 | − 8 | + 8 | Hoover (R) | 6,429,579 |
| 1930 | 72nd | 220 | 214 | 1 | + 53 | − 53 | 47 | 48 | 1 | + 8 | − 8 | | |
| 1932 | 73rd | 313 | 117 | 5 | + 97 | −101 | 59 | 36 | 1 | +12 | −12 | Roosevelt (D) | 7,068,817 |
| 1934 | 74th | 322 | 103 | 10 | + 9 | − 14 | 69 | 25 | 2 | +10 | −11 | | |
| 1936 | 75th | 333 | 89 | 13 | + 11 | − 14 | 75 | 17 | 4 | + 6 | − 8 | Roosevelt (D) | 11,073,102 |
| 1938 | 76th | 262 | 169 | 4 | − 71 | + 80 | 69 | 23 | 4 | − 6 | + 6 | | |
| 1940 | 77th | 267 | 162 | 6 | + 5 | − 7 | 66 | 28 | 2 | − 3 | + 5 | Roosevelt (D) | 4,964,561 |
| 1942 | 78th | 222 | 209 | 4 | − 45 | + 47 | 57 | 38 | 1 | − 9 | +10 | | |
| 1944 | 79th | 243 | 190 | 2 | + 21 | − 19 | 57 | 38 | 1 | 0 | 0 | Roosevelt (D) | 3,594,993 |
| 1946 | 80th | 188 | 246 | 1 | − 55 | + 56 | 45 | 51 | | −12 | +13 | Truman (D) | |
| 1948 | 81st | 263 | 171 | 1 | + 75 | − 75 | 54 | 42 | | + 9 | − 9 | Truman (D) | 2,188,054 |
| 1950 | 82nd | 234 | 199 | 2 | − 29 | + 28 | 48 | 47 | 1 | − 6 | + 5 | | |
| 1952 | 83rd | 213 | 221 | 1 | − 21 | + 22 | 47 | 48 | 1 | − 1 | + 1 | Eisenhower (R) | 6,621,242 |
| 1954 | 84th | 232 | 203 | | + 19 | − 18 | 48 | 47 | 1 | + 1 | − 1 | | |
| 1956 | 85th | 234 | 201 | | + 2 | − 2 | 49 | 47 | | + 1 | 0 | Eisenhower (R) | 9,567,720 |
| 1958 | 86th | 283 | 154 | | + 49 | − 47 | 64 | 34 | | +17 | −13 | | |
| 1960 | 87th | 263 | 174 | | − 20 | + 20 | 64 | 36 | | − 2 | + 2 | Kennedy (D) | 118,574[1] |
| 1962 | 88th | 258 | 176 | 1[2] | − 4 | + 2 | 67 | 33 | | + 4 | − 4 | | |
| 1964 | 89th | 295 | 140 | | + 38 | − 38 | 68 | 32 | | + 2 | − 2 | Johnson (D) | 15,951,378 |
| 1966 | 90th | 248 | 187 | | − 47 | + 47 | 64 | 36 | | − 3 | + 3 | | |
| 1968 | 91st | 243 | 192 | | − 4 | + 4 | 58 | 42 | | − 5 | + 5 | Nixon (R) | 510,314 |
| 1970 | 92nd | 255 | 180 | | + 12 | − 12 | 55 | 45 | | − 4 | + 2 | | |
| 1972 | 93rd | 243 | 192 | | − 12 | + 12 | 57 | 43 | | + 2 | − 2 | Nixon (R) | 17,999,528 |
| 1974 | 94th | 291 | 144 | | + 43 | − 43 | 61 | 38 | | + 3 | − 3 | | |
| 1976 | 95th | 292 | 143 | | + 1 | − 1 | 62 | 38 | | 0 | 0 | Carter (D) | 1,682,970 |
| 1978 | 96th | 277 | 158 | | − 11 | + 11 | 59 | 41 | | − 3 | + 3 | | |
| 1980 | 97th | 243 | 192 | | − 33 | + 33 | 47 | 53 | | −12 | +12 | Reagan (R) | 8,420,270 |
| 1982 | 98th | 269 | 166 | | + 26 | − 26 | 46 | 54 | | 0 | 0 | | |
| 1984 | 99th | 253 | 182 | | − 14 | + 14 | 47 | 53 | | + 2 | − 2 | Reagan (R) | 16,877,890 |
| 1986 | 100th | 258 | 177 | | + 5 | − 5 | 55 | 45 | | + 8 | − 8 | | |
| 1988 | 101st | 260 | 175 | | − 3 | − 3 | 55 | 45 | | + 1 | − 1 | Bush (R) | 7,077,023 |
| 1990 | 102nd | 267 | 165 | 1 | + 9 | − 8 | 56 | 44 | | + 1 | − 1 | | |
| 1992 | 103rd | 258 | 176 | 1 | − 10 | + 10 | 57 | 43 | | 0 | 0 | Clinton (D) | 5,805,444 |

1. Includes divided Alabama elector slate votes.
2. Vacancy — Rep. Clem Miller, D-Calif. (1959-62) died Oct. 6, 1962, but his name remained on the ballot and he received a plurality.

# Distribution of House Seats and Electoral Votes

*(Based on Censuses of 1950, 1960, 1970, 1980 and 1990)*

| State | U.S. House Seats | | | | | | | | Electoral Votes | | | | |
|---|---|---|---|---|---|---|---|---|---|---|---|---|---|
| | 1953-1963 | 1960 Census Changes | 1963-1973 | 1970 Census Changes | 1973-1983 | 1980 Census Changes | 1983-1993 | 1990 Census Changes | 1993-2003 | 1952, 1956, 1960 | 1964, 1968 | 1972, 1976, 1980 | 1984, 1988 | 1992, 1996, 2000 |
| Alabama | 9 | −1 | 8 | −1 | 7 | — | 7 | — | 7 | 11 | 10 | 9 | 9 | 9 |
| Alaska | 1 | — | 1 | — | 1 | — | 1 | — | 1 | 3 | 3 | 3 | 3 | 3 |
| Arizona | 2 | +1 | 3 | +1 | 4 | +1 | 5 | +1 | 6 | 4 | 5 | 6 | 7 | 8 |
| Arkansas | 6 | −2 | 4 | — | 4 | — | 4 | — | 4 | 8 | 6 | 6 | 6 | 6 |
| California | 30 | +8 | 38 | +5 | 43 | +2 | 45 | +7 | 52 | 32 | 40 | 45 | 47 | 54 |
| Colorado | 4 | — | 4 | +1 | 5 | +1 | 6 | — | 6 | 6 | 6 | 7 | 8 | 8 |
| Connecticut | 6 | — | 6 | — | 6 | — | 6 | — | 6 | 8 | 8 | 8 | 8 | 8 |
| Delaware | 1 | — | 1 | — | 1 | — | 1 | — | 1 | 3 | 3 | 3 | 3 | 3 |
| District of Columbia | — | — | — | — | — | — | — | — | — | — | 3 | 3 | 3 | 3 |
| Florida | 8 | +4 | 12 | +3 | 15 | +4 | 19 | +4 | 23 | 10 | 14 | 17 | 21 | 25 |
| Georgia | 10 | — | 10 | — | 10 | — | 10 | +1 | 11 | 12 | 12 | 12 | 12 | 13 |
| Hawaii | 1 | +1 | 2 | — | 2 | — | 2 | — | 2 | 3 | 4 | 4 | 4 | 4 |
| Idaho | 2 | — | 2 | — | 2 | — | 2 | — | 2 | 4 | 4 | 4 | 4 | 4 |
| Illinois | 25 | −1 | 24 | — | 24 | −2 | 22 | −2 | 20 | 27 | 26 | 26 | 24 | 22 |
| Indiana | 11 | — | 11 | — | 11 | −1 | 10 | — | 10 | 13 | 13 | 13 | 12 | 12 |
| Iowa | 8 | −1 | 7 | −1 | 6 | — | 6 | −1 | 5 | 10 | 9 | 8 | 8 | 7 |
| Kansas | 6 | −1 | 5 | — | 5 | — | 5 | −1 | 4 | 8 | 7 | 7 | 7 | 6 |
| Kentucky | 8 | −1 | 7 | — | 7 | — | 7 | −1 | 6 | 10 | 9 | 9 | 9 | 8 |
| Louisiana | 8 | — | 8 | — | 8 | — | 8 | −1 | 7 | 10 | 10 | 10 | 10 | 9 |
| Maine | 3 | −1 | 2 | — | 2 | — | 2 | — | 2 | 5 | 4 | 4 | 4 | 4 |
| Maryland | 7 | +1 | 8 | — | 8 | — | 8 | — | 8 | 9 | 10 | 10 | 10 | 10 |
| Massachusetts | 14 | −2 | 12 | — | 12 | −1 | 11 | −1 | 10 | 16 | 14 | 14 | 13 | 12 |
| Michigan | 18 | +1 | 19 | — | 19 | −1 | 18 | −2 | 16 | 20 | 21 | 21 | 20 | 18 |
| Minnesota | 9 | −1 | 8 | — | 8 | — | 8 | — | 8 | 11 | 10 | 10 | 10 | 10 |
| Mississippi | 6 | −1 | 5 | — | 5 | — | 5 | — | 5 | 8 | 7 | 7 | 7 | 7 |
| Missouri | 11 | −1 | 10 | — | 10 | −1 | 9 | — | 9 | 13 | 12 | 12 | 11 | 11 |
| Montana | 2 | — | 2 | — | 2 | — | 2 | −1 | 1 | 4 | 4 | 4 | 4 | 3 |
| Nebraska | 4 | −1 | 3 | — | 3 | — | 3 | — | 3 | 6 | 5 | 5 | 5 | 5 |
| Nevada | 1 | — | 1 | — | 1 | +1 | 2 | — | 2 | 3 | 3 | 3 | 4 | 4 |
| New Hampshire | 2 | — | 2 | — | 2 | — | 2 | — | 2 | 4 | 4 | 4 | 4 | 4 |
| New Jersey | 14 | +1 | 15 | — | 15 | −1 | 14 | −1 | 13 | 16 | 17 | 17 | 16 | 15 |
| New Mexico | 2 | — | 2 | — | 2 | +1 | 3 | — | 3 | 4 | 4 | 4 | 5 | 5 |
| New York | 43 | −2 | 41 | −2 | 39 | −5 | 34 | −3 | 31 | 45 | 43 | 41 | 36 | 33 |
| North Carolina | 12 | −1 | 11 | — | 11 | — | 11 | +1 | 12 | 14 | 13 | 13 | 13 | 14 |
| North Dakota | 2 | — | 2 | −1 | 1 | — | 1 | — | 1 | 4 | 4 | 3 | 3 | 3 |
| Ohio | 23 | +1 | 24 | −1 | 23 | −2 | 21 | −2 | 19 | 25 | 26 | 25 | 23 | 21 |
| Oklahoma | 6 | — | 6 | — | 6 | — | 6 | — | 6 | 8 | 8 | 8 | 8 | 8 |
| Oregon | 4 | — | 4 | — | 4 | +1 | 5 | — | 5 | 6 | 6 | 6 | 7 | 7 |
| Pennsylvania | 30 | −3 | 27 | −2 | 25 | −2 | 23 | −2 | 21 | 32 | 29 | 27 | 25 | 23 |
| Rhode Island | 2 | — | 2 | — | 2 | — | 2 | — | 2 | 4 | 4 | 4 | 4 | 4 |
| South Carolina | 6 | — | 6 | — | 6 | — | 6 | — | 6 | 8 | 8 | 8 | 8 | 8 |
| South Dakota | 2 | — | 2 | — | 2 | −1 | 1 | — | 1 | 4 | 4 | 4 | 3 | 3 |
| Tennessee | 9 | — | 9 | −1 | 8 | +1 | 9 | — | 9 | 11 | 11 | 10 | 11 | 11 |
| Texas | 22 | +1 | 23 | +1 | 24 | +3 | 27 | +3 | 30 | 24 | 25 | 26 | 29 | 32 |
| Utah | 2 | — | 2 | — | 2 | +1 | 3 | — | 3 | 4 | 4 | 4 | 5 | 5 |
| Vermont | 1 | — | 1 | — | 1 | — | 1 | — | 1 | 3 | 3 | 3 | 3 | 3 |
| Virginia | 10 | — | 10 | — | 10 | — | 10 | +1 | 11 | 12 | 12 | 12 | 12 | 13 |
| Washington | 7 | — | 7 | — | 7 | +1 | 8 | +1 | 9 | 9 | 9 | 9 | 10 | 11 |
| West Virginia | 6 | −1 | 5 | −1 | 4 | — | 4 | −1 | 3 | 8 | 7 | 6 | 6 | 5 |
| Wisconsin | 10 | — | 10 | −1 | 9 | — | 9 | — | 9 | 12 | 12 | 11 | 11 | 11 |
| Wyoming | 1 | — | 1 | — | 1 | — | 1 | — | 1 | 3 | 3 | 3 | 3 | 3 |

# Constitutional Provisions and Amendments on Elections

## Article I

### Section 2:

The House of Representatives shall be composed of Members chosen every second Year by the People of the several States, and the Electors in each State shall have the Qualifications requisite for Electors of the most numerous Branch of the State Legislature.

No Person shall be a Representative who shall not have attained to the age of twenty five Years, and been seven Years a Citizen of the United States, and who shall not, when elected, be an Inhabitant of that State in which he shall be chosen.

Representatives and direct Taxes shall be apportioned among the several States which may be included within this Union, according to their respective Numbers, which shall be determined by adding to the whole Number of free Persons, including those bound to Service for a Term of Years, and excluding Indians not taxed, three fifths of all other Persons. The actual Enumeration shall be made within three Years after the first Meeting of the Congress of the United States, and within every subsequent Term of ten Years, in such Manner as they shall by Law direct. The number of Representatives shall not exceed one for every thirty Thousand, but each State shall have at Least one Representative; and until such enumeration shall be made, the State of New Hampshire shall be entitled to chuse three, Massachusetts eight, Rhode-Island and Providence Plantations one, Connecticut five, New-York six, New Jersey four, Pennsylvania eight, Delaware one, Maryland six, Virginia ten, North Carolina five, South Carolina five, and Georgia three.

When vacancies happen in the Representation from any State, the Executive Authority thereof shall issue Writs of Election to fill such Vacancies....

### Section 3:

The Senate of the United States shall be composed of two Senators from each State, chosen by the Legislature thereof, for six Years; and each Senator shall have one Vote.

Immediately after they shall be assembled in Consequence of the first Election, they shall be divided as equally as may be into three Classes. The Seats of the Senators of the first Class shall be vacated at the Expiration of the second Year, of the second Class at the Expiration of the fourth Year, and of the third Class at the Expiration of the sixth Year, so that one third may be chosen every second Year; and if Vacancies happen by Resignation, or pointments until the next Meeting of the Legislature, which shall then fill such Vacancies.

No Person shall be a Senator who shall not have attained to the Age of thirty Years, and been nine Years a Citizen of the United States, and who shall not, when elected, be an Inhabitant of that State for which he shall be chosen....

### Section 4:

The Times, Places and Manner of holding Elections for Senators and Representatives, shall be prescribed in each State by the Legislature thereof; but the Congress may at any time by Law make or alter such Regulations, except as to the Places of chusing Senators.

The Congress shall assemble at least once in every Year, and such Meeting shall be on the first Monday in December, unless they shall by Law appoint a different Day.

### Section 5:

Each House shall be the Judge of the Elections, Returns and Qualifications of its own Members, and a Majority of each shall constitute a Quorum to do Business; but a smaller Number may adjourn from day to day, and may be authorized to compel the Attendance of absent Members, in such Manner, and under such Penalties as each House may provide....

## Article II

### Section 1:

The executive Power shall be vested in a President of the United States of America. He shall hold his Office during the Term of four Years, and, together with the Vice President, chosen for the same Term, be elected, as follows:

Each State shall appoint, in such Manner as the Legislature thereof may direct, a Number of Electors, equal to the whole Number of Senators and Representatives to which the State may be entitled in the Congress: but no Senator or Representative, or Person holding an Office of Trust or Profit under the United States, shall be appointed an Elector.

[The Electors shall meet in their respective States, and vote by Ballot for two Persons, of whom one at least shall not be an Inhabitant of the same State with themselves. And they shall make a List of all the Persons voted for, and of the Number of Votes for each; which List they shall sign and certify, and transmit sealed to the Seat of the Government of the United States, directed to the President of the Senate. The President of the Senate shall, in the Presence of the Senate and House of Representatives, open all the Certificates, and the Votes shall then be counted. The Person having the greatest Number of Votes shall be the President, if such Number be a Majority of the whole Number of Electors appointed; and if there be more than one who have such Majority, and have an equal Number of Votes, then the House of Representatives shall immediately chuse by Ballot one of them for President; and if no Person have a Majority, then from the five highest on the List the said House shall in like Manner chuse the President. But in chusing the President, the Votes shall be taken by States, the Representation from each State having one Vote; a quorum for this Purpose shall consist of a Member or Members from two thirds of the States, and a Majority of all the States shall be necessary to a Choice. In every Case, after the Choice of the President, the Person having the greatest Number of Votes of the Electors shall be the Vice President. But if there should remain two or more who have equal Votes, the Senate shall chuse from them by Ballot the Vice-President.]*

The Congress may determine the Time of chusing the Electors, and the Day on which they shall give their Votes; which Day shall be the same throughout the United States.

No person except a natural born Citizen, or a Citizen of the United States, at the time of the Adoption of this Constitution, shall be eligible to the Office of President; neither shall any person be eligible to that Office who shall not have attained to the Age of thirty five Years, and been fourteen Years a Resident within the United States.

In Case of the Removal of the President from Office, or of his Death, Resignation, or Inability to discharge the Powers and Duties of the said Office, the Same shall devolve on the Vice President, and the Congress may by Law provide for the Case of Removal, Death, Resignation or Inability, both of the President and Vice President, declaring what Officer shall then act as President, and such Officer shall act accordingly, until the Disability be removed, or a President shall be elected....

## Amendment XII

(Ratified July 27, 1804)

The Electors shall meet in their respective states and vote by ballot for President and Vice-President, one of whom, at least, shall not be an inhabitant of the same state with themselves; they shall name in their ballots the person voted for as President, and in distinct ballots the person voted for as Vice-President, and they shall make distinct lists of all persons voted for as President, and of all persons voted for as Vice-President, and of the number of votes for each, which lists they shall sign and certify, and transmit sealed to the seat of the government of the United States, directed to the President of the Senate;—The President of the Senate shall, in the presence of the Senate and House of Representatives, open all the certificates and the votes shall then be counted;—The person having the greatest number of votes for President, shall be the President, if such number be a majority of the whole number of Electors appointed; and if no person have such majority, then from

the persons having the highest numbers not exceeding three on the list of those voted for as President, the House of Representatives shall choose immediately, by ballot, the President. But in choosing the President, the votes shall be taken by states, the representation from each state having one vote; a quorum for this purpose shall consist of a member or members from two-thirds of the states, and a majority of all the states shall be necessary to a choice. [And if the House of Representatives shall not choose a President whenever the right of choice shall devolve upon them, before the fourth day of March next following, then the Vice-President shall act as President, as in the case of the death or other constitutional disability of the President.—]† The person having the greatest number of votes as Vice-President, shall be the Vice-President, if such number be a majority of the whole number of Electors appointed, and if no person have a majority, then from the two highest numbers on the list, the Senate shall choose the Vice President; a quorum for the purpose shall consist of two-thirds of the whole number of Senators, and a majority of the whole number shall be necessary to a choice. But no person constitutionally ineligible to the office of President shall be eligible to that of Vice-President of the United States.

## Amendment XIV

(Ratified July 9, 1868)

### Section 2:

Representatives shall be apportioned among the several States according to their respective numbers, counting the whole number of persons in each State, excluding Indians not taxed. But when the right to vote at any election for the choice of electors for President and Vice President of the United States, Representatives in Congress, the Executive and Judicial officers of a State, or the members of the Legislature thereof, is denied to any of the male inhabitants of such State, being twenty-one years of age, and citizens of the United States, or in any way abridged, except for participation in rebellion, or other crime, the basis of representation therein shall be reduced in the proportion which the number of such male citizens shall bear to the whole number of male citizens twenty-one years of age in such State.

### Section 3:

No person shall be a Senator or Representative in Congress, or elector of President and Vice President, or hold any office, civil or military, under the United States, or under any State, who, having previously taken an oath, as a member of Congress, or as an officer of the United States, or as a member of any State legislature, or as an executive or judicial officer of any State, to support the Constitution of the United States, shall have engaged in insurrection or rebellion against the same, or given aid or comfort to the enemies thereof. But Congress may by a vote of two-thirds of each House, remove such disability.

## Amendment XV

(Ratified February 3, 1870)

### Section 1:

The right of citizens of the United States to vote shall not be denied or abridged by the United States or by any State on account of race, color, or previous condition of servitude.

### Section 2:

The Congress shall have power to enforce this article by appropriate legislation.

*Superseded by the 12th Amendment.*
*† Changed to Jan. 20 by the 20th Amendment, ratified in 1933.*

## Amendment XVII
(Ratified April 8, 1913)

The Senate of the United States shall be composed of two Senators from each State, elected by the people thereof, for six years; and each Senator shall have one vote. The electors in each State shall have the qualifications requisite for electors of the most numerous branch of the State legislatures.

When vacancies happen in the representation of any State in the Senate, the executive authority of such State shall issue writs of election to fill such vacancies: *Provided*, That the legislature of any State may empower the executive thereof to make temporary appointments until the people fill the vacancies by election as the legislature may direct.

This amendment shall not be so construed as to affect the election or term of any Senator chosen before it becomes valid as part of the Constitution.

## Amendment XIX
(Ratified August 18, 1920)

The right of citizens of the United States to vote shall not be denied or abridged by the United States or by any State on account of sex.

Congress shall have power to enforce this article by appropriate legislation.

## Amendment XX
(Ratified January 23, 1933)

### Section 1:
The terms of the President and Vice President shall end at noon on the 20th day of January, and the terms of Senators and Representatives at noon on the 3d day of January, of the years in which such terms would have ended if this article had not been ratified; and the terms of their successors shall then begin.

### Section 2:
The Congress shall assemble at least once in every year, and such meeting shall begin at noon on the 3d day of January, unless they shall by law appoint a different day.

### Section 3:
If, at the time fixed for the beginning of the term of the President, the President elect shall have died, the Vice President elect shall become President. If a President shall not have been chosen before the time fixed for the beginning of his term, or if the President elect shall have failed to qualify, then the Vice President elect shall act as President until a President shall have qualified; and the Congress may by law provide for the case wherein neither a President elect nor a Vice President elect shall have qualified, declaring who shall then act as President, or the manner in which one who is to act shall be selected, and such person shall act accordingly until a President or Vice President shall have qualified.

### Section 4:
The Congress may by law provide for the case of the death of any of the persons from whom the House of Representatives may choose a President whenever the right of choice shall have devolved upon them, and for the case of the death of any of the persons from whom the Senate may choose a Vice President whenever the right of choice shall have devolved upon them.

### Section 5:
Sections 1 and 2 shall take effect on the 15th day of October following the ratification of this article.

## Amendment XXII
(Ratified February 27, 1951)

### Section 1:
No person shall be elected to the office of the President more than twice, and no person who has held the office of President, or acted as President, for more than two years of a term to which some other person was elected President shall be elected to the office of the President more than once. But this Article shall not apply to any person holding the office of President, when this Article was proposed by the Congress, and shall not prevent any person who may be holding the office of President, or acting as President, during the term within which this Article becomes operative from holding the office of President or acting as President during the remainder of such term.

## Amendment XXIII
(Ratified March 29, 1961)

### Section 1:
The District constituting the seat of Government of the United States shall appoint in such manner as the Congress may direct:

A number of electors of President and Vice President equal to the whole number of Senators and Representatives in Congress to which the District would be entitled if it were a State, but in no event more than the least populous State; they shall be in addition to those appointed by the States, but they shall be considered, for the purposes of the election of President and Vice President, to be electors appointed by a State; and they shall meet in the District and perform such duties as provided by the twelfth article of amendment.

## Amendment XXIV
(Ratified January 23, 1964)

### Section 1:
The right of citizens of the United States to vote in any primary or other election for President or Vice President, for electors for President or Vice President, or for Senator or Representative in Congress, shall not be denied or abridged by the United States or any State by reason of failure to pay any poll tax or other tax.

## Amendment XXV
(Ratified February 10, 1967)

### Section 1:
In case of the removal of the President from office or of his death or resignation, the Vice President shall become President.

### Section 2:
Whenever there is a vacancy in the office of the Vice President, the President shall nominate a Vice President who shall take office upon confirmation by a majority vote of both Houses of Congress.

### Section 3:
Whenever the President transmits to the President pro tempore of the Senate and the Speaker of the House of Representatives his written declaration that he is unable to discharge the powers and duties of his office, and until he transmits to them a written declaration to the contrary, such powers and duties shall be discharged by the Vice President as Acting President.

### Section 4:
Whenever the Vice President and a majority of either the principal officers of the executive departments or of such other body as Congress may by law provide, transmit

to the President pro tempore of the Senate and the Speaker of the House of Representatives their written declaration that the President is unable to discharge the powers and duties of his office, the Vice President shall immediately assume the powers and duties of the office as Acting President.

Thereafter, when the President transmits to the President pro tempore of the Senate and the Speaker of the House of Representatives his written declaration that no inability exists, he shall resume the powers and duties of his office unless the Vice President and a majority of either the principal officers of the executive department or of such other body as Congress may by law provide, transmit within four days to the President pro tempore of the Senate and the Speaker of the House of Representatives their written declaration that the President is unable to discharge the powers and duties of his office. Thereupon

Congress shall decide the issue, assembling within forty-eight hours for that purpose if not in session. If the Congress, within twenty-one days after receipt of the latter written declaration, or, if Congress is not in session, within twenty-one days after Congress is required to assemble, determines by two-thirds vote of both Houses that the President is unable to discharge the powers and duties of his office, the Vice President shall continue to discharge the same as Acting President; otherwise, the President shall resume the powers and duties of his office.

## Amendment XXVI
(Ratified July 1, 1971)
### Section 1:
The right of citizens of the United States, who are eighteen years of age or older, to vote shall not be denied or abridged by the United States or by any State on account of age.

# Population of the United States . . .

| | 1790 | 1800 | 1810 | 1820 | 1830 | 1840 | 1850 | 1860 | 1870 | 1880 | 1890 |
|---|---|---|---|---|---|---|---|---|---|---|---|
| Ala. | - | 1,250[1] | 9,046[1] | 127,901 | 309,527 | 590,756 | 771,623 | 964,201 | 996,992 | 1,262,505 | 1,513,401 |
| Alaska | - | - | - | - | - | - | - | - | - | 33,426 | 32,052 |
| Ariz. | - | - | - | - | - | - | - | - | 9,658 | 40,440 | 88,243 |
| Ark. | - | - | 1,062 | 14,273 | 30,388 | 97,574 | 209,897 | 435,450 | 484,471 | 802,525 | 1,128,211 |
| Calif. | - | - | - | - | - | - | 92,597 | 379,994 | 560,247 | 864,694 | 1,213,398 |
| Colo. | - | - | - | - | - | - | - | 34,277 | 39,864 | 194,327 | 413,249 |
| Conn. | 237,946 | 251,002 | 261,942 | 275,248 | 297,675 | 309,978 | 370,792 | 460,147 | 537,454 | 622,700 | 746,258 |
| Del. | 59,096 | 64,273 | 72,674 | 72,749 | 76,748 | 78,085 | 91,532 | 112,216 | 125,015 | 146,608 | 168,493 |
| D.C. | - | 8,144 | 15,471 | 23,336 | 30,261 | 33,745 | 51,687 | 75,080 | 131,700 | 177,624 | 230,392 |
| Fla. | - | - | - | - | 34,730 | 54,477 | 87,445 | 140,424 | 187,748 | 269,493 | 391,422 |
| Ga. | 82,548 | 162,686 | 252,433 | 340,989 | 516,823 | 691,392 | 906,185 | 1,057,286 | 1,184,109 | 1,542,180 | 1,837,353 |
| Hawaii | - | - | - | - | - | - | - | - | - | - | - |
| Idaho | - | - | - | - | - | - | - | - | 14,999 | 32,610 | 88,548 |
| Ill. | - | - | 12,282[3] | 55,211 | 157,445 | 476,183 | 851,470 | 1,711,951 | 2,539,891 | 3,077,871 | 3,826,352 |
| Ind. | - | 5,641[4] | 24,520[4] | 147,178 | 343,031 | 685,866 | 988,416 | 1,350,428 | 1,680,637 | 1,978,301 | 2,192,404 |
| Iowa | - | - | - | - | - | 43,112[5] | 192,214 | 674,913 | 1,194,020 | 1,624,615 | 1,912,297 |
| Kan. | - | - | - | - | - | - | - | 107,206 | 364,399 | 996,096 | 1,428,108 |
| Ky. | 73,677 | 220,955 | 406,511 | 564,317 | 687,917 | 779,828 | 982,405 | 1,155,684 | 1,321,011 | 1,648,690 | 1,858,635 |
| La. | - | - | 76,556 | 153,407 | 215,739 | 352,411 | 517,762 | 708,002 | 726,915 | 939,946 | 1,118,588 |
| Maine | 96,540 | 151,719 | 228,705 | 298,335 | 399,455 | 501,793 | 583,169 | 628,279 | 626,915 | 648,936 | 661,086 |
| Md. | 319,728 | 341,548 | 380,546 | 407,350 | 447,040 | 470,019 | 583,034 | 687,049 | 780,894 | 934,943 | 1,042,390 |
| Mass. | 378,787 | 422,845 | 472,040 | 523,287 | 610,408 | 737,699 | 994,514 | 1,231,066 | 1,457,351 | 1,783,085 | 2,238,947 |
| Mich. | - | - | 4,762[6] | 8,896[6] | 31,639[6] | 212,267 | 397,654 | 749,113 | 1,184,059 | 1,636,937 | 2,093,890 |
| Minn. | - | - | - | - | - | - | - | 6,077 | 172,023 | 439,706 | 780,773 | 1,310,283 |
| Miss. | - | 7,600[7] | 31,306[7] | 75,448 | 136,621 | 375,651 | 606,526 | 791,305 | 827,922 | 1,131,597 | 1,289,600 |
| Mo. | - | - | 19,783 | 66,586 | 140,455 | 383,702 | 682,044 | 1,182,012 | 1,721,295 | 2,168,380 | 2,679,185 |
| Mont. | - | - | - | - | - | - | - | - | 20,595 | 39,159 | 142,924 |
| Neb. | - | - | - | - | - | - | - | 28,841 | 122,993 | 452,402 | 1,062,656 |
| Nev. | - | - | - | - | - | - | - | 6,857[8] | 42,491 | 62,266 | 47,355 |
| N.H. | 141,885 | 183,858 | 214,460 | 244,161 | 269,328 | 284,574 | 317,976 | 326,073 | 318,300 | 346,991 | 376,530 |
| N.J. | 184,139 | 211,149 | 245,562 | 277,575 | 320,823 | 373,306 | 489,555 | 672,035 | 906,096 | 1,131,116 | 1,444,933 |
| N.M. | - | - | - | - | - | - | 61,547[9] | 93,516[9] | 91,874 | 119,565 | 160,282 |
| N.Y. | 340,120 | 589,051 | 959,049 | 1,372,812 | 1,918,608 | 2,428,921 | 3,097,394 | 3,880,735 | 4,382,759 | 5,082,871 | 6,003,174 |
| N.C. | 393,751 | 478,103 | 555,500 | 638,829 | 737,987 | 753,419 | 869,039 | 992,622 | 1,071,361 | 1,399,750 | 1,617,949 |
| N.D. | - | - | - | - | - | - | - | - | 4,837[10] | 2,405 | 36,909 | 190,983 |
| Ohio | - | 45,365[11] | 230,760 | 581,434 | 937,903 | 1,519,467 | 1,980,329 | 2,339,511 | 2,665,260 | 3,198,062 | 3,672,329 |
| Okla. | - | - | - | - | - | - | - | - | - | - | 258,657 |
| Ore. | - | - | - | - | - | - | 12,093 | 52,465 | 90,923 | 174,768 | 317,704 |
| Pa. | 434,373 | 602,365 | 810,091 | 1,049,458 | 1,348,233 | 1,724,033 | 2,311,786 | 2,906,215 | 3,521,951 | 4,282,891 | 5,258,113 |
| Puerto Rico | - | - | - | - | - | - | - | - | - | - | - |
| R.I. | 68,825 | 69,122 | 76,931 | 83,059 | 97,199 | 108,830 | 147,545 | 174,620 | 217,353 | 276,531 | 345,506 |
| S.C. | 249,073 | 345,591 | 415,115 | 502,741 | 581,185 | 594,398 | 688,507 | 703,708 | 705,606 | 995,577 | 1,151,149 |
| S.D. | - | - | - | - | - | - | - | - | 4,837[10] | 11,776 | 98,268 | 348,600 |
| Tenn. | 35,691 | 105,602 | 261,727 | 422,823 | 681,904 | 829,210 | 1,002,717 | 1,109,801 | 1,258,520 | 1,542,359 | 1,767,518 |
| Texas | - | - | - | - | - | - | 212,592 | 604,215 | 818,579 | 1,591,749 | 2,235,527 |
| Utah | - | - | - | - | - | - | 11,380 | 40,273[13] | 86,786 | 143,963 | 210,779 |
| Vt. | 85,425 | 154,465 | 217,895 | 235,981 | 280,652 | 291,948 | 314,120 | 315,098 | 330,551 | 332,286 | 332,422 |
| Va. | 691,737 | 807,557 | 877,683 | 938,261 | 1,044,054 | 1,025,227 | 1,119,348 | 1,219,630 | 1,225,163 | 1,512,565 | 1,655,980 |
| Wash. | - | - | - | - | - | - | - | 1,201 | 11,594[14] | 23,955 | 75,116 | 357,232 |
| W.Va. | 55,873 | 78,592 | 105,469 | 136,808 | 176,924 | 224,537 | 302,313 | 376,688 | 442,014 | 618,457 | 762,794 |
| Wis. | - | - | - | - | - | 30,945[15] | 305,391 | 775,881 | 1,054,670 | 1,315,497 | 1,693,330 |
| Wyo. | - | - | - | - | - | - | - | - | - | 9,118 | 20,789 | 62,555 |
| **Total** | 3,929,214 | 5,308,483 | 7,239,881 | 9,638,453 | 12,866,020[16] | 17,069,453[16] | 23,191,876 | 31,443,321 | 38,558,371 | 50,189,209 | 62,979,766[17] |

1. *Alabama. Population of those parts of Mississippi Territory now in Alabama.*
2. *Alaska. 1940 Census taken as of Oct. 1, 1939; 1930 Census, as of Oct. 1, 1929.*
3. *Illinois. Population of Illinois Territory, which comprised area constituting State of Illinois, almost all of Wisconsin, the western part of the upper peninsula of Michigan and the northeastern part of Minnesota.*
4. *Indiana. 1810 figure includes population of area separated in 1816; 1800 figure includes population (3,124) of those portions of Indiana Territory which were taken to form Michigan and Illinois Territories in 1805 and 1809, respectively, and that portion which was separated in 1816.*
5. *Iowa. Includes population of area constituting that part of Minnesota lying west of the Mississippi River and a line drawn from it source northwards to the Canadian boundary.*
6. *Michigan. Population of Michigan Territory as then constituted; boundaries changed in 1816, 1818, 1834 and 1836.*
7. *Mississippi. Population of those parts of present state included in Mississippi Territory as then constituted.*
8. *Nevada. Population of Nevada Territory as organized in 1861.*
9. *New Mexico. 1860 figure includes population of area taken to form part of Arizona Territory in 1863. 1850 figure is for Territory of New Mexico which included greater parts of present states of Arizona and New Mexico and smaller parts of Colorado and Nevada.*

# ...and Puerto Rico: 1790 to 1990

| 1900 | 1910 | 1920 | 1930 | 1940 | 1950 | 1960 | 1970 | 1980 | 1990 |
|---|---|---|---|---|---|---|---|---|---|
| 1,828.697 | 2,138,093 | 2,348,174 | 1,646,248 | 2,832,961 | 3,061,743 | 3,266,740 | 3,444,354 | 3,893,888 | 4,040,587 |
| 63,592 | 64,356 | 55,036 | 59,278[2] | 72,524[2] | 128,643 | 226,167 | 302,583 | 401,851 | 550,043 |
| 122,931 | 204,354 | 334,162 | 435,573 | 499,261 | 749,587 | 1,302,161 | 1,775,399 | 2,718,215 | 3,665,228 |
| 1,311,564 | 1,574,449 | 1,752,204 | 1,854,482 | 1,949,387 | 1,909,511 | 1,786,272 | 1,923,322 | 2,286,435 | 2,350,725 |
| 1,485,053 | 2,377,549 | 3,426,861 | 5,677,251 | 6,907,387 | 10,586,223 | 15,717,204 | 19,971,069 | 23,667,902 | 29,760,021 |
| 539,700 | 799,024 | 939,629 | 1,035,791 | 1,123,296 | 1,325,089 | 1,753,947 | 2,209,596 | 2,889,964 | 3,294,394 |
| 908,420 | 1,114,756 | 1,380,631 | 1,606,903 | 1,709,242 | 2,007,280 | 2,535,234 | 3,032,217 | 3,107,576 | 3,287,116 |
| 184,735 | 202,322 | 223,003 | 238,380 | 266,505 | 318,085 | 446,292 | 548,104 | 594,338 | 666,168 |
| 278,718 | 331,069 | 437,571 | 486,869 | 663,091 | 802,178 | 763,956 | 756,668 | 638,333 | 606,900 |
| 528,542 | 752,619 | 968,470 | 1,468,211 | 1,897,414 | 2,771,305 | 4,951,560 | 6,791,418 | 9,746,324 | 12,937,926 |
| 2,216,331 | 2,609,121 | 2,895,832 | 2,908,506 | 3,123,723 | 3,444,578 | 3,943,116 | 4,587,930 | 5,463,105 | 6,478,216 |
| 154,001 | 191,874 | 255,881 | 368,300 | 422,770 | 499,794 | 632,772 | 769,913 | 964,691 | 1,108,229 |
| 161,772 | 325,594 | 431,866 | 445,032 | 524,873 | 588,637 | 667,191 | 713,015 | 943,935 | 1,006,749 |
| 4,821,550 | 5,638,591 | 6,485,280 | 7,630,654 | 7,897,241 | 8,712,176 | 10,081,158 | 11,110,285 | 11,426,518 | 11,430,602 |
| 2,516,462 | 2,700,876 | 2,930,390 | 3,238,503 | 3,427,796 | 3,934,224 | 4,662,498 | 5,195,392 | 5,490,224 | 5,544,159 |
| 2,231,853 | 2,224,771 | 2,404,021 | 2,470,939 | 2,538,268 | 2,621,073 | 2,757,537 | 2,825,368 | 2,913,808 | 2,776,755 |
| 1,470,495 | 1,690,949 | 1,769,257 | 1,880,999 | 1,801,028 | 1,905,299 | 2,178,611 | 2,249,071 | 2,363,679 | 2,477,574 |
| 2,147,174 | 2,289,905 | 2,416,630 | 2,614,589 | 2,845,627 | 2,944,806 | 3,038,156 | 3,220,711 | 3,660,777 | 3,685,296 |
| 1,381,625 | 1,656,388 | 1,798,509 | 2,101,593 | 2,363,880 | 2,683,516 | 3,257,022 | 3,644,637 | 4,205,900 | 4,219,973 |
| 694,466 | 742,371 | 768,014 | 797,423 | 847,226 | 913,774 | 969,265 | 993,722 | 1,124,660 | 1,227,928 |
| 1,188,044 | 1,295,346 | 1,449,661 | 1,631,526 | 1,821,244 | 2,343,001 | 3,100,689 | 3,923,897 | 4,216,975 | 4,781,468 |
| 2,805,346 | 3,366,416 | 3,852,356 | 4,249,614 | 4,316,721 | 4,690,514 | 5,148,578 | 5,689,170 | 5,737,037 | 6,016,425 |
| 2,420,982 | 2,810,173 | 3,668,412 | 4,842,325 | 5,256,106 | 6,371,766 | 7,823,194 | 8,881,826 | 9,262,078 | 9,295,297 |
| 1,751,394 | 2,075,708 | 2,387,125 | 2,563,953 | 2,792,300 | 2,982,483 | 3,413,864 | 3,806,103 | 4,075,970 | 4,375,099 |
| 1,551,270 | 1,797,114 | 1,790,618 | 2,009,821 | 2,183,796 | 2,178,914 | 2,178,141 | 2,216,994 | 2,520,638 | 2,573,216 |
| 3,106,665 | 3,293,335 | 3,404,055 | 3,629,367 | 3,784,664 | 3,954,653 | 4,319,813 | 4,677,623 | 4,916,686 | 5,117,073 |
| 243,329 | 376,053 | 548,889 | 537,606 | 559,456 | 591,024 | 674,767 | 694,409 | 786,690 | 799,065 |
| 1,066,300 | 1,192,214 | 1,296,372 | 1,377,963 | 1,315,834 | 1,325,510 | 1,411,330 | 1,485,333 | 1,569,825 | 1,578,385 |
| 42,335 | 81,875 | 77,407 | 91,058 | 110,247 | 160,083 | 285,278 | 488,738 | 800,493 | 1,201,833 |
| 411,588 | 430,572 | 443,083 | 465,293 | 491,524 | 533,242 | 606,921 | 737,681 | 920,610 | 1,109,252 |
| 1,883,669 | 2,537,167 | 3,155,900 | 4,041,334 | 4,160,165 | 4,835,329 | 6,066,782 | 7,171,112 | 7,364,823 | 7,730,188 |
| 195,310 | 327,301 | 360,350 | 423,317 | 531,818 | 681,187 | 951,023 | 1,017,055 | 1,302,894 | 1,515,069 |
| 7,268,894 | 9,113,614 | 10,385,227 | 12,588,066 | 13,479,142 | 14,830,192 | 16,782,304 | 18,241,391 | 17,558,072 | 17,990,455 |
| 1,893,810 | 2,206,287 | 2,559,123 | 3,170,276 | 3,571,623 | 4,061,929 | 4,556,155 | 5,084,411 | 5,881,766 | 6,628,637 |
| 319,146 | 577,056 | 646,872 | 680,845 | 641,935 | 619,636 | 632,446 | 617,792 | 652,717 | 638,800 |
| 4,157,545 | 4,767,121 | 5,759,394 | 6,646 697 | 6,907,612 | 7,946,627 | 9,706,397 | 10,657,423 | 10,797,630 | 10,847,115 |
| 790,391 | 1,657,155 | 2,028,283 | 2,396,040 | 2,336,434 | 2,233,351 | 2,328,284 | 2,559,463 | 3,025,290 | 3,145,585 |
| 413,536 | 672,765 | 783,389 | 953,786 | 1,089,684 | 1,521,341 | 1,768,687 | 2,091,533 | 2,633,105 | 2,842,321 |
| 6,302,115 | 7,665,111 | 8,720,017 | 9,631,350 | 9,900,180 | 10,498,012 | 11,319,366 | 11,800,766 | 11,863,895 | 11,881,632 |
| 953,243[12] | 1,118,012 | 1,299,809 | 1,543,913 | 1,869,255 | 2,210,703 | 2,349,544 | 2,712,033 | 3,196,520 | 3,522,037 |
| 428,556 | 542,610 | 604,397 | 687,497 | 713,346 | 791,896 | 859,488 | 949,723 | 947,154 | 1,003,464 |
| 1,340,316 | 1,515,400 | 1,683,724 | 1,738,765 | 1,899,804 | 2,117,027 | 2,382,594 | 2,590,713 | 3,121,820 | 3,486,703 |
| 401,570 | 583,888 | 636,547 | 692,849 | 642,961 | 652,740 | 680,514 | 666,257 | 690,768 | 696,004 |
| 2,020,616 | 2,184,789 | 2,337,885 | 2,616,556 | 2,915,841 | 3,291,718 | 3,567,089 | 3,926,018 | 4,591,120 | 4,877,185 |
| 3,048,710 | 3,896,542 | 4,663,228 | 5,824,715 | 6,414,824 | 7,711,194 | 9,579,677 | 11,198,655 | 14,229,191 | 16,986,510 |
| 276,749 | 373,351 | 449,396 | 507,847 | 550,310 | 688,862 | 890,627 | 1,059,273 | 1,461,037 | 1,722,850 |
| 343,641 | 355,956 | 352,428 | 359,611 | 359,231 | 377,747 | 389,881 | 444,732 | 511,456 | 562,758 |
| 1,854,184 | 2,061,612 | 2,309,187 | 2,421,851 | 2,677,773 | 3,318,680 | 3,966,949 | 4,651,448 | 5,346,818 | 6,187,358 |
| 518,103 | 1,141,990 | 1,356,621 | 1,563,396 | 1,736,191 | 2,378,963 | 2,853,214 | 3,413,244 | 4,132,156 | 4,866,692 |
| 958,800 | 1,221,119 | 1,463,701 | 1,729,205 | 1,901,974 | 2,005,552 | 1,860,421 | 1,744,237 | 1,949,644 | 1,793,477 |
| 2,069,042 | 2,333,860 | 2,632,067 | 2,939,006 | 3,137,587 | 3,434,575 | 3,951,777 | 4,417,821 | 4,705,767 | 4,891,769 |
| 92,531 | 145,965 | 194,402 | 225,565 | 250,742 | 290,529 | 330,066 | 332,416 | 469,557 | 453,588 |
| 76,212,168 | 92,228,496 | 106,021,537 | 123,202,624 | 132,164,569 | 151,325,798 | 179,323,175 | 203,302,031 | 226,545,805 | 252,231,910 |

10. Dakotas. Population of Dakota Territory.
11. Ohio. Population of Territory northwest of the River Ohio.
12. Puerto Rico. Census taken as of Nov. 10, 1899 by War Department.
13. Utah. Population of Utah Territory exclusive of that part of present state of Colorado taken to form Colorado Territory in 1861.
14. Washington. 1860 figure includes population of Idaho and parts of Montana and Wyoming. 1850 figure of population of those parts of Oregon Territory taken to form part of Washington Territory in 1853 and 1859.
15. Wisconsin. Includes population of that part of Minnesota northeast of the Mississippi River.
16. Includes persons (6,100 in 1840 and 5,318 in 1830) on public ships in the service of the United States, not credited to any region, division, or state.
17. Includes population (325,464) of Indian Territory and Indian reservations specially enumerated in 1890 but not included in general report on population for 1890.

Source: Bureau of the Census, *Population and Housing Unit Counts 1990* (Washington, D.C.: Government Printing Office, 1993).

# Political Party Abbreviations

The following list provides a key to the political party abbreviations used in *Guide to U.S. Elections, Third Edition*. This list was developed by Congressional Quarterly from two sources for party designations: the Inter-University Consortium for Political and Social Research (ICPSR), for most election returns up to 1973; and Richard M. Scammon and Alice V. McGillivray's *America Votes* series, for most election returns after 1974. In cases of discrepancy, the ICPSR party designation was used.

The election data obtained from the ICPSR contain nearly 1,500 different party labels. In many cases the party labels represent combinations of multi-party support received by individual candidates. However, in preparing the returns for publication, approximately 1,000 of the party labels were eliminated because the candidate(s) did not receive at least 5 percent of the votes cast. The names of the parties appear below in the form they were obtained from ICPSR and Scammon.

| | | | | | |
|---|---|---|---|---|---|
| A-A | Anti-Adams | A-WOLF D | Anti-Wolf Democrat | D & F ALNC | Democrat and Farmers Alliance |
| A-AK R | Anti-Addicks Republican | BALLOT | Ballot Reform | DFL | Democrat Farmer-Labor |
| AB | Abolition | BARN D | Barnburner Democrat | D & G | Democrat and Greenback |
| A-BANK | Anti-Bank | BC | Butter Congressional | D-HANKER | Democrat-Hanker |
| AB-D | Abolition-Democrat | BENTON D | Benton Democrat | DI | Democratic-Independent |
| A-BEN D | Anti-Benton Democrat | B MOOSE | Bull Moose | D & I | Democrat and Independent |
| A-BOSS | Anti-Boss | BOLT D | Bolting Democrat | D & ID | Democrat and Independent Democrat |
| A-BROD D | Anti-Broderick Democrat | BRECK D | Breckinridge Democrat | | |
| AC | Anti-corruption | BROD D | Broderick Democrat | D IL | Democrat, Independent League |
| A-CB | Anti Carpet-Baggers | BRYAN | Bryan Party | | |
| ACP | A Connecticut Party | BRYAN D | Bryan Democrat | D & IL | Democrat and Independence League |
| AD | Adams Democrat | B-T R | Brindle-Tail Republican | | |
| A-D-FUS | Anti-Democrat-Fusion | B & T R | Black and Tan Republican | D IL A NP | Dem., Independent League, Amer., Nat'l. Progressive |
| AGA | American Grassroots Alternative | BUSINESS | Business Med | | |
| | | BUT D & N | Butler Democrat and National | D IL ANPI | Democrat, Independent League, American, Nat'l Progressive, Ind. |
| AG WHEEL | Agricultural Wheeler | | | | |
| A JAC | Andrew Jackson | BUT D & R | Butler Democrat and Greenback | D IL NPR | Democrat, Independent League, Nat'l Progressive |
| A-JAC | Anti-Jackson | | | | |
| A-JAC D | Anti-Jackson Democrat | BUT R | But. Republican | D-IP | Democrat-Independent Progressive |
| A-KN D | Anti-Know Nothing Democrat | C | Conservative | | |
| A-KN I | Anti-Know Nothing Independent | CALH D | Calhoun Democrat | D & I POP | Democrat and Independent Populist |
| | | CASS D | Cass Democrat | | |
| A-KN I D | Anti-Know Nothing Independent Democrat | CC | Change Congress | DISS D | Dissident Democrat |
| | | CD | Conservative Democrat | DISTRIB | Distributionist Candidate |
| AK R | Addicks Republican | CI/IC | Citizen Independent or Independent Citizen | D & KEY | Democrat and Keystone |
| A-LD D | Anti-Land Distribution Democrat | | | D K & PROG | Democrat, Keystone and Progressive |
| | | CIT | Citizens | | |
| A-LEC D | Anti-Lecompton Democrat | CIT & CO D | Citizen and County Democrat | D & L | Democrat and Liberal |
| A-LEC DR | Anti-Lecompton Democrat and Republican | CITY | City Party | D & LAB | Democrat and Labor |
| | | CITY FUS | City Fusion | D-LAB-PP | Democrat-Labor-Peoples |
| ALI | Alaskan Independent | CIV A | 'Civ. A' | D-LAF I | Democrat-La Follette Independent |
| ALL PP | All Peoples | CLAY D | Clay Democrat | | |
| ALNC | Alliance | CLAY R | Clay Republican | D & LIBN | Democrat and Liberation |
| A-LOT D | Anti-Lottery Democrat | CLEAN GV | Clean Government | D & LP | Democrat and Law Preservation and Liberty |
| AM | American | CLINT R | Clinton Republican | | |
| A-MACH | Anti-Machine | CLP | Commonwealth Land Party | | |
| A-MAINE | Anti-Maine Law | CLUNEY | Cluney Taxpayers Good Government | D LP & L | Democrat, Law Preservation and Liberty |
| A-MAS | Anti-Mason | | | | |
| A-MASC | Anti-Masonic | CNM | Cincinnatus Nonpartisan Movement | DN | Democratic National |
| A-MASDNR | Anti-Mason-Democrat-National Republican | | | DN & FS | D.N. and F.S. (Free Silver) |
| | | COALIT | Coalition | D-NG LAB | Democrat-National Green Labor |
| AM & EMANC | American and Emancipationist | CO D | County Democrat | | |
| | | COLORED | Colored | D NPR | Democrat National Progressive |
| AM I | American Independent | COLOR R | Colored Republican | | |
| AM LAB | American Labor | COM | Communist | D & NS | Democrat and National Silver |
| AM MO | American Party of Missouri | CONST | Constitution | DODD I | Dodd Independent |
| AM NAT | American National | CONSU | Consumer | D-OP | Democrat-Other Parties |
| A-MON D | Anti-Monopoly Democrat | CP | Commonwealth Party | DOUG D | Douglas Democrat |
| A-MONOP | Anti-Monopoly | CR | Conservative Republican | D & P | Democrat and Prohibition |
| AM R | American Republican | CREOLE | Creole Faction | D & POP | Democrat and Populist |
| AM&R | American and Republican | CS | Common Sense | D-POP I | Democrat-Populist Independent |
| A-NEB | Anti-Nebraska | CSI | Civil Service Independents | | |
| A-NEB D | Anti-Nebraska Democrat | CSR & D | 'CSR' and Democrat | DPOP PFS | Democrat, Populist, Prohibition & Free Silver |
| ANTI-CLINT | Anti-Clinton | CST | Constitutional | | |
| ANTI-CL R | Anti-Clinton Republican | CST U | Constitutional Union | D-PP | Democrat-Peoples |
| ANTI-FED | Anti-Federalist | D | Democrat | DPPC | Direct People's Candidate |
| AP | Action Party | D & AM | Democrat and American | D & PPI | Democratic and People's Independent |
| APOLLO | Apollo Hall | D & A-MASC | Democrat and Anti-Masonic | | |
| AR | Adams Republican | D AM IL | Democrat, American, Independence League | D PPI & PR | Democrat, People's Independent and Progressive |
| A-RENT | Anti-Rent | | | | |
| A-RPT D | Anti-Redemption Democrat | D & A-RENT | Democrat and Anti-Rent | | |
| A-TAM | Anti-Tammany | D & CD | Democrat and Co. Democrat | D & PRI | Democrat and Progressive Independent |
| A-TARIFF | Anti-Tariff | D CIT | Democratic Citizen | | |
| A-TAX | Anti-Tax | D & CIT | Democrat and Citizen | | |
| A-TRUST | Anti-Trust (A.T.) | D & CST | Democrat and Constitution | | |
| A VB D | Anti-Van Buren Democrat | DENVER I | Denver Independent Party | | |

| | | | | | |
|---|---|---|---|---|---|
| D PR & IL | Democrat, Progressive and Independence League | I DEMOC | Independent Democracy | LIBERT | Libertarian |
| D & PROG | Democrat and Progressive | I D-R | Independent Democratic Republican | LIF | Long Island First |
| D-PRO-TN | Democrat-Progressive-Townsend | ID & OPP | Independent Democrat and Opposition | LIN | Lin. |
| DPUS | D.P.U.S. | ID R & P | Independent Democratic Republican and Prohibition | LINCOLN | Lincoln |
| D-R [1] | Democratic-Republican | | | L-LAB D | Liberal-Labor-Democratic |
| D & REC | Democrat and Recovery | IFC | Independents for Change | LOCOFOCO | Locofoco |
| D REF | Democrat Reform | IFP | Independents for Perot | L & O W | Law and Order Whig |
| D & RESUB | Democrat and Resubmission | IG | Independent Greenback | LOW TAX D | Low Tax Democrat |
| D R & SOC | Democratic, Republican, Socialist | IG & R | Independent Greenback and Republican | LR | Liberal Republican |
| | | | | LRU | La Raza Unida |
| DR SOC P | Democratic, Republican, Socialist, Prohibition | I LEAGUE | Independence League | LU | Liberty Union |
| | | I LG | Independent League | LW & B | Light Wines and Beer |
| D SIL | Democratic (Silver) | IL & NPR | Independence League and National Progressive | LW R | Lily-White Republican |
| D & SILVER | Democrat and Silver | | | MCK SM | McKinley Sound Money |
| D SM | Democrat (S.M.) | I-N | Independent-National 'Ind. Cong.' | MID ROAD | Middle of the Road Populist |
| D SOC | Democratic Socialist | IND CONG | | MINN TAX | Minnesota Taxpayers |
| D & SOC | Democrat & Socialist | INDEP | Independence | MLP | Municipal League Party (M.L.) |
| D SOCIAL | Democratic Social | IND GOVT | Industrial Government | MOZART D | Mozart Democrat |
| D & UN LAB | Democrat and Union Labor | INDL | Industrialist | MR | Minstrel Republican |
| D-WM | Democrat-Working Man | INDUST | Industrial | N | National Party |
| ECR | Economic Recovery | I N-PART | Independent Non-Partisan | NA | New Alliance |
| EMANCIP | Emancipation | IP | Independent Party | NAM | Native American |
| ENVIRON | Environment | I-PO | Independent-Public Ownership | N AM | National American |
| EP | Elec. Prog. | | | NC R | North Carolina Republican |
| ER | Equal Right | INS | Independent Neighbors | ND | National Democrat |
| E TAX | Equal Tax | IPP CH | Independent People's Choice | NDPA | National Democratic Party of Alabama |
| FACP R | Father Coughlin's Principles, Republican | I PROG | Independent Progressive | | |
| | | I-PROG-R | Independent-Progressive-Republicans | NEB | Nebraska |
| F ALNC | Farmers' Alliance | | | NEB D | Nebraska Democrat |
| FB R | 'Free Bridge' Republican | I-PR-SOC | Independent-Progressive-Socialist | NEIGH | Neighborhood |
| FED | Federalist | | | NEW DEAL | New Deal |
| FEDL | Federal | IR, I-R | Independent Republican | NEW I | New Independent |
| FEDL AB | Federal Abolition | I.R. | I.R. | NEW LEAD | New Leadership |
| FEDR LAB | Federated Labor | I RAD R | Independent Radical Republican | NF | Nuclear Freeze |
| FF | Four Freedoms | | | NG | National Greenback |
| FILL AM | Fillmore American | IR & D | Independent Republican and Democrat | NON PART | Non Partisan |
| F-LAB | Farmer-Labor | | | NON PL | Nonpartisan League |
| FLA PP | Florida People's Party | I REF | Independent-Reform | NP | National Prohibition |
| F PLAY | Fair Play | I REF D | Independent Reform Democrat | N PROG | National Progressive |
| FREM AM | Fremont American | | | NR | National Republican |
| FS CLN | Free Soil Coalition | IR & P | Independent Republican and Prohibition | NR-A-MAS | National Republican-Anti-Mason |
| F SIL | Free Silver | | | | |
| F SIL R | Free Silver Republican | IRR U | Irregular Union | N SILVER | National Silver |
| F SOIL | Free Soil | IRR W | Irregular Whig | N SR | National States Rights |
| F SOIL D | Free Soil Democrat | IS | Illinois Solidarity | NULL | Nullifier |
| F SOIL W | Free Soil Whig | I SOC | Independent Socialist | NULL D | Nullifier Democrat |
| FS & SC | Free Soil and Scattering | IV | Independent Voters | NULL NR | Nullification-National Republican |
| FTP | For the People | I VT | Independent Vermonters Party | | |
| FUS | Fusion | | | N UNION | National Union |
| FUS-D-PO | Fusion-Democrat-Populist | I W | Independent Whig | OB | Open Book |
| FUS R | Fusion Republican | JAC | Jackson | OLD AGE | Old Age Pension |
| G | Greenback | JAC & AR | Jackson and Adams Republican | OLD R | Old Republican |
| GD | Greenback Democrat | | | OP | Occion Popular |
| G & D | Greenback and Democrat | JAC D | Jackson Democrat | OPP | Opposition |
| G LAB | Greenback Labor | JAC R | Jackson Republican | OPP D | Opposition Democrat |
| G LAB & P | Greenback Labor and Prohibition | JACS R | Jacksonian Republican | OPP R | Opposition Republican |
| | | JEFF | Jefferson | OPP & SC | Opposition and Scattering |
| G LAB R | Greenback Labor Republican | JEFF D | Jefferson-Democrat | P | Prohibition |
| GOLD D | Gold Democrat | JEFFS | Jeffersonian | P & D | Prohibition and Democrat |
| GOOD GOV | Good Government | JOBLESS | Jobless | P D-R & PR | Prohibition, Democrat-Republican and Progressive |
| G & P | Greenback and Prohibition | KEY | Keystone | | |
| G & R | Greenback and Republican | KN | Know-Nothing | P D SOC | Prohibition, Democrat, Socialist |
| GREEN | Green | K POP | Kolbite Populist | | |
| G & TAM | Greenback and Tammany | L | Liberal | PEACE D | Peace Democrat |
| HARD D | Hard Democratic | LAB | Labor | PERS LIB | Personal Liberty |
| HARD D & AM | Hard Democrat and American | LAB & POP | Labor and Populist | P & F ALNC | Prohibition and Farmer's Alliance |
| HC W | Henry Clay Whig | LAB-R | Labor-Republican | | |
| HE | Honest Elections | LAB REF | Labor Reform | PFP | Peace and Freedom |
| HG | Honest Government | LAB REF & P | Labor Reform and Prohibition | P-LAB | Population-Labor |
| HIG R | Higgins Republican | | | POP | Populist |
| HL | High Life | LAF | La Follette | POP & D | Populist and Democrat |
| H LIC | High License | LAF I | La Follette Independent | POP I | Populist Independent |
| HUNKER D | Hunker Democrat | LANCAST | Lancaster | POP & R | Populist and Republican |
| I | Independent | LAW ENF | Law Enforcement | POP SIL | Populist Silver |
| IA | Independent American | LAW ORD | Law and Order | POP & SL D | Populist and Silver Democrat |
| I ALNC | Independent Alliance | LAW PRES | Law Preservation | POPU GOV | Popular Government |
| IC | Independent Conservative | LD D | Land Distribution Democrat | PP | People's |
| I CIT AL | Independent Citizens Alliance | LFD | Lincoln Fair Deal | PP CAND | People's Candidate, The |
| ID | Independent Democrat | LIB | Liberty | PP & D | People's and Democrat |
| I & D | Independent and Democrat | LIBER W | Liberation Whig | PP-D-S-R | Peoples-Democrat-Silver-Republican |
| | | | | PP I | People's Independent |

| | | | | | |
|---|---|---|---|---|---|
| PPL DR S | People's Party Labor, Democratic Republican, Silver | RIL A NP | Republican Ind League, Amer. Nat'l Progressive | SO D | Southern Democrat |
| | | RIL & NPR | Republican, Independent League and National Progressive | SOFT D | Soft Democrat |
| PP & R | Peoples and Republican | | | SOFT D & AM | Soft Democrat and American |
| PRC TOWN | PRC, Townsend | | | SOJ | Scales of Justice |
| PRG SOC | Progressive Social | RIL P NP | Republican, Independent League, Prohibition, Nat'l Progressive | SO RTS | Southern Rights |
| PRI R | Primary Republican | | | SO RTS D | Southern Rights Democrat |
| PRO-BANK | Pro-Bank | | | SOR W | Southern Rights Whig |
| PROG | Progressive | R IL PR | Republican, Independence League and Progressive | SPP | Straight People Party |
| PROG-BMR | Progressive-Bull Moose-Roosevelt | | | SR | State Rights |
| | | R & IV | Republican and Independent Voters | SR D | State Rights Democrat |
| PROG & BUS | Progressive and Businessmen's | | | SR FT | State Rights Free Trader |
| | | R K & WASH | Republican, Keystone, and Washington | SR W | State Rights Whig |
| PROG D | Progressive Democrat | | | SSR D | State's Rights Democrat |
| PROG D & P | Progressive-Democrat and Prohibition | RKW & ROPR | Republican, Keystone, Washington and Roosevelt Progressive | SSR NULL | State's Rights Nullifier |
| | | | | STAL D | Stalwart Democrat |
| PROG & IL | Progressive and Independence League | | | STAL SIL | Stalwart Silver |
| | | R & LAB | Republican and Labor | STATE D | State Democrat |
| PROG-P | Progressive-Prohibition | R & LP | Republican and Law Preservation | STC D | State Credit Democrat |
| PROG R | Progressive Republican | | | STICKER | Sticker |
| PT | Protectionist | R MCK CIT | Republican, McKinley Citizen | TAFT | 'Taft for President' |
| PUB OWN | Public Ownership | R & ND | Republican and National Democrat | TAM | Tammany |
| PURE POL | Pure Politics | | | TAM D | Tammany Democrat |
| R | Republican | R & NG | Republican and National Greenback | TAM D & UL | Tammany Democrat and Union Labor |
| RAD | Radical | | | | |
| RAD R | Radical Republican | R & NP | Republican and Nonpartisan | TAM & NY D | Tammany and New York Democracy |
| R AM | Republican American | R NPR | Republican, Nat'l Progressive | | |
| R & A-MONO | Republican and Anti-Monopoly | R NPR AM | Republican, Nat'l Progressive, American | TAYLOR W | Taylor Whig |
| | | | | TCP-LI | Tax Cut Party-Long Island |
| R AM & PR | Republican, American and Progressive | RO | Roosevelt | TEMP | Temperance |
| | | ROBINSON | Robinson Citizens Party | TEMP REF | Temperance Reform |
| R & A-TAM | Republican and Anti-Tammany | ROB R | Rob. Republican | THIRD | The Third Party |
| | | R-OP | Republican-Other Parties | TOL | Toleration |
| R & A-TR | Republican and Anti-Trust Republican | RO PROG | Roosevelt Progressive | TOWN | Townsend |
| | | RO SOC D | Roosevelt Social Democrat | TOWN-C-L | Townsend-Coughlin-Labor |
| R & BM | Republican and Bull Moose | ROYAL OAK | Royal Oak | TOWN OAP | Townsend Old Age Pension |
| RBM & PR | Republican, Bull Moose and Progressive | RP | Rate Payers Against LILCO | TOWN SJ | Townsend Social Justice |
| | | R & P | Republican and Prohibition | TOWN-SJD | Townsend-Social Justice, Democratic |
| R & CF | Republican and City Fusion | RP & DC | Republican Party and Delegate Convention | | |
| RCF & LP | Republican City Fusion and Law Preservation | | | TCPT | Taxpayers Party to Cut Taxes |
| | | RPI | Ross Perot Independent | U | United |
| R CF & REC | Republican, City Fusion, and Recovery | R P NPR | Republican, Prohibition, Nat'l Progressive | U CIT | United Citizen |
| | | | | U LAB | United Labor |
| RCI | Rich County Independent | R POP FU | Republican Populist Fusion | ULTRA AB | Ultra Abolitionist |
| R CIT | Republican Citizens | RP & PROG | Republican, Prohibition, and Progressive | UN | Union |
| R CST & CF | Republican, Constitutional, and City Fusion | | | UN D | Union Democrat |
| | | R PR IL | Republican, Progressive, Independence League | UN LAB | Union Labor |
| R-D [1] | Republican-Democrat | | | UN LAB & D | Union Labor and Democrat |
| RDC | Republican Delegate Convention | R & PROG | Republican and Progressive | UNP R | Unpledged Republican |
| | | R-SIL R | Republican-Silver Republican | UN PROG | Union Progressive |
| R-D-P | Republican-Democrat-Prohibition | R & SOC | Republican and Socialist | UN R | Union Republican |
| | | R SOC & LP | Republican, Socialist, and Law Preservation | UN & SQD | Union and Square Deal |
| R-D-PR-C | Republican-Democrat-Progressive-Commonwealth | | | UNT | Unionist |
| | | R & SQDEAL | Republican and Square Deal | UN W | Union Whig |
| R-D-PROG | Republican-Democratic-Progressive | RT | Republican, Townsend | USLP | U.S. Labor Party |
| | | R & TEMP | Republican and Temperance | UT | Unity |
| R D P T | Republican, Democrat, Progressive, Townsend | RTL | Right to Life | U TAX | United Taxpayers |
| | | R & UL | Republican and Union Labor | UVD | Ultra-Veto Democrat |
| R D T | Republican, Democrat, Townsend | R-UNION | Republican-Union | VB D | Van Buren Democrat |
| | | R & VIC | Republican and 'Vic' | VB R | Van Buren Republican |
| READJ | Readjuster | R VIC & CF | Republican, 'Vic,' and City Fusion | VETS F | Veterans Farmer |
| REDEM D | Redemption Democrat | | | VETS V | Veterans Victory |
| REF | Reform | R & WASH | Republican and Washington | VI | Voice of Independence |
| REF D | Reform Democrat | R & YD | Republican and Young Democracy | VL | Voters League |
| REG | Regular | | | VR | Voter Rights |
| REG D | Regular Democrat | SEC | Secessionist | W | Whig |
| REPEAL | Repeal | SEC D | Secession Democrat | W & AM | Whig and American |
| REPEAL L | Repeal League | SEC W | Secessionist Whig | W & A-MASC | Whig and Anti-Masonic |
| R & F ALNC | Republican and Farmer's Alliance | SILENT | Silent Majority | W-A-RENT | Whig Anti-Rent |
| | | SIL-R | Silver Republican | WASH | Washington |
| R-FF | Republican-Federalist Fusion | SIL-R-D | Silver-Republican-Democrat | WCP AM | Workers (Communist) Party of America |
| R-F-LAB | Republican-Farmer Labor | SINGLE T | Single Tax | | |
| R F-L-P | Republican, Farmer-Labor-Prohibition | SIS | Staten Island Secession | WELFARE | Welfare |
| | | SM D | Sound Money Democrat | W FS | Whig Free Soil |
| RG | Republican Greenback | SOC | Socialist | WILDCAT | Wildcat |
| R-G-FUS | Republican-Greenback-Fusion | SOC & F-L | Socialist and Farmer-Labor | WILSON I | Wilson Independent |
| | | SOCIAL D | Social Democrat | WL | Workers League |
| R-GOLD D | Republican-Gold Democrat | SOC LAB | Socialist Labor | WM | Workingmen |
| R & ID | Republican and Independent Democrat | SOC & LP | Socialist and Law Preservation | WM PENN | William Penn |
| | | | | WMP/L | Workingman's Party or League |
| R & IL | Republican and Independence League | SOC & PROG | Socialist and Progressive | WOLF-D | Wolf Democrat |
| | | SOC WORK | Socialist Workers | WP AM | Workers Party of America |

| WRITE IN | Write In | YD & R | Young Democrat and Republican | YOUNGMAN | Youngman |
| YD | Young Democracy | | | | |

1. The party label D-R used in early 19th century returns refers to the party associated with Thomas Jefferson.

In California from 1913 to 1959, D-R refers to that state's system of crossfiling in primary elections for House, Senate and Governor. Democrats and Republicans would each run in the other party's primary in addition to their own. Frequently, the same candidate would win both nominations. In cases in which a Democrat won both primaries, the symbol D-R is used in the California vote returns in this book. Where a Republican won both primaries, the symbol R-D is used.

# Suggested Readings

## Political Parties

### Books

Alexander, Herbert E., and Monica Bauer. *Financing the 1988 Election*. Boulder, Colo.: Westview Press, 1991.

Alexander, Herbert E., and Anthony Corrado. *Financing the 1992 Election*. Armonk, N.Y.: M. E. Sharpe, forthcoming 1995.

Aldrich, John H. *Before the Convention: Strategies and Choices in Presidential Nomination Campaigns*. Chicago: University of Chicago Press, 1980.

Arnett, A. M. *The Populist Movement in Georgia*. 1922. Reprint. New York: Columbia University Press, 1971.

Bain, Richard C., and Judith H. Parris. *Convention Decisions and Voting Records*. Washington, D.C.: Brookings Institution, 1975.

Bibby, John F. *Governing by Consent: An Introduction to American Politics*. Washington, D.C.: CQ Press, 1992.

_____. *Politics, Parties, and Elections in America*. 2nd ed. Chicago: Nelson-Hall, 1992.

Blue, Frederick J. *The Free Soilers: Third Party Politics, 1848-1854*. Urbana, Ill.: University of Illinois Press, 1973.

Borden, Morton. *Parties and Politics in the Early Republic, 1789-1815*. Arlington Heights, Ill.: Davidson, Harlan, 1967.

Brock, William. *Parties and Political Conscience: American Dilemmas, 1840-1850*. Millwood, N.Y.: Kraus International Publications, 1979.

Brown, Stuart G. *First Republicans: Political Philosophy and Public Policy in the Party of Jefferson and Madison*. 1954. Reprint. Westport, Conn.: Greenwood Press, 1977.

Buell, Emmett H. and Lee Sigelman. *Nominating the President*. Knoxville: University of Tennessee Press, 1991.

Burner, David. *The Politics of Provincialism: The Democratic Party in Transition, 1918-1932*. 1968. Reprint. Cambridge: Harvard University Press, 1986.

Byrne, Gary C., and Paul Marx. *The Great American Convention: A Political History of Presidential Elections*. Palo Alto, Calif.: Pacific Books, 1976.

Cannon, James P. *The History of American Trotskyism from Its Origin in 1928 to the Founding of the Socialist Labor Workers Party*. New York: Pathfinders Press, 1972.

Chambers, W. N., and Walter D. Burnham, eds. *The American Party Systems: Stages of Political Development*. 2nd ed. New York: Oxford University Press, 1975.

Conway, M. Margaret. *Political Participation in the United States*, 2nd ed. Washington, D.C.: CQ Press, 1991.

Congressional Quarterly. *National Party Conventions 1831-1988*. Washington, D.C.: Congressional Quarterly, 1991.

Cotter, Cornelius P. *Party Organization in American Politics*. Pittsburgh: University of Pittsburgh Press, 1984.

Cunningham, Noble E. *Jeffersonian Republicans: The Formation of Party Organization, 1789-1801*. Chapel Hill, N.C.: University of North Carolina Press, 1967.

David, Paul T. *The Politics of National Party Conventions*. Washington, D.C.: Brookings Institution, 1960.

Davis, James W. *National Conventions: Nominations Under the Big Top*. Woodbury, N.Y.: Barron Educational Series, 1972.

_____. *National Conventions in an Age of Party Reform*. Westport, Conn.: Greenwood Press, 1983.

_____. *The President as Party Leader*. New York: Greenwood Press, 1992.

Dinkin, Robert J. *Voting in Revolutionary America: A Study of Elections in the Original Thirteen States, 1776-1789*. Westport, Conn.: Greenwood Press, 1982.

Duverger, Maurice. *Political Parties: Their Organization and Activity in the Modern State*. 3rd ed. New York: John Wiley and Sons, 1969.

Eldersveld, Samuel J. *Political Parties in American Society*. New York: Basic Books, 1982.

Fairlie, Henry. *The Parties: Republicans and Democrats in this Century*. New York: St. Martin's Press, 1978.

Farley, James A. *Behind the Ballots: the Personal History of a Politician*. 1938. Reprint. New York: Da Capo Press, 1973.

Fleischman, Harry. *Norman Thomas: A Biography: 1884-1968*. New York: W. W. Norton, 1969.

Fleishman, Joel L. *The Future of American Political Parties*. Englewood Cliffs, N.J.: Prentice-Hall, 1982.

Foner, Eric. *Free Soil, Free Labor, Free Men: The Ideology of the Republican Party Before the Civil War*. New York: Oxford University Press, 1971.

Fulton, Kenneth, ed. *Democrats in Convention 1972: Official Program for the Thirty-Sixth Quadrennial National Nominating Convention of the Democratic Party*. Washington, D.C.: Democratic National Committee, 1972.

Gillespie, J. David. *Politics at the Periphery: Third Parties in Two-Party America*. Columbia, S.C.: University of South Carolina Press, 1993.

Halstead, Murat. *Trimmers, Trucklers and Temporizers: Notes of Murat Halstead from the Political Convention of 1856*. Madison, Wis.: Wisconsin Historical Society Press, 1961.

Hertzke, Allen D. *Echoes of Discontent: Jesse Jackson, Pat Robertson, and the Resurgence of Populism*. Washington, D.C.: CQ Press, 1993.

Hicks, John D. *The Populist Revolt: A History of the Farmer's Alliance in the People's Party*. Minneapolis, Minn.: University of Minnesota Press, 1961.

Hofstadter, Richard. *The Idea of a Party System: The Rise of Legitimate Opposition in the United States, 1780-1840*. Berkeley, Calif.: University of California Press, 1969.

Holcombe, Arthur N. *Political Parties of Today: A Study in Republican and Democratic Politics*. New York: Harper and Row, 1974.

Jones, Charles O. *The Republican Party in American Politics*. New York: Macmillan, 1965.

Jones, Chester L. *Readings on Parties and Elections in the United States*. Westport, Conn.: Greenwood Press, 1970.

Kane, Joseph Nathan. *Famous First Facts*. 4th ed. New York: H. W. Wilson, 1981.

Keech, William R., and Donald R. Matthews. *The Party's Choice: With an Epilogue on the 1976 Nominations*. Washington, D.C.: Brookings Institution, 1977.

Keefe, William J. *Parties, Politics, and Public Policy in America*. 6th ed. Washington, D.C.: CQ Press, 1991.

Kessel, John H. *Presidential Campaign Politics*, 4th ed. Pacific Grove, Calif.: Brooks/Cole, 1992.

Kent, Frank R. *The Democratic Party: A History*. 1928. Reprint. New York: Johnson Reprint, 1968.

Kipnis, Ira. *American Socialist Movement, 1897-1912*. Westport, Conn.: Greenwood Press, 1968.

Kraut, Alan M., ed. *Crusaders and Compromisers: Essays on the Relationship of Antislavery Struggle to the Antebellum Party System*. Westport, Conn.: Greenwood Press, 1983.

Kruschke, Earl R. *Encyclopedia of Third Parties in the United States*. Santa Barbara, Calif: ABC-CLIO, 1991.

Ladd, Everett C., Jr. *Where Have All the Voters Gone? The Fracturing of American Political Parties*. 2nd ed. New York: W. W. Norton, 1982.

Ladd, Everett C., Jr., and Charles D. Hadley. *Transformations of the American Party System: Political Coalitions from the New Deal to the 1970s*. 2nd ed. New York: W. W. Norton, 1978.

Lamis, Alexander P. *The Two-Party South*, 2nd ed. New York: Oxford University Press, 1990.

La Palombara, Joseph, and M. Weiner. *Political Parties and Political Development*. Princeton, N.J.: Princeton University Press, 1966.

Lee, John H. *The Origin and Progress of the American Party in Politics: Embracing a Complete History of the Philadelphia Riots in May and July, 1844*. Salem, N.H.: Ayer, 1970.

Livermore, Shaw, Jr. *Twilight of Federalism: The Disintegration of the Federalist Party, 1815-1830*. Staten Island, N.Y.:

Gordian Press, 1972.

Lorant, Stefan. *The Glorious Burden: The American Presidency.* New York: Harper and Row, 1976.

Main, Jackson T. *Political Parties Before the Constitution.* New York: W. W. Norton, 1974.

Matthews, Donald R. *Perspectives on Presidential Selection.* Washington, D.C.: Brookings Institution, 1973.

McCormick, Richard P. *The Second American Party System: Party Formulation in the Jacksonian Era.* Chapel Hill: University of North Carolina Press, 1973.

McKay, Kenneth. *The Progressive Movement of 1924.* New York: Octagon Books, 1966.

McKee, Thomas H. *The National Conventions and Platforms of All Political Parties, 1789-1905: Convention, Popular and Electoral Vote.* New York: AMS Press, 1971.

Merriam, Charles E. *The American Party System: An Introduction to the Study of Political Parties in the United States.* 4th ed. New York: Macmillan, 1969.

Milkis, Sidney M. *The President and the Parties: The Transformation of the American Party System Since the New Deal.* New York: Oxford University Press, 1993.

Morgan, Wayne. *From Hayes to McKinley: National Party Politics, 1877-1896.* Syracuse, N.Y.: Syracuse University Press, 1969.

Morris, Richard B., ed. *Encyclopedia of American History.* 6th ed. New York: Harper and Row, 1982.

Nash, Howard P., Jr. *Third Parties in American Politics.* Washington, D.C.: Public Affairs Press, 1959.

Nichols, Roy F. *The Invention of the American Political Parties: A Study of Political Improvisation.* New York: Free Press, 1972.

Ostrogorski, Moisei. *Democracy and the Organization of Political Parties.* Brooklyn, N.Y.: Haskell Booksellers, 1970.

Parris, Judith H. *The Convention Problem: Issues in Reform of Presidential Nominating Procedures.* Washington, D.C.: Brookings Institution, 1972.

Pinchot, Amos R. E. *History of the Progressive Party, 1912-1916.* 1958. Reprint. New York: Westport, Conn.: Greenwood Press, 1978.

Pomper, Gerald M. *Nominating the President: The Politics of Convention Choice.* New York: Dodd and Mead, 1975.

―――. *Voters, Elections, and Parties: The Practice of Democratic Theory.* New Brunswick, N.J.: Transaction Books, 1988.

Porter, Kirk H., and Donald B. Johnson. *National Party Platforms, 1840-1972.* Urbana: University of Illinois Press, 1973.

Reeves, Richard. *Convention.* New York: Harcourt, Brace, Jovanovich, 1977.

Republican National Committee. *Official Report of the Proceedings of the Thirty-Fourth Republican National Convention.* Washington, D.C.: Republican National Committee, 1988.

Republican National Committee. *Official Report of the Proceedings of the Thirty-Fifth Republican National Convention.* Washington, D.C.: Republican National Committee, 1992.

Robinson, Edgar E. *The Evolution of American Political Parties.* 1924. Reprint. New York: Harcourt Brace Jovanovich, 1971.

Roseboom, Eugene H. *A History of Presidential Elections: From George Washington to Jimmy Carter.* 4th ed. New York: Macmillan, 1979.

Rosenstone, Steven J., Roy L. Behr and Edward H. Lazarus. *Third Parties in America: Citizen Response to Major Party Failure.* Princeton, N.J.: Princeton University Press, 1984.

Ross, Earle D. *The Liberal Republican Movement.* New York: AMS Press, 1971.

Rossiter, Clinton. *Parties and Politics in America.* Ithaca, N.Y.: Cornell University Press, 1960.

Sanford, Terry. *A Danger of Democracy: The Presidential Nominating Process.* Boulder, Colo.: Westview Press, 1981.

Schattschneider, E. E. *Party Government.* 1942. Reprint. Westport, Conn.: Greenwood Press, 1977.

Schefter, Martin. *Political Parties and the State: The American Historical Experience.* Princeton: Princeton University Press, 1994.

Schlesinger, Arthur M., Jr. *History of U.S. Political Parties.* 4 vols. 1973. Reprint. New York: Chelsea House, 1981.

Schlesinger, Arthur M., Jr., ed. *The Coming to Power: Critical Presidential Elections in American History.* New York: Chelsea House, 1981.

Schlesinger, Joseph A. *Political Parties and the Winning of Office.* Ann Arbor: University of Michigan Press, 1991.

Shafer, Byron. *Bifurcated Politics: Evolution and Reform in the National Party Convention.* Cambridge, Mass.: Harvard University Press, 1988.

Shafritz, Jay M. *The Dorsey Dictionary of American Government and Politics.* Chicago: The Dorsey Press, 1988.

Shannon, David A. *The Decline of American Communism: A History of the Communist Party in the United States Since 1945.* Chatham, N.J.: Chatham Booksellers, 1971.

Smallwood, Frank. *The Other Candidates: Third Parties in Presidential Elections.* Hanover, N.H.: University Press of New England, 1983.

Smith, Theodore C. *Liberty and Free Soil Parties in the Northwest.* New York: Arno Press, 1969.

Stanley, Harold W., and Richard G. Niemi. *Vital Statistics on American Politics.* 4th ed. Washington, D.C.: CQ Press, 1994.

Stedman, Murray S., Jr., and Susan W. Stedman. *Discontent at the Polls: A Study of Farmer and Labor Parties, 1827-1948.* New York: Russell and Russell Publishers, 1967.

Sundquist, James L. *Dynamics of the Party System: Alignment and Realignment of Political Parties in the United States.* rev. ed. Washington, D.C.: Brookings Institution, 1983.

Thompson, Kenneth W., and Burkett White. *The Presidential Nominating Process: The George Gund Lectures.* Lanham, Md.: University Press of America, 1983.

Timberlake, James H. *Prohibition and the Progressive Movement, 1912-1925.* New York: Random House, 1969.

Tocqueville, Alexis de. *Democracy in America.* New York: Vintage Books, 1990.

Van Buren, Martin. *Inquiry into the Origin and Course of Political Parties in the United States.* 1867. Reprint. New York: A. M. Kelley, 1967.

Wattenberg, Martin P. *The Decline of the American Political Parties 1952 to 1992.* Boston: Harvard University Press, 1994.

White, Theodore H. *America in Search of Itself: The Making of the President, 1956-1980.* New York: Harper and Row, 1982.

―――. *The Making of the President, 1960.* New York: Atheneum Publishers, 1961.

―――. *The Making of the President, 1964.* New York: Atheneum Publishers, 1965.

―――. *The Making of the President, 1968.* New York: Atheneum Publishers, 1969.

―――. *The Making of the President, 1972.* New York: Atheneum Publishers, 1973.

## Articles

Adkinson, Denny M. "The Electoral Significance of the Vice Presidency." *Presidential Studies Quarterly* 12 (Summer 1982): 330-336.

Angle, Paul M. "The Republican Convention of 1860." *Chicago History* (Spring 1960): 341.

Aldrich, John H. "A Dynamic Model of Presidential Nomination Campaigns." *American Political Science Review* 74 (September 1980): 651-669.

Black, Sloan W., Office of Kathy Vick, Secretary of the Democratic National Committee. "Information Guide to the Democratic National Committee." 1992.

Democratic National Committee, Research Department. "General Information about the DNC." December 1988.

Hurley, Patricia A. "Partisan Representation and the Failure of Realignment in the 1980s." *American Journal of Political Science* 33 (February 1989): 240-261.

Maisel, L. Sandy. "The Platform-Writing Process: Candidate-Centered Platforms in 1992," *Political Science Quarterly* (Winter 1993-94): 671.

McNitt, Andrew D. "The Effect of Preprimary Endorsement on Competition for Nominations: An Examination of Different

Nominating Systems." *Journal of Politics* 42 (February 1980): 257-266.

Miller, Warren E. "Party Identification, Realignment, and Party Voting: Back to the Basics." *American Political Science Review* 85 (June 1991): 557-568.

Polsby, Nelson W. "Decision Making at the National Conventions." *Western Political Quarterly* (September 1960): 609-619.

Schlesinger, Joseph A. "The New American Political Party." *American Political Science Review* 79 (December 1985): 1152-1169.

Stanley, Harold W., and Richard G. Niemi. "Partisanship and Group Support, 1952-1988." *American Politics Quarterly* 19 (April 1991): 189-210.

Wildavsky, Aaron B. "On the Superiority of National Conventions." *Review of Politics* (July 1962): 307-319.

Wilson, Woodrow. "There Ought Never to Be Another Presidential Nominating Convention: Excerpts from a Letter, February 5, 1913." *U.S. News & World Report,* Oct. 23, 1967, 124.

# Presidential Elections

## Books

Abramson, Paul R., John H. Aldrich and David W. Rohde. *Change and Continuity in the 1992 Elections.* Washington, D.C.: Congressional Quarterly, 1994.

Asher, Herbert. *Presidential Elections and American Politics: Votes, Candidates, and Campaigns since 1952.* 5th ed. Pacific Grove, Calif.: Brooks-Cole, 1992.

Bagby, Wesley. *The Road to Normalcy: The Presidential Campaign and Election of 1920.* New York: AMS Press, 1962.

Barber, James D. *The Presidential Character: Predicting Performance in the White House.* 4th ed. Englewood Cliffs, N. J.: Prentice-Hall, 1992.

Bartels, Larry M. *Presidential Primaries and the Dynamics of Public Choice.* Princeton, N.J.: Princeton University Press, 1988.

Best, Judith. *The Case Against Direct Election of the President: A Defense of the Electoral College.* Ithaca, N. Y.: Cornell University Press, 1975.

Black, Earl, and Merle Black. *The Vital South: How Presidential Elections Are Won.* Cambridge, Mass.: Harvard University Press, 1992.

Brams, Steven J. *The Presidential Election Game.* New Haven, Conn.: Yale University Press, 1978.

Burnham, Walter D. *Critical Elections and the Mainsprings of American Politics.* New York: W. W. Norton, 1971.

Ceaser, James, and Andrew Busch. *Upside Down and Inside Out: The 1992 Elections and American Politics.* Lanham, Md.: Rowman and Littlefield, 1993.

Congressional Quarterly. *Presidential Elections Since 1789.* 5th ed. Washington, D.C.: Congressional Quarterly, 1991.

Crotty, William, ed. *America's Choice: The Election of 1992.* Guilford, Conn.: Dushkin, 1993.

David, Paul T., and James W. Ceasar. *Proportional Representation in Presidential Nominating Politics.* Charlottesville, Va.: University Press of Virginia, 1980.

Davis, James W. *The Presidential Primaries: Road to the White House.* 1967. Reprint. Westport, Conn.: Greenwood Press, 1980.

Di Clerico, Robert E., and Eric M. Uslaner. *Few Are Chosen: Problems in Presidential Selection.* New York: McGraw-Hill, 1984.

Drew, Elizabeth. *Portrait of an Election: The 1980 Presidential Campaign.* New York: Simon and Schuster, 1981.

Durbin, Thomas, ed. *Nomination and Election of the President and Vice President of the United States, 1992, Including the Manner of Selecting Delegates to National Party Conventions.* Washington, D.C.: U.S. Government Printing Office, 1992.

Euchner, Charles. *Selecting the President.* Washington, D.C.: Congressional Quarterly, 1992.

Ewing, Cortez A. M. *Presidential Elections from Abraham Lincoln to Franklin Roosevelt.* 1940. Reprint. Westport, Conn.: Greenwood Press, 1972.

Flanigan, William H., and Nancy H. Zingale. *Political Behavior of the American Electorate.* 8th ed. Washington, D.C.: CQ Press, 1994.

Gammon, Samuel R., Jr. *The Presidential Campaign of 1832.* Reprint. 1922. Saint Clair Shores, Mich.: Scholarly Press, 1972.

Germond, Jack W., and Jules Witcover. *Blue Smoke and Mirrors: How Reagan Won and Why Carter Lost the Election of 1980.* New York: Viking Press, 1981.

Gray, Lee L. *How We Choose a President: the Election Year.* 5th ed. New York: St. Martin's Press, 1980.

Gunderson, Robert G. *The Log-Cabin Campaign.* 1957. Reprint. Westport, Conn.: Greenwood Press, 1977.

Haworth, Paul L. *The Hayes-Tilden Disputed Presidential Election of 1876.* 1906 Reprint. New York: AMS Press, 1979.

Hess, Stephen. *The Presidential Campaign: an Essay.* 3rd ed. Washington, D. C.: Brookings Institution, 1988.

Hill, David B., and Norman R. Luttberg. *Trends in American Electoral Behavior.* 2nd ed. Itasca, Ill.: Peacock, 1983.

Hirschfield, Robert S., ed. *Selection Election: A Forum on the American Presidency.* Hawthorne, N. Y.: Hawthorne, 1982.

Hoyt, Edwin P. *Jumbos and Jackasses: A Popular History of the Political Wars.* Garden City, N. Y.: Doubleday, 1960.

Jamieson, Kathleen Hall. *Packaging the Presidency: A History and Criticism of Presidential Campaign Advertising.* 2nd ed. New York: Oxford University Press, 1992.

Jennings, Jerry T., U.S. Bureau of the Census. *Voting and Registration in the Election of November 1992.* Washington, D.C.: Government Printing Office, 1993.

Jensen, Merrill, ed. *The Documentary History of the First Federal Elections, 1788-1790.* Madison, Wis.: Madison House, 1991.

Joint Center for Political Studies. *Picking a President: A Guide to Delegate Selection in the United States.* Washington, D.C.: Joint Center for Political Studies, 1980.

Keech, William R., ed. *Winners Take All: Report of the Twentieth Century Task Force on Reform of the Presidential Election Process.* New York: Holmes and Meier, 1978.

Kessel, John H. *Presidential Campaign Politics.* 4th ed. Pacific Grove, Calif.: Brook-Cole, 1992.

Key, V. O., Jr. *The Responsible Electorate: Rationality in Presidential Voting, 1936-1960.* Cambridge, Mass.: Harvard University Press, 1966.

Kirkpatrick, Samuel A., ed. *American Electoral Behavior: Change and Stability.* Beverly Hills, Calif.: Sage, 1976.

Kleppner, Paul. *Who Voted?: The Dynamics of Electoral Turnout, 1870-1980.* New York: Praeger, 1982.

Kleppner, Paul, and Walter D. Burnham. *The Evolution of American Electoral Systems.* Westport, Conn.: Greenwood Press, 1982.

Lazarsfeld, Paul F., et al. *The People's Choice: How the Voter Makes Up His Mind in a Presidential Campaign.* 3rd ed. New York: Columbia University Press, 1968.

Lipset, Seymour Martin. "The Significance of the 1992 Election." *PS: Political Science and Politics* 26 (March 1993): 7-16.

Longley, Lawrence D. *The Politics of Electoral College Reform.* New Haven, Conn.: Yale University Press, 1972.

Maisel, L. Sandy. *Parties and Elections in America: The Electoral Process.* 2nd ed. New York: McGraw-Hill, 1993.

Maisel, Louis, and Joseph Cooper, eds. *The Impact of the Electoral Process.* Beverly Hills, Calif.: Sage, 1977.

Mayhew, David R. *Divided We Govern: Party Control, Lawmaking & Investigations.* New Haven, Conn.: Yale University Press, 1991.

Mazmanian, Daniel A. *Third Parties in Presidential Elections.* Washington, D. C.: Brookings Institution, 1974.

McGillivray, Alice V. *Presidential Primaries and Caucuses: 1992. A Handbook of Election Statistics.* Washington, D.C.: Congressional Quarterly, 1992.

Michener, James A. *Presidential Lottery: The Reckless Gamble in Our Electoral System.* New York: Random House, 1969.

Moore, John. L. *Speaking of Washington: Facts, Firsts, and Folklore.* Washington, D.C.: Congressional Quarterly, 1993.

Nelson, Michael, ed.*The Presidency and the Political System,* 2nd ed. Washington, D.C.: CQ Press, 1988.

———. *The Elections of 1992.* Washington, D.C.: CQ Press, 1993.

Newman, Bruce I. *The Marketing of the President: Political Marketing as a Campaign Strategy.* Thousand Oaks, Calif.: Sage, 1994.

Norrander, Barbara. *Super Tuesday: Regional Politics and Presidential Primaries.* Lexington: University Press of Kentucky, 1992.

Overacker, Louise. *The Presidential Primary.* 1926. Reprint. New York: Arno, 1974.

Page, Benjamin I. *Choices and Echoes in Presidential Elections: Rational Man and Electoral Democracy.* Chicago: University of Chicago Press, 1978.

Peel, Roy V. *The 1928 Campaign: An Analysis.* 1931. Reprint. Salem, N. H.: Ayer, 1974.

———. *The 1932 Campaign: An Analysis.* 1935. Reprint. New York: Da Capo Press, 1973.

Peirce, Neal, and Lawrence D. Longley. *The People's President: The Electoral College and the Emerging Consensus for a Direct Vote Alternative.* Rev. ed. New Haven, Conn.: Yale University Press, 1981.

Petersen, Svend. *A Statistical History of the American Presidential Elections.* Westport, Conn.: Greenwood Press, 1981.

Polsby, Nelson W., and Aaron Wildavsky. *Presidential Elections: Contemporary Strategies of American Electoral Politics,* 8th ed. New York: Free Press, 1991.

Pomper, Gerald M. *The Election of 1992: Reports and Interpretations.* hatham, N.J.: Chatham House, 1993.

Ranney, Austin. *Federalization of Presidential Primaries.* Washington, D.C.: American Enterprise Institute, 1978.

Robinson, Edgar E. *The Presidential Vote, 1896-1932.* New York: Octagon Books, 1970.

———. *They Voted for Roosevelt: The Presidential Vote, 1932-1944.* 1947. Reprint. New York: Octagon Books, 1970.

Roseboom, Eugene H. *A History of Presidential Elections: From George Washington to Jimmy Carter.* 4th ed. New York: Macmillan, 1979.

Rosenstone, Steven J., Roy L. Behr and Edward Lazarus. *Third Parties in America: Citizen Response to Major Party Failure.* Princeton, N.J.: Princeton University Press, 1984.

Runyon, John H. *Source Book of American Presidential Campaign and Election Statistics, 1948-1968.* New York: Ungar, 1971.

Sayre, Wallace S. *Voting for President: The Electoral College and the American Political System.* Washington, D.C.: Brookings Institution, 1970.

Scammon, Richard M. *America Votes: A Handbook of Contemporary Election Statistics.* vols. 1 and 2. New York: Macmillan, 1956, 1958. *America Votes.* vols. 3-5. Pittsburgh: University of Pittsburgh, 1959, 1962, and 1964. *America Votes.* vols. 6-11. Washington, D.C.: Congressional Quarterly, 1966-75.

———. and Alice V. McGillivray. *America Votes.* vols. 12-20. Washington, D.C.: Congressional Quarterly, 1977-93.

Schlesinger, Arthur M., Jr., ed. *History of American Presidential Elections.* 4 vols. New York: McGraw Hill, 1971.

———. *The Coming to Power: Critical Presidential Elections in American History.* New York: Chelsea House, 1981.

Singer, Aaron, ed. *Campaign Speeches of American Presidential Candidates, 1928-1972.* New York: Ungar, 1976.

———. *Campaign Speeches of American Presidential Candidates, 1948-1984.* New York: Ungar, 1985.

Smith, Jeffrey A. *American Presidential Elections: Trust and the Rational Voter.* New York: Praeger Publishers, 1980.

Stanwood, Edward. *History of the Presidency.* 2 vols. rev. ed. Reprint. 1928. New York: Kelley, 1975.

Stavis, Ben. *We Were the Campaign: New Hampshire to Chicago for McCarthy.* Boston: Beacon Press, 1969.

Tate, Katherine. *From Protest to Politics: The New Black Voters in American Elections.* Cambridge: Harvard University Press, 1993.

Wattenberg, Martin P. *The Rise of Candidate-Centered Politics: Presidential Elections of the 1980s.* Cambridge: Harvard University Press, 1991.

Wayne, Stephen J. *The Road to the White House, 1992: The Politics of Presidential Elections.* New York: St. Martin's Press, 1992.

Weinbaum, M. G., and L. H. Gold. *Presidential Election, A Simulation with Readings.* 2nd ed. Hillsdale, Ill.: Dryden Press, 1974.

White, Theodore H. *America in Search of Itself: The Making of the President, 1956-1980.* New York: Harper and Row, 1982.

———. *The Making of the President, 1960.* New York: Atheneum Publishers, 1961.

———. *The Making of the President, 1964.* New York: Atheneum Publishers, 1965.

———. *The Making of the President, 1968.* New York: Atheneum Publishers, 1969.

———. *The Making of the President, 1972.* New York: Atheneum Publishers, 1973.

## Articles

Aldrich, John H. "Rational Choice and Turnout." *American Journal of Political Science* 37 (February 1993): 246-278.

Axelrod, Robert. "Where the Votes Come From: An Analysis of Electoral Coalitions, 1952-1968. *American Political Science Review* 66 (March 1972): 11-20.

Bayh, Birch. "Electing a President: The Case for Direct Popular Election." *Harvard Journal on Legislation* (January 1969): 1-12.

Brody, Richard, and Lee Sigelman. "Presidential Popularity and Presidential Elections: An Update and Extension." *Public Opinion Quarterly* 47 (Fall 1983): 325-329.

Brunk, Gregory G., and Paul A. Gough. "State Economic Conditions and the 1980 Presidential Election." *Presidential Studies Quarterly* 13 (Winter 1983): 62-69.

Cohen, Jeffrey Elliot, and David C. Nice. "Party Unity and Presidential Election Performance: 1936-1980." *Presidential Studies Quarterly* 12 (Summer 1982): 317-329.

Eshelman, Edwin D. "Congress and Electoral Reform: An Analysis of Proposals for Changing Our Method of Selecting a President." *Christian Century,* Feb. 5, 1969, 178-181.

Feerick, John D. "The Electoral College: Why It Ought to Be Abolished." *Fordham Law Review* (October 1968): 43.

Felson, Marcus, and Seymour Sudman. "The Accuracy of Presidential Preference Primary Polls." *Public Opinion Quarterly* 39 (Summer 1975): 232-236.

Freund, Paul A. "Direct Election of the President: Issues and Answers." *American Bar Association Journal* (August 1970): 733.

Gossett, William T. "Direct Popular Election of the President." *American Bar Association Journal* (March 1970): 230.

Kessel, John H. "The Seasons of Presidential Politics." *Social Science Quarterly* 58 (December 1977): 418-435.

Kirkpatrick, Samuel A., William Lyons and Michael R. Fitzgerald. "Candidates, Parties, and Issues in the American Electorate: Two Decades of Change." *American Politics Quarterly* 3 (July 1975): 247-283.

Lechner, Alfred J. "Direct Election of the President: The Final Step in the Constitutional Evolution of the Right to Vote." *Notre Dame Lawyer* (October 1971): 122-152.

Leighley, Jan E., and Jonathan Nagler. "Socioeconomic Class Bias in Turnout: 1964-1988: The Voters Remain the Same." *American Political Science Review* 86 (September 1992): 725-736.

Lengle, James I. "Divisive Presidential Primaries and Party Electoral Prospects, 1932-1976." *American Politics Quarterly* 8 (July 1980): 261-277.

Livingston, James. "The Presidency and the People." *Democracy* 3 (Summer 1983): 41-49.

Monroe, Kristen R., and Dona Laughlin Metcalf. "Economic Influences of Presidential Popularity Among Key Political and Socioeconomic Groups: A Review of the Evidence and Some New Findings." *Political Behavior* 5 (1983): 309-345.

Moran, Jack, and Mark Fenster. "Voter Turnout in Presidential Primaries: A Diachronic Analysis." *American Politics Quarterly* 10 (October 1982): 453-476.

Pomper, Gerald M. "The 1972 Presidential Election in the USA." *International Problems* (July 1972): 44-54.

Powell, G. Bingham, Jr. "American Voter Turnout in Comparative Perspective." *American Political Science Review* 80 (March 1986): 17-43.

"Presidential Primaries: Proposals for a New System." *Congressional Quarterly Weekly Report*, July 8, 1972, 1650-1655.

Roettger, Walter B., and Hugh Winebrenner. "The Voting Behavior of American Political Scientists: The 1980 Presidential Election." *Western Political Quarterly* 36 (March 1983): 134-148.

Rubin, Richard L. "The Presidency in the Age of Television." *Proceedings of the Academy of Political Science* 34 (1981): 138-152.

Sievers H. J. "Reform of the Electoral College." *America*, Nov. 16, 1968, 465.

# Gubernatorial and Congressional Elections

## Books

Barone, Michael, and Grant Ujifusa. *The Almanac of American Politics, 1990.* rev. ed. Washington, D.C.: National Journal, 1989.

Bartley, Numan V. *From Thurmond to Wallace: Political Tendencies in Georgia 1948-1968.* Baltimore: Johns Hopkins Press, 1970.

_____, and Hugh D. Graham. *Southern Elections: County and Precinct Data, 1950-1972.* Baton Rouge: Louisiana State University Press, 1977.

Bass, Jack, and Walter DeVries. *Transformation of Southern Politics: Social Change and Political Consequence Since 1945.* New York: New American Library, 1977.

Benjamin, Gerald. *Limiting Legislative Terms.* Washington, D.C.: Congressional Quarterly, 1992.

Bryce, James. *The American Commonwealth.* 1922. Reprint. New York: AMS Press, 1973.

Ceaser, James, and Andrew Busch. *Upside Down and Inside Out: The 1992 Elections and American Politics.* Lanham, Md.: Rowman and Littlefield, 1993.

Congressional Quarterly. *The People Speak: American Elections in Focus.* Washington, D.C.: Congressional Quarterly, 1990.

Congressional Quarterly. *Guide to the U.S. Supreme Court.* 2nd ed. Washington, D.C.: Congressional Quarterly, 1993.

Congressional Quarterly. *Politics in America 1994.* Washington, D.C.: Congressional Quarterly, 1993.

Congressional Quarterly. *American Leaders 1789-1994* Washington, D.C.: Congressional Quarterly, 1994.

Cosman, Bernard. *Five States for Goldwater: Continuity and Change in Southern Voting Patterns 1920-1964.* University, Ala.: University of Alabama Press, 1965.

Ewing, Cortez A. *Primary Elections in the South: Study in Uniparty Politics.* 1953. Reprint. Westport, Conn.: Greenwood Press, 1980.

Germond, Jack W., and Jules Witcover. *Mad as Hell: Revolt at the Ballot Box, 1992.* New York: Warner Books, 1993.

Grantham, Dewey W. *Democratic South.* 1963. Reprint. New York: W. W. Norton, 1965.

Heard, Alexander, and Donald S. Strong. *Southern Primaries and Elections 1920-1949.* 1950. Reprint. Salem, N.H.: Ayers, 1970.

Hollingsworth, Harold J., ed. *Essays on Recent Southern Politics.* Austin: University of Texas Press, 1970.

Jacobstein, Helen L. *The Segregation Factor in the Florida Democratic Gubernatorial Primary Election of 1956.* Gainesville: University of Florida Press, 1972.

Key, V. O. Jr. *Southern Politics in State and Nation.* New York: Alfred A. Knopf, 1949.

Kousser, J. Morgan. *The Shaping of Southern Politics: Suffrage Restrictions and the Establishment of the One Party South, 1880-1910.* New Haven, Conn.: Yale University Press, 1974.

Kurland, Gerald. *George Wallace: Southern Governor and Presidential Candidate.* Charlotteville, N.Y.: Sam Har Press, 1972.

Lamis, Alexander P. *The Two-Party South,* 2nd ed. New York: Oxford University Press, 1990.

McGillivray, Alice V. *Congressional and Gubernatorial Primaries: 1991-1992: A Handbook of Election Statistics.* Washing-

ton, D.C.: Congressional Quarterly, 1993.

Moreland, Laurence W., et al. *Contemporary Southern Political Attitudes and Behavior: Studies and Essays.* New York: Praeger Publishing, 1982.

Ornstein, Norman J., Thomas E. Mann and Michael J. Malbin. *Vital Statistics on Congress 1993-1994.* Washington, D.C.: Congressional Quarterly, 1994.

Paolucci, Henry. *The South and the Presidency: From Reconstruction to Carter, A Long Day's Task.* Whitestone, N.Y.: Griffon House Publishing, 1978.

Pomper, Gerald M., ed. *The Election of 1992: Reports and Interpretations.* Chatham, N.J.: Chatham House, 1993.

Reichley, A. James, ed. *Elections American Style.* Washington, D.C.: Brookings Institution, 1987.

Sale, Kirkpatrick. *Power Shift: The Rise of the Southern Rim and Its Challenge to the Eastern Establishment.* New York: Random House, 1975.

Scammon, Richard M. *America Votes: A Handbook of Contemporary Election Statistics.* vols. 1 and 2. New York: Macmillan, 1956, 1958. *America Votes.* vols. 3-5. Pittsburgh: University of Pittsburgh, 1959, 1962, and 1964. *America Votes.* vols. 6-11. Washington, D.C.: Congressional Quarterly, 1966-75.

_____. and Alice V. McGillivray. *America Votes.* vols. 12-20. Washington, D.C.: Congressional Quarterly, 1977-93.

_____. and Alice V. McGillivray. *America at the Polls 2: A Handbook of Presidential Election Statistics 1968-1984.* Washington, D.C.: Congressional Quarterly, 1988.

Sindler, Allan P., ed. *Change in the Contemporary South.* Durham, N.C.: Duke University Press, 1963.

_____. *Huey Long's Louisiana: State Politics 1920-1952.* 1956. Reprint. Baltimore: Johns Hopkins University Press, 1980.

Spence, James R. *The Making of a Governor: The Moore-Preyer-Lake Primaries of 1964.* Winston-Salem, N.C.: John H. Blair, 1968.

Steed, Robert P., and Laurence W. Moreland, eds. *Party Politics in the South.* New York: Praeger, 1980.

Tindale, George B. *The Disruption of the Solid South.* New York: W. W. Norton, 1972.

Will, George F. *Restoration: Congress, Term Limits, and the Recovery of a Deliberative Democracy.* New York: Free Press, 1992.

Woodward, C. Vann. *Origins of the New South, 1877-1913.* Baton Rouge: Louisiana State University Press, 1951.

_____. *Reunion and Reaction: The Compromise of 1877 and the End to Reconstruction.* 1985. Reprint. New York: Oxford University Press, 1991.

## Articles

"The American South, 1950-1970." *Journal of Politics* (February 1964).

Black, Merle, and Earl Black. "Republican Party Development in the South: The Rise of the Contested Primary." *Social Science Quarterly* (December 1976): 566-578.

Burnham, Walter D. "The Alabama Senatorial Election of 1962: Return of Inter-Party Competition." *Journal of Politics* (November 1964): 798-829.

Calvert, Randall L., and John A. Ferejohn. "Coattail Voting in Recent Presidential Elections." *American Political Science Review* 77 (June 1983): 407-419.

Campbell, James E. "Predicting Seat Gains from Presidential Coattails." *American Journal of Political Science* 30 (February 1986): 165-183.

Cosman, Bernard. "Republican in the South: Goldwater's Impact Upon Voting Alignment in Congressional, Gubernatorial and Senatorial Races." *Southwestern Social Science Quarterly* (June 1967): 13-23.

Eisenberg, Ralph. "1966 Politics in Virginia: The Democratic Senatorial Primary." *University of Virginia News Letter* (Jan. 15, 1967).

Ferejohn, John A., and Randall L. Calvert. "Presidential Coattails in Historical Perspective." *American Journal of Political Science* 28 (February 1984): 127-146.

McCrary, Peyton, Clark Miller and Dale Baum. "Class and

Party in Secession Crisis: Voting Behavior in the Deep South." *Journal of Interdisciplinary History* 8 (Winter 1977): 429-457.

Pettigrew, Thomas F. "Faubus and Segregation: An Analysis of Arkansas Voting." *Public Opinion Quarterly* (Fall 1960): 346-347.

"Post-Mortem of a Georgia Primary." *New South* (Summer 1969): 80-88.

Worsnop, Richard L. "Changing Southern Politics." *Editorial Research Reports* 1 (Jan. 19, 1966): 43-59.

# Gubernatorial Elections

## Books

Council of State Governments. *State Elective Officials and the Legislatures 1991-1992.* Lexington, Ky.: Council of State Governments, 1991.

_____. *Book of the States, 1992-1993,* vol. 29. Lexington, Ky.: Council of State Governments, 1992.

Haider, Donald H. *When Governments Come to Washington: Governors, Mayors, and Intergovernmental Lobbying.* New York: Free Press, 1974.

Jacob, Herbert. *Politics in the American States.* 3rd ed. Boston: Little, Brown, 1976.

Jewell, Malcolm E. *Parties and Primaries: Nominating State Governors.* New York: Praeger, 1984.

Lipson, Leslie. *The American Governor from Figurehead to Leader.* 1939. Reprint. Westport, Conn.: Greenwood Press, 1969.

Kallenbach, Joseph E., and Jessamine S. Kallenbach. *American State Governors, 1776-1976.* 3 vols. Dobbs Ferry, N.Y.: Oceana Publishing, 1977.

Mullaney, Marie M. *Biographical Directory of the Governors of the United States 1983-1988.* Westport, Conn.: Meckler Publishing, 1989.

_____. *Biographical Directory of the Governors of the United States 1988-1994.* Westport, Conn.: Greenwood Press, 1994.

Raimo, John, ed. *Biographical Directory of the Governors of the United States, 1978-1982.* Westport, Conn.: Meckler Publishing, 1983.

Ransone, Coleman B., Jr. *The American Governorship.* Westport, Conn.: Greenwood Press, 1982.

_____. *The Office of the Governor in the United States.* 1956. Reprint. Salem, N.C.: Ayer.

Sabato, Larry. *Goodbye to Good-time Charlie: The American Governorship Transformed.* Washington, D.C.: CQ Press, 1983.

Sobel, Robert, ed. *Biographical Directory of the Governors of the United States, 1789-1978.* 4 vols. Westport, Conn.: Meckler Publishing, 1978.

Spence, James R. *The Making of a Governor: The Moore Preyer-Lake Primaries, 1964.* Winston-Salem, N.C.: John F. Blair Publishing, 1968.

## Articles

Abrams, Burton A. "Political Power and the Market for Governors." *Public Choice* 37 (1981): 521-529.

Bibby, John F. "Political Parties and Federalism: The Republican National Committee Involvement in Gubernatorial and Legislative Elections." *Publius* 9 (Winter 1979): 229-236.

Bryan, Richard J. "Legislative Election of a Governor." *North Carolina Law Review* (December 1967): 128-142.

Eismeier, Theodore J. "Votes and Taxes: The Political Economy of the American Governorship." *Polity* 15 (Spring 1983): 368-379.

Jewell, Malcolm E. "Voting Turnout in State Gubernatorial Primaries." *Western Political Quarterly* 30 (June 1977): 236-254.

Patterson, Samuel C. "Campaign Spending in Contests for Governor." *Western Political Quarterly* 35 (December 1982): 457-477.

Penning, James M., and Corwin E. Smidt. "Public Funding of Gubernatorial Elections: The Views of State Legislatures." *American Politics Quarterly* 10 (July 1982): 315-332.

Pierson, James E. "Sources of Candidate Success in Gubernatorial Elections, 1910-1970." *Journal of Politics* 39 (November 1977): 939-958.

Reiter, Howard L. "Who Voted for Longley? Maine Elects an Independent Governor." *Polity* 10 (Fall 1977): 65-85.

# Senate Elections

## Books

Abramowitz, Alan I., and Jeffrey A. Segal. *Senate Elections.* Ann Arbor: University of Michigan Press, 1992.

Congressional Quarterly. *Guide to Congress.* 4th ed. Washington, D.C.: Congressional Quarterly, 1993.

Falco, Maria J. *Bigotry: Ethnic, Machine and Sexual Politics in a Senatorial Election.* Westport, Conn.: Greenwood Press, 1980.

Farrand, Max. *Records of the Federal Convention of 1787.* 4 vols. rev. ed. New Haven, Conn.: Yale University Press, 1967.

Huckshorn, Robert J. *Politics of Defeat: Campaigning for Congress.* Amherst, Mass.: University of Massachusetts Press, 1971.

Hutson, James H. *Supplement to Max Farrand's the Records of the Federal Convention of 1787.* New Haven, Conn.: Yale University Press, 1987.

Mann, Thomas E. *Unsafe at Any Margin: Interpreting Congressional Elections.* Washington, D.C.: American Enterprise Institute, 1978.

Matteson, David M. *The Organization of the Government under the Constitution.* New York: Da Capo Press, 1970.

Matthews, Donald R. *U.S. Senators and their World.* 1960. Reprint. Westport, Conn.: Greenwood Press, 1980.

Maurine, Christopher. *Black Americans in Congress.* New York: Crowell, 1976.

Miller, Warren, Arthur Miller and Edward Schneider. *American National Election Studies Data Sourcebook, 1952-1986.* Cambridge, Mass.: Harvard University Press, 1989.

Ranney, Austin. *The American Elections of 1984.* Washington, D.C.: American Enterprise Institute, 1985.

Rogers, Lindsay. *The American Senate.* 1926. Reprint. New York: Johnson Reprint, 1968.

## Articles

Abramowitz, Alan I. "A Comparison of Voting for U.S. Senator and Representative in 1978." *American Political Science Review* 74 (September 1980): 633-640.

_____. "Choices and Echoes in the 1978 U.S. Senate Elections: A Research Note." *American Journal of Political Science* 25 (February 1981): 112-118.

Abramson, Paul R., John H. Aldrich, and David W. Rohde. "Progressive Ambition among United States Senators: 1972-1988." *Journal of Politics* 49 (February 1987): 3-35.

Bernstein, Robert A. "Divisive Primaries Do Hurt: U.S. Senate Races, 1956-1972." *American Political Science Review* 71 (June 1977): 540-545.

Brookshire, Robert G., and Dean F. Duncan III. "Congressional Career Patterns and Party Systems." *Legislative Studies Quarterly* 8 (February 1983): 65-78.

Bullock, Charles S. III, and David W. Brady. "Party Constituency and Roll Call Voting in the U.S. Senate." *Legislative Studies Quarterly* 8 (February 1983): 29-43.

Burnstein, Paul. "Party Balance, Replacement of Legislators, and Federal Government Expenditures, 1941-1976." *Western Political Quarterly* 32 (June 1979): 203-208.

Delli Carpini, Michael X., and Ester R. Fuchs. "The Year of the Woman? Candidates, Voters, and the 1992 Elections." *Political Science Quarterly* 108 (Spring 1993): 29-36.

Kostroski, Warren. "The Effect of Number of Terms on the Re-Election of Senators, 1920-1970." *Journal of Politics* 40 (May 1978): 488-497.

Kuklinski, James H., and Darrell M. West. "Economic Expectations and Voting Behavior in the United States House and Senate Elections." *American Political Science Review* 75 (June 1981): 436-447.

Mann, Thomas E., and Raymond E. Wolfinger. "Candidates and Parties in Congressional Elections." *American Political Science Review* 74 (September 1980): 617-632.

Tuchel, Peter. "The Initial Re-election Chances of Appointed and Elected United States Senators." *Polity* 16 (Fall 1983): 138-142.

Uslaner, Eric M. "Party Reform and Electoral Disaggregation: A Paradox in Congress?" *Policy Studies Journal* 5 (Summer 1977): 454-459.

Westlye, Mark C. "Competitiveness of Senate Seats and Voting Behavior in Senate Elections." *American Journal of Political Science* 27 (May 1983): 253-283.

# House Elections

## Books

Campbell, James E. *The Presidential Pulse of Congressional Elections.* Lexington: University Press of Kentucky, 1991.

Commons, John R. *Proportional Representation.* 2nd ed. 1907. Reprint. New York: A. M. Kelley, 1967.

Congressional Quarterly. *Congressional Districts in the 1990s.* Washington, D.C.: Congressional Quarterly, 1993.

Congressional Quarterly. *Guide to Congress.* 4th ed. Washington, D.C.: Congressional Quarterly, 1993.

Crotty, William, ed. *America's Choice: The Election of 1992.* Guilford, Conn.: Dushkin, 1993.

Davidson, Roger H., and Walter J. Oleszek. *Congress and Its Members.* 4th ed. Washington, D.C.: CQ Press, 1994.

Dodd, Lawrence D., and Bruce I Oppenheimer, ed. *Congress Reconsidered.* 3rd ed. Washington, D.C.: CQ Press, 1985.

Farrand, Max. *Records of the Federal Convention of 1787.* Rev. ed. 4 vols. New Haven, Conn.: Yale University Press, 1967.

Fenno, Richard F., Jr. *Home Style: House Members in Their Districts.* Boston: Little, Brown, 1978.

Fiorina, Morris P. *Congress: Keystone of the Washington Establishment,* 2nd ed. New Haven, Conn.: Yale University Press, 1989.

Galloway, George B. *History of the House of Representatives.* 2nd. ed. New York: Crowell, 1976.

Grofman, Bernard, et al. *Reapportionment Policy.* Urbana, Ill.: Policy Studies Organization, University of Illinois at Urbana-Champagne, 1981.

Hacker, Andrew. *Congressional Districting: The Issue of Equal Representation.* Rev. ed. Washington, D.C.: Brookings Institution, 1964.

Hinckley, Barbara. *Congressional Elections.* Washington, D.C.: CQ Press, 1981.

Hutson, James H. *Supplement to Max Farrand's the Records of the Federal Convention of 1787.* New Haven, Conn.: Yale University Press, 1987.

Jacobson, Gary C. *The Electoral Origins of Divided Government: Competition in U.S. House Elections, 1946-1988.* Boulder, Colo.: Westview Press, 1990.

———. *The Politics of Congressional Elections,* 3rd ed. New York: Harper Collins, 1991.

Luce, Robert. *Legislative Principles; the Historic Theory of Lawmaking by Representative Government.* 1930. Reprint. New York: Da Capo Press, 1971.

McPhee, William N., and William A. Glasser, eds. *Public Opinion and Congressional Elections.* 1962. Reprint. Westport, Conn.: Greenwood Press, 1981.

Mann, Thomas E., and Norman J. Ornstein. *Renewing Congress.* Washington, D.C.: Brookings Institution, 1993.

Martis, Kenneth C. *The Historical Atlas of United States Congressional Districts 1789-1983.* New York: The Free Press, 1982.

Matteson, David M. *The Organization of the Government Under the Constitution.* New York: Da Capo Press, 1970.

Ornstein, Norman J., ed. *Congress in Change: Elections and Reform.* New York: Praeger, 1975.

O'Rourke, Timothy. *The Impact of Reapportionment.* New Brunswick, N.J.: Transaction Books, 1980.

Polsby, Nelson W., ed. *Reapportionment in the 1970s.* Berkeley, Calif.: University of California Press, 1971.

Rohde, David W. *Parties and Leaders in the Postreform House.* Chicago: University of Chicago Press, 1991.

Schmeckebier, Laurence F. *Congressional Apportionment.* 1941. Reprint. Westport, Conn.: Greenwood Press, 1976.

## Articles

Abramowitz, Alan I. "A Comparison of Voting for U.S. Senator and Representative in 1978." *American Political Science Review* 74 (September 1980): 633-640.

Alford, John R., and John R. Hibbing. "Increased Incumbency Advantage in the House." *Journal of Politics* 43 (November 1981): 1042-1061.

Baker, Gordon E. "Redistricting in the Seventies: The Political Thicket Deepens." *National Civic Review* (June 1972): 277-285.

Bond, Jon R. "The Influence of Constituency Diversity on Electoral Competition in Voting for Congress, 1974-1978." *Legislative Studies Quarterly* 8 (May 1983): 201-217.

Born, Richard. "House Incumbents and Inter-Election Vote Change." *Journal of Politics* 39 (November 1977): 1008-1034.

———. "Generational Replacement and the Growth of Incumbent Reelection Margins in the U.S. House." *American Political Science Review* 73 (September 1979): 811-817.

———. "The Influence of House Primary Election Divisiveness on General Election Margins, 1962-1976." *Journal of Politics* 43 (August 1981): 640-661.

———. "Reassessing the Decline of Presidential Coalitions: U.S. House Elections from 1952-80," *Journal of Politics* 46 (February 1984): 60-79.

Brookshire, Robert G., and Dean F. Duncan III. "Congressional Career Patterns and Party Systems." *Legislative Studies Quarterly* 8 (February 1983): 29-43.

Burnstein, Paul. "Party Balance, Replacement of Legislators, and Federal Government Expenditures, 1941-1976." *Western Political Quarterly* 32 (June 1979): 203-208.

Collie, Melissa P. "Incumbency, Electoral Safety and Turnover in the House of Representatives." *American Political Science Review* 75 (March 1981): 119-131.

"Congress in the Thicket: The Congressional Redistricting Bill of 1967." *George Washington Law Review* 36 (1967): 224-234.

"Congressional Redistricting: One Man, One Vote Demands Near Mathematical Precision." *De Paul Law Review* (Autumn 1969): 152-171.

Delli Carpini, Michael X., and Ester R. Fuchs. "The Year of the Woman? Candidates, Voters, and the 1992 Elections." *Political Science Quarterly* 108 (Spring 1993): 29-36.

Elving, Ronald D. "Redistricting: Drawing Power with a Map," *Editorial Research Reports,* Feb. 15, 1991, 99.

"Equal Representation and the Weighted Vote Alternative." *Yale Law Review* (Spring 1970): 311-321.

Fenno, Richard F., Jr. *Home Style: House Members in Their Districts.* Boston: Little, Brown, 1978.

Gazell, James A. "One Man, One Vote: Its Long Germination." *Western Political Quarterly* (September 1970): 445-462.

Gross, Donald A. "Representative Styles and Legislative Behavior." *Western Political Quarterly* 31 (September 1978): 359-371.

Irwin, William P. "Representation and Apportionment." *Parliamentary Affairs* (Summer 1968): 226-245.

———. "Representation and Election: The Reapportionment Cases in Retrospect." *Michigan Law Review* 67 (1969): 729-754.

Katz, Ellis. "Apportionment and Majority Rule." *Publius* (1971): 141-161.

Kuklinski, James H., and Darrell M. West. "Economic Expectations and Voting Behavior in the United States House and Senate Elections." *American Political Science Review* 75 (June 1981): 436-447.

Linton, Robert N. "Further Exploration in the Political Thicket: The Gerrymander and the Constitution." *Loyola Law Review* (October 1973): 1-47.

Lipset, Seymour Martin. "The Significance of the 1992 Election." *PS: Political Science and Politics* 26 (March 1993): 7-16.

Mann, Thomas E., and Raymond E. Wolfinger. "Candidates and Parties in Congressional Elections." *American Political Science Review* 74 (September 1980): 617-632.

Payne, James L. "Career Intentions and Electoral Performance of Members of the U.S. House." *Legislative Studies Quarterly* 7

(February 1982): 93-99.

———. "The Personal Electoral Advantage of House Incumbents, 1936-1976." *American Politics Quarterly* 8 (October 1980): 449-464.

Robeck, Bruce W. "State Legislator Candidacies for the U.S. House: Prospect for Success." *Legislative Studies Quarterly* 7 (November 1982): 507-514.

Rohde, David W. "Risk-Bearing and Progressive Ambition: The Case of the United States House of Representatives." *American Journal of Political Science* 23 (February 1979): 1-26.

Roll, C. W. "We, Some of the People: Apportionment in the Thirteen State Conventions Ratifying the Constitution." *American History* (June 1969): 21-40.

Sigelman, Lee. "Special Elections to the U. S. House: Some Descriptive Generalizations." *Legislative Studies Quarterly* (November 1981): 577-588.

Stone, Walter J. "The Dynamics of Constituency: Electoral Control in the House." *American Politics Quarterly* 8 (October 1980): 399-424.

Sullivan, John L. "Electoral Choice and Popular Control of Policy: The Case of the 1966 House Elections." *American Political Science Review* (December 1972): 1256-1268.

Uslaner, Eric M. "Party Reform and Electoral Disaggregation: A Paradox in Congress." *Policy Studies Journal* 5 (Summer 1977): 454-459.

Wattenberg, Martin P. "From Parties to Candidates: Examining the Role of the Media." *Public Opinion Quarterly* 46 (Summer 1982): 216-227.

Wollock, Andrea J. "Reapportionment Now." *State Legislatures* (January 1982): 7-13.

Wright, John R., and Richard G. Niemi. "Perceptions of Candidates' Issue Positions." *Political Behavior* 5 (1983): 209-223.

# Indexes

# Presidential Candidates Index

The Presidential Candidates Index includes all presidential candidates appearing in Presidential Elections, Popular Vote Returns, 1824-1984 (pp. 329-377).

The index includes candidates' names followed by the years of candidacy. To locate a candidate's returns, turn to pages 329-377 where the returns are arranged in chronological order. For major candidate returns, see pages 329-366; for minor candidate returns, see pages 367-377.

For other references to presidential candidates in the *Guide to U.S. Elections, Third Edition,* see the General Index, p. 1503.

# Gubernatorial Candidates Index

The Gubernatorial Candidates Index includes all candidates appearing in Gubernatorial Elections: Popular Vote Returns, 1789-1993 (pp. 667-716).

The index includes candidates' names followed by state abbreviations and the years of candidacy. To locate a candidate's returns, turn to pages 667-716 where the returns are arranged alphabetically by state *(State Abbreviations below)* and in chronological order of election for each state.

For other references to gubernatorial candidates in the *Guide to U.S. Elections, Third Edition,* see the General Index, page 1503.

## A

Aandahl, Fred G. (ND) - 1944, 1946, 1948
Abbett, Leon (NJ) - 1883, 1889
Abbott, Martha (VT) - 1974
Abernethy, Tom (AL) - 1954
Acker, Bert Lee (FL) - 1944, 1948
Ackerman, Lee (AZ) - 1960
Acuff, Roy (TN) - 1948
Adair, John A. M. (IN) - 1916
Adair, John (KY) - 1820
Adam, Andrew (ME) - 1990
Adams, Alva (CO) - 1884, 1886, 1896, 1904, 1906
Adams, Charles Francis (MA) - 1876
Adams, Jewett W. (NV) - 1882, 1886
Adams, John Quincy (MA) - 1833, 1867, 1868, 1869, 1870, 1871
Adams, Paul L. (NY) - 1966, 1970
Adams, Samuel (MA) - 1794, 1795, 1796
Adams, Sherman (NH) - 1948, 1950
Adams, Spencer B. (NC) - 1900
Adams, Tod R. (TX) - 1954
Adams, William H. (CO) - 1926, 1928, 1930
Adkins, Homer M. (AR) - 1940, 1942
Agnew, Spiro T. (MD) - 1966
Aiken, George D. (VT) - 1936, 1938
Akin (GA) - 1859
Alcorn, Hugh Meade (CT) - 1934
Alcorn, James L. (MS) - 1869, 1873
Aldrich, Chester H. (NE) - 1910, 1912
Aldrich, Walter J. (VT) - 1914
Alexander (NJ) - 1856
Alexander, Archibald (DE) - 1795
Alexander, Lamar (TN) - 1974, 1978, 1982
Alexander, Moses (ID) - 1908, 1914, 1916, 1922
Alfange, Dean (NY) - 1942
Alger, Fred M. Jr. (MI) - 1952
Alger, Horace C. (WY) - 1898
Alger, Russell A. (MI) - 1884
Allain, Bill (MS) - 1983
Allen (MO) - 1844

Allen, Byron G. (MN) - 1944
Allen, Charles H. (MA) - 1891
Allen, Frank G. (MA) - 1928, 1930
Allen, George W. (FL) - 1916
Allen, George F. (VA) - 1993
Allen, G. H. (CO) - 1896
Allen, Heman (VT) - 1829, 1831
Allen, Henry J. (KS) - 1914, 1918, 1920
Allen, Henry W. (LA) - 1864, 1865
Allen, James C. (IL) - 1860
Allen, John (KY) - 1808
Allen, Oscar K. (LA) - 1932
Allen, Philip (RI) - 1851, 1852, 1853
Allen, Samuel L. (MA) - 1833
Allen, William (OH) - 1873, 1875
Allen, William C. (SD) - 1934
Allin, Roger (ND) - 1894
Allis, Edward P. (WI) - 1877
Allred, James V. (TX) - 1934, 1936
Almond, J. Lindsay Jr. (VA) - 1957
Almond, Lincoln (RI) - 1978
Alschuler, Samuel (IL) - 1900
Alsop, John P. (IL) - 1892, 1896
Altgeld, John P. (IL) - 1892, 1896
Ameringer, Oscar (WI) - 1914
Ames, A. A. (MN) - 1886
Ames, Adelbert (MS) - 1873
Ames, Alfred K. (ME) - 1934
Ames, Oliver (MA) - 1886, 1887, 1888
Ammons, Elias M. (CO) - 1912
Ammons, Teller (CO) - 1936, 1938
Amsden, Charles H. (NH) - 1888, 1890
Anaya, Toney (NM) - 1982
Andersen, Elmer L. (MN) - 1960, 1962
Anderson, C. Elmer (MN) - 1952, 1954
Anderson, D.G. "Andy" (HI) - 1982, 1986
Anderson, Emmett T. (WA) - 1956
Anderson, Forrest H. (MT) - 1968
Anderson, Henry W. (VA) - 1921
Anderson, Hugh J. (ME) - 1843, 1844, 1845
Anderson, J. H. (ID) - 1898
Anderson, John Jr. (KS) - 1960, 1962
Anderson, Kenneth T. (KS) - 1950

Anderson, Sigurd (SD) - 1950, 1952
Anderson, Thomas J. (MN) - 1916
Anderson, T. J. (IA) - 1887
Anderson, Victor E. (NE) - 1954, 1956, 1958
Anderson, Wendell R. (MN) - 1970, 1974
Anderson, William R. (TN) - 1962
Andrew, John A. (MA) - 1860, 1861, 1862, 1863, 1864
Andrew, John F. (MA) - 1886
Andrews (GA) - 1855
Andrews, Charles B. (CT) - 1878
Andrews, John (CO) - 1990
Andrews, Lloyd (WA) - 1960
Andrews, Mark (ND) - 1962
Andrews, Reddin (TX) - 1910, 1912
Andrus, Cecil D. (ID) - 1966, 1970, 1974, 1986, 1990
Ansel, Martin F. (SC) - 1906, 1908
Anthony, George T. (KS) - 1876
Anthony, Henry B. (RI) - 1849, 1850
Apodaca, Jerry (NM) - 1974
Appleton, James (ME) - 1842, 1843, 1844
Archambault, Alberic A. (RI) - 1918, 1928
Archambault, Raoul Jr. (RI) - 1952
Ariyoshi, George R. (HI) - 1974, 1978, 1982
Armstrong (TN) - 1837
Armstrong, Alexander (MD) - 1923
Armstrong, Charles M. (CO) - 1936
Arn, Edward F. (KS) - 1950, 1952
Arnall, Ellis (GA) - 1942
Arnesen, Deborah Arnie (NH) - 1992
Arnold (WI) - 1904
Arnold, Lemuel H. (RI) - 1831, 1832, 1833
Arnold, Louis A. (WI) - 1922
Arnold, Olney (RI) - 1872, 1908, 1909
Arnold, Peleg (RI) - 1806, 1815
Aronson, John Hugo (MT) - 1952, 1956
Ashcroft, John (MO) - 1984, 1988
Ashe, Thomas S. (NC) - 1868
Ashelstrom, Charles A. (CO) - 1912
Ashley (MO) - 1836
Ashley, William H. (MO) - 1824
Askew, Reubin (FL) - 1970, 1974

Atiyeh, Victor G. (OR) - 1974, 1978, 1982
Atkinson (MO) - 1920
Atkinson, George W. (WV) - 1896
Atkinson, William Y. (GA) - 1894, 1896
Atkinson, W. P. (OK) - 1962
Atwater (CT) - 1878
Atwood, John (NH) - 1851, 1852
Austin, Horace (MN) - 1869, 1871
Austin, Richard B. (IL) - 1956
Auten, H. F. (AR) - 1898
Avenson, Donald D. (IA) - 1990
Avery, Carlos (MN) - 1924
Avery, William H. (KS) - 1964, 1966
Aycock, Charles B. (NC) - 1900
Ayers, Roy E. (MT) - 1936, 1940
Aylward, John A. (WI) - 1906, 1908
Ayres, Tom (SD) - 1926

## B

Babb, W. I. (IA) - 1895
Babbitt, Bruce (AZ) - 1978, 1980
Babcock, Tim (MT) - 1964, 1968
Bachelder, Nahum J. (NH) - 1902
Bacon, Gaspar G. (MA) - 1934
Bacon, Waler W. (DE) - 1940, 1944
Badger, William (NH) - 1834, 1835
Bafalis, L. A. (Skip) (DE) - 1982
Bagby, Arthur P. (AL) - 1837, 1839
Bagley, John J. (MI) - 1872, 1874
Bagwell, Paul D. (MI) - 1958, 1960
Bailey, Carl E. (AR) - 1936, 1938
Bailey, Ed F. (OR) - 1930
Bailey, Ernest H. (VT) - 1944
Bailey, John (MA) - 1834
Bailey, John W. (MI) - 1918
Bailey, M. S. (CO) - 1896
Bailey, Thomas L. (MS) - 1943
Bailey, W. (FL) - 1848
Bailey, W. J. (KS) - 1902
Baird, David Jr. (NJ) - 1931

---

## State Abbreviations

| | | | | | | | |
|---|---|---|---|---|---|---|---|
| Alabama | AL | Illinois | IL | Montana | MT | Rhode Island | RI |
| Alaska | AK | Indiana | IN | Nebraska | NE | South Carolina | SC |
| Arizona | AZ | Iowa | IA | Nevada | NV | South Dakota | SD |
| Arkansas | AR | Kansas | KS | New Hampshire | NH | Tennessee | TN |
| California | CA | Kentucky | KY | New Jersey | NJ | Texas | TX |
| Colorado | CO | Louisiana | LA | New Mexico | NM | Utah | UT |
| Connecticut | CT | Maine | ME | New York | NY | Vermont | VT |
| Delaware | DE | Maryland | MD | North Carolina | NC | Virginia | VA |
| Florida | FL | Massachusetts | MA | North Dakota | ND | Washington | WA |
| Georgia | GA | Michigan | MI | Ohio | OH | West Virginia | WV |
| Hawaii | HI | Minnesota | MN | Oklahoma | OK | Wisconsin | WI |
| Idaho | ID | Mississippi | MS | Oregon | OR | Wyoming | WY |
| | | Missouri | MO | Pennsylvania | PA | | |

# Gubernatorial Primary Candidates Index

The Gubernatorial Primary Candidates Index includes all candidates appearing in Gubernatorial Elections: Primary Returns, 1919-93 (pp. 719-773).

The index includes candidates' names followed by state abbreviations and the years of candidacy. To locate a candidate's returns, turn to pages 719-773 where the returns are arranged alphabetically by state *(State Abbreviations below)* and in chronological order of election for each state.

For other references to gubernatorial candidates in the *Guide to U.S. Elections, Third Edition,* see the General Index, page 1503.

---

## State Abbreviations

# Senate Candidates Index

The Senate Candidates Index includes all candidates appearing in Senate Popular Vote Returns, 1913-93 pp. 815-846).

The index includes candidates' names followed by state abbreviations and the years of candidacy. To locate a candidate's returns, turn to pages 815-846 where the returns are arranged alphabetically by state and in chronological order by class of senator for each state. *(Explanation of Senate classes, p. 780; State Abbreviations, below)* For other references to Senate candidates in the *Guide to U.S. Elections, Third Edition,* see the General Index, page 1503.

## A

Aandahl, Fred G. (ND) - 1952
Abdnor, James (SD) - 1980, 1986
Abel, Hazel H. (NE) - 1954
Abourezk, James (SD) - 1972
Abrams, Robert (NY) - 1992
Adams, Alva B. (CO) - 1924, 1932, 1938
Adams, Brock (WA) - 1986
Adams, Wilbur L. (DE) - 1934
Aiken, George D. (VT) - 1940, 1944, 1950, 1956, 1962, 1968
Aiken, Paul (KS) - 1950
Akaka, Daniel K. (HI) - 1990
Akins, Thomas J. (MO) - 1914
Alexander, Archibald S. (NJ) - 1948, 1952
Alexander, John G. (MN) - 1936
Alexander, Morton (CO) - 1924
Alexander, W. H. Bill (OK) - 1950
Allen, Henry J. (KS) - 1930
Allen, Jim (AL) - 1968, 1974
Allott, Gordon (CO) - 1954, 1960, 1966, 1972
Anaya, Toney (NM) - 1978
Andersen, Bill (TN) - 1988
Anderson, Clinton P. (NM) - 1948, 1954, 1960, 1966
Anderson, Wendell R. (MN) - 1978
Andrews, Charles O. (FL) - 1936, 1940
Andrews, Jackson M. (KY) - 1986
Andrews, Lloyd J. (WA) - 1964
Andrews, Mark (ND) - 1980, 1986
Archambault, Raoul (RI) - 1960
Arndt, Raymond W. (NE) - 1964
Arnold, James W. (GA) - 1932
Ashe, Victor (TN) - 1984
Ashurst, Henry F. (AZ) - 1916, 1922, 1928, 1934
Atcheson, Alex W. (TX) - 1916
Atchley, Forrest S. (NM) - 1958
Atkins, Hobart F. (TN) - 1952, 1958
Atkinson, C. D. (AR) - 1938
AuCoin, Les (OR) - 1992

Austin, Warren R. (VT) - 1931, 1934, 1940
Aylward Paul L. (KS) - 1962
Ayres, Tom (SD) - 1920, 1924

## B

Babbitt, Wayne H. (AR) - 1972
Babcock, Howard C. (FL) - 1936
Babcock, Tim (MT) - 1966
Bachman, Nathan L. (TN) - 1934, 1936
Bailey, Carl E. (AR) - 1937
Bailey, John W. (MI) - 1928
Bailey, Josiah W. (NC) - 1930, 1936, 1942
Baird, David (NJ) - 1918
Baker, Howard (TN) - 1940
Baker, Howard H. Jr. (TN) - 1964, 1966, 1972, 1978
Baker, Ray T. (NV) - 1926
Baker, Stuart D. (VA) - 1960
Baldwin, Raymond E. (CT) - 1946
Baldwin, Simeon (CT) - 1914
Ball, Joseph H. (MN) - 1942, 1948
Ball, Lewis Heisler (DE) - 1918
Bamberger, Ernest (UT) - 1922, 1928
Bancroft, Philip (CA) - 1938
Bankhead, John H. (AL) - 1918, 1930, 1936, 1942
Banks, L. A. (OR) - 1930
Bantz, William B. (WA) - 1958
Barbour, Haley (MS) - 1982
Barbour, W. Warren (NJ) - 1932, 1936, 1938, 1940
Bard, Guy Kurtz (PA) - 1952
Barkley, Alben W. (KY) - 1926, 1932, 1938, 1944, 1954
Barnett, Don (SD) - 1978
Barrett, Frank A. (WY) - 1952, 1958
Barry, Alex G. (OR) - 1938
Barth, Adam H. (WA) - 1914
Bartlett, Dewey F. (OK) - 1972
Bartlett, E. L. (AK) - 1958, 1960, 1966
Barton, Bruce (NY) - 1940

Barton, Joe L. (TX) - 1993
Bass, Perkins (NH) - 1962
Bass, Ross (TN) - 1964
Baucus, Max (MT) - 1978, 1984, 1990
Bauman, Rick (OR) - 1986
Baxter, James H. (DE) - 1978
Bayard, A. I. du Pont (DE) - 1952
Bayard, Thomas F. (DE) - 1922, 1928, 1930
Bayh, Birch (IN) - 1962, 1968, 1974, 1980
Beall, J. Glenn (MD) - 1952, 1958, 1964
Beall, J. Glenn Jr. (MD) - 1970, 1976
Bean, Martha E. (OR) - 1918
Beard, Robin L. (TN) - 1976
Beasley, Michael (AK) - 1990
Beckham, John C. W. (KY) - 1914, 1920
Beeckman, R. Livingston (RI) - 1922
Bell, Jeffrey (NJ) - 1978
Bellmon, Henry (OK) - 1968, 1974
Benavides, Tom R. (NM) - 1990
Bender, George H. (OH) - 1954, 1956
Benedict, Cleveland K. (WV) - 1982
Benedict, Cooper P. (WV) - 1964
Bennett, Robert F. (UT) - 1992
Bennett, Wallace F. (UT) - 1950, 1956, 1962, 1968
Bennion, Adams S. (UT) - 1944
Benson, Elmer A. (MN) - 1940, 1942
Bentley, Alvin M. (MI) - 1960
Benton, William (CT) - 1950, 1952
Bentsen, Lloyd (TX) - 1970, 1976, 1982, 1988
Berger, Victor L. (WI) - 1918
Berkstresser, H. E. (AL) - 1936
Berl, E. Ennalls (DE) - 1942
Berman, Dan (UT) - 1980
Bernard, Charles (AR) - 1968
Berry, Tom (SD) - 1938, 1942
Bethune, Ed (AR) - 1984
Betley, Joseph J. (NH) - 1944
Betley, Stanley J. (NH) - 1954
Bettman, Gilbert (OH) - 1932
Betts, James E. (OH) - 1980
Beveridge, Albert J. (IN) - 1914, 1922

Bible, Alan (NV) - 1954, 1956, 1962, 1968
Biden, Joseph R. Jr. (DE) - 1972, 1978, 1984, 1990
Bigelow, James E. (VT) - 1950
Bilbo, Theodore G. (MS) - 1934, 1940, 1946
Bingaman, Jeff (NM) - 1982, 1988
Bingham, Hiram (CT) - 1924, 1926, 1932
Birch, Alex C. (AL) - 1914
Bishop, Neil S. (ME) - 1970
Bjornson, Val (MN) - 1954
Black, Hugo L. (AL) - 1926, 1932
Black, John G. (AR) - 1978
Black, W. W. (WA) - 1914
Blaine, John J. (WI) - 926
Blakley, William A. (TX) - 1961
Blanton, Ray (TN) - 1972
Blatt, Genevieve (PA) - 1964
Blease, Cole L. (SC) - 1924
Blewett, Alex (MT) - 1964
Blount, Winton M. (Red) (AL) - 1972
Boggs, J. Caleb (DE) - 1960, 1966, 1972
Bond, Christopher S. (MO) - 1986, 1992
Bone, Homer T. (WA) - 1932, 1938
Bontrager, D. Russell (IN) - 1964
Boole, Ella A. (NY) - 1920
Booth, John P. (FL) - 1950
Booth, R. A. (OR) - 1914
Borah, William E. (ID) - 1918, 1924, 1930, 1936
Boren, David L. (OK) - 1978, 1984, 1990
Borough, Reuben W. (CA) - 1952
Boschwitz, Rudy (MN) - 1978, 1984, 1990
Bottolfsen, C. A. (ID) - 1944
Bottum, Joe (SD) - 1962
Boulter, Beau (TX) - 1988
Bourne, Jonathan Jr. (OR) - 1912
Bourquin, George M. (MT) - 1934
Boxer, Barbara (CA) - 1992
Bradford, W. S. (AZ) - 1916
Bradley, Bill (NJ) - 1978, 1984, 1990
Bradshaw, George M. (SD) - 1944
Bradshaw, Jean Paul (MO) - 1964
Brady, James H. (ID) - 1914

---

## State Abbreviations

| | | | | |
|---|---|---|---|---|
| **Alabama** . . . . . . . AL | **Illinois** . . . . . . . IL | **Montana** . . . . . . . MT | **Rhode Island** . . . . . . . RI |
| **Alaska** . . . . . . . AK | **Indiana** . . . . . . . IN | **Nebraska** . . . . . . . NE | **South Carolina** . . . . . . . SC |
| **Arizona** . . . . . . . AZ | **Iowa** . . . . . . . IA | **Nevada** . . . . . . . NV | **South Dakota** . . . . . . . SD |
| **Arkansas** . . . . . . . AR | **Kansas** . . . . . . . KS | **New Hampshire** . . . . . . . NH | **Tennessee** . . . . . . . TN |
| **California** . . . . . . . CA | **Kentucky** . . . . . . . KY | **New Jersey** . . . . . . . NJ | **Texas** . . . . . . . TX |
| **Colorado** . . . . . . . CO | **Louisiana** . . . . . . . LA | **New Mexico** . . . . . . . NM | **Utah** . . . . . . . UT |
| **Connecticut** . . . . . . . CT | **Maine** . . . . . . . ME | **New York** . . . . . . . NY | **Vermont** . . . . . . . VT |
| **Delaware** . . . . . . . DE | **Maryland** . . . . . . . MD | **North Carolina** . . . . . . . NC | **Virginia** . . . . . . . VA |
| **Florida** . . . . . . . FL | **Massachusetts** . . . . . . . MA | **North Dakota** . . . . . . . ND | **Washington** . . . . . . . WA |
| **Georgia** . . . . . . . GA | **Michigan** . . . . . . . MI | **Ohio** . . . . . . . OH | **West Virginia** . . . . . . . WV |
| **Hawaii** . . . . . . . HI | **Minnesota** . . . . . . . MN | **Oklahoma** . . . . . . . OK | **Wisconsin** . . . . . . . WI |
| **Idaho** . . . . . . . ID | **Mississippi** . . . . . . . MS | **Oregon** . . . . . . . OR | **Wyoming** . . . . . . . WY |
| | **Missouri** . . . . . . . MO | **Pennsylvania** . . . . . . . PA | |

Meacham, F. Todd (TN) - 1930, 1942
Mead, James M. (NY) - 1938, 1940
Means, Rice W. (CO) - 1924
Mecham, Evan (AZ) - 1962, 1992
Mechem, Edwin L. (NM) - 1954, 1964
Mechling, Thomas B. (NV) - 1952
Medalie, George Z. (NY) - 1932
Meek, Joseph T. (IL) - 1954
Meier, William H. (NE) - 1954
Mekota, John E. (NE) - 1946
Melcher, John (MT) - 1976, 1982, 1988
Metcalf, Jack (WA) - 1968, 1974
Metcalf, Jesse H. (RI) - 1924, 1930, 1936
Metcalf, Lee (MT) - 1960, 1966, 1972
Metcalfe, Richard L. (NE) - 1928
Metzenbaum, Howard M. (OH) - 1970, 1976, 1982, 1988
Meyers (AR) - 1914
Michaelson, Julius C. (RI) - 1982
Mikulski, Barbara A. (MD) - 1974, 1986, 1992
Miller, A. Grant (NV) - 1914, 1916
Miller, Andrew P. (VA) - 1978
Miller, Bert C. (ID) - 1948
Miller, Edward T. (MD) - 1962
Miller, Hugh (IN) - 1914
Miller, Jack (IA) - 1960, 1966, 1972
Miller, John E. (AR) - 1937
Miller, Milton A. (OR) - 1924
Miller, Oscar C. (VT) - 1916
Miller, Robert A. (OR) - 1938
Millikin, Eugene D. (CO) - 1942, 1944, 1950
Mills, Walter Thomas (CA) - 1916
Minton, Sherman (IN) - 1934, 1940
Mitchell, Albert K. (NM) - 1940
Mitchell, Elizabeth H. (ME) - 1984
Mitchell, George J. (ME) - 1982, 1988
Mitchell, Hugh B. (WA) - 1946
Mochary, Mary (NJ) - 1984
Mock, Fred M. (OK) - 1954
Moffett, Anthony T. (CT) - 1982
Monaghan, Joseph P. (MT) - 1936
Mondale, Walter F. (MN) - 1966, 1972
Mondell, F. W. (WY) - 1922
Monks, Robert A. G. (ME) - 1976
Monroney, A. S. Mike (OK) - 1950, 1956, 1962, 1968
Montoya, Joseph M. (NM) - 1964, 1970, 1976
Moody, Blair (MI) - 1952
Moore, A. Harry (NJ) - 1934
Moore, Arch A. Jr. (WV) - 1978
Moore, Edward H. (OK) - 1942
Moore, Frank L. (ID) - 1918
Moore, Joe A. (MS) - 1960
Moore, Minor (CA) - 1928
Moore, W. Henson (LA) - 1990
Morehead, John H. (NE) - 1918
Morehead, John M. (NC) - 1918
Morgan, Joe C. (VA) - 1930
Morgan, Robert B. (NC) - 1974, 1980
Morin, Gerard L. (NH) - 1954
Morrah, Bradley (SC) - 1966
Morris, Sam J. (NC) - 1942
Morrison, Frank B. (NE) - 1958, 1966, 1970
Morrison, Harold A. (ND) - 1952
Morrow, Dwight W. (NJ) - 1930
Morse, Wayne (OR) - 1944, 1950, 1956, 1962, 1968, 1972
Morton, Thruston B. (KY) - 1956, 1962
Moseley-Braun, Carol (IL) - 1992
Moses, George H. (NH) - 1918, 1920, 1926, 1932
Moses, John (ND) - 1944
Moss, Brian H. (UT) - 1988
Moss, Frank E. (UT) - 1958, 1964, 1970
Moyle, James H. (UT) - 1914
Moynihan, Daniel Patrick (NY) - 1976, 1982, 1988
Muenster, Ted (SD) - 1990
Mulkey, Fred W. (OR) - 1918
Mundt, Karl E. (SD) - 1948, 1954, 1960, 1966
Murchie, Robert C. (NH) - 1926
Murdock, Abe (UT) - 1940, 1946
Murdock, Victor (KS) - 1914
Murkowski, Frank H. (AK) - 1980, 1986, 1992
Murphy, Ed (MN) - 1942
Murphy, Francis P. (NH) - 1942
Murphy, George (CA) - 1964, 1970
Murphy, Richard Louis (IA) - 1932
Murray, James E. (MT) - 1934, 1936, 1942, 1948, 1954

Murray, Patty (WA) - 1992
Muskie, Edmund S. (ME) - 1958, 1964, 1970, 1976
Myers, Francis J. (PA) - 1944, 1950
Myers, Henry L. (MT) - 1916

## N

Nagle, P. S. (OK) - 1914
Neal, John R. (TN) - 1934, 1942, 1946
Needham, H. Clay (CA) - 1922
Neeley, George A. (KS) - 1914
Neely, Matthew M. (WV) - 1922, 1928, 1930, 1936, 1942, 1948, 1954
Nelson, Arthur E. (MN) - 1928, 1942
Nelson, Gaylord (WI) - 1962, 1968, 1974, 1980
Nelson, J. Bernard (AZ) - 1914
Nelson, Knute (MN) - 1912, 1918
Nelson, Martin A. (MN) - 1942
Nelson, Norris H. (ND) - 1926
Neuberger, Maurine B. (OR) - 1960
Neuberger, Richard L. (OR) - 1954
Neville, Keith (NE) - 1954
New, Harry S. (IN) - 1916
Newberry, Truman H. (MI) - 1918
Newbert, Earl (ME) - 1918
Newell, J. Benson (NM) - 1941
Newell, Jake F. (NC) - 1932
Newlands, Francis G. (NV) - 1908, 1914
Nice, Harry W. (MD) - 1940
Nicholson, Samuel D. (CO) - 1920
Nicholson, Will F. (CO) - 1948
Nickles, Don (OK) - 1980, 1986, 1992
Nixon, George S. (NV) - 1910
Nixon, Jay (MO) - 1988
Nixon, Richard M. (CA) - 1950
Noone, Albert W. (NH) - 1930
Norbeck, Peter (SD) - 1920, 1926, 1932
Norcross, David F. (NJ) - 1976
Norris, George W. (NE) - 1918, 1924, 1930, 1936, 1942
Nugent, John F. (ID) - 1918, 1920, 1926
Nunn, Louie B. (KY) - 1972
Nunn, Sam (GA) - 1972, 1978, 1984, 1990
Nye, Gerald P. (ND) - 1926, 1932, 1938, 1944, 1946
Nygaard, J. J. (ND) - 1938

## O

O'Brian, John Lord (NY) - 1938
O'Brien, Cornelius (IN) - 1944
O'Brien, Harry (ND) - 1950
O'Brien, Thomas C. (MA) - 1936
O'Connor, J. F. T. (ND) - 1922
O'Connor, Thomas J. Jr. (MA) - 1960
O'Conor, Herbert R. (MD) - 1946
O'Daniel, W. Lee (TX) - 1941, 1942
O'Dell, Gloria (KS) - 1992
Oddie, Tasker L. (NV) - 1920, 1926, 1932, 1938
Odlin, Reno (WA) - 1934
O'Dwyer, Paul (NY) - 1968
O'Hearn, Taylor Walters (LA) - 1962
Olds, Glenn (AK) - 1986
Olesen, Anna D. (MN) - 1922
Oliver, Craig (UT) - 1986
O'Mahoney, Joseph C. (WY) - 1934, 1940, 1946, 1952, 1954
O'Neal, David C. (IL) - 1980
O'Neal, W. R. (FL) - 1916, 1926
O'Rourke, John E. (MN) - 1942
Orvis, Ellis L. (PA) - 1916
Osborne, John E. (WY) - 1918
O'Shaunessy, George (RI) - 1918
O'Shea, Bernard G. (VT) - 1956
Otero, M. A. Jr. (NM) - 1936
Otjen, William J. (OK) - 1944
Ottinger, Richard L. (NY) - 1970
Ould, James P. Jr. (VA) - 1966
Overman, Lee S. (NC) - 1914, 1920, 1926
Overton, John H. (LA) - 1932, 1938, 1944
Owen, Robert L. (OK) - 1912, 1918
Owens, Wayne (UT) - 1974, 1992

## P

Packwood, Bob (OR) - 1968, 1974, 1980, 1986, 1992
Page, Carroll S. (VT) - 1916
Page, Lawrence C. (VA) - 1934
Paget, B. Lee (OR) - 1912
Palmer, A. Mitchell (PA) - 1914
Palmer, Hazel (MO) - 1958
Panken, Jacob (NY) - 1920
Park, James (KY) - 1944
Parker, Marshall (SC) - 1966, 1968
Parkinson, Thelma (NJ) - 1930
Parkman, Henry Jr. (MA) - 1940
Parmer, Hugh (TX) - 1990
Parran, Thomas (MD) - 1913
Parsons, Lester S. (VA) - 1946
Parsons, Paul G. (AL) - 1948
Pastore, John O. (RI) - 1950, 1952, 1958, 1964, 1970
Patterson, Pat J. (OK) - 1966
Patterson, Roscoe C. (MO) - 1928, 1934
Patton, E. Earl (GA) - 1968
Patton, Frank R. (NC) - 1936
Patton, George S. (CA) - 1916
Paulen, Ben S. (KS) - 1932
Payne, Frederick G. (ME) - 1952, 1958
Peabody, Endicott (MA) - 1966, (NH) 1986
Pearson, James B. (KS) - 1962, 1966, 1972
Pearson, William J. (CA) - 1922
Peddy, George E. B. (TX) - 1922
Peden, Katherine (KY) - 1968
Pell, Claiborne (RI) - 1960, 1966, 1972, 1978, 1984, 1990
Pennington, J. M. (AL) - 1938
Penrose, Boies (PA) - 1914, 1920
Pepper, Claude (FL) - 1936, 1938, 1944
Pepper, George Wharton (PA) - 1922
Percy, Charles H. (IL) - 1966, 1972, 1978, 1984
Perk, Ralph J. (OH) - 1974
Perry, H. H. (ND) - 1920
Peterson, Elly M. (MI) - 1964
Peterson, P. Kenneth (MN) - 1960
Petri, Thomas E. (WI) - 1974
Pfiefer, Paul E. (OH) - 1982
Pfost, Gracie (ID) - 1962
Phelan, James D. (CA) - 1914, 1920
Philip, Charles T. (CO) - 1924
Phipps, Lawrence C. (CO) - 1918, 1924
Picard, Frank A. (MI) - 1934
Pickett, Laurence M. (NH) - 1956
Pickrel, William G. (OH) - 1944
Pinchot, Gifford (PA) - 1914
Pine, William B. (OK) - 1924, 1930
Pittman, Key (NV) - 1910, 1912, 1916, 1922, 1928, 1934, 1940
Platt, Howard (SD) - 1926
Platt, Samuel (NV) - 1914, 1916, 1928, 1940
Poindexter, Miles (WA) - 1916, 1922
Pollard, J. P. (VA) - 1920
Pollard, Park H. (VT) - 1923
Pollock, William P. (SC) - 1918
Pomerene, Atlee (OH) - 1916, 1922, 1926
Poole, Van B. (FL) - 1982
Pope, James (ID) - 1932
Porter, Claude R. (IA) - 1920, 1926
Porter, Jack (TX) - 1948
Posey, John A. (AL) - 1944
Potter, Charles E. (MI) - 1952, 1958
Powell, Wesley (NH) - 1950, 1972
Powers, Ward S. (AZ) - 1946
Pratt, Judith A. (NM) - 1984
Pray, Charles N. (MT) - 1916
Pressler, Larry (SD) - 1978, 1984, 1990
Preus, J. A. O. (MN) - 1923
Price, Lawrence (MI) - 1916
Pritchard, George M. (NC) - 1930
Prouty, Charles A. (VT) - 1914
Prouty, Winston L. (VT) - 1958, 1964, 1970
Proxmire, William (WI) - 1957, 1958, 1964, 1970, 1976, 1982
Pryor, David (AR) - 1978, 1984, 1990
Pucinski, Roman (IL) - 1972
Purcell, W. E. (ND) - 1914
Purtell, William A. (CT) - 1952, 1958
Purvis, Melvin Jr. (SC) - 1984

## P

Pyle, Gladys (SD) - 1938

## Q

Quayle, Dan (IN) - 1980, 1986
Quinn, William F. (HI) - 1976

## R

Radcliffe, George L. (MD) - 1934, 1940
Raese, John R. (WV) - 1984
Rafferty (SD) - 1918
Rafferty, Max (CA) - 1968
Raggio, William J. (NV) - 1970
Ralston, Samuel M. (IN) - 1922
Ramp, B. F. (OR) - 1912
Randall, Blanchard Jr. (MD) - 1944
Randall, Charles H. (CA) - 1928
Randolph, Jennings (WV) - 1958, 1960, 1966, 1972, 1978
Rankin, Jeanette (MT) - 1918
Rankin, John E. (MS) - 1947
Rankin, Wellington D. (MT) - 1942
Ransdell, Joseph E. (LA) - 1918, 1924
Rappaport, Jim (MA) - 1990
Rasmuson, Elmer (AK) - 1968
Rauh, John (NH) - 1992
Ravenel, Charles D. (SC) - 1978
Rawlings, George C. Jr. (VA) - 1970
Redman, Futon J. (ME) - 1924, 1928, 1942
Reece, B. Carroll (TN) - 1948
Reed, Clyde M. (KS) - 1938, 1944
Reed, David A. (PA) - 1922, 1928, 1934
Reed, Eugene E. (NH) - 1918
Reed, James A. (MO) - 1916, 1922
Reed, Rick (HI) - 1992
Reese, George W. Jr. (LA) - 1960
Regan, John E. (MN) - 1940
Reid, Harry (NV) - 1974, 1986, 1992
Reinsch, Paul S. (WI) - 1920
Remmel, H. L. (AR) - 1916
Renk, Wilbur N. (WI) - 1964
Respess, James W. (VA) - 1964
Revercomb, Chapman (WV) - 1942, 1948, 1952, 1956, 1958
Reynolds, James G. (RI) - 1978
Reynolds, L. H. (AL) - 1920
Reynolds, Robert R. (NC) - 1932, 1938
Ribicoff, Abraham A. (CT) - 1952, 1962, 1974
Richards, R. O. (SD) - 1920
Richards, Richard (CA) - 1956, 1962
Richardson, H. L. (Bill) (CA) - 1974
Ricker, Allan W. (KS) - 1912
Ricker, Carroll Livingston (VA) - 1924
Riddick, Carl W. (MT) - 1922
Riegle, Donald W. Jr. (MI) - 1976, 1982, 1988
Rinehart (SD) - 1918
Ritchie, William (NE) - 1952
Rizley, Ross (OK) - 1948
Robb, Charles S. (VA) - 1988
Robb, Clarke T. (VA) - 1952, 1954
Roberts, Betty (OR) - 1974
Roberts, E. E. (NV) - 1918
Robertson, A. Willis (VA) - 1946, 1948, 1954, 1960
Robertson, Edward V. (WY) - 1942, 1948
Robertson, Michael (MA) - 1976
Robertson, R. E. (AK) - 1958
Robins, Raymond (IL) - 1914
Robinson, Arthur R. (IN) - 1926, 1928, 1934
Robinson, Joseph T. (AR) - 1918, 1924, 1930, 1936
Robinson, Rachel C. (PA) - 1922
Robinson, William I. (KS) - 1968
Robsion, John M. (KY) - 1930
Rockefeller, John D. (Jay) (WV) - 1984, 1990
Roehrick, John P. (IA) - 1986
Rogers, Bruce (WA) - 1916
Rogers, Will Jr. (CA) - 1946
Rogers, William N. (NH) - 1936
Rolde, Neil (ME) - 1990
Romer, Roy (CO) - 1966
Romney, Lenore (MI) - 1970
Roncalio, Teno (WY) - 1966
Rosa, Charles D. (WI) - 1926
Rose, Robert R. (WY) - 1924

## Y

## Z

# Senate Primary Candidates Index

The Senate Primary Candidates Index includes all candidates appearing in Senate Primary Returns, 1920-93 (pp. 851-911).

The index includes candidates' names followed by state abbreviations and the years of candidacy. To locate a candidate's returns, turn to pages 851-911 where the returns are arranged alphabetically by state and in chronological order by class of senator for each state. *(Explanation of Senate classes, p. 780; State Abbreviations, below)* For other references to Senate candidates in the *Guide to U.S. Elections, Third Edition,* see the General Index, page 1503.

## A

Abbott, John H. (CA) - 1986, 1988
Abdnor, James (SD) - 1980, 1986
Abercrombie, Neil (HI) - 1970
Abourezk, James (SD) - 1972
Abrams, Robert (NY) - 1992
Abzug, Bella (NY) - 1976
Accardo, Nick J. (LA) - 1992
Adams, Brock (WA) - 1986
Adams, Thomas B. (MA) - 1966
Addington, W. H. (KS) - 1986
Adkins, Homer M. (AR) - 1944
Aiken, George D. (VT) - 1956, 1962, 1968
Airy, Frederic W. (NJ) - 1960
Akaka, Daniel K. (HI) - 1990
Albough, William A. (MD) - 1964, 1982
Albright, Ernest G. (OK) - 1956
Alderson, Fleming N. (WV) - 1958
Alexander, Lee (NY) - 1974
Algood, Alice W. (TN) - 1988
Alioto, Kathleen Sullivan (MA) - 1978
Allen, Frank Tunney (LA) - 1972
Allen, James B. Jr. (AL) - 1986
Allen, Jim (AL) - 1968, 1974
Allen, Maryon Pittman (AL) - 1978
Allen, Melba T. (AL) - 1972
Allen, Oscar K. (LA) - 1936
Allen, William B. (CA) - 1992
Allott, Gordon (CO) - 1960, 1966, 1972
Allred, James (TX) - 1942
Allred, Thomas L. (NC) - 1984
Altvater, George (OR) - 1960
Anaya, Toney (NM) - 1978
Anderson, Andy (NV) - 1992
Anderson, Anson (ND) - 1958
Anderson, Ava A. (KS) - 1966
Anderson, Bill (TN) - 1988
Anderson, Blanche (MT) - 1958
Anderson, Clinton P. (NM) - 1960, 1966
Anderson, Doug (UT) - 1992
Anderson, Fred (NV) - 1958
Anderson, Henry L. (AL) - 1932, 1936

Anderson, Le Roy (MT) - 1960
Anderson, Mark E. (UT) - 1968
Anderson, Steve (OR) - 1978, 1986, 1990
Anderson, Tom (PA) - 1980
Anderson, Wendell R. (MN) - 1978
Andrews, Charles O. (FL) - 1936, 1940
Andrews, Jackson M. (KY) - 1980, 1986
Andrews, Lloyd J. (WA) - 1964
Andrews, Mark (ND) - 1980, 1986
Angell, Wayne (KS) - 1978
Antonovich, Michael D. (CA) - 1986
Apodaca, Jerry (NM) - 1982
Applegate, Ralph A. (OH) - 1988
Aragona, Xavier A. (MD) - 1974
Archambault, Raoul (RI) - 1960
Armstrong, Hepburn T. (WY) - 1958
Armstrong, William L. (CO) - 1978, 1984
Arn, Edward F. (KS) - 1962
Arndt, Raymond W. (NE) - 1964, 1966
Arnold, Burleigh (MO) - 1982
Arvidson, Gene (OR) - 1980
Ashe, Victor (TN) - 1984
Askew, James J. (MO) - 1986
Atchley, Forrest S. (NM) - 1958
Atkins, Hobart F. (TN) - 1958
AuCoin, Les (OR) - 1992
Austin, Richard H. (MI) - 1976
Auvil, Ken (WV) - 1984
Avery, William S. (KS) - 1968
Aylward, Paul (KS) - 1956, 1962

## B

Babb, Leslie R. (NH) - 1974
Babbitt, Wayne H. (AR) - 1972
Babcock, C. H. (NC) - 1962
Babcock, Tim M. (MT) - 1966
Bacaloff, James (OR) - 1966
Bachman, Nathan L. (TN) - 1924, 1934, 1936
Bagley, E. J. (GA) - 1980
Bailey, Carl E. (AR) - 1937

Bailey, Don (PA) - 1986
Bailey, Josiah W. (NC) - 1930, 1936, 1942
Bailey, J. W. (TX) - 1934
Baker, Albert J. (NE) - 1960
Baker, Deane (MI) - 1976, 1982
Baker, Gerald (IA) - 1978
Baker, Howard H. Jr. (TN) - 1964, 1966, 1972, 1978
Baker, John (AL) - 1978
Ball, Albert T. (OH) - 1962
Ballard, John S. (OH) - 1962
Ballenger, William S. (MI) - 1982
Bangerter, Bruce (UT) - 1974
Bankhead, John H. II (AL) - 1926, 1930, 1936, 1942
Bantz, William B. (WA) - 1958
Banuelos, Robert J. (CA) - 1988
Barbour, Haley (MS) - 1982
Barnes, Bill (AK) - 1966
Barnes, John (KS) - 1980
Barnes, Michael D. (MD) - 1986
Barnett, Don (SD) - 1978
Baron, Murray (NY) - 1968
Barr, Bob (GA) - 1992
Barrett, Frank A. (WY) - 1958, 1960
Barrows, Gordon H. (WY) - 1978
Bartlett, Dewey F. (OK) - 1972
Bartlett, E. L. (AK) - 1958, 1960, 1966
Bartlett, Roscoe G. (MD) - 1980
Bartley, David M. (MA) - 1984
Barton, T. H. (AR) - 1944
Bass, Doris M. (MO) - 1970
Bass, Perkins (NH) - 1962
Bass, Ross (TN) - 1964, 1966
Batchelor, George M. (UT) - 1980
Bates, Joe B. (KY) - 1956
Battle, Laurie C. (AL) - 1954
Baucom, John D. (MN) - 1970
Baucus, Max S. (MT) - 1978, 1984, 1990
Bauman, Rick (OR) - 1986
Baxter, James H. (DE) - 1978
Bayh, Birch (IN) - 1980
Beall, Forest W. (OK) - 1964

Beall, J. Glenn (MD) - 1958, 1964, 1970, 1976
Beals, Manny (NV) - 1986
Beard, Robin L. (TN) - 1982
Beard, Samuel S. (DE) - 1988
Beasley, Michael (AK) - 1984, 1990
Beck, Paul V. (OK) - 1956
Beck, Rodney W. (ID) - 1992
Beckjord, Walter E. (OH) - 1982
Beckworth, Lindley (TX) - 1952
Beilenson, Anthony C. (CA) - 1968
Belcher, A. P. (TX) - 1940
Belk, William I. (NC) - 1986
Bell, Alphonzo E. (CA) - 1976
Bell, Bob (OR) - 1992
Bell, Dale (SD) - 1980
Bell, Jeffrey (NJ) - 1978, 1982
Bellmon, Henry (OK) - 1968, 1974
Belluso, Nick M. (GA) - 1980
Benavides, Tom R. (NM) - 1990
Bender, George H. (OH) - 1956
Benedict, Cleveland K. (WV) - 1982
Benedict, Cooper P. (WV) - 1964
Bennett (SC) - 1948
Bennett, James G. (MD) - 1988
Bennett, Robert F. (UT) - 1992
Bennett, Terry (NH) - 1992
Bennett, Wallace F. (UT) - 1956, 1962, 1968
Bennett, William M. (CA) - 1968
Bentley, Alvin M. (MI) - 1960
Bentsen, Lloyd (TX) - 1970, 1976, 1982, 1988
Bergeson, Rollo (IA) - 1960
Bergland, David (CA) - 1980
Beringer, Raymond Warren (OH) - 1962
Berman, Dan (UT) - 1980
Bernard, Charles T. (AR) - 1968
Bernard, Sherman A. (LA) - 1974
Bernier-Nachtwey, E. F. (HI) - 1980, 1982
Bernstein, Mert (MO) - 1992
Berry, George (TN) - 1938
Bertroche, Joe (IA) - 1978
Bethune, Ed (AR) - 1984

---

## State Abbreviations

| | | | | | | | |
|---|---|---|---|---|---|---|---|
| **Alabama** | AL | **Illinois** | IL | **Montana** | MT | **Rhode Island** | RI |
| **Alaska** | AK | **Indiana** | IN | **Nebraska** | NE | **South Carolina** | SC |
| **Arizona** | AZ | **Iowa** | IA | **Nevada** | NV | **South Dakota** | SD |
| **Arkansas** | AR | **Kansas** | KS | **New Hampshire** | NH | **Tennessee** | TN |
| **California** | CA | **Kentucky** | KY | **New Jersey** | NJ | **Texas** | TX |
| **Colorado** | CO | **Louisiana** | LA | **New Mexico** | NM | **Utah** | UT |
| **Connecticut** | CT | **Maine** | ME | **New York** | NY | **Vermont** | VT |
| **Delaware** | DE | **Maryland** | MD | **North Carolina** | NC | **Virginia** | VA |
| **Florida** | FL | **Massachusetts** | MA | **North Dakota** | ND | **Washington** | WA |
| **Georgia** | GA | **Michigan** | MI | **Ohio** | OH | **West Virginia** | WV |
| **Hawaii** | HI | **Minnesota** | MN | **Oklahoma** | OK | **Wisconsin** | WI |
| **Idaho** | ID | **Mississippi** | MS | **Oregon** | OR | **Wyoming** | WY |
| | | **Missouri** | MO | **Pennsylvania** | PA | | |

# House Candidates Index

The House Candidates Index includes all candidates appearing in House Popular Vote Returns, 1824-1993 (pp. 943-1326).

The index includes candidates' names followed by state abbreviations and the years of candidacy. To locate a candidate's returns, turn to pages 943-1326 where the returns are arranged chronologically by year and alphabetically by state for each year. State abbreviations appear below.

## A

Aaker (MN) - 1900
Aandahl, Fred G. (ND) - 1950
Aaron, Samuel (NJ) - 1840
Aaron, Ward (NY) - 1824
Aarons, Morris (NY) - 1960
Abate, Frank (NJ) - 1992
Abbett, Edwin L. (NY) - 1890
Abbey, Frank E. (IL) - 1914
Abbey, George W. (MI) - 1886
Abbey, James B. (CA) - 1942, 1944
Abbitt, Watkins M. (VA) - 1948, 1950, 1952, 1954, 1956, 1958, 1960, 1962, 1964, 1966, 1968, 1970
Abbot, William S. (MA) - 1968
Abbott (WI) - 1852
Abbott, Amos (MA) - 1842, 1844, 1846
Abbott, Burnett J. (MI) - 1928
Abbott, Israel B. (NC) - 1886
Abbott, Jo (TX) - 1886, 1888, 1890, 1892, 1894
Abbott, Josiah G. (MA) - 1862, 1864, 1874
Abbott, Nehemiah (ME) - 1856
Abdella, James (NY) - 1980
Abdnor, James (SD) - 1972, 1974, 1976, 1978
Abele, Homer E. (OH) - 1958, 1962, 1964
Abercrombie, C. H. (OR) - 1912
Abercrombie, James (AL) - 1851, 1853
Abercrombie, James F. (AL) - 1914
Abercrombie, John W. (AL) - 1912, 1914
Abercrombie, Neil (HI) - 1986, 1990, 1992
Abernathy, Thomas G. (MS) - 1962
Abernethy, Charles L. (NC) - 1922, 1924, 1926, 1928, 1930, 1932
Abernethy, Thomas G. (MS) - 1942, 1944, 1946, 1948, 1950, 1952, 1954, 1956, 1958, 1960, 1964, 1966, 1968, 1970
Abernethy, Tom (AL) - 1962
Abourezk, James (SD) - 1970
Abraham, William C. (OH) - 1988
Abrahams, George (CA) - 1986
Abrams, Milton C. (UT) - 1984
Abrams, Samuel (MA) - 1930
Abramson, Irving (NJ) - 1942

Abramson, R. S. (LA) - 1972
Abt, Clark C. (MA) - 1986
Abzug, Bella S. (NY) - 1970, 1972, 1974, 1978, 1986
Acee (MS) - 1837
Acer, Christopher T. (NY) - 1970, 1974
Acers, N. F. (KS) - 1882
Acheson, A. W. (TX) - 1898, 1920
Acheson, Ernest F. (PA) - 1892, 1894, 1896, 1898, 1900, 1902, 1904, 1906
Achison, A. W. (TX) - 1890
Acker, Bert L. (FL) - 1940, 1942
Acker, Ephraim L. (PA) - 1870, 1874
Ackerman, Edwin D. (NY) - 1908
Ackerman, Ernest R. (NJ) - 1918, 1920, 1922, 1924, 1926, 1928, 1930
Ackerman, Gary L. (NY) - 1983, 1984, 1986, 1988, 1990, 1992
Ackerman, J. Waldo Jr. (IL) - 1960
Ackerman, Johann S. (IL) - 1956
Ackerman, Luther H. (PA) - 1958
Ackerson, Nels J. (IN) - 1980
Ackerty, Merrick W. (IN) - 1892
Acklen, Joseph H. (LA) - 1876, 1878, 1882
Acklen, William (AL) - 1847
Ackley, Charles W. (NJ) - 1934
Acklin, George W. (PA) - 1998
Acklin, J. A. (LA) - 1884
Acuff, Judd (TN) - 1938
Adair, Charles R. (MI) - 1922, 1940
Adair, Clark W. (NE) - 1904
Adair, E. Ross (IN) - 1950, 1952, 1954, 1956, 1958, 1960, 1962, 1964, 1966, 1968, 1970
Adair, J. Carlton (NV) - 1962
Adair, J. Leroy (IL) - 1932, 1934
Adair, John (KY) - 1831
Adair, John A. M. (IN) - 1906, 1908, 1910, 1912, 1914, 1924
Adair, Verdell (MD) - 1972
Adamowski, Benjamin S. (IL) - 1942
Adams (GA) - 1916
Adams (MO) - 1858
Adams (NJ) - 1912
Adams (NY) - 1842, 1872
Adams (PA) - 1848, 1850
Adams (VT) - 1872

Adams, Alfred (TN) - 1972
Adams, Allen C. (OK) - 1916
Adams, Allison L. (NY) - 1918
Adams, Alva B. (CO) - 1954, 1956
Adams, Alva (CO) - 1902
Adams, Augustus (IL) - 1878
Adams, Billy (GA) - 1976
Adams, Bob (WA) - 1992
Adams, Brock (WA) - 1964, 1966, 1968, 1970, 1972, 1974, 1976
Adams, C. E. (NE) - 1898
Adams, C. P. (MN) - 1882
Adams, Charles D. (OH) - 1880
Adams, Charles F. (MA) - 1852, 1858, 1860
Adams, Charles H. (NY) - 1874
Adams, Clifford R. (MN) - 1970
Adams, Clyde (FL) - 1976
Adams, David (TN) - 1835
Adams, Dennis (NJ) - 1984
Adams, Dennis Sr. (NJ) - 1976
Adams, Edson (CA) - 1974
Adams, Francis A. (NY) - 1908
Adams, G. (KY) - 1845
Adams, George (OH) - 1892, 1900
Adams, George E. (IL) - 1882, 1884, 1886, 1888, 1890
Adams, George M. (KY) - 1867, 1868, 1870, 1872, 1882
Adams, George Z. (CA) - 1986, 1988, 1990
Adams, Green (KY) - 1847, 1859
Adams, Henry C. (WI) - 1902, 1904
Adams, J. A. (WA) - 1900
Adams, J. M. (AL) - 1855
Adams, James A. (WI) - 1972
Adams, James F. (MO) - 1926
Adams, John J. (NY) - 1882, 1884
Adams, John (NH) - 1976
Adams, John (NY) - 1832
Adams, John Q. (NY) - 1896
Adams, John Quincy (MA) - 1830, 1833, 1834, 1836, 1838, 1840, 1842, 1844, 1846
Adams, Joseph S. (NC) - 1896
Adams, Ken (FL) - 1988
Adams, L. S. (AZ) - 1954
Adams, Mike (TN) - 1980

Adams, Monroe (NC) - 1938, 1940
Adams, Norman W. (OH) - 1946
Adams, Parmenio (NY) - 1824
Adams, Paul L. (MI) - 1942
Adams, Percy D. (NY) - 1890
Adams, Robert Jr. (PA) - 1893, 1894, 1896, 1898, 1900, 1902, 1904
Adams, S. C. (VA) - 1890
Adams, Samuel (PA) - 1878
Adams, Seth (MA) - 1870
Adams, Sherman (NH) - 1944
Adams, Silas R. (KY) - 1892, 1894
Adams, Spencer B. (NC) - 1898
Adams, Stanley G. (VA) - 1948
Adams, Stephen (MS) - 1845
Adams, Thomas J. (NY) - 1968
Adams, W. P. C. (WA) - 1894
Adams, Wayne N. (WA) - 1968
Adams, Wilbur (DE) - 1932
Adams, William (PA) - 1908, 1916, 1922
Adamson, William C. (GA) - 1896, 1898, 1900, 1902, 1904, 1906, 1908, 1910, 1912, 1914, 1916
Adanti, Michael J. (CT) - 1976
Addabbo, Joseph P. (NY) - 1960, 1962, 1964, 1966, 1968, 1970, 1972, 1974, 1976, 1978, 1980, 1982, 1984
Addams, William (PA) - 1824, 1826, 1828
Addonizio, G. George (NJ) - 1956, 1958
Addonizio, Hugh J. (NJ) - 1948, 1950, 1952, 1954, 1956, 1958, 1960
Ade, William H. (IN) - 1914
Adelman, Daniel (NY) - 1932
Adelman, Lynn S. (WI) - 1974
Adelman, William J. (IL) - 1970
Adkins, Burl C. (MI) - 1988, 1990
Adkins, Charles (IL) - 1924, 1926, 1928, 1930, 1932
Adkins, James (GA) - 1868
Adkins, Stockton (TN) - 1972
Adkinson, Ray (CA) - 1946
Adler, Charles S. (NY) - 1902, 1906
Adler, John H. (NJ) - 1990
Adler, John R. (CA) - 1980
Adler, Milton H. (NY) - 1956, 1958
Adney, Roy W. (IN) - 1926
Adrain, Garnett B. (NJ) - 1856, 1858

## State Abbreviations

| | | | | | | | |
|---|---|---|---|---|---|---|---|
| **Alabama** | AL | **Illinois** | IL | **Montana** | MT | **Rhode Island** | RI |
| **Alaska** | AK | **Indiana** | IN | **Nebraska** | NE | **South Carolina** | SC |
| **Arizona** | AZ | **Iowa** | IA | **Nevada** | NV | **South Dakota** | SD |
| **Arkansas** | AR | **Kansas** | KS | **New Hampshire** | NH | **Tennessee** | TN |
| **California** | CA | **Kentucky** | KY | **New Jersey** | NJ | **Texas** | TX |
| **Colorado** | CO | **Louisiana** | LA | **New Mexico** | NM | **Utah** | UT |
| **Connecticut** | CT | **Maine** | ME | **New York** | NY | **Vermont** | VT |
| **Delaware** | DE | **Maryland** | MD | **North Carolina** | NC | **Virginia** | VA |
| **Florida** | FL | **Massachusetts** | MA | **North Dakota** | ND | **Washington** | WA |
| **Georgia** | GA | **Michigan** | MI | **Ohio** | OH | **West Virginia** | WV |
| **Hawaii** | HI | **Minnesota** | MN | **Oklahoma** | OK | **Wisconsin** | WI |
| **Idaho** | ID | **Mississippi** | MS | **Oregon** | OR | **Wyoming** | WY |
| | | **Missouri** | MO | **Pennsylvania** | PA | | |

Blasi, Lawrence J. (IL) - 1960
Blass, Gregory J. (NY) - 1986
Blatchford, Joe (CA) - 1968
Blatnik, John A. (MN) - 1946, 1948, 1950, 1952, 1954, 1956, 1958, 1960, 1962, 1964, 1966, 1968, 1970, 1972
Blau, William (NY) - 1902
Blauvelt, John D. (NY) - 1900
Blaylock, Chet (MT) - 198-!
Blazer, David H. (NY) - 1972
Bleakley, O. D. (PA) - 1916
Bledsoe, Moses A. (NC) - 1880
Bledsoe, Stewart (WA) - 1972
Blee, John W. (IL) - 1890
Blessey, Gerald (MS) - 1976
Blevins, Lloyd (TN) - 1974, 1976
Bliley, Thomas J. Jr. (VA) - 1980, 1982, 1984, 1986, 1988, 1990, 1992
Blish, Zenas (OH) - 1846
Bliss (NJ) - 1878
Bliss (RI) - 1912
Bliss, Aaron T. (MI) - 1888, 1890
Bliss, Archibald M. (NY) - 1874, 1876, 1878, 1880, 1884, 1886
Bliss, George (OH) - 1852, 1854, 1862, 1864
Bliss, George R. (CA) - 1934, 1936
Bliss, Helen L. (NH) - 1974
Bliss, Hubert D. (NY) - 1948
Bliss, Philemon (OH) - 1854, 1856
Blitch, Iris Faircloth (GA) - 1954, 1956, 1958, 1960
Blizard, A. (TN) - 1870
Blobaum, Roger (IA) - 1970
Bloch, Adam F. (IL) - 1922
Bloch, Edward J. (NY) - 1984, 1986
Block, Charles (IL) - 1912
Block, Jacob W. (NY) - 1910
Block, Louis M. (NY) - 1916
Block, Richard R. (PA) - 1968
Bloedorn, Wallace A. (WI) - 1940
Blomgren, S. L. (SC) - 1922
Blood (NY) - 1862
Bloodworth, C. T. (AR) - 1908
Bloodworth, Ken (TN) - 1988, 1990
Bloom, Allan (IN) - 1972
Bloom, Max (NY) - 1950
Bloom, Sol (NY) - 1923, 1924, 1926, 1928, 1930, 1932, 1934, 1936, 1938, 1940, 1942, 1944, 1946, 1948
Bloom, William (PA) - 1900
Bloomer, John E. (NY) - 1954
Bloor, Ella Reeve (ND) - 1932
Blouin, Michael T. (IA) - 1974, 1976, 1978
Blount, George W. (NC) - 1874
Blount, James H. (GA) - 1872, 1874, 1876, 1878, 1880, 1882, 1884, 1886, 1888, 1890
Blount, Willie (TN) - 1825
Blow (MO) - 1902
Blow, Henry T. (MO) - 1862, 1864
Blow, Thomas (TX) - 1984, 1986
Bloxom, Roy D. (Bill) (CA) - 1984
Biford, Charles (KY) - 1898
Blue, Bill (MO) - 1984
Blue, Edna Mitchell (NY) - 1936, 1938
Blue, Fred O. (WV) - 1930, 1954
Blue, George R. (LA) - 1956
Blue, H. Clifton (NC) - 1970
Blue, Richard W. (KS) - 1894, 1896
Blue, William R. (MI) - 1968
Blum, David M. (MD) - 1960
Blum, Edward (TX) - 1992
Blum, Eugene A. (OH) - 1946
Blum, Tibby (NY) - 1974
Blume, John T. (NY) - 1982
Blume, Norbert (KY) - 1966
Blumetti, Robert (NY) - 1988
Blunt (NY) - 1862
Blust, John J. (NY) - 1938
Blute, Peter I. (MA) - 1992
Blvt, J. C. (NY) - 1848
Blvt, N. C. (NY) - 1848
Blyholder, Samuel S. (PA) - 1896
Blythe, A. (SC) - 1880
Boardman (NH) - 1829
Boardman, William (CT) - 1841
Boardman, William (NY) - 1864
Boardn (NY) - 1844
Boarman, Alexander (LA) - 1872
Boas (PA) - 1850
Boas, Roger (CA) - 1972
Boatner, Charles J. (LA) - 1884, 1888, 1890, 1892, 1894

Bober, Sam H. (SD) - 1950
Bobrowicz, Edmund V. (WI) - 1946
Boccio, Norman G. (IL) - 1992
Bock, Robert L. (KS) - 1950, 1954
Bockee, Abraham (NY) - 1828, 1832, 1834
Bockman, Robert H. (NY) - 1974
Bocock, Thomas S. (VA) - 1847, 1849, 1851, 1853, 1855, 1857, 1859
Boddie, Willis (NC) - 1827
Bodenhammer, B. F. (AR) - 1896
Bodfish, John D. W. (MA) - 1930, 1934, 1936, 1938
Bodine, Richard C. (IN) - 1982
Bodine, Robert N. (MO) - 1896
Bodle, Charles (NY) - 1832
Bodron, Ellis B. (MS) - 1968, 1972
Bodwell, Charles A. Jr. (CA) - 1920
Boehlert, Sherwood L. (NY) - 1982, 1984, 1986, 1988, 1990, 1992
Boehne, John W. (IN) - 1908, 1910
Boehne, John W. Jr. (IN) - 1928, 1930, 1932, 1934, 1936, 1938, 1940, 1942
Boehner, John A. (OH) - 1990, 1992
Boen (MN) - 1906
Boen, Haldor E. (MN) - 1892, 1894
Boerum, Bill (CA) - 1990
Boffa, Philip J. (IL) - 1953
Bogardus (NY) - 1828, 1850
Bogen, Gilbert (IL) - 1978
Bogert, Francis M. (CA) - 1975
Bogdanski, Joseph W. (CT) - 1950
Boggs, Corrine Claiborne (Lindy) (Mrs. Hale) (LA) - 1973, 1974, 1976, 1978, 1980, 1982, 1984, 1986, 1988
Boggs, Hale (LA) - 1940, 1946, 1948, 1950, 1952, 1954, 1956, 1958, 1960, 1962, 1964, 1966, 1968, 1970, 1972
Boggs, J. Caleb (DE) - 1946, 1948, 1950
Boggs, Thomas Hale Jr. (MD) - 1970
Bogle, Joseph M. (NC) - 1847
Bogle, W. S. (NC) - 1928, 1960
Bogy (NY) - 1852, 1862, 1863
Bogy, Bernard P. (MO) - 1920, 1922
Bohen, Frederick M. (NJ) - 1972, 1974
Bohlke, H. C. (WA) - 1924, 1928
Bohm (NJ) - 1912
Bohm, Ernest (NY) - 1922
Bohn (NJ) - 1914
Bohn, Frank P. (MI) - 1926, 1928, 1930, 1932
Bohnett, L. D. (CA) - 1914
Bohnsack, Kenneth F. (IL) - 1986
Bohrer, F. A. (MN) - 1882
Boies, John K. (MI) - 1882
Boies, William D. (IA) - 1918, 1920, 1922, 1924, 1926
Boileau, Gerald J. (WI) - 1930, 1932, 1934, 1936, 1938, 1940
Boise, Horace (IA) - 1902
Boiston, L. C. (VA) - 1876
Bokee, David A. (NY) - 1848
Bolan (RI) - 1912
Boland, Edward P. (MA) - 1952, 1954, 1956, 1958, 1960, 1962, 1964, 1966, 1968, 1970, 1972, 1974, 1976, 1978, 1980, 1982, 1984, 1986
Boland, John R. Jr. (PA) - 1940
Boland, Patrick J. (PA) - 1930, 1932, 1934, 1936, 1938, 1940
Bolding (MS) - 1872
Boldt, D. (MI) - 1920
Bolens, Harry W. (WI) - 1920
Boles (AR) - 1880
Boles, J. D. (TN) - 1968
Boles, Mrs. J. Durelle (TN) - 1970
Boles, Thomas (AR) - 1868, 1870
Bolger, Robert V. (PA) - 1930
Bolgny (LA) - 1862
Bolin, Andrew R. (OH) - 1888
Boll, John C. (WI) - 1910
Bollaert, Barbara (NY) - 1990
Bolles, John A. (MA) - 1852
Bolles, John A. (NY) - 1918
Bolles, Stephen (WI) - 1938, 1940
Bolling (VA) - 1835, 1847, 1851
Bolling, Richard (MO) - 1948, 1950, 1952, 1954, 1956, 1958, 1960, 1962, 1964, 1966, 1968, 1970, 1972, 1974, 1976, 1978, 1980
Bolling, Robert B. (VA) - 1870
Bolling, William B. (AL) - 1920
Bolognesi, William J. (MI) - 1962
Bolster, Charles S. (MA) - 1954
Bolte (MO) - 1900

Bolter, L. R. (IA) - 1876
Bolton, Chester C. (OH) - 1928, 1930, 1932, 1934, 1936, 1938
Bolton, Frances P. (OH) - 1940, 1942, 1944, 1946, 1948, 1950, 1952, 1954, 1956, 1958, 1960, 1962, 1964, 1966, 1968
Bolton, Oliver P. (OH) - 1952, 1954, 1962, 1964
Bolton, William P. (MD) - 1948, 1950, 1954
Boltwood, Lucius (MA) - 1842, 1844
Bolus, Robert C. (PA) - 1986
Bolz, Sanford (CA) - 1964
Bona, Monte R. (MI) - 1968
Bond (NY) - 1876
Bond, Arthur T. (MD) - 1976
Bond, Bill (CA) - 1974
Bond, Charles G. (NY) - 1920, 1922
Bond, Christopher (MO) - 1968
Bond, D. W. (MA) - 1872
Bond, Dick (CO) - 1990
Bond, Richard M. (WA) - 1968
Bond, Robert C. (NC) - 1845
Bond, Rufus H. (MA) - 1938
Bond, S. P. (GA) - 1900
Bond, Shadrack (IL) - 1824
Bond, Thomas (NY) - 1840
Bond, William K. (OH) - 1834, 1836, 1838
Bondy, James G. (KY) - 1958
Bone, Homer T. (WA) - 1920
Bonee, John L. (CT) - 1966
Boner, Bill (TN) - 1978, 1980, 1982, 1984, 1986
Boner, George W. (KY) - 1944
Boney, Tom (FL) - 1978
Bonfoey (MO) - 1912
Bongiovanni, Michael (NJ) - 1948, 1950
Bonham (IN) - 1876
Bonham, Edward (IL) - 1876
Bonham, Milledge L. (SC) - 1857, 1858, 1860
Bonilla, Henry (TX) - 1992
Bonin, Edward J. (PA) - 1952, 1954
Bonior, David E. (MI) - 1976, 1978, 1980, 1982, 1984, 1986, 1988, 1990, 1992
Bonitt, Edward J. (MO) - 1968
Bonjean, Roscoe (IL) - 1946
Bonker, Don (WA) - 1974, 1976, 1978, 1980, 1982, 1984, 1986
Bonner, Herbert C. (NC) - 1940, 1942, 1944, 1946, 1948, 1950, 1952, 1954, 1956, 1958, 1960, 1962, 1964
Bonner, J. Jordan (NC) - 1972
Bonner, Matthew (MO) - 1840
Bonner, Thomas N. (NE) - 1962
Bonnett, Lewis (IA) - 1882
Bonney, Stephen S. (IN) - 1982
Bonniwell, Eugene C. (PA) - 1910
Bonpane, Blase (CA) - 1992
Bonstein, William (WA) - 1904
Bonynge, Robert W. (CO) - 1900, 1902, 1904, 1906, 1908
Boody (NY) - 1882
Boody, Azariah (NY) - 1852
Boody, David A. (NY) - 1890
Boogaerts, John Jr. (NY) - 1974
Booham (PA) - 1854
Boohar, Charles W. (PA) - 1978
Booher, Charles F. (MO) - 1888, 1906, 1908, 1910, 1912, 1914, 1916, 1918
Booker, George W. (VA) - 1869
Booker, William B. (NY) - 1829
Boomer, George E. (WA) - 1914
Boon, George (IN) - 1833
Boon, Ratliff (IN) - 1824, 1826, 1828, 1831, 1833, 1835, 1837
Boone, A. Gordon (MD) - 1952, 1956
Boone, Andrew R. (KY) - 1874, 1876
Boone, Ratliff (MO) - 1844
Boone, Richard (AL) - 1968
Boone, W. K. (OH) - 1880
Boone, W. P. (KY) - 1872
Booth (AL) - 1876
Booth, S. M. (SD) - 1889
Booth, Samuel (NY) - 1868
Booth, Walter (CT) - 1849
Booth, Washington (MD) - 1870
Boothman, Melvin M. (OH) - 1886, 1888
Booze, William S. (MD) - 1894, 1896
Borah, William E. (ID) - 1896
Borchers, Charles M. (IL) - 1912, 1914, 1930
Borchers, Robert B. (IL) - 1950
Borchert, Ferdinand (MN) - 1892

Borden, James W. (IN) - 1851
Borden, Nathaniel B. (MA) - 1834, 1836, 1838, 1840
Borden, Newton W. (OR) - 1926
Borden, William W. (IN) - 1892
Bordwell, Charles E. (PA) - 1922
Boreing, Vincent (KY) - 1898, 1900, 1902
Boren, James H. (VA) - 1986
Boren, Lyle H. (OK) - 1936, 1938, 1940, 1942, 1944
Borgatti, Joseph J. (MA) - 1930
Borgman, Al (TN) - 1990
Bork, Bill (KS) - 1964
Bork, Norma K. (CA) - 1978, 1980
Borland, T. R. (VA) - 1894
Borland, William P. (MO) - 1908, 1910, 1912, 1914, 1916
Borman, Henry (SD) - 1930
Born, J. W. (WI) - 1904
Borneman, Henry S. (PA) - 1912
Bornhorst, William H. (KY) - 1924
Bornstein, Erwin L. (NY) - 1970
Borowsky, Benjamin (NY) - 1914
Borski, Robert A. (PA) - 1982, 1984, 1986, 1988, 1990, 1992
Borst, Peter (NY) - 1828
Bortin, Joe (CA) - 1964
Bosch, Albert H. (NY) - 1952, 1954, 1956, 1958
Bosch, Pat (AZ) - 1974, 1982
Bosco, Douglas H. (CA) - 1982, 1984, 1986, 1988, 1990
Bosley, John L. (KY) - 1894
Bosma, Charles F. (IN) - 1978
Bosone, Reva Beck (UT) - 1948, 1950, 1952, 1954
Bosse (MD) - 1886
Bossier, Pierre E. J. B. (LA) - 1842
Bossingham, William J. (IL) - 1938
Bostrom (WI) - 1936
Boswell, Charles H. (IN) - 1954
Boteler (MA) - 1853, 1855
Boteler, Alexander R. (VA) - 1859
Boteler, Alexander R. (WV) - 1872, 1874
Botkin, Jeremiah D. (KS) - 1894, 1896, 1898, 1900, 1902, 1910
Bottiglieri, Neal P. (NY) - 1958
Botts, John M. (VA) - 1839, 1841, 1843, 1845, 1847, 1849, 1851
Botts, W. H. (KY) - 1886
Bouchard, John D. (NY) - 1988
Boucher, Frederick C. (VA) - 1982, 1984
Boucher, Rick (VA) - 1986, 1988, 1990, 1992
Bouck (WI) - 1864
Bouck, Gabriel (WI) - 1874, 1876, 1878, 1880
Bouck, Joseph (NY) - 1830
Bouck, William (WA) - 1920
Bouck, William M. (WA) - 1930
Bougtr (PA) - 1854
Bouldin, James W. (VA) - 1834, 1835, 1837
Bouldin, Nathan (MS) - 1833
Bouldin, Thomas T. (VA) - 1829, 1831
Bouligny, John E. (LA) - 1859
Boulter, Beau (TX) - 1984, 1986, 1992
Boulton, D. H. (PA) - 1890
Bouma, O. J. (WI) - 1931
Bound, Franklin (PA) - 1884, 1886
Bouquard, Marilyn Lloyd (TN) - 1980, 1982
Bourke (NY) - 1878
Bourland, H. R. (KY) - 1890
Bourland, Jimmie Ray (MS) - 1988
Bourland, Kent (MI) - 1982
Bourne, James R. (NY) - 1950
Boutell, Henry Sherman (IL) - 1897, 1898, 1900, 1902, 1904, 1906, 1908
Boutelle, Charles A. (ME) - 1880, 1882, 1884, 1886, 1888, 1890, 1892, 1894, 1896, 1898, 1900
Boulton (MO) - 1862
Boulton (NJ) - 1912
Boulton (NY) - 1848
Boutwell, George S. (MA) - 1844, 1846, 1848, 1862, 1864, 1866, 1868
Bovee, Matthias J. (NY) - 1834
Bow, Frank T. (OH) - 1950, 1952, 1954, 1956, 1958, 1960, 1962, 1964, 1966, 1968, 1970
Bowden, George E. (VA) - 1886, 1888, 1890
Bowden, Rufus V. (CA) - 1916
Bowdle, Stanley E. (OH) - 1912, 1914, 1916

Butler, J. A. (TX) - 1920
Butler, J. C. (NY) - 1864
Butler, J. F. (CA) - 1916
Butler, James H. (MD) - 1876
Butler, James J. (MO) - 1900, 1902
Butler, Jasper N. (OK) - 1954
Butler, John B. (IA) - 1906
Butler, John C. (NY) - 1938, 1941, 1942, 1944, 1946, 1948, 1950
Butler, John M. (PA) - 1860, 1864
Butler, M. Caldwell (VA) - 1972, 1974, 1976, 1978, 1980
Butler, Michael E. (NY) - 1910
Butler, Mounce G. (TN) - 1904
Butler, N. L. (OR) - 1886
Butler, Paul T. (MI) - 1892
Butler, Percy (OK) - 1954, 1956
Butler, R. Gordon (RI) - 1962
Butler, Robert R. (OR) - 1928, 1930, 1932
Butler, Roderick R. (TN) - 1867, 1868, 1870, 1872, 1874, 1886, 1890
Butler, Roscoe (NC) - 1926
Butler, Sampson H. (SC) - 1838, 1840
Butler, Stanard Dow (NY) - 1942
Butler, Thomas B. (CT) - 1849, 1851
Butler, Thomas J. (PA) - 1920, 1924
Butler, Thomas S. (PA) - 1896, 1898, 1900, 1902, 1904, 1906, 1908, 1910, 1912, 1914, 1916, 1918, 1920, 1922, 1924, 1926
Butler, W. B. (TX) - 1954
Butler, W. H. (IA) - 1892
Butler, W. J. (OR) - 1924, 1932
Butler, Walter H. (IA) - 1890
Butler, William (SC) - 1840, 1843, 1844
Butler, William O. (KY) - 1839, 1841
Butman, Samuel (ME) - 1826, 1828
Butt, Cyrus M. (WI) - 1882, 1894
Buttenweiser, Joseph L. (NY) - 1914
Butterfield, Daniel (NY) - 1892
Butterfield, Franklin (NY) - 1832
Butterfield, Martin (NY) - 1858
Butterfield, Rob (CA) - 1988
Butterly, James J. (NY) - 1942
Butterworth, Benjamin (OH) - 1878, 1880, 1882, 1884, 1886, 1888
Buttimer, Thomas H. (MA) - 1904
Button, Daniel E. (NY) - 1966, 1968, 1970
Button, Jonas K. (NY) - 1864
Buttram, W. H. (TN) - 1912
Buttrick, E. S. (WV) - 1882
Butts, Alex P. (NY) - 1870
Butts, Lavern P. (IN) - 1918
Butts, Nathan T. (IN) - 1892
Buttz, Charles W. (SC) - 1874, 1876
Butzke, Jeffrey A. (NY) - 1986
Butzner, William W. (VA) - 1916
Buxton, Ingrid K. (WI) - 1992
Buxton, John C. (NC) - 1900
Buyer, Steve (IN) - 1992
Buzza, Richard A. (PA) - 1902, 1910
Byard, James J. Jr. (NY) - 1912
Byars (VA) - 1833
Byars, J. C. (VA) - 1908
Bybee, M. C. P. (TX) - 1944
Byers, Glen (TN) - 1980, 1982
Byers, W. A. (IA) - 1948
Byfield (IN) - 1880
Byington, Heratio (MA) - 1846
Byington, L. (OH) - 1846
Byk, Ephraim (NY) - 1904
Bynum, Jesse A. (NC) - 1833, 1835, 1857, 1839
Bynum, John Gray (NC) - 1847
Bynum, Joseph M. (MS) - 1888
Bynum, William D. (IN) - 1884, 1886, 1888, 1890, 1892, 1894
Byrd, A. Floyd (KY) - 1910
Byrd, Adam M. (MS) - 1902, 1904, 1906, 1908, 1910
Byrd, Garland T. (GA) - 1964
Byrd, H. C. (MD) - 1966
Byrd, J. M. (NC) - 1932
Byrd, Robert C. (WV) - 1952, 1954, 1956
Byrd, Roland (MS) - 1976, 1978
Byrne, Edward B. (PA) - 1966
Byrne, Emmet F. (IL) - 1956, 1958, 1960, 1964
Byrne, George (WV) - 1906
Byrne, James A. (PA) - 1952, 1954, 1956, 1958, 1960, 1962, 1964, 1966, 1968, 1970
Byrne, James F. (NY) - 1930
Byrne, James S. (NY) - 1944

Byrne, Joseph P. (NY) - 1932
Byrne, Leslie L. (VA) - 1992
Byrne, Patrick S. (WA) - 1906
Byrne, Richard P. (NY) - 1934
Byrne, Richard W. (MO) - 1958
Byrne, William Michael (DE) - 1902
Byrne, William T. (NY) - 1936, 1938, 1940, 1942, 1944, 1946, 1948, 1950
Byrnes, James F. (SC) - 1910, 1912, 1914, 1916, 1918, 1920, 1922
Byrnes, John W. (WI) - 1944, 1946, 1948, 1950, 1052, 1954, 1956, 1958, 1960, 1962, 1964, 1966, 1968, 1970
Byrnes, William (NY) - 1904
Byrns, Joseph W. Jr. (TN) - 1938, 1940
Byrns, Joseph W. (TN) - 1908, 1910, 1912, 1914, 1916, 1918, 1920, 1922, 1924, 1926, 1928, 1930, 1932, 1934
Byrns, Samuel (MO) - 1890
Byron, Alexander (MA) - 1962, 1964, 1986
Byron, Beverly D. (MD) - 1970, 1080, 1082, 1984, 1986, 1988, 1990
Byron, Goodloe E. (MD) - 1968, 1970, 1972, 1974, 1976
Byron, Robert D. (NY) - 1954
Byron, William D. (MD) - 1938, 1940
Byrum, Paul R. (MO) - 1936

## C

Cabaniss, Thomas B. (GA) - 1892
Cabell (NJ) - 1914
Cabell (VA) - 1833
Cabell, Earle (TX) - 1964, 1966, 1968, 1970, 1972
Cabell, Edward C. (FL) - 1845, 1846, 1848, 1850, 1852
Cabell, George C. (VA) - 1874, 1876, 1878, 1880, 1882, 1884, 1886
Cabell, Roy E. Jr. (VA) - 1956
Cable, Benjamin T. (IL) - 1890
Cable, Mrs. James A. (KS) - 1924
Cable, Jessie J. (TN) - 1982
Cable, John L. (OH) - 1912, 1920, 1922, 1928, 1930, 1932
Cable, Joseph (OH) - 1848, 1850
Cable, P. L. (IL) - 1870
Cabot, Joseph S. (MA) - 1828, 1830, 1833, 1834, 1836, 1838
Cacchione, Peter E. (NY) - 1934
Caddis, Charles (AL) - 1988
Cadenhead, Ed (OK) - 1966
Cadigan, Charles P. (WI) - 1934
Cadigan, John (WI) - 1924
Cadmus, Cornelius A. (NJ) - 1890, 1892
Cadmus, William E. (IL) - 1912
Cadmus, Wilmer A. (NJ) - 1922
Cadwalader, John (PA) - 1854
Cadwalader, John Jr. (PA) - 1882, 1904
Cady (NY) - 1844
Cady, Addison E. (NE) - 1896
Cady, Claude E. (MI) - 1932, 1934
Cady, Daniel (NY) - 1830
Cady, Ervin H. (IN) - 1912
Cady, Hiram H. (IL) - 1886
Cady, Virgil W. (WI) - 1914
Caesar, Joseph N. O. (NY) - 1984
Caffery, Frank J. (NY) - 1942
Caffery, Patrick T. (LA) - 1968, 1970
Cage, Harry (MS) - 1833
Cahal, Terry H. (TN) - 1841
Cahalane, John M. (OH) - 1918
Cahill, John F. (NJ) - 1922
Cahill, Maurice (IA) - 1928
Cahill, William T. (NJ) - 1958, 1960, 1962, 1964, 1966, 1968
Cahoon, William (VT) - 1828, 1830
Cain, Francis J. (NY) - 1974
Cain, G. M. (MS) - 1896
Cain, Herbert R. Jr. (PA) - 1966
Cain, John (VT) - 1868, 1870
Cain, Lucy (TX) - 1992
Cain, Richard H. (SC) - 1872, 1876
Caine, Edwin E. (NV) - 1916
Caine, Michael L. (CT) - 1920
Cairns (NJ) - 1912
Cairns, John J. Jr. (PA) - 1950
Cake (PA) - 1858
Cake, Henry L. (PA) - 1866, 1868
Calabrese, Anthony O. Jr. (OH) - 1966
Caldbeck, Matthew J. (VT) - 1946

Calder, William M. (NJ) - 1904, 1906, 1908, 1910, 1912
Calderhead, William A. (KS) - 1894, 1896, 1898, 1900, 1902, 1904, 1906, 1908, 1914
Calderwood, William G. (MN) - 1912
Caldwell (NY) - 1862
Caldwell (SC) - 1826
Caldwell (TN) - 1872
Caldwell, A. S. (IL) - 1922
Caldwell, Andrew J. (TN) - 1882, 1884
Caldwell, Ben F. (IL) - 1896, 1898, 1900, 1902, 1904, 1906
Caldwell, Charles M. (OH) - 1912
Caldwell, Charles Pope (NY) - 1914, 1916, 1918
Caldwell, Charles T. (WV) - 1892
Caldwell, David F. (NC) - 1868
Caldwell, George A. (KY) - 1843, 1845, 1849
Caldwell, Greene W. (NC) - 1841, 1849, 1851
Caldwell, Howard H. (CA) - 1914
Caldwell, Hugh L. (CO) - 1956
Caldwell, James H. (PA) - 1880, 1882
Caldwell, John (KS) - 1910
Caldwell, John A. (OH) - 1888, 1890, 1892
Caldwell, John H. (AL) - 1872, 1874
Caldwell, John R. (IA) - 1896
Caldwell, John W. (KY) - 1876, 1878, 1880
Caldwell, Joseph P. (NC) - 1849, 1851
Caldwell, Millard F. (FL) - 1932, 1934, 1936, 1938
Caldwell, Morrison H. (NC) - 1898
Caldwell, Patrick C. (SC) - 1840, 1843
Caldwell, Robert P. (TN) - 1870
Caldwell, Tod R. (NC) - 1865
Caldwell, William P. (TN) - 1874, 1876
Calhoon, John (KY) - 1827, 1835, 1837
Calhoun (GA) - 1853
Calhoun, Allan T. (VT) - 1924, 1926
Calhoun, B. A. (TX) - 1894, 1896
Calhoun, James M. (GA) - 1848
Calhoun, James S. (GA) - 1848
Calhoun, John (IL) - 1844, 1852
Calhoun, John N. (IA) - 1936
Calhoun, William B. (MA) - 1834, 1836, 1838, 1840
Califano, Richard C. (NY) - 1942
Caligiuri, Richard Edward (PA) - 1986, 1988, 1990
Calinger, Walter M. (NE) - 1986
Calise, Salvatore J. (NY) - 1986
Calkin, Hervey C. (NY) - 1868
Calkins - 1874
Calkins, Ephraim (MI) - 1852
Calkins, John T. (NY) - 1976
Calkins, Rolla C. (OK) - 1958
Calkins, William H. (IN) - 1876, 1878, 1880, 1882
Call, Jacob (IN) - 1824
Call, W. Douglas (NY) - 1984, 1992
Calla, Joseph J. Jr. (PA) - 1944
Callaghan, Denis J. (PA) - 1894
Callahan, Andrew J. (NJ) - 1924
Callahan, Daniel T. (MA) - 1912, 1914
Callahan, Dennis M. (OH) - 1972
Callahan, Ethelbert (IL) - 1864
Callahan, Frances X. (CA) - 1972
Callahan, Richard J. (NY) - 1966, 1968, 1970
Callahan, Sonny (AL) - 1984, 1986, 1988, 1990, 1992
Callahan, Vincent F. Jr. (VA) - 1976
Callan, Clair A. (NE) - 1958, 1962, 1964, 1966, 1968, 1970
Callas, George (NJ) - 1982
Callaway, Howard H. (GA) - 1964
Callaway, Oscar (TX) - 1910, 1912, 1914
Callen, Richard C. (CO) - 1932
Callender, Edward B. (MA) - 1906
Callery, Philip H. (NY) - 1914
Callihan, Mike (CO) - 1992
Callihan, Trudie (MI) - 1986
Callis, John B. (AL) - 1868
Callison, Preston H. (SC) - 1965
Calman, Everett E. (NY) - 1918
Calnen, Henry J. (CT) - 1926
Calpin, P. F. (PA) - 1910
Calse, Harry (PA) - 1924
Calvert (MD) - 1863
Calvert, Charles B. (MD) - 1861
Calvert, George (TX) - 1932
Calvert, Joseph W. (KY) - 1904, 1906

Calvert, Ken (CA) - 1992
Calvin, E. Elgie (CA) - 1956
Calvin, Samuel (PA) - 1848
Camacho, Julian (CA) - 1972, 1974
Camalier, Benjamin H. (MD) - 1900, 1902
Camardi, Lola (NY) - 1970
Cambreleng, Churchill C. (NY) - 1820, 1822, 1824, 1826, 1828, 1830, 1832, 1834, 1836, 1838
Camden (VA) - 1839, 1845
Cameron, Charles S. (AR) - 1868
Cameron, Don O. (OH) - 1944
Cameron, John A. (NC) - 1827, 1829
Cameron, Kenneth (NY) - 1934
Cameron, Ronald Brooks (CA) - 1962, 1964, 1966
Camerzell, Fritz (NJ) - 1982
Caminetti, Anthony (CA) - 1890, 1892, 1894, 1904
Cammarota, A. J. (PA) - 1956
Camp, A. Sidney (GA) - 1940, 1942, 1944, 1946, 1948, 1950, 1952
Camp, Billy Joe (AL) - 1982
Camp, Cyrus C. (PA) - 1878
Camp, Dave (MI) - 1990, 1992
Camp, Elisha (NY) - 1826, 1828
Camp, John G. (NY) - 1824, 1828
Camp, John H. (NY) - 1876, 1878, 1880
Camp, John N. Happy (OK) - 1968, 1970, 1972, 1974
Camp, Katherine L. (PA) - 1972
Camp, Silas (NY) - 1846
Camp, Thomas L. (GA) - 1946
Campbell (AL) - 1872
Campbell (GA) - 1840
Campbell (KY) - 1837
Campbell (NY) - 1844, 1848, 1874
Campbell (OK) - 1914
Campbell (PA) - 1848, 1862
Campbell (TN) - 1872
Campbell (VT) - 1880
Campbell (VA) - 1827
Campbell, Albert J. (MT) - 1898
Campbell, Alex (OH) - 1846
Campbell, Alexander (IL) - 1874, 1876, 1878
Campbell, Andrew J. (NY) - 1894
Campbell, B. C. (NC) - 1934
Campbell, Ben Nighthorse (CO) - 1986, 1988, 1990
Campbell, Braxton W. (OH) - 1904
Campbell, Brookins (TN) - 1853
Campbell, Bruce A. (IL) - 1910
Campbell, Carroll A. Jr. (SC) - 1978, 1980, 1982, 1984
Campbell, Charles M. (OK) - 1912
Campbell, Courtney (FL) - 1952, 1954
Campbell, Daniel (IA) - 1880, 1892
Campbell, Daniel (TN) - 1980, 1986
Campbell, David C. (GA) - 1838
Campbell, Ed. H. (IA) - 1928, 1930, 1932
Campbell, Edgar (PA) - 1946
Campbell, Edmund D. (VA) - 1952
Campbell, Edward (NY) - 1966
Campbell, Edward E. (IL) - 1922, 1924
Campbell, Emerson (OH) - 1930
Campbell, Ethan H. (MO) - 1960, 1962
Campbell, Felix (NY) - 1882, 1884, 1886, 1888
Campbell, Foster (LA) - 1988
Campbell, Frank T. (IA) - 1884
Campbell, George (OK) - 1950
Campbell, Guy E. (PA) - 1914, 1916, 1918, 1920, 1922, 1924, 1926, 1928, 1930, 1932, 1934
Campbell, Howard E. (PA) - 1944
Campbell, Howard O. (IN) - 1984
Campbell, J. B. (SC) - 1882
Campbell, J. C. (CA) - 1886
Campbell, J. E. (WA) - 1914
Campbell, J. Ike (NC) - 1920, 1922
Campbell, Jacob A. (PA) - 1876, 1878, 1880, 1882, 1884
Campbell, James (PA) - 1882
Campbell, James A. (NY) - 1930
Campbell, James E. (OH) - 1882, 1884, 1886, 1906
Campbell, James H. (PA) - 1854, 1856, 1858, 1860
Campbell, James R. (IL) - 1896, 1918
Campbell, John (SC) - 1828, 1830, 1836, 1838, 1840, 1843
Campbell, John A. (MA) - 1908
Campbell, John H. (PA) - 1844

Campbell, John P. (KY) - 1855
Campbell, John P. (MO) - 1842, 1846
Campbell, John W. (OH) - 1824
Campbell, John W. (OR) - 1912
Campbell, Joseph C. (IA) - 1918
Campbell, Julian H. (TN) - 1940
Campbell, Lee (OR) - 1912
Campbell, Lewis D. (OH) - 1840, 1842, 1844, 1848, 1850, 1852, 1854, 1856, 1858, 1870
Campbell, Lorne R. (VA) - 1953
Campbell, Neill (CA) - 1984
Campbell, Newman (IL) - 1852
Campbell, Nixon (MA) - 1920
Campbell, Philip P. (KS) - 1902, 1904, 1906, 1908, 1910, 1912, 1914, 1916, 1918, 1920
Campbell, Robert B. (SC) - 1826, 1834
Campbell, Stewart (IL) - 1932
Campbell, Terry L. (OK) - 1970
Campbell, Thomas (SC) - 1980
Campbell, Thomas E. (AZ) - 1912
Campbell, Thomas J. (TN) - 1841, 1843
Campbell, Thompson (IL) - 1850, 1852
Campbell, Timothy J. (NY) - 1886, 1888, 1890, 1892, 1894, 1896
Campbell, Tom (CA) - 1988, 1990
Campbell, Val B. (IL) - 1928
Campbell, William (NY) - 1824, 1844, 1846
Campbell, William B. (TN) - 1837, 1839, 1841, 1865
Campbell, William C. (IA) - 1906
Campbell, William D. (CA) - 1932, 1934, 1936, 1938, 1944
Campbell, William J. (WI) - 1934
Campbell, William W. (OH) - 1904, 1906, 1908
Campenni, Anthony L. (NJ) - 1976
Camper, Frank Sneed (TX) - 1922
Camper, John E. T. (MD) - 1948
Campolo, Anthony (PA) - 1976
Canada, A. J. "Joe" Jr. (VA) - 1986
Canaday, Delmar A. (OH) - 1948, 1952
Canaday, R. O. (NE) - 1940
Canaday, William P. (NC) - 1876, 1880, 1882
Canade, Austen D. (NY) - 1974
Canady, Charles T. (FL) - 1992
Canary, Kathryn (WI) - 1980
Canby, Richard S. (OH) - 1846
Candee, George (OH) - 1894
Candler, Allen D. (GA) - 1882, 1884, 1886, 1888
Candler, Ezekiel S. Jr. (MS) - 1900, 1902, 1904, 1906, 1908, 1910, 1912, 1914, 1916, 1918
Candler, John W. (MA) - 1880, 1882, 1888, 1890
Candler, Milton A. (GA) - 1874, 1876
Candler, W. W. (NC) - 1948
Candler, William G. (NC) - 1872
Candon, John B. (VT) - 1936, 1942
Canfield, Clar W. (PA) - 1890
Canfield, Gordon (NJ) - 1940, 1942, 1944, 1946, 1948, 1950, 1952, 1954, 1956, 1958
Canfield, Harry C. (IN) - 1920, 1922, 1924, 1926, 1928, 1930
Canfield, Roger (CA) - 1982, 1984
Canning, Charles (MN) - 1888
Cannon (KS) - 1882
Cannon (LA) - 1859
Cannon, Arthur P. (FL) - 1938, 1940, 1942, 1944
Cannon, Clarence (MO) - 1922, 1924, 1926, 1928, 1930, 1932, 1934, 1936, 1938, 1940, 1942, 1944, 1946, 1948, 1950, 1952, 1954, 1956, 1958, 1960, 1962
Cannon, Francis A. (WI) - 1914
Cannon, James J. (NJ) - 1944
Cannon, John C. (KS) - 1882
Cannon, Joseph G. (IL) - 1872, 1874, 1876, 1878, 1880, 1882, 1884, 1886, 1888, 1890, 1892, 1894, 1896, 1898, 1900, 1902, 1904, 1906, 1908, 1910, 1912, 1914, 1916, 1918, 1920
Cannon, LeGrand B. (NY) - 1866
Cannon, Marion (CA) - 1892
Cannon, Michael D. (VA) - 1976
Cannon, Quayle Jr. (UT) - 1944
Cannon, Raymond J. (WI) - 1932, 1934, 1936, 1938
Cannon, Richard M. (CA) - 1932

Cannon, V. S. (OK) - 1936
Cannon, W. L. (KY) - 1902
Cantando, Leonard L. (CA) - 1962
Canter, Julius D. (NJ) - 1952
Canter, N. MacKenzie III (VA) - 1990
Cantor, Bernard (TN) - 1972
Cantor, Jacob A. (NY) - 1894, 1912, 1914
Cantrell, Harvey E. (TN) - 1928
Cantrell, J. C. (KY) - 1926
Cantrill, James C. (KY) - 1908, 1910, 1912, 1914, 1916, 1918, 1920, 1922
Cantu, Mitchell (GA) - 1984
Cantwell (NY) - 1872
Cantwell, John M. (NY) - 1924
Cantwell, Maria (WA) - 1992
Cantwell, Percy J. (RI) - 1922
Cantwell, Thomas (NY) - 1910
Canwell, Al (WA) - 1952, 1954
Capatosto, Alice A. (NY) - 1968
Capehart, James (WV) - 1892
Capehart, Jones (WV) - 1890
Caperton (VA) - 1841
Capozzi, Alvin D. (PA) - 1964
Capozzoli, Louis J. (NY) - 1940, 1942
Cappelli, Michael R. (NY) - 1960
Cappiello, O. Arthur (PA) - 1954
Caprio, Frank (CA) - 1972
Capron, Adin B. (RI) - 1892, 1996, 1998, 1900, 1902, 1904, 1906, 1908
Capron, Wiley W. (NY) - 1912
Capstick, John H. (NJ) - 1914, 1916
Capua, S. Peter (FL) - 1974
Caputo, Bruce F. (NY) - 1976
Caputo, Vic (MI) - 1980
Capuzi, Louis F. (IL) - 1952
Car (MO) - 1852
Carasso, Max (NY) - 1978
Caraway, Thaddeus H. (AR) - 1912, 1914, 1916, 1918
Carbajal, Michael Jr. (NY) - 1974
Carberry, Glenn (CT) - 1988
Card (MI) - 1878
Carden, Cap R. (KY) - 1930, 1932, 1934
Carden, M. W. (AL) - 1902
Cardenas, Al (FL) - 1978
Carder (RI) - 1867
Cardin, Benjamin L. (MD) - 1986, 1988, 1990, 1992
Cardino, Joseph Jr. (NY) - 1988
Carew, John F. (NY) - 1912, 1914, 1916, 1918, 1920, 1922, 1924, 1926, 1928
Carey, Archibald James Jr. (IL) - 1950
Carey, Daniel J. (NY) - 1954
Carey, Henry (NY) - 1904, 1906
Carey, Hugh L. (NY) - 1960, 1962, 1964, 1966, 1968, 1970, 1972
Carey, Jacob S. Sr. (OH) - 1922
Carey, James C. Jr. (CA) - 1984
Carey, James F. (MA) - 1904, 1910
Carey, John (OH) - 1858, 1860
Carey, John I. (GA) - 1848
Carey, John L. (MI) - 1938
Carey, Robert (NJ) - 1902
Carey, William A. (MA) - 1942, 1944
Cargo, David F. (NM) - 1986
Carl, Douglas (MI) - 1988, 1992
Carlan, Andrew E. (NY) - 1980
Carlebach, William D. (NY) - 1956
Carleton (MA) - 1878
Carleton, Ezra C. (MI) - 1882, 1894
Carley, John (MO) - 1992
Carley, Patrick J. (NY) - 1926, 1928, 1930, 1932
Carley, Robert K. "Bob" (SC) - 1988
Carlin, Charles C. (VA) - 1908, 1910, 1912, 1914, 1916, 1918
Carlin, David R. Jr. (RI) - 1992
Carlin, John J. (NJ) - 1948
Carlisle (VA) - 1857
Carlisle, Charles A. (IN) - 1912
Carlisle, John G. (KY) - 1876, 1878, 1880, 1882, 1884, 1886, 1888
Carlisle, John S. (VA) - 1855
Carllee, R. B. (AR) - 1886
Carlson, Anthony (WY) - 1912
Carlson, Clifford D. (IL) - 1972, 1974
Carlson, Dave (AK) - 1982
Carlson, Dave (MN) - 1988
Carlson, Elmer G. (IA) - 1954
Carlson, Frank (KS) - 1934, 1936, 1938, 1940, 1942, 1944
Carlson, Gary K. (MT) - 1984
Carlson, Gerald R. (MI) - 1980, 1984
Carlson, Harry (NH) - 1944

Carlson, Lawrence M. (MN) - 1928
Carlson, Mrs. P. J. (IL) - 1926
Carlson, Peggy T. (OR) - 1948
Carlson, Ruth (Paula) (CA) - 1984
Carlson, Samuel A. (NY) - 1912, 1938
Carlson, William H. (CA) - 1896
Carlton (ME) - 1870
Carlton, Ezra C. (MI) - 1884
Carlton, Henry H. (GA) - 1886, 1888
Carlton, J. F. (AR) - 1912
Carlyle, F. Ertel (NC) - 1948, 1950, 1952, 1954
Carmack, Edward W. (TN) - 1896, 1898
Carman, E. Day (CA) - 1964
Carman, Gregory W. (NY) - 1978, 1980
Carmical (GA) - 1886
Carmichael (MD) - 1847
Carmichael, Archibald H. (AL) - 1934
Carmichael, James H. (MA) - 1910
Carmichael, Leander B. (NC) - 1855
Carmichael, Richard B. (MD) - 1833
Carmody, Dana Warren (CA) - 1978
Carmon, Henry P. (DE) - 1890
Carmony, Gerald C. (IN) - 1956
Carnahan, A. A. (KS) - 1884
Carnahan, A. S. J. (MO) - 1944, 1946, 1948, 1950, 1952, 1954, 1956, 1958
Carnahan, Charles C. (IL) - 1900
Carnahan, Russ (MO) - 1990
Carner, Grant C. (AR) - 1976
Carnes, Nicholas (NY) - 1948
Carney, Charles J. (OH) - 1970, 1972, 1974, 1976, 1978
Carney, Clarence S. (IA) - 1980
Carney, Claude S. (MI) - 1912, 1924
Carney, Cy Jr. (AR) - 1962
Carney, Herschel W. (MI) - 1946
Carney, J. J. (OK) - 1912
Carney, Joseph P. (WI) - 1910, 1918
Carney, William (NY) - 1978, 1980, 1982, 1984
Carnine, A. G. (IL) - 1938
Carnoy, Martin (CA) - 1984
Carns, William L. (NY) - 1932
Caron, Guy W. (AR) - 1908
Carothers, B. F. (TX) - 1853
Carothers, T. L. (CA) - 1884
Carp, Richard L. (Larry) (MO) - 1960
Carpenter (AL) - 1882
Carpenter (NY) - 1854
Carpenter, Alva (NY) - 1890
Carpenter, Charles T. (PA) - 1934
Carpenter, Cyrus C. (IA) - 1878, 1880
Carpenter, Edmund N. (PA) - 1918, 1824, 1826
Carpenter, Frank G. (OH) - 1914
Carpenter, G. J. (CA) - 1876
Carpenter, Lewis Cass (SC) - 1874, 1876
Carpenter, Noel (MO) - 1954
Carpenter, Oliver C. (NY) - 1936
Carpenter, Paul B. (CA) - 1964
Carpenter, R. R. (KY) - 1866
Carpenter, Raymond G. (NY) - 1966
Carpenter, Terry (NE) - 1932
Carpenter, W. H. (AR) - 1902
Carpenter, W. L. (IA) - 1886
Carpenter, Warren D. (AR) - 1988
Carpenter, William Randolph (KS) - 1932, 1934
Carpenter, Winfield S. (IN) - 1892
Carper, Thomas R. (DE) - 1982, 1984, 1986, 1988, 1990
Carr (IN) - 1870
Carr, Bob (MI) - 1974, 1976, 1978, 1980, 1982, 1984, 1986, 1988, 1990, 1992
Carr, D. R. (KY) - 1870, 1882
Carr, Edward Ellis (IL) - 1922
Carr, Edwin S. (IL) - 1930, 1932
Carr, Homer S. (MI) - 1922
Carr, John (IN) - 1831, 1833, 1835, 1839, 1841
Carr, John B. (MA) - 1950
Carr, John C. (MA) - 1952
Carr, M. Robert (MI) - 1972
Carr, Nathan Tracy (IN) - 1876
Carr, Samuel W. (NH) - 1835
Carr, Sherman S. (IL) - 1946
Carr, Thomas S. (MD) - 1950
Carr, William A. (PA) - 1904, 1910
Carr, Wooda N. (PA) - 1900, 1912, 1914
Carran, Edward F. (OH) - 1930
Carrano, Ralph J. (NY) - 1968
Carreau, Rene A. (NY) - 1942
Carrelas, Arthur (RI) - 1954

Carricarte, Michael A. (FL) - 1974
Carrick, Duncan (TX) - 1914
Carrick, Jonathan G. (ID) - 1912
Carrier, Chester O. (KY) - 1943, 1944
Carrigan, Charles E. (WV) - 1910
Carrigan, James D. (IL) - 1942
Carrigg, John J. (OH) - 1962
Carrigg, Joseph L. (PA) - 1952, 1954, 1956, 1958
Carrin (PA) - 1862
Carrington, John (NC) - 1990
Carrol (NY) - 1882
Carroll (MO) - 1882
Carroll (WA) - 1890
Carroll, Charles H. (NY) - 1824, 1842, 1844
Carroll, Dennis M. (CT) - 1950
Carroll, Edward P. (PA) - 1922, 1924, 1930
Carroll, James (MD) - 1839
Carroll, James H. (WI) - 1938
Carroll, John A. (CO) - 1946, 1948
Carroll, John M. (NY) - 1870
Carroll, John S. (HI) - 1966
Carroll, John S. (CO) - 1974
Carroll, Michael A. (IN) - 1982
Carroll, Otis S. (NY) - 1924
Carroll, Patrick D. (IN) - 1980
Carroll, T. Francis (PA) - 1922
Carroll, Thomas (WA) - 1892
Carroll, Thomas J. (PA) - 1928, 1930
Carroll, William D. (WI) - 1942, 1944
Carron, Joe (MO) - 1976
Carrott, Montgomery B. (IL) - 1942, 1960
Carryl (NY) - 1862
Carson (NJ) - 1916, 1918
Carson (WI) - 1872
Carson, Henderson H. (OH) - 1942, 1944, 1946, 1948
Carson, Joseph K. Jr. (OR) - 1926
Carson, Leslie J. Jr. (PA) - 1968
Carson, Robert (OH) - 1912
Carson, Samuel P. (NC) - 1825, 1827, 1829, 1831, 1833
Carss, William L. (MN) - 1918, 1920, 1922, 1924, 1926, 1928, 1930
Carswell, H. J. (GA) - 1930
Carswell, Porter W. (GA) - 1966
Carter (CT) - 1878
Carter (IN) - 1868
Carter (NJ) - 1880
Carter (TN) - 1872
Carter (VA) - 1843, 1844
Carter (WI) - 1876
Carter, Albert E. (CA) - 1924, 1926, 1928, 1930, 1932, 1934, 1936, 1938, 1940, 1942, 1944
Carter, Charles D. (OK) - 1907, 1908, 1910, 1912, 1914, 1916, 1918, 1920, 1922, 1924
Carter, Darwin (GA) - 1980
Carter, David K. (OH) - 1840, 1848, 1850
Carter, David M. (NC) - 1872
Carter, Elmer A. (NY) - 1950
Carter, Eugene (MS) - 1970
Carter, George (IA) - 1878
Carter, J. C. (KY) - 1972
Carter, J. N. (NE) - 1912
Carter, J. P. (AL) - 1950
Carter, James G. (MA) - 1846
Carter, John (SC) - 1824, 1826
Carter, Jonathan K. (ME) - 1992
Carter, Luther C. (NY) - 1858, 1860
Carter, M. C. (OK) - 1908
Carter, M. J. (IA) - 1906
Carter, Robert A. (FL) - 1970, 1972
Carter, S. J. (TN) - 1865
Carter, Samuel R. (PA) - 1900
Carter, Steven V. (IA) - 1948, 1950, 1956, 1958
Carter, Thomas C. (NC) - 1924
Carter, Thomas H. (MT) - 1889, 1890
Carter, Tim Lee (KY) - 1964, 1966, 1968, 1970, 1972, 1974, 1976, 1978
Carter, Timothy J. (ME) - 1836
Carter, Tom (TX) - 1986
Carter, Vincent M. (WY) - 1928, 1930, 1932
Carter, W. Beverly Jr. (PA) - 1954
Carter, W. T. (GA) - 1894
Carter, William B. (TN) - 1831, 1833, 1835, 1837, 1839
Carter, William H. (MA) - 1914, 1916
Cartier, Arthur J. B. (MA) - 1916, 1918, 1920, 1922, 1924
Cartland (NH) - 1827
Carton, John R. (VA) - 1878

Decker, George P. (NY) - 1910, 1912, 1914
Decker, N.H. (NY) - 1880
Decker, Percy W. (NY) - 1906
Decker, Perl D. (MO) - 1912, 1914, 1916, 1918
Decker, Robert S. (IL) - 1964
Decker, Teresa S. (MI) - 1986
DeCola, Fred S. (IL) - 1922
Decormier, Robert R. (NY) - 1948
Dedoncker, David (IL) - 1962
Dee, Martin (MT) - 1902
Deemer, Elias (PA) - 1900, 1902, 1904, 1906, 1908
Deemey, J. W. (ND) - 1922
Deen, Braswell (GA) - 1932, 1934, 1936
Deen, Carl K. (PA) - 1932
Deen, Richard L. (IN) - 1972
Deer, Ada E. (WI) - 1992
Deering, Harold F. (MN) - 1938
Deering, J. W. (ME) - 1894
Deering, Nathaniel C. (IA) - 1876, 1878, 1880
Deffebach, T. G. (SD) - 1908
Deford, J. E. (TN) - 1914
DeFazio, Peter A. (OR) - 1986, 1988, 1990, 1992
DeFazio, Thomas J. (IL) - 1986
DeForest, Lavergne B. (IL) - 1900
DeFosse, Daniel G. (IL) - 1982
DeFrance, Robert M. (PA) - 1868
Defrees, Joseph D. (IN) - 1864
Degener, Edward (TX) - 1869, 1871
Degenhardt, Gilbert (MO) - 1958
Degennaro, Carlo N. (NJ) - 1970
Degnan, John T. (NY) - 1942
Degnan, Joseph M. (NJ) - 1932
deGraffenried, Edward (AL) - 1948, 1950
DeGraff, John (NY) - 1826, 1836
DeGraff, William (NY) - 1902
DeHass (WV) - 1863
Dehoney, E. L. (TX) - 1882
Dehority, Edward C. (IN) - 1904
Dehr, Albert (CA) - 1976, 1980
Dehual (MN) - 1914
Dehunt, Jerome T. (NY) - 1922
Deighan, Neil F. (NJ) - 1962
Deimund, Linder (MO) - 1936
Deitch, Robert M. (NJ) - 1978
Deitman, William H. (PA) - 1960
Deitrick, Frederick S. (MA) - 1906, 1908, 1910, 1912, 1914, 1916, 1932
Deitz, William (NY) - 1824
DeJarnette, Daniel C. (VA) - 1859
DeJulio, Robert R. Jr. (OH) - 1990
Del Giorno, Peter J. (NY) - 1978, 1980
Del Rosso, Henry E. (NY) - 1954, 1964, 1966
DeLamater, Henry (NY) - 1846
Delamatyr, Gilbert (IN) - 1878, 1880
Delaney (KY) - 1847
Delaney (NJ) - 1918
Delaney, A. K. (WI) - 1886
Delaney, Edward K. (MN) - 1942
Delaney, James J. (NY) - 1944, 1946, 1948, 1950, 1952, 1954, 1956, 1958, 1960, 1962, 1964, 1966, 1968, 1970, 1972, 1974, 1976
Delaney, John J. (NY) - 1931, 1932, 1934, 1936, 1938, 1940, 1942, 1944, 1946, 1948
Delaney, Thomas S. (NY) - 1896
Delaney, Tom (WA) - 1956, 1958
Delano (MA) - 1888
Delano, Charles (MA) - 1858, 1860
Delano, Columbus (OH) - 1844, 1846, 1864, 1866
Delany, Hubert T. (NY) - 1929
Delaplaine, Isaac C. (NY) - 1860
DeLauro, Rosa (CT) - 1990, 1992
DeLay, Thomas D. (TX) - 1984, 1986, 1988, 1990, 1992
Delehanty, Thomas E. (ME) - 1954
DeLeon, Daniel (NY) - 1894, 1896
Delguidice, Michael J. (NY) - 1968
Delisle, Peter B. (MI) - 1906
Dellay, Vincent J. (NJ) - 1954, 1956
Dellenback, John (OR) - 1966, 1968, 1970, 1972, 1974
Dellet, James (AL) - 1833, 1839, 1843
DelliBovi, Alfred A. (NY) - 1978
Dellone, Mattie C. (NY) - 1930
Dellums, Ronald V. (CA) - 1970, 1972, 1974, 1976, 1978, 1980, 1982, 1984, 1986, 1988, 1990, 1992

Dellwo, Robert D. (WA) - 1950, 1952
Deloia, Angelo S. (NY) - 1962
Delong (NY) - 1842
Delong, James (NY) - 1846
Delzell, William A. (OR) - 1930
Demarest (NJ) - 1878, 1894, 1914
Demarest, Eugene E. (NJ) - 1954
Demarest, Horace A. (NY) - 1932
DeMars, Lewis (MN) - 1990
Demas, Henry (LA) - 1882
Demaulsby, I. (MD) - 1826
DeMauro, Peter (NY) - 1990
Dembufsky, Max (IL) - 1894
DeMell, Harry (NY) - 1980
Demers, James M. (NH) - 1986
Deming, Benjamin F. (VT) - 1832
Deming, Henry C. (CT) - 1863, 1865, 1867
Deming, O. S. (KY) - 1876
Demming, Henry C. (PA) - 1912
Dempsey (WI) - 1936
Dempsey, John J. (NM) - 1934, 1936, 1938, 1950, 1952, 1954, 1956
Dempsey, John T. (IL) - 1936
Dempsey, John T. (MI) - 1966
Dempsey, S. Wallace (NY) - 1914, 1916, 1918, 1920, 1922, 1924, 1926, 1928
Dempster, Milen C. (CA) - 1932
DeNardis, Lawrence J. (CT) - 1980, 1982, 1984
Denby, Edwin (MI) - 1904, 1906, 1908, 1910
Denholm, Frank E. (SD) - 1968, 1970, 1972, 1974
Denio, C. B. (CA) - 1875
Denison, Charles (PA) - 1862, 1864, 1866
Denison, Dudley C. (VT) - 1874, 1876
Denison, Edward E. (IL) - 1916, 1918, 1920, 1922, 1924, 1926, 1928, 1930, 1932
Denison, John D. Jr. (IA) - 1910
Denman, James (CA) - 1894
Denman, William F. (IA) - 1956
Denn, Gale A. (NY) - 1980
Dennerll, Norbert G. Jr. (OH) - 1964
Denney, Arthur J. (NE) - 1936
Denney, Robert V. (NE) - 1966, 1968
Dennis (MD) - 1855
Dennis, Andrew B. (IL) - 1922, 1924
Dennis, David W. (IN) - 1968, 1970, 1972, 1974
Dennis, Henry D. (IL) - 1892
Dennis, John (MD) - 1837, 1839
Dennis, John W. (NY) - 1918
Dennis, Littleton P. (MD) - 1833
Dennison, David (OH) - 1956, 1958, 1960
Dennison, Edward E. (IL) - 1914
Dennison, Fern Coste (NY) - 1972
Dennison, Joan Louise (MI) - 1990
Dennison, Margaret (OH) - 1970
Denny, George (KY) - 1878
Denny, George Jr. (KY) - 1894
Denny, George L. (IN) - 1948
Denny, Harmar (PA) - 1829, 1830, 1832, 1834
Denny, Harmar D. Jr. (PA) - 1950, 1952
Denny, Jacob F. (IN) - 1916
Denny, James W. (MD) - 1898, 1900, 1902
Denny, Walter McK. (MS) - 1894
Denson, William H. (AL) - 1892, 1894
Denston (NY) - 1858
Dent, Hayes (MS) - 1993
Dent, Jerry A. (MO) - 1978
Dent, John H. (PA) - 1958, 1960, 1962, 1964, 1966, 1968, 1970, 1972, 1974, 1976
Dent, Lewis (CA) - 1849
Dent, M. H. (WV) - 1906
Dent, S. Hubert Jr. (AL) - 1908, 1910, 1912, 1914, 1916, 1918
Dent, Thomas A. (NY) - 1954
Dent, William B. W. (GA) - 1853
Denton, E. Brady (MI) - 1976
Denton, George K. (IN) - 1916, 1918
Denton, J. A. (TN) - 1894
Denton, Phil (FL) - 1992
Denton, Winfield K. (IN) - 1946, 1948, 1950, 1952, 1954, 1956, 1958, 1960, 1962, 1964, 1966
Denver, James W. (CA) - 1854
Denver, James W. (OH) - 1870, 1884, 1886
Denver, Matthew R. (OH) - 1906, 1908, 1910
Derby, Marlyn A. (WA) - 1988, 1990
Dergance, Philip A. (KS) - 1948

Derham, Donald A. (NY) - 1970
Dermody, Joseph (NY) - 1938
Dermond, Philip C. (IN) - 1952
DeRouen, Rene L. (LA) - 1927, 1928, 1930, 1932, 1934, 1936, 1938
Derounian, Steven B. (NY) - 1952, 1954, 1956, 1958, 1960, 1962, 1964, 1966
Derrick (NJ) - 1918
Derrick, Butler C. (SC) - 1976, 1978, 1974, 1980, 1982, 1984, 1986, 1988, 1990, 1992
Derrick, George H. (CA) - 1914
Derry, George H. (NY) - 1922
Dershem, Frank L. (PA) - 1912, 1914
Derwinski, Edward J. (IL) - 1958, 1960, 1962, 1964, 1966, 1968, 1970, 1972, 1974, 1976, 1978, 1980
Desantis, John B. (PA) - 1916
Desborough, E. G. (NY) - 1974
Desha, L. B. (KY) - 1847
Desha, Robert (TN) - 1827, 1829
DeShazo, Al (AL) - 1980
Desmond, Andrew D. (NJ) - 1944
Desmond, John J. (IL) - 1964
Desmond, John J. (MA) - 1894
Dethloff, Edward C. (NY) - 1924
Detig, Robert H. (NY) - 1966
Dettry, William H. (PA) - 1906
Deupree, Harlan (OK) - 1937, 1938
Deuster, Peter V. (WI) - 1878, 1880, 1882, 1884
Deutsch, Peter (FL) - 1992
Devalle, A. F. (CA) - 1884
Devaney, Joe (TX) - 1982
Devany, John A. Jr. (NY) - 1944, 1946
Devens, John E. (AK) - 1990, 1992
Dever (GA) - 1872
Dever, John J. (IL) - 1926
Devereaux, Alvin (NY) - 1868
Devereaux, James P. (MI) - 1910
Devereux, James P. S. (MD) - 1950, 1952, 1954, 1956
Devereux, Thomas P. (NC) - 1882
Devery, John Patrick (NY) - 1944
Devine, Herbert W. (MI) - 1950
Devine, John E. Jr. (IL) - 1970, 1972
Devine, John M. (NE) - 1894
Devine, Samuel L. (OH) - 1958, 1960, 1962, 1964, 1966, 1968, 1970, 1972, 1974, 1976, 1978, 1980
Devine, Thomas C. (OH) - 1912, 1916
DeVisscher, Thomas D. (MA) - 1986
Devito, Anthony J. (NY) - 1968, 1970
Devitt, Edward J. (MN) - 1946, 1948
Devlin (IN) - 1858
Devlin, James (PA) - 1916
Devlin, William E. (NY) - 1924, 1930
DeVoe, Fred W. (NJ) - 1926
Devol (MO) - 1910
Dewalt, Arthur G. (PA) - 1914, 1916, 1918, 1926
Dewan, James T. (OH) - 1956
Dewar (GA) - 1914
Dewart (PA) - 1854, 1858
Dewart, Lewis (PA) - 1830
D'Ewart, Wesley A. (MT) - 1945, 1946, 1948, 1950, 1952
Dewart, William L. (PA) - 1856
Deweese, John T. (NC) - 1868
Dewey, Charles (IN) - 1835
Dewey, Charles S. (IL) - 1938, 1940, 1942, 1944
Dewey, Henry B. (WA) - 1912
DeWine, Michael (OH) - 1982, 1984, 1986, 1988
DeWitt, Bill (CA) - 1990
DeWitt, William C. (NY) - 1924
Dexter, Simon (NY) - 1830
Deyendorf, John F. (VA) - 1892
DeYoung, James E. (NY) - 1976
Dezendorf, John F. (VA) - 1878, 1880, 1882
Dial (OH) - 1854
Dial, A. Clayton (KS) - 1964
Dial, Joe (TX) - 1990
Diamond, Robert (NY) - 1950
Diamondstone, Peter (VT) - 1978, 1980
Diaz, Angel (NY) - 1992
Dibble, A. B. (CA) - 1856
Dibble, Henry C. (LA) - 1876
Dibble, Samuel (SC) - 1882, 1884, 1886, 1888
DiBiase, Carmine (PA) - 1984
Dible, Samuel (PA) - 1914

Dibrell, Anthony (TN) - 1839
Dibrell, George G. (TN) - 1874, 1876, 1878, 1880, 1882
DiCarlo, David C. (PA) - 1980
Dichter, David (NJ) - 1968
Dick, Archibald T. (PA) - 1834
Dick, Charles (OH) - 1898, 1900, 1902, 1918
Dick, Chuck (IA) - 1974
Dick, David (PA) - 1838
Dick, Frederick E. (RI) - 1992
Dick, John (PA) - 1852, 1854, 1856
Dick, Samuel B. (PA) - 1878
Dickens, E. Dana (NC) - 1930
Dickenson, A. C. (WA) - 1898
Dickenson, Edward (MA) - 1855
Dickenson, S. N. (WI) - 1886
Dicker, Herbert (NY) - 1970
Dickerman, Charles H. (PA) - 1902
Dickersin, E. J. (SC) - 1884
Dickerson (NJ) - 1918
Dickerson, David W. (TN) - 1843
Dickerson, J. G. (ME) - 1854
Dickerson, Philemon (NJ) - 1832, 1834, 1838, 1840
Dickerson, William W. (KY) - 1890
Dickes, Louis (IL) - 1902
Dickey (VT) - 1876, 1878
Dickey, F. B. (TN) - 1894
Dickey, F. Lyle (IL) - 1862
Dickey, Frank P. (TN) - 1892
Dickey, H. G. (OK) - 1952
Dickey, Henry L. (OH) - 1876, 1878
Dickey, Howard A. Jr. (KY) - 1960
Dickey, J. T. (GA) - 1900
Dickey, Jay (AR) - 1992
Dickey, Jesse C. (PA) - 1848, 1850
Dickey, John (PA) - 1843, 1846
Dickey, Oliver J. (PA) - 1868, 1870
Dickey, T. Lyle (IL) - 1866
Dickey, W. C. (KS) - 1928
Dickheiser, Saul J. (NY) - 1928
Dickie, Samuel (MI) - 1890
Dickinson (NJ) - 1864
Dickinson (PA) - 1886
Dickinson, A. C. (WA) - 1892
Dickinson, Bob (NV) - 1990
Dickinson, Clement C. (MO) - 1910, 1912, 1914, 1916, 1918, 1920, 1922, 1924, 1926, 1928, 1930, 1932
Dickinson, David W. (TN) - 1833
Dickinson, Edward (MA) - 1852, 1854
Dickinson, Edward F. (OH) - 1868, 1870
Dickinson, John (NY) - 1826, 1828, 1830, 1832
Dickinson, John Jr. (MA) - 1846
Dickinson, Lester J. (IA) - 1918, 1920, 1922, 1924, 1926, 1928
Dickinson, Rodolphus (MA) - 1839
Dickinson, Rodolphus (OH) - 1846, 1848
Dickinson, Samuel F. (MA) - 1828
Dickinson, William A. (VA) - 1936
Dickinson, William L. (AL) - 1964, 1966, 1968, 1970, 1972, 1974, 1976, 1978, 1980, 1982, 1984, 1986, 1988, 1990, 1992
Dickison, Richard (SC) - 1986
Dickman, Charles C. (IL) - 1936
Dicks, Norman D. (WA) - 1976, 1978, 1980, 1982, 1984, 1986, 1988, 1990, 1992
Dickson, Charles A. (IA) - 1906
Dickson, David (MS) - 1829, 1831, 1835
Dickson, E. E. (SC) - 1868
Dickson, Frank L. (IL) - 1904
Dickson, Frank S. (IL) - 1906, 1908
Dickson, Hugh L. (CA) - 1920
Dickson, J. L. (IL) - 1920
Dickson, John (NY) - 1830, 1832
Dickson, Samuel (NY) - 1854
Dickson, William A. (MS) - 1908, 1910
Dickstein, Samuel (NY) - 1922, 1924, 1926, 1928, 1930, 1932, 1934, 1936, 1938, 1940, 1942, 1944
Diefenderfer, Flora J. (PA) - 1920
Diehl, Harry E. (PA) - 1942
Diehl, Julius F. (MD) - 1926
Diehl, W. D. (Bill) (MT) - 1976
Diekema, Gerrit J. (MI) - 1907, 1908, 1910
Dielman, Fred (TX) - 1964
Dielmann, Harold L. (MO) - 1982
Dielmann, Henry B. (TX) - 1930
Dierkes, Edward (IL) - 1904
Dies, Martin (TX) - 1908, 1910, 1912, 1914, 1916

Dies, Martin Jr. (TX) - 1930, 1932, 1934, 1936, 1938, 1940, 1942, 1952, 1954, 1956
Dieterich, William H. (IL) - 1930
Dieterly, Duggan (CA) - 1992
Dietl, Richard (NY) - 1986
Dietrich, C. Elmer (PA) - 1934, 1936
Dietrich, John (TX) - 1992
Diette, Ernest J. Jr. (CT) - 1986
DiFazio, Lucien P. Jr. (CT) - 1976
Difenderfer, Robert E. (PA) - 1910, 1912
Diffenderffer (MO) - 1914
Digennaro, Vincent (NY) - 1956
Diggs, Charles C. Jr. (MI) - 1954, 1956, 1958, 1960, 1962, 1964, 1966, 1968, 1970, 1972, 1974, 1976, 1978
Diggs, E. E. (TX) - 1906, 1914
DiGiovanni, John (NY) - 1974
Dignan, Thomas S. (NJ) - 1940
Diiorio, Ralph (NY) - 1956
Dike, George W. (MA) - 1846
Dikeman, John (NY) - 1836
Dilbeck, William H. (CA) - 1990
Dill, Clarence C. (WA) - 1914, 1916, 1918, 1942
Dill, Charles C. (NY) - 1904
Dill, Harry V. (KY) - 1920
Dillard, Ann W. (OK) - 1930
Dillard, Barney E. Jr. (FL) - 1980
Dillemuth, Charles H. (LA) - 1960
Dillingham, Paul Jr. (VT) - 1843, 1844
Dillner, Arthur E. (IL) - 1952
Dillon (TN) - 1882
Dillon, Charles H. (SD) - 1912, 1914, 1916
Dillon, James C. (IL) - 1938
Dillon, Jim (Matt) (TX) - 1978
Dillon, John E. (IN) - 1904
Dillon, John J. (IL) - 1956
Dillon, M. J. (MN) - 1936
Dillon, Martin F. (NY) - 1902
Dillon, Walter K. (MO) - 1946, 1948
Dills, John (KY) - 1878
Dillw (DE) - 1846
Dilweg, LaVern R. (WI) - 1942, 1944
Dimarco, Antony (MD) — 1922
Di Micelli, Leonard (CA) - 1958
Dimitri, William A. Jr. (RI) - 1970
Dimk, E. S. (PA) - 1856
Dimmick, Milo M. (PA) - 1848, 1850
Dimmick, William H. (PA) - 1856, 1858, 1878
Dimmitt, James P. (IL) - 1878
Dimock, Davis Jr. (PA) - 1840
Dingell, John D. (MI) - 1932, 1934, 1936, 1938, 1940, 1942, 1944, 1946, 1948, 1950, 1952, 1954
Dingell, John D. Jr. (MI) - 1955, 1956, 1958, 1960, 1962, 1964, 1966, 1968, 1970, 1972, 1974, 1976, 1978, 1980, 1982, 1984, 1986, 1988, 1990, 1992
Dingeman, A. J. (CA) - 1942
Dingeman, Jim (MI) - 1990
Dingley, Edward N. (MI) - 1912, 1914
Dingley, Nelson Jr. (ME) - 1881, 1882, 1884, 1886, 1888, 1890, 1892, 1894, 1896, 1898
Dininny (NY) - 1888
Dinis, Edmund (MA) - 1968
Diniz, Jacinto F. (MA) - 1948
d'Innocenzo, Michael (NY) - 1984
Dinsmoor, James (IL) - 1872
Dinsmore, Hugh A. (AR) - 1892, 1894, 1896, 1898, 1900, 1902
Dinsmore, J. W. (KY) - 1912
Dinsmore, Robert S. (CA) - 1992
DioGuardi, Joseph J. (NY) - 1984, 1986, 1988, 1990
DiPerna, Paula (NY) - 1992
Director, Bruce (TX) - 1990
Director, Susan (TX) - 1986
Dirks, A. Stephen (UT) - 1982
Dirksen, Everett M. (IL) - 1932, 1934, 1936, 1938, 1940, 1942, 1944, 1946
DiSalle, Michael V. (OH) - 1946
Dishman (KY) - 1916
Dishongh, Lewis (NC) - 1833, 1835
Disney, David T. (OH) - 1848, 1850, 1852
Disney, Loren G. (OK) - 1907
Disney, Wesley E. (OK) - 1930, 1932, 1934, 1936, 1938, 1940, 1942
Disosway (NY) - 1854

Ditchen, John F. (OH) - 1904
Ditchey, Charles F. (PA) - 1922
Ditter, J. William (PA) - 1932, 1934, 1936, 1938, 1940, 1942
Ditucci, Cosmo J. (NY) - 1970
Ditus, Stan (NE) - 1980
Divelbiss, Carl W. (AZ) - 1950
Diven, Alexander S. (NY) - 1860
Dix, David (WV) - 1972
Dix, John W. (PA) - 1918
Dixon (CT) - 1869
Dixon (MD) - 1833
Dixon (RI) - 1833
Dixon (RI) - 1916
Dixon, Charles G. (IL) - 1894
Dixon, Emerald B. (MI) - 1930
Dixon, Henry Aldous (UT) - 1954, 1956, 1958
Dixon, J. N. (TX) - 1882
Dixon, James (CT) - 1845, 1847
Dixon, Joseph (NC) - 1870
Dixon, Joseph A. (OH) - 1936, 1938, 1940
Dixon, Joseph M. (MT) - 1902, 1904
Dixon, Julian C. (CA) - 1978, 1980, 1982, 1984, 1986, 1988, 1990, 1992
Dixon, Kelly (NC) - 1960
Dixon, L. P. (NC) - 1932
Dixon, Lincoln (IN) - 1904, 1906, 1908, 1910, 1912, 1914, 1916, 1918
Dixon, Mary C. (NY) - 1988
Dixon, Moses (NY) - 1828
Dixon, Mott C. (NY) - 1890
Dixon, Nathan F. (RI) - 1849, 1863, 1865, 1867, 1868, 1885, 1886
Dixon, Oliver O. (IN) - 1946
Dixon, Robert H. (NC) - 1918
Dixon, Sherwood (IL) - 1886
Dixon, T. B. (KY) - 1912
Dixon, Thurman B. (KY) - 1926
Dixon, W. O. (NC) - 1914, 1916, 1920
Dixon, W. R. (NC) - 1906
Dixon, William C. (OH) - 1934
Dixon, William W. (MT) - 1890, 1892
Dizotell, Forest (IL) - 1940
Doah, W. M. (VA) - 1920
Doan, Robert E. (OH) - 1890
Doan, William (OH) - 1838, 1840
Doan, William H. (OH) - 1878, 1882
Doane, George W. (NE) - 1892
Doane, Josial (IA) - 1882
Doane, Paul V. (MA) - 1980
Dobbin, James C. (NC) - 1845
Dobbins, Donald C. (IL) - 1932, 1934
Dobbins, James (NJ) - 1960
Dobbins, Samuel A. (NJ) - 1872, 1874
Dobbs, Jim (TX) - 1962
Dobler, Henry G. (IL) - 1922
Dobosh, Jack N. (NY) - 1974, 1976
Dobsevage, George (NY) - 1926
Dobson, David M. (IN) - 1847
Dock (PA) - 1848
Dockery, Alexander M. (MO) - 1882, 1884, 1886, 1888, 1890, 1892, 1894, 1896
Dockery, Alfred (NC) - 1845, 1851
Dockery, Oliver H. (NC) - 1868, 1870, 1872, 1882, 1884, 1898, 1900
Dockweiler, John F. (CA) - 1930, 1932, 1934, 1936, 1938
Dodd (NJ) - 1856
Dodd (NY) - 1862
Dodd, Christopher J. (CT) - 1974, 1976, 1978
Dodd, Craig (OK) - 1984
Dodd, Edward (NY) - 1854, 1856
Dodd, Hiram (AL) - 1948
Dodd, J. W. (AL) - 1934
Dodd, Thomas J. (CT) - 1952, 1954
Doddridge (VA) - 1825
Doddridge, Philip (VA) - 1829, 1831
Dodds, Francis H. (MI) - 1908, 1910
Dodge (NY) - 1848, 1856, 1888
Dodge, Clarence P. (CO) - 1912
Dodge, Frank L. (MI) - 1908, 1914, 1920, 1926
Dodge, Grenville M. (IA) - 1866
Dodge, James S. (IN) - 1892
Dodge, N. A. (TX) - 1900
Dodge, Rufus B. (MA) - 1902
Dodge, W. A. (TX) - 1908
Dodge, William (NY) - 1824, 1828
Dodge, William E. (NY) - 1864
Dodson (PA) - 1886
Dodson, George H. (OK) - 1916
Doe, Joseph B. Jr. (WI) - 1888

Doerfler, Ernest (NY) - 1950, 1954
Doherty (NJ) - 1892
Doherty, A. B. C. (MN) - 1936, 1938
Doherty, George T. (WI) - 1940
Doherty, James L. (IL) - 1954
Doherty, John (MN) - 1980
Doherty, John F. (WI) - 1898
Doherty, Philip J. (MA) - 1896
Doherty, Thomas A. (PA) - 1920
Dohr, William F. (CA) - 1982
Doig, Andrew (NY) - 1838, 1840
Dolan, John P. J. (MN) - 1928
Dolan, Joseph C. (PA) - 1956
Dolan, Thomas F. (IL) - 1950
Dolan, Thomas P. (PA) - 1906
Dole, Robert (KS) - 1960, 1962, 1964, 1966
Dolezal, Gerald (IL) - 1968
Dolgaard, Keith (AZ) - 1974
Doll, Ken (WV) - 1970
Dollinger, Isidore (NY) - 1948, 1950, 1952, 1954, 1956, 1958
Dolliver, James I. (IA) - 1944, 1946, 1948, 1950, 1952, 1954, 1956
Dolliver, Jonathan P. (IA) - 1888, 1890, 1892, 1894, 1896, 1898
Dombrowski, Leon A. (NY) - 1944
Domengeaux, James (LA) - 1940, 1942, 1944, 1946
Dominick, Fred H. (SC) - 1916, 1918, 1920, 1922, 1924, 1926, 1928, 1930
Dominick, Peter H. (CO) - 1960
Domme, Robert W. (KS) - 1958
Donahoe, John T. (IL) - 1908
Donahue (CT) - 1906
Donahue, Edward M. (CT) - 1980
Donahue, Louis A. (ME) - 1922
Donald, Clark M. (KY) - 1928
Donaldson, C. M. (OR) - 1898
Donaldson, Curt (NE) - 1982
Donaldson, Frank (AL) - 1968
Donaldson, Lisa A. (MI) - 1992
Donaldson, Michael C. (CA) - 1970
Donaldson, Presley G. (IL) - 1892
Donaugh, Carl C. (OR) - 1950
Donchess, James W. (NH) - 1988
Dondero, George A. (MI) - 1932, 1934, 1936, 1938, 1940, 1942, 1944, 1946, 1948, 1950, 1952, 1954
Donelon, James (LA) - 1980
Donges, John W. (NJ) - 1948
Dongvillo, Henry J. (MI) - 1966
Donihi, Robert M. (TN) - 1954
Donlan, Fraser P. (PA) - 1950
Donley, Charles C. (OH) - 1892
Donley, Joseph B. (PA) - 1868, 1870
Donley, Willis E. (WI) - 1934
Donlin, Patrick J. (OH) - 1978, 1980
Donlon, Mary (NY) - 1940
Donnally, Andrew (VA) - 1837
Donnan, William G. (IA) - 1870, 1872
Donnell, John A. (IA) - 1886
Donnell, Louis A. (KS) - 1950
Donnell, Richard S. (NC) - 1845, 1847
Donnelly (MN) - 1870, 1876, 1878
Donnelly (PA) - 1886, 1888
Donnelly, Brian J. (MA) - 1978, 1980, 1982, 1984, 1986, 1988, 1990
Donnelly, Edward L. (MA) - 1928, 1930
Donnelly, I. (MN) - 1884
Donnelly, Ignatius (MN) - 1862, 1864, 1866, 1868
Donnelly, Joseph G. (WI) - 1898, 1906
Donnelly, Neil (IL) - 1862
Donnelly, Tom (WA) - 1992
Donnelly, Thomas John (OH) - 1894, 1896
Donnelly, William M. (MI) - 1926, 1928, 1930
Donnelson (TN) - 1843
Donnohue (MO) - 1892
Donoghue, Arthur J. (IL) - 1906
Donoghue, Roger P. (MA) - 1897
Donohoe, Eugene D. (MI) - 1950
Donohoe, Michael (PA) - 1910, 1912, 1914, 1916
Donohue (MN) - 1916
Donohue, Charles (WI) - 1912
Donohue, Harold D. (MA) - 1946, 1948, 1950, 1952, 1954, 1956, 1958, 1960, 1962, 1964, 1966, 1968, 1970, 1972
Donohue, Michael (PA) - 1908
Donohue, Michael J. (IL) - 1984
Donovan (CT) - 1916
Donovan (MA) - 1886, 1888

Donovan (MO) - 1890
Donovan (NY) - 1886
Donovan, Andrew (IL) - 1912
Donovan, Cornelius (NY) - 1890
Donovan, Dennis D. (OH) - 1890, 1892
Donovan, James G. (NY) - 1950, 1952, 1954, 1956
Donovan, Jeremiah (CT) - 1912, 1914
Donovan, Jerome F. (NY) - 1918, 1920
Donovan, John C. (ME) - 1960
Donovan, John F. (WI) - 1902
Donovan, Joseph Francis (CA) - 1962
Donovan, Joseph O. (IL) - 1942
Donovan, Thomas F. (IL) - 1894
Donson, W. M. (KY) - 1898
Donworth, John P. (ME) - 1876
Doodridge (VA) - 1825
Doolan, Edward F. (MA) - 1952, 1954, 1956, 1958, 1960, 1962, 1964
Doole, D. (TX) - 1906
Dooley, Calvin (CA) - 1990, 1992
Dooley, Edwin B. (NY) - 1956, 1958, 1960
Dooley, Michael (IL) - 1990
Dooling, Peter J. (NY) - 1912, 1914, 1916, 1918, 1920
Doolittle, Dudley (KS) - 1912, 1914, 1916, 1918, 1940
Doolittle, Harvey (NY) - 1840
Doolittle, James R. (IL) - 1878
Doolittle, James R. (WI) - 1886
Doolittle, John T. (CA) - 1990, 1992
Doolittle, M. B. (IA) - 1880
Doolittle, Richard L. (PA) - 1968
Doolittle, William H. (WA) - 1892, 1894, 1896
Doon, Aloysius J. (MA) - 1918
Dopp, Arthur (WI) - 1904
Doran, James P. (MA) - 1922
Dore, C. F. (IL) - 1972
Doremus, Frank E. (MI) - 1910, 1912, 1914, 1916, 1918
Dorfman, Henry D. (NY) - 1948, 1952, 1954, 1956
Dorgan, Byron L. (ND) - 1974, 1980, 1982, 1984, 1986, 1988, 1990
Dorland (NY) - 1882
Dorlon, Robert (NY) - 1838
Dorn, D. A. (PA) - 1926, 1932
Dorn, Francis E. (NY) - 1948, 1949, 1950, 1952, 1954, 1956, 1958, 1960, 1962
Dorn, Frank A. (NY) - 1930
Dorn, W. J. Bryan (SC) - 1946, 1950, 1952, 1954, 1956, 1958, 1960, 1962, 1964, 1966, 1968, 1970, 1972
Dornan, Robert K. (CA) - 1976, 1978, 1980, 1984, 1986, 1988, 1990, 1992
Dornbach, George W. (PA) - 1912
Dornon, R. A. (PA) - 1908
Dorr (RI) - 1837
Dorr, Charles P. (WV) - 1896
Dorr, L. Bradley (NY) - 1908, 1912
Dorr, Thomas H. (WI) - 1924
Dorr, Thomas W. (RI) - 1839
Dorriblum, Jennie (PA) - 1924
Dorrier, Lindsay G. Jr. (VA) - 1982
Dorrity, Dan (MI) - 1980
Dorse, Bob (WA) - 1982
Dorse, Robert L. (WA) - 1984
Dorsett, James D. (NC) - 1924
Dorsey (MO) - 1882
Dorsey (OH) - 1854, 1856
Dorsey, Clement (MD) - 1824, 1826, 1829, 1833
Dorsey, Clinton G. (OH) - 1976
Dorsey, Frank J. G. (PA) - 1934, 1936, 1938
Dorsey, George W. E. (NE) - 1884, 1886, 1888, 1890
Dorsey, John L. Jr. (KY) - 1930
Dorsey, William (OH) - 1886
Dorsheimer, William (NY) - 1882
Dorwin (NY) - 1856
Dosland, Goodwin L. (IL) - 1938
Doss, Evan (MS) - 1978
Doss, W. G. (TN) - 1970
Dostal, Frank (NY) - 1916
Doster, F. (KS) - 1878
Doster, Robert M. (SC) - 1962, 1964
Doten, David C. (KS) - 1954
Dotson, Dalton (AR) - 1948
Dotts (PA) - 1884
Doty, Bessie (NJ) - 1976
Doty, Elizabeth G. (IL) - 1928
Doty, Ethan Allen (PA) - 1950

Fox, E. Frank (IA) - 1940, 1942
Fox, F. T. (KY) - 1855
Fox, George W. (PA) - 1910, 1912, 1916
Fox, Hamilton P. (MD) - 1956
Fox, Harry M. (PA) - 1974
Fox, Henry I. (KY) - 1912
Fox, J. Frank (MD) - 1916
Fox, James A. (MA) - 1890
Fox, John (NY) - 1866, 1868
Fox, John D. (MO) - 1962
Fox, John H. (NY) - 1978, 1984
Fox, Jon D. (PA) - 1992
Fox, L. R. (KY) - 1912
Fox, Leo P. (WI) - 1920
Fox, Martin S. (NJ) - 1952, 1954
Fox, Noel P. (MI) - 1938, 1940, 1950
Fox, Rosa Lee (IL) - 1970
Fox, William C. (CT) - 1930, 1932
Fox, William R. (OH) - 1894, 1902
Foxhall (NJ) - 1908
Foy, Francis H. (MA) - 1934, 1942
Frahn, Harry J. (AL) - 1948
Fraley, Elmer E. (WI) - 1946
Frambach, H. A. (WI) - 1892
France, James D. (IA) - 1948, 1950
Franchot, Peter (MD) - 1988
Franchot, Richard (NY) - 1860
Francis, Clarence (NY) - 1952
Francis, Frank (UT) - 1924
Francis, George B. (NY) - 1914, 1916
Francis, James A. (NY) - 1916
Francis, John J. (NJ) - 1944
Francis, John T. (OH) - 1984
Francis, Margaret (TN) - 1978
Francis, William B. (OH) - 1910, 1912, 1914, 1916, 1918
Francisco (MO) - 1894
Francisco, Michael A. (IL) - 1946
Francke, Carrie (MO) - 1984
Franco, Reuben D. (CA) - 1988, 1990, 1992
Frank, Augustus (NY) - 1858, 1860, 1862
Frank, Barney (MA) - 1980, 1982, 1984, 1986, 1988, 1990, 1992
Frank, David L. (NY) - 1926
Frank, E. L. (IL) - 1972, 1976
Frank, Gerry (CO) - 1978
Frank, Henry J. (NY) - 1922, 1924
Frank, M. P. (ME) - 1890
Frank, Nathan (MO) - 1886, 1888
Franke, Dorothy (OH) - 1972, 1974, 1976
Frankenfield, Don (SD) - 1990
Frankenfield, Robert F. (PA) - 1956
Frankhauser, William H. (MI) - 1920
Franklin (GA) - 1855
Franklin, Benjamin J. (MO) - 1874, 1876
Franklin, Brenda Lee (MA) - 1978
Franklin, Charles A. (CA) - 1956
Franklin, George T. (NY) - 1946
Franklin, J. H. (OK) - 1910
Franklin, John R. (MD) - 1853
Franklin, S. J. (NE) - 1922
Franklin, W. C. (VA) - 1908
Franklin, Webb (MS) - 1982, 1984, 1986
Franks, Bob (NJ) - 1992
Franks, E. F. (KY) - 1890
Franks, E. T. (KY) - 1896
Franks, Gary (CT) - 1990, 1992
Franks, Richard L. (MO) - 1974
Frantz, Frank (OK) - 1932
Frantz, Robert A. (OH) - 1974
Franz, Ed. (TX) - 1924
Franz, William J. (OH) - 1974
Frappier, J. H. (MO) - 1976
Fraser, Archie C. (MI) - 1938, 1940
Fraser, Donald M. (MN) - 1962, 1964, 1966, 1968, 1970, 1972, 1974, 1976
Fraser, Robert (MI) - 1890
Fraser, Willard E. (MT) - 1948, 1952
Fratt (WI) - 1874
Frawley (WI) - 1918
Frazce, John (NY) - 1830
Frazee (MS) - 1884
Frazee, W. D. (MS) - 1900
Frazer, R. (PA) - 1838
Frazer, W. D. (MS) - 1890
Frazier, A. Bradley (TN) - 1944
Frazier, Alvaader (NY) - 1990
Frazier, James A. (VA) - 1880
Frazier, James B. (TN) - 1954
Frazier, James B. Jr. (TN) - 1948, 1950, 1952, 1956, 1958, 1960
Frazier, William G. (IN) - 1976, 1978, 1980, 1992
Fream (NY) - 1856

Frear, James A. (WI) - 1912, 1914, 1916, 1918, 1920, 1922, 1924, 1926, 1928, 1930, 1932
Frederick, Benjamin Todd (IA) - 1882, 1884, 1886
Frederick, Theodore C. Jr. (PA) - 1948
Frederick, Walter E. (IN) - 1946
Fredericks, John D. (CA) - 1924
Fredericks, Thomas Jackson (PA) - 1912
Fredriksen, Arnold L. (MN) - 1956
Free, Arthur Monroe (CA) - 1920, 1922, 1924, 1926, 1928, 1930, 1932
Freed, C. William (PA) - 1922, 1924
Freedley, John (PA) - 1846, 1848, 1850
Freedman, Elliot Roy (CA) - 1992
Freedom, John G. (OH) - 1958, 1960, 1974, 1976
Freehill, Joseph H. (VA) - 1958
Freeland, J. A. (TX) - 1912
Freeland, William B. (PA) - 1946
Freeman (TN) - 1855
Freeman, A. H. (GA) - 1896, 1900
Freeman, Alexander H. (NJ) - 1840
Freeman, Allan C. (MA) - 1968
Freeman, Allen A. (IL) - 1958
Freeman, Andrew Yates (NY) - 1894
Freeman, Chapman (PA) - 1874, 1876
Freeman, Debra Hanania (MD) - 1978
Freeman, Frank (CA) - 1900
Freeman, George (AL) - 1865
Freeman, Howard F. (NC) - 1894
Freeman, J. J. (Tiny) (WA) - 1972
Freeman, J. Y. (TN) - 1932
Freeman, James C. (GA) - 1872
Freeman, John D. (MS) - 1851
Freeman, Michael O. (MN) - 1978
Freeman, N. H. (AL) - 1908
Freeman, Newman H. (AL) - 1916
Freeman, Porter (TN) - 1958
Freeman, Richard C. (OK) - 1980, 1982
Freeman, Richard P. (CT) - 1914, 1916, 1918, 1920, 1922, 1924, 1926, 1928, 1930
Freeman, Robert D. (OH) - 1964, 1966
Freeman, Ross R. (KS) - 1976
Freeman, Samuel (NE) - 1952, 1956
Freeman, Terry (OH) - 1980
Freeman, William G. (NJ) - 1954
Freer, Romeo H. (WV) - 1898
Freese, Arnold E. (CT) - 1932, 1934
Freiday, William (NJ) - 1942
Freidheim, J. B. (AR) - 1896
Freiman, Richard D. (CA) - 1990
Frelinghuysen, Peter H. B. Jr. (NJ) - 1952, 1954, 1956, 1958, 1960, 1962, 1964, 1966, 1968, 1970, 1972
French (KY) - 1837
French (MA) - 1886
French (MN) - 1906, 1908
French (NJ) - 1918
French (NY) - 1842, 1874, 1886
French, A. F. (NY) - 1916
French, Burton L. (ID) - 1902, 1904, 1906, 1910, 1912, 1916, 1918, 1920, 1922, 1924, 1926, 1928, 1930, 1932, 1934
French, Carlos (CT) - 1886
French, Charles J. (NH) - 1914, 1920
French, Eleanor C. (NY) - 1964
French, Ezra (ME) - 1858
French, James (NY) - 1840
French, John R. (NC) - 1868
French, Jonas H. (MA) - 1890
French, Richard (KY) - 1835, 1843, 1845, 1847
French, Robert (AL) - 1964
French, Samuel T. (NJ) - 1932
French, William H. (VT) - 1843, 1844
Frensdorf, Edward (MI) - 1912, 1930
Frenzel, Bill (MN) - 1970, 1972, 1974, 1976, 1978, 1980, 1982, 1984, 1986, 1988
Freschi, Raymond (CA) - 1966
Freshwater, Milton R. (IL) - 1888
Frethy, George C. (PA) - 1912
Freund, Gene (IA) - 1988
Frew (PA) - 1870
Frey (NY) - 1842
Frey, Louis Jr. (FL) - 1968, 1970, 1972, 1974, 1976
Frey, Louis G. (OH) - 1964
Frey, Oliver W. (PA) - 1934, 1936, 1938
Frey, William C. (AZ) - 1952
Frey, William J. (OH) - 1900
Frick, Henry (PA) - 1843
Fried, Eric (CA) - 1988

Friedel, Samuel N. (MD) - 1952, 1954, 1956, 1958, 1960, 1962, 1964, 1966, 1968
Friedman, Charles (FL) - 1974, 1976
Friedman, Don (CO) - 1976
Friedman, Esther (NY) - 1920, 1932
Friedman, Eugene F. (IL) - 1988
Friedman, Eugene M. (NJ) - 1962, 1964
Friedman, Herbert J. (IL) - 1906
Friedman, Nathaniel Jay (CA) - 1970
Friedman, Richard E. (IL) - 1962
Friedman, Samuel H. (NY) - 1934
Friend (FL) - 1868
Friend (NY) - 1858
Frierson, J. N. (SC) - 1868
Fries, Frank W. (IL) - 1936, 1938, 1940
Fries, George (OH) - 1844, 1846
Friloux, C. A. Jr. (TX) - 1956
Frink, Garry F. (MI) - 1968
Frisby (WI) - 1868, 1878
Frischer, Gerald G. (MO) - 1970
Fritsch, Joseph Jr. (NY) - 1936
Fritsche, Felix (NY) - 1912
Fritsche, L. A. (MN) - 1930
Frizell, William G. (OH) - 1908
Froehlich, Harold V. (WI) - 1972, 1974, 1976
Froehlich, Mark S. (OH) - 1988
Froehlich, William H. (WI) - 1902, 1910
Froehlicher, Hans Jr. (NJ) - 1930
Froeman (WI) - 1880
Fromowitz, Hyman (NY) - 1956
Frooks, Dorothy (NY) - 1934
Frost (MO) - 1918
Frost (WV) - 1863
Frost, Frank (CA) - 1982
Frost, Frank P. (NY) - 1902, 1904, 1906
Frost, Gene (MO) - 1936
Frost, J. E. (PA) - 1900
Frost, J. E. (WA) - 1912
Frost, Martin (TX) - 1978, 1980, 1982, 1984, 1986, 1988, 1990, 1992
Frost, Richard G. (MO) - 1876, 1878, 1880
Frost, Rufus S. (MA) - 1874, 1876
Frothingham (MA) - 1876
Frothingham, Louis A. (MA) - 1920, 1922, 1924, 1926
Frothingham, Richard Jr. (MA) - 1848, 1850
Fruchter, Henry (NY) - 1922
Frugone, Frank L. (NY) - 1904, 1906
Fry, Jacob Jr. (PA) - 1834, 1836
Fry, Joseph Jr. (PA) - 1826, 1828
Fry, Speed S. (KY) - 1865, 1880
Frye, Pliney S. (OK) - 1946
Frye, William P. (ME) - 1870, 1872, 1874, 1876, 1878, 1880
Fuchs, Joanne S. (NY) - 1976
Fugate, J. B. (KS) - 1878
Fugate, J. T. (TN) - 1908, 1922
Fugate, Thomas B. (VA) - 1948, 1950
Fuhrig, Joseph (CA) - 1980
Fulbright, J. William (AR) - 1942
Fulbright, James F. (MO) - 1922, 1924, 1926, 1928, 1930
Fulcrut, Vernon D. (MO) - 1946, 1950
Fulk, Kenneth R. (IA) - 1976
Fulkerson, Abram (VA) - 1880, 1882
Fulkerson, Frank B. (MO) - 1904, 1906
Fulkerson, George J. (MO) - 1962
Fulks, James H. (OH) - 1986
Fullam, John P. (PA) - 1954, 1956
Fullard, Thomas J. III (PA) - 1984
Fullenweider, Robert (AL) - 1914
Fuller (CT) - 1896
Fuller (ME) - 1860
Fuller (PA) - 1852, 1860
Fuller, Alvan T. (MA) - 1916, 1918
Fuller, Benoni S. (IN) - 1874, 1876
Fuller, Cecil R. (WA) - 1934
Fuller, Charles E. (IL) - 1902, 1904, 1906, 1908, 1910, 1912, 1914, 1916, 1918, 1920, 1922, 1924
Fuller, Claude A. (AR) - 1928, 1930, 1932, 1934, 1936
Fuller, E. S. (GA) - 1920
Fuller, George (PA) - 1844
Fuller, H. A. (NY) - 1920
Fuller, Hadwen C. (NY) - 1944, 1946, 1948
Fuller, Henry M. (PA) - 1850, 1854
Fuller, Jesse Jr. (NY) - 1912
Fuller, John F. (MA) - 1950
Fuller, L. F. (KS) - 1914
Fuller, Luther E. (VA) - 1936

Fuller, Nelson M. (NY) - 1942
Fuller, Philo C. (NY) - 1832, 1834
Fuller, Smith (PA) - 1864
Fuller, Thomas C. (NC) - 1865, 1868
Fuller, Thomas J. D. (ME) - 1848, 1850, 1852, 1854
Fuller, William (NY) - 1846
Fuller, William Elijah (IA) - 1884, 1886
Fuller, William K. (NY) - 1832, 1834
Fullerton (NY) - 1862
Fullerton, Dick (GA) - 1970
Fullerton, Hugh (IL) - 1864
Fullerton, Reese P. (NM) - 1942
Fullinwider, Patricia (AZ) - 1974, 1976
Fulmer, Hampton P. (SC) - 1920, 1922, 1924, 1926, 1928, 1930, 1932, 1934, 1936, 1938, 1940, 1942
Fulton (VA) - 1843
Fulton (WI) - 1874
Fulton, Andrew S. (VA) - 1847
Fulton, Arthur W. (IL) - 1912, 1916
Fulton, Elmer L. (OK) - 1907, 1908, 1910
Fulton, Frank M. (IL) - 1934, 1936
Fulton, James G. (PA) - 1942, 1944, 1946, 1948, 1950, 1952, 1954, 1956, 1958, 1960, 1962, 1964, 1966, 1968, 1970
Fulton, John H. (VA) - 1833, 1835
Fulton, Richard (TN) - 1962, 1964, 1966, 1968, 1970, 1972, 1974
Funk, Benjamin F. (IL) - 1892
Funk, Frank H. (IL) - 1920, 1922, 1924
Funk, James W. (UT) - 1920
Funk, Robert S. (CA) - 1936
Funkhouser, Alexander M. (IL) - 1900
Funsch, Richard O. (MO) - 1972
Funston, Edward H. (KS) - 1883, 1884, 1886, 1888, 1890, 1892
Fuqua, Don (FL) - 1962, 1964, 1966, 1968, 1970, 1972, 1974, 1976, 1978, 1980, 1982, 1984
Fuqua, W. M. (KY) - 1882
Furber (NJ) - 1918
Furchess, David M. (NC) - 1872, 1880
Furcolo, Foster (MA) - 1946, 1948, 1950
Furgeson, Charles (KY) - 1912
Furlong, Grant (PA) - 1924, 1942
Furlow, Allen J. (MN) - 1924, 1926
Furlow, W. A. S. (TN) - 1934
Furman, Robert (NY) - 1840
Furman, Willis B. (NE) - 1944
Furse, Elizabeth (OR) - 1992
Furst, Lyndon G. (MI) - 1980
Fusco, Dominick A. (NY) - 1960
Fussell, Sam (TX) - 1985
Fuzzell (TN) - 1900
Fyan, Robert W. (MO) - 1882, 1890, 1892

## G

Gaarenstroom, C. F. (MN) - 1932, 1938
Gabbard, Elmer E. (KY) - 1942, 1944
Gabbert, L. C. (MO) - 1922
Gableman, William N. (OH) - 1922
Gabler, Ray (TX) - 1968
Gabriel, Charles J. (MA) - 1960
Gabriel, G. W. (KS) - 1884
Gadd, Cyrus H. (WV) - 1952
Gaddle, D. W. (KY) - 1910
Gaddis, Albert (PA) - 1918
Gaddie (KY) - 1908
Gaddy, James M. (TX) - 1992
Gadrix, Ed (GA) - 1976
Gadsden, James (SC) - 1856
Gaffner, Robert H. (IL) - 1982, 1984, 1986, 1988, 1990
Gaffney, Alice E. (NY) - 1986, 1992
Gaffney, Edward (ID) - 1940
Gaffney, Hubert J. (MN) - 1934
Gaffney, James I. III (MA) - 1978
Gaffney, James P. (IA) - 1938
Gaffney, Michael (NY) - 1992
Gaffney, Warren N. (NJ) - 1930
Gage (WI) - 1876
Gage, A. W. (FL) - 1924
Gage, Gary G. (WA) - 1974
Gagen, August M. (MN) - 1926
Gagne, W. E. (Ted) (CA) - 1980
Gahn, Harry C. (OH) - 1920, 1922, 1924, 1926, 1936, 1944
Gain, Charles E. (OH) - 1894
Gaines, Franklin D. (KS) - 1974

Hartnett, Thomas F. (SC) - 1980, 1982, 1984
Hartnett, William E. (IL) - 1952
Hartranft, A. S. (PA) - 1880
Hartranft, Marshall V. (CA) - 1932
Hartridge, Julian (GA) - 1874, 1876
Hartsell, Charles (CO) - 1898
Hartstone, Roger (AZ) - 1990, 1992
Hartson, C. (CA) - 1867, 1868
Hartsuff, William (MI) - 1888
Hartwell, J. W. (VA) - 1884
Hartwig (MO) - 1888
Hartzell, Richard F. (PA) - 1944, 1946
Hartzell, William (IL) - 1870, 1874, 1876, 1880, 1886
Hartzell, William H. (IL) - 1928, 1930
Harvey (AL) - 1888
Harvey (NJ) - 1906
Harvey, A. M. (KS) - 1904
Harvey, J. Mark (MI) - 1914
Harvey, Jack (WI) - 1948, 1950
Harvey, James (MI) - 1960, 1962, 1964, 1966, 1968, 1970, 1972
Harvey, John (NH) - 1833
Harvey, Jonathan (NH) - 1824, 1827, 1829
Harvey, Paul (MS) - 1992
Harvey, Peter (MA) - 1868
Harvey, Ralph (IN) - 1948, 1950, 1952, 1954, 1956, 1958, 1960, 1962, 1964
Harvey, Ruth L. (VA) - 1968
Harvey, Samuel (PA) - 1828
Harvey, Thomas H. (WV) - 1894
Harvey, W. H. (TX) - 1910
Harvey, W. Scott (NC) - 1966, 1968
Harwell, W. D. (AL) - 1916
Harwood (MO) - 1884, 1886
Harwood (VA) - 1837
Harwood, H. L. (KY) - 1932
Hasbrook, Stephen (NY) - 1836
Hasbrouck (NY) - 1844, 1848, 1878
Hasbrouck, Abraham (NY) - 1824
Hasbrouck, Anthony (NY) - 1838
Hascall, Asa (NY) - 1826, 1836
Hascall, Augustus P. (NY) - 1850
Hascall, Charles C. (MI) - 1850
Hascall, M. S. (IN) - 1870
Haseltine (MO) - 1882
Haseman, Paul (CA) - 1982
Haskell, Dudley C. (KS) - 1876, 1878, 1880, 1882
Haskell, F. H. (ME) - 1920
Haskell, Harry G. Jr. (DE) - 1956, 1958
Haskell, Reuben L. (NY) - 1912, 1914, 1916, 1918
Haskell, Robert H. (NY) - 1904
Haskell, William Henry (MA) - 1940
Haskell, William T. (TN) - 1847
Haskett, Ray (SC) - 1990
Haskin, John B. (NY) - 1856, 1858
Haskins, Brad (MI) - 1990
Haskins, Dave (Buster) (TX) - 1980
Haskins, David K. (MI) - 1982
Haskins, Kittredge (VT) - 1900, 1902, 1904, 1906
Haskins, Terry E. (SC) - 1990
Haslett, Charles W. (OH) - 1916
Haslinger, Werner S. (OH) - 1940
Hass, Norman (CA) - 1960
Hassinger, John H. (VA) - 1922
Hastain (MO) - 1892
Hastert, Dennis (IL) - 1986, 1988, 1990, 1992
Hastie, Andrew (IA) - 1876
Hastings (ME) - 1858
Hastings (NY) - 1854
Hastings, Alcee L. (FL) - 1992
Hastings, D. R. (ME) - 1884
Hastings, George (NY) - 1852
Hastings, George A. (NY) - 1941
Hastings, James F. (NY) - 1968, 1970, 1972, 1974
Hastings, John (OH) - 1838, 1840
Hastings, L. W. (CA) - 1849
Hastings, R. P. (CA) - 1884
Hastings, Richard "Doc" (WA) - 1992
Hastings, S. Clinton (IA) - 1846
Hastings, S. D. (WI) - 1882
Hastings, W. G. (NE) - 1888
Hastings, Washington (DE) - 1882
Hastings, William S. (MA) - 1836, 1838, 1840
Hastings, William W. (OK) - 1914, 1916, 1918, 1920, 1922, 1924, 1926, 1928, 1930, 1932

Hasvold, G. L. (SD) - 1922
Haswell (KY) - 1916
Haswell, John P. Jr. (KY) - 1918, 1920
Haswell, Tyler (TX) - 1924
Hatch (NY) - 1854
Hatch (WI) - 1866
Hatch, Azel (NH) - 1833
Hatch, Bill (NH) - 1992
Hatch, Herschel H. (MI) - 1882
Hatch, Israel T. (NY) - 1856, 1858
Hatch, Jethro A. (IN) - 1894
Hatch, William H. (MO) - 1878, 1880, 1882, 1884, 1886, 1888, 1890, 1892, 1894
Hatchadorian, Matthew J. (OH) - 1984
Hatcher, Charles C. (IL) - 1924
Hatcher, Charles (GA) - 1980, 1982, 1984, 1986, 1988, 1990
Hatcher, F. T. (KY) - 1922
Hatcher, F. Tom (KY) - 1914
Hatcher, Harold C. (IL) - 1934
Hatcher, James G. (IL) - 1968
Hatcher, Robert A. (MO) - 1872, 1874, 1876
Hatem, Thomas J. (MD) - 1974
Hatfield (MA) - 1886
Hatfield, Charles S. (OH) - 1914
Hatfield, Clarence E. (KS) - 1922, 1924
Hatfield, Floyd (WA) - 1932
Hatfield, Guy W. (AR) - 1972
Hathaway (ME) - 1828
Hathaway (NY) - 1848, 1856, 1862
Hathaway, Howard (WA) - 1904
Hathaway, Medary M. (IN) - 1898
Hathaway, Mortimer D. (IL) - 1878
Hathaway, Nicholas (MA) - 1882
Hathaway, Samuel G. (NY) - 1832
Hathaway, William (MN) - 1966
Hathaway, William D. (ME) - 1962, 1964, 1966, 1968, 1970
Hathorn, A. C. (MS) - 1894
Hathorn, Henry H. (NY) - 1872, 1874
Hathorn, N. C. (MS) - 1896, 1898
Hathorn, Samuel M. (IN) - 1894
Hattabaugh, Murray R. (ID) - 1906
Hattery, Hiram D. (IN) - 1886
Hattery, Thomas H. (MD) - 1992
Hatton, Augustus R. (OH) - 1912
Hatton, J. B. (IA) - 1882
Hatton, Robert H. (TN) - 1859
Haugen, Elmer A. (MN) - 1936
Haugen, Gilbert N. (IA) - 1898, 1900, 1902, 1904, 1906, 1908, 1910, 1912, 1914, 1916, 1918, 1920, 1922, 1924, 1926, 1928, 1930, 1932
Haugen, Nils P. (WI) - 1887, 1888, 1890, 1892
Haughey, Thomas (AL) - 1868, 1869
Haughey, Tom (TX) - 1992
Haughton, John H. (NC) - 1845
Hauk, John C. (TN) - 1894
Hauser, Otto (WI) - 1934
Hauser, Warren A. (FL) - 1974
Havekost, John (NE) - 1922, 1936
Haven (NJ) - 1890
Haven (RI) - 1914
Haven, Solomon G. (NY) - 1850, 1852, 1854, 1856, 1860
Havenner, Franck R. (CA) - 1936, 1938, 1940, 1944, 1946, 1948, 1950, 1952
Havens (NJ) - 1914
Havens, H. E. (MO) - 1876
Havens, Harrison E. (MO) - 1870, 1872, 1874
Havice, Blaine L. Jr. (PA) - 1978
Havill, Ed (FL) - 1982
Hawes (NY) - 1852, 1854
Hawes, A. E. (KS) - 1944
Hawes, Albert G. (KY) - 1831, 1833, 1835
Hawes, Ferdinand B. (WA) - 1904
Hawes, Harry B. (MO) - 1920, 1922, 1924
Hawes, Richard (KY) - 1837, 1839
Hawk, Robert (NM) - 1978
Hawk, Robert M. A. (IL) - 1878, 1880
Hawke, Jack (NC) - 1970, 1972
Hawkes, Elizabeth (WI) - 1944
Hawkins (GA) - 1855
Hawkins (MO) - 1860
Hawkins (SC) - 1920
Hawkins (TN) - 1876, 1880, 1882, 1900
Hawkins, Al (OH) - 1988
Hawkins, Augustus F. (CA) - 1962, 1964, 1966, 1968, 1970, 1972, 1974, 1976, 1978, 1980, 1982, 1984, 1986, 1988
Hawkins, Carr (KY) - 1912

Hawkins, Charles (VA) - 1988
Hawkins, Charles A. (PA) - 1912, 1920
Hawkins, Dolan G. (MO) - 1976
Hawkins, Don (AL) - 1978
Hawkins, Frank H. (PA) - 1910
Hawkins, George C. (AL) - 1964
Hawkins, George S. (FL) - 1856, 1858
Hawkins, I. A. (IL) - 1886
Hawkins, Isaac R. (TN) - 1865, 1867, 1868
Hawkins, Joseph (NY) - 1828
Hawkins, Madison (NC) - 1870
Hawkins, Micajah T. (NC) - 1831, 1833, 1835, 1837, 1839, 1841
Hawkins, Nathan B. (IN) - 1908
Hawkins, P. B. (KY) - 1866
Hawkins, Philip W. (RI) - 1885
Hawkins, Ronald C. (IL) - 1992
Hawkins, Rush C. (NY) - 1864
Hawkins, S. W. (TN) - 1886
Hawks, Charles Jr. (WI) - 1938, 1940, 1942
Hawks, Rick (IN) - 1990
Hawley (CT) - 1876
Hawley, Cyrus (NY) - 1846
Hawley, Frank O. (IL) - 1910
Hawley, George A. (MO) - 1866
Hawley, Guy D. (OH) - 1934
Hawley, James H. Jr. (ID) - 1950
Hawley, John B. (IL) - 1868, 1870, 1872
Hawley, Joseph R. (CT) - 1872, 1873, 1875, 1878
Hawley, Robert B. (TX) - 1896, 1898
Hawley, Willis C. (OR) - 1906, 1908, 1910, 1912, 1914, 1916, 1918, 1920, 1922, 1924, 1926, 1928, 1930
Haworth, Rufus K. Jr. (NC) - 1954
Haws, J. H. Hobart (NY) - 1850
Hawson, Henry (CA) - 1918
Hawthorne, J. M. (WA) - 1918
Hawthorne, Lester A. (IL) - 1968, 1970
Hay (NY) - 1860
Hay, Andrew K. (NJ) - 1848
Hay, Frederick L. (MN) - 1900
Hay, James (VA) - 1896, 1898, 1900, 1902, 1904, 1906, 1908, 1910, 1912, 1914
Hay, John B. (IL) - 1872, 1880
Hay, William B. (OH) - 1912
Hayden, Carl (AZ) - 1911, 1912, 1914, 1916, 1918, 1920, 1922, 1924
Hayden, Edward D. (MA) - 1884, 1886
Hayden, Edward W. (PA) - 1914, 1920
Hayden, Frank E. (OH) - 1914
Hayden, Joel (MA) - 1842, 1844
Hayden, Moses (NY) - 1824
Hayden, Suzanne (PA) - 1990
Hayden, Thomas E. (CA) - 1910
Hayden, Tom (CA) - 1970
Hayes (ME) - 1860
Hayes (MA) - 1880
Hayes, A. Reed (PA) - 1962
Hayes, Bill (TX) - 1964
Hayes, Charles A. (IL) - 1983, 1984, 1986, 1988, 1990
Hayes, Cornelius J. (IL) - 1920
Hayes, Edward D. (MO) - 1918
Hayes, Edward R. (IA) - 1890
Hayes, Everis A. (CA) - 1904, 1906, 1908, 1910, 1912, 1914, 1916, 1918
Hayes, Gerald P. (WI) - 1920
Hayes, H. Clell (KY) - 1938, 1940
Hayes, Henry E. (IL) - 1950
Hayes, J. Byron (IN) - 1966
Hayes, James J. (PA) - 1928
Hayes, Jimmy (LA) - 1986, 1988, 1990, 1992
Hayes, John B. (IL) - 1940
Hayes, Kenneth P. (ME) - 1988
Hayes, Kyle (NC) - 1936
Hayes, L. L. (IL) - 1871
Hayes, Lawrence J. (IL) - 1952
Hayes, Max S. (OH) - 1904
Hayes, Philip C. (IL) - 1876, 1878
Hayes, Philip H. (IN) - 1974
Hayes, Rutherford B. (OH) - 1864, 1866, 1872
Hayes, Samuel L. (VA) - 1841
Hayes, Terry (AR) - 1990, 1992
Hayes, W. A. (ME) - 1834
Hayes, W. F. (IA) - 1938
Hayes, Walter I. (IA) - 1886, 1888, 1890, 1892, 1894
Hayes, Will (CA) - 1952
Hayes, William A. (ME) - 1844
Hayes, William A. (PA) - 1910, 1918
Haymond (VA) - 1827, 1851

Haymond, Thomas S. (VA) - 1849
Haymond, Wililam E. (WV) - 1900
Haymond, William Summerville (IN) - 1874, 1876
Haynes (NJ) - 1886, 1888
Haynes (OH) - 1856
Haynes (TN) - 1859, 1872
Haynes, Charles E. (GA) - 1824, 1826, 1828, 1830, 1832, 1834, 1836
Haynes, F. F. (MT) - 1942, 1944
Haynes, Gene A. (WV) - 1978
Haynes, Glenn (MS) - 1950
Haynes, J. L. (TX) - 1869, 1886
Haynes, Martin A. (NH) - 1882, 1884, 1886
Haynes, Oscar H. (IL) - 1974
Haynes, William E. (OH) - 1888, 1890
Haynie, C. M. (MS) - 1898
Hayns (TN) - 1851
Hayrin, Irham W. (IL) - 1862
Hays (PA) - 1826
Hays (VA) - 1843
Hays, Brooks (AR) - 1942, 1944, 1946, 1948, 1950, 1952, 1954, 1956, 1958
Hays, Brooks (NC) - 1972
Hays, Charles (AL) - 1869, 1870, 1872, 1874
Hays, David (KY) - 1918
Hays, Doug (KY) - 1926
Hays, Edward C. (IN) - 1942
Hays, Edward D. (MO) - 1920, 1922
Hays, Ellsworth O. (IA) - 1958
Hays, Frank J. (IN) - 1912
Hays, John B. (IL) - 1868, 1870
Hays, John Doug (KY) - 1992
Hays, John R. (NE) - 1900
Hays, Samuel (PA) - 1843
Hays, Thomas (KY) - 1880
Hays, W. K. (CA) - 1908
Hays, Wayne L. (OH) - 1948, 1950, 1952, 1954, 1956, 1958, 1960, 1962, 1964, 1966, 1968, 1970, 1972, 1974
Hays, William H. (KY) - 1868
Hayse, Sharon (AZ) - 1980
Hayt (NY) - 1872
Hayward (MO) - 1876
Hayward, J. Frank (MA) - 1902
Hayward, J. T. K. (MO) - 1870
Hayward, William (NE) - 1910
Haywood, G. W. (NC) - 1839
Haywood, Levi (MA) - 1866
Hayworth, Don (MI) - 1952, 1954, 1956, 1958, 1962
Hazard, Thomas P. (RI) - 1932
Hazel, Ignatius (MO) - 1868
Hazelbaker, H. K. (MT) - 1942
Hazeltine, Abner (NY) - 1832, 1834
Hazeltine, Ira S. (MO) - 1880
Hazelton, George C. (WI) - 1876, 1878, 1880, 1882
Hazelton, George H. (MI) - 1848
Hazelton, Gerry W. (WI) - 1870, 1872
Hazelwood, Edgar H. (NY) - 1932
Hazen, W. Dexter (OH) - 1950
Hazleton, John W. (NJ) - 1870, 1872
Hazlett, James M. (PA) - 1926
Hazltn (NJ) - 1854
Hazzard, John C. (DE) - 1934
Heacock, Joseph (PA) - 1916
Head, Frederick C. (PA) - 1914, 1916
Head, Hubbard (MI) - 1910
Head, John W. (TN) - 1874
Head, William F. (OK) - 1932
Headen, James H. (NC) - 1874
Heading, James G. (PA) - 1900
Headly, John F. (PA) - 1930
Headrick, William D. (IN) - 1926
Heady, William J. (KY) - 1863, 1876
Heald, Howard F. (OH) - 1934
Heald, Joshua T. (DE) - 1870
Heald, William H. (DE) - 1908, 1910
Healey, Arthur D. (MA) - 1922, 1924, 1928, 1932, 1934, 1936, 1938, 1940
Healey, Francis G. (NY) - 1962
Healey, James C. (NY) - 1955, 1956, 1958, 1960, 1962
Healey, John A. (NJ) - 1960
Healy, Gail (MS) - 1986
Healy, John E. (CA) - 1970
Healy, Joseph (NH) - 1824, 1825, 1827
Healy, Ned R. (CA) - 1944, 1946, 1948
Healy, Timothy (NY) - 1906, 1912
Heaps, William J. (MD) - 1914
Heard, John F. (MA) - 1858
Heard, John T. (MA) - 1850

Lloyd, Robin (VT) - 1980
Lloyd, Sherman P. (UT) - 1960, 1962, 1966, 1968, 1970, 1972
Lloyd, Wesley (WA) - 1932, 1934
Lloyd, William H. (MD) - 1942
Loan, Benjamin F. (MO) - 1862, 1864, 1866, 1876
Lobb, Mary Ellen (MO) - 1988
Lobeck (MN) - 1916, 1918
Lobeck, Charles O. (NE) - 1910, 1912, 1914, 1916, 1918
LoBiondo, Frank A. (NJ) - 1992
Lochrane (GA) - 1868
Lockard, Robert R. (IA) - 1984, 1986
Locke (FL) - 1884
Locke, Bobby (TX) - 1980
Locke, Bobby A. (TX) - 1976
Locke, Daniel W. (OH) - 1900
Locke, John (MA) - 1824, 1826
Locke, Thomas F. (ME) - 1930
Locker, Dale (OH) - 1981
Locket, H. E. (GA) - 1920
Lockey, Caleb P. (NC) - 1888
Lockhart, Andrew Francis (SD) - 1922
Lockhart, James (IN) - 1841, 1851, 1856
Lockhart, James A. (NC) - 1894, 1896
Lockley, Sidney L. (PA) - 1956
Lockwood (NY) - 1878, 1884
Lockwood (OH) - 1852
Lockwood, Daniel N. (NY) - 1876, 1890, 1892
Lockwood, E. (AL) - 1853
Lockwood, Frank C. (PA) - 1914
Lockwood, Leroy E. (MI) - 1892
Lockwood, M. L. (PA) - 1898, 1900
Lockwood, Stephen R. (NY) - 1918
Lockwood, Thomas (NY) - 1830, 1832
Lockwood, Walter A. (NY) - 1942
Lockwood, William F. (OH) - 1870
Lodge, Henry Cabot (MA) - 1884, 1886, 1888, 1890, 1892
Lodge, John Davis (CT) - 1946, 1948
LoDico, Carl C. (IL) - 1978
Lodise, Carmen (CA) - 1980
Loeb, Charles H. (OH) - 1956
Loebl, James D. (CA) - 1974
Loeffler, Tom (TX) - 1978, 1980, 1982, 1984
Loefflor, George H. Jr. (TX) - 1988
Loehr, Gordon E. (WI) - 1982
Loennecker, Martin G. (MI) - 1900
Loewenthal, Edward (IL) - 1904
Lofland, James R. (DE) - 1872, 1874
Loft, George W. (NY) - 1912, 1914
Loftin, W. C. (NC) - 1853
Loftis, James J. (NY) - 1930
Loftus, John J. (PA) - 1914
Logan (AL) - 1890
Logan (CO) - 1918
Logan, D. (OR) - 1860
Logan, David (OR) - 1859, 1868
Logan, Henry (PA) - 1834, 1836
Logan, John A. (IL) - 1858, 1860, 1866, 1868, 1870, 1914
Logan, R. G. (IL) - 1970
Logan, R. P. (ID) - 1914
Logan, Ralph H. (KY) - 1948
Logan, Stephen V. (IL) - 1848
Logan, W. Turner (SC) - 1920, 1922
Logue, J. Washington (PA) - 1912, 1914, 1916
Logue, John J. (PA) - 1966
Logue, Thomas A. (PA) - 1926
Lohr, H. J. (PA) - 1918
Lohr, Walter J. (NY) - 1934
Loisel, Victor (LA) - 1910
Lomax, Terrance J. Jr. (MA) - 1942
Lombardi, Peter O. (HI) - 1968
Lommen, Edwin E. (MN) - 1896
London (MO) - 1880, 1894
London, John M. (MO) - 1878
London, Meyer (NY) - 1910, 1912, 1914, 1916, 1918, 1920, 1922
Lonergan, Augustine (CT) - 1910, 1912, 1914, 1916, 1918, 1930
Lonergan, Mike (WA) - 1984
Long (AL) - 1886, 1894
Long (IN) - 1872
Long (MN) - 1914
Long (NY) - 1882
Long (OH) - 1860
Long (TN) - 1843
Long, A. J. (TX) - 1928
Long, Albert (WI) - 1912

Long, Alexander (OH) - 1862
Long, Ara E. S. (IN) - 1876, 1878
Long, Benjamin F. (OH) - 1904
Long, Brian (WA) - 1982
Long, Bruce (OR) - 1984, 1986
Long, Cathy (Mrs. Gillis) (LA) - 1985
Long, Charles W. (IN) - 1950
Long, Chester I. (KS) - 1892, 1894, 1896, 1898, 1900, 1902, 1924
Long, Clarence D. (MD) - 1962, 1964, 1966, 1968, 1970, 1972, 1974, 1976, 1978, 1980, 1982, 1984
Long, Clifford H. (IN) - 1938
Long, Edward H. C. (MD) - 1845
Long, Fred W. (PA) - 1896
Long, G. W. (KY) - 1890
Long, George S. (LA) - 1952, 1954, 1956
Long, Gillis W. (LA) - 1962, 1972, 1974, 1976, 1978, 1980, 1982, 1984
Long, Henry C. (MA) - 1912
Long, J. L. H. (OH) - 1876
Long, Jill (IN) - 1988, 1989, 1990, 1992
Long, John B. (TX) - 1890
Long, John D. (MA) - 1882, 1884, 1886
Long, John Jr. (NC) - 1825, 1827, 1829
Long, L. C. (MN) - 1894
Long, Lewis M. (IL) - 1936
Long, M. M. (VA) - 1952
Long, S. C. (MN) - 1892
Long, Speedy O. (LA) - 1964, 1966, 1968, 1970
Long, Stanley D. (NE) - 1946
Long, Thomas D. (MT) - 1908
Long, W. E. (TX) - 1932
Long, William L. (NC) - 1835, 1837, 1839
Long, Zadoc (ME) - 1838, 1840
Longaker, A. Brower (PA) - 1878
Longe, William T. (PA) - 1954
Longhi, Vincent J. (NY) - 1946, 1948, 1950
Longley (VA) - 1865
Longnecker, Henry C. (PA) - 1858, 1860
Longshore, Adolphus P. (AL) - 1892, 1912, 1920
Longshore, W. L. Jr. (AL) - 1956
Longstreet (GA) - 1826
Longworth, Nicholas (OH) - 1902, 1904, 1906, 1908, 1910, 1912, 1914, 1916, 1918, 1920, 1922, 1924, 1926, 1928, 1930
Longyear, John W. (MI) - 1862, 1864
Loofbourow, Frederick C. (UT) - 1930, 1932, 1934
Loomis (MO) - 1894, 1896
Loomis, Andrew W. (OH) - 1836
Loomis, Arphaxed (NY) - 1836
Loomis, Dwight (CT) - 1859, 1861
Loomis, George (WV) - 1882
Loomis, Luther (CT) - 1833, 1834
Loomis, S. B. (WI) - 1886
Loorem, Thomas F. (MA) - 1906
Lopez, Junio (NM) - 1962
Lorain (PA) - 1843
Lorenz, Mindy (CA) - 1992
Lord (IN) - 1866
Lord (NH) - 1829
Lord (NY) - 1828, 1854, 1856, 1862, 1876
Lord, Bert (NY) - 1934, 1936, 1938
Lord, C. A. (TX) - 1922
Lord, Frederick (NY) - 1846
Lord, Henry W. (MI) - 1880, 1882
Lord, Nathaniel J. (MA) - 1852, 1854
Lord, Otis P. (MA) - 1858, 1860, 1868
Lord, Ruth J. (MA) - 1856
Lord, Scott (NY) - 1874
Lord, William K. (PA) - 1902
Lore, Charles B. (DE) - 1882, 1884
Lore, Ludwig (NY) - 1916
Lore, Marvin E. (IL) - 1956
Loriks, Emil (SD) - 1938
Lorimer, William (IL) - 1894, 1896, 1898, 1900, 1902, 1904, 1906, 1908
Loring, Eleazer B. (MA) - 1884
Loring, George B. (MA) - 1858, 1876, 1878
Lorusso, Anthony P. (NY) - 1972
Losee, Frank E. (NY) - 1906
Loser, J. Carlton (TN) - 1956, 1958, 1960, 1962
Loss, Frank L. (MN) - 1970
Loth, John (PA) - 1964, 1970
Lothrop, Grover (SD) - 1944
Lotier, Victor A. (PA) - 1894
Lotsch, John L. (NY) - 1928
Lott, Charles (PA) - 1892
Lott, Edwin F. (PA) - 1890

Lott, Harry (LA) - 1872
Lott, Trent (MS) - 1972, 1974, 1976, 1978, 1980, 1982, 1984, 1986
Lotz, Charles E. (PA) - 1954, 1958
Lotz, Orlando J. (IN) - 1898
Louchery, Daniel L. (WV) - 1956
Loud, Eugene F. (CA) - 1890, 1892, 1894, 1896, 1898, 1900, 1902
Loud, George A. (MI) - 1902, 1904, 1906, 1908, 1910, 1912, 1914
Loud, Henry M. (MI) - 1886
Loud, Jacob H. (MA) - 1852
Loudenslager, Henry C. (NJ) - 1892, 1894, 1896, 1898, 1900, 1902, 1904, 1906, 1908, 1910
Loudon, D. W. C. (OH) - 1890
Loudon, Lotus H. (CA) - 1940
Loughman, M. Francis (NY) - 1904
Loughridge, William (IA) - 1866, 1868, 1872
Lounsberry, John (NY) - 1824
Lounsbery (NY) - 1886
Lounsbery, William (NY) - 1878
Loupe, R. C. (PA) - 1904
Louttit, James A. (CA) - 1884
Lovan (MO) - 1914
Love (MO) - 1888
Love, A. Kingsley (MD) - 1930, 1932, 1938
Love, Francis J. (WV) - 1946, 1948, 1950, 1952
Love, Frank (WV) - 1952
Love, J. R. (NC) - 1865
Love, James (KY) - 1833
Love, John (IN) - 1864
Love, Peter E. (GA) - 1859
Love, Richard (PA) - 1916
Love, Rodney M. (OH) - 1964, 1966
Love, Samuel L. (NC) - 1880
Love, Stephen H. (UT) - 1912
Love, Thomas C. (NY) - 1834
Love, Tom (KS) - 1992
Love, W. B. (NC) - 1922
Love, W. T. (NC) - 1954
Love, Walter B. (NC) - 1952
Love, William F. (MS) - 1896
Love, William I. (TN) - 1938
Lovejoy, Esther (OR) - 1920
Lovejoy, Owen (IL) - 1846, 1848, 1856, 1858, 1860, 1862
Lovejoy, Owen G. (IL) - 1888
Loveland, Sam C. (VT) - 1834
Loveless (IN) - 1876
Loveless, Herschel C. (IA) - 1954
Lovell (ND) - 1902
Lovell, Christopher (NY) - 1980
Lovell, Edward F. (NC) - 1898
Lovell, V. R. (NC) - 1912
Lovely, John A. (MN) - 1886
Loveridge (NY) - 1876
Lovering, Henry B. (MA) - 1882, 1884, 1886
Lovering, William C. (MA) - 1896, 1898, 1900, 1902, 1904, 1906, 1908
Lovett, Charles W. (MA) - 1930, 1932
Lovett, Woodrow (GA) - 1992
Lovette, Oscar B. (TN) - 1930, 1932
Lovingood, Joe Z. (FL) - 1966, 1968, 1970, 1974
Lovitt, Craig (IL) - 1968
Lovitt, R. A. (KS) - 1908
Lovre, Harold O. (SD) - 1948, 1950, 1952, 1954, 1956
Low (NY) - 1882
Low, Frederick F. (CA) - 1861
Low, Philip B. (NY) - 1894, 1896, 1898
Lowden, Frank O. (IL) - 1906, 1908
Lowe (MO) - 1854
Lowe (OH) - 1843
Lowe, Bob (CA) - 1972
Lowe, David P. (KS) - 1870, 1872
Lowe, J. G. (KS) - 1886
Lowe, Jacob B. (IN) - 1835
Lowe, Joseph G. (KS) - 1894
Lowe, Kenneth K. (MO) - 1960
Lowe, Lynn (AR) - 1966
Lowe, William M. (AL) - 1878, 1880
Lowe, Wyman C. (GA) - 1974
Lowell, Charles E. (MA) - 1900
Lowell, Joshua A. (ME) - 1838, 1840
Lowell, Sherman J. (NY) - 1932
Lowenberg, Henry A. (NY) - 1932
Lowenstein, Allard K. (NY) - 1968, 1970, 1972, 1974, 1976
Lowenthal, Margaret (LA) - 1986

Lowers, John F. (PA) - 1944
Lowery, Bill (CA) - 1980, 1982, 1984, 1986, 1988, 1990
Lowery, Bill G. (MS) - 1924
Lowery, Thomas J. (NY) - 1956
Lowey, Nita M. (NY) - 1988, 1990, 1992
Lowndes, Lloyd Jr. (MD) - 1872, 1874
Lowrance, Frank B. (KS) - 1904
Lowrey, Bill G. (MS) - 1920, 1922, 1926
Lowry (IN) - 1856, 1866, 1868
Lowry (NY) - 1882
Lowry, H. Graham (MA) - 1978
Lowry, J. H. (KY) - 1865, 1870
Lowry, J. M. (MO) - 1954
Lowry, James W. (KS) - 1946
Lowry, John (TN) - 1829
Lowry, Mike (WA) - 1978, 1980, 1982, 1984, 1986
Lowry, Robert (IN) - 1882, 1884, 1886
Lowry, Thomas C. (WA) - 1972
Loy, J. H. (IL) - 1910
Loy, William H. (WV) - 1974
Loyall, George (VA) - 1827, 1829, 1831, 1833, 1835
Loyd, M. B. (IL) - 1882
Loyd, William F. (OH) - 1894
Lozier, Lue C. (MO) - 1944
Lozier, Ralph F. (MO) - 1922, 1924, 1926, 1928, 1930, 1932
Luby, Jason (TX) - 1982
Lucas (OH) - 1843
Lucas (VA) - 1831, 1845, 1857
Lucas, Charles P. (OH) - 1968
Lucas, Edward A. (OH) - 1833, 1835
Lucas, Frank R. (NJ) - 1992
Lucas, Scott W. (IL) - 1934, 1936
Lucas, Thomas H. (MN) - 1892
Lucas, Thomas J. (IN) - 1886
Lucas, William (VA) - 1839, 1841, 1843
Lucas, William T. (CA) - 1904
Lucas, William V. (SD) - 1892
Lucas, Wilson H. (NC) - 1896
Lucas, Wingate H. (TX) - 1946, 1948, 1950, 1952
Lucca, Mariano A. (NY) - 1954, 1958, 1960
Luce, Charles T. (MA) - 1898, 1900, 1902
Luce, Clare Boothe (CT) - 1942, 1944
Luce, J. G. (VA) - 1908
Luce, John C. (OR) - 1892
Luce, Marjory L. (MN) - 1982
Luce, Robert (MA) - 1918, 1920, 1922, 1924, 1926, 1928, 1930, 1932, 1934, 1936, 1938, 1940
Lucero, Antonio (NM) - 1920
Lucey, Dennis B. (NY) - 1912
Lucey, Patrick J. (WI) - 1950
Lucier, Alvin A. (NH) - 1938
Luck, Charles W. (ID) - 1914
Luck, Oliver (WV) - 1990
Luckey, Henry C. (NE) - 1934, 1936, 1938, 1940
Luckey, Hugh M. (IL) - 1936
Luckey, James B. (OH) - 1878
Lucking, Alfred (MI) - 1902, 1904
Luckow, Edward L. (WI) - 1900
Lucy, Dennis B. (NY) - 1898
Ludeman, Cal R. (MN) - 1992
Ludington (WI) - 1874
Ludling, J. T. (LA) - 1878
Ludlow, C. O. (IL) - 1912
Ludlow, Louis (IN) - 1928, 1930, 1932, 1934, 1936, 1938, 1940, 1942, 1944, 1946
Ludlow, Willis H. (ID) - 1972
Ludwig, Carl J. (WI) - 1934
Ludwig, Earl (OH) - 1944, 1948
Ludwig, William H. (WI) - 1944
Luecke, John (MI) - 1936, 1938
Lufkin, Willfred W. (MA) - 1918, 1920
Luhring, Oscar R. (IN) - 1918, 1920, 1922
Lujan, Manuel (NM) - 1944
Lujan, Manuel Jr. (NM) - 1968, 1970, 1972, 1974, 1976, 1978, 1980, 1982, 1984, 1986
Luke, George W. (NJ) - 1968
Luken, Charles (OH) - 1990
Luken, Thomas A. (OH) - 1974, 1976, 1978, 1980, 1982, 1984, 1986, 1988
Lukens, Donald E. (OH) - 1966, 1968, 1986, 1988
Lukson, Lee (WA) - 1968
Luling, Charles (WI) - 1884, 1886
Luman (OH) - 1843
Lumina, Luke (MA) - 1992

## O

O'Day, Caroline (NY) - 1934, 1936, 1938, 1940
Oddo, Salvatore E. (IL) - 1974
Oddstad, Elma D. (CA) - 1958
Odegard, Robert J. (MN) - 1962, 1964
O'Dell (NY) - 1858
O'Dell, Benjamin B. Jr. (NY) - 1894, 1896
O'Dell, Moses F. (NY) - 1860, 1862
O'Dell, N. Holmes (NY) - 1874
O'Dell, Tracy (CA) - 1966
Oder, Henry A. Jr. (VA) - 1958
Odlum, Jacqueline Cochran (CA) - 1956
Odman, Robert (WA) - 1958
O'Doherty, Kieran (NY) - 1964
Odom, Archie C. (SC) - 1966
Odom, Christine P. (NC) - 1954
O'Donnall, Fred (IA) - 1878
O'Donnell, Daniel J. C. (PA) - 1924, 1926, 1942
O'Donnell, James (MI) - 1884, 1886, 1888, 1890, 1892
O'Donnell, P. M. (PA) - 1922, 1924
O'Donnell, Pierce (CA) - 1980
O'Donnell, Robert J. (OH) - 1924, 1926
O'Donnell, T. J. (CO) - 1890
O'Donovan, Jerome X. (NY) - 1988
O'Donovan, M. C. (PA) - 1906
Odum, Harry C. (IL) - 1942
Odum, J. T. (TN) - 1910
O'Dwyer, Paul (NY) - 1948
Oehmen, John S. (IL) - 1904
Oertling, Gus (LA) - 1926
O'Ferrall, Charles T. (VA) - 1882, 1884, 1886, 1888, 1890, 1892
Offenhender, Jacob M. (NY) - 1940
Officer, Charles B. (NH) - 1964, 1972
Offner, Paul (WI) - 1982
O'Flaherty, D. C. (VA) - 1898
O'Flanagan (KS) - 1882
Ogara, John (MA) - 1896
Ogdahl, Harmon T. (MN) - 1968
Ogden (LA) - 1849
Ogden (NJ) - 1834
Ogden (NY) - 1828, 1856, 1858
Ogden, A. R. (VA) - 1974, 1976
Ogden, Alan R. (VA) - 1978
Ogden, Charles F. (KY) - 1918, 1920
Ogden, Dan (CO) - 1976
Ogden, David (NY) - 1832
Ogden, Henry W. (LA) - 1894, 1896
Ogden, Isaac (NY) - 1830
Ogden, Michael S. (PA) - 1986
Ogden, William (MD) - 1896
Ogg, James B. (CA) - 1928
Ogier, Benson (OH) - 1936
Ogilivie, Thomas J. (TN) - 1892
Ogle (PA) - 1834
Ogle, Andrew Jackson (PA) - 1848, 1850
Ogle, Charles (PA) - 1836, 1838, 1840
Oglesby, Richard J. (IL) - 1858
Oglesby, Woodson R. (NY) - 1912, 1914, 1916
Ognibene, Thomas V. (NY) - 1986, 1990
O'Grady, Jack J. (IN) - 1948
O'Grady, James M. E. (NY) - 1898
O'Grady, Martin J. (NY) - 1988
Ogren, Oscar (IL) - 1918
O'Hagan, C. J. (NC) - 1870
O'Hair, Frank T. (IL) - 1912, 1914
O'Halloran, Edward J. (PA) - 1968
O'Halloran, Richard J. (IL) - 1930
O'Hanlon, J. (SC) - 1848
O'Hara, Barnatt (IL) - 1923
O'Hara, Barratt (IL) - 1948, 1950, 1952, 1954, 1956, 1958, 1960, 1962, 1964, 1966
O'Hara, Frederic S. (IL) - 1956
O'Hara, James (MI) - 1918
O'Hara, James (NE) - 1920
O'Hara, James E. (NC) - 1878, 1882, 1884, 1886
O'Hara, James F. (NY) - 1950
O'Hara, James G. (MI) - 1958, 1960, 1962, 1964, 1966, 1968, 1970, 1972, 1974
O'Hara, John Grady (TN) - 1958
O'Hara, John J. (MI) - 1934
O'Hara, Joseph P. (MN) - 1938, 1940, 1942, 1944, 1946, 1948, 1950, 1952, 1954, 1956
O'Hara, Thomas (MI) - 1902
O'Hara, Thomas A. (PA) - 1924, 1928
O'Hare, Bernard V. (PA) - 1928
Ohlendorf, Howard C. (MO) - 1964, 1974
Ohliger, Lewis P. (OH) - 1892

Ohlis, G. W. (PA) - 1916
Ojala, William R. (MN) - 1975
Ojeda, Miriam (CA) - 1984
O'Keefe (CT) - 1918
O'Keefe, Dan (CA) - 1978
O'Keefe, Esther Kathleen (IN) - 1922
O'Keefe, John A. (MA) - 1906
O'Keefe, Maurice P. (KS) - 1928
O'Keefe, Richard B. (MA) - 1946
O'Keefe, William W. (WI) - 1896
Okicki, Joseph F. (PA) - 1970
Okonski, Alvin E. (WI) - 1942, 1944, 1946, 1948, 1950, 1952, 1954, 1956, 1958, 1960, 1962, 1964, 1966, 1968, 1970, 1972
Olcott (NY) - 1860
Olcott, Jacob Vanvechten (NY) - 1904, 1906, 1908
Oldfield, Pearl Peden Mrs. (AR) - 1928
Oldfield, William A. (AR) - 1908, 1910, 1912, 1914, 1916, 1918, 1920, 1922, 1924, 1926
Oldham, George W. (WV) - 1924, 1926
Oldham, Wiley H. (OH) - 1874
Olds (OH) - 1832, 1834
Olds, Edson B. (OH) - 1848, 1850, 1852, 1854
O'Leary, Arthur F. (CT) - 1926
O'Leary, Denis (NY) - 1912
O'Leary, James A. (NY) - 1934, 1936, 1938, 1940, 1942
O'Leary, Jeremiah A. (NY) - 1920
O'Leary, Mark B. (IL) - 1914
O'Leary, Richard A. (NY) - 1952
O'Leary, Thomas C. (NY) - 1938
O'Leen, O. Henry (OR) - 1944
Oleson, Ole B. (WI) - 1892
Olessker, Karl (NY) - 1964
Oley, John H. (WV) - 1866
Olin, Abram B. (NY) - 1856, 1858, 1860
Olin, James R. (VA) - 1982, 1984
Olin, Jim (VA) - 1986, 1988, 1990
Olin, John M. (WI) - 1884
Olin, Vernon E. (NY) - 1954
Olinger, Henry W. (IL) - 1922
Olinger, R. J. (WA) - 1916
Oliphant, H. (PA) - 1838
Oliver, Andrew (NY) - 1852, 1854, 1856
Oliver, Daniel C. (NY) - 1916
Oliver, David S. (OH) - 1896
Oliver, Frank (NY) - 1922, 1924, 1926, 1928, 1930, 1932
Oliver, James C. (ME) - 1936, 1938, 1940, 1954, 1956, 1958, 1960
Oliver, John A. (PA) - 1870
Oliver, John E. (TN) - 1906
Oliver, Mordecai (MO) - 1852, 1854, 1868
Oliver, Robert C. (IN) - 1948
Oliver, Samuel (AL) - 1829
Oliver, Samuel Addison (IA) - 1874, 1876
Oliver, Thomas J. (WI) - 1910
Oliver, William (NY) - 1840
Oliver, William B. (AL) - 1914, 1916, 1918, 1920, 1922, 1924, 1926, 1928, 1930, 1932, 1934
Olmsted, Marlin E. (PA) - 1896, 1898, 1900, 1902, 1904, 1906, 1908, 1910
Olney (NY) - 1848
Olney, Richard (MA) - 1914, 1916, 1918, 1920
O'Laughlin, Joseph M. (MA) - 1976
Oloughlin, Kathryn E. Miss (KS) - 1932
Olpp, Archibald E. (NJ) - 1920, 1922
Olsen, Arnold (MT) - 1960, 1962, 1964, 1966, 1968, 1970, 1972
Olsen, Bob (TN) - 1975
Olsen, John E. (MI) - 1976
Olsen, Jon D. (HI) - 1968
Olsen, Kirsten (CA) - 1978, 1980
Olsen, Lawrence Wayne (NJ) - 1990
Olsen, Leslie O. (MO) - 1970
Olsen, Martin (WA) - 1896
Olson, Alec G. (MN) - 1962, 1964, 1966
Olson, Andrew H. (SD) - 1908
Olson, Andrew (IL) - 1920
Olson, Chuck (CA) - 1990
Olson, Curtis T. (MN) - 1950, 1952
Olson, Dawn (WA) - 1962
Olson, Jonas W. (IL) - 1894, 1902
Olson, Larry H. (MI) - 1972
Olson, Leslie O. (MO) - 1968
Olson, O. Martin (NY) - 1932
Olson, Ole H. (ND) - 1920
Olson, Robert C. (MN) - 1954

Olson, Robert C. Jr. (MN) - 1976
Olson, Virgil L. (KS) - 1976
Olver, John W. (MA) - 1991, 1992
O'Malley (MO) - 1900
O'Malley, Matthew V. (NY) - 1931
O'Malley, Patrick J. (MA) - 1948
O'Malley, Thomas (WI) - 1928, 1930, 1932, 1934, 1936, 1938
Omann, Bernie (MN) - 1992
O'Mara, Bill (NV) - 1978
O'Mara, Eugene J. (NJ) - 1928
O'Mauleby, William (MD) - 1866
Omdahl, John (ND) - 1940
Omdahl, Lloyd (ND) - 1976
O'Meara, Edward S. Jr. (ME) - 1988
O'Meara, John R. (MI) - 1958
O'Meara, Thomas J. (IA) - 1886
O'Merberg, Maynard J. (CA) - 1948
O'Neal (AL) - 1849
O'Neal (GA) - 1851
O'Neal, Emmet (KY) - 1934, 1936, 1938, 1940, 1942, 1944, 1946
O'Neal, H. F. (TX) - 1880
O'Neal, I. C. (VA) - 1876
O'Neal, James (NY) - 1918, 1920
O'Neal, John H. (IN) - 1886
O'Neal, Maston (GA) - 1964, 1966, 1968
O'Neal, Weden (KY) - 1890, 1892
O'Neal, William R. (FL) - 1908
O'Neall, John H. (IN) - 1888
O'Neil (CT) - 1902
O'Neil, A. F. (OH) - 1928
O'Neil, Frank M. (PA) - 1962
O'Neil, James F. (MI) - 1962
O'Neil, Joseph B. (CA) - 1942
O'Neil, Joseph H. (MA) - 1884, 1888, 1890, 1892
O'Neil, Patrick M. (NY) - 1972
O'Neil, Thomas J. (KS) - 1894
O'Neill (TX) - 1878
O'Neill, Bruce Michael (CA) - 1988
O'Neill, Charles (PA) - 1862, 1864, 1866, 1868, 1870, 1872, 1874, 1876, 1878, 1880, 1882, 1884, 1886, 1888, 1890, 1892
O'Neill, Edward L. (NJ) - 1934, 1936, 1938
O'Neill, Eugene T. (NY) - 1946
O'Neill, Francis A. (NY) - 1912
O'Neill, Francis G. (MA) - 1940
O'Neill, Francis P. (MA) - 1942
O'Neill, Harry P. (PA) - 1948, 1950, 1952
O'Neill, James F. (MA) - 1952, 1954
O'Neill, John (OH) - 1862
O'Neill, John J. (MO) - 1882, 1884, 1886, 1888, 1890, 1892
O'Neill, Megan (MI) - 1992
O'Neill, Paul J. (FL) - 1964
O'Neill, Thomas P. Jr. (MA) - 1952, 1954, 1956, 1958, 1960, 1962, 1964, 1966, 1968, 1972, 1974, 1976, 1978, 1980, 1982, 1984
O'Neill, Vincent E. (MI) - 1952
O'Neill, William E. (IL) - 1900
Oppenheim, J. Philip (IN) - 1978
Orchard, Ernest R. (MN) - 1952
Orchard, Ernie (MN) - 1954
Ordway, Albert (VA) - 1870
O'Reilly, Daniel (NY) - 1878, 1880
O'Reilly, Gerald (NY) - 1946
O'Reilly, Kathleen F. (MI) - 1980
O'Reilly, Maurice (IA) - 1950
O'Reilly, T. Bronson (NY) - 1956
O'Reilly, Timothy I. (CA) - 1954
Orenstein, Jeffrey R. (OH) - 1982
Organ, Rollin B. (IL) - 1898
Oriez, Charles A. (CO) - 1992
Orlikoski, Walter J. (IL) - 1940
Orlins, Steve A. (NY) - 1992
Orloski, Richard J. (PA) - 1982, 1990
Ormon, John M. (CT) - 1984
Ormsby, Caleb N. (MI) - 1848
Ormsby, Walter M. (NY) - 1962
Ornstein, Franklin (NY) - 1974
O'Rourke, Hugh (NY) - 1914
O'Rourke, James S. (IL) - 1926, 1928
O'Rourke, Jerome F. (MI) - 1960
O'Rourke, Peter (NY) - 1968
O'Rourke, Philip A. (CA) - 1954
O'Rourke, Vernon A. (PA) - 1942, 1944, 1946
O'Rourke, William J. (PA) - 1932
Orozco, Bill (CA) - 1966, 1968
Orr (MO) - 1914
Orr, Emmett (KY) - 1914

Orr, George (NY) - 1920
Orr, Jackson (IA) - 1870, 1872
Orr, James A. (CO) - 1910
Orr, James L. (SC) - 1848, 1850, 1853, 1854, 1856
Orr, James W. (TX) - 1964
Orr, Robert Jr. (PA) - 1826
Orr, Sample (MO) - 1864
Orr, Samuel (NY) - 1926, 1930, 1932, 1934
Orr, William (IL) - 1834
Orr, William P. (OH) - 1890
Orrick (MD) - 1841
Orth, Godlove S. (IN) - 1862, 1864, 1866, 1868, 1872, 1878, 1880, 1882
Ortiz, Solomon P. (TX) - 1982, 1984, 1986, 1988, 1990, 1992
Ortmeyer, D. H. (IN) - 1912
Orton (MO) - 1894, 1896
Orton (WI) - 1876
Orton, Bill (UT) - 1990, 1992
Orton, Duane (IA) - 1960
Orvis, E. E. (PA) - 1878
Orwig, Samuel H. (PA) - 1882
Osborn (NJ) - 1854
Osborn, Michael (TN) - 1970
Osborn, Robert A. (NY) - 1922
Osborne (NJ) - 1856
Osborne, A. B. (PA) - 1902
Osborne, Bartley P. (PA) - 1960
Osborne, Charles (NY) - 1942
Osborne, Edwin S. (PA) - 1884, 1886, 1888
Osborne, George (KY) - 1924
Osborne, Henry Z. (CA) - 1914, 1916, 1918, 1920, 1922
Osborne, James W. (NC) - 1853
Osborne, John E. (WY) - 1896
Osborne, Lithgow (NY) - 1932
Osborne, Thomas B. (CT) - 1839, 1841, 1843
Osborne, Thomas C. (NE) - 1926
Osborne, W. Ted (OH) - 1958, 1960
Osburn, Frank C. (PA) - 1892
O'Scannlain, Diarmuid (OR) - 1974
Osgood B. L. (TX) - 1904
Osgood, Charles (MA) - 1858
Osgood, Gayton P. (MA) - 1830, 1833, 1834, 1836, 1938, 1840, 1842
Osgood, Jason C. (NY) - 1868
Osgood, Jim (CA) - 1974
Osgood (IL) - 1856
Osgood, William N. (MA) - 1912, 1914
O'Shaunessy, George F. (RI) - 1910, 1912, 1914, 1916, 1922
O'Shea, Bernard (VT) - 1970
O'Shea, Bernard G. (VT) - 1964
O'Shea, George J. (MA) - 1962
O'Shea, Robert S. (IL) - 1972
Osheal, Shaemas (NY) - 1940
Oshel, Val (IL) - 1968, 1974
O'Shinskie, John (PA) - 1948
Oshlo, Richard (IA) - 1968
Osmer, James H. (PA) - 1878
Osmers, Frank C. Jr. (NJ) - 1938, 1940, 1952, 1954, 1956, 1958, 1960, 1962, 1964, 1966
Osser, Maurice S. (PA) - 1948, 1950
Osserman, Stanley (NY) - 1937
Osteen, William L. (NC) - 1968
Osterhaut, J. P. (TX) - 1876, 1884
Ostertag, Harold C. (NY) - 1950, 1952, 1954, 1956, 1958, 1960, 1962
Ostrander (NY) - 1874
O'Sullivan, Daniel E. (VT) - 1914
O'Sullivan, Eugene D. (NE) - 1948, 1950
O'Sullivan, Frank P. (CA) - 1954
O'Sullivan, Humphrey (MA) - 1912, 1924
O'Sullivan, Jeremiah J. (MA) - 1934
O'Sullivan, Jerry (IL) - 1968
O'Sullivan, Patrick B. (CT) - 1922, 1924
O'Sullivan, William Jr. (NJ) - 1980
Oswald, Louis William (IL) - 1946
Otero-Warren, Adelina (NM) - 1922
Otey, Peter (VA) - 1894, 1896, 1898, 1900
Otgen, Theobald (WI) - 1893
Otii, Joseph (OK) - 1916
Otis (MO) - 1914
Otis (NJ) - 1904
Otis (NY) - 1878
Otis, John (ME) - 1848
Otis, John G. (KS) - 1890
Otis, Lusien B. (IL) - 1872
Otis, Norton P. (NY) - 1900, 1902
Otjen, Theobald (WI) - 1892, 1894, 1896, 1898, 1900, 1902, 1904

Passmore, Edmond B. (IL) - 1918
Pasta, James (NY) - 1950
Pasternacki, Leo P. (WI) - 1920
Pastor, Ed (AZ) - 1991, 1992
Patchett, Randy (IL) - 1984, 1986
Patchin, John W. (MI) - 1912
Pate, Whit (OK) - 1966
Paterra, Frank J. (PA) - 1982
Paterson (NJ) - 1858
Paterson, Chat (OH) - 1950, 1952, 1954, 1958, 1960, 1964
Paterson, Thomas A. (NY) - 1906
Pates, James S. (PA) - 1926, 1928, 1930
Patman, Bill (TX) - 1980, 1982, 1984
Patman, Cornelius (NY) - 1836
Patman, Wright (TX) - 1928, 1930, 1932, 1934, 1936, 1938, 1940, 1942, 1944, 1946, 1948, 1950, 1952, 1954, 1956, 1958, 1960, 1962, 1964, 1966, 1968, 1970, 1972, 1974
Paton, Clarence (CA) - 1942
Patrick (OH) - 1858
Patrick, Clyde T. (OK) - 1940, 1948
Patrick, Fred L. (OK) - 1928, 1936
Patrick, Luther (AL) - 1936, 1938, 1940, 1944
Patridge, Alden (VT) - 1830
Patrosso, Mark (CA) - 1990
Pattangall, William R. (ME) - 1904, 1914
Pattee, James Howard (IL) - 1905
Patten, Edward J. (NJ) - 1962, 1964, 1966, 1968, 1970, 1972, 1974, 1976, 1978
Patten, Harold A. (AZ) - 1948, 1950, 1952
Patten, Thomas G. (NY) - 1910, 1912, 1914, 1916
Patten, William A. (CT) - 1942
Patter, H. N. (TX) - 1851
Patterakis, Chris (CA) - 1978
Patterson (GA) - 1840
Patterson (KY) - 1908
Patterson (NJ) - 1872
Patterson (NY) - 1878
Patterson (PA) - 1862, 1884
Patterson, A. A. (IL) - 1906
Patterson, Alfred L. (MI) - 1980
Patterson, Claude (MO) - 1974
Patterson, E. W. (KS) - 1932
Patterson, Edith McClure (OH) - 1932
Patterson, Edward W. (KS) - 1934, 1936, 1938
Patterson, Edward W. (NY) - 1926
Patterson, Ellis E. (CA) - 1944, 1946, 1948
Patterson, Francis F. Jr. (NJ) - 1920, 1922, 1924
Patterson, G. Brown (FL) - 1900
Patterson, George R. (PA) - 1900, 1902, 1904
Patterson, George W. (NY) - 1876
Patterson, Gilbert B. (NC) - 1902, 1904
Patterson, Henry J. (MI) - 1904
Patterson, Hobart M. (NC) - 1942
Patterson, J. B. (KS) - 1936
Patterson, J. L. (NC) - 1902
Patterson, J. O. Jr. (TN) - 1972
Patterson, James O'H. (SC) - 1904, 1906, 1908
Patterson, James T. (CT) - 1946, 1948, 1950, 1952, 1954, 1956, 1958, 1960, 1970
Patterson, James W. (NH) - 1863, 1865
Patterson, Jerry (TX) - 1984
Patterson, Jerry M. (CA) - 1974, 1976, 1978, 1980, 1982, 1984
Patterson, Josiah (TN) - 1890, 1892, 1894, 1896
Patterson, Josiah S. (GA) - 1838
Patterson, Knox (UT) - 1928
Patterson, Lafayette L. (AL) - 1928, 1930
Patterson, Liz J. (SC) - 1986, 1988, 1990, 1992
Patterson, Lucy B. (NC) - 1922
Patterson, Lucy P. (TX) - 1982
Patterson, Malcolm R. (TN) - 1900, 1902, 1904
Patterson, R. E. (PA) - 1900
Patterson, R. William (OH) - 1956, 1960
Patterson, Roscoe C. (MO) - 1920, 1922
Patterson, Samuel (NC) - 1837
Patterson, T. H. (WI) - 1902
Patterson, Thomas J. (NY) - 1842
Patterson, Thomas M. (CO) - 1876, 1878
Patterson, Violet L. (MI) - 1948
Patterson, Walter (NY) - 1826
Patterson, William (NY) - 1836

Patterson, William (OH) - 1832, 1834
Patteson, Camm (VA) - 1878
Pattison (IL) - 1876
Pattison, Edward W. (NY) - 1970, 1974, 1976, 1978
Pattison, John M. (OH) - 1888, 1890, 1892
Pattison, John W. (OH) - 1930
Pattison, W. M. (CA) - 1908
Patton (PA) - 1884
Patton (TN) - 1876
Patton, Billy (TX) - 1964
Patton, Charles E. (PA) - 1910
Patton, David H. (IN) - 1890
Patton, E. E. (TN) - 1930, 1934
Patton, Frank C. (NC) - 1938
Patton, George S. (CA) - 1894
Patton, Gerard B. (CT) - 1988
Patton, James J. (PA) - 1914
Patton, John D. (PA) - 1860, 1882, 1886
Patton, John H. (IA) - 1912
Patton, John M. (VA) - 1831, 1833, 1835, 1837
Patton, Milton (KY) - 1000
Patton, Nat (TX) - 1934, 1936, 1938, 1940, 1942
Patton, Robert L. (NC) - 1892
Patton, William (PA) - 1874
Patton, William D. (PA) - 1960
Pauken, Tom (TX) - 1978, 1980, 1991
Paul, A. M. (OR) - 1906
Paul, D. B. (NC) - 1912
Paul, James C. N. (PA) - 1958
Paul, John (VA) - 1878, 1880, 1882, 1910, 1916, 1918, 1920, 1922
Paul, Joshua H. (UT) - 1928, 1930
Paul, Ron (TX) - 1974, 1976, 1978, 1980, 1982
Paul, William B. (HI) - 1974
Paulitsch, Fred (NY) - 1912
Paulson, Nathan J. (NY) - 1944
Pavatt (TN) - 1843
Pavatt, Stephen C. (TN) - 1839
Pavey, Charles W. (IL) - 1880
Pavis, Frank A. (NY) - 1948
Pavott (TN) - 1853
Paxon, Bill (NY) - 1988, 1990, 1992
Paxton, Floyd (WA) - 1966, 1974
Paxton, Harry W. (OH) - 1896
Paxton, J. Hays (IL) - 1930
Paxton, Thomas B. (OH) - 1924
Payne (NY) - 1884
Payne, Donald M. (NJ) - 1988, 1990, 1992
Payne, H. B. (PA) - 1876
Payne, Henry B. (OH) - 1874, 1876
Payne, Howard E. (KS) - 1934
Payne, John W. (IN) - 1843
Payne, Lawrence O. (OH) - 1952
Payne, Lewis F. Jr. (VA) - 1988, 1990, 1992
Payne, Melvin L. (NY) - 1936
Payne, Oliver H. (OH) - 1866
Payne, Sereno E. (NY) - 1882, 1884, 1889, 1890, 1892, 1894, 1896, 1898, 1900, 1902, 1904, 1906, 1908, 1910, 1912, 1914
Payne, Thomas P. (MI) - 1960, 1962
Payne, William W. (AL) - 1841, 1843, 1845
Paynter, Lemuel (PA) - 1836, 1838
Paynter, Thomas H. (KY) - 1888, 1890, 1892
Payson, Lewis E. (IL) - 1880, 1882, 1884, 1886, 1888, 1890
Payton, Roger A. (CA) - 1990
Peabody, Frank A. (ME) - 1926
Peace, T. W. (TN) - 1906
Peach (CT) - 1910
Peacock, M. A. (WA) - 1914
Peacock, Raymond J. (IL) - 1934
Peacock, Robert R. (NJ) - 1960, 1962
Peacock, William (IL) - 1900
Peake, J. D. (VA) - 1928
Peale (MO) - 1902
Pearce (MS) - 1884
Pearce, Charles E. (MO) - 1896, 1898
Pearce, Dutee J. (RI) - 1825, 1827, 1829, 1831, 1833, 1835, 1837
Pearce, George (CA) - 1871
Pearce, James Alfred (MD) - 1835, 1837, 1839, 1841
Pearce, Rice A. (TN) - 1892
Pearl, F. M. (KS) - 1908
Pearre, George Alexander (MD) - 1898, 1900, 1902, 1904, 1906, 1908
Pearse, Frederick M. P. (NJ) - 1932
Pearson (MN) - 1926

Pearson, Albert J. (OH) - 1890, 1892
Pearson, Claude (NC) - 1904
Pearson, Greg (CO) - 1966
Pearson, Herron (TN) - 1934, 1936, 1938, 1940
Pearson, James (IA) - 1928, 1930
Pearson, John James (PA) - 1836
Pearson, Johnny (CA) - 1988
Pearson, Joseph E. (OH) - 1874
Pearson, L. L. (MS) - 1898
Pearson, Richard M. (NC) - 1835
Pearson, Richmond (NC) - 1894, 1896, 1898
Pearson, Roger (CT) - 1988
Pease (WI) - 1866
Pease, Don J. (OH) - 1976, 1978, 1980, 1982, 1984, 1986, 1988, 1990
Pease, Edward E. (NY) - 1898
Pease, Edward G. (OH) - 1912
Pease, John M. (SD) - 1900
Peaslee, Charles H. (NH) - 1847, 1849, 1851
Peaslee, Clarence L. (PA) - 1910
Peaslee, John B. (OH) - 1900
Peavey, Hubert H. (WI) - 1922, 1924, 1926, 1928, 1930, 1932, 1934
Pechtel, Curtis T. (WI) - 1966
Peck (CT) - 1918
Peck (NY) - 1856, 1860
Peck (VT) - 1849
Peck, Carey (CA) - 1978, 1980
Peck, Erasmus D. (OH) - 1870
Peck, George W. (MI) - 1854, 1856
Peck, George W. (WI) - 1900
Peck, H. J. (MN) - 1896
Peck, Hiram D. (OH) - 1894
Peck, James A. (NY) - 1978
Peck, James K. (PA) - 1942
Peck, Jared V. (NY) - 1852
Peck, Lucius B. (VT) - 1846, 1848
Peck, Luther (NY) - 1836, 1838
Peck, Wilbur L. (IA) - 1930
Peckham, George W. (CA) - 1908
Peckham, Rufus W. (NY) - 1852
Pecora, Frank A. (PA) - 1992
Peddie, Thomas B. (NJ) - 1876
Peden, Preston E. (OK) - 1946
Pedersen, Steve (IL) - 1990
Pedicone, Gus A. (PA) - 1972
Peebles (MN) - 1908
Peel (AR) - 1880
Peel, Inez B. (PA) - 1942
Peel, Samuel W. (AR) - 1882, 1884, 1886, 1888, 1890
Peel, W. M. (AR) - 1894
Peelle, Stanton J. (IN) - 1880, 1882, 1884
Peeples, H. L. (GA) - 1900
Peery, George C. (VA) - 1922, 1924, 1926
Peet (CT) - 1880
Peet, Robert Melvin (IA) - 1916
Pegram (VA) - 1839
Peil, Norman A. (PA) - 1946
Peirce, Robert B. F. (IN) - 1880, 1882
Pelagatti, Gustine J. (PA) - 1970
Pelham, Charles (AL) - 1872
Pelham, J. P. (AL) - 1902
Pell (NY) - 1886
Pell, Herbert C. Jr. (NY) - 1918, 1920
Pellet, Elizabeth E. (CO) - 1942
Pelley, James H. (OH) - 1966
Pelly, Thomas M. (WA) - 1952, 1954, 1956, 1958, 1960, 1962, 1964, 1966, 1968, 1970
Pelosi, Nancy (CA) - 1987, 1988, 1990, 1992
Pelt, John L. (NJ) - 1978
Pelton, Guy R. (NY) - 1854, 1856
Pemberton (MO) - 1912
Pemberton, Gladys (NY) - 1976
Pemberton, Samuel J. (NC) - 1896
Pena, Sergio S. (NY) - 1968
Penberthy, Larry (WA) - 1990
Pence, La Fayette (CO) - 1892, 1894
Pence, Mike (IN) - 1988, 1990
Pence, Richard F. (VA) - 1958
Pendarvis, Ed (SC) - 1984
Pendell, Thomas (NY) - 1922, 1934
Pender, J. L. (IN) - 1882
Pender, J. T. (PA) - 1908
Pendery, Harry H. (CA) - 1992
Pendergast, Joseph E. (IL) - 1914
Pendergast, William G. (NY) - 1948
Pendleton (FL) - 1886
Pendleton (NY) - 1828

Pendleton (OH) - 1832
Pendleton (VA) - 1849, 1855, 1865
Pendleton, A. V. (IN) - 1874
Pendleton, C. M. (KY) - 1888
Pendleton, Edmund H. (NY) - 1826, 1830, 1832, 1834
Pendleton, George C. (TX) - 1892, 1894
Pendleton, George H. (OH) - 1854, 1856, 1858, 1860, 1862, 1866
Pendleton, James M. (RI) - 1870, 1873
Pendleton, John O. (WV) - 1888, 1890, 1892
Pendleton, John S. (VA) - 1845, 1847
Pendleton, Nathan (CT) - 1827
Pendleton, Nathanael G. (OH) - 1838, 1840
Pendleton, Norman W. (CA) - 1912
Pendleton, Phillip Childs (PA) - 1932
Pendleton, Walter (WV) - 1896
Penington, John B. (DE) - 1886, 1888
Penn, Alexander G. (LA) - 1851
Pennell, W. M. (ME) - 1910
Penner, Larry (NY) - 1978
Penniman, Ebenezer J. (MI) - 1850, 1862
Penningroth, Charles (IA) - 1936
Pennington (KY) - 1916
Pennington (NJ) - 1830, 1832, 1834
Pennington, Alexander C. M. (NJ) - 1852, 1854
Pennington, Dennis (IN) - 1833
Pennington, Henry F. (MI) - 1884
Pennington, Levi T. (IN) - 1906
Pennington, William (NJ) - 1858, 1860
Penny (MO) - 1894
Penny, Timothy J. (MN) - 1982, 1984, 1986, 1988, 1990, 1992
Pennybacker, E. B. (WV) - 1944
Pennybacker, Isaac S. (VA) - 1837
Penrose (CT) - 1882
Penrose, Boies Jr. (PA) - 1936, 1939
Pentoney, Francis A. (MA) - 1934
Pentz (MD) - 1884
Peoples, Charles E. (OH) - 1892, 1898
Pepper, Claude (FL) - 1962, 1964, 1966, 1968, 1970, 1972, 1974, 1976, 1978, 1980, 1982, 1984, 1986, 1988
Pepper, George W. (OH) - 1878
Pepper, Irvin S. (IA) - 1910, 1912
Pepple, Worth W. (IN) - 1904
Perce, Legrand W. (MS) - 1869, 1870
Percifield, Anderson (IN) - 1904
Percival, Robert (IA) - 1880
Perdue J. M. (TX) - 1892, 1894
Perez, John J. (CA) - 1974
Perham, Sidney (ME) - 1862, 1864, 1866
Periconi, Joseph F. (NY) - 1970
Perkins (NH) - 1845
Perkins (TN) - 1882
Perkins, Bishop (NY) - 1852
Perkins, Bishop K. (KS) - 1882, 1884, 1886, 1888, 1890
Perkins, Carl C. (KY) - 1984, 1986, 1988, 1990
Perkins, Carl D. (KY) - 1948, 1950, 1952, 1954, 1956, 1958, 1960, 1962, 1964, 1966, 1968, 1970, 1972, 1974, 1976, 1978, 1980, 1982
Perkins, Chester A. (IN) - 1928
Perkins, Frank C. (NY) - 1930
Perkins George W. (MA) - 1898
Perkins, George D. (IA) - 1890, 1892, 1894, 1896
Perkins, James Breck (NY) - 1900, 1902, 1904, 1906, 1908
Perkins, James W. (TN) - 1950
Perkins, Jared (NH) - 1851, 1853
Perkins, John Jr. (LA) - 1853
Perkins, Melvin (MD) - 1978
Perkins, Randolph (NJ) - 1920, 1922, 1924, 1926, 1928, 1930, 1932, 1934
Perkins, Sampson (MA) - 1843
Perkins, Vincent H. (IL) - 1897
Perley (NY) - 1884
Perlman, Jesse B. (NY) - 1932
Perlman, Max (NY) - 1924
Perlman, Nathan D. (NY) - 1922, 1924, 1926
Perlman, Nathan S. (NY) - 1920
Perrill, Augustus L. (OH) - 1844, 1846
Perrin, Arthur R. (NY) - 1936
Perrin, J. Nick (IL) - 1904, 1918
Perrin, Solomon (NY) - 1934
Perrine, Lewis (NY) - 1902
Perrini, Joseph J. (NY) - 1952, 1956, 1958
Perry (NJ) - 1904, 1906

Richter, Francis C. (SD) - 1966
Richter, Frank J. (OH) - 1944
Richter, Leonard G. (OH) - 1960, 1962
Ricker, Clarence C. (PA) - 1910
Ricketts, Edwin D. (OH) - 1914, 1916, 1918, 1920, 1922, 1924, 1928
Riddering Albert A. (MI) - 1944, 1946
Riddick, Carl W. (MT) - 1918, 1920
Riddle (NJ) - 1910
Riddle, Albert G. (OH) - 1860
Riddle, Claude (CA) - 1906
Riddle, George (OH) - 1894
Riddle, George Read (DE) - 1850, 1852, 1854
Riddle, Haywood Y. (TN) - 1876
Riddle, Thomas P. (IN) - 1930
Ridenhower, Ray (TX) - 1940
Rider, Ira Edgar (NY) - 1902
Rider, Myron (MI) - 1870
Ridge, Tom (PA) - 1982, 1984, 1986, 1988, 1990, 1992
Ridgely (MD) - 1837
Ridgely, Edwin R. (KS) - 1896, 1898
Ridgely, Henry M. (DE) - 1830
Ridgway, Joseph (OH) - 1836, 1838, 1840, 1843
Ridgway, Robert (VA) - 1865, 1869
Ridgway, Thomas S. (IL) - 1884, 1889
Riding, Maurice C. (TN) - 1936, 1938
Ridpath, John Clark (IN) - 1896
Riegle, Donald W. Jr. (MI) - 1966, 1968, 1970, 1972, 1974
Riegle, Franklin P. (OH) - 1916
Riehlman, R. Walter (NY) - 1946, 1948, 1950, 1952, 1954, 1956, 1958, 1960, 1962, 1964
Riehm, Curtis G. (IA) - 1960
Rielly (PA) - 1872
Riemer, Wolfgang J. (NY) - 1962
Ries, W. F. (OH) - 1910
Riesner, Daniel J. (NY) - 1940
Rife, John W. (PA) - 1888, 1890
Rigdon (OH) - 1832
Rigdon, D. B. (GA) - 1906
Rigg, Edward L. (ID) - 1906
Riggins, Elisha A. (IN) - 1894
Riggle, Paul (PA) - 1964, 1966, 1968
Riggs, Bob (MN) - 1974
Riggs, E. L. (ID) - 1912
Riggs, Frank (CA) - 1990, 1992
Riggs, James M. (IL) - 1882, 1884
Riggs, Jetur R. (NJ) - 1858
Riggs, L. Alton (AZ) - 1966
Riggs, Lewis (NY) - 1840
Riggs, Samuel A. (KS) - 1872, 1883
Righter (NJ) - 1876
Rigney, Hugh M. (IL) - 1936, 1938
Riley, Bernard J. (NY) - 1918, 1928
Riley, Charles J. (MO) - 1940
Riley, Corinne B. (SC) - 1962
Riley, James J. (MD) - 1980
Riley, John J. (SC) - 1944, 1946, 1950, 1952, 1954, 1956, 1958, 1960
Riley, John W. (IN) - 1990
Riley, Martha (WI) - 1922
Riley, Phillip A. (NY) - 1914
Riley, Reuben A. (IN) - 1878
Riley, Robert A. (OH) - 1962
Riley, T. S. (WV) - 1906
Riley, Thomas H. (IL) - 1912
Riley, Tom (IA) - 1968, 1974, 1976
Rinaker, John I. (IL) - 1874, 1894, 1896
Rinaldo, Matthew J. (NJ) - 1972, 1974, 1976, 1978, 1980, 1982, 1984, 1986, 1988, 1990
Rinaldo, Samuel (NY) - 1890
Rinehart, John B. G. (NY) - 1912
Ring, Carl E. (NJ) - 1950
Ring, J. (VA) - 1890
Ring, James H. (PA) - 1970
Ring, John W. (CT) - 1938
Ringdal (MN) - 1898
Ringer, Darrell (KS) - 1984
Ringgold, Tim (PA) - 1986
Ringland (PA) - 1834
Ringle, John (WI) - 1886
Ringo, George (CA) - 1912
Rinkenberger, George H. (IL) - 1928
Rinker, Glenn (FL) - 1982
Riordan, Daniel J. (NY) - 1898, 1906, 1908, 1910, 1912, 1914, 1916, 1918, 1920, 1922
Riordan, Obrien (CA) - 1970
Ripley, Eleazer W. (LA) - 1834, 1836

Ripley, James W. (ME) - 1826, 1828
Ripple, James L. (OH) - 1974
Rippman, J. G. Harry (PA) - 1932
Rippon, Donald J. (PA) - 1968, 1972
Rippon, Thomas R. (PA) - 1978
Ririe, Joseph (UT) - 1930
Risenhoover, Theodore (OK) - 1974, 1976
Rising, Spencer (IL) - 1886
Risk, Charles F. (RI) - 1936, 1938, 1940
Risk, William L. (IN) - 1912
Risley, Elijah (NYL) - 1848
Risley, Hanson A. (NY) - 1866
Risley, Theodore G. (IL) - 1898
Ristow, Harold C. (WI) - 1964
Ritchey, M. H. (MO) - 1878
Ritchey, Paul E. (PA) - 1988
Ritchey, Thomas (OH) - 1846, 1852
Ritchie, Byron F. (OH) - 1892, 1894
Ritchie, David (PA) - 1852, 1854, 1856
Ritchie, James M. (OH) - 1880
Ritchie, Jess M. (CA) - 1954
Ritchie, John (MD) - 1870, 1872
Ritchie, John E. (MD) - 1886
Ritchie, John E. (MD) - 1984
Ritchie, R. S. (NC) - 1974
Ritenauer, Fred M. (OH) - 1974
Ritner, Roy W. (OR) - 1936
Rittenband, Richard M. (CT) - 1972
Rittenhouse, E. Stanley (VA) - 1976
Ritter, Al (OR) - 1992
Ritter, Burwell C. (KY) - 1865, 1867
Ritter, Donald L. (PA) - 1978, 1980, 1982, 1984, 1986, 1988, 1990, 1992
Ritter, John (PA) - 1843, 1844
Ritter, Milo (OK) - 1958
Ritter, Tom (MI) - 1984
Rivers, L. Mendel (SC) - 1940, 1942, 1944, 1946, 1948, 1950, 1952, 1954, 1956, 1958, 1960, 1962, 1964, 1966, 1968, 1970
Rivers, Norman J. (MI) - 1988
Rivers, Ralph J. (AK) - 1958, 1960, 1962, 1964, 1966
Rivers, Thomas (TN) - 1855
Rives, Alexander (VA) - 1870
Rives, Francis E. (VA) - 1837, 1839
Rives, George E. (VA) - 1884
Rives, J. Henry (VA) - 1882
Rives, William C. (VA) - 1825, 1827, 1829
Rives, Zeno J. (IL) - 1904, 1906
Rixey, John F. (VA) - 1896, 1898, 1900, 1902, 1904, 1906
Rizley, Ross (OK) - 1940, 1942, 1944, 1946
Roach, John J. (NY) - 1904, 1906
Roach, John L. (IL) - 1952
Roach, Leonard (CA) - 1936
Roach, Milton J. (KY) - 1870
Roach, Sidney C. (MO) - 1920, 1922, 1924
Roach, William D. (IN) - 1970
Roads (MA) - 1888
Roads, Samuel Jr. (MA) - 1902
Roane (VA) - 1834
Roane, Francis J. (MA) - 1938, 1940
Roane, John (VA) - 1827, 1829, 1835
Roane, John J. (VA) - 1831, 1833, 1835
Roark, Charles W. (KY) - 1928
Roark, Lester D. (NC) - 1986
Robb, Edward (MO) - 1896, 1898, 1900, 1902, 1904
Robb, Holland L. (NC) - 1960
Robb, John H. (NM) - 1960
Robb, Scotty (OK) - 1978
Robb, W. H. (IA) - 1896
Robb, Winifred E. (IA) - 1922
Robbie, Joseph (MN) - 1956, 1958
Robbins (NJ) - 1880
Robbins, Charles E. (NY) - 1916
Robbins, Charles H. (PA) - 1914
Robbins, Edward E. (PA) - 1896, 1916, 1918
Robbins, Gaston A. (AL) - 1892, 1894, 1898
Robbins, George (NJ) - 1854, 1856
Robbins, John Jr. (PA) - 1848, 1850, 1852, 1874
Robbins, Joseph (IL) - 1876
Robbins, Joseph A. (PA) - 1924
Robbins, Mark A. (CA) - 1992
Robbins, Robert J. (MI) - 1960
Robbins, William M. (NC) - 1872, 1874, 1876, 1882
Rober, William B. (PA) - 1870
Roberson, Samuel D. (NY) - 1898
Roberts (MS) - 1847
Roberts (NY) - 1852

Roberts (PA) - 1858, 1884, 1886
Roberts (VA) - 1853
Roberts, Anthony E. (PA) - 1843, 1854, 1856
Roberts, Carlos E. (AL) - 1924, 1926
Roberts, Charles B. (MD) - 1874, 1876
Roberts, Charles E. (AL) - 1922
Roberts, Charles H. (NY) - 1924, 1940
Roberts, Charles H. (PA) - 1970
Roberts, Christine (CA) - 1992
Roberts, Clarence M. (MD) - 1922
Roberts, Clint (SD) - 1980, 1982
Roberts, Clyde M. (NC) - 1964
Roberts, Courtney (TX) - 1972
Roberts, D. Jr. (VT) - 1850
Roberts, D. W. (TX) - 1890
Roberts, David (NY) - 1992
Roberts, David G. (ME) - 1960
Roberts, Don (IN) - 1936
Roberts, Edward F. (PA) - 1938
Roberts, Edwin E. (NV) - 1910, 1912, 1914, 1916
Roberts, Ellis H. (NY) - 1870, 1872, 1874
Roberts, Elmer C. (KY) - 1950
Roberts, Ernest W. (MA) - 1898, 1900, 1902, 1904, 1906, 1908, 1910, 1912, 1914, 1916
Roberts, F. (NC) - 1906
Roberts, Frank C. (CA) - 1914
Roberts, Frederick M. (CA) - 1946
Roberts, George Henry (NY) - 1894
Roberts, Gordon (OH) - 1986, 1988
Roberts, Harry (WY) - 1970
Roberts, Henry (PA) - 1878
Roberts, J. W. (AL) - 1904
Roberts, Jack E. (CA) - 1974
Roberts, John (VT) - 1838
Roberts, Kenneth A. (AL) - 1950, 1952, 1954, 1956, 1958, 1960, 1962, 1964
Roberts, Kirby J. (TX) - 1990
Roberts, Leader (NY) - 1840
Roberts, Louis F. (NY) - 1916
Roberts, Melvin P. (ME) - 1938
Roberts, Matthew (OH) - 1850
Roberts, Noel F. (NJ) - 1988
Roberts, Pat (KS) - 1980, 1982, 1984, 1986, 1988, 1990, 1992
Roberts, Phil (KY) - 1894
Roberts, Ray (TX) - 1961, 1962, 1964, 1966, 1968, 1970, 1972, 1974, 1976, 1978
Roberts, Robert W. (MS) - 1843, 1845
Roberts, Thomas J. (KY) - 1968
Roberts, Victor W. (IL) - 1978
Roberts, William P. (IL) - 1942
Roberts, William R. (NY) - 1870, 1872
Robertson (MN) - 1918
Robertson (MO) - 1898
Robertson, A. Willis (VA) - 1932, 1934, 1936, 1938, 1940, 1942, 1944
Robertson, Alice M. (OK) - 1920, 1922
Robertson, Charles A. (OR) - 1940
Robertson, Charles R. (ND) - 1940, 1942, 1944, 1946
Robertson, D. Mott (VA) - 1892
Robertson, Edward W. (LA) - 1876, 1878, 1880, 1886
Robertson, Ernest (VA) - 1954
Robertson, F. C. (WA) - 1900
Robertson, Harrison M. (KY) - 1954
Robertson, James (MN) - 1928
Robertson, John (VA) - 1833, 1834, 1835, 1837
Robertson, Joyce M. (CA) - 1986
Robertson, Norm (NJ) - 1982
Robertson, Paul (MD) - 1946
Robertson, Samuel M. (LA) - 1887, 1888, 1890, 1892, 1894, 1896, 1898, 1900, 1902, 1904
Robertson, Thomas A. (KY) - 1882, 1884
Robertson, William H. (NY) - 1866
Robeson, Edward J. Jr. (VA) - 1950, 1952, 1954, 1956
Robeson, George M. (NJ) - 1878, 1880, 1882
Robie, Reuben (NY) - 1850
Robins, James B. (GA) - 1892
Robinson (IN) - 1874
Robinson (NE) - 1852
Robinson (MO) - 1912
Robinson (NY) - 1860, 1888
Robinson (PA) - 1860, 1888
Robinson (SD) - 1902
Robinson (VT) - 1834

Robinson, Ben T. (KY) - 1918
Robinson, Blackwell P. (NC) - 1962
Robinson, Charles (KS) - 1886
Robinson, Charles A. (IN) - 1896, 1898
Robinson, Charles H. S. (MA) - 1912, 1914, 1916
Robinson, Charles R. (AL) - 1934, 1936
Robinson, Chas. (TX) - 1992
Robinson, Christopher (RI) - 1859, 1861
Robinson, Clinton (MN) - 1912
Robinson, David L. (IL) - 1980
Robinson, E. L. (WV) - 1908
Robinson, Edward (ME) - 1838
Robinson, F. P. (TN) - 1924
Robinson, Frederick (MA) - 1846
Robinson, George D. (MA) - 1876, 1878, 1880, 1882
Robinson, Gilbert A. (NY) - 1962
Robinson, Harvey R. (PA) - 1962
Robinson, Henry A. (MI) - 1886
Robinson, Henry C. (NY) - 1892
Robinson, J. Chester (AL) - 1962
Robinson, J. Kenneth (VA) - 1962, 1970, 1972, 1974, 1976, 1978, 1980, 1982
Robinson, J. Will (UT) - 1932, 1934, 1936, 1938, 1940, 1942, 1944, 1946
Robinson, James A. (TX) - 1988
Robinson, James C. (FL) - 1968
Robinson, James C. (IL) - 1858, 1860, 1862, 1870, 1872
Robinson, James M. (IN) - 1898, 1900, 1902, 1904
Robinson, James N. (IN) - 1896
Robinson, James S. (OH) - 1880, 1882
Robinson, James W. (OH) - 1872, 1874
Robinson, Joel (FL) - 1982
Robinson, John B. (PA) - 1890, 1892, 1894, 1896, 1898
Robinson, John L. (IN) - 1847, 1849, 1851
Robinson, John S. (NE) - 1898, 1900, 1902
Robinson, John S. (VT) - 1836
Robinson, Joseph (IN) - 1849
Robinson, Joseph E. (PA) - 1920
Robinson, Joseph T. (AR) - 1902, 1904, 1906, 1908, 1910
Robinson, L. B. (TX) - 1944
Robinson, Leonidas D. (NC) - 1916, 1918
Robinson, Lucius (NY) - 1870
Robinson, Maurice G. (IN) - 1940
Robinson, Milton Stapp (IN) - 1874, 1876
Robinson, Orville (NY) - 1842
Robinson, Richard (CA) - 1986
Robinson, S. W. (MS) - 1892
Robinson, Stephen A. (OH) - 1908
Robinson, T. B. (MO) - 1876, 1878
Robinson, Thomas (ME) - 1843
Robinson, Thomas J. B. (IA) - 1922, 1924, 1926, 1928, 1930, 1932
Robinson, Thomas Jr. (DE) - 1838, 1840
Robinson, Thomas T. (IL) - 1888
Robinson, Tommy F. (AR) - 1984, 1986, 1988
Robinson, W. B. (NY) - 1918, 1920, 1922, 1924, 1930
Robinson, W. C. (AL) - 1894
Robinson, W. G. (TX) - 1890
Robinson, W. S. (NC) - 1904
Robinson, William (IN) - 1912
Robinson, William (NC) - 1888
Robinson, William E. (NY) - 1866, 1880, 1882
Robinson, William H. (IL) - 1870
Robinson, William I. (KS) - 1960
Robison (MI) - 1874, 1876
Robison (MO) - 1902
Robison, David F. (PA) - 1854
Robison, Howard W. (NY) - 1958, 1960, 1962, 1964, 1966, 1968, 1970, 1972
Robles, Mario Jr. (CT) - 1988
Robles, Ernest Z. (CA) - 1972
Robsion, John M. (KY) - 1918, 1920, 1922, 1924, 1926, 1928, 1934, 1936, 1938, 1940, 1942, 1944, 1946
Robson, W. S. (TX) - 1898
Robtsn (NJ) - 1844
Roche, Anthony M. (MA) - 1946, 1948
Roche, Dan (MI) - 1986
Rocheteau, Ralph Carlos (FL) - 1988
Rochford, Dennis J. (PA) - 1980
Rock, Michael J. (VT) - 1940
Rock, Rudolph (OH) - 1886
Rock, Sherman N. (NC) - 1964
Rock, Thomas (NY) - 1918
Rockee, Abraham (NY) - 1834

Speer, Emory (GA) - 1877, 1878, 1880, 1882
Speer, Leonidas E. (OH) - 1936
Speer, Peter M. (PA) - 1910, 1912
Speer, R. Milton (PA) - 1870, 1872, 1880
Speer, Thomas J. (GA) - 1870
Speers, Grover H. (MO) - 1974
Speers, H. W. Grady Jr. (VA) - 1964
Speers, Harry (TN) - 1924
Speers, Ronald T. (ME) - 1970
Speiden, John G. (AZ) - 1956, 1958
Speight, J. C. (KY) - 1932
Speight, J. J. (AL) - 1914
Speight, Jesse (NC) - 1829, 1831, 1833, 1835
Speir, C. E. (FL) - 1912
Spellman, Gladys Noon (MD) - 1974, 1976, 1978, 1980
Spellman, James P. (CA) - 1982
Spelman, Harold J. (IL) - 1956
Spen (NY) - 1852
Spence (MD) - 1872, 1876
Spence (WI) - 1936
Spence, Arthur T. (WI) - 1934
Spence, Ben L. (NC) - 1946
Spence, Betty C. (IL) - 1974
Spence, Brent (KY) - 1928, 1930, 1932, 1934, 1936, 1938, 1940, 1942, 1944, 1946, 1948, 1950, 1952, 1954, 1956, 1958, 1960
Spence, Floyd D. (SC) - 1970, 1972, 1974, 1976, 1978, 1980, 1982, 1984, 1986, 1988, 1990, 1992
Spence, George S. (TN) - 1956
Spence, John S. (MD) - 1824, 1831
Spence, Lavosier (OH) - 1899
Spence, O. M. (TN) - 1954
Spence, Thomas (MD) - 1843
Spence, W. A. (IL) - 1936
Spencer (NJ) - 1834
Spencer (NY) - 1848, 1874
Spencer (OH) - 1860
Spencer, A. B. (PA) - 1900
Spencer, A. B. (TX) - 1924
Spencer, Ambrose (NY) - 1828, 1830, 1832
Spencer, Charles S. (NY) - 1866
Spencer, Colin G. (NC) - 1930
Spencer, Dale B. (IN) - 1932
Spencer, Elizabeth W. (MD) - 1982
Spencer, James (NY) - 1836
Spencer, James G. (MS) - 1894
Spencer, John W. (IN) - 1902
Spencer, Joshua A. (NY) - 1834, 1836
Spencer, Joshua M. (IN) - 1902
Spencer, Louis N. (PA) - 1900
Spencer, Nelson E. (NY) - 1930
Spencer, R. C. (IA) - 1908
Spencer, R. C. (WI) - 1890
Spencer, Richard (MD) - 1829, 1831
Spencer, Terence J. (NY) - 1972
Spencer, Virginia A. (NY) - 1938
Spencer, William B. (LA) - 1874
Spencer, William F. (IN) - 1922
Sperrazzo, Jim (CA) - 1968
Sperry, Francis C. (IL) - 1948
Sperry, Lewis (CT) - 1890, 1892
Sperry, Nehemiah D. (CT) - 1894, 1896, 1898, 1900, 1902, 1904, 1906, 1908
Spessard, Harvey R. (MD) - 1906
Speziale, John A. (CT) - 1952
Spicely, W. F. (IN) - 1876
Spicer, Keith (MN) - 1984
Spicer, William S. (AR) - 1956
Spiegel, Jacob R. (PA) - 1898
Spiegelberg, George A. (NY) - 1934
Spiegelman, Lee Arnold (FL) - 1976
Spight, Thomas (MS) - 1898, 1900, 1902, 1904, 1906, 1908
Spillane, William D. (HI) - 1978
Spillers, C. Lee (WV) - 1956
Spillman, O. S. (NE) - 1914
Spilman, I. R. (IL) - 1908
Spilman, James P. (KY) - 1914
Spingarn, Joel Elias (NY) - 1908
Spingler, Bill (CA) - 1986
Spink, Cyrus (OH) - 1858
Spink, John C. (OH) - 1850
Spinner, Francis E. (NY) - 1854, 1856, 1858
Spinner, Frank C. (NY) - 1968, 1970
Spinney, Elvington P. (ME) - 1928
Spinney, Samuel R. (MA) - 1854
Spinola, Francis B. (NY) - 1886, 1888, 1890

Spinosa, Tom (CA) - 1974, 1976, 1978, 1980, 1984
Spiridellis, Ona (NJ) - 1992
Spiro, Herbert (TX) - 1992
Spitler, Merrill (MO) - 1942
Spittal, Herman (PA) - 1920
Spitz, Henry H. (NY) - 1928
Spitzer (NY) - 1876
Spitzli, George H. (NY) - 1914
Spofford (ME) - 1874
Spofford, Richard S. (MA) - 1884
Spohn, J. V. (TX) - 1890
Sponsler (PA) - 1872
Spoo, James (NV) - 1988
Spooner (WI) - 1854
Spooner, Frank (LA) - 1976
Spooner, Henry J. (RI) - 1881, 1882, 1884, 1886, 1888, 1890
Spooner, William R. (NY) - 1902
Sporkin, Charles H. (PA) - 1954, 1956
Spotts, Charles E. (PA) - 1918
Sprague (NY) - 1850
Sprague (RI) - 1833
Sprague, Albert P. (NE) - 1920
Sprague, Charles F. (MA) - 1896, 1898
Sprague, Charles S. (NY) - 1910
Sprague, David (CO) - 1986
Sprague, Frederick H. (NC) - 1870
Sprague, Hugh A. (MO) - 1970
Sprague, Peleg (ME) - 1824, 1826, 1828
Sprague, Peter J. (NY) - 1970
Sprague, Philip A. (IN) - 1970
Sprague, Seth (MA) - 1842
Sprague, William (MI) - 1848
Sprague, William (RI) - 1835
Sprague, William P. (OH) - 1870, 1872
Spratt, George (WI) - 1908
Spratt, John (SC) - 1982
Spratt, John M. Jr. (SC) - 1984, 1986, 1988, 1990, 1992
Spratt, William E. (MO) - 1922
Sprenkle, John A. (PA) - 1918
Sprigade, Herman E. (NY) - 1924
Sprigg, James C. (KY) - 1841, 1843
Sprigg, Michael C. (MD) - 1826, 1829, 1831
Spriggs (OH) - 1858
Spriggs, John P. (OH) - 1888
Spriggs, John T. (NY) - 1868, 1878, 1882, 1884, 1886
Sprik, Dale R. (MI) - 1978, 1980, 1993
Spring (MO) - 1882
Spring, Giles (IL) - 1843
Springer, Arthur (TX) - 1898
Springer, Gerald N. (OH) - 1970
Springer, Raymond S. (IN) - 1938, 1940, 1942, 1944, 1946
Springer, William (MI) - 1906, 1908
Springer, William L. (IL) - 1950, 1952, 1954, 1956, 1958, 1960, 1962, 1964, 1966, 1968, 1970
Springer, William M. (IL) - 1874, 1876, 1878, 1880, 1882, 1884, 1886, 1888, 1890, 1892, 1894
Springmeyer, George (NV) - 1912
Sproesser, Albert M. (MD) - 1912
Sproul, Elliott W. (IL) - 1920, 1922, 1924, 1926, 1928, 1930, 1932
Sproul, J. D. (CA) - 1900
Sproul, William H. (KS) - 1922, 1924, 1926, 1928
Sproule, George B. (MT) - 1902
Sprunk, Gary (AZ) - 1988
Spry, William (UT) - 1918
Spurry, John (MA) - 1833
Squire (NY) - 1848
Squires, William H. (NY) - 1904
Stabler, Paul R. (GA) - 1992
Stachl, George (IA) - 1896
Stack (CO) - 1918
Stack, Daniel J. (IL) - 1978
Stack, Edmund J. (IL) - 1906, 1910
Stack, Edward J. (FL) - 1978, 1982
Stack, John M. (WV) - 1978
Stack, Michael J. (PA) - 1934, 1936
Stackhouse, Eli T. (SC) - 1890
Stacy (MN) - 1876
Stacy, Consider A. (MI) - 1858
Staebler, Neil (MI) - 1962
Stafford, Chas. B. (IL) - 1904
Stafford, E. (MO) - 1864
Stafford, Edward R. (OH) - 1932
Stafford, James S. (VA) - 1968
Stafford, Jefferson (VA) - 1984

Stafford, Robert T. (VT) - 1960, 1962, 1964, 1966, 1968, 1970
Stafford, W. T. (KY) - 1912
Stafford, William H. (WI) - 1902, 1904, 1906, 1908, 1912, 1914, 1916, 1918, 1920, 1922, 1926, 1928, 1930
Staggers, Harley O. (WV) - 1948, 1950, 1952, 1954, 1956, 1958, 1960, 1962, 1964, 1966, 1968, 1970, 1972, 1974, 1976, 1978
Staggers, Harley O. Jr. (WV) - 1982, 1984, 1986, 1988, 1990, 1992
Stahl, Andrew F. (WI) - 1920
Stahl, Scott (OH) - 1930
Stahle, James A. (PA) - 1894, 1896
Stahlnecker, William G. (NY) - 1884, 1886, 1888, 1890
Staighton, Jonathan C. (IL) - 1878
Stakes, Louis (OH) - 1976
Stalbaum, Lynn E. (WI) - 1964, 1966, 1968
Stalbaum, Merrill E. (WI) - 1972
Staley, Edward (OH) - 1912
Staley, Joe (TX) - 1970
Stalker, Gale H. (NY) - 1922, 1924, 1926, 1928, 1930, 1932
Stallard, H. H. (OK) - 1910, 1912, 1914, 1916
Stallings, Jesse F. (AL) - 1892, 1894, 1896, 1898
Stallings, Richard H. (ID) - 1982, 1984, 1986, 1988, 1990
Stallwood, Burton (RI) - 1982
Stallworth, James A. (AL) - 1855, 1857, 1859
Stanard, Edwin O. (MO) - 1872, 1874
Stanard, Mrs. Stillman J. (IL) - 1964
Stanberry (OH) - 1832
Stanberry, Henry (OH) - 1836
Stanberry, James R. (OH) - 1844
Stanbery, Henry R. (OH) - 1898
Stanbery, William (OH) - 1828, 1830
Standifee, L. J. (AL) - 1870
Standifer, James (TN) - 1825, 1827, 1829, 1831, 1833, 1835, 1837
Standiford, Elisha D. (KY) - 1872
Stanek, John A. (IL) - 1934
Stangeland, Arlan (MN) - 1977, 1978, 1980, 1982, 1984, 1986, 1988, 1990
Stanley, Augustus O. (KY) - 1902, 1904, 1906, 1908, 1910, 1912
Stanley, Frank B. (TX) - 1904
Stanley, George S. (MI) - 1904
Stanley, John V. (ID) - 1916
Stanley, M. C. (OK) - 1976
Stanley, Thomas B. (VA) - 1946, 1948, 1950, 1952
Stanley, Thornton (AL) - 1970
Stanley, Winifred C. (NY) - 1942
Stanly, Edward (NC) - 1837, 1839, 1841, 1843, 1849, 1851
Stannard, Sarah (AZ) - 1992
Stant, Frederick T. Jr. (VA) - 1968
Stanton (KY) - 1849, 1916
Stanton, Benjamin (OH) - 1850, 1854, 1856, 1858
Stanton, Charles (NY) - 1928, 1932
Stanton, Elsie (OH) - 1938, 1944
Stanton, Frederick P. (TN) - 1845, 1847, 1849, 1851, 1853
Stanton, J. William (OH) - 1964, 1966, 1968, 1970, 1972, 1974, 1976, 1978, 1980
Stanton, James V. (OH) - 1968, 1970, 1972, 1974
Stanton, Richard H. (KY) - 1849, 1851, 1853, 1855
Stanton, W. H. (PA) - 1876
Staplekamp, Judson W. (WI) - 1934
Staples (TN) - 1904
Staples (VA) - 1855
Staples, David H. (ME) - 1944
Staples, E. W. (ME) - 1896
Starbird, C. R. (AR) - 1948
Starbird, Charles M. (ME) - 1926
Starbuck (NY) - 1860
Starin, John H. (NY) - 1876, 1878
Staring, George B. (NY) - 1908
Stark, Albert G. (CT) - 1853
Stark, Fortney H. (Pete) (CA) - 1972, 1974, 1976, 1978, 1980, 1982, 1984, 1986
Stark, James H. (GA) - 1843
Stark, John Paul (CA) - 1980, 1982, 1984, 1988
Stark, Judson L. (IN) - 1944

Stark, Pete (CA) - 1988, 1990, 1992
Stark, William L. (NE) - 1894, 1896, 1898, 1900, 1902, 1916
Starke (MS) - 1845
Starke, Jay (VA) - 1990
Starkey, Frank T. (MN) - 1944, 1946
Starkey, Hiram E. (NY) - 1912
Starkloff, Carl E. (MO) - 1942
Starkweather (OH) - 1860
Starkweather, David A. (OH) - 1838, 1844, 1846
Starkweather, George (NY) - 1846
Starkweather, Harvey G. (OR) - 1928, 1932
Starkweather, Henry H. (CT) - 1867, 1869, 1871, 1873, 1875
Starkweather, Samuel (OH) - 1844
Starling, Alton H. (Bill) (FL) - 1984
Starnes, Joe (AL) - 1934, 1936, 1938, 1940, 1942
Starr, George (NY) - 1868
Starr, John F. (NJ) - 1862, 1864
Starr, Julius S. (IL) - 1884
Starr, Mark (NY) - 1950, 1962
Starr, Mike (IL) - 1992
Starr, Western (IL) - 1908
Staskiewicz, Ronald L. (NE) - 1992
Stassen, Harold (MN) - 1986
States, Michael A. (AK) - 1992
Staton, David M. (WV) - 1978
Staton, David Michael (WV) - 1982
Staton, Mick (WV) - 1980
Staton, R. Hilliard (NC) - 1912
Staton, Robert H. (IN) - 1966
Stauffer, John K. (PA) - 1914
Stauffer, Randolph (PA) - 1944
Stauffer, S. Walter (PA) - 1952, 1954, 1956, 1958
Staum, John R. M. (MD) - 1924
Staunton (TN) - 1843
Staver, Daniel (OR) - 1908
Stayart, L. W. (TX) - 1946
Stayles (NY) - 1844
Steadman, Martin J. (NY) - 1966
Steagall, Henry B. (AL) - 1918, 1920, 1922, 1926, 1928, 1930, 1932, 1934, 1936, 1938, 1940, 1942
Stearn, Mrs. Edith Shaffer (FL) - 1944
Stearns, Cliff (FL) - 1988, 1990, 1992
Stearns, Darrel H. (VA) - 1970
Stearns, Elisha (CT) - 1835
Stearns, Foster (NH) - 1938, 1940, 1942
Stearns, J. Thomas (NY) - 1890
Stearns, Willard M. (MI) - 1888
Stebbins (NY) - 1874
Stebbins, C. E. (IL) - 1906
Stebbins, Charles Jr. (NY) - 1868
Stebbins, Henry G. (NY) - 1862, 1864
Stebbins, Homer A. (NY) - 1934, 1936, 1938, 1940
Stebbins, Lucien (NE) - 1920
Stecher, Jack E. (OH) - 1980
Steck (PA) - 1888
Steck, A. C. (IA) - 1900
Steckler, Ferne M. (NY) - 1972
Stedman (CT) - 1871
Stedman, Charles M. (NC) - 1910, 1912, 1914, 1916, 1918, 1920, 1922, 1924, 1926, 1928
Stedman, Seymorse (IL) - 1923
Steed, Tom (OK) - 1948, 1950, 1952, 1954, 1956, 1958, 1960, 1962, 1964, 1966, 1968, 1970, 1972, 1974, 1976, 1978
Steedman (OH) - 1860
Steeholm, Hardy (NY) - 1940
Steel (MO) - 1896
Steele (IN) - 1860
Steele (NJ) - 1908
Steele (TN) - 1872
Steele (VT) - 1872
Steele (VA) - 1833, 1839
Steele (WI) - 1878
Steele, Bill (CA) - 1986
Steele, David (VA) - 1837
Steele, G. Fred Jr. (NC) - 1966, 1968
Steele, George W. (IN) - 1880, 1882, 1884, 1886, 1888, 1894, 1896, 1898, 1900
Steele, Henry J. (PA) - 1914, 1916, 1918
Steele, John B. (NY) - 1860, 1862
Steele, John D. (FL) - 1964
Steele, John N. (MD) - 1835
Steele, Leslie J. (GA) - 1926, 1928
Steele, Philip L. (CT) - 1992
Steele, Robert H. (CT) - 1970, 1972
Steele, Thomas J. (IA) - 1914, 1916, 1918

# General Index

The General Index includes page references to all sections of the *Guide to U.S. Elections, Third Edition,* except the popular vote returns, which are indexed separately in candidate indexes. The six candidates indexes are: Presidential Candidates Index, p. 1367; Gubernatorial Candidates Index, pp. 1368-1380; Gubernatorial Primary Candidates Index, pp. 1381-1387; Senate Candidates Index, pp. 1388-1394; Senate Primary Candidates Index, pp. 1395-1401; and House Candidates Index, pp. 1402-1501. Italic numbers in the General Index refer to photographs or illustrations.

## A

**Aandahl, Fred G.**
Governor, North Dakota, 655
**Abbett, Leon**
Governor, New Jersey, 653
**Abbott, Joseph C.**
Senator, North Carolina, 802
**Abdnor, James**
Senator, South Dakota, 807
**Abel, Hazel H.**
Senator, Nebraska, 799
**Abernethy, Thomas G.**
House seat challenge, 919
**Abolitionist movement.** *See* **Slavery**
**Abourezk, James**
Senator, South Dakota, 806
**Adair, John**
Governor, Kentucky, 646
Senator, Kentucky, 793
**Adams, Alva**
Governor, Colorado, 641
**Adams, Alva B.**
Senator, Colorado, 787
**Adams, Brock**
Senator, Washington, 810
**Adams, Charles Francis**
biography, 563
at Free Soil convention, **(1848)** 42
at Liberal Republican convention, **(1872)** 56
Vice President, Free Soil Party nominee, **(1848)** 42, 275
**Adams, James H.**
Governor, South Carolina, 658
**Adams, Jewett W.**
Governor, Nevada, 652
**Adams, John**
background, 424, 590
biography, 563
President
Electoral College vote, **(1789)** 359, **(1792)** 360, **(1796)** 361, **(1800)** 362
nominations, **(1796, 1800)** 9, 289
Vice President
attitude toward office, 484
electoral vote, **(1789, 1792)** 9, 288
**Adams, John Quincy**
background, 418, 424, 590
biography, 563
House membership after presidency, 590, 917
President
election by House, 1825, 11, 292-293, 348, 349
Electoral College vote, **(1820)** 367, **(1824)** 368, **(1828)** 369
nominations, **(1824, 1828)** 11
popular vote, **(1824, 1828)** 429
Senator, Massachusetts, 795
**Adams, John Quincy II**
Vice President, Straight-Out Democratic Party nominee, **(1872)** 276
**Adams, Robert H.**
Senator, Mississippi, 797
**Adams, Samuel**
biography, 563
Governor, Massachusetts, 648
President, Electoral College vote, **(1796)** 361
Governor, Arkansas, 640
**Adams, Sherman**
Governor, New Hampshire, 653
**Adams, Stephen**
Senator, Mississippi, 797

**Adams, William H.**
Governor, Colorado, 641
**Addams, Jane**
at Progressive convention, **(1912)** 81
**Adet, Pierre**
role in 1796 presidential election, 289
**Adkins, Homer M.**
Governor, Arkansas, 640
**Agnew, Spiro Theodore**
biography, 563
Governor, Maryland, 648
at Republican conventions, **(1968)** 121, **(1972)** 130
Vice President
Electoral College vote, **(1968, 1972)** 412
Republican Party nominee, **(1968)** 121, 281, 328, **(1972)** 130, 281
resignation, 330, 355, 606
**Agran, Lawrence A.**
Democratic convention ballots, **(1992)** 255
presidential primary vote, **(1992)** 552, 554-560
**Ahern, Frank**
presidential primary vote, **(1976)** 530, **(1980)** 533, 537, **(1988)** 546, 551
**Aiken, George D.**
Governor, Vermont, 661
Senator, Vermont, 809
**Aiken, John W.**
President
popular vote, **(1936, 1940)** 473
Socialist Labor Party nominee, **(1936, 1940)** 279
Vice President
Socialist Labor Party nominee, **(1932)** 279
**Aiken, William**
Governor, South Carolina, 658
**Ailes, Roger**
on 1988 campaign tactics, 335
**Akaka, Daniel K.**
Senator, Hawaii, 790
**Alabama**
apportionment paradox, 929
city commissioners election case, 938
preferential primary system, 628
**Albaugh, Arla A.**
Vice President, Socialist Labor Party nominee, **(1944)** 279
**Albert, Carl**
at Democratic conventions, **(1968)** 124, **(1976)** 134
**Alcorn, James L.**
Governor, Mississippi, 650
Senator, Mississippi, 797
**Aldrich, Chester H.**
Governor, Nebraska, 652
**Aldrich, Nelson W.**
Senator, Rhode Island, 805
**Alexander, Herbert E.**
convention cost estimates, 13
**Alexander, Lamar**
Governor, Tennessee, 660
**Alexander, Moses**
Governor, Idaho, 644
**Alexander, Nathaniel**
Governor, North Carolina, 655
**Alger, Russell A.**
Governor, Michigan, 649
at Republican convention, **(1888)** 66
ballots, **(1888)** 211
Senator, Michigan, 796
**Allain, Bill**
Governor, Mississippi, 650

**Allee, James F.**
Senator, Delaware, 788
**Allen, Frank G.**
Governor, Massachusetts, 649
**Allen, George F**
Governor, Virginia, 662
**Allen, H. C.**
presidential primary vote, **(1940)** 505
**Allen, Henry J.**
Governor, Kansas, 645
Senator, Kansas, 792
**Allen, Henry T.**
Democratic convention ballots, **(1924)** 227
**Allen, Henry W.**
Governor, Louisiana, 647
**Allen, James B.**
Senator, Alabama, 785
**Allen, John B.**
Senator, Washington, 810
**Allen, Maryon Pittman**
Senator, Alabama, 785
**Allen, Oscar K.**
Governor, Louisiana, 647
**Allen, Philip**
Governor, Rhode Island, 657
Senator, Rhode Island, 805
**Allen, Seymour E.**
President, National Party nominee, **(1932)** 279
**Allen, William**
Democratic convention ballots, **(1876)** 205
Governor, Ohio, 656
Senator, Ohio, 803
**Allen, William V.**
Senator, Nebraska, 798, 799
**Allen, Willis**
presidential primary vote, **(1940)** 505
**Allin, Roger**
Governor, North Dakota, 655
**Allison, William B.**
Republican convention ballots, **(1888)** 211, **(1896)** 214
Senator, Iowa, 792
**Allott, Gordon**
Senator, Colorado, 787
**Allred, James V.**
Governor, Texas, 660
**Almond, James Lindsay Jr.**
Governor, Virginia, 662
**Alston, Joseph**
Governor, South Carolina, 658
**Alston, Robert F. W.**
Governor, South Carolina, 658
**Altgeld, John P.**
Governor, Illinois, 644
**Amendments to the Constitution**
12th, 9, 290, 345, 347, 349, 484, 1347
14th, 415, 918, 928, 1347
15th, 415, 630, 916, 1347
17th, 779, 780, 1348
19th, 415, 916, 1348
20th, 779, 781, 1348
22nd, 576, 625, 1348
23rd, 415, 916, 1348
24th, 415, 630, 916, 1348
25th, 347, 354-355, 1348-1349
26th, 415, 916, 1349
**America First Party**
nominees, **(1944)** 279, **(1952)** 280, **(1972)** 281, **(1992)** 283
*See also* **Tax Cut Party**
**American Independent Party**
convention, **(1968)** 125-126
platform, **(1968)** 126
historical profile, 259-260

lifespan (chart), 258
nominees, **(1968)** 125, 281, **(1972)** 281, **(1976, 1980)** 282, **(1988)** 283
percentage of vote, 1968 (chart), 26
**American Labor Party**
nominees, **(1952)** 280
**American National Party**
nominees, **(1986)** 276
**American Party**
nominees, **(1880)** 277, **(1920)** 278, **(1924)** 279, **(1980)** 282, **(1984-1992)** 283
**American Party (American Independent)**
historical profile, 259-260
nominees, **(1968)** 281
**American Party (Know-Nothings)**
convention, **(1856)** 47
platform, **(1856)** 47
historical profile, 260
lifespan (chart), 258
nominees, **(1856)** 276
percentage of vote, 1856 (chart), 26
**American Prohibition Party**
nominees, **(1884)** 277
**American Third Party**
nominees, **(1956)** 280
**American Vegetarian Party**
nominees, **(1952, 1956)** 280
*See also* **Vegetarian Party**
**Ames, Adelbert**
Governor, Mississippi, 650
Senator, Mississippi, 797
**Ames, Benjamin**
Governor, Maine, 647
**Ames, Oliver**
Governor, Massachusetts, 649
**Ammons, Elias M.**
Governor, Colorado, 641
**Ammons, Teller**
Governor, Colorado, 641
**Anaya, Toney**
Governor, New Mexico, 654
**Andersen, Elmer L.**
Governor, Minnesota, 650
**Anderson, Alexander**
Senator, Tennessee, 807
**Anderson, C. Elmer**
Governor, Minnesota, 650
**Anderson, Charles**
Governor, Ohio, 656
**Anderson, Clinton P.**
Senator, New Mexico, 801
**Anderson, Forrest H.**
Governor, Montana, 651
**Anderson, Hugh J.**
Governor, Maine, 647
**Anderson, John B.,** *142*
biography, 563
President
National Unity Campaign nominee **(1980)**, 151, 282, 332
percentage of vote, 1980 (chart), 26
popular vote, **(1980)** 465, **(1984)** 477
primary vote, **(1980)** 531-537
at Republican conventions
ballots, **(1980)** 249
platform opposition, **(1976)** 138
**Anderson, John Jr.**
Governor, Kansas, 646
**Anderson, Joseph**
Senator, Tennessee, 807
**Anderson, Sharon**
presidential primary, **(1992)** 556, 560
**Anderson, Sigurd**
Governor, South Dakota, 659